World Dictionaries In Print 1983

This edition of WORLD DICTIONARIES IN PRINT 1983 was prepared
by the R. R. Bowker Company's Department of
Bibliography in collaboration with the
Publications Systems Department.

Senior staff of the Department of Bibliography includes:
Peter Simon, Database Manager.
Emilia Tomaszewski, Senior Product Manager.
Jane Tiarsmith, Project Manager.
Brian Phair, Project Coordinator.

Michael B. Howell, Manager, Systems Development.

Andrew H. Uszak, Senior Vice President, Data Services/Systems.
Gertude Jennings, Manager, Product Research and Development,
Data Services.

World Dictionaries In Print 1983

A Guide to General and Subject Dictionaries
in World Languages.

SUBJECT INDEX

TITLE INDEX

AUTHOR/EDITOR/COMPILER INDEX

LANGUAGE INDEX

R. R. BOWKER COMPANY

New York & London

Published by the R. R. Bowker Company (a XEROX Information Company)
205 East Forty-second Street, New York, NY 10017
Copyright © 1983 Xerox Corporation

International Standard Book Number: 0-8352-1615-2
International Standard Serial Number: 0000-0604
Printed and bound in the
United States of America

Contents

FOREWORD VII

PREFACE IX

HOW TO USE WORLD DICTIONARIES IN PRINT 1983 XI

KEY TO ABBREVIATIONS XIII

KEY TO CURRENCY SYMBOLS XV

SUBJECT INDEX 1

TITLE INDEX 219

AUTHOR/EDITOR/COMPILER INDEX 367

LANGUAGE INDEX 449

KEY TO PUBLISHERS' AND DISTRIBUTORS'
   ABBREVIATIONS 527

Foreword

In recent years our economic and strategic interests in an ever greater variety of countries and the increase in foreign students at all levels of our educational system have created new demands for foreign language dictionaries. At the same time new technologies, increased specialization, and the analysis and documentation of languages scarcely studied a few years ago have led to rapid growth in the number and kinds of dictionaries available. In this environment the scope of *World Dictionaries In Print* will come as little surprise, but few of us will have expected to see so many unfamiliar titles. So much is coming out today that it is hard to keep up, but many of these titles were published in other countries and have never before even been listed in the bibliographies of the English speaking world.

Good, general translating dictionaries for the major European languages and some others are produced in the United States and Great Britain, but foreign language dictionaries on specialized subjects and dictionaries of less commonly studied languages are often published only in the countries where that language is spoken. Also, even when a good translating dictionary has been done here, people for whom English is a second language may prefer a dictionary compiled in their own country with their particular needs and cultural background in mind. For example, a Spanish dictionary meant for English speakers may leave the English idioms and slang unexplained and may save space by omitting English plurals and irregular verb forms.

Should foreign books be purchased in the U.S. or abroad some of these foreign works have American distributors whose addresses will be found in the list of publishers of *World Dictionaries In Print*. Others can be obtained only through a specialist dealer in the United States or overseas. Unfortunately some people will shy away from the second group, thinking it will be too much trouble. None will deny that an extensive foreign acquisitions program or one that concentrates on Third World countries can be difficult to monitor, but buying the occasional reference book should in most cases be no harder than getting a title from a small press, a non-profit organization, or a government agency. Each of these will have a distribution system tailored to its clientele or to the convenience of a small staff, and similarly each country will have its own distribution system, partly as the result of historical accident, partly in an effort to reach its book buying public effectively and economically. There is no one right way

to acquire the specialized domestic book or the foreign reference book. In either case your strategy will probably be to weigh your convenience and the probable costs and choose a dealer accordingly. If a general dealer cannot supply the book you want, you will go on to try a specialist or go direct. The only additional factor to consider in buying foreign books is that some of the dealers are overseas.

If you are buying only a few titles and those are standard reference books of the type described in *World Dictionaries In Print*, you may well prefer the convenience of using a dealer in North America, although the price will probably be somewhat higher than the original publisher's price. Distribution rights to some titles have been sold to American publishers. Then the distributor's address will be found in the list of publishers and the title should be available just like any other title from that publisher.

If the rights have not been sold, the book will often still be available from specialized booksellers. There are specialists in reference books, and increasingly in many large cities there are specialists in foreign language grammars and dictionaries who can supply basic needs from their stock. There are of course also book importers who specialize in a particular language or country. Most of these dealers also maintain a stock and many will order from overseas any item they do not have available. Since this can take longer than going to the foreign dealer first, size of stock as well as price should be considered in choosing a dealer.

Finally, there are the larger international booksellers, a few in this country and some older companies in Europe. Some few claim to cover the world, most in fact cover part of Western Europe or North America and part or all of some other continent. Except that delivery times may be a bit longer, they present no more problems than do American dealers and indeed many of them now have subsidiaries or offices here. They can be a good choice especially for those starting or expanding a dictionary collection and needing titles from a variety of countries. ·

BUYING FROM THE FOREIGN BOOK DEALER

If you have an interest or expertise in some specific part of the world, or if it seems likely that you will continue for some years to order the publications of a particular country or area, you may want to establish a relationship with a dealer in that area. Paying the original price plus postage is usually cheaper than paying an importer's markup (there is little discounting among foreign book dealers, though there may be some differences in postage charges). The foreign dealer is often a better source of information than the domestic one. Many large dealers and some smaller ones will provide regular customers with information about new titles and series, remainders, prepublication offers, etc. They will also often provide dollar equivalents on invoices, though at a time when the dollar is rising you may wish to get a more current figure from a newspaper or a bank. Delivery time varies greatly from country to country — as little as three weeks from some parts of Western Europe, particularly if the dealer uses air freight, as much as six months from some parts of Asia. Of course orders can be sent air mail and payments certainly should be, but for books air mail is generally too expensive to use regularly, though it may well be worth it for the occasional purchase. Other problems that may be encountered include an inability to correspond in English, billing problems arising from currency conversion or transit time, requests for prepayment (understandable in view of some long delivery times), slow or no response to claims, and the usual shipping problems increased by the greater distance and by revolutions, earthquakes, scorpions, and other "usual tropical wear and tear," as catalogs sometimes say.

For the countries with a well developed export book trade, mostly, but not exclusively, the industrialized nations, any of the approaches described is likely to work. For other countries, mostly in the Third World but also in Eastern Europe, no approach works very well, and it may be a problem finding any dealer at all. Some of the smaller developing nations will probably not have an importer in this country and the dictionary specialists may not have their publications. The international bookseller who specializes in African or Asian or Latin American books is probably your next step, and, if that too fails, you may wish to try a dealer in the individual country. Unfortunately, where there is little local publishing and the book trade is based primarily on imports, there may be no one interested in the exporter's small profit after a long wait. Dealers may also not want to spend money answering your inquiries and claims. All of this is understandable, but none the less frustrating. If as a last resort you approach the publisher directly, you will likely get either a pro forma invoice or no answer at all. Publishers in very small countries and specialized publishers seem to respond most often, but only where English is an established language or when you write in the language of the country.

When you have decided on an approach, consult one of the lists of specialized booksellers and exporters. The recommendations of experienced people will obviously be of use. The Library of Congress publishes a list of its blanket order dealers in *LC Acquisitions Trends* and lists of dealers have appeared at various times in the library literature. Advertising can be helpful and correspondence or phone calls can clear up questions about stock or postage charges. Like other companies, booksellers have their ups and downs, but the consensus on major dealers has shown less change than might be expected over the last twenty years. Remember though that the large institutions choose dealers for a variety of reasons, not all of which may be applicable to a smaller institution or individual. If you can work out a good relationship with a small importer near you or a specialized bookseller, that may meet your occasional needs at least as well as a big dealer with blanket order plans and a computerized serials system.

FURTHER READING

A. J. Walford's *Guide to Foreign Language Courses and Dictionaries* (3rd ed., London: Library Association, 1977) supplements the standard guides to reference books as an evaluative tool. Siegfred Taubert's *Book Trade of the World* (New York: Bowker, 1972–) is an interesting survey of the various national book trades, usefully supplemented by Herbert R. Lottman's occasional reports on foreign publishing and book fairs in *Publishers Weekly*. Theodore Samore, ed., *Acquisition of Foreign Materials for U.S. Libraries* (2nd ed., Metuchen: Scarecrow, 1982) and *Acquisitions from the Third World*, a special issue of *Library Acquisitions: Practice and Theory* (6:79–238) are both good surveys of acquisitions problems. Finally, the *American Book Trade Directory* (New York: Bowker, annually), *Publishers, Distributors and Wholesalers of the United States* (New York: Bowker, annually), and *Who Distributes What and Where* (New York: Bowker, 1983) provide addresses and through their many indexes help to identify specialist booksellers.

JAMES CAMPBELL
North Europe Bibliographer
University of Virginia, Charlottesville, Virginia

James Campbell's education includes: B.A., Washington and Lee University; M.L.S., University of Pittsburgh; graduate work in German and comparative literature at the University of Erlangen (Fulbright Grant) and University of North Carolina at Chapel Hill (Honorary Woodrow Wilson Fellow). His professional experience includes: 1968–1973, Instructor in German, University of Pittsburgh; 1973–1976, Humanities Bibliographer, Alexander Library, Rutgers University; 1976–present, North Europe Bibliographer, University of Virginia. Currently Chair, Publications Committee, ACRL Western European Specialists Section.

Preface

Bowker's regular inquiries in the academic, professional and business worlds to ascertain reference book needs brought forth in all these domains a demand for comprehensive, reliable, current international information on dictionaries. Physicians, scientists, technicians of all kinds and individuals engaged in the study of languages *all over the world* now more than ever need up-to-date wordbooks. The professional and the businessman, the scholar and the traveler is no longer confined to the borders of his own country. The Italian merchant finds himself doing business in Portugal, the German oceanographer is doing research off the coast of California, the United States mechanical engineer is studying robotics in Japan. Technical dictionaries in bilingual or trilingual combinations such as these and a myriad more are included in *World Dictionaries In Print: A Guide To General And Subject Dictionaries In World Languages.* Over 238 languages and 5,854 subjects are covered for dictionaries published in approximately 100 countries around the world.

World Dictionaries In Print 1983: A Guide To General And Subject Dictionaries In World Languages represents one more example of the R. R. Bowker Company's continuing efforts to provide diverse users with bibliographic reference works aimed at meeting their special needs. This comprehensive collection of nearly 14,000 titles provides a comprehensive listing of the output of international publishing of dictionaries, wordbooks, glossaries and thesauri. All titles listed are currently in-print.

World Dictionaries In Print 1983 includes general language dictionaries in English as well as the languages of Europe, Asia and Africa; special purpose dictionaries such as slang and pronunciation dictionaries, and usage manuals; translating dictionaries in two or more languages as well as subject dictionaries which focus on the specialized vocabulary of a particular area of study. This single source volume includes scientific, technical, medical, religious, legal, social science, business and other subject and general dictionaries that have been published in the world's languages. *World Dictionaries In Print 1983* does *not* include works dealing with people, places and things which because of their alphabetical or "dictionary" arrangement are called dictionaries. *World Dictionaries In Print 1983* is a basic resource needed for reference, research, collection development, acquisitions and interlibrary loan and cataloging.

ACQUISITION OF DATA

This edition of World Dictionaries in Print was produced from data stored on magnetic tape, edited by computer programs and set in type by computer controlled videocomposition.

More than 4000 dictionary and reference book publishers in over 100 countries received at least two mailings from Bowker editors to collect the information published in *World Dictionaries In Print*. Close to 50 percent of the titles are published outside the United States. Titles published in foreign countries with no exclusive distributor within the United States could not be found in *Books In Print*. The remaining titles in *World Dictionaries In Print* were selected from Bowker's *Books In Print* and *Associations' Publications In Print* databases.

SURVEY OF PROFESSIONALS, LIBRARIANS AND INFORMATION

In addition to our regular personal inquiries among the users of Bowker reference works, it is our established routine to consult the potential user before publishing a specific work. The surveys we make seek to establish a definite need for the reference work as well as to obtain practical direction from potential users as to content and format. This interaction has been most satisfying since it has resulted in direct hands on influence on the final design of *World Dictionaries In Print 1983*.

We surveyed by questionnaire college, university and public libraries specializing in scientific, technical, business, legal, religious and health science information. Over 75 percent of those queried responded affirmatively to questions asking whether they would purchase *World Dictionaries In Print*, offered invaluable suggestions incorporated in its final design and with comments such as these confirmed the validity of our concept:

"We have really needed something like this. Content and format are great." "... A must for every college library. It is a subject bibliography, a cataloging tool, a buying guide in some areas and a lot of other uses." "It provides the especially difficult to obtain information on where to purchase the dictionary, in-print status, current price."

ARRANGEMENT AND CONTENT

World Dictionaries In Print 1983 contains five indexes. The Subject Index lists nearly 14,000 entries under 5,854 Library of Congress subject headings, with 8,370 cross-references. Full bibliographic information is provided including the current price, when available, in the currency of the country.

The Title Index lists 13,623 publications arranged alphabetically by title and provides full bibliographic and publisher information.

The Author, Editor, Compiler Index lists 13,255 authors, editors and compilers alphabetically by the author's name. Each entry contains the name of author(s), title, subtitle and publisher, for easy reference back to the more complete entry in the Title Index.

A special feature of this publication is the Language Index, which lists all non-English dictionaries alphabetically by title, under 238 language headings. The format of all languages was standardized according to the latest Library of Congress Subject Headings. Bibliographic information provided includes the title, subtitle, author(s) and publisher for reference back to the Author and Title entries. This index provides access to all dictionaries in world languages listed in *World Dictionaries In Print*. Where dictionaries cover two or more languages, titles are listed under each language.

The Key to Publishers and Distributors Abbreviations contains complete name, address and ordering information for over 2,549 publishers and distributors in the United States and abroad whose titles are listed in *World Dictionaries In Print*.

A more complete description of all indexes and the elements contained in each can be found in the section entitled "How To Use *World Dictionaries In Print 1983*" beginning on page xi.

ACKNOWLEDGEMENTS

We extend our thanks to James Campbell, North Europe Bibliographer, University of Virginia for providing us with his excellent essay: "Suggestions for Acquiring Foreign Reference Books."

World Dictionaries In Print 1983 was produced from a concept developed by Gertrude Jennings, Manager, Product Research and Development for Bowker's Data Services Division. She, Peter Simon, Database Manager and Emilia Tomaszewski, Senior Product Manager were responsible for the design, planning and production of this publication. Special thanks to Jane Tiarsmith, Project Manager and Brian Phair, Project Coordinator for their diligent work and contributions to this publication.

Our appreciation is extended to Michael B. Howell, Manager, Systems Development and Philip Pan, Applications Manager for their special contributions. Our thanks to Frank McWade, Manager, Data Processing, and Jack Murphy, Computer Operator Specialist for their support and cooperation in the processing of the data used in this publication.

GERTRUDE JENNINGS
Manager, Product Research and Development

PETER SIMON
Database Manager

EMILIA TOMASZEWSKI
Senior Product Manager

How To Use World Dictionaries In Print 1983

INFORMATION INCLUDED IN THE SUBJECT INDEX

The users of *World Dictionaries In Print 1983* can access information in the Subject Index where 13,623 complete entries appear alphabetically under 5,854 Library of Congress Subject Headings, with 8,370 cross-references. Entry information includes, when available, title, subtitle, author(s), editor(s), translator(s), number of volumes, edition, Library of Congress number, series information, page numbers, language, whether or not illustrated, grade range, year of publication, type of binding if other than cloth over boards, price and currency, International Standard Book Number (ISBN), publishers' order number, imprint and publisher. When an entry includes the prices for both the hardcover and paperback editions, the publication date in the entry refers to the hardcover binding, however, when the paperback binding is the only one included in the entry, the publication date is the paperback publication date.

TITLE INDEX

The title index of *World Dictionaries In Print 1983* includes 13,623 titles alphabetically arranged. Initial articles of titles in all languages are deleted from this index. Numerals are written out in most cases and are filed alphabetically. For example:

> Seven Hundred Russian Idioms
> Seven Thousand Words

Each entry contains the same complete bibliographic information found in the subject index.

AUTHOR/EDITOR/COMPILER INDEX

This index is arranged alphabetically by author, editor or compiler name. When two authors or editors are responsible for a book, full bibliographic information is included in the author entry for the author or editor name first, and a cross reference directs the user from the second author or editor to the primary entry. If two or more authors are responsible for a certain publication, only the name of the first is given followed by et al. Bibliographic information provided in this index includes, when available, author(s), title, subtitle, imprint and publisher.

LANGUAGE INDEX

The Language Index includes 13,542 titles arranged alphabetically under 238 headings for world languages. Languages have been styled using the latest Library of Congress Subject Headings for consistency and accuracy. Each entry in this index includes, when available, title, subtitle, author(s), imprint, and publisher.

GENERAL EDITORIAL POLICIES

In order to ensure that the essential information in these listings is uniform, complete and easy to find, the following editorial policies have been maintained:

Titles of single volumes as part of a set are supplied if the volumes are sold singly. Titles of volumes can also be listed under the main title of the set, with "see" references provided from the individual title to the set title. Some series are also listed.

Every effort is made by most contributing publishers to prepare their material with consideration for its accuracy throughout the life of *World Dictionaries In Print 1983*. In spite of these efforts, a number of changes in price will occur and a number of titles in this edition will become unavailable. All prices are subject to change without notice.

Most prices are list prices and are given in the currency of the country of publication. A Key to Currency Symbols appears on page xiii.

Publishers' and distributors' names are abbreviated. A key to these abbreviations can be found in the Key to Publishers' and Distributors' Abbreviations at the end of this volume. Entries in the "Key" are arranged alphabetically by the abbreviation used in the bibliographic entries. The full name, editorial address, telephone number, ordering address (if different from the editorial address), Standard Address Numbers (SAN) and ISBN Prefix follow the abbreviation. SAN is a unique identification code for each address of each organization served by the book industry.

For Example: Garsi Edit

Garsi Editorial
Londres 17, Madrid 28
Spain

We have made every effort to identify foreign publishers, but in some instances were unable to do so. If we have listed a title with the name of a foreign book importer, that does not mean that the book might not be available from other importers of books in those languages.

In some cases an entry may appear twice in an index with two different publishers. In our foreign data acquisitions efforts we have included many titles that may also be exclusively distributed by a United States publisher. In those cases, we have often provided the user with both entries to show the original information from the publisher as well as the availability of the title in the United States.

The R. R. Bowker Company has used its best efforts in collecting and preparing material for inclusion in *World Dictionaries In Print 1983*, but does not assume, and hereby disclaims any liability to any party for any loss or damage caused by errors or omissions in *World Dictionaries In Print 1983* whether such errors or omissions result from negligence, accident or any other cause.

Key To Abbreviations

a	after price, specially priced library edition available
abr.	abridged
adpt.	adapted
Amer.	American
annot.	annotation(s), annotated
ans.	answer(s)
app.	appendix
approx.	approximately
assn.	association
auth.	author
bd.	bound
bdg.	binding
bds.	boards
bibl(s).	bibliography (ies)
bk(s).	book, books
bklet(s).	booklets
Bro.	Brother
coll.	college
comm.	commission, committee
co.	company
cond.	condensed
comp(s).	compiler(s)
corp.	corporation
dept.	department
diag(s).	diagram(s)
dir.	director
dist.	distributed
Div.	Division
doz.	dozen
ea.	each
ed.	editor, edited, edition
eds.	editions, editors
educ.	education
elem.	elementary
ency.	encyclopedia
Eng.	English
enl.	enlarged
exp.	expurgated
fac.	facsimile
fasc.	fascicule
fict.	fiction
fig(s).	figure(s)
for.	foreign
Fr.	French
frwd.	foreword
g	after price, guaranteed juvenile binding
gen.	general
Ger.	German
Gr.	Greek
gr.	grade, grades
hdbk.	handbook
Heb.	Hebrew
i	invoice price
i.t.a.	initial teaching alphabet
Illus.	illustrated, illustration(s), illustrator(s)
in prep.	in preparation
incl.	includes, including
inst.	institute
intro.	introduction
It.	Italian
Jr.	Junior
jt. auth.	joint author
jt. ed.	joint editor

k	kindergarten audience level
l.p.	long playing
ltd. ed.	limited edition
lab.	laboratory
lang(s).	language(s)
Lat.	Latin
lea.	leather
lib.	library
lit.	literature, literary
math.	mathematics
mod.	modern
mor.	morocco
MS, MSS	manuscript, manuscripts
natl.	national
no., nos.	number, numbers
o.p.	out of print
orig.	original text, not a reprint
o.s.i.	out of stock indefinitely
pap.	paper
photos	photographs, photographer
PLB	publisher's library binding
Pol.	Polish
pop. ed.	popular edition
Port.	Portuguese
prep.	preparation
probs.	problems
prog. bk.	programmed book
ps	preschool audience level
pseud.	pseudonym
pt(s).	part, parts
pub.	published, publisher, publishing
pubn.	publication
ref(s).	reference(s)
repr.	reprint
reprod(s).	reproduction(s)
rev.	revised
rpm.	revolution per minute (phono records)
Rus.	Russian
s & l	signed & limited
scp	single copy, direct to the consumer price
sec.	section
sel.	selected
ser.	series
Soc.	Society
sols.	solutions
Span.	Spanish
Sr. (after given name)	Senior
Sr. (before given name)	Sister
St.	Saint
subs.	subsidiary
subsc.	subscription
suppl.	supplement
t	after price, tentative price
tech.	technical
text ed.	text edition
tr.	translator, translated, translation
univ.	university
vol(s).	volume, volumes
wkbk.	workbook
x	after price, short discount (20% or less)
YA	young adult audience level
yrbk.	yearbook

Key To Currency Symbols

SYMBOL	UNIT	COUNTRY
Arg.$	peso	Argentina
As.	annas	Pakistan
Aus.$	dollars	Australia
B.	bahts	Thailand
B.$	dollars	Borneo (Brunei)
Bl.	balboas	Panama
Bol.$	peso	Bolivia
Bs.	bolivares	Venezuela
C.$	cordobas	Nicaragua
Can.$	dollars	Canada
Col.	colones	Costa Rica, El Salvador
Col.$	peso	Colombia
Cr.$	cruzeiros	Brazil
ctms.	centimes; centimos; centesimos	various
cvs.	centavos	various
d.	pence	Great Britain
DH.	dirhams	Morocco
DM.	marks	West Germany
din.	dinars	Yugoslavia
$	dollars; pesos	various
Dr.	drachmas	Greece
E.	pounds	Gt. Britain
EAs.	shillings	East Africa
Esc.	escudos	Portugal
Eth.$	dollars	Ethiopia
F.	franc	France
fl.	florins or guilders	The Netherlands, Surinam
FMG.	francs	Malagasy Republic
Fmk.	marks; markkas	Finland
Fr.	francs	Belgium, Switzerland
Fr. CFA	francs	African Financial Community
Ft.	forints	Hungary
Gde.	gourdes	Haiti
G.$	dollars	Guyana
g.	guaranies	Paraguay
HK.$	dollars	Hong Kong
I.D.	dinars	Iran, Iraq
Jam.$	dollar	Jamaica
K.	kwacha	Zambia
Kcs.	koruny	Czechoslovakia
Kop.	kopecks	U.S.S.R.

SYMBOL	UNIT	COUNTRY
Kr.	kroner; kronor	Scandinavian countries
L.	lempira; lira	Honduras, Italy
Le.	Leones	Sierra Leone
lei	lei	Romania
lv.	leva	Bulgaria
M.	marks	East Germany
M.$	dollars	Malaya
Mex.$	pesos	Mexico
Mils.	mils	Cyprus
$m.n.	moneda nacional	various
n.	ngwee	Zambia
NC.	New Cedis	Ghana
NT.$	dollars	Taiwan
N.Z.$	dollars	New Zealand
p.	pesewas; pence	Ghana, Gt. Britain
P.	pesos	various
P.T.	piasters	Egypt, Syria, Turkey
pf.	pfennigs	Germany
£E	pounds	Egypt
I£	pounds	Israel
£L	pounds	Lebanon, Libya
£N	pounds	Nigeria
£S	pounds	Syria
ptas.	pesetas	Spain
Q.	quetzales	Guatemala
R.	rands	South Africa
RD.$	peso	Dominican Republic
Rhod.$	dollars	Rhodesia
Rps.	rupiahs	Indonesia
Rs.	riels; rupees; rials	Cambodia, Ceylon, India, Pakistan, Iran
Rub.	rubles	U.S.S.R.
S/	sucres, soles	Ecuador, Peru
S.	schillings	Austria
S.$	dollars	Singapore
s.	shillings	Gt. Britain
TL.	pounds	Turkey
T.T.$	dollars	Trinidad
Urg.$	Pesos	Uruguay
VN.$	dollars	Vietnam
Won	won (hwan)	Korea
Yen	yen	Japan
Zl.	zlotys	Poland

Subject Index

A

A-C CARRIER CONTROL SYSTEMS
see Carrier Control Systems
ABANDONMENT (MARINE INSURANCE)
see Insurance, Marine
ABBREVIATIONS
see also Acronyms; Code Names; Shorthand; Signs and Symbols
also subdivision Abbreviations under subjects, e.g. Law–Abbreviations
Abbreviations Used by FAO for International Congresses, Commissions, Etc. (Terminology Bulletin Ser.: No. 27, R. 2). 144p. 1979. pap. $9.75 (ISBN 0-686-72305-8, F2056, FAO). Unipub.
Allen, E. F. Dictionary of Abbreviations & Symbols. $18.50 (ISBN 0-87559-167-1). Shalom.
Alvarez de la Brana, Ramon. Siglas & Abreviaturas Latinas con su Significado por Orden Alfabetico de un Catalogo de las Abreviaturas. LC 78-366525. xi, 215p. (Lat.). 1978. write for info. (ISBN 3-487-06454-5). Olms Verlag.
Azzaretti, M. Dictionnaire International d'abreviations Scientifiques et Techniques. 300p. (Eng., Fr., Span., Ital. & Ger.). 1978. 120.00 F. Maison Dictionnaire.
--Dictionnaire International d'abreviation Scientifiques et Techniques. 300p. (Eng., Fr., Span., Ital., Ger. & Rus.). 1978. 150.00 F. Maison Dictionnaire.
Bluvshtein, V. O. Slovar Angliishkikh & Amerikanskikh Sokrashchenii. 767p. (Eng. & Rus.). 1957. $4.50 (Pub. by GINS). Four Continent.
--Slovar Nemetskikh Sokrashchenii. 442p. (Rus.). 1958. $2.25 (Pub. by GINS). Four Continent.
Buttress, F. A., ed. World Guide to Abbreviations of Organizations. 6th ed. 500p. 1980. $115.00x (ISBN 0-8103-2024-X). Gale.
Capelli. Dizionario di Abbreviature Latine e Italiane. (Ital. & Lat.). L.16.00. Hoepli.
Capelli, A. Dizionario di abbreviature latine ed italiane. (Illus.). lxxiv, 536p. (Lat. & Ital.). 1979. L.8000.00 (ISBN 88-203-0221-7). Hoepli.

Chassant, Alphonse A. Dictionnaire des Abbreviations Latines et Francaises Usitees dans les Inscriptions Lapidaires et Metalliques, les Manuscrits et les Chartes de Moyen Age. 5th ed. LC 73-3365. (Illus., Fr.). 1973. Repr. of 1884 ed. lib. bdg. $22.50 (ISBN 0-8337-0547-4). B Franklin.
Chassant, Louis A. Dictionnaire des Abreviations Latines & Francaise: Usitees dans les Inscriptions du Moyen-Age. 5th ed. (Lat. & Fr.). $28.50. Lenox.
--Dictionnaire des Abreviations Latines & Francaises: Usitees dans les Inscriptions du Moyen Age. (Lat. & Fr.). DM.26.80. Olms Verlag.
Crowley, Ellen, ed. Acronyms, Initialisms & Abbreviations Dictionary, 2 pts, Vol. 1. 8th ed. 1701p. 1982. $110.00x (ISBN 0-8103-0505-4). Gale.
--Reverse Acronyms, Initialisms, & Abbreviations Dictionary. 8th ed. (The Acronyms, Initialisms, & Abbreviations Dictionary Ser.: Vol. 3). 1600p. 1982. $130.00x (ISBN 0-8103-0507-0). Gale.
De Sola, R. Abbreviations Dictionary. 6th ed. 1981. $38.00 (ISBN 0-444-00380-0). Elsevier.
Dictionary of Abbreviations in Information Science. 406p. 1976. $50.00x (ISBN 0-686-44776-X, Pub. by Collets). State Mutual Bk.
Dubois, M. Dictionnaire de sigles nationaux et internationaux. 405p. (Fr.). 1977. 130.00 F. Maison Dictionnaire.
Dubois, Michel. Dictionnaire de Sigles Nationaux & Internationaux. 2nd ed. 479p. (Fr.). 1977. 100.00 F. Maison Dictionnaire.
Freyberger, G. Abkurzungen der Kernkraftwerkstechnik. LC 79-376298. 199p. (Eng. & Ger.). 1979. write for info. (ISBN 3-521-06120-5). Thiemeg.
Gendrel, M. Dictionnaire des Principaux Sigles Utilises dans le Monde Juridique de A-Z. (Fr.). 460.00 F. Bruylant.
Gomez de Cadiz, Javier. Diccionario de Siglas. LC 77-471470. 62p. (Span.). 1976. 50.00 ptas (ISBN 8-420-30051-9). Alas.
Kohler, Rolf & Mayr, Ernst. EDV-Abkurzungen. LC 79-342495. 332p. (Ger.). 1978. write for info. (ISBN 3-8009-1262-7). Siemens AG.

Krist, Thomas. Taschen-Lexikon Internationale Abkurzungen & Kurzzeichen. LC 80-474810. 144p. (Eng. & Ger.). 1979. DM.9.80 (ISBN 3-87807-110-8). Technik Tabel.
Loland, Stale & Thorsen, Arnold. Norsk Forkortingsbok. LC 77-463699. 68p. (Norwegian.). 1976. Kr.35.00 (ISBN 8-20200-892-1). J W Cappelens.
Nyblom, Ake. Engelsk-Svensk Elteknisk Forkortningslista. LC 75-547472. 24p. (Eng. & Swedish.). 1975. Kr.19.00 (ISBN 91-7284-026-9). Ingenjorsforlaget.
Oestling, Sven E. Foerkortningslexikon. LC 76-512672. 32p. (Swedish.). 1975. write for info (ISBN 9-171-82159-7). Utrikespolitiska.
Paxton, John, ed. Dictionary of Abbreviations. 384p. 1973. $15.00x (ISBN 0-87471-188-6). Rowman.
--Everyman's Dictionary of Abbreviations: With Supplement. rev. ed. 408p. 1981. $20.00x (ISBN 0-8476-6973-4). Rowman.
Pugh, Eric, compiled by. Pugh's Dictionary of Acronyms & Abbreviations. LC 81-14029. 348p. 1982. $87.50x (ISBN 0-89774-012-2). Oryx Pr.
Rogers, Walter T. Dictionary of Abbreviations. LC 68-30662. 1969. Repr. of 1913 ed. $37.00x (ISBN 0-8103-3338-4). Gale.
Rybicki, Stephen A., ed. Abbreviations: A Reverse Guide to Standard & Generally Accepted Abbreviated Forms. LC 74-143239. (Reverse Dictionary Ser.: No. 1). 1971. $17.50 (ISBN 0-87650-010-6). Pierian.
Schwartz, Robert J. Complete Dictionary of Abbreviations. $9.95i (ISBN 0-690-20620-8). T Y Crowell.
Slovar Sokrashchenii Po Informatike. 406p. (Rus.). 1974. $9.75 (Pub. by Izd. Mexdunarod. Tsentral' Nauchin. & Tekhn. Informatsii). Four Continent.
Sundby, Dag, ed. Den Nye Forkortningsordboken. LC 76-514223. 87p. (Norweigan.). 1975. Kr.33.00 (ISBN 8-251-60275-0). Schibsted.
Touati, Maurice A. Lexique Francais des Abreviations: Formules Medico-Chirugicales Courantes. 142p. (Fr.). 1969. 24.00 F. Maloine.

Walter, Frank K. Abbreviations & Technical Terms Used in Book Catalogues & in Bibliographies. LC 77-6174. 1977. Repr. of 1917 ed. lib. bdg. $12.50 (ISBN 0-89341-152-3). Longwood Pr.
Walther, Johann L. Lexicon Diplomaticum Abbreviationes Syllabarum et Vocum in Diplomatibus et Codicibus a Seculo Octo a Sextum-Decimum Usque Occurentes Exponens, 2 vols. in 1. folio ed. (Lat.). 1967. Repr. of 1756 ed. $87.00 (ISBN 0-8337-3680-9). B Franklin.
Wennrich, Peter. Anglo-American & German Abbreviations in Environmental Protection. 624p. (Eng. & Ger.). 1979. $60.00x (ISBN 0-89664-096-5, Pub. by K G Saur). Gale.
ABBREVIATIONS, MEDICAL
see Medicine–Abbreviations
ABERRATION, CHROMATIC AND SPHERICAL
see Optical Instruments
ABIGAR LANGUAGE
see Nuer Language
ABNORMAL CHILDREN
see Exceptional Children
ABNORMAL PSYCHOLOGY
see Psychology, Pathological
ABSENTEE VOTING
see Voting
ABSTINENCE
see Temperance
ABUA-OGBIA LANGUAGES
Wolff, Hans. A Comparative Vocabulary of Aubuan Dialects. 293p. 1969. $5.95x (ISBN 0-89771-003-7). State Mutual Bk.
ABUSE
see Invective
ACCIDENTS–PREVENTION
see also Industrial Safety
also subdivisions Safety Appliances or Safety Measures under subjects, e.g. Railroads–Safety Appliances, Automobiles–Safety Measures
De Villiers-Sidani, Maria E. Lexique de la Prevention des Accidents. (Illus.). 173p. (Fr.). 1973. Can.$2.00. Quebec Off.
De Villiers-Sidani, Maria E., et al. Lexique de Prevention des Accidents. 137p. (Eng. & Fr.). 1980. pap. $4.95 (ISBN 0-686-97398-4, M-9225). French & Eur.
ACCOUNTING
see also Bookkeeping; Cost Accounting; Depreciation

also subdivision Accounting under names of industries, professions, trades, etc., e.g. Printing–Accounting
Accountants International Study Group. Comparative Glossary of Accounting Terms in Canada, the United Kingdom & the United States. 1975. $3.50 (333). Can Inst Chart Accts.
Terminology for Accountants. 1976. $8.50 (219). Can Inst Chart Accts.

ACCOUNTING–DICTIONARIES
Abdeen, Adnan. A Dictionary of Accounting & Finance. (Arabic & Eng.). 1980. $30.00 (275-1). Intl Bk Ctr.
--English-Arabic Dictionary for Accounting & Finance. LC 79-41213. (Eng. & Arabic.). 1981. $23.95x (ISBN 0-471-27673-1, Pub. by Wiley-Interscience). Wiley.
Blanes Prieto, Joaquin. Diccionario de terminos contables. 118p. (Span.). 1970. $5.30. CECSA.
Canadian Institute of Chartered Accountants. Terminology for Accountants. 1976 ed. LC 77-370287. 92p. (Eng.). 1976. write for info. (ISBN 0-88800-002-2). Canadian Inst Chart.
Cholvis, F. Diccionario de Contabilidad. 469p. (Span.). 1977. $65.00 (ISBN 0-686-92515-7, S-33738). French & Eur.
--Diccionario de Contabilidad, 2 vols. 3rd ed. 778p. (Span.). 1974. write for info. Ateneo Edit.
Cholvis, Francisco. Diccionario de contabilidad. 760p. (Span.). Arg.$760.00. Contabilidad Moderna.
Codera Martin, Jose M. Diccionario De Contabilidad. 2nd ed. (Span.). leatherette $16.50 (ISBN 84-368-0061-3, S-50180). French & Eur.
--Diccionario de Contabilidad. 3rd ed. 272p. (Span.). 1980. 700.00 ptas. Piramide.
--Diccionario de contabilidad. 4th ed. 272p. (Span.). 1982. pap. 800.00 ptas (ISBN 84-368-0061-3). Piramide.
Colasse. Lexique de Comptabilite et de Gestion. (Fr.). 1975. pap. $14.95 (ISBN 0-686-56768-4, M-6079). French & Eur.
Enriquez Palomic, R. Lexico basico del contador. 2nd ed. 160p. (Span.). 1968. $2.24; Mex.$28.00. Trillas.
Estes, Ralph W. A Dictionary of Accounting. 176p. 1981. text ed. $16.50x (ISBN 0-262-05024-2); pap. $4.95 (ISBN 0-262-55009-1). MIT Pr.
Fryd, Ejnar, ed. Fransk-Dansk, Dansk-Fransk Specialordbog. LC 78-377405. 199p. (Danish & Fr.). 1977. Kr.175.00. For Stat Rev.
Garza Bores, Jaime. Diccionario Tecnico de Terminologia Comercial Cantable y Bancaria. (Span.). $6.95 (ISBN 0-686-56677-7, S-25235). French & Eur.
--Diccionario tecnico de terminologia comercial, contable y bancaria: Espanol-Ingles, Ingles-Espanol. (Span. & Eng.). $1.60; Mex.$20.00. Diana.
Glossaire Europeen de Terminologie Juridique et Administrative. Budgeting & Auditing. German-Italian, No. 26. 144p. (Ger. & Ital.). 1980. pap. $19.95 (ISBN 3-468-49076-3, M-9493). French & Eur.
Houghton, Diane & Wallace, Ralph G. Students' Accounting Vocabulary. 278p. 1980. pap. text ed. $15.00x (ISBN 0-566-00330-9). Gower Pub Ltd.
March, Robert T. Accounting Language. LC 77-12041. 1978. lib. bdg. $12.90 (ISBN 0-89471-017-6); pap. $2.95 (ISBN 0-89471-016-8). Running Pr.
Nagel, Kurt. Lexikon EDV und Rechnungswesen. (Ger.). 1977. $28.50 (ISBN 3-470-58181-9, M-7203). French & Eur.
Ramos-Ramos, Abiud. Vocabulario Tecnico De Contabilidad Moderna. LC 77-11200. (Span.). 1978. pap. $8.75 (ISBN 0-8477-2629-0). U of PR Pr.
Running Press Glossary of Accounting Language. LC 77-12041. 78p. (Eng.). 1978. $9.80 (ISBN 0-89471-017-6); pap. $1.95 (ISBN 0-89471-016-8). Running Pr.
Seone, Joaquin R. Diccionario de contabilidad, organizacion, administracion, control & ciencia afines, 7 vols. 3400p. (Span.). 1972. $45.00. Difusion.
Sylvain, Fernand. Dictionnaire de la comptabilite. (Fr.). 1977. $17.50 (220). Can Inst Chart Accts.
Union Europeenne Des Experts Compatables, Economiques et Financiers. Accounting Dictionary - U.E.C. Lexicon: American-French-German-Spanish-Dutch. 2nd ed. LC 63-31440. (Eng., Fr., Ger., Span. & Dutch.). 1974. $107.50x (ISBN 3-8021-0073-5). Intl Pubns Serv.

ACCOUNTING–FORMS, BLANKS, ETC.
see Business–Forms, Blanks, etc.

ACOUSTIC ENGINEERING
see Acoustical Engineering

ACOUSTICAL ENGINEERING
see also Architectural Acoustics; Electro-Acoustics; Telecommunication
Applied Technical Dictionary: Acoustics. $50.00x (ISBN 0-569-08535-7, Pub. by Collets). State Mutual Bk.
Clason, W. E. Elsevier's Dictionary of Cinema, Sound & Music. (Eng., Fr., Span., Ital., Dutch, & Ger., Polyglot). 1956. $117.00 (ISBN 0-444-40117-2). Elsevier.
Piraux, Henri. Diccionario General De Acustica y Electro Acustica. 374p. (Espn.). 1967. $14.95 (ISBN 84-283-0153-0, S-50237). French & Eur.
Reichardt, W. Acoustics Dictionary. Date not set. lib. bdg. $28.50 (ISBN 90-247-2707-3, Pub. by Martinus Nijhoff Netherlands). Kluwer Academic.
Reichardt, Walter. Technicka Akustika. LC 80-465612. 268p. (Eng., Rus., Span. & Slovak.). 1978. 50.00 Kcs. VEB Verlat Technik.
--Technische Akustik. LC 80-491210. 268p. (Eng., Ger., Fr., Rus., Span., Pol., Hungarian, & Slovak.). 1979. M.30.00. VEB Verlag Technik.

ACOUSTICS
see Architectural Acoustics; Sound

ACQUISITION OF LANGUAGE
see Children–Language

ACROGENS
see Ferns

ACRONYMS
Brunner, Victor. Diccionario de Siglas en Comercio Exterior. LC 77-566386. (Illus.). 125p. (Span.). 1977. Arg.$70.00. Liv Nobel.
Crowley, Ellen, ed. Acronyms, Initialisms & Abbreviations Dictionary, 2 pts, Vol. 1. 8th ed. 1701p. 1982. $110.00x (ISBN 0-8103-0505-4). Gale.
--Reverse Acronyms, Initialisms, & Abbreviations Dictionary. 8th ed. (The Acronyms, Initialisms, & Abbreviations Dictionary Ser.: Vol. 3). 1600p. 1982. $130.00x (ISBN 0-8103-0507-0). Gale.
French & International Acronyms & Initialisms Dictionary. 2nd ed. 1977. pap. $30.00x (ISBN 0-930624-00-9). Marlin.
Jones, David J., ed. The Australian Dictionary of Acronyms & Abbreviations. LC 78-312706. 156p. 1977. write for info. (ISBN 0-909325-08-1). Second Back Row.
--The Australian Dictionary of Acronyms & Abbreviations. 2nd, rev. ed. LC 82-126656. 220p. 1981. write for info. (ISBN 0-909325-24-3). Second Back Row.
Pugh, Eric. Third Dictionary of Acronyms & Abbreviations: More Abbreviations in Management, Technology, & Information Science. 1977. $17.50 (ISBN 0-208-01535-3, Linnet). Shoe String.
Pugh, Eric, compiled by. Pugh's Dictionary of Acronyms & Abbreviations. LC 81-14029. 348p. 1982. $87.50x (ISBN 0-89774-012-2). Oryx Pr.
Vaillancourt, Pauline M. International Directory of Acronyms in Library, Information & Computer Sciences. LC 80-18352. xi, 518p. 1980. $45.00 (ISBN 0-8352-1152-5). Bowker.

ACTING
see also Mime
Dunn, Charles W., ed. The Actors' Analects. LC 79-8837. (Studies in Oriental Culture Ser). (Illus.). 306p. 1970. $24.00x (ISBN 0-231-03391-5). Columbia U Pr.

ACTING–COSTUME
see Costume

ACTUARIAL SCIENCE
see Insurance, Life

AD VALOREM TARIFF
see Tariff

ADAGES
see Maxims; Proverbs

ADAMAWA DIALECT
see Fulah Language

ADDITIVES, FOOD
see Food Additives

ADDRESS, TITLES OF
see Titles of Honor and Nobility

ADJECTIVE LAW
see Procedure (Law)

ADMINISTRATION
see Administrative Law; Civil Service; Management; Political Science
also subdivision Politics and Government under names of countries, states, cities, etc.

ADMINISTRATION, BUSINESS
see Business

ADMINISTRATION, NURSING SERVICE
see Nursing Service Administration

ADMINISTRATION, PUBLIC
see Public Administration

ADMINISTRATION OF CRIMINAL JUSTICE
see Criminal Justice, Administration Of

ADMINISTRATION OF JUSTICE
see Justice, Administration Of

ADMINISTRATIVE LAW
see also Civil Service; Constitutional Law; Local Government; Public Administration; Rule of Law
Barrillon, Raymond. Droit Administratif. LC 79-361007. 191p. (Fr.). 1979. 29.00 F (ISBN 2-130-35777-6). Pr Univ Fr.
Guarino, Giuseppe. Dizionario Amministrativo. LC 78-367131. xvi, 671p. (Ital.). 1978. L.1600.00. Giuffre.

ADOLESCENCE
Hudson, Kenneth. Dictionary of the Teenage Revolution & its Aftermath. 320p. 1983. E12.95 (ISBN 0-333-28517-4). Macmillan London.

ADULT EDUCATION
Densmore, Dana. Speech Is the Form of Though - With a New Glossary. (Reprinted from Cell 16). 1970. $0.50 (015). Know Inc.
Terminology of Adult Education. (IBE Data Ser.). 154p. 1980. pap. $10.50 (ISBN 92-3-001683-7, U950, UNESCO). Unipub.

ADVERTISING
see also Marketing; Packaging; Public Relations; Publicity
also subdivided by topic, e.g. Advertising–Banks and Banking
Conseil International de la Langue Francaise. Vocabulaire de la Publicite. (Fr.). 1976. 31.20 F. Hachette.

ADVERTISING–DICTIONARIES
Ayer Glossary of Advertising & Related Terms: 1977. rev. ed. LC 72-185383. 1977. $11.95x (ISBN 0-910190-10-0). Ayer Pr.
Gruber, Clemens. Dictionary of Advertising & Marketing. (Eng. & Ger.). 1977. pap. $15.75 (ISBN 3-1900-6312-5). Adler.
--Woerterbuch der Werbung und des Marketing. (Eng. & Ger.). 1977. pap. $15.00 (ISBN 3-19-006312-5, M-6942). French & Eur.
Herbin, Pierre. Vocabulaire de la Publicite. 148p. (Fr.). 30.00 F. Bourdine.
International Chain of Industrial & Technical Advertising Agencies. Dictionary of Advertising & Marketing Terms in Six Languages: English-Spanish-French-German-Italian-Japanese. Black, George, ed. 300p. 1982. lib. bdg. cancelled (ISBN 0-930624-03-3). Marlin.
Practical Dictionary for Press & Advertising. 256p. (Ger. , Eng. & Fr.). 1972. pap. $15.00x (ISBN 0-8002-1334-3). Intl Pubns Serv.
Urdang, Laurence, ed. Dictionary of Advertising Terms. LC 76-45506. (Orig.). 1979. pap. text ed. $15.95 (ISBN 0-87251-042-5). Crain Bks.

ADVERTISING–RETAIL TRADE
see Advertising

ADVERTISING, CONSUMER
see Advertising

ADVERTISING, RETAIL
see Advertising

AERODYNAMICS
see also Aeronautics
Anglo-Russkii Slovar Po Aerogidrodinamike. 710p. (Eng. & Rus.). 1970. $5.50 (Pub. by Sov Entsiklopediia). Four Continent.
Dictionary of Aerodynamics. 250p. (Eng. & Chinese.). 1974. pap. $5.95 (ISBN 0-686-92380-4, M-9595). French & Eur.
Kotik, M. G. Anglo-Russkii Slovar Po Aerogidrodinamike. 422p. (Eng. & Rus.). 1960. $3.65 (Pub. by Glav. Red. Inostr. Tekhn. Slovrei Fizmatgiza). Four Continent.

AERODYNAMICS, SUBSONIC
see Aerodynamics

AERONAUTICAL SPORTS
see Airplanes–Models

AERONAUTICS
see also Aerodynamics
Turchin, P. E. Russko-Frantsuzskii Aviatsionno-Tekhnicheskii Slovar. 624p. (Rus. & Fr.). 1968. $7.25 (Pub. by Sov. Entsiklopedia). Four Continent.

AERONAUTICS–ABBREVIATIONS
Murashkevich, A. M. Slovar Anglo-Amerikanskikh Sokrashchenii Po Aviatsionnoi & Raketno-Kosmicheskoi Tekhnike. 440p. (Rus. & Eng.). 1969. $5.50 (Pub. by Voenizdat). Four Continent.

AERONAUTICS–DICTIONARIES
Daoud, Hesham O. Daoud's Aviation Dictionary. 1972. pap. $8.00 (ISBN 0-911720-55-3, Pub. by Daouds). Aviation.
Darcy, H. L., ed. Luftfahrtechisches Worterbuch, Deutsch-English. (Dictionary of Aviation Ser.). 312p. (Ger. & Eng.). 1960. $33.50 (ISBN 3-11-000723-1, M-7545, Pub. by Walter de Gruyter, Inc.). French & Eur.
Demaison, H. Dictionnaire Technologique: Aeronautique, Vol. 3. 671p. (Eng., Fr., & Span.). 1978. 350.00 F. Maison Dictionnaire.
Dictionnaire des Techniques Aeronautiques & Spatiales. LC 78-394540. 374p. (Eng. , Fr. & Ger.). 1978. write for info. (ISBN 2-0401-0124-1). Bordas.
Dictionnaire des Techniques Aeronautiques et Spatiales-- Trilingue: Francais, Anglais, Allemand: 24,000 Entrees Dans Chaque Langue. 1200p. (Fr., Eng. & Ger.). 1978. $175.00 (ISBN 2-04-010124-1, M-6131). French & Eur.
Domanski, Jerzy. Tysiac Slow o Samolocie i Lotnictwie. LC 79-392676. 422p. (Pol., Warsaw, Poland). 1978. 70.00 Zl. Wydaw. Min. Obrony Narodowej.
Dorian, A. & Osenton, J. Fachwoerterbuch der Luftfahrt. (Eng., Fr., Span., Ital., Port & Ger., Dictionary of Aviation). 1964. $75.00 (ISBN 3-486-30971-4, M-7389, Pub. by R. Oldenbourg). French & Eur.
Dragovic, J. English-Russian-Serbocroatian Aviations Dictionary. 460p. (Eng., Rus. & Serbocroation.). 1973. Leatherette $35.00 (ISBN 0-686-92266-2, M-9632). French & Eur.
English-Chinese Dictionary of Aeronautical Engineering. 367p. (Eng. & Chinese.). 1975. Leatherette $25.00 (ISBN 0-686-92353-7, M-9257). French & Eur.
Fernandez-Martinez, F. Diccionario Tecnico de Aeronautica. (Span.). 1983. write for info. Paraninfo.
Foye, James & Crane, Dale. Aviation Technical Dictionary. 1978. pap. $3.95 (ISBN 0-89100-089-5). Aviation Maint.

Gentle, E. J. & Reithmaier, L. W. Aviation-Space Dictionary. 6th ed. LC 80-67567. (Illus.). 1980. $18.95 (ISBN 0-8168-3002-9). Aero.

Guilbert, Louis. La Formation du Vocabulaire de L'Aviation. 712p. (Fr.). 1966. $37.50 (ISBN 0-686-57276-9, F-135660). French & Eur.

Gunston, Bill. Jane's Aerospace Dictionary. 492p. 1980. $34.95 (ISBN 0-86720-573-3). Jane's Pub Inc.

Henry, Louis. Dictionnaire Aerotechnique Anglais-Francais. 3rd ed. 576p. (Fr.). 51.40 F. Petit.

Hiebeler, Toni. Lexikon der Aero & Astronautik Einschliesslich Raketentechnik: Lexikon der Alpen. (Ger.). 1972. write for info. (ISBN 3-920902-07-6). Sokoll.

Instituto Americano. Vocabulario Tecnologico Aeronautico. 2nd ed. LC 77-556591. 77p. (Eng. & Span.). 1976. write for info. (ISBN 8-4353-0618-6). Inst Amer.

Konarski, M. M. Russian-English Dictionary of Modern Terms in Aeronautics & Rocketry. (Rus. & Eng.). 1962. $88.00 (ISBN 0-08-009658-1). Pergamon.

Lexikon der Aero und Astronautik Enischliesslich Raketentechnik. (Ger.). 1972. write for info. (ISBN 3-920902-07-6, M-7282). French & Eur.

Ministry of Education. Scientific Terms, Aeronautics: Japanese-English, English-Japanese. 235p. (Japanese & Eng.). 1973. leatherette $19.95 (ISBN 0-686-92173-9, M-9347). French & Eur.

Osenton, J. Fachwoerterbuch der Luftfahrt. (Eng., Fr., Span., Ital., Portuguese & Ger.). 1964. DM.75.00 (ISBN 3-486-30971-4). Oldenbourg Verlag.

Rosario. Diccionario de Terminos Aerauticos. (Eng. & Span.). write for info. (A-37343). French & Eur.

Schlomann, A. Illustrierter Technische Woerterbucher: Luffahrts, Vol. 17. (Illus., Ger., Eng., Fr., Rus., Span. & It., Aeronautics). 1956. $62.50 (ISBN 0-686-56488-X, M-7475, Pub. by R. Oldenbourg). French & Eur.

--Illustrierter Technische Woerterbucher: Luffahrts, Vol. 17. (Illus., Ger., Eng., Fr., Rus., Span. & Ital.). 1956. $62.50. Oldenbourg Verlag.

Societe Nationale Industrielle Aerospatiale, ed. Dictionnaire Des Techniques Aeronautiques et Spatiales. 2nd ed. Orig. Title: Aerospace Technical Dictionary. 1152p. (Eng., Fr. & Ger.). 1978. $165.00x (ISBN 2-04-010124-1). Intl Pubns Serv.

Stepanets, A. T. Illiustrirovannyi Aviatsionnyi Slovar Dlia Molodezhi. 454p. (Rus.). 1964. $4.85 (Pub. by Dosaaf). Four Continent.

Wragg, David. A Dictionary of Aviation. LC 74-75382. 286p. 1974. $9.95 (ISBN 0-8119-0236-6). Fell.

Wragg, David W. Dictionary of Aviation. 286p. 1973. $17.95x (ISBN 0-8464-0331-5). Beekman Pubs.

Zimaity, M. A. Aeronautic Engineering Dictionary: English-French-German-Arabic. Abd-el-Washed, ed. 369p. (Eng., Fr., Ger. & Arabic). 1976. $45.00 (ISBN 0-686-92564-5, M-9764). French & Eur.

AERONAUTICS–MEDICAL ASPECTS
see Aviation Medicine
AERONAUTICS–TERMINOLOGY
Balter, Deborah J. Primary Aeronautical Language Manual. 1980. pap. $30.95 (ISBN 0-941456-00-5). Aviation.

Diccionario Tecnic Aeronautico Espanol-Ingles: Tomo 2. 106p. (Span. & Eng.). 1980. pap. write for info. (ISBN 84-300-3349-1). Autor.

Diccionario Tecnico Aeronautico Espanol-Ingles-Espanol, 6 vols. 1628p. (Span. & Eng.). 1980. pap. write for info. (ISBN 84-300-3345-9). Autor.

Diccionario Tecnico Aeronautico Espanol-Ingles, Tomo 1. 227p. (Span. & Eng.). 1980. pap. write for info. (ISBN 84-300-3347-5). Autor.

Diccionario Tecnico Aeronautico Espanol-Ingles, Tomo 3. 459p. (Span. & Eng.). 1980. pap. write for info. (ISBN 84-300-3351-3). Autor.

Diccionario Tecnico Aeronautico Ingles-Espanol, Tomo 1. 247p. (Eng. & Span.). 1980. pap. write for info. (ISBN 84-300-3346-7). Autor.

Diccionario Tecnico Aeronautico Ingles-Espanol, Tomo 3. 479p. (Eng. & Span.). 1980. pap. write for info. (ISBN 84-300-3350-5). Autor.

Diccionario Tecnico Aeronautico Ingles-Espanol, Tomo 200246207x. 110p. (Eng. & Span.). 1980. pap. write for info. (ISBN 84-300-3348-3). Autor.

Rosario, et al. Diccionario de Terminos Aeronauticos: Ingles-Espanol & Espanol-Ingles. (Eng. & Span.). 1983. write for info. ptas. Paraninfo.

AESTHETICS
see Esthetics
AFFECTION
see Love
AFGHAN LANGUAGE
see Pushto Language
AFGHANISTAN
see also names of regions, cities, etc. in Afghanistan
Hanifi, M. Jamil. Historical & Cultural Dictionary of Afghanistan. LC 75-40249. (Historical & Cultural Dictionaries of Asia Ser.: No. 5). 1976. $15.00 (ISBN 0-8108-0892-7). Scarecrow.

AFRICA
see also names of countries or regions of Africa, e.g. Egypt, Congo, Ghana, Sahara, etc. geographic subdivisions of Africa e.g. Africa, East; Africa, Sub-Saharan
Nunez, Benjamin. Dictionary of Afro-Latin American Civilization. LC 79-7731. (Illus.). xxxv, 525p. 1980. lib. bdg. $45.00 (ISBN 0-313-21138-8, NAL/). Greenwood.

AFRICA–JUVENILE LITERATURE
Hornburger. African Countries & Cultures. 1981. $13.95 (ISBN 0-679-20507-1). McKay.

AFRICA–LANGUAGES
Dalgish, Gerard M. A Dictionary of Africanisms: Contributions of Sub-Saharan Africa to the English Language. LC 82-9366. xviii, 203p. 1982. lib. bdg. $35.00 (ISBN 0-313-23585-6, DDA/). Greenwood.

Fischer, A. Lumko English-Xhosa Dictionary. (Eng. & Khosa). 1982. $39.95x (ISBN 0-19-570290-5). Oxford U Pr.

AFRICA–POLITICS AND GOVERNMENT
Phillips, Claude S. The African Political Dictionary. (Clio Dictionaries in Political Science: No. 5). (Illus.). 300p. 1983. lib. bdg. $20.75 (ISBN 0-87436-036-6); pap. $10.75 (ISBN 0-87436-040-4). ABC-Clio.

AFRICA, CENTRAL–HISTORY
Kalck, Pierre. Historical Dictionary of the Central African Republic. O'Toole, Thomas, tr. LC 80-21199. (African Historical Dictionaries Ser.: No. 27). 194p. 1980. $13.00 (ISBN 0-8108-1360-2). Scarecrow.

AFRICAN LANGUAGES
see also names of languages, e.g. Bantu Languages; Fulah Language; also subdivision Languages under names of African countries, regions, etc., e.g. Nigeria–Languages
Barth, Heinrich, ed. Collection of Vocabularies of Central African Languages, 2 vols. 1971. Repr. of 1862 ed. Set. $120.00x (ISBN 0-7146-1914-0, F Cass Co). Biblio Dist.

Bleek, Dorothea F. A Bushman Dictionary. (American Oriental Society: Vol. 41). 1956. pap. $11.00x (ISBN 0-940490-41-2). Am Orient Soc.

Hendrix, Melvin K. An International Bibliography of African Lexicons. LC 81-16533. 370p. 1982. $22.50 (ISBN 0-8108-1478-1). Scarecrow.

Hoeftmann, Hildegard. The Structure of Lelemi Language. 130p. 1973. $17.50x (ISBN 0-8002-1344-0). Intl Pubns Serv.

Kotapish, Carl & Kotapish, Sharon. A Darai-English, English-Darai Glossary. LC 76-904757. xi, 152p. (Eng. & Darai). 1975. Rs.20.00. Summer Inst Abor.

Murphy, John D. Luganda-English Dictionary. (Publications in the Languages of Africa Ser.: No. 2). (Luganda & Eng.). 1973. $36.95 (ISBN 0-8132-0525-5). Cath U Pr.

Tisserant, C. Dictionnaire Banda-Francais. 611p. (Fr. & Banda). 1931. 66.20 F. Institut Ethnologie.

Tisserant, Ch. Dictionnaire Banda-Francais. 611p. (Banda-Fr.). 1931. $32.50 (ISBN 0-686-56789-7, M-6585, Pub. by Institut Ethnologie). French & Eur.

Turvey, B., compiled by. Kwanyama-English Dictionary. LC 78-306064. xvii, 162p. (Kuanyama & Eng.). 1977. write for info. (ISBN 0-85494-315-3). Witwatersrand.

Wynne, R. C. English-Mbukushu Dictionary. 615p. (Eng. & Mbukushu). 1980. text ed. $45.00x (ISBN 0-86127-203-X, Pub. by Avebury England). Humanities.

AFRICAN LYMPHONA
see Burkitt's Lymphoma
AFRIKAANS LANGUAGE
Coetzee, A. African-English, English-African Dictionary. (African & Eng.). $22.50 (ISBN 0-87559-000-4); thumb indexed $27.50 (ISBN 0-87559-001-2). Shalom.

DuPlessis, E. Die Kennis Gids tot Moderne Afrikaans. LC 80-468749. 240p. (Afrikaans). 1979. write for info. (ISBN 0-7981-0916-5). Human & Rousseau.

Kriel, T. Popular Northern Sotho Dictionary. 2nd ed. LC 77-363921. 342p. (Eng. & Sotho). 1976. write for info. (ISBN 0-627-00932-8). Van Schaik.

Kritzinger, M. S. Afrikaans-English, English-Afrikaans Dictionary. 12th, rev., enl. ed. (Afrikaans & Eng.). $60.00 (ISBN 0-627-01082-2). Heinman.

Munnik, Eulalie. Afrikaanse Verklarende Woordeboek vir Biologie. LC 80-451787. 152p. (Afrikaan). 1979. R.3.80 (ISBN 0-620-03588-9). Knaggs Assoc.

Viljoen, Johannes J. Ndonga, Afrikaans, English: Dreitalige Woordeboek. LC 76-479622. 89p. (Ndonga, Afrikaans & Eng.). 1975. write for info. (ISBN 0-627-00328-1). Van Schaik.

Ziervogel, D. Groot Noord-Sotho-Woordeboek. LC 76-516085. 1536p. (Sotho). 1975. write for info. (ISBN 0-627-00366-4). Van Schaik.

AFRO-AMERICAN AUTHORS
This heading used beginning January 1976. See Negro Authors for earlier works.
see also American Literature–Afro-American Authors
New York Public Library. Dictionary Catalog of the Schomburg Collection of Negro Literature & History, Supplement 1974. 1976. lib. bdg. $105.00 (ISBN 0-8161-0062-4, Hall Library). G K Hall.

AFRO-AMERICAN DIALECT
see Black English
AFRO-AMERICAN ENGLISH
see Black English
AFRO-AMERICAN LITERATURE (ENGLISH)
see American Literature–Afro-American Authors
AFRO-AMERICANS–HISTORY
This heading used beginning January 1976. See Negroes–History for earlier works.
The Dictionary Catalog of the Vivian G. Harsh Collection of Afro-American History & Literature: Chicago Public Library, 4 vols. 1978. Set. lib. bdg. $352.00 (ISBN 0-8161-0252-X, Hall Library). G K Hall.

Howard University Library, Washington, D.C. Dictionary Catalog of the Jesse E. Moorland Collection of Negro Life & History, First Supplement, 3 vols. 1976. lib. bdg. $350.00 (ISBN 0-8161-0944-3, Hall Library). G K Hall.

AGE OF ROCKS
see Geology, Stratigraphic
AGGREGATES
see Set Theory
AGRARIAN QUESTION
see Agriculture–Economic Aspects
AGRIBUSINESS
see Agriculture–Economic Aspects
AGRICULTURAL ASSOCIATIONS
see Agricultural Societies
AGRICULTURAL BANKS
see Banks and Banking
AGRICULTURAL BOTANY
see Botany, Economic
AGRICULTURAL CLUBS
see Agricultural Societies
AGRICULTURAL ECONOMICS
see Agriculture–Economic Aspects
AGRICULTURAL EDUCATION
Elements of the Structure & Terminology of Agricultural Education in India. 82p. 1982. pap. $11.50 (ISBN 92-3-101866-3, U1170, UNESCO). Unipub.

AGRICULTURAL ENGINEERING
see also Drainage; Irrigation
Dictionnaire Technique de la Mecanisation Agricole. (Fr. , Eng. , Ger. , Span. & Ital., Technical Dictionary of Agricultural Mechanics). 1968-70. pap. $59.95 (ISBN 0-686-56723-4, M-6155). French & Eur.

Dictionnaire Technique de la Mecanisation Agricole: Francais-Anglais-Allemand-Espagnol-Italien, 3 vols. (Fr. , Eng. , Ger. , Span. & Ital.). 125.00 F. Centre Nat. Et. Machin Agricole.

Farrall, Arthur W. & Basselman, James A. Dictionary of Agricultural & Food Engineering. LC 78-71856. 1979. $17.50 (ISBN 0-8134-2023-7, 2023). Interstate.

Lexique Methodique Illustre du Machinisme Agricole, 1. (Illus., Fr.). 36.00 F. Centre Nat. & Machin Agricole.

Wahed, Abd El. Agricultural Engineering Dictionary: English-French-German-Arabic. 446p. (Eng., Fr., Ger. & Arabic). 1977. $45.00 (ISBN 0-686-92251-4, M-9761). French & Eur.

AGRICULTURAL LAWS AND LEGISLATION
Arlt, Reiner, et al, eds. Lexikon Recht der Landwirtschaft der Deutschen Demokratischen Republik. LC 76-487653. 397p. (Ger.). 1975. M.10.50. Staatsdruk.

AGRICULTURAL MECHANICS
see Agricultural Engineering
AGRICULTURAL PESTS
see also Fungi in Agriculture; Insects, Injurious and Beneficial; Plant Diseases; Weeds
also subdivision Diseases and Pests under names of crops, etc., Fruit–Diseases and Pests
Kwizda, R. Vocabularium Nocentium Florae. 4th ed. (Lat.). 1963. pap. $23.50 (ISBN 0-387-80646-6). Springer-Verlag.

Merino-Rodriguez, Manuel, ed. Lexicon of Plant Pests & Diseases. (Eng., Lat., Fr., Span., Ital. & Ger., Polyglot). 1966. $70.25 (ISBN 0-444-40393-0). Elsevier.

AGRICULTURAL SOCIETIES
Faure, Robert. Le Dictionnaire de L'agriculture. 8th ed. LC 76-469040. 295p. (Fr.). 1976. 98.00 F. Doc Univers.

AGRICULTURE
see also Botany, Economic; Drainage; Field Crops; Food Industry and Trade; Forests and Forestry; Fruit; Grain; Grasses; Horticulture; Insects, Injurious and Beneficial; Irrigation; Livestock; Pastures; Soil Science; Soils; Trees; Vegetables
also headings beginning with the word Agricultural, and names of agricultural products
Ergo, A. B., et al. Thesaurus des Symboles Agrobioclimatiques, Geographiques & Techniques, 4. 531p. (Fr.). 1974. 535.00 F. Centre Informatique Develop.

Henry, J. M. & Ergo, A. B. Thesaurus des Symboles Agrobioclimatiques, Geographiques & Techniques, 3. 270p. (Fr.). 1973. 450.00 F. Centre Informatique Develop.

Petit, J. L., et al. Thesaurus des Symboles Agrobioclimatiques, Geographiques & Techniques, 2 vols. (Illus.). 686p. (Fr.). 1971. 2240.00 F. Centre Informatique Develop.

Vocabulaire d'initation aux Etudes Agronomiques. (Fr.). 5.40 F. C. R. E. D. I. F.

AGRICULTURE–BIBLIOGRAPHY

Dictionary Catalog of the National Agricultural Library, 1862-1965, 73 Vols. 56500p. Set. $1460.00x (ISBN 0-87471-001-4). Rowman.

AGRICULTURE–DICTIONARIES, INDEXES, ETC.

Abbreviations Used by FAO for International Congresses, Commissions, Etc. (Terminology Bulletin Ser.: No. 27, R. 2). 144p. 1979. pap. $9.75 (ISBN 0-686-72305-8, F2056, FAO). Unipub.

Carena, A. Dizionario di agricoltura, 2 vols. xii, 1914p. (Ital.). 1956. L.40000.00 (ISBN 88-02-01492-2). UTET.

Chihabi. Agriculture, Forestry, & Allied Terminology Dictionary: English-Arabic with Arabic Glossary. Khatib, A., ed. (Eng. & Arabic.). 1978. $40.00x (ISBN 0-86685-072-4). Intl Bk Ctr.

Commission of the European Communities, Directorate-General for Research, Science & Education, ed. Agricultural Economics & Rural Sociology: Multilingual Thesaurus. 2nd ed. Incl. Vol. 1. German. 80p. (Ger.); Vol. 2. English. 84p. pap. 68.00 (ISBN 0-686-81238-7); Vol. 3. French. 84p. (Fr.); Vol. 4. Italian. 78p. (Italian.); Vol. 5. Quadrilingual Index. 130p. (Eng., Fr., Ger. & Ital.). 1979. Set. pap. $200.00x (ISBN 3-598-10097-3, Pub. by K G Saur); 16 microfiches incl. Gale.

Dabbs, Jack A. Glossary of Agricultural Terms, English-Bengali. LC 79-626525. (Eng. & Bengali.). 1969. $3.00 (ISBN 0-911494-05-7). Dabbs.

Dalal-Clayton, D. B., ed. Black's Agricultural Dictionary. (Illus.). 512p. 1981. $28.50x (ISBN 0-389-20261-4, 07079). B&N Imports.

Deane, Samuel. The New England Farmer; or, Georgical Dictionary. LC 72-5043. (Technology & Society Ser.). 543p. 1972. Repr. of 1822 ed. $25.00 (ISBN 0-405-04695-2). Ayer Co.

Diccionari de agriculatura ruso-espanol. (Rus. & Span.). Mex.$30.00. Cultura Popular.

Diccionario de agricultura ruso-espanol. (Rus. & Span.). $1.00. Pueblos Unidos.

Dictionary of Soil Science & Soil Engineering Terms. (Hebrew, Eng. , Ger. & Fr.). IL.8.00. Massada Pr.

Dictionnaire-Annuaire de l'agriculture. 152p. (Fr.). 1975. 89.00 F. Faure.

Dictionnaire d'Agriculture. (Fr.). 1976. $45.00 (ISBN 0-686-57095-2, M-6119). French & Eur.

Dictionnaire d'agriculture. (Fr.). 1976. write for info. C. I. L. F.

Farrall, Arthur W. & Basselman, James A. Dictionary of Agricultural & Food Engineering. LC 78-71856. 1979. $17.50 (ISBN 0-8134-2023-7, 2023). Interstate.

Favati, F. Dizionario di Agricoltura. (Illus.). x, 990p. (Ital.). 1983. write for info. Ed Calderini.

Favati, Franco. Dizionario di agricoltura: English-italian e italiano-inglese. (Illus.). x, 990p. (Eng. & Ital.). 1973. L.20000.00 (ISBN 88-206-0667-4). Edagricole.

Gorgoni, G. Vocabolario agronomico nel dialetto della provincia de Lecce. viii, 515p. (Ital.). L.23000.00. Forni.

Habibi, B. Deutsch-Persisches Fachwoerterbuch Fuer Naturwissenschaft, Medezin und Landwirtschaft. 240p. (Ger. & Persian.). 1964. pap. $17.50 (ISBN 3-447-00354-5, M-7331, Pub. by Harrassowitz). French & Eur.

Haensch, G. Dictionary of Agriculture. 3rd ed. 1963. $29.80 (ISBN 0-444-40266-7). Elsevier.

--Dictionary of Agriculture in German, French, Spanish, & Russian. 4th ed. De Anton, Haberkamp G., ed. 1000p. (Ger., Fr., Span. & Rus.). 1976. $110.75 (ISBN 0-444-99849-7). Elsevier.

Haensch, Guenther. Woerterbuch der Landwirtschaft. 4th ed. (Ger., Eng., Fr. & Span., Dictionary of Agriculture). 1975. pap. $99.50 (ISBN 3-405-10950-7, M-6984). French & Eur.

Haensch, Gunther. Dictionnaire Agricole Allemand-Anglais-Francais-Espagnol-Russe. 4th ed. (Illus.). 746p. (Ger., Eng., Fr., Span. & Rus.). 1975. 260.00 F. pap. $170.00. Maison Rustique.

Haensch, Gunther & Haberkamp, Gisela. Dictionnaire Agricole Allemand, Anglais, Francais, Espagnol, Russe. 4th ed. 746p. (Ger., Eng., Fr., Span. & Rus., Agriculture Dictionary, German, English, French, Spanish, Russian). 1975. $69.95 (ISBN 0-686-56783-8, M-6579, Pub. by Maison Rust). French & Eur.

--Dictionnaire agricole Allemand, Anglais, Francais, Espanol, Russe. 4th ed. 746p. (Ger., Fr., Span., Rus.). 1975. 69.95 F. Maison Rustique.

Istilah pertanian, bahasa Ingeris-bahasa Malaysia, bahasa Malaysia-bahasa Inggeris. LC 80-942013. xviii, 276p. (Eng. & Malay.). 1980. M.$pap. 4.00. Dewan Bahasa.

Khatib, Ahmad. Arabic-English Dictionary of Agricultural Terms & Allied Terminology. (Arabic & Eng.). pap. $10.00x (ISBN 0-86685-274-3). Intl Bk Ctr.

--A Dictionary of Agricultural & Allied Terminology. 88p. (Arabic & Eng.). pap. $10.00 (274-3). Intl Bk Ctr.

Landwirtschaftliches Woerterbuch in Acht Sprachen, 2 vols. (Ger. , Eng. , Rus. , Bulg. , Hungarian , Czech. & Pol., Dictionary of Agriculture in Eight Languages). 1971. $225.00 (ISBN 3-405-11076-9, M-7532, Pub. by BLV). French & Eur.

Lexikon der Neuzeitlichen Landwirtschaft, 3 vols. 776p. (Ger.). 1973. DM.75.00 (ISBN 3-7736-8002-3). Girardet.

Lexikon der Neuzeitlichen Landwirtschaft, Vol. 1. 9th ed. (Ger.). 1973. $25.00 (ISBN 3-7736-8003-1, M-7242). French & Eur.

Lexikon der Neuzeitlichen Landwirtschaft, Vol. 2. 9th ed. (Ger.). 1974. $25.00 (ISBN 3-7736-8004-X, M-7243). French & Eur.

Lexikon der Neuzeitlichen Landwirtschaft, Vol. 3. 9th ed. (Ger.). 1974. $25.00 (ISBN 3-7736-8005-8, M-7244). French & Eur.

Lexikon der Neuzeittlichen Landwirtschaft: Bd 1, Tierernaehrung, Tierzucht, Tierhaltung. 257p. (Ger.). 1974. DM.29.00 (ISBN 3-7736-8003-1). Girardet.

Lexikon der Neuzeittlichen Landwirtschaft: Bd 2, Ackerbau, Pflanzenbau, Gruenlandwirtschaft. 252p. (Ger.). 1974. DM.29.00 (ISBN 3-7736-8004-X). Girardet.

Mauroy, L. N. Dictionnaire d'Agriculture. Migne, J. P., ed. (Nouvelle Encyclopedie Theologique Ser.: Vol. 28). 726p. (Fr.). Repr. of 1862 ed. lib. bdg. $92.50x (ISBN 0-89241-271-2). Caratzas Pub Co.

Miyayama, H., et al. A Glossary of Agricultural Terms. 261p. (Eng. & Japanese.). 1975. $39.95 (ISBN 0-686-92558-0, M-9345). French & Eur.

Nelvik, Nikolai. Norsk Landbruksordbok, 2 vols. LC 79-377494. (Eng. & Norwegian.). 1979. write for info. (ISBN 8-2521-0870-9). Samlaget.

Sanchez Monge y Parellada, Enrique. Diccionario de Plantas Agricolas. 468p. (Span.). 1981. 2250.00 ptas (ISBN 84-7479-098-0). Minist Agricultura.

Soroa. Diccionario de agricultura. (Span.). 1375.00 ptas. Labor.

Thesaurus of Agricultural Terms. 2nd ed. LC 78-61381. 1978. lib. bdg. $27.50x (ISBN 0-912700-45-9). Oryx Pr.

Winburne, John N., et al, eds. Dictionary of Agricultural & Allied Terminology. 906p. 1962. $24.95x (ISBN 0-87013-067-6). Mich St U Pr.

AGRICULTURE–ECONOMIC ASPECTS

Lexikon der Neuzeittlichen Landwirtschaft: Bd 3, Belriebswirtschaft, Markt, Recht. 267p. (Ger.). 1974. DM.29.00 (ISBN 3-7736-8005-8). Girardet.

University of California - Berkeley. Dictionary Catalog of the Giannini Foundation of Agricultural Economics Library, 12 vols. 1971. $1140.00 (ISBN 0-8161-0908-7, Hall Library). G K Hall.

AGRICULTURE–LAWS AND LEGISLATION

see Agricultural Laws and Legislation

AGRICULTURE–POLITICAL ASPECTS

see Agriculture and Politics

AGRICULTURE–CHINA

A Chinese-English Dictionary of China's Rural Economy. (Chinese & Eng.). 1979. $70.00 (ISBN 0-85198-381-2, CAB 6, CAB). Unipub.

AGRICULTURE–INDIA

Elements of the Structure & Terminology of Agricultural Education in India. 82p. 1982. pap. $11.50 (ISBN 92-3-101866-3, U1170, UNESCO). Unipub.

AGRICULTURE AND POLITICS

Bremer, R., et al. Woerterbuch der Agrarpolitik. 175p. (Ger.). 1961. DM.9.80 (ISBN 3-490-01315-8). Parey.

AGRONOMY

see Agriculture

AGROSTOLOGY

see Grasses

AGUE

see Malaria

AIR–POLLUTION

American Lung Association. A Glossary on Air Pollution. 8p. avail. (0450). Am Lung Assn.

Thesaurus Pollution Atmospherique. 158p. (Fr.). 1973. 107.00 F. I. F. C. E.

AIR, MOISTURE OF

see Humidity

AIR CONDITIONING

see also Refrigeration and Refrigerating Machinery; Ventilation also specific subject with or without subdivision air-conditioning, e.g. Dwellings–Air conditioning

American Society of Heating, Refrigerating & Air-Conditioning Engineers. Automatic Control Terminology for Heating, Ventilating, Air Conditioning & Refrigeration Equipment. (Illus.). $14.00 (ST8578); members $7.00. Am Heat Ref & Air Eng.

Applied Technical Dictionary: Air Conditioning & Refrigeration. (Eng. , Ger. , Fr , Rus. & Slovak.). $69.00x (ISBN 0-569-08534-9, Pub. by Collets). State Mutual Bk.

Booth, K. M. Dictionary of Refrigeration & Air Conditioning. 1970. $29.90x (ISBN 0-444-20069-X, Pub. by Applied Science). Burgess-Intl Ideas.

Booth, K. M., ed. Dictionary of Refrigeration & Air Conditioning. 1971. $30.75 (ISBN 0-444-20069-X). Elsevier.

European Heating & Ventilating Associations, ed. The International Dictionary of Heating, Ventilating, & Air Conditioning. LC 79-41714. 416p. 1982. $79.95x (ISBN 0-419-11650-8, NO. 6553, E&FN Spon England). Methuen Inc.

Haeder, Walter & Reichow, Guenther. Lexikon der Heizungs, Lueftungs & Klimatechnik. (Ger.). 1978. write for info. (ISBN 3-7864-1448-3). Langenscheidt.

Heinrich, Gunter. Woerterbuch Klima & Kaltetechnik. LC 79-349127. 404p. (Eng., Ger., Fr & Rus.). 1978. 74.00 F (ISBN 3-87144-303-4). Verlag Harri Deutsch.

Technical Dictionary: Refrigeration & Air Conditioning. (Eng. , Fr. , Ger. & Arabic.). 1979. $35.00x (ISBN 0-686-44746-8, Pub. by Collets). State Mutual Bk.

AIR NAVIGATION

see Aeronautics

AIR POLLUTION

see Air–Pollution

AIRPLANES–AERODYNAMICS

see Aerodynamics

AIRPLANES–MAINTENANCE AND REPAIR

Crane, Dale, et al. Aircraft Technical Dictionary. 2nd ed. (Aviation Maintenance Training Course Ser.). pap. write for info. (ISBN 0-89100-124-7). Aviation Maintenance.

AIRPLANES–MODELS

Thies, Werner. Modellflug-Lexikon. LC 80-470206. 269p. (Ger.). 1977. DM.28.00 (ISBN 3-88180-001-8). Verlag Technik.

AKKADIAN (EAST SEMITIC) LANGUAGE

see Assyro-Babylonian Language

AKUAPEM LANGUAGE

see Twi Language

AKWAPIM LANGUAGE

see Twi Language

ALBANIAN LANGUAGE

Albanian-English & English Albanian Dictionary. (Albanian & Eng.). $27.50 (ISBN 0-87557-001-1, 001-1). Saphrograph.

Cordignano, F. Dizionario Italiano-Albanese. xii, 758p. (Ital. & Albanian.). L.26000.00. Forni.

Drizari, Nelo. Albanian-English, English-Albanian Dictionary. LC 57-9330. (Albanian & Eng.). $20.00 (ISBN 0-8044-0130-6). Ungar.

Kici, Gasper. Albanian-English Dictionary. (Albanian & Eng.). 1976. $15.00 (ISBN 0-686-17904-8). G Kici.

Kici, Gasper & Aliko, Hysni. English-Albanian Dictionary. (Eng. & Albanian.). 1969. $15.00 (ISBN 0-686-04914-4). G Kici.

Kostallari, A. Karmannyi Russko-Albanskii Slovar. 428p. (Rus. & Albanian.). 1959. $1.50. Four Continent.

ALCHEMY

see also Magic

Gettings, Fred. Dictionary of Occult, Hermetic & Alchemical Sigils. 1981. $40.00 (ISBN 0-7100-0095-2). Routledge & Kegan.

Testi, Gino. Dizionario di alchimia e di chimica antiquaria. (Illus.). 300p. (Ital.). 1950. L.4000.00. Edizioni Mediterranee.

ALCOHOL INTOXICATION

see Alcoholism

ALCOHOLIC BEVERAGE INDUSTRY

see Brewing Industry; Distilling Industries; Wine and Wine Making

ALCOHOLIC BEVERAGES

see also Temperance; Wine and Wine Making

Allison, Norman & Allison, Sonia. Drinks Dictionary. LC 78-317531. (Illus.). 154p. 1978. E2.25 (ISBN 0-00-435220-3); pap. write for info. (ISBN 0-00-435221-1). W Collins Sons.

ALCOHOLISM

Keller, M., et al. A Dictionary of Words About Alcohol. 2nd, Rev. ed. LC 81-620046. xxviii, 291p. 1982. $19.50x (ISBN 0-911290-12-5). Rutgers Ctr Al.

ALCORAN

see Koran

ALEUT LANGUAGE

Lee, Charles A. Aleutian Indian & English Dictionary. facsimile ed. 23p. (Aleut.). Repr. of 1896 ed. pap. $9.95 (ISBN 0-8466-0101-X, SJS101). Shorey.

ALGEBRA

see also Mathematical Analysis

Howson, A. G. A Handbook of Terms Used in Algebra & Analysis. LC 71-178281. (Illus.). 260p. 1972. $35.50 (ISBN 0-521-08434-2); pap. $14.95 (ISBN 0-521-09695-2). Cambridge U Pr.

ALGEBRA OF LOGIC

see Logic, Symbolic and Mathematical

ALGERIA–HISTORY
Heggoy, Alf A. & Crout, Robert R. Historical Dictionary of Algeria. LC 80-24126. (African Historical Dictionaries Ser.: No. 28). x, 247p. 1981. $15.00 (ISBN 0-8108-1376-9). Scarecrow.

ALGOL (COMPUTER PROGRAM LANGUAGE)
Breuer, Hans. Dictionary for Computer Languages. (Automatic Programming Information Centre Studies in Data Processing: Vol. 6). 1966. $65.00 (ISBN 0-12-132950-X). Acad Pr.

ALGORITHMIC LANGUAGE
see ALGOL (Computer Program Language)

ALIENS
Institut International de Terminologie Juridique & Administrative. Niederlassungsrecht. 145p. (Ger. & Fr.). 1976. DM.15.80. Langen AG.

ALIMENTATION
see Nutrition

ALKORAN
see Koran

ALLERGY
Wilken-Jensen, K. Lexikon Allergologicum. 1965. $16.25 (ISBN 0-08-011838-0). Pergamon.

ALLEYS
see Streets

ALLUSIONS
see also Terms and Phrases
Smith, Eric. A Dictionary of Classical Allusion in English Literature. LC 83-12273. 256p. 1983. $39.50x (ISBN 0-389-20430-7). B&N Imports.

ALMANACS
see also Calendars; Chronology; Yearbooks
Urdang, Laurence. The World Almanac Dictionary of Dates. 320p. 1982. $8.95 (ISBN 0-911818-26-X). World Almanac.
Wittman, Alfred. Fachwoerterbuch der Datenverarbeitung. 3rd ed. (Eng., Fr. & Ger.). 1977. DM.67.50 (ISBN 3-486-39063-5). Oldenbourg Verlag.

ALMS AND ALMS-GIVING
see Charities

ALPHABET
see also Initial Teaching Alphabet
also subdivision Alphabet, or Writing under groups of languages, or under particular languages, e.g. Greek Languages–Alphabet, Chinese Language–Writing
Daughters of St. Paul. ABC's Dictionary. write for info. Dghtrs St Paul.

ALPHABET, INITIAL TEACHING
see Initial Teaching Alphabet

ALPS–DESCRIPTION AND TRAVEL–GUIDEBOOKS
Bibelriether, Hans, et al, eds. Lexikon fuer Bergfreunde. LC 77-337290. (Illus.). 256p. (Ger.). 1978. 29.80 F (ISBN 3-7658-0259-X). Bucher.

ALTERATION, CHROMATIC
see Chromatic Alteration (Music)

ALUMINUM
see also Aluminum Foil; Silicates
Kehler. Surface Treatment of Aluminum--A Glossary of Technical Terms. 1981. $11.50 (ISBN 0-9960034-1-X). Heyden.
Surface Treatment of Aluminum: Glossary of Technical Terms. LC 76-356688. 50p. (Eng. , Fr. & Ger.). 1975. write for info. (ISBN 3-87017-121-9). Aluminum Verlag.

ALUMINUM FOIL
Surface Treatment of Aluminum: Glossary of Technical Terms. LC 76-356688. 50p. (Eng. , Fr. & Ger.). 1975. write for info. (ISBN 3-87017-121-9). Aluminum Verlag.

AMARIGNA LANGUAGE
see Amharic Language

AMATEUR JOURNALISM
see Journalism

AMATEUR MOVING-PICTURES
Pollet, R. Lexique du cinema d'Amateur: Anglais-Francais Francais-Anglais. 127p. (Eng. & Fr.). 1971. 50.00 F. Maison Dictionnaire.

AMATEURISM IN SPORTS
see Professionalism in Sports

AMERICA–BIBLIOGRAPHY
Deak, Etienne. Grand Dictionnaire d'Americanismes: Contenant les Principaux Termes Americains avec Leur Equivalent Exact en Francais. 5th ed. 839p. (Fr. & Eng.). 1973. 22.50x (ISBN 0-8002-1466-8). Intl Pubns Serv.
De Alcedo, Antonio. Geographical & Historical Dictionary of America & the West Indies, 5 Vols. Thompson, George A., tr. LC 70-146788. (Research & Source Works Ser: No. 627). 1971. Repr. of 1812 ed. Set. lib. bdg. $220.00 (ISBN 0-8337-3525-X). B Franklin.
Newberry Library - Chicago. Dictionary Catalog of the Edward E. Ayer Collection of Americana & American Indians, 16 Vols. 1961. Set. $1120.00 (ISBN 0-8161-0586-3, Hall Library). G K Hall.

AMERICA–HISTORY
New York Public Library, Research Libraries. Dictionary Catalog of the History of the Americas Collection, First Supplement, 9 vols. 1974. Set. lib. bdg. $945.00 (ISBN 0-8161-0771-8, Hall Library). G K Hall.

AMERICA–HISTORY–BIBLIOGRAPHY
New York Public Library, Research Libraries. Dictionary Catalog of the History of the Americas Collection, 28 Vols. 1961. Set. lib. bdg. $2200.00 (ISBN 0-8161-0540-5, Hall Library). G K Hall.

AMERICAN ABORIGINES
see Indians; Indians of North America; Indians of South America, and similar headings

AMERICAN CIVIL WAR
see United States–History–Civil War, 1861-1865

AMERICAN COMPOSERS
see Composers, American

AMERICAN DRAMA–AFRO-AMERICAN AUTHORS–HISTORY AND CRITICISM
Woll, Allen. Dictionary of the Black Theatre: Broadway, Off-Broadway, & Selected Harlem Theatre. LC 82-21090. (Illus.). 416p. 1983. lib. bdg. $39.95 (ISBN 0-313-22561-3, WDB/). Greenwood.

AMERICAN DRAMA–BIBLIOGRAPHY
Brown University. Dictionary Catalog of the Harris Collection of American Poetry & Plays, Brown University, 13 vols. 1972. Set. lib. bdg. $1620.00 (ISBN 0-8161-0974-5, Hall Library). G K Hall.

AMERICAN ENGLISH
see English Language in the United States

AMERICAN INDIANS
see Indians; Indians of North America; Indians of South America, and similar headings

AMERICAN LITERATURE–AFRO-AMERICAN AUTHORS
see also Afro-American Authors
The Dictionary Catalog of the Vivian G. Harsh Collection of Afro-American History & Literature: Chicago Public Library, 4 vols. 1978. Set. lib. bdg. $352.00 (ISBN 0-8161-0252-X, Hall Library). G K Hall.

AMERICAN LITERATURE–BIBLIOGRAPHY–CATALOGS
New York Public Library, Research Libraries. Dictionary Catalog of the Albert A. & Henry W. Berg Collection of English & American Literature, First Supplement. 1975. lib. bdg. $105.00 (ISBN 0-8161-0014-4, Hall Library). G K Hall.
--Dictionary Catalog of the Henry W. & Albert A. Berg Collection of English & American Literature, 5 Vols. 1969. Set. lib. bdg. $465.00 (ISBN 0-8161-0870-6, Hall Library). G K Hall.

AMERICAN LITERATURE–HISTORY AND CRITICISM–19TH CENTURY
Byers, John R., Jr. & Owen, James J. A Concordance to the Five Novels of Nathaniel Hawthorne. LC 79-7910. 951p. 1979. lib. bdg. $138.00 (ISBN 0-8240-9545-6). Garland Pub.

Irey, Eugene F. A Concordance to Melville's Moby Dick. LC 82-9387. 2031p. 1982. lib. bdg. $275.00 (ISBN 0-8240-9398-4). Garland Pub.

AMERICAN POETRY–BIBLIOGRAPHY
Brown University. Dictionary Catalog of the Harris Collection of American Poetry & Plays, Brown University, 13 vols. 1972. Set. lib. bdg. $1620.00 (ISBN 0-8161-0974-5, Hall Library). G K Hall.

AMERICAN PORTRAITS
see Portraits

AMERICAN WIT AND HUMOR
Levinson, Leonard L. Left-Handed Dictionary. (Orig.). 1964. pap. $2.50 (ISBN 0-02-040550-2, Collier). Macmillan.
--Webster's Unafraid Dictionary. (Orig.). 1967. pap. $2.95 (ISBN 0-02-040540-5, Collier). Macmillan.

AMERICAN WIT AND HUMOR–MARRIAGE AND FAMILY LIFE
Goliard, Roy. Scholar's Glossary of Sex. (Illus., Orig.). 1968. pap. $1.95 (ISBN 0-685-11982-3, 20). Heineman.

AMERICAN WIT AND HUMOR, PICTORIAL
Battista, O. A. Dictionary of Quotoons. LC 66-12694. $9.95 (ISBN 0-915054-04-4). Research Servs Corp.

AMERICANISMS
Clapin, Sylvia. New Dictionary of Americanisms. LC 68-17985. 1968. Repr. of 1902 ed. $42.00x (ISBN 0-8103-3244-2). Gale.
Deak, Etienne & Deak, Simone. Dictionnaire des Americanismes. 6th ed. 928p. (Fr. & Eng.). 1974. 65.00 F. Dauphin.
Diccionario de Americanismos. 576p. (Span.). 1980. 675.00 ptas (ISBN 84-241-1504-X). Everest.
Horlacher, Friedrich W. Piccolo Dizionario Americano Italiano. LC 78-343989. 111p. (Eng. & Ital.). 1976. L.1800.00. Nuova Vallecchi.
Kenyon, John S. & Knott, Thomas A. Pronouncing Dictionary of American English. 2nd ed. 1953. $7.95 (ISBN 0-87779-047-7). Merriam-Webster Inc.
Landau, Sidney & Bogus, Ronald, eds. Doubleday Roget's Thesaurus in Dictionary Form. LC 76-7696. 564p. 1977. $9.95 (ISBN 0-385-01236-5); thumb-indexed $11.95 (ISBN 0-385-12379-5). Doubleday.
Malaret, Augusto. Diccionario De Americanismos. 1977. lib. bdg. $75.00 (ISBN 0-8490-1717-3). Gordon Pr.
Mathews, Mitford M., ed. Americanisms: A Dictionary of Selected Americanisms on Historical Principles. LC 69-19279. (Orig.). 1966. pap. $1.95 (ISBN 0-226-51012-3, P229, Phoen). U of Chicago Pr.
Morinigo, Marcos A. Diccionario de Americanismos. (Span.). $35.00 (ISBN 0-686-56690-4, S-12121). French & Eur.
--Diccionario de Americanismos. (Span.). $20.00. SEI.
Partridge, Eric. Dictionary of Slang & Unconventional English. 7th ed. 1970. $45.00 (ISBN 0-02-594970-5). Macmillan.
Pickering, John. A Vocabulary; or, Collection of Words & Phrases, Which Have Been Supposed to Be Peculiar to the United States of America; to Which Is Prefixed an Essay on the Present State of the English Language in the United States, 2 vols. in 1. Bd. with A Letter to John Pickering on the Subject of His Vocabulary or Collection of Words & Phrases. Webster, Noah. LC 70-178096. vii, 266p. 1972. Repr. of 1817 ed. lib. bdg. $24.00 (ISBN 0-8337-2752-4). B Franklin.
Watts, Peter. A Dictionary of the Old West. 1977. $12.95 (ISBN 0-394-49043-4). Knopf.
Wentworth, Harold & Flexner, Stuart B. Dictionary of American Slang. 2nd ed. LC 75-8644. 766p. 1975. $15.34i (ISBN 0-690-00670-5). T Y Crowell.
--Pocket Dictionary of American Slang. abr. ed. 1968. pap. $3.95 (ISBN 0-671-78976-7). PB.

Williams, Roger. Key into the Language of America. 5th ed. LC 70-157500. Repr. of 1643 ed. $43.00x (ISBN 0-8103-3723-1). Gale.

AMHARIC LANGUAGE
Leslau, Wolf. Concise Amharic Dictionary. LC 73-90668. (Amharic.). 1976. $69.50x (ISBN 0-520-02660-8). U of Cal Pr.

AMIENS–NOTRE DAME (CATHEDRAL)
Debrie, Rene. Lexique Picard des Parlers Ouest-Amienois. LC 76-451761. 424p. (Fr.). 1975. write for info. Univers Picardie.

AMMUNITION–LAW AND LEGISLATION
see Firearms–Laws and Regulations

AMPLIFIERS (ELECTRONICS)
Clason, W., ed. Elsevier's Dictionary of Amplification Modulation Reception & Transmission. (Eng., Fr. & Span.). 1963. $63.50 (ISBN 0-444-40113-X). Elsevier.

ANA
see Aphorisms and Apothegms; Epigrams; Maxims; Proverbs; Quotations

ANAESTHESIA
see Anesthesia

ANAGRAMS
Curl, Michael. The Anagram Dictionary. 288p. 1982. $30.00x (ISBN 0-7091-9674-1, Pub. by Robert Hale England). State Mutual Bk.
Edwards, R. J., compiled by. Crossword Anagram Dictionary. (Illus.). 1979. $6.95 (ISBN 0-8317-1882-X, Mayflower Bks). Smith Pubs.
Hunter, Samuel D. The Dictionary of Anagrams. 160p. 1982. $12.95 (ISBN 0-7100-9006-4). Routledge & Kegan.

ANALOGIES, ELECTROMECHANICAL
see Electromechanical Analogies

ANALOGY
Castillo, Gonzalo. Diccionario de Similes & Analogias. (Span.). pap. $2.50 (BCA). Lectorum Pubns.
--Diccionario de similes y analogias. (Span.). Mex.$12.00. EDIMEX.
Maquet, Charles. Dictionnaire Analogique. 591p. (Fr.). 1971. 16.00 F. Larousse.
--Dictionnaire Analogique. 11th ed. 600p. (Fr.). 1971. 49.00 F. Larousse.
Niobey. Dictionnaire Analogique de Poche. (Fr.). 1980. pap. 10.25 F (Dist. by Continental Bk Co). Larousse.

ANALYSIS (MATHEMATICS)
see Mathematical Analysis

ANALYSIS, CHROMATOGRAPHIC
see Chromatographic Analysis

ANALYSIS, MICROSCOPIC
see Microscope and Microscopy

ANALYSIS, SPECTRUM
see Spectrum Analysis

ANALYSIS SITUS
see Topology

ANATOMY–DICTIONARIES
Chatain, Yves. Terminologia Anatomica. 316p. (Span.). 1967. $5.00. Norma.
Lovasy, Ernest & Veillon, Emmanuel. Dictionnaire des Termes d'anatomie, d'embryologie & d'histologie. 624p. (Fr.). 1954. 40.00 F. Maloine.
Lovasy, Ernst. Dictionnaire des Termes d'Anatomie, d'Embryologie et d'Histologie. 624p. (Fr.). 1954. $17.50 (ISBN 0-686-57022-7, M-6380). French & Eur.
Mezhdunarodnaia Anatomicheskaia Nomenklatura. 224p. (Rus.). 1976. $5.50 (Pub. by Ganatleba). Four Continent.

ANATOMY, HUMAN
see also Body, Human
also names of organs and regions of the body, e.g. Heart, Pelvis, Skull
Layman, Dale P. The Terminology of Anatomy & Physiology: A Programmed Approach. LC 82-13448. 293p. 1983. pap. $10.95 (ISBN 0-471-86262-2, Pub. by Wiley Med). Wiley.
Piscitelli, N. Dizionario di anatomia e fisiologia umana. (Illus.). 128p. (Ital.). L.3000.00. Ist Geo Agostini.

Piscitelli, Nicola. Diccionario Atlas De Anatomia Humana. 256p. (Span.). 1974. pap. $13.25 (ISBN 84-307-8290-7, S-50259). French & Eur.

ANATOMY, MICROSCOPIC
see Histology

ANCESTRY
see Genealogy

ANCIENT GEOGRAPHY
see Geography, Ancient

ANDHRA LANGUAGE
see Telugu Language

ANECDOTES
Vega, V. Diccionario ilustrado de anecdotas. 3rd ed. (Illus.). 900p. (Span.). write for info. G Gili.

ANESTHESIA
Klein, Sanford L. Glossary of Anesthesia. 1984. pap. text ed. price not set (ISBN 0-87488-973-1). Med Exam.

ANGLO-AMERICAN LAW
see Law–United States

ANGLO-DUTCH WAR, 1672-1674
see Dutch War, 1672-1678

ANGLO-NORMAN DIALECT
Stone, Louise W., et al, eds. An Anglo-Norman Dictionary. (Publications of the Modern Humanities Research Association: Vol. 8). avail. Modern Humanities Res.

ANGLO-SAXON LANGUAGE–DICTIONARIES–ENGLISH
Borden, Arthur R., Jr. A Comprehensive Old-English Dictionary. LC 81-40837. 1612p. 1982. lib. bdg. $101.75 (ISBN 0-8191-2254-8). U Pr of Amer.
Bosworth, Joseph. A Compendious Anglo-Saxon & English Dictionary. 1979. Repr. of 1860 ed. lib. bdg. $30.00 (ISBN 0-89341-478-6). Longwood Pr.
Bosworth, Joseph, et al, eds. An Anglo-Saxon Dictionary. (Anglo-Saxon & Eng.). 1972. Repr. of 1898 ed. $110.00x (ISBN 0-19-863101-4); 1921 supplement & addenda $85.00x (ISBN 0-19-863112-X). Oxford U Pr.
Hall, John R. & Meritt, Herbert D. Concise Anglo-Saxon Dictionary. 4th ed. 1961. $59.95 (ISBN 0-521-05179-7). Cambridge U Pr.
Sweet, Henry. Student's Dictionary of Anglo-Saxon. (Anglo-Saxon). 1896. $27.50x (ISBN 0-19-863107-3). Oxford U Pr.

ANGLO-SAXON LANGUAGE–GLOSSARIES, VOCABULARIES, ETC.
Barney, Stephen A., et al. Word-Hoard: An Introduction to Old English Vocabulary. LC 76-47003. 1977. pap. $5.95x (ISBN 0-300-02110-0). Yale U Pr.
Oliphant, Robert. Harley Latin-Old English Glossary. (Janua Linguarum, Ser. Practica: No. 20). (Lat. & Eng.). 1966. pap. text ed. $36.00x (ISBN 90-2790-639-4). Mouton.
Padelford, Frederick M. Old English Musical Terms. LC 76-22346. 1976. Repr. of 1899 ed. lib. bdg. $15.00 (ISBN 0-89341-012-8). Longwood Pr.
Tinkler, John D. Vocabulary & Syntax of the Old English Version in the Paris Psalter. LC 68-29824. (Janua Linguarum, Ser. Practica: No. 67). (Illus.). 92p. (Orig., Old Eng.). 1971. pap. text ed. $16.00x (ISBN 90-2791-895-3). Mouton.
Wright, T. Anglo-Saxon & English Vocabularies, 2 vols. Set. $95.20 (ISBN 3-534-04078-3). Adler.
Wright, Thomas. Anglo-Saxon & Old English Vocabularies, 2 vols. Set. lib. bdg. $300.00 (ISBN 0-87968-432-1). Gordon Pr.

ANGLO-SAXON POETRY
Bessinger, J. B., Jr., ed. A Concordance to the "Anglo-Saxon Poetic Records". LC 77-6186. (Concordances Ser.). 1978. $65.00x (ISBN 0-8014-1146-7). Cornell U Pr.

ANGOLA
Martin, Phyllis M. Historical Dictionary of Angola. LC 80-15662. (African Historical Dictionaries Ser.: No. 26). 196p. 1980. $14.00 (ISBN 0-8108-1322-X). Scarecrow.

ANIMAL BEHAVIOR
see Animals, Habits and Behavior Of

ANIMAL DISEASES
see Veterinary Medicine

ANIMAL FOLKLORE
see Animal Lore

ANIMAL FOOD
Piccioni, Marcello. Dictionnaire des Aliments pour les Animaux. (Illus). 620p. (Fr.). 1965. 110.00 F. Maison Rustique.

ANIMAL HUSBANDRY
see Livestock

ANIMAL LORE
see also Animals, Mythical
Clebert, Jean Paul. Dictionnaire du Symbolisme Animal. (Illus.). 455p. (Fr.). 75.00 F. Albin-Michel.

ANIMAL NUTRITION
Committee on Animal Nutrition, National Research Council. Nutritional Energetics of Domestic Animals & Glossary of Energy Terms. 54p. (Orig.). 1981. pap. text ed. $5.25 (ISBN 0-309-03127-3). Natl Acad Pr.

ANIMAL-ORIGIN FOOD
see Animal Food

ANIMAL SYMBOLISM
see Animal Lore

ANIMALS
see also Mammals; Vertebrates
also names of kinds of animals, e.g. Bears, cats, deer, etc.
Burton, Maurice. Le Dictionnaire En Couleurs Des Animaux. 400p. (Fr.). 1974. $57.00 (ISBN 0-686-56875-3, M-6653). French & Eur.
--Le Dictionnaire en Couleurs des Animaux. (Illus.). 400p. (Fr.). 145.00 F. Elsevier Sequoia.
Diccionario Monografico del Reino Animal. 286p. (Span.). 1980. $19.95 (ISBN 84-7153-385-5, S-32725). French & Eur.
Dictionnaire des Animaux. (Illus., Fr.). 40.00 F. Deux Coqs.
Dizionario degli animali. (Illus.). 48p. (Ital.). L.3500.00. Dami.
Gack & Jahn. Herder - Lexikon Tiere. 342p. (Ger.). 1976. pap. $15.95 (ISBN 3-451-17371-9, M-7459, Pub. by Herder). French & Eur.
--Herder-Lexikon Tiere. 342p. (Ger.). 1976. pap. $15.95 (ISBN 3-451-17371-9). Herder.
Gozmany, L., et al, eds. Septemlingual Dictionary of the Names of European Animal, 2 vols. (Eng., Rus., Span., Ger., Hungarian, Fr., & Lat.). 1979. Set. $230.00 (ISBN 0-9960010-0-X, Pub. by Kiado Hungary). Heyden.
Gozmany, Laslo. Septemligual Dictionary of the Names of European Animals, 2 vols. 2188p. 1980. $500.00x (ISBN 0-569-08577-2, Pub. by Collet's). State Mutual Bk.
Gozmany, Laszlo, ed. Septemlingual Dictionary of the Names of European Animals, 2 vols. 2228p. 1979. Set. $200.00x (ISBN 963-05-1381-1). Intl Pubns Serv.
Husson, Roger. Dictionnaire de Biologie Animale. 2nd ed. 280p. (Fr.). 1970. 44.00 F. Gauthier-Villars.
Lexikon der Neuzeittlichen Landwirtschaft: Bd 1, Tierernaehrung, Tierzucht, Tierhaltung. 257p. (Ger.). 1974. DM.29.00 (ISBN 3-7736-8003-1). Girardet.
Piccioni, M., ed. Diccionario de Alimentacion Animal. 820p. (Span.). 1970. write for info. (S-36852). French & Eur.
Rousselet, Blanc P. Dictionnaire des Animaux. 250p. (Fr.). 1981. $12.95 (ISBN 0-686-97634-7, M-9771). French & Eur.

ANIMALS (IN RELIGION, FOLK-LORE, ETC.)
see Animal Lore

ANIMALS–FOOD
see Animals, Food Habits of

ANIMALS–JUVENILE LITERATURE
Burton, Maurice, ed. Young People's Animal Encyclopedia, 24 vols. LC 72-83306. (Illus.). 48p. (gr. 4-9). 1980. Set. PLB $226.60 (ISBN 0-516-00300-3). Childrens.

ANIMALS, AQUATIC
see Fresh-Water Biology; Marine Fauna

ANIMALS, CRUELTY TO
see Animals, Treatment Of

ANIMALS, DISEASES OF
see Veterinary Medicine

ANIMALS, EDIBLE
see Animal Food

ANIMALS, EXPERIMENTAL
see Laboratory Animals

ANIMALS, FICTITIOUS
see Animals, Mythical

ANIMALS, FOOD HABITS OF
Picconi, Marcello. Dictionnaire des Aliments pour les Animaux. 620p. (Fr.). 1965. $42.50 (ISBN 0-686-57077-4, M-6452). French & Eur.

ANIMALS, FOSSIL
see Paleontology

ANIMALS, HABITS AND BEHAVIOR OF
see also Animals, Food Habits of
also names of particular animals
Heymer, Armin. The Ethological Dictionary: In English, French & German. LC 77-78418. (Illus.). 238p. (Eng., Fr. & Ger.). 1979. Repr. of 1977 ed. lib. bdg. $35.00 (ISBN 0-8240-7005-4, Garland STPM Pr). Garland Pub.
Immelmann, Klaus. Woerterbuch der Verhaltensforschung. LC 78-342717. 133p. (Eng. & Ger.). 1975. DM.12.00 (ISBN 3-463-00616-2). Kindler.
Meyer, Peter K. Taschenlexikon der Verhaltenskunde. LC 77-462747. 240p. (Ger.). 1976. DM.12.80 (ISBN 3-506-99191-4). Schoningh.
Smith, Stevenson & Guthrie, Edwin R. General Psychology in Terms of Behavior. LC 22-444. (Psychology Ser.). 1970. Repr. of 1921 ed. $18.00 (ISBN 0-384-56175-6). Johnson Repr.

ANIMALS, IMAGINARY
see Animals, Mythical

ANIMALS, MYTHICAL
see also Animal Lore
Malaret, A. Lexicon de fauna y flora. (Span.). 1961. write for info. Inst Caro y Cuervo.

ANIMALS, PREHISTORIC
see Paleontology

ANIMALS, PROTECTION OF
see Animals, Treatment Of

ANIMALS, RESPIRATION OF
see Respiration

ANIMALS, RESTRAINT OF
see Animals, Treatment of

ANIMALS, SEA
see Marine Fauna

ANIMALS, TREATMENT OF
Glossaire de Termes Relatifs aus Pratiques Commerciales Restrictes. 100p. (Fr.). 1965. 6.00 F. O. C. D. E.

ANIMALS AS FOOD
see Animal Food

ANIMALS IN FOLK-LORE
see Animal Lore

ANIMALS IN RESEARCH
see Laboratory Animals

ANNALS
see Chronology, Historical; History

ANNIVERSARIES
Collison, Robert L., ed. Dictionary of Dates. LC 77-95116. Repr. of 1961 ed. lib. bdg. $23.00x (ISBN 0-8371-2495-6, CODD). Greenwood.

ANNOTATIONS AND CITATIONS (LAW)
see also Citation of Legal Authorities
Germa, Pierre. Larousse des Citations: Francaises et Etrangeres. (Fr.). 1975. $33.00 (Dist. by Continental Bk Co). Larousse.
Petit, Karl. Le Dictionnaire des Citations. (Fr.). 1960. write for info. Bout.
Serand, Pierre & De Sacy, Samuel S. Dictionnaire des Citations Francaises. (Fr.). write for info. Larousse.

ANNUALS
see Almanacs; Calendars; Yearbooks

ANONYMS AND PSEUDONYMS
see also Anagrams
Cushing, William. Initials & Pseudonyms: A Dictionary of Literary Disguises, 2 Vols. 936p. 1982. Repr. of 1888 ed. Set. $79.00x (ISBN 0-8103-3962-5). Gale.
Halkett & Laing. A Dictionary of Anonymous & Pseudonymous Publications in the English Language: Vol. 1, 1475-1640. Horden, John, ed. 1980. $150.00 (ISBN 0-582-55521-3). Longman.

ANIMALS, EDIBLE
see Animal Food

Masanov, I. F. Slovar Psevdonimov Russkikh Pisatelei: Uchenykh & Obshchestvennykh Deiatelei, 4 vols. (Rus.). 1960. $35.00 set (Pub. by Izd Vsesoiuzn Knizhn Palaty). Four Continent.
Mossman, Jennifer, ed. Pseudonyms & Nicknames Dictionary. rev. 2nd ed. LC 80-13274. 1982. $160.00x (ISBN 0-8103-0547-X). Gale.
Rogers, P. P. & Lapuente, F. A. Diccionario De Seudonimos Literarios Espanoles, Con Algunas Iniciales. 610p. (Span.). 1977. $38.95 (ISBN 84-249-1352-3, S-50152); pap. $32.95 (ISBN 84-249-1351-5, S-31444). French & Eur.

ANTEDILUVIAN ANIMALS
see Paleontology

ANTENNAS (ELECTRONICS)
Diccionario tecnico, radio, antenas, video, radar: Espanol-ingles. (Span. & Eng.). Arg.$3.00. Cosmopolita.

ANTHROPO-GEOGRAPHY
Fulvi, Fulvio. Dizionario di Termini Della Geografia Umana. LC 80-475625. 149p. (Ital.). 1978. L.3900.00. Patron.

ANTHROPOLOGY
see also Anthropo-Geography; Archaeology; Civilization; Language and Languages; Man; Social Change; Women
also names of races, tribes etc., and subdivision Race Question under names of countries, e.g. United States–Race Question
Bielecki, Tadeusz, ed. Maly Slownik Antropologiczny. LC 77-500992. (Illus.). 511p. (Pol.). 1976. 100.00 Zl. Wiedza Powszechna.

ANTHROPOLOGY–DICTIONARIES
Diccionario de Antropologia. 200p. (Span.). 1980. 450.00 ptas. Bellaterra.
Duroux, Paul-Emile. Dictionnaire des Anthropologistes. 336p. (Fr.). 1974. pap. $35.00 (ISBN 0-686-57130-4, M-6182). French & Eur.
--Dictionnaire des Anthropologistes. 336p. (Fr.). 1974. 90.00 F. Delarge.
Jehan, L. F. Dictionnaire d'Anthropologie ou Histoire Naturelle del'Homme et des Races Humaines. Migne, J. P., ed. (Nouvelle Encyclopedie Theologique Ser.: Vol. 42). 800p. (Fr.). Repr. of 1853 ed. lib. bdg. $101.50x (ISBN 0-89241-281-X). Caratzas Pub Co.
Martinez Cruz, Abelardo. Lexico De Antropologia. 3rd ed. 184p. (Span.). 1975. pap. $8.75 (ISBN 84-7222-754-5, S-50038). French & Eur.
Pearson, Roger. Dictionary of Anthropology. (Orig.). 1984. write for info. (ISBN 0-89874-510-1). Krieger.
Winick, Charles. Dictionary of Anthropology. Repr. of 1956 ed. lib. bdg. $29.75x (ISBN 0-8371-2094-2, WIDA). Greenwood.
--Dictionary of Anthropology. (Quality Paperback: No. 131). 1977. pap. $5.95 (ISBN 0-8226-0131-1). Littlefield.
Winick, Charles, tr. Diccionario de antropologia. 660p. (Span.). 1969. $7.00. Troquel.

ANTHROPONOMY
see Names, Personal

ANTI-CORROSIVE PAINT
see Corrosion and Anti-Corrosives

ANTILLES, LESSER
Gastmann, Albert. Historical Dictionary of the French & Netherlands Antilles. LC 78-19070. (Latin American Historical Dictionaries Ser.: No. 18). 1978. lib. bdg. $13.00 (ISBN 0-8108-1153-7). Scarecrow.

ANTIMILITARISM
see Militarism

ANTIQUES–DICTIONARIES
Antique Collectors' Club. Pictorial Dictionary of British Nineteenth Century Furniture Design. 583p. 1980. $69.50 (ISBN 0-902028-47-2). Antique Collect.
Barber, Edward A. & Lockwood, Luke V. The Ceramic Furniture & Silver Collectors' Glossary. (Architecture & Decorative Art Ser.). 1976. pap. $6.95 (ISBN 0-306-80049-7). Da Capo.

Benzon, Gorm R. Gyldendals Antikvitetshandbog, 2 vols. LC 76-488522. (Illus., Danish.). 1976. Kr.296.00 (ISBN 8-700-09561-3). Gyldendal Norsk.

Bernasconi, J. R. Collector's Glossary of Antiques & Fine Arts. (Illus.). 1971. $17.50x (ISBN 0-900361-34-4). Intl Pubns Serv.

Bernasconi, John R. Collector's Glossary. 3rd ed. $24.50 (ISBN 0-900361-34-4). Transatlantic.

Bonnaffe, Edmond. Dictionnaire des Amateurs Francais au Dix-Septieme Siecle. (Bibliography & Reference Ser.: No. 138). (Fr.). 1968. Repr. of 1884 ed. $26.50 (ISBN 0-8337-0335-8). B Franklin.

Romand, Didier. Dictionnaire du Marche de l'Art: Meubles, Objects, Curiosities. LC 78-384890. (Illus.). 415p. (Fr.). 1978. 135.00 F (ISBN 2-859-17007-3). Amateur.

Savage, George. Dictionary of Antiques. 2nd ed. (Illus.). 1978. $20.00 (ISBN 0-8317-0011-4, Mayflower Bks). Smith Pubs.

Ziegler, K. & Sontheimer, W., eds. Lexikon der Antike, 5 vols. 800p. (Ger.). 1975. pap. $79.00 per vol. M Rosenberg.

ANTIQUITIES
see also Archaeology
also subdivision Antiquities under names of countries, cities, etc
Lamer, Hans. Woerterbuch der Antike. 8th ed. (Ger.). 1976. $23.00 (ISBN 3-520-09608-0, M-7042). French & Eur.
ANTIQUITIES, BYZANTINE
see Byzantine Antiquities
ANTIQUITIES, GRECIAN
see Greece-Antiquities
Daremberg, Charles & Saglio, E. Dictionnaire des Antiquites Grecques & Romaines, 10 vols. (Illus.). 8464p. (Fr.). 1962. S.15400.00. Akadem Druck-U Verlagsanstalt.
ANTIQUITIES, ROMAN
see Rome-Antiquities
Daremberg, Charles & Saglio, E. Dictionnaire des Antiquites Grecques & Romaines, 10 vols. (Illus.). 8464p. (Fr.). 1962. S.15400.00. Akadem Druck-U Verlagsanstalt.
ANTISEPTIC MEDICATION
Neuman, Maur. Dictionnaire des Medicaments. 432p. (Fr.). 1971. 66.00 F. Heures de France.
ANTITHESIS (IN RELIGION, FOLK-LORE, ETC.)
see Polarity (In Religion, Folk-Lore, etc.)
APACHE INDIANS
see Indians of North America-Southwest, New
APHORISMS AND APOTHEGMS
see also Epigrams; Maxims; Proverbs; Quotations
Felitsyna, V. P. & Prokhorov, Iu. E. Russkie Poslovitsy, Pogovorki i Krylatye Vyrazheniia. 240p. (Rus.). 1979. $5.50 (Pub. by Russkii Iazyk). Four Continent.
Sintes. Diccionario de Aforismos, Proverbios & Refranes. (Span.). $19.50 (SOP). Lectorum Pubns.
--Diccionario de aforismos, proverbios y refrances. 4th ed. 894p. (Span.). 1968. 500.00 ptas. Sintes.
Sintes Pros, Jorge. Diccionario de aforismos, proverbios y refrances. 5th ed. 896p. (Span.). 1982. 2200.00 ptas (ISBN 84-302-0440-7). Sintes.
APHRODISIACS
Wedeck, Harry E., ed. Dictionary of Aphrodisiacs. LC 61-12626. 1961. $10.00 (ISBN 0-8022-1828-8). Philos Lib.
APOLLINAIRE, GUILLAUME, 1880-1918
Bates, Scott. Dictionnaire des Mots Libres d'Apollinaire. 160p. (Fr.). 1975. 45.00 F. 30.00 F. Filipacchi.
APOLOGETICS
see also Faith and Reason

also subdivision Doctrinal and Controversial works under names of particuliar denominations, and also subdivision Apologetic Works under religious denominations, e.g. Catholic Church-Apologetic Works
Cheve, C. F. Dictionnaire des Apologistes Involuntaires, 2 vols. Migne, J. P., ed. (Nouvelle Encyclopedie Theologique Ser.: Vols. 38-39). 1494p. (Fr.). Repr. of 1853 ed. lib. bdg. $189.50x (ISBN 0-89241-279-8). Caratzas Pub Co.
Jehan, L. F. Dictionnaire d'Apologetique, 2 vols. Migne, J. P., ed. (Nouvelle Encyclopedie Theologique Ser.: Vols. 51-52). 1702p. (Fr.). Repr. of 1855 ed. lib. bdg. $215.00x (ISBN 0-89241-289-5). Caratzas Pub Co.
APOTHEGMS
see Aphorisms and Apothegms
APPARATUS, CHEMICAL
see Chemical Apparatus
APPARATUS, ORTHOPEDIC
see Orthopedic Apparatus
APPARATUS, SCIENTIFIC
see Scientific Apparatus and Instruments
APPLE (COMPUTER)
Noonan, Larry. Basic BASIC-English Dictionary for the Apple, PET & TRS-80. (Illus.). 154p. $17.95 (ISBN 0-686-88421-3, 1521). TAB Bks.
APPLIED SCIENCE
see Technology
APPRAISAL
see Assessment
APPRAISAL OF BOOKS
see Criticism; Literature-History and Criticism
AQUARIUMS
Favre, Henri. Larousse Dictionary of the Fresh-Water Aquarium. Vevers, Gwynne, tr. LC 77-11664. 1978. $6.95 (ISBN 0-8120-5192-0). Barron.
Frey, Hans. Das Grosse Lexikon der Aquaristik. LC 77-551968. 859p. (Ger.). 1976. write for info. (ISBN 3-7888-0243-X). Neumann-Neudamm.
ARAB CIVILIZATION
see Civilization, Arab
ARABIA
Mac Guckin De Slane, tr. from Arabic. Wafayat al-a yan: Ibn Khallikan's Biographical Dictionary, 4 vols. (Eng. & Arabic). $110.00 set (129-1). Intl Bk Ctr.
Von Ronart, Nandy & Ronart, Stephan. Lexikon der Arabischen Welt. 1100p. (Ger.). 1978. DM.230.00 (ISBN 3-7608-0138-2). Artemis Verlag.
ARABIA-SOCIAL LIFE AND CUSTOMS
Dozy, R. Dictionnaire detaille des noms des vetements chez les Arabes. 445p. (Arabic & Fr.). $20.00 (104-5). Intl Bk Ctr.
ARABIC LANGUAGE
Adnani, Muhammad. Dictionary of Common Language Errors & Their Corrections: Arabic-Arabic. (Arabic). $20.00x (ISBN 0-86685-104-6). Intl Bk Ctr.
Dozy, R. Glossaire des Mots Espagnols et Portugais Derives de L'arabe. (Span., Port. & Arabic). 1974. $20.00x (ISBN 0-86685-105-4). Intl Bk Ctr.
Learn Arabic for English Speakers. (Arabic & Eng.). pap. $10.50 (ISBN 0-87557-004-6, 004-6). Saphrograph.
Schmidt, J. Vocabulaire d'Arabe Moderne: Economie-Politique-Actualite, Vol. 1. 627p. (Fr. & Arabic). 1979. 100.00 F. Maison Dictionnaire.
--Vocabulaire d'Arabe moderne: Economie-Politique-Actualite, Vol. 2. 670p. (Arabic & Fr.). 1982. 120.00 F. Maison Dictionnaire.
Wahba, Magdi & Muhandes, Kamel. A Dictionary of Literary & Linguistic Terms. 266p. (Arabic., With Arabic-English glossary). $30.00 (131-3). Intl Bk Ctr.
ARABIC LANGUAGE-DIALECTS
Dictionnaire Arabe-Francais. LC 77-980964. 155p. (Fr. & Arabic). 1977. write for info. N'Damena Tchad.

Harrell, Richard S. & Sobelman, Harvey, eds. A Dictionary of Moroccan Arabic: Moroccan-Arabic English-Moroccan. (Richard Slade Harrell Arabic Ser.). 528p. (Moroccan, Arabic & Eng.). 1963. pap. $19.95 (ISBN 0-87840-008-7). Georgetown U Pr.
Krolkoff, Georg. Langenscheidts Taschenbuecher Arabisch-Deutsch. (Arabic & Ger.). 1975. DM.14.80 (ISBN 3-468-10060-4). Langenscheidt.
Roth-Laly, Arlette. Lexique des Parlers Arabes-Tchado-Soudanais. 148p. (Fr., Arabic & Sudanese). 1972. 35.50 F. CNRS.
--Lexique des Parlers Arabes-Tchado-Soudanais. 164p. (Fr., Arabic & Sudanese). 1969. 35.50 F. CNRS.
--Lexique des Parlers Arabes-Tchado-Soudanais, 3. 144p. (Arabic, Sudanese & Fr.). 1971. 34.20 F. CNRS.
Schukry, K. Langenscheidts Taschenwoerterbuecher Deutsch-Arabisch. (Ger. & Arabic). 1978. DM.14.80 (ISBN 3-468-10065-5). Langenscheidt.
Sieny, Mahmoud. Syntax of Urban Hijazi Arabic. (Arabic). $12.00x (ISBN 0-86685-051-1). Intl Bk Ctr.
Stowasser, Karl & Ani, Moukhtar, eds. A Dictionary of Syrian Arabic: English-Arabic. (Richard Slade Harrell Arabic Ser). 202p. (Eng. & Arabic). 1964. pap. $9.95 (ISBN 0-87840-010-9). Georgetown U Pr.
ARABIC LANGUAGE-DICTIONARIES
ABC Dictionary I, Arabic Italian. (Arabic & Ital.). $7.99. Intl Bk Ctr.
ABC Dictionary I, Arabic-Spanish. (Arabic & Span.). $7.99 (ISBN 0-86685-308-1). Intl Bk Ctr.
Abdallah. Abdallah Dictionary of International Relations & Conference Terminology in English-Arabic. (Eng. & Arabic). 1982. $40.00x (ISBN 0-86685-289-1). Intl Bk Ctr.
Abdel-Massih, Ernest T. A Sample Lexicon of Pan-Arabic. LC 75-18985. (Arabic). 1975. pap. text ed. $7.00x (ISBN 0-932098-10-X). Ctr for NE & North African Stud.
Addi, Al-Sayyid. Dictionary of Persian Loan Words in the Arabic Language. (Persian & Arabic). 1980. $21.00x (ISBN 0-86685-128-3). Intl Bk Ctr.
Al-Adnani, Muhammad. A Dictionary of Common Language Errors & their Corrections. 368p. (Arabic). $20.00 (894-5). Intl Bk Ctr.
Al-Amir Al-Nasiruddin, Amin. Ar-Rafed. 200p. (Arabic). 1971. $18.00 (101-1). Intl Bk Ctr.
Al-Bustani, Abdullah. Al-Wafi. (Arabic). $40.00 (095-3). Intl Bk Ctr.
Al-Bustani, Butros. Qutr Al-Muhit, 2 vols. 2452p. (Arabic). $45.00 (097-X). Intl Bk Ctr.
Al-Bustani, Butrus. Arabic-Arabic Dictionary Muhit Al Muhit. (Arabic). $50.00x (ISBN 0-86685-096-1). Intl Bk Ctr.
Al-Sayyid'Addi Shir. A Dictionary of Persian Loan Words in the Arabic Language. 194p. (Arabic & Persian). $21.00 (128-3). Intl Bk Ctr.
Al-Sharif Al-Juriani. Kitab Al-Ta'rifat: Book of Definitions. 336p. (Arabic). $16.00 (0-3). Intl Bk Ctr.
Al-Yaziji, Ibrahim. Naj'ati Ur-Ra'id wa-Shar'Atu al-Warid fi al-Mutaradifi wa al-Mu tawarid. 555p. (Arabic). $30.00 (102-X). Intl Bk Ctr.
Arabic-English Dictionary. (Arabic & Eng.). $19.50 (ISBN 0-87557-002-X, 002-X). Saphrograph.
Arabic-English Dictionary: Hava's Al: Faraid. (Arabic & Eng.). 1974. $35.00x (ISBN 2-7214-2106-9). Intl Bk Ctr.
Arabic-English, English-Arabic Student's Dictionary, 2 vols. (Illus., Arabic & Eng.). Set. $50.00 (ISBN 2-7214-2879-9). Heinman.
Arabic Pocket Dictionary. (Arabic & Eng.). 10.00 (ISBN 0-685-11992-0). Heinman.

Arabisch, 2 vols. Incl. Teil I. Arabisch-Deutsch. Krotkoff, G. 624p. DM.18.80 (10060); Teil II. Deutsch-Arabisch. Schukry, K. & Humberdrotz, R. 456p. DM.18.80 (10065). (Langenscheidts Taschenwoerterbuecher Ser.). (Arabic & Ger.). DM.beide Teile in einem Band 29.80 (11060). Langenscheidt.
Assaran, Hassan. Arabic-English Dictionary of Basic Scientific & Technical Terms: "Al Mustalah". 1967. $20.00x (ISBN 0-86685-299-9). Intl Bk Ctr.
Ba'Alabaki, Munir. English-Arabic Pocket Dictionary: Al-Mawrid Al Quareb. (Eng. & Arabic). 1980. pap. $5.95x (ISBN 0-86685-062-7). Intl Bk Ctr.
Ba'Albaki, Munir. English-Arabic Dictionary: Al-Mawrid. (Eng. & Arabic). 1983. $48.00 (ISBN 0-86685-059-7). Intl Bk Ctr.
--English-Arabic Dictionary: Al-Mawrid Al-Waset. (Eng. & Arabic). $25.00x (ISBN 0-86685-060-0). Intl Bk Ctr.
--English-Arabic Student Dictionary: Al-Muyassar. (Eng. & Arabic). $12.00x (ISBN 0-86685-061-9). Intl Bk Ctr.
Barakat, Gamal. English-Arabic Dictionary of Diplomacy & Related Terminology. (Eng. & Arabic). 1982. $25.00x (ISBN 0-86685-290-5). Intl Bk Ctr.
Biella, Joan C. Dictionary of Old South Arabic: Sabaen Dialect. LC 81-8946. (Harvard Semitic Studies). (Arabic). 1982. $33.00 (ISBN 0-89130-455-X, 04-04-25). Scholars Pr CA.
Blachere, Regis & Chouemi, Moustafa. Dictionnaire Arabe-Francais-Anglais, 12 vols. (Arabic, Fr. & Eng.). 1970. 650.00 F. Maison & Larose.
--Dictionnaire Arabe-Francais-Anglais, 1, Pts. 1-12. (Arabic, Fr. & Eng.). 1967. $350.00 (ISBN 0-686-56918-0, M-6034). French & Eur.
--Dictionnaire Arabe-Francais-Anglais, 2, Pts. 13-24. (Arab., Fr. & Eng.). 1970. $350.00 (ISBN 0-686-56919-9, M-6035). French & Eur.
Bustani, Butros. Muhit al-Muhit. 997p. (Arabic). $50.00 (096-1). Intl Bk Ctr.
Cameron, D. Arabic-English Dictionary. (Arabic & Eng.). 1979. $16.00x (ISBN 0-86685-084-8). Intl Bk Ctr.
Chaldean Arabic, English Picture Dictionary. (Arabic & Eng.). pap. $4.95x (ISBN 0-86685-132-1). Intl Bk Ctr.
Cherbonneau, Auguste. Arabic-French Dictionary, 2 vols. (Arabic & Fr.). Set. $30.00x (ISBN 0-86685-103-8). Intl Bk Ctr.
Chouemi, M. & Pellat, C. H. Al-Kamil Dictionnaire Arabe-Francais-Anglais. 64p. (Arabic, Fr. & Eng.). 1981. write for info. (M-9286). French & Eur.
Concise Dictionary of Islamic Terms: English-Arabic. 1979. $6.95x (ISBN 0-86685-276-X). Intl Bk Ctr.
Corriente Cordoba, Federico. Diccionario espanol-arabe. 2nd ed. 480p. (Span. & Arabic). 1980. 800.00 ptas (ISBN 84-7472-023-0). Inst Hispano-Arabe.
Cowan, J. Milton, ed. Dictionary of Modern Written Arabic. 4th, rev. ed. 1300p. (Arabic & Eng.). 1979. $115.00x (ISBN 3-447-02002-4). Intl Pubns Serv.
Dahdah, Antoine. Dictionary of Arabic Grammar in Charts & Tables. (Illus., Arabic). 1982. $30.00x (ISBN 0-86685-292-1). Intl Bk Ctr.
Dar El Mashreq. Arabic-English Students Dictionary. (Arabic & Eng.). 1974. $15.00x (ISBN 2-7214-2107-7). Intl Bk Ctr.
--Munjid al Tulab. 950p. (Arabic). student dict. $15.00 (2128-2). Intl Bk Ctr.
Daykin, Vernon. Technical Arabic. 132p. (Arabic). 1980. $15.00x (ISBN 0-686-94054-7, Pub. by Lund Humphries England). State Mutual Bk.

Debahy, M. Dictionary of Hebrew Verbs. 96p. (Arabic & Hebrew.). $15.00 (123-2). Intl Bk Ctr.
Denizeau, Claude. Dictionnaire des Parlers Arabes de Syrie, Libyan & Palestine. 580p. (Arabic.). 1961. 120.00 F. Maison & Larose.
--Dictionnaire des Parlers Arabes de Syrie, Liban et Palestine. 581p. (Fr. & Arabic.). 1961. pap. $49.95 (ISBN 0-686-57090-1, M-6112). French & Eur.
Dictionary Arabic-Chinese. 1505p. (Arabic & Chinese.). 1978. $45.00 (ISBN 0-686-92338-3, M-9288). French & Eur.
Dictionnaire Moderne Francais-Arabe. 868p. (Fr. & Arabic.). 1979. leatherette $29.95 (ISBN 0-686-97332-1, M-9749). French & Eur.
Doniach, N. S., ed. Oxford English-Arabic Dictionary of Current Usage. (Eng. & Arabic.). 1972. $49.50x (ISBN 0-19-864312-8). Oxford U Pr.
Dozy, R. Dictionaire Detaille des Noms de Vetements Chez Les Arabes. (Arabic & Fr.). $20.00x. Intl Bk Ctr.
--Supplement Aux Dictionnaire Arabe (Arabic-French, 2 vols. (Arabic & Fr.). 1969. $80.00x (ISBN 0-86685-106-2). Intl Bk Ctr.
El-Baz, Farouk. Say It in Arabic. LC 67-17506. (Arabic.). 1968. lib. bdg. $8.50x (ISBN 0-88307-557-1). Gannon.
Elias. Elias Arabic-English Modern Dictionary. (Arabic & Eng.). $29.00 (ISBN 0-686-18362-2); pap. $6.50 pocket size (ISBN 0-686-18363-0). Kazi Pubns.
--Elias English-Arabic & Arabic-English Pocket Dictionary. (Arabic & Eng.). pap. $15.95 (ISBN 0-686-18361-4). Kazi Pubns.
--Elias English-Arabic Modern Dictionary. (Arabic & Eng.). $29.00 (ISBN 0-686-18364-9); pap. $6.50 pocket size (ISBN 0-686-18365-7). Kazi Pubns.
Elias, ed. English Arabic, Arabic-English Pocket Dictionary. (Eng. & Arabic.). $7.50x (ISBN 0-686-00859-6). Colton Bk.
Elias, E. A. Arabic-English, English-Arabic Dictionary, 2 vols. rev. & enl. ed. (Arabic & Eng.). Set. $70.00 (ISBN 0-685-55017-6). Heinman.
--English-Arabic; Arabic-English Dictionary. (Eng. & Arabic.). $12.00x (ISBN 0-86685-173-9). Intl Bk Ctr.
Elias, Elias. Arabic-English Modern Dictionary. (Arabic & Eng.). 1981. $30.00x (ISBN 0-86685-287-5). Intl Bk Ctr.
--Elias' English-Arabic Dictionary. (Eng. & Arabic.). 1979. $25.00x (ISBN 0-86685-288-3). Intl Bk Ctr.
Elihai, Yohanan. Dictionnaire de l'Arabe Parle Palestinien. 418p. (Fr. & Arabic.). 1974. pap. $22.50 (ISBN 0-686-57132-0, M-6185). French & Eur.
El Mashreq, Dar. Arabic Dictionary: Al Munjid fi al-Lugha Wal 'Alam. (Arabic.). $48.00x (ISBN 2-7214-2124-7). Intl Bk Ctr.
English-Arabic Student Dictionary: Dar el Mashreq. (Eng. & Arabic.). $12.00x (ISBN 2-7214-2123-9). Intl Bk Ctr.
Fagnan, E. Additions Aux Dictionnaires Arabes (Arabic-French) 194p. (Arabic & Fr.). 1969. $20.00x (ISBN 0-86685-107-0). Intl Bk Ctr.
Field, Claud. Dictionary of Arabic-Persian Quotes. (Arabic, Persian & Eng.). $18.00x (ISBN 0-86685-168-2). Intl Bk Ctr.
First Picture Dictionary - English-Arabic. (Illus., Eng. & Arabic.). $2.50x (ISBN 0-86685-202-6). Intl Bk Ctr.
Freyha, Anis. Dictionary of Non-Classical Vocables in Spoken Arabic. (Arabic.). 1973. $16.00x (ISBN 0-86685-098-8). Intl Bk Ctr.
Freytag, George W. Lexicon Arabico-Latinum, 4 vols. (Arabic & Lat.). $95.00x (ISBN 0-86685-124-0). Intl Bk Ctr.
--Lexicon Arabico-Latinum, 4 vols. 2257p. (Arabic & Lat.). Repr. of 1830 ed. $95.00 (124-0). Intl Bk Ctr.
Georr, Khalil. Dictionnaire Arabe moderne Larousse. 1360p. (Arabic.). 1973. 25.00 F. Larousse.
Hava, J. Al-Faraid: Arabic-English Dictionary. 915p. (Arabic & Eng.). $25.00 (2106-9). Intl Bk Ctr.
Hava, J. G. Al-Faraid Arabic-English Dictionary. 3rd ed. 915p. (Arabic & Eng.). 1970. $30.00x (ISBN 2-7214-2106-9). Intl Pubns Serv.
Henni, Mustapha. Dictionary Des Terms Economiques et Commerciaux (French-English-Arabic) (Fr., Eng. & Arabic.). $25.00x (ISBN 0-86685-111-9). Intl Bk Ctr.
Institute for Language Study. Vest Pocket Arabic. LC 74-17006. (Illus.). 252p. (Arabic.). 1979. pap. $3.50 (ISBN 0-06-464907-5, BN 4907, BN). B&N NY.
Ismat, Shafiq. Police Dictionary: English-Arabic Dictionary. (Eng. & Arabic.). 1980. $25.00x (ISBN 0-86685-068-6). Intl Bk Ctr.
Jannota, Elpidio. Dizionario italiano-arabo moderno, 2 vols. (Ital. & Arabic.). 1964. L.31500.00. Ist Poligrafico.
Jaschke, R. English Arabic Conversational Dictionary. (Arabic & Eng.). $6.95. Iaconi.
Johannsen, H. Management Glossary: (English-Arabic) 238p. (Eng. & Arabic.). 1972. $16.00x (ISBN 0-86685-069-4). Intl Bk Ctr.
Jurjani, Al Sharif. Kitab al-Ta Rifat (Book of Definitions) Arabic-Arabic Dictionary. (Arabic.). 1969. $16.00x (ISBN 0-86685-100-3). Intl Bk Ctr.
Karmi, Hasan. English-Arabic Dictionary: Al-Manar. (Eng. & Arabic.). 1971. lib. bdg. $25.00x (ISBN 0-86685-070-8). Intl Bk Ctr.
Karmi, Hassan. Al Manar: English-Arabic Dictionary. 904p. (Eng. & Arabic.). $25.00 (070-8); student ed. $12.00 (071-6). Intl Bk Ctr.
Kaye, Alan S. A Dictionary of Nigerian Arabic. LC 81-71736. (Bibliotheca Afroasiatica Ser.: Vol. 1). 104p. (Orig., Nigerian Arabic.). 1982. $26.00x (ISBN 0-89003-100-2); pap. $19.50x (ISBN 0-89003-101-0). Undena Pubns.
Kazirmski, A. Arabe Francais Dictionnaire, 2 vols. (Arabic & Fr.). Repr. of 1860 ed. $80.00x (ISBN 0-86685-110-0). Intl Bk Ctr.
Kropacek, Lubos. Arabsko-Cesky Cesko-Arabsky Slovnik. LC 75-585137. 529p. (Czech. & Arabic.). 1975. 22.50 Kcs. SNTC.
Krotkoff, G. Langenscheidts Taschenwoerterbuch Arabisch: Teil I, Arabisch-Deutsch. 624p. (Arabian & Ger.). DM.19.80 (10060). Langenscheidt.
Krotkoff, G., et al. Langenscheidts Taschenwoerterbuch Arabisch, 2 vols. in 1. (Arabian & Ger.). DM.29.80 (11060). Langenscheidt.
Lane, Edward W., ed. Arabic-English Lexicon, 8 Vols. (Arabic & Eng.). Set. $360.00 (ISBN 0-8044-0272-8). Ungar.
Larousse Arab Dictionary. (Illus.). 1400p. (Arabic.). $30.00. Intl Bk Ctr.
Liban, Libr d. ABC Dictionary I: Arabic & Span. (Arabic & Span.). 1983. $7.95x. Intl Bk Ctr.
Libr. du Liban. ABC Dictionary I: Arabic & Fr. (Arabic & Fr.). 1983. $7.95x (ISBN 0-86685-310-3). Intl Bk Ctr.
--ABC Dictionary I: Arabic & Ger. (Arabic & Ger.). 1983. $7.95x (ISBN 0-86685-309-X). Intl Bk Ctr.
Libr du Liban. ABC Dictionary Tamhidi: Arabic & Eng. (Arabic & Eng.). 1983. $7.95x (ISBN 0-86685-314-6). Intl Bk Ctr.
--ABC Dictionary Tamhidi: Arabic & Fr. (Arabic & Fr.). 1983. $7.95x (ISBN 0-86685-315-4). Intl Bk Ctr.
--ABC Dictionary Tamhidi: Arabic & Ital. (Arabic & Ital.). 1983. $7.95x (ISBN 0-86685-316-2). Intl Bk Ctr.
--ABC Dictionary Tamhidi: Arabic Ger. (Arabic & Ger.). 1983. $7.95x (ISBN 0-86685-313-8). Intl Bk Ctr.
--ABC Dictionary Tamhidi: Arabic-Spanish. (Arabic & Span.). 1983. $7.95x (ISBN 0-86685-312-X). Intl Bk Ctr.
--My Illustrated Dictionary: Arabic & Fr. (Arabic & Fr.). 1983. $9.00x (ISBN 0-86685-321-9). Intl Bk Ctr.
--My Illustrated Dictionary: Arabic & Ger. (Arabic & Ger.). 1983. $9.00x (ISBN 0-86685-318-9). Intl Bk Ctr.
--My Illustrated Dictionary: Arabic & Ital. (Arabic & Ital.). 1983. $9.00x (ISBN 0-86685-319-7). Intl Bk Ctr.
--My Illustrated Dictionary: Arabic & Span. (Arabic & Span.). 1983. $9.00x (ISBN 0-86685-320-0). Intl Bk Ctr.
--My Illustrated Dictionary: Arabic Eng. (Arabic & Eng.). 1983. $9.00x (ISBN 0-86685-317-0). Intl Bk Ctr.
Modern Arab Dictionary. (Arabic.). $29.95 (ISBN 2-03-020540-0, 3680); pap. $14.95 (ISBN 2-03-020540-0). Larousse.
Mokri, M. Al-Hadiyati 'l-Hamidiyah. 400p. (Arabic & Kurdish.). $28.00 (126-7). Intl Bk Ctr.
--Kurdish-Arabic Dictionary: Al-Hadiyati 'l-Hamidiyah. (Arabic.). 1975. $28.00x (ISBN 0-86685-126-7). Intl Bk Ctr.
Munjid fi al Lugha wal A'Alam. (Illus.). 900p. (Arabic.). $48.00 (2124-7). Intl Bk Ctr.
Nasr, Raja. Colloquial Arabic: An Oral Approach. (Arabic.). 1968. $11.00x (ISBN 0-86685-044-9). Intl Bk Ctr.
--English Colloquial Arabic Dictionary. 1972. $18.00x (ISBN 0-86685-079-1). Intl Bk Ctr.
Nasr, Raja T. An English Colloquial Arabic Dictionary in Phonetic Script. 285p. 1974. text ed. $30.00 (ISBN 0-685-50128-0). Transatlantic.
Qamus, Madd A. & Edward, Wm. An Arabic-English Lexicon, 8 vols. (Arabic & Eng.). Set. $295.00x. Intl Bk Ctr.
Roth-Laly, Arlette. Lexique des Parlers Arabes-Tchado-Soudanais. 294p. (Arabic, Chad & Soudanese.). 1969. pap. 50.00 F (ISBN 2-22201-164-7). Editions du CNRS.
--Lexique des Parlers Arabes-Tchado-Soudanais: K-Y. 148p. (Arabic & Sudanese.). 1972. pap. 50.00 F (ISBN 2-22201-428-X). CNRS.
Russian-Arabic Dictionary. 1056p. (Rus. & Arabic.). 1979. Leatherette $26.95 (ISBN 0-686-97414-X, M-9073). French & Eur.
Sabek, Jerwan. English-French-Arabic Trilingual Dictionary. (Eng., Fr. & Arabic.). $35.00x (ISBN 0-86685-116-X). Intl Bk Ctr.
Saisse, Louis. Dictionaire Francais-Arabe. (Fr. & Arabic.). 1980. pap. $8.95x (ISBN 0-86685-112-7). Intl Bk Ctr.
Salmone, Anthony. Arabic-English Advanced Learners Dictionary. (Arabic & Eng.). $30.00x (ISBN 0-86685-089-9). Intl Bk Ctr.
Schregle, Gotz. Deutsch-Arabisches Worterbuch. LC 79-366306. xii, 1472p. (Ger. & Arabic.). 1977. write for info. Lib Liban.
Schukry, K. & Humberdrotz, R. Langenscheidts Taschenwoerterbuch Arabisch: Teil II, Deutsch-Arabisch. 456p. (Ger. & Arabic.). DM.19.80 (10065). Langenscheidt.
Sharbatov, G. Sh. Russko-Arabskii Uchebnyi Slovar. 1196p. (Rus. & Arabic.). 1979. $16.95 (Pub. by Russki Iazyk). Four Continent.
Simonet, Francisco J. Glosario de voces Ibericas y Latinas. 628p. (Span. & Arabic.). $18.00 (113-5). Intl Bk Ctr.
Skoss, Solomon, ed. Hebrew-Arabic Dictionary of the Bible Known As Kitab Jami-Al-Alfaz, 2 vols. (Yale Oriental Researches Ser.: No. XX, XXI). (Hebrew & Arabic.). 1945. $50.00x ea.; $95.00x set (ISBN 0-686-57837-6). Elliots Bks.
Spiro, Socrates. Arabic-English Dictionary: Colloquial Arabic of Egypt. (Arabic & Eng.). 1973. $30.00x (ISBN 0-86685-090-2). Intl Bk Ctr.
--English-Arabic Dictionary: Colloquial Arabic of Egypt. (Eng. & Arabic.). 1974. $20.00x (ISBN 0-86685-080-5). Intl Bk Ctr.
Steingass, F. Arabic-English Learners Dictionary. (Arabic & Eng.). 1972. $35.00x (ISBN 0-86685-087-2). Intl Bk Ctr.
--English-Arabic Learner's Dictionary. (Eng. & Arabic.). 1972. $20.00x (ISBN 0-86685-081-3). Intl Bk Ctr.
--A Learner's Arabic-English Dictionary. (Arabic & Eng.). 1978. $24.00x (ISBN 0-8364-0312-6). South Asia Bks.
Tulab, Munjid al & Mashreq, Dar el. Arabic Student Dictionary. (Arabic.). 1979. $15.00x (ISBN 2-7214-2118-2). Intl Bk Ctr.
Valderrama Martinez, Fernando. Glosario Espanol-Arabe. 333p. (Span. & Arabic.). 1980. 300.00 ptas. Albir.
--Glosario Espanol-Arabe y Arabe-Espanol. 333p. (Span. & Arabic.). 1980. pap. 6.00 ptas. pap. 300.00 ptas. Albir.
Van Wagoner, Merrill Y., et al. English-Arabic Vocabulary: Students Pronouncing Dictionary. LC 80-81198. 452p. (Orig., Eng. & Arabic.). 1980. pap. text ed. $10.00x (ISBN 0-87950-028-X). Spoken Lang Serv.
Wafi, Al & Bustani, Butros. A Concise Arabic Dictionary. (Arabic.). 1980. $40.00x (ISBN 0-86685-095-3). Intl Bk Ctr.
Wahrmund, Adolf. Handworterbuch der Neu-Arabischen und Deutschen Sprache, 3 vols. (Arabic & Ger.). 1974. Set. text ed. $50.50x (ISBN 0-8426-0776-5). Verry.
--Handworterbuch der neu Arabischen und Deutschen Sprache, 3 vols. 2826p. (Ger. & Arabic.). Repr. $70.00 set (178-X). Intl Bk Ctr.
Wehr, Hans. Arabic-English Dictionary. rev. 3rd ed. Cowan, J Milton, ed. LC 75-24236. (Arabic & Eng.). 1976. pap. $12.00x (ISBN 0-87950-001-8). Spoken Lang Serv.
--A Dictionary of Modern Written Arabic. 4th rev. ed. Cowan, J. M., ed. 1300p. (Arabic.). 1980. $115.00x (ISBN 0-87950-002-6). Spoken Lang Serv.
--A Dictionary of Modern Written Arabic. Cowan, J. M., ed. xvii, 1110p. (Arabic & Eng.). E12.00 (ISBN 0-245-53120-3). Harrap.
--A Dictionary of Modern Written Arabic. 4th & enl. ed. Cowan, J. Milton, ed. LC 80-466867. xviii, 1301p. (Arabic & Eng.). 1979. write for info. (ISBN 3-447-02002-4). Harrassowitz.
Wortabet, J. & Porter, H., eds. English-Arabic, Arabic-English Dictionary. 880p. (Eng. & Arabic.). $30.00 (ISBN 0-8044-0875-0). Ungar.
Wortabet, John. Arabic-English Pocket Dictionary. 1980. pap. $5.50x (ISBN 0-86685-093-7). Intl Bk Ctr.
--English-Arabic; Arabic-English Dictionary. (Eng. & Arabic.). 1979. $16.00x (ISBN 0-86685-120-8). Intl Bk Ctr.
--English-Arabic; Arabic-English Pocket Dictionary. (Eng. & Arabic.). pap. $10.00x (ISBN 0-86685-121-6). Intl Bk Ctr.
--English-Arabic Pocket Dictionary. (Eng. & Arabic.). 1980. pap. $5.50x (ISBN 0-86685-083-X). Intl Bk Ctr.
Wortabet, William. Arabic-English Dictionary. (Arabic & Eng.). 1968. $18.00x (ISBN 0-86685-092-9). Intl Bk Ctr.

ARABIC LANGUAGE–WRITING
see Writing, Arabic

ARABIC LITERATURE–TRANSLATIONS INTO ENGLISH

Landau, Jacob. A Word Count of Modern Arabic Prose. 485p. (Arabic & Eng.). 1959. $10.00x (275-4). Intl Bk Ctr.

Wahba, Magdi & Muhandes, Kamel. A Dictionary of Literary & Linguistic Terms. 266p. (Arabic., With Arabic-English glossary). $30.00 (131-3). Intl Bk Ctr.

Wahba, Magdi, compiled by. A Dictionary of Literary Terms. 616p. (Arabic, Fr. & Eng.). $28.00 (117-8). Intl Bk Ctr.

ARABIC PHILOSOPHY

see Philosophy, Islamic

ARAMAIC INSCRIPTIONS

see Inscriptions, Aramaic

ARAMAIC LANGUAGE

see also Syriac Language

Buxtorf, Johann. Lexicon Chaldaicum Talmudicum & Rabbinicum. LC 78-359320. (Aramaic & Lat.). 1977. write for info. (ISBN 3-487-06386-7). Olms Verlag.

Hebrew-English Lexicon of the Bible. LC 74-26705. 296p. (Orig., Hebrew & Eng.). 1975. pap. $7.50 (ISBN 0-8052-0481-4). Schocken.

Jastrow, Marcus. Hebrew-Aramaic-English Dictionary, a Dictionary of Talmud Babli & Talmud Yerushalmi Targum & Midrash, 2 Vols. (Hebrew, Aramaic & Eng.). $68.50 (ISBN 0-87559-019-5). Shalom.

ARAPAHO INDIANS

see Indians of North America–The West

ARBITRATION, INTERNATIONAL

see also Disarmament

American Arbitration Association. Dictionary of Arbitration & Its Terms. LC 70-94692. 334p. 1970. lib. bdg. $21.00 (ISBN 0-379-00386-4). Oceana.

ARBORICULTURE

see Forests and Forestry; Trees

ARCH

see Arches

ARCHAEOLOGICAL SPECIMENS

see Antiquities

ARCHAEOLOGY

see also Antiquities; Art, Primitive; Christian Art and Symbolism; Epitaphs; Gems; Heraldry; Inscriptions; Numismatics

also subdivision Antiquities under names of countries, regions, cities, etc., e.g. Crete–Antiquities

Gay, Victor. Glossaire Archeologique du Moyen-Age & de la Renaissance, 2 vols. (Illus., Fr.). 1928. 243.00 F. Kraus.

Marois, Roger. Vocabulaire Francais-Anglais d'archeologie Prehistorique. 116p. (Fr. & Eng.). 1972. Can.$7.95. Quebec P. U.

ARCHAEOLOGY–DICTIONARIES

Apelt, M. German-English Dictionary: Art History-Archaeology. (Eng. & Ger.). Date not set. text ed. $25.00 (ISBN 0-686-46538-5). Heinman.

Bray & Trump. Dictionary of Archaeology. rev. ed. 1982. pap. $6.95. Penguin.

Bray, W. & Trump, D. Lexikon der Archaeologie, 2 vols. (Ger.). 1975. Set. pap. $29.95 (ISBN 3-499-16187-7, M-7276). French & Eur.

Bray, Warwick & Trump, David. Diccionario De Arqueologia. 276p. (Span.). 1976. pap. $17.95 (ISBN 84-335-9301-3, S-50363). French & Eur.

--Dizionario di archeologia. (Ital.). 1974. L.2000.00. Mondadori.

Cartailhac, Emile. Dictionnaire Archeologique de la Gaul. 160p. (Fr.). 1923. 10.00 F. Nationale.

--Dictionnaire Archeologique de la Gaule. 472p. (Fr.). 1923. 10.00 F. Biblio Nationale.

Champion, Sara. Dictionary of Terms & Techniques in Archaeology. (Illus.). 144p. 1982. pap. $7.95 (ISBN 0-89696-162-1, An Everest House Book). Dodd.

Champion, Sarah. A Dictionary of Terms & Techniques in Archaeology. LC 80-66774. (Illus.). 144p. (Eng.). 1980. $15.95 (ISBN 0-87196-445-7). Facts on File.

Cooper, William R. Archaic Dictionary. LC 73-76018. 1969. Repr. of 1876 ed. $66.00x (ISBN 0-8103-3885-8). Gale.

De Laborde, Leon. Glossaire Francais du Moyen Age: L'usage de l'archeologue & de l'amateur des Arts. 562p. (Fr.). 1975. 110.00 F. Slatkine.

Dictionnaire prehistoire. (Illus., Fr.). pap. $8.50 (ISBN 0-685-13882-8). Larousse.

Franz, L. & Neumann, A. R., eds. Lexikon Zur & Freuhgeschictlicher Fundstaetten Oesterreichs. (Ger.). 1965. DM.58.00 (ISBN 3-7749-0255-0). Habelt.

Gay. Glossaire archeologique du moyer age et de la Renaissance, 2 tomes. (Fr.). Set. $167.00 (ISBN 0-685-34006-6). French & Eur.

Trump, David. The Penguin Dictionary of Archaeology. rev. ed. (Reference Ser.). (Illus.). 1972. pap. $6.95 (ISBN 0-14-051116-4). Penguin.

Whitehouse, Ruth, ed. The Macmillan Dictionary of Archaeology. 608p. 1983. E19.95 (ISBN 0-333-27190-4). Macmillan.

ARCHAEOLOGY, MEDIEVAL

Gay, Victor. Glossaire Archeologique du Moyen-Age & de la Renaissance, 2 vols. (Illus.). 1290p. (Fr.). 1927. 585.00 F. Picard.

ARCHES

Huber, Rudolf & Rieth, Renate, eds. Glossarium Artis: Fasz 3, Bogen & Arkaden-Arcs et Arcades. 167p. (Ger.). 1973. DM.35.00 (ISBN 3-484-60048-9). Max Niemeyer.

--Glossarium Artis: Fasz 6, Gewoelbe & Kuppeln-Voutes et Coupoles. 250p. (Ger.). 1974. DM.35.00 (ISBN 3-484-60051-9). Niemeyer.

ARCHITECTS

De Fontenay, Louis-Abel. Dictionnaire des Artistes ou Notice Historique: Raisonnee des Architectes, Peintres & Graveurs, 2 vols. (Fr.). 1972. 240.00 F. Minkoff.

Diccionario Universal del Arte y De los Artistas: Arquitectos. 323p. (Span.). 1970. leatherette $25.50 (ISBN 84-252-0381-3, S-50282). French & Eur.

Sturgis, Russell. Dictionary of Architecture & Building, Biographical & Descriptive, 3 Vols. LC 66-26997. (Illus.). 1966. Repr. of 1902 ed. Set. $79.00x (ISBN 0-8103-3075-X). Gale.

ARCHITECTURAL ACOUSTICS

see also Electro-Acoustics

Cormier, France-Pauline. Vocabulaire de l'electroacoustique de l'acoustique. 186p. (Fr.). 1973. Can.$2.50. Quebec Off.

Lexique Trilingue des Termes D'Usage Courant En Electrotechnique, Electronique, Acoustique, Optique et Controle Par Ultrasons. 340p. (Fr., Trilingual Lexicon of Currently Used Terms in Electrotechnics, Electronics, Acoustics, Optics and Control by Ultra-Sound). 1966. pap. $35.00 (ISBN 0-686-56793-5, M-6373). French & Eur.

Pujolle, Jean. Lexique Guide D'acoustique Architecturale. (Illus.). 152p. (Fr.). 1971. 92.00 F. Eyrolles.

ARCHITECTURAL ENGINEERING

see Building; Strength of Materials

ARCHITECTURAL LIBRARIES

New York Public Library Research Libraries. Dictionary Catalog of the Art & Architecture Division, The Research Libraries of The New York Public Library, 30 vols. 1975. Set. lib. bdg. $2950.00 (ISBN 0-8161-1157-X, Hall Library). G K Hall.

ARCHITECTURE

see also Arches; Building; Building Materials; Buildings; Castles; Cathedrals; Concrete Construction; Factories; Lighting; Strength of Materials

also headings beginning with the word Architectural

Auger, Jules. Vocabulaire Architecturale. 28p. (Fr.). 1975. Can.$2.30. Montreal P. U.

Bucksch, H. Woerterbuch fuer Architektur, Hochbau & Baustoffe. 2nd ed. 1137p. (Eng. & Ger.). 1976. DM.220.00 (ISBN 3-7625-0714-7). Bauverlag.

--Woerterbuch fuer Architektur, Hochbau & Baustoffe: Band 1, Deutsch-Englisch. 2nd ed. 942p. (Ger. & Eng.). 1980. DM.220.00 (ISBN 3-7625-1399-6). Bauverlag.

Calsat, Jean-Henri. Vocabulaire International des Termes d'urbanisme & d'architecture: Francais-Allemand-Anglais. (Illus.). 350p. (Fr., Ger. & Eng.). 1970. 250.00 F. Eyrolles.

Diccionario de Arquitectos de la Antiguedad a Nuestros Dias. (Span.). 1981. pap. write for info. G Gili.

Wells, Roy A. Some Royal Arch Terms Examined. LC 79-301402. (Illus.). 64p. (Eng.). 1978. E2.95 (ISBN 0-85318-106-3). Lewis Ltd.

ARCHITECTURE–BIBLIOGRAPHY

Sturgis, Russell. Dictionary of Architecture & Building, Biographical & Descriptive, 3 Vols. LC 66-26997. (Illus.). 1966. Repr. of 1902 ed. Set. $79.00x (ISBN 0-8103-3075-X). Gale.

ARCHITECTURE–DATA PROCESSING

Society of American Registered Architects. Obtaining a Computer & Computer Terminology. $1.50; members $1.00. Soc Am Reg Architects.

ARCHITECTURE–DICTIONARIES

Abd-El-Gawad, Tawfik. Technical Dictionary: Archtiecture & Building. 1319p. (Eng., Fr., Ger. & Arabic.). 1976. $35.00x (ISBN 0-686-44745-X, Pub. by Collets). State Mutual Bk.

Acharya, Prasanna K. A Dictionary of Hindu Architecture: Treating of Sanskrit Architectural Terms. LC 79-912314. xxi, 861p. (Eng. & Hindu.). 1979. write for info. Bharatiya Publishing House.

Barry, W. R., ed. Architectural, Construction, Manufacturing & Engineering Glossary of Terms. 519p. 1979. pap. $40.00 (ISBN 0-930284-05-4). Am Assn Cost Engineers.

Bassegoda Muste, B. Diccionario poliglota de la arquitectura. 366p. (Span., Ger., Fr., Eng. & Ital.). 1976. pap. $35.00. Imported Bks.

Bassegoda Muste, Buenaventura. Nuevo Glosario, Diccionario Poliglota de la Arquitectura. 366p. (Span., Ger., Catalan, Fr., Eng. & Ital.). 1976. pap. $44.95 (ISBN 84-600-0588-7, S-50134). French & Eur.

Bucksch. Dictionnaire pour l'Architecture le Batiment et les Materiaux de Construction: Allemand-Francais, Vol. 1. 819p. (Ger. & Fr.). 1977. 930.00 F. Maison Dictionnaire.

--Dictionnaire pour l'architecture le Batiment et les Materiaux de Construction: Francais-Allemand, Vol. 2. 675p. (Fr. & Ger.). 1979. 930.00 F. Maison Dictionnaire.

Bucksch, Herbert. Dictionary of Architecture, Building Construction & Materials, Vol. II. 1137p. (Eng. & Ger.). 1976. $175.00 (ISBN 3-7625-0714-7, M-7130). French & Eur.

--Dictionary of Architecture, Building Construction & Materials, Vol. I. 942p. (Eng. & Ger.). 1974. $175.00 (ISBN 3-7625-0357-5, M-7131). French & Eur.

--Dictionary of Architecture, Building Construction & Materials, 2 vols. 1974-76. plastic bdg. $120.00x ea. Vol. 1, Ger.-Eng (ISBN 3-7625-0357-5). Vol. 2, Eng.-Ger (ISBN 3-7625-0714-7). Intl Pubns Serv.

Buksch, Herbert. Woerterbuch fuer Architektur, Hochbau & Baustoffe. LC 77-578817. (Ger. & Fr.). 1977. DM.29.00 (ISBN 3-762-50786-4). Bauverlag.

Calsat, Jean-Henri & Sydler, Jean P. Vocabulaire International des Termes d'Urbanisme et d'Architecture. 350p. (Fr., Ger. & Eng.). 1970. $95.00 (ISBN 0-686-56935-0, M-6057). French & Eur.

Calsat, Jean-Henri & Sydler, Jean-Pierre. Vocabulaire International des Termes d'urbanisme & d'architecture: Francais-Allemand-Anglais. 368p. (Fr., Ger. & Eng.). 1970. 139.65 F. Ste. Diff. Tech. Bat. T. P.

Cowan, Henry J. A Dictionary of Architectural Science. LC 73-15839. (Illus.). 354p. 1973. pap. $18.95x (ISBN 0-470-18070-6). Halsted Pr.

De Marsy, Francois-Marie. Dictionnaire Abrege de Peinture & d'Architecture, 2 vols. (Fr.). Kr.100.00. Minkoff.

Dewan Bahasa dan Pustaka. Istilah Senibina, Perancangan dan Ukur Kuantiti. LC 79-941288. xv, 217p. (Eng. & Malay.). 1978. M.$3.50. Dewan Bahasa.

Diccionario de Arquitectos de la Antiguedad a Nuestros Dias. (Span.). 1981. pap. write for info. G Gili.

Diccionario de Arquitectura. 460p. (Span.). 1974. 75.00 ptas. Tesoro Edit.

Diccionario Universal del Arte y De los Artistas: Arquitectos. 323p. (Span.). 1970. leatherette $25.50 (ISBN 84-252-0381-3, S-50282). French & Eur.

Dictionnaire Pour l'Architecture, le Batiment et les Materiaux de Construction, 2 vols. 820p. (Ger. & Fr.). 1977. band I $236.00 (ISBN 3-7625-0786-4, M-7095). French & Eur.

Dictionnaire Pour l'Architecture, le Batiment et les Materiaux de Construction, 2 vols. 688p. (Ger. & Fr.). 1979. band II $236.00 (ISBN 3-7625-0787-2, M-7096). French & Eur.

Dictionnaire pour L'Architecture, le Batiment et les Mateiaux de Construction: Band I, Deutsch-Franzosisch. 820p. (Ger. & Fr.). 1980. DM.290.00 (ISBN 3-7625-0787-2). Bauverlag.

Dictionnaire pour l'Architecture, le Batiment et les Materiaux de Constrction: Band II, Franzosisch-Deutsch. 688p. (Fr. & Ger.). 1979. DM.290.00 (ISBN 3-7625-0787-2). Bauverlag.

English-Chinese Architectural Engineering Dictionary. 441p. (Eng. & Chinese.). 1973. $14.95 (ISBN 0-686-92620-X, M-9254). French & Eur.

Fleming, John, et al. The Penguin Dictionary of Architecture. rev. ed. (Reference Ser.). 1973. pap. $5.95 (ISBN 0-14-051013-3). Penguin.

Gaward, Abd El. Architecture & Building Dictionary: English-French-German-Arabic. 465p. (Eng., Fr., Ger. & Arabic.). 1976. Leatherette $45.00 (ISBN 0-686-92255-7, M-9753). French & Eur.

Harris, Cyril M. Dictionary of Architecture & Construction. 1975. $42.50 (ISBN 0-07-026756-1, P&RB). McGraw.

Harris, John & Lever, Jill. Illustrated Glossary of Architecture: Eight Fifty to Eighteen Thirty. (Illus.). 314p. 1979. pap. $9.95 (ISBN 0-571-09074-5). Faber & Faber.

Hatje, G. Diccionario ilustrado de la arquitectura contemporanes. 3rd ed. (Span.). 1980. pap. 700.00 ptas. G Gili.

Hatje, Gerd. Diccionario Ilustrado De la Arquitectura Contemporanea. 3rd ed. Sabater, Gerd, ed. 358p. (Span.). 1975. pap. $29.25 (ISBN 84-252-0860-2, S-50278). French & Eur.

Knell, Heiner. Ullstein Lexikon der Kunst und Architektur. (Ger.). 1976. $20.00 (ISBN 3-550-06013-0, M-7673, Pub. by Ullstein Verlag/VVA). French & Eur.

Meikleham, Robert. A Dictionary of Architecture, 3 vols. 1980. Set. lib. bdg. $500.00 (ISBN 0-8490-3122-2). Gordon Pr.

Neve, Richard. City & Country Purchaser & Builder's Dictionary. LC 69-16762. Repr. of 1726 ed. $19.50x (ISBN 0-678-05616-1). Kelley.

Oudin, Bernard. Dizionario degli architetti. (Illus.). 280p. (Ital.). 1971. L.20000.00. ISEDI.

Paniagua, J. R. Vocabulario Basico de la Arquitectura. 375p. (Span.). 1978. pap. $17.95 (ISBN 84-376-0134-7, S-37345). French & Eur.

Parker, John Henry. A Concise Glossary of Terms Used in Grecian, Roman, Italian, & Gothic Architecture. 1980. Repr. of 1896 ed. lib. bdg. $35.00 (ISBN 0-89341-372-0). Longwood Pr.

Perez Calvo, Carlos E. Diccionario Ilustrado de Arquitectura. LC 79-122250. (Illus.). 231p. (Span.). 1979. write for info. Plaza Janes.

Pevesner, Nikolaus. Diccionario de Arquitectura. 651p. (Span.). 1981. write for info. Alianza Ed.

Pevsner, N. Lexikon der Weltarchitektur, 2 vols. (Ger.). 1976. Set. pap. $25.00 (ISBN 3-499-16199-0, M-7216). French & Eur.

Pevsner, Nikolaus, et al. Diccionario de arquitectura. Bustamente, Agustin, tr. 651p. (Span. & Eng.). 1981. write for info. Alianza Ed.

--Diccionario de Arquitectura. (Span.). 1979. pap. pns (S-50087). French & Eur.

--A Dictionary of Architecture. LC 75-27325. (Illus.). 554p. 1976. $25.00 (ISBN 0-87951-040-4). Overlook Pr.

Pevsner, Nikolaus, et al, eds. Lexikon der Weltarchitektur. (Ger.). 1971. DM.22.50 (ISBN 3-7913-0319-8); $30.00 (ISBN 3-7913-0318-X). Prestel-Verlag.

Putnam, R. E. & Carlson, G. E. Architectural & Building Trades Dictionary. 3rd ed. 512p. 1983. $17.95 (ISBN 0-442-27461-0). Van Nos Reinhold.

Putnam, Robert & Carlson, G. E. Architectural & Building Trades Dictionary. 3rd ed. (Illus.). 1974. $15.50 (ISBN 0-8269-0402-5). Am Technical.

Ravazzini, Giacomo. Dizionario di architettura. LC 78-365683. (Illus.). viii, 250p. (Ital.). 1976. L.4200.00 (ISBN 88-205-0092-2). Cisalpino.

Reau, L. Diccionario poligloto de terminos de Arte y Arquitectura. (Span.). write for info. Fondo Cult.

Research Libraries of the New York Public Library. Dictionary Catalog of the Art & Architecture Division, Supplement 1974. 1976. lib. bdg. $80.00 (ISBN 0-8161-0061-6, Hall Library). G K Hall.

Saylor, Henry H. Dictionary of Architecture. LC 52-8260. 221p. 1952. pap. $11.95 (ISBN 0-471-75601-6). Wiley.

Sturgis, R. A Dictionary of Architecture & Building, 3 vols. $300.00 (ISBN 0-8490-0032-7). Gordon Pr.

Sturgis, Russell. Dictionary of Architecture & Building, Biographical & Descriptive, 3 Vols. LC 66-26997. (Illus.). 1966. Repr. of 1902 ed. Set. $79.00x (ISBN 0-8103-3075-X). Gale.

Szolginia, Witold. Architektura & Budownictwo. LC 76-515661. (Illus.). vii, 478p. (Pol.). 1975. 160.00 Zl. Wydawnictwa Naukowo.

Viollet-Le-Duc. Dictionnaire Raisonne de l'Architecture Francaise, du XIe au Siecles, 10 tomes. facsimile ed. (Fr.). Repr. of 1868 ed. Set. $250.00 (ISBN 0-685-36003-2). French & Eur.

Ware, D. & Beatty, B. Diccionario de Arquitectura. 4th ed. (Illus.). 204p. (Span.). 1974. write for info. G Gili.

Woerterbuch Fuer Architektur: Hochbau und Baustoffe. (Fr. & Ger.). 1979. $232.00 (ISBN 0-686-56608-4, M-6923). French & Eur.

Zhitomirskii, M. M. Nemetsko-Russkii Arkhitekturnyi Slovar. 208p. (Ger. & Rus.). 1957. $1.95 (Pub. by GINS). Four Continent.

ARCHITECTURE–EARLY WORKS TO 1800

Neve, Richard. City & Country Purchaser & Builder's Dictionary. LC 69-16762. Repr. of 1726 ed. $19.50x (ISBN 0-678-05616-1). Kelley.

ARCHITECTURE–PICTORIAL WORKS

Harris, John & Lever, Jill. Illustrated Glossary of Architecture: Eight Fifty to Eighteen Thirty. (Illus.). 314p. 1979. pap. $9.95 (ISBN 0-571-09074-5). Faber & Faber.

ARCHITECTURE–NEAR EAST

Aurenche, Oliver, ed. Dictionnaire Illustre Multilingue de l'Architecture du Proche Orient Ancien. LC 78-392938. (Illus.). 391p. (Fr.). 1977. $250.00 F. Boccard.

Aureneche, Olivier. Dictionnaire Illustre Multilinque De L'architecture du Procher-Orient Ancien. 392p. (Fr.). 1978. $125.00 (ISBN 0-686-56729-3, M-6017). French & Eur.

ARCHITECTURE, COLONIAL

see also Architecture, Domestic–United States

Isham, Norman M. Early American Houses & a Glossary of Colonial Architectural Terms, 2 vols. LC 67-27458. (Architecture & Decorative Art Ser). 1967. Repr. of 1939 ed. lib. bdg. $19.50 (ISBN 0-306-70973-2). Da Capo.

ARCHITECTURE, DOMESTIC

see also House Construction

Laframbois, Yves. L' Architecture Traditionnelle au Quebec: Glossaire Illustre de la Maison aux 17e & 18e Siecles. LC 75-517455. (Illus.). 319p. (Fr.). 1975. write for info. (ISBN 0-7759-0457-0). Edns Homme.

ARCHITECTURE, DOMESTIC–GREAT BRITAIN

Smith, Roge T. Gothic Architecture in England with an Illustrated Glossary of Technical Terms. (Illus.). 164p. 1983. $91.85 (ISBN 0-86650-059-6). Gloucester Art.

ARCHITECTURE, DOMESTIC–UNITED STATES

Isham, Norman M. Early American Houses & a Glossary of Colonial Architectural Terms, 2 vols. LC 67-27458. (Architecture & Decorative Art Ser). 1967. Repr. of 1939 ed. lib. bdg. $19.50 (ISBN 0-306-70973-2). Da Capo.

ARCHITECTURE, GOTHIC

see also Cathedrals

Smith, Roge T. Gothic Architecture in England with an Illustrated Glossary of Technical Terms. (Illus.). 164p. 1983. $91.85 (ISBN 0-86650-059-6). Gloucester Art.

ARCHITECTURE, MODERN

Hatje, Gerd. Diccionario ilustrado de la arquitectura contemporanea. 4th ed. Mantero, Jose M., tr. (Illus.). 360p. (Span.). 1982. pap. 860.00 ptas (ISBN 84-252-0860-2). G Gili.

ARCHITECTURE, NAVAL

see Ship-Building

ARCHITECTURE, RURAL

see Architecture, Domestic

ARCHIVES

see also Diplomatics; Libraries; Manuscripts

Brachmann-Teubner, Elisabeth. Lexikon Archivwesen der DDR. LC 76-478503. 319p. (Ger.). 1976. M.12.00. Staatsdruk.

Evans, Frank B., et al. A Basic Glossary for Archivists, Manuscript Curators, & Records Managers. 19p. 1974. pap. $2.00 (ISBN 0-931828-02-3). Soc Am Archivists.

ARCHIVES–CANADA

Provincial Archives & Victoria, British Columbia. Dictionary Catalogue of the Library of the Provincial Archives of British Columbia, 8 vols. 1971. Set. lib. bdg. $760.00 (ISBN 0-8161-0912-5, Hall Library). G K Hall.

ARCHIVES–ITALY

Cecchetti, Bartolomeo. Saggio di un dizionario del linguaggio archivistico veneto. LC 79-353675. 74p. (Ital.). 1978. write for info. Forni.

ARGENTINE REPUBLIC

see also names of cities, towns, etc. in the Argentine Republic

Bioy Casares, Adolfo. Breve Diccionario del Argentino Exquisito. 162p. (Span.). 1978. $10.50 (ISBN 0-686-56668-8, S-33074). French & Eur.

Casullo, Fernando H. Diccionario de Voces Lunfardas & Vulgares. LC 76-151616. 219p. (Span.). 1976. write for info. Plus Ultra SA.

ARGOT

see Slang

ARGUMENTATION

see Debates and Debating; Logic; Oratory

ARISTOCRACY

see also Democracy; Nobility also subdivision Nobility under names of countries

Aubert de la Chenaye-Desbois, Francais. Dictionnaire de la Noblesse, 10 vols. 9800p. (Fr.). 1978. Set. $155.00 (ISBN 0-686-56904-0, M-6015). French & Eur.

ARISTOTLE–DICTIONARIES, INDEXES, ETC.

Kappes, Matthias. Aristoteles-Lexikon, 2 vols. LC 75-172191. (Bibliography & Reference Ser.: No. 82). 78p. (Philosophy Monographs, No. 437). 1971. Repr. of 1894 ed. Set. lib. bdg. $19.00 (ISBN 0-8337-1893-2). B Franklin.

ARITHMETIC

see also Accounting; Metric System

Erdsneker, Barbara & Haller, Margaret. Civil Service Arithmetic & Vocabulary. LC 81-7988. 256p. 1981. lib. bdg. $12.00 (ISBN 0-668-05116-7, 4872-7); pap. $8.00 (ISBN 0-668-04872-7). Arco.

ARMAGH, IRELAND (ECCLESIASTICAL PROVINCE)

Kurochkin, V. D., et al. Slovar Spravochnik Nazvanii Obraztsov Vooruzheniia & Boevoi Tekhniki Kapitalisticheskikh Stran & Osnovnykh Firm Proizvodiashikh Vooruzhenie. 200p. (Rus.). 1966. $1.50 (Pub. by Voenizdat). Four Continent.

ARMENIAN LANGUAGE

Bedrossian, Mathias. Armenian-English Dictionary. (Armenian & Eng.). $35.00x (ISBN 0-86685-122-4). Intl Bk Ctr.

Calfa, Ambroise. Dictionnaire Armenien-Francais, 2 vols. 1038p. (Armenian & Fr.). 1973. Set. pap. $49.95 (ISBN 0-686-56934-2, M-6056). French & Eur.

--Dictionnaire Armenien-Francais, 2 vols. 1038p. (Armenian & Fr.). 1973. 120.00 F. Klincksieck.

Froundiian-Dirair. Armenisch-Deutsches Woerterbuch. (Armenian & Ger.). 1952. $45.00 (ISBN 3-486-41021-0, Pub. by Oldenbourg). French & Eur.

--Armenisch-Deutsches Woerterbuch. (Armenian & Ger.). 1952. DM.45.00 (ISBN 3-486-41021-0). Oldenbourg Verlag.

Gamrekeli, N., et al. Nemetsko-Gruzinsko-Russkii Frazeologicheskii Slovar. 566p. (Ger., Gr. & Rus.). 1973. $4.35 (Pub. by Ganatleba). Four Continent.

Garibian, A. Russko-Armianskii Slovar. 1340p. (Rus. & Armenian.). 1977. $16.75 (Pub. by Hayastan). Four Continent.

Garibian, A. S. Russko-Armianskii Slovar. 1421p. (Rus. & Armenian.). 1968. $14.25 (Pub. by Hayastan). Four Continent.

Koushakdjian, M. Armenian-English - English-Armenian Dictionary. 2nd, rev. ed. (Armenian & Eng.). $45.00 (ISBN 0-686-68934-8). Heinman.

Russko-Armianskii Frazeologicheskii Slovar. 616p. (Rus. & Armenian.). 1975. $7.25 (Pub. by Gos. Un-Tet). Four Continent.

Yacobian, A. H. English-Armenian, Armenian English Dictionary. (Eng. & Armenian.). $24.50 (ISBN 0-87559-004-7); thumb indexed $29.50 (ISBN 0-87559-005-5). Shalom.

ARMORIC LANGUAGE

see Breton Language

ARMS, COATS OF

see Devices; Heraldry

ARMS CONTROL

see Disarmament

ARMY

see Military Art and Science also France–Army; United States–Army, and similar headings

ART

see also Archaeology; Architecture; Art Objects; Bronzes; Caricature; Christian Art and Symbolism; Costume; Drawing; Engraving; Esthetics; Expressionism (Art); Gems; Graphic Arts; Impressionism (Art); Jewelry; Miniature Painting; Performing Arts; Pictures; Portraits; Printing As a Graphic Art; Sculpture also subdivision Art under special headings, e.g., jesus christ–art; also Animals in Art; Birds in Art; Nude in Art; Sea in Art, and similar headings

Huber, Rudolf & Rieth, Renate, eds. Glossarium Artis: Deutsch-Franzoesisches Woerterbuch zur Kunst. (Ger. & Fr.). write for info. Max Niemeyer.

--Glossarium Artis: Fasz 1, Burgen & Feste Plaetze. 200p. (Ger.). 1977. DM.35.00 (ISBN 3-484-60053-5). Max Niemeyer.

--Glossarium Artis: Fasz 2, Liturgische Geraete-Objets Liturgiques. 160p. (Ger.). 1972. DM.35.00 (ISBN 3-484-60047-0). Max Niemeyer.

--Glossarium Artis: Fasz 3, Bogen & Arkaden-Arcs et Arcades. 167p. (Ger.). 1973. DM.35.00 (ISBN 3-484-60048-9). Max Niemeyer.

--Glossarium Artis: Fasz 4, Paramente & Buecher der Christlichen Kirchen. 203p. (Ger.). DM.35.00 (ISBN 3-484-60049-7). Max Niemeyer.

--Glossarium Artis: Fasz 6, Gewoelbe & Kuppeln-Voutes et Coupoles. 250p. (Ger.). 1974. DM.35.00 (ISBN 3-484-60051-9). Niemeyer.

Iaponsko-Russkii Politekhnicheskii Slovar. 496p. (Japanese & Rus.). 1976. $9.95 (Pub. by Russkii Iazyk). Four Continent.

ART–ANALYSIS, INTERPRETATION, APPRECIATION

see Art Criticism; Esthetics; Pictures

ART–CATALOGS

Research Libraries of the New York Public Library. Dictionary Catalog of the Art & Architecture Division, Supplement 1974. 1976. lib. bdg. $80.00 (ISBN 0-8161-0061-6, Hall Library). G K Hall.

ART–CRITICISM

see Art Criticism

ART–DICTIONARIES, INDEXES, ETC.

Apelt, M. German-English Dictionary: Art History-Archaeology. (Eng. & Ger.). Date not set. text ed. $25.00 (ISBN 0-686-46538-5). Heinman.

Bilzer, B. Begriffslexikon der Bildenden Kuenste, 2 vols. 320p. (Ger.). 1971. Set. pap. $25.50 (ISBN 3-499-16142-7, M-7305). French & Eur.

Boeing & Haeusgen. Herder-Lexikon Kunst. 240p. (Ger.). 1974. pap. $25.95 (ISBN 3-451-16459-0, M-7458, Pub. by Herder). French & Eur.

--Herder-Lexikon Kunst. 240p. (Ger.). 1974. $15.95 (ISBN 3-451-16458-2). Herder.

Boeing-Haeusgen, Ursula. Diccionario Rioduero: Arte. 620p. (Span.). 1978. leatherette $26.95 (ISBN 84-220-0873-4, S-50170). French & Eur.

Bradley, John W. Dictionary of Miniaturists, Illustrators, Calligraphers, & Copyists, with References to Their Works, & Notices of Their Patrons, from the Establishment of Christianity to the 18th Century, 3 vols. LC 61-35160. 1973. Repr. of 1887 ed. Set. lib. bdg. $85.00 (ISBN 0-8337-0353-6). B Franklin.

Cabanne, Pierre. Dictionnaire International des Arts. LC 80-106368. (Illus., Fr.). 1979. write for info (ISBN 2-040-10638-3). Bordas.

--Dictionnaire International des Arts, 2 vols. 1456p. (Fr.). 1979. $135.00 set (Dist. by Continental Bk Co). Bordas.

Capou, Gerard. Le Dictionnaire des Mots Cles du Dessin de la Peinture, de l'Estampe. LC 80-450957. 89p. (Fr.). 1979. 35.00 F. Capou.

Cognia, Raymond & Elgar, Frank. Illustrated Dictionary of Impressionism. (Pocket Art Ser.). (Illus., Eng.). (gr. 10-12). 1979. pap. $3.95 (ISBN 0-8120-0986-X). Barron.

Crespi, Irene & Ferrario, Jorge. Lexico tecnico de las artes plasticas. (Illus.). 208p. (Span.). write for info. EUDEBA.

Diccionario de Arte & Artistas. 600p. (Span.). 1979. write for info. Parramon Edns.

Diccionario de Arte & Artistas. (Span.). 1980. $7.00; 600.00 ptas. Parramon Edns.

Diccionario Universal del Arte, 5 vols. 2nd ed. 1808p. (Span.). 1981. pap. 13450.00 ptas (ISBN 84-7017-621-8). Argos-Vergara.

Diccionario Universal del Arte: A-CH, Vol. 1. 2nd ed. 376p. (Span.). 1981. pap. 2690.00 ptas (ISBN 84-7017-622-6). Argos-Vergara.

Diccionario Universal del Arte: D-H, Vol. 2. 2nd ed. 352p. (Span.). 1981. pap. 2690.00 ptas (ISBN 84-7017-623-4). Argos-Vergara.

Diccionario Universal del Arte: I-M, Vol. 3. 2nd ed. 368p. (Span.). 1981. pap. 2690.00 ptas (ISBN 84-7017-624-2). Argos-Vergara.

Diccionario Universal del Arte: N-R, Vol. 4. 2nd ed. 344p. (Span.). 1981. pap. 2690.00 ptas (ISBN 84-7017-625-0). Argos-Vergara.

Diccionario Universal del Arte: S-Z, Vol. 5. 2nd ed. 368p. (Span.). 1981. pap. 2690.00 ptas (ISBN 84-7017-626-9). Argos-Vergara.

Diccionario Universal del Arte y De los Artistas: Arte Occidental y del Proximo Oriente, II. 300p. (Span.). 1969. leatherette $25.50 (ISBN 0-686-77260-1, S-50284). French & Eur.

Diccionario Universal del Arte y De los Artistas: Arte Occidental y del Proximo Oriente, I. 300p. (Span.). 1969. leatherette $25.50 (ISBN 84-252-0578-6, S-50285). French & Eur.

Dictionnaire Iconologique. (Fr.). 1972. write for info. Minkoff Repr.

Dictionnaire Universal de l'Art et des Artistes, 3 tomes. (Fr.). Set. $341.25 (ISBN 0-685-36013-X). French & Eur.

Dizionario dell'arte. (Illus., Ital.). L.19800.00. Mondadori.

Ehresmann, Julia M., ed. Pocket Dictionary of Art Terms. LC 74-143464. (Illus.). 1971. pap. $3.95 (ISBN 0-8212-0748-2, 712019). NYGS.

Fairholt, Frederick W. A Dictionary of Terms in Art. $59.95 (ISBN 0-8490-0047-5). Gordon Pr.

Fairholt, Frederick W., ed. Dictionary of Terms in Art. LC 68-30630. (Illus.). 1969. Repr. of 1854 ed. $37.00x (ISBN 0-8103-3071-7). Gale.

Fischborn, Gabriele. Woerterbuch der Darstellenden Kuenste: Russiche-Deutsch. LC 77-569863. 248p. (Ger. & Rus.). 1976. M.18.00. VEB Verlag Enzyklopadie.

Garzena, B. Dizionario delle arti figurative. (Illus.). 162p. (Ital.). L.2500.00. Zanichelli.

Gautier, T. F. Dictionnaire des Confreries & Corporations d'Arts & Metiers. Migne, J. P., ed. (Nouvelle Encyclopedie Theologique Ser.: Vol. 50). 562p. (Fr.). Repr. of 1854 ed. lib. bdg. $72.00x (ISBN 0-89241-288-7). Caratzas Pub Co.

Grund. Benezit Dictionary of Artists, 10 Vols. 1976. $500.00 (ISBN 0-686-43137-5). Apollo.

Hall, James. Dictionary of Subjects & Symbols in Art. 2nd, rev. ed. LC 74-6578. (Icon Editions). (Illus.). 1979. o. p. $15.95i (ISBN 0-06-433316-7, HarpT); pap. $8.95i (ISBN 0-06-430100-1, IN-100, HarpT). Har-Row.

Harris, John. Lexicon Techicum, or, a Universal English Dictionary of Arts & Sciences, 2 Vols. (Illus.). 1967. Repr. of 1710 ed. Set. $195.00 (ISBN 0-384-21473-8). Johnson Repr.

Jahn, Johannes. Woerterbuch der Kunst. 8th ed. (Ger.). 1975. $20.00 (ISBN 3-520-16508-2, M-6986). French & Eur.

--Woerterbuch der Kunst. 8th ed. LC 76-463394. (Illus.). viii, 806p. (Ger.). 1975. write for info. (ISBN 3-520-16508-2). Kroener.

--Woerterbuch der Kunst. 9th ed. LC 80-473856. (Illus.). viii, 834p. (Ger.). 1979. write for info. (ISBN 3-520-16509-0). Kroener.

Karin, Thomas. Diccionario del Arte Actual. 224p. (Span.). 1978. pap. $16.50 (ISBN 84-335-7561-9, S-50064). French & Eur.

Kozaklewicz, Stefana. Slownik Terminologiczny Sztuk Pieknych. 2d ed. LC 76-529202. (Illus.). 522p. (Pol.). 1976. 120.00 Zl. Panstwowe Wydawnicto Iskry.

Lapoulide, J. Diccionario Grafico de Arte y Oficios Artisticos, 4 vols. 1600p. (Span.). 1963. Set. $125.00 (ISBN 84-7186-037-6, S-12333). French & Eur.

Leutzeler, H. Bildwoerterbuch der Kunst. 2nd ed. 404p. (Ger.). 1962. $22.50 (ISBN 3-427-85012-9, M-7310, Pub. by F. Duemmlers). French & Eur.

Lindemann, G. Lexikon der Kunststile. 360p. (Ger.). 1970. pap. $15.95 (ISBN 3-499-16132-X, M-7251). French & Eur.

MacDonald. Dictionary of Canadian Artists, 6 Vols. 1977. $100.00 (ISBN 0-686-43129-4). Apollo.

Masciotta, Michelangelo. Dizionario di termini artistici. 272p. (Ital.). L.4000.00. Monnier.

Mayer, Ralph. A Dictionary of Art Terms & Techniques. LC 80-8854. (Illus.). 464p. 1981. pap. $6.95 (ISBN 0-06-463531-7, EH 531, EH). B&N NY.

--A Dictionary of Art Terms & Techniques. 1981. $25.00x (ISBN 0-7136-1095-6, Pub. by Lewis Pubs). State Mutual Bk.

--Dictionary of Art Terms & Techniques. (Illus.). 1969. $14.37i (ISBN 0-690-23673-5). T Y Crowell.

Morales Marin, Jose L. Diccionario de terminos artisticos. 400p. (Span.). 1982. pap. 1800.00 ptas (ISBN 84-85656-36-9). Unali.

Muller, Joseph-Emile. Illustrated Dictionary of Expressionism. LC 78-50723. (Pocket Art Ser.). (Illus.). (gr. 10-12). 1978. pap. $3.95 (ISBN 0-8120-0985-1). Barron.

Murray, Peter & Murray, Linda. Diccionario De Artes y Artistas. 600p. (Span.). 1978. $17.25 (ISBN 84-342-0144-5, S-50013). French & Eur.

--The Penguin Dictionary of Art & Artists. lib. bdg. $11.50x (ISBN 0-88307-415-X). Gannon.

New York Public Library Research Libraries. Dictionary Catalog of the Art & Architecture Division, The Research Libraries of The New York Public Library, 30 vols. 1975. Set. lib. bdg. $2950.00 (ISBN 0-8161-1157-X, Hall Library). G K Hall.

Pierre, Jose. An Illustrated Dictionary of Pop Art. LC 78-50723. (Pocket Art Ser.). (Illus.). (gr. 10-12). 1978. pap. $3.95 (ISBN 0-8120-0984-3). Barron.

--An Illustrated Dictionary of Surrealism. (Pocket Art Ser.). (Illus.). (gr. 10-12). 1978. pap. $3.95 (ISBN 0-8120-0987-8). Barron.

Reau, L. Diccionario poligloto de terminos de Arte y Arquitectura. (Span.). write for info. Fondo Cult.

Reynolds, Kimberley & Seddon, Richard. Illustrated Dictionary of Art Terms: A Handbook for the Artist & Art Lover. 190p. 1981. $35.00x (ISBN 0-85223-207-1, Pub. by Ebury Pr England). State Mutual Bk.

Schaffran, Emerich, ed. Dictionary of European Art. 1958. $4.75 (ISBN 0-8022-1497-5). Philos Lib.

Thomas, Denis. Dictionary of Fine Arts. (Illus.). 208p. E6.95 (ISBN 0-600-32995-X). Newnes Bks.

Von Heinecken, Karl H. Dictionnaire Des Artistes, Dont Nous Avons Des Estampes, Avec une Notice Detailee De Leurs Ouvrages Graves, 4 vols. LC 4-7666. (Fr). 1970. Repr. of 1790 ed. Set. $280.00 (ISBN 0-384-22089-4). Johnson Repr.

Walker, John A. Glossary of Art, Architecture, & Design Since 1945. 2nd ed. 1977. $19.50 (ISBN 0-208-01543-4, Linnet). Shoe String.

Wallace, Grocet. The New York Historical Society's Dictionary of Artists in America, 1564-1860. 1979. $65.00 (ISBN 0-686-43145-6). Apollo.

Watelet, Claude-Henri & Levesque, Pierre-Charles. Dictionnaire des Arts de Peinture, Sculpture & Gravure, Vol. 2. (Fr.). 1972. 118.00 F. Olms Verlag.

ART–EARLY WORKS TO 1800

Harris, John. Lexicon Techicum, or, a Universal English Dictionary of Arts & Sciences, 2 Vols. (Illus.). 1967. Repr. of 1710 ed. Set. $195.00 (ISBN 0-384-21473-8). Johnson Repr.

ART–HISTORY

Here are entered general works on art history. For works on the history of art of specific nationalities or countries see Art, Chinese; Art, French; Art, Jewish; etc., with or without the subdivision History.

Apelt, M. L. German-English Dictionary: Art History, Archaelogy. 240p. (Ger. & Eng.). 1982. pap. $24.00. M Rosenberg.

Bossaglia, Rossana. Dizionario di terminologia di storia dell'arte. (Illus.). 143p. (Ital.). 1970. L.1000.00. Bignami.

Diccionario Universal del Arte y De los Artistas: Estilos y Tendencias En el Arte Occidental. 320p. (Span.). 1969. leatherette $25.50 (ISBN 0-686-57358-7, S-50283). French & Eur.

Franklin, Alfred. Dictionnaire Historique des Arts: Metiers & Professions Exerces dans Paris, Depuis 13 Siecle. 882p. (Fr.). 1977. 230.00 F. Lafitte Repr.

Le Roux, Hubert. Dictionnaire de Poitiers, Ville d'art & d'histoire. (Illus.). 298p. (Fr.). 1976. 59.50 F. H. Le Roux.

ART–HISTORY–20TH CENTURY

see Art, Modern–20th Century

ART–MARKETING

Romand, Didier & Schurr, Gerard. Dictionnaire du Marche de l'art. new ed. 420p. (Fr.). 1978. write for info. Amateur.

ART–SUBJECTS

see Art–Themes, Motives, Etc.

ART–TECHNIQUE

see also subdivision Technique under painting, sculpture and similar headings

Mayer, Ralph. A Dictionary of Art Terms & Techniques. 1981. $25.00x (ISBN 0-7136-1095-6, Pub. by Lewis Pubs). State Mutual Bk.

ART–THEMES, MOTIVES, ETC.

Cecchini, Norma & Plessi, Giuseppe. Dizionario Sinottico di Iconologia. LC 77-466702. (Illus.). xxx, 471p. (Ital.). 1976. L.24500.00. Patron.

ART, BRITISH

Ormond, Richard & Rogers, Malcolm, eds. Dictionary of British Portraiture. 1981. Vol. 3: The Victorians: Historical Figures Born Between 1800-1860. $62.50x (ISBN 0-19-520182-5); Vol. 4: The Twentieth Century: Historical Figures Born Before 1900. $62.50x (ISBN 0-19-520183-3). Oxford U Pr.

ART, CANADIAN

MacDonald. Dictionary of Canadian Artists, 6 Vols. 1977. $100.00 (ISBN 0-686-43129-4). Apollo.

ART, CHINESE

Munsterberg, Hugo. Dictionary of Chinese & Japanese Art. LC 79-83856. 1981. lib. bdg. $40.00 (ISBN 0-87817-248-3). Hacker.

ART, CHRISTIAN

see Christian Art and Symbolism

ART, DECORATIVE

see also Bronzes; Needlework also Art, African; Art, Byzantine, and similar headings

Honour, Hugh & Fleming, John. Dictionary of the Decorative Arts. LC 76-50163. (Illus.). 1977. $29.95i (ISBN 0-06-011936-5, HarpT). Har-Row.

Marmol, F. Dictionnaire des Filigranes Classes en Groupe Alphabetique. (Fr.). 1900. DM.31.80. Olms Verlag.

ART, EARLY CHRISTIAN

see Christian Art and Symbolism

ART, ECCLESIASTICAL

see Christian Art and Symbolism

ART, ENGLISH

see Art, British

ART, EUROPEAN

Schaffran, Emerich, ed. Dictionary of European Art. 1958. $4.75 (ISBN 0-8022-1497-5). Philos Lib.

ART, FRENCH

Bonnaffe, Edmond. Dictionnaire des Amateurs Francais au Dix-Septieme Siecle. (Bibliography & Reference Ser.: No. 138). (Fr.). 1968. Repr. of 1884 ed. $26.50 (ISBN 0-8337-0335-8). B Franklin.

De La Chavignerie, Emile B. & Auvray, Louis. Dictionnaire General, 5 vols. Rosenblum, Robert, ed. LC 78-68412. (Dictionnaire General Ser.). 2000p. 1979. Repr. of 1885 ed. lib. bdg. $303.00 (ISBN 0-8240-3539-9). Garland Pub.

Franklin, Alfred. Dictionnaire Historique des Arts, Metlers & Professions Exerces dans Paris Depuis le Treizieme Siecle. 882p. (Fr.). $40.00. Lenox.

Mireur, H. Dictionnaire des Ventes d'art Faites en France & a l'etranger, 1. (Illus., Fr.). 1912. DM.118.00. Olms Verlag.

--Dictionnaire des Ventes d'art Faites en France & a l'etranger, 2. (Illus., Fr.). 1912. DM.118.00. Olms Verlag.

--Dictionnaire des Ventes d'art Faites en France & a l'etranger, 3. (Illus., Fr.). 1912. DM.118.00. Olms Verlag.

--Dictionnaire des Ventes d'art Faites en France & a l'etranger, 4. (Illus., Fr.). 1912. DM.118.00. Olms Verlag.

--Dictionnaire des Ventes d'art Faites en France & a l'etranger, 5. (Illus., Fr.). 1912. DM.118.00. Olms Verlag.

--Dictionnaire des Ventes d'art Faites en France & a l'etranger, 6. (Illus., Fr.). 1912. DM.118.00. Olms Verlag.

ART, FRENCH–BIBLIOGRAPHY

Janson, H. W. An Iconographic Index to Stanislas Lami's Dictionnaire des Sculpteurs de l'Ecole Francaise au Dix-Neuvieme Siecle. LC 82-48768. 230p. 1983. lib. bdg. $75.00 (ISBN 0-8240-9399-2). Garland Pub.

ART, GERMAN

Thieme, Ulrich & Becker, Felix, eds. Allegemeines Lexikon der Bildenden Kunstler von der Antike bis zur Gegenwart, 37 vols. (Ger.). 1906-50. Repr. $2750.00 set (ISBN 0-403-07236-0). Somerset Pub.

ART, GRAPHIC

see Graphic Arts

ART, HINDU

Shukla, Lalit K. Study of Hindu Art & Architecture with Special Reference to Terminology. (Chowkamba Sanskrit Studies Ser.: Vol. 82). (Illus.). 1972. $32.00x (ISBN 0-8426-0382-4). Verry.

ART, JAPANESE

Munsterberg, Hugo. Dictionary of Chinese & Japanese Art. LC 79-83856. 1981. lib. bdg. $40.00 (ISBN 0-87817-248-3). Hacker.

ART, MODERN–20TH CENTURY

see also Expressionism (Art); Modernism (Art); Pop Art; Surrealism

Charmet, Raymond. Dictionnaire de l'art Contemporain. (Illus.). 250p. (Fr.). 1965. 17.60 F. Larousse.

O'Dwyer, R. & Le Page, R. Glossary of Modern Art. pap. $1.45 (ISBN 0-685-19403-5, 99, WL). Citadel Pr.

Osborne, Harold, ed. The Oxford Companion to Twentieth-Century Art. (Illus.). 1982. $39.95 (ISBN 0-19-866119-3). Oxford U Pr.

ART, MODERNIST
see Modernism (Art)
ART, OCCIDENTAL
see Art
ART, POP
see Pop Art
ART, PRIMITIVE
see also Idols and Images
also subdivision Antiquities under names of countries, etc.
Diccionario Universal del Arte y De los Artistas: Arte Oriental, Precolombino y De los Pueblos Primitivos. 315p. (Span.). 1969. leatherette $25.50 (ISBN 84-252-0598-0, S-50286). French & Eur.
ART, RENAISSANCE
Lexikon der Kunstslile: Bd 1, Von der Griechischen Archaik bis zur Renaissance. (Ger. & Gr.). 1978. DM.8.80 (ISBN 3-499-16132-X). Rowohlt.
ART CRITICISM
Franklin, Alfred L. Dictionnaire Historique des Arts, Metiers & Professions: Exercees dans Paris Depuis le 13 Siecle. 856p. (Fr.). 1906. DM.138.00. Olms Verlag.
Grassi, Luigi & Pepe, Mario. Dizionario della critica d'arte, 2 vols. (Illus.). xx, 676p. (Ital.). 1978. L.50000.00 (ISBN 88-02-02578-9). UTET.
Marquez Villagas, Luis. Un Lexico de la artesania. 144p. (Span.). 1961. 60.00 ptas (CSIC). Univ Granada.
ART DEALERS
Romand, Didier & Schurr, Gerald. Le Dictionnaire du Marche de l'Art. 416p. (Fr.). 1978. pap. $55.00 (ISBN 0-686-56728-5, M-6490). French & Eur.
ART INDUSTRIES AND TRADE–DICTIONARIES
Bernasconi, John R. Collector's Glossary. 3rd ed. $24.50 (ISBN 0-900361-34-4). Transatlantic.
Equipo Reactor De Ceac. Diccionario de la Decoracion. 792p. (Span., Fr., Eng., Ger. & Ital.). 1973. $44.25 (ISBN 84-329-5010-6, S-12256). French & Eur.
ART LIBRARIES
see also Architectural Libraries
Smithsonian Institution, Washington, D. C. Dictionary Catalog of the Library of the Freer Gallery of Art, 6 Vols. 1967. Set. lib. bdg. $530.00 (ISBN 0-8161-0799-8, Hall Library). G K Hall.
ART OBJECTS
Here are entered works on decorative art objects. Works on old decorative or utilitarian objects having aesthetic, historic and financial value are entered under Antiques.
Mayer, E. Dictionnaire des Valeurs de Meubles & Objets d'art. (Illus.). 450p. (Fr.). 1973. 99.00 F. Fischbacher.
Mayer, Enrique. Le Dictionnaire des Meubles & Objets D'art 1965 & 1966. 112p. (Fr.). 1967. 120.00 F. Mayer.
--Le Dictionnaire des Meubles & Objets d'art, 1963 & 1964. 320p. (Fr.). 1965. 99.00 F. Mayer Ed.
ARTHROPATHY
see Joints–Diseases
ARTICLES OF WAR
see Military Law
ARTIFICIAL TEETH
see Prosthodontics
ARTISTS–DICTIONARIES
Antique Collector's Club. The Dictionary of British Artists: 1880-1940. 567p. 1977. $59.50 (ISBN 0-902028-36-7). Antique Collect.
Archibald, E. H. Dictionary of Sea Painters. (Illus.). 453p. 1980. $79.50 (ISBN 0-902028-84-7). Antique Collect.
Benezit, E. Dictionnaire des Peintres, Sculpteurs, Dessinateurs et Graveurs, 10 vols. new, rev. ed. (Illus., Fr.). 1976. $495.00 set (ISBN 2-7000-0149-4). Hacker.
Bradley, John W. Dictionary of Miniaturists, Illustrators, Calligraphers, & Copyists, with References to Their Works, & Notices of Their Patrons, from the Establishment of Christianity to the 18th Century, 3 vols. LC 61-35160. 1973. Repr. of 1887 ed. Set. lib. bdg. $85.00 (ISBN 0-8337-0353-6). B Franklin.
Diccionario de Arte & Artistas. 600p. (Span.). 1979. write for info. Parramon Edns.
Diccionario de Arte & Artistas. (Span.). 1980. $7.00; 600.00 ptas. Parramon Edns.
Diccionario Universal del Arte y De los Artistas: Arte Occidental y del Proximo Oriente, II. 300p. (Span.). 1969. leatherette $25.50 (ISBN 0-686-77260-1, S-50284). French & Eur.
Diccionario Universal del Arte y De los Artistas: Arte Occidental y del Proximo Oriente, I. 300p. (Span.). 1969. leatherette $25.50 (ISBN 84-252-0578-6, S-50285). French & Eur.
Houfe, Simon. The Dictionary of British Book Illustrators & Caricaturists: 1800-1914. (Illus.). 520p. 1980. $62.50 (ISBN 0-902028-73-1). Antique Collect.
Laclotte, Michel & Smith, Alistair, eds. Larousse Dictionary of Painters. LC 81-81046. (Illus.). 480p. 1981. $50.00 (ISBN 0-88332-265-X, 8191). Larousse.
Mackay, James. Dictionary of Western Sculptors in Bronze. 414p. 1977. $49.50 (ISBN 0-902028-55-3). Antique Collect.
Mackey, James. Dictionary of Western Sculptors in Bronze. (Illus.). 1977. $49.50 (ISBN 0-902028-55-3). Apollo.
Mallalien, H. L. The Dictionary of Watercolors Artists, Vol. I. (Illus.). 1976. $45.00 (ISBN 0-902028-48-0). Apollo.
--The Dictionary of Watercolors Artists, Vol. II. (Illus.). 1979. $45.00 (ISBN 0-902028-63-4). Apollo.
Mallalieu, H. L. The Dictionary of Watercolour Artists up to 1920: Vol. 1, The Text. 298p. 1978. $44.50 (ISBN 0-902028-48-0). Antique Collect.
--The Dictionary of Watercolour Artists up to 1920: Vol. 2, The Plates. (Illus.). 268p. 1980. $44.50 (ISBN 0-902028-63-4). Antique Collect.
Murray, Peter & Murray, Linda. Diccionario De Artes y Artistas. 600p. (Span.). 1978. $17.25 (ISBN 84-342-0144-5, S-50013). French & Eur.
--The Penguin Dictionary of Art & Artists. lib. bdg. $11.50x (ISBN 0-88307-415-X). Gannon.
Redgrave, Samuel. A Dictionary of Artists of the English School. 500p. 1970. Repr. of 1878 ed. $20.00 (ISBN 0-87556-249-3). Saifer.
Schenck, A. Kuenstlerlexikon. 320p. (Ger.). 1973. pap. $12.95 (ISBN 3-499-16165-6, M-7523, Pub. by Rowohlt). French & Eur.
--Kuenstlerlexikon. 320p. (Ger.). 1973. pap. $12.95 (ISBN 3-499-16165-6). Rowohlt.
Strickland, Walter G. Dictionary of Irish Artists, 2 vols. (Illus.). 1358p. 1969. Repr. of 1913 ed. $90.00x set (ISBN 0-7165-0602-5, Pub. by Irish Academic Pr Ireland). Biblio Dist.
Wood, Christopher. The Dictionary of Victorian Painters. (Illus.). 764p. 1979. $74.50 (ISBN 0-902028-72-3). Antique Collect.
ARTISTS–GREAT BRITAIN
Dolman, Bernard. The Dictionary of Contemporary British Artists, 1929. 551p. 1981. $39.50 (ISBN 0-902028-99-5). Antique Collect.
Graves, Algernon. Dictionary of Artists: London Exhibitions 1760-1893. 3rd rev. ed. $24.00 (ISBN 0-912729-04-X). Newbury Bks.
--The Royal Academy of Arts, a Complete Dictionary of Contributors & Their Work from Its Foundation in 1769 to 1904, Compiled with the Sanction of the President & Council of the Royal Academy, 8 vols. in 4. LC 76-118750. 1972. Repr. of 1905 ed. Set. lib. bdg. $181.00 (ISBN 0-8337-1425-2). B Franklin.
Houfe, Simon. The Dictionary of British Book Illustrators & Caricaturists: 1800-1914. (Illus.). 520p. 1980. $62.50 (ISBN 0-902028-73-1). Antique Collect.
Johnson & Greutyner. The Dictionary of British Artists Eighteen Eighty to Nineteen Forty. (Illus.). 1980. $59.50 (ISBN 0-902028-36-7). Apollo.
Redgrave, Samuel. Dictionary of Artists of the English School. 2nd rev. ed. $12.00 (ISBN 0-912728-16-7). Newbury Bks.
ARTISTS–IRELAND
Strickland, Walter G. Dictionary of Irish Artists, 2 vols. (Illus.). 1358p. 1969. Repr. of 1913 ed. $90.00x set (ISBN 0-7165-0602-5, Pub. by Irish Academic Pr Ireland). Biblio Dist.
ARTISTS, WOMEN
see Women Artists
ARTS, THE
Diccionario Manual de Bellas Artes. 320p. (Span.). 1979. write for info. Biblograf.
Diccionario Monografico de Bellas Artes. 288p. (Span.). 750.00 ptas (ISBN 84-7153-381-2). Biblograf SP.
Koch, Willi A. Musisches Lexikon. LC 77-457599. (Illus., Ger.). 1976. DM.48.00 (ISBN 3-520-80303-8). Kroener.
ARTS, THE–CRITICISM
see Art Criticism
ARTS, DECORATIVE
see Art, Decorative; Handicraft
also subjects referred to under these headings
ARTS, FINE
see Art; Arts, the
ARTS, GRAPHIC
see Graphic Arts
ARTS, USEFUL
see Technology
ARTS IN THE CHURCH
see Christian Art and Symbolism
ARYAN LANGUAGES
see Indo-European Languages
ARYANS
see Indo-Europeans
ASANTE LANGUAGE
see Twi Language
ASCORBIC ACID
see Vitamins
ASHANTI LANGUAGE
see Twi Language
ASIA
see also names of regions, countries, cities, etc. in Asia
Anthony, John D. Historical & Cultural Dictionary of the Sultanate of Oman & the Emirates of Eastern Arabia. LC 76-42216. (Historical & Cultural Dictionaries of Asia Ser.: No. 9). 1976. $13.00 (ISBN 0-8108-0975-3). Scarecrow.
ASIA–RELIGION
Rice, Edward. Eastern Definitions. LC 77-19359. (Illus.). 1980. pap. $8.95 (ISBN 0-385-15631-6, Anch). Doubleday.
ASIA, SOUTHEASTERN–LANGUAGES
Freiberger, Nancy & Vy Thi Be. Nung Fan Slihng Vocabulary. 353p. 1976. pap. $9.00x (ISBN 0-88312-793-8); microfiche $3.75 (ISBN 0-88312-337-1). Summer Inst Ling.
Wojowasito, Soewojo. A Kawi Lexicon. Mills, Roger F., ed. LC 78-57221. (Michigan Papers on South & Southeast Asia: No. 17). xv, 629p. (Orig.). 1980. pap. $16.00x (ISBN 0-89148-017-X). Ctr S&SE Asian.
ASSAM
Cordier, Henri. Bibliotheca Indosinica. Dictionnaire bibliographique des ouvrages relatifs a la peninsule indo-chinoise, 5 vols. in 3. (Span. & Indonesian.). 1912-32. Set. $197.00 (ISBN 0-8337-0676-4). B Franklin.
ASSASSINATION
Maurais, J. Lexique des Epices et Assaisonnements: Anglais-Francais. 73p. (Eng. & Fr.). 1979. pap. $5.95 (ISBN 0-7754-2593-1, M-9236). French & Eur.
ASSESSMENT
Here are entered works on tax assessment. Works on the technique of property valuation for other than taxation purposes are entered under specific headings with subdivision Valuation, e.g. Real Property–Valuation. Works on assessment in a particular field of taxation are entered under the heading covering taxation in that field, e.g. Real Property Tax.
see also Real Property–Valuation
Institute of Business Appraiser. Glossary of Value Terms. $5.00; $2.00. Inst Busn Appraisers.
ASSINIBOIN INDIANS
see Indians of North America–The West
ASSOCIATION FOOTBALL
see Soccer
ASSOCIATIONS, INSTITUTIONS, ETC.
see also Meetings
also names of specific types of associations, institutions, etc. e.g., Corporations; Public Institutions; Trade and Professional Associations; subdivision Societies under appropriate subjects
Gomez de Cadiz, Javier. Diccionario de Sigles de Organismos Nacionales e Internacionales. 64p. (Span.). 1976. pap. $1.75 (ISBN 84-203-0051-9, S-50584). French & Eur.
Marion, Marcel. Dictionnaire des Institutions de la France aux XVII & XVIII Siecles. 573p. (Fr.). 1968. $27.50. Lenox.
Spillner, P. Internationales Woerterbuch der Abkuerzungen Von Organisationen, 3 vols. 1295p. (Ger. & Eng., International Dictionary of Abbreviations of Organizations). 1972. $120.00 (ISBN 3-7940-1098-1, M-7484, Pub. by Vlg. Dokumentation). French & Eur.
Spillner, Paul. International Dictionary of Abbreviations of Organizations, 3 vols. 2nd ed. (Eng. & Ger.). 1970. $120.00 (ISBN 3-7940-1398-0, M-7481, Pub. by Verlag Dokumentation SVK). French & Eur.
ASSOCIATIONS, INTERNATIONAL
see International Agencies
ASSURANCE (INSURANCE)
see Insurance
ASSYRO-BABYLONIAN LANGUAGE
see also Sumerian Language
Gelb, Ignace J. Glossary of Old Akkadian. (Materials for the Assyrian Dictionary Ser: No. 3). 1957. pap. text ed. $12.00x (ISBN 0-226-62307-6). U of Chicago Pr.
Muss-Arnolt, William. A Concise Dictionary of the Assyrian Languages, 2 vols. LC 78-72752. (Ancient Mesopotamian Texts & Studies). (Assyrian.). Repr. of 1905 ed. $97.50 set (ISBN 0-404-18195-3). AMS Pr.
Oppenheim, A. Leo, ed. The Assyrian Dictionary of the Oriental Institute of the University of Chicago, Vol. 5, G. LC 56-58292. (Assyrian & Eng.). 1956. lib. bdg. $14.50x (ISBN 0-918986-11-7). Oriental Inst.
--The Assyrian Dictionary of the Oriental Institute of the University of Chicago, Vol. 6, H. LC 56-58292. (Assyrian & Eng.). 1956. lib. bdg. $21.00x (ISBN 0-918986-12-5). Oriental Inst.
Oppenheim, A. Leo & Reiner, Erica, eds. Assyrian Dictionary of the Oriental Institute of the University of Chicago. Incl. Vol. 1, A, Pt. 2. 1976. Repr. of 1968 ed. 42.00x (ISBN 0-918986-07-9); Vol. 3, D. 1977. Repr. of 1959 ed. 17.00x (ISBN 0-918986-09-5); Vol. 4, E. 1974. Repr. of 1958 ed. 31.00x (ISBN 0-918986-10-9); Vol. 7, I-J. 1974. Repr. of 1960 ed. 25.00x (ISBN 0-918986-13-3); Vol. 9, L. 1978. Repr. of 1973 ed. 35.00x (ISBN 0-918986-15-X); Vol. 10, M, Pts 1 & 2. LC 56-58292. 1978. 110.00x (ISBN 0-918986-16-8); Vol. 16, S. 1977. Repr. of 1962 ed. 22.00x (ISBN 0-918986-18-4). LC 56-58292. (Assyrian.). Oriental Inst.
--The Assyrian Dictionary of the Oriental Institute of the University of Chicago, Vol. 1, A, Pt. 1. LC 56-58292. (Assyrian.). 1964. lib. bdg. $29.00x (ISBN 0-918986-06-0). Oriental Inst.
Oppenheim, A. Leo, et al, eds. The Assyrian Dictionary of the Oriental Institute of the University of Chicago, Vol. 2, B. LC 56-58292. (Assyrian.). 1966. lib. bdg. $28.00x (ISBN 0-918986-08-7). Oriental Inst.

ASTROLOGY–DICTIONARIES
Brau, Jean-Louis. Dictionnaire de l'astrologie. LC 77-559018. (Illus.). 222p. (Fr.). 1977. 16.90 F (ISBN 2-03-075477-3). Larousse FR.
--Dictionnaire de l'astrologie. (Illus.). 222p. (Fr.). 1977. 17.60 F. Larousse.
Capone, Federico. Dizionario astrologico. 224p. (Ital.). 1978. L.7500.00. Capone C.
Curcio, Michele. Dictionnaire de l'astrologie. LC 77-451302. (Illus.). 290p. (Fr.). 1976. 39.00 F (ISBN 2-203-22107-0). Casterman.
Fleming-Mitchell, Leslie. Astrology Terms. LC 77-597. (Orig.). 1977. lib. bdg. $12.90 (ISBN 0-914294-69-5); pap. $2.95 (ISBN 0-914294-70-9). Running Pr.
Francis, James J. The New English Astrological Thesaurus. LC 76-47426. 1977. pap. $1.95 (ISBN 0-87707-179-9). CSA Pr.
Gouchou, Henry J. Le Dictionnaire Astrologique. 670p. (Fr.). 1975. $67.50 (ISBN 0-686-57307-2, M-6284). French & Eur.
--Le Dictionnaire Astrologique. 670p. (Fr.). 1975. 170.00 F. Dervy Livres.
Johndro. Astrological Dictionary. $2.00. Am Fed Astrologers.
Leo. Complete Dictionary of Astrology. $7.95 (Inner Traditions). Am Fed Astrologers.
Leo, Alan & Robson. Alan Leo's Dictionary of Astrology. $6.50 (Pub. by Sun Pub). Am Fed Astrologers.
Leo, Alan & Robson, Vivian E. Alan Leo's Dictionary of Astrology. 205p. 1981. pap. $10.50 (ISBN 0-89540-101-0, SB-101). Sun Pub.
Wedeck, H. E. Dictionary of Astrology. (Illus.). 288p. 1973. pap. $3.95 (ISBN 0-8065-0371-8). Citadel Pr.
Wilson, James. Dictionary of Astrology. LC 79-16506. (Illus.). 1970. Repr. $15.00 (ISBN 0-87728-086-X). Weiser.
--Dictionary of Astrology. LC 79-16506. $15.00 (Samuel Weiser Inc.). Am Fed Astrologers.

ASTRONAUTICAL INSTRUMENTS
Angelo, Joseph A., Jr. Dictionary of Space Technology. LC 81-3144. (Illus.). 392p. 1982. $19.95x (ISBN 0-87196-583-6). Facts on File.

ASTRONAUTICS–DICTIONARIES
Angelo, Joseph A., Jr. Dictionary of Space Technology. LC 81-3144. (Illus.). 392p. 1982. $19.95x (ISBN 0-87196-583-6). Facts on File.
Astronautical Multilingual Dictionary: International Academy of Astronautics. (Eng. , Ger. , Fr. , Ital. , Span. , Rus. & Czech.). 1970. $149.00 (ISBN 0-444-40830-4). Elsevier.
De Galiana, Thomas. Diccionario de la astronautica. (Span.). 100.00 ptas. Plaza Janes.
Dictionnaire des Techniques Aeronautiques et Spatiales-- Trilingue: Francais, Anglais, Allemand: 24,000 Entrees Dans Chaque Langue. 1200p. (Fr., Eng. & Ger.). 1978. $175.00 (ISBN 2-04-010124-1, M-6131). French & Eur.
Guilbert. Le Vocabulaire de L'astronautique: Enquete Linguistique a travers la Presse d'information a L'occasion De Cinq Exploits de Cosmonautes. (Publ. de l'Univ. de Rouen Fac. des Lettres et Sc. Hum.). (Fr.). $15.95 (ISBN 0-685-36683-9). French & Eur.
Guilbert, L. Le Vocabulaire De L'astronautique. 361p. (Fr.). pap. $45.00 (ISBN 0-686-57265-3, F-137130). French & Eur.
Hiebeler, Toni. Lexikon der Aero & Astronautik Einschliesslich Raketentechnik: Lexikon der Alpen. (Ger.). 1972. write for info. (ISBN 3-920902-07-6). Sokoll.
Hyman, Charles J. German-English, English-German Astronautics Dictionary. LC 65-20216. 273p. (Ger. & Eng.). 1968. $30.00x (ISBN 0-306-10748-1, Consultants). Plenum Pub.
Konarski, M. M. Russian-English Space Technology Dictionary. LC 72-99990. (Rus. & Eng.). 1970. $77.00 (ISBN 0-08-015617-7). Pergamon.
McLaughlin, Charles. Space Age Dictionary. 2nd ed. (Illus.). 1963. $11.95x (ISBN 0-442-05284-7). Van Nos Reinhold.
Mateu Sancho, Pedro. Diccionario de la astronomia y astronautica. (Illus.). 346p. (Span.). 400.00 ptas. Destino.
--Diccionario de la Astronomica y Astronautica. 350p. (Span.). 1962. $37.50 (ISBN 84-233-0114-1, S-12334). French & Eur.

ASTRONOMICAL PHYSICS
see Astrophysics

ASTRONOMY
see also Almanacs; Astrophysics; Chronology; Cosmogony; Geodesy; Outer Space; Space Environment; Space Sciences; Spectrum Analysis
Herrmann, Joachim. Meyers Grosses Sternbuch fur Kinder. (Illus.). 126p. (Ger.). write for info. (ISBN 3-411-01909-3). Biblio Inst.

ASTRONOMY–DICTIONARIES
Becker, Udo. Herder-Lexikon. LC 75-514614. 239p. (Ger.). 1975. DM.19.80 (ISBN 3-451-16463-9). Herder.
Chiu, Hong-Yee, ed. Chinese-English & English-Chinese Astronomical Dictionary. LC 65-10966. 173p. (Chinese & Eng.). 1966. $30.00x (ISBN 0-306-10739-2, Consultants). Plenum Pub.
Dictionary of Astronomy. 103p. (Eng. & Chinese.). 1974. pap. $3.95 (ISBN 0-686-92284-0, M-9574). French & Eur.
Hopkins, Jeanne, ed. Glossary of Astronomy & Astrophysics. 2nd, rev. & enl. ed. LC 80-5226. (Phoenix Ser.). x, 196p. 1982. pap. $10.00 (ISBN 0-226-35169-6). U of Chicago Pr.
--Glossary of Astronomy & Astrophysics. rev. ed. LC 80-5226. 224p. 1980. lib. bdg. $17.50x (ISBN 0-226-35171-8). U of Chicago Pr.
Illingworth, Valerie. The Anchor Dictionary of Astronomy. LC 79-6538. (Illus.). 448p. (Orig.). 1980. pap. $7.50 (ISBN 0-385-15936-6, Anch). Doubleday.
Illingworth, Valerie, ed. Facts on File: Dictionary of Astronomy. (Illus.). 1979. $17.50 (ISBN 0-87196-326-4). Facts on File.
Kleczek, Josip. Astronomical Dictionary: In Six Languages. (Eng., Fr., Ger., Ital., Rus. & Czech.). 1962. $109.00 (ISBN 0-12-411950-6). Acad Pr.
Maddison, Robert. A Dictionary of Astronomy. 208p. E5.95 (ISBN 0-600-32996-8). Newnes Bks.
Mateu Sancho, Pedro. Diccionario de la astronomia y astronautica. (Illus.). 346p. (Span.). 400.00 ptas. Destino.
--Diccionario de la Astronomica y Astronautica. 350p. (Span.). 1962. $37.50 (ISBN 84-233-0114-1, S-12334). French & Eur.
Meinikov, O. English-Russian Astronomical Dictionary. 504p. (Eng. & Rus.). 1980. $15.00x (ISBN 0-569-06519-4, Pub. by Collet's). State Mutual Bk.
Melnikov, O. A., et al, eds. Anglo-Russkii Astronomicheskii Slovar. 504p. (Eng. & Rus.). 1971. $4.75 (Pub. by Sov Entsiklopediia). Four Continent.
Mitton, Jacqueline. Key Definitions in Astronomy. LC 82-183. (Quality Paperback: No. 375). 174p. (Orig.). 1982. pap. text ed. $4.95 (ISBN 0-8226-0375-6). Littlefield.
Nicolson, Iain, ed. Dictionary of Astronomy. (Illus.). 250p. 1980. pap. $4.95 (ISBN 0-06-463524-4, EH 524). B&N NY.
Popovici, Calin. Dictionar de Astronomie Astronautica. LC 77-567521. 439p. (Romanian.). 1977. 28.00 lei. Editura Stiintifica.
Schnitzler, Ilse. Lexikon Fuer Planetenbilder. (Ger.). 1975. $25.00 (ISBN 3-920807-07-3, M-7196). French & Eur.
Tver, David F. Dictionary of Astronomy, Space & Atmospheric Phenomena. 1979. text ed. $19.95 (ISBN 0-442-24045-7). Van Nos Reinhold.
Tver, David F., et al. Dictionary of Astronomy, Space & Atmospheric Phenomena. 288p. 1982. pap. text ed. $12.95 (ISBN 0-442-28422-5). Van Nos Reinhold.
Vega, Vincente. Diccionario Ilustrado de Efemerides, 2 vols. 1901p. (Span.). 1968. Set. leatherette $47.95 (ISBN 84-252-0600-6, S-12366); pap. $38.95 (ISBN 84-252-0600-6, S-50279). French & Eur.
Vocabulaire d'Astronomie. (Fr., Eng. & Ger.). 1978. pap. $39.95 (ISBN 0-686-57249-1, M-6555). French & Eur.
Vocabulaire d'astronomie: Francais-Anglais-Allemand. (Fr. , Eng. & Ger.). 1978. 85.00 F. C. I. L. F.

ASTRONOMY–DIRECTORIES
Lindner, K. & Neumann, K. H. Jugendlexikon Astronomie & Raumfahrt. (Illus.). 256p. (Ger.). 1982. M.12.00. Bibl Inst Leipzig.

ASTROPHYSICS
see also Spectrum Analysis
Hopkins, Jeanne, ed. Glossary of Astronomy & Astrophysics. 2nd, rev. & enl. ed. LC 80-5226. (Phoenix Ser.). x, 196p. 1982. pap. $10.00 (ISBN 0-226-35169-6). U of Chicago Pr.
--Glossary of Astronomy & Astrophysics. rev. ed. LC 80-5226. 224p. 1980. lib. bdg. $17.50x (ISBN 0-226-35171-8). U of Chicago Pr.

ATHEISM
Karmannyi Slovar Ateista. 280p. (Rus.). 1979. $2.85 (Pub. by Politizdat). Four Continent.

ATHENS–ANTIQUITIES
Travlos, John. Pictorial Dictionary of Ancient Athens. LC 79-91823. (Illus.). 590p. 1980. Repr. of 1971 ed. lib. bdg. $100.00 (ISBN 0-87817-267-X). Hacker.

ATHLETIC MEDICINE
see Sports Medicine

ATHLETICS–MEDICAL ASPECTS
see Sports Medicine

ATLASES
Hanle, Adolf. Meyers Neues Lexikon Weltatlas. 354p. (Ger.). write for info. (ISBN 3-411-01759-7). Biblio Inst.

ATLASES, AMERICAN
see Atlases

ATMOSPHERE
see also Meteorology
also headings beginning with the word Atmospheric
Gavande, S. A. & Bornemisza, Elemer. Terminologia Moderna de Energia de Agua en el Sistema Suelo-Planta Atmosfera. 6p. (Span.). 1969. write for info. IICA.
Tver, David F., et al. Dictionary of Astronomy, Space & Atmospheric Phenomena. 288p. 1982. pap. text ed. $12.95 (ISBN 0-442-28422-5). Van Nos Reinhold.

ATMOSPHERIC HUMIDITY
see Humidity

ATOMIC ENERGY
see also Atomic Power; Nuclear Engineering
American Nuclear Society. Trial Use Nuclear Glossary. Incl. ANS-6.5, ANS-19.2, ANS-50 Glossaries. $25.00. Am Nuclear Soc.
Hoefling, Oskar, ed. Lexikon der Schulphysik: Bd 5, Atomphysik. (Ger.). 1978. DM.58.00 (ISBN 3-7614-0110-8). Aulis Verlag.

ATOMIC ENERGY–DICTIONARIES
Anglo-Ispano-Russko-Frantsuzskii Slovar Nauchnykh & Tekhnicheskikh Terminov Po Atomnoi Energii. 216p. (Eng. , Span. , Rus. & Fr.). 1958. $5.50 (Pub. by United Nations Publications). Four Continent.
Carpovich, Eugene A. Russian-English Atomic Dictionary: Physics, Mathematics, Nucleonics. rev. ed. 2nd ed. LC 57-8256. (Rus. & Eng.). 1959. $15.00 (ISBN 0-911484-00-0). Tech Dict.
Charles, Victorin. Diccionario Atomico. 296p. (Span.). 1962. $14.95 (ISBN 0-686-56708-0, S-33057). French & Eur.
Franzen, F. & Hard, L. Woerterbuch der Kernenergie. viii, 240p. (Ger.). 1957. DM.23.90 (ISBN 3-18-400034-6). Brandstetter.
Markus, John. Diccionario de Electronica y Tecnica Nuclear. 1052p. (Span. & Eng.). $75.95 (ISBN 84-267-0003-9, S-14264). French & Eur.
Mataix, M. Diccionario de eletronica y energia nuclear ingles-espanol. 772p. (Eng. & Span.). 620.00 ptas. Danae.
Mataix Lord, Mariano. Diccionario De Electronica, Informatica y Centrales Nucleares. 660p. (Fr. & Eng.). 1978. leather $59.95 (ISBN 84-267-0350-X, S-30687). French & Eur.

ATOMIC MEDICINE
see Nuclear Medicine

ATOMIC NUCLEI
see Nuclear Physics

ATOMIC POWER
see also Atomic Energy; Atomic Power Plants
Brandenberger, E. & Stattmann, F. Nuclear Power Dictionary, Vol. 63. 456p. (Eng. & Ger.). 1978. pap. $52.50 (ISBN 3-521-06112-4, M-7572, Verlag Karl Thiemig). French & Eur.
Larsson, Lars G. & Lorveberg, Sven. Karnkraft Fran A til O. LC 80-468740. 136p. (Swedish.). 1979. write for info. (ISBN 9-1728-4108-7). Ingenjorsforlaget.
V. Franzen, F. Woerterbuch der Kerenergie. (Eng. & Ger., Dictionary of Nuclear Energy). 1957. $20.00 (ISBN 0-686-56618-1, M-6987). French & Eur.

ATOMIC POWER ENGINEERING
see Nuclear Engineering

ATOMIC POWER PLANTS
Stattmann, F. Dictionary of Power Plant Engineering: Nuclear Power Plants, Pt. II. 316p. (Ger. & Fr.). 1973. $15.95 (ISBN 3-521-06081-0, M-7102). French & Eur.

ATOMS
see also Nuclear Physics
Charles, Victorin, tr. Diccionario atomico. 296p. (Span.). 1962. Arg.$2.00. Leru.
Doskoboinik, D. I., et al, eds. Anglo-Russkii Iadernyi Slovar. 400p. (Eng. & Rus.). 1960. $4.80 (Pub. by Glav. Red. Inostr. Nauchn. Tekhn. Slovarei Fizmatgiza). Four Continent.

ATOMS, NUCLEI OF
see Nuclear Physics

ATYPICAL CHILDREN
see Exceptional Children

AUDIO-VISUAL AIDS
see Audio-Visual Materials

AUDIO-VISUAL EQUIPMENT
Here are entered general works on projects, screens, sound equipment, pointers, tables, exhibit boards, etc.
see also names of particular equipment, e.g. Moving picture projectors; Record changers
Rosenberg, Kenyon C. & Feinstein, Paul T. Dictionary of Library & Educational Technology. 2nd, rev., & enl. ed. 300p. 1983. lib. bdg. write for info. (ISBN 0-87287-396-X). Libs Unl.

AUDIO-VISUAL MATERIALS
see also Moving-Pictures
also subdivision Audio-visual aids, or study and teaching under subjects, e.g. Music
Dictionary of Audio Visual Terms. 1983. text ed. $24.95. Butterworth.
Heinrichs, Heribert. Lexikon der Audio-Visuellen Bildungsmittel. (Ger.). 1971. $28.00 (ISBN 3-466-30097-5, M-7275). French & Eur.
Heinrichs, Heribert, ed. Lexikon der Audio-Visuellen Bildungsmittel. xvi, 404p. (Ger.). 1971. DM.35.00 (ISBN 3-466-30097-5). Koesel.
Pessis-Pasternak, Guitta. Dictionnaire de l'audio-Visual. 372p. (Fr.). 1976. Can.$10.00. Flammarion.
--Dictionnaire de l'audio-Visual: Francais-Anglais. 384p. (Fr. & Eng.). 1976. 38.00 F. Flammarion.
--Dictionnaire de l'Audio-Visuel: Francais-Anglais, Anglais-Francais. 384p. (Fr. & Eng.). 1976. pap. $15.95 (ISBN 0-686-57070-7, M-6442). French & Eur.

AUDIOLOGY
see also Deafness

Nicolosi, Lucille, et al. Terminology of Communication Disorders: Speech, Language, Hearing. (Illus.). 288p. 1978. pap. $17.50 (ISBN 0-683-06500-9). Williams & Wilkins.

AUROBINDO, SRI, 1872-1950

Aurobindo. Glossary of Terms in Sri Aurobindo's Writings. 1979. $9.50 (ISBN 0-89744-980-0, Pub. by Sri Aurobindo Ashram Trust India); pap. $7.50 (ISBN 0-89744-981-9, Pub. by Sri Aurobindo Ashram Trust India). Auromere.

AUSTEN, JANE, 1775-1817

Apperson, G. L. Jane Austen Dictionary. LC 73-15997. 1932. lib. bdg. $10.75 (ISBN 0-8414-2922-7). Folcroft.

Schapera, I. Kinship Terminology in Jane Austen's Novels. (Royal Anthropological Institute of Great Britain & Ireland Occasional Paper Ser.: No.33). 24p. 1977. pap. text ed. $5.50x (ISBN 0-391-01112-X). Humanities.

AUSTRALIA–COMMERCE

Yorston, Keith. The Australian Commercial Dictionary. LC 73-163182. 340p. 1972. $12.50x (ISBN 0-455-16550-5). Intl Pubns Serv.

AUSTRALIA–HISTORY

Murphy, B. Dictionary of Australian History. 340p. 1982. $19.00 (ISBN 0-07-072946-8). McGraw.

AUSTRALIA–POLITICS AND GOVERNMENT

Jaensch, Dean & Teichmann, Max E. The Macmillan Dictionary of Australian Politics. LC 81-461270. 264p. 1979. pap. write for info. (ISBN 0-333-29883-7). Macmillan Aust.

AUSTRALIAN ABORIGINES–LANGUAGES

see Australian Languages

AUSTRALIAN ENGLISH

see English Language in Australia

AUSTRALIAN LANGUAGES

Geytenbeek, Brian & Geytenbeek, Helen. Gidabal Grammar & Dictionary. (AIAS Linguistics Ser.: No. 17). (Orig.). 1971. pap. text ed. $10.50x (ISBN 0-85575-019-7). Humanities.

Hall, Harold A. A Partial Vocabulary of the Ngalooma Aboriginal Tribe. (AIAS Linguistics Ser.: No. 18). 1971. pap. text ed. $6.00x (ISBN 0-85575-020-0). Humanities.

Harber, K., ed. Heinemann Australian Dictionary. 1976. text ed. 14.50x (ISBN 0-686-65318-1, 00511). Heinemann Ed.

Loving, Dick. Awa Dictionary. LC 76-382715. xliv, 203p. (Awa & Eng.). 1975. write for info. (ISBN 0-85883-137-6). Linguistic Circle.

Parlier, Jim & Parlier, Jaki. Managalasi Language: Managalasi Dictionary. LC 82-130942. viii, 504p. (Eng. & Managalasi.). 1981. pap. write for info. (ISBN 0-7263-0761-0). Summer Inst Abor.

AUSTRIA

see also names of cities, regions, etc. in Austria, e.g. Vienna

Jungmair, Otto, ed. Woerterbuch zur Oberoesterreichischen Volksmundart. LC 80-487672. 351p. (Ger.). 1978. S.280.00. Selbstverlag Inst.

Zedtwitz, Hans G. Jurdicia Lexikon: Das Kleine Oesterreicher Rechtswoerterbuch. LC 75-590427. 223p. (Ger.). 1974. S.175.00. Juridica Verlag.

AUSTRONESIAN LANGUAGES

see also Malayan Languages; Melanesian Languages; Polynesian Languages

Korigodsky, R. N., et al. Indonesian-Russian Dictionary. 1171p. (Indonesian & Rus.). 1961. leatherette $14.25 (ISBN 0-686-87187-1, M-9098). French & Eur.

Wurm, Stefan A. & Wilson, Basil. English Finderlist of Reconstructions in Austronesian Languages. LC 79-342769. xxxii, 246p. (Proto-Austronesian & Eng.). 1975. write for info. (ISBN 0-85883-129-5). Linguistic Circle.

AUTHORITY

Vajda, Georges. Le Dictionnaire des Autorites. 226p. (Fr.). 1963. pap. 49.00 F (ISBN 2-22200-635-X). CNRS.

AUTHORS

see also Anonyms and Pseudonyms also particular classes of writers, e.g. Dramatists, Historians, Poets; also names of authors, e.g. Shakespeare, William

Diccionario de Autoridades, 3 vols. 2104p. (Span.). Set. $120.00 (ISBN 84-249-1334-5, S-12251). French & Eur.

Steiner, G., et al, eds. Lexikon Fremdsprachiger Schriftsteller, 3 vols. 1828p. (Ger.). 1981. M.60.00. Bibl Inst Leipzig.

AUTHORS–CORRESPONDENCE, REMINISCENCES, ETC.

Browning, D. S. Everyman's Dictionary of Literary Biography. 3rd ed. (Everyman's Reference Library). 812p. 1969. $13.50 (ISBN 0-460-03008-6, Pub by J M Dent England). Biblio Dist.

AUTHORS, AFRO-AMERICAN

see Afro-American Authors

AUTHORS, FRENCH

Favre, Yves-Alain A. Dictionnaire des Auteurs de Langue Francais. (Fr.). 1978. write for info. Flammarion.

Malignon, J. Dictionnaire des Ecrivains Francais. 576p. (Fr.). 1971. $29.95 (ISBN 0-686-57029-4, M-6388). French & Eur.

Tilander, Gunnar. Lexique du Roman de Renart. 163p. (Fr.). 1971. 35.00 F. Champion.

AUTHORS, GERMAN

Albrecht, Guenther. Lexikon Deutschsprachiger Schriftsteller, Vol. 1. (Ger.). 1974. $45.00 (ISBN 3-589-00091-0, M-7204). French & Eur.

--Lexikon Deutschsprachiger Schriftsteller, Vol. 2. (Ger.). 1974. $45.00 (ISBN 3-589-00092-9, M-7205). French & Eur.

Albrecht, Guenther, et al, eds. Lexikon Deutschsprachiger Schriftsteller: Bd 1. 262p. (Ger.). 1974. DM.12.80 (ISBN 3-589-00061-9). Scriptor Verlag.

--Lexikon Deutschsprachiger Schriftsteller: Bd 3. 248p. (Ger.). 1974. DM.12.80 (ISBN 3-589-00063-5). Scriptor Verlag.

--Lexikon Deutschsprachiger Schriftsteller: Bd 4. 262p. (Ger.). 1974. DM.12.80 (ISBN 3-589-00064-3). Scriptor Verlag.

--Lexikon Deutschsprachiger Schriftsteller: Bd 1. 509p. (Ger.). 1974. DM.29.00 (ISBN 3-589-00091-0). Scriptor Verlag.

AUTHORS, LATIN-AMERICAN

Medina, Jose T. Diccionario de Anonimos y Seudonimos Hispanoamericanos, 2 vols. in 1. LC 73-78355. (Span.). 1973. Repr. of 1925 ed. $38.50x (ISBN 0-87917-026-3). Ethridge.

Ocampo de Gomez, Aurora & Prado Velazquez, Ernesto. Diccionario de Escritores Mexicanos. (Span.). $69.95 (ISBN 0-686-56696-3, S-6745). French & Eur.

AUTHORS, RUSSIAN

Masanov, I. F. Slovar PsevdonimovRusskikh Pisatelei: Uchenykh & Obshchestvennykh Deiatelei, 4 vols. (Rus.). 1960. $35.00 set (Pub. by Izd. Vsesoiuzn Knizhn Palaty). Four Continent.

AUTHORS AND PRINTERS

see Authorship–Handbooks, Manuals, etc.; Printing–Style Manuals

AUTHORSHIP–HANDBOOKS, MANUALS, ETC.

see also Printing–Style Manuals

Seaton, A. G. Writer's Dictionary. new ed. LC 77-166289. 1000p. 1973. $20.00 (ISBN 0-685-38709-7). St Martin.

AUTO MECHANICS

see Automobile Mechanics

AUTOBIOGRAPHY

see also Biography (As a Literary Form)

Winslow, Donald J. Life-Writing: A Glossary of Terms in Biography, Autobiography & Related Forms. (Biography Monographs). 60p. (Orig.). pap. text ed. $5.00x (ISBN 0-8248-0748-0). UH Pr.

AUTOBIOGRAPHY–TECHNIQUE

see Autobiography

AUTOCODES

see Programming Languages (Electronic Computers)

AUTOGENOUS WELDING

see Welding

AUTOGRAPHIC PROCESSES

see Copying Processes

AUTOMATED INFORMATION NETWORKS

see Information Networks

AUTOMATIC COMPUTERS

see Computers

AUTOMATIC CONTROL–DICTIONARIES

Anglo-Russkii Slovar Po Avtomatike & Kontrol'noizmeritel'nym Priboram. 380p. (Eng. & Rus.). 1957. $3.25 (Pub. by Gosizdat Tekhnikoteoretich. Lit.). Four Continent.

Broadbent, D. T. & Masubuchi, M. Multilingual Glossary of Automatic Control Technology: English-French-German-Russian-Italian-Spanish-Japanese. 230p. (Eng., Fr., Ger., Rus., Ital., Span. & Japanese.). 1981. $45.00 (ISBN 0-08-027607-5). Pergamon.

Clason, W., ed. Elsevier's Dictionary of Automatic Control. (Eng., Fr., Ger. & Rus.). 1961. $37.25 (ISBN 0-444-40752-9). Elsevier.

Control Terminology (A Glossary of Common Control Terms, No. 13. (Tech Tip). 100 copies $6.50. NA Heating & AC Wholesalers.

Khramov, A. V., ed. Russko-Anglo-Nemetsko-Frantsuzskii Slovar Terminov Po Avtomaticheskomu Upravleniiu. 229p. (Rus., Eng., Fr. & Ger.). 1963. $4.80 (Pub. by An Arm SSR). Four Continent.

Radet for Teknisk Terminologi. Ordbok for Automatiseringsteknikk. 143p. (Eng. & Dutch.). 1979. Kr.80.00 (ISBN 8-2002-6067-4). Universitesforlaget.

Sykora, Jiri. Automatizacna Technika. LC 76-511586. 1023p. (Eng., Fr., Rus., Pol. & Slovak.). 1975. 140.00 Kcs. Alfa-Vydavatel.

Sykora, Jiri, ed. Dictionary of Automatical Technique. 1023p. (Eng., Ger., Fr., Rus., Span., Pol., Madasko & Sloven.). 1975. $150.00 (ISBN 0-686-92413-4, M-9892). French & Eur.

Terminological Dictionary of Automatic Control. 641p. 1977. Leatherette $19.95 (ISBN 0-686-92164-X, M-9059). French & Eur.

AUTOMATIC DATA PROCESSING

see Electronic Data Processing

AUTOMATIC DATA PROCESSORS

see Computers

AUTOMATIC DATA STORAGE

see Information Storage and Retrieval Systems

AUTOMATIC DIGITAL COMPUTERS

see Electronic Digital Computers

AUTOMATIC DRAFTING

see Computer Graphics

AUTOMATIC FACTORIES

see Automation

AUTOMATIC PRODUCTION

see Automation

AUTOMATIC PROGRAMMING LANGUAGES

see Programming Languages (Electronic Computers)

AUTOMATION

Field, R. M. A Glossary of Office Automation Terms. 32p. 1982. pap. text ed. $15.00 (ISBN 0-914548-42-5). Soc Tech Comm.

Tver, David F. & Bolz, Roger W. Robotics Sourcebook & Dictionary. 304p. 1983. $29.95 (ISBN 0-8311-1152-6). Indus Pr.

AUTOMATION–DICTIONARIES

American Society of Mechanical Engineers. Terminology for Automatic Control: MC85.1-1963. incl. supplements $6.00 (NX0036); members $4.80; Supplement MC85.1a-1966 $1.75 (N00052); Supplement MC85.1b-1972 $1.75 (N00037). ASME.

Anglo-Russkii Slovar Po Avtomatike & Kontrol'noizmeritel'nym Priboram. 380p. (Eng. & Rus.). 1957. $3.25 (Pub. by Gosizdat Tekhnikoteoretich. Lit.). Four Continent.

Carlson, Don, ed. Automation in Housing & Systems Building News: Dictionary of Industrialized Manufactured Housing. (Illus.). 1981. $15.00 (ISBN 0-9607408-0-5). Automation in Housing Mag.

Fach Lexikon ABC Automatisierung. 739p. (Ger.). 1976. $22.50 (ISBN 3-87144-243-7, M-7377, Pub. by Verlag Harri Deutsch). French & Eur.

Ortega Garcia, Luiz Miguel. Diccionario Tecnico-Comercial y Profesional de Automocion. 214p. (Span.). 1982. 1500.00 ptas (ISBN 84-86104-00-9). Tecnipublicaciones.

Sykora, Jiri. Dictionary of Automation Techniques. 1024p. 1980. $80.00x (Pub. by Collet's). State Mutual Bk.

--Dictionary of Automation Techniques. 1024p. 1975. $95.00x (ISBN 0-569-08528-4, Pub. by Collets). State Mutual Bk.

AUTOMOBILE DRIVERS

see also Automobile Driving

Vebel, C. Diccionario del perfecto automobilista. (Span.). 120.00 ptas. Grijalbo.

AUTOMOBILE DRIVING

Diccionario tecnico automovilismo, mecanica automotriz: Espanol-Ingles. (Span. & Eng.). Arg.$3.00. Cosmopolita.

Diccionario tecnico, automovilismo, mecanica automotriz: Ingles-espanol. (Eng. & Span.). Arg.$3.00. Cosmopolita.

AUTOMOBILE ENGINEERING

DeCoster, Jean. Dictionary for Automotive Engineering. 280p. 1983. $38.00 (ISBN 3-598-10430-8, Pub. by K G Saur). Shoe String.

Society of Automotive Engineers. Vehicle Dynamics Terminology. 24p. 1978. $5.00 (ISBN 0-89883-379-5, HS-J670E). Soc Auto Engineers.

Vollnhals, Otto. Woerterbuch des Kraftfahrzeugwesens. (Ger. & Ital.). 1975. $92.00 (ISBN 3-7736-5120-1, M-6936). French & Eur.

AUTOMOBILE ENGINEERING–DICTIONARIES

Bosch, R., ed. Technical Dictionary for Automotive Engineering, 2 vols. (Eng. & Ger.). 1976. $68.00 (ISBN 0-9961072-5-8, Pub. by VDI W Germany). Heyden.

Diccionario tecnico-grafico del automovil. (Span.). 1967. 200.00 ptas. Bluma.

Kondo, K. Elsevier's Dictionary of Automobile Engineering. 1977. $127.75 (ISBN 0-444-41590-4). Elsevier.

Shaw, Frank. Dictionary of Automotive Engineering. LC 78-40918. 1979. E9.00 (ISBN 0-408-00409-6). Newnes Bks.

AUTOMOBILE MECHANICS

Diccionario tecnico automovilismo, mecanica automotriz: Espanol-Ingles. (Span. & Eng.). Arg.$3.00. Cosmopolita.

Diccionario tecnico, automovilismo, mecanica automotriz: Ingles-espanol. (Eng. & Span.). Arg.$3.00. Cosmopolita.

AUTOMOBILE OPERATION

see Automobile Driving

AUTOMOBILE RACING–JUVENILE LITERATURE

Olney, Ross R. Illustrated Auto Racing Dictionary for Young People. LC 78-59243. (Illustrated Dictionary Ser.). (Illus.). (gr. 4 up). 1978. PLB $7.29 (ISBN 0-8178-5762-1). Harvey.

--Illustrated Auto Racing Dictionary for Young People. (Treehouse Bks). (Illus.). (gr. 4 up). 1981. pap. $2.50 (ISBN 0-13-450742-8). P-H.

AUTOMOBILE WORKERS

see Automobile Mechanics

AUTOMOBILES

see also Motorcycles also names of automobiles under Automobiles–Types; Automobiles, Foreign–Types, e.g. Automobiles–Types–Ford; Automobiles, Foreign–Types–Volkswagen; also headings beginning with the word automobile

Block, C., et al. Geillustrrerd Woordenboek Voor de Autombieltechniek en Zes Talen. 502p. (Dutch, Rus., Eng., Ger. & Ital.). 1978. $145.00 (ISBN 90-201-1070-5, M-9475). French & Eur.

AUTOMOBILES–CONSTRUCTION

see Automobiles–Design and Construction

AUTOMOBILES–DESIGN AND CONSTRUCTION
Bosch. Fachwoerterbuch Kraftfahrtechnik, 2 vols, Vol. 1. 354p. (Ger. & Eng., Technical Dictionary for Automotive Engineering). 1976. $85.00 (ISBN 3-18-419044-7, M-7638, Pub. by VDI Verlag GMBH). French & Eur.
––Fachwoerterbuch Kraftfahrtechnik, 2 vols, Vol. 2. 369p. (Ger. & Eng., Technical dictionary of automotive engineering). 1977. $59.95 (ISBN 3-18-419046-3, M-7639, Pub. by VDI Verlag GMBH). French & Eur.
Dictionnaire Illustre des Petites Voitures. (Illus.). 1976p. (Fr.). write for info. Rossel Edns.

AUTOMOBILES–DICTIONARIES
Balbastre & Ferrer, Josep. Diccionari tecnic de l'automovil. 151p. (Span.). 1972. 90.00 ptas. Portic.
Baudoin, Anne-Marie. Vocabulaire Francais-Anglais De L'automobile: Le Moteur. 174p. (Eng. & Fr.). 1973. pap. $9.95 (ISBN 0-686-56909-1, M-6025). French & Eur.
––Vocabulaire Francais-Anglais de l'automobile. (Illus.). 174p. (Fr. & Eng.). 1973. Can.$2.50. Quebec Off.
Blok, C. & Jezewski, W. Dictionnaire Illustre de l'Automobile "Kluwer," en 6 Langues. 504p. (Fr., Eng., Ger., Ital., Rus. & Dutch.). 1979. $145.00 (ISBN 0-686-56923-7, M-6039). French & Eur.
Blok, Czesaw & Jezewski, Wiesaw. Automobily. (Illus.). 502p. (Rus., Eng., Fr., Ital., & Ger.). 1979. 70.00 Kcs (ISBN 8-320-60049-9). Wydawnictwa.
Blok, Czeslaw & Jezewski, Wieslaw. Illustrated Automobile Dictionary. (Illus.). 1978. lib. bdg. $89.00 (ISBN 9-0201-1070-5, Pub. by Kluwer Tech Netherlands). Kluwer Academic.
Blok, Jezewski. Diccionario tecnico ilustrado del automovil. Diorki, tr. 500p. (Span.). 1981. 6000.00 ptas (ISBN 84-85647-06-8). Aneto Edns.
Bosch. Fachwoerterbuch Kraftfahrtechnik, 2 vols, Vol. 1. 354p. (Ger. & Eng., Technical Dictionary for Automotive Engineering). 1976. $85.00 (ISBN 3-18-419044-7, M-7638, Pub. by VDI Verlag GMBH). French & Eur.
––Fachwoerterbuch Kraftfahrtechnik, 2 vols, Vol. 2. 369p. (Ger. & Eng., Technical dictionary of automotive engineering). 1977. $59.95 (ISBN 3-18-419046-3, M-7639, Pub. by VDI Verlag GMBH). French & Eur.
Burger, E., ed. Technical Dictionary of Automatization & Programming: English, French, German, Russian,- Slovene. 479p. (Eng., Fr., Ger., Rus. & Slovene.). 1976. $95.00 (ISBN 0-686-92330-8, M-9889). French & Eur.
Carnelutti, Daniel. Dictionnaire Technique de l'automobile. (Illus.). 580p. (Fr.). 55.00 F. Spes SA.
Chrysler Corporation. Glossary of Automotive Terminology: French-English English-French. 230p. (Fr. & Eng.). 1977. $9.95 (ISBN 0-89883-195-4, SP-423). members $7.95. Soc Auto Engineers.
––Glossary of Automotive Terminology: Spanish-English English-Spanish. 380p. (Span. & Eng.). 1978. $12.50 (ISBN 0-89883-208-X, SP-436); members $9.75. Soc Auto Engineers.
Cristea, Petre. Dictionar Tehnic Auto de Buzunar in Sapte Limbi. LC 76-503037. 441p. (Eng., Romanian, Ger., Fr., Ital., Span. & Rus.). 1975. 21.00 lei. Editura Stiintifica.
Diccionario del automovil. 1158p. (Span.). 800.00 ptas. CEAC.
Diccionario del automovil II. 7th ed. 920p. (Span.). 1982. 1820.00 ptas (ISBN 84-329-1010-4). Ceac.
Dictionary of Automobile Terms. (Hebrew, Eng. , Fr. & Ger.). IL.8.00. Massada Pr.
Dinkel, John. The Road & Track Illustrated Auto Dictionary. (Illus.). 96p. 1981. pap. $3.95 (ISBN 0-393-00028-1). Norton.

Equipo Reactor de Ceac. Manual del Automovil en 5 Idiomas: Diccionario Idiomatico del Automovil. 240p. (Span., Fr., Eng., It. & Ger.). 1974. $8.50 (ISBN 84-329-1403-7, S-50224). French & Eur.
Equipo Reactor de CEAC, ed. Diccionario del Automovil. 916p. (Span.). 1978. $37.50 (ISBN 84-329-1010-4, S-14232). French & Eur.
Guerber, R. Diccionario del automovil. 3rd ed. (Illus.). 238p. (Span.). write for info. G Gili.
Guerber, Robert. Dictionnaire de l'automobile. 174p. (Fr.). 1967. 28.00 F. Flammarion.
––Dictionnaire de L'Automobile. 174p. (Fr.). 1967. pap. $12.50 (ISBN 0-686-57320-X, M-6303). French & Eur.
Guerber, Roger. Diccionario del Automovil. 4th ed. 237p. (Span., Eng., Fr. & Ger.). 1972. pap. $16.75 (ISBN 84-252-0065-2, S-14249). French & Eur.
Jetikov. Dictionnaire Russe-Francais de l'automobile & du Tracteur. (Rus. & Fr.). 34.10 F. Mir.
Kirkeby, Willy. Bil-og Trafikkteknisk Ordbok. LC 79-374320. (Eng. & Norwegian.). 1979. Kr.98.00 (ISBN 8-2573-0079-9). Kunnskapsforlaget.
Lima, Robert F., ed. Arco Motor Vehicle Dictionary: English & Spanish. LC 76-77605. 368p. (Eng. & Span.). 1980. pap. $7.95 (ISBN 0-668-04982-0, 4982-0). Arco.
Mereneiano & Frederic i Ricart, Antoni. Vocabulari Automobilistic. (Span.). 1972. write for info. Claret.
Schrader, Halwart. Oldtimer-Lexikon. LC 76-473673. 187p. (Ger.). 1976. DM.18.00 (ISBN 3-405-11397-0). BLV-Verlag.
Schuurmans, G., ed. Elseviers Automobile Dictionary. (Eng., Fr., Span., Port., Ger., Rus. & Japanese.). 1960. $139.75 (ISBN 0-444-40517-8). Elsevier.
Sikora, G. Technical Automotive Dictionary: Russian-English-German-French-Bulgarian. 624p. (Rus., Eng., Ger., Fr. & Bulgarian.). 1977. leatherette $95.00 (ISBN 0-686-92472-X, M-9828). French & Eur.
Vebel, Christian. Dictionnaire du Parfait Automobiliste. 256p. (Fr.). write for info. Pensee Moderne.
Vollnhals, Otto. Woerterbuch des Kraftfahreugwesens. LC 75-515768. 618p. (Ital. & Ger.). 1975. DM.108.00 (ISBN 3-7736-5120-1). Girardet.
Zlatovski, George. Dictionnaire Technique de L'Automobile. Russek, P. R., ed. 184p. (Fr., Eng. & Ger.). 1973. pap. $22.50 (ISBN 0-686-57262-9, M-6575). French & Eur.
Zlatovski, George & Russek, P. R. Dictionnaire Technique de l'automobile. 184p. (Fr.). 1973. 50.00 F. Bordas-Dunod.
Zurita Ruiz, Jose. Diccionario Basico de la Construccion. 16th ed. 248p. (Span.). 1976. pap. $8.95 (ISBN 84-329-2905-0, S-50223). French & Eur.

AUTOMOBILES–DIESEL MOTORS
see Automobiles–Motors
AUTOMOBILES–DRIVING
see Automobile Driving
AUTOMOBILES–ELECTRONIC EQUIPMENT
Society of Automotive Engineers. Glossary of Automotive Electronic Terms. 8p. $5.00 (ISBN 0-89883-392-2, J1213); members $4.00. Soc Auto Engineers.
AUTOMOBILES–ENGINES
see Automobiles–Motors
AUTOMOBILES–MOTORS
Abd-El-Wahed. Automotive Engineering Dictionary: English-French-German-Arabic. 436p. (Eng., Fr., Ger. & Arabic.). 1978. $45.00 (ISBN 0-686-92337-5). French & Eur.
Baudoin, Anne-Marie. Vocabulaire Francais-Anglais De L'automobile: Le Moteur. 174p. (Eng. & Fr.). 1973. pap. $9.95 (ISBN 0-686-56909-1, M-6025). French & Eur.

AUTOMOBILES–SAFETY MEASURES
Society of Automotive Engineers. SAE Motor Vehicle, Safety & Environmental Terminology. 179p. pap. $9.50 (ISBN 0-89883-370-1, HS-215); pap. $7.95 members. Soc Auto Engineers.
––Society of Vehicle Safety & Environmental Terminology Handbook. 184p. 1976. $9.50 (ISBN 0-89883-370-1, HS-215); members $7.95. Soc Auto Engineers.
AUTOMOBILES–DIESEL
see Automobiles–Motors
AUTOMOTIVE VEHICLES
see Motor Vehicles
AUTOSUGGESTION
see Hypnotism
AVIATION
see Aeronautics
AVIATION MEDICINE
see also Space Medicine
Giurdzhian, A. A., et al, eds. Anglo-Russkii Slovar Po Aviatsionno-Kosmicheskoi Meditsine. 388p. (Rus. & Eng.). 1972. $5.60 (Pub. by Voenizdat). Four Continent.
AVOCATIONS
see Hobbies
AZERBAIJANI LANGUAGE
Orudzhev, A. Azerbaidzhansko-Russkii Frazeogicheskii (Idiomaticheskii) Slovar. 278p. (Rus.). 1976. $3.95 (Pub. by Elm). Four Continent.
Russko-Azerbaidzhanskii Slovar, 3 vols. (Rus. & Azerbaijani). 1971. $28.95 set (Pub. by Elm). Four Continent.
AZERI LANGUAGE
see Azerbaijani Language
AZTEC LANGUAGE
Denison, T. S. A Mexican-Aryan Comparative Vocabulary. (Span.). 1976. lib. bdg. $59.95 (ISBN 0-8490-0613-9). Gordon Pr.
Karttunen, Frances. An Analytical Dictionary of Nahuatl. (Texas Linguistics Ser.). 385p. 1983. text ed. $35.00x (ISBN 0-292-70365-1). U of Tex Pr.
Macazaga Ordono, Cesar. Diccionario de la Lengua Nahuatl. LC 80-106467. 122p. (Eng., Aztec & Span.). 1979. write for info. Innovacion.
––Diccionario de la Lengua Nahuatl. (Illus.). 128p. (Span.). 1979. Mex.$pap. 3.95. Innovacion.
Santamaria, Francisco J. Diccionario de Mejicanismos. (Span.). $39.50 (ISBN 0-686-56689-0, S-12355). French & Eur.
Simeon, Remi. Diccionario de la Lengua Nahuatl o Mexicana. LC 79-116666. xcvi, 782p. (Aztec & Span.). 1977. write for info. Siglo Veintiuno.

B

BABYLONIAN LANGUAGE
see Assyro-Babylonian Language
BACK PACKING
see Backpacking
BACKPACKING
Larson, Randy. Illustrated Backpacking & Hiking Dictionary for Young People. (Treehouse Bks). (Illus.). (gr. 4 up). 1981. pap. 2.50 (ISBN 0-13-450759-2). P-H.
BACKWARD CHILDREN
see Slow Learning Children
BAHA'I FAITH
see Bahaism
BAHAISM
Mahmoudi, Jalil. A Concordance to the Hidden Words of Baha'u'llah. (Orig.). 1980. pap. $6.95 (ISBN 0-87743-148-5, 368-052). Baha'i.
BAHASA INDONESIA
see Indonesian Language
BAHNER LANGUAGE
Banker, John, et al. Bahnar Dictionary. 202p. (Orig., Bahnar.). 1979. pap. $9.00x (ISBN 0-88312-997-3); microfiche (3) $3.00 (ISBN 0-686-96898-0). Summer Inst Ling.
BAKERS AND BAKERIES
Daniel, A. R. Baker's Dictionary. 2nd ed. 1971. $18.50 (ISBN 0-444-20121-1). Elsevier.
BALANCE OF NATURE
see Ecology

BALANCE OF TRADE
see also Mercantile System
Codera Martin, J. M. Diccionario de Derecho Mercantil. 288p. (Span.). write for info. (ISBN 8-43680-115-6, #230018). Piramide.
BALLADS, FRENCH
Poirion, Daniel. Lexique de Charles d'Orleans dans les Ballades. 160p. (Fr.). 1967. 18.00 F. Droz.
BALLET–DICTIONARIES
Beaumont, Cyril W. A French-English Dictionary of Technical Terms Used in Classical Ballet. LC 79-307143. iv, 44p. (Eng. & Fr.). 1977. E0.60. Imp Soc Tchrs Da.
Dictionnaire de Ballet Moderne. (Fr.). $43.25 (ISBN 0-685-35976-X). French & Eur.
Grant, Gail. Technical Manual & Dictionary of Classical Ballet. 3rd, rev. ed. (Illus.). 160p. 1982. pap. $2.95 (ISBN 0-486-21843-0). Dover.
Kersley, Leo & Sinclair, Janet. A Dictionary of Ballet Terms. (Paperbacks Ser.). 1979. pap. $5.95 (ISBN 0-306-80094-2). Da Capo.
Koegler, Horst. The Concise Oxford Dictionary of Ballet. 2nd ed. (Illus.). 1982. pap. $14.95 (ISBN 0-19-311330-9). Oxford U Pr.
Mara, Thalia. The Language of Ballet. LC 78-181477. (Illus.). 120p. pap. $4.95 (ISBN 0-87127-038-2). Dance Horiz.
Rossi, Luigi. Dizionario di balletto. 251p. (Ital.). 1978. L.7000.00. Edizioni Della Danza.
BALLET–JUVENILE LITERATURE
Jaffe, Evan. Illustrated Ballet Dictionary. LC 78-73753. (Illustrated Culture Dictionary). (Illus.). (gr. 4 up). 1979. PLB $7.29 (ISBN 0-8178-6155-6). Harvey.
BALTO-SLAVIC LANGUAGES
see Slavic Languages
BALTO-SLAVIC PHILOLOGY
see Slavic Philology
BAMBARA LANGUAGE
Bailleul, Charles. Petit Dictionnaire-Bambara-Francais Francais-Bambara. 339p. (Bambara & Fr.). 1981. text ed. $36.00x (ISBN 0-86127-220-X, Pub. by Avebury England). Humanities.
BANGALA LANGUAGE
Odhner, John D. English-Lingala Manual. LC 80-6174. 206p. (Orig., Eng. & Bangala). 1981. lib. bdg. $19.50 (ISBN 0-8191-1554-1); pap. text ed. $10.00 (ISBN 0-8191-1555-X). U Pr of Amer.
BANJO
Banjo Chord Dictionary. 1981. $2.50. Alfred Pub.
Lambard, Neil. Pocket Dictionary of Banjo Chords. page. $1.50 (ISBN 0-934286-19-1). Kenyon.
BANKING
see Banks and Banking
BANKING LAW
Committee on Developments in Business Financing of the Section of Corporation, et al. Term Loan Handbook. 300p. 1983. $55.00 (ISBN 0-686-89076-0). HarBraceJ.
BANKS AND BANKING
see also Checks; Credit; Development Banks; Money
Klaus, Hans A. Franzoesische Fachausdruecke im Bankgeschaft: Franzoesisch-Deutsch, Deutsch-Franzoesisch. LC 75-513804. 248p. (Fr. & Ger.). 1975. 26.00 F (ISBN 3-258-01279-2). Haupt Verlag.
BANKS AND BANKING–DICTIONARIES
Achterberg, E. & Lanz, K. Enzyklopadisches Lexikon Fur des Geld, Bank und Borsen Wesen, 2 vols. (Ger.). 1967. $240.00 set (ISBN 3-7819-0030-4, M-7364, Pub. by Fritz Knapp Verlag). French & Eur.
American Bankers Association. Bank Card Standards Manual Glossary. 1980. $6.50 (207224); members $5.00. Am Bankers.
Assiouly, E. Banking & Financial Dictionary: English-French-Arabic. 338p. (Eng., Fr. & Arabic.). 1980. pap. $75.00 (ISBN 0-686-92351-0, M-9767). French & Eur.

Banca Mas Sarda, Servicio de Estudios. Diccionario de Banca & Borsa: Catala-Castella-Diccionario de Banca & Bolsa. LC 76-454176. 69p. (Catalan & Span.). 1975. write for info. (ISBN 8-438-30008-1). Alba.

Batz, Laila. Banking Language. LC 77-610. (Orig.). 1977. lib. bdg. $12.90 (ISBN 0-914294-67-9); pap. $2.95 (ISBN 0-914294-68-7). Running Pr.

Davids, Lewis E. Dictionary of Banking & Finance. (Littlefield, Adams Quality Paperback: No. 336). 1979. pap. $7.95 (ISBN 0-8226-0336-5). Littlefield.

––Dictionary of Banking & Finance. 229p. 1980. Repr. of 1978 ed. $15.00x (ISBN 0-8476-6132-6). Rowman.

Feldbausch, F. Bankwoerterbuch Englisch-Deutsch, Deutsch-Englisch. 400p. (Eng. & Ger., Dictionary of Banking). $38.50 (ISBN 3-478-51240-9, M-7304, Pub. by Vlg. Moderne Industrie). French & Eur.

Feldbausch, Friedrich K. Banking Dictionary: German-English & English-German. 388p. (Ger. & Eng.). 1972. $22.50x (ISBN 3-258-02439-1). Intl Pubns Serv.

Garza Bores, Jaime. Diccionario Tecnico de Terminologia Comercial Cantable y Bancaria. (Span.). $6.95 (ISBN 0-686-56677-7, S-25235). French & Eur.

Glossary of Fiduciary Terms. 1968. $2.00 (ISBN 0-89982-137-5, 360300); 1-24 copies $6.00 ea.; 25-99 copies $5.25 ea.; over 100 copies $4.50 ea. Am Bankers.

Institute of Financial Education. Glossary of Savings Association Terminology. 68p. 1983. softcover $4.95. Inst Finan Educ.

Istituto per l'Enciclopedia della Banca e della Borsa. Dizionario di banca e di borsa: Vol. 1, A-D. 584p. (Ital.). 1979. L.15000.00. Giuffre.

Kafitz, Franz. Lexikon des Wirtschaftsrechnens. 2nd ed. (Ger.). 1976. $15.00 (ISBN 3-470-71192-5, M-7210). French & Eur.

Klaus, Hans. Banking Dictionary of English-American & German Terms. 5th ed. 234p. (Eng. & Ger.). 1980. pap. $34.95x (ISBN 3-258-02983-0). Intl Ideas.

Martinez Cerezo, A. Diccionario de Banca. 4th ed. 208p. (Span.). write for info. (ISBN 8-43680-028-1, 250013). Piramide.

Martinez Cerezo, Antonio. Diccionario de banca. 5th ed. 208p. (Span.). 1980. 500.00 ptas (Dist. Grupo Editorial). Piramide.

Pegna, Vera. Dizionario Italiano-Francese e Francese-Italiano di termini in uso in economia, borsa, finanza. 512p. (Ital. & Fr.). 1969. L.5000.00. Etas Libri.

Perry, F. E. A Dictionary of Banking. 304p. 1979. text ed. $28.50x (ISBN 0-7121-0428-3, Pub. by Macdonald & Evans England). Intl Ideas.

Ricci, J. Elsevier's Banking Dictionary. 2nd ed. (Eng., Fr., Ital., Span., Dutch & Ger.). 1980. $64.00 (ISBN 0-444-41834-2). Elsevier.

Ricour, Pierre. Lexique Anglais-Francais De la Banque et De la Monnaie. 87p. (Eng. & Fr.). 1973. pap. $2.95 (ISBN 0-686-57208-4, M-6486). French & Eur.

Ricour, Pierre & Cousineau, Rene. Lexique de la Banque & de la Monnaie. LC 79-353044. 87p. (Eng. & Fr.). 1978. write for info. (ISBN 0-7754-2667-9). Edit Quebec.

Rosenberg, Jerry M. Dictionary of Banking & Finance. LC 81-21961. 690p. 1982. $24.95 (ISBN 0-471-08096-9, Pub. by Wiley-Interscience). Wiley.

––Dictionary of Banking & Finance. 690p. 1983. pap. $14.95 (ISBN 0-471-88039-6, Pub. by Wiley-Interscience). Wiley.

Ugo, Monetti. Dizionarietto di tecnica bancaria, mercantile con appendice trilingue. (Ital.). L.750.00. RIREA.

BANKS AND BANKING–DIRECTORIES
Gil Esteban, Rafael. English-Spanish Banking Dictionary. LC 78-323192. 270p. (Eng. & Span.). 1978. write for info. (ISBN 8-440-04115-2). Autores Propias.

BANKS AND BANKING–HISTORY
Banking Terminology. 1-4 copies $33.75 ea. (626600); members $22.50; bulk price avail. Am Bankers.

BANKS AND BANKING–LAWS AND LEGISLATION
see Banking Law

BANKS AND BANKING–GERMANY
Bank-Lexikon. Handwoerterbuch fur der Bank & Sparkassenwesen. LC 79-355716. (Illus., Ger.). 1978. DM.96.00 (ISBN 3-409-46105-1). Gabler.

BANNOCK INDIANS
see Indians of North America–Northwest, Pacific

BANTU LANGUAGES
see also Bangala Language; Congo Language; Ganda Language; Kikuyu Language; Sotho Language; Swahili Language; Xosa Language; Zulu Language
Helmlinger, Paul. Dictionnaire Duala-Francais. 666p. (Fr.). 1972. 105.00 F. S. E. L. A. F.

––Lexique Francais-Duala: Dictionnaire Duala-Francais. 666p. (Fr.). 1972. 105.00 F. S. E. L. A. F.

Hoeftmann, Hildegard. The Structure of Lelemi Language. 130p. 1973. $17.50x (ISBN 0-8002-1344-0). Intl Pubns Serv.

BASEBALL–JUVENILE LITERATURE
Remmers, Mary. Little League Baseball Lingo. rev. ed. (Illus.). 64p. (gr. 2 up). 1981. pap. $2.95 (ISBN 0-88319-059-1). Hart Graphics.

Walker, Henry. Illustrated Baseball Dictionary for Young People. LC 70-102354. (Illustrated Dictionary Ser.). (Illus.). (gr. 5 up). 1970. PLB $7.29 (ISBN 0-8178-4592-5). Harvey.

BASHKIR LANGUAGE
Karimova, G. R. Russko-Bashkirskii Slovar. 600p. (Rus. & Bashkirsh.). 1954. $2.70 (Pub. by GINS). Four Continent.

BASIC (COMPUTER PROGRAM LANGUAGE)
Noonan, Larry. The Basic-BASIC English Dictionary. 150p. 1982. pap. $10.95 (ISBN 0-918398-54-1). Dilithium Pr.

BASKETBALL–JUVENILE LITERATURE
Clark, Steve. Illustrated Basketball Dictionary for Young People. LC 77-77859. (Illustrated Dictionary Ser.). (Illus.). (gr. 5 up). 1977. PLB $7.29 (ISBN 0-8178-5642-0). Harvey.

BASQUE LANGUAGE
Aberlaitz & Buenaventura de Oreyegui, P. Diccionario Vasco-Castellano, Castellano-Vasco De Voces Comunes a Dos O Mas Dialectos Del Euskera. (Span.). $25.50 (ISBN 84-248-0014-1, S-21917). French & Eur.

Azkue, Resurreccion M. Diccionario Vasco-Espanol-Frances, 2 vols. (Span. & Fr.). Set. leatherette $68.00 (ISBN 84-248-0015-X, S-12384). French & Eur.

Eiguren, Joe V. English-Basque Dictionary. (Eng. & Basque.). $5.95. L Fereday Schol.

Estornes Lasa, Bernardo, et al. Diccionario Aunamendi Espanol-Vasco: Tomo 7, Conch-Corr. 196p. (Span.). 1982. pap. 550.00 ptas (ISBN 84-7025-213-5). Aunamendi Edit.

Kintana, Xabier. Euskal Histegi Modernoa. LC 77-564729. xxiv, 731p. (Basque, & Span.). 1977. write for info. (ISBN 8-472-77058-3). Cinsa Coord.

Kintana, Xabier, et al, eds. Euskal Histegi Modernoa. LC 77-564729. xxiv, 731p. (Basque, & Span.). 1977. write for info. (ISBN 8-47277-058-3). Coord Iniciat.

Lhande, Pierre. Dictionnaire Basque Francais. 1117p. (Basque & Fr.). 1938. $79.95 (ISBN 0-686-57020-0, M-6377). French & Eur.

––Dictionnaire Basque Francais. (Illus.). 1117p. (Fr.). 1938. 200.00 F. Beauchesne.

Lopez, Issac M. Basque-Spanish Dictionary. (Basque & Span.). 1974. lib. bdg. $69.95 (ISBN 0-685-51638-5). Revisionist Pr.

Lopez Mendizabal, Isaac. La Lengua Vasca. LC 77-571017. 351p. (Basque & Span.). 1977. write for info. (ISBN 8-470-25126-0). Aunamendi Edit.

––La Lengua Vasca: Gramatica, Conversacion, Diccionario Vasco-Castellano, Castellano-Vasco. LC 77-571017. 351p. (Basque). 1977. write for info. (ISBN 8-47025-126-0). Aunamendi Edit.

Lopez Mendizabal, Isaac. Diccionario Vasco-Castellano. 6th ed. 452p. (Castella). 1976. $25.50 (ISBN 84-7025-026-4, S-50439). French & Eur.

Natur Zientziak. LC 77-459840. liv, 483p. (Basque.). 1976. write for info. (ISBN 8-4724-0064-6). Aranzazu.

Oyeregui, Buenaventura de. Diccionario Vasco-Castellano, Castellano-Vasco De Voces Comunes a Dos O Mas Dialectos Del Euskera. 2nd ed. 372p. (Castella). 1978. pap. $7.50 (ISBN 0-686-57354-4, S-50454). French & Eur.

Querexeta Gallostequi, Jaime. Diccionario Onomastico y Heraldico Vasco, 6 vols. (Span.). 1974. Set. leather $205.00 (ISBN 84-248-0011-7, S-50375). French & Eur.

Reguero, Marina & Goyoaga, Ricardo. Vocabulario de las lenguas ibericas. 192p. (Span.). 1982. pap. 480.00 ptas (ISBN 84-7465-048-8). Nuestra Cultura.

BASS, ELECTRIC
see Guitar

BATTERIES, ELECTRIC
see Electric Batteries

BATTLES
see also Naval Battles
also names of battles, e.g. Gettysburg, Battle of; subdivision Campaigns or Campaigns and Battles under names of wars, e.g. European War, 1914-1918 campaigns; United States–History–Civil war, 1861-1865–Campaigns and Battles
Bruce, George. Harbottle's Dictionary of Battles. 3rd rev. ed. 304p. 1981. $14.95 (ISBN 0-442-22336-6); pap. $7.95 (ISBN 0-442-22335-8). Van Nos Reinhold.

Harbottle, T. B. Dictionary of Battles. $69.95 (ISBN 0-8490-0033-5). Gordon Pr.

Harbottle, Thomas B. Dictionary of Battles. LC 66-22672. 1966. Repr. of 1905 ed. $33.00x (ISBN 0-8103-3004-0). Gale.

Young, Brigadier P. Dictionary of Battles, Vol. 1. (Illus.). 1978. $15.00 (ISBN 0-8317-2260-6, Mayflower Bks). Smith Pubs.

Young, Brigadier P. & Calvert, Brigadier M. Dictionary of Battles, Vol. 2. LC 78-23518. (Illus.). 1979. $15.00 (ISBN 0-8317-2261-4, Mayflower Bks). Smith Pubs.

BEACH-LA-MAR JARGON
see also Pidgin English
Camden, William G. A Descriptive Dictionary: Bislama to English. LC 79-304384. xviii, 138p. (Eng. & Bislama.). 1977. write for info. (ISBN 0-9596774-0-2). Camden Aus.

BEAUTIFUL, THE
see Esthetics

BEAUTY
see Beauty, Personal; Esthetics

BEAUTY, PERSONAL
see also Beauty Culture; Cosmetics; Costume; Hairdressing; Perfumes
Prevot, Floriane. Dictionnaire de la Beaute Feminine. 268p. (Fr.). 1972. $9.95 (ISBN 0-686-56816-8, M-6594). French & Eur.

BEAUTY CULTURE
see also Beauty, Personal; Cosmetics; Hairdressing
Colletti, Anthony B. Dictionary of Cosmetology & Related Sciences. (Illus.). 1981. $25.00x (ISBN 0-912126-58-2). Sheridan.

––A Dictionary of Cosmetology & Related Services. Chiranky, Gary, ed. 1981. text ed. $23.57 (ISBN 0-912126-58-2, 1275-00). Keystone Pubns.

BEAUVOIR, SIMONE DE, 1908-
Berghe, Christian van den. Dictionnaire des Idees dans L'oeuvre de Simone de Beauvoir. (Collection Dictionnaires Des Idees, Litterature Francaise: No. 1). (Fr.). 1966. $16.00x (ISBN 0-686-20917-6). Mouton.

BECHE-DE-MER JARGON
see Beach-La-Mar Jargon

BEEF
Lexique du Boeuf. LC 79-356928. 140p. (Eng. & Fr.). 1977. write for info. (ISBN 0-7754-2796-9). Edit Quebec.

BEETLES
Annett, Ross H., Jr. & Samuelson, G. Allen. Dictionary of Coleoptera Collections of North America: Canada Through Panama. 1969. $6.95 (ISBN 0-916846-05-9). World Natural Hist.

BEHAVIOR
see Etiquette

BEHAVIOR (PSYCHOLOGY)
see Animals, Habits and Behavior Of; Human Behavior

BEHAVIOR, VERBAL
see Verbal Behavior

BEHAVIOR OF CHILDREN
see Etiquette for Children and Youth

BELGIUM–HISTORY
De Seyn, Eugene. Dictionnaire de L'histoire de Belgique. (Fr.). 512p. (Fr.). 250.00 F. Halbart Wahle.

BELT CONVEYORS
see Conveying Machinery

BENEVOLENT INSTITUTIONS
see Charities; Hospitals

BENGALI LANGUAGE
Bengali-English Dictionary. (Bengali). $22.50 (ISBN 0-87557-109-3, 109-3). Saphrograph.

Dabbs, Jack A. Short Bengali-English, English-Bengali Dictionary. 3rd ed. LC 78-149931. $5.00 (ISBN 0-911494-01-4). Dabbs.

English-Bengali Dictionary. (Bengali). $22.50 (ISBN 0-87557-110-7, 110-7). Saphrograph.

Learn Bengali: For English Speakers. (Begali). pap. $9.50 (ISBN 0-87557-005-4, 005-4). Saphrograph.

Litton. Russko-Bengal'skii Slovar. 760p. (Rus. & Bengali.). 1972. $6.30 (Pub. by Sov. Entsiklopediia). Four Continent.

Litton, D. Karmannyi Bengal'sko-Russkii Slovar. 532p. (Rus. & Bengali.). 1960. $1.95 (Pub. by Gosizdat Natsional Slovarei). Four Continent.

BENIN
Decalo, Samuel. Historical Dictionary of Dahomey. LC 75-42168. (African Historical Dictionaries Ser.: No. 7). 1976. $14.00 (ISBN 0-8108-0833-1). Scarecrow.

BEOWULF–CONCORDANCES
Bessinger, J. B., Jr., ed. Concordance to Beowulf. (Concordances Series). 407p. (Prog. Bk.). 1969. $34.50x (ISBN 0-8014-0480-0). Cornell U Pr.

Cook, Albert S. Concordance to Beowulf. LC 74-46. 1911. lib. bdg. $30.00 (ISBN 0-8414-3456-5). Folcroft.

BERBER LANGUAGES
Abdel-Massih, Ernest T. A Computerized Lexicon of Tamazight: Berber Dialect of Ayt Seghrouchen. LC 77-32220. (Berber.). 1971. pap. text ed. $9.00x (ISBN 0-932098-06-1). Ctr for NE & North African Stud.

BETON
see Concrete

BEVERAGES
see also Alcoholic Beverages
also names of beverages, e.g. Cocoa, Coffee, Tea
Mariani, John F. The Dictionary of American Food & Drink. 352p. 1983. $17.95 (ISBN 0-89919-199-1). Ticknor & Fields.

BHOTANA LANGUAGE
see Tibetan Language

BIBLE–CHRONOLOGY

Calmet, A. Dictionnaire Historique, Archeologique, Philologique, Chronologique Geographique et Literal de la Bible, 4 vols. Migne, J. P., ed. (Encyclopedie Theologique Ser. (First Series): Vols. 1-4). 2602p. (Fr.). Repr. of 1846 ed. lib. bdg. $332.50x (ISBN 0-89241-231-3). Caratzas Pub Co.

BIBLE–COMMENTARIES–N. T. EPISTLES OF PAUL

Morton, A. Q. & Michaelson, Sidney. Critical Concordance to the Letter of Paul to the Romans. Baird, J. Arthur & Freedman, David Noel, eds. (Computer Bible Ser: Vol. XIII). 1977. pap. $27.50 (ISBN 0-935106-08-1). Biblical Res Assocs.

BIBLE–CONCORDANCES

Andersen, Francis I. & Forbes, A. Dean. A Linguistic Concordance of Ruth & Jonah: Hebrew Vocabulary & Idiom. (Computer Bible Ser.: Vol. IX). 1976. pap. $15.00 (ISBN 0-935106-12-X). Biblical Res Assocs.

Bagster, Samuel. Bagster's Keyword Concordance. 96p. 1983. Repr. $5.95 (ISBN 0-8007-1335-4). Revell.

Baker's Pocket Bible Concordance. (Direction Bks). 1973. pap. $5.95 (ISBN 0-8010-0616-3). Baker Bk.

Englishman's Greek Concordance of the New Testament: Numerically Coded to Strong's Exhaustive Concordance. rev. ed. (Gr.). 1980. pap. $23.95 (ISBN 0-8010-3357-8). Baker Bk.

Englishman's Hebrew & Chaldee Concordance of the Old Testament. 1792p. (Hebrew). 1980. softcover $29.95 (ISBN 0-8010-3360-8). Baker Bk.

The Englishman's Hebrew Chaldee Concordance of the Old Testament. (Hebrew & Eng.). 1980. pap. $35.95 (ISBN 0-8054-1387-1). Broadman.

Findeisen, Barbara. A Course in Miracles Concordance. 457p. $15.00 (ISBN 0-942494-45-8). Coleman Graphics.

Goodrick, Edward W. & Kohlenberger, John R., III. The NIV Handy Concordance. 384p. (Orig.). 1982. pap. $4.95 (ISBN 0-310-43662-1). Zondervan.

Katz, Eliezer. A Classified Concordance, 4 vols. Incl. Vol. 1. The Torah. 415p. 1964. $25.00x (ISBN 0-8197-0382-6); Vol. 2. The Early Prophets. 702p. 1967. 20.00x (ISBN 0-8197-0383-4); Vol. 3. The Later Prophets. 683p. 1970. 20.00x (ISBN 0-8197-0384-2). Bloch.

Katz, Eliezer, ed. Classified Concordance: To the Bible & Its Various Subjects, Vol. 4. 1000p. (Hebrew & Eng.). 1974. $30.00x (ISBN 0-8197-0385-0). Bloch.

Knoch, A. E., ed. Concordant Literal New Testament with Keyword Concordance. 1983. text ed. $15.00 (ISBN 0-910424-14-4). Concordant.

Martin, R. A. Syntactical & Critical Concordance to the Greek Text of Baruch & the Epistle of Jeremiah. (Computer Bible Ser: Vol. XII). (Gr.). 1977. pap. $15.00 (ISBN 0-935106-09-X). Biblical Res Assocs.

Mendelkern, Solomon. Concordance of the Bible. (Hebrew & Lat.). 1977. Repr. of 1896 ed. $14.50 (ISBN 0-685-81426-2). Feldheim.

Morton, A. Q. & Michaelson, Sidney. A Critical Concordance to the Acts of the Apostles. (Computer Bible Ser.: Vol. VII). 1976. pap. $15.00 (ISBN 0-935106-14-6). Biblical Res Assocs.

Morton, A. Q., et al. Critical Concordance to the Letter of Paul to the Colossians. Baird, J. Arthur & Freedman, David, eds. (Computer Bible Ser: Vol. 24). (Orig.). 1981. pap. text ed. $20.00 (ISBN 0-935106-19-7). Biblical Res Assocs.

––Critical Concordance to the Letter of Paul to the Philippians. Baird, J. Arthur & Freedman, David, eds. (Computer Bible Ser: Vol. 23). (Orig.). 1980. pap. text ed. $20.00 (ISBN 0-935106-18-9). Biblical Res Assocs.

––A Critical Concordance to I & II Corinthians. (Computer Bible Ser.: Vol. XIX). 1979. pap. $30.00 (ISBN 0-935106-01-4). Biblical Res Assocs.

New Combined Bible Dictionary & Concordance. (Direction Bks). 1973. pap. $3.95 (ISBN 0-8010-6680-8). Baker Bk.

Oxford Concordance: King James Version. write for info. Oxford U Pr.

Radday, Yehuda T. An Analytical Linguistic Concordance to the Book of Isaiah. (Computer Bible Ser: Vol. II). 1975. pap. $20.00 (ISBN 0-935106-15-4). Biblical Res Assocs.

––An Analytical, Linguistic Key-Word-in-Context Concordance to the Book of Judges. (Computer Bible Ser.: Vol. XI). 1977. pap. $20.00 (ISBN 0-935106-10-3). Biblical Res Assocs.

Radday, Yehuda T. & Leb, G. M. An Analytical, Linguistic, Key-Word-in-Context Concordance to Esther, Ruth, Canticles, Ecclesiastes & Lamentations. Baird, J. Arthur & Freedman, David Noel, eds. (The Computer Bible Ser.: Vol. XVI). 1978. pap. $25.00 (ISBN 0-935106-04-9). Biblical Res Assocs.

Smith, Jacob B., ed. Greek-English Concordance. 430p. (Gr. & Eng.). 1955. $24.95 (ISBN 0-8361-1368-3). Herald Pr.

Stegenga, J. Greek-English Analytical Concordance of the Greek-English New Testament. (Gr. & Eng.). 1963. $14.95 (ISBN 0-910710-01-5). Hellenes.

Strong, James. Strong's Exhaustive Concordance. $17.95 (ISBN 0-8010-8228-5); pap. $13.95 (ISBN 0-8010-8108-4). Baker Bk.

––Strong's Exhaustive Concordance. LC 78-73138. 1978. pap. $16.95 (ISBN 0-8054-1134-8). Broadman.

Thayer, Joseph H. Greek-English Lexicon of the New Testament: A Dictionary Numerically Coded to Strong's Exhaustive Concordance. (Gr. & Eng.). 1977. pap. $14.95 (ISBN 0-8010-8838-0). Baker Bk.

Vigram, George V. The Englishman's Greek Concordance of the New Testament. rev. ed. (Gr. & Eng.). 1982. pap. $29.95 (ISBN 0-8054-1388-X). Broadman.

Young. Youngs Analytical Concordance to the Bible. $18.50x (ISBN 0-686-12407-3); thumb-indexed $22.50 (ISBN 0-686-12408-1). Church History.

Young, Robert. Young's Analytical Concordance to the Bible. 1955. $19.95 (ISBN 0-8028-8084-3); deluxe ed. $22.95 (ISBN 0-8028-8085-1). Eerdmans.

BIBLE–CRITICISM, HIGHER
see Bible–Criticism, Interpretation, etc.

BIBLE–CRITICISM, INTERPRETATION, ETC.
Here are entered works on the Bible as a whole. Works on the New Testament as a whole and on portions of the New Testament precede works on the Old Testament.
Kasher, M. M. Encyclopedia of Biblical Interpretation, 9 vols. Set. $35.00 ea. (ISBN 0-87068-315-2). Ktav.

BIBLE–CRITICISM, INTERPRETATION, ETC.–N. T.
Darton, Michael, ed. A Modern Concordance to the New Testament. LC 75-34831. 1977. $12.95 (ISBN 0-385-07901-X). Doubleday.

BIBLE–CRITICISM, INTERPRETATION, ETC.–N. T. COLOSSIANS
see Bible–Criticism, Interpretation, etc.–N. T. Epistles

BIBLE–CRITICISM, INTERPRETATION, ETC.–N. T. CORINTHIANS
see Bible–Criticism, Interpretation, Etc.–N. T. Epistles

BIBLE–CRITICISM, INTERPRETATION, ETC.–N. T. EPHESIANS
see Bible–Criticism, Interpretation, Etc.–N. T. Epistles

BIBLE–CRITICISM, INTERPRETATION, ETC.–N. T. EPISTLES
Here are entered books on the Epistles as a whole, or on one or more of the following, Colossians, Corinthians, Ephesians, Galatians, Hebrews, James, Epistles of John, Jude, Peter, Philemon, Romans, Thessalonians, Timothy, Titus.
Morton, A. Q., et al. A Critical Concordance to I & II Corinthians. (Computer Bible Ser.: Vol. XIX). 1979. pap. $30.00 (ISBN 0-935106-01-4). Biblical Res Assocs.

––A Critical Concordance to the Epistle of Paul to the Galatians. Baird, J. Arthur & Freedman, David, eds. (The Computer Bible Ser.: Vol. XXI). (Orig.). 1980. pap. text ed. $20.00 (ISBN 0-935106-16-2). Biblical Res Assocs.

––A Critical Concordance to the Letter of Paul to the Ephesians. Baird, J. Arthur & Freedman, David, eds. (The Computer Bible Ser.: Vol. XXII). (Orig.). 1980. pap. text ed. $20.00 (ISBN 0-935106-17-0). Biblical Res Assocs.

BIBLE–CRITICISM, INTERPRETATION, ETC.–N. T. EPISTLES OF JOHN
see Bible–Criticism, Interpretation, Etc.–N. T. Epistles

BIBLE–CRITICISM, INTERPRETATION, ETC.–N. T. GALATIANS
see Bible–Criticism, Interpretation, Etc.–N. T. Epistles

BIBLE–CRITICISM, INTERPRETATION, ETC.–N. T. GOSPELS
Here are entered works on the gospels as a whole, or on one or more of the gospels: John, Luke, Mark, Matthew.
Kunst, H. Evangelisches Staatslexikon. 2nd rev. ed. (Ger.). 1975. $125.00 (ISBN 3-7831-0463-7, M-7373, Pub. by Kreuz Vlg.). French & Eur.

BIBLE–CRITICISM, INTERPRETATION, ETC.–N. T. HEBREWS
see Bible–Criticism, Interpretation, Etc.–N. T. Epistles

BIBLE–CRITICISM, INTERPRETATION, ETC.–N. T. JAMES
see Bible–Criticism, Interpretation, Etc.–N. T. Epistles

BIBLE–CRITICISM, INTERPRETATION, ETC.–N. T. JOHN
see Bible–Criticism, Interpretation, etc.–N. T. Gospels

BIBLE–CRITICISM, INTERPRETATION, ETC.–N. T. JUDE
see Bible–Criticism, Interpretation, Etc.–N. T. Epistles

BIBLE–CRITICISM, INTERPRETATION, ETC.–N. T. LUKE
see Bible–Criticism, Interpretation, Etc.–N. T. Gospels

BIBLE–CRITICISM, INTERPRETATION, ETC.–N. T. MARK
see Bible–Criticism, Interpretation, Etc.–N. T. Gospels

BIBLE–CRITICISM, INTERPRETATION, ETC.–N. T. MATTHEW
see Bible–Criticism, Interpretation, Etc.–N. T. Gospels

BIBLE–CRITICISM, INTERPRETATION, ETC.–N. T. PETER
see Bible–Criticism, Interpretation, Etc.–N. T. Epistles

BIBLE–CRITICISM, INTERPRETATION, ETC.–N. T. PHILEMON
see Bible–Criticism, Interpretation, Etc.–N. T. Epistles

BIBLE–CRITICISM, INTERPRETATION, ETC.–N. T. ROMANS
see Bible–Criticism, Interpretation, Etc.–N. T. Epistles

BIBLE–CRITICISM, INTERPRETATION, ETC.–N. T. THESSALONIANS
see Bible–Criticism, Interpretation, Etc.–N. T. Epistles

BIBLE–CRITICISM, INTERPRETATION, ETC.–N. T. TIMOTHY
see Bible–Criticism, Interpretation, Etc.–N. T. Epistles

BIBLE–CRITICISM, INTERPRETATION, ETC.–N. T. TITUS
see Bible–Criticism, Interpretation, Etc.–N. T. Epistles

BIBLE–CRITICISM, INTERPRETATION, ETC.–O. T
Holladay, William L. A Concise Hebrew & Aramaic Lexicon of the Old Testament. (Hebrew & Aramaic). 1971. $20.00 (ISBN 0-8028-3413-2). Eerdmans.

BIBLE–DICTIONARIES
Armstrong, Terry, et al, eds. A Reader's Hebrew-English Lexicon of the Old Testament: (Genesis-Deuteronomy, Vol. 1. (Hebrew & Eng.). 1978. $9.95 (ISBN 0-310-37020-5). Zondervan.

Bauer. Diccionario De Teologia Biblica. 2nd ed. 582p. (Span.). 1976. $38.95 (ISBN 84-254-0360-X, S-50203). French & Eur.

Botterweck, G. Johannes & Ringgren, Helmer, eds. Theological Dictionary of the Old Testament, 4 vols. Incl. Vol. I. (ISBN 0-8028-2325-x); Vol. II. (ISBN 0-8028-2326-2); Vol. III. (ISBN 0-8028-2327-0). 1978. $22.50ea (ISBN 0-686-77203-2). Eerdmans.

––Theological Dictionary of the Old Testament, Vol. 4. 560p. 1981. $22.50 (ISBN 0-8028-2328-9). Eerdmans.

Bryant, Al. New Compact Bible Dictionary. 1967. $8.95 (ISBN 0-310-22080-7); pap. $4.95 (ISBN 0-310-22082-3). Zondervan.

Bryant, T. A., compiled by. Today's Dictionary of the Bible. 678p. (Orig.). 1982. $15.95 (ISBN 0-87123-569-2, 230569). Bethany Hse.

Buckland, A. R. Diccionario Biblico. Broch. (Port.). 1981. pap. $4.50 (ISBN 0-8297-1172-4). Life Pubs Intl.

––Diccionario Biblico: Enc. (Port.). 1981. pap. $6.50 (ISBN 0-8297-0836-7). Life Pubs Intl.

Buttrick, George A. & Crim, Keith R., eds. The Interpreter's Dictionary of the Bible, 5 vols. LC 62-9387. 1976. Set. $99.50 (ISBN 0-687-19268-4). Abingdon.

Calmet, A. Dictionnaire Historique, Archeologique, Philologique, Chronologique Geographique et Literal de la Bible, 4 vols. Migne, J. P., ed. (Encyclopedie Theologique Ser. (First Series): Vols. 1-4). 2602p. (Fr.). Repr. of 1846 ed. lib. bdg. $332.50x (ISBN 0-89241-231-3). Caratzas Pub Co.

Concordia Bible Dictionary. 176p. 1963. text ed. $4.75 (ISBN 0-570-03186-9, 12-2213). Concordia.

Cruden, Alexander. Cruden's Pocket Dictionary of Bible Terms. (Direction Bks). 1976. pap. $5.95 (ISBN 0-8010-2380-7). Baker Bk.

David Ben Abraham. The Hebrew-Arabic Dictionary of the Bible, Known As Kitab Jami al-Alfaz (Agron, 2 vols. Skoss, Solomon L., ed. LC 78-63565. (Yale Oriental Ser. Researches: Nos. 20-21). (Hebrew & Arabic). Repr. of 1945 ed. Set. $97.50 (ISBN 0-404-60290-8). AMS Pr.

Davidson, Benjamin. Analytical Hebrew & Chaldee Lexicon. (Hebrew). $24.95 (ISBN 0-310-20290-6, Pub. by Bagster). Zondervan.

Davis. Davis Dictionary of the Bible. $21.95 (ISBN 0-8054-1124-0). Broadman.

Davis, John D. Davis Dictionary of the Bible. 1954. $18.95 (ISBN 0-8010-2805-1). Baker Bk.

Dheilly, Joseph. Dictionnaire Biblique. 1284p. (Fr.). 1964. $22.50 (ISBN 0-686-57092-8, M-6114). French & Eur.

Dictionnaire Des Paralleles, Concordances et Analogies Bibliques. 300p. (Fr.). 1981. Repr. of 1856 ed. lib. bdg. $120.00 (ISBN 0-8287-1511-4). Clearwater Pub.

Earle, Ralph. Word Meanings in the New Testament: I & II Corinthians, Galatians & Ephesians, Vol. 4. 1979. $9.95 (ISBN 0-8010-3349-7). Baker Bk.
Eastwood, J. & Wright, W. Aldis. A Glossary of the English Bible Words. 564p. 1981. Repr. of 1866 ed. lib. bdg. $75.00 (ISBN 0-89760-210-2). Telegraph Bks.
Eddison, John. Dictionary of Bible Words. LC 79-302346. 126p. 1977. E1.95 (ISBN 0-85421-539-5). Scripture Union.
Fohrer, Georg, et al, eds. Hebrew & Aramaic Dictionary of the Old Testament. Johnstone, W. A., tr. from Ger. LC 73-82430. viii, 344p. (Hebrew & Aramaic.). 1973. text ed. $16.00x (ISBN 3-11-004572-9). De Gruyter.
Furst, Gesenius. Hebrew-English Dictionary: Hebrew & Chaldee Lexicon to the Old Testament. rev. ed. Mitchell, Edward C., ed. (Hebrew & Eng.). $42.50 (ISBN 0-87559-021-7); thumb indexed $42.50 (ISBN 0-87559-022-5). Shalom.
Gesenius, Wilhelm. Hebrew & Chaldee Lexicon: Keyed to Strong's Exhaustive Concordance. Tregelles, Samuel P., tr. (Hebrew & Chaldee.). kivar $18.95 (ISBN 0-8010-3736-0). Baker Bk.
Gesenius, William. Hebrew & English Lexicon to the Old Testament. 2nd ed. Brown, Francis, et al, eds. Robinson, Edward, tr. (Hebrew & Eng.). 1959. $34.95x (ISBN 0-19-864301-2). Oxford U Pr.
Haag, Herbert. Diccionario De la Biblia. 7th ed. 1080p. (Span.). 1977. $50.00 (ISBN 84-254-0077-5, S-50196). French & Eur.
Hebrew-English Lexicon of the Bible. LC 74-26705. 296p. (Orig., Hebrew & Eng.). 1975. pap. $7.50 (ISBN 0-8052-0481-4). Schocken.
Inglis, James. Topical Dictionary of Bible Texts. (Direction Bks.). pap. $3.95 (ISBN 0-8010-5030-8). Baker Bk.
International Bible Dictionary. 1977. (Pub. by Logos); pap. $6.95 (ISBN 0-88270-235-1). Bridge Pub.
Kittel, Gerhard & Friedrich, Gerhard, eds. Theological Dictionary of the New Testament, 10 vols. Incl. Vol. 1. 1964. 27.50 (ISBN 0-8028-2243-6); Vol. 2. 1965. 27.50 (ISBN 0-8028-2244-4); Vol. 3. 1966. 29.95 (ISBN 0-8028-2245-2); Vol. 4. 1967. 29.95 (ISBN 0-8028-2246-0); Vol. 5. 1968. 29.95 (ISBN 0-8028-2247-9); Vol. 6. 1969. 27.50 (ISBN 0-8028-2248-7); Vol. 7. 1970. 29.95 (ISBN 0-8028-2249-5); Vol. 8. 1972. 25.00 (ISBN 0-8028-2250-9); Vol. 9. 1973. 27.50 (ISBN 0-8028-2322-X); Vol. 10. 1976. 25.00 (ISBN 0-8028-2323-8). $279.80 set (ISBN 0-8028-2324-6). Eerdmans.
Lamsa, George M. Idioms in the Bible Explained. 3rd ed. pap. $1.00 (ISBN 0-686-09905-2). Aramaic Bible.
McElrath, William N. Bible Dictionary for Young Readers. LC 65-15604. (Illus.). (gr. 4-11). 1965. $8.95 (ISBN 0-8054-4404-1). Broadman.
--Mi Primer Diccionario Biblico. McElrath, Ruth G., tr. from Eng. (Illus.). 128p. (Span.). 1980. pap. $2.85 (ISBN 0-311-03656-2). Casa Bautista.
McKenzie, John L. & Maggioni, B. Dizionario biblico. 1100p. (Ital.). L.18000.00. Cittadella.
Nelson, Wilton M., ed. Diccionario Ilustrado de la Biblia. (Illus.). 735p. (Span.). 1974. $27.95 (ISBN 0-89922-033-9); pap. $18.95 (ISBN 0-89922-099-1). Edit Caribe.
New Combined Bible Dictionary & Concordance. (Direction Bks). 1973. pap. $3.95 (ISBN 0-8010-6680-8). Baker Bk.
Obermayer, Heinz. Diccionario Biblico Manual. 352p. (Span.). 1975. pap. $7.95 (ISBN 84-7263-094-3, S-50212). French & Eur.
Preuschen, Erwin. Griechisch-Deutsches Taschenwoerterbuch zum Neuen Testament. 6th ed. LC 77-484567. 197p. (Gr. & Ger.). 1976. DM.19.80 (ISBN 3-110-06960-1). De Gruyter.
Rand, W. W. Diccionario De la Santa Biblia. (Illus.). 768p. (Span.). 1969. pap. $12.95 (ISBN 0-89922-003-7). Edit Caribe.
Skoss, Solomon, ed. Hebrew-Arabic Dictionary of the Bible Known As Kitab Jami-Al-Alfaz, 2 vols. (Yale Oriental Researches Ser.: No. XX, XXI). (Hebrew & Arabic.). 1945. $50.00x ea.; $95.00x set (ISBN 0-686-57837-6). Elliots Bks.
Smith, William. New Smith's Bible Dictionary. rev. ed. Lemmons, Reuel G., et al, eds. LC 66-20927. 1966. $9.95 (ISBN 0-385-04869-6); thumb-indexed $10.95 (ISBN 0-385-04872-6). Doubleday.
--New Smith's Bible Dictionary. rev. ed. LC 78-69668. 1979. pap. $8.95 (ISBN 0-385-14652-3, Galilee). Doubleday.
--Smith's Dictionary of the Bible, 4 vols. 1981. Repr. $95.00 (ISBN 0-8010-8211-0). Baker Bk.
Van Deursen, A. Illustrated Dictionary of Bible Manners & Customs. (Illus.). 1979. pap. $3.95 (ISBN 0-8065-0707-1). Citadel Pr.
Watts, John D. Lists of Words Occurring Frequently in the Hebrew Bible. (Hebrew & Eng.). 1960. pap. $2.95 (ISBN 0-8028-1214-7). Eerdmans.
Young, Robert. Young's Analytical Concordance to the Bible. 1955. $19.95 (ISBN 0-8028-8084-3); deluxe ed. $22.95 (ISBN 0-8028-8085-1). Eerdmans.

BIBLE–GLOSSARIES, VOCABULARIES, ETC.
see Bible–Dictionaries

BIBLE–HIGHER CRITICISM
see Bible–Criticism, Interpretation, etc.

BIBLE–HISTORY
This head is used for work on the History of Bible texts or versions. For works on historical events see Bible–History of Biblical Events, or Bible–History of Contemporary Events.
Calmet, A. Dictionnaire Historique, Archeologique, Philologique, Chronologique Geographique et Literal de la Bible, 4 vols. Migne, J. P., ed. (Encyclopedie Theologique Ser. (First Series): Vols. 1-4). 2602p. (Fr.). Repr. of 1846 ed. lib. bdg. $332.50x (ISBN 0-89241-231-3). Caratzas Pub Co.

BIBLE–HISTORY OF BIBLICAL EVENTS–CHRONOLOGY
see Bible–Chronology

BIBLE–INDEXES, TOPICAL
Cruden, Alexander. Cruden's Concordance: Handy Reference Edition. (Baker's Paperback Reference Library). 344p. 1982. pap. $6.95 (ISBN 0-8010-2478-1). Baker Bk.
Katz, Eliezer. A Classified Concordance, 4 vols. Incl. Vol. 1. The Torah. 415p. 1964. $25.00x (ISBN 0-8197-0382-6); Vol. 2. The Early Prophets. 702p. 1967. 20.00x (ISBN 0-8197-0383-4); Vol. 3. The Later Prophets. 683p. 1970. 20.00x (ISBN 0-8197-0384-2). Bloch.

BIBLE–INTERPRETATION
see Bible–Criticism, Interpretation, etc.

BIBLE–LITERARY CRITICISM
see Bible–Criticism, Interpretation, etc.

BIBLE–MIRACLES
see Miracles

BIBLE–PRINTING
see Bible–History

BIBLE–STUDY–N. T.
Earle, Ralph. Word Meanings in the New Testament: I & II Corinthians, Galatians & Ephesians, Vol. 4. 1979. $9.95 (ISBN 0-8010-3349-7). Baker Bk.

BIBLE–TEACHINGS
see Bible–Theology

BIBLE–THEOLOGY
see also names of specific doctrines, with or without the subdivision Biblical Teaching
Bauer, Johannes B. Bibeltheologisches Woerterbuch, 2 vols. 3rd ed. (Ger.). 1967. Set. $150.00 (ISBN 3-222-10240-6, M-7308, Pub. by Styria). French & Eur.

BIBLE–THEOLOGY–O. T.
Botterweck, G. Johannes & Ringgren, Helmer, eds. Theological Dictionary of the Old Testament, 4 vols. Incl. Vol. I. (ISBN 0-8028-2325-4); Vol. II. (ISBN 0-8028-2326-2); Vol. III. (ISBN 0-8028-2327-0). 1978. $22.50ea (ISBN 0-686-77203-2). Eerdmans.

BIBLE–TRANSLATING
Bratcher, R. G., et al. A New Testament Wordbook for Translators. (Translational Articles Ser.). 1966. pap. $1.00x (ISBN 0-8267-0020-9, 08638). United Bible.

BIBLE–TRANSLATIONS
see Bible–Versions

BIBLE–VERSIONS
Here are entered works on Versions of the Bible in any language except English. For English Version see subdivision Versions, English.
McKibben-Stockwell. Nuevo Lexico Griego Espanol. 316p. (Span.). 1981. pap. $10.50 (ISBN 0-311-42058-3, Edit Mundo). Casa Bautista.
Smith, Richard H. A Concise Coptic-English Lexicon. 81p. 1983. $10.95x (ISBN 0-8028-3581-3). Eerdmans.

BIBLE–VERSIONS–THEORY, METHODS, ETC.
see Bible–Translating

BIBLE TRANSLATING
see Bible–Translating; Bible–Versions

BIBLICAL ARAMAIC LANGUAGE
see Aramaic Language

BIBLICAL RESEARCH
see Bible–Criticism, Interpretation, etc.

BIBLIOGRAPHY
see also Anonyms and Pseudonyms; Archives; Bookbinding; Books; Indexing; Information Storage and Retrieval Systems; Libraries; Library Science; Manuscripts; Reference Books
also names of literature, e.g. American Literature; also names of persons, places and subjects, with or without the subdivision bibliography
Orne, Jerrold. Language of the Foreign Book Trade: Abbreviations, Terms, Phrases. 3rd ed. $20.00 (ISBN 0-8389-0219-7). ALA.

BIBLIOGRAPHY–DICTIONARIES
see also Library Science–Dictionaries
Barbeau, Victor. Dictionnaire Bibliographique du Canada. 246p. (Fr.). 1974. Can.$25.00. Acad Can Fr.
Kuhn, Peter. Deutsche Woerterbucher. LC 79-369972. viii, 266p. (Ger.). 1978. write for info. (ISBN 3-484-10323-X). Niemeyer.
Maldonado, Tomas. Universita la Sperimentazione Dipartimentale. LC 80-499795. 147p. (Ital.). 1978. L.3.500. Guaraldi.
Mitchell Library, the Library of New South Wales. (Sydney, Australia) Dictionary Catalog of Printed Books, 38 Vols. 1968. Set. lib. bdg. $3590.00 (ISBN 0-8161-0790-4, Hall Library); lib. bdg. $130.00 1st suppl. (ISBN 0-8161-0848-X). G K Hall.
Orne, Jerrold. Language of the Foreign Book Trade: Abbreviations, Terms, Phrases. 3rd ed. $20.00 (ISBN 0-8389-0219-7). ALA.
Walter, Frank K. Abbreviations & Technical Terms Used in Book Catalogues & in Bibliographies. LC 77-6174. 1977. Repr. of 1917 ed. lib. bdg. $12.50 (ISBN 0-89341-152-3). Longwood Pr.
Wuster, Eugen, et al. International Bibliography of Standardized Vocabularies. 2nd & rev. ed. International Information Centre for Terminology, ed. LC 78-13537. xxiv, 540p. (Eng., Fr. & Ger.). 1979. write for info. (ISBN 0-89664-075-2). K G Saur.

BIBLIOGRAPHY–RARE BOOKS
see also Manuscripts
New York Public Library, Research Libraries. Dictionary Catalog of the Rare Book Division: First Supplement. 1973. $110.00 (ISBN 0-8161-1089-1, Hall Library). G K Hall.
--Dictionary Catalog of the Rare Book Division, 21 vols. 1971. Set. $1996.00 (ISBN 0-8161-0782-3, Hall Library). G K Hall.

BIBLIOGRAPHY–REFERENCE BOOKS
see Reference Books

BIBLIOGRAPHY, CRITICAL
see Criticism; Literature–History and Criticism
also subdivision History and Criticism under names of literatures, e.g. American Literatures–History and Criticism

BICHELAMAR JARGON
see Beach-La-Mar Jargon

BILLS OF FARE
see Menus

BINDING OF BOOKS
see Bookbinding

BIOASTRONAUTICS
see Space Medicine

BIOCHEMISTRY
see Biological Chemistry

BIOENGINEERING
see also Agricultural Engineering; Human Engineering; Sanitary Engineering
Dictionary Catalog of the Applied Life Studies Library, First Supplement, 2 vols. 1982. Set. lib. bdg. $235.00 (ISBN 0-8161-0390-9, Hall Library). G K Hall.

BIOGRAPHY–BIBLIOGRAPHY
Ethier-Blais, Jean. Dictionnaire de Moi-Meme. (Fr.). 1976. Can.$6.50. Presse.

BIOGRAPHY–DICTIONARIES, INDEXES, ETC.
Dictionnaire des Personnages. 3rd ed. 776p. (Fr.). 1970. $85.00 (ISBN 0-686-56859-1, M-6637). French & Eur.
Dictionnaire des Personnages de Tous les Temps & de Tous les Pays. (Fr.). $81.50 (ISBN 0-685-36081-4). French & Eur.
Kurian, George. Dictionary of Biography. 560p. (Orig.). 1980. pap. $3.50 (ISBN 0-440-31889-0, LE). Dell.
Meyers Grosses Personenlexikon. (Ger.). $46.00 (ISBN 3-411-01152-1, M-7559, Pub. by Bibliographisches Institut). French & Eur.
Meyers Grosses Personenlexikon. (Ger.). $46.00 (ISBN 3-411-01152-1). Biblio Inst.
Ruffner, James, et al, eds. Eponyms Dictionaries Index: A Compilation of Terms Based on Names of Actual or Legendary Persons. LC 76-20341. 1977. $104.00x (ISBN 0-8103-0688-3). Gale.
Sitzmann, Edourd. Dictionnaire de Biographie des Hommes Celebres: Depuis les Temps les Plus Recules Jusqu'a nos Jours. (Fr.). 1973. write for info. Berger Levrault.
Thomas, Joseph. Universal Pronouncing Dictionary of Biography & Mythology, 2 Vols. 5th ed. LC 76-137298. Repr. of 1930 ed. Set. $225.00 (ISBN 0-404-06386-1). AMS Pr.
Thorne, J. O. & Collocott, T. C., eds. Chambers Biographical Dictionary. LC 78-56110. 1974. $25.00 (ISBN 0-8467-0510-9, Pub. by Two Continents). Am Map.

BIOGRAPHY–HISTORY AND CRITICISM
see Biography (As a Literary Form)

BIOGRAPHY (AS A LITERARY FORM)
see also Autobiography
Winslow, Donald J. Life-Writing: A Glossary of Terms in Biography, Autobiography & Related Forms. (Biography Monographs). 60p. (Orig.). pap. text ed. $5.00x (ISBN 0-8248-0748-0). UH Pr.

BIOLOGICAL CHEMISTRY
see also Chromatographic Analysis; Enzymes
Jakubke, H. D. Lexikon Biochemie. (Ger.). 1976. $25.00 (ISBN 3-527-25662-8, M-7285). French & Eur.
Jakubke, Hans D. & Jeschkeit, Hans. Lexikon biochemie. LC 77-460833. 605p. (Ger.). 1976. write for info. (ISBN 3-527-25662-8). Verlag Chemie.
Kossel, Hans. Herder Lexikon. LC 80-471281. 271p. (Ger.). 1978. write for info. (ISBN 3-451-17378-6). Herder.

Stenesh, J. Dictionary of Biochemistry. LC 75-23037. 344p. 1975. $42.50 (ISBN 0-471-82105-5, Pub. by Wiley-Interscience). Wiley.

Theilman, K. Dictionary of Biochemistry. 742p. 1980. $90.00x (ISBN 0-686-44721-2, Pub. by Collets). State Mutual Bk.

Thielmann. Woerterbuch der Biochemie. 724p. (Eng., Span., Fr., Rus. & Ger.). 1978. DM.58.00 (ISBN 3-87144-346-8). Verlag Harri Deutsch.

Thielmann, K. Dictionary of Biochemistry. (Ger., Eng., Fr., Rus. & Span.). 1978. pap. $36.00 (ISBN 3-87144-346-8, M-7129). French & Eur.

--Woerterbuch der Biochemie. 724p. (Ger., Eng., Fr., Rus. & Span.), Dictionary of Biochemistry). 1978. $38.00 (ISBN 0-686-56646-7, M-7041). French & Eur.

Von Thielmann, K. Woerterbuch der Biochemie. LC 79-354449. 742p. (Eng., Fr., Rus., & Span.). 1977. M.48.00. VEB Verlag Enzyklopädie.

BIOLOGICAL ENGINEERING
see Bioengineering
BIOLOGICAL FORM
see Morphology
BIOLOGICAL STRUCTURE
see Morphology
BIOLOGY–DICTIONARIES
Abercrombie, M., et al. Diccionario De Biologia. 242p. (Span.). 1978. pap. $16.75 (ISBN 0-686-57336-6, S-50068). French & Eur.

--Dicionario de Biologia. (Port.). Esc.495.00. Pub Euro Am.

--The Penguin Dictionary of Biology. 1978. $12.95 (ISBN 0-670-27222-1). Viking Pr.

Afanaseva, I. N., et al. Anglo-russki i biologicheski i slovar. LC 80-461323. 732p. (Eng. & Rus.). 1979. 8.00 Rub. Russkii Iazyk.

Aguayo, Carlos A. & Biaggi, Virgilio. Diccionario De Biologia Animal. LC 76-41882. (Span.). 1977. $15.00 (ISBN 0-8477-2318-6). U of PR Pr.

Ahlheim, Karl H. Die Biologie: Ein Lexikon der Gesamten Schulbiologie. 464p. (Ger.). DM.19.80 (ISBN 3-411-01366-4). Biblio Inst.

Anglo-Russkii Biologicheskii Slovar. LC 80-461323. 732p. (Eng. & Rus.). 1979. 8.00 Rub. Russkii Iazyk.

Anglo-Russkii Biologischeskii Slovar. 736p. (Eng. & Rus.). 1979. $15.95 (Pub. by Russkii Iazyk). Four Continent.

Bergfeld, R. Herder-Lexikon Biologie. 238p. (Ger.). 1975. pap. $24.95 (ISBN 3-451-16453-1, M-7453, Pub. by Herder). French & Eur.

--Herder-Lexikon Biologie. 238p. (Ger.). 1975. pap. $24.95 (ISBN 3-451-16453-1). Herder.

Bergfeld, Rainer. Diccionario Rioduero: Biologia. 2nd ed. 244p. (Span.). 1977. $9.95 (ISBN 84-220-0683-9, S-50169). French & Eur.

--Diccionarios Rioduero: Biologia. 3rd ed. Arroyo Marcos, Gloria, tr. 244p. (Span.). 1981. pap. 600.00 ptas (ISBN 84-220-0683-9). Catolica Edit.

Blain, Mireille. Trois Cent Cinquante Definitions Biologiques Raisonnees. LC 77-472766. 86p. (Fr.). 1976. 28.50 F (ISBN 2-7181-6364-X). Doc Univers.

Carpovich, Eugene A. Russian-English Biological & Medical Dictionary. 2nd ed. LC 58-7915. (Rus. & Eng.). 1960. $25.00 (ISBN 0-911484-01-9). Tech Dict.

Cihui, Y. Dongwuxue. English-Chinese Biology Dictionary. 477p. (Eng. & Chinese.). 1975. $25.00 (ISBN 0-686-92343-X, M-9277). French & Eur.

Craciun, Teofil. Mic Dictionar de Biologie. LC 77-452607. 414p. (Romanian.). 1976. 16.00 lei. Albatros.

Dictionnaire de la Biologie--B.L.V. 496p. (Eng., Ger., Fr. & Span.). 1976. $95.00 (ISBN 0-686-57097-9, M-6121). French & Eur.

Dietrich, G. & Mueller-Hegemann, A., eds. Jugendlexikon Biologie. (Illus.). 408p. (Ger.). 1981. M.22.00. Bibl Inst Leipzig.

Dizionario di biologia. 352p. (Ital.). L.3600.00. Zanichelli.

Encyclopedia of Biology Terms. 1984. $6.95 (ISBN 0-8120-2511-3). Barron.

English-Russian Biological Dictionary. 3rd, rev. & enl. ed. LC 78-40145. (Eng. & Rus.). 1978. E100.00 (ISBN 0-08-023163-2); $50.00. Pergamon.

Fachlexikon ABC Biologie. 2nd ed. (Ger.). 1972. leatherette $49.95 (ISBN 3-87144-001-9, M-7378, Pub. by Harri Deutsch). French & Eur.

Forth, E. & Schewitzer, E., eds. Meyers Taschenlexikon Bionik. 375p. (Ger.). 1976. M.16.00. Bibl Inst Leipzig.

Grandis, Valentino & Donati, Mario. Dizionario tedesco-italiano di biologia e medicina. xil, 710p. (Ger. & Ital.). 1964. L.7000.00 (ISBN 88-7011-010-9). Rosenberg & Sel.

Gray, Peter. Dictionary of the Biological Sciences. 1967. $26.95 (ISBN 0-442-15590-5). Van Nos Reinhold.

Gray, Peter, ed. Student Dictionary of Biology. 1973. pap. $4.95x (ISBN 0-442-22816-3). Van Nos Reinhold.

Haensch, G. & Haberkamp De Anton, G. Dictionary of Biology in English, French, German & Spanish. 2nd, rev. & enl. ed. (Eng., Fr., Ger. & Span.). 1981. $106.50 (ISBN 0-444-41968-3). Elsevier.

Haensch, Guenther. Dictionary of Biology. (Eng., Ger., Fr. & Span.). 1976. pap. $78.00 (ISBN 3-405-10950-7, M-7128). French & Eur.

--Woerterbuch der Biologie. (Eng., Ger., Fr. & Span., Dictionary of Biology). 1976. pap. $78.00 (ISBN 3-405-10933-7, M-7040). French & Eur.

Haensch, Gunther. Dictionary de la Biologie. LC 77-451261. xii, 483p. (Eng., Ger., Fr. & Span.). 1976. DM.98.00 (ISBN 3-405-10933-7). BLV Verlag.

Haensch, Gunther & Haberkamp, Gisela. Diccionario de Biologia en Quatre Lenguas: Aleman, Ingles, Frances y Espanol. 496p. (Span., Eng., Fr. & Ger.). 1976. $70.00 (ISBN 84-7214-090-3, S-50222). French & Eur.

Holmes, Sandra. Henderson's Dictionary of Biological Terms. 9th ed. 521p. text ed. $35.00 (ISBN 0-442-24865-2). Van Nos Reinhold.

Husson, Roger. Dictionnaire de Biologie Animale. 2nd ed. 280p. (Fr.). 1970. 44.00 F. Gauthier-Villars.

Istilah biologi, bahasa Inggeris-bahasa Malaysia, bahasa Malaysia-Bahasa Inggeris. LC 81-941148. xxii, 388p. (Eng. & Malay.). 1980. M.$pap. 6.00. Dewan Bahasa.

Jacobs, Werner. Woerterbuch der Biologie. (Ger.). 1976. pap. $15.00 (ISBN 3-437-30195-0, M-7039). French & Eur.

Jimenez Ortega, Javier. Diccionario de Biologia. 322p. (Span.). 1979. Mex.$140.00. Porrua.

Lender, T., et al. Diccionario de Biologia. Serrano, Merce & Vallespinos, Ferran, trs. 208p. (Span.). 1982. pap. 1000.00 ptas (ISBN 84-253-1372-4). Grijalbo.

Lepine, Pierre. Dictionnaire Francais-Anglais des Termes Medicaux & Biologiques. 2nd ed. 896p. (Fr. & Eng.). 1974. 160.00 F. Flammarion.

--Dictionnaire Francais-Anglais et Anglais-Francais des Termes Medicaux et Biologiques. 2nd ed. 896p. (Fr. & Eng.). 1974. $65.00 (ISBN 0-686-57292-0, M-4665). French & Eur.

Manuila, A & Nicole, M. Dictionnaire Francais de Medicine el de Biologie, Vol. 2. (Fr.). 1971. $175.00 (ISBN 0-686-57033-2, M-6393). French & Eur.

Manuila, A. & Nicole, M. Dictionnaire Francais de Medicine et de Biologie, Vol. 1. 866p. (Fr.). 1970. $175.00 (ISBN 0-686-57032-4, M-6392). French & Eur.

Manuila, A., et al. Dictionnaire Francais de Medicine el de Biologie, Vol. 4. 580p. (Fr.). 1975. $130.00 (ISBN 0-686-57035-9, M-6395). French & Eur.

Manuila, Nicole A. Dictionnaire Francais de Medecine & de Biologie, 1 A-D. 866p. (Fr.). 1970. 500.00 F. Masson.

--Le Dictionnaire Francais de Medecine & de Biologie, 2. (Fr.). 1971. 500.00 F. Masson.

--Dictionnaire Francais de Medecine & de Biologie, 3 N-Z. 1200p. (Fr.). 1972. 600.00 F. Masson.

--Dictionnaire Francais de Medecine & de Biologie, 4. 580p. (Fr.). 1975. 380.00 F. Masson.

Mauila, A., et al. Dictionnaire Francais de Medicine el de Biologie, Vol. 3. 1200p. (Fr.). 1972. $195.00 (ISBN 0-686-57034-0, M-6394). French & Eur.

Munnik, Eulalie. Afrikaanse Verklarende Woordeboek vir Biologie. LC 80-451787. 152p. (Afrikaan.). 1979. R.3.80 (ISBN 0-620-03588-9). Knaggs Assoc.

Roe, Keith E. & Frederick, Richard G. Dictionary of Theoretical Concepts in Biology. LC 80-19889. 312p. 1981. $17.50 (ISBN 0-8108-1353-X). Scarecrow.

Steen, Edwin B. Dictionary of Biology. LC 70-156104. (EH); pap. $5.95 (ISBN 0-06-463321-7). B&N NY.

--Dictionary of Biology. LC 70-156104. 630p. 1971. text ed. $17.50x (ISBN 0-686-83546-8). B&N Imports.

Straub, Ferenc B. & Adam, Gyorgy. Biologiai Lexikon. LC 76-506702. (Hungarian.). 1975. 165.00 Ft (ISBN 963-05-0529-0). Akademiai Kiado.

Tootil, Elizabeth, ed. Dictionary of Biology. LC 81-125830. (Illus.). 282p. (Eng.). 1980. E5.95. Intl Bk Ctr.

Tootill, Elizabeth, ed. The Facts on File Dictionary of Biology. 288p. 1981. $14.95 (ISBN 0-87196-510-0). Facts on File.

Vaillancourt, J. Lexique Anglais-Francais. LC 79-347577. 427p. (Eng. & Fr.). 1978. Can.$13.25 (ISBN 0-7766-8004-8). Edns Ottawa.

Vaillancourt, Jean. Lexique Anglais-Francais: Termes Techniques a l'usage des Biologistes. (Eng. & Fr.). 1978. Can.$pap. 12.00 (ISBN 0-7766-8004-8). U of Toronto Pr.

BIOLOGY–ECOLOGY
see Ecology
BIOLOGY–NOMENCLATURE
see Botany–Nomenclature
BIOLOGY–TERMINOLOGY
see also Botany–Terminology
Ayers, Donald M. Bioscientific Terminology. LC 74-163010. 336p. 1972. pap. $5.95x (ISBN 0-8165-0305-2). U of Ariz Pr.

Borror, Donald J. Dictionary of Word Roots & Combining Forms. LC 60-15564. 134p. 1960. pap. 4.95 (ISBN 0-87484-053-8). Mayfield Pub.

Holmes, Sandra. Henderson's Dictionary of Biological Terms. 9th ed. 521p. text ed. $35.00 (ISBN 0-442-24865-2). Van Nos Reinhold.

Jeffrey, Charles. Biological Nomenclature. 2nd ed. LC 77-90821. 72p. 1978. $13.00x (ISBN 0-8448-1264-1). Crane-Russak Co.

Savory, Theodore. Latin & Greek for Biologists. 42p. (Lat. & Gr.). 1971. $39.00x (ISBN 0-900541-47-4, Pub. by Meadowfield Pr England). State Mutual Bk.

BIOMEDICAL ENGINEERING
Von Roald, Albert & Hahnewald, Harry. Medizintechnik. LC 79-359051. 596p. (Eng., Fr., Rus., Span. & Pol.). 1978. M.55.00. VEB Verlag Technik.

BIONOMICS
see Ecology
BIOSCIENCES
see Life Sciences

BIOTECHNOLOGY
see Human Engineering
BIRD NAMES
see Birds–Nomenclature
BIRD WATCHING
Weaver, Peter. The Birdwatcher's Dictionary. (Illus.). 160p. (YA) 1981. $17.50 (ISBN 0-85661-028-3, Pub. by T & A D Poyser England). Buteo.

BIRDS
Cuisin, Michel. Dictionnaire des Oiseaux. (Illus.). 250p. (Fr.). 1969. 17.60 F. Larousse.

--Dictionnaire oiseaux. (Illus., Fr.). pap. $8.50 (ISBN 0-685-13879-8, 3729). Larousse.

BIRDS–NOMENCLATURE
Gotch, A. F. Birds: Their Latin Names Explained. (Illus.). 228p. 1981. $22.50 (ISBN 0-7137-1175-2, Pub. by Blandford Pr England). Sterling.

Hoffmann, Alfred. Glossar der Heute Chinesischen Vogelnamen. LC 75-516973. xvi, 366p. (Ger. & Chinese.). 1975. DM.52.00 (ISBN 3-447-01693-0). Harrassowitz.

--Neue Chinesische Vogelnamen. LC 79-361040. x, 113p. (Ger. & Chinese.). 1978. write for info. (ISBN 3-447-01980-8). Harrassowitz.

BIRTH CONTROL
Lucas, Caroline & Turner, Carann. Population-Family Planning Thesaurus: An Alphabetical & Hierarchical Display of Terms Drawn from Population-Related Literature in the Social Sciences. 2nd ed. Long, Karen & Turner, Carann, eds. 286p. 1978. pap. $20.00 spiral bdg., incl. 1981 suppl. (ISBN 0-89055-049-2). Carolina Pop Ctr.

BIRTH-RATE
see Population
BISHOPS–ROME
see Popes
BLACK CARIB INDIANS
see Indians of Central America
BLACK ENGLISH
Dillard, J. L. Lexicon of Black English. LC 76-30389. 1977. pap. $6.95 (ISBN 0-8264-0125-2). Continuum.

Folb, Edith A. Black Vernacular Vocabulary: A Study of Intra-Inter-Cultural Concerns & Usage. (CAAS Monographs: No. V). 53p. (Orig.). 1972. pap. $3.00x (ISBN 0-934934-14-2). Ctr Afro-Am Stud.

BLACK LITERATURE (AMERICAN)
see American Literature–Afro-American Authors
BLACK MASS
see Satanism
BLACKFEET INDIANS
see Indians of North America–Northwest, Pacific
BLAKE, WILLIAM, 1757-1827
Erdman, David V., ed. Concordance to the Writings of William Blake. 2 Vols. (Concordances Ser.). 3463p. 1968. $85.00x (ISBN 0-8014-0120-8). Cornell U Pr.

BLAZONRY
see Heraldry
BLIND, LIBRARIES FOR THE
American Foundation for the Blind (New York) Dictionary Catalog of the M. C. Migel Memorial Library, 2 Vols. 1966. Set. lib. bdg. $150.00 (ISBN 0-8161-0705-X, Hall Library). G K Hall.

BLUE COLLAR WORKERS
see Labor and Laboring Classes
BLUES (SONGS, ETC.)
Arnaudon, Jean-Claude. Dictionnaire du Blues. (Illus., Fr.). write for info. Filipacchi.

BOAT HANDLING
see Boats and Boating
BOATS AND BOATING
see also Sailing; Ships; Yachts and Yachting
De Kerchove, R. Small Craft Dictionary. Date not set. price not set (ISBN 0-442-21890-7); pap. price not set (ISBN 0-442-25420-2). Van Nos Reinhold.

Dictionnaire a l'Usage des Plaisanciers. 160p. (Fr. & Eng.). 1969. pap. $15.50 (ISBN 0-686-57258-0, M-6569). French & Eur.

Gruss, Robert. Dictionnaire de Marine, Francais et Anglais. 368p. (Fr. & Eng.). 1978. $49.95 (ISBN 0-686-57319-6, M-6302). French & Eur.

Noel, John V. The Boating Dictionary: Sail & Power. 304p. 1981. text ed. $16.95 (ISBN 0-442-26048-2). Van Nos Reinhold.

Paasch, Henri. Dictionnaire Anglais-Francais et Francais-Anglais des Termes et Locutions Maritimes. 2nd ed. 320p. (Fr. & Eng.). 1974. pap. $23.50 (ISBN 0-686-57065-0, M-6437). French & Eur.

BODY, HUMAN
see also Anatomy, Human; Mind and Body
Florez, L. Lexico del cuerpo humano en Colombia. (Span.). 1966. write for info. Inst Caro y Cuervo.

BODY AND MIND
see Mind and Body
BODY AND SOUL (PHILOSOPHY)
see Mind and Body
BOHEMIAN HYMNS (LANGUAGE, NEWSPAPERS, ETC.)
see Czech Language
BOILER-SCALE
see Steam-Boilers
BOLIVIA
Fernandez Naranjo, Nicolas. Diccionario de Bolivianismos. 247p. (Span.). 1980. write for info. Cochabamba.

BOLIVIA-HISTORY
Heath, Dwight D. Historical Dictionary of Bolivia. LC 73-172476. (Latin American Historical Dictionaries Ser.: No. 4). 1972. $15.00 (ISBN 0-8108-0451-4). Scarecrow.

BONDING (TECHNOLOGY)
see Sealing (Technology)
BONS MOTS
see Wit and Humor
BOOK INDUSTRIES AND TRADE
see also Bookbinding; Booksellers and Bookselling; Paper Making and Trade; Publishers and Publishing
Mora, Imre. Husznyelvu Kiadoi Szotar. LC 77-477898. 389p. (Eng., Ger. & Hungarian.). 1977. 175.00 Ft (ISBN 9-6305-0996-2). Akademiai Kiado.

BOOK INDUSTRIES AND TRADE-DICTIONARIES
American Dictionary of Printing & Bookmaking. LC 66-27215. 1967. Repr. of 1894 ed. $42.00x (ISBN 0-8103-3345-7). Gale.

Mora, Imre. Husznyelvu Kiadoi Szotar. LC 77-477898. 389p. (Eng., Ger. & Hungarian.). 1977. 175.00 Ft (ISBN 9-6305-0996-2). Akademiai Kiado.

Orne, Jerrold. Language of the Foreign Book Trade: Abbreviations, Terms, Phrases. 3rd ed. $20.00 (ISBN 0-8389-0219-7). ALA.

Peters, Jean, ed. The Bookman's Glossary. 6th ed. 200p. 1983. $21.95 (ISBN 0-8352-1686-1). Bowker.

BOOK OF THE DEAD-DICTIONARIES, INDEXES, ETC.
Budge, Ernest A. A Hieroglyphic Vocabulary to the Theban Recension of the Book of the Dead. LC 73-18846. Repr. of 1911 ed. $26.50 (ISBN 0-404-11335-4). AMS Pr.

BOOK PRIZES
see Literary Prizes
BOOK RARITIES
see Bibliography-Rare Books
BOOK SALES
see Booksellers and Bookselling
BOOK TRADE
see Book Industries and Trade; Booksellers and Bookselling; Publishers and Publishing
BOOKBINDING
Glaister, Geoffrey. Glaister's Glossary of the Book: Terms Used in Paper-Making, Printing, Bookbinding, & Publishing. LC 76-47975. 1979. $75.00 (ISBN 0-520-03364-7). U of Cal Pr.

BOOKKEEPING
see also Accounting; Cost Accounting; Depreciation; Office Equipment and Supplies

also subdivision Accounting under specific industries, professions, trades, etc.
Colasse. Lexique de Comptabilite & de Gestion. (Fr.). 1975. 23.00 F. Ecole Electricite.

Lexique EUC Woerterbuch des Rechnungswesens. 1100p. (Ger.). 1974. write for info. (ISBN 3-8021-0073-5). IdW Verlag.

BOOKS
see also Bibliography; Copyright; Libraries; Manuscripts; Publishers and Publishing
also headings beginning with the word Book
Martinez de Sousa, J. Diccionario de Tipografia & del Libro. (Span.). 1981. 1300.00 ptas (ISBN 8-42831-132-3). Paraninfo.

BOOKS-APPRAISAL
see Criticism; Literature-History and Criticism
BOOKS-HISTORY
see also Printing-History
Eroles, Emili. Diccionario Historico del Libro. 336p. (Span.). 1981. 1500.00 ptas (ISBN 84-7304-062-7). Milla Lib.

BOOKS, LARGE TYPE
see Large Type Books
BOOKS, RARE
see Bibliography-Rare Books
BOOKS, REFERENCE
see Reference Books
BOOKS FOR THE BLIND
see Blind, Libraries for the
BOOKS OF KNOWLEDGE
see Encyclopedias and Dictionaries
BOOKSELLERS AND BOOKSELLING
see also Copyright; Publishers and Publishing
Bories, J. & Bonassies, F. Dictionnaire Pratique de la Presse, de l'imprimerie & de la Librairie, 2 vols. 1238p. (Fr.). 1972. $70.00. Gregg.

BOOTS AND SHOES
Technisches Woerterbuch Fuer Die Schuhindustrie: German-English & English-German. LC 67-73812. 304p. (Ger. & Eng.). 1966. 17.50x (ISBN 3-7785-0040-6). Intl Pubns Serv.

BOOTS AND SHOES-TRADE AND MANUFACTURE
Knebel, Gerhard. Technical Dictionary for the Shoe Industry. (Eng. & Ger.). 1966. pap. $29.95 (ISBN 3-7785-0040-6, M-7641, Pub. by Huethig). French & Eur.

BOSTON-FIRST CHURCH OF CHRIST, SCIENTIST
Concordance to Christian Science Hymnal & Hymnal Notes. 1961. $8.50 (ISBN 0-87510-023-6). Chr Science.

BOTANICAL NOMENCLATURE
see Botany-Nomenclature
BOTANISTS
see also Horticulturists
Desmond, Ray. Dictionary of British & Irish Botanists & Horticulturists: Including Plant Collectors & Botanical Artists. 3rd ed. 747p. 1977. $99.50x (ISBN 0-8476-1392-5). Rowman.

Desmond, Ray, ed. Dictionary of British & Irish Botanists & Horticulturists. 3rd ed. 764p. 1977. write for info (ISBN 0-85066-089-0). Taylor & Francis.

BOTANY-BIO-BIBLIOGRAPHY
see also Botanists
Desmond, Ray, ed. Dictionary of British & Irish Botanists & Horticulturists. 3rd ed. 764p. 1977. write for info (ISBN 0-85066-089-0). Taylor & Francis.

BOTANY-CLASSIFICATION
Elgin, Peter. Talk & Taxonomy. LC 81-160082. ix, 125p. (Eng.). 1980. fl.pap. 30.00 (ISBN 9-02-722510-9). Benjamins.

BOTANY-DICTIONARIES
Anell, Ivar. Vad Betyder Vaxtens Latinska Namn. LC 76-470315. 159p. (Eng., Danish, Finnish, Fr., Lat., Norwegian, & Swedish.). 1976. Kr.55.00 (ISBN 9-1370-6121-6). Forum Bok.

Bastian, Hartmut. Ullstein Lexikon der Pflanzenwelt. (Ger.). 1973. $27.50 (ISBN 0-686-56471-5, M-7675, Pub. by Ullstein Verlag VA). French & Eur.

Belmont, Abel. Dictionnaire Historique & Artistique de la Rose. (Illus.). 207p. (Fr.). 30.00 F. Lechevalier.

Boerner, F. Taschenwoerterbuch der Botanischen Pflanzennamem. 2nd ed. 435p. (Ger.). 1966. $39.95 (ISBN 3-489-56322-0, M-7631, Pub. by P. Parey). French & Eur.

--Taschenwoerterbuch der Botanischen Pflanzennamem. 2nd ed. 435p. (Ger.). 1966. $39.95 (ISBN 3-489-56322-0). Parey.

Cook, J. Gordon. ABC of Plant Terms. 293p. 1968. $39.00x (ISBN 0-900541-56-3, Pub. by Meadowfield Pr England). State Mutual Bk.

Desmond, Ray, ed. Dictionary of British & Irish Botanists & Horticulturists. 3rd ed. 764p. 1977. write for info (ISBN 0-85066-089-0). Taylor & Francis.

Diccionario Axon de zoologia y botanica. (Span.). Arg.$11.00. Plus Ultra.

Diccionario De Botanica. 256p. (Span.). 1973. leatherette $11.50 (ISBN 84-307-8268-0, S-50258). French & Eur.

Diccionario Monografico del Reino Vegetal. 288p. (Span.). 750.00 ptas (ISBN 84-7153-387-1). Biblograf SP.

Diccionario Monografico del Reino Vegetal. (Span.). 750.00 ptas (ISBN 84-7153-386-3). Biblograf.

Diccionario Monografico del Reino Vegetal 'Vox' 288p. (Span.). 1980. write for info. (ISBN 84-7153-386-3). Biblo SP.

Font Quer. Diccionario de botanica. (Span.). 990.00 ptas. Labor.

Font Quer, Pio. Diccionario de Botanico. 1264p. (Span.). 1979. 2.200 ptas. Labor SA.

Gatin, Charles Louis. Dictionnaire Aide Memoire de Botanique. 867p. (Fr.). 1924. $99.50 (ISBN 0-686-56785-4, M-6581, Pub. by Lechevalier). French & Eur.

Gatin, Charles-Louis. Dictionnaire Alde-Memoire de Botanique. (Illus.). 867p. (Fr.). 1924. 260.00 F. Lechevalier.

Gatin, Charles Louis. Dictionnaire de Botanique. (Fr.). 1966. write for info. Kraus.

Genaust, Helmut. Etymologisches Woerterbuch der Botanischen Pflanzennamen. 390p. (Ger.). 1976. $62.50 (ISBN 3-7643-0755-2, M-7368, Pub. by Birkhaeuser). French & Eur.

Grebenshchikov, O. S. Geobotanic Dictionary. (Rus., Eng., Ger. & Fr.). 1979. lib. bdg. $36.00x (ISBN 3-87429-164-2). Lubrecht & Cramer.

Har, R. & Synge, P. M. Diccionario Ilustrado en Color de Plantas de Jardin con Plantas de Interior y de Invernadero. 364p. (Span.). 1977. $60.00 (ISBN 84-252-0376-7, S-12330). French & Eur.

Howes, F. N. Dictionary of Useful & Everyday Plants & Their Common Names. LC 73-91701. 300p. 1974. $34.50 (ISBN 0-521-08520-9). Cambridge U Pr.

Jackson, Benjamin D. Glossary of Botanic Terms, with Their Derivation & Accent. 4th rev. ed. 1960. Repr. of 1928 ed. $27.50x (ISBN 0-02-847110-5). Hafner.

Jehan, L. F. Dictionnaire de Botanique. Migne, J. P., ed. (Nouvelle Encyclopedie Theologique Ser.: Vol. 8). 758p. (Fr.). Repr. of 1860 ed. lib. bdg. $105.00x (ISBN 0-89241-258-5). Caratzas Pub Co.

Lemee, Albert. Dictionnaire Descriptif & Synonymique des Genres de Plantes Phanerogmes, 7. 693p. (Fr.). 1939. 65.00 F. Lechevalier.

--Dictionnaire Descriptif & Synonymique des Genres de Plantes Phanerogames, 8. 273p. (Fr.). 1941. 45.00 F. Lechevalier.

--Dictionnaire Descriptif & Synonymique des Genres de Plantes Phanerogames, 9. 287p. (Fr.). 1951. 65.00 F. Lechevalier.

--Dictionnaire Descriptif & Synonymique des Genres de Plantes Phanerogames, 10. 219p. (Fr.). 1959. 75.00 F. Lechevalier.

Lexis Veinte-dos: Apendice Botanica. 7th ed. 280p. (Span.). 1982. pap. 600.00 ptas (ISBN 84-226-1041-8). Circulo Lect.

Lexis Veinte-dos: Apendice Botanica. 2nd ed. 288p. (Span.). 1981. pap. 550.00 ptas (ISBN 84-226-1218-6). Circulo Lect.

Lexix Veinte-Dos: Apendice, Botanica. 3rd ed. 288p. (Span.). 1982. pap. 600.00 ptas (ISBN 84-226-1218-6). Circulo Lect.

Little, R. J. & Jones, C. E. A Dictionary of Botany. 416p. 1980. text ed. $22.50 (ISBN 0-442-24169-0). Van Nos Reinhold.

Macura, P. Dictionary of Botany, 2 vols. 1982. Set. $213.00 (ISBN 0-686-94134-9); Vol. 1. write for info.; Vol. 2: General Terms. $110.75 (ISBN 0-444-41977-2). Elsevier.

--Elsevier's Dictionary of Botany, Vol. 1: Plant Names. LC 79-15558. 580p. 1979. $110.75 (ISBN 0-444-41787-7). Elsevier.

Macura, Paul. Russian-English Botanical Dictionary. 678p. (Rus. & Eng.). 1982. $49.95 (ISBN 0-89357-092-3). Slavica.

Malaret, A. Lexicon de fauna y flora. (Span.). 1961. write for info. Inst Caro y Cuervo.

Marzell. Woerterbuch der Deutschen Pflanzennamen. (Ger.). fascs. 1-22 $550.00 (ISBN 0-686-56642-4, M-7031). French & Eur.

Miller, P. The Gardener's Dictionary. 1969. Repr. of 1754 ed. $64.00 (ISBN 3-7682-0613-0). Lubrecht & Cramer.

Musmarra, Alfio. Dizionario botanico. 1184p. (Ital.). 1973. L.12000.00 (ISBN 88-206-0730-1). Edagricole.

Pont Quer, Pio. Diccionario De Botanica. 1244p. (Span.). 1977. $59.95 (ISBN 84-335-5804-8, S-50066). French & Eur.

Tosco, U. Dizionario di botanica: A-L. (Illus.). 96p. (Ital.). L.3000.00. Ist Geo Agostini.

--Dizionario di Botanica: M-Z. (Illus.). 96p. (Ital.). L.3000.00. Ist Geo Agostini.

Tosco, Uberto. Diccionario de botanica. 2nd ed. Gil, Francisco, tr. 255p. (Span.). 1980. pap. 500.00 ptas (ISBN 84-307-8268-0). Teide.

--Dictionnaire de Botanique: Vol. 1, A-H. (Fr.). write for info. Atlas.

--Dictionnaire de Botanique: Vol. 2, I-Z. (Fr.). write for info. Atlas.

Tozzetti, Ottaviano T. Dizionario botanico italiano. xiv, 558p. (Ital.). L.26000.00. Forni.

Usher, George. A Dictionary of Botany. 408p. 1979. text ed. $19.00x (ISBN 0-8448-1387-7). Crane-Russak Co.

Willis, J. C. A Dictionary of the Flowering Plants & Ferns Vol. 1: Generic & Family Names. 8th ed. LC 72-83581. 1300p. 1973. $99.00 (ISBN 0-521-08699-X). Cambridge U Pr.

BOTANY-NOMENCLATORS
see Botany-Nomenclature
BOTANY-NOMENCLATURE
see also Botany-Terminology; Plant Names, Popular
Genaust, Helmut. Etymologisches Woerterbuch der Botanischen Pflanzennamen. 390p. (Ger.). 1976. $62.50 (ISBN 3-7643-0755-2, M-7368, Pub. by Birkhaeuser). French & Eur.

Stearn, William T. Botanical Latin: History, Grammar, Syntax, Terminology & Vocabulary. (Illus., Lat.). 1966. $18.95x (ISBN 0-02-852900-6). Hafner.

BOTANY-NOMENCLATURE (POPULAR)
see Plant Names, Popular
BOTANY-PATHOLOGY
see Plant Diseases
BOTANY-TAXONOMY
see Botany-Classification
BOTANY-TERMINOLOGY
see also Botany-Nomenclature
Cook, J. Gordon. ABC of Plant Terms. 293p. 1968. $39.00x (ISBN 0-900541-56-3, Pub. by Meadowfield Pr England). State Mutual Bk.

A Guide to the Use of Terms in Plant Pathology: Terminology Sub-Committee of the Federation of British Plant Pathologists. 55p. 1973. pap. $30.00x (ISBN 0-85198-290-5, Pub. by CAB Bks England). State Mutual Bk.
Stearn, William T. Botanical Latin: History, Grammar, Syntax, Terminology & Vocabulary. (Illus., Lat.). 1966. $18.95x (ISBN 0-02-852900-6). Hafner.
Viktorov, D. P. Kratkii Slovar Botanicheskikh Terminov. 213p. (Rus.). 1957. $00.95 (Pub. by Sov. Nauka). Four Continent.
--Kratkii Slovar Botanicheskikh Terminov. 178p. (Rus.). 1964. $1.40 (Pub. by Nauka). Four Continent.

BOTANY–ASIA
Thompson, Reginald C. A Dictionary of Assyrian Botany. LC 78-72767. (Ancient Mesopotamian Texts & Studies). (Assyrian.). Repr. of 1949 ed. $45.00 (ISBN 0-404-18221-6). AMS Pr.

BOTANY, AGRICULTURAL
see Botany, Economic

BOTANY, ECONOMIC
see also Forest Products; Grain; Grasses; Plants, Useful; Poisonous Plants; Weeds
Uphof, J. C. Dictionary of Economic Plants. 2nd, rev. & enl. ed. 1968. $28.00 (ISBN 3-7682-0001-9). Lubrecht & Cramer.

BOTANY, MEDICAL
see also Herbs
Debuigne, Gerard. Dictionnaire des Plantes Qui Guerissent. 250p. (Fr.). 1972. pap. $6.95 (ISBN 0-686-56860-5, M-6638). French & Eur.
Duquesne, J. Dictionnaires des Plantes Medicinales. (Illus.). 556p. (Fr.). 1975. 49.00 F. Chiron.

BOTANY, SYSTEMATIC
see Botany–Classification

BOTSWANA
Stevens, Richard P. Historical Dictionary of the Republic of Botswana. LC 75-16489. (African Historical Dictionaries Ser.: No. 5). 189p. 1975. $13.00 (ISBN 0-8108-0857-9). Scarecrow.

BOTTLED GAS
see Liquefied Petroleum Gas

BOTTOM DEPOSITS (OCEANOGRAPHY)
see Sedimentation and Deposition

BOUTAN LANGUAGE
see Tibetan Language

BOY SCOUTS
Low-Income Glossary. $0.15 ea. (SL3638). BSA.

BRACHYGRAPHY
see Abbreviations; Shorthand

BRACKISH WATER BIOLOGY
see Marine Biology; Marine Fauna

BRAIDISM
see Hypnotism

BRAND NAMES
see Trade-Marks

BRANDS (COMMERCE)
see Trade-Marks

BRAZIL
see also names of cities, towns and areas in Brazil, e.g. Rio de Janeiro; Amazon River and Valley
Leite, Yara M. Dicionario Juridico Brasileiro: Contendo Termos, Expressoes Idiomaticas & Brocardos Usuais em Direito. 3rd ed. LC 77-570484. 223p. (Port.). 1976. Cr.$70.00. Saraiva SA.
Leite, Yara Muller. Dicionario de Acoes & de Procedimentos Judiciais. LC 79-115699. vii, 692p. (Port.). 1979. Cr.$590.00. Saraiva SA.
Malta, Christovao P. Dicionario de Direito do Trabalho. LC 76-452001. 535p. (Port.). 1975. Cr.$115.00. Rio Grafica.
Sidou, J. Vocabulario do Cheque. LC 76-464726. 333p. (Port.). 1975. write for info. Editora Revista.
Valle, Gerson. Vocabulario Trabalhista: Direito do Trabalho, Processo do Trabalho, Previdencia Socail. LC 76-463962. 288p. (Port.). 1975. Cr.$60.00. Rio Grafica.

BRAZIL–DESCRIPTION AND TRAVEL
Dicionario de Geografia do Brasil. 544p. (Port.). $23.00. Imported Bks.

BRAZIL–HISTORIOGRAPHY
Dicionario de Historia do Brasil. 618p. (Port.). 1973. $25.00. Imported Bks.

BRAZIL–HISTORY
Levine, Robert M. Historical Dictionary of Brazil. LC 78-10178. (Latin American Historical Dictionaries Ser.: No. 19). 1979. lib. bdg. $14.50 (ISBN 0-8108-1178-2). Scarecrow.

BREADSTUFFS
see Grain

BREAKERS
see Ocean Waves

BREATHING
see Respiration

BRETON LANGUAGE
Dictionanaire Francais-Breton. (Fr. - Bret.). 1979. $15.00 (ISBN 0-686-56718-8, M-6141). French & Eur.
Dictionnaire Breton-Francais, Francais-Breton. (Fr. & Breton.). 1979. $29.95 (ISBN 0-686-56717-X, M-6118). French & Eur.
Dictionnaire Etymologiqe du Moyen-Breton. 225p. (Fr.). 80.00 F. Slatkine.
Ernault, Emile Jean M. Glossaire Moyen-Breton, 2 vols. LC 77-553414. xxviii, 833p. (Fr.). 1976. 290.00 F. Lafitte Repr.
Le Du, Jean & Le Berre, Yves. Dictionnaire Pratique Francais-Breton. 87p. (Fr.). 1976. 8.00 F. Rennes, C. R. D. P.
Loth, Joseph. Vocabulaire du Vieux Breton. 258p. (Fr.). 1970. 36.00 F. Champion.

BREVIARIES
see Liturgies

BREWING
see also Enzymes
European Brewery Convention. Elsevier's Dictionary of Brewing. 1983. $83.00 (ISBN 0-444-42131-9). Elsevier.
Hartong, Bernard D. Elsevier's Dictionary of Barley, Malting, & Brewing. (Eng., Ger., Fr., Danish, Ital., & Span., Polyglot). 1961. $76.75 (ISBN 0-444-40270-5). Elsevier.
Schmitt, Tilman. Fachworterbuch der Brauerei & Abfullpraxis. LC 78-344854. viii, 200p. (Eng. & Ger.). 1977. DM.25.00 (ISBN 3-418-00637-X). Carl KG.

BREWING INDUSTRY
Downard, William L. Dictionary of the History of the American Brewing & Distilling Industries. LC 79-6826. (Illus.). xxv, 268p. 1980. lib. bdg. $45.00 (ISBN 0-313-21330-5, DOD/). Greenwood.

BRIC-A-BRAC
see Art Objects

BRICKLAYING
see also Masonry
Glossary of Terms Relating to Brick Masonry. Rev. ed. (No.2). 1975. $0.50. Brick Inst Amer.

BRIDGE (GAME)
see Contract Bridge

BRIDGE CONSTRUCTION
see Masonry

BRIEFHAND
see Shorthand

BRITISH LITERATURE
see English Literature (Collections); Irish Literature (Collections); Scottish Literature (Collections); and subdivisions under these headings, e.g. English Literature–History and Criticism

BRITISH POETRY
see English Poetry (Collections); Irish Poetry (Collections); Irish Poetry (English) (Collections); Scottish Poetry (Collections); Welsh Poetry (Collections); and subdivisions under these headings, e.g. English Poetry–History and Criticism

BRITISH PORCELAIN
see Porcelain

BRITISH PORTRAITS
see Portraits

BROADCASTING
see also Radio Broadcasting; Television Broadcasting
Conseil International de la Langue Francaise. Vocabulaire de la Radiodifussion. (Fr.). 1973. 15.40 F. Hachette.
National Association of Broadcasters. Standard Definition of Broadcast Research Terms. $2.00. Natl Assn Broadcasters.
Saur, Karl O. Klipp & Klar. LC 79-375153. 208p. (Ger.). 1978. DM.17.80 (ISBN 3-411-01711-2). Biblio Inst.

BRONZES
Mackay, James. Dictionary of Western Sculptors in Bronze. 414p. 1977. $49.50 (ISBN 0-902028-55-3). Antique Collect.
Mackey, James. Dictionary of Western Sculptors in Bronze. (Illus.). 1977. $49.50 (ISBN 0-902028-55-3). Apollo.

BRUTALITY
see Cruelty

BUCKET-SHOPS
see Speculation

BUDDHISM
see also Zen Buddhism
also headings beginning with the word Buddhist
Ling, T. O. A Dictionary of Buddhism. LC 72-37231. 244p. 1972. $7.95 (ISBN 0-684-12763-6, ScribT). Scribner.
Ling, Trevor. A Dictionary of Buddhism: Indian & South-East Asia. (Bagchi Indological Ser.: No. 2). 202p. 1981. text ed. $14.00x (ISBN 0-391-02587-2, Pub. by K P Bagchi India). Humanities.
Nyanatiloka. Buddhist Dictionary. LC 77-87508. Repr. of 1950 ed. $20.00 (ISBN 0-404-16846-9). AMS Pr.
Soothill, W. E. & Hodous, L. A Dictionary of Chinese Buddhist Terms. (Chinese & Eng.). 1977. $35.00 (ISBN 0-89684-194-4, Pub. by Motilal Banarsidass India). Orient Bk Dist.

BUDDHISM–CHINA
Soothill, William E. & Hodous, L., eds. Dictionary of Chinese Buddhist Terms, with Sanskrit & English Equivalents & a Sanskrit-Pali Index. (Chinese, Sanskrit & Eng.). 1977. text ed. $50.00x (ISBN 0-8426-1030-8). Verry.

BUILDER'S PLANT
see Construction Equipment

BUILDING
see also Arches; Architecture; Bricklaying; Building Trades; Concrete Construction; Construction Equipment; Construction Industry; Foundations; House Construction; Masonry; Materials
Barbier, Maurice & Cadiergues, Roger. Dictionnaire Technique du Batiment & des Travaux Publics. 6th ed. (Illus.). 148p. (Fr.). 1978. 60.00 F. Eyrolles.
Diccionario de la construccion. 246p. (Span.). pap. 90.00 ptas. CEAC.
Diccionario de la Construcion (II) 2nd ed. 642p. (Span.). 1981. 1115.00 ptas (ISBN 84-329-2608-6). Ceac.
Diccionario para Obras Publicas, Edificacion & Maquinaria en Obra. 1114p. (Ger. & Span.). 1962. DM.108.00 (ISBN 3-7625-1160-8). Bauverlag.
Dictionnaire pour les Travaux Publics & l'equipement des Chantiers de Construction. 5th ed. 420p. (Eng. & Fr.). 1976. DM.38.00 (ISBN 3-7625-0533-0). Bauverlag.
Dictionnaire pour les Travaux Publics & l'equipement des Chantiers de Construction. 5th ed. 548p. (Fr. & Eng.). 1976. DM.48.00 (ISBN 3-7625-0534-9). Bauverlag.
Killer, W. K. Bautechnisches Englisch im Bild: Illustrated Technical German for Builders. 5th ed. (Illus.). 183p. (Eng. & Ger.). 1981. DM.24.00 (ISBN 3-7625-1477-1). Bauverlag.
Sizaire, Pierre. Dictionnaire Technique de la Construction Electrique. (Illus.). 172p. (Fr.). 1968. 67.00 F. Eyrolles.
Wallnig, G. & Evered, H. Deutsch fuer Baufachleute. (Illus.). 102p. (Eng. & Ger., Fr. & Span.). 1979. DM.16.00 (ISBN 3-7625-0462-8). Bauverlag.
--Deutsch fur Baufachleute fuer Daenen, Norweger & Sshweden. (Illus.). 110p. (Danish, Ger., Norwegian & Swedish.). 1982. DM.20.00 (ISBN 3-7625-1467-4). Bauverlag.
--Englisch fuer Baufachleute: Band 1. 6th ed. 101p. (Eng., Ger. & Fr.). 1978. DM.16.00 (ISBN 3-7625-0807-0). Bauverlag.
--Englisch fur Baufachleute: Band 2. 2nd ed. viii, 192p. (Eng., Ger. & Fr.). 1977. DM.38.00 (ISBN 3-7625-0807-0). Bauverlag.
Zurita Ruiz, Jose. Diccionario basico de la construccion. 246p. (Span.). 1982. 390.00 ptas (ISBN 84-329-2805-4). Ceac.
--Diccionario basico de la construccion II. 246p. (Span.). 1982. pap. 340.00 ptas (ISBN 84-329-2905-0). Ceac.

BUILDING–AMATEURS' MANUALS
Crowdis, Kay & Crowdis, David. Designing & Building Your Own Home. (Illus.). 240p. 1980. text ed. $14.95 (ISBN 0-8359-1272-8). Reston.

BUILDING–CONTRACTS AND SPECIFICATIONS
Fletcher, Leonard, et al. Construction Contract Dictionary. LC 81-16935. 128p. 1981. $25.00x (ISBN 0-902132-65-2, 6632, Pub. by E & Fn. Spon England). Methuen Inc.

BUILDING–DETAILS
Lates, Ernest M., et al. Dictionar Poliglot. LC 79-393899. xviii, 827p. (Eng., Romanian, Ger., Fr. & Rus.). 1979. 91.00 lei. Editura Stiintifica.

BUILDING–DICTIONARIES
Abd-El-Gawad, Tawfik. Technical Dictionary: Archtiecture & Building. 1319p. (Eng., Fr., Ger. & Arabic.). 1976. $35.00x (ISBN 0-686-44745-X, Pub. by Collets). State Mutual Bk.
Avramenko, Boris I. Ital'iansko-Russkii i Rusko-Ital'ianskii Stroitel'nyi Slovar. 480p. (Ital. & Rus.). 1978. 4.20 Rub. Russkii Iazyk.
Barbier, et al. Diccionario tecnico ilustrado de edificacion y obras publicas. (Illus.). 177p. (Span.). write for info. G Gili.
Barbier, Maurice. Diccionario Tecnico Ilustrado De Edificacion y Obras Publicas. 177p. (Span.). 1976. pap. $11.50 (ISBN 84-252-0327-9, S-50273). French & Eur.
--Dictionnaire Technique du Batiment & des Travaux Publics. LC 76-456147. 150p. (Eng. & Fr.). 1976. 47.00 F. Eyrolles.
Barry, W. R., ed. Architectural, Construction, Manufacturing & Engineering Glossary of Terms. 519p. 1979. pap. $40.00 (ISBN 0-930284-05-4). Am Assn Cost Engineers.
Benito Bacho, Jose. Diccionario de la Construccion y Obras Publicas Ingles-Espanol, 2 vols. 268p. (Span. & Eng.). 1975. Set. $38.95 (ISBN 84-85198-10-7, S-50117). French & Eur.
--Diccionario de la Construccion y Obras Publicas, Tomo 2: Span. 110p. (Span.). 1975. $18.95 (ISBN 84-85198-09-3, S-50119). French & Eur.
--Diccionario de la Construcion y de Obras Publicas, Tomo I: Ingles. 168p. (Span.). 1975. $18.95 (ISBN 84-85198-00-X, S-50118). French & Eur.
Brooks, Hugh. Encyclopedia of Building & Construction Terms. LC 82-21565. 416p. 1983. $50.00 (ISBN 0-13-275511-4). P-H.
Bucksch, H. Woerterbuch Bau: Ingenieurbau & Baumaschinen. 3rd ed. 934p. (Eng. & Ger.). 1965. DM.38.00 (ISBN 3-7625-1411-9). Bauverlag.
--Woerterbuch fuer Architektur, Hochbau & Baustoffe. 2nd ed. 1137p. (Eng. & Ger.). 1976. DM.220.00 (ISBN 3-7625-0714-7). Bauverlag.
--Woerterbuch fuer Architektur, Hochbau & Baustoffe: Band 1, Deutsch-Englisch. 2nd ed. 942p. (Ger. & Eng.). 1980. DM.220.00 (ISBN 3-7625-1399-6). Bauverlag.
Bucksch, Hector. Dictionnaire pour les Travaux Publics, le Batiment et l'Equipement des Chantiers de Construction. 7th ed. 420p. (Eng. & Fr.). 1979. $42.50 (ISBN 0-686-56930-X, M-6051). French & Eur.
Bucksch, Herbert & Galan e Hidalgo, Arturo. Diccionario frances-espanol de la construccion y obras publicas. 564p. (Fr. & Span.). 1969. 700.00 ptas. ETA.

Bucksch, Herbert & Galan e Hildalgo, Arturo. Diccionario Frances-Espanol de la Construccion y Obras Publicas. 564p. (Fr. & Span.). 1975. $35.95 (ISBN 84-7146-047-5, S-50133). French & Eur.

Chaballe, L. Y. & Vandenberghe, J. P. Elsevier's Dictionary of Building Tools & Materials. (Eng., Fr., Span., Ger. & Dutch.). 1982. $138.50 (ISBN 0-444-42047-9). Elsevier.

Cowan, Henry J. A Dictionary of Architectural Science. LC 73-15839. (Illus.). 354p. 1973. pap. $18.95x (ISBN 0-470-18070-6). Halsted Pr.

Dictionnaire Pour les Travaux Publics et l'Equipement des Chartiers de Construction, 2 vols. 875p. (Ger. & Fr.). 1976. leatherette, band I $112.00 (ISBN 3-7625-0379-6, M-7097). French & Eur.

Dictionnaire Pour les Travaux Publics et l'Equipement des Chartiers de Construction, 2 vols. 911p. (Ger. & Fr.). 1978. leatherette, band II $112.00 (ISBN 3-7625-0999-9, M-7098). French & Eur.

English-Chinese Architectural Engineering Dictionary. 441p. (Eng. & Chinese.). 1973. $14.95 (ISBN 0-686-92620-X, M-9254). French & Eur.

Equipo Reactor de Ceac. Diccionario de la Construccion. 650p. (Span.). 1978. pap. $26.50 (ISBN 84-329-2608-6, S-50225). French & Eur.

Frommhold, Hanns. Bauworterbuch. LC 79-358361. viii, 299p. (Ger.). 1978. DM.75.00 (ISBN 3-8041-1529-2). Werner Verlag.

Fullana Llompart, Miguel. Diccionario De L'art I Els Oficis De la Construccion. 440p. (Catalan.). 1974. $35.95 (ISBN 84-273-0372-6, S-50000). French & Eur.

Gaward, Abd El. Architecture & Building Dictionary: English-French-German-Arabic. 465p. (Eng., Fr., Ger. & Arabic.). 1976. Leatherette $45.00 (ISBN 0-686-92255-7, M-9753). French & Eur.

Grabbe, Hans J. Bauherren-Lexikon. LC 76-488016. 251p. (Eng. & Ger.). 1976. DM.29.50 (ISBN 3-528-08657-2). Vieweg.

Hurlimann, Ernst. Lexikon fur den Bauherrn. LC 76-459881. 224p. (Ger.). 1975. write for info. (ISBN 3-478-04250-X). Verlag Moderne.

Lefebvre, M. Nouveau Dictionnaire du Batiment: Anglais-Francais Francais-Anglais. 1971 ed. (Illus.). 450p. (Eng. & Fr.). 300.00 F. Maison Dictionnaire.

Lefebvre, Marcel. Dictionnaire du Batiment: Francais-Anglais. 356p. (Fr. & Eng.). 1965. write for info. LEMEAC.

--Nouveau Dictionnaire Du Batiment. 411p. (Fr.). 1971. pap. $25.00 (ISBN 0-686-57010-3, M-6351). French & Eur.

Lehtipuu, Irma. Englantilais-Suomalainen Asunto ja Rakennusalan Sanasto. LC 79-392967. 247p. (Eng. & Finnish.). 1978. write for info. (ISBN 9-5110-5150-4). Otava.

Lexique Des Termes Du Batiment. 212p. (Fr.). 1963. pap. $14.95 (ISBN 0-686-57014-6, M-6361). French & Eur.

Lexique des Termes du Batiment. (Illus.). 212p. (Fr.). 1963. 32.00 F. Massin.

Lexique Du Batiment. (Fr.). $14.95 (ISBN 0-686-57015-4, M-6364). French & Eur.

Machado. Diccionario Tecnico de la Construccion, Edificacion & Obras Publicas. (Fr. & Span.). 1969. 00.1400.00 ptas (ISBN 8-42830-245-6). Paraninfo.

Machado, M. Diccionario Tecnico De la Construccion, Edificacion y Obras Publicas Frances-Espanol y Espanol-Frances. 576p. (Fr. & Span.). 1969. leatherette $35.95 (ISBN 84-283-0245-6, S-50242). French & Eur.

--Diccionario tecnico de la construccion: Edificacion y obras publicas; francesa-espanol y espanol-frances. 578p. (Fr. & Span.). 1969. 500.00 ptas. Paraninfo.

Neve, Richard. City & Country Purchaser & Builder's Dictionary. LC 69-16762. Repr. of 1726 ed. $19.50x (ISBN 0-678-05616-1). Kelley.

Profor. Initiation Au Vocabulaire Du Batiment et Des Travaux Publics. 176p. (Fr.). 1979. $37.50 (ISBN 0-686-57088-X, M-6467). French & Eur.

Putnam, R. E. & Carlson, G. E. Architectural & Building Trades Dictionary. 3rd ed. 512p. 1983. $17.95 (ISBN 0-442-27461-0). Van Nos Reinhold.

Sakharov. Dictionnaire Francais-Russe du Batiment. (Fr. & Rus.). 1976. 280.00 F. MIR.

Scott, John S. Dictionary of Building. rev. ed. (Reference Ser.). 392p. 1964. pap. $4.95 (ISBN 0-14-051015-X). Penguin.

Steiger, Eduard & Busch, Karl F. Bautechnik. LC 78-340416. 375p. (Ger.). 1976. M.15.00. Bibl Inst Leipzig.

Tekniska Nomenklaturcentralen. Byggordsamling. LC 77-464415. 164p. (Eng. & Swedish.). 1976. Kr.57.00 (ISBN 9-1719-6063-5). Tek Nomen.

--Plan och Byggtermer. LC 76-522778. 198p. (Swedish.). 1975. Kr.50.00 (ISBN 91-7196-058-9). Tek Nomen.

Volkart, K. H. Gips-Woerterbuch. 176p. (Ger., Eng. & Fr.). 1971. DM.85.00 (ISBN 3-7625-0460-1). Bauverlag.

Voronin, V. V., et al. Russko-Frantsuzskii Stroitelnyi Slovar. 464p. (Fr. & Rus.). 1978. $7.25 (Pub. by Russkii Iazyk). Four Continent.

Wallnig, G. & Evered, H. L' Anglais Dans le Batiment: Text En Anglais Avec un Glossaire Illustre. 100p. (Eng., Fr. & Ger.). 1970. pap. $19.95 (ISBN 0-686-57255-6, M-6564). French & Eur.

--German for Building Specialists, (L'allemand Dans le Batiment, el Aleman En la Construccion) 102p. (Ger. & Eng.). 1979. $12.95 (ISBN 3-7625-0462-8, M-7420, Pub. by Bauverlag). French & Eur.

--German for Building Specialists: L'Allemand dans le Batiment, el Aleman en la construccion. 102p. (Ger. & Fr.). 1979. DM.12.95 (ISBN 3-7625-0462-8). Bauverlag.

Wallnig, Gunter & Evered, H. L' Anglais Dans le Batiment: Texte En Anglais Avec un Glossaire Illustre, 2. 192p. (Eng., Fr & Ger.). 1976. pap. $37.50 (ISBN 0-686-57256-4, M-6565). French & Eur.

Wallnig, Gunter & Evered, Harry. El Ingles en la Construccion. 104p. (Eng.-Span.). 1975. pap. $26.95 (ISBN 84-7146-082-3, S-50131). French & Eur.

BUILDING–EARLY WORKS TO 1800

Neve, Richard. City & Country Purchaser & Builder's Dictionary. LC 69-16762. Repr. of 1726 ed. $19.50x (ISBN 0-678-05616-1). Kelley.

BUILDING–MATERIALS

see Building Materials

BUILDING–SPECIFICATIONS

see Building–Contracts and Specifications

BUILDING, CONCRETE

see Concrete Construction

BUILDING, HOUSE

see House Construction

BUILDING AND LOAN ASSOCIATIONS

Institute of Financial Education. Glossary of Savings Association Terminology. 68p. 1983. softcover $4.95. Inst Finan Educ.

BUILDING INDUSTRY

see Construction Industry

BUILDING MATERIALS

see also Cement; Ceramics; Concrete; Plastics; Strength of Materials; Tiles; Wood

Bucksch. Dictionnaire pour l'Architecture le Batiment et les Materiaux de Construction: Allemand-Francais, Vol. 1. 819p. (Ger. & Fr.). 1977. 930.00 F. Maison Dictionnaire.

--Dictionnaire pour l'architecture le Batiment et les Materiaux de Construction: Francais-Allemand, Vol. 2. 675p. (Fr. & Ger.). 1979. 930.00 F. Maison Dictionnaire.

Bucksch, H. Woerterbuch fuer Architektur, Hochbau & Baustoffe. 2nd ed. 1137p. (Eng. & Ger.). 1976. DM.220.00 (ISBN 3-7625-0714-7). Bauverlag.

--Woerterbuch fuer Architektur, Hochbau & Baustoffe: Band 1, Deutsch-Englisch. 2nd ed. 942p. (Ger. & Eng.). 1980. DM.220.00 (ISBN 3-7625-1399-6). Bauverlag.

Bucksch, Hector. Dictionnaire Francais-Allemand pour le Travaux Publics le Batiment & l'equipement des Chantiers de Construction. (Illus.). 912p. (Fr. & Ger.). 1970. 375.00 F. Eyrolles.

--Dictionnaire Francais-Anglais pour les Travaux Publics: Le Batiment & l'equipement des Chantiers de Construction. 6th ed. (Illus.). 550p. (Fr. & Eng.). 1977. 130.00 F. Eyrolles.

Bucksch, Herbert. Dictionary of Architecture, Building Construction & Materials, Vol. II. 1137p. (Eng. & Ger.). 1976. $175.00 (ISBN 3-7625-0714-7, M-7130). French & Eur.

--Dictionary of Architecture, Building Construction & Materials, Vol. I. 942p. (Eng. & Ger.). 1974. $175.00 (ISBN 3-7625-0357-5, M-7131). French & Eur.

--Dictionary of Architecture, Building Construction & Materials, 2 vols. 1974-76. plastic bdg. $120.00x ea. Vol. 1, Ger.-Eng (ISBN 3-7625-0357-5). Vol. 2, Eng.-Ger (ISBN 3-7625-0714-7). Intl Pubns Serv.

Dictionary of Floor, Wall & Ceiling Covering. (Hebrew, Eng. , Fr. & Ger.). IL.7.00. Massada Pr.

Dictionnaire Pour l'Architecture, le Batiment et les Materiaux de Construction, 2 vols. 820p. (Ger. & Fr.). 1977. band I $236.00 (ISBN 3-7625-0786-4, M-7095). French & Eur.

Dictionnaire Pour l'Architecture, le Batiment et les Materiaux de Construction, 2 vols. 688p. (Ger. & Fr.). 1979. band II $236.00 (ISBN 3-7625-0787-2, M-7096). French & Eur.

Grigorovich, M. V., et al. Slovar Po Mineral Nomu Syriu Dlia Promyshlennosti Stroitelnykh Materialov. 87p. (Rus.). 1976. $1.35 (Pub. by Nedra). Four Continent.

Lates, Ernest M., et al. Dictionar Poliglot. LC 79-393899. xviii, 827p. (Eng., Romanian, Ger., Fr. & Rus.). 1979. 91.00 lei. Editura Stiintifica.

Volkart, K. H. Gypsum & Plaster Dictionary. 176p. (Eng., Ger. & Fr.). 1971. $47.50x (ISBN 3-7625-0460-1). Intl Pubns Serv.

BUILDING MATERIALS–SPECIFICATIONS

see Building–Contracts and Specifications

BUILDING SOCIETIES

see Building and Loan Associations

BUILDING TRADES

see also Building; Construction Industry;
also Bricklayers, Carpenters, and similar headings

Putnam, Robert & Carlson, G. E. Architectural & Building Trades Dictionary. 3rd ed. (Illus.). 1974. $15.50 (ISBN 0-8269-0402-5). Am Technical.

Schwicker, Angelo C. International Dictionary of Building Construction: English-French-German-Italian. 1280p. (Eng., Fr., Ger. & Ital.). 1975. lib. bdg. $60.00x (ISBN 0-87936-004-6). Scholium Intl.

Wallnig, G. & Evered, H. L' Anglais Dans le Batiment: Text En Anglais Avec un Glossaire Illustre. 100p. (Eng., Fr. & Ger.). 1970. pap. $19.95 (ISBN 0-686-57255-6, M-6564). French & Eur.

Wallnig, Gunter & Evered, H. L' Anglais Dans le Batiment: Texte En Anglais Avec un Glossaire Illustre, 2. 192p. (Eng., Fr. & Ger.). 1976. pap. $37.50 (ISBN 0-686-57256-4, M-6565). French & Eur.

BUILDINGS

see also Architecture; Building also names of particular types of building and construction e.g. Dwellings; School-houses; Concrete Construction

Bucksch. Dictionnaire pour l'Architecture le Batiment et les Materiaux de Construction: Allemand-Francais, Vol. 1. 819p. (Ger. & Fr.). 1977. 930.00 F. Maison Dictionnaire.

--Dictionnaire pour l'architecture le Batiment et les Materiaux de Construction: Francais-Allemand, Vol. 2. 675p. (Fr. & Ger.). 1979. 930.00 F. Maison Dictionnaire.

BUILDINGS–ACOUSTICS

see Architectural Acoustics

BUILDINGS–DETAILS

see Building–Details

BUILDINGS–MATERIALS

see Building Materials

BULGARIAN LANGUAGE

Andreichina, K., et al. Russian-Bulgarian Phraseological Dictionary. Vlasova, ed. 582p. (Rus. & Bulgarian.). 1980. $65.00 (ISBN 0-686-97416-6, M-9830). French & Eur.

Atanassova, T., et al. Bulgarian-English Dictionary. 2nd ed. 1050p. (Bulgarian & Eng.). 1980. $55.00x (ISBN 0-569-08665-5, Pub. by Collets). State Mutual Bk.

Bodey, Jozsef. Magyar-Bolgar Szotar. LC 77-474283. 584p. (Hungarian & Bulgarian.). 1975. 35.00 Ft (ISBN 9-6320-5050-9). Terra.

--Magyar-Bolgar Szotar. LC 77-474283. 584p. (Hungarian & Bulgarian.). 1975. 35.00 Ft (ISBN 9-63205-050-9). Terra.

Bulgarian-Russian Dictionary (M-9095) 519p. (Bulgarian & Rus.). 1977. $4.95 (ISBN 0-686-87184-7). French & Eur.

Cavaletto, M., et al. Dizionario Italiano-Bulgaro. 967p. (Ital. & Bulgarian.). 1979. leatherette $35.00 (ISBN 0-686-97340-2, M-9835). French & Eur.

Chukalov, S. K. Russko-Bolgarskii Slovar. 911p. (Rus. & Bulgarian.). 1972. $7.95 (Pub. by Sov. Entsiklopediia). Four Continent.

Desov, A. English-Bulgarian Concise Technical Dictionary. (Eng. & Bulgarian.). $17.50 (ISBN 0-686-91776-6). Heinman.

Harlakova, Ivanka & Stankova, Elena. English-Bulgarian Dictionary. 2nd ed. 392p. (Eng. & Bulgarian.). 1978. $30.00x (ISBN 0-686-44692-5, Pub. by Collets). State Mutual Bk.

Karmannyi Russko-Bolgarskii Slovar. 464p. (Rus. & Bulgarian.). 1978. $1.95 (Pub. by Russkii Iazyk). Four Continent.

Langenscheidts Universal-Woerterbuch Bulgarisch. 560p. (Bulgarian & Ger.). DM.6.80 (18080). Langenscheidt.

Langenscheidts Universal-Woerterbuecher Bulgarisch-Deutsch. (Bulgarian & Ger.). 1978. DM.5.80 (ISBN 3-468-18080-2). Langenscheidt.

Leonidova, M. A. Karmannyi Bolgarsko-Russkii Slovar. 534p. (Rus. & Bulgarian.). 1961. $1.75 (Pub. by Gosizdat Inostr. & Natsional). Four Continent.

--Karmannyi Russko-Bolgarskii Slovar. 474p. (Rus. & Bulgarian.). 1960. $1.25. Four Continent.

Parashkevov, Boris, et al. Bulgarialais-Suomalainen Sanakirja. LC 76-501852. 91p. (Bulgarian & Swedish.). 1975. write for info. (ISBN 951-662-159-7). Gaudeamus.

Russev, R. Bulgarian-English Dictionary. (Bulgarian & Eng.). pap. text ed. $27.50 (ISBN 0-685-20185-6, 006-2). Saphrograph.

Russev, Rusi, ed. Bulgarian-English Dictionary. (Bulgarian & Eng.). 1953. $12.00 (ISBN 0-8044-0506-9). Ungar.

Varma, B. Kanti. Bulgarian-Hindi Dictionary. 706p. (Bulgarian & Hindi.). 1978. leatherette $50.00 (ISBN 0-686-92526-2, M-9836). French & Eur.

Voinov, M. Latin-Bulgarian Dictionary. 840p. (Lat. & Bulgarian.). 1980. $45.00 (ISBN 0-686-97420-4, M-9831). French & Eur.

BULGARIAN LANGUAGE TO 1100
see *Church Slavic Language*

BULLS AND BEARS
see *Stock-Exchange*

BURKITT'S LYMPHOMA
Histopathological Definition of Burkitt's Tumour. (WHO Bulletin Reprint: Vol. 40, No. 4). (Summary in French & Russian). 1969. pap. $2.00 (ISBN 92-4-056000-9). World Health.

BURMA
see *also names of cities and towns in Burma*
Cordier, Henri. Bibliotheca Indosinica. Dictionnaire bibliographique des ouvrages relatifs a la peninsule indo-chinoise, 5 vols. in 3. (Span. & Indonesian). 1912-32. Set. $197.00 (ISBN 0-8337-0676-4). B Franklin.

Maring, Joel M. & Maring, Ester G. Historical & Cultural Dictionary of Burma. LC 73-1477. (Historical & Cultural Dictionaries of Asia Ser.: No. 4). 1973. $15.00 (ISBN 0-8108-0596-0). Scarecrow.

BURMESE LANGUAGE
Esche, Annemarie. Woerterbuch Burmesisch-Deutsch. LC 76-476865. 546p. (Ger. & Burmese.). 1976. M.65.00. VEB Verlag Enzyklopadie.

Novikov, N. N., et al. Russko-Birmanskii Slovar. 880p. (Rus. & Burmese.). 1966. $7.50 (Pub. by Sov. Entsiklopediia). Four Continent.

U Chin Vei, et al. Karmannyi Russko-Birmanskii Slovar. (Rus. & Burmese.). 1962. $2.50 (Pub. by GINS). Four Continent.

BURNS, ROBERT, 1759-1796
Cuthbertson, John. Complete Glossary to the Poetry & Prose of Robert Burns. 1886. $22.50 (ISBN 0-8337-0747-7). B Franklin.

Reid, J. B. Complete Word & Phrase Concordance to the Poems & Songs of Robert Burns. LC 68-58477. (Bibliography & Reference Ser.: No. 252). 1969. Repr. of 1889 ed. $30.50 (ISBN 0-8337-2932-2). B Franklin.

Scots Words from Burns. LC 75-329215. 53p. 1976. $5.75x (ISBN 0-284-98564-3). Intl Pubns Serv.

BURUNDI (AFRICAN STATE)
Weinstein, Warren. Historical Dictionary of Burundi. LC 76-13594. (African Historical Dictionaries Ser.: No. 8). 1976. $19.50 (ISBN 0-8108-0962-1). Scarecrow.

BUSINESS
see *also Accounting; Advertising; Bookkeeping; Commerce; Commercial Law; Corporations; Credit; Industrial Management; Marketing; Merchants; Occupations; Office Management; Real Estate Business; Secretaries; Small Business; Trade-Marks*
Guarino, Giuseppe. Dizionario amministrativo. xvi, 672p. (Ital.). 1978. L.16000.00. Giuffre.

Zavada. Satzlexikon der Handelskorrespondenz. 356p. (Ger. & Eng.). 1982. DM.25.00. Brandstetter.

Zavada & Eberle. Satzlexikon der Handelskorrespondenz. 435p. (Ger. & Port.). 1982. DM.30.00. Brandstetter.

Zavada & Hartgenbush. Satzlexikon der Handelskorrespondenz. 430p. (Ger. & Fr.). 1982. DM.30.00. Brandstetter.

Zavada & Schraffl. Satzlexikon der Handelskorrespondenz. 388p. (Ger. & Ital.). 1982. DM.30.00. Brandstetter.

Zavada & Weis. Satzlexikon der Handelskorrespondenz. 405p. (Ger. & Span.). 1982. DM.30.00. Brandstetter.

BUSINESS–DICTIONARIES
Administrative & Financial Terms. (FAO Terminology Bulletin: No. 23, Rev. 1). 169p. 1982. pap. $12.75 (ISBN 92-5-001120-2, F2212, FAO). Unipub.

Ammer, Christine & Ammer, Dean. Dictionary of Business & Economics. rev. & expanded ed. 1983. $29.95 (ISBN 0-02-900790-9). Free Pr.

Ammer, Christine & Ammer, Dean S. Dictionary of Business & Economics. LC 76-41625. 1977. $27.95 (ISBN 0-02-900590-6). Free Pr.

Anderla, Georges & Schmidt-Anderla, Georgette. Business Dictionary: English-French, French-English. 2nd ed. 524p. (Eng. & Fr.). 1979. $62.50x (ISBN 2-7034-0153-1). Intl Pubns Serv.

Arisi Rota, Umberto. Dizionario aziendale. 428p. (Ital.). L.9000.00. Buffetti.

Bajic, B., et al. Technical-Economical Dictionary for Business Purposes. 1700p. (Eng., Fr., Ger. & Serbocroation.). 1973. $95.00 (ISBN 0-686-92638-2, M-9689). French & Eur.

Berenyi, John. The Modern American Business Dictionary: Including Reaganomics & an Appendix of Business Slang. LC 81-22342. 288p. 1982. $22.50 (ISBN 0-688-00986-7). Morrow.

--The Modern American Business Dictionary: Including Reagonomics & an Appendix of Business Slang. LC 81-21185. 288p. 1982. pap. $7.50 (ISBN 0-688-00987-5). Quill NY.

Berman, Ben. The Dictionary of Business & Credit Terms. Andover, James J., ed. LC 82-14231. 208p. 1983. $19.95 (ISBN 0-934914-45-1). NACM.

Brownstone, David M., et al. The VNR Dictionary of Business & Finance. 320p. 1980. text ed. $18.95 (ISBN 0-442-20949-5). Van Nos Reinhold.

Chu, Hsiu-Feng, et al. English-Chinese Chinese-English Dictionary of Business Terms. 476p. (Orig.). 1973. pap. $7.95x (ISBN 0-917056-85-X, Pub. by Chih-Wen Pub Co China). Cheng & Tsui.

Clark, Donald T. & Gottfried, Bert A., eds. University Dictionary of Business & Finance. (Apollo Eds.). 1972. pap. $4.95i (ISBN 0-8152-0143-5, A143). T Y Crowell.

Colin, Francoise, et al. Harrap's French & English Business Dictionary. 507p. (Fr. & Eng.). 1981. $48.00. Imported Bks.

Collin, Francoise, et al, eds. Harrap's French & English Business Dictionary. 222p. (Fr. & Eng.). 1983. $45.00 (ISBN 0-686-44824-3). Natl Textbk.

Coveney, James. Glossary of English & German Management Terms. (English for Special Purposes Bk.). (Eng. & Ger.). 1977. pap. text ed. $6.95x (ISBN 0-582-55525-6). Longman.

Davids, L. E. Instant Business Dictionary. (Career Institute Instant Reference Library). 1971. $3.95 (ISBN 0-531-02012-6). Watts.

De Renty, Ivan. The Businessman's Everyday English to Spanish Dictionary: El Mundo De Negocios. (Eng. & Span.). 1978. pap. $9.95 (ISBN 84-7143-118-1, 8138). Larousse.

Dietl, C. Woerterbuch des Wirtschafts, Rechts und Handelssprache. (Eng. & Ger., Dictionary of Economic, Legal & Commercial Terms). 1970. $33.00 (ISBN 3-87527-003-7, M-6939). French & Eur.

Edler, Florence. Glossary of Mediaeval Terms of Business, 1200-1600. 1934. $32.00 (ISBN 0-527-01690-X). Kraus Repr.

Eichborn, R. Kleine Eichborn, Taschenwoerterbuch der Wirtschaftssprache, Vol. 1. (Ger. & Eng., English-German Dictionary of Commercial Terms). 1975. $33.50 (ISBN 3-921392-00-4, M-7495, Pub. by Siebenpunkt Vlg.). French & Eur.

Emolumento, V. Dizionario Commerciale Francese-Italiano. 533p. (Fr. & Ital.). 1978. pap. $37.50 (ISBN 88-7075-024-8, M-9281). French & Eur.

Enciclopedia simultanea de correspondencia comercial en seis idiomas. 495p. (Eng., Span., Fr., Ital., Ger. & Port.). 1976. Mex.$16.50. Distein.

Filkins, James H. & Caruth, Donald L. Lexicon of American Business Terms. pap. $1.95 (ISBN 0-671-18705-8). Monarch Pr.

Franklin, Alfred L. Dictionnaire Historique des Arts, Metiers & Professions: Exercees dans Paris Depuis le 13 Siecle. 856p. (Fr.). 1906. DM.138.00. Olms Verlag.

Ghattas, Nabih. Dictionary of Economics, Business & Finance: English-Arabic with Arabic Glossary. (Eng. & Arabic.). $25.00x (ISBN 0-86685-169-0). Intl Bk Ctr.

Ginguay, Michael. Diccionario De Informatica. 184p. (Span.). 1972. pap. $23.50 (ISBN 84-311-0004-4, S-50130). French & Eur.

Giordano, Albert G. Concise Dictionary of Business Terminology. 464p. 1981. text ed. $14.95 (ISBN 0-13-166553-7, Spec); pap. text ed. $5.95 (ISBN 0-13-166546-4). P-H.

Grossmann. Englisches Handelsvokabularium Nach Sachgebieten. 330p. (Ger. & Eng., English Commercial Vokabulary Subjects). 1950. pap. $15.95 (ISBN 3-87217-001-5, 7360, Pub. by Th. Grossmann). French & Eur.

Henni, Mustapha. Dictionaire Des Termes Economiques et Commerciaux: Francais-Arabe. (Fr. & Arabic.). $18.00x (ISBN 0-86685-109-7). Intl Bk Ctr.

Herbst, R. Dictionary of Commericial, Financial & Legal Terms in Two Languages. (Eng. & Ger.). $78.25 ea. Vol. A, Eng. & Ger. Vol. B, Ger. & Eng (ISBN 3-85942-004-6). Adler.

Herbst, Robert & Readett, Alan G. The Herbst Dictionaries of Commercial, Financial & Legal Terms: English-German. (The Two-Language Ser.: Vol. A). 688p. (Eng. & Ger.). 1975. text ed. $69.95 (ISBN 0-686-92254-9). Birkhauser.

Herbst, Robert & Readett, Alan G., eds. The Herbst Dictionaries of Commercial, Financial & Legal Terms: Deutsch-Englisch. (The Two-Language Ser.: Vol. B). 906p. (Ger. & Eng.). 1976. text ed. $69.95x (ISBN 0-686-92258-1). Birkhauser.

Horner, C. F. & Liebster, L. M. THe Hamlyn Pocket Dictionary of Business Terms. LC 81-131528. 317p. 1980. Epap. 1.25 (ISBN 0-600-31599-1). Hamlyn Pub.

IBM. Diccionario De Siglas Relacionadas Con la Informatica. 200p. (Span.). 1974. pap. $9.95 (ISBN 84-360-2250-5, S-50370). French & Eur.

Johannsen, Hano & Page, G. Terry. The International Dictionary of Business. 376p. 1981. $17.95 (ISBN 0-13-470823-7); pap. $7.95 (ISBN 0-13-470815-6). P-H.

Kershaw, F. & Russon, S. German for Business Studies. 203p. (Ger.). pap. $7.95 (ISBN 0-582-36186-9, M-9203). French & Eur.

Kettridge. French-English, English-French Dictionary of Commercial & Financial Terms. (Fr. & Eng.). $21.50 (ISBN 0-685-36684-7). French & Eur.

Koszyk, K. Woerterbuch zur Publizistik. (Ger.). 1970. $28.00 (ISBN 3-7940-4281-6, M-6901). French & Eur.

Laurendeau, F., et al, eds. Harrap's French & English Business Dictionary. 514p. (Fr. & Eng.). E20.00 (ISBN 0-245-53594-2). Harrap.

Lebel, Wilfrid. Le Dictionnaire des Affaires. (Fr.). 1967. 4.00 F. Homme.

Lewis, Terence, et al, eds. Harrap's English-Brazilian Portuguese Business Dictionary. 250p. (Port. & Eng.). E35.00. Harrap.

Lexikon der Geschaeftsbriefe in vier Sprachen. 700p. (Ger.). 1972. DM.210.00 (ISBN 3-478-52340-0). Verlag Moderne.

Liebster, Leo & Horner, Colin. Pocket Dictionary of Business Terms. 320p. E1.25 (ISBN 0-600-31599-1); Epap. 12.50 shrink-wrap pack of 10 copies (ISBN 0-600-04831-4). Newnes Bks.

Moore, Norman D. Dictionary of Business, Finance, & Investment. LC 74-29447. (Illus). 560p. 1975. lib. bdg. $14.95x (ISBN 0-915610-00-0). Investor's Syst.

Munniksma, F., ed. International Business Dictionary in Nine Languages. 1974. $45.00x (ISBN 90-267-0394-5, 1526). Esperanto League North Am.

Peron. A Dictionary of Business Terms. (Fr. & Eng.). $30.95 (ISBN 2-03-020609-1). Larousse.

Peron, Michel, et al. Dictionnaire francais-anglais, anglais-francais des affaires: A French-English English-French Dictionary of Business Terms. rev. ed. 512p. (Fr. & Eng.). 1974. $30.95 (ISBN 2-03-020609-1, 3764). Larousse.

Poulsen, Sven-Olaf. Ordbog for Korrespondenter, Dansk-Tysk. LC 79-353149. 411p. (Danish & Ger.). 1977. Kr.110.00 (ISBN 8-787-69700-9). Kjaer Bogtryk.

Quadrilingual Business Dictionary. (Eng., Fr., Ger. & Span.). 1981. $60.00x (ISBN 0-686-75659-2, Pub. by European Schoolbks England). State Mutual Bk.

Renty, Ivan de. Lexique de L'Anglais des Affaires. 352p. (Eng. & Fr.). 1977. pap. $5.95 (ISBN 0-686-57286-6, M-4761). French & Eur.

--Lexique Quadrilingue Des Affaires. 702p. (Eng., Fr., Ger. & Span.). 1977. $29.95 (ISBN 0-686-57205-X, M-6483). French & Eur.

Rice, Michael D. Prentice-Hall Dictionary of Business, Finance & Law. LC 83-3022. 362p. 1983. $39.95 (ISBN 0-13-696583-0). P-H.

Robb, Louis. Dictionary of Modern Business. (Span. & Eng.). 1960. $30.00 (ISBN 0-910136-00-9). Anderson Kramer.

Romeuf, Jean & Guinot, Jean P. Diccionario del Jefe de Empresa. 644p. (Span.). 1966. $44.95 (ISBN 84-335-6524-9, S-14191). French & Eur.

Rosenberg, Jerry M. Dictionary of Business & Management. LC 78-7796. 1978. pap. $9.95 (ISBN 0-471-09885-X). Wiley.

--Dictionary of Business & Management. 2nd. ed. LC 82-24743. 631p. 1983. $29.95 (ISBN 0-471-86730-6, Pub. by Wiley-Interscience). Wiley.

Rover, M. French for Business Studies. 95p. (Fr. & Eng.). 1980. pap. $5.95 (ISBN 0-582-35900-7, M-9207). French & Eur.

Sachs, Rudolf. British & American Business in Key Words. 186p. (Eng. & Ger.). 1975. $25.00 (ISBN 3-7819-2010-0, M-7313, Pub. by Fritz Knapp Verlag). French & Eur.

--British & American Business in Keywords. LC 81-117456. 186p. 1980. pap. write for info. (ISBN 3-7819-2016-X). Knapp Verlag.

--British & American Business Terms. 144p. (Orig.). 1975. pap. text ed. $12.95x (ISBN 0-7121-0242-6, Pub. by Macdonald & Evans England). Intl Ideas.

Suarez, Andres Santiago. Diccionario Economico De la Empresa. 384p. (Span.). 1977. leatherette $19.95 (ISBN 84-368-0067-2, S-50181). French & Eur.

Systems Research Institute Staff. Dictionary of Administration & Management. LC 78-56093. 752p. 1981. $24.95 (ISBN 0-912352-04-3). Systems Res.

Tver, David F., compiled by. Dictionary of Business & Science. 3rd ed. 632p. 1974. $22.50x (ISBN 0-87201-172-0). Gulf Pub.

Wortman, Leon A. A Deskbook of Business Management Terms. LC 78-23257. 1979. $24.95 (ISBN 0-8144-5470-4). Am Mgmt.

Zavada & Eberle. Diccionario Fraseologico Comercial. 435p. (Ger. & Port.). 1978. $27.50 (ISBN 0-686-92497-5, M-9026). French & Eur.

Zavada, Dusan. Slovak-English Business Correspondence Dictionary. 560p. (Slovak & Eng.). 1980. $30.00 (ISBN 0-569-08524-1, Pub. by Collet's). State Mutual Bk.

BUSINESS–FORMS, BLANKS, ETC.
Diego Hernandez, Juan. Diccionario de Formularios Generales, 6 vols. 700p. (Span.). 1981. pap. 3000.00 ptas. Coleccion Nereo.

--Diccionario de Formularios Generales: Tomo 7, 7 vols. 756p. (Span.). 1981. pap. 3000.00 ptas (ISBN 84-85565-08-8). Coleccion Nereo.

Diego Hernandez, Juan & Rodriguez Segui, Alejandro. Diccionario de Formularios Generales, 4 vols. 800p. (Span.). 1980. 3000.00 ptas (ISBN 84-85565-05-3). Coleccion Nereo.

BUSINESS–STUDY AND TEACHING
see *Business Education*
BUSINESS, CHOICE OF
see *Vocational Guidance*
BUSINESS ADMINISTRATION
see *Business*
BUSINESS CORPORATIONS
see *Corporations*
BUSINESS CORRESPONDENCE
see *Commercial Correspondence*
BUSINESS EDUCATION
see also *Accounting; Bookkeeping; Commercial Law; Secretaries; Shorthand; Typewriting*
Oran, Daniel & Shafritz, Jay M. The MBA's Dictionary. LC 83-4524. 448p. 1983. $26.95 (ISBN 0-8359-4146-9); pap. $15.95 (ISBN 0-8359-4145-0). P-H.

BUSINESS ENGLISH
see *English Language–Business English*
BUSINESS LAW
see also *Commercial Law*
Becker, H. Dictionnaire trilingue du Droit des Affaires pour le Commerce & l'industrie: Allemand-Anglais-Francais & index. 2nd ed. 992p. (Ger., Eng. & Fr.). 1980. 420.00 F. Maison Dictionnaire.

Conte, Giuseppe. Dizionario giuridico-economico: Vol. 1, Italiano-tedesco. vii, 356p. (Ital. & Ger.). 1971. L.11000.00. Giuffre.

--Dizionario giuridico-economico: Vol. 2, Tedesco-italiano. 458p. (Ger. & Ital.). 1969. L.11000.00. Giuffre.

Ross, Martin J. & Ross, Jeffrey S. New Encyclopedic Dictionary of Business Law: With Forms. 2nd ed. LC 81-78. 349p. 1981. $32.95 (ISBN 0-13-612630-8, Busn). P-H.

BUSINESS LETTERS
see *Commercial Correspondence*
BUSINESS LITERATURE SEARCHING
see *Information Storage and Retrieval Systems–Business*
BUSINESS MACHINES
see *Electronic Office Machines; Office Equipment and Supplies*
BUSINESS-REPLY MAIL
see *Postal Service*
BUSINESS SPANISH
see *Spanish Language–Business Spanish*
BY-PRODUCTS
see *Waste Products*
BYRON, GEORGE GORDON NOEL BYRON, 6TH BARON, 1788-1824
Hagelman, Charles W., Jr. & Barnes, Robert J., eds. Concordance to Byron's Don Juan. (Concordances Ser.). 981p. 1967. $52.50x (ISBN 0-8014-0169-0). Cornell U Pr.
BYZANTINE ANTIQUITIES
Harvard University Dumbarton Oaks Research Library. Dictionary Catalogue of the Byzantine Collection of the Dumbarton Oaks Research Library, 12 vols. 1975. Set. lib. bdg. $1335.00 (ISBN 0-8161-1150-2, Hall Library). G K Hall.

C

CABLES, ELECTRIC
see *Electric Cables; Electronic Cables*
CACTUS
Backeberg, Curt. Cactus Lexicon. 1981. $60.00x (ISBN 0-686-78783-8, Pub. by RHS Ent England). State Mutual Bk.
CADASTRAL SURVEYS
see *Real Property*
CAESAR, C. JULIUS, 100 B.C.-44 B.C.
Kunzer, Paul E. Caesar Vocabularies. (Bk. I- Iv). $1.00 ea (NO. 9). Am Classical.
CAESARS
see *Roman Emperors*
CALABRIA–DESCRIPTION AND TRAVEL
Rohlfs, Gerhard. Nuovo Dizionario Dialettale Della Calabria. LC 77-476371. (Illus.). 945p. (Ital.). 1977. L.30000.00. Longo A.
CALCULATING-MACHINES, ELECTRONIC
see *Computers*
CALENDAR, DANISH
Host. Danish Pocket Dictionary. 6th ed. (Eng. & Danish.). 1978. pap. text ed. $7.00x (ISBN 87-146-1178-3, D711). Vanous.
CALENDARS
see also *Almanacs*
Collison, Robert L., ed. Dictionary of Dates. LC 77-95116. Repr. of 1961 ed. lib. bdg. $23.00x (ISBN 0-8371-9495-6, CODD). Greenwood.
CALVIN, JEAN, 1509-1564
Battles, Ford L. & Miller, Charles. A Concordance to Calvin's Institutio. LC 73-206014. (Bibliographia Tripotamopolitana Ser.: No. 8). 1974. $80.00x (ISBN 0-931222-07-9). C E Barbour.
CAMBODIA
Headley, Robert K. Cambodian-English Dictionary, 2 vols. (Publications in the Languages of Asia Ser.: No. 3). (Cambodian & Eng.). 1977. Set. $51.95 (ISBN 0-8132-0509-3). Cath U Pr
CAMBODIAN LANGUAGE
see *Khmer Language*
CAMERALISM
see *Mercantile System*
CAMEROONS–HISTORY
Le Vine, Victor T. & Nye, Roger. Historical Dictionary of Cameroon. LC 74-901. (African Historical Dictionaries Ser.: No. 1). 1974. $13.00 (ISBN 0-8108-0707-6). Scarecrow.
CAMORRA
see *Mafia*
CANADA
see also *names of cities, provinces, regions, etc. in Canada, e.g. Quebec; British Columbia; Northwest, Canadian*
Avis, Walter S. Canadian Intermediate Dictionary. (Illus.). 1980. Can.$12.95 (ISBN 0-7715-1982-6). U of Toronto Pr.
Avis, Walter S., et al. Canadian Junior Dictionary. 2nd ed. 1976. Can.$14.95 (ISBN 0-7715-1989-3); $10.50 (ISBN 0-7715-1988-5). U of Toronto Pr.
Dulong. Dictionnaire Correctif du Francais au Canada. 256p. (Fr.). 1968. write for info. Laval P. U.
Sandilands, John. Western Canadian Dictionary & Phrase-Book. 1977. Can.$5.00 (ISBN 0-88864-021-8). U of Toronto Pr.
Societe du Parler Francais au Canada. Glossaire du Parler Francais au Canada. 710p. (Fr.). 1968. Can.$18.00. Laval P. U.
CANADA–SOCIAL LIFE AND CUSTOMS
Avis, Walter S., et al. A Dictionary of Canadianisms. 1967. Can.$19.95 (ISBN 0-7715-1970-2); $25.00 (ISBN 0-7715-1972-9). U of Toronto Pr.
CANADIANS
see also *French-Canadians*
Leibman, Dan. Young Canada Dictionary. (Illus.). 1980. pap. write for info. (ISBN 0-17-600751-2). Nelson & Sons Group.

CANARY ISLANDS
Viera Clavijo, Jose. Diccionario de historia natural de las Islas Canarias. 586p. (Span.). 1982. 3500.00 ptas (ISBN 84-7133-434-8). Muralla.
CANON LAW
see also *Ecclesiastical Law*
also special legal headings with Canon Law added in parentheses, e.g. Marriage (Canon Law)
Naz, R. Dictionnaire de Droit Canonique, 7 vols. (Fr.). 1965. Set. $695.00 (ISBN 0-686-57057-X, M-6423). French & Eur.
CANTAL, FRANCE (DEPARTMENT)
Nauton, P., ed. Vocabulaire du Cantal du Nord & de la Margeride Auvergnate d'Apres l'ALMC. LC 76-451549. 73p. (Fr.). 1975. write for info. Cercle Occitan.
CAOUTCHOUC
see *Rubber*
CAPE DUTCH
see *Afrikaans Language*
CAPITAL EQUIPMENT
see *Industrial Equipment*
CAPITAL FORMATION
see *Saving and Investment*
CAPITALISM
Suarez Suarez, A. S., et al. Diccionario Economico de la Empresa. 2nd ed. 384p. (Span.). write for info. (ISBN 8-43680-067-2, 250022). Piramide.
CARBON
see also *Diamonds*
Lexique International De Petrographie Des Charbons. 2nd ed. 160p. (Eng. & Fr.). 1963. $32.50 (ISBN 0-686-57016-2, M-6366). French & Eur.
Lexique International De Petrographie Des Charbon: Supplement. 250p. (Fr.). 1971. pap. $32.50 (ISBN 0-686-57017-0, M-6367). French & Eur.
CARBONATED BEVERAGES
see *Beverages*
CARCINOMA
see *Tumors*
CARD GAMES
see *Cards*
CARDINALS
Berton, C. Dictionnaire des Cardinaux. Migne, J. P., ed. (Troisieme et Derniere Encyclopedie Theologique Ser.: Vol. 31). 912p. (Fr.). Repr. of 1857 ed. lib. bdg. $115.00x (ISBN 0-89241-310-7). Caratzas Pub Co.
CARDS
see also *Fortune-Telling*
also names of card games, e.g. Cribbage, Contract Bridge
Tissot, Livio. Dizionario primierotto. (Illus.). 368p. (Ital.). 1976. L.12000.00. Manfrini.
CARE OF SOULS
see *Pastoral Counseling*
CAREER EDUCATION
see *Vocational Education*
CAREERS
see *Occupations; Professions; Vocational Guidance*
CARGO HANDLING
Course, A. G. & Oram, R. B. Glossary of Cargo Handling Terms. 1981. $12.00x (ISBN 0-85174-080-4, Pub. by Nautical England). State Mutual Bk.
--Glossary of Cargo Handling Terms. 2nd ed. 96p. 1974. pap. $7.50x (ISBN 0-85174-080-4). Sheridan.
CARIBBEAN AREA
see also *West Indies*
Nunez, Benjamin. Dictionary of Afro-Latin American Civilization. LC 79-7731. (Illus.). xxxv, 525p. 1980. lib. bdg. $45.00 (ISBN 0-313-21138-8, NAL/). Greenwood.
CARIBBEAN COOKERY
see *Cookery, Caribbean*
CARICATURE
see also *Wit and Humor*
Walker, Mort. The Lexicon of Comicana. (Illus.). 96p. (Orig.). 1980. pap. $4.95 (ISBN 0-940420-00-7). Comicana.
CARPENTRY–TOOLS
Salaman, R. A. Dictionary of Tools Used in the Woodworking & Allied Trades c. 1700-1970. LC 75-35059. 1976. $49.50 (ISBN 0-684-14535-9, ScribT). Scribner.

CARRIAGES AND CARTS
Berkebile, Don H. Carriage Terminology: An Historical Dictionary. LC 77-118. (Illus.). 487p. 1979. $35.00x (ISBN 0-87474-166-1). Smithsonian.
CARRIER CONTROL SYSTEMS
Dictionnaire des Sigles Economiques & Sociaux. (Fr.). 25.00 F. Liaisons Sociales.
CARS (AUTOMOBILES)
see *Automobiles*
CARS, RAILROAD
see *Railroads–Cars*
CARS AND CAR BUILDING
see *Railroads–Cars*
CARTOGRAPHY
see also *Topographical Drawing*
American Congress on Surveying & Mapping. Automation Terms in Cartography. 23p. 1973. $3.00 (C120). Am Congrs Survey.
Eden, P., ed. Dictionary of Land Surveyors & Local Cartographers of Great Britain & Ireland. 528p. 1981. $14.00x (ISBN 0-7129-0900-1, Pub. by Dawson). State Mutual Bk.
International Cartographic Association. Glossary of Terms in Computer Assisted Cartography. 166p. 1980. $8.00 (C155). Am Congrs Survey.
Meynen, E. Multilingual Dictionary of Technical Terms in Cartography. 572p. (Eng. & Ger.). 1973. pap. $88.00 (ISBN 3-515-00127-1, M-7564, Pub. by F. Steiner). French & Eur.
Tooley, R. V. Tooley's Dictionary of Mapmakers. LC 79-1936. 696p. 1979. $120.00x (ISBN 0-8451-1701-7). A R Liss.
CARTOMANCY
see *Fortune-Telling*
CARTONS
see *Paper Coatings*
CARTOON DRAWING
see *Caricature*
CARTS
see *Carriages and Carts*
CARTULARIES
see *Archives; Diplomatics*
CASTILIAN LANGUAGE
see *Spanish Language*
CASTING
see *Founding*
CASTINGS, METAL
see *Metal Castings*
CASTLES
Dictionnaire des Chateaux de France. 2nd ed. (Illus.). 250p. (Fr.). 1970. write for info. Larousse.
CAT
see *Cats*
CAT, DOMESTIC
see *Cats*
CATALAN LANGUAGE
Alberti & Santiago, Gubern. Diccionari castella-catala, catala-castella. 4th ed. 1183p. (Span.). 1969. 500.00 ptas. Alberti.
Alberti, Santiago. Diccionari Castella-Catala, Catala-Castella, Mitja. 2nd ed. 584p. (Catalan & Castel.). 1978. $19.95 (ISBN 84-400-0761-2, S-31551). French & Eur.
--Diccionari Castella-Catala, Catala-Castella Petit. LC 75-512211. 338p. (Span. & Catalan.). 1975. write for info. (ISBN 8-472-46057-6). Alberti.
--Diccionari De la Llengua Catalan. 3rd ed. 412p. (Catalan.). 1978. pap. $13.95 (ISBN 84-7246-058-4, S-50208). French & Eur.
--Diccionari de la Llengua Catalana. LC 75-406972. 411p. (Span.). 1975. 350.00 ptas (ISBN 8-472-46058-4). Alberti.
Alcover, Antoni M. & Moll, Francesc de B. Diccionari I Catala-Valencia-Balear, 10 vols. 2nd ed. 9850p. (Catalan.). 1975. Set. $200.00 (ISBN 84-273-0025-5, S-31549). French & Eur.
Arimany Coma, Miguel. Diccionari Catala General Usual. 4th ed. 1418p. (Catalan). 1976. $35.95 (ISBN 84-7211-097-4, S-50049). French & Eur.
--Diccionari Manual Castella-Catala. 2nd ed. 413p. (Castella & Catalan.). 1975. $8.75 (ISBN 84-7211-084-2, S-50358). French & Eur.

--Diccionari Manual Catala-Castella. 2nd ed. 535p. (Catalan & Castella.). 1975. $8.75 (ISBN 84-7211-078-8, S-50357). French & Eur.

--Diccionari Manual Catala-Castella i Castella-Catala. 9th ed. 956p. (Catalan & Castella.). 1976. $16.50 (ISBN 84-7211-088-5, S-50360). French & Eur.

--Diccionari Practic Castella-Catala, Catala-Castella. 3rd ed. 456p. (Castella & Catalan.). 1976. $9.95 (ISBN 84-7211-087-7, S-50356). French & Eur.

--Diccionari Practic Catala-Frances. 2nd ed. 256p. (Catalan & Span.). 1977. pap. $5.25 (ISBN 84-7211-048-6, S-50413). French & Eur.

--Diccionari Usual Catala-Castella i Castella-Catala. 7th ed. 958p. (Catalan & Castella.). 1976. $23.95 (ISBN 84-7211-080-X, S-50361). French & Eur.

Arimany Coma, Miquel. Diccionari Basic Catala-Castella, Castella-Catala. 9th ed. 390p. (Catala & Span.). 1975. pap. $3.95 (ISBN 84-7211-085-0, S-50359). French & Eur.

Brew Vocabulari Catala-Castella-Angles de Comerc Exterior. 43p. (Span. , Catalan & Eng.). write for info. (S-37580). French & Eur.

Calbet Corbella, Josep Maria. Diccionari de metges catalans. 224p. (Span.). 1981. pap. 1000.00 ptas (ISBN 84-232-0186-4). Dalmau.

Canigo Diccionari Castella-Catala, Catala-Castella. 878p. (Span. & Catala.). pap. $17.95 (ISBN 84-303-0089-9, S-31565). French & Eur.

Castellanos i Llorenc, Carlos. Diccionari Catala-Frances, Frances-Catala. LC 79-125113. 1095p. (Fr. & Catalan.). 1979. 1000.00 ptas (ISBN 8-485-19409-8). Encic Catalan.

Collins. Diccionario castellano-ingles. (Span. & Eng.). Arg.$9.00. Albatros.

Colomer del Castillo, Jordi. Diccionari Ingles-Catala, Catala-Ingles. 3rd ed. 253p. (Eng. & Catalan.). 1978. pap. $8.75 (ISBN 84-7306-091-1, S-50414). French & Eur.

Coromines i Vegneaux, Joan. Diccionari etimologie i complementari de la llengua catalana, Tomo 3. 1056p. (Span.). 1982. write for info. (ISBN 84-7256-204-2). Curial.

Coromines i Vigneaux, Joan. Diccionari etimologic i complementari de la llengua catalana, Tomo 2. 2nd ed. 1120p. (Span.). 1981. 4500.00 ptas (ISBN 84-7256-191-7). Curial.

Diccionari escolar de la llengua catalana 'Vox' 510p. (Span.). 1981. 450.00 ptas (ISBN 84-7153-334-0). Biblo SP.

Diccionari Escolarde la Llengua Catalana. 512p. (Span.). write for info. Biblograf SP.

Diccionari Fondamental de la Llengua Catalana. 448p. (Catalan.). 495.00 ptas. (ISBN 84-7153-333-2). Biblograf SP.

Diccionari Practic de Sinonims Catalans: Mots i Frases. 2nd ed. 640p. (Catalan.). 1972. $9.95 (ISBN 84-7211-075-3, S-50047). French & Eur.

Diccionario Escolar de la llengua Catalana 'Vox' 2nd ed. 512p. (Span.). 1982. write for info. (ISBN 84-7153-334-0). Biblograf.

Diccionario Fundamental de la Llengua Catalana 'Vox' 443p. (Span.). 1980. 425.00 ptas (ISBN 84-7153-333-2). Biblo SP.

Elies I Busqueta, Pere. Canigo: Dicionario Catalan-Castellano, Castellano-Catalan. (Illus.). (Fr. ?. (Catalan & Span.). 1975. write for info. (ISBN 8-430-30089-9). Sopena.

Fabra, Pompeu. Diccionari General de la Llengua Catalana. LC 79-349036. xxxi, 1779p. (Catalan.). 1978. write for info. (ISBN 8-435-00120-2). Edhasa.

Ferrer-Pastor, Francesc. Vocabulari Castella-Valencia & Valencia-Castella. LC 80-117607. 1075p. (Span. & Catalan.). 1979. write for info. (ISBN 8-485-10436-6). Estel Edit.

Franquesa, Manuel. Diccionari De Sinonims. 1248p. (Catalan.). 1970. $40.50 (ISBN 0-686-57365-X, S-50185). French & Eur.

Lllllull Marti, Antoni. Vocabularis Tematics. LC 79-127295. ii, 117p. (Catalan.). 1979. write for info. (ISBN 8-450-03005-6). Organismos Ofic.

Miracle, Josep. Diccionari Catala-Castella, Castella-Catala. 2nd ed. LC 77-458925. xi, 1122p. (Span. & Catalan.). 1976. write for info. (ISBN 8-485-08300-8). Poseidon SA.

Miracle Montserrat, Josep. Diccionari Manual de la Llengua Catalana. 1401p. (Catalan.). 1975. $19.95 (ISBN 84-298-0594-X, S-31550). French & Eur.

Moll Casanovas, Fransesc de B. Diccionari Catala-Castella I Castella-Catala. 816p. (Catala & Span.). 1978. $46.00 (ISBN 84-273-0257-6, S-50362). French & Eur.

Moll Y Cassanovas, Francisco de. Diccionari Catala-Castella. LC 78-351223. 395p. (Span. & Catalan.). 1977. 1100.00 ptas (ISBN 8-427-30238-X). Moll Edit.

Pey Estrany, Santiago. Diccionari De Sinonims I Antonims. 4th ed. 840p. (Catalan.). 1977. pap. $13.95 (ISBN 84-307-7329-0, S-50235). French & Eur.

Raspall de Cauhe, Joana, et al. Diccionari Usual de Sinonims Catalans: Mots i Frases. 572p. (Catalan.). 1975. $17.50 (ISBN 84-7211-111-3, S-50048). French & Eur.

Romeu, Xavier. Brei Diccionari Ideologic: Amb Vocabulari Catala-Castella & Castella-Catala. LC 76-465853. (Illus.). 267p. (Catalan.). 1976. write for info. (ISBN 8-430-77321-5). Edit Teide.

Vox. Diccionari Fondamental de la Llengua Catalana. Gali I Herrera, Jordi, prologue by. LC 79-110126. (Illus.). 430p. (Catalan.). 1979. write for info. (ISBN 8-471-53333-2). Biblo Sp.

--Diccionari Manual Castella-Catala, Catala-Castella, 2 vols. 3rd ed. LC 79-112856. 614p. (Span. & Catalan.). 1977. 425.00 ptas (ISBN 8-471-53198-4). Biblo Sp.

Xuriguera, J. B. Nou Diccionari de la Llengua Catalana. 836p. (Catalan.). 1975. $18.95 (ISBN 84-7263-111-7, S-50211). French & Eur.

CATALAN POETRY
Fabra, Pompeu. Diccionario General de la Lengua Catalana. 1779p. (Span.). 1981. 850.00 ptas (ISBN 84-350-0120-2). Edhasa.

CATALOGING OF MUSIC
Research Libraries of the New York Public Library. Second Edition of the Dictionary Catalog of the Music Collection. 1983. lib. bdg. $6000.00 (ISBN 0-8161-0374-7, Hall Library). G K Hall.

CATALOGS
see Library Catalogs;
also subdivision Catalogs under specific subjects, e.g. Engravings-Catalogs; Manuscripts-Catalogs

CATALOGS, DICTIONARY
see also Subject Headings
Michigan State University,(East Lansing) Dictionary Catalog of the G. Robert Vincent Library. 1975. $75.00 (ISBN 0-8161-1149-9, Hall Library). G K Hall.

Miksa, Frances. Subject in the Dictionary Catalog From Cutter to the Present. 496p. 1983. $55.00 (ISBN 0-8389-0367-3). ALA.

New York Public Library Research Libraries. Dictionary Catalog of the Art & Architecture Division, The Research Libraries of The New York Public Library, 30 vols. 1975. Set. lib. bdg. $2950.00 (ISBN 0-8161-1157-X, Hall Library). G K Hall.

New York Public Library, Research Libraries. Dictionary Catalog of the Dance Collection, Performing Arts Research Center, 10 vols. 1974. Set. lib. bdg. $820.00 (ISBN 0-8161-1124-3, Hall Library). G K Hall.

Princeton University. Dictionary Catalog of the Princeton University Plasma Physics Laboratory Library, First Supplement. 1973. lib. bdg. $150.00 (ISBN 0-8161-1032-8, Hall Library). G K Hall.

CATALOGS, LIBRARY
see Library Catalogs

CATHEDRALS
see also Architecture, Gothic; also subdivision Churches under names of cities, e.g. New York (City)-Churches
Dictionnaires des Cathedrales de France. (Illus.). 256p. (Fr.). 1971. write for info. Larousse.

CATHOLIC CHURCH-DICTIONARIES
Hardon, John A. Modern Catholic Dictionary. LC 77-82945. 1980. $19.95 (ISBN 0-385-12162-8). Doubleday.

Thesaurus Doctrine Catholicae: Documentis Magisteri Eccleslasticae, Ordine Methodico. 812p. (Fr.). 51.00 F. Beauchesne.

CATHOLIC CHURCH-DOCTRINAL AND CONTROVERSIAL WORKS-DEBATES, ETC.
Pinard, C. Dictionnaire des Objections Populaires contre le Dogme, la Morale, la Discipline et L'histoire de Eglise Catholique. Migne, J. P., ed. (Troisieme et Derniere Encyclopedie Theologique Ser.: Vol. 33). 756p. (Fr.). Repr. of 1858 ed. lib. bdg. $96.50x (ISBN 0-89241-312-3). Caratzas Pub Co.

CATHOLIC CHURCH-DOCTRINAL AND CONTROVERSIAL WORKS-PROTESTANT AUTHORS
Wright, Charles & Neil, Charles, eds. The Protestant Dictionary: Containing Articles on the History, Doctrines, & Practices of the Christian Church. LC 73-155436. 1971. Repr. of 1933 ed. $56.00x (ISBN 0-8103-3388-0). Gale.

CATHOLIC CHURCH-ENCYCLOPEDIAS
see Catholic Church-Dictionaries

CATHOLIC CHURCH-LITURGY AND RITUAL
see also Chants (Plain, Gregorian, etc.)
Podhradsky, Gerhard. New Dictionary of the Liturgy. 1967. $6.95 (ISBN 0-8189-0101-2). Alba.

CATHOLICS
Scott, Thomas. The Interpreter, Wherein Three Principal Terms of State Are Clearly Unfolded. LC 74-80194. (English Experience Ser.: No. 673). 1974. Repr. of 1624 ed. $3.50 (ISBN 90-221-0281-5). Walter J Johnson.

CATS
Rousselet-Blanc, Pierre, ed. Larousse du chat. (Larousse des animaux familiers). (Illus.). 240p. (Fr.). 1975. $43.95x (ISBN 2-03-014852-0). Larousse.

CATULLUS, C. VALERIUS
McCarren, V. P., ed. A Critical Concordance to Catullus. (Lat. & Eng.). 1977. text ed. $66.00x (ISBN 90-04-05224-0). Humanities.

CAUCASIAN LANGUAGES
Russko-Chechenskii Slovar. 728p. (Rus.). 1978. $10.95 (Dist. by Four Continent Bk) Russkii Iazyk.

CB RADIO
see Citizens Band Radio

CEBU DIALECT
Wolff, John V. Dictionary of Cebuano Visayan, Vols 1 & 2. 120p. 1972. $8.00 (ISBN 0-87727-087-2, DP 87). Cornell SE Asia.

Yap, Elsa P. & Bunye, Maria V. Cebuano-Visayan Dictionary. McKaughan, Howard P., ed. LC 74-152461. (PALI Language Texts: Philippines). 576p. (Orig.). 1971. pap. text ed. $14.00x (ISBN 0-87022-093-4). UH Pr

CELDAL LANGUAGE
see Tzeltal Language

CELL, VOLTAIC
see Electric Batteries

CELL BIOLOGY
see Cytology

CELLULAR BIOLOGY
see Cytology

CELTIC LANGUAGES
see also Breton Language; Cornish Language; Gaelic Language; Irish Language; Manx Language; Welsh Language
Jakobsen, Jakob. An Etymological Dictionary of the Norn Language in Shetland, 2 vols. LC 78-72630. (Celtic Language & Literature: Goidelic & Brythonic). (Celtic.). Repr. of 1932 ed. Set. $87.50 (ISBN 0-404-17554-6). AMS Pr.

CEMENT
see also Concrete
ACI Committee 116. Cement & Concrete Terminology. 1978. pap. $12.95 (ISBN 0-685-85102-8, SP-19). ACI.

Cement & Concrete Thesaurus. 1969. pap. $14.95 (ISBN 0-685-85158-3, CCT). ACI.

Conseil International de la Langue Francaise. Vocabulaire du Beton. 192p. (Fr.). 1976. 98.00 F. Eyrolles.

Van Amerongen, C. Dictionary of Cement. 202p. (Ger. & Eng.). 1967. $44.00 (ISBN 3-7625-1171-3, M-7127). French & Eur.

CEMENT INDUSTRIES
Zement-Woerterbuch: Herstellung & Technologie. (Eng. & Ger.). write for info. (ISBN 3-7625-1341-4). Bauverlag.

CENTRIFUGAL REGULATORS
see Governors (Machinery)

CERAMIC MATERIALS
Hamer, Frank. Potter's Dictionary of Materials & Techniques. (Illus.). 400p. 1975. $30.00 (ISBN 0-8230-4210-3). Watson-Guptill.

CERAMICS
Here are entered general works on the technology of fired earth products, or clay products intended for industrial and technical use. Works on earthenware, chinaware, and art objects are entered under Pottery or Pottery Craft.; Particular objects and types are entered under their specific names, e.g. Bricks; clay; pipe; Refractory Materials; Tiles; Vases.
see also Pottery Craft
Institut de Ceramique Francaise. Thesaurus Ceramique. 2nd ed. 163p. (Fr.). 1974. 170.00 F. Francaise, Institut Ceramique.

CERAMICS-DICTIONARIES
Alvaro Zamora, Maria Isabel. Lexico de Ceramica & Alfareria Aragonesas. 210p. (Fr.). 1981. 750.00 ptas (ISBN 84-85264-40-1). Portico.

CERAMICS-MATERIALS
see Ceramic Materials

CEREAL PRODUCTS
Schneeweiss, R. Dictionary of Cereal Processing & Cereal Chemistry. (Eng., Fr., Ger. & Rus.). 1982. $121.50 (ISBN 0-444-42049-5). Elsevier.

CEREALS
see Grain

CEREMONIES
see Etiquette; Manners and Customs

CHAD
Decalo, Samuel. Historical Dictionary of Chad. LC 77-23585. (African Historical Dictionaries Ser.: No. 13). 1977. $20.00 (ISBN 0-8108-1046-8). Scarecrow.

Dictionnaire Arabe-Francais. LC 77-980964. 155p. (Fr. & Arabic.). 1977. write for info. N'Damena Tchad.

CHAIRS
Oirschot, Anton van. Het Stoelenboek. LC 78-384766. (Illus.). 128p. (Dutch.). 1978. fl.7.90 (ISBN 9-025-26367-4). Helmond.

CHALDEAN LANGUAGE
see Aramaic Language

CHAMORRO LANGUAGE
Topping, Donald. Spoken Chamorro: With Gramatical Notes & Glossary. 2nd ed. LC 80-14596. (PALI Language Texts: Micronesia). 376p. (Orig., Chamorro). 1980. pap. text ed. $11.00x (ISBN 0-8248-0417-1). UH Pr.

Topping, Donald M., et al. Chamorro-English Dictionary. LC 74-16907. (PALI Language Texts: Micronesian). 365p. (Orig., Chamorro & Eng.). 1975. pap. text ed. $10.00x (ISBN 0-8248-0353-1). UH Pr.

CHAMPIGNONS
see Mushrooms

CHANGE
Dictionnaire des Changements de Noms. (Fr.). write for info. Lib.

CHANGE, SOCIAL
see Social Change

CHANTING
see Chants (Plain, Gregorian, etc.)

CHANTS (PLAIN, GREGORIAN, ETC.)
D'Ortigue, M. J. Dictionnaire Liturgique, Historique et Theorique de Plainchant et de Musique d'Eglise. LC 79-155353. (Music Ser). (Fr.). 1971. Repr. of 1854 ed. lib. bdg. $75.00 (ISBN 0-306-70165-0). Da Capo.

CHARACTER
Heymer, A. Diccionario de Etologia. De Haro Vera, Andres, tr. 284p. (Span.). 1981. 1500.00 ptas (ISBN 84-282-0668-6). Omega SA.

CHARITABLE INSTITUTIONS
see Charities

CHARITIES
see also Hospitals; Public Welfare also subdivision Civilian Relief under names of wars, e.g. World War, 1939-1945–Civilian Relief
Martin-Doisy, F. Dictionnaire d'Economic Charitable, 4 vols. Migne, J. P., ed. (Troisieme et Derniere Encyclopedie Theologique Ser.: Vols. 5-8). 3616p. (Fr.). Repr. of 1857 ed. lib. bdg. $456.00x (ISBN 0-89241-292-5). Caratzas Pub Co.

CHARTS
Dictionary Chart. $1.30 (P4). Am Classical.

CHATEAUX
see Castles

CHECKS
Sidou, J. Vocabulario do Cheque. LC 76-464726. 333p. (Port.). 1975. write for info. Editora Revista.

CHEESE
see also Cookery (Dairy Products)
Courtine, Robert H. Dictionnaire des Fromages. 250p. (Fr.). 1972. pap. $6.95 (ISBN 0-686-56807-9, F-A16). French & Eur.
--Dictionnaire des Fromages. 250p. (Fr.). 1972. 17.60 F. Larousse.
Gosetti, Fernanda. Dizionari dei Formaggi: Tutte le Notizie le Ricette come & con che Cosa Servirli. LC 78-400002. 293p. (Eng. & Ital.). 1977. L.5000.00. Marietti.
--Dizionario dei formaggi. (Ital.). L.5000.00. Marietti.
--Dizionario dei formaggi. (Illus.). 296p. (Ital.). 1977. L.5000.00. AMZ.
Hasselfeldt, Othmar. Internationes Kaselexikon. LC 77-575279. 141p. (Ger.). 1977. DM.5.80 (ISBN 3-436-02465-1). Fischer Taschen.

CHEIROMANCY
see Palmistry

CHEMICAL ADDITIVES IN FOOD
see Food Additives

CHEMICAL APPARATUS
Haley, Gessner G. Diccionario de quimica y de productos quimicos. 2nd, Rev. ed. (Span.). pap. write for info. Omega SA.

CHEMICAL ENGINEERING
see also Chemistry, Technical; Metallurgy
Bureau de l'Information Scientifique & Technique. Thesaurus Genie Chimique. LC 78-374404. vi, 199p. (Fr.). 1977. 350.00 F (ISBN 2-222-02176-6). Doc Scient.

CHEMICAL ENGINEERING–DICTIONARIES
Carpovich, Eugene A. Russian-English Chemical Dictionary. 2nd ed. LC 61-11700. (Rus. & Eng.). 1963. $25.00 (ISBN 0-911484-03-5). Tech Dict.
Clason, W. Elsevier's Dictionary of Chemical Engineering, 2 Vols. (Eng., Fr., Span., Ital., Dutch, & Ger.). 1969. Set. $170.25 (ISBN 0-444-40736-7); Vol. 1. $85.00 (ISBN 0-444-40714-6); Vol. 2. $85.00 (ISBN 0-444-40715-4). Elsevier.
DeVries, Louis & Kolb, Helga. Dictionary of Chemistry & Chemical Engineering, 2 vols. 2nd ed. Incl. Vol. 1. German-English. 1978. 150.00x (ISBN 0-686-53141-8); Vol. 2. English-German. LC 77-138815. 150.00x (ISBN 0-89573-025-1). (Ger. & Eng.). 1979. Verlag Chemie.
Dictionary Industrial Chemistry: English-Chinese. 81p. (Eng. & Chinese.). 1977. pap. $1.95 (ISBN 0-686-92273-5, M-9585). French & Eur.
Dictionary of Industrial Chemistry. 24p. (Eng. & Chinese.). 1973. pap. $1.95 (ISBN 0-686-92145-3, M-9570). French & Eur.
Dictionary of Industrial Chemistry. 164p. (Chinese & Eng.). 1979. pap. $3.95 (ISBN 0-686-92529-7, M-9576). French & Eur.
Dictionary of Industrial Organic Chemistry. 56p. (Eng. & Chinese.). 1973. pap. $1.95 (ISBN 0-686-92279-4, M-9584). French & Eur.
Dictionnaire Technique Russe-Francais de la Preparation. 129p. (Fr. & Rus.). 1973. pap. $19.95 (ISBN 0-686-56771-4, M-6160). French & Eur.
English-Chinese Dictionary of Chemistry & Chemical Engineering. 1458p. (Eng. & Chinese.). 1978. leatherette $49.95 (ISBN 0-686-92360-X, M-9248). French & Eur.
Ernst, R. Dictionary of Chemical Terms, 2 vols. Vol. 1, Ger-Eng. $33.70 (ISBN 3-8709-7011-1); Vol. 2, Eng-Ger. $41.20 (ISBN 3-8709-7012-X). Adler.
Vries, Louis de. Dictionary of Chemistry & Chemical Engineering, Vol. 1. (Eng. & Ger.). 1970. pap. $125.00 (ISBN 3-527-25303-3, M-7126). French & Eur.
--Dictionary of Chemistry & Chemical Engineering, Vol. 2. (Eng. & Ger.). 1972. pap. $125.00 (ISBN 3-527-25358-0, M-7125). French & Eur.

CHEMICAL FORMULAE
see Chemistry–Notation

CHEMICAL INSTRUMENTS
see Chemical Apparatus

CHEMICAL PROCESSES
Rosendahl, Fritz. Handbuch der Namensverfahren in der Chemischen Technik. LC 78-366424. 335p. (Ger.). 1976. write for info. (ISBN 2-225-46079-5). Vulkan Verlag.

CHEMICAL SYMBOLS
see Abbreviations; Chemistry–Notation

CHEMICAL TECHNOLOGY
see Chemistry, Technical

CHEMICALS–LAW AND LEGISLATION
OECD. Chemical Control Legislation Glossary. 170p. 1982. pap. $13.50x (ISBN 92-64-12364-4). OECD.

CHEMICALS–MANUFACTURE AND INDUSTRY
see also Chemistry, Technical also specific chemical industries
Lexique des Termes Techniques Concernant le Material d'Une Usine d'Acetylene Dissous. 78p. (Fr., Lexicon of Technical Terms Concerning the Materials of Dissolved Acetylene Manufacturing). 1970. pap. $29.95 (ISBN 0-686-56759-5, M-6363). French & Eur.

CHEMISTRY
see also Alchemy; Biological Chemistry; Color; Crystallography; Electrochemistry; Explosives; Pharmacy; Spectrum Analysis also headings beginning with the word Chemical
Borucki, Hans, et al. Die Chemie: Ein Lexikon der Gesamten Schulchemie. 424p. (Ger.). DM.19.80 (ISBN 3-411-01367-2). Biblio Inst.
Chemie & Chemische Technik Englisch-Deutsch. 720p. (Eng. & Ger.). 1978. M.70.00. VEB Technik.
Donadini, Jean-Claude & Donadini, G. Lexique Technique des Produits Chimiques, 2 vols. 15th ed. 2140p. (Fr.). 1976. 350.00 F. Rous.
Gross, Helmut. Chemie & Chemische Technik Russisch-Deutsch. 832p. (Rus. & Ger.). 1980. M.48.00. VEB Technik.
--Kleines Woerterbuch der Chemie & Chemischen Technik. LC 79-393988. 108p. (Rus. & Ger.). 1979. M.7.00. VEB Verlag Technik.
Gross, Helmut & Hildebrand, Helmut. Chemie & Chemische Technik. 2nd ed. LC 77-550181. (Rus. & Ger.). 1976. M.48.00. VEB Verlag Technik.
Institut fur Angewandte Sprachwissenschaft. Russisch-Deutsches Woerterbuch der Chemie & Chemischen. 2nd ed. LC 78-382767. 832p. (Rus. & Ger.). 1977. write for info. VEB Verlag Technik.
Masterton, William L., et al. Chemistry. 1980. text ed. write for info. (ISBN 0-03-056214-7, CBS C). SCP.

CHEMISTRY–APPARATUS
see Chemical Apparatus

CHEMISTRY–DICTIONARIES
Anglo-Russkii Slovar Po Khimii & Tekhnologii Polimerov: Okolo 30000 Terminov. 536p. (Eng. & Rus.). 1977. $9.95 (Pub. by Russkii Iazyk). Four Continent.
Ballentyne, D. W. & Walker, L. E. Diccionario de Leyes y Efectos Cientificos En Quimica-Fisica Matematicas. 216p. (Span.). $14.95 (ISBN 0-686-56711-0, S-33054). French & Eur.
Barcelo, J. R. Diccionario Terminologico de Quimica. 1100p. (Span.). 1974. write for info. Alhambra.
--Spanish-English, English-Spanish Chemical Vocabulary. (Span. & Eng.). pap. $7.50 (ISBN 84-205-0696-6). Heinman.
Barcelo, Jose R. Diccionario Terminologico de Quimica. LC 76-480438. xi, 774p. (Eng. & Span.). 1976. write for info. (ISBN 8-4205-0521-8). Edit Alhambra.
Barcelo Matutano, Jose. Diccionario terminologico de Quimaca. 2nd ed. 788p. (Span.). 1982. pap. 3160.00 ptas (ISBN 84-205-0521-8). Alhambra.
Barcelo Matutano, Jose R. Diccionario Terminologico de Quimica. 2nd ed. 1100p. (Span., Ger. & Eng.). 1976. pap. $46.00 (ISBN 84-205-0521-8, S-50090). French & Eur.
Basinski, Antoni. Slownik Polskiej Terminologii Chemicznej. LC 75-404572. 278p. (Pol.). 1975. write for info. Wydawnictwa Naukowo.
Bennett, Harry, ed. Concise Chemical & Technical Dictionary. 3rd ed. 1974. $56.50 (ISBN 0-8206-0026-1). Chem Pub.
Bevan, Stanley C., et al. A Concise Etymological Dictionary of Chemistry. ix, 140p. 1976. $18.50 (ISBN 0-85334-653-4, Pub. by Applied Sci England). Elsevier.
Bubnikova, M. Rusko-Sesky Chemicky Slovnik. LC 80-466659. 494p. (Rus. & Czech.). 1978. 57.00 Kcs. Russkii Iazyk.
Bureau International de Documentation de Chemin de Fer. Chemins de Fer Glossary. (Fr., Ger., Ital., Span. & Swedish.). 1960. $13.50 (ISBN 0-444-40751-0). Elsevier.
Callaham, Ludmilla I. Russian-English Chemical & Polytechnical Dictionary. 3rd ed. LC 75-5982. 852p. (Rus. & Eng.). 1975. $58.50x (ISBN 0-471-12998-4, Pub. by Wiley-Interscience). Wiley.
--Russian-English Chemical & Polytechnical Dictionary. 3rd ed. LC 75-5982. xxviii, 852p. (Eng. & Rus.). 1975. $58.50 (ISBN 0-471-12998-4). Wiley.
Carpovich, Eugene A. Russian-English Chemical Dictionary. 2nd ed. LC 61-11700. (Rus. & Eng.). 1963. $25.00 (ISBN 0-911484-03-5). Tech Dict.
Concise Dictionary of Chemistry & Chemical Technology. 128p. 1975. $30.00x (ISBN 0-686-44771-9, Pub. by Collets). State Mutual Bk.
Cooke, E. I. & Cooke, R. W. Gardner's Chemical Synonyms & Trade Names: A Dictionary & Commercial Handbook Containing Over 35,500 Definitions & Identifications. 8th ed. 776p. 1980. $99.50x (ISBN 0-291-39678-X, Pub. by Tech Pr). State Mutual Bk.
Cornubert, Raymond. Dictionnaire Chimique. 6th ed. (Eng. & Fr.). 1970. $17.50x (ISBN 2-04-007334-5). Intl Pubns Serv.
--Dictionnaire de Chimie Allemand-Francais. 3rd ed. 240p. (Fr. & Ger.). 1977. pap. $29.65 (ISBN 0-686-56964-4, M-6088). French & Eur.
Daintith, John, ed. Dictionary of Chemistry. 1982. pap. $5.72i (ISBN 0-06-463559-7, EH-559). Har-Row.
--Dictionary of Chemistry. (Illus.). 240p. 1982. pap. $5.72i (ISBN 0-06-463559-7). B&N NY.
--The Facts on File Dictionary of Chemistry. 224p. 1981. $14.95 (ISBN 0-87196-513-5). Facts on File.
DeVries, Louis & Kolb, Helga. Dictionary of Chemistry & Chemical Engineering, 2 vols. 2nd ed. Incl. Vol. 1. German-English. 1978. 150.00x (ISBN 0-686-53141-8); Vol. 2. English-German. LC 77-138815. 150.00x (ISBN 0-89573-025-1). (Ger. & Eng.). 1979. Verlag Chemie.
Duval, C. Dictionnaire de la Chimie et de Ses Applications. 3rd ed. 1100p. (Fr.). 1977. $225.00 (ISBN 0-686-56741-2, M-6183). French & Eur.
English-Chinese Dictionary of Chemistry & Chemical Engineering. 1458p. (Eng. & Chinese.). 1978. leatherette $49.95 (ISBN 0-686-92360-X, M-9248). French & Eur.
Ernst. Woerterbuch der Chemie: Band II, English-Deutsch. 1056p. (Eng. & Ger.). 1982. DM.55.00. Brandstetter.
Ernst, I. & Ernst von Morgenstern, F. Woerterbuch der Chemie, Vol. 1. 891p. (Eng. & Ger., English-German Dictionary of Chemistry). $36.00 (ISBN 3-87097-011-1, M-7037). French & Eur.
--Woerterbuch der Chemie, Vol. 2. 892p. (Eng. & Ger., English-German Dictionary of Chemistry). $44.00 (ISBN 3-87097-012-X, M-7036). French & Eur.
Ernst, R. Dictionary of Chemical Terms, 2 vols. Vol. 1, Ger-Eng. $33.70 (ISBN 3-8709-7011-1); Vol. 2, Eng-Ger. $41.20 (ISBN 3-8709-7012-X). Adler.
Ernst, Richard. Dictionary of Chemistry, Vol. 1. (Eng. & Ger.). 1961. $36.00 (ISBN 3-87097-011-1, M-7124). French & Eur.
--Dictionary of Chemistry, Vol. 2. (Eng. & Ger.). 1963. $44.00 (ISBN 3-87097-012-X, M-7123). French & Eur.
Escobar, Guillermo. Vocabulario Lengua General Quichua. 5th ed. 221p. (Quichua.). 1951. $3.00; S/95.00. U. San Marcos.
Fachlexikon ABC Chemie, 2 vols. 1590p. (Ger.). 1976. Set. letherette $79.95 (ISBN 3-87144-002-7, M-7379, Pub. by Verlag Harri Deutsch). French & Eur.
Fouchier, J. & Billet, F. Chemical Dictionary. 3rd ed. (Fr., Ger. & Eng.). 1972. $106.50 (ISBN 0-444-41090-2). Elsevier.
Fromherz, H. & King, A. English-German Chemical Terminology: An Introduction to Chemistry in English & German. 5th, rev. ed. 588p. (Eng. & Ger.). 1968. DM.55.00. Verlag Chemie.
--Franzoesische und Deutsche Chemische Fachuasdruecke. 568p. (Fr. & Ger.). 1968. DM.52.50 (ISBN 3-527-25094-8). Verlag Chemie.
--French-English Chemical Terminology: An Introduction to Chemistry in French & English. 561p. (Fr. & Ger.). 1968. $52.50 (ISBN 0-686-56475-8, M-7417, Pub. by Vlg. Chemie). French & Eur.
--French-English Chemical Terminology: An Introduction to Chemistry in French & English. 561p. (Fr. & Ger.). 1968. DM.52.50. Verlag Chemie.
Giua Lollini, Clara & Giua, Michele. Dizionario tedesco-italiano per le scienze chimiche e affini. viii, 798p. (Ger. & Ital.). 1962. L.6500.00 (ISBN 88-7011-011-7). Rosenberg & Sel.

Godman, Arthur. Illustrated Dictionary of Chemistry. (Illustrated Dictionaries Ser.). (Illus.). 256p. 1982. text ed. $7.95x (ISBN 0-582-55550-7). Longman.
Grant, Julius. Hackh's Chemical Dictionary. 4th ed. 1968. 63.25 (ISBN 0-07-024064-7, P&RB). McGraw.
Gross & Hildebrand. Kleines Woerterbuch Chemie & Chemische Technik. 128p. (Eng. & Ger.). 1976. DM.14.80 (ISBN 3-87144-218-6). Verlag Harri Deutsch.
--Kleines Woerterbuch Chemie & Chemische Technik. 96p. (Ger. & Eng.). 1980. DM.14.80 (ISBN 3-87144-219-4). Verlag Harri Deutsch.
Gross, H. Woerterbuch Chemie und Chemische Technik, Vol. 2. (Ger.). $68.00 (ISBN 0-686-56616-5, M-6965). French & Eur.
Gross, H. & Hildebrand, H. Kleines Worterbuch der Chemie und Chem. Technik, Vol. 2. 128p. (Ger. & Eng., Dictionary of Chemistry and Chemical Engineering). $9.95 (ISBN 3-87144-219-4, M-7510, Pub. by Verlag Harri Deutsch). French & Eur.
Gross, Helmut. Kleines Woerterbuch der Chemie & Chemischen Technik Russisch-Deutsch. 108p. (Rus. & Ger.). 1979. M.7.00. VEB Technik.
Haley, Gessner G. Diccionario de quimica y de productos quimicos. 2nd, Rev. ed. (Span.). pap. write for info. Omega SA.
Hampel, Clifford & Hawley, Gessner. Glossary of Chemical Terms. 300p. 1976. text ed. $17.95x (ISBN 0-442-23238-1); pap. text ed. $9.95x (ISBN 0-442-23243-8). Van Nos Reinhold.
Hawley, Gessner. Condensed Chemical Dictionary. 10th ed. 1472p. 1981. pap. $42.50 (ISBN 0-442-23244-6). Van Nos Reinhold.
Iashunskaia, F. I., et al, eds. Anglo-Russkii Slovar Po Kauchuku, Rezine & Khimicheskim Voloknam. 260p. (Rus. & Eng.). 1962. $3.75 (Pub. by Glav. Red. Instr. Nauchn. Tekhn. Slovrei Fizmatgiza). Four Continent.
Ibeas, Franco. Diccionario Tecnologico Ingles-Espanol: Electricidad, Electronica, Telecomunicacion, & Materias Afinas con la Fisica, Optica & Quimica. 452p. (Eng. & Span.). 1974. E950.00 (ISBN 84-205-0492-0). Alhambra.
Jehan, L. F. Dictionnaire de Chimie et de Mineralogie. Migne, J. P., ed. (Encyclopedie Theologique Ser.: Vol. 46). 830p. (Fr.). Repr. of 1851 ed. lib. bdg. $105.00x (ISBN 0-89241-250-X). Caratzas Pub Co.
Kleines Woerterbuch der Chemie & Chemischen Technik Deutsch-Englisch. 96p. (Ger. & Eng.). 1980. M.11.00. VEB Technik.
Kleines Woerterbuch der Chemie & Chemischen Technik Englisch-Deutsch. 128p. (Eng. & Ger.). 1975. M.11.00. VEB Technik.
Kryt, Dobromila & Semniuk, Bazyli, eds. English-Polish Polish-English Chemical Dictionary. LC 79-393179. 912p. (Eng. & Pol.). 1979. 32.50x (ISBN 83-204-0004-X). Intl Pubns Serv.
Lexikon Chemischer Kurzbezeichnungen von Arzneistoffen. 104p. (Ger.). 1970. DM.16.50 (ISBN 3-7741-9909-4). Govi Verlag.
Lexique Technique des Produits Chimiques, 2 vols. 15th ed. (Fr.). 300.00 F. Officielles, Ed. Vente Publ.
Macedo, Horacio. Dicionario Escolar de Quimica. (Port.). Cr.$1450.00. Edit Atica.
Marks, Robert W. Diccionario y manual de la nueva fisica y quimica. (Illus.). 262p. (Span.). $1.50. Edit Pr Serv.
Marler, E. E., compiled by. Pharmacological & Chemical Synonyms: A Collection of Names of Drugs, Pesticides & Other Compounds Drawn from the Medical Literature of the World. 7th ed. 1983. $76.75 (ISBN 0-444-90227-9). Elsevier.
Ministry of Education. Scientific Terms, Chemistry: Japanese-English, English-Japanese. 630p. (Japanese & Eng.). 1974. $25.00 (ISBN 0-686-92209-3, M-9335). French & Eur.
Nekriach, E. F. Russko-Ukrainskii Khimicheskii Slovar. 204p. (Rus. & Ukrainian.). 1959. $1.50 (Pub. by An Arm SSR). Four Continent.
Ottokar, Peter. Diccionario Rioduero: Quimica. 2nd ed. 272p. (Span.). 1977. leatherette $11.95 (ISBN 84-220-0726-6, S-50172). French & Eur.
--Diccionario Rioduero: Quimica. 3rd ed. Arroyo Marcos, Gloria, tr. 272p. (Span.). 1981. pap. 600.00 ptas (ISBN 84-220-0726-6). Catolica Edit.
Patterson, A. M. German-English Dictionary for Chemists. 3rd ed. (Ger. & Fr.). 1950. $32.50 (ISBN 0-471-66990-3, Pub. by Wiley-Interscience). Wiley.
Peristilahan Kimia dan Farmasi. LC 78-940182. x, 288p. (Eng. & Indonesian.). 1976. write for info. Penerbit Jaya.
Peter, O. Herder-Lexikon Chemie. 3rd ed. 256p. (Ger.). 1975. pap. $15.95 (ISBN 3-451-16465-5, M-7454, Pub. by Herder). French & Eur.
--Herder-Lexikon Chemie. 3rd ed. 256p. (Ger.). 1975. pap. $15.95 (ISBN 3-451-16465-5). Herder.
Sharp, D. W., ed. Miall's Dictionary of Chemistry. (Illus.). 528p. text ed. 60.00x (ISBN 0-582-35152-9). Longman.
Sobecka, Z., et al, eds. Dictionary of Chemistry & Chemical Technology in Six Languages. rev. ed. 1966. 130.00 (ISBN 0-08-011600-0). Pergamon.
Technik-Worterbuch: Chemie & Chemische Technik. 720p. (Ger.). 1980. vinyl $90.00x (ISBN 0-569-07861-X, Pub. by Collet's). State Mutual Bk.
Technische Universitat Dresden, ed. German-English Dictionary of Chemistry & Chemical Technology-Chemie und Chemische Technik: Deutsch-Englisch. 633p. (Ger. & Eng.). 1980. $45.00x (ISBN 0-8002-2765-4). Intl Pubns Serv.
Technishe Universitaet, Dresden, ed. English-German Dictionary of Chemistry & Chemical Technology. 2nd ed. LC 76-455777. (Eng. & Ger.). 1978. 47.50x (ISBN 0-8002-0401-8). Intl Pubns Serv.
Theilman, K. Dictionary of Biochemistry. 742p. 1980. $90.00x (ISBN 0-686-44721-2, Pub. by Collets). State Mutual Bk.
Thompson, Reginald C. A Dictionary of Assyrian Chemistry & Geology. LC 78-72768. (Ancient Mesopotamian Texts & Studies). (Assyrian.). Repr. of 1936 ed. $24.50 (ISBN 0-404-18222-4). AMS Pr.
Titova, I. A. Polsko-Ruskii Khimicheskii Slovar. 459p. (Rus. & Pol.). 1970. $6.75 (Pub. by Sov Entsiklopediia). Four Continent.
Turtoi, Dumitru, et al. Dictionar de Chimie si Inginerie Chimica Rus-Roman. LC 79-363446. 654p. (Rus. & Romanian.). 1978. 36.00 lei. Editura Stiintifica.
Villavecchia, G. V. & Eigenmann, G. Nuovo dizionario di merceologia e chimia applicata, Vol. 7. (Illus.). vii, 372p. (Ital.). 1977. L.10000.00 (ISBN 88-203-0892-4). Hoepli.
Villavecchia, G. V., et al. Dizionario di merceologia e chimica applicata. vi, 490p. (Ital.). 1976. L.10000.00 (ISBN 88-203-1045-7). Hoepli.
--Nuovo dizionario di merceologia e chimica applicata, Vol. 1. (Illus.). xvi, 516p. (Ital.). 1973. L.10000.00 (ISBN 88-203-0528-3). Hoepli.
--Nuovo dizionario di merceologia e chimica applicata, Vol. 2. (Illus.). vi, 506p. (Ital.). 1973. L.10000.00 (ISBN 88-203-0529-1). Hoepli.
--Nuovo dizionario di merceologia e chimica applicata, Vol. 3. (Illus.). vi, 506p. (Ital.). 1973. L.10000.00 (ISBN 88-203-0530-5). Hoepli.
--Nuovo dizionario di merceologia e chimica applicata, Vol. 4. (Illus.). vi, 506p. (Ital.). 1973. L.10000.00 (ISBN 88-203-0531-3). Hoepli.
--Nuovo dizionario di merceologia e chimica applicata, Vol. 5. (Illus.). vi, 506p. (Ital.). 1974. L.10000.00 (ISBN 88-203-0532-1). Hoepli.
Vries, Louis de. Dictionary of Chemistry & Chemical Engineering, Vol. 1. (Eng. & Ger.). 1970. pap. $125.00 (ISBN 3-527-25303-3, M-7126). French & Eur.
--Dictionary of Chemistry & Chemical Engineering, Vol. 2. (Eng. & Ger.). 1972. pap. $125.00 (ISBN 3-527-25358-0, M-7125). French & Eur.
Woerterbuch Chemie und Chemische Technik, Vol. 1. 1600p. (Ger.). 1975. $78.00 (ISBN 3-87144-141-4, M-6966). French & Eur.
Woerterbuch der Chemie: Band I, D - E. 727p. (Ger.). 1982. DM.45.00. Brandstetter.
Yamada, Hiroshi. Sanyo's Tri-Lingual Glossary of Chemical Terms. 1977. 150.00 (ISBN 0-685-51744-6). Sadtler Res.

CHEMISTRY–NOTATION

Siemens. Quantities, Formulae, Definitions. 1979. $4.95 (ISBN 0-471-26120-3, Wiley Heyden). Wiley.

CHEMISTRY–TERMINOLOGY

Cooke, E. I. & Cooke, R. W. Gardner's Chemical Synonyms & Trade Names: A Dictionary & Commercial Handbook Containing Over 35,500 Definitions & Identifications. 8th ed. 776p. 1980. $99.50x (ISBN 0-291-39678-X, Pub. by Tech Pr). State Mutual Bk.
Dictionary of Chemical Terminology. 562p. (Pol. , Ger. , Eng. , Fr. & Rus.). 1974. $16.95 (Pub. by Vyd. Naukowo-Techniczne). Four Continent.
Fromherz, H. & King, A. English-German Chemical Terminology: An Introduction to Chemistry in English & German. 5th rev. ed. 588p. (Eng. & Ger.). 1968. 55.00 (ISBN 0-686-56603-3, M-7362, Pub. by Vlg. Chemie). French & Eur.
Fromherz, Hans & King, Alexander. English-German Chemical Terminology: An Introduction to Chemistry in English & German. 5th ed. LC 68-26705. 609p. (Eng. & Ger.). 1968. $46.30x (ISBN 3-527-25093-X). Verlag Chemie.
--French-English Chemical Terminology: An Introduction to Chemistry in French & English. 580p. (Fr. & Eng.). 1968. $46.30x (ISBN 3-527-25095-6). Verlag Chemie.
--French-German Chemical Terminology: An Introduction to Chemistry in French & German. LC 68-54575. 587p. (Fr. & Ger.). 1969. $46.30x (ISBN 3-527-25094-8). Verlag Chemie.
Godman, Arthur. Barnes & Noble Thesaurus of Chemistry. (Illus.). 256p. (gr. 11-12). 1983. $13.41i (ISBN 0-06-015175-7); pap. $6.68i (ISBN 0-06-463578-3, EH 578). B&N NY.
Haisman & Muller. Glossay of Clinical Chemistry Terms. (Eng.). E4.95. Butterworth.
Hampel, Clifford A. & Hawley, Gessner G. Glossary of Chemical Terms. 2nd ed. 1982. text ed. $19.95 (ISBN 0-442-23871-1). Van Nos Reinhold.
Hawley, Gessner. Condensed Chemical Dictionary. 10th ed. 1472p. 1981. pap. $42.50 (ISBN 0-442-23244-6). Van Nos Reinhold.
Kryt, D. Dictionary of Chemical Terminology. (Eng., Ger., Fr., Pol. & Rus.). 1980. $83.00 (ISBN 0-444-99788-1). Elsevier.

CHEMISTRY, BIOLOGICAL
see Biological Chemistry

CHEMISTRY, CLINICAL

Haisman, P. & Muller, B. R. Glossary of Clinical Chemistry Terms. 133p. 1974. $13.95 (ISBN 0-407-72700-0). Butterworth.
Hood, W. A-Z of Clinical Chemistry. LC 80-23908. 386p. 1980. 24.95x (ISBN 0-470-27029-2). Halsted Pr.

CHEMISTRY, INDUSTRIAL
see Chemical Engineering; Chemistry, Technical

CHEMISTRY, INORGANIC
see also Metals
also names and classes of inorganic compounds

Hebrew Nomenclature of Inorganic Chemistry. (Eng. & Hebrew.). IL.5.00. Massada Pr.

CHEMISTRY, MEDICAL AND PHARMACEUTICAL
see also Chemistry, Clinical; Drugs; Materia Medica; Pharmacy; Poisonous Plants

Lexikon Chemischer Kurzbezeichnungen Von Arzneistoffen. (Ger.). 1970. pap. $13.95 (ISBN 3-7741-9909-4, M-7283). French & Eur.

CHEMISTRY, ORGANIC
see also Surface Active Agents
also names of classes of organic compounds, e.g. Alkaloids; Carbohydrates; Proteins; also names of individual organic substances, e.g. Benzene

Buckingham, J., et al, eds. Dictionary of Organic Compounds, 7 Vols. 5th ed. 1982. Set. 1950.00x (ISBN 0-412-17000-0, NO.6611, Pub. by Chapman & Hall). Methuen Inc.
Orchin, Milton, et al. The Vocabulary of Organic Chemistry. LC 79-25930. 1980. $43.50x (ISBN 0-471-04491-1, Pub. by Wiley-Interscience). Wiley.

CHEMISTRY, ORGANIC–TABLES, ETC.

Buckingham, J. B., et al, eds. Dictionary of Organic Compounds: First Supplement. 1983. $175.00 (ISBN 0-412-17010-8, NO. 6798, Pub. by Chapman & Hall). Methuen Inc.

CHEMISTRY, PATHOLOGICAL
see Chemistry, Medical and Pharmaceutical

CHEMISTRY, PHARMACEUTICAL
see Chemistry, Medical and Pharmaceutical

CHEMISTRY, TECHNICAL
see also Ceramics; Chemical Engineering; Chemicals–Manufacture and Industry; Cleaning Compounds; Corrosion and Anti-Corrosives; Electrochemistry; Oxygen–Industrial Applications; Textile Chemistry
also particular industries and products, e.g. Clay Industries; Dyes and Dyeing; Petroleum Products

Abd-El-Wahed, A. M. Chemical Technology Dictionary: English, French-German-Arabic. 383p. (Eng., Fr., Ger. & Arabic.). 1974. $45.00 (ISBN 0-686-92502-5, M-9759). French & Eur.

CHEMISTRY, TECHNICAL–DICTIONARIES

Concise Dictionary of Chemistry & Chemical Technology. 128p. 1975. $30.00x (ISBN 0-686-44771-9, Pub. by Collets). State Mutual Bk.
Osteroth, Dieter & Von Baeckmann, Walter G. Chemisch-Technisches Lexikon. LC 79-385912. xi, 304p. (Eng. & Ger.). 1979. write for info. (ISBN 0-387-08891-1). Springer-Verlag.
Sobecka, Z., et al, eds. Dictionary of Chemistry & Chemical Technology in Six Languages. rev. ed. 1966. 130.00 (ISBN 0-08-011600-0). Pergamon.
Technishe Universitaet, Dresden, ed. English-German Dictionary of Chemistry & Chemical Technology. 2nd ed. LC 76-455777. (Eng. & Ger.). 1978. 47.50x (ISBN 0-8002-0401-8). Intl Pubns Serv.

CHEMISTRY, TEXTILE
see Textile Chemistry

CHESS–DICTIONARIES

Brace, Edward R. An Illustrated Dictionary of Chess. (Illus.). 320p. (Ger.). E4.50 (ISBN 0-600-32920-8). Newnes Bks.
Ibero, Ramon. Diccionario de Ajedrez. 192p. (Span.). 1977. pap. $8.75 (ISBN 84-270-0413-3, S-30996). French & Eur.
Le Lionnais, Francois. Dictionnaire des Echecs. (Fr.). 1974. 176.80 F. PUF.
Maget, E. Dictionnaire de Echecs. 429p. (Fr.). 1974. $67.50 (ISBN 0-686-57023-5, M-6381). French & Eur.

CHEYENNE INDIANS
see Indians of North America–The West

CHEYENNE LANGUAGE
English-Cheyenne Dictionary: A Dictionary of the Cheyenne Language. (Eng. & Cheyenne.). 1976. 4.95 (ISBN 0-686-26100-3); pap. write for info. MT Coun Indian.

CHICANOS
see Mexican Americans

CHILD ABUSE
Giovannoni, Jeanne M. & Becerra, Rosina. Defining Child Abuse. LC 79-7180. (Illus.). 1979. 24.95 (ISBN 0-02-911750-X). Free Pr.

CHILD BEHAVIOR
see Child Psychology; Etiquette for Children and Youth

CHILD HEALTH
see Children–Care and Hygiene

CHILD MENTAL HEALTH
see Child Psychiatry

CHILD NEGLECT
see Child Abuse

CHILD PSYCHIATRY
see also Child Psychology
Lafon, Robert. Vocabulaire de Psychopedagogic et de Psychiatrie de l'Enfant. 4th ed. LC 79-381763. xix, 1060p. (Fr.). 1979. 182.00 F. Pr Univ Fr.
––Vocabulaire De Psychopedagogie et De Psychiatrie De L'enfant. 3rd ed. 868p. (Fr.). 1973. $57.50 (ISBN 0-686-57282-3, F-19440). French & Eur.
Vocabulaire de Psychopedagogie & de Psychiatrie de l'enfant. 3rd ed. 868p. (Fr.). 1973. 145.60 F. PUF.

CHILD PSYCHOLOGY
see also Child Psychiatry; Educational Psychology; Learning, Psychology of
Glossaire de Pedologie. 173p. (Fr.). 1972. 50.00 F. Biosphere.
Moor, Lise. English-French-German Glossary for Psychiatry, Child Psychiatry & Abnormal Psychology. 2nd ed. LC 75-450548. (Eng., Fr. & Ger.). 1969. 8.75x (ISBN 0-8002-0766-1). Intl Pubns Serv.

CHILD STUDY
see Child Psychology

CHILDHOOD
see Children

CHILDREN
see also Etiquette for Children and Youth; Exceptional Children
Bauer, Karl W. & Hengst, Heinz. Kritische Stichwoerter zur Kinderkultur. 366p. (Ger.). 1978. write for info. (ISBN 3-770-51634-6). W Fink.
Lamblin, L. Le Larousse des Enfants. (Fr.). 1978. $22.75 (Dist. by Continental Bk Co). Larousse.
Plaisance, Georges. Lexique Pedologique Trilingue. 355p. (Fr.). 1958. 44.00 F. CDU.

CHILDREN–CARE AND HYGIENE
see also Nurses and Nursing
Groothoff, Hans. Lexikon Fuer Eltern und Erzieher. (Ger.). 1973. $20.00 (ISBN 3-7831-0320-7, M-7199). French & Eur.

CHILDREN–ETIQUETTE
see Etiquette for Children and Youth

CHILDREN–HEALTH
see Children–Care and Hygiene

CHILDREN–HYGIENE
see Children–Care and Hygiene

CHILDREN–LANGUAGE
Alden, Moe J., et al. The Vocabulary of First-Grade Children. 136p. 1981. $21.50x (ISBN 0-398-04623-9). C C Thomas.
Iwamura, Susan. The Verbal Games of Pre-School Children. LC 79-22384. 1979. $25.00x (ISBN 0-312-83877-8). St Martin.
The Magic World of Words: The New Macmillan Very First Dictionary. 2nd ed. (Illus.). (gr. 4-7). 1980. 8.95 (ISBN 0-02-578980-5). Macmillan.

CHILDREN–MENTAL DISORDERS
see Child Psychiatry

CHILDREN–PSYCHOLOGY
see Child Psychology

CHILDREN–RECREATION
see Games

CHILDREN–SPEECH
see Children–Language

CHILDREN–VOCABULARY
see Children–Language

CHILDREN, ABNORMAL AND BACKWARDS
see Exceptional Children; Slow Learning Children

CHILDREN, DEAF
see also Deaf–Means of Communication
Guilfoyle, George R. & Silverman-Dresner, Toby. Vocabulary Norms for Deaf Children. LC 72-83498. (Lexington School Ser.: Book 7). 1972. softcover $8.00 (ISBN 0-88200-060-8, C2344). Alexander Graham.

CHILDREN, DEAF–EDUCATION
see Deaf–Education

CHILDREN, EXCEPTIONAL
see Exceptional Children

CHILDREN, RETARDED
see Slow Learning Children

CHILDREN'S ALMANACS
see Almanacs

CHILDREN'S COURTS
see Juvenile Courts

CHILDREN'S ENCYCLOPEDIAS AND DICTIONARIES
Anderson, Anne. Little Beginner's Dictionary. 1973. Can.$pap. 5.00. U of Toronto Pr.
Daughters of St. Paul. ABC's Dictionary. write for info. Dghtrs St Paul.
DTV Junior Lexikon, 10 vols. (Ger.). 1974. Set. pap. 62.50 (ISBN 3-423-05951-6, M-7340. Pub. by DTV/KNO). French & Eur.
Jenkins, William A. & Schiller, Andrew. My First Picture Dictionary. rev. ed. LC 78-13248. (Illus.). (gr. k-3). 1977. PLB 11.28 (ISBN 0-688-51786-2). Lothrop.
Lippman, Peter. One & Only Wacky Wordbook. (Golden Storybk.). (Illus.). (gr. 2-7). 1979. $3.95 (ISBN 0-307-13739-2, Golden Pr); PLB 10.69 (ISBN 0-307-63379-9). Western Pub.
Maxwell, Christine. The Children's Dictionary. 480p. write for info. Wheaton.
Merriam Company, ed. Webster's Intermediate Dictionary. LC 70-38974. (Illus.). 960p. (gr. 7-9). 1977. 8.95 (ISBN 0-87779-279-8). Merriam-Webster Inc.
Mi Primer Diccionario Escolar. 4th ed. 480p. (Span.). 1975. pap. $2.95 (ISBN 84-319-0028-8, S-27087). French & Eur.
Morris, William, ed. Xerox Intermediate Dictionary. (Illus.). 800p. (gr. 4-6). 1973. Repr. 9.95 (ISBN 0-448-02849-2, G&D). Putnam Pub Group.
Scarry, Richard. Mi Primer Gran Diccionario Infantil. 4th ed. 90p. (Span.). 1978. leatherette $13.95 (ISBN 84-02-03836-0, S-26637). French & Eur.
Schulz, Charles M. The Charlie Brown Dictionary. (gr. 1 up). 1977. pap. $5.95 (ISBN 0-590-09898-5). Scholastic Inc.
Trevaskis, John & Hyman, Robin. Boys & Girls First Dictionary. 2nd ed. (Illus.). 1979. Can.$pap. 4.95 (ISBN 0-7730-1071-8); pap. $1.50 (ISBN 0-7730-1073-4). U of Toronto Pr.
Walt Disney's Winnie-the-Pooh Dictionary. (Look-Look Bks.). (Illus.). (ps). 1981. $1.25 (ISBN 0-307-11868-1, Golden Pr); PLB $6.08 (ISBN 0-307-61868-4). Western Pub.
Weston, John, compiled by. The Oxford Children's Dictionary in Colour. (gr. 3-9). 1976. text ed. 11.95x (ISBN 0-19-910209-0). Oxford U Pr.

CHILDREN'S ETIQUETTE
see Etiquette for Children and Youth

CHILDREN'S LIBRARIES
see School Libraries

CHILDREN'S WIT AND HUMOR
see Wit and Humor, Juvenile

CHILE
see also names of cities, towns, etc. in Chile
Rodriguez, Zorobabel. Diccionario de Chilenismos. LC 73-124394. xii, 487p. (Span.). 1979. write for info. Universidad & Acad.

CHILE–POLITICS AND GOVERNMENT
Caffarena de Jiles, Elena. Diccionario de jurisprudencia chilena: Recopilacionde conceptos y definiciones. 346p. (Span.). 1959. $2.00. Juridica-Andres Belio.

Fuentes, Jordi & Cortes, Lia. Diccionario politico de Chile. 532p. (Span.). write for info. Orbe Edns.

CHILLS AND FEVER
see Malaria

CHIMNEYS
Standard Glossary of Terms Relating to Chimneys, Vents & Heat Producing Appliances. (Eighty-Ninety Ser). 1972. pap. 2.00 (ISBN 0-685-58178-0, 97M). Natl Fire Prot.

CHINA–ANTIQUITIES
Xinglian, Zhang. A Glossary of Chinese Archaeology. Shuhan, Zhao, ed. 199p. (Orig., Chinese & Eng.). 1983. $4.95 (ISBN 0-8351-1210-1); pap. $3.95 (ISBN 0-8351-1082-6). China Bks.

CHINA–BIBLIOGRAPHY
Cordier, Henri. Bibliotheca Sinica, dictionnaire bibliographique des ouvrages relatifs a l'Empire chinois, 6 vols. in 5. 2nd ed. LC 68-58196. (Bibliography & Research Ser.: No. 250). (Span., Chinese & Fr.). 1969. Repr. of 1922 ed. $200.00 (ISBN 0-8337-0671-3). B Franklin.

CHINA–BIOGRAPHY
Goodrich, L. Carrington & Fang, Chaoying, eds. Dictionary of Ming Biography, 1364-1644, 2 vols. (Illus.). 1976. $140.00x set (ISBN 0-685-62034-4). Vol. 1, 1054pgs (ISBN 0-231-03801-1). Vol. 2, 634pgs (ISBN 0-231-03833-X). Columbia U Pr.

CHINA–ECONOMIC CONDITIONS
Broadbent, K. Dictionary of China's Rural Economy. 406p. (Chinese & Eng.). 1978. $125.00 (ISBN 0-85198-381-2, M-9712). French & Eur.

CHINA–HISTORY
Here are entered general works on Chinese history. Smaller periods are listed chronologically at the end of the History subject headings.
Dillon, Michael. A Dictionary of Chinese History. 240p. 1979. $27.50x (ISBN 0-7146-3107-8, F Cass Co). Biblio Dist.
Dittmar, P. Woerterbuch der Chinesischen Revolution. 224p. (Ger.). 1975. pap. $5.95 (ISBN 0-686-56644-0, M-7035). French & Eur.

CHINA–POLITICS AND GOVERNMENT
Bilancia, Philip R. Dictionary of Chinese Law & Government. LC 73-80618. 832p. (Chinese & Eng.). 1981. $45.00x (ISBN 0-8047-0864-9). Stanford U Pr.
Hucker, Charles O. A Dictionary of Official Titles in Imperial China: Governmental Nomenclature from Antiquity to 1850. Date not set. price not set. Stanford U Pr.

CHINA–POLITICS AND GOVERNMENT–1949-
Doolin, Dennis & Ridley, Charles. A Chinese-English Dictionary of Communist Chinese Terminology. LC 70-170210. (Publications Ser.: No. 124). 569p. (Chinese & Eng.). 1973. 30.00x (ISBN 0-8179-6241-7). Hoover Inst Pr.

CHINA (PORCELAIN)
see Porcelain

CHINAWARE
see Porcelain

CHINESE ART
see Art, Chinese

CHINESE LANGUAGE
Anderson, Olov B. A Companion Volume to R. H. Mathews' Chinese-English Dictionary. 2nd ed. LC 78-320299. 335p. (Chinese & Eng.). 1978. E7.50 (ISBN 9-144-15221-3) (ISBN 0-7007-0081-1). Curzon Pr.
––A Concordance to Five Systems of Transcription for Standard Chinese. 230p. (Chinese). 1982. pap. text ed. $22.50 (ISBN 0-7007-0080-3, Pub. by Curzon Pr England). Apt Bks.
DObson, W. A. A Dictionary of the Chinese Particles. (Chinese). 1974. Can.$50.00 (ISBN 0-8020-2119-0). U of Toronto Pr.
Hoffman, Alfred. Glosar der Wichtigsten Saugetiere Chinas. xi, 103p. (Ger. & Chinese). 1978. write for info. (ISBN 3-447-02001-6). Harrassowitz.

Hoffmann, Alfred. Glossar der Heute Chinesischen Vogelnamen. LC 75-516973. xvi, 366p. (Ger. & Chinese.). 1975. DM.52.00 (ISBN 3-447-01693-0). Harrassowitz.
––Neue Chinesische Vogelnamen. LC 79-361040. x, 113p. (Ger. & Chinese.). 1978. write for info. (ISBN 3-447-01980-8). Harrassowitz.
Karlgren, Bernhard. Schrift & Sprache der Chinesen. LC 74-34031. x, 119p. (Chinese). 1975. write for info. (ISBN 0-387-07108-3). Springer-Verlag.
McNaughton, William. Reading & Writing Chinese: A Guide to the Chinese Writing System. LC 77-77699. (Chinese). 1979. $17.50 (ISBN 0-8048-1188-1). C E Tuttle.
Mei-Wah Choy, Rita. Read & Write Chinese: A Simplified Guide to the Chinese Characters. rev. ed. 336p. (Chinese.). 1982. pap. text ed. $9.95 (ISBN 0-941340-09-0). China West.
Wieger, L. Chinese Characters, Their Origin, Etymology, History, Classification & Signification. 2nd ed. Davrout, L., tr. (Chinese). 1927. pap. $12.50 (ISBN 0-486-21321-8). Dover.

CHINESE LANGUAGE–CONVERSATION AND PHRASE BOOKS
Chinese-English Expressions for Travellers. 90p. (Chinese & Eng.). 1983. pap. $3.95 (ISBN 0-8044-6993-8). Ungar.
Huihua, Jianyi H. Simple Chinese Conversation. (Chinese). pap. $6.50 (ISBN 0-87557-010-0, 010-0). Saphrograph.
Montanaro, John S. Chinese-English Phrase Book for Travellers. 304p. (Chinese & Eng.). 1981. pap. $8.95 (ISBN 0-471-08298-8, Pub. by Wiley Pr). Wiley.

CHINESE LANGUAGE–DIALECTS
Cowles, Roy T. The Cantonese Speaker's Dictionary. 1600p. (Chinese). 1965. text ed. $27.50x (ISBN 0-8188-0139-5). Paragon.

CHINESE LANGUAGE–DICTIONARIES
Araushkin, N. S., et al. Karmannyi Kitaisko-Russkii Slovar. 210p. (Rus.). 1975. $1.95 (Pub. by Russkii Iazyk). Four Continent.
Beijing Foreign Institute. The Pinyin Chinese-English Dictionary. Wu Jingrong, ed. LC 79-2477. 976p. (Chinese & Eng.). 1979. $68.95x (ISBN 0-471-27557-3, Pub. by Wiley-Interscience); pap. $16.95 (ISBN 0-471-86796-9). Wiley.
Bergman, Peter, ed. The Basic English-Chinese, Chinese-English Dictionary with PINYIN Transliteration. (Eng. & Chinese.). 1979. text ed. 12.00x (ISBN 0-391-01287-8). Humanities.
Chao, Yuen R. & Yang, Lien-Sheng. Concise Dictionary of Spoken Chinese. LC 47-5464. (Harvard-Yenching Institute Publications Ser). 1947. 17.50x (ISBN 0-674-15800-8). Harvard U Pr.
The Chinese-English Dictionary. 976p. (Chinese & Eng.). 1981. $49.95 (ISBN 962-07-0005-8, M-9400). French & Eur.
Chinese-English Dictionary. 976p. (Chinese & Eng.). 1982. 30.00x (ISBN 0-8044-0097-0). Ungar.
Chinese-English Dictionary. 976p. (Chinese & Eng.). 1979. pap. $60.00x (ISBN 0-686-44768-9, Pub. by Collets). State Mutual Bk.
Chinese-English Dictionary of Current Affairs. 594p. (Chinese & Eng.). 1977. leatherette $25.00 (ISBN 0-686-92562-9, M-9247). French & Eur.
Chinese-English Dictionary of Military Terms. 366p. (Chinese & Eng.). 1977. $25.00 (ISBN 0-686-97446-8, M-9275). French & Eur.
Chinese-English, English-Chinese Dictionary, 2 vols. (Chinese & Eng.). Set. 40.00 (ISBN 0-685-79110-6). Heinman.

Chinese-English Translation Assistance Group, ed. Chinese Dictionaries: An Extensive Bibliography of Dictionaries in Chinese & Other Languages. LC 82-923. xvi, 448p. (Chinese & Eng.). 1982. lib. bdg. 49.95 (ISBN 0-313-23505-8, MDC/). Greenwood.
Chinese Pocket Dictionary. (Chinese & Eng.). 15.00 (ISBN 0-686-77962-2). Heinman.
Chinese-Russian Phonetic Dictionary. 319p. (Chinese & Rus.). 1957. leatherette $4.95 (ISBN 0-686-92615-3, M-9126). French & Eur.
Chiu, Hong-Yee, ed. Chinese-English & English-Chinese Astronomical Dictionary. LC 65-10966. 173p. (Chinese & Eng.). 1966. $30.00x (ISBN 0-306-10739-2, Consultants). Plenum Pub.
Chu, Hsiu-Feng, et al. English-Chinese Chinese-English Dictionary of Business Terms. 476p. (Orig.). 1973. pap. $7.95x (ISBN 0-917056-85-X, Pub. by Chih-Wen Pub Co China). Cheng & Tsui.
Couvreur. Dictionnaire Classique de la Langue Chinoise. 1080p. (Chinese.). 1966. write for info. Mason & Larose.
Couvveur, F. S. Dictionnaire Classique de la Langue Chinoise. 1080p. (Fr. & Chinese.). 1966. $35.00 (ISBN 0-686-56810-9, M-6588). French & Eur.
Dictionnaire Chinois-Francais. 673p. (Fr. & Chinese.). 1979. $25.00 (ISBN 0-686-97329-1, M-9268). French & Eur.
Dictionnaire Francais-Chinois. 1498p. (Fr. & Chinese.). 1979. $49.95 (ISBN 962-04-0090-9, M-9262). French & Eur.
Dictionnaire Francais-Chinois. 956p. (Fr. & Chinese.). 1979. leatherette $19.95 (ISBN 0-686-97330-5, M-9256). French & Eur.
Dobson, W. A. Dictionary of the Chinese Particles, with a Prolegomenon in Which the Problems of the Particles are Considered & They are Classified by Their Grammaticel Functions. LC 73-91242. (Chinese.). 1974. $75.00x (ISBN 0-8020-2119-0). U of Toronto Pr.
Doolin, Dennis & Ridley, Charles. A Chinese-English Dictionary of Communist Chinese Terminology. LC 70-170210. (Publications Ser.: No. 124). 569p. (Chinese & Eng.). 1973. 30.00x (ISBN 0-8179-6241-7). Hoover Inst Pr.
Eckardt, Andre. Chinesisch-Koreanisch-Deutsch Woerterbuch. 224p. (Chinese, Ger. & Korean.). 1966. write for info. (ISBN 3-87276-115-3). Groos Verlag.
Eitel, Ernes J. Chinese Dictionary: Cantonese Dialect, 3 pts. (Chinese.). 1976. Repr. of 1958 ed. $140.00 (ISBN 0-518-19009-9). Ayer Co.
English-Chinese & Chinese-English Dictionary. (Eng. & Chinese.). 1977. $7.95 (ISBN 0-8351-0725-6). China Bks.
English-Chinese Architectural Engineering Dictionary. 441p. (Eng. & Chinese.). 1973. $14.95 (ISBN 0-686-92620-X, M-9254). French & Eur.
English-Chinese Dictionary of Civil & Architectural Engineering Terms. 706p. (Eng. & Chinese.). 1979. $29.95 (ISBN 0-686-97359-3, M-9271). French & Eur.
English-Chinese Dictionary of Construction Engineering. 251p. (Eng. & Chinese.). 1980. leatherette $14.95 (ISBN 0-686-97360-7, M-9279). French & Eur.
English-Chinese Dictionary of Medicine. 1675p. (Eng. & Chinese.). 1979. text ed. $24.95 (ISBN 0-8351-1048-6). China Bks.
English-Chinese Dictionary of Physical Geography. 279p. (Eng. & Chinese.). 1980. $25.00 (ISBN 0-686-97362-3, M-9292). French & Eur.
English-Chinese Dictionary of Scientific & Technology Abreviations. 587p. (Eng. & Chinese.). 1979. pap. $9.95 (ISBN 0-686-97363-1, M-9250). French & Eur.
English-Chinese Glossary of Electronic & Electrical Engineering. 636p. (Eng. & Chinese.). 1980. $29.95 (ISBN 0-686-97364-X, M-9255). French & Eur.
English-Chinese Maritime Dictionary. 678p. (Eng. & Chinese.). 1979. $14.95 (ISBN 0-686-97365-8, M-9251). French & Eur.
English-Chinese Medical Dictionary. 1665p. (Eng. & Chinese.). 1980. $95.00 (ISBN 0-686-97366-6, M-9264). French & Eur.
English-Chinese Microbiological Dictionary. 138p. (Eng. & Chinese.). 1979. pap. $3.95 (ISBN 0-686-97368-2, M-9573). French & Eur.
Fenn, Courtenay H., ed. Five Thousand Dictionary: A Chinese-English Pocket Dictionary & Index to the Character Cards of the College of Chinese Studies. rev. ed. LC 43-754. 1942. 20.00x (ISBN 0-674-30550-7); pap. 8.95 (ISBN 0-674-30551-5, HP35). Harvard U Pr.
General Chinese-English Dictionary. 926p. (Chinese & Eng.). 1979. $9.95 (ISBN 0-686-92471-1, M-9583). French & Eur.
Hemeling, Karl E. English-Chinese Dictionary: Standard Chinese, 3 vols. (Chinese & Eng.). 1976. Repr. of 1958 ed. $165.00 (ISBN 0-518-19001-3). Ayer Co.
Herring, J. A. The Foursquare Dictionary. 605p. 1969. 12.50x (ISBN 0-89955-232-3, Pub. by Mei Ya China). Intl Schol Bk Serv.
Hung, W. S. A New English-Chinese Law Dictionary. 162p. (Eng. & Chinese.). 1979. $17.50 (ISBN 962-204-001-2, M-9558). French & Eur.
Jameson, E. W., Jr. A Short Dictionary of Simplified Chinese Characters. 3rd ed. (Chinese & Eng.). 1975. pap. $6.95 (ISBN 0-9606576-2-2). E W Jameson Jr.
Japanese-Chinese Dictionary. 2587p. (Japanese & Chinese.). 1979. leatherette $49.95 (ISBN 0-686-97413-1, M-9267). French & Eur.
Japanese-Chinese Dictionary. 569p. (Japanese & Chinese.). 1980. pap. $7.95 (ISBN 0-686-97415-8, M-9252). French & Eur.
Japanese-Chinese Loanword Dictionary (M-9259) 748p. (Japanese & Chinese.). Date not set. Leatherette $25.00 (ISBN 0-686-97404-2, M-9259). French & Eur.
Karlgren, Bernhard. Analytic Dictionary of Chinese & Sino-Japanese. (Chinese & Japanese.). $12.00 (ISBN 0-8446-5208-3). Peter Smith.
Kimball, Richard L. China Beginner's Traveler's Dictionary. (Chinese.). 1980. pap. $6.95 (ISBN 0-8351-0732-9). China Bks.
--China Beginner's Traveler's Dictionary. 154p. $6.95 (ISBN 0-8351-0732-9). Eurasia Pr NY.
Kotov, A. V. Kitaisko-Russkii Slovar-Minimum. 432p. (Rus.). 1974. $2.95 (Pub. by Russkii Iazyk). Four Continent.
Kwon, Hyogmyou. Basic Chinese-Korean Character Dictionary. LC 79-322885. xxvi, 556p. (Chinese & Korean.). 1978. write for info. (ISBN 3-447-01884-4). Harrassowitz.
Learn Chinese: For English Speakers. (Chinese.). pap. 9.50 (ISBN 0-87557-009-7, 092-6). Saphrograph.
Learner's Chinese-English Dictionary. (Chinese & Eng.). pap. $14.95. Iaconi.
Lee, Bennett & Barme, Geremie. China Traveler's Phrasebook. (Chinese.). 1980. pap. $5.95 (ISBN 0-8351-0729-9). China Bks.
Liang, Shi-Chiu. A New Practical Chinese-English Dictionary. 1355p. 1973. $32.00x (ISBN 0-917056-53-1, Pub. by Far East Bk Co China). Cheng & Tsui.
--A New Practical Chinese-English Dictionary. 1355p. 1973. pap. $16.95x (ISBN 0-917056-54-X, Pub. by Far East Bk Co China). Cheng & Tsui.
Liang, Shi-Chiu, ed. A New Practical Chinese-English Dictionary. 1355p. 1973. $45.00x (ISBN 0-917056-52-3, Pub. by Far East Bk Co China). Cheng & Tsui.
--A New Practical English-Chinese Dictionary. 2401p. 1980. pap. $25.00x (ISBN 0-917056-56-6, Pub. by Far East Bk Co China). Cheng & Tsui.
Liu, Eric S. Frequency Dictionary of Chinese Words. (Linguistic Structures, First Ser.). (Chinese.). 1973. pap. text ed. 57.50x (ISBN 90-2792-627-1). Mouton.
Makkai, Adam. A Dictionary of American Idioms in Chinese. Gates & Boatner, eds. 396p. (Chinese & Eng.). Date not set. pap. $14.95 (ISBN 0-8120-2386-2). Barron.
Martin, Helmut, et al. Vocabulaire Usuel du Chinois Moderne. LC 78-358753. vvi, 328p. (Chinese.). 1977. write for info. (ISBN 3-468-49025-9). Langen Kommand.
Mathews, Robert H. Chinese-English Dictionary: A Chinese-English Dictionary Compiled for the China Inland Mission. rev. ed. (Harvard-Yenching Institute Publications Ser.). 1250p. 1943. text ed. 32.50x (ISBN 0-674-12350-6). Harvard U Pr.
Mathias, J. & Hixson, Sandra. A Compilation of Chinese Dictionaries. (Chinese.). 1975. $4.50 (ISBN 0-88710-020-1). Far Eastern Pubns.
Matthews, B. & Tan, K. English-Chinese Picture Dictionary. (Illus., Chinese & Eng.). $5.00. Iaconi.
Midoux, Marcel. Vocabulaire Usuel du Chinois Moderne, 2: Chinois-Francais. (Illus.). 276p. (Chinese & Fr.). 1970. 19.00 F. Geuthner.
--Vocabulaire Usuel du Chinois Moderne, 3: Chinois-Francais. (Illus.). 254p. (Chinese & Fr.). 1971. 20.00 F. Geuthner.
Model English-Chinese Dictionary with Illustrative Examples. (Illus.). 1674p. (Eng. & Chinese.). 1979. leatherette $19.95 (ISBN 0-686-97401-8). French & Eur.
New English-Chinese Dictionary. 1252p. (Eng. & Chinese.). 1979. $17.95 (ISBN 0-686-97423-9, M-9290). French & Eur.
A New English-Chinese Dictionary. 1542p. (Eng. & Chinese.). 1982. $18.50x (ISBN 0-8044-0138-1). Ungar.
Nouveau Dictionnaire: Francais-Chinois. 846p. (Fr. & Chinese.). 1980. leatherette $9.95 (ISBN 0-686-97425-5, M-9278). French & Eur.
Nouveau Dictionnaire Francais-Chinois. 1499p. (Fr. & Chinese.). 1981. $25.95 (ISBN 962-04-0090-9, M-9372). French & Eur.
Piasek, Martin. Chinesisch-Deutsches Woerterbuch. 3rd ed. (Chinese & Ger.). 1975. $28.95 (ISBN 0-686-56599-1, 7320, Pub. by Max Heuber). French & Eur.
A Pocket Concise Chinese-English Dictionary. 620p. (Chinese , Eng.). 1978. pap. $6.95 (ISBN 0-686-92467-3, M-9182). French & Eur.
A Pocket English-Chinese Dictionary. (Eng. & Chinese.). 1980. pap. $4.95 (ISBN 0-8351-0727-2). China Bks.
A Pocket English-Chinese Dictionary. 451p. (Eng. & Chinese.). 1980. pap. text ed. $4.95 (ISBN 0-686-92473-8, M-9580). French & Eur.
A Practical English-Chinese Dictionary. 1674p. (Eng. & Chinese.). 1979. leatherette $19.95 (ISBN 0-686-97443-3, M-9291). French & Eur.
Quo, James C. Concise Chinese - English Dictionary Romanized. LC 60-14372. (Chinese & Eng.). 1961. $4.95 (ISBN 0-8048-0116-9). C E Tuttle.
Rose-Innes, Arthur. Beginners Dictionary of Chinese-Japanese Characters. (Chinese & Japanese.). $15.00 (ISBN 0-8446-5657-7). Peter Smith.
Rudenberg, Werner. Chinesisch-Deutsches Woerterbuch. 3rd ed. 821p. (Chinese & Ger.). 1963. $196.00x (ISBN 0-686-56600-9, M-7321). De Gruyter.
Season, S. M. Chinese-English Idioms & Phrases. 311p. (Chinese & Eng.). 1978. leatherette $14.95 (ISBN 0-686-92616-1, M-9246). French & Eur.
Shiratori, T. Chinese-English-Japanese Glossary of Chemical Terms. (Chinese, Eng. & Japanese.). write for info. (M-9351). French & Eur.
Simon, W. A Beginner's Chinese English Dictionary of the National Language (Gwpyeu) 1200p. (Chinese & Eng.). 1980. $55.00x (ISBN 0-85331-013-0, Pub. by Lund Humphries England). State Mutual Bk.
Soothill, William E. & Hodous, L., eds. Dictionary of Chinese Buddhist Terms, with Sanskrit & English Equivalents & a Sanskrit-Pali Index. (Chinese, Sanskrit & Eng.). 1977. text ed. $50.00x (ISBN 0-8426-1030-8). Verry.
Tamura, S. & Shiratori, F. Chinese-English-Japanese Glossary of Chemical Terms. 661p. (Chinese, Eng. & Japanese.). 1977. $49.95 (ISBN 962-04-0028-3, M-9263). French & Eur.
The Trictionary. 432p. (Chinese , Span. & Eng.). softcover $12.95. Bilingual Pubns.
Wei, S. S. Chinese Idioms, English Idioms, English Synonyms Practical Dictionary. (Chinese & Eng.). 17.50 (ISBN 0-686-31874-9). Heinman.
Wieger, L. Chinese Characters, Their Origin, Etymology, History, Classification & Signification. 2nd ed. Davrout, L., tr. (Chinese.). 1927. pap. $12.50 (ISBN 0-486-21321-8). Dover.
Wieger, Leon. Chinese Characters. 2nd ed. Davrout, L., tr. (Chinese.). 1965. 22.50 (ISBN 0-8188-0094-1). Paragon.
Wilhelm, Hellmut. German-Chinese Dictionary. (Ger. & Chinese.). 1976. Repr. of 1958 ed. $175.00 (ISBN 0-518-19006-4). Ayer Co.
Williams, Samuel W. Chinese-English Dictionary. (Eng. & Chinese.). 1976. Repr. of 1958 ed. $65.00 (ISBN 0-518-19007-2). Ayer Co.
Xin Ying-Han-Cidian Editing Committee. A New English-Chinese Dictionary. 1648p. 1975. $29.95 (ISBN 0-917056-59-0, Pub. by Joint Pub Co China). Cheng & Tsui.
Zhou Long Ru. English-Chinese Dictionary of Abbreviation & Acronyms. 1290p. (Eng. & Chinese.). 1980. $9.95 (ISBN 0-8351-1106-7). China Bks.

CHINESE LANGUAGE–PRONUNCIATION

Chen, Janet. A Practical English-Chinese Pronouncing Dictionary. (Chinese & Eng.). $22.50. Iaconi.

CHINESE LANGUAGE–READERS

Beijing Language Institute. Vocabulary List-Key to Exercise for Practical Chinese Reader. (Practical Chinese Reader Ser.: No. 1 & 2). 75p. (Orig.). 1982. pap. $1.95 (ISBN 0-8351-1148-2). China Bks.

CHINESE LANGUAGE–VOCABULARY

Andre, Yvonne. Vocabulaire de Base du Chinois Moderne. 160p. (Chinese.). 1965. 40.00 F. Klincksieck.
Kennedy, George A. Minimum Vocabularies of Written Chinese. (Chinese.). $2.50 (ISBN 0-88710-048-1). Far Eastern Pubns.
Midoux, Marcel. Vocabulaire Usuel du Chinois Moderne. 4th ed. 1141p. (Chinese.). 1971. 88.00 F. Pubns Orient.

CHINESE LANGUAGE–WRITING

McNaughton, William. Reading & Writing Chinese: A Guide to the Chinese Writing System. LC 77-77699. (Chinese.). 1979. $17.50 (ISBN 0-8048-1188-1). C E Tuttle.
Rose-Innes, Arthur. Beginners' Dictionary of Chinese-Japanese Characters & Compounds. (Chinese & Japanese.). 1977. pap. $7.95 (ISBN 0-486-23467-3). Dover.

**CHINESE LITERATURE-
BIBLIOGRAPHY**
Cordier, Henri. Bibliotheca Sinica,
dictionnaire bibliographique des
ouvrages relatifs a l'Empire
chinois, 6 vols. in 5. 2nd ed. LC
68-58196. (Bibliography &
Research Ser.: No. 250). (Span.,
Chinese & Fr.). 1969. Repr. of
1922 ed. $200.00 (ISBN 0-8337-
0671-3). B Franklin.
CHINESE PAINTING
see Painting, Chinese
CHINESE PHILOSOPHY
see Philosophy, Chinese
**CHINESE POETRY-HISTORY
AND CRITICISM**
Stimson, Hugh M. T'ang Poetic
Vocabulary. $8.95 (ISBN 0-88710-
121-6). Far Eastern Pubns.
CHINESE QUESTION
see China-History
CHINOOK INDIANS
*see Indians of North America-
Northwest, Pacific*
CHINOOK JARGON
Gibbs, George. Alphabetical
Vocabulary of the Chinook
Language. LC 72-168141. (Library
of American Linguistics: No. 13).
(Chinook.). Repr. of 1863 ed.
$10.00 (ISBN 0-404-50993-2).
AMS Pr.
--Dictionary of the Chinook Jargon,
or Trade Languages of Oregon. LC
76-168142. (Library of American
Linguistics: No. 12). (Chinook.).
Repr. of 1863 ed. $10.00 (ISBN 0-
404-50992-4). AMS Pr.
CHIPPEWA LANGUAGE
Baraga, R. R. Dictionary of the
Otchipwe Language. (Chippwe.).
Repr. $20.00 (ISBN 0-87018-002-
9). Ross.
CHIROMANCY
see Palmistry
CHIVALRY-ROMANCES
see Romances
CHOICE OF PROFESSION
see Vocational Guidance
CHOLESTEROL
Kraus, Barbara. The Dictionary of
Sodium, Fats, & Cholesterol.
(Illus.). 384p. Date not set. pap.
6.95 (ISBN 0-399-50945-3,
Perigee). Putnam Pub Group.
CHRESTOMATHIES
see Readers
**CHRISTIAN ART AND
SYMBOLISM**
*see also Cathedrals; Jewish Art and
Symbolism
also subdivision Art under various
subjects, e.g. Jesus Christ-Art*
Huber, Rudolf & Rieth, Renate, eds.
Glossarium Artis: Fasz 4,
Paramente & Buecher der
Christlichen Kirchen. 203p. (Ger.).
DM.35.00 (ISBN 3-484-60049-7).
Max Niemeyer.
Jouve, E. G. Dictionnaire
d'Esthetique Chretienne ou
Theorie du Beau dans l'Art
Chretien. Migne, J. P., ed.
(Troisieme et Derniere
Encyclopedie Theologique Ser.:
Vol. 17). 646p. (Fr.). Repr. of
1856 ed. lib. bdg. $82.50x (ISBN
0-89241-300-X). Caratzas Pub Co.
Urech, Edouard. Lexikon Christlicher
Symbole. (Illus.). 256p. (Ger.).
DM.12.50 (ISBN 3-76737-609-1).
F Bahn.
Van Voss, M. Heerma. Agypten, die
21: Dynastie. (Iconography of
Religions Ser.: XVI/9). (Illus.). viii,
18p. (Ger.). 1982. pap. write for
info. (ISBN 90-04-06826-0). E J
Brill.
CHRISTIAN CONVERTS
see Converts
CHRISTIAN DEMOCRACY
Quantin, M. Dictionnaire Raisonne
de Diplomatie Chretienne, Vol. 47.
Migne, J. P., ed. (Encyclopedie
Theologique Ser.). 578p. (Fr.).
Repr. of 1846 ed. lib. bdg. $74.00x
(ISBN 0-89241-251-8). Caratzas
Pub Co.
**CHRISTIAN DEVOTIONAL
LITERATURE**
see Devotional Literature
CHRISTIAN DOCTRINE
see Theology, Doctrinal
CHRISTIAN ETHICS
see also Sin; Social Ethics

*also subdivision Moral and Religious
Aspects under specific subjects, e.g.
Amusements-Moral and Religious
Aspects*
Stoeckle, Bernhard. Woerterbuch
Christlicher Ethik. 284p. (Ger.).
1975. DM.9.90 (ISBN 3-451-
07533-4). Herder.
**CHRISTIAN ETHICS-
DICTIONARIES**
Stoeckle, Bernard, ed. The Concise
Dictionary of Christian Ethics.
1979. $19.50 (ISBN 0-8245-0300-
7). Crossroad NY.
Stoeckle, Bernhard. Woerterbuch
christlicher Ethik. LC 75-520505.
284p. (Ger.). 1975. write for info.
(ISBN 3-451-07533-4). Herder.
CHRISTIAN EVIDENCES
see Apologetics
CHRISTIAN LITERATURE
see also Devotional Literature
Jouhanneaud, P. Dictionnaire
d'Anecdotes Chretiennes. Migne,
J. P., ed. (Nouvelle Encyclopedie
Theologique Ser.: Vol. 10). 610p.
(Fr.). Repr. of 1857 ed. lib. bdg.
$78.00x (ISBN 0-89241-260-7).
Caratzas Pub Co.
**CHRISTIAN LITERATURE,
EARLY**
Brunet, G. Dictionnaire des
Apocryphes, 2 vols. Migne, J. P.,
ed. (Troisieme et Derniere
Encyclopedie Theologique Ser.:
Vols. 23-24). 1310p. (Fr.). Repr. of
1858 ed. lib. bdg. $167.50x (ISBN
0-89241-305-0). Caratzas Pub Co.
CHRISTIAN NAMES
see Names, Personal
CHRISTIAN SCIENCE
*see also Boston-First Church of
Christ, Scientist*
A Complete Concordance to the
Writings of Mary B. Eddy. $27.00
(ISBN 0-87952-092-2). First
Church.
CHRISTIAN SYMBOLISM
see Christian Art and Symbolism
CHRISTIANITY
*see also Councils and Synods;
Ecumenical Movement; Miracles
also headings beginning with the
word Christian and Church; and
names of Christian churches and
sects, e.g. Catholic Church, Lutheran
Church, Huguenots*
Assfalg, Julius & Krueger, P. Kleines
Woerterbuch Des Christlichen
Orients. 1st ed. (Ger.). 1975.
$52.00 (ISBN 3-447-01707-4, M-
7514, Pub. by Harrassowitz).
French & Eur.
Brosse, La. Diccionario del
Cristianismo. 1104p. (Span.). 1976.
$53.95 (ISBN 84-254-0777-X, S-
50202). French & Eur.
Brosse, Olivier. Diccionario del
Cristianismo. 1101p. (Span.). 1974.
1500.00 ptas (ISBN 84-254-0777-
X). Herder SA.
Cross, F. L. & Livingstone, Elizabeth
A. The Oxford Dictionary of the
Christian Church. 1974. 60.00x
(ISBN 0-19-211545-6). Oxford U
Pr.
Diccionario. Grandes Temas de la fe
Cristiana. 400p. (Span.). 1981.
1200.00 ptas (ISBN 84-236-1511-
1). Don Bosco Ed.
Henry, Antonir Marie & LaBrosse,
Olivier De, eds. Dictionnaire de la
Foi Chretienne, 2 vols. 792p. (Fr.).
1968. pap. $47.50 (ISBN 0-686-
56818-4, M-6596). French & Eur.
Pieterse, Liberius. English-Urdu
Dictionary of Christian
Terminology. Slomp, Jan, ed. LC
77-930423. xxviii, 108p. (Eng. &
Urdu.). 1976. write for info.
Christian Study Centre.
Urech, Edouard. Dictionnaire des
Symboles Chretiens. (Illus.). 190p.
(Fr.). 1972. 63.00 F. Delachaux.
**CHRISTIANITY-APOLOGETIC
WORKS**
see Apologetics
**CHRISTIANITY-
CONTROVERSIAL LITERATURE**
see also Atheism
Pinard, C. Dictionnaire des
Objections Populaires contre le
Dogme, la Morale, la Discipline et
L'histoire de Eglise Catholique.
Migne, J. P., ed. (Troisieme et
Derniere Encyclopedie
Theologique Ser.: Vol. 33). 756p.
(Fr.). Repr. of 1858 ed. lib. bdg.
$96.50x (ISBN 0-89241-312-3).
Caratzas Pub Co.

CHRISTIANITY-EVIDENCES
see Apologetics
**CHRISTIANITY AND
PHILOSOPHY**
see Philosophy and Religion
**CHRISTIANITY IN (AFRICA,
ASIA, ETC.)**
see Christians in (Africa, Asia, etc.)
CHRISTIANS IN ASIA
Assfalg, Julius & Krueger, P. Kleines
Woerterbuch Des Christlichen
Orients. 1st ed. (Ger.). 1975.
$52.00 (ISBN 3-447-01707-4, M-
7514, Pub. by Harrassowitz).
French & Eur.
**CHROMATIC ALTERATION
(MUSIC)**
Banjo Chord Dictionary. 1981. $2.50.
Alfred Pub.
Organ Chord Dictionary. 1981. $2.50
(ISBN 0-88284-156-4). Alfred Pub.
Piano Chord Dictionary. 1981. $2.50
(ISBN 0-88284-155-6). Alfred Pub.
CHROMATICS
see Color
**CHROMATOGRAPHIC
ANALYSIS**
see also Thin Layer Chromatography
Denney, R. C. A Dictionary of
Chromatography. 2nd ed. 224p.
1982. E15.00 (ISBN 0-333-31667-
3). Macmillan London.
Denney, Roland C. Dictionary of
Chromatography. 2nd ed. 229p.
1982. $43.95 (ISBN 0-471-87477-
9, Pub. by Wiley-Interscience).
Wiley.
**CHROMATOGRAPHY, THIN
LAYER**
see Thin Layer Chromatography
CHRONOGRAMS
see Anagrams
CHRONOLOGY
*see also Almanacs; Clocks and
Watches*
Chesnel De La Charbouclais, L. P.
Dictionnaire de Geologie... et
Dictionnaire de Chronologie
Universelle par M. Champagnac,
Vol. 50. Migne, J. P., ed.
(Encyclopedie Theologique Ser.).
728p. (Fr.). Repr. of 1849 ed. lib.
bdg. $192.50x (ISBN 0-89241-253-
4). Caratzas Pub Co.
CHRONOLOGY, BIBLICAL
see Bible-Chronology
CHRONOLOGY, HISTORICAL
*see also Calendars; History-
Yearbooks
also subdivision History-Chronology
under names of countries, e.g. United
States-History-Chronology*
Benedictines de la Congregation de
Saint-Maur. Dictionnaire de l'art
de Verifier les Dates. Migne, J. P.,
ed. (Nouvelle Encyclopedie
Theologique Ser.: Vol. 49). 680p.
(Fr.). Repr. of 1854 ed. lib. bdg.
$86.50x (ISBN 0-89241-287-9).
Caratzas Pub Co.
Haydn, Joseph T. Haydn's
Dictionary of Dates & Universal
Information Relating to All Ages &
Nations. 1968. Repr. of 1911 ed.
$89.00 (ISBN 0-403-00083-1).
Scholarly.
Parker, K. Vocabulario de la Cronica
Troyana. 327p. (Span.). 1958.
150.00 ptas. U de Salamanca.
World Almanac Editors. World
Almanac Dictionary of Dates.
Laurence Urdang, Inc., ed. LC 81-
71772. 320p. 24.95x (ISBN 0-582-
28372-8). Longman.
CHRONOPHOTOGRAPHY
see Cinematography
CHURCH BUILDINGS
see Churches
CHURCH COUNCILS
see Councils and Synods
CHURCH DISCIPLINE
Dictionnaire d'Histoire & de
Geographie Ecclesiastiques. 128p.
(Fr.). 1975. 87.00 F. Letouzey &
Ane.
**CHURCH HISTORY-
DICTIONARIES**
Aubert, Roger & Van Cauwenberg.
Dictionnaire d'histoire & de
Geographie Ecclesiastiques, 16
vols. (Fr.). 4464.00 F. Letouzey &
Ane.
Aubert, Roger, et al. Dictionnaire
d'histoire & de Geographie
Ecclesiastiques. 176p. (Fr.). 88.00
F. Letouzey & Ane.
Dictionnaire d'Histoire & de
Geographie Ecclesiastiques. 128p.
(Fr.). 1975. 87.00 F. Letouzey &
Ane.

Grosse, E. Dictionnaire
d'Antiphilosophisme ou Refutation
des Erreurs du 18e Siecle. Migne,
J. P., ed. (Troisieme et Derniere
Encyclopedie Theologique Ser.:
Vol. 18). 770p. (Fr.). Repr. of
1856 ed. lib. bdg. $97.50x (ISBN
0-89241-301-8). Caratzas Pub Co.
Guerin, L. F. Dictionnaire de
l'Histoire Universelle de l'Eglise, 6
vols. Migne, J. P., ed. (Troisieme
et Derniere Encyclopedie
Theologique Ser.: Vols. 51-56).
4187p. (Fr.). Repr. of 1873 ed. lib.
bdg. $532.50x (ISBN 0-89241-322-
0). Caratzas Pub Co.
**CHURCH HISTORY-PRIMITIVE
AND EARLY CHURCH, ca. 30-600**
Sevestre, A. Dictionnaire de
Patrologie, 4 vols. in 5. Migne, J.
P., ed. (Nouvelle Encyclopedie
Theologique Ser.: Vols. 20-23b).
3830p. (Fr.). Repr. of 1859 ed. lib.
bdg. $485.00x (ISBN 0-89241-267-
4). Caratzas Pub Co.
**CHURCH HISTORY-18TH
CENTURY**
Grosse, E. Dictionnaire
d'Antiphilosophisme ou Refutation
des Erreurs du 18e Siecle. Migne,
J. P., ed. (Troisieme et Derniere
Encyclopedie Theologique Ser.:
Vol. 18). 770p. (Fr.). Repr. of
1856 ed. lib. bdg. $97.50x (ISBN
0-89241-301-8). Caratzas Pub Co.
CHURCH LATIN
see Latin Language-Church Latin
CHURCH LAW
see Ecclesiastical Law
CHURCH SLAVIC LANGUAGE
Lysaght, T. Material Towards the
Compilation of a Concise Old
Church Slavonic-English
Dictionary. LC 79-322674. xiv,
472p. (Eng. & Slavic.). 1978. write
for info. (ISBN 0-7055-0668-1).
Victoria University Press.
Lysaght, T. A. Material Towards the
Compilation of a Concise Old
Church Slavonic-English
Dictionary. LC 79-322674. xiv,
472p. (Slavic & Eng.). 1978. write
for info. (ISBN 0-7055-0668-1).
Price Milburn.
CHURCHES
*see also Cathedrals; Parishes
also names of individual churches;
subdivision Churches under names of
cities*
Huber, Rudolf & Rieth, Renate, eds.
Glossarium Artis: Fasz 4,
Paramente & Buecher der
Christlichen Kirchen. 203p. (Ger.).
DM.35.00 (ISBN 3-484-60049-7).
Max Niemeyer.
CHWEE LANGUAGE
see Twi Language
CHWI LANGUAGE
see Twi Language
**CICERO, MARCUS TULLIUS,
106-43 B.C.**
Kunzer, Paul E. Cicero Vocabularies.
(Bk. I Iv). $1.00 ea. (NO. B10).
Am Classical.
CINEMA
see Moving-Pictures
CINEMATOGRAPHY
*see also Amateur Moving-Pictures;
Television Film*
Alvey, Glenn, Jr. Dizionario dei
termini cinematografici. 180p.
(Ital.). 1952. L.2000.00. Edizioni
Mediterranee.
Beaver, Frank. Dictionary of Film
Terms. (Illus.). 320p. 1983. text
ed. 15.95 (ISBN 0-07-004216-0,
C); pap. text ed. 9.95 (ISBN 0-07-
004212-8). McGraw.
De Poorter, Wim. Filmlexikon. LC
77-572112. 102p. (Dutch). 1976.
fl.14.50 (ISBN 9-0236-5349-1).
Nygh Ditmar.
Pozsonyi, Gabor. Filmgyartas es
Filmtechnika. LC 78-391538.
220p. (Eng., Hungarian, Fr., Ger.
& Rus.). 1975. 50.00 Ft (ISBN 9-
6305-0592-4). Akademiai Kiado.
Salazar Lopez, Jose M. Diccionario
legislativo de cinematografia y
teatro. (Span.). 300.00 ptas.
Nacional Editora.
CIPHERS (LETTERING)
see Monograms
CIRCUITS, ELECTRIC
see Electric Circuits
**CITATION OF LEGAL
AUTHORITIES**
*see also Annotations and Citations
(Law)*

Bryson, William H. A Dictionary of Sigla & Abbreviations to & in Law Books Before 1607. LC 75-5675. (Virginia Legal Studies). 224p. 1975. $20.00x (ISBN 0-8139-0615-6). U Pr of Va.

CITIES AND TOWNS
see also Streets
also headings beginning with the word City, Municipal and Urban; names of individual cities and towns
Capdevila Font, Juan. Diccionario de Citas. 132p. (Span.). 1977. pap. $13.95 (ISBN 84-85117-43-3, S-50580). French & Eur.
De Fleurian, Dominique, et al. Dictionnaire National des Communes de France. 20th ed. (Illus.). 1150p. (Fr.). 1977. 98.00 F. Albin-Michel.
Dictionnaire des Communes. (Illus.). 862p. (Fr.). write for info. Larousse.
Dictionnaire des Communes de la Haute-Saone, 3. 450p. (Fr.). 1971. write for info. M. Bon.
Dictionnaire des Communes de la Haute-Saone, 4. (Fr.). 1972. write for info. M. Bon.
Dictionnaire des Communes de la Haute-Saone, 1. 400p. (Fr.). 1969. write for info. M. Bon.
Dictionnaire des Communes de la Haute-Saone, 2. 416p. (Fr.). 1970. write for info. M. Bon.
Dictionnaire des Communes de la Haute-Saone, 5. (Fr.). 1973. write for info. M. Bon.
Dictionnaire National des Communes de France. rev. ed. 1416p. (Fr.). 1977. 98.00 F. Albin-Michel.
Gache, Roberto. Glosario de la farsa urbana. 120p. (Span.). Arg.$2.40. Centro Ed.
Rousset, A. Dictionnaire Geographique, Historique & Statistique des Communes: Franche-Comte & des Hameaux qui en Dependent, 6 vols. 3602p. (Fr.). 1970. 600.00 F. Guenegaud.

CITIES AND TOWNS–PLANNING
see City Planning

CITIES AND TOWNS–SURVEYING
see Surveying

CITIES AND TOWNS–GERMANY
Sieferl, Fritz, ed. Das Lexikon der Deutschen Staedte & Gemeinden. 576p. (Ger.). 1975. DM.29.00 (ISBN 3-87220-336-3). Fackelverlag.
Siefert, Fritz, ed. Das Lexikon der Deutschen Staedte & Gemeinden. 584p. (Ger.). 1973. DM.26.00 (ISBN 3-517-00453-7). Suedwest.

CITIZENS BAND RADIO
APR Industries Division of Aero Products Research, Inc., ed. The Complete CB Dictionary. 1977. pap. $2.98 (ISBN 0-912682-17-5). Aero Products.
Bradley, William J. CB Fact Book & Language Dictionary. (Illus.). pap. $1.95 (ISBN 0-89552-011-7). DMR Pubns.
Dills, Lanie. The Official CB Slanguage Language Dictionary. 1981. pap. $3.75 (ISBN 0-930414-00-4). Burrows & Baker.
Jacobs, Michael. Complete CB Slang Dictionary. 3rd ed. 1977. pap. 1.50 (ISBN 0-89596-208-X, Success). Merit Pubns.
Murray, Joan. A CB Picture Dictionary. LC 80-1725. (Illus.). 64p. (gr. 5 up). PLB $8.95a (ISBN 0-385-14783-X). Doubleday.

CITIZENS RADIO SERVICE
see Citizens Band Radio

CITY AND TOWN LIFE
Flynn & Montoto. Spanish for Urban Workers. (Span.). $9.95; pap. $7.75. Camino Real.

CITY GOVERNMENT
see Municipal Government

CITY LIFE
see City and Town Life

CITY PLANNING
see also Housing; Urban Transportation; Zoning
Calsat, Jean-Henri. Vocabulaire International des Termes d'urbanisme & d'architecture: Francais-Allemand-Anglais. (Illus.). 350p. (Fr., Ger. & Eng.). 1970. 250.00 F. Eyrolles.
Calsat, Jean-Henri & Sydler, Jean P. Vocabulaire International des Termes d'Urbanisme et d'Architecture. 350p. (Fr., Ger. & Eng.). 1970. $95.00 (ISBN 0-686-56935-0, M-6057). French & Eur.
International Vocabulary of Town Planning & Architecture. LC 70-860237. (Illus.). 366p. (Fr., Ger. & Eng.). 1970. $55.00x (ISBN 0-8002-1582-6). Intl Pubns Serv.
Petroni & Kenigsberg. Diccionario de urbanismo. (Span.). Arg.$9.00. Cesarini.
Vocabulaire de l'urbanisme. 53p. (Fr.). 1971. 16.05 F. C. N. I. P. E.

CITY PLANNING–BIBLIOGRAPHY
U. S. Department of Housing & Urban Development, Washington, D. C. Dictionary Catalog of the United States Department of Housing & Urban Development Library & Information Division, 19 vols. 1972. Set. lib. bdg. $1805.00 (ISBN 0-8161-1007-7, Hall Library). G K Hall.

CITY PLANNING–ZONE SYSTEM
see Zoning

CITY SURVEYING
see Surveying

CITY TRANSIT
see Local Transit

CITY TRANSPORTATION
see Urban Transportation

CIVIC PLANNING
see City Planning

CIVICS
Here are entered general works and works about the United States in particular. For works dealing with specific states see names of individual states, with or without the subdivision Politics and Government.
see also Civil Rights
Karcsay, Sandor. Ungarisch-Deutsches Woerterbuch der Rechts & Verwaltungssprache: Teil I, Ungarisch-Deutsch. xix, 487p. (Hungarian & Ger.). 1969. DM.48.00. Recht & Wirtschaft.
--Ungarisch-Deutsches Woerterbuch der Rechts & Verwaltungssprache: Teil II, Deutsch-Ungarisch. xvii, 427p. (Ger. & Hungarian.). 1972. DM.48.00. Recht & Wirtschaft.

CIVIL ENGINEERING
see also Arches; Dams; Drainage; Foundations; Hydraulic Engineering; Irrigation; Marine Engineering; Masonry; Mining Engineering; Public Works; Railroad Engineering; Rivers; Roads; Sanitary Engineering; Streets; Strength of Materials; Surveying; Water-Supply Engineering
also subdivision Public Works under names of countries, cities, etc. e.g. United States–Public Works
Lates, Ernest M., et al. Dictionar Poliglot. LC 79-393899. xviii, 827p. (Eng., Romanian, Ger., Fr & Rus.). 1979. 91.00 lei. Editura Stiintifica.

CIVIL ENGINEERING–DICTIONARIES
American Society of Civil Engineers, compiled By. Definitions of Surveying & Associated Terms. (Manual & Report on Engineering Practice Ser.: No. 34). 216p. 1978. pap. $8.00 (ISBN 0-87262-211-8). Am Soc Civil Eng.
Bucksch, H. Dictionary of Civil Engineering & Construction Machinery & Equipment, 2 vols. 7th ed. 420p. 1979. Vol. 1, Eng.-Fr. 35.00x (ISBN 0-8002-2313-6); Vol. 2, Fr.-Eng. 45.00x (ISBN 0-8002-2314-4). Intl Pubns Serv.
--Woerterbuch fuer Bautechnik & Baumaschinen: Band I, Deutsch-Englisch. 1184p. (Ger. & Eng.). 1982. DM.160.00 (ISBN 3-7625-2032-1). Bauverlag.
--Woerterbuch fuer Bautechnik & Baumaschinen: Band II, Englisch-Deutsch. 1219p. (Eng. & Ger.). 1982. DM.160.00 (ISBN 3-7625-2034-8). Bauverlag.
--Woerterbuch fuer Bautechnik und Baumaschinen. 4th ed. (Ger. & Fr.). 1976. pap. $112.00 (ISBN 0-686-56607-6, M-6922). French & Eur.
Bucksch, Herbert. Dictionary of Civil Engineering & Construction Machinery & Equipment, Vol. 1. 5th ed. 420p. (Fr. & Eng.). 1976. $30.00 (ISBN 3-7625-0533-0, M-7120). French & Eur.
--Dictionary of Civil Engineering & Construction Machinery & Equipment, Vol. 1. 7th ed. (Eng. & Ger.). 1978. leatherette $135.00 (ISBN 3-7625-0950-6, M-7122). French & Eur.
--Dictionary of Civil Engineering & Construction Machinery & Equipment, Vol. 2. 5th ed. 548p. (Fr. & Eng.). 1976. $40.00 (ISBN 3-7625-0534-9, M-7119). French & Eur.
--Dictionary of Civil Engineering & Construction Machinery & Equipment, Vol. 2. 7th ed. (Eng. & Ger.). 1978. leatherette $135.00 (ISBN 3-7625-0951-4, M-7121). French & Eur.
Building Industry & Civil Engineering Society. Dictionary of Technical Information, Vol. 41. 210p. 1980. $15.00x (ISBN 0-569-08243-9, Pub. by Collet's). State Mutual Bk.
Dictionary of Civil Engineering & Construction Machinery & Equipment, 2 vols. 4th ed. 1180p. 1978. plastic bdg. 90.00x ea. Vol. 1, Ger-Eng (ISBN 3-7625-0502-0). Vol. 2, Eng.-Ger (ISBN 3-7625-0950-6). Intl Pubns Serv.
English-Chinese Dictionary of Civil & Architectural Engineering Terms. 706p. (Eng. & Chinese.). 1979. $29.95 (ISBN 0-686-97359-3, M-9271). French & Eur.
Huerlimann, Ernst. Lexikon Feurden Bauherrn. (Ger.). 1975. $28.50 (ISBN 3-478-04250-X, M-7202). French & Eur.
Research & Education Association. Technical Dictionary for Civil Engineers. 1408p. 1981. 32.65 (ISBN 0-87891-531-1). Res & Educ.
Robb, Louis A. Engineers' Dictionary, Spanish-English, English-Spanish. 2nd ed. (Span. & Eng.). 1949. $49.50 (ISBN 0-471-72501-3, Pub. by Wiley-Interscience). Wiley.
Scott, John S. Dictionary of Civil Engineering. 3rd ed. LC 80-24419. 308p. 1982. 22.95x (ISBN 0-470-27087-X). Halsted Pr.
Steinig, Karl. Woerterbuch fuer Strassenbau und Strassenverkehe. (Fr. & Ger.). 1970. $92.00 (ISBN 3-7812-0560-6, M-6921). French & Eur.

CIVIL ENGINEERING–ESTIMATES AND COSTS
see Engineering–Estimates and Costs

CIVIL GOVERNMENT
see Political Science

CIVIL LAW
see also Roman Law
Diccionario indice de jurisprudencia civil 1947-1956. (Span.). 1958. 400.00 ptas. Bosch Casa.
Pallares, Eduardo. Diccionario de Derecho Procesal Civil. 877p. (Span.). $37.50 (ISBN 0-686-56687-4, S-12340). French & Eur.

CIVIL LAW–ROME
see Roman Law

CIVIL LAW (ROMAN LAW)
see Roman Law

CIVIL-MILITARY RELATIONS
see Militarism

CIVIL RIGHTS
Lexique Francais-Arabe de la Protection Civile & du Secourisme. (Fr. & Arabic.). 14.00 F. France Selection.
Mosler, Hermann, et al, eds. Woerterbuch des Voelkerrechts: Bd 2, Ibero-Amerikanismus bis Quirin-Fall. (Ger.). 1961. DM.225.00 (ISBN 3-11-001031-3). De Gruyter.
--Woerterbuch des Voelkerrechts: Bd 3, Rapollo-Vertrag bis Zypern. (Ger.). 1962. DM.50.00 (ISBN 3-11-001033-X). De Gruyter.
Pallares, Eduardo. Diccionario de Derecho Procesal Civil. 13th ed. 880p. (Span.). 1981. Mex.$500.00. Porrua.
Quintano Heilpern. Diccionario juridico aleman-espanol de derecho comparado: Con vocabulario juridico espanol-aleman. (Ger. & Span.). 525.00 ptas. Rev Derecho Pri.
Strupp, Karl, et al, eds. Woerterbuch des Voelkerrechts: Bd 1, Aachener Kongress-Hussar Fall. (Ger.). 1960. DM.225.00 (ISBN 3-11-001030-5). De Gruyter.

CIVIL SERVICE
see also Administrative Law
also subdivision Officials and Employees–Appointments, Qualifications, Tenure, etc. under the names of countries, cities, etc. e.g. United States–Officials and Employees–Appointments, Qualifications, Tenure, etc.
Bierfelder, Wilhelm, ed. Handwoerterbuch des Oeffentlichen Dienstes. LC 77-457292. (Illus., Ger.). DM.228.00 (ISBN 3-503-01424-1). Schmidt Verlag.

CIVIL SERVICE–EXAMINATIONS
see Civil Service Examinations

CIVIL SERVICE EXAMINATIONS
Here are entered general works and works on United States civil service examinations. Examinations for specific cities in the United States or for countries other than the United States are entered under the appropriate subdivisions.
Rudman, Jack. Civil Service Vocabulary. (Career Examination Ser.: C-S 10). (Cloth bdg. avail. on request). pap. 6.00 (ISBN 0-8373-3760-7). Natl Learning.
Turner, David R. Vocabulary, Spelling & Grammar. 9th ed. LC 70-153705. (Orig.). 1975. pap. $6.00 (ISBN 0-668-00077-5). Arco.

CIVIL WAR–UNITED STATES
see United States–History–Civil War, 1861-1865

CIVILIZATION
Includes works treating of culture or civilization in general. Literature dealing with the culture of peoples and races ordinarily classed as civilized and not confined to one country are entered under the headings Civilization, Greek; Civilization, Germanic; Civilization, Homeric; etc.; Works on the civilization of a single country are entered under the name of the country with the subdivision Civilization, e.g. United States–Civilization; Works treating of the culture of uncivilized tribes are entered under the name of the tribe.
see also Anthropology; Archaeology; Art; Culture; Education; Inventions; Manners and Customs; Renaissance; Social Problems; Social Sciences
Wiener, Philip P., ed. Dictionary of the History of Ideas, 5 vols. LC 72-7943. 1973. Set. text ed. $275.00 (ISBN 0-684-13293-1, ScribR); pap. $100.00 (ISBN 0-684-16418-3). Scribner.

CIVILIZATION, AMERICAN
see Latin America–Civilization

CIVILIZATION, ARAB
Ronart, Nandy. Lexikon der Arabischen Welt. (Ger.). $184.00 (ISBN 3-7608-0138-2, M-7277). French & Eur.

CIVILIZATION, GREEK
see also Hellenism
Dictionnaire de la Civilisation Grecque. 500p. (Fr.). 1966. $36.95 (ISBN 0-686-57098-7, M-6122). French & Eur.
Rachet, G. & Rachet, M. F. Dictionnaire civilisation Grecque. (Illus., Fr.). pap. $8.50 (ISBN 0-685-13861-5, 3715). Larousse.
Winniczuk, Lida. Maly Slownik Kultury Antycznej. LC 76-523030. (Illus.). 674p. (Pol.). 1976. 110.00 Zl. Wiedza Powszechna.

CIVILIZATION, INDO-EUROPEAN
see Indo-Europeans

CIVILIZATION, ROMAN
see Rome–Civilization

CLASSES (MATHEMATICS)
see Set Theory

CLASSICAL ANTIQUITIES–DICTIONARIES
see Classical Dictionaries

CLASSICAL ATLASES
see Classical Geography

CLASSICAL DANCING
see Modern Dance

CLASSICAL DICTIONARIES

Blackman, R. D. A Dictionary of Foreign Phrases & Classical Quotations. Repr. of 1893 ed. 25.00 (ISBN 0-686-20089-6). Quality Lib.

Hammond, N. G. & Scullard, H. H., eds. Oxford Classical Dictionary. 2nd ed. 1970. 45.00 (ISBN 0-19-869117-3). Oxford U Pr.

Jones, Hugh P., ed. A New Dictionary of Foreign Phrases & Classical Quotations. 532p. 1981. Repr. of 1902 ed. lib. bdg. $75.00 (ISBN 0-89984-264-X). Century Bookbindery.

Kroh, Paul. Woerterbuch der Antike: Mit Beruecks Ihres Fortwirkens. Bux, E. & Schoene, W., eds. LC 76-475045. 832p. (Ger.). 1976. DM.25.00 (ISBN 3-520-09608-0). Kroener.

Lempriere, J. A. A Classical Dictionary, 2 vols. Set. lib. bdg. 250.00 (ISBN 0-87968-878-5). Gordon Pr.

Le Mot Juste. (Fr.). $3.50. Longman.

Le Mot Juste: A Dictionary of Foreign & Classical Words & Phrases. write for info. (ISBN 0-333-30583-3). Macmillan.

Seyffert, Oskar. Dictionary of Classical Antiquities. rev. ed. Nettleship, ed. (Illus.). 18.00 (ISBN 0-8446-2910-3). Peter Smith.

Smith, William, ed. Dictionary of Greek & Roman Biography & Mythology, 3 Vols. LC 11-24983. (Gr. & Lat.). Repr. of 1890 ed. Set. $210.00 (ISBN 0-404-06130-3). AMS Pr.

--Dictionary of Greek & Roman Geography, 2 Vols. LC 4-14843. (Gr.). Repr. of 1873 ed. Set. $125.00 (ISBN 0-404-06134-6). AMS Pr.

Starnes, DeWitt T. & Talbert, Ernest W. Classical Myth & Legend in Renaissance Dictionaries. LC 73-11753. (Illus.). 517p. 1973. Repr. of 1955 ed. lib. bdg. 39.75x (ISBN 0-8371-7086-9, STCM). Greenwood.

Stephanus, Charles. Dictionarium Historicum, Geographicum, Poeticum. LC 75-27859. (Renaissance & the Gods Ser.: Vol. 16). (Illus.). 1976. Repr. of 1596 ed. lib. bdg. 80.00 (ISBN 0-8240-2065-0). Garland Pub.

Vial, Claude. Lexique d'antiquites Grecques. 272p. (Fr.). 1972. 20.60 F. Colin.

Warrington, John. Everyman's Classical Dictionary. 3rd rev. ed. (Everyman's Reference Library). 537p. 1978. Repr. of 1969 ed. $11.00 (ISBN 0-460-03004-3, Pub. by J. M. Dent England). Biblio Dist.

Wright, F. A., ed. Lempriere's Classical Dictionary. new rev. ed. 1969. Repr. of 1788 ed. $22.00 (ISBN 0-7100-1734-0). Routledge & Kegan.

CLASSICAL GEOGRAPHY

see also Geography, Ancient

Smith, William, ed. Dictionary of Greek & Roman Geography, 2 Vols. LC 4-14843. (Gr.). Repr. of 1873 ed. Set. $125.00 (ISBN 0-404-06134-6). AMS Pr.

CLASSICAL MYTHOLOGY

see Mythology, Classical

CLASSICAL PHILOLOGY

Here are entered treatises on the theory, methods and history of classical scholarship.

see also Greek Language; Hellenism

Vocabulaire des Animaux Marins en Latin Classique. 154p. (Fr.). 1947. 32.00 F. Klincksieck.

CLASSIFICATION-BOOKS-CHINA

Cordier, Henri. Bibliotheca Sinica, dictionnaire bibliographique des ouvrages relatifs a l'Empire chinois, 6 vols. in 5. 2nd ed. LC 68-58196. (Bibliography & Research Ser.: No. 250). (Span., Chinese & Fr.). 1969. Repr. of 1922 ed. $200.00 (ISBN 0-8337-0671-3). B Franklin.

CLASSIFICATION-BOTANY

see Botany-Classification

CLASSIFICATION-DISEASES

see Nosology

CLASSIFICATION-PLANTS

see Botany-Classification

CLAY

see also Ceramics

Passebecq, Andre. L'argile pour votre Sante. LC 80-471204. 129p. (Fr.). 1978. 27.00 F (ISBN 2-7033-0192-8). Dangles.

CLEANING COMPOUNDS

see also Soap and Soap Trade

International Fabricare Institute. Terms Related to Soap & Detergents. (Fabric Care Ser.). $0.25 (FC-20). Intl Fabricare Inst.

CLEANING PREPARATIONS

see Cleaning Compounds

CLEANSERS (COMPOUNDS)

see Cleaning Compounds

CLEMENS, SAMUEL LANGHORNE, 1835-1910

Emberson, Frances G. Mark Twain's Vocabulary. 1978. Repr. of 1935 ed. lib. bdg. 10.00 (ISBN 0-8495-1316-2). Arden Lib.

--Mark Twain's Vocabulary. 53p. 1980. Repr. of 1935 ed. lib. bdg. $12.50 (ISBN 0-89987-206-9). Darby Bks.

--Mark Twain's Vocabulary. LC 73-16345. 1935. lib. bdg. $15.00 (ISBN 0-8414-3922-2). Folcroft.

CLIMATE

see Climatology

CLIMATOLOGY

see also Meteorology; Weather

also names of countries, cities, etc. with or without the subdivision Climate

Villeneuve, G. O. & Ferland, M. G. Glossaire De Meteorologie et De Climatologie. LC 75-501061. 560p. (Fr.). 1974. $29.95 (ISBN 0-686-57246-7, M-6552). French & Eur.

Villeneuve, Georges O. & Ferland, Michel G. Glossaire de Meteorologie & de Climatologie. 550p. (Fr.). 1974. DM.20.00. Laval P. U.

CLINICAL CHEMISTRY

see Chemistry, Clinical

CLINICAL ENGINEERING

see Biomedical Engineering

CLINICAL MEDICINE

see Medicine, Clinical

CLINICAL PSYCHOLOGY

Benesch, Hellmuth. Woerterbuch zur klinischen Psychologie, 2 vols. (Ger.). DM.22.80. Deutscher Taschenbuch.

CLINICAL RADIOLOGY

see Radiology, Medical

CLINICS

see also Group Medical Practice

Cooper, Hellen H. Vocabulario Ingles-Espanol para Servicio Clinico. (Eng. & Span.). $0.80; Mex.$10.00. Pax.

CLOCKS AND WATCHES

Britten, F. J. Britten's Watch & Clock Maker's Handbook, Dictionary & Guide. 16th rev. ed. Good, Richard, ed. LC 78-3539. (Illus.). 1978. $69.95 (ISBN 0-668-04638-4). Arco.

--Watch & Clockmakers' Handbook, Dictionary & Guide. (Illus.). 499p. 1978. Repr. of 1907 ed. $29.50 (ISBN 0-902028-46-4). Antique Collect.

CLOCKS AND WATCHES-REPAIRING AND ADJUSTING

Tardy. Dictionnaire des Horlogers Francais. (Illus.). 350p. (Fr.). 195.00 F. Tardy-Lengelle.

CLOTH

see Textile Fabrics

CLOTHIERS

see Clothing Trade

CLOTHING

see Costume

CLOTHING AND DRESS-CLEANING

see Dry Cleaning

CLOTHING TRADE

Schierbaum, Wilfried, ed. Bekleidungslexikon. LC 78-381510. (Illus.). 338p. (Ger.). 1978. DM.58.00 (ISBN 3-7949-0305-6). Schiele & Schoen.

COACHES

see Carriages and Carts

COAL-DICTIONARIES

Lexique International de Petrographie des Charbons. 2nd ed. (Illus.). 160p. (Fr.). 1963. 67.70 F. CNRS.

Lexique International de Petrographie des Charbons. 250p. (Fr.). 1971. 67.40 F. CNRS.

Todd, A. H. Lexicon of Terms Relating to the Assessment & Classification of Coal Resources. 140p. 1983. $55.00x (ISBN 0-8448-1438-5). Crane-Russak Co.

COAL MINES AND MINING

Preston, Dennis. Bituminous Coal Mining Vocabulary of the Eastern United States. (Publication of the American Dialect Society: No. 59). (Illus.). 96p. (Orig.). 1973. pap. $7.70 (ISBN 0-8173-0659-5). U of Ala Pr.

Todd, A. H. Lexicon of Terms Relating to the Assessment & Classification of Coal Resources. 140p. 1982. $99.00x (ISBN 0-86010-403-6, Pub. by Graham & Trotman England). State Mutual Bk.

COAL OIL

see Petroleum

COASTAL SIGNALS

see Signals and Signaling

COATED PAPER

see Paper Coatings

COATS OF ARMS

see Devices; Heraldry

COCHITI INDIANS

see Indians of North America-Southwest, New

CODE NAMES

see also Acronyms

Ruffner, Frederick G., Jr. & Thomas, Robert C., eds. Code Names Dictionary: A Guide to Code Names, Slang, Nicknames, Journalese, & Similar Terms. LC 63-21847. 1963. $38.00x (ISBN 0-8103-0685-9). Gale.

COGNITION

Battro, A. M. Dictionnaire d'Epistemologie Genetique. 188p. (Fr.). 1966. $29.00 (ISBN 90-277-0002-8, Pub. by Reidel Holland). Kluwer Academic.

COIFFURE

see Hairdressing

COIN COLLECTING

see Numismatics-Collectors and Collecting

COINAGE OF WORDS

see Words, New

COINS

Here are entered lists of coins, specimens, etc. Works about coins are entered under the heading numismatics.

De Salzade, M. Dictionnaire historique des monnoies tant anciennes que modernes. LC 79-359296. (Illus.). 187p. (Fr.). 1978. 32.00 F. Thimonier.

Dictionary & Auction Catalogues of the Library of the American Numismatic Society: Third Supplement. 1978. lib. bdg. $195.00 (ISBN 0-8161-0247-3, Hall Library). G K Hall.

COINS-COLLECTORS AND COLLECTING

see Numismatics-Collectors and Collecting

COINS, GREEK

Florance, A. Geographical Lexicon of Greek Coin Inscriptions. (Gr.). 1978. pap. $10.00 (ISBN 0-89005-232-8). Ares.

Icard, S. Dictionary of Greek Coin Inscriptions. (Gr. & Eng.). 1979. 30.00 (ISBN 0-916710-42-4); pap. 20.00 (ISBN 0-916710-43-2). Obol Intl.

Icard, Severin. Dictionary of Greek Coin Inscriptions. (Gr. & Eng.). 1979. Repr. of 1920 ed. lib. bdg. $42.50 (ISBN 0-915262-31-2). S J Durst.

COINS, ROMAN

Stevenson. Dictionary Roman Coins. 1982. Repr. of 1892 ed. lib. bdg. 40.00 (ISBN 0-686-45266-6, Pub. by B A Seaby England). S J Durst.

COLEOPTERA

see Beetles

COLLEGE ATHLETICS

see Track-Athletics

COLLEGE EMPLOYEES

see Universities and Colleges-Employees

COLLEGE FACULTY

see College Teachers

COLLEGE LIBRARIES

see Libraries, University and College

COLLEGE LIFE

see College Students

COLLEGE STUDENTS

Hall, Benjamin H. Collection of College Words & Customs. LC 68-17995. 1968. Repr. of 1856 ed. $42.00x (ISBN 0-8103-3282-5). Gale.

COLLEGE TEACHERS

Abel, Emily K. Terminal Degree: The Job Crisis in Higher Education. 250p. 1984. $24.95 (ISBN 0-686-89487-1). Praeger.

COLLEGES

see Universities and Colleges

COLLOIDS

Anglo-Russkii Slovar Po Kholodil Noi i Kriogennoi Tekhnike. 468p. (Rus. & Eng.). 1978. $8.95 (Pub. by Russkii Iazyk). Four Continent.

COLLOQUIAL ENGLISH

see English Language-Conversation and Phrase Books; English Language-Spoken English

COLOMBIA

Florez, L. Lexico del cuerpo humano en Colombia. (Span.). 1966. write for info. Inst Caro y Cuervo.

COLOMBIA-DESCRIPTION AND TRAVEL

Florez, L. Lexico de la casa popular urbano en Bolivar, Colombia. (Span.). 1962. write for info. Inst Caro y Cuervo.

COLONIAL ARCHITECTURE

see Architecture, Colonial

COLOR

see also Colors; Dyes and Dyeing

Lexikon in Farbe. (Ger.). 1974. DM.725.00 (ISBN 3-85012-018-X). Andreas & Andreas.

COLOR-TERMINOLOGY

Federation of Societies for Coatings Technology, Definitions Committee, ed. Glossary of Color Terms. 96p. $6.00 (ISBN 0-686-95498-X). Fed Soc Coat Tech.

COLORS

see also Color

Cohen, Viviane. Dictionnaire des Couleurs. (Illus., Fr.). 1973. write for info. Paris Livre de Odege.

--Dictionnaire des Couleurs. (Illus.). 24p. (Fr.). 1973. write for info. Livre de Paris.

COLUMBIA UNIVERSITY-TEACHERS COLLEGE

Columbia University, Teachers College Library. Dictionary Catalog of the Teachers College Library, Columbia University, Third Supplement. 1977. lib. bdg. $1050.00 (ISBN 0-8161-0017-9, Hall Library). G K Hall.

COLUMNISTS

see Journalists

COMANCHE INDIANS

see Indians of North America-The West

COMEDY

Dictionnaires des Comediens Francais, 2 vols. (Fr.). 1969. write for info. Slatkine.

COMIC LITERATURE

see Comedy

COMMENTATORS

see Journalists

COMMERCE

see also Balance of Trade; Business; Communication and Traffic; Inland Navigation; Insurance, Marine; Maritime Law; Merchant Marine; Merchants; Money; Shipping; Trade-Marks

also subdivision Commerce under names of countries, cities, etc.; names of articles of commerce, e.g. Cotton, Leather, Lumber; headings beginning with the word Commercial

Brunner, Victor. Diccionario de Siglas en Comercio Exterior. LC 77-566386. (Illus.). 125p. (Span.). 1977. Arg.$70.00. Liv Nobel.

Eksportno-Importnyi Slovar, 3 vols. (Rus.). 1954. $18.00 set (Pub. by Vneshtorgizdat). Four Continent.

Falk, Bernard & Wolf, Jakob. Handlexikon fuer Handel & Absatz. LC 80-469758. (Illus.). 750p. (Ger.). 1979. DM.48.00 (ISBN 3-478-24150-2). Verlag Moderne Industrie.

Israelevich, E. E. English-Russian Dictionary of Finance & World Trade. 544p. (Eng. & Rus.). $10.50. Imported Bks.

Lexique Commente de la Douane & du Commerce Exterieur. 307p. (Fr.). 1973. 500.00 F. Editorial Office.

COMMERCE–DICTIONARIES

Bagma, L. T. Kratkii Nemetsko-Russkii Vneshnetorgovyi Slovar. 480p. (Ger. & Rus.). 1954. $2.95 (Pub. by Vneshtorgizdat). Four Continent.

Becker, H. Dictionnaire trilingue du Droit des Affaires pour le Commerce & l'industrie: Allemand-Anglais-Francais & index. 2nd ed. 992p. (Ger., Eng. & Fr.). 1980. 420.00 F. Maison Dictionnaire.

Birkhauser-Boston Publishing. The Herbst-Readett Three-Language Dictionaries of Commerce, Finance & Law, 3 Vols. (Eng., Ger. & Fr.). 1983. Vol. 1 1979 English-German-French. $98.95 (ISBN 0-686-87520-6); Vol. 2 1982 German-English-French. $98.95 (ISBN 0-686-87521-4); Vol. 3 1983 French-English-German. $98.95 (ISBN 0-686-87522-2). Birkhauser.

Budic, D. W. Diccionario del comercia exterior. (Span.). Arg.$15.00. Ergon.

Centre International Du Droit Des Affaires (CIDA) Lexique Pratique Commercial. (Fr.). 1973. pap. $25.00x (ISBN 2-85273-001-4). Marlin.

C.I.D.A. Lexique Commercial: Tout le vocabulaire des affaires. 450p. (Eng. & Fr.). 1974. 80.00 F. Maison Dictionnaire.

Clara, Cenni. Dizionarietto fraseologico commerciale italiano-inglese. 184p. (Ital.). L.2500.00. Trevisini.

Clara, Cenni & Clotilde, Sandri. Dizionarietto fraseologico commerciale italiano-francese. 152p. (Ital. & Fr.). L.2000.00. Trevisini.

Diccionario de terminos comerciales. 623p. (Span.). 1963. 500.00 ptas. Hispano Europa.

Dictionnaire Commerciale. 297p. (Fr.). 1979. pap. $49.95 (ISBN 2-85319-069-2, M-9307). French & Eur.

Duse, Ada. Dizionario commerciale fraseologico italiano-inglese, inglese-italiano. 736p. (Ital. & Eng.). 1975. L.5000.00. Bignami.

--Dizionario fraseologico commerciale italiano-francese e francese-italiano. 538p. (Ital. & Fr.). 1973. L.5000.00. Bignami.

Emolumento, Vincenzo. Dizionario commerciale francese-italiano. 536p. (Fr. & Ital.). 1978. L.8000.00 (ISBN 88-7075-024-8). Editrice Bibliografica.

--Dizionario commerciale italiano-francese. 656p. (Ital. & Fr.). 1975. L.8000.00 (ISBN 88-7075-006-X). Bibliografica.

Frias, A. Diccionario comercial: Espanol-ingles e ingles-espanol. 2nd ed. 304p. (Span. & Eng.). 1965. 120.00 ptas. Juventud.

Frias-Sucre, Alejandro. Diccionario comercial Ingles-Espanol, Espanol-Ingles. 304p. (Span.). 1981. write for info. (ISBN 84-261-1223-4). Fed Gremios.

Frias-Sucre Giraud, Alejandro. Diccionario Comercial Espanol-Ingles: El Secretario. 4th ed. 144p. (Span. & Eng.). 1981. 1200.00 ptas (ISBN 84-261-1223-4). Juventud.

--Diccionario Comercial Espanol-Ingles y Ingles-Espanol. 3rd ed. 145p. (Span. & Eng.). 1977. $10.75 (ISBN 84-261-1223-4, S-14158). French & Eur.

Gaballi Prat, P. Diccionario De Terminos Comerciales. 634p. (Eng. & Span.). 1963. $32.95 (ISBN 84-255-0295-0, S-31618). French & Eur.

Giraud, Alejandro F. S. Diccionario Comercial Ingles-Espanol, Espanol-Ingles. 304p. (Eng. & Span.). 1981. write for info. (ISBN 84-261-1223-4). Editorial Juventud.

Grossmann & Friedmann. Kaufmannisches Grundworte Buch Fur Schule und Praxis. 280p. (Ger. -Eng., Dictionary of Commerce for School and Practice). $14.50 (ISBN 3-87217-300-6, M-7494, Pub. by Fachverlag Th. Grossmann). French & Eur.

Hakki, Mamdouh. Dictionnaire Des Terms Juridiques et Commerciaux (Francais-Arabe) 1973. $20.00x (ISBN 0-86685-108-9). Intl Bk Ctr.

Hamblock, Dieter. Englisch in Wirtschaft und Handel, Vol. 2. (Eng. & Ger.). 1977. DM.15.95 (ISBN 3-7736-3351-3). Girardet.

--Englische in Wirtschaft und Handel, Vol. 1. (Eng. & Ger.). 1977. DM.pap. 15.95 (ISBN 3-7736-3350-5). Girardet.

Hansen, Mamdouh. A Dictionary of Economics & Commerce. 496p. (Eng. & Arabic., With Eng. & Arabic Glossary). $20.00 (066-X). Intl Bk Ctr.

Hanson, J. L. Dictionary of Economics & Commerce. 5th ed. 472p. 1981. pap. $17.50x (ISBN 0-7121-0424-0). Intl Ideas.

Henni, Mustapha. Dictionnaire des termes economiques et commerciaux. 412p. (Arabic, Fr. & Eng.). $20.00 (109-7). Intl Bk Ctr.

Herbst, Robert. Dictionary of Commerce, Finance & Law. (Eng. & Ger.). 1975. $92.00 (ISBN 3-85942-003-8, M-7118). French & Eur.

Herbst, Robert & Readett, Alan G. The Herbst Dictionaries of Commercial, Financial & Legal Terms Vol. I. (The Herbst Dictionaries; 3-Language Ser.). 1138p. (Eng., Ger. & Fr.). 1979. text ed. $98.95 (ISBN 3-85942-000-3). Birkhauser.

Herbst, Robert & Readett, Alan G., eds. The Herbst Dictionaries of Commercial, Financial & Legal Terms Vol. 2. (The Herbst Dictioaries; 3-Language Ser.). 1106p. (Ger., Eng. & Fr.). 1979. text ed. $98.95 (ISBN 3-85942-006-2). Birkhauser.

--Herbst Dictionary of Commercial, Financial & Legal Terms. (Three-Language Ser.: Vol. 3). 980p. (Fr., Eng. & Ger.). 1979. text ed. $98.95 (ISBN 3-85942-002-X). Birkhauser.

--Herbst Dictionay of Commercial, Financial & Legal Terms. (Two-Language Ser.: Vol. A). 688p. (Eng. & Ger.). 1975. text ed. $69.95 (ISBN 0-686-97268-6). Birkhauser.

Isaacs, Alan. The Multilingual Commercial Dictionary. 485p. 1978. $25.00. Facts on File.

Jannini Pasquale, A. Vocabolario commerciale italiano-francese e francese-italiano, Caputo Cataldo. xii, 260p. (Ital. & Fr.). 1978. L.8000.00. Monnier.

Kettridge, J. O. French-English & English-French Dictionary of Commercial & Financial Terms. 655p. (Fr. & Eng.). 1978. $32.00. Routledge & Kegan.

Kohls, S. Oekonomisches Woerterbuch Aussenwirtschaft. 619p. (Ger., Rus., Eng., Fr. & Span., Dictionary of Economics (Foriegn Trade)). 1972. $38.00 (ISBN 3-87106-018-6, M-7574, Pub. by Ruceken Vlg). French & Eur.

Kohls, V. Economics & Foreign Trade Dictionary. 619p. 1980. $90.00x (ISBN 0-686-72095-4, Pub. by Collet's). State Mutual Bk.

Kolpakov, B. T., et al. Kratkii Vneshnetorgovyi Slovar. 544p. (Rus.). 1954. $1.50 (Pub. by Vneshtorgizdat). Four Continent.

Lamming, Anne, compiled by. A Co-operator's Dictionary: Basic List of Co-operative & Commercial Terms for Use at Primary Level in Developing Countries. LC 77-3716170. 59p. (Eng.). 1977. E1.00 (ISBN 0-904380-26-2). Intl Coop All.

Libr. du Liban, ed. A Dictionary of Economics & Commerce. (Eng. & Arabic.). pap. $7.95 (0-76-7). Intl Bk Ctr.

Lugo-Guernelli, A., et al. Manuel De Gramatica Comercial. 204p. (Eng. & Span.). 1976. pap. $9.95 (ISBN 84-7119-018-4, S-50369). French & Eur.

Martius, T. Dictionary of International Trade Fairs, 3 vols. 1267p. 1980. $70.00x set (ISBN 0-569-05140-1, Pub. by Collet's). State Mutual Bk.

Michel, Raoul & Pardel-Lans, Humbert. Dictionnaire-Formulaire Commercial. 152p. (Fr.). 1953. 7.00 F. Foucher.

Mitra, Ashok. Terms of Trade & Class Relations: An Essay in Political Economy. 208p. 1977. $30.00x (ISBN 0-7146-3083-7, F Cass Co). Biblio Dist.

Mormile, Mario. Dictionnaire Commercial: Italien-Francais Francais-Italien. 650p. (Ital. & Fr.). 1978. 150.00 F. Maison Dictionnaire.

--Dizionario commerciale italiano-francese e francese-italiano. 622p. (Ital. & Fr.). 1979. L.18000.00. Bulzoni.

--Dizionario Commerciale Italiano-Francese, Francese-Italiano. LC 79-352644. xxv, 622p. (Fr. & Ital.). 1978. L.18000.00. Maison Dictionnaire.

Multilengua Diccionario de Cartas Comerciales en Cuatro Idiomas, 3 vols. 972p. (Eng., Span., Ger. & Fr.). 1975. Set. $120.00 (ISBN 84-221-0412-1, S-50102). French & Eur.

Munniksma, F., ed. International Business Dictionary in Nine Languages. 1974. $45.00x (ISBN 90-267-0394-5, 1526). Esperanto League North Am.

Oekonomisches Woerterbuch Aussenwirtschaft. (Ger. , Rus. , Span. , Eng. & Fr.). M.48.00. Wissenschaftliche.

Orozco, C. R. Spanish-English, English-Spanish Commercial Dictionary. (Span. & Eng.). 1969. 23.00 (ISBN 0-08-006381-0); pap. 12.00 (ISBN 0-08-006380-2). Pergamon.

Postlethwayt, Malachy. Universal Dictionary of Trade & Commerce, 2 Vols. 4th ed. LC 67-29516. Repr. of 1774 ed. Set. 250.00x (ISBN 0-678-00551-6). Kelley.

Potonnier. Woerterbuch fuer Wirtschaft, Recht & Handel: Band I, Deutsch-Franzoesisch. 1616p. (Ger. & Fr.). 1982. DM.130.00. Brandstetter.

--Woerterbuch fuer Wirtschaft, Recht & Handel: Band II, Franzoesisch-Deutsch. 1502p. (Fr. & Ger.). 1982. DM.100.00. Brandstetter.

Potonnier, Georges E. & Potonnier, Brigitte. Woerterbuch Wirtschaft Recht Handel: Deutsch-Franzoesisch, Vol. 2. 1486p. (Fr. & Ger.). 1970. 330.00 F. Maison Dictionnaire.

Rossi, Gualtiero. Dizionario inglese-italiano e italiano-inglese con glossario bilingue di economia e organizzazione aziendale. xxxii, 2044p. (Eng. & Ital.). L.24000.00. Zanichelli.

Ruhland, Jean. Dictionnaire Francais-Allemand-Anglais pour le Commerce Exterieur. (Fr., Ger. & Eng.). 60.00 F. Ruhland.

Sachs, Rudolf. British & American Business in Keywords. LC 76-450966. vi, 186p. (Eng. & Ger.). 1975. DM.32.00 (ISBN 3-7819-2010-0). Knapp Verlag.

Servotte, Josef V. Dictionnaire Commercial & Financier en Quatre Langues: Francais-Neerlandais-Anglais-Allemand. 5th ed. 960p. (Fr., Dutch, Eng. & Ger.). write for info. Erasme.

--Dictionnaire Commercial & Financier: Francais-Anglais. (Fr. & Eng.). 1977. write for info. Marabout.

Servotte, Jozef V. Commercial & Financial Dictionary in Four Languages. rev. 4th ed. Orig. Title: Dictionnaire Commercial et Financier en 4 Langues. 968p. (Fr., Dutch, Eng. & Ger.). 1972. 52.50x (ISBN 90-02-11109-6). Intl Pubns Serv.

Shevchenko, V. S., et al. Kratkii Cheshsko-Russkii i Russko-Cheshskii Vneshnetorgovyi Slovar. (Rus. & Czech.). 1955. $2.50 (Pub. by Vneshtorgizdat). Four Continent.

Weis, Erich & Haberfellner, Eva. Vocabulaire Commercial Francais-Allemand. LC 77-576772. 271p. (Fr.). 1976. DM.14.80 (ISBN 3-125-23410-7). Klett.

Yorston, Keith. The Australian Commercial Dictionary. LC 73-163182. 340p. 1972. $12.50x (ISBN 0-455-16550-5). Intl Pubns Serv.

Zorin, I. N. Russko-Kitaiskii Obschcheekonomicheskii i Vneshnetorgovyi Slovar. 708p. (Rus.). 1961. $4.25 (Pub. by Vneshtorgizdat). Four Continent.

COMMERCE–TERMINOLOGY

Edler, Florence. Glossary of Mediaeval Terms of Business, 1200-1600. 1934. $32.00 (ISBN 0-527-01690-X). Kraus Repr.

Evjen, H. Norwegian-Spanish Dictionary of Commerce. (Norwegian & Span.). 1974. write for info. (ISBN 82-573-0107-8). Kunnskapsforlaget.

Gabrielsen, Daae. Norwegian-English Dictionary of Commerce. (Norwegian & Eng.). 1978. write for info. (ISBN 82-573-0108-6). Kunnskapsforlaget.

--Norwegian-French Dictionary of Commerce. (Norwegian & Fr.). 1975. write for info. (ISBN 82-573-0094-2). Kunnskapsforlaget.

--Norwegian-German Dictionary of Commerce. (Norwegian & Ger.). 1971. write for info. (ISBN 82-573-0092-6). Kunnskapsforlaget.

Garza Bores, Jaime. Diccionario tecnico de terminologia comercial, contable y bancaria: Espanol-Ingles, Ingles-Espanol. (Span. & Eng.). $1.60; Mex.$20.00. Diana.

Varela Colmeiro, G. Diccionario comercial y economico moderno: Ingles-espanol. 256p. (Eng. & Span.). 1964. 300.00 ptas. Inter-Ciencia.

COMMERCIAL CORNERS

see Speculation; Stock-Exchange

COMMERCIAL CORRESPONDENCE

see also English Language–Business English

Langenscheidts Satz-Lexikon des Englischen Geschaeftsbriefes. (Ger. & Eng.). 1978. DM.19.80 (ISBN 3-468-39150-1). Langenscheidt.

Lexikon der Geschaeftsbriefe in Vier Sprachen, 3 vols. (Ger. , Eng. , Fr. & Ital., Lexicon of Commercial Letters in Four Languages). 1972. Set. $168.00 (ISBN 3-478-52340-0, M-7257). French & Eur.

COMMERCIAL CORRESPONDENCE–COPYING PROCESSES

see Copying Processes

COMMERCIAL CORRESPONDENCE, FRENCH

Hakki, Mamdouh. Dictionnaire des termes juridiques et commerciaux. (Fr. & Arabic.). 1973. $20.00 (108-9). Intl Bk Ctr.

Henni, Mustapha, compiled by. Dictionnaire des Termes Techniques et Commerciaux. 386p. (Arabic, Fr. & Eng.). $25.00 (11-9). INtl Bk Ctr.

Langenscheidts Satz-Lexikon des Franzoesischen Geschaeftsbriefes. (Ger. & Fr.). 1978. DM.19.80 (ISBN 3-468-39150-1). Langenscheidt.

COMMERCIAL CORRESPONDENCE, SPANISH

Burfeindt-Moral, H. & Moral-Arroyo, J.. A. Langenscheidts Satz-Lexikon des Spanischen Geschaeftsbriefes. (Ger. & Span.). 1978. DM.19.80 (ISBN 3-468-39340-7). Langenscheidt.

COMMERCIAL CREDIT

see Credit

COMMERCIAL EDUCATION

see Business Education

COMMERCIAL FISHING

see Fisheries

COMMERCIAL LAW

Here are entered general works and works on commercial law in the United States. For commercial law of other countries, see subdivisions below.

see also Banking Law; Business; Business Law; Checks; Maritime Law; Mortgages; Real Property; Sales; Trade-Marks

Codera Martin, Jose. Diccionario De Derecho Mercantil. 286p. (Span.). 1979. leatherette $22.50 (ISBN 84-368-0115-6, S-50178). French & Eur.

COMMERCIAL LAW–GREAT BRITAIN

Postlethwayt, Malachy. Universal Dictionary of Trade & Commerce, 2 Vols. 4th ed. LC 67-29516. Repr. of 1774 ed. Set. 250.00x (ISBN 0-678-00551-6). Kelley.

COMMERCIAL SCHOOLS
see Business Education

COMMODORE (COMPUTER)
Noonan, Larry. Basic BASIC-English Dictionary for the Apple, PET & TRS-80. (Illus.). 154p. $17.95 (ISBN 0-686-88421-3, 1521). TAB Bks.

COMMON MARKET COUNTRIES
see European Economic Community

COMMONPLACES
see Terms and Phrases

COMMONS (SOCIAL ORDER)
see Labor and Laboring Classes

COMMUNICATION
Here are entered works on human communication, including both the primary techniques of language, pictures, etc., and the secondary techniques which facilitate the process, such as the press and radio.
see also Communication and Traffic; Cybernetics; Information Science; Information Theory; Language and Languages; Mass Media
Bodson, Dennis, ed. & frwd. by. Fiberoptics & Lightwave Communications Vocabulary. LC 80-26168. 156p. (Orig.). 1983. pap. text ed. 12.95 (ISBN 0-07-606706-8, R-030). McGraw.

COMMUNICATION–DICTIONARIES
Connors, Tracy D. Longman Dictionary of the Mass Media & Communication. LC 82-92. (Public Communication Ser.). (Illus.). 256p. 1982. text ed. 24.95x (ISBN 0-582-28337-X); pap. text ed. 12.95x (ISBN 0-582-28336-1). Longman.
Delson, Donn & Michalove, Ed. Delson's Dictionary of Cable, Video & Satellite Terms. Posner, Neil, ed. LC 82-17767. (Entertainment Communications Ser.: Vol. 3). (Orig.). 1982. pap. $6.95 (ISBN 0-9603574-3-2, A-4). Bradson.
Fages, Jean-Baptiste. Diccionario de los Medios de Comunicacion: Tecnica, Semiologia, Linguistica. 288p. (Span.). 1978. pap. $18.95 (ISBN 84-7366-022-6, S-50121). French & Eur.
Jefkins, Frank. Dictionary of Marketing & Communication. 1973. text ed. $19.95x (ISBN 0-7002-0218-8). Intl Ideas.
Weik, Martin H. Communications Standard Dictionary. 928p. 1982. text ed. $29.50 (ISBN 0-442-21933-4). Van Nos Reinhold.

COMMUNICATION AND TRAFFIC
see also Aeronautics; Broadcasting; Commerce; Inland Navigation; Mass Media; Postal Service; Radio; Railroads; Roads; Shipping; Tariff; Telecommunication; Traffic Engineering
Bein, Gerhard. Woerterbuch Des Internationalen Verkehrs (Dictionary of International Traffic) 233p. (Ger. & Eng.). 1968. 9.00x (ISBN 0-8002-1306-8). Intl Pubns Serv.
Eichborn, R. Woerterbuch fuer Wirtschaft-Recht-Verwaltungs & Umgangssprache: Vol.I, Englisch-Deutsch. rev. ed. 1150p. (Eng. & Ger.). 1983. $124.00. M Rosenberg.
--Woerterbuch fuer Wirtschaft-Recht-Verkehr-Verwaltungs & Umgangssprache: Vol. II, Deutch-Englisch. 1150p. (Ger. & Eng.). 1982. $124.00. M Rosenberg.

COMMUNICATION IN EDUCATION
see also Education
Terminology of Adult Education. (IBE Data Ser.). 154p. 1980. pap. $10.50 (ISBN 92-3-001683-7, U950, UNESCO). Unipub.

COMMUNICATION IN MEDICINE
see also Medical Libraries
American Medical Record Association. Medical Terminology Outline: 1980. 68p. $6.00 (3003A). Am Med Record Assn.

Steen, Edwin B. Abbreviations in Medicine. 4th ed. 1978. pap. $12.95 (ISBN 0-7216-0766-7, Pub. by Bailliere-Tindall). Saunders.

COMMUNICATION SKILLS (ELEMENTARY EDUCATION)
see English Language–Study and Teaching (Elementary)

COMMUNICATION THEORY
see Information Theory

COMMUNICATIONS SYSTEMS, POLICE
see Police Communication Systems

COMMUNICATIVE DISORDERS
Nicolosi, Lucille. Terminology of Communication Disorders: Speech, Language, & Hearing. 2nd ed. (Illus.). 338p. 1982. $18.50 (ISBN 0-683-06499-1). Williams & Wilkins.

COMMUNISM–DICTIONARIES
Biard, Roland. Dictionnaire de L'Extreme-Gauche. 384p. (Fr.). 1978. 59.00 F. Belfond.
--Dictionnaire de l'Extreme-Gauche: De 1945 a Nos Jours. LC 78-399569. 411p. (Fr.). 1978. 50.00 F (ISBN 2-7144-1131-2). Belfond.
Bottomore, Tom & Harris, Laurence, eds. A Dictionary of Marxist Thought. 544p. 1983. $35.00 (ISBN 0-686-47014-1); prepub. $27.50 until 12/31/83. Harvard U Pr.
Colby, Roy. Communism-English Dictionary. 123p. 1973. pap. $1.00 pocketsize (ISBN 0-88279-030-7). Western Islands.
Gottschalg, J. & Wolter, G., eds. Jugendlexikon Wissenschaftlicher Kommunismus. 2nd ed. (Illus.). 188p. (Ger.). 1981. DM.9.80. Bibl Inst Leipzig.
Gould, L. Harry. Marxist Glossary. 99p. 1980. pap. text ed. 2.95 (ISBN 0-89380-018-X). Proletarian Pubs.
Jacobson, Howard B., ed. Mass Communications Dictionary. LC 60-53157. 1961. 6.00 (ISBN 0-8022-0785-5). Philos Lib.
Russell, James. Marx-Engels Dictionary. LC 80-786. (Illus.). xxv, 140p. 1981. lib. bdg. 22.50x (ISBN 0-313-22035-2, RME/). Greenwood.
Sole Tura, Jorge. Diccionario del Comunismo. 96p. (Espn.). 1977. pap. $2.25 (ISBN 84-7235-299-4, S-50082). French & Eur.

COMMUNIST PARTIES
Fejto, Francois. Dictionnaire des Partis Communistes & des Mouvements Revolutionnaires. 236p. (Fr.). 1971. 31.00 F. Casterman.

COMMUNITY HEALTH
see Public Health

COMMUNITY POWER
Press, Charles & VerBerg, Kenneth. State & Community Governments in the Federal System. LC 78-22064. 1979. text ed. $21.95x (ISBN 0-471-02725-1); tchrs.' manual $6.00 (ISBN 0-471-04909-3). Wiley.

COMMUNITY PSYCHIATRY
see Social Psychiatry

COMPANIES
see Corporations

COMPARATIVE GRAMMAR
see Grammar, Comparative and General

COMPARATIVE MORPHOLOGY
see Morphology

COMPETITIVE EXAMINATIONS
see Civil Service Examinations

COMPLEXION
see Beauty, Personal; Cosmetics

COMPOSERS
Slonimsky, Nicolas. Lexicon of Musical Invective: Critical Assaults on Composers Since Beethoven's Time. 2nd ed. LC 65-26270. 331p. 1969. pap. $7.95 (ISBN 0-295-78579-9, WP52). U of Wash Pr.

COMPOSERS–DICTIONARIES
see Music–Bio-Bibliography

COMPOSERS, AMERICAN
Butterworth, Neil. A Dictionary of American Composers. LC 81-43331. 600p. 1983. lib. bdg. 75.00 (ISBN 0-8240-9311-9). Garland Pub.

COMPOSITION (RHETORIC)
see Rhetoric

also subdivision Composition and Exercises under names of languages

COMPUTATIONAL LINGUISTICS
see Programming Languages (Electronic Computers)

COMPUTER CONTROL
see Automation

COMPUTER GRAPHICS
Hubbard, Stuart W. The Computer Graphics Glossary. LC 82-42918. 96p. 1983. pap. $18.50 (ISBN 0-89774-072-6). Oryx Pr.

COMPUTER INPUT-OUTPUT EQUIPMENT
Bennett, John, et al, eds. Visual Display Terminal: Usability Issues & Health Concerns. 1983. $32.00 (ISBN 0-13-942482-2). P-H.

COMPUTER LANGUAGES
see Programming Languages (Electronic Computers)

COMPUTER PROGRAM LANGUAGES
see Programming Languages (Electronic Computers)

COMPUTER PROGRAMMING
see Programming (Electronic Computers)

COMPUTER SOFTWARE
see Programming (Electronic Computers); Programming Languages (Electronic Computers)
also similar headings

COMPUTERS
Here are entered works on modern electronic computers first developed after 1945. Works on calculators, as well as all mechanical computers of pre-1945 vintage, are entered under Calculating-Machines.
see also Electronic Data Processing; Electronic Digital Computers; Information Storage and Retrieval Systems
also headings beginning with the word Computer
Burton, Philip E. A Dictionary of Minicomputing & Microcomputing. 368p. 1983. pap. 17.95 (ISBN 0-8240-7286-3). Garland Pub.
Clason, W. E. Elsevier's Dictionary of Computers, Automatic Control & Data Processing. 2nd ed. (Eng., Fr., Span., & Ital., Polyglot). 1971. $85.00 (ISBN 0-444-40928-9). Elsevier.
Maronski, J. & Rupinska, M. Computer Networks Terminology. 73p. 1980. pap. $7.50 (ISBN 83-01-01179-3, M-9061). French & Eur.
Mayer, JoAnne C. & Sippl, Charles J. Essential Computer Dictionary & Speller for Secretaries, Managers, & Office Personnel. (Illus.). 256p. 1980. text ed. 14.95 (ISBN 0-13-284364-1, Spec); pap. 6.95 (ISBN 0-13-284356-0). P-H.

COMPUTERS–DICTIONARIES
Anderson, R. G. Dictionary of Data Processing & Computer Terms. 112p. 1982. pap. text ed. $13.95x (ISBN 0-7121-0429-1). Intl Ideas.
Bly, Robert W. A Dictionary of Computer Words. (Illus.). 208p. (gr. 7 up). 1983. pap. $3.95 (ISBN 0-440-01920-6, Banbury). Dell.
Bola Glossary of Electronic Data Processing & Computer Terms: English-Spanish & Spanish-English. (Span. & Eng.). $29.95. Iaconi.
Bola Publications. Bola Glossary of Electronic Data Processing & Computer Terms English-Spanish & Spanish-English. LC 82-71113. (Glossary Ser.: Vol. 1). 200p. (Orig., Span. & Eng.). 1982. pap. $29.95 (ISBN 0-943118-00-X). Bola Pubns.
Burger, E. Technical Dictionary of Data Processing, Computers & Office Machines, English, German, French, Russian. (Eng., Ger., Fr. & Rus.). 1970. $130.00 (ISBN 0-08-006425-6). Pergamon.
Chandor, Anthony. Diccionario de Computadores. 402p. (Span.). 1975. leather $28.50 (ISBN 84-335-6411-0, S-31859). French & Eur.
Chandor, Anthony, et al. The Penguin Dictionary of Computers. 2nd ed. 1977. pap. $4.95. Penguin.
Dataordbok: Computers, Automatic, Control & Data Processing. (Eng. & Swedish.). 1983. Kr.195.00 (ISBN 91-86236-16-4). EC Print AB.

Dictionary of Measurement Technology for Computers. 161p. (Eng. & Chinese.). 1977. pap. $3.95 (ISBN 0-686-92302-2, M-9565). French & Eur.
Drieux, Jean P. & Jarlaud, Alain. Let's Talk D. P. Computer Lexicon. 116p. (Eng., Amer. & Fr.). 1977. pap. $11.95 (ISBN 0-686-57123-1, M-6171). French & Eur.
Fisher, R. & Krchten, P. English-French Dictionary of Computer Science. (Eng. & Fr.). Date not set. text ed. $25.00 (ISBN 0-686-46529-6). Heinman.
Freedman, Alan. The Computer Glossary: It's Not Just a Glossary. 3rd ed. (Illus.). 324p. 1983. $14.95 (ISBN 0-941878-02-3). Computer Lang.
Freedman, Alan & Morrison, Irma L. The Computer Glossary: It's Not Just a Glossary. 320p. 1983. pap. $14.95 (ISBN 0-13-164483-1). P-H.
Galland, Frank J., ed. Dictionary of Computing: Data Communications, Hardware & Software Basics, Digital Electronics. 330p. 1982. $34.95x (ISBN 0-471-10468-X, Pub. by Wiley-Interscience); pap. $19.95x (ISBN 0-471-10469-8). Wiley.
Giarratano, Joseph C. Timex-Sinclair One Thousand Pocket Dictionary. 1983. pap. 4.95 (ISBN 0-88022-028-7). Que Corp.
Isaacs, Alan. The Multilingual Computer Dictionary. 332p. (Eng., Fr., Ger., Span., Ital. & Port.). 1981. $27.00. Facts on File.
Isaacs, Alan, ed. The Multilingual Computer Dictionary. 336p. 1981. $22.50 (ISBN 0-87196-431-7). Facts on File.
--Multilingual Computer Dictionary. (Eng., Fr., Span., Ital. & Port.). 1980. $22.50. Facts on File.
Kassel, Hans. Lexikon Datens & Datensicherung. LC 79-373659. 157p. (Ger.). 1978. write for info. (ISBN 3-8009-1257-0). Siemens AG.
Kelly-Bootle, Stan. The Devil's DP Dictionary. (Illus.). 160p. 1981. pap. 8.50 (ISBN 0-07-034022-6, P&RB). McGraw.
Lomax, J. D. Data Dictionary Systems. (Illus.). 1977. pap. $45.00x (ISBN 0-85012-191-4). Intl Pubns Serv.
National Computing Centre, ed. Thesaurus of Computing Terms. 8th ed. 1977. pap. 82.50x (ISBN 0-85012-169-8). Intl Pubns Serv.
The Personal Computer Glossary. 1982. $2.95 (ISBN 0-88284-233-1). Alfred Pub.
Prenis, John. Computer Terms. LC 77-343. (Orig.). 1977. lib. bdg. 12.90 (ISBN 0-914294-75-X); pap. 2.95 (ISBN 0-914294-76-8). Running Pr.
--The Running Press Glossary of Computer Terms: An Insider's Guide to the Language of the Experts. (Eng.). pap. $2.95. Running Pr.
Prenis, John, ed. The Computer Dictionary: A User-Friendly Guide to Language, Terms, & Jargon. (Illus.). 128p. 1983. lib. bdg. $12.90 (ISBN 0-89471-232-2); pap. $4.95 (ISBN 0-89471-231-4). Running Pr.
Pyle, Ian & Glazer, Edward, eds. Dictionary of Computing. 450p. 1983. $34.95 (ISBN 0-19-853905-3). Oxford U Pr.
--Dictionary of Computing. 450p. 1983. $34.95 (ISBN 0-19-853905-3). Oxford U Pr.
Schmalz, Larry C. & Sippl, Charles J. Computer Glossary for Students & Teachers. (Apollo Eds.). pap. $3.25i (ISBN 0-8152-0411-6, A-411). T Y Crowell.
Shishmarev, A. I. & Zamorin, A. P. Explanatory Dictionary of Computing Machinery & Data Processing. 416p. 1978. $60.00x (ISBN 0-686-44717-4, Pub. by Collets). State Mutual Bk.
Shismarev, A. I. & Zamorin, A. P. Explanatory Dictionary of Computing Machinery & Data Processing. 416p. 1978. Leatherette $7.95 (ISBN 0-686-92229-8, M-9080). French & Eur.

Sippl, Charles J. & Sippl, Roger J. Computer Dictionary. 3rd ed. LC 79-91696. 1980. pap. 15.95 (ISBN 0-672-21652-3, 21652). Sams.

Slownik Informatyki Polsko-Angielsko-Rosyjski. LC 77-469027. 159p. (Eng. , Rus. & Pol.). 1976. 50.00 Zl. Wydawnictwa Naukowo.

Spencer, Donald. Computer Dictionary for Everyone. 1981. pap. $5.95 (ISBN 0-684-16946-0, ScribT). Scribner.

Spencer, Donald D. Computer Dictionary. 2nd ed. LC 78-31738. 1979. pap. $6.95 (ISBN 0-89218-038-2). Camelot Pub.

--The Illustrated Computer Dictionary. Rev. ed. 187p. 1983. pap. $8.95 (ISBN 0-686-46828-7). Merrill.

--Illustrated Computer Dictionary for Young People. LC 81-21795. (Illus.). 1982. $8.95x (ISBN 0-89218-052-8). Camelot Pub.

Stokes, Adrian V. Concise Encyclopedia of Computer Terminology. 289p. 1980. text ed. $37.50x (ISBN 0-905897-32-3). Gower Pub Ltd.

Technical Committee on Computer Controlled Environmental Testing of the Inst. of Environ. Sciences. Glossary of Computer Controlled Environmental Testing Terminology. LC 62-38584. 27p. 1977. pap. text ed. $3.00 (ISBN 0-915414-53-8). Inst Environ Sci.

Toth, Rudolf. Terminoloski Komparativni Srpskohrvatsko. LC 77-476859. 224p. (Eng. & Hungarian.). 1976. write for info. Ekonomski Fakultet.

Vaillancourt, Pauline M. International Directory of Acronyms in Library, Information & Computer Sciences. LC 80-18352. xi, 518p. 1980. $45.00 (ISBN 0-8352-1152-5). Bowker.

Webster's New World Dictionary of Computer Terms. Date not set. $5.95 (ISBN 0-671-46866-9). S&S.

Weik, Martin H. Standard Dictionary of Computers & Information Processing. rev., 2nd ed. 1977. 23.95 (ISBN 0-8104-5099-2). Hayden.

Weik, Martin H. Standard Dictionary of Computers & Information Processing. 2nd, rev. ed. 390p. 1977. $23.95 (ISBN 0-686-98126-X). Telecom Lib.

Windsor, A. T., ed. Using the ICL Data Dictionary: Proceedings of the ICL DDS User Group. 160p. 1980. text ed. $29.95 (ISBN 0-906812-06-2). Birkhauser.

Yakubaitis, E. A. English-Russian Glossary of Computer Systems & Networks Terminology. 270p. (Eng. & Rus.). 1981. $40.00x (ISBN 0-686-44705-0, Pub. by Collets). State Mutual Bk.

COMPUTERS--HANDBOOKS, MANUALS, ETC.
CAD-CAM Glossary. $19.25 (ISBN 0-686-40545-5). Prod Intl.

Windsor, A. T., ed. Using the ICL Data Dictionary: Proceedings of the ICL DDS User Group. 160p. 1980. text ed. $29.95 (ISBN 0-906812-06-2). Birkhauser.

COMPUTERS--JUVENILE LITERATURE
Bly, Robert W. A Dictionary of Computer Words. (Illus.). 208p. (gr. 7 up). 1983. pap. $3.95 (ISBN 0-440-01920-6, Banbury). Dell.

COMPUTERS--PROGRAMMING
see Programming (Electronic Computers)

COMPUTERS, ELECTRONIC
see Computers; Electronic Digital Computers

COMPUTING MACHINES (COMPUTERS)
see Computers

CONCEPTS
Cirlot, Juan E. Diccionario de los Ismos. (Span.). $18.00 (ARG). Lectorum Pubns.

Laffal, Julius. Concept Dictionary of English. LC 72-97927. 1973. text ed. 16.95 (ISBN 0-686-77072-2). Gallery Pr.

CONCERTS--PROGRAMS
Daae, E. English-Norwegian, Norwegian-English, Lommeordbok. 568p. (Eng. & Norwegian.). 1980. pap. $8.95 (ISBN 82-573-0152-3, M-9462). French & Eur.

CONCHOLOGY
see Mollusks

CONCORDANCES
see also Bible--Concordances
also subdivision Concordances under names of authors, e.g. Shakespeare, William--Concordances

Cruden, Alexander. Cruden's Unabridged Concordance. $17.95 (ISBN 0-8010-2351-8). Baker Bk.

Kasten, Lloyd & Anderson, Jean. Concordance to the Celestina (1499) (Spanish Ser.: No. 1). 338p. 1976. 12.50 (ISBN 0-942260-10-4). Hispanic Seminary.

CONCRETE
see also Cement; Prestressed Concrete

ACI Committee 116. Cement & Concrete Terminology. 1978. pap. $12.95 (ISBN 0-685-85102-8, SP-19). ACI.

Cement & Concrete Thesaurus. 1969. pap. $14.95 (ISBN 0-685-85158-3, CCT). ACI.

Conseil International De la Langue Francais. Vocabulaire Du Beton. 192p. (Fr.). 1976. pap. $39.95 (ISBN 0-686-56961-X, M-6084). French & Eur.

Dictionary of Concrete Terms. (Hebrew, Eng. , Fr. & Ger.). IL.8.00. Massada Pr.

Federation Internationale de la Precontrainte. Multi-Lingual Dictionary of Concrete. 1976. $89.50 (ISBN 0-444-41237-9). Elsevier.

CONCRETE, PRESTRESSED
see Prestressed Concrete
CONCRETE BUILDING
see Concrete Construction
CONCRETE CONSTRUCTION
see also Prestressed Concrete; Prestressed Concrete Construction

Gerwick, Ben C., Jr. & Peters, V. P., eds. Russian-English Dictionary of Prestressed Concrete & Concrete Construction. 120p. (Rus. & Eng.). 1966. 33.00x (ISBN 0-677-00260-2). Gordon.

CONDITIONED RESPONSE
see also Verbal Behavior

Zeier, Hans. Woerterbuch der Lerntheorien & der Verhaltenstherapie. LC 76-482355. (Illus.). 189p. (Ger.). 1976. DM.14.80 (ISBN 3-463-00655-3). Kindler.

CONDOLENCE, ETIQUETTE OF
see Etiquette
CONFERENCES
see Congresses and Conventions; Meetings
CONFIGURATIONS
Electrical Generating Systems Marketing Association. Glossary of Department of Defense Configuration Management Terminology & Definitions. 1972. $3.00 (CMTD1); members $1.25. Elec Gen Syst.

CONFLAGRATIONS
see Fires
CONGENITAL DISEASES
see Medical Genetics
CONGO (BRAZZAVILLE)
Thompson, Virginia & Adloff, Richard. Historical Dictionary of the People's Republic of the Congo (Congo-Brazzaville) LC 74-14975. (African Historical Dictionaries Ser.: No. 2). 1974. $13.00 (ISBN 0-8108-0762-9). Scarecrow.

CONGO LANGUAGE
Craven, Henry & Barfield, John. English-Congo & Congo-English Dictionary. facs. ed. LC 75-157365. (Black Heritage Library Collection). (Eng. & Congo). 1883. $17.75 (ISBN 0-8369-8803-5). Ayer Co.

Laman, Karl Edward. Dictionnaire Kikongo-Francais. 1278p. (Fr.). 1936. $24.00. Gregg.

CONGRESSES AND CONVENTIONS
Glossary of Conference Terms, English, French, Arabic. (Eng. , Fr. & Arabic.). 1978. pap. $6.00 (ISBN 92-3-101566-4, U840, UNESCO). Unipub.

Vocabulaire des Conferences: Francais-Anglais-Arabe: Francais-Anglais-Arabic.). 1974. 12.00 F. Unesco.

CONGREVE, WILLIAM, 1670-1729
Mann, David D., ed. A Concordance to the Plays of William Congreve. LC 72-13384. (Concordances Ser.). 888p. 1973. $49.50x (ISBN 0-8014-0767-2). Cornell U Pr.

CONNECTICUT--GENEALOGY
Gannett, Henry. A Geographic Dictionary of Connecticut & Rhode Island, 2 vols. in 1. LC 78-59123. 98p. 1978. Repr. of 1894 ed. 9.50 (ISBN 0-8063-0820-6). Genealog Pub.

CONRAD, JOSEPH, 1857-1924
Bender, Todd K. A Concordance to Conrad's the Mirror of the Sea & the Inheritors. 340p. 1983. lib. bdg. $45.00 (ISBN 0-8240-9110-8). Garland Pub.

Higdon, David & Bender, Todd K. A Concordance to Conrad's Under Western Eyes. LC 82-48434. (Conrad Concordances Ser.). 283p. 1982. lib. bdg. $50.00 (ISBN 0-8240-9234-1). Garland Pub.

CONSERVATION OF ENERGY RESOURCES
see Energy Conservation
CONSERVATION OF MANUSCRIPTS
see Manuscripts--Conservation and Restoration
CONSERVATION OF NATURAL RESOURCES
see also Energy Conservation; Soil Conservation; Water

Holum, John R. Topics & Terms in Environmental Problems. LC 77-12805. 1977. $39.95x (ISBN 0-471-01982-8, Pub. by Wiley-Interscience). Wiley.

CONSERVATION OF POWER RESOURCES
see Energy Conservation
CONSERVATION OF RESOURCES
see Conservation of Natural Resources
CONSERVATION OF THE SOIL
see Soil Conservation
CONSTANTS
see Units
CONSTITUTIONAL LAW
see also Administrative Law; Civil Rights; Democracy; Legislation; Rule of Law
also subdivision Constitutional Law under names of countries, e.g. United States--Constitutional Law

Barrillon, Raymond. Dictionnaire de la Constitution: Les Institutions de la Ve Republique. 2nd ed. xxxiv, 538p. (Fr.). 1978. write for info. Cujas.

CONSTITUTIONAL LIMITATIONS
see Constitutional Law
CONSTRUCTION
see Architecture; Building; Engineering
CONSTRUCTION, CONCRETE
see Concrete Construction
CONSTRUCTION, HOUSE
see House Construction
CONSTRUCTION EQUIPMENT
see also Pumping Machinery

Bucksch, H. Woerterbuch fuer Bautechnik & Baumaschinen: Band I, Deutsch-Englisch. 1184p. (Ger. & Eng.). 1982. DM.160.00 (ISBN 3-7625-2032-1). Bauverlag.

--Woerterbuch fuer Bautechnik & Baumaschinen: Band II, Englisch-Deutsch. 1219p. (Eng. & Ger.). 1982. DM.160.00 (ISBN 3-7625-2034-8). Bauverlag.

Bucksch, Herbert. Dictionary of Civil Engineering & Construction Machinery & Equipment, Vol. 1. 5th ed. 420p. (Fr. & Eng.). 1978. $30.00 (ISBN 3-7625-0533-0, M-7120). French & Eur.

--Dictionary of Civil Engineering & Construction Machinery & Equipment, Vol. 1. 7th ed. (Fr. & Ger.). 1978. leatherette $135.00 (ISBN 3-7625-0950-6, M-7122). French & Eur.

--Dictionary of Civil Engineering & Construction Machinery & Equipment, Vol. 2. 5th ed. 548p. (Fr. & Eng.). 1976. $40.00 (ISBN 3-7625-0534-9, M-7119). French & Eur.

--Dictionary of Civil Engineering & Construction Machinery & Equipment, Vol. 2. 7th ed. (Eng. & Ger.). 1978. leatherette $135.00 (ISBN 3-7625-0951-4, M-7121). French & Eur.

Dictionary of Civil Engineering & Construction Machinery & Equipment, 2 vols. 4th ed. 1180p. 1978. plastic bdg. 90.00x ea. Vol. 1, Ger-Eng (ISBN 3-7625-0502-0). Vol. 2, Eng.-Ger (ISBN 3-7625-0950-6). Intl Pubns Serv.

CONSTRUCTION INDUSTRY
Here are entered works dealing comprehensively with the construction business, including finance, planning, management, and skills.
see also Building; Building Trades

American Institute of Architects. Glossary of Construction Industry Terms. pap. $2.00 (ISBN 0-913962-18-X). Am Inst Arch.

Benito Bacho, Jose. Diccionario de la Construccion y Obras Publicas Ingles-Espanol, 2 vols. 268p. (Span. & Eng.). 1975. Set. $38.95 (ISBN 84-85198-10-7, S-50117). French & Eur.

--Diccionario de la Construccion y Obras Publicas, Tomo 2: Span. 110p. (Span.). 1975. $18.95 (ISBN 84-85198-09-3, S-50119). French & Eur.

--Diccionario de la Construcion y de Obras Publicas, Tomo 1: Ingles. 168p. (Span.). 1975. $18.95 (ISBN 84-85198-00-X, S-50118). French & Eur.

Brooks, Hugh. Encyclopedia of Building & Construction Terms. LC 82-21565. 416p. 1983. $50.00 (ISBN 0-13-275511-4). P-H.

Bucksch, Herbert. Dictionary of Architecture, Building Construction & Materials, Vol. II. 1137p. (Eng. & Ger.). 1976. $175.00 (ISBN 3-7625-0714-7, M-7130). French & Eur.

--Dictionary of Architecture, Building Construction & Materials, Vol. I. 942p. (Eng. & Ger.). 1974. $175.00 (ISBN 3-7625-0357-5, M-7131). French & Eur.

Harris, Cyril M. Dictionary of Architecture & Construction. 1975. $42.50 (ISBN 0-07-026756-1, P&RB). McGraw.

Lange, K. & Ferval, L. International Construction Terminology. 120p. (Eng. & Fr.). 1979. $14.50 (ISBN 3-7625-1235-3, M-7479, Pub. by Bauverlag). French & Eur.

--International Construction Terminology. 120p. (Eng. & Fr.). 1979. $14.50 (ISBN 3-7625-1235-3). Bauverlag.

Der Sprach-Brockhaus: Deutsches Bildwoerterbuch von A-Z. 835p. (Ger.). DM.30.00 (ISBN 3-7653-0023-3). F A Brockhaus.

Vukicevic, B., ed. Dictionary of Construction Industries. 516p. (Eng. & Serbocroation). 1981. $95.00 (ISBN 0-686-92430-4, M-9686). French & Eur.

CONSTRUCTION INDUSTRY--CONTRACTS AND SPECIFICATIONS
see Building--Contracts and Specifications
CONSTRUCTION INDUSTRY--LAW AND LEGISLATION
Bucksch, H. Woerterbuch fur Bau & Grundstucksrecht & Raumordnung. (Ger. & Eng.). 1982. write for info. (ISBN 3-7625-1413-5). Bauverlag.

--Woerterbuch fur Baurecht, Grundstucksrecht & Raumordnung: Band I, Deutsch-Englisch. 1400p. (Ger. & Eng.). 1982. DM.380.00. Bauverlag.

--Woerterbuch fur Baurecht, Grunstucksrecht & Raumordnung: Band II, Englisch-Deutsch. 1400p. (Eng. & Ger.). 1982. DM.380.00. Bauverlag.

CONSTRUCTION MACHINERY
see Construction Equipment
CONSTRUCTION OF ROADS
see Road Construction
CONSUMER ADVERTISING
see Advertising
CONSUMER BEHAVIOR
see Consumers

CONSUMERS
Here are entered works on consumer behavior. Consumers' guides are entered under Consumer Education; works on the economic theory of consumption under Consumption (economics).
Pujol, R. Dictionnaire du Consommateur. 288p. (Fr.). write for info. Gonthier.

CONTACT VERNACULARS
see Languages, Mixed

CONTAINER TRANSPORTATION
see Containerization

CONTAINERIZATION
Truck Trailer Manufacturers Association. Nomenclature & Terminology of Tank Trailers & Containers. (Recommended Practices: RP No. 36-75). 1975. $3.00. Truck Trailer Mfrs.

CONTAMINATION OF ENVIRONMENT
see Pollution

CONTEMPORARY ART
see Art, Modern–20th Century

CONTEMPORARY SCULPTURE
see Sculpture, Modern–20th Century

CONTEMPT OF COURT
Sternberg, Jacques. Dictionnaire du Mepris. (Fr.). write for info. Calmann Levy.

CONTRACT BRIDGE
Versini, Georges. Dictionnaire du Bridge. (Fr.). 1968. write for info. PUF.

CONTRACTIONS
see Abbreviations; Paleography

CONTRARIETY IN RELIGION, FOLK-LORE, ETC.)
see Polarity (In Religion, Folk-Lore, etc.)

CONTROL, INVENTORY
see Inventory Control

CONTROL OF INDUSTRIAL PROCESSES
see Process Control

CONTROL SYSTEMS, CARRIER
see Carrier Control Systems

CONTROL THEORY
Seone, Joaquin R. Diccionario de contabilidad, organizacion, administracion, control & ciencia afines, 7 vols. 3400p. (Span.). 1972. $45.00. Difusion.

CONUNDRUMS
see Riddles

CONVENTIONS (CONGRESSES)
see Congresses and Conventions

CONVERSION
see also Converts
Cheve, C. F. Dictionnaire des Conversions. Migne, J. P., ed. (Nouvelle Encyclopedie Theologique Ser.: Vol. 33). 836p. (Fr.). Repr. of 1852 ed. lib. bdg. $106.00x (ISBN 0-89241-275-5). Caratzas Pub Co.

CONVERTS
see also Buddhist converts, Muslim converts, etc. for works on converts to religions other than Christianity
Cheve, C. F. Dictionnaire des Conversions. Migne, J. P., ed. (Nouvelle Encyclopedie Theologique Ser.: Vol. 33). 836p. (Fr.). Repr. of 1852 ed. lib. bdg. $106.00x (ISBN 0-89241-275-5). Caratzas Pub Co.

CONVEYING MACHINERY
Conveyor Equipment Manufacturers Association & American National Standards Institute. Conveyor Terms & Definitions. 4th ed. (CEMA Standards: No. 102). (Illus.). 93p. 1982. $7.00. Conveyor Equip Mfrs.
Vibrating Equipment Terms & Definitions. 7p. 1981. $1.00. Conveyor Equip Mfrs.

COOK-BOOKS
see Cookery

COOKERY
see also Diet; Gastronomy; Menus
Atkinson, David. Menu French. LC 78-323348. (Illus.). 94p. (Fr.). 1978. E1.00 (ISBN 0-902692-17-8). Oxford Poly Pr.
Diccionario de la cocina clasica american y europea, Tomo 3. 230p. (Span.). 1981. pap. 3000.00 ptas (ISBN 84-248-0731-6). Encicl Vasca.
Jean-Charles, Jehanne. Le Lexique des Bons Petits Plats. 222p. (Fr.). 1970. 19.40 F. Presses Cite.

COOKERY–DICTIONARIES
Bickel, Walter, ed. Hering's Dictionary of Classical & Modern Cookery. 5th ed. 1974. $27.95 (ISBN 3-8057-0232-9, Pub. by Virtuea Col Ltd. England). CBI Pub.
Borra, Edoardo, et al. Sana Alimentazione. LC 77-456792. xxx, 826p. (Ital.). 1976. L.15.000. Edizioni Paoline.
Combes, Steve. Dictionary of Cuisine French. 2nd ed. 1973. 12.50x (ISBN 0-214-15569-2). Intl Pubns Serv.
Dahl, C. Food & Menu Dictionary. LC 77-123002. 160p. 1972. $12.50 (ISBN 0-8436-0556-1). CBI Pub.
Dr. Gabler's die Sprache der Chefs. 227p. (Ger.). 1977. $15.95 (ISBN 3-409-90031-4, M-7352, Pub. by Betriebswirtschaftlicher Vlg.). French & Eur.
Four Language Culinary Dictionary: French, Hungarian, English, German. (Fr., Hungarian, Eng. & Ger.). pap. 9.50 saddle stitched bdg. (ISBN 0-87557-099-2, 099-2). Saphrograph.
Gorys, Erhard. Heimerans Kuchenlexikon. LC 76-453925. 558p. (Ger.). 1975. write for info. (ISBN 3-8063-1093-9). Kochbuch Verlag.
Hering, R. Hering's Dictionary of Classical & Modern Cookery. rev. ed. $30.00x (ISBN 0-685-47437-2). Corner.
Hering, Richard. Hering's Dictionary of Classical & Modern Cookery. rev. ed. Bickel, Walter, tr. from Ger. (Illus.). 1977. text ed. 42.95 (ISBN 0-911202-08-0). Radio City.
Kolpas, Norman. The Gourmet's Lexicon. 1982. 3.95 (ISBN 0-686-83115-2, Perigee). Putnam Pub Group.
Mercier, Jean. Lexique Anglais-Francais du Programmateur de Cuisiniere. 29p. (Eng. & Fr.). 1973. Can.$0.50. Quebec Off.
Servi, Vera. Cookbook Dictionary. LC 79-15334. 1982. $10.95 (ISBN 0-913290-21-1). Camaro Pub.

COOKERY (BUTTERMILK)
see Cookery (Dairy Products)

COOKERY (CHEESE)
see Cookery (Dairy Products)

COOKERY (DAIRY PRODUCTS)
Gosetti, Fernanda. Dizionari dei Formaggi: Tutte le Notizie le Ricette come & con che Cosa Servirli. LC 78-400002. 293p. (Eng. & Ital.). 1977. L.5000.00. Marietti.

COOKERY (MILK)
see Cookery (Dairy Products)

COOKERY (SOUR CREAM AND MILK)
see Cookery (Dairy Products)

COOKERY (WINE)
Sharman, Fay. The Taste of France: A Dictionary of French Food & Wine. Chadwick, Brian & Boehm, Klaus, eds. (Eng.). 1982. $10.95 (ISBN 0-395-32561-7). HM.

COOKERY, AUSTRIAN
Ulrich, Gertrude A. One Hundred Eleven Viennese Dishes. pap. 3.95 (ISBN 0-87557-103-4, 103-4). Saphrograph.

COOKERY, CARIBBEAN
De Brissiere, P. Caribbean Cookery. (Chinese & Eng.). pap. 3.95 (ISBN 0-87557-100-X, 100-X). Saphrograph.

COOKERY, CHINESE
Fifty Chinese Recipes. pap. 3.95 (ISBN 0-87557-105-0, 105-05). Saphrograph.
Jackson, Lenli. One Hundred Simple Chinese Recipes. pap. 3.95 (ISBN 0-87557-104-2, 104-2). Saphrograph.

COOKERY, FRENCH
Dumas, Alexandre. Dumas on Food. Davidson, Alan & Davidson, Jane, trs. (Illus.). 327p. (Fr.). 1982. $14.95x (ISBN 0-7181-1842-1). U Pr of Va.
Picard, R. French Dishes, Easy & Delicious. pap. 3.95 (ISBN 0-87557-101-8, 101-8). Saphrograph.
Sharman, Fay. The Taste of France: A Dictionary of French Food & Wine. Chadwick, Brian & Boehm, Klaus, eds. (Eng.). 1982. $10.95 (ISBN 0-395-32561-7). HM.

COOKERY, HEBREW
see Cookery, Jewish

COOKERY, HUNGARIAN
Az Inyesmester Nagy Szakacsko-Nyve: The Art of Hungarian Cooking. 19.50 (ISBN 0-87557-097-6, 097-6). Saphrograph.
De Biro, Elizabeth. Hungarian Cooking. 9.50 (ISBN 0-87557-098-4, 098-4). Saphrograph.
Erdfly-Markovics, L. Hungarian Kitchen Parade. pap. 3.95 (ISBN 0-87557-102-6, 102-6). Saphrograph.

COOKERY, JEWISH
Shosteck, Patti. A Lexicon of Jewish Cooking. rev. ed. 1981. pap. $6.95 (ISBN 0-8092-5995-8). Contemp Bks.

COOKERY, MICROWAVE
see Microwave Cookery

COOKERY, RUSSIAN
Gorina, R. Russian Fare. pap. $3.95 (ISBN 0-87557-106-9, 106-9). Saphrograph.

COOKERY, SCANDINAVIAN
Savonius, M. Scandinavian Smorgasbord, Soups, Savouries & Sweets. pap. $3.95 (ISBN 0-87557-107-7, 107-7). Saphrograph.

COOKING UTENSILS
see Kitchen Utensils

COOLING APPLIANCES
see Refrigeration and Refrigerating Machinery

COOPERATION, INTERNATIONAL
see International Cooperation

COOPERATIVE BUILDING ASSOCIATIONS
see Building and Loan Associations

COOPERATIVE EDUCATION
see Education, Cooperative

COPPER ENGRAVING
see Engraving

COPTIC LANGUAGE
see also Egyptian Language
Cerny, Jaroslav. Coptic Etymological Dictionary. LC 69-10192. 350p. 1976. $175.00 (ISBN 0-521-07228-X). Cambridge U Pr.
Crum, Walter E., ed. Coptic Dictionary. 1939. $98.00x (ISBN 0-19-864404-3). Oxford U Pr.
Smith, Richard H. A Concise Coptic-English Lexicon. 81p. 1983. $10.95x (ISBN 0-8028-3581-3). Eerdmans.

COPYING PROCESSES
see also Photocopying Processes
Deutsches Komitee fur Reprographie. Woerterbuch der Reprographie. LC 76-456115. 273p. (Eng., Fr. & Ger.). 1975. write for info. Aussant & Schrift.
Deutsches Komittee fuer Reprographie. Woerterbuch der Reprographie: Begriffe und Definitionen. 3rd rev. ed. 273p. (Ger., Eng. & Fr., Dictionary of Reprography: Terms & Definitions). 1976. pap. $44.00 (ISBN 0-686-56614-9, M-6961). French & Eur.

COPYRIGHT
see also Trade-Marks
Glucksmann, A., et al. Meyers Taschenlexikon Urheberrecht. 556p. (Ger.). 1980. M.22.00. Bibl Inst Leipzig.
WIPO Glossary of the Terms of the Law of Copyright & Neighboring Rights. 281p. 1980. pap. $38.25 (ISBN 92-805-0016-3, WIPO69, WIPO). Unipub.

CORNEILLE, PIERRE, 1606-1684
Godefroy, Frederic. Lexique Compare de la Langue de Corneille, 2 vols. (Fr.). 1971. 144.00 F. Kraus.
Marty-Lavezux, Charles J. Lexique de la Langue de Pierre Corneille, 2 vols. (Fr.). 1970. $42.50. Lenox.

CORNERS, COMMERCIAL
see Speculation; Stock-Exchange

CORNISH LANGUAGE
Cornish-English Dictionary. (Cornish & Eng.). $10.95 (ISBN 0-686-10840-X). British Am Bks.
Cornish-English Dictionary. 1974. 22.50 (ISBN 0-87557-011-9, 001-9). Saphrograph.

CORPORATION RESERVES
see Depreciation

CORPORATIONS
Here are entered works on business associations organized as legal persons. For works dealing with United States corporations see the subdivision United States which follows.
Gautier, T. F. Dictionnaire des Confreries & Corporations d'Arts & Metiers. Migne, J. P., ed. (Nouvelle Encyclopedie Theologique Ser.: Vol. 50). 562p. (Fr.). Repr. of 1854 ed. lib. bdg. $72.00x (ISBN 0-89241-288-7). Caratzas Pub Co.

CORPORATIONS, BUSINESS
see Corporations

CORRELATION OF FORCES
see Force and Energy

CORRESPONDENCE
see Commercial Correspondence; Letters

CORRESPONDENT BANKS
see Banks and Banking

CORRESPONDENTS, FOREIGN
see Journalists

CORROSION AND ANTI-CORROSIVES
see also Paint
Gross, Helmut. Korrosion & Korrosionsschutz Deutsch-Russisch. 240p. (Ger. & Rus.). 1982. M.22.00. VEB Technik.
Melnikova, M. M. & Smirnov, I. P. English-Russian Dictionary of Electrochemistry & Corrosion. 496p. (Eng. & Rus.). 1976. $9.95 (ISBN 0-686-92367-7, M-9121). French & Eur.

COSMETICS
see also Beauty, Personal; Beauty Culture; Perfumes
Cariere, G., ed. Dictionary of Surface-Active Agents, Cosmetics & Toiletries. (Eng., Fr., Ger., Span., Ital., Dutch & Pol.). 1978. $36.25 (ISBN 0-444-99809-8). Elsevier.
Carriere, G. Dictionary of Surface Active Agents, Cosmetics & Toiletries. LC 77-8552. 198p. (Eng., Fr., Ger., Span., Ital., Pol. & Dutch). 1978. write for info. (ISBN 0-444-99809-8). Elsevier.
European Directories, ed. The Dictionary of Toiletry & Cosmetic Manufacturers in Western Europe. 1981. $100.00x (ISBN 0-686-78875-3, Pub. by European Directories England). State Mutual Bk.
Feinberg, H. Cosmetics-Perfumery Thesaurus. 1972. 17.95 (ISBN 0-02-469030-9). Macmillan Info.
Winter, Ruth. The Consumer's Dictionary of Cosmetic Ingredients. rev. ed. 1976. pap. $4.95 (ISBN 0-517-52737-5). Crown.

COSMETOLOGY
see Beauty Culture

COSMOGONY
Jehan, L. F. Dictionnaire De Cosmogonie et De Paleontologie. Migne, J. P., ed. (Nouvelle Encyclopedie Theologique Ser.: Vol. 48). 732p. (Fr.). Repr. of 1854 ed. lib. bdg. $93.00x (ISBN 0-89241-286-0). Caratzas Pub Co.

COST ACCOUNTING
Munz, Max & Winkel, Harald. Lexikon der Kostenrechnung. LC 77-567449. (Illus.). 234p. (Ger.). 1977. DM.24.00 (ISBN 3-470-58153-3). Kiehl.

COST OF MEDICAL CARE
see Medical Care, Cost of

COSTA RICA
Creedman, Theodore S. Historical Dictionary of Costa Rica. LC 77-6390. (Latin American Historical Dictionaries Ser.: No. 16). 1977. $14.00 (ISBN 0-8108-1040-9). Scarecrow.
--Historical Dictionary of Costa Rica. 1977. $10.00 ea. Intl Guatemala.
Gagini, Carlos & Soto, Victor M. Diccionario de Costarriquenismos. 3rd ed. Cuervo, Rufino J., prologue by. LC 77-459051. 243p. (Span.). 1975. write for info. Costa Rica.
Garro, Joaquin. Habla Que el Tiempo se Lleva? LC 79-126852. 129p. (Span., Costa Rica). 1978. write for info. Costa Rica.

COSTUME
see also Cosmetics; Dressmaking; Fashion; Jewelry; Veils

also individual articles of apparel, e.g. Hosiery; Gloves
Vincenzo, Coratelli. Dizionarietto del costume della moda e dell'acconciatura. 112p. (Ital.). L.1000.00. San Marco.
Wilcox, R. Turner. Dictionary of Costume. LC 68-12503. (Illus.). 1963. lib. rep. ed. $32.50 (ISBN 0-684-15150-2, ScribT). Scribner.

COSTUME–HISTORY
Wilcox, R. Turner. Dictionary of Costume. LC 68-12503. (Illus.). 1963. lib. rep. ed. $32.50 (ISBN 0-684-15150-2, ScribT). Scribner.

COSTUME–EUROPE
Yarwood, Doreen. Costume of the Western World. (Illus.). 192p. 1981. $18.50x (ISBN 0-312-17013-0). St Martin.

COSTUME–GREAT BRITAIN
Fairholt, Fredrick W. A Glossary of Costume in England, Vol. 11. (Illus.). 1976. Repr. write for info. (ISBN 0-7158-1142-8). Charles River Bks.

COSTUME–UNITED STATES
Yarwood, Doreen. Costume of the Western World. (Illus.). 192p. 1981. $18.50x (ISBN 0-312-17013-0). St Martin.

COSTUME, ANCIENT
see Costume–History

COSTUME, MEDIEVAL
see Costume–History

COSTUME, THEATRICAL
see Costume

COSTUME DESIGN
Fashion Vocabulary & Dictation. 1969. pap. $10.95 (ISBN 0-672-96058-3). Bobbs.

COUNCILS AND SYNODS
see also Popes
Peltier, A. C. Dictionnaire Universel et Complet des Conciles, 2 vols. Migne, J. P., ed. (Encyclopedie Theologique Ser.: Vols. 13-14). 1378p. (Fr.). Repr. of 1846 ed. lib. bdg. $175.00x (ISBN 0-89241-236-4). Caratzas Pub Co.
Poussin, J. C. & Garnier, J. C. Dictionnaire de la Tradition Pontificale, Patristique et Conciliaire, 2 vols. Migne, J. P., ed. (Troisieme et Derniere Encyclopedie Theologique Ser.: Vol. 12-13). 1464p. (Fr.). Repr. of 1855 ed. lib. bdg. $186.00x (ISBN 0-89241-296-8). Caratzas Pub Co.

COUNSELING
see also Pastoral Counseling; Vocational Guidance
Harper, Frederick D. Dictionary of Counseling Techniques & Terms. LC 81-82985. 62p. 1981. pap. text ed. $4.95 (ISBN 0-935392-02-5). Douglass Pubs.

COUNSELING, PASTORAL
see Pastoral Counseling

COUNTERINSURGENCY
see Insurgency

COUNTING-OUT RHYMES
Abrahams, Roger D. & Rankin, Lois, eds. Counting Out Rhymes: A Dictionary. (AFS Bibliographical & Special Ser.: Vol. 33). 263p. 1980. text ed. $19.95x (ISBN 0-292-71057-7). U of Tex Pr.

COUNTRY LIFE
see also Agricultural Societies
Beedell, Suzanne & Hargreaves, Barbara. The Complete Guide to Country Living. $19.95 (ISBN 0-7153-7665-9). David & Charles.

COUPLES PSYCHOTHERAPY
see Family Psychotherapy

COURT, CONTEMPT OF
see Contempt of Court

COURTESY
see also Etiquette
Prevot, Floriane. Dictionnaire du Savoir-Vivre Moderne. (Fr.). 1970. 27.00 F. Casterman.

COWBOY SLANG
see Cowboys–Language

COWBOYS–LANGUAGE
Dana, Bill. Cowboy-English, English-Cowboy Dictionary. 96p. (Orig.). 1982. pap. $1.95 (ISBN 0-345-30155-2). Ballantine.

COWPER, WILLIAM, 1731-1800
Neve, John. Concordance to the Poetical Works of William Cowper. 1967. Repr. of 1887 ed. $21.00 (ISBN 0-8337-2519-X). B Franklin.

CRAFTS (HANDICRAFTS)
see Handicraft

CRANE, STEPHEN, 1871-1900
Crosland, Andrew. A Concordance to The Complete Poetry of Stephen Crane. $72.00 (ISBN 0-685-77427-9). Bruccoli.

CREDIT
see also Banks and Banking
Berman, Ben. The Dictionary of Business & Credit Terms. Andover, James J., ed. LC 82-14231. 208p. 1983. $19.95 (ISBN 0-934914-45-1). NACM.

CREOLE DIALECTS
Chaudenson, Robert. Le Lexique du Parler Creole de la Reunion, 2 vols. (Illus.). 1252p. (Fr. & Creole.). 1973. 220.00 F. Champion.
Faine. Dictionnaire Francais-Creole. 488p. (Fr. & Creole.). 1974. 300.00 F. Maison Dictionnaire.
Faine, Jules. Dictionnaire Francais-Creole. 480p. (Fr. Creole.). 1975. pap. $39.95 (ISBN 0-686-57291-2, M-4608). French & Eur.
--Dictionnaire Francais-Creole. 480p. (Fr.). 1975. 27.50 F. Lemeac.
Ferrer-Pastor, Francesc. Vocabulari Castella-Valencia & Valencia-Castella. LC 80-117607. 1075p. (Span. & Catalan.). 1979. write for info. (ISBN 8-485-10436-6). Estel Edit.
Frizzi, Giuseppe. Dizionario dei Frizzetti Popolari Firoentini. LC 76-488668. vii, 267p. (Ital.). 1975. L.9000.00. Multigrafica.
Hall, Robert A., et al, eds. Haitian Creole Grammar, Texts, Vocabulary. LC 53-9364. (Haitian Creole.). Repr. of 1953 ed. 38.00 (ISBN 0-527-01095-2). Kraus Repr.
Hessmann, Pierre. Namenforschung im Ostniederlandisch-Westfalischen Grengebiet. LC 78-375124. 104p. (Ger. & Dutch.). 1978. fl.20.00 (ISBN 9-0620-3380-6). Rodopi.
Kagaine, Elga & Rage, S. Ergemes Izloksnes Vardnica. LC 79-394141. (Illus., Latvian & Riga.). 1977. 3.50 Rub. Zinatne.
Lyse, Peter. Attved Tyrifjorden. LC 77-452595. (Illus.). 270p. (Norwegian.). 1976. Kr.39.50 (ISBN 8-20009-423-5). Universitetsforlaget.
Nougayrol, Pierre, et al. Dictionnaire Elementaire Creole Haitien-Francais. Bentolila, Alain, ed. 511p. (Haitian & Fr.). 1976. $29.95 (ISBN 0-686-57060-X, M-6430). French & Eur.
Otero, Anibal. Vocabulario de San Jorge de Piquin. LC 77-566102. 225p. (Span.). 1977. 500.00 ptas (ISBN 8-47191-009-8). Univers Santiago.
Plomteux, Hugo. I Dialetti della Liguria Orientale Odierna, 2 vols. LC 76-514874. (Illus.). 1174p. (Ital.). 1975. L.24000.00. Patron.
Raddi, Renzo. A Firenze si Parla Cosi: Frasario Moderno del Vernacolo Fiorentino. LC 76-468656. xxvii, 290p. (Ital., Firenze). 1976. L.5000.00. Libreria.
Rohlfs, Gerhard. Nuovo Dizionario Dialettale Della Calabria. LC 77-476371. (Illus.). 945p. (Ital.). 1977. L.30000.00. Longo A.
Sandefur, John R. & Sandefur, Joy L., eds. Beginnings of a Ngukurr-Bamyili Creole Dictionary: Work Papers of SIL-AAB, Series B; vol. 4. LC 80-509176. v, 136p. (Creole & Eng.). 1979. write for info. (ISBN 0-86892-190-4). Summer Inst Abor.

CRESTS
see Heraldry

CRETE
Gaya Nuno, Benito. Lexicon Creticum: Estudios sobre Escritura & lengua cretense; inscripciones monumentales; faistos, arkolochori, mallia. 84p. (Span.). 1953. 60.00 ptas (CSIC). Inst. Antonio de Nebrija.

CRIME AND CRIMINALS
Here are entered general works. For books dealing with crime and criminals in specific areas see the appropriate geographic subdivision, e.g. Crime and Criminals–United States.
see also Assassination
also headings beginning with the word Criminal
Adler, J. A. Elsevier's Dictionary of Criminal Science. (Eng., Fr., Span., Ital., Port., Dutch, Swedish, & Ger., Polyglot). 1960. $127.75 (ISBN 0-444-40003-6). Elsevier.
De Sola, Ralph. Crime Dictionary. 240p. 1982. $22.50 (ISBN 0-87196-443-0). Facts on File.
Gobello, Jose. Diccionario Lunfardo Ilustrado. (Span.). $55.00 (ISBN 0-686-56669-6, S-33076). French & Eur.
Kaiser. Kleines Kriminologisches Woerterbuch. (Ger.). 1974. pap. $7.95 (ISBN 0-686-56620-3, M-7501, Pub. by Herder). French & Eur.
--Kleines Kriminologishes Woerterbuch. (Ger.). 1974. pap. $7.95. Herder.
Reouven, Rene. Diccionario de los Asesinos. 386p. (Span.). 1976. pap. $13.95 (ISBN 84-7235-262-5, S-50083). French & Eur.
Williams, Vergil L. Dictionary of American Penology: An Introductory Guide. LC 77-94751. 1979. lib. bdg. 45.00x (ISBN 0-313-20327-X, WAP/). Greenwood.

CRIME AND CRIMINALS–BIBLIOGRAPHY
Beckman, Erik. The Criminal Justice Dictionary. 2nd, rev. ed. LC 78-72049. 1983. 22.95 (ISBN 0-87650-153-6); pap. 16.95 (ISBN 0-87650-152-8). Pierian.

CRIME AND CRIMINALS–SPAIN
Sanchez Ordonez, Angel. Diccionario Penal: Libro del Opositor C. G. P. LC 76-461919. (Illus.). 304p. (Span.). 1975. write for info. (ISBN 8-485-03319-1). Lemos.

CRIMES AND MISDEMEANORS
see Criminal Law

CRIMINAL JUSTICE, ADMINISTRATION OF
see also Crime and Criminals; Criminal Law; Juvenile Courts; Juvenile Delinquency; Police; Prisons; Punishment
Martin, Julian A. & Astone, Nicholas A. Criminal Justice Vocabulary. 312p. 1980. lexotone $29.50x (ISBN 0-398-03987-9). C C Thomas.
Walsh, Dermot & Poole, Adrian. A Dictionary of Criminology. LC 83-4611. 1983. $20.00 (ISBN 0-7100-9549-X). Routledge & Kegan.

CRIMINAL LAW
see also Contempt of Court; Criminal Justice, Administration of; Punishment
Antoniu, George, et al. Dictionar Juridic Penal. LC 76-471534. 286p. (Romanian.). 1976. 21.00 lei. Editura Stiintifica.

CRIMINALS
see Crime and Criminals

CRIMINOLOGY
see Crime and Criminals

CRITICISM
Here are entered works on the principles of criticism in general and of literary criticism in particular. Criticism in a specific field is entered under the appropriate heading, e.g. Art Criticism; English Literature–History and Criticism; English Poetry–History and Criticism; Literature–History and Criticism; Music–History and Criticism. Criticism of the work of an individual is entered under the name of the individual.
see also Bible–Criticism, Interpretation, etc.; Esthetics; Literature–History and Criticism also Criticism in specific fields e.g. Art Criticism; English Literature–History and Criticism; also names of individuals, with or without the subdivision Criticism and Interpretation
Berardi, Roberto. Dizionario di termini della critica letteraria. 234p. (Ital.). L.3500.00. Monnier.
Fowler, Roger, ed. A Dictionary of Modern Critical Terms. 218p. 1973. 18.00x (ISBN 0-7100-7543-X); pap. 5.95 (ISBN 0-7100-7544-8). Routledge & Kegan.
Le Sage, Laurent. Dictionnaire des Critiques Litteraires. 218p. (Fr.). 1969. write for info. Pa St U Pr.

CROATIAN LANGUAGE
see Serbo-Croatian Language

CROATO-SERBIAN LANGUAGE
see Serbo-Croatian Language

CROPS
see Agriculture; Field Crops; Plants, Cultivated

CROSS-WORD PUZZLES
see Crossword Puzzles

CROSSWORD PUZZLES
Charron, Jacqueline. Dictionnaire Raisonne des Mots-Croises. 315p. (Fr.). 1977. Can.$8.00. Homme.
Denis-Papin, Maurice. Dictionnaire Analoqique & de Synonymes pour la Resolution des Problemes des Mots Croises. 6th ed. (Fr.). 1970. 16.00 F. Albin Michel.
--Dictionnaire des Mots Croises. rev. ed. 384p. (Fr.). 1978. 29.00 F. Albin Michel.
--Dictionnaire des Mots Croises & Jeux Divers. 384p. (Fr.). 1973. 22.00 F. Albin Michel.
Dictionnaire de Mots Croises. (Fr.). 1978. pap. 25.00 F. Larousse.
Dictionnaire des Mots Croises. (Fr.). 1978. 25.00 F. Larousse.
Lasnier, Paul. Dictionnaire des Mots Croises: Noms Communs. 317p. (Fr.). 1975. Can.$7.00. Homme.
Noel-Henrard, L. & Noel-Henrard, M. Dictionnaire Marabout des Mots Croises, 1. (Fr.). 17.50 F. Marabout.
--Dictionnaire Marabout des Mots Croises, 2. (Fr.). 17.50 F. Marabout.
Piquette, Robert, et al. Dictionnaire des Mots Croises. 300p. (Fr.). 1966. 8.00 F. Homme.
Running Press, ed. The Scrabble Trade Mark Crossword Games Scorebook. 128p. (Orig.). 1980. lib. bdg. $12.90 (ISBN 0-89471-104-0); pap. $3.95 (ISBN 0-89471-105-9). Running Pr.

CROSSWORD PUZZLES–GLOSSARIES, VOCABULARIES, ETC.
Bailie, J. M., ed. The Hamlyn Crossword dictionary. rev. ed. LC 78-324843. 301p. (Eng.). 1978. E2.95 (ISBN 0-600-31923-7). Hamlyn Pub.
Bailie, John, ed. The Crossword Dictionary. 304p. (Eng.). E3.95 (ISBN 0-600-31923-7). Newnes Bks.
--Pocket Crossword Dictionary. 320p. (Span.). Epap. 1.25 (ISBN 0-600-32145-2). Newnes Bks.
Baus, Herbert M. The Experts Crossword Puzzle Dictionary. LC 72-84960. pap. $6.95 (ISBN 0-385-04788-6, Dolp). Doubleday.
--Master Crossword Puzzle Dictionary: The Unabridged Wordbank. LC 79-7681. (Eng.). 1981. write for info. (ISBN 0-385-17515-9). Doubleday.
Brown, John E. & Brown, Margaret H. The Crossworder's List Book. LC 77-14662. 1978. pap. $4.95 (ISBN 0-312-17690-2). St Martin.
Crossword Dictionary. (Purse Books). 1964. pap. $0.69 (ISBN 0-440-61529-1). Dell.
Crossword Puzzle Dictionary. pap. $1.99 (ISBN 0-686-00469-8). Dennison.
Denis-Papin, Maurice. Dictionnaire Des Mots Croises. 384p. (Fr.). 1978. pap. $11.95 (ISBN 0-686-56883-4, F-137060). French & Eur.
Diccionario auxiliar del crucigramista. (Span.). 60.00 ptas. Bruguera.
Diccionario de Crucigramas. 448p. (Span.). 1974. write for info. (ISBN 84-252-0783-5). G Gili.
Diccionario para resolver palabras cruzadas. (Span.). Arg.$3.00. Cosmopolita.
Dictionnaire Complet des Mots Croises. (Fr.). $9.95 (ISBN 0-686-56804-4, F-136830). French & Eur.
Finnegan, Edward G., ed. New Webster's Crossword Puzzle Dictionary: Vest Pocket Edition. 1978. pap. $1.95 (ISBN 0-8326-2221-4, 6430). Delair.
Fried, Jerome, compiled by. The Bantam Crossword Dictionary. 1979. pap. $2.75 (ISBN 0-553-14828-1). Bantam.
Halikas, Coraline E. Just Words. (Word Game & Crossword Puzzle Aid Ser.). 274p. (Orig.). 1982. pap. $14.95x (ISBN 0-686-35739-6). Ili-Cor Pubns.

Hershey, Douglas M. The Ultimate Crossword Puzzle Index. LC 81-3591. (Illus.). 192p. 1981. pap. $7.95 (ISBN 0-498-02557-8). A S Barnes.

Hill, Norman. Webster's Red Seal Crossword Dictionary. 272p. 1982. pap. $2.95 (ISBN 0-446-31186-3). Warner Bks.

Kowit, Steve. Cross Word Dictionary. 5th ed. 1977. pap. 1.50 (ISBN 0-89596-212-8, Success). Merit Pubns.

Larousse & Co. Dictionnaire Complet des Mots Croises. (Fr., Fr) 27.50 (ISBN 2-03-020294-0, 3617). Larousse.

Litero. Diccionario De Crucigramas. 435p. (Span.). 1974. pap. $7.50 (ISBN 84-252-0783-5, S-50276). French & Eur.

Melnicove, Betty F. Crossword Puzzle Dictionary. pap. $2.50 (ISBN 0-06-461007-1, D-7). B&N NY.

Melnicove, Bettye F. New Webster's Crossword Puzzle Dictionary. 1978. pap. $2.50 (ISBN 0-449-24071-1, Crest). Fawcett.

Menacho, Mary. A Practical Dictionary of Crosswords. pap. cancelled (ISBN 0-912314-07-9). Academy Pr-Santa.

Merriam Webster Editorial Staff. Webster's Official Crossword Puzzle Dictionary. LC 81-38341. 757p. 1981. 12.95 (ISBN 0-87779-021-3). Merriam-Webster Inc.

Moore, Thurston. The Original Word Game Dictionary. LC 83-42631. 272p. 1983. $16.95 (ISBN 0-8128-2926-3); pap. $7.95 (ISBN 0-8128-6191-4). Stein & Day.

Mots croises. (Fr.). 1978. pap. text ed. 9.75 (ISBN 2-03-029307-5). Larousse.

Newman, Frank E. New Practical Dictionary for Crossword Puzzles. LC 74-5608. (Eng.). 1975. $7.95 (ISBN 0-385-14776-7). Doubleday.

Newman, Frank Eaton. New Practical Dictionary for Crossword Puzzles. rev. ed. LC 74-5608. 336p. 1975. $7.95 (ISBN 0-385-05280-4). Doubleday.

Powell-Froissard, Lily. The Spanish-English, English-Spanish Crossword Puzzle Book. (Span. & Eng.). 1979. pap. $2.95 (ISBN 0-8065-0676-8). Citadel Pr.

Pulliam & Grundman. The New York Times Crossword Puzzle Dictionary. expanded ed. LC 76-50913. 1977. $19.95 (ISBN 0-8129-0668-3). Times Bks.

Pulliam, Tom & Grundman, Claire, eds. The New York Times Crossword Puzzle Dictionary. 704p. 1976. pap. $9.95 (ISBN 0-446-37262-5). Warner Bks.

Rafferty, Kathleen, ed. The Dell Crossword Dictionary. 384p. 1983. pap. $5.95 (ISBN 0-440-56314-3, Dell Trade Pbks). Dell.

--Dell Crossword Puzzle Dictionary. 384p. 1983. pap. $2.95 (ISBN 0-440-16314-5). Dell.

Room, Adrian. Dictionary of Cryptic Crossword Clues. 288p. 1983. 16.95 (ISBN 0-7100-9415-9). Routledge & Kegan.

Sisson, A. F. Unabridged Crossword Puzzle Dictionary. 1963. $8.95 (ISBN 0-385-02843-1); thumb-indexed edition $10.95 (ISBN 0-385-01350-7). Doubleday.

Swanfeldt, Andrew. Apollo Crossword Puzzle Dictionary. (Apollo Eds.). 1971. pap. $6.95i (ISBN 0-8152-0303-9, A303G). T y Crowell.

--Crossword Puzzle Dictionary. 4th, rev, new ed. LC 76-57994. 1977. $14.37i (ISBN 0-690-00426-5); thumb-indexed $15.34i (ISBN 0-690-01198-9). T y Crowell.

--The Swanfeldt Famous Crossword Puzzle Dictionary. 736p. 1982. pap. $7.64i (EH 552, EH). B&N NY.

Tuazon & Schaffer. The New Comprehensive A-Z Crossword Dictionary. 1982. pap. $3.95 (ISBN 0-380-00168-3, 50492-8). Avon.

Tuazon, Redentor M. & Schaffer. The New Comprehensive A-Z Crossword Dictionary. LC 72-79971. 600p. 1973. 5.95 (ISBN 0-448-01525-0, G&D). Putnam Pub Group.

Turell, Baldovi F. Diccionario Auxiliar del Crucigramista. 671p. (Span.). 1970. Mex.$0.86. Bruguera MX.

Turell Baldovi, Fausto. Diccionario auxiliar del crucigramista II. 256p. (Span.). 1982. pap. write for info. (ISBN 84-02-09116-4). Bruguera.

Webster's New World Crossword Puzzle Dictionary. 1983. pap. write for info. (ISBN 0-671-46870-7). S&S.

Webster's Official Crossword Puzzle Dictionary. (Eng.). 1981. $12.95 (ISBN 0-87779-021-3, 72446). Merriam.

Weeterau, Bruce. Complete Word-Finder Crossword Dictionary. 1981. pap. $3.95 (ISBN 0-451-09910-9, E9910, Sig). NAL.

Whitfield, Jane S., compiled by. Websters New World Crossword Puzzle Dictionary. LC 75-926. $7.95 (ISBN 0-529-05176-1, 190); thumb-indexed $8.95 (ISBN 0-529-05278-4, 190-I). Collins Pubs.

Wilson, Tom & Morehead, Loy. New American Crossword Puzzle Dictionary. 1971. pap. 3.50 (ISBN 0-451-12648-3, Sig). NAL.

CROW INDIANS
see Indians of North America-The West
CRUDE OIL
see Petroleum
CRUELTY
see also Animals, Treatment of
Estrany, Santiago. Vocabulari de Barbarismes. 87p. (Span.). 1982. 220.00 ptas (ISBN 8-43077-431-9). Teide.
CRUELTY TO CHILDREN
see Child Abuse
CRYOGENICS
see Low Temperatures; Refrigeration and Refrigerating Machinery
CRYPTANALYSIS
see Cryptography
CRYPTOGRAPHY
Migne, J. P., ed. Dictionnaire de Paleographie, de Cryptographie, de Dactylologie. (Nouvelle Encyclopedie Theologique Ser.: Vol. 47). 668p. (Fr.). Repr. of 1854 ed. lib. bdg. $85.00x (ISBN 0-89241-285-2). Caratzas Pub Co.
CRYSTALLINE SEMICONDUCTORS
see Semiconductors
CRYSTALLOGRAPHY
see also Geology; Mineralogy also names of minerals
Backhaus. Woerterbuch Kristallografie. 132p. (Eng., Fr., Rus. & Ger.). 1983. DM.20.00 (ISBN 3-87144-744-7). Verlag Harri Deutsch.
Technical Dictionary of Crystallography. 132p. 1980. $40.00x (ISBN 0-686-72093-8, Pub. by Collet's). State Mutual Bk.
CUB SCOUTS
see Boy Scouts
CULTIVATED PLANTS
see Plants, Cultivated
CULTURAL CHANGE
see Social Change
CULTURAL EVOLUTION
see Social Change
CULTURAL EXCHANGE PROGRAMS
see Cultural Relations
CULTURAL RELATIONS
Salon, A. Vocabulaire Critique des relations culturelles internationales. 175p. (Fr.). 1978. 80.00 F. Maison Dictionnaire.
CULTURE
see also Civilization; Education
Eliot, T. S. Notes Towards the Definition of Culture. 8.95 (ISBN 0-15-167277-6). HarBraceJ.
Langenbucher, W. R., ed. Kulturpolitisches Woerterbuch. (Ger.). 1982. $24.00. M Rosenberg.
Lexikon der Voelker & Kulturen: Bd 1. (Ger.). 1972. DM.9.80 (ISBN 3-499-16158-3). Rowohlt.
Lexikon der Voelker & Kulturen: Bd 2. (Ger.). 1978. DM.9.80 (ISBN 3-499-16159-1). Rowohlt.

Lexikon der Voelker & Kulturen: Bd 3. (Ger.). 1978. DM.9.80 (ISBN 3-499-16160-5). Rowohlt.
Stoehr, W. Lexikon der Voelker und Kulturen, 3 vols. (Ger.). 1972. pap. $25.00 (ISBN 3-499-16158-3, M-7218). French & Eur.
CUPOLAS
see Domes
CUPS AND SAUCERS
see Porcelain
CURE OF SOULS
see Pastoral Counseling
CURIOSA
see also subdivision Curiosa and Miscellany under names of persons, and under particular subjects
Ward, Philip. A Dictionary of Common Fallacies. 2nd ed. (Oleander Reference Bks.: Vols. 3 & 4). 1980. 17.50 ea. Vol. 1 (ISBN 0-900891-63-7). Vol. 2 (ISBN 0-900891-64-5). Set. 35.00 (ISBN 0-900891-65-3). Oleander Pr.
CURIOSITIES AND WONDERS
A general and miscellaneous form heading, not to be confused with Curiosa which stands for literary and bibliographical curiosities.
Chesnel De la Charbouclais, L. P. Dictionnaire des Merveilles et Curiosites de Nature et De Art. Migne, J. P., ed. (Nouvelle Encycliopedie Theologique Ser.: Vol. 44). 634p. (Fr.). Repr. of 1853 ed. lib. bdg. $81.00x (ISBN 0-89241-283-6). Caratzas Pub Co.
Dictionnaire Illustre des Merveiles Naturelles. (Illus.). 464p. (Fr.). write for info. Reader's Digest.
Vega, Vicente. Diccionario Ilustrado de Rarezas, Inverosimilitudes y Curiosidades. 4th ed. 622p. (Span.). 1971. leatherette $24.75 (ISBN 84-252-0203-5, S-12368). French & Eur.
CURRENCY
see Money
CURRENT METERS (FLUD DYNAMICS)
see Flow Meters
CURRENTS, OCEANIC
see Ocean Currents
CUSTOMARY LAW
Lexique Commente de la Douane & du Commerce Exterieur. 307p. (Fr.). 1973. 500.00 F. Editorial Office.
CUSTOMS (LAW)
see Customary Law
CUSTOMS (TARIFF)
see Tariff
CUSTOMS, SOCIAL
see Manners and Customs; also subdivision Social Life and Customs under ethnic groups, e.g. Indians, Jews, and under names of countries, cities, etc.
CUSTOMS DUTIES
see Tariff
CUTLERY
Heiler, T. Diccionario tecnico ilustrado de herramientas de corte para el trabajo de metales: Espanol-aleman-ingles-frances-italiano. (Illus.). 474p. (Span., Ger., Eng., Fr. & Ital.). write for info. G Gili.
Heiler, Toni. Dictionnaire Technique Illustre des Outlis Coupants: L'usinage des Metaux; Francais-Allemand-Anglais-Italien-Espagnol. (Illus.). 474p. (Fr., Ger., Eng., Ital. & Span.). 1965. 156.00 F. Eyrolles.
CUTTER, CHARLES AMMI, 1837-1903
Miksa, Frances. Subject in the Dictionary Catalog From Cutter to the Present. 496p. 1983. $55.00 (ISBN 0-8389-0367-3). ALA.
CYBERNETICS
see also Computers; Information Theory; System Analysis
Junge, Hans D. Technische Kybernetik Grundlagen & Anwendungen Deutsch-Englisch. 560p. (Ger. & Eng.). 1982. M.70.00. VEB Technik.
Kotz, Samuel. Russian-English Dictionary & Reader in the Cybernetical Sciences. 1966. $49.00 (ISBN 0-12-422450-4). Acad Pr.
Lexikon der Kybernetik, 4 vols. 590p. (Ger.). 1980. Set. $395.00x (ISBN 0-686-44730-1, Pub. by Collets). State Mutual Bk.

Mueller, A., ed. Lexikon der Kybernetik. 224p. (Ger.). 1964. DM.46.00 (ISBN 3-87715-022-5). Quickborner Team.
Oppermann, Alfred. Woerterbuch Kybernetik. (Ger. & Eng., Dictionary of Cybernetics). 1969. pap. $22.50 (ISBN 3-7940-3258-6, M-6915). French & Eur.
Slovar Po Kibernetike. 624p. (Rus.). 1979. $8.95 (Pub. by Sov. Entsiklopediia). Four Continent.
Sydow, A. Cibernetical Dictionary: E-G-F-R-Slovene. 171p. (Eng., Ger., Fr., Rus. & Slovene). 1974. $75.00 (ISBN 0-686-92219-0, M-9895). French & Eur.
--Dictionary of Cybernetics. 172p. 1980. $35.00x (ISBN 0-569-08527-6, Pub. by Collet's). State Mutual Bk.
Sydow, Achim. Kybernetik. LC 78-387093. 138p. (Eng. & Ger.). 1976. DM.20.00. VEB Verlag Technik.
CYCLING
see also Motorcycles
Novozhilov, S. N., et al. Velosipeday i sport. LC 80-482184. 96p. (Rus., Fr., Eng., Ger. & Span.). 1979. 0.40 Rub. Russky Yazyk.
CYCLOPEDIAS
see Encyclopedias and Dictionaries
CYMRIC LANGUAGE
see Welsh Language
CYTOGENETICS-DICTIONARIES
Rieger, R., et al. Glossary & Genetics & Cytogenetics. 4th rev. ed. LC 76-16183. (Illus.). 1976. soft cover $16.00 (ISBN 3-540-07668-9). Springer-Verlag.
Terminologia Fitogenetica & Citogenetica. (Span.). $3.20; Mex.$40.00. Herrero.
CYTOLOGY
Klishov, A. A. Kratkii Tsitologicheskii Slovar. 116p. (Rus.). 1968. $1.50 (Pub. by Meditsina). Four Continent.
CZECH LANGUAGE
Belic, Jaromir & Kamis, Adolf. Maly Starocesky Slovnik. LC 79-399115. 707p. (Czech., Prague). 1979. 43.00 Kcs. S. P. N.
Benes, Josef & Puba, Vaclay. Muzeologicky slovnik. LC 79-367213. 169p. (Czech.). 1978. write for info. SNTC.
Benesova, Hana. Cesko-Italsky Slovnik na Cesty. LC 76-532562. (Illus.). 288p. (Czech. & Ital.). 1976. 17.00 Kcs. SNTC.
Brain, James L. A Short Dictionary of Science Terms for Swahili Speakers. (Foreign & Comparative Studies Program, African Special Publications: No. 4). 70p. (Orig., Swahili.). 1969. pap. text ed. $4.50x (ISBN 0-686-74011-4). Syracuse U Foreign Comp.
Caha, J. & Kramsky, J. English-Czech Dictionary. 878p. (Eng. & Czech.). 1980. $50.00x (ISBN 0-569-00405-5, Pub. by Collet's). State Mutual Bk.
Chermak, A. Czech-English, English-Czech Dictionary. (Czech. & Eng.). 27.50 (ISBN 0-87557-012-7, 012-7). Saphrograph.
--English-Czech, Czech-English Dictionary. (Eng. & Czech.). 27.50 (ISBN 0-87557-012-7). Saphrograph.
Czech-English, English-Czech Pocket Dictionary. (Czech. & Eng.). 11.00 (ISBN 0-685-68787-2). Heinman.
Czech-English, English-Czech Pocket Dictionary. 1223p. (Czech. & Eng.). 1980. $16.95 (ISBN 0-88254-542-6, Pub. by Artia Czechoslovakia). Hippocrene Bks.
Czech-English, English-Czech Pocket Dictionary. 1223p. (Czech. & Eng.). 1980. $16.95 (ISBN 0-88254-542-6). Artia.
Dlugi, D. A., et al. Karmannyi Cheshsko-Russkii i Russko-Cheshskii Slovar. 476p. (Rus. & Czech.). 1970. $2.50 (Pub. by Sov Entsiklopediia). Four Continent.
Dobrovolny, Bohumil. Piirucni Slovnik Vedy a Techniky. LC 80-488092. 253p. (Czech.). 1979. 25.00 Kcs. Prace.
Felix, Jiri. Cesko-Rumunsky & Rumunsko-Cesky Slovnik na Cesty. LC 80-451473. 328p. (Czech. & Romanian.). 1979. 18.00 Kcs. SNTC.

Hais, Karel. Anglico-Cesko a Cesko-Anglico Kapesni-Slovnik: English-Czech, Czech-English Dictionary. 570p. (Eng. & Czech). 1974. $13.50. Imported Bks.

Hampl, Zdenek. Portugalsko-Cesky Slovnik. LC 76-508331. 883p. (Czech. & Port.). 1975. 45.00 Kcs. SNTC.

Hampl, Zdenek & Holsan, Jiri. Portugalsko-Cesko-Portugalsky Kapesni Slovnik. LC 77-551645. 497p. (Czech. & Port.). 1976. 29.00 Kcs. SNTC.

Horalek, Karel. Skolni Rusko-Cesky Slovnik. LC 79-389285. 1263p. (Rus. & Czech). 1977. 54.00 Kcs. SNTC.

Kabesch, Friedrich. Langenscheidts Taschenwoerterbuch Tschechisch: Teil II, Deutsch-Tschechisch. 478p. (Ger. & Czech). DM.19.80 (10365). Langenscheidt.

--Langenscheidts Taschenwoerterbuecher Deutsch-Tschechisch. 500p. (Ger. & Czech). 1977. DM.14.80 (ISBN 3-468-10365-4). Langenscheidt.

Kolafova, V. & Slaba, D. Czech-English-Czech Dictionary. (For Travel Ser.). 394p. (Czech. & Eng.). 1979. text ed. $6.00x (ISBN 0-89918-302-6, C302). Vanous.

Kopeckeho, L. V., ed. Skolni Rusko-Cesky Slovnik, 2 vols. 6th ed. LC 77-551653. xvi, 1134p. (Rus. & Czech). 1976. 54.00 Kcs. SNTC.

Kopetskov, L. V., et al. Russko-Cheshskii Slovar, 2 vols. (Rus.). 1977. $23.50 set (Pub. by Russkii Iazyk). Four Continent.

Kropacek, Lubos. Arabsko-Cesky Cesko-Arabsky Slovnik. LC 75-585137. 529p. (Czech. & Arabic). 1975. 22.50 Kcs. SNTC.

Langenscheidts Taschenwoerterbuecher Tschechisch. 1100p. (Czech). 1977. DM.23.80 (ISBN 3-468-11360-9). Langenscheidt.

Langenscheidts Universal-Woerterbuch Tschechisch. 560p. (Czech. & Ger.). DM.6.80 (18360). Langenscheidt.

Langenscheidts Universal-Woerterbuecher Tschechisch-Deutsch. (Czech. & Ger.). 1978. DM.5.80 (ISBN 3-468-18360-7). Langenscheidt.

Learn Czech for English Speakers. (Czech. & Eng.). pap. 9.50 (ISBN 0-87557-013-5, 013-5). Saphrograph.

Marvan, Jiri. Reverse Dictionary of Czech. LC 73-11586. (Czech. & Eng.). Date not set. 22.50x (ISBN 0-271-01164-5). Pa St U Pr.

Mrazek, Jindrich. Slovnik Zakladnich Odbornych Cesko-Nemeckych Vyrazu ze Silnicni a Mestske Dopravy. LC 75-545516. 215p. (Czech. & Ger., Praha, Czechoslovakia). 1975. write for info. SNTL.

Muller, Vaclav. Maly Divadelni Slovnik. LC 77-553272. 132p. (Czech.). 1977. write for info. Kultura.

Osicka, V. & Poldauf, I., eds. English-Czech Dictionary. 636p. (Eng. & Czech). 1980. $50.00x (ISBN 0-569-06529-1, Pub. by Collet's). State Mutual Bk.

Poldauf, I., ed. Czech-English Dictionary. 1235p. (Czech. & Eng.). 1980. $50.00x (ISBN 0-569-00404-7, Pub. by Collet's). State Mutual Bk.

--Czech-English, English Czech Dictionary. 9th ed. (Czech. & Eng.). 25.00 (ISBN 0-686-77982-7). Heinman.

Poldauf, J. Czech-English-Czech Dictionary. 4th ed. (Czech. & Eng.). 1980. text ed. $20.00x (ISBN 0-89918-253-4, C253). Vanous.

Prazak, Josef M. Latinsko-Cesky Slovnik, 2 vols. 2nd ed. LC 76-502083. (Lat. & Czech). 1975. 94.00 Kcs. SNTC.

Prirucni Slovnik Jazyka Ceskeho: Zarabcty-Zzonka, Vol. 8. (Czech). $215.00 set (EG). Statni.

Prirucni Slovnik Naucny, 4 vols. (Czech). 1963-1967. $195.00 (ISBN 0-8277-3051-9). Pergamon.

Rosendorfsky, Jaroslav. Dizionario ceco-italiano. 820p. (Czech. & Ital.). L.2000.00. Ist Univers Orient.

--Dizionario italiano-ceco. 716p. (Ital. & Czech). L.2000.00. Ist Univers Orient.

Roucka, Bohuslav. Pracovni Heslar Ceskeho Pravnehistorickeho Terminologickeho Slovniku. LC 78-366665. ii, 773p. (Czech., Prague). 1975. write for info. Ustav Statu a Prava Ceskoslovenske Akademie Ved.

Rozkovcova, L. Z. & Hanusova, S. Stary. Rustina pro Vedecke a Odborne Pracovniky, 2 vols. 208p. (Rus. & Czech). 1977. 27.00 Kcs. Academia.

Tschechisch, 2 vols. Incl. Teil I. Tschechisch-Deutsch. Ulbrich, Rolf. 576p. DM.18.80 (10360); Teil II. Deutsch-Tschechisch. Kabesch, Friedrich. 478p. DM.18.80 (10365). (Langenscheidts Taschenwörterbucher Ser.). (Czech. & Ger.). DM.29.80 (11360). Langenscheidt.

Ulbrich, Rolf. Langenscheidts Taschenwoerterbuch Tschechisch: Teil I, Tschechisch-Deutsch. 576p. (Czech. & Ger.). DM.19.80 (10360). Langenscheidt.

--Langenscheidts Taschenwoerterbuecher Tschechisch-Deutsch. 600p. (Czech. & Ger.). 1977. DM.14.80 (ISBN 3-468-10360-3). Langenscheidt.

Ulbrich, Rolf & Kabesch, Friedrich. Langenscheidts Taschenwoerterbuch Tschechisch-Deutsch, 2 vols. in 1. (Czech. & Ger.). DM.29.80 (11360). Langenscheidt.

Vencovska, Marta. Cesko-Rusky Slovnik na Cesty, 2 vols. LC 77-563463. (Illus., Czech. & Rus.). 1976. 20.00 Kcs. SNTC.

Vilikovska. Slovak-English Dictionary. 3rd ed. (Slovak & Eng.). 1971. text ed. $10.00x (ISBN 0-89918-259-3, C259). Vanous.

Vomackova, Libuse. Cesko-Francouzsky Technicky Slovnik. LC 80-458243. 907p. (Czech. & Fr.). 1978. $95.00. SNTC.

Vydava Treti Trida Ceske Akademie Ved a Umeni. Prirucni Slovnik Jazyka Ceskeho, 8 vols. (Czech). $215.00 set (EG) Vol. 1 A-J. Vol. 2, K-M. Vol. 3, N-O. Vol. 4, Pt. 1, P-Prusvitne. Vol. 4 Pt. 2, Prusvitneti-R. Vol. 5, S-S. Vol. 6, T-Vuzek. Vol. 7, Vy-Zap. Statni.

D

DACTYLOGRAPHY
see Fingerprints
DACTYLOLOGY
see Deaf–Means of Communication
DAHOMEY
see Benin
DAIRYING–DICTIONARIES
Dictionary of Dairy Terminology. (Eng. , Fr. , Ger. & Span.). Date not set. $83.00 (ISBN 0-444-42101-7). Elsevier.
DAKOTA INDIANS
see Indians of North America–The West
DAKOTA LANGUAGE
Riggs, Stephen R. Dakota-English Dictionary. facsimile ed. (Dakota & Eng.). 1968. Repr. of 1882 ed. buckram bdg. 20.00 (ISBN 0-87018-050-9). Ross.
Williamson, J. P. English-Dakota Dictionary. (Eng. & Dakota). Repr. 15.00 (ISBN 0-87018-061-4). Ross.
DALMATIAN LANGUAGE (SLAVIC)
see Serbo-Croatian Language
DAMS
Dictionary of Dams. (Hebrew, Eng. , Fr. & Ger.). IL.5.00. Massada Pr.
DANCING–DICTIONARIES
Baril, Jacques. Dictionnaire de Danse. 288p. (Fr.). 1964. pap. $14.95 (ISBN 0-686-56812-5, M-6590). French & Eur.

Desrat, G. Dictionnaire de la Danse, Historique, Theorique, Pratique & Bibliographique. LC 79-347641. (Illus.). vi, 484p. (Fr.). 1977. DM.68.00 (ISBN 3-487-06327-1). Olms Verlag.
DANCING–LIBRARIES AND MUSEUMS
see Music Libraries
DANCING–INDIA
Krishan Rao, V. S. Dictionary of Bharatnatya. 1981. $15.00x (ISBN 0-8364-0698-2, Orient Longman). South Asia Bks.
Menon, K. P. Dictionary of Kathakali. 1980. $11.00 (ISBN 0-8364-0573-0, Orient Longman). South Asia Bks.
Rao, Krishna. A Dictionary of Bharata Natya. (Illus.). 100p. 1980. text ed. $15.95x (ISBN 0-86131-155-8, Pub. by Orient Longman Ltd India). Apt Bks.
DANISH LANGUAGE
Borum, Oscar A. & Von Eyben, W. E. Juridisk Ordbog. LC 77-459744. 254p. (Danish). 1976. Kr.92.00 (ISBN 8-712-08818-8). Gad Forlag.
Espersen, Johan C. Bornholmsk Ordbog. LC 75-400668. xxi, 683p. (Danish). 1975. write for info. Rosenkilde.
Holmboe, Henrik. Dansk Retrogradordbog. LC 78-363861. 259p. (Danish). 1978. Kr.106.20 (ISBN 8-75001-793-4). Akademisk Forlag.
Muschinsky, Lars J. & Schnack, Karsten, eds. Paedagogisk Opslangsbog: Alfabetisk Ordnet. LC 79-371231. (Illus.). 285p. (Danish). 1977. Kr.74.50 (ISBN 8-772-41417-0). Ejlers Forlag.
DANISH LANGUAGE–DICTIONARIES
Albertus, Flemming G. Gjellerups Gronne Ordbog. LC 78-343138. (Danish). 1977. Kr.34.50 (ISBN 8-71301-300-9). Gjellerup Forlag.
Bailey, I. E. Dansk-Engelsk Handels-og Fagordbog. 514p. (Danish & Eng.). 1973. $75.00 (ISBN 87-570-0533-8, M-8411). French & Eur.
Bang, Jorgen. Femmedordbog. 11th ed. LC 77-561717. 480p. (Danish). 1976. Kr.56.00 (ISBN 8-71940-170-1). Berlingske Forlag.
Benzon, Gorm R. Gyldendals Antikvitetshandbog, 2 vols. LC 76-488522. (Illus., Danish). 1976. Kr.296.00 (ISBN 8-700-09561-3). Gyldendal Norsk.
Berlitz Editors. Berlitz Pocket Dictionaries: Danish-English. 300p. (Danish & Eng.). 1982. pap. 4.95 (ISBN 0-686-92980-2, Berlitz). Macmillan.
Blinkenberg, A. & Hoybye, P. Dansk-Fransk Ordbog. 2058p. (Danish & Fr.). 1975. leatherette $175.00 (ISBN 0-686-92500-9, M-1278). French & Eur.
Blinkenberg, A. P. & Hoybye, Poul. Dansk-Fransk Ordbog. 3rd ed. Thiele, Margrethe, ed. LC 77-467208. (Fr. & Dan.). 1975. Kr.180.00 (ISBN 8-71703-231-8). Erhvervso.
Bork, E. & Kaper, E. Dansk-Tysk Ordbog. 626p. (Danish & Ger.). 1981. $24.95 (ISBN 87-01-93141-5, M-1283). French & Eur.
Bork, Egon & Kaper, Egon. Dansk-Tysk Ordbog. LC 76-458154. 531p. (Danish & Ger.). 1975. Kr.55.00 (ISBN 8-70009-141-3). Gyldendal Norsk.
Bruun, Erik. Dansk Sprogbrug. LC 79-389408. 588p. (Danish). 1978. Kr.110.00 (ISBN 8-70130-201-9). Gyldendal Norsk.
Danish Pocket Dictionary. (Danish & Eng.). 7.50 (ISBN 8-7146-1178-3). Heinman.
Dansk-Engelsk Teknisk Ordbog. 393p. (Danish & Eng.). 1981. $49.95 (ISBN 87-11-04027-0, M-1289). French & Eur.
Dansk-Spansk Ordborg. 489p. (Danish & Span.). 1980. $29.95 (ISBN 87-01-71901-7, S-39031). French & Eur.
Dehn-Nielsen, Henning. Fogtdals et-binds leksikon i farver. Sejersen, Gorm, ed. LC 80-459104. (Illus.). 656p. (Danish). 1979. Kr.298.00 (ISBN 8-74270-116-3). Fogtdals Boger.

De Vries, Geerte. Van Goor's Deens Woordenboek, 2 vols. LC 76-477773. (Dutch & Danish). 1976. fl.85.00 (ISBN 9-00002-195-2). Goor.
Diccionario Lexicon Espanol-Danes & Espanol-Danes. 384p. (Span. & Danish). 1974. leatherette $4.95 (ISBN 84-303-0160-7, S-50407); pap. $4.50 (ISBN 84-303-0159-3, S-50406). French & Eur.
Dissing, Borge & Lave, Rud. Dansk-Tysk Ordbog. LC 79-383402. (Illus.). 347p. (Ger. & Danish). 1978. write for info. Gyldendal Norsk.
Falk, H. S. & Torp, Alf. Norwegisch-Daenisches Etymologisches Woerterbuch, Vol. 1. 2nd ed. (Norwegian & Danish). 1960. $55.00 (ISBN 3-533-00505-4, M-7570, Pub. by Carl Winter). French & Eur.
--Norwegisch-Daenisches Etymologisches Woerterbuch, Vol. 1. 2nd ed. (Norwegian & Danish). 1960. $55.00 (ISBN 3-533-00505-4). Winter Univ.
--Norwegisch-Daenisches Etymologisches Woerterbuch, Vol. 2. 2nd ed. (Norwegian & Danish). 1960. $55.00 (ISBN 3-533-00506-2, M-7571, Pub. by Carl Winter). French & Eur.
--Norwegisch-Daenisches Etymologisches Woerterbuch, Vol. 2. 2nd ed. (Norwegian & Danish). 1960. $55.00 (ISBN 3-533-00506-2). Winter Univ.
--Norwegisch Daenisches Etymologisches Woerterbuch: Mit Literatur-Nachweisen Strittiger Etymologien Sowie Deutschem und Altnordischen Woerterverzeichnis, 2 Vols. 2nd ed. 1722p. (Norwegian & Danish). 1960. Set. $80.00x (ISBN 8-200-00085-0, Dist. by Columbia U Pr). Universitet.
Grue-Sorensen, K. & Winther-Jensen, Thyge, eds. Paedagogikkens Hvem Hvad Hvor. LC 78-379066. (Illus.). 295p. (Danish). 1978. Kr.75.00 (ISBN 8-756-72555-8). Politikens Forlag.
Gubba, W. Juridisk Ordbog, Dansk-Tysk: Supplement & Forkortelsesliste. 68p. (Danish & Ger.). 1978. write for info. Guba.
Henningsen, H. Langenscheidts Taschenwoerterbuch Danisch, 2 vols. in 1. (Danish & Ger.). DM.29.80 (11100). Langenscheidt.
--Langenscheidt's Taschenwoerterbuch Danisch: Teil I, Danisch-Deutsch. 557p. (Danish & Ger.). DM.19.80 (10100). Langenscheidt.
--Langenscheidts Taschenwoerterbuch Danisch: Teil II, Deutsch-Danisch. 548p. (Ger. & Danish). DM.19.80 (10105). Langenscheidt.
--Langenscheidts Taschenwoerterbuecher Daenisch. (Danish). 1978. DM.23.80 (ISBN 3-468-11100-2). Langenscheidt.
Kjaer, L. Ove. Dansk-Latinsk: Ordbog. 580p. (Danish & Lat.). 1979. $29.95 (ISBN 0-686-92574-2, M-1277). French & Eur.
Krymova, N. I., et al. Russko-Datskii Slovar. 906p. (Rus.). 1956. $4.75 (Pub. by GINS). Four Continent.
Lademanns Leksikon, 20 vols. (Danish). 1970-1976. $850.00 (ISBN 0-8277-3066-7). Pergamon.
Langenscheidt Danish-English Lilliput Dictionary. 615p. (Danish & Eng.). plastic $1.50 (ISBN 3-468-96467-6). Langenscheidt.
Mengel, J. Dansk-Italiensk Ordborg. 660p. (Danish & Ital.). 1979. $39.95 (ISBN 0-686-92569-6, M-1292). French & Eur.
Molde, Bertil. Dansk-Svensk Ordbok. Ferlov, Niels, ed. 726p. (Danish & Swedish). 1980. Kr.170.00 (ISBN 91-24-29601-5). Esselte Studium.
Poulsen, O. Dansk-Tysk Ordbog for Korrespondenter. 415p. (Danish & Ger.). 1980. $39.95 (ISBN 87-87697-10-6, M-1273). French & Eur.

Schibsbye, K. & Kossmann, H. Danish-English Dictionary. rev. ed. Rona, G. & Raylor, R., eds. (Danish & Eng.). $32.50 (ISBN 0-87559-006-3); thumb indexed $37.50 (ISBN 0-87559-007-1). Shalom.

Sorensen, N. C. Dansk-Fransk Ordbog. 484p. (Danish & Fr.). 1980. $24.95 (ISBN 87-01-33721-1, M-1284). French & Eur.

Sorensen, Niels C. Dansk-Fransk Ordbog. LC 76-511464. 515p. (Danish & Fr.). 1975. Kr.60.00 (ISBN 8-70049-461-5). Gyldendal Norsk.

Vangmark, H. Dansk-Russik Ordborg. 238p. (Danish & Rus.). 1979. $39.95 (ISBN 87-429-7608-1). French & Eur.

Vinterberg, H. & Bodelsen, C. A. Dansk-Engelsk Ordbog. 1846p. (Danish & Eng.). 1981. $95.00 (ISBN 87-00-67161-4, M-1281). French & Eur.

Vinterberg, H. & Axelsen, J., eds. Danish-English, English-Danish Dictionary, 2 vols. 8th & 10th ed. (Danish & Eng.). Set. 50.00 (ISBN 0-685-36173-X). Vol. 1, Danish-English (ISBN 8-7001-1282-8). Vol. 2, English-Danish (ISBN 8-7013-3451-4). Heinman.

Vinterberg, H., et al. Danish Dictionary: Rode Ordbog-Gyldendals, Danish-English. 11th ed. (Danish & Eng.). 1981. text ed. $20.00x (ISBN 8-7001-1282-8, D705). Vanous.

--Danish Dictionary: Rode Ordbog-Gyldendals, English-Danish. 9th ed. (Danish & Eng.). 1979. text ed. $20.00x (ISBN 8-7008-0381-2, D704). Vanous.

--Dansk-Engelsk Ordboger. 538p. (Danish & Eng.). 1981. $24.95 (ISBN 0-686-92581-5, M-1272). French & Eur.

Warren, A. Dansk-Tysk Teknisk Ordborg. 279p. (Danish & Ger.). 1977. $49.95 (ISBN 87-11-03797-0, M-1290). French & Eur.

Warrern, A. Danish-English, English-Danish Technical Dictionary, 2 vols. new, rev. ed. (Danish & Eng.). Set. 80.00 (ISBN 8-7110-3767-9). Danish-Eng (ISBN 87-11-03767-9). Eng.-Danish (ISBN 87-11-03867-5). Heinman.

Widman, Karen. Dansk-Svensk Ordbok. 309p. (Danish & Swedish). write for info. (ISBN 91-24-14367-7). Esselte Studium.

DANO-NORWEGIAN LANGUAGE
see Danish Language; Norwegian Language
DARK AGES
see Middle Ages
DARWINISM
see Evolution
DATA BASE MANAGEMENT
Trilingual Dictionary. 216p. 1982. pap. $35.00 (ISBN 0-686-87246-0, IB101, Pub. by Intergovernmental Bureau). Unipub.
DATA PROCESSING
see Electronic Data Processing; Information Storage and Retrieval Systems
DATA TERMINALS (COMPUTERS)
see Computer Input-Output Equipment
DATA TRANSMISSION SYSTEMS
Sippl, Charles J. Data Communications Dictionary. 533p. 1980. pap. text ed. $12.95 (ISBN 0-442-21931-8). Van Nos Reinhold.
DATES
see Chronology, Historical
DATES, BOOKS OF
see Calendars
DAY DREAMS
see Fantasy
DAY RELEASE (GREAT BRITAIN)
see Education, Cooperative
DEAF
see also Children, Deaf
Gallaudet College Library, Washington, D. C. Dictionary Catalog on Deafness & the Deaf, 2 vols. 1970. Set. lib. bdg. $190.00 (ISBN 0-8161-0877-3, Hall Library). G K Hall.
DEAF-EDUCATION
see also Deaf-Means of Communication

Vaughan, Wm. A Vocabulary Arranged for the Instruction of the Deaf & Dumb. 69.95 (ISBN 0-8490-1265-1). Gordon Pr.

Watson, T. J. An Illustrated Vocabulary for the Use of the Deaf & Dumb. 69.95 (ISBN 0-8490-0383-0). Gordon Pr.

DEAF-MEANS OF COMMUNICATION
Boatner, M., et al, eds. Dictionary of American Idioms for Deaf. 1976. $9.95 (ISBN 0-8120-0612-7). Barron.

Boatner, M. T., et al, eds. Dictionary of American Idioms for the Deaf. 1976. $14.95 (ISBN 0-8120-5103-3). Barron.

Darton, Harvey. Plates Illustrative of the Vocabulary for the Deaf & Dumb. 69.95 (ISBN 0-8490-0841-7). Gordon Pr.

Guilfoyle, George R. & Silverman-Dresner, Toby. Vocabulary Norms for Deaf Children. LC 72-83498. (Lexington School Ser.: Book 7). 1972. softcover $8.00 (ISBN 0-88200-060-8, C2344). Alexander Graham.

Gustason, Gerilee, et al. Signing Exact English. 1980 ed. LC 80-80571. (Illus.). 460p. (gr. k-12). 1980. text ed. 24.00x (ISBN 0-916708-02-0); pap. text ed. 18.00x (ISBN 0-916708-03-9). Modern Signs.

O'Rourke, Terrence J. A Basic Vocabulary of American Sign Language for Parents & Children. (Illus.). 240p. 1978. $12.95 (SL040); pap. $8.95. Natl Assn Deaf.

Ward, Jill. Ward's Natural Sign Language Thesaurus of Useful Signs N' Synonyms. Joyce, John, ed. LC 77-93547. (Illus.). 1978. 27.00 (ISBN 0-917002-18-0, 446). Joyce Media.

DEAF MUTES
see Deaf
DEAFNESS
Here are entered works on the lack of sense of hearing, including the lack combined with the inability to speak, i.e. deaf-mutism. Works on the inability to speak whether from any functional or physical case other than deafness are entered under Mutism.
Boatner, Maxine & Gates, John. Dictionary of Idioms for the Deaf. 1975. pap. $8.95 (E001). Natl Assn Deaf.

Gallaudet College Library, Washington, D. C. Dictionary Catalog on Deafness & the Deaf, 2 vols. 1970. Set. lib. bdg. $190.00 (ISBN 0-8161-0877-3, Hall Library). G K Hall.

DEAFNESS IN CHILDREN
see Children, Deaf
DEATH
see also Hell
Lope Blanch, Juan M. Vocabulario Mexicano Relativo a la Muerte. 183p. (Span.). 1964. Mex.$20.00. UNAM.

Sabatier, Robert. Diccionario Ilustrado de la Muerte. 612p. (Span.). 1970. pap. $24.75 (ISBN 84-252-0351-1, S-50581). French & Eur.

DEBATES AND DEBATING
see also Oratory
Ministere des Communications Assemblee Nationale. Lexique du Journal des Debats. 7th ed. (Fr.). 1974. Can.$2.00. Quebec Off.

--Lexique du Journal des Debats. 8th ed. 232p. (Fr.). 1976. Can.$3.00. Quebec Off.

--Lexique du Journal des Debats. 6th ed. 146p. (Fr.). 1972. Can.$1.50. Quebec Off.

DECENNALIA
see Roman Emperors
DECISION-MAKING, JUDICIAL
see Judicial Process
DECORATIVE ARTS
see Art, Decorative
also the specific subjects referred to under these headings
DEDUCTION (LOGIC)
see Logic
DEDUCTIVE LOGIC
see Logic
DEEP-SEA DEPOSITS
see Sedimentation and Deposition
DEEP-SEA EXPLORATION
see Marine Biology; Marine Fauna

DEFECTIVE SPEECH
see Speech, Disorders Of
DE GAULLE, CHARLES
see Gaulle, Charles De, Pres. France, 1890-1970
DEGREES OF LATITUDE AND LONGITUDE
see Geodesy
DEITIES
see Gods
DELAWARE LANGUAGE
Brinton, Daniel G. Lenape-English Dictionary. LC 77-153000. iii, 77p. (Eng. & Lenape.). 1977. write for info. Waletittin.

--A Lenape-English Dictionary. LC 76-43670. 236p. (Eng. & Lenape.). 1979. write for info. (ISBN 0-404-15764-5). AMS Pr.

Brinton, Daniel G. & Anthony, Albert S., eds. A Lenape-English Dictionary. LC 76-43670. (Eng. & Lenape.). Repr. of 1888 ed. $22.50 (ISBN 0-404-15764-5). AMS Pr.

Goddard, Ives. Delaware Verbal Morphology: A Descriptive & Comparative Study. Hankamer, Jorge, ed. LC 78-66556. (Outstanding Dissertations in Linguistics Ser.). 1979. lib. bdg. 29.00 (ISBN 0-8240-9685-1). Garland Pub.

DELINQUENCY, JUVENILE
see Juvenile Delinquency
DELUSIONS
see Superstition
DEMOCRACY
see also Aristocracy; Socialism
Haro Tecglen, Eduardo. Diccionario del Democrata. LC 77-569550. (Illus.). 92p. (Span.). 1977. 70.00 ptas (ISBN 8-472-35313-3). Dopesa.
DEMOGRAPHY
see also Population
also subdivision Population under names of countries
Chanlett, Eliska. A Glossary of Selected Demographic Terms. LC 77-71130. (Occasional Publications Ser.). 1974. pap. text ed. 3.50 (ISBN 0-89383-060-7). Intl Program Labs.

Dizionario demografico multilingue. xix, 166p. (Ital.). 1959. L.1200.00. Giuffre.

Pressat, Roland. Dictionnaire de Demographie. 1st ed. LC 79-123891. vi, 295p. (Fr.). 1979. write for info. (ISBN 2-13-036008-4). Pr Univ Fr.
DENDROLOGY
see Trees
DENMARK
Linder, Bernhard & Paltorp, Adam S. Lademanns Rejsleleksikon Danmark. LC 76-478984. (Illus., Danish.). 1976. Kr.550.00 (ISBN 8-715-07133-2). Lademann Forlag.
DENTAL MEDICINE
see Teeth-Diseases
DENTAL PATHOLOGY
see Teeth-Diseases
DENTAL PROSTHESIS
see Prosthodontics
DENTAL SURGERY
see Dentistry
DENTISTRY
see also Periodontia; Prosthodontics
Aeschlimann, Werner H. Zahnarztliches aus dem Dictionnaire des Sciences Medicales. LC 75-507861. 75p. (Fr.). 1975. 20.00 F (ISBN 3-260-03859-0). Juris Druckg.

Bucksch, Herbert. Dental dictionary. LC 79-315800. 846p. (Eng. & Ger.). 1978. write for info. (ISBN 3-921280-24-9). Verlag Neuer.

Durante Avellanal, Ciro. Diccionario odontologico. (Span.). $23.00; Arg.$120.00. Mundi.

Ehrlich, Ann. Cavity Classification & Related Terminology. (Illus.). 1978. $4.25 (ISBN 0-940012-04-9). Colwell Co.

--Introduction to Dental Terminology. (Illus.). 1978. $3.95 (ISBN 0-940012-10-3). Colwell Co.

Fowler, Jennifer. Heinemann Modern Dictionary for Dental Students. 184p. (Eng. & Fr.). 1973. $29.95 (ISBN 0-686-56750-1, M-6257). French & Eur.

Heinemann Modern Dictionary for Dental Students. (Illus.). 1973. text ed. $16.95x (ISBN 0-433-10701-4). Intl Ideas.

Rice. Introduction to Dental Terminology. 1982. pap. $12.95 (ISBN 0-8151-7239-7). Year Bk Med.

Roucoules, Leon. Terminologie Fondamentale en Odonto-Stomatologie. LC 77-469099. 259p. (Eng. & Fr.). 1977. write for info. (ISBN 2-224-00328-5). Maloine.

Terminologie Fondamentale En Odonto-Stomatologie et Lexique: Francais-Anglais, Anglais-Francais. 259p. (Fr. & Eng.). 1977. $27.50 (ISBN 0-686-57210-6, M-6492). French & Eur.

Vieillefosse, Roger. Dictionnaire de Pharmacologie Dentaire. 228p. (Fr.). 1970. 58.00 F. Maloine.

Viellefosse, Roger. Dictionnaire de Pharmacologie Dentaire. 228p. (Fr.). 1970. $24.95 (ISBN 0-686-57245-9, M-6550). French & Eur.

Woolley, LeGrand H. Medical-Dental Terminology: Syllabus. 2nd ed. 1974. pap. text ed. 6.10 (ISBN 0-89420-003-8, 217705); cassette recordings 177.70 (ISBN 0-89420-162-X, 196700). Natl Book.

Zwemer, Thomas J., et al. Boucher's Clinical Dental Terminology: A Glossary of Accepted Terms in All Disciplines of Dentistry. 3rd ed. LC 81-18843. (Illus.). 378p. 1982. text ed. 27.95 (ISBN 0-8016-0712-4). Mosby.

DENTISTRY, PROSTHETIC
see Prosthodontics
DENTURES
see Prosthodontics
DEPOSITION AND SEDIMENTATION
see Sedimentation and Deposition
DEPOSITS, DEEP-SEA
see Sedimentation and Deposition
DEPRECIATION
Glossary of Depreciation Terms. 44p. 1980. $3.50. NARUC.
DERMATOLOGY
see also Pediatric Dermatology
Robinson, Harry M., Jr. & Burnett, Joseph W. A Dictionary of Dermatologic Therapy. LC 78-62796. 1978. text ed. $25.00 (ISBN 0-914316-15-X). Yorke Med.
DESCARTES, RENE, 1596-1650
Morris, John, ed. Descartes Dictionary. LC 73-137789. 1971. 10.00 (ISBN 0-8022-2046-0). Philos Lib.
DESCENT
see Genealogy
DESCRIPTION (RHETORIC)
Centre de Documentatio de. Lexique Thematique des Des Descripteurs & Identificateurs. new ed. 151p. (Fr.). 1976. 75.00 F. Centre Documentation.
DESIGN
see also Costume Design; Printing-Layout and Typography; Printing As a Graphic Art
Barber, Bruce T. Designer's Dictionary Two. (Illus.). 407p. 1981. $28.00 (ISBN 0-911380-54-X). Signs of Times.

Beguin, Andre. Dictionnaire Technique et Critique du Dessin. (Fr.). 1978. $99.50 (ISBN 0-686-56911-3, M-6027). French & Eur.
DETERGENTS
see Cleaning Compounds
DEVELOPMENT BANKS
Scharf, T. & Shetty, M. C. Dictionary of Development Banking: A Compilation of Terms in English, French, & German with Definitions in English. LC 72-83212. (Eng., Fr. & Ger.). 1973. $42.00 (ISBN 0-444-41028-7). Elsevier.
DEVELOPMENTAL DYSLEXIA
see Reading Disability
DEVICES
see also Heraldry; Mottoes; Symbolism
Chassant, Louis A. & Tausin, Henri. Dictionnaire des Devises Heraldiques. 1624p. (Fr.). write for info. Olms Verlag.
DEVIL-WORSHIP
see Satanism
DEVOTIONAL LITERATURE
Cruden, Alexander. Cruden's Unabridged Concordance. LC 54-11084. $17.95 (ISBN 0-8054-1123-2). Broadman.

DEVOTIONAL THEOLOGY
see Devotional Literature; Meditations
also subdivision Prayer-Books and Devotions under names of Christian denominations, religious orders, classes of persons, etc.

DHYANA (SECT)
see Zen Buddhism

DIABETES
Brown, Joseph F. Diabetes Dictionary & Guide. LC 77-92938. (Illus.). 1978. 14.95 (ISBN 0-9601484-1-8). Press West.

DIAGNOSIS
see also Medicine, Clinical; Pathology
also subdivisions Diseases–Diagnosis or Diseases under names of organs and regions of the body, e.g. Lungs–diseases–diagnosis; also subdivisions Diagnosis under particular diseases, e.g. Tuberculosis–Diagnosis
Blacque-Belair, Alain & Fossey, Bernard M. de. Dictionnaire de Diagnostic Clinique et Topographique. 1250p. (Fr.). 1969. $55.00 (ISBN 0-686-56921-0, M-6037). French & Eur.
Dictionnaire des Symptomes. 602p. (Fr.). 1978. 88.00 F. Edito Serv.
Gomez, Joan. Diccionario de Sintomas. 681p. (Span.). 1980. 800.00 ptas. Acervo.
--A Dictionary of Symptoms. rev. ed. LC 82-42525. (Illus.). 324p. 1983. pap. $5.95 (ISBN 0-8128-1949-7). Stein & Day.
Isler, C. Isler's Pocket Dictionary of Diagnostic Tests, Procedures & Terms. 1980. pap. 8.95 (ISBN 0-87489-189-2). Med Economics.

DIAGNOSTIC PSYCHOLOGICAL TESTING
see Clinical Psychology

DIAGRAMS, STATISTICAL
see Statistics–Graphic Methods

DIALECTIC (LOGIC)
see Logic

DIALECTIC (RELIGION)
see Polarity (In Religion, Folk-Lore, etc.)

DIALECTIC LOGIC
see Logic

DIALECTS
see Creole Dialects; Franco-Provencal Dialects; Grammar, Comparative and General; Languages, Mixed
also subdivisions Dialects; Idioms, Corrections, Errors; Provincialisms under names of languages
Pinelli, Stefano. Piccolo Dizionario del Dialetto Bresciano. LC 77-467177. (Illus.). 109p. (Ital.). 1976. write for info. Grafo.

DIAMONDS
see also Gems
Gaal, Robert A. The Diamond Dictionary. 2nd ed. (Illus.). 1977. 16.95 (ISBN 0-87311-008-0). Gemological.

DIANETICS
Hubbard, L. Ron. Dianetics & Scientology Technical Dictionary. $32.00 (ISBN 0-686-30803-4). Church Scient NY.
--Dianetics & Scientology Technical Dictionary. 1975. $37.00 (ISBN 0-88404-037-2). Bridge Pubns Inc.

DICKENS, CHARLES, 1812-1870
Fitzgerald, Percy H. The Pickwickian Dictionary & Cyclopaedia. LC 71-148777. Repr. of 1902 ed. $27.50 (ISBN 0-404-08778-7). AMS Pr.
Williams, Mary. Dickens Concordance. LC 74-31478. 1907. lib. bdg. $12.50 (ISBN 0-8414-9373-1). Folcroft.

DICKINSON, EMILY ELIZABETH, 1830-1886
Rosenbaum, Stanford P., ed. Concordance to the Poems of Emily Dickinson. LC 64-25335. (Concordances Ser.). 921p. 1964. $55.00x (ISBN 0-8014-0362-6). Cornell U Pr.

DICTIONARIES
see Encyclopedias and Dictionaries; also particular languages or subjects with or without the subdivision dictionaries

DICTIONARIES, CLASSICAL
see Classical Dictionaries

DICTIONARIES, PICTURE
see Picture Dictionaries

DICTIONARIES, POLYGLOT
see also Polyglot Glossaries, Phrase Books, etc.
Abrahamian, R. Pekhleviisko-Persidsko-Armiano-Russko-Angliiskii Slovar. 336p. (Rus. & Eng. & Armenian.). 1965. $3.65 (Pub. by Mitk). Four Continent.
Ahlsved, Karl-Johan, et al. Lexicon Forestale. LC 80-487653. xix, 592p. (Eng., Finnish, Ger., Swedish, & Rus.). 1979. Fmk.350.00 (ISBN 9-5100-9174-X). Suomen Standard.
Albota, Mihail. Dictionar Poliglot de Geodezie: Fotogrammetrie si Cartografie. LC 76-477531. xv, 325p. (Eng., Ger., Fr., Rus. & Romanian.). 1976. 41.00 lei. Editura Stiintifica.
Al-Kasimi, Ali M. Linguistics & Bilingual Dictionaries. 1977. text ed. 20.50x (ISBN 90-04047-87-5). Humanities.
Anell, Ivar. Vad Betyder Vaxtens Latinska Namn. LC 76-470315. 159p. (Eng., Danish, Finnish, Fr., Lat., Norwegian, & Swedish.). 1976. Kr.55.00 (ISBN 9-1370-6121-6). Forum Bok.
Arva, Gyorgy. Etlapiras. LC 77-473040. 513p. (Eng., Czech. & Hungarian.). 1975. 71.00 Ft (ISBN 9-6322-0195-7). Kozgazdasagi.
Aurenche, Oliver, ed. Dictionnaire Illustre Multilingue de l'Architecture du Proche Orient Ancien. LC 78-392938. (Illus.). 391p. (Fr.). 1977. $250.00 F. Boccard.
Aurousseau, Paul. International Hospital Vade Mecum & English, French, Spanish Glossary. LC 78-675029. 340p. (Eng., Fr. & Span.). 1977. 0.257 F. Editions Sedip F.Galula.
Avfallsordlista. LC 78-361963. xxvii, 210p. (Eng , Fr. & Swedish.). 1977. Kr.40.00 (ISBN 9-1719-6062-7). Tek Nomen.
Aymard Lapalu, Nicole. Safety at Work & Pollution Control. LC 76-376744. 320p. (Eng., Fr., Ger. & Span.). 1975. write for info. (ISBN 2-7213-0051-2). Elp.
Band-Kuzmany, K. R. Glossary of the Theatre. (Eng., Fr., Ital. & Ger.). 1970. $30.00 (ISBN 0-444-40716-2). Elsevier.
Bassegoda Muste, B. Diccionario poliglota de la arquitectura. 366p. (Span., Ger., Fr., Eng & Ital.). 1976. pap. $35.00. Imported Bks.
Bergman, P. H. Concise Dictionary of Twenty-Six Languages in Simultaneous Translation. pap. 2.95 (ISBN 0-451-11478-7, AE1478, Sig). NAL.
Biass-Ducroux, Francoise. Glossary of Genetics. (Eng., Fr., Span., Ital., Ger. & Rus.). 1970. $72.50 (ISBN 0-444-40712-X). Elsevier.
Blok, Czeslaw. Ilustrowany Slownik Samochodowy. LC 76-526304. 867p. (Eng., Pol., Rus. & Fr.). 1976. 250.00 Zl. Wydawnictwa.
Boleslaw, Adamczyk. Pieciojezyczny Slownik Gleboznawczy. LC 76-532466. 264p. (Eng., Fr., Ger., Pol. & Rus.). 1976. 120.00 Zl. Panstwowe Zaklad W.
Bosch, Ten. Dutch-English-French-German Engineering Dictionary. 11th ed. (Dutch, Eng., Fr. & Ger.). 45.00 (ISBN 90-2010-132-3). Heinman.
Brunhuber, E. Giesserei-Fachwoerterbuch. 802p. (Ger., Eng., Fr. & Ital.). 1977. DM.120.00 (ISBN 3-7949-0283-1). Schiele & Schon.
--Giesserei-Lexikon 1978. 960p. (Ger.). 1977. DM.62.50 (ISBN 3-7949-0282-3). Schiele & Schon.
Brunhuber, Ernst. Giesserei-Fachworterbuch. LC 78-350030. 729p. (Eng., Fr., Ger. & Ital.). 1977. DM.148.00 (ISBN 3-7949-0283-1). Schiele & Schon.
Brunius, Niklas. Teaterord. LC 77-578501. 179p. (Eng., Danish, Finnish, Icelandic, Norwegian & Swedish.). 1975. write for info. Nord Teater.
Burger, E. Technical Dictionary of Data Processing, Computers & Office Machines, English, German, French, Russian. (Eng., Ger., Fr. & Rus.). 1970. $130.00 (ISBN 0-08-006425-6). Pergamon.
Burger, Erich. Automatizovany Zber Dat Programovanie. LC 78-373214. 479p. (Eng., Fr. & Rus.). 1976. 80.00 Kcs. Alfa-Vydavatel.
--Datenerfassung Programmierung. LC 77-484881. 388p. (Eng., Ger., Fr. & Rus.). 1976. M.38.00. VEB Verlag Technik.
Capdevila Font, Juan. Diccionario Simultaneo en 6 Idiomas. 192p. (Span., Eng., Fr., Ital., Ger. & Port.). 1975. pap. $6.75 (ISBN 84-85117-14-X, S-31467). French & Eur.
Capdevilla Font, Juan. Diccionario Simultaneo en 21 Idiomas. 416p. (Span., Eng., Fr., Ger., Ital., Port., Catalan, Czech, Danish, Esparanto, Finnish, Gr., Dutch, Hungarian, Malaysian, Pol., Rumanian, Rus., Swedish & Turkish.). 1977. pap. $18.75 (ISBN 0-686-57350-1, S-31466). French & Eur.
Cesky a Sovensky Terminologicky Slovnik z Fytopatologie a Ochrany Rostlin. LC 79-356902. 392p. (Czech. & Slovak.). 1977. write for info. SNTC.
Clason, W. Elsevier's Dictionary of Chemical Engineering, 2 Vols. (Eng., Fr., Span., Ital., Dutch, & Ger.). 1969. Set. $170.25 (ISBN 0-444-40736-7); Vol. 1. $85.00 (ISBN 0-444-40714-6); Vol. 2. $85.00 (ISBN 0-444-40715-4). Elsevier.
Clason, W. E. Elsevier's Dictionary of Nuclear Science & Technology. 2nd rev. ed. (Eng., Fr., Span., Ital., Dutch & Ger.). 1970. $121.50 (ISBN 0-444-40810-X). Elsevier.
Costaz, Louis. Dictionnaire Syraique-Francais-Anglais. 423p. (Syrian & Eng.). 1963. 25.00 F. Dar El-Machreq.
Craeybeckx, A. S. Elsevier's Dictionary of Photography. (Eng., Fr., & Ger.). 1965. $113.00 (ISBN 0-444-40146-6). Elsevier.
Cristea, Petre. Dictionar Tehnic Auto de Buzunar in Sapte Limbi. LC 76-503037. 441p. (Eng., Romanian, Ger., Fr., Ital., Span. & Rus.). 1975. 21.00 lei. Editura Stiintifica.
Deutsches Komitee fur Reprographie. Woerterbuch der Reprographie. LC 76-456115. 273p. (Eng., Fr. & Ger.). 1975. write for info. Aussant & Schrift.
Diccionario demografico plurilingue. 115p. (Span.). 1958. $1.00. ONU.
Dictionarium Tetraglotten Seu Voces Latinae Omnes, et Graecae Eis Respondentes, Cum Gallica & Teutonica (Quam Passim Flandricam Vocant) Earum Interpretatione: Dictionarum Tetraglotten A.D. MDLXII Ed, 2 vols. (Monumenta Lexicographica Neerlandica Ser.: No. 2). (Fr. , Lat. & Ger.). 1972. 120.00x (ISBN 90-2797-063-7). Mouton.
Dizionario assicurativo: Tedesco-francese-inglese-italiano. (Ger. , Fr. , Eng. & Ital.). L.5000.00. Centro St Assic.
Elkhaden, Saad. The York Dictionary of English-French-German-Spanish Literary Terms & Their Origin. LC 77-364336. 154p. (Eng., Fr., Ger. & Span.). 1976. $6.95 (ISBN 0-919966-01-2). York Pr CA.
Evered, H. & Wallnig, G. Duits voor Bouwkundigen-Saksaa Rakentajille. 102p. (Ger., Dutch & Finnish.). 1978. DM.18.00 (ISBN 3-7625-0916-6). Bauverlag.
Fachwortschatz Mathematik. LC 77-552687. 96p. (Eng & Ger.). 1976. M.5.00. VEB Verlag Enzyklopadie.
Fekete, Ivan. Epuletgepeszet. LC 76-504896. 211p. (Eng., Ger & Rus.). 1975. 48.00 Ft (ISBN 963-05-0560-6). Akademiai Kiado.
Feutry, Michel. Technological Dictionary. LC 78-346108. (Fr. & Ger.). 1976. 160.00 F (ISBN 2-85608-000-6). Maison Dictionnaire.
Four Language Culinary Dictionary: French, Hungarian, English, German. (Fr. , Hungarian, Eng. & Ger.). pap. 9.50 saddle stitched bdg. (ISBN 0-87557-099-2, 099-2). Saphrograph.
Frederick Muller, Ltd., ed. Multilingual Dictionary of Printing & Publishing. 1981. $30.00x (ISBN 0-584-95569-3, Pub. by Muller Ltd). State Mutual Bk.
--Multilingual Energy Dictionary. 1981. $30.00x (ISBN 0-584-95568-5, Pub. by Muller Ltd). State Mutual Bk.
Ghaleb, Edouard. Dictionnaire des Sciences de la Nature (Dictionary of the Natural Sciences, 3 vols. (Illus.). 1643p. (Arabic, Lat., Fr., Eng., Ger. & Ital.). 1966. Set. 172.50x (ISBN 0-8002-1208-8). Intl Pubns Serv.
Gheorghita, Stefan. Dictionar Poliglot de Matematica, Mecanica si Astronomie. LC 78-387413. xvi, 664p. (Eng., Rus., Ger., Fr. & Romanian.). 1978. 67.00 lei. Editura Stiintifica.
Gives, L., et al. Dizionario inglese-italiano-francese-tedesco. 296p. (Eng., Ital., Fr. & Ger.). 1973. L.1600.00. De Bono.
--Dizionario italiano-inglese-francese-tedesco. 304p. (Ital., Eng., Fr. & Ger.). 1973. L.1600.00. De Bono.
Goedecke, Werner. Woerterbuch der Wirkstoffprufung. LC 80-475766. (Eng., Ger. & Fr.). 1979. write for info. (ISBN 3-18-400434-1). VDI-Verlag.
Graafinen Sanakirja. 308p. (Finnish , Rus. & Ger.). 1979. write for info. (ISBN 9-5100-9086-7). Soderstrom.
Hartong, Bernard D. Elsevier's Dictionary of Barley, Malting, & Brewing. (Eng., Ger., Fr., Danish, Ital., & Span., Polyglot). 1961. $76.75 (ISBN 0-444-40270-5). Elsevier.
Heinrich, Gunter. Woerterbuch Klima & Kaltetechnik. LC 79-349127. 404p. (Eng., Ger., Fr & Rus.). 1978. 74.00 F (ISBN 3-87144-303-4). Verlag Harri Deutsch.
Heymer, Armin. The Ethological Dictionary: In English, French & German. LC 77-78418. (Illus.). 238p. (Eng., Fr & Ger.). 1979. Repr. of 1977 ed. lib. bdg. $35.00 (ISBN 0-8240-7005-4, Garland STPM Pr). Garland Pub.
International Gas Union, ed. Elsevier's Dictionary of the Gas Industry, 2 vols. (Polyglot). 1961. Set. $95.75 (ISBN 0-444-40758-8); Incl. suppl. pap. $138.50 (ISBN 0-686-85926-X). Elsevier.
International Institute of Refrigeration. New International Dictionary of Refrigeration. LC 76-373634. xxxvii, 560p. (Eng., Danish, Fr., Ger., Ital., Rus. & Span.). 1976. 3000.00 F (IIR). Unipub.
Isaacs, Alan, ed. The Multilingual Computer Dictionary. 336p. 1981. $22.50 (ISBN 0-87196-431-7). Facts on File.
--The Multilingual Dictionary of Printing & Publishing. 336p. 1981. $22.50 (ISBN 0-87196-444-9). Facts on File.
--The Multilingual Energy Dictionary. 288p. 1981. $22.50 (ISBN 0-87196-430-9). Facts on File.
James, Glenn. Mathematics Dictionary. 4th ed. LC 76-233. vii, 509p. (Eng., Fr., Ger., Rus. & Span.). 1976. write for info. (ISBN 0-442-24091-0). Van Nos Reinhold.
Jorgensen, V. Tams. Snaak Friisk: Interfriisk Leksikon. LC 78-398618. (Norwegian.). 1977. DM.7.50 (ISBN 3-88007-063-6). Verein Nord.
Kardanov, B. M., et al. Russko-Kabardinsko-Cherkesskii Slovar. 1054p. (Rus.). 1955. $5.85 (Pub. by GINS). Four Continent.
Kleczek, Josip. Astronomical Dictionary: In Six Languages. (Eng., Fr., Ger., Ital., Rus. & Czech.). 1962. $109.00 (ISBN 0-12-411950-6). Acad Pr.
Klimek, Adolf. Polovodicove Soucastky. LC 77-472717. 444p. (Eng. & Czech., Praha, Czechoslovakia). 1977. 30.00 Kcs. SNTL.

Koelle, Sigismund W. Polyglotta Africana. LC 65-82544. 1963. Repr. of 1854 ed. 42.50x (ISBN 3-201-00766-8). Intl Pubns Serv.

Kosik, Vaclav. Cesko, Slovensko, Latinsko, Anglicko, Nemecko, Rusky, Slovnik Plevelu. LC 76-507633. 149p. (Czech., Slovak, Lat., Eng., Ger. & Rus.). 1975. write for info. SNTC.

Kratkii Terminologicheskii Spravochnik po Ekonomike Geologorazvedochnykh Rabot. LC 79-398743. 203p. (Eng. , Rus. & Bulgarian.). 1979. 100.00 Zl. Wydawnictwa.

Kwizda, R. Vocabularium Nocentium Florae. 4th ed. (Lat.). 1963. pap. $23.50 (ISBN 0-387-80646-6). Springer-Verlag.

Lange, K., et al. Englische & Franzoesisch Fachsprache im Auslandsbau. 131p. (Fr., Eng. & Ger.). 1980. DM.24.00 (ISBN 3-7625-1235-3). Bauverlag.

Last, J. T. Polyglotta Africana Orientalis. 251p. 1972. Repr. of 1885 ed. 13.50x (ISBN 0-8002-1333-5). Intl Pubns Serv.

Lenczewska, Bronislawa. Slownik Terminow z Zakresu Informatyki. LC 77-557144. 116p. (Eng. & Pol.). 1977. 15.00 Zl. Politekens Forlag.

Lexique General. (Eng. , Fr. , Span. & Rus., ST/DCS/1/Rev. 1). pap. $35.00 (ISBN 0-686-94816-5, UN). Unipub.

Logie, Gordon & Hemstead, Hemel, eds. International Planning Glossary. LC 77-367067. (Eng., Fr., Ital., Dutch, Ger., Swedish, Finnish, Dannish & Norwegian.). 1975. E3.00 (ISBN 0-9504753-0-0). Intl Plan Glos.

Lokshina, S. M. Kratkii Slovar Inostrannykh Slov. 360p. (Rus.). $1.80 (Pub. by Russkii Iazyk). Four Continent.

Medina, G. Diccionario ideografico poliglot0. (Span.). 250.00 ptas. Aguilar SP.

Meinck, F. & Mohle, K. Dictionary of Water & Sewage Engineering. 2nd ed. (Ger., Eng., Fr., & Ital.). 1977. $127.75 (ISBN 0-444-99811-X). Elsevier.

Meinck, Fritz. Woerterbuch fur das Wasser & Abwasserfach. LC 78-337966. 737p. (Eng., Fr. & Ital.). 1977. write for info. (ISBN 3-486-35352-7). Oldenbourg Verlag.

Merino-Rodriguez, Manuel, ed. Lexicon of Plant Pests & Diseases. (Eng., Lat., Fr., Span., Ital. & Ger., Polyglot). 1966. $70.25 (ISBN 0-444-40393-0). Elsevier.

Metallurgisk Ordbok. LC 77-468526. 347p. (Eng. & Ger., Norsk Verks). 1976. write for info. (ISBN 8-2902-0400-0). Norsk Verkstedsindustris Standardiseringssentral.

Mora, Imre. Husznyelvu Kiadoi Szotar. LC 77-477898. 389p. (Eng., Ger. & Hungarian.). 1977. 175.00 Ft (ISBN 9-6305-0996-2). Akademiai Kiado.

Nash, Rose. Multilingual Lexicon of Linguistics & Philology: English, Russian, German, French. LC 68-31044. (Miami Linguistics Ser: No. 3). (Eng., Rus., Ger. & Fr.). 1968. $19.95x (ISBN 0-87024-095-1). U of Miami Pr.

Niermeyer, J. F. Lexique Latin Medieval-Francais-Anglais. (Lat., Fr. & Eng.). 20.00 F. Brill.

Pallas, Peter S. Linguarum Totius Orbis Vocabularia Comparativa. LC 78-380313. (Lat. & Rus.). 1977. DM.100.00 (ISBN 3-87118-285-0). Buske.

Pallegoix, Jean-Baptiste. Dictionarium Linguae Thai Slve Slamensis Interpretatione Latina, Gallica & Anglica. 902p. (Lat., Fr. & Eng.). 1972. $24.00. Gregg.

Papa-Sotir, Mihai. Dictionar Poliglot de Industrie Alimentara. LC 78-344895. xiv, 619p. (Eng., Romanian, Ger., Fr. & Rus.). 1977. 56.00 lei. Editura Stiintifica.

Pesonen, Niilo. Laaketieteen Sanairja. LC 76-486173. 559p. (Eng. & Finnish.). 1976. Fmk.100.00 (ISBN 9-5100-7479-9). Werner Soderstrom.

Petzold, Armin. Silikatova Technika. LC 80-490689. 271p. (Eng., Rus. & Slovak.). 1977. 47.00 Kcs. Alfa-Vydavatel.

Pipics, Z. The Librarian's Practical Dictionary in Twenty-Two Languages. 386p. 1980. $90.00x (ISBN 0-686-72094-6, Pub. by Collet's). State Mutual Bk.

Platts, John T. A Dictionary of Urdu Classical Hindi & English. LC 78-670100. (Hindi & Eng.). 1977. Repr. of 1884 ed. 50.00x (ISBN 0-8002-0243-0). Intl Pubns Serv.

Pozsonyi, Gabor. Filmgyartas es Filmtechnika. LC 78-391538. 220p. (Eng., Hungarian, Fr., Ger. & Rus.). 1975. 50.00 Ft (ISBN 9-6305-0592-4). Akademiai Kiado.

Quadrilingual Business Dictionary. (Eng. , Fr. , Ger. & Span.). 1981. $60.00x (ISBN 0-686-75659-2, Pub. by European Schoolbks England). State Mutual Bk.

Reichardt, Walter. Technicka Akustika. LC 80-465612. 268p. (Eng., Rus., Span. & Slovak.). 1978. 50.00 Kcs. VEB Verlat Technik.

--Technische Akustik. LC 80-491210. 268p. (Eng., Ger., Fr., Rus., Span., Pol., Hungarian, & Slovak.). 1979. M.30.00. VEB Verlag Technik.

Reiff, Filipp. Novye Parallel'nye Slovari Iazykov Russkago, Frantsuzskago, Nemetskago i Angliiskago, 4 vols. 4th ed. Incl. Vol. 1. Russkii Slovar. 832p. 1884; Vol. 2. Dictionnaire Francais. 832p. 1885; Vol. 3. Deutsches Woerterbuch. 816p. 1884; Vol. 4. English Dictionary. 848p. 1884. (Rus., Fr., Ger. & Eng.). $100.00 set. Four Continent.

Richling, Christel. Woerterbuch der Kabeltechnik. LC 77-46358. 610p. (Eng., Fr & Ger.). 1976. DM.60.00 (ISBN 3-87097-072-3). Brandstetter.

Rudakova, I. F. Uchebny Slovar Obschetekhnich: Leksiki. 190p. (Rus., Ger., Fr., & Eng.). 1976. $1.00 (237-B, Pub. by Russkii Iazyk). Four Continent.

Rudakova, I. F., et al. Uchebnyi Slovar Obshchetekhnich: Russko-Anglo-Frantsuzsko-Nemetskii. 190p. (Rus., Eng., Fr. & Ger.). 1976. $1.00 (Pub. by Russkii Iazyk). Four Continent.

Russko-Anglo-Azerbaidzhansko-Kirgozsko-Turkmensko-Uzbekskii Terminologicheskii Slovar Po Avtomati cheskomu Upravleniiu. 642p. (Rus. & Eng.). 1977. $12.50 (Pub. by Elm). Four Continent.

Ruysch, W. A. Elsevier's Multilingual Dictionary of Insurance Technology. (Eng., Dutch, Fr., Ger., Span. & Ital.). write for info (ISBN 0-685-82355-5). Elsevier.

Sandri-White, Alex. Boobytraps of the German Language. (Ger.). $5.95 (ISBN 0-685-22759-6). Aurea.

Scharnow, Ulrich. Transpress Lexikon Seefahrt. LC 77-471655. 608p. (Eng., Rus & Ger., Berlin, East Germany). 1976. M.32.00. Transpress Verlag fur Verkehrswesen.

Schulz, Joachim. Woerterbuch der Datentechnick. LC 77-514536. 134p. (Eng., Rus & Ger.). 1977. DM.50.00 (ISBN 3-87097-075-8). Brandstetter.

Seven Languages Dictionary. 829p. (Fr. , Ger. , Hebrew, Ital. , Port. , Rus. & Span.). 1978. $10.50. Imported Bks.

Shumaker, David, ed. Seven Language Dictionary. LC 78-16509. 828p. (Eng., Fr., Ger., Hebrew, Ital., Port., & Rus.). 1978. write for info. (ISBN 0-517-26296-7). Crown.

Siunchev, Kh. I, et al, eds. Russko-Karachaevo-Balkarskii Slovar. 744p. (Rus.). 1955. $7.50 (Pub. by Sov. Entsiklopediia). Four Continent.

Sliosberg, A. Elsevier's Dictionary of Pharmaceutical Science & Techniques, 2 vols. Incl. Vol. 1: Pharmaceutical Technology. 1968. 132.00 (ISBN 0-444-40544-5); Vol. 2: Materia Medica. 1980. $123.50 (ISBN 0-444-41664-1). Set. $255.50 (ISBN 0-686-85925-1). Elsevier.

Slownik Informatyki Polsko-Angielsko-Rosyjski. LC 77-469027. 159p. (Eng. , Rus. & Pol.). 1976. 50.00 Zl. Wydawnictwa Naukowo.

Sobecka, Z., et al, eds. Dictionary of Chemistry & Chemical Technology in Six Languages. rev. ed. 1966. 130.00 (ISBN 0-08-011600-0). Pergamon.

Sozanskiej, Ewa. Slownik Elektroniczny Polsko-Angielsko-Rosyjski. LC 78-384390. vii, 254p. (Eng., Pol. & Rus.). 1977. 100.00 Zl. Wydawnictwa Naukowo.

Specialized Dictionaries, Bi & Multilingual. (Eng.). 1979. write for info. M Rosenberg.

Stepanek, Josef. Woerterbuch Industrieofen & Indudtrielle Warmeanlagen. LC 76-454323. viii, 444p. (Eng., Span. & Fr.). 1975. DM.78.00 (ISBN 3-8027-2484-4). Vulkan Verlag.

Sube, R. & Eisenreich, G., eds. Physics Dictionary, 3 vols. (Eng., Ger., Fr & Rus.). 1974. $260.00 (ISBN 3-87144-143-0). Adler.

Suomen Standardisoimislitto. Sahkotieteellinen Sanasto. LC 77-481554. 167p. (Eng., Finnish, Fr., Ger., Rus. & Swedish.). 1976. write for info. Suomen Standard.

Surface Treatment of Aluminum: Glossary of Technical Terms. LC 76-356688. 50p. (Eng. , Fr. & Ger.). 1975. write for info. (ISBN 3-87017-121-9). Aluminum Verlag.

Sveriges Standardiseringskommission. Dataordboken. LC 78-393289. 476p. (Eng., Fr., Ger., & Swedish.). 1977. Kr.114.60 (ISBN 9-1716-2052-4). Standard Sver.

Sykora, Jiri. Automatizacna Technika. LC 76-511586. 1023p. (Eng., Fr., Rus., Pol. & Slovak.). 1975. 140.00 Kcs. Alfa-Vydavatel.

Tekniska Nomenklaturcentralen. Komunalteknisk Ordlista. LC 77-454090. 214p. (Eng. Danish, Finnish & Norwegian.). 1976. Kr.50.00 (ISBN 9-1719-6061-9). Tek Nomen.

--Plan och Byggtermer. LC 76-522778. 198p. (Swedish.). 1975. Kr.50.00 (ISBN 91-7196-058-9). Tek Nomen.

Toth, Rudolf. Terminoloski Komparativni Srpskohrvatsko. LC 77-476859. 224p. (Eng. & Hungarian.). 1976. write for info. Ekonomski Fakultet.

Tutzaver, Otto E. & Tutzaver, Ingrid M. Dictionary of environmental protection, 3 vols. LC 80-458477. (Eng., Fr., & Ger.). 1979. DM.70.00 (ISBN 3-452-18481-1). Heymanns Verlag.

Vasil'Eva, A. S. Russkikh Glagolov. (Russkii iazyk Ser.). (Rus., Eng., Fr., Ital. & Span.). 1980. pap. $2.95. Four Continent.

Velte, Herbert. Budo-Lexikon: 1500 Fachausdruecke Fernoestl. LC 77-475498. (Illus.). 137p. (Ger.). 1976. DM.9.80 (ISBN 3-8068-0383-8). Falken Verlag.

Vicens Carrio, J. Lexicon comercial internacional: Espanol, frances, ingles, italiano, portugues y aleman. (Span., Fr., Eng., Ital., Port. & Ger.). 800.00 ptas. Reverte SA.

Von Berger, Karl. Mykologisches Worterbuch. LC 80-479189. 432p. (Eng., Fr., Span., Lat., Czech., Pol., & Rus.). 1980. write for info. (ISBN 3-437-20220-0). Fischer Verlag.

Von Roald, Albert & Hahnewald, Harry. Medizintechnik. LC 79-359051. 596p. (Eng., Fr., Rus., Span. & Pol.). 1978. M.55.00. VEB Verlag Technik.

Von Thielmann, K. Woerterbuch der Biochemie. LC 79-354449. 742p. (Eng., Fr., Rus., & Span.). 1977. M.48.00. VEB Verlag Enzyklopadie.

Voros, Arpad. Onteszet. LC 79-244881. 435p. (Eng., Hungarian, Fr., Ger. & Rus.). 1978. 95.00 Ft (ISBN 9-6305-1597-0). Akademiai Kiado.

Wallnig, G. & Evered, H. Engels voor Bouwkundigen-Englantia Rakentajille. 95p. (Eng., Ger., Finnish & Dutch.). 1980. DM.18.00 (ISBN 3-7625-1226-4). Bauverlag.

--Englisch fuer Baufachleute: Band 1. 6th ed. 101p. (Eng., Ger. & Fr.). 1978. DM.16.00 (ISBN 3-7625-0807-0). Bauverlag.

--Englisch fur Baufachleute: Band 2. 2nd ed. viii, 192p. (Eng., Ger. & Fr.). 1977. DM.38.00 (ISBN 3-7625-0807-0). Bauverlag.

Walter, Frank K. Abbreviations & Technical Terms Used in Book Catalogues & in Bibliographies. LC 77-6174. 1977. Repr. of 1917 ed. lib. bdg. $12.50 (ISBN 0-89341-152-3). Longwood Pr.

Weber, Fritz W. Elsevier's Dictionary of High Vacuum Science & Technology. (Eng., Ger., Fr., Ital., Span. & Rus.). 1968. $106.50 (ISBN 0-444-40625-5). Elsevier.

Wilhelm, Evelyne. Bien Manger dans Quinze Pays. LC 79-390204. 205p. (Eng. & Fr.). 1979. 39.00 F (ISBN 2-86418-029-4). Encre.

Wilken-Jensen, K. Lexikon Allergologicum. 1965. $16.25 (ISBN 0-08-011838-0). Pergamon.

Williams, Edwin B. & Senn, Alfred. Diccionario multilingue. 304p. (Span.). $1.50. Edit Pr Serv.

Wittmann, Alfred. Dictionary of Data Processing. LC 76-28194. (Eng. & Fr.). 1977. write for info. Elsevier.

Woerterbuch der Kraftuebertragungselemente-Deutsch-Spanisch-Franzoesisch-Englisch-Italienisch-Niederlandisch-Schwedisch-Finnisch: Bd 1, Zahnraeder. 116p. (Ger. , Span. , Fr. , Eng. , Ital. , Dutch, Swedish & Finnish.). 1976. DM.39.50 (ISBN 3-7830-0104-8). Krausskopf.

Zlotnicki, T. Lexicon Medicum. 1603p. 1980. $150.00x (ISBN 0-569-07372-3, Pub. by Collet's). State Mutual Bk.

DICTIONARIES, RHYMING

see English Language–Rime–Dictionaries

DICTIONARY CATALOGS

see Catalogs, Dictionary

DIDACTICS

see Teaching

DIEQUENO LANGUAGE

Couro, Ted & Hutcheson, Christina. Dictionary of Mesa Grande Diegueno. 1973. pap. 5.50 (ISBN 0-939046-14-8). Malki Mus Pr.

DIET

see also Animal Food; Beverages; Cookery; Menus; Nutrition

Bergeson, Sandy. Dieter's Dictionary: Chubby Webster's. (Illus.). 1983. pap. $4.95 (ISBN 0-943084-09-1). Print Mat.

DIET IN DISEASE

Rose, Jim & Gilbert, Jayne. Dietetic Policies & Procedures Manual for Long Term Care Facilities. 400p. Date not set. price not set. Aspen Systems.

DIET THERAPY

see Diet in Disease

DIETETICS

see Diet; Diet in Disease; Nutrition

DIGITAL COMPUTERS, ELECTRONIC

see Electronic Digital Computers

DINING CARS

see Railroads–Cars

DINOSAURIA

Glut, Donald F. The Dinosaur Dictionary. (Illus.). 218p. 1976. pap. $6.95 (ISBN 0-8065-0519-2). Citadel Pr.

--The Dinosaur Dictionary. 1972. $12.50 (ISBN 0-8065-0283-5). Citadel Pr.

--The New Dinosaur Dictionary. (Illus.). 256p. 1982. $19.95 (ISBN 0-8065-0782-9). Citadel Pr.

DINOSAURIA–JUVENILE LITERATURE

Rosenbloom, Joseph. A Dictionary of Dinosaurs. LC 80-18525. (Illus.). 96p. (gr. 4 up). 1980. PLB 8.29 (ISBN 0-671-34038-7). Messner.

Sattler, Helen R. The Illustrated Dinosaur Dictionary. (Illus.). 1983. 17.00 (ISBN 0-686-46202-5). Lothrop.

--The Illustrated Dinosaur Dictionary. (Illus.). 1983. 17.00 (ISBN 0-686-46202-5). Lothrop.

Sattler, Helen Roney. The Illustrated Dinosaur Dictionary. LC 82-22947. (Illus.). 316p. 1983. $17.00 (ISBN 0-688-00479-2). Lothrop.

DIOLA LANGUAGE
Wintz, E. Dictionnaire Francais-Dyola. 280p. (Fr.). 1968. $18.00. Gregg.

DIPLOMACY
Fouk al-Ada, Samuhi. A Dictionary of Diplomacy & International Affairs. 566p. (Arabic, Fr. & Eng.). $30.00 (114-3). Intl Bk Ctr.

DIPLOMACY–DICTIONARIES
Barakat, Gamal. English-Arabic Dictionary of Diplomacy & Related Terminology. (Eng. & Arabic.). 1982. $25.00x (ISBN 0-86685-290-5). Intl Bk Ctr.

Sandahl, P. & De Bea, L. Dictionnaire Politique & Diplomatique. 3rd ed. (Fr.). 1976. 340.00 F. Bruylant.

Sandahl, Pierre & Bea, Louise de. Dictionnaire Politique et Diplomatique. 194p. (Fr.). 1976. pap. $14.95 (ISBN 0-686-57214-9, M-6503). French & Eur.

DIPLOMATIC PROTESTS
see Diplomacy

DIPLOMATICS
see also Archives; Manuscripts; Paleography; Seals (Numismatics)
Walther, Johann L. Lexicon Diplomaticum Abbreviationes Syllabarum et Vocum in Diplomatibus et Codicibus a Seculo Octo a Sextum-Decimum Usque Occurentes Exponens, 2 vols. in 1 folio ed. (Lat.). 1967. Repr. of 1756 ed. $87.00 (ISBN 0-8337-3680-9). B Franklin.

DIPSOMANIA
see Alcoholism

DIRECT TAXATION
see Taxation

DIRECTORS, MOVING-PICTURE
see Moving-Picture Producers and Directors

DISABILITY, READING
see Reading Disability

DISARMAMENT
see also Arbitration, International; Militarism
Language Services Division of the Foreign Office of the Federal Republic of Germany, ed. Disarmament Terminology: English, German, French, Spanish, Russian. (Terminological Ser.: Vol. 1). 645p. 1982. pap. $45.00 (ISBN 3-11-008858-4). De Gruyter.

Razoruzhenie: Spravochnik. 160p. (Rus.). 1980. $00.85 (Pub. by Politizdat). Four Continent.

DISCIPLINE, ECCLESIASTICAL
see Church Discipline

DISCOVERERS
see Discoveries (In Geography)

DISCOVERIES (IN GEOGRAPHY)
see also Voyages and Travels
also subdivision Discovery and Exploration under names of countries, etc.
Jouffroy, A. Dictionnaire des Inventions et Decouvertes Anciennes et Modernes, 2 vols. Migne, J. P., ed. (Nouvelle Encyclopedie Theologique Ser.: Vols. 35-36). 1424p. (Fr.). Repr. of 1860 ed. lib. bdg. $181.00x (ISBN 0-89241-277-1). Caratzas Pub Co.

DISCOVERIES (IN GEOGRAPHY)–DICTIONARIES
Langnas, Isaac A. Dictionary of Discoveries. LC 68-8064. (Illus.). 1968. Repr. of 1959 ed. lib. bdg. 15.00x (ISBN 0-8371-0526-9, LADD). Greenwood.

DISCOVERIES (IN SCIENCE)
see Inventions; Patents; Science

DISEASE (PATHOLOGY)
see Pathology

DISEASE, DIET IN
see Diet in Disease

DISEASES–CLASSIFICATION
see Nosology

DISEASES, MENTAL
see Mental Illness; Psychology, Pathological

DISEASES OF ANIMALS
see Veterinary Medicine

DISEASES OF PLANTS
see Plant Diseases

DISEASES OF THE BLOOD, DISEASES OF THE BRAIN, DISEASES OF THE HEART
see subdivision Diseases under specific subjects, e.g. Blood–Diseases; Brain–Diseases

DISNEY, WALT, 1901-1966
Disney, Walt. Diccionario Disney. 112p. (Span.). 1973. pap. $5.95 (ISBN 84-305-0601-2, S-24118). French & Eur.

DISORDERS OF LOCOMOTION
see Locomotion, Disordered

DISORDERS OF SPEECH
see Speech, Disorders Of

DISPERSOIDS
see Colloids

DISPOSAL OF REFUSE
see Refuse and Refuse Disposal

DISSENTERS
Miquel I Verges, Jose Maria. Diccionario de Insurgentes. (Span.). $55.00 (ISBN 0-686-56698-X, S-12335). French & Eur.

DISTILLING INDUSTRIES
Downard, William L. Dictionary of the History of the American Brewing & Distilling Industries. LC 79-6826. (Illus.). xxv, 268p. 1980. lib. bdg. $45.00 (ISBN 0-313-21330-5, DOD/). Greenwood.

DISTRICT NURSES
see Nurses and Nursing

DISTRICTING (IN CITY PLANNING)
see Zoning

DIVERS
see also Diving
Undersea Medical Society, Inc. Glossary of Diving & Hyperbaric Terms. $2.50. Undersea Med.

DIVINE HEALING
see Christian Science; Miracles

DIVING
see also Divers; Swimming
Hourcastagne, Andre. Lexique du Secourisme & de la Plongee Autonome. (Fr.). 8.00 F. France Selection.

DIVORCE–JUVENILE LITERATURE
Glass, Stuart. A Divorce Dictionary: A Book for You & Your Children. (Illus.). 80p. (gr. 7 up). 1980. 7.95 (ISBN 0-316-31581-8). Little.

DO-IT-YOURSELF WORK
see specific fields of activity for do-it-yourself manuals in such fields, e.g. House Painting; Interior Decoration

DOCTORS
see Physicians

DOCTRINAL THEOLOGY
see Theology, Doctrinal

DOCTRINES
see Theology, Doctrinal

DOCUMENT COPYING
see Photocopying Processes

DOCUMENTATION
see also Archives; Bibliography; Copying Processes; Indexing; Information Services; Information Storage and Retrieval Systems; Library Science; Museums; Photocopying Processes; Translating Services
Terminology of Documentation: A Selection of 1200 Basic Terms Published in English, French, German, Spanish & Russian. 274p. (Eng. , Fr. , Ger. , Span. & Rus.). 1976. pap. $24.25 (ISBN 92-3-001232-7, U673, UNESCO). Unipub.

DOCUMENTS, CONSERVATION OF
see Archives; Manuscripts–Conservation and Restoration

DOG
see Dogs

DOGMATIC THEOLOGY
see Theology, Doctrinal

DOGS
Here are entered works on dogs in general. For works on specific breeds of dogs see subdivision breeds, further subdivided by specific names, e.g. Dogs–Breeds–Dalmatians.
Rousselet-Blanc, Pierre & Rousselet-Blanc, Josette. Dictionnaire du Chien. 267p. (Fr.). 1976. $27.50 (ISBN 0-686-56869-9, M-6647). French & Eur.

DOGS–DICTIONARIES
Rousselet-Blanc, Pierre & Rousselet-Blanc, Josette. Dictionnaire du Chien. (Illus.). 267p. (Fr.). 1976. write for info. Laffont.

Sarkany, Pal, ed. Nemzetkozi Kutya Enciklopedia. LC 77-560281. (Illus.). 741p. (Hungarian.). 1976. 210.00 Ft (ISBN 9-632-05052-5). Terra.

Spira, Harold R. Canine Terminology. (Illus.). 147p. 1983. 29.95 (ISBN 0-06-312047-X). Howell Bk.

DOLLS
Hillier, Mary. Pollock's Dictionary of English Dolls. 1983. $19.95 (ISBN 0-517-54922-0). Crown.

DOMES
Huber, Rudolf & Rieth, Renate, eds. Glossarium Artis: Fasz 6, Gewoelbe & Kuppeln-Voutes et Coupoles. 250p. (Ger.). 1974. DM.35.00 (ISBN 3-484-60051-9). Niemeyer.

DOMESTIC ANIMALS–DISEASES
see Veterinary Medicine

DOMESTIC APPLIANCES
see Household Appliances

DOMESTIC ARCHITECTURE
see Architecture, Domestic

DOMESTIC ECONOMY
see Home Economics

DOMESTIC RELATIONS
see also Family
Zanzucchi, Anne M. Family Portrait, from a Mother's Diary. Szczesniak, Lenny, tr. from It. LC 81-80031. Orig. Title: Giorno per Giorno. 100p. 1981. pap. 2.95 (ISBN 0-911782-19-2). New City.

DOMESTIC SCIENCE
see Home Economics

DOMESTICATION
see Plants, Cultivated

DOMINICAN REPUBLIC
Brache, Jose A. Cinco Mil Seiscientos Refranes & Frases de Uso Comun Entre los Dominicanos. Pichardo, Nicolas, ed. LC 80-100004. xiv, 311p. (Span.). 1978. write for info. Galaxia.

DOMINION OF THE SEA
see Maritime Law

DONKEYS
Donkey & Mule Terms & Their Definitons. 1p. $0.15. Am Donkey.

DOSTOEVSKII, FEDOR MIKHAILOVICH, 1821-1881
Chapple, Richard. A Dostoevsky Dictionary. 512p. 1983. $35.00 (ISBN 0-88233-727-0). Ardis Pubs.

DOUBLE ENTRY BOOKKEEPING
see Bookkeeping

DOUGLAS FAMILY
Volkart, K. Gips-Woerterbuch. 176p. (Ger.). 1971. DM.68.00 (ISBN 3-7625-0460-1). Bauverlag.

DRAFTING, MECHANICAL
see Mechanical Drawing

DRAINAGE
Here are entered only works relating to land drainage, as distinguished from sewerage and house drainage.
see also Sewerage
Bucksch, Hector. Dictionnaire des Canalisations: Francais-Allemand. 288p. (Fr. & Ger.). 1969. write for info. Eyrolles.

Multilingual Technical Dictionary on Irrigation & Drainage. (Eng. & Turkish.). 1972. $12.00; members $8.00. US Comm Irrigation.

Multilir gual Technical Dictionary on Irrigation & Drainage. (Eng. & Ger., French translation of terms only). 1971. $40.00; members $30.00. US Comm Irrigation.

Multilingual Technical Dictionary on Irrigation & Drainage. (Eng. & Fr.). 1967. $15.00; members $7.50. US Comm Irrigation.

Multilingual Technical Dictionary on Irrigation & Drainage, Suppl. 1. 1980. $7.00; members $5.00. US Comm Irrigation.

DRAMA–DICTIONARIES
De Chamfort, Nicolas. Dictionnaire Dramatique, 3 vols. (Fr.). 1967. write for info. Slatkine.

DRAMA–STUDY AND TEACHING
Foster, John, compiled by. Shakespeare Word-Book, Being a Glossary of Archaic Forms & Varied Usages of Words Employed by Shakespeare. LC 68-15123. 1969. Repr. of 1908 ed. 17.50x (ISBN 0-8462-1234-X). Russell.

DRAVIDIAN LANGUAGES
see also Tamil Language

Burrow, Thomas & Emeneau, Murray B. Dravidian Etymological Dictionary. 1961. 69.00x (ISBN 0-19-864310-1). Oxford U Pr.

DRAWING
see also Caricature; Drawings; Graphic Methods; Map Drawing; Mechanical Drawing; Topographical Drawing
also Birds in Art; Dogs–Pictures, Illustrations, Etc., and similar headings
De Fiore, Gaspare. Dizionario del disegno. (Illus.). 616p. (Ital.). 1967. L.6500.00. La Scuola.

Diccionario de pintura y dibujo. (Span.). 150.00 ptas. Tesoro.

Zaidenberg, Arthur. Dictionary of Drawing. LC 81-65858. (Illus.). 192p. 1982. $15.00 (ISBN 0-8453-4701-2). Cornwall Bks.

DRAWING–INSTRUCTION
Beguin, Andre. Dictionnaire Technique & Critique du Dessin. (Fr.). 1978. 247.50 F. Vander Oyez.

DRAWING–INSTRUCTION–JUVENILE LITERATURE
Boughner, Howard. Dictionary of Things to Draw. (gr. 1-7) 1979. PLB 3.99 (ISBN 0-448-13125-0, G&D); pap. 1.50 (ISBN 0-448-14991-5). Putnam Pub Group.

DRAWINGS
see also Engravings
Kolesnikova, A. & Lulchak, L. Dictionnaire Illustre: Francais-Russe. 856p. (Fr. & Rus.). 1977. $17.95 (ISBN 0-686-92566-1, M-9070). French & Eur.

DREAMS
see also Fantasy; Psychoanalysis
Boushahla, Jo J. & Reidel-Geubtner, Virginia. The Dream Dictionary: The Key to Your Unconscious. 192p. 1983. $18.95 (ISBN 0-8298-0695-4); pap. $9.95 (ISBN 0-8298-0696-2). Pilgrim NY.

Chetwynd, Tom. Le Dictionnaire des Reves. 315p. (Fr.). 1975. 34.00 F. Seghers.

Greer, R. Dictionary of One Thousand Dreams. $1.00 (ISBN 0-685-02610-8, 00545193). Stein Pub.

Kurth, Hanns. Diccionario de los suenos. Rada, Carmen, tr. 296p. (Span.). 1982. 525.00 ptas (ISBN 84-226-1484-7). Circulo Lect.

Lucky Number Lottery Guide. (Illus.). 240p. 1982. pap. 2.95 (ISBN 0-87637-370-8). Hse of Collectibles.

Robinson, Stearn. Dreamer's Dictionary. 1975. pap. $3.96 (ISBN 0-446-30610-X). Warner Bks.

Robinson, Stearn & Corbett, Tom. Dreamer's Dictionary: Complete Guide to Interpreting Your Dreams. LC 72-6612. 256p. 1974. $9.95 (ISBN 0-8008-2270-6). Taplinger.

Yancy, Wallace. The Dream Dictionary. 1981. $6.95 (ISBN 0-8062-1685-9). Carlton.

DRENTHE, NETHERLANDS
Hadderingh, H. Drents Woordenboek. LC 79-385034. (Illus.). 344p. (Dutch.). 1979. fl.35.00 (ISBN 9-06397-019-6). Interbk Intl.

DRESS DESIGN
see Costume Design

DRESSMAKING
see also Needlework; Sewing
Ladbury, Ann. The Dressmaker's Dictionary. LC 82-8725. (Illus.). 360p. 1983. $19.95 (ISBN 0-668-05653-3, 5653). Arco.

DRILL AND MINOR TACTICS
Here are entered general works, including works for home guards, boy scouts, bands, etc. Manuals, handbooks and regulations intended for the army of a particular country are entered under name of the country, with subheading Army.
see also Military Art and Science
Plaisance, Georges. Dictionnaire Des Forets. 5th ed. (Fr.). 1975. pap. $22.50 (ISBN 0-686-56725-0, M-6457). French & Eur.

DRINKS
see Beverages

DRIVING, AUTOMOBILE
see Automobile Driving

DROP-FORGING
see Forging

DRUG ABUSE
see also Alcoholism; Marihuana
Lingeman, Richard R. Drugs from A
to Z: A Dictionary. 2nd ed.
(McGraw-Hill Paperbacks). 320p.
(Orig.). 1974. text ed. 9.95 (ISBN
0-07-037913-0, SP); pap. 5.95
(ISBN 0-07-037912-2). McGraw.

DRUG ADDICTION
see Drug Abuse

DRUG HABIT
see Drug Abuse

DRUGS
see also Botany, Medical; Materia
Medica; Pharmacy
also names of particular drugs and
groups of drugs, e.g. Narcotics,
Stimulants
Rosner, Fred. Moses Maimonides
Glossary of Drug Names.
(Memoirs Ser.: No. 135). 1979.
$20.75 (ISBN 0-87169-135-3). Am
Philos.

DRUGS–DICTIONARIES
Albanese, Joseph. The Nurses' Drug
Reference. 2nd ed. (Illus.). 1184p.
1981. 28.50x (ISBN 0-07-000767-
5); pap. 21.50 (ISBN 0-07-000768-
3). McGraw.
Elsevier's Geneesmiddelengids. LC
75-595997. 399p. (Eng. & Dutch.).
1975. fl.22.50 (ISBN 90-10-01263-
8). Elsevier Nederland.
Fisher, Richard B. & Christie, George
A. A Dictionary of Drugs: The
Medicines You Use. rev. ed. LC
76-12241. 1976. $7.95x (ISBN 0-
8052-3638-4). Schocken.
Gerecke, Klaus. Arzneimittel-
Verzeichnis. LC 79-344736. (Ger.).
1977. M.5.80. VEB Verlag
Technik.
Graa, Albert, ed. Vocabularium
Pharmaceuticum. 2nd ed. 125p.
(Eng., Ger., Fr. & Ital.). 1964. text
ed. 13.50x (ISBN 0-8002-3024-8).
Intl Pubns Serv.
Kleemann, Axel. Pharmazeutische.
LC 80-453717. xv, 555p. (Ger.).
1978. DM.200.00 (ISBN 3-13-
558401-1). Thieme Verlag.
Lingeman, Richard R. Drugs from A
to Z: A Dictionary. 2nd ed.
(McGraw-Hill Paperbacks). 320p.
(Orig.). 1974. text ed. 9.95 (ISBN
0-07-037913-0, SP); pap. 5.95
(ISBN 0-07-037912-2). McGraw.
Rosenstein, E., ed. Diccionario De
Especialidades Farmaceuticas. 28th
Mexican ed. (Span.). 1982. pap.
$52.00x (ISBN 968-460-017-8).
Drug Intl Pubns.
Touitou, Yvan & Perlemuter, Leon.
Dictionnaire Pratique de
Pharmacologie Clinique. LC 76-
675973. vi, 1196p. (Fr.). 1976.
167.00 F (ISBN 2-225-43550-2).
Masson & Cie.
USAN & the USP Dictionary of
Drug Names: 1983. 1982. $35.00
(ISBN 0-686-37681-1). USPC.
Van Gemert, G. A. & De
Maesschalck, A.
Geneesmiddelenzakboekje. LC 76-
677126. 144p. (Eng. & Dutch.).
1976. fl.16.50 (ISBN 9-0100-1588-
2). Agon Elsevier.
Verbeke, Ronald. Un Dictionnaire
Critique des Drogues. 160p. (Fr.).
1978. $39.95 (ISBN 0-686-57243-
2, M-6548). French & Eur.

DRUGS, DERMATOLOGIC
see Dermatology

DRUNKENNESS
see Alcoholism; Temperance

DRY CLEANING
Asmussen, H. Ordbog for Rensning
Vask og Rengoring. LC 79-344243.
112p. (Eng. & Dutch.). 1978.
Kr.54.10 (ISBN 8-7751-1064-4).
Tek Inst.

DRYING
Dryer Felt Terminology. 1966. $4.00
(014-14). members $2.67. TAPPI.
Drying & Related Ventilating
Terminology. 1972. $3.00 (014-
16); members $2.00. TAPPI.
Hall. Dictionary of Drying. 1979.
$52.25 (ISBN 0-8247-6652-0).
Dekker.

DUMB (DEAF MUTES)
see Deaf

DUNGEONS
see Prisons

DUPLICATING PROCESSES
see Copying Processes

DUTCH LANGUAGE
Harrison, Francis. The English &
Low-Dutch School-Master. LC 72-
1876. 144p. (Eng. & Dutch.). 1976.
write for info. (ISBN 0-404-03137-
4). AMS Pr.
Oirschot, Anton van. Het
Stoelenboek. LC 78-384766.
(Illus.). 128p. (Dutch.). 1978.
fl.7.90 (ISBN 9-025-26367-4).
Helmond.
Quak, Arend. Wortkonkordanz zu
den Altmittel- &
Altniederfraenkischen Psalmen &
Glossen. 182p. (Dutch.). 1975.
fl.25.00. Rodopi.

DUTCH LANGUAGE–
DICTIONARIES
Athenum Woordenboek: Espanol-
Holandes, Holandes-Espanol. 382p.
(Span. & Dutch.). 1979. pap. $5.25
(ISBN 84-303-0801-6, S-35068).
French & Eur.
Berlitz Editors. Berlitz Pocket
Dictionaries: Dutch-English. 300p.
(Eng. & Dutch.). 1982. pap. $4.95
(ISBN 0-686-92990-X, Berlitz).
Macmillan.
Booij, G, et al. Lexikon van de
Taalwetenschap. LC 76-502048.
(Illus.). 187p. (Dutch.). 1975.
fl.9.90. Spectrum NL.
Broers, A. & Smit, J. English-Dutch
Dictionary. Born, R., ed. 674p.
(Eng. & Dutch.). 1980. pap. $24.95
(ISBN 90-01-81264-3, M-9748).
French & Eur.
Bruggencate, K. T. Dutch-English
Dictionary. Gerritsen, J., et al, eds.
1048p. (Dutch & Eng.). 1980.
$24.95 (ISBN 90-01-96819-8, M-
9746). French & Eur.
––English-Dutch Dictionary.
Gerritsen, J., et al, eds. 898p.
(Eng. & Dutch.). 1980. $24.95
(ISBN 90-01-96818-X, M-9747).
French & Eur.
Bruggencate, K. Ten. Dutch-English,
English-Dutch Dictionary, 2 vols.
(Dutch & Eng.). Set. 50.00 (ISBN
9-0019-6819-8). Dutch-Eng. Eng.-
Dutch (ISBN 90-01-96818-X).
Heinman.
Buchner, Greet. Milieuvriendelijk van
A tot Z. LC 79-365782. 117p.
(Dutch.). 1979. fl.12.50 (ISBN 9-
0603-0246-X). Driehoek.
Buydens, John. Groot Systematisch
en Klankalfabetisch
Rijmwoordenboek. LC 78-362599.
363p. (Dutch.). 1977. fl.520.00
(ISBN 9-02890-291-0).
Nederlandse Boek.
Cassell. Cassell's New Dutch
Dictionary: English-Dutch, Dutch-
English. 729p. (Eng. & Dutch.).
1982. 34.95 (ISBN 0-02-522940-
0). Macmillan.
De Poorter, Wim. Filmlexikon. LC
77-572112. 102p. (Dutch.). 1976.
fl.14.50 (ISBN 9-0236-5349-1).
Nygh Ditmar.
De Vries, Geerte. Van Goor's Deens
Woordenboek, 2 vols. LC 76-
477773. (Dutch & Danish.). 1976.
fl.85.00 (ISBN 9-00002-195-2).
Goor.
Diccionario Lexicon Holandes-
Espanol y Espanol-Holandes.
384p. (Dutch & Span.). 1974. pap.
$4.50 (ISBN 84-303-0161-5, S-
50408); pap. $4.95 leatherette
(ISBN 84-303-0162-3, S-50409).
French & Eur.
Diccionario Universal Herder
Holandes-Espanol, Espanol-
Holandes. 264p. (Dutch & Span.).
1977. leatherette $4.50 (ISBN 84-
254-0779-6, S-50412). French &
Eur.
Dijk, G. Economische Begrippen. LC
78-383140. 144p. (Dutch.). 1978.
fl.9.75 (ISBN 9-027-52020-8).
NIB.
Dijkhoff, Mario. Bokabulario
Papiamentu-Ulandes. LC 79-
340768. 56p. (Eng. & Dutch.).
1978. fl.12.50 (ISBN 9-0601-1085-
4). Walburg Pers.
Dreniasova, T. N. Karmannyi
Niderlandsko-Russkii Slovar. 392p.
(Rus. & Dutch.). 1977. $1.80 (Pub.
by Russkii Iazyk). Four Continent.
Fockman, Andreae & Sybrandus,
Johannes. Fockema Andreae's
Rechtsgeleerd Handwoordenboek.
Algra, N. E., rev. by. LC 78-
343297. 713p. (Dutch.). 1977.
fl.write for info. Tjeenk Willink.

Glossarium Harlemense: Circa 1440.
(Monumenta Lexicographica
Neelandica, Ser. I: Vol. I). 422p.
1973. text ed. 120.00x (ISBN 0-
686-27746-5). Mouton.
Grootaers, Ludovic. Dictionnaire
Classique: Francais-Neerlandais,
Neerlandais-Francais. 22nd ed.
1050p. (Fr. & Dutch.). 1969.
$29.95 (ISBN 0-686-57317-X, M-
6300). French & Eur.
––Le Nouveau Dictionnaire
Francais-Neerlandais, Nederlands-
Francais. 18th ed. 826p. (Fr. &
Dutch.). 1969. $65.00 (ISBN 0-
686-57318-8, M-6301). French &
Eur.
Hadderingh, H. Drents
Woordenboek. LC 79-385034.
(Illus.). 344p. (Dutch.). 1979.
fl.35.00 (ISBN 9-06397-019-6).
Interbk Intl.
Haesendock, Francois M. Judo;
Encyclopedie in Beeld. LC 78-
353537. (Illus.). 272p. (Dutch.).
1976. fl.245.00 (ISBN 9-002-
13418-5). Standard.
Hugo Pocket Dictionary: Dutch-
English, English-Dutch. 624p.
1969. 3.50 (ISBN 0-8226-0502-3,
502). Littlefield.
Jong, F. J. Economisch Woorden
Boek: Engels-Frans-Duits-
Nederlands. 685p. (Eng., Fr., Ger.
& Dutch.). 1980. $75.00 (ISBN 90-
247-2243-8, M9474). French &
Eur.
Kiel, Cornelis. Dictionarium
Teutonicolatinum. LC 76-459868.
xii, 246p. (Lat.). 1975. DM.68.00
(ISBN 3-487-05227-X). Olms
Verlag.
Koenen, Matthijs J. & Drewes, J. B.
Verklarend Handwoordenboek der
Nederlandse Taal. LC 78-375038.
xii, 1696p. (Dutch.). 1975. write
for info. (ISBN 0-949964-77-8).
Academia Edms.
Langendorf, Hans. Legal Dictionary:
Part 1, Dutch-German. 365p.
(Dutch & Ger.). 1977. $26.00
(ISBN 90-26-8070-74). Kluwer
Academic.
––Woerterbuch der Deutschen &
Niederlaendischen Rechtssprache:
Lexikon fuer Justiz, Verwaltung,
Wirtschaft & Handel. LC 78-
376399. (Ger. & Dutch.). 1976.
DM.55.00 (ISBN 3-406-06672-0).
Kluwer Group.
Langenscheidt Dutch-English Lilliput
Dictionary. 640p. (Dutch & Eng.).
plastic $1.50 (ISBN 3-468-96476-
5). Langenscheidt.
Langenscheidt English-Dutch Lilliput
Dictionary. 637p. (Dutch & Eng.).
plastic $1.50 (ISBN 3-468-96477-
3). Langenscheidt.
Langenscheidts Universal-
Woerterbuch Niederlandisch.
560p. (Dutch & Ger.). DM.6.80
(18231). Langenscheidt.
Noordzij, Nel. Woordenboek van
magic, okkultisme &
parapsychologi. LC 76-456275.
110p. (Dutch.). 1976. fl.12.50
(ISBN 9-02613-015-5). Fontein.
Norsk-Nederlansk-Norsk. 379p.
(Norwegian & Dutch.). 1981.
$14.95 (ISBN 82-573-0164-7, M-
9459). French & Eur.
Paardekooper, Petrus C. ABN-
Uitspraakgids. LC 80-499677. xvii,
250p. (Dutch.). 1978. write for
info. (ISBN 9-02912-020-7).
Heideland-Orbis.
Peek, H. Standaard Nederlands-
Engels Technisch Woordenboek.
LC 75-539819. 388p. (Eng. &
Dutch.). 1975. fl.35.00 (ISBN 90-
02-12737-5). Standaard Uitgeverij.
Pimentel, Jitschak. Woordenboek
Hebreeuws-Nederlands. LC 78-
388662. 480p. (Hebrew & Dutch.).
1978. fl.49.00 (ISBN 9-0601-0322-
X). Strengholt.
––Woordenboek Hebreeuws-
Nederlands. LC 78-388662. 480p.
(Hebrew & Dutch.). 1978. fl.49.00
(ISBN 9-06010-322-X). Strengholt.
Pirog, Zh. I., et al. Karmannyi
Russko-Niderlandskii Slovar. 496p.
(Rus. & Dutch.). 1977. $2.50 (Pub.
by Russkii Iazyk). Four Continent.
Radet for Teknisk Terminologi.
Ordbok for
Automatiseringsteknikk. 143p.
(Eng. & Dutch.). 1979. Kr.80.00
(ISBN 8-2002-6067-4).
Universitesforlaget.

Renier, Fernand G. Dutch-English,
English-Dutch Dictionary. (Dutch
& Eng.). 19.50 (ISBN 0-87557-
014-3, 014-3). Saphrograph.
Schoell, K. Dutch-Norwegian &
Norwegian-Dutch Pocket
Dictionary. (Dutch & Norwegian.).
1981. write for info. (ISBN 82-
573-0164-7). Kunnskapsforlaget.
Schuurmans, Stekhovenn G. Kluwer's
Universeel Technisch Woorenboek
Nederlands Frans. LC 77-568049.
xii, 643p. (Fr. & Dutch.). 1977.
write for info. (ISBN 9-0201-0609-
0). Kluwer Technische.
Schuurmans Stekhoven, G. Dutch-
English, English-Dutch
Engineering Dictionary, 2 vols.
(Dutch & Eng.). 125.00 set (ISBN
90-2010-602-3). Heinman.
Siekmann, Rob. Prisma
Voetbalwoordenboek. LC 79-
398681. 159p. (Dutch.). 1978.
write for info. (ISBN 9-027-40962-
5). Spectrum NL.
Slagmolen, Gerrit. Muzieklexicon, 2
vols. LC 74-336503. (Dutch.).
1974. fl.15.00 (ISBN 9-022-91367-
8). Bruna.
Van Dale, Johan H. Groot
Woordenboek der Nederlandse
Taal, 2 vols. 10th ed. Kruyskamp,
C., ed. LC 76-461655. xli, 3230p.
(Dutch.). 1976. fl.168.00 (ISBN 9-
02471-829-5). Nyhoff.
Van De Wiele, F. J. Langenscheidts
Taschenwoerterbuch
Niederlaendisch: Teil I,
Niederlaendisch-Deutsch. 527p.
(Dutch & Ger.). DM.19.80
(10231). Langenscheidt.
Van Gelderen, ed. Duits-Nederland
Woordenboek. 972p. (Ger.). 1980.
pap. $24.95 (ISBN 90-01-96814-7,
M-9745). French & Eur.
Van Gemert, G. A. & De
Maesschalck, A.
Geneesmiddelenzakboekje. LC 76-
677126. 144p. (Eng. & Dutch.).
1976. fl.16.50 (ISBN 9-0100-1588-
2). Agon Elsevier.
Van Kampen, V. Dizionario Italiano-
Olandese, Olandese-Italiano. 486p.
(Ital. & Dutch.). 1980. leatherette
$5.95 (ISBN 0-686-97344-5, M-
9171). French & Eur.
Van Meerhaeghe, Marcel A. Lexicon
Van de Economie. LC 77-557822.
170p. (Dutch.). 1977. write for
info. (ISBN 9-020-70684-5).
Stenfert Kroese.
Van Nierop, Maarten. Nieuwe
Woorden. LC 76-504980. 327p.
(Dutch.). 1975. fl.22.75 (ISBN 9-
06158-054-4). Scheltens.
Wallis, W. H. Neederland-Duits:
Wolter's Woorden Boek. 956p.
(Ger.). 1981. $24.95 (ISBN 90-01-
96815-5, M-9744). French & Eur.
Willemze, Theo. Spectrum
Muzieklexicon, 4 vols. LC 76-
500562. (Illus., Dutch.). 1975.
fl.40.00 (ISBN 9-027-48298-5).
Spectrum NL.

DUTCH WAR, 1672-1678
Sterkenburg, P. Een Glossarium van
Zeventiende-Eeuws Nederlands.
LC 76-505834. lix, 152p. (Dutch.).
1975. fl.25.00 (ISBN 9-00181-210-
4). Tjeenk Willink.

DUTIES
see Tariff; Taxation

DWELLINGS–HEATING AND
VENTILATION
see Heating

DYEING
see Dyes and Dyeing

DYES AND DYEING
see also Textile Chemistry
Ponting, Ken. A Dictionary of Dyes
& Dyeing. 216p. 1982. $35.00x
(ISBN 0-7135-1311-X, Pub. by
Bell & Hyman England). State
Mutual Bk.

DYOLA LANGUAGE
see Diola Language

DYSLEXIA, DEVELOPMENTAL
see Reading Disability

E

EARLY CHRISTIAN
LITERATURE
see Christian Literature, Early

EARLY PRINTED BOOKS
see Bibliography–Rare Books

EARTH, EFFECT OF MAN ON
see Man–Influence on Nature
EARTH SCIENCE
see Earth Sciences; Geology
EARTH SCIENCES
see also Atmosphere; Climatology; Geography; Geology; Geophysics; Hydrology; Meteorology; Oceanography
A Dictionary of Earth Sciences. (A Helix Bks.: No. 377). (Illus.). 301p. 1983. pap. text ed. $9.95 (ISBN 0-8226-0377-2). Rowman & Allanheld.
Franz, L. Lexikon Zur - und Fruehgeschichtlicher Fundstaetten Oesterreichs. (Ger.). 1965. $47.00 (ISBN 3-7749-0255-0, M-7193). French & Eur.
Geowissenschaften. LC 77-466982. (Fr. & Ger.). 1975. write for info. Schweizerbart.
Icart, Antoine. Je Sais Tout Sur le Monde & la Nature. LC 77-574200. 115p. (Eng. & Fr.). 1977. write for info. (ISBN 2-01-000928-2). Hachette-Jeunesse.
Jacks, G. V. & Tavernier, R. Vocabulaire Multilingue de la Science du Sol: Anglais-Francais-Espagnol-Allemand-Portugais-Italien-Neerlandais-Suedois-Russe. 3rd ed. 430p. (Eng., Fr., Span., Ger., Port., Ital., Dutch, Swedish & Rus.). 1968. 22.50 F. F. A. O.
Stiegeler, Stella E. A Dictionary of Earth Sciences. LC 76-41042. (Illus.). 1977. $20.00x (ISBN 0-87663-725-X, Pica Pr). Universe.
Watznauer. Woerterbuch Geowissenschaften. 400p. (Eng. & Ger.). 1982. DM.58.00 (ISBN 3-87144-635-1). Verlag Harri Deutsch.
--Woerterbuch Geowissenschaften. 400p. (Ger. & Eng.). 1982. DM.58.00 (ISBN 3-87144-636-X). Verlag Harri Deutsch.
Watznauer, A. Dictionary of Geosciences, 2 vols. (Eng. & Ger.). Date not set. English-German. $57.50 (ISBN 0-444-99702-4); German-English. $57.50 (ISBN 0-444-99701-6). Elsevier.
--Woerterbuch Geowissenschaften, Vol. 1. (Eng. & Ger., English-German Dictionary of Geo-Sciences). 1973. $38.00 (ISBN 3-87144-139-2, M-6917). French & Eur.
Watznauer, Adolf. Geowissenschaften Deutsch-Englisch. 372p. (Ger. & Eng.). 1981. M.46.00. VEB Technik.
--Geowissenschaften Englisch-Deutsch. 400p. (Eng. & Ger.). 1981. M.46.00. VEB Technik.
EAST GERMANY
see Germany, East
EAST INDIAN PHILOSOPHY
see Philosophy, Indic
EASTERN GERMANY
see Germany, East
EATING
see Gastronomy
EBON LANGUAGE
see Marshall Language
EBONITE
see Rubber
ECCLESIASTICAL ART
see Christian Art and Symbolism
ECCLESIASTICAL DISCIPLINE
see Church Discipline
ECCLESIASTICAL DIVISIONS
see Ecclesiastical Geography
ECCLESIASTICAL GEOGRAPHY
see also Geography, Historical
Aubert, Roger & Van Cauwenberg. Dictionnaire d'histoire & de Geographie Ecclesiastiques, 16 vols. (Fr.). 4464.00 F. Letouzey & Ane.
Aubert, Roger, et al. Dictionnaire d'histoire & de Geographie Ecclesiastiques. 176p. (Fr.). 88.00 F. Letouzey & Ane.
ECCLESIASTICAL LAW
see also Canon Law
also subdivision Government under denominations, e.g. Church of England–Government
Prompsault, J. H. Dictionnaire Raisonne de Droit et de Jurisprudence en Matiere Civile Ecclesiastique, 3 vols. Migne, J. P., ed. (Encyclopedie Theologique Ser.: Vols. 36-38). 1948p. (Fr.). Repr. of 1849 ed. lib. bdg. $248.00x (ISBN 0-89241-244-5). Caratzas Pub Co.

ECCLESIASTICAL RITES AND CEREMONIES
see Liturgies
ECKANKAR
Twitchell, Paul. Eckankar Dictionary. LC 75-306747. 160p. (Orig.). 1981. pap. 9.00 (ISBN 0-914766-74-0, 0154). IWP Pub.
ECOLOGY
see also Conservation of Natural Resources
Allaby, ed. Dictionary of the Environment. (Eng.). Epap. 5.95. Macmillan.
Allaby, Michael. A Dictionary of the Environment. 1977. text ed. $17.95 (ISBN 0-442-20288-1). Van Nos Reinhold.
Becker, U. Herder - Lexikon Umwelt. 216p. (Ger.). 1976. $17.95 (ISBN 3-451-16457-4, M-7460, Pub. by Herder). French & Eur.
--Herder-Lexikon Umwelt. 216p. (Ger.). 1976. $17.95 (ISBN 3-451-16457-4). Herder.
Becker, Udo. Diccionario Rioduero: Ecologia. 216p. (Span.). 1975. leatherette $7.50 (ISBN 84-220-0714-2, S-50165). French & Eur.
Buchner, Greet. Milieuvriendelijk van A tot Z. LC 79-365782. 117p. (Dutch.). 1979. fl.12.50 (ISBN 9-0603-0246-X). Driehoek.
Conseil International de la Langue Fran c04aise, ed. Vocabulaire de L'Environnement. (Fr.). 1976. pap. $14.95 (ISBN 0-686-57283-1, M-4648). French & Eur.
Conseil International de la Langue Francaise. Vocabulaire de l'environnement. new ed. (Fr.). 1976. 37.60 F. Hachette.
--Vocabulaire d'ecologie. (Fr.). 1974. 23.70 F. Hachette.
Gilpin, Alan. Dictionary of Environmental Terms. 191p. 1976. $14.95x (ISBN 0-7022-1010-2); pap. $8.95x (ISBN 0-7022-1011-0). U of Queensland Pr.
Lewis, Walter H. Ecology Field Glossary: A Naturalist's Vocabulary. LC 77-71856. 1977. lib. bdg. 25.00 (ISBN 0-8371-9547-0, LEF/). Greenwood.
Lincoln, R. J. & Boxshall, G. A. A Dictionary of Ecology, Evolution & Systematics. LC 81-18013. 350p. 1982. $47.50 (ISBN 0-521-23957-5). Cambridge U Pr.
Miljoleksikon. LC 75-546754. 121p. (Norwegian.). 1975. Kr.32.00. Norges Natur.
Monkhouse & Small. Dictionary of the Natural Environment. (Eng.). Epap. 3.95. E. Arnold.
Monkhouse, F. Dictionary of Natural Environment with English-Arabic Glossary. $16.00x (ISBN 0-86685-078-3). Intl Bk Ctr.
Monkhouse, F. J. & Small, John. Dictionary of Natural Environment. 326p. 1978. pap. text ed. $9.95 (ISBN 0-7131-5958-8). E Arnold.
Tischler, Wolfgang. Okologie. LC 76-457603. 125p. (Ger.). 1975. DM.9.80 (ISBN 3-437-20142-5). Fischer Verlag.
U. S. Army Natick Laboratories. Glossary of Environmental Terms (Terrestrial) LC 73-2851. 149p. 1973. Repr. of 1968 ed. $34.00x (ISBN 0-8103-3277-9). Gale.
ECONOMETRICS
Olmi, Andre & July, Fortune. Lexique du Calcul Economique & de l'econometrie. 192p. (Fr.). 1970. 39.00 F. E. M. E.
ECONOMIC BOTANY
see Botany, Economic
ECONOMIC DEVELOPMENT
Here are entered general works on the theory and policy of economic development. Works restricted to a particular area are entered under the name of the area.
see also Development Banks; Saving and Investment
Mitra, Ashok. Terms of Trade & Class Relations: An Essay in Political Economy. 208p. 1977. $30.00x (ISBN 0-7146-3083-7, F Cass Co). Biblio Dist.
Tezenas Du Montcel, Henri. Dictionnaire des Sciences de la Gestion. 368p. (Fr.). 1972. Can.$12.50. Hurtubise H. M. H.
ECONOMIC ENTOMOLOGY
see Insects, Injurious and Beneficial

ECONOMIC GROWTH
see Economic Development
ECONOMIC POLICY
see also Economic Development; Labor Supply; Mercantile System; Monetary Policy; Social Policy; Tariff also subdivisions Commercial Policy and Economic Policy under names of countries
Back, H., et al. Dictionary of Politics & Economics. 1037p. (Eng., Fr. & Ger., Dictionnaire de Politique et d'Economie - Lexikon fur Politik und Wirschaft). 1967. $37.00 (ISBN 3-11-000892-0, M-7104). French & Eur.
Borisov, E. F., ed. Politekonomicheskii Slovar. 267p. (Rus.). 1972. $3.35 (Pub. by Politizdat). Four Continent.
De Togore, Roca. Diccionario de economia y dissiplinas a fines, aleman-espanol. 500p. (Span.). 1965. 500.00 ptas. InterCiencia.
Heller. Diccionario de economia politica. (Span.). 500.00 ptas. Labor.
Lexikon des Steuer & Wirtschaftsrechts. (Ger., Munich, Germany). 1973. DM.29.80 (ISBN 3-8092-0000-X). WRS Verlag.
Logie, Gordon & Hemstead, Hemel, eds. International Planning Glossary. LC 77-367067. (Eng., Fr., Ital., Dutch, Ger., Swedish, Finnish, Dannish & Norwegian.). 1975. E3.00 (ISBN 0-9504753-0-0). Intl Plan Glos.
Napoleoni, Claudio. Diccionario de Economia Politica, 2 vols. 1668p. (Span.). 1982. 4850.00 ptas (ISBN 8-4718-9163-8). Ortells Ferriz.
--Diccionario de economia politicia. (Span.). 925.00 ptas. Castilla.
Russko-Ukrainskii Slovar Sotsial'No-Ekonomicheskoi Terminologii. 412p. (Rus. & Ukrainian.). 1976. $3.95 (Pub. by Ukr. Entsiklopediia). Four Continent.
Zahn, H. Dictionary of Politics & Economic Policy. 384p. (Ger., Eng. & Fr.). 1975. $49.50 (ISBN 0-7121-5514-7, M-7105). French & Eur.
Zahn, Hans E. Woerterbuch zur Politik und Wirtschaftpolitik. (Ger., Eng. & Fr.). 1976. $76.00 (ISBN 3-7819-2011-9, M-6904). French & Eur.
Zhamin, V. A., ed. Politicheskaia Ekonomiia Slovar. 464p. (Rus.). 1979. $6.50 (Pub. by Politizdat). Four Continent.
ECONOMIC STATISTICS
see Economic History (for collections of statistics), Statistics (for works on the theory and methodology of economic statistics)
ECONOMIC THEORY
see Economics
ECONOMICS
see also Balance of Trade; Banks and Banking; Business; Capitalism; Commerce; Communication and Traffic; Credit; Demography; Econometrics; Economic Development; Economic Policy; Employment (Economic Theory); Finance; Finance, Public; Labor and Laboring Classes; Land Use; Marxian Economics; Mercantile System; Money; Population; Saving and Investment; Socialism; Speculation; Tariff; Taxation
Bernard, Yves & Colli, Jean-Claude. Vocabulaire Economique & Financier. 384p. (Fr.). 1976. 17.00 F. Seuil.
Diccionario de Economia Politica. 1650p. (Span.). 1982. 2500.00 ptas (ISBN 8-43007-463-5). Autores-Editores.
Dictionnaire des Sigles Economiques & Sociaux. (Fr.). 25.00 F. Liaisons Sociales.
Ghattas, Nabih. Dictionary of Economic Business & Finance. 977p. (Eng. & Arabic., With Arabic glossary). $25.00 (271-9). Intl Bk Ctr.
--Dictionary of Economics, Business & Finance: English-Arabic with Arabic Glossary. (Eng. & Arabic.). $25.00x (ISBN 0-86685-169-0). Intl Bk Ctr.
Gottschalg, J. & Just, K., eds. Jugendlexikon Politische Okonomie. 220p. (Eng.). 1981. M.9.80. Bibl Inst Leipzig.

Hansen, Mamdouh. A Dictionary of Economics & Commerce. 496p. (Eng. & Arabic., With Eng. & Arabic Glossary). $20.00 (066-X). Intl Bk Ctr.
Henni, Mustapha. Dictionnaire des termes economiques et commerciaux. 412p. (Arabic, Fr. & Eng.). $20.00 (109-7). Intl Bk Ctr.
Kohls, Siegfried, ed. Oekonomisches Woerterbuch Aussenwirtschaft (Dictionary of External Exonomic Relations & Trade) 619p. (Ger., Rus., Eng., Fr. & Span.). 1972. $25.00x (ISBN 3-87106-018-6). Intl Pubns Serv.
Libr. du Liban, ed. A Dictionary of Economics & Commerce. (Eng. & Arabic.). pap. $7.95 (0-76-7). Intl Bk Ctr.
Thesaurus du Management & de L'economie, 2 vols. 2nd ed. LC 77-461651. (Eng. & Fr.). 1975. 2025.00 F (ISBN 2-9500-2031-3). Bureau Marcel.
Van Dijk, Marcel & Sandeau, Georges. Thesaurus du Management & de l'economie, 2 vols. 150p. (Fr.). 1975. 225.00 F. M. Van Dijk.
ECONOMICS–BIBLIOGRAPHY
Rolland-Thomas, Paule & Coulombe, Victor. Vocabulaire Technique de la Bibliotheconomie. 187p. (Fr.). 1969. Can.$5.00. Assoc. Canad. Biblio. Lang. Fr.
ECONOMICS–COLLECTED WORKS
Lambert, Denis-Clair. Dictionnaire Francais-Anglais de l'economie. 264p. (Fr. & Eng.). 1975. 34.00 F. Ouvrieres.
ECONOMICS–DICTIONARIES
Ammer, Christine & Ammer, Dean. Dictionary of Business & Economics. rev. & expanded ed. 1983. $29.95 (ISBN 0-02-900790-9). Free Pr.
Ammer, Christine & Ammer, Dean S. Dictionary of Business & Economics. LC 76-41625. 1977. $27.95 (ISBN 0-02-900590-6). Free Pr.
Anikin, A. V., ed. Anglo-Russkii Eknomicheskii Slovar. 728p. (Rus.). 1977. $14.50 (Pub. by Russkii Iazyk). Four Continent.
Bannock, Graham, et al. Dizionario di economia. vii, 154p. (Ital.). 1977. L.3900.00. Laterza.
Barca, Luciano. Dizionario di politica economica. 256p. (Ital.). 1979. L.3500.00. Editori Riuniti.
Barraine, Raymond. Nouveau Dictionnaire de Droit et de Sciences Economiques. 540p. (Fr.). 1974. $39.95 (ISBN 0-686-56779-X, M-6023). French & Eur.
Becher, H. Woerterbuch der Spanischen und Deutschen Rechts und Wirtschaftssprache, Vol. 1. (Span. & Ger.). 1971. $85.00 (ISBN 3-406-00469-5, M-6956). French & Eur.
Becher, Herbert J. Woerterbuch der Recht & Wirtshaftssprache: Teil II, Deutsch-Spanisch. viii, 814p. (Ger. & Span.). 1979. DM.148.00. Recht & Wirtschaft.
--Woerterbuch der Rechts & Wirtschaftssprache: Teil I, Spanisch-Deutsch. viii, 933p. (Span. & Ger.). 1978. DM.175.00. Recht & Wirtschaft.
Becker, Ursula. Rechtsworterbuch Fur Die Gewerbliche Wirtschaft. 600p. (Ger., Eng. & Fr., Dictionary of Industrial Economics). 1978. $145.00 (ISBN 3-7819-2015-1, M-7599, Pub. by Fritz Knapp Verlag). French & Eur.
Bernard, Yves. Diccionario Economico & Financiero. LC 80-9262. xi, 1274p. (Span.). 1975. write for info. (ISBN 8-470-19071-7). Assn Prog Direc.
Bernard, Yves & Colli, Jean-Claude. Vocabulaire Economique et Financier: Coll. Points Economie. 384p. (Fr.). 1976. pap. $10.95 (ISBN 0-686-56915-6, M-6031). French & Eur.
Bernard, Yves & Suarez Campos, Jose M. Vocabulario Economico & Financiero. 488p. (Span.). 1981. 1300.00 ptas (ISBN 84-7019-077-6). Assn Prog Direc.

Bernard, Yves, et al. Dictionnaire Economique et Financier. Lewandowski, Dominique, ed. 1200p. (Fr.). 1975. $119.95 (ISBN 0-686-57297-1, M-4643). French & Eur.
--Dictionnaire Economique & Financier. 1200p. (Eng., Fr. & Ger.). 1975. 250.00 F. Seuil.
Birou, Alain. Lexico De Economia. 6th ed. 200p. (Span.). 1977. pap. $8.75 (ISBN 84-7222-751-0, S-50040). French & Eur.
Bljach & Bagma. Deutsch-Russisches Oekonomisches Woerterbuch. (Rus. & Ger.). M.43.50. Wissenschaftliche.
Boeing, G. Herder - Lexikon Wirtschaft. 2nd ed. 256p. (Ger.). 1975. pap. $25.95 (ISBN 3-451-16460-4, M-7462, Pub. by Herder). French & Eur.
--Herder-Lexikon Wirtschaft. 2nd ed. 256p. (Ger.). 1975. pap. $25.95 (ISBN 3-451-16460-4). Herder.
Bortnikov, V. B., et al. Russko-Moldavskii Ekonomicheskii Slovar. 363p. (Rus. & Moldavian.). 1973. $2.65 (Pub. by Kartia Moldoveniaske). Four Continent.
Bouvier-Ajam, Maurice, et al. Dictionnaire Economique & Social. LC 75-508274. 765p. (Fr.). 1975. 59.00 F. Edns Sociales.
Branciard, Michel. Dictionnaire Economique & Social: Dictionnaire Thomas Suavet. 11th ed. LC 79-368728. 582p. (Fr.). 1978. 110.00 F (ISBN 2-7082-0209-X). Ouvrieres.
Bubic, S. Dictionary of Economic Terms. 1040p. (Eng. & Serbocroation.). 1975. $95.00 (ISBN 0-686-92261-1, M-9699). French & Eur.
Clifford Vaughn, F. Glossary of Economics. (Eng., Fr., Ger. & Rus.). 1966. $24.50 (ISBN 0-444-40129-6). Elsevier.
Compagnol, Marcello G. Dizionario Merli geografico, storico, economico: Vol. 1, Lettera AZ. (Illus.). 176p. (Ital.). 1975. L.25000.00. ERGA.
Congdon, TIm, et al. Diccionario de economia. Menduina, Antonio, tr. 323p. (Span.). 1982. 800.00 ptas (ISBN 84-253-1375-9). Grijalbo.
Cotta, Alain. Dictionnaire de la Science Economique. 3rd ed. 448p. (Fr.). pap. $22.50 (ISBN 0-686-56965-2, M-6092). French & Eur.
--Dictionnaire de la Science Economique. 3rd ed. 448p. (Fr.). 50.00 F. Delarge.
Crane, David. A Dictionary of Canadian Economics. (Eng.). 1980. Can.$pap. 18.95 (ISBN 0-88830-174-X); pap. $8.95 (ISBN 0-88830-173-1). Hurtig.
--A Dictionary of Canadian Economics. LC 80-143762. ix, 372p. 1980. Can.$18.95 (ISBN 0-88830-174-X); pap. $8.95 (ISBN 0-88830-173-1). Hurtig.
Decsi, Gyula & Karcsay, Sandor. Woerterbuch der Rechts & Wirtschaftssprache: Teil I, Deutsch-Russisch. (Ger. & Rus.). write for info. Recht & Wirtschaft.
--Woerterbuch der Rechts & Wirtschaftssprache: Teil II, Russisch-Deutsch. (Rus. & Ger.). write for info. Recht & Wirtschaft.
De Jong, Frits J., et al, eds. Quadrilingual Economics Dictionary. 1981. lib. bdg. 48.00 (ISBN 90-247-2243-8, Pub. by Martinus Nijhoff Netherlands). Kluwer Academic.
Delattre, J. & DeVernisy, G. Vocabulaire Barometre Dans le Langage Economique. 3rd ed. 160p. (Eng. & Fr.). 1967. pap. $9.95 (ISBN 0-686-56982-2, M-6109). French & Eur.
Delattre, J. & Vernisy, G. Le Vocabulaire Barometre dans le Langage Economique. 3rd ed. 160p. (Fr.). 1967. 12.00 F. Georg.
De Togore, Roca. Diccionario de economia y dissiplinas a fines, aleman-espanol. 500p. (Span.). 1965. 500.00 ptas. InterCiencia.
Dictionnaire Economique & Financier. 248p. (Fr.). 1972. 4.00 F. Homme.
Dictionnaire Francais-Anglais de l'Economie. 264p. (Fr. & Eng.). 1975. pap. $14.95 (ISBN 0-686-56989-X, M-6329). French & Eur.
Dictionnaire Juridique & Economique, 1: Francais-Allemand. 2nd ed. (Fr. & Ger.). 1967. 81.00 F. Litec.
Dietl, C. Woerterbuch des Wirtschafts, Rechts und Handelssprache. (Eng. & Ger., Dictionary of Economic, Legal & Commercial Terms). 1970. $33.00 (ISBN 3-87527-003-7, M-6939). French & Eur.
Dietl, Clara E. & Lorenz, Egon. Woerterbuch fuer Recht, Wirtschaft & Politik: Teil II, Deutsch-Englisch. (Ger. & Eng.). 1983. write for info. Recht & Wirtschaft.
Dijk, G. Economische Begrippen. LC 78-383140. 144p. (Dutch.). 1978. fl.9.75 (ISBN 9-027-52020-8). NIB.
Doucet. Dictionnaire Juridique et Economique: Anglais-Francais Francais-Anglais. 770p. (Eng. & Fr.). 1979. 350.00 F. Maison Dictionnaire.
Doucet, M. Dictionnaire Juridique & Economique Francais-Allemand & Allemand Francais, 2 vols. 4th ed. Klaus, E. W., ed. (Fr. & Ger.). 8600.00 F. Bruylant.
--Dictionnaire Juridique & Economique Francais-Allemand & Allemand-Francais, Vol. 1. 4th ed. Fleck, K., ed. (Fr. & Ger.). 1980. 1800.00 F. Bruylant.
--Dictionnaire Juridique & Economique Francias-Allemand & Allemand-Francais, Vol. 2. Fleck, K., ed. (Fr. & Ger.). 1980. 1140.00 F. Bruylant.
Douret, Michel. Dictionnaire Juridique et Economique, 1: Francais-Allemand. 2nd ed. (Fr. & Ger.). 1967. $39.95 (ISBN 0-686-57122-3, M-6170). French & Eur.
Dowling, Noel. Dictionary of Economic Definitions for the Leaving Certificate. LC 77-380100. (Illus.). 45p. (Eng.). 1977. 0.45p. Educ Co Ire.
Dreuihe. Dictionnaire Anglais-Francais et Lexique Francais-Anglais des termes Politiques Juridiques et Economiques. (Eng. & Fr.). 1981. pap. $22.95 (ISBN 0-686-92584-X, M-9628). French & Eur.
Eichborn & Fuentes. Wirtschaftswoerterbuch Spanisch-Deutsch. (Span. & Ger.). 1974. $120.00 (ISBN 3-430-12390-9, M-7685, Pub. by Econ). French & Eur.
Eichborn, R. Kleine Eichborn, Taschenwoerterbuch der Wirtschaftssprache, Vol. 2. (Ger. & Eng., German-English Dictionary of Economic Terms). 1975. $33.50 (ISBN 3-921392-01-2, M-7496, Pub. by Siebenpunkt Vlg.). French & Eur.
--Wirtschafts-Woerterbuch. 4th ed. 2169p. (Ger. & Eng., Dictionary of Economics). write for info (M-7687, Pub. by Econ Vlg.). French & Eur.
--Woerterbuch fuer Wirtschaft-Recht-Verkehr-Verwaltungs & Umgangssprache: Vol.I, Englisch-Deutsch. rev. ed. 1150p. (Eng. & Ger.). 1983. $124.00. M Rosenberg.
--Woerterbuch fuer Wirtschaft-Recht-Verkehr-Verwaltungs & Umgangssprache: Vol. II, Deutch-Englisch. 1150p. (Ger. & Eng.). 1982. $124.00. M Rosenberg.
Eichborn, R. & Fuentes, A. Wirtschafts-Woerterbuch. 2nd ed. 2174p. (Ger. & Span.). $120.00 (ISBN 3-430-12388-7, M-7686, Pub. by Econ Vlg.). French & Eur.
Eichborn, R. V. Dictionary of Economics, 2 vols. Incl. Vol. 1. English & German. 168.00 (ISBN 3-921392-06-3); plastic bdg. 59.95 (ISBN 3-92139-047-8); Vol. 2. German & English. 168.00 (ISBN 3-921392-07-1); plastic bdg. 59.95 (ISBN 3-92139-055-9). (Eng. & Ger.). 1982. Adler.
Englisch fuer die Seewirtschaft Aufbaukurs Stufe IIa. (Eng. & Ger.). M.21.80. Wissenschaftliche.
Eynern, Gert V. Woerterbuch zur Politischen Oekonomie. 2nd ed. (Ger.). 1977. pap. $19.95 (ISBN 3-531-21148-X, M-6902). French & Eur.
Freyd-Wadham, H. Englisches Wirtschaftsalphabet. 6th ed. 156p. (Eng. & Ger., English Economic Terms With German Vocabulary). 1975. $9.95 (ISBN 3-87217-006-6, Pub. by Th. Grossmann). French & Eur.
Fryd, Ejnar. Tysk-Dansk, Dansk-Tysk Specialordbog. LC 75-582435. 175p. (Ger. & Danish.). 1975. Kr.115.00. For Stat Rev.
Gablers Wirtschaftslexikon. 10th ed. (Ger.). 1979. DM.248.00 (ISBN 3-409-96542-4). Gabler.
Geigant, Friedrich. Lexikon der Volkswirtschaft. (Ger.). 1975. $32.00 (ISBN 3-478-37050-7, M-7217). French & Eur.
Geigant, Friedrich, et al. Lexikon der Volkswirtschaft. LC 75-508655. 580p. (Ger.). 1975. write for info. (ISBN 3-478-37050-7). Verlag Moderne Industrie.
Greenwald, Douglas, et al. The McGraw-Hill Dictionary of Modern Economics. 3rd ed. (Illus.). 656p. 1983. 49.95 (ISBN 0-07-024376-X, P&RB). McGraw.
Guenter, H. Jugendlexikon Wirtschaft. 192p. (Ger.). 1976. $5.95 (ISBN 3-499-16189-3, M-7492, Pub. by Rowohlt). French & Eur.
--Jugenlexikon Wirtschaft. 192p. (Ger.). 1976. $5.95 (ISBN 3-499-16189-3). Rowohlt.
Haensch, G. & Casero, F. Wirtschaftssprache Spanisch-Deutsch. (Span. & Ger.). 1971. $32.00 (ISBN 3-19-006203-X, M-7684, Pub. by M. Hueber). French & Eur.
--Wirtschaftssprache Spanisch-Deutsch. (Span. & Ger.). 1971. $32.00 (ISBN 3-19-006203-X). Hueber.
Haensch, G. & Renner, R. Wirtschaftssprache Franzoesisch-Deutsch. 540p. (Fr. & Ger.). 1975. $32.00 (ISBN 3-19-006202-1, M-7683, Pub. by M. Hueber). French & Eur.
--Wirtschaftssprache Franzoesisch-Deutsch. 540p. (Fr. & Ger.). 1975. $32.00 (ISBN 3-19-006202-1). Hueber.
Haffner, Friedrich. Grundbegriffe der Marxistischen Politischen Oekonomie des Kapitalismus. LC 79-340061. 160p. (Ger.). 1978. DM.9.80 (ISBN 3-7678-0441-7). Colloguium Verlag.
Handwoerterbuch der Volkwirtschaft. LC 80-460492. (Ger.). 1978. write for info. Gabler.
Hanson, J. L. Dictionary of Economics & Commerce. 5th ed. 472p. 1981. pap. $17.50x (ISBN 0-7121-0424-0). Intl Ideas.
Henni, Mustapha. Dictionaire Des Termes Economiques et Commerciaux: Francais-Arabe. (Fr. & Arabic.). $18.00x (ISBN 0-86685-109-7). Intl Bk Ctr.
--Dictionary Des Terms Economiques et Commerciaux (French-English-Arabic) (Fr., Eng. & Arabic.). $25.00x (ISBN 0-86685-111-9). Intl Bk Ctr.
Herbst, R. Dictionary of Commercial, Financial & Legal Terms, 3 vols. (Eng., Fr & Ger.). $98.60 ea.; Vol. I. (ISBN 3-85942-000-3); Vol. II. (ISBN 3-85942-006-2); Vol. III. Adler.
--Dictionary of Commercial, Financial & Legal Terms, 3 Vols. (Eng, Fr, & Ger.). Set. $330.00 (ISBN 0-686-76877-9); Vol. 1. $125.00 ea. (ISBN 3-8594-2000-3). Vol. 2 (ISBN 3-8594-2006-2). Vol. 3 (ISBN 3-8594-2002-X). Heinman.
James, Simon, compiled by. A Dictionary of Economic Quotations. LC 81-6632. 244p. 1981. $23.50x (ISBN 0-389-20230-4). B&N Imports.
Jong, F. J. Economisch Woorden Boek: Engels-Frans-Duits-Nederlands. 685p. (Eng., Fr., Ger. & Dutch.). 1980. $75.00 (ISBN 90-247-2243-8, M9474). French & Eur.
Kohls, V. Economics & Foreign Trade Dictionary. 619p. 1980. $90.00x (ISBN 0-686-72095-4, Pub. by Collet's). State Mutual Bk.
Koszyk, K. Woerterbuch zur Publizistik. (Ger.). 1970. $28.00 (ISBN 3-7940-4281-6, M-6901). French & Eur.
Kozlov, G. A., et al, eds. Kratkii Ekonomicheskii Slovar. 390p. (Rus.). 1958. $2.75 (Pub. by Politizdat). Four Continent.
Kratkii Ekonomicheskii Slovar Piatiletki Effektivnosti & Kachestva. 264p. (Rus.). 1978. $2.70 (Pub. by Politizdat Ukrainy). Four Continent.
Langendorf, Hans & Stein, P. A. Woerterbuch der Recht & Wirtschaftssprache: Teil I, Niederlandisch-Deutsch. 365p. (Dutch & Ger.). 1976. DM.55.00. Recht & Wirtschaft.
--Woerterbuch der Rechts & Wirtschaftssprache: Teil II, Deutsch-Niederlaendisch. 365p. (Ger. & Dutch.). 1976. DM.55.00. Recht & Wirtschaft.
Lerche, Mario R. Deutsch-Spanisches Glossarium Finanzieller & Wirtschaftlicher Fachausdrueck. LC 77-574052. 460p. (Ger. & Span.). 1970. DM.22.00 (ISBN 3-7819-2012-7). Knapp Verlag.
Lopatnikov, L. I. Kratkii Ekonomiko-Matematicheskii Slovar. 360p. (Rus.). 1979. $5.25 (Pub. by Nauka). Four Continent.
--Populiarnyi Ekonomiko-Matematicheskii Slovar. 165p. (Rus.). 1973. $1.95 (Pub. by Znanie). Four Continent.
Malthus, Thomas R. Definitions in Political Economy. LC 70-21333. Repr. of 1827 ed. 25.00x (ISBN 0-678-00018-2). Kelley.
Mathieu, Gilbert. Vocabulaire De L'economie. (Fr.). pap. $17.50 (ISBN 0-686-57041-3, M-6401). French & Eur.
--Vocabulaire de l'economie. (Fr.). 40.00 F. Delarge.
Mayer, G. Dizionario di economia. (Ital.). L.3000.00. Bulzoni.
Mentzel, Wolfgang & Wittlesberger, Helmut. Kleines Wirtschafts-Woerterbuch. LC 78-349791. (Illus.). 379p. (Ger.). 1977. DM.12.90 (ISBN 3-451-07629-2). Herder.
Moechel, G. Oekonomisches Woerterbuch Russisch-Deutsch. 3rd ed. 692p. (Rus. & Ger.). 1976. $43.50 (ISBN 3-87106-011-9, M-7575, Pub. by Vlg. Die Wirtschaft). French & Eur.
Moiseev, A. V. Ekonomicheskii Slovar Spravochnik Rabochego. (Rus.). 1979. $1.50 (Pub. by Politizdat). Four Continent.
Moreno Pacheo, Miguel. Economic Terminology. (Eng. & Span.). 1967. $30.00 (ISBN 3-1900-6205-6). Adler.
New Japanese-English Dictionary of Economic Terms. 580p. (Japanese & Eng.). 1977. Leatherette $45.00 (ISBN 0-686-92411-8, M-9334). French & Eur.
Nichols, Peter & Vibes, Pierre. Vocabulaire Anglais-Francais de Terminologie, Economique & Juridique. 104p. (Eng. & Fr.). 1971. 16.00 F. L. G. D. J.
Nikitin, V. T. Kratkii Ekonomicheskii Slovar-Spravochnik Mastera i Nachal'nika Tsekha. 279p. (Rus.). 1968. $5.25 (Pub. by Ekonomika). Four Continent.
Noble, C. E. Australian Economic Terms. LC 78-320336. x, 200p. (Eng.). 1977. Aus.$4.95 (ISBN 0-582-68442-0). Longman.
Noehring. Woerterbuch Wirtschaft. 784p. (Eng. & Ger.). 1981. DM.29.80 (ISBN 3-87144-652-1). Verlag Harri Deutsch.
Oekonomisches Lexikon: A-G. (Ger.). M.33.00. Wissenschaftliche.
Oekonomisches Lexikon: H-P. (Ger.). M.33.00. Wissenschaftliche.
Oekonomisches Lexikon: Q-Z. (Ger.). M.33.00. Wissenschaftliche.
Oekonomisches Woerterbuch Englisch-Deutsch. (Eng. & Ger.). M.76.80. Wissenschaftliche.
Olivera. Diccionario de economia y cooperativismo. 254p. (Span.). 1970. 40.00 ptas. Albatros.

Olivera, J. Diccionario de economia y cooperativismo. (Span.). Arg.$25.00. Hachette-Jeunesse.
Olmi, Andre & July, Fortune. Lexique du Calcul Economique & de l'econometrie. 192p. (Fr.). 1970. 39.00 F. E. M. E.
Osmowej, M. N. Polish-Russian Dictionary of Economics. 494p. (Pol. & Rus.). 1977. leatherette $19.50 (ISBN 0-686-92093-7, M-9121). French & Eur.
Pacheco, M. Economic Terminology: English-Spanish. 480p. (Eng. & Span.). 1967. DM.19.95 (ISBN 3-19-006205-6). Hueber.
Pacheco Moreno, Miguel. Economic Terminology. 480p. (Eng. & Span.). DM.17.50. Hueber.
Palgrave, Robert H. Dictionary of Political Economy, 3 vols. LC 74-31358. 1976. Repr. of 1910 ed. Set. $191.00x (ISBN 0-8103-4210-3). Gale.
Papi, Giuseppe U. Dizionario di economia. iv, 1512p. (Ital.). 1972. L.20000.00 (ISBN 88-02-01493-0). UTET.
Parsenow, Gunther. Fachwoerterbuch Fur Recht und Wirtschaft. 504p. (Swedish & Ger.). 1975. $68.00 (ISBN 3-452-18010-7, M-7399, Pub. by Carl Heymanns Verlag KG). French & Eur.
Pearce, D. W. The Macmillan Dictionary of Modern Economics. 450p. (Eng.). 1981. E14.95 (ISBN 0-333-26962-4). Macmillan London.
Phelizon, Jean F. Lexique des Termes Economiques. 2nd ed. LC 76-477732. (Illus.). 184p. (Fr.). 1975. 30.00 F. Tech Vulgar.
Phelizon, Jean-Francois. Lexique des Termes Economiques. new ed. 192p. (Fr.). 1977. 23.00 F. Tech Vulgar.
Polsko-Russkii Ekonomicheskii Slovar. 496p. (Pol. & Rus.). 1977. $9.50 (0-22, Pub. by Russkii Iazyk). Four Continent.
Potonnier. Woerterbuch fuer Wirtschaft, Recht & Handel: Band I, Deutsch-Franzoesisch. 1616p. (Ger. & Fr.). 1982. DM.130.00. Brandstetter.
--Woerterbuch fuer Wirtschaft, Recht & Handel: Band II, Franzoesisch-Deutsch. 1502p. (Fr. & Ger.). 1982. DM.100.00. Brandstetter.
Potonnier, Georges. Woerterbuch fuer Wirtschaft: Recht und Handel, Vol. 1. (Ger. & Fr.). 1970. $56.00 (ISBN 3-87097-030-8, M-6919). French & Eur.
--Woerterbuch fuer Wirtschaft: Recht und Handel, Vol. 2. (Fr. & Ger.). 1970. $80.00 (ISBN 3-87097-031-6, M-6918). French & Eur.
Potonnier, Georges E. & Potonnier, Brigitte. Woerterbuch Wirtschaft Recht Handel: Deutsch-Franzoesisch, Vol. 2. 1486p. (Fr. & Ger.). 1970. 330.00 F. Maison Dictionnaire.
Recktenwald, Horst C. Woerterbuch der Wirtschaft. 7th ed. (Ger.). 1975. $20.00 (ISBN 3-520-11407-0, M-6941). French & Eur.
Rektenwald, Horst C. Woerterbuch der Wirtschaft. 7th ed. LC 76-454037. (Illus.). xvi, 555p. (Ger.). 1975. DM.25.00 (ISBN 3-520-11407-0). Kroener.
Renner, et al. Economic Terminology German-English. 2nd ed. (Ger. & Eng.). 1970. $27.50 (ISBN 3-1900-6201-3). Adler.
Rittershofer, Werner. Das Lexikon Wirtschaft, Gesellschaft, Gewerkschaften. LC 76-457119. (Illus.). 379p. (Ger.). 1975. DM.18.00 (ISBN 3-7663-0095-4). Bund.
Romain, Alfred. Dictionary of German & English Legal & Economic Terminology, Vol. 1. (Eng. & Ger.). 1976. $78.00 (ISBN 3-406-03370-9, M-7101). French & Eur.
--Dictionary of German & English Legal & Economic Terminology, Vol. 2. (Ger. & Fr.). 1975. $78.00 (ISBN 3-406-03371-7, M-7100). French & Eur.
--Woerterbuch der Rechts & Wirtschaftssprache: Teil II, Deutsch-Englisch. viii, 848p. (Ger. & Eng.). 1980. DM.138.00. Recht & Wirtschaft.
--Woerterbuch der Rechts & Wirtschaftssprache: Teil I, Englisch-Deutsch. viii, 760p. (Eng. & Ger.). 1979. DM.98.00. Recht & Wirtschaft.
Russian-Chinese Dictionary of Export & Economics. 708p. (Rus. & Chinese.). 1961. leatherette $6.95 (ISBN 0-686-92108-9, M-9068). French & Eur.
Russisch fuer Oekonomen: Lehrbuch fuer die Sprachkundigenausbildung IIb. (Rus.). M.18.00. Wissenschaftliche.
Santos, F. N. Dicionario Ingles-Portugues de Economia. (Eng. & Port.). Esc.450.00. Pub Euro Am.
Schuler, A. Economics Dictionary. 784p. 1980. $95.00x (ISBN 0-686-44670-4, Pub. by Collets). State Mutual Bk.
Seldon, Arthur & Pennance, F. G. Diccionario De Economia. 2nd ed. 560p. (Span.). 1975. pap. $26.25 (ISBN 84-281-0294-5, S-50019). French & Eur.
--Diccionario de Economia. 2nd ed. 554p. (Span.). 1975. $35.95 (ISBN 84-281-0034-9, S-12358). French & Eur.
Sellien, R. Dr. Gablers Wirtschafts - Lexikon. 2565p. (Ger.). 1975. $189.00 (ISBN 3-409-32992-7, M-7351, Pub. by Betriebswirtschaftlicher Vlg.). French & Eur.
Sellien, R. & Sellien, H., eds. Doktor Gabler's Wirtschafts-Lexikon, 2 vols. LC 75-522546. (Illus., Ger.). 1975. DM.224.00 (ISBN 3-409-30932-2). Gabler.
Sloan, Harold S. & Zurcher, Arnold J. Dictionary of Economics. 5th ed. LC 70-118099. text ed. $15.00x (ISBN 0-06-480799-1). B&N Imports.
--Dictionary of Economics. LC 70-118099. pap. text ed. $5.95 (ISBN 0-06-463266-0, EH 266, EH). B&N NY.
Slovar Ekonomicheskikh Terminov. 598p. (Rus.). 1975. $3.60 (Pub. by Liesma). Four Continent.
Stefanelli, Renzo. Capire l'Economiea: Dizionario Critico del Capitalismo Contemporaneo. LC 78-337064. (Ital.). 1977. L.5500.00. De Donato.
Suarvet, Thomas H. Dictionnaire Economique et Social. 526p. (Fr.). 1973. $19.95 (ISBN 0-686-57227-0, M-6526). French & Eur.
Suavet, Thomas. Dictionnaire Economique & Social. 526p. (Fr.). 1973. 42.00 F. Ouvrieres.
Terceiro, J. B. Diccionario de economia. 2nd ed. 208p. (Span.). 1970. 150.00 ptas. Zyx.
Thomik, Rudolf. Fachwoerterbuch fuer Wirtschaft, Handel & Finanzen. 3rd ed. LC 77-562019. 685p. (Ger.). 1977. DM.74.00. Heymanns Verlag.
--Fachwoerterbuch Fur Wirtschaft, Handel und Finanzen. 685p. (Fr. & Ger.). 1977. $59.95 (ISBN 3-452-18138-3, 7400, Pub. by Carl Heymanns Verlag KG). French & Eur.
Trioke-Strambaci, H. & Helffrich-Mariani, E. Woerterbuch des Italienisch-Deutschen Privat & Wirtschaftsrechts: Band I, Deutsch-Italienisch. xix, 1332p. (Ger. & Ital.). 1982. DM.148.00. Recht & Wirtschaft.
Troike-Strambaci, H. & Helffrich-Mariani, E. Woerterbuch des Italienisch-Deutschen Privat & Wirtschaftsrechts: Band II, Italienish-Deutsch. xix, 1332p. (Ital. & Ger.). 1982. DM.148.00. Recht & Wirtschaft.
Van Meerhaeghe, Marcel A. Lexicon Van de Economie. LC 77-557822. 170p. (Dutch.). 1977. write for info. (ISBN 9-020-70684-5). Stenfert Kroese.
Varela Colmeiro, G. Diccionario comercial y economico moderno: Ingles-espanol. 256p. (Eng. & Span.). 1964. 300.00 ptas. Inter-Ciencia.
Vocabulaire de L'economie. 3rd ed. LC 79-360009. 62p. (Fr.). 1978. write for info. (ISBN 0-7754-2244-4). Edit Quebec.
Von Eynern, Gert & Boehret, Carl, eds. Woerterbuch zur Politischen Oekonomie. LC 78-393797. 582p. (Ger.). 1977. DM.26.00 (ISBN 3-531-21148-X). Westdeutscher.
Vuitton, Jacques & Vuitton, Philippe. Nouveau Lexique d'Economie: Economie, Droit, Gestion, Finance. LC 79-385411. (Illus.). 185p. (Fr.). 1978. 37.00 F. Doc Univers.
Wilson, Howard. Glossary of Economic Terms. 1964. pap. $1.00 (ISBN 0-910022-22-4). ARA.
Wortman, Leon A. A Deskbook of Business Management Terms. LC 78-23257. 1979. $24.95 (ISBN 0-8144-5470-4). Am Mgmt.
Zahn, Hans E. English-German Glossary of Financial & Economic Terms. (Eng. & Ger.). 1977. 56.00x (ISBN 3-7819-2013-5). Intl Pubns Serv.
--Euro Dictionary of Economics & Business. xiii, 702p. (Ger., Eng. & Fr.). 1973. $72.50x (ISBN 3-78192-009-7). Rothman.
--Euro-Wirtschafts Worterlrich in Drei Sprachen. 716p. (Ger., Eng. & Fr., Euro-Dictionary of Economics in Three Languages). 1973. $99.50 (ISBN 3-7819-2009-7, M-7372, Pub. by Fritz Knapp Verlag). French & Eur.

ECONOMICS–EXAMINATIONS, QUESTIONS, ETC.

Seldon, Arthur & Pennanee, F. G., trs. Diccionario de economia. 560p. (Span.). 1968. 750.00 ptas. Oikos Tau.

ECONOMICS–JUVENILE LITERATURE

Guenter, H. Jugendlexikon Wirtschaft. 192p. (Ger.). 1976. $5.95 (ISBN 3-499-16189-3, M-7492, Pub. by Rowohlt). French & Eur.
--Jugenlexikon Wirtschaft. 192p. (Ger.). 1976. $5.95 (ISBN 3-499-16189-3). Rowohlt.

ECONOMICS–TERMINOLOGY

Buracas, A. English-Lithuanian Dictionary of Economic Terms. 488p. (Eng. & Lithuanian.). 1980. $4.95 (Pub. by Mokslas). Four Continent.
Dietl, C. Woerterbuch des Wirtschafts, Rechts und Handelssprache. (Eng. & Ger., Dictionary of Economic, Legal & Commercial Terms). 1970. $33.00 (ISBN 3-87527-003-7, M-6939). French & Eur.
Eichborn & Fuentes. Wirtschaftswoerterbuch Spanisch-Deutsch. (Span. & Ger.). 1974. $120.00 (ISBN 3-430-12390-9, M-7685, Pub. by Econ). French & Eur.
Gunston, C. A. Deutsch-Englishes Glossarium. 1292p. (Ger. & Eng., German-English Glossary of Financial and Economic Terms). 1977. $69.50 (ISBN 3-7819-2014-3, 7328, Pub. by Fritz Knapp Verlag). French & Eur.
Haensch, G. & Casero, F. Wirtschaftssprache Spanisch-Deutsch. (Span. & Ger.). 1971. $32.00 (ISBN 3-19-006203-X, M-7684, Pub. by M. Hueber). French & Eur.
--Wirtschaftssprache Spanisch-Deutsch. (Span. & Ger.). 1971. $32.00 (ISBN 3-19-006203-X). Hueber.
Haensch, G. & Renner, R. Wirtschaftssprache Franzoesisch-Deutsch. 540p. (Fr. & Ger.). 1975. $32.00 (ISBN 3-19-006202-1, M-7683, Pub. by M. Hueber). French & Eur.
--Wirtschaftssprache Franzoesisch-Deutsch. 540p. (Fr. & Ger.). 1975. $32.00 (ISBN 3-19-006202-1). Hueber.
Nasr, Zacharia, ed. A Dictionary of Economics & Commerce. 320p. (Eng., Fr. & Arabic.). 1980. E17.50 (ISBN 0-333-23109-0). Macmillan London.
Pearce, D. W. The Dictionary of Modern Economics. 2nd ed. 480p. (Eng.). 1983. E17.95 (ISBN 0-333-36122-9); pap. $5.95 (ISBN 0-333-35173-8). Macmillan London.
Piernas, J. Vocabulario de Economia. (Span.). 10.00 ptas. Espasa Calpe.
Romain, Alfred. Dictionary of German & English Legal & Economic Terminology, Vol. 1. (Eng. & Ger.). 1976. $78.00 (ISBN 3-406-03370-9, M-7101). French & Eur.
--Dictionary of German & English Legal & Economic Terminology, Vol. 2. (Ger. & Fr.). 1975. $78.00 (ISBN 3-406-03371-7, M-7100). French & Eur.

ECONOMICS–VOCATIONAL GUIDANCE

Woerterbuch der Berufs und Wirtschaftspaedagogik. 320p. (Ger.). 1973. pap. $7.95 (ISBN 0-686-56645-9, M-7038). French & Eur.

ECONOMICS, INTERNATIONAL

Kohls, S., ed. Dictionary of International Economics: German, Russian, English, French, Spanish. 620p. (Ger., Rus., Eng., Fr. & Span.). 1976. $32.50x (ISBN 90-286-0505-3). Sijthoff & Noordhoff.

ECONOMICS, VOCATIONAL OPPORTUNITIES IN

see Economics–Vocational Guidance

ECUMENICAL MOVEMENT

Congar, Yves & Siegwalt, Gerard. Vocabulaire Oecumenique. 428p. (Fr.). 51.00 F. Cerf.

EDIBLE FUNGI

see Mushrooms, Edible

EDIBLE MUSHROOMS

see Mushrooms, Edible

EDITING

see also Authorship–Handbooks, Manuals, Etc.

Miettinen, Liisa. Toimitustyon Terminologiaa. LC 77-469600. 39p. (Finnish.). 1975. Fmk.6.50 (ISBN 9-5110-2130-3). Otava.
Moreau, Pierre & Masson, Andre. Vocabulaire Redaction. 64p. (Fr.). 1969. 4.50 F. Hachette.
Vinoly, A. & Vinoly, J. Diccionario-guia de redaccion. 200p. (Span.). 70.00 ptas. Teide.
Vinoly, A. J. Diccionario-Guia de Redaccion. 3rd ed. 200p. (Span.). 1976. pap. $5.50 (ISBN 84-307-7091-7, S-12219). French & Eur.
Vocabulaire & Redaction. (Fr.). 7.75 F. Ligel.
Vocabulaire & Redaction. (Fr.). 6.30 F. Ligel.

EDITORS (JOURNALISM)

see Journalists

EDUCATION

see also Adult Education; Agricultural Education; Business Education; Communication in Education; Culture; Learning, Psychology of; Libraries; Physical Education and Training; Schools; Students; Teachers; Teaching; Technical Education; Universities and Colleges; Vocational Education also subdivision Study and Teaching under special subjects; subdivision Education under names of denominations, sects, etc., e.g. Catholic Church–Education, and under special classes of people and social groups, e.g. Deaf–Education; and headings beginning with the word Educational

Laeng. Vocabulario de Pedagogia. 310p. (Span.). $3.86; 250.00 ptas. Herder SA.
Laeng, Mauro. Vocabulario de Pedagogia. 3rd ed. Genovart Rosello, C., ed. 308p. (Span.). 1982. pap. 600.00 ptas (ISBN 84-254-0581-5). Herder SA.
Woerterbuch der Schulpaedagogik. 384p. (Ger.). 1976. $12.90 (ISBN 3-451-09001-5). Herder.

EDUCATION–BIBLIOGRAPHY

Columbia University. Dictionary Catalog of the Teachers College Library, 36 vols. 1970. Set. lib. bdg. $3750.00 (ISBN 0-8161-0855-2, Hall Library). G K Hall.

EDUCATION–DICTIONARIES

Arimany Coma, Miguel. Diccionari Escolar Catala Arimany. 4th ed. 310p. (Catalan.). 1978. pap. $7.95 (ISBN 84-7211-117-2, S-50050). French & Eur.
Aschersleben, Karl. Handlexikon der Schulpaedagogik. LC 80-450953. 255p. (Ger.). 1979. write for info. (ISBN 3-170-05394-9). Kohlhammer.

Baumgartel. Diccionario de pedagogia. 2nd ed. 238p. (Span.). Col.$12.00. Paulinas.
Becher, H. Woerterbuch der Deutschen und Spanischen Rects und Wirtschaftssprache, Vol. 2. (Ger. & Span.). 1972. $79.95 (ISBN 3-406-00470-9, M-7022). French & Eur.
Botiakova, V. V., et al. Russko-Angliiskii Shkol'No-Pedagogicheskii Slovar. 455p. (Rus. & Eng.). 1959. $3.90 (Pub. by Iaroslavsk. Knizhn. Izd.). Four Continent.
Brocher, Tobias. Lexikon der Sozialerziehung. (Ger.). 1972. $15.95 (ISBN 3-7831-0378-9, M-7221). French & Eur.
Conte, Giuseppe. Woerterbuch der Deutschen und Italienischen Wirtschafts und Rechtssprache, Vol. 1. 2nd ed. (Ital. & Ger.). 1971. $30.00 (ISBN 3-406-01195-0, M-7028). French & Eur.
--Woerterbuch der Deutschen und Italienischen Wirtschafts und Rechtssprache, Vol. 2. 2nd ed. (Ger. & Ital.). 1969. $30.00 (ISBN 3-406-00887-9, M-7027). French & Eur.
De Landsheere, Gilbert. Dictionnaire de l'Evaluation et de la Recherche en Education. 352p. (Fr.). 1979. $62.50 (ISBN 0-686-56981-4, M-6108). French & Eur.
Diccionario Enciclopedico Escolar Basico. 808p. (Span.). 1974. pap. $26.95 (ISBN 84-01-60131-2, S-50044). French & Eur.
An English-Chinese Glossary of Social Sciences & Education. 238p. (Eng. & Chinese.). 1975. Leatherette $9.95 (ISBN 0-686-92309-X, M-9562). French & Eur.
Foulquie, Paul. Diccionario De Pedagogia. 464p. (Span.). 1976. $44.95 (ISBN 84-281-0328-3, S-50016). French & Eur.
--Diccionario De Pedogogia. 464p. (Span.). 1976. pap. $37.50 (ISBN 0-686-57334-X, S-50015). French & Eur.
--Dictionnaire de la Langue Pedagogique. 496p. (Fr.). 124.80 F. PUF.
Garcia Hoz, Victor. Diccionario de Pedagogia Labor, 2 vols. 3rd ed. 444p. (Span.). 1974. Set. $44.00 (ISBN 84-335-3715-6, S-12488). French & Eur.
Gieber, Robert L. An English-French Glossary of Educational Terminology. LC 80-5652. 212p. (Eng. & Fr.). 1980. lib. bdg. $20.25 (ISBN 0-8191-1344-1); pap. text ed. $10.25 (ISBN 0-8191-1345-X). U Pr of Amer.
Goliakova, N. V., et al. Russko-Frantsuzskii Shkol'No-Pedagogicheskii Slovar. 544p. (Fr. & Rus.). 1969. $3.30 (Pub. by Sov. Entsiklopediia). Four Continent.
Grue-Sorensen, K. & Winther-Jensen, Thyge, eds. Paedagogikkens Hvem Hvad Hvor. LC 78-379066. (Illus.). 295p. (Danish.). 1978. Kr.75.00 (ISBN 8-756-72555-8). Politikens Forlag.
Hawes, Gene R. & Hawes, Lynne S. The Concise Dictionary of Education. (A Hudson Group Bk.). 256p. 1982. text ed. $18.95 (ISBN 0-442-26298-1). Van Nos Reinhold.
Hehlmann, Wilhelm. Woerterbuch der Paedagogik. 9th ed. (Ger.). 1971. pap. $17.50 (ISBN 3-520-09409-6, M-6976). French & Eur.
Hu, C. T. & Beach, Beatrice. Russian-Chinese-English Glossary of Education. LC 73-108419. 1970. text ed. $10.95x (ISBN 0-8077-1529-8). Tchrs Coll.
Joubrel, H. & Bertrand, P., trs. Diccionario de educacion infantil. 224p. (Span.). 1968. Arg.$1.40. Leru.
Jourbel, H. & Bertrand, P. Diccionario de Educacion Infantil. 224p. (Span.). 1968. $22.50 (ISBN 0-686-56709-9, S-33056). French & Eur.
Kairov, I. A., ed. Pedagogicheskii Slovar, 2 vols. (Rus.). 1960. $10.75 set (980, Pub. by Izd. Akademii Ped. Nauk). Four Continent.
Kaluza, B. Herder - Lexikon Paedagogik. 216p. (Ger.). 1976. pap. $15.95 (ISBN 3-451-16466-3, M-7447, Pub. by Herder). French & Eur.
--Herder-Lexikon Paedagogik. 216p. (Ger.). 1976. pap. $15.95 (ISBN 3-451-16466-3). Herder.
Kaluza, Bjorn, ed. Herder Lexikon Paedogogik. LC 76-481667. (Illus.). 209p. (Ger.). 1976. write for info. (ISBN 3-451-16466-3). Herder.
Koeck, Peter & Ott, Hans. Woerterbuch fuer Erziehung & Unterricht. 2nd ed. 656p. (Ger.). 1979. DM.44.80. Auer.
Laeng, Mauro & Auandani, Guy. Vocabulaire de Pedagogie Moderne. 256p. (Fr.). 1974. 34.00 F. Centurion.
Lamanna, Paolo E. & Goretti, Maria. Dizionario di pedagogia, psicologia, storia dell'educazione. 130p. (Ital.). L.2200.00. Monnier.
Langendorf, Hans. Woerterbuch der Deutschen und Nierderlaendischen Rechtssprache, Vol. 1. (Dutch & Ger.). 1976. $44.00 (ISBN 3-406-06672-0, M-7025). French & Eur.
--Woerterbuch der Deutschen und Nierderlaendischen Rechtssprache, Vol. 2. (Dutch & Ger.). 1976. $44.00 (ISBN 3-406-06673-9, M-7026). French & Eur.
Lexikon der Paedagogik: Bd 1, 3 Aubl. (Ger.). 1971. DM.95.00 (ISBN 3-451-01041-0). Herder.
Lexikon der Paedagogik: Bd 2, 3 Aufl. 512p. (Ger.). 1974. DM.95.00 (ISBN 3-451-01042-9). Herder.
Lexikon der Paedagogik: Bd 3, 3 Aufl. (Ger.). 1974. DM.95.00 (ISBN 3-451-01043-7). Herder.
Lexikon der Paedagogik: Bd 4, 3 Aufl. 496p. (Ger.). 1975. DM.95.00 (ISBN 3-451-01044-5). Herder.
Luzuriaga, Lorenzo. Diccionario de pedagogia. (Span.). write for info. Losada.
Maier, Karl E. Paedagogisches Taschenlexikon. Eckinger, Ludwig, ed. LC 79-391256. (Illus.). 462p. (Ger.). 1978. DM.29.00 (ISBN 3-523-67002-0). Wolf Verlag.
Mialaret, Gaston. Vocabulaire De L'Education. 488p. (Fr.). 1979. $62.50 (ISBN 0-686-57048-0, M-6410). French & Eur.
Mialaret, Gaston, ed. Vocabulaire de l'Education. LC 79-385192. xxii, 457p. (Fr.). 1979. 160.00 F (ISBN 2-130-35643-5). Pr Univ Fr.
Ministere de L'education. Lexique de L'education au Nouveau-Brunswick. LC 77-550177. 98p. (Fr.). 1976. write for info. Ministere de L'education.
Moore, Byron C., et al. A Dictionary of Special Education Terms. 128p. 1980. lexotone $12.75x (ISBN 0-398-04009-5). C C Thomas.
Multilingual Vocabulary of Educational Radio & Television Terms. 189p. (Orig., Eng. , Fr. , Ger. , Ital. , Dutch, Span. & Swedish.). 1971. pap. $11.25x (ISBN 3-19-006291-9). Intl Pubns Serv.
Muschinsky, Lars J. & Schnack, Karsten, eds. Paedagogisk Opslagsbog: Alfabetisk Ordnet. LC 79-371231. (Illus.). 285p. (Danish.). 1977. Kr.74.50 (ISBN 8-772-41417-0). Ejlers Forlag.
Nagel, Kurt. Lexikon EDV und Rechnungswesen. (Ger.). 1977. $28.50 (ISBN 3-470-58181-9, M-7203). French & Eur.
Nagy, Sandor, ed. Pedagogiai Lexikon. LC 77-483334. (Illus., Hungarian.). 1976. 124.00 Ft (ISBN 9-630-50851-6). Akademiai Kiado.
Niermann, Johannes. Woerterbuch der DDR Paedagogik. (Ger.). 1974. pap. $13.50 (ISBN 3-494-02036-1, M-7032). French & Eur.
Niklis, Werner S., ed. Handwoerterbuch der Schulpaedagogik. LC 75-516726. 459p. (Ger.). 1975. write for info. (ISBN 3-781-50267-8). Klinkhardt.
Paulik, Helmut. Lexikon der Ausbildungspraxis. (Ger.). 1975. pap. $30.00 (ISBN 3-478-11610-4, M-7274). French & Eur.
Paulik, Helmut, ed. Lexikon der Ausbildungspraxis. 276p. (Ger.). 1975. DM.36.00 (ISBN 3-478-11610-4). Verlag Mod Ind.
Paulik, Helmut, et al, eds. Lexikon der Ausbildungspraxis. LC 80-478372. 253p. (Ger.). 1980. write for info. (ISBN 3-478-11612-0). Verlag Moderne Industrie.
Quintana Cabanas, Jose M. La Pedagogia Moderna. LC 79-126501. 196p. (Span.). 1978. 150.00 ptas (ISBN 8-427-91316-8). Noguer SA.
Rafael. Diccionario pedagogico, 4 vols. 2nd ed. (Span.). Bs.0.90. Min. Educ.
Rauch, Eberhard & Anzinger, Wolfgang. Woerterbuch Kritische Erziehung. (Ger.). 1975. DM.7.80 (ISBN 3-596-26301-8). Fischer Taschen.
Raymond, D. Dictionnaire d'Education. Migne, J. P., ed. (Nouvelle Encyclopedie Theologique Ser.: Vol. 34). 856p. (Fr.). Repr. of 1853 ed. lib. bdg. $108.50x (ISBN 0-89241-276-3). Caratzas Pub Co.
Rischer, Klaus. Lexikon fuer Berufs & Arbeitspaedagogik: Ueber 2400 Haupt- & Hinweisstichworte. LC 77-474241. 162p. (Ger.). 1976. DM.18.60 (ISBN 3-470-71401-0). Kiehl.
Roth, Leo, ed. Handlexikon zur Erziehungswissenschaft. LC 76-465106. (Illus.). 488p. (Ger.). 1976. DM.58.00 (ISBN 3-431-01703-7). Ehrenwirth.
Rowntree, Derek. A Dictionary of Education. 362p. 1982. text ed. $18.50x (ISBN 0-389-20263-0). B&N Imports.
Schorb, Alfons O. Paedagogisches Taschenlexikon: A-Z. 8th ed. LC 75-518208. 258p. (Ger.). 1975. DM.9.80. Kamp Verlag.
Schwendtke, Arnold. Woerterbuch der Schulpaedagogik. 4th ed. (Ger.). 1976. pap. $10.95 (ISBN 3-451-09001-5, M-6960). French & Eur.
Shaw, Marie-Jose. The Dictionary. (Sound Filmstrip Kits Ser.). (gr. 3-6). 1981. tchrs ed. $24.00 (ISBN 0-8209-0441-4, FCW-18). ESP.
Slovar Terminov Pedagogiki. 472p. (Latvian & Rus.). 1978. $4.50 (Pub. by Liesma). Four Continent.
Speichert, H. Kritisches Lexikon der Erzeihungswissenschaft und Bildungspolitik. 400p. (Ger.). 1975. pap. $7.98 (ISBN 3-499-16190-7, M-7522, Pub. by Rowohlt). French & Eur.
--Kritisches Lexikon der Erzeihungswissenschaft und Bildungspolitik. 400p. (Ger.). 1975. pap. $7.98 (ISBN 3-499-16190-7). Rowohlt.
Speichert, Horst, ed. Kritisches Lexikon der Erziehungswissenschaft & Bildungspolitik. 4th ed. LC 76-454595. (Ger.). 1975. DM.9.80 (ISBN 3-499-16190-7). Verlag.
Thesaurus de l'education de l'Unesco: Francais-Anglais. 264p. (Fr. & Eng.). 1974. 32.00 F. Unesco.
Torres, Rosa E. Terminologia de la Education. LC 78-111426. 210p. (Span.). 1978. write for info. Minist Ed La Paz.
Turell Baldovi, Fausto. Diccionario Auxiliar del Crucigramista. 3rd ed. (Span.). 1978. pap. $8.75 (ISBN 84-02-00817-8, S-50154). French & Eur.
Willmann-Institut. Woerterbuch der Paedagogik. 1150p. (Ger.). 1978. DM.128.00 (ISBN 3-451-17641-6). Herder.
Willmann-Institut Muenchen. Woerterbuch der Paedagogik, 3 vols. LC 78-355189. (Ger.). 1977. DM.98.00 (ISBN 3-451-17641-6). Herder.
Woerterbuch der Berufs & Wirtschaftspaedagogik. 320p. (Ger.). 1973. DM.9.90 (ISBN 3-451-09009-0). Herder.
Woerterbuch der Paedagogik, 3 vols, Vols. 1-3. (Ger.). 1977. Set. pap. $105.00 (ISBN 3-451-17641-6, M-6971). French & Eur.
Woerterbuch der Schulpaedagogik. 384p. (Ger.). 1976. $12.90 (ISBN 3-451-09001-5). Herder.
Wulf, Christoph. Woerterbuch der Erziehung. 717p. (Ger.). 1976. DM.28.00 (ISBN 3-492-02098-4). Piper Co.
Zoepfl, Helmut & Bittner, Gerhard. Kleines Lexikon der Paedagogik & Didaktik. 7th ed. Tschamler, Herbert, ed. 398p. (Ger.). 1976. DM.28.80 (ISBN 3-40300-472-4). Auer.
Zoepfl, Helmut, ed. Kleines Lexikon der Paedagogik & Didaktik. LC 75-521594. 398p. (Ger.). 1975. DM.28.80 (ISBN 3-403-00472-4). Auer.
Zoepfl, Herbert. Kleines Lexikon der Paedagogik und Didatik. 7th ed. (Ger.). 1976. $22.95 (ISBN 3-403-00472-4, M-7502, Pub. by Auer). French & Eur.
--Kleines Lexikon der Paedagogik und Didatik. 7th ed. (Ger.). 1976. $22.95 (ISBN 3-403-00472-4). Auer.

EDUCATION–PSYCHOLOGY
see Educational Psychology

EDUCATION–TERMINOLOGY

Beach, Mark. Words for the Wise: A Field Guide to Academic Terms. LC 79-51616. (Illus., Orig.). 1979. pap. $4.95 (ISBN 0-9602664-0-2). Coast to Coast.
National Information Center for Educational Media. NICSEM Special Education Thesaurus. 2nd ed. LC 80-83509. 1980. pap. $16.00 (ISBN 0-89320-048-4). Univ SC Natl Info.
Terminology: Special Education. 1978. pap. $15.75 (ISBN 92-3-001564-4, U844, UNESCO). Unipub.
Terminology: UNESCO: IBE Education Thesaurus. 1978. pap. $15.75 (ISBN 92-3-101531-1, U842, UNESCO). Unipub.
Thesarus of ERIC Descriptors. 9th ed. LC 80-52477. 512p. 1982. lib. bdg. $35.00x (ISBN 0-89774-019-X). Oryx Pr.
Walker, W. G., et al. Glossary of Educational Terms: Usage in Five English Speaking Countries. 1973. $12.00x (ISBN 0-7022-0802-7). U of Queensland Pr.

EDUCATION–AUSTRALIA

McLaren, J. Dictionary of Austrialian Education. 1974. $12.00x (ISBN 0-7022-0956-2). U of Queensland Pr.

EDUCATION–GERMANY

Zoepfl, Helmut & Bittner, Gerhard. Kleines Lexikon der Paedagogik & Didaktik. 7th ed. Tschamler, Herbert, ed. 398p. (Ger.). 1976. DM.28.80 (ISBN 3-40300-472-4). Auer.

EDUCATION–GREAT BRITAIN

Izbicki. Education A-Z. LC 78-323295. 196p. (Eng.). 1978. E2.95 (ISBN 0-00-412069-8); pap. write for info. (ISBN 0-00-412070-1). W Collins Sons.

EDUCATION, AGRICULTURAL
see Agricultural Education

EDUCATION, BILINGUAL

Newhouse, Dora. Homonyms-Homonimos: Sound-Alikes. LC 77-82190. (Illus., Eng. & Span.). 1978. pap. $6.95 (ISBN 0-918050-27-8). Newhouse Pr.

EDUCATION, BUSINESS
see Business Education

EDUCATION, COOPERATIVE

Here are entered works dealing with the plan of instruction under which students spend alternating periods in school and in a practical occupation.

Dictionary of Work Study Terms. (Hebrew & Eng.). IL.7.00. Massada Pr.

EDUCATION, ELEMENTARY

Jourbel, H. & Bertrand, P. Diccionario de Educacion Infantil. 224p. (Span.). 1968. $22.50 (ISBN 0-686-56709-9, S-33056). French & Eur.
Wittgenstein, Ludwig. Dizionario per le scuole elementari. Antiseri, D., tr. 284p. (Ital.). 1978. L.8000.00. Armando.

EDUCATION, INDUSTRIAL
see Technical Education

EDUCATION, PHYSICAL
see Physical Education and Training

EDUCATION, PRESCHOOL
Schinzler, Engelbert, ed. Woerterbuch der Vorschulerziehung. LC 76-470196. 335p. (Ger.). 1976. DM.12.90 (ISBN 3-451-09035-X). Herder.
Woerterbuch der Vorschulerzeihung. 336p. (Ger.). 1976. DM.12.90 (ISBN 3-451-09035-X). Herder.
Woerterbuch der Vorschulerziehung. (Ger.). 1976. pap. $10.50 (ISBN 0-686-56611-4, M-6944). French & Eur.

EDUCATION, TECHNICAL
see Technical Education

EDUCATION, VOCATIONAL
see Vocational Education

EDUCATION AND SOCIOLOGY
see Educational Sociology

EDUCATION OF ADULTS
see Adult Education

EDUCATION OF THE DEAF
see Deaf–Education

EDUCATIONAL ADMINISTRATION
see School Management and Organization

EDUCATIONAL LITERATURE SEARCHING
see Information Storage and Retrieval Systems–Education

EDUCATIONAL PSYCHOLOGY
see also Child Psychology; Learning, Psychology Of
Woerterbuch der Paedagogischen Psychologie: Lexikon der Paedagogik. 304p. (Ger.). 1974. $9.90 (ISBN 3-451-09016-3). Herder.

EDUCATIONAL SOCIOLOGY
Schwendtke, Arnold. Woerterbuch der Sozialarbeit & Sozialpaedagogik. 312p. (Ger.). 1977. DM.18.80 (ISBN 3-494-02072-8). Quelle & Meyer.

EDUCATIONAL TECHNOLOGY
see also Teaching–Aids and Devices
Glossary on Educational Technology. (Eng. & Ger.). 1973. DM.9.80 (ISBN 3-7940-5134-3). Saur Verlag.

EGG (BIOLOGY)
see Embryology

EGYPT–CIVILIZATION
Posener, Georges. Dictionnaire de la Civilisation Egytienne. 326p. (Fr.). 1970. $47.50 (ISBN 0-686-57085-5, M-6462). French & Eur.

EGYPT–HISTORY–TO 640
Cooper, William R. Archaic Dictionary. LC 73-76018. 1969. Repr. of 1876 ed. $66.00x (ISBN 0-8103-3885-8). Gale.

EGYPTIAN HIEROGLYPHICS
see Egyptian Language–Writing, Hieroglyphic

EGYPTIAN LANGUAGE
see also Coptic Language
Faulkner, R. O. A Concise Dictionary of Middle Egyptian. 348p. (Egyptian.). 1976. $37.00x (ISBN 0-900416-32-7, Pub. by Griffith Inst). State Mutual Bk.
Lesko, Leonard H., ed. Dictionary of Late Egyptian, Vol. 1 of 3 Vols. (Egyptian.). 1982. lib. bdg. $35.00x (ISBN 0-930548-03-5); pap. text ed. $20.00x (ISBN 0-930548-04-3). B C Scribe.
Lorton, David. The Juridical Terminology of International Relations in Egyptian Texts Through Dynasty XVIII. LC 73-8114. (Near Eastern Studies). 208p. 1974. $16.00x (ISBN 0-8018-1535-5). Johns Hopkins.

EGYPTIAN LANGUAGE–WRITING, HIEROGLYPHIC
Budge, E. Wallis. Egyptian Hieroglyphic Dictionary, Vols. 1 & 2. LC 77-86708. 1978. pap. $12.00 ea. Vol. 1 (ISBN 0-486-23615-3). Vol. 2 (ISBN 0-486-23616-1). Dover.

EGYPTIAN MYTHOLOGY
see Mythology, Egyptian

EGYPTIAN STUDIES
see Egyptology

EGYPTOLOGY
Helck, Wolfgang & Otto, Eberhard. Kleines Woerterbuch der Aegyptologie. 2nd ed. (Ger.). 1970. $35.00 (ISBN 3-447-00064-3, M-7509, Pub. by Harrassowitz). French & Eur.
--Lexikon der Aegyptologie. 80p. (Ger.). 1973. DM.38.00 (ISBN 3-447-01521-7). Harrassowitz.
--Lexikon der Aegyptologie: Bd II, Lfg 10. 80p. (Ger.). 1975. DM.46.00 (ISBN 3-447-01728-7). Harrassowitz.
--Lexikon der Aegyptologie: Bd II, Lfg 11. 80p. (Ger.). 1976. DM.46.00 (ISBN 3-447-01746-5). Harrassowitz.
--Lexikon der Aegyptologie: Bd II, Lfg 12. 80p. (Ger.). 1976. DM.46.00 (ISBN 3-447-01749-X). Harrassowitz.
--Lexikon der Aegyptologie: Bd II, Lfg 13. 80p. (Ger.). 1976. DM.46.00 (ISBN 3-447-01819-4). Harrassowitz.
--Lexikon der Aegyptologie: Bd II, Lfg 14. 80p. (Ger.). 1976. DM.46.00 (ISBN 3-447-01825-9). Harrassowitz.
--Lexikon der Aegyptologie: Bd II, Lfg 9. 80p. (Ger.). 1975. DM.46.00 (ISBN 3-447-01708-2). Harrassowitz.
--Lexikon der Aegyptologie: Bd 1, Lfg 1. (Ger.). 1972. DM.38.00 (ISBN 3-447-01441-5). Harrassowitz.
--Lexikon der Aegyptologie: Bd 1, Lfg. 2. 80p. (Ger.). 1973. DM.38.00 (ISBN 3-447-01481-4). Harrassowitz.
--Lexikon der Aegyptologie: Bd 1, Lfg. 3. 80p. (Ger.). 1973. DM.38.00 (ISBN 3-447-01499-7). Harrassowitz.
--Lexikon der Aegyptologie: Bd 1, Lfg 4. 80p. (Ger.). 1973. DM.38.00 (ISBN 3-447-01508-X). Harrassowitz.
--Lexikon der Aegyptologie: Bd 1, Lfg 6. 80p. (Ger.). 1974. DM.38.00 (ISBN 3-447-01557-8). Langenscheidt.
--Lexikon der Aegyptologie: Bd 1, Lfg 7. 80p. (Ger.). 1974. DM.38.00 (ISBN 3-447-01605-1). Harrassowitz.
--Lexikon der Aegyptologie: Bd 1, Lfg 8. xxxvi, 76p. (Ger.). 1975. DM.80.00 (ISBN 3-447-01619-1). Harrassowitz.

EL SALVADOR
see Salvador

ELECTRIC ANALOGIES IN MECHANICS
see Electromechanical Analogies

ELECTRIC BASS
see Guitar

ELECTRIC BATTERIES
Bogenschuetz, A. Fachwoerterbuch fuer Batterien und Energie-Direktumwandlung. 200p. (Ger. & Eng.). 1968. DM.29.95 (ISBN 3-87097-002-2). Brandstetter.

ELECTRIC CABLES
Retzlaff, Ewald. Kurzzeichen-Lexikon fur Kabel & Isoierte Leitungen Nach VDE IEC & CEE. LC 76-454451. 65p. (Eng. & Ger.). 1975. DM.12.00 (ISBN 3-8007-1105-2). VDE Verlag.
Richling, Christel. Woerterbuch der Kabeltechnik. (Ger., Eng. & Fr., Dictionary of Cable Engineering). 1976. pap. $48.00 (ISBN 3-87097-072-3, M-6988). French & Eur.
--Woerterbuch der Kabeltechnik. LC 77-46358. 610p. (Eng., Fr. & Ger.). 1976. DM.60.00 (ISBN 3-87097-072-3). Brandstetter.

ELECTRIC CIRCUITS
see also Electronic Circuits
Dictionary of Electrical Circuits. 203p. (Eng. & Chinese.). 1975. pap. $3.95 (ISBN 0-686-92288-3, M-9572). French & Eur.

ELECTRIC COMMUNICATION
see Telecommunication

ELECTRIC ENGINEERING
see also Electric Lighting; Electric Machinery; Electro-Acoustics; Electromechanical Devices; Radio
Colella, Antonio. Nuovo Dizionario di Elettrotecnica & di elettronica. 2nd ed. LC 79-382317. 541p. (Ital.). 1977. L.30000.00. Il Rostro.
Dictionary of Electronics Engineering. 785p. (Eng. & Chinese.). 1976. $12.95 (ISBN 0-686-92369-3). French & Eur.
Institute of Signage Research. Glossary. $7.50 (ISR); $5.00, members. Natl Elec Sign.
Klimek, Adolf. Polovodicove Soucastky. LC 77-472717. 444p. (Eng. & Czech., Praha, Czechoslovakia). 1977. 30.00 Kcs. SNTL.
Nyblom, Ake. Engelsk-Svensk Elteknisk Forkortningslista. LC 75-547472. 24p. (Eng. & Swedish.). 1975. Kr.19.00 (ISBN 91-7284-026-9). Ingenjorsforlaget.
Piraux, H. Dizionario Inglese-Italiano dei Termini Relativi All'Elettronica: All'Elettrotecnica e Alle Applicazioni Connesse. 534p. (Eng. & Ital.). 1977. pap. $29.95 (ISBN 0-686-92527-0, M-9195). French & Eur.
Piraux, Henri. Dictionnaire Allemand-Francais des Termes Relatifs a l'Electrorechnique, l'Electronique, et aux Applications Connexes. 4th ed. 254p. (Fr. & Ger.). 1976. pap. $31.95 (ISBN 0-686-57080-4, M-6455). French & Eur.

ELECTRIC ENGINEERING–DICTIONARIES
Athenstaedt, William. Elektrotechnik Elektronik. LC 79-349122. 964p. (Rus. & Ger.). 1978. write for info. VEB Verlag Technik.
Budig, Peter K. Elektrotechnik Elektronik. LC 77-454020. 724p. (Eng. & Ger.). 1975. M.55.00. VEB Verlag Technik.
--Fachwoerterbuch Elektrotechnik, Elektronik. (Eng. & Ger., Dictionary of Electrical Engineering and Electronics). 1976. $86.50 (ISBN 3-7785-0357-X, M-7394, Pub. by Huethig). French & Eur.
Clason, W. E. Elsevier's Electrotechnical Dictionary. (Eng., Fr., Span., Ital., Dutch & Ger.). 1965. $113.00 (ISBN 0-444-40118-0). Elsevier.
Condruc, Mihai. Dictionar de Electrotehnica. LC 80-490952. 868p. (Fr. & Romanian.). 1979. 49.00 lei. Editura Stiintifica.
--Dictionar de Electrotehnik. LC 76-467628. 841p. (Fr., & Romanian.). 1976. 48.00 lei. Editura Stiintifica.
Diccionario tecnico electrotecnia; luminotecnia; espanol-ingles. (Span. & Eng.). Arg.$3.00. Cosmopolita.
Diccionario tecnico, electrotecnia, luminotecnia: Ingles-espanol. (Eng. & Span.). Arg.$3.00. Cosmopolita.
Electrical Generating Systems Marketing Association. Glossary of Standard Industry Terminology & Definitions. 1980. $5.00 (GDT4); members $2.00. Elec Gen Syst.
English-Chinese Glossary of Electronic & Electrical Engineering. 636p. (Eng. & Chinese.). 1980. $29.95 (ISBN 0-686-97364-X, M-9255). French & Eur.
Goedecke, W. Woerterbuch der Elektrotechnik, Fernmeldetechnik und Elektonik, Vol. 1. (Ger., Eng. & Fr., Dictionary of Electrical Engineering, Telecommunication Engineering & Electronics). 1966-68. $56.00 (ISBN 3-87097-013-8, M-7018). French & Eur.
--Woerterbuch der Elektrotechnik, Fernmeldetechnik und Elektronik, Vol. 2. (Fr., Eng. & Ger., Dictionary of Electrical Engineering, Telecommuunications Engineering & Electronics). 1966-68. $56.00 (ISBN 3-87097-014-6, M-7019). French & Eur.
Haberle, Gregor D. & Haberle, Heinz O. Kurzlexikon der Elektrotechnik. LC 79-387542. 104p. (Ger.). 1979. DM.15.00 (ISBN 3-87234-054-9). Frankfurt Fachverlag.
Junge, Hans D. Brockhaus ABC Elektrotechnik. LC 78-399295. 667p. (Ger.). 1978. M.17.30. F A Brockhaus.
Miladinovic, Tomislav. Woerterbuch der Elektrotechnik und Elektronik. (Ger. & Rus.). 1970. $92.00 (ISBN 3-7736-5285-2, M-7016). French & Eur.
Ministry of Education Science & Culture. Scientific Terms Electrical Engineering. 675p. (Eng. & Japanese.). 1979. $39.95 (ISBN 0-686-97433-6, M-9330). French & Eur.
Piraux, H. French-Eng., Eng-French Dictionary of Electrotechnic Electronics & Allied Fields, 2 Vols. (Fr. & Eng.). Set. 90.00 (ISBN 0-685-12017-1). Heinman.
Schattner, Friedrich. Dictionar de Electrotehnica. LC 75-407648. 700p. (Ger. & Romanian.). 1975. 39.00 lei. Editura Stiintifica.
--Dictionar de Electrotehnica. LC 79-386549. 815p. (Ger. & Romanian.). 1979. 48.00 lei. Editura Stiintifica.
Schlomann, A. Illustrierte Technische Woerterbucher: Elektrotechnik und Elektrochemie, Vol. 2. (Illus., Ger., Eng., Fr., Rus., Span. & Ital., Illustrated Dictionary of Electrical Engineering & Electro-Ehemistry). 1963. $105.00 (ISBN 0-686-56483-9, M-7470, Pub. by R. Oldenbourg). French & Eur.
--Illustrierte Technische Woerterbucher: ELektrotechnik und Elektrochemie, Vol. 2. (Illus., Ger., Eng., Fr., Rus., Span. & Ital.). 1963. $105.00. Oldenbourg Verlag.
Schwenkhagen, H. Woerterbuch Elektrotechnik & Elektronik. LC 78-381882. 839p. (Eng. & Ger.). 1978. DM.160.00 (ISBN 3-7736-5072-8). Girardet.
--Woerterbuch Elektrotechnik und Elektronik. 2nd ed. (Ger. & Eng., Dictionary of Electrical Engineering and Electronics). 1967. $128.00 (ISBN 0-686-56610-6, M-6927). French & Eur.
Schwenkhagen, H. F. & Meinhhold, H. Woerterbuch Elektrotechnik und Elektronik. (Ger. & Eng., Dictionary of Electrical Engineering and Electronics). 1978. $128.00 (ISBN 3-7736-5072-8, M-6928). French & Eur.
Sizaire, P. Dictionnaire Technique De la Construction Electrique. 172p. (Fr.). 1968. $29.95 (ISBN 0-686-57222-X, M-6520). French & Eur.
Suomen Standardisoimislitto. Sahkotieteellinen Sanasto. LC 77-481554. 167p. (Eng., Finnish, Fr., Ger., Rus. & Swedish.). 1976. write for info. Suomen Standard.
Wennrich, P. Anglo-Amerikanische Abkuerzungen und Kurzwoerter der Elektrotechnik. 307p. (Ger. & Eng., Anglo-American Abbreviations and Acronyms of Electrical Engineering). 1973. pap. $25.00 (ISBN 3-7940-3100-8, M-7296, Pub. by Vlg. Dokumentation). French & Eur.
Wernicke, H. Dictionary of Electronics, Communications & Electrical Engineering, 2 vols. 1300p. Vol. 1. $32.50 ea. (ISBN 0-685-05199-4); Vol. 2. $36.00 ea. (ISBN 0-685-05200-1). Adler.

ELECTRIC HOUSEHOLD APPLIANCES
see Household Appliances

ELECTRIC LIGHT
see Electric Lighting

ELECTRIC LIGHT AND POWER INDUSTRY
see Electric Utilities

ELECTRIC LIGHTING
see also Lighting
Diccionario tecnico electrotecnia; luminotecnia; espanol-ingles. (Span. & Eng.). Arg.$3.00. Cosmopolita.
Diccionario tecnico, electrotecnia, luminotecnia: Ingles-espanol. (Eng. & Span.). Arg.$3.00. Cosmopolita.

ELECTRIC MACHINERY
Bezner, Heinrich. Electrical Machines Dictionary. LC 80-452859. 544p. (Eng. & Ger.). 1978. DM.80.00 (ISBN 3-87097-087-1). Brandstetter.

ELECTRIC MECHANICAL DEVICES
see Electromechanical Devices

ELECTRIC METERS
Mercier, Jean. Lexique Anglais-Francais du Compteur d'electricite. 42p. (Eng. & Fr.). 1973. Can.$1.00. Quebec Off.
Office de la Langue Francaise. Lexique Anglais-Francais du Compteur d'electricite. 56p. (Eng. & Fr.). 1972. Can.$1.00. Quebec Off.

ELECTRIC POWER INDUSTRY
see Electric Utilities

ELECTRIC POWER-PLANTS
see also Atomic Power Plants; Electric Utilities; Steam Power-Plants
Load Cell Terminology & Test Procedure Recommendations. 20p. 1979. $2.50 (SM-1). Scale Mfrs.

ELECTRIC POWER POOLING
see Electric Utilities
ELECTRIC RELAYS
Sauer, Hans. Relais Lexikon. LC 76-453351. 242p. (Ger.). 1975. write for info. Vertrieb.
ELECTRIC UTILITIES
Here are entered economic works on the sale and distribution of electricity for lighting and power purposes. Technical works are entered under Electric Engineering; Electric Lighting; Electric power Etc.
Edison Electric Institute. Glossary of Electric Utility Terms. 86p. 1970. $1.25 (01704000). Edison Electric.
ELECTRICAL ENGINEERING
see Electric Engineering
ELECTRICITY
see also Magnetism; Radioactivity; Thermoelectricity
also headings beginning with Electric and Electro
Dictionary of Physics: No. 2, Electricity & Magnetism. (Hebrew, Eng. , Fr. & Ger.). IL.8.00. Massada Pr.
Hoefling, Oskar, ed. Lexikon der Schulphysik: Bd 3, Elektrizitaet & Magnetismus-1.Tlbd, A-K. vi, 201p. (Ger.). 1978. DM.46.00 (ISBN 3-7614-0168-X). Aulis Verlag.
--Lexikon der Schulphysik: Bd 3, Elektrizitaet & Magnetismus-2.Tlbd, L-Z. vi, 201p. (Ger.). 1978. DM.46.00 (ISBN 3-7614-0169-8). Aulis Verlag.
Marec, Eugene. Dictionnaire de l'electricien Praticien. (Illus.). 330p. (Fr.). 1955. 16.00 F. Bailliere.
ELECTRICITY–DICTIONARIES
Besse, B., et al. Lexique Anglais-Francais de L'Aciere Electrique. 135p. (Eng. & Fr.). 1975. pap. $8.95 (ISBN 0-686-92555-6, M-9239). French & Eur.
Breitsameter. Lexikon der Schulphysik: Elektrizitaet und Magnetismus A-K, Vol. 3A. (Ger.). $42.50 (ISBN 3-7614-0168-X, M-7224). French & Eur.
--Lexikon der Schulphysik: Elektrizitaet und Magnetismus L-Z, Vol. 3B. (Ger.). $42.50 (ISBN 3-7614-0169-8, M-7225). French & Eur.
Budig, Peter-Klaus, ed. Electricity & Electronics Technical Dictionary. 2nd, rev. ed. 724p. (Eng. & Ger.). 1979. $62.50x (ISBN 0-8002-2468-X). Intl Pubns Serv.
Colella, A. Nuovo Dizionario di Elettrotecnic e di Elettronica: Italiano-Inglese, Inglese-Italiano. 541p. (Ital. & Eng.). 1977. $95.00 (ISBN 0-686-92200-X, M-9296). French & Eur.
Ibeas, Franco. Diccionario Tecnologico Ingles-Espanol: Electricidad, Electronica, Telecomunicacion, & Materias Afinas con la Fisica, Optica & Quimica. 452p. (Eng. & Span.). 1974. E950.00 (ISBN 84-205-0492-0). Alhambra.
Mercier, Jean. Lexique Anglais-Francais Des Appareils De Mesures Electriques. 44p. (Eng. & Fr.). 1973. pap. $1.95 (ISBN 0-686-57044-8, M-6405). French & Eur.
--Lexique Anglais-Francais Du Compteur D'electricite: Principes et Pieces Composantes. 42p. (Eng. & Fr.). 1973. pap. $3.50 (ISBN 0-686-57046-4, M-6407). French & Eur.
Piraux, H. Dictionnaire des termes relatifs a electrotechnique, l'electronique et aux applications connexes, 2 vols. 387p. (Eng. & Fr.). 1978. Vol. 1: English-French. 49.00 F. Vol. 2: French-English. $49.00. Eyrolles.
Understanding Electricity & Electrical Terms. 48p. $5.00. Natl Assn Elect Dist.
ELECTRICITY–MECHANICAL ANALOGIES
see Electromechanical Analogies
ELECTRO-ACOUSTICS
Cormier, France-Pauline. Vocabulaire de l'electroacoustique de l'acoustique. 186p. (Fr.). 1973. Can.$2.50. Quebec Off.
Peraux, Henry. Diccionario general de acustica y electroacustica. 376p. (Span.). 1967. 300.00 ptas. Paraninfo.
Piraux. Diccionario General de Acustica & Electroacustica. (Span.). 1967. 550.00 ptas (ISBN 8-42830-799-7). Paraninfo.
ELECTROCHEMICAL APPARATUS
see Chemical Apparatus
ELECTROCHEMISTRY
see also Electric Batteries
Melnikova, M. M. & Smirnov, I. P. English-Russian Dictionary of Electrochemistry & Corrosion. 496p. (Eng. & Rus.). 1976. $9.95 (ISBN 0-686-92367-7, M-9121). French & Eur.
Melnikova, M. M., et al, eds. Anglo-Russkii Slovar Po Elektrokhimii i Korrozii. (Eng. & Rus.). 1976. $5.50 (Pub. by Russkii Iazyk). Four Continent.
Schlomann, A. Illustrierte Technische Woerterbucher: Elektrotechnik und Elektrochemie, Vol. 2. (Illus., Ger., Eng., Fr., Rus., Span. & Ital., Illustrated Dictionary of Electrical Engineering & Electro-Ehemistry). 1963. $105.00 (ISBN 0-686-56483-9, M-7470, Pub. by R. Oldenbourg). French & Eur.
--Illustrierte Technische Woerterbucher: ELektrotechnik und Elektrochemie, Vol. 2. (Illus., Ger., Eng., Fr., Rus., Span. & Ital.). 1963. $105.00. Oldenbourg Verlag.
ELECTROMECHANICAL ANALOGIES
Weiss-Ballesteros. Diccionario ingles-espanol, tecnico-electromecanico. (Eng. & Span.). 340.00 ptas. Index.
ELECTROMECHANICAL DEVICES
see also Electric Machinery
Ballesteros, Luis W. Diccionario Tecnico De Electromecanica: Ingles-Espanol. 1976. pap. $13.50x (ISBN 968-18-0522-4). Intl Learn Syst.
Ballesteros Weis, L. Diccionario Tecnico de electromecanica: Ingles-espanol. 298p. (Eng. & Span.). Mex.$4.00; $50.00. Limusa.
ELECTROMYOGRAPHY
American Association of Electromyography & Electrodiagnosis. Glossary of EMG Terms. $5.00. Am Assn Electromyography.
ELECTRON OPTICS
see also Electronics; Quantum Electronics
Lexique Trilingue des Termes D'Usage Courant En Electrotechnique, Electronique, Acoustique, Optique et Controle Par Ultrasons. 340p. (Fr., Trilingual Lexicon of Currently Used Terms in Electrotechnics, Electronics, Acoustics, Optics and Control by Ultra-Sound). 1966. pap. $35.00 (ISBN 0-686-56793-5, M-6373). French & Eur.
ELECTRONIC ANALOG COMPUTERS–INPUT-OUTPUT EQUIPMENT
see Computer Input-Output Equipment
ELECTRONIC BRAINS
see Computers
ELECTRONIC CABLES
Richling, Drewitz. Woerterbuch der Kabeltechnik: Deutsch-Englisch-Franzoesisch. 610p. (Ger., Eng. & Fr.). 1982. DM.60.00. Brandstetter.
ELECTRONIC CALCULATING-MACHINES
see Computers
ELECTRONIC CIRCUITS
see also Semiconductors
Douglas-Young, John. Illustrated Encyclopedic Dictionary of Electronic Circuits. LC 82-23067. 444p. 1983. $27.95 (ISBN 0-13-450734-7). P-H.
ELECTRONIC COMPUTER–PROGRAMMING
see Programming (Electronic Computers)
ELECTRONIC COMPUTERS
see Computers
ELECTRONIC DATA PROCESSING
see also Data Transmission Systems; Data Base Management; Programming (Electronic Computers); Programming Languages (Electronic Computers)
also subdivision Data Processing under subjects, e.g. Business–Data Processing
Amglo-Russko-Nemetsko-Frantsuzskii Tolkovyi Slovar Po Vychislitel Noi Tekhnike & Obrabotke Dannykh. 416p. (Eng. , Rus. , Ger. & Fr.). 1978. $7.95 (Pub. by Russkii Iazyk). Four Continent.
Burger, Erich. Automatizovany Zber Dat Programovanie. LC 78-373214. 479p. (Eng., Fr. & Rus.). 1976. 80.00 Kcs. Alfa-Vydavatel.
Kohler, Rolf & Mayr, Ernst. EDV-Abkurzungen. LC 79-342495. 332p. (Ger.). 1978. write for info. (ISBN 3-8009-1262-7). Siemens AG.
Leong-Hong, Belkis W. & Plagman, Bernard K. Data Dictionary-Directory Systems: Aministration, Implementation & Usage. members $25.95; (W7) $27.95. Data Process Mgmt.
Schulze, Hans H. Rororo-Lexikon zur Datenverarbeitung. LC 80-453504. 258p. (Ger.). 1978. DM.7.80 (ISBN 3-499-16220-2). Rowohlt.
Viet, Jean. Thesaurus for Information Processing in Sociology. 1971. pap. text ed. 20.00x (ISBN 90-2796-941-8). Mouton.
ELECTRONIC DATA PROCESSING–DICTIONARIES
Anderson, R. G. Dictionary of Data Processing & Computer Terms. 112p. 1982. pap. text ed. $13.95x (ISBN 0-7121-0429-1). Intl Ideas.
Averbach. Diccionario de electronica, proceso de datos. (Span.). 1970. 200.00 ptas. Iber Euro Edns.
Bola Publications. Bola Glossary of Electronic Data Processing & Computer Terms English-Spanish & Spanish-English. LC 82-71113. (Glossary Ser.: Vol. 1). 200p. (Orig., Span. & Eng.). 1982. pap. $29.95 (ISBN 0-943118-00-X). Bola Pubns.
Brinkmann & Schmidt. Woerterbuch der Datentechnik. 733p. (Ger. & Eng.). 1982. DM.60.00. Brandstetter.
Brinkmann, Karl H. Dictionary of Dataprocessing. (Ger. & Eng.). 1974. $59.95 (ISBN 3-87097-059-6, M-7117). French & Eur.
Brinkmann, Karl-Heinz, et al. Data Systems Dictionary. 2nd, rev. & enl. ed. LC 80-470062. 399p. (Ger. & Eng.). 1979. DM.55.00 (ISBN 3-87097-095-2). Brandstetter.
Buerger, E. Woerterbuch Datenerfassung-Programmierung. (Eng., Ger., Fr. & Rus., Dictionary of Data Processing & Programming). 1976. $56.00 (ISBN 3-87144-265-8, M-6967). French & Eur.
Burger, E. Technical Dictionary of Data Processing, Computers & Office Machines, English, German, French, Russian. (Eng., Ger., Fr. & Rus.). 1970. $130.00 (ISBN 0-08-006425-6). Pergamon.
Burger, Erich. Datenerfassung Programmierung. LC 77-484881. 388p. (Eng., Ger., Fr. & Rus.). 1976. M.38.00. VEB Verlag Technik.
Burger, Habil E. Dictionary of Automatic Data Processing. 480p. 1980. $75.00x (Pub. by Collet's). State Mutual Bk.
Burger, Ing H. Dictionary of Automatic Data Processing. 480p. (Eng., Ger., Fr., Rus. & Slovak.). 1976. $80.00x (ISBN 0-569-08521-7, Pub. by Collets). State Mutual Bk.
Camarao, Paulo C., et al. Great technical dictionary. LC 79-122945. 303p. (Eng. & Port.). 1979. Cr.$250.00. Ao Livro Tecnico.
Camille, Claude & Dehaine, Michael. Harrap's French & English Dictionary of Data Processing, 2 vols. in 1. 2nd ed. ii, 261p. (Fr. & Eng.). 1980. E16.00. Harrap.
Camille, Claude & Dehaine, Michel. Harrap's English-French Dictionary of Data Processing. 2nd ed. LC 78-300149. 137p. (Eng. & Fr.). 1976. E13.00 (ISBN 0-245-52293-X). Harrap.
Drieux, Jean-Pierre & Jarlaud, Alain. Let's Talk D. P. Lexique D'informatique. LC 78-360973. 116p. (Eng. & Fr.). 1977. write for info. (ISBN 2-04-008033-3). Bordas.
Frid, Lena. Dataordbok. LC 81-451744. 144p. (Eng. & Swedish.). 1980. write for info. (ISBN 9-1970-3442-8). EC Print AB.
Ginguay, Michel. Dictionnaire D'informatique Anglais-Francais. 5th ed. LC 79-381483. 208p. (Eng. & Fr.). 1979. 68.00 F (ISBN 2-225-63459-9). Masson & Cie.
Gould. IFIP Sachwoerterbuch der Datenverarbeitung. (Illus.). 170p. (Eng., Rus. & Ger.). 1977. DM.24.80 (ISBN 3-87144-335-2). Verlag Harri Deutsch.
Gould, I. IFIP-Sach Worterbuch der Datenverarbeitung. 170p. (Ger.). 1977. $19.95 (ISBN 3-87144-335-2, M-7467, Pub. by Verlag Harri Deutsch). French & Eur.
Guckler, G. Zweisprachiges Woerterbuch Fuer Angenaeherte Operationelle Analyse Semantischer Entsprechungen Mittels EDV. 300p. (Ger. & It.). 1975. pap. $30.00 (ISBN 3-87808-053-0, M-7693, Pub. by G. Narr). French & Eur.
Hofmann, Egon. Dictionary of Dataprocessing. 4th ed. (Eng. & Ger.). 1976. $15.95 (ISBN 3-19-006288-9, M-7115). French & Eur.
IFIP. IFIP Fachtworterbuch der Informationsverabeitung. (Ger.). 1968. $22.00 (ISBN 0-7204-2027-X, North Holland). Elsevier.
Isaacs, Alan, ed. The Multilingual Computer Dictionary. 336p. 1981. $22.50 (ISBN 0-87196-431-7). Facts on File.
Kelly-Bootle, Stan. The Devil's DP Dictionary. (Illus.). 160p. 1981. pap. 8.50 (ISBN 0-07-034022-6, P&RB). McGraw.
Lenczewska, Bronislawa. Slownik Terminow z Zakresu Informatyki. LC 77-557144. 116p. (Eng. & Pol.). 1977. 15.00 Zl. Politekens Forlag.
Leong-Hong, Belkis W. & Plagman, Bernard K. Data Dictionary-Directory Systems: Aministration, Implementation & Usage. members $25.95; (W7) $27.95. Data Process Mgmt.
Linse. Woerterbuch der Datentechnik. 394p. (Ger. & Fr.). 1982. DM.50.00. Brandstetter.
Loebel & Mueller. Lexikon der Datenverarbeitung. 704p. (Ger.). 1975. $62.00 (ISBN 3-478-33206-0, M-7264). French & Eur.
Lomax, J. D. Data Dictionary Systems. (Illus.). 1977. pap. $45.00x (ISBN 0-85012-191-4). Intl Pubns Serv.
Malstrom, Robert C. SRA Data Processing Glossary. 281p. 1979. pap. write for info. (ISBN 0-574-21250-7, 13-4250). SRA.
Maynard. Dictionary of Data Processing. 2nd ed. 1982. text ed. $29.95 (ISBN 0-408-00591-2). Butterworth.
Mueller, Peter. Lexikon der Datenverarbeitung. (Ger.). 1968. $55.00 (ISBN 3-478-33205-2, M-7265). French & Eur.
Norsk Sprakrad. Norsk Dataordbok. LC 77-552785. 184p. (Eng. & Norwegian.). 1976. Kr.49.50 (ISBN 8-2000-2403-2). Universitetsforlaget.
Oppermann, A. Woerterbuch der Datenverarbeitung. 2nd ed. 343p. (Eng. & Ger., Dictionary of Dataprocessing). 1973. $28.00 (ISBN 3-7940-3099-0, M-7034). French & Eur.
Oppermann, Alfred. Dictionary of Dataprocessing. 2nd ed. (Ger. & Eng.). 1973. pap. $30.00 (ISBN 3-7940-3099-0, M-7116). French & Eur.
Ross, Ronald G. Data Dictionaries & Data Administration: Concepts & Practices for Data Resource Management. 384p. 1981. $25.95 (ISBN 0-8144-5596-4). Am Mgmt.

Russian-English Dictionary of Data Processing Terminology. 359p. (Rus. & Eng.). 1971. text ed. $6.95 (ISBN 0-686-92123-2, M-9127). French & Eur.

Salto Dolla, Angel. Diccionario de terminos de proceso de datos: Definicion de 2500 terminos de informatica y vocabulario completo espanol-ingles e ingles-espanol. 350p. (Span. & Eng.). 1971. 320.00 ptas. Paraninfo.

Schmid, Hans & Von Muller, Peter. EDV-Taschenlexikon: In Zusammenarbeit Mit Guido Lobel. LC 76-481702. 227p. (Eng. & Ger.). 1976. DM.19.80. Verlag Moderne Industrie.

Schmoll, G. Wortschatz der Information und Dokumentation. 160p. (Ger.). $15.95 (ISBN 3-7940-4037-6, M-7690, Pub. by Vlg. Dokumentation). French & Eur.

Schulz. Woerterbuch der Datentechnik: Russisch-Deutsch-Englisch. 364p. (Rus., Ger. & Eng.). 1982. DM.50.00. Brandstetter.

Schulz, Joachim. Data Systems Dictionary. (Eng., Rus., Ger.). 1978. DM.pap. 39.95 (ISBN 3-87097-075-8). Brandstetter.

--Data Systems Dictionary: English-Russian-German. (Eng., Rus. & Ger.). 1978. pap. $39.95 (ISBN 3-87097-075-8, M-7325, Pub. by Brandstetter Verlag). French & Eur.

--Woerterbuch der Datentechnick. LC 77-514536. 134p. (Eng., Rus. & Ger.). 1977. DM.50.00 (ISBN 3-87097-075-8). Brandstetter.

Shain, M. & Longley, D. A Dictionary of Information Technology. 1982. $75.00x (ISBN 0-686-42940-0, Pub. by Macmillan England). State Mutual Bk.

Shishmarev, A. I. & Zamorin, A. P. Explanatory Dictionary of Computing Machinery & Data Processing. 416p. 1978. $60.00x (ISBN 0-686-44717-4, Pub. by Collets). State Mutual Bk.

Sveriges Standardiseringskommission. Dataordboken. LC 78-393289. 476p. (Eng., Fr., Ger., & Swedish.). 1977. Kr.114.60 (ISBN 9-1716-2052-4). Standard Sver.

Thesaurus. (INIS Ser.: Rev. 20). 756p. 1981. pap. $46.50 (ISBN 92-0-178081-8, IN13-R20, IAEA). Unipub.

Tollet, Gustav. Atk-Sanakirja. LC 77-568115. ix, 140p. (Eng. & Finnish.). 1975. write for info. (ISBN 9-1576-2112-8). Tietojen.

UNESCO Thesaurus, Vols. 1 & 2. 1978. $93.50 (ISBN 92-3-101469-2, U816, UNESCO). Unipub.

Welk, Martin H. Standard Dictionary of Computers & Information Processing. 2nd, rev. ed. 390p. 1977. $23.95 (ISBN 0-686-98126-X). Telecom Lib.

Wittman, A. & Klos, J. Dictionary of Data Processing. 3rd. rev. ed. 1977. $89.50 (ISBN 0-444-99823-3). Elsevier.

Wittmann, Alfred. Dictionary of Data Processing. LC 76-28194. (Eng. & Fr.). 1977. write for info. Elsevier.

ELECTRONIC DATA PROCESSING DEPARTMENTS–MANAGEMENT

Ross, Ronald G. Data Dictionaries & Data Administration: Concepts & Practices for Data Resource Management. 384p. 1981. $25.95 (ISBN 0-8144-5596-4). Am Mgmt.

ELECTRONIC DIGITAL COMPUTERS

see also Computer Graphics

Agnew, Irene, ed. Glossary of English & Russian Computer & Automated Control Systems Terminology. (Eng. & Rus.). 1978. soft covers $15.00 (ISBN 0-686-31723-8). Agnew Tech-Tran.

ELECTRONIC DIGITAL COMPUTERS–DICTIONARIES

Burger, E. Technical Dictionary of Data Processing, Computers & Office Machines, English, German, French, Russian. (Eng., Ger., Fr. & Rus.). 1970. $130.00 (ISBN 0-08-006425-6). Pergamon.

Prenis, John. Computer Terms. LC 77-343. (Orig.). 1977. lib. bdg. 12.90 (ISBN 0-914294-75-X); pap. 2.95 (ISBN 0-914294-76-8). Running Pr.

Sippl, Charles J. & Sippl, Roger J. Computer Dictionary. 3rd ed. LC 79-91696. 1980. pap. 15.95 (ISBN 0-672-21652-3, 21652). Sams.

Spencer, Donald D. Computer Dictionary. 2nd ed. LC 78-31738. 1979. pap. $6.95 (ISBN 0-89218-038-2). Camelot Pub.

--Computer Dictionary for Everyone. rev. ed. 1980. $11.95 (ISBN 0-684-16305-5, ScribT). Scribner.

ELECTRONIC DIGITAL COMPUTERS–INPUT-OUTPUT EQUIPMENT

see Computer Input-Output Equipment

ELECTRONIC MUSIC

Eimert, Herbert. Das Lexikon der Elektronischen Musik. 426p. (Ger.). 1973. $27.50 (ISBN 3-7649-2083-1, M-7260). French & Eur.

ELECTRONIC OFFICE MACHINES

see also Computers

Burger, E. Technical Dictionary of Data Processing, Computers & Office Machines, English, German, French, Russian. (Eng., Ger., Fr. & Rus.). 1970. $130.00 (ISBN 0-08-006425-6). Pergamon.

ELECTRONIC OPTICS

see Electron Optics

ELECTRONIC ORGAN

Irwin, Stevens. Dictionary of Electronic Organ Stops. 1969. pap. $9.95 (ISBN 0-02-871120-3). Assoc-Mus.

ELECTRONIC PULSE TECHNIQUES

see Pulse Techniques (Electronics)

ELECTRONICS

see also Cybernetics; Electronic Cables; Electronic Circuits; High-Fidelity Sound Systems; Microelectronics; Modulation (Electronics); Pulse Techniques (Electronics); Quantum Electronics; Semiconductors

D'Agostino, Francisco J. Vocabulario Ingles-Espanol de Electronica. (Eng. & Span.). write for info. ARBO.

Markus, John. Diccionario de Electronica & Tecnica Nuclear. (Illus.). 1052p. (Span.). write for info. (ISBN 84-267-0003-9). Marcombo.

--Vocabulario Ingles-Espanol de Electronica & Tecnica Nuclear. 196p. (Eng. & Span.). write for info. (ISBN 84-267-0247-3). Marcombo.

Markus, John, tr. Diccionario de electronica y tecnica nuclear. 1052p. (Span.). 1972. 2400.00 ptas. Marcombo.

Proulx, G. J. Dictionnaire D'electronique & Tele-Communication: Anglais-Francais. 582p. (Eng. & Fr.). 1959. Can.$8.50. Beauchemin.

Vocabulario de Electronica. 56p. (Span.). 1981. 180.00 ptas (ISBN 84-353-0009-9). Inst Amer.

ELECTRONICS–DICTIONARIES

Arnaud, Jean F. Diccionario De la Electronica. 3rd ed. 368p. (Span.). 1976. pap. $5.25 (ISBN 84-01-90304-1, S-14211). French & Eur.

--Dictionnaire de l'electronique. 3rd ed. (Illus.). 250p. (Fr.). 1971. 17.60 F. Larousse.

Arnaud, Jean-Francois. Diccionario de la electronica. (Span.). 100.00 ptas. Plaza Janes.

Arsenijevic, N. S. German-Serbocroatian Electrotechnical Dictionary. 150p. (Ger. & Serbocroatian.). 1971. Leatherette $24.95 (ISBN 0-686-92462-2, M-963X3). French & Eur.

Bezner. Elektromaschinen-Woerterbuch. 558p. (Ger. & Eng.). 1982. DM.80.00. Brandstetter.

Birdmann, G. English-German, German, English Solid State Physics & Electronics Dictionary. 1103p. (Eng. & Ger.). 1980. $100.00x (ISBN 0-569-07204-2, Pub. by Collet's). State Mutual Bk.

Brand, John R. Handbook of Electronic Formulas, Symbols, & Definitions. 1979. text ed. $15.95 (ISBN 0-442-20999-1). Van Nos Reinhold.

Brosset, Raymond & Fondaneche, Pierre. Dictionnaire Memento D'electronique. 3rd ed. 512p. (Fr.). 1969. $39.95 (ISBN 0-686-56929-6, M-6047). French & Eur.

--Dictionnaire Memento d'electronique. 3rd ed. 512p. (Fr.). 1969. 95.00 F. Bordas-Dunod.

Budig, Peter K. Elektrotechnik Elektronik Deutsch-Englisch. 770p. (Ger. & Eng.). 1982. M.98.00. VEB Technik.

--Fachwoerterbuch Elektrotechnik, Elektronik. (Eng. & Ger., Dictionary of Electrical Engineering and Electronics). 1976. $86.50 (ISBN 3-7785-0357-X, M-7394, Pub. by Huethig). French & Eur.

Budig, Peter-Klaus, ed. Electricity & Electronics Technical Dictionary. 2nd, rev. ed. 724p. (Eng. & Ger.). 1979. $62.50x (ISBN 0-8002-2468-X). Intl Pubns Serv.

Carter, Harley. Diccionario de Electronica. 416p. (Span.). 1962. $19.95 (ISBN 0-686-56716-1, S-33049). French & Eur.

Carter, Harley, tr. Diccionario de electronica. 416p. (Span.). 1962. Arg.$2.60. Leru.

Clason, W., ed. Electronics Dictionary: Russian Supplement. 1963. $32.70 (ISBN 0-444-40127-X). Elsevier.

--Electronics Dictionary: Swedish Supplement. 1960. $9.60 (ISBN 0-444-40121-0). Elsevier.

Clason, W. E. Elsevier's Dictionary of Electronics & Waveguides. 2nd ed. (Eng., Fr., Span., Ital., Dutch & Ger., Polyglot). 1965. $106.50 (ISBN 0-444-40119-9). Elsevier.

Colella, Antonio. Nuovo dizionario di elettrotecnica e elettronica italiano-inglese, inglese-italiano. (Illus.). 540p. (Ital. & Eng.). L.30000.00. Il Rostro.

Conrad, W. BI-Taschenlexikon Elektronik-Funktechnik. (Illus.). 400p. (Ger.). 1982. M.15.00. Biblio Inst.

Diccionario de electronica, radio y TV. (Span.). 135.00 ptas. Afha Intl.

Diccionario Electromecanico Ingles-Espanol. 298p. (Eng & Span.). 1969. pap. $18.95 (ISBN 84-7087-002-5, S-12420). French & Eur.

Diccionario internacional de electronica. (Span.). write for info. Cultura Popular.

Diccionario y tablas electronicas. (Span.). $6.50. Minerva.

Dictionary of Telecommunications & Electronics. (Hebrew & Eng.). IL.7.00. Massada Pr.

Dictionnaire International Electrotechnique: Francais-Russe-Anglais-Allemand-Italien-Suedois-Hollandais-Polonais. (Fr. , Rus. , Eng. , Ger. , Ital. , Swedish, Dutch & Pol.). write for info. Mir.

Dictionnaire International Electrotechnique: Francais-Russe-Anglais-Allemand-Espagnol-Suedois-Hollandais-Polonais. (Fr. , Rus. , Eng. , Ger. , Span. , Swedish, Dutch & Pol.). write for info. Mir.

Dictionnaire Technique Anglais-Francais d'electronique. 82p. (Eng & Fr.). 1967. 45.00 F. Chiron.

Electronics Dictionary. 254p. (Pol. , Eng. & Rus.). $59.00x (ISBN 0-686-44676-3, Pub. by Collets). State Mutual Bk.

Fiandaca, G. Dizionario di elettronica: Tedesco-italiano. 408p. (Ger. & Ital.). 1962. L.10000.00. Il Rostro.

Franz, Georg I. Fachworter der Elektronik. LC 76-488356. 86p. (Ger.). 1976. DM.4.80 (ISBN 3-7723-0402-8). Franzis Verlag.

Freeman, Roger L. English-Spanish, Spanish-English Dictionary of Communications & Electronic Terms. (Eng. & Span.). 1972. $39.50 (ISBN 0-521-08080-0). Cambridge U Pr.

Geiler, L. B., et al, eds. Anglo-Russkii Elektrotekhnicheskii Slovar. 704p. (Eng. & Rus.). 1955. $5.95 (Pub. by Gosizdat Tekhn. Teoret.). Four Continent.

Ginzburg, M. L., et al. Nemetsko-Russkii Elektrotekhnicheskii Slovar. 1066p. (Rus.). 1959. $12.75 (Pub. by Gosizdat Fizmatlit). Four Continent.

Gluzman, I. S. Anglo-Russkii Slovar Zheleznodorozhnoi Automatike, Telemekhanike & Sviazi. 427p. (Rus. & Eng.). 1958. $5.25 (Pub. by Gosizdat Fizmat. Lit.). Four Continent.

Goedecke. Woerterbuch der Elektrotechnik Fernmeldetechnik & Elektronik: Band I, Deutsch-Englisch-Franzoesisch. 908p. (Ger., Eng. & Fr.). 1982. DM.70.00. Brandstetter.

--Woerterbuch der Elektrotechnik Fernmeldetechnik & Elektronik: Band II, Franzoesisch-Englisch-Deutsch. 908p. (Fr., Eng. & Ger.). 1982. DM.70.00. Brandstetter.

--Woerterbuch der Elektrotechnik Fernmeldetechnik & Elektronik: Band III, Englisch-Deutsch-Franzoesisch. 1252p. (Eng., Ger. & Fr.). 1982. DM.80.00. Brandstetter.

Goedecke, W. Woerterbuch der Elektrotechnik, Fernmeldetechnik und Elektonik, Vol. 1. (Ger., Eng. & Fr., Dictionary of Electrical Engineering, Telecommunication Engineering & Electronics). 1966-68. $56.00 (ISBN 3-87097-013-8, M-7018). French & Eur.

--Woerterbuch der Elektrotechnik, Fernmeldetechnik und Elektronik, Vol. 2. (Fr., Eng. & Ger., Dictionary of Electrical Engineering, Telecommuunications Engineering & Electronics). 1966-68. $56.00 (ISBN 3-87097-014-6, M-7019). French & Eur.

Gorokhov, P. K. Russko-Nemetskii Radiotekhnicheskii Slovar. 390p. (Rus. & Ger.). 1961. $3.60 (Pub. by Glav. Red. Inostr. Nauchno-Tekhn. Slovarei Fizmata). Glav. Red. Inostr. Nauchno-Tekhn. Slovarei Fizmata.

Grenier, Jean Guy. Dictionnaire Anglais-Francais D'electrotechnique. 260p. (Eng. & Fr.). 1976. C.$12.00. Lanaudiere.

Gross, Helmut. Elektrotechnik Elektronik Russisch-Deutsch. 964p. (Rus. & Ger.). 1982. M.60.00. VEB Technik.

--Kleines Woerterbuch der Elektrotechnik Elektronik Russisch-Deutsch. 128p. (Rus. & Ger.). 1980. M.7.00. VEB Technik.

Handel, S. Diccionario De Electronica. 470p. (Span.). 1976. $39.75 (ISBN 84-335-6408-0, S-50070). French & Eur.

--Dizionario di Elettronica Italiano-Inglese, Inglese-Italiano. 284p. (Eng. & Ital.). 1966. $39.95 (ISBN 0-686-92632-3, M-9192). French & Eur.

Handel, Saul. Dizionario di elettronica. Suriani, E., tr. (Illus.). 284p. (Ital.). 1966. L.3600.00. Zanichelli.

--Dizionario di elettronica. Suriani, E., tr. (Illus.). 286p. (Ital.). 1967. L.13000.00. Zanichelli.

Hyman, Charles J. German-English, English-German Electronics Dictionary. LC 64-7757. 182p. (Ger. & Eng.). 1965. $35.00x (ISBN 0-306-10710-4, Consultants). Plenum Pub.

Ibeas, Franco. Diccionario Tecnologico Ingles-Espanol: Electricidad, Electronica, Telecomunicacion, & Materias Afinas con la Fisica, Optica & Quimica. 452p. (Eng. & Span.). 1974. E950.00 (ISBN 84-205-0492-0). Alhambra.

Institute of Electrical & Electronics Engineers, Inc. IEEE Standard Dictionary of Electrical & Electronics Terms. 2nd ed. LC 77-92333. 1977. $37.50x (ISBN 0-471-04264-1, Pub. by Wiley-Interscience). Wiley.

International Electrotechnical Com. Vocabulario Electronico Internacional. 318p. (Span.). 1975. $14.95 (ISBN 84-237-0148-4, S-50247). French & Eur.

International Electrotechnical Vocabulary: Electronics. 335p. (Eng. , Fr. & Rus.). 1956. leatherette $9.95 (ISBN 0-686-92485-1, M-9071). French & Eur.
International Electrotechnical Vocabulary, Machines & Transformers. 212p. (Eng. , Fr. & Rus.). 1958. leatherette $4.95 (ISBN 0-686-92488-6, M-9072). French & Eur.
Izak, Miklos. Hiradastechnikai Kislexikon. LC 78-399684. 435p. (Hungarian.). 1976. write for info. Mueszaki Konyv.
Junge. Woerterbuch fuer den Hobbyelektroniker. 250p. (Ger.). 1983. DM.19.80 (ISBN 3-87144-676-9). Verlag Harri Deutsch.
Junge, Hans D. Brockhaus ABC Elektronik. LC 79-391270. 751p. (Ger.). 1978. M.18.60. R Brockhaus.
--Woerterbuch fur den Hobby-Elektroniker Englisch-Deutsch. 240p. (Eng. & Ger.). 1982. M.28.00. VEB Technik.
Knaeps, E. & Zacharias, D. Woerterbuch der Elektronik. 104p. (Ger. & Fr.). 1976. pap. $9.95 (ISBN 3-7723-6231-1, M-7020). French & Eur.
Lexique Trilingue des Termes d'usage Courant: Electrotechnique, Electronique, Acoustique, Optique, Controle. 340p. (Fr.). 1966. 72.00 F. Ste. Publications Mecaniques.
Markus, John. Diccionario de Electronica y Tecnica Nuclear. 1052p. (Span. & Eng.). $75.95 (ISBN 84-267-0003-9, S-14264). French & Eur.
--Vocabulario Ingles-Espanol de Electronica y Tecnica Nuclear. 2nd ed. 196p. (Span. & Eng.). pap. $16.75 (ISBN 84-267-0247-3, S-30684). French & Eur.
Marquet, Lluis. Diccionari d'electrionica. 177p. (Span.). 1971. 90.00 ptas. Portic.
Marquet, Luis. Diccionari d'Electronica. 208p. (Catalan.). 1977. pap. $4.50 (ISBN 84-7306-116-0, S-50184). French & Eur.
Mataix, M. Diccionario de eletronica y energia nuclear ingles-espanol. 772p. (Eng. & Span.). 620.00 ptas. Danae.
Mataix, Mariano. Diccionario de Electronica, Informatica & Centrales Nucleares. 660p. (Span.). 1978. 2400.00 ptas (ISBN 8-42670-350-X). Marcombo.
Mataix Lord, Mariano. Diccionario De Electronica, Informatica y Centrales Nucleares. 660p. (Fr. & Eng.). 1978. leather $59.95 (ISBN 84-267-0350-X, S-30687). French & Eur.
Mezhdunarodnyi Elektrotekhnicheskii Slovar: Gruppa 07 (Elektronika) 335p. (Rus.). 1959. $3.50 (Pub. by Gosizdat Fiziko-Matematich. Literatury). Four Continent.
Mezhdunarodnyi Elektrotekhnicheskii Slovar: Gruppa 10 (Mashiny & Transformatory) (Rus.). $2.25 (Pub. by Gosizdat Fiziko Matematich. Literatury). Four Continent.
Mezhdunarodnyi Elektrotekhnicheskii Slovar: Gruppa 65 (Radiologiia & Radiologicheskaia Fizika) 252p. (Rus.). 1966. $3.50 (Pub. by Sov Entsiklopediia). Four Continent.
Miladinovic, Tomislav. Woerterbuch der Elektrotechnik und Elektronik. (Ger. & Rus.). 1970. $92.00 (ISBN 3-7736-5285-2, M-7016). French & Eur.
Moellerke, Georg. Concise Electronics Dictionary. LC 75-332199. 149p. (Eng. & Ger.). 1975. 16.00 F. A T Fachverlag.
Morelli, Marcello. Dizionario di informatica e degli elaboratori elettronici. (Illus.). 216p. (Ital.). 1978. L.5000.00 (ISBN 88-204-0203-3). Angeli.
Muchow, Helmut. Festkorperelektronik. 212p. (Rus. & Ger.). 1974. M.20.00. VEB Technik.
Opperman, Alfred. Dictionary of Electronics. 692p. (Eng. & Ger.). 1980. $120.00x (ISBN 0-686-98305-X, K G Saur). Gale.
Piraux. Dictionaire Francais-Anglais d'electro-technique et d'electronique. (Fr.). $32.50 (ISBN 0-685-36687-1). French & Eur.
Piraux, H. Dictionnaire des termes relatifs a electrotechnique, l'electronique et aux applications connexes, 2 vols. 387p. (Eng. & Fr.). 1978. Vol. 1: English-French. 49.00 F. Vol. 2: French-English. $49.00. Eyrolles.
--French-Eng., Eng-French Dictionary of Electrotechnic Electronics & Allied Fields, 2 Vols. (Fr. & Eng.). Set. 90.00 (ISBN 0-685-12017-1). Heinman.
Piraux, H., et al. Diccionario ingles-espanol de electrotecnia y electronica. 534p. (Span. & Eng.). 1966. 600.00 ptas. ETA.
Piraux, Henri. Dictionnaire Allemand-Francais des Termes Relatifs a l'Electrorechnique, l'Electronique, et aux Applications Connexes. 4th ed. 254p. (Fr. & Ger.). 1976. pap. $31.95 (ISBN 0-686-57080-4, M-6455). French & Eur.
--Dictionnaire Allemand-Francais des Termes Relatifs a l'electrotechnique: L'electrotechnique & aux Applications Connexes. 4th ed. (Illus.). 254p. (Ger. & Fr.). 1976. 72.00 F. Eyrolles.
--Dictionnaire Francais-Anglais des Termes Relatifs a l'electronique: L'electronique & aux Applications Connexes. 6th ed. (Illus.). 204p. (Fr. & Eng.). 1978. 82.00 F. Eyrolles.
Piraux, Henry. Dizionario inglese-italiano dei termini relativi all'elettrotecnica. 544p. (Eng. & Ital.). L.6400.00. Signorelli C.
Proulx, G. J. Dictionnaire d'Electrique et Tele-Communication: Anglais-Francais. 582p. (Fr. & Eng.). 1979. $15.95 (ISBN 0-686-57089-8, M-6469). French & Eur.
Ramirez Villareal, Humberto. Diccionario Ilustrado de Electronica. 192p. (Span.). $12.95 (ISBN 0-686-56678-5, S-25248). French & Eur.
Ramirez Villarreal, Humberto. Diccionario ilustrado de electronica: Espanol-ingles e ingles-espanol. (Illus.). 192p. (Span. & Eng.). $3.60; Mex.$45.00. Diana.
Rodgers, Harold R., et al, eds. Arlington Dictionary of Electronics. (Illus.). 1971. text ed. $16.95x (ISBN 0-8464-0146-0). Beekman Pubs.
Saarikoski, Lea. Englantilais-Suomaainen Elektromikka ja Instrumentointisanasto. LC 77-469166. 123p. (Eng. & Finnish.). 1976. Fmk.18.00 (ISBN 9-5110-2382-9). Otava.
Saiz, M. Diccionario de Electronica, Radio & TV: Ingles-Espanol. 144p. (Eng. & Span.). pap. $4.50. Lectorum Pubns.
Santano. Diccionario de Electronica. (Span.). 1983. write for info. Paraninfo.
Schneider, Leonhard. Woerterbuch der Elektronik. (Ger. & Pol.). 1977. pap. $13.50 (ISBN 3-7723-6431-4, M-7021). French & Eur.
Schwenkhagen, H. Woerterbuch Elektrotechnik und Elektronik. 2nd ed. (Ger. & Eng., Dictionary of Electrical Engineering and Electronics). 1967. $128.00 (ISBN 0-686-56610-6, M-6927). French & Eur.
Schwenkhagen, H. F. & Meinhhold, H. Woerterbuch Elektrotechnik und Elektronik. (Ger. & Eng., Dictionary of Electrical Engineering and Electronics). 1978. $128.00 (ISBN 3-7736-5072-8, M-6928). French & Eur.
Sizaire, Pierre. Dictionnaire Technique de la Construction Electrique. (Illus.). 172p. (Fr.). 1968. 67.00 F. Eyrolles.
Sozanskiej, Ewa. Slownik Elektroniczny Polsko-Angielsko-Rosyjski. LC 78-384390. vii, 254p. (Eng., Pol. & Rus.). 1977. 100.00 Zl. Wydawnictwa Naukowo.
Standards Council, Society for Technical Communication. Abbreviations & Symbols for Terms Used in Electronics. 1975. pap. $8.00 (ISBN 0-914548-19-0). Soc Tech Comm.
Taschenlexikon Elektronik, Funktechnik. 320p. (Ger.). 1974. $12.50 (ISBN 3-87144-176-7, M-7630, Pub. by Verlag Harri Deutsch). French & Eur.
Technik-Worterbuch: Elektronik, Elektrotechnik. 1980. $120.00x (ISBN 0-686-72091-1, Pub. by Collet's). State Mutual Bk.
Wanke & Havlicek. English Fuer Elektrotechniker & Elektroniker. xv, 368p. (Eng. & Ger.). DM.40.00. Brandstetter.
Wernicke, H. Dictionary of Electronics, Communications & Electrical Engineering, 2 vols. 1300p. Vol. 1. $32.50 ea. (ISBN 0-685-05199-4); Vol. 2. $36.00 ea. (ISBN 0-685-05200-1). Adler.

ELECTRONICS–EXAMINATIONS, QUESTIONS, ETC.

Mataix, Mariano. Diccionario de Electronica, Informatica & Centrales Nucleares. 660p. (Span.). 1978. 2400.00 ptas (ISBN 8-42670-350-X). Marcombo.

ELECTRONICS–MATERIALS

see also Semiconductors

Dictionary of Terms for Vacuum Science & Technology, Surface Science, Thin Film Technology, Vacuum Metallurgy, Electronic Materials. 1980. $5.00. Am Vacuum Soc.

ELECTRONICS–NOTATION

Brand, John R. Handbook of Electronic Formulas, Symbols, & Definitions. 1979. text ed. $15.95 (ISBN 0-442-20999-1). Van Nos Reinhold.

ELECTRONICS–TABLES, CALCULATIONS, ETC.

Diccionario y tablas electronicas. (Span.). $6.50. Minerva.

ELECTROPHONIC MUSIC

see Electronic Music

ELECTROPHOTOGRAPHY

Electrophotography Definitions & Standardization of Terms. 1965. $3.00 (399-1); members $2.00. TAPPI.

ELEMENTARY EDUCATION

see Education, Elementary

ELEMENTARY PARTICLES (PHYSICS)

see Particles (Nuclear Physics)

ELEUTH LANGUAGE

see Aleut Language

ELIOT, GEORGE, PSEUD., I.E. MARIAN EVANS, AFTERWARDS CROSS, 1819-1880

Mudge, Isadore G. & Sears, Minnie E. George Eliot Dictionary. LC 76-27710. 1924. lib. bdg. $21.00 (ISBN 0-8414-6114-7). Folcroft.

ELUARD, PAUL, 1895-1952

Guyard, Marie-Renee. Le Vocabulaire Politique de Paul Eluard. 286p. (Fr.). 68.00 F. Klincksieck.

EMBOMMA LANGUAGE

see Congo Language

EMBRYOLOGY

Lovasy, Ernest & Veillon, Emmanuel. Dictionnaire des Termes d'anatomie, d'embryologie & d'histologie. 624p. (Fr.). 1954. 40.00 F. Maloine.
Lovasy, Ernst. Dictionnaire des Termes d'Anatomie, d'Embryologie et d'Histologie. 624p. (Fr.). 1954. $17.50 (ISBN 0-686-57022-7, M-6380). French & Eur.

EMERGENCIES

see Medical Emergencies

EMERGENCY MEDICAL SERVICES

Diccionario de Medicina de Urgencia. 2nd ed. 208p. (Span.). 1977. $6.95 (ISBN 84-352-0174-0, S-13672). French & Eur.

EMERSON, RALPH WALDO, 1803-1882

Birrell, Augustine. Emerson: A Lecture. 1978. Repr. of 1903 ed. lib. bdg. $8.50 (ISBN 0-8495-0422-8). Arden Lib.

EMOTIONS

see also Love

Poujol, F. A. Dictionnaire des Facultes Intellectuelles et Affectives de l'ame ou l'on Traite des Passions, des Vertus, des Vices, Des Defauts. Migne, J. P., ed. (Encyclopedie Theologique Ser.: Vol. 39). 560p. (Fr.). Repr. of 1849 ed. lib. bdg. $72.00x (ISBN 0-89241-245-3). Caratzas Pub Co.

EMOTIONS IN LITERATURE

Miles, Josephine. Wordsworth & the Vocabulary of Emotion. 1965. lib. bdg. 18.00x (ISBN 0-374-95681-2). Octagon.

EMPLOYMENT (ECONOMIC THEORY)

Logie, G. Glossary of Employment & Industry. (International Planning Glossaries Ser.: Vol. 3). 1982. $57.50 (ISBN 0-444-42064-9). Elsevier.

EMPLOYMENT MANAGEMENT

see Personnel Management

ENAMEL PAINTS

see Paint; Painting, Industrial

ENCYCLOPEDIAS AND DICTIONARIES

Encyclopedias and dictionaries of a particular subject are entered under the subject with subdivisions Dictionaries, Dictionaries, Juvenile or, in the case of countries, cities, etc. or ethnic groups, dictionaries and encyclopedias e.g. Botany–Dictionaries; Catholic Church–Dictionaries Juvenile.

see also Children's Encyclopedias and Dictionaries; Dictionaries, Polyglot; Handbooks, Vade-Mecums, etc.; Lexicography; Picture Dictionaries

also particular subjects with or without the subdivision Dictionaries

Bartlett, John R. Dictionary of Americanism: A Glossary of Words & Phrases, Usually Regarded As Peculiar to the United States. 1976. Repr. of 1848 ed. $69.00 (ISBN 0-403-06365-5, Regency). Scholarly.
Beebe, Brooke M. & Rosenblatt, Ruth Y. The Dictionary. LC 77-730283. (Illus.). (gr. 3-5). 1977. pap. text ed. $125.00 (ISBN 0-89290-121-7, A151-SAR). Soc for Visual.
Bergeron, Leandre. The Quebecois Dictionary. 206p. 1983. $28.00x (ISBN 0-88862-548-0); pap. $17.95x (ISBN 0-88862-547-2). Enslow Pubs.
Bergflexner, Stuart, ed. Oxford American Dictionary. 1982. pap. $3.95 (ISBN 0-380-60772-7, 60772-7). Avon.
Bolander, B. O. The Instant Quotation Dictionary. (Career Institute Instant Reference Library). 314p. 1969. $3.95 (ISBN 0-531-02006-1). Watts.
Byrne, Josefa H. Mrs. Byrne's Dictionary of Unusual, Obscure, & Preposterous Words, Gathered from Numerous & Diverse Authoritative Sources. Byrne, Robert, ed. & intro. by. 1974. $12.50 (ISBN 0-8216-0203-9). Univ Bks.
Chambers Compact Dictionary. LC 77-83851. 1978. $3.95 (ISBN 0-8467-0394-7, Pub. by Two Continents). Am Map.
Chambers Everyday Dictionary. LC 77-84354. 1978. $6.95 (ISBN 0-8467-0395-5, Pub. by Two Continents); pap. text ed. $3.95 (ISBN 0-8467-0396-3). Am Map.
Chambers Twentieth Century Dictionary. LC 77-83852. 1978. $10.95 (ISBN 0-8467-0393-9, Pub. by Two Continents). Am Map.
Creswell, Thomas J. Usage in Dictionaries & Dictionaries of Usage. 212p. 1975. $10.00 (55774); members $9.25. NCTE.
Dehn-Nielsen, Henning. Fogtdals et-binds leksikon i farver. Sejersen, Gorm, ed. LC 80-459104. (Illus.). 656p. (Danish.). 1979. Kr.298.00 (ISBN 8-74270-116-3). Fogtdals Boger.
Diccionario Lexikon. 368p. (Span.). 1974. Mex.$17.50. Fernandez.
Dictionaries, Vols. II-III. (J). 1980-81. $14.00. Dict Soc NA.
Dictionaries, Vol. 1. 164p. (J). 1979. $9.00. Dict Soc NA.
Dictionary Chart. $1.30 (P4). Am Classical.

Edwards, Eliezer E. Words, Facts & Phrases: A Dictionary of Curious, Quaint, & Out-of-the-Way Matters. LC 68-21768. 1968. Repr. of 1881 ed. $42.00x (ISBN 0-8103-3087-3). Gale.
Fine Paper Dictionary, 1982. 6th ed. 512p. 1982. pap. 45.00 (ISBN 0-686-17578-6). Grade Finders.
Forte, Imogene & MacKenzie, Joy. Dictionary Dynamite. (Choose-A-Card Ser.). (gr. 2-6). 1979. pap. text ed. $5.95 (ISBN 0-913916-85-4, IP85-4). Incentive Pubns.
Haydn, Joseph T. Dictionary of Names & Universal Information. Repr. 89.00 (ISBN 0-403-00083-1). Scholarly.
Hobar, Donald, ed. Papers of the Dictionary Society of North America, 1977. 93p. members $5.50 (ISBN 0-686-95920-5); members $7.00 (ISBN 0-686-99671-2). Ind St Univ.
--Papers of the Dictionary Society of North America 1977. 93p. 1982. $7.00; members $5.50. Dict Soc NA.
Illustriertes Woerterbuch. 3rd ed. (Illus.). 192p. (Ger. , Eng. , Fr. & Span., Illustrated Dictionary). 1962. $29.95 (ISBN 3-8036-0250-5, M-7477, Pub. by Gebrueder Weiss). French & Eur.
Jesperson, Otto. International Dictionary. (Ger., Fr. & Eng.). 1930. $9.95 (ISBN 3-533-01130-5, M-7480, Pub. by Carl Winter). French & Eur.
--International Dictionary. (Ger., Fr. & Eng.). 1930. $9.95 (ISBN 3-533-01130-5). Winter Univ.
Langenscheidt Little Webster Lilliput Dictionary. 640p. plastic $1.50 (ISBN 0-686-40190-5). Langenscheidt.
Langenscheidt New Muret-Sanders Encyclopedic Dictionary. Incl. Part I, Vol. 1, A-M (English-German) 883p. (Eng. & Ger.). 70.00 (ISBN 3-468-01120-2); Part II, Vol. 2, N-Z (English-German) 960p. (Eng. & Ger.). 70.00 (ISBN 3-468-01122-9); Part II, Vol. 1, A-K (German-English) 973p. (Eng. & Ger.). 80.00 (ISBN 3-468-01124-5); Part II, Vol. 2, L-Z (German-English) 1048p. (Eng. & Ger.). 80.00 (ISBN 3-468-01126-1). Langenscheidt.
McMasters, Dale. The Dictionary. (Language Arts Ser.). 24p. (gr. 6 up). 1980. wkbk. $5.00 (ISBN 0-8209-0308-6, D-1). ESP.
March, Francis, et al. March's Thesaurus & Dictionary of the English Language. 2nd ed. LC 79-92443. 1324p. 1980. $19.95 (ISBN 0-89659-107-7); pap. $10.95 (ISBN 0-89659-161-1). Abbeville Pr.
Masarykuv Slovnik Naucny, 7 vols. (Bohemian.). 1925-1933. Set. $435.00 (ISBN 0-8277-3050-0). Pergamon.
Meydan-Larousse, 13 vols. (Turkish.). 1970-76. $1050.00 (ISBN 0-8277-3069-1). Pergamon.
Meyers Neues Lexikon, 8 vols. (Ger.). 1978-81. 445.00 (ISBN 3-411-01750-3). Pergamon.
Michell, Gillian, ed. Papers of the Dictionary Society of North America 1979. 179p. 1982. members $6.50 (ISBN 0-686-95917-5); non-members $8.00 (ISBN 0-686-99669-0). Ind St Univ.
--Papers of the Dictionary Society of North America 1979. 179p. 1981. $8.00; members $6.50. Dict Soc NA.
My First Dictionary. (Illus.). 342p. (gr. k-3). 1980. 9.95 (ISBN 0-395-29210-7). HM.
News Dictionary: Vol. 7, 1970. annual 1971. $14.95 (ISBN 0-87196-091-5). Facts on File.
News Dictionary: Vol. 8, 1971. annual 1972. $14.95 (ISBN 0-87196-093-1). Facts on File.
Ostrowski, Roza & Trojanwska, Izabella. Bedekr Kaszubski. LC 80-466240. (Illus.). 513p. (Pol., Gdansk). 1978. 180.00 Zl. Wydawn.
Ouseg, H. L. Twenty-One Language Dictionary: International Dictionary. write for info. Philos Lib.
Paton, John. Knowledge Encyclopedia. LC 80-471792. (Illus.). 415p. (Eng.). 1979. E7.95 (ISBN 0-7112-0004-1). Windward.
Rapetti, Sergio, et al. Piccolo lessico universale. LC 79-342345. 369p. (Ital.). 1976. L.3500.00. Nuova Vallecchi.
Romeo, Luigi. Ecce Homo! A Lexicon of Man. xv, 163p. 1979. $18.00x (ISBN 90-272-2006-9). Benjamins North Am.
Room, Adrian. Room's Dictionary of Confusibles. 1979. 16.00 (ISBN 0-7100-0120-7). Routledge & Kegan.
--Room's Dictionary of Distinguishables. 220p. 1981. 12.95 (ISBN 0-7100-0775-2). Routledge & Kegan.
Shaw, Marie-Jose. The Dictionary. (Sound Filmstrip Kits Ser.). (gr. 3-6). 1981. tchrs ed. $24.00 (ISBN 0-8209-0441-4, FCW-18). ESP.
Underwood, Peter. Dictionary of the Supernatural: An A to Z of Hauntings, Possession, Witchcraft, Demonology & Other Occult Phenomena. LC 79-303952. (Illus.). 389p. (Eng.). 1978. E5.50 (ISBN 0-245-52784-2). Harrap.
Watson, Owen, ed. Longman's Modern English Dictionary. 2nd ed. LC 77-368512. (Illus.). xv, 1286p. (Eng.). 1976. E5.50 (ISBN 0-582-55512-4). Longman England.
Webster's Encyclopedia of Dictionaries: 1975 Large Print. $24.50x (ISBN 0-685-70713-X). Wehman.
West, M. P. & Endicott, J. G. New Method Dictionary. $27.50 (ISBN 0-87559-106-X); thumb index $32.00 (ISBN 0-87559-139-6). Shalom.
Wood, Clement. Wood's New World Unabridged Rhyming Dictionary. 1056p. $15.00 (ISBN 0-529-03390-9, 1084). Collins Pubs.

ENCYCLOPEDIAS AND DICTIONARIES–BIBLIOGRAPHY

Brewer, Annie M., ed. Dictionaries, Encyclopedias, & Other Word-Related Books, 3 vols. 3rd ed. LC 81-20247. 1982. Vol. 1: English. $110.00x (ISBN 0-8103-1191-7); Vol. 2: Polyglot. $160.00x (ISBN 0-8103-1192-5); Vol. 3: Foreign. $160.00x (ISBN 0-8103-1193-3). Gale.
Molho, Emanuel. The Dictionary Catalogue. LC 80-67876. 196p. $4.95 (ISBN 0-8288-0150-9). French & Eur.
World Dictionaries in Print, 1983. 450p. 1983. $99.50 (ISBN 0-8352-1615-2). Bowker.
Zaunmuller, Wolfram. Bibliographisches Handbuch der Sprachworterbucher: Ein Internationales Verzeichnis Von 5600 Worterbuchern der Jahre 1460-1958 Fur Mehr Als 500 Sprachen und Dialekte. LC 59-1510. 264p. (Ger.). 1958. 50.00x (ISBN 3-7772-5812-1). Intl Pubns Serv.

ENCYCLOPEDIAS AND DICTIONARIES–HISTORY AND CRITICISM

Collison, Robert. A History of Foreign-Language Dictionaries. 216p. 1982. $60.00x (ISBN 0-233-97310-9, Pub. by A Deutsch England). State Mutual Bk.
Malkiel, Yakov. Etymological Dictionaries: A Tentative Typology. LC 75-11866. 160p. 1976. lib. bdg. $19.00x (ISBN 0-226-50292-9). U of Chicago Pr.

ENCYCLOPEDIAS AND DICTIONARIES, CHINESE

MacGowan, J. English & Chinese Dictionary of the Amoy Dialect. (Chinese & Eng.). 1978. Repr. of 1883 ed. $25.00 (ISBN 0-89986-343-4). Oriental Bk Store.
MacIver, D. Chinese-English Dictionary: Hakka-Dialect. (Chinese & Eng.). 1982. Repr. of 1926 ed. $35.00 (ISBN 0-89986-344-2). Oriental Bk Store.
Tan, K. T. Chinese-English Dictionary: Taiwan Dialect. (Chinese & Eng.). 1978. $50.00 (ISBN 0-89986-342-6). Oriental Bk Store.

ENCYCLOPEDIAS AND DICTIONARIES, FRENCH

Balay, Maurice. Lexique Informatique. 128p. (Fr.). 1971. pap. $9.95 (ISBN 0-686-56908-3, M-6021). French & Eur.
Bureau, Jacques. Dictionnaire de l'Informatique. 250p. (Fr.). 1972. pap. $6.95 (ISBN 0-686-56932-6, M-6053). French & Eur.
Diderot, Denis & D'Alembert, eds. Encyclopedie ou dictionnaire raisonne des sciences, des arts et des metiers, 35 Vols. (Illus.). 1967. Repr. of 1751 ed. Set. $4208.75 (ISBN 3-7728-0116-1). Adler.
Gastmann, Albert. Historical Dictionary of the French & Netherlands Antilles. LC 78-19070. (Latin American Historical Dictionaries Ser.: No. 18). 1978. lib. bdg. $13.00 (ISBN 0-8108-1153-7). Scarecrow.
Ginguay, M. Dictionnaire d'Informatique: Anglais-Francais. 172p. (Eng. & Fr.). 1977. pap. $27.50 (ISBN 0-686-57299-8, F-137100). French & Eur.
Ginguay, Michel & Lauret, Annette. Lexique d'Informatique. 244p. (Fr.). 1973. pap. $32.50 (ISBN 0-686-57198-3, M-6273). French & Eur.
Grande Encyclopedie Larousse, 22 vols. (Illus.). 13000p. (Fr.). 1972-1981. incl. suppl. $1250.00 set (ISBN 0-8277-3030-6). Pergamon.
Guilbert, Louis. Grand Larousse de la Langue Francaise, 7 vols. (Fr.). 1975. Set. $495.00 (ISBN 0-686-57308-0, M-6287). French & Eur.
Larouse de la Langue Francaise, 2 vols. (Fr.). 1977. $98.50 (ISBN 2-03-020287-8). Pergamon.

ENCYCLOPEDIAS AND DICTIONARIES, GERMAN

Das Bertelsmann Lexikon, 10 vols. (Ger.). 1980-1981. Set. $720.00 (ISBN 0-8277-3001-2). Pergamon.
Bilder-Conversations-Lexikon fur das Deutsche Volk, 4 vols. LC 79-363849. (Illus., Ger.). 1977. DM.234.00. F A Brockhaus.
Duden-Lexikon in Drei Banden, 3 vols. LC 80-481771. (Illus.). 2016p. (Ger.). 1980. DM.26.00 (ISBN 3-411-01777-5). Biblio Inst.
Freeman, Henry G. Pocket Dictionary Iron & Steel. LC 76-354255. (Eng. & Ger.). $11.25x ea.; Vol. 1. German-English. (ISBN 3-19-006214-5); Vol. 2. English-German. (ISBN 3-19-006215-3). Intl Pubns Serv.
Der Grosse Brockhaus, 12 Vols. 18th ed. (Illus., Ger.). 1977-81. $895.00 (ISBN 3-7653-0039-X). Pergamon.
Meyers grosses Handlexikon in Farbe. 12th ed. LC 76-450981. (Illus.). 1147p. (Ger.). 1975. DM.34.00 (ISBN 3-411-01344-3). Biblio Inst.
Meyers Universallexikon. LC 80-451635. (Illus., Ger.). 1978. M.29.80. Bibl Inst Leipzig.
Neue Herder, 14 vols. Incl. Grossa Atlas. (Ger.). 1973-1975. Set. $955.00 (ISBN 0-685-40123-5). Pergamon.
Rall, Dietrich, et al. Diccionario de Valencias Verbales. Aleman-Espanol. (Tuebinger Beitraege zur Linguistik: No. 134). 292p. (Orig., Span. & Ger.). 1980. pap. $18.00x (ISBN 3-87808-134-0). Benjamins North Am.
Springer, Otto, ed. Langenscheidt's New Muret-Sanders German-English Encyclopedic Dictionary: Part 2, Vol. 2, L-Z. (Eng. & Ger.). 1975. $80.00x (ISBN 3-468-01126-1). Am Map.

ENCYCLOPEDIAS AND DICTIONARIES, JEWISH

see Jews–Dictionaries and Encyclopedias

ENCYCLOPEDIAS AND DICTIONARIES, SPANISH

Diccionario De la Lengua Espanola. (Span.). 1979. $70.00 (ISBN 0-8277-3007-1). Pergamon.
Diccionario Enciclopedia Universal, 10 vols. 5036p. (Span. , Ger. , Fr. , Ital. & Eng.). Set. $270.00 (ISBN 0-686-57349-8, S-12271). French & Eur.
Diccionario Enciclopedico: Gran Omeba, 12 vols. (Span.). $325.00 (ISBN 0-686-56680-7, S-33046). French & Eur.
Diccionario Enciclopedico Tomo IX: Suplemento A-Z. 2nd ed. 808p. (Span.). 1979. 3600.00 ptas. Labor SA.
Diccionario nuevo Larousse manual ilustrado. (Span.). (gr. 9). 1977. Repr. 19.95 (ISBN 2-03-020546-X, 21121). Larousse.
Lexicolabor: Diccionario Enciclopedico Ilustrado, 4 vols. 2216p. (Span.). 1977. Set. $295.00 (ISBN 84-335-0344-8, S-50443). French & Eur.
Mi Primer Diccionario Escolar. 4th ed. 480p. (Span.). 1975. pap. $2.95 (ISBN 84-319-0028-8, S-27087). French & Eur.
Multidiccionario. 544p. (Span.). 1979. $29.95 (ISBN 84-278-0559-4, S-50514). French & Eur.
Nuevo Diccionario Ilustrado de la Lengua Espanola. 1232p. (Span.). $20.95 (ISBN 84-303-0047-3, S-12227). French & Eur.
Rall, Dietrich, et al. Diccionario de Valencias Verbales. Aleman-Espanol. (Tuebinger Beitraege zur Linguistik: No. 134). 292p. (Orig., Span. & Ger.). 1980. pap. $18.00x (ISBN 3-87808-134-0). Benjamins North Am.
Rances, Atilano. Diccionario Ilustrado De la Lengua Espanola. 640p. (Span.). 1974. $9.95 (ISBN 84-303-0051-1, S-12346). French & Eur.
Scarry, Richard. Mi Primer Gran Diccionario Infantil. 4th ed. 90p. (Span.). 1978. leatherette $13.95 (ISBN 84-02-03836-0, S-26637). French & Eur.
Spanish-English Dictionary. $14.50 (ISBN 0-685-00817-7, 076-3). Saphrograph.
Victorica, Ricardo. Errores y Omisiones del Diccionario de Anonimos y Seudonimos Hispanoamericanos de Jose Toribio Medina. LC 73-78356. 338p. (Span.). 1973. Repr. of 1928 ed. $24.50x (ISBN 0-87917-027-1). Ethridge.
Vox--Lexis-22, Diccionario Enciclopedia, 23 vols. 6704p. (Span.). 1977. Set. leatherette $250.00 (ISBN 84-7153-400-2, S-31569). French & Eur.
Zendrera, Concepcion. Mi Diccionario Ilustrado. 2nd ed. 20p. (Span.). 1974. $4.95 (ISBN 84-261-0358-8, S-16498). French & Eur.

ENDLESS PUNISHMENT

see Hell

ENDOWED CHARITIES

see Charities

ENEMY ALIENS

see Aliens

ENERGY

see Force and Energy; Power Resources

ENERGY CONSERVATION

Here are entered general works on the conservation of all forms of energy. Works on the conservation of a specific form of energy are entered under that form, e.g. Petroleum Conservation. Works on the conservation of energy as a physical concept are entered under Force and Energy.

Institut Francais du Petrole. Thesaurus Economie de l'energie. 232p. (Fr.). 1974. 194.00 F. Technip.
Kut, David. Dictionary of Applied Energy Conservation: An Illustrated Dictionary of Terms. (Illus.). 300p. 1983. 32.00 (ISBN 0-89397-131-6). Nichols Pub.

ENERGY RESOURCES

see Power Resources

ENGINEERING

see also Agricultural Engineering; Arches; Architecture; Bioengineering; Biomedical Engineering; Building Materials; Chemical Engineering; Civil Engineering; Dams; Drainage; Electric Engineering; Engines; Environmental Engineering; Hydraulic Engineering; Irrigation; Marine Engineering; Masonry; Mechanical Drawing; Mechanics; Mensuration; Mining Engineering; Nuclear Engineering; Railroad Engineering; Rivers; Roads; Sanitary Engineering; Strength of Materials; Surveying; Ventilation; Water-Supply Engineering

Russisch fuer Ingenieur & Fashschulen. (Rus.). M.12.00 (674 947 1). Wissenschaftliche.

ENGINEERING-DICTIONARIES

Barry, W. R., ed. Architectural, Construction, Manufacturing & Engineering Glossary of Terms. 519p. 1979. pap. $40.00 (ISBN 0-930284-05-4). Am Assn Cost Engineers.

Benito y Bacho, Jose de & Hernandez, Manuel B. Diccionario de la Constuccion & Obras Publicas, 2 vols. LC 76-453130. (Eng. & Span.). write for info. (ISBN 8-4851-9800-X). Lib Tec Bell.

Bosch, Ten. Dutch-English-French-German Engineering Dictionary. 11th ed. (Dutch, Eng. & Fr. & Ger.). 45.00 (ISBN 90-2010-132-3). Heinman.

Brockhaus der Naturwissenschaften und der Technik. 832p. (Ger.). $35.00 (ISBN 3-7653-0019-5, M-7314, Pub. by Wiesbaden). French & Eur.

Carcamo, L. Dictionnaire pour Ingenieurs et Techniciens: Francais-Espagnol, Espagnol-Francais. 1106p. (Fr. & Span.). 1981. $95.00 (ISBN 0-686-92423-1, M-7669). French & Eur.

Clauser, H. R. Diccionario De Materiales y Procesos De Ingenieria. 820p. (Span.). 1970. $98.00 (ISBN 84-335-6404-8, S-50067). French & Eur.

De Vries & Herrmann. Technical & Engineering Dictionary: Band II, English-German. 1154p. (Eng. & Ger.). 1982. DM.120.00. Brandstetter.

--Technical & Engineering Dictionary: Band I, German-English. 1178p. (Ger. & Eng.). 1982. DM.120.00. Brandstetter.

DeVries, Louis. German-English Technical & Engineering Dictionary. 2nd ed. (Ger. & Eng.). 1966. 63.95 (ISBN 0-07-016631-5, P&RB). McGraw.

Engineering Index, Inc. Engineering Index Thesaurus. LC 72-78325. 1972. 19.50 (ISBN 0-02-468550-X). Macmillan Info.

English-Chinese Dictionary of Construction Engineering. 251p. (Eng. & Chinese.). 1980. leatherette $14.95 (ISBN 0-686-97360-7, M-9279). French & Eur.

Ernst, Richard. Dictionary of Engineering & Technology, 2 vols. Rev. ed. (Ger. & Eng.). 1980. Vol 1: German-English, 1092p. $69.00; Vol. 2: English-German, 1170p. $69.00. Oxford U Pr.

--Dictionary of Engineering & Technology: With Extensive Treatment of the Most Modern Techniques & Processes, Vol. 2, English-German. 4th, rev. & enl. ed. 1178p. (Eng. & Ger.). 1975. text ed. 69.00x (ISBN 0-19-520109-4). Oxford U Pr.

Ernst, Richard, ed. Dictionary of Engineering & Technology, Vol. 1. 4th ed. 1981. 69.00x (ISBN 0-19-520269-4). Oxford U Pr.

Fachlexikon ABC Technik und Naturwissenschaft, Vols. 1 & 2. (Ger.). 1970. Set. leatherette $55.00 (ISBN 3-87144-004-3, M-7384). French & Eur.

Fekete, Ivan. Epuletgepeszet. LC 76-504896. 211p. (Eng., Ger. & Rus.). 1975. 48.00 Ft (ISBN 963-05-0560-6). Akademiai Kiado.

Freeman, H. Taschenwoerterbuch Kraftfahrzeugtechnik. 377p. (Ger. & Eng., Dictionary of Automotive Engineering). 1968. $12.50 (ISBN 3-19-006270-6, M-7635, Pub. by M. Hueber). French & Eur.

--Taschenwoerterbuch Kraftfahrzeugtechnik. 377p. (Ger. & Eng.). 1968. $12.50 (ISBN 3-19-006270-6). Hueber.

Freeman, Henry G. Fachenglisch Fur Technik und Industrie. 303p. (Ger. & Eng., English for Engineering and Industry). 1974. $22.50 (ISBN 3-452-17766-1, M-7376, Pub. by Carl Heymanns Verlag KG). French & Eur.

--Pocket Dictionary of Automotive Engineering: Taschenwoerterbuch Kraftfahrzeugtechnik. LC 71-362034. 380p. (Ger. & Eng.). 1968. 12.50x (ISBN 3-19-006270-6). Intl Pubns Serv.

Gaimaro, Oscar. Diccionario de los ingenios. (Span.). write for info. Alonso Edns.

Halbauer, S. Russisch-Deutsches Woerterbuch Fuer Naturwissenschaftler und Ingenieure. 170p. (Ger. & Rus.). 1971. $9.95 (ISBN 0-686-56466-9, M-7607, Pub. by M. Hueber). French & Eur.

--Russisch-Deutsches Woerterbuch Fuer Naturwissenschaftler und Ingenieure. 170p. (Ger. & Rus.). 1971. $9.95. Hueber.

Heck, Hans. Knaurs Lexikon der Technik. (Ger.). $55.00 (ISBN 3-426-04577-X, M-7520, Pub. by Druckenmueller). French & Eur.

Heller, C. Dictionary of Engineering Mechanics. (Eng. & Rus.). 1965. $14.75 (ISBN 0-444-40274-8). Elsevier.

Kovalenko, Y. G. English-Russian Dictionary of Reliability & Quality Control. LC 77-70279. (Eng. & Rus.). 1977. text ed. 72.00 (ISBN 0-08-021933-0). Pergamon.

Meinck, Fritz. Woerterbuch fur das Wasser & Abwasserfach. LC 78-337966. 737p. (Eng., Fr. & Ital.). 1977. write for info. (ISBN 3-486-35352-7). Oldenbourg Verlag.

Mugica Urdangarin, Luis M. Diccionario General y Tecnico: Hiztegi Orokor-Teknikoa, 2 vols. #1220p. (Span. & Vasco). 1977. Set. $80.00 (ISBN 84-85288-07-6, S-50100). French & Eur.

Naxerova, A. Technisches Woerterbuch, Vol. 2. (Czech. & Ger.). 1972. $40.00 (ISBN 3-87097-056-1, M-7650, Pub. by Brandstetter). French & Eur.

--Technisches Woerterbuch, Vol. 2. (Czech. & Ger.). 1972. $40.00 (ISBN 3-87097-056-1). Brandstetter.

Neubert, Gunter, ed. Technical Dictionary of Hydraulics & Pneumatics. 1973. text ed. 40.00 (ISBN 0-08-016958-9). Pergamon.

O'Bannon, Loran. Dictionary of Ceramic Science & Engineering. 330p. 1983. $45.00 (ISBN 0-306-41324-8, Plenum Pr). Plenum Pub.

Oppermann, A. Woerterbuch der Modernen Technik. (Ger. & Eng., Dictionary of Modern Engineering). $112.00 (ISBN 3-7940-6001-6, M-6982). French & Eur.

Oppermann, Alfred. Dictionary of Modern Engineering, Vol. 1. 3rd ed. (Eng. & Ger.). 1971. $113.00 (ISBN 3-7940-6001-6, M-7109). French & Eur.

--Dictionary of Modern Engineering, Vol. 2. 3rd ed. (Ger. & Eng.). 1974. $113.00 (ISBN 3-7940-6002-4, M-7108). French & Eur.

Oppermann, Alfred, ed. Dictionary of Modern Engineering, 2 vols. 3rd ed. Incl. Vol. 1. English-German. 912p. (Eng. & Ger.). 1972. 80.00 (ISBN 3-7940-6001-6); Vol. 2. German-English. 952p. (Ger. & Eng.). 1974. 80.00 (ISBN 3-7940-6002-4). $160.00x set (ISBN 3-7940-6003-2, Pub. by K G Saur). Gale.

Orlando-Meyer, Salvatore. Technisches Woerterbuch, Vol. 1. 2nd ed. (Ital. & Ger.). 1977. $40.00 (ISBN 3-87097-079-0, M-7651, Pub. by Brandstetter). French & Eur.

--Technisches Woerterbuch, Vol. 1. 2nd ed. (Ital. & Ger.). 1977. $40.00 (ISBN 3-87097-079-0). Brandstetter.

--Technisches Woerterbuch, Vol. 2. 2nd ed. (Ital. & Ger.). 1977. $40.00 (ISBN 3-87097-080-4, M-7652, Pub. by Brandstetter). French & Eur.

--Technisches Woerterbuch, Vol. 2. 2nd ed. (Ital. & Ger.). 1977. $40.00 (ISBN 3-87097-080-4). Brandstetter.

Pabst, Martin. Technologisches Woerterbuch Franzoisisch. 550p. (Port. & Ger.). 1971. leatherette $92.00 (ISBN 0-686-56470-7, M-7662, Pub. by Verlag W. Girardet). French & Eur.

--Technologisches Woerterbuch Franzoisisch. 550p. (Port. & Ger.). 1971. leatherette $92.00. Girardet.

Perucca, Eligio. Dizionario d'ingegneria. (Illus.). xx, 976p. (Ital.). 1968. L.55000.00 (ISBN 88-02-01486-8). UTET.

--Dizionario d'ingegneria. 2nd ed. (Illus.). 1028p. (Ital.). 1969. L.55000.00 (ISBN 88-02-01487-6). UTET.

--Dizionario d'ingegneria. 3rd ed. (Illus.). xvi, 984p. (Ital.). 1970. L.55000.00 (ISBN 88-02-01488-4). UTET.

--Dizionario d'ingegneria. 4th ed. (Illus.). xvi, 1028p. (Ital.). 1972. L.55000.00 (ISBN 88-02-01489-2). UTET.

--Dizionario d'ingegneria. 5th ed. (Illus.). xvi, 940p. (Ital.). 1973. L.55000.00 (ISBN 88-02-01490-6). UTET.

--Dizionario d'ingegneria. 6th ed. (Illus.). xvi, 976p. (Ital.). 1974. L.55000.00 (ISBN 88-02-01491-4). UTET.

--Dizionario d'ingegneria. 7th ed. (Ital.). 1975. L.55000.00 (ISBN 88-02-02396-4). UTET.

--Dizionario d'ingegneria. 8th ed. (Illus.). xvi, 1040p. (Ital.). 1976. L.55000.00 (ISBN 88-02-02998-9). UTET.

--Dizionario d'ingegneria. 9th ed. (Illus.). xvi, 1024p. (Ital.). 1977. L.55000.00 (ISBN 88-02-02445-6). UTET.

--Dizionario d'ingeneria. 10th ed. (Illus.). xvi, 972p. (Ital.). 1978. L.55000.00 (ISBN 88-02-02526-6). UTET.

Radic, S., ed. Technological Engineering Dictionary German-Serbocroatian. 495p. (Ger. & Serbocroation.). 1981. $95.00 (ISBN 0-686-92294-8, M-9687). French & Eur.

Robb, Louis A. Diccionario para Ingenieros Espanol-Ingles, Ingles-Espanol. 664p. (Span. & Eng.). 1977. $42.75 (ISBN 84-7051-048-7, S-31339). French & Eur.

--Diccionario para ingenieros: Ingles-espanol, espanol-ingles. 664p. (Eng. & Span.). $10.15. CECSA.

Schmidt, J. J. Vocabulaire Francais-Arabe de l'ingenieur & du Technicien, 1. 136p. (Fr. & Arabic.). 1973. 45.00 F. Maisonneuve & Larose.

Schuurmans Stekhoven, G. Dutch-English, English-Dutch Engineering Dictionary, 2 vols. (Dutch & Eng.). 125.00 set (ISBN 90-2010-602-3). Heinman.

Stellhorn, Kurt. Technologisches Woerterbuch Franzoisisch. 3rd ed. (Fr. & Ger.). 1965. leatherette $86.00 (ISBN 3-7736-5221-6, M-7660, Pub. by Verlag W. Girardet). French & Eur.

--Technologisches Woerterbuch Franzoisisch. 3rd ed. (Fr. & Ger.). 1965. leatherette $86.00 (ISBN 3-7736-5221-6). Girardet.

Technologisches Woerterbuch Spanisch. 564p. (Span. & Ger.). 1967. leatherette $99.50 (ISBN 3-7736-5410-3, M-7664, Pub. by Verlag W. Girardet). French & Eur.

Technologisches Woerterbuch Spanisch. 564p. (Span. & Ger.). 1967. leatherette $99.50 (ISBN 3-7736-5410-3). Girardet.

Ten Bosch's Quadralingual Engineering Dictionary. 692p. (Dutch, Eng. , Fr. & Ger.). $40.00. Imported Bks.

Von Bahder, Egon. Technologisches Woerterbuch. (Rus. & Ger.). 1970. $72.00 (ISBN 3-7736-5280-1, M-7656, Pub. by Girardet). French & Eur.

--Technologisches Woerterbuch. (Rus. & Ger.). 1970. $72.00 (ISBN 3-7736-5280-1). Girardet.

Zhong Wai Publishing Company. An English-Chinese Dictionary of Engineering & Technology. 1036p. (Eng. & Chinese.). 1981. $69.95x (ISBN 0-471-09371-8). Wiley.

ENGINEERING-ESTIMATES AND COSTS

Barry, W. R., ed. Architectural, Construction, Manufacturing & Engineering Glossary of Terms. 519p. 1979. pap. $40.00 (ISBN 0-930284-05-4). Am Assn Cost Engineers.

ENGINEERING-GRAPHIC METHODS
see Engineering Graphics

ENGINEERING-HANDBOOKS, MANUALS, ETC.
Engineers Joint Council Editors. Thesaurus of Engineering & Scientific Terms. rev. ed. LC 68-6569. 1967. flexible cover $50.00 (ISBN 0-87615-163-2). AAES.

ENGINEERING-MATERIALS
see Materials

ENGINEERING, AGRICULTURAL
see Agricultural Engineering

ENGINEERING, ARCHITECTURAL
see Building; Strength of Materials

ENGINEERING, BIOMEDICAL
see Biomedical Engineering

ENGINEERING, CHEMICAL
see Chemical Engineering

ENGINEERING, CIVIL
see Civil Engineering

ENGINEERING, CLINICAL
see Biomedical Engineering

ENGINEERING, ELECTRICAL
see Electric Engineering

ENGINEERING, HYDRAULIC
see Hydraulic Engineering

ENGINEERING, INDUSTRIAL
see Industrial Engineering

ENGINEERING, MARINE
see Marine Engineering

ENGINEERING, MEDICAL
see Biomedical Engineering

ENGINEERING, MINING
see Mining Engineering

ENGINEERING, MUNICIPAL
see Municipal Engineering

ENGINEERING, RAILROAD
see Railroad Engineering

ENGINEERING, SANITARY
see Sanitary Engineering

ENGINEERING, TRAFFIC
see Traffic Engineering

ENGINEERING, WATER-SUPPLY
see Water-Supply Engineering

ENGINEERING CYBERNETICS
see Automation

ENGINEERING DRAWING
see Mechanical Drawing

ENGINEERING GRAPHICS
see also Computer Graphics; also subdivision Graphic Methods under specific subjects
Lexikon der Grafischen Technik. 656p. (Ger.). 1977. DM.36.00 (ISBN 3-7940-4078-3). Saur Verlag.

ENGINEERING GRAPHICS-DATA PROCESSING
see Computer Graphics

ENGINEERING INSTRUMENTS
Ramalingom, T. Dictionary of Instrument Science. LC 81-14724. 588p. 1982. $24.95x (ISBN 0-471-86396-3, Pub. by Wiley-Interscience). Wiley.

ENGINEERING MATERIALS
see Materials

ENGINES
see also Fuel; Gas and Oil Engines; Locomotives; Pumping Machinery; Steam-Boilers; Tractors
Uhlig, Siegfried. Einfuhrung in das Technische Russisch Maschinenbau: Lehrmaterial fuer den Fremdsprachenunterricht. 382p. (Ger. & Rus.). 1976. M.7.00. VEB Technik.

ENGLAND-HISTORY
see Great Britain-History

ENGLISH ART
see Art, British

ENGLISH AS A FOREIGN LANGUAGE
see English Language-Study and Teaching-Foreign Students

ENGLISH DRAMA-HISTORY AND CRITICISM-TO 1500
Partridge, A. C. Orthography in Shakespeare & Elizabethan Drama: A Study of Colloquial Contractions, Elision, Prosody, & Punctuation. LC 64-17222. viii, 200p. 1964. $14.50x (ISBN 0-8032-0143-5). U of Nebr Pr.

ENGLISH DRAMA-HISTORY AND CRITICISM-18TH CENTURY
Partridge, A. C. Orthography in Shakespeare & Elizabethan Drama: A Study of Colloquial Contractions, Elision, Prosody, & Punctuation. LC 64-17222. viii, 200p. 1964. $14.50x (ISBN 0-8032-0143-5). U of Nebr Pr.

ENGLISH LANGUAGE
Dow, Francis D. Partially Naturalised French Words in Modern English. LC 76-370523. 65p. (Eng. & Fr.). 1976. E1.00 (ISBN 0-903745-02-X). Dow.
--Partially Naturalised French Words in Modern English. LC 76-370523. 65p. (Eng. & Fr.). E1.00 (ISBN 0-903745-02-X). Dow.
Fowler, Henry W. Dictionary of Modern English Usage. 2nd ed. Gowers, Ernest, ed. (YA) (gr. 9 up). 1965. 15.95 (ISBN 0-19-500153-2); with thumb index 18.95 (ISBN 0-19-500154-0). Oxford U Pr.
Pinkerton, Edward C. Word for Word. LC 77-20391. xxxii, 432p. 1982. $39.95 (ISBN 0-930454-06-5). Verbatim.
Watts, Peter. A Dictionary of the Old West. 1977. $12.95 (ISBN 0-394-49013-4). Knopf.

ENGLISH LANGUAGE-MIDDLE ENGLISH, 1100-1500-DICTIONARIES
Carter, Henry H. Dictionary of Middle English Musical Terms. Gerhard, George B., et al, eds. LC 61-63413. (Indiana University Humanities Ser: No. 45). 1961. 39.00 (ISBN 0-527-15150-5). Kraus Repr.
Halliwell-Phillipps, James O., ed. Dictionary of Archaic & Provincial Words, Obsolete Phrases, Proverbs, & Ancient Customs from the 14th Century, 2 Vols. 11th ed. LC 10-30948. 1971. Repr. of 1889 ed. Set. 90.00 (ISBN 0-384-21083-X). Johnson Repr.
Mayhew, A. L. & Skeat, W. W. Concise Dictionary of Middle English from A. D. 1150-1580. LC 77-20783. (Middle English.). 1888. lib. bdg. $25.00 (ISBN 0-8414-6220-8). Folcroft.
Stratmann, Francis H. A Dictionary of the Old English Language: Compiled from Writings of the XII, XIII, XIV, & XV Centuries. LC 73-4631. 1973. lib. bdg. $85.00 (ISBN 0-8414-7511-3). Folcroft.
Stratmann, Franz H. A Supplement to the Dictionary of the English Language of the 12th, 13th, 14th, & 15th Centuries. 3rd ed. LC 76-30620. 1977. Repr. of 1881 ed. lib. bdg. $15.00 (ISBN 0-8414-7554-7). Folcroft.

ENGLISH LANGUAGE-MIDDLE ENGLISH, 1100-1500-GLOSSARIES
Wright, T. Anglo-Saxon & English Vocabularies, 2 vols. Set. $95.20 (ISBN 3-534-04078-3). Adler.

ENGLISH LANGUAGE-EARLY MODERN, 1500-1700
Galfridus Anglicus. Promptorium Parvulorum Sive Clericorum, Dictionarius Anglolatinus Princeps, 3 Pts. Repr. of 1865 ed. $37.00 ea. Johnson Repr.
Galfridus, Anglicus. Promptorium Parvulorum Sive Clericorum, Lexicon Anglo-Latinum Princeps, 3 Vols. LC 70-168091. (Camden Society, London. Publications, First Ser.: Nos. 25, 54, 89). (Lat.). Repr. of 1865 ed. Set $84.00 (ISBN 0-404-50209-1); $28.00 ea. AMS Pr.
Halliwell-Phillipps, James O., ed. Dictionary of Archaic & Provincial Words, Obsolete Phrases, Proverbs, & Ancient Customs from the 14th Century, 2 Vols. 11th ed. LC 10-30948. 1971. Repr. of 1889 ed. Set. 90.00 (ISBN 0-384-21083-X). Johnson Repr.

ENGLISH LANGUAGE-ABBREVIATIONS
see Abbreviations
ENGLISH LANGUAGE-ACRONYMS
see Acronyms
ENGLISH LANGUAGE-AMERICANISMS
see Americanisms

ENGLISH LANGUAGE-ANALYSIS AND PARSING
see English Language-Grammar
ENGLISH LANGUAGE-ANTONYMS
see English Language-Synonyms and Antonyms
ENGLISH LANGUAGE-BUSINESS ENGLISH
Adam, J. H., ed. Longman Dictionary of Business English. 528p. 1982. 15.95 (ISBN 0-582-55558-2). Longman.
Attal, Jean-Pierre. Business English Vocabulary. LC 80-460081. 269p. (Fr. & Eng.). 1979. write for info. (ISBN 2-7081-0409-8). Edns Organisation.
Davids, Lewis E. Instant Business Dictionary. LC 78-150232. 1970. $3.95 (ISBN 0-911744-07-X). Career Inst.
De Renty, Ivan. Lexique de l'Anglais des affaires. 352p. (Fr. & Eng.). pap. $8.00. Imported Bks.
--Lexique de l'anglais des Affaires. 320p. (Fr.). 1977. 10.50 F. L. G. F.
--Lexique Quadrilingue des Affaires: Anglais-Francais-Allemand-Espagnol. 702p. (Eng., Fr., Ger. & Span.). 1977. 72.00 F. Hachette.
Janis, J. Harold. Modern Business Language & Usage in Dictionary Form. LC 80-1656. (Illus.). 504p. 1984. $19.95 (ISBN 0-385-14489-X). Doubleday.
Peron, Michel & Withnell, William. Dictionnaire des Affaires: Francais-Anglais. 512p. (Fr. & Eng.). 1969. 57.00 F. Larousse.

ENGLISH LANGUAGE-COMPOSITION AND EXERCISES
Here are entered works of an elementary character containing exercises in, and treatises on English composition. More advanced works on English composition are entered under the headings English Language-Rhetoric and English Language-Style.
see also English Language-Grammar; English Language-Rhetoric; English Language-Text-Books for Foreigners
The Hamlyn Guide to English Usage. 1980. pap. 3.95 (ISBN 0-600-33189-X). Larousse.
Levine, Harold. Vocabulary & Composition: Through Pleasurable Reading, Book 4. (gr. 11-12). 1978. wkbk $8.17 (ISBN 0-87720-376-8); pap. text ed. $7.17 (ISBN 0-87720-378-4). AMSCO Sch.

ENGLISH LANGUAGE-CONJUGATION
see English Language-Verb
ENGLISH LANGUAGE-CONVERSATION AND PHRASE BOOKS
Armengol, Joseph, et al, eds. English-Spanish Guide for Medical Personnel. (Eng. & Span.). 1966. pap. $7.00 (ISBN 0-87488-721-6). Med Exam.
Beitler, L. & McDonald, B. English for the Medical Professions. 1982. $6.96 (ISBN 0-07-004521-6). McGraw.
Diccionario de habla inglesa: Ingles-espanol, espanol-ingles. 536p. (Eng. & Span.). $1.50. Edit Pr Serv.
Gavrilovets, A. V. Russko-Angliiskii Slovar-Razgovornik: Letnie Olimpiiskie Vidy Sporta. 352p. (Rus.). 1979. $3.50 (Pub. by Russkii Iazyk). Four Continent.

ENGLISH LANGUAGE-DIAGRAMING
see English Language-Grammar
ENGLISH LANGUAGE-DIALECTS
see also Americanisms; English Language-Provincialisms; Pidgin English
Atwood, E. Bagby. The Regional Vocabulary of Texas. LC 62-9784. (Illus.). 286p. 1969. pap. $6.95 (ISBN 0-292-77008-1). U of Tex Pr.
Beeton, Douglas R. & Dorner, Helene T. A Dictionary of English Usage in Southern Africa. 1976. 19.95x (ISBN 0-19-570069-4). Oxford U Pr.

Cassidy, Frederick G. & Le Page, R. B., eds. Dictionary of Jamaican English. 2nd ed. LC 78-17799. 1980. $82.50 (ISBN 0-521-22165-X). Cambridge U Pr.
Clark, James M. The Vocabulary of Anglo-Irish. LC 73-12699. (Eng. & Irish.). 1917. lib. bdg. $15.00 (ISBN 0-8414-3394-1). Folcroft.
Craigie, William A. & Hulbert, James R., eds. Dictionary of American English on Historical Principles, 4 Vols. LC 36-21500. 1938-1944. Set. $250.00x (ISBN 0-226-11741-3); Vol. 1. o.s.i. (ISBN 0-226-11737-5). U of Chicago Pr.
Everhart, Jim. Illustrated Texas Dictionary of the English Language, 5 Vols. pap. $2.95 ea.; Vol. 1. (ISBN 0-8220-1477-7); Vol. 2. (ISBN 0-8220-1478-5); Vol. 3. (ISBN 0-8220-1479-3); Vol. 4. (ISBN 0-8220-1480-7); Vol. 5. (ISBN 0-8220-1487-4). Cliffs.
Foscue, Virginia O. A Preliminary Survey of the Vocabulary of White Alabamians. (Publications of the American Dialect Society Ser., No. 56). 48p. 1971. pap. $2.80 (ISBN 0-8173-0656-0, Am Dialect Soc). U of Ala Pr.
Harder, K. B. The Vocabulary of Marble Playing. Bd. with The Position of the Charleston Dialect. McDavid, R. I. (Publications of the American Dialect Society: No. 23). 61p. 1955. pap. $5.95 (ISBN 0-8173-0623-4). U of Ala Pr.
Hirst, T. O. A Grammar of the Dialect of Kendal (Wesmoreland) Descriptive & Historical with Specimens & a Glossary. 175p. 1968. Repr. of 1906 ed. 37.50x (ISBN 0-8002-0880-3). Intl Pubns Serv.
Horwill, H. W. An Anglo-American Interpreter: A Vocabulary & Phrase Book. LC 72-169624. 1939. lib. bdg. $10.00 (ISBN 0-8414-5130-3). Folcroft.
Jamieson, John. Etymological Dictionary of the Scottish Language, 5 Vols. rev. ed. Longmuir, John & Donaldson, David, eds. LC 70-144425. (Gaelic.). Repr. of 1887 ed. Set. $325.00 (ISBN 0-404-59470-0). AMS Pr.
Long, William H. A Dictionary of the Isle of Wight Dialect, & of Provincialisms Used in the Island, with Illustrative Anecdotes & Tales. LC 76-9101. 1976. Repr. of 1886 ed. lib. bdg. $20.00 (ISBN 0-8414-5740-9). Folcroft.
Mackay, Charles. Dictionary of Lowland Scotch. LC 68-17998. (Scottish.). 1968. Repr. of 1888 ed. $45.00x (ISBN 0-8103-3284-1). Gale.
Major, Alan. A New Dictionary of Kent Dialect. 1981. $39.00x (ISBN 0-905270-27-4, Pub. by Meresborough England). State Mutual Bk.
Ordman. The New Zealand Dictionary. 1339p. 1983. 9.95 (ISBN 0-86863-373-9, Pub. by Heinemann Pubs New Zealand). Intl Schol Bk Serv.
Warrack, A. Scots Dictionary. LC 65-16666. (Alabama Linguistic & Philological Ser: Vol. 6). 717p. 1965. $25.00 (ISBN 0-8173-0400-2). U of Ala Pr.
Wilkes, G. A. A Dictionary of Australian Colloquialisms. 1978. 28.00x (ISBN 0-424-00034-2, Pub. by Sydney U Pr). Intl Schol Bk Serv.
Wright, John, ed. The English Dialect Dictionary: Being the Complete Vocabulary of All Dialect Words...During the Last Two Hundred Years, 6 vols. 1970. Repr. of 1905 ed. Set. text ed. 525.00x (ISBN 0-19-580497-X). Oxford U Pr.

ENGLISH LANGUAGE-DICTIONARIES
see also English Language-Dictionaries, Juvenile;

also subdivisions Etymology; Glossaries, Vocabularies, etc.; Idioms, Corrections, Errors; Rime; Synonyms and Antonyms; Terms and Phrases under English Language
Abo, Takaji, et al. Marshallese-English Dictionary. LC 76-26156. (PALI Language Texts-Micronesia). 624p. (Marshallese & Eng.). 1976. pap. text ed. $12.50x (ISBN 0-8248-0457-0). UH Pr.
Allee, John G., ed. Webster's Dictionary for Everyday Use. 445p. 1971. pap. $3.25 (ISBN 0-06-463330-6, EH 330, EH). B&N NY.
Allen, F. Sturges. Allen's Synonyms & Antonyms. 3.95 (ISBN 0-06-463328-4, EH 328, EH). B&N NY.
Amankwaah, J. W. & Rytz, O., eds. Gonja-English Dictionary & Spelling Book. LC 79-303260. v, 273p. (Gonja & Eng.). 1977. write for info. Inst Afr Stu.
The American College Dictionary. tan buckram bdg. with index o.s.i. 7.95 (ISBN 0-394-40001-1); tan buckram bdg., without index 6.95 (ISBN 0-394-40002-X). Random.
American Heritage. The Word Book. LC 76-698. 1976. 3.95 (ISBN 0-395-24521-4). HM.
The American Heritage Desk Dictionary. 1981. 9.95 (ISBN 0-395-31256-6). HM.
The American Heritage Dictionary. rev. ed. 1983. pap. $4.95 (ISBN 0-440-10068-2). Dell.
The American Heritage Dictionary. rev. ed. 1983. pap. $9.95 (ISBN 0-440-50079-6, Dell Trade Pbks). Dell.
American Heritage Dictionary: College Edition. (Eng.). write for info. HM.
The American Heritage Dictionary of the English Language: New College Edition. LC 76-86995. (gr. 9 up). 1981. 12.95 (ISBN 0-395-20359-7); thumb-indexed 13.95 (ISBN 0-395-20360-0); large format ed. thumb-indexed 17.95 (ISBN 0-395-09066-0); pap. text ed. 1.20 user's guide (ISBN 0-395-20515-8). HM.
American Heritage Editors, ed. American Heritage School Dictionary. LC 72-75557. 1977. 9.95 (ISBN 0-395-24792-6). HM.
American Heritage Staff. Concise American Heritage Dictionary. LC 76-4047. 1980. 6.95 (ISBN 0-395-24522-2). HM.
Anderson, Olov B. A Companion Volume to R. H. Mathews' Chinese-English Dictionary. 2nd ed. LC 78-320299. 335p. (Chinese & Eng.). 1978. E7.50 (ISBN 9-144-15221-3) (ISBN 0-7007-0081-1). Curzon Pr.
Anglo-Latyshsko-Russkii Frazeologicheskii Slovar. 718p. (Eng. & Rus.). 1977. $3.25 (Pub. by Liesma). Four Continent.
Appel, L. Lexique des Fruits et Legumes. 133p. (Fr. & Eng.). Date not set. pap. $9.95 (ISBN 0-686-97410-7, M-9238). French & Eur.
Bailey, Nathan. Universal Etymological English Dictionary. 1969. Repr. of 1721 ed. $100.00 (ISBN 3-4870-2625-2). Adler.
Baker, W. M. Bell's Acrostic Dictionary. LC 77-141772. 1971. Repr. of 1927 ed. $30.00x (ISBN 0-8103-3379-1). Gale.
Ballard, Richard. Talking Dictionary. (Michigan Learning Modules Ser.: No. 21). 1978. write for info. (ISBN 0-914004-24-7). Ulrich.
Barnhart, Clarence. Dictionary of New English. 572p. (Eng.). 1973. $110.00. Colin.
Barnhart, Clarence L., ed. Scott, Foresman Advanced Dictionary. rev. ed. 1978. $19.95 (ISBN 0-385-14852-6). Doubleday.
--Scott, Foresman Intermediate Dictionary. (Illus.). 1978. $19.95 (ISBN 0-385-14853-4). Doubleday.
--Thorndike Barnhart Handy Dictionary. 1971. pap. $2.25 (ISBN 0-553-20012-7, 12839-6). Bantam.
Barnhart, Clarence L., et al. Second Barnhart Dictionary of New English. LC 79-6815. 1980. 19.95i (ISBN 0-06-010154-7, HarpT). Har-Row.

Beeching, Cyril L. A Dictionary of Eponyms. 2nd ed. 160p. 1983. $20.00 (ISBN 0-85157-329-0, Pub. by Bingley England). Shoe String.

Bell, Francis L. Tanga-English, English-Tanga Dictionary. LC 78-311012. xxx, 156p. (Tanga & Eng.). 1977. Aus.$3.00. Univ Syd Aust Lang.

Bennett, Archie, ed. New Illustrated Grosset Dictionary. LC 76-42144. (Illus.). (gr. k-5). 1977. pap. 6.95 (ISBN 0-448-14384-4, G&D). Putnam Pub Group.

Bennett, Roger G. Naturgeografisk ordbok: Engelsk-Norsk. LC 78-398859. 84p. (Eng. & Norwegian.). 1976. write for info. Berg Inst Sociol.

Benson, Morton. Englesko-srpskohrvatski Recnik. LC 79-343879. xiv, 669p. (Serbo-Croation & Eng.). 1978. write for info. Beogradski.

Bergflexner, Stuart, et al, eds. The Oxford American Dictionary. 832p. 1980. pap. $5.95 (ISBN 0-380-51052-9, 55897-1). Avon.

Bergquist, Sidney R., ed. New Webster's Dictionary of the English Language (Handy School & Office Edition) LC 75-15424. 1975. $4.95 (ISBN 0-8326-0033-4, 6501). Delair.

--New Webster's Dictionary of the English Language (Modern Desk Edition) LC 76-3282. (Illus.). 1976. $8.95 (ISBN 0-8326-0040-7, 6603). Delair.

Bernstein, Theodore M. Bernstein's Reverse Dictionary. LC 75-8283. 384p. 1975. $16.95 (ISBN 0-8129-0566-0). Times Bks.

Bevington, J. Macmillan Colour Dictionary. (Illus.). write for info. (ISBN 0-333-28859-9). Macmillan.

Bildwoerterbuch Deutsch-Englisch-Franzosisch. 941p. (Ger. , Eng. & Fr.). write for info. (ISBN 3-411-01830-5). Biblio Inst.

Blachere, Regis & Chouemi, Moustafa. Dictionnaire Arabe-Francais-Anglais, 12 vols. (Arabic, Fr. & Eng.). 1970. 650.00 F. Maison & Larose.

Borelli, A., et al. Dizionario inglese. (Eng.). L.18000.00. Ist Geo Agostini.

Bornstein, Harry & Saulnier, Karen L., eds. The Comprehensive Signed English Dictionary. LC 82-21044. (Illus.). x, 454p. 1983. $24.95 (ISBN 0-913580-81-3). Gallaudet Coll.

Bremner, John B. Words, Words, Words: A Dictionary for Writers & Others Who Care About Words. LC 80-256. 1980. $26.00x (ISBN 0-231-04492-5); pap. $10.95 (ISBN 0-231-04493-3). Columbia U Pr.

Brinton, Daniel G. Lenape-English Dictionary. LC 77-153000. iii, 77p. (Eng. & Lenape.). 1977. write for info. Waletittin.

--A Lenape-English Dictionary. LC 76-43670. 236p. (Eng. & Lenape.). 1979. write for info. (ISBN 0-404-15764-5). AMS Pr.

Brinton, Daniel G. & Anthony, Albert S., eds. A Lenape-English Dictionary. LC 76-43670. (Eng. & Lenape.). Repr. of 1888 ed. $22.50 (ISBN 0-404-15764-5). AMS Pr.

Bromberg, Murray, et al. Five Hundred & Four Absolutely Essential Words. rev. ed. LC 74-5052. 1975. pap. $4.95 (ISBN 0-8120-0525-2). Barron.

Brown, Charles P. Dictionary of Telugu & English: Explaining English Idioms & Phrases in Telugu, 2 vols. (Eng. & Telugu.). 1976. Repr. of 1958 ed. $195.00 (ISBN 0-518-19008-0). Ayer Co.

Bullokar, John. English Expositor: Teaching the Interpretation of the Hardest Words Used in Our Language. 1971. Repr. of 1616 ed. $32.00 (ISBN 3-4870-4070-0). Adler.

Burchfield, R. W. A Supplement to the Oxford English Dictionary, Volume 2 H-N. 1976. 110.00x (ISBN 0-19-861123-4). Oxford U Pr.

Burchfield, R. W., ed. Supplement to the Oxford English Dictionary Vol. 1: A-G. 1972. 110.00x (ISBN 0-19-861115-3). Oxford U Pr.

Burchfield, Robert W., ed. A Supplement to the Oxford English Dictionary, Vol. 3. 1982. 110.00x (ISBN 0-19-861124-2). Oxford U Pr.

Burridge, Shirley, ed. Oxford Elementary Learner's Dictionary of English. (Illus., Orig.). 1981. pap. text ed. 9.95x (ISBN 0-19-431253-4). Oxford U Pr.

Camden, William G. A Descriptive Dictionary: Bislama to English. LC 79-304384. xviii, 138p. (Eng. & Bislama.). 1977. write for info. (ISBN 0-9596774-0-2). Camden Aus.

Carver, D. J., et al, eds. Collins English Learner's Dictionary. 640p. 1974. $13.95x (ISBN 0-00-433111-7, Pub. by Collins ELT Scotland). State Mutual Bk.

Cawdrey, Robert. A Table Alphabeticall of English Wordes. LC 73-25889. (English Experience Ser.: No. 226). 132p. 1970. Repr. of 1604 ed. $11.50 (ISBN 90-221-0226-2). Walter J Johnson.

Chambers Mini Dictionary. 1983. pap. $3.95 (ISBN 0-686-40772-5, Pub by Salem Hse Ltd). Merrimack Pub Cir.

Chambers Twentieth Century Dictionary. 1983. $19.95 (ISBN 0-686-40766-0, Pub. by Michael Joseph). Merrimack Pub Cir.

The Christian Student Dictionary. (Illus.). 862p. 1982. text ed. $12.95 (ISBN 0-89084-172-1). Bob Jones Univ Pr.

Ciardi, John. A Browser's Dictionary. LC 79-1658. 464p. 1980. 17.26i (ISBN 0-06-010766-9, HarpT). Har-Row.

--A Second Browser's Dictionary: Native's Guide to the Unknown American Language. LC 82-48658. 420p. 1983. 16.30i (ISBN 0-06-015125-0, HarpT). Har-Row.

Cockeram, Henry. English Dictionary: An Interpreter of Hard English Words. 1970. Repr. of 1626 ed. $39.50 (ISBN 3-4870-2632-5). Adler.

Coles, E. An English Dictionary. Repr. of 1676 ed. $55.00 (ISBN 3-4870-4748-9). Adler.

Collin, P. H., ed. Harrap's Easy English Dictionary. (Eng.). write for info. (ISBN 0-245-53660-4); pap. write for info. (ISBN 0-245-53624-8). Harrap.

--Harrap's English Dictionary. 608p. (Eng.). write for info. (ISBN 0-245-53660-4); pap. write for info. (ISBN 0-245-53624-8). Harrap.

--Harrap's Two Thousand Word English Dictionary. (Illus.). vi, 271p. (Eng.). write for info. (ISBN 0-245-53834-8). Harrap.

Collins English Learner's Dictionary. 622p. (Eng.). write for info. (ISBN 91-24-25707-9). Esselte Studium.

Collison, R. L. Dictionaries of English & Foreign Languages. 2nd ed. 1971. 20.50x (ISBN 0-02-843110-3). Hafner.

Collocott, T. C., ed. Chambers' English Dictionary. (Quality Paperback: No. 166). 380p. 1965. pap. 2.95 (ISBN 0-8226-0166-4). Littlefield.

Cooper, W. R. An Archaic Dictionary. 59.95 (ISBN 0-87968-653-7). Gordon Pr.

Copperud, Roy H. Dicionario de Ingles Coloquial. (Eng.). write for info. Difel Editorial, S. A.

Coulson, J., et al, eds. The Oxford Illustrated Dictionary. 2nd rev. ed. 1975. 29.50x (ISBN 0-19-861118-8). Oxford U Pr.

Cowie, A. P. & Mackin, Ronald. Oxford Dictionary of Current Idiomatic English: Verbs with Prepositions & Particles, Vol. 1. 1975. 13.95x (ISBN 0-19-431145-7). Oxford U Pr.

Cronin. Vocabulary One Thousand. xi, 180p. (Eng.). Epap. 5.80. HarBraceJ.

Davidenko, R. A. An Explanatory Dictionary for Students of English. 664p. (Eng. & Rus.). 1977. $8.50 (Pub. by Ganatleba). Four Continent.

--An Explanatory Dictionary for Students of English. 664p. (Eng.). 1977. $8.50 (Pub by Ganatleba). Four Continent.

Davids, Lewis E. Instant Business Dictionary. LC 78-150232. 1970. $3.95 (ISBN 0-911744-07-X). Career Inst.

Davies, Thomas L. Supplementary English Glossary. LC 68-23468. 1968. Repr. of 1881 ed. $47.00x (ISBN 0-8103-3245-0). Gale.

Dels Prats, Alfonso T. Diccionario de Dificultades del Ingles. 368p. (Span. & Eng.). 1976. write for info. (ISBN 84-261-5814-5). Editorial Juventud.

Diccionario Corona Ingles. 9th ed. 720p. (Span.). 1982. 625.00 ptas (ISBN 84-241-1272-5). Everest.

Diccionario de modismos ingleses. (Span.). Arg.$27.60. Sopena.

The Dictionary Dictionary. (Eng.). 1967. $13.95 (ISBN 0-7715-1977-X). Gage.

Dictionary of American English. (Gem Reference Ser.). 1980. $2.95 (ISBN 0-529-05687-9, GR 13). Collins Pubs.

Dictionary of American Idioms Workbook, Vol. 2. 1984. pap. price not set (ISBN 0-8120-2515-6). Barron.

Dictionary of Contemporary English (DCE) 1344p. (Eng.). DM.33.50 (50810); DM.Wkbk. 6.80; DM.Cassette 19.00. Langenscheidt.

Dictionary of Space English. 80p. (Eng.). 1978. 18.00 F. Garnier.

Dictionary of the English Language. (Eng.). 1978. write for info. Belin.

Dictionnaire Anglais Chambers: Essential Dictionary. (Eng.). $10.50 (Dist. by Continental Bk Co). Lib. Fernand Nathan.

Dictionnaire Anglais Chambers: 20th Century Dictionary. (Eng.). $32.25. Lib. Fernand Nathan.

Drill, Douglas D. Doubtful Dictionary. Wilson-Fulkerson, Roberta, ed. (Illus.). 1979. pap. $6.95 (ISBN 0-89262-023-4). Career Pub.

Dubois Charlier, et al. Dictionnaire d'Anglais Niveau 1. (Fr.). 1975. write for info. Larousse.

Dubois-Charlier, F. Dictionnaire D'anglais. LC 77-559350. xvii, 868p. (Eng. & Fr.). 1975. 29.00 F (ISBN 2-03-040531-0); pap. $11.50 text ed. Larousse FR.

Dubois-Charlier, Francois, et al. Dictionnaire d'anglais. LC 77-559350. xvii, 868p. (Eng. & Fr.). 1975. write for info. Larousse.

Dunn, John A. A Practical Dictionary of the Coast Tsimshian Language. LC 79-321726. x, 155p. (Eng. & Tsimshian.). 1978. write for info. Natl Mus Can.

Dyche, Thomas. A New General English Dictionary. 1971. Repr. of 1723 ed. $114.25 (ISBN 3-4870-4398-X). Adler.

Eastman, P. D. Cat in the Hat Beginner Book Dictionary. LC 64-1157. (Illus.). (gr. k-6). 1964. $5.95 (ISBN 0-394-81009-0). Beginner.

Ehrlich, Eugene & Murphy, Daniel. Basic Vocabulary Builder. (McGraw-Hill Paperbacks). 192p. (Orig.). 1975. pap. 3.95 (ISBN 0-07-019105-0, SP). McGraw.

Ehrlich, Eugene, et al, eds. Oxford American Dictionary. 1980. 14.95 (ISBN 0-19-502795-7). Oxford U Pr.

Elementary Dictionary of English. 283p. (Eng.). DM.13.80 (50800). Langenscheidt-Longman.

English Dictionary. (Eng.). 1980. NT.$3.95. Reed Ltd.

English-English Dictionary. 640p. 14.00 (ISBN 0-87557-017-8, 017-8). Saphrograph.

Evans, Ivor H., ed. Brewer's Dictionary of Phrase & Fable. 1248p. 1982. $50.00x (ISBN 0-304-30706-8, Pub. by Cassell England). State Mutual Bk.

Everyday Dictionary. (Eng.). 1982. $12.95; pap. $7.95. Times Books.

Falconer, William. Universal Dictionary of the Marine. LC 72-87321. (Illus.). Repr. of 1780 ed. lib. bdg. 37.50x (ISBN 0-678-05655-2). Kelley.

Farmer, Johns. The Public School Word-Book. 1900. $30.00 (ISBN 0-8274-3224-0). R West.

Field, John. English Field-Names: A Dictionary. LC 76-148407. (Illus.). xxx, 120p. 1973. $25.00 (ISBN 0-8103-2010-X). Gale.

Fillenbaum, Samuel & Rapoport, Amnon. Structures in the Subjective Lexicon: An Experimental Approach to the Study of Semantic Fields. 1971. $46.00 (ISBN 0-12-256250-X). Acad Pr.

Finkenstaedt, Thomas. A Chronological English Dictionary. Listing 80,000 Words in Order of Their Earliest Known Occurrence. 1412p. 1970. 120.00x (ISBN 3-533-02076-2). Intl Pubns Serv.

Finnegan, Edward G., ed. New Webster's Dictionary of the English Language (College Edition) LC 75-18559. (Illus.). 1975. $14.95 (ISBN 0-8326-0035-0, 6602). Delair.

--New Webster's Dictionary (Vest Pocket Edition) LC 75-18560. 1976. pap. $1.75 (ISBN 0-8326-0036-9, 6401). Delair.

Fitzgerald, E. M., ed. Chambers Mini Dictionary. 1980. pap. 2.95 (ISBN 0-550-10701-0, Pub. by W. R. Chambers). Hippocrene Bks.

Fowler, H. W. A Dictionary of Modern English Usage. 2nd ed. 1983. pap. 8.95 (ISBN 0-19-281389-7, GB 725, GB). Oxford U Pr.

Fox, Charles El. Dictionary of Nggela. 271p. (Nggela.). 1955. $2.50. Anthro AucMus.

Frank, Roberta & Cameron, Angus, eds. A Plan for the Dictionary of Old English. LC 72-97152. (Toronto Old English Ser.). 1973. $35.00x (ISBN 0-8020-3303-2). U of Toronto Pr.

Franklin, K. J., et al. A Kewa Dictionary with Supplementary Grammatical & Anthropological Materials. LC 81-453278. (Illus.). 514p. (Kewa & Eng.). 1978. Aus.$16.00 (ISBN 0-85883-182-1). Linguistic Circle.

Funk And Wagnalls Editors. Funk & Wagnalls Standard College Dictionary. new updated ed. LC 72-13007. (Funk & W Bk.). 1632p. 1977. $9.95i (ISBN 0-308-10309-2); thumb indexed $10.95i (ISBN 0-308-10310-6). T Y Crowell.

Funk & Wagnalls Standard College Dictionary. 1978. Can.$12.95 (ISBN 0-88902-440-5); $14.95 (ISBN 0-88902-573-8). Fitzhenry.

Funk & Wagnalls Standard Desk Dictionary. rev. ed. (Illus.). 890p. 1980. $8.95 (ISBN 0-308-10352-1); thumb indexed $9.95 (ISBN 0-308-10353-X). T Y Crowell.

Fyle, Clifford N., compiled by. A Krio-English Dictionary. (Krio & Eng.). 1980. text ed. 65.00x (ISBN 0-19-864409-4). Oxford U Pr.

Garmonsway, G. N., ed. The Penquin English Dictionary. LC 80-460939. xiv, 842p. (Eng.). E5.95 (ISBN 0-7139-0199-3). Lane.

Gem English Learner's Dictionary. (Eng.). write for info. (ISBN 0-671-42047-X). S&S.

Goldstein, Sam. The Birdicide of Cock Robin, & Other Murderous Words Ending in Cide. (Weirdictionaries Ser.). (Illus.). 68p. (Orig.). 1982. pap. $3.95 cancelled (ISBN 0-938338-04-8). Winds World Pr.

Great Encyclopedic Dictionary. (Eng.). 1966. Can.$29.95 (ISBN 0-88850-023-8). Reader's Digest.

Gregorich, Barbara. Dictionary Skills. (Horizons II Ser.). (Illus.). 24p. (gr. 3-4). 1980. wkbk. $2.50 (ISBN 0-89403-605-X). EDC.

The Grosset Webster Dictionary. (Illus.). 672p. 1981. pap. 6.95 (ISBN 0-686-81504-1, G&D). Putnam Pub Group.

Guinagh, Kevin, tr. & compiled by. Dictionary of Foreign Phrases & Abbreviations. 3rd ed. 288p. 1982. $28.00 (ISBN 0-8242-0675-4). Wilson.

Gurainik, David B., ed. Webster's New World Dictionary: Student's Edition. 1976. $17.28 (ISBN 0-13-944652-4). P-H.

Guralnik, David. Webster's New World Dictionary of the American Language. 704p. 1982. pap. $3.50 (ISBN 0-446-31192-8). Warner Bks.

Guralnik, David B. Webster's New World Dictionary of the American Language. 704p. 1983. pap. $8.95 (ISBN 0-446-37914-X). Warner Bks.

Guralnik, David B., ed. Webster's New World Dictionary for Young Readers: New Rev. Color Edition. LC 78-59178. (Illus.). (gr. 4-9). $9.95 (ISBN 0-529-05625-9, 103N). Collins Pubs.

--Webster's New World Dictionary: Modern Desk Edition. LC 79-52089. (Illus.). 1979. gold-stamped hardcovers $4.95 (ISBN 0-529-05333-0, 166N); thumb indexed $5.95 (ISBN 0-529-05340-3, 166N-I). Collins Pubs.

--Webster's New World Dictionary: Second College Edition, Revised School Printing. (Eng.). $10.98; pap. $4.32. P-H.

--Webster's New World Dictionary: Student Edition. (Eng.). 1983. $10.59; pap. $4.32. P-H.

Haensch, Guenther. Diccionario Ingles. 1012p. (Eng. & Span.). 1981. 950.00 ptas (ISBN 84-254-1156-4). Herder SA.

Hargreaves, Roger. Mr. Men Picture Dictionary. (Mr. Men Bks.). (Illus.). 256p. (ps-1). Date not set. pap. 7.95 (ISBN 0-8431-1300-6). Price Stern.

Hawkins, ed. Oxford Paperback Dictionary. (Eng.). Epap. 2.25. Oxford U Pr.

Hawkins, Joyce M., compiled by. The Oxford Minidictionary. 1982. pap. 3.95 (ISBN 0-19-861138-2). Oxford U Pr.

Heimbach, Ernest E., compiled by. White-Hmong English Dictionary. (Linguistic Ser.: No. IV). 497p. 1979. Repr. of 1969 ed. $6.50 (ISBN 0-87727-075-9, DP 75). Cornell SE Asia.

Hill, Robert, ed. Dictionary of Difficult Words. 1959. 5.00 (ISBN 0-8022-0722-7). Philos Lib.

Hill, Robert H. Dictionary of Difficult Words. 1975. pap. 3.95 (ISBN 0-451-11803-0, AE1803, Sig). NAL.

Holm, John A. & Shilling, Alison W. The Dictionary of Bahamian English. LC 82-83045. 270p. 1982. 42.00 (ISBN 0-936368-03-9). Lexik Hse.

Holt Staff. Holt Intermediate Dictionary of American English. (gr. 4-9). 1967. text ed. 7.92 (ISBN 0-03-067320-8); tchrs' manual incl. regional pronunciation record. 2.28 (ISBN 0-03-060406-0). HR&W.

--Winston Dictionary for Schools. (gr. 5-9). 1967. text ed. 4.84 (ISBN 0-03-063485-7); text ed. 5.36 indexed (ISBN 0-03-065960-4). HR&W.

Hornberger, Esteban S. & Hornberger, H. N. Diccionario Trilingue, 3 vols. LC 79-102496. (Eng., Quechua, & Span.). 1978. write for info. LCA.

Hornby, A. S. Oxford Advanced Learner's Dictionary of Current English. 3rd ed. (Illus.). 1974. text ed. 14.95x (ISBN 0-19-431101-5). Oxford U Pr.

--Oxford Student's Dictionary of American English. (Illus.). 1983. pap. 11.95 (ISBN 0-19-431140-6). Oxford U Pr.

Hornby, A. S. & Parnwell, E. C. The Oxford English-Reader's Dictionary. 638p. (Eng.). DM.18.80 (49003). Langenscheidt.

Hornby, A. S. & Parnwell, E. C., eds. The Progressive English Dictionary. 2nd ed. 1972. pap. 2.95x (ISBN 0-19-431120-1). Oxford U Pr.

Hornby, A. S., et al. Oxford student's dictionary of Current English. LC 78-323797. v, 774p. 1978. write for info. (ISBN 0-19-431114-7). Oxford U Pr.

Hornby, Albert S. & Parnwell, E. C., eds. English-Reader's Dictionary. 2nd ed. 1969. pap. 5.95x (ISBN 0-19-431116-3). Oxford U Pr.

The Houghton Mifflin Canadian Dictionary of the English Language. (Eng.). 1980. $13.95 (ISBN 0-395-29653-6); $16.95 (ISBN 0-395-29654-4). HM.

Hudson, Kenneth. The Dictionary of Even More Diseased English. 320p. (Eng.). 1983. E12.95 (ISBN 0-333-34170-8). Macmillan.

Illustrated Heritage Dictionary & Information Book. 1977. 34.95 (ISBN 0-395-25441-8). HM.

Institute for Language Study. Vest Pocket English. LC 58-59519. (Illus.). 188p. 1979. pap. $2.95 (ISBN 0-06-464908-3, BN 4908, BN). B&N NY.

The Intermediate Dictionary. (Eng.). 1972. $12.95 (ISBN 0-7715-1974-5). Gage Ed Pub.

Isaacs, Alan, ed. Multilingual Commercial Dictionary. 496p. 1980. $22.50 (ISBN 0-87196-425-2). Facts on File.

Johnson, Samuel. Dictionary of the English Language, 2 Vols. facsimile ed. LC 74-181906. Repr. of 1755 ed. $100.00 (ISBN 0-404-09840-1). AMS Pr.

--A Dictionary of the English Language. facsimile ed. LC 79-14941. (Illus.). 2320p. 1980. Repr. of 1755 ed. $95.00 (ISBN 0-405-12414-7). Ayer Co.

--Dictionary of the English Language, 2 vols. 1978. Set. $220.00x (ISBN 0-86685-125-9). Intl Bk Ctr.

--A Dictionary of the English Language, 2 vols. facsimile ed. 2285p. (Eng.). Repr. $220.00 set (125-9). Intl Bk Ctr.

Johnstone, Thomas M. Harsusi Lexicon & English-Harsusi Word-list. LC 77-364070. xxviii, 181p. (Harsusi & Eng.). 1977. E13.00 (ISBN 0-19-713580-3). Oxford U Pr.

Jones, Daniel, ed. Everyman's English Pronouncing Dictionary: Completely Revised. (Everyman's Reference Library Ser.). 592p. 1981. Repr. of 1977 ed. $13.50 (ISBN 0-460-03029-9, Pub. by J. M. Dent England). Biblio Dist.

Jong, F. J. Economisch Woorden Boek: Engels-Frans-Duits-Nederlands. 685p. (Eng., Fr., Ger. & Dutch.). 1980. $75.00 (ISBN 90-247-2243-8, M9474). French & Eur.

Kennedy, John. A Stem Dictionary of the English Language. 1890. 30.00 (ISBN 0-8274-3506-1). R West.

Kersey, J. A New English Dictionary. Repr. of 1702 ed. $38.00 (ISBN 3-4870-5349-7). Adler.

Kettridge, J. O. French for English Idioms & Figurative Phrases. (Fr. & Eng.). 1966. Repr. of 1940 ed. 16.00 (ISBN 0-7100-1669-7). Routledge & Kegan.

Kirkeby, Willy. Norsk-Engelsk Ordbok. 3rd ed. LC 79-374954. 514p. (Eng. & Norwegian.). 1978. Kr.55.00 (ISBN 8-2573-0006-3). Kunnskapsforlaget.

Kirkpatrick, E. M., ed. Chambers Universal Learners' Dictionary. 928p. 1980. $25.00x (ISBN 0-550-10632-4, Pub. by W & R Chambers Scotland). State Mutual Bk.

Kirkpatrick, E. M., et al, eds. Chambers Second Learners' Dictionary. LC 78-325064. viii, 376p. (Eng.). 1978. E1.50 (ISBN 0-550-10631-6). W & R Chambers.

Klatt, E. & Klatt, G. Langenscheidts Taschenwoerterbuch Englisch: Teil II, Deutsch-Englisch. 639p. (Ger. & Eng.). DM.16.80 (10126). Langenscheidt.

Klatt, E. & Roy, D. Langenscheidts Taschenwoerterbuch Englisch: Teil I, Englisch-Deutsch. 640p. (Eng. & Ger.). DM.16.80 (10120). Langenscheidt.

Klatt, E., et al. Langenscheidts Taschenwoerterbuch Englisch, 2 vols. in 1. (Eng. & Ger.). DM.23.80 (11121). Langenscheidt.

Kobylkova, Andela. Anglicko-Cesky Lekarsky Slovnik. LC 76-509268. 227p. (Eng. & Czech.). 1975. 10.50 Kcs. SNTC.

Kriel, T. Popular Northern Sotho Dictionary. 2nd ed. LC 77-363921. 342p. (Eng. & Sotho.). 1976. write for info. (ISBN 0-627-00932-8). Van Schaik.

Laffal, Julius. Concept Dictionary of English. LC 72-97927. 1973. text ed. 16.95 (ISBN 0-686-77072-2). Gallery Pr.

Laird, Charles. Webster's New World Thesaurus. 544p. 1982. pap. $2.95 (ISBN 0-446-31203-7). Warner Bks.

Laird, Charlton. Webster's New World Thesaurus. (Eng.). $12.93; pap. $8.94. P-H.

Lambdin, William. Doublespeak Dictionary. 295p. 1981. pap. 2.95 (ISBN 0-523-41194-4). Pinnacle Bks.

Landau, Sidney & Bogus, Ronald. Webster Illustrated Contemporary Dictionary. LC 82-45499. 1024p. 1982. $12.95 (ISBN 0-385-18306-2). Doubleday.

Landau, Sidney & Bogus, Ronald, eds. Doubleday Dictionary: For Home, School & Office. LC 74-3543. 936p. 1975. $9.95 (ISBN 0-385-04099-7); thumb-indexed $10.95 (ISBN 0-385-03368-0). Doubleday.

--Doubleday Roget's Thesaurus in Dictionary Form. LC 76-7696. 564p. 1977. $9.95 (ISBN 0-385-01236-5); thumb-indexed $11.95 (ISBN 0-385-12379-5). Doubleday.

Langenscheidt's Lilliput Little Webster Dictionary. 640p. 1972. $1.50 (ISBN 0-685-31362-X). Am Map.

Langenscheidt's Universal Webster Dictionary. 416p. 1972. $2.95 (ISBN 0-685-31338-7). Am Map.

Langenscheidts Universal-Woerterbuch Englisch. 560p. (Eng. & Ger.). DM.6.80 (18121). Langenscheidt.

Lass, Abranam & Lass, Betty. Dictionary of Pronunciation. LC 75-36252. 356p. 1976. $15.95 (ISBN 0-8129-0614-4). Times Bks.

Lawrence, Erma. Haida Dictionary. Edenso, Christine & Cogo, Robert, eds. LC 78-101871. 464p. (Eng. & Haida.). 1977. write for info. Society for the Preservation of Haida Language & Literature.

Laycock, Donald C. The Complete Enochian Dictionary. LC 80-476863. 272p. (Eng. & Enochian.). 1978. write for info. (ISBN 0-905919-01-7). Askin Pub.

Lee, W. R. Study Dictionary of Social English. Newson, B., ed. (Pergamon Institute of English Dictionaries Ser.). 160p. 1983. $14.95 (ISBN 0-08-024561-7); pap. $7.50 (ISBN 0-08-024560-9). Pergamon.

Leland, Louis S. Kiwi: Yankee Dictionary. 115p. 1980. pap. $5.95 (ISBN 0-86868-001-X). Bradt Ent.

Lilliput Dictionary: Little Webster. 640p. (Eng.). $1.50 (124). Langenscheidt.

Lysaght, T. Material Towards the Compilation of a Concise Old Church Slavonic-English Dictionary. LC 79-322674. xiv, 472p. (Eng. & Slavic.). 1978. write for info. (ISBN 0-7055-0668-1). Victoria University Press.

Lysaght, T. A. Material Towards the Compilation of a Concise Old Church Slavonic-English Dictionary. LC 79-322674. xiv, 472p. (Slavic & Eng.). 1978. write for info. (ISBN 0-7055-0668-1). Price Milburn.

McAdam, E. L. & Milne, G., eds. Johnson's Dictionary: A Modern Selection. 480p. (Eng.). 1982. Epap. 3.95 (ISBN 0-333-32984-8). Macmillan London.

The Macmillan Contemporary Dictionary. (Illus.). 1979. pap. 6.95 (ISBN 0-686-65754-3). Macmillan.

Macmillan Dictionary. (Illus., Eng.). write for info. Macmillan London.

Macmillan Dictionary for Children. LC 81-13651. 756p. 1982. 12.95 (ISBN 0-02-578790-X). Macmillan.

The Macmillan New Dictionary. (Illus.). 1979. pap. 6.95 (ISBN 0-686-67747-1, Collier). Macmillan.

Macmillan Pub. Co. Macmillan Dictionary. 1973. 8.40 (ISBN 0-02-195000-8). Macmillan.

--Macmillan School Dictionary. 1974. 7.00 (ISBN 0-02-195050-4). Macmillan.

Macmillan School Dictionary. (Illus., Eng.). 1981. write for info. Macmillan London.

Macmillan School Dictonary. (Illus., Eng.). 1981. write for info. Macmillan London.

Macmillan Very First Dictionary: A Magic World of Words. LC 82-22901. (Illus.). 280p. (ps-2). 1983. 10.95 (ISBN 0-02-761730-0). Macmillan.

Manser, M. H., ed. Pocket Thesaurus of English Words. 336p. (Eng.). Epap. 1.25 (ISBN 0-600-38779-8). Hamlyn-Amer.

--Thesaurus of English Words. 224p. (Eng.). E5.00 (ISBN 0-600-33213-6). Hamlyn-Amer.

Maurais, J. Lexique des Epices et Assaisonnements: Anglais-Francais. 73p. (Eng. & Fr.). 1979. pap. $5.95 (ISBN 0-7754-2593-1, M-9236). French & Eur.

Mayhew, A. I. & Skeat, Walter W. Concise Dictionary of Middle English from A.D. 1150 to 1580. LC 78-3583. xv, 272p. (Eng.). 1978. $35.00 (ISBN 0-8482-4963-1). Norwood Edns.

Menon, K. P. A Dictionary of Kathakali. LC 80-903797. (Illus.). vi, 80p. (Eng.). 1979. Rs.45.00 (Orient Longman). South Asia Bks.

Merriam Company, ed. Webster's New Ideal Dictionary. (Illus.). 1978. 6.95 (ISBN 0-87779-249-6). Merriam-Webster Inc.

--Webster's Third New International Dictionary, Unabridged: The Great Library of the English Language. Incl. Regular-Paper Style. blue sturdite 69.95 (ISBN 0-87779-201-1); Tan Imperial Buckram. deluxe binding 79.95 (ISBN 0-87779-206-2). (Illus.). 2728p. (Sprinkled edges, indexed). 1981. Merriam-Webster Inc.

Merriam Webster Dictionary. 1981. pap. 8.95 (ISBN 0-671-79073-0). PB.

The Merriam-Webster Dictionary. 1978. pap. 8.95 (ISBN 0-671-79073-0, Wallaby). PB.

The Merriam-Webster Dictionary for Large Print Users. (General Ser.). 1977. lib. bdg. $29.50 (ISBN 0-8161-6459-2, Large Print Bks). G K Hall.

Merriam-Webster Editorial Staff. Webster's Elementary Dictionary. (Illus.). (gr. 1-6). 1980. 9.95 (ISBN 0-87779-475-8). Merriam-Webster Inc.

--Webster's Ninth New Collegiate Dictionary. 8th ed. 1568p. 1983. gray lexotone 15.95 (ISBN 0-87779-508-8); thumb-indexed red linen 14.95 (ISBN 0-87779-409-X); thumb-indexed brown skivertex 14.95 (ISBN 0-87779-509-6). Merriam-Webster Inc.

--Webster's School Dictionary. (Illus.). (gr. 8-12). 1980. 10.95 (ISBN 0-87779-280-1). Merriam-Webster Inc.

--Webster's Vest Pocket Dictionary. 380p. 1981. pap. $2.25 (ISBN 0-87779-190-2). Merriam-Webster Inc.

Merriam Webster Editorial Staff, ed. Six Thousand Words: A Supplement to Webster's Third New International Dictionary. 240p. 1976. 8.50 (ISBN 0-87779-007-8). Merriam-Webster Inc.

Merriam-Webster Editorial Staff, ed. Webster's Concise Family Dictionary. 848p. 1975. 7.95 (ISBN 0-87779-039-6). Merriam-Webster Inc.

Merriam Webster "Mod" Dictionary. 1981. pap. 3.50 (ISBN 0-671-47344-1). PB.

The Merriam-Webster Thesaurus. 1981. 7.95 (ISBN 0-671-79095-1, Wallaby). PB.

Messinger, Heinz & Ruedenberg, Werner, eds. Langenscheidts Handwoerterbuecher Englisch. (Eng.). DM.28.00 (ISBN 3-468-80012-6). Langenscheidt.

Meyer, George A. The Two Word Verb: A Dictionary of the Verb Preposition Phrases in American English. (Janua Linguarum Series Didactica: No. 19). 268p. 1975. text ed. 55.00x (ISBN 90-2793-323-5). Mouton.
Morehead, Philip D. & Morehead, Andrew T. The New American Webster Handy College Dictionary. 1981. pap. 2.50 (ISBN 0-451-12537-1). NAL.
Morris, William & Morris, Mary. Harper Dictionary of Contemporary Usage. LC 73-4112. 672p. 1975. 23.99i (ISBN 0-06-013062-8, HarpT). Har-Row.
Nelson-Webster Vest Pocket Dictionary. 1978. 0.95 (ISBN 0-8407-5637-2). Nelson.
Nelson's New Compact Webster's Dictionary. 1978. 2.45 (ISBN 0-8407-5633-X). Nelson.
New Century Vest-Pocket: Webster Dictionary. rev. ed. 304p. 1975. pap. 2.95 (ISBN 0-8329-1536-X). New Century.
New Oxford Illustrated Dictionary, 2 vols. (Illus.). 1920p. (Eng.). 1976. Aus.$99.95. Oxford U Pr.
New Webster's Dictionary. pap. $1.99 (ISBN 0-686-00475-2). Dennison.
The New Webster's Quick Reference Dictionary. 1981. pap. $1.95 (ISBN 0-8326-0051-2, 6604). Delair.
New World Dictionary Editors. Misspeller's Dictionary. 1983. write for info. (ISBN 0-671-46864-2). S&S.
New York Times. The New York Times Everyday Dictionary. Paikeday, Thomas M., ed. LC 81-84903. 832p. (Orig.). 1982. $12.95 (ISBN 0-8129-0910-0); pap. $7.95 (ISBN 0-8129-6318-0). Times Bks.
Newman, Paul. Sabon Kamus na Hausa Zuwa Turanci. LC 79-104420. xii, 151p. (Hausa & Eng.). 1977. write for info. (ISBN 0-19-575303-8). Oxford U Pr.
Nunberg, Geoffrey, ed. The American Heritage Dictionary. 1982. 13.95 (ISBN 0-686-81876-8). HM.
The Official Scrabble Player's Dictionary. (gr. 10 up). 1979. pap. 5.95 (ISBN 0-671-49517-8). PB.
Ogden, C. K., ed. The General Basic English Dictionary. 438p. 1970. Repr. of 1940 ed. 15.00x (ISBN 0-87471-362-5). Rowman.
Orsman, H. W., ed. Heinemann New Zealand Dictionary. 1339p. 1981. 13.50x (ISBN 0-86863-373-9, 00564). Heinemann Ed.
--Heinemann New Zealand Dictionary. LC 80-466872. ix, 1339p. (Eng.). 1979. write for info. (ISBN 0-86863-373-9). Heinemann Ed Bks.
The Oxford Dictionary for Writers & Editors. 1981. 12.95x (ISBN 0-19-212970-8). Oxford U Pr.
Oxford English Dictionary: Compact Edition, 2 vols. boxed set with magnifying glass 150.00 (ISBN 0-686-75482-4). Oxford U Pr.
Oxford English Dictionary: Compact Edition, 2 vols. compact ed. 16569p. 1971. 100.00 (ISBN 0-918414-08-3). Readex Bks.
Oxford Picture Dictionary. (Illus.). $4.00; charts $30.00; wkbk. $3.75; cassettes $14.95. Iaconi.
Oxford Picture Dictionary of American English. (Illus.). 95p. (Eng. & Fr.). 1978. pap. $5.50. Oxford U Pr.
Pacific College Dictionary. 936p. (Eng.). 1981. $19.00 (ISBN 9-97163-188-1). Pan Pacific Bk.
Pacific School Dictionary. 496p. (Eng.). 1979. $6.00 (ISBN 9-97163-023-0). Pan Pacific Bk.
Paikeday, Thomas. Compact Dictionary of Canadian English. 1976. pap. $4.25 (ISBN 0-03-923309-X). HRW.
Parnwell, E. C. Oxford Picture Dictionary of American English: English-Japanese Edition. (Illus., Eng. & Japanese.). 1978. pap. $8.80. Oxford U Pr.
--Oxford Picture Dictionary of American English. (Illus.). 1978. pap. 3.95 ea.; pap. monolingual ed. (ISBN 0-19-502332-3); pap. English-Spanish ed. (ISBN 0-19-502333-1); pap. french indexed ed. (ISBN 0-19-502334-X). Oxford U Pr.
Phythian, B. A., ed. A Concise Dictionary of Correct English. (Littlefield, Adams Quality Paperback Ser.: No. 349). 1979. pap. 5.50 (ISBN 0-8226-0349-7). Littlefield.
--Concise Dictionary of Correct English. 166p. 1979. 12.50x (ISBN 0-8476-6212-8). Rowman.
Pillai, T. R. English-Malayalam Dictionary. Chandrasekhara, M. S., ed. 904p. (Eng. & Malayalam.). 1980. write for info. DC Bks.
Pillai, T. Ramalingam. English-English-Malayalam Dictionary. Krishna, N. V., rev. by. 3333p. (Eng. & Malayalam.). 1976. write for info. DC Bks.
--English-English-Malayalam Dictionary. Octavo, M. S., ed. 1200p. (Eng. & Malayalam.). 1983. write for info. DC Bks.
Pineiro, J. Compendio de Dificultades de la Lengua Inglesa. 276p. (Eng. & Span.). 1978. 9695.00 ptas (ISBN 84-7153-367-7). Biblograf SP.
Pink, M. Alderton. A Dictionary of Correct English. 1977. Repr. of 1928 ed. lib. bdg. 22.50 (ISBN 0-8492-2055-6). R West.
Pitman, Isaac. Pitman Dictionary of English & Shorthand. (New Era Edition). 1974. 32.00 (ISBN 0-8224-0024-3). Pitman Learning.
Pitman Two Thousand Student Dictionary. 1980. NT.$4.50. Pitman Bks.
The Pocket Dictionary. LC 78-13455. 1978. pap. 1.95 (ISBN 0-395-26661-0). HM.
Pocket Dictionary of Synonyms & Antonyms. 1960. pap. 2.95 (ISBN 0-394-51933-7). Random.
Pocket English Dictionary. 320p. (Eng.). Epap. 1.00 . (ISBN 0-600-37091-7). Newnes Bks.
Pollmann, Friedrich. Macmillan Lensing New Basic Dictionary. LC 78-302181. (Illus.). viii, 247p. 1976. E1.00 (ISBN 0-333-21213-4). Macmillan London.
Poolman & Scott, Christopher. New Basic Dictionary. 256p. write for info. Macmillan London.
Powell, J. Quileute Dictionary, 10 vols. LC 79-307128. xvii, 519p. (Eng. & Quileute.). 1976. write for info. Univ Idaho.
Prizzi, Elaine & Hoffman, Jeanne. Diction Harry's Magical, Marvelous, Motivational Dictionary Kit. (gr. 3-6). 1982. pap. 9.95 (ISBN 0-8224-2252-2). Pitman Learning.
Proctor, Paul, ed. Longman Dictionary of Contemporary English. (Illus.). 1979. text ed. 14.95x (ISBN 0-582-52571-3); pap. text ed. 11.95x (ISBN 0-582-55608-2). Longman.
Quo, J. C. English-Chinese Dictionary Romanized. 323p. (Eng. & Chinese.). 1964. pap. $6.95 (ISBN 0-686-92269-7, M-9591). French & Eur.
The Random House College Dictionary. rev. ed. Date not set. thumb-indexed ed. incl. Pocket Thesaurus $14.95 (ISBN 0-394-52760-7); thumb-indexed ed. incl. Bad Speller's Dictionary $14.95 (ISBN 0-394-52762-3). Random.
The Random House College Dictionary. thumb-indexed ed. incl. pocket thesaurus $14.95 (ISBN 0-394-43600-8); deluxe ed. $14.95 thumb-indexed ed. incl. Bad Speller's Dictionary (ISBN 0-394-52762-3). Random.
The Random House Dictionary of the English Language. 1966. 49.95 (ISBN 0-394-47176-8). Random.
Random House, Inc. The Random House Dictionary: Concise Edition. 1980. 4.95 (ISBN 0-394-51200-6). Random.
Rauk, M. English-Estonian Dictionary for Schools. 444p. (Eng. & Estonian.). 1977. $3.95 (Pub. by Valgus). Four Continent.
Reece, Laurie. Dictionary of the Walbiri (Walpiri) Language of Central Australia. LC 76-370309. (Eng. & Walbiri.). 1975. Aus.$3.50. Univ Syd Aust Lang.
Reisner, Thomas A. A Dictionary of Superseded Accentuations in 18th Century English. (European University Studies: Series 14, Anglo-Saxon Language & Literature. Vol. 40). 171p. 1976. pap. write for info. (ISBN 3-261-01961-1). P Lang Pubs.
Ridout, Ronald, ed. Nelson ELT Pocket Dictionary. 352p. (Eng.). E1.75 (ISBN 0-17-555210-X). Nelson & Sons Group.
Riese, Alan W. & LaSalle, Herbert J. All About the Dictionary. (Orig.). (gr. 8-11). 1976. pap. text ed. $6.58 (ISBN 0-87720-330-X). AMSCO Sch.
The Right Word: A Concise Thesauras. LC 78-3461. (gr. 9 up). 1978. 3.95 (ISBN 0-395-26672-6). HM.
Ristic, Syetomir & Simic, Zivojin, eds. Englesko-srpskohrvatski Recnik. LC 76-523250. xxx, 807p. (Serbo-Croatian & Eng.). 1975. write for info. Prosveta.
Rogers, May. The Waverley Dictionary. 75.00 (ISBN 0-8490-1279-1). Gordon Pr.
Roget's Thesaurus. 1981. pap. $2.95 (ISBN 0-671-43675-9). PB.
Rott, N. V., ed. Malaiziisko-Russko-Angliiskii Slovar. 400p. (Malay, Rus. & Eng.). 1977. $7.75 (Pub. by Russkii Iazyk). Four Continent.
Ruffner, James, et al, eds. Eponyms Dictionaries Index: A Compilation of Terms Based on Names of Actual or Legendary Persons. LC 76-20341. 1977. $104.00x (ISBN 0-8103-0688-3). Gale.
Ruhland, Jean. Dictionnaire Trilingue. 220p. (Fr., Ger. & Eng.). 1977. 60.00 F. Ruhland.
Senior, H. W., ed. A Vocabulary of the Limbu Language of Eastern Nepal. LC 78-908311. 86p. (Eng. & Limbu.). 1977. Repr. of 1908 ed. Rs.65.00. Radha.
Shaw, Harry. Dictionary of Problem Words & Expressions. 1975. 24.95 (ISBN 0-07-056489-2, P&RB). McGraw.
Shaw, John R. & Shaw, Janet. The New Horizon Ladder Dictionary of the English Language for Young Readers. rev. ed. (Illus.). 686p. 1973. pap. 2.95 (ISBN 0-451-12421-9, Sig). NAL.
Shorter Oxford English Dictionary. 1973. 125.00 (ISBN 0-19-861126-9); 2 vols. indexed ed. 135.00 (ISBN 0-19-861127-7). Oxford U Pr.
Six Thousand Words: Supplement to Webster's Third New International Dictionary. (Eng.). 1976. $8.50 (ISBN 0-87779-007-8, 72422). Merriam.
Stanislawski, Jan. Wielki Slownik Polsko-Angielski, 2 vols. LC 79-338334. (Pol. & Eng.). 1978. 1600.00 Zl. Wiedza Powszechna.
Stein, Jess, ed. The Random House Dictionary. (Orig.). 1981. pap. $2.25 (ISBN 0-345-29096-8). Ballantine.
--Student's Webster Dictionary. 48p. 1981. pap. $1.95 (ISBN 0-89531-021-X, 0114-72). Sharon Pubns.
Stratmann, Franz H. A Supplement of the Dictionary of the English Language of the XII, XIII, XIV, & XV Centuries. 3rd ed. 93p. 1980. Repr. of 1881 ed. lib. bdg. 22.50 (ISBN 0-8492-8111-3). R West.
Swannell, Julia, ed. Little Oxford Dictionary. 5th ed. 1980. 8.95 (ISBN 0-19-861128-5). Oxford U Pr.
Sykes, J. B., ed. The Concise Oxford Dictionary of Current English. 7th ed. 1982. 19.95 (ISBN 0-19-861131-5); Thumb-Indexed 24.95 (ISBN 0-19-861132-3). Oxford U Pr.
--The Pocket Oxford Dictionary of Current English. 6th ed. 1978. 12.95 (ISBN 0-19-861129-3). Oxford U Pr.
Tharp, James A. A Rhade-English Dictionary with English-Rhade Finder List. LC 81-157706. ix, 271p. (Eng. & Rade.). 1980. write for info. (ISBN 0-85883-217-8). Linguistic Circle.
Tu Dien Mien Dich Hoc. LC 79-984056. (Eng. , Fr. & Vietnamese.). 1976. write for info. Y Hoc.
Turvey, B., compiled by. Kwanyama-English Dictionary. LC 78-306064. xvii, 162p. (Kuanyama & Eng.). 1977. write for info. (ISBN 0-85494-315-3). Witwatersrand.
Universal Webster Dictionary. 560p. (Eng.). $2.95 (099). Langenscheidt.
University of the State of New York, State Education Department. Iontenwennaweienstahkhwa. LC 77-624515. xi, 93p. (Eng. & Mohawk.). 1977. write for info. State U NY Pr.
Urdang, Laurence, ed. The New York Times Everyday Reader's Dictionary of Misunderstood, Misused, Mispronounced Words. LC 74-184644. 196p. 1972. pap. $7.95 (1975) (ISBN 0-8129-0232-7); pap. $4.95 (ISBN 0-8129-6244-3). Times Bks.
Urdang, Lawrence & Hoequist, Charles, Jr., eds. Ologies & Isms: A Thematic Dictionary. 2nd ed. 365p. 1981. $72.00x (ISBN 0-8103-1055-4). Gale.
Vest Pocket Webster Dictionary. rev. ed. 304p. pap. $2.95 (ISBN 0-8329-1536-X). New Century.
Viljoen, Johannes J. Ndonga, Afrikaans, English: Dreitalige Woordeboek. LC 76-479622. 89p. (Ndonga, Afrikaans & Eng.). 1975. write for info. (ISBN 0-627-00328-1). Van Schaik.
Waldhorn, Arthur, ed. Concise Dictionary of American Language. 1956. 4.50 (ISBN 0-8022-1793-1). Philos Lib.
Warner Educational Services, ed. The Super Dictionary. LC 78-55453. (Illus.). 1978. 9.95 (ISBN 0-03-043756-3). HR&W.
Warrack, A. Scots Dictionary. LC 65-16666. (Alabama Linguistic & Philological Ser: Vol. 6). 717p. 1965. $25.00 (ISBN 0-8173-0400-2). U of Ala Pr.
Webster, Noah. American Dictionary of the English Language. facsimile ed. (Facsimile Reprint). 1967. Repr. of 1828 ed. lib. bdg. $30.00 (ISBN 0-912498-03-X). Found Am Christ.
--An American Dictionary of the English Language: To Which Are Prefixed, an Introductory Dissertation of the Origin, History & Connection of the Language of Western Asia & Europe & A...Grammar of the English Language, 2 Vols. LC 77-117409. Repr. of 1828 ed. Set. 80.00 (ISBN 0-384-66333-8); Set. deluxe ed. 190.00 deluxe ed. (ISBN 0-384-66336-2). Johnson Repr.
Webster's Concise Family Dictionary. 1975. $6.95 (ISBN 0-87779-039-6, 72423). Merriam.
Webster's Dictionary of Synonyms-Forty-One. (Eng.). 1978. $10.95 (ISBN 0-87779-241-0, 72410). Merriam.
Webster's New Collegiate Dictionary. (Eng.). 1981. $14.95 (ISBN 0-87779-409-X, 72407). Merriam.
Webster's New Collegiate Dictionary. (Eng.). 1981. $13.95 (ISBN 0-87779-408-1, 72420). Merriam.
Webster's New Compact Dictionary. 1979. 2.95 (ISBN 0-8407-4081-6). Nelson.
Webster's New Twentieth Century Dictionary. unabridged. 2nd ed. (Illus.). 1979. deluxe color ed., thumb indexed $59.95 (ISBN 0-529-04852-3, 86N-I). Collins Pubs.
Webster's New World Dictionary. 1983. $16.95 (ISBN 0-671-47035-3). S&S.
Webster's New World Dictionary. 2nd ed. 1728p. $16.95 (ISBN 0-671-47035-3). S&S.
Webster's New World Dictionary: Basic School Edition. 3rd ed. (Eng.). 1983. $10.98. P-H.

Webster's New World Dictionary: Compact School & Office Edition. LC 76-58966. 1977. $3.49 (ISBN 0-529-05344-6, 134R). Collins Pubs.

Webster's New World Dictionary: Compact School & Office Edition. (Eng.). $3.93. P-H.

Webster's New World Dictionary of the American Language. second concise ed. LC 79-50954. 1979. $8.95 (ISBN 0-529-05267-9, 83N); thumb-indexed $9.95 (ISBN 0-529-05268-7, 83N-I); pap. $4.95 (ISBN 0-529-05281-4, M37ON). Collins Pubs.

Webster's New World Dictionary: Second College Ed. (Illus.). deluxe ed. $18.95 (ISBN 0-529-05328-4, 65B-I). Collins Pubs.

Webster's New World Dictionary: Students Edition. LC 76-4634. 1976. $9.95 (ISBN 0-529-05375-6, 79). Collins Pubs.

Webster's New World Handy Pocket Dictionary. LC 76-48828. 1977. with slip-on vinyl jacket $1.95 (ISBN 0-529-05323-3, 171N); prepack of 20 $39.00 (ISBN 0-529-05335-7, 171NP). Collins Pubs.

Webster's New World Quick Reference Dictionary. LC 70-147261. 1977. $1.00 (ISBN 0-529-03091-8, 172); prepack of 20 $20.00 (ISBN 0-529-05336-5, 172P). Collins Pubs.

Webster's New World Vest Pocket Dictionary. LC 76-48830. 1977. imitation lea. $0.99 (ISBN 0-529-04686-5, 183N); 30-copy prepack $26.70 (ISBN 0-529-04804-3, 183NP). Collins Pubs.

Webster's School Thesaurus. (Eng.). 1978. $8.95 (ISBN 0-87779-178-3, 72435). Merriam.

Websters Seventh New Collegiate Dictionary. (Eng.). 1976. $16.95 (ISBN 0-87779-314-X, 72406). Merriam.

Webster's Super New School & Office Dictionary. 1978. pap. $2.50 (ISBN 0-449-23249-2, Crest). Fawcett.

Webster's Third New International Dictionary. (Illus.). 1981. $69.65 (ISBN 0-87779-201-1, 72448). Merriam.

West, Michael P. & Kingdon, Roger. An International Reader's Dictionary. 2nd ed. LC 79-104746. x, 401p. (Eng.). 1978. write for info. (ISBN 0-582-52566-7). Longman England.

Wheatley, Henry B. A Dictionary of Reduplicated Words in the English Language. LC 75-22169. 1975. Repr. of 1866 ed. lib. bdg. $15.00 (ISBN 0-8414-9407-X). Folcroft.

Wijewardena, Hema. Kalamanakarana Paribhasika Sabda Sangrahaya. LC 79-904454. viii, 496p. (Eng. & Sinhalese.). 1978. Rs.27.00. Dewan Bahasa.

Williams, Edwin B., ed. The Scribner-Bantam English Dictionary. 1979. pap. $2.25 (ISBN 0-553-13217-2, B14408-1). Bantam.

The Winston Canadian Dictionary for Schools. 1965. $8.10 (ISBN 0-03-923504-1); pap. $4.50 (ISBN 0-03-923312-X). HRW.

The Winston Dictionary of Canadian English. 1969. $11.14 (ISBN 0-03-923512-2). HRW.

The Winston Dictionary of Canadian English. 1975. $8.91 (ISBN 0-03-923516-5). HRW.

Witty, F. R. Pacific Junior Dictionary. 352p. (Eng.). 1975. $5.40 (ISBN 9-97163-001-X). Pan Pacific Bk.

Witty, F. R., ed. Nelson Canadian Elementary School Dictionary. LC 77-365319. 252p. 1975. Can.$3.00 (ISBN 0-17-600410-6). Nelson & Sons Group.

World Pub. Co. Prentice-Hall Students Edition of the Concise Webster's New World Dictionary of the American Language. 1971. 7.80 (ISBN 0-13-944561-7). P-H.

Wright, Peter. Language of British Industry. 207p. 1974. text ed. $20.00x (ISBN 0-333-15359-6). Verry.

Wurm, Stefan A. & Wilson, Basil. English Finderlist of Reconstructions in Austronesian Languages. LC 79-342769. xxxii, 246p. (Proto-Austronesian & Eng.). 1975. write for info. (ISBN 0-85883-129-5). Linguistic Circle.

Wyld, Henry C., ed. The Universal Dictionary of the English Langauge. rev. ed. 1447p. 1978. 45.00 (ISBN 0-7100-2333-2). Routledge & Kegan.

Wynne, R. C. English-Mbukusha dictionary. LC 80-487422. xxxii, 615p. (Eng. & Mbukusha.). 1980. E24.00 (ISBN 0-86127-203-X). Avebury Pub Co.

Wynne, Ronald C. English-Mbukushu Dictionary. LC 80-487422. xxxii, 615p. (Mbukushu & Eng.). 1980. E24.00 (ISBN 0-86127-203-X). Avebury Pub Co.

Zvidadze, Givi. A Dictionary of Contemporary English. 400p. 1983. text ed. $27.00x (ISBN 0-686-89414-6). Humanities.

ENGLISH LANGUAGE–DICTIONARIES–HISTORY AND CRITICISM

see English Language–Lexicography

ENGLISH LANGUAGE–DICTIONARIES–AFRIKAANS

Coetzee, A. African-English, English-African Dictionary. (African & Eng.). $22.50 (ISBN 0-87559-000-4); thumb indexed $27.50 (ISBN 0-87559-001-2). Shalom.

Kritzinger, M. S. Afrikaans-English, English-Afrikaans Dictionary. 12th, rev., enl. ed. (Afrikaans & Eng.). $60.00 (ISBN 0-627-01082-2). Heinman.

ENGLISH LANGUAGE–DICTIONARIES–ALBANIAN

Drizari, Nelo. Albanian-English, English-Albanian Dictionary. LC 57-9330. (Albanian & Eng.). $20.00 (ISBN 0-8044-0130-6). Ungar.

Kici, Gasper. Albanian-English Dictionary. (Albanian & Eng.). 1976. $15.00 (ISBN 0-686-17904-8). G Kici.

Kici, Gasper & Aliko, Hysni. English-Albanian Dictionary. (Eng. & Albanian.). 1969. $15.00 (ISBN 0-686-04914-4). G Kici.

ENGLISH LANGUAGE–DICTIONARIES–ALEUT

Lee, Charles A. Aleutian Indian & English Dictionary. facsimile ed. 23p. (Aleut.). Repr. of 1896 ed. pap. $9.95 (ISBN 0-8466-0101-X, SJS101). Shorey.

ENGLISH LANGUAGE–DICTIONARIES–ANGLO-SAXON

Bosworth, Joseph. A Compendious Anglo-Saxon & English Dictionary. 1979. Repr. of 1860 ed. lib. bdg. $30.00 (ISBN 0-89341-478-6). Longwood Pr.

Nowell, L. Vocabularium Saxonicum. Marckwardt, A., ed. (Lat.). Repr. of 1952 ed. 15.00 (ISBN 0-527-67800-7). Kraus Repr.

Sweet, Henry. Student's Dictionary of Anglo-Saxon. (Anglo-Saxon.). 1896. $27.50x (ISBN 0-19-863107-3). Oxford U Pr.

ENGLISH LANGUAGE–DICTIONARIES–ARABIC

Abcarius, J. John. An English-Arabic Reader's Dictionary. 1974. $18.00x (ISBN 0-86685-063-5). Intl Bk Ctr.

Abcarius, John. An English-Arabic Readers' Dictionary. 700p. (Arabic & Eng.). $18.00 (063-5). Intl Bk. Ctr.

Abdeen, Adnan. English-Arabic Dictionary for Accounting & Finance. LC 79-41213. (Eng. & Arabic.). 1981. $23.95x (ISBN 0-471-27673-1, Pub. by Wiley-Interscience). Wiley.

--English-Arabic Dictionary of Accounting & Finance. 1981. $30.00x (ISBN 0-86685-275-1). Intl Bk Ctr.

Arabic-English, English-Arabic Student's Dictionary, 2 vols. (Illus., Arabic & Eng.). Set. $50.00 (ISBN 2-7214-2879-9). Heinman.

Arabic Pocket Dictionary. (Arabic & Eng.). 10.00 (ISBN 0-685-11992-0). Heinman.

Assaran, Hassan. Arabic-English Dictionary of Basic Scientific & Technical Terms: "Al Mustalah". 1967. $20.00x (ISBN 0-86685-299-9). Intl Bk Ctr.

Ba'Alabaki, Munir. English-Arabic Pocket Dictionary: Al-Mawrid Al Quareb. (Eng. & Arabic.). 1980. pap. $5.95x (ISBN 0-86685-062-7). Intl Bk Ctr.

Ba'Albaki, Munir. English-Arabic Dictionary: Al-Mawrid. 1982. 48.00x (ISBN 0-86685-059-7). Intl Bk Ctr.

--English-Arabic Dictionary: Al-Mawrid. (Eng. & Arabic.). 1983. $48.00 (ISBN 0-86685-059-7). Intl Bk Ctr.

--English-Arabic Pocket Dictionary: Al Mawrid. (Arabic & Eng.). 1978. $4.00x (ISBN 0-86685-325-1). Intl Bk Ctr.

--A Modern English-Arabic Dictionary, 4 eds. (Illus., Eng. & Arabic.). Al-Mawrid. $48.00 (059-7); Al-Mawrid Al-Waset. medium size $25.00 (060-0); Al-Mawrid Al-Muyassar. student dict. (575p) $12.00 (061-9); Al-Mawrid Al-Qareb. pocket dict. (484p) $5.95 (062-7). Intl Bk Ctr.

Bagder, George P. An English-Arabic Lexicon. $80.00x (ISBN 0-86685-064-3). Intl Bk Ctr.

Bakalla. Dictionary of Modern Linguistic Terms: English-Arabic, Arabic-English. (Arabic & Eng.). 1975. $20.00 (ISBN 0-86685-304-9). Intl Bk Ctr.

Berlitz Editors. Berlitz Arabic for Travellers. 192p. (Arabic.). 1982. 4.95 (ISBN 0-02-964180-2, Berlitz). Macmillan.

Biella, Joan C. Dictionary of Old South Arabic: Sabaen Dialect. LC 81-8946. (Harvard Semitic Studies). (Arabic.). 1982. $33.00 (ISBN 0-89130-455-X, 04-04-25). Scholars Pr CA.

Clarity, B. A Dictionary of Iraqi Arabic. 202p. (Eng. & Arabic.). $8.00. Intl Bk Ctr.

Concise Dictionary of Islamic Terms: English-Arabic. 1979. $6.95x (ISBN 0-86685-276-X). Intl Bk Ctr.

Dar el Mashreq. Arabic-English Dictionary. simplified ed. (Illus.). 747p. (Arabic & Eng.). 1974. student dict. $12.00 (310-7). Intl Bk Ctr.

--Student Arabic-English Dictionary. (Illus.). 440p. (Engl. & Arabic.). Arabic script $11.00 (2123-9). Intl Bk Ctr.

A Dictionary of Arab Grammatical Terms: The Monitor. 200p. (Arabic & Eng.). $15.00 (119-4). Intl Bk Ctr.

Elias. Arabic-English Collegiate Dictionary. (Arabic & Eng.). $12.50 (ISBN 0-686-27676-0). Colton Bk.

--Elias Arabic-English Modern Dictionary. (Arabic & Eng.). $29.00 (ISBN 0-686-18362-2); pap. $6.50 pocket size (ISBN 0-686-18363-0). Kazi Pubns.

--Elias English-Arabic & Arabic-English Pocket Dictionary. (Arabic & Eng.). pap. $15.95 (ISBN 0-686-18361-4). Kazi Pubns.

--Elias English-Arabic Modern Dictionary. (Arabic & Eng.). $29.00 (ISBN 0-686-18364-9); pap. $6.50 pocket size (ISBN 0-686-18365-7). Kazi Pubns.

--English-Arabic Collegiate Dictionary. (Eng. & Arabic.). $12.50 (ISBN 0-686-27677-9). Colton Bk.

Elias, ed. English Arabic, Arabic-English Pocket Dictionary. (Eng. & Arabic.). $7.50x (ISBN 0-686-00859-6). Colton Bk.

Elias, A. E. English Arabic, Arabic-English Dictionary. (Arabic & Eng.). student simplified ed. $15.00; pocket ed. $12.00. Intl Bk Ctr.

Elias, E. Elias Pocket Dictionary: English, Arabic. (Eng. & Arabic.). leatherette $16.95 (ISBN 0-686-92306-5, M-9365). French & Eur.

Elias, E. A. Arabic-English, English-Arabic Dictionary, 2 vols. rev. & enl. ed. (Arabic & Eng.). Set. $70.00 (ISBN 0-685-55017-6). Heinman.

--English-Arabic; Arabic-English Dictionary. (Eng. & Arabic.). $12.00x (ISBN 0-86685-173-9). Intl Bk Ctr.

Elias, E. A., ed. Arabic-English, English-Arabic Collegiate Dictionary, Vol. 1-2. (Illus., Arabic & Eng.). Date not set. Set. text ed. $35.00 (ISBN 0-686-46526-1). Heinman.

--Arabic-English, English-Arabic School Dictionary. (Illus., Arabic & Eng.). Date not set. text ed. $20.00 (ISBN 0-686-46527-X). Heinman.

Elias, Edward. English-Arabic Dictionary, Romanized. (Eng. & Arabic.). $22.50 (ISBN 0-87559-002-0); thumb indexed $27.50 (ISBN 0-87559-003-9). Shalom.

Elias, Elias. Arabic-English Modern Dictionary. (Arabic & Eng.). 1981. $30.00x (ISBN 0-86685-287-5). Intl Bk Ctr.

--Elias English-Arabic Practical Dictionary of the Colloquial Arabic of the Middle Jacket. (Arabic & Eng.). 1971. $8.95x (ISBN 0-86685-296-4). Intl Bk Ctr.

--Modern Arabic-English Dictionary. (Illus.). 970p. (Arabic & Eng.). 1981. $30.00. Intl Bk Ctr.

Elias English-Arabic Practical Dictionary of the Arabic of the Middle East. (Eng. & Arabic.). $8.95 (ISBN 0-86685-296-4). Intl Bk Ctr.

Elias, M. Elias' Pocket Dictionary Arabic-English. 533p. (Eng. & Arabic.). 1981. $12.95 (ISBN 0-686-91623-9, M-9750). French & Eur.

English-Arabic Dictionary. (Eng. & Arabic.). 19.50 (ISBN 0-87557-003-8, 003-8). Saphrograph.

English-Arabic Pocket Dictionary. (Eng. & Arabic.). $4.00 (ISBN 0-86685-325-1). Intl Bk Ctr.

Field, Claud. Dictionary of Arabic-Persian Quotes. 352p. (Arabic, Persian & Eng.). $18.00 (168-2). Intl Bk Ctr.

Harrell, Richard S. & Sobelman, Harvey, eds. A Dictionary of Moroccan Arabic: Moroccan-Arabic English-Moroccan. (Richard Slade Harrell Arabic Ser.). 528p. (Moroccan, Arabic & Eng.). 1963. pap. $19.95 (ISBN 0-87840-008-7). Georgetown U Pr.

Hava, J. Al-Faraid: Arabic-English Dictionary. 915p. (Arabic & Eng.). $25.00 (2106-9). Intl Bk Ctr.

Hava, J. G. Al-Faraid Arabic-English Dictionary. 3rd ed. 915p. (Arabic & Eng.). 1970. $30.00x (ISBN 2-7214-2106-9). Intl Pubns Serv.

Henni, Mustapha. Dictionary Des Terms Economiques et Commerciaux (French-English-Arabic) (Fr., Eng. & Arabic.). $25.00x (ISBN 0-86685-111-9). Intl Bk Ctr.

Hitti, Jusuf. Medical English-Arabic Dictionary. (Illus.). 1973. $35.00x (ISBN 0-86685-067-8). Intl Bk Ctr.

Jaschke, Richard. English-Arabic Conversational Dictionary. (Eng. & Arabic.). pocket dictionary using phonetic letters $6.95x. Intl Bk Ctr.

Jaschke, Richard, ed. English-Arabic Conversational Dictionary, with Supplement. LC 54-11491. (Eng. & Arabic.). 1978. pap. $7.95 (ISBN 0-8044-6311-5). Ungar.

Karmi, Hasan. English-Arabic Dictionary: Al-Manar. (Eng. & Arabic.). 1971. lib. bdg. $25.00x (ISBN 0-86685-070-8). Intl Bk Ctr.

Karmi, Hassan. Al Manar: English-Arabic Dictionary. 904p. (Eng. & Arabic.). $25.00 (070-8); student ed. $12.00 (071-6). Intl Bk Ctr.

Lane, Edward W., ed. Arabic-English Lexicon, 8 Vols. (Arabic & Eng.). Set. $360.00 (ISBN 0-8044-0272-8). Ungar.

Lane, Edward W., compiled by. An Arabic-English Lexicon: Madd al Qamus, 8 vols. 3064p. (Arabic & Eng.). $295.00 (087-2). Intl Bk Ctr.

Libr du Liban. ABC Dictionary Tamhidi: Arabic & Eng. (Arabic & Eng.). 1983. $7.95x (ISBN 0-86685-314-6). Intl Bk Ctr.

--My Illustrated Dictionary: Arabic Eng. (Arabic & Eng.). 1983. $9.00x (ISBN 0-86685-317-0). Intl Bk Ctr.
Modern Arab Dictionary. (Eng. & Arabic.). write for info. (608-122). Pan Amer Pub.
Nasr, Raja. English Colloquial Arabic Dictionary. 1972. $18.00x (ISBN 0-86685-079-1). Intl Bk Ctr.
--An English-Colloquial Arabic Dictionary. 382p. (Eng. & Arabic.). 1982. $18.00 (079-1). Intl Bk Ctr.
Percy Badger, George. An English-Arabic Lexicon. 1250p. (Eng. & Arabic.). $80.00 (064-3). Intl Bk Ctr.
Qamus, Madd A. & Edward, Wm. An Arabic-English Lexicon, 8 vols. (Arabic & Eng.). Set. $295.00x. Intl Bk Ctr.
Qazi, M. A. Concise Dictionary of Islamic Terms. (Eng. & Arabic.). pap. $6.95 (276-X). Intl Bk Ctr.
Sabek, Jerwan. English-French-Arabic Trilingual Dictionary. (Eng., Fr. & Arabic.). $35.00x (ISBN 0-86685-116-X). Intl Bk Ctr.
Salmone, Anthony. An Advanced Learner's Arabic-English Dictionary. 1461p. (Arabic & Eng.). $30.00 (089-9). Intl Bk Ctr.
Spiro, Socrates. Arabic-English Dictionary: Colloquial Arabic of Egypt. (Arabic & Eng.). 1973. $30.00x (ISBN 0-86685-090-2). Intl Bk Ctr.
--An Arabic-English Dictionary of the Colloquial Arabic of Egypt. 680p. (Arabic & Eng.). 1973. $30.00 (090-2). Intl Bk Ctr.
--English-Arabic Dictionary: Colloquial Arabic of Egypt. (Eng. & Arabic.). 1974. $20.00x (ISBN 0-86685-080-5). Intl Bk Ctr.
--An English-Arabic Dictionary of the Colloquial Arabic of Egypt. 586p. (Eng. & Arabic.). 1975. $20.00 (080-5). Intl Bk Ctr.
Steingass, F. Arabic-English Learners Dictionary. (Arabic & Eng.). 1972. $35.00x (ISBN 0-86685-087-2). Intl Bk Ctr.
--English-Arabic Dictionary. 464p. (Eng. & Arabic.). 1978. Repr. of 1882 ed. 22.00 (ISBN 0-89684-148-0). Orient Bk Dist.
--English-Arabic Learner's Dictionary. (Eng. & Arabic.). 1972. $20.00x (ISBN 0-86685-081-3). Intl Bk Ctr.
--A Learner's Arabic-English Dictionary. (Arabic & Eng.). 1978. $24.00x (ISBN 0-8364-0312-6). South Asia Bks.
--A Learner's Arabic-English Dictionary. 1243p. (Arabic & Eng.). $35.00 (091-0). Intl Bk Ctr.
--A Learner's English-Arabic Dictionary. 466p. (Eng. & Arabic.). 1978. $20.00 (081-3). Intl Bk Ctr.
Stowasser, Karl & Ani, Moukhtar, eds. A Dictionary of Syrian Arabic: English-Arabic. (Richard Slade Harrell Arabic Ser). 202p. (Eng. & Arabic.). 1964. pap. $9.95 (ISBN 0-87840-010-9). Georgetown U Pr.
Tulab, Munjid al & Mashreq, Dar el. Arabic Student Dictionary. (Arabic.). 1979. $15.00x (ISBN 2-7214-2118-2). Intl Bk Ctr.
Van Wagoner, Merrill. English-Arabic Vocabulary. 452p. (Eng. & Arabic.). 1980. $10.00x. Intl Bk Ctr.
Van Wagoner, Merrill Y., et al. English-Arabic Vocabulary: Students Pronouncing Dictionary. LC 80-81198. 452p. (Orig., Eng. & Arabic.). 1980. pap. text ed. $10.00x (ISBN 0-87950-028-X). Spoken Lang Serv.
Wafi, Al & Bustani, Butros. A Concise Arabic Dictionary. (Arabic.). 1980. $40.00x (ISBN 0-86685-095-3). Intl Bk Ctr.
Wahba, Magdi. A Dictionary of Literary Terms (English-French-Arabic) 1974. $28.00x (ISBN 0-86685-117-8). Intl Bk Ctr.
Wehr, H. Arabic-English Dictionary. (Arabic & Eng.). $12.50. Iaconi.
Wehr, Hans & Cowan, J. M. Arabic-English Dictionary. 1110p. (Eng. & Arabic.). pap. $19.00. Imported Bks.
Woodhead, Daniel. A Dictionary of Modern Iraqi Arabic. 509p. (Arabic & Eng.). pap. $10.00 (003-6). Intl Bk Ctr.
Woodhead, Daniel & Beene, Wayne, eds. A Dictionary of Iraqi Arabic: Arabic-English. (Richard Slade Harrell Arabic Ser). 509p. (Arabic & Eng.). 1967. pap. 9.50 (ISBN 0-87840-003-6). Georgetown U Pr.
Wortabet, J. & Porter, H., eds. English-Arabic, Arabic-English Dictionary. 880p. (Eng. & Arabic.). $30.00 (ISBN 0-8044-0875-0). Ungar.
Wortabet, John. Arabic-English Pocket Dictionary. 1980. pap. $5.50x (ISBN 0-86685-093-7). Intl Bk Ctr.
--English-Arabic; Arabic-English Dictionary. (Eng. & Arabic.). 1979. $16.00x (ISBN 0-86685-120-8). Intl Bk Ctr.
--English-Arabic, Arabic-English Dictionary. 900p. (Arabic & Eng.). 1979. $16.00 (120-8); pap. $10.00 pocket size (121-6). Intl Bk Ctr.
--English-Arabic Pocket Dictionary. (Eng. & Arabic.). 1980. pap. $5.50x (ISBN 0-86685-083-X). Intl Bk Ctr.
Wortabet, John & Porter, Harvey. Wortabet's Pocket English-Arabic Dictionary. 448p. (Eng. & Arabic.). pap. $5.50 (083-X). Intl Bk Ctr.
Wortabet, William. Arabic-English Dictionary. (Arabic & Eng.). 1968. $18.00x (ISBN 0-86685-092-9). Intl Bk Ctr.
Wortabet, William & Porter, Harvey, eds. Arabic-English Dictionary. 800p. (Arabic & Eng.). $18.00 (092-9); pocket dict. (431 p $5.50 (093-7). Intl Bk Ctr.

ENGLISH LANGUAGE–DICTIONARIES–ARAMAIC

Jastrow, Marcus. Hebrew-Aramaic-English Dictionary, a Dictionary of Talmud Babli & Talmud Yerushalmi Targum & Midrash, 2 Vols. (Hebrew, Aramaic & Eng.). $68.50 (ISBN 0-87559-019-5). Shalom.

ENGLISH LANGUAGE–DICTIONARIES–ARMENIAN

Bedrossian, Mathias. Armenian-English Dictionary. (Armenian & Eng.). $35.00x (ISBN 0-86685-122-4). Intl Bk Ctr.
Bedrossian, Matthias. New Dictionary of Armenian-English. 816p. (Eng. & Armenian.). $35.00 (122-4). Intl Bk Ctr.
Koushakdjian, M. Armenian-English - English-Armenian Dictionary. 2nd, rev. ed. (Armenian & Eng.). $45.00 (ISBN 0-686-68934-8). Heinman.
Kratkii Anglo-Gruzinskii Slovar. 154p. (Rus.). 1975. $2.25 (Pub. by Metsniereba). Four Continent.
Yacobian, A. H. English-Armenian, Armenian English Dictionary. (Eng. & Armenian.). $24.50 (ISBN 0-87559-004-7); thumb indexed $29.50 (ISBN 0-87559-005-5). Shalom.
Yerevan. Anglo-Armianskii Shkolnyi Slovar. 204p. (Eng. & Armenian.). 1968. $1.75 (Pub. by Luys). Four Continent.

ENGLISH LANGUAGE–DICTIONARIES–AUSTRALIAN LANGUAGES

Johnston, Grahame, ed. The Australian Pocket Oxford Dictionary. (Australian.). 1977. 16.95x (ISBN 0-19-550537-9). Oxford U Pr.

ENGLISH LANGUAGE–DICTIONARIES–BANTU

Barlow, A. R. English-Kikuyu Dictionary. Benson, T. G., tr. 340p. (Eng. & Kikuyu.). 1975. $24.95x (ISBN 0-19-864407-8). Oxford U Pr.

ENGLISH LANGUAGE–DICTIONARIES–BENGALI

Dabbs, Jack A. Short Bengali-English, English-Bengali Dictionary. 3rd ed. LC 78-149931. (Bengali & Eng.). Date not set. $4.00 (ISBN 0-911494-01-4). Dabbs.
--Short Bengali-English, English-Bengali Dictionary. 3rd ed. LC 78-149931. $5.00 (ISBN 0-911494-01-4). Dabbs.
Odhner, John D. English-Lingala Manual. LC 80-6174. 206p. (Orig., Eng. & Bangala.). 1981. lib. bdg. $19.50 (ISBN 0-8191-1554-1); pap. text ed. $10.00 (ISBN 0-8191-1555-X). U Pr of Amer.

ENGLISH LANGUAGE–DICTIONARIES–BULGARIAN

Atanassova, T., et al. Bulgarian-English Dictionary. 2nd ed. 1050p. (Bulgarian & Eng.). 1980. $55.00x (ISBN 0-569-08665-5, Pub. by Collets). State Mutual Bk.
Atnassova, T., et al. Bulgarian-English Dictionary. 1050p. (Bulgarian & Eng.). 1980. $65.00 (ISBN 0-686-97393-3, M-9829). French & Eur.
Desov, A. English-Bulgarian Concise Technical Dictionary. (Eng. & Bulgarian.). $17.50 (ISBN 0-686-91776-6). Heinman.
Harlakova, Ivanka & Stankova, Elena. English-Bulgarian Dictionary. 2nd ed. 392p. (Eng. & Bulgarian.). 1978. $30.00x (ISBN 0-686-44692-5, Pub. by Collets). State Mutual Bk.

ENGLISH LANGUAGE–DICTIONARIES–CHINESE

Beijing Foreign Institute. The Pinyin Chinese-English Dictionary. Wu Jingrong, ed. LC 79-2477. 976p. (Chinese & Eng.). 1979. $68.95x (ISBN 0-471-27557-3, Pub. by Wiley-Interscience); pap. $16.95 (ISBN 0-471-86796-9). Wiley.
Bergman, Peter. The Basic English-Chinese, Chinese-English Dictionary. 135p. (Eng. & Chinese.). 1980. $16.00. Imported Bks.
Bergman, Peter M., compiled by. The Basic English-Chinese, Chinese-English Dictionary. (Chinese & Eng.). (YA) 1980. pap. 2.25 (ISBN 0-451-11688-7, AE1688, Sig). NAL.
Chan, Shau Wing. Concise English-Chinese Dictionary. rev. ed. (Eng. & Chinese.). 1955. pap. $6.95x (ISBN 0-8047-0384-1). Stanford U Pr.
Chen, Janet. A Practical English-Chinese Pronouncing Dictionary. (Chinese & Eng.). $22.50. Iaconi.
Chen, Janey. Practical English-Chinese Pronouncing Dictionary. LC 78-77122. (Eng. & Chinese.). 1970. $22.50 (ISBN 0-8048-0663-2). C E Tuttle.
Chen, Janey & Simms, Ena. A Practical English-Chinese Pronouncing Dictionary. 601p. (Chinese & Eng., Chinese characters, romanized Mandarin & Cantonese). 1980. $29.00. C E Tuttle.
Chiang Ker-Chiu. Practical English-Cantonese Dictionary. (Eng. & Cantonese.). $25.00x (ISBN 0-686-00881-2). Colton Bk.
Chinese-English Dictionary. $12.00 (ISBN 0-685-00818-5, 007-0). Saphrograph.
The Chinese-English Dictionary. 976p. (Chinese & Eng.). 1981. $49.95 (ISBN 962-07-0005-8, M-9400). French & Eur.
Chinese-English Dictionary. 976p. (Chinese & Eng.). 1982. $30.00x (ISBN 0-8044-0097-0). Ungar.
Chinese-English Dictionary. 976p. (Chinese & Eng.). 1979. pap. $60.00x (ISBN 0-686-44768-9, Pub. by Collets). State Mutual Bk.
Chinese-English, English-Chinese Dictionary, 2 vols. (Chinese & Eng.). Set. 40.00 (ISBN 0-685-79110-6). Heinman.
Chinese-English Expressions for Travellers. 90p. (Chinese & Eng.). 1983. pap. $3.95 (ISBN 0-8044-6993-8). Ungar.
Chi Wen-Shun, ed. Chinese-English Dictionary of Contemporary Usage. (Chinese & Eng.). 1977. $27.50x (ISBN 0-520-02655-1). U of Cal Pr.
Chu, Hsiu-Feng, et al. English-Chinese Chinese-English Dictionary of Business Terms. 476p. (Orig.). 1973. pap. $7.95x (ISBN 0-917056-85-X, Pub. by Chih-Wen Pub Co China). Cheng & Tsui.
A Concise English-Chinese Dictionary. 1211p. (Eng. & Chinese.). 1962. $9.95 (ISBN 0-686-92460-6, M-9563). French & Eur.
Cowles, Roy T. The Cantonese Speaker's Dictionary. 1600p. (Chinese.). 1965. text ed. $27.50x (ISBN 0-8188-0139-5). Paragon.
Daehler, David J., ed. English-Chinese Glossary for Elementary Chinese. LC 77-83819. (CT Language Ser.). (Eng. & Chinese.). 1977. pap. text ed. $2.50 (ISBN 0-917056-05-1). Cheng & Tsui.
English-Chinese & Chinese-English Dictionary. (Eng. & Chinese.). 1977. $7.95 (ISBN 0-8351-0725-6). China Bks.
An English-Chinese Dictionary of Abreviations & Acronyms. 1162p. (Eng. & Chinese.). 1979. lib. bdg. $9.95 (ISBN 0-686-92171-2, M-9555). French & Eur.
Glossary of Current Chinese-English Phrases. 594p. (Chinese & Eng.). 1972. $9.95 (ISBN 0-8351-0600-4). China Bks.
Hemeling, Karl E. English-Chinese Dictionary: Standard Chinese, 3 vols. (Chinese & Eng.). 1976. Repr. of 1958 ed. $165.00 (ISBN 0-518-19001-3). Ayer Co.
Hornby, A. S., et al. The Advanced Learner's Dictionary of Current English with Chinese Translation. (Illus.). 1354p. (Eng. & Chinese.). $25.00. Imported Bks.
--Oxford Advanced Learner's Dictionary of Current English with Chinese Translations. (Illus., Chinese & Eng.). 1980. text ed. 17.50x (ISBN 0-19-580003-6). Oxford U Pr.
A Junior English-Chinese Dictionary. 1023p. (Eng. & Chinese.). 1977. pap. $5.95 (ISBN 0-686-92475-4, M-9557). French & Eur.
Karlgren, Bernhard. Analytical Dictionary of Chinese & Sino-Japenese. LC 74-75625. 448p. (Chinese, Sino-Japanese & Eng.). 1974. pap. $7.00 (ISBN 0-486-21887-2). Dover.
Learner's Chinese-English Dictionary. (Chinese & Eng.). 1979. 14.95 (ISBN 0-8351-0641-1). China Bks.
Learner's Chinese-English Dictionary. 666p. (Chinese & Eng.). 1979. pap. $14.95 (ISBN 0-8351-0641-1). China Bks.
Liang, Shi-Chiu. A New Practical Chinese-English Dictionary. 1355p. 1973. $32.00x (ISBN 0-917056-53-1, Pub. by Far East Bk Co China). Cheng & Tsui.
--A New Practical Chinese-English Dictionary. 1355p. 1973. pap. $16.95x (ISBN 0-917056-54-X, Pub. by Far East Bk Co China). Cheng & Tsui.
Liang, Shi-Chiu, ed. A New Practical Chinese-English Dictionary. 1355p. 1973. $45.00x (ISBN 0-917056-52-3, Pub. by Far East Bk Co China). Cheng & Tsui.
--A New Practical English-Chinese Dictionary. 2401p. 1980. pap. $25.00x (ISBN 0-917056-56-6, Pub. by Far East Bk Co China). Cheng & Tsui.
Lo-Tien, F. Beginner's Translation Handbook: English-Chinese. 364p. 1974. pap. $3.95 (ISBN 0-686-92139-9, M-9581). French & Eur.
Makkai, Adam. A Dictionary of American Idioms in Chinese. Gates & Boatner, eds. 396p. (Chinese & Eng.). Date not set. pap. $14.95 (ISBN 0-8120-2386-2). Barron.
Mathews, B. English-Chinese Picture Dictionary. (Illus.). 48p. (Eng. & Chinese.). $2.50. G Brash.
Matthews, B. English-Chinese Picture Dictionary. (Illus.). 48p. (Chinese & Eng.). 1983. pap. $4.50 (ISBN 9971-947-00-5). Hippocrene Bks.
Model English-Chinese Dictionary with Illustrative Examples. (Illus.). 1674p. (Eng. & Chinese.). 1979. leatherette $19.95 (ISBN 0-686-97401-8). French & Eur.
A New Chinese-English Dictionary. 718p. (Chinese & Eng.). 1979. Leatherette $14.95 (ISBN 0-686-92174-7, M-9554). French & Eur.

New English-Chinese Dictionary. 1252p. (Eng. & Chinese.). 1979. $17.95 (ISBN 0-686-97423-9, M-9290). French & Eur.

A New English-Chinese Dictionary. 1542p. (Eng. & Chinese.). 1982. $18.50x (ISBN 0-8044-0138-1). Ungar.

A New English-Chinese Dictionary. 1688p. (Eng. & Chinese.). 1975. leatherette $24.95 (ISBN 0-686-92166-6, M-9556). French & Eur.

A New English-Chinese Dictionary. 1688p. (Eng. & Chinese.). 1976. Leatherette $19.95 (ISBN 0-686-92177-1, M-9553). French & Eur.

A New English-Chinese Dictionary. 1702p. (Chinese & Eng.). 1975. $17.50 (ISBN 0-8351-0596-2); PLB $29.95 (ISBN 0-8351-0597-0). China Bks.

A New Practical English-Chinese Dictionary. 2410p. (Eng. & Chinese.). $14.95 (ISBN 0-686-92368-5, M-9552). French & Eur.

The Pinyin Chinese-English Dictionary. (Chinese & Eng.). $61.00. Iaconi.

A Pocket Chinese-English Dictionary: Zhong Hua Edition. 620p. (Chinese & Eng.). 1978. $8.95 (ISBN 0-8351-0601-2); pap. $5.95 (ISBN 0-8351-0602-0). China Bks.

A Pocket English-Chinese Dictionary. (Eng. & Chinese.). 1980. pap. $4.95 (ISBN 0-8351-0727-2). China Bks.

A Pocket English-Chinese Dictionary. 451p. (Chinese & Eng.). 1980. $4.95 (ISBN 0-8351-0727-2). China Bks.

A Pocket English-Chinese Dictionary. (Chinese & Eng.). pap. $2.25. Iaconi.

A Practical English-Chinese Dictionary. 1674p. (Eng. & Chinese.). 1979. leatherette $19.95 (ISBN 0-686-97443-3, M-9291). French & Eur.

Quo, James. Concise English-Chinese Dictionary Romanized. (Chinese & Eng.). $4.95. Iaconi.

Quo, James C. Concise Chinese-English Dictionary, Romanized. 225p. (Chinese & Eng.). pap. $7.75 pocket size. C E Tuttle.

--Concise English-Chinese Dictionary. LC 55-11585. (Eng. & Chinese.). 1960. $4.95 (ISBN 0-8048-0117-7). C E Tuttle.

--Concise English-Chinese Dictionary, Romanized. 324p. (Eng. & Chinese., Avail. in Chinese characters). pap. $7.75. Imported Bks.

--English-Chinese Dictionary, Romanized. 323p. (Eng. & Chinese.). 15.00 (ISBN 0-87557-008-9, 008-9). Saphrograph.

Rose-Innes, Arthur. Beginner's Dictionary of Chinese-Japanese Characters. 510p. (Chinese, Japanese & Eng.). 1959. pap. $7.95. Dover.

Simon, W. A Beginner's Chinese English Dictionary of the National Language (Gwpyeu) 1200p. (Chinese & Eng.). 1980. $55.00x (ISBN 0-85331-013-0, Pub. by Lund Humphries England). State Mutual Bk.

A Student English-Chinese Dictionary. (Illus.). 978p. (Orig., Chinese & Eng.). 1983. pap. text ed. $7.95 (ISBN 9971-9060-3-1). Hippocrene Bks.

Supplementary Indexes to Lin Yutang's Chinese-English Dictionary of Modern Usage. LC 79-319125. 105p. (Chinese & Eng.). 1978. write for info. (ISBN 9-622-01160-8). Chinese U Pr.

The Trictionary. 432p. (Chinese, Span. & Eng.). softcover $12.95. Bilingual Pubns.

Watters, David & Watters, Nancy. An English-Kham, Kham-English Glossary. 126p. (Eng. & Kham.). 1973. pap. $2.00x (ISBN 0-88312-756-3); $2.25. Summer Inst Ling.

Wei, S. Practical Dictionary of Chinese Idioms, English Idioms, English Synonyms. (Illus., Chinese & Eng.). $16.50. Iaconi.

Wieger, L. Chinese Characters, Their Origin, Etymology, History, Classification & Signification. 2nd ed. Davrout, L., tr. (Chinese.). 1927. pap. $12.50 (ISBN 0-486-21321-8). Dover.

Williams, Samuel W. Chinese-English Dictionary. (Eng. & Chinese.). 1976. Repr. of 1958 ed. $65.00 (ISBN 0-518-19007-2). Ayer Co.

Xin Ying-Han-Cidian Editing Committee. A New English-Chinese Dictionary. 1648p. 1975. $29.95 (ISBN 0-917056-59-0, Pub. by Joint Pub Co China). Cheng & Tsui.

Zhou Long Ru. English-Chinese Dictionary of Abbreviation & Acronyms. 1290p. (Eng. & Chinese.). 1980. $9.95 (ISBN 0-8351-1106-7). China Bks.

ENGLISH LANGUAGE–DICTIONARIES–COPTIC

Crum, Walter E., ed. Coptic Dictionary. 1939. $98.00x (ISBN 0-19-864404-3). Oxford U Pr.

ENGLISH LANGUAGE–DICTIONARIES–CORNISH

Jago, Frederick W. An English-Cornish Dictionary. LC 78-72629. (Celtic Language & Literature: Goidelic & Brythonic). (Eng. & Cornish.). Repr. of 1887 ed. $34.50 (ISBN 0-404-17553-8). AMS Pr.

ENGLISH LANGUAGE–DICTIONARIES–CROATIAN

Bogadek, F. A. New English-Croatian & Croatian-English Dictionary. 531p. (Eng. & Croatian.). 1944. $25.00. Hafner.

Bogadek, Francis A. New English-Croatian, Croatian-English Dictionary. 3rd ed. (Eng. & Croatian.). 1971. Repr. of 1944 ed. 25.95x (ISBN 0-02-841580-9). Hafner.

Croatian-English, English-Croatian Pocket Dictionary. (Croation & Eng.). 10.00 (ISBN 0-685-58554-9). Heinman.

Filipovic, R. Croatian-English, English-Croatian Small Pocket Dictionary. (Croatian & Eng.). 1981. pap. $10.00x (ISBN 0-89918-727-7, Y-727). Vanous.

Filipovic, Rudolf. English-Croatian or Serbian Dictionary. 1436p. (Eng. & Serbocroatian.). 1980. $150.00x (ISBN 0-569-08646-9, Pub. by Collets). State Mutual Bk.

ENGLISH LANGUAGE–DICTIONARIES–CZECH

Caha, J. & Kramsky, J. English-Czech Dictionary. 878p. (Eng. & Czech.). 1980. $50.00x (ISBN 0-569-00405-5, Pub. by Collet's). State Mutual Bk.

Caha, J., ed. English-Czech Dictionary. 878p. (Eng. & Czech.). 1964. $10.75 (Pub. by State Pedag. Publ. House). Four Continent.

Chermak, A. English-Czech, Czech-English Dictionary. (Eng. & Czech.). 27.50 (ISBN 0-87557-012-7). Saphrograph.

Czech-English, English-Czech Pocket Dictionary. (Czech. & Eng.). 11.00 (ISBN 0-685-68787-2). Heinman.

Czech-English, English-Czech Pocket Dictionary. 1223p. (Czech. & Eng.). 1980. $16.95 (ISBN 0-88254-542-6, Pub. by Artia Czechoslovakia). Hippocrene Bks.

Czech-English, English-Czech Pocket Dictionary. 1223p. (Czech. & Eng.). 1980. $16.95 (ISBN 0-88254-542-6). Artia.

Hais, K. English-Czech & Czech-English Pocket Dictionary. 570p. (Eng. & Czech.). 1974. $5.50 (Pub. by State Pedag. Publ. House). Four Continent.

Kolafova, V. & Slaba, D. Czech-English-Czech Dictionary. (For Travel Ser.). 394p. (Czech. & Eng.). 1979. text ed. $6.00x (ISBN 0-89918-302-6, C302). Vanous.

Osicka, V. & Poldauf, I., eds. English-Czech Dictionary. 636p. (Eng. & Czech.). 1980. $50.00x (ISBN 0-569-06529-1, Pub. by Collet's). State Mutual Bk.

Poldauf, I., ed. Czech-English Dictionary. 1235p. (Czech. & Eng.). 1980. $50.00x (ISBN 0-569-00404-7, Pub. by Collet's). State Mutual Bk.

--Czech-English, English Czech Dictionary. 9th ed. (Czech. & Eng.). 25.00 (ISBN 0-686-77982-7). Heinman.

ENGLISH LANGUAGE–DICTIONARIES–DAKOTA

Riggs, Stephen R. Dakota-English Dictionary. facsimile ed. (Dakota & Eng.). 1968. Repr. of 1882 ed. buckram bdg. 20.00 (ISBN 0-87018-050-9). Ross.

ENGLISH LANGUAGE–DICTIONARIES–DANISH

Bach, H. & Florant, J. Luftartsteknisk Ordbog Engelsk-Dansk. 255p. (Eng. & Danish.). 1968. $35.00 (ISBN 0-686-92484-3, M-1280). French & Eur.

Berlitz. Berlitz Pocket Dictionaries: Danish-English-Danish. (Eng. & Danish.). pap. $4.95 (ISBN 0-02-964550-6). Macmillan.

Berlitz Editors. Berlitz Pocket Dictionaries: Danish-English. 300p. (Danish & Eng.). 1982. pap. 4.95 (ISBN 0-686-92980-2, Berlitz). Macmillan.

Berulfsen, B. Engelsk-Norsk Ordbok. 430p. 1978. $24.95 (ISBN 82-573-0007-1, M-9455). French & Eur.

Danish-English-Danish Ser. (Berlitz Pocket Dictionaries). (Danish & Eng.). $4.95 (ISBN 0-02-964550-6). Macmillan.

Langenscheidt Danish-English Lilliput Dictionary. 615p. (Danish & Eng.). plastic $1.50 (ISBN 3-468-96467-6). Langenscheidt.

Langenscheidt English-Danish Lilliput Dictionary. 615p. (Danish & Eng.). plastic $1.50 (ISBN 3-468-96467-6). Langenscheidt.

Langenscheidt's Lilliput Danish-English Dictionary. 640p. (Danish & Eng.). 1972. $1.50 (ISBN 0-685-31350-6). Am Map.

Langenscheidt's Lilliput English-Danish Dictionary. 640p. (Danish & Eng.). 1972. $1.50 (ISBN 0-685-31374-3). Am Map.

Lilliput Dictionary. 640p. (Danish & Eng.). $1.50 (106). Langenscheid-Hachette.

Lilliput Dictionary. 640p. (Eng. & Danish.). $1.50 (107). Langenscheidt.

Nielsen, B. K., et al. Engelsk-Dansk-Ordbog. (Eng. & Danish.). 1981. $95.00 (ISBN 87-01-44971-0, M-1270). French & Eur.

Vinterberg, H. & Axelsen, J., eds. Danish-English, English-Danish Dictionary, 2 vols. 8th & 10th ed. (Danish & Eng.). Set. 50.00 (ISBN 0-685-36173-X). Vol. 1, Danish-English (ISBN 8-7001-1282-8). Vol. 2, English-Danish (ISBN 8-7013-3451-4). Heinman.

Vinterberg, H., et al. Danish Dictionary: Rode Ordbog-Gyldendals, Danish-English. 11th ed. (Danish & Eng.). 1981. text ed. $20.00x (ISBN 8-7001-1282-8, D705). Vanous.

--Danish Dictionary: Rode Ordbog-Gyldendals, English-Danish. 9th ed. (Danish & Eng.). 1979. text ed. $20.00x (ISBN 8-7008-0381-2, D704). Vanous.

Warren, A. Engelsk-Dansk Teknisk Ordbog. 393p. (Eng. & Danish.). 1981. $49.95 (ISBN 87-11-04029-7, M-8413). French & Eur.

ENGLISH LANGUAGE–DICTIONARIES–DUTCH

Berlitz. Berlitz Pocket Dictionaries: Dutch-English-Dutch. (Eng. & Dutch.). pap. $4.95 (ISBN 0-02-964540-9). Macmillan.

Berlitz Editors. Berlitz Pocket Dictionaries: Dutch-English. 300p. (Eng. & Dutch.). 1982. pap. $4.95 (ISBN 0-686-92990-X, Berlitz). Macmillan.

Broers, A. & Smit, J. English-Dutch Dictionary. Born, R., ed. 674p. (Eng. & Dutch.). 1980. pap. $24.95 (ISBN 90-01-81264-3, M-9748). French & Eur.

Bruggencate, K. T. Dutch-English Dictionary. Gerritsen, J., et al, eds. 1048p. (Dutch & Eng.). 1980. $24.95 (ISBN 90-01-96819-8, M-9746). French & Eur.

--English-Dutch Dictionary. Gerritsen, J., et al, eds. 898p. (Eng. & Dutch.). 1980. $24.95 (ISBN 90-01-96818-X, M-9747). French & Eur.

Bruggencate, K. Ten. Dutch-English, English-Dutch Dictionary, 2 vols. (Dutch & Eng.). Set. 50.00 (ISBN 9-0019-6819-8). Dutch-Eng. Eng.-Dutch (ISBN 90-01-96818-X). Heinman.

Capitol's Concise Dictionary of Seven Languages. (gr. 9-12). 1978. $29.95 (ISBN 0-8120-5333-8). Barron.

Cassell. Cassell's Dutch Dictionary: English-Dutch Dutch-English. 1364p. (Eng. & Dutch.). $34.95 (ISBN 0-02-522940-0). Macmillan.

--Cassell's New Dutch Dictionary: English-Dutch, Dutch-English. 729p. (Eng. & Dutch.). 1982. 34.95 (ISBN 0-02-522940-0). Macmillan.

Dutch-English-Dutch. (Berlitz Pocket Dictionaries Ser.). (Eng. & Dutch.). $4.95 (ISBN 0-02-964550-6). Macmillan.

Hugo Pocket Dictionary: Dutch-English, English-Dutch. 624p. 1969. 3.50 (ISBN 0-8226-0502-3, 502). Littlefield.

Jansonius, H. Dutch-English (Only) New Great Dictionary, 3 vols. 2nd ed. (Dutch & Eng.). Set. 225.00 (ISBN 90-6110-032-1). Heinman.

Kramers. Dutch-English, English-Dutch Dictionary, 2 vols. 36th, rev., enl. ed. (Dutch & Eng.). 35.00 (ISBN 9-0100-2541-1). Heinman.

Kramer's Engels Woordenboek, 2 vols. 1330p. (Dutch & Eng.). Set. fl.35.00. Elsevier.

Langenscheidt Dutch-English Lilliput Dictionary. 640p. (Dutch & Eng.). plastic $1.50 (ISBN 3-468-96476-5). Langenscheidt.

Langenscheidt English-Dutch Lilliput Dictionary. 637p. (Dutch & Eng.). plastic $1.50 (ISBN 3-468-96477-3). Langenscheidt.

Langenscheidt's Lilliput Dutch-English Dictionary. 640p. (Dutch & Eng.). 1972. $1.50 (ISBN 0-685-31373-5). Am Map.

Langenscheidt's Lilliput English-Dutch Dictionary. 640p. (Dutch & Eng.). 1972. $1.50 (ISBN 0-685-31372-7). Am Map.

Lilliput Dictionary. 640p. (Dutch & Eng.). $1.50 (108). Langenscheidt.

Lilliput Dictionary. 640p. (Eng. & Dutch.). $1.50 (109). Langenscheidt.

Renier, Fernand. Dutch-English Dictionary. (Dutch & Eng.). 1982. pap. 7.95 (ISBN 0-7100-9352-7). Routledge & Kegan.

Renier, Fernand G. Dutch-English, English-Dutch Dictionary. (Dutch & Eng.). 19.50 (ISBN 0-87557-014-3, 014-3). Saphrograph.

Schuurmans Stekhoven, G. Dutch-English, English-Dutch Engineering Dictionary, 2 vols. (Dutch & Eng.). 125.00 set (ISBN 90-2010-602-3). Heinman.

Van Baars & Van der Schoot. Engels-Nederlands Woodenboek. 359p. (Eng. & Dutch.). 1969. pap. $5.50. Spectrum Pub.

Van Wely, F. P. Cassell's Dutch Dictionary: English-Dutch, Dutch-English. LC 77-81889. (Eng. & Dutch.). 1978. 19.95 (ISBN 0-02-522890-0). Macmillan.

Verhoeff, Schot E. Standaard Nieuw Engels-Nederlands Woordenboek. LC 76-478704. 1437p. (Eng. & Dutch.). 1975. 450.00 F (ISBN 9-0021-2736-7). Standaard Uitgeverij.

Verhoeff-Schot, E. & Cauberghe, J. R. Standard Niew Engels-Nederlands, Nederlands-Engels Woordenboek. LC 76-478704. 1437p. (Dutch & Eng.). 1975. fl.450.00 (ISBN 9-00212-736-7). Standaard Uitgeverij.

Visser, G. J. Nederlands-Engels Woordenboek. 323p. (Dutch & Eng.). 1981. pap. $5.00. Spectrum Pub.

ENGLISH LANGUAGE–DICTIONARIES–EFIK

Adams, R. F. English-Efik Dictionary. (Eng. & Efik.). $27.50 (ISBN 0-87559-056-X); thumb indexed $32.50 (ISBN 0-87559-057-8). Shalom.

ENGLISH LANGUAGE–DICTIONARIES–ESKIMO

English-Eskimo, Eskimo-English Dictionary. (Eng. & Eskimo.). $22.50 (ISBN 0-87559-061-6); thumb indexed $27.50 (ISBN 0-87559-062-4). Shalom.

Thibert, A. Eskimo-English, English-Eskimo Dictionary. rev. ed. (Eskimo & Eng.). pap. 12.50 (ISBN 0-685-12011-2). Heinman.

Wells, Roger & Kelley, John W., eds. English-Eskimo & Eskimo-English Vocabularies. LC 74-5889. (Eng. & Eskimo.). Repr. of 1890 ed. $11.50 (ISBN 0-404-11698-1). AMS Pr.

Wells, Roger, Jr., compiled by. English-Eskimo & Eskimo-English Vocabularies. Kelly, John W., tr. LC 82-51153. 72p. (Inupiaq & Eng.). 1982. pap. $6.95 (ISBN 0-8048-1403-1). C E Tuttle.

ENGLISH LANGUAGE–DICTIONARIES–ESPERANTO

Butler, Montagu C. Esperanto-English Dictionary. (Esperanto & Eng.). 1967. $8.95x (ISBN 0-685-71601-5, 1065). Esperanto League North Am.

ENGLISH LANGUAGE–DICTIONARIES–FINNISH

Alanne, V. S. Finnish Dictionary: Suomalais-Englantilainen, Vol. 1. 3rd ed. (Finnish & Eng.). 1980. $85.00x (ISBN 95-100-1069-3, F563). Vanous.

--Finnish-English General Dictionary. 1111p. (Eng. & Finnish.). 1980. $75.00 (ISBN 951-0-01069-3, M-9658). French & Eur.

Berlitz. Berlitz Pocket Dictionaries: Finnish-English-Finnish. (Eng. & Finnish.). pap. $4.95 (ISBN 0-02-964580-8). Macmillan.

Berlitz Editors. Berlitz Pocket Dictionaries: Finnish-English. 300p. (Eng. & Finnish.). 1982. pap. $4.95 (ISBN 0-686-92984-5, Berlitz). Macmillan.

Finnish-English-Finnish. (Berlitz Pocket Dictionaries Ser.). (Eng. & Finnish.). $4.95 (ISBN 0-02-964580-8). Macmillan.

Finnish Pocket Dictionary. (Finnish & Eng.). 13.00 (ISBN 9-5100-7468-3). Heinman.

Hurme, R., et al. English-Finnish General Dictionary. 1183p. (Eng. & Finnish.). 1981. $75.00 (ISBN 951-0-08553-7, M-9659). French & Eur.

Hurme, Raija & Pesonen, Maritta. Englantilais-suomalainen Suursanakirja: English-Finnish General Dictionary. LC 80-461357. xl, 1182p. (Finnish-Eng.). 1978. Fmk.190.00 (ISBN 9-510-0855-45); pap. $173.00 (ISBN 9-510-0855-37). Soderstrom.

Vuolle, Aino. Suomalais-Englantilainen Sanakirja. LC 76-478143. 484p. (Finnish & Eng.). 1975. write for info. (ISBN 9-5164-359-63). Femi Suuri.

Wuole, A. Finnish-English, English-Finnish Dictionary. (Finnish & Eng.). $24.50 (ISBN 0-87559-010-1); thumb indexed $29.00 (ISBN 0-87559-011-X). Shalom.

Wuolle, A. English-Finnish Dictionary. 512p. (Eng. & Finnish.). 1980. leatherette $19.95 (ISBN 951-0-08500-6, M-9653). French & Eur.

--Finnish-English, English-Finnish Dictionary, 2 Vols. 11th ed. (Finnish & Eng.). Set. 37.50. Finnish-Eng (ISBN 9-5100-9469-2). Eng.-Finnish (ISBN 951-0-08500-6). Heinman.

--Finnish-English, English-Finnish Dictionary. 2nd, rev. ed. (Eng. & Finnish.). Date not set. text ed. $30.00 (ISBN 0-686-46544-X). Heinman.

Wuolle, Aino. Finnish Small Dictionary: Finnish-English, Vol. 2. 11th ed. (Finnish & Eng.). 1979. text ed. $20.00x (ISBN 95-100-9469-2, F558). Vanous.

ENGLISH LANGUAGE–DICTIONARIES–FRENCH

Atkins, B. T., et al, eds. Collins Robert Dictionary: French-English-English-French. Duval, A. & Milnet, R. C. (Fr. & Eng.). $16.95 (ISBN 0-686-28358-9, CFD1); thumb index avail. (ISBN 0-00-433479-5). Collins Pubs.

Beguin, J., et al. Vocabulaire Technique des Assurances sur la Vie, Vol. 2. 335p. (Eng. & Fr.). 1979. pap. $9.95 (ISBN 2-551-03302-0, M-9245). French & Eur.

Beguin, L., et al. Vocabulaire Technique des Assurances sur la Vie, Vol. 1. 309p. (Eng. & Fr.). 1979. pap. $9.95 (ISBN 0-7754-2396-3, M-9244). French & Eur.

Belle-Isle, Gerald J. Dictionnaire Technique General Anglais-Francais. 2nd ed. 555p. (Eng. & Fr.). 1977. 24.00 F. Beauchemin.

Berlitz. Berlitz Pocket Dictionaries: French-English-French. (Fr. & Eng.). pap. $4.95 (ISBN 0-02-964500-X). Macmillan.

Berlitz Editors. Berlitz French for Travellers. 192p. (Fr.). 1982. pap. 4.95 (ISBN 0-686-92978-0, Berlitz). Macmillan.

--Berlitz Pocket Dictionaries: French-English. 300p. (Eng. & Fr.). 1982. pap. $4.95 (ISBN 0-686-93004-5, Berlitz). Macmillan.

Blachere, Regis & Chouemi, Moustafa. Dictionnaire Arabe-Francais-Anglais, 1, Pts. 1-12. (Arabic, Fr. & Eng.). 1967. $350.00 (ISBN 0-686-56918-0, M-6034). French & Eur.

--Dictionnaire Arabe-Francais-Anglais, 2, Pts. 13-24. (Arab., Fr. & Eng.). 1970. $350.00 (ISBN 0-686-56919-9, M-6035). French & Eur.

Boudier, J. F. & Luquet, F. M. Dictionnaire Laitier: French-English-French. 220p. (Fr. & Eng.). 1981. leatherette $69.95 (ISBN 2-85206-092-2, M-9627). French & Eur.

Camille, Cl. & Dehaine, M. Dictionnaire de l'Informatique, Francais-Anglais. 248p. (Fr. & Eng.). 1972. $22.50 (ISBN 0-686-56936-9, M-6058). French & Eur.

Capitol's Concise Dictionary of Seven Languages. (gr. 9-12). 1978. $29.95 (ISBN 0-8120-5333-8). Barron.

Cassell's Compact French-English, English-French Dictionary. 672p. (Fr. & Eng.). 1981. pap. $3.95 (ISBN 0-440-31128-4, LE). Dell.

Chaffurin, L. & Mergault, J. Dictionnaire Bilingue Larousse, Francais-Anglais, Anglais-Francais. (Apollo). (Fr. & Eng.). $10.50 (ISBN 0-685-13856-9, 3767). Larousse.

Chauffurin, L. Petit Dictionnaire bilingue Larousse, francais-anglais et English-French. (Adonis). (Fr. & Eng.). plastic bdg. $6.25 (ISBN 0-685-14032-6, 3768). Larousse.

Collins French-English English-French Dictionary. 512p. (Orig., Fr. & Eng.). 1982. pap. $2.95 (ISBN 0-425-05449-7). Berkley Pub.

Collins Pocket French Dictionary. 528p. 1983. $7.95 (ISBN 0-671-49220-9). S&S.

Collins, Robert. French-English English-French Dictionary. (Fr. & Eng.). 1978. Can.$pap. 22.95 (ISBN 0-00-216695-X); $24.95 (ISBN 0-00-216696-8). U of Toronto Pr.

Collins-Robert Concise French-English & English-French Dictionary. 960p. (Fr. & Eng.). $10.95 (ISBN 0-671-44958-3). S&S.

Collins Robert French-English & English-French Dictionary. 1498p. (Fr. & Eng.). write for info. (ISBN 0-671-41935-8); write for info. thumb-indexed (ISBN 0-671-41936-6). S&S.

Collins Robert French-English, English-French Dictionary. 1490p. (Fr. & Eng.). 1978. $19.00; indexed $20.00. Imported Bks.

Cotgrave, Randle. Dictionary of the French & English Tongues. (Fr. & Eng.). 1971. Repr. of 1611 ed. $128.00 (ISBN 0-685-05204-4). Adler.

Cruikshank, Eleanor P. French-English Instant Vocabulary. 88p. (Fr. & Eng.). 1980. pap. $4.00 (ISBN 0-9605284-0-7). Cruikshank.

Cusset, Francis. English-French & French-English Technical Dictionary. rev. ed. (Eng. & Fr.). 1967. $28.50 (ISBN 0-8206-0043-1). Chem Pub.

Delamarre. Dictionnaire Francais-Anglais et Anglais-Francais des Termes Techniques De Medecine. (Fr. & Eng.). $49.95 (ISBN 0-685-36680-4). French & Eur.

Delmas-Harrap. Dictionnaire des Affaires Francais-Anglais, Anglais-Francais. (Fr. & Eng.). $65.50 (ISBN 0-685-36681-2). French & Eur.

Douglas, J. H., et al, eds. Cassell's Concise French-English, English-French Dictionary. abr. ed. LC 77-7667. 658p. (Fr. & Eng.). 1977. 9.95 (ISBN 0-02-522670-3). Macmillan.

Dubois, M. M. Dictionnaire moderne Larousse francais-anglais et anglais-francais. new rev. ed. (Fr. & Eng.). 29.95 (ISBN 0-88332-003-7, 3769). Larousse.

Dubois, Marguerite-Marie. Dictionnaire de Locutions, Francais-Anglais. 392p. (Fr. & Eng.). 1973. $22.50 (ISBN 0-686-57125-8, M-6173). French & Eur.

English-French Dictionary. (Eng. & Fr.). 14.50 (ISBN 0-87557-022-4, 021-6). Saphrograph.

English-French, French-English Dictionary. (Eng. & Fr.). write for info. (608-70). B&N.

Ferrar, H., et al. The Concise Oxford French Dictionary: French-English, English-French. 863p. (Eng. & Fr.). $24.00. Imported Bks.

Forbes, Patricia & Smith, Muriel H. Harrap's Concise French & English Dictionary. 2nd ed. Collin, P. H., ed. LC 78-320359. 933p. (Fr. & Eng.). 1978. E4.95 (ISBN 0-245-52829-6). Harrap.

French-English & English-French Dictionary. (Fr. & Eng.). pap. $1.99 (ISBN 0-686-02351-X). Dennison.

French-English Dictionary. (Fr. & Eng.). 14.50 (ISBN 0-87557-021-6, 021-6). Saphrograph.

Gem Language Dictionaries: French-English & English-French. (Fr. & Eng.). write for info. (ISBN 0-671-41957-9). S&S.

Gieber, Robert L. An English-French Glossary of Educational Terminology. LC 80-5652. 212p. (Eng. & Fr.). 1980. lib. bdg. $20.25 (ISBN 0-8191-1344-1); pap. text ed. $10.25 (ISBN 0-8191-1345-X). U Pr of Amer.

Girard, Denis. Dictionnaire Francais-Anglais et Anglais-Francais. 1464p. (Fr.-Eng.). 1972. $27.50 (ISBN 0-686-57300-5, M-6274). French & Eur.

Girard, Denis, et al. Cassell's French Dictionary: French-English, English-French. Rev. ed. 1436p. (Eng. & Fr.). 1977. $16.95; indexed $18.95. Imported Bks.

Girard, Denis, et al, eds. Cassell's French Dictionary. LC 77-7669. (Fr.). 1977. indexed 18.95 (ISBN 0-02-522620-7); plain 16.50 (ISBN 0-02-522610-X). Macmillan.

Glossaire Europeen de Terminologie Juridique & Administrative: No. 15 Termes de Droit Anglais des Obligations, Anglais-Francais. 36p. (Eng. & Fr.). Date not set. pap. $9.95 (ISBN 0-686-97408-5, M-9482). French & Eur.

Hall, Robert A., Jr. & Langbaum, Francesca V. French Vest Pocket Dictionary. (Fr.). 1954. pap. 2.95 (ISBN 0-394-40054-2). Random.

Hamlyn French-English Dictionary. (Fr. & Eng.). 1977. pap. 4.95 (ISBN 0-600-36563-8, 8086). Larousse.

Harrap's French-English Dictionary of Slang & Colloquialisms. (Fr. & Eng.). 1975. $14.95 (ISBN 0-686-57323-4, M-6308). French & Eur.

Harrap's New Collegiate French Dictionary: English-French, French-English. 1450p. (Fr. & Eng.). 1978. $19.50. Imported Bks.

Harrap's New Standard Francais-Anglais, 1: A-I. (Fr.-Eng.). 1972. $32.50 (ISBN 0-8442-1876-6, M-6309). French & Eur.

Harrap's New Standard Francais-Anglais, 2: J-Z. 1162p. (Fr.-Eng.). 1972. $32.50 (ISBN 0-8442-1898-7, M-6310). French & Eur.

Harrap's Standard Anglais-Francais. 1530p. (Fr.-Eng.). 1970. $49.95 (ISBN 0-686-57324-2, M-6311). French & Eur.

Hochman, ed. Kettridge's English-French - French-English Dictionary. (Eng. & Fr.). 1971. pap. 3.50 (ISBN 0-451-11804-9, AE1804, Sig). NAL.

Hugo Pocket Dictionary: French-English, English-French. (Fr. & Eng.). 1973. 3.50 (ISBN 0-8226-0503-1, 503). Littlefield.

INIS Thesaurus: Version Francaise. (INIS Reference Ser.: No. 13). 840p. 1979. pap. write for info. (ISBN 92-0-278079-X, IAEA-INIS-13, IAEA). Unipub.

Jean's Pocket Dictionaries: French-English. 224p. (Orig., Fr. & Eng.). 1981. pap. 2.25 (ISBN 0-8437-1725-4). Hammond Inc.

Kendris, C. Dictionary of Five-Hundred-One French Verbs Fully Conjugated. 527p. (Fr. & Eng.). $11.75; pap. $5.00. Barron.

Kettridge's French-English, English-French Dictionary. 700p. (Fr. & Eng.). pap. $2.50. NAL.

Langbaum, Francesca L., ed. The Random House Basic Dictionary French. (Fr. & Eng.). 1981. pap. $1.50 (ISBN 0-345-29617-6). Ballantine.

Langenscheidt English-French Lilliput Dictionary. 640p. (Fr. & Eng.). plastic $1.50 (ISBN 3-468-96408-0). Langenscheidt.

Langenscheidt French-English Lilliput Dictionary. 640p. (Fr. & Eng.). plastic $1.50 (ISBN 3-468-96407-2). Langenscheidt.

Langenscheidt's Lilliput English-French Dictionary. 640p. (Eng. & Fr.). 1972. $1.50 (ISBN 0-685-31353-0). Am Map.

Langenscheidt's Universal French-English, English-French Dictionary. 12th ed. 464p. (Eng. & Fr.). 1972. $2.95x (ISBN 0-685-31346-8). Am Map.

Larousse & Co. Larousse de poche French-English & English-French. (Fr. & Eng.). pap. $6.95 (ISBN 2-03-029203-6, 1009). Larousse.

Larousse And Co. Mon Premier Larousse francais-anglais, anglais-francais en couleurs. (Fr. & Eng.). (gr. 6-9). $23.75 (ISBN 2-03-051431-4, 3794). Larousse.

Larousse Bi-Lingual French-English, English French Dictionary. (Apollo). (Fr. & Eng.). 10.50 (ISBN 2-03-020903-1, 3767). Larousse.

Larousse French-English Dictionary. (Fr. & Eng.). 1981. pap. 3.95 (ISBN 0-671-47166-X). PB.

Larousse Modern French-English, English-French Dictionary. (Fr. & Eng.). 29.95 (ISBN 2-03-020602-4, 3776). Larousse.

Lilliput Dictionary. 640p. (Fr. & Eng., New York). $1.50 (102). Langenscheidt.

Lilliput Dictionary. 640p. (Eng. & Fr.). $1.50 (103). Langenscheidt.

Lipton, Gladys. French Bilingual Dictionary. (Illus., Fr. & Eng.). 1979. pap. $5.00; Pocket ed., 335p. pap. $3.25. Barron.

--French Bilingual Dictionary: Compact Ed. rev. ed. LC 78-20788. (Illus., Fr. & Eng.). (gr. 7-12). 1979. pap. $3.25 (ISBN 0-8120-2007-3). Barron.

Mansion, J. E. Harrap's Concise Student French & English Dictionary. new ed. Collin, P. H., et al, eds. (Fr. & Eng.). (gr. 9-12). 1978. Repr. text ed. 9.95 (ISBN 0-8442-1872-3, 1872-4). Natl Textbk.

--Harrap's New Collegiate French & English Dictionary. rev. ed. Ledesert, D. H., ed. LC 75-182800. (Fr. & Eng.). (gr. 9-12). 1967. Repr. text ed. 14.95 (ISBN 0-8442-1873-1, 1873-4). Natl Textbk.

--Harrap's New Standard French & English Dictionary, 4 vols. Rev. ed. (Fr. & Eng.). 1980. Vols. 1-2: Eng.-Fr. $90.00; Vols. 3-4: Fr.-Eng. $90.00; of 4 vols. $169.00 set. Imported Bks.

--Harrap's New Standard French & English Dictionary, Part One, French-English (A-I) rev. ed. Ledesert, D. H. & Ledesert, R. P., eds. (Fr. & Eng.). 1972. Repr. text ed. 32.50 (ISBN 0-8442-1876-6, 1874-4). Natl Textbk.

--Harrap's New Standard French & English Dictionary, Part One, French-English (J-Z) rev. ed. Ledesert, D. H. & Ledesert, R. P., eds. (Fr. & Eng.). 1972. Repr. 32.50 (ISBN 0-8442-1884-7, 1875-4). Natl Textbk.

--Harrap's Standard French & English Dictionary, Part 2, English-French (A-Z) rev. ed. (Fr. & Eng.). 1962. Repr. text ed. 49.50 (ISBN 0-8442-1898-7, 1876-4). Natl Textbk.

--Harrap's Super-Mini French & English Dictionary. abridged ed. Forbes, Patricia & Ledesert, Margaret, eds. (Fr. & Eng.). (gr. 7-12). 1977. pap. 2.75 (ISBN 0-8442-1871-5, 1871-4). Natl Textbk.

Marcy, Teresa & Marcy, Michel. Cortina-Grosset Basic French Dictionary. Berberi, Dilaver & Berberi, Edel A., eds. LC 73-18522. 384p. (Fr.). 1975. pap. $3.50 (ISBN 0-448-14031-4, G&D). Putnam Pub Group.

Muller, Wilhelm. Customs Dictionary: German-English-French-Italian. LC 72-311634. 277p. (Ger., Eng., Fr. & Ital.). 1971. 17.50x (ISBN 3-8029-8565-6). Intl Pubns Serv.

Murray, Joseph P. Selective English Old-French Glossary As a Basis for Studies in Old French Onomatology & Synonymics. LC 77-128932. (Carl Ser.: No. 40). (Fr. & Eng.). Repr. of 1950 ed. $16.00 (ISBN 0-404-50340-3). AMS Pr.

Nouveau Larousse Francais-Anglais, English-French. (Mars). (Eng. & Fr.). $24.50 (ISBN 2-03-020812-4, 4083). Larousse.

Nuss, A. M. Export for Marketing French. 96p. (Fr. & Eng.). 1979. pap. $13.95 (ISBN 0-582-35157-X, M-9208). French & Eur.

Peron, Michel, et al. Dictionnaire francais-anglais, anglais-francais des affaires: A French-English English-French Dictionary of Business Terms. rev. ed. 512p. (Fr. & Eng.). 1974. $30.95 (ISBN 2-03-020609-1, 3764). Larousse.

Petit, Charles & Savage, William. Dictionnaire Classique Anglais-Francais et Francais-Anglais. 686p. (Eng. & Fr.). 1967. pap. $27.50 (ISBN 0-686-57072-3, M-6444). French & Eur.

Piraux, H. French-Eng., Eng-French Dictionary of Electrotechnic Electronics & Allied Fields, 2 Vols. (Fr. & Eng.). Set. 90.00 (ISBN 0-685-12017-1). Heinman.

Practical Dictionary for Press & Advertising. 256p. (Ger. , Eng. & Fr.). 1972. pap. $15.00x (ISBN 0-8002-1334-3). Intl Pubns Serv.

Ratcliff, Ronald E. & Peck, Michael A. Dictionary of Naval Terminology-Dictionnaire de Terminologie Navale: English-French; Anglais-Francais. (Illus.). 160p. (Orig.). 1983. pap. text ed. $39.00x (ISBN 2-85206-200-3, Pub. by Technique Doc France). Sheridan.

Rudler, G. & Anderson, N. C., eds. French-English, English-French Gem Dictionary. (Gem Foreign Language Ser.). (Fr. & Eng.). 1952. $2.95 (ISBN 0-00-458617-4, G2). Collins Pubs.

Sabek, Jerwan. English-French-Arabic Trilingual Dictionary. (Eng., Fr. & Arabic.). $35.00x (ISBN 0-86685-116-X). Intl Bk Ctr.

Steiner, Roger J. The Bantam New College French & English Dictionary. 736p. (Fr. & Eng.). pap. $2.75 (ISBN 0-553-14890-7). Bantam.

--The New College French & English Dictionary. (Fr. & Eng.). (gr. 7-12). 1972. pap. text ed. $8.58 (ISBN 0-87720-463-2). AMSCO Sch.

Switzer, Richard & Gochberg, Herbert S., eds. New Century Vest Pocket French Dictionary. rev. ed. (Orig., Fr.). 2.95 (ISBN 0-686-86497-2). New Century.

Urwin, Kenneth, ed. A Short Old French Dictionary for Students. 108p. (Fr.). 1972. pap. $7.50x (ISBN 0-631-07970-X, Pub. by Basil Blackwell). Biblio Dist.

Villers, M. Vocabulaire de l'Informatique de Gestion: Anglais-Francais. 31p. (Eng. & Fr.). 1980. pap. $3.95 (ISBN 2-551-03899-5, M-9228). French & Eur.

Violette, Louis. Dictionnaire Samoa-Francais-Anglais et Francais-Samoa-Anglais. LC 75-35215. (Fr. & Eng.). Repr. of 1879 ed. $44.50 (ISBN 0-404-14238-9). AMS Pr.

Williams, Rosalind. Practical French-English, English-French Dictionary. (Hippocrene Practical Language Dictionaries Ser.). 400p. (Orig., Eng. & Fr.). 1983. pap. $6.95 (ISBN 0-88254-815-8). Hippocrene Bks.

World Wide French Language Dictionary French-English. 512p. (Fr. & Eng.). $7.95; pap. $3.95 (ISBN 0-8329-9682-3). New Century.

ENGLISH LANGUAGE–DICTIONARIES–GAELIC

Dwelly. Illustrated Gaelic-English Dictionary. 8th ed. (Illus., Gaelic & Eng.). $35.00x (ISBN 0-686-00868-5). Colton Bk.

I.A.R.R. Abair faclan. LC 80-508491. viii, 162p. (Gaelic & Eng.). 1979. pap. write for info. (ISBN 0-906675-00-6). Mingulay.

Jamieson, John. Etymological Dictionary of the Scottish Language, 5 Vols. rev. ed. Longmuir, John & Donaldson, David, eds. LC 70-144425. (Gaelic.). Repr. of 1887 ed. Set. $325.00 (ISBN 0-404-59470-0). AMS Pr.

Mackay, Charles. Dictionary of Lowland Scotch. LC 68-17998. (Scottish.). 1968. Repr. of 1888 ed. $45.00x (ISBN 0-8103-3284-1). Gale.

MacLennan, Malcolm. Gaelic Dictionary: Gaelic-English English-Gaelic. 632p. (Gaelic & Eng.). 1980. 45.00 (ISBN 0-08-025713-5); pap. 22.00 (ISBN 0-08-025712-7). Pergamon.

--A Pronouncing & Etymological Dictionary of the Gaelic Language. LC 80-494565. xv, 613p. (Eng. & Gaelic.). 1979. E12.00 (ISBN 0-08-025713-5); write for info. (ISBN 0-08-025712-7). Aberdeen U Pr.

ENGLISH LANGUAGE–DICTIONARIES–GERMAN

Barker, M. L. & Homeyer, H., eds. The Pocket Oxford German Dictionary, 2 vols. in 1. Incl. Pt. 1. German-English. 3rd ed. (Eng. & Ger.). 1975; Pt. 2. English-German. Carr, C. T., compiled by. (Eng. & Ger.). 1975. (Ger.). pap. 5.95x (ISBN 0-19-864138-9). Oxford U Pr.

Berlitz. Berlitz Pocket Dictionaries: German-English-German. (Ger. & Eng.). pap. $4.95 (ISBN 0-02-964530-1). Macmillan.

Berlitz Editors. Berlitz Pocket Dictionaries: German-English. 300p. (Eng. & Ger.). 1982. pap. $4.95 (ISBN 0-686-93007-X, Berlitz). Macmillan.

Bertelsmann Dictionary English-German, German-English. (Ger. & Eng.). 1975. $29.95 (ISBN 3-570-01438-X, M-7444, Pub. by Bertelsmann Lexikon/VVA). French & Eur.

Betteridge, H. T. Cassell's German-English, English-German Dictionary. (Eng. & Ger.). 1978. $16.95; indexed $18.95. Imported bks.

Breuer, K. German-English, English-German Technical Pocket Dictionary. 6th. ed. (Ger. & Eng.). pap. 22.50 (ISBN 0-685-25495-X). Heinman.

Briese, K. English-German Dictionary. 624p. (Eng. & Ger.). 1980. $20.00x (ISBN 0-569-06892-4, Pub. by Collet's). State Mutual Bk.

Brockhaus Illustrated Dictionary: English-German, German-English. Rev. ed. (Illus.). 1450p. (Ger. & Eng.). 1976. $39.00. Imported Bks.

Capitol's Concise Dictionary of Seven Languages. (gr. 9-12). 1978. $29.95 (ISBN 0-8120-5333-8). Barron.

Cassell's German Dictionary: German-English, English-German. (Ger. & Eng.). standard $17.95 (ISBN 0-02-522920-6); thumb-indexed $19.95 (ISBN 0-02-522930-3); concise $9.95 (ISBN 0-02-522650-9). Macmillan.

Cassell's New Compact German Dictionary. 560p. (Ger.). 1981. pap. $3.95 (ISBN 0-440-31100-4, LE). Dell.

Cassell's New Compact German-English, English-German Dictionary. 542p. (Eng. & Ger.). pap. $3.00. Dell.

Clark, J. M., ed. German-English, English-German Gem Dictionary. (Gem Foreign Language Ser.). (Ger. & Eng.). 1953. leatheroid $2.95 (ISBN 0-00-458619-0, G3). Collins Pubs.

Collins German-English & English-German Dictionary. 1582p. (Ger. & Eng.). write for info. (ISBN 0-671-42046-1); write for info. thumb-indexed (ISBN 0-671-42045-3). S&S.

Collins German-English English-German Dictionary. 416p. (Orig., Ger. & Eng.). 1983. pap. $2.95 (ISBN 0-425-05450-0). Berkley Pub.

Collins Pocket German Dictionary. 448p. 1983. $7.95 (ISBN 0-671-49222-5). S&S.

DeVries, Louis & Jacolev, Leon. German-English Science Dictionary. 4th ed. (Ger. & Eng.). 1978. 26.95 (ISBN 0-07-016602-1, P&RB). McGraw.

Eggeling, H. F. Dictionary of Modern German Prose Usage. (Ger.). 1961. $34.00x (ISBN 0-19-864110-9). Oxford U Pr.

English-German -- German-English Welding Engineering Dictionary. 396p. (Eng. & Fr.). 1980. $75.00x (ISBN 0-569-05715-9, Pub. by Collet's). State Mutual Bk.

English-German Dictionary. (Eng. & Ger.). 14.50 (ISBN 0-87557-026-7, 026-7X). Saphrograph.

Ernst, R. German-English, English-German Dictionary of Industrial Technics, 2 vols. 4th, rev., enl. ed. (Ger. & Eng.). Set. $150.00 (ISBN 0-686-77968-1). German-english (ISBN 3-87097-096-0). English-german (ISBN 3-87097-068-5). Heinman.

Fischer, Eric & Elliott, Francis E. A German & English Glossary of Geographical Terms. LC 76-20474. (American Geographical Society Library Ser: No. 5). 111p. (Ger. & Eng.). 1976. Repr. of 1950 ed. lib. bdg. $15.00x (ISBN 0-8371-8994-2, ELGG). Greenwood.

Freeman, Henry. Technisches Taschen Woerterbuch: Deutsch-Englisch, Englisch-Deutsch, 2 vols. (Ger. & Eng.). 1978. DM.pap. 17.50 ea. Hueber.

Freeman, Henry G. Dictionary of Metal-Cutting Machine Tools, 2 vols. (Eng. & Ger.). 1965. $61.75 ea. (ISBN 3-7736-5095-7). Adler.

--Technical Pocket Dictionary, English-German, German-English, 2 vols. 2nd ed. (Eng. & Ger.). $12.00 ea. Ger.-Eng (ISBN 3-1900-6212-9). Eng.-Ger (ISBN 3-1900-6213-7). Adler.

--Tool Dictionary. 2nd ed. (Ger. & Eng.). 1960. $78.00 (ISBN 3-7736-5052-3). Adler.

Freeman, Henry G., compiled by. DIN Definitions: German-English with an English-German Vocabulary. 2nd rev. ed. (Ger. & Eng.). 80.00 (ISBN 3-4101-0804-1). Heinman.

Friedrich, Wolf. Dictionary of Tourism: German-English & English-German. LC 71-520026. (Ger. & Eng.). 1970. 5.00x (ISBN 0-8002-1259-2). Intl Pubns Serv.

Gem Language Dictionaries: German-English & English-German. (Ger. & Eng.). write for info. (ISBN 0-671-41958-7). S&S.

German Dictionary. (Eng. & Ger.). write for info. (608-94). Pan Amer Pub.

German-English & English-German Dictionary. (Ger. & Eng.). pap. $1.99 (ISBN 0-686-00471-X). Dennison.

German-English Dictionary. (Ger. & Eng.). 14.50 (ISBN 0-87557-025-9, 026-7). Saphrograph.

German-English-German. (Berlitz Pocket Dictionaries Ser.). (Ger. & Eng.). $4.95 (ISBN 0-02-964530-1). Macmillan.

Glucksman, Paul H., ed. World-Wide German Dictionary. (Ger.). 1978. pap. $2.50 (ISBN 0-449-30850-2, Prem). Fawcett.

Grosses Schulwoerterbuch English-German, 2 vols. 1439p. (Eng. & Ger.). 1983. pap. $10.90 per vol. M Rosenberg.

Hamlyn German-English Dictionary. (Ger. & Eng.). 1977. pap. 4.95 (ISBN 0-600-36564-6, 8088). Larousse.

Handwoerterbuch Deutsch-Englisch. 699p. (Ger. & Eng.). 1983. pap. $16.00. M Rosenberg.

Hoffmann, E. Dictionary for the Glass Industry: Fachwoerterbuch fuer die Glasindustrie, 2 Pts. (Pt, 1, Ger-Eng, Pt, 2, Eng-Ger). 1963. $26.60 (ISBN 0-387-03007-7). Springer-Verlag.

Hugo Pocket Dictionary: German-English, English-German. 622p. (Ger. & Eng.). 1969. 3.50 (ISBN 0-8226-0504-X, 504). Littlefield.

Hyman, Charles J. German-English, English-German Astronautics Dictionary. LC 65-20216. 273p. (Ger. & Eng.). 1968. $30.00x (ISBN 0-306-10748-1, Consultants). Plenum Pub.

IWT Verlag Editors. Microelectronics Dictionary. (Eng. & Ger.). 1980. $23.00 (ISBN 0-9961073-2-0, Pub. by VDI W Germany). Heyden.

Jean's Pocket Dictionaries: German-English. 224p. (Orig., Ger. & Eng.). 1981. pap. 2.25 (ISBN 0-8437-1726-2). Hammond Inc.

Jones, Stephen. Practical English-German, German-English Dictionary. (Hippocrene's Practical Language Dictionary Ser.). 400p. (Orig., Eng. & Ger.). 1983. pap. $6.95 (ISBN 0-88254-813-1). Hippocrene Bks.

Klaften, E. B. German-English, English-German Mathematical Dictionary. (Ger. & Eng.). pap. 15.00 (ISBN 0-686-77978-9). Heinman.

Klaften, E. B. & Allison, F. C. German-English, English-German Patent Terminological Dictionary. (Ger. & Eng.). 50.00 (ISBN 0-685-12020-1). Heinman.

Klatt, Edmund. Langenscheidt's Standard Dictionary. 1278p. (Eng. & Ger.). $14.50. Imported Bks.

Kniepkamp, H. P. Legal Dictionary. (Ger. & Eng.). $26.50 (ISBN 3-7678-0013-6). Adler.

Koehler, Friedrich. Woerterbuch der Amerikanismen. 3rd ed. (Ger.). 1972. $25.00 (ISBN 3-500-25340-7, M-7044). French & Eur.

Kohler, Friedrich. Ro Ro Ro Woerterbuch: Deutsch-Englisch, Englisch-Deutsch, 2 vols. (Eng. & Ger.). DM.pap. 3.60 ea. Rowohlt.

Langenscheidt English-German Lilliput Dictionary. 575p. (Eng. & Ger.). plastic $1.50 (ISBN 3-468-96404-8). Langenscheidt.

Langenscheidt New Muret-Sanders Encyclopedic Dictionary: German-English, 2 vols. 2020p. (Eng. & Ger.). 1974. $180.00 set. Imported Bks.

Langenscheidt's Lilliput English-German Dictionary. 640p. (Eng. & Ger.). 1972. $1.50 (ISBN 0-685-31336-0). Am Map.

Langenscheidt's Lilliput German-English Dictionary. 640p. (Eng. & Ger.). 1972. $1.50 (ISBN 0-685-31337-9). Am Map.

Lilliput Dictionary. 640p. (Eng. & Ger.). $1.50 (101). Langenscheidt.

Messinger, H. Langenscheidts Grosswoerterbuch: Englisch-Deutsch. 1104p. (Eng. & Ger.). DM.88.00 (02120). Langenscheidt.

Messinger, H. & Ruedenberger, H. Langenscheidts Grosse Schulwoerterbuecher Englisch-Deutsch. 1400p. (Eng. & Ger.). 1977. DM.19.80 (ISBN 3-468-07121-3). Langenscheidt.
Messinger, Heinz. Langenscheidt's Comprehensive English-German Dictionary. 1134p. (Eng. & Ger.). $36.00. Imported Bks.
--Langenscheidts Grosse Schulwoerterbuch Deutsch-Englisch. 1328p. (Eng. & Ger.). DM.23.80 (07126). Langenscheidt.
--Langenscheidts Grosswoerterbuch Englisch-Deutsch. (Eng. & Ger.). 1971. DM.78.00 (ISBN 3-468-02120-8). Langenscheidt.
--Langenscheidt's New College German Dictionary: German-English, English-German. 1390p. (Ger. & Eng.). 1973. $16.95. Imported Bks.
Messinger, Heinz & Rudenberg, Werner. Langenscheidts Grosse Schulwoerterbuch Englisch-Deutsch. 07121p. (Eng. & Ger.). DM.23.80. Langenscheidt.
--Langenscheidt's New College German Dictionary (German-English, English-German) 1400p. (Eng. & Ger.). 1973. $16.95 (ISBN 0-685-30210-5); thumb indexed $18.95 (ISBN 0-685-30211-3). Am Map.
Moulton, Jenni H., ed. The Random House Basic Dictionary German. (Ger. & Eng.). 1981. pap. $1.50 (ISBN 0-345-29619-2). Ballantine.
Muller, Wilhelm. Customs Dictionary: German-English-French-Italian. LC 72-311634. 277p. (Ger., Eng., Fr. & Ital.). 1971. 17.50x (ISBN 3-8029-8565-6). Intl Pubns Serv.
New College Dictionary English-German. 1400p. (Eng. & Ger.). 1983. pap. $16.95. M Rosenberg.
Ottenheimer, ed. German-English, English-German Dictionary. (Ger. & Eng.). pap. $2.50 (ISBN 0-06-465028-6, DI 2, BN). B&N NY.
Pons Globalwoerterbuch Englisch-Deutsch, 2 vols. 1178p. (Eng. & Ger.). pap. $10.90. M Rosenberg.
Putnam's Contemporary German Dictionary. (Ger. & Eng.). 1980. pap. $2.25 (ISBN 0-425-04362-2). Berkley Pub.
Reisewoerterbuch Deutsch-Englisch. 239p. (Ger. & Eng.). $5.90. M Rosenberg.
Sawers, Robin, ed. Harrap's Concise German & English Dictionary. 1120p. (Ger. & Eng.). E6.95 (ISBN 0-245-53869-0). Harrap.
Schoeffler, Weis. Woerterbuch der Englischen und Deutschen Sprache, Vol. 1. (Ger. & Eng., Dictionary of the English & German Language). pap. $17.95 (ISBN 3-12-518100-3, M-7015). French & Eur.
--Woerterbuch der Englischen und Deutschen Sprache, Vol. 2. (Ger. & Eng., Dictionary of the English & German Language). pap. $17.95 (ISBN 3-12-518200-X, M-7014). French & Eur.
Schoffler & Weis. Pons Globalworterbuch. LC 78-400567. (Eng. & Ger.). 1978. DM.21.80 (ISBN 3-12-517130-X). Klett.
Smith, Josefa J., et al, eds. Cortina-Grosset Basic German Dictionary. LC 73-18523. 384p. (Ger.). 1975. pap. $3.50 (ISBN 0-686-96722-4, G&D). Putnam Pub Group.
Springer, O. New Muret-Sanders Encyclopedic Dictionary: Part II, German-English, 2 vols. 1040p. (Ger. & Eng.). 1983. pap. $80.00 ea. M Rosenberg.
Springer, O., ed. New Muret-Sanders Encyclopedic Dictionary: Part I, English-German, 2 vols. 958p. (Eng. & Ger.). 1983. pap. $70.00 ea. M Rosenberg.
Springer, Otto. Der Grosse Muret-Sanders: Teil I, Englisch-Deutsch, 2 vols. 1843p. (Eng. & Ger.). 1963. DM.178.00 set; Band A-M. (01120); Band N-Z. (01122). Langenscheidt.
Springer, Otto, ed. Langenscheidt's New Muret-Sanders English-German Dictionary, 2 vols, Part I. Incl. Vol. 1. A-M. 924p. 1962. 70.00x (ISBN 3-468-01120-2); Vol. 2. N-Z. 958p. 1963. 70.00x (ISBN 0-685-31317-4). (Eng. & Ger.). Hippocrene Bks.
Technik-Worterbuch: Optik & Optischer Geratebau. 432p. 1980. vinyl $90.00x (ISBN 0-686-72097-0, Pub. by Collet's). State Mutual Bk.
Terrell, Peter, et al. Collins German Dictionary: German-English, English-Ger. 1600p. (Ger. & Eng.). 1980. $20.00. Imported Bks.
Traupman, John C. New College German & English Dictionary. (Ger. & Eng.). (gr. 9-12). 1981. reference $12.00 (ISBN 0-87720-584-1). AMSCO Sch.
Traupman, John C., ed. The Bantam New College German & English Dictionary. 768p. (Orig., Ger. & Eng.). (gr. 7-12). 1981. pap. $2.50 (ISBN 0-553-14155-4). Bantam.
Tuttle's Watch-Pocket Dictionary. Eng.-Japanese $2.00 (ISBN 0-8048-0600-4). C E Tuttle.
Universal Woerterbuch Englisch-Deutsch. (Eng. & Ger.). 1983. $4.10. M Rosenberg.
Unseld, D. W. Medical Dictionary. (Ger. & Eng.). 1982. $39.50 (ISBN 3-8047-0661-4). Adler.
Wahrig, G. German-English Dictionary. 661p. (Ger. & Eng.). 1980. $35.00x (ISBN 0-569-05717-5, Pub. by Collet's). State Mutual Bk.
Walther, R. Technical Dictionary of Production Engineering: Vol. 2, German-English. (Ger. & Eng.). $49.00 (ISBN 0-08-016960-0). Pergamon.
Webel, A. A German-English Dictionary of Technical, Scientific & General Terms. 3rd ed. (Ger. & Eng.). 1969. Repr. of 1952 ed. $37.50 (ISBN 0-7100-2258-1). Routledge & Kegan.
Weis, E., et al. Pons Schoffler Weis English-German, German-English Dictionary. 1060p. (Eng. & Ger.). 1979. $52.50 (ISBN 3-12-517120-2, M-9361). French & Eur.
Wernicke, H. Dictionary of Electronics, Communications & Electrical Engineering, 2 vols. 1300p. Vol. 1. $32.50 ea. (ISBN 0-685-05199-4); Vol. 2. $36.00 ea. (ISBN 0-685-05200-1). Adler.
World Wide German Language Dictionary German-English. 544p. (Ger. & Eng.). $7.95 (ISBN 0-8329-0144-X); pap. $3.95 (ISBN 0-8329-9687-4). New Century.
Zahn, Hans E. English-German Glossary of Financial & Economic Terms. (Eng. & Ger.). 1977. 56.00x (ISBN 3-7819-2013-5). Intl Pubns Serv.

ENGLISH LANGUAGE–DICTIONARIES–GREEK

Brown, C. N. Modern English-Greek Dictionary. 420p. (Gr. & Eng.). 1976. $12.50 (ISBN 0-686-92187-9, M-9592). French & Eur.
Divry, G. C. Modern English-Greek-English Desk Dictionary with Thumb Index. 768p. (Gr. & Eng.). 1979. $19.95 (ISBN 0-686-97405-0, M-9443). French & Eur.
--New English-Greek-English Handy Dictionary. 511p. (Eng. & Gr.). 1978. $9.95 (ISBN 0-686-92414-2, M-9439). French & Eur.
English-Greek Pocket Dictionary. (Eng. & Gr.). pap. $8.50 (ISBN 0-685-77571-2, 030-5). Saphrograph.
Gelis, D. N., ed. Greek-English, English-Greek Medical Dictionary. 4th rev. ed. (Illus., Gr. & Eng.). 1978. 75.00 (ISBN 0-686-91764-2). Heinman.
Hionides, H. T. Greek-English, English-Greek Technical Dictionary, Vol.1-2. rev. ed. (Eng. & Gr.). Date not set. Set. text ed. $50.00 (ISBN 0-686-46533-4). Heinman.
Hoffman, Horace Addison. Everyday Greek: Greek Words in English, Including Scientific Terms. (Midway Reprint). 1976. pap. $8.00x (ISBN 0-226-34787-7). U of Chicago Pr.
Langenscheidt Modern Greek-English Lilliput Dictionary. 640p. (Eng. & Ger.). plastic $1.50 (ISBN 3-468-96472-2). Langenscheidt.
Langenscheidt's Lilliput Modern Greek-English Dictionary. (Eng. & Ger.). 1972. $1.50 (ISBN 0-685-87395-1). Am Map.
Liddell & Scott. An Intermediate Greek-English Lexicon. 910p. (Gr. & Eng.). 1980. $35.00. Oxford U Pr.
Liddell, H. G. & Scott, Robert, eds. Abridged Greek-English Lexicon. (Gr. & Eng.). 1957. $24.95x (ISBN 0-19-910207-4). Oxford U Pr.
--Intermediate Greek-English Lexicon. (Gr. & Eng.). 1959. text ed. 30.00x (ISBN 0-19-910206-6). Oxford U Pr.
Liddell, Henry G. & Scott, Robert, eds. Greek-English Lexicon. 9th ed. (Gr. & Eng.). 1940. 79.00x (ISBN 0-19-864214-8). Oxford U Pr.
Parkhurst. Greek & English Lexicon. 680p. (Gr. & Eng.). Repr. of 1769 ed. loose leaf bdg. $29.95 (ISBN 0-89957-549-8). AMG Pubs.
Patsis, C. Greek-English, English-Greek Dictionary, 2 vols. (Gr. & Eng.). Set. 50.00 (ISBN 0-685-79111-4). Heinman.
Pocket-Shorter Dictionary. 600p. (Gr. & Eng.). $5.95 (087). Langenscheidt.
Schaeffer, Rudolph F., ed. Greek English Derivative Dictionary. (Gr. & Eng.). $1.95 (B6). Am Classical.

ENGLISH LANGUAGE–DICTIONARIES–GREEK, MODERN

Berlitz Editors. Berlitz Greek for Travellers. 192p. (Gr.). 1982. pap. 4.95 (ISBN 0-686-92956-X, Berlitz); pap. 4.95 (ISBN 0-02-964040-7). Macmillan.
Divry, George C., ed. Divry's New Modern Greek-English & English-Greek Handy Dictionary. rev. ed. (Gr. & Eng.). 1978. pocket ed. $4.20 (ISBN 0-685-09029-9); with thumb indexes $5.50 (ISBN 0-685-09030-2); lea. $8.50 (ISBN 0-685-09031-0). Divry.
Divry's Modern English-Greek & Greek-English Desk Dictionary. (Eng. & Gr.). 1982. $9.50 (ISBN 0-685-81638-9); thumb indexed $12.00 (ISBN 0-685-81639-7). Divry.
Feyerabend, Karl, ed. Langenscheidt's Pocket Greek Dictionary, Classical Greek-English. (Langenscheidt Pocket Dictionaries Ser.). 428p. (Eng. & Gr.). 1969. $5.95 (ISBN 0-685-31349-2). Am Map.
Greek-English Dictionary "Modern". (Gr. & Eng.). $15.00 (ISBN 0-87557-029-1, 028-3Y). Saphrograph.
Greek-English, English-Greek Pocket Dictionary. (Gr. & Eng.). 9.00 (ISBN 0-685-58555-7). Heinman.
Greek-English Pocket Dictionary. (Gr. & Eng.). pap. 8.50 (ISBN 0-685-77570-4, 030-5X). Saphrograph.
Jannaris, A. N. A Concise Dictionary of the English & Modern Greek Languages. xvi, 436p. (Eng. & Gr.). 1981. lib. bdg. $35.00x (ISBN 0-89241-333-6); pap. text ed. $20.00x (ISBN 0-89241-339-5). Caratzas Pub Co.
Kykkotis, I. Modern English-Greek & Greek-English Dictionary. 652p. (Eng. & Gr.). 1980. $40.00x (ISBN 0-85331-046-7, Pub. by Lund Humphries England). State Mutual Bk.
Lilliput Dictionary. 640p. (Modern Gr. & Eng.). $1.50 (114). Langenscheidt.
Pring, J. T., ed. The Oxford Dictionary of Modern Greek: English-Greek. (Gr. Eng.). 1982. $15.95x (ISBN 0-19-864136-2). Oxford U Pr.
--The Oxford Dictionary of Modern Greek: Greek-English, English-Greek. (Gr. & Eng.). 1982. 19.95 (ISBN 0-19-864137-0). Oxford U Pr.
Rogers, Thomas. Greek Word Roots: A Practical List with Greek & English Derivatives. 32p. (Gr. & Eng.). 1981. pap. $1.95 (ISBN 0-8010-7707-9). Baker Bk.
Vassiliades, G., ed. Penguin-Hellenews English-Greek Dictionary. (Eng. & Gr.). 1978. $35.00 (ISBN 0-89241-051-5). Caratzas Pub Co.

ENGLISH LANGUAGE–DICTIONARIES–HEBREW

Alcalay, Reuben. Complete English-Hebrew, Hebrew-English Dictionary, 3 vols. 7180p. (Eng. & Hebrew.). 1980. Repr. of 1965 ed. $69.00 set (ISBN 0-89961-003-X). Vol. 1 (ISBN 0-89961-017-X). Vol. 2 (ISBN 0-89961-007-2). Vol. 3 (ISBN 0-89961-008-0). SBS Pub.
--The Massada English-Hebrew Student Dictionary. 734p. (Eng. & Hebrew.). 1980. Repr. $18.95 (ISBN 0-89961-006-4). SBS Pub.
Alcalay, Rueben. The Complete English-Hebrew Dictionary, 2 vols. 2150p. (Eng. & Hebrew.). 1981. IL.60.00 set; Vol. I, A-L. (35-2093); Vol. II, M-Z. (35-2094). Massada Pr.
--The Complete Hebrew-English Dictionary. 1456p. (Hebrew & Eng.). 1981. IL.43.00 (35-2091). Massada Pr.
--The Massada Student Dictionary English-Hebrew. 736p. (Eng. & Hebrew.). 1978. IL.13.00 (002198). Massada Pr.
Berlitz Editors. Berlitz Hebrew for Travellers. 192p. (Hebrew.). 1982. pap. $4.95 (ISBN 0-02-964050-4, Berlitz). Macmillan.
Dov Ben Abba. The Signet Hebrew-English - English-Hebrew Dictionary. (Orig., Hebrew & Eng.). 1978. pap. $2.95 (ISBN 0-451-09654-1, E9654, Sig). NAL.
Feyerabend, Karl, ed. Langenscheidt's Pocket Hebrew Dictionary, Hebrew-English. (Langenscheidt Pocket Dictionaries Ser.). 400p. (Eng. & Hebrew.). 1969. $5.95 (ISBN 0-685-31348-4). Am Map.
Furst, Gesenius. Hebrew-English Dictionary: Hebrew & Chaldee Lexicon to the Old Testament. rev. ed. Mitchell, Edward C., ed. (Hebrew & Eng.). $42.50 (ISBN 0-87559-021-7); thumb indexed $42.50 (ISBN 0-87559-022-5). Shalom.
Gesenius, William. Hebrew & Chaldee Lexicon, Tregelles Translation. (Hebrew & Chaldee.). 1949. $12.95 (ISBN 0-8028-8029-0). Eerdmans.
Goldberg, Nathan. New Functional Hebrew-English, English-Hebrew Dictionary. (Hebrew & Eng.). (gr. 9-12). 1958. $5.00x (ISBN 0-87068-379-9). Ktav.
Hebrew Pocket Dictionary. (Hebrew & Eng.). $12.50 (ISBN 0-685-12022-8). Heinman.
Jastrow, Marcus. Hebrew-Aramaic-English Dictionary, a Dictionary of Talmud Babli & Talmud Yerushalmi Targum & Midrash, 2 Vols. (Hebrew, Aramaic & Eng.). $68.50 (ISBN 0-87559-019-5). Shalom.
The Megiddo Modern Dictionary: English-Hebrew to Hebrew-English, 2 Vols. 2000p. (Eng. & Hebrew.). 1982. lib. bdg. $125.00 (ISBN 0-686-97939-7, M-9904). French & Eur.
Simon & Schuster Gem Ben-Yehuda's Hebrew-English & English-Hebrew Dictionary. (Hebrew & Eng.). write for info. vinyl jacket (ISBN 0-671-46098-6). S&S.
Sivan, Reuben & Levenston, Edward A. The New Bantam-Meggido Hebrew & English Dictionary. 736p. (Eng. & Hebrew.). pap. $2.95 (ISBN 0-553-14420-0). Bantam.
Sivan, Reuven & Levenston, Edward A. The New Bantam-Megiddo Hebrew & English Dictionary. LC 77-75289. (Hebrew & Eng.). 1977. $24.95 (ISBN 0-8052-3666-X). Schocken.

Waldstein, A. Hebrew-English, English-Hebrew Dictionary. (Hebrew & Eng.). $18.50 (ISBN 0-87559-016-0); thumb indexed $23.50 (ISBN 0-87559-017-9). Shalom.

ENGLISH LANGUAGE–DICTIONARIES–HINDI

Bahri, Hardev. Comprehensive English-Hindi Dictionary, 2 vols. rev. 2nd ed. 2200p. (Eng. & Hindi.). 1969. $40.00x (ISBN 0-8002-0533-2). Intl Pubns Serv.

Bulke. English Hindi Dictionary. (Eng. & Hindi.). 1979. $15.00 (ISBN 0-89744-967-3). Auromere.

Chaturvedi, Mahendra & Bhola, Nath T. A Practical Hindi-English Dictionary. 700p. (Hindi & Eng.). 1974. $14.00x (ISBN 0-88386-380-4). South Asia Bks.

English-Hindi Dictionary. (Eng. & Hindi.). large ed. $27.50 (ISBN 0-87557-034-8); small ed. $19.50 (ISBN 0-686-66962-2, 033-XX). Saphrograph.

Hindi-English Dictionary. (Hindi & Eng.). $27.50 (ISBN 0-87557-033-X, 034-8); large ed. $24.50 (ISBN 0-685-59369-X). Saphrograph.

Meenakshi Hindi-English Dictionary. (Hindi & Eng.). 1981. $13.50x (ISBN 0-8364-0790-3, Pub. by Meenakshi). South Asia Bks.

Pathak, R. C. Concise English Hindi Dictionary. (Eng. & Hindi.). 1979. $6.50 (ISBN 0-89744-972-X). Auromere.

--Concise Hindi-English Dictionary. (Eng. & Hindi.). 1979. $6.50 (ISBN 0-89744-971-1). Auromere.

--Hindi English Dictionary. (Hindi & Eng.). 1979. $11.00 (ISBN 0-89744-969-X). Auromere.

Pathak, R. C., ed. Hindi-English - English-Hindi Standard Illustrated Dictionary, 2 vols. (Illus., Hindi & Eng.). Set. $40.00 (ISBN 0-686-68936-4). Vol. 1, Hindi-Eng., 1512pp. Vol. 2. Eng.-Hindi, Heinman.

Pradeeps Standard Oxford Dictionary: English to English, Panjabi & Hindi, with Pronunciations & Idioms. 1983. $15.00x (ISBN 0-8364-0991-4, Pub. by Pradeep Co). South Asia Bks.

Shanney, A. T. Hindi-English Dictionary: With Pronounciations Romanized. (Hindi & Eng.). $27.50 (ISBN 0-87559-113-2). Shalom.

Suryakanta. Sanskrit-Hindi-English Dictionary. (Sanskrit, Hindi & Eng.). 1976. $47.50x (ISBN 0-8002-1950-3). Intl Pubns Serv.

Vira, Raghu. A Comprehensive English-Hindi Dictionary of Governmental & Educational Words & Phrases. 1761p. (Eng. & Hindi.). 1976. $40.00x (ISBN 0-8002-0664-9). Intl Pubns Serv.

ENGLISH LANGUAGE–DICTIONARIES–HINDUSTANI

English-Hindustani Dictionary. (Eng. & Hindustani.). pap. $17.50 (ISBN 0-87557-036-4, 036-4). Saphrograph.

Platts, John T. Dictionary of Urdu, Classical Hindi, & English. (Urdu., Hindu & Eng.). 1930. $82.00x (ISBN 0-19-864309-8). Oxford U Pr.

ENGLISH LANGUAGE–DICTIONARIES–HUNGARIAN

Andras, L. T. & Murval, M. How to Say It in Hungarian: An English-Hungarian Phrase-Book with Lists of Words. 6th ed. (Illus., Eng. & Hungarian.). 1979. $6.50 (ISBN 9-6317-4194-X). Heinman.

Magy, Tamas. Utiszotar, Angol-Magyar. LC 79-345136. 313p. (Hungarian & Eng.). 1978. 33.00 Ft (ISBN 9-632-05069-X). Terra.

Nagy, E. & Klar, J., eds. English-Hungarian Technical Dictionary. 792p. (Eng. & Hungarian.). 1980. $70.00x (ISBN 0-686-72096-2, Pub. by Collet's). State Mutual Bk.

Orszagh, I. Pocket English-Hungarian Dictionary. (Eng. & Hungarian.). 1980. $20.00x (ISBN 0-569-00408-X, Pub. by Collet's). State Mutual Bk.

--Pocket Hungarian-English Dictionary. (Hungarian & Eng.). 1980. $20.00x (ISBN 0-569-00344-X, Pub. by Collet's). State Mutual Bk.

Orszagh, L. Hungarian-English, English-Hungarian Concise Dictionary (1976-79, 2 vols. rev & enl ed. (Hungarian & Eng.). $55.00 set (ISBN 0-685-29277-0). Vol. 1, Hungarian-English, 9th ed. Vol. 2, English-Hungarian, 10th ed (ISBN 9-6305-2464-3). Heinman.

Orszagh, Laszlo. Hungarian-English: English Hungarian Dictionary, 2 vols. 13th rev. ed. (Hungarian & Eng.). Set. $20.00x (ISBN 963-05-2019-2). Heinman.

Orszagh, Laszlo, ed. English-Hungarian Dictionary. 13th ed. 608p. (Eng. & Hungarian.). 1982. $6.25x (ISBN 963-05-2975-0). Intl Pubns Serv.

Orszagh, V. A Concise English-Hungarian Dictionary. 1091p. (Eng. & Hungarian.). 1980. $50.00 (ISBN 0-569-00407-1, Pub. by Collet's). State Mutual Bk.

--A Concise Hungarian-English Dictionary. 1180p. (Hungarian & Eng.). 1980. $50.00x (ISBN 0-569-00343-1, Pub. by Collet's). State Mutual Bk.

--English-Hungarian Dictionary, 2 vols. 2336p. (Eng. & Hungarian.). 1980. $99.00x (ISBN 0-569-00359-8, Pub. by Collet's). State Mutual Bk.

--Hungarian-English Dictionary, 2 vols. 2160p. (Hungarian & Eng.). 1980. $125.00x (ISBN 0-569-00409-8, Pub. by Collet's). State Mutual Bk.

Razso, Imre. English-Hungarian Technical Dictionary-Angol-Magyar Muszaki Szotar. (Eng. & Hungarian.). $29.50 (ISBN 0-87557-041-0, 041-0). Saphrograph.

Tamas, Magay. Hungarian Dictionary for Tourists. 5th ed. (Hungarian & Eng.). 1980. $6.00x (ISBN 96-320-5110-6, H300). Vanous.

Willerfest, Biro. English-Hungarian, Hungarian-English Dictionary-Angol-Magyar-Angol Szotar. (Eng. & Hungarian.). $19.50 (ISBN 0-87557-039-9, 042-2). Saphrograph.

ENGLISH LANGUAGE–DICTIONARIES–ICELANDIC AND OLD NORSE

Bogason, S. O. English-Icelandic Dictionary. (Eng. & Icelandic.). $75.00 (ISBN 0-685-29251-7). Heinman.

Sigurdsson, A. & Bogason, S. O. Icelandic-English - English-Icelandic Dictionary, 2 vols. 3rd ed. (Icelandic & Eng.). Set. $155.00 (ISBN 0-686-68938-0). Heinman.

Taylor, A. Icelandic-English-Icelandic, Pocket Dictionary. 176p. (Icelandic & Eng.). 1980. pap. $11.00x (ISBN 0-89918-103-1, IC103). Vanous.

Zoega, Geir T. Concise Dictionary of Old Icelandic. (Icelandic.). 1910. $39.00x (ISBN 0-19-863108-1). Oxford U Pr.

ENGLISH LANGUAGE–DICTIONARIES–INDIAN LANGUAGES

Baraga, R. R. Dictionary of the Otchipwe Language. (Chippwe.). Repr. $20.00 (ISBN 0-87018-002-9). Ross.

La Fleche, Francis. A Dictionary of the Osage Language. Repr. of 1932 ed. $49.00 (ISBN 0-403-03580-5). Scholarly.

Miller, Wick R. Newe Natekwinappeh: Shoshoni Stories & Dictionary. (Utah Anthropological Papers: No. 94). (Shoshoni.). Repr. of 1972 ed. $24.00 (ISBN 0-404-60694-6). AMS Pr.

Rand, Silas T. Dictionary of the Languages of the Micmac Indians, Who Reside in Nova Scotia, New Brunswick, Prince Edward Island, Cape Breton & Newfoundland. Repr. of 1888 ed. $40.00 (ISBN 0-384-49565-6). Johnson Repr.

Zeisberger, David. Zeisberger's Indian Dictionary: English, German, Iroquois - the Onandaga & Algonquin - the Delaware. LC 76-43905. 248p. (Eng., Ger. & Iroquois.). Repr. of 1887 ed. $42.50 (ISBN 0-404-15802-1). AMS Pr.

ENGLISH LANGUAGE–DICTIONARIES–INDONESIAN

Baihaki, Achmad, et al. Dafoar islilah pertanian, 2 vols. LC 81-941728. (Eng. & Indonesian.). 1979. write for info. Pustaka Antara.

Deshpande, P. G. A Modern English-Gujarati Dictionary. 820p. (Eng. & Gujarati.). 1983. $29.95 (ISBN 0-19-561140-3). Oxford U Pr.

Echols, John M. & Shadily, Hassan. An English-Indonesian Dictionary. LC 72-5638. 660p. (Eng. & Indonesian.). 1975. $49.50x (ISBN 0-8014-0728-1); softcover $27.50x (ISBN 0-8014-9859-7). Cornell U Pr.

Hassan, Irene. Tausug-English Dictionary. LC 78-317697. 789p. (Eng. & Tausug.). 1975. write for info. Jolu, Sulu.

Karim, A. Common English Words & Idioms with Their Equivalents in Bahasa Indonesia. (Indonesian.). 1978. pap. $8.50 (ISBN 0-8048-1283-7). C E Tuttle.

Kramer, A. L., Sr. English-Indonesian, Indonesian-English Dictionary. (Eng. & Indonesian.). $24.50 (ISBN 0-87559-066-7); thumb indexed $29.50 (ISBN 0-87559-067-5). Shalom.

--Van Goor's Concise Indonesian Dictionary: English-Indonesian Indonesian-English. LC 66-23535. (Indonesian.). 1966. Repr. $8.95 (ISBN 0-8048-0611-X). C E Tuttle.

Schmidgall-Tellings, A. Ed. & Stevens, Alan. Contemporary Indonesian-English Dictionary. LC 80-20994. xvi, 388p. (Indonesian & Eng.). 1981. $28.95x (ISBN 0-8214-0424-5, 82-83152); pap. $14.95x (ISBN 0-8214-0435-0, 82-83160). Ohio U Pr.

Siregar, A. Hamid. Kamus Inggeris Indonesia: Dictionary English-Indonesia for School, Office & Home. LC 74-940821. 313p. (Indonesian & Eng.). 1974. write for info. Pustaka Antara.

ENGLISH LANGUAGE–DICTIONARIES–IRISH

De Bhaldraithe, Tomas. English-Irish Dictionary. LC 79-304424. 25p. (Eng. & Gaelic.). 1978. E0.30. Oifig An Tsolathair.

De Bhaldraithe, Tomas & Claithe, Baile A. English-Irish Dictionary: Terminological Additions & Corrections. LC 79-304424. 25p. (Eng. & Gaelic.). 1978. E0.30. Govt Publications Sale Office.

De Bhardraithe, T. English-Irish Dictionary. (Eng. & Irish.). 1959. $12.50x (ISBN 0-686-00860-X). Colton Bk.

Dinneen, Patrick S. English-Irish Dictionary. rev. ed. Murcava, L. O., ed. (Eng. & Irish.). $22.50 (ISBN 0-87559-072-1); thumb indexed $27.50 (ISBN 0-87559-040-3). Shalom.

Ireland Department of Education. Focloir Modulach. LC 80-484412. 25p. (Eng. & Gaelic.). 1978. write for info. Le Ceannach Direach on Oifig Dhiolta Foilseachan Rialtais.

O'Reilly, Edward. An Irish-English Dictionary. (Irish & Eng.). 75.00 (ISBN 0-8490-0424-1). Gordon Pr.

ENGLISH LANGUAGE–DICTIONARIES–ITALIAN

Berlitz. Berlitz Pocket Dictionaries: Italian-English-Italian. (Eng. & Ital.). pap. $4.95 (ISBN 0-02-964520-4). Macmillan.

Berlitz Editors. Berlitz Italian for Travellers. 192p. (Ital.). 1982. $8.95 (ISBN 0-02-965180-8, Berlitz); pap. $4.95 (ISBN 0-02-963940-9). Macmillan.

--Berlitz Pocket Dictionaries: Italian-English. 300p. (Eng. & Ital.). 1982. pap. $4.95 (ISBN 0-686-93001-0, Berlitz). Macmillan.

Bocchetta, Vittore & Young, Ruth E., eds. New Century Vest-Pocket Italian Dictionary. (Ital.). 1967. $2.95 (ISBN 0-8329-1535-1). New Century.

Bocchetta, Vittore E., ed. New Century World-Wide Italian Dictionary: Italian-English, English-Italian. (Orig., Ital. & Eng.). $7.95 (ISBN 0-8329-9696-3). New Century.

Bussi, Luciano & Cognazzo, Maria. Nuovo Dizionario Inglese-Italiano Delle Science Mediche. 864p. (Eng. & Ital.). 1980. $78.00 (ISBN 0-913298-55-7). S F Vanni.

Capitol's Concise Dictionary of Seven Languages. (gr. 9-12). 1978. $29.95 (ISBN 0-8120-5333-8). Barron.

Cassells, et al. Cassell's Italian Dictionary: Italian-English, English-Italian. LC 77-7405. (Ital. & Eng.). 1977. index $23.95 (ISBN 0-02-522540-5); plain $19.95 (ISBN 0-02-522530-8). Macmillan.

Collins Italian-English English-Italian Dictionary. 416p. (Orig., Ital. & Eng.). 1983. pap. $2.95 (ISBN 0-425-05451-9). Berkley Pub.

Denti, Renzo. Dizionario Tecnico Italiano-Inglese, Inglese-Italiano. 9th rev. ed. 1811p. (Eng. & Ital.). 1979. $78.00x (ISBN 88-203-1052-X). S F Vanni.

English-Italian, Italian-English Dictionary, 1 vol. (Eng. & Ital.). $19.50 (ISBN 0-685-33020-6, 045-3). Saphrograph.

English-Italian, Italian-English Dictionary. 1960p. (Ital. & Eng.). 1981. $62.00. Oxford U Pr.

Gem Language Dictionaries: Italian-English & English-Italian. (Ital. & Eng.). write for info. (ISBN 0-671-41956-0). S&S.

Grande Dizionario Hazon-Garzanti Inglese-Italiano Italiano-Inglese. (Eng. & Ital.). 1976. $45.00x (ISBN 0-686-19963-4). Intl Learn Syst.

Gualtieri, Franceso M. Dizionario inglese moderno. (Illus.). 1400p. (Eng.). L.12000.00. Trevisini.

Hall, Robert A., ed. The Random House Basic Dictionary Italian. (Ital. & Eng.). 1981. pap. $1.50 (ISBN 0-345-29618-4). Ballantine.

Hall, Robert A., Jr. Italian Vest Pocket Dictionary. (Ital.). 1957. pap. $3.50 (ISBN 0-394-40060-7). Random.

Hamlyn Italian-English Dictionary. (Ital. & Eng.). 1977. pap. $4.95 (ISBN 0-600-36566-2, 8089). Larousse.

Hazon, M. Dizionario Garzanti: Italiano-Inglese, Inglese-Italiano. 1024p. (Eng. & Ital.). 1980. $19.95 (ISBN 0-686-97642-8, M-9187). French & Eur.

--Grande Dizionario Hazon Garzanti Inglese-Italiano, Italiano-Inglese. 2112p. (Eng. & Ital.). 1980. $49.95 (ISBN 0-686-97429-8, M-9186). French & Eur.

--Italian-English, English-Italian (Grande) Dictionary. 27th, rev. ed. (Eng. & Ital.). Date not set. text ed. $60.00 (ISBN 0-686-46532-6). Heinman.

Hugo Pocket Dictionary: Italian-English, English-Italian. 622p. (Ital. & Eng.). 1971. $3.50 (ISBN 0-8226-0505-8, 505). Littlefield.

Institute for Language Study. Vest Pocket Italian. LC 58-8919. (Illus.). 128p. (Ital.). 1979. pap. $2.45 (ISBN 0-06-464903-2, BN 4903, BN). B&N NY.

Isopel, May, ed. Italian-English, English-Italian Gem Dictionary. (Gem Foreign Language Ser.). (Ital. & Eng.). 1954. $2.95 (ISBN 0-00-458625-5, G1). Collins Pubs.

Italian Bilingual Dictionary. (Illus.). 436p. (Eng. & Ital.). 1980. pap. $3.50 pocket ed. Barron.

Italian-English Dictionary, 1 vol. (Ital. & Eng.). $19.50 (ISBN 0-685-33019-2, 045-3). Saphrograph.

Italian-English-Italian. (Berlitz Pocket Dictionaries Ser.). (Ital. & Eng.). $4.95 (ISBN 0-02-964520-4). Macmillan.

Langenscheidt English-Italian Lilliput Dictionary. 640p. (Eng. & Ital.). plastic $1.50 (ISBN 3-468-96415-3). Langenscheidt.

Langenscheidt's Lilliput English-Italian Dictionary. 640p. (Eng. & Ital.). 1972. $1.50 (ISBN 0-685-31370-0). Am Map.
Langenscheidt's Lilliput Italian-English Dictionary. 640p. (Eng. & Ital.). 1972. $1.50 (ISBN 0-685-31371-9). Am Map.
Langenscheidt's Universal Italian-English, English-Italian Dictionary. 384p. (Eng. & Ital.). 1972. $2.95 (ISBN 0-685-31344-1). Am Map.
Lilliput Dictionary. 640p. (Ital. & Eng.). $1.50 (110). Langenscheidt.
Lilliput Dictionary. 640p. (Eng. & Ital.). $1.50 (111). Langenscheidt.
Lucchesi, Mario. Dizionario Medico Ragionato Inglese-Italiano: Termini, Abbreviazioni, Sigle, Eponimi e Sinonimi Medici, Medico-Biologici e Delle Specializzazioni Mediche. 1490p. (Eng. & Ital.). 1978. $98.00x (ISBN 0-913298-52-2). S F Vanni.
Maiocchi, Annamaria F. & De Bichiacchi, Ada. Harrap's Compact Italian & English Dictionary. 667p. (Eng. & Ital.). E5.95 (ISBN 0-245-59636-4). Harrap.
Marolli, G. Italian-English, English-Italian Technical Dictionary. 11th, enl. ed. (Illus., Ital. & Eng.). 1980. $100.00 (ISBN 8-8005-1040-X). Heinman.
Melzi, Robert C. The Bantam New College Italian & English Dictionary. 736p. (Orig., Ital. & Eng.). 1976. pap. $2.75 (ISBN 0-553-20267-7). Bantam.
--The New College Italian & English Dictionary. (Orig., Ital. & Eng.). (gr. 7-12). 1976. pap. text ed. $9.92 (ISBN 0-87720-592-2). AMSCO Sch.
Mondadori's Pocket Italian-English, English-Italian Dictionary. 600p. (Eng. & Ital.). pap. $2.50. Imported Bks.
Muller, Wilhelm. Customs Dictionary: German-English-French-Italian. LC 72-311634. 277p. (Ger., Eng., Fr. & Ital.). 1971. 17.50x (ISBN 3-8029-8565-6). Intl Pubns Serv.
Musu-Boy, R. Dizionario Italiano-Inglese, Inglese-Italiano. 463p. (Ital. & Eng.). 1979. leatherette $4.95 (ISBN 0-686-97343-7, M-9177). French & Eur.
Putnam's Contemporary Italian Dictionary. (Ital. & Eng.). pap. $2.25 (ISBN 0-425-04363-0). Berkley Pub.
Ragazzini & Gagliardelli. Italian-English, English-Italian Commercial Dictionary. (Ital. & Eng.). $50.00 (ISBN 0-685-25202-7). Heinman.
The Random House Basic Dictionary. (Eng. & Ital.). write for info. (608-103). Pan Amer Pub.
Rebora, Piero, et al. Cassell's Italian Dictionary: Italian-English, English-Italian. Rev. ed. 1150p. (Eng. & Ital.). 1979. $16.95; indexed $18.95. Imported bks.
Reynolds, Barbara. Cambridge Italian Dictionary, 2 vols. LC 74-77384. (Ital.). 1962. Vol. 1. Italian-English 1962. $175.00 (ISBN 0-521-06059-1); Vol. 2, English-italian 1981. $225.00 (ISBN 0-521-08708-2). Cambridge U Pr.
Skey, Malcolm, ed. English-Italian, Italian-English Dictionary. (Eng. & Ital.). 1981. $49.95x (ISBN 0-19-431158-9). Oxford U Pr.
World Wide Italian Language Italian-English. 544p. (Ital. & Eng.). $7.95 (ISBN 0-8329-9696-3). New Century.

ENGLISH LANGUAGE–DICTIONARIES–JAPANESE

Basic Words in Japanese. (Eng. & Japanese.). write for info. (454-6). Pan Am Bk Co.
Berlitz Editors. Berlitz Japanese for Travellers. 192p. (Japanese.). 1982. pap. $4.95 (ISBN 0-02-964070-9, Berlitz). Macmillan.
Corwin, Charles, et al. A Dictionary of Japanese & English Idiomatic Equivalents. LC 68-11818. 302p. (Japanese & Eng.). 1980. $18.75 (ISBN 0-87011-111-6). Kodansha.
Dixson, et al. My First English-Japanese Picture Dictionary. (Illus., Eng. & Japanese.). (gr. 1-6). 1978. pap. text ed. $4.50 (ISBN 0-88345-260-X). Regents Pub.
Hepburn, James C. A Japanese & English Dictionary with an English & Japanese Index. LC 81-52935. 704p. (Japanese & Eng.). 1982. Repr. of 1867 ed. $29.50 (ISBN 0-8048-1441-4). C E Tuttle.
Inoue, Jukichi. Inoue's Smaller Japanese-English Dictionary. LC 81-52936. 968p. (Japanese & Eng.). 1982. $13.95 (ISBN 0-8048-1440-6). C E Tuttle.
Institute for Language Study. Vest Pocket Japanese. (Illus.). 240p. (Japanese.). 1979. pap. $2.95 (ISBN 0-06-464906-7, BN 4906, BN). B&N NY.
Kai. All Romanized English-Japanese Dictionary. (Japanese & Eng.). $6.95. Iaconi.
Kawamoto, Shigeo & Nishiwaki, Junzaburo, eds. The Kodansha English-Japanese Dictionary. Narita, Shigehisa & Shimizu, Mamoru, trs. 1557p. (Japanese & Eng.). 1980. pap. $22.50 flexible soft-binding (ISBN 0-87011-420-4). Kodansha.
The Kodansha English-Japanese Dictionary. 1572p. (Eng. & Japanese.). 1983. 1900.00 Yen. Kodansha.
Martin, Samuel. Basic Japanese Conversation Dictionary: English-Japanese & Japanese-English. LC 57-8797. (Eng. & Japanese.). $3.95 (ISBN 0-8048-0057-X). C E Tuttle.
Nelson, Andrew N. The Modern Reader's Japanese-English Character Dictionary. rev. ed. 1109p. (Japanese & Eng.). 1980. $42.00. C E Tuttle.
New English-Japanese Dictionary. LC 81-101348. (Illus.). xxi, 2477p. (Eng. & Japanese.). 1980. 10000.00 Yen. Kenkyusha.
The Oxford-Duden Pictorial English-Japanese Dictionary. (Illus.). 848p. (Eng. & Japanese.). 1983. $29.95 (ISBN 0-19-864149-4). Oxford U Pr.
Oxford Picture Dictionary of American English: English-Japanese. (Eng. & Japanese.). write for info. (608-106). Pan Amer Pub.
Parnwell, E. C. Oxford Picture Dictionary of American English: English-Japanese Edition. (Illus., Orig.). 1981. pap. text ed. $6.95x (ISBN 0-19-581877-6). Oxford U Pr.
Rose-Innes, Arthur. Beginner's Dictionary of Chinese-Japanese Characters. 510p. (Chinese, Japanese & Eng.). 1959. pap. $7.95. Dover.
Tuttle's Watch-Pocket Dictionary. Eng.-Japanese $2.00 (ISBN 0-8048-0600-4). C E Tuttle.

ENGLISH LANGUAGE–DICTIONARIES–KHMER

Cambodian-English, English-Cambodian Dictionary. (Cambodian & Eng.). $22.00. Iaconi.
Headley, R. Cambodian-English Dictionary, 2 vols. (Cambodian & Eng.). $25.00. Iaconi.
Huffman, Franklin E. Cambodian English. 152p. (Eng. & Cambodian.). 1977. $5.95 (ISBN 0-300-02070-8). Yale U Pr.
Huffman, Franklin E. & Proum, Im. Cambodian-English Glossary. (Linguistic Ser.). 160p. (Eng. & Khmerz.). 1981. pap. $7.95x. Yale U Pr.
--English-Khmer Dictionary. LC 78-7705. (Linguistic Ser.). (Eng. & Khmer.). 1978. text ed. $40.00x (ISBN 0-300-02261-1). Yale U Pr.
Jacob, J. Concise Cambodian-English Dictionary. (Cambodian & Eng.). $59.00. Iaconi.
Soeur, Samnang, tr. English-Khmer Phrasebook with Useful Word List: For Cambodians. LC 80-66143. 140p. (Eng. & Cambodian.). 1980. pap. text ed. $5.00x (ISBN 0-87281-115-8). Ctr Appl Ling.

ENGLISH LANGUAGE–DICTIONARIES–KOREAN

Basic Words in Korean. (Eng. & Korean.). write for info. (454-4). Pan Amer Pub.
Jones, B. J. English-Korean Dictionary for Practical Conversation. LC 83-81486. (Korean.). 1983. price not set (ISBN 0-930878-22-1). Hollym Corp.
--Standard English-Korean Dictionary for Foreigners. LC 81-84204. (Illus.). 386p. (Korean & Eng.). 1982. $7.95 (ISBN 0-930878-21-3). Hollym Intl.
Jones, B. J., ed. Standard English-Korean Dictionary: For Foreigners. LC 81-84204. 369p. (Korean.). $5.50 (ISBN 0-930878-21-3). Hollym Corp.
Pong Kook Lee. Standard English-Korean Dictionary for Foreigners. Jones, B. J., ed. 386p. (Korean & Eng.). 1982. pap. 6.95 (ISBN 0-89346-223-3). Hollym Intl.
Song, M. E. English Korean Dictionary Romanized. (Eng. & Korean.). $27.50 (ISBN 0-87559-174-4). Shalom.
Underwood. Concise English-Korean Dictionary Romanized. (Korean & Eng.). $3.95. Iaconi.
Underwood, Joan V. Concise English-Korean Dictionary Romanized. LC 55-5891. (Eng. & Korean.). 1960. $3.95 (ISBN 0-8048-0118-5). C E Tuttle.

ENGLISH LANGUAGE–DICTIONARIES–LAMBA

Doke, Clement M. English-Lamba Dictionary. (Eng. & Lamba.). $22.00 (ISBN 0-87559-055-1). Shalom.

ENGLISH LANGUAGE–DICTIONARIES–LAO

Kerr, Allen. Comprehensive Lao-English Dictionary, 2 vols. (Lao & Eng.). $42.00. Iaconi.
Luangpraseut, Kamchong, tr. English-Lao Phrasebook with Useful Word List: For Laotians. (Eng. & Lao.). 1980. pap. text ed. $5.00x (ISBN 0-87281-117-4). Ctr Appl Ling.
Marcus, Russell. English-Lao, Lao-English Dictionary. LC 77-116487. (Eng. & Laotian.). 1970. $10.50 (ISBN 0-8048-0909-7). C E Tuttle.

ENGLISH LANGUAGE–DICTIONARIES–LATIN

Cassell. Cassell's Latin Dictionary: Latin-English, English Latin. Simpson, D. P., ed. (Lat. & Eng.). standard $17.95 (ISBN 0-02-522570-7); thumb-indexed $19.95 (ISBN 0-02-522580-4); concise $9.95 (ISBN 0-02-522630-4). Macmillan.
Cassell's New Compact Latin Dictionary. 384p. (Lat.). 1981. pap. $3.95 (ISBN 0-440-31101-2, LE). Dell.
Cassell's New Latin-English, English-Latin Dictionary. (Eng. & Lat.). pap. $3.00. Dell.
Galfridus Anglicus. Promptorium Parvulorum Sive Clericorum, Dictionarius Anglolatinus Princeps, 3 Pts. Repr. of 1865 ed. $37.00 ea. Johnson Repr.
Galfridus, Anglicus. Promptorium Parvulorum Sive Clericorum, Lexicon Anglo-Latinum Princeps, 3 Vols. LC 70-168091. (Camden Society, London. Publications, First Ser.: Nos. 25, 54, 89). (Lat.). Repr. of 1865 ed. Set. $84.00 (ISBN 0-404-50209-1); $28.00 ea. AMS Pr.
Gem Language Dictionaries: Latin-English & English-Latin. (Lat. & Eng.). write for info. (ISBN 0-671-41961-7). S&S.
Glare, P. G. W., ed. Oxford Latin Dictionary: Fascicle 6-a-Calcitro. (Lat.). 1978. pap. $49.50x (ISBN 0-19-864219-9). Oxford U Pr.
Handford, S. A. & Herberg, M., eds. Langenscheidt's Pocket Latin Dictionary, Latin-English, English-Latin. (Langenscheidt Pocket Dictionaries Ser.). 480p. (Eng. & Lat.). 1969. $5.95 (ISBN 0-685-31347-6). Am Map.
Kidd, D. A. Latin-English, English-Latin Dictionary. (Lat. & Eng.). $19.50 (ISBN 0-87557-050-X, 052-6). Saphrograph.
Langenscheidt English-Latin Lilliput Dictionary. 640p. (Eng. & Lat.). plastic $1.50 (ISBN 3-468-96484-6). Langenscheidt.
Langenscheidt's Lilliput English-Latin Dictionary. 640p. (Eng. & Lat.). 1972. $1.50 (ISBN 0-685-31355-7). Am Map.
Langenscheidt's Lilliput Latin-English Dictionary. 640p. (Eng. & Lat.). 1972. $1.50 (ISBN 0-685-31369-7). Am Map.
Langenscheidt's Universal Latin-English, English-Latin Dictionary. 456p. (Eng. & Lat.). 1972. $2.95 (ISBN 0-685-31343-3). Am Map.
Latin-English & English-Latin Dictionary. (Lat. & Eng.). pap. $1.99 (ISBN 0-686-00473-6). Dennison.
Latin-English, English-Latin. (Cassell's Concise Dictionaries). (Eng. & Lat.). $8.95 (522630-4). Inst Mod Lang.
Latin-English, English-Latin Dictionary. (Lat. & Eng.). pap. $2.50 (ISBN 0-686-79571-7, DI 6, BN). B&N NY.
Lewis, Charlton T. Elementary Latin Dictionary. (Eng. & Lat.). 1891. $23.00x (ISBN 0-19-910205-8). Oxford U Pr.
Lilliput Dictionary. 640p. (Eng. & Lat.). $1.50 (113). Langenscheidt.
Simpson, D. P. Cassell's Latin Dictionary: Latin-English, English-Latin. 883p. (Eng. & Lat.). 1979. indexed $18.95. Imported Bks.
Simpson, D. P., compiled by. Cassell's Concise Latin-English, English-Latin Dictionary. abr. ed. LC 77-7660. (Lat. & Ger.). 1977. $9.95 (ISBN 0-02-522630-4). Macmillan.
Simpson, D. P., ed. Cassell's Latin Dictionary: Latin-English, English-Latin. (Lat. & Eng.). 1977. indexed $18.95 (ISBN 0-02-522580-4); plain $16.95 (ISBN 0-02-522570-7). Macmillan.
Traupman, John C. New College Latin & English Dictionary. (Lat. & Eng.). (gr. 7-12). 1966. pap. text ed. $7.67 (ISBN 0-87720-560-4). AMSCO Sch.
Traupman, John C., ed. New College Latin & English Dictionary. (Language Library). (Orig., Lat. & Eng.). 1970. pap. $2.95 (ISBN 0-553-20255-3). Bantam.
Woodhouse, S. C., ed. Latin-English & English-Latin Dictionary. (Routledge Pocket Dictionaries Ser.). 496p. (Orig., Lat. & Eng.). 1982. pap. $8.95 (ISBN 0-7100-9267-9). Routledge & Kegan.

ENGLISH LANGUAGE–DICTIONARIES–LATVIAN

Raskevics, J., et al. English-Latvian-Russian Dictionary. 718p. (Eng., Latvian & Rus.). 1977. $50.00x (ISBN 0-686-82324-9, Pub. by Collets). State Mutual Bk.

ENGLISH LANGUAGE–DICTIONARIES–LITHUANIAN

Baravikas, V., et al. Kratkii Shkol'Nyi Anglo-Litovskii i Litovsko-Angliiskii Slovar. 329p. (Rus.). 1970. $2.25 (Pub. by Shviesa). Four Continent.
Laucka, A., et al. English-Lithuanian Dictionary. 1096p. (Eng. & Lithuanian.). 1978. $11.95 (Pub. by Mokslas). Four Continent.
Litovsko-Russkii Slovar. 392p. (Rus.). 1956. $1.95 (Pub. by Gosizdat Polit. & Nauchn.Lit. SSR.). Four Continent.
Litovsko-Russkii Slovar. 893p. (Rus.). 1971. $7.95 (Pub. by Mintis). Four Continent.
Piesarskas, B. & Baravykas, V. Lithuanian-English, English-Lithuanian Dictionary, 2 vols. (Lithuanian & Eng.). 30.00 set (ISBN 0-685-39857-9). Heinman.
Piesarskas, B., et al. Lithuanian-English Dictionary. 912p. (Lithuanian & Eng.). 1979. $8.50 (Pub. by Vilnius). Four Continent.

ENGLISH LANGUAGE–DICTIONARIES–MALAY

Awang, Sudjai H. & Yusoff, Khan. Kamus Lengkap: Penyunting. LC 77-940970. (Illus.). 1244p. (Maylay & Eng.). 1977. write for info. Pustaka Antara.
Dewan Bahasa dan Pustaka. Kamus dwibahasa, bahasa Inggeris-bahasa Malaysia. LC 79-941803. xv, 1457p. (Eng. & Malay.). 1979. M.$25.00. Dewan Bahasa.

Hornby, Albert S. Kamus pembaca, Inggeris-Malayu. LC 81-940893. (Illus.). 409p. (Eng. & Malay.). 1980. write for info. (ISBN 0-19-580771-5). Oxford U Pr.

Istilah percetakan, penerbitan, dan komunikasi massa, Inggeris-Malaysia-Inggeris. LC 79-102377. xiv, 594p. (Malay & Eng.). 1978. M.$7.00. Dewan Bahasa.

McManus, Edwin G., et al. Palauan-English Dictionary. LC 76-9058. (Pali Language Texts: Micronesia). (Palauan & Eng.). 1977. pap. text ed. $16.00x (ISBN 0-8248-0450-3). UH Pr.

Marsden, William. Malay-English Dictionary. (Eng. & Malayian.). 1976. Repr. of 1958 ed. $92.00 (ISBN 0-518-19003-X). Ayer Co.

Senarai istilah seni lukis, bahasa Inggeris-bahasa Malaysia. LC 81-940245. xi, 37p. (Eng. & Malay.). 1980. M.$1.20. Dewan Bahasa.

ENGLISH LANGUAGE–DICTIONARIES–MAORI

Biggs, Bruce, ed. The Complete English-Maori Dictionary. (Eng. & Maori.). 1981. 29.95x (ISBN 0-19-647989-4). Oxford U Pr.

Reed, A. W. & Brougham, A. E., eds. The Concise Maori Handbook. LC 80-497775. (Illus.). 587p. (Eng. & Maori.). 1978. pap. write for info. (ISBN 0-589-01111-1). Reed Ltd.

ENGLISH LANGUAGE–DICTIONARIES–MARATHI

Molesworth, James T. A Dictionary-Marathi & English. 2nd ed. (Marathi & Eng.). 1973. Repr. of 1857 ed. 295.00x (ISBN 0-8002-0173-6). Intl Pubns Serv.

ENGLISH LANGUAGE–DICTIONARIES–MICRONESIAN LANGUAGES

Lee, Kee-Dong. Kusaiean-English Dictionary. (PALI Language Texts-Micronesia). 330p. (Kusaiiean & Eng.). 1976. pap. text ed. $12.00x (ISBN 0-8248-0413-9). UH Pr.

ENGLISH LANGUAGE–DICTIONARIES–MOCHA

Harrison, Sheldon P. & Albert, Salich. Mokilese-English Dictionary. LC 76-41796. (PALI Language Tests Ser.: Micronesia). 182p. (Orig., Mokilese & Eng.). 1976. pap. text ed. $9.50x (ISBN 0-8248-0512-7). UH Pr.

ENGLISH LANGUAGE–DICTIONARIES–MONGOLIAN

Hangin, John G. A Concise English-Mongolian Dictionary. (Uralic & Altaic Ser: Vol. 89). (Eng. & Mongolian.). 1970. pap. text ed. 11.50x (ISBN 0-87750-079-7). Res Ctr Lang Semiotic.

ENGLISH LANGUAGE–DICTIONARIES–NORWEGIAN

Ansteinsson, J. & Andreassen, A. T. Norwegian-English, English-Norwegian Technical Dictionary, 2 Vols. (Norwegian & Eng.). Set. 60.00 (ISBN 8-2702-8007-0). Heinman.

Berlitz. Berlitz Pocket Dictionaries: Norwegian-English-Norwegian. (Eng. & Norwegian.). pap. $4.95 (ISBN 0-02-964560-3). Macmillan.

Berlitz Editors. Berlitz Pocket Dictionaries: Norwegian-English. 300p. (Eng. & Norwegian.). 1982. pap. $4.95 (ISBN 0-686-92987-X, Berlitz). Macmillan.

Berulfsen, B. English-Norsk Dictionary: Gyldendals. new ed. (Eng. & Norwegian.). 1978. $20.00x (ISBN 8-2573-0007-1, N481); Norsk-English. $22.00x (ISBN 8-2573-0006-3, N-482). Vanous.

Berulfsen, B. & Berulfsen, T. English-Norwegian Dictionary. (Eng. & Norwegian.). 1981. write for info. (ISBN 82-573-0161-2). Kunnskapsforlaget.

--Norwegian Dictionary: Engelsk-Norwegina. rev. ed. 433p. (Norwegian & Eng.). 1981. $22.00x (ISBN 82-573-0161-2, N481). Vanous.

Berulfsen, B. & Svenkerud, A. Norwegian Deluxe Dictionary: English-Norse. (Norwegian & Eng.). 1968. $100.00x (ISBN 82-02-09060-1, N461). Vanous.

Berulfsen, B. & Scavenius, H., eds. McKay's Modern Norwegian-English & English-Norwegian Dictionary. (Modern Dictionaries Ser.). (Norwegian & Eng.). 1953. 14.95 (ISBN 0-679-10076-8). McKay.

--McKay's Modern Norwegian-English & English-Norwegian Dictionary. (Modern Dictionaries Ser.). (Norwegian & Eng.). 1953. 14.95 (ISBN 0-679-10076-8). McKay.

Bjerke, L. & Soraas, H., eds. Norwegian Dictionary: English-Norwegian. (Norwegian & Eng.). 1963. $30.00x (ISBN 0-686-31692-4, N434). Vanous.

Daae, E. English-Norwegian, Norwegian-English, Lommeordbok. 568p. (Eng. & Norwegian.). 1980. pap. $8.95 (ISBN 82-573-0152-3, M-9462). French & Eur.

Dietrichson, Jan W. & Verland, Orm. English-Norwegian, Norwegian-English. 7th ed. LC 78-387531. 448p. (Eng. & Norwegian.). 1978. Kr.19.50 (ISBN 8-257-30054-3). Kunnskapsforlaget.

Kirkeby, W. & Berulfsen, B. Norwegian-English, English-Norwegian Dictionary, 2 vols. 4th rev. ed. (Norwegian & Eng.). 45.00 set (ISBN 82-573-0007-1). Norwegian-Eng (ISBN 82-573-0006-3). Eng.-Norwegian (ISBN 82-573-0007-1). Heinman.

Kirkeby, W. A. Norwegian-English Dictionary. (Norwegian & Eng.). 1977. write for info. (ISBN 82-573-0006-3). Kunnskapsforlaget.

--Norwegian-English Dictionary. Large ed. (Norwegian & Eng.). 1979. write for info. (ISBN 82-573-0135-3). Kunnskapsforlaget.

Kirkeby, W. A. & Utgabes, S. Norsk-Engelsk Ordbok. 1276p. (Norweigian & Eng.). 1979. $95.00 (ISBN 82-573-0079-9, M-9458). French & Eur.

Kirkely, Willie. Norsk-Engelsk Ordbok. 4th ed. 514p. (Norwegian & Eng.). 1981. $22.00x (ISBN 82-573-0006-3, N482). Vanous.

Myklestad, J. Meyer & Soras, H. English-Norwegian, Norwegian-English Dictionary, Norwegian-English Dictionary. (Eng. & Norwegian.). 19.50 (ISBN 0-87557-054-2, 054-2). Saphrograph.

Norwegian-English-Norwegian. (Berlitz Pocket Dictionaries Ser.). (Eng. & Norwegian.). $4.95 (ISBN 0-02-964560-3). Macmillan.

Norwegian Pocket Dictionary. (Norwegian & Eng.). 10.00 (ISBN 82-517-8010-1). Heinman.

Scarry, R. Min Forste Ordbok: English & Norwegian. (Illus., Eng. & Norwegian.). $15.00x (ISBN 0-686-31678-9, N504). Vanous.

Slette, T. Norwegian-English Dictionary. 1326p. (Norwegian & Eng.). 1977. $100.00x (ISBN 82-521-0692-7, N-537). Vanous.

ENGLISH LANGUAGE–DICTIONARIES–NUBIAN

Murray, G. W. English-Nubian Comparative Dictionary. Hooton, E. A. & Bates, Natica I., eds. (Harvard African Studies: Vol. 4). (Eng. & Nubian.). 1923. 37.00 (ISBN 0-527-01027-8). Kraus Repr.

ENGLISH LANGUAGE–DICTIONARIES–NUKUORO

Carroll, Vern & Soulik, Tobias. Nukuoro Lexicon. LC 73-78975. (PALI Language Texts: Polynesia). 859p. (Orig., Pali.). 1973. pap. text ed. $17.50x (ISBN 0-8248-0250-0). UH Pr.

ENGLISH LANGUAGE–DICTIONARIES–NYANJA

Price, Thomas. English-Nyanja Dictionary. (Eng. & Nyanja.). $22.50 (ISBN 0-87559-114-0). Shalom.

ENGLISH LANGUAGE–DICTIONARIES–PAPAGO

Saxton, Dean & Saxton, Lucille. Papago & Pima to English, English to Papago & Pima Dictionary. 2nd ed. Cherry, R. L., ed. (Papago, Pima & Eng.). 1983. text ed. $19.95x (ISBN 0-8165-0826-7). U of Ariz Pr.

ENGLISH LANGUAGE–DICTIONARIES–PERSIAN

English-Persian Dictionary: Romanized. (Eng. & Persian.). 19.50 (ISBN 0-87557-058-5, 058-5). Saphrograph.

Fazl-i-Ali. Dictionary of Persian & English Languages. 668p. (Persian & Eng.). 1979. Repr. of 1885 ed. 39.00 (ISBN 0-89684-266-5, Pub. by Cosmo Pubns India). Orient Bk Dist.

Field, Claud. Dictionary of Arabic-Persian Quotes. 352p. (Arabic, Persian & Eng.). $18.00 (168-2). Intl Bk Ctr.

Haim, S. Persian-English, English-Persian Shorter Dictionary, 2 vols. rev., enl. ed. (Persian & Eng.). Set. 50.00 (ISBN 0-686-77974-6). Heinman.

Lambton, Ann K. Persian Vocabulary. (Persian.). 1954-1962. pap. $24.95x (ISBN 0-521-09154-3). Cambridge U Pr.

Steingass. Persian-English Dictionary. (Persian & Eng.). $75.00. Iaconi.

Steingass, F. Comprehensive Persian-English Dictionary. 1540p. (Persian & Eng.). 1975. $65.00x (ISBN 0-86685-130-5). Intl Bk Ctr.

Wollaston, A. N. English Persian Dictionary. 462p. (Eng. & Persian.). 1978. Repr. of 1842 ed. 28.00 (ISBN 0-89684-156-1, Pub. by Cosmo Pubns India). Orient Bk Dist.

--An English-Persian Dictionary Compiled from Original Sources. 2nd ed. (Eng. & Persian.). 1904. text ed. 21.00x (ISBN 0-391-01068-9). Humanities.

ENGLISH LANGUAGE–DICTIONARIES–PIMA

Saxton, Dean & Saxton, Lucille. Papago & Pima to English, English to Papago & Pima Dictionary. 2nd ed. Cherry, R. L., ed. (Papago, Pima & Eng.). 1983. text ed. $19.95x (ISBN 0-8165-0826-7). U of Ariz Pr.

ENGLISH LANGUAGE–DICTIONARIES–POLISH

Billip, K. English-Polish & Polish-English Minimum Dictionary. 543p. (Eng. & Pol.). 1979. $2.85. Wiedza Powszechna.

Borkowski, Pioter. English-Polish Dictionary of Idioms & Phrases. 244p. (Orig., Eng. & Pol.). 1983. pap. 6.95. Hippocrene Bks.

Borkowski, Piotr. English-Polish Dictionary of Idioms & Phrases. 206p. (Orig., Eng. & Pol.). 1982. pap. $6.95 (ISBN 0-903705-46-X). Hippocrene Bks.

Bulas, Kazimierz, et al. The Kosciuszko Foundation English-Polish, Polish-English Dictionary, 2 vols. (Poland's Millennium Ser.). (Eng. & Pol.). 1973. English-Polish. text ed. 12.50 (ISBN 0-917004-00-0); Polish-English. text ed. 12.50 (ISBN 0-917004-16-7). Kosciuszko.

Bullas, K. & Whitfield, F. J. Dictionary English-Polish, Polish-English, 2 vols. (Eng. & Pol.). 1969. Set. $38.50 (ISBN 0-685-05192-7). Adler.

Czerni, S. & Skrzynska, M. Polish Science & Technology Dictionary: Polish-English. 3rd rev. ed. (Pol. & Eng.). 1976. $35.00x (ISBN 0-89918-537-1, P-537). Vanous.

A Dictionary of Adam Mickiewicz's Language: Vol. 3, H-K. (Pol. & Eng.). 1977. $38.38 (Pub. by Ossolineum). Four Continent.

A Dictionary of Adam Mickiewicz's Language: Vol. 5, N-O. 678p. (Pol. & Eng.). 1977. $41.70 (Pub. by Ossolineum). Four Continent.

A Dictionary of Adam Mickiewicz's Language: Vol. 6, P. 620p. (Pol. & Eng.). 1977. $39.15 (Pub. by Ossolineum). Four Continent.

A Dictionary of Adam Mickiewicz's Language: Vol. 7, P-R. 578p. (Pol. & Eng.). 1977. $38.35 (Pub. by Ossolineum). Four Continent.

A Dictionary of Adam Mickiewicz's Language: Vol. 4, L-M, Vol. 4. 506p. (Pol. & Eng.). 1977. $41.70 (Pub. by Ossolineum). Four Continent.

English-Polish & Polish-English Compact Dictionary. Rev. ed. 542p. (Eng. & Pol.). 1977. $5.50. Imported Bks.

English-Polish-English Dictionary. (Eng. & Pol.). 15.00 (ISBN 0-87557-060-7). Saphrograph.

Grzebieniowski, T. Illustrated English-Polish Polish-English Dictionary. 908p. (Pol. & Eng.). 1978. $9.95 (Pub. by Wiedza Powszechna). Four Continent.

Grzebieniowski, Tadeusz, ed. Illustrated English-Polish Polish-English Dictionary. rev. & enl. ed. (Illus.). 908p. (Eng. & Pol.). 1978. 13.50x (ISBN 0-8002-2262-8). Intl Pubns Serv.

Grzebieniowski, Takeusz. Ilustrowany slownik angielsko-polski, polsko-angielski. LC 79-361868. (Illus.). 903p. (Eng. & Pol.). 1978. 200.00 Zl. Wiedza Powszechna.

Grzebienowski, Tadeus Z. Polish-English, English-Polish Dictionary. (Illus., Pol. & Eng.). 1980. 16.95 (ISBN 0-88254-477-2). Hippocrene Bks.

A Handy English-Polish Dictionary. 914p. (Eng. & Pol.). 1980. $20.00x (ISBN 0-569-07422-3, Pub. by Collet's). State Mutual Bk.

Kierst, W. English-Polish, Polish-English Dictionary. (Eng. & Pol.). 29.50 (ISBN 0-87557-060-7, 060-7). Saphrograph.

Kryt, Dobromila & Semniuk, Bazyli, eds. English-Polish Polish-English Chemical Dictionary. LC 79-393179. 912p. (Eng. & Pol.). 1979. 32.50x (ISBN 83-204-0004-X). Intl Pubns Serv.

Pogonowski, Iwo. Concise Polish-English-English-Polish Dictionary. 436p. (Orig., Pol. & Eng.). 1983. pap. 3.95 (ISBN 0-88254-799-2). Hippocrene Bks.

--Dictionary Polish-English, English-Polish Slovnik. 648p. (Eng. & Pol.). $16.50. Hippocrene Bks.

Shorter Technological Dictionary: English-Polish, Polish-English. (Pol. & Eng.). $7.95 (Pub. by Wydaw. Naukowo-Tech.). Four Continent.

Stanislawski, J. English-Polish & Polish-English Dictionary. 879p. (Eng. & Pol.). E12.95. McKay.

--The Great English-Polish Dictionary. 1405p. (Eng. & Pol.). 1979. leatherette $75.00 (ISBN 0-686-97431-X, M-9329). French & Eur.

--The Great Polish-English Dictionary. 1728p. (Pol. & Eng.). 1980. leatherette $75.00 (ISBN 83-214-0107-4, M-9368). French & Eur.

--Polish-English & English-Polish Dictionary. (New Pronouncing Dictionaries). (Pol. & Eng.). (YA) (gr. 9 up). 12.95 (ISBN 0-679-10082-2). McKay.

--Polish-English, English-Polish Dictionary (1975, 4 vols. (Pol. & Eng.). 1978. Set. 120.00 (ISBN 0-685-85757-3). Heinman.

--Polish-English, English-Polish Practical Dictionary, 2 vols. (Pol. & Eng.). Set. 50.00 (ISBN 0-685-79114-9). Heinman.

--A Practical Polish-English Dictionary. 1030p. (Pol. & Eng.). 1978. Leatherette $19.95 (ISBN 0-686-92364-2, M-9134). French & Eur.

Stanislawski, J. & Billip, K. Polish Practical Dictionary (English-Polish) (Pol. & Eng.). 1981. $20.00x (ISBN 0-89918-533-9, P-533). Vanous.

Stanislawski, J., ed. The Great English-Polish Dictionary, 2 vols. 607p. (Eng. & Pol.). 1980. vinyl $99.00x (ISBN 0-569-00671-6, Pub. by Collet's). State Mutual Bk.

--The Great Polish-English Dictionary, 2 vols. (Pol. & Eng.). 1980. vinyl $60.00x (ISBN 0-569-02649-0, Pub. by Collet's). State Mutual Bk.

Stanislawski, J., et al. A Practical English-Polish Dictionary. 913p. (Eng. & Pol.). 1976. leatherette $19.95 (ISBN 0-686-92102-X, M-9328). French & Eur.

Stanislawski, Jan. A Practical English-Polish Dictionary. LC 77-578742. 913p. (Pol.). 1981. $17.50x (ISBN 83-214-0245-3). Intl Pubns Serv.

Stanislawski, Jan, ed. Great English-Polish Dictionary. 1178p. (Eng. & Pol.). 1977. 40.00x (ISBN 0-8002-1469-2). Intl Pubns Serv.

Stanisljawski, J., et al. Polish-English Practical Dictionary. 1030p. (Pol. & Eng.). 1978. $20.00x (ISBN 0-89918-532-0, P-532). Vanous.

ENGLISH LANGUAGE–DICTIONARIES–POLYGLOT

Bergman, Peter M. Concise Dictionary of Twenty-Six Languages. 408p. (Eng.). pap. $2.50 indexed. Imported Bks.

Capitol's Concise Dictionary. 1416p. (Eng. , Swedish , Dutch , Ger. , Ital. & Span.). 1972. $35.95 (ISBN 84-7183-079-5, S-50438). French & Eur.

Clason, W., ed. Dictionary of Library Science Information & Documentation. rev. ed. (Eng., Fr., Span., Ital., Dutch, Ger., & Arabic.). 1977. $95.75 (ISBN 0-444-41475-4). Elsevier.

Graa, Albert, ed. Vocabularium Pharmaceuticum. 2nd ed. 125p. (Eng., Ger., Fr. & Ital.). 1964. text ed. 13.50x (ISBN 0-8002-3024-8). Intl Pubns Serv.

Hoffman, Johannes P. Dictionary of Packaging: German-English-French. 2nd, rev. ed. LC 72-352784. 353p. (Ger., Eng. & Fr.). 1971. 62.50 (ISBN 0-8002-0745-9). Intl Pubns Serv.

Hoyer-Kreuter. Technological Dictionary in Three Languages, 3 vols. Schlomann, Alfred, ed. Incl. Vol. 1. German-English-French; Vol. 2. English-German-French; Vol. 3. French-German-English. (Ger., Fr. & Eng.). Set. $135.00 (ISBN 0-8044-0202-7). Ungar.

International Institution for Production Engineering Research. Dictionary of Production Engineering: German-English-French, 8 vols. Incl. Vol. 1. Forging & Drop Forging. 108p. 1962. 30.00x (ISBN 3-7736-5920-2); Vol. 2. Grinding - Surface Roughness. 140p. 1963. 30.00x (ISBN 3-7736-5930-X); Vol. 3. Sheet Metal Forming. 136p. 1965. 30.00x (ISBN 3-7736-5940-7); Vol. 4. Fundamental Terms of Cutting. 124p. 1969. 30.00x (ISBN 3-7736-5946-6); Vol. 5. Cold Extrusion & Upsetting. 157p. 1969. 30.00x (ISBN 3-7736-5945-8); Vol. 6. Planing, Slotting, Broaching, Turning. 1972. 30.00x (ISBN 3-7736-5946-6); Vol. 7. 30.00x (ISBN 3-7736-5947-4); Milling, Sawing, Gear Manufacturing. 359p. 1979. 42.50x (ISBN 3-7736-5948-2). (Ger., Eng. & Fr.). Intl Pubns Serv.

Orne, Jerrold. Language of the Foreign Book Trade: Abbreviations, Terms, Phrases. 3rd ed. $20.00 (ISBN 0-8389-0219-7). ALA.

Pfannkuch, Hans-Olaf. Elsevier's Dictionary of Hydrogeology. (Eng., Fr., & Ger.). 1969. $42.75 (ISBN 0-444-40717-0). Elsevier.

Scharf, T. & Shetty, M. C. Dictionary of Development Banking: A Compilation of Terms in English, French, & German with Definitions in English. LC 72-83212. (Eng., Fr. & Ger.). 1973. $42.00 (ISBN 0-444-41028-7). Elsevier.

ENGLISH LANGUAGE–DICTIONARIES–PORTUGUESE

Aliandro, H. Dicionario Ingles-Portugues. 402p. (Eng. & Port.). 1980. pap. $8.95 (ISBN 0-686-97638-X, M-9215). French & Eur.

Aliandro, Hygino. Portuguese-English Dictionary. 311p. (Port. & Eng.). 1978. pap. $4.80. Imported Bks.

Altman, M. Dicionario Tecnico Contabil: Portugues-Ingles, Ingles-Portugues. 126p. (Port. & Eng.). 1980. pap. $14.95 (ISBN 0-686-97637-1, M-9355). French & Eur.

Basic Words in Portuguese. (Eng. & Port.). write for info. (454-8). Pan Am Bk Co.

Berlitz. Berlitz Pocket Dictionaries: Portuguese-English-Portuguese. (Port. & Eng.). pap. $4.95 (ISBN 0-02-964440-2). Macmillan.

Berlitz Editors. Berlitz Portuguese for Travellers. 192p. (Port.). 1982. pap. 4.95 (ISBN 0-02-963960-3, Berlitz). Macmillan.

Collins GEM Dictionary: Portuguese-English, English-Portuguese. 768p. (Port. & Eng.). $3.95. Imported Bks.

De Morais, Armando. Dicionario De Ingles-Portugues. 1966. $16.00x (ISBN 0-686-19950-2). Intl Learn Syst.

De Pina, Araujo A. Portuguese-English, English-Portuguese Technical Dictionary, 2 vols. (Port. & Eng.). Set. 115.00 (ISBN 0-685-79115-7). Heinman.

Dicionario Ingles-Portugues. (Dicionarios Academicos). 1974. $6.50x (ISBN 0-686-19951-0). Intl Learn Syst.

Dicionario Ingles-Portugues. (Dicionarios Academicos). 1974. $6.50x (ISBN 0-686-19951-0). Intl Learn Syst.

Dicionario Portuges-Ingles. (Dicionarios Academicos). 1975. $6.50x (ISBN 0-686-19952-9). Intl Learn Syst.

Dicionario Portuges-Ingles. (Dicionarios Academicos). 1975. $6.50x (ISBN 0-686-19952-9). Intl Learn Syst.

Dicionario Portugues-Ingles. (Dicionarios Escolares). (Port. & Eng.). 1973. 19.50x (ISBN 0-686-19953-7). Intl Learn Syst.

Dixson & Fox. Meu Primeiro Dicionario Ilustrado de Ingles. (Illus.). 67p. (Port. & Eng.). (gr. 2-6). pap. $6.50. Imported Bks.

Ferreira, J. A. Portuguese-English, English-Portuguese Dictionary. (Port. & Eng.). 30.00 (ISBN 0-685-12039-2). Heinman.

Ferreira, J. Albino. English-Portuguese Dictionary. rev. ed. De Morais, O., ed. (Eng. & Port.). $32.50 (ISBN 0-87559-027-6); thumb indexed $37.50 (ISBN 0-87559-028-4). Shalom.

Gem Language Dictionaries: Portuguese-English & English-Portuguese. (Port. & Eng.). write for info. (ISBN 0-671-41946-3). S&S.

Langenscheidt English-Portuguese Lilliput Dictionary. 640p. (Eng. & Port.). plastic $1.50 (ISBN 3-468-96463-3). Langenscheidt.

Langenscheidt Portuguese-English Lilliput Dictionary. 640p. (Eng. & Port.). plastic $1.50 (ISBN 3-468-96462-5). Langenscheidt.

Langenscheidt's Lilliput English-Portuguese Dictionary. 640p. (Eng. & Port.). 1972. $1.50 (ISBN 0-685-31367-0). Am Map.

Langenscheidt's Lilliput Portuguese-English Dictionary. 640p. (Eng. & Port.). 1972. $1.50 (ISBN 0-685-31368-9). Am Map.

Langenscheidt's Universal Portuguese-English, English-Portuguese Dictionary. 8th ed. 384p. (Eng. & Port.). 1972. $2.95 (ISBN 0-685-31342-5). Am Map.

Lilliput Dictionary. 640p. (Port. & Eng.). $1.50 (116). Langenscheidt.

Lilliput Dictionary. 640p. (Eng. & Port.). $1.50 (117). Langenscheidt.

Martins, M. J. Portuguese-English, English-Portuguese Dictionary, 2 vols. (Port. & Eng.). Set. 45.00 (ISBN 0-685-58543-3). Heinman.

Michaelis. Concise Dictionary Portuguese-English. (Port. & Eng.). $25.00. Iaconi.

--Portuguese-English, English-Portuguese Basic Dictionary. (Eng. & Port.). Date not set. text ed. $35.00 (ISBN 0-686-46534-2). Heinman.

New Michaelis Illustrated Dictionary: English-Portuguese, Portuguese English, 2 vols. (Illus., Port. & Eng.). 1976. Vol. 1 Eng.-Port. $42.00; Vol. 2 Port.-Eng. $45.00. Imported Bks.

Pietzschke, F., ed. Portuguese-English, English-Portuguese Illustrated Dictionary: The New Michaelis, 2 vols. (Port. & Eng.). Set. 125.00 (ISBN 0-685-58551-4). Portuguese-english, 28th Ed (ISBN 3-7653-0050-0). English-portuguese, 30th Ed (ISBN 3-7653-0051-9). Heinman.

Portuguese-English-Portuguese. (Berlitz Pocket Dictionaries Ser.). (Port. & Eng.). $4.95 (ISBN 0-02-964440-2). Macmillan.

Richardson & Pereira. McKay's Modern Portuguese-English, English-Portuguese Dictionary. 347p. (Port. & Eng.). 1976. $11.00. Imported Bks.

Richardson, Elbert L., et al, eds. McKay's Modern Portuguese-English & English-Portuguese Dictionary. (Modern Dictionaries). (Port. & Eng.). 1943. 10.95 (ISBN 0-679-10077-6). McKay.

Taylor, James L. Harrap Portuguese-English Dictionary. xx, 662p. (Port. & Eng.). E17.50 (ISBN 0-245-57228-7). Harrap.

ENGLISH LANGUAGE–DICTIONARIES–ROMANIAN

Andronescu, Serban C. English-Romanian Dictionary. (Eng. & Romanian.). Date not set. price not set (ISBN 0-917944-03-8). Am Inst Writing Res.

Levitchi, V. & Bantas, T. English-Romanian Dictionary. 1068p. (Eng. & Rumanian.). 1980. $55.00x (ISBN 0-569-07472-X, Pub. by Collet's). State Mutual Bk.

Panovf, Irina. Dictionar englez-roman. LC 79-344523. 422p. (Eng. & Romanian.). 1978. 16.50 lei. Editura Stiintificia.

Schonkron, M. Rumanian-English & Dictionary. (Rumanian & Eng.). $25.00. Iaconi.

Schonkron, M., ed. Rumanian-English, English-Rumanian Dictionary, with Supplement. (Rumanian & Eng.). $25.00 (ISBN 0-8044-0546-8). Ungar.

ENGLISH LANGUAGE–DICTIONARIES–RUSSIAN

Akhmanova, et al. Russian-English Dictionary. 510p. (Rus. & Eng.). $4.00. Imported Bks.

Akhmanova, O. S. & Wilson, E. English-Russian Dictionary. 639p. (Rus. & Eng.). 1979. $9.95 (ISBN 0-686-97370-4, M-9115). French & Eur.

Akhmanova, Ol'ga Sergeevna. Anglo-Russkii Slovar. LC 80-465947. 639p. (Eng. & Rus.). 1978. write for info. Russkii Iazyk.

Akmanova, A. English-Russian Dictionary. 590p. (Eng. & Rus.). 1980. $25.00x (ISBN 0-569-00012-2, Pub. by Collet's). State Mutual Bk.

Alekhina, A. I. Kratikii Russko-Angliiskii i Anglo-Russkii Frazeologicheskii Slovar' (BGU im. V. I. Lenina Ser.). 400p. (Rus. & Eng.). 1980. $4.50 (Q-36). Four Continent.

Anpilogova, B. G., et al. Essential Russian-English Dictionary. (Progress Ser.). 180p. (Rus. & Eng.). $1.50 (98 F). Four Continent.

Arakin, T. English-Russian Dictionary. 988p. (Eng. & Rus.). 1980. $35.00x (ISBN 0-569-00013-0, Pub. by Collets). State Mutual Bk.

Arakin, V. D. English-Russian Dictionary. (Eng. & Rus.). 1980. leatherette $19.95 (ISBN 0-686-97371-2, M-9107). French & Eur.

Beniukh, O. P. Karmannyi Anglo-Russkii Slovar. 832p. (Eng. & Rus.). 1973. $2.00 (Pub. by Sov Entsiklopediia). Four Continent.

--Karmannyi Anglo-Russkii Slovar. 832p. (Eng. & Rus.). 1973. $2.00 (Pub. by Russkii Iazyk). Four Continent.

Beniukh, O. P., et al. Karmannyi Anglo-Russkii Slovar. 832p. (Eng. & Rus.). 1977. $2.25 (Pub. by Russkii Iazyk). Four Continent.

--Karmannyi Anglo-Russkii Slovar' (Russkii iazyk Ser.). 832p. (Rus. & Eng.). $2.00 (C-102). Four Continent.

Beniukh, O. P., et al, eds. Karmannyi Russko-Angliiskii Slovar' (Sov. Entsiklopediia Ser.). 784p. (Rus. & Eng.). 1977. $2.00. Four Continent.

Bratus, B. V., et al. Russian Word-Collocations: Learner's Dictionary. (Russkii iazyk Ser.). 368p. (Rus. & Eng.). 1979. $5.95 (D-205 A). Four Continent.

Congrat-Butlar, Stefan, ed. Russian Vest Pocket Dictionary. (Rus.). 1974. $2.95 (ISBN 0-394-40068-2). Random.

Coulson, Jessie, et al, eds. The Pocket Oxford Russian Dictionary: Russian-English - English-Russian. (Rus. & Eng.). 1981. pap. $10.95x (ISBN 0-19-864122-2). Oxford U Pr.

Daum, V. & Schenk. Dictionary of Russian Verbs (Russian-English) 750p. (Rus. & Eng.). 1980. $75.00x (ISBN 0-569-08093-2, Pub. by Collet's). State Mutual Bk.

English-Russian, Russian-English Dictionary. 464p. (Eng. & Rus.). 1978. $4.75 (ISBN 0-686-92374-X, M-9094). French & Eur.

Folomkina, A. & Weiser, H. The Learner's English-Russian Dictionary. 472p. (Eng. & Rus.). 1975. $3.00. Russki Iazyk.

Folomkina, S. & Weiser, H. Learner's English-Russian Dictionary. (Eng. & Rus.). 1963. pap. 9.95 (ISBN 0-262-56002-X). MIT Pr.

--The Learner's English-Russian Dictionary. 471p. (Eng. & Rus.). 1975. leatherette $9.95 (ISBN 0-686-92469-X, M-9118). French & Eur.

Folomkina, S. K., et al. Anglo-Russkii Uchebnyi Slovar' 655p. (Eng. & Rus.). 1970. $3.25. Four Continent.

Folomkina, V. & Weiser, T. Learner's English-Russian Dictionary. 655p. (Eng. & Rus.). 1980. $15.00x (ISBN 0-569-05869-4, Pub. by Collet's). State Mutual Bk.

Galperin, I. R., ed. Bol'Shoi Anglo-Russkii Slovar, 2 vols. (Rus. & Eng.). 1977. $35.00 set. Four Continent.

--A Supplement to the New English-Russian Dictionary. (Russkii iazyk Ser.). 432p. (Rus. & Eng.). 1980. $6.95 (D-209A). Four Continent.

Gem Language Dictionaries: Russian-English & English-Russian. (Rus. & Eng.). write for info. (ISBN 0-671-41960-9). S&S.

Harrison, W. & LeFlemming, Svetlana. Russian-English & English-Russian Dictionary. (Routledge Pocket Dictionaries Ser.). 580p. (Orig.). 1981. pap. $8.95 (ISBN 0-7100-0800-7). Routledge & Kegan.

Harrison, William & Le Fleming, Svetlana. Russian-English, English-Russian Dictionary. 1973. $14.00 (ISBN 0-7100-6960-X). Routledge & Kegan.

Hugo Pocket Dictionary: Russian-English, English-Russian. 658p. (Rus. & Eng.). 1975. $3.50 (ISBN 0-8226-0506-6, 506). Littlefield.

Hugo Pocket Dictionary: Russian-English, English-Russian. 657p. (Rus. & Eng.). 1969. $3.95 (ISBN 0-686-92547-5, M-9011). French & Eur.

Kunin, A. V., et al. Anglo-Russkii Frazeologicheskii Slovar. 1456p. (Eng. & Rus.). 1956. $5.25 (294). Four Continent.

Langenscheidt Russian-English Lilliput Dictionary. 640p. (Eng. & Rus.). plastic $1.50 (ISBN 3-468-96453-6). Langenscheidt.

Langenscheidt's Lilliput English-Russian Dictionary. 640p. (Eng. & Rus.). 1972. $1.50 (ISBN 0-685-31365-4). Am Map.

Langenscheidt's Lilliput Russian-English Dictionary. 640p. (Eng. & Rus.). 1972. $1.50 (ISBN 0-685-31366-2). Am Map.

Langenscheidt's Universal Russian-English, English-Russian Dictionary. 415p. (Eng. & Rus.). 1972. $2.95 (ISBN 0-685-31341-7). Am Map.

Lapidus, A., et al. The Learner's Russian-English Dictionary: For Foreign Students of Russian. 552p. (Rus. & Eng.). $4.65. Four Continent.

Lapidus, B. A. & Shevtsoka, S. V. The Learner's Russian-English Dictionary. 550p. (Eng. & Rus.). 1977. leatherette $9.95 (ISBN 0-686-92466-5, M-9117). French & Eur.

Lapidus, B. A., et al. The Learner's Russian-English Dictionary. 552p. (Rus. & Eng.). 1977. $3.95 (Pub. by Russkii Iazyk). Four Continent.

The Learner's English-Russian Dictionary: For English Speaking Students. (Russkii iazyk Ser.). 472p. (Eng. & Rus.). 1975. $3.00 (D-202 A). Four Continent.

Lilliput Dictionary. 640p. (Rus. & Eng.). $1.50 (118). Langenscheidt.

Miuller, V. K., ed. Anglo-Russkii Slovar. 888p. (Eng. & Rus.). 1977. $14.25. Four Continent.

Muller, V. English-Russian Dictionary. 888p. (Eng. & Rus.). 1980. vinyl $42.00x (ISBN 0-569-08362-1, Pub. by Collet's). State Mutual Bk.

Muller, V. K., ed. English-Russian Dictionary. rev. ed. (Eng. & Rus.). 1973. $24.75 (ISBN 0-525-09881-X, 02403-720). Dutton.

Muller, Vladimir K. English-Russian Dictionary. 6th ed. (Eng. & Rus.). 19.50 (ISBN 0-685-20186-4, 066-6). Saphrograph.

New English-Russian Dictionary, 2 vols. 1685p. (Eng. & Rus.). 1980. Set. $80.00x (ISBN 0-569-07330-8, Pub. by Collet's). State Mutual Bk.

O'Brien. New Russian-English & English-Russian Dictionary. 710p. (Rus. & Eng.). $6.00. Imported Bks.

Parsons, Charles. Russian-English Dictionary of irovat' Verbs. 34p. (Orig., Rus. & Eng.). 1983. $10.00x (ISBN 0-917564-14-6). Translation Research.

--Russian-English Dictionary of....ost' Words. 64p. (Orig., Rus. & Eng.). 1978. pap. text ed. $10.00x (ISBN 0-917564-05-7). Translation Research.

Pochertsova, L. D., et al, eds. English-Russian Phrase Book. (Vyscha shkola Ser.). 335p. (Eng. & Rus.). 1979. $4.95 (C-94). Four Continent.

Rankin, N. A. The Pocket Oxford English-Russian Dictionary. (Eng. & Rus.). 1981. text ed. 11.95x (ISBN 0-19-864127-3). Oxford U Pr.

Romanov, A. S. Romanov Russian-English Dictionary. (Rus. & Eng.). pap. 4.95 (ISBN 0-671-49619-0). PB.

Romanov's Pocket Russian-English, English-Russian Dictionary. (Rus. & Eng.). pap. $2.75. Imported Bks.

Rozenberg, M. B. English-Russian Dictionary of Refrigeration & Low Temperature Technology. 2nd, rev. ed. $73.00 (ISBN 0-08-024737-7). Pergamon.

Russian-English Dictionary. (Russkii iazyk Ser.). 520p. (Rus. & Eng.). 1979. $3.95 (O-50). Four Continent.

Ruzicka, R. A Dictionary of Russian Verbs. Daum, E. & Schenk, W., eds. 752p. (Rus. & Eng.). 1974. $17.50 (O-26). Hippocrene Bks.

Segal, Louis. English-Russian Dictionary. 3rd ed. (Rus. & Eng.). 1958. text ed. $19.95x (ISBN 0-8464-0380-3). Beekman Pubs.

Smirnitskii, A. I. Russko-Angliiskii Slovar. (Russkii iazyk Ser.). 768p. (Rus. & Eng.). 1977. $14.25 (D-215 A). Four Continent.

Smirnitskii, T. Russian-English Dictionary. 766p. (Rus. & Eng.). 1980. $42.00x (ISBN 0-569-00006-8, Pub. by Collet's). State Mutual Bk.

Smirnitsky, A. I. Russian English Dictionary. rev. ed. (Rus. & Eng.). 1973. $24.75 (ISBN 0-525-19520-3, 02403-720). Dutton.

Steinfeldt, E. Russian Word Count. (Progress Ser.). 228p. (Rus. & Eng.). guide for tchrs. $3.00 (C-35). Four Continent.

Taube, A. M. Russian-English Dictionary. 832p. (Rus. & Eng.). 1980. vinyl bds. $25.00x (ISBN 0-569-06453-8, Pub. by Collet's). State Mutual Bk.

U. S. War Department. Dictionary of Spoken Russian: Russian-English: English-Russian. (Rus. & Eng.). 1959. pap. $8.95 (ISBN 0-486-20496-0). Dover.

Voinova, L. A., et al, eds. Frazeologicheskii Slovar' Russkogo Iazyka. (Russkii iazyk Ser.). 544p. (Rus.). 1978. $11.95 (C-33). Four Continent.

Wilson, E. A. The Modern Russian Dictionary for English Speakers: English-Russian. LC 81-12141. 1200p. (Rus. & Eng.). 1983. 39.50 (ISBN 0-08-020554-2). Pergamon.

Zaimovskii, S. G. Concise English-Russian, Russian-English Dictionary. 464p. (Eng. & Rus.). 1980. $20.00x (ISBN 0-569-06089-3, Pub. by Collet's). State Mutual Bk.

--Kratkii Anglo-Russkii i Russko-Angliiskii Slovar' (Russkii iazyk Ser.). 464p. (Rus. & Eng.). 1978. $3.10 (O-134). Four Continent.

Zaimovsky, S. G. Russian-English, English-Russian Dictionary. pap. $8.50 (ISBN 0-685-20192-9, 069-0). Saphrograph.

Zalizniak, A. A., ed. Grammaticheskii Slovar' Russkogo Iazyka. (Russkii iazyk Ser.). 892p. (Rus.). 1977. $14.95 (D-207A). Four Continent.

ENGLISH LANGUAGE–DICTIONARIES–SANSKRIT

Apte, V. S. Practical Sanskrit-English Dictionary. rev. ed. (Sanskrit & Eng.). 1978. Repr. $28.00 (ISBN 0-89684-294-0). Orient Bk Dist.

--The Student's English-Sanskrit Dictionary. (Eng. & Sanskrit.). 1974. Repr. 9.95 (ISBN 0-8426-0507-X). Orient Bk Dist.

--Student's English-Sanskrit Dictionary. 501p. (Sanskrit & Eng.). 1973. text ed. $9.50x (ISBN 0-8426-0507-X). Verry.

Apte, Vaman S. Practical Sanskrit-English Dictionary. new ed. (Sanskrit & Eng.). 1975. $40.00x (ISBN 0-8426-0996-2). Verry.

Gode, P. K., et al, eds. Practical Sanskrit-English Dictionary. Rev. & enl. ed. LC 78-911335. (Sanskrit & Eng.). write for info. Prasarnmitr.

MacDonnell, Arthur A. Practical Sanskrit Dictionary: With Transliteration Accentuation & Etymological Analysis Throughout. (Sanskrit.). 1924. $37.50x (ISBN 0-19-864303-9). Oxford U Pr.

Monier-Williams. Sanskrit-English Dictionary. (Sanskrit & Eng.). 1973. $37.00x (ISBN 0-8364-0464-5). South Asia Bks.

Monier-Williams, Monier. English Sanskrit Dictionary. (Eng. & Sanskrit.). 1979. $30.00x (ISBN 0-89744-966-5). Auromere.

--English-Sanskrit Dictionary. (Eng. & Sanskrit.). 1976. Repr. of 1851 ed. Set. text ed. 34.00x (ISBN 0-391-01069-7). Humanities.

--English-Sanskrit Dictionary. (Eng. & Sanskrit.). 1976. Repr. of 1851 ed. 27.50x (ISBN 0-8002-0205-8). Intl Pubns Serv.

Monier-Williams, Monier, et al. Sanskrit-English Dictionary. rev. ed. (Sanskrit & Eng.). 1899. $105.00x (ISBN 0-19-864308-X). Oxford U Pr.

Sanskrit-Thai-English Dictionary. 1339p. (Sanskrit, Thai & Eng.). 10.00x (ISBN 0-8002-1951-1). Intl Pubns Serv.

Sen, Chitrabhanu. A Dictionary of the Vedic rituals. LC 78-901425. 172p. (Eng. & Sanskrit.). 1978. $20.00; Rs.100.00. Concept Pub. Co.

Suryakanta. Sanskrit-Hindi-English Dictionary. (Sanskrit, Hindi & Eng.). 1976. $47.50x (ISBN 0-8002-1950-3). Intl Pubns Serv.

Williams, M. Sanskrit-English Dictionary. (Sanskrit & Eng.). 1979. $55.00 (ISBN 0-89684-314-9). Orient Bk Dist.

Williams, M. Monier. Dictionary of English & Sanskrit. LC 73-495007. (Eng. & Sanskrit.). 1971. Repr. of 1851 ed. 17.50x (ISBN 0-8002-0172-8). Intl Pubns Serv.

Williams, Monier, ed. Sanskrit-English Dictionary: Etymologically & Philologically Arranged with Special Reference to Cognate Indo-European Languages. LC 73-495007. 1333p. (Sanskrit & Eng.). 1981. Repr. of 1899 ed. 50.00x (ISBN 0-8002-0204-X). Intl Pubns serv.

Williams, Monier, et al. Sanskrit-English Dictionary. 1367p. (Sanskrit & Eng.). 1981. Repr. $45.00 (ISBN 0-89581-173-1). Lancaster-Miller.

Wllliams, Monier. A Dictionary, English & Sanskrit. 4th ed. (Eng. & Sanskrit.). 1976. 35.00 (ISBN 0-89684-193-6). Orient Bk Dist.

ENGLISH LANGUAGE–DICTIONARIES–SERBO-CROATIAN

Benson, M. English-Serbocroatian Dictionary. 669p. (Eng. & Serbocroatian.). 1981. $75.00 (ISBN 0-686-97376-3, M-9635). French & Eur.

--Serbocroatian-English Dictionary. 770p. (Serbocroatian & Eng.). 1980. $75.00 (ISBN 0-686-97438-7, M-9630). French & Eur.

Benson, Morton. English - SerboCroatian Dictionary. LC 78-64520. (Eng. & Serbocroatian.). 1979. $35.50x (ISBN 0-8122-7764-3). U of Pa Pr.

Brkic, S. Serbocroatian-English Dictionary. 416p. (Serbocroatian & Eng.). 1980. pap. $14.95 (ISBN 0-686-97436-0, M-9631). French & Eur.

Brozovic, Blanka & Gercan, Oktavija. English-Serbocroatian & Serbocroatian-English Dictionary. 7th ed. (Eng. & Serbocroatian.). 1980. pap. 8.00x (ISBN 0-686-31617-7). Intl Learn Syst.

Cvetanovic, Ratimir J. English-Serbocroatian, Serbocroatian-English Dictionary. (Eng. & Serbocroatian.). 19.50 (ISBN 0-87557-074-7, 074-7). Saphrograph.

Drvodelic, Milan. English-Croatian or Serbian Dictionary. 5th ed. (Eng. & Serbocroatian.). 1978. 30.00x (ISBN 0-686-19962-6). Intl Learn Syst.

Filipovic, Rudolf. English-Croatian or Serbian Dictionary. 1436p. (Eng. & Serbocroatian.). 1980. $150.00x (ISBN 0-569-08646-9, Pub. by Collets). State Mutual Bk.

Filipovic, Rudolf, et al. English-Serbocroatian Dictionary. 10th ed. (Eng. & Serbocroatian.). 1975. 80.00x (ISBN 0-686-19960-X). Intl Learn Syst.

Grujic, B. Serbocroatian-English, English-Serbocroatian Dictionary. Rev. & enl. ed. (Serbocroatian & Eng.). 25.00 (ISBN 0-685-65374-9). Heinman.

--Serbocroatian-English-Serbocroatian Dictionary: Short Grammar. 33rd ed. 624p. (Serbocroatian & Eng.). 1982. text ed. $18.00x (ISBN 0-89918-647-5, Y-647). Vanous.

Grujic, J. English-Serbo-Croat & Serbo-Croat-English Dictionary. 620p. (Eng. & Serbocroatian.). 1980. $40.00x (ISBN 0-569-03165-6, Pub. by Collet's). State Mutual Bk.

Grujic, V. C. English-Serbocroat & Serbocroat-English Dictionary. 620p. (Eng. & Serbocroatian.). 1971. $65.00x (ISBN 0-686-44712-3, Pub. by Collets). State Mutual Bk.

Ristic, Svetomir & Simic, Zivojin. English-Serbocroatian Dictionary. (Eng. & Serbocroatian.). 1975. 29.95x (ISBN 0-686-19961-8). Intl Learn Syst.

Simic, Z. English-Serbocroatian Dictionary. 446p. (Eng. & Serbocroatian.). 1979. pap. text ed. $14.95 (ISBN 0-686-97375-5, M-9634). French & Eur.

--Yugoslavian Dictionary: English-Serbocroatian. 446p. (Eng. & Serbocroatian.). 1977. pap. text ed. $6.50x (ISBN 0-89918-784-6). Vanous.

ENGLISH LANGUAGE–DICTIONARIES–SIAMESE

Michell, Edward B. Siamese-English Dictionary. (Siamese & Eng.). 1976. Repr. of 1958 ed. $39.50 (ISBN 0-518-19004-8). Ayer Co.

ENGLISH LANGUAGE–DICTIONARIES–SLOVAK

Komac & Skerlj. Yugoslavian Pocket Dictionary: Slovene-English, English-Slovenski. (Eng. & Slovenian.). 1979. $15.00x (ISBN 0-89918-778-1, Y-778). Vanous.

Lysaght, T. Dictionary, Material Towards the Compilation of a Concise Old Church Slavonic English. $25.00. VicUni.

Slovak-English, English-Slovak Dictionary. 791p. (Slovak & Eng.). 1981. 14.95 (ISBN 0-88254-543-4, Pub. by Slovart Czechoslovakia). Hippocrene Bks.

Smejkalova, J., et al. Czechoslovakian Dictionary: English-Slovak & Slovak-English. 5th ed. 793p. (Czech. & Eng.). 1979. $9.50x (ISBN 0-89918-170-8, C-170). Vanous.

--Slovak-English-Slovak Pocket Dictionary. (Slovak & Eng.). 1979. text ed. $9.50x (ISBN 0-89918-170-8, C170). Vanous.

ENGLISH LANGUAGE–DICTIONARIES–SLOVENIAN

Grad, A., et al. English-Slovene Dictionary. 1120p. (Eng. & Slovene.). 1979. $49.95 (ISBN 0-686-97378-X, M-9695). French & Eur.

Komac & Skeri, J. Modern Dictionary Slovene-English, English-Slovene. 787p. (Eng. & Slovene.). 1981. leatherette $17.50 (ISBN 0-686-97403-4, M-9701). French & Eur.

Kotnik, J. & Grad, A. Slovene-English, English-Slovene Dictionary, 2 vols. new ed. (Slovene & Eng.). Set. 75.00 (ISBN 0-685-55016-8). Heinman.

Simko, P. English-Slovak Dictionary. 1442p. (Eng. & Slovak.). 1980. $70.00x (ISBN 0-569-03737-9, Pub. by Collet's). State Mutual Bk.

Skerlj, R., et al. Yugoslavian-English Slovene Dictionary. 1122p. (Eng. & Slovenian.). 1979. text ed. $35.00x (ISBN 0-89918-704-8, Y704). Vanous.

Vilikovska, J. & Vilikovsky, P. Slovak-English Dictionary. 522p. (Slovak & Eng.). 1980. $39.50x (ISBN 0-569-08530-6, Pub. by Collet's). State Mutual Bk.

ENGLISH LANGUAGE–DICTIONARIES–SOTHO

English Sotho-Sotho English Dictionary. (Eng. & Sotho.). $21.00 (ISBN 0-87559-031-4); thumb indexed $27.00 (ISBN 0-87559-032-2). Shalom.

ENGLISH LANGUAGE–DICTIONARIES–SPANISH

A Beginner's Bilingual Pictorial Dictionary. 358p. (Span. & Eng.). pap. $5.25 (T01). Bilingual Ed Serv.

Amador, E. M. Martinez. Diccionario Ingles-Espanol, Espanol-Ingles. 1504p. (Span. & Eng.). $47.95 (ISBN 84-303-0105-4, S-2789). French & Eur.

American Heritage. Diccionario Ingles. 1981. 9.95 (ISBN 0-395-31254-X); pap. 7.95 (ISBN 0-395-31255-8). HM.

Appleton-Cuyas Dictionary: English-Spanish, Spanish-English. (Span. & Eng.). write for info. (608-11). Pan Amer Pub.

Armengol, Joseph, et al, eds. English-Spanish Guide for Medical Personnel. (Eng. & Span.). 1966. pap. $7.00 (ISBN 0-87488-721-6). Med Exam.

Bantam New College Dictionary: English-Spanish, Spanish-English. (Span. & Eng.). write for info. (608-39). Pan Amer Pub.

Basic Words in Spanish. (Eng. & Span.). write for info. (454-3). Pan Amer Pub.

Beginner's Spanish-English Dictionary. (Span. & Eng., Large format). $12.95; pap. $10.95; in 2 vols. $15.95. Iaconi.

Benedetto, U. Spanish-English, English-Spanish Dictionary, 2 Vols. (Span. & Eng.). Set. 100.00 (ISBN 8-4716-6211-6). Heinman.

Berlitz. Berlitz Pocket Dictionaries: Spanish-English-Spanish. (Span. & Eng.). pap. $4.95 (ISBN 0-02-964510-7). Macmillan.
Berlitz Editors. Berlitz Latin-American Spanish for Travellers. 192p. (Span.). 1982. 8.95 (ISBN 0-02-965510-2, Berlitz); pap. 4.95 (ISBN 0-02-963950-6). Macmillan.
--Berlitz Pocket Dictionaries: Spanish-English. 300p. (Eng. & Span.). 1982. pap. $4.95 (ISBN 0-686-92998-5, Berlitz). Macmillan.
--Berlitz Spanish for Travellers. 192p. (Span.). 1982. 8.95 (ISBN 0-02-965190-5, Berlitz); pap. 4.95 (ISBN 0-02-963970-0). Macmillan.
Bohigas Rosell, Mauricio. Diccionario Ingles-Espanol, Spanish-English. 1370p. (Eng. & Span.). 1974. $7.95 (ISBN 84-7183-007-8, S-12385). French & Eur.
Brew Vocabulari Catala-Castella-Angles de Comerc Exterior. 43p. (Span. , Catalan & Eng.). write for info. (S-37580). French & Eur.
Brown, R. F., ed. Spanish-English, English-Spanish Gem Dictionary. (Gem Foreign Language Ser.). (Span. & Eng.). 1957. $2.95 (ISBN 0-00-458653-0, G4). Collins Pubs.
Bruguera Grane, Francisco. Diccionario Ingles-Espanol, Espanol-Ingles. 3rd ed. 680p. (Eng. & Span.). 1979. pap. $4.95 (ISBN 84-02-00835-6, S-50345). French & Eur.
Caldwell, Pablo. Diccionario de Modismos Ingleses. 496p. (Eng. & Span.). 1973. $17.50 (ISBN 0-686-56672-6, S-33065). French & Eur.
Calvert, G. H. Spanish Dictionary. (Routledge Pocket Dictionaries Ser.). 560p. 1980. pap. 7.95 (ISBN 0-7100-0558-X). Routledge & Kegan.
Capitol's Concise Dictionary of Seven Languages. (gr. 9-12). 1978. $29.95 (ISBN 0-8120-5333-8). Barron.
Cassell. Cassell's Spanish Dictionary: Spanish-English, English-Spanish. Peers, Edqan A., ed. (Span. & Eng.). standard $17.95 (ISBN 0-02-522900-1); thumb-indexed $19.95 (ISBN 0-02-522910-9); concise $9.95 (ISBN 0-02-522660-6). Macmillan.
Cassell's Compact Spanish-English Dictionary. 444p. (Span. & Eng.). 1981. pap. $2.95 (ISBN 0-440-31129-2, LE). Dell.
Cassell's Concise Spanish-English English-Spanish Dictionary. (Span. & Eng.). 1977. 9.95 (ISBN 0-02-522660-6). Macmillan.
Cassell's French Dictionary: French-English, English-French. (Fr. & Eng.). standard $17.95 (ISBN 0-02-522610-X); thumb-indexed $19.95 (ISBN 0-02-522620-7); concise $9.95 (ISBN 0-02-522670-3). Macmillan.
Cassell's Spanish Dictionary: English-Spanish, Spanish-English. (Span. & Eng.). write for info. (608-35). Pan Amer Pub.
Castillo, Bond. University of Chicago Spanish-English Dictionary. (Span. & Eng.). pap. $2.95. Iaconi.
Castillo, Carlos & Bond, Otto F. Spanish-English Dictionary. (Span. & Eng.). 1981. pap. 3.50 (ISBN 0-671-47762-5). PB.
--University of Chicago Spanish Dictionary. 3rd rev. enl. ed. (Span.). 1977. $12.50 (ISBN 0-226-09673-4, Phoen); pap. $4.95 (ISBN 0-226-09674-2). U of Chicago Pr.
The Cat in the Hat Beginner Book Dictionary in Spanish & English. (Span. & Eng.). $8.95. Lectorum Pubns.
Collins Contemporary Dictionary: English-Spanish, Spanish-English. (Span. & Eng.). write for info. (608-64). Pan Am Bk Co.
Collins English-Spanish & Spanish-English Dictionary. 1242p. (Eng. & Span.). write for info. (ISBN 0-671-41939-0); write for info. thumb-indexed (ISBN 0-671-41938-2). S&S.
Collins Pocket Spanish Dictionary. 448p. 1983. $7.95 (ISBN 0-671-49221-7). S&S.
Collins Spanish Dictionary: English-Spanish, Spanish-English. (Span. & Eng.). write for info. indexed (608-23). Pan Amer Pub.
Constantinon, P. English-Spanish Dictionary. (Eng. & Span.). $14.50 (ISBN 0-87559-172-8). Shalom.
Cortina & Grosset. Basic Spanish Dictionary: English-Spanish, Spanish-English. (Eng. & Span.). write for info. (608-63). Pan Amer Pub.
Cuyas, A., ed. New Appleton's Cuyas English-Spanish & Spanish-English Dictionary. 5th ed. (Eng. & Span.). 1972. 18.95 (ISBN 0-13-611749-X); thumb-indexed 19.95 (ISBN 0-13-611756-2). P-H.
Cuyas, Arturo. English-Spanish to Spanish-English Dictionary. rev. ed. 548p. (Span. & Eng.). 1982. pap. 2.50 (ISBN 0-13-615559-6). P-H.
Cuyas Armengol, Arturo. Diccionario Manual Ingles-Espanol, Spanish-English. 2nd ed. 768p. (Eng. & Span.). 1975. $5.95 (ISBN 84-7183-044-2, S-12389). French & Eur.
--Diccionario Manual Ingles-Espanol, Spanish-English. 35th ed. 768p. (Eng. & Span.). 1978. pap. $4.50 (ISBN 84-7183-005-1, S-12389). French & Eur.
--Gran Diccionario Cuyas Ingles-Espanol, Spanish-English. 6th ed. 1640p. (Eng. & Span.). 1977. $26.95 (ISBN 84-7183-008-6, S-12386). French & Eur.
Di Benedetto, Ubaldo, ed. New Comprehensive English-Spanish, Spanish-English Dictionary, 2 Vols. 3100p. (Eng. & Span.). 1977. Set. 60.00x (ISBN 84-7166-211-6). Intl Pubns Serv.
Diccionario bilingue ilustrado, 3 vols. (Illus., Span. & Eng.). Vol. 1. $5.90 (TB6); Vol. 2. $5.90 (TB7); Vol. 3. $8.95 (TB8). Bilingual Ed Serv.
Diccionario De Bolsillo, Ingles-Espanol y Spanish-English. 640p. (Eng. & Span.). 1978. pap. $3.50 (ISBN 84-7183-080-9, S-50350). French & Eur.
Diccionario de modismos ingleses y norteamericanos. 294p. (Eng. & Span.). 1975. $19.95 (ISBN 0-685-55464-3, 21048). Larousse.
Diccionario Espanol-Ingles, Ingles-Espanol. 800p. (Eng. & Span.). 1979. pap. $6.95 (ISBN 84-346-0310-1, S-29129). French & Eur.
Diccionario Everest Punto English-Spanish Spanish-English. (Eng. & Span.). 2.95 (ISBN 84-241-1211-3, 22882). Larousse.
Diccionario Everest-Vertice: English-Spanish, Spanish-English. (Span. & Eng.). write for info. (608-25). Pan Amer Pub.
Diccionario Ingles-Espanol y Espanol-Ingles, 2 vols. 6th ed. 3000p. (Eng. & Span.). 1977. Set. $75.00 (ISBN 84-7166-211-6, S-12391). French & Eur.
Diccionario Iter Espanol-Ingles. 700p. (Span. & Eng.). (gr. 7-12). 3.75 ptas (DI52). Cruzada.
Diccionario Larousse Moderno Espanol-Ingles, English-Spanish. (Span. & Eng.). 29.95 (ISBN 2-03-020605-9, 21914). Larousse.
Diccionario Manual Amador Ingles-Espanol, Espanol-Ingles. 944p. (Span. & Eng.). $17.95 (ISBN 84-303-0116-X, S-50395). French & Eur.
Diccionario Mini Sopena Ingles-Espanol. 320p. (Eng. & Span.). 1975. pap. $1.75 (ISBN 84-303-0115-1, S-50398). French & Eur.
Diccionario moderno Larousse. (Eng. & Span.). write for info. (608-63). Pan Am Bk co.
Diccionario Punto. (Span.). pap. 2.95 (ISBN 84-241-1211-3). Larousse.
Diccionario Universal Herder Ingles-Espanol, Espanol-Ingles. 4th ed. 340p. (Eng. & Span.). 1977. leatherette $4.50 (ISBN 84-254-0781-8, S-12395). French & Eur.
Dictionario Basico: Primary Dictionary. 96p. 1983. pap. $2.25 (ISBN 0-515-07390-3). Jove Pubns.
Diez Mateo, Felix & Hochleitner, Frida. Diccionario Manual Ingles-Espanol, Espanol-Ingles. 1008p. (Eng. & Span.). 1971. $9.95 (ISBN 84-239-4720-3, S-50351). French & Eur.
Douglas, J. M. & Lomo, A., eds. Divry's New Spanish-English & English-Spanish Handy Dictionary. (Span. & Eng.). 1965. pocket size, flexible $3.50 (ISBN 0-685-09033-7); thumb indexed $5.00 (ISBN 0-685-09034-5). Divry.
Eastman, P. D. Cat in the Hat Beginner Book Dictionary in English & Spanish. LC 66-1068°. (Illus., Span. & Eng.). (gr. k-3). 1966. $8.95 (ISBN 0-394-81542-4); PLB $8.99 (ISBN 0-394-91542-9). Beginner.
English-Spanish Dictionary. (Eng. & Span.). 14.50 (ISBN 0-87557-077-1, 077-1). Saphrograph.
English-Spanish Technical Dictionary. (Span. & Eng.). $37.50 (ISBN 0-87559-188-4). Shalom.
Finnegan, Edward G., ed. New Webster's English-Spanish Dictionary: Vest Pocket Edition. 1980. pap. $1.75 (ISBN 0-8326-0050-4, 6454). Delair.
Follet World-Wide Dictionary. (Eng. & Span.). write for info. (608-5). Pan Amer Pub.
Follet World Wide Dictionary: Spanish-English, English-Spanish. (Span. & Eng.). write for info. (608-7). Pan Am Bk Co.
Follett-Velazquez Spanish & English Dictionary. 1488p. (Span. & Eng.). $17.95. Cruzada Span Pubns.
Follett World-Wide Spanish-English Dictionary. 640p. (Span. & Eng.). $7.95. Cruzada Span Pubns.
Folley, T. Spanish Aide-Memoire: English-Spanish Vocabulary. pap. $6.50x (ISBN 0-392-08443-0, SpS). Sportshelf.
Francisco, Padill. Diccionario de anglicismos, barbaricismos, pachuquismos & otras locuci o01nes. (Span. & Eng.). $7.00. Iaconi.
Freeman, Roger L. English-Spanish, Spanish-English Dictionary of Communications & Electronic Terms. (Eng. & Span.). 1972. $39.50 (ISBN 0-521-08080-0). Cambridge U Pr.
Frias-Sucre Girard, Alejandro. Diccionario Comercial Ingles-Espanol. 137p. (Eng. & Span.). $9.50. Lectorum Pubns.
Frias-Sucre Giraud, A. Spanish-English, English-Spanish Commercial Dictionary: "the Secretary". rev. & enl. ed. (Eng. & Span.). $17.50 (ISBN 8-4261-1223-4). Heinman.
Garcia Merayo, F. Glosario De Informatica: Terminologia Ordenada Segun el Vocablo Ingles y Su Acepcion En Espanol. 290p. (Eng. & Span.). 1971. pap. $28.50 (ISBN 84-314-0001-3, S-50368). French & Eur.
Garcia-Pelayo, Ramon. Diccionario Moderno Espanol-Ingles, English-Spanish. 1992p. (Span. & Eng.). 1976. $25.00 (ISBN 0-686-57189-4, M-6261). French & Eur.
Gem Language Dictionaries: Spanish-English & English-Spanish. (Span. & Eng.). write for info (ISBN 0-671-41959-5). S&S.
Gonzalez Gutierrez, Orlando. Diccionario de Expresiones Idiomaticas y Modismo Ingleses. 2nd ed. 328p. (Span. & Eng.). 1976. $35.00 (ISBN 0-686-56683-1, S-33043). French & Eur.
Hamlyn Spanish-English Dictionary. (Span. & Eng.). 1977. pap. 4.95 (ISBN 0-600-36565-4, 8087). Larousse.
Harper English-Spanish, Spanish-English Dictionary. (No. 5027). (Span. & Eng.). write for info. (608-44). Pan Amer Pub.
Hinojosa, Ida N., ed. New Century World-Wide Spanish Dictionary: Spanish: Spanish-English, English-Spanish. rev. ed. (Span., Eng). 1965. $7.95 (ISBN 0-8329-9711-0); pap. $3.95 (ISBN 0-8329-9712-9). New Century.
Hugo Pocket Dictionary: Spanish-English, English-Spanish. 610p. (Span. & Eng.). 1975. 3.50 (ISBN 0-8226-0507-4, 507). Littlefield.
International Dictionary Simon & Schuster. (Span. & Eng.). write for info. (608-72). Pan Amer Pub.
Kantrowitz, Martin P. Que Paso? (Eng. & Span.). $3.00. Camino Real.
Kendris, Christopher. Two Thousand & One Words You Need to Know to Pass Any Spanish Test. (Span.). 1984. pap. $2.95 (ISBN 0-8120-2537-7). Barron.
Kercheville, F. M. A Preliminary Glossary of New Mexican Spanish. LC 34-27896. 102p. (Span.). 1982. lib. bdg. $29.95x (ISBN 0-89370-727-9). Borgo Pr.
Kloe, Donald R. A Dictionary of Onomatopoeic Sounds, Tones, & Noises in English & Spanish. LC 77-2627. (Eng. & Span.). 1977. $25.50 (ISBN 0-87917-059-X). Ethridge.
--A Dictionary of Onomatopoeic Sounds, Tones, & Noises in English & Spanish. LC 77-2627. (Eng. & Span.). 1977. $25.50 (ISBN 0-87917-059-X). Ethridge.
Laita, Luis M. Cortina-Grosset Basic Spanish Dictionary. Berberi, Dilaver & Berberi, Edel A., eds. LC 73-18525. 384p. (Span.). 1975. $3.95 (ISBN 0-448-11559-X, G&D). Putnam Pub Group.
Langenscheidt English-Spanish Lilliput Dictionary. 640p. (Eng. & Span.). plastic $1.50 (ISBN 3-468-96423-4). Langenscheidt.
Langenscheidt's Lilliput English-Spanish Dictionary. 640p. (Eng. & Span.). 1972. $1.50 (ISBN 0-685-31351-4). Am Map.
Langenscheidt's Lilliput Spanish-English Dictionary. 640p. (Eng. & Span.). 1972. $1.50 (ISBN 0-685-31352-2). Am Map.
Langenscheidt's Universal Spanish-English, English-Spanish Dictionary. 15th ed. 464p. (Eng. & Span.). 1972. $2.95 (ISBN 0-685-31340-9). Am Map.
Lazzati, Santiago. Diccionario del Verbo Castellano: Como Se Conjugan los Verbos Americanos. 438p. (Span.). 1977. pap. $13.50 (ISBN 0-686-56657-2, S-12049). French & Eur.
Lilliput Dictionary. 640p. (Span. & Eng.). $1.50 (104). Langenscheidt.
Lilliput Dictionary. 640p. (Eng. & Span.). $1.50 (105). Langenscheidt.
Lipton, Gladys & Munoz, Olivia. Spanish Bilingual Dictionary: Compact Guide. rev. ed. LC 78-27770. (Illus., Span. & Eng.). (gr. 7-12). 1979. pap. $3.95 (ISBN 0-8120-2540-7). Barron.
Macarulla, D. Diccionario Lexicon Ingles-Espanol, Espanol-Ingles. 384p. (Eng. & Span.). 1974. pap. $3.25 (ISBN 84-303-0110-0, S-31391). French & Eur.
Mac Cragh, Esteban. Nuevo Diccionario Ingles-Espanol y Espanol-Ingles. 3rd ed. 376p. (Eng. & Span.). 1979. $9.50 (ISBN 84-261-0079-1, S-12401). French & Eur.
Merino, Jose. Diccionario Tematico Ingles-Espanol, Espanol-Ingles. 604p. (Eng. & Span.). 1978. pap. $17.95 (ISBN 84-283-0918-3, S-31559). French & Eur.
Merino Bustamante, Jose. Vocabulario Ingles-Espanol, Espanol-Ingles. 186p. (Eng. & Span.). 1977. pap. $3.50 (ISBN 84-205-0565-X, S-50346). French & Eur.
Mi primer diccionario ilustrado. (Illus.). 95p. (Span. & Eng.). (gr. 2 up). pap. $3.95 (T102). Bilingual Ed Serv.
New Century Velazquez Spanish-English Dictionary. rev. ed. (Span. & Eng.). 1977. 16.95 (ISBN 0-8329-0472-4). New Century.
New Webster's Quick Reference English-Spanish Dictionary. (Quick Reference Ser.). (Orig.). 1981. pap. $1.95 (ISBN 0-8326-0054-7, 6607). Delair.
The New World English-Spanish, Spanish-English Dictionary. 592p. (Eng. & Span.). write for info. (ISBN 0-671-41836-X); pap. $6.95 (ISBN 0-671-41837-8). S&S.
The New World English-Spanish, Spanish-English Dictionary. (Span. & Eng.). $9.95; pap. $6.95. Iaconi.

Oxford Picture Dictionary of American English: English-Spanish. (Span. & Eng.). write for info. (608-107). Pan Amer Pub.
Padilla, Francisco. Bilingual Dictionary of Anglicismos, Barbarismos, Pachuquismos y Otras Locuciones En el Barrio. LC 80-83981. 214p. (Orig., Span. & Eng.). pap. $7.00 (ISBN 0-9605292-0-9). Padilla.
Parnwell, E. Oxford Picture Dictionary of American English & Spanish. (Illus., Span. & Eng.). $4.00. Iaconi.
Parnwell, E. C. English-Spanish picture dictionary. (Illus.). 96p. (Eng. & Span.). 1980. write for info. Fondo Educativo.
Peers, Edgar A., ed. Cassell's Spanish Dictionary: Spanish-English, English-Spanish. LC 77-7403. (Span. & Eng.). 1977. 18.95 (ISBN 0-02-522910-9); plain 16.95 (ISBN 0-02-522900-1). Macmillan.
A Phrase & Sentence Dictionary Spanish-English. (Span. & Eng.). write for info. (608-109). Pan Amer Pub.
Putnam's Contemporary Spanish Dictionary. (Span. & Eng.). 1980. pap. $2.50 (ISBN 0-425-04387-8). Berkley Pub.
Pyramid Primary Dictionary, 2 vols. (Span. & Eng.). Vol. 1: Spanish. write for info. (608-21); Vol. 2: English. write for info. (608-22). Pan Amer Pub.
Ramondino, Salvatore, ed. New World Spanish-English & English-Spanish Dictionary. LC 67-17418. (Illus., Span. & Eng.). (YA) (gr. 9up). 1973. thumb-indexed $7.95 (ISBN 0-529-04719-5, 2677N-I). pap. $5.95 (ISBN 0-529-05181-8, 2677P). Collins Pubs.
--New World Spanish-English, English-Spanish Dictionary. (Span. & Eng.). pap. 3.50 (ISBN 0-451-11312-8, E9043, Sig). NAL.
Ramos-Ramos, Abiud. Vocabulario Tecnico De Contabilidad Moderna. LC 77-11200. (Span.). 1978. pap. $8.75 (ISBN 0-8477-2629-0). U of PR Pr.
The Random House Basic Dictionary. (Eng. & Span.). write for info. (608-100). Pan Amer Pub.
Robb, Louis. Dictionary of Modern Business. (Span. & Eng.). 1960. $30.00 (ISBN 0-910136-00-9). Anderson Kramer.
Robb, Louis A. Dictionary of Legal Terms: Spanish-English,English-Spanish. (Span. & Eng.). 1976. pap. 10.95x (ISBN 968-18-0384-1). Intl Learn Syst.
Robertson. Diccionario Ingles-Espanol, Espanol-Ingles. 894p. (Eng. & Span.). $12.25 (ISBN 84-303-0107-0, S-50396); pap. $9.95 (ISBN 84-303-0108-9, S-50397). French & Eur.
Serrano Mesa, Eleesbaan. Diccionario Ingles-Espanol, Espanol-Ingles. 9th ed. 640p. (Eng. & Span.). 1977. leatherette $5.25 (ISBN 84-7105-019-6, S-50353). French & Eur.
Simon & Schuster International Dictionary: English-Spanish, Spanish-English. (Eng. & Span.). 1973. thumb-indexed 15.95 (ISBN 0-671-21267-2). S&S.
Simon & Schuster's International Dictionary English-Spanish. 1065p. (Eng. & Span.). $29.95. Lectorum Pubns.
Simon & Schuster's International Dictionary: English-Spanish & Spanish-English. 1632p. (Eng. & Span.). thumb-indexed $39.95 (ISBN 0-671-21267-2). S&S.
Sola, Donald F. & Agard, Frederick B. Spanish Pocket Dictionary. (Span.). 1954. 2.95 (ISBN 0-394-40064-X). Random.
Sola, Donald P., ed. The Random House Basic Dictionary Spanish. (Span. & Eng.). 1981. pap. $1.50 (ISBN 0-345-29620-6). Ballantine.
Spanish Bilingual Dictionary. (Span. & Eng.). (gr. 4-9). $4.95. Iaconi.
Spanish Bilingual Dictionary. (Span. & Eng.). write for info. (608-54). Pan Amer Pub.
Spanish-English & English-Spanish Dictionary. (Span. & Eng.). pap. $1.99 (ISBN 0-686-00482-5). Dennison.
Spanish-English, English-Spanish Dictionary. (Span. & Eng.). pap. $2.50 (ISBN 0-06-465027-8, DI 3, BN). B&N NY.
Spanish-English-Spanish. (Berlitz Pocket Dictionaries Ser.). (Span. & Eng.). $4.95 (ISBN 0-02-964510-7). Macmillan.
Torrents dels Prats, Alfonso. Diccionario De Dificultades Del Ingles. 500p. (Eng. & Span.). 1976. $18.75 (ISBN 84-261-5814-5, S-31568). French & Eur.
--Diccionario de Modismos Inglese y Norteamericanos. 2nd ed. 304p. (Eng. & Span.). 1979. $16.25 (ISBN 84-261-0838-5, S-12364). French & Eur.
The Trictionary. 432p. (Chinese , Span. & Eng.). softcover $12.95. Bilingual Pubns.
U. S. War Department. Dictionary of Spoken Spanish: Spanish-English, English-Spanish. (Span. & Eng.). pap. $5.95 (ISBN 0-486-20495-2). Dover.
University of Chicago Dictionary. (Span. & Eng.). write for info. (608-4). Pan Amer Pub.
Velasquez Dictionary: English-Spanish, Spanish-English. (Span. & Eng.). write for info. (608-6). Pan Am Bk Co.
Velasquez Spanish-English Dictionary. Revised ed. (Span. & Eng.). $12.95. Camino Real.
Velazquez, et al, eds. The Spanish & English, English & Spanish Dictionary - Self Pronouncing. rev. ed. LC 72-94281. (Span. & Eng.). 1973. thumb-indexed 20.95 (ISBN 0-13-615534-0). P-H.
Velazquez, Mariana. Velazquez Spanish & English Dictionary. 1486p. (Span. & Eng.). $16.95 (ISBN 0-8329-0472-4). New Century.
Velazquez Spanish-English Dictionary: Indexed. (Span. & Eng.). 16.95 (ISBN 0-8329-0472-4). New Century.
Velazquez Spanish-English, English-Spanish Dictionary. (Span. & Eng.). $19.95. Iaconi.
Vox-Diccionario Ingles-Espanol, Espanol-Ingles. 4th ed. 1450p. (Eng. & Span.). 1978. leatherette $24.95 (ISBN 84-7153-151-8, S-12417). French & Eur.
Vox-Diccionario Manual Ingles-Espanol, Espanol-Ingles. 8th ed. 1008p. (Eng. & Span.). 1979. leatherette $15.95 (ISBN 84-7153-181-X, S-12491). French & Eur.
Williams, Edwin B. New College Spanish & English Dictionary. (Span. & Eng.). (gr. 7-12). 1968. pap. text ed. $8.58 (ISBN 0-87720-511-6). AMSCO Sch.
Williams, Edwin B., ed. Bantam New College Spanish & English Dictionary. (Language Library). (Orig., Span. & Eng.). 1970. pap. $2.75 (ISBN 0-553-20085-2, C13718-2). Bantam.
The World Dictionary. (Span. & Eng.). write for info. (608-37). Pan Amer Pub.
World Wide Spanish Language Dictionary Spanish-English. 640p. (Span. & Eng.). $7.95; pap. $3.95 (ISBN 0-8329-9712-9). New Century.

ENGLISH LANGUAGE–DICTIONARIES–SWAHILI

Nassir, Abdilahi. A Concise Dictionary of English-Swahili Idioms. LC 76-980032. (Eng. & Swahili.). 1975. write for info. Shungways Publishers.
Swahili-English Dictionary. (Swahili & Eng.). $35.00. Iaconi.

ENGLISH LANGUAGE–DICTIONARIES–SWEDISH

Bergstrom, Mats & Carlson, Ingvar. Engelsk-Svensk Ordbog. LC 77-471718. 451p. (Eng. & Swedish.). 1976. Kr.42.00 (ISBN 9-1275-7032-0). Natur & Kultur.
Berlitz. Berlitz Pocket Dictionaries: Swedish-English-Swedish. (Swedish & Eng.). pap. $4.95 (ISBN 0-02-964570-0). Macmillan.
Berlitz Editors. Swedish-English, English-Swedish Pocket Dictionary. LC 74-1987. (Swedish & Eng.). 1974. pap. 2.95 (ISBN 0-02-964410-0, Berlitz). Macmillan.
Bruzelius, Andre, et al, eds. Concise English-Swedish Dictionary of Legal Terms. 175p. (Eng. & Swedish.). $39.95 (ISBN 0-686-80959-9). French & Eur.
Capitol's Concise Dictionary of Seven Languages. (gr. 9-12). 1978. $29.95 (ISBN 0-8120-5333-8). Barron.
Danielsson, B. Modern English-Swedish Dictionary. 394p. (Eng. & Swedish.). 1980. $19.95 (ISBN 91-518-1296-7, M-9451). French & Eur.
Danielsson, Bror. Engelsk-Svensk Ordbok (Prisma Modern) 5th ed. 396p. 1980. text ed. $17.50x (ISBN 91-518-0550-2, SW205); Svensk-engelsk, 4th Ed. 1982. text ed. $20.00x (ISBN 9-1518-1297-5, SW-204). Vanous.
English-Swedish-English Dictionary. 275p. (Eng. & Swedish.). 1981. pap. $9.95 (ISBN 91-518-1438-2, M-9449). French & Eur.
Engstroem, E. Swedish-English, English-Swedish Technical Dictionary, 2 vols. rev. enl ed. (Swedish & Eng.). Set. 115.00 (ISBN 0-685-42614-9). Heinman.
Hill's English-Swedish, Swedish-English Pocket Dictionary. 244p. (Eng. & Swedish.). 1981. $15.00x (ISBN 0-561-00191-X, Pub. by Bailey & Swinfen South Africa). State Mutual Bk.
Karre, K. Swedish Karre Dictionary, Vol. 1: Svensk-Engelsk. (Swedish & Eng.). 1976. $50.00x (ISBN 91-24-14308-1, SW132). Vanous.
--Swedish Karre Dictionary, Vol. 2: Engelsk-Svensk. 3rd ed. (Swedish & Eng.). 1981. text ed. $60.00x (ISBN 91-24-29824-7, SW133). Vanous.
Nojd, Ruben. English-Swedish Dictionary. (Eng. & Swedish.). 16.00 (ISBN 0-87557-083-6, 083-6). Saphrograph.
Nojd, Ruben & Tornberg, Astrid. McKay's Modern English-Swedish, Swedish-English Dictionary. 470p. (Eng. & Swedish.). $9.95. Imported Bks.
Prisma-Lagersson, R. Swedish-English Modern Dictionary, Vol. 1. 4th ed. (Swedish & Eng.). 1982. $20.00x (ISBN 91-518-1297-5, SW204). Vanous.
Santesson, R. & Kaerre, Karl K. Swedish-English, English-Swedish Dictionary, 2 vols. (Swedish & Eng.). Set. 120.00 (ISBN 0-686-77012-9). Vol. 1 (ISBN 9-1242-9824-7). Vol. 2 (ISBN 9-1241-4308-1). Heinman.
Swedish-English-Swedish. (Berlitz Pocket Dictionaries Ser.). (Eng. & Swedish.). $4.95 (ISBN 0-02-964570-0). Macmillan.
Swedish Pocket Dictionary. (Swedish & Eng.). 7.50 (ISBN 8-4399-8784-6). Heinman.
Tornberg, Astrid, et al. McKay's Modern Swedish-English & English-Swedish Dictionary. (Modern Dictionaries Ser.). (Swedish & Eng.). 1954. 9.95 (ISBN 0-679-10079-2). McKay.

ENGLISH LANGUAGE–DICTIONARIES–TAGALOG

Enriquez & Bautista. English-Tagalog-Visayan Pocket Dictionary. (Eng. & Tagalog.). $4.00x (ISBN 0-686-05265-X). Colton Bk.
Enriquez & Guzman. English-Tagalog, Tagalog-English Pocket Dictionary. (Eng. & Tagalog.). $3.50x (ISBN 0-686-00861-8). Colton Bk.
Enriquez & Quimba. English-Tagalog-Ilocano Pocket Dictionary. (Eng. & Tagalog.). $4.00x (ISBN 0-686-05264-1). Colton Bk.
Guzman, Maria O. Tagalog-English - English-Tagalog Dictionary. rev. ed. (Tagalog & Eng.). pap. 22.50 (ISBN 0-686-68939-9). Heinman.
Panganiban. Concise English-Tagalog Dictionary. (Tagalog & Eng.). $9.50. Iaconi.
Panganiban, J. Villar. Concise English-Tagalog Dictionary. LC 69-13501. (Eng. & Tagalog.). 1969. bds. $9.50 (ISBN 0-8048-0119-3). C E Tuttle.
Ramos, T. Tagalog Dictionary. (Tagalog.). $7.50. Iaconi.
Villa Panganiban, Jose. Concise English-Tagalog Dictionary. 170p. (Eng. & Tagalog.). 1969. $10.75. Imported Bks.

ENGLISH LANGUAGE–DICTIONARIES–TAHITIAN

Andrews, Edmund & Andrews, Irene D. A Comparative Dictionary of the Tahitian Language: Tahitian-English with an English-Tahitian Finding List. LC 75-35171. (Eng. & Tahitian.). Repr. of 1944 ed. $23.00 (ISBN 0-404-14201-X). AMS Pr.
Clairmont, Leonard. Tahitian-English, English Tahitian Dictionary. (Tahitian & Eng.). $17.50 (ISBN 0-87559-053-5). Shalom.

ENGLISH LANGUAGE–DICTIONARIES–THAI

Robertson, Richard G., ed. Robertson's Practical English-Thai Dictionary. LC 79-87787. (Eng. & Thai.). 1969. bds. $6.75 (ISBN 0-8048-0706-X). C E Tuttle.
Robertson, S. Practical English-Thai Dictionary. (Thai & Eng.). $6.25. Iaconi.
Sanskrit-Thai-English Dictionary. 1339p. (Sanskrit, Thai & Eng.). 10.00x (ISBN 0-8002-1951-1). Intl Pubns Serv.
Sethaputra, So, compiled by. New Model English - Thai Dictionary. (Illus.). 879p. (Eng. & Thai.). 1973. 17.50x (ISBN 0-8002-1748-9). Intl Pubns Serv.
--New Model English - Thai Dictionary. (Illus.). 879p. (Eng. & Thai.). 1973. 17.50x (ISBN 0-8002-1748-9). Intl Pubns Serv.

ENGLISH LANGUAGE–DICTIONARIES–TIBETAN

Chandra Das, S. Tibetan-English Dictionary: With Sanskrit Synonyms. Sanberg, Graham & Heyde, A. William, eds. 1389p. (Tibetan & Eng.). 1976. Repr. 35.00 (ISBN 0-89581-177-4). Lancaster-Miller.
Das, S. C. & Kazi, I. D. Tibetan-English, English-Tibetan Dictionary, 2 vols. (Tibetan & Eng.). Set. 70.00 (ISBN 0-686-77964-9). Heinman.
Dass, S. C. Tibetan-English Dictionary. (Tibetan & Eng.). 1979. 42.00 (ISBN 0-89684-329-7). Orient Bk Dist.
Goldstein, Melvyn C. Tibetan-English Dictionary of Modern Tibetan. (Tibetan & Eng.). 1975. 27.95x (ISBN 0-685-89505-X). Himalaya Hse.
Jaschke, H. A. Tibetan-English Dictionary. (Tibetan & Eng.). 1980. 22.50 (ISBN 0-8426-0962-8). Orient Bk Dist.
Tibetan-English Dictionary. (Tibetan & Eng.). $35.00. Iaconi.

ENGLISH LANGUAGE–DICTIONARIES–TURKISH

Alderson, A. D., ed. The Oxford English-Turkish Dictionary. 2nd ed. Iz, Fahir. (Eng. & Turkish.). 1978. text ed. 39.95x (ISBN 0-19-864123-0). Oxford U Pr.
Alderson, A. D. & Iz, Fahir, eds. Concise Oxford Turkish Dictionary. (Turkish.). 1959. 29.00x (ISBN 0-19-864109-5). Oxford U Pr.
Avery, Robert, et al, eds. Turkish, English-English, Turkish Dictionary (the Redhouse Portable Dictionary) (Turkish & Eng.). 15.00 (ISBN 0-685-80306-6). Heinman.
Goodenough, Ward H. & Sugita, Hiroshi. Trukese-English Dictionary. LC 79-54277. (Memoir Ser.: Vol. 141). (Turkish.). 1980. $10.00 (ISBN 0-87169-141-8). Am Philos.
Iz, Fahir & Hony, H. C. The Oxford English-Turkish Dictionary. 2nd ed. LC 78-40230. xvi, 619p. (Eng. & Turkish.). 1978. E10.00 (ISBN 0-19-864123-0). Oxford U Pr.
Langenscheidt English-Turkish Lilliput Dictionary. 670p. (Eng. & Turkish.). plastic $1.50 (ISBN 3-468-96532-X). Langenscheidt.
Langenscheidt Turkish-English Lilliput Dictionary. 608p. (Eng. & Turkish.). plastic $1.50 (ISBN 3-468-96533-8). Langenscheidt.

Langenscheidt's Lilliput English-Turkish Dictionary. 640p. (Eng. & Turkish.). 1972. $1.50 (ISBN 0-685-31363-8). Am Map.
Langenscheidt's Universal Turkish-English, English-Turkish Dictionary. 9th ed. 408p. (Eng. & Turkish.). 1972. $2.95 (ISBN 0-685-31339-5). Am Map.
Lilliput Dictionary. 640p. (Turkish & Eng.). $1.50 (122). Langenscheidt.
Lilliput Dictionary. 640p. (Eng. & Turkish.). $1.50 (123). Langenscheidt.
Portable Redhouse Turkish-English, English-Turkish Dictionary. (Turkish & Eng.). 1975. 9.00x (ISBN 0-686-16857-7). Intl Learn Syst.
Redhouse Cagdas Turkce-Ingilizce. 430p. (Turkish & Eng.). 1983. $30.00 (440). Redhouse Pr.
Redhouse English-Turkish Dictionary. (Eng. & Turkish.). 1974. 33.00x (ISBN 0-686-16859-3). Intl Learn Syst.
Redhouse Ingilizce-Turkce Sozlugu. rev. 9th ed. viii, 1152p. (Eng. & Turkish.). 1983. $30.00 (396). Redhouse Pr.
Redhouse Ingilizce-Turkce, Turkce-Ingilizce elsozlugu. 503p. (Eng. & Turkish.). 1982. $8.00 (401). Redhouse Pr.
Redhouse, James W. Turkish-English Dictionary, 3 pts. (Turkish & Eng.). 1976. Repr. of 1958 ed. Set. $250.00 (ISBN 0-518-19005-6). Ayer Co.
Redhouse Turkce-Ingilizce sozlugu. 5th ed. xxiii, 1292p. (Turkish & Eng.). 1981. $35.00 (369). Redhouse Pr.
Redhouse Turkish-English Dictionary. (Turkish & Eng.). 1968. 41.00x (ISBN 0-686-16860-7). Intl Learn Syst.
Sak, Ziya. English-Turkish, Turkish-English Dictionary. (Eng. & Turkish.). 19.50 (ISBN 0-87557-085-2, 085-2). Saphrograph.
Shorter Redhouse Turkish-English Dictionary. (Turkish & Eng.). 1971. 11.50x (ISBN 0-686-16858-5). Intl Learn Syst.
Turkish-English, English-Turkish Dictionary: New Red House, 2 Vols. (Turkish & Eng.). Set. 75.00 (ISBN 0-685-12051-1). Heinman.

ENGLISH LANGUAGE–DICTIONARIES–UKRAINIAN

Andrusyshen, C. H., ed. Ukrainian-English Dictionary. 1200p. (Ukrainian & Eng.). 1981. pap. $19.50 (ISBN 0-8020-6421-3). U of Toronto Pr.
Anglo-Ukrainskii Slovar. 448p. (Eng. & Ukrainian.). 1978. $3.95 (Pub. by Radianska Shkola). Four Continent.
Barantsev, K. T. Anglo-Ukrainskii Frazeologicheskii Slovar. 1052p. (Eng. & Ukranian.). 1969. $9.00 (Pub. by Radianska Shkola). Four Continent.
Podveska, M. L. & Balla, M. J. English-Ukrainian Dictionary. 664p. (Eng. & Ukrainian.). 1980. $30.00x (ISBN 0-569-08127-0, Pub. by Collet's). State Mutual Bk.
Podvesko, M. L., ed. English-Ukrainian Dictionary. 2nd ed. (Eng. & Ukrainian.). 24.50 (ISBN 0-87557-089-5, 089-5). Saphrograph.
Podvesko, M. L., compiled by. Ukrainian-English, English-Ukrainian Dictionary, 2 vols. (Ukranian & Eng.). 45.00 set (ISBN 0-686-91769-3). Heinman.
Ukrainian-English, English-Ukrainian Pocket Dictionary. (Ukranian & Eng.). 12.50 (ISBN 0-685-58556-5). Heinman.
Zhluktenko, I. O., ed. English-Ukrainian Dictionary. (Rad. Shkola Ser.). 446p. (Eng. & Ukrainian.). 1978. $3.95 (O-38). Four Continent.

ENGLISH LANGUAGE–DICTIONARIES–URDU

Barker, M. A., et al. Urdu-English Vocabulary: Student's Dictionary. LC 79-92847. 382p. (Urdu & Eng.). 1980. pap. text ed. $10.00x (ISBN 0-87950-438-2). Spoken Lang Serv.
English URDV Dictionary. 24.50 (ISBN 0-686-36513-5). Saphrograph.
Hameed Khan, A., ed. Ferozsons Concise Dictionary. LC 78-931279. 647p. (Eng. & Urdu.). 1978. Rs.45.00. Ferozsons.
Pakistani. English-Urdu Dictionary. (Eng. & Urdu.). 29.00 (ISBN 0-686-18359-2). Kazi Pubns.
Platts, John T. Dictionary of Urdu, Classical Hindi, & English. (Urdu., Hindu & Eng.). 1930. $82.00x (ISBN 0-19-864309-8). Oxford U Pr.
Urdu-English Dictionary. (Urdu & Eng.). 22.00 (ISBN 0-686-18358-4). Kazi Pubns.

ENGLISH LANGUAGE–DICTIONARIES–VENDA

Marole, L. T. & De Goma, F. S. English-Venda Dictionary. (Eng. & Venda.). $22.50 (ISBN 0-87559-185-X); thumb indexed $26.00 (ISBN 0-686-66534-1). Shalom.
Wentzel, Petrus J. Drietalige Elementere Woordeboek. LC 77-460273. ix, 525p. (Eng. & Afrikaan.). 1976. write for info. (ISBN 0-86981-069-3). U Sth Africa.

ENGLISH LANGUAGE–DICTIONARIES–VIETNAMESE

Anh-Viet, Tu Dien. English-Vietnamese Dictionary. 1560p. (Eng. & Vietnamese.). 1975. $99.00x (ISBN 0-686-44716-6, Pub. by Collets). State Mutual Bk.
Basic words in Vietnamese. (Eng. & Vietnamese.). write for info. (454-7). Pan Am Bk Co.
Duong Thanh Binh & Cage, William. Vietnamese-English Phrasebook with Useful Word List. 74p. (Eng. & Vietnamese.). pap. $5.00. Ctr Appl Ling.
English-Vietnamese Dictionary Romanized. (Eng. & Vietnamese.). $17.50 (ISBN 0-87559-012-8); thumb indexed $22.50 (ISBN 0-87559-013-6). Shalom.
English-Vietnamese Pocket Dictionary. (Eng. & Vietnamese.). pap. $7.50 (ISBN 0-87559-164-7). Shalom.
Gage, William & Duong Thanh Binh. Vietnamese-English Phrasebook with Useful Word List: For English Speakers. LC 75-24857. (Vietnamese Refugee Education Ser.: No. 2). 142p. (Vietnamese & Eng.). 1975. pap. $4.00x (ISBN 0-87281-044-5). Ctr Appl Ling.
Hieu, Nguyen-Trung, ed. Practical English-Vietnamese Idioms for Teachers & Students. (Eng. & Vietnamese.). 1981. $6.50 (ISBN 0-533-04431-6). Vantage.
Hoa, Dinh Nguyen. Vietnamese-English Dictionary. (Vietnamese & Eng.). $16.95. Iaconi.
Le-Ba-Kong & Le-Ba-Khanh, eds. Vietnamese-English, English Vietnamese Dictionary. (Vietnamese & Eng.). $30.00 (ISBN 0-8044-0310-4). Ungar.
Nguyen-Dinh-Hoa. Essential English-Vietnamese Dictionary. LC 82-80014. 328p. (Eng. & Vietnamese.). 1983. $22.50 (ISBN 0-8048-1444-9). C E Tuttle.
--Vietnamese-English Dictionary. 563p. (Eng. & Vietnamese.). $18.00. C E Tuttle.
Nguyen-Dinh-Hoa, ed. Vietnamese-English Dictionary. LC 66-17773. (Eng. & Vietnamese.). 1966. $16.95 (ISBN 0-8048-0618-7). C E Tuttle.
Nguyen Hy Quang. English-Vietnamese Phrasebook with Useful Word List: For Vietnamese Speakers. LC 75-24856. (Vietnamese Refugee Education Ser.: No. 1). (Eng. & Vietnamese.). 1975. pap. text ed. $5.00x (ISBN 0-87281-043-7). Ctr Appl Ling.
Tu-Dien Dictionary. (Eng. & Vietnamese.). write for info. (608-55). Pan Amer Pub.
Tu-Dien Tieu-Chuan Anh-Viet. Standard Pronouncing English-Vietnamese Dictionary. (Vietnamese & Eng.). pap. $8.75. Iaconi.
Tu-Dien Tuie-Chuan Viet-Anh. Standard Pronouncing Vietnamese English Dictionary. (Vietnamese & Eng.). pap. $7.50. Iaconi.
Vietnamese English Conversational Dictionary. (Vietnamese & Eng.). $4.95. Iaconi.
Vietnamese-English Pocket Dictionary. (Vietnamese & Eng.). pap. $7.50 (ISBN 0-87559-165-5). Shalom.

ENGLISH LANGUAGE–DICTIONARIES–WELSH

Evans, H. Meurig & Thomas, W. O. The Complete Welsh-English, English-Welsh Dictionary. Y Geiriadur Mawr. 8th ed. (Welsh & Eng.). 1979. text ed. 30.50x (ISBN 0-391-01734-9). Humanities.
--Welsh-English, English-Welsh Dictionary. (Welsh & Eng.). 20.50 (ISBN 0-87557-091-7, 091-7). Saphrograph.
Meurig, H. & Thomas, W. O. Y Geiriadur Mawr: The Complete Welsh-English, English-Welsh Dictionary. Williams, S. J., ed. 859p. (Welsh & Eng.). 1981. $35.00 (ISBN 0-686-97426-3, M-9434). French & Eur.

ENGLISH LANGUAGE–DICTIONARIES–YIDDISH

Harkovy, A. English-Yiddish Dictionary. $22.50 (ISBN 0-87559-192-2). Shalom.
Hoffman, Paul & Freedman, Matt. Dictionary, Schmictionary. LC 83-3050. (Illus.). 160p. (Orig.). 1983. pap. write for info. (ISBN 0-688-02162-X). Quill NY.
Markowitz, Endel. Encyclopedia Yiddishanica. LC 79-114831. (Eng. & Yiddish.). 1979. write for info. (ISBN 0-933910-02-9). Haymark.
Weinreich, Uriel. Modern English-Yiddish, Yiddish-English Dictionary. (Eng. & Yiddish.). 1968. 44.95 (ISBN 0-07-069038-3, P&RB). McGraw.
--Modern English-Yiddish Yiddish-English Dictionary. LC 77-76038. (Eng. & Yiddish.). 1978. pap. $18.95 (ISBN 0-8052-0575-6). Schocken.
--Modern English-Yiddish, Yiddish-English Dictionary. LC 67-23848. 789p. (Eng. & Yiddish.). 1968. write for info (ISBN 0-914512-25-0). Yivo Inst.

ENGLISH LANGUAGE–DICTIONARIES–ZULU

Doke, C. M. English & Zulu Dictionary: English-Zulu, Zulu-English. (Zulu & Eng.). 1958. pap. 14.25x (ISBN 0-85494-010-3). Intl Learn Syst.
Doke, C. M., ed. Zulu-English, English-Zulu Dictionary. rev. ed. (Zulu & Eng.). pap. 20.00 (ISBN 0-85494-010-3). Heinman.
Zulu-English & Zulu Dictionary. (Zulu & Eng.). 19.50 (ISBN 0-685-77569-0, 096-8). Saphrograph.

ENGLISH LANGUAGE–DICTIONARIES, JUVENILE

Amery & Mila. First One Thousand Words-English, 4 Bks. (First Thousand Words Ser.). (gr. 1-9). 1979. $10.95 ea. (Usborne-Hayes). English ed. EDC.
Barnhart, Clarence L. & Barnhart, Robert K., eds. The World Book Dictionary, 2 Vols. LC 82-45610. (Illus.). 2554p. (gr. 4-12). 1983. lib. bdg. write for info. (ISBN 0-7166-0283-0). World Bk.
Beginning Dictionary. LC 78-27760. (Illus.). (gr. 3-6). 1979. text ed. $7.98 (ISBN 0-395-27400-1). HM.
Bennett, A. Y. Picture Dictionary, ABCs, Telling Time, Counting Rhymes, Riddles & Finger Plays. (Illus.). (gr. k-3). 1970. 5.95 (ISBN 0-448-02813-1, G&D). Putnam Pub Group.
Bennett, Archie. The New Color Picture Dictionary for Children. LC 76-42144. (Illus.). (gr. 1-4). 1978. $8.95 (ISBN 0-8326-2214-1, 6391). Delair.
--The New Color Picture Dictionary for Children. (Illus.). 252p. (Eng.). 1981. $12.95 (ISBN 0-516-00820-X). Childrens.
The Children's Dictionary. LC 78-27636. (Illus.). (gr. 3-6). 1979. 11.95 (ISBN 0-395-27512-1). HM.
Daniel, Charlie & Daniel, Becky. My Very Own Dictionary. (gr. 1-4). 1978. 5.50 (ISBN 0-916456-17-X, GA81). Good Apple.
Dent's Primary Dictionary. (Eng.). 1970. $4.95 (ISBN 0-460-90925-8); $2.65 (ISBN 0-460-90925-8). Dent.
Dictionnaire Anglais Chambers: Junior Learners' Dictionary. (Fr.). $7.15 (Dist. by Continental Bk Co). Lib. Fernand Nathan.
Gurainik, David B., ed. Webster's New World Dictionary: Student's Edition. 1976. $17.28 (ISBN 0-13-944652-4). P-H.
Hornby, A. S., compiled by. Oxford Student's Dictionary of Current English. 1978. pap. text ed. 6.95x (ISBN 0-19-431114-7). Oxford U Pr.
Macmillan Dictionary for Children. rev. ed. (Illus.). (gr. 2 up). 1977. 12.95 (ISBN 0-02-578750-0). Macmillan.
Merriam Company, ed. Webster's Intermediate Dictionary. LC 70-38974. (Illus.). 960p. (gr. 7-9). 1977. 8.95 (ISBN 0-87779-279-8). Merriam-Webster Inc.
Morgan, Joyce L. & Wilbur, Beverley. Dent's Primary Dictionary. (Eng.). 1959. pap. $1.75 (ISBN 0-460-90923-1). Dent.
Morris, William. The Ginn Beginning Dictionary. (Eng.). 1975. Can.$9.95 (ISBN 0-7702-0000-1). Ginn.
O'Donnell & Townes. Words I Like to Read & Write: Grades 1-2 Picture Dictionary. (Illus., Eng.). $5.46 (516324-9). Har-Row.
--Words I Like to Read & Write: Grades 2-4 Picture Dictionary. (Illus., Eng.). $8.22 (516425-7). Har-Row.
Oftedal, Laura & Jacob, Nina. My First Dictionary. (Illus.). (gr. k-3). 1948. 4.50 (ISBN 0-448-02962-6, G&D). Putnam Pub Group.
Perry, Day & Wolfe, Josephine B., eds. Dictionary of Basic Words. LC 73-86343. (Illus.). 640p. (gr. 2-8). 1969. PLB $19.95 (ISBN 0-516-00810-2). Childrens.
Pheby, J. A., ed. The Oxford-Duden Pictorial English Dictionary. (Illus.). 1981. text ed. 19.95x (ISBN 0-19-864140-0). Oxford U Pr.
Reid, Hale & Crane, Helen. My Picture Dictionary. (Illus., Eng.). 1963. Can.$2.95 (ISBN 0-7702-0098-2). Ginn.
--My Second Picture Dictionary. (Illus., Eng.). 1963. Can.$8.95 (ISBN 0-7702-0098-2). Ginn.
Schimpff, Jill W. Open Sesame Picture Dictionary: Featuring Jim Henson's Sesame Street Muppets, Children's Television Workshop. 1982. pap. text ed. 4.95x (ISBN 0-19-503035-4). Oxford U Pr.
Student Dictionary with Merriam-Webster Phonetic Key. 1976. pap. $3.00 (ISBN 0-685-22408-2). Youth Ed.
Ulrich, George. Beginning Dictionary. Hamilton, David R., ed. (Illus., Eng.). 1979. $9.75 (ISBN 0-395-28977-7). HM.
--Children's Dictionary. (Illus., Eng.). 1979. $12.95 (ISBN 0-395-28978-5). HM.
Watters, Garnette & Courtis, S. A. Picture Dictionary for Children. (Illus.). (gr. 1-3). pap. 3.95 (ISBN 0-448-14002-0, G&D). Putnam Pub Group.
The Winston Primary Dictionary. 1972. $5.20 (ISBN 0-03-923500-9). HRW.
Wright, Wendell W., ed. The Rainbow Dictionary for Young Reader. (Illus.). $7.95 (ISBN 0-529-05399-3). Collins Pubs.

ENGLISH LANGUAGE–ERRORS

see English Language–Idioms, Corrections, Errors

ENGLISH LANGUAGE–ETYMOLOGY

Shipley, Joseph T. Dictionary of Early English. (Quality Paperback: No. 150). 1977. pap. 5.95 (ISBN 0-8226-0150-8). Littlefield.

ENGLISH LANGUAGE–ETYMOLOGY–DICTIONARIES

Brewer, E. Cobham. Brewer's Dictionary of Phrase & Fable: Centenary Edition. rev. ed. Evans, Ivor, pref. by. LC 81-47407. 1248p. 1981. 24.95i (ISBN 0-06-014903-5, HarpT). Har-Row.

Kennedy, John. Stem Dictionary of the English Language. LC 78-142547. 1971. Repr. of 1870 ed. $45.00x (ISBN 0-8103-3377-5). Gale.
Klein, Ernest. Comprehensive Etymological Dictionary of the English Language. 1971. $85.00 (ISBN 0-444-40930-0). Elsevier.
Morris, William & Morris, Mary. Morris Dictionary of Word & Phrase Origins. LC 77-3763. 1977. bds. 21.10i (ISBN 0-06-013058-X, HarpT). Har-Row.
Onions, Charles T., et al, eds. Oxford Dictionary of English Etymology. 1966. 39.95 (ISBN 0-19-861112-9). Oxford U Pr.
Palmer, Abram. Folk-Etymology: A Dictionary of Verbal Corruptions or Words Perverted in Form. LC 68-26365. (Studies in Language, No. 41). 1969. Repr. of 1882 ed. lib. bdg. 59.95x (ISBN 0-8383-0279-3). Haskell.
Palmer, Abram S. Folk-Etymology, a Dictionary of Verbal Corruptions or Words Perverted in Form or Meaning, by False Derivation or Mistaken Analogy. LC 68-57636. (Illus.). 1969. Repr. of 1882 ed. lib. bdg. 29.25x (ISBN 0-8371-1153-6, PAFE). Greenwood.
Scardigli, Piergiuseppe & Gervasi, Teresa. Avviamento All'etimologia Inglese e Tedesca: Dizionario Comparativo dell'Elemento Germanico Commune ad Entrabe le Lingue. LC 79-361495. xv, 406p. (Eng. & Ger.). 1978. L.9500.00. Monnier.
Shipley, Joseph T. Dictionary of Word Origins. 2nd ed. Repr. of 1945 ed. lib. bdg. 32.00 (ISBN 0-8371-1966-9, SHWO). Greenwood.
--Dictionary of Word Origins. (Quality Paperback: No. 121). 1979. pap. 5.95 (ISBN 0-8226-0121-4). Littlefield.
Skeat, Walter W., ed. Concise Etymological Dictionary of the English Language. 1911. 26.50x (ISBN 0-19-863105-7). Oxford U Pr.
--Etymological Dictionary of the English Language. rev. & enl. ed. 1910. 69.00x (ISBN 0-19-863104-9). Oxford U Pr.
Smith, Robert W. Dictionary of English Word-Roots. 373p. 1966. 9.00x (ISBN 0-87471-238-6). Rowman.
--Dictionary of English Word-Roots: English-Roots & Roots-English with Examples & Exercises. (Quality Paperback: No. 98). (Orig.). 1980. pap. 4.95 (ISBN 0-8226-0098-6). Littlefield.
Weekley, E. Etymological Dictionary of Modern English, 2 Vols. Set. 25.00 (ISBN 0-8446-3142-6). Peter Smith.
Weekley, Ernest. Etymological Dictionary of Modern English, 2 Vols. 1967. pap. text ed. $6.50 ea.; Vol. 1. pap. text ed. (ISBN 0-486-21873-2); Vol. 2. pap. text ed. (ISBN 0-486-21874-0). Dover.

ENGLISH LANGUAGE–EXAMINATIONS, QUESTIONS, ETC.
Rudman, Jack. Civil Service Vocabulary. (Career Examination Ser.: C-S 10). (Cloth bdg. avail. on request). pap. 6.00 (ISBN 0-8373-3760-7). Natl Learning.
--Vocabulary. (Teachers License Examination Ser.: G-5). (Cloth bdg. avail. on request). pap. 10.00 (ISBN 0-8373-8195-9). Natl Learning.
Turner, David R. Vocabulary, Spelling & Grammar. 9th ed. LC 70-153705. (Orig.). 1975. pap. $6.00 (ISBN 0-668-00077-5). Arco.

ENGLISH LANGUAGE–EXERCISES
see English Language–Composition and Exercises

ENGLISH LANGUAGE–FIGURES OF SPEECH
see Figures of Speech

ENGLISH LANGUAGE–FOREIGN WORDS AND PHRASES
Bentley, Harold W. A Dictionary of Spanish Terms in English, with Special Reference to the American Southwest. LC 73-1936. 243p. (Span. & Eng.). 1973. Repr. of 1932 ed. lib. bdg. 20.00x (ISBN 0-374-90582-7). Octagon.
Borror, Donald J. Dictionary of Word Roots & Combining Forms. LC 60-15564. 134p. 1960. pap. 4.95 (ISBN 0-87484-053-8). Mayfield Pub.
Carroll, David. The Dictionary of Foreign Terms in the English Language. 1979. pap. $4.95 (ISBN 0-8015-2053-3, Hawthorn). Dutton.
Guinagh, Kevin, tr. & compiled by. Dictionary of Foreign Phrases & Abbreviations. 3rd ed. 288p. 1982. $28.00 (ISBN 0-8242-0675-4). Wilson.
Jacobs, Sidney J. The Jewish Word Book. 356p. (Eng. & Hebrew.). 1982. $12.50 (ISBN 0-8246-0249-8). Jonathan David.
Kogan Page, Ltd. & Buchanan-Brown, John, eds. Le Mot Juste: A Dictionary of Classical & Foreign Words & Phrases. LC 80-6122. 176p. 1981. pap. 2.95 (ISBN 0-394-74690-2, V-690, Vin). Random.
Newmark, Maxim. Dictionary of Foreign Words & Phrases. Repr. of 1957 ed. lib. bdg. 18.50x (ISBN 0-8371-2103-5, NEFW). Greenwood.
Rosten, Leo. Joys of Yiddish. 1968. $19.95 (ISBN 0-07-053975-8, GB). McGraw.
Steffanides, George F. The Scientist's Thesaurus. 4th ed. 156p. 1978. pap. $3.00 (ISBN 0-9600114-0-4, TX-7-128). Steffanides.

ENGLISH LANGUAGE–GLOSSARIES, VOCABULARIES, ETC.
see also Crossword Puzzles–Glossaries, Vocabularies, etc.
Bacquet, Paul. Le Vocabulaire Anglais. 128p. (Fr.). 1974. 9.60 F. PUF.
Bliss, A. J. A Dictionary of Foreign Words & Phrases in Current English. 400p. 1983. 18.00 (ISBN 0-7100-1092-3); pap. 9.95 (ISBN 0-7100-9521-X). Routledge & Kegan.
Bornstein, Scott. Vocabulary Mastery. (Illus.). 272p. (YA) (gr. 9-12). 1982. $19.95 (ISBN 0-9602610-1-X). Bornstein Memory.
Bouscaren, Christian. Le Vocabulaire Anglais au Baccalaureat. 152p. (Fr. & Eng.). 1972. 11.90 F. Ophrys.
Byrne, Josefa Heifetz. Mrs. Byrne's Dictionary of Unusual, Obscure, & Preposterous Words. Byrne, Robert, ed. & intro. by. 1976. pap. $5.95 (ISBN 0-8065-0498-6). Citadel Pr.
Davies, T. L. A Supplementary English Glossary. 1875. 25.00 (ISBN 0-8274-3557-6). R West.
Davies, T. Lewis. English Glossary: A Supplementary. 736p. 1980. Repr. of 1881 ed. lib. bdg. $125.00 (ISBN 0-8495-1119-4). Arden Lib.
Dictionaries & Vocabularies Nineteen Sixty-Six to Nineteen Seventy-Seven. 170p. 1978. pap. $12.50 (ISBN 0-686-79528-8, F2185, FAO). Unipub.
Du Gran, Claurene. Wordsmanship. 95p. 1981. $9.95 (ISBN 0-930454-11-1). Verbatim.
Frazer, Joan, et al. Thirty-Thousand Selected Words Organized by Letter, Sound & Syllable. 1978. text ed. $15.95 (ISBN 0-88450-799-8, 3083-B); pap. text ed. $10.95 (ISBN 0-88450-798-X, 2506-B). Communication Skill.
Funk, Wilfred & Lewis, Norman. Thirty Days to a More Powerful Vocabulary. LC 72-94340. (Funk & W Bk.). (gr. 9-12). 1970. text ed. $12.45 (ISBN 0-308-40079-8, 430180). T Y Crowell.
Glazier. Least You Should Know About Vocabulary. (Eng.). Epap. 6.95. HR&W.
Glossar Deutsch-Englisch. 68p. (Ger. & Eng.). pap. $4.10. M Rosenberg.
Glossar Deutsch-Englisch. 46p. (Ger. & Eng.). pap. $3.50. M Rosenberg.
Glossar Englisch. (Eng.). 1983. $2.50. M Rosenberg.
Glossary. LC 78-107662. (Illus.). iv, 55p. (Eng.). 1978. write for info. (ISBN 0-87588-142-4). United Federation Doll Clubs.
Holt, Alfred H. Phrase & Word Origins: A Study of Familiar Expressions. 2nd ed. Orig. Title: Phrase Origins. 1961. pap. $4.50 (ISBN 0-486-20758-7). Dover.
Hugon, Paul D. The Modern Word-Finder: A Living Guide to Modern Usage, Spelling, Synonyms, Pronunciation, Grammar, Word Origins, & Authorship. LC 73-20139. 420p. 1974. Repr. of 1934 ed. $45.00x (ISBN 0-8103-3970-6). Gale.
Hunsberger, I. Moyer. The Quintessential Dictionary. 512p. 1978. $15.00 (ISBN 0-89104-247-4). A & W Pubs.
Kantrowitz, Nathan & Kantrowitz, Joanne. Stateville Names: A Prison Vocabulary. (Maledicta Press Publications Ser.: Vol. 12). Date not set. 15.00 (ISBN 0-916500-12-8). Maledicta.
Kurtz, M., et al. Ten Thousand Legal Words. 1971. $6.56 (ISBN 0-07-035669-6, G). McGraw.
Lee, Donald W. Harbrace Vocabulary Guide. 2nd ed. 184p. (Orig.). 1970. pap. text ed. 9.95 (ISBN 0-15-534471-4, HC); instr. key avail. (ISBN 0-15-534472-2, HC). HarBraceJ.
Levine, Harold. Vocabulary for the High School Student. 2nd ed. (gr. 10-12). 1982. wkbk. $7.00 (ISBN 0-87720-437-3). AMSCO Sch.
Nabel, H. L., et al. Shuter's New Basic English Dictionary for Xhosa Speakers. LC 81-455769. (Illus.). viii, 246p. 1979. R.pap. 2.85 (ISBN 0-86985-423-2). Shuter & Shooter.
Norback, C. & Norback, P. The Must Words: The Six Thousand Most Important Words for a Successful & Profitable Vocabulary. 312p. 1983. pap. 5.95 (ISBN 0-07-047141-X, GB). McGraw.
Nurnberg & Rosenblum. Adult Approach to Vocabulary Building. Epap. 1.40. Mentor Bks.
Readers Digest Editors. Family Word Finder. LC 75-18006. 896p. 1975. 18.45 (ISBN 0-89577-023-7). RD Assn.
Richey, Jim. Drugstore Language. (Survival Vocabulary Ser.). (Illus.). 48p. (gr. 7-12). 1978. pap. 2.95 (ISBN 0-915510-28-6). Janus Bks.
--Supermarket Language. (Survival Vocabulary Ser.). (Illus.). 48p. (gr. 7-12). 1978. pap. 2.95 (ISBN 0-915510-27-8). Janus Bks.
Six Thousand Words: No. 76. $8.50 (ISBN 0-87779-007-8). Ency Brit Ed.
Smith, Henry P. Glossary of Terms & Phrases. LC 79-175746. x, 521p. 1972. Repr. of 1889 ed. $45.00x (ISBN 0-8103-3816-5). Gale.
Trench, Richard C. A Select Glossary of English Words Used Formerly in Senses Different from Their Present. Palmer, A. Smythe, ed. 1979. Repr. of 1906 ed. lib. bdg. $25.00 (ISBN 0-8495-5138-2). Arden Lib.
Webster's Collegiate Thesaurus. (Eng.). 1976. $11.95 (ISBN 0-87779-069-8, 72421). Merriam.
Webster's Third Interntaional Dictionary. (Eng.). 1981. $85.00 (ISBN 0-87779-206-2, 72449). Merriam.

ENGLISH LANGUAGE–GLOSSARIES, VOCABULARIES, ETC.–POLYGLOT
Gurung, Deu B., et al. Gurung-Nepali-English Glossary. 223p. (Nepalese & Eng.). 1976. pap. $3.00x (ISBN 0-88312-854-3); $3.00 (ISBN 0-88312-391-6). Summer Inst Ling.
Gustafsson, Uwe. English-Kotiya Oriya, Kotiya Oriya-English Glossary. 1974. pap. $2.00x (ISBN 0-88312-748-2). Summer Inst Ling.

ENGLISH LANGUAGE–GRAMMAR
see also English Language–Text-Books for Foreigners
Curme, George O. A Grammar of the English Language. 1983. $40.00 set (ISBN 0-930454-03-0). Verbatim.
--A Grammar of the English Language: Parts of Speech, Vol. 1. LC 77-87423. 400p. 1983. $20.00 (ISBN 0-930454-02-2). Verbatim.
Koch, Harry W. An Easy Guide to English Grammar & Vocabulary. rev. ed. 119p. 1980. pap. 5.00 (ISBN 0-913164-84-4). Ken-Bks.
Miller, Walter J. & Morsecluley, Elizabeth. Vocabulary, Spelling & Grammar. 10th ed. 256p. 1983. pap. $5.95 (ISBN 0-668-05806-4). Arco.
Watson & Folliet. Round the World-English. (Round the World Ser.). (gr. 1-9). 1980. $10.95 (ISBN 0-86020-485-5, Usborne-Hayes). French ed (ISBN 0-86020-488-X). Spanish ed (ISBN 0-86020-484-7). EDC.

ENGLISH LANGUAGE–HISTORY
Bray, J. W. A History of English Critical Terms. 59.95 (ISBN 0-8490-0325-3). Gordon Pr.
Frank, Roberta & Cameron, Angus. A Plan for the Dictionary of Old English. 1973. Can.$25.00 (ISBN 0-8020-3303-2). U of Toronto Pr.
Johnson, Samuel. Dictionary of the English Language: In Which the Words Are Deduced from Their Originals & Illustrated in Their Different Significations by Examples from the Best Writers, 2 Vols. 1968. Repr. of 1755 ed. Set. $257.50 (ISBN 3-4870-1935-3). Adler.

ENGLISH LANGUAGE–HOMOGRAPHS
see English Language–Homonyms

ENGLISH LANGUAGE–HOMONYMS
Ellyson, Louise. A Dictionary of Homonyms: New Word Patterns. 166p. 1979. lib. bdg. $8.95x (ISBN 0-88411-136-9). Amereon Ltd.
Hagan, S. F. Which I Which? A Manual of Homophones. write for info. (ISBN 0-333-27235-8). Macmillan.
Newhouse, Dora. The Encyclopedia of Homonyms 'Sound-Alikes' LC 76-27486. 1977. 16.95 (ISBN 0-918050-01-4). Newhouse Pr.
--Homonyms. LC 77-82190. viii, 247p. (Eng. & Span.). 1978. write for info. Newhouse Pr.
Townsend, W. C. Handbook of Homophones. 121p. 1975. pap. $1.50x (ISBN 0-88312-772-5); microfiche $2.25x (ISBN 0-88312-350-9). Summer Inst Ling.
Webster's Synonyms, Antonyms, Homonyms. pap. $1.99 (ISBN 0-671-41838-6). Dennison.

ENGLISH LANGUAGE–HOMOPHONES
see English Language–Homonyms

ENGLISH LANGUAGE–IDIOMS, CORRECTIONS, ERRORS
Almeida, Dauster C. Dicionario de Expressoes Idiomaticas Ingles-Portugues. LC 80-109558. 198p. (Eng. & Port.). 1979. Cr.$230.00. Auer.
Bellenger, W. A. A Dictionary of Idioms, French & English. 331p. (Fr. & Eng.). 1983. Repr. of 1830 ed. lib. bdg. $125.00 (ISBN 0-89760-052-5). Telegraph Bks.
Boatner, M., et al, eds. Dictionary of American Idioms for Deaf. 1976. $9.95 (ISBN 0-8120-0612-7). Barron.
Boatner, M. T., et al, eds. Dictionary of American Idioms for the Deaf. 1976. $14.95 (ISBN 0-8120-5103-3). Barron.
--Dictionary of American Idioms. 1976. $14.95. Barron.
Carbonell, Basset D. Diccionario de Modismos Ingleses. 2nd ed. LC 77-475058. 223p. (Eng & Span.). 1976. write for info. (ISBN 8-4850-6508-5). Dos Continentes.
Cowie, A. P. & Mackin, Ronald. Oxford Dictionary of Current Idiomatic English: Verbs with Prepositions & Particles, Vol. 1. 1975. 13.95x (ISBN 0-19-431145-7). Oxford U Pr.

Dels Prats, Alfonso T. Diccionario de Modismos Ingleses & Norteamericanos. 368p. (Span. & Eng.). 1979. write for info. (ISBN 84-261-0838-5). Editorial Juventud.

Denoeu, F., et al. French & English Idioms. (Fr. & Eng.). 1982. $7.95 (ISBN 0-8120-0435-3). Barron.

Engeroff, K. & Lovelace-Kaeufer, C. English-German Dictionary of Idioms. (Eng. & Ger.). $22.75 (ISBN 3-1900-6217-X). Adler.

Fowler, Henry W. Dictionary of Modern English Usage. 2nd ed. Gowers, Ernest, ed. (YA) (gr. 9 up). 1965. 15.95 (ISBN 0-19-500153-2); with thumb index 18.95 (ISBN 0-19-500154-0). Oxford U Pr.

Fowler, W. S. Dictionary of Idioms. 112p. (Eng.). E1.95 (ISBN 0-17-555381-5). Nelson & Sons Group.

Freeman, William. Concise Dictionary of English Idioms. rev ed. 1976. pap. $5.95 (ISBN 0-87116-094-3). Writer.

Gonzalez Gutierrez, O. Diccionario de expresiones idiomaticas y modismos ingleses. 328p. (Span. & Span.). write for info. EUDEBA.

Hall, R. & Hall, F. Italian & English Idioms. (Eng. & Ital.). 1982. $9.95 (ISBN 0-8120-0467-1). Barron.

Hall, Robert R., Jr. & Hall, Frances A. Two Thousand & One Italian & English Idioms: 2001 Locuzione Italiane e Inglese. LC 81-66403. (Ital. & Eng.). 1981. pap. text ed. $9.95 (ISBN 0-8120-0467-1). Barron.

Hieu, Nguyen-Trung, ed. Practical English-Vietnamese Idioms for Teachers & Students. (Eng. & Vietnamese.). 1981. $6.50 (ISBN 0-533-04431-6). Vantage.

Hudson, Kenneth. The Dictionary of Even More Diseased English. 416p. 1983. E12.95 (ISBN 0-333-34867-2). MacMillan London.

Idiomatic Expressions English-Spanish. (Eng. & Span.). write for info. (608-111). Pan Amer Pub.

Karim, A. & Lucy, T. A Dictionary of English Bahasa Malaysia Idiomatic Phrases. LC 78-942330. 145p. (Eng., Bahasa & Malay.). 1978. write for info. Jaya Ciencia.

Kennedy, W. G. & Silva, Maria. Expressoes Idiomaticas Inglesas: English Idioms. 132p. (Port. & Eng.). pap. $2.75. Imported Bks.

Laurence Urdang Associates Under the Editorial Supervision of the Longman Dictionary Department. Longman Dictionary of English Idioms. (Illus.). 404p. 1979. 18.95 (ISBN 0-582-55524-8). Longman.

McArthur, Tom & Atkins, Beryl. Dictionary of English Phrasal Verbs & Their Idioms. 256p. 1982. $15.00x (ISBN 0-00-370200-6, Pub. by Collins ELT Scotland). State Mutual Bk.

McKaskill, S. G. Dictionary of Good English. 173p. 1981. Epap. 2.95 (ISBN 0-333-30883-2). Macmillan London.

Major, Clarence. Dictionary of Afro-American Slang. LC 74-130863. 128p. 1970. pap. 1.95 (ISBN 0-7178-0269-8). Intl Pub Co.

Makkai, Adam. A Dictionary of American Idioms in Chinese. Gates & Boatner, eds. 396p. (Chinese & Eng.). Date not set. pap. $14.95 (ISBN 0-8120-2386-2). Barron.

Manser, Martin H. That's What People Say! A Dictionary of Common Speech Idioms. (Illus.). write for info. (ISBN 0-333-33298-9). Macmillan.

Rechtschaffen, Bernard & Marck, Louis. Two Thousand & One German & English Idioms: 2001 Deutsche und Englische Idiome. (Ger. & Eng.). 1984. pap. $9.95 (ISBN 0-8120-0474-4). Barron.

Savaiano, E. & Wing, L. Spanish & English Idioms: 2001 Modismos Espanoles & Ingleses. (Span. & Eng.). 1977. $6.95 (ISBN 0-8120-0438-8). Barron.

Savaiano, E. & Winget, L. Spanish-English Idioms: 2001 Modisomos Espanoles & Ingleses (Pocket Size) (Span. & Eng.). 1976. $3.95 (ISBN 0-8120-0711-5). Barron.

Shaw, Harry. Dictionary of Problem Words & Expressions. 1975. 24.95 (ISBN 0-07-056489-2, P&RB). McGraw.

Taylor, Ronald J. & Gottschalk, W. German-English Dictionary of Idioms. (Eng. & Ger.). $30.00 (ISBN 3-19-006216-1). Adler.

Torrens dels Prats, A. Diccionario de modismos ingleses y norteamericanos. 296p. (Span. & Eng.). 1969. pap. 290.00 ptas. Juventud.

Two Thousand & One Spanish & English Idioms. (Span. & Eng.). write for info. (608-66). Pan Amer Pub.

Vizetelly, Frank H. Desk-Book of Errors in English. LC 74-3021. 1974. Repr. of 1920 ed. $34.00x (ISBN 0-8103-3637-5). Gale.

Wahba, Magdi. A Dictionary of Modern Political Idiom. ix, 747p. (Eng., Fr. & Arabic.). 1978. $25.00 (79-960201). Lib Liban.

Wallace, Michael J. Dictionary of English Idioms. 256p. 1983. $15.00x (ISBN 0-00-370014-3, Pub. by Collins ELT Scotland). State Mutual Bk.

Wei, S. Practical Dictionary of Chinese Idioms, English Idioms, English Synonyms. (Illus., Chinese & Eng.). $16.50. Iaconi.

Wei, S. S. Chinese Idioms, English Idioms, English Synonyms Practical Dictionary. (Chinese & Eng.). 17.50 (ISBN 0-686-31874-9). Heinman.

Wood, F. T. Dictionary of English Colloquial Idioms. Hill, R., rev. by. 304p. 1982. write for info. (ISBN 0-333-27839-9). Macmillan.

Wood, F. T. & Hill, Robert. Dictionary of English Colloguial Idioms. 328p. 1979. Epap. 4.55 (ISBN 0-333-25450-3). Macmillan LOndon.

ENGLISH LANGUAGE–LEXICOGRAPHY

Attiyate, Y. H. Lexique CN: Anglais-Allemand-Francais. (Illus.). 526p. (Eng., Ger. & Fr.). 1977. 65.00 F. Iron Age Metalworking Int.

Burkett, Eva M. American Dictionaries of the English Language Before 1861. LC 78-11677. 1979. lib. bdg. $18.00 (ISBN 0-8108-1179-0). Scarecrow.

Parkhurst. Greek & English Lexicon. 680p. (Gr. & Eng.). Repr. of 1769 ed. loose leaf bdg. $29.95 (ISBN 0-89957-549-8). AMG Pubs.

Picoche. La Lexicologie. (Fr.). $19.00 (Dist. by Continental Bk Co). Lib. Fernand Nathan.

ENGLISH LANGUAGE–METRICS AND RHYTHMICS

see English Language–Versification

ENGLISH LANGUAGE–NOUN

Sparkes, Ivan G., ed. A Dictionary of Collective Nouns & Group Terms. LC 75-4117. 213p. 1975. $42.00x (ISBN 0-8103-2016-9, Pub. by White Lion Publishers). Gale.

Verma, M. K. Structure of the Noun Phrase in English & Hindi. (Eng. & Hindi.). 1971. $8.50 (ISBN 0-89684-322-X). Orient Bk Dist.

ENGLISH LANGUAGE–OBSOLETE WORDS

Halliwell-Phillipps, James O. Dictionary of Archaic & Provincial Words, Obsolete Phrases, Proverbs, & Ancient Customs, from the Fourteenth Century, 2 Vols. 3rd ed. LC 76-168221. Repr. of 1855 ed. Set. $35.00 (ISBN 0-404-03055-6). AMS Pr.

--Dictionary of Archaic & Provincial Words, Obsolete Phrases, Proverbs, & Ancient Customs, from the Fourteenth Century, 2 vols. LC 66-27837. 1968. Repr. of 1847 ed. Set. $86.00x (ISBN 0-8103-3283-3). Gale.

ENGLISH LANGUAGE–ORTHOGRAPHY AND SPELLING

see also Spellers; Spelling Reform

Bailie, John, ed. The Good Spelling Dictionary. 176p. Epap. 75.00p (ISBN 0-600-38293-1); pap. $9.00 (ISBN 0-600-04982-5). Newnes Bks.

Davidson, Jessica. How to Improve Your Spelling & Vocabulary. (gr. 7 up). 1980. PLB $8.90 (ISBN 0-531-04133-6). Watts.

Dougherty, Margaret M., et al, eds. Instant Spelling Dictionary. (Career Institute Instant Reference Library). (gr. 9 up). 1967. $3.95 (ISBN 0-531-01697-8). Watts.

Emery, Donald W. Variant Spellings in Modern American Dictionaries. rev. ed. LC 73-83843. (Orig.). 1973. pap. 5.70 (ISBN 0-8141-5630-4); pap. 4.00 members (ISBN 0-686-86489-1). NCTE.

Lawrence, Marjorie K., et al. Grammar & Orthography, Bks. 1-4. Smeeth, William B., ed. (gr. 1-6). 1966. pap. text ed. $1.67 ea. (Pub. by Lawrence); word study supplement $0.80 (ISBN 0-87505-308-4). Borden.

Miller, Walter J. & Morsecluley, Elizabeth. Vocabulary, Spelling & Grammar. 10th ed. 256p. 1983. pap. $5.95 (ISBN 0-668-05806-4). Arco.

New World Dictionary Editors. Misspeller's Dictionary. 1983. write for info. (ISBN 0-671-46864-2). S&S.

Olivares, Dennis A. The Spelling Helper Dictionary. Berdell, Dorothy K., ed. 1979. $6.95 (ISBN 0-686-26693-5). Denco Intl.

Smalley, W. A., et al. Orthography Studies. 1964. $3.00 (ISBN 0-686-14418-X, 08508). Am Bible.

--Orthography Studies. 1964. $3.00x (ISBN 0-8267-0027-6, 08508). United Bible.

Stein, Jess, ed. The Random House Basic Speller-Divider. 1981. pap. $1.50 (ISBN 0-345-29255-3). Ballantine.

Venezky, Richard L. Structure of English Orthography. (Janua Linguarum, Ser. Minor: No. 82). 1970. pap. text ed. $14.00x (ISBN 90-2790-707-2). Mouton.

ENGLISH LANGUAGE–ORTHOGRAPHY AND SPELLING–PROGRAMMED INSTRUCTION

Gilboy, Robert C. Spell It Fast! The Quick Way to Spell Using Sixty Stimulating Word Lists. LC 81-1146. pap. $5.95 (ISBN 0-87491-071-4). Acropolis.

ENGLISH LANGUAGE–PARSING

see English Language–Grammar

ENGLISH LANGUAGE–PERIPHRASTIC VERB

see English Language–Verb

ENGLISH LANGUAGE–PHONETICS

Venezky, Richard L. Structure of English Orthography. (Janua Linguarum, Ser. Minor: No. 82). 1970. pap. text ed. $14.00x (ISBN 90-2790-707-2). Mouton.

ENGLISH LANGUAGE–PHRASES AND TERMS

see English Language–Terms and Phrases

ENGLISH LANGUAGE–PREFIXES

see English Language–Suffixes and Prefixes

ENGLISH LANGUAGE–PREPOSITIONS

Fernald, James C. Funk & Wagnall's Standard Handbook of Synonyms, Antonyms & Prepositions. rev. ed. LC 47-11924. (Funk & W Bk.). (gr. 9-12). 1947. $13.41i (ISBN 0-308-40024-0, 420140). T y Crowell.

ENGLISH LANGUAGE–PRIMERS

see Readers

ENGLISH LANGUAGE–PRONUNCIATION

Here are entered works on the pronunciation of words (as distinct from that of particular sounds or letters) especially with reference to best usage.

Bender, James F. N. B. C. Handbook of Pronunciation. 3rd, rev. ed. Crowell, Thomas, Jr., ed. 1964. $14.37i (ISBN 0-690-57472-X). T Y Crowell.

Bronstein, Arthur J. Pronunciation of American English. (Illus.). 1960. 18.95 (ISBN 0-13-730887-6). P-H.

Dzhouiz, D. Slovar Angliiskogo Proiznosheniia. 538p. (Eng.). 1963. $3.85 (Pub. by GINS). Four Continent.

English Language Institute. Vocabulary in Context. (Intensive Course in English Ser.). 1964. pap. $5.95x (ISBN 0-472-08305-8). U of Mich Pr.

Lass, Abraham & Lass, Betty. Dictionary of Pronunciation. LC 75-36252. 356p. 1976. $15.95 (ISBN 0-8129-0614-4). Times Bks.

Noory, Samuel. Dictionary of Pronunciation. 4th ed. LC 81-66273. 512p. 1981. $19.95 (ISBN 0-8453-4722-5). Cornwall Bks.

A Pronouncing Dictionary of American English: No. 47. $7.95 (ISBN 0-87779-047-7). Ency Brit Ed.

ENGLISH LANGUAGE–PROSODY

see English Language–Versification

ENGLISH LANGUAGE–PROVINCIALISMS

Davies, Thomas L. Supplementary English Glossary. LC 68-23468. 1968. Repr. of 1881 ed. $47.00x (ISBN 0-8103-3245-0). Gale.

Halliwell-Phillipps, James O. Dictionary of Archaic & Provincial Words, Obsolete Phrases, Proverbs, & Ancient Customs, from the Fourteenth Century, 2 Vols. 3rd ed. LC 76-168221. Repr. of 1855 ed. Set. $35.00 (ISBN 0-404-03055-6). AMS Pr.

--Dictionary of Archaic & Provincial Words, Obsolete Phrases, Proverbs, & Ancient Customs, from the Fourteenth Century, 2 vols. LC 66-27837. 1968. Repr. of 1847 ed. Set. $86.00x (ISBN 0-8103-3283-3). Gale.

Langker, R. Flash in New South Wales, 1788-1850. LC 81-205617. 61p. (Eng.). 1980. write for info. Univ Syd Aust Lang.

Palmer, Abram. Folk-Etymology: A Dictionary of Verbal Corruptions or Words Perverted in Form. LC 68-26365. (Studies in Language, No. 41). 1969. Repr. of 1882 ed. lib. bdg. 59.95x (ISBN 0-8383-0279-3). Haskell.

Palmer, Abram S. Folk-Etymology, a Dictionary of Verbal Corruptions or Words Perverted in Form or Meaning, by False Derivation or Mistaken Analogy. LC 68-57636. (Illus.). 1969. Repr. of 1882 ed. lib. bdg. 29.25x (ISBN 0-8371-1153-6, PAFE). Greenwood.

Pettman, Charles. Africanderisms. LC 68-18007. 1968. Repr. of 1913 ed. $47.00x (ISBN 0-8103-3289-2). Gale.

Watts, Peter. A Dictionary of the Old West. 1977. $12.95 (ISBN 0-394-49013-4). Knopf.

ENGLISH LANGUAGE–READERS

see Readers

ENGLISH LANGUAGE–REVERSE DICTIONARIES

see English Language–Synonyms and Antonyms

ENGLISH LANGUAGE–RHETORIC

see also English Language–Composition and Exercises

De Bono, Edward. Wordpower. 1977. pap. 4.95i (ISBN 0-06-090568-9, CN 568, CN). Har-Row.

Lanham, Richard A. A Handlist of Rhetorical Terms: A Guide for Students of English Literature. LC 68-31636. 1968. pap. $5.95x (ISBN 0-520-01414-6). U of Cal Pr.

Smith, Forrest G. Dictionary of Freshman Composition. LC 70-78633. (Quality Paperback: No. 239). (Orig.). 1969. pap. 3.95 (ISBN 0-8226-0239-3). Littlefield.

Woodson, Linda. A Handbook of Modern Rhetorical Terms. LC 79-17400. (Orig.). 1979. pap. 4.60 (ISBN 0-8141-2019-9); pap. 3.30 members (ISBN 0-686-86419-0). NCTE.

ENGLISH LANGUAGE–RIME

Pocket Rhyming Dictionary. 1960. pap. 2.95 (ISBN 0-394-40062-3). Random.

ENGLISH LANGUAGE–RIME–DICTIONARIES

Barker, Ronnie. Fletcher's Book of Rhyming Slang. (Illus.). 1982. pap. $10.00x (ISBN 0-330-25980-6, Pub. by Pan Bks). State Mutual Bk.

Cahn, Sammy. The Songwriter's Rhyming Dictionary. (Illus.). 224p. 1983. $17.95 (ISBN 0-87196-765-0). Facts on File.
Lees, Gene. A Modern Rhyming Dictionary. 360p. (YA) 1981. $14.95 (ISBN 0-89524-129-3, 8601). Cherry Lane.
Levens, Peter. Manipulus Vocabulorum. (Camden Society, London. Publications, First Series: No. 95). Repr. of 1867 ed. $28.00 (ISBN 0-404-50195-8). AMS Pr.
Modglin, Nel. The Rhymer & Other Helps for Poets. 147p. 1977. $5.95 (ISBN 0-8059-2421-3). Dorrance.
Ottenheimer. New Rhyming Dictionary of One & Two Syllable Rhymes. pap. $2.50 (ISBN 0-06-461009-8, BN). B&N NY.
Reed, Langford. Writer's Rhyming Dictionary. $7.95 (ISBN 0-87116-044-7). Writer.
Stillman, F. Whitfield's University Rhyming Dictionary: English Language Rime. 283p. 1964. pap. $3.95 (ISBN 0-8152-0080-3, M-9049). French & Eur.
Stillman, Frances & Whitfield, Jane S. Poet's Manual & Rhyming Dictionary. LC 65-11650. 1965. $12.45i (ISBN 0-690-64572-4). T Y Crowell.
Walker, J. Walker's Rhyming Dictionary of the English Language: In Which the Whole Language is Arranged According to its Terminations. rev. & enl. ed. 558p. 1979. Repr. of 1924 ed. 14.95 (ISBN 0-7100-2247-6). Routledge & Kegan.
Whitfield, Jane. Songwriters Rhyming Dictionary. 1974. pap. $5.00 (ISBN 0-87980-293-6). Wilshire.
Whitfield, Jane S. Whitfield's University Rhyming Dictionary. Stillman, Frances, ed. 284p. 1981. pap. $4.95 (ISBN 0-06-463538-4, EH 538, EH). B&N NY.
--Whitfield's University Rhyming Dictionary. Stillman, Frances, ed. (Apollo Eds.). pap. $3.95i (ISBN 0-8152-0080-3, A80). T Y Crowell.
Wood, Clement, ed. Complete Rhyming Dictionary. 1936. $10.95 (ISBN 0-385-00046-4). Doubleday.

ENGLISH LANGUAGE–SLANG
see also English Language–Terms and Phrases; Pidgin English
Rose, Howard N. A Thesaurus of Slang. LC 72-167144. xii, 120p. Repr. of 1934 ed. $34.00x (ISBN 0-8103-3115-2). Gale.

ENGLISH LANGUAGE–SLANG–DICTIONARIES
Barker, Ronnie. Fletcher's Book of Rhyming Slang. (Illus.). 1982. pap. $10.00x (ISBN 0-330-25980-6, Pub. by Pan Bks). State Mutual Bk.
Clapin, Sylvia. New Dictionary of Americanisms. LC 68-17985. 1968. Repr. of 1902 ed. $42.00x (ISBN 0-8103-3244-2). Gale.
Elting, John R. & Cragg, Dan. A Dictionary of Soldier Talk. 480p. 1983. $24.95 (ISBN 0-684-17862-1, ScribT). Scribner.
Franklyn, Julian. A Dictionary of Rhyming Slang. rev ed. 1975. 16.00 (ISBN 0-7100-8051-4); pap. 7.95 (ISBN 0-7100-8052-2). Routledge & Kegan.
Fraser, Edward & Gibbons, John. Soldier & Sailor Words & Phrases. LC 68-30635. 1968. Repr. of 1925 ed. $40.00x (ISBN 0-8103-3281-7). Gale.
Grose, Francis. A Classical Dictionary of the Vulgar Tongue. facsimile ed. Partridge, E., ed. LC 70-179523. (Select Bibliographies Reprint Ser). Repr. of 1963 ed. $21.00 (ISBN 0-8369-6652-X). Ayer Co.
Holt, Alfred H. Phrase & Word Origins: A Study of Familiar Expressions. 2nd ed. Orig. Title: Phrase Origins. 1961. pap. $4.50 (ISBN 0-486-20758-7). Dover.
Major, Clarence. Dictionary of Afro-American Slang. LC 74-130863. 128p. 1970. pap. 1.95 (ISBN 0-7178-0269-8). Intl Pub Co.
Marks, Georgette A. The New English-French Dictionary of Slang & Colloquialisms. LC 74-32524. 299p. (Eng. & Fr.). 1975. $12.95 (ISBN 0-87690-149-6). Dutton.
Marks, Georgette A. & Johnson, Charles B. Harrap's English-French Dictionary of Slang & Colloquialisms. LC 75-329804. 299p. (Eng. & Fr.). 1975. E7.25 (ISBN 0-245-52267-0). Harrap.
Morinigo, Marcos A. Diccionario de americanismos. 738p. (Span. & Eng.). 800.00 ptas. Teide.
Partridge, Eric. Dictionary of Slang & Unconventional English. 7th ed. 1970. $45.00 (ISBN 0-02-594970-5). Macmillan.
--Smaller Slang Dictionary. 1968. 16.95 (ISBN 0-7100-1938-6); pap. 7.95 (ISBN 0-7100-8331-9). Routledge & Kegan.
Spears, Richard A. Slang & Euphemism: Abridged Edition. 1982. pap. 4.50 (ISBN 0-451-11889-8, AE1889, Sig). NAL.
Wentworth, Harold & Flexner, Stuart B. Dictionary of American Slang. 766p. DM.48.00 (49016). Langenscheidt.
--Pocket Dictionary of American Slang. abr. ed. 1968. pap. $3.95 (ISBN 0-671-78976-7). PB.

ENGLISH LANGUAGE–SPELLERS
see Spellers

ENGLISH LANGUAGE–SPELLING
see English Language–Orthography and Spelling

ENGLISH LANGUAGE–SPELLING REFORM
see Spelling Reform

ENGLISH LANGUAGE–SPOKEN ENGLISH
The Hamlyn Guide to English Usage. 1980. pap. 3.95 (ISBN 0-600-33189-X). Larousse.

ENGLISH LANGUAGE–STUDY AND TEACHING
Lemon. Glossary for the Study of English. E3.00. Oxford U Pr.

ENGLISH LANGUAGE–STUDY AND TEACHING–FOREIGN STUDENTS
Allen, Virginia F. Techniques in Teaching Vocabulary. (Illus., Orig.). 1983. pap. 3.95x (ISBN 0-19-503231-4). Oxford U Pr.

ENGLISH LANGUAGE–STUDY AND TEACHING (ELEMENTARY)
Justus, Fred. Jumbo Vocabulary Development Yearbook: Grade 1. (Jumbo Vocabulary Ser.). 96p. (gr. 1). 1979. $14.00 (ISBN 0-8209-0050-8, JVDY 1). ESP.
--Jumbo Vocabulary Development Yearbook: Grade 2. (Jumbo Vocabulary Ser.). 96p. (gr. 2). 1980. $14.00 (ISBN 0-8209-0051-6, JVDY 2). ESP.
--Jumbo Vocabulary Fun Yearbook. (Jumbo Vocabulary Ser.). 96p. (gr. 3). 1980. $14.00 (ISBN 0-8209-0058-3, JVFY 3). ESP.
McMaster, Dale. Vocabulary Development. (Language Arts Ser.). 24p. (gr. 6-9). 1976. wkbk. $5.00 (ISBN 0-8209-0312-4, VD-4). ESP.
McMasters, Dale. Vocabulary Study. (Language Arts Ser.). 24p. (gr. 5-7). 1976. wkbk. $5.00 (ISBN 0-8209-0311-6, VD-3). ESP.
Shaw, Marie-Jose. Jumbo Vocabulary Development Yearbook: Grade 3. (Jumbo Vocabulary Ser.). 96p. (gr. 3). 1980. $14.00 (ISBN 0-8209-0052-4, JVDY 3). ESP.
--Jumbo Vocabulary Development Yearbook: Grade 4. (Jumbo Vocabulary Ser.). 96p. (gr. 4). 1980. $14.00 (ISBN 0-8209-0053-2, JVDY 4). ESP.
--Jumbo Vocabulary Development Yearbook: Grade 5. (Jumbo Vocabulary Ser.). 96p. (gr. 5). 1981. $14.00 (ISBN 0-8209-0054-0, JVDY 5). ESP.
Vaughn, Jim. Jumbo Vocabulary Development Yearbook: Grade 7. (Jumbo Vocabulary Ser.). 96p. (gr. 7-9). 1981. $14.00 (ISBN 0-8209-0056-7, JVDY J). ESP.

ENGLISH LANGUAGE–STUDY AND TEACHING (HIGHER)
Hornby, A. S. Oxford Advanced Learner's Dictionary of Current English. 3rd ed. (Illus.). 1974. text ed. 14.95x (ISBN 0-19-431101-5). Oxford U Pr.
Scott, Christopher. A Learner's First Dictionary. 176p. (Orig., Eng.). write for info. Macmillan London.

ENGLISH LANGUAGE–STUDY AND TEACHING (SECONDARY)
Vaughn, Jim. Jumbo Vocabulary Development Yearbook: Grade 10. (Jumbo Vocabulary Ser.). 96p. (gr. 10-12). 1981. $14.00 (ISBN 0-8209-0057-5, JVDY S). ESP.

ENGLISH LANGUAGE–SUFFIXES AND PREFIXES
Urdang, Laurence, ed. Suffixes: And Other Word-Final Elements of English. 320p. 1982. $60.00x (ISBN 0-8103-1123-2). Gale.

ENGLISH LANGUAGE–SYLLABICATION
Finnegan, Edward G., ed. New Webster's Word Divider: Vest Pocket Edition. LC 76-6038. 1978. pap. $1.95 (ISBN 0-8326-0041-5, 6450). Delair.

ENGLISH LANGUAGE–SYNONYMS AND ANTONYMS
Bernstein, Theodore M. Bernstein's Reverse Dictionary. LC 75-8283. 384p. 1975. $16.95 (ISBN 0-8129-0566-0). Times Bks.
Colligan, Louise. How to Use the Thesaurus. (gr. 7-12). 1978. pap. $1.50 (ISBN 0-590-11860-9). Scholastic Inc.
Devlin. A Dictionary of Synonyms & Antonyms. 384p. 1982. pap. $2.95 (ISBN 0-446-31028-X). Warner Bks.
Fernald, James C. Funk & Wagnall's Standard Handbook of Synonyms, Antonyms & Prepositions. rev. ed. LC 47-11924. (Funk & W Bk.). (gr. 9-12). 1947. $13.41i (ISBN 0-308-40024-0, 420140). T y Crowell.
Finnegan, Edward G., ed. New Webster's Vest Pocket Thesaurus. LC 78-52347. 1978. pap. $1.75 (ISBN 0-8326-0045-8, 6440). Delair.
Gem Dictionary of Synonyms. (Gem Reference Ser.). 1964. $2.95 (ISBN 0-529-05651-8, GR12). Collins Pubs.
Hamlyn Pocket Thesaurus of English Words. 1979. pap. 3.95 (ISBN 0-600-38779-8). Larousse.
Laffal, Julius. Concept Dictionary of English. LC 72-97927. 1973. text ed. 16.95 (ISBN 0-686-77072-2). Gallery Pr.
Laird, Charlton. Webster's New World Thesaurus. 544p. 1983. pap. $8.95 (ISBN 0-446-37053-3). Warner Bks.
Laird, Charlton, ed. Webster's New World Thesaurus. 688p. $8.95 (ISBN 0-529-03961-3, 2694N); thumb indexed $9.95 (ISBN 0-529-05187-7, 2694N-1); pap. $5.95 (ISBN 0-529-04805-1, M383). Collins Pubs.
--Webster's New World Thesaurus. pap. 8.95 (ISBN 0-452-00627-9, F627, Mer). NAL.
Landau, Sidney & Bogus, Ronald, eds. Doubleday Roget's Thesaurus in Dictionary Form. LC 76-7696. 564p. 1977. $9.95 (ISBN 0-385-01236-5); thumb-indexed $11.95 (ISBN 0-385-12379-5). Doubleday.
Lewis, Norman. Roget's Thesaurus in Dictionary Form. 1983. pap. $2.25 (ISBN 0-425-06400-X, Medallion). Berkley Pub.
Merriam Webster Dictionary of Synonyms. 1981. pap. 3.50 (ISBN 0-671-46893-6). PB.
Merriam-Webster Editorial Staff. Webster's New Dictionary of Synonyms. 942p. 1978. thumb-indexed 12.95 (ISBN 0-87779-241-0). Merriam-Webster Inc.
--Webster's School Thesaurus. 1978. 9.95 (ISBN 0-87779-178-3). Merriam-Webster Inc.
Nechas, James W. Synonomy, Repitition & Restatement in the Vocabulary of Herman Melville's Moby Dick. 286p. 1980. Repr. of 1978 ed. lib. bdg. $30.00 (ISBN 0-8414-6311-5). Folcroft.
Nelson's New Compact Roget's Thesaurus. 1978. 2.45 (ISBN 0-8407-5634-8). Nelson.
New American Roget's Thesaurus in Dictionary Form. rev. ed. 1978. pap. 2.95 (ISBN 0-451-12539-8, Sig). NAL.
The New Roget's Thesaurus in Dictionary Form. 512p. 1983. pap. $2.95 (ISBN 0-425-06400-X). Berkley Pub.
New Webster's Quick Reference Thesaurus. (Quick Reference Ser.). (Orig.). 1981. pap. $1.95 (ISBN 0-8326-0052-0, 6605). Delair.
Pocket Dictionary of Synonyms & Antonyms. 1960. pap. 2.95 (ISBN 0-394-51933-7). Random.
Rodale, J. I. Synonym Finder. rev. ed. 1978. 19.95 (ISBN 0-87857-236-8); deluxe ed. 21.95 (ISBN 0-87857-244-9). Rodale Pr Inc.
Roget, Peter M. Roget's International Thesaurus. 4th ed. LC 62-12806. 1977. $12.50i (ISBN 0-690-00010-3); thumb indexed $13.95i (ISBN 0-690-00011-1). T y Crowell.
--Roget's Thesaurus of English Words & Phrases. Dutch, R. A., ed. 1965. $11.95 (ISBN 0-312-68880-6); thumb indexed $13.50 (ISBN 0-312-68845-8). St Martin.
--Roget's Thesaurus of Words & Phrases. 774p. 1960. 6.95 (ISBN 0-448-01607-9, G&D). Putnam Pub Group.
--Thesaurus of English Words & Phrases. rev. ed. Roget, John L. & Roget, Samuel R., eds. $35.00 (ISBN 0-87559-049-7); thumb indexed $40.00 (ISBN 0-87559-050-0). Shalom.
Roget's II: The New Thesaurus. 1980. Plain-edged. 9.95 (ISBN 0-395-29604-8); Thumb-indexed. 10.95 (ISBN 0-395-29605-6). HM.
Roget's Thesaurus of Synonyms & Antonyms. Date not set. pap. $2.95 (ISBN 0-87505-254-1). Borden.
Roget's Thesaurus of Synonyms & Antonyms. pap. $2.95 (ISBN 0-686-17306-6). Dennison.
Schiller, Andrew & Jenkins, William A. Junior Thesaurus: In Other Words II. rev. ed. LC 77-84159. (Illus.). (gr. 3-6). 1978. PLB 12.68 (ISBN 0-688-51827-3). Lothrop.
Smith, Charles J. Synonyms Discriminated. Smith, Percy H., ed. LC 78-126007. 1970. Repr. of 1903 ed. $42.00x (ISBN 0-8103-3010-5). Gale.
Smith, V. J. Dictionary of Synonyms & Antonyms. $32.50 (ISBN 0-87559-045-4); thumb indexed $31.00 (ISBN 0-87559-046-2). Shalom.
Soule, Richard & Howson, G., eds. Dictionary of English Synonyms & Synonymous Parallel Expressions. rev. ed. $32.50 (ISBN 0-87559-043-8); thumb indexed $37.50 (ISBN 0-87559-044-6). Shalom.
Townley, Helen M. & Gee, Ralph C. Thesaurus-Making: Grow Your Own Word-Stock. (Grafton Ser.). 208p. 1981. lib. bdg. $32.00 (ISBN 0-86531-107-2). Westview.
Urdang & Manser, eds. Dictionary of Synonyms & Antonyms. Epap. 1.95. Pan Bks.
Urdang, Laurence. The Basic Book of Synonyms & Antonyms. 1978. pap. 2.75 (ISBN 0-451-11688-7, AE1688, Sig). NAL.
--A Basic Dictinary of Synonyms & Antonyms. 1979. 9.95 (ISBN 0-525-66604-4). Lodestar Bks.
--A Basic Dictionary of Synonyms & Antonyms. LC 79-4064. 1979. 9.95 (ISBN 0-525-66604-4). Lodestar Bks.
Urdung, Lawrence, ed. The Random House Basic Dictionary-Synonyms & Antonyms. 1981. pap. $1.50 (ISBN 0-345-29712-1). Ballantine.
Webster's Synonyms, Antonyms, Homonyms. pap. $1.99 (ISBN 0-671-41838-6). Dennison.
Wei, S. Practical Dictionary of Chinese Idioms, English Idioms, English Synonyms. (Illus., Chinese & Eng.). $16.50. Iaconi.
Wei, S. S. Chinese Idioms, English Idioms, English Synonyms Practical Dictionary. (Chinese & Eng.). 17.50 (ISBN 0-686-31874-9). Heinman.

ENGLISH LANGUAGE–SYNTAX
Curme, George O. A Grammar of the English Language: Syntax, Vol. 2. LC 77-87422. 640p. 1983. $20.00 (ISBN 0-930454-01-4). Verbatim.

ENGLISH LANGUAGE–TERMS AND PHRASES
see also English Language–Slang

Bray, J. W. A History of English Critical Terms. 1977. lib. bdg. 59.95 (ISBN 0-8490-1974-5). Gordon Pr.

Brown, Charles P. Dictionary of Telugu & English: Explaining English Idioms & Phrases in Telugu, 2 vols. (Eng. & Telugu.). 1976. Repr. of 1958 ed. $195.00 (ISBN 0-518-19008-0). Ayer Co.

Colcord, Joanna C. Sea Language Comes Ashore. Dorsen, Richard M., ed. (International Folklore Ser.). 1977. Repr. of 1945 ed. lib. bdg. $12.00x (ISBN 0-405-10089-2). Ayer Co.

Diccionario de americanismos. (Eng. & Span.). write for info. Tres Americas.

Dubois, Marguerite-Marie. Dictionnaire de Locutions: Francais-Anglais. 392p. (Fr.). 1973. 60.00 F. Larousse.

Duffy, Charles & Petit, Henry. Dictionary of Literary Terms. rev. ed. pap. $2.00 (ISBN 0-910294-02-X). Brown Bk.

Evans, Ivor H., ed. Brewer's Dictionary of Phrase & Fable. 1248p. 1982. $50.00x (ISBN 0-304-30706-8, Pub. by Cassell England). State Mutual Bk.

Fairchild, Henry P. Dictionary of Sociology & Related Sciences. LC 76-110377. Repr. of 1955 ed. lib. bdg. 22.75x (ISBN 0-8371-4581-3, FADS). Greenwood.

Haller, Margaret A. Essential Vocabulary for College-Bound Students. LC 82-1732. 208p. (Orig.). (YA) (gr. 10 up). 1982. pap. $5.95 (ISBN 0-668-05417-4, 5417). Arco.

Holt, Alfred H. Phrase & Word Origins: A Study of Familiar Expressions. 2nd ed. Orig. Title: Phrase Origins. 1961. pap. $4.50 (ISBN 0-486-20758-7). Dover.

Horwill, H. W. An Anglo-American Interpreter: A Vocabulary & Phrase Book. LC 72-169624. 1939. lib. bdg. $10.00 (ISBN 0-8414-5130-3). Folcroft.

Hyamson, Albert M. Dictionary of English Phrases: Phraseological Allusions, Catchwords, Stereotyped Modes of Speech & Metaphors, Nicknames, Sobriquets, Derivations from Personal Names. LC 66-22673. 1970. Repr. of 1922 ed. $37.00x (ISBN 0-8103-3852-1). Gale.

Kettridge, J. O. French for English Idioms & Figurative Phrases. (Fr. & Eng.). 1966. Repr. of 1940 ed. 16.00 (ISBN 0-7100-1669-7). Routledge & Kegan.

Kwong Ki Chaou. Dictionary of English Phrases with Illustrative Sentences. LC 74-136559. (Illus.). 1971. Repr. of 1881 ed. $63.00 (ISBN 0-8103-3386-4). Gale.

LaRoche, Nancy & Urdang, Laurence, eds. Picturesque Expressions: A Thematic Dictionary. LC 80-22705. 300p. 1980. $55.00x (ISBN 0-8103-1122-4). Gale.

Mager, N. H. & Mager, S. K. The Morrow Book of New Words: 8500 Terms Not Yet in Standard Dictionaries. LC 81-14205. 256p. 1982. 13.50 (ISBN 0-688-00685-X); pap. 6.50 (ISBN 0-688-00927-1). Morrow.

Marwick, Lawrence. A Glossary of Current Terminology. LC 79-12383. 188p. (Eng. & Hebrew.). 1980. write for info. (ISBN 0-8444-0308-3). Govt Print.

Mathews, Mitford M., ed. Americanisms: A Dictionary of Selected Americanisms on Historical Principles. LC 69-19279. (Orig.). 1966. pap. $1.95 (ISBN 0-226-51012-3, P229, Phoen). U of Chicago Pr.

Neves, Alfredo N. Diccionario de Americanismos. (Span. & Eng.). $12.50. SPA.

Partridge, Eric. A Dictionary of Catch Phrases. LC 77-8750. 1979. pap. $11.95 (ISBN 0-8128-6037-3). Stein & Day.

--A Dictionary of Cliches. 5th ed. 1978. pap. 8.95 (ISBN 0-7100-0049-9). Routledge & Kegan.

Rofe, Leslie G. Behind the Headlines. LC 77-568757. 207p. (Fr.). 1975. 24.00 F. Belin.

Schur, Norman W. English English: A Descriptive Dictionary. LC 77-20390. 332p. 1980. $24.95 (ISBN 0-930454-05-7). Verbatim.

ENGLISH LANGUAGE–TEXT-BOOKS FOR FOREIGNERS

Beitler, L. & McDonald, B. English for the Medical Professions. 1982. $6.96 (ISBN 0-07-004521-6). McGraw.

Croft, K. Science Readings for Students of English As a Second Language, with Exercises for Vocabulary Development. 1968. 2.75 (ISBN 0-07-013883-4, I). McGraw.

Mouthany, J. R. English Without Teacher & Dictionary: English-Arabic. $7.95x (ISBN 0-86685-058-9). Intl Bk Ctr.

ENGLISH LANGUAGE–TEXT-BOOKS FOR FOREIGNERS–CHINESE

Montanaro, John S. Chinese-English Phrase Book for Travellers. 304p. (Chinese & Eng.). 1981. pap. $8.95 (ISBN 0-471-08298-8, Pub. by Wiley Pr). Wiley.

ENGLISH LANGUAGE–TEXT-BOOKS FOR FOREIGNERS–GERMAN

Lehnert, Martin. Altenglisches Elementarbuch Einfuehrung, Grammatik, Texte Mit Uebersetzung und Woerterbuch. rev. 9th ed. (Sammlung Goeschen). (Ger.). 1978. $7.15x (ISBN 3-11-007643-8). De Gruyter.

ENGLISH LANGUAGE–TEXT-BOOKS FOR FOREIGNERS–HUNGARIAN

Hugo, Latzko. Angol Nyelvkonyv: English Language Book for Self-Learners & Student with Teachers. 180p. (Eng. & Hungarian.). pap. 7.50 (ISBN 0-87557-093-3, 093-3). Saphrograph.

ENGLISH LANGUAGE–TEXT-BOOKS FOR FOREIGNERS–SPANISH

English Language Institute. Vocabulary in Context. (Intensive Course in English Ser.). 1964. pap. $5.95x (ISBN 0-472-08305-8). U of Mich Pr.

Newhouse, Dora. Homonyms-Homonimos: Sound-Alikes. LC 77-82190. (Illus., Eng. & Span.). 1978. pap. $6.95 (ISBN 0-918050-27-8). Newhouse Pr.

Prieto, Muriel H. Vocabulary Made Easy for Spanish Speakers: Teacher's Guide. LC 76-3732. 1978. pap. text ed. $3.00 (ISBN 0-8477-2635-5). U of PR Pr.

ENGLISH LANGUAGE–TRANSLATING

Rey, Jean. Dictionnaire Selectif & Commente des Difficultes de la Version Anglais. 288p. (Fr. & Eng.). 1973. 27.00 F. Ophrys.

ENGLISH LANGUAGE–USAGE

Dictionary of Contemporary & Colloquial Usage. 40p. (Eng.). 1978. 15.00 F. Garnier.

Mager, Nathan H. & Mager, Sylvia K. Encyclopedic Dictionary of English Usage. 1974. 14.95 (ISBN 0-13-275792-3, Reward). P-H.

Morris, William & Morris, Mary. Harper Dictionary of Contemporary Usage. LC 73-4112. 672p. 1975. 23.99i (ISBN 0-06-013062-8, HarpT). Har-Row.

Pink, M. Alderton. A Dictionary of Correct English. 1977. Repr. of 1928 ed. lib. bdg. 22.50 (ISBN 0-8492-2055-6). R West.

Rakhmanov, I. V., ed. Slovar Naibolee Upotrebitel'Nykh Slov Anglii-Skogo, Nemetskogo & Frantsuzskogo Iazykov. 582p. (Rus., Ger. & Fr.). 1960. $2.40 (Pub. by Izd. Inostr. & Natsional'Nal'Nykh Slovarei). Four Continent.

The Right Word II. (Eng.). $3.95. HM.

Shaw, Harry. Dictionary of Problem Words & Expressions. 1975. 24.95 (ISBN 0-07-056489-2, P&RB). McGraw.

Stratton, Clarence. Handbook of English. LC 74-19222. 1975. Repr. of 1940 ed. $45.00x (ISBN 0-8103-4112-3). Gale.

Strong, William. Basic Usage & Vocabulary. 1983. pap. text ed. $4.95 (ISBN 0-394-33615-1, RanC). Random.

Timmons, Christine & Gibney, Frank, eds. Britannica Book of English Usage. LC 79-7706. (Encyclopedia Britannica Ser.). (Illus.). 672p. 1980. $17.95 (ISBN 0-385-14193-9). Doubleday.

Von Friederich, Wolf. Dictionary of English Words in Context. LC 80-482234. 379p. 1979. DM.36.00 (ISBN 3-559-22638-4). Lensing Verlag.

The Word Book II. (Eng.). $3.95. HM.

The Word Desk Set II. (Eng.). $12.95. HM.

The Written Word II. (Eng.). $4.95. HM.

ENGLISH LANGUAGE–VERB

Kaczmarski, Stanisaw P. A Glossary of Polish & English Verb Forms. LC 79-345099. 199p. (Pol. & Eng.). 1978. 20.00 Zl. Panstwowy Zaklad W.

Kaczmarski, Stanislaw P. A Glossary of Polish & English Verb Forms. LC 77-352469. 199p. (Eng. & Pol.). 1976. write for info. Panstwowe Zaklad W.

Kendris. Dictionnaire De Deux Cent Un Verbes Anglais Conjugues Completement a Tous les Temps & a Toutes les Personnes. (Fr.). Date not set. pap. $3.95 (ISBN 0-8120-0550-3). Barron.

McArthur, Tom & Atkins, Beryl. Dictionary of English Phrasal Verbs & Their Idioms. 256p. 1982. $15.00x (ISBN 0-00-370200-6, Pub. by Collins ELT Scotland). State Mutual Bk.

--Dictionary of English Phrasal Verbs & Their Idioms. 160p. (Eng.). 1976. $4.20 (ISBN 9-97163-154-7). Pan Pacific Bk.

Meyer, George A. The Two Word Verb: A Dictionary of the Verb Preposition Phrases in American English. (Janua Linguarum Series Didactica: No. 19). 268p. 1975. text ed. 55.00x (ISBN 90-2793-323-5). Mouton.

ENGLISH LANGUAGE–VERSIFICATION

Malof, Joseph. A Manual of English Meters. LC 78-823. 1978. Repr. of 1970 ed. lib. bdg. 24.25 (ISBN 0-313-20293-1, MAMEM). Greenwood.

Stillman, Frances & Whitfield, Jane S. Poet's Manual & Rhyming Dictionary. LC 65-11650. 1965. $12.45i (ISBN 0-690-64572-4). T Y Crowell.

Wood, Clement, ed. Complete Rhyming Dictionary. 1936. $10.95 (ISBN 0-385-00046-4). Doubleday.

ENGLISH LANGUAGE–VOCABULARIES

see English Language–Glossaries, Vocabularies, etc.

ENGLISH LANGUAGE–VOCABULARY

see Vocabulary

ENGLISH LANGUAGE–WORDS–HISTORY

see also English Language–Obsolete Words

Asimov, Isaac. Words of Science. (Illus.). (gr. 7 up). 1959. 10.95 (ISBN 0-395-06571-2). HM.

--Words of Science & the History Behind Them. (Illus.). (RL 7). 1969. pap. 1.95 (ISBN 0-451-61799-1, MJ1799, Ment). NAL.

Shipley, Joseph T. Dictionary of Early English. (Quality Paperback: No. 150). 1977. pap. 5.95 (ISBN 0-8226-0150-8). Littlefield.

ENGLISH LANGUAGE IN AUSTRALIA

Morris, Edward E. Austral English. LC 68-18003. 1968. Repr. of 1898 ed. $58.00x (ISBN 0-8103-3287-6). Gale.

ENGLISH LANGUAGE IN SOUTH AFRICA

Branford, Jean. A Dictionary of South African English. 2nd ed. 1980. 22.50x (ISBN 0-19-570177-1). Oxford U Pr.

ENGLISH LANGUAGE IN THE UNITED STATES

see also Americanisms; Black English

Boatner, M., et al, eds. Dictionary of American Idioms for Deaf. 1976. $9.95 (ISBN 0-8120-0612-7). Barron.

Boatner, M. T., et al, eds. Dictionary of American Idioms for the Deaf. 1976. $14.95 (ISBN 0-8120-5103-3). Barron.

--Dictionary of American Idioms. 1976. $14.95. Barron.

Parnwell, E. C. Oxford Picture Dictionary of American English. (Illus.). 1978. pap. 3.95 ea.; pap. monolingual ed. (ISBN 0-19-502332-3); pap. English-Spanish ed. (ISBN 0-19-502333-1); pap. french indexed ed. (ISBN 0-19-502334-X). Oxford U Pr.

Tescher & Bills. Spanish & English of the United States Hispanos. (Span. & Eng.). $9.55. Camino Real.

Whitford, Harold C. & Dixson, Robert J. Handbook of American Idioms & Idiomatic Usage. rev. ed. 188p. (gr. 9 up). 1973. pap. 4.25 (ISBN 0-88345-196-4, 18014). Regents Pub.

Wood, Gordon R. Vocabulary Change: A Study of Variation in Regional Words in Eight of the Southern States. LC 76-86183. 407p. 1971. 19.50x (ISBN 0-8093-0433-3). S Ill U Pr.

ENGLISH LANGUAGE IN THE UNITED STATES–DIALECTS

see also Black English

Bentley, Harold W. A Dictionary of Spanish Terms in English, with Special Reference to the American Southwest. LC 73-1936. 243p. (Span. & Eng.). 1973. Repr. of 1932 ed. lib. bdg. 20.00x (ISBN 0-374-90582-7). Octagon.

Cassidy, Frederic G. The ADS Dictionary - How Soon? Bd. with The Linguistic Atlas of New England Revisited. (Publications of the American Dialect Society: No. 39). 27p. 1963. pap. $1.25 (ISBN 0-8173-0639-0). U of Ala Pr.

Haskell, Ann S. The Lexicon of the Sports & Racing Car Enthusiast. Bd. with Words Relating to Plants & Animals in the Mammoth Cave Region. Wilson, Gordon; Terms of Abuse for Some Chicago Social Groups. Pederson, Lee A. (Publications of the American Dialect Society: No. 42). 48p. 1964. pap. $3.50 (ISBN 0-8173-0642-0). U of Ala Pr.

Hench, Atcheson L. The Use of the Dictionary of American English & the Dictionary of Americanisms. Bd. with Bilingualism Among American Slovaks: Analysis of Loans. Meyerstein, Goldie P; A Cleburne County, Arkansas Word List. Skillman, Billy G; Low German in Mexico. Moelleken, Wolfgang W. (Publications of the American Dialect Society: No. 46). 41p. 1966. pap. $4.20 (ISBN 0-8173-0646-3). U of Ala Pr.

King, A. T. Oil Refinery Terms in Oklahoma. Bd. with State-Wide Dialect Collecting. Criswell, E. H; Problems Confronting the Investigator of Gullah. Turner, L. D. (Publications of the American Dialect Society: No. 9). 99p. 1948. pap. $5.50 (ISBN 0-8173-0609-9). U of Ala Pr.

Nixon, P. J. A Glossary of Virginia Words. (Publications of the American Dialect Society: No. 5). 46p. 1946. pap. $3.50 (ISBN 0-8173-0605-6). U of Ala Pr.

ENGLISH LANGUAGE IN THE UNITED STATES–DICTIONARIES

Boetner, Maxine & Gates, John E. A Dictionary of American Idioms. rev. ed. Makkai, Adam, ed. LC 75-42110. 1984. $14.95 (ISBN 0-8120-5102-5); pap. $9.95 (ISBN 0-8120-0612-7). Barron.

Follett, Wilson. Modern American Usage: A Guide. Barzun, Jacques, ed. 443p. 1966. 12.95 (ISBN 0-8090-6950-4); pap. 9.95 (ISBN 0-8090-0139-X). Hill & Wang.

Garcia Becerra, Manuel. Diccionario escolar americano. (Span.). Mex.$6.00. Iztaccihuatl.

Guralnik, David B., et al, eds. Webster's New World Dictionary of the American Language: Second College Edition. (Illus.). 1980. $10.95 (ISBN 0-529-05324-1, 60B); thumb-indexed $11.95 (ISBN 0-529-05326-8, 60BI); lea. gift ed. $45.00 (ISBN 0-529-05329-2, 62BI); pap. $8.50 (ISBN 0-529-05327-6, 60BP). Collins Pubs.

Malmstrom, Jean. Webster's Third on Non-Standard Usage. Bd. with Social Aspects of Bilingualism in San Antonio, Texas. Sawyer, Janet B; Names in Gardening. Bryant, Margaret M. (Publications of the American Dialect Society: No. 41). 69p. 1964. pap. $5.00 (ISBN 0-8173-0641-2). U of Ala Pr.

Mathews, Mitford M., ed. Americanisms: A Dictionary of Selected Americanisms on Historical Principles. LC 69-19279. (Orig.). 1966. pap. $1.95 (ISBN 0-226-51012-3, P229, Phoen). U of Chicago Pr.

Morehead, Albert H., et al, eds. New American Roget's College Thesaurus in Dictionary Form. (gr. 9 up). 1957. 4.95 (ISBN 0-448-01605-2, G&D); thumb-indexed ed. 4.95 (ISBN 0-448-01622-2). Putnam Pub Group.

Pickering, John. A Vocabulary; or, Collection of Words & Phrases, Which Have Been Supposed to Be Peculiar to the United States of America; to Which Is Prefixed an Essay on the Present State of the English Language in the United States, 2 vols. in 1. Bd. with A Letter to John Pickering on the Subject of His Vocabulary or Collection of Words & Phrases. Webster, Noah. LC 70-178096. vii, 266p. 1972. Repr. of 1817 ed. lib. bdg. $24.00 (ISBN 0-8337-2752-4). B Franklin.

Torrents dels Prats, Alfonso. Diccionario de ingles-americano. 336p. 1983. pap. 950.00 ptas (ISBN 84-261-1948-4). Juventud.

Webster, Noah. An American Dictionary of the English Language: To Which Are Prefixed, an Introductory Dissertation of the Origin, History & Connection of the Language of Western Asia & Europe & A...Grammar of the English Language, 2 Vols. LC 77-117409. Repr. of 1828 ed. Set. 80.00 (ISBN 0-384-66333-8); Set. deluxe ed. 190.00 deluxe ed. (ISBN 0-384-66336-2). Johnson Repr.

Wentworth, Harold & Flexner, Stuart B. Dictionary of American Slang. 2nd ed. LC 75-8644. 766p. 1975. $15.34i (ISBN 0-690-00670-5). T Y Crowell.

ENGLISH LANGUAGE IN THE UNITED STATES–PRONUNCIATION

Bronstein, Arthur J. Pronunciation of American English. (Illus.). 1960. 18.95 (ISBN 0-13-730887-6). P-H.

Kenyon, John S. & Knott, Thomas A. Pronouncing Dictionary of American English. 2nd ed. 1953. $7.95 (ISBN 0-87779-047-7). Merriam-Webster Inc.

ENGLISH LITERATURE–BIBLIOGRAPHY–CATALOGS

New York Public Library, Research Libraries. Dictionary Catalog of the Albert A. & Henry W. Berg Collection of English & American Literature, First Supplement. 1975. lib. bdg. $105.00 (ISBN 0-8161-0014-4, Hall Library). G K Hall.

--Dictionary Catalog of the Henry W. & Albert A. Berg Collection of English & American Literature, 5 Vols. 1969. Set. lib. bdg. $465.00 (ISBN 0-8161-0870-6, Hall Library). G K Hall.

ENGLISH LITERATURE–DICTIONARIES, INDEXES, ETC.

Donker, Marjorie & Muldrow, George M. Dictionary of Literary-Rhetorical Conventions of the English Renaissance. LC 81-4266. xvi, 268p. 1982. lib. bdg. 35.00 (ISBN 0-313-23000-5, DER/). Greenwood.

Lazarus, Arnold & Smith, H. Wendell. A Glossary of Literature & Composition. rev ed. 326p. (Orig.). 1983. pap. $13.00 (ISBN 0-8141-1852-6, 18526); pap. $11.50 members. NCTE.

Smith, Eric. A Dictionary of Classical Allusion in English Literature. LC 83-12273. 256p. 1983. $39.50x (ISBN 0-389-20430-7). B&N Imports.

ENGLISH LITERATURE–HISTORY AND CRITICISM–EARLY MODERN, 1500-1700

Starnes, DeWitt T. & Talbert, Ernest W. Classical Myth & Legend in Renaissance Dictionaries. LC 73-11753. (Illus.). 517p. 1973. Repr. of 1955 ed. lib. bdg. 39.75x (ISBN 0-8371-7086-9, STCM). Greenwood.

ENGLISH LITERATURE–HISTORY AND CRITICISM–19TH CENTURY

Bender, Todd K. A Concordance to Conrad's the Mirror of the Sea & the Inheritors. 340p. 1983. lib. bdg. $45.00 (ISBN 0-8240-9110-8). Garland Pub.

Higdon, David & Bender, Todd K. A Concordance to Conrad's Under Western Eyes. LC 82-48434. (Conrad Concordances Ser.). 283p. 1982. lib. bdg. $50.00 (ISBN 0-8240-9234-1). Garland Pub.

ENGLISH LITERATURE–HISTORY AND CRITICISM–20TH CENTURY

Bender, Todd K. A Concordance to Conrad's the Mirror of the Sea & the Inheritors. 340p. 1983. lib. bdg. $45.00 (ISBN 0-8240-9110-8). Garland Pub.

Higdon, David & Bender, Todd K. A Concordance to Conrad's Under Western Eyes. LC 82-48434. (Conrad Concordances Ser.). 283p. 1982. lib. bdg. $50.00 (ISBN 0-8240-9234-1). Garland Pub.

ENGLISH POETRY (COLLECTIONS)–TO 1100

see Anglo-Saxon Poetry

ENGLISH POETRY–DICTIONARIES, INDEXES, ETC.

Langland, William. Piers Plowman Glossary, Pt. 4. Skeat, W. W., ed. (EETS, OS Ser.: No. 81). Repr. of 1884 ed. 29.00 (ISBN 0-527-00060-4). Kraus Repr.

ENGLISH PORCELAIN

see Porcelain

ENGRAVERS

Engen, Rodney K. Dictionary of Victorian Engravers, Print Publishers & Their Works. (Illus.). 1979. 60.00x (ISBN 0-914146-86-6). Somerset Hse.

ENGRAVING

see also Engravings; Gems; Printing As a Graphic Art

Watelet, Claude-Henri & Levesque, Pierre-Charles. Dictionnaire des Arts de Peinture & Gravure, 5 vols. (Fr.). 1972. Kr.500.00. Minkoff Repr.

ENGRAVING–HISTORY

Engen, Rodney K. Dictionary of Victorian Engravers, Print Publishers & Their Works. (Illus.). 1979. 60.00x (ISBN 0-914146-86-6). Somerset Hse.

ENGRAVINGS

see also Sporting Prints

Engen, Rodney K. Dictionary of Victorian Engravers, Print Publishers & Their Works. (Illus.). 1979. 60.00x (ISBN 0-914146-86-6). Somerset Hse.

ENHARMONIC ORGAN

see Organ

ENIGMAS

see Curiosities and Wonders; Riddles

ENSEMBLES (MATHEMATICS)

see Set Theory

ENTOMOLOGY

Foote, ed. Thesaurus of Entomology. 1977. $15.00 (ISBN 0-686-22689-5); members $9.00. Entomol Soc.

Forest Products Research Society. Glossary of Terms Related to the Drying of Wood. 81p. $7.00 (607-61); members $5.00. Forest Prod.

Jacobs, Werner. Systematische Zoologie Insekten. LC 76-483862. 377p. (Ger.). 1975. write for info. (ISBN 3-437-30195-0). Fischer Verlag.

Leftwich, A. W. A Dictionary of Entomology. LC 75-27143. 364p. 1976. $27.50x (ISBN 0-8448-0820-2). Crane-Russak Co.

Quintanilla, R. H. & Fraga, C. P. Glosario de terminos entomologicos. 120p. (Span.). write for info. EUDEBA.

Seguy, Eugene. Dictionnaire des Termes Techniques d'Entomologies Elementaire. 465p. (Fr.). 1967. $79.95 (ISBN 2-7205-0466-1, M-6512). French & Eur.

--Dictionnaire des Termes Techniques d'entomologie Elementaire. (Illus.). 465p. (Fr.). 1967. 200.00 F. Lechevalier.

Torre-Bueno, J. R. dela. A Glossary of Entomology. 1973. 14.00 (ISBN 0-934454-45-0). Lubrecht & Cramer.

Tuxen, S. L., ed. Taxonomist's Glossary of Genitalia in Insects. 1970. text ed. $27.50 (ISBN 0-934454-76-0). Lubrecht & Cramer.

ENTOMOLOGY, ECONOMIC

see Insects, Injurious and Beneficial

ENTOZOA

see Worms, Intestinal and Parasitic

ENVIRONMENT

see Ecology; Anthropo-Geography; Man–Influence on Nature

ENVIRONMENT AND STATE

see Environmental Policy

ENVIRONMENTAL, SPACE

see Space Environment

ENVIRONMENTAL CONTROL

see Environmental Engineering; Environmental Policy

ENVIRONMENTAL ENGINEERING

see also Environmental Health; Environmental Policy; Environmental Protection; Environmental Testing; Human Engineering; Lighting; Pollution; Sanitary Engineering

Milovanov, E. L. & Veistman, E. A., eds. English-Russian Dictionary of Environmental Control. 338p. (Eng. & Rus.). 1981. $29.50 (ISBN 0-08-023576-X). Pergamon.

Villate, Jose T. Dictionary of Environmental Engineering & Related Sciences. LC 78-67002. (Coleccion Diccionrios). Orig. Title: Diccionario De Ingenieria Ambiental y Ciencias Afines. 445p. (Eng. & Span.). 1979. $25.00 (ISBN 0-89729-209-X). Ediciones.

--Dictionary of Environmental Engineering & Related Sciences. LC 78-67002. xvi, 445p. (Span.). 1979. write for info. (ISBN 0-89729-209-X). Edns Universal.

ENVIRONMENTAL HEALTH

see also Environmental Engineering; Pollution; Public Health

European Parliament - Translation Division. Terminology of Environmental Hygiene, 2 vols. 148p. (Eng., Fr., Ital., Ger. & Dutch.). 1971-72. 5.00x ea (ISBN 0-8002-1350-5). Intl Pubns Serv.

Frick, G. William. Environmental Glossary. 2nd ed. LC 82-83908. 310p. 1982. text ed. 28.00 (ISBN 0-86587-096-9). Gov Insts.

ENVIRONMENTAL HEALTH ENGINEERING

see Sanitary Engineering

ENVIRONMENTAL MANAGEMENT

see Environmental Engineering; Environmental Policy

ENVIRONMENTAL POLICY

Frick, G. William. Environmental Glossary. 2nd ed. LC 82-83908. 310p. 1982. text ed. 28.00 (ISBN 0-86587-096-9). Gov Insts.

Landy, Marc, ed. Environmental Impact Statement Glossary: A Reference Source for EIS Writers, Reviewers & Citizens. LC 79-19586. 547p. 1979. 75.00x (ISBN 0-306-65185-8, IFI Plenum). Plenum Pub.

Tutzaver, Otto E. & Tutzaver, Ingrid M. Dictionary of environmental protection, 3 vols. LC 80-458477. (Eng., Fr., & Ger.). 1979. DM.70.00 (ISBN 3-452-18481-1). Heymanns Verlag.

ENVIRONMENTAL POLLUTION

see Pollution

ENVIRONMENTAL PROTECTION

see also Conservation of Natural Resources; Environmental Engineering; Environmental Policy

Ahlhaus, Otto E., et al. Tachenlexikon Umweltschultz. LC 80-470211. 288p. (Ger.). 1979. DM.10.00 (ISBN 3-590-14362-2). Pr Univ Fr.

Anglo-Russkii Slovar Po Okhrane Okruzhaiushchei Sredy. 368p. (Rus. & Eng.). 1980. $5.95 (Pub. by Russkii Iazyk). Four Continent.

Glossaire Europeen de Terminologie Juridique et Administrative: Environment Policy Protection & Management of the Environment, No. 29. 160p. (Ger. & Eng.). pap. $22.50 (ISBN 0-686-92511-4, M-9496). French & Eur.

Lindeke, Wolfgang. Dictionary of Ventilation & Health. 186p. 1980. $25.00x (ISBN 0-569-08522-5, Pub. by Collet's). State Mutual Bk.

Milovanov, E. L., et al. Anglo-russki i slovar po okhrane okruzha i ushche i sredy. LC 81-473924. 366p. (Eng. & Rus.). 1980. write for info. Russki Iazyk.

Wennrich, Peter. Anglo-American & German Abbreviations in Environmental Protection. 624p. (Eng. & Ger.). 1979. $60.00x (ISBN 0-89664-096-5, Pub. by K G Saur). Gale.

ENVIRONMENTAL TESTING

Institute of Environmental Science. Glossary of Computer Controlled Environmental Testing Terminology. 27p. non-member $3.00 (ISBN 0-915414-53-8); member $2.40; $2.00, for shipping & handling. Inst Environ Sci.

ENZYMES

Barrett, Alan & McDonald, J. Ken. Mammalian Proteases: a Glossary & Bibliography: Vol. 1: Endopeptidases. 1980. $32.00 (ISBN 0-12-079501-9). Acad Pr.

EPIGRAMS

see also Aphorisms and Apothegms; Maxims; Proverbs; Quotations

Beeching, Cyril L. A Dictionary of Eponyms. 1979. $13.00 (ISBN 0-85157-283-9, Pub. by Bingley England). Shoe String.

EPIGRAPHY

see Inscriptions

EPILEPSY

Gastaut, H. Dictionary of Epilepsy: Part I - Definitions. (Also avail. in French, Russian & Spanish). 1973. $8.00 (ISBN 92-4-154027-3). World Health.

--Dizionario dell'epilessia. De Fiore, E. & Vizioli, R., trs. 156p. (Ital.). 1976. L.6000.00. Il Pensiero.

--Woerterbuch der Epilepsie. (Ger.). 1975. pap. $22.50 (ISBN 3-7773-0380-1, M-7013). French & Eur.

EPITAPHS

Bourasse, J. J. Dictionnaire d'Epigraphie Chretienne, 2 vols. Migne, J. P., ed. (Nouvelle Encyclopedie Theologique Ser.: Vols. 30-31). 1262p. (Fr.). Repr. of 1852 ed. lib. bdg. $161.00x (ISBN 0-89241-273-9). Caratzas Pub Co.

EPITHETS

see also Names; Nicknames

Gorbachevich, S., et al. Slovar Epitetov Russkogo Literaturnogo Iazyka. 568p. (Rus.). 1979. $7.95 (Pub. by Nauka). Four Continent.

EQUILIBRIUM, THERMAL

see Heat; Thermodynamics

EQUIPMENT, INDUSTRIAL

see Industrial Equipment

EQUITORIAL GUINEA

Liniger-Goumaz, Max. Historical Dictionary of Equatorial Guinea. LC 79-15914. (African Historical Dictionaries Ser.: No. 21). 246p. 1979. $14.00 (ISBN 0-8108-1230-4). Scarecrow.

ERAS

see Chronology

ERGONOMICS

see Human Engineering

EROSION CONTROL

see Soil Conservation

EROTIC LITERATURE–DICTIONARIES

Guiraud, Pierre. Dictionnaire Historique, Stylistique, Rhetorique, Etomologique, de la Litterature Erotique. LC 377481. 639p. (Fr.). 1978. 90.00 F (ISBN 2-228-12040-5). Payot.

EROTICA

Breton, Andre. Lexico Sucinto del Erotismo. 110p. (Span.). 1974. pap. $6.75 (ISBN 84-339-0419-1, S-50153). French & Eur.

Le Pennec, Marie F. Petit Glossaire du Language Erotique aux XVIIe & XVIIIe Siecles. LC 79-379970. 110p. (Fr.). 1979. 35.00 F (ISBN 2-863-80004-3). Borderie.

ERRORS, LOGICAL
see Fallacies (Logic)

ERSE
see Gaelic Language; Irish Language

ESKIMO LANGUAGE
Dorais, Louis J. Lexique Analytique du Vocabulaire Inuit Moderne au Quebec-Labrador. LC 79-363935. 136p. (Fr. & Inupiaq.). 1978. Can.$9.00 (ISBN 0-7746-6850-4, Dist. by Four Continent Bk). Univ Laval.
English-Eskimo, Eskimo-English Dictionary. (Eng. & Eskimo.). $22.50 (ISBN 0-87559-061-6); thumb indexed $27.50 (ISBN 0-87559-062-4). Shalom.
Ray, P. N. & Murdoch, John. Vocabulary of the Eskimos of Point Barrow & Cape Smyth. facs. ed. 13p. Repr. of 1885 ed. pap. $2.95 (ISBN 0-8466-0093-5, S93). Shorey.
Schneider, Lucien. Dictionnaire Esquimau-Francais du Parler de l'Ungava & Contrees Limitrophes. 2nd ed. 446p. (Fr.). 1970. Can.$15.00. Laval P. U.
--Dictionnaire Francais-Esquimau du Parier: l'Ungava & Contrees Limitrophes, 2. 430p. (Fr. & Eskimo.). 1970. Can.$15.00. Laval P. U.
Thibert, A. Eskimo-English, English-Eskimo Dictionary. rev. ed. (Eskimo & Eng.). pap. 12.50 (ISBN 0-685-12011-2). Heinman.
Webster, Donald H. & Zibell, Wilfried. Inupiat Eskimo Dictionary. LC 76-632478. Orig. Title: Inupiat Dialect of Eskimo. (Illus.). 212p. (Eng. & Eskimo.). 1970. pap. $2.20 (ISBN 0-88312-377-0); microfiche $3.00. Summer Inst Ling.
Wells, Roger & Kelley, John W., eds. English-Eskimo & Eskimo-English Vocabularies. LC 74-5889. (Eng. & Eskimo.). Repr. of 1890 ed. $11.50 (ISBN 0-404-11698-1). AMS Pr.
Wells, Roger, Jr., compiled by. English-Eskimo & Eskimo-English Vocabularies. Kelly, John W., tr. LC 82-51153. 72p. (Inupiaq & Eng.). 1982. pap. $6.95 (ISBN 0-8048-1403-1). C E Tuttle.

ESKIMOS
Schneider, Lucien. Dictionnaire des Infixes de l'esquimau de l'Ungava. 144p. (Fr.). 1972. Can.$2.00. Quebec Off.

ESP
see Psychical Research

ESPERANTO (ARTIFICIAL LANGUAGE)
Butler, Montagu C. Esperanto-English Dictionary. (Esperanto & Eng.). 1967. $8.95x (ISBN 0-685-71601-5, 1065). Esperanto League North Am.
Diccionario Lexicon Esperanto-Espanol, Espanol-Esperanto. 400p. (Esperanto & Span.). leatherette $4.95 (ISBN 84-303-0148-8, S-50403); pap. $4.50 (ISBN 84-303-0147-X, S-50402). French & Eur.
Duc-Goninaz, Michel. Vocabulaire Esperanto. 108p. (Fr. & Esperanto.). 1971. 13.30 F. Ophrys.
Haferkorn, R. Technisches Woerterbuch Deutsch-Esperanto. (Ger. & Esperanto.). 1967. Can.$1.80 (ISBN 0-919186-01-7). U of Toronto Pr.
Learn Esperanto for English Speakers. (Esperanto & Eng.). pap. $9.50 (ISBN 0-87557-019-4, 019-4). Saphrograph.
Leger, Albault A. Dictionnaire Francais-Esperanto. 736p. (Fr. & Esperanto.). 1961. 21.00 F. Esperanto.
Millidge, Edward A. Esperanto-English Dictionary. (Esperanto & Eng.). $24.50 (ISBN 0-87557-018-6, 018-6). Saphrograph.
Wells, J. C. Esperanto Dictionary. (Teach Yourself Ser.). (Esperanto.). 1974. pap. 6.95 (ISBN 0-679-10205-1). McKay.

ESPIONAGE
Pastor Petit, Domingo. Diccionario del espionaje. (Span.). 100.00 ptas. Plaza Janes.

ESTHETICS
see also Art; Color; Criticism; Expressionism (Art); Impressionism (Art); Sculpture; Surrealism
Giraldi, Giovanni. Dizionario di estetica & di linguistica generale. LC 76-503182. (Illus.). 946p. (Ital.). 1975. L.25000.00. Pergamena.
Jouve, E. G. Dictionnaire d'Esthetique Chretienne ou Theorie du Beau dans l'Art Chretien. Migne, J. P., ed. (Troisieme et Derniere Encyclopedie Theologique Ser.: Vol. 17). 646p. (Fr.). Repr. of 1856 ed. lib. bdg. $82.50x (ISBN 0-89241-300-X). Caratzas Pub Co.

ESTIMATES
see subdivision Estimates and Estimates and Costs under technical subjects, e.g. Building–Estimates; Engineering–Estimates and Costs

ESTONIAN LANGUAGE
Arumaa, P., et al. Russko-Estonskii Slovar, 2 vols. (Rus. & Estonian.). 1975. $14.95 set (Pub. by Valgus). Four Continent.
Mukhel, V. Kratkii Estonsko-Russkii Slovar. 681p. (Rus. & Estonian.). 1973. $2.75 (Pub. by Tallinn). Four Continent.
--Russko-Estonskii Slovar. 708p. (Rus. & Estonian.). 1955. $3.30 (Pub. by Estonsk. Gos. Izd.). Four Continent.
Rauk, M. English-Estonian Dictionary for Schools. 444p. (Eng. & Estonian.). 1977. $3.95 (Pub. by Valgus). Four Continent.
Reitsak, A. Russko-Estonskii Razgovornik. 256p. (Rus. & Estonian.). 1976. $1.00 (Pub. by Valgus). Four Continent.
Saagpakk, Paul F. Estonian-English Dictionary. LC 81-43606. (Yale Linguistic Ser.). 1216p. (Estonian & Eng.). 1982. $150.00x (ISBN 0-300-02849-0). Yale U Pr.
Silvert, J. Estonian-English Dictionary. (Estonian & Eng.). $35.00 (ISBN 0-87559-009-8); thumb indexed $40.00 (ISBN 0-87559-186-8). Shalom.
Tamm, J. Estonsko-Russkii Slovar. 757p. (Estonian & Rus.). 1977. $8.50 (Pub. by Valgus). Four Continent.
Wieselgren, Per. Svensk-Estnisk Ordbok. LC 77-458507. xxx, 630p. (Swedish & Estonian.). 1976. Kr.170.00. Fyris.

ETERNAL PUNISHMENT
see Hell

ETHICAL THEOLOGY
see Christian Ethics

ETHICS–DICTIONARIES
Hartman, Robert S. Terminos Fundamentales en Etica. 43p. (Span.). 1972. write for info. Univ Aut Nuevo.
Heymer, Armin. Vocabulaire Ethologique: Allemand-Anglais-Francais. (Illus.). 237p. (Ger., Eng. & Fr.). 1977. 92.00 F. PUF.
Hoffe, Otfried. Lexikon der Ethik. LC 77-566300. 287p. (Ger.). 1977. DM.14.80 (ISBN 3-406-06752-2). Beck Verlag.
Mathews, Shailer & Smith, Gerald B., eds. Dictionary of Religion & Ethics. LC 70-145713. 1971. Repr. of 1921 ed. $45.00x (ISBN 0-8103-3196-9). Gale.
Slovar Po Etike. 392p. (Rus.). 1975. $2.90 (Pub. by Politizdat). Four Continent.

ETHICS, CHRISTIAN
see Christian Ethics

ETHICS, MEDICAL
see Medical Ethics

ETHICS, SOCIAL
see Social Ethics

ETHIOPIA–HISTORY
Prouty, Chris & Rosenfeld, Eugene. Historical Dictionary of Ethiopia. LC 81-8729. (African Historical Dictionaries Ser.: No. 32). 454p. 1981. $25.00 (ISBN 0-8108-1448-X). Scarecrow.

ETHNOLOGY–DICTIONARIES
Bell, Francis L. Tanga-English, English-Tanga Dictionary. LC 78-311012. xxx, 156p. (Tanga & Eng.). 1977. Aus.$3.00. Univ Syd Aust Lang.
Calamegriaule, Genevieve. Dictionnaire Dogon: Ethnologique & Linguistique. 296p. (Fr.). 1968. 45.00 F. S. E. L. A. F.
Folkman, D. & Folkman, E. Dictionary of Races or Peoples. 75.00 (ISBN 0-8490-0045-9). Gordon Pr.
Heymer, A. Ethnologisches Woerterbuch. 256p. (Ger., Eng. & Fr., Ethnological Dictionary). 1977. 22.50 (ISBN 3-489-66366-7, M-7367, Pub. by P. Parey). French & Eur.
--Ethnologisches Woerterbuch. 256p. (Ger., Eng. & Fr.). 1977. DM.22.50 (ISBN 3-489-66366-7). Parey.
Heymer, Armin. Vocabulaire Ethnologique. 237p. (Ger., Eng. & Fr.). 1977. $37.50 (ISBN 0-686-57329-3, M-6317). French & Eur.
Hirschberg, Walter. Woerterbuch der Voelkerkunde. (Ger.). 1965. $17.50 (ISBN 3-520-20501-7, M-6945). French & Eur.
Migne, J. P., ed. Dictionnaire d'Ethnographie. (Nouvelle Encyclopedie Theologique Ser.: Vol. 37). 964p. (Fr.). Repr. of 1853 ed. lib. bdg. $121.50x (ISBN 0-686-82875-5). Caratzas Pub Co.
Ortutay, Gyula, ed. Magyar Neprajzi Lexikon. LC 77-569808. (Illus., Hungarian.). 1977. 187.00 Ft (ISBN 9-630-51285-8). Akademiai Kiado.
Panoff & Perrin. Dizionario di etnologia. (Ital.). L.2800.00. Newton-Compton.
Panoff, Michel & Perrin, Michel. Dictionnaire de l'ethnologie. 224p. (Fr.). 1973. 20.00 F. Payot.
Schoenfeld, M. Woerterbuch der Altgermanischen Personen und Voelkernamen. 2nd ed. 309p. (Ger.). 1965. $32.00 (ISBN 3-533-00512-7, M-7045). French & Eur.
Vulcanescu, Romulus. Dictionar de Etnologie. LC 80-475520. 436p. (Romanian.). 1979. 19.50 lei. Albatros.
Vuorela, Toivo. Kansanperinteen Sanakirja. LC 79-373974. (Illus.). 542p. (Finnish.). write for info. (ISBN 9-510-08803-X). Soderstrom.

ETHNOLOGY–AFRICA
Novelli, Tina. Dizionario Etnologico Africano, 3 vols. LC 76-463596. (Illus., Ital.). L.9000.00. Jaca Bk.
--Etnologico africano, 3 vols. (Ital.). 1976. L.9000.00. Jaca Bk.

ETHNOLOGY–EGYPT
Klunzinger, Karl B. Upper Egypt: Its People & Its Products. LC 76-44747. Repr. of 1878 ed. $31.50 (ISBN 0-404-15866-8). AMS Pr.

ETHNOLOGY–NEAR EAST
Lewin, Bernhard. A Vocabulary of the Hudailian Poems. (Acta Regiae Societatis Scientarum et Litterarum Goteborg, Humaniora: No. 13). 1978. pap. text ed. 28.00x (ISBN 91-85252-16-6). Humanities.

ETHOLOGY
see Character; Human Behavior

ETHOLOGY (ZOOLOGY)
see Animals, Habits and Behavior of

ETIQUETTE
see also Courtesy; Etiquette for Children and Youth; Manners and Customs
also subdivision; social life and custom under names of countries
Ganning, London. A Dictionary of Bad Manners. 1982. 14.95 (ISBN 0-395-32509-9). HM.
Mazzucato, Fluffy M. Dizionario delle buone maniere. (Illus.). 304p. (Ital.). L.5000.00; L.pap. 2500.00. Bietti.
Torres Calvo, Angel. Diccionario de textos sociales pontificios. (Span.). 600.00 ptas. Bibliografica.

ETIQUETTE–JUVENILE LITERATURE
see Etiquette for Children and Youth

ETIQUETTE FOR CHILDREN AND YOUTH
Barnhart, Clarence L., ed. Scott, Foresman Beginning Dictionary. (Illus.). $15.95 (ISBN 0-385-13330-8). Doubleday.

ETYMOLOGY
see Language and Languages–Etymology;
also subdivisions Etymology and Semantics under particular languages or groups of languages
Tischler, Johann. Hethitisches Etymologisches Glossar. Neumann, Guenther, ed. LC 79-384968. (Fr.). 1977. S.240.00 (ISBN 3-851-24537-7). Inst Verg Sprach.

EUPHEMISM
Rawson, Hugh. A Dictionary of Euphemisms & Other Double Talk. 320p. 1981. $15.95 (ISBN 0-517-54518-7). Crown.

EUROPE
see also European Economic Community
also names of countries, cities and geographic areas in Europe
Busturia, Daniel. Diccionario terminoligico de la Comunidades Europeas. 680p. (Span.). 1982. 3200.00 ptas (ISBN 84-7019-084-9). Assn Prog Direc.
Paxton, ed. Dictionary of the European Community. (Eng.). Epap. 4.95. Macmillan.
Paxton, John. A Dictionary of the European Communities. 2nd ed. 288p. (Eng.). 1982. E20.00 (ISBN 0-333-33438-8). Macmillan LOndon.

EUROPE–HISTORY
Here are entered general works on European history. For works covering shorter periods of time see chronological subdivisions below.
Berenger, Jean. Lexique Historique de l'Europa Danublenne, XVIe.-XXe. Siecle. (Illus.). 256p. (Fr.). 1976. 26.00 F. Colin.
Glossar zur Fruehmittelalterlichen Geschichte im Oestlichen Europa: Lfg 2, Quellensiglenverzeichnis, Aba-Alania. 64p. (Ger.). 1974. DM.32.00 (ISBN 3-515-01786-0). Buch Vertrieb.
Glossar zur Fruehmittelalterlichen Geschichte im Oestlichen Europa: Lfg 3, Alanorum Montes-Antes. 64p. (Ger.). 1974. DM.32.00 (ISBN 3-515-01950-2). Buch Vertrieb.
Glossar zur Fruehmittelalterlichen Geschichte im Oestlichen Europa: Lfg 5, Atto-Avari. 64p. (Ger.). 1975. DM.32.00 (ISBN 3-515-02026-8). Buch Vertrieb.
Glossar zur Fruehmittelalterlichen Geschichte im Oestlichen Europa: Lfg 6, Avari (Arabes)-Baioaria. 64p. (Ger.). 1976. DM.32.00 (ISBN 3-515-02346-1). Buch Vertrieb.
Glossar zur Fruehmittelalterlichen Geschichte im Oestlichen Europa: Lfg 1, Einleitung, Abkuerzungen & Literatursiglenverzeichnis. 64p. (Ger.). 1974. DM.32.00 (ISBN 3-515-01982-0). Buch Vertrieb.
Miroglio, Abel & Miroglio, Yvonne D. L'Europe & ses population. LC 78-777166. 828p. (Fr.). 1978. write for info. (ISBN 9-02472-082-6). Nyhoff.
Otto, Norbert & Wojtecki, Dieter. Glossar zur Fruehmittelalterlichen Geschichte im Oestlichen Europa. 64p. (Ger.). 1975. DM.32.00 (ISBN 3-515-01977-4). Buch Vertrieb.
--Glossar zur Fruehmittelalterlichen Geschichte im Oestlichen Europa: Lfg 7, Baioariae Marcha-Behin Redaktion. 64p. (Ger.). 1976. DM.32.00 (ISBN 3-515-02479-4). Buch Vertrieb.
Williams, E. N. Facts on File Dictionary of European History: 1485-1789. 1980. lib. bdg. $22.50 (ISBN 0-87196-327-2). Facts on File.
--The Penguin Dictionary of English & European History 1485-1789. (Reference Ser.). 480p. 1980. pap. 6.95 (ISBN 0-14-051084-2). Penguin.

EUROPE, EASTERN–POLITICS AND GOVERNMENT
McCrea, Barbara P. & Plano, Jack C. The Soviet & East European Political Dictionary. (Clio Dictionaries in Political Science Ser.: No. 4). 350p. (gr. 10-12). 1983. lib. bdg. $20.75 (ISBN 0-87436-333-0); pap. $10.75 (ISBN 0-87436-347-0). ABC-Clio.

EUROPEAN ART
see Art, European

EUROPEAN COMMON MARKET (1955-)
see European Economic Community
EUROPEAN ECONOMIC COMMUNITY
Dictionnaire du Marche Commun. (Fr.). 1978. write for info. Joly.
Parker, G. & Parker, B., eds. Dictionary of the European Communities. (Eng.). Epap. 3.95. Butterworth.
Paxton, John. A Dictionary of the European Communities. 2nd ed. LC 82-10375. 290p. 1983. $27.50x (ISBN 0-312-20099-4). St Martin.
Paxton, John, ed. A Dictionary of the European Economic Community. LC 77-3595. 304p. 1977. lib. bdg. $20.00x (ISBN 0-87196-370-1). Facts on File.
EUROPEAN ECONOMIC ORGANIZATION
Dictionnaire du Marche Commun, 4 vols. (Fr.). 1978. Set. $250.00 (ISBN 0-686-56746-3, M-6135). French & Eur.
EUROPEAN PORCELAIN
see Porcelain
EUROPEAN WAR, 1914-1918-LANGUAGE (NEW WORDS, SLANG, ETC.)
Fraser, Edward & Gibbons, John. Soldier & Sailor Words & Phrases. LC 68-30635. 1968. Repr. of 1925 ed. $40.00x (ISBN 0-8103-3281-7). Gale.
EUROPEAN WAR, 1939-1945
see World War, 1939-1945
EUSKARA LANGUAGE
see Basque Language
EVALUATION OF LITERATURE
see Criticism; Literature-History and Criticism
EVANGELICAL RELIGION
see Evangelicalism
EVANGELICALISM
Kunst, H. Evangelisches Staatslexikon. 2nd, rev. ed. (Ger.). 1975. DM.125.00 (ISBN 3-7831-0463-7). Kreuz.
EVERLASTING PUNISHMENT
see Hell
EVIDENCES, CHRISTIAN
see Apologetics
EVIDENCES OF CHRISTIANITY
see Apologetics
EVOLUTION
see also Embryology; Origin of Species
Lincoln, R. J. & Boxshall, G. A. A Dictionary of Ecology, Evolution & Systematics. LC 81-18013. 350p. 1982. $47.50 (ISBN 0-521-23957-5). Cambridge U Pr.
EXAMINATIONS, MEDICAL
see Diagnosis
EXCEPTIONAL CHILDREN
Reinartz, Erika & Masendorf, Friedrich. Kleines Woerterbuch der Sonderpaedagogik: Englisch-Deutsche. LC 76-454597. 177p. (Eng. & Ger.). 1975. DM.12.80 (ISBN 3-786-43456-5). Marhold.
EXCHANGES, STOCK
see Stock-Exchange
EXERCISE THERAPY
Passebecq, Andre. L'argile pour votre Sante. LC 80-471204. 129p. (Fr.). 1978. 27.00 F (ISBN 2-7033-0192-8). Dangles.
EXISTENTIALISM
Nauman, St. Elmo, Jr. The New Dictionary of Existentialism. 1972. pap. $2.95 (ISBN 0-8065-0281-9). Citadel Pr.
EXPERIMENTAL ANIMALS
see Laboratory Animals
EXPLORATION OF THE DEEP SEA
see Marine Biology; Marine Fauna
EXPLOSIVES
Meyer, Rudolph. Explosives. 2nd ed. (Illus.). 440p. 1981. $60.00x (ISBN 3-527-25933-3). Verlag Chemie.
EXPORTS
see Commerce; Tariff
EXPRESSIONISM
see also Surrealism
Perez Rioja, J. A. Diccionario de simbolos y mitos: Las ciencias y las artes en su expresion figurada. 2nd ed. (Illus.). 434p. (Span.). 320.00 ptas. Tecnos SA.
EXPRESSIONISM (ART)
Muller, Joseph-Emile. Illustrated Dictionary of Expressionism. LC 78-50723. (Pocket Art Ser.). (Illus.). (gr. 10-12). 1978. pap. $3.95 (ISBN 0-8120-0985-1). Barron.

EXTRATERRESTRIAL ENVIRONMENT
see Space Environment
EYE
see also Vision
Cassin, Barbara & Solomon, Sheila. Dictionary of Eye Terminology. (Illus., Orig.). 1983. $14.95 (ISBN 0-937404-07-1). Triad Pub FL.
EYE-DISEASES AND DEFECTS
see also Ophthalmology
Marsico, Vincenzo. Dizionario delle malattie, sindromi e sintori oculari. 158p. (Ital.). 1968. L.7000.00. Minerva Medica.

F

FABRICS
see Textile Fabrics
FACETIAE
see Wit and Humor;
see American Wit and Humor, English Wit and Humor, and similar headings subdivided by subject, e.g. American Wit and Humor-Sports
FACTOR TABLES
Costa, Vasco & Frances, Osvaldo. Diccionario de unidades y tablas de conversion. 2nd ed. 168p. (Span.). write for info. G Gili.
FACTORIES
Slovar Terminov PoElektroprovodu & Avtomatizatsii Promyshlennykh Ustanovo. 154p. (Rus. & Eng. & Azerbaidian.). 1966. $2.70 (Pub. by Izd. An Az. SSR). Four Continent.
FACTORY BUILDINGS
see Factories
FACULTY (EDUCATION)
see College Teachers; Teachers
FAITH
see also Atheism; Faith and Reason
Dizionario dei temi della fede. 511p. (Ital.). 1977. L.7000.00. SEI.
FAITH AND REASON
see also Philosophy and Religion
LeNoir, C. P. Dictionnaire des Droits et de la Raison. Migne, J. P., ed. (Troisieme et Derniere Encyclopedie Theologique Ser.: Vol. 57). 952p. (Fr.). Repr. of 1860 ed. lib. bdg. $120.00x (ISBN 0-89241-323-9). Caratzas Pub Co.
--Dictionnaire des Harmonies de la Raison et de la Foi. Migne, J. P., ed. (Troisieme et Derniere Encyclopedie Theologique Ser.: Vol. 19). 876p. (Fr.). Repr. of 1856 ed. lib. bdg. $110.50x (ISBN 0-89241-302-6). Caratzas Pub Co.
FALLACIES (LOGIC)
Jouffroy, A. Dictionnaire des Erreurs Sociales. Migne, J. P., ed. (Nouvelle Encyclopedie Theologique Ser.: Vol. 19). 664p. (Fr.). Repr. of 1852 ed. lib. bdg. $84.50x (ISBN 0-89241-266-6). Caratzas Pub Co.
FALLIBILITY
D'lachkov, A. I., et al, eds. Kratkii Defektologicheskii Slovar. 398p. (Rus.). 1964. $3.50 (Pub. by Prosveschchenie). Four Continent.
FAMILY
see also Children; Domestic Relations; Fathers; Marriage; Mothers
Zanzucchi, Anne M. Family Portrait, from a Mother's Diary. Szczesniak, Lenny, tr. from It. LC 81-80031. Orig. Title: Giorno per Giorno. 100p. 1981. pap. 2.95 (ISBN 0-911782-19-2). New City.
FAMILY-LAW
see Domestic Relations
FAMILY COURTS
see Juvenile Courts
FAMILY GROUP THERAPY
see Family Psychotherapy
FAMILY HISTORIES
see subdivision genealogy under countries, e.g., United States-Genealogy; and individual families, e.g. Lee Family
FAMILY LAW
see Domestic Relations

FAMILY MEDICINE
International Planned Parenthood Federation. ed. Defining Family Health Needs, Standards of Care & Priorities: With Particular Reference to Family Planning. (Occasional Essay Ser.: No. 4). 1977. $10.00x (ISBN 0-686-87089-1, Pub. by Intl Planned Parent). State Mutual Bk.
FAMILY PLANNING
see Birth Control
FAMILY PRACTICE (MEDICINE)
see Family Medicine
FAMILY PSYCHOTHERAPY
Pinney, Edward L., Jr. & Slipp, Samuel. Glossary of Group & Family Therapy. LC 82-4193. 120p. 1982. $15.00 (ISBN 0-87630-300-9). Brunner-Mazel.
FAMILY THERAPY
see Family Psychotherapy
FANCY DRESS
see Costume
FANTASY
Bernard, Jean-Louis. Dictionnaire de l'insolite & du Fantastique. 356p. (Fr.). 1974. 30.00 F. Dauphin.
FAO
see Food and Agriculture Organization of the United Nations
FARE, BILLS OF
see Menus
FARM CROPS
see Field Crops
FARM LIFE CLUBS
see Agricultural Societies
FARM MECHANICS
see Agricultural Engineering
FARMERS' ORGANIZATIONS
see Agricultural Societies
FARMING
see Agriculture
FARRIERY
see Horses; Veterinary Medicine
FASCISM-ITALY
Cannistraro, Philip V., ed. Historical Dictionary of Fascist Italy. LC 81-4493. (Illus.). xxix, 657p. 1982. lib. bdg. $49.95 (ISBN 0-313-21317-8, CFA/). Greenwood.
FASHION
see also Costume; Costume Design; Dressmaking
Calasibetta, Charlotte M. Fairchild's Dictionary of Fashion. Davis, Lorraine & Goble, Ermina S., eds. LC 74-84805. (Illus.). 700p. 1975. $50.00 (ISBN 0-87005-133-4). Fairchild.
Fashion Vocabulary & Dictation. 1969. pap. $10.95 (ISBN 0-672-96058-3). Bobbs.
Gioello & Berke. Fashion Production Terms. LC 78-62289. (The Languages of Fashion Ser.). (Illus.). 1979. lib. bdg. $25.00 (ISBN 0-87005-200-4). Fairchild.
FASHION DESIGN
see Costume Design
FAT
Here is entered material on fat in its relation to the animal organism. Works on the technological aspects of fats in general are entered under the heading Oils and Fats.
Kraus, Barbara. The Dictionary of Sodium, Fats, & Cholesterol. (Illus.). 384p. Date not set. pap. 6.95 (ISBN 0-399-50945-3, Perigee). Putnam Pub Group.
FATHERS
Cloutier, Francois. Dictionnaire des Parents. 250p. (Fr.). 1969. 3.00 F. Edns Du Jour.
FATS
see Fat
FAULKNER, WILLIAM, 1897-1962-DICTIONARIES, INDEXES, ETC.
Brown, Calvin S. A Glossary of Faulkner's South. LC 75-43308. (Illus.). 1976. $24.00x (ISBN 0-300-01944-0); pap. $6.95x (ISBN 0-300-02240-9). Yale U Pr.
Runyon, Harry. Faulkner Glossary. 1966. pap. $2.25 (ISBN 0-8065-0152-9, 228). Citadel Pr.
FAUNA
see Animals; Fresh-Water Biology
FAUNA, PREHISTORIC
see Paleontology
FEE SYSTEM (TAXATION)
see Taxation
FEEBLE MINDED
see Mental Deficiency
FEEDING
see Animal Nutrition

FEEDING BEHAVIOR
see Animals, Food Habits of
FEELINGS
see Emotions
FELONY
see Criminal Law
FELT WORK
Dryer Felt Terminology. 1966. $4.00 (014-14); members $2.67. TAPPI.
FELTWORK
see Felt Work
FEMALE
see Women
FEMINISM
see also Women-Social Conditions
Sau Sanchez, Victoria. Un Diccionario ideóligico feminista. 280p. (Span.). 1981. pap. 580.00 ptas (ISBN 84-7426-072-8). Icaria Edit.
--Un Diccionario Ideologico Feminista. 280p. (Span.). 580.00 ptas (ISBN 8-47426-072-8). Icaria Edit.
FERMENTS
see Enzymes
FERNS
Olson, Wilson W. The Fern Dictionary. $4.70. LA Intl Fern.
FERROUS METAL INDUSTRIES
see Iron Industry and Trade
FEUDAL CASTLES
see Castles
FIAT MONEY
see Paper Money
FIBER OPTICS
Bodson, Dennis, ed. & frwd. by. Fiberoptics & Lightwave Communications Vocabulary. LC 80-26168. 156p. (Orig.). 1983. pap. text ed. 12.95 (ISBN 0-07-606706-8, R-030). McGraw.
Glossary of Fiber Optics Terms. (Eng. , Fr , Span. & Ger.). $35.00 (ISBN 0-686-32959-7). Info Gatekeepers.
Weik, Martin H. Fiber Optics & Lightwave Communications Standard Dictionary. 320p. 1980. text ed. $18.50 (ISBN 0-442-25658-2). Van Nos Reinhold.
FICTITIOUS ANIMALS
see Animals, Mythical
FICTITIOUS NAMES
see Anonyms and Pseudonyms
FIELD ATHLETICS
see Track-Athletics
FIELD CROPS
see also Grain; Horticulture
also names of specific crops, e.g. Cotton, Hay
Lexikon der Neuzeittlichen Landwirtschaft: Bd 2, Ackerbau, Pflanzenbau, Gruenlandwirtschaft. 252p. (Ger.). 1974. DM.29.00 (ISBN 3-7736-8004-X). Girardet.
FIELD OF VISION, MEASUREMENT OF
see Perimetry
FIELD SPORTS
see Sports
FIFTH COLUMN
see Subversive Activities
FIGHTING
see Battles; Karate; Military Art and Science; Naval Art and Science
FIGHTING, HAND-TO-HAND
see Hand-To-Hand Fighting
FIGURES OF SPEECH
see also particular figures of speech, e.g. Metaphor, Simile
De Dony, Ivon P. Lexico de lenguaje figurado. 2nd ed. 262p. (Span.). 1951. $15.00. Club de Lectores.
Lanham, Richard A. A Handlist of Rhetorical Terms: A Guide for Students of English Literature. LC 68-31636. 1968. pap. $5.95x (ISBN 0-520-01414-6). U of Cal Pr.
FIJIAN LANGUAGE
see also Melanesian Languages
Hazlewood, David. A Fijian & English & an English & Fijian Dictionary. 2nd ed. LC 75-35119. (Eng. & Fijian). Repr. of 1872 ed. $28.00 (ISBN 0-404-14136-6). AMS Pr.
FILICINEAE
see Ferns
FILM, TELEVISION
see Television Film
FILMS
see Moving-Pictures

FINANCE
see also Banks and Banking; Commerce; Credit; Finance, Public; Insurance; International Finance; Investments; Money; Saving and Investment; Speculation; Stock-Exchange
also subdivision Finance under special subjects, e.g. Corporations–Finance; Railroads–Finance
Bernard, Yves & Colli, Jean-Claude. Vocabulaire Economique & Financier. 384p. (Fr.). 1976. 17.00 F. Seuil.
Mancera. Terminologia del Contador. 7th ed. 401p. (Span.). Mex.$50.00. Banca Comercio.
Vocabulaire des Finances Locales. 78p. (Fr.). 1973. 16.05 F. C. N. I. P. E.

FINANCE–DICTIONARIES
Abdeen, Adnan. A Dictionary of Accounting & Finance. (Arabic & Eng.). 1980. $30.00 (275-1). Intl Bk Ctr.
--English-Arabic Dictionary of Accounting & Finance. 1981. $30.00x (ISBN 0-86685-275-1). Intl Bk Ctr.
Assiouly, E. Banking & Financial Dictionary: English-French-Arabic. 338p. (Eng., Fr. & Arabic.). 1980. pap. $75.00 (ISBN 0-686-92351-0, M-9767). French & Eur.
Bellisco Hernandez, Manuel. Diccionario de Banca y Bolsa, Tomo I: Ingles-Espanol. 170p. (Eng. & Span.). 1977. pap. $15.75 (ISBN 84-85198-02-6, S-50120). French & Eur.
Beltran. Diccionario de banca y bolsa. (Span.). write for info. Labor.
Bernard, Yves & Colli, Jean-Claude. Vocabulaire Economique et Financier: Coll. Points Economie. 384p. (Fr.). 1976. pap. $10.95 (ISBN 0-686-56915-6, M-6031). French & Eur.
Bernard, Yves & Suarez Campos, Jose M. Vocabulario Economico & Financiero. 488p. (Span.). 1981. 1300.00 ptas (ISBN 84-7019-077-6). Assn Prog Direc.
Bernard, Yves, et al. Dictionnaire Economique et Financier. Lewandowski, Dominique, ed. 1200p. (Fr.). 1975. $119.95 (ISBN 0-686-57297-1, M-4643). French & Eur.
--Dictionnaire Economique & Financier. 1200p. (Eng., Fr. & Ger.). 1975. 250.00 F. Seuil.
Birkhauser-Boston Publishing. The Herbst-Readett Three-Language Dictionaries of Commerce, Finance & Law, 3 Vols. (Eng., Ger. & Fr.). 1983. Vol. 1 1979 English-German-French. $98.95 (ISBN 0-686-87520-6); Vol. 2 1982 German-English-French. $98.95 (ISBN 0-686-87521-4); Vol. 3 1983 French-English-German. $98.95 (ISBN 0-686-87522-2). Birkhauser.
Blanes Prieto, Joaquin. Diccionario de Terminos Contables. 2nd ed. 388p. (Eng. & Span.). 1972. pap. $21.95 (ISBN 0-686-57342-0, S-28549). French & Eur.
Brownstone, David M., et al. The VNR Dictionary of Business & Finance. 320p. 1980. text ed. $18.95 (ISBN 0-442-20949-5). Van Nos Reinhold.
Bueschgen, Hans E., ed. Handwoerterbuch der Finanzwirtschaft. LC 77-460396. (Illus., Ger.). 1976. DM.220.00 (ISBN 3-791-08010-5). Poeschel.
Clark, Donald T. & Gottfried, Bert A., eds. University Dictionary of Business & Finance. (Apollo Eds.). 1972. pap. $4.95i (ISBN 0-8152-0143-5, A143). T Y Crowell.
Davids, Lewis E. Dictionary of Banking & Finance. (Littlefield, Adams Quality Paperback: No. 336). 1979. pap. $7.95 (ISBN 0-8226-0336-5). Littlefield.
--Dictionary of Banking & Finance. 229p. 1980. Repr. of 1978 ed. $15.00x (ISBN 0-8476-6132-6). Rowman.
Diccionario Bursatil. 195p. (Span.). 1977. pap. $17.50 (ISBN 84-85307-01-1, S-50126). French & Eur.
Dictionnaire Economique & Financier. 248p. (Fr.). 1972. 4.00 F. Homme.
Ewald, Peter K. Encyclopedia of Finance & Investment Terms. 1983. pap. price not set (ISBN 0-8120-2522-9). Barron.
Finansovo-Kreditynyi Slovar, 2 vols. (Rus.). 1964. $10.00 set (Pub. by Finansy). Four Continent.
Freshman, Samuel K. Real Estate Finance & Syndication Glossary. 3rd., rev. ed. LC 79-2801. 109p. 1979. 5.95 (ISBN 0-9600708-3-4). Law & Cap Dynamics.
Garmendia Miangolarra, J. Ignacio de. Diccionario De Bolsa. 208p. (Span.). 1977. leatherette $14.95 (ISBN 84-368-0057-5, S-50182). French & Eur.
Garza Bores, Jaime. Diccionario tecnico de terminologia comercial, contable y bancaria: Espanol-Ingles, Ingles-Espanol. (Span. & Eng.). $1.60; Mex.$20.00. Diana.
Ghattas, Nabih. Dictionary of Economic Business & Finance. 977p. (Eng. & Arabic., With Arabic glossary). $25.00 (271-9). Intl Bk Ctr.
--Dictionary of Economics, Business & Finance: English-Arabic with Arabic Glossary. (Eng. & Arabic.). $25.00x (ISBN 0-86685-169-0). Intl Bk Ctr.
Glossaire de la Finance. 284p. (Fr. & Eng.). 1976. $22.50 (ISBN 0-686-57009-X, M-6350). French & Eur.
Gunston, C. A. Deutsch-Englishes Glossarium. 1292p. (Ger. & Eng., German-English Glossary of Financial and Economic Terms). 1977. $69.50 (ISBN 3-7819-2014-3, 7328, Pub. by Fritz Knapp Verlag). French & Eur.
Herbst, Robert. Dictionary of Commerce, Finance & Law. (Eng. & Ger.). 1975. $92.00 (ISBN 3-85942-003-8, M-7118). French & Eur.
--Woerterbuch der Handels, Finanz und Rechtssprache. 2nd ed. (Ger., Eng. & Fr., Dictionary of Commercial, Fininancial & Legal Terms). 1975. $92.00 (ISBN 3-85942-001-1, M-7002). French & Eur.
Herbst, Robert & Readett, Alan G. The Herbst Dictionaries of Commercial, Financial & Legal Terms: English-German. (The Two-Language Ser.: Vol. A). 688p. (Eng. & Ger.). 1975. text ed. $69.95 (ISBN 0-686-92254-9). Birkhauser.
--The Herbst Dictionaries of Commercial, Financial & Legal Terms Vol. I. (The Herbst Dictionaries; 3-Language Ser.). 1138p. (Eng., Ger. & Fr.). 1979. text ed. $98.95 (ISBN 3-85942-000-3). Birkhauser.
Herbst, Robert & Readett, Alan G., eds. The Herbst Dictionaries of Commercial, Financial & Legal Terms: Deutsch-Englisch. (The Two-Language Ser.: Vol. B). 906p. (Ger. & Eng.). 1976. text ed. $69.95x (ISBN 0-686-92258-1). Birkhauser.
--The Herbst Dictionaries of Commercial, Financial & Legal Terms Vol. 2. (The Herbst Dictioaries; 3-Language Ser.). 1106p. (Ger., Eng. & Fr.). 1979. text ed. $98.95 (ISBN 3-85942-006-2). Birkhauser.
--Herbst Dictionary of Commercial, Financial & Legal Terms. (Three-Language Ser.: Vol. 3). 980p. (Fr., Eng. & Ger.). 1979. text ed. $98.95 (ISBN 3-85942-002-X). Birkhauser.
--Herbst Dictionay of Commercial, Financial & Legal Terms. (Two-Language Ser.: Vol. A). 688p. (Eng. & Ger.). 1975. text ed. $69.95 (ISBN 0-686-97268-6). Birkhauser.
Israelevich, E. E. English-Russian Dictionary of Finance & World Trade. 544p. (Eng. & Rus.). $10.50. Imported Bks.
Kafitz, Franz. Lexikon des Wirtschaftsrechnens. 2nd ed. (Ger.). 1976. $15.00 (ISBN 3-470-71192-5, M-7210). French & Eur.
Kettridge, J. O. French-English & English-French Dictionary of Commercial & Financial Terms, Phrases & Practice. 2nd ed. (Fr. & Eng.). 1969. Repr. of 1968 ed. $30.00 (ISBN 0-7100-1671-9). Routledge & Kegan.
--French-English & English-French Dictionary of Commercial & Financial Terms. 655p. (Fr. & Eng.). 1978. $32.00. Routledge & Kegan.
--French-English & English-French Dictionary of Financial & Mercantile Terms, Phrases & Practice. 288p. (Fr. & Eng.). 1971. Repr. of 1934 ed. 20.00 (ISBN 0-7100-1667-0). Routledge & Kegan.
Kettridge, Julius O. Financial & Mercantile Dictionary. (Fr. & Eng.). $13.95 (ISBN 0-685-11187-3). French & Eur.
Lefebvre, Marcel. Glossaire de la Finance. 284p. (Fr.). 1976. Can.$15.95. Lemeac.
Martinez Cerezo, Antonio. Diccionario De Banca. 3rd ed. 208p. (Span.). 1976. leatherette $13.95 (ISBN 84-368-0028-1, S-50179). French & Eur.
Rice, Michael D. Prentice-Hall Dictionary of Business, Finance & Law. LC 83-3022. 362p. 1983. $39.95 (ISBN 0-13-696583-0). P-H.
Rosenberg, Jerry M. Dictionary of Banking & Finance. LC 81-21961. 690p. 1982. $24.95 (ISBN 0-471-08096-9, Pub. by Wiley-Interscience). Wiley.
--Dictionary of Banking & Finance. 690p. 1983. pap. $14.95 (ISBN 0-471-88039-6, Pub. by Wiley-Interscience). Wiley.
Seone, Joaquin R. Diccionario de contabilidad, organizacion, administracion, control & ciencia afines, 7 vols. 3400p. (Span.). 1972. $45.00. Difusion.
Servotte, Josef V. Dictionnaire Commercial & Financier en Quatre Langues: Francais-Neerlandais-Anglais-Allemand. 5th ed. 960p. (Fr., Dutch, Eng & Ger.). write for info. Erasme.
--Dictionnaire Commercial & Financier: Francais-Anglais. (Fr. & Eng.). 1977. write for info. Marabout.
Thomik, Rudolf. Fachwoerterbuch Fur Wirtschaft, Handel und Finanzen. 685p. (Fr. & Ger.). 1977. $59.95 (ISBN 3-452-18138-3, 7400, Pub. by Carl Heymanns Verlag KG). French & Eur.
Thomson, F. J. Elsevier's Dictionary of Financial Terms. LC 79-11810. 496p. (Eng., Ger., Span., Fr., Ital., Dutch.). 1980. $113.00 (ISBN 0-444-41775-3). Elsevier.
Walmsley, Julian. A Dictionary of International Finance. LC 79-17753. 270p. 1979. lib. bdg. 27.50 (ISBN 0-313-20974-X, WIF/). Greenwood.
Zahn, Hans E. English-German Glossary of Financial & Economic Terms. (Eng. & Ger.). 1977. 56.00x (ISBN 3-7819-2013-5). Intl Pubns Serv.

FINANCE, INTERNATIONAL
see International Finance

FINANCE, PUBLIC
see also Money; Paper Money; Tariff; Taxation
also subdivision Finance under special subjects, e.g. Education–Finance; World War, 1939-1945–Finance
Martinez Cachero, Luis A. Diccionario de Hacienda & Derecho Fiscal. LC 75-521721. 205p. (Span.). 1976. write for info. (ISBN 8-436-80035-4). Piramide.

FINANCIAL ACCOUNTING
see Accounting

FINDING LISTS
see Library Catalogs

FINE ARTS
see Art; Arts, the

FINGER ALPHABET
see Deaf–Means of Communication

FINGER GAMES
see Finger Play

FINGER PLAY
Bennett, A. Y. Picture Dictionary, ABCs, Telling Time, Counting Rhymes, Riddles & Finger Plays. (Illus.). (gr. k-3). 1970. 5.95 (ISBN 0-448-02813-1, G&D). Putnam Pub Group.

FINGERPRINTS
Migne, J. P., ed. Dictionnaire de Paleographie, de Cryptographie, de Dactylologie. (Nouvelle Encyclopedie Theologique Ser.: Vol. 47). 668p. (Fr.). Repr. of 1854 ed. lib. bdg. $85.00x (ISBN 0-89241-285-2). Caratzas Pub Co.

FINLAND
Vuorela, Toivo. Kansanperinteen Sanakirja. LC 79-373974. (Illus.). 542p. (Finnish.). write for info. (ISBN 9-510-08803-X). Soderstrom.

FINNISH LANGUAGE
Branch, Michael, et al. A Student's Glossary of Finnish. LC 80-14030. (Illus.). 378p. (Finnish.). 1980. Fmk.147.00 (ISBN 9-510-08746-7). Soderstrom.
Kielitoimisto. Udissanasto Kahdeksankymmenta. LC 80-463931. 194p. (Finnish.). 1979. write for info. (ISBN 9-51009-287-8). Soderstorm.
Kotimaisten Kielten Tutkimuskekus. Uudissanasto Kahdeksankymmenta. LC 80-463931. 194p. (Finnish.). 1979. write for info. (ISBN 9-51009-287-8). Soderstrom.
Learn Finnish for English Speakers. (Finnish & Eng.). pap. 10.50 (ISBN 0-87557-020-8, 020-8). Saphrograph.
Uudissanasto. LC 80-463931. 194p. (Finnish.). 1979. write for info. (ISBN 9-5100-9287-8). Soderstrom.

FINNISH LANGUAGE–DICTIONARIES
Alanne, V. S. Finnish Dictionary: Suomalais-Englantilainen, Vol. 1. 3rd ed. (Finnish & Eng.). 1980. $85.00x (ISBN 95-100-1069-3, F563). Vanous.
--Finnish-English General Dictionary. 1111p. (Eng. & Finnish.). 1980. $75.00 (ISBN 951-0-01069-3, M-9658). French & Eur.
Berlitz Editors. Berlitz Pocket Dictionaries: Finnish-English. 300p. (Eng. & Finnish.). 1982. pap. $4.95 (ISBN 0-686-92984-5, Berlitz). Macmillan.
Cannelin, Aulis, et al. Suomalais-Ruotsalainen Suursanakirja. 3rd. ed. LC 77-471720. xv, 1140p. (Finnish & Swedish.). 1976. Fmk.write for info. (ISBN 9-51007-012-2). Werner Soderstrom.
Colussi, G. Finnish-Italian Dictionary. 302p. (Finnish & Italian.). 1978. $29.95 (ISBN 951-0-08233-3, M-9650). French & Eur.
--Finnish-Italian-Finnish Dictionary. 532p. (Ital. & Finnish.). 1981. pap. $14.95 (ISBN 951-0-07998-7, M-9640). French & Eur.
Diccionario Lexicon Finlandes-Espanol, Espanol-Finlandes. 400p. (Finnish & Span.). leatherette $4.95 (ISBN 84-303-0150-X, S-50405); pap. $4.50 (ISBN 84-303-0149-6, S-50404). French & Eur.
Eliseev, I. S. Karmannyi Russko-Finskii Slovar. 304p. (Rus. & Finnish.). 1978. $2.85 (Pub. by Russkii Iazyk). Four Continent.
Farbregd & Kamarainen. Finnish-Norwegian Norwegian-Finnish Pocket Dictionary. (Finnish & Norwegian.). 1978. write for info. (ISBN 82-573-0116-7). Kunnskapsforlaget.
Farbregd, T., et al. Finnish-Norwegian-Finnish Dictionary (Suomi-Noria-Suomi) 636p. (Finnish & Norwegian.). 1981. pap. $18.95 (ISBN 951-0-10498-1, M-9644). French & Eur.
Farbregd, Turid & Kamarainen, Aili. Suomi-Norja-Suomi: Taskusanakirja. LC 79-350054. 636p. (Finnish & Nor.). 1978. write for info. (ISBN 9-51008-527-8). Soderstrom.
Finnish Pocket Dictionary. (Finnish & Eng.). 13.00 (ISBN 9-5100-7468-3). Heinman.

Finnish Pocket Dictionary, Finnish-English - English-Finnish. 465p. (Eng. & Finnish.). 1980. pap. text ed. $13.00x (ISBN 9-5100-7468-3, F559). Vanous.
Finnish-Swedish-Finnish Dictionary. 272p. (Finnish & Swedish.). 1981. pap. $9.95 (ISBN 91-518-1442-0, M-9444). French & Eur.
Gersov, A. S. Finnish-Danish-Finnish Dictionary: Suomi-Tanska-Suomi. 315p. (Finnish & Danish.). 1976. pap. $14.95 (ISBN 951-0-07507-8, M-9648). French & Eur.
Hagfors, E., et al. French-Finnish Dictionary. 599p. (Fr. & Finnish.). 1980. leatherette $24.95 (ISBN 951-0-04682-5, M-9657). French & Eur.
Hiltunen, A. Finnish-Russian-Finnish Dictionary (Suomi-Venaja-Suomi) 543p. (Finnish & Rus.). 1981. pap. $19.95 (ISBN 951-0-09631-8, M-9643). French & Eur.
Hirvensalo, L. Finnish-German-Finnish Dictionary (Suomi-Saksa-Suomi) 610p. (Finnish & Ger.). 1980. pap. $14.95 (ISBN 951-0-08070-5, M-9646). French & Eur.
Hurme, R. & Pesonen, M. Finnish Deluxe Dictionary: English-Finnish. 2nd ed. (Eng. & Finnish.). 1978. $85.00x (ISBN 9-5100-5699-5, F-565). Vanous.
Hurme, R., et al. English-Finnish General Dictionary. 1183p. (Eng. & Finnish.). 1981. $75.00 (ISBN 951-0-08553-7, M-9659). French & Eur.
Karttunen, Kaarina. Nykyslangin Sanakirja. LC 79-398529. 333p. (Finnish.). 1979. write for info. (ISBN 9-51009-050-6). Soderstrom.
Koistinen, R. M. Finnish-French-Finnish Dictionary (Suomi-Ranska-Suomi) 438p. (Fr. & Finnish.). 1981. pap. $14.95 (ISBN 951-0-08071-3). French & Eur.
Kratkii Russko-Finskii Slovar. 384p. (Rus. & Finnish.). 1946. $3.20 (Pub. by GINS). Four Continent.
Krawczykiewicz, A. Suomi-Poula Suomi Dictionary: Finnish-Polish-Finnish. 687p. (Finnish & Pol.). 1979. pap. $18.95 (ISBN 951-0-08000-4, M-9638). French & Eur.
Kuusiena, M. E., et al, eds. Russko-Finskii Slovar. 1000p. (Rus. & Finnish.). 1963. $10.95 (Pub. by GINS). Four Continent.
Laanpere, H. Finnish-Esthonian-Finnish Dictionary: Suomi-Eesti-s. 499p. (Finnish & Estonian.). 1977. pap. $15.95 (ISBN 951-0-07765-8, M-9641). French & Eur.
Lampen, L. Finnish-Swedish Dictionary. 571p. (Finnish & Swedish.). 1980. leatherette $24.95 (ISBN 951-0-08620-7, M-9655). French & Eur.
--Finnish-Swedish-Finnish Dictionary (Suomi-Ruotsi-Suomi) 623p. (Finnish & Swedish.). 1980. pap. $15.95 (ISBN 951-0-07771-2, M-09647). French & Eur.
--Swedish-Finnish Dictionary. 548p. (Swedish & Finnish.). 1980. Leatherette $24.95 (ISBN 951-0-08621-5, M-9656). French & Eur.
Lampeu, Lea. Ruotsalais-Suomalaines. LC 79-361738. 547p. (Swedish & Finnish., Helsinki, Finland). 1978. write for info. WSOY.
Langenscheidts Universal-Woerterbuch Finnisch. 560p. (Finnish & Ger.). DM.6.80 (18141). Langenscheidt.
Miettinen, Liisa. Toimitustyon Terminologiaa. LC 77-469600. 39p. (Finnish.). 1975. Fmk.6.50 (ISBN 9-5110-2130-3). Otava.
Neuvonen, E. K. Finnish-Spanish-Finnish Dictionary. 452p. (Finnish & Span.). 1980. pap. $14.95 (ISBN 951-0-07202-8, S-37816). French & Eur.
Nurmela, T. Finnish-French Dictionary. 683p. (Finnish & Fr.). Date not set. $24.95 (ISBN 951-0-05012-1, M-9651). French & Eur.
Nyirkos, I. Finnish-Hungarian-Finnish Dictionary (Suomi-Unkari-Suomi) 712p. (Finnish & Hungarian.). 1979. pap. $19.95 (ISBN 951-0-07860-3). French & Eur.
Nyirkos, Istvan. Suomi-Unkari-Suomi: Taskusanakirja. LC 78-346065. 712p. (Finnish & Hungarian.). 1977. Fmk.44.00 (ISBN 9-51007-860-3). Soderstrom.
--Unkarilais-Suomalainen Sanakirja. LC 78-389367. 392p. (Hungarian & Finnish.). 1977. write for info. (ISBN 9-51717-114-5). Suoma Kirja.
Nykysuomen Laitos. Nykysuomen Sivistyssankirja: Vierasperaiset Sanat. LC 77-576667. 464p. (Finnish.). 1977. write for info. (ISBN 9-51008-134-5). Suoma Kirja.
Parashkevov, Boris, et al. Bulgarialais-Suomalainen Sanakirja. LC 76-501852. 91p. (Bulgarian & Swedish.). 1975. write for info. (ISBN 951-662-159-7). Gaudeamus.
Rahinantti, K. Finnish-Portuguese-Finnish Dictionary. 359p. (Finnish & Port.). 1975. pap. $16.95 (ISBN 0-686-92218-2, M-9649). French & Eur.
Rahinantti, Kristina, et al. Suomi-Portugali-Suomi. LC 75-546478. xvi, 359p. (Port. & Finnish.). 1975. Fmk.20.00 (ISBN 951-0-06884-5). Werner Soderstrom.
Riikon, E. & Tuomikowski, A. Finnish Dictionary: English-Finnish. 10th ed. (Finnish & Eng.). 1979. text ed. $55.00x (ISBN 95-110-4266-1, F560). Vanous.
Salamaa, Elsa. Maly Slownik Finsko-Polski & Polski-Finski. LC 76-503222. 106p. (Finnish & Pol.). 1975. Fmk.26.00 (ISBN 9-51261-007-8). Kirjayhtyma.
Saukkonen, Pauli. Nykvsuomen Saneiston Yleisyystilastoa Sanennloppuisessa Aakkosjarjestykessa. LC 78-386714. xxiv, 111p. (Finnish.). 1977. write for info. (ISBN 9-51420-45-81). Oulun Yliopisto.
Vakharos, I., et al. Finsko-Russkii Slovar. 815p. (Finnish & Rus.). 1977. $25.50 (Pub. by Russkii Iazyk). Four Continent.
Vesikansa, Jouko. Tasmennyssanasto. LC 77-480112. 127p. (Finnish.). 1976. Fmk.27.50 (ISBN 9-5100-7425-X); write for info. (ISBN 9-5100-7424-1). Werner Soderstrom.
Walega, Stanislaw. Slownik Finsko-Polski. LC 78-376750. 658p. (Finnish & Pol.). 1978. Fmk.135.00. Wiedza Powszechna.
Wuole, A. Finnish-English, English-Finnish Dictionary. (Finnish & Eng.). $24.50 (ISBN 0-87559-010-1); thumb indexed $29.00 (ISBN 0-87559-011-X). Shalom.
Wuolle. Finnish-English-Finnish Dictionary. 470p. (Finnish & Eng.). 1980. pap. $13.95 (ISBN 0-686-92371-5, M-9639). French & Eur.
Wuolle, A. English-Finnish Dictionary. 512p. (Eng. & Finnish.). 1980. leatherette $19.95 (ISBN 951-0-08500-6, M-9653). French & Eur.
--Finnish-English, English-Finnish Dictionary, 2 Vols. 11th ed. (Finnish & Eng.). Set. 37.50. Finnish-Eng (ISBN 9-5100-9469-2). Eng.-Finnish (ISBN 951-0-08500-6). Heinman.
--Finnish-English, English-Finnish Dictionary. 2nd, rev. ed. (Eng. & Finnish.). Date not set. text ed. $30.00 (ISBN 0-686-46544-X). Heinman.
Wuolle, Aino. Finnish Small Dictionary: English-Finnish, Vol. 1. (Finnish & Eng.). 1980. text ed. $20.00x (ISBN 9-5100-8500-6, F557). Vanous.
--Finnish Small Dictionary: Finnish-English, Vol. 2. 11th ed. (Finnish & Eng.). 1979. text ed. $20.00x (ISBN 95-100-9469-2, F558). Vanous.

FINNISH LANGUAGES
see also Estonian Language; Finnish Language; Finno-Ugrian Languages
Swanljung, Ritva. Rakennusalan Sanastot ja Sanastohankkeet Suomessa. LC 77-483474. (Finnish.). 1975. write for info. (ISBN 9-5138-0250-7). Valtion.

FINNO-HUNGARIAN LANGUAGES
see Finno-Ugrian Languages

FINNO-UGRIAN LANGUAGES
see also Estonian Language; Hungarian Language; Lapp Language
Budenz, Jozsef. Comparative Dictionary of the Finno-Ugric Elements in the Hungarian Vocabulary. LC 66-64927. (Uralic & Altaic Ser: Vol. 78). (Finnish & Hungarian., Repr. of 1881 ed). 1966. pap. text ed. $22.00x (ISBN 0-87750-029-0). Res Ctr Lang Semiotic.
Collinder, Bjorn. Fenno-Ugric Vocabulary: An Etymological Dictionary of the Uralic Languages. 158p. (Finnish & Hungarian.). 1977. pap. text ed. $41.00x (ISBN 3-87118-187-0, Pub. by Helmut Buske Verlag Hamburg). Benjamins North Am.

FIOTI LANGUAGE
see Congo Language

FIRE EXTINCTION
Fire Terminology. 4th ed. 67p. 1970. 4.00 (ISBN 0-685-46056-8, FSD-3A). Natl Fire Prot.
Institution of Fire Engineers. Dictionary of Fire Technology. 3rd, rev. ed. LC 80-510226. 170p. (Eng.). 1979. $4.00 (ISBN 0-903345-03-X). Inst Fire Eng.
Kuvshinoff, B. W., et al, eds. Fire Sciences Dictionary. LC 77-3489. 439p. 1977. $25.00x (ISBN 0-471-51113-7, Pub. by Wiley-Interscience). Wiley.

FIRE FIGHTING
see Fire Extinction

FIRE LOSSES
see Fires

FIRE PREVENTION
see also Fire Extinction
also subdivision Fires and Fire Prevention under various classes of institutions and buildings, e.g. Schools–Fires and Fire Prevention
Kuvshinoff, B. W., et al, eds. Fire Sciences Dictionary. LC 77-3489. 439p. 1977. $25.00x (ISBN 0-471-51113-7, Pub. by Wiley-Interscience). Wiley.

FIREARMS
Sybertz, Gustav. Technical Dictionary for Weaponry. (Ger. & Eng.). 1969. pap. $120.00 (ISBN 3-7888-0081-X, M-7642, Pub. by Neumann-Neudamm). French & Eur.

FIREARMS–LAWS AND REGULATIONS
Arms Control Association. A Glossary of Arms Control Terms. free. Arms Control.

FIREARMS CONTROL
see Firearms–Laws and Regulations

FIRES
see also Fire Extinction; Fire Prevention
also subdivision Fires and Fire Prevention under various classes of institutions and buildings, e.g. Schools–Fires and Fire Prevention; Particular conflagrations are entered under names of place, e.g. London–Fire, 1666
National Fire Protection Association. Fire Terms: A Guide to Their Meaning & Use. $11.00 (SPP-60). Natl Fire Prot.

FIRST CHURCH OF CHRIST, SCIENTIST
see Boston–First Church of Christ, Scientist

FISH
see Fishes

FISH BY-PRODUCTS
see Fishery Products

FISH WASTE
see Fishery Products

FISHERIES
see also Fishes
Bensch, Erhard. Schiffbau, Schiffahrt, Fischereitechnik-Russisch-Englisch-Deutsch. 784p. (Rus., Eng. & Ger.). 1981. M.98.00. VEB Technk.
Dipl-Ling, V. & Bensch, Erhard. Dictionary of Shipbuilding, Shipping & Fisheries. 784p. 1980. vinyl $150.00x (ISBN 0-686-30016-5, Pub. by Collet's). State Mutual Bk.
Glossary of Inland Fishery Terms. (EIFAC Occasional Papers: No. 12). 129p. 1979. pap. $9.50 (ISBN 92-5-000724-8, F1558, FAO). Unipub.
Post, G., ed. Glossary of Fish Health Terms. American Fisheries Society, Fish Health Section. 48p. 1977. $5.00. Am Fisheries Soc.
Trilingual Dictionary of Fisheries Technological Terms-Curing. (FAO Fisheries Ser.: No. 12). 91p. 1980. pap. $11.50 (ISBN 0-686-68188-6, F483, FAO). Unipub.

FISHERY METHODS
see Fisheries

FISHERY PRODUCTS
Multilingual Dictionary of Fish & Fish Products. 1978. $60.00 (ISBN 0-85238-086-0, FN 64, FNB). Unipub.
OECD. Multilingual Dictionary of Fish & Fish Products. 1978. $59.00 (ISBN 0-685-63442-6). State Mutual Bk.
OECD, ed. Multilingual Dictionary of Fish & Fish Products. 2nd ed. 446p. 1978. 42.50x (ISBN 0-85238-086-0). Intl Pubns Serv.

FISHES
see also Aquariums; Fisheries
also names of classes, orders, etc. of fishes, e.g. Bass, salmon
Allyn, Rube. Dictionary of Fishes. LC 52-334. (Orig.). pap. 4.95 (ISBN 0-8200-0101-5). Great Outdoors.
Multilingual Dictionary of Fish & Fish Products. 1978. $60.00 (ISBN 0-85238-086-0, FN 64, FNB). Unipub.
OECD. Multilingual Dictionary of Fish & Fish Products. 1978. $59.00 (ISBN 0-685-63442-6). State Mutual Bk.

FISHES–NOMENCLATURE
OECD, ed. Multilingual Dictionary of Fish & Fish Products. 2nd ed. 446p. 1978. 42.50x (ISBN 0-85238-086-0). Intl Pubns Serv.

FISHING–DICTIONARIES
Dictionary of Fishing Terms: Japanese-English, English-Japanese. 443p. (Japanese & Eng.). 1980. $39.95 (ISBN 0-686-92534-3, M-9344). French & Eur.
Glossary of UK Fishing Gear Terms. 1980. $39.50x (ISBN 0-686-64737-8, Pub. by Fishing News England). State Mutual Bk.
Glossary of United Kingdom Fishing Gear Terms. 115p. 1982. $47.25 (ISBN 0-85238-119-0, FN95, FNB). Unipub.
Schreiner, Jean, et al. Le Nouveau Dictionnaire de la Peche. 384p. (Fr.). 1975. $35.95 (ISBN 0-686-57331-5). French & Eur.
Veronese, Ugo. Dizionario del pescatore italiano di acqua dolce. (Illus.). 384p. (Ital.). L.8500.00. Bietti.

FISHING–IMPLEMENTS AND APPLIANCES
Glossary of United Kingdom Fishing Gear Terms. 115p. 1982. $47.25 (ISBN 0-85238-119-0, FN95, FNB). Unipub.

FISK UNIVERSITY, NASHVILLE
Fisk University Library (Nashville) Dictionary Catalog of the Negro Collection of the Fisk University Library, 6 vols. 1974. Set. lib. bdg. $490.00 (ISBN 0-8161-1055-7, Hall Library). G K Hall.

FLATWARE, SILVER
see Silverware

FLAUBERT, GUSTAVE, 1821-1880
Carlut, Charles. A Concordance to Flaubert's Bouvard et Pecuchet. LC 79-7915. 1021p. 1980. lib. bdg. $110.00 (ISBN 0-8240-9518-9). Garland Pub.

FLEMISH LANGUAGE
see Dutch Language

FLESH FOODS
see Animal Food

FLIGHT–MEDICAL ASPECTS
see Aviation Medicine

FLORA
see Plants

FLORENCE
Frizzi, Giuseppe. Dizionario dei Frizzetti Popolari Firoentini. LC 76-488668. vii, 267p. (Ital.). 1975. L.9000.00. Multigrafica.
Raddi, Renzo. A Firenze si Parla Cosi: Frasario Moderno del Vernacolo Fiorentino. LC 76-468656. xxvii, 290p. (Ital., Firenze). 1976. L.5000.00. Libreria.

FLORIDA–HISTORY–BIBLIOGRAPHY
Dictionary Catalog of the P. K. Yonge Library of Florida History, the University of Florida, Gainesville. 1977. lib. bdg. $380.00 (ISBN 0-8161-0019-5, Hall Library). G K Hall.
FLOW METERS
American Society of Mechanical Engineers. Glossary of Terms Used in the Measurement of Fluid Flow in Pipes: ANSI-ASME MFC-1M-1979. $4.50 (J00065); members $3.60. ASME.
FLOW OF WATER
see Hydraulics
FLOWERS
see also Plants
also names of flowers, e.g. Carnations, Roses, Violets
Hay, Roy & Synge, Patrick M. The Color Dictionary of Flowers & Plants for Home & Garden. (Illus.). 584p. 1982. pap. $11.95 (ISBN 0-517-52456-2). Crown.
Synge, P. & Hay, R. Dictionary of Garden Plants & Flowers in Colour: May 1981. 1981. $60.00x (ISBN 0-686-78769-2, Pub. by RHS Ent England). State Mutual Bk.
FLOWMETERS
see Flow Meters
FLUID METERS
see Flow Meters
FLUID POWER TECHNOLOGY
see also Hydraulic Machinery; Pneumatic Machinery
American National Standards Institute & National Fluid Power Association. Glossary of Terms for Fluid Power (Includes Supplement B93.2a) ANSI-B93.2m. 1971. $24.00; $16.00, NFPA member. Natl Fluid Power.
--Supplement to the Glossary of Terms for Fluid Power: ANSI-B93.2a. 1978. $12.00; $8.00, NFPA member. Natl Fluid Power.
National Fluid Power Association. Glossary of Terms for Compressed Air Dryers (Included in Supplement to the Glossary of Terms, ANSI-B93.2a-1978) NFPA-T3.27.1. 1981. $10.50; $7.00, NFPA member. Natl Fluid Power.
--Glossary of Terms for Fluid Power Quick Disconnect Couplings (Included in Supplement to the Glossary of Terms) NFPA-T3.20.1. 1981. $10.50; $7.00, NFPA member. Natl Fluid Power.
--Glossary of Terms for Hydraulic Fluid Power Filters & Separator: NFPA-T3.10.3m. rev. ed. 1980. $10.50; $7.00, NFPA member. Natl Fluid Power.
FOLK COSTUME
see Costume
FOLK CUSTOMS
see Manners and Customs
FOLK-LORE–DICTIONARIES
Papahagi, Tache. Mic Dictionar Folkloric: Spicuiri Folklorice si Etnografice Comparate. LC 80-478266. xxxiv, 545p. (Romanian.). 1979. 28.00 lei. Minerva Yugo.
Younis. Dictionary of Folklore: English-Arabic. (Arabic & Eng.). 1983. $30.00 (ISBN 0-86685-307-3). Intl Bk Ctr.
FOLK-LORE, JAPANESE
Kotowaza Daijiten: Comprehensive Dictionary of Japanese Phrase, Fable & Proverb. 2016p. (Japanese.). 1982. 9800.00 Yen. Shogakukan.
FOLK-LORE, MEDICAL
see Folk Medicine
FOLK-LORE OF ANIMALS
see Animal Lore
FOLK LORE OF NUMBERS
see Counting-Out Rhymes
FOLK-LORE OF POLARITY
see Polarity (In Religion, Folk-Lore, etc.)
FOLK MEDICINE
Rinzler, Carol A. The Dictionary of Medical Folklore. LC 78-69518. 1979. $14.37i (ISBN 0-690-01704-9). T Y Crowell.
FOLKWAYS
see Manners and Customs
FOOD–DICTIONARIES
Arva, Gyorgy. Etlapiras. LC 77-473040. 513p. (Eng., Czech. & Hungarian.). 1975. 71.00 Ft (ISBN 9-6322-0195-7). Kozgazdasagi.
Ashley, Richard & Duggal, Heidi. Dictionary of Nutrition. 1976. pap. 3.50 (ISBN 0-671-49407-4). PB.
Bender, Arnold E. Dictionary of Nutrition & Food Technology. 4th ed. 1975. text ed. $29.95 (ISBN 0-408-00143-7). Butterworth.
Bourdet, Francoise. Understanding French Cookery: A Guide to French Recipes & Cooking Terms. LC 78-318824. iivi, 58p. (Eng. & Fr.). 1978. E0.95 (ISBN 0-901571-92-X). Kingsmead Pr.
Commission of the European Communities, Directorate-General for Scientific & Technical Information & Information Management, ed. Food: Multilingual Thesaurus. Incl. Vol. 1. German. 129p. (Ger.); Vol. 2. English. 145p. pap. 95.00 (ISBN 0-686-81239-5); Vol. 3. French. 144p. (Fr.); Italian. 132p. (Ital.); Vol. 5. Quadrilingual Index. 168p. (Eng., Fr., Ger. & Ital.). 1979. pap. $240.00x (ISBN 3-598-10103-1, Pub. by K G Saur). Gale.
Dahl, C. Food & Menu Dictionary. LC 77-123002. 160p. 1972. $12.50 (ISBN 0-8436-0556-1). CBI Pub.
Diccionario de los Alimentos: Vitaminas, Calories, Coccion, Conservacion, Etc. 2nd ed. 758p. (Span.). 1979. pap. $41.95 (ISBN 84-352-0338-7, S-13671). French & Eur.
Esser, William L. Dictionary of Man's Foods. (Illus.). 1983. pap. 3.95 (ISBN 0-914532-06-5). Natural Hygiene.
--Dictionary of Natural Foods. (Illus.). 1983. pap. 4.95 (ISBN 0-914532-30-8). Natural Hygiene.
Gelb, Barbara L. The Dictionary of Food & What's in It for You. 1979. pap. $3.50 (ISBN 0-345-29479-3). Ballantine.
Hauser, Gaylord & Berg, Ragnar. Dictionary of Foods. 156p. 1971. pap. 2.25 (ISBN 0-87904-008-4). Lust.
Igoe, Robert S. The Dictionary of Food Ingredients. 192p. 1982. text ed. $17.95 (ISBN 0-442-24002-3). Van Nos Reinhold.
Lindberg, G. U. Multilingual Dictionary of Names of Marine Food-Dishes of World Fauna. 562p. 1980. 79.00x (ISBN 0-686-44732-8, Pub. by Collets). State Mutual Bk.
Mariani, John F. The Dictionary of American Food & Drink. 352p. 1983. $17.95 (ISBN 0-89919-199-1). Ticknor & Fields.
Maurel, Rosie. Dictionnaire des Aliments. (Fr.). 15.50 F. Table Ronde.
Wilhelm, Evelyne. Bien Manger dans Quinze Pays. LC 79-390204. 205p. (Eng. & Fr.). 1979. 39.00 F (ISBN 2-86418-029-4). Encre.
FOOD ADDITIVES
Benarde, Melvin A. The Food Additives Dictionary. 96p. 1981. pap. $4.95 (ISBN 0-671-42837-3, Wallaby). S&S.
Winter, Ruth. A Consumer's Dictionary of Food Additives. 1978. pap. $4.95 (ISBN 0-517-53161-5). Crown.
FOOD ALLERGY
see Allergy
FOOD AND AGRICULTURE ORGANIZATION OF THE UNITED NATIONS
Administrative & Financial Terms. (FAO Terminology Bulletin: No. 23, Rev. 1). 169p. 1982. pap. $12.75 (ISBN 92-5-001120-2, F2212, FAO). Unipub.
FOOD ANIMALS
see Animal Food
FOOD HABITS OF ANIMALS
see Animals, Food Habits of
FOOD INDUSTRY AND TRADE
see also Food Additives
also individual processed food and processing industries, e.g. Cheese and Dairying; Meat Industry and Trade
Baniecki, Henryk. Encyklopedia Techniki. LC 79-354168. vii, 928p. (Pol.). 1978. 300.00 Zl. Wydawnictwa Naukowo.
Clement, Jean M. Dictionnaire des Industries Alimentaires. LC 78-366424. (Illus.). xiii, 348p. (Fr.). 1978. 78.00 F (ISBN 2-225-46079-5). Masson & Cie.
Clement, Jean-Michel. Dictionnaire des Industries Alimentaires. 361p. (Fr.). 1978. $32.50 (ISBN 0-686-56949-0, M-6071). French & Eur.
Papa-Sotir, Mihai. Dictionar Poliglot de Industrie Alimentara. LC 78-344895. xiv, 619p. (Eng., Romanian, Ger., Fr. & Rus.). 1977. 56.00 lei. Editura Stiintifica.
FOOD OF ANIMALS
see Animals, Food Habits of
FOOD PROCESSING
see Food Industry and Trade
FOOD SERVICE
Here are entered works on quantity preparation and service of food for outside the home. Works dealing solely with quantity food preparation are entered under Quantity Cookery.
Morton, Ian & Morton, C. Elsevier's Dictionary of Food Science & Technology. 1977. $42.75 (ISBN 0-444-41559-9). Elsevier.
FOOD TRADE
see Food Industry and Trade
FOOTBALL–DICTIONARIES
Shefski, Bill. Football Language. LC 77-12492. 1978. lib. bdg. 12.90 (ISBN 0-89471-021-4); pap. 2.95 (ISBN 0-89471-020-6). Running Pr.
--Running Press Glossary of Football Language. LC 77-12492. 120p. (Eng.). 1978. $2.50 (ISBN 0-89471-020-6). Running Pr.
Sirages, H. Elsevier's Football Dictionary. (Eng. & Ger.). 1980. $40.50 (ISBN 0-444-41890-3). Elsevier.
FOOTBALL–JUVENILE LITERATURE
Olgin, Joseph. Illustrated Football Dictionary for Young People. LC 74-82014. (Illustrated Dictionary Ser.). (Illus.). 128p. (gr. 5 up). 1974. PLB 7.29 (ISBN 0-8178-5182-8). Harvey.
FOOTWEAR
see Boots and Shoes
FORCE AND ENERGY
see also Mechanics
Bogenschuetz. Fachwoerterbuch fuer Batterien & Energie-Direktumwandlung. 200p. (Eng. & Ger.). 1982. DM.22.00. Brandstetter.
Bogenschuetz, A. Fachwoerterbuch fuer Batterien und Energie-Direktumwandlung. 200p. (Ger. & Eng.). 1968. DM.29.95 (ISBN 3-87097-002-2). Brandstetter.
Conrad, W., et al. BI-Taschenlexikon Energie. (Illus.). 346p. (Ger.). 1981. M.15.00. Bibl Inst Leipzig.
Counihan, Martin. A Dictionary of Energy. (Illus.). 200p. 1981. 14.95 (ISBN 0-7100-0847-3). Routledge & Kegan.
Frederick Muller, Ltd., ed. Multilingual Energy Dictionary. 1981. $30.00x (ISBN 0-584-95568-5, Pub. by Muller Ltd). State Mutual Bk.
Slesser, Malcolm. Dictionary of Energy. 320p. (Eng.). 1982. E25.00 (ISBN 0-333-31825-0). Macmillan London.
Slesser, Malcom, et al, eds. Dictionary of Energy. 400p. 1982. E15.00 (ISBN 0-333-31825-0). Macmillan London.
FORCE PUMPS
see Pumping Machinery
FOREIGN AFFAIRS
see International Relations; see subdivisions Foreign Relations under names of countries
FOREIGN COMMERCE
see Commerce
FOREIGN POLICY
see International Relations
FOREIGN RELATIONS
see International Relations
FOREIGN TRADE
see Commerce
FOREIGNERS
see Aliens
FORENAMES
see Names, Personal
FORENSIC PSYCHOLOGY
see Psychology, Forensic
FOREST ENTOMOLOGY
see Entomology
FOREST MANAGEMENT
see Forests and Forestry
FOREST PLANTING
see Forests and Forestry
FOREST PRODUCTS
see also Lumber Trade; Rubber; Wood
Forest Products Research Society. Thesaurus of Forest Products Terms. 167p. $30.00 (685T1). Forest Prod.
FOREST REPRODUCTION
see Forests and Forestry
FORESTATION
see Forests and Forestry
FORESTS AND FORESTRY
see also Landscape Gardening; Lumber Trade; Trees; Wood
Ahlsved, Karl-Johan, et al. Lexicon Forestale. LC 80-487653. xix, 592p. (Eng., Finnish, Ger., Swedish, & Rus.). 1979. Fmk.350.00 (ISBN 9-5100-9174-X). Suomen Standard.
Bruttini, Alberto. Dictionnaire de Sylviculture: Francais-Allemand-Anglais-Espagnol-Italien. (Illus.). 384p. (Fr., Ger., Eng., Span. & Ital.). 1930. 70.00 F. Lechevalier.
Dictionary of Forestry. 274p. (Eng. & Chinese.). 1977. pap. $5.95 (ISBN 0-686-92384-7, M-9594). French & Eur.
Jacobi, C. Vocabulaire Forestier Francais-Allemand-Danois. 207p. (Fr., Ger. & Danish.). 1907. 25.00 F. Picard.
Khatib, Ahmed. Chihabi's Dictionary of Agricultural & Forestry Terms. (Illus.). 300p. (Eng. & Arabic.). 1978. $40.00 (072-4). Intl Bk Ctr.
Lagrenade, Marcel. Lexique Forestier: Anglais-Francais. (Illus., Eng. & Fr.). 1978. Can.$pap. 19.50 (ISBN 0-88905-005-8). Dotmar.
Linnard, W. Russian-English Forestry & Wood Dictionary. 109p. (Rus. & Eng.). 1966. $30.00x (ISBN 0-686-45635-1, Pub. by CAB Bks England). State Mutual Bk.
Litschauer, R. Vocabularium Polyglottum Vitae Silvarum. 126p. (Lat., Eng., Ger., Fr., Span. & Rumanian.). 1955. $21.50 (ISBN 0-686-56473-1, M-7679, Pub. by P. Parey). French & Eur.
--Vocabularium Polyglottum Vitae Silvarum. 126p. (Lat., Eng., Ger., Fr., Span. & Romanian.). 1955. $21.50. Parey.
Martinot Lagarde. Lexique de Sylviculture Allemand-Francais. (Ger. & Fr.). 5.00 F. Genie Rural.
Metro, Andre. Dictionnaire Forestier Multilingue. 434p. (Fr.). 1976. $79.95 (ISBN 0-686-57047-2, M-6409). French & Eur.
--Dictionnaire Forestier Multilingue. 434p. (Fr.). 1976. 200.00 F. C. I. L. F.
Pavlov, Ernst A. & Semenova, Olga I. Nemetsko-Russkii Slovar po Lesnomu Khoziaistvu. LC 80-466812. 477p. (Ger. & Rus.). 1978. 4.20 Rub. Russkii Iazyk.
Plaisance, Georges. Dictionnaire des Forets. 5th ed. (Fr.). 1975. 54.00 F. G. Plaisance.
Society of American Foresters. Terminology of Forest Science, Technology, Practice & Products (with 1978 Addendum) 1971. $21.00 set; Addendum only $3.00. Soc Am Foresters.
Tekniska Nomenklaturcentralen. Skogsordlista. LC 80-485348. 676p. (Eng. & Swedish.). 1978. write for info. (ISBN 9-1719-6071-6). Tek Nomen.
V. Weck, Johannes. Woerterbuch der Forstwirtschaft. (Ger., Eng., Fr., Span. & Rus., Dictionary of Forestry). 1966. $99.50 (ISBN 3-405-10494-7, M-7005). French & Eur.
Weck, J. Dictionary of Forestry. (Eng., Ger., Fr., Span. & Rus.). 1966. $106.50 (ISBN 0-444-40626-3). Elsevier.
Weck, Johannes, et al. Woerterbuch der Forstwirtschaft Deutsch-Englisch-Franzoesisch-Spanisch-Russisch. (Ger., Eng., Fr., Span. & Rus.). 1966. DM.128.00 (ISBN 3-405-10494-7). BLV Verlag.
FORESTS AND FORESTRY–BIBLIOGRAPHY
Yale University. Henry S. Graves Memorial Library. Dictionary Catalogue of the Yale Forestry Library, 12 Vols. 1962. Set. lib. bdg. $1140.00 (ISBN 0-8161-0631-2, Hall Library). G K Hall.

FORGING
Garcia Mercadal, Jose. Diccionario Lengua Espanola Forja. 24th ed. 488p. (Span.). 1977. $4.50 (ISBN 84-7105-026-9, S-50034). French & Eur.
Serrano Mesa, Eleesbaan. Diccionario Ingles-Espanol, Espanol-Ingles Forja. 17th ed. 488p. (Eng. & Span.). 1977. $4.50 (ISBN 84-7105-098-6, S-50352). French & Eur.

FORM IN BIOLOGY
see Morphology

FORMS (BUSINESS)
see Business–Forms, Blanks, etc.

FORMULA TRANSLATION (COMPUTER PROGRAM LANGUAGE)
see FORTRAN (Computer Program Language)

FORMULAS (MATHEMATICS)
see Mathematics–Formulae

FORSTER, EDWARD MORGAN, 1879-1970
Borrello, Alfred. An E. M. Forster Glossary. LC 74-188548. 1972. $15.00 (ISBN 0-8108-0475-1). Scarecrow.

FORTRAN (COMPUTER PROGRAM LANGUAGE)
Breuer, Hans. Dictionary for Computer Languages. (Automatic Programming Information Centre Studies in Data Processing: Vol. 6). 1966. $65.00 (ISBN 0-12-132950-X). Acad Pr.
Fleming-Redish. The McMaster Glossary of Fortran Seventy-Seven. 64p. 1983. pap. text ed. $3.95 (ISBN 0-8403-3052-9). Kendall-Hunt.

FORTUNE-TELLING
see also Dreams; Palmistry
Scouezec. Diccionario De Atres Adivinatorias. 226p. (Span.). 1973. pap. $7.95 (ISBN 84-270-0220-3, S-50042). French & Eur.

FOSSILS
see Paleontology

FOUNDATIONS
see also Concrete; Masonry; Soil Mechanics
Barker, John. Dictionary of Soil Mechanics & Foundation Engineering. 1981. pap. text ed. 30.00x (ISBN 0-86095-885-X). Longman.

FOUNDING
see also Metal Castings
Brunhuber, E. Giesserei - Fachwoerterbuch. 802p. (Ger., Eng., Fr. & Ital., Dictionary of Foundry). 1977. 120.00 (ISBN 3-7949-0283-1, M-7424, Pub. by Fachverlag, Schiele & Schon). French & Eur.
--Giesserei - Lexikon 1978. 960p. (Ger.). 1977. 62.50 (ISBN 3-7949-0282-3, M-7425, Pub. by Fachverlag, Schiele & Schon). French & Eur.
Brunhuber, Ernst. Giesserei-Fachworterbuch. LC 78-350030. 729p. (Eng., Fr., Ger. & Ital.). 1977. DM.148.00 (ISBN 3-7949-0283-1). Schiele & Schon.
Centre Technique des Industries de la Fonderie. Vocabulaire de Fonderie Anglais-Francais. LC 77-577539. 75p. (Eng. & Fr.). 1976. 24.00 F (ISBN 2-7119-0032-0). Ed Tech Ind.
--Vocabulaire de Fonderie Francais-Allemand. LC 77-570223. 100p. (Fr. & Ger.). 1976. 36.00 F (ISBN 2-7119-0033-9). Ed Tech Ind.
Dictionary of Foundry Terms. (Hebrew, Eng. , Fr. & Ger.). IL.8.00. Massada Pr.
Pahlitzsch, G. Woerterbucher der Fertigungstechnik: Bd 1, Schmieden-Freiformschmieden & Gesenkschmieden. 108p. (Ger.). 1962. DM.45.00 (ISBN 3-7736-5920-2). Girardet.
--Woerterbucher der Fertigungstechnik Deutsch-Englisch-Franzoesisch: Bd 2, Schleifen Oberflaechenrauheit. 139p. (Ger., Eng. & Fr.). 1963. DM.45.00 (ISBN 3-7736-5930-X). Girardet.
--Woerterbucher der Fertigungstechnik Deutsch-Englisch-Franzoesisch: Bd 3, Blechbearbeitung. 136p. (Ger., Eng. & Fr.). 1965. DM.45.00 (ISBN 3-7736-5940-7). Girardet.
--Woerterbucher der Fertigungstechnik Deutsch-Englisch-Franzoesisch: Bd 4, Grundbegriffe des Spanens. 123p. (Ger., Eng. & Fr.). 1969. DM.45.00 (ISBN 3-7736-5941-5). Girardet.
--Woerterbucher der Fertigungstechnik Deutsch-Englisch-Franzoesisch: Bd 5, Kaltfliesspressen & Kaltstauchen. 157p. (Ger., Eng. & Fr.). 1969. DM.45.00 (ISBN 3-7736-5945-8). Girardet.
--Woerterbucher der Fertigungstechnik Deutsch-Spanisch-Italienisch-Portugiesisch: Bd 1R, Schmieden-Freiformschmieden & Gesenkschmieden. 114p. (Ger., Span., Ital. & Port.). 1967. DM.45.00 (ISBN 3-7736-5801-X). Girardet.
Standke, Wolfgang, compiled by. Foundry Dictionary: German-English & English-German. (Ger. & Eng.). 1971. 21.50x (ISBN 3-87260-002-8). Intl Pubns Serv.
Vocabulaire de la Fonderie: Anglais-Francais. (Eng. & Fr.). 22.40 F. Techniques Fonderie.
Vocabulaire de la Fonderie: Francais-Anglais. (Fr. & Eng.). 33.38 F. Techniques Fonderie.
Vocabulary de la Fonderie, Francais-Anglais. (Fr. & Eng., French-English Vocabulary of Foundries). pap. $14.95 (ISBN 0-686-56719-6, M-6557). French & Eur.
Vocabulary de la Fonderie, Francais-Anglais. (Fr. & Eng., French-English Vocabulary of Foundries). pap. $12.50 (ISBN 0-686-56720-X, M-6556). French & Eur.
Voros, Arpad. Onteszet. LC 79-244881. 435p. (Eng., Hungarian, Fr., Ger. & Rus.). 1978. 95.00 Ft (ISBN 9-6305-1597-0). Akademiai Kiado.

FOUNDRY PRACTICE
see Founding

FOURIER, FRANCOIS MARIE CHARLES, 1772-1837
Silberling, E. Dictionnaire De Sociologie Phalansterienne: Guide Des Oeuvres Completes De Charles Fourier. (Fr.). 1964. Repr. of 1911 ed. $29.50 (ISBN 0-8337-3266-8). B Franklin.

FRANCE
see also names of cities, towns and geographic areas in France
Barrillon, Raymond. Dictionnaire de la Constitution: Les Institutions de la Ve Republique. 2nd ed. xxxiv, 538p. (Fr.). 1978. write for info. Cujas.
Castellana, Georges. Dictionnaire Francais-Nicois. LC 78-380119. 421p. (Fr.). 1978. 60.00 F. Serre.
Gonfroy, Gerard. Dictionnaire Normatif Limousin-Francais. LC 77-479648. 229p. (Fr.). 1976. write for info. Lemouzi.
Marion, Marcel. Dictionnaire des Institutions de la France aux XVII & XVIII Siecles. 573p. (Fr.). 1968. $27.50. Lenox.
Ogee, Jean, et al. Dictionnaire Historique & Geographique de la Province de Bretagne, 2 vols. 1520p. (Fr.). 1973. 450.00 F. Floch.
Pothion, Jean. Dictionnaire des Bureaux de Poste Francais. (Fr.). write for info. Poste Aux Lettres.
Stein, Henri. Dictionnaire Topographique de la France. Hubert, J., ed. 738p. (Fr.). 1954. pap. $25.00 (ISBN 0-686-57226-2, M-6525). French & Eur.

FRANCE–BIOGRAPHY
Dictionnaire des Groupes Industriels & Financiers en France. 360p. (Fr.). 1978. $17.95 (ISBN 0-686-57102-9, M-6127). French & Eur.
Dictionnaire des Personnages de Tous les Temps & de Tous les Pays. (Fr.). $81.50 (ISBN 0-685-36081-4). French & Eur.

FRANCE–CIVILIZATION
Franklin, Afred L. Dictionnaire Historique Des Arts, Metiers & Professions Exerces Dans Paris Depuis Le Treizieme Siecle. (Biblio. & Ref. Ser.: No. 198). (Fr.). 1968. Repr. of 1906 ed. $49.00 (ISBN 0-8337-1231-4); $40.00 (ISBN 0-685-06747-5). B Franklin.

FRANCE–COLONIES
Decalo, Samuel. Historical Dictionary of Niger. LC 79-15704. (African Historical Dictionaries Ser.: No. 20). 376p. 1979. $20.50 (ISBN 0-8108-1229-0). Scarecrow.

FRANCE–COMMERCE
Franklin, Alfred. Dictionnaire Historique des Arts, Metlers & Professions Exerces dans Paris Depuis le Treizieme Siecle. 882p. (Fr.). $40.00. Lenox.

FRANCE–DESCRIPTION AND TRAVEL–GUIDEBOOKS
Michelin Guides & Maps. Dictionnaire des Communes de France (Guide to French Townships) (Fr.). 1979. 45.00 (ISBN 2-06-007500-9). Michelin.

FRANCE–ECONOMIC CONDITIONS
Dictionnaire des Groupes Industriels & Financiers en France. 360p. (Fr.). 1978. $17.95 (ISBN 0-686-57102-9, M-6127). French & Eur.

FRANCE–EXECUTIVE DEPARTMENTS
Fleurian, Dominique de. Dictionnaire National des Communes de France. 20th ed. Simond, Jacques & Frenay, Jacques, eds. 1150p. (Fr.). 1977. $39.95 (ISBN 0-686-57184-3, M-6254). French & Eur.

FRANCE–HISTORICAL GEOGRAPHY
Moreau, Joseph. Dictionnaire de Geographie Historique de la Gaule et de la France. 426p. (Fr.). 1972. pap. $37.50 (ISBN 0-686-56815-X, M-6593). French & Eur.

FRANCE–HISTORY–DICTIONARIES
Cabourdin, Guy & Viard, Georges. Lexique historique de la France d'Ancien regime. LC 79-381603. (Illus.). 324p. (Fr.). 1978. 65.00 F. A Colin.
Lalanne, Ludovic. Dictionnaire Historique De la France, 2 Vols. 2nd ed. (Fr.). 1967. Repr. of 1877 ed. $93.00 (ISBN 0-8337-1985-8). B Franklin.
--Dictionnaire Historique de la France Contenant l'histoire Civile, Politique, 2 vols. (Fr.). 1967. $65.00. Lenox.
Marion, Marcel, ed. Dictionnaire Des Institutions De la France Aux Dix-Septieme et Dix-Huitieme Siecles. LC 68-6230. (Bibliography & Reference Ser.: No. 214). (Fr.). 1968. Repr. of 1923 ed. $39.00 (ISBN 0-8337-2216-6). B Franklin.
Marx, Roland. Lexique Historique de la Grande-Bretagne XVIe. & XXe. Siecle. (Illus.). 216p. (Fr.). 1976. 26.00 F. Colin.
Ogee, Jean, et al. Dictionnaire Historique & Geographique de la Province de Bretagne, 2 vols. 1520p. (Fr.). 1973. 450.00 F. Floch.

FRANCE–HISTORY–THIRD REPUBLIC, 1870-1940
Pierrard, Pierre. Dictionnaire de la Troisieme Republique. (Illus.). 250p. (Fr.). 1968. 17.60 F. Larousse.

FRANCE–INTELLECTUAL LIFE
Beaud, Michel & Bellon, Bertrand. Dictionnaire des Groupes Industriels & Financiers en France. (Illus.). 361p. (Fr.). 1978. 45.00 F. Seuil.

FRANCE–LAWS, STATUTES, ETC.
Marion, Marcel. Dictionnaire des Institutions de la France aux 17 & 18 Siecles. 564p. (Fr.). 1972. 65.00 F. Picard.

FRANCE–NOBILITY
Saint-Simon, F. Dictionnaire de la Noblesse Francais. (Illus.). 1214p. (Fr.). 1975. 240.00 F. Contrepoint.
Sereville, Etienne De & Saint-Simon, F. de. Dictionnaire de la Noblesse Francais. 1214p. (Fr.). 1975. $95.00 (ISBN 0-686-56753-6, M-6513). French & Eur.
Sereville, Etienne de & Saint-Simon, Fernand de. Supplement au Dictionnaire de la Noblesse Francaise. 668p. (Fr.). 1977. $65.00 (ISBN 0-686-56752-8, M-6514). French & Eur.

FRANCE–PARLEMENT (PARIS)
Jolly, Jean. Dictionnaire des Parlementaires Francais: Vol. 3, 1889-1940. 380p. (Fr.). 1962. 41.60 F. PUF.
--Dictionnaire des Parlementaires Francais: Vol. 4, 1889-1940. 316p. (Fr.). 1968. 48.80 F. PUF.

FRANCE–POLITICS AND GOVERNMENT
Coston, Henry. Dictionnaire de la Politique Francaise, 2 vols. (Illus.). 1088p. (Fr.). 1970. 240.00 F. Coston.
--Dictionnaire de la Politique Francaise, 3. (Fr.). 1976. 150.00 F. Coston.
Dioudonnat, Pierre-Marie & Bragadir, Sabine. Dictionnaire des 10,000 Dirigeants Politiques Francais. 756p. (Fr.). 1978. $69.50 (ISBN 0-686-56727-7, M-6164). French & Eur.
Kuscinski, A. Dictionnaire des Conventionnels. (Fr.). 1973. 250.00 F. Francais, Ed. Du Vexin.
Lalanne, Ludovic. Dictionnaire Historique De la France, 2 Vols. 2nd ed. (Fr.). 1967. Repr. of 1877 ed. $93.00 (ISBN 0-8337-1985-8). B Franklin.
--Dictionnaire Historique de la France Contenant l'histoire Civile, Politique, 2 vols. (Fr.). 1967. $65.00. Lenox.

FRANCE–SOCIAL LIFE AND CUSTOMS
Davau, M. R., et al, eds. Dictionnaire Bordas: Dictionnaire du Francais Vivant. 1530p. (Fr.). 1980. E12.95 (ISBN 2-45538-828-X). Harrap.

FRANCESCO D'ASSISI, SAINT, 1182-1226
Giovanni, Boccali. Concordantiae verbales opuscolorum S. Francisci et S. Clarae Assisiensium. 960p. (Lat.). 1976. L.30000.00. LIEF.

FRANCIS OF ASSISI, SAINT
see Francesco D'Assisi, Saint, 1182-1226

FRANCO-PROVENCAL DIALECTS
see also Provencal Language
Duraffour, Antonin. Glossaire des Patois Franco-Provencaux. (Illus.). 758p. (Fr.). 447.00 F. CNRS.

FRANKLIN, BENJAMIN, 1706-1790
MacLaurin, Lois M. Franklin's Vocabulary. 1928. 35.00 (ISBN 0-8274-2371-3). R West.

FRATERNITIES
see Secret Societies

FREEHOLD
see Real Property

FREEMASONS
Diccionario Enciclopedico de la Masoneria. (Span.). $40.95 (ISBN 0-686-56654-8, S-14860). French & Eur.
Mellor, Allec. Dictionnaire de la Franc-Maconnerie et des Francs-Macons. 400p. (Fr.). 1971. $27.50 (ISBN 0-686-57043-X, M-6403). French & Eur.
Pocket Lexicon of Freemasonry. 1.50 (ISBN 0-685-19495-7). Powner.

FREEMASONS–HISTORY
Castell Blanch, Emilio. Claves de la Masoneria. LC 78-391684. (Illus.). 576p. (Span.). 1978. 300.00 ptas (ISBN 8-472-35344-3). Dopesa.

FREEZING
see Refrigeration and Refrigerating Machinery

FRENCH ART
see Art, French

FRENCH AUTHORS
see Authors, French

FRENCH-CANADIANS
Dunn, Oscar. Glossaire Franco-Canadien. LC 77-552917. 196p. (Fr.). 1976. Can.$9.95 (ISBN 0-7746-6779-6). Univ Laval.

FRENCH LANGUAGE
Belisle, Louis-Alexandre. Dictionnaire General de la Langue Francaise au Canada. (Illus.). 1487p. (Fr.). 1976. Can.$25.00. Beauchemin.
Dow, Francis D. Partially Naturalised French Words in Modern English. LC 76-370523. 65p. (Eng. & Fr.). 1976. E1.00 (ISBN 0-903745-02-X). Dow.
Golian, Milan. L'aspect Verbal en Francais. (Hamburger Phonetische Beitrage Ser.: No. 29). 269p. (Orig., Fr.). 1979. pap. text ed. $19.00x (ISBN 3-87118-390-3, Pub. by Helmut Buske Verlag Hamburg). Benjamins North Am.
Lefebvre, Jean-Jacques. Dictionnaire Beauchemin Canadien. (Fr.). 1968. Can.$12.00. Beauchemin.

Prefontaine, Robert & Cote-Prefont, Gisele. Dictionnaire. (Fr.). 1968. write for info. Beauchemin.
Thesaurus, 3: Liste Alphabetique. 2nd ed. 257p. (Fr.). 1975. 100.00 F. E. D. F.

FRENCH LANGUAGE–TO 1500

Godefroy, Frederic. Lexique de l'ancien Francais. 544p. (Fr.). 1976. 80.00 F. Champion.
Murray, Joseph P. Selective English Old-French Glossary As a Basis for Studies in Old French Onomatology & Synonymics. LC 77-128932. (Carl Ser.: No. 40). (Fr. & Eng.). Repr. of 1950 ed. $16.00 (ISBN 0-404-50340-3). AMS Pr.

FRENCH LANGUAGE–TO 1500–DICTIONARIES

Baldinger, Kurt. Dictionnaire Etymologique de l'ancien Francais. 144p. (Fr.). 1974. Can.$14.00. Laval P. U.
--Dictionnaire Etymologique de l'ancien Francais. (Fr.). 1974. Can.$14.00. Laval P. U.
Baldinger, Kurt & Straka, Georges. Dictionnaire Etymologique de l'ancien Francais, 1. 120p. (Fr.). 1971. 92.00 F. Klincksieck.
Baldinger, Kurt, et al. Dictionnaire Etymologique de l'ancien Francais. 112p. (Fr.). 1974. Can.$14.00. Laval P. U.
De Gorog, Ralph. Lexique Francais Moderne - Ancien Francais. LC 72-91996. 488p. (Fr.). 1973. $25.00x (ISBN 0-8203-0312-7). U of Ga Pr.
Godefroy, Frederic. Dictionnaire de L'ancienne Langue Francaise, 10 vols. (Fr.). 1961. 2364.00 F. Kraus.
--Lexique de l'ancien Francais. 544p. (Fr.). 1976. $39.95 (ISBN 0-686-57305-6, M-6282). French & Eur.
--Lexique de l'ancien Francais. 544p. (Fr.). 1901. DM.78.00. Olms.
Greimas, Julien A. Dictionnaire de l'Ancien Francais. 4th ed. (Fr.). 1970. 57.20 F. Larousse.
Mellerio, Louis. Lexique de Ronsard. 250p. (Fr.). 1974. DM.54.00. Olms.

FRENCH LANGUAGE–ABBREVIATIONS
see Abbreviations

FRENCH LANGUAGE–BUSINESS FRENCH

De Renty, Ivan. Lexique Quadrilingue des Affaires: Anglais-Francais-Allemand-Espagnol. 702p. (Eng., Fr., Ger. & Span.). 1977. 72.00 F. Hachette.
Peron, Michel & Withnell, William. Dictionnaire des Affaires: Francais-Anglais. 512p. (Fr. & Eng.). 1969. 57.00 F. Larousse.

FRENCH LANGUAGE–CONVERSATION AND PHRASE BOOKS

Ellison, Al. Ellison's French Menu Reader. (Fr.). 1977. $2.95 (ISBN 0-930580-00-1). Ellison Ent.

FRENCH LANGUAGE–DIALECTS

Albertini, Jean. Dictionnaire Francais-Corse. 349p. (Fr.). 1974. 76.00 F. C. E. R. C.
Andrews, James B. Vocabulaire Francais-Mentonnais. 174p. (Fr.). 1977. 75.00 F. Lafitte Repr.
Banitt, Menahem. Le Glossaire de Bale, 2 vols. 670p. (Fr.). 1972. fl.128.00. Brill.
Boris, Gilbert & Denizeau, M. Lexique du Parler des Marazig. 686p. (Fr.). 1958. 66.00 F. Imprimerie Nat.
Bos, Alphonse. Glossaire de la Langue d'Oll. 495p. (Fr.). 1974. 200.00 F. Laffitte Reprints.
Ceccald, Mathieu. Dictionnaire Corse-Francais (Pierre d'Evisa) 98p. (Fr.). 1974. write for info. CNRS.
Cellard, J. & Key, A. Dictionnaire du Francais non Conventionnel. 893p. (Fr.). 1980. $65.00 (ISBN 2-01-007382-7). French & eur.
Charbot, Nicolas & Blanchet, Hector. Dictionnaire des Patols du Dauphine. 448p. (Fr.). 1973. 150.00 F. Lafitte Repr.
Costa, Jean. Vocabulaire Analogique de la Langue Corse. 376p. (Fr.). 1972. 35.00 F. C. E. R. C.
Couzinie, J. Dictionnaire de la Langue Romano-Casteaise & des Contrees Limitrophes. 563p. (Fr.). 1976. 210.00 F. Lafitte Repr.
Debrie, Rene. Lexique Picard des Parlers Ouest-Amienois. LC 76-451761. 424p. (Fr.). 1975. write for info. Univers Picardie.
De Chambure, Eugene. Glossaire du Morvan. Taverdet, Gerard, pref. by. LC 80-463586. xxii, 966p. (Fr.). 1978. 350.00 F. Lafitte Repr.
Decour, Armand. Vocabulaire du Patols de Bettant, 2. 209p. (Fr.). 1975. 20.00 F. Decour.
De Foucauld, Charles. Dictionnaire Touareg-Francais, 4 vols. 2040p. (Fr.). 1952. 70.00 F. Imprimerie Nat.
De Landberg, C. & Zettersteen, K. V. Glossaire Datinois, 3 vols. 2976p. (Fr.). 1942. 360.00 F. Brill.
Les Dialectes Romans de France a la Lumiere des Atlas Regionaux. (Fr.). 1973. 201.00 F (ISBN 2-22201-540-5). CNRS.
Dubois, J. Dictionnaire du Francais Contemporain. 1263p. (Fr.). 1980. $19.95 (ISBN 2-03-320101-5, M-9357). French & Eur.
Dunn, Oscar. Glossaire Franco-Canadien: Vocabulaire de Locutions Vicieuses Usitees au Canada. 198p. (Fr.). 1976. 9.75 F. Laval P. U.
Duraffour, Antonin. Glossaire des Patois Franco-Provencaux. (Illus.). 758p. (Fr.). 1969. 320.40 F. CNRS.
Favre, Christophe & Balet, Robert. Lexique du Parler de Saviese. (Illus.). 1252p. (Fr.). 1973. 220.00 F. Champion.
Girodet, J. Dictionnaire du Bon Francais. 896p. (Fr.). 1981. lib. bdg. $37.50 (ISBN 2-04-010580-8, M-9362). French & Eur.
Gonfroy, Gerard. Dictionnaire Normatif Limousin-Francais. 300p. (Fr.). 1972. 34.00 F. Lemouzi.
Lalanne, Charles C. Glossaire du Patois Poitavin. 303p. (Fr.). 1976. 105.00 F. Lafitte Repr.
Lexique Patois-Francais du Parler de Vaux-Bugey, 1919-1940, 2 vols. 508p. (Fr.). 1942. 72.00 F. Klincksieck.
Malvezin, Pierre. Glossaire de la Langue d'Oc. 285p. (Fr.). 1975. 130.00 F. Laffitte Reprints.
Musset, Georges. Glossaire des Patois & des Parlers de l'Aunis & de la Saintonge, 5 vols. 2612p. (Fr.). 1977. 950.00 F. Lafitte Repr.
Onofrio, Jean B. Essai d'un Glossaire des Patois de Lyonnais, Forez & Beaujolais. LC 76-467468. (Illus.). lxxxii, 455p. (Fr.). 1975. write for info. (ISBN 2-717-10090-3). Horvath.
--Glossaire de Patois: Lyonnais, Forez & Beaujolais. 550p. (Fr.). 1974. 180.00 F. Horvath.
Palay, Simin. Dictionnaire du Bernais & du Gascon Modernes. 45p. (Fr.). 1980. pap. 35.00 F (ISBN 2-22202-708-X). CNRS.
Palay, Simon. Dictionnaire du Bearnais & du Gascon Modernes. 1052p. (Fr.). 1980. 290.00 F (ISBN 2-22201-608-8). CNRS.
Simin. Dictionnaire du Bearnais & du Gascon Moderne. 1044p. (Fr.). 1974. write for info. CNRS.
Vermesse, Louis & Lille. Vocabulaire du Patois Lillois. 238p. (Fr.). 1977. 85.00 F. Lafitte Repr.

FRENCH LANGUAGE–DICTIONARIES

Achard, Claude F. Dictionnaire de la Provence & du Comte Venaissin, 2 vols. 1162p. (Fr.). 1971. 235.00 F. Slatkine.
--Vocabulaire Francois-Provencal, 2 vols. 1425p. (Fr.). 300.00 F. Slatkine.
Albertini, Jean. Dictionnaire Francais-Corse. 349p. (Fr. & Corse.). 1974. pap. $39.95 (ISBN 0-686-56891-5, M-6001). French & Eur.
--Dictionnaire Francais-Corse. 349p. (Fr.). 1974. 76.00 F. C. E. R. C.
Alcala Zamora. Diccionario bilingue frances-espanol-aleman. Rev. ed. (Illus.). 960p. (Fr., Span. & Ger.). 100.00 ptas. 75.00 ptas ptas. Sopena.
Alletz, Pons Auguste. Dictionnaire des Richesses de la Langue Francoise: Neologisme qui s'y Introduit. 512p. (Fr.). 1968. 90.00 F. Slatkine.
Appel, L. Lexique des Fruits et Legumes. 133p. (Fr. & Eng.). Date not set. pap. $9.95 (ISBN 0-686-97410-7, M-9238). French & Eur.
Argaw, Makonnen. Lexique Queze-Amharique. 432p. (Fr.). 1974. 65.00 F. Publ. Orientalistes France.
Aurox, Sylvain & Weil, Yvonne. Nouveau vocabulaire des etudes philosophiques. LC 78-390296. 255p. (Fr.). 1975. 19.00 F (ISBN 2-01-002450-8). Hachette-Jeunesse.
Avril, J. T. Dictionnaire Provencal-Francais. 651p. (Fr.). 1978. 110.00 F. Slatkine.
--Vocabulaire Francais-Provencal: Dictionnaire Provencal-Francais. 651p. (Fr.). 1970. 110.00 F. Slatkine.
Bacon, F., et al. Petit Lexique de la Manutentio n. Anglais-Francais. Chartrand, P., ed. 37p. (Eng. & Fr.). 1974. pap. $5.95 (ISBN 0-686-92075-9, M-9226). French & Eur.
Bailleul, Charles. Petit Dictionnaire-Bambara-Francais Francais-Bambara. 339p. (Bambara & Fr.). 1981. text ed. $36.00x (ISBN 0-86127-220-X, Pub. by Avebury England). Humanities.
Bailly, Anatole. Dictionnaire Abrege Grec-Francais. 1012p. (Gr. & Fr.). 1969. pap. $39.95 (ISBN 0-686-56906-7, M-6019). French & Eur.
--Dictionnaire Abrege Grec-Francais. 1012p. (Gr. & Fr.). 1969. $58.00. Hachette-Jeunesse.
--Dictionnaire Grec-Francais. 2230p. (Gr.-Fr.). 1967. pap. $95.00 (ISBN 0-686-56907-5, M-6020). French & Eur.
--Dictionnaire Grec-Francais. 2230p. (Gr. & Fr.). 1967. 123.00 F. Hachette-Jeunesse.
Balmas, E. & Wagner, R. L. Vocabolario del francese moderno. (Illus.). 2517p. (Fr.). 1979. L.21000.00. Ist Geo Agostini.
Balmas, Enea. Dizionario pratico della lingua francese. (Illus.). 1950p. (Fr.). 1979. L.16000.00. Ist Geog Agostini.
--Dizionario pratico della lingua francese. 1936p. (Fr.). 1974. L.15000.00. Ghisetti & Corvi.
Barbier, Paul. Lexique d'Erquinghem-Lys. 70p. (Fr.). 1978. 20.00 F. Ste. Linguistique Picarde.
Barthe, Roger. Lexique Francais-Occitan. 240p. (Fr.). 1974. 30.00 F. R. Barthe.
--Lexique Occitan-Francais. 240p. (Fr.). 1973. 32.00 F. Lemouzi.
Baudouin, Alphonse. Glossaire du Patois de la Foret de Clairvaux. 342p. (Fr.). 1970. 60.00 F. Slatkine.
Bergeron, L. Dictionnaire de la Langue Quebecoise. 574p. (Fr.). 1980. pap. $75.00 (ISBN 0-686-92606-4, M-9360). French & Eur.
Berthe, Leon-Noel. Dictionnaire des Correspondants de l'academie. (Fr.). 1969. write for info. Eveche D'Arras.
Bielas, Leon. Slownik Minimum Francusko-Polski. LC 77-502306. 558p. (Pol. & Fr.). 1976. 30.00 Zl. Wiedza Powszechna.
Bildwoerterbuch Deutsch-Englisch-Franzosisch. 941p. (Ger. , Eng. & Fr.). write for info. (ISBN 3-411-01830-5). Biblio Inst.
Blachere, Regis & Chouemi, Moustafa. Dictionnaire Arabe-Francais-Anglais, 12 vols. (Arabic, Fr. & Eng.). 1970. 650.00 F. Maison & Larose.
Blanchard, E. Dictionnaire du Bon Langage. 8th ed. 318p. (Fr.). write for info. LIDEC.
Blinkenberg, A. P. & Hoybye, Poul. Dansk-Fransk Ordbog. 3rd ed. Thiele, Margrethe, ed. LC 77-467208. (Fr. & Dan.). 1975. Kr.180.00 (ISBN 8-71703-231-8). Erhvervso.
Bonaffe, Edmond. Dictionnaire des Amateurs Francais au 17 Siecle. 535p. (Fr.). 1967. $25.00. Lenox.
Bornecque, Henri & Cauet, Fernand. Dictionnaire Latin-Francais. 560p. (Fr. & Lat.). 1953. $39.95 (ISBN 0-686-56926-1, M-6044). French & Eur.
Bos, Aphonse. Glossaire de la Langue d'Oll. 495p. (Fr.). 1974. 110.00 F. Slatkine.
Bossicart, Claude. Dictionnaire de l'effusion. (Fr.). 85.00 F. Dryade.
Boursin, E. & Challamel, Auguste. Dictionnaire de la Revolution Francaise. (Fr.). 1971. 163.50 F. Kraus.
Boussinot, Roger. Dictionnaire des Synonymes, Analogies & Antonymes. 1031p. (Fr.). 1977. 58.00 F. Bordas-Dunod.
Bridel, Philippe Cyriaque & Favrat, Louis. Glossaire du Patois de la Suisse Romande. 565p. (Fr.). 1970. 100.00 F. Slatkine.
Burger, Andre. Lexique Complet de la Langue de Villon. 110p. (Fr.). 1974. 16.00 F. Droz.
Cahen, Jacques-Gabriel. Vocabulaire de Racine. 252p. (Fr.). 1970. 50.00 F. Slatkine.
Calfa, Ambroise. Dictionnaire Armenien-Francais, 2 vols. 1038p. (Armenian & Fr.). 1973. Set. pap. $49.95 (ISBN 0-686-56934-2, M-6056). French & Eur.
--Dictionnaire Armenien-Francais, 2 vols. 1038p. (Armenian & Fr.). 1973. 120.00 F. Klincksieck.
Calvin, Jean. Glossaire Dictionnaire des Locutions Obscures & des Mots Vieillis: Recontrent dans les Oeuvres de Calvin. 45p. (Fr.). 1968. 10.00 F. Slatkine.
Caprile, Jean P. Lexique Tumak-Francais Tchad. LC 76-459019. iv, 137p. (Eng., Tumak, & Fr.). 1975. write for info. Reimer.
Cassells. French Concise Dictionary. 1977. 9.95 (ISBN 0-02-522670-3). Macmillan.
Castellana, Georges. Dictionnaire Francais Nicois. 422p. (Fr.). 1977. Can.$90.00. Serre.
Castellanos i Llorenc, Carlos. Diccionari Catala-Frances, Frances-Catala. LC 79-125113. 1095p. (Fr. & Catalan.). 1979. 1000.00 ptas (ISBN 8-485-19409-8). Encic Catalan.
Ceccald, Mathieu. Dictionnaire Corse-Francais, Pierre d'Evisa. 464p. (Fr.). 1974. write for info. Klincksieck.
--Dictionnaire Corse-Francais (Pierre d'Evisa) 98p. (Fr.). 1974. write for info. CNRS.
Ceccaldi, Mathieu. Dictionnaire Corse-Francais, Pierre d'Evisa. 464p. (Corsican & Fr.). 1974. pap. $29.95 (ISBN 0-686-56944-X, M-6066). French & Eur.
Celerier, P. & Maillard, J. P. Dictionnaire des Structures Fondamentales du Francais. (Fr.). $13.50 (Dist. by Continental Bk Co). Cle International.
Cenacmoncaut, Justin E. Dictionnaire Gascon-Francais du Departement du Gers. 155p. (Fr.). 1971. 30.00 F. Slatkine.
Centre National De la Recherche Scientifique & Imbs, Paul, eds. Tresor De la Langue Francaise: Dictionnaire De la Langue Du 19th et Du 20th Siecle (1789-1960, 14 vols. 2000p. (Fr.). 1972. $55.00x ea. Intl Pubns Serv.
Cerlogne, Jean B. Dictionnaire du Patols Valdotain. 321p. (Fr.). 1971. 75.00 F. Slatkine.
Charbot, Nicolas & Blanchet, Hector. Dictionnaire des Patols du Dauphine, 2 vols. 457p. (Fr.). 1973. 100.00 F. Slatkine.
Cheneviere, Adolphe & Frank, Felix. Lexique de la Langue de Bonaventure Des Periers. 251p. (Fr.). 1971. 55.00 F. Slatkine.
Choppy, Jacques. Dictionnaire de l'Industrie Routiere. LC 77-573401. (Illus.). 143p. (Fr.). 1977. 55.00 F. Eyrolles.
Clapin, Sylva. Dictionnaire Canadien-Francais. 394p. (Canadian & Fr.). 1974. $17.50 (ISBN 0-686-56809-5, M-6587). French & Eur.
--Dictionnaire Canadien-Francais. xlvi, 394p. (Fr.). 1974. Can.$12.00 (ISBN 2-7637-6723-0). Soc Dev Liv.
--Dictionnaire Canadien-Francais. (Fr.). 1974. write for info. Laval.

Compendios de Divulgacion Filologica, 11 vols. Incl. Vol. 1. Ortografia Practica Espanola. Gili Gaya, S. 104p. pap. 195.00 ptas (ISBN 84-7153-255-7); Vol. 2. Resumen Practico de Gramatica Espanola. Gili Gaya, S. 112p ptas (ISBN 84-7153-256-5); Vol. 3. Nociones de Gramatica Historica Espanola. Gili Gaya, S. 104p. pap. 195.00 ptas (ISBN 84-7153-257-3); Vol. 5. Resumen Practico de Gramatica Francesa. 132p. pap. 195.00 ptas (ISBN 84-7153-263-8); Vol. 7. Ortografia Practica Francesa. 240p. pap. 250.00 ptas (ISBN 84-7153-264-6); Vol. 8. Ortografia Practica Catalana. 126p. pap. 225.00 ptas (ISBN 84-7153-266-2); Vol. 9. Vocabulario Basico Infantil. 64p. pap. 195.00 ptas (ISBN 84-7153-369-3). (Span.). Biblograf.

Comte Jaubert. Glossaire du Centre de la France, 2 vols. 915p. (Fr.). 1970. 190.00 F. Slatkine.

Conso, P., et al. Dictionnaire du Francais Vivant: Collection "Dunod Entreprise". 448p. (Fr.). 1979. 45.00 F (Dist. by Continental Bk Co). Bordas.

Constantin, Aime & Desormaux, Joseph. Dictionnaire Savoyard. (Illus.). 514p. (Fr.). 1973. 100.00 F. Slatkine.

Constantin, Aime & Desormeaux, Joseph. Dictionnaire Savoyard. 443p. (Fr.). 1973. 160.00 F. Lafitte Repr.

Dansel, Michel. Dictionnaire des Inconnus aux Noms Communs. LC 79-123074. 247p. (Fr.). 1979. write for info. (ISBN 2-86418-033-2). Encre.

Dauzat, A., et al. Nouveau Dictionnaire etymologique. (Fr., Fr). 27.50 (ISBN 2-03-020210-X, 3612). Larousse.

Davau, M. R., et al, eds. Dictionnaire Bordas: Dictionnaire du Francais Vivant. 1530p. (Fr.). 1980. E12.95 (ISBN 2-45538-828-X). Harrap.

Davaux, M., et al. Dictionnaire du Francais Vivant: Nouvelle Edition. 1360p. (Fr.). 1980. 23.75 F (Dist. by Continental Bk Co). Bordas.

Deak, Etienne & Deak, Simone. Dictionnaire des Americanismes. 6th ed. 928p. (Fr.). 1974. $25.00 (ISBN 0-686-56976-8, M-6103). French & Eur.

Debrie, Rene. Lexique Picard du Berger. LC 78-376584. 23p. (Fr.). 1977. 10.00 F. Eklitra.

--Lexiques Picards du Cidrier & du Meunier. 424p. (Fr.). 1977. 15.00 F. Eklitra.

De Foucauld, Charles. Dictionnaire Touareg-Francais, 4 vols. 2040p. (Fr.). 1952. 70.00 F. Imprimerie Nat.

Delboulle, Achille. Glossaire de la Vallee d'Yeres, 2 vols. 424p. (Fr.). 1969. 75.00 F. Slatkine.

Delvau, Alfred. Dictionnaire de la Langue Verte. 600p. (Fr.). 1972. 120.00 F. Slatkine.

Denizeau, Claude. Dictionnaire des Parlers Arabes de Syrie, Liban et Palestine. 581p. (Fr. & Arabic.). 1961. pap. $49.95 (ISBN 0-686-57090-1, M-6112). French & Eur.

De Regnier, Henri. Lexique de la Langue de Jean de La Fontaine, 2 vols. (Fr.). 1970. $55.00. Lenox.

--Lexique de la Langue de La Rochefoucauld. 446p. (Fr.). 1883. DM.98.00. Olms.

De Rochefort, Cesar. Dictionnaire General & Curieux Contenant les Principaux Mots: Les Plus Usitez en la Langue Francoise. 850p. (Fr.). 1972. 300.00 F. Slatkine.

De Roquefort, Jean-Baptiste B. Glossaire de la Langue Romane, 3 vols. 1915p. (Fr.). 1978. 400.00 F. Slatkine.

De Somaize, Antoine B. Le Dictionnaire des Preccleuses, 2 vols. (Fr.). 75.00 F. Kraus.

Desrosiers, G. & Boulay, J. Vocabulaire des assurances Sociales. 21p. (Fr.). 1971. pap. $3.95 (ISBN 0-7754-2274-6, M-9231). French & Eur.

Devigne, Paul. Glossaire du Patois Thierachien. 240p. (Fr.). 1978. 60.00 F. Ste. Linguistique Picarde.

De Vinols De Montfleury, Jules-Gabriel. Vocabulaire Patois Vellavien-Francais. 227p. (Fr.). 1975. 100.00 F. Lafitte Repr.

Dictionanaire Francais-Breton. (Fr. - Bret.). 1979. $15.00 (ISBN 0-686-56718-8, M-6141). French & Eur.

Dictionnaire Actif Nathan. (Fr.). $14.55 (Dist. by Continental Bk Co). Lib. Fernand Nathan.

Dictionnaire Breton-Francais, Francais-Breton. (Fr. & Breton.). 1979. $29.95 (ISBN 0-686-56717-X, M-6118). French & Eur.

Dictionnaire Chinois-Francais des Locutions et Proverbes. 565p. (Chinese & Fr.). 1980. $14.95 (ISBN 0-686-92595-5). French & Eur.

Dictionnaire de Franglais. 175p. (Fr.). 1980. pap. $16.50 (ISBN 0-686-92565-3, M-8980). French & Eur.

Dictionnaire de l'academie Francois, 2 vols. 878p. (Fr.). 1968. 800.00 F. Slatkine.

Dictionnaire de Poche Francais-Norvegien. (Fr. & Norwegian.). 11.00 F. Berlitz.

Dictionnaire des Communes (de France) (Fr.). $20.95 (ISBN 0-685-36659-6). French & Eur.

Dictionnaire des Communes de la Haute-Saone, 6. (Fr.). 1974. write for info. M. Bon.

Dictionnaire des Mots Contemporains. (Fr.). 1979. pns (M-6128). French & Eur.

Dictionnaire du francais contemporain: Manuel et travaux pratique. (Fr.). $18.95 (ISBN 0-685-92177-8, 4078). Larousse.

Dictionnaire du Francais Contemporain (DFC) 1119p. (Fr.). DM.29.80 (49005). Larousse-Langenscheidt.

Dictionnaire du Francais Facile. 86p. (Fr.). 1974. write for info. Hachette.

Dictionnaire du Francais Fondamental pour l'Afrique. 440p. (Fr.). 1974. write for info. Didier.

Dictionnaire du Francais Vivant. 1342p. (Fr.). 2500.00 ptas (ISBN 84-7153-150-X). Biblograf SP.

Dictionnaire Francais Azed. 940p. (Fr.). 1978. 20.60 F. Hatier.

Dictionnaire Francais-Francais des Mots Rare et Precieux. (Fr.). $8.50 (ISBN 0-685-36677-4). French & Eur.

Dictionnaire Francais-Serbo-Croate. 632p. (Fr. , Serbo & Croatian.). pap. $19.95 (ISBN 0-686-57109-6, M-6142). French & Eur.

Dictionnaire Francais-Vietnamien. 1276p. (Fr. & Vietnamese.). 1981. 260.00 F. Maison Dictionnaire.

Dictionnaire Image d'enfants. (Illus.). 14p. (Fr.). 1974. write for info. Mesure.

Dictionnaire Inverse de la Langue Francais. (Illus.). 504p. (Fr.). 1965. write for info. Mouton-De.

Dictionnaire Larousse de Poche. (Fr.). pap. 10.50 F. L. G. F.

Dictionnaire Larousse de Poche. new ed. (Fr.). 1967. pap. 10.00 F. Larousse FR.

Dictionnaire Marabout Universite. (Fr.). 19.50 F. Marabout.

Dictionnaire Marabout Universite, 3 vols. (Fr.). 34.50 F. Marabout.

Dictionnaire Moderne Francais-Arabe. 868p. (Fr. & Arabic.). 1979. leatherette $29.95 (ISBN 0-686-97332-1, M-9749). French & Eur.

Dictionnaire Pratique Quillet, 4 vols. 2416p. (Fr.). 1978. 875.00 F. Quillet.

Dictionnaire Quillet De la Langue Francais, 4 vols. 2132p. (Fr.). Set. $195.00 (ISBN 0-686-57114-2, M-6153). French & Eur.

Dictionnaire Quillet de la Langue Francaise, 4 vols. 2132p. (Fr.). 1978. 545.00 F. Quillet.

Dictionnaire Scolaire du Francais. 320p. (Fr.). DM.14.80 (46500). Langenscheidt.

Dictionnaire Vidal. (Fr.). 1976. 96.00 F. O. V. P.

Dictionnaire Vidal, 1982. 58th ed. 1168p. (Fr.). 1982. $75.00x (ISBN 2-85091-058-9). Intl Pubns Serv.

Dictionnaires. (Fr.). 15.00 F. I. P. E. C.

Dider, Marcel. Mes Dix Mille Mots. (Illus.). 792p. (Fr.). E5.75. Harrap.

Didler, M. Le Dictionnaire Pour L'Ecole: Mes 10,000 Mots. (Fr.). 1977. $14.95 (ISBN 0-8120-5207-2). Barron.

Dordillon, Ildefonse. Dictionnaire de la Langue des Iles Marquises. 598p. (Fr. & Marquise.). 1932. $27.50 (ISBN 0-686-56819-2, M-6597). French & Eur.

Dottin, Georges & Langouet, J. Glossaire du Parler de Piechatel. 373p. (Fr.). 1970. 70.00 F. Slatkine.

Dournon, Jean-Yves. Dictionnaire des 1001 Tournures: La Correspondance Pratique. (Illus.). 434p. (Fr.). 1977. 5.50 F. L. G. F.

--Dictionnaire Pratique d'orthographe & des Difficultes du Francais. 650p. (Fr.). 1975. 46.50 F. Hachette.

Dow, Francis D. Partially Naturalised French Words in Modern English. LC 76-370523. 65p. (Eng. & Fr.). E1.00 (ISBN 0-903745-02-X). Dow.

Dubois & Dubois-Charlier, F. Dictionnaire du Francais Langue Etrangere: Niveau I. (Fr.). 1977. $15.00 (Dist. by Continental Bk Co). Larousse.

Dubois, C. Pluri Dictionnaire. new ed. (Illus., Fr.). 1974. 31.50x (ISBN 2-03-020124-3, 3677). Larousse.

Dubois, J. Dictionnaire du Francais Contemporain. (Illus., Fr.). 1980. $17.75 (Dist. by Continental Bk Co). Larousse.

--Dictionnaire du Francais Langue Etrangere. (Fr.). 1977. write for info. Larousse.

--Larousse de la Langue Francaise Lexis, Illustre. (Illus., Fr.). 1979. $43.95 (Dist. by Continental Bk Co). Larousse.

Dubois, J. & Dubois-Charlier, F. Dictionnaire du Francais Langue Etrangere: Niveau II. (Fr.). 1979. $15.00 (Dist. by Continental Bk Co). Larousse.

Dubois, J. & Giacomo, M. Dictionnaire de Linguistique. 516p. (Fr.). 1974. $27.50 (ISBN 2-03-020299-1, 1002). Larousse.

Dubois, Jean & Lagane, Rene. Dictionnaire du Francais Classique. 608p. (Fr.). 1971. $22.50 (ISBN 0-686-57298-X, F-133960). French & Eur.

--Dictionnaire du Francais Classique. 608p. (Fr.). 1971. write for info. Larousse.

--Dictionnaire du Francais Contemporain. (Fr.). 1971. write for info. Larousse.

Dubois, Jean, ed. Lexis: Dictionnaire De la Langue Francaise. 2032p. (Fr.). 1975. $47.50 (ISBN 0-686-57019-7, M-6376). French & Eur.

--Lexis-Dictionnaire de la langue francaise. 1939p. (Fr.). 1975. $56.25 (ISBN 2-03-020285-1, 3924). Larousse.

--Lexis-Dictionnaire de la Langue Francaise. (Fr.). 1979. $56.25 (ISBN 0-686-60644-2, 2427). Larousse.

--Lexis: Dictionnaire de la Langue Frances. LC 76-455682. lxxix, 1950p. (Fr.). 1975. 139.00 F (ISBN 2-030-20285-1). Larousse.

Dubois, Jean & Duboise-Charlier, Francoise, eds. Larousse de Base: Dictionnaire d'Apprentissage du Francais. LC 78-380974. viii, 1023p. (Fr.). 1977. 30.00 F (ISBN 2-030-20144-8). Larousse FR.

Dubois, Jean, et al, eds. Dictionnaire du Francais Contemporain. LC 77-468961. xxii, 1263p. (Fr.). 1975. 34.00 F (ISBN 2-030-29321-0). Larousse FR.

Dubois, M. Claude. Petit Larousse en Couleur 1980. (Fr.). 1980. $56.75 (Dist. by Continental Bk Co). Larousse.

--Petit Larousse 1980. (Fr.). 1980. $31.25 (Dist. by Continental Bk Co). Larousse.

Dugast, Idelette. Lexique de la Langue Turen: Parler des Banen du sud-ouest du Cameroun. (Fr.). 1967. 51.00 F. S. E. L. A. F.

Dulong. Dictionnaire Correctif du Francais au Canada. 256p. (Fr.). 1968. write for info. Laval P. U.

Dumeril, E. Dictionnaire du Patols Normand. 326p. (Fr.). 1969. write for info. Slatkine.

Dupuis, Hector. Dictionnaire des Synonymes & des Antonymes. 607p. (Fr.). 1975. Can.$8.95. Fides.

Dupuis, Hector & Legare, Romain. Dictionnaire des Synonymes & des Antonymes. 608p. (Fr.). 1975. 54.00 F. Ecole.

--Dictonnaire des Synonymes et des Antonymes. 608p. (Fr.). 1975. $22.50 (ISBN 0-686-57129-0, M-6180). French & Eur.

Eckhardt, S. Dictionnaire de Poche Francais-Hongrois. 6th ed. 480p. (Fr. & Hungarian.). 1977. 10.00 F. Terra.

--Dictionnaire Usuel Hongrois-Francais. 376p. (Hungarian & Fr.). 1973. 35.00 F. Terra.

Eckhardt, Sandor. Magyar-Francia Szotar, 2 vols. LC 79-337569. xvi, 2558p. (Fr. & Hungarian.). 1978. 500.00 Ft (ISBN 9-6305-1297-1). Akademiai Kiado.

--Magyar-Francia Szotar, 2 vols. 2nd ed. LC 79-337569. xvi, 2558p. (Hungarian & Fr.). 1978. 500.00 Ft (ISBN 9-63051-297-1). Akademiai Kiado.

Edon, Georges. Dictionnaire Francais-Latin. (Fr. & Lat.). $37.50 (ISBN 0-686-57201-7, M-6703). French & Eur.

Elihai, Yohanan. Dictionnaire de l'Arabe Parle Palestinien. 418p. (Fr. & Arabic.). 1974. pap. $22.50 (ISBN 0-686-57132-0, M-6185). French & Eur.

Ernault, Emile. Glossaire Moyen-Breton, 2 vols. 870p. (Fr.). 175.00 F. Slatkine.

Ernault, Emile Jean M. Glossaire Moyen-Breton, 2 vols. LC 77-553414. xxviii, 833p. (Fr.). 1976. 290.00 F. Lafitte Repr.

Esnault. Dictionnaire des Argots Francais. (Fr.). $16.50 (ISBN 0-685-36663-4). French & Eur.

Fabre, Antonin. Lexique de la Langue de Chapelain. 77p. (Fr.). 1971. 20.00 F. Slatkine.

Faine. Dictionnaire Francais-Creole. 488p. (Fr. & Creole.). 1974. 300.00 F. Maison Dictionnaire.

Faine, Jules. Dictionnaire Francais-Creole. 480p. (Fr. Creole.). 1975. pap. $39.95 (ISBN 0-686-57291-2, M-4608). French & Eur.

--Dictionnaire Francais-Creole. 480p. (Fr.). 1975. 27.50 F. Lemeac.

Farsi, S. Kamusi Vocabulaire. LC 79-105083. 428p. (Fr. & Swahili.). 1978. write for info. Edns St Paul.

Ferrar, H., et al, eds. The Concise Oxford French Dictionary. (Fr.). 1980. 27.50 (ISBN 0-19-864126-5). Oxford U Pr.

Five Thousand French Words. (Fr.). write for info. (ISBN 0-671-41964-1). S&S.

Fortin, A., et al. Petit Lexique du Soudage. Anglais-Francais. Chartrand, P., ed. 47p. (Eng. & Fr.). 1974. pap. $2.95 (ISBN 0-686-92078-3, M-9227). French & Eur.

Francois, Dom Jean. Dictionnaire Roman, Wallon, Celtique & Tudesque: Servir a l'intelligence des Anciennes lois & Contrats, des Chartes. 380p. (Fr.). 100.00 F. Slatkine.

Franklin, Afred L. Dictionnaire Historique Des Arts, Metiers & Professions Exerces Dans Paris Depuis Le Treizieme Siecle. (Biblio. & Ref. Ser.: No. 198). (Fr.). 1968. Repr. of 1906 ed. $49.00 (ISBN 0-8337-1231-4); $40.00 (ISBN 0-685-06747-5). B Franklin.

French Dictionary. (Teach Yourself Ser.). (Fr.). 1977. pap. 5.95 (ISBN 0-679-10245-0). McKay.

Froimont, J. Dictionnaire de Poche Explicatif. 528p. (Fr.). 65.00 F. Erasme.

Fuchs, Maximilien. Lexique du Journal des Goncourt. 190p. (Fr.). 1972. 45.00 F. Slatkine.

Furetiere, Antoine. Dictionnaire Universel, 3 vols. 1650p. (Fr.). 1970. 1000.00 F. Slatkine.

--Dictionnaire Universel: Contenant Generalement tous les Mots Francois, 2. (Fr.). 1972. DM.298.00. Olms.

--Dictionnaire Universel: Contenant Generalement tous les Mots Francois, 3. (Fr.). 1972. DM.298.00. Olms.
--Dictionnaire Universel: Contenant Generalement tous les Mots Francois, 4. (Fr.). 1972. DM.298.00. Olms.
--Dictionnaire Universel d'Antoine Furetiere, 3 vols. (Illus.). 2504p. (Fr.). 1978. 690.00 F. Ste. Nouv. Littre.
Furetiere, Antoine & La Haye. Dictionnaire Universel: Contenant Generalement tous les Mots Francois, 1. (Fr.). 1972. DM.298.00. Olms.
Gaden, Henri. Lexique Poular-Francais: Le Poular Dialecte Peul du Fouta Senegalais. 280p. (Fr.). 1967. $16.00. Gregg.
Gaffiot, Felix. Dictionnaire Abrege Latin-Francais. 1720p. (Lat. & Fr.). 1970. pap. $15.95 (ISBN 0-686-57186-X, M-6258). French & Eur.
--Dictionnaire Abrege Latin-Francais. 1720p. (Lat. & Fr.). 1970. $40.00. Hachette Jeunesse.
--Dictionnaire Latin-Francais. (Lat. & Fr.). 1967. pap. $32.50 (ISBN 0-686-57187-8, M-6259). French & Eur.
--Dictionnaire Latin-Francais. (Lat. & Fr.). 1967. 83.00 F. Hachette.
Galisson, R. & Coste, D., eds. Dictionnaire de Didactique des Largues. 612p. (Fr.). 1976. $22.50 (ISBN 0-686-56813-3, M-6591). French & Eur.
Galley, Samuel. Dictionnaire Francais-Fang. 594p. (Fr.). 1978. 45.00 F. Messeiller.
Gamillscheg, Ernst. Etymologisches Woerterbuch der Franzoesischen Sprache. 2nd ed. (Fr & Ger.). 1969. 195.00 (ISBN 0-686-56604-1, M-7370, Pub. by Carl Winter). French & Eur.
Gary, Leger. Dictionnaire Patois-Francais a l'usage du Departement du Tarn & des Departements Circonvoisins. (Fr.). 1978. 150.00 F. Lafitte Repr.
Genouvrier, Emile, et al. Nouveau Dictionnaire des Synonymes. (Fr.). 1977. $19.95 (ISBN 0-686-57192-4, M-6266). French & Eur.
Georgin. Dictionnaire Grec-Francais. (Gr. & Fr.). 1978. 30.00 F. Hatier.
Georgin, Ch. Dictionnaire Grec-Francais. (Gr. & Fr.). pap. $14.95 (ISBN 0-686-57194-0, M-6268). French & Eur.
Gilbert, Pierre. Dictionnaire des Mots Nouveaux. 572p. (Fr.). 49.00 F. Tchou.
Giraudeau & Gore, Francis. Dictionnaire Francais-Tibetain. 310p. (Fr. & Tibetan.). 1956. 120.00 F. Maisonneuve, A.
Giraudeau, A. & Gore, Francis. Dictionnaire Francais-Tibetain (Tibet Oriental) 310p. (Fr. & Tibetian.). 1956. $49.95 (ISBN 0-686-57301-3, M-6275). French & Eur.
Girodet, Jean. Logos: Grand Dictionnaire de la Langue Francaise, 3 vols. LC 78-391601. xv, 3113p. (Fr.). 1978. 510.00 F (ISBN 2-040-07060-5). Bordas.
Girodet, Jean, ed. Logos-Grand Dictionnaire de la Langue Francaise, 3 vols. 3113p. (Fr.). E110.00 set (ISBN 0-245-53130-0). Harrap.
Gougenheim, G. Dictionnaire du Francais Fondamental. (Fr.). $8.75 (Dist. by Continental Bk Co). Didier.
Gougenheim, Georges. Dictionnaire Fondamental. 256p. (Fr.). 1958. 17.10 F. Didier.
Grad, A. Dictionary French-Slovene. 1402p. (Fr. & Slovene.). 1975. $35.00 (ISBN 0-686-92263-8, M-9693). French & Eur.
--Dictionnaire Moderne: Slovene-French-Slovene. 745p. (Slovenian & Fr.). 1978. leatherette $14.95 (ISBN 0-686-92561-0, M-9705). French & Eur.
Gras, Louis-Pierre. Dictionnaire du Patols Forezien. 302p. (Fr.). 1970. write for info. Slatkine.
Greimas, Algirdas J. & Courtes, Joseph. Semiotique: Dictionnaire Raisonne de la Theorie du Language. LC 80-462606. vi, 422p. (Fr.). 1979. 90.00 F (ISBN 2-010-05221-8). Hachette-Jeunesse.
Grujic, B. Dictionnaire Serbocrate-Francais, Francais-Serbocroate, suivi d'une courte grammaire de Langue Francaise. 631p. (Serbocroatian & Fr.). Date not set. $19.95 (ISBN 0-686-92591-2). French & Eur.
Guignard, Theodore. Dictionnaire Laotien Francais. 1034p. (Laotian & Fr.). 1971. $28.00. Gregg.
Guilbert. Le Vocabulaire de L'astronautique: Enquete Linguistique a travers la Presse d'information a L'occasion De Cinq Exploits de Cosmonautes. (Publ. de l'Univ. de Rouen Fac. des Lettres et Sc. Hum.). (Fr.). $15.95 (ISBN 0-685-36683-9). French & Eur.
Guilbert, L., et al. Grand Larousse de la Langue Francaise: Tome I, 7 vols. (Fr.). 1971. $67.80 ea. (Dist. by Continental Bk Co); $450.00 set. Larousse.
--Grand Larousse de la Langue Francaise: Tome VII, 7 vols. (Fr.). 1978. $67.80 ea. (Dist. by Continental Bk Co); $450.00 set. Larousse.
Guillemaut, Lucien. Dictionnaire Patois. 351p. (Fr.). 1970. 60.00 F. Slatkine.
Hamel, Bernard. Dictionnaire de Poche, 1: Francais-Polonais. 490p. (Fr. & Pol.). 1971. 24.00 F. Polonaises.
--Dictionnaire de Poche, 2: Polonais-Francais. 514p. (Pol. & Fr.). 1971. 24.00 F. Polonaises.
Hargous, Henri. Vocabulario Fundamental de la Lengua Francesa. 55p. (Fr.). Mex.$5.00. UNAM.
Hatzfeld, Adolphe & Darmesteter, Arsene. Dictionnaire General de la Langue Francaise: Commencement du 17 Siecle Jusqu'a nos Jours, 2 vols. 1468p. (Fr.). 1964. 230.00 F. Delagrave.
Hatzfeld, Adophe & Darmesteter, Arsene. Dictionnaire General de la Langue Francaise du Commencement du 17e Siecle Jusqu' a Nos Jours, 2 vols. 1468p. (Fr.). 1964. Set. $89.95 (ISBN 0-686-57290-4, F-134240). French & Eur.
Hausmann, F. J., frwd. by. New Diesterweg-Larousse: Dictionnaire du Francais Langue Etrangere. 1104p. (Fr.). DM.29.80. Diesterweg.
--Newu Diesterweg-Larousse: Dictionnaire du Francais Langue Etrangere. 928p. (Fr.). DM.26.80. Diesterweg.
Haust, Jean. Dictionnaire Francais-Liegois. (Fr. & Walloon.). 1974. write for info. Vaillant-Carmanne.
--Dictionnaire Liegeois. (Illus., Walloon.). 1933. write for info. Vaillant-Carmanne.
Helmlinger, Paul. Dictionnaire Duala-Francais. 666p. (Fr.). 1972. 105.00 F. S. E. L. A. F.
Henstock, Colin. Harrap's First French Dictionary. 133p. (Fr. & Eng.). E2.95 (ISBN 0-245-59978-9). Harrap.
Honnorat, Simon-Jude. Dictionnaire Provencal-Francais ou Dictionnaire de la Langue D'oc Ancienne & Moderne, 3 vols. 2365p. (Fr.). 1971. 500.00 F. Slatkine.
Hunter, Alfred C. Lexique de la Langue de Jean Chapelain. 160p. (Fr.). 1967. 30.00 F. Droz.
Jaba, Auguste. Dictionnaire Kurde-Francais. LC 76-472421. xviii, 463p. (Fr. & Kurdish.). 1975. DM.98.00 (ISBN 3-7648-0409-2). Biblio-Verlag.
Jarnier, Robert. Dictionnaire Bordas. 60p. (Fr.). 1974. DM.6.50. Bordas-Dunod.
Jaubert, Hippolyte-Francois. Glossaire du Centre de la France, 2 vols. 915p. (Fr.). 1970. 190.00 F. Slatkine.
Jesse, A. Physics Terminology. 129p. (Fr. Ger. & Eng.). 1980. pap. $24.95 (ISBN 3-7625-0963-8, M-9310). French & Eur.
Jong, F. J. Economisch Woorden Boek: Engels-Frans-Duits-Nederlands. 685p. (Eng., Fr., Ger. & Dutch.). 1980. $75.00 (ISBN 90-247-2243-8, M9474). French & Eur.
Jossier, Sophie. Dictionnaire des Patols de l'Yonne. 130p. (Fr.). 1970. 30.00 F. Slatkine.
Kahlmann, Andre. Petit Dictionnaire du Francais que l'on n'Apprend Pas a l'Ecole. 38p. (Fr.). 1977. Kr.42.00 (ISBN 91-24-27154-3). Esselte Studium.
Kiwanis-Club. Le Dictionnaire Franco-Montcellien. (Illus.). 117p. (Fr.). 1976. 15.00 F. Kiwanis-Club.
Klaus, Hans A. Franzoesische Fachausdruecke im Bankgeschaeft: Franzoesisch-Deutsch, Deutsch-Franzoesisch. LC 75-513804. 248p. (Fr. & Ger.). 1975. 26.00 F (ISBN 3-258-01279-2). Haupt Verlag.
Kornrumpf, H. J. Dictionnaire Europa Francais-Turc. 384p. (Fr. & Turkish.). 1966. 11.00 F. Larousse.
Kupisz, K. & Kielski, B. Dictionnaire Pratique Francais-Polonais. 1036p. (Fr. & Polish.). 1976. $19.95 (ISBN 0-686-92636-6, M-9327). French & Eur.
Labourasse, Henri A. Glossaire Abrege Patois de la Meuse. 570p. (Fr.). 1970. 100.00 F. Slatkine.
Lacombe, Francois. Dictionnaire de la Langue Romane ou du Vieux Langue Francois, 2 vols. 1200p. (Fr.). 1978. 250.00 F. Slatkine.
Lagrenade, Marcel. Lexique Aborite. (Fr.). 1974. Can.$pap. 5.75 (ISBN 0-88905-003-1). Dotmar.
Laman, Karl Edward. Dictionnaire Kikongo-Francais. 1278p. (Fr.). 1936. $24.00. Gregg.
Lamizet, Bernard. Dictionnaire des Synonymes & Antonymes. (Fr.). 1978. 6.00 F. Garnier-Flammarion.
Lange-Kowal, E. E. Langenscheidts Taschenwoerterbuch Franzoesisch: Teil I, Franzoesisch-Deutsch. 576p. (Fr. & Ger.). DM.16.80 (10151). Langenscheidt.
Lange-Kowal, E. E., et al. Langenscheidts Taschenwoerterbuch Franzoesisch, 2 vols. in 1. (Fr. & Ger.). DM.23.80 (11151). Langenscheidt.
Langenscheidts Handwoerterbuecher: Franzoesisch, 2 Teile in 1. (Fr.). 1978. DM.44.00 (ISBN 3-468-05151-4). Langenscheidt.
Langenscheidts Universal-Woerterbuch Franzoesisch. 560p. (Fr. & Ger.). DM.6.80 (18151). Langenscheidt.
Larousse & Co. Dictionnaire du vocabulaire essentiel. (Illus., Fr.). pap. $12.25 (ISBN 0-685-13873-9, 3753). Larousse.
--Larousse de poche. (Fr.). pap. $6.95 (ISBN 2-03-020166-9, 1008). Larousse.
--Larousse des debutants. (Illus., Fr.). $16.25 (ISBN 2-03-020151-0, 3752). Larousse.
--Nouveau Larousse Eementaire. (Illus., Fr.). $23.95 (ISBN 0-685-14003-2). Larousse.
Larousse And Co. Nouveau Petit Larousse en couleurs. (Illus., Fr.). 1974. $75.00 (ISBN 2-03-020111-1, 3676). Larousse.
--Petit Dictionnaire francais Larousse. (Illus., Fr.). $9.95 (ISBN 0-685-14034-2, 3754). Larousse.
Larousse de la Langue Francaise, 2 vols. (Fr.). 1977. $98.50 set (ISBN 2-03-020287-8). Pergamon.
La Rue, Jean. Dictionnaire d'Argot et des Principales Locutions Populaires. 189p. (Fr.). 1975. pap. $5.95 (ISBN 0-686-92571-8, F-136760). French & Eur.
Laureilhe, Marie T. Le Thesaurus: Son Role, sa Structure, son Elaboration. LC 77-575129. (Illus.). 48p. (Fr.). 1977. 20.00 F (ISBN 2-901-11904-2). Assoc Biblio.
Lebaigue, Charles. Dictionnaire Latin-Francais. 1382p. (Fr. & Lat.). $33.50 (ISBN 0-686-56999-7, M-6340). French & Eur.
Le Du, Jean & Le Berre, Yves. Dictionnaire Pratique Francais-Breton. 87p. (Fr.). 1976. 8.00 F. Rennes, C. R. D. P.
Leger, Albault A. Dictionnaire Francais-Esperanto. 736p. (Fr. & Esperanto.). 1961. 21.00 F. Esperanto.
Le Maistre. Dictionnaire Jersias-Francais, 2 tomes. (Fr.). Set. $86.50 (ISBN 0-685-36662-6). French & Eur.
Lemaitre, Yves. Lexique du Tahitien Contemporain: Tahitien-Francais. 201p. (Tahitian & Fr.). 1973. 27.00 F. Orstom.
Le Pennec, Marie F. Petit Glossaire du Language Erotique aux XVIIe & XVIIIe Siecles. LC 79-379970. 110p. (Fr.). 1979. 35.00 F (ISBN 2-863-80004-3). Borderie.
Lerond, A. Dictionnaire de la Prononciation. 589p. (Fr.). 1980. text ed. $20.95 (ISBN 2-03-340101-4, M-9124). French & Eur.
Lespy, Jean-Desire & Raymond, Paul. Dictionnaire Bearnais Ancien & Moderne, 2 vols. 878p. (Fr.). 1970. 150.00 F. Slatkine.
Lhande, Pierre. Dictionnaire Basque Francais. 1117p. (Basque & Fr.). 1938. $79.95 (ISBN 0-686-57020-0, M-6377). French & Eur.
Librairie A. Quillet. Dictionnaire Quillet de la Langue Francaise, 4 vols. LC 76-460437. (Fr.). 1978. write for info. Librairie Aritide.
Librairie Larousse. Larousse de Poche: Precis de Grammaire. LC 80-105478. lv, 543p. (Fr.). 1979. write for info. (ISBN 2-253-00344-1). Lib Gen Fr.
Linguistic Society of America & Woodard, C. M. Census of French & Provencal Dialect Dictionaries in American Libraries. $2.00. Linguistic Soc Am.
Lipsik, Frank. Le Dictionnaire des Varietes, A-Z. (Illus.). 188p. (Fr.). 1977. 29.00 F. Menges.
Littre. Dictionnaire de la Langue Francaise. Beaujean & Geraud-Venzac, eds. (Fr.). $24.95 (ISBN 0-685-36652-9). French & Eur.
Littre, Emile. Dictionnaire de La Langue Francaise, 7 tomes. (Fr.). $21.95 (ISBN 0-685-11141-5); Set. $245.00 (ISBN 0-685-11142-3). French & Eur.
Livet, Charles L. Lexique de la Langue de Moliere, 1. 532p. (Fr.). 1970. DM.298.00. Olms.
--Lexique de la Langue de Moliere, 2. 666p. (Fr.). 1970. DM.298.00. Olms.
--Lexique de la Langue de Moliere, 3. 824p. (Fr.). 1970. DM.298.00. Olms.
MacClelland. Vocabulaire de Lais de Marie de France. 204p. (Fr.). 1978. 58.50 F. Ottawa U.
Magnien, Victor & Lacroix, M. Dictionnaire Grec-Francais. 2168p. (Gr. & Fr.). 1969. 157.00 F. Belin.
Mai-Aru & Anisson du Perron, J. Dictionnaire Francais-Tahitien et Tahitien-Francais. 380p. (Fr. & Tahitian.). 1973. $17.50 (ISBN 0-686-57025-1, M-6383). French & Eur.
Mai-Aru, Mai-Arii & Anisson du Perron, J. Dictionnaire Francais-Tahitien. 380p. (Fr. & Tahitian.). 1973. 40.00 F. Pensee Moderne.
Mallement De Messanges, Claude. Dictionnaire de Halles. (Fr.). 1972. 150.00 F. Slatkine.
Malvezin, Pierre. Glossaire de la Langue d'Oc. 285p. (Fr.). 1976. 70.00 F. Slatkine.
Malzac, R. P. Dictionnaire Francais-Malgache. 861p. (Fr. & Malgache.). 1953. pap. $32.50 (ISBN 0-686-57030-8, M-6390). French & Eur.
--Dictionnaire Francais-Malgache. 861p. (Fr.). 1953. 70.00 F. Maritimes Outremer.
Marchand. Premier Dictionnaire Nathan. (Fr.). $8.95 (Dist. by Continental Bk Co). Lib. Fernand Nathan.
Marchand, Frank. Dictionnaire Actif Nathan. (Illus.). 288p. (Fr.). 1976. 36.00 F. Nathan.
Mathieu, Gustave. La Sante Grace a la Dietetique. LC 77-477672. 271p. (Fr.). 1975. 38.00 F (ISBN 2-85256-021-6). Doc Scient.
Matore, Georges & Matore, Geneve. Le Vocabulaire & la Societe Sous Louis Phillippe. 385p. (Fr.). 1967. 70.00 F. Slatkine.

Messinger, Heinz & Ruedenberg, Werner, eds. Langenscheidts Handwoerterbuecher Franzoesisch. (Fr.). DM.28.00 (ISBN 3-468-80015-0). Langenscheidt.
Mignard, Thomas. Vocabulaire Raisonne & Compare du Dialecte & du Patols de la Province de Bourgogne. 335p. (Fr.). 1970. 70.00 F. Slatkine.
Mineau, Robert & Racinoux, Lucien. Glossaire des Vieux Parlers du Departement de la Vilenne. (Illus.). 497p. (Fr.). 1975. 165.00 F. Quiniste.
Mirambel, Andre. Petit Dictionnaire Francais-Grec Moderne et Grec Moderne-Francais. 486p. (Fr. & Gr.). 1969. $29.95 (ISBN 0-686-57051-0, M-6413). French & Eur.
Missir, Emile. Dictionnaire Francais-Romaneique. 1060p. (Fr. & Romanian.). 1955. 110.00 F. Klincksieck.
Moisy, Henri. Dictionnaire du Patois Normand. 864p. (Fr.). 1969. write for info. Slatkine.
Moreschi, Xavier. Lexique Francais-Corse. 175p. (Fr.). 1973. 18.00 F. Corses.
Moulis, Adelin. Dictionnaire Languedocien-Francais. (Fr.). 1978. 75.00 F. Moulis, Ad.
Mousseau, Jacques & Moreau, Pierre F. L'Inconscient. LC 77-466781. 538p. (Eng. & Fr.). 1976. 72.50 F (ISBN 2-7256-0109-6). Retz.
Nardin, Pierre. Lexique Compare des Fabilaux de Jean Bedel. 188p. (Fr.). 1942. 50.00 F. Slatkine.
Nougayrol, Pierre, et al. Dictionnaire Elementaire Creole Haitien-Francais. Bentolila, Alain, ed. 511p. (Haitian & Fr.). 1976. $29.95 (ISBN 0-686-57060-X, M-6430). French & Eur.
Nouveau Dictionnaire du Francais Contemporain Illustre. 1290p. (Fr.). $27.00 (Dist. by Continental Bk Co). Larousse.
Nouveau Larousse Elementaire. (Fr.). 1967. $18.50 (Dist. by Continental Bk Co). Larousse.
Pauliat, Paul. Dictionnaire Bilingue Apollo. (Fr.). 1976. 18.00 F. Larousse.
Pernot, Hubert. Dictionnaire Grec Moderne Francais. 544p. (Gr. & Fr.). 1970. 25.50 F. Garnier.
Pessoneaux, Emile. Dictionnaire Grec-Francais. 896p. (Fr. & Gr.). 1953. $35.95 (ISBN 0-686-57071-5, M-6443). French & Eur.
Pessonneaux, Emile. Dictionnaire Grec-Francais. 896p. (Gr. & Fr.). 1953. 90.00 F. Belin.
Petit Dictionnaire Francais. (Fr.). $9.50 (Dist. by Continental Bk Co). Larousse.
Petit Dictionnaire Francais: Nouvelle Edition. (Fr.). 1978. $7.95 (Dist. by Continental Bk Co). Larousse.
Petit Dictionnaire Moderne: Nouvelle Edition. (Fr.). 1979. $9.95 (Dist. by Continental Bk Co). Larousse.
Phelizon, Jean F. Lexique des Termes Economiques. 2nd ed. LC 76-477732. (Illus.). 184p. (Fr.). 1975. 30.00 F. Tech Vulgar.
Piat. Dictionnaire Francais-Langue. 1000p. (Fr.). 1978. 180.00 F. Ramoun.
--Dictionnaire Francais-Langue d'Oc. 1000p. (Fr.). $75.00 (ISBN 0-686-56730-7, M-6451). French & Eur.
Piat, L. Dictionnaire Francais-Occitanien. 1000p. (Fr.). 1978. 250.00 F. Berenguie.
Planque, B. & Chabaud, N. La Pratique d'un Dictionnaire. (Fr.). 1977. $23.75 (Dist. by Continental Bk Co). Larousse.
Pleasants, Jeanne V. Phonetic French Dictionary: Contrasting French-English Sounds. 1959p. (Fr. & Eng.). pap. text ed. 5.95 (ISBN 0-940630-01-X, T-7010). Playette Corp.
Popelar, Inge. Das Akademiewoerterbuch von 1694: Das Woerterubch des Honnete Homme? LC 77-456424. vii, 235p. (Fr.). 1976. write for info. (ISBN 3-484-52057-4). Niemeyer.
Pryce, D. K. Les Idiotismes du Francais Fondamental, Premier Degre. (Illus.). 192p. (Fr.). E2.50 (ISBN 0-245-51978-5). Harrap.
Rampa, Lobsang T. Dictionnaire de Rampa. (Fr.). 1972. Can.$3.00. Presse.
Regnier, Adolphe. Lexique de la Langue de la Bruyere. 381p. (Fr.). 1970. DM.74.00. Olms.
--Lexique de la Langue du Cardinal de Retz. 439p. (Fr.). 1896. DM.98.00. Olms.
Reinhorm, Marc. Dictionnaire Laotien-Francais, 2 vols. (Laotian & Fr.). 215.00 F. C. N. R. S.
Reinhorn, Marc. Dictionnaire Laotien-Francais, 2 vols. 2000p. (Fr. & Laotian.). 1970. Set. $85.00 (ISBN 0-686-57204-1, M-6481). French & Eur.
--Dictionnaire Laotien-Francais, 2 vols. 2000p. (Fr. & Laotian.). 1970. 300.00 F (ISBN 2-22201-295-3). CNRS.
Remy, Maurice. Dictionnaire du Francais Moderne. (Fr.). write for info. Hatier.
Rey-Debove, G. Dictionnaire des Anglicismes. (Fr.). 1980. $44.95 (ISBN 0-686-92557-2, M-3259). French & Eur.
Richardson, Leonard T. Lexique de la Langue des Oeuvres Burlesques de Scarron. 286p. (Fr.). 1976. DM.56.00. Olms.
Richelet, Pierre. Dictionnaire Francois. 1148p. (Fr.). 1973. DM.356.00 F. Olms.
--Dictionnaire Francois, 2 vols. 1040p. (Fr.). 1970. 200.00 F. Slatkine.
Rietstap, Johannes B. Armorial general precede d'un dictionnaire des termes du Blason, Pt. 1. (Fr.). 1934. DM.135.00 (M-7298). Olms Verlag.
--Armorial general precede d'un dictionnaire des termes du Blason, Pt. 2. (Fr.). 1934. DM.135.00 (M-7299). Olms Verlag.
Robert. Dictionnaire Alphabetique et Analogique de la Langue Francaise, 7 vols. (Illus., Fr.). Set. $437.50 (ISBN 0-685-11140-7). French & Eur.
Robert, Paul. Dictionnaire Alphabetique & Analogique de la Langue Francais. Ray, A. & ReyDebove, J., eds. LC 77-569782. xxxi, 2171p. (Fr.). 1977. 158.00 F (ISBN 2-850-36030-9). Soc Nouveau.
--Dictionnaire Alphabetique & Analogique de la Langue Francais, 7 vols. 6000p. (Fr.). 1964. 1430.00 F. Ste. Nouv. Littre.
--Dictionnaire Alphabetique & Analogique de la Langue Francais, 6 vols. (Fr.). 1964. 1380.00 F. Ste. Nouv. Littre.
--Dictionnaire Alphabetique & Analogique de la Langue Francais, 6 vols. 534p. (Fr.). 1970. 150.00 F. Ste. Nouv. Littre.
--Le Micro-Robert: Dictionnaire Du Francais Primordial. 1231p. (Fr.). 1971. $14.95 (ISBN 0-686-57209-2, M-6487). French & Eur.
Robert, Paul, ed. The Robert Dictionaries. Incl. Le Micro Robert en Poche, 2 vols. 1171p; Le Micro Robert, 2 vols. in 1. 1230p; Le Petit Robert. rev. ed. 1972p; Le Grand Robert, 7 vols. 6530p. Set. $295.00x (ISBN 0-684-14004-7); suppl. only (ISBN 0-684-14085-3); Dictionnaire Universel des Noms Propres, 4 vols. (Illus.). 3200p. (Fr.). 1974. Scribner.
Rouaix, Paul. Dictionnaire des Idees Suggerees par les Mots. 32nd ed. 540p. (Fr.). 51.00 F. Colin.
Ruelle, Pierre. Le Vocabulaire Professional du Houilleur Borain. 200p. (Fr.). 1953. 280.00 F. Acad Royale.
Ruhland, Jean. Dictionnaire Trilingue. 220p. (Fr., Ger. & Eng.). 1977. 60.00 F. Ruhland.
Sacleux, Charles. Dictionnaire Francais-Swahili. 2nd ed. 755p. (Fr. & Swahili.). 1959. 53.00 F. Institut Ethnologie.
--Dictionnaire Swahili-Francais. 2nd ed. 1594p. (Swahili & Fr.). 1960. 86.10 F. Inst Ethnol.
Saras, Marcel. Dictionar Francez-Roman: Pentru uzul Elevilor. 2nd ed. LC 77-457298. 413p. (Romanian & Fr.). 1976. 17.00 lei. Editura Stiintifica.
Schneider, Lucien. Dictionnaire Esquimau-Francais du Parler de l'Ungava & Contrees Limitrophes. 2nd ed. 446p. (Fr.). 1970. Can.$15.00. Laval P. U.
--Dictionnaire Francais-Esquimau du Parier: l'Ungava & Contrees Limitrophes, 2. 430p. (Fr. & Eskimo.). 1970. Can.$15.00. Laval P. U.
Schuurmans, Stekhoven G. & Piriou-Vandamme, M. Kluwer's Universeel Technisch Woordenboek Frans-Nederlands. LC 75-406354. xiv, 622p. (Fr. & Dutch.). 1975. fl.73.75 (ISBN 90-201-0608-2). Kluwer Technische.
Setton, C., et al. Dictionnaire Hachette de la Langue Francaise. 1813p. (Fr.). 1980. $65.00 (ISBN 0-686-97331-3, M-9373). French & Eur.
Silvy, Antoine. Dictionnaire Montagnais Francais. 192p. (Fr.). 1974. 9.95 F. Quebec P. U.
Societe du Paler Francais au Canada. Glossaire du Parler Francais au Canada. LC 68-143461. 710p. (Fr.). 1968. $25.00 (ISBN 0-686-57223-8, M-6521). French & Eur.
Sommer, Edouard. Lexique Francais-Latin. 480p. (Fr. & Lat.). 1967. 11.30 F. Hachette-Jeunesse.
Sommer, Jean E. Lexique de la Langue de Mme de Sevigne, 1. (Fr.). 1973. DM.97.00. Olms.
--Lexique de la Langue de Mme de Sevigne, 2. (Fr.). 1973. DM.97.00. Olms.
Sorensen, Niels C. Dansk-Fransk Ordbog. LC 76-511464. 515p. (Danish & Fr.). 1975. Kr.60.00 (ISBN 8-70049-461-5). Gyldendal Norsk.
Stephanova, L., et al. Dictionnaire Bulgare-Francais. 978p. (Bulgarian & Fr.). 1973. leatherette $45.00 (ISBN 0-686-92575-0, M-9834). French & Eur.
Switzer, Robert, ed. World-Wide French Dictionary. (Fr.). 1978. pap. $2.95 (ISBN 0-449-30849-9, Prem). Fawcett.
Szwykowski, Ludwik, et al. Maly Slownik Francusko-Polski. LC 77-578114. xxviii, 326p. (Fr. & Pol.). 1977. 110.00 Zl. Wiedza Powszechna.
Talvitie, Jyrki K. Ranskalais-Suomalainen Tekniikan ja Kaupan Sanakirja. LC 79-338502. 296p. (Fr. & Finnish.). 1978. write for info. (ISBN 9-5190-3536-2). Tietoteos.
Tedjini, Abulgacim. Dictionnaire Francais-Marocain. 394p. (Fr.). 1949. 22.00 F. Maritimes Outre-Mer.
Tedjini, Abulqacim. Dictionnaire. (Fr.). 1948. 22.00 F. Maritimes Outremer.
Thesaurus I. R. S. I. D. 242p. (Fr.). 1971. 70.00 F. Francais, (Comptor) Siderurg.
Thibault, Adrien. Glossaire du Pays Biaiaois. 387p. (Fr.). 1970. 65.00 F. Slatkine.
Thoburn, et al. Mon Premier Dictionnaire en 2000 mots & 2000 Images. (Fr.). $19.50 (Dist. by Continental Bk Co). Casterman.
Thomas, A. V. Dictionnaire des Difficultes de la Langue Francaise. (Fr., Fr). 23.50 (ISBN 0-685-13865-8, 3611). Larousse.
--Dictionnaire des Difficultes de la Langue Francaise. 12th ed. 448p. (Fr.). 1971. pap. $6.00 (Dist. by Continental Bk Co). Larousse.
Tisserant, C. Dictionnaire Banda-Francais. 611p. (Fr & Banda.). 1931. 66.20 F. Institut Ethnologie.
Tisserant, Ch. Dictionnaire Banda-Francais. 611p. (Banda-Fr.). 1931. $32.50 (ISBN 0-686-56789-7, M-6585, Pub. by Institut Ethnologie). French & Eur.
Tissier, Jean. Dictionnaire Berrichon. 117p. (Fr.). 1970. 25.00 F. Slatkine.
Toesca, Maurice. Dictionnaire de la Contradiction. 234p. (Fr.). 1969. pap. $10.95 (ISBN 0-686-56825-7, M-6603). French & Eur.
Touati, Maurice A. Lexique Francais: La Reparation Juridique du Dommage Corporel. 268p. (Fr.). 1976. 68.00 F. Maloine.
Tresor de la Langue Francaise: Dictionnaire de la langue du 19e & du 20e siecle, Tome 7. 1380p. (Fr.). 1979. 114.00 F (Dist. by Continental Bk Co). Klincksieck.
Troupeau, Gerard. Lexique Index du Kitab de Sibawayhl. 268p. (Fr.). 1976. 64.00 F. Klincksieck.
Universal French Dictionary. 560p. (Fr.). $2.95 (091). Langenscheidt.
Vallieres, P., et al. Lexique des Produits de la Peche: Anglais-Francais. 35p. (Eng. & Fr.). 1980. pap. $3.95 (ISBN 2-551-03722-0, M-9223). French & Eur.
Vautherin, Auguste. Glossaire du Patois de Chatenois avec Vocables des Autres: Localites du Territoire de Belfort & des Environs. 548p. (Fr.). 1970. 95.00 F. Slatkine.
Vayssier, Aime R. Dictionnaire Patois-Francais du Departement de l'Aveyron. 704p. (Fr.). 1971. 120.00 F. Slatkine.
Vermesse, Louis & Douai. Dictionnaire du Patols de la Flandre Francaise. (Fr.). 1969. write for info. Slatkine.
Vermesse, Louis & Lille. Vocabulaire du Patois Lillois. 242p. (Fr.). 1978. 50.00 F. Slatkine.
Vernet, Pierre & Alexandre, Charles. Dictionnaire Elementaire Creole Haitien-Francais. (Illus.). 511p. (Fr.). 1976. 75.00 F. Hatier.
Vest-Pocket French. (Fr.). pap. 2.95 (ISBN 0-8329-1532-7). New Century.
Vest Pocket French Dictionary. rev. & enl. ed. 288p. (Fr.). pap. $2.95 (ISBN 0-8329-1532-7). New Century.
Vitu, Auguste C. Le Jargon du XVe Siecle: Etude Philologique. LC 78-375979. 542p. (Fr.). 1977. 120.00 F. Slatkine.
Vocabulaire des Termes: Essentiels Utilises pour la Transmissien Ligne; Francais-Espagnol-Russe-Allemand-Italien-Neerlandais-Polonais-Portugais-Suedois. (Fr. , Span. , Rus. , Ger. , Ital. , Dutch, Pol. , Port. & Swedish.). 1959. 11.20 F. U. I. T.
Weymuth, E. Langenscheidts Taschenwoerterbuch Franzoesisch: Teil II, Deutsch-Franzoesisch. 640p. (Ger. & Fr.). DM.16.80 (10156). Langenscheidt.
Wintz, E. Dictionnaire Francais-Dyola. 280p. (Fr.). 1968. $18.00. Gregg.
World-Wide French Dictionary: Indexed. (Fr.). 7.95 (ISBN 0-8329-9681-5). New Century.
Zandreitere, I., et al. Frantsuzsko-Latviiskii Slovar. 772p. (Fr. & Latvian.). 1957. $3.50 (Pub. by Latv Valsts). Four Continent.
Zeliqzon, Leon. Dictionnaire des Patols Romans de la Moselle. (Illus.). 735p. (Fr.). 1924. 32.33 F. Strasbourg, U.

FRENCH LANGUAGE–DICTIONARIES–ARABIC

Al-Chihabi, Emir. Dictionnaire des Termes Agricoles: Francais-Arabe. 2nd. ed. (Arabic & Fr.). $40.00 (ISBN 0-86685-305-7). Intl Bk Ctr.
Badawi, A. A Dictionary of the Social Sciences. LC 79-120007. xvi, 591p. (Eng., Fr. & Arabic.). 1978. write for info. Lib Liban.
Barthelemy, Adrien. Dictionnaire Arabe-Francais: Dialectes de Syrie. (Illus.). 68p. (Arabic & Fr.). 1969. 15.00 F. Geuthner.
Belot, P. Dictionnaire Al-Fara-id Arabe-Francais. 18th ed. (Illus.). 1114p. (Arabic & Fr.). 1964. 15.00 F. Dar El-Machreq.
Blachere, Regis & Chouemi, Moustafa. Dictionnaire Arabe-Francais-Anglais, 1, Pts. 1-12. (Arabic, Fr. & Eng.). 1967. $350.00 (ISBN 0-686-56918-0, M-6034). French & Eur.
--Dictionnaire Arabe-Francais-Anglais, 2, Pts. 13-24. (Arab., Fr. & Eng.). 1970. $350.00 (ISBN 0-686-56919-9, M-6035). French & Eur.
Cherbonneau, Auguste. Arabic-French Dictionary, 2 vols. (Arabic & Fr.). Set. $30.00x (ISBN 0-86685-103-8). Intl Bk Ctr.

--Dictionnaire Arabe-Francais: Langue ecrite, 2 vols. 436p. (Arabic & Fr.). $30.00 (103-8). Intl Bk Ctr.
Dozy, R. Dictionaire Detaille des Noms de Vetements Chez Les Arabes. (Arabic & Fr.). $20.00x. Intl Bk Ctr.
--Glossaire des mots Espagnols derives de l'Arabe. 426p. (Arabic & Fr.). $20.00 (105-4). Intl Bk Ctr.
--Supplement aux dictionnaires Arabes, 2 vols. 1721p. (Arabic & Fr.). $80.00 set (106-2). Intl Bk Ctr.
Elihai, Yohanan. Dictionnaire de L'arabe Parte Palestinien: Francais-Arabe. 418p. (Fr. & Arabic.). 1974. 52.00 F. Klincksieck.
Gasselin, E. Dictionnaire Francais-Arabe(Arabe Parle-Arabe Grammatical, 2 vols. (Fr. & Arabic.). 1974. Repr. of 1880 ed. text ed. $75.00x (ISBN 0-8426-0757-9). Verry.
Institut Dominicain d'Etudes Orientales du Caire, ed. Melanges: Tables generales (1954-1977, Tomes 1-14. (Fr. & Arabic.). 1980. Tomes 1-13 (168 p . $13.00 (283-2); Tome 14 (516 p . $40.00 (284-0). Intl Bk Ctr.
Jomier, Jacques & Institut Francais D'Archeologie Orientale. Lexique Pratique Francais-Arabe. 231p. (Fr. & Arabic.). 1976. 35.00 F. Francais, Inst. Archeo. Orient.
Kazimirski, A. B. Dictionnaire Arabe-Francais, 2 vols. (Arabic & Fr.). Repr. of 1860 ed. $80.00 set (110-0). Intl Bk Ctr.
Kazirmski, A. Arabe Francais Dictionnaire, 2 vols. (Arabic & Fr.). Repr. of 1860 ed. $80.00x (ISBN 0-86685-110-0). Intl Bk Ctr.
Libr. du Liban. ABC Dictionary I: Arabic & Fr. (Arabic & Fr.). 1983. $7.95x (ISBN 0-86685-310-3). Intl Bk Ctr.
Libr du Liban. ABC Dictionary Tamhidi: Arabic & Fr. (Arabic & Fr.). 1983. $7.95x (ISBN 0-86685-315-4). Intl Bk Ctr.
--My Illustrated Dictionary: Arabic & Fr. (Arabic & Fr.). 1983. $9.00x (ISBN 0-86685-321-9). Intl Bk Ctr.
Naggary-Bey, M. Dictionnaire Francais-Arabe, 6 vols. in 3. (Fr. & Arabic.). 1974. $90.00x set (ISBN 0-8426-0756-0). Verry.
Sabek, Jerwan. English-French-Arabic Trilingual Dictionary. (Eng., Fr. & Arabic.). $35.00x (ISBN 0-86685-116-X). Intl Bk Ctr.
Saisse, Louis. Dictionaire Francais-Arabe. (Fr. & Arabic.). 1980. pap. $8.95x (ISBN 0-86685-112-7). Intl Bk Ctr.
--Dictionnaire Francais-Arabe. 425p. (Fr. & Arabic.). pap. $8.95 student dict. (112-7). Intl Bk Ctr.
Sedira, Ben. Dictionnaire Arabe-Francais. 628p. (Arabic & Fr.). 1980. write for info. (M-9305). French & Eur.
--Dictionnaire Francais-Arabe. 828p. (Fr. & Arabic.). 1980. write for info. (M-9306). French & Eur.
Wahba, Magdi. A Dictionary of Literary Terms (English-French-Arabic) 1974. $28.00x (ISBN 0-86685-117-8). Intl Bk Ctr.

FRENCH LANGUAGE–DICTIONARIES–CHINESE

Dictionnaire Chinois-Francais. 673p. (Fr. & Chinese.). 1979. $25.00 (ISBN 0-686-97329-1, M-9268). French & Eur.
Dictionnaire de Poche Francais-Chinois. 558p. (Fr. & Chinese.). 1975. pap. $4.95 (ISBN 0-686-92470-3, M-9579). French & Eur.
Dictionnaire de Poche Francais-Chinois. 560p. (Fr. & Chinese.). 1977. 8.70 F. Pekin.
Dictionnaire Francais-Chinois. 1498p. (Fr. & Chinese.). 1979. $49.95 (ISBN 962-04-0090-9, M-9262). French & Eur.
Dictionnaire Francais-Chinois. 956p. (Fr. & Chinese.). 1979. leatherette $19.95 (ISBN 0-686-97330-5, M-9256). French & Eur.
Nouveau Dictionnaire: Francais-Chinois. 846p. (Fr. & Chinese.). 1980. leatherette $9.95 (ISBN 0-686-97425-5, M-9278). French & Eur.
Nouveau Dictionnaire Francais-Chinois. 1499p. (Fr. & Chinese.). 1981. $25.95 (ISBN 962-04-0090-9, M-9372). French & Eur.
Un Petit Dictionnaire Francais-Chinois. 177p. (Fr. & Chinese.). 1978. pap. $3.95 (ISBN 0-686-92073-2, M-9280). French & Eur.
Vocabulaire Methodique Chinois-Francais a l'usage des Interpretes. (Chinese & Fr.). 1971. 25.00 F. Asie-Orientale Cent. Pub.

FRENCH LANGUAGE–DICTIONARIES–DANISH

Dictionnaire Danois-Francais. 640p. (Danish & Fr.). write for info. Larousse.
Dictionnaire de Poche Francais-Danois. (Fr. & Danish.). 11.00 F. Berlitz.
Dictionnaire Lilliput Bilingue Francais-Danois. 640p. (Fr. & Danish.). 7.50 F. Larousse FR.

FRENCH LANGUAGE–DICTIONARIES–DUTCH

Dictionnaire de Poche Francais-Neerlandais. (Fr. & Dutch.). 11.00 F. Berlitz.
Dictionnaire de Poche: Francais-Neerlandias. 15th ed. 330p. (Fr. & Dutch.). 1977. 30.00 F. Erasme.
Dictionnaire Lilliput Bilingue Francais-Neerlandais. 640p. (Fr. & Dutch.). 7.50 F. Larousse FR.
Dictionnaire Neerlandais-Francais. 640p. (Dutch & Fr.). 7.50 F. Larousse FR.
Froimont, J. Dictionnaire des Synonymes: Francais-Neerlandais. 428p. (Fr. & Dutch.). 195.00 F. Erasme.
Grootaers, Ludovic. Dictionnaire Classique Francais-Neerlandais. 22nd ed. LC 75-505480. 10019p. (Dutch & Fr.). 1975. write for info. Vander.
--Dictionnaire Classique: Francais-Neerlandais, Neerlandais-Francais. 22nd ed. 1050p. (Fr. & Dutch.). 1969. $29.95 (ISBN 0-686-57317-X, M-6300). French & Eur.
--Le Nouveau Dictionnaire Francais-Neerlandais, Nederlands-Francais. 18th ed. 826p. (Fr. & Dutch.). 1969. $65.00 (ISBN 0-686-57318-8, M-6301). French & Eur.
Van Grieken, J. E. Dictionnaire du Traducteur: Francais-Neerlandais. 1760p. (Fr. & Dutch.). 1484.00 F. Administratives.

FRENCH LANGUAGE–DICTIONARIES–ENGLISH

Atkins, B. T., et al, eds. Collins Robert Dictionary: French-English-English-French. Duval, A. & Milnet, R. C. (Fr. & Eng.). $16.95 (ISBN 0-686-28358-9, CFD1); thumb index avail. (ISBN 0-00-433479-5). Collins Pubs.
Atkins, Beryl T., et al. Collins-Robert French-English, English-French dictionary. LC 79-359393. xxix, 781p. (Fr. & Eng.). 1978. E9.95 (ISBN 0-00-433479-5). W Collins Sons.
--Collins-Robert French-English Dictionary. LC 79-359393. xxix, 717p. (Eng. & Fr.). 1978. write for info. (ISBN 0-00-433478-7). W Collins Pubs.
Badawi, A. A Dictionary of the Social Sciences. LC 79-120007. xvi, 591p. (Eng., Fr. & Arabic.). 1978. write for info. Lib Liban.
Bell, John. Dictionnaire Anglais-Francais. (Illus.). 960p. (Eng. & Fr.). 1959. 18.00 F. Garnier.
Belle-Isle, J. G. Dictionnaire technique general. 2nd ed. 554p. (Fr. & Eng.). 1977. $45.00. Imported Bks.
Berlitz Editors. Berlitz French for Travellers. 192p. (Fr.). 1982. pap. 4.95 (ISBN 0-686-92978-0, Berlitz). Macmillan.
--Berlitz Pocket Dictionaries: French-English. 300p. (Eng. & Fr.). 1982. pap. $4.95 (ISBN 0-686-93004-5, Berlitz). Macmillan.
Blachere, Regis & Chouemi, Moustafa. Dictionnaire Arabe-Francais-Anglais, 1, Pts. 1-12. (Arabic, Fr. & Eng.). 1967. $350.00 (ISBN 0-686-56918-0, M-6034). French & Eur.
--Dictionnaire Arabe-Francais-Anglais, 2, Pts. 13-24. (Arab., Fr. & Eng.). 1970. $350.00 (ISBN 0-686-56919-9, M-6035). French & Eur.
Boudier, J. F. & Luquet, F. M. Dictionnaire Laitier: French-English-French. 220p. (Fr. & Eng.). 1981. leatherette $69.95 (ISBN 2-85206-092-2, M-9627). French & Eur.
Brommer. Lexique Anglais-Francais des Termes Appartenant aux Techniques en Usage a I. G. N. 122p. (Eng. & Fr.). 1958. 13.00 F. I. G. N.
Cassell. Cassell's French Dictionary: Concise French-English English-French. (Fr. & Eng.). $9.95 (ISBN 0-02-522670-3). Macmillan.
--Cassell's French Dictionary: Standard French-English English-French. (Fr. & Eng.). $17.95 (ISBN 0-02-522610-X). Macmillan.
--Cassell's French Dictionary: Thumb-indexed French-English English-French. (Fr. & Eng.). $19.95 (ISBN 0-02-522620-7). Macmillan.
Cassell's Compact French-English, English-French Dictionary. 672p. (Fr. & Eng.). 1981. pap. $3.95 (ISBN 0-440-31128-4, LE). Dell.
Centre de Documentation de L'armement. Lexique des Mots-cles, Descripteurs & Identificateurs, Francais-Anglais: Utiliser pour la Recherche Documentaire, 3 vols. 2001p. (Fr. & Eng.). 1976. 200.00 F. Centre Documentation Armement.
Chaffurin, L. & Mergault, J. Dictionnaire Bilingue Larousse, Francais-Anglais, Anglais-Francais. (Apollo). (Fr. & Eng.). $10.50 (ISBN 0-685-13856-9, 3767). Larousse.
Chaffurin, Louis & Mergault, Jean. Dictionnaire Bilingue Apollo Francais-Anglais. 768p. (Fr. & Eng.). 1971. 18.70 F. Larousse.
Chauffurin, L. Petit Dictionnaire bilingue Larousse, francais-anglais et English-French. (Adonis). (Fr. & Eng.). plastic bdg. $6.25 (ISBN 0-685-14032-6, 3768). Larousse.
Clifton, Ebenezer & Mac Laughlin, Horace J. Dictionnaire Anglais-Francais. (Illus.). 1260p. (Eng. & Fr.). 1968. 56.00 F. Garnier.
Collin, P. H., et al. Harrap's Shorter French & English Dictionary. 1781p. (Fr. & Eng.). 1982. E9.95 (ISBN 0-245-53926-3). Harrap.
Collins French-English English-French Dictionary. 512p. (Orig., Fr. & Eng.). 1982. pap. $2.95 (ISBN 0-425-05449-7). Berkley Pub.
Collins Pocket French Dictionary. 528p. 1983. $7.95 (ISBN 0-671-49220-9). S&S.
Collins, Robert. French-English Dictionary. (Fr. & Eng.). $19.95. Iaconi.
Colpron, Gilles. Les Anglicismes au Quebec. 247p. (Fr. & Eng.). 1979. $17.50 (ISBN 0-686-56957-1, M-6080). French & Eur.
Cortina. Cortina-Ace Basic French Dictionary. (Foreign Language Dictionary Ser.). 384p. (Fr.). 1983. pap. $3.50 (ISBN 0-441-04999-0). Ace Bks.
Cotgrave, Randle. A Dictionarie of the French & English Tongues. LC 77-171741. (English Experience Ser.: No. 367). 992p. (Fr. & Eng.). 1971. Repr. of 1611 ed. $105.00 (ISBN 90-221-0367-6). Walter J Johnson.
--Dictionary of the French & English Tongues. (Fr. & Eng.). 1971. Repr. of 1611 ed. $128.00 (ISBN 0-685-05204-4). Adler.
Coveney & Moore. Glossary of French & English Management Terms. xii, 146p. (Fr. & Eng.). E3.50. Longman.
Cruikshank, Eleanor P. French-English Instant Vocabulary. 88p. (Fr. & Eng.). 1980. pap. $4.00 (ISBN 0-9605284-0-7). Cruikshank.
Cusset, Francis. English-French & French-English Technical Dictionary. rev. ed. (Eng. & Fr.). 1967. $28.50 (ISBN 0-8206-0043-1). Chem Pub.
--Vocabulaire Technique Anglais-Francais. 9th ed. 434p. (Eng. & Fr.). 1977. 118.50 F. Berger-Levrault.
De Gorog, Ralph. Dictionnaire inverse de l'ancien francais. LC 81-18874. (Medieval & Renaissance Texts & Studies: No. 4). 256p. (Fr.). 1981. 13.50 (ISBN 0-86698-010-5). Medieval & Renaissance NY.
Delmas-Harrap. Dictionnaire des Affaires Francais-Anglais, Anglais-Francais. (Fr. & Eng.). $65.50 (ISBN 0-685-36681-2). French & Eur.
Deneubourg, Debleser M. Vocabulaire, Orthographe, Conjugaison, Analyse. (Illus.). 210p. (Fr.). 1974. 178.00 F. Wesmael-Charlier.
Deneubourg, N. Vocabulaire, Orthographe, Conjugalson, Analyse. 208p. (Fr.). 1974. 210.00 F. Wesmael-Charlier.
--Vocabulaire, Orthographe, Conlugalson, Analyse. (Illus.). 274p. (Fr.). 1976. 243.00 F. Wesmael-Charlier.
Dictionary of Idioms French-English: Dictionnaire des locutions. (Fr. & Eng.). 33.95 (ISBN 2-03-021101-X, 3681). Larousse.
Dictionnaire Anglais-Francais. 640p. (Eng. & Fr.). 1978. 7.50 F. Larousse.
Dictionnaire Bilingue "Apollo". (Fr. & Eng.). 1973. $7.25 (Dist. by Continental Bk Co). Larousse.
Dictionnaire de Poche Francais-Anglais. (Fr. & Eng.). 11.00 F. Berlitz.
Dictionnaire Europa Francais-Anglais. 460p. (Fr. & Eng.). 1978. 11.00 F. Larousse.
Dictionnaire Francais-Serbo-Croate. 632p. (Fr. & Serbo-Croatian.). 1978. 39.20 F. Vander.
Dictionnaire Gemeaux: Francais-Anglais. (Fr. & Eng.). 19.50 F. Hatier.
Dictionnaire Larousse Bilingue de Poche. (Fr. & Eng.). 1968. $3.95 (Dist. by Continental Bk Co). Larousse.
Dictionnaire Larousse Bilingue de Poche: Francais-Anglais. 500p. (Fr. & Eng.). pap. 11.70 F. Larousse FR.
Dictionnaire Larousse: Francais-Anglais. (Fr. & Eng.). pap. 10.50 F. L. G. F.
Dictionnaire Larousse Moderne Francais-Anglais. (Illus.). 1552p. (Fr. & Eng.). 1968. Can.$7.95. Edns Francaises.
Dictionnaire Lilliput Bilingue Francais-Anglais. 640p. (Fr. & Eng.). 7.50 F. Larousse FR.
Dictionnaire Polonais-Francais. 1076p. (Pol. & Fr.). 1978. 55.80 F. Vander.
Dictionnaire Poucet Anglais-Francais. (Eng. & Fr.). 5.15 F. Hatier.
Dictionnaire Poucet Francais-Anglais. (Fr. & Eng.). 1978. pap. 5.15 F. Hatier.
Dictionnaires Bilingues Francais-Anglais. 500p. (Fr. & Eng.). $6.50 (Dist. by Continental Bk Co). Larousse.
Dictionnaires Bilingues Larousse Francais-Anglais. (Fr. & Eng.). $9.95 (Dist. by Continental Bk Co). Larousse.
Dictionnaires Modernes Larousse Francais-Anglais. 1290p. (Fr. & Eng.). $32.50 (Dist. by Continental Bk Co). Larousse.
Dion, Gerard. Dictionnaire Canadien des Relations du Travall Francais-Anglais. (Fr. & Eng.). 1976. write for info. Laval P. U.
Douglas, J. H., et al, eds. Cassell's Concise French-English, English-French Dictionary. abr. ed. LC 77-7667. 658p. (Fr. & Eng.). 1977. 9.95 (ISBN 0-02-522670-3). Macmillan.

Dubois, Charlier F. Dictionnaire Francais-Anglais des Debutantes. (Fr. & Eng.). 1978. $8.95 (Dist. by Continental Bk Co). Larousse.
Dubois, M. M. Dictionnaire moderne Larousse francais-anglais et anglais-francais. new rev. ed. (Fr. & Eng.). 29.95 (ISBN 0-88332-003-7, 3769). Larousse.
--Dictionnaire Moderne "Saturne". (Fr. & Eng.). 1979. $27.00 (Dist. by Continental Bk Co). Larousse.
Dubois, Marguerite-Marie. Dictionnaire de Locutions, Francais-Anglais. 392p. (Fr. & Eng.). 1973. $22.50 (ISBN 0-686-57125-8, M-6173). French & Eur.
Dubois, Marie M. Dictionnaire Moderne Saturne: Francais-Anglais. 10th ed. 1552p. (Fr. & Eng.). 1972. 70.00 F. Larousse FR.
Dubois, Marie-Marguerite. Dictionnaire Moderne Saturne: Francais-Anglais, Anglais-Francais. 10th ed. 1552p. (Fr. & Eng.). 1972. $29.95 (ISBN 0-686-57126-6, M-6174). French & Eur.
Dubois-Charlier, F., et al. Dictionnaire d'Anglais. 868p. (Fr.). 1975. pap. text ed. $11.50 (ISBN 2-03-040531-0). Larousse.
Eastman, P. D. Cat in the Hat Beginner Book Dictionary in French & English. LC 65-22650. (Illus., Fr. & Eng.). (gr. 2-3). 1965. $8.95 (ISBN 0-394-81063-5). Beginner.
Editions Berlitz S. A. English-French Dictionary. rev. ed. LC 78-78078. 335p. (Eng. & Fr.). 1979. $2.95 (ISBN 0-02-964500-X, Pub by Berlitz). Macmillan.
Falconer, William. Universal Dictionary of the Marine. LC 72-87321. (Illus.). Repr. of 1780 ed. lib. bdg. 37.50x (ISBN 0-678-05655-2). Kelley.
Fedou, R. Lexique Histoire du Moyen-Age. (Fr.). pap. $16.50 (ISBN 0-686-92260-3, M-8981). French & Eur.
Fonteneau, M. & Theureau, S. Mon Dictionnaire Francais-Anglais. (Fr. & Eng.). 1969. $15.95 (Dist. by Continental Bk Co). Larousse.
Forbes, Patricia & Ledesert, Margaret, eds. Harrap's Mini Pocket French & English Dictionary. 544p. (Fr. & Eng.). E1.25 (ISBN 0-245-53135-1). Harrap.
--Harrap's New Pocket French & English Dictionary. 525p. (Fr. & Eng.). 1969. E2.95 (ISBN 0-245-59812-X). Harrap.
Gerber, Barbara & Storzer, Gerald. French Idioms on the Way. (Illus., Fr.). 1984. pap. $4.95 (ISBN 0-8120-2108-8). Barron.
Girard, Denis. Dictionnaire Francais-Anglais. (Illus.). 1464p. (Fr. & Eng.). 1972. 68.00 F. Garnier.
--Dictionnaire Francais-Anglais et Anglais-Francais. 1464p. (Fr.-Eng.). 1972. $27.50 (ISBN 0-686-57300-5, M-6274). French & Eur.
Girard, Denis, et al, eds. Cassell's French Dictionary. LC 77-7669. (Fr.). 1977. indexed 18.95 (ISBN 0-02-522620-7); plain 16.50 (ISBN 0-02-522610-X). Macmillan.
Hall, Robert A., Jr. & Langbaum, Francesca V. French Vest Pocket Dictionary. (Fr.). 1954. pap. 2.95 (ISBN 0-394-40054-2). Random.
Hamlyn. French Dictionary. 320p. (Fr. & Eng.). Epap. 1.00 (ISBN 0-600-36563-8). Hamlyn-Amer.
Hamlyn French-English Dictionary. (Fr. & Eng.). 1977. pap. 4.95 (ISBN 0-600-36563-8, 8086). Larousse.
Harrap's French-English Dictionary of Slang & Colloquialisms. (Fr. & Eng.). 1975. $14.95 (ISBN 0-686-57323-4, M-6308). French & Eur.
Harrap's New Standard Francais-Anglais, 1: A-I. (Fr.-Eng.). 1972. $32.50 (ISBN 0-8442-1876-6, M-6309). French & Eur.
Harrap's New Standard Francais-Anglais, 2: J-Z. 1162p. (Fr.-Eng.). 1972. $32.50 (ISBN 0-8442-1898-7, M-6310). French & Eur.
Harrap's Standard Anglais-Francais. 1530p. (Fr.-Eng.). 1970. $49.95 (ISBN 0-686-57324-2, M-6311). French & Eur.
Henstock, Colin. Dictionnaire Fondamental Harrap: Francais-Anglais. 136p. (Fr. & Eng.). 1973. 15.00 F. Bordas-Dunod.
Hochman, ed. Kettridge's English-French - French-English Dictionary. (Eng. & Fr.). 1971. pap. 3.50 (ISBN 0-451-11804-9, AE1804, Sig). NAL.
Hughes, Charles A. Ace's French Phrase Book & Dictionary. (Ace's Foreign Phrase Bk). 192p. (Eng. & Fr.). 1981. pap. $1.95 (ISBN 0-441-25208-7). Ace Bks.
Hugo Pocket Dictionary: French-English, English-French. (Fr. & Eng.). 1973. 3.50 (ISBN 0-8226-0503-1, 503). Littlefield.
Institute for Language Study. Vest Pocket French. (Illus.). 128p. (Fr.). 1979. pap. $1.95 (ISBN 0-06-464901-6, BN 4901, BN). B&N NY.
Jean's Pocket Dictionaries: French-English. 224p. (Orig., Fr. & Eng.). 1981. pap. 2.25 (ISBN 0-8437-1725-4). Hammond Inc.
Kettridge, Julius O. Financial & Mercantile Dictionary. (Fr. & Eng.). $13.95 (ISBN 0-685-11187-3). French & Eur.
Kuentz, Eugene. Dictionnaire Anglais-Francais. 824p. (Eng. & Fr.). 1973. 23.50 F. Ecole.
Kuentz, Eugene & Saillens, Emile. Dictionnaire Anglais-Francais. (Eng. & Fr.). 1970. 20.00 F. Licet.
--Dictionnaire Anglais-Francais. 872p. (Eng. & Fr.). 1978. 23.50 F. Magnard.
Langbaum, Francesca L., ed. The Random House Basic Dictionary French. (Fr. & Eng.). 1981. pap. $1.50 (ISBN 0-345-29617-6). Ballantine.
Langenscheidt English-French Lilliput Dictionary. 640p. (Fr. & Eng.). plastic $1.50 (ISBN 3-468-96408-0). Langenscheidt.
Langenscheidt French-English Lilliput Dictionary. 640p. (Fr. & Eng.). plastic $1.50 (ISBN 3-468-96407-2). Langenscheidt.
Langenscheidt Staff, ed. Langenscheidt's New Pocket French Dictionary: French-English, English-French. (Langenscheidt Pocket Dictionaries Ser.). 640p. (Fr. & Eng.). 1970. $5.95 (ISBN 0-685-31331-X). Am Map.
Langenscheidt's Lilliput French-English Dictionary. 640p. (Eng. & Fr.). 1972. $1.50 (ISBN 0-685-31354-9). Am Map.
Larousse And Co. Mon Premier Larousse francais-anglais, anglais-francais en couleurs. (Fr. & Eng.). (gr. 6-9). $23.75 (ISBN 2-03-051431-4, 3794). Larousse.
Larousse Bi-Lingual French-English, English French Dictionary. (Apollo). (Fr. & Eng.). 10.50 (ISBN 2-03-020903-1, 3767). Larousse.
Larousse De Poche. (Fr.). pap. $4.95 (ISBN 0-671-48896-1). PB.
Larousse French-English Dictionary. (Fr. & Eng.). 1981. pap. 3.95 (ISBN 0-671-47166-X). PB.
Larousse Modern French-English, English-French Dictionary. (Fr. & Eng.). 29.95 (ISBN 2-03-020602-4, 3776). Larousse.
Laurence Urdang Associates. Hamlyn French Dictionary. LC 77-377030. 305p. (Eng. & Fr.). 1976. E0.75 (ISBN 0-600-36563-8). Hamlyn-Amer.
Lipton, G. French Bilingual Dictionary: A Beginner's Guide in Words & Pictures. (Fr. & Eng.). 1974. $4.95 (ISBN 0-8120-0470-1). Barron.
Lipton, Gladys. French Bilingual Dictionary: Compact Ed. rev. ed. LC 78-20788. (Illus., Fr. & Eng.). (gr. 7-12). 1979. pap. $3.25 (ISBN 0-8120-2007-3). Barron.
Lipton, Gladys C. French Bilingual Dictionary: A Beginner's Guide in Words & Pictures. LC 78-20788. ix, 355p. (Eng. & Fr.). 1979. $2.95 (ISBN 0-8120-2007-3). Barron.
Malgorn, Guy. Dictionnaire technique Anglais-Francais. 5th ed. (Fr. & Eng.). 1972. $38.00. Imported Bks.
Mansion, J. E. Harrap's Concise Student French & English Dictionary. new ed. Collin, P. H., et al, eds. (Fr. & Eng.). (gr. 9-12). 1978. Repr. text ed. 9.95 (ISBN 0-8442-1872-3, 1872-4). Natl Textbk.
--Harrap's New Collegiate French & English Dictionary. rev. ed. Ledesert, D. H., ed. LC 75-182800. (Fr. & Eng.). (gr. 9-12). 1967. Repr. text ed. 14.95 (ISBN 0-8442-1873-1, 1873-4). Natl Textbk.
--Harrap's New Standard French & English Dictionary, 2 vols. (Fr. & Eng.). 1973. $35.95 ea. (ISBN 0-7720-0546-X); $35.95 ea. (ISBN 0-7720-0546-X). Clarke Ltd.
--Harrap's New Standard French & English Dictionary: A-I, French-English, Vol. 1. Ledesert, D. M. & Ledesert, R. P., eds. xxx, 567p. (Fr. & Eng.). E20.00 (ISBN 0-245-50972-0). Harrap.
--Harrap's New Standard French & English Dictionary: A-K, English-French, Vol. 3. Ledesert, D. M. & Ledesert, R. L., eds. xxiii, 638p. (Fr. & Eng.). E20.00 (ISBN 0-245-51859-2). Harrap.
--Harrap's New Standard French & English Dictionary: J-Z, French-English, Vol. 2. Ledesert, D. M. & Ledesert, R. P., eds. x, 546p. (Fr. & Eng.). E20.00 (ISBN 0-245-50973-9). Harrap.
--Harrap's New Standard French & English Dictionary: L-Z, English-French, Vol. 4. Ledesert, D. M. & Ledesert, R. P., eds. iv, 727p. (Fr. & Eng.). E20.00 (ISBN 0-245-51860-6). Harrap.
--Harrap's New Standard French & English Dictionary, Part One, French-English (A-I) rev. ed. Ledesert, D. H. & Ledesert, R. P., eds. (Fr. & Eng.). 1972. Repr. text ed. 32.50 (ISBN 0-8442-1876-6, 1874-4). Natl Textbk.
--Harrap's New Standard French & English Dictionary, Part One, French-English (J-Z) rev. ed. Ledesert, D. H. & Ledesert, R. P., eds. (Fr. & Eng.). 1972. Repr. 32.50 (ISBN 0-8442-1884-7, 1875-4). Natl Textbk.
--Harrap's Standard French & English Dictionary. xii, 1488p. (Fr. & Eng.). E17.00 (ISBN 0-245-57661-4). Harrap.
--Harrap's Standard French & English Dictionary, Part 2, English-French (A-Z) rev. ed. (Fr. & Eng.). 1962. Repr. text ed. 49.50 (ISBN 0-8442-1898-7, 1876-4). Natl Textbk.
--Harrap's Super-Mini French & English Dictionary. abridged ed. Forbes, Patricia & Ledesert, Margaret, eds. (Fr. & Eng.). (gr. 7-12). 1977. pap. 2.75 (ISBN 0-8442-1871-5, 1871-4). Natl Textbk.
Mansion, J. E., et al. Harrap's Shorter French & English Dictionary. (Fr. & Eng.). 1967. $19.95 (ISBN 0-7720-0142-1); $12.95 (ISBN 0-7720-0143-X). Harrap Co.
Marcy, Teresa & Marcy, Michel. Cortina-Grosset Basic French Dictionary. Berberi, Dilaver & Berberi, Edel A., eds. LC 73-18522. 384p. (Fr.). 1975. pap. $3.50 (ISBN 0-448-14031-4, G&D). Putnam Pub Group.
Marks, G. Harrap's Dictionnaire d'argot: French to English, English to French Slang Dictionary. 555p. (Fr. & Eng.). 1981. pap. $24.50 (ISBN 0-245-53601-9, M-6308). French & Eur.
Maurais, J. Lexique des Epices et Assaisonnements: Anglais-Francais. 73p. (Eng. & Fr.). 1979. pap. $5.95 (ISBN 0-7754-2593-1, M-9236). French & Eur.
Maurais, J. & Giroux, S. Lexiques des Boissons Gazeuses. 63p. (Eng. & Fr.). 1979. pap. $4.95 (ISBN 0-686-92432-0, M-9241). French & Eur.
Mergault, J. Nouveau Larousse "Mars". (Fr. & Eng.). 1971. $16.75 (Dist. by Continental Bk Co). Larousse.
Nouveau Larousse Francais-Anglais, English-French. (Mars). (Eng. & Fr.). $24.50 (ISBN 2-03-020812-4, 4083). Larousse.
Nuss, A. M. Export for Marketing French. 96p. (Fr. & Eng.). 1979. pap. $13.95 (ISBN 0-582-35157-X, M-9208). French & Eur.
Nutting, Teresa & Marcy, Michel. Cortina-Grosset Basic French Dictionary. LC 73-18522. xi, 368p. (Eng. & Fr.). 1975. $3.95. G&D.
The Oxford-Duden Pictorial French-English Dictionary. (Illus.). 880p. (Fr. & Eng.). 1983. $29.95 (ISBN 0-19-864153-2). Oxford U Pr.
Patit, Charles & Savage, William. Dictionnaire Classique Anglais-Francais. 686p. (Eng. & Fr.). 1967. write for info. Hac.
Patterson, A. M. German-English Dictionary for Chemists. 3rd ed. (Ger. & Fr.). 1950. $32.50 (ISBN 0-471-66990-3, Pub. by Wiley-Interscience). Wiley.
Pereira, Milton S. & Pereira, Maria S., eds. Harrap's Modern Portuguese & English Dictionary, 2 pts. 347p. (Port. & Eng.). E5.25 (ISBN 0-245-56866-2). Harrap.
Peron, Michel, et al. Dictionnaire Francais-Anglais, Anglais-Francais des affaires. 476p. (Fr. & Eng.). 1968. 29.80 F. Larousse.
Perreau & Langford. Concise French-American Dictionary of Figurative & Idiomatic Language. (Fr. & Eng.). $17.95 (ISBN 0-685-36686-3). French & Eur.
Petit, Charles & Savage, William. Dictionnaire Classique Anglais-Francais et Francais-Anglais. 686p. (Eng. & Fr.). 1967. pap. $27.50 (ISBN 0-686-57072-3, M-6444). French & Eur.
Petit Dictionnaire Bilingue "Adonis". (Fr. & Eng.). 1941. $3.95 (Dist. by Continental Bk Co). Larousse.
Petits Dictionnaires Bilingues Larousse Francais-Anglais. 500p. (Fr. & Eng.). $5.75 (Dist. by Continental Bk Co). Larousse.
Pierret, Albert & Basiaux. Vocabulaire, Phraseologie, Lecture, Informations. (Illus.). 144p. (Fr.). 1975. 228.00 F. Wesmael-Charlier.
--Vocabulaire, Phraseologie, Lecture Mentale. 132p. (Fr.). 1977. 182.00 F. Wesmael-Charlier.
Pierret, Albert, et al. Vocabulaire, Phraseologie, Lecture, Informations. (Illus.). 272p. (Fr.). 1975. 192.00 F. Wesmael-Charlier.
Piraux. Dictionnaire Francais-Anglais d'electro-technique et d'electronique. (Fr.). $32.50 (ISBN 0-685-36687-1). French & Eur.
Piraux, H. French-Eng., Eng-French Dictionary of Electrotechnic Electronics & Allied Fields, 2 Vols. (Fr. & Eng.). Set. 90.00 (ISBN 0-685-12017-1). Heinman.
Pocket-Shorter Dictionary. 600p. (Fr. & Eng.). $5.95 (086). Langenscheidt.
Quemner. Dictionaire Juridique Francais-Anglais, Anglais-Francais, 2 vols. in 1. (Fr. & Eng.). $75.00 (ISBN 0-685-36688-X). French & Eur.
Ratcliff, Ronald E. & Peck, Michael A. Dictionary of Naval Terminology-Dictionnaire de Terminologie Navale: English-French; Anglais-Francais. (Illus.). 160p. (Orig.). 1983. pap. text ed. $39.00x (ISBN 2-85206-200-3, Pub. by Technique Doc France). Sheridan.
Rudler, G. & Anderson, N. C., eds. French-English, English-French Gem Dictionary. (Gem Foreign Language Ser.). (Fr. & Eng.). 1952. $2.95 (ISBN 0-00-458617-4, G2). Collins Pubs.
Sabek, Jerwan. English-French-Arabic Trilingual Dictionary. (Eng., Fr. & Arabic.). $35.00x (ISBN 0-86685-116-X). Intl Bk Ctr.
Schuwer, Philippe. Dictionnaire de l'edition: Francais-Anglais. (Fr. & Eng.). 1977. 130.00 F. Cercle Librairie.
Standard French Dictionary. 1200p. (Fr. & Eng.). $11.95 (320). Langenscheidt.

Steiner, Roger, ed. Bantam New College French & English Dictionary. 736p. (Orig., Fr. & Eng.). 1972. pap. 2.75 (ISBN 0-553-14890-7). Bantam.

Steiner, Roger J. The New College French & English Dictionary. (Fr. & Eng.). (gr. 7-12). 1972. pap. text ed. $8.58 (ISBN 0-87720-463-2). AMSCO Sch.

Switzer, Richard & Gochberg, Herbert S., eds. New Century Vest Pocket French Dictionary. rev. ed. (Orig., Fr.). 2.95 (ISBN 0-686-86497-2). New Century.

Thuiluer. Lexique Anglais-Francais: Termes Appartenant aux Techniques en Usage a I. G. N. Premiere Partie, 2 vols. 464p. (Eng. & Fr.). 1958. 28.60 F. I. G. N.

Unwin, Kenneth. Langenscheidt's Standard French Dictionary: French-English, English-French. Orig. Title: Standard French Dictionary. 1216p. (Fr. & Eng.). 1974. $11.95 (ISBN 0-88254-285-0). Am Map.

Villiers, M., et al. Vocabulaire de la Vente Promotionelle: Anglais-Francais. 30p. (Eng. & Fr.). 1975. pap. $3.95 (ISBN 0-7754-3244-X, M-9242). French & Eur.

Vinay, Jean-Paul, et al. The Canadian Dictionary-French-English. (Fr. & Eng.). 1962. Can.$8.95 (ISBN 0-7710-8715-2); $5.95 (ISBN 0-7710-8715-2). McClelland.

Vincent, Jean. Dictionnaire Anglais-Francais. (Eng. & Fr.). 1978. pap. 11.00 F. Garnier-Flammarion.

--Dictionnaire Anglais-Francais. 394p. (Eng. & Fr.). 1964. 9.50 F. Garnier-Flammarion.

Williams, Rosalind. Practical French-English, English-French Dictionary. (Hippocrene Practical Language Dictionaries Ser.). 400p. (Orig., Eng. & Fr.). 1983. pap. $6.95 (ISBN 0-88254-815-8). Hippocrene Bks.

FRENCH LANGUAGE–DICTIONARIES–FINNISH

Dictionnaire de Poche Francais-Finnois. (Fr. & Finnish.). pap. 11.00 F. Berlitz.

Hagford, Edvin & Sundelin, Seppo. Dictionnaire Scolaire Francais-Finnois. 610p. (Fr. & Finnish.). 1974. 16.00 F. 40.65 F. Soderstrom.

Hagfors, E., et al. French-Finnish Dictionary. 599p. (Fr. & Finnish.). 1980. leatherette $24.95 (ISBN 951-0-04682-5, M-9657). French & Eur.

Koistinen, R. M. Finnish-French-Finnish Dictionary (Suomi-Ranska-Suomi) 438p. (Fr. & Finnish.). 1981. pap. $14.95 (ISBN 951-0-08071-3). French & Eur.

Koistinen, Raila-Maarit & Lasslo, Helene. Dictionnaire Finnois-Francais-Finnois. 393p. (Finnish & Fr.). 1973. 7.00 F. 20.32 F. Soderstrom.

Nurmela, T. Finnish-French Dictionary. 683p. (Finnish & Fr.). Date not set. $24.95 (ISBN 951-0-05012-1, M-9651). French & Eur.

Nurmela, Tauno. Dictionnaire Finnois-Francais. 694p. (Finnish & Fr.). 1976. 15.00 F. 40.65 F. Soderstrom.

Pesonen, Pentti. Ranskalais-Suomalainen-Sanakirja. LC 79-355820. 746p. (Fr. & Finnish.). 1978. write for info. Otava.

FRENCH LANGUAGE–DICTIONARIES–GERMAN

Bertaux. Dictionnaire Classique Francais-Allemand. 2nd ed. 1310p. (Fr. & Ger.). 1970. write for info. Hachette.

Bertaux, Pierre. Franzosisch-Deutsches, Deutsch-Franzosisches Woerterbuch, Vol. 1. (Ger. & Fr.). 1966. 69.95 (ISBN 3-87097-000-6, M-7411, Pub. by Brandstetter). French & Eur.

--Franzosisch-Deutsches, Deutsch-Franzosisches Woerterbuch, Vol. 1. (Ger. & Fr.). 1966. DM.69.95 (ISBN 3-87097-000-6). Brandstetter.

--Franzosisch-Deutsches, Deutsch-Franzosisches Woerterbuch, Vol. 2. (Ger. & Fr.). 1966. DM.69.95 (ISBN 3-87097-001-4). Brandstetter.

Cardoso, Ersillo. Dictionnaire Poucet Allemand-Francais. (Ger. & Fr.). 1978. 5.15 F. Hatier.

Chatelanat, Charles & Henzi, Theodor. Vocabulaire de Base Allemand-Francais. 214p. (Ger. & Fr.). 1972. 19.00 F. Hachette.

Clediere, Jean, et al. Dictionnaire Francais-Allemand. LC 75-512974. (Illus.). 1094p. (Fr. & Ger.). 1975. 45.00 F (ISBN 2-030-20811-6). Larousse FR.

Cusset, Francis. Vocabulaire Technique Allemand-Francais. 8th ed. 474p. (Ger. & Fr.). 1977. 66.50 F. Berger-Levrault.

Dictionnaire Allemand-Francais. 640p. (Ger. & Fr.). 1978. 7.50 F. Larousse.

Dictionnaire de Poche Francais-Allemand. (Fr. & Ger.). pap. 11.00 F. Berlitz.

Dictionnaire Europa: Francais-Allemand. 424p. (Fr. & Ger.). 1959. 11.00 F. Larousse.

Dictionnaire Gemeaux Francais-Allemand. (Fr. & Ger.). 19.50 F. Hatier.

Dictionnaire Larousse Bilingue de Poche: Francais-Allemand. 500p. (Fr. & Ger.). 11.70 F. Larousse FR.

Dictionnaire Larousse: Francais-Allemand. (Fr. & Ger.). pap. 10.50 F. L. G. F.

Dictionnaire Lilliput Bilingue Francais-Allemand. 640p. (Fr. & Ger.). 1961. 7.50 F. Larousse FR.

Dictionnaire Poucet Francais-Allemand. (Fr. & Ger.). 1978. pap. 5.15 F. Hatier.

Dubois, F. & Werny, P. Dictionnaire Francais-Allemand des Locutions. (Fr. & Ger.). 1976. $23.95 (ISBN 0-686-57124-X, M-6172). French & Eur.

Eckel, Denis & Hofer, Manfred. Dictionnaire Allemand-Francais. (Illus.). 1324p. (Ger. & Fr.). 1970. 64.00 F. Garnier.

Eckel, Denis & Manfred, Hofer. Dictionnaire Allemand-Francais et Francais-Allemand. 1324p. (Fr. & Ger.). 1970. $25.95 (ISBN 0-686-57131-2, M-6184). French & Eur.

Gem Language Dictionaries: French-German & German-French. (Fr. & Ger.). write for info. (ISBN 0-671-41943-9). S&S.

Grappin, P. Dictionnaire moderne Larousse, francais-allemand et allemand-francais. (Fr. & Ger.). $39.95 (ISBN 2-03-020603-2, 3778). Larousse.

--Dictionnaire Moderne Saturne: Francais-Allemand. 9th ed. 1744p. (Fr. & Ger.). 1971. 70.00 F. Larousse FR.

Knauer, Karl. Bertelsmann Woerterbuch Deutsch-Franzoesisch, Franzoesisch-Deutsch. 640p. (Ger. & Fr.). 1974. $17.50 (ISBN 3-570-01486-X, M-7307, Pub. by Bertelsmann Lexikon VVA). French & Eur.

Lange-Koval, Ernst E. & Wilhelm, Kurt. Dictionnaire Pratique Mercure Francais-Allemand. 3rd ed. 1206p. (Fr. & Ger.). 1964. 62.00 F. Larousse.

Lange-Kowal, Ernst E. Langenscheidts Grosse Schulwoerterbuecher Franzoesisch-Deutsch. 1400p. (Fr. & Ger.). 1977. DM.19.80 (ISBN 3-468-07151-5). Langenscheidt.

Lange-Kowal, Ernst E. & Beaucaire, Louis. Langenscheidts Grosse Schulwoerterbuch Franzoesisch-Deutsch. 1200p. (Fr. & Ger.). DM.23.80 (07151). Langenscheidt.

Lange-Kowal, Ernst Erwin. Langenscheidts Handwoerterbuch: Franzoesisch. 4th ed. Beaucaire, Louis, ed. LC 78-373125. (Ger. & Fr.). 1977. write for info. (ISBN 3-468-04151-9). Langenscheidt.

Larousse & Co. Larousse de poche, francais-allemand et allemand-francais. (Fr. & Ger.). pap. $6.95 (ISBN 0-685-13959-X). Larousse.

Pinloche, A. Dictionnaire Francais-Allemand, Deutsch-Franzosisch. 805p. (Fr. & Ger.). Date not set. pap. $6.50 (ISBN 0-686-97409-3, M-9043). French & Eur.

Pinloche, A. & Jolivet, A. Dictionnaire Bilingue Larousse, Francais-Alemand et Allemand-Francais. (Apollo). (Fr. & Ger.). $10.50 (ISBN 0-685-13853-4, 3779). Larousse.

Pinoche, Jolivet A. Dictionnaire Bilingue Apollo Francais-Allemand. (Fr. & Ger.). 18.70 F. Larousse.

Roepke, F. Franzoesisch-Deutsches Glossarium. 540p. (Ger. & Fr.). 1964. $36.00 (ISBN 3-7819-2007-0, M-7413, Pub. by Fritz Knapp Verlag). French & Eur.

Rotteck. Dictionnaire Allemand-Francais. (Illus.). 980p. (Ger. & Fr.). 1970. 18.00 F. Garnier.

Rotteck, ed. Dictionnaire Allemand-Francais, Francais-Allemand. 980p. (Fr. & Ger.). 1970. pap. $7.50 (ISBN 0-686-57093-6, M-6115). French & Eur.

Sachs & Villatte. Langenscheidts Grosswoerterbuch Franzoesisch: Tl 1, Franzoesisch-Deutsch. (Fr. & Ger.). 1978. DM.68.00 (ISBN 3-468-02150-X). Langenscheidt.

Sachs, Karl & Villatte, Cesaire. Langenscheidts Grosswoerterbuch: Teil I, Franzoesisch-Deutsch. 1047p. (Fr. & Ger.). 1979. DM.118.00 (02151). Langenscheidt.

Villain, Siefried P. Dictionnaire Allemand-Francais. 460p. (Ger. & Fr.). 1964. 9.50 F. Garnier-Flammarion.

Villain, Siegfried P. Dictionnaire Allemand-Francais. 612p. (Ger. & Fr.). 1960. 11.00 F. Garnier-Flammarion.

Weis, E. & Mattutat, H. Woerterbuch der Franzoesischen und Deutschen Sprache, Vol. 1. (Fr. & Ger.). $18.95 (ISBN 3-215-01824-1, M-7004). French & Eur.

--Woerterbuch der Franzoesischen und Deutschen Sprache, Vol. 2. (Ger. & Fr.). $18.95 (ISBN 3-215-01825-X, M-7003). French & Eur.

Weis, Erich & Mattutat, Heinrich. Dictionnaire Allemand-Francais. 570p. (Ger. & Fr.). 1977. $29.95 (ISBN 0-686-57259-9, M-6570). French & Eur.

--Dictionnaire Allemand-Francais. 570p. (Ger. & Fr.). 1977. 75.00 F. Bordas-Dunod.

--Dictionnaire Francais-Allemand. 480p. (Fr. & Ger.). 1976. 75.00 F. Bordas-Dunod.

--Dictionnaire Francais-Allemand. 1022p. (Fr. & Ger.). 1977. 139.00 F. Bordas-Dunod.

--Dictionnaire Francais-Allemand et Allemand-Francais. 1022p. (Fr. & Ger.). 1977. $55.00 (ISBN 0-686-57260-2, M-6571). French & Eur.

Weiss, Erich. Pons-Grosswoerterbuch, 2 vols. Mattutat, Heinrich & Nugue, Christian, eds. LC 79-337909. (Ger. & Fr.). 1978. DM.56.00 (ISBN 3-125-17220-9). Klett.

Werny, Paul & Snyckers, Alexandre. Dictionnaire des Locutions Francais-Allemand. LC 77-568508. viii, 636p. (Ger. & Fr.). 1976. 60.00 F (ISBN 2-030-21103-6). Larousse FR.

FRENCH LANGUAGE–DICTIONARIES–HEBREW

Cohn, M. M. Dictionnaire francais-hebreu. (Fr. & Hebrew.). $35.95 (ISBN 0-685-13874-7). Larousse.

Cohn, Marc M. Dictionnaire Francais-Hebreu. 760p. (Fr. & Hebrew.). 1966. $27.50 (ISBN 0-686-56955-5, M-6077). French & Eur.

--Dictionnaire Francais-Hebreu. 760p. (Fr. & Hebrew.). 1966. 69.00 F. Larousse.

--Nouveau Dictionnaire Hebreu-Francais. 792p. (Fr. & Hebrew.). 1974. $32.50 (ISBN 0-686-56956-3, M-6078). French & Eur.

Darmesteter, Arsene. Le Glosses & Glossaires Hebreux-Francais. 52p. (Hebrew & Fr.). 1878. 30.00 F. Champion.

Hadar, Joseph. Dictionnaire Hebrau-Francais, 2 vols. 832p. (Hebrew & Fr.). 1973. IL.18.70 (2114). Massada Pr.

Lambert, Mayer & Brandin, Louis. Glossaire Hebreu-Francais. 315p. (Hebrew & Fr.). 1975. 75.00 F. Slatkine.

--Glossaire Hebreu-Francais du XIIIe. Siecle. 315p. (Hebrew & Fr.). 1977. 75.00 F. Slatkine.

Marchand-Ennery, Rabbin. Dictionnaire Hebreu-Francais. 302p. (Hebrew & Fr.). 1976. 18.00 F. Colbo.

Nouveau Dictionnaire Francais-Hebreu. (Fr. & Hebrew.). 1973. 35.85 (ISBN 0-685-55772-3). Larousse.

Nouveau Dictionnaire hebreu-francais. (Hebrew & Fr.). 1973. 39.25 (ISBN 0-685-55771-5). Larousse.

FRENCH LANGUAGE–DICTIONARIES–ITALIAN

Cusatelli, G. & Brunacci, G. Dizionario Garzanti: Francese-Italiano, Italiano-Francese. Salati, U. & Dominicis, F., eds. 2029p. (Fr. & Ital.). 1980. $49.95 (ISBN 0-686-92560-2, M-6143). French & Eur.

Dictionnaire de Poche Francais-Italien. (Fr. & Ital.). 11.00 F. Berlitz.

Dictionnaire Europa Francais-Italien. 352p. (Fr. & Ital.). 1960. 11.00 F. Larousse.

Dictionnaire Garzanti Francais-Italien. 2046p. (Fr. & Ital.). 1978. 108.00 F. Bordas-Dunod.

Dictionnaire Garzanti Francais-Italien, Italien-Francais. 2046p. (Fr. & Ital.). 1969. $39.95 (ISBN 0-686-57110-X, M-6143). French & Eur.

Dictionnaire Gemeaux: Francais-Italien. (Fr. & Ital.). 30.00 F. Hatier.

Dictionnaire Italien-Francais. 640p. (Ital. & Fr.). write for info. Larousse FR.

Dictionnaire Larousse Bilingue de Poche: Francais-Italien. (Fr. & Ital.). pap. 11.70 F. Larousse FR.

Dictionnaire Larousse: Francais-Italien. (Fr. & Ital.). pap. 10.50 F. L. G. F.

Dictionnaire Lilliput Bilingue Francais-Italien. 640p. (Fr. & Ital.). 7.50 F. Larousse FR.

Dizionario Garzantil Italiano-Francese, Francese-Italiano. 1020p. (Ital. & Fr.). 1979. $19.95 (ISBN 0-686-97334-8, M-9191). French & Eur.

Ghiotti, et al. Dictionnaire Italien-Francais, Francais-Italien de la Langue d'Aujourd'hui. (Fr. & Ital.). 1976. $27.50 (ISBN 0-686-57196-7, M-6270). French & Eur.

Herselin, Jacqueline. Dictionnaire Italien-Francais. (Ital. & Fr.). 1969. write for info. Garnier.

Larousse & Co. Larousse de poche, francais-italien et italien-francais. (Fr. & It.). pap. $6.95 (ISBN 0-685-13960-3, 1012). Larousse.

Laurent, G. Dizionario Italiano-Francese, Francese-Italiano. 413p. (Fr. & Ital.). 1979. leatherette $5.95 (ISBN 0-686-97341-0, M-9173). French & Eur.

Padovani, G. & Silvestri, R. Dictionnaire Bilingue Larousse, Francais-Italien et Italien-Francais. (Apollo). (Fr.). $10.50 (ISBN 0-685-13854-2, 3784). Larousse.

Padovani, Giuseppe & Silvestri, Richard. Dictionnaire Bilingue Apollo Francais-Italien. 768p. (Fr. & Ital.). 1971. 18.70 F. Larousse.

Rouede, Denis. Dictionnaire Italien-Francais. (Illus.). 1256p. (Ital. & Fr.). 1970. write for info. Garnier.

Rouede, Pierre & Rouede, Denise. Dictionnaire Italien-Francais et Francais-Italien. 1256p. (Fr. & Ital.). 1970. $25.00 (ISBN 0-686-57211-4, M-6493). French & Eur.

FRENCH LANGUAGE–DICTIONARIES–NORWEGIAN

Daae, E. Francais-Norvegien-Francais Lommerorbok. 455p. (Fr. & Norwegian.). 1981. pap. $12.95 (ISBN 82-573-0162-0, M-9461). French & Eur.

Dedichen, L. Fransk-Norsk Ordbok. 373p. (Fr.). 1979. $29.95 (ISBN 82-573-0068-3, M-9457). French & Eur.

Dedichen, Line. French-Norwegian Dictionary. (Fr. & Norwegian.). 1973. write for info. (ISBN 82-573-0068-3). Kunnskapsforlaget.

Gabrielsen, Daae. Norwegian-French Dictionary of Commerce. (Norwegian & Fr.). 1975. write for info. (ISBN 82-573-0094-2). Kunnskapsforlaget.

Lesoil, M. Norwegian-French Dictionary. (Norwegian & Fr.). 1970. write for info. (ISBN 82-573-0074-8). Kunnskapsforlaget.

FRENCH LANGUAGE–DICTIONARIES–POLYGLOT

Renoux, Y. & Yates, J. Glossary of International Treaties. (Eng., Fr., Span., Ital., Dutch & Rus.). 1970. $28.00 (ISBN 0-444-40813-4). Elsevier.

Violette, Louis. Dictionnaire Samoa-Francais-Anglais et Francais-Samoa-Anglais. LC 75-35215. (Fr. & Eng.). Repr. of 1879 ed. $44.50 (ISBN 0-404-14238-9). AMS Pr.

Vocabulaire de l'oceanologie. LC 77-456565. (Illus.). 431p. (Eng. , Ger. , Rus. & Fr.). 1976. 75.00 F (ISBN 2-85319-028-5). Hachette-Jeunesse.

FRENCH LANGUAGE–DICTIONARIES–PORTUGUESE

Burtin Vinholes, S., et al. Dicionario Frances-Portugues, Portugues-Frances. 27th ed. LC 78-379871. 836p. (Fr. & Port.). 1975. write for info. Editora Globo.

Cardoso, Ersilio. Dictionnaire Portugais-Francais. 544p. (Port. & Fr.). 1978. 11.00 F. Garnier.

--Grande Dicionario Frances-Portugues. (Fr. & Port.). Cr.$25.74. Difel Difusao.

Cardoso, Ersillo. Dictionnaire Portugais-Francais. 1820p. (Port. & Fr.). 1963. 58.40 F. Garnier.

Da Fonseca, F. Peixoto. Dictionnaire Bilingue Larousse, Francais-Portugais et Portugais-Francais. (Apollo). (Fr. & Port.). $10.50 (ISBN 2-03-020909-0, 3791). Larousse.

De Azevedo, Domingos. Dictionnaire Francais-Portugais. 1506p. (Fr. & Port.). 1955. 100.00 F. Garnier.

--Dictionnaire Portugais-Francais. 1500p. (Port. & Fr.). 1978. 100.00 F. Garnier.

Dictionnaire Europa Francais-Portugais. 460p. (Fr. & Port.). 1978. 11.00 F. Larousse.

Dictionnaire Lilliput Bilingue Francais-Portugais. 640p. (Fr. & Port.). 7.50 F. Larousse FR.

Dictionnaire Portugais-Francais. 640p. (Port. & Fr.). 1978. 7.50 F. Larousse.

Difel. Dicionario Frances-Portuques. (Fr. & Port.). write for info. Difel Editorial, S. A.

Fournier, J. & Laborde, G. Le Mot et L'idee, Francais-Portugais, Portugais-Francais. 120p. (Fr.-Port.). $6.95 (ISBN 0-686-57185-1, M-6256). French & Eur.

Mendes Campos, Aluizio. Dicionario Frances-Portugues de Locucoes. (Fr. & Port.). Cr.$2000.00. Edit Atica.

Peixoto da Fonseca, Fernando V. Dictionnaire Bilingue Apollo Francais-Portugais. 758p. (Fr. & Port.). 1958. 18.70 F. Larousse.

FRENCH LANGUAGE–DICTIONARIES–PROVENCAL

Mistral, Frederic. Le Tresor de Felibridge: Dictionnaire Provencal-Francais, 2 vols. 2375p. (Fr.). Set. $195.00 (ISBN 0-686-56736-6, M-6414). French & Eur.

Taupiac, Jacme. Pichon Diccionari Frances-Occitan. LC 80-454080. (Illus.). 304p. (Fr.). 1977. 75.00 F. Inst Occit Tlse.

FRENCH LANGUAGE–DICTIONARIES–RUSSIAN

De Chtcherba. Dictionnaire Russe-Francais. 9th ed. (Rus. & Fr.). 31.85 F. Mir.

Dictionnaire Bilingue Francais-Russe et Russe-Francais. (Fr. & Rus.). $10.50 (ISBN 2-03-020904-X, 2715, Apollo). Larousse.

Dolgopolova. Dictionnaire de Poche Russe-Francais. (Rus. & Fr.). 6.00 F. MIR.

Gamchina, K. Dictionnaire Francais-Russe. 911p. (Fr. & Rus.). 1977. $19.95 (ISBN 0-686-92572-6, M-9066). French & Eur.

Ganchina, K. A. Dictionnaire Francais-Russe. (Fr. & Rus.). 1978. 32.85 F. MIR.

Kolesnikova, A. D., et al. Frantsuzsko-Russkii Illiustrirovannyi Slovar. (Illus.). 856p. (Fr. & Rus.). 1977. $7.25 (Pub. by Sov Entsiklopediia). Four Continent.

Noctuel & Calmann-Levy. Dictionnaire Francais-Russe. (Fr. & Rus.). 1978. 9.15 F. Labiche.

Pauliat, Paul. Dictionnaire Francais-Russe. 473p. (Fr. & Rus.). 1976. 27.60 F. Larousse.

Potozkaia, Varvara. Dictionnaire Francais-Russe. (Fr. & Rus.). 1978. 10.95 F. MIR.

--Dictionnaire Russe-Francais. (Rus. & Fr.). 7.00 F. Mir.

Retsker, I. I., ed. Frantsuzsko-Russkii Frazeologicheskii Slovar. 1112p. (Fr. & Rus.). 1963. $8.95 (Pub. by Gosizdat Inostr Natsional Lit). Four Continent.

Voronine, V. V., et al. Dictionnaire Russe-Francais du Batiment. Denissov, A. I., ed. 462p. (Rus. & Fr.). 1978. leatherette $13.25 (ISBN 0-686-92634-X, M-9064). French & Eur.

FRENCH LANGUAGE–DICTIONARIES–SPANISH

Alcala-Zamora. Alcala-Zamora, Diccionario Frances-Espanol, Espanol-Frances. 960p. (Span. & Fr.). pap. $9.95 (ISBN 84-303-0094-5, S-50399). French & Eur.

--Alcala-Zamora, Diccionario Frances-Espanol, Espanol-Frances. 960p. (Span. & Fr.). $12.25 (ISBN 84-303-0093-7, S-50400). French & Eur.

Amador, E. M. Martinez. Diccionario Frances-Espanol, Espanol-Frances. 1568p. (Span. & Fr.). 1974. $47.95 (ISBN 84-303-0091-0, S-13282). French & Eur.

--Diccionario Manual Amador Frances-Espanol y Espanol-Frances. 944p. (Span. & Fr.). 1975. $17.95 (ISBN 84-303-0100-3, S-50401). French & Eur.

Arimany Coma, Miguel. Diccionari Practic Catala-Frances. 2nd ed. 256p. (Catalan & Span.). 1977. pap. $5.25 (ISBN 84-7211-048-6, S-50413). French & Eur.

Azkue, Resurreccion M. Diccionario Vasco-Espanol-Frances, 2 vols. (Span. & Fr.). Set. leatherette $68.00 (ISBN 84-248-0015-X, S-12384). French & Eur.

Corbiere, A. & Lautier. Dictionnaire Espagnol-Francais. 1046p. (Span. & Fr.). 25.20 F. Dessain & Tolra.

Corbiere, Lautier. Dictionnaire Francais-Espagnol. 932p. (Fr. & Span.). 1966. 23.10 F. Dessain & Tolra.

Cuyas Armengol, Arturo. Diccionario De Bolsillo Frances-Espanol, Espagnol-Francais. 670p. (Span. & Fr.). 1971. pap. $3.50 (ISBN 84-7183-048-5, S-50391). French & Eur.

--Diccionario Manual Frances-Espanol, Espagnol-Francais. 36th ed. 830p. (Span. & Fr.). 1977. $5.95 (ISBN 84-7183-047-7, S-50390). French & Eur.

Denis, Serge & Maraval, M. Dictionnaire Espagnol-Francais. 1774p. (Span. & Fr.). 66.00 F. Hachette.

Denis, Serge & Maraval, Marcel. Dictionnaire Espagnol-Francais. 1774p. (Fr. & Eng.). 1968. pap. $26.50 (ISBN 0-686-56983-0, M-6110). French & Eur.

Denis, Serge, et al. Le Dictionnaire Espagnol-Francais. 904p. (Span. & Fr.). 1976. $90.00. Hachette Jeunesse.

--Le Dictionnaire Espagnol-Francais et Francais-Espagnol. new ed. 904p. (Span. & Fr.). 1976. $36.95 (ISBN 0-686-56984-9, M-6111). French & Eur.

De Toro, M. & Gisbert. Dictionnaire Bilingue Larousse, Francais-Espagnol, Espanol-Frances. (Apollo). (Fr. & Span.). $10.50 (ISBN 0-685-13857-7, 3774). Larousse.

De Toro, Miguel & De Toro, Gisbert. Dictionnaire Bilingue Apollo Francais-Espagnol. 792p. (Fr. & Span.). 1978. 18.70 F. Larousse.

De Toro Gisbert, M. Dictionnaire Bilingue: Francais-Espagnol, Espagnol-Francais. 546p. (Fr. & Span.). 1968. pap. text ed. $7.95 (ISBN 0-686-97445-X, S-36345). French & Eur.

Diccionario Cuyas: Spanish-French, French-Spanish. (Span. & Fr.). $6.00x (ISBN 0-686-00850-2). Colton Bk.

Diccionario Manual Frances-Espanol Espanol-Frances Vox. 10th ed. 922p. (Fr. & Span.). 1982. 725.00 ptas (ISBN 84-7153-186-0). Biblo SP.

Diccionario Universal Herder Frances-Espanol, Espanol-Frances. 5th ed. 368p. (Fr. & Span.). 1977. leatherette $4.50 (ISBN 84-254-0780-X, S-12394). French & Eur.

Dictionnaire de Poche Francais-Espagnol. (Fr. & Span.). 11.00 F. Berlitz.

Dictionnaire Espagnol-Francais. 640p. (Span. & Fr.). 7.50 F. Larousse.

Dictionnaire Europa Francais-Espagnol. 460p. (Fr. & Span.). 1978. 11.00 F. Larousse.

Dictionnaire Gemeaux: Francais-Espagnol. (Fr. & Span.). 19.50 F. Hatier.

Dictionnaire Larousse Bilingue de Poche: Francais-Espagnol. 500p. (Fr. & Span.). 11.70 F. Larousse FR.

Dictionnaire Larousse: Francais-Espagnol. (Fr. & Span.). pap. 10.50 F. L. G. F.

Dictionnaire Lilliput Bilingue Francais-Espagnol. 640p. (Fr. & Span.). 7.50 F. Larousse FR.

Dictionnaire Poucet Espagnol-Francais. (Span. & Fr.). 1978. pap. 5.15 F. Hatier.

Diez Mateo, Felix & Hochleitner, Frida. Diccionario Manual Frances-Espanol, Espanol-Frances. 992p. (Span. & Fr.). 1971. $9.95 (ISBN 84-239-4721-1, S-50389). French & Eur.

Garcia-Pelayo, R. Dictionnaire Moderne "Saturne". (Span. & Eng.). 1976. $35.00 (Dist. by Continental Bk Co). Larousse.

Garcia-Pelayo, R. & Testas, J. Dictionnaire moderne Larousse, francais-espagnol et espagnol-francais. (Span. & Fr.). $39.95 (ISBN 2-03-020601-6, 3773). Larousse.

Garcia-Pelayo, R., ed. Dictionnaire Moderne: Francaise-Espagnol, Espagnol-Francais. (Fr. & Span.). $35.00 (ISBN 2-03-020601-6, S-32371). French & Eur.

Garcia-Pelayo, Ramon & Testas, Jean. Dictionnaire Moderne Saturne: Francais-Espagnol. 3rd ed. 1758p. (Fr. & Span.). 1971. 70.00 F. Larousse FR.

Gimenez Sales, Miguel. Diccionario Espanol-Frances, Espagnol-Francais. 736p. (Span. & Fr.). 1975. pap. $3.95 (ISBN 84-02-04265-1, S-50394). French & Eur.

Gimeno, E. Diccionario Lexicon Frances-Espanol, Espanol-Frances. 384p. (Fr. & Span.). 1975. leatherette $3.75 (ISBN 84-303-0099-6, S-31393). French & Eur.

Haensch, Gunther. Diccionario Manual Herder Frances-Espanol, Espanol-Frances. 644p. (Span. & Fr.). 1976. $16.75 (ISBN 84-254-1049-5, S-50392). French & Eur.

Larousse And Co. Petit Dictionnaire bilingue Larousse, francais-espagnol, espanol-frances. (Adonis). (Fr. & Span., Fr & Span). plastic bdg. 6.95 (ISBN 0-685-14033-4, 3775). Larousse.

Larrieu, Robert. Dictionnaire Espagnol-Francais. 512p. (Span. & Fr.). 1961. $11.00. Garnier.

--Dictionnaire Espagnol-Francais. (Span. & Fr.). 9.50 F. Garnier-Flammarion.

Puy-Costa, M. Dictionnaire Pratique Mercure Francais-Espagnol. 2nd ed. 1024p. (Fr. & Span.). 1966. 62.00 F. Larousse.

Salva, Vicente. Dictionnaire Espagnol-Francais. (Illus.). 948p. (Span. & Fr.). 1959. 18.00 F. Garnier-Flammarion.

Salva, Vicente & Larrieu, Robert. Dictionnaire Espagnol-Francais. (Illus.). 1580p. (Span. & Fr.). 1951. 26.00 F. Garnier.

Salva, Vicente & Larrieu, Robert, eds. Dictionnaire Espagnol-Francais et Francais-Espagnol. 1580p. (Fr.-Span.). 1951. $22.50 (ISBN 0-686-57295-5, F-140811). French & Eur.

Vox-Diccionario Abreviado Frances-Espanol, Espanol-Frances. 8th ed. 672p. (Fr. & Span.). 1978. leatherette $7.25 (ISBN 84-7153-216-6, S-12414). French & Eur.

FRENCH LANGUAGE–DICTIONARIES–SWEDISH

Dictionnaire de Poche Francais-Suedois. (Fr. & Swedish.). 11.00 F. Berlitz.

French-Swedish-French Dictionary. 370p. (Fr. & Swedish.). 1980. pap. $9.95 (ISBN 0-686-97383-6, M-9445). French & Eur.

FRENCH LANGUAGE–DICTIONARIES, JUVENILE

Didier, Marcel. Mes dix millet mots. (Fr.). (gr. 3-6). 1977. text ed. $14.95 (ISBN 0-8120-5207-2). Barron.

Mon Grand Dictionnaire Francais-Anglais. (Fr. & Eng.). $13.50 (ISBN 0-685-11402-3). French & Eur.

FRENCH LANGUAGE–ETYMOLOGY

Baldinger, Kurt. Dictionnaire Etymologique de l'ancien Francais. 144p. (Fr.). 1974. Can.$14.00. Laval P. U.

--Dictionnaire Etymologique de l'ancien Francais. (Fr.). 1974. Can.$14.00. Laval P. U.

Baldinger, Kurt & Straka, Georges. Dictionnaire Etymologique de l'ancien Francais, 1. 120p. (Fr.). 1971. 92.00 F. Klincksieck.

Baldinger, Kurt, et al. Dictionnaire Etymologique de l'ancien Francais. 112p. (Fr.). 1974. Can.$14.00. Laval P. U.

Bloch, Oscar & Von Wartburg, Walther. Dictionnaire Etymologique de la Langue Francaise. 6th ed. 684p. (Fr.). 1975. 166.40 F. PUF.

Bloch, Oscar & Wartburg, Walther Von. Dictionnaire Etymologique de la Langue Francaise. 6th ed. 684p. (Fr.). 1975. $83.95 (ISBN 0-686-57293-9, F-C1016). French & Eur.

Caillon, Octave. Dictionnaire Etymologique. (Fr.). 1967. 44.00 F. Ligel.

Dauzat, A., et al. Nouveau Dictionnaire etymologique. (Fr., Fr). 27.50 (ISBN 2-03-020210-X, 3612). Larousse.

Dauzat, Albert. Nouveau Dictionnaire Etymologique. 6th ed. 856p. (Fr.). 1971. $23.50 (ISBN 0-686-57269-6, F-135950). French & Eur.

Dauzat, Albert, et al. Dictionnaire Etymologique. 805p. (Fr.). 1971. 20.00 F. Larousse.

De Castelbajac, Bernadette. Qui a dit Quoi? Dictionanaire des Mots & des Phrases qui Ont Une Historire. LC 80-453759. 277p. (Fr.). 1978. 36.00 F (ISBN 2-235-00575-6). Tallandier.

Dictionnaire Etymologiqe du Moyen-Breton. 225p. (Fr.). 80.00 F. Slatkine.

Du Puitspelu, Nizier. Dictionnaire Etymologique du Patols Lyonnais. 595p. (Fr.). 1970. 100.00 F. Slatkine.

Gostony, Colman G. Dictionnaire d'etymologie Sumerienne & Grammaire Comparee. 204p. (Fr.). 1975. 130.00 F. Boccard.

Grandgagnage, Charles-Marie. Dictionnaire Etymologique de la Langue Wallonne, 3 vols. 1275p. (Fr. & Waloon.). 1969. 220.00 F. Slatkine.

Heylli, Edmond G. Dictionnaire des Racines Semitiques. 567p. (Fr.). 1971. 100.00 F. Slatkine.

Lancombe, Michel & Monceaux, Jean-Pierre. Lexique Etymologique des Termes Medicaux. 20p. (Fr.). 1971. 25.00 F. Lamarre Poinot.

Losique, Serge. Dictionnaire Etymologique des Noms de Pays & de Peuples. 243p. (Fr.). 1971. 48.00 F. Klincksieck.

Menage, Gilles. Dictionnaire Etymologique de la Langue Francaise avec les Origines Francaises, 2 vols. 950p. (Fr.). 1973. 750.00 F. Slatkine.

Quitard, Pierre-Marie. Dictionnaire Etymologique: Historique & Anecdotique des Proverbes & des Locutions Proverbiales de la Langue Francaise. 715p. (Fr.). 1968. 130.00 F. Slatkine.

FRENCH LANGUAGE–GLOSSARIES, VOCABULARIES, ETC.

Banitt, Menahem. Le Glossaire de Bale, 2 vols. 670p. (Fr.). 1972. fl.128.00. Brill.

Becker. Glossaire sur la T. V. A. (Fr.). 327.00 F. Office Intern. Librairie.

Carton, J. B. Glossaire Picard du Parler de Long. (Fr.). 15.00 F. Eklitra.

Centre Culturel Occitan Pais Nissart. Glossari Ilustrat. (Illus.). 16p. (Fr.). 8.00 F. Centre Cult. Pais Nissart.

De Landberg, C. & Zettersteen, K. V. Glossaire Datinois, 3 vols. 2976p. (Fr.). 1942. 360.00 F. Brill.

Dictionnaire du Patols du Bas-Limousin. 375p. (Fr.). 1971. write for info. Slatkine.

Juilland, Alphonse. Dictionnaire Inverse De la Langue Francaise. (Janua Linguarum, Ser. Practica: No. 7). (Fr.). 1965. text ed. 81.00x (ISBN 90-2790-626-2). Mouton.

Laureilhe, Marie-Therese. Le Thesaurus. (Illus.). 48p. (Fr.). 1977. 20.00 F. Ecole Biblio.

Leirie, Michel. Glossaire: Mots sans Memoire. 160p. (Fr.). 1969. 22.00 F. Gallimard.

Roepke & Haefner. Deutsch-Franzoesisches Glossarium: Finanzieller und Wirtschaftlicher Fachausdruеke. 6th ed. 475p. (Ger. & Fr.). 1982. 325.00 F. Maison Dictionnaire.

Roepke, F. Franzoesisch-Deutsches Glossarium. 540p. (Ger. & Fr.). 1964. $36.00 (ISBN 3-7819-2007-0, M-7413, Pub. by Fritz Knapp Verlag). French & Eur.

Schonberg, James. The Comparative Trilby Glossary, French-English. 60p. (Fr. & Eng.). 1983. Repr. of 1895 ed. lib. bdg. $30.00 (ISBN 0-89984-614-9). Century Bookbindery.

Societe du Parler Francais au Canada. Glossaire du Parler Francais au Canada. 710p. (Fr.). 1968. Can.$18.00. Laval P. U.

Thesaurus Verrier, 2 vols. (Fr.). 1971. 160.00 F. Inst Verre.

FRENCH LANGUAGE–GRAMMAR

Caput, J. P. & Caput, J. Dictionnaire des Verbe Francais. (Fr.). 1979. $13.50 (Dist. by Continental Bk Co). Larousse.

Caput, Jean & Caput, Josette. Dictionnaire des Verbes Francais. 2nd ed. (Fr.). 1970. 57.20 F. Larousse.

Dagneaud, Robert. Le Vocabulaire Grammatical. 247p. (Fr.). 1965. 32.50 F. CDU.

Dictionnaire des Difficultes Grammaticale & Lexicologiques. 760p. (Fr.). 48.00 F. Scientifiques & Litteraires.

Richardson, Henry B. Outline of French Grammar with Vocabularies. rev. ed. (Fr.). 1950. text ed. 12.50x (ISBN 0-89197-327-3); pap. text ed. 4.95x (ISBN 0-89197-328-1). Irvington.

FRENCH LANGUAGE–GRAMMAR, COMPARATIVE

Dictionnaire des Difficultes Grammaticales & Lecicologiques. 760p. (Fr.). 550.00 F. Samson, CED.

FRENCH LANGUAGE–IDIOMS, CORRECTIONS, ERRORS

Bellenger, W. A. A Dictionary of Idioms, French & English. 331p. (Fr. & Eng.). 1983. Repr. of 1830 ed. lib. bdg. $125.00 (ISBN 0-89760-052-5). Telegraph Bks.

Cassell. Cassell's Colloquial French. 160p. (Fr.). pap. $3.95 (ISBN 0-02-079420-7). Macmillan.

Denoeu, F., et al. French & English Idioms. (Fr. & Eng.). 1982. $7.95 (ISBN 0-8120-0435-3). Barron.

Gerber, Barbara & Storzer, Gerald. French Idioms on the Way. (Illus., Fr.). 1984. pap. $4.95 (ISBN 0-8120-2108-8). Barron.

Gerber, Barbara L. & Storzer, Gerald H. Dictionary of Modern French Idioms, 2 vols. LC 76-24743. (Reference Library of the Humanities Ser.: Vol. 63). (Fr. & Eng.). 1977. Set. lib. bdg. 110.00 (ISBN 0-8240-9935-4). Garland Pub.

Kettridge, J. O. French Idioms & Figurative Phrases. (Fr.). pap. 9.50 (ISBN 0-87557-024-0, 024-0). Saphrograph.

Lafleur, Bruno. Dictionnaire des locutions idiomatiques Fran c04aises. (Fr.). Can.$14.95. Soc Dev Liv.

Thomas, A. V. Dictionnaire des Difficultes de la Langue Francaise. (Fr., Fr). 23.50 (ISBN 0-685-13865-8, 3611). Larousse.

FRENCH LANGUAGE–LEXICOGRAPHY

Attiyate, Y. H. Lexique CN: Anglais-Allemand-Francais. (Illus.). 526p. (Eng., Ger. & Fr.). 1977. 65.00 F. Iron Age Metalworking Int.

Dictionnaire des Difficultes Grammaticale & Lexicologiques. 760p. (Fr.). 48.00 F. Scientifiques & Litteraires.

Dictionnaire des Difficultes Grammaticales & Lecicologiques. 760p. (Fr.). 550.00 F. Samson, CED.

Ducroz, Jean M. & Charles, Marie C. Lexique Soncy Francais. 282p. (Fr.). 1978. 65.00 F. Harmattan.

Feuillet, L. Lexique Francais-Grec. 496p. (Fr. & Gr.). 1976. 35.20 F. Belin.

Helmlinger, Paul. Lexique Francais-Duala: Dictionnaire Duala-Francais. 666p. (Fr.). 1972. 105.00 F. S. E. L. A. F.

Lexicologie & Lexicographie Francaises & Romanes. 294p. (Fr & Ital.). 1959. 42.00 F (ISBN 2-22200-359-8). CNRS.

Trenel, Jacques. Lexique Francais-Latin. 694p. (Fr. & Lat.). 1978. 30.40 F. Belin.

FRENCH LANGUAGE–OLD FRENCH

see French Language–To 1500

FRENCH LANGUAGE–ORTHOGRAPHY AND SPELLING

Dictionnaire du Vocabulaire Orthographique. 7th ed. (Fr.). 1971. 8.00 F. Larousse.

Gallet, Francois. Dictionnaire Phonetique d'Orthographe. (Fr.). 1978. 67.50 F. PenseeUniv.

Lamizet, Bojana. Dictionnaire Orthographique Suivi d'Une Liste des Verbes Irreguliers. LC 75-517895. 411p. (Fr.). 1975. 11.50 F. Garnier.

Lamizet, Bojana & Lamizet, Bernard. Dictionnaire Orthographique. (Fr.). 1974. 11.50 F. Garnier.

Rat, Maurice. Dictionnaire Orthographique Garnier. new ed. 384p. (Fr.). 14.00 F. Garnier.

Ters, Francois. Vocabulaire Orthographique de Base. 228p. (Fr.). 46.00 F. OCDL.

Ters, Francois, et al. Vocabulaire Orthographique de Base. 304p. (Fr.). 321.00 F. Messeiller.

FRENCH LANGUAGE–PHONETICS

Pleasants, Jeanne V. Phonetic French Dictionary: Contrasting French-English Sounds. 1959p. (Fr. & Eng.). pap. text ed. 5.95 (ISBN 0-940630-01-X, T-7010). Playette Corp.

FRENCH LANGUAGE–PRONUNCIATION

Lerond, A. Dictionnaire de la Prononciation. (Fr.). 1980. $17.75 (Dist. by Continental Bk Co). Larousse.

Martinet, Andre & Walter, Henriette. Dictionnaire de la Prononciation Francaise Dans Son Usage Reel. 932p. (Fr.). 1973. $95.00 (ISBN 0-686-56802-8, M-4739). French & Eur.

--Dictionnaire de la Prononciation Francaise dans son Usage Reel. 932p. (Fr.). 1973. 236.00 F. France Expansion.

Warnant, Leon. Dictionnaire de la Prononciation Francais. 3rd ed. (Fr.). 1968. 750.00 F. Duculot.

--Dictionnaire de la Prononciation Francais. 236p. (Fr.). 1967. 225.00 F. Duculot.

--Dictionnaire de la Prononciation Francais. 3rd ed. 654p. (Fr.). 1968. C.$21.00. Renouveau Pedagogique.

--Dictionnaire de la Prononciation Francaise, Vol. 1. 3rd ed. (Fr.). 1968. pap. $35.00 (ISBN 0-686-56824-9, M-6602). French & Eur.

FRENCH LANGUAGE–RIME–DICTIONARIES

Le Fevre, Jean. Dictionnaire de Rimes Francaises. 562p. (Fr.). 1973. 120.00 F. Slatkine.

Warnant, Leon. Dictionnaire des rimes orales et ecrites. new ed. 553p. (Fr.). 1972. $23.50 (ISBN 2-03-020271-1, 3546). Larousse.

FRENCH LANGUAGE–SLANG–DICTIONARIES

Caradec, Francois. Dictonnaire Du Francais Argotique et Populaire. 255p. (Fr.). 1977. pap. $6.95 (ISBN 0-686-56879-6, M-4968). French & Eur.

Kahlmann, Andre. Petit Dictionnaire du Francais gue l'on n'Apprend pas a l'Ecole. LC 78-396931. 38p. (Fr.). 1977. write for info. (ISBN 9-124-27154-3). Esselte Studium.

La Rue, Andre. Dictionnaire d'argot. (Fr.). write for info. Flammarion.

LeBreton, Auguste. L Argot Chez les Vrais de Vrais. LC 76-454371. (Illus.). 510p. (Fr.). 1975. 45.00 F. Presses Cite.

Sandir-White, Alex. Dictionary of French Slang. (Fr. & Eng.). $4.95. Aurea.

FRENCH LANGUAGE–SUFFIXES AND PREFIXES

Peytard, Jean. Recherches sur la Prefixation en Francais Contemporain, 3 vols. LC 77-456063. (Illus.). 790p. (Fr.). 1975. write for info. F (ISBN 2-252-01690-6). Klincksieck.

FRENCH LANGUAGE–SYNONYMS

Bailly, R. Dictionnaire des synonymes. (Fr., Fr). 23.50 (ISBN 0-685-13870-4, 3621). Larousse.

Bar, E. Dictionnaire des Synonymes. 406p. (Fr.). 1968. 14.00 F. Garnier.

Benac, Henri. Dictionnaire des Synonymes. new ed. 1026p. (Fr.). 1975. 46.50 F. Hachette.

--Dictionnaire des Synonymes. (Fr.). Can.$13.60. Renouveau Pedagogique.

Bertrand Du Chazaud, Henri. Dictionnaire des Synonymes. LC 79-122880. iv, 468p. (Fr.). 1979. 85.00 F (ISBN 2-85036-025-2). Soc Nouveau.

Denis-Papin, Maurice. Dictionnaire Analogique et de Synonymes Pour la Resolution des Problemes des Mots Croises. 6th ed. (Fr.). 1970. pap. $6.95 (ISBN 0-686-56786-2, M-6582, Pub. by Albin Michel). French & Eur.

De Noter, R. & Vuillermoz, P. Dictionnaire des Synonymes. 284p. (Fr.). 1969. 33.20 F. PUF.

Dictionnaire des Synonymes. 17th ed. 640p. (Fr.). 1971. 51.00 F. Larousse.

Dupuis, Hector. Dictionnaire des Synonymes & des Antonymes. 607p. (Fr.). 1975. Can.$8.95. Fides.

--Dictionnaire des synonymes et des antonymes. 2nd rev. ed. Legare, Romain, rev. by. 608p. (Fr.). 1975. Can.$15.95. Soc Dev Liv.

Dupuis, Hector & Legare, Romain. Dictionnaire des Synonymes & des Antonymes. 608p. (Fr.). 1975. 54.00 F. Ecole.

Froimont, J. Dictionnaire des Synonymes: Francais-Neerlandais. 428p. (Fr. & Dutch.). 195.00 F. Erasme.

Genouvrier, E. Dictionnaire des Synonymes de Poche. (Fr.). 1977. pap. $7.25 (Dist. by Continental Bk Co). Larousse.

FRENCH LANGUAGE–TECHNICAL FRENCH

Belle-Isle, J. G. Dictionnaire technique general. 2nd ed. 554p. (Fr. & Eng.). 1977. $45.00. Imported Bks.

Cusset, Francis. Vocabulaire Technique Allemand-Francais. 8th ed. 474p. (Ger. & Fr.). 1977. 66.50 F. Berger-Levrault.

--Vocabulaire Technique Anglais-Francais. 9th ed. 434p. (Eng. & Fr.). 1977. 118.50 F. Berger-Levrault.

Malgorn, Guy. Dictionnaire technique Anglais-Francais. 5th ed. (Fr. & Eng.). 1972. $38.00. Imported Bks.

FRENCH LANGUAGE–TERMS AND PHRASES

Dubois, Marguerite-Marie. Dictionnaire de Locutions: Francais-Anglais. 392p. (Fr.). 1973. 60.00 F. Larousse.

Gabillon, Aime. Dictionnaire des Mots, des Phrases, des Images. (Illus.). 128p. (Fr.). 1963. 36.00 F. RST.

Kettridge, J. O. French for English Idioms & Figurative Phrases. (Fr. & Eng.). 1966. Repr. of 1940 ed. 16.00 (ISBN 0-7100-1669-7). Routledge & Kegan.

Rakhmanov, I. V., ed. Slovar Naibolee Upotrebitel'Nykh Slov Anglii-Skogo, Nemetskogo & Frantsuzskogo Iazykov. 582p. (Rus., Ger. & Fr.). 1960. $2.40 (Pub. by Izd. Inostr. & Natsional'Nal'Nykh Slovarei). Four Continent.

Rat, M. Dictionnaire des Locutions Francaises. (Fr., Fr). 23.50 (ISBN 0-685-13866-6, 3613). Larousse.

Rat, Maurice. Dictionnaire des Locutions Francaises. 7th ed. 464p. (Fr.). 1970. 49.00 F. Larousse.

FRENCH LANGUAGE–TEXT-BOOKS FOR FOREIGNERS

see also French Language–Conversation and Phrase Books

Lumeka, Placide-Raphael. Vocabulaire Alphabetique & Analogique Destine aus Ecollers Africains Francophones. 229p. (Fr.). 1972. 40.00 F. Lang, H.

Patterson, W. R. Learn French for English Speakers. 230p. (Fr. & Eng.). pap. 9.50 (ISBN 0-87557-023-2, 023-2). Saphrograph.

Stone, R. G., et al. A Glossary of English Equivalents of Terms Commonly Used in French Auctions, Catalogues, & Stamp Trade. (Fr. & Eng.). $2.00. France & Col Philatelist.

FRENCH LANGUAGE–VERB

Caput, J. P. & Caput, J. Dictionnaire des verbes francais. (Fr., Fr). 27.50 (ISBN 0-685-13871-2, 3622). Larousse.

Kendris, Christopher. Diccionario De Dos Cientos Uno Verbos Franceses Conjugados en Todos sus Tiempos & Personas. LC 68-8677. (Orig., Span. & Fr.). 1972. pap. $3.95 (ISBN 0-8120-0393-4). Barron.

FRENCH LANGUAGE–VOCABULARY

Baker, H. H. A Classified French Vocabulary. 96p. (Fr.). Epap. 1.75. Harrap.

Ballereau, Emile & Bouquet, Georges. Le Vocabulaire Vivant. (Illus.). 192p. (Fr.). 1961. 9.75 F. SUDEL.

Ballot, Marc M. & Fougerouse. Le Vocabulaire par la Vie des Mots. 152p. (Fr.). 1958. 10.00 F. Lavauzelle.

Borel, Pierre. Vocabulaire Systematique Francais-Allemand. 171p. (Fr. & Ger.). 1959. 9.80 F. Francke.

Buissonnier, Solange. Vocabulaire & Elocution les Debutants. (Illus., Fr.). 1969. 4.70 F. Hachette.

De Bazin, Jean. Vocabulaire de la Princesse de Cleves. new ed. 56p. (Fr.). 1974. 19.26 F. Nizet.

Dictionnaire Orthographique du Vocabulaire de Base. 324p. (Fr.). 1.20 F. Desoer.

Dottrens, Robert & Massarenti, Dino. Vocabulaire Fondamentale du Francais. 4th ed. (Illus.). 64p. (Fr.). 1963. 18.00 F. Delachaux.

Dubois, Jean. Vocabulaire Politique & Social en France de 1869 a 1872. 460p. (Fr.). 1963. 40.00 F. Larousse FR.

Essential French Vocabulary. (Fr.). $3.10. Longman.

Girolami-Boulinier, Andree. Vocabulaire & Language. 3rd ed. (Illus.). 156p. (Fr.). 1976. 41.00 F. Delachaux.

Haygood, James D. Le Vocabulaire Fondamentale du Francais. 160p. (Fr.). 1948. 12.00 F. Droz.

Lelu, Adolphe & Kluber, Louis. Vocabulaire & Exercices Francais. (Illus.). 96p. (Fr.). 11.00 F. Hatier.

——Vocabulaire & Exercices Francais. (Illus.). 302p. (Fr.). 15.25 F. Hatier.

——Vocabulaire & Exercices Francais. (Illus.). 366p. (Fr.). 9.00 F. Hatier.

——Vocabulaire & Exercices Francais. (Illus.). 256p. (Fr.). 14.95 F. Hatier.

——Vocabulaire & Exercices Francais. (Illus.). 256p. (Fr.). 6.20 F. Hatier.

Mackey, William Francis & Savard, J. G. Vocabulaire Disponible du Francais en France & en Acadie. (Fr.). 134.30 F. Didier.

Malzac, R. P. Vocabulaire Francais-Malgache. 446p. (Fr.). 1952. 18.00 F. Maritimes Outremer.

Marthaler, Andre. Le Vocabulaire Vivant. (Illus.). 208p. (Fr.). 1961. 15.00 F. Payot.

——Le Vocabulaire Vivant, 1. (Illus.). 155p. (Fr.). 1970. 9.00 F. Payot.

——Le Vocabulaire Vivant, 3. 240p. (Fr.). 1967. 16.00 F. 13.00 F. Payot.

Masson, Arthur. Vocabulaire. 3rd ed. 64p. (Fr.). 1967. 4.90 F. Hachette.

Matore, Georges. Dictionnaire du Vocabulaire Essentiel. 5th ed. 360p. (Fr.). 1970. pap. $10.95 (ISBN 0-686-56874-5, M-6652). French & Eur.

——Dictionnaire du Vocabulaire Essentiel. 5th ed. (Illus.). 360p. (Fr.). 26.00 F. Larousse.

Moreu-Rey, E. Vocabulario Basico Frances. 112p. (Fr.). 40.00 ptas. Teide.

Moreu Rey, Enrico. Vocabulario Basico Frances. 5th ed. 112p. (Fr.). 1981. 125.00 ptas (ISBN 84-307-7062-3). Teide.

Schmitt, Roger & Filbert, Pierre. Vocabulaire & Style. 5th ed. 160p. (Fr.). 20.25 F. Nathan.

Thesaurus Normalisation, 1: Liste Alphabetique Structuree Francais-Anglais. 281p. (Fr. & Eng.). 1976. 705.60 F. A. F. N. O. R.

Thesaurus Normalisation, 2: Index Bilingue Francais-Anglais par Mots Vedettes. 193p. (Fr. & Eng.). 1976. 600.00 F. A. F. N. O. R.

Thesaurus Normalisation, 3: Table de Correspondance Anglais-Francais. 124p. (Eng. & Fr.). 1976. 600.00 F. A. F. N. O. R.

Vocabulaire & Redaction. (Fr.). 7.75 F. Ligel.

Vocabulaire & Redaction. (Fr.). 6.30 F. Ligel.

Vocabulaire, Dans: Larousse pour Tous. (Illus.). 832p. (Fr.). 23.90 F. Larousse FR.

Vocabulario T. Frances. (Fr.). 40.00 ptas. Bruno.

Vocabularios Frances-Espanol-Ingles. (Fr. , Span. & Eng.). $0.80; Mex.$10.00. Novaro.

Wagner, Rene L. Le Vocabulaire Francais, 1. 192p. (Fr.). 1967. 19.00 F. Didier Erudition.

——Le Vocabulaire Francais, 2. (Fr.). 1970. 19.00 F. Didier Erudition.

FRENCH LITERATURE–DICTIONARIES

Barbier. Dictionnaire Des Ouvrages Anonymes, 4 Vols. (Fr.). Set. $325.00 (ISBN 0-685-11143-1, F-12410). French & Eur.

Bonnefoy, Claude, et al. Dictionnaire de Litterature Francais Contemporaine. 411p. (Fr.). 1977. $39.95 (ISBN 0-686-56924-5, M-6042). French & Eur.

Dictionnaire des Oeuvres: Index. 5th ed. (Fr.). 1969. $295.00 (ISBN 0-686-56851-6, M-6629). French & Eur.

FRENCH LITERATURE–HISTORY AND CRITICISM–19TH CENTURY

Carlut, Charles. A Concordance to Flaubert's Bouvard et Pecuchet. LC 79-7915. 1021p. 1980. lib. bdg. $110.00 (ISBN 0-8240-9518-9). Garland Pub.

FRENCH MUSIC
see Music, French

FRENCH SCULPTURE
see Sculpture–France

FRENCH WIT AND HUMOR

Webb, Barbara. Dictionnaire a l'usage des Plaisanciers. 160p. (Fr.). 1969. 33.00 F. Maritimes Outre mer.

FRESH-WATER BIOLOGY
see also Aquariums

Russian-English Glossary of Hydrobiology. 113p. (Rus. & Eng.). 1958. $35.00x (ISBN 0-306-10599-3, Consultants). Plenum Pub.

FRIESIAN LANGUAGE

Dykstra, J. K. Op 't Aljemint. 2nd ed. LC 79-389433. 343p. (Friesian.). 1978. fl.25.00 (ISBN 9-06273-079-5). AFUK-LEARMIDDELFUNS.

Mutinelli, Fabio. Lessico Vento. LC 79-388187. 425p. (Ital., Sala Bolgonese). 1978. write for info. Forni.

FRISIAN LANGUAGE
see Friesian Language

FROISSART, JEAN, 1338-1410

La Magna, Giovanni. Dizionario sintattico latino: Italiano-latino e latino-italiano. 180p. (Ital. & Lat.). L.2000.00. Signorelli C.

Pinoche, Jacqueline. Le Vocabulaire Psychologique dans les Chroniques de Froissart, 1. (Fr.). 1976. 92.00 F. Klincksieck.

Wilcox, R. Dictionary of Costume. 1979. $37.00 (ISBN 0-7134-0856-1, Pub. by Batsford England). David & Charles.

FRUIT

Appel, L. Lexique des Fruits et Legumes. 133p. (Fr. & Eng.). Date not set. pap. $9.95 (ISBN 0-686-97410-7, M-9238). French & Eur.

Appel, Louise. Lexique Anglais-Francais Des Fruits et Legumes. rev. ed. 128p. (Eng. & Fr.). 1974. pap. $9.95 (ISBN 0-686-56897-4, M-6007). French & Eur.

FRUITS
see Fruit

FUCHSIA

Ewart, Ron. Fuchsia Lexicon. 280p. 1982. $29.95 (ISBN 0-442-22283-1). Van Nos Reinhold.

FUCUS

Papok, K. K. & Ragozin, N. A. Tekhnicheskii Slovar Spravochnik po Toplivu i Maslam. 766p. (Rus.). 1963. $6.50 (Pub. by Gostoptekhizda r). Four Continent.

FUEL
see also Heating

Papok, K. K. & Ragozin, N. A. Tekhnicheskii Slovar Spravochnik Po Toplivu & Maslam. 766p. (Rus.). 1963. $6.50 (Pub. by Gostoptekhizdat). Four Continent.

FULAH LANGUAGE

Gaden, Henri. Lexique Poular-Francais: Le Poular Dialecte Peul du Fouta Senegalais. 280p. (Fr.). 1967. $16.00. Gregg.

FUNDAMENTAL THEOLOGY
see Apologetics

FUNDS
see Finance

FUNGI
see also Lichens; Mushrooms

Ainsworth & Bisby. Dictionary of the Fungi. 663p. 1971. $69.00x (ISBN 0-85198-075-9, Pub. by CAB Bks England). State Mutual Bk.

Ainsworth & Bisby's. Dictionary of the Fungi. 663p. 1978. $75.00 (ISBN 0-85198-075-9, M-9711). French & Eur.

Ainsworth, G. C. Ainsworth & Bisby's Dictionary of the Fungi, Including the Lichens. 6th ed. LC 74-883641. (Illus.). 673p. 1971. 27.50x (ISBN 0-85198-075-9). Intl Pubns Serv.

FUNGI, EDIBLE
see Mushrooms, Edible

FUNGI IN AGRICULTURE
see also Plant Diseases

Ainsworth & Bisby. Dictionary of the Fungi. 663p. 1971. $69.00x (ISBN 0-85198-075-9, Pub. by CAB Bks England). State Mutual Bk.

FURNACES

Stepanek, Josef. Woerterbuch Industrieofen & Indudtrielle Warmeanlagen. LC 76-454323. viii, 444p. (Eng., Span. & Fr.). 1975. DM.78.00 (ISBN 3-8027-2484-4). Vulkan Verlag.

FURNITURE–BUILDING
see Furniture Making

FURNITURE–CATALOGS

Filbee, Marjorie. Dictionary of Country Furniture. 208p. 1981. $30.00x (ISBN 0-900305-17-7, Pub. by Ebury Pr England). State Mutual Bk.

FURNITURE–DICTIONARIES

Antique Collectors' Club. Pictorial Dictionary of British Nineteenth Century Furniture Design. 583p. 1980. $69.50 (ISBN 0-902028-47-2). Antique Collect.

Barber, Edward A. & Lockwood, Luke V. The Ceramic Furniture & Silver Collectors' Glossary. (Architecture & Decorative Art Ser.). 1976. pap. $6.95 (ISBN 0-306-80049-7). Da Capo.

Filbee, Marjorie. The Connoisseur Dictionary of Country Furniture. new ed. (Illus.). 1977. 12.95 (ISBN 0-900305-17-7). Hearst Bks.

——Dictionary of Country Furniture. 208p. 1981. $30.00x (ISBN 0-900305-17-7, Pub. by Ebury Pr England). State Mutual Bk.

Gloag, John. A Short Dictionary of Furniture. 1976. pap. $14.95 (ISBN 0-04-749009-8). Allen Unwin.

Jay, E. Pictorial Dictionary of Nineteeth Century Furniture Design. (Illus.). 1980. $69.50 (ISBN 0-902028-47-2). Apollo.

Lockwood, Luke V. Furniture Collector's Glossary. LC 67-27460. (Architecture & Decorative Art Ser.). 1967. Repr. of 1940 ed. lib. bdg. $15.00 (ISBN 0-306-70968-6). Da Capo.

Mayer, E. Dictionnaire des Valeurs de Meubles & Objets d'art. (Illus.). 450p. (Fr.). 1973. 99.00 F. Fischbacher.

Mayer, Enrique. Le Dictionnaire des Meubles & Objets D'art 1965 & 1966. 112p. (Fr.). 1967. 120.00 F. Mayer.

——Le Dictionnaire des Meubles & Objets d'art, 1963 & 1964. 320p. (Fr.). 1965. 99.00 F. Mayer Ed.

VonZweck, Dina. Woman's Day Dictionary of Furniture. 1983. pap. $4.95 (ISBN 0-8065-0842-6). Citadel Pr.

FURNITURE–FRANCE

Viollet-Le-Duc, Eugene E. Dictionnaire Raisonne Du Mobilier Francais De L'epoque Carlovingienne a la Renaissance, 6 Vols. 2nd ed. LC 76-153606. (Illus., Fr.). Repr. of 1875 ed. Set. lib. bdg. $345.00 (ISBN 0-404-09750-2); lib. bdg. $57.50 ea. Vol. 1 (ISBN 0-404-09751-0). Vol. 2 (ISBN 0-404-09752-9). Vol. 3 (ISBN 0-404-09753-7). Vol. 4 (ISBN 0-404-09754-5). Vol. 5 (ISBN 0-404-09755-3). Vol. 6 (ISBN 0-404-09756-1). AMS Pr.

FURNITURE–GREAT BRITAIN

Antique Collectors' Club. Pictorial Dictionary of British Nineteenth Century Furniture Design. 583p. 1980. $69.50 (ISBN 0-902028-47-2). Antique Collect.

Edwards, Ralph. The Shorter Dictionary of English Furniture. (Illus.). 684p. (Eng.). E50.00 (ISBN 0-600-43082-0). Newnes Bks.

Joy, Edward. Pictorial Dictionary of British Nineteenth Century Furniture Designs. (Illus.). 578p. 1980. 59.50 (ISBN 0-686-65051-4). Hacker.

FURNITURE BUILDING
see Furniture Making

FURNITURE MAKING

Pallini, L. Dizionario sintetico da tavolo. (Illus.). xvi, 790p. (Ital.). L.11000.00. Vallardi F.

FUTURES
see Speculation

FYOTI LANGUAGE
see Congo Language

G

GABON

Gardinier, David E. Historical Dictionary of Gabon. LC 81-5290. (African Historical Dictionaries Ser.: No. 30). 284p. 1981. $15.00 (ISBN 0-8108-1435-8). Scarecrow.

GAELIC LANGUAGE
see also Celtic Languages; Irish Language; Manx Language

Dwelly. Illustrated Gaelic-English Dictionary. 8th ed. (Illus., Gaelic & Eng.). $35.00x (ISBN 0-686-00868-5). Colton Bk.

Mackay, Charles. Dictionary of Lowland Scotch. LC 68-17998. (Scottish.). 1968. Repr. of 1888 ed. $45.00x (ISBN 0-8103-3284-1). Gale.

MacLennan, Malcolm. Gaelic Dictionary: Gaelic-English English-Gaelic. 632p. (Gaelic & Eng.). 1980. 45.00 (ISBN 0-08-025713-5); pap. 22.00 (ISBN 0-08-025712-7). Pergamon.

O'Donaill. Foclair Gaeilge Bearla (Irish-English Dictionary) (Irish & Eng.). $25.00x (ISBN 0-686-28280-9). Colton Bk.

Vendryes, Joseph. Lexique Etymologique de l'Irlandais Ancien. 272p. (Fr. & Gaelic). 1975. 70.00 F. CNRS.

Warrack, Alexander. Chambers Scots Dictionary. (Gaelic). Repr. of 1911 ed. $14.95 (ISBN 0-550-11801-2, Pub. by Two Continents). Am Map.

GALA LANGUAGE
see Bangala Language

GALVANIC BATTERIES
see Electric Batteries

GALVANISM
see Electricity

GAMBIA

Gailey, Harry A. Historical Dictionary of the Gambia. LC 75-5882. (African Historical Dictionaries Ser.: No. 4). 180p. 1975. $13.00 (ISBN 0-8108-0810-2). Scarecrow.

GAMES
see also Cards; Puzzles; Sports; Video Games
also specific games, e.g. Baseball, Contract Bridge, Tennis

Cuddon, J. A. The International Dictionary of Sports & Games. LC 79-20983. (Illus.). 898p. 1980. $29.95 (ISBN 0-8052-3733-X). Schocken.

Denis-Papin, Maurice. Dictionnaire des Mots Croises & Jeux Divers. 384p. (Fr.). 1973. 22.00 F. Albin Michel.

GANDA LANGUAGE

Luganda-English Dictionary. (Luganda & Eng.). $35.00. Iaconi.

Nosova, O. P. Kratkii Lugunda-Russkii & Russko-Lugunda Slovar. 520p. (Rus. & Luganda). 1969. $3.95 (Pub. by Sov Entsiklopediia). Four Continent.

GAOLS
see Prisons

GARBAGE
see Refuse and Refuse Disposal

GARCIA LORCA, FEDERICO, 1899-1936

Pollin, Alice M. & Smith, Philip H., eds. A Concordance to the Plays & Poems Federico Garcia Lorca. LC 73-20817. (Concordances Ser.). 1216p. 1975. $59.50x (ISBN 0-8014-0808-3). Cornell U Pr.

GARDEN ARCHITECTURE
see Architecture, Domestic; Landscape Gardening

GARDENING–BIBLIOGRAPHY

Massachusetts Horticultural Society, Boston. Dictionary Catalog of the Library of the Massachusetts Horticultural Society, 3 Vols. 1963. Set. lib. bdg. $250.00 (ISBN 0-8161-0648-7, Hall Library). G K Hall.

GARDENING–DICTIONARIES

Jahn, H. Herder-Lexikon Pflanzen. 256p. (Ger.). 1975. pap. $15.95 (ISBN 3-451-17370-0, M-7448, Pub. by Herder). French & Eur.

——Herder-Lexikon Pflanzen. 256p. (Ger.). 1975. pap. $15.95 (ISBN 3-451-17370-0). French & Eur.

Miller, P. The Gardener's Dictionary. 1969. Repr. of 1754 ed. $64.00 (ISBN 3-7682-0613-0). Lubrecht & Cramer.

Neues Grosses Gartenlexikon. (Ger.). 1973. $32.00 (ISBN 3-517-00442-1, M-7567, Pub. by Suedwest). French & Eur.

Neues Grosses Gartenlexikon. (Ger.). 1973. $32.00 (ISBN 3-517-00442-1). Suedwest.

Synge, Patrick M., ed. Dictionary of Gardening - Supplement. 1969. 74.00x (ISBN 0-19-869116-5). Oxford U Pr.

GAS
see also Gas Manufacture and Works; Petroleum
Belodvorskii, Iu. M. Kratkii Slovar Gazovika. 187p. (Rus.). 1955. $1.65 (Pub. by Ministertvo Kommun Khoz). Four Continent.

GAS, BOTTLED
see Liquefied Petroleum Gas

GAS, NATURAL
see also Gas Industry; Liquefied Petroleum Gas; Oil Fields
Chaballe, L. Y. & Masuy, L. Elsevier's Oil & Gas Field Dictionary. (in 6 languages plus Arabic suppl.). 1980. $127.75 (ISBN 0-444-41833-4). Elsevier.

GAS AND OIL ENGINES
Crouse, William H. & Anglin, Donald L. Pocket Automotive Dictionary, with Metric Conversion Table. new ed. (Automotive Technology Ser). 1976. pap. text ed. 4.95 (ISBN 0-07-014752-3, G). McGraw.

GAS ENGINES
see Gas and Oil Engines

GAS INDUSTRY
Here are entered general works on industries based on natural or manufactured gas.
see also Gas, Natural; Gas Manufacture and Works
also other headings beginning with the word Gas
American Gas Association. Glossary for the Gas Industry. rev. ed. 83p. 1975. pap. $3.50 (F50000). Am Gas Assn.
Commisssion of the European Communities. Oil & Gas Multilingual Glossary. 500p. 1979. $44.00x (ISBN 0-86010-170-3, Pub. by Graham & Trotman England). State Mutual Bk.
International Gas Union, compiled by. Supplement to Elsevier's Dictionary of the Gas Industry: Polygot. LC 61-8851. 216p. 1973. $42.75 (ISBN 0-444-40757-X). Elsevier.
Von Baeckmann, Walter G. Lexikon der Gastechnik. LC 79-366542. 346p. (Ger.). 1978. DM.38.00 (ISBN 3-8027-2262-0). Vulkan Verlag.

GAS MANUFACTURE AND WORKS
see also Gas Industry
International Gas Union, ed. Elsevier's Dictionary of the Gas Industry, 2 vols. (Polyglot). 1961. Set. $95.75 (ISBN 0-444-40758-8); Incl. suppl. pap. $138.50 (ISBN 0-686-85926-X). Elsevier.

GAS-TURBINES
Dictionary of Gas Turbine Installation. 170p. (Eng. & Chinese). 1973. pap. $3.95 (ISBN 0-686-92296-4, M-9566). French & Eur.

GASCON DIALECT
Palay, Simin. Dictionnaire du Bernais & du Gascon Modernes. 45p. (Fr.). 1980. pap. 35.00 F (ISBN 2-22202-708-X). CNRS.
Palay, Simon. Dictionnaire du Bearnais & du Gascon Modernes. 1052p. (Fr.). 1980. 290.00 F (ISBN 2-22201-608-8). CNRS.
Simin. Dictionnaire du Bearnais & du Gascon Moderne. 1044p. (Fr.). 1974. write for info. CNRS.

GASEOUS PLASMA
see Plasma (Ionized Gases)

GASOLINE ENGINES
see Gas and Oil Engines

GASTRONOMY
see also Cookery; Menus
Dictionnaire Gastronomique. 2nd ed. 225p. (Fr.). 1974. 22.00 F. Union Helvi.
Neiger, Elisabetta. Dizionario gastronomico. 139p. (Ital.). L.3000.00. Buffetti.
Simon, Andre L. & Howe, Robin. Dictionary of Gastronomy. 2nd ed. LC 78-16260. (Illus.). 400p. 1979. 37.95 (ISBN 0-87951-081-1). Overlook Pr.

GAUL
Cartailhac, Emile. Dictionnaire Archeologique de la Gaul. 160p. (Fr.). 1923. 10.00 F. Nationale.

GAUL-HISTORY
Moreau, Joseph. Dictionnaire de Geographie Historique de la Gaule et de la France. 426p. (Fr.). 1972. pap. $37.50 (ISBN 0-686-56815-X, M-6593). French & Eur.

GAULLE, CHARLES DE, PRES. FRANCE, 1890-1970
Dictionnaire Commente de l'oeuvre de General de Gaulle. 880p. (Fr.). 1975. $30.00 (ISBN 0-686-56811-7, M-6589). French & Eur.

GAZETTEERS
see Geography-Dictionaries

GELS
see Colloids

GEMS
Here are entered books on engraved stones and jewels, interesting from the point of view of antiquities or art. Works on mineralogical interest are entered under Precious Stones.
see also Jewelry
Diccionario de gemologia. (Span.). 480.00 ptas. Jover.
Read. Dictionary of Gemmology. 1982. text ed. $34.95 (ISBN 0-408-00571-8). Butterworth.

GEMSTONES
see Precious Stones

GENEALOGICAL RESEARCH
see Genealogy

GENEALOGY
see also Heraldry
also names of families, e.g. Adams Family; and names of places with or without the subdivision Genealogy, e.g. United States - Genealogy
Arthur, William. An Etymological Dictionary of Family Christian Names. 59.95 (ISBN 0-8490-0135-8). Gordon Pr.
Suess, Jared H. Central European Geneological Terminology. LC 80-112612. xi, 168p. (Eng.). 1978. write for info. Everton Pubs.
Tanguay, Cyprien & Senechal. Dictionnaire Genealogique des Familles Canadiennes: Depuis la Fondation de la Colonie Jusqu'a nos Jours, 7 vols. (Fr.). 1975. Can.$210.00. Elysee.

GENEALOGY-RESEARCH
see Genealogy

GENERAL PRACTICE (MEDICINE)
see Family Medicine

GENERATIVE ORGANS
Tuxen, S. L., ed. Taxonomist's Glossary of Genitalia in Insects. 1970. text ed. $27.50 (ISBN 0-934454-76-0). Lubrecht & Cramer.

GENETICS-DICTIONARIES
Biass-Ducroux, Francoise. Glossary of Genetics. (Eng., Fr., Span., Ital., Ger. & Rus.). 1970. $72.50 (ISBN 0-444-40712-X). Elsevier.
King, Robert C. Dizionario di genetica. vi, 372p. (Ital.). 1974. L.10000.00. ISEDI.
L'Heritier, Philippe. Dictionnaire de Genetique. LC 79-386405. 259p. (Fr.). 1979. 55.00 F (ISBN 2-225-52657-5). Masson & Cie.
Rieger, R., et al. Glosario de Genetica y Citogenetica II. Puertas Gallego, M. J., tr. 512p. (Span.). 1982. map. 920.00 ptas (ISBN 84-205-0875-6). Alhambra.
--Glossary & Genetics & Cytogenetics. 4th rev. ed. LC 76-16183. (Illus.). 1976. soft cover $16.00 (ISBN 3-540-07668-9). Springer-Verlag.
Wiesner, E. & Willer, S. Lexikon der Genetik der Hundekrankheiten. (Illus.). 480p. (Ger.). 1983. 29.50 (ISBN 3-8055-3616-X). S. Karger.

GENTOO LANGUAGE
see Telugu Language

GEODESY
see also Surveying
Albota, Mihail. Dictionar Poliglot de Geodezie: Fotogrammetrie si Cartografie. LC 76-477531. xv, 325p. (Eng., Ger., Fr., Rus. & Romanian). 1976. 41.00 lei. Editura Stiintifica.
Kuzmin, B. S., ed. Kratkii Topografo-Geodezicheskii Slovar. 280p. (Rus.). 1973. $4.75 (Pub. by Nedra). Four Continent.
Piskunova, I. A. Nemetsko-Russkii Geodezicheskii Slovar. 210p. (Rus.). 1965. $2.95 (Pub. by Nedra). Four Continent.

GEOGNOSY
see Geology

GEOGRAPHICAL ATLASES
see Atlases

GEOGRAPHICAL DICTIONARIES
see Geography-Dictionaries

GEOGRAPHICAL DISTRIBUTION OF MAN
see Anthropo-Geography

GEOGRAPHICAL NAMES
see Names, Geographical

GEOGRAPHY
see also Anthropo-Geography; Atlases; Classical Geography; Discoveries (In Geography); Ecclesiastical Geography; Voyages and Travels
also subdivision Description and Travel under names of countries, e.g. France-Description and Travel; and subdivision Description, Geography under names of countries of antiquity, e.g. Greece-Description, Geography; and subdivision Maps under names of places, e.g. France-Maps
Capot-Rey, Robert & Blaudin De The, Bernard. Glossaire des Principaux Termes Geographiques & Logiques Sahariens. (Illus.). 84p. (Fr.). 1963. 10.00 F. Sahariennes Inst. Rech.
Ergo, A. B., et al. Thesaurus des Symboles Agrobioclimatiques, Geographiques & Techniques, 4. 531p. (Fr.). 1974. 535.00 F. Centre Informatique Develop.
Hanle, Adolf. Die Geographie: Ein Lexikon der Gesamten Schul-Erdkunde. (Illus.). 420p. (Ger.). DM.19.80 (ISBN 3-411-01731-7). Biblio Inst.
Henry, J. M. & Ergo, A. B. Thesaurus des Symboles Agrobioclimatiques, Geographiques & Techniques, 3. 270p. (Fr.). 1973. 450.00 F. Centre Informatique Develop.
Kuzmin, B. S., ed. Kratkii Topografo-Geodezicheskii Slovar. 280p. (Rus.). 1973. $4.75 (Pub. by Nedra). Four Continent.
Moore. Diccionario de geografia. (Span.). write for info. Dossat.
Petit, J. L., et al. Thesaurus des Symboles Agrobioclimatiques, Geographiques & Techniques, 2 vols. (Illus.). 686p. (Fr.). 1971. 2240.00 F. Centre Informatique Develop.

GEOGRAPHY-ATLASES
see Atlases

GEOGRAPHY-DICTIONARIES
Aubakirov, Z., et al. Russko-Kazakhskii Tolkovyi Geograficheskii Slovar. 203p. (Rus.). 1966. $2.70 (Pub. by Nauka). Four Continent.
Barbier De Meynard, Achille. Dictionnaire Geographique, Historique & Literaire: La Perse & des Contrees Adjacentes, 8 vols. 640p. (Fr.). 1970. fl.96.00. Philo Pr.
Boccaccio, Giovanni. Dizionario geografico. (Ital.). 1978. L.7000.00. Fogola.
Brommer, ed. Lexique Anglais-Francais des Termes Appartenant Aux Techniques En Usage a I.G.N. Pt.2. 122p. (Fr. & Eng., English-French Lexicon of Terms Pertaining to Techniques Used at I.G.N). 1958. pap. $7.95 (ISBN 0-686-56778-1, M-6356). French & Eur.
Compagnol, Marcello G. Dizionario Merli geografico, storico, economico: Vol. 1, Lettera AZ. (Illus.). 176p. (Ital.). 1975. L.25000.00. ERGA.
Cotti-Cometti, G. & George, P. Dizionario della geografica: Geografica umana, Vol. 1. 256p. (Ital.). 1971. L.3000.00. CESVIET.
Deschamps, Pierre. Dictionnaire de Geographie Ancienne et Moderne. 2nd ed. 1008p. (Fr.). 1965. $85.00 (ISBN 0-686-56814-1, M-6592). French & Eur.
Dey, Nundo Lal. The Geographical Dictionary of Ancient & Mediaeval India. LC 42-31336. (Illus.). 272p. 1971. Repr. of 1927 ed. 19.50x (ISBN 0-8002-1453-6). Intl Pubns Serv.
Egli, Jakob. Etymologisch Geographisches Lexikon. (Ger.). 1970. $62.50 (ISBN 3-500-21620-X, M-7371, Pub. by Saendig-Walluf). French & Eur.

English-Chinese Dictionary of Physical Geography. 279p. (Eng. & Chinese). 1980. $25.00 (ISBN 0-686-97362-3, M-9292). French & Eur.
Fischer, Eric & Elliott, Francis E. A German & English Glossary of Geographical Terms. LC 76-20474. (American Geographical Society Library Ser: No. 5). 111p. (Ger. & Eng.). 1976. Repr. of 1950 ed. lib. bdg. $15.00x (ISBN 0-8371-8994-2, ELGG). Greenwood.
Forster, Klaus. Pronouncing Dictionary of English-Place Names. 308p. 1981. 30.00 (ISBN 0-7100-0756-6). Routledge & Kegan.
Fulvi, Fulvio. Dizionario di termini della geografia umana. 150p. (Ital.). 1978. L.3900.00. Patron.
George, Pierre. Dictionnaire de la Geographie. 2nd ed. 460p. (Fr.). 1974. $47.50 (ISBN 0-686-57193-2, M-6267). French & Eur.
Graesse, Johann G. Orbis Latinus: Lexikon lateinischer geographischer Namen des Mittelalters und der Neuzeit, 3 vols. new ed. Plechl, Helmut, ed. 1800p. (Lat. & Ger.). 1970. $275.00x (ISBN 3-7814-0087-5). Intl Pubns Serv.
Istilah geografi, Inggeris-Malaysia-Inggeris. LC 76-941849. xvi, 511p. (Eng. & Malay.). 1976. M.$6.50. Dewan Bahasa.
Klein, Johannes. Diccionario Rioduero: Paises De la Tierra. 296p. (Span.). 1978. leatherette $15.75 (ISBN 84-220-0876-9, S-50165). French & Eur.
Klein, M. Herder - Lexikon Geographie. 238p. (Ger.). 1975. pap. $15.95 (ISBN 3-451-16451-5, M-7456, Pub. by Herder). French & Eur.
--Herder-Lexikon Geographie. 238p. (Ger.). 1975. pap. $15.95 (ISBN 3-451-16451-5). Herder.
Klein, Margit & Klein, Johannes. Diccionario Rioduero: Geografia. 2nd ed. (Span.). 1977. leatherette $15.75 (ISBN 84-220-0670-7, S-50173). French & Eur.
Knox, Alexander. Glossary of Geographical & Topographical Terms. LC 68-30592. 1968. Repr. of 1904 ed. $27.00 (ISBN 0-8103-3236-1). Gale.
Lexique d'amenagement du Territoire. (Fr.). 1973. 10.70 F. C. N. I. P. E.
Monkhouse, F. J. Diccionario De Terminos Geograficos. 560p. (Span.). 1978. $48.00 (ISBN 84-281-0386-0, S-50017). French & Eur.
--Dizionario di geografia. Manzoni, M., tr. (Illus.). 400p. (Ital.). 1974. L.13000.00. Zanichelli.
Moore. Dizionario di geografia. (Ital.). L.3000.00. Newton-Compton.
Moore, W. C. Diccionario de Geografia. 158p. (Span.). 1972. $11.95 (ISBN 84-237-0340-1, S-50246). French & Eur.
Moore, W. G. A Dictionary of Geography: Definitions & Explanations of Terms Used in Physical Geography. LC 77-94144. (Illus.). 260p. 1978. text ed. $19.50x (ISBN 0-06-494934-6). B&N Imports.
Ogee, Jean, et al. Dictionnaire Historique & Geographique de la Province de Bretagne, 2 vols. 1520p. (Fr.). 1973. 450.00 F. Floch.
Riccardi, Mario. Glossario geografico. (Ital.). L.3500.00 (ISBN 88-7006-903-6). Japadre.
Rousset, A. Dictionnaire Geographique, Historique & Statistique des Communes: Franche-Comte & des Hameaux qui en Dependent, 6 vols. 3602p. (Fr.). 1970. 600.00 F. Guenegaud.
Stein, Henri. Dictionnaire Topographique de la France. Hubert, J., ed. 738p. (Fr.). 1954. pap. $25.00 (ISBN 0-686-57226-2, M-6525). French & Eur.
Thesaurus des Termes Geographiques. 96p. (Fr.). 1971. 69.00 F. Technip.

Thuillier. Lexique Anglais-Francais des Termes Appartenant Aux Technques En Usage I.G.N, 2 vols, Pt. 1. 464p. (Fr. & Eng., English-French Lexicon of Terms Pertaining to Techniques Used at I.G.N.). 1958. pap. $14.95 (ISBN 0-686-56781-1, M-6357). French & Eur.
Vasmer, Max. Woerterbuch der Russischen Gewaessernamen: Bd 1, A-E. (Ger.). 1961. DM.168.00 (ISBN 3-447-00971-3). Harrassowitz.
Whitten, D. G. & Brooks, J. R. Dizionario di geologia. (Ital.). 1978. L.5500.00. Mondadori.
Woerterbuch der Russichen Gewaessernamen: Lfg 1. (Ger.). 1961. DM.46.00 (ISBN 3-447-00976-4). Borntaeger.
Woerterbuch der Russichen Gewaessernamen: Lfg 2. (Ger.). DM.46.00 (ISBN 3-447-00977-2). Harrassowitz.
Woerterbuch der Russichen Gewaessernamen: Bd 2, Z-K. (Ger. & Rus.). DM.154.00 (ISBN 3-447-00972-1). Harrassowitz.
Woerterbuch der Russichen Gewaessernamen: Lfg 4. (Ger. & Rus.). DM.46.00 (ISBN 3-447-00979-9). Harrassowitz.
Woerterbuch der Russischen Gewaessernamen: Bd 3, L-P. (Ger. & Rus.). DM.166.00 (ISBN 3-447-00973-X). Harrassowitz.
Woerterbuch der Russischen Gewaessernamen: Bd 4, R-U. (Ger. & Rus.). 1968. DM.132.00 (ISBN 3-447-00974-8). Harrassowitz.
Woerterbuch der Russischen Gewaessernamen: Bd 5, F-Ja. (Ger. & Rus.). 1969. DM.74.00 (ISBN 3-447-00975-6). Harrassowitz.
Woerterbuch der Russischen Gewaessernamen: Lfg 3. (Ger. & Rus.). DM.46.00 (ISBN 3-447-00978-0). Harrassowitz.
Woerterbuch der Russischen Gewaessernamen: Lfg 5. (Ger.). DM.46.00 (ISBN 3-447-00980-2). Harrassowitz.
Woerterbuch der Russischen Gewaessernamen: Lfg 6. (Ger. & Rus.). DM.32.00 (ISBN 3-447-00981-0). Harrassowitz.
Woerterbuch der Russischen Gewaessernamen: Lfg 7. (Ger. & Rus.). DM.46.00 (ISBN 3-447-00982-9). Harrassowitz.
Woerterbuch der Russischen Gewaessernamen: Lfg 8. (Ger. & Rus.). DM.46.00 (ISBN 3-447-00983-7). Harrassowitz.
Woerterbuch der Russischen Gewaessernamen: Lfg 9. (Ger. & Rus.). DM.74.00 (ISBN 3-447-00984-5). Harrassowitz.
Woerterbuch der Russischen Gewaessernamen: Lfg 10. (Ger. & Rus.). DM.44.00 (ISBN 3-447-00985-3). Harrassowitz.
WOerterbuch der Russischen Gewaessernamen: Lfg 11. (Ger. & Rus.). DM.44.00 (ISBN 3-447-00986-1). Harrassowitz.
Woerterbuch der Russischen Gewaessernamen: Lfg 12. (Ger. & Rus.). DM.44.00 (ISBN 3-447-00987-X). Harrassowitz.
Woerterbuch der Russischen Gewaessernamen: Lfg 13. (Ger. & Rus.). DM.44.00 (ISBN 3-447-00988-8). Harrassowitz.
Woerterbuch der Russischen Gewaessernamen: Lfg 14. (Ger. & Rus.). DM.30.00 (ISBN 3-447-00989-6). Harrassowitz.
Woerterbuch der Russischen Gewaessernamen: Lfg 15. iv, 190p. (Ger. & Rus.). DM.50.00 (ISBN 3-447-01494-6). Harrassowitz.
Zavala Cubillos, Armando. Diccionario Estudios de geografia. 200p. (Span.). 1961. Arg.$1.10. Leru.

GEOGRAPHY–EARLY WORKS
see Classical Geography; Geography, Ancient; Geography, Medieval

GEOGRAPHY–GAZETTEERS
see Geography–Dictionaries

GEOGRAPHY–TERMINOLOGY
see also Names, Geographical
Soto Mora, Consuelo & Fuentes Aguilar, Luis. Glosario de terminos geograficos. (Illus.). 232p. (Span.). 1966. Mex.$55.00. UNAM.

GEOGRAPHY–TO 400 A.D.
see Geography, Ancient

GEOGRAPHY–400-1400
see Geography, Medieval

GEOGRAPHY, ANCIENT
Here are entered works on the geography of the ancient world in general. Works confined to the geography of Greece and Rome are entered under Classical Geography.
Dey, Nundo Lal. The Geographical Dictionary of Ancient & Mediaeval India. LC 42-31336. (Illus.). 272p. 1971. Repr. of 1927 ed. 19.50x (ISBN 0-8002-1453-6). Intl Pubns Serv.

GEOGRAPHY, CLASSICAL
see Classical Geography

GEOGRAPHY, ECCLESIASTICAL
see Ecclesiastical Geography

GEOGRAPHY, HISTORICAL
see also Classical Geography; Ecclesiastical Geography; Geography, Ancient; Geography, Medieval; also names of countries, regions, etc., or subdivision Historical Geography, or Description, Geography under names of countries, regions, etc.
Adams, I. H. Agrarian Landscape Terms: A Glossary for Historical Geography. (Special Publication of the Institute of British Geographers: No. 9). 1980. $23.00 (ISBN 0-12-044180-2). Acad Pr.

GEOGRAPHY, LINGUISTIC
see Linguistic Geography

GEOGRAPHY, MEDIEVAL
Dey, Nundo Lal. The Geographical Dictionary of Ancient & Mediaeval India. LC 42-31336. (Illus.). 272p. 1971. Repr. of 1927 ed. 19.50x (ISBN 0-8002-1453-6). Intl Pubns Serv.

GEOGRAPHY, SOCIAL
see Anthropo-Geography

GEOGRAPHY, URBAN
see Cities and Towns

GEOLOGICAL PHYSICS
see Geophysics

GEOLOGY
see also Crystallography; Geophysics; Hydrogeology; Mineralogy; Mountains; Oceanography; Paleography; Paleontology; Petrology; Rocks; Sedimentation and Deposition
Heckman, Carol, et al, eds. GeoRef Thesaurus & Guide to Indexing. 2nd ed. LC 78-65083. 1978. pap. $35.00 (ISBN 0-913312-07-X) (ISBN 0-913312-40-1). Am Geol.

GEOLOGY–DICTIONARIES
American Geological Institute. Dictionary of Geological Terms. 3rd ed. LC 82-45315. (Illus.). 480p. 1984. $19.95 (ISBN 0-385-18100-0, Anchor Pr); pap. $7.95 (ISBN 0-385-18101-9, Anch). Doubleday.
Bates, Robert L. & Jackson, Julia A., eds. Glossary of Geology. 2nd ed. LC 79-57360. 749p. 1980. $60.00 (ISBN 0-913312-15-0). Am Geol.
Brain, James L. A Short Dictionary of Science Terms for Swahili Speakers. (Foreign & Comparative Studies Program, African Special Publications: No. 4). 70p. (Orig., Swahili.). 1969. pap. text ed. $4.50x (ISBN 0-686-74011-4). Syracuse U Foreign Comp.
Brun-Durand, Justin. Dictionnaire Topographique & Historique de la Drome. 580p. (Fr.). 1973. 120.00 F. Chantemerle.
Cagnacci-Schwicker, A. Woerterbuch fuer Metallurgie, Mineralogie, Geologie, Bergbau & die Oelindustrie. 1530p. (Eng., Fr., Ger. & Ital.). 1970. DM.110.00 (ISBN 3-7625-0751-1). Bauverlag.
Cagnacci-Schwicker, Angelo. Dictionnaire International de Metallurgie, Mineralogie, Geologie et Industries Extractives, 2 vols. 1530p. (Fr.). 1969. Set. $95.00 (ISBN 0-686-56933-4, M-6054). French & Eur.
--Woerterbuch fuer Metallurgie, Mineralogie, Geologie, Bergbau & die Oelindustrie Englische-Franzosisch-Deutsch-Italienisch. 1530p. (Eng., Fr., Ger. & Ital.). 1970. DM.110.00 (ISBN 3-7625-0751-1). Bauverlag.
Cailleux, E. Elements de Geologie En Six Langues. 191p. (Fr., Ger., Rus., Span. & Eng., Elements of Geology in Six Languages). 1965. pap. $19.95 (ISBN 0-686-56735-8, M-6055). French & Eur.
Challinor, John. A Dictionary of Geology. 5th ed. 365p. 1978. text ed. $22.00x (ISBN 0-7083-0675-6). Verry.
--A Dictionary of Geology. 5th ed. LC 78-4530. xvii, 365p. (Eng.). 1978. $14.95 (ISBN 0-19-520063-2). Oxford U Pr.
Chesnel De La Charbouclais, L. P. Dictionnaire de Geologie... et Dictionnaire de Chronologie Universelle par M. Champagnac, Vol. 50. Migne, J. P., ed. (Encyclopedie Theologique Ser.). 728p. (Fr.). Repr. of 1849 ed. lib. bdg. $192.50x (ISBN 0-89241-253-4). Caratzas Pub Co.
Diccionario Rioduero: Geologia y Mineralogia. 2nd ed. (Span.). 1978. leatherette $9.95 (ISBN 0-686-57363-3). French & Eur.
Dobovskaia, I. K. Frantsuzsko-Russkii Geologicheskii Slovar. 406p. (Fr. & Rus.). 1958. $2.90 (Pub. by Gosfizmat). Four Continent.
Dybovskaia, V. & Kirillova, I. Dictionnaire Geologique: Francais-Russe. 406p. (Fr. & Rus.). 1958. leatherette $4.95 (ISBN 0-686-92570-X, M-9099). French & Eur.
Four Languages Dictionary of Geological Terms. 703p. (Eng., Fr., Ger. & Rus.). 1980. $19.95 (ISBN 0-686-97380-1). French & Eur.
Gagnacci-Schwicker, A. & Schwicker. International Dictionary of Metallurgy, Mineralogy, Geology & the Mining & Oil Industries. 1530p. (Eng., Fr., Ger. & Ital.). 1970. $88.00 (ISBN 3-7625-0751-1, M-7482, Pub. by Bauverlag). French & Eur.
--International Dictionary of Metallurgey, Mineralogy, Geology & the Mining & Oil Industries. 1530p. (Eng., Fr., Ger. & Ital.). 1970. $88.00 (ISBN 3-7625-0751-1). Bauverlag.
Garcin, E. Dictionnaire Historique & Topographique de la Ancienne & Moderne, 2 vols. 1232p. (Fr.). write for info. Chantemerle.
Gary, M., et al. Glossary of Geology. 1717p. (Eng. & Rus.). 1977. $75.00 (ISBN 0-686-92556-4, M-9113). French & Eur.
Geologicheskii Slovar, 2 vols. (Rus.). 1973. $35.00 set (Pub. by Nedra). Four Continent.
Geri, M., ed. Tolkovyi Slovar' Angliskikh Geologicheskikh Terminov, 3 vols. (Rus. & Eng.). 1977. $37.50 set (Pub. by Prosveshchenie). Four Continent.
Heckman, Carol, et al, eds. GeoRef Thesaurus & Guide to Indexing. 2nd ed. LC 78-65083. 1978. pap. $35.00 (ISBN 0-913312-07-X) (ISBN 0-913312-40-1). Am Geol.
Klein, J. Herder-Lexikon Geologie und Mineralogie. 238p. (Ger.). 1975. $15.95 (ISBN 3-451-16452-3, M-7457, Pub. by Herder). French & Eur.
--Herder-Lexikon Geologie und Mineralogie. 238p. (Ger.). 1975. $15.95. Herder.
Krishtofovich, A. N. Geologicheskii Slovar, 2 Vols. (Rus.). 1960. $15.00 set (Pub. by Gos. Nauch. Tekhn. Izd. Lit. Po Geologii & Okhrane Nedr.). Four Continent.
Lexique Stratigraphique International. (Fr. & Eng.). pap. $37.50 (ISBN 0-686-57018-9, M-6369). French & Eur.
Manzoni, Marcello. Dizionario di geologia. (Illus.). 234p. (Ital.). 1968. L.13000.00. Zanichelli.
Mihailescu, Nicolae. Lexikon Geologie Geografie Mine Petrol. LC 76-506712. (Romanian.). 1975. 88.00 lei. Editura Stiintifica.
Murawski, H. Geologisches Woerterbuch. 7th ed. (Ger.). 1977. DM.pap. 10.95 (ISBN 3-432-84107-8). Deutscher Taschenbuch Verlag.
--Geologisches Woerterbuch. (Ger.). 1972. DM.pap. 10.95. Deutscher Taschenbuch Verlag.
Pascenkova, N. A., et al. Czechoslovakian-Russian Dictionary of Geology. 248p. (Czech. & Rus.). 1960. $41.95 (ISBN 0-686-92454-1, M-9067). French & Eur.
--Czechoslovakian-Russian Dictionary of Geology. 248p. (Czech. & Rus.). 1960. $41.95 (ISBN 0-686-92454-1, M-9067). French & Eur.
Petrov, V. S. & Tulin, S. A. Russian-Czechoslovakian Polytechnical Dictionary. 639p. (Rus. & Czech.). 1962. leatherette $6.95 (ISBN 0-686-92116-X, M-9074). French & Eur.
Riley, Sharon J., ed. GeoRef Thesaurus & Guide to Indexing. 3rd ed. 468p. 1981. $45.00 (ISBN 0-913312-53-3). Am Geol.
Rosenfeld, V. Kleines Fachwoerterbuch Geologie. 197p. (Ger.). 1966. $14.50 (ISBN 3-443-39048-X, M-7500, Pub. by Borntaeger). French & Eur.
Thesaurus di Scienze della Terra. LC 79-350721. 119p. (Eng., Fr., Ger. & Ital.). 1977. L.4000.00. Patron.
Thompson, Reginald C. A Dictionary of Assyrian Chemistry & Geology. LC 78-72768. (Ancient Mesopotamian Texts & Studies). (Assyrian.). Repr. of 1936 ed. $24.50 (ISBN 0-404-18222-4). AMS Pr.
Verbic, Ing S. English-Serbocroat & Serbocroat-English Geological & Mining Dictionary. 528p. (Eng. & Serbocroatian.). 1981. $90.00x (ISBN 0-686-44714-X, Pub. by Collets). State Mutual Bk.
Watt, Alec. Barnes & Noble Thesaurus of Geology. (Illus.). 192p. (gr. 11-12). 1983. $13.41i (ISBN 0-06-015177-3, EH 579); pap. $6.68i (ISBN 0-06-463579-1, EH 579). B&N NY.
Watznauer, A. Woerterbuch Geowissenschaften, Vol. 2. (Ger. & Eng., German-English Dictionary of Geo-Sciences). 1973. $45.00 (ISBN 3-87144-140-6, M-6916). French & Eur.
Woerterbuch fuer Metallurgie, Mineralogie, Geologie, Bergbau und die Oelindustrie. (Eng., Fr., Ger. & Ital., Dictionary of Metallurgy, Mineralogy, Geology, Mining and Oil Industry). 1970. $88.00 (ISBN 3-7625-0751-1, M-6912). French & Eur.
Wyllie, R. J. & Argall, George O., Jr., eds. World Mining Glossary of Mining, Processing & Geological Terms. LC 74-20169. (A World Mining Book). 432p. 1975. 47.50 (ISBN 0-87930-031-0). Miller Freeman.

GEOLOGY–EXAMINATIONS, QUESTIONS, ETC.
Pipkin, Bernard & Cummings, David. Environmental Geology: Practical Exercises. (Illus.). 240p. 1983. pap. $14.95 (ISBN 0-89863-058-4). Star Pub CA.

GEOLOGY–MEXICO
Suplemento a la Segunda Edicion Del Diccionario Pornua De Historia, Biografia y Geografia de Mexico. 496p. (Span.). $17.50 (ISBN 0-686-56693-9, S-12280). French & Eur.

GEOLOGY–NEAR EAST
Thompson, Reginald C. A Dictionary of Assyrian Chemistry & Geology. LC 78-72768. (Ancient Mesopotamian Texts & Studies). (Assyrian.). Repr. of 1936 ed. $24.50 (ISBN 0-404-18222-4). AMS Pr.

GEOLOGY–SOUTH AMERICA
Nunez, Benjamin. Terminos Topograficos en la Argentina Colonial, 1516-1810. 351p. (Span.). 1965. Mex.$2.00. Inst. Pan. Georg.

GEOLOGY, HISTORICAL
see Geology, Stratigraphic; Paleontology

GEOLOGY, STRATIGRAPHIC
see also Paleontology
Stratigraficheskii Slovar SSSR. (Rus.). 1977. $8.75 (Pub. by Nedra). Four Continent.
Stratigraficheskii Slovar SSSR. 592p. (Rus.). 1979. $10.95 (Pub. by Nedra). Four Continent.

GEOLOGY, STRUCTURAL
see also Geomorphology; Mountains; Plate Tectonics
Sommerville, Paul. Dictionary of Geotechnics. 1983. text ed. $49.95 (ISBN 0-408-00437-1). Butterworth.

GEOMETRY

see also Topology

C.I.L.F. Vocabulaire de sciences et techniques spatiales. 193p. (Ger. & Eng.). 1978. 125.00 F. Maison Dictionnaire.

GEOMORPHOLOGY

Baulig, Henri. Vocabulaire Franco-Anglo-Allemand de Geomorphologie. 230p. (Fr., Eng. & Ger.). 1970. 26.90 F. Strasbourg, U.

C.I.L.F. Vocabulaire de la geomorphologie. 200p. (Fr.). 1979. 100.00 F. Maison Dictionniare.

GEOPHYSICS

see also Geology; Magnetism; Meteorology; Oceanography; Plate Tectonics

Elektrorazvedka: Spravochnik Geofizika. 520p. (Rus.). 1979. $9.95 (Pub. by Nedra). Four Continent.

GEOPHYSICS–DICTIONARIES

Pashchenko, N. A., et al. Kratkii Cheshsko-Russkii Geofizicheskii Slovar. 248p. (Rus. & Czech.). 1960. $2.00 (Pub. by Glav. Red. Nauchn. Tekhn. Slovarei Fizmata). Four Continent.

GEOSCIENCE

see Earth Sciences

GEOTECHNIQUE

see Soil Mechanics

GEOTECTONICS

see Geology, Structural

GERMAN ART

see Art, German

GERMAN AUTHORS

see Authors, German

Albrecht, Guenther, et al, eds. Lexikon Deutschsprachiger Schriftsteller: Bd 2. 254p. (Ger.). 1974. DM.12.80 (ISBN 3-589-00062-7). Scriptor Verlag.

GERMAN DRAMA–HISTORY AND CRITICISM

Gellinek, Christian. Hugo Grotius Drama Concordance. LC 83-70923. (Studies in German Literature, Linguistics, & Culture: Vol. 7). (Illus.). 800p. 1983. $29.50x (ISBN 0-938100-23-8). Camden Hse.

GERMAN HEBREW

see Yiddish Language

GERMAN LANGUAGE

see also Low German Language

Althaus, Hans P., et al, eds. Lexikon der Germanistischen Linguistik. (Ger.). 1973. DM.106.00 (ISBN 3-484-10186-5). Niemeyer.

Bluvshtein, V. O. Slovar Nemetskikh Sokrashchenii. 442p. (Rus.). 1958. $2.25 (Pub. by GINS). Four Continent.

Dictionnaire de Deux Cent un Verbes Allemandes. (Fr. & Ger.). Date not set. $6.95 (ISBN 0-8120-2118-5). Barron.

Goetze, Alfred. Fruehneuhochdeutsches Glossar. 7th ed. (Kleine Texte, No. 101). (Ger.). 1971. Repr. of 1967 ed. bds. $9.90x (ISBN 3-11-003527-8). De Gruyter.

Inghult, Goran. Die Semantische Struktur Desubstantivischer Bildungen auf Maessig. LC 76-458533. 206p. (Ger.). 1975. Kr.50.00. Almqvist.

Larousse Elementaire a L'usage des Allemand. 672p. (Ger.). DM.18.80 (49009). Langenscheidt.

Leopold, Max. Die Vorsilbe ver & Ihre Geschichte. LC 77-562245. viii, 284p. (Ger.). 1977. DM.49.80 (ISBN 3-48706-181-3). Olms Verlag.

Schaefer, Michael. Die Adjektive auf Isch in der Deutschen Gegenwartssprache. LC 78-355176. (Illus.). 208p. (Ger.). 1977. write for info. (ISBN 3-53302-656-6). Winter Univ.

GERMAN LANGUAGE–OLD HIGH GERMAN, 750-1050

Raven, F. A. Die Schwachen Verben des Althochdeutschen, Vol. 2. LC 64-23934. 224p. (Ger.). 1967. $24.60 (ISBN 0-8173-0801-6). U of Ala Pr.

GERMAN LANGUAGE–CONVERSATION AND PHRASE BOOKS

Gamrekeli, N., et al. Nemetsko-Gruzinsko-Russkii Frazeologicheskii Slovar. 566p. (Ger., Gr. & Rus.). 1973. $4.35 (Pub. by Ganatleba). Four Continent.

GERMAN LANGUAGE–DIALECTS

Ciani, Maria G. Lexikon zu Lycophron. LC 79-342190. 359p. (Gr.). 1975. write for info. (ISBN 3-487-05593-7). Olms Verlag.

Conrath, Karl. Die Volkssprache der Unteren Saar & der Obermosel: Ein Moselfrankisches Woerterbuch. LC 75-522113. xix, 308p. (Ger.). 1975. write for info. MG Schmitz.

Endres, Edmund. Moselfraenkische Mundart. LC 80-471656. 94p. (Ger.). 1979. write for info. (ISBN 3-79270-488-9). Rheinland Verlag.

Ilmberger, Josef. Die Bairische Fibel. LC 77-573555. 223p. (Ger., Munich). 1977. DM.28.00 (ISBN 3-405-11719-4). B. L. V.

Martin, Ernst & Lienhart, Hans. Woerterbuch der Elsaessischen Mundarten. (Ger.). 1974. DM.435.00 (ISBN 3-11-003338-0). De Gruyter.

Siebenbuergisch-Saechsisches Woerterbuch, 3 vols. Incl. Vol. 1 (a-c) 851p. 1924. 61.00x (ISBN 3-11-009500-9); Vol 2 (d-f) 548p. 1911-25. 35.50x (ISBN 3-11-009501-7); Vol 3 (g). 355p. 1971. 42.25x (ISBN 3-11-003707-6). (Ger.). De Gruyter.

GERMAN LANGUAGE–DICTIONARIES

Agricola, C. & Agricola, E. Woerter & Gegenwoerter. 4th ed. 280p. (Ger.). 1982. M.9.80. Bibl Inst Leipzig.

Agricola, E., et al, eds. Woerter & Wendungen. 818p. (Ger.). 1982. M.22.00. Bibl Inst Leipzig.

Ahlhaus, Otto E., et al. Tachenlexikon Umweltschultz. LC 80-470211. 288p. (Ger.). 1979. DM.10.00 (ISBN 3-590-14362-2). Pr Univ Fr.

Albertus, F. Tysk-Dansk: Dansk-Tysk Ordbog. 532p. (Danish & Ger.). 1982. $19.95 (ISBN 0-686-92489-4, M-1293). French & Eur.

Albrecht, Gunter E. & Reichardt, Hans D. Modellbahnlexikon. LC 75-519566. 232p. (Eng. & Ger.). 1975. DM.26.00 (ISBN 3-87094-406-4). Alba Buchverlag.

Alcala Zamora. Diccionario bilingue frances-espanol-aleman. Rev. ed. (Illus.). 960p. (Fr., Span. & Ger.). 100.00 ptas. 75.00 ptas ptas. Sopena.

Alheim, Karl-Heinz, ed. Duden Woerterbuch Medizinischer Fachausdruecke, 3 vols. LC 79-384676. 751p. (Ger.). 1979. write for info. (ISBN 3-41101-747-3). Thieme Verlag.

Altgriechisch, 2 Vols. Incl. Teil I. Altgriechisch-Deutsch. Menge, H. 528p. DM.16.80 (10030); Teil II. Deutsch-Altgriechisch. Guthling, O. 551p. DM.16.80 (10035). (Langenscheidts Taschenwoerterbucher Ser.). (Gr. & Ger.). DM.beide Teile in einem Band 23.80 (11030). Langenscheidt.

Althaus, H. P., et al, eds. Lexikon der Germanistischen. 2nd rev. ed. 870p. (Ger.). 1980. pap. $74.00. M Rosenberg.

Amery, et al. The First Thousand Words in German. (Illus.). 62p. (Ger.). (gr. 1-4). $7.95 (1095). Adler Bks.

Angerstein, Wilfried. Lexikon der Radiologischen Technik in der Mediazin. LC 80-471099. 576p. (Ger.). 1979. write for info. (ISBN 3-13-484603-9). Thieme Verlag.

Angerstein, Winifred. Lexikon der Radiologischen Technik in der Medizin. LC 75-595971. 480p. (Eng. & Ger.). 1975. DM.44.00 (ISBN 3-13-484602-0). Thieme Verlag.

Appel, Reinhold. Lexikon fur Tennisfreunde. Baumann, Ernst, ed. LC 78-363843. (Illus.). 256p. (Ger.). 1977. 29.80 F (ISBN 3-7658-0254-9). Bucher.

Arabisch, 2 vols. Incl. Teil I. Arabisch-Deutsch. Krotkoff, G. 624p. DM.18.80 (10060); Teil II. Deutsch-Arabisch. Schukry, K. & Humberdrotz, R. 456p. DM.18.80 (10065). (Langenscheidts Taschenwoerterbucher Ser.). (Arabic & Ger.). DM.beide Teile in einem Band 29.80 (11060). Langenscheidt.

Areisin, L. & Mueller-Hegemann, A., eds. Jugendlexikon Jugend zu Zweit. 3rd ed. (Illus.). 243p. (Ger.). 1982. M.9.80. Bibl Inst Leipzig.

Aresin, L. & Mueller-Hegemann, A., eds. Jugendlexikon Junge Ehe. (Illus.). 192p. (Ger.). 1982. M.9.80. Bibl InstLeipzig.

Arnold, Hans J. Stellwerksdienst. LC 76-472929. 119p. (Ger., Berlin, East Germany). 1976. M.4.80. Transpress Verlag fur Verkehrswesen.

Aschersleben, Karl. Handlexikon der Schulpaedogogik. LC 80-450953. 255p. (Ger.). 1979. write for info. (ISBN 3-170-05394-9). Kohlhammer.

Attiyate, Y. H. Lexique CN: Anglais-Allemand-Francais. (Illus.). 526p. (Eng., Ger. & Fr.). 1977. 65.00 F. Iron Age Metalworking Int.

Augst, Gerhard. Lexikon zur Wortbildung, 3 vols. LC 76-457738. 1306p. (Ger.). 1975. write for info. (ISBN 3-87808-624-5). Narr.

Austeda, Franz. Lexikon der Philosophie. LC 79-380526. ix, 340p. (Ger.). 1979. S.380.00 (ISBN 3-85119-156-0). Hollinek.

Bacmeister, Arnold. Das Grosse Lexikon der Fischwaid. (Ger.). 1969. $65.00 (ISBN 3-87372-001-9, M-7324, Pub. by Jfland). French & Eur.

Bauer, Karl W. & Hengst, Heinz. Kritische Stichwoerter zur Kinderkultur. 366p. (Ger.). 1978. write for info. (ISBN 3-770-51634-6). W Fink.

Becker, Udo. Herder-Lexikon. LC 75-514614. 239p. (Ger.). 1975. DM.19.80 (ISBN 3-451-16463-9). Herder.

Berger, K. Mykologisches Worterbuch. 432p. (Ger. & Eng. & Fr. & Span. & Lat. & Czech. & Pol. & Rus.). 1980. write for info. (M-9435). French & Eur.

Bertelsmann Lexikon, 10 vols. (Ger.). 1972-74. Set. $1225.00 (ISBN 0-686-56596-7, M-7306, Pub. by Bertelsmann). French & Eur.

Bertelsmann Lexikon, 10 vols. (Ger.). 1972-74. Set. DM.1225.00. C Bertelsmann.

Bertholet, Alfred. Woerterbuch der Religionen. LC 76-483576. x, 659p. (Ger.). 1976. DM.25.00 (ISBN 3-520-12503-X). Kroener.

Bezner, Heinrich. Electrical Machines Dictionary. LC 80-452859. 544p. (Eng. & Ger.). 1978. DM.80.00 (ISBN 3-87097-087-1). Brandstetter.

Bibliographisches Institut. Meyers Lexikon A-Z. LC 75-522777. 1060p. (Ger.). 1975. M.14.00. Bibl Inst Leipzig.

Biedermann, Hans. Handlexikon der magischen Kunste. LC 76-466579. (Illus.). 374p. (Ger.). 1976. DM.9.80 (ISBN 3-426-00421-6). Droemersche Knaur.

Bierfelder, Wilhelm, ed. Handwoerterbuch des Oeffentlichen Dienstes. LC 77-457292. (Illus.). (Ger.). DM.228.00 (ISBN 3-503-01424-1). Schmidt Verlag.

Bildwoerterbuch Deutsch-Englisch-Franzosisch. 941p. (Ger. , Eng. & Fr.). write for info. (ISBN 3-411-01830-5). Biblio Inst.

Bilginer, Sadettin. Deutsch-Turkisches Woerterbuch fur Technische Berufe. 2nd ed. 448p. (Ger. & Turkish.). 1966. DM.leatherette 55.00 (ISBN 3-7736-5270-4). Girardet.

Bischoff, Walter. Das Kleine Bergbaulexikon. LC 76-487997. 203p. (Ger.). 1976. DM.48.00 (ISBN 3-7739-0185-2). Verlag Glockauf.

--Das Kleine Bergbaulexikon. LC 79-395530. 254p. (Ger.). 1979. write for info. (ISBN 3-7739-0248-4). Verlag Gluckauf.

Blumenberg, Franz-Jurgen. Herder-Lexikon: Psychologie Sachwoerterbuch. LC 77-477664. (Illus.). 238p. (Ger.). 1975. DM.19.80 (ISBN 3-451-16467-1). Herder.

Bonin, Werner F. Lexikon der Parapsychologie & ihrer Grenzgebiete. LC 77-452317. vii, 587p. (Ger.). 1976. 48.00 F. Scherz AG.

Bonnefoi, Alexandre. Woerterbuch des Arbeits & Sozialrechts: Deutsch-Franz Dictionnaire de Droit du Trava il & de Droit Social. LC 76-469011. 395p. (Fr. & Ger.). 1975. DM.45.00 (ISBN 3-19-006293-5). Hueber.

Bork, E. & Kaper, E. Tysk-Dansk Ordbog. 550p. (Ger. & Danish.). 1981. $24.95 (ISBN 0-686-92483-5, M-1282). French & Eur.

Bork, Egon & Kaper, Egon. Dansk-Tysk Ordbog. LC 76-458154. 531p. (Danish & Ger.). 1975. Kr.55.00 (ISBN 8-70009-141-3). Gyldendal Norsk.

Boscher, Winfried, et al. Woerterbuch Vietnamesisch-Deutsch. LC 78-375203. 738p. (Ger. & Vietnamese.). 1978. M.48.00. VEB Verlag Enzyklopadie.

Brachmann-Teubner, Elisabeth. Lexikon Archivwesen der DDR. LC 76-478503. 319p. (Ger.). 1976. M.12.00. Staatsdruk.

Brauner, Rudolf. Von Bach zur Elektronik. LC 78-347055. 96p. (Ger.). 1977. S.60.00 (ISBN 3-853-85001-4). Prugg.

Brautigam, Kurt. So Werd bei uns Geredd. LC 80-491003. 168p. (Ger.). 1979. DM.16.80 (ISBN 3-87804-072-5). SVA Verlag.

Breitung, Eusebius. Deutsch-Japanisches Woerterbuch. LC 79-349548. 1277p. (Ger. & Japanese.). 1977. write for info. Buske.

Brockhaus Bildwoerterbuecher. (Ger.). write for info. F A Brockhaus.

Brockhaus Bildwoerterbuecher in vier Sprachen. (Eng. , Fr. , Ital. & Ger.). DM.48.00; $28.00. F A Brockhaus.

Der Brockhaus in Zwei Baenden. 1440p. (Ger.). DM.89.00 F (ISBN 3-7653-0037-3). F A Brockhaus.

Broeger, Achim. Meyers Grosses Kinderlexikon. (Illus.). 323p. (Ger.). DM.29.80 (ISBN 3-411-01797-X). Biblio Inst.

Bueschgen, Hans E., ed. Handwoerterbuch der Finanzwirtschaft. LC 77-460396. (Illus., Ger.). 1976. DM.220.00 (ISBN 3-791-08010-5). Poeschel.

Buksch, Herbert. Woerterbuch fuer Architektur, Hochbau & Baustoffe. LC 77-578817. (Ger. & Fr.). 1977. DM.29.00 (ISBN 3-762-50786-4). Bauverlag.

Butzmann, G., ed. Jugendlexikon UdSSR. (Illus.). 352p. (Ger.). 1981. M.14.80. Bibl Inst Leipzig.

Butzmann, G., et al, eds. Jugendlexikon A-Z. (Illus.). 752p. (Ger.). 1982. M.42.00. Bibl Inst Leipzig.

Claessens, Dieter. Jugendlexikon Gesellschaft: Einfache Antworten afu Schwierige Fragen. LC 76-469431. (Illus.). 184p. (Ger.). 1976. DM.5.80 (ISBN 3-499-16195-8). Rowohlt.

Clauss, Gunter. Woerterbuch der Psychologie. LC 77-458138. (Illus.). 596p. (Ger.). 1976. M.18.00. Biblio Inst.

Cortina. Cortina-Ace Basic German Dictionary. (Foreign Language Dictionary Ser.). 384p. 1982. pap. $2.95 (ISBN 0-441-05002-6). Ace Bks.

Daum, Edmund & Schenk, W. Deutsch-Russisches Woerterbuch. 15th ed. (Ger. & Rus.). 1976. $13.50 (ISBN 0-686-56602-5, M-7333, Pub. by Max Hueber). French & Eur.

Davary, Gholam D. Baktrisch: Ein Woerterbuch. 308p. (Ger.). 1982. DM.56.00 (ISBN 3-87276-270-2). Groos Verlag.

Debenjak, D. Modern Dictionary Slovene-German-Slovene. 608p. (Slovene & Ger.). 1981. leatherette $14.95 (ISBN 0-686-97402-6, M-9702). French & Eur.

Der Duden in 10 Baenden das Standardwerk zur Deutschen Sprache, 10 vols. Incl. Vol. 1. Die Rechtschreibung. 792p. 1983. DM.29.80 (ISBN 3-411-00901-2); Vol. 2. Das Stilwoerterbuch. Drosdowski, Guenther. 846p. 1983. DM.29.80 (ISBN 3-411-00902-0); Vol. 3. Das Bildwoerterbuch. 784p. 1983. DM.29.80 (ISBN 3-411-00913-6); Vol. 4. Die Grammtik. Grebe, Paul, et al. 763p. 1983. DM.29.80 (ISBN 3-411-00914-4); Vol. 5. Das Fremdwoerterbuch. Mueller, Wolfgang, et al. 816p. 1983. DM.29.80 (ISBN 3-411-20905-4); Vol. 6. Das Aussprachewoerterbuch. Mangold, Max. 791p. 1983. DM.29.80 (ISBN 3-411-00916-0); Vol. 7. Das Herkunftswoerterbuch. Drosdowski, Guenther & Grebe, Paul. 816p. 1983. DM.29.80 (ISBN 3-411-00907-1); Vol. 8. Die Sinn & Sachverwandten Woerter & Wendungen. Mueller, Wolfgang. 797p. 1983. DM.29.80 (ISBN 3-411-00918-7); Vol. 9. Die Zweifelsfaelle der Deutschen Sprache. Berger, Dieter, et al. 784p. 1983. DM.29.80 (ISBN 3-411-00919-5); Vol. 10. Das Bedeutungswoerterbuch. Mueller, Wolfgang, et al. 815p. 1983. DM.29.80 (ISBN 3-411-00910-1). (Ger.). Bibliographisches Institut.

De Renty, Ivan. Lexique Quadrilingue des Affaires: Anglais-Francais-Allemand-Espagnol. 702p. (Eng., Fr., Ger. & Span.). 1977. 72.00 F. Hachette.

Deutsch-Ungarisches Woerterbuch. 376p. (Ger. & Hungarian.). 1955. 2.50 Ft. Akademiai Kiado.

Deutsches Woerterbuch. (Ger.). 1977. $7.50 (ISBN 3-411-01702-3, M-7338, Bibliogr. Institut). French & Eur.

Deutsches Woerterbuch, 3 vols. (Ger.). 1977. DM.7.50 (ISBN 3-411-01702-3). Biblio Inst.

Deutsches Woerterbuch in 3 Banden: Band I, Deutsches Woerterbuch, A-F. (Ger.). write for info. (ISBN 3-411-01831-3). Biblio Inst.

Deutsches Woerterbuch in 3 Banden: Band 2, Deutsches Woerterbuch. (Ger.). write for info. (ISBN 3-411-01832-1). Biblio Inst.

Deutsches Woerterbuch in 3 Banden: Band 3, Deutsches Woerterbuch, O-Z. (Ger.). write for info. (ISBN 3-411-01833-X). Biblio Inst.

De Vries, Louis. German-English Science Dictionary. 4th ed. LC 78-6465. xxxviii, 628p. (Eng. & Ger.). 1978. $14.50 (ISBN 0-07-016602-1). McGraw.

Dictionar Frazeologic German-Roman. LC 75-540143. 538p. (Ger. & Romanian.). 1975. 18.00 lei. Editura Stiintifica.

Dictionnaire Duden-Larousse: Tout Allemand. (Fr. & Ger.). 38.50 F. Larousse.

Dissing, Borge & Lave, Rud. Dansk-Tysk Ordbog. LC 79-383402. (Illus.). 347p. (Ger. & Danish.). 1978. write for info. Gyldendal Norsk.

Dominninghaus, Hans. Lexikon der Kunststoffe, 2 vols. LC 78-364503. 576p. (Ger.). 1978. write for info. (ISBN 3-453-49070-3). Heyne W Verlag.

Dorsch, Friedrich. Psychologisches Woerterbuch. LC 76-472620. (Illus.). 774p. (Ger.). 1976. write for info. (ISBN 3-456-80320-6). H Huber.

Dreschler, Hanno, et al. Gesellschaft & Staat: Lexikon der Politik. LC 79-388088. (Illus.). xx, 604p. (Ger.). 1979. DM.38.00 (ISBN 3-797-10078-7). Signal-Verlag.

Drosdowski, Gunther. Fremdwoerterbuch: Herkunft & Bedeutung der Fremdwoerter. 466p. (Ger.). DM.19.80 (ISBN 3-411-01121-1). Biblio Inst.

DTV Junior Lexikon, 10 vols. (Ger.). 1974. Set. DM.pap. 62.50 (ISBN 3-423-05951-6). Deutscher Taschenbuch Verlag.

Duden. Was Bedeuted Das? 444p. (Ger.). write for info (ISBN 91-24-20301-7). Esselte Studium.

Duden-Das Grosse Woerterbuch der Deutschen Sprache in 6 Baenden, 6 vols. 3000p. (Ger.). DM.64.00 ea. (ISBN 3-411-01354-0). Biblio Inst.

Der Duden in 10 Banden Das Standardwerk zur Deutschen Sprache: Duden Band I, Die Rechtschreibung der Deutschen Sprache & der Fremdwoerter. 792p. (Ger.). DM.29.80 (ISBN 3-411-00901-2). Biblio Inst.

Duden, Konrad. Sammlung Duden: Band I, Vollstaendiges Orthographisches Woerterbuch der Deutschen Sprache. 202p. (Ger.). DM.6.80 (ISBN 3-411-01041-X). Biblio Inst.

Duden, R. Duden-Stilwoerterbuch. 5th rev. ed. (Der Grosse Duden: Vol. 2). (Ger.). $15.95 (ISBN 3-411-00902-0). Adler.

Dudenredaktion Manheim. Der Kleine Duden, Fremdenwoerterbuch. LC 78-340908. 448p. (Ger.). 1977. write for info. Biblio Inst.

Eckardt, Andre. Chinesisch-Koreanisch-Deutsch Woerterbuch. 224p. (Chinese, Ger. & Korean.). 1966. write for info. (ISBN 3-87276-115-3). Groos Verlag.

--Deutsch-Koreanisches Woerterbuch. 2nd ed. 332p. (Korean & Ger.). 1976. DM.58.00 (ISBN 3-87276-149-8). Groos Verlag.

--Koreanisch-Deutsches Woerterbuch. 2nd ed. 332p. (Korean & Ger.). 1976. DM.69.99 (ISBN 3-87276-149-8). Groos Verlag.

Eckert, Werner. Einfuehrung in die Deutsche Wortbildungslehre. LC 75-51569. (Illus.). 160p. (Ger.). 1975. DM.14.80 (ISBN 3-50301-210-9). Schmidt Verlag.

Editions Berlitz. German-English, English-German Dictionary: Woerterbuch Deutsch-Englisch, Englisch-Deutsch. Rev ed. LC 78-78082. 359p. (Ger. & Eng.). 1979. E0.95 (ISBN 0-02-964530-1, Pub. by Berlitz). Macmillan.

Emde, Heiner. Das Lexikon der Politik. LC 76-461039. 170p. (Ger.). 1975. DM.4.80 (ISBN 3-453-41123-4). Heyne W Verlag.

Engert, M. & Stephan, H., eds. Lexikon RGW. 282p. (Ger.). 1981. M.18.00. Bibl Inst Leipzig.

Esche, Annemarie. Woerterbuch Burmesisch-Deutsch. LC 76-476865. 546p. (Ger. & Burmese.). 1976. M.65.00. VEB Verlag Enzyklopadie.

Falk, Bernard & Wolf, Jakob. Handlexikon fuer Handel & Absatz. LC 80-469758. (Illus.). 750p. (Ger.). 1979. DM.48.00 (ISBN 3-478-24150-2). Verlag Moderne Industrie.

Das Farbige Duden Schuelerlexikon. 768p. (Ger.). $24.50 (1094). Adler Bks.

Fetz, Friedrich, ed. Lexikon des Alpinen Schifahrens. LC 77-457896. 156p. (Ger.). 1975. S.150.00 (ISBN 3-85123-028-0). Inn Verlag.

Finke, K. & Goock, R. Das Moderne Kinder-Lexikon in Farbe.Unsere Welt in Wort Und Bild: Unsere Welt in Wort & Bild. (Illus.). 320p. (Ger.). $20.30 (1099). Adler Bks.

Five Thousand German Words. (Ger.). write for info. (ISBN 0-671-41965-X). S&S.

Fleischer, W. Wortbildung der Deutschen Gegenwartssprache. 4th ed. 363p. (Ger.). 1976. M.26.00. Bibl Inst Leipzig.

Franz, Georg I. Fachworter der Elektronik. LC 76-488356. 86p. (Ger.). 1976. DM.4.80 (ISBN 3-7723-0402-8). Franzis Verlag.

Frey, Hans. Das Grosse Lexikon der Aquaristik. LC 77-551968. 859p. (Ger.). 1976. write for info. (ISBN 3-7888-0243-X). Neumann-Neudamm.

Frohlich, Gerd, et al. Phytopathologie & Pflanzenschutz. LC 79-377360. 295p. (Eng. & Ger.). 1979. DM.19.80 (ISBN 3-437-20207-3). Fischer Verlag.

Frommhold, Hanns. Bauworterbuch. LC 79-358361. viii, 299p. (Ger.). 1978. DM.75.00 (ISBN 3-8041-1529-2). Werner Verlag.

Froundiian-Dirair. Armenisch-Deutsches Woerterbuch. (Armenian & Ger.). 1952. $45.00 (ISBN 3-486-41021-0, Pub. by Oldenbourg). French & Eur.

--Armenisch-Deutsches Woerterbuch. (Armenian & Ger.). 1952. DM.45.00 (ISBN 3-486-41021-0). Oldenbourg Verlag.

Fryd, E. Tysk-Dansk Dansk-Tysk Special Ordbog. 175p. (Ger. & Danish.). 1974. $35.00 (ISBN 0-686-92491-6, M-1274). French & Eur.

Fryd, Ejnar. Tysk-Dansk, Dansk-Tysk Specialordbog. LC 75-582435. 175p. (Ger. & Danish.). 1975. Kr.115.00. For Stat Rev.

Gatzlaff-Halsig, Margot. Woerterbuch Deutsch-Hindi. LC 78-359321. 646p. (Ger. & Hindi.). 1977. M.60.00. VEB Verlag Enzyklopadie.

Gaugler, Eduard, ed. Handwoerterbuch des Personalwesens. LC 76-483335. (Illus., Ger.). 1975. DM.220.00 (ISBN 3-791-08009-1). Poeschel Verlag.

Geowissenschaften. LC 77-466982. (Fr. & Ger.). 1975. write for info. Schweizerbart.

Gerescher, Konrad. Politik Aufgespiesst: Heiteres Lexikon der Politischen Missbildung. LC 77-481880. 58p. (Ger.). 1976. write for info. (ISBN 3-87998-010-1). Gauke.

German Dictionary. 320p. (Ger.). Epap. 1.25 (ISBN 0-600-36564-6). Newnes Bks.

Goeschel, H. & Zwahr, A., eds. Meyers Universal Lexikon, Vol. 1. 3rd ed. 720p. (Ger.). 1980. M.35.00. Bibl Inst Leipzig.

--Meyers Universal Lexikon, Vol. 2. 3rd ed. 744p. (Ger.). 1981. M.35.00. Bibl Inst Leipzig.

--Meyers Universal Lexikon, Vol. 3. 3rd ed. 704p. (Ger.). 1981. M.35.00. Bibl Inst Leipzig.

--Meyers Universal Lexikon, Vol. 4. 3rd ed. (Ger.). M.35.00. Bibl Inst Leipzig.

Goetze, Alfred & Mitzka, Walther, eds. Truebners Deutsches Woerterbuch, 8 vols. (Ger.). 1947-57. Set. $240.00x (ISBN 3-11-000319-8). De Gruyter.

Goldhahn, Irmgard. Kleines Medizinisches Fremdworterbuch. LC 76-477700. 122p. (Ger.). 1976. M.9.50. Thieme Verlag.

Goock, Roland. Neues Taschenlexikon. LC 75-519004. 192p. (Ger.). 1975. write for info. (ISBN 3-87644-045-9). Prae Heinz.

Gorys, Erhard. Heimerans Kuchenlexikon. LC 76-453925. 558p. (Ger.). 1975. write for info. (ISBN 3-8063-1093-9). Kochbuch Verlag.

Gotze, Alfred. Trubners Deutsches Woerterbuch, 8 vols. 4851p. (Ger.). 1939. Set. $283.00 (ISBN 3-11-000319-8, M-7671, Pub. by de Gruyter). French & Eur.

Grabbe, Hans J. Bauherren-Lexikon. LC 76-488016. 251p. (Eng. & Ger.). 1976. DM.29.50 (ISBN 3-528-08657-2). Vieweg.

Grabmueller, Klaus, pref. by. Vocabulaius Teutonico-Latinus. LC 77-46995. xxxiv, 622p. (Lat.). 1976. write for info. (ISBN 3-487-05883-9). Olms Verlag.

Grebe, Paul. Bedeutungswoerterbuch: Bedeutung & Gebrauch der Woerter. 447p. (Ger.). DM.19.80 (ISBN 3-411-01125-4). Biblio Inst.

--Sammlung Duden: Band III, Akten zur Geschichte der Deutschen Einheitsschreibung. 48p. (Ger.). DM.6.80 (ISBN 3-411-01043-6). Biblio Inst.

Grimm, J. & Grimm, W. Deutsches Woerterbuch. (Ger.). 1965. DM.18.00 (7983059). Herzel Verlag.

Gross. Woerterbuch, 2 vols. (Ger.). DM.98.00 ea. Verlag Harri Deutsch.

--Woerterbuch Chemie & Chemische Technik, 2 vols. Incl. Vol. 1. 700p. (Eng. & Ger.). 1976 (ISBN 3-87144-141-4); Vol. 2. 700p. (Ger. & Eng.). 1980 (ISBN 3-87144-142-2). (Ger. & Eng.). DM.98.00 ea. Verlag Harri Deutsch.

Der Grosse Brockhaus, 12 vols. 18th ed. (Ger.). 1977. Set. $995.00 (ISBN 3-7653-0039-X, M-7326, Pub. by Brockhaus). French & Eur.

Der Grosse Brockhaus. 400p. (Ger.). write for info. (ISBN 3-7653-0329-1). F A Brockhaus.

Der Grosse Brockhaus: Band 14, Ergaenzungen A-Z. (Ger.). 1982. write for info. (ISBN 3-7653-0331-3). F A Brockhaus.

Der Grosse Brockhaus: Band 15. (Ger.). DM.128.00 (ISBN 3-7653-0332-1). F A Brockhaus.

Der Grosse Brockhaus: Band 15-20. (Ger.). 1983. write for info. (ISBN 3-7653-0330-5). F A Brockhaus.

Der Grosse Duden. 23rd ed. 768p. (Ger.). 1982. M.16.80. Bibl Inst Leipzig.

Grosse, Walter G., et al, eds. Versicherungsenzykolpaedie. LC 77-574020. 3109p. (Ger.). 1976. DM.165.00 (ISBN 3-409-85531-9). Gabler.

Das Grosse Woerterbuch der Deutschen Sprache, 6 vols. 3000p. (Ger.). 1983. $32.00. M Rosenberg.

Grosses Fremdwoerterbuch. 4th ed. 832p. (Ger.). 1982. M.24.00. Bibl Inst Leipzig.

Grossman, Paul & Lang, Viktor, eds. Kleines Lexikon zur Politischen Bildung. LC 75-516868. 181p. (Ger.). 1975. DM.5.80 (ISBN 3-87364-033-3). Hornung-Verlag.

Gubba, W. Jurdisk Ordbog. LC 79-366377. 72p. (Ger. & Danish.). 1978. write for info. Guba.

Haas, Peter. Management-Taschenlexikon. LC 80-477370. (Illus.). 189p. (Ger.). 1978. DM.9.80. Verlag Moderne Industrie.

Haberle, Gregor D. & Haberle, Heinz O. Kurzlexikon der Elektrotechnik. LC 79-387542. 104p. (Ger.). 1979. DM.15.00 (ISBN 3-87234-054-9). Frankfurt Fachverlag.

Haferkorn, R. Technisches Woerterbuch Deutsch-Esperanto. (Ger. & Esperanto.). 1967. Can.$1.80 (ISBN 0-919186-01-7). U of Toronto Pr.

Halasz, ed. Langenscheidts Handwoerterbuecher: Tl 2, Deutsch-Ungarisch. 1978 ed. (Ger. & Hungarian.). DM.38.00 (ISBN 3-468-04385-6). Langenscheidt.

Handwoerterbuch der Volkwirtschaft. LC 80-460492. (Ger.). 1978. write for info. Gabler.

Harrap & Dudenredaktion. Duden-Was Bedeutet Das? Kleines Bedeutungswoerterbuch der Deutschen Sprache. (Illus.). 444p. (Ger.). E3.00 (ISBN 0-245-50332-3). Harrap.

Hartfiel, Guenter. Woerterbuch der Soziologie. LC 77-458366. vi, 715p. (Ger.). 1976. DM.22.00 (ISBN 3-520-41002-8). Kroener.

Hasselfeldt, Othmar. Internationes Kaselexikon. LC 77-575279. 141p. (Ger.). 1977. DM.5.80 (ISBN 3-436-02465-1). Fischer Taschen.

Heinisch, Kurt F. Kautschuk-Lexikon. 2nd ed. LC 79-361675. (Illus.). 572p. (Ger.). 1978. DM.75.00. Gentner.

Helbig, G. & Schenkel, W. Woerterbuch zur Valenz & Distribution Deutscher Verben. 6th ed. 458p. (Ger.). 1982. M.22.00. Bibl Inst Leipzig.

Hembus, Joe. Western Lexikon. LC 79-396669. 816p. (Ger.). 1978. DM.12.80 (ISBN 3-453-00767-0). Heyne W Verlag.

Henschel, E. & Pretzel, U., eds. Lexers Mittlehochdeutsches Taschenwoerterbuch: Mit Bearbeiteten & Erweiterten Nachtraegen. 36th ed. 504p. (Ger.). 1980. M.24.00 (796 739 0). Hirzel Verlag.

Hentschel, Erwin. Tiernamen & Zoologische Fachworter. LC 77-451749. 528p. (Eng. & Ger.). 1976. DM.19.80 (ISBN 3-437-20130-1). Fischer Verlag.
Herbst, Robert & Readett, Alan G., eds. Herbst Dictionay of Commercial, Financial & Legal Terms. (Two-Language Ser.: Vol. A). 688p. (Eng. & Ger.). 1975. text ed. $69.95 (ISBN 0-686-97268-6). Birkhauser.
Herschelmann, Ferdinand. Meyers Grosses Jahreslexikon: Berichtszeitraum. 328p. (Ger.). 1979. write for info. (ISBN 3-411-01946-8). Biblio Inst.
Herstig, David. Hebraeisch-Deutches Woerterbuch. (Hebrew & Ger.). 1971. $17.50 (ISBN 3-19-006289-7). Hueber.
--Hebraeisch-Deutsches Woerterbuch. (Hebrew & Ger.). 1971. $17.50 (ISBN 3-19-006289-7, M-7441, Pub. by Max Hueber). French & Eur.
Heupel, Carl. Linguistisches Woerterbuch. LC 79-363518. (Illus.). 161p. (Ger.). 1978. DM.12.80 (ISBN 3-423-03040-2). Deutscher Taschenbuch.
Heyne, Moritz. Deutsche Woerterbuch, 3 vols. 2nd ed. (Ger.). 1970. Set. DM.195.00 (ISBN 3-7776-0053-9). Hirzel Verlag.
--Deutsches Woerterbuch, 3 vols. 2nd ed. (Ger.). 1970. Set. $195.00 (ISBN 3-7776-0053-9, M-7334, Pub. by Hirzel). French & Eur.
Hirschelmann, Ferdinand. Meyers Grosses Jahreslexikon. 328p. (Ger.). 1982. write for info. (ISBN 3-411-01964-6). Biblio Inst.
Hoffe, Otfried. Lexikon der Ethik. LC 77-566300. 287p. (Ger.). 1977. DM.14.80 (ISBN 3-406-06752-2). Beck Verlag.
Hoftmann, Hildegard, et al. Woerterbuch Swahili-Deutsch. LC 79-384471. 402p. (Ger. & Swahili.). 1979. DM.42.00. VEB Verlag Enzyklopadie.
Hurlimann, Ernst. Lexikon fur den Bauherrn. LC 76-459881. 224p. (Ger.). 1975. write for info. (ISBN 3-478-04250-X). Verlag Moderne.
Immelmann, Klaus. Woerterbuch der Verhaltensforschung. LC 78-342717. 133p. (Eng. & Ger.). 1975. DM.12.00 (ISBN 3-463-00616-2). Kindler.
Institut fur Grafische Technik. Lexikon der Grafischen Technik. LC 78-341716. 656p. (Ger.). 1977. write for info. (ISBN 3-7940-4078-3). Saur Verlag.
Isaacs, Alan, ed. Multilingual Commercial Dictionary. 496p. 1980. $22.50 (ISBN 0-87196-425-2). Facts on File.
Jacob, U. & Petersein, G. T. BI-Taschenlexikon Heimtiere. (Illus.). 352p. (Ger.). 1982. M.15.00. Bibl Inst Leipzig.
Jahn, Johannes. Woerterbuch der Kunst. 8th ed. LC 76-463394. (Illus.). viii, 806p. (Ger.). 1975. write for info. (ISBN 3-520-16508-2). Kroener.
--Woerterbuch der Kunst. 9th ed. LC 80-473856. (Illus.). viii, 834p. (Ger.). 1979. write for info. (ISBN 3-520-16509-0). Kroener.
Jakob, Ludwig. Lexikon der Onologie. LC 79-386617. 415p. (Eng. & Ger.). 1979. write for info. Meininger.
Jakubke, Hans D. & Jeschkeit, Hans. Lexikon biochemie. LC 77-460833. 605p. (Ger.). 1976. write for info. (ISBN 3-527-25662-8). Verlag Chemie.
Johnson, Victor. An Advanced Modern German Vocabulary. 63p. (Ger.). 1980. Epap. 1.65. Harrap Co.
Jong, F. J. Economisch Woorden Boek: Engels-Frans-Duits-Nederlands. 685p. (Eng., Fr., Ger. & Dutch.). 1980. $75.00 (ISBN 90-247-2243-8, M9474). French & Eur.
Junge, Hans D. Brockhaus ABC Elektronik. LC 79-391270. 751p. (Ger.). 1978. M.18.60. R Brockhaus.
--Brockhaus ABC Elektrotechnik. LC 78-399295. 667p. (Ger.). 1978. M.17.30. F A Brockhaus.
Jungmair, Otto, ed. Woerterbuch zur Oberoesterreichischen Volksmundart. LC 80-487672. 351p. (Ger.). 1978. S.280.00. Selbstverlag Inst.
Kabesch, Friedrich. Langenscheidts Taschenwoerterbuch Tschechisch: Teil II, Deutsch-Tschechisch. 478p. (Ger. & Czech.). DM.19.80 (10365). Langenscheidt.
--Langenscheidts Taschenwoerterbuecher Deutsch-Tschechisch. 500p. (Ger. & Czech.). 1977. DM.14.80 (ISBN 3-468-10365-4). Langenscheidt.
Kadar, I. & Ratz, O. Langenscheidts Handwoerterbuch Ungarisch HALASZ: Teil II, Deutsch-Ungarisch. 775p. (Ger. & Hungarian.). DM.44.00 (04385). Langenscheidt.
Kahlo, Gerhard, et al. Woerterbuch Deutsch-Indonesisch. LC 77-463622. xxiv, 400p. (Ger. & Indonesian.). 1975. M.38.00. VEB Verlag Enzyklopadie.
Kaluza, Bjorn, ed. Herder Lexikon Paedogogik. LC 76-481667. (Illus.). 209p. (Ger.). 1976. write for info. (ISBN 3-451-16466-3). Herder.
Keller, Howard H. German Root Lexicon. LC 72-85112. (Miami Linguistics Ser: No. 11). 128p. (Ger.). 1973. $12.95x (ISBN 0-87024-244-X). U of Miami Pr.
Keupper, H. Woerterbuch der Deutschen Umgangsprache: Vol. 4, Berufsschelten & Verwandtes. (Ger.). 1983. $19.00. M Rosenberg.
Killer, W. K. Illustrated Technical German for Builders. 4th ed. 183p. (Eng. & Ger.). 1977. $15.95 (ISBN 3-7625-0898-4). Bauverlag.
Kinder Duden: Mein Erster Duden. (Illus.). 160p. (Ger.). $6.40 (1096). Adler Bks.
Kirchner, Joachim, ed. Lexicon des Buchwesen: Bd 4, Bilderatlas zum Buchwesen Teil 2. xlvii, 343p. (Ger.). 1956. DM.90.00 (ISBN 3-7772-5613-7). Hiersemann.
--Lexikon des Buchwesens. 1688p. (Ger.). 1956. DM.360.00 (ISBN 3-7772-5214-X). Hiersemann.
--Lexikon des Buchwesens: Bd 1, Text A-K. viii, 405p. (Ger.). 1952. DM.90.00 (ISBN 3-7772-5215-8). Hiersemann.
--Lexikon des Buchwesens: Bd 2, Text L-Z. vii, 519p. (Ger.). 1953. DM.90.00 (ISBN 3-7772-5311-1). Hiersemann.
--Lexikon des Buchwesens: Bd 3, Bilderatlas zum Buchwesen Teil 1. xxxix, 320p. (Ger.). 1955. DM.90.00 (ISBN 3-7772-5504-1). Hiersemann.
Klatt, Edmund, et al, eds. Langenscheidt's Taschenworterbuch. 6th ed. 1264p. (Ger.). 1970. $10.95 (ISBN 3-468-11121-5). Am Map.
Kleemann, Axel. Pharmazeutische. LC 80-453717. xv, 555p. (Ger.). 1978. DM.200.00 (ISBN 3-13-558401-1). Thieme Verlag.
Klein, Heijo. DuMont's Kleines Sachworterbuch der Druektechnik & Grafischen Kunst. LC 75-505939. 193p. (Eng. & Ger.). 1975. write for info. (ISBN 3-7701-0760-8). DuMont Buch.
--DuMont's Kleines Sachworterbuch der Drucktechnik & Grafischen Kunst. LC 77-564784. 205p. (Eng. & Ger.). 1977. write for info. (ISBN 3-7701-0760-8). DuMont Buchverlag.
Klein, M. Herder - Lexikon Gemeinschaftskunde. (Ger.). pap. $15.95 (ISBN 3-451-16465-5, M-7455, Pub. by Herder). French & Eur.
--Herder-Lexikon Gemeinschaftskunde. (Ger.). pap. $15.95 (ISBN 3-451-16465-5). Herder.
Der Kleine Duden: Deutsches Woerterbuch. 445p. (Ger.). DM.10.80 (ISBN 3-411-01961-1). Bibl io Inst.
Der Kleine Duden: Fremdwoerterbuch. 448p. (Ger.). DM.10.80 (ISBN 3-411-01703-1). Biblio Inst.
Der Kleine Wahrig: Woerterbuch der deutschen Sprache. 943p. (Ger.). 1982. $14.90. M Rosenberg.
Klimke, Reiner & Savelsberg, Jorg. Lexikon fur Pferdefreunde. LC 76-468179. 255p. (Ger.). 1976. 29.80 F (ISBN 3-7658-0221-2). Bucher.
Knaura Lexikon, A-Z. (Ger.). $17.50 (ISBN 0-686-56627-0, M-7518, Pub. by Druckenmuellar). French & Eur.
Knaurs Lexicon A-Z. (Illus.). 1056p. (Ger.). $17.00. M Rosenberg.
Knaurs Lexicon der sinnverwandten Woerter. 560p. (Ger.). 1983. $12.40. M Rosenberg.
Knaurs Lexikon A-Z. (Illus.). 1056p. (Ger.). 1983. pap. $17.00. M Rosenberg.
Knerr, Richard. Lexikon der Mathematik. LC 79-368679. 484p. (Ger.). 1978. DM.12.80 (ISBN 3-596-26376-X). Fischer Taschen.
Knoll, Ludwig. Lexikon der praktischen Psychologie. LC 79-398496. 488p. (Ger.). 1979. DM.36.00 (ISBN 3-7857-0231-0). Luebbe.
Koblischke, H. Grosses Abkuerzungsbuch. 2nd ed. 508p. (Ger.). 1980. M.24.00. Bibl Inst Leipzig.
--Kleines Abkuerzungsbuch. 3rd ed. 144p. (Ger.). 1981. M.9.80. Bibl Inst Leipzig.
Koch, Willi A. Musisches Lexikon. LC 77-457599. (Illus., Ger.). 1976. DM.48.00 (ISBN 3-520-80303-8). Kroener.
Koester, Rudolf. Ullstein Lexikon der Deutschen Sprache. (Ger.). 1969. $20.00 (ISBN 3-550-06016-5, M-7672, Pub. by Ullstein Verlag/VVA). French & Eur.
Kollnig, Karl Rudolf. Politisch-Soziologisches Woerterbuch. LC 75-516317. 254p. (Ger.). 1975. DM.9.80. Kamp Verlag.
Kondakov, Nikolai I., et al. Woerterbuch der Logik. LC 79-380114. 554p. (Ger.). 1978. M.22.00. Bibl Inst Leipzig.
Kossel, Hans. Herder Lexikon. LC 80-471281. 271p. (Ger.). 1978. write for info. (ISBN 3-451-17378-6). Herder.
Kremnitz, Walter A. Lexikon der Mythologie Aegyptens, Persiens & des Orients. LC 76-460759. (Illus.). 140p. (Ger.). 1975. write for info. Ambro Lacus.
Krichbaum, Jorg. Dumonts Kleines Lexikon der Phantastischen Malerei. LC 77-579484. (Illus.). 329p. (Ger.). 1977. write for info. (ISBN 3-770-10908-2). DuMont Buchverlag.
Krist, Thomas. Taschen-Lexikon Internationale Abkurzungen & Kurzzeichen. LC 80-474810. 144p. (Eng. & Ger.). 1979. DM.9.80 (ISBN 3-87807-110-8). Technik Tabel.
Krolkoff, Georg. Langenscheidts Taschenwoerterbuecher Arabisch-Deutsch. (Arabic & Ger.). 1975. DM.14.80 (ISBN 3-468-10060-4). Langenscheidt.
Kruger, Sabine. Zum Fachwortschatz. LC 80-467779. vii, 523p. (Ger.). 1979. DM.90.00 (ISBN 3-18-150037-2). VDI Verlag.
Krywalski, Diether. Knaurs Lexikon der Weltliteratur. LC 80-462297. 942p. (Ger.). 1979. DM.39.80 (ISBN 3-426-26011-5). Droemersche Knaur.
Kuepper, H. Woerterbuch der Deutschen Umgangssprache: Vol. 5, 10000 neue Ausdruecke Sachschelten. (Ger.). 1983. $19.00. M Rosenberg.
--Woerterbuch der Deutschen Umgangssprache: Vol. 6, Jugenddeutsch A-Z. (Ger.). 1983. $21.00. M Rosenberg.
Kuhn, Peter. Deutsche Woerterbucher. LC 79-369972. viii, 266p. (Ger.). 1978. write for info. (ISBN 3-484-10323-X). Niemeyer.
Kurth, Hanns. Lexikon der Modernen Konservation. (Ger.). 1973. $16.95 (ISBN 3-87718-502-9, M-7247). French & Eur.
Langenscheidt Comprehensive German Dictionary. 1104p. (Ger.). $42.50 (ISBN 0-340-14967-1). Langenscheidt.
Langenscheidt Condensed Muret-Sanders German Dictionary. 1293p. (Ger.). $70.00 (ISBN 3-468-02125-9). Langenscheidt.
Langenscheidts Grosswoerterbuch Altgriechisch: Tl 1, Altgriechisch-Deutsch. (Gr. & Ger.). 1978. DM.58.00 (ISBN 3-468-02030-9). Langenscheidt.
Langenscheidts Grosswoerterbuch Lateinisch: Tl 1, Lateinisch-Deutsch. (Lat. & Ger.). 1978. DM.58.00 (ISBN 3-468-02200-X). Langenscheidt.
Langenscheidts Grosswoerterbuch Lateinisch: Tl 2, Deutsch-Lateinisch. (Ger. & Lat.). 1978. DM.58.00 (ISBN 3-468-02205-0). Langenscheidt.
Langenscheidts Lilliput-Woerterbuch Deutsch-Lateinisch. 640p. (Ger. & Lat.). DM.3.00 (20013). Langenscheidt.
Langenscheidts Lilliput-Woerterbuch Lateinisch-Deutsch. 640p. (Lat. & Ger.). DM.3.00 (20014). Langenscheidt.
Langenscheidts Lilliput-Woerterbuecher Altgriechisch-Deutsch. (Gr. & Ger.). 1978. DM.2.20 (ISBN 3-468-20032-3). Langenscheidt.
Langenscheidts Lilliput-Woerterbuecher Deutsch-Lateinisch. (Ger. & Lat.). 1978. DM.2.20 (ISBN 3-468-20013-7). Langenscheidt.
Langenscheidts Lilliput-Woerterbuecher Lateinisch-Deutsch. (Lat. & Ger.). 1978. DM.2.20 (ISBN 3-468-20014-5). Langenscheidt.
Langenscheidts Schulwoerterbuecher Lateinisch-Deutsch. (Lat. & Ger.). 1978. DM.10.80 (ISBN 3-468-13200-X). Langenscheidt.
Langenscheidts Taschenwoerterbuecher Deutsch-Lateinisch. (Ger. & Lat.). 1978. DM.13.80 (ISBN 3-468-10205-4). Langenscheidt.
Langenscheidts Universal-Woerterbuch Bulgarisch. 560p. (Bulgarian & Ger.). DM.6.80 (18080). Langenscheidt.
Langenscheidts Universal-Woerterbuecher Bulgarisch-Deutsch. (Bulgarian & Ger.). 1978. DM.5.80 (ISBN 3-468-18080-2). Langenscheidt.
Langenscheidts Universal-Woerterbuecher Islaendisch-Deutsch. (Icelandic & Ger.). 1978. DM.5.80 (ISBN 3-468-18170-1). Langenscheidt.
Langenscheidts Universal-Woerterbuecher Lateinisch-Deutsch. (Lat. & Ger.). 1978. DM.5.80 (ISBN 3-468-18200-7). Langenscheidt.
Langenscheidts Universal-Woerterbuecher Neugriechisch-Deutsch. (Gr. & Ger.). 1978. DM.5.80 (ISBN 3-468-18200-7). Langenscheidt.
Langenscheidts Universal-Woerterbuecher Rumaenisch-Deutsch. (Romanian & Ger.). 1978. DM.5.80 (ISBN 3-468-18280-5). Langenscheidt.
Langenscheidts Universal-Woerterbuecher Serbokroatisch-Deutsch. (Serbo-Croatian & Ger.). 1978. DM.5.80 (ISBN 3-468-18311-9). Langenscheidt.
Langenscheidts Universal-Woerterbuecher Slowakisch-Deutsch. (Slavic & Ger.). 1978. DM.5.80 (ISBN 3-468-18320-8). Langenscheidt.
Langenscheidts Universal-Woerterbuecher Tschechisch-Deutsch. (Czech. & Ger.). 1978. DM.5.80 (ISBN 3-468-18360-7). Langenscheidt.
Langenscheidts Universal-Woerterbuecher Tuerkisch-Deutsch. (Turkish & Ger.). 1978. DM.5.80 (ISBN 3-468-18371-2). Langenscheidt.
Langenscheidts Universal-Woerterbuecher Ungarisch-Deutsch. (Hungarian & Ger.). 1978. DM.5.80 (ISBN 3-468-18381-X). Langenscheidt.
Lateinisch-Deutsch, Deutsch-Lateinisch. (Langenscheidts Schulwoerterbuecher Ser.). 512p. (Ger. & Lat.). DM.12.80 (13200). Langenscheidt.
Lehmann, Ulrich. Palaontologisches Woerterbuch. LC 77-560773. viii, 439p. (Ger.). 1977. DM.18.80 (ISBN 3-432-83572-8). Enke.

Leping, A. A., ed. Russko-Nemetskii Slovar. 568p. (Rus.). 1957. $1.70 (Pub. by GINS). Four Continent.

Leping, E. I., ed. Russko-Nemetskii Slovar. 848p. (Rus. & Ger.). 1978. $15.95 (Pub. by Russkii Iazyk). Four Continent.

Lerche, Mario R. Deutsch-Spanisches Glossarium Finanzieller & Wirtschaftlicher Fachausdrueck. LC 77-574052. 460p. (Ger. & Span.). 1970. DM.22.00 (ISBN 3-7819-2012-7). Knapp Verlag.

Lexikon 2000, Vol. 1. (Ger.). 1970. $86.00 (ISBN 3-8075-1001-X, M-7189, Pub. by Wissen). French & Eur.

Lexikon 2000, Vol. 2. (Ger.). 1970. $86.00 (ISBN 3-8075-1002-8, M-7188, Pub. by Wissen). French & Eur.

Lexikon 2000, Vol. 3. (Ger.). 1971. $86.00 (ISBN 3-8075-1003-6, M-7187, Pub. by Wissen). French & Eur.

Lexikon 2000, Vol. 4. (Ger.). 1971. $86.00 (ISBN 3-8075-1004-4, M-7186, Pub. by Wissen). French & Eur.

Lexikon 2000, Vol. 5. (Ger.). 1971. $86.00 (ISBN 3-8075-1005-2, M-7185, Pub. by Wissen). French & Eur.

Lexikon 2000, Vol. 6. (Ger.). 1971. $86.00 (ISBN 3-8075-1006-0, M-7184, Pub. by Wissen). French & Eur.

Lexikon 2000, Vol. 7. (Ger.). 1972. $86.00 (ISBN 3-8075-1007-9, M-7183, Pub. by Wissen). French & Eur.

Lexikon 2000, Vol. 8. (Ger.). 1972. $86.00 (ISBN 3-8075-1008-7, M-7182, Pub. by Wissen). French & Eur.

Lexikon 2000, Vol. 9. (Ger.). 1972. $86.00 (ISBN 3-8075-1009-5, M-7181, Pub. by Wissen). French & Eur.

Lexikon 2000, Vol. 10. (Ger.). 1972. $86.00 (ISBN 3-8075-1010-9, M-7180, Pub. by Wissen). French & Eur.

Lexikon 2000, Vol. 11. (Ger.). 1973. $86.00 (ISBN 3-8075-1011-7, M-7179, Pub. by Wissen). French & Eur.

Lexikon 2000, Vol. 12. (Ger.). 1973. $86.00 (ISBN 3-8075-1012-5, M-7178, Pub. by Wissen). French & Eur.

Lexikon 2000, Vol. 13. (Ger.). 1973. $86.00 (ISBN 3-8075-1013-3, M-7177, Pub. by Wissen). French & Eur.

Lexikonredaktion. BI-Handlexikon, 2 vols, Vol. 1. (Illus.). 704p. (Ger.). 1982. M.32.00. Bibl Inst Leipzig.

Lexikonredaktion, ed. BI-Handlexikon, 2 vols, Vol. 2. (Illus.). 688p. (Ger.). 1982. M.32.00. Bibl Inst Leipzig.

--Meyers Grosses Handlexikon in Farbe. 1147p. (Ger.). M.42.00 (ISBN 3-411-01784-8). Biblio Inst.

Lexikonredaktion des Bibliographischen Instituts, ed. Duden-Lexikon in Drei Banden, 3 vols. (Illus.). 2016p. (Ger.). DM.32.00 ea. Vol. 1 (ISBN 3-411-01778-3). Vol. 2 (ISBN 3-411-01778-3). Vol. 3 (ISBN 3-411-01779-1). Biblio Inst.

--Meyers Grosses Standardlexikon in 3 Banden, 3 vols. (Illus.). 2200p. (Ger.). M.294.00 set (ISBN 3-411-01970-0); DM.98.00 ea. Bd. 1, A-Gh (ISBN 3-411-01971-9). Bd. 2, Gi-Pd (ISBN 3-411-01972-7). Bd. 3, Pe-Zz (ISBN 3-411-01973-5). Biblio Inst.

Lexikothek: Bd 10, Torp-Z. (Ger.). 1978. DM.118.00 (ISBN 3-570-06560-X). C Bertelsmann.

Lexikothek: Bd 2, Bez-Dit. (Ger.). 1978. DM.118.00 (ISBN 3-570-06552-9). C Bertelsmann.

Lexikothek: Bd 3, Diu-Gass. (Ger.). 1978. DM.118.00 (ISBN 3-570-06553-7). C Bertelsmann.

Lexikothek: Bd 4, Gast-Hz. (Ger.). 1978. DM.118.00 (ISBN 3-570-06554-5). C Bertelsmann.

Lexikothek: Bd 5, I-Kreb. (Ger.). 1978. DM.118.00 (ISBN 3-570-06555-3). C Bertelsmann.

Lexikothek: Bd 6, Kred-Mit. (Ger.). 1978. DM.118.00 (ISBN 3-570-06556-1). C Bertelsmann.

Lexikothek: Bd 7, Miv-Phyo. (Ger.). 1978. DM.118.00 (ISBN 3-570-06557-X). C Bertelsmann.

Lexikothek: Bd 8, Phys-Schlo. (Ger.). 1978. DM.118.00 (ISBN 3-570-06558-8). C Bertelsmann.

Lexikothek: Bd 9, Schlu-Toro. (Ger.). 1978. DM.118.00 (ISBN 3-570-06559-6). C Bertelsmann.

Lexikothek: Das Bertelsmann Lexikon in 10 Baenden. (Ger.). 1978. DM.118.00 (ISBN 3-570-06551-0). C Bertelsmann.

libr. du Liban. ABC Dictionary I: Arabic & Ger. (Arabic & Ger.). 1983. $7.95x (ISBN 0-86685-309-X). Intl Bk Ctr.

Libr du Liban. ABC Dictionary Tamhidi: Arabic Ger. (Arabic & Ger.). 1983. $7.95x (ISBN 0-86685-313-8). Intl Bk Ctr.

--My Illustrated Dictionary: Arabic & Ger. (Arabic & Ger.). 1983. $9.00x (ISBN 0-86685-318-9). Intl Bk Ctr.

Livescu, Jean & Savin, Emilia. Dictionar Roman-German: Pentru uzul Elevilor. LC 77-464118. 493p. (Ger. & Romanian.). 1976. 19.00 lei. Editura Stiintifica.

Mackensen, Lutz. Deutsches Woerterbuch. (Ger.). 1977. $38.50 (ISBN 3-517-00637-8, M-7339, Pub. by Suedwest). French & Eur.

--Deutsches Woerterbuch. (Ger.). 1977. DM.38.50 (ISBN 3-517-00637-8). Suedwest.

Mein Erster Brockhaus. 142p. (Ger.). DM.28.00 (ISBN 3-7653-0335-6). F A Brockhaus.

Menge & Guethling. Langenscheidts Grosswoerterbuch Deutsch-Lateinisch. (Ger. & Lat.). 1978. DM.58.00 (ISBN 3-468-02205-0). Langenscheidt.

--Langenscheidts Grosswoerterbuch Lateinisch-Deutsch. (Lat. & Ger.). 1978. DM.58.00 (ISBN 3-468-02200-X). Langenscheidt.

Menge & Guthling. Langenscheidts Grossworterbuch Altgriechisch-Deutsch. xxiv, 762p. (Gr. & Ger.). DM.68.00 (02030). Langenscheidt.

Menge, H. Langenscheidts Taschenwoerterbuecher Altgriechisch-Deutsch. (Gr. & Ger.). DM.13.80 (ISBN 3-468-10030-2). Langenscheidt.

Menge, Hermann. Lateinisch, 2 vols. rev. ed. Pertsch, E., rev. by. (Langenscheidts Taschewoerterbuecher Ser.). (Lat. & Ger.). Teil 1: Lateinisch-Deutsch (576p.) DM.16.80 (10200); Teil 2: Deutsch-Lateinisch (460p.) DM.16.80 (10205); DM.beide Teile in einem Band 23.80 (11200). Langenscheidt.

Menge, Hermann & Guethling, Otto. Langenscheidts Grosswoerterbuch: Lateinisch-Deutsch, 2 vols. 1553p. (Lat. & Ger.). DM.78.00; Teil I, Lateinisch-Deutsch. (02200); Teil II, Deutsch-Lateinisch. (02205). Langenscheidt.

Meras, Albert A. & Miller, Maud. Kleiner Wortschatz. 2nd ed. Ridgeway, W. R., rev. by. 64p. (Ger.). 1956. 0.95p (ISBN 0-245-56653-8). Harrap.

Meyers Grosses Taschenlexikon in 24 Banden. (Ger.). write for info. (ISBN 3-411-01920-4). Biblio Inst.

Meyers Grosses Universallexikon-Jahrbucher. 328p. (Ger.). 1980. write for info. (ISBN 3-411-01862-3). Biblio Inst.

Meyers Grosses Universallexikon-Jahrbucher. 328p. (Ger.). write for info. (ISBN 3-411-01892-5). Biblio Inst.

Meyers Grosses Universallexikon-Jahrbucher. 328p. (Ger.). 1981. write for info. (ISBN 3-411-01864-X). Biblio Inst.

Meyers Grosses Universallexikon-Jahrbucher: Luxusausgabe. 328p. (Ger.). 1982. write for info. (ISBN 3-411-01894-1). Biblio Inst.

Meyers Kinderlexikon: Mein Erstes Lexikon. (Illus.). 256p. (Ger.). $10.00 (1098). Adler Bks.

Meyers Kinderlexikon: Mein erstes Lexikon. (Illus.). 259p. (Ger.). DM.16.80 (ISBN 3-411-01774-0). Biblio Inst.

Meyers Neues Lexikon Jahrbucher. 328p. (Ger.). write for info. (ISBN 3-411-01769-4). Biblio Inst.

Meyers Neues Lexikon Jahrbucher. 328p. (Ger.). write for info. (ISBN 3-411-01789-9). Biblio Inst.

Meyers Neues Lexikon Jahrbucher. 328p. (Ger.). write for info. (ISBN 3-411-01948-4). Biblio Inst.

Moeller, Hilke. Thraenen-Samen & Steckdosenschnauze. Von Grieffenberg, C. R. & Schnurres, Wolfdietrich, eds. LC 77-455717. (Ger.). 1975. 26.00 F (ISBN 3-26003-966-X). Jurisdruck.

Mory, Ludwig, et al. Brukmanns' Zinn-Lexikon. LC 79-351818. (Illus.). 324p. (Ger.). 1977. DM.58.00 (ISBN 3-765-41361-5). Bruckmann KG.

Muller, Wolfgang. Die Richtige Wortwahl: Ein Vergleichendes Woerterbuch Sinnverwandter Ausdruecke. 480p. (Ger.). DM.19.80 (ISBN 3-411-01370-2). Biblio Inst.

Mylius, Klaus. Woerterbuch Sanskrit-Deutsch. LC 76-506569. 583p. (Ger. & Sanskrit.). 1975. M.86.00. VEB Verlag Enzyklopadie.

Der Neue Brockhaus. 653p. (Ger.). DM.120.00 (ISBN 3-7653-0310-0). F A Brockhaus.

Der Neue Brockhaus Lexikon & Woerterbuch in funf Baenden & Einem Atlas: Band 1. 700p. (Ger.). DM.108.00 (ISBN 3-7653-0300-3). F A Brockhaus.

Neue Herder: Lexikon, 14 vols. (Ger.). 1968-73. Set. $995.00 (ISBN 0-686-56635-1, M-7568, Pub. by Herder). French & Eur.

Neue Herder: Lexikon, 14 vols. (Ger.). 1968-73. Set. $995.00 (ISBN 0-686-56635-1). Herder.

Neugriechisch, 2 vols. Incl. Teil I. Neugriechisch-Deutsch. Wendt, H. F. 552p. DM.18.80 (10210); Teil II. Deutsch-Neugriechisch. Steinmetz, A. 487p. DM.18.80 (10215). (Langenscheidts Taschenworterbucher Ser.). (Ger. & Gr.). DM.beide Teile in einem Band 29.80 (11210). Langenscheidt.

Paul, H. Deutsches Woerterbuch Tuebingen. 841p. (Ger.). 1983. pap. $24.00. M Rosenberg.

Paul, Hermann. Deutsches Woerterbuch. 7th ed. (Ger.). 1976. $29.95 (ISBN 3-484-10057-5, M-7335, Pub. by Max Niemeyer). French & Eur.

--Deutsches Woerterbuch. 7th ed. (Ger.). 1976. fl.29.95 (ISBN 3-484-10057-5). Niemeyer.

Pertsch, Dietrich. Lateinisch-Deutsch. rev. & enl. ed. (Langenscheidts Grosse Schulwoerbuecher Ser.). 1344p. (Lat. & Ger.). 1983. DM.23.80 (07202). Langenscheidt.

Pertsch, Erich. Langenscheidts Grosses Schulwoerterbuch Lateinisch-Deutsch. 1344p. (Lat. & Ger.). DM.23.80 (07202). Langenscheidt.

--Langenscheidts Handwoerterbuch Lateinisch-Deutsch. 652p. (Lat. & Ger.). DM.34.00 (04200). Langenscheidt.

--Langenscheidts Schulwoerterbuecher Lateinisch-Deutsch. 1400p. (Lat. & Ger.). 1977. DM.19.80 (ISBN 3-468-07201-5). Langenscheidt.

Pertsch, Erich & Lange-Kowal, Ernst E. Langenscheidts Schulwoerterbuch Lateinisch-Deutsch. 512p. (Lat. & Ger.). DM.13.80 (13200). Langenscheidt.

Pertsch, Erich, compiled by. Lateinisch-Deutsch. (Langenscheidts Handwoerterbuecher Ser.). 652p. (Lat. & Ger.). DM.32.00 (04200). Langenscheidt.

Preuss, Gisela. Das Grosse Duden-Schulerlexikon: Ein Nachschlagewerk fuer Jeden Schueler. (Illus.). 704p. (Ger.). DM.write for info. (ISBN 3-411-01773-2). Biblio Inst.

--Das Wissen von A-Z: Ein Allgemeines Lexikon fur die Schule. (Illus.). 568p. (Ger.). DM.write for info. (ISBN 3-411-01780-5). Biblio Inst.

Rittmann, Herbert. Deutsches Munzsammler-Lexikon. LC 79-34554. (Illus.). 447p. (Ger.). 1977. write for info. (ISBN 3-87045-116-5). Battenberg.

Ruhland, Jean. Dictionnaire Trilingue. 220p. (Fr., Ger. & Eng.). 1977. 60.00 F. Ruhland.

Sammlung Duden: Band II, Regeln & Woerterverzeichnis fuer die Deutsch Rechtschreibung. 47p. (Ger.). DM.6.80 (ISBN 3-411-01042-8). Biblio Inst.

Scarry, Richard. Mein Allerschoenstes Woerterbuch. (Illus.). 78p. (Ger., Eng. & Fr.). $8.35 (1097). Adler Bks.

Schregle, Gotz. Deutsch-Arabisches Worterbuch. LC 79-366306. xii, 1472p. (Ger. & Arabic.). 1977. write for info. Lib Liban.

Schukry, K. Langenscheidts Taschenwoerterbuecher Deutsch-Arabisch. (Ger. & Arabic.). 1978. DM.14.80 (ISBN 3-468-10065-5). Langenscheidt.

Schwartz, Erwin, et al. Woerterbuch fuer die Grundschule. 96p. (Ger.). 1978. DM.5.90 (ISBN 3-14-190586-X). Westermann.

Skripecz, Ratz S., et al. Langenscheidts Handwoerterbuch Ungarisch HALASZ: Teil I, Ungarisch-Deutsch. 1064p. (Hungarian & Ger.). DM.48.00 (04381). Langenscheidt.

Smith, Josefa J., et al, eds. Cortina-Grosset Basic German Dictionary. LC 73-18523. 384p. (Ger.). 1975. pap. $3.50 (ISBN 0-686-96722-4, G&D). Putnam Pub Group.

Sommerfeldt, K. E. & Schreiber, H. Woerterbuch zur Valenz & Distribution Deutscher Adjektive. 3rd ed. 435p. (Ger.). 1982. M.22.00. Bibl Inst Leipzig.

Sommerfeldt, Karl-Ernst. Woerterbuch zur Valenz & Distribution der Substantive. LC 80-479437. 432p. (Ger.). 1977. M.16.00. Bibl Inst Leipzig.

Der Sprach Brockhaus. (Illus.). 835p. (Ger.). $22.80. Imported Bks.

Steuerwald, K. Langenscheidts Taschenwoerterbuch Tuerkisch: Teil I, Tuerkisch-Deutsch. 552p. (Turkish & Ger.). DM.19.80 (10370). Langenscheidt.

Steuerwald, K. & Koprulu, Cemal. Langenscheidts Taschenwoerterbuch Tuerkisch-Deutsch, 2 vols. in 1. (Turkish & Ger.). DM.29.80 (11370). Langenscheidt.

--Langenscheidts Taschenwoerterbuch Tuerkisch: Teil II, Deutsch-Tuerkisch. 616p. (Ger. & Turkish.). DM.19.80 (10375). Langenscheidt.

Steuerwald, Karl. Langenscheidts Taschenwoerterbuecher Tuerkisch-Deutsch. (Turkish & Ger.). 1978. DM.14.80 (ISBN 3-468-10370-0). Langenscheidt.

Strutz. Five Hundred & One German Verbs: Written in Japanese. (Japanese & Ger.). Date not set. pap. $4.25 (ISBN 0-8120-2182-7). Barron.

Sydow, Achim. Kybernetik. LC 78-387093. 138p. (Eng. & Ger.). 1976. DM.20.00. VEB Verlag Technik.

Taschenwoerterbuch. 1278p. (Ger.). $10.95 (11121). Langenscheidt.

Tomsic, F. German-Slovene Dictionary. 989p. (Ger. & Slovene.). 1980. $49.95 (ISBN 0-686-97384-4, M-9696). French & Eur.

Tschechisch, 2 vols. Incl. Teil I. Tschechisch-Deutsch. Ulbrich, Rolf. 576p. DM.18.80 (10360); Teil II. Deutsch-Tschechisch. Kabesch, Friedrich. 478p. DM.18.80 (10365). (Langenscheidts Taschenworterbucher Ser.). (Czech. & Ger.). DM.29.80 (11360). Langenscheidt.

Ulbrich, Rolf. Langenscheidts Taschenwoerterbuch Tschechisch: Teil I, Tschechisch-Deutsch. 576p. (Czech. & Ger.). DM.19.80 (10360). Langenscheidt.

--Langenscheidts Taschenwoerterbuecher Tschechisch-Deutsch. 600p. (Czech. & Ger.). 1977. DM.14.80 (ISBN 3-468-10360-3). Langenscheidt.

Ulbrich, Rolf & Kabesch, Friedrich. Langenscheidts Taschenwoerterbuch Tschechisch-Deutsch, 2 vols. in 1. (Czech. & Ger.). DM.29.80 (11360). Langenscheidt.

Ulrich, Winfried. Woerterbuch: Linguistische Grundbegriffe. 2nd ed. LC 77-460610. (Illus.). 173p. (Ger.). 1975. DM.13.80 (ISBN 3-554-80336-7). Hirt.

Universal German Dictionary. 560p. (Ger.). $2.95 (092). Langenscheidt.

Veb. Inst. Leipzig. Bi-Lexikon A-Z. 1072p. (Ger.). 1982. M.18.00 (5772135). Bibl Inst Leipzig.

Vest Pocket German Dictionary. rev. & enl. ed. 344p. (Ger.). pap. $2.95 (ISBN 0-8329-1533-5). New Century.

Vischer, Ruediger. Lateinische Wortkunde fuer Anfaenger & Fortgeschrittene. LC 79-383471. 224p. (Ger. & Lat.). 1977. write for info. (ISBN 3-519-07407-9). Teubner.

Wahrig. DTV Woerterbuch der deutschen Sprache. 942p. (Ger.). pap. $17.90. Imported Bks.

Wahrig, G., ed. DTV-Woerterbuch der deutschen Sprache. 943p. (Ger.). pap. $9.25. M Rosenberg.

Wahrig, Gerhard. Deutsches Woerterbuch. 2nd ed. (Ger.). 1975. $30.95 (ISBN 3-570-01631-5, M-7336, Pub. by Bertelsmann Lexikon VVA). French & Eur.

--Deutsches Woerterbuch. 2nd ed. (Ger.). 1975. DM.30.95 (ISBN 3-570-01631-5). C Bertelsmann.

Wahrig, Gerhard, et al. Brockhaus-Wahrig Deutsches Woerterbuch in Sechs Baenden: Band 1-3. 800p. (Ger.). DM.128.00 (ISBN 3-7653-0312-7). F A Brockhaus.

Wahrig-Gerhard. Fremdwoerter Lexikon. (Ger.). 1976. DM.15.95 (ISBN 3-570-01631-5). C Bertelsmann.

Wahrmund, Adolf. Handworterbuch der Neu-Arabischen und Deutschen Sprache, 3 vols. (Arabic & Ger.). 1974. Set. text ed. $50.50x (ISBN 0-8426-0776-5). Verry.

--Handworterbuch der neu Arabischen und Deutschen Sprache, 3 vols. 2826p. (Ger. & Arabic). Repr. $70.00 set (178-X). Intl Bk Ctr.

Walde, Alois. Vergleichendes Woerterbuch der Indogermanischen Sprachen, 3 vols. Pokorny, Julius, ed. (Ger.). 1973. Repr. of 1932 ed. Set. $224.00x (ISBN 3-11-004556-7). De Gruyter.

Wallnig, G. & Evered, H. Deutsch fuer Baufachleute. (Illus.). 102p. (Eng. & Ger., Fr. & Span.). 1979. DM.16.00 (ISBN 3-7625-0462-8). Bauverlag.

--Deutsch fur Baufachleute fuer Daenen, Norweger & Sshweden. (Illus.). 110p. (Danish, Ger., Norwegian & Swedish). 1982. DM.20.00 (ISBN 3-7625-1467-4). Bauverlag.

Warneck, Johannes G. Toba-Batak-Deutsches Worterbuch. LC 79-353140. xii, 332p. (Ger. & Toba-Batak). 1977. fl.98.80 (ISBN 9-0247-2018-4). Nyhoff.

Weber, Albert. Grammatiken und Woerterbuecher des Schweizer Deutschen. 2nd ed. 354p. (Ger.). 1968. $14.50 (ISBN 3-85865-029-3, M-7431, Pub. by Hans Rohr). French & Eur.

Weigand, Karl. Deutsches Woerterbuch, 2 vols. 6th ed. (Ger.). 1968. Set. $252.00x (ISBN 3-11-000383-X, M-7337). De Gruyter.

Weissling, Heinrich. Taschenworterbuch Deutsch-Ungarisch. LC 76-472365. 272p. (Ger. & Hungarian). 1975. M.5.80. VEB Verlag Enzyklopaedie.

Weissling, Heinrich, ed. Taschenworterbuch Deutsch-Ungarisch. LC 76-472365. 272p. (Ger. & Hungarian). 1975. M.5.80. VEB Verlag Enzyklopaedie.

Die Welt Von A-Z, 2 vols. (Illus.). 1264p. (Ger.). $66.70 (1102). Adler Bks.

Wendt, H. F., ed. Langenscheidts Taschenwoerterbuecher Neugriechisch-Deutsch. (Gr. & Ger.). 1978. DM.14.80 (ISBN 3-468-10210-0). Langenscheidt.

Woerterbuch als Fehlerquelle. 48p. (Ger.). 1970. DM.4.80 (ISBN 3-87118-019-X). Buske.

Woerterbuch der deutschen Gegenwartssprache, 6 vols. (Ger.). 1978. Vol. 1-5. $24.00 ea.; Vol. 6. $19.80 ea. M Rosenberg.

Woerterbuch der Deutschen Gegenwartssprache: Vol. 6. 480p. (Ger.). pap. $19.80. M Rosenberg.

Woerterbuch der Deutschen Gegenwartssprache: Vols. 1-5, 6 vols. 800p. (Ger.). pap. $24.00 ea. M Rosenberg.

Woerterbuch der Deutschen Sprache mit Rechtschreiblehre. 256p. (Ger.). 1966. DM.3.80 (ISBN 3-8036-0251-3). Gebrueder Weiss.

Woerterbuch der Deutschen Umgangssprache: Vol. 3, Hochdeutsch-Umgangsdeutsch A-Z. (Ger.). 1983. $13.50. M Rosenberg.

Woerterbuch zum Deutschen Sprachgebrauch: Woerter & Wendungen. 818p. (Ger.). 1972. pap. $11.00. M Rosenberg.

Woeter & Wendungen: Woerterbuch zum Deutschen Sprachgebrauch. 818p. (Ger.). 1972. $11.00. M Rosenberg.

Zellweger, Rudolf. Le Vocabulaire Allemand du Bacheller. 3rd ed. 80p. (Fr.). 1967. 8.00 F. Payot.

Ziefle, Helmut W. Dictionary of Modern Theological German. LC 82-70464. 360p. (Orig., Ger.). 1982. pap. $9.95 (ISBN 0-8010-9929-3). Baker Bk.

Zotter, Josefa, ed. Cortina-Grosset Basic German Dictionary. (Ger.). 1977. pap. $2.95 (ISBN 0-448-14029-2, G&D). Putnam Pub Group.

GERMAN LANGUAGE–DICTIONARIES–CHINESE

Deutsch-Chinesisches Handworterbuch. 1197p. (Ger. & Chinese). 1980. $54.00 (ISBN 0-686-92250-6, M-9270). French & Eur.

Deutsch-Chinesisches Standard Handworterbuch. 1364p. (Ger. & Chinese). 1979. $49.95 (ISBN 0-686-92450-9, M-9265). French & Eur.

Piasek, Martin. Chinesisch-Deutsches Woerterbuch. 3rd ed. (Chinese & Ger.). 1975. $28.95 (ISBN 0-686-56599-1, 7320, Pub. by Max Heuber). French & Eur.

--Chinesisch-Deutsches Woerterbuch. 3rd ed. (Chinese & Ger.). 1975. DM.28.95. Hueber.

Rudenberg, Werner. Chinesisch-Deutsches Woerterbuch. 3rd ed. 821p. (Chinese & Ger.). 1963. $196.00x (ISBN 0-686-56600-9, M-7321). De Gruyter.

Wilhelm, Hellmut. German-Chinese Dictionary. (Ger. & Chinese). 1976. Repr. of 1958 ed. $175.00 (ISBN 0-518-19006-4). Ayer Co.

GERMAN LANGUAGE–DICTIONARIES–DANISH

Hennigsen, H. Danisch, 2 vols. (Langenscheidts Taschenwoerterbucher). (Ger. & Danish). Teil 1: Danisch-Deutsch (557p.) DM.mit Lautschrift 18.80 (10100); Teil 2: Deutsch-Danisch (548p.) DM.18.80 (10105); DM.beide Teile in einem Band 29.80 (11100). Langenscheidt.

Langenscheidts Taschenwoerterbuecher Deutsch-Daenisch. (Ger. & Danish). 1978. DM.14.80 (ISBN 3-468-10105-8). Langenscheidt.

Langenscheidts Universal-Woerterbuch Danisch. 560p. (Danish & Ger.). DM.6.80 (18101). Langenscheidt.

Langenscheidts Universal-Woerterbuecher Daenisch-Deutsch. (Danish & Ger.). 1978. DM.5.80 (ISBN 3-468-18101-9). Langenscheidt.

Warrern, A. Tysk-Dansk Teknisk Ordbog. 259p. (Ger. & Danish). 1974. $49.95 (ISBN 0-686-92486-X, M-1291). French & Eur.

GERMAN LANGUAGE–DICTIONARIES–DUTCH

Beersmans, Frans. Langenscheidts Taschenwoerterbuch Niederlaendisch: Teil II, Deutsch-Niederlaendisch. 542p. (Ger. & Dutch). DM.19.80 (10236). Langenscheidt.

Langendorf, Hans. Legal Dictionary: Part 1, Dutch-German. 365p. (Dutch & Ger.). 1977. $26.00 (ISBN 90-26-8070-74). Kluwer Academic.

Niederlaendisch, 2 vols. rev. ed. Incl. Teil I. Niederlaendisch-Deutsch. Van de Wiele, F. J., rev. by. 527p. DM.18.80 (10231); Teil II. Deutsch-Niederlaendisch. Beersmans, Frans, rev. by. 544p. DM.18.80 (10236). (Langenscheidts Taschenworterbucher Ser.). (Ger. & Dutch). DM.beide Teile in einem Band 29.80 (11231). Langenscheidt.

Schneider, Jan, ed. Langenscheidts Taschenwoerterbuecher Niederlandisch-Deutsch. (Dutch & Ger.). 1978. DM.14.80 (ISBN 3-468-10230-5). Langenscheidt.

Van Beckum, J. H., ed. Langenscheidts Handwoerterbuecher: Tl 1, Gelderen, 1 van: Niederlandisch-Deutsch. (Dutch & Ger.). 1975. DM.38.00 (ISBN 3-468-04230-2). Langenscheidt.

Van Beckum, J. H. & Wallis, H., eds. Langenscheidts Handwoerterbuecher: Tl 2, Gelderen, 1 van, Deutsch-Niederlandisch. (Ger. & Dutch). 1975. DM.38.00 (ISBN 3-468-04235-3). Langenscheidt.

Van De Wiele, F. J. J. & Beersmans, Frans. Langenscheidts Taschenwoerterbuch Niederlandisch-Deutsch, 2 vols. in 1. (Dutch & Ger.). DM.29.80 (11231). Langenscheidt.

Van Gelderen, de Duits-Neederland Woordenboek. 972p. (Ger.). 1980. pap. $24.95 (ISBN 90-01-96814-7, M-9745). French & Eur.

Van Gelderen, I. & Wallis, W. H. Langenscheidts Handwoerterbuch Niederlaendisch Wolters: Teil I, Niederlaendisch-Deutsch. 976p. (Dutch & Ger.). DM.42.00 (04230). Langenscheidt.

Wallis, W. H. Neederland-Duits: Wolter's Woorden Boek. 956p. (Ger.). 1981. $24.95 (ISBN 90-01-96815-5, M-9744). French & Eur.

Worgt, Gerhard, ed. Taschenwoerterbuch Deutsch-Niederlaendisch. LC 78-349037. xxiv, 359p. (Ger. & Dutch). 1977. M.5.80. VEB Verlag Enzyklopadie.

GERMAN LANGUAGE–DICTIONARIES–ENGLISH

Barker, M. L. & Homeyer, H., eds. The Pocket Oxford German Dictionary, 2 vols. in 1. Incl. Pt. 1. German-English. 3rd ed. (Eng. & Ger.). 1975; Pt. 2. English-German. Carr, C. T., compiled by. (Eng. & Ger.). 1975. pap. 5.95x (ISBN 0-19-864138-9). Oxford U Pr.

Basic German-English Dictionary & Grammar. 176p. (Ger.). 1976. pap. text ed. $5.95 (ISBN 0-88436-183-7, 45258). EMC.

Bein, G. German-English Dictionary of International Transport. 232p. (Ger. & Eng.). 1980. $15.00x (ISBN 0-569-05117-7, Pub. by Collet's). State Mutual Bk.

Berlitz Editors. Berlitz Pocket Dictionaries: German-English. 300p. (Ger. & Eng.). 1982. pap. $4.95 (ISBN 0-686-93007-X, Berlitz). Macmillan.

Bertelsmann Dictionary English-German, German-English. (Ger. & Eng.). 1975. $29.95 (ISBN 3-570-01438-X, M-7444, Pub. by Bertelsmann Lexikon/VVA). French & Eur.

Bertelsmann Dictionary: English-German, German-English. (Ger. & Eng.). 1975. DM.29.95 (ISBN 3-570-01438-X). C Bertelsmann.

Bildwoerterbuch Deutsch-Englisch. 864p. (Ger. & Eng.). 1983. $18.00. M Rosenberg.

Birdmann, G. English-German, German, English Solid State Physics & Electronics Dictionary. 1103p. (Eng. & Ger.). 1980. $100.00x (ISBN 0-569-07204-2, Pub. by Collet's). State Mutual Bk.

Briese, K. English-German Dictionary. 624p. (Eng. & Ger.). 1980. $20.00x (ISBN 0-569-06892-4, Pub. by Collet's). State Mutual Bk.

Brockhaus Bildwoerterbuch Englisch-Deutsch. (Eng. & Ger.). 1983. pap. $24.00. M Rosenberg.

Clark, J. M., ed. German-English, English-German Gem Dictionary. (Gem Foreign Language Ser.). (Ger. & Eng.). 1953. leatheroid $2.95 (ISBN 0-00-458619-0, G3). Collins Pubs.

Collins German-English English-German Dictionary. 416p. (Orig., Ger. & Eng.). 1983. pap. $2.95 (ISBN 0-425-05450-0). Berkley Pub.

Collins Pocket German Dictionary. 448p. 1983. $7.95 (ISBN 0-671-49222-5). S&S.

Comprehensive German Dictionary. 1104p. (Ger. & Eng.). $42.50 (02120). Langenscheidt.

Deutsch-Englisch, Englisch-Deutsch. (Langenscheidts Schulworterbucher Ser.). 576p. (Ger. & Eng.). DM.12.80 (13120). Langenscheidt.

DeVries, Louis. German-English Technical & Engineering Dictionary. 2nd ed. (Ger. & Eng.). 1966. 63.95 (ISBN 0-07-016631-5, P&RB). McGraw.

DeVries, Louis & Jacolev, Leon. German-English Science Dictionary. 4th ed. (Ger. & Eng.). 1978. 26.95 (ISBN 0-07-016602-1, P&RB). McGraw.

Engeroff, K. & Lovelace-Kaeufer, C. English-German Dictionary of Idioms. (Eng. & Ger.). $22.75 (ISBN 3-1900-6217-X). Adler.

Englisch, 2 vols. Incl. Englisch-Deutsch. Messinger, Heinz & Rudenberg, Werner. 1440p (07121); Deutsch-Englisch. Messinger, Heinz. 1328p (07126). (Langenscheidts Grosse Schulworterbucher Ser.). (Eng. & Ger.). DM.23.80 ea. Langenscheidt.

Englisch, 2 vols. rev. ed. Incl. Teil I. Englisch-Deutsch. Klatt, E. Roy, D., rev. by. 640p. DM.16.80 (10120); Teil II. Deutsch-Englisch. Klatt, E. & Klatt, G. Messinger, Heinz, rev. by. 639p. DM.16.80 (10126). (Langenscheidts Taschenworterbucher Ser.). (Eng. & Ger.). DM.beide Teile in einem Band 23.80 (11121). Langenscheidt.

Fischer, Eric & Elliott, Francis E. A German & English Glossary of Geographical Terms. LC 76-20474. (American Geographical Society Library Ser: No. 5). 111p. (Ger. & Eng.). 1976. Repr. of 1950 ed. lib. bdg. $15.00x (ISBN 0-8371-8994-2, ELGG). Greenwood.

Freeman, Henry G., compiled by. DIN Definitions: German-English with an English-German Vocabulary. 2nd rev. ed. (Ger. & Eng.). 80.00 (ISBN 3-4101-0804-1). Heinman.

German-English & English-German Dictionary. (Ger. & Eng.). pap. $1.99 (ISBN 0-686-00471-X). Dennison.

Glossar & Erlaeuterungen zur Grammatik Deutsch-Englisch. 72p. (Ger. & Eng.). 1983. $3.25. M Rosenberg.

Glossar Deutsch-Englisch. 50p. (Ger. & Eng.). 1983. pap. $2.90. M Rosenberg.

Glossar Deutsch-Englisch. 46p. (Ger. & Eng.). pap. $3.50. M Rosenberg.

Grossmann, T. & Friedmann, G. Kaufmannisches Grundwoerterbuch fuer Schule und Praxis: Deutsch-Englisch. 280p. (Ger. & Eng.). pap. $9.40. M Rosenberg.

Grosswoerterbuch der Englischen & Deutschen Sprache. 1300p. (Eng. & Ger.). 1983. pap. $60.00. M Rosenberg.

Gunston, C. A. Deutsch-Englishes Glossarium. 1292p. (Ger. & Eng., German-English Glossary of Financial and Economic Terms). 1977. $69.50 (ISBN 3-7819-2014-3, 7328, Pub. by Fritz Knapp Verlag). French & Eur.
Hamlyn German-English Dictionary. (Ger. & Eng.). 1977. pap. 4.95 (ISBN 0-600-36564-6, 8088). Larousse.
Hugo Pocket Dictionary: German-English, English-German. 622p. (Ger. & Eng.). 1969. 3.50 (ISBN 0-8226-0504-X, 504). Littlefield.
Institute for Language Study. Vest Pocket German. LC 58-8920. (Illus.). 128p. (Ger.). 1979. pap. $2.45 (ISBN 0-06-464902-4, BN 4902, BN). B&N NY.
Jean's Pocket Dictionaries: German-English. 224p. (Orig., Ger. & Eng.). 1981. pap. 2.25 (ISBN 0-8437-1726-2). Hammond Inc.
Jones, Stephen. Practical English-German, German-English Dictionary. (Hippocrene's Practical Language Dictionary Ser.). 400p. (Orig., Eng. & Ger.). 1983. pap. $6.95 (ISBN 0-88254-813-1). Hippocrene Bks.
Keller, Howard H. A German Word Family Dictionary: Together with English Equivalents. LC 76-19988. (Ger. & Eng.). 1978. $14.95 (ISBN 0-520-03291-8). U of Cal Pr.
Klaften, E. B. & Allison, F. C. German-English, English-German Patent Terminological Dictionary. (Ger. & Eng.). 50.00 (ISBN 0-685-12020-1). Heinman.
Klatt, E. & Roy, D. Langenscheidts Taschenwoerterbuecher Englisch-Deutsch. (Eng. & Ger.). 1970. DM.13.80 (ISBN 3-468-10120-1). Langenscheidt.
Klatt, Edmund, et al. Langenscheidt's Standard German Dictionary: German-English, English-German. Orig. Title: Standard German Dictionary. 1264p. (Ger. & Eng.). 1974. $11.95 (ISBN 0-685-39723-8). Am Map.
Langenscheidt English-German Lilliput Dictionary. 575p. (Eng. & Ger.). plastic $1.50 (ISBN 3-468-96404-8). Langenscheidt.
Langenscheidt German-English Lilliput Dictionary. 576p. (Eng. & Ger.). plastic $1.50 (ISBN 3-468-96403-X). Langenscheidt.
Langenscheidt-Redaktion. Langenscheidts Schulwoerterbuch Englisch-Deutsch. 576p. (Eng. & Ger.). DM.13.80 (13120). Langenscheidt.
Langenscheidt Staff, ed. Langenscheidt's New Pocket German Dictionary: German-English, English-German. (Langenscheidt Pocket Dictionaries Ser.). 702p. (Ger. & Eng.). 1970. $5.95 (ISBN 0-685-31330-1). Am Map.
Langenscheidt Taschenwoerterbuch Englisch komplett. 1278p. (Ger.). $10.95 (ISBN 3-468-10126-0). Langenscheidt.
Langenscheidts Lilliput-Woerterbuch Deutsch-Englisch. 640p. (Ger. & Eng.). DM.3.00 (20003). Langenscheidt.
Langenscheidts Lilliput-Woerterbuch Englisch-Deutsch. 640p. (Eng. & Ger.). DM.3.00 (20004). Langenscheidt.
Langenscheidts Lilliput-Woerterbuecher Deutsch-Englisch. (Ger. & Eng.). 1978. DM.2.20 (ISBN 3-468-20003-X). Langenscheidt.
Langenscheidts Lilliput-Woerterbuecher Englisch-Deutsch. (Eng. & Ger.). 1978. DM.2.20 (ISBN 3-468-20004-8). Langenscheidt.
Langenscheidts Schulwoerterbuecher Englisch-Deutsch. (Eng. & Ger.). 1978. DM.10.80 (ISBN 3-468-13120-8). Langenscheidt.
Langenscheidt's Universal German-English, English-German Dictionary. 35th ed. (Universal Dictionaries Ser.). 512p. (Eng. & Ger.). $2.95 (ISBN 3-468-18121-3). Am Map.
Langenscheidts Universal-Woerterbuecher Englisch-Deutsch. (Eng. & Ger.). 1978. DM.5.80 (ISBN 3-468-18121-3). Langenscheidt.
Laurence Urdang Associates, Ltd., compiled by. Hamlyn German Dictionary: German-English, English-German. 306p. (Eng. & Ger.). 1976. 0.75p (ISBN 0-600-36564-6). Hamlyn-Amer.
Lilliput German-English Dictionary. 640p. (Ger. & Eng.). $1.50 (100). Langenscheidt.
Messinger, Heinz. Der Kleine Muret-Sanders: Deutsch-Englisch. 1296p. (Ger. & Eng.). 1982. DM.148.00 (02125). Langenscheidt.
--Langenscheidt Grosswoerterbuch: Englisch-Deutsch. 1104p. (Ger. & Eng.). DM.88.00 (02120). Langenscheidt.
--Langenscheidts Handwoerterbuch: Teil II, Deutsch-Englisch. 702p. (Ger. & Eng.). DM.34.00 (04126). Langenscheidt.
--Langenscheidts Handwoerterbuecher: Tl 2, Deutsch-Englisch. (Ger. & Eng.). 1978. DM.28.00 (ISBN 3-468-04125-X). Langenscheidt.
Messinger, Heinz & Rudenberg, Werner. Langenscheidt's New College German Dictionary (German-English, English-German) 1400p. (Eng. & Ger.). 1973. $16.95 (ISBN 0-685-30210-5); thumb indexed $18.95 (ISBN 0-685-30211-3). Am Map.
Messinger, Heinz & Ruedenberg, Werner. Langenscheidts Handwoerterbuch: Englisch-Deutsch Deutsch-Englisch, 2 vols. in 1. 1471p. (Eng. & Ger.). DM.49.00 (05122). Langenscheidt.
--Langenscheidts Handwoerterbuch: Teil I, Englisch-Deutsch. 760p. (Eng. & Ger.). DM.34.00 (04121). Langenscheidt.
--Langenscheidts Handwoerterbuecher: Tl 1, Englisch-Deutsch. (Eng. & Ger.). 1978. DM.28.00 (ISBN 3-468-04120-9). Langenscheidt.
Messinger, Heinz, ed. Condensed Muret-Sanders German-English Dictionary. 1st ed. 1296p. (Eng. & Ger.). 1983. $70.00x (ISBN 3-468-02125-9). Gale.
Messinger, Heinz & Rudenberg, Werner, eds. Englisch, 2 vols. (Langenscheidts Hanworterbucher Ser.). (Eng. & Ger.). Teil 1: Englisch-Deutsch (760p.) DM.32.00 (04121); Teil 2: Deutsch-Englisch. DM.32.00 (04126); DM.beide Teile in einem Band (1471p.) 48.00 (05122). Langenscheidt.
Mosse, Walter M. Theological German Vocabulary. (Ger.). 1968. lib. bdg. 14.50x (ISBN 0-374-95966-8). Octagon.
Moulton, Jenni H., ed. The Random House Basic Dictionary German. (Ger. & Eng.). 1981. pap. $1.50 (ISBN 0-345-29619-2). Ballantine.
New College German Dictionary (Plain Edition) 1416p. (Ger. & Eng.). $16.95 (074). Langenscheidt.
New College German Dictionary (Thumb-Indexed) 1416p. (Ger. & Eng.). $18.95 (073). Langenscheidt-Hachette.
New Condensed Muret-Sanders German Dictionary. 1296p. (Ger. & Eng.). $70.00 (33071). Langenscheidt.
New Muret-Sanders Encyclopedic Dictionary: Pt. I, vol. 1, A-M. 1050p. (Eng. & Ger.). $70.00 (01120). Langenscheidt.
New Muret-Sanders Encyclopedic Dictionary: Pt. II, vol. 1, A-K. 1050p. (Ger. & Eng.). $80.00 (01124). Langenscheidt.
New Muret-Sanders Encyclopedic Dictionary: Pt. I, vol. 2, N-Z. 1050p. (Eng. & Ger.). $70.00 (01122). Langenscheidt.
New Muret-Sanders Encyclopedic Dictionary: Pt. II, vol. 2, L-Z. 1050p. (Ger. & Eng.). $80.00 (01126). Langenscheidt.
Ottenheimer, ed. German-English, English-German Dictionary. (Ger. & Eng.). pap. $2.50 (ISBN 0-06-465028-6, DI 2, BN). B&N NY.
Oxford-Duden Bildwoerterbuch Deutsch & Englisch. 864p. (Ger.). DM.39.00 (ISBN 3-411-01765-1). Biblio Inst.
Pocket-Shorter Dictionary. 600p. (Ger. & Eng.). $5.95 (085). Langenscheidt.
Pons. Global Woerterbuch: English-German, German-English, 2 vols. (Ger. & Eng.). $10.90 ea. M Rosenberg.
Rechtschaffen, Bernard & Marck, Louis. Two Thousand & One German & English Idioms: 2001 Deutsche und Englische Idiome. (Ger. & Eng.). 1984. pap. $9.95 (ISBN 0-8120-0474-4). Barron.
Reisewoerrterbuch: German-English, English-German. 239p. (Ger. & Eng.). plastic cover $5.90. M Rosenberg.
Renner, R. & Sachs, R. Wirtschaftssprache Deutsch-Englisch, Englisch-Deutsch. 544p. (Ger. & Eng.). $21.00. M Rosenberg.
Ritter, U. P. & Zinn, K. G. Grundwortschatz wirtschaftswissenshcaftlicher Begriffe: Deutsch- Englisch, Englisch-Deutsch. 2nd ed. 199p. (Ger. & Eng.). 1980. pap. $9.25 (UTB644). M Rosenberg.
Sawers, Robin, ed. Harrap's Concise German & English Dictionary. 1120p. (Ger. & Eng.). E6.95 (ISBN 0-245-53869-0). Harrap.
Schmidt, Walter. Taschenworterbuch. LC 77-554903. xiv, 347p. (Eng. & Ger.). 1977. M.5.80. VEB Verlag Enzyklopadie.
Schmidt, Walter, ed. Taschenwoerterbuch Englisch-Deutsch. LC 77-554903. 347p. (Ger.). 1977. DM.5.85. VEB Verlag Enzyklopadie.
Schoeffler, Weis. Woerterbuch der Englischen und Deutschen Sprache, Vol. 1. (Ger. & Eng., Dictionary of the English & German Language). pap. $17.95 (ISBN 3-12-518100-3, M-7015). French & Eur.
--Woerterbuch der Englischen und Deutschen Sprache, Vol. 2. (Ger. & Eng., Dictionary of the English & German Language). pap. $17.95 (ISBN 3-12-518200-X, M-7014). French & Eur.
Schoffler-Weiss. German-English, English-German Dictionary. 1062p. (Ger. & Eng.). 1981. $16.95. M Rosenberg.
Springer, Otto. Der Grosse Muret-Sanders: Teil II, Deutsch-Englisch, 2 vols. 2021p. (Ger. & Eng.). 1975. DM.198.00 set; Band A-K. (01124); Band L-Z. (01126). Langenscheidt.
Springer, Otto, ed. Der Neue Muret-Sanders, 2 pts. Incl. Teil I. Englisch-Deutsch. 1962-63. Band A-M (883p.) DM.168.00 (0112-0); Band N-Z (viii, 960p.) DM.168.00 (0112-1); Teil II. Deutsch-Englisch. 1974-75. Band A-K (973p.) DM.198.00 (01124); Band N-Z (viii, 1048p.) DM.198.00 (01126). (Ger. & Eng.). Langenscheidt.
Standard German Dictionary. 1200p. (Ger. & Eng., New York). $11.95 (319). Langenscheidt.
Strutz, H. Dictionary of Five Hundred One German Verbs Fully Conjugated. 523p. (Ger. & Eng.). 1972. pap. $5.00. Barron.
Taylor, Ronald J. & Gottschalk, W. German-English Dictionary of Idioms. (Eng. & Ger.). $30.00 (ISBN 3-19-006216-1). Adler.
Terrel, P., et al. Collins German-English, English-German Dictionary. 790p. (Ger. & Eng.). $19.95 (ISBN 0-671-42045-3); pap. $8.95 (ISBN 0-671-42046-1, M-9309). French & Eur.
Traupman, John C. New College German & English Dictionary. (Ger. & Eng.). (gr. 9-12). 1981. reference $12.00 (ISBN 0-87720-584-1). AMSCO Sch.
Traupman, John C., ed. The Bantam New College German & English Dictionary. 768p. (Orig., Ger. & Eng.). (gr. 7-12). 1981. pap. $2.50 (ISBN 0-553-14155-4). Bantam.
Wahrig, G. German-English Dictionary. 661p. (Ger. & Eng.). 1980. $35.00x (ISBN 0-569-05717-5, Pub. by Collet's). State Mutual Bk.
Walther, R. Technical Dictionary of Production Engineering: Vol. 2, German-English. (Ger. & Eng.). $49.00 (ISBN 0-08-016960-0). Pergamon.
Weis, E., et al. Pons Schoffler Weis English-German, German-English Dictionary. 1060p. (Eng. & Ger.). 1979. $52.50 (ISBN 3-12-517120-2, M-9361). French & Eur.
Weis, Erich & Mattutat, Heinrich, eds. Harrap's Schoeffler-Weis German & English Dictionary, 2 PTS. 1077p. (Eng. & Ger.). E9.95 (ISBN 0-245-59813-8). Harrap.
Wildhagen. Englisch-Deutsches, Deutsch-Englisches Woerterbuch, Vol. 1. 2nd ed. (Ger. & Eng.). 1973. DM.52.00 (ISBN 3-87097-046-4). Brandstetter.
--Englisch-Deutsches, Deutsch-Englisches Woerterbuch, Vol. 2. 2nd ed. (Ger. & Eng.). 1972. DM.72.00 (ISBN 3-87097-047-2). Brandstetter.
Wildhagen & Hereaucourt. English-German, German-English Dictionary, 2 vols. rev. ed. (Ger. & Eng.). 1972. Vol. 1: English-German, 1148p. $32.50; Vol. 2: German-English, 1524p. $45.00. M Rosenberg.
Wiidhagen, Heraucourt. Englisch-Deutsches Deutsch-Englisches Woerterbuch: Band II, Deutsch-Englisch. 1524p. (Eng. & Ger.). 1982. DM.90.00. Brandstetter.
--Englisch-Deutsches Deutsch-Englisches Woerterbuch: Band I, Englisch-Deutsch. 1180p. (Eng. & Ger.). 1982. DM.65.00. Brandstetter.
Zotter, Josefa. Cortina-Grosset Basic German Dictionary. LC 73-18523. xiii, 366p. (Eng. & Ger.). 1975. $3.95 (ISBN 0-448-11557-3). G&D.

GERMAN LANGUAGE–DICTIONARIES–FINNISH

Hirvensalo, L. Finnish-German-Finnish Dictionary (Suomi-Saksa-Suomi) 610p. (Finnish & Ger.). 1980. pap. $14.95 (ISBN 951-0-08070-5, M-9646). French & Eur.
Katara, P., et al. Finnish-German Great Dictionary. 1443p. (Ger. & Finnish.). 1981. $39.95 (ISBN 951-0-10060-9, M-9660). French & Eur.
Rosentahl, A., et al. Deutsch-Finnisches Schulworterbuch. 673p. (Ger. & Finnish.). 1976. $24.95 (ISBN 951-0-05140-3, M-9637). French & Eur.

GERMAN LANGUAGE–DICTIONARIES–FRENCH

Bertaux, Pierre. Franzosisch-Deutsches, Deutsch-Franzosisches Woerterbuch, Vol. 1. (Ger. & Fr.). 1966. 69.95 (ISBN 3-87097-000-6, M-7411, Pub. by Brandstetter). French & Eur.
--Franzosisch-Deutsches, Deutsch-Franzosisches Woerterbuch, Vol. 1. (Ger. & Fr.). 1966. DM.69.95 (ISBN 3-87097-000-6). Brandstetter.
--Franzosisch-Deutsches, Deutsch-Franzosisches Woerterbuch, Vol. 2. (Ger. & Fr.). 1966. DM.69.95 (ISBN 3-87097-001-4). Brandstetter.
Bertraux, Lepointe. Franzoesisch-Deutsches-Deutsch-Franzoesisches Woerterbuch: Band II, Deutsch-Franzoesisch. 1392p. (Ger. & Eng.). 1982. DM.65.00. Brandstetter.
--Franzosisch-Deutsches-Deutsch-Franzosisches Woerterbuch: Band I, Franzoesisch-Deutsch. 1312p. (Fr. & Ger.). 1982. DM.65.00. Brandstetter.
Dubois, F. & Werny, P. Dictionnaire Francais-Allemand des Locutions. (Fr. & Ger.). 1976. $23.95 (ISBN 0-686-57124-X, M-6172). French & Eur.
Duden Francais Bildworterbuch Deutsch & Franzoesisch. (Illus.). 872p. (Ger. & Fr.). M.39.00 (ISBN 3-411-01954-9). Biblio Inst.

Eckel, Denis & Manfred, Hofer. Dictionnaire Allemand-Francais et Francais-Allemand. 1324p. (Fr. & Ger.). 1970. $25.95 (ISBN 0-686-57131-2, M-6184). French & Eur.

Franzoesisch, 2 vols. Incl. Teil I. Franzoesisch-Deutsch. Lange-Kowal, Ernst E., compiled by. 640p. DM.34.00 (04151); Teil II. Deutsch-Franzoesisch. rev. ed. Wilhelm, Kurt & Lange-Kowal, Ernst E., eds. 700p. 1983. DM.34.00 (04157). (Langenscheidts Handworterbucher Ser.). (Fr. & Ger.). DM.beide Teile in einem Band (1364p.) 49.00 (05153). Langenscheidt.

Franzoesisch, 2 vols. Incl. Teil I. Franz oesisch-Deutsch. Lange-Kowal, Ernst E. 1200p (07151); Deutsch-Franzoesisch. rev. ed. Lange-Kowal, Ernst E., rev. by. 1312p. 1982 (07157). (Langenscheidts Grosse Schulworterbucher Ser.). (Fr. & Ger.). DM.23.80 ea. Langenscheidt.

Franzoesisch, 2 vols. rev. ed. Incl. Teil I. Franzoesisch-Deutsch. Lange-Kowal, E. E. 576p. DM.16.80 (10151); Teil II. Deutsch-Franz oesisch. Weymuth, E. 640p. DM.16.80 (10156). (Langenscheidts Taschenworterbucher Ser.). (Fr. & Ger.). 1982. DM.beide Teile in einem Band 23.80 (11151). Langenscheidt.

Franzoesisch-Deutsch, Deutsch-Franzoesisch. (Langenscheidts Schulworterbucher Ser.). 576p. (Ger. & Fr.). DM.12.80 (13150). Langenscheidt.

Grappin, P. Dictionnaire moderne Larousse, francais-allemand et allemand-francais. (Fr. & Ger.). $39.95 (ISBN 2-03-020603-2, 3778). Larousse.

Knauer, Karl. Bertelsmann Woerterbuch Deutsch-Franzoesisch, Franzoesisch-Deutsch. 640p. (Ger. & Fr.). 1974. $17.50 (ISBN 3-570-01486-X, M-7307, Pub. by Bertelsmann Lexikon VVA). French & Eur.

--Bertelsmann Woerterbuch Deutsch-Franzoesisch, Franzoesisch-Deutsch. 640p. (Fr. & Ger.). 1974. DM.17.50 (ISBN 3-570-01486-X). C Bertelsmann.

Lange-Kowal & Ernst, E. Langenscheidts Taschenwoerterbuecher Franzoesisch-Deutsch. (Fr. & Ger.). 1978. DM.13.80 (ISBN 3-468-10150-3). Langenscheidt.

Lange-Kowal, Ernst E. Langenscheidts Grosse Schulwoerterbuch Deutsch-Franzoesisch. 1312p. (Ger. & Fr.). DM.23.80 (07157). Langenscheidt.

--Langenscheidts Handwoerterbuch: Teil II, Deutsch-Franzoesisch. 700p. (Ger. & Fr.). DM.34.00 (04157). Langenscheidt.

Lange-Kowal, Ernst E. & Beaucaire, Louis. Langenscheidts Handwoerterbuch: Franzoesisch-Deutsch Deutsch-Franzoesisch, 2 vols. in 1. 1320p. (Fr. & Ger.). DM.49.00 (05153). Langenscheidt.

--Langenscheidts Handwoerterbuch: Teil I, Franzoesisch-Deutsch. 640p. (Fr. & Ger.). DM.34.00 (04151). Langenscheidt.

Lange-Kowal, Ernst E. & Hartig, Paul. Langenscheidts Schulwoerterbuch Franzoesisch-Deutsch. 576p. (Fr. & Ger.). DM.13.80 (13150). Langenscheidt.

Lange-Kowal, Ernst E., ed. Langenscheidts Handwoerterbuecher: Tl 1, Franzoesisch-Deutsch. (Fr. & Ger.). 1978. DM.28.00 (ISBN 3-468-04151-9). Langenscheidt.

Langenscheidt Grossworterbucher Franzosisch, 2 pts. Rev. ed. Incl. Teil I. Franz o06sisch-Deutsch. Sachs, Karl & Villatte, C e01saire, eds. xxxii, 1047p. DM.108.00 (02151); Teil II. Deutsch-Franz o06sisch. Gottschalk, Walter & Bentot, Gaston, eds. xxxii, 1080p. DM.108.00 (02156); DM.nachtrag 1979 7.80 (02159). (Ger. & Fr.). 1979. Langenscheidt.

Langenscheidts Grosswoerterbuch Franzoesisch: Tl 2, Deutsch-Franzoesisch. (Ger. & Fr.). 1978. DM.78.00 (ISBN 3-468-02155-0). Langenscheidt.

Langenscheidts Lilliput-Woerterbuch Deutsch-Franzoesisch. 640p. (Ger. & Fr.). DM.3.00 (20001). Langenscheidt.

Langenscheidts Lilliput-Woerterbuch Franzoesisch-Deutsch. 640p. (Fr. & Ger.). DM.3.00 (20002). Langenscheidt.

Langenscheidts Lilliput-Woerterbucher Franzoesisch-Deutsch. (Fr. & Ger.). 1978. DM.2.20 (ISBN 3-468-20002-1). Langenscheidt.

Langenscheidts Lilliput-Woerterbuecher Deutsch-Franzoesisch. (Ger. & Fr.). 1978. DM.2.20 (ISBN 3-468-20001-3). Langenscheidt.

Langenscheidts Schulwoerterbuecher Franzoesisch-Deutsch. (Fr. & Ger.). 1978. DM.10.80 (ISBN 3-468-13150-X). Langenscheidt.

Langenscheidts Universal-Woerterbuecher Franzoesisch-Deutsch. (Fr. & Ger.). 1978. DM.5.80 (ISBN 3-468-18151-5). Langenscheidt.

Larousse & Co. Larousse de poche, francais-allemand et allemand-francais. (Fr. & Ger.). pap. $6.95 (ISBN 0-685-13959-X). Larousse.

Pinloche, A. Dictionnaire Francais-Allemand, Deutsch-Franzosisch. 805p. (Fr. & Ger.). Date not set. pap. $6.50 (ISBN 0-686-97409-3, M-9043). French & Eur.

Pinloche, A. & Jolivet, A. Dictionnaire Bilingue Larousse, Francais-Alemand et Allemand-Francais. (Apollo). (Fr. & Ger.). $10.50 (ISBN 0-685-13853-4, 3779). Larousse.

Roepke, F. Deutsch-Franzosisches Glossarium. 588p. (Ger. & Fr.). 1966. $35.00 (ISBN 3-7819-2006-2, M-7329, Pub. by Fritz Knapp Verlag). French & Eur.

Rotteck, ed. Dictionnaire Allemand-Francais, Francais-Allemand. 980p. (Fr. & Ger.). 1970. pap. $7.50 (ISBN 0-686-57093-6, M-6115). French & Eur.

Sachs, Karl & Villatte, Cesaire. Langenscheidts Grosswoerterbuch: Teil II, Deutsch-Franzoesisch. Gottschalk, Walter & Bentot, Gaston, eds. 1080p. (Ger. & Fr.). 1979. DM.118.00 (02156). Langenscheidt.

Weis, E. & Mattutat, H. Woerterbuch der Franzoesischen und Deutschen Sprache, Vol. 1. (Fr. & Ger.). $18.95 (ISBN 3-215-01824-1, M-7004). French & Eur.

--Woerterbuch der Franzoesischen und Deutschen Sprache, Vol. 2. (Ger. & Fr.). $18.95 (ISBN 3-215-01825-X, M-7003). French & Eur.

Weis, Erich & Mattutat, Heinrich. Dictionnaire Allemand-Francais. 570p. (Ger. & Fr.). 1977. $29.95 (ISBN 0-686-57259-9, M-6570). French & Eur.

--Dictionnaire Francais-Allemand et Allemand-Francais. 1022p. (Fr. & Ger.). 1977. $55.00 (ISBN 0-686-57260-2, M-6571). French & Eur.

Wilhelm, Kurt. Langenscheidts Grosse Schulwoerterbuecher Deutsch-Franzoesisch. 1400p. (Ger. & Fr.). 1977. DM.19.80 (ISBN 3-468-07156-6). Langenscheidt.

Wilhelm, Kurt, ed. Langenscheidts Handwoerterbuecher: Tl 2, Deutsch-Franzoesisch. (Ger. & Fr.). 1978. DM.28.00 (ISBN 3-468-04155-1). Langenscheidt.

GERMAN LANGUAGE–DICTIONARIES–ITALIAN

Altenberg, G. A. & Ubaldi, V. Dizionario Italiano-Tedesco, Tedesco-Italian. 395p. (Ger. & Ital.). 1979. leatherette $6.95 (ISBN 0-686-97349-6, M-9176). French & Eur.

Dizionario illustrato tedesco-italiano. (Illus.). 828p. (Ger. & Ital.). L.12000.00. Longanesi.

Frenzel, Herbert & Frenzel, Walter. Langenscheidts Handwoerterbuch Italienisch: Teil II, Deutsch-Italienisch. Macchi, Vladimiro, ed. 656p. (Ital. & Ger.). DM.39.80 (04186). Langenscheidt.

Frenzel, Herbert & Frenzel, Walter, eds. Langenscheidts Handwoerterbuecher: Tl 2, Deutsch-Italienisch. (Ger. & Ital.). 1978. DM.33.00 (ISBN 3-468-04185-3). Langenscheidt.

Giovannelli, Paolo, ed. Langenscheidts Handwoerterbuecher: Tl 1, Italienisch-Deutsch. (Ital. & Ger.). 1978. DM.33.00 (ISBN 3-468-04180-2). Langenscheidt.

Guarnieri, M. & Guarnieri, O. Dizionario Tecnico Tedesco-Italiano, Italiano-Tedesco Garzanti. 2032p. (Ger. & Ital.). 1979. $75.00 (ISBN 0-686-97355-0, M9184). French & eur.

Italienisch, 2 vols. Incl. Teil I. Italienish-Deutsch. Giovanelli, Paolo & Frenzel, Walter, eds. 568p. DM.39.80 (04180); Teil II. Deutsch-Italienisch. rev. ed. Frenzel, Herbert & Frenzel, Walter, eds. 656p. 1982. DM.39.80 (04186). (Langenscheidts Handworterbucher Ser.). (Ger. & Ital.). DM.biede Teile in einem Band 72.00 (05181). Langenscheidt.

Italienisch, 2 vols. Incl. Teil I. Italienisch-Deutsch. Macchi, V. 640p. DM.17.80 (10181); Teil II. Deutsch-Italienisch. Frenzel, W. 606p. DM.17.80 (10186). (Langenscheidts Taschenworterbucher Ser.). (Ital. & Ger.). DM.26.80 set (11181). Langenscheidt.

Langenscheidts Lilliput-Woerterbuch Deutsch-Italienisch. 640p. (Ger. & Ital.). DM.3.00 (20005). Langenscheidt.

Langenscheidts Lilliput-Woerterbuch Italienisch-Deutsch. 640p. (Ital. & Ger.). DM.3.00 (20006). Langenscheidt.

Langenscheidts Lilliput-Woerterbuecher Deutsch-Italienisch. (Ger. & Ital.). 1978. DM.2.20 (ISBN 3-468-20005-6). Langenscheidt.

Langenscheidts Lilliput-Woerterbuecher Italienisch-Deutsch. (Ital. & Ger.). 1978. DM.2.20 (ISBN 3-468-20006-4). Langenscheidt.

Langenscheidts Taschenwoerterbuecher Italienisch-Deutsch. (Ital. & Ger.). 1978. DM.13.80 (ISBN 3-468-10180-5). Langenscheidt.

Langenscheidts Universal-Woerterbuecher Italienisch-Deutsch. (Ital. & Ger.). 1978. DM.5.80 (ISBN 3-468-18181-7). Langenscheidt.

Lexikographischen Institut Sansoni, ed. Langenscheidts Grosswoerterbuch: Teil II, Deutsch-Italiensch. Macchi, Vladimiro. 938p. (Ger. & Ital.). DM.78.00 (02185). Langenscheidt.

Macchi, V. & Frenzel, W. Langenscheidts Taschenworterbuch Italienisch-Deutsch, 2 vols. in 1. (Ital. & Ger.). DM.27.80 (11181). Langenscheidt.

Macchi, Vladimiro, ed. Langenscheidts Grossworterbucher Italienisch, 2 vols. (Ger. & Ital.). Teil 1: Italienisch-Deutsch (xix, 786p.) DM.68.00 (02180); Teil 2: Deutsch-Italienisch (xvii, 938p.) DM.68.00 (02185). Langenscheidt.

Sansoni. Das Grosse Woerterbuch der Italienischen & Deutschen Sprache: Band I, Italienisch-Deutsch. 1472p. (Ital. & Ger.). 1982. DM.280.00. Brandstetter.

--Das Grosse Woerterbuch der Italienischen & Deutschen Sprache: Band II, Deutsch-Italienisch. 1596p. (Ger. & Ital.). 1982. DM.280.00. Brandstetter.

Schlegelmich, A. Worterbuch der Technik: Italienisch-Deutsch. 630p. (Ital. & Ger.). 1981. $95.00 (ISBN 3-7736-5110-4, M-122653). French & Eur.

Storni, Bruno. Schwierigkeiten des Deutsch-Italienischen Wortschatzes. Giovannelli, Paolo, ed. LC 76-455176. 335p. (Ital. & Ger.). 1975. DM.32.00 (ISBN 3-125-21500-5). Klett.

Von Macchi, Vladimiro. Langenscheidts Grosswoerterbuch Italienisch. 786p. (Ger. & Ital.). 1977. DM.48.00 (ISBN 3-468-02180-1). Langenscheidt.

--Langenscheidts Grosswoerterbuch Italienisch. 938p. (Ger. & Ital.). 1977. DM.48.00 (ISBN 3-468-02185-2). Langenscheidt.

Woerterbuch der Italienisch & Deutschen Sprache: Bd 1: Italienisch-Deutsch. (Ital. & Ger.). 1970. DM.280.00 (ISBN 3-87097-033-2). Brandstetter.

Woerterbuch der Italienisch & Deutschen Sprache: Bd 2: Deutsch-Italienisch. 1596p. (Ger. & Ital.). 1972. DM.280.00 (ISBN 3-87097-034-0). Brandstetter.

Woerterbuch der Italienischen und Deutschen Sprache, Vol. 1. (Ital. & Ger.). 1970. $225.00 (ISBN 3-87097-033-2, M-6992). French & Eur.

Woerterbuch der Italienischen und Deutschen Sprache, Vol. 2. (Ger. & Ital.). 1972. $225.00 (ISBN 3-87097-034-0, M-6991). French & Eur.

GERMAN LANGUAGE–DICTIONARIES–NORWEGIAN

Haukoy & Zickfeldt. German-Norwegian Dictionary. (Ger. & Norwegian.). 1976. write for info. (ISBN 82-573-0077-2). Kunnskapsforlaget.

Langenscheidts Handwoerterbuecher Norwegisch-Deutsch. (Norwegian & Ger.). 1978. DM.38.00 (ISBN 3-468-05240-5). Langenscheidt.

Langenscheidts Universal-Woerterbuecher Norwegisch-Deutsch. (Norwegian & Ger.). 1978. DM.5.80 (ISBN 3-468-18240-6). Langenscheidt.

Paulsen, Gerd. Norwegian-German Dictionary. (Norwegian & Ger.). 1979. write for info. (ISBN 8-25730-121-3). Kunnskapsforlaget.

Strom, D. & Strom, J. A. German-Norwegian Dictionary of Technical Terms. (Ger. & Norwegian.). 1983. write for info. (ISBN 82-573-0170-1). Kunnskapsforlaget.

--Norwegian-German Dictionary of Technical Terms. (Norwegian & Ger.). 1979. write for info. (ISBN 82-573-0136-1). Kunnskapsforlaget.

Von Trygue Alsos. Deutsch-Norwegisch-Deutsch. 553p. (Ger. & Norwegian.). 1981. pap. $7.95 (ISBN 82-573-0082-9, M-9438). French & Eur.

GERMAN LANGUAGE–DICTIONARIES–POLISH

Brzeska, Wanda & Brzeski, Alojzy. Ilustrowany Slownik Niemiecko-Polski. LC 75-547124. (Illus.). 995p. (Pol.). 1975. 150.00 Zl. Wiedza Powszechna.

Brzeska, Wanda, et al. Ilustrowany Slownik Niemiecko-Polski. LC 75-547124. 995p. (Ger. & Pol.). 1975. 150.00 Zl. Wiedza Powszechna.

Bzdega, A., et al. Podreczny Slownik Polsko-Niemiecki (Manual Dictionary Polish-German) 1018p. (Pol. & Ger.). 1977. leatherette $19.95 (ISBN 0-686-87194-4, M-0129). French & Eur.

Chodera & Kubica, eds. Langenscheidts Handwoerterbuecher Deutsch-Polnisch. (Ger. & Pol.). 1978. DM.38.00 (ISBN 3-468-04265-5). Langenscheidt.

Jozwicki, J. Minimum-Worterbuch: Deutsch-Polnisch, Polnisch-Deutsch. 557p. (Ger. & Pol.). 1980. pap. $4.95 (ISBN 83-214-0099-X). French & Eur.

Koch, Z. J. Polnisch-Deutsches Wissenschaftlich-Technishes Worterbuch. 598p. (Pol. & Ger.). 1980. $75.00 (ISBN 83-204-0021-X, M-9217). French & Eur.

Langenscheidts Handwoerterbuecher Polnisch-Deutsch. (Pol. & Ger.). 1966. DM.38.00 (ISBN 3-468-04261-2). Langenscheidt.

Langenscheidts Universal-Woerterbuecher Polnisch-Deutsch. (Pol. & Ger.). 1978. DM.5.80 (ISBN 3-468-18260-0). Langenscheidt.

Piprek, J. & Ippoldt, J. Grobworterbuch Polnisch-Deutsch. 2121p. (Ger. & Pol.). 1979. leatherette $75.00 (ISBN 83-214-0011-6, M-9128). French & Eur.

Piprek, Jan & Ippoldt, Juliusz. Wielki Slownik Polsko-Niemiecki: Grosswoerterbuch Polnische-Deutsch, 2 vols. LC 79-348368. (Pol. & Ger.). 1977. 650.00 Zl. Wiedza Powszechna.

Schimitzek, S., et al. Kleinworterbuch Deutsch-Polnisch (Handy German-Polish Dictionary) 652p. (Ger. & Pol.). 1977. $12.95 (ISBN 0-686-87188-X, M-9133). French & Eur.

Walewski, Stanislaw. Langenscheidts Taschenwoerterbuch Polnisch: Teil I, Polnisch-Deutsch. 624p. (Pol. & Ger.). DM.19.80 (10260). Langenscheidt.

--Polnisch, 2 vols. (Langenscheidts Taschenworterbucher Ser.). (Ger. & Pol.). Teil 1: Polnisch-Deutsch (624p.) DM.18.80 (10260); Teil 2: Deutsch-Polnisch (590p.) DM.18.80 (10265); DM.beide Teile in einem Band 29.80 (11260). Langenscheidt.

Wypych, Konrad. Deutsch Lehnwoerter in der Polnischen Bergbausprache. LC 77-463784. 267p. (Pol. & Ger.). 1976. DM.38.00. MG Schmitz.

GERMAN LANGUAGE–DICTIONARIES–POLYGLOT

Berset, F. Handelskorrenpondenz in Vier Sprachen. 253p. (Ger., Eng., Fr. & Span.). 1982. pap. $14.00. M Rosenberg.

Fachworterbuch Polygrafie: English-Deutsch-French-Russian-Spanish-Polish-Hungarian-Slowakian. 1019p. (Eng. & Deutsch & Fr. & Rus. & Span & Pol. & Hungarian & Slowakian.). 1980. leatherette $125.00 (ISBN 3-87150-141-7, M-11292). French & Eur.

Hoyer-Kreuter. Technological Dictionary in Three Languages, 3 vols. Schlomann, Alfred, ed. Incl. Vol. 1. German-English-French; Vol. 2. English-German-French; Vol. 3. French-German-English. (Ger., Fr. & Eng.). Set. $135.00 (ISBN 0-8044-0202-7). Ungar.

GERMAN LANGUAGE–DICTIONARIES–PORTUGUESE

Irmen, F. Langenscheidts Taschenwoerterbuch Portugiesisch: Teil I, Portugiesisch-Deutsch. 640p. (Port. & Ger.). DM.19.80 (10271). Langenscheidt.

--Langenscheidts Taschenwoerterbuecher Portugiesisch-Deutsch. (Port. & Ger.). 1978. DM.14.80 (ISBN 3-468-10270-4). Langenscheidt.

Langenscheidts Universal-Woerterbuecher Portugiesisch-Deutsch. (Port. & Ger.). 1978. DM.5.80 (ISBN 3-468-18270-8). Langenscheidt.

GERMAN LANGUAGE–DICTIONARIES–RUSSIAN

Bernstein, L. B. Deutsch-Russisches Worterbuch fur Wasserbau. 579p. (Rus. & Ger.). 1961. leatherette $19.95 (ISBN 0-686-92359-6, M-9100). French & Eur.

Bielfeldt, Hans H. Deutsch-Russiches Woerterbuch: S-Z, 3 vols, Vol. 3. Loetzsch, Ronald, ed. (Ger. & Rus.). 1984. M.38.00. Akad Verl Ath.

--Deutsch-Russisches Woerterbuch: A-G. Loetzsch, R., et al, eds. 1250p. (Ger. & Rus.). 1983. M.38.00 (LSV 0875). Akad Verl Ath.

--Deutsch-Russisches Woerterbuch: H-R, 3 vols, Vol. 2. Loetzsch, Ronald, ed. 1150p. (Ger. & Rus.). 1983. M.38.00. Akad Verl Ath.

Birkfellner, Gerhard, ed. Teutscher, & Reussischer, Dictionarium: Dictionarium Vindobonense. 960p. (Ger. & Rus.). 1983. M.120.00. Akad Verl Ath.

Blattner, Karl. Russisch, 2 vols. rev. ed. Incl. Teil I. Russisch-Deutsch. Orschel, H., rev. by. 568p. DM.18.80 (10290); Teil II. Deutsch-Russisch. Braun, M. & Pollok, K., eds. 604p. DM.18.80 (10295). (Langenscheidts Taschenworterbucher Ser.). (Ger. & Rus.). DM.biede Teile in einem Band 29.80 (11290). Langenscheidt.

Blattner, Karl & Orschel, H. Langenscheidts Taschenwoerterbuch Russisch: Teil I, Russisch-Deutsch. 568p. (Rus. & Ger.). DM.19.80 (10290). Langenscheidt.

Blattner, Karl, et al. Langenscheidts Taschenwoerterbuch Russisch, 2 vols. in 1. (Rus. & Ger.). DM.29.80 (11290). Langenscheidt.

Braun, M. & Pollok, K. Langenscheidts Taschenwoerterbuch Russisch: Teil II, Deutsch-Russisch. 604p. (Ger. & Rus.). DM.19.80 (10295). Langenscheidt.

Bunin, D. A., et al. Deutsch-Russisches Worterbuch fur Eisenbahnwessen. 531p. (Ger. & Rus.). 1957. $7.95 (ISBN 0-686-92383-9, M-9060). French & Eur.

Daum, Edmund & Schenk, W. Deutsch-Russisches Woerterbuch. 15th ed. (Ger. & Rus.). 1976. DM.13.50. Hueber.

--Russisch-Deutsches Woerterbuch. 7th ed. (Rus. & Ger.). 1976. $17.50 (ISBN 3-19-006219-6, M-7606, Pub. by Max Hueber). French & Eur.

--Russich-Deutsches Woerterbuch. 7th ed. (Ger. & Rus.). 1976. $17.50 (ISBN 3-19-006219-6). Hueber.

Gorski, N. N., et al. Deutsch-Russisches Worterbuch fur Ozeanographie. 240p. (Ger. & Rus.). 1957. leatherette $4.95 (ISBN 0-686-92378-2, M-9104). French & Eur.

Grischen, N. Deutsch-Russische Wirtschaftssprache. 480p. (Ger. & Rus.). 1969. $27.50 (ISBN 3-19-006207-2, M-7332, Pub. by M. Hueber). French & Eur.

--Deutsch-Russische Wirtschaftssprache. 480p. (Ger. & Rus.). 1969. DM.27.50 (ISBN 3-19-006207-2). Hueber.

Kratkii Russko-Nemetskii Frazeologicheskii Slovar. (Rus. & Ger.). 1977. $5.95 (Pub. by Russkii Iazyk). Four Continent.

Langenscheidts Universal-Woerterbuecher Russisch-Deutsch. (Rus. & Ger.). 1978. DM.5.80 (ISBN 3-468-18290-2). Langenscheidt.

Martschenko, W. G. Deutsch-Russisches Meteorologisches Worterbuch. 392p. (Ger. & Rus.). 1973. leatherette $12.95 (ISBN 0-686-92387-1, M-9092). French & Eur.

Mineralogy Dictionary, German-Russian, 2 Vols. 633p. (Ger. & Rus.). 1976. $19.95 (ISBN 0-686-87191-X, M-9112). French & Eur.

Nemetsko-Russkii Frazeologicheskii Slovar. 904p. (Ger. & Rus.). 1956. $3.30 (Pub. by GINS). Four Continent.

Orschel, H. Langenscheidts Taschenwoerterbuecher Russisch-Deutsch. (Rus. & Ger.). 1978. DM.14.80 (ISBN 3-468-10290-9). Langenscheidt.

Pawlow, E. A. & Semjonowa, O. I. Deutsch-Russisches Worterbuch der Forstund Holzwirtschaft. 477p. (Ger. & Rus.). 1978. $9.95 (ISBN 0-686-92498-3, M-9058). French & Eur.

Rahmanoba. German-Russian Dictionary. 556p. (Ger. & Rus.). 1957. $4.95 (ISBN 0-686-92465-7, M-9105). French & Eur.

Rakhmanov, I. V., ed. Nemetsko-Russkii Slovar. 557p. (Ger. & Rus.). 1956. $1.95 (Pub. by GINS). Four Continent.

--Nemetsko-Russkii Slovar. 556p. (Ger. & Rus.). 1958. $1.65 (Pub. by GINS). Four Continent.

Scharow, W. A. & Nowitschkowa, A. L. Deutsch-Russisches Worterbuch der Rechentechnik und Datenverarbeitung. 400p. (Ger. & Rus.). 1976. leatherette $12.50 (ISBN 0-686-92365-0, M-9057). French & Eur.

Sommerau, E. F. Nemetsko-Russkii Meditsinskii Slovar. 460p. (Ger. & Rus.). 1958. $4.95 (Pub. by Medgiz). Four Continent.

Strakhova, A. A., et al, eds. Russko-Nemetskii Slovar. 920p. (Rus.). 1960. $7.50 (Pub. by GINS). Four Continent.

Sulima-Samujillo, A. P., et al. Deutsch-Russisches Worterbuch fur Eisenbahnwesen. 536p. (German & Rus.). 1960. write for info. (M-9069). French & Eur.

Toporov, V. N. Prusskii Iazyk Slovar: E-H. 352p. (Ger. & Rus.). 1978. $8.50 (Pub. by Nauka). Four Continent.

Toprov, V. N. Prusskii Iazyk Slovar: I-L. 384p. (Ger. & Rus.). 1979. $7.95 (Pub. by Nauka). Four Continent.

GERMAN LANGUAGE–DICTIONARIES–SPANISH

Alvarez-Prada, Enrique. Langenscheidts Handwoerterbuch Spanisch: Teil II, Deutsch-Spanisch. 768p. (Span. & Ger.). DM.39.80 (04345). Langenscheidt.

Amador, E. F. Martinez. Diccionario Aleman-Espanol, Espanol-Aleman. 1616p. (Ger. & Span.). $50.95 (ISBN 84-303-0117-8, S-12381). French & Eur.

Amador, E. M. Martinez. Diccionario Manual Aleman-Espanol, Spanisch-Deutsch. 17th ed. 936p. (Ger. & Span.). 1977. $5.95 (ISBN 84-7183-002-7, S-50382). French & Eur.

--Diccionario Manual Amador Aleman-Espanol, Espanol-Aleman. 1400p. (Ger. & Span.). $17.95 (ISBN 84-303-0118-6, S-50385). French & Eur.

Diccionario Cuyas: Spanish-German, German-Spanish. (Span. & Ger.). $6.00x (ISBN 0-686-00851-0). Colton Bk.

Diccionario Iter Aleman-Espanol, Espanol-Aleman. 512p. (Ger. & Span.). 1977. leatherette $6.75 (ISBN 84-303-0127-5, S-50377); pap. $5.95 (ISBN 84-303-0126-7, S-50376). French & Eur.

Diccionario Lexicon, Aleman-Espanol, Espanol-Aleman. 400p. (Ale. -Espn.). $5.75 (ISBN 0-686-57343-9, S-31392). French & Eur.

Diccionario Universal Herder Aleman-Espanol, Espanol-Aleman. 4th ed. 388p. (Ger. & Span.). 1977. leatherette $4.50 (ISBN 84-254-0782-6, S-50378). French & Eur.

Haberkamp de Anton, G. Langenscheidts Taschenwoerterbuch Spanisch: Teil I, Spanisch-Deutsch. 544p. (Span & Ger.). DM.18.80 (10341). Langenscheidt.

Haberkamp de Anton, G. & Willers, D. H. Langenscheidts Taschenwoerterbuch Spanisch, 2 vols. in 1. (Span. & Ger.). DM.27.80 (11341). Langenscheidt.

Haensch, Gunther. Diccionario Moderno Herder Aleman-Espanol, Espanol-Aleman. 684p. (Ger. & Span.). 1977. $16.75 (ISBN 84-254-0652-8, S-50379). French & Eur.

Langenscheidts Lilliput-Woerterbuch Deutsch-Spanisch. 640p. (Ger. & Span.). DM.3.00 (20017). Langenscheidt.

Langenscheidts Lilliput-Woerterbuch Spanisch-Deutsch. 640p. (Span. & Ger.). DM.3.00 (20018). Langenscheidt.

Langenscheidts Lilliput-Woerterbuecher Deutsch-Spanisch. (Ger. & Span.). 1978. DM.2.20 (ISBN 3-468-20017-X). Langenscheidt.

Langenscheidts Lilliput-Woerterbuecher Spanisch-Deutsch. (Span. & Ger.). 1978. DM.2.20 (ISBN 3-468-20018-8). Langenscheidt.

Langenscheidts Reisewoerterbuecher Spanisch-Deutsch. (Span. & Ger.). DM.9.80 (ISBN 3-468-14340-0). Langenscheidt.

Langenscheidts Universal-Woerterbuecher Spanisch-Deutsch. (Span. & Ger.). 1978. DM.5.80 (ISBN 3-468-18341-0). Langenscheidt.

Lerche, Mario R. Deutsch-Spanisches Glossarium. 460p. (Ger. & Span.). 1967. $17.50 (ISBN 3-7819-2012-7, S-7347, Pub. by Fritz Knapp Verlag). French & Eur.

Mink, H. Diccionario Tecnico Aleman-Espanol, Espanol-Aleman, 2 vols. 3rd ed. 2530p. (Span. & Ger.). 1978. Set. $120.00 (ISBN 84-254-0704-4, S-50189). French & Eur.

Mueller, Heinz & Haensch, Guenther, eds. Langenscheidts Handwoerterbuecher: Tl 1, Spanisch-Deutsch. (Span. & Ger.). 1978. DM.33.00 (ISBN 3-468-04340-6). Langenscheidt.

Muller. Diccionario Aleman-Espanol, Espanol-Aleman. 900p. (Ger. & Span.). leatherette $12.25 (ISBN 84-303-0119-4, S-50384). French & Eur.

Muller, F. Atheneum Worterbuch: Aleman-Espanol, Espanol-Aleman. 383p. (Ger. & Span.). 1979. pap. $5.25 (ISBN 84-303-0800-8, S-35066). French & Eur.

Muller, Hans. Diccionario Lexicon Aleman-Espanol, Espanol-Aleman. 384p. (Ger. & Span.). 1977. pap. $4.50 (ISBN 84-303-0124-0, S-31392). French & Eur.

Muller, Heinz & Haensch, Gunther. Langenscheidts Handwoerterbuch Spanisch: Teil I, Spanisch-Deutsch. 640p. (Span. & Ger.). DM.39.80 (04340). Langenscheidt.

Muller, Heinz, et al. Langenscheidts Handwoerterbuch Spanisch-Deutsch, 2 vols. in 1. (Span. & Ger.). DM.72.00 (05340). Langenscheidt.

Slaby & Grossmann. Woerterbuch der Spanischen & Deutschen Sprache: Band II, Deutsch-Spanisch. 1256p. (Ger. & Span.). 1982. DM.100.00. Brandstetter.

--Woerterbuch der Spanischen & Deutschen Sprache: Band I, Spanisch-Deutsch. 1188p. (Span. & Ger.). 1982. DM.100.00. Brandstetter.

Slaby, R. J. & Grossman, R., eds. Spanish & German Dictionary, 2 vols. Incl. Vol. 1. Spanish-German. 17.00 (ISBN 0-8044-0581-6); Vol. 2. German-Spanish. 28.00 (ISBN 0-8044-0582-4). 2172p. (Span. & Ger.). Set. $45.00 (ISBN 0-8044-0580-8). Ungar.

Slaby, Rudolf. Diccionario De las Lenguas Espanola y Alemana, 2 vols. 3rd ed. 2422p. (Ger. & Span.). 1977. Set. $110.00 (ISBN 84-254-0694-3, S-50380). French & Eur.

--Woerterbuch der Deutschen und Spanischen Sprache, Vol. 1. 3rd ed. (Ger. & Span.). 1975. $76.00 (ISBN 3-87097-067-7, M-7024). French & Eur.

--Woerterbuch der Deutschen und Spanischen Sprache, Vol. 2. 2nd ed. (Ger. & Span.). 1973. $66.00 (ISBN 3-87097-040-5, M-7023). French & Eur.

Spanisch, 2 vols. Incl. Teil I. Spanisch-Deutsch. Mueller, Heinz & Haensch, Guenther. 640p. DM.39.80 (03340); Teil II. Deutsch-Spanisch. Alvarez-Prada, Enrique. 768p. DM.39.80 (04345). (Langenscheidts HandworterbucherSer.). (Span. & Ger.). DM.beide Teile in einem Band 72.00 (05340). Langenscheidt.

Spanisch, 2 vols. Incl. Teil I. Spanisch-Deutsch. rev. ed. Haberkamp de Anton, G., ed. 544p. 1980. DM.17.80 (10341); Teil II. Deutsch-Spanisch. Willers, D. H. 511p. DM.17.80 (10345). (Langenscheidts Taschenworterbucher Ser.). (Span. & Ger., Unter Berucksichtigung der Sudamerikanismen). DM.beide Teile in einem Band 26.80 (11341). Langenscheidt.

Strutz, Henry. Zwei Hundert Eins Spanische Verben. (Ger. & Span.). 1981. pap. $3.95 (ISBN 0-8120-0688-7). Barron.

Von Baumgart, Arturo E. Langenscheidts Fachwoerterbuecher Deutsch-Spanisch. (Ger. & Span.). 1960. DM.39.00 (ISBN 3-468-49150-6). Langenscheidt.

Willers, D. H. Langenscheidts Taschenwoerterbuch Spanisch: Teil II, Deutsch-Spanisch. 511p. (Ger. & Span.). DM.18.80 (10345). Langenscheidt.

Willers, H. Langenscheidts Taschenwoerterbuecher Spanisch-Deutsch. (Span. & Ger.). 1978. DM.13.80 (ISBN 3-468-10340-9). Langenscheidt.

GERMAN LANGUAGE–DICTIONARIES–SWEDISH

German-Swedish-German Dictionary. (Ger. & Swedish.). $9.95 (ISBN 0-686-92401-0, M-9448). French & Eur.

Kornitzky, H. Langenscheidts Taschenwoerterbuch Schwedisch, 2 vols. in 1. (Swedish & Ger.). DM.29.80 (11300). Langenscheidt.

––Langenscheidts Taschenwoerterbuch Schwedisch: Teil II, Deutsch-Schwedisch. 510p. (Ger. & Swedish.). DM.19.80 (10305). Langenscheidt.

––Langenscheidts Taschenwoerterbuch Schwedisch: Teil I, Schwedisch-Deutsch. 573p. (Swedish & Ger.). DM.19.80 (10300). Langenscheidt.

––Schwedisch, 2 vols. (Langenscheidts Taschenworterbucher Ser.). (Ger. & Swedish.). Teil 1: Schwedisch-Deutsch (xvi, 557p.) DM.18.80 (10300); Teil 2: Deutsch-Schwedisch (xv, 510p.) DM.18.80 (10305); DM.Beide Teile in einem Band 29.80 (11300). Langenscheidt.

Langenscheidts Handwoerterbuch Schwedisch PRISMA. 640p. (Swedish & Ger.). DM.48.00 (04300). Langenscheidt.

Langenscheidts Taschenwoerterbuecher Schwedisch-Deutsch. (Swedish & Ger.). 1978. DM.14.80 (ISBN 3-468-10300-X). Langenscheidt.

GERMAN LANGUAGE–ETYMOLOGY

Corominas, Joan. Breve Diccionario Etimologico de la Lengua Castellana. (Span.). pap. $32.00 (GRD). Lectorum Pubns.

Jacobs, Werner. Systematische Zoologie Insekten. LC 76-483862. 377p. (Ger.). 1975. write for info. (ISBN 3-437-30195-0). Fischer Verlag.

GERMAN LANGUAGE–FOREIGN WORDS AND PHRASES

Gurst, G., et al, eds. Kleines Fremdwoerterbuch. 7th ed. 400p. (Ger.). 1982. M.9.80. Bibl Inst Leipzig.

Roehrich, L. Lexikon der Sprichwoertlichen Redensarten, 2 vols. (Illus.). 1256p. (Ger.). $130.00 set. M Rosenberg.

Stoetzer, U., ed. Grosses Woerterbuck der Deutschen Aussprache. 592p. (Ger.). 1982. M.26.00. Bibl Inst Leipzig.

GERMAN LANGUAGE–GLOSSARIES, VOCABULARIES, ETC.

Banvard, Paul & Kuhn, Pierre. Vocabulaire Progressif de l'allemand. (Illus.). 224p. (Ger.). 1976. 47.50 F. CDU.

Borel, Pierre. Vocabulaire Systematique Francais-Allemand. 171p. (Fr. & Ger.). 1959. 9.80 F. Francke.

Chassard, Jean & Weil, Gonthier. Vocabulaire Allemand. (Ger.). 1969. 13.60 F. Hachette.

Glossar & Erlaeuterungen zur Grammatik Deutsch-Englisch. 72p. (Ger. & Eng.). 1983. $3.25. M Rosenberg.

Glossar Deutsch-Englisch. 50p. (Ger. & Eng.). 1983. pap. $2.90. M Rosenberg.

Glossar Deutsch-Englisch. 68p. (Ger. & Eng.). 4ap. $4.10. M Rosenberg.

Johnson, Arta F. How to Read German Church Records Without Knowing Much German. LC 80-128394. (Illus.). 48p. (Ger.). 1980. write for info. Johnson.

Michea, Rene. Vocabulaire Allemand Progressif & livret d'exercices. 40p. (Fr. & Eng.). 1959. 21.70 F. Didier.

Roepke & Haefner. Deutsch-Franzoesisches Glossarium: Finanzieller und Wirtschaftlicher Fachausdrueke. 6th ed. 475p. (Ger. & Fr.). 1982. 325.00 F. Maison Dictionnaire.

Roepke, F. Deutsch-Franzosisches Glossarium. 588p. (Ger. & Fr.). 1966. $35.00 (ISBN 3-7819-2006-2, M-7329, Pub. by Fritz Knapp Verlag). French & Eur.

Scheid, O. N. Vocabulaire Allemand par l'image. 80p. (Ger.). 1971. 15.00 F. Bordas-Dunod.

Schmidt, Karl A. Easy Ways to Enlarge Your German Vocabulary. LC 73-92020. (Orig., Ger. & Eng.). 1974. $4.50 (ISBN 0-486-23044-9). Dover.

Vocabularios Aleman-Espanol-Polaco. (Ger. , Span. & Pol.). $0.80; Mex.$10.00. Novaro.

Wadepuhl, Walter & Morgan, Bayard. Minimum Standard German Vocabulary. (Ger.). 1982. pap. text ed. 4.95x (ISBN 0-89197-549-7). Irvington.

Zahn, Hans E. Englisch-Deutsches Glossarium. 528p. (Eng. & Ger., English - German Glossary). 1977. $78.50 (ISBN 3-7819-2013-5, M-7355, Pub. by Fritz Knapp Verlag). French & Eur.

GERMAN LANGUAGE–GRAMMAR

Bohusch, Otmar. Lexikon der Grammatischen Terminologie. 336p. (Ger.). DM.22.80 (ISBN 3-40300-298-5). Auer.

Eggeling, H. F. Dictionary of Modern German Prose Usage. (Ger.). 1961. $34.00x (ISBN 0-19-864110-9). Oxford U Pr.

Konrad, Roselinde. Reviewing German Grammar & Building Vocabulary. LC 80-6238. 415p. (Ger.). 1981. pap. text ed. $19.75 (ISBN 0-8191-1605-X). U Pr of Amer.

GERMAN LANGUAGE–IDIOMS, CORRECTIONS, ERRORS

Borovski, Conrad. Active German Idioms. 64p. (Ger. & Eng.). 1974. DM.pap. 8.00. Hueber.

Cassell, Cassell's Colloquial German. 176p. (Ger.). pap. $3.95 (ISBN 0-02-079410-X). Macmillan.

Duden, R. Duden-Stilwoerterbuch. 5th rev. ed. (Der Grosse Duden: Vol. 2). (Ger.). $15.95 (ISBN 3-411-00902-0). Adler.

Engeroff, K. & Lovelace-Kaeufer, C. English-German Dictionary of Idioms. (Eng. & Ger.). $22.75 (ISBN 3-1900-6217-X). Adler.

Rechtschaffen, Bernard & Marck, Louis. Two Thousand & One German & English Idioms: 2001 Deutsche und Englische Idiome. (Ger. & Eng.). 1984. pap. $9.95 (ISBN 0-8120-0474-4). Barron.

Taylor, Ronald J. & Gottschalk, W. German-English Dictionary of Idioms. (Eng. & Ger.). $30.00 (ISBN 3-19-006216-1). Adler.

GERMAN LANGUAGE–ORTHOGRAPHY AND SPELLING

Woerterbuch zur Rechtschreibung. (Ger.). DM.5.20 (ISBN 3-12-216800-6). Klett.

GERMAN LANGUAGE–PRONUNCIATION

Krech, Hans. Woerterbuch der Deutschen Aussprache. 2nd ed. 549p. (Ger.). 1967. $19.95 (ISBN 0-686-56643-2, M-7033). French & Eur.

GERMAN LANGUAGE–SLANG–DICTIONARIES

Juncker. Junckers Worterbuch German-American Slang. Seiffhart, Arthur, ed. (Eng. & Ger.). 1968. $3.00 (ISBN 0-685-06570-7). Assoc Bk.

Kuepper, Heinz. ABC-Komiker bis Zwitschergemuese. LC 79-366187. xxiii, 229p. (Ger.). 1978. DM.24.80 (ISBN 3-88228-001-8). Deutsche Sprache.

Nusser, Peter, ed. Anzeigenwerbung: Ein Reader fuer Studenten & Lehrer der Deutscher Sprache & Literatur. LC 77-460308. 274p. (Ger.). 1975. DM.19.80 (ISBN 3-77051-224-3). Fink Verlag.

Puchner, Guenter. Sprechen Sie Rotwelsch. LC 76-456534. 62p. (Ger.). 1975. write for info. (ISBN 3-77650-202-9). Heimeran.

GERMAN LANGUAGE–SPOKEN GERMAN

Eichborn, R. Woerterbuch fuer Wirtschaft-Recht-Verkehr-Verwaltungs & Umgangssprache: Vol.I, Englisch-Deutsch. rev. ed. 1150p. (Ger. & Eng.). 1983. $124.00. M Rosenberg.

––Woerterbuch fuer Wirtschaft-Recht-Verkehr-Verwaltungs & Umgangssprache: Vol. II, Deutch-Englisch. 1150p. (Ger. & Eng.). 1982. $124.00. M Rosenberg.

Rakhmanov, I. V., ed. Slovar Naibolee Upotrebitel'Nykh Slov Anglii-Skogo, Nemetskogo & Frantsuzskogo Iazykov. 582p. (Rus., Ger. & Fr.). 1960. $2.40 (Pub. by Izd. Inostr. & Natsional'Nal'Nykh Slovarei). Four Continent.

GERMAN LANGUAGE–STUDY AND TEACHING

Grimm, Jacob & Grimm, Wilhelm. Deutsches Woerterbuch, 33 vols. (Ger.). 1973. Repr. Set. $3150.00 (ISBN 0-685-30396-9). Adler.

Hausmann, Franz J. Einfuehrung in die Benutzung der Neufranzoesischen Woerterbucher. LC 77-478069. 166p. (Fr. & Ger.). 1977. write for info. (ISBN 3-484-50090-5). Niemeyer Verlag.

GERMAN LANGUAGE–SYNONYMS AND ANTONYMS

Farrell, R. B. Dictionary of German Synonyms. 3rd ed. LC 75-36175. (Ger.). 1977. $54.50 (ISBN 0-521-21189-1); pap. $14.95 (ISBN 0-521-29068-6). Cambridge U Pr.

Farrell, Ralph B. Dictionary of German Synonyms. 3rd ed. LC 75-36175. ix, 412p. (Eng. & Ger.). 1977. $17.00 (ISBN 0-521-21189-1); $7.50 (ISBN 0-521-29068-6). Cambridge U Pr.

Goerner, H. & Kempcke, G., eds. Synonymwoerterbuch. 7th ed. 643p. (Ger.). 1982. M.22.00. Bibl Inst Leipzig.

GERMAN LANGUAGE–TEXTBOOKS FOR FOREIGNERS

see also German Language–Conversation and Phrase Books

Strasak & Sulek. Technisches Deutsch fuer Auslaender. 156p. (Ger.). DM.16.00. Brandstetter.

GERMAN LITERATURE–HISTORY AND CRITICISM

Braasch, Theodor. Vollstaendiges Woerterbuch Zur Sogenannten Caedmonschen Genesis. (Ger.). 1933. $17.95 (ISBN 3-533-00946-7, M-7682, Pub. by Carl Winter). French & Eur.

––Vollstaendiges Woerterbuch Zur Sogenannten Caedmonschen Genesis. (Ger.). 1933. $17.95 (ISBN 3-533-00946-7). Winter Univ.

GERMAN MUSIC
see Music, German

GERMAN POETRY–HISTORY AND CRITICISM

Capelle, Carl. Volistaendiges Woerterbuch Ueber die Gedichte des Homores und der Homeriden. 9th ed. (Ger.). 1968. $48.00 (ISBN 3-534-03408-2, M-7681, Pub. by Wissenschaftl Buchgesells). French & Eur.

GERMAN PORCELAIN
see Porcelain

GERMANIC LANGUAGES

see also Danish Language; Dutch Language; English Language; Friesian Language; German Language; Icelandic and Old Norse Languages; Low German Language; Norwegian Language; Scandinavian Languages; Swedish Language

Jones, William J. Lexicon of French Borrowings in the German Vocabulary. (Studia Linguistica Germanica Ser.: No. 12). (Fr. & Ger.). 1976. $79.50x (ISBN 3-11-004769-1). De Gruyter.

GERMANY

Here are entered works on Germany for the pre-1949 period, the Territories under Allied Occupation, and East Germany and West Germany, collectively, for the post-1949 period.
see also Germany, East; Germany, West;
also specific cities, areas, etc. in Germany

Endres, Edmund. Moselfraenkische Mundart. LC 80-471656. 94p. (Ger.). 1979. write for info. (ISBN 3-79270-488-9). Rheinland Verlag.

Hanle, Adolf. Meyers Neues Lexikon Weltatlas. 354p. (Ger.). write for info. (ISBN 3-411-01759-7). Biblio Inst.

GERMANY–DESCRIPTION AND TRAVEL

Siefert, Fritz. Das Lexikon der Deutschen Staedt und Gemeinden. (Ger.). 1973. $25.00 (ISBN 3-517-00453-7, M-7261). French & Eur.

GERMANY–HISTORY

Blaschke, Karlheinz, et al. Lexikon Staedte & Wappen der Deutschen Demokratischen Republik. 1st ed. LC 80-460533. (Illus.). 526p. (Ger.). 1979. M.25.00. VEB Verlag Enzyklopadie.

Taddey, Gerhard. Lexikon der Deutschen Geschichte. (Ger.). 1977. $99.50 (ISBN 3-520-81301-7, M-7263). French & Eur.

Taddey, Gerhard, ed. Lexikon der Deutschen Geschichte. 1120p. (Ger.). 1977. DM.125.00 (ISBN 3-520-81301-7). Kroener.

GERMANY–HISTORY–1789-1900

Here are entered works in the period between 1789 and 1900 either as a whole or in part, except those subdivisions immediately below.

Fest, Wilfried. Dictionary of German History 1806-1945. LC 78-54658. 1979. $27.50x (ISBN 0-312-20103-6). St Martin.

GERMANY–HISTORY–20TH CENTURY

Fest, Wilfried. Dictionary of German History 1806-1945. LC 78-54658. 1979. $27.50x (ISBN 0-312-20103-6). St Martin.

GERMANY–HISTORY, NAVAL

Witthoeft, Hans. Lexikon der Deutschen Marinegeschichte. (Ger.). 1977. $35.00 (ISBN 3-7822-0144-2, M-7262). French & Eur.

GERMANY–NAVY

Witthoeft, Hans J., ed. Lexikon der Deutschen Marinegeschichte. 300p. (Ger.). 1977. DM.44.00 (ISBN 3-7822-0144-2). Koehlers Verlag.

GERMANY, DEMOCRATIC REPUBLIC OF
see Germany, East

GERMANY, EAST

Here are entered works on the present Democratic Republic, and works on the eastern part of the former jurisdiction, Germany.

Arlt, Reiner, et al, eds. Lexikon Recht der Landwirtschaft der Deutschen Demokratischen Republik. LC 76-487653. 397p. (Ger.). 1975. M.10.50. Staatsdruk.

Blaschke, Karlheinz, et al. Lexikon Staedte & Wappen der Deutschen Demokratischen Republik. 1st ed. LC 80-460533. (Illus.). 526p. (Ger.). 1979. M.25.00. VEB Verlag Enzyklopadie.

GERMANY, EAST–POLITICS AND GOVERNMENT

Tautz, G. BI-Taschenlexikon Orden, Preise & Medaillen Staatliche Auszeichnungen der DDR. 199p. (Ger.). 1980. M.16.00. Bibl Inst Leipzig.

GERMANY, EASTERN
see Germany, East

GERMANY, FEDERAL REPUBLIC OF
see Germany, West

GERMANY, WEST

Here are entered works on the present Federal Republic, and works on the western part of the former jurisdiction, Germany.

Institut International de Terminologie Juridique & Administrative. Niederlassungsrecht. 145p. (Ger. & Fr.). 1976. DM.15.80. Langen AG.

Wacker, Wilhelm H., ed. Steuerlexikon. LC 75-514753. xii, 486p. (Ger.). 1975. DM.45.80 (ISBN 3-800-60472-8). Vahlen.

GERMANY, WESTERN
see Germany, West

GESTURE LANGUAGE
see Deaf–Means of Communication

GIKUYU LANGUAGE
see Kikuyu Language

GILBERT, WILLIAM SCHWENCK, SIR, 1836-1911

Dunn, George E. A Gilbert & Sullivan Dictionary. LC 72-10177. 1972. Repr. of 1936 ed. lib. bdg. $25.00 (ISBN 0-8414-0683-9). Folcroft.

GIMBALA LANGUAGE
see Congo Language

GIPSIES

Moreno Castro, Pablo-Carrillo & Reyes, Juan R. Diccionario Gitano. 82p. (Span.). 1981. 900.00 ptas (ISBN 84-300-4410-8). Piquenas Edit.

GLADNESS
see Happiness

GLASS–DICTIONARIES
Newman, Harold. An Illustrated
Dictionary of Glass. (Illus.). 1978.
$29.95 (ISBN 0-500-23262-8).
Thames Hudson.
VonZweck, Dina. Woman's Day
Dictionary of Glass. 1983. pap.
$4.95 (ISBN 0-8065-0841-8).
Citadel Pr.
GLASS, ORNAMENTAL
Society of Glass Decorations.
Glossary of Decorating
Terminology. (Publications). 1982.
$50.00; $13.00, members. Soc
Glass Decorators.
GLASS MANUFACTURE
see also Optical Instruments
Hoffman, E. Fachwoerterbuch fuer
die Glasindustriel. 160p. (Ger. &
Eng.). 1963. DM.36.00 (ISBN 3-
540-03007-7). Springer-Verlag.
Hoffmann, E. Fachwoerterbuch Fuer
die Glasindustriel. 160p. (Ger. &
Eng., Dictionary doe the Glass
Industry). 1963. 36.00 (ISBN 3-
540-03007-7, M-7396, Pub. by
Springer). French & Eur.
ICG. Dictionary of Glass Making.
402p. (Eng., Fr. & Ger.). 1983.
$106.50 (ISBN 0-444-42048-7).
Elsevier.
GLASS TRADE
Hoffmann, E. Fachwoerterbuch Fuer
die Glasindustriel. 160p. (Ger. &
Eng., Dictionary doe the Glass
Industry). 1963. 36.00 (ISBN 3-
540-03007-7, M-7396, Pub. by
Springer). French & Eur.
GLOBULAR PROTEINS
see Proteins
GNOMES (MAXIMS)
*see Aphorisms and Apothegms;
Maxims; Proverbs*
GOBBLEDYGOOK
see Languages, Mixed
GODS
see also Myth
Chastel, Pierre. Lexique des Dieux.
110p. (Fr.). 1968. 12.00 F.
Delpire.
**GOETHE, JOHANN WOLFGANG
VON, 1749-1832**
Dobel, Richard, ed. Lexikon der
Goethe-Zitate. viii, 654p. (Ger.).
1978. DM.78.00 (ISBN 3-7608-
0139-0); $150.00 (ISBN 3-7608-
0140-4). Artemis Verlag.
GOLF
Langdon, David. How to Talk Golf:
David Langdon's A-Z of Golfing
Terms. LC 76-353017. (Illus.).
80p. (Eng.). 1975. E1.75 (ISBN 0-
413-34250-6). Spon Ltd.
Taylor, Hugh. Golf Dictionary.
$7.50x (ISBN 0-392-12072-0,
SpS). Sportshelf.
GOLF COURSES
United States Golf Association.
Dictionary of Turfgrass Terms.
$0.50 (016). US Golf Assn.
GOLF-LINKS
see Golf Courses
GONJA LANGUAGE
Amankwaah, J. W. & Rytz, O., eds.
Gonja-English Dictionary &
Spelling Book. LC 79-303260. v,
273p. (Gonja & Eng.). 1977. write
for info. Inst Afr Stu.
GORKHALI LANGUAGE
see Nepali Language
GOTHIC ARCHITECTURE
see Architecture, Gothic
GOVERNMENT
*see Civics; Political Science;
also subdivision Politics and
Government under names of
countries, states, etc., e.g. United
States–Politics and government; New
York (state) State Politics and
Government*
GOVERNMENT EMPLOYEES
see Civil Service
GOVERNORS (MACHINERY)
Standard Terminology & Definition
for Filled Thermal Systems for
Remote Sensing Temperature
Regulators: FCI 70-1. $2.00. Fluid
Controls.
Standard Terminology for Regulators:
FCI 71-1. $2.00. Fluid Controls.
GRAIN
Vocabolario degli accademici della
Crusca. 1260p. (Ital.). 1976.
L.90000.00. Licosa.
Vocabolario degli accademici della
Crusca. 1260p. (Ital.). 1976.
L.78000.00. Licosa.
GRAMMAR
*see Grammar, Comparative and
General;*

*also subdivision Grammar under
names of languages, e.g. English
Language–Grammar*
**GRAMMAR, COMPARATIVE
AND GENERAL**
see also Language and Languages
Bohusch, Otmar. Lexikon der
Grammatischen Terminologie.
(Ger.). 1972. $27.50 (ISBN 3-403-
00298-5, M-7254). French & Eur.
Kiefer, Ferenc, ed. Morphologie &
Generative Grammatik. LC 76-
450339. (Illus.). xix, 289p. (Ger.).
1975. DM.44.00 (ISBN 3-799-
70628-3). Akad Verl Ath.
Millan Contreras. Diccionario
Internacional Abreviado de Siglas,
Contracciones & Abreviaturas.
(Span.). 1974. 350.00 ptas (ISBN
8-42830-539-0). Paraninfo.
Millan Contreras, Donato.
Diccionario Internacional de
Siglas, Contracciones &
Abreviaturas. 240p. (Span.). 1974.
200.00 ptas (ISBN 84-283-0539-0).
Paraninfo.
Osterreichisches Linguistisches
Programm. Wortbildung Diachron,
Synchron. Panagl, Oswald, ed. LC
78-356489. (Illus.). 157p. (Ger.).
1976. S.200.00 (ISBN 3-851-
24533-4). Inst Verg Sprach.
Pallas, Peter S. Linquarum Totius
Orbis Vocabularia Comparativa,
Vol. 1. 411p. (Rus.). 1977. Repr.
of 1786 ed. lib. bdg. $49.00x
(ISBN 3-87118-285-0, Pub. by
Helmut Buske Verlag Hamburg).
Benjamins North Am.
--Linquarum Totius Orbis
Vocabularia Comparativa, Vol. 2.
491p. (Rus.). 1978. Repr. of 1789
ed. lib. bdg. $57.00x (ISBN 3-
87118-286-9, Pub. by Helmut
Buske Verlag Hamburg).
Benjamins North Am.
Turner, L. D. Notes on the Sounds &
Vocabulary of Gullah.
(Publications of the American
Dialect Society: No. 3). 28p. 1945.
pap. $2.50x (ISBN 0-8173-0603-
X). U of Ala Pr.
**GRAMMAR, COMPARATIVE
AND GENERAL–PHONOLOGY**
Wang, W. The Lexicon in
Phonological Change.
(Monographs on Linguistics
Analysis: No. 5). 1977. 62.00
(ISBN 90-279-7814-X). Mouton.
Wiedert, Alfons. Tai-Khamti
Phonology & Vocabulary. LC 77-
479800. 92p. (Khamti.). 1977.
write for info (ISBN 3-515-02582-
0). Steiner Verlag.
GRAPHIC ARTS
*see also Bookbinding; Drawing;
Engraving; Printing As a Graphic
Art; Prints*
Born, Ernst. Lexikon Fuer Die
Graphische Industrie. 2nd ed.
(Ger.). $95.00 (ISBN 3-87641-184-
X, M-7201). French & Eur.
Comte, Rene & Pernin, Andre.
Lexique des Industries Graphiques.
125p. (Fr.). 1974. 35.00 F. Comp
Fr Edns.
Definitions of Graphic Arts Terms.
1964. $4.00 (399-2); members
$2.67. TAPPI.
GRAPHIC ARTS–DICTIONARIES
Comte, R. & Pernin, A. Lexique des
Industries Graphiques. (Fr.).
1975. pap. $17.50 (ISBN 0-686-
56959-8, M-6082). French & Eur.
Dictionary for the Graphic Arts:
German-English, English-German.
(Ger. & Eng.). 1979. plastic bdg.
26.25 (ISBN 3-87641-198-9).
Perfect Graphic.
Dictionary for the Graphic Arts in
Eight Languages: German-English-
French-Spanish-Russian-
Hungarian-Polish-Slowak. (Ger. ,
Eng. , Fr. , Span. , Rus. , Pol. ,
Hungarian & Slovak.). 1979. plastic
bdg. 109.00 (ISBN 3-87641-192-0).
Perfect Graphic.
Mintz, Patricia. Dictionary of
Graphic Arts Terms: A
Communication Tool for People
Who Buy Type & Printing. 328p.
1981. text ed. $17.95 (ISBN 0-
442-26711-8). Van Nos Reinhold.
Muller, W., ed. Dictionary of the
Graphic Arts Industry. (Eng., Ger.,
Fr., Rus., Span., Pol., Slovak &
Hungarian.). 1981. $117.00 (ISBN
0-444-99745-8). Elsevier.

Thompson, Philip & Davenport,
Peter, eds. Dictionary of Graphic
Cliches. LC 79-2094. (Illus.). 1979.
$30.00x (ISBN 0-312-20108-7). St
Martin.
GRAPHIC DATA PROCESSING
see Computer Graphics
GRAPHIC METHODS
Garland, Ken. Illustrated Graphics
Glossary. 192p. 1981. $30.00x
(ISBN 0-09-141511-X, Pub. by
Barrie & Jenkins England). State
Mutual Bk.
GRAPHICS, COMPUTER
see Computer Graphics
GRAPHICS, ENGINEERING
see Engineering Graphics
GRAPHOLOGY
International Graphoanalysis Society.
Dictionary of Stroke Structures in
Graphoanalysis. $35.25 (G1029).
Intl Graphoanalysis.
GRAPHOLOGY–DICTIONARIES
Stamp, L. & Perevod, A. S. Slovar
Obshchegeo graficheskikh
Terminov, 2 vols. (Rus.). 1974.
$14.95 set (Pub. by Progress).
Four Continent.
Vels. Diccionario de grafologia. 450p.
(Span.). 1972. 320.00 ptas. Cedel.
GRAPHS
see Graphic Methods
GRASSES
see also Pastures
also names of grasses
Dictionary of Turfgrass Terms. $1.00
(2003). Pro Golfers.
GRATES
see Furnaces
GRAVES
see Epitaphs
GRAY, THOMAS, 1716-1771
Cook, Albert S. A Concordance to
English Poems of Thomas Gray.
LC 74-8062. Repr. of 1908 ed. lib.
bdg. $20.00 (ISBN 0-8414-3355-0).
Folcroft.
GREAT BRITAIN–ANTIQUITIES
Adkins, Lesley & Adkins, Roy A. A
Thesaurus of British Archaeology.
LC 81-12898. (Illus.). 320p. 1982.
$27.50x (ISBN 0-389-20245-2).
B&N Imports.
**GREAT BRITAIN–ARMED
FORCES–MEDALS, BADGES,
DECORATIONS, ETC.**
Fraser, Edward & Gibbons, John.
Soldier & Sailor Words & Phrases.
LC 68-30635. 1968. Repr. of 1925
ed. $40.00x (ISBN 0-8103-3281-7).
Gale.
GREAT BRITAIN–ARMY
Fraser, Edward & Gibbons, John.
Soldier & Sailor Words & Phrases.
LC 68-30635. 1968. Repr. of 1925
ed. $40.00x (ISBN 0-8103-3281-7).
Gale.
GREAT BRITAIN–COMMERCE
Postlethwayt, Malachy. Universal
Dictionary of Trade & Commerce,
2 Vols. 4th ed. LC 29-29516.
Repr. of 1774 ed. Set. 250.00x
(ISBN 0-678-00551-6). Kelley.
GREAT BRITAIN–HISTORY
*Here are entered works on the
history of Great Britain as a whole.
For works on specific periods see the
period subdivisions.*
Kenyon, J. P., ed. A Dictionary of
British History. LC 82-42759.
415p. 1983. $20.00 (ISBN 0-8128-
2910-7). Stein & Day.
Williams, E. N. The Penguin
Dictionary of English & European
History 1485-1789. (Reference
Ser.). 480p. 1980. pap. 6.95 (ISBN
0-14-051084-2). Penguin.
**GREAT BRITAIN–HISTORY–
OUTLINES, SYLLABI, ETC.**
Marwick, Arthur, et al, eds. The
Illustrated Dictionary of British
History. (Illus.). 320p. 1981.
$19.95 (ISBN 0-500-25072-3).
Thames Hudson.
**GREAT BRITAIN–NAVY–
HISTORY**
Cooper, Richard & Uden, Grant.
British Ships & Seamen. (Illus.).
591p. 1981. lib. bdg. $40.00x
(ISBN 0-312-20028-5). St Martin.

**GREAT BRITAIN–POLITICS
AND GOVERNMENT–18TH
CENTURY**
Ormond, Richard & Rogers,
Malcolm. Dictionary of British
Portraiture: Vol. 2, the Later
Georgians to the Early Victorians;
Historical Figures Born Between
1700 & 1800. Kilmurray, Elaine,
ed. 1979. text ed. 49.50x (ISBN 0-
19-520181-7). Oxford U Pr.
GREAT SCHISM
see Schism
GREECE–ANTIQUITIES
Blumner, Hugo. Technologie und
Terminologie des Gewerbe und
Kunste bei Griechen und Romern,
4 vols. Finley, Moses, ed. LC 79-
4963. (Ancient Economic History
Ser.). (Illus., Ger.). 1980. Repr. of
1875 ed. Set. lib. bdg. $128.00x
(ISBN 0-405-12350-7); $32.00x ea.
Vol. 1 (ISBN 0-405-12351-5). Vol.
2 (ISBN 0-405-12352-3). Vol. 3
(ISBN 0-405-12484-8). Vol. 4
(ISBN 0-405-12485-6). Ayer Co.
Paris, Pierre. Dictionnaire des
Antiquites Grecques. (Fr.). 1909.
68.00 F. Boccard.
--Lexique Des Antiquites Grecques.
(Fr.). 1909. pap. $23.50 (ISBN 0-
686-57066-9, M-6438). French &
Eur.
Smith, William. Dictionary of Greek
& Roman Antiquities, 2 vols. LC
77-6173. 1977. Repr. of 1890 ed.
lib. bdg. 65.00 (ISBN 0-89341-166-
3). Longwood Pr.
GREECE–BIOGRAPHY
Smith, William, ed. Dictionary of
Greek & Roman Biography &
Mythology, 3 Vols. LC 11-24983.
(Gr. & Lat.). Repr. of 1890 ed. Set.
$210.00 (ISBN 0-404-06130-3).
AMS Pr.
GREECE–CIVILIZATION
see Civilization, Greek
**GREECE–DESCRIPTION,
GEOGRAPHY**
Smith, William, ed. Dictionary of
Greek & Roman Geography, 2
Vols. LC 4-14843. (Gr.). Repr. of
1873 ed. Set. $125.00 (ISBN 0-
404-06134-6). AMS Pr.
Tischler, Johann. Kleinasiatische
Hydronymie: Semantik &
Morphologie Analyse der
Geichicher Gewaessernamen. LC
78-394985. ix, 191p. (Ger.). 1977.
write for info (ISBN 3-882-26001-
7). Reichert.
**GREECE–ECONOMIC
CONDITIONS**
Korver, Jan. De Terminologie van
het Crediet-Wezen in het
Grieksch. Finley, Moses, ed. LC
79-4987. (Ancient Economic
History Ser.). (Dutch.). 1980.
Repr. of 1934 ed. lib. bdg. $14.00x
(ISBN 0-405-12372-8). Ayer Co.
GREECE–HISTORY
Devambez, Pierre. Diccionario de la
Civilizacion Griega. (Span.).
1972. $37.50 (ISBN 84-233-0645-
3, S-50367). French & Eur.
Snell, Bruno & Erbse, Hartmut.
Lexikon des Fruehgriechischen
Epos: Lfg 1. 96p. (Ger. & Gr.).
1955. DM.60.00 (ISBN 3-525-
25015-0). Vandenhoeck.
--Lexikon des Fruehgriechischen
Epos: Lfg 2. 96p. (Ger. & Gr.).
1956. DM.60.00 (ISBN 3-525-
25016-9). Vandenhoeck.
--Lexikon des Fruehgriechischen
Epos: Lfg 3. 96p. (Ger. & Gr.).
1959. DM.60.00 (ISBN 3-525-
25017-7). Vandenhoeck.
--Lexikon des Fruehgriechischen
Epos: Lfg 4. 96p. (Ger. & Gr.).
1965. DM.60.00 (ISBN 3-525-
25018-5). Vandenhoeck.
--Lexikon des Fruehgriechischen
Epos: Lfg 5. 96p. (Ger. & Gr.).
1967. DM.60.00 (ISBN 3-525-
25501-2). Vandenhoeck.
--Lexikon des Fruehgriechischen
Epos: Lfg 6. 96p. (Ger. & Gr.).
1969. DM.60.00 (ISBN 3-525-
25502-0). Vandenhoeck.
--Lexikon des Fruehgriechischen
Epos: Lfg 7. 97p. (Ger. & Gr.).
1973. DM.60.00 (ISBN 3-525-
25503-9). Vandenhoeck.
--Lexikon des Fruehgriechischen
Epos: Lfg 8. 112p. (Ger. & Gr.).
1976. DM.86.00 (ISBN 3-525-
25504-7). Vandenhoeck.
GREEK CIVILIZATION
see Civilization, Greek; Hellenism

GREEK INSCRIPTIONS
see Inscriptions, Greek
GREEK LANGUAGE
see also Classical Philology; Hellenism; Inscriptions, Greek

Joint Association of Classical Teachers. Greek Vocabulary. (Gr.). 1980. pap. $5.95 (ISBN 0-521-23277-5). Cambridge U Pr.

Tischler, Johann. Kleinasiatische Hydronymie: Semantik & Morphologie Analyse der Geichicher Gewaessernamen. LC 78-394985. ix, 191p. (Ger.). 1977. write for info (ISBN 3-882-26001-7). Reichert.

GREEK LANGUAGE–DICTIONARIES

Altgriechisch, 2 Vols. Incl. Teil I. Altgriechisch-Deutsch. Menge, H. 528p. DM.16.80 (10030); Teil II. Deutsch-Altgriechisch. Guthling, O. 551p. DM.16.80 (10035). (Langenscheidts Taschenwoerterbucher Ser.). (Gr. & Ger.). DM.beide Teile in einem Band 23.80 (11030). Langenscheidt.

Annaratone, Alessandro & La Magna, Giovanni. Vocabolario greco-italiano. xii, 1602p. (Gr. & Ital.). L.18400.00. Signorelli C.

Bailly, Anatole. Dictionnaire Abrege Grec-Francais. 1012p. (Gr. & Fr.). 1969. pap. $39.95 (ISBN 0-686-56906-7, M-6019). French & Eur.

--Dictionnaire Abrege Grec-Francais. 1012p. (Gr. & Fr.). 1969. $58.00. Hachette-Jeunesse.

--Dictionnaire Grec-Francais. 2230p. (Gr.-Fr.). 1967. pap. $95.00 (ISBN 0-686-56907-5, M-6020). French & Eur.

--Dictionnaire Grec-Francais. 2230p. (Gr. & Fr.). 1967. 123.00 F. Hachette-Jeunesse.

Balagur, Miguel. Diccionario griego-espanol. (Gr. & Span.). 300.00 ptas. Bibliografica.

Bauer, Walter. Griechisch-Deutsches Woerterbuch zu den Schriften des Neuen Testaments und der uebrigen urchristlichen Literatur. 5th rev. ed. (Gr. & Ger.). 1981. Repr. $54.00x (ISBN 3-11-002073-4). De Gruyter.

Berlitz Editors. Berlitz Greek for Travellers. 192p. (Gr.). 1982. pap. 4.95 (ISBN 0-686-92956-X, Berlitz); pap. 4.95 (ISBN 0-02-964040-7). Macmillan.

Bonazzi, Benedetto. Dizionario greco-italiano. v, 1232p. (Gr. & Ital.). L.7000.00. Morano.

Brighenti, Eliseo. Dizionario greco moderno-italiano e italiano-greco moderno: Vol. 1, Greco moderno-italiano. xvi, 696p. (Gr. & Ital.). 1976. L.6300.00 (ISBN 88-205-0045-0). Cisalpino.

Byl, Simon. Vocabulaire Grec de Base. 132p. (Gr.). 20.00 F. Dessain & Tolra.

Chantraine, Pierre. Dictionnaire Etymologique de la Langue Grecque. 609p. (Gr.). 1976. 300.00 F. Klincksieck.

--Dictionnaire Etymologique de la Langue Grecque, 2. (Gr.). 110.00 F. Klincksieck.

--Dictionnaire Etymologique de la Langue Grecque, 3. 360p. (Gr.). 1975. 180.00 F. Klincksieck.

--Dictionnaire Etymologique de la Langue Grecque, 4. 200p. (Gr.). 1977. 140.00 F. Klincksieck.

Collin, Paul. Vocabulaire Grec. 328p. (Gr.). 1963. 24.25 F. Dessain & Tolra.

Cotolulis, Socratis. Dictionar Roman-Grec. LC 76-515769. 534p. (Romanian & Gr.). 1975. 22.50 lei. Editura Stiintifica.

De Sommevoire, Alexis & Da Parigi, Tomaso. Tesoro Della Linqua Greca-Volgare Ed Italiana, cioe Ricchissimo dizzionario greco-volgare et italiano, 2 vols. (Gr. & Ital.). Repr. of 1709 ed. lib. bdg. $175.00x (ISBN 0-686-72425-9). Pt. 1, Italian-Greek, Viii, 513 Pages. Pt. 2, Greek-Italian, Xxviii, 461 Pages. Caratzas Pub Co.

Diccionario Manual Griego-Espanol Vox. 16th ed. 724p. (Gr. & Span.). 1982. 795.00 ptas (ISBN 84-7153-192-5). Biblo SP.

Dizionario greco moderno-italiano e italiano-greco moderno: Vol. 2, Italiano-greco moderno. 672p. (Ital. & Gr.). 1976. L.6000.00 (ISBN 88-205-0046-9). Cisalpino.

Dizionario greco moderno-italiano, italiano-greco moderno. 304p. (Gr. & Ital.). L.3000.00. Malipiero.

Dizionario italiano-greco moderno. 304p. (Ital. & Gr.). L.3000.00. Malipiero.

Estienne, Henri. Thesaurus Graecae Linguae, 9 vols. 10800p. (Lat. & Gr.). 1954. S.11000.00. Akad Druck.

Frisk, Hjalmar. Griechiesches Etymologisches Woerterbuch, Vol. 1. (Gr. & Ger.). 1960. $95.00 (ISBN 3-533-00652-2). Winter Univ.

--Griechisches Etymologiches Woerterbuch, Vol. 3. (Gr. & Ger.). 1972. $45.00 (ISBN 3-533-02203-X). Winter Univ.

--Griechisches Etymologisches Woerterbuch, Vol. 1. (Gr. & Ger.). 1960. $95.00 (ISBN 3-533-00652-2, M-7434, Pub. by Carl Winter). French & Eur.

--Griechisches Etymologisches Woerterbuch, Vol. 2. (Gr. & Ger.). 1960. $132.00 (ISBN 3-533-00653-0, M-7435, Pub. by Carl Winter). French & Eur.

--Griechisches Etymologisches Woerterbuch, Vol. 3. (Gr. & Ger.). 1972. $45.00 (ISBN 3-533-02203-X, M-7436, Pub. by Carl Winter). French & Eur.

--Griechishes Etymologishes Woerterbuch, Vol. 2. (Gr. & Ger.). 1960. $132.00 (ISBN 3-533-00653-0). Winter Univ.

Gazes, Anthimos, ed. Lexikon tes Hellenikes Glosses Tritomon: Lexicon of the Greek Language in Three Volumes, 3 vols. 2627p. (Gr.). 1980. Repr. of 1835 ed. lib. bdg. $450.00x (ISBN 0-89241-136-8). Caratzas Pub Co.

Gemoll, Guglielmo. Vocabolario greco-italiano. 1202p. (Gr. & Ital.). L.14500.00. Sandron.

Georgin. Dictionnaire Grec-Francais. (Gr. & Fr.). 1978. 30.00 F. Hatier.

Georgin, Ch. Dictionnaire Grec-Francais. (Gr. & Fr.). pap. $14.95 (ISBN 0-686-57194-0, M-6268). French & Eur.

Gresk-Norsk-Gresk Lommeordbok. 381p. (Gr. & Norwegian.). 1981. pap. $14.95 (ISBN 82-573-0163-9, M-9460). French & Eur.

Guthling, O. Langenscheidts Taschenwoerterbuch Altgriechisch: Teil II, Deutsch-Altgriechisch. 547p. (Ger. & Gr.). DM.17.80 (10035). Langenscheidt.

Hoffman, Horace Addison. Everyday Greek: Greek Words in English, Including Scientific Terms. (Midway Reprint). 1976. pap. $8.00x (ISBN 0-226-34787-7). U of Chicago Pr.

Ioannidia, A. A. Russko-Novogrecheskii Slovar. 819p. (Rus. & Gr.). 1966. $7.95 (Pub. by Sov. Entsiklopediia). Four Continent.

Khorikov, I. P. Novogrechesko-Russkii Slovar. 854p. (Rus. & Gr.). 1979. $22.95 (Pub. by Russkii Iazyk). Four Continent.

Lampe, G. W., ed. A Patristic Greek Lexicon. 1616p. (Gr.). 1976. 5200.00 F. Brepols.

--Patristic Greek Lexicon Nineteen Sixty-One to Sixty-Eight. (Gr.). 149.00x (ISBN 0-19-864213-X). Oxford U Pr.

Langenscheidts Grosswoerterbuch Altgriechisch: Tl 1, Altgriechisch-Deutsch. (Gr. & Ger.). 1978. DM.58.00 (ISBN 3-468-02030-9). Langenscheidt.

Langenscheidts Lilliput-Woerterbuecher Altgriechisch-Deutsch. (Gr. & Ger.). 1978. DM.2.20 (ISBN 3-468-20032-3). Langenscheidt.

Langenscheidts Taschenwoerterbuecher Neugriechisch. (Gr.). 1978. DM.23.80 (ISBN 3-468-11210-6). Langenscheidt.

Langenscheidts Universal-Woerterbuch Neugriechisch. 560p. (Gr. & Ger.). DM.6.80 (18210). Langenscheidt.

Langenscheidts Universal-Woerterbuecher Neugriechisch-Deutsch. (Gr. & Ger.). 1978. DM.5.80 (ISBN 3-468-18200-7). Langenscheidt.

Liddell, H. G., et al. Dizionario illustrato greco-italiano. (Illus.). xvi, 1568p. (Gr. & Ital.). 1975. L.23800.00. Monnier.

Menge & Guthling. Langenscheidts Grosswoerterbuch Altgriechisch-Deutsch. xxiv, 762p. (Gr. & Ger.). DM.68.00 (02030). Langenscheidt.

Menge, H. Langenscheidts Taschenwoerterbuch Altgriechisch: Teil I, Altgriechisch-Deutsch. 528p. (Gr. & Ger.). DM.17.80 (10030). Langenscheidt.

--Langenscheidts Taschenwoerterbuecher Altgriechisch-Deutsch. (Gr. & Ger.). DM.13.80 (ISBN 3-468-10030-2). Langenscheidt.

Menge, H. & Guthling, O. Langenscheidts Taschenwoerterbuch Altgriechisch, 2 vols. in 1. (Gr. & Ger.). DM.24.80 (11030). Langenscheidt.

Moulton, Harold K., ed. The Analytical Greek Lexicon Revised. rev. ed. (Gr.). 1978. $15.95 (ISBN 0-310-20280-9). Zondervan.

Mystakidis, Antonis. Nygrekisk-Svensk Ordbok. Frangos, Eftychia, ed. 234p. (Gr. & Swedish.). 1980. Kr.115.00 (ISBN 91-24-20176-6). Esselte Studium.

Neugriechisch, 2 vols. Incl. Teil I. Neugriechisch-Deutsch. Wendt, H. F. 552p. DM.18.80 (10210); Teil II. Deutsch-Neugriechisch. Steinmetz, A. 487p. DM.18.80 (10215). (Langenscheidts Taschenworterbucher Ser.). (Ger. & Gr.). DM.beide Teile in einem Band 29.80 (11210). Langenscheidt.

Pabon, Jose M. Vox-Diccionario Manual Griego-Espanol. 11th ed. 724p. (Gr. & Span.). 1979. leatherette $17.25 (ISBN 84-7153-192-5, S-12136). French & Eur.

Pabon, Jose M. & Fernandez Galiano, M. Diccionario Manual Griego-Espanol. 724p. (Gr. & Span.). 925.00 ptas (ISBN 84-7153-192-5). Biblograf SP.

Patsis, C. Greek-English, English-Greek Dictionary, 2 vols. (Gr. & Eng.). Set. 50.00 (ISBN 0-685-79111-4). Heinman.

Pernot, Hubert. Dictionnaire Grec Moderne Francais. 544p. (Gr. & Fr.). 1970. 25.50 F. Garnier.

Pessoneaux, Emile. Dictionnaire Grec-Francais. 896p. (Fr. & Gr.). 1953. $35.95 (ISBN 0-686-57071-5, M-6443). French & Eur.

Petinis, Lambros. Dictionar Grec-Roman. LC 77-481194. 439p. (Gr. & Romanian.). 1976. 19.00 lei. Editura Stiintifica.

Preisigke, Friedrich. Fachwoerter des Oeffentlichen Verwaltungsdienstes Aegyptens in den Griechischen Papyrusurkunden der Ptolemaeisch-Romischen Zeit. LC 78-347087. x, 186p. (Ger. & Gr.). 1975. DM.33.80 (ISBN 3-487-05896-0). Olms Verlag.

Rocci, Lorenzo. Vocabolario greco-italiano. xx, 2076p. (Gr. & Ital.). 1976. L.26800.00. Dante Alighieri.

Sal'nov, N. Al. Russko-Novogrecheskii Karmannyi Slovar. 352p. (Rus. & Ger.). 1965. $1.60 (Pub. by Sov. Entsiklopediia). Four Continent.

Sebastian Yarza, Florencio I. Diccionario griego-espanol. 1644p. (Gr. & Span.). 1974. 1000.00 ptas. Sopena.

Steinmetz, A. Langenscheidts Taschenwoerterbuch Neugriechisch: Teil II, Deutsch-Neugriechisch. 487p. (Ger. & Gr.). DM.19.80 (10215). Langenscheidt.

Theodorakis, Mikis. Lexique de la Resistance Grecque: Journal de Resistance. 324p. (Fr.). 1971. 43.85 F. Flammarion.

Valmin, Natan & Frangos, Eftychia. Svensk-Nygrekisk Ordbok. 279p. (Swedish & Gr.). 1980. Kr.115.00 (ISBN 91-24-20265-7). Esselte Studium.

Wendt, H. F. Langenscheidts Taschenwoerterbuch Neugriechisch: Teil I, Neugriechisch-Deutsch. 552p. (Gr. & Ger.). DM.19.80 (10210). Langenscheidt.

Wendt, H. F., ed. Langenscheidts Taschenwoerterbuecher Neugriechisch-Deutsch. (Gr. & Ger.). 1978. DM.14.80 (ISBN 3-468-10210-0). Langenscheidt.

Wharton, E. R. Etymological Lexicon of Classical Greek. LC 74-7787. 192p. (Gr.). 1975. Repr. $10.00 (ISBN 0-89005-033-3). Ares.

GREEK LANGUAGE–GLOSSARIES, VOCABULARIES, ETC.

American Classical League. The Golden Greek Glossary. (Gr.). $1.00 (NO. L3). Am Classical.

Cheadle, John R. Basic Greek Vocabulary. (Gr.). 1969. text ed. $6.95 (ISBN 0-312-06790-9). St Martin.

Cousin, Jean. Vocabulaire Grec de la Terminologie Rhetorique: Dans; Etudes sur Quintillen. 1023p. (Gr.). 1967. fl.160.00 (Pub. by B R Gruner Netherlands). Humanities.

Dornseiff, F. & Hansen, Bernard. Reverse Lexicon of Greek Proper Names. (Gr.). 1978. Repr. 30.00 (ISBN 0-89005-251-4). Ares.

Fontoynont, Victor. Vocabulaire Grec. 8th ed. 200p. (Gr.). 1974. 35.00 F. Picard.

Fontoynont-Ribot. Vocabulario Griego. 4th ed. 214p. (Span.). 80.00 ptas. Sal Terrae.

Leonard, P. Vocabulaire Pratique du Grec. 152p. (Gr.). 1968. 125.00 F. Duculot.

Saunier, Joannes. Vocabulaire Grec. 220p. (Gr.). 1977. 19.80 F. Gigord.

Villarroel, Raul. Vocabulario Griego-Argentino. (Gr. & Span.). write for info. Castellvi.

GREEK LANGUAGE–HISTORY

Mugler, Charles. Dictionnaire Historique de la Terminologique Optique des Grecs. 460p. (Gr.). 1964. 280.00 F. Klincksieck.

GREEK LANGUAGE–TERMS AND PHRASES

Maxwell, Stuart P. Studies in Greek Colour Terminology, Vol. 2. (Mnemosyne Supplement Ser.: No. 67). 90p. 1981. pap. text ed. 15.25x (ISBN 90-04-06407-9, Pub. by E J Brill Holland). Humanities.

Stuart, Maxwell P. Studies in Greek Colour Terminology, Vol. 1. (Mnemosyne Supplement Ser.: No. 65). 254p. 1981. pap. text ed. 35.50x (ISBN 90-04-06406-0, Pub. by E J Brill Holland). Humanities.

GREEK LANGUAGE (KOINE)
see Greek Language, Hellenistic (300 B.C.-600 A.D.)

GREEK LANGUAGE, BIBLICAL–DICTIONARIES

Alsop, John R. An Index to Bauer Arndt, Gingrich Greek Lexicon. 2nd ed. (Gr.). Date not set. $11.95 (ISBN 0-310-44031-9). Zondervan.

Berry, George R. Berry's Greek-English New Testament Lexicon with Synonyms: Numerically Coded to Strong's Exhaustive Concordance. 208p. (Orig., Gr. & Eng.). 1980. pap. $5.95 (ISBN 0-8010-0791-7). Baker Bk.

--A Dictionary of New Testament Greek Synonyms. (Gr.). 1979. $4.95 (ISBN 0-310-21161-1). Zondervan.

Gingrich, F. Wilbur, ed. Shorter Lexicon of the Greek New Testament. LC 65-24434. 1965. $10.00x (ISBN 0-226-29520-6). U of Chicago Pr.

Guerra y Gomez, Manuel. Diccionario Morfologico del Nuevo Testamento. LC 79-108693. 443p. (Span.). 1978. 1500.00 ptas (ISBN 8-470-09048-8). Aldecoa.

Holly, David. A Complete Categorized Greek-English New Testament Vocabulary. (Gr. & Eng.). 1980. pap. $6.95 (ISBN 0-8010-4224-0). Baker Bk.

Kittel, Gerhard & Friedrich, Gerhard, eds. Theological Dictionary of the New Testament, 10 vols. Incl. Vol. 1. 1964. 27.50 (ISBN 0-8028-2243-6); Vol. 2. 1965. 27.50 (ISBN 0-8028-2244-4); Vol. 3. 1966. 29.95 (ISBN 0-8028-2245-2); Vol. 4. 1967. 29.95 (ISBN 0-8028-2246-0); Vol. 5. 1968. 29.95 (ISBN 0-8028-2247-9); Vol. 6. 1969. 27.50 (ISBN 0-8028-2248-7); Vol. 7. 1970. 29.95 (ISBN 0-8028-2249-5); Vol. 8. 1972. 25.00 (ISBN 0-8028-2250-9); Vol. 9. 1973. 27.50 (ISBN 0-8028-2322-X); Vol. 10. 1976. 25.00 (ISBN 0-8028-2323-8). $279.80 set (ISBN 0-8028-2324-6). Eerdmans.

Pitkin, ed. Index to the Theological Dictionary to the New Testament. (Theological Dictionary to the N. T. Ser.). 1976. text ed. $25.00 (ISBN 0-8028-2323-8). Eerdmans.

Preuschen, Erwin. Griechisch-Deutsches Taschenwoerterbuch zum Neuen Testament. 6th ed. LC 77-484561. 197p. (Gr. & Ger.). 1976. DM.19.80 (ISBN 3-110-06960-1). De Gruyter.

Smith, Jacob B., ed. Greek-English Concordance. 430p. (Gr. & Eng.). 1955. $24.95 (ISBN 0-8361-1368-3). Herald Pr.

Stegenga, J. Greek-English Analytical Concordance of the Greek-English New Testament. (Gr. & Eng.). 1963. $14.95 (ISBN 0-910710-01-5). Hellenes.

Thayer, Joseph H. Thayer's Greek-English Lexicon of the New Testament. LC 78-67264. (Gr. & Eng.). 1978. pap. $16.95 (ISBN 0-8054-1376-6). Broadman.

Young, Robert. Young's Analytical Concordance to the Bible. 1955. $19.95 (ISBN 0-8028-8084-3); deluxe ed. $22.95 (ISBN 0-8028-8085-1). Eerdmans.

GREEK LANGUAGE, BIBLICAL–GLOSSARIES, VOCABULARIES, ETC.
Hickie, W. J. Greek-English Lexicon of the New Testament. (Direction Bks.). (Gr. & Eng.). 1977. pap. $4.95 (ISBN 0-8010-4164-3). Baker Bk.

Holly, David. A Complete Categorized Greek-English New Testament Vocabulary. 141p. (Eng. & Gr.). 1978. $12.50 (ISBN 0-85150-119-2). Attic Pr.

Moulton, James H. & Milligan, George. Vocabulary of the Greek New Testament. (Gr.). 1949. $24.95 (ISBN 0-8028-2178-2). Eerdmans.

GREEK LANGUAGE, HELLENISTIC (300 B.C.-600 A.D.)
Lampe, G. W., ed. Patristic Greek Lexicon, Fascicle 5. (Gr.). 1968. 22.00x (ISBN 0-19-864212-1). Oxford U Pr.

Maxwell, Stuart P. Studies in Greek Colour Terminology, Vol. 2. (Mnemosyne Supplement Ser.: No. 67). 90p. 1981. pap. text ed. 15.25x (ISBN 90-04-06407-9, Pub. by E J Brill Holland). Humanities.

Stuart, Maxwell P. Studies in Greek Colour Terminology, Vol. 1. (Mnemosyne Supplement Ser.: No. 65). 254p. 1981. pap. text ed. 35.50x (ISBN 90-04-06406-0, Pub. by E J Brill Holland). Humanities.

GREEK LANGUAGE, MODERN
Learn Greek for English Speakers. (Gr. & Eng.). pap. 9.50 (ISBN 0-87557-031-3, 031-3). Saphrograph.

Shipp, G. P. Modern Greek Evidence for the Ancient Greek Vocabulary. LC 80-670068. (Gr.). 1980. 43.00x (ISBN 0-424-00076-8, Pub. by Sydney U Pr). Intl Schol Bk Serv.

GREEK LANGUAGE, MODERN–CONVERSATION AND PHRASE BOOKS
Tsirpanlis, Constantine N. Modern Greek Idiom & Phrase Book. 320p. (Orig., Gr. & Eng.). $8.95. Barron.

GREEK LANGUAGE, MODERN–DICTIONARIES
Divry, G. C. Modern English-Greek-English Desk Dictionary with Thumb Index. 768p. (Gr. & Eng.). 1979. $19.95 (ISBN 0-686-97405-0, M-9443). French & Eur.

Divry, George C., ed. Divry's New Modern Greek-English & English-Greek Handy Dictionary. rev. ed. (Gr. & Eng.). 1978. pocket ed. $4.20 (ISBN 0-685-09029-9); with thumb indexes $5.50 (ISBN 0-685-09030-2); lea. $8.50 (ISBN 0-685-09031-0). Divry.

Divry's Modern English-Greek & Greek-English Desk Dictionary. (Eng. & Gr.). 1982. $9.50 (ISBN 0-685-81638-9); thumb indexed $12.00 (ISBN 0-685-81639-7). Divry.

Feuillet, L. Lexique Francais-Grec. 496p. (Fr. & Gr.). 1976. 35.20 F. Belin.

Greek-English, English-Greek Pocket Dictionary. (Gr. & Eng.). 9.00 (ISBN 0-685-58555-7). Heinman.

Greek-English Pocket Dictionary. (Gr. & Eng.). pap. 8.50 (ISBN 0-685-77570-4, 030-5X). Saphrograph.

Institute for Language Study. Vest Pocket Modern Greek. LC 60-53247. (Illus.). 184p. (Modern Greek.). 1979. pap. $2.95 (ISBN 0-06-464904-0, BN4904, BN). B&N NY.

Kykkotis, I. Modern English-Greek & Greek-English Dictionary. 652p. (Eng. & Gr.). 1980. $40.00x (ISBN 0-85331-046-7, Pub. by Lund Humphries England). State Mutual Bk.

Magnien, Victor & Lacroix, M. Dictionnaire Grec-Francais. 2168p. (Gr. & Fr.). 1969. 157.00 F. Belin.

Mirambel, Andre. Petit Dictionnaire Francais-Grec Moderne et Grec Moderne-Francais. 486p. (Fr. & Gr.). 1969. $29.95 (ISBN 0-686-57051-0, M-6413). French & Eur.

Pessonneaux, Emile. Dictionnaire Grec-Francais. 896p. (Gr. & Fr.). 1953. 90.00 F. Belin.

Pring, J. T., ed. The Oxford Dictionary of Modern Greek: Greek-English, English-Greek. (Gr. & Eng.). 1982. 19.95 (ISBN 0-19-864137-0). Oxford U Pr.

Rogers, Thomas. Greek Word Roots: A Practical List with Greek & English Derivatives. 32p. (Gr. & Eng.). 1981. pap. $1.95 (ISBN 0-8010-7707-9). Baker Bk.

Theophilakis, E. Greek-Norwegian Norwegian-Greek Pocket Dictionary. (Gr. & Norwegian.). 1981. write for info. (ISBN 82-573-0005-5). Kunnskapsforlaget.

GREEK LITERATURE–DICTIONARIES
DuCange, Charles Du Fresne. Glossarium Ad Scriptores Mediae et Infimae Graecitatis. LC 60-21441. 1280p. (Lat.). 1958. Repr. of 1688 ed. 135.00x (ISBN 0-8002-1276-2). Intl Pubns Serv.

GREEK MYTHOLOGY
see Mythology, Greek
GREEN BERETS
see United States–Army
GREENLANDIC LANGUAGE
see Eskimo Language
GREGORIAN CHANT
see Chants (Plain, Gregorian, etc.)
GROOMING, PERSONAL
see Beauty, Personal
GROOMING FOR WOMEN
see Beauty, Personal
GROS VENTRE INDIANS
see Indians of North America–The West
GROSVENTRE LANGUAGE
see Hidatsa Language
GROTIUS, HUGO, 1583-1645
Gellinek, Christian. Hugo Grotius Drama Concordance. LC 83-70923. (Studies in German Literature, Linguistics, & Culture: Vol. 7). (Illus.). 800p. 1983. $29.50x (ISBN 0-938100-23-8). Camden Hse.

GROUND WATER
see Water, Underground
GROUP MEDICAL PRACTICE
see also Clinics
Medical Group Practice Terminology with Accompanying Definitions. Center for Research in Ambulatory Health Care Administration. LC 81-65571. 58p. (Orig.). 1981. pap. 15.00 three ring binder (ISBN 0-933948-09-3). Med Group Mgmt.

GRYPHONS
see Animals, Mythical

GUATEMALA
Aquilar Pelaez, V. Diccionario Geografico de Guatemala. (Span.). 1930. $40.00 ea.; pap. $27.50 ea. Intl Guatemala.

Carvalho Neto, Paulo de. Diccionario d Teoria Folklorica. (Span.). 1977. $13.50. Intl Guatemala.

GUATEMALA–HISTORY
Moore, Richard A. Historical Dictionary of Guatemala. rev. ed. 1973. $10.00 ea. Intl Guatemala.

Sandoval, Lisandro. Semantica Guatemala O Diccionario De Guatemaltequisma, 2 vols. (Span.). 1941-1942. $85.00ea. Intl Guatemala.

GUATEMALAN LEGENDS
see Legends, Guatemalan
GUESTS
see Etiquette
GUIDANCE, STUDENT
see Vocational Guidance
GUIDANCE, VOCATIONAL
see Vocational Guidance
GUINEA (REGION)
O'Toole, Thomas E. Historical Dictionary of Guinea: Republic of Guinea-Conakry. LC 77-28145. (African Historical Dictionaries Ser.: No. 16). 1978. $13.00 (ISBN 0-8108-1112-X). Scarecrow.

GUINEA-BISSAU–HISTORY
Lobban, Richard. Historical Dictionary of the Republics of Guinea-Bissau & Cape Verde. LC 79-18227. (African Historical Dictionaries Ser.: No. 22). 209p. 1979. $14.00 (ISBN 0-8108-1240-1). Scarecrow.

GUITAR
Cafagna, C. & Gangi, M. Dizionario chitarristico italiano. (Ital.). L.5000.00. Berben.

GUJARATI LANGUAGE
Deshpande, P. G. A Modern English-Gujarati Dictionary. 820p. (Eng. & Gujarati.). 1983. 29.95 (ISBN 0-19-561140-3). Oxford U Pr.

GUJRI LANGUAGE
see Urdu Language
GUM ELASTIC
see Rubber
GUN CONTROL
see Firearms–Laws and Regulations
GUNS
see Firearms
GURJARI LANGUAGE
see Urdu Language
GYMNASTICS
see also Physical Education and Training
Guraedy, Ila. Illustrated Gymnastics Dictionary for Young People. LC 79-93357. (Illustrated Dictionary Ser.). (Illus.). 120p. (gr. 4 up). 1980. PLB 7.29 (ISBN 0-8178-0002-6). Harvey.

GYMNASTICS, MEDICAL
see Exercise Therapy
GYNECOLOGY
Hughes, Edward C. Obsteric-Gynecological Terminology. 1972. text ed. $14.00x (ISBN 0-8036-4725-5). Davis Co.

GYNECOLOGY–DICTIONARIES
Brigato, Giovanni & Pisano, Giorgio. Dizionario eponimico ostetrico-ginecologico. xi, 562p. (Ital.). 1977. L.15000.00. Piccin.

GYPSIES
see Gipsies

H

HABITS OF ANIMALS
see Animals, Habits and Behavior Of
HACKS (CARRIAGES)
see Carriages and Carts
HADES
see Hell
HAGIOGRAPHY
Here are entered works on the lives of the saints, and how to write them. The lives themselves are entered under the heading Saints.
Petin, L. M. Dictionnaire Hagiographique, 2 vols. Migne, J. P., ed. (Encyclopedie Theologique Ser.: Vols. 40-41). 1580p. (Fr.). Repr. of 1850 ed. lib. bdg. $240.00x (ISBN 0-89241-246-1). Caratzas Pub Co.

HAIDA INDIANS
see Indians of North America–Northwest, Pacific

HAIDA LANGUAGE
Lawrence, Erma. Haida Dictionary. Edenso, Christine & Cogo, Robert, eds. LC 78-101871. 464p. (Eng. & Haida.). 1977. write for info. Society for the Preservation of Haida Language & Literature.

HAIRDRESSING
see also Costume
Vincenzo, Coratelli. Dizionarietto del costume della moda e dell'acconciatura. 112p. (Ital.). L.1000.00. San Marco.

HAITI–HISTORY
Perusse, Roland I. Historical Dictionary of Haiti. LC 76-30264. (Latin American Historical Dictionaries Ser: No. 15). (Illus.). 1977. $13.00 (ISBN 0-8108-1006-9). Scarecrow.

HALL-MARKS
see also Clocks and Watches; Jewelry; Pewter
Barber, Edward A. & Lockwood, Luke V. The Ceramic Furniture & Silver Collectors' Glossary. (Architecture & Decorative Art Ser.). 1976. pap. $6.95 (ISBN 0-306-80049-7). Da Capo.

Dictionnaire des Poincons de l'Orfevrerie Provinciale Francaise. LC 77-565816. (Illus., Fr.). 1976. 240.00 F. Droz.

French, Hollis. Silver Collector's Glossary & a List of Early American Silversmiths & Their Marks. LC 67-27454. (Architecture & Decorative Art Ser.). 1967. lib. bdg. $19.50 (ISBN 0-306-70969-4). Da Capo.

MacDonald-Taylor, Margaret. Dictionary of Marks. (Illus.). 1962. pap. $6.25 (ISBN 0-8015-2089-4, 0607-180, Hawthorn). Dutton.

HAMMERED STRINGED INSTRUMENTS
see Stringed Instruments
HAND-TO-HAND FIGHTING
see also Self-Defense
Velte, Herbert. Budo-Lexikon: 1500 Fachausdruecke Fernoestl. LC 77-475498. (Illus.). 137p. (Ger.). 1976. DM.9.80 (ISBN 3-8068-0383-8). Falken Verlag.

HANDBOOKS, VADE-MECUMS, ETC.
Corson, Betty M., ed. The New Secretary's Deskbook. LC 74-34544. 844p. (Eng.). 1975. write for info. (ISBN 0-03-923299-9). HR&W Canada.

HANDICAPPED–EMPLOYMENT
Vocational Rehabilitation & the Employment of the Disabled. 182p. pap. 8.75 (ISBN 92-2-002571-X, ILO177, ILO). Unipub.

HANDICAPPED–REHABILITATION
see Vocational Rehabilitation
HANDICAPPED CHILDREN–EDUCATION
Ling, Daniel & Ling, Agnes H. Basic Vocabulary & Language Thesaurus for Hearing-Impaired Children. LC 76-52826. 1977. $6.00 (ISBN 0-88200-078-0, C1437). Alexander Graham.

HANDICRAFT
see also Bookbinding; Jewelry; Lace and Lace Making; Needlework; Occupational Therapy; Occupations; Pottery Craft
De Kerchove, R. Small Craft Dictionary. Date not set. price not set (ISBN 0-442-21890-7); pap. price not set (ISBN 0-442-25420-2). Van Nos Reinhold.

Lammar, Jutta. Der Grosse Ravensburger Werkkunstbuch. LC 76-470410. (Illus.). 424p. (Ger.). 1975. DM.29.80 (ISBN 3-473-42348-3). Maier Verlag.

Stoutenburgh, John L., ed. Dictionary of Arts & Crafts. 1956. 6.00 (ISBN 0-8022-1661-7). Philos Lib.

HANDLING OF MATERIALS
see Materials Handling
HANDWRITING
see Graphology; Paleography
HAPPINESS
McDonald, Marianne. Terms for happiness in Euripides. LC 79-312780. 335p. (Eng.). 1978. write for info. (ISBN 3-525-25149-1). Vandenhoeck.

HARD OF HEARING CHILDREN
see Children, Deaf

HAUSA LANGUAGE
Newman, Paul. Sabon Kamus na Hausa Zuwa Turanci. LC 79-104420. xii, 151p. (Hausa & Eng.). 1977. write for info. (ISBN 0-19-575303-8). Oxford U Pr.
HAVASUPAI INDIANS
see Indians of North America–Southwest, New
HAWAII
Nishiyama, Kazuo & Katayama, Hiroshi. Hawaii's Real Estate Industry & Technical Terminology in English & Japanese. 201p. (Japanese & Eng.). $8.32. Honolulu Japanese.
HAWAIIAN LANGUAGE
Helbig, W. Ray. Let's Learn a Little Hawaiian. (Eng. & Hawaiian.). 1970. soft bdg. 2.50 (ISBN 0-930492-07-2). Hawaiian Serv.
Leenhardt, Maurice. Vocabulaire & Grammaire de la Langue Houailou. 414p. (Hawaiian.). 1935. 66.20 F. Inst Ethnol.
Soper, J. H., ed. Hawaiian Phrase Book. LC 68-13868. (Hawaiian.). 1968. pap. $3.50 (ISBN 0-8048-0241-6). C E Tuttle.
HAWAIIAN LANGUAGE–DICTIONARIES–ENGLISH
Andrews. Dictionary of the Hawaiian Language. (Hawaiian & Eng.). $17.50. Iaconi.
Andrews, Lorrin. A Dictionary of the Hawaiian Language. LC 72-89745. (Hawaiian.). 1973. $17.50 (ISBN 0-8048-1087-7). C E Tuttle.
Burningham, Robin. Illustrated Hawaiian Word Book. (Illus.). 104p. (Orig., Hawaiian.). 1982. pap. $5.95 (ISBN 0-935848-12-6). Bess Pr.
Hitchcock. An English-Hawaiian Dictionary. (Hawaiian & Eng.). $7.25. Iaconi.
Hitchcock, Harvey R. English-Hawaiian Dictionary. LC 68-13870. (Hawaiian & Eng.). (gr. 7 up). 1968. Repr. $7.25 (ISBN 0-8048-0168-1). C E Tuttle.
Judd, Henry P. The Hawaiian Language & Hawaiian-English Dictionary. LC 78-101212. (Eng. & Hawaiian.). 1966. soft bdg. 4.95 (ISBN 0-930492-06-4). Hawaiian Serv.
Pukui, Mary K. & Elbert, Samuel H. Hawaiian Dictionary. rev. ed. Orig. Title: Hawaiian-English Dictionary English-Hawaiian Dictionary. 639p. (Hawaiian & Eng.). 1971. $20.00 (ISBN 0-87022-662-2). UH Pr.
Pukui, Mary K., et al. The Pocket Hawaiian Dictionary: With a Concise Hawaiian Grammar. LC 74-78865. 286p. (Hawaiian.). 1975. pap. $2.95 (ISBN 0-8248-0307-8). UH Pr.
Rehg, Kenneth L. & Sohl, Damian G. Ponapean-English Dictionary. LC 79-19451. (Pali Language Texts: Micronesia). 265p. (Ponapean & Eng.). 1979. pap. text ed. $14.00x (ISBN 0-8248-0562-3). UH Pr.
HAWTHORNE, NATHANIEL, 1804-1864
Byers, John R., Jr. & Owen, James J. A Concordance to the Five Novels of Nathaniel Hawthorne. LC 79-7910. 951p. 1979. lib. bdg. $138.00 (ISBN 0-8240-9545-6). Garland Pub.
HEAD-GEAR
see Costume
HEAD NURSE
see Nursing Service Administration
HEADDRESS
see Hairdressing
HEADINGS, SUBJECT
see Subject Headings
HEALTH
Here are entered works on optimal physical, mental, and social well-being, as well as how to achieve and preserve it. Works on personal body care and cleanliness are entered under Hygiene. Works on muscular efficiency and physical endurance are entered under Physical fitness.
see also Diet; Environmental Health; Hygiene; Nutrition; Public Health; Temperance
also subdivision Care and Hygiene under parts of the body, or under age groups dependent on the assistance of others, e.g. Eye–Care and Hygiene; Infants–Care and Hygiene; and subdivision Health and Hygiene under classes of persons or ethnic groups, e.g. Students–Health and Hygiene; Afro-Americans–Health and Hygiene
Der Gesundheits-Brockhaus. 848p. (Ger.). DM.48.00 (ISBN 3-7653-0026-8). F A Brockhaus.
McMurtray, Frances. Allied Health Reading Vocabulary Workbook. 122p. 1978. pap. text ed. $5.95x (ISBN 0-89641-008-0). American Pr.
HEALTH–DICTIONARIES
Diccionario Manual de Medicina & Salud. 288p. (Span.). 1979. 595.00 ptas. Biblograf.
Diccionario Monografico de Medicina & Salud. 380p. (Span.). 750.00 ptas (ISBN 84-7153-380-4). Biblograf SP.
Gardner, A. Ward. Good Housekeeping Dictionary of Symptoms. 256p. 1982. pap. $2.95 (ISBN 0-441-29822-2). Ace Bks.
Lexikon-Institut Bertelsmann. Lexikon der Medizin & Gesundheit. 850p. (Ger.). 1975. DM.39.00 (ISBN 3-570-04598-6). C Bertelsmann.
Lexis Veinte-dos: Medicina y Salud. 7th ed. 288p. (Span.). 1982. pap. 600.00 ptas. Circulo Lect.
Lindeke, Wolfgang. Dictionary of Ventilation & Health. 186p. 1980. $25.00x (ISBN 0-569-08522-5, Pub. by Collet's). State Mutual Bk.
The New American Medical Dictionary & Health Manual. 1982. pap. $4.50x (ISBN 0-451-12027-2, Pub. by NAL). Formur Intl.
Saponaro, A. Diccionario de los Sintomas: Los Testa de su Salud. 333p. (Span.). 1973. $29.95 (ISBN 0-686-92559-9, S-35094). French & Eur.
HEALTH, COMMUNITY
see Public Health
HEALTH, PUBLIC
see Public Health
HEALTH, RURAL
Matthews, C. M. Health & Culture in a South Indian village. LC 80-900413. (Illus.). 498p. (Eng. & Tamil.). 1979. Rs.125.00. Orient Bk Dist.
HEALTH COMMUNICATION
see Communication in Medicine
HEALTH OF CHILDREN
see Children–Care and Hygiene
HEALTH SERVICES
see Public Health
HEARING DISORDERS IN CHILDREN
see also Children, Deaf
Ling, Daniel & Ling, Agnes H. Basic Vocabulary & Language Thesaurus for Hearing-Impaired Children. LC 76-52826. 1977. $6.00 (ISBN 0-88200-078-0, C1437). Alexander Graham.
HEARING-IMPAIRED CHILDREN
see Children, Deaf
HEART
National Heart, Lung & Blood Institute. A Handbook of Heart Terms. LC 81-12490. (Illus.). 64p. 1982. $6.95x (ISBN 0-89490-052-8). Enslow Pubs.
HEAT
see also Thermodynamics; Thermoelectricity
Hoefling, Oskar, ed. Lexikon der Schulphysik: Waerme & Wetter. (Ger.). 1978. DM.46.00 (ISBN 3-7614-0108-6). Aulis Verlag.
HEAT–TRANSMISSION
Begell, William, ed. Glossary of Terms in Heat Transfer, Fluid Flow & Related Topics. LC 82-3153. (A Hemisphere Engineering Paperback Ser.). 112p. (Eng., Rus., Ger., Fr. & Japanese.). 1983. pap. 29.95 (ISBN 0-89116-261-5). Hemisphere Pub.
HEAT TRANSFER
see Heat–Transmission
HEAT TREATMENT OF METALS
see Metals–Heat Treatment
HEATING
see also Fuel; Furnaces; Stoves; Ventilation
American Society of Heating, Refrigerating & Air-Conditioning Engineers. Automatic Control Terminology for Heating, Ventilating, Air Conditioning & Refrigeration Equipment. (Illus.). $14.00 (ST8578); members $7.00. Am Heat Ref & Air Eng.
Control Terminology (A Glossary of Common Control Terms, No. 13. (Tech Tip). 100 copies $6.50. NA Heating & AC Wholesalers.
Doring, G. & Rudolphi. Tiefkuhl Lexikon. 239p. (Ger.). $10.95 (ISBN 3-87150-020-8, M-7666, Pub. by Deutscher Fachverlag). French & Eur.
European Heating & Ventilating Associations, ed. The International Dictionary of Heating, Ventilating, & Air Conditioning. LC 79-41714. 416p. 1982. $79.95x (ISBN 0-419-11650-8, NO. 6553, E&FN Spon England). Methuen Inc.
Haeder, Walter & Reichow, Guenther. Lexikon der Heizungs, Lueftungs & Klimatechnik. (Ger.). 1978. write for info. (ISBN 3-7864-1448-3). Langenscheidt.
HEBREW LANGUAGE–DICTIONARIES
Ben-Yehuda, Eliezer, ed. Dictionary & Thesaurus of the Hebrew Language, 8 Vols. Set. $150.00 (ISBN 0-498-07038-7, Yoseloff); lea. bd. set o.p. $250.00 (ISBN 0-498-08915-0). A S Barnes.
Board of Jewish Education. Miloni: Illustrated Dictionary for Children. (Illus.). 206p. (Hebrew.). pap. $9.00 (11-500). Board Jewish Educ.
--My Little Dictionary. (Illus.). 36p. (Hebrew.). $4.50 (11-551). Board Jewish Educ.
Cross, Frank M., Jr. & Freedman, David N. Early Hebrew Orthography: A Study of the Epigraphic Evidence. (American Oriental Ser.: Vol. 36). (Hebrew.). 1952. pap. $9.00x (ISBN 0-940490-36-6). Am Orient Soc.
Davidson, Benjamin. Analytical Hebrew & Chaldee Lexicon. (Hebrew.). $24.95 (ISBN 0-310-20290-6, Pub. by Bagster). Zondervan.
Debahy, M. Dictionary Hebrew Verbs. 1974. $15.00x (ISBN 0-86685-123-2). Intl Bk Ctr.
--Dictionary of Hebrew Verbs. 96p. (Arabic & Hebrew.). $15.00 (123-2). Intl Bk Ctr.
Diccionario hebreo-espanol. (Hebrew & Span.). 100.00 ptas. Perpetuo.
Ducach, Juan. Nuevo Diccionario Castellano-Hebreo, 2 vols. 720p. (Castilian & Hebrew.). 1971. IL.16.50 (36-0000). Massada Pr.
Einspahr, Bruce, compiled by. Index to the Brown, Driver & Briggs Hebrew Lexicon. LC 76-25479. (Hebrew.). 1976. 23.95 (ISBN 0-8024-4082-7). Moody.
Even-Shoshan, Abraham, ed. Condensed Hebrew Dictionary. (Illus.). 824p. (Hebrew.). 1982. text ed. $35.00 (ISBN 965-17-0103-X). K Sefer.
--The Student's Dictionary. (Illus.). 592p. (Hebrew.). 1982. text ed. $12.00 (ISBN 965-17-0105-6). K Sefer.
Feyerabend, K. Langenscheidts Taschenwoerterbuch Hebraisch. 306p. (Hebrew & Ger.). DM.19.80 (10040). Langenscheidt.
Gesenius, Friedrich H. Guilielmi Gesenii Thesaurus Philologicus Linguae Hebraeae, 3 vols. LC 78-392234. 1522p. (Hebrew & Lat.). 1977. DM.780.00. Biblio-Verlag.
Herlitz, G., ed. Juedisches Lexikon, 5 vols. (Illus.). 4482p. (Ger.). 1982. pap. $320.00. M. Rosenberg.
Jastrow, Marcus. Hebrew-Aramaic-English Dictionary, a Dictionary of Talmud Babli & Talmud Yerushalmi Targum & Midrash, 2 Vols. (Hebrew, Aramaic & Eng.). $68.50 (ISBN 0-87559-019-5). Shalom.
Klatzkin. Thesaurus Philosophicus Linguae Hebraica, 4 pts. in 2 vols. (Hebrew.). $47.50 (ISBN 0-87306-118-7). Feldheim.
Learn Hebrew for English Speakers. (Hebrew & Eng.). pap. 9.50 romanized (ISBN 0-87557-032-1, 032-1). Saphrograph.
Levenston, Edward A. & Sivan, Reuven. The New Bantam-Megiddo Hebrew Dictionary. 736p. (Hebrew.). 1975. pap. $2.95 (ISBN 0-553-02094-3, G14420-0). Bantam.
Nouveau Dictionnaire Francais-Hebreu. (Fr. & Hebrew.). 1973. 35.85 (ISBN 0-685-55772-3). Larousse.
Nouveau Dictionnaire hebreu-francais. (Hebrew & Fr.). 1973. 39.25 (ISBN 0-685-55771-5). Larousse.
Pavoncello, Nello. Elef Millim. LC 79-367877. 60p. (Hebrew & Ital.). 1979. L.00.2000.00 (ISBN 8-88502-709-1). Carucci.
--Mille Parole Fondamentali. LC 79-367877. 60p. (Hebrew & Ital.). 1979. L.2000.00 (ISBN 8-8850-2709-1). Carucci.
Pimentel, Jitschak. Woordenboek Hebreeuws-Nederlands. LC 78-388662. 480p. (Hebrew & Dutch.). 1978. fl.49.00 (ISBN 9-0601-0322-X). Strengholt.
--Woordenboek Hebreeuws-Nederlands. LC 78-388662. 480p. (Hebrew & Dutch.). 1978. fl.49.00 (ISBN 9-06010-322-X). Strengholt.
Shoshan, A. Even & Yarden, Dov, eds. Milon Kis: A Hebrew Pocket Dictionary. (Illus.). 662p. (Hebrew.). $5.00 (11-575). Board Jewish Educ.
Shoshan, Abraham E., ed. The Complete Hebrew Dictionary Supplement to the 3 Volume Set. (Illus.). 352p. (Hebrew.). 1983. $25.00 (ISBN 9-651-7015-60). K Sefer.
--The Complete Hebrew Dictionary Supplement Volume to Seven Volume Set. (Illus.). 352p. (Hebrew.). 1983. $30.00 (ISBN 9-651-7015-52). K Sefer.
HEBREW LANGUAGE–DICTIONARIES–ENGLISH
Alcalay, Reuben. Complete English-Hebrew, Hebrew-English Dictionary, 3 vols. 7180p. (Eng. & Hebrew.). 1980. Repr. of 1965 ed. $69.00 set (ISBN 0-89961-017-X). Vol. 1 (ISBN 0-89961-003-X). Vol. 2 (ISBN 0-89961-007-2). Vol. 3 (ISBN 0-89961-008-0). SBS Pub.
--The Massada English-Hebrew Student Dictionary. 734p. (Eng. & Hebrew.). 1980. Repr. $18.95 (ISBN 0-89961-006-4). SBS Pub.
Armstrong, Terry, et al, eds. A Reader's Hebrew-English Lexicon of the Old Testament: (Genesis-Deuteronomy, Vol. 1. (Hebrew & Eng.). 1978. $9.95 (ISBN 0-310-37020-5). Zondervan.
Bantam Hebrew-English, English-Hebrew Dictionary. (Hebrew & Eng.). $2.95 (235-5). Bantam.
Berlitz Editors. Berlitz Hebrew for Travellers. 192p. (Hebrew.). 1982. pap. $4.95 (ISBN 0-02-964050-4, Berlitz). Macmillan.
Dov Ben Abba. The Signet Hebrew-English - English-Hebrew Dictionary. (Orig., Hebrew & Eng.). 1978. pap. $2.95 (ISBN 0-451-09654-1, E9654, Sig). NAL.
Ettinger, David. Hebrew-English Pictorial Dictionary. (Hebrew & Eng.). $27.50 (ISBN 0-87559-018-7). Shalom.
Even-Shoshan, Abraham, ed. The Complete Hebrew Dictionary in Seven Volumes. (Illus.). 3236p. (Eng. & Hebrew.). text ed. $140.00 (ISBN 965-17-0083-1). K Sefer.
--The Complete Hebrew Dictionary in Three Volumes. (Illus.). 1664p. (Eng. & Hebrew.). text ed. $80.00 (ISBN 965-17-0084-X). K Sefer.
Furst, Gesenius. Hebrew-English Dictionary: Hebrew & Chaldee Lexicon to the Old Testament. rev. ed. Mitchell, Edward C., ed. (Hebrew & Eng.). $42.50 (ISBN 0-87559-021-7); thumb indexed $42.50 (ISBN 0-87559-022-5). Shalom.
Gesenius, William. Hebrew & Chaldee Lexicon, Tregelles Translation. (Hebrew & Chaldee.). 1949. $12.95 (ISBN 0-8028-8029-0). Eerdmans.

--Hebrew & English Lexicon to the Old Testament. 2nd ed. Brown, Francis, et al, eds. Robinson, Edward, tr. (Hebrew & Eng.). 1959. $34.95x (ISBN 0-19-864301-2). Oxford U Pr.

Goldberg, Nathan. New Functional Hebrew-English, English-Hebrew Dictionary. (Hebrew & Eng.). (gr. 9-12). 1958. $5.00x (ISBN 0-87068-379-9). Ktav.

--New Illustrated Hebrew-English Dictionary for Young Readers. (Illus., Hebrew & Eng.). (gr. 4-7). 1958. pap. 6.95x (ISBN 0-87068-370-5). Ktav.

Hebrew-English Lexicon of the Bible. LC 74-26705. 296p. (Orig., Hebrew & Eng.). 1975. pap. $7.50 (ISBN 0-8052-0481-4). Schocken.

Hebrew Pocket Dictionary. (Hebrew & Eng.). $12.50 (ISBN 0-685-12022-8). Heinman.

Jacobs, Sidney J. The Jewish Word Book. 356p. (Eng. & Hebrew). 1982. $12.50 (ISBN 0-8246-0249-8). Jonathan David.

Kamrat, Mordechai & Samuel, Edwin, eds. Roots: A Hebrew-English Word List. (Illus.). 308p. (Eng. & Hebrew). 1982. pap. text ed. $7.50 (ISBN 965-17-0118-8). K Sefer.

Levenston, Edward A. & Sivan, Reuban, eds. The Megiddo Modern Dictionary: English-Hebrew, Hebrew-English, 3 Vols. (Eng. & Hebrew). 1983. $75.00 (ISBN 0-686-43009-3, Carta Maps & Guides Pub Israel). Hippocrene Bks.

--The Megiddo Modern Dictionary: English-Hebrew, Hebrew-English, 3 vols. (Hebrew & Eng.). 1983. $75.00 (ISBN 0-686-43009-3). Carta Pub Co.

Pocket-Shorter Dictionary. 600p. (Hebrew & Eng.). $5.95 (088). Langenscheidt.

Sivan, Reuven & Levenston, Edward A. The New Bantam-Megiddo Hebrew & English Dictionary. LC 77-75289. (Hebrew & Eng.). 1977. $24.95 (ISBN 0-8052-3666-X). Schocken.

Waldstein, A. Hebrew-English, English-Hebrew Dictionary. (Hebrew & Eng.). $18.50 (ISBN 0-87559-016-0); thumb indexed $23.50 (ISBN 0-87559-017-9). Shalom.

Young, Robert. Young's Analytical Concordance to the Bible. 1955. $19.95 (ISBN 0-8028-8084-3); deluxe ed. $22.95 (ISBN 0-8028-8085-1). Eerdmans.

HEBREW LANGUAGE-DICTIONARIES-GERMAN

Feierabend, K. Langenscheidts Taschenwoerterbuecher Hebraeisch-Deutsch. (Hebrew & Ger.). 1978. DM.14.80 (ISBN 3-468-10040-X). Langenscheidt.

Feyerabend, K. Hebraisch-Deutsch: Zum Alten Testament. (Langenscheidts Taschenworterbucher Ser.). 306p. (Ger. & Hebrew.). DM.18.80 (10040). Langenscheidt.

Herstig, David. Deutsch-Hebraeisches Woerterbuch. (Ger. & Hebrew). 1971. $17.50 (ISBN 3-19-006285-4, M-7330, Pub. by Max Hueber). French & Eur.

--Deutsch-Hebraeisches Woerterbuch. (Ger. & Hebrew). 1971. DM.17.50 (ISBN 3-447-00354-5). Hueber.

--Hebraeisch-Deutches Woerterbuch. (Hebrew & Ger.). 1971. $17.50 (ISBN 3-19-006289-7). Hueber.

--Hebraeisch-Deutsches Woerterbuch. (Hebrew & Ger.). 1971. $17.50 (ISBN 3-19-006289-7, M-7441, Pub. by Max Hueber). French & Eur.

Lavy, Jaacom. Langenscheidt's Hebrew-German Dictionary. 638p. (Ger. & Hebrew). 1978. $32.00 (ISBN 0-685-64071-X). Am Map.

Lavy, Jaacov. Hebraisch, 2 vols. (Langenscheidts Handworterbucher Ser.). (Ger. & Hebrew). Teil 1: Hebraisch-Deutsch (639p.) DM.78.00 (04160); Teil 2: Deutsch-Hebraisch (xxiii, 824p.) DM.88.00 (04165). Langenscheidt.

--Langenscheidts Handwoerterbuch Hebraisch: Teil II, Deutsch-Hebraisch. 823p. (Hebrew & Ger.). DM.88.00 (04165). Langenscheidt.

--Langenscheidts Handwoerterbuch Hebraisch: Teil I, Hebraisch-Deutsch. 639p. (Hebrew & Ger.). DM.78.00 (04160). Langenscheidt.

HEBREW LANGUAGE-GLOSSARIES, VOCABULARIES, ETC.

Payne, J. Barton. Hebrew Vocabularies. (Hebrew). pap. $3.95 (ISBN 0-8010-6949-1). Baker Bk.

HELL

Collin de Pianci, Santiago. Diccionario de los infiernos. (Span.). Arg.$7.00. Rueda.

HELLENISM

Kleines Woerterbuch Des Hellenismus. 1st ed. (Ger. & Gr.). 1972. $30.95 (ISBN 0-686-56625-4, M-7515, Pub. by Harrassowitz). French & Eur.

HELLENISTIC GREEK

see Greek Language, Hellenistic (300 B.C.-600 A.D.)

HELMINTHOLOGY

see also Worms, Intestinal and Parasitic

Pozniak, G. I., ed. Dictionary of Helminthology & Plant Nematology. 108p. (Rus. & Eng.). 1979. $35.00 (ISBN 0-85198-447-9). French & EUr.

Pozniak, G. J. Russian-English Dictionary of Helminthology & Plant Nematology. 108p. (Rus. & Eng.). 1979. $60.00x (ISBN 0-85198-447-9, Pub. by CAB Bks England). State Mutual Bk.

HELMINTHS

see Worms, Intestinal and Parasitic

HEMATOLOGY

Samson, P. Glossary of Hematological & Seriological Terms. (Illus.). 128p. 1973. text ed. $13.95 (ISBN 0-407-72720-5). Butterworth.

HERALDRY

see also Devices; Genealogy; Mottoes; Nobility; Seals (Numismatics); Titles of Honor and Nobility

Brault, Gerard J. Early Blazon: Heraldic Terminology in the Twelfth & Thirteenth Centuries; with Special Reference to Arthurian Literature. (Illus.). 1972. text ed. 45.00x (ISBN 0-19-822337-4). Oxford U Pr.

Briggs, Geoffrey, ed. Civic & Corporate Heraldry: A Dictionary of Impersonal Arms of England, Wales, & Northern Ireland. (Illus.). 432p. 1971. $32.00x (ISBN 0-685-29194-4). Gale.

Cadenas y Vicent, Vicente de. Diccionario heraldico. 2nd ed. LC 78-362955. (Illus.). 295p. (Span.). 1976. 1000.00 ptas (ISBN 8-40004-294-8). Consejo Superior.

Chassant, A. & Tausin, H. Dictionnaire des Devises Historiques & Heraldiques. 1728p. (Fr.). write for info. Slatkine.

Dayre De Mailhol, C. P. Dictionnaire Historique & Heraldique, 2 vols. 2120p. (Fr.). write for info. Slatkine.

De Mailhol, D. Dictionnaire Historique & Heraldique. (Fr.). write for info. Fac.

Gough, H. A Glossary of Terms Used in Heraldry. 59.95 (ISBN 0-8490-0239-7). Gordon Pr.

Lizaso, Domingo. Diccionario onomastico y heraldico vasco: Tomo 7. 592p. (Span.). 1982. pap. 2390.00 ptas (ISBN 84-248-0741-3). Encicl Vasca.

Pasini, Frassoni F. Dizionario storico araldico dell'antico ducato di Ferrara. 793p. (Ital.). L.35000.00. Forni.

Piero, Guelfi C. Dizionario araldico. (Illus.). vi, 586p. (Ital.). 1966. L.9500.00. Forni.

Puttock, A. G. Dictionary of Heraldry & Related Subjects. LC 76-137421. (Illus.). 256p. 1970. 15.00 (ISBN 0-8063-0449-9). Genealogy Pub.

Rentzmann, Wilhelm. Numismatisches Wappen-Lexicon, 2 vols. in 1. LC 78-380299. (Illus., Ger., Berlin). 1978. M.30.00. Transpress Verlag fur Verkehrswesen.

Rietstap, Johannes B. Armorial General Precede d'un Dictionnaire des Termes du Blason, Pt. 1. (Fr.). 1934. $135.00 (ISBN 0-686-56594-0, M-7298, Pub. by Olms). French & Eur.

--Armorial General Precede d'un Dictionnaire des Termes du Blason, Pt. 2. (Fr.). 1934. $135.00 (ISBN 0-686-56595-9, M-7299, Pub. by Olms). French & Eur.

HERALDRY-JUVENILE LITERATURE

Parker, James. Glossary of Terms Used in Heraldry. LC 77-94021. (Illus.). (gr. 9 up). 1970. $29.50 (ISBN 0-8048-0715-9). C E Tuttle.

HERBAGE

see Grasses

HERBALS

see Botany, Medical; Herbs

HERBERT, GEORGE, 1593-1633

Di Cesare, Mario A. & Mignani, Rigo, eds. A Concordance to the Complete Writings of George Herbert. LC 76-56642. (Cornell Concordances Ser.). 1977. $59.50x (ISBN 0-8014-1106-8). Cornell U Pr.

Mann, Cameron. Concordance to the English Poems of George Herbert. LC 77-4939. 1927. lib. bdg. $19.00 (ISBN 0-8414-6186-4). Folcroft.

HERBS

see also Botany, Medical

Clair, Colin. Dictionnaire des Herbes & des Epices. 259p. (Fr.). 1963. 14.00 F. Denoel.

--Dictionnaire des Herbes et des Epices. 259p. (Fr.). 1963. pap. $6.95 (ISBN 0-686-56842-7, M-6621). French & Eur.

Stuart, Malcolm. Van Nostrand Reinhold Color Dictionary of Herbs & Herbalism. 160p. 1982. pap. $12.95 (ISBN 0-442-28338-5). Van Nos Reinhold.

HERBS-THERAPEUTIC USE

see Botany, Medical

HERDSMEN

see Shepherds

HEREDITARY DISEASES

see Medical Genetics

HEREDITY OF DISEASE

see Medical Genetics

HERESIES AND HERETICS

For general descriptive and historical works. Works on heresy in the abstract are entered under the heading Heresy.

Nelli, Rene. Dictionnaire Des Heresies Meridionales. 384p. (Fr.). $18.50 (ISBN 0-686-56886-9, F-21110). French & Eur.

--Dictionnaire des Heresies Meridionales. (Illus.). 384p. (Fr.). 44.10 F. Privat.

Pluquet, F. A. Dictionnaire des Heresies des Erreurs et des Schismes, 2 vols. Migne, J. P., ed. (Encyclopedie Theologique Ser.: Vols. 11-12). 1374p. (Fr.). Repr. of 1847 ed. lib. bdg. $175.00x (ISBN 0-89241-235-6). Caratzas Pub Co.

HERMETIC ART AND PHILOSOPHY

see Alchemy; Magic; Occult Sciences

HEROINES

see Women

HERPETOLOGY

A, Peters J. Dictionary of Herpetology: Description of Words & Terms. (Illus.). 392p. 1981. lib. bdg. 15.00x (ISBN 0-02-850230-2). Lubrecht & Cramer.

HERRICK, ROBERT, 1591-1674

MacLeod, Malcolm L. A Concordance to the Poems of Robert Herrick. LC 77-13605. 1977. Repr. lib. bdg. $35.00 (ISBN 0-8414-6219-4). Folcroft.

HESIODUS

Hofinger, M. Lexicon Hesiodeum: Cum Indice Inverso. LC 79-345373. xi, 745p. (Gr.). 1978. write for info. Brill Verlag.

HEXAPODA

see Insects

HI-FI SYSTEMS

see High-Fidelity Sound Systems

HIDATSA INDIANS

see Indians of North America--The West

HIDATSA LANGUAGE

Matthews, Washington. Ethnography & Philology of the Hidatsa Indians: U. S. Geological & Geographical Survey of the Territories, Miscellaneous Publication, No. 7. LC 3-8072. 1971. Repr. of 1877 ed. $25.00 (ISBN 0-384-35892-6). Johnson Repr.

--Ethnography & Philology of the Hidatsa Indians: U. S. Geological & Geographical Survey of the Territories, Miscellaneous Publication, No. 7. LC 3-8072. 1971. Repr. of 1877 ed. $25.00 (ISBN 0-384-35892-6). Johnson Repr.

HIEROGLYPHICS

see also Alphabet; Egyptian Language--Writing, Hieroglyphic

Feldman-Konrad, N. I. Iaponsko-Russkii Uchebnyi Slovar Ieroglifov. 683p. (Japanese & Rus.). 1977. $15.50 (Pub. by Russkii Iazyk). Four Continent.

HIGH-FIDELITY SOUND SYSTEMS

Howard W. Sams Editorial Staff. Dictionary of Audio & Hi-Fi. LC 74-79354. 1975. pap. 7.50 (ISBN 0-672-21084-3). Sams.

HIGH SEAS, JURISDICTION OVER

see Maritime Law

HIGHWAY ENGINEERING

see Highway Research; Road Construction; Roads; Traffic Engineering

HIGHWAY LAW

see Cycling

HIGHWAY RESEARCH

Choppy, Jacques. Dictionnaire de l'Industrie Routiere. LC 77-573401. (Illus.). 143p. (Fr.). 1977. 55.00 F. Eyrolles.

Morilla, Abad I. Diccionario de Ingenieria de Caminos. LC 79-117965. 358p. (Span.). 1979. write for info. (ISBN 8-4368-0119-9). Piramide.

HIGHWAYS

see Roads

HIKING

see also Backpacking

Larson, Randy. Illustrated Backpacking & Hiking Dictionary for Young People. (Treehouse Bks). (Illus.). (gr. 4 up). 1981. pap. 2.50 (ISBN 0-13-450759-2). P-H.

HINDI LANGUAGE

see also Hindustani Language; Urdu Language

Dymshits, Z. M., et al. Karmannyi Russko-Khindi Slovar. 867p. (Rus). 1958. $1.85 (Pub. by GINS). Four Continent.

Gatzlaff-Halsig, Margot. Woerterbuch Deutsch-Hindi. LC 78-359321. 646p. (Ger. & Hindi.). 1977. M.60.00. VEB Verlag Enzyklopadie.

Handoo, Jawaharlal & Handoo, Lalita. Hindu-Kashmiri Common Vocabulary. LC 76-902046. vii, 292p. (Kashmiri & Hindi.). 1975. Rs.20.00. Ctr Inst Ind Lang.

Hindi Pocket Dictionary, 2 vols. (Hindi & Eng.). 15.00 set (ISBN 0-685-30576-7). Heinman.

Platts, John T. A Dictionary of Urdu Classical Hindi & English. LC 78-670100. (Hindi & Eng.). 1977. Repr. of 1884 ed. 50.00x (ISBN 0-8002-0243-0). Intl Pubns Serv.

Pradeeps Standard Oxford Dictionary: English to English, Panjabi & Hindi, with Pronunciations & Idioms. 1983. $15.00x (ISBN 0-8364-0991-4, Pub. by Pradeep Co). South Asia Bks.

Suryakanta. Sanskrit-Hindi-English Dictionary. (Sanskrit, Hindi & Eng.). 1976. $47.50x (ISBN 0-8002-1950-3). Intl Pubns Serv.

Ul'Tsiferov, O. G. Khindi-Russkii Uchebnyi Slovar. 744p. (Rus.). 1962. $2.75 (Pub. by GINS). Four Continent.

HINDU ART

see Art, Hindu

HINDU LAW

Mansoor. Introduction, Key to Text, Vocabularies. (Legal & Documentary Ser.). 1965. write for info. E J Brill.

HINDUSTANI LANGUAGE

see also Hindi Language; Urdu Language

Learn Hindustani. (Hindustani.). pap. 9.50 (ISBN 0-87557-037-2, 037-2). Saphrograph.
Platts, John T. Dictionary of Urdu, Classical Hindi, & English. (Urdu., Hindu & Eng.). 1930. $82.00x (ISBN 0-19-864309-8). Oxford U Pr.

HIPPOLOGY
see Horses

HISPANOAMERICANISM
see Pan-Hispanism

HISPANOS
see Mexican Americans

HISTOLOGY
see also Microscope and Microscopy also names of particular tissues or organs, e.g. Muscle, Nerves
Lovasy, Ernest & Veillon, Emmanuel. Dictionnaire des Termes d'anatomie, d'embryologie & d'histologie. 624p. (Fr.). 1954. 40.00 F. Maloine.
Lovasy, Ernst. Dictionnaire des Termes d'Anatomie, d'Embryologie et d'Histologie. 624p. (Fr.). 1954. $17.50 (ISBN 0-686-57022-7, M-6380). French & Eur.
Wawrzyniak, Marka. Mianownictwo Histologiczne. LC 80-463674. 209p. (Pol. & Lat.). 1979. 160.00 Zl (ISBN 8-3200-0033-5). Panstowy Zaklad W.

HISTOLOGY, PATHOLOGICAL
Law, J. & Oliver, H. J. Glossary of Histopathological Terms. (Illus.). 128p. 1972. text ed. $13.95 (ISBN 0-407-72730-2). Butterworth.

HISTORICAL ATLASES
see Classical Geography

HISTORICAL CHRONOLOGY
see Chronology, Historical

HISTORICAL DICTIONARIES
see History–Dictionaries

HISTORICAL GEOGRAPHY
see Geography, Historical

HISTORICAL RECORD PRESERVATION
see Archives

HISTORY
Here are entered general works about history, its methods, philosophy, etc. For works on the history of specific places or periods, see World History; History, Ancient; History, modern, etc.
see also Anthropo-Geography; Archaeology; Battles; Chronology; Civilization; Culture; Diplomacy; Diplomatics; Discoveries (In Geography); Genealogy; Geography, Historical; Heraldry; Military History; Numismatics; Political Science; Revolutions; Seals (Numismatics)
also subdivisions Antiquities, Foreign Relations, History and Politics and Government under names of countries, states, cities, etc.
Forstmann, Wilfried, et al. Die Geschichte: Ein Sachlexikon fuer die Schule. (Illus.). 503p. (Ger.). DM.19.80 (ISBN 3-411-01799-6). Biblio Inst.

HISTORY–ATLASES
see Classical Geography

HISTORY–CHRONOLOGY
see Chronology, Historical

HISTORY–DICTIONARIES
Abaev, V. I. Istoriko-Etimologicheskii Slovar Osetinskogo. 360p. (Rus.). 1979. $8.25 (Pub. by Nauka). Four Continent.
Allard, Guy & Granoble. Dictionnaire Historique, Chronologique, Geographique, Genealogique, Heraldique, Juridique, Politique & Botanographique du Daup, 2 vols. 754p. (Fr.). 1970. 150.00 F. Slatkine.
Arnaldi, G. Dizionario dei termini storiografici. 120p. (Ital.). L.2500.00. Zanichelli.
Barbier De Meynard, Achille. Dictionnaire Geographique, Historique & Literaire: La Perse & des Contrees Adjacentes, 8 vols. 640p. (Fr.). 1970. fl.96.00. Philo Pr.
Bayer, Erich. Woerterbuch zur Geschichte. 3rd ed. (Ger.). 1974. pap. $19.95 (ISBN 3-520-28903-2, M-6905). French & Eur.
--Woerterbuch zur Geschichte. (Ger.). 1974. DM.22.00 (ISBN 3-520-28903-2). Kroener.
Bayle, Pierre. Dictionnaire Historique & Critique, 16 vols. 9546p. (Fr.). 1969. 1800.00 F. Slatkine.
--Dictionnaire Historique & Critique. (Illus.). 236p. (Fr.). 1974. 15.00 F. Sociales.
Brun-Durand, Justin. Dictionnaire Topographique & Historique de la Drome. 580p. (Fr.). 1973. 120.00 F. Chantermerle.
Chabrol, G. M. Dictionnaire Historique des Fiefs: Chateilenies & Paroisses de la Haute & de la Basse Auvergne. 1060p. (Fr.). 1973. 330.00 F. Guenegaud.
Coler, Christfried. Diccionario por Fechas de Historia Universal. 2nd ed. 480p. (Span.). 1977. $50.95 (ISBN 84-261-5799-8, S-50366). French & Eur.
Compagnol, Marcello G. Dizionario Merli geografico, storico, economico: Vol. 1, Lettera AZ. (Illus.). 176p. (Ital.). 1975. L.25000.00. ERGA.
Cook, Chris. Dictionary of Historical Terms. 384p. (Eng.). 1983. E12.95 (ISBN 0-333-28470-4); pap. $6.95 (ISBN 0-333-35190-8). Macmillan London.
Coston, Henry. Dictionnaire des Dynasties Bourgeoises & du Monde des Affaires. (Illus.). 599p. (Fr.). 1975. 120.00 F. A. Moreau.
Davis, Robert R., Jr. Lexicon of Historical & Political Terms. pap. 1.95 (ISBN 0-671-18706-6, 18706). Monarch Pr.
--Lexicon of Historical & Political Terms. Reed, R., ed. LC 81-83626. (Illus.). 125p. 1982. pap. 7.95 (ISBN 0-88247-612-2). R & E Res Assoc.
Dayre De Mailhol, C. P. Dictionnaire Historique & Heraldique, 2 vols. 2120p. (Fr.). write for info. Slatkine.
De Mailhol, D. Dictionnaire Historique & Heraldique. (Fr.). write for info. Fac.
Dictionnaire Historique, Literaire & Statistique, 2 vols. 1620p. (Fr.). 1973. write for info. Lafitte Repr.
Dizionario di cultura universale, 5 vols. (Ital.). 1974. L.100000.00. Vallardi F.
Franz, L. & Neumann, A. R., eds. Lexikon Zur & Freuhgeschictlicher Fundstaetten Oesterreichs. (Ger.). 1965. DM.58.00 (ISBN 3-7749-0255-0). Habelt.
Harbottle, Thomas B. Dictionary of Historical Allusions. LC 68-23163. 1968. Repr. of 1904 ed. $34.00x (ISBN 0-8103-3088-1). Gale.
Haydn, Joseph T. Haydn's Dictionary of Dates & Universal Information Relating to All Ages & Nations. 1968. Repr. of 1911 ed. $89.00 (ISBN 0-403-00083-1). Scholarly.
Herbert. Dictionnaire Pittoresque & Historique: Ou Description d'architecture, Peinture, Sculpture, Gravure, 2 vols. (Fr.). 1972. 150.00 F. Minkoff Repr.
Lalanne, Ludovic. Dictionnaire Historique de la France. 1971p. (Fr.). 1974. 350.00 F. Slatkine.
--Dictionnaire Historique de la France, 2 vols. 1884p. (Fr.). 1978. 300.00 F. Slatkine.
Lexikon der Geschichte. (Ger.). 1976. DM.29.40 (ISBN 3-453-41149-8). Heyne W Verlag.
Lexikon der Geschicte, 3 vols. (Ger.). 1976. Set. pap. $25.00 (ISBN 3-453-41149-8, M-7255). French & Eur.
Marchand, Prosper. Dictionnaire Historique. 702p. (Fr.). DM.228.00. Olms.
Masquet, Georges. Dictionnaire des Grands Evenements de L'histoire. 315p. (Fr.). 1973. pap. 8.95 (ISBN 0-686-56796-X, M-174, Pub. by Hachette). French & Eur.
--Dictionnaire des Grands Evenements de l'histoire. (Illus.). 315p. (Fr.). 1973. 20.00 F. Hachette.
--Dictionnaire des Grands Evenements de l'Historie. 315p. (Fr.). 1973. pap. $8.95. Hachette-Jeunesse.
Mourre, Michel. Dizionario Mondadori di storia universale, 2 vols. (Ital.). L.30000.00. Mondadori.
Palmer, Alan. The Penguin Dictionary of Twentieth Century History: Nineteen Hundred to Nineteen Seventy-Eight. (Reference Ser.). 1979. pap. 5.95 (ISBN 0-14-051085-0). Penguin.
Pedio, Tommaso. Dizionario dei patrioti lucani artefici ed oppositori (1700-1870) Vol. 1, A-C. xxiv, 520p. (Ital.). 1969. L.8000.00. Soc Bari.
--Dizionario dei patrioti lucani artefici ed oppositori (1700-1870) Vol. 2, D-I. 590p. (Ital.). 1972. L.8500.00. Soc Bari.
Pskovskii Oblastnoi Slovar S Istoricheskimi Dannymi, Vol. 2. 244p. (Rus.). 1973. $4.50 (Pub. by LGU). Four Continent.
Pskovskii Oblastnoi Slovar S Istoricheskimi Dannymi, Vol. 3. 180p. (Rus.). 1976. $3.90 (Pub. by LGU). Four Continent.
Pskovskii Oblastnoi Slovar S Istorischeskmi Dannymi, Vol. 4. 184p. (Rus.). 1979. $3.95 (Pub. by LGU). Four Continent.
Rogger, M. R., tr. Dizionario dell'antichita classica. (Illus.). 352p. (Ital.). L.3300.00. Zanichelli.
Romero, J. L. Diccionario de historia universal. (Span.). Arg.$22.00. Atlantida.
Rosa, U. Glossario storico popolare piemontese. 118p. (Ital.). L.4800.00. Forni.
Rousset, A. Dictionnaire Geographique, Historique & Statistique des Communes: Franche-Comte & des Hameaux qui en Dependent, 6 vols. 3602p. (Fr.). 1970. 600.00 F. Guenegaud.
Wetterau, Bruce. The Macmillan Concise Dictionary of World History. 672p. 1983. 39.95 (ISBN 0-02-626110-3). Macmillan.

HISTORY–YEARBOOKS
Epstein, Howard M. & Kanner, Gerald B., eds. News Dictionary: Vol. 5, 1968. annual LC 65-17649. (Illus.). 1969. $14.95 (ISBN 0-87196-087-7). Facts on File.
Paneth, Donald. News Dictionary 1980. 400p. 1981. $14.95 (ISBN 0-87196-111-3). Facts on File.
Sobel, Lester A., et al. News Dictionary: Vol. 1, 1964. annual LC 65-17649. (Orig.). 1965. $14.95 (ISBN 0-87196-079-6). Facts on File.
Sobel, Lester A., et al, eds. News Dictionary: Vol. 2, 1965. annual LC 65-17649. (Orig.). 1966. $14.95 (ISBN 0-87196-081-8). Facts on File.
--News Dictionary: Vol. 3, 1966. annual LC 65-17649. (Orig.). 1967. $14.95 (ISBN 0-87196-083-4). Facts on File.
--News Dictionary: Vol. 4, 1967. annual LC 65-17649. 1968. $14.95 (ISBN 0-87196-085-0). Facts on File.
Trotsky, Judith, ed. News Dictionary 1974, Vol. 11. annual LC 65-17649. 500p. 1975. lib. bdg. $14.95 (ISBN 0-87196-099-0). Facts on File.

HISTORY, ANCIENT–DICTIONARIES
Andresen, Carl, et al. Lexikon der Alten Welt. (Ger.). 1965. DM.320.00 (ISBN 3-7608-0137-4). Artemis Verlag.
Cooper, William R. Archaic Dictionary. LC 73-76018. 1969. Repr. of 1876 ed. $66.00x (ISBN 0-8103-3885-8). Gale.
Garcin, E. Dictionnaire Historique & Topographique de la Ancienne & Moderne, 2 vols. 1232p. (Fr.). write for info. Chantemerle.

HISTORY, JUVENILE
see World History–Juvenile Literature;
also subdivision Juvenile Literature, or History, Juvenile under names of countries

HISTORY, LOCAL
see Local History

HISTORY, MEDIEVAL
see Middle Ages–History

HISTORY, MILITARY
see Military History

HISTORY, MODERN–CHRONOLOGY
see Chronology, Historical

HISTORY, MODERN–DICTIONARIES
De Launay, Jacques & Lousse, Emile. Dictionnaire d'Histoire Contemporaine 1776-1969. 550p. (Fr.). 1973. 16.00 F. Rencontre.
Garcin, E. Dictionnaire Historique & Topographique de la Ancienne & Moderne, 2 vols. 1232p. (Fr.). write for info. Chantemerle.
Palmer. Diccionario de historia moderna. (Span.). 265.00 ptas. Labor SA.
Palmer, Alan W. Dictionary of Modern History. (Reference Ser.). (Orig.). (YA) (gr. 11 up). 1964. pap. 5.95 (ISBN 0-14-051026-5). Penguin.

HISTORY, MODERN–20TH CENTURY
see also World War, 1939-1945
Palmer, Alan. Facts on File Dictionary of Twentieth Century History. 403p. 1980. $22.50 (ISBN 0-686-60214-5). Facts on File.
--The Penguin Dictionary of Twentieth Century History: Nineteen Hundred to Nineteen Seventy-Eight. (Reference Ser.). 1979. pap. 5.95 (ISBN 0-14-051085-0). Penguin.
Sobel, Lester A., ed. News Dictionary: 1973, Vol. 10. annual 500p. 1974. lib. bdg. $14.95 (ISBN 0-87196-097-4). Facts on File.

HISTORY, UNIVERSAL
see World History

HISTORY, MODERN–YEARBOOKS
see History–Yearbooks

HISTRIONICS
see Acting

HITTITE LANGUAGE
Friedrich, Johannes & Kammenhuber, Annelies. Hethitisches Woerterbuch. 2nd ed. (Ger.). 1975. write for info. Winter Univ.
Hoffner, Harry A., Jr. An English-Hittite Glossary. 1967. 10.50x (ISBN 0-8002-1398-X). Intl Pubns Serv.
Hoffner, Harry A., Jr. & Guterbock, Hans G., eds. The Hittite Dictionary of the Oriental Institute of the University of Chicago, Vol. 3, Fasc. 1, L. LC 79-53554. (Hittite.). 1980. pap. 9.00x (ISBN 0-918986-27-3). Oriental Inst.
Linguistic Society of America & Sturtevant, E. H. Hittite Glossary. 2nd ed. (William Dwight Whitney Linguistic Ser.: W2). $2.00. Linguistic Soc Am.
Tischler, Johann. Hethitisches Etymologisches Glossar. Neumann, Guenther, ed. LC 79-384968. (Ger.). 1977. S.240.00 (ISBN 3-851-24537-7). Inst Verg Sprach.

HOBBIES
Junge. Woerterbuch fuer den Hobbyelektroniker. 250p. (Ger.). 1983. DM.19.80 (ISBN 3-87144-676-9). Verlag Harri Deutsch.

HOLLAND
see Netherlands

HOLLOW-WARE, SILVER
see Silverware

HOLOGRAPHY
Anglo-Russkii Slovar Po Kvantovoi Elektronike i Golografii. 504p. (Eng. & Rus.). 1977. $6.75 (Pub. by Russkii Iazyk). Four Continent.

HOLY SEE
see Popes

HOME APPLIANCES
see Household Appliances

HOME COMPUTERS
see Microcomputers

HOME CONSTRUCTION
see House Construction

HOME DESIGN
see Architecture, Domestic

HOME ECONOMICS
see also Cookery; Food Service; Fuel; Heating; Laundry and Laundry Industry; Needlework; Sewing; Ventilation
Brown, Philomena. A Basic Dictionary of Home Economics. 64p. 1982. $25.00x (ISBN 0-7135-1317-9, Pub. by Bell & Hyman England). State Mutual Bk.
Chappat, Djenane. Diccionario de la Limpieza. 234p. (Span.). 1970. pap. $3.50 (ISBN 84-206-1282-0, S-12249). French & Eur.
Five Hundred Terms of Home Economic. (Hebrew & Eng.). IL.7.00. Massada Pr.

HOMEOPATHY
Clarke, John H. A Dictionary of Practical Materia Medica. 1980. $125.00x (ISBN 0-85032-139-5, Pub. by Daniel Co England). State Mutual Bk.
A Dictionary of Practical Materia Medica, 3 vols. 2585p. 1980. text ed. $119.95x (ISBN 0-8464-1004-4). Beekman Pubs.
Dictionnaire Homeopatheque d'Urgerce. 11th ed. 765p. (Fr.). 1978. $35.00 (ISBN 0-686-56732-3, M-6461). French & Eur.
Dictionnaire Homeopathique d'urgence. 11th ed. 765p. (Fr.). 1978. write for info. Ste. Ind. D'imprimere.
Maury, Emmerick A. Dictionnaire Familial d'homeopathie. 216p. (Fr.). 30.00 F. Delarge.
--Dictionnaire Familial D'homoeopathie. LC 77-675217. 210p. (Fr.). 1976. 25.00 F. Edns Univers.

HOMER
Owen, William B. & Goodspeed, Edgar J. Homeric Vocabularies: Greek & English Word-Lists for the Study of Homer. LC 68-31669. (Gr. & Eng.). (YA) (gr. 9 up). 1969. pap. $3.95x (ISBN 0-8061-0828-2). U of Okla Pr.

HOMER-DICTIONARIES
Autenrieth, Georg. A Homeric Dictionary for Schools & Colleges. Flagg, Isaac, ed. Keep, Robert P., tr. (Illus.). (YA) (gr. 9 up). 1979. pap. $8.95x (ISBN 0-8061-1289-1). U of Okla Pr.
Cunliffe, Richard J. A Lexicon of the Homeric Dialect. 1977. pap. $14.95x (ISBN 0-8061-1430-4). U of Okla Pr.

HOMES (INSTITUTIONS)
see Charities
HOMILIES
see Sermons
HOMOEOPATHY
see Homeopathy
HONDURAS-HISTORY
Meyer, Harvey K. Historical Dictionary of Honduras. (Illus.). 1976. $15.00 ea. Intl Guatemala.
HONORARY TITLES
see Titles of Honor and Nobility
HOPI INDIANS
see Indians of North America-Southwest, New
HORROR FILMS
Jung, Fernand & Weil, Georg. Der Horror-Film. LC 77-474725. 527p. (Eng. & Ger.). 1977. DM.54.00 (ISBN 3-88144-122-0); write for info. Roloff.
Stanley, John. The Creature Features Movie Guide or An A to Z Encyclopedia to Fantastic Films or Is There a Mad Doctor in the House? LC 81-67664. (Illus.). 208p. (Orig.). (gr. 8 up). 1981. pap. $8.95 (ISBN 0-940064-00-6). Creatures at Large.
HORSE
see Horses
HORSEMANSHIP-DICTIONARIES
Baranowski, Zdzislaw. Woerterbuch Pferd und Reiter. (Eng., Fr. & Ger., Dictionary of Horses and Horsemanship). 1977. $24.95 . (ISBN 0-273-00937-0, M-6910). French & Eur.
Baronowski, Zdzislaw. Woerterbuch Pferd & Reiter. 176p. (Ger.). 1976. DM.18.00 (ISBN 0-273-00937-0). Pitman Bks.
Cassart, C. & Moirant, R. Dictionnaire du Cheval et du Chevalier. 288p. (Fr.). 1979. $49.95 (ISBN 0-686-56942-3, M-6064). French & Eur.
Muller, Hanns. Pocket Dictionary of Horseman's Terms in English, German, French & Spanish. (Fr.) 1971. $5.25 (ISBN 0-685-00343-4). Transatlantic.
Saint Riquier, Marc & Delporte, Jacques. Lexique de l'homme a Cheval. (Fr.). 1975. 47.00 F. Amphora.
Saint-Riquier, Marc de. Lexique de l'homme a Cheval. (Fr.). $25.00 (ISBN 0-686-57287-4, M-4669). French & Eur.
Vansteenwyk, Elizabeth Van. Illustrated Horseback Riding Dictionary for Young People. 119p. (gr. 4 up). 1980. pap. $2.50 (ISBN 0-13-450908-0). P-H.

Vocabulari de Fusteria: Generalitat de Catalunya. 58p. (Span.). 1982. pap. 320.00 ptas (ISBN 84-500-5206-8). Organ Ofic Adm.
HORSEMANSHIP-JUVENILE LITERATURE
Van Steenwyk, Elizabeth. Illustrated Riding Dictionary for Young People. LC 80-81789. (Illustrated Dictionaries Ser.). (Illus.). 128p. (gr. 5 up). 1981. PLB $7.29 (ISBN 0-8178-0015-8). Harvey.
HORSES
Rossdale, Peter D. & Wreford, Susan M. Horses' Health A to Z. LC 73-89678. 256p. 1974. $19.95 (ISBN 0-668-03414-9). Arco.
HORSES-DICTIONARIES
Baranowski, Zdzislaw. The International Horseman's Dictionary. (Illus.). $9.10 (ISBN 0-85131-262-4, Dist. by Sporting Book Center). J A Allen.
--Woerterbuch Pferd und Reiter. (Eng., Fr. & Ger., Dictionary of Horses and Horsemanship). 1977. $24.95 (ISBN 0-273-00937-0, M-6910). French & Eur.
Cassart, C. & Moirant, R. Dictionnaire du Cheval et du Chevalier. 288p. (Fr.). 1979. $49.95 (ISBN 0-686-56942-3, M-6064). French & Eur.
Klimke, Reiner & Savelsberg, Jorg. Lexikon Fur Pferdefreunde. LC 76-468179. 255p. (Ger.). 1976. 29.80 F (ISBN 3-7658-0221-2). Bucher.
Lexikon Fuer Pferdefreunde. (Ger.). 1976. $25.00 (ISBN 3-7658-0221-2, M-7197). French & Eur.
Lexikon fuer Pferdefreunde. 256p. (Ger.). 1976. DM.32.80 (ISBN 3-7658-0221-2). Bucher Verlag.
Muhlmann, Hans G. Woerterbuch ser Pferdekunde. LC 77-554222. 383p. (Ger.). 1976. write for info. Verlag Sankt.
HORTICULTURE
see also Agricultural Pests; Horticulturists; Insects, Injurious and Beneficial; Landscape Gardening
American Association of Nurserymen. Technical Glossary of Horticultural & Landscape Terminology. $9.95; educators $6.00; 10 or more $5.00. Am Nurserymen.
Ballard, Edward B., et al, eds. A Technical Glossary of Horticultural & Landscape Terminology. LC 78-165521. 1971 (ISBN 0-686-26652-8). text ed. $5.50 (ISBN 0-935336-00-1); tchrs' ed. $4.00 (ISBN 0-935336-00-1). Horticult Research.
Bourke, D. O. French-English Horticultural Dictionary. 196p. 1974. $59.00x (ISBN 0-85198-308-1, Pub. by CAB Bks England). State Mutual Bk.
--Horticultural Dictionary: French-English. (Fr. & Eng.). 1974. $49.95 (ISBN 0-85198-308-1, M-9713). French & Eur.
Ministry of Agriculture & Fisheries-Netherlands & Nijdam, J., eds. Elsevier's Dictionary of Horticulture. (Eng., Fr., Dutch, Ger., Danish, Swedish, Span., Ital., & Lat.). 1970. $89.50 (ISBN 0-444-40812-6). Elsevier.
HORTICULTURE-BIBLIOGRAPHY
Massachusetts Horticultural Society, Boston. Dictionary Catalog of the Library of the Massachusetts Horticultural Society, 3 Vols. 1963. Set. lib. bdg. $250.00 (ISBN 0-8161-0648-7, Hall Library). G K Hall.
--Dictionary Catalog of the Library of the Massachusetts Horticultural Society, First Supplement. 1972. lib. bdg. $105.00 (ISBN 0-8161-1038-7, Hall Library). G K Hall.
HORTICULTURISTS
Desmond, Ray. Dictionary of British & Irish Botanists & Horticulturists: Including Plant Collectors & Botanical Artists. 3rd ed. 747p. 1977. $99.50x (ISBN 0-8476-1392-5). Rowman.
Desmond, Ray, ed. Dictionary of British & Irish Botanists & Horticulturists. 3rd ed. 764p. 1977. write for info (ISBN 0-85066-089-0). Taylor & Francis.
HOSPITAL ADMINISTRATION
see Hospitals-Administration
HOSPITAL MANAGEMENT
see Hospitals-Administration

HOSPITALS
see also Clinics; Medicine, Clinical; Nurses and Nursing; Nursing Homes
also subdivision Hospitals under names of cities, e.g. New York (City)-Hospitals
Aurousseau, Paul. International Hospital Vade Mecum & English, French, Spanish Glossary. LC 78-675029. 340p. (Eng., Fr. & Span.). 1977. 0.257 F. Editions Sedip F.Galula.
Glosario de terminos hospitalarios. (Span.). write for info. OPS.
HOSPITALS-ACCOUNTING
American Medical Record Association. Glossary of Hospital Terms. 2nd rev. ed. 128p. 1974. $5.75 (ISBN 0-686-68577-6, 14911). Healthcare Fin Man Assn.
HOSPITALS-ADMINISTRATION
Hospital Administration Terminology. 48p. (Orig.). 1982. pap. $10.75 (ISBN 0-87258-367-8, AHA-001110). Am Hospital.
HOSPITALS-MANAGEMENT AND REGULATION
see Hospitals-Administration
HOSPITALS-NURSES
see Nurses and Nursing
HOTEL ADMINISTRATION
see Hotel Management
HOTEL MANAGEMENT
Molina Aranda, Fernando. Diccionario Tecnico Hostelero. 245p. (Span.). 1972. pap. $12.25 (ISBN 84-85087-02-X, S-50021). French & Eur.
HOTELS, TAVERNS, ETC.-ACCOUNTING
American Hotel & Motel Association. Expense & Payroll Dictionary. $8.50; members $6.00. Am Hotel & Motel Assn.
--Uniform System of Accounts & Expense Dictionary for Small Hotels & Motels. (Illus.). 157p. 1981. Repr. $15.00 (ISBN 0-86612-001-7). Educ Inst Am Hotel.
HOTELS, TAVERNS, ETC.-MANAGEMENT
see Hotel Management
HOURS (TIME)
see Chronology
HOUSE CONSTRUCTION
see also House Painting
Crowdis, Kay & Crowdis, David. Designing & Building Your Own Home. (Illus.). 240p. 1980. text ed. $14.95 (ISBN 0-8359-1272-8). Reston.
HOUSE DRAINAGE
see Sewerage
HOUSE PAINTING
see also Painting, Industrial
Goodier, J. H. Dictionary of Painting & Decorating. 308p. 1974. $39.50x (ISBN 0-85264-224-5, Pub. by Griffin England). State Mutual Bk.
HOUSE PLANTS
Hay, Roy, et al. Diccionario Ilustrado en Color De Plantas De Interior. 231p. (Span.). 1976. $60.00 (ISBN 84-252-0892-0, S-50277). French & Eur.
HOUSEHOLD APPLIANCES
French Language Bureau. Lexique Anglais-Francais des Petits Appareils Electromenagers. LC 76-471924. 183p. (Eng. & Fr.). 1975. write for info. (ISBN 0-7754-2280-0). Edit Quebec.
HOUSEHOLD GOODS
see Household Appliances; Kitchen Utensils
HOUSEHOLD MANAGEMENT
see Home Economics
HOUSEHOLD UTENSILS
see Kitchen Utensils
HOUSEKEEPING
see Home Economics
HOUSES
see Architecture, Domestic
HOUSING
Logie, G. Glossary of Populations & Housing. (International Planning Glossaries: Vol. 1). (Eng., Fr., Ital., Dutch, Ger. & Swedish.). 1978. $53.25 (ISBN 0-444-41730-3). Elsevier.
United States League of Savings Associations. Housing-Planning Glossary. $6.00 (15388). US League Savings Assns.
HUALAPAI INDIANS
see Indians of North America-Southwest, New
HUMAN ANATOMY
see Anatomy, Human

HUMAN BEHAVIOR
Statt, D. Dictionary of Human Behavior. 1981. text ed. $15.50 (ISBN 0-686-69149-0, Pub. by Har-Row Ltd England). Har-Row.
HUMAN BODY
see Body, Human
HUMAN ENGINEERING
European Coal & Steel Community, Luxembourg, ed. Ergonomics Glossary: Terms Commonly Used in Ergonomics. 264p. (Eng., Fr. & Ger.). 1982. $47.50x (ISBN 90-313-0500-6). Intl Pubns Serv.
HUMAN GEOGRAPHY
see Anthropo-Geography
HUMAN RIGHTS
see Civil Rights
HUMANE SOCIETIES
see Animals, Treatment Of
HUMANE TREATMENT OF ANIMALS
see Animals, Treatment of
HUMIDITY
Terms Defining Humidity of Air. 1978. $4.00 (014-23); members $2.67. TAPPI.
HUMOR
see Wit and Humor
HUNGARIAN LANGUAGE
Barczi, Geza. A Pesti Nyelv. LC 78-374048. 37p. (Hungarian.). 1977. 24.00 Ft (ISBN 9-63750-112-6). Magyar Tarsasag.
HUNGARIAN LANGUAGE-DICTIONARIES
A Szotarszerk Bizottsag Vezetoje Toth Lajos. Magyar-Orosz Katonai Szotar. LC 78-377454. 1177p. (Hungarian & Rus.). 1977. 355.00 Ft (ISBN 9-6305-1022-7). Akademiai Kiado.
Akademie Verlages Budapest, ed. Taschenlexikon Ungarn. (Illus.). 280p. (Hungarian.). 1981. M.12.00. Bibl Inst Leipzig.
Bakos, Ferenc, et al. Idegen Szavak Szotara. LC 77-554987. 544p. (Hungarian.). 1975. 35.00 Ft (ISBN 9-6320-5037-1). Terra.
Bakos, Forenc & Fabian, Pal. Idegen Szavak Szotara. LC 77-554987. 544p. (Hungarian.). 1976. 35.00 Ft (ISBN 9-63205-037-1). Terra.
Bodey, Jozsef. Magyar-Bolgar Szotar. LC 77-474283. 584p (Hungarian & Bulgarian.). 1975. 35.00 Ft (ISBN 9-6320-5050-9). Terra.
--Magyar-Bolgar Szotar. LC 77-474283. 584p. (Hungarian & Bulgarian.). 1975. 35.00 Ft (ISBN 9-63205-050-9). Terra.
Budenz, Jozsef. Comparative Dictionary of the Finno-Ugric Elements in the Hungarian Vocabulary. LC 66-64927. (Uralic & Altaic Ser: Vol. 78). (Finnish & Hungarian., Repr. of 1881 ed.) 1966. pap. text ed. $22.00x (ISBN 0-87750-029-0). Res Ctr Lang Semiotic.
Deutsch-Ungarisches Woerterbuch. 376p. (Ger. & Hungarian.). 1955. 2.50 Ft. Akademiai Kiado.
Dictionnaire Franco-Hongrois. (Fr. & Hungarian.). 1978. 15.00 F. Voyages.
Eckhardt, S. Dictionnaire de Poche Francais-Hongrois. 6th ed. 480p. (Fr. & Hungarian.). 1977. 10.00 F. Terra.
--Dictionnaire Usuel Hongrois-Francais. 376p. (Hungarian & Fr.). 1973. 35.00 F. Terra.
--Hungarian-French Concise Dictionary. 1092p. (Hungarian & Fr.). 1973. leatherette $39.95 (ISBN 0-686-92492-4, M-9324). French & Eur.
Eckhardt, Sandor. Magyar-Francia Szotar, 2 vols. LC 79-337569. xvi, 2558p. (Fr. & Hungarian.). 1978. 500.00 Ft (ISBN 9-6305-1297-1). Akademiai Kiado.
--Magyar-Francia Szotar, 2 vols. 2nd ed. LC 79-337569. xvi, 2558p. (Hungarian & Fr.). 1978. 500.00 Ft (ISBN 9-63051-297-1). Akademiai Kiado.
Galdi, Laszlo. Orosz-Magyar Szotar. 3rd ed. LC 80-467905. 1120p. (Hungarian & Rus.). 1978. 135.00 Ft (ISBN 9-63051-821-X). Akademiai Kiado.
Gobel, Marianne T. Slovak-Magyar Szotar. 3rd ed. LC 78-347303. 480p. (Hungarian & Slovak.). 1976. 35.00 Ft (ISBN 9-63205-043-6). Terra.

Hadrovics, Laszlo. Magyar-Szerbhorvat Szotar. LC 76-533581. 655p. (Hungarian & Serbo-Croatian.). 1976. 26.00 Ft (ISBN 9-63205-042-8). Terra.
--Szerbhorvat-Magyar Szotar. 4th ed. LC 77-501008. lxiv, 688p. (Serbo-Croatian & Hungarian.). 1976. 26.00 Ft (ISBN 9-63205-041-X). Terra.
Hadrovics, Laszlo & Hadrovics, Galdi. Magyar-Orosz Keziszotar. 4th ed. LC 79-339814. 712p. (Hungarian & Rus.). 1978. 100.00 Ft (ISBN 9-63051-532-6). Akademiai Kiado.
Hadrovics, Laszlo, et al. Magyar-Orosz Kez Iszotar. LC 79-339814. 712p. (Hungarian & Rus.). 1978. 100.00 Ft (ISBN 9-6305-1532-6). Akademiai Kiado.
--Magyar-Szerbhorvat Szotar. LC 76-533581. 655p. (Hungarian & Serbo-Croatian.). 1976. 26.00 Ft (ISBN 963-205-042-8). Terra.
--Szerbhorvat-Magyar Szotar. LC 77-501008. lxiv, 688p. (Hungarian & Serbo-Croatian.). 1976. 26.00 Ft (ISBN 9-6320-5041-X). Terra.
Halasz, ed. Langenscheidts Handwoerterbuecher: Tl 2, Deutsch-Ungarisch. 1978 ed. (Ger. & Hungarian.). DM.38.00 (ISBN 3-468-04385-6). Langenscheidt.
Herczeg, Gyula. Magyar-Olasz Szotar. LC 78-397749. 768p. (Ital. & Hungarian.). 1978. 35.00 Ft (ISBN 9-6320-5072-X). Terra.
--Magyar-Olasz Szotar. 5th ed. LC 78-397749. 768p. (Hungarian & Ital.). 1978. 35.00 Ft (ISBN 9-63205-072-X). Terra.
--Olasz-Magyar Szotar, 2 vols. LC 78-399851. (Hungarian, & Ital.). 1978. 510.00 Ft (ISBN 9-6305-1613-6). Akademiai Kiado.
--Olasz-Magyar-Szotar. 5th ed. LC 78-399544. 896p. (Ital. & Hungarian.). 1978. 35.00 Ft (ISBN 9-63205-073-8). Terra.
--Olasz-Magyar Szotar: Vocabolario Italiano-Ungherese, 2 vols. 3rd ed. Kolttay-Kastner, Jeno, ed. LC 78-399851. xv, 1781p. (Ital. & Hungarian.). 1978. 510.00 Ft (ISBN 9-63051-613-6). Akademiai Kiado.
Hernadi, Miklos. Koezhelyszotar. LC 78-346072. (Illus.). 363p. (Hungarian.). 1976. 30.00 Ft (ISBN 9-63280-426-0). Gondolat.
--Kozhelyszotar. LC 78-346072. 363p. (Hungarian.). 1976. 30.00 Ft (ISBN 9-632-80426-0). Gondolat.
Juhasz, Jozsef. Magyar Ertelmezo Keziszotar. LC 76-532553. xv, 1550p. (Hungarian.). 1975. 260.00 Ft (ISBN 963-05-0731-5). Akademiai Kiado.
Juhasz, Jozsef, et al, eds. Magyar Ertelmezo Keziszotar. LC 76-532553. (Illus.). xv, 1550p. (Hungarian.). 1975. 260.00 Ft (ISBN 9-63050-731-5). Akademiai Kiado.
Kadar, I. & Ratz, O. Langenscheidts Handwoerterbuch Ungarisch HALASZ: Teil II, Deutsch-Ungarisch. 775p. (Ger. & Hungarian.). DM.44.00 (04385). Langenscheidt.
Kiraly, Rudolf. Portugal-Magyar Szotar. LC 78-396058. 728p. (Port. & Hungarian.). 1978. 108.00 Ft (ISBN 9-6305-1382-X). Akademiai Kiado.
Kotet, I. Hungarian-Vietnamese Dictionary. 864p. (Hungarian & Vietnamese.). 1974. $95.00 (ISBN 963-05-0366-2, M-9325). French & Eur.
Langenscheidts Universal-Woerterbuch Ungarisch. 560p. (Hungarian & Ger.). DM.6.80 (18381). Langenscheidt.
Langenscheidts Universal-Woerterbuecher Ungarisch-Deutsch. (Hungarian & Ger.). 1978. DM.5.80 (ISBN 3-468-18381-X). Langenscheidt.
Laszlo, Orszagh. A Concise English-Hungarian Dictionary, 2 vols. 1052p. (Eng. & Hungarian.). 1981. Vol. 1: Eng.-Hunagarian. 24.00 Ft. Vol. 2: Hungarian-Eng. $31.00. Akademiai Kiado.
Lee-Delisle, Dora. English-Hungarian, Hungarian-English Medical Dictionary. (Eng. & Hungarian.). $18.50 (ISBN 0-87557-040-2, 042-2X). Saphrograph.
Lorinczy, Eva B. Uj Magyar Tajszotar. LC 80-480571. (Hungarian.). 1979. 207.00 Ft (ISBN 9-6305-1810-4). Akademiai Kiado.
Magyar Tudomanyos Akademia Nyelvtudomany Intezeteben. Magyar Tajszotar. Lorinczy, Eva B., ed. LC 80-480571. (Hungarian.). 1979. 207.00 Ft (ISBN 9-63051-810-4). Akademiai Kiado.
Morei, Ferenc & Binet, Agnes V. Ablak-Zsir Kepes Gyermeklexikon. (Illus.). 160p. (Hungarian.). (gr. 1 up). $6.00 (3002). Adler Bks.
Nagy, Gabor O., et al. Magyar Szinonimaszotar. LC 78-397301. 593p. (Hungarian.). 1978. 147.00 Ft (ISBN 9-6305-1607-1). Akademiai Kiado.
Nyirkos, I. Finnish-Hungarian-Finnish Dictionary (Suomi-Unkari-Suomi) 712p. (Finnish & Hungarian.). 1979. pap. $19.95 (ISBN 951-0-07860-3). French & Eur.
Nyirkos, Istvan. Suomi-Unkari-Suomi: Taskusanakirja. LC 78-346065. 712p. (Finnish & Hungarian.). 1977. Fmk.44.00 (ISBN 9-51007-860-3). Soderstrom.
--Unkarilais-Suomalainen Sanakirja. LC 78-389367. 392p. (Hungarian & Finnish.). 1977. write for info. (ISBN 9-51717-114-5). Suoma Kirja.
Ol'dal, G. I. Russko-Vengerskii Slovar. 368p. (Rus.). 1961. $00.95 (Pub. by Gosizdat Inostr Natsional Slovarei). Four Continent.
Ol'Dal, G. I., et al. Karmannyi Vengersko-Russkii Slovar. 405p. (Rus.). 1969. $1.50 (Pub. by GINS). Four Continent.
Orszagh. Hungarian Deluxe Dictionary: English-Hungarian, Vol. 1. 6th ed. (Hungarian & Eng.). 1980. $95.00x (ISBN 96-305-0554-1, H-331). Vanous.
--Hungarian Deluxe Dictionary: Hungarian-English, Vol. 2. 5th ed. (Hungarian & Eng.). 1977. $75.00x (ISBN 96-305-0067-1, H-330). Vanous.
Orszagh, I. Pocket English-Hungarian Dictionary. (Eng. & Hungarian.). 1980. $20.00x (ISBN 0-569-00408-X, Pub. by Collet's). State Mutual Bk.
--Pocket Hungarian-English Dictionary. (Hungarian & Eng.). 1980. $20.00x (ISBN 0-569-00344-X, Pub. by Collet's). State Mutual Bk.
Orszagh, L. English-Hungarian Dictionary. (Eng. & Hungarian.). $24.50 (ISBN 0-686-65153-7, 043-7). Saphrograph.
--Hungarian-English Dictionary, 2 vols. (Hungarian & Eng.). $29.50 (ISBN 0-87557-042-9, 042-9). Saphrograph.
--Hungarian-English, English-Hungarian Concise Dictionary (1976-79, 2 vols. rev & enl ed. (Hungarian & Eng.). $55.00 set (ISBN 0-685-29277-0). Vol. 1, Hungarian-English, 9th ed. Vol. 2, English-Hungarian, 10th ed (ISBN 9-6305-2464-3). Heinman.
Orszagh, L., ed. Magyar-Angol Szotar, Hungarian-English Dictionary. rev. ed. (Hungarian & Eng.). $29.50 (ISBN 0-87557-042-9, 042-9). Saphrograph.
Orszagh, Laszlo. Hungarian Concise Dictionary: English-Hungarian. 9th ed. (Hungarian & Eng.). 1981. $25.00x (ISBN 96-305-2464-3, H-269). Vanous.
--Hungarian-English: English Hungarian Dictionary, 2 vols. 13th rev. ed. (Hungarian & Eng.). Set. $20.00x (ISBN 963-05-2019-2). Heinman.
--Hungarian Pocket Dictionary: Hungarian-English, Vol. 2. 12th ed. 462p. (Hungarian & Eng.). 1979. $8.50x (ISBN 96-305-1256-4, H273). Vanous.
Orszagh, Laszlo, ed. English-Hungarian Dictionary. 13th ed. 608p. (Eng. & Hungarian.). 1982. $6.25x (ISBN 963-05-2975-0). Intl Pubns Serv.
Orszagh, V. A Concise English-Hungarian Dictionary. 1091p. (Eng. & Hungarian.). 1980. $50.00 (ISBN 0-569-00407-1, Pub. by Collet's). State Mutual Bk.
--A Concise Hungarian-English Dictionary. 1180p. (Hungarian & Eng.). 1980. $50.00x (ISBN 0-569-00343-1, Pub. by Collet's). State Mutual Bk.
--English-Hungarian Dictionary, 2 vols. 2336p. (Eng. & Hungarian.). 1980. $99.00x (ISBN 0-569-00359-8, Pub. by Collet's). State Mutual Bk.
--Hungarian-English Dictionary, 2 vols. 2160p. (Hungarian & Eng.). 1980. $125.00x (ISBN 0-569-00409-8, Pub. by Collet's). State Mutual Bk.
Orszagn, L. Angol-Magyar Szotar English-Hungarian Dictionary. 791p. (Eng. & Hungarian.). $22.50 (ISBN 0-87557-043-7, 043-7). Saphrograph.
Sandri-White, Alex. Dictionary of Hungarian Slang. (Hungarian.). $5.95 (ISBN 0-685-22762-6). Aurea.
Skripecz, Ratz S., et al. Langenscheidts Handwoerterbuch Ungarisch HALASZ: Teil I, Ungarisch-Deutsch. 1064p. (Hungarian & Ger.). DM.48.00 (04381). Langenscheidt.
Szabo, Miklos. Orosz-Magyar Szotar Iskolak Szamara, 2 vols. LC 80-467907. (Eng., Rus. & Hungarian.). 1978. 21.50 Ft (ISBN 9-6305-1611-X). Akademiai Kiado.
UJ Magyar Lexikon, 7 vols. (Hungarian.). 1960-1972. Set. $350.00 (ISBN 0-8277-3103-5). Pergamon.
Varsanyi, Istvan. Lengyel-Magyar Szotar. LC 76-533514. xvi, 784p. (Pol. & Hungarian.). 1976. 35.00 Ft (ISBN 963-205-048-7). Terra.
--Magyar-Lengyel Szotar. LC 77-457358. 928p. (Hungarian & Pol.). 1976. 35.00 Ft (ISBN 9-6320-5049-5). Terra.
--Magyar-Lengyel Szotar. LC 77-457358. 928p. (Hungarian & Pol.). 1976. 35.00 Ft (ISBN 9-63205-049-5). Terra.
Weissling, Heinrich. Taschenworterbuch Deutsch-Ungarisch. LC 76-472365. 272p. (Ger. & Hungarian.). 1975. M.5.80. VEB Verlag Enzyklopadie.
Weissling, Heinrich, ed. Taschenwoerterbuch Deutsch-Ungarisch. LC 76-472365. 272p. (Ger. & Hungarian.). 1975. M.5.80. VEB Verlag Enzyklopaedie.
Willerfest, Biro. English-Hungarian, Hungarian-English Dictionary-Angol-Magyar-Angol Szotar. (Eng & Hungarian.). $19.50 (ISBN 0-87557-039-9, 042-2). Saphrograph.

HUNGARIAN LANGUAGE–GRAMMAR

Whitney, A. H. Learn Hungarian for English Speakers. 264p. (Hungarian.). pap. $9.50 (ISBN 0-87557-044-5, 044-5). Saphrograph.

HUNTING–DICTIONARIES

Burnand, Tony. Dictionnaire Chasse. (Dictionnaires de l'homme du vingtieme siecle). (Fr., Fr). 1970. $8.50 (ISBN 0-685-13859-3, 3711). Larousse.
--Dictionnaire de la Chasse. 250p. (Fr.). 1970. pap. $7.50 (ISBN 0-686-56817-6, M-6595, Pub. by Larousse). French & Eur.
--Dictionnaire de la chasse. 250p. (Fr.). 1970. pap. 7.50 F. Larousse.
Conseil International de la Langue Francaise. Vocabulaire de la Chasse & de la Venerie. (Fr.). 1974. 16.60 F. Hachette.
Frevert, W. Woerterbuch der Jaegerei. 4th ed. (Ger.). 1975. $12.00 (ISBN 3-490-05612-4, M-6990). French & Eur.
Kehrein, Franz. Woerterbuch der Weidmannssprache. (Ger.). 1969. $36.00 (ISBN 3-500-26250-3, M-6943). French & Eur.
Kirchoff, Anne. Woerterbuch der Jagel. (Ger., Eng. & Fr., Dictionary of Hunting). 1976. $27.50 (ISBN 3-405-11571-X, M-6989). French & Eur.
Rodero, Jose M. Diccionario de caza. 512p. (Span.). 1955. 290.00 ptas. Juventud.
Ugolini, Luigi. Dizionario del cacciatore italiano. (Illus.). 336p. (Ital.). L.8500.00. Bietti.

HUSBANDRY

see Agriculture

HYDRAULIC CEMENT

see Cement

HYDRAULIC ENGINEERING

see also Drainage; Hydraulic Machinery; Hydraulics; Irrigation; Pumping Machinery; Rivers; Water-Supply Engineering

Bernshtein, L. B. Nemetsko-Russkii Gidrotekhnicheskii Slovar. 579p. (Ger. & Rus.). 1961. $7.75 (Pub. by Fizmatgiz). Four Continent.
Mertz De Mertzenteld, R., et al. Dictionnaire Technologique Feutry: Mecanique-Metallurgie-Hydraulique, Vol. 1. 750p. (Eng., Fr. & Ger.). 1976. 250.00 F. Maison Dictionnaire.
Robb, Louis A. Engineers' Dictionary, Spanish-English, English-Spanish. 2nd ed. (Span. & Eng.). 1949. $49.50 (ISBN 0-471-72501-3, Pub. by Wiley-Interscience). Wiley.

HYDRAULIC MACHINERY

see also Pumping Machinery

Troskolanski, A. T. Dictionary of Hydraulic Machinery. (Eng., Ger., Span., Fr. & Ital. & Rus.). Date not set. $117.00 (ISBN 0-444-99728-8). Elsevier.

HYDRAULIC POWER PLANTS

see Water-Power

HYDRAULICS

see also Fire Extinction; Hydraulic Engineering

Institute for Power System. Hydraulic Standards, Lexicon & Data. 200p. 1979. $35.00x (ISBN 0-85461-005-7). State Mutual Bk.
Lexique Francais-Anglais: Termes d'usage Courant en Hydraulique & Pneumatique. 42p. (Fr. & Eng.). 14.00 F. Ste. Publications Mecaniques.
Neubert, G. Dictionary of Hydraulics & Pneumatics: English-German-Russian-Slovene. 226p. (Eng., Ger., Rus. & Slovene.). 1973. $75.00 (ISBN 0-686-92602-1, M-9896). French & Eur.
Neubert, Gunter. Dictionary of Hydraulics & Pneumatics. 226p. 1980. $40.00x (ISBN 0-569-08523-3, Pub. by Collet's). State Mutual Bk.
Nichil, P. Lexique Francais-Anglais et Anglais-Francais des Termes d'usage Courant En Hydraulique et Pneumatique. 42p. (Fr. & Eng., French-English, English-French Lexicon of Commonly Used Terms in Hydraulics and Pneumatics). 1974. pap. $8.95 (ISBN 0-686-56790-0, M-6426). French & Eur.

HYDROBIOLOGY

see Fresh-Water Biology; Marine Biology

HYDROCARBONS

Paruit, Bernard. Illustrated Glossary of Process Equipment: English-French-Spanish Edition. (Illus.). 324p. 1982. $39.95x (ISBN 0-87201-691-9). Gulf Pub.

HYDROGEOLOGY

Castany, G. Dictionnaire Francais d'Hydrogeologie. LC 78-359598. (Illus.). 249p. (Fr.). 1977. 75.00 F. Bureau Recherches.
Pfannkuch, Hans-Olaf. Elsevier's Dictionary of Hydrogeology. (Eng., Fr., & Ger.). 1969. $42.75 (ISBN 0-444-40717-0). Elsevier.

HYDROLOGY

see also Hydrogeology; Oceanography; Water also headings beginning with the word Water

Chebotarev, A. I. Gidrologicheskii Slovar. 308p. (Rus.). 1978. $6.50 (Pub. by GIdrometeoizdat). Four Continent.
Chebotarev, L. Gidrologicheskii Slovar. 221p. (Rus.). 1964. $2.40 (Pub. by Gidrometeorologich Izd.). Four Continent.

Cicchini, Joelle, ed. Thesaurus Hydrologie. LC 76-472957. iv, 134p. (Fr.). 1975. 30.00 F (ISBN 2-901560-00-8). Serv Doc Cart.

C.I.L.F. Vocabulaire de l'Hydrologie et de la meteorologie. 239p. (Fr.). 1978. 80.00 F. Maison Dictionnaire.

Conseil International de la Language Francaise. Vocabulaire de l'Hydrologie et de la Meteorologie. LC 79-353461. (Illus.). 239p. (Fr.). 1978. 65.00 F (ISBN 2-85319-048-X). Maison Dictionnaire.

Dictionary of Hydrology Terms. (Hebrew, Eng. , Fr. & Ger.). IL.8.00. Massada Pr.

Glossaire International d'Hydrologie. 393p. (Fr.). 1974. pap. $29.95 (ISBN 0-686-57304-8, M-6281). French & Eur.

Glossaire International d'hydrologie. 393p. (Fr.). 1974. 64.00 F. Unesco.

Lexique Trilinque des Termes de l'Eau. 224p. (Fr., Trilingual Lexicon of Water Terminology). 1975. pap. $29.95 (ISBN 0-686-56724-2, M-6372). French & Eur.

Spenger, O. A. Gidrologicheskii Slovar na Inostrannykh Iazykakh. 216p. (Rus.). 1959. $2.95 (Pub. by Gidrometeoizdat). Four Continent.

HYDROPHYTES
see Fresh-Water Biology
HYGIENE
Here are entered works on personal body care and cleanliness. Works on optimal physical, mental, and social well-being, as well as how to achieve and preserve it, are entered under Health.
see also Health
also subdivision Care and hygiene under parts of the body, and under age groups dependent on the assistace of others, e.g. Eye-Care and hygiene; Infants-Care and hygiene; and subdivision Health and hygiene under classes of persons or ethnic groups, e.g. Students-Health and hygiene; Afro-Americans-Health and hygiene

Capron, Gustave & Boisselier, Jackie. Dictionnaire de Prevention, 3 vols. (Illus.). 249p. (Fr.). 1976. 58.00 F. Soc Corp Hygiene.

Chappat, Djenane, tr. Diccionario de limpieza. 240p. (Span.). 1970. 60.00 ptas. Alianza Ed.

HYGIENE, PUBLIC
see Public Health
HYGIENE, RURAL
see Health, Rural
HYGIENE, SOCIAL
see Public Health
HYMNS-DICTIONARIES, INDEXES, ETC.
Julian, J., ed. A Dictionary of Hymnology: Origin & History of Christian Hymns, 4 vols. 1977. Set. lib. bdg. $600.00 (ISBN 0-8490-1719-X). Gordon Pr.

HYPERBARIC OXYGENATION
Undersea Medical Society, Inc. Glossary of Diving & Hyperbaric Terms. $2.50. Undersea Med.

HYPERBOREAN LANGUAGES
see also Aleut Language; Eskimo Language
Bogoraz, Vladimir G. Koryak Texts. LC 73-3540. (American Ethnological Society. Publications: No. 5). Repr. of 1917 ed. $16.75 (ISBN 0-404-58155-2). AMS Pr.

HYPNOSIS
see Hypnotism
HYPNOTISM
see also Mind and Body; Psychoanalysis
Marchesan, Marco. Dizionario di ipnopsicologia. 230p. (Ital.). 1971. L.5000.00 (ISBN 88-85021-01-8). Ist. Indagini Psicologiche.

HYPOACOUSTIC CHILDREN
see Children, Deaf
HYPOTHECATION
see Mortgages

I

IBERIANS
Kruger, Fritz, tr. El lexico rural del noroeste iberico. 142p. (Span.). 1947. 60.00 ptas (CSIC). Inst. Antonio de Nebrija.

Simonet, Francisco J. Glosario de voces ibericas y latinas: Tomo 2. 425p. (Span. & Lat.). 1982. pap. 1500.00 ptas (ISBN 84-363-0546-9). Atlas Edns.

IBIZA
Planells Cardona, Mariano. Diccionario de secretos de Ibiza. 320p. (Span.). 1982. pap. 700.00 ptas (ISBN 84-86000-07-6). Obelisco.

IBO LANGUAGE
Njoku, John E. A Dictionary of Igbo Names, Culture & Proverbs. LC 78-66416. 1978. pap. text ed. $7.00 (ISBN 0-8191-0134-6). U Pr of Amer.

ICE-MANUFACTURE
see Refrigeration and Refrigerating Machinery
ICELANDIC AND OLD NORSE LANGUAGES
see also Norwegian Language
Skadberg, Kare & Ulset, Tor. Merknader til en dell Norrone Tekster. LC 75-542801. 255p. (Norse & Icelandic). 1975. Kr.34.00 (ISBN 8-27000-020-5). Univers Oslo.

ICELANDIC AND OLD NORSE LANGUAGES-DICTIONARIES
Cleasby, Richard & Vigfusson, Gudbrand, eds. Icelandic-English Dictionary. 2nd ed. (Icelandic & Eng.). 1957. $125.00x (ISBN 0-19-863103-0). Oxford U Pr.

Langenscheidts Universal-Woerterbuch Islaendisch. 560p. (Icelandic & Ger.). DM.6.80 (18170). Langenscheidt.

Langenscheidts Universal-Woerterbuecher Islaendisch-Deutsch. (Icelandic & Ger.). 1978. DM.5.80 (ISBN 3-468-18170-1). Langenscheidt.

Sigurdsson, A. Icelandic-English Dictionary. 3rd ed. (Icelandic & Eng.). $80.00 (ISBN 0-686-64772-6). Heinman.

Sigurdsson, Arngrimur. Icelandic-English Dictionary. (Icelandic & Eng.). $42.50 (ISBN 0-87559-166-3). Shalom.

Zoega, Geir T. Concise Dictionary of Old Icelandic. (Icelandic). 1910. $39.00x (ISBN 0-19-863108-1). Oxford U Pr.

ICELANDIC LANGUAGE
see Icelandic and Old Norse Languages; Icelandic Language, Modern
ICELANDIC LANGUAGE, MODERN
Einarsson, Stefan. Icelandic Grammar, Text & Glossary. 2nd ed. 538p. 1949. $25.00x (ISBN 0-8018-0187-7). Johns Hopkins.

Icelandic Pocket Dictionary. (Icelandic & Eng.). $12.50 (ISBN 0-685-36175-6). Heinman.

Johannesson, Alex. Islaendisches Etymologisches Woerterbuch. 1406p. (Icelandic & Ger.). 1956. $232.00 (ISBN 3-7720-0429-6, M-7485, Pub. by Francke). French & Eur.

ICHTHYOLOGY
see Fishes
ICONOGRAPHY
see Art; Christian Art and Symbolism; Idols and Images; Portraits
IDEA (PHILOSOPHY)
Wiener, Philip P., ed. Dictionary of the History of Ideas. 1980. pap. $100.00 5-volume boxed edition (ISBN 0-684-16418-3, ScribR). Scribner.

IDENTIFICATION
see also Fingerprints
Centre de Documentatio de. Lexique Thematique des Des Descripteurs & Identificateurs. new ed. 151p. (Fr.). 1976. 75.00 F. Centre Documentation.

IDEOGRAPHY
see Chinese Language-Writing
IDOLATRY
see Idols and Images
IDOLS AND IMAGES
Cecchini, Norma. Dizionario sinottico di iconologia. (Illus.). xxx, 472p. (Ital.). 1976. L.24500.00. Patron.

IGBO LANGUAGE
see Ibo Language
ILLUMINATION
see Lighting

ILLUMINATION OF BOOKS AND MANUSCRIPTS-CATALOGS
New York Public Library, Research Libraries. Dictionary Catalog & Shelf List of the Spencer Collection of Illustrated Books & Manuscripts & Fine Bindings, 2 vols. 1970. Set. lib. bdg. $190.00 (ISBN 0-8161-0862-5, Hall Library). G K Hall.

ILLUSTRATED BOOKS-BIBLIOGRAPHY
New York Public Library, Research Libraries. Dictionary Catalog & Shelf List of the Spencer Collection of Illustrated Books & Manuscripts & Fine Bindings, 2 vols. 1970. Set. lib. bdg. $190.00 (ISBN 0-8161-0862-5, Hall Library). G K Hall.

ILLUSTRATORS
Peppin, Brigid. Book Illustrators of the Twentieth Century. rev. ed. (Illus.). 544p. 1982. cancelled (ISBN 0-668-04366-0). Arco.

ILLYRIAN LANGUAGE (SLAVIC)
see Serbo-Croatian Language
ILOKANOS
Constantino. Ilokano Dictionary. (Ilokano). $10.00. Iaconi.

Constantino, Ernesto. Ilokano Dictionary. McKaughan, Howard P., ed. (PALI Language Texts: Philippines). 510p. (Orig.). 1971. pap. text ed. $12.00x (ISBN 0-87022-152-3). UH Pr.

IMAGE OF GOD
Provenzal, Dino. Dizionario delle immagini. (Illus.). xxiv, 1064p. (Ital.). 1954. L.3200.00 (ISBN 88-203-0218-7). Hoepli.

IMAGES AND IDOLS
see Idols and Images
IMAGINARY ANIMALS
see Animal Lore; Animals, Mythical
IMMUNOLOGY
Del Giacco, G. S. Glossario di immunologia. 142p. (Ital.). 1975. L.8000.00. Minerva Medica.

Halliday, W. J. Glossary of Immunological Terms. 102p. 1971. $13.95 (ISBN 0-407-72740-X). Butterworth.

Herbert, W. J. & Wilkinson, P. C. Diccionario de Inmunologia. 256p. (Span.). 1974. E750.00 (ISBN 84-7092-106-1). Jims.

Slopek, Stefan. Slownik Immunologiczny Ilustrowany. LC 77-567783. 339p. (Pol.). 1977. 120.00 Zl. Panstowy Zaklad W.

Tu Dien Mien Dich Hoc. LC 79-984056. (Eng. , Fr. & Vietnamese.). 1976. write for info. Y Hoc.

IMPORT CONTROLS
see Tariff
IMPORTS
see Commerce; Tariff
IMPRESSIONISM (ART)
Cognia, Raymond & Elgar, Frank. Illustrated Dictionary of Impressionism. (Pocket Art Ser.). (Illus., Eng.). (gr. 10-12). 1979. pap. $3.95 (ISBN 0-8120-0986-X). Barron.

Serullaz, Maurice. Lexikon des Impressionismus. (Ger.). 1975. $25.00 (ISBN 3-8046-0011-5, M-7208). French & Eur.

INCA LANGUAGE
see Quechua Language
INDEXING
Buchanan, Brian W. Glossary of Indexing Terms. 144p. 1976. $14.00 (ISBN 0-208-01377-6, Linnet). Shoe String.

INDEXING VOCABULARIES
see Subject Headings
INDIA-ANTIQUITIES
Lal Dey, Nando. The Geographical Dictionary of Ancient & Medieval India. 262p. 1979. Repr. of 1927 ed. $27.50 (ISBN 0-89684-150-2). Orient Bk Dist.

INDIA-DESCRIPTION AND TRAVEL
Dey, Nundo Lal. The Geographical Dictionary of Ancient & Mediaeval India. LC 42-31336. (Illus.). 272p. 1971. Repr. of 1927 ed. 19.50x (ISBN 0-8002-1453-6). Intl Pubns Serv.

INDIA-DICTIONARIES AND ENCYCLOPEDIAS
Garrett, John. Classical Dictionary of India, 2 vols. in 1. 1973. Repr. of 1873 ed. $51.50 (ISBN 0-8337-1289-6). B Franklin.

Kurian, George T. Historical & Cultural Dictionary of India. LC 76-16186. (Historical & Cultural Dictionaries of Asia Ser.: No. 8). 1976. $17.50 (ISBN 0-8108-0951-6). Scarecrow.

Sharma, Jagdish S. The National Geographical Dictionary of India. LC 72-929631. 350p. 1972. $11.25x (ISBN 0-8002-0942-7). Intl Pubns Serv.

Watt, George. A Dictionary of the Economic Products of India, 6 vols. in 10. 5450p. 1972. Repr. of 1889 ed. Set. $300.00x (ISBN 0-8002-0198-1). Intl Pubns Serv.

--A Dictionary of the Economic Products of India, 6 vols. 1978. Repr. of 1889 ed. Set. $324.00 (ISBN 0-89955-259-5, Pub. by Intl Bk Dist). Intl Schol Bk Serv.

INDIA-ECONOMIC CONDITIONS
Watt, George. A Dictionary of the Economic Products of India, 6 vols. in 10. 5450p. 1972. Repr. of 1889 ed. Set. $300.00x (ISBN 0-8002-0198-1). Intl Pubns Serv.

--A Dictionary of the Economic Products of India, 6 vols. 1978. Repr. of 1889 ed. Set. $324.00 (ISBN 0-89955-259-5, Pub. by Intl Bk Dist). Intl Schol Bk Serv.

INDIA-HISTORY
Bhattacharya, Sachchidananda. A Dictionary of Indian History. LC 77-1105. 1977. Repr. of 1972 ed. lib. bdg. $58.50x (ISBN 0-8371-9515-2, BHDI). Greenwood.

INDIA-HISTORY-EARLY TO 1000 A.D
Dey, Nundo Lal. Geographical Dictionary of Ancient & Mediaeval India. 3rd ed. (Illus.). 262p. 1971. $22.00x (ISBN 0-8426-0332-8). Verry.

INDIA-LANGUAGES
Gerow, Edwin. A Glossary of Indian Figures of Speech. (Publications in Near & Middle East Ser. A: No. 16). 436p. 1971. text ed. $48.00x (ISBN 90-2791-759-0). Mouton.

INDIA-POLITICS AND GOVERNMENT-1765-1947
Kaushik, P. D. Congress Ideology & Programme. 1964. $7.50x (ISBN 0-8188-1064-5). Paragon.

INDIA-RUBBER
see Rubber
INDIAN LANGUAGES
see Indians-Languages; Indians of Mexico-Languages; Indians of North America-Languages
INDIAN NATIONAL CONGRESS
Kaushik, P. D. Congress Ideology & Programme. 1964. $7.50x (ISBN 0-8188-1064-5). Paragon.

INDIANS-BIBLIOGRAPHY
Newberry Library - Chicago. Dictionary Catalog of the Edward E. Ayer Collection of Americana & American Indians, 16 Vols. 1961. Set. $1120.00 (ISBN 0-8161-0586-3, Hall Library). G K Hall.

INDIANS-ETHNOLOGY
see Indians of North America
also indians of South America and similar headings
INDIANS-LANGUAGES
see also Indians of North America-Languages; Indians of South America-Languages
Bykova, E. M., et al. Bengal'sko-Russkii Slovar. 908p. (Rus. & Bengali.). 1957. $5.50 (Pub. by Gosizdat Inostr. Natsion. Slovarei). Four Continent.

INDIANS-ORIGIN
Villafuerte, Carlos. Diccionario de Toponimos Indigenas de Catamarca. 93p. (Span.). 1979. write for info. Plus Ultra S. A.

INDIANS IN ART
see subdivision Pictorial Works under Indians; Indians Of North America and similar headings
INDIANS OF CENTRAL AMERICA
De Castillo Mathieu, Micolas. Lexico Caribe en el Caribe Negro de Honduras Britanica. LC 77-472040. 70p. (Cariban.). 1975. write for info. Instituto Caro & Cuervo.

INDIANS OF CENTRAL AMERICA-ETHNOLOGY
see Indians of Central America
INDIANS OF CENTRAL AMERICA-ORIGIN
see Indians-Origin

INDIANS OF MEXICO—LANGUAGES
see also Aztec Language; Maya Language; Papago Language; Popoluca Language (Vera Cruz)
Reid, et al. Diccionario Totonaco de Xicotepec de Juarez. (Vocabularios Indigenas Ser.: No. 17). (Span.). 1974. pap. $12.00x (ISBN 0-88312-752-0); microfiche $4.50 (ISBN 0-88312-552-8). Summer Inst Ling.
Turner, Paul & Turner, Shirley. Dictionary of Chontal to Spanish-English, & Spanish to Chontal. LC 78-164366. (Span., Eng. & Chontal.). 1971. pap. $3.95x (ISBN 0-8165-0338-9). U of Ariz Pr.

INDIANS OF MEXICO—ORIGIN
see Indians—Origin

INDIANS OF NORTH AMERICA
Here are entered works on the Indians of North America in general. For works of specific tribes or groups of tribes see subdivisions—Eastern States,—Northwest, Pacific,— Southwest, New,—Southwest, Old,— The West.
see also Eskimos
Leitch, Barbara A. A Concise Dictionary of Indian Tribes of North America. LePoer, Kendall, ed. LC 78-21347. 1980. $59.95 (ISBN 0-917256-09-3). Ref Pubns.
Nanooch, Henry, et al. Plains Cree Dictionary. 2nd rev. ed. (Illus., Cree.). 1976. Can.$22.00 (ISBN 0-919864-19-8). U of Toronto Pr.
Travers, Milton A. One of the Keys: The Wampanoag Contribution. LC 75-10246. 64p. (Eng. & Wampanoag.). 1975. $4.95 (ISBN 0-8158-0326-5). Chris Mass.
Waldman, Harry, ed. Dictionary of Indians of North America, 3 vols. 1978. Set. $145.00 (ISBN 0-403-01799-8). Scholarly.

INDIANS OF NORTH AMERICA—ANTIQUITIES
Barnett, Franklin. Dictionary of Prehistoric Indian Artifacts of the American Southwest. LC 73-82865. (Illus.). 288p. 1973. pap. $8.95 (ISBN 0-87358-120-2). Northland.

INDIANS OF NORTH AMERICA—BIBLIOGRAPHY
Huntington Free Library & Reading Room. Dictionary Catalog of the American Indian Collection. 1977. lib. bdg. $380.00 (ISBN 0-8161-0065-9, Hall Library). G K Hall.
Newberry Library - Chicago. Dictionary Catalog of the Edward E. Ayer Collection of Americana & American Indians, First Supplement, 3 vol. 1970. Set. lib. bdg. $315.00 (ISBN 0-8161-0810-2, Hall Library). G K Hall.
--Dictionary Catalog of the Edward E. Ayer Collection of Americana & American Indians, 16 Vols. 1961. Set. $1120.00 (ISBN 0-8161-0586-3, Hall Library). G K Hall.

INDIANS OF NORTH AMERICA—ETHNOLOGY
see Indians of North America

INDIANS OF NORTH AMERICA—LANGUAGES
Bruno Natlis, Elena. Estudio Comparativo de Vocabularios Tobas y Pilagas. 107p. (Span.). 1965. pap. $49.95 (ISBN 0-686-56659-9, S-33083). French & Eur.
Faries, R. & Watkins, E. A. A Dictionary of the Cree Language. (Cree.). 1938. Can.$24.00. Anglican Church.
Matthews, Washington. Grammar & Dictionary of the Language of the Hidatsa. LC 76-44080. (Shea's American Linguistics, Ser. 2: Nos. 1 & 2). Repr. of 1873 ed. $27.50 (ISBN 0-404-15787-4). AMS Pr.
Uhlenbeck, Christianus C. & Van Gulik, R. H. A Blackfoot-English Vocabulary. LC 76-44086. (Verhardelingen der Koninklijke Akademie Van Wetenschappen Te Amsterdam. Afdeeling Letterkunde. Nieuwe Reeks: 33, No. 2). (Blackfoot & Eng.). Repr. of 1934 ed. $35.50 (ISBN 0-404-15795-5). AMS Pr.

--An English-Blackfoot Vocabulary. LC 76-44087. (Verhandelingen der Koninklijke Akademie Van Wetenschappen Te Amsterdam. Afdeeling Letterkunde. Nieuwe Reeks: 29, No. 4). 261p. (Eng. & Blackfoot.). 1979. Repr. of 1930 ed. $26.50 (ISBN 0-404-15796-3). AMS Pr.

INDIANS OF NORTH AMERICA—LANGUAGES—DICTIONARIES
Byington, Cyrus. A Dictionary of the Choctaw Language. (Choctaw.). Repr. of 1915 ed. $49.00 (ISBN 0-403-03579-1). Scholarly.
Dictionary of Chinook Jargon. (Shorey Indian Ser.). 42p. Repr. pap. $4.95 (ISBN 0-8466-0005-6, S5). Shorey.
La Fleche, Francis. A Dictionary of the Osage Language. Repr. of 1932 ed. $49.00 (ISBN 0-403-03580-5). Scholarly.
Matthews, Washington. Grammar & Dictionary of the Language of the Hidatsa. LC 76-44080. (Shea's American Linguistics, Ser. 2: Nos. 1 & 2). Repr. of 1873 ed. $27.50 (ISBN 0-404-15787-4). AMS Pr.
Miller, Wick R. Newe Natekwinappeh: Shoshoni Stories & Dictionary. (Utah Anthropological Papers: No. 94). (Shoshoni.). Repr. of 1972 ed. $24.00 (ISBN 0-404-60694-6). AMS Pr.
Rand, Silas T. Dictionary of the Languages of the Micmac Indians, Who Reside in Nova Scotia, New Brunswick, Prince Edward Island, Cape Breton & Newfoundland. Repr. of 1888 ed. $40.00 (ISBN 0-384-49565-6). Johnson Repr.
Zeisberger, David. Zeisberger's Indian Dictionary: English, German, Iroquois - the Onandaga & Algonquin - the Delaware. LC 76-43905. 248p. (Eng., Ger. & Iroquois.). Repr. of 1887 ed. $42.50 (ISBN 0-404-15802-1). AMS Pr.

INDIANS OF NORTH AMERICA—LEGENDS
Miller, Wick R. Newe Natekwinappeh: Shoshoni Stories & Dictionary. (Utah Anthropological Papers: No. 94). (Shoshoni.). Repr. of 1972 ed. $24.00 (ISBN 0-404-60694-6). AMS Pr.

INDIANS OF NORTH AMERICA—MYTHOLOGY
see Indians of North America—Legends

INDIANS OF NORTH AMERICA—ORIGIN
see Indians—Origin

INDIANS OF NORTH AMERICA—NORTHWEST, PACIFIC
Uhlenbeck, Christianus C. & Van Gulik, R. H. A Blackfoot-English Vocabulary. LC 76-44086. (Verhardelingen der Koninklijke Akademie Van Wetenschappen Te Amsterdam. Afdeeling Letterkunde. Nieuwe Reeks: 33, No. 2). (Blackfoot & Eng.). Repr. of 1934 ed. $35.50 (ISBN 0-404-15795-5). AMS Pr.
--An English-Blackfoot Vocabulary. LC 76-44087. (Verhandelingen der Koninklijke Akademie Van Wetenschappen Te Amsterdam. Afdeeling Letterkunde. Nieuwe Reeks: 29, No. 4). 261p. (Eng. & Blackfoot.). 1979. Repr. of 1930 ed. $26.50 (ISBN 0-404-15796-3). AMS Pr.

INDIANS OF NORTH AMERICA—SOUTHWEST, NEW
Seiler, Hansjakob & Hioki, Kojiro. Cahuilla Dictionary. 1979. pap. $15.00 (ISBN 0-939046-04-0). Malki Mus Pr.

INDIANS OF NORTH AMERICA—THE WEST
Matthews, Washington. Ethnography & Philology of the Hidatsa Indians: U. S. Geological & Geographical Survey of the Territories, Miscellaneous Publication, No. 7. LC 3-8072. 1971. 284p. Repr. of 1877 ed. $25.00 (ISBN 0-384-35892-6). Johnson Repr.

--Grammar & Dictionary of the Language of the Hidatsa. LC 76-44080. (Shea's American Linguistics, Ser. 2: Nos. 1 & 2). Repr. of 1873 ed. $27.50 (ISBN 0-404-15787-4). AMS Pr.
Miller, Wick R. Newe Natekwinappeh: Shoshoni Stories & Dictionary. (Utah Anthropological Papers: No. 94). (Shoshoni.). Repr. of 1972 ed. $24.00 (ISBN 0-404-60694-6). AMS Pr.

INDIANS OF NORTH AMERICA—UNITED STATES
see Indians of North America

INDIANS OF SOUTH AMERICA—LANGUAGES
see also Quechua Language
Brewer, Forrest & Brewer, Jean. Vocabulario Mexicano de Tetelcingo. (Vocabularios Indigenas Ser.: No. 8). 274p. (Span.). 1962. pap. $4.00x (ISBN 0-88312-658-3); microfiche $3.00x (ISBN 0-88312-363-0). Summer Inst Ling.
Collard, Howard & Collard, Elizabeth. Vocabulario Mayo, Vol. 6. rev. ed. 225p. (Span.). 1974. pap. $4.00x (ISBN 0-88312-657-5); microfiche $4.00 (ISBN 0-88312-318-5). Summer Inst Ling.
Gerdel, Florence & Slocum, Marianna. Vocabulario Tzeltal de Bachajon. (Vocabularios Indigenas Ser.: No. 13). 215p. (Span.). 1965. $3.00 (ISBN 0-88312-589-7). Summer Inst Ling.
Schoenhals, Alvin & Schoenhals, Louise. Vocabulario Mixe de Totontepec. (Vocabularios Indigenas Ser.: No. 14). 353p. (Span.). 1965. pap. $5.00x (ISBN 0-88312-659-1); microfiche $3.75 (ISBN 0-88312-319-3). Summer Inst Ling.

INDIANS OF SOUTH AMERICA—ORIGIN
see Indians—Origin

INDIANS OF THE UNITED STATES
see Indians of North America

INDIANS OF THE WEST INDIES—ORIGIN
see Indians—Origin

INDIC INSCRIPTIONS
see Inscriptions, Indic

INDIC LANGUAGES
Here are entered works on the languages of India in general, and works not confined to the Indo-Aryan languages, or to any other special group or language.
see also Dravidian Languages; Indo-Aryan Languages
Verma, M. K. Structure of the Noun Phrase in English & Hindi. (Eng. & Hindi.). 1971. $8.50 (ISBN 0-89684-322-X). Orient Bk Dist.

INDIC PHILOSOPHY
see Philosophy, Indic

INDIRECT TAXATION
see Tariff; Taxation

INDO-ARYAN LANGUAGES
see also Pali Language; Sanskrit Language
Hunter, W. W. A Comparative Dictionary of the Languages of India & High Asia. 218p. 1978. Repr. of 1868 ed. $26.00x (ISBN 0-89684-144-8). Orient Bk Dist.
Turner, Sir Ralph. A Comparative Dictionary of the Indo-Aryan Languages. (Indo-Aryan.). 1966. text ed. $74.00x (ISBN 0-19-713550-1). Oxford U Pr.

INDO-EUROPEAN LANGUAGES
see also Albanian Language; Armenian Language; Celtic Languages; Germanic Languages; Greek Language
Buck, Carl D. Dictionary of Selected Synonyms in the Principal Indo-European Languages. LC 49-11769. 1949. $80.00x (ISBN 0-226-07932-5). U of Chicago Pr.
Denison, T. S. A Mexican-Aryan Comparative Vocabulary. (Span.). 1976. lib. bdg. $59.95 (ISBN 0-8490-0613-9). Gordon Pr.
Pokorny, Julius. Indogermanisches Etymologisches Woerterbuch, 2 vols, Vols. 1 & 2. 1648p. (Ger.). 1969. $240.00 set (ISBN 3-7720-0526-8, M-7478, Pub. by Francke). French & Eur.

INDO-EUROPEAN LINGUISTICS
see Indo-European Philology

INDO-EUROPEAN PHILOLOGY
see also names of languages and literatures belonging to the Indo-European group
Beard, R. The Indo-European Lexicon: Synchronic Theory. (North Holland Linguistic Ser.: Vol. 44). 1981. $47.00 (ISBN 0-444-86214-5). Elsevier.
Kuipers, A. H. A Dictionary of Proto-Circassian Roots. (PDR Press Publication on North Caucasian Languages: No. 1). 1975. pap. text ed. $13.75x (ISBN 90-316-0018-0). Humanities.

INDO-EUROPEANS
Benveniste, Emile. Vocabulaire des Institutions Indo-Europeennes, 2. 344p. (Fr.). 1969. 45.00 F. Minuit.

INDO-GERMANIC LANGUAGES
see Indo-European Languages

INDO-GERMANIC PEOPLES
see Indo-Europeans

INDONESIAN LANGUAGE
see also Malay Language
Baried, Baroroh, ed. Kamus Istilah Filologi. LC 78-944676. iv, 124p. (Indonesian., Jakarta). 1977. write for info. Universitas Gadjah Mada.
Belkina, E. S. Russko-Indoneziiskii Slovar. 624p. (Rus. & Indonesian.). 1972. $7.85 (Pub. by Sov. Entsiklopediia). Four Continent.
Bulygin, N. F. Karmannyi Indoneziisko-Russkii Slovar. 310p. (Rus. & Indonesian.). 1959. $1.25 (Pub. by GINS). Four Continent.
Bulygin, N. F., et al. Karmannyi Russko-Indoneziiskii Slovar. 576p. (Rus. & Indonesian.). 1958. $1.75 (Pub. by GINS). Four Continent.
Echols, John M. & Shadily, Hassan. An Indonesian-English Dictionary. 2nd ed. 431p. (Eng. & Indonesian.). 1963. $30.00x (ISBN 0-8014-0112-7). Cornell U Pr.
Kahlo, Gerhard, et al. Woerterbuch Deutsch-Indonesisch. LC 77-463622. xxiv, 400p. (Ger. & Indonesian.). 1975. M.38.00. VEB Verlag Enzyklopadie.
Korigodskii, V. N., et al. Indoneziisko-Russkii Slovar. 1171p. (Rus. & Indonesian.). 1961. $5.75 (Pub. by Gosizdat Inostr Natsional Slovarei). Four Continent.
Kramer, Van Goor's Concise Indonesian Dictionary. (Indonesian.). $8.95. Iaconi.
Kramer, A. L., Sr. English-Indonesian, Indonesian-English Dictionary. (Eng. & Indonesian.). $24.50 (ISBN 0-87559-066-7); thumb indexed $29.50 (ISBN 0-87559-067-5). Shalom.
--Van Goor's Concise Indonesian Dictionary: English-Indonesian Indonesian-English. LC 66-23535. (Indonesian.). 1966. $8.95 (ISBN 0-8048-0611-X). C E Tuttle.
Lordkipanidze, A. G., et al. Russko-Indoneziiskii Uchebnyi Slovar. 707p. (Rus. & Indonesian.). 1963. $2.95 (Pub. by GINS). Four Continent.
Poerwadarminta, W. Kamus Umum Bahasa Indonesia. LC 76-941594. 1156p. (Eng. & Indonesian.). 1976. write for info. P N Balai Pustaka.
Sarumpaet, J. Modern Usage in Bahasa Indonesia. LC 80-484867. vii, 264p. (Indonesian & Eng.). 1980. write for info (ISBN 0-85896-484-8). Pitman Ltd.
Teselkin, A. S., et al. Indoneziisko-Russkii Uchebnyi Slovar. 577p. (Rus. & Indonesian.). 1974. $2.35 (Pub. by Sov Entsiklopediia). Four Continent.
Ushakova, L. I., et al. Indoneziisko-Russkii Uchebnyi Razgovornik. 541p. (Rus. & Indonesian.). 1963. $1.75 (Pub. by Gosizdat Inostr Natsional Slovarei). Four Continent.

INDONESIAN LANGUAGES
see Austronesian Languages

INDUSTRIAL ACCIDENTS—PREVENTION
see Industrial Safety

INDUSTRIAL ADMINISTRATION
see Industrial Management

INDUSTRIAL ARTS—DICTIONARIES
Anglo-Russkii Politekhnicheskii Slovar. (Rus.). $19.95. Russki Iazyk.

Diccionario politecnico de las lenguas espanola e inglesa, 2 vols. 3rd ed. (Span. & Eng.). 3000.00 ptas. Castilla.

Ernst, R. German-English, English-German Dictionary of Industrial Technics, 2 vols. 4th, rev., enl. ed. (Ger. & Eng.). Set. $150.00 (ISBN 0-686-77968-1). German-english (ISBN 3-87097-096-0). English-german (ISBN 3-87097-068-5). Heinman.

Feutry, Michel, et al, eds. Dictionary of Industrial Technology: English-French-German-Portuguese-Spanish. $90.00 (ISBN 2-85608-000-6). Heinman.

Franklin, Afred L. Dictionnaire Historique Des Arts, Metiers & Professions Exerces Dans Paris Depuis Le Treizieme Siecle. (Biblio. & Ref. Ser.: No. 198). (Fr.). 1968. Repr. of 1906 ed. $49.00 (ISBN 0-8337-1231-4); $40.00 (ISBN 0-685-06747-5). B Franklin.

Novodvorkis, A. I. Anglo-Litovskii Politekhnicheskii Slovar. 172p. (Eng. & Lith.). 1958. $1.65 (Pub. by Gospolitnauchizdat). Four Continent.

INDUSTRIAL CHEMISTRY
see Chemical Engineering; Chemistry, Technical

INDUSTRIAL DRAWING
see Mechanical Drawing

INDUSTRIAL EDUCATION
see Technical Education

INDUSTRIAL ENGINEERING
see also Automation; Human Engineering; Production Engineering; Quality Control

American Institute of Industrial Engineers. Industrial Engineering Terminology Index. (Industrial Engineering Terminology: 663). $11.00; $8.80, with membership. Inst Indus Eng.

American Society of Mechanical Engineers. Z Ninety Four Industrial Engineering Terminology: 1972 Index. $11.00 (N00073); members $8.80. ASME.

Ernst, R. Woerterbuch der Industriellen Technik, Vol. 1. (Ger. & Eng.), Dictionary of Industrial Engineering). 1974. $80.00 (ISBN 3-87097-060-X, M-7001). French & Eur.

--Woerterbuch der Industriellen Technik, Vol. 2. (Eng. & Ger., Dictionary of Industrial Engineering). 1975. $80.00 (ISBN 3-87097-068-5, M-7000). French & Eur.

--Woerterbuch der Industriellen Technik, Vol. 3. (Ger. & Fr.). 1965. $64.00 (ISBN 3-87097-005-7, M-6999). French & Eur.

--Woerterbuch der Industriellen Technik, Vol. 4. (Fr. & Ger.). 1968. $56.00 (ISBN 3-87097-006-5, M-6998). French & Eur.

--Woerterbuch der Industriellen Technik, Vol. 5. 2nd ed. (Ger. & Span.). 1973. $56.00 (ISBN 3-87097-069-3, M-6997). French & Eur.

--Woerterbuch der Industriellen Technik, Vol. 7. (Port. & Ger.). 1963. $48.00 (ISBN 3-87097-009-X, M-6995). French & Eur.

--Woerterbuch der Industriellen Technik, Vol. 8. (Port. & Ger.). 1967. $48.00 (ISBN 3-87097-010-3, M-6994). French & Eur.

INDUSTRIAL EQUIPMENT
see also Office Equipment and Supplies

Paruit, Bernard. Illustrated Glossary of Process Equipment: Chinese-English-French Edition. (Illus.). 400p. 1983. text ed. $40.00x (ISBN 0-87201-692-7). Gulf Pub.

INDUSTRIAL MANAGEMENT
see also Business; Marketing; Office Management; Personnel Management

Lee, John & Chandler, Alfred D., eds. Pitman's Dictionary of Industrial Administration: A Comprehensive Encyclopedia of the Organization, Administration, & Management of Modern Industry, 2 vols. LC 79-7552. (History of Management Thought & Practice Ser.). 1980. Repr. of 1928 ed. Set. lib. bdg. $125.00 (ISBN 0-405-12336-1); lib. bdg. $62.50x ea. Vol. 1 (ISBN 0-405-12337-X). Vol. 2 (ISBN 0-405-12338-8). Ayer Co.

Moiseev, Anatolii V. Ekonomicheskii Slovar-Spravochnik Rabochego. 4th ed. LC 79-387742. (Illus.). 231p. (Rus.). 1979. 0.45 Rub. Politizdat.

INDUSTRIAL MANAGEMENT-DICTIONARIES

Allen, Louis A. COMVOC, the Louis A. Allen Common Vocabulary of Professional Management. 5th ed. LC 79-110056. vii, 108p. (Eng.). 1978. write for info. Palo Alto, Ca.

Electrical Generating Systems Marketing Association. Glossary of Department of Defense Configuration Management Terminology & Definitions. 1972. $3.00 (CMTD1); members $1.25. Elec Gen Syst.

INDUSTRIAL MATERIALS
see Materials

INDUSTRIAL PAINTING
see Painting, Industrial

INDUSTRIAL PLANTS
see Factories

INDUSTRIAL PROCESS CONTROL
see Process Control

INDUSTRIAL PROCESSING
see Manufacturing Processes

INDUSTRIAL PROPERTY
see also Marks of Origin; Trade-Marks

Industrial Property Glossary. 1979. pap. $20.00 (ISBN 0-685-96910-X, WIPO58, WIPO). Unipub.

Kase, Francis J., ed. Dictionary of Industrial Property, Legal & Related Terms: English, Spanish, French & German. 232p. (Eng., Span., Fr. & Ger.). 1980. $50.00x (ISBN 90-286-0619-X). Sijthoff & Noordhoff.

INDUSTRIAL RELATIONS-DICTIONARIES

Becker, Esther, ed. Dictionary of Personnel & Industrial Relations. 1958. $10.00 (ISBN 0-8022-0088-5). Philos Lib.

Dion, Gerard. Glossary of Terms Used in Industrial Relations. 2nd ed. (Eng. & Fr.). 1975. pap. $16.00 (ISBN 0-7746-6733-8). Univ Laval.

Doherty, Robert E. Industrial & Labor Relations Terms: A Glossary. 4th rev. ed. LC 79-18839. (ILR Bulletin: No. 44). 40p. 1979. pap. $2.50 (ISBN 0-87546-075-5). ILR Pr.

Roberts, Harold S. Roberts' Dictionary of Industrial Relations. rev. ed. LC 78-175029. 616p. 1971. $22.00 (ISBN 0-87179-135-8). BNA.

INDUSTRIAL SAFETY

Klost, Walter. Arbeitsschutzlexikon. LC 80-465045. (Illus.). 186p. (Ger.). 1979. write for info. Verlag Moderne.

Tarrants, William E., ed. Dictionary of Terms Used in the Safety Profession. 1980. Repr. of 1971 ed. $25.00 (ISBN 0-939874-41-5). ASSE.

INDUSTRIAL VACUUM
see Vacuum Technology

INDUSTRY-DICTIONARIES

Becker, H. Dictionnaire trilingue du Droit des Affaires pour le Commerce & l'industrie: Allemand-Anglais-Francais & index. 2nd ed. 992p. (Ger., Eng. & Fr.). 1980. 420.00 F. Maison Dictionnaire.

Cote, N. & Gaumond, J. Nomenclature des Appelations d'emploi dans L' Industrie Papetiere Quebecoise: Anglais-Francais. 114p. (Eng. & Fr.). 1977. pap. $6.95 (ISBN 0-7754-2765-9, M-9234). French & Eur.

Diccionario Tecnico & Industrial Italiano-Espanol. 678p. (Ital. & Span.). 1974. 750.00 ptas. L Carcamo.

Diccionario tecnico industrial: Vol. 2, Aleman-espanol. 584p. (Ger. & Span.). write for info. G Gili.

Dictionnaire de l'industrie Francaise. (Fr.). 1976. 150.00 F. U. F. A. P.

Ernst. Woerterbuch der Industriellen Technik: Band III, Deutsch-Franzoesisch. 1233p. (Ger. & Fr.). 1982. DM.130.00. Brandstetter.

--Woerterbuch der Industriellen Technik: Band IV, Franzoesisch-Deutsch. 1182p. (Fr. & Ger.). 1982. DM.130.00. Brandstetter.

--Woerterbuch der Industriellen Technik: Band IX, Franzoesisch-Englisch. 1085p. (Fr. & Eng.). 1982. DM.140.00. Brandstetter.

--Woerterbuch der Industriellen Technik: Band VII, Deutsch-Portugiesisch. 450p. (Ger. & Port.). 1983. DM.100.00. Brandstetter.

--Woerterbuch der Industriellen Technik: Band V, Deutsch-Spanisch. 1035p. (Ger. & Span.). 1982. DM.80.00. Brandstetter.

--Woerterbuch der Industriellen Technik: Band VIII, Portugiesch-Deutsch. 587p. (Port. & Ger.). 1982. DM.60.00. Brandstetter.

--Woerterbuch der Industriellen Technik: Band VI, Spanisch-Deutschg) 1073p. (Span. & Ger.). 1982. DM.80.00. Brandstetter.

Ernst, R. Diccionario tecnico industrial: Vol. 1, Espanol-aleman. 480p. (Span. & Ger.). write for info. G Gili.

--Dictionnaire de la Technique Industrielle: Allemand-Francais. 3rd ed. 1233p. (Ger. & Fr.). 1979. 430.00 F. Maison Dictionnaire.

Ernst, Richard. Dictionnaire General de la Technique Industrielle: Francais-Anglais. 1080p. (Fr. & Eng.). 1982. 465.00 F. Maison Dictionnaire.

Ferraris, E. Dictionnaire de l'Industrie des matieres plastiques. 1977 ed. 320p. (Fr., Eng., & Ger.). 150.00 F. Maison Dictionnaire.

Freeman, Henry G. Fachenglisch Fur Technik und Industrie. 303p. (Ger. & Eng., English for Engineering and Industry). 1974. $22.50 (ISBN 3-452-17766-1, M-7376, Pub. by Carl Heymanns Verlag KG). French & Eur.

Ketchian, Sonia. Dictionnaire Petrolier des Techniques de Diagraphique, Forage et Production. 376p. (Rus., Fr., Eng. & Ger.), Oil Industry Dictionary of Diagraphy, Sinking, and Production Techniques). 1965. $65.00 (ISBN 0-686-56756-0, M-6326). French & Eur.

Logie, G. Glossary of Employment & Industry. (International Planning Glossaries Ser.: Vol. 3). 1982. $57.50 (ISBN 0-444-42064-9). Elsevier.

Soap & Detergent Association. A Handbook of Industry Terms. 2nd ed. 62p. 1981. free. Soap & Detergent.

Woerterbuch der Industriellen Technik: Band I, Deutsch-Englisch. ix, 1092p. (Ger. & Eng.). 1983. DM.130.00. Brandstetter.

Woerterbuch der Industriellen Technik: Band II, Englisch-Deutsch. ix, 1092p. (Eng. & Ger.). 1983. DM.140.00. Brandstetter.

Wright, Peter. Language of British Industry. 207p. 1974. text ed. $20.00x (ISBN 0-333-15359-6). Verry.

INDUSTRY (PSYCHOLOGY)
see Work

INEBRIETY
see Alcoholism

INFANT EDUCATION
see Education, Preschool

INFIRMARIES
see Hospitals

INFORMATION CENTERS
see Information Services

INFORMATION NETWORKS

Carl, W. H. Dictionnaire de poche du teletraitement des donnees. 290p. (Eng., Ger., & Fr.). 1982. 210.00 F. Maison Dictionnaire.

INFORMATION SCIENCE
see also Documentation; Electronic Data Processing; Information Services; Information Storage and Retrieval Systems; Library Science

Dictionary of Abbreviations in Information Science. 406p. 1976. $50.00x (ISBN 0-686-44776-X, Pub. by Collets). State Mutual Bk.

IFIP. IFIP Fachtworterbuch der Informationsverabeitung. (Ger.). 1968. $22.00 (ISBN 0-7204-2027-X, North Holland). Elsevier.

Leong-Hong, Belkis W. & Plagman, Bernard K. Data Dictionary-Directory Systems: Administration Implementation & Usage. LC 81-21875. 328p. 1982. $31.95x (ISBN 0-471-05164-0, Pub. by Wiley-Interscience). Wiley.

Longley, Dennis & Shain, Michael. Dictionary of Information Technology. 379p. 1982. $34.95 (ISBN 0-471-89574-1, Pub. by Wiley-Interscience). Wiley.

--Dictionary of Information Technology. 400p. (Eng.). 1982. E20.00 (ISBN 0-333-32762-4); pap. $6.95 (ISBN 0-333-34806-0). Macmillan London.

Meadows, A. J., et al. Dictionary of New Information Technology. 256p. 1982. $29.00x (ISBN 0-7126-0019-1, Pub. by Century Pub Co). State Mutual Bk.

Pooch, H. Fachwoerterbuch des Nachrichtenwese. 280p. (Ger.). 1976. DM.pap. 22.50 (ISBN 3-7949-0234-3). Schiele & Schon.

Pugh, Eric. Third Dictionary of Acronyms & Abbreviations: More Abbreviations in Management, Technology, & Information Science. 1977. $17.50 (ISBN 0-208-01535-3, Linnet). Shoe String.

Shain, M. & Longley, D. A Dictionary of Information Technology. 1982. $75.00x (ISBN 0-686-42940-0, Pub. by Macmillan England). State Mutual Bk.

Shain, Michael & Longley, David. Dictionary of Information Technology. 450p. (Ger.). 1982. E15.00 (ISBN 0-333-32762-4). Macmillan London.

Slovar Sokrashchenii Po Informatike. 406p. (Rus.). 1974. $9.75 (Pub. by Izd. Mexdunarod. Tsentral' Nauchin. & Tekhn. Informatsii). Four Continent.

Terminologicheskii Slovar Po Informatike: Na 14-i Iazykakh. 752p. (Rus.). 1975. $29.85. Four Continent.

TerminologicheskiiSLovar Po Informatike. 752p. (Rus.). 1975. $29.85 (Pub. by Izd. Mezhdunarod. Tsentra & Tekhn. Informatsii). Four Continent.

A Thesaurus for Informatics. (Illus.). 167p. 1982. pap. $35.00 (ISBN 0-686-87240-1, IB100, Pub. by Intergovernmental Bureau). Unipub.

Vaillancourt, Pauline M. International Directory of Acronyms in Library, Information & Computer Sciences. LC 80-18352. xi, 518p. 1980. $45.00 (ISBN 0-8352-1152-5). Bowker.

INFORMATION SERVICES
see also Archives; Documentation; Information Storage and Retrieval Systems; Libraries

Carmara Oficial de Comercio, Industria y Navegacion Barcelona. Diccionari d'Informatica. 2nd ed. 214p. (Span.). 1982. pap. 500.00 ptas (ISBN 84-500-7912-8). Organ Ofic Adm.

INFORMATION STORAGE AND RETRIEVAL SYSTEMS
see also Computers; Data Base Management; Electronic Data Processing; Information Networks

Frizzi, Graziano. Dizionarietto di informatica. 112p. (Ital.). 1972. L.1500.00. Bucalo.

Guilhaumou, Jean. Lexique de l'informatique. 3rd ed. 122p. (Fr.). 1976. 36.00 F. E. M. E.

Lancaster, F. Wilfrid. Vocabulary Control for Information Retrieval. LC 78-186528. (Illus.). xiv, 233p. 1972. text ed. $27.50 (ISBN 0-87815-006-4). Info Resources.

Lomax, J. D. Data Dictionary Systems. (Illus.). 1977. pap. $45.00x (ISBN 0-85012-191-4). Intl Pubns Serv.

INFORMATION STORAGE AND RETRIEVAL SYSTEMS–BUSINESS
Warner-Eddison Associates. Words That Mean Business: Three Thousand Terms for Access to Business Information. 235p. 1981. $49.95 (ISBN 0-918212-55-3). Neal-Schuman.

INFORMATION STORAGE AND RETRIEVAL SYSTEMS–EDUCATION
Viet, Jean, ed. Eudised Multilingual Thesaurus for Information Processing in the Field of Education. 391p. (Orig.). 1974. pap. text ed. $17.50x (ISBN 0-686-22571-6). Mouton.

INFORMATION STORAGE AND RETRIEVAL SYSTEMS–MEDICINE
Current Procedural Terminology. 4th ed. 1970. pap. $12.00 (ISBN 0-89970-029-2, OP-041). AMA.

INFORMATION THEORY
see also Data Transmission Systems; Language and Languages; Semantics; Telecommunication
Chandor, Anthony. Dizionario di informatica. Rapelli, G., tr. xvi, 356p. (Ital.). 1972. L.13000.00. Zanichelli.

INFORMATIONS
Amkreutz, Carl. Abreviation du traitement de l'informatique. 2nd ed. 210p. (Eng., Ger., & Fr.). 1982. 160.00 F. Maison Dictionnaire.
--Dictionnaire du Traitement de l'information: Francais-Allemand-Anglais. 900p. (Fr., Ger. & Eng.). 1972. 85.00 F. Carl Amkreutz.
--Dictionnaire du traitement de l'informatique. 2nd ed. 1944p. (Eng., Fr., & Ger.). 1981. 600.00 F. Maison Dictionnaire.
Balay, Maurice. Lexique Informatique. 128p. (Fr.). 1971. 11.00 F. Bordas-Dunod.
Buerger. Woerterbuch Informationsverarbeitung. 461p. (Eng., Fr., Rus. & Ger.). 1979. DM.98.00 (ISBN 3-87144-265-8). Verlag Harri Deutsch.
Bureau, Jacques. Dictionnaire de l'informatique. (Illus.). 250p. (Fr.). 1972. 17.60 F. Larousse.
Burger, Erich. Informationsverarbeitung-Englisch-Deutsch-Franzoesisch-Russisch. 464p. (Eng., Ger., Fr. & Rus.). 1980. M.48.00. VEB Technik.
Camille, Claude & Dehaine, Michel. Dictionnaire de l'informatique: Francais-Anglais. 248p. (Fr. & Eng.). 1972. 59.00 F. Bordas-Dunod.
Dictionnaire d'informatique: Anglais-Francais. 3rd ed. 172p. (Eng. & Fr.). 1975. write for info. Masson.
Dictionnaire d'informatique: Francais-Anglais. 152p. (Fr. & Eng.). 1976. write for info. Masson.
Dictionnaire du Traitement de l'information: Francais-Allemand. 900p. (Fr. & Ger.). 85.00 F. Pioton.
Ginguay, Michel & Lauret, Annette. Lexique d'informatique. (Illus.). 244p. (Fr.). 1973. 73.00 F. Masson & Cie.
Le Garff, Andre. Dictionnaire de l'informatique. 584p. (Fr.). 1975. 202.80 F. PUF.
Nania, G. Dictionnaire d'informatique: Francais-Anglais-Italien-Espagnol-Portugais. 1000p. (Fr., Eng., Ital., Span. & Port.). 1982. 450.00 F. Maison Dictionnaire.
Nania, Georges. Dictionnaire d'informatique. 1000p. (Fr., Eng., Ital., Span. & Port.). 1983. 450.00 F. Maison Dictionnaire.
Valensi, Serge. Lexique Usuel d'informatique. 63p. (Fr.). 1976. 27.50 F. S. C. M.

INITIAL TEACHING ALPHABET
Alexenberg, Melvin & Alexenberg, Miriam. Alef Bet Picture Dictionary. (Illus.). (gr. 1-3). 1963. $5.00 (ISBN 0-914080-06-7). Shulsinger Sales.

INITIALISMS
see Acronyms

INITIALS
see also Monograms

Crowley, Ellen, ed. Reverse Acronyms, Initialisms, & Abbreviations Dictionary. 8th ed. (The Acronyms, Initialisms, & Abbreviations Dictionary Ser.: Vol. 3). 1600p. 1982. $130.00x (ISBN 0-8103-0507-0). Gale.
Cushing, William. Initials & Pseudonyms: A Dictionary of Literary Disguises, 2 Vols. 936p. 1982. Repr. of 1888 ed. Set. $79.00x (ISBN 0-8103-3962-5). Gale.
Dictionnaire Initiatique. (Fr.). write for info. Herve-Masson.
Martinez de Sousa, J. Diccionario Internacional de Siglas. 472p. (Span.). write for info. (ISBN 8-43680-083-4, 270009). Piramide.

INJURIES
see Sports–Accidents and Injuries

INJURIES (LAW)
see Personal Injuries

INJURIOUS INSECTS
see Insects, Injurious and Beneficial

INLAND NAVIGATION
see also Lakes; Rivers
Berna, Henri. Dictionnaire Technique et Administratif De la Navigation Interieure. 393p. (Fr.). 1977. $82.50 (ISBN 0-686-56914-8, M-6030). French & Eur.

INLAND RULES OF THE ROAD
see Inland Navigation

INNUIT
see Eskimos

INNUIT LANGUAGE
see Eskimo Language

INORGANIC CHEMISTRY
see Chemistry, Inorganic

INPUT EQUIPMENT (COMPUTERS)
see Computer Input-Output Equipment

INPUT-OUTPUT EQUIPMENT (COMPUTERS)
see Computer Input-Output Equipment

INSCRIPTIONS
see also Epitaphs; Monograms; Seals (Numismatics)
Gignoux, Phillipe. Glossaire des Inscriptions Pehlevies et Parthes. (Fr.). 1972. $17.50x (ISBN 0-8002-1459-5). Intl Pubns Serv.

INSCRIPTIONS–CRETE
Gaya Nuno, Benito. Lexicon Creticum: Estudios sobre Escritura & lengua cretense; inscripciones monumentales; faistos, arkolochori, mallia. 84p. (Span.). 1953. 60.00 ptas (CSIC). Inst. Antonio de Nebrija.

INSCRIPTIONS, ARAMAIC
Aufrecht, Walter E. & Hurd, John. A Synoptic Concordance of Aramaic Inscriptions. (International Concordance Library: Vol. I). 1975. pap. $20.00 (ISBN 0-935106-24-3). Biblical Res Assocs.

INSCRIPTIONS, GREEK
see also Inscriptions, Linear B
Icard, Severin. Dictionary of Greek Coin Inscriptions. (Gr. & Eng.). 1979. Repr. of 1920 ed. lib. bdg. $42.50 (ISBN 0-915262-31-2). S J Durst.

INSCRIPTIONS, INDIC
Sircar, D. C. Indian Epigraphical Glossary. 1966. $13.95 (ISBN 0-89684-222-3). Orient Bk Dist.

INSCRIPTIONS, LINEAR B
see also Inscriptions–Crete
Pomponas, Giannes K. Lexiko tes Mykenaikes Hellenikes. LC 79-121485. (Gr.). 1978. write for info. Ekdoseis Filon.

INSECTS
see also Entomology
also Ants; Butterflies; Moths; Wasps; and similar headings
Leftwich, A. W. A Dictionary of Entomology. LC 75-27143. 364p. 1976. $27.50x (ISBN 0-8448-0820-2). Crane-Russak Co.

INSECTS–ANATOMY
Tuxen, S. L., ed. Taxonomist's Glossary of Genitalia in Insects. 1970. text ed. $27.50 (ISBN 0-934454-76-0). Lubrecht & Cramer.

INSECTS, DESTRUCTIVE AND USEFUL
see Insects, Injurious and Beneficial

INSECTS, INJURIOUS AND BENEFICIAL
see also Agricultural Pests

also subdivision Diseases and Pests under names of Crops, Plants, Trees, etc. e.g. Fruit–Diseases and Pests; also specific names of insect pests
Leftwich, A. W. A Dictionary of Entomology. LC 75-27143. 364p. 1976. $27.50x (ISBN 0-8448-0820-2). Crane-Russak Co.

INSPECTION OF SCHOOLS
see School Management and Organization

INSTITUTIONS, ASSOCIATIONS, ETC.
see Associations, Institutions, etc.

INSTITUTIONS, CHARITABLE AND PHILANTHROPIC
see Charities

INSTITUTIONS, INTERNATIONAL
see International Agencies; International Cooperation

INSTRUCTION
see Education; Teaching; also subdivision Instruction and Study under Music and under names of musical instruments

INSTRUCTIONAL MATERIALS
see Teaching–Aids and Devices

INSTRUCTIONAL TECHNOLOGY
see Educational Technology

INSTRUCTORS
see College Teachers

INSTRUMENT INDUSTRY
see also Scientific Apparatus and Instruments
Scientific Apparatus Makers Association. Process Measurement & Control Terminology: 20.1-1973. $2.00; bulk prices avail. Sci Apparatus.

INSTRUMENTAL MUSIC
Barlow, Harold & Morgenstern, Sam, eds. Dictionary of Musical Themes. rev. ed. (Illus.). 1976. $14.95 (ISBN 0-517-52446-5). Crown.

INSTRUMENTATION AND ORCHESTRATION
see also Musical Instruments
Read, Gardner. Thesaurus of Orchestral Devices. Repr. of 1953 ed. lib. bdg. $45.00x (ISBN 0-8371-1884-0, REOD). Greenwood.

INSTRUMENTS, ENGINEERING
see Engineering Instruments

INSTRUMENTS, MUSICAL
see Musical Instruments

INSTRUMENTS, OPTICAL
see Optical Instruments

INSTRUMENTS, SCIENTIFIC
see Scientific Apparatus and Instruments
CEI. Dizionario della strumentazione nucleare. 188p. (Ital.). L.1100.00. AEEI.

INSULTS
see Invective

INSURANCE
Classon, Sigvard. Socialfoersaekringslexikon. LC 75-577397. 142p. (Swedish). 1975. Kr.22.00 (ISBN 9-138-01724-5). LiberFoerlag.
Diccionario basico de seguros. rev. ed. (Span.). write for info. Mex. de Seguros.
Garrido y Comas, Juan J. Diccionario practico de seguros. 216p. (Span.). 130.00 ptas. Ariel.
Johnsoh, John R., intro. By. Real Estate Securities & Title Insurance Terminology. (Orig.). 1980. pap. $3.95 (ISBN 0-914256-12-2). Real Estate Pub.
Reavis, Marshall W. Handbook of Insurance Terms & Concepts. 208p. 1983. pap. $14.95 (ISBN 0-88462-630-X, 4101-10). Develop Sys Corp.

INSURANCE–AGENTS–DIRECTORIES
see Insurance–Directories
Sell. Diccionario para especialistas de seguros. (Span.). write for info. Rev. Mex. de Seguros.

INSURANCE–DICTIONARIES
Castelo Matran, Julio. Diccionario Basico De Seguros. 312p. (Span.). 1978. pap. $18.50 (ISBN 84-7100-049-0, S-50036). French & Eur.
--Diccionario Basico De Seguros. 4th ed. 312p. (Span.). 1981. 700.00 ptas (ISBN 84-7100-049-0). Mapfre.
Davids, Lewis E. Dictionary of Insurance. 5th ed. (Quality Paperback Ser: No. 62). (Orig.). 1977. pap. $5.95 (ISBN 0-8226-0062-5). Littlefield.

--Dictionary of Insurance. 6th Rev. ed. 1983. pap. $8.95 (ISBN 0-8226-0381-0). Rowman & Allanheld.
Glossaire Europeen de Terminologie Jurdique et Administrative. Motor, Insurance, German-Italian, No. 27. 152p. (Ger. & Ital.). 1980. pap. $19.95 (ISBN 0-686-97437-9, M-9494). French & Eur.
Green, Thomas E. & Osler, Robert W. Glossary of Insurance Terms. 240p. 1980. pap. text ed. $11.95 (ISBN 0-930868-06-4). Merritt Co.
Grosse, Walter G., et al, eds. Versicherungsenzykolpaedie. LC 77-574020. 3109p. (Ger.). 1976. DM.165.00 (ISBN 3-409-85531-9). Gabler.
Heinze. Fachwoerterbuch des Versicherungswesen, Vol. 1. (Ger. & Eng., Dictionary of Insurance Terms). 1961. $12.50 (ISBN 3-87097-016-2, M-7392, Pub. by Brandstetter). French & Eur.
--Fachwoerterbuch des Versicherungswesen, Vol. 1. (Ger. & Eng.). 1961. DM.12.50 (ISBN 3-87097-016-2). Brandstetter.
Heinze, S. Fachwoerterbuch des Versicherungswesen. (Ger. & Eng., Dictionary of Insurance Terms, English-German). 1961. $12.00 (ISBN 3-87097-017-0, M-7393, Pub. by Brandstetter). French & Eur.
--Fachwoerterbuch des Vesicherungswesen, Vol. 2. (Ger. & Eng.). 1961. DM.12.00 (ISBN 3-87097-017-0). Brandstetter.
Keim, Marianne. Insurance Language. LC 77-12037. 1978. lib. bdg. $12.90 (ISBN 0-89471-019-2); pap. $2.95 (ISBN 0-89471-018-4). Running Pr.
Lesobre, J. & Sommer, H. Vocabulaire Technique Des Assurances: Anglais-Francais, Francais-Anglais. 255p. (Eng.-Fr.). 1972. $27.50 (ISBN 0-686-57013-8, M-6354). French & Eur.
Lipperheide, Manfred, et al. Fachbegriffe der Versicherungwirtschaft. LC 75-537357. 288p. (Ger.). 1974. write for info. Deutsch Spark.
Molnar. Diccionario de seguros. (Span.). write for info. Rev. Mex. de Seguros.
Mueller Lutz, H. & Castelo Matran, Julio. Diccionario de Seguros. 3rd ed. 282p. (Span.). 1981. 600.00 ptas (ISBN 84-7100-004-0). Mapfre.
Mueller-Lutz, H. L. Diccionario De Seguros. 282p. (Span., Ger., Eng. & Fr.). 1977. pap. $15.75 (ISBN 84-7100-004-0, S-50035). French & Eur.
Palacios. Diccionario de la legislacion de seguros. (Span.). write for info. Rev. Mex. de Seguros.
Ruysch, W. A. Elsevier's Multilingual Dictionary of Insurance Technology. (Eng., Dutch, Fr., Ger., Span. & Ital.). write for info (ISBN 0-685-82355-5). Elsevier.
Sommer, Henri. Vocabulaire Technique des Assurances & Reassurances Anglais-Francais. 255p. (Eng. & Fr.). 1972. 54.00 F. Berger-Levrault.

INSURANCE–DIRECTORIES
Garrido y Comas. Diccionario practico de seguros. (Span.). write for info. Rev. Mex. de Seguros.

INSURANCE, LIFE
Beguin, J., et al. Vocabulaire Technique des Assurances sur la Vie, Vol. 2. 335p. (Eng. & Fr.). 1979. pap. $9.95 (ISBN 2-551-03302-0, M-9245). French & Eur.
Beguin, L., et al. Vocabulaire Technique des Assurances sur la Vie, Vol. 1. 309p. (Eng. & Fr.). 1979. pap. $9.95 (ISBN 0-7754-2396-3, M-9244). French & Eur.
De Grandpre, Jean-Paul. Vocabulaire Bilingue des Assurances sur la Vie. 39p. (Fr.). 1969. Can.$1.00. Quebec Off.
Grandpre, Jean-Paul. Vocabulaire des Assurances Sur la Vie. 16p. (Fr.). 1973. Can.$0.50. Quebec Off.
Karlsruhe. Diccionario tecnico del seguro de vida. (Span.). write for info. Rev. Mex. de Seguros.

INSURANCE, MARINE
Bes, J. Chartering & Shipping Terms: Time-Sheet Supplements, Vols. 2 & 3. Set. $70.00 (ISBN 0-685-11999-8). Heinman.
Brown, R. H. Diccionario de terminos maritimos en seguros. Gonzalez Hevia, Raul, tr. 552p. (Span.). 1980. 2600.00 ptas (ISBN 84-7100-095-4). Mapfre.
INSURANCE, MUTUAL
see Insurance
INSURANCE, POSTAL LIFE
see Insurance, Life
INSURANCE, SOCIAL
see Social Security
INSURANCE, STATE AND COMPULSORY
see Social Security
INSURANCE, TRANSPORTATION
see Insurance, Marine
INSURANCE, WORKING-MEN'S
see Social Security
INSURANCE COMPANIES– DIRECTORIES
see Insurance–Directories
INSURGENCY
see also Subversive Activities
Miguel y Verges, Jose Maria. Diccionario de Insurgentes. 2nd ed. 628p. (Span.). 1980. Mex.$750.00. Porrua.
INSURRECTIONS
see Revolutions
INTAGLIO PRINTS
see Engravings
INTANGIBLE PROPERTY
see Copyright; Patents; Trade-Marks
INTEGRATED DATA PROCESSING
see Electronic Data Processing
INTELLECT
see also Intelligence Tests; Logic
Poujol, F. A. Dictionnaire des Facultes Intellectuelles et Affectives de l'ame ou l'on Traite des Passions, des Vertus, des Vices, Des Defauts. Migne, J. P., ed. (Encyclopedie Theologique Ser.: Vol. 39). 560p. (Fr.). Repr. of 1849 ed. lib. bdg. $72.00x (ISBN 0-89241-245-3). Caratzas Pub Co.
INTELLECTUALS
see also Professions; also subdivision Intellectual Life under names of countries, cities, etc., e.g. France–Intellectual Life
Condal, Elias. Dizionario dell'intellettuale di sinistra. 119p. (Ital.). 1970. L.1500.00. Savelli.
Wurmser, Andre. Dictionnaire pour l'intelligence des Choses. (Fr.). 6.00 F. Sagittaire.
INTELLIGENCE
see Intellect
INTELLIGENCE LEVELS– TESTING
see Intelligence Tests
INTELLIGENCE TESTING
see Intelligence Tests
INTELLIGENCE TESTS
Kennon, L. H. Tests of Literary Vocabulary for Teachers of English. LC 70-176966. (Columbia University. Teachers College. Contributions to Education: No. 223). Repr. of 1926 ed. $17.50 (ISBN 0-404-55223-4). AMS Pr.
INTEMPERANCE
see Alcoholism; Temperance
INTERCONNECTED ELECTRIC UTILITY SYSTEMS
see Electric Utilities
INTERCULTURAL RELATIONS
see Cultural Relations
INTERIOR DECORATION– ENCYCLOPEDIAS, YEARBOOKS
Goodier, J. H. Dictionary of Painting & Decorating. 308p. 1974. $39.50x (ISBN 0-85264-224-5, Pub. by Griffin England). State Mutual Bk.
Pegler, Martin M. Dictionary of Interior Design. (Illus.). 260p. 1983. $25.00 (ISBN 0-87005-447-3). Fairchild.
INTERMITTENT FEVER
see Malaria
INTERNAL COMBUSTION ENGINES
see Gas and Oil Engines
INTERNAL MEDICINE
see also Hematology
American Society of Internal Medicine. Procedural Terminology for Internists. $3.00 (312). Am Soc Intern Med.
INTERNATIONAL ADMINISTRATION
see International Agencies

INTERNATIONAL AGENCIES
Here are entered works on public international organizations and agencies of international government. Particular organizations are entered under their respective names.
Broad Terms for United Nations Programmes & Activities, 1979. 186p. 1980. pap. $13.00 (ISBN 0-686-68945-3, UN79/0/1, UN). Unipub.
INTERNATIONAL ARBITRATION
see Arbitration, International
INTERNATIONAL CONFERENCES, CONGRESSES AND CONVENTIONS
see Congresses and Conventions
INTERNATIONAL COOPERATION
Here are entered general works on international cooperative activities with or without the participation of governments.
see also Arbitration, International; Congresses and Conventions; International Agencies
International Cooperation in Terminology. (Infoterm Ser.: Vol. 3). 333p. 1975. pap. text ed. $35.00x (ISBN 3-7940-5503-9, Pub. by K G Saur). Gale.
INTERNATIONAL FINANCE
Walmsley, Julian. Dictionary of International Finance. 356p. (Eng.). 1979. E12.95 (ISBN 0-333-23109-0). Macmillan London.
INTERNATIONAL INSTITUTIONS
see International Cooperation
INTERNATIONAL LAW
see also Aliens; Arbitration, International; International Cooperation; Maritime Law; Military Law
also subdivisions Laws and Legislation and Laws and Regulations under topics of international concern
Gilbertson, G. Harrap's German & English Glossary of Terms in International Law. xii, 355p. (Eng. & Ger.). E25.00 (ISBN 0-245-53524-1). Harrap.
Paenson, I. Manual of the Terminology of Public International Law & International Organizations. (Fr. & Span. & Rus. & Eng.). $110.00 (ISBN 90-65-44052-6). Kluwer Academic.
INTERNATIONAL LAW– HISTORY
Lorton, David. The Juridical Terminology of International Relations in Egyptian Texts Through Dynasty XVIII. LC 73-8114. (Near Eastern Studies). 208p. 1974. $16.00x (ISBN 0-8018-1535-5). Johns Hopkins.
INTERNATIONAL MONETARY FUND
International Monetary Fund, Bureau of Language Services. IMF Glossary: English-French-Spanish. rev. ed. (Eng., Fr. & Span.). 1980. pap. $5.00 (ISBN 0-939934-04-3). Intl Monetary.
INTERNATIONAL ORGANIZATIONS
see International Agencies
INTERNATIONAL RELATIONS
Here are entered works dealing with the theory of international intercourse. Historical accounts are entered under the headings World Politics; United States–Politics and Government; etc. Works dealing with foreign relations from the point of view of an individual state are entered under the name of the state with subdivision Foreign Relations.
see also Arbitration, International; Congresses and Conventions; Cultural Relations; Diplomacy; Disarmament; International Cooperation; International Law
also subdivision Foreign Relations under names of countries, e.g. France–Foreign Relations; also names of international alliances, congresses, treaties, etc. e.g. Holy Alliance; Versailles, Treaty of, 1918
Abdallah. Abdallah Dictionary of International Relations & Conference Terminology in English-Arabic. (Eng. & Arabic). 1982. $40.00x (ISBN 0-86685-289-1). Intl Bk Ctr.

Wolfe, Lucienne V. English-French Glossary. LC 77-601793. 645p. (Eng. & Fr.). 1976. $7.90. Govt Print.
INTERNATIONAL RELATIONS– DICTIONARIES
Fouk al-Ada, Samuhi. A Dictionary of Diplomacy & International Affairs. 566p. (Arabic, Fr. & Eng.). $30.00 (114-3). Intl Bk Ctr.
Haensch, Guenther. Woerterbuch der Internationalen Beziehungen und der Politik. 2nd ed. (Ger., Eng., Fr. & Span., Dictionary of International Relations & Politics). pap. $40.00 (ISBN 3-19-006211-0, M-6993). French & Eur.
Plano & Othon. Diccionario de relaciones internacionales. 465p. (Span.). $2.80; Mex.$35.00. Limusa.
Plano, Jack C. & Olton, Roy. The International Relations Dictionary. 3rd ed. LC 82-3996. (Clio Dictionaries in Political Science Ser.: No. 2). 488p. 1982. text ed. $22.50 (ISBN 0-87436-332-2); pap. $10.75 (ISBN 0-87436-336-5). ABC-Clio.
Woyke, Wichard, ed. Handwoerterbuch Internationale Politik. LC 80-482177. xiv, 412p. (Ger.). 1980. DM.write for info. (ISBN 3-810-00287-9). Leske-Budrich.
INTERNATIONAL SYSTEM OF UNITS
see Metric System
INTERNATIONAL TRADE
see Commerce
INTERPRETATION, BIBLICAL
see Bible–Criticism, Interpretation, etc.
INTERPRETIVE DANCING
see Modern Dance
INTERVALS (MUSIC)
see Musical Intervals and Scales
INTESTINAL AND PARASITIC WORMS
see Worms, Intestinal and Parasitic
INTESTINAL WORMS
see Worms, Intestinal and Parasitic
INTOXICANTS
see Alcoholic Beverages
INTOXICATION
see Alcoholism; Temperance
INVASION OF PRIVACY
see Privacy, Right of
INVECTIVE
The Insult Dictionary: How to Get What You Want in Five Nasty Languages. 1981. pap. $4.95 (ISBN 0-686-29649-4). Natl Textbk.
Languirand, Jacques. Le Dictionnaire Insolite. (Fr.). write for info. Jour, Ed. Du.
Roback, A. A. A Dictionary of International Slurs. LC 76-5696. (Maledicta Press Publications Ser.: Vol. 5). 1979. pap. $15.00 (ISBN 0-916500-05-5). Maledicta.
INVENTIONS
see also Patents
Jouffroy, A. Dictionnaire des Inventions et Decouvertes Anciennes et Modernes, 2 vols. Migne, J. P., ed. (Nouvelle Encyclopedie Theologique Ser.: Vols. 35-36). 1424p. (Fr.). Repr. of 1860 ed. lib. bdg. $181.00x (ISBN 0-89241-277-1). Caratzas Pub Co.
INVENTORY CONTROL
Wallace, Tom. Dictionary. 4th ed. LC 79-90362. 30p. 1980. pap. $7.50 ref. (ISBN 0-935406-00-X). Am Prod & Inventory.
INVENTORY MANAGEMENT
see Inventory Control
INVESTMENT AND SAVING
see Saving and Investment
INVESTMENT COMPANIES
see Investment Trusts
INVESTMENT IN REAL ESTATE
see Real Estate Investment
INVESTMENT TRUSTS
Investment Funds Institute of Canada-L' Institut Des Fonds D' Investissement Du Canada. Glossary of Mutual Fund Terms. free. Inv Funds Inst CN.
INVESTMENTS
see also Building and Loan Associations; Investment Trusts; Mortgages; Real Estate Investment; Speculation; Stock-Exchange

Brownstone, David M. & Franck, Irene M. The VNR Investor's Dictionary. 320p. 1980. $16.95 (ISBN 0-442-21578-9). Van Nos Reinhold.
Johnsich, John R., intro. by. Title Insurance & Real Estate Securities Terminology. (Orig.). 1980. pap. $3.95 (ISBN 0-914256-11-4). Real Estate Pub.
Luecke, Wolfgang. Investigationslexikon. Bloech, Juergen, ed. LC 75-514621. (Illus.). 403p. (Ger.). 1975. DM.59.80 (ISBN 3-800-60482-5). Vahlen.
Schwilling, Werner. Lexikon der Geldenlage. (Ger.). 1974. $35.00 (ISBN 3-478-51560-2, M-7258). French & Eur.
Thole, B. L. & Gilissen, Theodor. Dictionary of Stock Market Terms in Four Languages. (Eng., Fr., Ger. & Dutch.). $18.50 (ISBN 0-87559-068-3). Shalom.
INVESTMENTS–CANADA
Canadian Securities Institute. Investment Terms & Definitions. 56p. first ten copies $1.25; eleven copies & over $1.00. Can Securities Inst.
IRANIAN LANGUAGES
see Kurdish Language; Ossetic Language; Persian Language; Pushto Language
IRELAND
Lewis, Samuel. Topographical Dictionary of Ireland, 3 Vols. LC 75-102611. (Irish Culture & History Ser). 1970. Repr. of 1837 ed. Set. $150.00x (ISBN 0-8046-0788-5, Pub by Kennikat). Assoc Faculty Pr.
IRELAND–HISTORY
Hickey, D. J. & Doherty, J. E. Dictionary of Irish History Since 1800. 615p. 1981. $38.50x (ISBN 0-389-20160-X). B&N Imports.
IRISH LANGUAGE
see also Celtic Languages; Gaelic Language
Dictionary of the Irish Language. 2500p. (Gaelic). 1982. $250.00 (ISBN 0-686-96570-1, Pub by Royal Irish Ireland). State Mutual Bk.
Dinneen. Irish-English Dictionary. (Irish & Eng.). $25.00x (ISBN 0-686-12048-5). Colton Bk.
Dinneen, Patrick S., rev. by. Irish-English Dictionary. (Irish & Eng.). $22.50 (ISBN 0-87559-070-5); thumb indexed $27.50 (ISBN 0-685-32982-8, 071-3). Shalom.
IRISH LANGUAGE–TO 1100
Vendryes, Joseph. Lexique Etymologique de L'Irlandais Ancien: Fascicule R-S. 272p. (Fr.). 1975. 70.00 F (ISBN 2-22201-629-0). CNRS.
—Lexique Etymologique de L'Irlandais Ancien: Fascicule T-U. 211p. (Fr.). 1978. 110.00 F (ISBN 2-22202-227-4). CNRS.
—Lexique Etymologique de l'Irlandais Ancien, 1. 106p. (Fr. & Gaelic.). 1959. 20.00 F. CNRS.
Vendryes, Joseph & Bachellery, E. Lexique Etymologique de L'Irlandais Ancien: Lettre B. 120p. (Fr.). 1981. 90.00 F (ISBN 2-22202-800-0). CNRS.
IRISH LEGENDS
see Legends, Irish
IRON–DICTIONARIES
Abd-El-Wahed, A. M. Iron & Steel Industry Dictionary. 441p. (Eng., Fr., Ger. & Arabic.). 1974. $45.00 (ISBN 0-686-92487-8, M-9760). French & Eur.
Freeman, H. Taschenwoerterbuch Eisen und Stahl. 600p. (Ger. & Eng., Dictionary of Iron and Steel). 1966. $12.50 (ISBN 3-19-006215-3, M-7634, Pub. by M. Hueber). French & Eur.
—Taschenwoerterbuch Eisen und Stahl. 600p. (Ger. & Eng.). 1966. $12.50 (ISBN 3-19-006215-3). Hueber.
Freeman, Henry G. Pocket Dictionary Iron & Steel. LC 76-354255. (Eng. & Ger.). $11.25x ea.; Vol. 1. German-English. (ISBN 3-19-006214-5); Vol. 2. English-German. (ISBN 3-19-006215-3). Intl Pubns Serv.

IRON INDUSTRY AND TRADE
Iron & Steel Institute. Iron & Steel Dictionary: German-English & English-German. 2nd ed. 1962. $22.50x (ISBN 3-514-00197-9). Intl Pubns Serv.
--Iron & Steel Dictionary: German-French & French-German. (Ger. & Fr.). 1962. $22.50x (ISBN 3-514-00209-6). Intl Pubns Serv.
--Iron & Steel Dictionary: German-Italian & Italian-German. (Ger. & Ital.). 1969. $22.50x (ISBN 3-514-00012-3). Intl Pubns Serv.
--Iron & Steel Dictionary: German-Spanish & Spanish-German. 2nd ed. (Ger. & Span.). 1966. $22.50x (ISBN 3-514-00011-5). Intl Pubns Serv.
IRONING
see Laundry and Laundry Industry
IRONWORK
see Forging; Welding
IRRIGATION
see also Dams
Multilingual Technical Dictionary on Irrigation & Drainage. (Eng. & Turkish.). 1972. $12.00; members $8.00. US Comm Irrigation.
Multilingual Technical Dictionary on Irrigation & Drainage. (Eng. & Ger., French translation of terms only). 1971. $40.00; members $30.00. US Comm Irrigation.
Multilingual Technical Dictionary on Irrigation & Drainage. (Eng. & Fr.). 1967. $15.00; members $7.50. US Comm Irrigation.
Multilingual Technical Dictionary on Irrigation & Drainage, Suppl. 1. 1980. $7.00; members $5.00. US Comm Irrigation.
ISI-XOSA
see Xosa Language
ISLAM
see also Koran
also special headings with Islam added in parentheses; subdivision Islam under special topics, e.g. Marriage–Islam; headings beginning with the words Islamic and Muslim
Hughes. Dictionary of Islam. $29.00 (ISBN 0-686-18366-5). Kazi Pubns.
Hughes, Thomas P. A Dictionary of Islam, 2 vols. 1980. Set. lib. bdg. $199.95 (ISBN 0-8490-3121-4). Gordon Pr.
--Dictionary of Islam. LC 71-14622. (Illus.). 1976. Repr. of 1885 ed. $30.00x (ISBN 0-8002-0207-4). Intl Pubns Serv.
--A Dictionary of Islam. 1976. Repr. $35.00x (ISBN 0-8364-0395-9). South Asia Bks.
Kreiser, Klaus, et al, eds. Lexikon der Islamischen Welt. (Ger.). 1974. DM.36.00 (ISBN 3-17-001802-7). Kohlhammer.
--Lexikon der Islamischen Welt: Bd 2, Gram-Nom. 212p. (Ger.). 1974. DM.12.00 (ISBN 3-17-002161-3). Kohlhammer.
--Lexikon der Islamischen Welt: Bd 3, Nor-Z. 192p. (Ger.). 1974. DM.12.00 (ISBN 3-17-002162-1). Kohlhammer.
--Lexikon der Islamischen Welt: Bd 1, A-Grab. 212p. (Ger.). 1974. DM.12.00 (ISBN 3-17-002160-5). Kohlhammer.
ISLAMIC LITERATURE
see also Koran
Feroz-ul-Lughat (Urdu) Dictionary. (Urdu.). $39.50 (ISBN 0-686-83586-7). Kazi Pubns.
ISLAMIC PHILOSOPHY
see Philosophy, Islamic
ISLE OF WIGHT
Long, William H. A Dictionary of the Isle of Wight Dialect, & of Provincialisms Used in the Island, with Illustrative Anecdotes & Tales. LC 76-9101. 1976. Repr. of 1886 ed. lib. bdg. $20.00 (ISBN 0-8414-5740-9). Folcroft.
I.T.A
see Initial Teaching Alphabet
ITALIAN LANGUAGE
Cecchini, Norma & Plessi, Giuseppe. Dizionario Sinottico di Iconologia. LC 77-466702. (Illus.). xxx, 471p. (Ital.). 1976. L.24500.00. Patron.
Isaacs, Alan, ed. Multilingual Commercial Dictionary. 496p. 1980. $22.50 (ISBN 0-87196-425-2). Facts on File.
Lexicologie & Lexicographie Francaises & Romanes. 294p. (Fr. & Ital.). 1959. 42.00 F (ISBN 2-22200-359-8). CNRS.
Melillo, Michelle. Concordanze dei dialetti di Puglia, 2 vols. 916p. (Ital.). 1975. L.50000.00. Atlantica.
Migliorini, Bruno. Parole & Storia. LC 75-545498. 163p. (Ital.). 1975. L.3000.00. Rizzoli Edit.
Plomteux, Hugo. I Dialetti della Liguria Orientale Odierna, 2 vols. LC 76-514874. (Illus.). 1174p. (Ital.). 1975. L.24000.00. Patron.
Raddi, Renzo. A Firenze si Parla Cosi: Frasario Moderno del Vernacolo Fiorentino. LC 76-468656. xxvii, 290p. (Ital., Firenze). 1976. L.5000.00. Libreria.
Rohlfs, Gerhard. Nuovo Dizionario Dialettale Della Calabria. LC 77-476371. (Illus.). 945p. (Ital.). 1977. L.30000.00. Longo A.
Thesaurus di Scienze della Terra. LC 79-350721. 119p. (Eng. , Fr. , Ger. & Ital.). 1977. L.4000.00. Patron.
ITALIAN LANGUAGE–CONVERSATION AND PHRASE BOOKS
Hayward, Arthur L. & McFarlane, C. Learn Italian for English Speakers. (Ital. & Eng.). $9.50 (ISBN 0-87557-046-1, 046-1). Saphrograph.
Hughes, Charles A. Grosset's Italian Phrase Book & Dictionary for Travelers. 300p. (Orig., Ital.). 1971. pap. $3.50 (ISBN 0-448-00653-7, G&D). Putnam Pub Group.
ITALIAN LANGUAGE–DICTIONARIES
ABC Dictionary I, Arabic Italian. (Arabic & Ital.). $7.99. Intl Bk Ctr.
Accattatis, Luigi. Dizionario del dialetto calabrese, 3 vols. 1330p. (Ital.). L.48000.00. Brenner.
--Vocabolario del dialetto calabrese. 1300p. (Ital.). 1978. L.46500.00. Pellegrini.
Aguilera Cerni, Vincente, ed. Diccionario del Arte Moderno: Conceptos, Ideas, Tendencias. LC 80-110365. 569p. (Ital.). 1979. 2800.00 ptas (ISBN 8-473-66108-7). Toreres.
Alessio, Luigi. Vocabolario dell'argot. 100p. (Ital.). L.700.00. Petrini.
Alinei, M. Dizionario inverso italiano. (Ital.). L.10000.00. Il Mulino.
Amendola, Joao. Dictionario Italiano Portugues. Behar, Macim & Moretti, Mario, eds. LC 76-464505. 1037p. (Ital. & Port.). 1976. Cr.$150.00. Hemus-Livraria.
Angelini, Gino. Nuovo dizionario latino-italiano. xii, 1828p. (Lat. & Ital.). 1975. L.10000.00. Dante Alighieri.
Angiloini, Francesco. Vocabolario milanese-italiano. xl, 1056p. (Ital.). 1978. L.21000.00. Imago Libri.
Angiolini, Francesco. Vocabolario milanese-italiano coi segni per la pronuncia. xxxviii, 1054p. (Ital.). L.28000.00. Forni.
Annaratone, Alessandro & La Magna, Giovanni. Vocabolario greco-italiano. xii, 1602p. (Gr. & Ital.). L.18400.00. Signorelli C.
Arrighi, Cletto. Dizionario milanese-italiano. xii, 904p. (Ital.). 1978. L.9000.00 (ISBN 88-203-0964-5). Hoepli.
Atzeni, E. Vocabolario domestico sardo-italiano. 96p. (Ital.). L.3800.00. Forni.
Azzolini, Giambattista. Vocabolario vernacolo-italiano pei destrette roveretano e trentino. 1156p. (Ital.). 1976. L.30000.00. Manfrini.
Badellino, Oreste. Dizionario italiano-latino. 1480p. (Ital. & Lat.). 1972. L.17500.00 (ISBN 88-7011-007-9). Rosenberg & Sel.
--Dizionario italiano-latino: Edizione speciale. 213p. (Ital. & Lat.). 1972. L.25000.00 (ISBN 88-7011-008-7). Rosenberg & Sel.
Bajec, A. & Kalan, P. Dizionario Italian-Slovar. 843p. (Ital. & Slovene.). 1980. $49.95 (ISBN 0-686-97337-2, M-9692). French & Eur.
Baldelli, Ignazio & Mazzetti, Alberto. Vocabolario minimo della lingua italiana per stranieri. iv, 194p. (Ital.). 1974. L.3200.00. Monnier.
Baldelli, Ignazio, et al. Vocabolario minimo della lingua italiana per stranieri con dizionarietto somalo. vi, 222p. (Ital.). 1978. L.4500.00. Monnier.
Bazzarelli, E. Dizionario Motta della lingua italiana, 2 vols. (Illus.). 1800p. (Ital.). L.69600.00. Motta.
Bazzetta de Vemenia, Nino. Dizionario del gergo milanese e lombardo. (Illus.). 112p. (Ital.). L.4200.00. Forni.
Bellini, L. Dizionario della lingua italiano. (Ital.). L.135000.00. Rizzoli Edit.
Benesova, Hana. Cesko-Italsky Slovnik na Cesty. LC 76-532562. (Illus.). 288p. (Czech. & Ital.). 1976. 17.00 Kcs. SNTC.
Benveniste, Emile. Vocabolario delle istituzioni indoeuropee: Vol. 1, Economia-parentela-societa. Liborio, M. A., tr. xix, 286p. (Ital.). 1976. L.12000.00. Einaudi.
Bianchi, Raffaello. Il Vocabolario Latino-Italiano & Italiano-Latino. LC 77-578107. (Illus.). 619p. (Ital. & Lat.). 1977. L.5000.00. Monnier.
Bianchi, Raffaello & Lelli, Onorio. Vocabolario Latino-italiano, italiano-latino. (Illus.). iv, 620p. (Lat. & Ital.). 1973. L.5000.00. Monnier.
Biava. Dizionario italiano-portoghese. 292p. (Ital. & Port.). 1976. L.2300.00. Vallardi A.
Biava, A. Dizionario Italiano-Portoghese, Portoghese-Italiano. 318p. (Ital. & Port.). 1980. leatherette $5.95 (ISBN 0-686-97345-3, M-9172). French & Eur.
Bildwoerterbuch Italienisch: Dizionario Figurato. (Illus.). 896p. (Ital. & Ger.). DM.29.80 (ISBN 3-411-00973-X). Biblio Inst.
Bindoni, Vincenzo & Netto, G. Vocabolarietto del dialetto trevigiano 1884. 112p. (Ital.). 1978. L.2500.00. Canova.
Biundi, Giuseppe. Dizionario siciliano-italiano. 600p. (Ital.). L.18000.00. Forni.
Biundi, Giuseppe & Rigoli, A. Dizionario siciliano-italiano. xvi, 540p. (Ital.). 1978. L.6000.00. Il Vespro.
Bobbio, Norberto & Matteuci, Nicola, eds. Dizionario di Politica. LC 77-467442. xi, 1097p. (Ital.). 1976. L.3200.00. UTET.
Bocchetta, V., ed. Vest Pocket Italian Dictionary. 288p. (Ital.). pap. $2.95 (ISBN 0-8329-1535-1). New Century.
Bocchetta, Vittore E., ed. World-Wide Italian Dictionary. (Ital.). 1977. pap. $2.50 (ISBN 0-449-30840-5, Prem). Fawcett.
Boerio, Giuseppe. Dizionario del dialetto veneziano. 976p. (Ital.). L.25000.00. Giunti-Martello.
Bonazzi, Benedetto. Dizionario greco-italiano. v, 1232p. (Gr. & Ital.). L.7000.00. Morano.
Bortolan, D. Vocabolario dei dialetto antico vicentino. 312p. (Ital.). L.13000.00. Forni.
--Vocabolario del dialetto antico vicentino. 312p. (Ital.). L.13000.00. Forni.
Bottiglioni, G. Dizionario delle parlate corse. (Ital.). L.10000.00. Stem Mucchi.
Brighenti, Eliseo. Dizionario greco moderno-italiano e italiano-greco moderno: Vol. 1, Greco moderno-italiano. xvi, 696p. (Gr. & Ital.). 1976. L.6300.00 (ISBN 88-205-0045-0). Cisalpino.
Brunati, G. Dizionarietto degli uomini illustri della riviera di Sabo. 184p. (Ital.). L.7800.00. Forni.
Brunoli, A. Dizionario Avicolo Internazionale. (Illus.). viii, 300p. (Ital.). 1983. write for info. Ed Calderini.
Brunoli, Alberto. Dizionario avicolo internazionale. 330p. (Ital.). L.4000.00 (ISBN 88-206-0904-5). Edagricole.
Budgay. Dizionario turco-italiano. 194p. (Turkish & Ital.). 1976. L.2300.00. Vallardi A.
Bugday, M. Celalettin. Dizionario Italiano-Turco, Turco-Italiano. 410p. (Ital. & Turkish.). 1979. leatherette $5.95 (ISBN 0-686-97351-8, M-9178). French & Eur.
Busa, Vittorio. Dizionario italiano di vocaboli e modi usati in poesia: Per le Scuole superiori. 68p. (Ital.). L.1910.00. Mori.
Calonghi, et al, eds. Dizionario della lingua latina: Latino-italiano e italiano-latino. 1329p. (Lat. & Ital.). 1968. L.15000.00 (ISBN 88-7011-006-0). Rosenberg & Sellier.
Calonghi, Ferruccio. Dizionario latino-italiano. 1480p. (Lat. & Ital.). 1972. L.17500.00 (ISBN 88-7011-009-5). Rosenberg & Sel.
Campanini, Giuseppe, et al. Vocabolario latino-italiano-latino. 1506p. (Lat. & Ital.). 1976. L.14500.00. Paravia.
Cantamessa, Giuseppe & Messina, Giuseppe. Dizionario della lingua italiana. 1424p. (Ital.). L.6000.00. Signorelli C.
Carletti, Ernesto. Dizionario tascabile illustrato. (Illus.). 104p. (Ital.). 1978. L.2800.00. Citta Nuova.
Casaccia, G. Dizionario genovese-italiano. 871p. (Ital.). L.30000.00. Brenner.
Castiglioni, Luigi. Vocabolario Della Lingua Latina. 15th ed. Brambilla, A. & Campagna, G., eds. LC 76-485030. xii, 2493p. (Lat. & Ital.). 1976. L.18000.00. Loescher.
Cavaletto, M., et al. Dizionario Italiano-Bulgaro. 967p. (Ital. & Bulgarian.). 1979. leatherette $35.00 (ISBN 0-686-97340-2, M-9835). French & Eur.
Cavallaro, Giovanni. Dizionario siciliano-italiano. (Ital.). L.1450.00. Bonanno.
Ceppellini, Vincenzo. Dizionario grammaticale. 650p. (Ital.). 1968. L.5000.00. Ist Geo Agostini.
Cherubini, Francesco. Vocabolario milanese-italiano. 2400p. (Ital.). L.56000.00. Brenner.
Cinti, Decio. Dizionario dei sinonimi e dei contrari. 632p. (Ital.). L.5500.00. Ist Geo Agostini.
Coletti Gruenbaum, Hanne. Dizionario persiano-italiano classico, moderno, familiare. xvi, 960p. (Persian & Ital.). 1978. L.25000.00. Coletti.
Colli, G. Dizionario italiano illustrato per l'uso essenziale della lingua. (Illus.). 862p. (Ital.). 1978. L.8500.00 (ISBN 88-05-03624-2). SEI.
Colombo, P. Vocabolario della lingua italiana. (Illus.). 544p. (Ital.). L.3500.00 (CEB). Capitol-Dischi.
--Vocabolario della lingua italiana. (Illus.). 912p. (Ital.). L.8000.00 (CEB). Capitol-Dischi.
Comitato Del Folklore Cremonese. Dizionario del dialetto cremonese. (Illus.). xxiii, 389p. (Ital.). L.15000.00. Libreria Convegno.
Condrea-Derer, Doina. Dictionar Roman-Italian: Pentru uzul Elevilor. LC 79-353106. 364p. (Romanian & Ital.). 1978. 17.50 lei. Editura Stiintifica.
Conti, Elio. Vocabolario metaurense. xv, 362p. (Ital.). L.17500.00. Forni.
Cordignano, F. Dizionario Italiano-Albanese. xii, 758p. (Ital. & Albanian.). L.26000.00. Forni.
Cusatelli, G. Dizionario Garzanti della Lingua Italiana. 1008p. (Ital.). 1979. $19.95 (ISBN 0-686-97335-6, M-9189). French & Eur.
--Dizionario Garzanti della Lingua Italiana. 2008p. (Ital.). 1980. $49.95 (ISBN 0-686-97336-4, M-9190). French & Eur.
Cusatelli, G., ed. Dizionario Garzanti della Lingua Italiana. 968p. (Ital.). write for info. (M-9188). French & Eur.
Cutolo, Alessandro. Vocabolario della lingua italiana. (Illus.). 1250p. (Ital.). L.28000.00. Euro Co.
D'Ambra, R. Vocabolario napolitano-toscano. xi, 551p. (Ital.). L.25000.00. Forni.
D'Arbela, Edmondo, et al. Vocabolario latino-italiano e italiano-latino. viii, 2030p. (Lat. & Span.). L.16800.00. Signorelli C.
De Felice, Emido & Duro, Aldo. Dizionario della lingua e della civita italiana contemporanea. 2250p. (Ital.). 1975. L.18500.00. Palumbo.

Denti, Renzo. Dizionario Tecnico Italiano-Inglese. LC 76-470277. 1799p. (Eng. & Ital.). 1976. write for info. Hoepli.
De Ruggiero, Ettore. Dizionario epigrafico di antichita romane, 3 vols. 4358p. (Ital.). 1961. L.254000.000. L'Erma.
De Vincentiis, D. L. Vocabolario del dialetto tarantino in corrispondenza della lingua italiana. 320p. (Ital.). L.11500.00. Forni.
Devoto, G. & Oli, G. C., eds. Dizionario della Lingua Italiano. 2712p. (Ital.). write for info. (M-9196). French & Eur.
Devoto, Giacomo & Oli, Giancarlo. Dizionario della lingua italiana. (Illus.). xvi, 2712p. (Ital.). 1974. L.22800.00. Monnier.
--Vocabolario della lingua italiana. vi, 1200p. (Ital.). 1979. L.8800.00. Monnier.
--Vocabolario ilustrato della lingua italiana, 2 vols. 3104p. (Ital.). 1978. L.42500.00. Sel Rdrs Digest.
Dizionarietto della malavita napoletana. 47p. (Ital.). L.500.00. Colonnese.
Dizionario Completo Italiano-Portoghese (Brasiliano), Portoghese (Brasiliano)-Italiano: Con L'etimologia Delle Voci Italiane e Portoghesi (Brasiliane), la Loro Esatta Traduzione, Frasi e Modi Di Dire, 2 vols. (Ital. & Port.). 1978. Set. $82.00x (ISBN 0-686-70496-7); (ISBN 88-203-1010-4). S F Vanni.
Dizionario del Concilio Ecumenico Vaticano Secondo. 1800p. (Ital.). L.36000.00; L.pap. 30000.00. Scode.
Dizionario della lingua italiana, 2 vols. 2008p. (Ital.). 1977. L.23500.00. Garzanti Edit.
Dizionario della lingua italiana. (Illus.). 2008p. (Ital.). 1971. L.pap. 17500.00. Garzanti Edit.
Dizionario della lingua italiana. (Illus.). 1008p. (Ital.). 1976. L.5000.00. Garzanti Edit.
Dizionario della lingua italiana. (Illus.). 1008p. (Ital.). 1971. L.6800.00. Garzanti Edit.
Dizionario della lingua italiana. (Illus.). 1062p. (Ital.). L.4800.00. Bietti.
Dizionario della lingua italiana. (Illus.). 1032p. (Ital.). 1971. L.13000.00. Garzanti Edit.
Dizionario Garzanti Della Lingua Italiana. (Orig., Ital.). L.12.00. Speedimpex.
Dizionario Garzanti Della Lingua Italiana. (Ital.). L.17.00. Speedimpex.
Dizionario greco moderno-italiano e italiano-greco moderno: Vol. 2, Italiano-greco moderno. 672p. (Ital. & Gr.). 1976. L.6000.00 (ISBN 88-205-0046-9). Cisalpino.
Dizionario greco moderno-italiano, italiano-greco moderno. 304p. (Gr. & Ital.). L.3000.00. Malipiero.
Dizionario illustrato della lingua italiana. (Illus.). xvi, 1216p. (Ital.). 1978. L.10000.00. Sansoni.
Dizionario illustrato della lingua italiana. (Illus.). 1304p. (Ital.). L.9000.00. Ist Geo Agostini.
Dizionario illustrato della lingua italiana, 2 vols. (Illus.). 1280p. (Ital.). L.15000.00. Curcio.
Dizionario italiano-greco moderno. 304p. (Ital. & Gr.). L.3000.00. Malipiero.
Dizionario italiano illustrato. (Illus.). 866p. (Ital.). L.8500.00. SEI.
Dizionario italiano illustrato. (Illus.). 1472p. (Ital.). 1974. L.14000.00. Ist Geog Agostini.
Dizionario italiano-latino. 576p. (Ital. & Lat.). L.1500.00. Malipiero.
Dizionario italiano-serbocroato sloveno. 304p. (Ital. & Serbo-Croation.). L.3000.00. Malipiero.
Dizionario latino-italiano e italiano-latino. 304p. (Lat. & Ital.). L.2000.00. Malipiero.
Dizionario Sandron della lingua italiana. (Illus.). xvi, 2160p. (Ital.). 1976. L.18500.00. Sandron.
Dizionario serbocroato-italiano e sloveno-italiano. 304p. (Serbo-Croation, Slovenian & Ital.). L.3000.00. Malipiero.
Dobrovolskaia, I. A. Karmannyi Ital'iansko-Russkii Slovar. 408p. (Rus. & Ital.). 1959. $1.10 (Pub. by GINS). Four Continent.
Dobrovolskaia, I. A., et al. Karmannyi Russko-Ital'ianskii Slovar. (Ital. & Rus.). $1.85 (Pub. by Sov Entsiklopediia). Four Continent.
Ercolani, Libero. Vocabolario romagnolo-italiano, italiano-romagnolo. 920p. (Ital. & Rumanian.). 1971. L.20000.00. Edn Girasole.
Facco, Giannina & Facco, Maria. Vocabolarietto figurato. (Illus.). 380p. (Ital.). 1979. L.3800.00. Edipem.
Fadanelli. Dizionario italiano-russo. 138p. (Ital. & Rus.). 1976. L.2300.00. Vallardi A.
Fadanelli, R. Dizionario Italiano-Russo, Russo-Italiane. 286p. (Ital. & Rus.). leatherette $5.95 (ISBN 0-686-92582-3). French & Eur.
Falcucci, F. D. Vocabolario dei dialetti della Corsica. 474p. (Ital.). 1972. L.30000.00. Licosa.
--Vocabolario dei dialetti della Corsica. xxiii, 473p. (Ital.). 1972. L.12000.00. Licosa.
Fanfani, Pietro. Vocabolario dell'uso toscano, 2 vol. 1036p. (Ital.). L.18000.00. Le Lettere.
Ferrari, G. B. Vocabolario reggiano-italiano. 935p. (Ital.). L.29000.00. Forni.
Ferraro, Giuseppe. Dizionario monferrino. 137p. (Ital.). L.5500.00. Forni.
Ferri, L. Vocabolario ferrarese-italiano. 310p. (Ital.). L.18000.00. Forni.
Finamore, G. Vocabolario dell'uso abruzzese. 328p. (Ital.). 1967. L.8500.00. Dante Alighieri.
--Vocabolario dell'uso abruzzese. 322p. (Ital.). L.10800.00. Forni.
Frenzel, W. Langenscheidts Taschenwoerterbuch Italienisch: Teil II, Deutsch-Italienisch. 606p. (Ger. & Ital.). DM.18.80 (10186). Langenscheidt.
Frisoni, Giuseppe. Dizionario moderno genovese-italiano e italiano-genovese. 538p. (Ital.). L.19500.00. Forni.
Frizzi, Giuseppe. Dizionario dei Frizzetti Popolari Firoentini. LC 76-488668. vii, 267p. (Ital.). 1975. L.9000.00. Multigrafica.
Fusella, L. & Girace, A. Dizionario pratico e frasario per conversazione italiano-amarica. (Ital.). 1937. L.1500.00. Ist Univers Orient.
Gabrielli, Aldo. Dizionario dei sinonimi e dei contrari. (Ital.). L.23000.00. Ist Edit Ital.
--Dizionario dei verbi italiani regolari ed irregolari. (Ital.). L.10000.00. Ist Edit Ital.
--Dizionario linguistico moderno. 1192p. (Ital.). L.12000.00. Edn Scol Mond.
Gaffiot, F. Dizionario illustrato latino-italiano. (Illus.). 1576p. (Lat. & Ital.). 1973. L.15000.00. Piccin.
Gavuzzi, G. Vocabolario italiano-piemontese. viii, 696p. (Ital.). 1971. L.24000.00. Bottega d'Erasmo.
Gemoll, Guglielmo. Vocabolario greco-italiano. 1202p. (Gr. & Ital.). L.14500.00. Sandron.
Gere, S. V., et al. Italiansko-Russkii Slovar. 744p. (Rus. & Ital.). 1947. $5.20 (Pub. by Gosizdat Inostr. Natsional Slovarei). Four Continent.
Giacchi, Pirro. Dizionario del vernacolo fiorentino. 123p. (Ital.). 1966. L.3500.00. Multigrafica.
Giammarco, Ernesto. Dizionario abruzzese e molisano: A-E, Vol. 1. xl, 750p. (Ital.). 1968. L.25000.00. Ateneo & Bizzarri.
--Dizionario abruzzese e molisano: F-M, Vol. 2. 496p. (Ital.). 1969. L.25000.00. Ateneo & Bizzarri.
--Dizionario abruzzese e molisano: N-R, Vol. 3. 560p. (Ital.). 1977. L.25000.00. Ateneo & Bizzarri.
Giampaolo, Barosso. Dizionarietto della lingua italiana lussuosa. (Illus.). 216p. (Ital.). 1977. L.5500.00. Rizzoli Edit.
Gomez, Joan. Dizionario dei sintomi. Ferrario, E. V., tr. (Illus.). 496p. (Ital.). 1977. L.2800.00. Garzanti Edit.
Grad, A. Dizionario Moderno Slovene-Italian-Slovene. 445p. (Ital. & Slovene.). 1979. leatherette $14.95 (ISBN 0-686-97353-4, M9704). French & Eur.
Grassi. Vocabolario della lingua italiana. 540p. (Ital.). 1976. L.2000.00. Vallardi A.
Grassi, C. Vocabolarietto della Lingua Italiana. (Ital.). write for info. French & Eur.
Groff, Lionello. Dizionario trentino-italiano. 206p. (Ital.). L.3500.00. Monauni.
Herczeg, Gyula. Magyar-Olasz Szotar. LC 78-397749. 768p. (Ital. & Hungarian.). 1978. 35.00 Ft (ISBN 9-6320-5072-X). Terra.
--Olasz-Magyar Szotar, 2 vols. LC 78-399851. (Hungarian, & Ital.). 1978. 510.00 Ft (ISBN 9-6305-1613-6). Akademiai Kiado.
--Olasz-Magyar-Szotar. 5th ed. LC 78-399544. 896p. (Ital. & Hungarian.). 1978. 35.00 Ft (ISBN 9-63205-073-8). Terra.
--Olasz-Magyar Szotar: Vocabolario Italiano-Ungherese, 2 vols. 3rd ed. Kolttay-Kastner, Jeno, ed. LC 78-399851. xv, 1781p. (Ital. & Hungarian.). 1978. 510.00 Ft (ISBN 9-63051-613-6). Akademiai Kiado.
Horlacher, Friedrich W. Piccolo Dizionario Americano Italiano. LC 78-343989. 111p. (Eng. & Ital.). 1976. L.1800.00. Nuova Vallecchi.
Italian Dictionary. 320p. (Ital.). Epap. 1.25 (ISBN 0-600-36566-2). Newnes Bks.
Jannota, Elpidio. Dizionario italiano-arabo moderno, 2 vols. (Ital. & Arabic.). 1964. L.31500.00. Ist Poligrafico.
Karmannyi Italiansko-Russkii Slovar. 408p. (Ital. & Rus.). 1959. $1.10. Four Continent.
Kobert, R. Vocabularium syriacum. v, 215p. (Lat.). 1956. L.7000.00; L.pap. 5000.00. Pont Ist Biblico.
Lana, Italo. Vocabolario Della Lingua Latina: Italiano-Latino, Latino-Italiano. LC 80-457571. xvi, 1870p. (Lat. & Ital.). 1978. write for info. Paravia.
Langenscheidts Handwoerterbuecher: Italienisch, 2 Teile in 1. (Ital.). 1978. DM.55.00 (ISBN 3-468-05180-8). Langenscheidt.
Langenscheidts Universal-Woerterbuch Italienisch. 560p. (Ital. & Ger.). DM.6.80 (18181). Langenscheidt.
Libr du Liban. ABC Dictionary Tamhidi: Arabic & Ital. (Arabic & Ital.). 1983. $7.95x (ISBN 0-86685-316-2). Intl Bk Ctr.
--My Illustrated Dictionary: Arabic & Ital. (Arabic & Ital.). 1983. $9.00x (ISBN 0-86685-319-7). Intl Bk Ctr.
Liddell, H. G., et al. Dizionario illustrato greco-italiano. (Illus.). xvi, 1568p. (Gr. & Ital.). 1975. L.23800.00. Monnier.
Lini, L. Dizionario italo-indonesiano. 818p. (Ital. & Indonesian.). L.18000.00. EMI.
Lipparini, L. Vocabolario latino-italiano e italiano-latino. 1008p. (Lat. & Ital.). L.10000.00. Malipiero.
Livadic. Dizionario Italiano-Serbo Croato. 554p. (Ital. & Serbo-Croation.). L.2300.00. Vallardi A.
Livadic, P., ed. Dizionario Italiano-Serbocroato, Serbocroato-Italiano. 500p. (Ital. & Serbocroatian.). 1980. leatherette $5.95 (ISBN 0-686-92461-4, M-9180). French & Eur.
Luciano, L. & Traina, A. Vocabolario fraseologico italiano-latino. xxiii, 1092p. (Ital. & Lat.). 1962. L.10600.00. Patron.
Macchi, V. Langenscheidts Taschenwoerterbuch Italienisch: Teil I, Italienisch-Deutsch. 640p. (Ital. & Ger.). DM.19.80 (10181). Langenscheidt.
Malagoli, Giuseppe. Vocabolarietto del vernacolo pisano. (Illus.). 112p. (Ital.). 1937. L.3000.00. Nistri-Lischi.
Malara, G. Vocabolario dialettale calabro-reggino-italiano. xx, 496p. (Ital.). L.16000.00. Forni.
Malaspina, Carlo. Vocabolario parmigiano-italiano, 4 vols. 1888p. (Ital.). L.75000.00. Forni.
Malchiori, G. Battista. Vocabolario bresciano-italiano. 732p. (Ital.). L.32000.00. Forni.
Maragliano, Alessandro. Dizionario Dialettale Vogherese. LC 76-457376. xlvi, 794p. (Ital.). 1976. L.14000.00. Patron.
Maranesi, Ernesto & Papini, P. Vocabolario modenese-italiano. xxiii, 448p. (Ital.). L.18000.00. Forni.
Marri, Fabio. Glossario al milanese di Bonvesin. 220p. (Ital.). 1977. L.6700.00. Patron.
Mazzucchi, P. Dizionario polesano-italiano. 308p. (Pol. & Ital.). L.10800.00. Forni.
Merlo Pick, Vittorio. Vocabolario italiano-kiswahili. (Ital. & Swahili.). 1978. L.25000.00. EMI.
--Vocabolario kiswahili-italiano. 496p. (Swahili & Ital.). 1978. L.12000.00. EMI.
--Vocabolario swahili-italiano e italiano-swahili. (Swahili & Ital.). L.7000.00. EMI.
Meschiari, E. Vocabolario mirandolese-italiano. (Ital.). L.3000.00. La Vela.
Messinger, Heinz & Ruedenberg, Werner, eds. Langenscheidts Handwoerterbuecher Italienisch. (Ital.). DM.28.00 (ISBN 3-468-80018-5). Langenscheidt.
Migliorini, Bruno. Vocabolario della lingua italiana. (Illus.). xviii, 1638p. (Ital.). 1978. L.16800.00. Paravia.
Migliorini, Bruno & Pellegrini, G. Dizionario del feltrino rustico. (Ital.). L.7000.00. Liviana.
Molossi, L. Vocabolario topografico dei ducati di Parma, Piacenza e Guastalla, 2 vols. (Illus.). 924p. (Ital.). L.42000.00. Forni.
Monti, Pietro. Vocabolario dei dialette della citta e diocesi di Como. xlviii, 483p. (Ital.). L.21000.00. Forni.
Moretti, Giovanni. Vocabolario del dialetto de Magione. xxxii, 672p. (Ital.). L.20000.00. Univ Perugia.
Morri, A. Vocabolario romagnolo-italiano. vi, 926p. (Ital. & Rumanian.). L.36000.00. Forni.
Mortillaro, Vincenzo. Nuovo dizionario siciliano-italiano. 1200p. (Ital.). L.30000.00. Soc St Catanese.
--Nuovo dizionario siciliano-italiano. 1220p. (Ital.). L.44000.00. Forni.
Natta, F. Vocabolario sallustiano. 206p. (Ital.). 1972. L.26500.00. L'Erma.
Neiger, E. Terminologia Turistico Alberghiera. vi, 788p. (Ital.). 1983. write for info. Ed Calderini.
Nelida, Caffarello. Dizionario di antichita classiche. (Illus.). xii, 532p. (Ital.). 1971. L.22000.00. Olschki.
Neri, A. Vocabolario del dialetto modenese. xvi, 335p. (Ital.). 1973. L.9800.00. Forni.
Nicchi, E. Dizionario dei comuni. 800p. (Ital.). 1978. L.8000.00. La Tribuna.
Nichea, Niccolo. Vocabolario croato serbo-italiano de M. Deanovic e J. Jerej. 48p. (Serbo-Croatian & Ital.). 1967. L.3000.00. Del Bianco.
Nicotra, V. Dizionario siciliano-italiano. 926p. (Ital.). L.33000.00. Forni.
Nieri, I. Vocabolario lucchese. xlviii, 286p. (Ital.). L.14500.00. Forni.
Novelli, Tina. Dizionario Etnologico Africano, 3 vols. LC 76-463596. (Illus., Ital.). L.9000.00. Jaca Bk.
Nuovo dizionario della lingua italiana. (Illus.). 1280p. (Ital.). L.12500.00. Curcio.
Nurigiani, Giorgio. Vocabolario italiano-macedone. 752p. (Ital. & Macedonian.). 1969. L.7000.00. Lint.
Nuzzo, Mario. Dizionario della lingua italiana. (Illus.). 1724p. (Ital.). 1977. L.18000.00. Marotta.
Onatskyj, E. Vocabolario ucraino-italiano. 1736p. (Ukranian & Ital.). 1941. L.4000.00. Ist Univers Orient.

Paganini, A. Vocabolario domestico genovese-italiano. (Illus.). 297p. (Ital.). L.15500.00. Forni.
Paganini, Angelo. Vocabolario Domestico Genovese-Italiano. LC 79-391544. (Illus.). 297p. (Ital.). 1977. write for info. Forni.
Palazzi, F. Novissimo Dizionario della Lingua Italiana. Folena, G., ed. 1624p. (Ital.). 1981. $75.00 (ISBN 0-686-97427-1, M-9363). French & Eur.
Pallotta, Gino. Dizionario Politico e Parlamentare Italiano. LC 77-454206. 302p. (Ital.). 1976. L.2500.00. Newton Compton.
Panzini, Alfredo, et al. Dizionario moderno. xxiv, 1096p. (Ital.). 1963. L.10000.00 (ISBN 88-203-0228-4). Hoepli.
Paolo, Marchi G. Concordanze verghiane. 318p. (Ital.). 1972. L.4300.00. Fiorini.
Papias. Vocabularium. 400p. (Ital.). 1968. L.30000.00. Bottega d'Erasmo.
Parlagreco. Dizionario portoghese-italiano. 434p. (Port. & Ital.). 1974. L.14000.00. Vallardi A.
Parlagreco, C. Dizionario Portoghese-Italiano, Italiano-Portoghese. 1138p. (Port. & Ital.). 1979. $35.00 (ISBN 0-686-97354-2, M-9183). French & Eur.
Pavoncello, Nello. Elef Millim. LC 79-367877. 60p. (Hebrew & Ital.). 1979. L.00.2000.00 (ISBN 8-88502-709-1). Carucci.
--Mille Parole Fondamentali. LC 79-367877. 60p. (Hebrew & Ital.). 1979. L.2000.00 (ISBN 8-8850-2709-1). Carucci.
Pecorini, Giorgio. Dizionario della scuola democratica. 160p. (Ital.). 1977. L.3500.00. Emme.
Peri, A. Vocabolario cremonese-italiano. viii, 704p. (Ital.). L.25000.00. Forni.
Perugini, Angelo. Dizionario Italiano-Latino. LC 78-337088. x, 2322p. (Ital. & Lat.). 1976. write for info. Libr Ed Vat.
--Dizionario italiano-latino. xii, 2322p. (Ital. & Lat.). 1977. L.35000.00 (ISBN 88-209-1227-9). Libr Ed Vat.
Pettoello, Pietro. Vocabolario per le favole de Fedro. 84p. (Ital.). L.600.00. Loescher.
Pinelli, Stefano. Piccolo Dizionario del Dialetto Bresciano. LC 77-467177. (Illus.). 109p. (Ital.). 1976. write for info. Grafo.
Pinguentini, Gianni. Nuovo dizionario del dialetto triestino. (Illus.). 574p. (Ital.). L.12000.00. Nuova Cappelli.
Pittano, Giuseppe. Dizionario elementare. 864p. (Ital.). 1978. L.6500.00. Edipem.
--Dizionario elementare: Per la Scuola elementare. (Ital.). L.7500.00. Edipem.
--Dizionario elementare: Per la Scuola elementare. (Ital.). L.6500.00. Edipem.
--Dizionario latino-italiano e italiano-latino. 1696p. (Lat. & Ital.). L.22000.00. Edn Scol Mond.
Pons, Teofilo. Dizionario del dialetto valdese della Val Germanasca. 280p. (Ital.). L.7000.00. Soc Studi Valdesi.
Prati, Angelico. Dizionario etimologico italiano. (Illus.). 1100p. (Ital.). 1969. L.18000.00. Multigrafica.
--Vocabolari delle parlate italiante. 68p. (Ital.). 1966. L.3500.00. Forni.
Provenzal, Dino. Dizionario delle voci. xii, 540p. (Ital.). 1957. L.2500.00 (ISBN 88-203-0219-5); L.pap. 1800.00 (ISBN 88-203-0220-9). Hoepli.
Pulgram, Ernst. Italic, Latin, Italian. LC 79-312793. 400p. (Lat. & Ital.). 1978. pap. write for info. (ISBN 3-533-02769-4). C Winter.
Purves, John. Italian Dictionary. (Routledge Pocket Dictionaries Ser.). 862p. (Ital.). 1980. pap. $8.95 (ISBN 0-7100-0602-0). Routledge & Kegan.
Rapetti, Sergio, et al. Piccolo lessico universale. LC 79-342345. 369p. (Ital.). 1976. L.3500.00. Nuova Vallecchi.
Reynolds, Barbara. Concise Cambridge Italian Dictionary. (Ital.). 1974. $44.50 (ISBN 0-521-07273-5). Cambridge U Pr.
Ricci, V. Vocabolario trentino-italiano. vi, 522p. (Ital.). L.18000.00. Forni.
Roccella, Remingio. Vocabolario della lingua parlata in Piazza Armerina. 292p. (Ital.). L.11800.00. Forni.
Rocci, Lorenzo. Vocabolario greco-italiano. xx, 2076p. (Gr. & Ital.). 1976. L.26800.00. Dante Alighieri.
Rohlfs, Gerhard. Nuovo dizionario dialettale della Calabria. 1000p. (Ital.). 1979. L.30000.00. Longo A.
--Vocabolario dei dialette salentini, 3 vols. (Illus.). 1300p. (Ital.). 1976. L.60000.00. Congedo.
Rosamani, Enrico. Vocabolario Marinaresco Giuliano-Dalmata. LC 76-512031. xxiv, 200p. (Ital.). 1975. write for info. Olschki.
Rosendorfsky, Jaroslav. Dizionario ceco-italiano. 820p. (Czech. & Ital.). L.2000.00. Ist Univers Orient.
--Dizionario italiano-ceco. 716p. (Ital. & Czech.). L.2000.00. Ist Univers Orient.
Rossi, A. Dizionario italiano moderno. (Ital.). L.4300.00. Malipiero.
Rozental, D. E. Russko-Ital'ianskii Ucxhebnyi Slovar. 712p. (Rus. & Ital.). 1966. $2.75 (Pub. by Sov. Entsiklopediia). Four Continent.
Sacerdote, Gustavo. Langenscheidts Taschenwoerterbuecher Italienisch. (Ital.). 1978. DM.21.80. Langenscheidt.
Sacerdoti. Dizionario italiano-latino. 208p. (Ital. & Lat.). 1976. L.2000.00. Vallardi A.
Sacerdoti, N. Dizionario Italiano-Latino, Latino-Italiano. 391p. (Ital & Lat.). 1977. leatherette $5.95 (ISBN 0-686-92629-3, M-9175). French & Eur.
Samarani, B. Vocabolario cremasco-italiano. 280p. (Ital.). L.9000.00. Forni.
Sanna, Carlo. Il Gergo della Camorra. LC 78-370722. (Illus.). 128p. (Ital.). 1978. L.2400.00. Il Vespro.
Scarry, Richard. Primo Dizionario. (Ital.). 1976. $9.00x (ISBN 0-686-16891-7). Intl Learn Syst.
Sciarone Abondio, Giuseppe. Vocabolario fondamentale della lingua italiana. 288p. (Ital.). 1977. L.11000.00. Minerva Italica.
Sella, Pietro. Dizionario latino-italiano: Stato della Chiesa-Veneto-Abruzzi. xxxii, 687p. (Lat. & Ital.). 1965. L.10000.00 (ISBN 88-210-0387-6). Biblioteca Apostolica Vaticana.
--Glossario latino-emiliano. xxiv, 407p. (Ital.). 1973. L.11000.00 (ISBN 88-210-0415-5). Biblio Apost.
Servolini, L. L. Dizionario illustrato degli incisori italiani. (Illus., Ital.). L.34500.00. Goerlich.
Shogakukan Iwa Chujiten: Comprehensive Italian-Japanese Dictionary. 1744p. (Ital. & Japanese.). 1983. 5800.00 Yen. Shogakukan.
Skvorzova & Maizel. Dizionario italiano-russo. 954p. (Ital. & Rus.). 1963. L.4000.00. Editori Riuniti.
Soja, Stanislaw, et al. Maly Slownik Wlosko-Polski, 2 vols. LC 77-562532. (Ital. & Pol.). 1977. 130.00 Zl. Wiedza Powszechna.
--Maly Slownik Wlosko-Polski & Polsko-Wloski, 2 vols. 3rd ed. LC 77-562532. (Pol. & Ital.). 1977. 130.00 Zl. Wiedza Powszechna.
Spaltro, Enzo. Dizionario di psicologia del lavoro. LC 79-378075. 205p. (Ital.). 1976. L.5000.00. Ghisoni.
Spano, Giovanni. Vocabolario sardo-italiano e italiano-sardo, 2 vols. 992p. (Ital.). L.39000.00. Forni.
Spiller. Vocabolario del milanese d'oggi. (Illus.). 208p. (Ital.). L.4500.00. Rizzoli Edit.
Spinelli, Vincenzo & Casasanta, Mario. Dizionario completo italiano-portoghese (brasiliano) e portoghese (brasiliano)-italiano. xxiv, 896p. (Ital. & Port.). 1978. L.15000.00 (ISBN 88-203-1010-4). Hoepli.
--Dizionario completo italiano-portoghese (brasiliano) e portoghese (brasiliano)-italiano. xii, 1040p. (Ital. & Port.). 1976. L.12000.00 (ISBN 88-203-0216-0). Hoepli.
Stanciulescu-Cuza, Mariana. Dictionar Frazeologic Italian-Roman. LC 75-406132. 363p. (Romanian & Ital.). 1975. 13.50 lei. Editura Stiintifica.
Stefanelli, Renzo. Capire l'Economiea: Dizionario Critico del Capitalismo Contemporaneo. LC 78-337064. (Ital.). 1977. L.5500.00. De Donato.
Tamburin, Vincenzo M. Dizionario del dialetto di Cortina d'Ampezzo. (Illus.). 212p. (Ital.). 1973. L.5000.00. Pozza.
Tiraboschi, Antonio. Vocabolario dei dealetti bergamashi. (Ital.). L.13000.00. Forni.
--Vocabolario dei deatetti bergamashi, 3 vols. 1676p. (Ital.). L.48000.00. Forni.
Tommaseo, Niccolo. Dizionario dei sinonimi della lingua italiana, 4 vols. (Ital.). 1973. L.15000.00. Nuova Vallecchi.
Tommaseo, Niccolo & Bellini, Bernardo. Dizionario della lingua italiana, 20 vols. 14824p. (Ital.). 1977. L.90000.00. Rizzoli Edit.
Tonetti, F. Dizionario del dialetto valsesiano. 334p. (Ital.). L.9800.00. Forni.
Tosi, Carlo P. Dizionario della lingua italiana. (Illus.). xii, 1730p. (Ital.). L.16000.00. Principato.
Ungarelli, Gaspare. Vocabolario del dialetto bolognese. 412p. (Ital.). 1965. L.12000.00. Multigrafica.
Universal Italian Dictionary. 560p. (Ital.). $2.95 (093). Langenscheidt.
Vaccaro, Gennaro. Vocabolario romanesco-belliano e italiano-romanesco. lxii, 819p. (Ital.). 1969. L.13000.00. Romana Libri.
--Vocabolario romanesco-trilussiano e italiano-romanesco. 404p. (Ital.). 1971. L.10000.00. Romana Libri.
Valla, Nicola. Vocabularium vulgare. 95p. (Ital.). 1966. L.6000.00. Bottega d'Erasmo.
Valle, Guglielmo. Vocabolario dei piccoli. (Illus.). 190p. (Ital.). L.3500.00. La Scuola.
Vandelli, Canzio. Dizionario fraseologico di russo-italiano e viceversa. (Rus. & Ital.). 1977. L.24000.00. Mondini Siccardi.
Venturino, B. Dizionario borana-italiano. (Ital.). L.2500.00. EMI.
Vianello, Natale. Vocabolario latino-italiano, italiano-latino. xii, 884p. (Lat. & Ital.). 1975. L.6000.00. Dante Alighieri.
Vidari, Giovanni, et al. Vocabolario del dialetto de Vigevano. xii, 444p. (Ital.). 1972. L.18000.00. Olschki.
Viterbo, E. Vocabolario della lingua oromonica. 241p. (Ital.). L.350.00 (ISBN 88-203-0824-X). Hoepli.
Vollnhals, Otto. Woerterbuch des Kraftfahreugwesens. LC 75-515768. 618p. (Ital. & Ger.). 1975. DM.108.00 (ISBN 3-7736-5120-1). Girardet.
Volpe, P. P. Vocabolario napolitano-italiano. lv, 438p. (Ital.). L.14500.00. Forni.
Von Allmen, J. Vocabolario biblico. 548p. (Ital.). 1975. L.7000.00. AVE.
Zingarelli, Nicola. Vocabolario della lingua italiana. (Illus.). xxxii, 2044p. (Ital.). 1970. L.pap. 26000.00. Zanichelli.
--Vocabolario della lingua italiana. (Illus.). 1248p. (Ital.). L.8400.00; L.pap. 6800.00. Zanichelli.

ITALIAN LANGUAGE–DICTIONARIES–DANISH

Anderson, K. & Mafera, G. Italiensk-Dansk Ordbog. 485p. (Ital. & Danish.). 1980. $29.95 (ISBN 87-01-83431-2, M-1286). French & Eur.
Dizionario danese-italiano e italiano-danese. 304p. (Danish & Ital.). L.3000.00. Malipiero.
Dizionario italiano-danese. 576p. (Ital. & Danish.). L.1800.00. Malipiero.

ITALIAN LANGUAGE–DICTIONARIES–DUTCH

Dizionario italiano-olandese. 576p. (Ital. & Dutch.). L.1800.00. Malipiero.
Dizionario olandese-italiano e italiano. 304p. (Dutch & Ital.). L.3000.00. Malipiero.
Van Cappen. Dizionario italiano-olandese. 540p. (Ital. & Dutch.). L.2300.00. Vallardi A.
Van Kampen, V. Dizionario Italiano-Olandese, Olandese-Italiano. 486p. (Ital. & Dutch.). 1980. leatherette $5.95 (ISBN 0-686-97344-5, M-9171). French & Eur.

ITALIAN LANGUAGE–DICTIONARIES–ENGLISH

Berberi, Dilaver & Berberi, Edel A., eds. Cortina-Grosset Basic Dictionary: Italian. (Ital.). 1977. pap. $2.95 (ISBN 0-448-14030-6, G&D). Putnam Pub Group.
Berlitz Editors. Berlitz Italian for Travellers. 192p. (Ital.). 1982. $8.95 (ISBN 0-02-965180-8, Berlitz); pap. $4.95 (ISBN 0-02-963940-9). Macmillan.
--Berlitz Pocket Dictionaries: Italian-English. 300p. (Eng. & Ital.). 1982. pap. $4.95 (ISBN 0-686-93001-0, Berlitz). Macmillan.
Bocchetta, Vittore & Young, Ruth E., eds. New Century Vest-Pocket Italian Dictionary. (Ital.). 1967. $2.95 (ISBN 0-8329-1535-1). New Century.
Bocchetta, Vittore E., ed. New Century World-Wide Italian Dictionary: Italian-English, English-Italian. (Orig., Ital. & Eng.). $7.95 (ISBN 0-8329-9696-3). New Century.
Bussi, Luciano & Cognazzo, Maria. Nuovo Dizionario Inglese-Italiano Delle Science Mediche. 864p. (Eng. & Ital.). 1980. $78.00 (ISBN 0-913298-55-7). S F Vanni.
Cassell. Cassell's Italian Dictionary: Standard Italian-English English-Italian. (Ital. & Eng.). $17.95 (ISBN 0-02-522530-8). Macmillan.
--Cassell's Italian Dictionary: Thumb-indexed Italian-English English-Italian. (Ital. & Eng.). $19.95 (ISBN 0-02-522540-5). Macmillan.
Cassells. Italian-English Dictionary. (Ital. & Eng.). 1977. standard $23.95 (ISBN 0-02-052254-1); indexed $17.95 (ISBN 0-02-052253-3). Macmillan.
Cassells, et al. Cassell's Italian Dictionary: Italian-English, English-Italian. LC 77-7405. (Ital. & Eng.). 1977. index $23.95 (ISBN 0-02-522540-5); plain $19.95 (ISBN 0-02-522530-8). Macmillan.
Cecioni, C. G. Vocabolario inglese-italiano e italiano-inglese. 1056p. (Ital. & Eng.). L.11000.00. Malipiero.
Collins Italian-English English-Italian Dictionary. 416p. (Orig., Ital. & Eng.). 1983. pap. $2.95 (ISBN 0-425-05451-9). Berkley Pub.
Cortina. Cortina-Ace Basic Italian Dictionary. (Foreign Language Dictionary Ser.). 384p. 1982. pap. $2.95 (ISBN 0-441-05003-4). Ace Bks.
Denti, Renzo. Dizionario italiano-inglese e inglese-italiano tecnico. xvi, 1812p. (Ital. & Eng.). 1979. L.18000.00 (ISBN 88-203-1052-X). Hoepli.
--Dizionario Tecnico Italiano-Inglese, Inglese-Italiano. 9th rev. ed. 1811p. (Eng. & Ital.). 1979. $78.00x (ISBN 88-203-1052-X). S F Vanni.
Diccionario universal: Italiano-espanol, espanol-italiano. 364p. (Ital. & Span.). $0.77; 50.00 ptas. Herder SA.
Dizionario Garzanti Italiano-Inglese & Inglese-Italiano. (Orig., Eng. & Ital.). L.12.00. Speedimpex.
Dizionario inglese-italiano e italiano-inglese. 304p. (Eng. & Ital.). L.2000.00. Malipiero.
Dizionario inglese-italiano e italiano-inglese. (Eng. & Ital.). 1975. L.17500.00. Sansoni.
Dizionario inglese-italiano, italiano-inglese: Adattamento e ristrutturazione dell'originale. lxv, 1894p. (Eng. & Ital.). 1977. L.18000.00. SEI.
Dizionario italiano-inglese. (Ital. & Eng.). L.1500.00. Mondadori.
Dizionario italiano-inglese. 576p. (Ital. & Eng.). L.1500.00. Malipiero.

Dizionario italiano-inglese e inglese-italiano. 1100p. (Ital. & Eng.). 1975. L.6800.00. Garzanti Edit.
Dizionario italiano-inglese e inglese-italiano. 1072p. (Ital. & Eng.). 1975. L.5000.00. Garzanti Edit.
Dizionario italiano-inglese inglese-italiano. (Ital. & Eng.). L.2000.00. Mondadori.
English-Italian, Italian-English Dictionary, 1 vol. (Eng. & Ital.). $19.50 (ISBN 0-685-33020-6, 045-3). Saphrograph.
Gatto, Massimo. Dizionario fraseologico e grammaticale italiano-inglese. 306p. (Ital. & Eng.). L.2000.00. Sandron.
Grande Dizionario Hazon-Garzanti Inglese-Italiano Italiano-Inglese. (Eng. & Ital.). 1976. $45.00x (ISBN 0-686-19963-4). Intl Learn Syst.
Gualtieri, F. M. Dizionario italiano-inglese e inglese-italiano. xii, 680p. (Ital. & Eng.). 1967. L.3200.00. Casanova F & C.
Hall, Robert A., ed. The Random House Basic Dictionary Italian. (Ital. & Eng.). 1981. pap. $1.50 (ISBN 0-345-29618-4). Ballantine.
Hall, Robert A., Jr. Italian Vest Pocket Dictionary. (Ital.). 1957. pap. $3.50 (ISBN 0-394-40060-7). Random.
Hamlyn Italian-English Dictionary. (Ital. & Eng.). 1977. pap. $4.95 (ISBN 0-600-36566-2, 8089). Larousse.
Hazon. Dizionario Garzanti Italiano-Inglese & Inglese-Italiano. (Ital. & Eng.). L.30.00. Speedimpex.
--Dizionario Garzanti Italiano-Inglese & Inglese-Italiano. (Eng. & Ital.). L.45.00. Speedimpex.
Hazon, M. Dizionario Garzanti: Italiano-Inglese, Inglese-Italiano. 1024p. (Eng. & Ital.). 1980. $19.95 (ISBN 0-686-97642-8, M-9187). French & Eur.
--Grande Dizionario Hazon Garzanti Inglese-Italiano, Italiano-Inglese. 2112p. (Eng. & Ital.). 1980. $49.95 (ISBN 0-686-97429-8, M-9186). French & Eur.
Hazon, M., ed. Dizionario Hazon Garzanti: Inglese-Italiano, Italiano-Inglese. 1686p. (Eng. & Ital.). write for info. (M-9185). French & Eur.
Hazon, Mario. Dizionario inglese-italiano e italiano-inglese: Edizione scholastica. (Illus.). 1686p. (Eng. & Ital.). 1975. L.16000.00. Garzanti Edit.
Hughes, Charles A. Ace's Italian Phrase Book & Dictionary. (Ace's Foreign Phrase Bk). 192p. 1981. pap. $1.95 (ISBN 0-441-37488-3). Ace Bks.
--Aces's Italian Phrase Book & Dictionary. 1982. pap. $2.25 (ISBN 0-441-37490-5). Ace Bks.
Hugo Pocket Dictionary: Italian-English, English-Italian. 622p. (Ital. & Eng.). 1971. $3.50 (ISBN 0-8226-0505-8, 505). Littlefield.
IBM. Glossario della Elabarione dei Dati: Inglese-Italiano, Italiono-Inglese. 221p. (Eng. & Ital.). 1978. pap. $35.00 (ISBN 0-686-92478-9, M-9294). French & Eur.
Institute for Language Study. Vest Pocket Italian. LC 58-8919. (Illus.). 128p. (Ital.). 1979. pap. $2.45 (ISBN 0-06-464903-2, BN 4903, BN). B&N NY.
Isopel, May, ed. Italian-English, English-Italian Gem Dictionary. (Gem Foreign Language Ser.). (Ital. & Eng.). 1954. $2.95 (ISBN 0-00-458625-5, G1). Collins Pubs.
Italian Bilingual Dictionary: A Beginner's Guide in Words & Pictures. (Eng. & Ital.). 1979. $3.50. Barron.
Italian-English Dictionary, 1 vol. (Ital. & Eng.). $19.50 (ISBN 0-685-33019-2, 045-3). Saphrograph.
Concise English-Italian Italian-English Dictionary. (Eng. & Ital.). $12.95. Longman.
Jean's Pocket Dictionaries: Italian-English. 224p. (Orig., Ital. & Eng.). 1981. pap. $2.25 (ISBN 0-8437-1727-0). Hammond Inc.
Langenscheidt Italian-English Lilliput Dictionary. 640p. (Eng. & Ital.). plastic $1.50 (ISBN 3-468-96416-1). Langenscheidt.
Lipton, Gladys & Colinari, John. Italian Bilingual Dictionary: A Beginner's Guide in Words & Pictures. LC 79-10831. (Ital. & Eng.). (gr. 9-12). 1980. pap. text ed. $3.50 (ISBN 0-8120-0885-5). Barron.
Lysle & Gualtieri. Dizionario delle lingue italiana e inglese, 2 vols. 3320p. (Ital.). L.16000.00. Casanova F & C.
McAllister, J. Vocabolario italiano-inglese, inglese-italiano. 1232p. (Ital. & Eng.). L.15000.00 (CEB); L.pap. 7500.00. Capitol-Dischi.
Macchi, Vladimiro, ed. Inglese-italiano, italiano-inglese. LC 80-500584. xii, 997p. (Ital. & Eng.). 1980. L.2000.00. Sansoni.
Marolli, G. Italian-English, English-Italian Technical Dictionary. 11th, enl. ed. (Illus., Ital. & Eng.). 1980. $100.00 (ISBN 8-8005-1040-X). Heinman.
Melzi, Robert C. The Bantam New College Italian & English Dictionary. 736p. (Orig., Ital. & Eng.). 1976. pap. $2.75 (ISBN 0-553-20267-7). Bantam.
--The New College Italian & English Dictionary. (Orig., Ital. & Eng.). (gr. 7-12). 1976. pap. text ed. $9.92 (ISBN 0-87720-592-2). AMSCO Sch.
Motta, Giuseppe. Dizionario Commerciale Inglese-Italiano, Italiano-Inglese: Economia, Legge, Finanza, Banca, Etc. 1051p. (Eng. & Ital.). 1978. $48.00x (ISBN 0-913298-50-6). S F Vanni.
--Dizionario italiano-inglese e inglese-italiano. x, 1052p. (Ital. & Eng.). L.12400.00. Signorelli C.
Musu, Boy. Dizionario italiano-inglese. 508p. (Ital. & Eng.). L.2000.00. Vallardi A.
Musu-Boy, R. Dizionario Italiano-Inglese, Inglese-Italiano. 463p. (Ital. & Eng.). 1979. leatherette $4.95 (ISBN 0-686-97343-7, M-9177). French & Eur.
Orlandi, Giuseppe. Dizionario italiano-inglese e inglese-italiano: Edizione minore. xiv, 1184p. (Ital. & Eng.). L.7600.00. Signorelli C.
Pipitone, Francesco. Dizionario fraseologico e grammaticale della lingua inglese. 662p. (Ital. & Eng.). L.7000.00. Galeati.
Purves, J. Italian-English, English-Italian Pocket Dictionary. 833p. (Ital. & Eng.). 1980. pap. $13.95 (ISBN 0-7100-0602-0, M-9364). French & Eur.
Ragazzini & Gagliardelli. Italian-English, English-Italian Commercial Dictionary. (Ital. & Eng.). $50.00 (ISBN 0-685-25202-7). Heinman.
Ragazzini, Giuseppe. Dizionario inglese-italiano e italiano-inglese. xxxii, 1864p. (Ital.). 1967. L.26000.00; L.pap. 21800.00. Zanichelli.
Ragazzini, Giuseppe & Biagi, Adele. Dizionario inglese-italiano. 1150p. (Eng. & Ital.). 1972. L.8400.00; L.pap. 6800.00. Zanichelli.
Ragazzini, Giuseppe & Biagi, Adele, eds. Concise English-Italian Italian-English Dictionary. LC 73-17088. 1214p. (Eng. & Ital.). 1973. pap. text ed. $12.95x (ISBN 0-582-55505-1). Longman.
Reynolds, Barbara. Cambridge Italian Dictionary, 2 vols. LC 74-77384. (Ital.). 1962. Vol. 1. Italian-English 1962. $175.00 (ISBN 0-521-06059-1); Vol. 2, English-italian 1981. $225.00 (ISBN 0-521-08708-2). Cambridge U Pr.
--The Concise Cambridge Italian Dictionary. 792p. (Ital.). 1975. pap. $8.95 (ISBN 0-14-051064-8). Penguin.
Sani, Luciano. Vocabolario inglese-italiano e italiano-inglese. xlii, 918p. (Eng. & Ital.). 1977. L.8000.00. Dante Alighieri.
--Vocabolario inglese-italiano, italiano-inglese. xxviii, 2316p. (Eng. & Ital.). L.19000.00. Dante Alighieri.
Skey, Malcolm, ed. English-Italian, Italian-English Dictionary. (Eng. & Ital.). 1981. $49.95x (ISBN 0-19-431158-9). Oxford U Pr.

ITALIAN LANGUAGE–DICTIONARIES–FINNISH

Colussi. Dizionario italiano-finlandese. 460p. (Ital. & Finnish.). L.2300.00. Vallardi A.
Colussi, G. Finnish-Italian-Finnish Dictionary. 532p. (Ital. & Finnish.). 1981. pap. $14.95 (ISBN 951-0-07998-7, M-9640). French & Eur.
Colussi, G., ed. Dizionario Italiano-Finlandes, Finlandes-Italiano. (Ital. & Finnish.). leatherette $5.95 (ISBN 0-686-92443-6, M-9170). French & Eur.

ITALIAN LANGUAGE–DICTIONARIES–FRENCH

Balmas, Enea. Vocabolario del francese moderno. 2536p. (Ital. & Fr.). 1979. L.21000.00. Ghisetti & Corvi.
Bertet, Amato, et al. Dizionario italiano-francese e francese-italiano. (Illus.). xii, 1824p. (Ital. & Fr.). L.11500.00. Paravia.
Boch, Raol. Dizionario Francese Italiano, Italiano Francese. LC 79-348264. (Illus.). xxix, 2175p. (Fr. & Ital.). 1978. write for info. Zanichelli.
Boch, Raoul. Dizionario del francese fondamentale. 248p. (Fr. & Ital.). 1975. L.3600.00. Zanichelli.
--Dizionario francese-italiano italiano-francese. 2208p. (Fr. & Ital.). 1978. L.21600.00. Zanichelli.
Cassiani, Ernesto. Dizionario moderno italiano-francese e francese-italiano. xvi, 2238p. (Ital. & Fr.). L.18000.00. SEI.
Cassone, F. Vocabolario italiano-francese-italiano. 1408p. (Ital. & Fr.). L.14500.00 (CEB); L.pap. 7500.00. Capitol-Dischi.
Denti, Renzo. Dizionario tecnico francese-italiano e italiano-francese. xx, 1840p. (Fr. & Ital.). 1977. L.15000.00 (ISBN 88-203-0937-8). Hoepli.
Dictionnaire Garzanti Francais-Italien, Italien-Francais. 2046p. (Fr. & Ital.). 1969. $39.95 (ISBN 0-686-57110-X, M-6143). French & Eur.
Dizionario francese-italiano e italiano-francese. (Fr. & Ital.). 1975. L.18000.00. Garzanti Edit.
Dizionario francese-italiano e italiano-francese, 2 vols. 2048p. (Fr. & Ital.). 1975. L.28000.00. Garzanti Edit.
Dizionario francese-italiano e italiano-francese. 304p. (Fr. & Ital.). L.2000.00. Malipiero.
Dizionario francese-italiano italiano-francese. (Fr. & Ital.). L.2000.00. La Mondadori.
Dizionario Garzantil Italiano-Francese, Francese-Italiano. 1020p. (Ital. & Fr.). 1979. $19.95 (ISBN 0-686-97334-8, M-9191). French & Eur.
Dizionario italiano-francese. 576p. (Ital. & Fr.). L.1500.00. Malipiero.
Dizionario italiano-francese. (Ital. & Fr.). L.1500.00. Mondadori.
Dizionario italiano-francese e francese-italiano. 1024p. (Ital. & Fr.). 1974. L.5000.00. Garzanti Edit.
Dizionario italiano-francese e francese-italiano. 1024p. (Ital. & Fr.). 1975. L.6800.00. Garzanti Edit.
Filippi & La Tour. Dizionario francese-italiano e italiano-francese. (Fr. & Ital.). L.3500.00. Giunti-Martello.
Gatto, Massimo. Dizionario fraseologico e grammaticale italiano-francese. 376p. (Ital. & Fr.). L.2200.00. Sandron.
Ghiotti, et al. Dictionnaire Italien-Francais, Francais-Italien de la Langue d'Aujourd'hui. (Fr. & Ital.). 1976. $27.50 (ISBN 0-686-57196-7, M-6270). French & Eur.
Ghiotto, Candido, et al. Dizionario italiano-francese francese-italiano della lingua d'oggi. 1230p. (Ital. & Fr.). 1977. L.9500.00. Petrini.
Grimod, Francesco & Caselli, G. Vocabolario italiano-francese e francese-italiano. xii, 2216p. (Ital. & Fr.). 1977. L.15000.00. Dante Alighieri.
Larousse & Co. Larousse de poche, francais-italien et italien-francais. (Fr. & It.). pap. $6.95 (ISBN 0-685-13960-3, 1012). Larousse.
Laurent, Claire. Dizionario italiano-francese. 190p. (Ital. & Fr.). 1975. L.2000.00. Vallardi A.
Laurent, G. Dizionario Italiano-Francese, Francese-Italiano. 413p. (Fr. & Ital.). 1979. leatherette $5.95 (ISBN 0-686-97341-0, M-9173). French & Eur.
Padovani, G. & Silvestri, R. Dictionnaire Bilingue Larousse, Francais-Italien et Italien-Francais. (Apollo). (Fr.). $10.50 (ISBN 0-685-13854-2, 3784). Larousse.
Paoli, Bruno A. Dizionario moderno italiano-francese e francese-italiano. 1584p. (Ital. & Fr.). L.8000.00. Edn Scol Mond.
Rostan, Edwin. Vocabolario francese-italiano e italiano-francese. 1184p. (Fr. & Ital.). L.12000.00. Malipiero.
Rouede, Pierre & Rouede, Denise. Dictionnaire Italien-Francais et Francais-Italien. 1256p. (Fr. & Ital.). 1970. $25.00 (ISBN 0-686-57211-4, M-6493). French & Eur.
Sbrulli, G. & Biffoli, T. Dizionario italiano-francese-italiano. xvi, 1056p. (Ital. & Fr.). L.7000.00. Valmartina.
Simone, R. Dizionario italiano-francese e francese-italiano. 640p. (Ital. & Fr.). 1975. L.2500.00. La Nuova Italia.

ITALIAN LANGUAGE–DICTIONARIES–GERMAN

Altenberg. Dizionario italiano-tedesco. 246p. (Ital. & Ger.). 1975. L.2300.00. Vallardi A.
Altenberg, G. A. & Ubaldi, V. Dizionario Italiano-Tedesco, Tedesco-Italian. 395p. (Ger. & Ital.). 1979. leatherette $6.95 (ISBN 0-686-97349-6, M-9176). French & Eur.
Bidoli, Emilio & Cosciani, Guido. Dizionario tedesco-italiano. xxii, 1282p. (Ger. & Ital.). 1970. L.16000.00. Paravia.
Ciardi Dupre, Giovanni & Escher, Angelica. Dizionario italiano-tedesco e tedesco-italiano. x, 1762p. (Ital. & Ger.). 1978. L.21000.00 (ISBN 88-05-04137-8). SEI.
Cosciani, Guido. Dizionario italiano-tedesco. xxiv, 1096p. (Ital. & Ger.). 1970. L.16000.00. Paravia.
David, S. Vocabolario italiano-tedesco-italiano, 2 vols. cviii, 2656p. (Ital. & Ger.). L.35000.00 (CEB). Capitol-Dischi.
--Vocabolario italiano-tedesco-italiano. (Illus.). 1406p. (Ital. & Ger.). 1977. L.12500.00 (CEB). Capitol-Dischi.
David, Sante, ed. Vocabolario Italiano-Tedesco, Tedesco-Italiano. LC 79-354933. liii, 1351p. (Ger. & Ital.). 1977. L.00.12500.00. Capitol Edit.
Deidda, A. Vocabolario tedesco-italiano e italiano-tedesco. 2496p. (Ger. & Ital.). L.22000.00. Malipiero.
Dizionario illustrato italiano-tedesco. (Illus.). 776p. (Ital. & Ger.). 1974. L.12000.00. Longanesi.
Dizionario italiano-tedesco. 576p. (Ital. & Ger.). L.1500.00. Malipiero.
Dizionario italiano-tedesco. (Ital. & Ger.). L.1500.00. Mondadori.
Dizionario tedesco-italiano e italiano-tedesco. 304p. (Ger. & Ital.). L.2000.00. Malipiero.
Dizionario tedesco-italiano e italiano-tedesco. (Ger. & Ital.). 1975. L.20000.00. Sansoni.
Frenzel, W. & Macchi, V., eds. Langenscheidts Taschenwoerterbuch der Italienischen & Deutschen Sprache. LC 79-385348. 1244p. (Ger. & Ital.). 1978. write for info. Langenscheidt.
Giovannelli. Dizionario italiano-tedesco e tedesco-italiano. 1224p. (Ital. & Ger.). L.13600.00. Signorelli C.
Giovannelli, Paolo & Frenzel, Walter. Langenscheidts Handwoerterbuch Italienisch-Deutsch, 2 vols. in 1. (Ital. & Ger.). DM.72.00 (05181). Langenscheidt.
--Langenscheidts Handwoerterbuch Italienisch: Teil I, Italienisch-Deutsch. 568p. (Ital. & Ger.). DM.39.80 (04180). Langenscheidt.

Guarnieri, M. & Guarnieri, O. Dizionario Tecnico Tedesco-Italiano, Italiano-Tedesco Garzanti. 2032p. (Ger. & Ital.). 1979. $75.00 (ISBN 0-686-97355-0, M9184). French & eur.
Gullino Kuhn, A. Dizionario italiano-tedesco e tedesco-italiano. xxii, 950p. (Ital. & Ger.). 1967. L.5400.00. Casanova F & C.
Introito & Porta. Vocabolario italiano-tedesco. x, 112p. (Ital. & Ger.). 1971. L.8500.00. Bottega d'Erasmo.
Langenscheidt. Dizionario italiano-tedesco tedesco-italiano. 112p. (Ital. & Ger.). L.18000.00. Signorelli C.
--Dizionario pratico tedesco-italiano italiano-tedesco. 624p. (Ger. & Ital.). L.6800.00. Signorelli C.
Lanzara, A. Dizionario tedesco-italiano. 744p. (Ger. & Ital.). L.34000.00. Forni.
Lexikographischen Institut Sansoni, ed. Langenscheidts Grosswoerterbuch: Teil I, Italienisch-Deutsch. 786p. (Ital. & Ger.). DM.78.00 (02180). Langenscheidt.
Lysle & Pontevideo. Dizionario italiano-tedesco e tedesco-italiano. 2200p. (Ital. & Ger.). L.12000.00. Casanova F & C.
Macchi, Vladimiro, ed. Tedesco-Italiano, Italiano-Tedesco. LC 77-579817. xvi, 938p. (Ital. & Ger.). 1976. L.18000.00. Sansoni.
Meyer, A. & Orlando, S. Dizionario tecnico italiano-tedesco e tedesco-italiano, 2 vols. 2860p. (Ital. & Ger.). L.25000.00 (ISBN 88-203-0936-X). Hoepli.
Schlegelmich, A. Worterbuch der Technik: Italienisch-Deutsch. 630p. (Ital. & Ger.). 1981. $95.00 (ISBN 3-7736-5110-4, M-122653). French & Eur.

ITALIAN LANGUAGE–DICTIONARIES–NORWEGIAN
Ulleland, M. Italian-Norwegian Dictionary. (Norwegian & Ital.). 1981. write for info. (ISBN 82-573-0149-3). Kunnskapsforlaget.
--Italiensk-Norsk Ordbok. 412p. (Ital. & Norwegian.). 1981. pap. $39.95 (ISBN 82-573-0149-3, M-9464). French & Eur.

ITALIAN LANGUAGE–DICTIONARIES–SPANISH
Alvisi & Arce. Vocabolario spagnolo-italiano e italiano-spagnolo. 928p. (Ital. & Span.). L.16000.00. Malipiero.
Amador, E. M. Martinez. Diccionario Italiano-Espanol, Espanol-Italiano. 1440p. (Span. & Ital.). $50.95 (ISBN 84-303-0133-X, S-12383). French & Eur.
Ambruzzi, Lucio. Nuovo dizionario italiano-spagnolo. xx, 1332p. (Ital. & Span.). 1978. L.16000.00. Paravia.
Carbonell, Sebastiano. Dizionario fraseologico completo italiano-spagnolo e spagnolo-italiano: Parte italiana-spagnola. (Illus.). xvi, 840p. (Ital. & Span.). 1977. L.12000.00 (ISBN 88-203-0225-X). Hoepli.
--Dizionario fraseologico completo italiano-spagnolo e spagnolo-italiano: Parte spagnola-italiana. xii, 1524p. (Span. & Ital.). 1979. L.18000.00 (ISBN 88-203-0224-1). Hoepli.
Diccionario Cuyas: Spanish-Italian, Italian-Spanish. (Span. & Ital.). $6.00x (ISBN 0-686-00857-X). Colton Bk.
Diccionario Iter Italiano-Espanol, Espanol-Italiano. 712p. (Ital. & Span.). leatherette $6.95 (ISBN 84-303-0139-9, S-50434); pap. $5.95 (ISBN 84-303-0138-0, S-50435). French & Eur.
Diccionario Lexicon Italiano-Espanol, Espanol-Italiano. 400p. (Span. & Ital.). pap. $3.50 (ISBN 84-303-0136-4, S-31394). French & Eur.
Diccionario Universal Herder Italiano-Espanol, Espanol-Italiano. 5th ed. 364p. (Span. & Ital.). 1977. pap. $4.50 (ISBN 84-254-0558-0, S-50433). French & Eur.
Dizinario italiano-spagnolo. (Ital. & Span.). L.1500.00. Malipiero.
Dizionario spagnolo-italiano e italiano-spagnolo. 304p. (Span. & Ital.). L.2000.00. Malipiero.
Frisoni, Gaetano. Dizionario moderno italiano-spagnolo e spagnolo-italiano: Vol. 1, Italiano-spagnolo. xii, 1118p. (Ital. & Span.). 1977. L.7500.00 (ISBN 88-203-0229-2). Hoepli.
--Dizionario moderno italiano-spagnolo e spagnolo-italiano: Vol. 2, Spagnolo-italiano. xii, 748p. (Span. & Ital.). 1977. L.5000.00 (ISBN 88-203-0230-6). Hoepli.
--Dizionario Moderno Spagnuolo-Italiano, Italiano-Spagnuolo, 2 vols. 1865p. (Span. & Ital.). Set. $44.00x (ISBN 0-913298-51-4). S F Vanni.
Garcia. Dizionario italiano-spagnolo. 232p. (Ital. & Span.). 1975. L.2000.00. Vallardi A.
Garcia, A. Dizionario Italiano-Spagnolo, Spagnolo-Italiano. 437p. (Span. & Ital.). 1980. leatherette $5.95 (ISBN 0-686-97347-X, S-31237). French & Eur.
Migliori, Enrico. Dizionario spagnolo-italiano e italiano-spagnolo. (Span. & Ital.). L.3500.00. Giunti-Martello.
Ortiz De Burgos, Jose. Diccionario Manual Italiano-Espanol, Spagnuolo-Italiano. 16th ed. 960p. (Span. & Ital.). 1977. $5.95 (ISBN 84-7183-045-0, S-50432). French & Eur.

ITALIAN LANGUAGE–DICTIONARIES–SWEDISH
Dizionario italiano-svedese. 576p. (Ital. & Swedish.). L.1800.00. Malipiero.
Dizionario svedes-italiano e italiano-svedese. 304p. (Swedish & Ital.). L.3000.00. Malipiero.
Gaft & Bassoli. Dizionario italiano-svedese. 530p. (Ital. & Swedish.). L.2300.00. Vallardi A.
Gareff, G. & Bassoli, F. Dizionario Italiano-Svedese, Svedese-Italiano. 442p. (Ital. & Swedish.). 1973. Leatherette $5.95 (ISBN 0-686-92541-6, M-9174). French & Eur.
Italian-Swedish-Italian Dictionary. 279p. (Ital. & Swedish.). 1978. pap. $9.95 (ISBN 0-686-92481-9, M-9446). French & Eur.

ITALIAN LANGUAGE–GLOSSARIES, VOCABULARIES, ETC.
Durand, Roger H. & Greco, Salvatore. Vocabulaire Italien par l'image. 96p. (Ital.). 1969. 15.00 F. Bordas-Dunod.
Edler, Florence. Glossary of Mediaeval Terms of Business, 1200-1600. 1934. $32.00 (ISBN 0-527-01690-X). Kraus Repr.
Tommaseo, Niccolo & Rigutini, G. Dizionario dei sinonimi della lingua italiana, 2 vols. (Ital.). 1974. L.60000.00. Vallardi F.
Vaccaro, Gennaro. Dizionario delle parole nuovissime e difficili. 497p. (Ital.). 1967. L.6000.00. Romana Libri ALfabeto.
Vocabularios Portugues-Espanol-Italiano. (Port. , Span. & Ital.). $0.80; Mex.$10.00. Novaro.

ITALIAN LANGUAGE–GRAMMAR
Cesana, Gianni. Dizionario ragionato di sinonimi e dei contrari. 662p. (Ital.). L.7500.00. De Vecchi Italy.

ITALIAN LANGUAGE–HISTORY
Rezasco, G. Dizionario del linguaggio italiano storico e amministrativo. xlvii, 128p. (Ital.). L.55000.00. Forni.

ITALIAN LANGUAGE–IDIOMS, CORRECTIONS, ERRORS
Cassell. Cassell's Colloquial Italian. 192p. (Ital.). pap. $3.95 (ISBN 0-02-079440-1). Macmillan.
Hall, R. & Hall, F. Italian & English Idioms. (Eng. & Ital.). 1982. $9.95 (ISBN 0-8120-0467-1). Barron.
Hall, Robert R., Jr. & Hall, Frances A. Two Thousand & One Italian & English Idioms: 2001 Locuzione Italiane e Inglese. LC 81-66403. (Ital. & Eng.). 1981. pap. text ed. $9.95 (ISBN 0-8120-0467-1). Barron.

ITALIAN LANGUAGE–PHONETICS
Magni, Mauro. Dizionario degli errori. 416p. (Ital.). L.8500.00. Edit Vecchi.

ITALIAN PAINTING
see Painting, Italian

ITALIAN PAINTINGS
see Paintings, Italian

ITALY
see also names of cities, towns and geographic areas in Italy
Maldonado, Tomas. Universita la Sperimentazione Dipartimentale. LC 80-499795. 147p. (Ital.). 1978. L.3.500. Guaraldi.

ITALY–HISTORY
Cannistraro, Philip V., ed. Historical Dictionary of Fascist Italy. LC 81-4493. (Illus.). xxix, 657p. 1982. lib. bdg. $49.95 (ISBN 0-313-21317-8, CFA/). Greenwood.
Racine, Pierre. Lexique Historique de l'Italie XVIe.-XXe. Siecle. (Illus.). 384p. (Fr.). 1977. 39.00 F. Colin.

J

JAILS
see Prisons

JAPAN–DICTIONARIES AND ENCYCLOPEDIAS
Papinot, E. Historical & Geographical Dictionary of Japan. LC 71-152116. (Illus.). 1972. pap. $10.50 (ISBN 0-8048-0996-8). C E Tuttle.

JAPAN–ECONOMIC CONDITIONS
Lewin, B. Kleines Woerterbuch der Japanologie. 596p. (Ger. & Japanese.). 1968. $38.00 (ISBN 3-447-00530-0, M-7512, Pub. by Harrassowitz). French & Eur.

JAPAN–SOCIAL LIFE AND CUSTOMS
Lewin, B. Kleines Woerterbuch der Japanologie. 596p. (Ger. & Japanese.). 1968. $38.00 (ISBN 3-447-00530-0, M-7512, Pub. by Harrassowitz). French & Eur.

JAPANESE ART
see Art, Japanese

JAPANESE FOLK-LORE
see Folk-Lore, Japanese

JAPANESE LANGUAGE
Breitung, Eusebius. Deutsch-Japanisches Woerterbuch. LC 79-349548. 1277p. (Ger. & Japanese.). 1977. write for info. Buske.
Gluskina, A. E., et al. Kratkii Russko-Iaponskii Slovar. 1000p. (Rus. & Japanese.). 1950. $5.75 (Pub. by GINS). Four Continent.
Karlgren, Bernhard. Analytic Dictionary of Chinese & Sino-Japanese. (Chinese & Japanese.). $12.00 (ISBN 0-8446-5208-3). Peter Smith.
Kokugo Daijiten: Comprehensive Dictionary of the Japanese Language. 2640p. (Japanese.). 1981. 8800.00 Yen. Shogakukan.
Langenscheidts Universal-Woerterbuch Japanisch. 560p. (Japanese & Ger.). DM.6.80 (18190). Langenscheidt.
Martinez Duenas, Luis M. & Kato Yda, Manuel M. Diccionario espanol-japones. 1160p. (Span. & Japanese.). 1982. 450.00 ptas (ISBN 84-85786-53-X). Edi-Seis.
A New Dictionary of Kanji Usage. (Kanji.). 1982. $28.95 (ISBN 0-8120-5493-8). Barron.
Zarubin, S. F. Russko-Iaponskii Slovar. 818p. (Rus. & Japanese.). 1964. $16.50 (Pub. by Sov. Entsiklopediia). Four Continent.

JAPANESE LANGUAGE–CONVERSATION AND PHRASE BOOKS
Japanese-Chinese Dictionary. 2587p. (Japanese & Chinese.). 1979. leatherette $49.95 (ISBN 0-686-97413-1, M-9267). French & Eur.
Japanese-Chinese Dictionary. 569p. (Japanese & Chinese.). 1980. pap. $7.95 (ISBN 0-686-97415-8, M-9252). French & Eur.
Japanese-Chinese Loanword Dictionary (M-9259) 748p. (Japanese & Chinese.). Date not set. Leatherette $25.00 (ISBN 0-686-97404-2, M-9259). French & Eur.
Kratkii Iaponsko-Russkii Razgovornik. 240p. (Rus. & Japanese.). 1957. $1.95 (Pub. by Iskra Revoliutsii). Four Continent.
Thorlin, Eldora & Brannen, Noah. Everyday Japanese. LC 69-19854. 180p. (Japanese.). 1969. $3.95 (ISBN 0-8348-0037-3). Weatherhill.
Thorlin, Eldora S. Japanese Word & Phrase Book for Tourists. LC 76-113904. (Japanese & Eng.). 1970. flexible leatherette bdg. $5.95 (ISBN 0-8048-0876-7). C E Tuttle.

JAPANESE LANGUAGE–DICTIONARIES–ENGLISH
Berlitz Editors. Berlitz Japanese for Travellers. 192p. (Japanese.). 1982. pap. $4.95 (ISBN 0-02-964070-9, Berlitz). Macmillan.
Ceadel, Eric B. Japanese-English Dictionary, 2 vols. (Japanese & Eng.). romanized $35.00 (ISBN 0-87557-048-8, 048-8). Saphrograph.
Corwin, Charles, et al. A Dictionary of Japanese & English Idiomatic Equivalents. LC 68-11818. 302p. (Japanese & Eng.). 1980. $18.75 (ISBN 0-87011-111-6). Kodansha.
Daniels, F. J. Basic English: Writer's Japanese-English Word Book. (Eng. & Japanese.). 1969. $35.00 (ISBN 0-89346-100-8, Pub. by Hokuseido Pr). Heian Intl.
Dixson, et al. My First English-Japanese Picture Dictionary. (Illus., Eng. & Japanese.). (gr. 1-6). 1978. pap. text ed. $4.50 (ISBN 0-88345-260-X). Regents Pub.
English-Japanese Dictionary (Romanized) (Eng. & Japanese.). $19.50 (ISBN 0-87557-047-X, 048-X). Saphrograph.
Hepburn, James C. A Japanese & English Dictionary with an English & Japanese Index. LC 81-52935. 704p. (Japanese & Eng.). 1982. Repr. of 1867 ed. $29.50 (ISBN 0-8048-1441-4). C E Tuttle.
Inoue, Jukichi. Inoue's Smaller Japanese-English Dictionary. LC 81-52936. 968p. (Japanese & Eng.). 1982. $13.95 (ISBN 0-8048-1440-6). C E Tuttle.
Institute for Language Study. Vest Pocket Japanese. (Illus.). 240p. (Japanese.). 1979. pap. $2.95 (ISBN 0-06-464906-7, BN 4906, BN). B&N NY.
Japanese-English Dictionary: Romanized. (Japanese & Eng.). $19.50 (ISBN 0-686-65152-9, 047-X). Saphrograph.
Kai, Hyojun R. All-Romanized English-Japanese Dictionary. LC 73-90232. 732p. (Eng. & Japanese.). 1973. pap. $6.95 (ISBN 0-8048-1118-0). C E Tuttle.
Kawamoto, Shigeo & Nishiwaki, Junzaburo, eds. The Kodansha English-Japanese Dictionary. Narita, Shigehisa & Shimizu, Mamoru, trs. 1557p. (Japanese & Eng.). 1980. pap. $22.50 flexible soft-binding (ISBN 0-87011-420-4). Kodansha.
The Kodansha Japanese-English Dictionary. 1250p. (Japanese & Eng.). 1983. 1900.00 Yen. Kodansha.
Martin, Samuel. Basic Japanese Conversation Dictionary: English-Japanese & Japanese-English. LC 57-8797. (Eng. & Japanese.). $3.95 (ISBN 0-8048-0057-X). C E Tuttle.
Nelson, Andrew. Modern Reader's Japanese-English Character Dictionary. LC 61-11973. (Japanese & Eng.). 1962. $35.00 (ISBN 0-8048-0408-7). C E Tuttle.
Parnwell, E. C. Oxford Picture Dictionary of American English: English-Japanese Edition. (Illus., Orig.). 1981. pap. text ed. $6.95x (ISBN 0-19-581877-6). Oxford U Pr.
Rose-Innes, Arthur. Beginners Dictionary of Chinese-Japanese Characters. (Chinese & Japanese.). $15.00 (ISBN 0-8446-5657-7). Peter Smith.
Shogakukan Iwa Chujiten: Comprehensive Italian-Japanese Dictionary. 1744p. (Ital. & Japanese.). 1983. 5800.00 Yen. Shogakukan.
Shogakukan Random House Eiwa Daijiten. 3072p. (Eng. & Japanese.). 1979. 9800.00 Yen. Shogakukan.

JAPANESE LANGUAGE–TEXTBOOKS FOR FOREIGNERS
Gardner, Elizabeth F. & Martin, Samuel E. An Introduction to Modern Japanese Orthography: Kana. (Japanese.). $3.00 (ISBN 0-88710-039-2). Far Eastern Pubns.

Learn Japanese for English Speakers. (Japanese & Eng.). pap. $9.50 (ISBN 0-87557-049-6, 049-6). Saphrograph.

JAPANESE LANGUAGE–VOCABULARY
The Kodansha Japanese-Russian Dictionary. 1154p. (Japanese & Rus.). 1983. 5800.00 Yen. Kodansha.

Martin, S. Basic Japanese Conversation Dictionary. (Japanese.). $3.95. Iaconi.

Miura, Akira. English Loanwords in Japanese: A Selection. LC 78-65031. (Japanese & Eng.). 1979. $11.50 (ISBN 0-8048-1248-9). C E Tuttle.

Rose-Innes, A. Vocabulary of Common Japanese Words. (Japanese.). $3.00 (ISBN 0-88710-123-2). Far Eastern Pubns.

Vocabularios Japones-Espanol-Ruso. (Japanese, Span. & Rus.). $0.80; Mex.$10.00. Novaro.

JAPANESE LANGUAGE–WRITING
Rose-Innes, Arthur. Beginners' Dictionary of Chinese-Japanese Characters & Compounds. (Chinese & Japanese.). 1977. pap. $7.95 (ISBN 0-486-23467-3). Dover.

JARGONS
see Languages, Mixed
JAVANESE LANGUAGE
Horne, Elinor C. Javanese-English Dictionary. (Linguistic Ser). (Javanese & Eng.). 1974. text ed. $55.00x (ISBN 0-300-01689-1). Yale U Pr.

JAZZ MUSIC–DICTIONARIES
Berindei, Mihai. Dictionar de Jazz. LC 78-353033. (Illus.). 298p. (Romanian.). 1976. 23.50 lei. Editura Stiintifica.

Ortiz Oderigo. Diccionario del jazz. (Span.). Arg.$30.00. Ricordi.

Panassie, Hugues & Gautier. Dictionnaire du Jazz. rev. ed. (Illus.). 363p. (Fr.). 1971. write for info. Albin Michel.

Panassie, Hugues & Gautier, Madeleine. Dictionnaire du Jazz. 363p. (Fr.). 1971. pap. $18.95 (ISBN 0-686-56870-2, M-6648). French & Eur.

JESTS
see Wit and Humor
JEWELRY
see also Gems; Hall-Marks
McNeil, Donald S., ed. Jewelers' Dictionary. 3rd ed. LC 76-26012. 268p. 1979. $39.95x (ISBN 0-931744-01-6). Jewelers Circular.

Newman, Harold. An Illustrated Dictionary of Jewelry. (Illustrated Dictionary Ser.). (Illus.). 1981. $29.95 (ISBN 0-500-23309-8). Thames Hudson.

JEWELRY TRADE
McNeil, Donald S., compiled by. The Jewelers' Dictionary. 1976. $39.95 (ISBN 0-685-84983-X). Jewelers Circular.

JEWELS
see Gems; Jewelry; Precious Stones
JEWISH ART AND SYMBOLISM
Samuel, Edith. Your Jewish Lexicon. 192p. (Orig. Hebrew). 1982. $10.00 (ISBN 0-8074-0054-8); pap. $5.95 (ISBN 0-8074-0061-0). UAHC.

JEWISH LANGUAGE
see Yiddish Language
JEWISH LITERATURE–BIBLIOGRAPHY
New York Public Library, Research Libraries. Dictionary Catalog of Jewish Collection, 14 Vols. Set. $1190.00 (ISBN 0-8161-0409-3, Pub. by Hall Library). G K Hall.

JEWISH PORTRAITS
see Portraits
JEWISH SYMBOLISM AND ART
see Jewish Art and Symbolism
JEWISH WIT AND HUMOR
Rosten, Leo. Joys of Yiddish. 1968. $19.95 (ISBN 0-07-053975-8, GB). McGraw.

JEWS–BIBLIOGRAPHY
New York Public Library, Research Libraries. Dictionary Catalog of Jewish Collection, 14 Vols. 1960. Set. $1190.00 (ISBN 0-8161-0409-3, Pub. by Hall Library). G K Hall.

––Dictionary Catalog of the Jewish Collection, First Supplement, 8 vols. 5424p. 1975. Set. lib. bdg. $840.00 (ISBN 0-8161-0773-4, Hall Library). G K Hall.

JEWS–DICTIONARIES AND ENCYCLOPEDIAS
see also Judaism–Dictionaries
Bridger & Wolk. The New Jewish Encyclopedia. rev. ed. LC 76-15251. (Illus.). 542p. 1976. $14.95 (ISBN 0-87441-120-3). Behrman.

Harkavy, Alexander. Harkavy's Complete Dictionary. 1123p. 1898. $12.50 (ISBN 0-88482-666-X). Hebrew Pub.

JOB SATISFACTION
Hutar, Laddie F. Job Success Dictionary: A Hutar Guide to Becoming a More Valuable Employee & Earning More. (Illus.). pap. $2.00 (ISBN 0-918896-02-9). Hutar.

JOBS
see Occupations; Professions
Genette, Francis. Dictionnaire Marabout du Bricolage. (Illus.). 414p. (Fr.). 16.50 F. Marabout.

JOHNSON, SAMUEL, 1709-1784
Clifford, James L. Dictionary Johnson. 384p. 1981. pap. $6.95 (ISBN 0-07-011379-3, GB). McGraw.

––Dictionary Johnson: The Middle Years of Samuel Johnson. (Illus.). 1979. $17.95 (ISBN 0-07-011378-5, GB). McGraw.

Naugle, Helen H., ed. A Concordance to the Poems of Samuel Johnson. LC 72-13383. (Concordances Ser). 578p. 1973. $39.50x (ISBN 0-8014-0769-9). Cornell U Pr.

Wallis, John E. Doctor Johnson & His English Dictionary. 1978. Repr. of 1945 ed. lib. bdg. $10.00 (ISBN 0-8495-5643-0). Arden Lib.

JOINERY
see also Furniture Making; Woodwork
Dictionary of Joinery Terms: Doors, Windows, Shutters. (Hebrew, Eng. , Fr. & Ger.). IL.8.00. Massada Pr.

JOINTS–DISEASES
Huskisson & Hart. Joint Disease. 3rd ed. 192p. 1982. pap. $21.50 (ISBN 0-7236-0465-7). Wright-PSG.

JOKES
see Wit and Humor
JONSON, BEN, 1573-1637
Di Cesare, Mario A. & Fogel, Ephim, eds. A Concordance to the Poems of Ben Jonson. LC 78-59630. (Concordances Ser). 1978. $57.00x (ISBN 0-8014-1217-X). Cornell U Pr.

JOURNALISM
see also Editing; Musical Criticism; Newspapers
Kutuzov, A. I. Slovar Russko-Suahkili Gazetnoi Leksiki. 174p. (Rus. & Swahili.). 1963. $2.10 (Pub. by In-Tut Mezhdunarod. Otnoshenii). Four Continent.

Lenzi, Mario. Dizionario di giornalismo. 260p. (Ital.). 1974. L.5000.00. Mursia.

Lopez de Zuazo, A. Diccionario del Periodismo. 2nd ed. 244p. (Span.). write for info. (ISBN 8-43680-053-2, 270003). Piramide.

Lopez De Zuazo Algar, Antonio. Diccionario del Periodismo. 2nd ed. 256p. (Span.). 1978. leatherette $16.75 (ISBN 84-368-0053-2, S-50177). French & Eur.

––Diccionario del periodismo. 3rd ed. 256p. (Span.). 1981. pap. 800.00 ptas (ISBN 84-368-0053-2). Piramide.

Martinez de Sousa, J. Diccionario General de Periodismo. (Span.). 1981. 2000.00 ptas (ISBN 8-42831-117-X). Paraninfo.

Martinez de Sousa, Jose. Diccionario General del Periodismo. 596p. (Span.). 1980. 1200.00 ptas (ISBN 84-283-1117-X). Paraninfo.

Pepper, W. H. Diccionario de terminos periodisticos y graficos. (Span.). Arg.$14.00. Sudamer.

JOURNALISM–BIOGRAPHY
see Journalists

JOURNALISM–HANDBOOKS, MANUALS, ETC.
Kent, Ruth. Language of Journalism: A Glossary of Print-Communications Terms. LC 71-100624. (Illus.). 1970. $8.00x (ISBN 0-87338-091-6); pap. $4.00x (ISBN 0-87338-092-4). Kent St U Pr.

JOURNALISTS
Muller, Jean. Dictionnaire Abrege des Imprimeurs-Editeurs du 16 Siecle. 150p. (Fr.). 1970. DM.80.00. Koerner.

Sgard, Jean. Dictionnaire des Journalistes. (Illus., Fr.). 1976. 25.00 F. Club Livre Select.

Sgard, Jean & Gilot, Michel. Dictionnaire des Journalistes, 1600-1789. 391p. (Fr.). 1976. pap. $75.00 (ISBN 0-686-57221-1, M-6516). French & Eur.

JOURNEYS
see Voyages and Travels
JOYCE, JAMES, 1882-1941
Hart, Clive. A Concordance to Finnegans Wake. rev. ed. 1963. $35.00x (ISBN 0-911858-27-X). Appel.

JUDAEO-GERMAN
see Yiddish Language
JUDAISM–DICTIONARIES
see also Jews–Dictionaries and Encyclopedias
Glustrom, Simon. Language of Judaism. rev. ed. 1973. pap. $7.95x (ISBN 0-87068-224-5). Ktav.

Koehler, Ludwig & Baumgartner, Walter. Lexicon in Veteris Testamenti Libros: Hebrew-Aramaic Lexicon, Incl. Supplement. (Hebrew & Aramaic.). 1951-53. $49.50x (ISBN 0-8028-2176-6). Eerdmans.

Maier, Johann & Schaefer, Peter. Kleines Lexikon des Judentums. (Illus.). 300p. (Ger.). DM.24.50 (ISBN 3-76737-616-4). F Bahn.

Markowitz, Endel. Encyclopedia Yiddishanica. LC 79-114831. (Eng. & Yiddish.). 1980. write for info. (ISBN 0-933910-02-9). Haymark.

Runes, Dagobert D. Dictionary of Judaism. 236p. 1981. $5.95 (ISBN 0-8065-0787-X). Citadel Pr.

Runes, Dagobert D., ed. Concise Dictionary of Judaism. LC 77-88933. 124p. Repr. of 1966 ed. lib. bdg. $65.00 (ISBN 0-8371-2109-4, RUDJ). Greenwood.

Schonfield, Hugh J. Popular Dictionary of Judaism. 1966. pap. $1.75 (ISBN 0-8065-0075-1, 232). Citadel Pr.

JUDAISM–JUVENILE LITERATURE
Goldman, Alex J. Child's Dictionary of Jewish Symbols. (gr. 1-4). $5.00 (ISBN 0-685-09470-7). Feldheim.

JUDGMENTS
see also Jurisdiction
Castan, Pascual. Los Terminos Judiciales. 184p. (Span.). 1964. 200.00 ptas. Dist. Anfora.

––Los Terminos Judiciales. 184p. (Span.). 1964. 200.00 ptas. Dist. Arenzadi.

Diez-Picazo, Luis. Dictamenes Juridicos. 490p. (Span.). 2000.00 ptas (ISBN 8-47398-126-X). Civitas.

JUDICIAL BEHAVIOR
see Judicial Process
JUDICIAL DECISION-MAKING
see Judicial Process
JUDICIAL PROCESS
see also Judgments
Perez Caballero, Arelio. Diccionario juridico peruano. 190p. (Span.). 1972. S/2.40. Mejia.

JUDO
see also Karate
Haesendonck, Francois M. Judo: Encyclopedie in Beeld. LC 78-353537. (Illus.). 272p. (Dutch.). 1976. fl.245.00 (ISBN 9-002-13418-5). Standard.

JUNK
see Waste Products
JURIDICAL PSYCHOLOGY
see Psychology, Forensic
JURISDICTION
see also Judgments
Capitant, H. Vocabulario Juridico. 652p. (Span.). 1972. write for info. Depalma.

JURISPRUDENCE
see also Law; Public Law

Caffarena de Jiles, Elena. Diccionario de jurisprudencia chilena: Recopilaciondе conceptos y definiciones. 346p. (Span.). 1959. $2.00. Juridica-Andres Belio.

JURISTIC PSYCHOLOGY
see Psychology, Forensic
JUSTICE
Brassine, Jules. Dictionnaire Juridique Flammand-Francais. (Flemish & Fr.). 252.00 F. Bruylant.

Dictionnaire Juridique. (Fr. & Arabic.). $40.00 (ISBN 0-86685-303-0). Intl Bk Ctr.

Dictionnaire Juridique & Economique, 1: Francais-Allemand. 2nd ed. (Fr. & Ger.). 1967. 81.00 F. Litec.

Doucet. Dictionnaire Juridique et Economique: Anglais-Francais Francais-Anglais. 770p. (Eng. & Fr.). 1979. 350.00 F. Maison Dictionnaire.

Doucet, M. Dictionnaire Juridique & Economique Francais-Allemand & Allemand Francais-Anglais, 2 vols. 4th ed. Klaus, E. W., ed. (Fr. & Ger.). 8600.00 F. Bruylant.

––Dictionnaire Juridique & Economique Francais-Allemand & Allemand-Francais, Vol. 1. 4th ed. Fleck, K., ed. (Fr. & Ger.). 1980. 1800.00 F. Bruylant.

––Dictionnaire Juridique & Economique Francias-Allemand & Allemand-Francais, Vol. 2. Fleck, K., ed. (Fr. & Ger.). 1980. 1140.00 F. Bruylant.

Gendrel, M. Dictionnaire des Principaux Sigles Utilises dans le Monde Juridique de A-Z. (Fr.). 460.00 F. Bruylant.

Guillien, Raymond & Vincent, Jean. Lexique de Termes Juridiques. 3rd ed. 354p. (Fr.). 1978. 30.00 F. Dalloz.

LeDocte, E. Dictionnaire les termes juridiques en quatre langues: Francais-Neerlandais-Anglais-Allemand. 3rd ed. 800p. (Fr., Dutch, Eng. & Ger.). 1982. 520.00 F. Maison Dictionnaire.

Lexique de Termes Juridiques. (Fr.). 1981. 490.00 F. Bruylant.

Malka, Elie. Dictionnaire Pratique des Termes Juridiques: Francais-Arabe. 88p. (Fr. & Arabic.). 1972. 16.00 F. France Selection.

Nichols, Peter & Vibes, Pierre. Vocabulaire Anglais-Francais de Terminologie, Economique & Juridique. 104p. (Eng. & Fr.). 1971. 16.00 F. L. G. D. J.

Tortora, Giovanni. Dictionnaire Juridique: Italien-Francais Francais-Italien. 700p. (Ital. & Fr.). 1982. 240.00 F. Maison Dictionnaire.

JUSTICE, ADMINISTRATION OF
see also Criminal Justice, Administration of
Glossaire Europeen de Terminologie Juridique & Administrative, 2. 68p. (Fr.). 1969. 15.00 F. Bordas-Dunod.

Institut International de Terminologie Juridique & Administrative. Glossaire Europeen de Terminologie Juridique & Administrative, 1. 64p. (Fr.). 1969. 15.00 F. Bordas-Dunod.

––Glossaire Europeen de Terminologie Juridique & Administrative, 3. 48p. (Fr.). 1969. 15.00 F. Bordas-Dunod.

––Glossaire Europeen de Terminologie Juridique & Administrative, 5. 72p. (Fr.). 1969. 15.00 F. Bordas-Dunod.

––Glossaire Europeen de Terminologie Juridique & Administrative, 6. 64p. (Fr.). 1969. 15.00 F. Bordas-Dunod.

––Glossaire Europeen de Terminologie Juridique & Administrative, 8. 64p. (Fr.). 1969. 15.00 F. Bordas-Dunod.

JUVENILE AUTOMOBILE DRIVERS
see Automobile Drivers
JUVENILE COURTS
Glossary of Selected Legal Terms for Juvenile Justice Personnel. 10p. 1978. $2.00 (GLT). Natl Juv & Family Ct Judges.

JUVENILE DELINQUENCY
see also Juvenile Courts

Altieri de Barreto, Carmen G. El Lexico De la Delincuencia En Puerto Rico. (UPREX, C. Sociales: No. 18). (Span.). pap. $1.85 (ISBN 0-8477-0018-6). U of PR Pr.

JUVENILE ENCYCLOPEDIAS
see Children's Encyclopedias and Dictionaries

K

KAFFIR LANGUAGE
see Xosa Language
KANT, IMMANUEL, 1724-1804
Stockhammer, Morris. Kant Dictionary. LC 76-155974. 1971. $10.00 (ISBN 0-8022-1649-8). Philos Lib.
Verneaux, Roger. Le Vocabulaire de Kant, 1. (Fr.). 1973. 36.00 F. Aubier-Montaigne.
KARA-KIRGHIZ LANGUAGE
see Kirghiz Language
KARATE
Thomas, Raymond. Diccionario del Budo: Artes Marciales. 128p. (Span., Japanese, Chinese, Korean, & Other Oriental Languages.). 1978. pap. $4.50 (ISBN 84-203-0069-1, S-50092). French & Eur.
KASANDSI LANGUAGE
see Bangala Language
KAZAKH LANGUAGE
Bekmukhametov, E. Russko-Kazakhskii Terminologicheskii Slovar, 4 Vols. (Rus.). 1959. $7.00 set (Pub. by Izd. An Kaz. SSR). Four Continent.
Shnitnikov, Boris N. Kazakh-English Dictionary. (Orig., Kazakh & Eng.). 1966. pap. text ed. $36.00x (ISBN 90-2790-367-0). Mouton.
KECHUA LANGUAGE
see Quechua Language
KENYA–HISTORY
Ogot, Bethwell A. Historical Dictionary of Kenya. LC 81-1815. (African Historical Dictionaries Ser.: No. 29). 299p. 1981. $16.00 (ISBN 0-8108-1419-6). Scarecrow.
KERAMICS
see Ceramics
KERESAN INDIANS
see Indians of North America–Southwest, New
KHAS LANGUAGE
see Nepali Language
KHMER LANGUAGE
Huffman, Franklin E. & Proum, Im. Cambodian-English Glossary. (Linguistic Ser.). 160p. (Eng. & Khmerz.). 1981. pap. $7.95x. Yale U Pr.
Jacob, Judith. A Concise Cambodian-English Dictionary. (Eng. & Khmerz.). 1974. $59.00x (ISBN 0-19-713574-9). Oxford U Pr.
Soeur, Samnang, tr. English-Khmer Phrasebook with Useful Word List: For Cambodians. LC 80-66143. 140p. (Eng. & Cambodian.). 1980. pap. text ed. $5.00x (ISBN 0-87281-115-8). Ctr Appl Ling.
KHOTAN
Bailey, Harold W. Dictionary of Khotan Saka. LC 77-80825. 1979. $210.00 (ISBN 0-521-21737-7). Cambridge U Pr.
KI-KONGO LANGUAGE
see Congo Language
KICKAPOO INDIANS
see Indians of North America–The West
KIFIOTI LANGUAGE
see Congo Language
KIKUYU LANGUAGE
Barlow, A. R. English-Kikuyu Dictionary. Benson, T. G., tr. 340p. (Eng. & Kikuyu.). 1975. $24.95x (ISBN 0-19-864407-8). Oxford U Pr.
KILARI LANGUAGE
see Congo Language
KINDNESS TO ANIMALS
see Animals, Treatment Of
KINESIOTHERAPY
see Exercise Therapy
KINGALA LANGUAGE
see Congo Language
KIOWA INDIANS
see Indians of North America–The West
KIPLING, RUDYARD, 1865-1936
Younge, W. A. A Kipling Dictionary. $75.00 (ISBN 0-8490-0473-X). Gordon Pr.

KIRGHIZ LANGUAGE
Iudakhin, K. K., ed. Russko-Kirgizskii Slovar. 990p. (Rus.). 1957. $9.90 (Pub. by GINS). Four Continent.
KIRGHIZ-KAISSAK LANGUAGE
see Kazakh Language
KISWAHILI LANGUAGE
see Swahili Language
KITCHEN UTENSILS
Lantz, Louise K. Dictionary & Price Guide to Kitchenware Collectibles. (Illus.). 160p. 1981. pap. $6.95 (ISBN 0-686-32593-1). Everybodys Pr.
KITCHENS
Diccionario de cocina. (Span.). 250.00 ptas. Bruguera.
Diccionario de la cocina clasica americana y europea, Tomo 1. 234p. (Span.). 1981. pap. 3000.00 ptas (ISBN 84-248-0729-4). Encicl Vasca.
Diccionario de la cocina clasica americana y europea, Tomo 2. 230p. (Span.). 1981. pap. 3000.00 ptas (ISBN 84-248-0730-8). Encicl Vasca.
Diccionario de la cocina clasica americana y europea, Tomo 4. 230p. (Span.). 1981. pap. 3000.00 ptas (ISBN 84-248-0732-4). Encicl Vasca.
Diccionario de la cocina clasica americana y europea, Tomo 5. 230p. (Span.). 1981. pap. 3000.00 ptas (ISBN 84-248-0733-2). Encicl Vasca.
Diccionario de la cocina clasica americana y europea: Obra completa, 5 vols. (Span.). 1981. pap. 15000.00 ptas (ISBN 84-248-0728-6). Encicl Vasca.
Diccionario de la cocina clasica mejicana y europea: Obra completa, 5 vols. 1154p. (Span.). 1981. pap. 15000.00 ptas (ISBN 84-248-0722-7). Encicl Vasca.
Diccionario de la cocina clasica mejicana y europea: Tomo 1. 234p. (Span.). 1981. pap. 3000.00 ptas (ISBN 84-248-0723-5). Encicl Vasca.
Diccionario de la cocina clasica mejicana y europea: Tomo 2. 230p. (Span.). 1981. pap. 3000.00 ptas (ISBN 84-248-0724-3). Encicl Vasca.
Diccionario de la cocina clasica mejicana y europea: Tomo 3. 230p. (Span.). 1981. pap. 3000.00 ptas (ISBN 84-248-0725-1). Encicl Vasca.
Diccionario de la cocina clasica mejicana y europea: Tomo 4. 230p. (Span.). 1981. pap. 3000.00 ptas (ISBN 84-248-0726-X). Encicl Vasca.
Diccionario de la cocina clasica mejicana y europea: Tomo 5. 230p. (Span.). 1981. pap. 3000.00 ptas (ISBN 84-248-0727-8). Encicl Vasca.
KITUBA LANGUAGE
see Congo Language
KNITTING
National Knitted Outerwear Association. Knitting Dictionary. rev. ed. (Illus.). text ed. $10.00. Natl Knit Outwear.
KNITTING, MACHINE
Gartshore, Linda. The Machine Knitter's Dictionary. (Illus.). 192p. 1983. pap. $9.95 (ISBN 0-312-50221-4). St Martin.
KNOT THEORY
Stoltzfus, N. Unraveling the Integral Knot Concordance Group. LC 77-10133. (Memoirs Ser.: No. 192). 1977. $12.00 (ISBN 0-8218-2192-X, MEMO 192). Am Math.
KNOTS (TOPOLOGY)
see Knot Theory
KNOWLEDGE, BOOKS OF
see Encyclopedias and Dictionaries
KNOWLEDGE, THEORY OF–DICTIONARIES
Battro, A. M. Dictionnaire d'Epistemologie Genetique. 188p. (Fr.). 1966. $29.00 (ISBN 90-277-0002-8, Pub. by Reidel Holland). Kluwer Academic.
Meyers Standardlexikon Des Gesamten Wissens. (Ger.). 1975. $15.95 (ISBN 3-411-01346-X, M-7562, Pub. by Bibliographisches Institut). French & Eur.

Meyers Standardlexikon Des Gesamten Wissens. (Ger.). 1975. $15.95 (ISBN 3-411-01346-X). Biblio Inst.
Miers, Horst E. Lexikon des Geheimwissens. (Ger.). leatherette $68.00 (ISBN 3-7626-0028-7, M-7214). French & Eur.
KORAN
Penrice, John. A Dictionary & Glossary of the Koran. (Arabic). 1982. text ed. $18.95x (ISBN 0-7007-0001-3, Pub. by Curzon Pr England). Apt Bks.
--Dictionary & Glossary of the Koran. (Arabic & Eng.). $20.00x (ISBN 0-86685-088-0). Intl Bk Ctr.
--Dictionary & Glossary of the Koran. 166p. (Arabic & Eng.). 1968. $20.00 (088-0). Intl Bk Ctr.
--Dictionary & Glossary of the Koran, with Copious Grammatical References & Explanations. LC 70-90039. (Arabic). 1969. Repr. of 1873 ed. $17.00x (ISBN 0-8196-0252-3). Biblo.
--A Dictionary & Glossary of the Koran with Grammatical References & Explanations. 1980. lib. bdg. $55.00 (ISBN 0-8490-3123-0). Gordon Pr.
KOREAN LANGUAGE
Abbreviated Russian-Korean Dictionary. 648p. (Rus. & Korean.). $4.95 (ISBN 0-686-97385-2, M-9055). French & Eur.
Dictionary Korean-Chinese. 1274p. (Korean & Chinese.). 1978. $30.00 (ISBN 0-686-92316-2, M-9289). French & Eur.
Eckardt, Andre. Chinesisch-Koreanisch-Deutsch Woerterbuch. 224p. (Chinese, Ger. & Korean.). 1966. write for info. (ISBN 3-87276-115-3). Groos Verlag.
--Deutsch-Koreanisches Woerterbuch. 2nd ed. 332p. (Korean & Ger.). 1976. DM.58.00 (ISBN 3-87276-149-8). Groos Verlag.
--Koreanisch-Deutsches Woerterbuch. 2nd ed. 332p. (Korean & Ger.). 1976. DM.69.99 (ISBN 3-87276-149-8). Groos Verlag.
Grant, Bruce K. A Guide to Korean Characters: Reading & Writing Hangul & Hanja. 400p. (Korean & Eng.). 1979. $21.95 (ISBN 0-930878-13-2). Hollym Intl.
--A Guide to Korean Characters: Reading & Writing Hangul & Hanja. 367p. (Korean.). $16.70 (ISBN 0-930878-13-2). Hollym Corp.
Jones, B. J. English-Korean Dictionary for Practical Conversation. LC 83-81486. (Korean.). 1983. price not set (ISBN 0-930878-22-1). Hollym Corp.
--Standard English-Korean Dictionary for Foreigners. LC 81-84204. (Illus.). 386p. (Korean & Eng.). 1982. $7.95 (ISBN 0-930878-21-3). Hollym Intl.
Jones, B. J., ed. Standard English-Korean Dictionary: For Foreigners. LC 81-84204. 369p. (Korean.). $5.50 (ISBN 0-930878-21-3). Hollym Corp.
Korean Dictionary, 2 vols. 4100p. (Korean.). $80.00 (Dist. by Koryo Bks Importing, Inc) Sam-Sung Pub.
Martin, Samuel E., et al. Korean-English Dictionary. (Linguistic Ser.). (Korean & Eng.). 1967. text ed. $75.00x (ISBN 0-300-00753-1). Yale U Pr.
Mazur, I. N. Kratkii Russko-Koreiskii Slovar. 648p. (Rus. & Korean.). 1959. $2.95 (Pub. by GINS). Four Continent.
KUNG-FU
see Karate
KURDISH LANGUAGE
Jaba, Auguste. Dictionnaire Kurde-Francais. LC 76-472421. xviii, 463p. (Fr. & Kurdish.). 1975. DM.98.00 (ISBN 3-7648-0409-2). Biblio-Verlag.
Mokri, M. Al-Hadiyati 'I-Hamidiyah. 400p. (Arabic & Kurdish.). $28.00 (126-7). Intl Bk Ctr.
--Kurdish-Arabic Dictionary: Al-Hadiyati 'l-Hamidiyah. (Arabic). 1975. $28.00x (ISBN 0-86685-126-7). Intl Bk Ctr.

KURMANJI LANGUAGE
see Kurdish Language
KUTENAI INDIANS
see Indians of North America–Northwest, Pacific
KWAKIUTAL INDIANS
see Indians of North America–Northwest, Pacific
KWAKIUTL LANGUAGE
Boas, Franz. Kwakiutl Grammar - with a Glossary of Suffixes. LC 74-7939. (Kwankiutl.). Repr. of 1947 ed. $24.50 (ISBN 0-404-11826-7). AMS Pr.

L

LAADI LANGUAGE
see Congo Language
LABOR AND LABORING CLASSES
see also Job Satisfaction; Machinery in Industry; Occupations; Professions; Socialism
also classes of laborers, e.g. Coal-Miners, Railroads–Employees; subdivisions Economic Conditions and Social Conditions under names of countries, cities, etc., e.g. U. S.–Economic Conditions
Bayod Serrat, Ramon. Diccionario Laboral. 546p. (Span.). 1969. pap. $6.95 (ISBN 84-290-0937-X, S-50139). French & Eur.
Denisov, A. I., ed. Trudovoe Pravo: Entsiklopedicheskii Slovar. 576p. (Rus.). 1963. $4.60 (Pub. by Sov. Entsiklopediia). Four Continent.
Dion, Gerard. Dictionnaire Canadien des Relations du Travail: Francais-Anglais. 682p. (Eng. & Fr.). 1976. $49.95 (ISBN 0-686-57118-5, M-6163). French & Eur.
ILO Thesaurus: Labour, Employment & Training Terminology. 2nd ed. 223p. 1980. $13.70 (ISBN 92-2-001982-5). Intl Labour Office.
Lasso de La Vega, Javier & Rubert Candau, Jose M., eds. Diccionario Enciclopedias Labor, 9 vols. 7th ed. 6500p. (Span.. Fr., Port., Eng. & Ger.). 1978. Set. leatherette $550.00 (ISBN 84-335-0322-7, S-12269). French & Eur.
Roth, Rainer. Lexikon der Arbeits und Soziallere. (Ger.). 1976. $26.00 (ISBN 3-403-00593-3, M-7278). French & Eur.
Roth, Rainer A. & Selzer, Helmut M., eds. Lexikon zur Arbeits & Soziallehre. 384p. (Ger.). 1976. DM.32.80 (ISBN 3-403-00593-3). Habelt.
LABOR FORCE
see Labor Supply
LABOR LAWS AND LEGISLATION
Bonnefoi, Alexandre. Woerterbuch des Arbeits & Sozialrechts: Deutsch-Franz Dictionnaire de Droit du Trava il & de Droit Social. LC 76-469011. 395p. (Fr. & Ger.). 1975. DM.45.00 (ISBN 3-19-006293-5). Hueber.
Malta, Christovao P. Dicionario de Direito do Trabalho. LC 76-452001. 535p. (Port.). 1975. Cr.$115.00. Rio Grafica.
Valle, Gerson. Vocabulario Trabalhista: Direito do Trabalho, Processo do Trabalho, Previdencia Socail. LC 76-463962. 288p. (Port.). 1975. Cr.$60.00. Rio Grafica.
LABOR-MANAGEMENT RELATIONS
Graham, William. The Scots Word Book. 2nd ed. LC 79-301141. 194p. (Eng.). 1978. E4.60 (ISBN 0-902859-47-1). Ramsay Head Pr.
LABOR MARKET
see Labor Supply
LABOR SUPPLY
Lexicon por una Comision de Trabajo del CIMAC: Conseil International des Machines a Combustion. 96p. (Span.). write for info. (ISBN 84-600-0836-3). Marcombo.

LABORATORY ANIMALS
Altman, Philip L. & Katz, Dorothy D., eds. Inbred & Genetically Defined Strains of Laboratory Animals. Incl. Pt. 1. Mouse & Rat. 65.00 (ISBN 0-913822-12-4); Pt. 2. Hamster, Guinea Pig, Rabbit & Chicken. 50.00 (ISBN 0-913822-13-2). LC 78-73555. (Biological Handbooks: Vol. 3). (Illus.). 1979. Set. $100.00 (ISBN 0-913822-14-0). FASEB.

LABORERS
see Labor and Laboring Classes

LACE AND LACE MAKING
Clifford, C. R., ed. Lace Dictionary: Including Historic & Commercial Terms, Technical Terms, Native & Foreign. (Illus.). 156p. 1981. Repr. of 1913 ed. $30.00x (ISBN 0-8103-4311-8). Gale.
Earnshaw, Pat. A Dictionary of Lace. (Illus.). 240p. (Orig.). 1983. pap. $14.95 (ISBN 0-85263-602-4, 3380389, Pub. by Shire Pubns England). Seven Hills Bks.

LA FONTAINE, JEAN DE, 1621-1695
Tyler, J. Allen & Parrish, Stephen M., eds. A Concordance to the Fables & Tales of Jean De la Fontaine. LC 73-8388. (Concordances Ser.). 1104p. (Fr. & Eng.). 1974. $55.00x (ISBN 0-8014-0811-3). Cornell U Pr.

LAKES
Slovar Gidronimov Ukrainy. 784p. (Ukrainian.). 1978. $12.95 (Pub. by Naukova Dumka). Four Continent.

LAMPS
Gaudillat, Louis. Lexique Officiel des Lampes Radio. 21st ed. 96p. (Fr.). 1963. 20.00 F. Radio.

LAND
see Land Use

LAND–VALUATION
see Real Property–Valuation

LAND DRAINAGE
see Drainage

LAND SURVEYING
see Surveying

LAND USE
see also Agriculture; Real Estate Business; Real Property; Zoning
British Columbia, Ministry of Lands, Parks & Housing. Land Allocation Terminology. LC 81-478975. 71p. (Eng.). 1979. write for info. (ISBN 0-7719-8201-1). Minist Prov Sec.
Orellana, E. Diccionario ingles-espanol de las ciencias de la tierra. 325p. (Eng. & Span.). 1967. 600.00 ptas. Interciencia.

LAND USE, URBAN–PLANNING
see City Planning

LAND VALUATION
see Real Property–Valuation

LANDSCAPE
American Association of Nurserymen. Technical Glossary of Horticultural & Landscape Terminology. $9.95; educators $6.00; 10 or more $5.00. Am Nurserymen.

LANDSCAPE GARDENING
Ballard, Edward B., et al, eds. A Technical Glossary of Horticultural & Landscape Terminology. LC 78-165521. 1971 (ISBN 0-686-26652-8). text ed. $5.50 (ISBN 0-935336-00-1); tchrs' ed. $4.00 (ISBN 0-935336-00-1). Horticult Research.

LANDSCAPE PAINTING
Grant, Maurice H. A Dictionary of British Landscape Painters: From the 16th to the 20th Century. (Illus.). 236p. 1970. $40.00x (ISBN 0-85317-250-1). Intl Pubns Serv.

LANDSCAPE PAINTING–GREAT BRITAIN
Grant, Maurice. A Dictionary of British Landscape Painters: From the 16th Century to the Early 20th Century. 236p. 1976. Repr. of 1952 ed. text ed. $30.00x (ISBN 0-85317-250-1, Pub. by A & C Black England). Humanities.

LANGUAGE, LEGAL
see Law–Language

LANGUAGE, PHILOSOPHY OF
see Languages–Philosophy

LANGUAGE, PSYCHOLOGY OF
see Psycholinguistics

LANGUAGE ACQUISITION
see Children–Language

LANGUAGE AND LANGUAGES
Here are entered works on language in general, works on the origin and history of language, and surveys of languages; Works dealing with the scientific study of human speech, including phonetics, phonemics, morphology and syntax, are entered under Linguistics. Works on the philosophy and psychology of language are entered under Languages–Philosophy, and Languages–Psychology, respectively.
see also Children–Language; Communication; Languages–Philosophy; Linguistics; Philology; Programming Languages (Electronic Computers); Psycholinguistics; Rhetoric; Semantics; Sociolinguistics; Speech
also names of particular languages or groups of cognate languages, e.g. English Language, Semitic Languages
Costello, Nancy A. Katu Vocabulary. 124p. (Katu.). 1971. microfiche $2.25. Summer Inst Ling.
Ducrot, Oswald & Todorov, Tzvetan. Encyclopedic Dictionary of the Sciences of Language. Porter, Catherine, tr. LC 78-23901. 400p. 1979. pap. $10.95x (ISBN 0-8018-2857-0). Johns Hopkins.
The Insult Dictionary: How to Get What You Want in Five Nasty Languages. 1981. pap. $4.95 (ISBN 0-686-29649-4). Natl Textbk.
The Lover's Dictionary: How to Be Amorous in Five Delectable Languages. 1981. pap. $4.95 (ISBN 0-686-29648-6). Natl Textbk.
Schuh, Russell G. A Dictionary of Ngizim. (U.C. Publications in Linguistics: Vol. 99). 256p. 1981. $12.50x (ISBN 0-520-09636-3). U of Cal Pr.
Tischler, Johann. Kleinasiatische Hydronymie: Semantik & Morphologie Analyse der Geichicher Gewaessernamen. LC 78-394985. ix, 191p. (Ger.). 1977. write for info (ISBN 3-882-26001-7). Reichert.

LANGUAGE AND LANGUAGES–DICTIONARIES
see also Dictionaries, Polyglot; Polyglot Glossaries, Phrase Books, etc.
Castell, Edmund. Lexicon Heptaglotton, 2 vols. LC 70-870022. 1544p. 1970. Repr. of 1686 ed. Set. $175.00x (ISBN 3-201-00074-4). Intl Pubns Serv.
Collinder, Bjorn. Fenno-Ugric Vocabulary: An Etymologic Dictionary of the Uralic Languages. 2nd ed. LC 78-387096. 217p. (Uralic.). 1977. write for info. (ISBN 3-87118-187-0). Buske.
Dictionnaire des Costumes, Croyances & Langages. 131p. (Fr.). 1976. write for info. Reprints.
Douglas, W. H. Illustrated Topical Dictionary of the Western Desert Language: 1959. 2nd rev. ed. (AIAS Research Regional Studies: No. 11). 1977. pap. text ed. $3.75x (ISBN 0-85575-061-8). Humanities.
Hartmann, R. R. & Stork, F. C., eds. Dictionary of Language & Linguistics. LC 72-6251. 302p. 1976. pap. $29.95 (ISBN 0-470-15200-1). Halsted Pr.
Lithgow, David & Lithgow, Daphne. Muyuw Dictionary. (Muyuw.). 1974. pap. $2.50x o. p. (ISBN 0-7263-0205-8); microfiche $2.25 (ISBN 0-88312-332-0). Summer Inst Ling.
Living Language Dictionaries & Manuals. (Living Language Course Ser). pap. $3.00 ea. Crown.
Pensinger, Brenda. Diccionario Mixteco del Este De Jamiltepec. (Vocabularios Indigenas Ser.: No. 18). 156p. (Span.). 1974. $7.00 (ISBN 0-88312-751-2); microfiche $2.25x (ISBN 0-88312-586-2). Summer Inst Ling.
Pipics, Z. The Librarian's Practical Dictionary in Twenty-Two Languages. 386p. 1980. $90.00x (ISBN 0-686-72094-6, Pub. by Collet's). State Mutual Bk.
Robinson, Dow F. Manual for Bilingual Dictionaries, 3 vols. 1969. o. p. $5.00 (ISBN 0-685-40975-9); Set. microfiche $9.00; Vol. I. microfiche $3.00 (ISBN 0-88312-327-4); Vol. II. microfiche $3.00 (ISBN 0-88312-328-2); Vol. III. microfiche $3.00 (ISBN 0-88312-329-0). Summer Inst Ling.
Slovar Iazyka Pushkina, 4 vols. (Rus.). 1961. $40.00 set (Pub. by GINS). Four Continent.
Stark, Frederick. Phrase Dictionaries for the American Tourist, 6 bks. Incl. German for the American Tourist. (Ger. & Eng.). pap. (ISBN 0-8326-2409-8, 6570); Spanish for the English-Speaking Tourist. (Span. & Eng.). pap. (ISBN 0-8326-2410-1, 6571); French for the English-Speaking Tourist. (Fr. & Eng.). pap. (ISBN 0-8326-2411-X, 6572); Italian for the English-Speaking Tourist. (Ital. & Eng.). pap. (ISBN 0-8326-2412-8, 6573); Greek for the English-Speaking Tourist. (Gr. & Eng.). pap. (ISBN 0-8326-2413-6, 6574); Russian for the English-Speaking Tourist. (Rus. & Eng.). pap. (ISBN 0-8326-2414-4, 6575). 128p. (Orig., Ger., Span., Fr., Ital., Gr. & Rus.). 1981. pap. $2.50 ea. Delair.
Stoudt, Betty. Vocabulario Mixteco de San Miguel el Grande. (Vocabularios Indigenas Ser.: No. 12). (Span.). 1965. pap. $3.00 (ISBN 0-88312-660-5); microfiche $1.60x (ISBN 0-88312-580-3). Summer Inst Ling.
Urdang, Laurance, ed. Allusions, Cultural, Literary, Biblical, & Historical: A Thematic Dictionary. 1982. $52.00x (ISBN 0-8103-1124-0). Gale.
Varios. Diccionario Enciclopedico De las Ciencias Del Lenquaje. (Span.). $32.95 (ISBN 0-686-56652-1, S-30990). French & Eur.
Walford, Alberto J. & Screen, J. E., eds. A Guide to Foreign Language Courses & Dictionaries. LC 77-26283. 1978. lib. bdg. $25.00 (ISBN 0-313-20100-5, WGL/). Greenwood.
Zlotnicki, T. Lexicon Medicum. 1603p. 1980. $150.00x (ISBN 0-569-07372-3, Pub. by Collet's). State Mutual Bk.

LANGUAGE AND LANGUAGES–ETYMOLOGY
see also Names;
also subdivision Etymology under names of languages
Abaev, V. I. Istoriko-Etimologicheskii Slovar Osetinskogo. 360p. (Rus.). 1979. $8.25 (Pub. by Nauka). Four Continent.
Alessio, Giovanni. Lexicon etymologicum: Supplemento ai dizionario etimologici latini e romanzi. 689p. (Lat. & Ital.). 1976. L.60000.00. Licosa.
Chantraine, Pierre. Dictionnaire Etymologique de la Langue Grecque. 609p. (Gr.). 1976. 300.00 F. Klincksieck.
--Dictionnaire Etymologique de la Langue Grecque, 2. (Gr.). 110.00 F. Klincksieck.
--Dictionnaire Etymologique de la Langue Grecque, 3. 360p. (Gr.). 1975. 180.00 F. Klincksieck.
--Dictionnaire Etymologique de la Langue Grecque, 4. 200p. (Gr.). 1977. 140.00 F. Klincksieck.
Corblet, Jules. Glossaire Etymologique & Comparatif du Patois Picard Ancien & Moderne. 645p. (Fr.). 140.00 F. Slatkine.
Corominas, Joan & Pascual, J. A. Diccionario Critico Etimologico Castellano & Hispanico, 2 vols. (Span.). 1979. 3.25 ptas. $3.500. Gredos.
Coromines i Vegneaux, Joan. Diccionari etimologie i complementari de la llengua catalana, Tomo 3. 1056p. (Span.). 1982. write for info. (ISBN 84-7256-204-2). Curial.
Coromines i Vigneaux, Joan. Diccionari etimologic i complementari de la llengua catalana, Tomo 2. 2nd ed. 1120p. (Span.). 1981. 4500.00 ptas (ISBN 84-7256-191-7). Curial.
Coromines i Vigneaux, Joan & Pascual, J. A. Diccionario critico etimologico castellano & hispanico, Tomo 3. 904p. (Span.). 1980. write for info. (ISBN 84-249-1365-5). Gredos.
Corripio, Fernando. Diccionario Etimologico Abreviado. 320p. (Span.). 1974. 80.00 ptas. Bruguera.
--Diccionario Etimologico Abreviado. (Span.). pap. $2.95 (BRG). Lectorum Pubns.
--Diccionario Etimologico General de la Lengua Castellana. 512p. (Span.). 1974. 425.00 ptas. Bruguera.
Cortelazzo, Manlio & Zolli, Paolo. Dizionario etimologico della lingua italiana: Vol. 1, A-C. xxviii, 308p. (Ital.). 1979. L.13000.00. Zanichelli.
Devoto. Avviamento All'Etimologia Italiana: Dizionario Etimologico. (Ital.). L.10.00. Oscar.
Diez Mateo, Felix. Diccionario Espanol Etimologico. (Span.). $3.50 (CANT). Lectorum Pubns.
--Diccionario espanol etimologico: El pequeno academico. (Span.). 1972. write for info. Cantabrica.
Dorais, Louis J. Lexique Analytique du Vocabulaire Inuit Moderne au Quebec-Labrador. LC 79-363935. 136p. (Fr. & Inupiaq.). 1978. Can.$9.00 (ISBN 0-7746-6850-4, Dist. by Four Continent Bk). Univ Laval.
Durante, Dino & Turato, Gianfranco. Dizionario etimologico veneto-italiano. xvi, 720p. (Ital.). 1976. L.20000.00. Erredici.
Else, Gerald F. Basic Latin Vocabulary Along Etymological Lines. 15p. (Lat. & Eng.). $0.90 (NO. B14). Am Classical.
Ernout, Alfred & Meillet, Antoine. Dictionnaire Etymologique de la Langue Latine. 4th ed. 946p. (Lat.). 1967. 280.00 F. Klincksieck.
Etimologicheskii Slovar Slavianskikh Iazykov: Vyp. 4. 236p. (Rus.). 1977. $4.65 (Pub. by Nauka). Four Continent.
Etimologicheskii Slovar Slavianskikh Iazykov: Vyp. 7. 224p. (Rus.). 1980. $3.95 (Pub. by Nauka). Four Continent.
Gamillscheg, Ernst. Etymologisches Woerterbuch der Franzoesischen Sprache. 2nd ed. (Fr. & Ger.). 1969. DM.195.00. Winter Univ.
Garcia de Diego, Vicente. Diccionario etimologica espanol e hispanico. (Span.). 500.00 ptas. SAETA.
Hunt, Cecil. A Dictionary of Word Makers: Pen Pictures of the People Behind Our Language. LC 72-13203. Repr. of 1949 ed. lib. bdg. $15.00 (ISBN 0-8414-1153-0). Folcroft.
Joan-Pascual, J. A. Diccionario Critico Etimologico Castellano & Hispanico, Tomo 4. 960p. (Span.). 1981. write for info. ptas (ISBN 84-249-0066-9). Gredos.
Johannesson, Alex. Islaendisches Etymologisches Woerterbuch. 1406p. (Icelandic & Ger.). 1956. $232.00 (ISBN 3-7720-0429-6, M-7485, Pub. by Francke). French & Eur.
Lokotsch, Karl. Etymologisches Woerterbuch der Europaeischen Woerter Orientalischen Ursprungs. 2nd ed. (Ger.). 1975. pap. $43.50 (ISBN 3-533-02427-X, M-7369, Pub. by Carl Winter). French & Eur.
--Etymologisches Woerterbuch der Europaeischen Woerter Orientalischen Ursprungs. 2nd ed. (Ger.). 1975. pap. $43.50 (ISBN 3-533-02427-X). Winter Univ.
Malkiel, Yakov. Etymological Dictionaries: A Tentative Typology. LC 75-11866. 160p. 1976. lib. bdg. $19.00x (ISBN 0-226-50292-9). U of Chicago Pr.
Pokorny, Julius. Indogermanisches Etymologisches Woerterbuch, 2 vols, Vols. 1 & 2. 1648p. (Ger.). 1969. $240.00 set (ISBN 3-7720-0526-8, M-7478, Pub. by Francke). French & Eur.
Prati, Angelico. Vocabolario etimologico italiano. 1100p. (Ital.). 1970. L.7800.00. Garzanti Edit.

Richardson, Henry B. Etymological Vocabulary to the Libro De Buen Amor of Juan Ruiz, Arcipreste De Hita. LC 72-1684. (Yale Romanic Studies: No. 2). (Span.). Repr. of 1930 ed. $14.50 (ISBN 0-404-53202-0). AMS Pr.
Sevortian, E. V. Etimologicheskii Slovar Tiurkskikh Iazykov. 767p. (Turkish & Rus.). 1974. $15.95 (Pub. by Nauka). Four Continent.
--Etimologicheskii Slovar Tiurkskikh Iazykov. 352p. (Rus. & Turkish.). 1978. $9.75 (Pub. by Nauka). Four Continent.
Shagirov, A. K. Etimologicheskii Slovar Adygskikh (Cherkesskikh) 224p. (Rus.). 1978. $5.95 (Pub. by Nauka). Four Continent.
Smith, W. B. De la Toponymie Bretonne, Dictionnaire Etymologique. (Fr.). Repr. of 1940 ed. $9.00 (ISBN 0-527-00824-9). Kraus Repr.
Vendryes, Joseph. Lexique Etymologique de L'Irlandais Ancien: Fascicule R-S. 272p. (Fr.). 1975. 70.00 F (ISBN 2-22201-629-0). CNRS.
--Lexique Etymologique de L'Irlandais Ancien: Fascicule T-U. 211p. (Fr.). 1978. 110.00 F (ISBN 2-22202-227-4). CNRS.
--Lexique Etymologique de l'Irlandais Ancien, 1. 106p. (Fr. & Gaelic.). 1959. 20.00 F. CNRS.
Vendryes, Joseph & Bachellery, E. Lexique Etymologique de L'Irlandais Ancien: Lettre B. 120p. (Fr.). 1981. 90.00 F (ISBN 2-22202-800-0). CNRS.
Verrier, A. J. & Onillon, Rene. Glossaire Etymologique & Historique des Patois & des Parlers de l'Anjou, 2 vols. 1157p. (Fr.). 1970. 200.00 F. Slatkine.
Wartburg, Walter von. Franzoesisch Etymologisches Woerterbuch. 2nd ed. (Fr.). 1948. $38.50 (ISBN 3-16-926772-8, M-7414, Pub. by Francke). French & Eur.
Zambaldi, Francesco. Vocabolario etimologico italiano. xiv, 630p. (Ital.). 1913. L.7500.00. Dante Alighieri.

LANGUAGE AND LANGUAGES–FOREIGN ELEMENTS
Mawson, C. O. Dictionary of Foreign Terms. 2nd ed. (Everyday Handbooks Ser.). 384p. 1979. pap. $4.95 (ISBN 0-06-463494-9). B&N NY.
Phythian, B. A., ed. A Concise Dictionary of Foreign Expressions. LC 82-13895. 158p. 1982. text ed. $15.50x (ISBN 0-389-20327-0). B&N Imports.

LANGUAGE AND LANGUAGES–GRAMMAR, COMPARATIVE
see Grammar, Comparative and General

LANGUAGE AND LANGUAGES–PHILOSOPHY
see Languages–Philosophy

LANGUAGE AND LANGUAGES–PHONETIC TRANSCRIPTIONS
Anderson, Olov B. A Concordance to Five Systems of Transcription for Standard Chinese. 230p. (Chinese.). 1982. pap. text ed. $22.50 (ISBN 0-7007-0080-3, Pub. by Curzon Pr England). Apt Bks.

LANGUAGE AND LANGUAGES–PRINTING
see Printing–Style Manuals

LANGUAGE AND LANGUAGES–PSYCHOLOGY
see Psycholinguistics

LANGUAGE AND LANGUAGES–STUDY AND TEACHING
Brewer, Forrest & Brewer, Jean. Vocabulario Mexicano de Tetelcingo. (Vocabularios Indigenas Ser.: No. 8). 274p. (Span.). 1962. pap. $4.00x (ISBN 0-88312-658-3); microfiche $3.00x (ISBN 0-88312-363-0). Summer Inst Ling.
Galisson, R. & Coste, D., eds. Dictionnaire de Didactique des Langues. LC 77-462328. 612p. (Fr.). 1976. write for info. (ISBN 2-010-03576-3). Hachette-Jeunesse.
Gerdel, Florence & Slocum, Marianna. Vocabulario Tzeltal de Bachajon. (Vocabularios Indigenas Ser.: No. 13). 215p. (Span.). 1965. $3.00 (ISBN 0-88312-589-7). Summer Inst Ling.
Larson, Mildred L. Vocabulario Aguaruna de Amazonas. (Peruvian Linguistic Ser: No. 3). 211p. (Span.). 1966. pap. $3.00x (ISBN 0-88312-653-2). Summer Inst Ling.
Minor, Eugene E. & Minor, Dorothy. Vocabulario Huitoto Muinane. (Peruvian Linguistic Ser: No. 5). 139p. (Span.). 1970. pap. $3.00x (ISBN 0-88312-656-7); microfiche $2.25x (ISBN 0-88312-362-2). Summer Inst Ling.
Pride, Leslie & Pride, Kitty. Vocabulario Chatino de Tataltepec. (Vocabularios Indigenas Ser.: No. 15). 103p. (Span.). 1970. pap. $3.00x (ISBN 0-88312-655-9); microfiche $2.25 (ISBN 0-88312-317-7). Summer Inst Ling.
Schoenhals, Alvin & Schoenhals, Louise. Vocabulario Mixe de Totontepec. (Vocabularios Indigenas Ser.: No. 14). 353p. (Span.). 1965. pap. $5.00x (ISBN 0-88312-659-1); microfiche $3.75 (ISBN 0-88312-319-3). Summer Inst Ling.
Walford, Alberto J. & Screen, J. E., eds. A Guide to Foreign Language Courses & Dictionaries. LC 77-26283. 1978. lib. bdg. $25.00 (ISBN 0-313-20100-5, WGL/). Greenwood.

LANGUAGE AND SOCIETY
see Sociolinguistics

LANGUAGE ARTS
see also Communication; English Language; Reading; Speech
Dicionario Melhoramentos da lingua Portuguesa. 2nd ed. 1035p. (Port.). 1977. $22.00. Imported Bks.
Minsheu, John. Ductor in Linguas: The Guide into Tongues. LC 78-14754. xxi, 543p. (Eng. & Span.). 1978. Repr. of 1617 ed. lib. bdg. $120.00x (ISBN 0-8201-1321-2). Schol Facsimiles.
Moldenhauer, Janice. Developing Dictionary Skills. (gr. 3-8). 1979. $5.95 (ISBN 0-916456-48-X, GA120). Good Apple.
Wahrig, G. Deutsches Woerterbuch und Lexicon der deutsches Sprachlehre. 1500p. (Ger.). simulated leather $24.00. M Rosenberg.

LANGUAGE ARTS–STUDY AND TEACHING
see Language Arts

LANGUAGE GEOGRAPHY
see Linguistic Geography

LANGUAGES–PHILOSOPHY
Capdevila Font, Juan. Diccionario Ideologico Manual de la Lengua Espanola. 900p. (Span.). 1976. $18.75 (ISBN 84-85117-22-0, S-50264). French & Eur.
Diccionario Ilustrado Danae de la Lengua Espanola. (Span.). pns leatherette (ISBN 84-7060-397-3, S-50207). French & Eur.

LANGUAGES–PSYCHOANALYSIS
see Psycholinguistics

LANGUAGES–PSYCHOLOGY
see Psycholinguistics

LANGUAGES–SOCIOLOGICAL ASPECTS
see Sociolinguistics

LANGUAGES, MIXED
see also Creole Dialects; Pidgin English
Dictionnaire du Francais Argotique & Populaire. (Illus.). 255p. (Fr.). 1977. write for info. Larousse.
Glossaire des Patois de la Suisse Romande. (Fr.). 1978. 30.00 F. Droz.
Steele, Guy L. The Hacker's Dictionary. LC 83-47573. 96p. (Orig.). 1983. pap. $4.76I (ISBN 0-06-091082-8, CN 1082, CN). Har-Row.

LANGUAGES, MODERN
Here are entered works dealing with the living literary languages of Europe.
see also Philology
Gonfroy, Gerard. Dictionnaire Normatif Limousin-Francais. LC 77-479648. 229p. (Fr.). 1976. write for info. Lemouzi.
Living Language Dictionaries & Manuals. (Living Language Course Ser). pap. $3.00 ea. Crown.

LANGUAGES, MODERN–GLOSSARIES, VOCABULARIES, ETC.
see Polyglot Glossaries, Phrase Books, etc.

LANGUAGES, OCCIDENTAL
see Languages, Modern

LANGUAGES, ORIENTAL
see Oriental Languages

LANGUAGES, SEMITIC
see Semitic Languages

LANGUAGES, WESTERN
see Languages, Modern

LANGUE D'OC
see Provencal Language

LANGUE D'OIL
see French Language

LAO LANGUAGE
Guignard, Theodore. Dictionnaire Laotien Francais. 1034p. (Laotian & Fr.). 1971. $28.00. Gregg.
Kerr, Allen. Lao-English Dictionary, 2 vols. (Publications in the Languages of Asia Ser.: No. 2). (Laotian & Eng.). 1973. Set. $44.95 (ISBN 0-8132-0526-3). Cath U Pr.
Marcus, Russell. English-Lao, Lao-English Dictionary. LC 77-116487. (Eng. & Laotian.). 1970. $10.50 (ISBN 0-8048-0909-7). C E Tuttle.
Reinhorm, Marc. Dictionnaire Laotien-Francais, 2 vols. (Laotian & Fr.). 215.00 F. C. N. R. S.
Reinhorn, Marc. Dictionnaire Laotien-Francais, 2 vols. 2000p. (Fr. & Laotian.). 1970. Set. $85.00 (ISBN 0-686-57204-1, M-6481). French & Eur.
--Dictionnaire Laotien-Francais, 2 vols. 2000p. (Fr. & Laotian.). 1970. 300.00 F (ISBN 2-22201-295-3). CNRS.
Russell, Marcus. English-Lao, Lao-English Dictionary. (Lao & Eng.). $10.50. Iaconi.

LAPP LANGUAGE
Nielsen, Konrad & Nesheim, Asbjorn, eds. Lapp Dictionary, 5 vols. 3221p. 1980. $250.00x set (ISBN 82-00-14201-9). Universitet.

LARGE PRINT BOOKS
see Large Type Books

LARGE TYPE BOOKS
Chadsey, Charles P. & Wentworth, Harold, eds. The Grosset Webster Large-Type Dictionary. (Illus.). 1978. pap. $5.95 (ISBN 0-448-14636-3, G&D). Putnam Pub Group.
The Merriam-Webster Dictionary for Large Print Users. (General Ser.). 1977. lib. bdg. $29.50 (ISBN 0-8161-6459-2, Large Print Bks). G K Hall.

LARI LANGUAGE
see Congo Language

LARYNX
Larrauri, A. Dictionary of Oto-Rhino-Laryngology in Five Languages. LC 71-501781. 1008p. (Eng., Fr., Span., Ger. & Ital.). 1971. $65.00x (ISBN 0-8002-0197-3). Intl Pubns Serv.

LASER PHOTOGRAPHY
see Holography

LASTS (SHOES)
see Boots and Shoes

LATIN AMERICA
see also names of Latin-American countries and geographic areas of Latin America, e.g. Brazil; Caribbean Area; South America; names of cities, towns, and geographic areas in specific countries
Schwauss, Maria. Woerterbuch der Regionalen Umgangssprache in Lateinamerika. LC 77-562131. 692p. (Ger. & Span.). 1977. M.52.00. VEB Verlag Enzyklopadie.

LATIN AMERICA–BIBLIOGRAPHY
Levine, Robert M. Race & Ethnic Relations in Latin America & the Caribbean: An Historical Dictionary & Bibliography. LC 80-15179. 260p. 1980. $14.50 (ISBN 0-8108-1324-6). Scarecrow.

LATIN AMERICA–CIVILIZATION
Nunez, Benjamin. Dictionary of Afro-Latin American Civilization. LC 79-7731. (Illus.). xxxv, 525p. 1980. lib. bdg. $45.00 (ISBN 0-313-21138-8, NAL/). Greenwood.

LATIN AMERICA–CIVILIZATION–STUDY AND TEACHING
Nunez, Benjamin. Dictionary of Afro-Latin American Civilization. LC 79-7731. (Illus.). xxxv, 525p. 1980. lib. bdg. $45.00 (ISBN 0-313-21138-8, NAL/). Greenwood.

LATIN AMERICA–POLITICS AND GOVERNMENT
Rossi, Ernest E. & Plano, Jack C. The Latin American Political Dictionary. LC 79-27128. (Clio Dictionaries in Political Science Ser.: No. 1). 261p. 1981. $19.75 (ISBN 0-87436-324-1); pap. $9.75 (ISBN 0-87436-327-6). ABC-Clio.

LATIN AMERICA–SOCIAL CONDITIONS
Levine, Robert M. Race & Ethnic Relations in Latin America & the Caribbean: An Historical Dictionary & Bibliography. LC 80-15179. 260p. 1980. $14.50 (ISBN 0-8108-1324-6). Scarecrow.

LATIN-AMERICAN AUTHORS
see Authors, Latin-American

LATIN-AMERICAN LITERATURE–BIBLIOGRAPHY
Foster, David W., ed. Dictionary of Contemporary Latin American Authors. LC 75-17988. 250p. 1975. pap. $6.95x (ISBN 0-87918-021-8). ASU Lat Am St.

LATIN LANGUAGE–ABBREVIATIONS
see Abbreviations

LATIN LANGUAGE–CHURCH LATIN
Galfridus Anglicus. Promptorium Parvulorum Sive Clericorum, Dictionarius Anglolatinus Princeps, 3 Pts. Repr. of 1865 ed. $37.00 ea. Johnson Repr.

LATIN LANGUAGE–DICTIONARIES
Ahlberg, Axel W., et al. Latinsk-Svensk Ordbok. 430p. (Lat. & Swedish.). 1968. Kr.200.00 (ISBN 91-24-62108-0). Esselte Studium.
Alvarez de la Brana, Ramon. Siglas & Abreviaturas Latinas con su Significado por Orden Alfabetico de un Catalogo de las Abreviaturas. LC 78-366525. xi, 215p. (Lat.). 1978. write for info. (ISBN 3-487-06454-5). Olms Verlag.
Angelini, Gino. Nuovo dizionario latino-italiano. xii, 1828p. (Lat. & Ital.). 1975. L.10000.00. Dante Alighieri.
Angelini, Gino, et al. Dizionario latino. xii, 1908p. (Lat.). 1975. L.16000.00. Dante Alighieri.
Badellino, Oreste. Dizionario italiano-latino. 1480p. (Ital. & Lat.). 1972. L.17500.00 (ISBN 88-7011-007-9). Rosenberg & Sel.
--Dizionario italiano-latino: Edizione speciale. 213p. (Ital. & Lat.). 1972. L.25000.00 (ISBN 88-7011-008-7). Rosenberg & Sel.
Bertaux, Felix & Lepointe, Emile. Dictionnaire Redige en Caracteres Latins: Allemand-Francais. (Ger. & Fr.). 1972. 76.00 F. Hachette.
--Dictionnaire Redige en Caracteres Latins: Francais-Allemand. 1310p. (Ger. & Fr.). 1967. 68.50 F. Hachette.
Bianchi, E., et al. Dizionario illustrato della lingua latina. (Illus.). xx, 2582p. (Lat.). 1973. L.2300.00. Monnier.
--Dizionario illustrato della lingua latina, 2 vols. xxxvi, 2482p. (Lat.). 1973. L.19000.00. Monnier.
Bianchi, Raffaello. Il Vocabolario Latino-Italiano & Italiano-Latino. LC 77-578107. (Illus.). 619p. (Ital. & Lat.). 1977. L.5000.00. Monnier.
Bianchi, Raffaello & Lelli, Onorio. Vocabolario Latino-italiano, italiano-latino. (Illus.). iv, 620p. (Lat. & Ital.). 1973. L.5000.00. Monnier.
Blanco Garcia, Vicente. Diccionario latino-espanol y espanol-latino. (Span.). 175.00 ptas. Aguilar SP.
Blanquez. Diccionario Latino-Espanol, Espanol-Latino, 3 vols. 2703p. (Lat. & Span.). Set. leatherette $75.00 (ISBN 84-303-0151-8, S-50419). French & Eur.
Blanquez Fraile, Agustin. Diccionario manual latino-espanol y espanol-latino. 672p. (Lat. & Span.). 150.00 ptas. Sopena.
Buxtorf, Johann. Lexicon Chaldaicum Talmudicum & Rabbinicum. LC 78-359320. (Aramaic & Lat.). 1977. write for info. (ISBN 3-487-06386-7). Olms Verlag.

Calonghi, et al, eds. Dizionario della lingua latina: Latino-italiano e italiano-latino. 1329p. (Lat. & Ital.). 1968. L.15000.00 (ISBN 88-7011-006-0). Rosenberg & Sellier.
Calonghi, Ferruccio. Dizionario latino-italiano. 1480p. (Lat. & Ital.). 1972. L.17500.00 (ISBN 88-7011-009-5). Rosenberg & Sel.
Campanini, Giuseppe, et al. Vocabolario latino-italiano-latino. 1506p. (Lat. & Ital.). 1976. L.14500.00. Paravia.
Cassells. Latin Concise Dictionary. (Lat.). 1977. $9.95 (ISBN 0-02-052263-0). Macmillan.
Castiglioni, Luigi. Vocabolario Della Lingua Latina. 15th ed. Brambilla, A. & Campagna, G., eds. LC 76-485030. xii, 2493p. (Lat. & Ital.). 1976. L.18000.00. Loescher.
Castiglioni, Luigi & Mariotti, Scevola. Vocabolario della lingua latina: Latino-italiano e italiano-latino. 2500p. (Lat. & Ital.). 1966. L.25000.00. Loescher.
Chaudhary, Abdul G. The Law Latin Lexicon. LC 79-930806. 248p. (Eng. & Lat.). 1979. Rs.35.00. Khyber Law Publishers.
D'Arbela, Edmondo, et al. Vocabolario latino-italiano e italiano-latino. viii, 2030p. (Lat. & Span.). L.16800.00. Signorelli C.
De Andrea. Diccionario manual latino-castellano y castellano-latino. (Lat. & Span.). Arg.$21.60. Sopena.
Diccionario Abreviado Latino-Espanol Espanol-Latino. 316p. (Lat. & Span.). 350.00 ptas (ISBN 84-7153-221-2). Biblograf SP.
Diccionario Abreviado Latino-Espanol Espanol-Latino 'Spes' 9th ed. 316p. (Lat. & Span.). 1980. write for info. (ISBN 84-7153-221-2). Biblo SP.
Diccionario abreviado Latino-Espanol Espanol-Latino Vox. 11th ed. 316p. (Lat. & Span.). 1982. 325.00 ptas (ISBN 84-7153-221-2). Biblo SP.
Diccionario Basico Latino-Espanol. 9th ed. 830p. (Lat. & Span.). 1981. 385.00 ptas (ISBN 84-7153-223-9). Biblo SP.
Diccionario Basico Latino-Espanol Espanol-Latino. 830p. (Lat. & Span.). 625.00 ptas (ISBN 84-7153-223-9). Biblograf SP.
Diccionario basico latino-espanol, espanol-latino. (Span. & Lat.). $8.60. Imported Bks.
Diccionario basico Latino-Espanol Espanol-Latino. 10th ed. 830p. (Lat. & Span.). 1982. 550.00 ptas (ISBN 84-7153-223-9). Biblo SP.
Diccionario Everest Cima Latin. 6th ed. (Illus.). 756p. (Lat.). 1982. 475.00 ptas (ISBN 8-42411-442-6). Everest.
Diccionario Everest Cima Latin-Espanol. 5th ed. 756p. (Lat. & Span.). 1981. 390.00 ptas (ISBN 84-241-1442-6). Everest.
Diccionario Everest Cima Latin (II) 756p. (Lat.). 1982. 475.00 ptas (ISBN 8-42411-442-6). Everest.
Diccionario Everest Cima latino-espanol, espanol-latino. (Span.). 125.00 ptas. Everest.
Diccionario Ilustrado Latino-Espanol Espanol-Latino. (Illus.). 800p. (Lat. & Span.). 1981. 825.00 ptas (ISBN 84-7153-197-6). Biblograf SP.
Diccionario Ilustrado Latino-Espanol Espanol-Latino. 14th ed. (Illus.). 800p. (Span. & Lat.). 1982. pap. 725.00 ptas (ISBN 84-7153-197-6). Biblo SP.
Dizionario italiano-latino. 576p. (Ital. & Lat.). L.1500.00. Malipiero.
Dizionario latino-italiano e italiano-latino. 304p. (Lat. & Ital.). L.2000.00. Malipiero.
Du Cange, Charles D. Glossarium ad Scriptores Mediae & Infimae Graecitatis. 1280p. (Lat.). 1958. S.1500.00. Akad Druck.
Echauri Martinez, Eustaquio. Diccionario Basico Latino-Espanol, Espanol-Latino. 8th ed. LC 80-100210. 829p. (Lat. & Span.). 1978. 235.00 ptas (ISBN 8-471-53223-9). Biblo Sp.
Estienne, Henri. Thesaurus Graecae Linguae, 9 vols. 10800p. (Lat. & Gr.). 1954. S.11000.00. Akad Druck.
Estienne, Robert. Dictionariolum Puerorum Tribus Linguis: Lat., Ang. & Gall. Conscriptum. LC 72-194. (English Experience Ser.: No. 351). 616p. (Lat., Eng. & Fr.). 1971. Repr. of 1552 ed. $76.00 (ISBN 90-221-0351-X). Walter J Johnson.
Forcellini, Egidio. Lexicon totius latinitatus, 6 vols. 5816p. (Lat.). 1965. L.460000.00. Lib Edit Greg.
Freytag, George W. Lexicon Arabico-Latinum, 4 vols. (Arabic & Lat.). $95.00x (ISBN 0-86685-124-0). Intl Bk Ctr.
--Lexicon Arabico-Latinum, 4 vols. 2257p. (Arabic & Lat.). Repr. of 1830 ed. $95.00 (124-0). Intl Bk Ctr.
Fumagalli, Giuseppe. Lexicon typographicum Italiae. (Illus.). xlvii, 587p. (Lat.). 1966. L.65000.00. Olschki.
Gaffiot, F. Dizionario illustrato latino-italiano. (Illus.). 1576p. (Lat. & Ital.). 1973. L.15000.00. Piccin.
Gaffiot, Felix. Dictionnaire Abrege Latin-Francais. 1720p. (Lat. & Fr.). 1970. $40.00. Hachette Jeunesse.
--Dictionnaire Latin-Francais. (Lat. & Fr.). 1967. 83.00 F. Hachette.
Gesenius, Friedrich H. Guilielmi Gesenii Thesaurus Philologicus Linguae Hebraeae, 3 vols. LC 78-392234. 1522p. (Hebrew & Lat.). 1977. DM.780.00. Biblio-Verlag.
Glare, G. P., ed. Oxford Latin Dictionary, Fascicle 4. Gorgonia-Libero. (Lat.). 1973. pap. $49.50x (ISBN 0-19-864217-2). Oxford U Pr.
Glare, P. G. Oxford Latin Dictionary: Fascicle 8. (Lat.). 1982. pap. $48.00x (ISBN 0-19-864221-0). Oxford U Pr.
Glare, P. G., ed. Oxford Latin Dictionary, Fascicle 3: Demiurgus-Gorgoneus. (Lat.). 1971. pap. $49.50x (ISBN 0-19-864216-4). Oxford U Pr.
Grabmueller, Klaus, pref. by. Vocabulaius Teutonico-Latinus. LC 77-46995. xxxiv, 622p. (Lat.). 1976. write for info. (ISBN 3-487-05883-9). Olms Verlag.
Graesse, Johann G. Orbis Latinus: Lexikon lateinischer geographischer Namen des Mittelalters und der Neuzeit, 3 vols. new ed. Plechl, Helmut, ed. 1800p. (Lat. & Ger.). 1970. $275.00x (ISBN 3-7814-0087-5). Intl Pubns Serv.
Hastrup, T. Latin-Dansk Ordbog. 307p. (Lat. & Danish.). 1981. $24.95 (ISBN 87-01-67511-7, M-1288). French & Eur.
Isambaev, M. Russko-Latino-Kazakhskii Terminologicheskii Slovar. 506p. (Rus. & Lat.). 1960. $2.40 (Pub. by Izd. An Kaz. SSR). Four Continent.
Kiel, Cornelis. Dictionarium Teutonicolatinum. LC 76-459868. xii, 246p. (Lat.). 1975. DM.68.00 (ISBN 3-487-05227-X). Olms Verlag.
Lana, Italo. Vocabolario latino. xvi, 1870p. (Span.). 1978. L.18500.00. Paravia.
Langenscheidts Grosswoerterbuch Lateinisch: Tl 1, Lateinisch-Deutsch. (Lat. & Ger.). 1978. DM.58.00 (ISBN 3-468-02200-X). Langenscheidt.
Langenscheidts Grosswoerterbuch Lateinisch: Tl 2, Deutsch-Lateinisch. (Ger. & Lat.). 1978. DM.58.00 (ISBN 3-468-02205-0). Langenscheidt.
Langenscheidts Lilliput-Woerterbuch Deutsch-Lateinisch. 640p. (Ger. & Lat.). DM.3.00 (20013). Langenscheidt.
Langenscheidts Lilliput-Woerterbuch Lateinisch-Deutsch. 640p. (Lat. & Ger.). DM.3.00 (20014). Langenscheidt.
Langenscheidts Lilliput-Woerterbuecher Deutsch-Lateinisch. (Ger. & Lat.). 1978. DM.2.20 (ISBN 3-468-20013-7). Langenscheidt.
Langenscheidts Lilliput-Woerterbuecher Lateinisch-Deutsch. (Lat. & Ger.). 1978. DM.2.20 (ISBN 3-468-20014-5). Langenscheidt.
Langenscheidts Schulwoerterbuecher Lateinisch-Deutsch. (Lat. & Ger.). 1978. DM.10.80 (ISBN 3-468-13200-X). Langenscheidt.
Langenscheidts Taschenwoerterbuecher Deutsch-Lateinisch. (Ger. & Lat.). 1978. DM.13.80 (ISBN 3-468-10205-4). Langenscheidt.
Langenscheidts Universal-Woerterbuch Lateinisch. 560p. (Lat. & Ger.). DM.6.80 (18200). Langenscheidt.
Langenscheidts Universal-Woerterbuecher Lateinisch-Deutsch. (Lat. & Ger.). 1978. DM.5.80 (ISBN 3-468-18200-7). Langenscheidt.
Lateinisch-Deutsch, Deutsch-Lateinisch. (Langenscheidts Schulwoerterbuecher Ser.). 512p. (Ger. & Lat.). DM.12.80 (13200). Langenscheidt.
Latham, R. E., compiled by. Dictionary of Medieval Latin from British Sources: Fascicule I, A-B. (Medieval Lat.). 1975. pap. $55.00x (ISBN 0-19-725948-0); Fascicule 2 C. pap. $198.00x 1981 (ISBN 0-19-725968-5). Oxford U Pr.
Lewis, Charlton T. & Short, Charles. Latin Dictionary: Founded on Andrews Edition of Freund's Latin Dictionary. (Lat.). 1879. $69.00x (ISBN 0-19-864201-6). Oxford U Pr.
Lipparini, L. Vocabolario latino-italiano e italiano-latino. 1008p. (Lat. & Ital.). L.10000.00. Malipiero.
Llauro Padrosa, J. Diccionario latino-espanol. 2nd ed. (Lat. & Span.). 150.00 ptas. SAETA.
Llauro Padrose, J. & Marques Casanovas, J. Diccionario espanol-latino. (Span. & Lat.). 200.00 ptas. SAETA.
Macchi, L. Diccionario latino. (Lat.). Arg.$40.00. Don Bosco Ed.
MacDonald, Gerald, ed. Vocabulario De Romance En Latin: Antonio De Nebrija. LC 72-96003. 214p. (Lat. & Span.). 1973. $19.95 (ISBN 0-87722-018-2). Temple U Pr.
Mariano, Cosimo. Nuovo dizionario italiano-latino. viii, 1646p. (Ital. & Lat.). 1975. L.10000.00. Dante Alighieri.
Martinez Burgos, Matias & Ayala Lopez, Manuel. Diccionario escolar latino-espanol y espanol-latino. (Span.). 200.00 ptas. Bibliografica.
Menge & Guethling. Langenscheidts Grosswoerterbuch Deutsch-Lateinisch. (Ger. & Lat.). 1978. DM.58.00 (ISBN 3-468-02205-0). Langenscheidt.
--Langenscheidts Grosswoerterbuch Lateinisch-Deutsch. (Lat. & Ger.). 1978. DM.58.00 (ISBN 3-468-02200-X). Langenscheidt.
Menge, H. Langenscheidts Taschenwoerterbuecher Lateinisch. (Lat.). 1978. DM.21.80 (ISBN 3-468-11200-9). Langenscheidt.
Menge, H. & Pertsch, E. Langenscheidts Taschenwoerterbuch Lateinisch, 2 vols. in 1. (Lat. & Ger.). DM.24.80 (11200). Langenscheidt.
--Langenscheidts Taschenwoerterbuch Lateinisch: Teil I, Lateinisch-Deutsch. 576p. (Lat. & Ger.). DM.17.80 (10200). Langenscheidt.
Menge, Hermann. Langenscheidts Taschenwoerterbuch Lateinisch: Teil II, Deutsch-Lateinisch. 460p. (Ger. & Lat.). DM.17.80 (10205). Langenscheidt.
--Lateinisch, 2 vols. rev. ed. Pertsch, E., rev. by. (Langenscheidts Taschewoerterbuecher Ser.). (Lat. & Ger.). Teil 1: Lateinisch-Deutsch (576p.) DM.16.80 (10200); Teil 2: Deutsch-Lateinisch (460p.) DM.16.80 (10205); DM.beide Teile in einem Band 23.80 (11200). Langenscheidt.
Menge, Hermann & Guethling, Otto. Langenscheidts Grosswoerterbuch: Lateinisch-Deutsch, 2 vols. 1553p. (Lat. & Ger.). DM.78.00; Teil I, Lateinisch-Deutsch. (02200); Teil II, Deutsch-Lateinisch. (02205). Langenscheidt.
Michel, J. & Gester, Michel. Lexique de base du Latin. 236p. (Fr. & Lat.). 1967. 236.00 F. Sikkel.
Mugica. Diccionario manual latino-espanol y espanol-latino. 7th ed. 640p. (Lat. & Span.). 230.00 ptas. Razon y Fe.
Pertsch, Dietrich. Lateinisch-Deutsch. rev. & enl. ed. (Langenscheidts Grosse Schulwoerbuecher Ser.). 1344p. (Lat. & Ger.). 1983. DM.23.80 (07202). Langenscheidt.
Pertsch, Erich. Langenscheidts Grosses Schulwoerterbuch Lateinisch-Deutsch. 1344p. (Lat. & Ger.). DM.23.80 (07202). Langenscheidt.
--Langenscheidts Handwoerterbuch Lateinisch-Deutsch. 652p. (Lat. & Ger.). DM.34.00 (04200). Langenscheidt.
--Langenscheidts Schulwoerterbuecher Lateinisch-Deutsch. 1400p. (Lat. & Ger.). 1977. DM.19.80 (ISBN 3-468-07201-5). Langenscheidt.
Pertsch, Erich & Lange-Kowal, Ernst E. Langenscheidts Schulwoerterbuch Lateinisch-Deutsch. 512p. (Lat. & Ger.). DM.13.80 (13200). Langenscheidt.
Pertsch, Erich, compiled by. Lateinisch-Deutsch. (Langenscheidts Handwoerterbuecher Ser.). 652p. (Lat. & Ger.). DM.32.00 (04200). Langenscheidt.
Perugini, Angelo. Dizionario Italiano-Latino. LC 78-337088. x, 2322p. (Ital. & Lat.). 1976. write for info. Libr Ed Vat.
--Dizionario italiano-latino. xii, 2322p. (Ital. & Lat.). 1977. L.35000.00 (ISBN 88-209-1227-9). Libr Ed Vat.
Pittano, Giuseppe. Dizionario latino-italiano e italiano-latino. 1696p. (Lat. & Ital.). L.22000.00. Edn Scol Mond.
Prazak, Josef M. Latinsko-Cesky Slovnik, 2 vols. 2nd ed. LC 76-502083. (Lat. & Czech.). 1975. 94.00 Kcs. SNTC.
Pulgram, Ernst. Italic, Latin, Italian. LC 79-312793. 400p. (Lat. & Ital.). 1978. pap. write for info. (ISBN 3-533-02769-4). C Winter.
Russko-Latinsko-Uzbekskii Slovar. 188p. (Rus. , Lat. & Uzbek.). 1978. $3.95 (Pub. by Meditsina). Four Continent.
Sacerdoti. Dizionario italiano-latino. 208p. (Ital. & Lat.). 1976. L.2000.00. Vallardi A.
Sacerdoti, N. Dizionario Italiano-Latino, Latino-Italiano. 391p. (Ital. & Lat.). 1977. leatherette $5.95 (ISBN 0-686-92629-3, M-9175). French & Eur.
Schaeffer, Randolph F. & Carr, W. L., eds. Latin English Derivative Dictionary. (Lat. & Eng.). $1.95 (B5). Am Classical.
Sella, Pietro. Dizionario latino-italiano: Stato della Chiesa-Veneto-Abruzzi. xxxii, 687p. (Lat. & Ital.). 1965. L.10000.00 (ISBN 88-210-0387-6). Biblioteca Apostolica Vaticana.
--Glossario latino-emiliano. xxiv, 407p. (Ital.). 1973. L.11000.00 (ISBN 88-210-0415-5). Biblio Apost.
Simonet, Francisco J. Glosario de voces ibericas y latinas: Tomo 1. 424p. (Span. & Lat.). 1982. pap. 1500.00 ptas (ISBN 84-363-0545-0). Atlas Edns.
--Glosario de voces ibericas y latinas: Obras completa. 849p. (Span. & Lat.). 1982. pap. 3000.00 ptas (ISBN 84-363-0547-7). Atlas Edns.
Sommer, Edouard. Lexique Francais-Latin. 480p. (Fr. & Lat.). 1967. 11.30 F. Hachette-Jeunesse.
Spes--Diccionario Abreviado Latino-Espanol, Espanol-Latino. 9th ed. 316p. (Lat. & Span.). 1978. leatherette $7.25 (ISBN 84-7153-221-2, S-12409). French & Eur.
Tucker, T. G. Etymological Dictionary of Latin. (Lat.). 1976. $25.00 (ISBN 0-89005-172-0). Ares.
Universal Latin Dictionary. 560p. (Lat.). $2.95 (094). Langenscheidt.

Vianello, Natale. Vocabolario latino-italiano, italiano-latino. xii, 884p. (Lat. & Ital.). 1975. L.6000.00. Dante Alighieri.
Vischer, Ruediger. Lateinische Wortkunde fuer Anfaenger & Fortgeschrittene. LC 79-383471. 224p. (Ger. & Lat.). 1977. write for info. (ISBN 3-519-07407-9). Teubner.
Vives. Diccionario de bolsillo latino-espanol & espanol-latino. (Span. & Lat.). write for info. Coculsa.
Vocabular Latina. 119p. (Lat. , Eng. , Fr. & Ger.). write for info. Esselte Studium.
Voinov, M. Latin-Bulgarian Dictionary. 840p. (Lat. & Bulgarian.). 1980. $45.00 (ISBN 0-686-97420-4, M-9831). French & Eur.
Wilson, A. Latin Dictionary. (Teach Yourself Ser.). (Lat.). 1974. pap. $4.95 (ISBN 0-679-10204-3). McKay.

LATIN LANGUAGE–DICTIONARIES–ENGLISH

Cassell. Cassell's Latin Dictionary: Concise Latin-English English-Latin. (Lat. & Eng.). $9.95 (ISBN 0-02-522630-4). Macmillan.
--Cassell's Latin Dictionary: Standard Latin-English English-Latin. (Lat. & Eng.). $17.95 (ISBN 0-02-522570-7). Macmillan.
Cassells. Latin-English Dictionary. (Lat. & Eng.). 1977. standard $16.95 (ISBN 0-686-63973-1); index $19.95 (ISBN 0-02-052258-4). Macmillan.
Galfridus Anglicus. Promptorium Parvulorum Sive Clericorum, Dictionarius Anglolatinus Princeps, 3 Pts. Repr. of 1865 ed. $37.00 ea. Johnson Repr.
Kidd, D. A. Latin-English, English-Latin Dictionary. (Lat. & Eng.). $19.50 (ISBN 0-87557-050-X, 052-6). Saphrograph.
Langenscheidt English-Latin Lilliput Dictionary. 640p. (Eng. & Lat.). plastic $1.50 (ISBN 3-468-96484-6). Langenscheidt.
Latin-English & English-Latin Dictionary. (Lat. & Eng.). pap. $1.99 (ISBN 0-686-00473-6). Dennison.
Latin-English, English-Latin Dictionary. (Lat. & Eng.). pap. $2.50 (ISBN 0-686-79571-7, DI 6, BN). B&N NY.
Pocket-Shorter Dictionary. 600p. (Lat. & Eng.). $5.95 (089). Langenscheidt.
Simpson, D. P., compiled by. Cassell's Concise Latin-English, English-Latin Dictionary. abr. ed. LC 77-7660. (Lat. & Ger.). 1977. $9.95 (ISBN 0-02-522630-4). Macmillan.
Simpson, D. P., ed. Cassell's Latin Dictionary: Latin-English, English-Latin. (Lat. & Eng.). 1977. indexed $18.95 (ISBN 0-02-522580-4); plain $16.95 (ISBN 0-02-522570-7). Macmillan.
Smith, William & Lockwood, J. L., eds. Chambers Murray Latin-English Dictionary. 3rd ed. (Lat. & Eng., Totally Recast Version). 1976. Repr. of 1934 ed. $15.75x (ISBN 0-06-496367-5). B&N Imports.
Traupman, John C. New College Latin & English Dictionary. (Lat. & Eng.). (gr. 7-12). 1966. pap. text ed. $7.67 (ISBN 0-87720-560-4). AMSCO Sch.
Traupman, John C., ed. New College Latin & English Dictionary. (Language Library). (Orig., Lat. & Eng.). 1970. pap. $2.95 (ISBN 0-553-20255-3). Bantam.
Woodhouse, S. C., ed. Latin-English & English-Latin Dictionary. (Routledge Pocket Dictionaries Ser.). 496p. (Orig., Lat. & Eng.). 1982. pap. $8.95 (ISBN 0-7100-9267-9). Routledge & Kegan.

LATIN LANGUAGE–DICTIONARIES–FRENCH

Bornecque, Henri & Cauet, Fernand. Dictionnaire Latin-Francais. 560p. (Fr. & Lat.). 1953. $39.95 (ISBN 0-686-56926-1, M-6044). French & Eur.
Cotton, Gerard. Vocabulaire Raisonne Latin-Francais. 332p. (Lat. & Fr.). 19.40 F. Dessain & Tolra.
De Cahors, Jean E. Dictionnaire Hatier-Beauchemin: Francais-Latin. (Fr. & Lat.). 1957. Can.$2.95. Beauchemin.
Decahors, Jean-Elie. Dictionnaire Francais-Latin. 864p. (Fr. & Lat.). 1957. 19.50 F. Hatier.
Edon, Georges. Dictionnaire Francais-Latin. (Fr. & Lat.). $37.50 (ISBN 0-686-57201-7, M-6703). French & Eur.
--Dictionnaire Francais-Latin. 1800p. (Fr. & Lat.). 1978. 92.00 F. Belin.
Estienne, Robert. Dictionnaire Francais-Latin. 680p. (Fr. & Lat.). 1972. 300.00 F. Slatkine.
Gaffiot, Felix. Dictionnaire Abrege Latin-Francais. 1720p. (Lat. & Fr.). 1970. pap. $15.95 (ISBN 0-686-57186-X, M-6258). French & Eur.
--Dictionnaire Abrege Latin-Francais Illustre. (Illus.). 720p. (Lat. & Fr.). 1969. C.$9.35. Renouveau Pedagogique.
--Dictionnaire Latin-Francais. (Lat. & Fr.). 1967. pap. $32.50 (ISBN 0-686-57187-8, M-6259). French & Eur.
Gariel, A. Dictionnaire Hatier-Beauchemin: Latin-Francais. (Lat. & Fr.). 1960. Can.$2.95. Beauchemin.
Geoffroy. Dictionnaire Francais-Latin. 1200p. (Fr. & Lat.). 1978. 21.40 F. Delalain.
--Dictionnaire Latin-Francais. 1200p. (Lat. & Fr.). 21.40 F. Delalain.
Goelzer, Henri. Dictionnaire Francais-Latin. 640p. (Fr. & Lat.). 1966. 11.50 F. Garnier-Flammarion.
--Dictionnaire Francais-Latin. 744p. (Fr. & Lat.). 1967. 21.00 F. Garnier.
--Dictionnaire Latin-Francais. 704p. (Lat. & Fr.). 1966. 11.50 F. Garnier.
--Dictionnaire Latin-Francais. 792p. (Lat. & Fr.). 1967. pap. 21.00 F. Garnier.
--Dictionnaire Latin-Francais. 734p. (Lat. & Fr.). pap. 35.50 F. Garnier.
Lebaigue, Charles. Dictionnaire Latin-Francais. 1382p. (Fr. & Lat.). $33.50 (ISBN 0-686-56999-7, M-6340). French & Eur.
Quicherat, Louis. Dictionnaire Francais-Latin. (Fr. & Lat.). 1967. $86.80. Hachette-Jeinesse.
Sommer, Edouard. Lexique Latin-Francais. 512p. (Fr.). 1967. 29.00 F. Hachette.
Trenel, Jacques. Lexique Francais-Latin. 694p. (Fr. & Lat.). 1978. 30.40 F. Belin.

LATIN LANGUAGE–GLOSSARIES, VOCABULARIES, ETC.

Babeliowsky, J. K. Basiswoordenlijst Latijn. LC 76-526797. 273p. (Dutch & Lat.). 1975. write for info. (ISBN 9-012-00872-7). Staatsdruk.
Bodson, Arthur. Vocabulaire Latin. 48p. (Lat.). 1974. 42.00 F. Sciences Lettres.
Else, Gerald F. Basic Latin Vocabulary Along Etymological Lines. 15p. (Lat. & Eng.). $0.90 (NO. B14). Am Classical.
Hellegouarch, Jean. Le Vocabulaire Latin des Relations & des Partis Politiques sous la Republique. (Lat.). 109.00 F. Belles Lettres.
Lodge, Gonzalez. The Vocabulary of High School Latin. LC 73-177003. (Columbia University. Teachers College. Contributions to Education: No. 9). (Lat.). Repr. of 1912 ed. $17.50 (ISBN 0-404-55009-6). AMS Pr.
Oliphant, Robert. Harley Latin-Old English Glossary. (Janua Linguarum, Ser. Practica: No. 20). (Lat. & Eng.). 1966. pap. text ed. $36.00x (ISBN 90-2790-639-4). Mouton.
Paschall, Dorothy M. Vocabulary of Mental Aberration in Roman Comedy & Petronius. (Language Dissertations: No. 27). 1939. pap. $9.00 (ISBN 0-527-00773-0). Kraus Repr.
Simonet, Francisco J. Glosario de voces ibericas y latinas: Tomo 2. 425p. (Span. & Lat.). 1982. pap. 1500.00 ptas (ISBN 84-363-0546-9). Atlas Edns.
Wilson, John & Parsons, C. Basic Latin Vocabulary. (Lat.). 1969. text ed. $7.95 (ISBN 0-312-06825-5). St Martin.

LATIN LANGUAGE–GRAMMAR

see also Latin Language–Syntax

Lewis, Carolyn D. Medical Latin. (Lat.). (YA) (gr. 12). $6.00x (ISBN 0-8338-0040-X). M Jones.

LATIN LANGUAGE–SUFFIXES AND PREFIXES

Zellmer, Ernst. Die Lateinischen Woerter auf -Ura. LC 78-374219. 293p. (Ger.). 1976. write for info. Selbstverlag Inst.

LATIN LANGUAGE–SYNTAX

Nelli, Bruno. Dizionario sintattico latino. 280p. (Lat.). 1968. L.6000.00. Giardini Pisa.

LATIN LANGUAGE, MEDIEVAL AND MODERN–DICTIONARIES

Lexicon Latinitatis Medii Aevi: Praesertim ad res Ecclesiasticas Investigandas Pertinens. 1040p. (Lat.). 1975. 3750.00 F. Brepols.
Papias, Gramarian. Papiae Elementarium. De Angelis, V., ed. LC 77-578447. (Lat. & Ital.). 1977. write for info. Cisalpino.

LATIN LANGUAGE, MEDIEVAL AND MODERN–GLOSSARIES, VOCABULARIES, ETC.

Galfridus Anglicus. Promptorium Parvulorum Sive Clericorum, Dictionarius Anglolatinus Princeps, 3 Pts. Repr. of 1865 ed. $37.00 ea. Johnson Repr.
Galfridus, Anglicus. Promptorium Parvulorum Sive Clericorum, Lexicon Anglo-Latinum Princeps, 3 Vols. LC 70-168091. (Camden Society, London. Publications, First Ser.: Nos. 25, 54, 89). (Lat.). Repr. of 1865 ed. Set. $84.00 (ISBN 0-404-50209-1); $28.00 ea. AMS Pr.

LATIN LITERATURE (SELECTIONS: EXTRACTS, ETC.)

Cree, A. Cree's Dictionary of Latin Quotations. LC 78-51482. (Eng. & Lat.). 1979. $16.00 (ISBN 0-912728-12-4). Newbury Bks.

LATIN LITERATURE–DICTIONARIES

Kunzer, Paul E. Vergil Vocabularies. (Bk. I- II). $1.00ea (8). Am Classical.

LATIN LITERATURE–HISTORY AND CRITICISM

Paschall, Dorothy M. Vocabulary of Mental Aberration in Roman Comedy & Petronius. (Language Dissertations: No. 27). 1939. pap. $9.00 (ISBN 0-527-00773-0). Kraus Repr.

LATIN POETRY–HISTORY AND CRITICISM

Virgil. Virgil Eclogues & a Special Vocabulary to Virgil. Greenough, J. B. & Kittredge, G. L., eds. (College Classical Ser). 1977. lib. bdg. $20.00x (ISBN 0-89241-027-2). Caratzas Pub Co.

LATVIAN LANGUAGE

Anglo-Latyshsko-Russkii Frazeologicheskii Slovar. 718p. (Eng. & Rus.). 1977. $3.25 (Pub. by Liesma). Four Continent.
Kagaine, Elga & Rage, S. Ergemes Izloksnes Vardnica. LC 79-394141. (Illus., Latvian & Riga.). 1977. 3.50 Rub. Zinatne.
Millers, Antonia. Grammar, Vocabulary, Exercises of the Latvian Language for the Use of Students. LC 79-89077. (Latvian & Eng.). $10.00x (ISBN 0-912852-26-7). Echo Pubs.
Turkina, Phil E. Latvian-English Dictionary. (Latvian & Eng.). $19.50 (ISBN 0-87557-052-6, 052-6). Saphrograph.
Zandreitere, I., et al. Frantsuzsko-Latviiskii Slovar. 772p. (Fr. & Latvian.). 1957. $3.50 (Pub. by Latv Valsts). Four Continent.

LAUNDRY AND LAUNDRY INDUSTRY

Institute of Industrial Launderers. Glossary of Commonly Used Terms. $12.00 (ILP-TE-01); members $8.00. Inst Indus Launderer.
International Fabricare Institute. Chemical Terms for Washroom Procedures. (Special Reporter-Laundry Library). $1.00. Intl Fabricare Inst.

LAW

see also Jurisdiction; Jurisprudence; Justice; Justice, Administration Of; Legislation
also names of legal systems, e.g. Canon Law, Common Law, Roman Law; special branches of law, e.g. Constitutional Law, Criminal Law, Maritime Law; specific legal topics, e.g. Contracts, Mortgages, Sanctions (Law); subdivision Laws and Legislation under subjects, e.g. Postal Service–Law

Bola Publications. Bola Glossary of Civil Procedural Law: Spanish-English & English-Spanish. LC 82-72320. (Bola Glossary Ser.: Vol. 2). 100p. (Orig., Span. & Eng.). pap. $19.95 (ISBN 0-943118-01-8). Bola Pubns.
Dictionnaire du Droit des Societes a Responsabille, 6 vols. (Fr.). write for info. JolY.
Dictionnaire du Droit des Societes a Responsabille. (Fr.). 1978. write for info. Joly.
Klost, Walter. Arbeitsschutzlexikon. LC 80-465045. (Illus.). 186p. (Ger.). 1979. write for info. Verlag Moderne.
Leite, Yara M. Dicionario Juridico Brasileiro: Contendo Termos, Expressoes Idiomaticas & Brocardos Usuais em Direito. 3rd ed. LC 77-570484. 223p. (Port.). 1976. Cr.$70.00. Saraiva SA.
Martinez Cachero, Luis A. Diccionario de Hacienda & Derecho Fiscal. LC 75-521721. 205p. (Span.). 1976. write for info. (ISBN 8-436-80035-4). Piramide.
Wacker, Wilhelm H., ed. Steuerlexikon. LC 75-514753. xii, 486p. (Ger.). 1975. DM.45.80 (ISBN 3-800-60472-8). Vahlen.

LAW–ABBREVIATIONS

Bryson, William H. A Dictionary of Sigla & Abbreviations to & in Law Books Before 1607. LC 75-5675. (Virginia Legal Studies). 224p. 1975. $20.00x (ISBN 0-8139-0615-6). U Pr of Va.
Sprudzs, Adolf. Benelux Abbreviations & Symbols: Law & Related Subjects. LC 74-140620. 129p. 1971. lib. bdg. $20.00 (ISBN 0-379-00120-9). Oceana.

LAW–BIBLIOGRAPHY

see also Legal Literature

American Arbitration Association. Dictionary of Arbitration & Its Terms. LC 70-94692. 334p. 1970. lib. bdg. $21.00 (ISBN 0-379-00386-4). Oceana.

LAW–DATA PROCESSING

Congressional Information Service, Inc. Staff, ed. CIS Online User Guide & Thesaurus. 400p. 1982. loose-leaf $75.00 (ISBN 0-686-43131-6). Cong Info.

LAW–DICTIONARIES

see also Law–Terms and Phrases

Al-Wahab, Ibrahim. Law Dictionary (English-Arabic) 320p. (Eng. & Arabic.). 1972. $20.00x (ISBN 0-86685-082-1). Intl Bk Ctr.
Anderson, R. Anglo-Scandinavian Law Dictionary. 1977. pap. $15.00x (ISBN 82-00-02365-6, Dist. by Columbia U Pr). Universitet.
Anderson, Ralph J. Anglo-Scandinavian Law Dictionary of Legal Terms. LC 77-481598. 137p. (Eng. & Scandinavian.). 1977. Kr.59.00 (ISBN 8-20002-365-6). Universitets.
Anderson, William, ed. Ballentine's Law Dictionary with Pronunciations. 3rd ed. LC 68-30931. 1429p. write for info. Lawyers Co-Op.
Antolinez, Crescencio. Fachworterbuch Fur Recht und Verwaltung. (Span. & Ger.). 1970. leatherette $35.00 (ISBN 3-452-17065-9, M-7398, Pub. by Carl Heymanns Verlag KG). French & Eur.
Backe, Torild, et al. Concise Swedish-English Glossary of Legal Terms. 164p. (Swedish & Eng.). 1973. text ed. $13.50x (ISBN 0-8377-0305-0). Rothman.
Bahri, Hardev. Bahri's Law Dictionary. LC 78-912999. x, 290p. (Eng. & Hindi.). 1978. $5.00. Haredeva Bahari.

Becher, H. Woerterbuch der Deutschen und Spanischen Rects und Wirtschaftssprache, Vol. 2. (Ger. & Span.). 1972. $79.95 (ISBN 3-406-00470-9, M-7022). French & Eur.

--Woerterbuch der Spanischen und Deutschen Rechts und Wirtschaftssprache, Vol. 1. (Span. & Ger.). 1971. $85.00 (ISBN 3-406-00469-5, M-6956). French & Eur.

Becher, Herbert J. Woerterbuch der Recht & Wirtshaftssprache: Teil II, Deutsch-Spanisch. viii, 814p. (Ger. & Span.). 1979. DM.148.00. Recht & Wirtschaft.

--Woerterbuch der Rechts & Wirtschaftssprache: Teil I, Spanisch-Deutsch. viii, 933p. (Span. & Ger.). 1978. DM.175.00. Recht & Wirtschaft.

Beseler, D. & Jacobs, B. Technical Dictionary of Anglo-American Legal Terminology. 3rd ed. 385p. (Ger. & Eng.). 1971. $110.00 (ISBN 3-11-002187-0, M-7636, Pub. by de Gruyter). French & Eur.

Beseler, D. v. & Jacobs, B., eds. Law Dictionary: Technical Dictionary of Anglo-American Legal Terminology, German-English. 3rd rev. ed. 385p. (Ger. & Eng.). 1971. $56.00x (ISBN 3-11-006775-7); pap. $45.00x (ISBN 3-11-002187-0). De Gruyter.

Beseler, Dora Von & Jacobs, Barbara. Law Dictionary: Fachwoerterbuch der anglo-amerikanischen Rechtssprache, Englisch-Deutsch. 3rd. rev. ed. (Ger.). 1976. $123.25x (ISBN 3-11-006774-9); pap. $111.00x (ISBN 3-11-001698-2). De Gruyter.

Birkhauser-Boston Publishing. The Herbst-Readett Two-Language Dictionaries of Finance, Commerce & Law, 2 vols. (Eng. & Ger.). 1976. Vol. 1 1975 English-German. $24.95 (ISBN 0-686-87523-0); Vol. 2 1976 German-English. $24.95 (ISBN 3-85942-004-6). Birkhauser.

Black, Henry C. Black's Law Dictionary. 5th ed. Nolan, Joseph R. & Connolly, Michael J., eds. LC 79-12547. 1511p. 1979. text ed. $18.95 (ISBN 0-8299-2041-2); deluxe ed. $37.50 (ISBN 0-8299-2045-5). West Pub.

--Black's Law Dictionary: Abridged Fifth Edition. Nolan, Joseph R., et al, eds. 854p. pap. text ed. $11.95 (ISBN 0-314-77135-2). West Pub.

Bonnefoi, Alexandre. Woerterbuch des Arbeits und Sozialrechtd. (Ger. & Fr.). 1975. $55.00 (ISBN 3-19-006293-5, M-6938). French & Eur.

Borum, Oscar A. & Von Eyben, W. E. Juridisk Ordbog. LC 77-459744. 254p. (Danish.). 1976. Kr.92.00 (ISBN 8-712-08818-8). Gad Forlag.

Brassine, J. Rechtskundig Woerdenboek: Dictionnaire Juridique. 248p. (Flemmish & Fr.). 1935. 267.00 F. Bruylant.

Bruzelius, Anders, et al. Kortfattad Engelsk-svensk Juridisk Ordbok. LC 81-188653. 16p. (Eng. & Swedish.). 1980. Kr.130.00 (ISBN 9-14-030185-0). Liber Gleerup.

Bruzelius, Andre, et al, eds. Concise English-Swedish Dictionary of Legal Terms. 175p. (Eng. & Swedish.). $39.95 (ISBN 0-686-80959-9). French & Eur.

Burke, John. Osborne's Concise Law Dictionary. 6th ed. LC 77-375736. vii, 396p. (Eng.). E3.25 (ISBN 0-421-20820-1). Sweet Max.

Burton, William C. Legal Thesaurus. Trade ed. 1983. $19.95 (ISBN 0-02-691020-9). Macmillan.

Bysiewicz, Shirley R. Monarch's Dictionary of Legal Terms. 192p. (Orig.). 1983. pap. $7.95 (ISBN 0-671-09232-4). Monarch Pr.

Centre de Formation et de Perfectionnement des Journalistes. Petit Lexique des Termes Judiciares: A l'Usage des Journalistes. LC 77-456720. 27p. (Fr.). 1975. write for info. Centre Formation.

Columbia University Law Library, New York. Dictionary Catalog of the Columbia University Law Library, 28 Vols. 1969. Set. lib. bdg. $2750.00 (ISBN 0-8161-0800-5, Hall Library). G K Hall.

Conte, Giuseppe. Woerterbuch der Deutschen und Italienischen Wirtschafts und Rechtssprache, Vol. 1. 2nd ed. (Ital. & Ger.). 1971. $30.00 (ISBN 3-406-01195-0, M-7028). French & Eur.

--Woerterbuch der Deutschen und Italienischen Wirtschafts und Rechtssprache, Vol. 2. 2nd ed. (Ger. & Ital.). 1969. $30.00 (ISBN 3-406-00887-9, M-7027). French & Eur.

Coughlin, George G. Dictionary of Law. 224p. 1982. pap. $5.72i (ISBN 0-06-463539-2, EH-539). Har-Row.

Curzon, L. B. A Dictionary of Law. 384p. 1979. pap. $18.95x (ISBN 0-7121-0380-5, Pub. by Macdonald & Evans England). Intl Ideas.

Decsi, Gyula & Karcsay, Sandor. Woerterbuch der Rechts & Wirtschaftssprache: Teil I, Deutsch-Russisch. (Ger. & Rus.). write for info. Recht & Wirtschaft.

--Woerterbuch der Rechts & Wirtschaftssprache: Teil II, Russisch-Deutsch. (Rus. & Ger.). write for info. Recht & Wirtschaft.

De Pina, Rafael. Diccionario de Derecho. 4th ed. 392p. (Span.). 1975. write for info. Porrua.

Dictionnaire de Droit, 2 vols. 2nd ed. (Fr.). 1966. Set. $17.50 (ISBN 0-686-57096-0, M-6120). French & Eur.

Dictionnaire Juridique: Francais-Italien. (Fr. & Ital.). 80.00 F. Navarre.

Dietl, C. Woerterbuch des Wirtschafts, Rechts und Handelssprache. (Eng. & Ger., Dictionary of Economic, Legal & Commercial Terms). 1970. $33.00 (ISBN 3-87527-003-7, M-6939). French & Eur.

Dietl, Clara E. & Lorenz, Egon. Woerterbuch fuer Recht, Wirtschaft & Politik: Teil II, Deutsch-Englisch. (Ger. & Eng.). 1983. write for info. Recht & Wirtschaft.

Doucet, Michel. Woerterbuch der Deutschen und Franzoesischen Rechtssprache, Vol. 1. 2nd ed. (Ger. & Fr.). 1966. $28.00 (ISBN 3-406-00969-7, M-7030). French & Eur.

--Woerterbuch der Deutschen und Franzoesischen Rechtssprache, Vol. 2. 2nd ed. (Ger. & Fr.). 1977. $54.00 (ISBN 3-406-01196-9, M-7029). French & Eur.

Douret, Michel. Dictionnaire Juridique et Economique, 1: Francais-Allemand. 2nd ed. (Fr. & Ger.). 1967. $39.95 (ISBN 0-686-57122-3, M-6170). French & Eur.

Egbert, Lawrence D. Multilingual Law Dictionary: English, French, Spanish, German. LC 77-25072. 551p. (Eng., Fr., Span. & Ger.). 1978. lib. bdg. 50.00 (ISBN 0-379-00589-1). Oceana.

Eichborn, R. Woerterbuch fuer Wirtschaft-Recht-Verkehr-Verwaltungs & Umgangssprache: Vol.I, Englisch-Deutsch. rev. ed. 1150p. (Eng. & Ger.). 1983. $124.00. M Rosenberg.

--Woerterbuch fuer Wirtschaft-Recht-Verkehr-Verwaltungs & Umgangssprache: Vol. II, Deutch-Englisch. 1150p. (Ger. & Eng.). 1982. $124.00. M Rosenberg.

Faruqi, Harith. Law Dictionary (Arabic-English) 288p. (Arabic & Eng.). 1972. $30.00x (ISBN 0-86685-085-6). Intl Bk Ctr.

--Law Dictionary (English-Arabic) rev. ed. 1972. $35.00x (ISBN 0-86685-065-1). Intl Bk Ctr.

Favata, Angelo. Dizionario dei termini giuridici. 500p. (Ital.). 1978. L.4000.00. La Tribuna.

Finnegan, Edward G., ed. New Webster's Law for Everyone: Vest Pocket Edition. 1980. pap. $1.75 (ISBN 0-8326-0049-0, 6452). Delair.

Fockman, Andreae & Sybrandus, Johannes. Fockema Andreae's Rechtsgeleerd Handwoordenboek. Algra, N. E., rev. by. LC 78-343297. 713p. (Dutch.). 1977. fl.write for info. Tjeenk Willinik.

Geissler, E. A. & Wolff, Lise. Legal Dictionary. 200p. 1980. $45.00x (ISBN 0-686-44720-4, Pub. by Collets). State Mutual Bk.

Gilmer, Wesley. The Law Dictionary. rev. ed. 1981. pap. $6.95 (ISBN 0-684-17329-8, ScribT). Scribner.

Glossaire Europeen de Terminologe Juridique et Administrative: Local Government, No. 14. (Ger, & Eng.). write for info. (M-9481). French & Eur.

Glossaire Europeen de Terminologie Juridique & Administrative: No. 15 Termes de Droit Anglais des Obligations, Anglais-Francais. 36p. (Eng. & Fr.). Date not set. pap. $9.95 (ISBN 0-686-97408-5, M-9482). French & Eur.

Glossaire Europeen de Terminologie Juridque et Administrative. 127p. (Ger. & Eng.). 1973. pap. $14.95 (ISBN 3-468-49068-2, M-9485). French & Eur.

Glossaire Europeen de Terminologie Juridique et Administrative, No. 5. (Organization Administrative). (Fr.). write for info. (M-9601). French & Eur.

Glossaire Europeen de Terminologie Juridique et Administrative: Amenagement du Territiore, No 9. (Fr. & Ger.). write for info. (M-9605). French & Eur.

Glossaire Europeen de Terminologie Juridique et Administrative: Budget, No. 7. (Ger. & Fr.). write for info. (M-9603). French & Eur.

Glossaire Europeen de Terminologie Juridique et Administrative: Civil Service Organizations, No. 22. 83p. (Ger. & Eng.). 1976. pap. $14.95 (ISBN 0-686-92436-3, M-9489). French & Eur.

Glossaire Europeen de Terminologie Juridique et Administrative: Driot Administratif, No. 4. (Et Procedure Contentieuses). (Ger. & Fr.). write for info. (M-9499). French & Eur.

Glossaire Europeen de Terminologie Juridiqe et Administrative: Droits des Collectivites Locales, No. 6. (Ger. & Fr.). write for info. (M-96902). French & Eur.

Glossaire Europeen de Terminologie Juridique et Administrative: Driot de al Fonction Publique, No. 8. (Ger. & Fr.). write for info. (M-9604). French & Eur.

Glossaire Europeen de Terminologie Juridique et Administrative: Droit du Mariage, No. 19. 96p. (Ger. & Fr.). 1973. pap. $14.95 (ISBN 0-686-92449-5, M-9486). French & Eur.

Glossaire Europeen de Terminologie Juridique et Administrative: Droits D'Etablissement, No. 21. 146p. (Ger. & Fr.). 1976. pap. $18.95 (ISBN 0-686-92444-4, M-9488). French & Eur.

Glossaire Europeen de Terminologie Juridique et Administrative: Eductions et Enseignment, No. 23. 168p. (Ger. & Fr.). pap. $18.95 (ISBN 0-686-92507-6, M-9490). French & Eur.

Glossaire Europeen de Terminologie Juridique et Administrative: Environment Policy Protection & Management of the Environment, No. 29. 160p. (Ger. & Eng.). pap. $22.50 (ISBN 0-686-92511-4, M-9496). French & Eur.

Glossaire Europeen de Terminologie Juridique et Administrative: Jeunesse, No. 11. (Allemand-Francais Ser.). 109p. (Ger. & Fr.). 1972. pap. $12.95 (ISBN 0-686-92456-8, M-9478). French & Eur.

Glossaire Europeen de Terminologie Juridique et Administrative: Local Government, No. 20. 96p. (Ger. & Ital.). 1975. pap. $14.95 (ISBN 0-686-92446-0). French & Eur.

Glossaire Europeen de Terminologie Juridique et Administrative: Law of Establishment, No. 13. 100p. (Fr.). 1973. pap. $12.95 (ISBN 0-686-92453-3, M-9480). French & Eur.

Glossaire Europeen de Terminologie Juridique et Administrative: Marches Publics, No. 10. 72p. (Ger. & Fr.). 1972. pap. $12.95 (ISBN 0-686-92459-2, M-9479). French & Eur.

Glossaire Europeen de Terminologie Juridique et Administrative: Renumeration, No. 3. (Ger. & Fr.). write for info. (M-9498). French & Eur.

Glossaire Europeen de Terminologie Juridique et Administrative: Regional Policy, Ger. & Ital. 111p. (Fr.). write for info. (M-9484). French & Eur.

Glossaire Europeen de Terminologie Juridique et Administrative: Terminologie Administrative et Secretariat, No. 1. (Ger. & Fr.). write for info. (M-9495). French & Eur.

Glossaire Europeen de Terminologie Juridique et Administrative: Terminologie de Reunions, No. 2. (Ger, & Ital.). write for info. (M-9497). French & Eur.

Goehler, Erich. Lexikon des Nebenstrafrechts. 2nd ed. (Ger.). 1977. pap. $44.00 (ISBN 3-406-01806-8, M-7245). French & Eur.

Gordon, Frank S. & Hemnes, Thomas. The Legal Word Book. 1978. 7.95 (ISBN 0-395-26662-9). HM.

Gould Editorial Dept. Dictionary of Criminal Justice Terms. 500p. 1982. text ed. 8.95 looseleaf (ISBN 0-87526-276-7). Gould.

Grapp, Valera. Paralegal's Encyclopedic Dictionary. 1979. 29.50 (ISBN 0-13-648675-4). P-H.

Gritschneder, Otto. Ullstein Lexikon des Rechts. (Ger.). 1971. $20.00 (ISBN 3-550-06018-1, M-7677, Pub. by Ullstein Verlag/VVA). French & Eur.

Gubba, W. Jurdisk Ordbog. LC 79-366377. 72p. (Ger. & Danish.). 1978. write for info. Guba.

--Juridisk Ordbog, Dansk-Tysk: Supplement & Forkortelsesliste. 68p. (Danish & Ger.). 1978. write for info. Guba.

Guillen, Raymond & Vincent, Jean, eds. Lexique de Termes Juridiques. 4th ed. LC 78-381853. viii, 406p. (Fr.). 1978. 30.00 F (ISBN 2-247-01448-8). Dalloz.

Hemphill, Charles F., Jr. & Hemphill, Phyllis. Dictionary of Practical Law. 1979. text ed. 12.95 (ISBN 0-13-210567-5, Spec); pap. text ed. 4.95 (ISBN 0-13-210559-4). P-H.

Herbst, R. Dictionary of Commercial, Financial & Legal Terms, 3 vols. (Eng., Fr & Ger.). $98.60 ea.; Vol. I. (ISBN 3-85942-000-3); Vol. II. (ISBN 3-85942-006-2); Vol. III. Adler.

--Dictionary of Commercial, Financial & Legal Terms, 3 Vols. (Eng, Fr, & Ger.). Set. $330.00 (ISBN 0-686-76877-9); Vol. 1. $125.00 ea. (ISBN 3-8594-2000-3). Vol. 2 (ISBN 3-8594-2006-2). Vol. 3 (ISBN 3-8594-2002-X). Heinman.

Herbst, Robert. Dictionary of Commerce, Finance & Law. (Eng. & Ger.). 1975. $92.00 (ISBN 3-85942-003-8, M-7118). French & Eur.

--Woerterbuch der Handels, Finanz und Rechtssprache. 2nd ed. (Ger., Eng. & Fr., Dictionary of Commercial, Fininancial & Legal Terms). 1975. $92.00 (ISBN 3-85942-001-1, M-7002). French & Eur.

Herbst, Robert & Readett, Alan G. The Herbst Dictionaries of Commercial, Financial & Legal Terms: English-German. (The Two-Language Ser.: Vol. A). 688p. (Eng. & Ger.). 1975. text ed. $69.95 (ISBN 0-686-92254-9). Birkhauser.

--The Herbst Dictionaries of Commercial, Financial & Legal Terms Vol. I. (The Herbst Dictionaries; 3-Language Ser.). 1138p. (Eng., Ger. & Fr.). 1979. text ed. $98.95 (ISBN 3-85942-000-3). Birkhauser.

Herbst, Robert & Readett, Alan G., eds. The Herbst Dictionaries of Commercial, Financial & Legal Terms: Deutsch-Englisch. (The Two-Language Ser.: Vol. B). 906p. (Ger. & Eng.). 1976. text ed. $69.95x (ISBN 0-686-92258-1). Birkhauser.
--The Herbst Dictionaries of Commercial, Financial & Legal Terms Vol. 2. (The Herbst Dictioaries; 3-Language Ser.). 1106p. (Ger., Eng. & Fr.). 1979. text ed. $98.95 (ISBN 3-85942-006-2). Birkhauser.
--Herbst Dictionary of Commercial, Financial & Legal Terms. (Three-Language Ser.: Vol. 3). 980p. (Fr., Eng. & Ger.). 1979. text ed. $98.95 (ISBN 3-85942-002-X). Birkhauser.
--Herbst Dictionay of Commercial, Financial & Legal Terms. (Two-Language Ser.: Vol. A). 688p. (Eng. & Ger.). 1975. text ed. $69.95 (ISBN 0-686-97268-6). Birkhauser.
Hung, W. S. A New English-Chinese Law Dictionary. 162p. (Eng. & Chinese.). 1979. $17.50 (ISBN 962-204-001-2, M-9558). French & Eur.
Hung, William. A New English-Chinese Law Dictionary. LC 80-113867. 162p. (Eng. & Chinese.). 1979. HK.$60.00 (ISBN 9-622-04001-2). M Stevenson.
Jordana de Pozas, Luis & Merlin, Olivier. Dictionnaire Juridique, Francais-Espagnol, Espagnol-Francais. 608p. (Fr. & Span.). 1968. $45.00 (ISBN 0-686-57112-6, M-6148). French & Eur.
Jowitt, William A. Jowitt's Dictionary of English Law. 2nd ed. LC 78-302082. vii, 1935p. 1977. write for info. (ISBN 0-421-23090-8). Sweet & Maxwell.
Karcsay, Sandor. Ungarisch-Deutsches Woerterbuch der Rechts & Verwaltungssprache: Teil I, Ungarisch-Deutsch. xix, 487p. (Hungarian & Ger.). 1969. DM.48.00. Recht & Wirtschaft.
--Ungarisch-Deutsches Woerterbuch der Rechts & Verwaltungssprache: Teil II, Deutsch-Ungarisch. xvii, 427p. (Ger. & Hungarian.). 1972. DM.48.00. Recht & Wirtschaft.
--Woerterbuch der Ungarischen Rechts und Verwaltungssprache, Vol. 1. 2nd ed. (Ger. & Hungarian.). 1969. $38.00 (ISBN 3-406-03325-3, M-6947). French & Eur.
Keyes, W. Noel. Keyes Encyclopedic Dictionary of Procurement Law: Definitions of Legal Terms & Concepts in Private Procurement & Public Procurement of Federal, State & Local Governments, Their Contractors & Subcontractors. LC 75-9984. 500p. 1976. text ed. 100.00x looseleaf (ISBN 0-379-00311-2); suppl. 20.00 ea. Oceana.
Kniepkamp, H. P. Legal Dictionary. (Ger. & Eng.). $26.50 (ISBN 3-7678-0013-6). Adler.
Langendorf, Hans. Legal Dictionary: Part 1, Dutch-German. 365p. (Dutch & Ger.). 1977. $26.00 (ISBN 90-26-8070-74). Kluwer Academic.
--Woerterbuch der Deutschen & Niederlaendischen Rechtssprache: Lexikon fuer Justiz, Verwaltung, Wirtschaft & Handel. LC 78-376399. (Ger. & Dutch.). 1976. DM.55.00 (ISBN 3-406-06672-0). Kluwer Group.
--Woerterbuch der Deutschen und Nierderlaendischen Rechtssprache, Vol. 1. (Dutch & Ger.). 1976. $44.00 (ISBN 3-406-06672-0, M-7025). French & Eur.
--Woerterbuch der Deutschen und Nierderlaendischen Rechtssprache, Vol. 2. (Dutch & Ger.). 1976. $44.00 (ISBN 3-406-06673-9, M-7026). French & Eur.
Langendorf, Hans & Stein, P. A. Woerterbuch der Recht & Wirtschaftssprache: Teil I, Niederlandisch-Deutsch. 365p. (Dutch & Ger.). 1976. DM.55.00. Recht & Wirtschaft.
--Woerterbuch der Rechts & Wirtschaftssprache: Teil II, Deutsch-Niederlaendisch. 365p. (Ger. & Dutch.). 1976. DM.55.00. Recht & Wirtschaft.
Law Dictionary for Laymen. LC 80-65097. 1980. write for info. (ISBN 0-89648-074-7); pap. write for info. (ISBN 0-89648-075-5). Citizens Law.
Le Docte, E. Dictionnaire des Termes Juridique en Quartre Langues: Francais, Neerlandais, Anglais, Allemand. (Fr., Dutch, Eng. & Ger.). 1978. $95.00 (ISBN 0-686-57008-1, M-6349). French & Eur.
--Dictionnaire des Termes Juridiques en Quatre Langues: Francais-Neerlandais-Anglais-Allemand. (Fr., Dutch, Eng. & Ger.). 1978. 240.00 F. Vander Oyez.
Le Docte, E., ed. Legal Dictionary in Four Languages. 2nd ed. 696p. 1978. 75.00x (ISBN 0-8377-0808-7). Oyez.
--Legal Dictionary in Four Languages. 2nd ed. xix, 696p. 1978. lib. bdg. 80.00x. Rothman.
Lexikon des Rechts. 3706p. (Ger.). 1978. write for info. H Luchterhand.
Luggauer, Karl. Der Wortschatz des Juristen: Ein Lern & Lesebuch Juristischen Sprachausdrucks. LC 76-465150. 206p. (Ger.). 1976. write for info. (ISBN 3-853-66138-6). Heyn.
Matteucci, M. Dictionnaire Juridique. (Fr.-It.). $39.95 (ISBN 0-686-57042-1, M-6402). French & Eur.
Mayrand, Albert. Dictionnaire de Maximes & Locutions Latines Utilisees en Droit Quebecois. 235p. (Fr.). 1972. Can.$8.95. Guerin.
Menghi, A. Nuovo dizionario di terminologia giuridica. 308p. (Ital.). 1977. L.4500.00. Cortina M.
Merlin, Olivier. Dictionnaire Juridique: Francais-Espagnol. 608p. (Fr. & Span.). 1968. 100.00 F. Navarre.
Millet, Robert. Dictionnaire de la Loi. 176p. (Fr.). 1965. 2.50 F. Homme.
Murray, John. The Media Law Dictionary. LC 78-63257. 1978. pap. text ed. $8.00 (ISBN 0-8191-0616-X). U Pr of Amer.
Najjar. Law Dictionary French-Arabic: Dictionnaire Juridique. (Arabic & Fr.). 1983. $40.00x (ISBN 0-86685-303-0). Intl Bk Ctr.
Neumann, Hugo. Dictionnaire Juridique Francais-Allemand, Allemand-Francais. Quemner, Thomas A., ed. 592p. (Fr.-Ger.). 1964. $59.95 (ISBN 0-686-57058-8, M-6425). French & Eur.
Norton-Kyshe, J. W. Dictionary of Legal Quotations. 75.00 (ISBN 0-8490-0037-8). Gordon Pr.
Norton-Kyshe, James W. Dictionary of Legal Quotations. LC 68-30648. 1968. Repr. of 1904 ed. $34.00x (ISBN 0-8103-3189-6). Gale.
Oran, Daniel. Oran's Dictionary of the Law. 333p. 1980. pap. text ed. $6.95 (ISBN 0-8299-2062-5). West Pub.
--Oran's Dictionary of the Law. New ed. (Illus.). 512p. 1982. pap. $9.95 (ISBN 0-314-68800-5). West Pub.
Palermo, Antonio & Palermo, Carlo. Dizionario giuridico del lavoro e delle assicurazioni sociali. 1550p. (Ital.). 1972. L.15000.00. La Tribuna.
Pallares, Eduardo. Diccionario Teorico y Practico del Juicio de Amparo. 321p. (Span.). $17.50 (ISBN 0-686-56705-6, S-21916). French & Eur.
Parsenow, Gunther. Fachwoerterbuch Fur Recht und Wirtschaft. 504p. (Swedish & Ger.). 1975. $68.00 (ISBN 3-452-18010-7, M-7399, Pub. by Carl Heymanns Verlag KG). French & Eur.
Pina, Rafael de. Diccionario de Derecho. 355p. (Span.). $25.95 (ISBN 0-686-56688-2, S-12345). French & Eur.
Potonnier. Woerterbuch fuer Wirtschaft, Recht & Handel: Band I, Deutsch-Franzoesisch. 1616p. (Ger. & Fr.). 1982. DM.130.00. Brandstetter.
--Woerterbuch fuer Wirtschaft, Recht & Handel: Band II, Franzoesisch-Deutsch. 1502p. (Fr. & Ger.). 1982. DM.100.00. Brandstetter.
Potonnier, Georges. Woerterbuch fuer Wirtschaft: Recht und Handel, Vol. 1. (Ger. & Fr.). 1970. $56.00 (ISBN 3-87097-030-8, M-6919). French & Eur.
--Woerterbuch fuer Wirtschaft: Recht und Handel, Vol. 2. (Fr. & Ger.). 1970. $80.00 (ISBN 3-87097-031-6, M-6918). French & Eur.
Potonnier, Georges E. & Potonnier, Brigitte. Woerterbuch Wirtschaft Recht Handel: Deutsch-Franzoesisch, Vol. 1. 2nd, rev. ed. 1616p. (Ger. & Fr.). 1982. 430.00 F. Maison Dictionnaire.
--Woerterbuch Wirtschaft Recht Handel: Deutsch-Franzoesisch, Vol. 2. 1486p. (Fr. & Ger.). 1970. 330.00 F. Maison Dictionnaire.
Quemner. Dictionnaire Juridique Francais-Anglais, Anglais-Francais, 2 vols. in 1. (Fr. & Eng.). $75.00 (ISBN 0-685-36688-X). French & Eur.
Quemner, T. A. French-English, English-French Legal Dictionary. new ed. Baleyte, Jean & Kurgansky, Alexander, eds. (Fr. & Eng.). 75.00 (ISBN 0-685-01106-2). Heinman.
Quemner, Thomas A. Dictionnaire Juridique: Frances-Allemand. 592p. (Fr. & Ger.). 1964. 130.00 F. Navarre.
--Legal Dictionary: French-English & English-French. (Fr. & Eng.). 1969. 62.50x (ISBN 0-8002-1647-4). Intl Pubns Serv.
Radin, Max & Greene, Lawrence G., eds. Law Dictionary. 2nd, rev. ed. LC 74-123997. (Illus.). 1970. 17.50 (ISBN 0-379-00465-8). Oceana.
Ramirez Gronda, J. D. Diccionario juridico. 6th ed. 328p. (Span.). Arg.$12.00. Claridad.
Redden, Kenneth R. & Veron, Enid L. Modern Legal Glossary. 576p. 1980. 19.00 (ISBN 0-87215-237-5). Michie Co.
Reifferscheid, Adolph & Benseler, Frank. Lexikon des Rechts. 4947p. (Ger.). 1978. DM.80.00. H Luchterhand.
Renner, R. & Tooth, J. Rechtssprache Englisch-Deutsch. 526p. (Ger.). 1971. $35.00 (ISBN 3-19-006280-3, M-7597, Pub. by M. Hueber). French & Eur.
--Rechtssprache Englisch-Deutsch. 526p. (Ger.). 1971. $35.00 (ISBN 3-19-006280-3). Hueber.
Robb, Louis A. Diccionario de Terminos Legales Espanol-Ingles e Ingles-Espanol: Spanish-English, English-Spanish Dictionary of Legal Terms. (Span. & Eng.). pap. 14.95 (ISBN 0-88332-134-3). Larousse.
--Dictionary of Legal Terms: Spanish-English,English-Spanish. (Span. & Eng.). 1976. pap. 10.95x (ISBN 968-18-0384-1). Intl Learn Syst.
Rodd, Louis. Diccionario de terminos legales. (Span. & Eng.). $7.95. Iaconi.
Romain, Alfred. Dictionary of German & English Legal & Economic Terminology, Vol. 1. (Eng. & Ger.). 1976. $78.00 (ISBN 3-406-03370-9, M-7101). French & Eur.
--Dictionary of German & English Legal & Economic Terminology, Vol. 2. (Ger. & Fr.). 1975. $78.00 (ISBN 3-406-03371-7, M-7100). French & Eur.
--Woerterbuch der Rechts & Wirtschaftssprache: Teil II, Deutsch-Englisch. viii, 848p. (Ger. & Eng.). 1980. DM.138.00. Recht & Wirtschaft.
--Woerterbuch der Rechts & Wirtschaftssprache: Teil I, Englisch-Deutsch. viii, 760p. (Eng. & Ger.). 1979. DM.98.00. Recht & Wirtschaft.
Roshton, M. Legal Secretary's Concise Dictionary. 1974. $5.50 (ISBN 0-685-42669-6). Claitors.
Rothenberg, Robert. The Plain-Language Law Dictionary. (Reference Ser.). 1981. pap. 7.95 (ISBN 0-14-051109-1). Penguin.
Roucka, Bohuslav. Pracovni Heslar Ceskeho Pravnehistorickeho Terminologickeho Slovniku. LC 78-366665. ii, 773p. (Czech., Prague). 1975. write for info. Ustav Statu a Prava Ceskoslovenske Akademie Ved.
Sprudzs, Adolf. Italian Abbreviations & Symbols: Law & Related Subjects. LC 70-95307. 124p. 1969. $20.00 (ISBN 0-379-00451-8). Oceana.
Sturgess, H. & Hewitt, A. A Dictionary of Legal Terms & Citations. 75.00 (ISBN 0-87968-408-9). Gordon Pr.
Touati, Maurice A. Lexique Francais De la Reparation Juridique Du Dommage Corporel. 268p. (Fr.). 1976. $32.50 (ISBN 0-686-57233-5, M-6534). French & Eur.
Trioke-Strambaci, H. & Helffrich-Mariani, E. Woerterbuch des Italienisch-Deutschen Privat & Wirtschaftsrechts: Band I, Deutsch-Italienisch. xix, 1332p. (Ger. & Ital.). 1982. DM.148.00. Recht & Wirtschaft.
Troike-Strambaci, H. & Helffrich-Mariani, E. Woerterbuch des Italienisch-Deutschen Privat & Wirtschaftsrechts: Band II, Italienish-Deutsch. xix, 1332p. (Ital. & Ger.). 1982. DM.148.00. Recht & Wirtschaft.
Velden, F. J. Beknopt Juridisch Woordenboek Frans-Nederlands. LC 78-349929. viii, 140p. (Dutch & Fr.). 1977. write for info. (ISBN 9-026-80975-1). Kluwer Group.
Woerterbuch der Ungarischen Rechts und Verwaltungssprache, Vol. 2. 2nd ed. (Ger. & Hungarian.). 1972. $38.00 (ISBN 3-406-03326-1, M-6946). French & Eur.
Yogis, John. Law Dictionary: The Canadian Edition. (Barron's Educational Ser.). (Orig.). 1983. pap. text ed. $6.95 (ISBN 0-8120-2116-9). Barron.
Zedtwitz, Hans G. Juridicia Lexikon: Das Kleine Oesterreicher Rechtswoerterbuch. LC 75-590427. 223p. (Ger.). 1974. S.175.00. Juridica Verlag.

LAW–DIRECTORIES
see Lawyers–Directories

LAW–LANGUAGE

Bander, Edward J. Dictionary of Selected Legal Terms & Maxims, Vol. 58. 2nd ed. LC 79-19266. (Legal Almanac Ser.: No. 58). 140p. 1979. 5.95 (ISBN 0-379-11119-5). Oceana.
Chaudhary, Abdul G. The Law Latin Lexicon. LC 79-930806. 248p. (Eng. & Lat.). 1979. Rs.35.00. Khyber Law Publishers.
Gilmer, Wesley. Cochran's Law Lexicon. 5th ed. LC 72-95860. 429p. 1973. Repr. text ed. $9.00 (ISBN 0-87084-148-3). Anderson Pub Co.

LAW–PRACTICE
see Procedure (Law)

LAW–TERMS AND PHRASES

Alessandrino, Igino. Dizionario delle contravvenzioni. xvi, 640p. (Ital.). L.9000.00. Patron.
American Association for State & Local History. Glossary of Legal Terminology: An Aid to Geneologists. $1.00 (55); members $0.75. AASLH.
Beseler, D. & Jacobs, B. Technical Dictionary of Anglo-American Legal Terminology. 3rd ed. 385p. (Ger. & Eng.). 1971. $110.00 (ISBN 3-11-002187-0, M-7636, Pub. by de Gruyter). French & Eur.
Bieber, Doris M. Dictionary of Legal Abbreviations Used in American Law Books. LC 78-60173. 337p. 1979. lib. bdg. $19.50 (ISBN 0-930342-61-5); pap. text ed. $7.95 (ISBN 0-930342-96-8). W S Hein.
Bruzelius, Andre, et al, eds. Concise English-Swedish Dictionary of Legal Terms. 175p. (Eng. & Swedish.). $39.95 (ISBN 0-686-80959-9). French & Eur.

Burton, William C. & DeCosta, Steven E. The Legal Thesaurus. LC 80-83803. 1980. $35.00 (ISBN 0-02-691000-4). Free Pr.

Bysiewicz, Shirley R. Monarch's Dictionary of Legal Terms. 192p. (Orig.). 1983. pap. $7.95 (ISBN 0-671-09232-4). Monarch Pr.

Dictionary of Law. rev. ed. LC 75-40443. 144p. 1976. lib. bdg. 12.90 (ISBN 0-914294-44-X); pap. 3.95 (ISBN 0-914294-43-1). Running Pr.

Dictionary of Legal Terms. (Eng. & Span.). write for info. Lectorum Pubns.

Dietl, C. Woerterbuch des Wirtschafts, Rechts und Handelssprache. (Eng. & Ger., Dictionary of Economic, Legal & Commercial Terms). 1970. $33.00 (ISBN 3-87527-003-7, M-6939). French & Eur.

Glass, G. Englische Rechtssprache: Mustertexte & Fachausdruecke unter Einbeziehung von Amerikanismen. 80p. (Eng. & Ger.). 1982. DM.24.00 (ISBN 3-7625-1487-9). Bauverlag.

Guillien, Raymond & Vincent, Jean. Lexique des Termes Juridiques. 3rd ed. 354p. (Fr.). 1978. pap. $14.95 (ISBN 0-686-57321-8, M-6304). French & Eur.

Heimanson, Rudolph. Dictionary of Political Science & Law. LC 67-14401. 188p. 1967. 12.00 (ISBN 0-379-00325-2). Oceana.

Herbst, R. Dictionary of Commericial, Financial & Legal Terms in Two Languages. (Eng. & Ger.). $78.25 ea. Vol. A, Eng. & Ger. Vol. B, Ger. & Eng (ISBN 3-85942-004-6). Adler.

Herbst, Robert. Woerterbuch der Handels, Finanz und Rechtssprache. 2nd ed. (Ger., Eng. & Fr., Dictionary of Commercial, Fininancial & Legal Terms). 1975. $92.00 (ISBN 3-85942-001-1, M-7002). French & Eur.

Hexner, Erwin. Studies in Legal Terminology. vi, 150p. 1981. Repr. of 1941 ed. lib. bdg. 20.00x (ISBN 0-8377-0635-1). Rothman.

Menghi, A. Nuovo Dizionario di Terminologia Giuridica. (Ital.). 1979. pap. $25.00 (ISBN 0-686-92407-X, M-(354). French & Eur.

Renner, Ruediger & Tooth, Jeffery. Legal Terminology English & German. (Eng. & Ger.). 1971. $38.50 (ISBN 3-1900-6280-3). Adler.

--Legal Terminology English-German. 526p. (Eng. & Ger.). 1971. 22.50x (ISBN 3-19-006280-3). Intl Pubns Serv.

Robb, Louis A. Diccionario de terminos legales espanol-ingles e ingles-espanol. 228p. (Span. & Eng.). Mex.$3.20; $40.00. Limusa.

--Diccionario de Terminos Legales, Espanol-Ingles. 228p. (Span. & Eng.). 1967. Mex.$4.50. Limusa.

--Diccionario de Terminos Legales Espanol-Ingles. 228p. (Span. & Eng.). pap. $8.95 (LIM). Lectorum Pubns.

--Dictionary of Legal Terms, Spanish-English & English-Spanish. (Span. & Eng.). 1955. $27.95 (ISBN 0-471-72534-X, Pub. by Wiley-Interscience). Wiley.

Romain, Alfred. Dictionary of German & English Legal & Economic Terminology, Vol. 1. (Eng. & Ger.). 1976. $78.00 (ISBN 3-406-03370-9, M-7101). French & Eur.

--Dictionary of German & English Legal & Economic Terminology, Vol. 2. (Ger. & Fr.). 1975. $78.00 (ISBN 3-406-03371-7, M-7100). French & Eur.

Ross, Louis A. Diccionario de Terminos Legales Espanol-Ingles. (Span. & Eng.). $7.30. Camino Real.

Shorthand Guide to Legal Terminology. 1982 ed. 700p. 7.00. Gould.

Volkell, Randolph Z. Quick Legal Terminology. LC 79-13647. (Self-Teaching Guides Ser.). 1979. pap. text ed. $7.50 (ISBN 0-471-03786-9, Pub. by Wiley Pr.). Wiley.

LAW–BELGIUM
Sprudzs, Adolf. Benelux Abbreviations & Symbols: Law & Related Subjects. LC 74-140620. 129p. 1971. lib. bdg. $20.00 (ISBN 0-379-00120-9). Oceana.

LAW–CANADA
Page, Dominique. Petit Dictionnaire de Droit Quebecois & Canadien. LC 77-476465. 165p. (Fr.). 1975. Can.$write for info. (ISBN 0-7755-0542-0). Fides.

LAW–FRANCE
Ragueau, Francois. Glossaire du Droit Francais. 616p. (Fr.). 1969. 150.00 F. Slatkine.

LAW–NORWAY
Gulbransen, Egil. Juridisk Leksikon. LC 78-376208. 237p. (Norwegian). 1977. Kr.79.00 (ISBN 8-251-80150-8). Tanum-Norli.

LAW–SPAIN
Lopez de Haro, Carlos. Diccionario de Reglas, Aforismos & Principios de Derecho. LC 77-452232. 254p. (Span.). 1975. 450.00 ptas (ISBN 8-429-00609-5). Reus SA.

Yanguas & Miranda, Jose. Diccionario de los fueros & leyes de Navarra. 377p. (Span.). 300.00 ptas. pap. 230.00 ptas. Aranzadi Edit.

LAW–UNITED STATES
Coughlin, George G. Dictionary of Law. 224p. 1982. pap. $5.72i (ISBN 0-06-463539-2, EH-539). Har-Row.

LAW–UNITED STATES–BIBLIOGRAPHY
Gifis, Steven H. Law Dictionary. rev. ed. LC 74-18126. 240p. 1975. pap. $4.95 (ISBN 0-8120-0543-0). Barron.

LAW, ADMINISTRATIVE
see Administrative Law
LAW, AGRICULTURAL
see Agricultural Laws and Legislation
LAW, ANGLO-AMERICAN
see Law–United States
LAW, BANKING
see Banking Law
LAW, BUSINESS
see Business Law
LAW, CIVIL
see Civil Law
LAW, COMMERCIAL
see Commercial Law
LAW, CONSTITUTIONAL
see Constitutional Law
LAW, CRIMINAL
see Criminal Law
LAW, ECCLESIASTICAL
see Ecclesiastical Law
LAW, HINDU
see Hindu Law
LAW, INDUSTRIAL
see Labor Laws and Legislation
LAW, INTERNATIONAL
see International Law
LAW, LABOR
see Labor Laws and Legislation
LAW, MARITIME
see Maritime Law
LAW, MEDICAL
see Medical Laws and Legislation
LAW, MERCHANT
see Commercial Law
LAW, MILITARY
see Military Law
LAW, PUBLIC
see Public Law
LAW, ROMAN
see Roman Law
LAW AND SCIENCE
see Science and Law
LAW BOOKS
see Law–Bibliography; Legal Literature
LAW ENFORCEMENT OFFICERS
Martin, Julian A. Law Enforcement Vocabulary. 262p. 1973. $13.75x (ISBN 0-398-02599-1). C C Thomas.

Seitzinger, Jack M. & Kelley, Thomas M. Police Terminology: Programmed Manual for Criminal Justice Personnel. (Illus.). 152p. 1974. spiral $11.75x (ISBN 0-398-02947-4). C C Thomas.

LAW LIBRARIES
Columbia University Law Library, New York. Dictionary Catalog of the Columbia University Law Library, First Supplement, 7 vols. 1973. Set. lib. bdg. $900.00 (ISBN 0-8161-0802-1, Hall Library). G K Hall.

LAW LISTS
see Lawyers–Directories
LAW OF NATIONS
see International Law
LAW OF THE SEA
see Maritime Law
LAWBOOKS
see Law–Bibliography; Legal Literature
LAWN TENNIS
see Tennis
LAWYERS–DIRECTORIES
Roessler, Rudolf. Woerterbuch des Steuerrechts. (Ger.). 1971. $54.00 (ISBN 3-448-00204-6, M-6934). French & Eur.

LAYOUT
see Printing–Layout and Typography
LEARNING, PSYCHOLOGY OF
see also Conditioned Response; Learning Disabilities
Welles, E. R. The Learning Incorporated Dictionary of Learning Handicaps. 3rd ed. 1970. prepaid 1.00 ea. (ISBN 0-913692-01-8). Learning Inc.

LEARNING DISABILITIES
see also Reading Disability
Bush, Clifford L. & Andrews, Robert C. Dictionary of Reading & Learning Disabilities. LC 79-57293. 179p. 1978. pap. $13.40x (ISBN 0-87424-153-7). Western Psych.

Manset & Maine. The Learning Inc. Dictionary of Learning Handicaps. $0.75. Assn Child & Adult Learn.

LEARNING DISORDERS
see Learning Disabilities
LEATHER INDUSTRY AND TRADE
see also Bookbinding; Boots and Shoes
Rama, Louis. Dictionnaire Technique de la Maroquinerie. (Illus.). xxxviii, 532p. (Fr.). 1975. write for info. Centre Technique.

LEBANON–DESCRIPTION AND TRAVEL
Freyha, Annis. Arabic-Arabic Dictionary of the Names of Towns & Villages in Lebanon. 1974. $16.00x (ISBN 0-86685-099-6). Intl Bk Ctr.

LEBANON–HISTORY
Freyha, Anis. Dictionary of Modern Lebanese Proverbs. (Arabic & Eng.). 1974. $25.00x (ISBN 0-86685-086-4). Intl Bk Ctr.

--A Dictionary of the Names of Towns & Villages in Lebanon. 210p. (Arabic). $16.00 (099-6). Intl Bk Ctr.

LEBANON–SOCIAL LIFE AND CUSTOMS
Freyha, Anis. A Dictionary of Modern Lebanese Proverbs. 758p. (Arabic & Eng.). 1974. $25.00 (ISBN 0-86685-086-4, 086-4). Intl Bk Ctr.

LEBESGUE MEASURE
see Measure Theory
LEGAL ABBREVIATIONS
see Law–Abbreviations
LEGAL BIBLIOGRAPHY
see Law–Bibliography
LEGAL CITATION
see Citation of Legal Authorities
LEGAL CITATIONS
see Annotations and Citations (Law)
LEGAL DIRECTORIES
see Lawyers–Directories
LEGAL LANGUAGE
see Law–Language
LEGAL LITERATURE
see also Law–Bibliography
Legal Terms. $1.30 (P6). Am Classical.

LEGAL PROCEDURE
see Procedure (Law)
LEGAL PSYCHOLOGY
see Psychology, Forensic
LEGAL STYLE
see Law–Language
LEGENDS, GUATEMALAN
Carvalho Neto, Paulo de. Diccionario d Teoria Folklorica. (Span.). 1977. $13.50. Intl Guatemala.

LEGENDS, INDIAN
see Indians of North America–Legends
LEGENDS, IRISH
Coghlan, Ronan. Dictionary of Irish Myth & Legend. LC 80-497675. (Gaelic). 1979. Epap. 1.80 (ISBN 0-9505767-1-9). Donard Pub Co.

LEGENDS, MAORI
see Legends, Polynesian

LEGENDS, POLYNESIAN
Williams, H. W. Dictionary of the Maori Language. 500p. (Maori). 1975. $7.50. Govern.

LEGERDEMAIN
see Magic
LEGION OF MARY
Diccionario de Legislacion de Navarra, Vol. 2. (Span.). 1981. pap. 2800.00 ptas (ISBN 84-235-0514-6). Diput Foral.

LEGISLATION
see also Law
also legislation on particular subjects; e.g. Factory Laws and Legislation
Diccionario de legislacion. (Span.). 8750.00 ptas. pap. 8000.00 ptas. Apendice 1951-66. 13140.00 ptas. pap. 11520.00 ptas. Aranzadi Edit.

Diccionario de legislacion administrativa y fiscal de Navarra. 1912p. (Span.). 1969. 1600.00 ptas. Apendice 1969-70. 200.00 ptas. Apendice 1970-71. 180.00 ptas. Aranzadi Edit.

Diccionario Esedal de la legislacion peruana. 552p. (Span.). 1972. S/200.00. Esedal.

Klost, Walter. Arbeitsschutzlexikon. LC 80-465045. (Illus.). 186p. (Ger.). 1979. write for info. Verlag Moderne.

LENAPE LANGUAGE
see Delaware Language
LENNI LENAPE LANGUAGE
see Delaware Language
LENSLESS PHOTOGRAPHY
see Holography
LEPCHA LANGUAGE
Mainwaring, G. B. & Grunwedal, Albert, eds. Dictionary of the Lepcha language. LC 80-905482. xvi, 552p. (Lepcha). 1979. Rs.130.00. Radha.

LESOTHO
Haliburton, Gordon. Historical Dictionary of Lesotho. LC 76-49550. (African Historical Dictionaries Ser.: No. 10). (Illus.). 1977. $15.00 (ISBN 0-8108-0993-1). Scarecrow.

LETTERS
Lexique des Lettres Commerciales en Quatre Langues, 3 vols. 735p. (Fr.). 1972. 260.00 F. Multi Ling Verlag A. G.

Zavada. Satzlexikon der Handelskorrespondenz. 356p. (Ger. & Eng.). 1982. DM.25.00. Brandstetter.

Zavada & Eberle. Satzlexikon der Handelskorrespondenz. 435p. (Ger. & Port.). 1982. DM.30.00. Brandstetter.

Zavada & Hartgenbush. Satzlexikon der Handelskorrespondenz. 430p. (Ger. & Fr.). 1982. DM.30.00. Brandstetter.

Zavada & Schraffl. Satzlexikon der Handelskorrespondenz. 388p. (Ger. & Ital.). 1982. DM.30.00. Brandstetter.

Zavada & Weis. Satzlexikon der Handelskorrespondenz. 405p. (Ger. & Span.). 1982. DM.30.00. Brandstetter.

LETTERS OF THE ALPHABET
see Alphabet
LEXICOGRAPHY
see also Encyclopedias and Dictionaries–History and Criticism; Language and Languages–Etymology
Dictionaries, Vols. II-III. (J). 1980-81. $14.00. Dict Soc NA.

Dictionaries, Vol. 1. 164p. (J). 1979. $9.00. Dict Soc NA.

Gili Gaya, Samuel. Tesoro Lexicografico 1492-1726. 712p. (Span.). 1974. 240.00 ptas. $260.00. CSIS.

Glossarium Harlemense: Circa 1440. (Monumenta Lexicographica Neelandica, Ser. I: Vol. I). 422p. 1973. text ed. 120.00x (ISBN 0-686-27746-5). Mouton.

Guckler, Gudrun. Zweisprachiges Woerterbuch fuer Angenaeherte Operationelle Analyse. LC 75-522118. x, 300p. (Ger.). 1975. write for info. (ISBN 3-878-08053-0). Narr.

Hartmann, R. R., ed. Dictionaries & Their Users. (Papers from the 1978 Seminar on Lexicography). 1979. pap. $20.00 (ISBN 0-686-46740-X). Heinman.

Lexicologie & Lexicographie Francaises & Romanes. 294p. (Fr. & Ital.). 1959. 42.00 F (ISBN 2-22200-359-8). CNRS.

National Conference on Dictionary Making in Indian Languages & Misra, Bal G. Lexicography in India. LC 81-901003. xv, 253p. (Indic.). 1970. 27.00 Rub. Central Institute of Indian Languages.

LEXICOLOGY
see also Semantics; Vocabulary
Guilbert, Louis. La Creativite lexicale. (Collection langue et langage). 285p. (Fr.). 1975. pap. $23.95 (ISBN 2-03-070340-0). Larousse.
Hirschelmann, Ferdinand. Meyers Grosses Jahreslexikon. 328p. (Ger.). 1981. write for info. (ISBN 3-411-01963-8). Biblio Inst.
Lexicologie & Lexicographie Francaises & Romanes. 294p. (Fr. & Ital.). 1959. 42.00 F (ISBN 2-22200-359-8). CNRS.
Merino-Rodriguez, M., ed. Lexicon of International & National Units. (Eng., Ger., Span., Fr., Ital., Dutch, Port., Pol. & Japanese.). 1966. $70.25 (ISBN 0-444-40392-2). Elsevier.

LIABILITY FOR PERSONAL INJURIES
see Personal Injuries
LIBRARIANSHIP
see Library Science
LIBRARIES
see also Archives; Information Services
Kunze, Horst & Rueckl, Gotthard, eds. Lexikon des Bibliothekswesens. (Ger.). 1975. DM.102.00 (ISBN 3-7940-4210-7). Saur Verlag.
Massa De Gil, Beatriz. Diccionario Tecnico de Biblioteconomia. 387p. (Span.). 1965. Mex.$10.75. Trillas.
Massa de Gil, Beatriz, et al. Diccionario tecnico de biblioteconomia espanol-ingles, ingles-espanol. 3rd ed. 390p. (Span. & Eng.). 1964. $9.60; Mex.$120.00. Trillas.
Rigsbibliotekareembedet. Bibliotekskoder. LC 76-476911. 16p. (Eng. & Danish.). 1975. write for info. Bibliotekscentralen.

LIBRARIES-ADMINISTRATION
see Library Science
LIBRARIES-CATALOGS
see Library Catalogs
LIBRARIES-ORGANIZATION
see Libraries; Library Science
LIBRARIES-REFERENCE BOOKS
see Reference Books
LIBRARIES, ARCHITECTURAL
see Architectural Libraries
LIBRARIES, ART
see Art Libraries
LIBRARIES, COLLEGE
see Libraries, University and College
LIBRARIES, LAW
see Law Libraries
LIBRARIES, MEDICAL
see Medical Libraries
LIBRARIES, MUSIC
see Music Libraries
LIBRARIES, PHONORECORD
see Phonorecord Libraries
LIBRARIES, SCHOOL
see School Libraries
LIBRARIES, SPECIAL
American Numismatic Society, New York. Dictionary & Auction Catalogues of the Library of the American Numismatic Society: First Supplement 1962-67. 1967. lib. bdg. $105.00 (ISBN 0-8161-0788-2, Hall Library). G K Hall.
LIBRARIES, UNIVERSITY AND COLLEGE
McGill University, Blacker - Wood Library of Zoology & Ornithology. A Dictionary Catalogue of the Blacker - Wood Library of Zoology & Ornithology, 9 vols. 6300p. 1966. Set. lib. bdg. $810.00 (ISBN 0-8161-0719-X, Hall Library). G K Hall.
LIBRARIES FOR THE BLIND
see Blind, Libraries for the
LIBRARY CATALOGS
see also Catalogs, Dictionary
Columbia University. Dictionary Catalog of the Library of the School of Library Service, 1st Suppl, 4 vols. 1976. Set. lib. bdg. $460.00 (ISBN 0-8161-1166-9, Hall Library). G K Hall.

--Dictionary Catalog of the Teachers College Library, First Supplement, 5 vols. 1971. Set. lib. bdg. $525.00 (ISBN 0-8161-0958-3, Hall Library). G K Hall.
--Dictionary Catalog of the Teachers College Library, Second Supplement, 2 vols. 1973. Set. lib. bdg. $260.00 (ISBN 0-8161-1039-5, Hall Library). G K Hall.
Massachusetts Horticultural Society, Boston. Dictionary Catalog of the Library of the Massachusetts Horticultural Society, First Supplement. 1972. lib. bdg. $105.00 (ISBN 0-8161-1038-7, Hall Library). G K Hall.
New York Public Library, Research Libraries. Dictionary Catalog of the Music Collection, 33 Vols. 1964. Set. lib. bdg. $3135.00 (ISBN 0-8161-0709-2, Hall Library). G K Hall.
Pontifical Institute of Medieval Studies, Ontario. Dictionary Catalogue of the Library of the Pontifical Institute of Medieval Studies, 5 vols. 1972. Set. lib. bdg. $485.00 (ISBN 0-8161-0970-2, Hall Library). G K Hall.
Princeton University. Dictionary Catalog of the Princeton University Plasma Physics Laboratory Library, 4 vols. 1970. Set. lib. bdg. $380.00 (ISBN 0-8161-0881-1, Hall Library). G K Hall.
Provincial Archives & Victoria, British Columbia. Dictionary Catalogue of the Library of the Provincial Archives of British Columbia, 8 vols. 1971. Set. lib. bdg. $760.00 (ISBN 0-8161-0912-5, Hall Library). G K Hall.
Smithsonian Institution, Washington, D. C. Dictionary Catalog of the Library of the Freer Gallery of Art, 6 Vols. 1967. Set. lib. bdg. $530.00 (ISBN 0-8161-0799-8, Hall Library). G K Hall.
U. S. Department of the Interior, Washington, D. C. Dictionary Catalog of the Department Library, 37 Vols. 1967. Set. $3515.00 (ISBN 0-8161-0715-7, Hall Library). G K Hall.
University of California - Berkeley. Dictionary Catalog of the Giannini Foundation of Agricultural Economics Library, 12 vols. 1971. $1140.00 (ISBN 0-8161-0908-7, Hall Library). G K Hall.
University of Washington at Seattle. The Dictionary Catalog of the Pacific Northwest Collection of the University of Washington Libraries, 6 vols. 1972. Set. lib. bdg. $640.00 (ISBN 0-8161-0985-0, Hall Library). G K Hall.
U.S. Department of the Interior, Washington D.C. Dictionary Catalog of the Department Library, Third Sup, 8 Vols., 4th Supp. 1973. Set. lib. bdg. $420.00 (ISBN 0-8161-1054-9, Hall Library); lib. bdg. $790.00 1975 (ISBN 0-8161-0016-0). G K Hall.
LIBRARY SCIENCE
see also Bibliography; Information Storage and Retrieval Systems
also headings beginning with the word Library
Kunze, H. & Rueckl, G., eds. Lexikon des Bibliothekswesens, 2 vols. 2nd ed. (Ger.). 1975. M.48.00. Bibl Inst Leipzig.
LIBRARY SCIENCE-DICTIONARIES
Clason, W., ed. Dictionary of Library Science Information & Documentation. rev. ed. (Eng., Fr., Span., Ital., Dutch, Ger., & Arabic.). 1977. $95.75 (ISBN 0-444-41475-4). Elsevier.
Columbia University. Dictionary Catalog of the Library of the School of Library Service, 7 Vols. 1962. Set. lib. bdg. $665.00 (ISBN 0-8161-0634-7, Hall Library). G K Hall.
Diccionario de Bibliotecologia. 2nd ed. 458p. (Span.). 1976. $44.95 (ISBN 0-686-56656-4, S-12239). French & Eur.
Dictionary of Library Terms. (Hebrew, Eng. , Fr. & Ger.). IL.8.00. Massada Pr.

Harrod, L. M. The Librarians' Glossary & Reference Book: Of Terms Used in Librarianship Documentation & the Book Trade. (Grafton Library Ser.). 904p. 1982. Repr. of 1977 ed. 49.95x (ISBN 0-233-96744-3). Lexington Bks.
Istilah perpustakaan, Inggeris-Malaysia-Inggeris. LC 79-102563. xvi, 421p. (Eng. & Malay.). 1978. M.$5.50. Dewan Bahasa.
Kahla, Martti. Kirjastotermien Sanakirja. LC 80-460426. vi, 127p. (Finnish & Rus.). 1979. write for info. (ISBN 9-5170-7031-4). Neuvost.
Kunze, Horst. Lexikon des Bibliothekswesens, 2 vols, Vols. 1 & 2. 2nd ed. (Ger.). 1974. $82.00 (ISBN 3-7940-4210-7, M-7209). French & Eur.
Mezer, A. V. Slovarnyi Ukazatel Po Knigovedeniiu. 927p. (Rus.). 1924. $11.00 (Pub. by Kolos). Four Continent.
Pipics, Zoltan. Librarians Practical Dictionary in 22 Languages (Worterbuch Des Bibliothekars in 22 Sprachen). 6th ed. LC 73-695. 1974. $64.50 (ISBN 3-7940-4109-7, Pub by Verlag Dokumentation). Bowker.
Vaillancourt, Pauline M. International Directory of Acronyms in Library, Information & Computer Sciences. LC 80-18352. xi, 518p. 1980. $45.00 (ISBN 0-8352-1152-5). Bowker.
Young, Hartsill. A.L.A. Glossary of Library & Information Science. 1983. text ed. $50.00 (ISBN 0-8389-0371-1). ALA.
LIBYA
Hahn, Lorna. Historical Dictionary of Libya. LC 81-5228. (African Historical Dictionaries Ser.: No. 33). 132p. 1981. $13.00 (ISBN 0-8108-1442-0). Scarecrow.
LIBYAN LANGUAGES
see Berber Languages
LICENSED BEVERAGE INDUSTRY
see Distilling Industries
LICHENS
Ainsworth, G. C. Ainsworth & Bisby's Dictionary of the Fungi, Including the Lichens. 6th ed. LC 74-883641. (Illus.). 673p. 1971. 27.50x (ISBN 0-85198-075-9). Intl Pubns Serv.
LIE DETECTORS AND DETECTION
Mercier, L. S. Dictionnaire d'un Polygraphe. (Fr.). 1978. 17.70 F. U. G. E.
Muller, Wolfgang. Polygrafie-Englisch-Deutsch-Franzoesisch-Russisch-Spanisch-Polnisch-Ungarisch-Solwakisch. 1020p. (Eng., Ger., Fr., Rus., Span., Pol., Hungarian & Czech.). 1981. M.110.00. VEB Technik.
LIFE INSURANCE
see Insurance, Life
LIFE-LONG EDUCATION
see Adult Education
LIFE SCIENCE ENGINEERING
see Bioengineering
LIFE SCIENCES
see also Agriculture; Medicine
McGraw-Hill Editors. Dictionary of the Life Sciences. (Illus.). 1976. 32.50 (ISBN 0-07-045262-8, P&RB). McGraw.
Martin, E. A. Dictionary of Life Sciences. 2nd ed. 416p. (Eng.). 1983. E17.50 (ISBN 0-333-34867-2). Macmillan London.
Martin, Sue. Dictionary of the Life Sciences. LC 76-41041. $20.00x (ISBN 0-87663-724-1). Universe.
LIGATURE (MUSIC)
see Musical Notation
LIGHT, ELECTRIC
see Electric Lighting
LIGHTING
see also Electric Lighting; Lamps
American Association for State & Local History. A Glossary of Old Lamps & Lighting Devices. $1.00 (30); members $0.75. AASLH.
Zimmermann, Ralf. Dictionary of Lighting. 362p. 1980. $70.00x (ISBN 0-569-08526-8, Pub. by Collet's). State Mutual Bk.
LIMITATION OF ARMAMENT
see Disarmament
LIMITATIONS (LAW)
see Real Property

LIMITATIONS, CONSTITUTIONAL
see Constitutional Law
LIMITED COMPANIES
see Corporations
LINCOLN, ABRAHAM, PRES. U. S., 1809-1865
Lincoln, Abraham. Lincoln Dictionary. Winn, Ralph, ed. pap. $1.45 (ISBN 0-685-19407-8, 43, WL). Citadel Pr.
LINE-ENGRAVING
see Engraving
LINEAR B INSCRIPTIONS
see Inscriptions, Linear B
LINEAR SYSTEM THEORY
see System Analysis
LINGALA LANGUAGE
see Bangala Language
LINGUA FRANCA
see Languages, Mixed
LINGUISTIC GEOGRAPHY
Masica, Colin P. Defining a Linquistic Area: South Asia. LC 74-16677. 256p. 1976. lib. bdg. $16.00x (ISBN 0-226-50944-3). U of Chicago Pr.
LINGUISTICS
Here are entered works dealing with the scientific study of human speech, including phonetics, phonemics, morphology, and syntax. Works dealing with language in general, the origin and history of language and surveys of languages, are entered under the heading Language and Languages.
see also Grammar, Comparative and General; Phonetics; Sociolinguistics
Abraham, Werner & Meno Blanco, Francisco. Diccionario de Terminologia Linguistica Actual. 510p. (Span.). 1981. write for info. (ISBN 84-249-0079-0); pap. write for info. (ISBN 84-249-0080-4). Gredos.
Al-Khuli, Muhammad A. Dictionary of Theoretical Linguistics: English-Arabic with Arabic-English Glossary. (Arabic & Eng.). 1983. $30.00 (ISBN 0-86685-306-5). Intl Bk Ctr.
Althaus, Hans. Lexikon der Grammatischen Linguistik. (Ger.). 1973. $95.00 (ISBN 3-484-10186-5, M-7256). French & Eur.
Althaus, Hans P., et al, eds. Lexikon der Germanistischen Linguistik. (Ger.). 1973. DM.106.00 (ISBN 3-484-10186-5). Niemeyer.
Arunabharathi, N. Glossary of Linguistics. LC 77-900957. xi, 82p. (Eng. & Tamil.). 1976. Rs.6.00. Tamil Nuulagam.
Aschmann, Herman & Aschmann, Bessie. Diccionario Totonaco De Papantla. (Vocabularios Indigenas Ser.: No. 16). 268p. (Span.). 1973. pap. $5.00x (ISBN 0-88312-750-4); microfiche $3.00x (ISBN 0-88312-585-4). Summer Inst Ling.
Bakalla. Dictionary of Modern Linguistic Terms: English-Arabic, Arabic-English. (Arabic & Eng.). 1975. $20.00 (ISBN 0-86685-304-9). Intl Bk Ctr.
Beaudet, Albert. Dictionnaire Anglo-Francais des Nouveautes Linguistiques. 198p. (Fr.). 1972. 4.95 F. Fides.
Booij, G, et al. Lexikon van de Taalwetenschap. LC 76-502048. (Illus.). 187p. (Dutch.). 1975. fl.9.90. Spectrum NL.
Bulakhov, M. G. Vostochnoslavianskie Iazykovedy. (Rus.). 1978. $15.75. Four Continent.
Calamegriaule, Genevieve. Dictionnaire Dogon: Ethnologique & Linguistique. 296p. (Fr.). 1968. 45.00 F. S. E. L. A. F.
Center for Applied Linguistics, Washington D.C. Dictionary Catalog of the Library of the Center for Applied Linguistics, Washington, D. C, 4 vols. 1974. Set. lib. bdg. $355.00 (ISBN 0-8161-1114-6, Hall Library). G K Hall.
Constantinescu-Dobridor, G. Mic Dictionar de Terminologie Lingvistica. LC 80-471399. 463p. (Romanian.). 1980. 6.50 lei. Albatros.
DeJoia, Alex & Stenton, Adrian. Terms in Systemic Linguistics. LC 80-5089. 1980. $20.00 (ISBN 0-312-79180-1). St Martin.

Denisova, M. A. Lingvisticheskii Slovar. 276p. (Rus.). 1978. $4.90 (Pub. by Russkii Iazyk). Four Continent.

Dictionary of Modern Linguistic Terms (English-Arabic) (Eng. & Arabic.). 1975. $20.00 (ISBN 0-86685-304-9). Intl Bk Ctr.

Dictionary of Theoretical Linguistics (English-Arabic) Arabic-English Glossary. (Eng. & Arabic.). $30.00 (ISBN 0-86685-306-5). Intl Bk Ctr.

Dubois, J. & Giacomo, M. Dictionnaire de Linguistique. 516p. (Fr.). 1974. $27.50 (ISBN 2-03-020299-1, 1002). Larousse.

Dubois, J., et al. Dictionnaire de Linguistique. (Fr.). 1977. pap. text ed. $21.00 (Dist. by Continental Bk Co). Larousse.

Dubois, Jean, et al. Dictionnaire de Linguistique. 516p. (Fr.). 1972. 57.20 F. Larousse.

Glosario de terminos linguisticos. 132p. (Span.). 1982. pap. write for info. (ISBN 84-369-0934-8). Serv Pub Minist.

Gusmani, Roberto. Lydisches Woerterbuch. (Ger.). 1964. $49.95 (ISBN 3-533-00655-7, M-7546, Pub. by Carl Winter). French & Eur.

––Lydisches Woerterbuch. (Ger.). 1964. $49.95 (ISBN 3-533-00655-7). Winter Univ.

Hamp, Eric L. Glossary of American Technical Linguistic Usage, 1925-1950. 3rd ed. 1966. 10.50x (ISBN 0-8002-1460-9). Intl Pubns Serv.

Hartmann, R. R. & Stork, F. C., eds. Dictionary of Language & Linguistics. LC 72-6251. 302p. 1976. pap. $29.95 (ISBN 0-470-15200-1). Halsted Pr.

Heupel, Carl. Linguistisches Woerterbuch. LC 79-363518. (Illus.). 161p. (Ger.). 1978. DM.12.80 (ISBN 3-423-03040-2). Deutscher Taschenbuch.

Jehan, L. F. Dictionnaire de Linguistique et de Philologie Comparee. Migne, J. P., ed. (Troisieme et Derniere Encyclopedie Theologique Ser.: Vol. 34). 724p. (Fr.). Repr. of 1864 ed. lib. bdg. $92.50x (ISBN 0-89241-313-1). Caratzas Pub Co.

Jota, Zelio dos Santos. Dicionarios de Linguistica. 3rd ed. LC 76-461651. 353p. (Port.). 1976. Cr.$90.00. Prensa Acad.

Kenesbaev, S., et al. Russko-Kazakhsii Slovar Lingvisticheskikh Terminov. 206p. (Rus.). 1966. $1.85 (Pub. by An Arm SSR). Four Continent.

Landerman, Peter. Vocabulario Quechua del Pastaza. (Peruvian Linguistic Ser.: No. 8). 165p. (Span.). 1973. pap. $2.50x (ISBN 0-88312-664-8); microfiche $2.25 (ISBN 0-88312-366-5). Summer Inst Ling.

Lepsius, Richard. Standard Alphabet for Reducing Unwritten Languages & Foreign Graphic Systems to a Uniform Orthography in European Letters. 2nd ed. Kemp, J. Alan, ed. (Amsterdam Classics in Linguistics Ser.: Vol. 5). 462p. 1981. $48.00x (ISBN 90-272-0876-X). Benjamins North Am.

Lewandowski, Theodor, et al. Diccionario de linguistica. Bernardez, Enrique & Garcia, M. Luz, trs. 464p. (Span.). 1982. pap. 2000.00 ptas (ISBN 84-376-0363-3). Edns Catedra.

Lewin, Bernhard. A Vocabulary of the Hudailian Poems. (Acta Regiae Societatis Scientarum et Litterarum Goteborg, Humaniora: No. 13). 1978. pap. text ed. 28.00x (ISBN 91-85252-16-6). Humanities.

Lope Blanch, J. M. El Lexico indigena en el espanol de Mexico. 74p. (Span.). Mex.$1.20; $12.00. Col. de Mexico.

Marouzeau, Jules. Lexique De la Terminologie Linguistique. 3rd ed. LC 53-5692. 280p. (Fr., Ger., Eng. & Ital.). 1969. Repr. of 1951 ed. $7.50x (ISBN 0-8002-0840-4). Intl Pubns Serv.

Mayrhofer, Manfred. Kurzgefasstes Etymologisches Des Altindischen, Vol. 3. (Ger. & Sanskrit.). 1976. $130.00 (ISBN 3-533-02466-0). Winter Univ.

––Kurzgefasstes Etymologisches Woerterbuch Des Altindischen, Vol. 2. (Ger. & Sanskrit.). 1963. $92.00 (ISBN 3-533-00657-3, M-7530, Pub. by Carl Winter). French & Eur.

––Kurzgefasstes Etymologisches Woerterbuch Des Altindischen, Vol. 2. (Ger. & Sanskrit.). 1963. $92.00 (ISBN 3-533-00657-3). Winter Univ.

––Kurzgefasstes Etymologisches Woerterbuch Des Altindischen, Vol. 3. (Ger. & Sanskrit.). 1976. $130.00 (ISBN 3-533-02466-0, M-7531, Pub. by Carl Winter). French & Eur.

Mounin, Georges. Diccionario de linguistica. Pochtar, Ricardo, tr. 288p. (Span.). 1982. pap. 1500.00 ptas (ISBN 84-335-4005-X). Labor SA.

––Dictionnaire de la Linguistique. (Illus.). 384p. (Fr.). 1974. 130.00 F. PUF.

Nash. Multinlingual Lexicon of Linguistics & Philology. (Miami Linguistic Ser.). (Polyglot.). $52.50 (ISBN 0-685-36678-2). French & Eur.

Nuessel, Frank H., Jr., ed. Linguistic Approaches to the Romance Lexicon. LC 78-12654. 123p. 1978. pap. text ed. 5.50 (ISBN 0-87840-046-X). Georgetown U Pr.

Pei, Mario & Gaynor, Frank. Dictionary of Linguistics. (Quality Paperback: No. 177). 1980. pap. 4.95 (ISBN 0-8226-0177-X). Littlefield.

Pei, Mario & Gaynor, Frank, eds. Dictionary of Linguistics. 1960. 6.00 (ISBN 0-685-77553-4). Philos Lib.

Pei, Mario A. Glossary of Linguistic Terminology. LC 66-21013. 299p. 1966. $30.00x (ISBN 0-231-03012-6). Columbia U Pr.

Pensinger, Brenda. Diccionario Mixteco del Este De Jamiltepec. (Vocabularios Indigenas Ser.: No. 18). 156p. (Span.). 1974. $7.00 (ISBN 0-88312-751-2); microfiche $2.25x (ISBN 0-88312-586-2). Summer Inst Ling.

Press, Margaret L. Chemehuevi: A Grammar & Lexicon. (U. C. Publications in Linguistics Ser.: Vol. 92). 1980. pap. $16.50x (ISBN 0-520-09600-2). U of Cal Pr.

Provenzal, Dino. Dizionario dei dubbi linguistici. vii, 380p. (Ital.). 1967. L.2000.00 (ISBN 88-203-0217-9). Hoepli.

Rosiello, L. & Loi, I. Dizionario di linguistica. viii, 368p. (Ital.). 1979. L.13000.00. Zanichelli.

Rozental, D. E., et al. Slovar-Spravochni k Lingvisticheskikh Terminov. 544p. (Rus.). 1976. $3.50 (Pub. by Prosveschchenie). Four Continent.

Seebold, Elmar. Vergleichendes und Etymologisches Worterbuch der Germanischen Starken Verben. (Janua Linguarum, Ser. Practica: No. 85). (Ger., Ger.). 1970. pap. text ed. 87.00x (ISBN 0-686-22397-7). Mouton.

Steible, Daniel J., ed. Concise Handbook of Linguistics. LC 67-11578. 1967. 6.00 (ISBN 0-8022-1635-8). Philos Lib.

Stoudt, Betty. Vocabulario Mixteco de San Miguel el Grande. (Vocabularios Indigenas Ser.: No. 12). (Span.). 1965. pap. $3.00 (ISBN 0-88312-660-5); microfiche $1.60x (ISBN 0-88312-580-3). Summer Inst Ling.

Tinkler, John D. Vocabulary & Syntax of the Old English Version in the Paris Psalter. LC 68-29824. (Janua Linguarum, Ser. Practica: No. 67). (Illus.). 92p. (Orig., Old Eng.). 1971. pap. text ed. $16.00x (ISBN 90-2791-895-3). Mouton.

Ulrich, W. Woerterbuch – Linguistische Grundbegriffe. 2nd ed. (Ger.). 1975. pap. $12.95 (ISBN 3-554-80336-7, M-6914). French & Eur.

Ulrich, Winfried. Woerterbuch: Linguistische Grundbegriffe. 2nd ed. LC 77-460610. (Illus.). 173p. (Ger.). 1975. DM.13.80 (ISBN 3-554-80336-7). Hirt.

Von Ulrich, Winfried. Woerterbuch Linguistische Grundbegriffe. 176p. (Ger.). 1975. DM.14.80 (ISBN 3-554-80336-7). Hirt.

Ward, Kendall K. & Kaltenborn, Arthur L. Guides for American-English Pronunciation. (Illus.). 256p. 1971. photocopy ed. spiral $19.75x (ISBN 0-398-02019-1). C C Thomas.

LINGUISTICS–ADDRESSES, ESSAYS, LECTURES

Dubois, Jean. Diccionario de Linguistica. (Span.). 1979. pap. pns (S-50086). French & Eur.

LINGUISTICS–BIBLIOGRAPHY

Center for Applied Linguistics, Washington D.C. Dictionary Catalog of the Library of the Center for Applied Linguistics, Washington, D. C, 4 vols. 1974. Set. lib. bdg. $355.00 (ISBN 0-8161-1114-6, Hall Library). G K Hall.

Crystal, David. A First Dictionary of Linguistics & Phonetics. (Language Library Ser.). 404p. 1980. lib. bdg. $34.00 (ISBN 0-86531-051-3, Pub. by Andre Deutsch). Westview.

LINGVO INTERNACIA (ARTIFICIAL LANGUAGE)
see Esperanto (Artificial Language)
LINKS, GOLF
see Golf Courses
LIPAN INDIANS
see Indians of North America–Southwest, New
LIP-READING
see Deaf–Means of Communication
LIQUEFIED PETROLEUM GAS

Canadian Society of Petroleum Geologists. Lexicon of Canadian Stratigraphy Arctic Archipelago, Vol. 1. 1981. $8.00; pap. $6.00. Can Soc Petro Geo.

––Lexicon of Canadian Stratigraphy Yukon-MacKenzie, Vol. 2. 1981. $22.00; $20.00. Can Soc Petro Geo.

LIQUOR INDUSTRY
see Distilling Industries
LITERARY CRITICISM
see Criticism
LITERARY PRIZES

Tissier, Jean. Dictionnaire Berrichon avec Citations Litteraires. 112p. (Fr.). 1978. 50.00 F. Lafitte Repr.

LITERARY PROPERTY
see Copyright
LITERARY TERMS
see Literature–Terminology
LITERATURE–BIBLIOGRAPHY

Halkett & Laing. A Dictionary of Anonymous & Pseudonymous Publications in the English Language: Vol. 1, 1475-1640. Horden, John, ed. 1980. $150.00 (ISBN 0-582-55521-3). Longman.

LITERATURE–BIO-BIBLIOGRAPHY

Steiner, G. & Greiner-Mai, H., eds. BI-Taschenlexikon Fremdsprachige Schriftsteller. 4th ed. 736p. (Ger.). 1982. M.25.00. Bibl Inst Leipzig.

LITERATURE–BIOGRAPHY
see Authors
LITERATURE–DICTIONARIES

Aarnes, Asbjorn. Litteraert Lekxikon. LC 77-555382. 278p. (Norwegian.). 1977. write for info. Tanum-Norli.

Barbier De Meynard, Achille. Dictionnaire Geographique, Historique & Literaire: La Perse & des Contrees Adjacentes, 8 vols. 640p. (Fr.). 1970. fl.96.00. Philo Pr.

Bede, Jean-Albert & Edgerton, William, eds. Columbia Dictionary of Modern European Literature. 2nd ed. 800p. 1980. $55.00x (ISBN 0-231-03717-1). Columbia U Pr.

Brewer, E. C. The Dictionary of Phrase & Fable. Date not set. $7.98 (ISBN 0-517-25921-4). Outlet Bk Co.

Capdevila Font, Juan. Diccionario de la Literatura Universal. 536p. (Span.). 1977. $22.50 (ISBN 84-85117-41-7, S-50261). French & Eur.

Cuddon, J. A. A Dictionary of Literary Terms. LC 76-47853. 1977. $17.95 (ISBN 0-385-12713-8). Doubleday.

Dictionnaire Historique, Literaire & Statistique, 2 vols. 1620p. (Fr.). 1973. write for info. Lafitte Repr.

Duffy, Charles & Petit, Henry. Dictionary of Literary Terms. rev. ed. pap. $2.00 (ISBN 0-910294-02-X). Brown Bk.

Elkhaden, Saad. The York Dictionary of English-French-German-Spanish Literary Terms & Their Origin. LC 77-364336. 154p. (Eng., Fr., Ger. & Span.). 1976. $6.95 (ISBN 0-919966-01-2). York Pr CA.

Fitzgerald, Percy. The Pickwickian Dictionary & Cyclopedia. LC 74-7473. Repr. of 1900 ed. lib. bdg. $50.00 (ISBN 0-8414-4179-0). Folcroft.

Helmut, H. Woerterbuch des Buches. (Ger.). 1976. pap. $15.95 (ISBN 3-465-00186-9, M-6937). French & Eur.

Krywalski, Diether. Knaurs Lexikon der Weltliteratur. LC 80-462297. 942p. (Ger.). 1979. DM.39.80 (ISBN 3-426-26011-5). Droemersche Knaur.

Parnaso. Diccionario Sopena De Literatura. 1820p. (Span.). $54.00 (ISBN 84-303-0247-6, S-50140). French & Eur.

Perez-Rioja, Jose A. Diccionario Literario Universal. LC 77-466197. 989p. (Span.). 1977. write for info. (ISBN 8-4309-0690-8). Tecnos SA.

Shipley, Joseph T. Diccionario de la Literatura Mundial. 2nd ed. 564p. (Span.). 1974. $37.50 (ISBN 84-233-0781-6, S-12359). French & Eur.

Timofeev, L. I., et al, eds. Kratkii Slovar' Literaturovedcheskikh Terminov. (Prosveshchenie Ser.). 224p. (Rus.). 1978. $1.95 ()-21). Four Continent.

Timofeev, Leonid I. & Turev, S. V. Kratkii Slovar Literaturovedcheskikh Terminov. LC 79-378589. 233p. (Rus.). 1978. $0.55 (Pub. by Proveschchenie). Four Continent.

Vox. Diccionario Monografico de Bellas Artes. (Span.). 1979. leatherette $17.50 (ISBN 84-7153-381-2, S-36147). French & Eur.

Wahba, Magdi. A Dictionary of Literary Terms (English-French-Arabic) 1974. $28.00x (ISBN 0-86685-117-8). Intl Bk Ctr.

Wilpert, Gero von. Lexikon der Weltliteratur: Werke, Vol. 2. 2nd ed. (Ger.). 1968. $77.00 (ISBN 3-520-80801-3, M-7211). French & Eur.

LITERATURE–EVALUATION
see Criticism; Literature–History and Criticism
LITERATURE–HISTORY AND CRITICISM
see also Authors

Thrall, W. F. & Hibbard, A. A Handbook to Literature. 582p. 1980. Repr. lib. bdg. $40.00 (ISBN 0-89987-807-5). Darby Bks.

LITERATURE–PRIZES
see Literary Prizes
LITERATURE–TERMINOLOGY

Abrams, M. H. A Glossary of Literary Terms. 4th ed. LC 80-26095. 220p. 1981. pap. text ed. 10.95 (ISBN 0-03-054166-2, HoltC). HR&W.

Anderson, Robert & Eckhard, Ronald. Lexicon of Literary Terms. 160p. 1975. pap. 3.50 (ISBN 0-671-18749-X). Monarch Pr.

Dictionnaire des Frequences: Vocabulaire Literaire des 19 & 20 Siecles, 1, 4 vols. 2284p. (Fr.). 1976. 280.00 F. Klincksieck.

Dictionnaire des Frequences: Vocabulaire Literaire des 19 & 20 Siecles, 2. 575p. (Fr.). 1976. 74.00 F. Klincksieck.

Dictionnaire des Frequences: Vocabulaire Literaire des 19 & 20 Siecles, 3. 352p. (Fr.). 1976. 60.00 F. Klincksieck.

Dictionnaire des Frequences: Vocabulaire Literaire des 19 & 20 Siecle, 4. 98p. (Fr.). 1976. 12.00 F. Klincksieck.

Elkhadem, Saad. The York Dictionary of English-French-German-Spanish Literary Terms & Their Origin. (Eng., Fr., Ger., & Span.). 1976. pap. $9.95 (ISBN 0-919966-04-7); pap. $6.95 (ISBN 0-919966-01-2). York Pr CA.

Escarpit, Robert. Dictionnaire International des Termes Literaires. 86p. (Fr.). 1973. write for info. Mouton-De.

Loane, George G. Short Handbook of Literary Terms. LC 72-188273. 1972. lib. bdg. $15.00 (ISBN 0-8414-0600-6). Folcroft.

Ruttkowski, Wolfgang V. & Blake, R. E. Glossaire de Termes Litteraires. 68p. (Fr.). 1969. 9.40 F. Francke.

Scott, A. F. Current Literary Terms: A Concise Dictionary of Their Origin & Use. 334p. (Eng.). 1979. E10.00 (ISBN 0-333-03566-6); pap. $3.50 (ISBN 0-333-26101-1). Macmillan London.

Scott, A. F., ed. Current Literary Terms. 324p. Repr. of 1980 ed. lib. bdg. $16.95x (ISBN 0-312-17956-1). St Martin.

Shaw, Harry. Concise Dictionary of Literary Terms. (McGraw-Hill Paperbacks). Orig. Title: Dictionary of Literary Terms. 224p. 1976. pap. 4.95 (ISBN 0-07-056483-3, SP). McGraw.

Slovar Sovremennogo Russkogo Literaturnogo Iazyka: I-K, Vol. 5. 1915p. (Rus.). 1956. $15.00 (Pub. by An Arm SSR). Four Continent.

Slovar Sovremennogo Russkogo Literaturnogo Iazyka: O, Vol. 8. 1840p. (Rus.). 1959. $15.00 (Pub. by An Arm SSR). Four Continent.

Slovar Sovremennogo Russkogo Literaturnogo Iazyka: Zh-Z, Vol. 4. 1363p. (Rus.). 1955. $15.00 (Pub. by An Arm SSR). Four Continent.

Yelland, H. L., et al. Handbook of Literary Terms. LC 79-14512. 1980. bds. $10.00 laminated (ISBN 0-87116-118-4). Writer.

LITERATURE, COMIC
see Comedy

LITERATURE, COMPARATIVE–ENGLISH AND CLASSICAL
Starnes, DeWitt T. & Talbert, Ernest W. Classical Myth & Legend in Renaissance Dictionaries. LC 73-11753. (Illus.). 517p. 1973. Repr. of 1955 ed. lib. bdg. 39.75x (ISBN 0-8371-7086-9, STCM). Greenwood.

LITERATURE, LEGAL
see Legal Literature

LITERATURE AS A PROFESSION
see Authors; Journalism; Journalists

LITHOLOGY
see Petrology

LITHUANIAN LANGUAGE
Napalis, I., et al. Orfograficheskii Slovar Litovskogo Iazyka Dlia Shkol. 244p. (Rus.). 1958. $1.35 (Pub. by Izd Pedag Lit). Four Continent.

Peteraitis, Vilius. Lithuanian-English Dictionary. (Lithuanian & Eng.). $27.50 (ISBN 0-87559-037-3); thumb indexed $31.00 (ISBN 0-87559-038-1). Shalom.

Robinson, David F. Lithuanian Reverse Dictionary. ix, 209p. (Lithuanian.). 1976. soft cover $11.95 (ISBN 0-89357-034-6). Slavica.

Serafini Amato, Loredana. La Distribuzione della Posposizione nel Lituano Antico. LC 78-401196. 74p. (Eng. & Lithuanian.). 1976. write for info. Ist Univers Orient.

Vaitkavichiute, V. A. Polsko-Litovskii Slovar. 1024p. (Pol. & Lithuanian.). 1979. $9.95 (Pub. by Mokslas). Four Continent.

LITHUANIAN LITERATURE
Fraenkel, Ernst. Litauisches Etymologisches Woerterbuch, Vol. 1. (Lithuanian & Ger.). 1960. $152.00 (ISBN 3-533-00650-6, M-7541, Pub. by Westdeutscher Verlag/VVA). French & Eur.

--Litauisches Etymologisches Woerterbuch, Vol. 2. (Lithuanian & Ger.). 1965. $195.00 (ISBN 3-533-00651-4, M-7542, Pub. by Westdeutscher Verlag/VVA). French & Eur.

LITURGICAL LATIN
see Latin Language–Church Latin

LITURGICS
see also Chants (Plain, Gregorian, etc.); Christian Art and Symbolism
Hughes, Dom A., compiled by. Liturgical Terms for Music Students: A Dictionary. LC 70-166236. 1972. Repr. of 1940 ed. $14.00 (ISBN 0-403-01363-1). Scholarly.

Lehmann, Arnold O. Lehmann's Little Dictionary of Liturgical Terms. 1980. 3.75 (ISBN 0-8100-0127-6, 15N0371). Northwest Pub.

LITURGIES
see also Liturgies
also subdivision Liturgy and Ritual, or name of ritual, under names of churches, e.g. Catholic Church–Liturgy and Ritual; Church of England–Book of Common Prayer
Huber, Rudolf & Rieth, Renate, eds. Glossarium Artis: Fasz 2, Liturgische Geraete-Objets Liturgiques. 160p. (Ger.). 1972. DM.35.00 (ISBN 3-484-60047-0). Max Niemeyer.

Lee, Frederick G. A Glossary of Liturgical & Ecclesiastical Terms. LC 76-174069. (Tower Bks). (Illus.). xl, 452p. 1972. Repr. of 1877 ed. $38.00x (ISBN 0-8103-3949-8). Gale.

LITURGY
see Liturgics

LIVESTOCK
see also Donkeys; Horses; Pastures; Range Management; Sheep
also headings beginning with the word Livestock
Mason, I. L. A Dictionary of Livestock Breeds. 268p. 1969. cloth $50.00x (ISBN 0-85198-007-4, Pub. by CAB Bks England). State Mutual Bk.

LIVESTOCK–DISEASES
see Veterinary Medicine

LOAN ASSOCIATIONS
see Building and Loan Associations

LOBSTERS
Merriam, Kendall A. Illustrated Dictionary of Lobstering. LC 78-61525. (Illus., Orig.). 1978. pap. $6.95 (ISBN 0-87027-192-X). Cumberland Pr.

LOCAL ADMINISTRATION
see Local Government

LOCAL GOVERNMENT
Here are entered works which deal with local government of districts, counties, townships, etc. Works dealing with government of municipalities only are entered under Municipal Government; those dealing with government of counties only are entered under County Government.
see also Cities and Towns; Mayors; Municipal Government; Public Administration
Modica, Enzo. Dizionario delle Autonomie Locali. LC 77-575264. xi, 851p. (Ital.). 1977. L.1200.00. Editori Riuniti.

Noel, Bernard. Dictionnaire de la Commune, Vol. 1. (Fr.). 1978. pap. $6.95 (ISBN 0-686-57059-6, M-6428). French & Eur.

LOCAL HISTORY
Here are entered works on the writing and compiling of local histories. Works concerned with local history of specific areas are entered under names of countries, states, etc. with subdivision History, Local, or under names of places with or without the subdivision History.
Blaschke, Karlheinz, et al. Lexikon Staedte & Wappen der Deutschen Demokratischen Republik. 1st ed. LC 80-460533. (Illus.). 526p. (Ger.). 1979. M.25.00. VEB Verlag Enzyklopadie.

LOCAL TRANSIT
American Public Transit Association. Glossary of Reliability, Availability, & Maintainability Terminology for Rail Rapid Transit. $3.00; 1st. copy free, members; add'l $1.50 ea. Am Public Transit.

LOCKSMITHING
Mayers, Keith. A Dictionary of Locksmithing. 1980. pap. 6.50 (ISBN 0-9604860-0-3). Mayers-Joseph.

LOCOMOTION, DISORDERED
Fusari, Alberto. Dizionario di Terminologia Ortopedica & Traumatologia. LC 77-675054. 285p. (Ital.). 1975. L.1500.00. Gaggi.

LOCOMOTIVES
Wright, Roy V., ed. Locomotives from the Nineteen Sixteen Locomotive Dictionary. (Train Shed Cyclopedia Ser., No. 18). (Illus.). 1974. pap. 4.95 (ISBN 0-912318-47-3). N K Gregg.

LOCOMOTIVES–HISTORY
Fowler, George L., ed. Locomotive Dictionary. (Illus.). 684p. 1972. Repr. of 1906 ed. lib. bdg. 24.95 buckram (ISBN 0-912318-20-1). N K Gregg.

LODGES
see Secret Societies

LOGIC
see also Fallacies (Logic)
Greenstein, Carol. Dictionary of Logical Terms & Symbols. 1982. pap. text ed. $9.95 (ISBN 0-442-22836-8). Van Nos Reinhold.

Kondakov, N. I. Logicheskii Slovar. Gorskii, D. P., ed. 656p. (Rus.). 1971. $11.75 (Pub. by Nauka). Four Continent.

--Vvedenie v Logiku. 465p. (Rus.). 1967. $6.85 (Pub. by Nauka). Four Continent.

Kondakov, Nikolai I., et al. Woerterbuch der Logik. LC 79-380114. 554p. (Ger.). 1978. M.22.00. Bibl Inst Leipzig.

Prior, Arthur N. The Doctrine of Propositions & Terms. Geach, P. T. & Kenny, A. J., eds. LC 76-9375. 1976. $9.00x (ISBN 0-87023-214-2). U of Mass Pr.

The, Liang G. Kamus Logika. LC 75-940899. 209p. (Indonesian.). 1975. write for info. Nur Cahaya.

LOGIC, DEDUCTIVE
see Logic

LOGIC, SYMBOLIC AND MATHEMATICAL
see also Set Theory
Feys, R. & Fitch, F., eds. Dictionary of Symbols of Mathematical Logic. (Studies in Logic: Vol. 20). 1973. $22.00 (ISBN 0-7204-2250-7, North Holland). Elsevier.

Greenstein, Carol. Dictionary of Logical Terms & Symbols. 1978. text ed. $13.95 (ISBN 0-442-22834-1). Van Nos Reinhold.

LOGIC AND FAITH
see Faith and Reason

LOGISTICS
Cavinato, Joseph L., ed. Transportation-Logistics Dictionary. 2nd ed. 323p. 1982. $14.00 (ISBN 0-87408-022-3). Traffic Serv.

LONDON–ROYAL ACADEMY OF ARTS
Graves, Algernon. The Royal Academy of Arts, a Complete Dictionary of Contributors & Their Work from Its Foundation in 1769 to 1904, Compiled with the Sanction of the President & Council of the Royal Academy, 8 vols. in 4. LC 76-118750. 1972. Repr. of 1905 ed. Set. lib. bdg. $181.00 (ISBN 0-8337-1425-2). B Franklin.

LOVE
see also Marriage
The Lover's Dictionary: How to Be Amorous in Five Delectable Languages. 1981. pap. $4.95 (ISBN 0-686-29648-6). Natl Textbk.

Nanxe, Aline de. Diccionario Del Amor. 122p. (Span.). 1969. pap. $3.50 (ISBN 84-290-1061-0, S-50136). French & Eur.

Teppe, Julien. Vocabulaire de la Vie Amoureuse. 224p. (Fr.). 1973. 24.00 F. Pavillon.

Vocabula amatoria. 280p. (Ital.). L.6000.00. Le Lettere.

LOW GERMAN LANGUAGE
see also Friesian Language
Hessmann, Pierre. Namenforschung im Ostniederlandisch-Westfalischen Grengebiet. LC 78-375124. 104p. (Ger. & Dutch.). 1978. fl.20.00 (ISBN 9-0620-3380-6). Rodopi.

LOW GERMAN LANGUAGE–TO 1500
Inghult, Goran. Die Semantische Struktur Desubstantivischer Bildungen auf Maessig. LC 76-458533. 206p. (Ger.). 1975. Kr.50.00. Almqvist.

LOW GERMAN LANGUAGE–DICTIONARIES
Thiessen, John & Thiessen, Jack. Mennonite Low-German Dictionary. LC 79-304075. 70p. (Eng. & Ger.). 1977. write for info. (ISBN 3-7708-0579-8). Elwert.

LOW INCOME HOUSING
see Housing

LOW TEMPERATURES
Anglo-Russkii Slovar Po Kholodil Noi i Kriogennoi Tekhnike. 468p. (Rus. & Eng.). 1978. $8.95 (Pub. by Russkii Iazyk). Four Continent.

LPG
see Liquefied Petroleum Gas

LU-GANDA
see Ganda Language

LUDICROUS, THE
see Wit and Humor

LUGANDA LANGUAGE
see Ganda Language

LUMBER TRADE
see also Woodwork
Saario, Hilkka. Timber Trade Terminology. LC 78-392222. 51p. (Eng. & Finnish.). 1975. write for info. (ISBN 9-5166-2165-1). Gaudeamus.

LUMMI LANGUAGE
Gibbs, George. Alphabetical Vocabularies of the Clallam & Lumni. LC 75-168115. (Library of American Linguistics: No. 11). Repr. of 1863 ed. $10.00 (ISBN 0-404-50991-6). AMS Pr.

LUTHERAN CHURCH–MISSOURI SYNOD
see Evangelical Lutheran Synod of Missouri, Ohio and other states

M

MACEDONIA
Giannelli, Ciro. Un Lexique Macedonien du XV Siecle. 71p. (Fr.). 1958. 17.10 F. Inst Etudes Slaves.

MACHINE DATA STORAGE AND RETRIEVAL SYSTEMS
see Information Storage and Retrieval Systems

MACHINE LANGUAGE
see Programming Languages (Electronic Computers)

MACHINE QUILTING
see Quilting

MACHINE TOOLS–DICTIONARIES
Freeman, Henry G. Fachwoerterbuch Spanende Werkzeugmaschinen. 527p. (Ger. & Eng., Dictionary of Machine Tools). 1965. leatherette 72.00 (ISBN 3-7736-5090-6, M-7403, Pub. by Verlag W. Gerardet). French & Eur.

--Spanende Werkzeugmaschinen, Deutsch-Englische Begriffserlauterungen und Kommentare. 617p. (Ger. & Eng., Machine Tools, German-English Explanations and Comments). 1973. $75.00 (ISBN 3-7736-5082-5, M-7624, Pub. by Verlag W. Girardet). French & Eur.

--Spanende Werkzeugmaschinen, Deutsch-Englische Begriffserlauterungen und Kommentare. 617p. (Ger. & Eng.). 1973. $75.00 (ISBN 3-7736-5082-5). Girardet.

Lexicue Trilingue des Termes d'usage Courant En Machines Outils; les Tours, Pt. 1. 74p. (Fr., Trilingual Lexicon of Common Terms in Machine Tools; Wheels). 1961. pap. $12.50 (ISBN 0-686-56791-9, M-6374). French & Eur.

Lexique Trilinque des Termes d'Usage Courant En Machines Outils, les Perceuses, Pt. 2. 96p. (Fr., Trilingual Lexicon of Commonly Used Terms in Machine Tools; Drilling Tools). pap. $12.50 (ISBN 0-686-56792-7, M-6375). French & Eur.

Michauz, Jean P. Dictionnaire de L'outillage et de la Machine-Outil. LC 78-354894. 179p. (Fr.). 1976. 20.00 F (ISBN 2-7080-0444-1). Ophrys.

MACHINERY–DICTIONARIES
Abd-El-Wahed, A. M. Machine Tools Dictionary: English-French-German-Arabic. 334p. (Eng., Fr., Ger. & Arabic). 1977. $45.00 (ISBN 0-686-92135-6, M-9757). French & Eur.

Carpovich, Eugene A. Russian-English Metals & Machines Dictionary. LC 60-12013. (Rus. & Eng.). 1960. $15.00x (ISBN 0-911484-02-7). Tech Dict.

Diccionario Para Obras Publicas, Edificacion y Maquinaria en Obra. (Ger. & Span.). 1962. $86.00 (ISBN 3-7625-1160-8, M-7132). French & Eur.
Freeman, H. G. Special Dictionary Machinery. 8th ed. 207p. (Eng. & Ger.). 1971. $44.25 (ISBN 3-7736-5031-0). Adler.
Freeman, Henry G. Fachwoerterbuch Spanende Werkzeugmaschinen. 527p. (Ger. & Eng.). 1965. DM.leatherette 72.00 (ISBN 3-7736-5090-6). Girardet.
Lanecki, Francois & Dupre, Celine. Vocabulaire Francais-Anglais De la Machine a Coudre Industrielle. 85p. (Fr.-Eng.). 1973. pap. $3.50 (ISBN 0-686-56991-1, M-6331). French & Eur.
Lexique Francais-Anglais et Anglais-Francais des Termes d'usage Courant en Machines Outils et Machines Similaires. 56p. (Fr., French-English, English-French Lexicon of Commonly Used Terms in Machine Tools and Similar Machines). 1960. pap. $6.95 (ISBN 0-686-56794-3, M-6365). French & Eur.
Lexique Francais-Anglais: Termes d'usage Courant en Machines-Outlis & Machines Similaires. 56p. (Fr. & Eng.). 1960. 11.00 F. Ste. Publications Mecaniques.
Lexique Trillingue des Termes d'usage Courant en Machines. (Illus.). 74p. (Fr.). 1961. 21.00 F. Ste. Publications.
Lexique Trillingue des Termes d'usage Courant en Machines: Les Perceuses. 96p. (Fr.). 1963. 21.00 F. Ste. Publications Mecaniques.
Schlomann, A. Illustrierte Technische Woerterbucher: Maschinenelemente, Vol. 1. (Illus., Ger., Eng., Fr., Rus., Span. & It., Illustrated dictionary elements of machinery & tools). 1968. $59.95 (ISBN 0-686-56482-0, M-7469, Pub. by R. Oldenbourg). French & Eur.
--Illustrierte Technische Woerterbucher: Maschinenelemente, Vol. 1. (Illus., Ger., Eng., Fr., Rus., Span. & Ital.). 1968. $59.95. Oldenbourg Verlag.
Simons, Eric N. A Dictionary of Machining. (Illus.). 240p. 1973. 15.00 (ISBN 0-685-27907-3). Philos Lib.
Welling, Manfred S. German-English Glossary of Plastics Machiney Terms. 280p. (Ger. & Eng.). 1981. text ed. 14.00x (ISBN 0-02-949800-7, Pub. by Hanser International). Macmillan.

MACHINERY IN INDUSTRY
see also Automation
Lanecki, Francois & Dupre, Celine. Vocabulaire Francais-Anglais de la Machine a Coudre Industrielle. 85p. (Fr. & Eng.). 1973. Can.$1.50. Quebec Off.

MAFIA
Pallotta, Gino. Dizionario Storico Della Mafia. LC 77-576985. (Illus.). 134p. (Ital.). 1977. L.2000.00. Newton Compton.

MAGIC
Here are entered works dealing with occult science (supernatural arts). Works on modern parlor magic, legerdemain, prestidigitation, etc. are entered under the heading Conjuring.
see also Alchemy; Idols and Images; Occult Sciences
Bersez, Jacques. Dictionnaire Pratique & Explicatif des Produits Magiques & Articles Usuels. (Illus.). 125p. (Fr.). 1977. 63.00 F. Bersez.
Chardans, J. L. & Vega, Vicente. Diccionario Ilustrado de Trucos. 700p. (Span.). 1970. leatherette $24.75 (ISBN 84-252-0206-X, S-14532). French & Eur.
Dizionario dei sogni e cabala del lotto. (Illus., Ital.). L.2700.00. Malipiero.
Lamb, Geoffrey. Illustrated Magic Dictionary. (Illus.). 160p. 1980. 7.95 (ISBN 0-525-66689-3). Lodestar Bks.

MAGIC–JUVENILE LITERATURE
Goma, Eulalia. Diccionario Magico Infantil. 7th ed. 50p. (Span.). 1978. $10.75 (ISBN 84-324-0190-0, S-26065). French & Eur.
--Diccionario Magico Infantil En Seis Lenguas. 2nd ed. 96p. (Span., Catalan, Vasco, Gallic, Fr. & Eng.). 1978. $20.25 (ISBN 84-324-0249-4, S-50028). French & Eur.

MAGICIANS
Disney, Walt. Dictionnaire Magique. (Illus., Fr.). 1978. 19.50 F. Nathan.
Goma, Eulalia. Diccionario Magico Infantil. 10th ed. 50p. (Span.). 1982. 500.00 ptas (ISBN 84-324-0190-0). Vilamala.
--Diccionario Magico Infantil. 9th ed. 50p. (Span.). 1981. 430.00 ptas (ISBN 84-324-0190-0). Vilamala.

MAGNETISM
see also Electricity
also headings beginning with the word Magnetic
Breitsameter. Lexikon der Schulphysik: Elektrizitaet und Magnetismus A-K, Vol. 3A. (Ger.). $42.50 (ISBN 3-7614-0168-X, M-7224). French & Eur.
--Lexikon der Schulphysik: Elektrizitaet und Magnetismus L-Z, Vol. 3B. (Ger.). $42.50 (ISBN 3-7614-0169-8, M-7225). French & Eur.
Dictionary of Physics: No. 2, Electricity & Magnetism. (Hebrew, Eng. , Fr. & Ger.). IL.8.00. Massada Pr.
Hoefling, Oskar, ed. Lexikon der Schulphysik: Bd 3, Elektrizitaet & Magnetismus-1.Tlbd, A-K. vi, 201p. (Ger.). 1978. DM.46.00 (ISBN 3-7614-0168-X). Aulis Verlag.
--Lexikon der Schulphysik: Bd 3, Elektrizitaet & Magnetismus-2.Tlbd, L-Z. vi, 201p. (Ger.). 1978. DM.46.00 (ISBN 3-7614-0169-8). Aulis Verlag.

MAGYAR LANGUAGE
see Hungarian Language

MAIL SERVICE
see Postal Service

MAINE–GENEALOGY
Noyes, Sybil, et al. Genealogical Dictionary of Maine & New Hampshire. LC 79-88099. 795p. 1983. Repr. of 1939 ed. 30.00 (ISBN 0-8063-0502-9). Genealog Pub.

MAITLAND CLUB, GLASGOW
Volkart, K. Gips-Woerterbuch. 176p. (Ger.). 1971. DM.68.00 (ISBN 3-7625-0460-1). Bauverlag.

MAKAH INDIANS
see Indians of North America–Northwest, Pacific

MAKE-UP (COSMETICS)
see Cosmetics

MALABAR LANGUAGE
see Malayalam Language

MALACOLOGY
see Mollusks

MALAGASY LANGUAGE
Malzac, R. P. Dictionnaire Francais-Malgache. 861p. (Fr.). 1953. 70.00 F. Maritimes Outremer.
--Vocabulaire Francais-Malgache. 446p. (Fr.). 1952. 18.00 F. Maritimes Outremer.

MALARIA
Terminologia del Paludismo & de la Erradicacion del Paludismo. 161p. (Span.). 1964. $3.25. OMS.
Terminology of Malaria & of Malaria Eradication: Report of a Drafting Committee. 127p. (Eng. , Fr. , Rus. & Span.). 1963. pap. $6.40 (ISBN 92-4-154014-1). World Health.

MALARIAL FEVER
see Malaria

MALAWI
Crosby, Cynthia A. Historical Dictionary of Malawi. LC 80-18. (African Historical Dictionaries Ser.: No. 25). 280p. 1980. lib. bdg. $15.00 (ISBN 0-8108-1287-8). Scarecrow.

MALAY LANGUAGE
see also Indonesian Language
Marsden, William. Malay-English Dictionary. (Eng. & Malayian.). 1976. Repr. of 1958 ed. $92.00 (ISBN 0-518-19003-X). Ayer Co.
Newell, Leonard E. A Batad Ifugao Vocabulary. (Language & Literature Ser.). 1968. $15.00. HRAFP.

MALAY-POLYNESIAN LANGUAGES
see Austronesian Languages

MALAYALAM LANGUAGE
see also Tamil Language
Pilla, T. Ramalingam. Sailee Nihantu: Dictionary of Idioms & Phrases. 1008p. (Malayalam.). 1975. write for info. DC Bks.
Pillai, C. Madhavan. Abhinava Malayala Nikhantu: New Malayalam Dictionary, 2 vols. (Malayalam.). 1980. write for info. DC Bks.
Pillai, T. R. English-Malayalam Dictionary. Chandrasekhara, M. S., ed. 904p. (Eng. & Malayalam.). 1980. write for info. DC Bks.
Pillai, T. Ramalingam. English-English-Malayalam Dictionary. Krishna, N. V., rev. by. 3333p. (Eng. & Malayalam.). 1976. write for info. DC Bks.
--English-English-Malayalam Dictionary. Octavo, M. S., ed. 1200p. (Eng. & Malayalam.). 1983. write for info. DC Bks.

MALAYAN LANGUAGES
see also Austronesian Languages; Indonesian Language; Javanese Language; Malagasy Language; Malay Language; Philippine Languages
McManus, Edwin G., et al. Palauan-English Dictionary. LC 76-9058. (Pali Language Texts: Micronesia). (Palauan & Eng.). 1977. pap. text ed. $16.00x (ISBN 0-8248-0450-3). UH Pr.
Richards, A. J., ed. An Iban-English Dictionary. (Illus., Iban & Eng.). 1982. 65.00x (ISBN 0-19-864325-X). Oxford U Pr.

MALAYSIA
Rott, N. V., ed. Malaiziisko-Russko-Angliiskii Slovar. 400p. (Malay, Rus. & Eng.). 1977. $7.75 (Pub. by Russkii Iazyk). Four Continent.

MALEMBA LANGUAGE
see Congo Language

MALGACHE LANGUAGE
see Malagasy Language

MALI
Imperato, Pascal J., ed. Historical Dictionary of Mali. LC 76-55775. (African Historical Dictionaries Ser.: No. 11). (Illus.). 1977. $15.00 (ISBN 0-8108-1004-2). Scarecrow.

MALRAUX, ANDRE, 1901-1976–DICTIONARIES, INDEXES, ETC.
Juilland, Ileana. Dictionnaire Des Idees Dans L'oeuvre D'andre Malraux. 325p. (Fr.). 1968. $29.95 (ISBN 0-686-56887-7, F-111080). French & Eur.
Julland, Ileana. Dictionnaire Des Idees Dans L'oeuvre D'Andre Malraux: Collection Dictionaries Des Idees Dans les Litteratures Occidentales, Litterature Francaise: Dictionnnaires D'auteurs. (No. 2). (Fr.). 1968. 17.00x (ISBN 0-686-21240-1). Mouton.

MAMMALS
Gotch, A. F. Mammals: Their Latin Names Explained. (Illus.). 1979. $18.95 (ISBN 0-7137-0939-1, Pub. by Blandford Pr England). Sterling.
Hoffman, Alfred. Glosar der Wichtigsten Saugetiere Chinas. xi, 103p. (Ger. & Chinese.). 1978. write for info. (ISBN 3-447-02001-6). Harrassowitz.

MAN
see also Anthropology; Men; Women
Romeo, Luigi. Ecce Homo! A Lexicon of Man. xv, 163p. 1979. $18.00x (ISBN 90-272-2006-9). Benjamins North Am.
Russell, Bertrand. Diccionario del Hombre Contemporaneo. (Span.). pap. $17.50 (ISBN 0-686-56655-6). French & Eur.
--Diccionario del hombre contemporaneo. (Span.). Arg.$23.00. Rueda.

MAN–INFLUENCE ON NATURE
see also Environmental Policy; Pollution
Khatib, Ahmad. A Dictionary of Natural Environment. 59p. (Eng. & Arabic.). 1979. pap. $7.95 (073-2). Intl Bk Ctr.
Monkhouse, F. A Dictionary of the Natural Environment. (Illus.). 381p. (Eng. & Arabic.). 1978. $16.00 (078-3). Intl Bk Ctr.

MAN-TO-MAN COMBAT
see Hand-To-Hand Fighting

MANAGEMENT
see also Business; Hospitals–Administration; Industrial Management; Office Management; Organization; Personnel Management; Planning; School Management and Organization
also subdivision management under specific subjects, e.g. Railroads–Management
Altfelder, Klaus. Lexikon der Unternehmensfuehrung. (Ger.). 1973. $65.00 (ISBN 3-470-56191-5, M-7219). French & Eur.
Antolinez, Crescencio. Fachworterbuch Fur Recht und Verwaltung. (Span. & Ger.). 1970. leatherette $35.00 (ISBN 3-452-17065-9, M-7398, Pub. by Carl Heymanns Verlag KG). French & Eur.
Diccionario de terminos administrativos. (Span. & Eng.). write for info. (608-105). Pan Amer Pub.
Pugh, Eric. Third Dictionary of Acronyms & Abbreviations: More Abbreviations in Management, Technology, & Information Science. 1977. $17.50 (ISBN 0-208-01535-3, Linnet). Shoe String.
Rosenberg, Jerry M. Dictionary of Business & Management. 2nd. ed. LC 82-24743. 631p. 1983. $29.95 (ISBN 0-471-86730-6, Pub. by Wiley-Interscience). Wiley.
Thesaurus du Management & de L'economie, 2 vols. 2nd ed. LC 77-461651. (Eng. & Fr.). 1975. 2025.00 F (ISBN 2-9500-2031-3). Bureau Marcel.

MANAGEMENT–ABBREVIATIONS
Pugh, Eric, compiled by. Pugh's Dictionary of Acronyms & Abbreviations. LC 81-14029. 348p. 1982. $87.50x (ISBN 0-89774-012-2). Oryx Pr.

MANAGEMENT–DICTIONARIES
Altfelder, Klaus, et al. Lexikon der Unternehmensfuehrung. 292p. (Ger.). 1973. DM.58.00 (ISBN 3-470-56191-5). Kiehl.
Bolado, Victor H. Management Terminology: English-Spanish & Spanish-English. 192p. (Eng. & Span.). 1981. $9.95 (ISBN 0-89962-034-5). Todd & Honeywell.
Colasse. Lexique de Comptabilite & de Gestion. (Fr.). 1975. 23.00 F. Ecole Electricite.
--Lexique de Comptabilite et de Gestion. (Fr.). 1975. pap. $14.95 (ISBN 0-686-56768-4, M-6079). French & Eur.
Conveney, James & Amey, Julian. Glossary of Spanish & English Management Terms. 138p. (Span. & Eng.). pap. $6.95 (C-107S). Biling Rev Pr.
Conveney, James & Moore, Shiela J. Lexique De Termes Anglais-Francais De Gestion: Les Cycle Au Superieur, Ecoles Superieures De Gestion. 160p. (Eng. & Fr.). 1972. pap. $9.95 (ISBN 0-686-56963-6, M-6087). French & Eur.
Coveney & Moore. Glossary of French & English Management Terms. 146p. (Fr. & Eng.). 1972. pap. $8.50 pocket size. Imported Bks.
--Glossary of French & English Management Terms. xii, 146p. (Fr. & Eng.). E3.50. Longman.
Coveney & Amey, eds. Glossary of Spanish & English Management Terms. (Span. & Eng.). E3.50. Longman.
Coveney, James & Amey, J. Glossary of Spanish & English Management Terms. (English for Special Purposes Bk.). (Span. & Eng.). 1978. pap. text ed. 6.95x (ISBN 0-582-55541-8). Longman.
Coveney, James & Moore, Sheila J. Lexique de Termes Anglais-Francais de Gestion. 160p. (Eng. & Fr.). 1972. 23.50 F. Colin.
Coveney, James & Moore, Shelia J., eds. Glossary of French & English Management Terms. (English for Special Purposes Bk.). 158p. (Fr. & Eng.). 1972. pap. text ed. 6.95x (ISBN 0-582-55502-7). Longman.
Coveny, James & Degens, Christina. Glossary of German & English Management Terms. (Ger. & Eng.). pap. $6.95. Longman.

De Silva, Dharmasena. Kalamanakarana Paribhasika Sabda Sangrahaya. LC 79-904454. viii, 496p. (Eng.). 1978. Rs.27.00. Kojamba.

Dictionnaire du Style & des Usages Administratifs. 484p. (Fr.). 43.50 F. Sodi.

Dubac, R. Vocabulaire de gestion. 135p. (Eng. & Fr.). 1974. 60.00 F. Maison Dictionnaire.

Dubuc, Robert. Vocabulaire de Gestion. 135p. (Fr.). 1974. Can.$3.96. Radio-Canada.

Eichborn, R. Woerterbuch fuer Wirtschaft-Recht-Verkehr-Verwaltungs & Umgangssprache: Vol.I, Englisch-Deutsch. rev. ed. 1150p. (Eng. & Ger.). 1983. $124.00. M Rosenberg.

--Woerterbuch fuer Wirtschaft-Recht-Verkehr-Verwaltungs & Umgangssprache: Vol. II, Deutch-Englisch. 1150p. (Ger. & Eng.). 1982. $124.00. M Rosenberg.

Eriksson, Erick R. & Baeckbom, Roy. Modernt Foertagsekonomiskt Lexikon. LC 78-349746. (Illus.). 350p. (Swedish). 1977. Kr.94.00 (ISBN 9-15-180888-9). Prisma.

Glossary of French & English Management Terms. (Fr. & Eng.). $6.95. Longman.

Glossary of German & English Management Terms. (Ger. & Eng.). pap. $8.50. Imported Bks.

Glossary of Spanish & English Management Terms. (Span. & Eng.). $6.95. Longman.

Haas, Peter. Management-Taschenlexikon. LC 80-477370. (Illus.). 189p. (Ger.). 1978. DM.9.80. Verlag Moderne Industrie.

Hano & Robertson, Andrew B., trs. Diccionario de management. 240p. (Span.). 1972. 350.00 ptas. Oikos Tau.

Johannsen, H. Management Glossary: (English-Arabic) 238p. (Eng. & Arabic.). 1972. $16.00x (ISBN 0-86685-069-4). Intl Bk Ctr.

Johannsen, H. & Page, G. T., eds. International Dictionary of Management. 2nd ed. 1981. pap. 29.95 (ISBN 0-686-86508-1, Pub by Kogan Pg). Nichols Pub.

Johannsen, H., et al. Diccionario de Management. 244p. (Span.). 1972. $23.95 (ISBN 84-281-0220-1, S-31465). French & Eur.

Kerler, Richard. Begriffe des Managements. LC 75-517995. (Illus.). 126p. (Ger.). 1975. DM.3.80 (ISBN 3-581-66261-2). Humboldt Taschen.

Lauzel, Pierre. Lexique de la Gestion. 240p. (Fr.). 1970. 39.00 F. E. M. E.

Linnert, Peter. Lexikon Angloamerikanischer und Deutscher Managementbegriffe. (Ger.). 1972. $75.00 (ISBN 3-921099-00-5, M-7286). French & Eur.

Management Dictionary. (Ger. & Eng.). 1978. 4th ed. $26.00 (ISBN 3-11-004863-9); 5th ed. $29.25x (ISBN 3-11-007708-6). De Gruyter.

Rosenberg, Jerry M. Dictionary of Business & Management. LC 78-7796. 1978. pap. $9.95 (ISBN 0-471-09885-X). Wiley.

Seone, Joaquin R. Diccionario de contabilidad, organizacion, administracion, control & ciencia afines, 7 vols. 3400p. (Span.). 1972. $45.00. Difusion.

Sommer-Schoenfeld, Management Dictionary, Deutsch-English: Fachwoerterbuch Fuer Betriebswirtschaft Wirtschafts-und Steuerrecht und Datenverarbeitung. 4th ed. 290p. (Ger. & Eng.). 1978. $24.50x (ISBN 3-11-002663-5). De Gruyter.

Sommer, Werner & Schoenfeld, Hanns-Martin. Management Dictionary. 5th rev. enl. ed. 621p. 1979. text ed. $34.25x (ISBN 0-686-77467-1). De Gruyter.

Sommer, Werner & Schoenfeld, Hans-Martin. Management Dictionary: Fachwoerterbuch fuer Betriebswirtschaft, Wirtschafts und Steuerrecht und Datenverarbeitung. 4th ed. LC 78-190431. (English-Deutsch). 328p. (Eng. & Ger.). 1972. $17.75x (ISBN 3-11-001981-7). De Gruyter.

Spreutels, Marcel. Dictionnaire du Style et des Usages Administratifs. 484p. (Fr.). 1979. $19.95 (ISBN 0-686-57225-4, M-6523). French & Eur.

Tezenas Du Montcel, Henri. Dictionnaire des Sciences de la Gestion. 332p. (Fr.). 1972. 50.00 F. Delarge.

Van Dijk, Marcel & Sandeau, Georges. Thesaurus du Management & de l'economie, 2 vols. 150p. (Fr.). 1975. 225.00 F. M. Van Dijk.

Villers, M. Vocabulaire de l'Informatique de Gestion: Anglais-Francais. 31p. (Eng. & Fr.). 1980. pap. $3.95 (ISBN 2-551-03899-5, M-9228). French & Eur.

Von Linnert, et al. Lexikon der Managementbegriffe. (Ger.). 1977. DM.9.80 (ISBN 3-453-49068-1). Heyne W Verlag.

Weinzierl, Emil. Begriffswoerterbuch zur Betriebswirtschafts & Managementlehre. LC 77-567493. 187p. (Ger.). 1976. S.135.00 (ISBN 3-85122-063-3). Industrieverlag.

Wortman, Leon A. A Deskbook of Business Management Terms. LC 78-23257. 1979. $24.95 (ISBN 0-8144-5470-4). Am Mgmt.

--A Deskbook of Business Management Terms. 1982. $14.95 (ISBN 0-8144-7571-X). Am Mgmt.

MANAGEMENT, INDUSTRIAL
see Industrial Management

MANCHU LANGUAGE
Norman, Jerry. A Concise Manchu-English Lexicon. LC 77-14307. (Publications on Asia of the School for International Studies: No. 32). 336p. (Manchu & Eng.). 1979. $25.00x (ISBN 0-295-95574-0). U of Wash Pr.

Sravnitelnyi Slovar Tunguso-Manchzhurskikh Iazykov: Materialy & Etimologicheskomu Slovariu, 2 vols. (Rus.). 1975. $37.50 set (Pub. by Nauka). Four Continent.

MANDAN INDIANS
see Indians of North America–The West

MANDEL'SHTAM, OSIP EMIL'EVICH, 1891-1938?
Koubourlis, Demetrius J. & Parrish, Stephen M., eds. A Concordance to the Poems of Osip Mandelstam. LC 73-8387. (Concordances Ser.). 704p. (Rus. & Eng.). 1974. $42.50x (ISBN 0-8014-0806-7). Cornell U pr.

MANGAIAN LANGUAGE
Christian, F. W. Vocabulary of the Mangaian Language. (Mangaian.). Repr. of 1924 ed. pap. 8.00 (ISBN 0-527-02114-8). Kraus Repr.

MANIFOLDING
see Copying Processes

MANJU LANGUAGE
see Manchu Language

MANNERS AND CUSTOMS
see also Costume; Etiquette; Sports; Students

Affre, Henri & Rodez. Dictionnaire des Institutions, Moeurs & Costumes du Rouergue. 470p. (Fr.). 150.00 F. Lafitte Repr.

Dictionnaire des Costumes, Croyances & Langages. 131p. (Fr.). 1976. write for info. Reprints.

Klein, J. R. Vocabulaire des Moeurs de la Vie Parisienne Sous le Second Empire. 342p. (Fr.). 1977. 78.40 F. Vander.

MANOBO LANGUAGE–DICTIONARIES–ENGLISH
Elkins, Richard E. Manobo-English Dictionary. LC 68-63364. (Oceanic Linguistics Special Publications: No. 3). 376p. (Manobo & Eng.). 1968. pap. text ed. $10.00x (ISBN 0-87022-225-2). UH Pr.

MANSLAUGHTER
see Assassination

MANUAL ALPHABETS
see Deaf–Means of Communication

MANUFACTURES–DIRECTORIES
European Directories, ed. The Dictionary of Toiletry & Cosmetic Manufacturers in Western Europe. 1981. $100.00x (ISBN 0-686-78875-3, Pub. by European Directories England). State Mutual Bk.

MANUFACTURING ENGINEERING
see Production Engineering

MANUFACTURING PROCESSES
see also Materials; Process Control; Woodwork

Standard Terms Used in the Soda Pulping Process. 1961. $1.00 (1202); members $0.67. TAPPI.

Standard Terms Used in the Sulfate Pulping Process. 1961. $1.00 (1203); members $0.67. TAPPI.

MANUKUTUBA LANGUAGE
see Congo Language

MANUSCRIPT DEPOSITORIES
see Archives

MANUSCRIPTS
see also Diplomatics; Paleography

Evans, Frank B., et al. A Basic Glossary for Archivists, Manuscript Curators, & Records Managers. 19p. 1974. pap. $2.00 (ISBN 0-931828-02-3). Soc Am Archivists.

Haenel, G. F. Dictionnaire des Manuscrits, Ou Recueil De Catalogues De Manuscrits Existants Dans les Pri Cipales Bibliotheques D'europe, 2 vols. Migne, J. P., ed. (Nouvelle Encyclopedie Theologique Ser.: Vols. 40-41). 1624p. (Fr.). Repr. of 1853 ed. lib. bdg. $205.50x (ISBN 0-89241-280-1). Caratzas Pub Co.

Kasten, Lloyd & Nitti, John. Concordances & Texts of the Royal Scriptorium Manuscripts of Alfonso X, el Sabio, 2 vols. (Spanish Ser.: No. 2). 1978. 150.00x (ISBN 0-942260-11-2). Hispanic Seminary.

Meyer, Karl H. Altkirchenslavisch-Griechisches Woerterbuch Des Codex Supraliensis. (Gr.). $25.00 (ISBN 0-685-71713-5). J J Augustin.

MANUSCRIPTS–BIBLIOGRAPHY
New York Public Library, Research Libraries. Dictionary Catalog & Shelf List of the Spencer Collection of Illustrated Books & Manuscripts & Fine Bindings, 2 vols. 1970. Set. lib. bdg. $190.00 (ISBN 0-8161-0862-5, Hall Library). G K Hall.

--Dictionary Catalog of the Manuscript Division, 2 Vols. 1967. Set. lib. bdg. $150.00 (ISBN 0-8161-0750-5, Hall Library). G K Hall.

MANUSCRIPTS–CONSERVATION AND RESTORATION
Haenel, G. F. Dictionnaire des Manuscrits, Ou Recueil De Catalogues De Manuscrits Existants Dans les Pri Cipales Bibliotheques D'europe, 2 vols. Migne, J. P., ed. (Nouvelle Encyclopedie Theologique Ser.: Vols. 40-41). 1624p. (Fr.). Repr. of 1853 ed. lib. bdg. $205.50x (ISBN 0-89241-280-1). Caratzas Pub Co.

MANUSCRIPTS–RESTORATION
see Manuscripts–Conservation and Restoration

MANX LANGUAGE
Fargher, Douglas. Fargher's English-Manx Dictionary. 928p. 1979. $90.00x (ISBN 0-904980-23-5, Pub. by Shearwater England). State Mutual Bk.

Fargher, Douglas C. Fargher's English Manx Dictionary. 1979. text ed. 67.75x (ISBN 0-904980-23-5). Humanities.

MAORI LANGUAGE
see also Tahitian Language

Barham, I. H. Vocabulary & Science Structure of Maori Children. (Maori.). $1.25. Nzcer.

MAORI LANGUAGE–DICTIONARIES
Concise Maori Dictionary. (Eng., Auckland, New Zealand). 1980. NT.$3.95. Reed Ltd.

Ngata, Apirana N. Complete Manual of Maori Grammar & Conversation, with Vocabulary. 5th rev. enl. ed. LC 75-35261. (Maori.). Repr. of 1939 ed. $19.00 (ISBN 0-404-14433-0). AMS Pr.

Ryan, P. New Dictionary of Modern Maori. (Maori.). $2.65. Hein.

Ryan, P. M., ed. New Dictionary of Modern Maori. 104p. (Maori.). 1983. pap. 4.95 (ISBN 0-86863-565-0, Pub. by Heinemann Pub New Zealand). Intl Schol Bk Serv.

MAORI LEGENDS
see Legends, Polynesian

MAP DRAWING
see also Cartography; Topographical Drawing

Tooley, R. V. Tooley's Dictionary of Mapmakers. LC 79-1936. 696p. (Orig.). 1981. pap. $40.00 (ISBN 0-8451-1702-5). A R Liss.

MAPS–BIBLIOGRAPHY
New York Public Library, Research Libraries. Dictionary Catalog of the Map Division, 10 vols. 1971. Set. lib. bdg. $950.00 (ISBN 0-8161-0783-1, Hall Library). G K Hall.

MAPS, HISTORICAL
see Classical Geography

MARCHING
see Drill and Minor Tactics

MARICOPA INDIANS
see Indians of North America–Southwest, New

MARIE DE L'INCARNATION, MOTHER, 1599-1672
L'Heureux, Mother Aloysius G. Mystical Vocabulary of Venerable Mere Marie De L'Incarnation & Its Problems. LC 72-94190. (Catholic University of America Studies in Romance Languages & Literatures Ser: No. 53). (Fr.). Repr. of 1956 ed. $18.75 (ISBN 0-404-50353-5). AMS Pr.

MARIHUANA
Abel, Ernest L. A Marihuana Dictionary: Words, Terms, Events & Persons Relating to Cannabis. LC 81-13427. xi, 136p. 1982. lib. bdg. 25.00 (ISBN 0-313-23252-0, ABM/). Greenwood.

MARIJUANA
see Marihuana

MARINE ARCHITECTURE
see Ship-Building

MARINE BIOLOGY
see also Marine Fauna; Sedimentation and Deposition

English-Japanese Marine Terms Dictionary. 542p. (Eng. & Japanese.). $95.00 (ISBN 0-686-92390-1, M-93491). French & Eur.

MARINE BOILERS
see Steam-Boilers

MARINE DEPOSITION
see Sedimentation and Deposition

MARINE ENGINEERING
see also Steam-Boilers

Claviez, Wolfram. Seemaennisches Woerterbuch. (Ger.). 1973. $38.50 (ISBN 3-7688-0166-7, M-7620, Pub. by Delius, Klaving & Co.). French & Eur.

Gil, L. S. Diccionario Tecnico-Maritimo Ingles-Espanol & Espanol-Ingles. 708p. (Eng. & Span.). 1980. pap. write for info. (ISBN 84-205-0772-5). Edit Alhambra.

Institute of Marine Engineers. Glossary of Marine Technology Terms. 178p. 1980. pap. $15.00x (ISBN 0-434-90840-1). Sheridan.

--Glossary of Marine Technology Terms. 256p. 1980. $35.00x (Pub. by Heinemann England). State Mutual Bk.

Masuda, M., ed. Dictionary of Marine Engineering Terms: Japanese-English, English-Japanese. 313p. (Japanese & Eng.). 1980. $35.00 (ISBN 0-686-92525-4, M-9339). French & Eur.

MARINE FAUNA
see also Fishes

Vocabulaire des Animaux Marins en Latin Classique. 154p. (Fr.). 1947. 32.00 F. Klincksieck.

MARINE INSURANCE
see Insurance, Marine

MARINE LAW
see Maritime Law

MARINE PAINTING
Archibald, E. H. Dictionary of Sea Painters. (Illus.). 453p. 1980. $79.50 (ISBN 0-902028-84-7). Antique Collect.

Wilson, Arnold. A Dictionary of British Marine Painters. (Illus.). 1980. Repr. of 1967 ed. text ed. 40.00x (ISBN 0-85317-051-7, Pub. by A & C Black England). Humanities.

MARINE SHIPPING
see Shipping
MARINE TECHNOLOGY
see Marine Engineering
MARINE TRANSPORTATION
see Shipping
MARINE ZOOLOGY
see Marine Fauna
MARINERS
see Seamen
MARITIME DISCOVERIES
see Discoveries (In Geography)
MARITIME HISTORY
see subdivisions Navy or History, Naval under names of countries, e.g. United States–History, Naval and Great Britain–Navy
MARITIME LAW
see also Commercial Law; Insurance, Marine
Amich, Julian. Diccionario maritimo. 2nd ed. 427p. (Span.). 1971. 380.00 ptas. Juventud.
Bes, J. Chartering & Shipping Terms: Time-Sheet Supplements, Vols. 2 & 3. Set. $70.00 (ISBN 0-685-11999-8). Heinman.
Garcia de Paredes y Castro, Jose & Barbudo Duarte, Enrique. Diccionario maritimo ingles-espanol y espanol-ingles. 256p. (Eng. & Span.). 1965. 340.00 ptas. Fragata.
Navarro Dagnino, J. Vocabulario Maritimo Ingles-Espanol. 3rd ed. 152p. (Eng. & Span.). write for info. G Gili.
Navarro Dagnino, Juan. Vocabulario maritimo ingles-espanol y espanol-ingles. 5th ed. 152p. (Eng. & Span.). 1980. pap. 280.00 ptas (ISBN 84-252-0225-6). G Gili.
Paasch, Henri. Dictionnaire Anglais-Francais Des Termes & Locutions Maritimes. 2nd ed. 320p. (Fr.). 1974. 53.00 F. Maritimes Outre mer.

MARITIME SHIPPING
see Shipping
MARKETING
see also Merchandising
also Subdivision Marketing under Names of Commodities, E.g. Farm Produce–Marketing; Fruit–Marketing
Delson, Donn. The Dictionary of Marketing & Related Terms in the Motion Picture Industry. LC 79-67865. (Entertainment Communication Ser.: Vol. 1). 70p. (Orig.). 1979. pap. text ed. $7.95 (ISBN 0-9603574-0-8). Bradson.
Giomot, Sylvain. Dictionnaire de la Publicite et du Marketing: Anglais-Francais Francais-Anglais. 500p. (Eng. & Fr.). 1979. 110.00 F. Maison Dictionnaire.
Gruber, Clemens. Dictionary of Advertising & Marketing. (Eng. & Ger.). 1977. pap. $15.75 (ISBN 3-1900-6312-5). Adler.
--Woerterbuch der Werbung und des Marketing. (Eng. & Ger.). 1977. pap. $15.00 (ISBN 3-19-006312-5, M-6942). French & Eur.
Hart, Norman A. & Stapleton, John. Glossary of Marketing Terms. 2nd ed. 156p. 1981. $30.00x (ISBN 0-434-91861-X, Pub. by Heinemann England). State Mutual Bk.
--Glossary of Marketing Terms. 1981. pap. $11.50 (ISBN 0-434-91861-X, Pub. by W Heinemann England). David & Charles.
International Chain of Industrial & Technical Advertising Agencies. Dictionary of Advertising & Marketing Terms in Six Languages: English-Spanish-French-German-Italian-Japanese. Black, George, ed. 300p. 1982. lib. bdg. cancelled (ISBN 0-930624-03-3). Marlin.
Jefkins, Frank. Dictionary of Marketing & Communication. 1973. text ed. $19.95x (ISBN 0-7002-0218-8). Intl Ideas.
Nuss, A. M. Export for Marketing French. 96p. (Fr. & Eng.). 1979. pap. $13.95 (ISBN 0-582-35157-X, M-9208). French & Eur.
Nyssen, Hubert. Lexique du Marketing. 86p. (Fr.). 1971. pap. $7.50 (ISBN 0-686-57064-2, M-6435). French & Eur.

--Lexique du Marketing. (Fr.). 1971. 12.00 F. Delpire.
Rabassa Asenjo, B. & Garcia Tous, M. R. Diccionario de Marketing. 168p. (Span.). write for info. (ISBN 8-43680-075-3, 250027). Piramide.
Rabassa Asenjo, Bernardo & Garcia Tous, M. R. Diccionario de Marketing. 168p. (Span.). 1978. $14.95 (ISBN 84-368-0075-3, S-50176). French & Eur.
Roche, Francois. Lexique du Marketing. 3rd ed. 108p. (Fr.). 1970. 32.00 F. E. M. E.
San Juan Rubio, Roman. Terminos Internacionales en la Gestion de Compras & Ventas. 44p. (Span.). 70.00 ptas. APD.
Shapiro, Irving J. Dictionary of Marketing Terms. 4th ed. (Littlefield, Adams Quality Paperback Ser.: No. 363). 280p. (Orig.). 1981. pap. 7.95 (ISBN 0-8226-0363-2). Littlefield.
--Dictionary of Marketing Terms. 4th ed. LC 80-25669. 280p. 1981. 16.50x (ISBN 0-8476-6967-X). Rowman.

MARKS, POTTERS'
see Pottery–Marks
MARKS OF ORIGIN
see also Trade-Marks
MacDonald-Taylor, Margaret. Dictionary of Marks. (Illus.). 1962. pap. $6.25 (ISBN 0-8015-2089-4, 0607-180, Hawthorn). Dutton.
--A Dictionary of Marks. 320p. (Illus.). 1981. $25.00x (ISBN 0-900305-11-8, Pub. by Ebury Pr England). State Mutual Bk.

MARKS ON PLATE
see Hall-Marks
MARLOWE, CHRISTOPHER, 1564-1593
Fehrenbach, Robert J., et al, eds. A Concordance to the Plays, Poems, & Translations of Christopher Marlowe. LC 81-67175. (A Cornell Concordance). 1710p. 1982. 45.00 F. Salkine. $75.00x (ISBN 0-8014-1420-2). Cornell U Pr.

MARRIAGE
see also Domestic Relations; Family
Glossaire Europeen de Terminologie Juridique et Administrative: Droit du Mariage, No. 19. 96p. (Ger. & Fr.). 1973. pap. $14.95 (ISBN 0-686-92449-5, M-9486). French & Eur.

MARRIAGE–EUROPE
Pressot, Marcel. Vocabulaire des Quinze Joles du Mariage. 145p. (Fr.). 1974. 45.00 F. Slatkine.

MARSHALL LANGUAGE
Abo, Takaji, et al. Marshallese-English Dictionary. LC 76-26156. (PALI Language Texts-Micronesia). 624p. (Marshallese & Eng.). 1976. pap. text ed. $12.50x (ISBN 0-8248-0457-0). UH Pr.
Bender, Byron W. Spoken Marshallese. (PALI Language Texts: Micronesian). (Orig., Marshallese & Eng.). 1969. pap. text ed. $13.00x (ISBN 0-87022-070-5). UH Pr.

MARTIAL ARTS
see also Hand-To-Hand Fighting
Lopez Dominguez, Mario. Diccionario de las Artes Marciales. 250p. (Span.). 1981. 250.00 ptas (ISBN 84-7494-032-X). Ramos-Majos.

MARTYRS
Russo-Alesi, Anthony I. Martyrology Pronouncing Dictionary. LC 79-167151. 1973. Repr. of 1939 ed. $30.00x (ISBN 0-8103-3272-8). Gale.

MARXIAN ECONOMICS
Bischoff, Joachim. Grundbegriffe der Marxistischen Theorie. 1st ed. LC 79-397548. 263p. (Ger.). 1978. DM.16.00 (ISBN 3-87975-136-6). VSA Verlag.

MARXISM
see Socialism
MASCULINITY (PSYCHOLOGY)
Vincent, P. Dictionnaire de la Virilite. 370p. (Fr.). 1973. $12.50 (ISBN 0-686-57247-5, M-6553). French & Eur.
Vincent, Paul. Dictionnaire de la Virilite. (Illus.). 370p. (Fr.). 1973. 28.00 F. Maloine.

MASONIC ORDERS
see Freemasons

MASONRY
see also Arches; Bricklaying; Cement; Concrete; Foundations
Glossary of Terms Relating to Brick Masonry. Rev. ed. (No.2). 1975. $0.50. Brick Inst Amer.
International Masonry Institute. Masonry Glossary. 100p. 1981. $12.95 (ISBN 0-8436-0134-5). CBI Pub.
Ligou, Daniel. Dictionnaire Universel de la Franc-Maconnerie, 2 vols. 1518p. (Fr.). 1975. 300.00 F. Prisme.

MASONS (SECRET ORDER)
see Freemasons
MASS CASUALTIES–TREATMENT
see Emergency Medical Services
MASS COMMUNICATION
see Communication; Communication and Traffic; Mass Media; Telecommunication
MASS FEEDING
see Food Service
MASS MEDIA
see also Moving-Pictures; Newspapers; Radio Broadcasting; Television Broadcasting
Connors, Tracy D. Longman Dictionary of the Mass Media & Communication. LC 82-92. (Public Communication Ser.). (Illus.). 256p. 1982. text ed. 24.95x (ISBN 0-582-28337-X); pap. text ed. 12.95x (ISBN 0-582-28336-1). Longman.
Divers. Dictionnaire de la presse ecrite et audiovisuelle. 580p. (Span., Fr., Ital., Port. & Romanian). 1981. 160000.00 F. Maison Dictionnaire.
Escarpit, Denise. Press, Radio & Television. LC 76-472541. 349p. (Eng., Ger., Fr., & Span.). 1975. 28.00 F (ISBN 2-7213-0050-4). Elp.
Fages, Jean B. & Pagano, Christian. Dictionnaire des Media. 350p. (Fr.). Can.$12.50. Hurtubise H. M. H.
Fages, Jean Baptiste & Pagano, Christian. Dictionnaire des Media. 364p. (Fr.). 1971. pap. $22.50 (ISBN 0-686-56848-6, M-6626). French & Eur.
--Dictionnaire des Media. 364p. (Fr.). 1971. 50.00 F. Delarge.
Istilah percetakan, penerbitan, dan komunikasi massa, Inggeris-Malaysia-Inggeris. LC 79-102377. xiv, 594p. (Malay & Eng.). 1978. M.$7.00. Dewan Bahasa.
Jacobson, Howard B., ed. Mass Communications Dictionary: A Reference Work of Common Terminologies for Press, Print, Broadcast, Film, Advertising & Communications Research. Repr. of 1961 ed. lib. bdg. 25.00x (ISBN 0-8371-2124-8, JAMC). Greenwood.

MASS PSYCHOLOGY
see Social Psychology
MASS TRANSIT
see Local Transit
MASSACHUSETTS–GENEALOGY
Gannett, Henry. A Geographic Dictionary of Massachusetts. LC 78-59121. 126p. 1978. Repr. of 1894 ed. 12.00 (ISBN 0-8063-0818-4). Genealog Pub.

MATERIA MEDICA
see also Aphrodisiacs; Drugs; Pharmacy; Therapeutics
also names of drugs
Clarke, John H. A Dictionary of Practical Materia Medica. 1980. $125.00x (ISBN 0-85032-139-5, Pub. by Daniel Co England). State Mutual Bk.
Leonard, C. Henri & Christy, Thomas. Dictionary of Materia Medica & Therapeutics. 1980. lib. bdg. 75.00 (ISBN 0-8490-3120-6). Gordon Pr.

MATERIAL HANDLING
see Materials Handling
MATERIAL SCIENCE
see Materials
MATERIALS
see also Building Materials; Manufacturing Processes
Clauser. Diccionario de materiales y procesos de ingenieria. (Span.). 2310.00 ptas. Labor SA.

MATERIALS–HANDLING AND TRANSPORTATION
see Materials Handling

MATERIALS–TESTING
Goedecke, Werner. Woerterbuch der Wirkstoffprufung. LC 80-475766. (Eng., Ger. & Fr.). 1979. write for info. (ISBN 3-18-400434-1). VDI-Verlag.

MATERIALS, STRENGTH OF
see Strength of Materials
MATERIALS HANDLING
see also Cargo Handling; Conveying Machinery; Pallets (Shipping, Storage, etc.)
American National Standards Institute. Terms & Conveyors Definitions: ANSI-CEMA No. 102, ANSI MH4.1. 1975. $5.00 (VI-18). Material Handling.

MATHEMATICAL ANALYSIS
see also Algebra; Programming (Electronic Computers)
Buchholz, W., et al. Iterated Inductive Definitions & Subsystems of Analysis: Recent Proof-Theoretical Studies. (Lecture Notes in Mathematics Ser.: Vol. 897). 383p. 1982. pap. $20.00 (ISBN 0-387-11170-0). Springer-Verlag.

MATHEMATICAL DRAWING
see Mechanical Drawing
MATHEMATICAL FORMULAE
see Mathematics–Formulae
MATHEMATICAL LOGIC
see Logic, Symbolic and Mathematical
MATHEMATICAL SETS
see Set Theory
MATHEMATICAL SYMBOLS
see Abbreviations
MATHEMATICS
see also Algebra; Arithmetic; Geometry; Graphic Methods; Logic, Symbolic and Mathematical; Mensuration; Metric System; Numerals; Set Theory
also headings beginning with the word Mathematical
Fachredaktionen des Bibliographischen Instituts, ed. Duden-Rechnen & Mathematik. 1056p. (Ger.). DM.39.00 (ISBN 3-411-00920-9). Biblio Inst.
Gibson, Carol, ed. The Facts on File Dictionary of Mathematics. 224p. 1981. prepub. $14.95 (ISBN 0-87196-512-7). Facts on File.
Herland. Dictionary of Mathematical Sciences: Band II, Englisch-German. 349p. (Eng. & Ger.). 1982. DM.65.00. Brandstetter.
--Dictionary of Mathematical Sciences: Band I, German-English. 323p. (Ger. & Eng.). 1982. DM.60.00. Brandstetter.
Scheid, Harald, et al. Die Mathematik II: Ein Lexikon zur Schulmathematik Sekundarstufe II. (Illus.). 468p. (Ger.). 1982. DM.19.80 (ISBN 3-411-01959-X). Biblio Inst.
--Die Mathematik I: Ein Lexikon zur Schulmathematik Sekundarstufe. (Illus.). 539p. (Ger.). 1981. DM.19.80 (ISBN 3-411-01912-3). Biblio Inst.

MATHEMATICS–ADDRESSES, ESSAYS, LECTURES
Millet, Kenneth C. Piecewise Linear Concordances & Isotopies. LC 74-18328. (Memoirs Ser.: No. 153). 74p. 1974. pap. $9.00 (ISBN 0-8218-1853-8, MEMO-153). Am Math.

MATHEMATICS–DICTIONARIES
Alsina, Claudi. Vocabulari Catala De Matematica Basica. 48p. (Catalan.). 1977. pap. $8.75 (ISBN 84-85008-06-5, S-50127). French & Eur.
Ballentyne, D. W. & Walker, L. E. Diccionario de Leyes y Efectos Cientificos En Quimica-Fisica Matematicas. 216p. (Span.). $14.95 (ISBN 0-686-56711-0, S-33054). French & Eur.
Bendick, Jeanne & Levin, Marcia. Mathematics Illustrated Dictionary: Facts, Figures & People, Including the New Math. (Illus.). (gr. 7 up). 1982. 8.95 (ISBN 0-07-004460-0, GB). McGraw.
Boursin, Jean-Louis. DEMO: Dictionnaire Elementaire de Mathematiques Modernes. 320p. (Fr.). 1972. $21.95 (ISBN 0-686-56927-X, M-6045). French & Eur.

Chambadal, L. L. Dizionario di matematica moderna. (Ital.). L.7500.00. Mursia.

Chambadal, Lucien. Diccionario De las Matematicas Modernas. 2nd ed. 264p. (Span.). 1976. pap. $5.25 (ISBN 84-01-90307-6, S-12248). French & Eur.

--Diccionario de las matematicas modernas. (Span.). $100.00. Plaza Janes.

--Dictionnaire des Mathematiques Modernes. rev. ed. 250p. (Fr.). 1972. pap. $6.95 (ISBN 0-686-56847-8, M-6625). French & Eur.

--Dictionnaire des Mathematiques Modernes. (Illus.). 250p. (Fr.). 1972. 17.60 F. Larousse.

Costa, Vasco & Frances, Osvald. Diccionario De Unidadaes y Tablas De Conversion. 3rd ed. 168p. (Span.). 1977. pap. $8.75 (ISBN 84-252-0214-0, S-50579). French & Eur.

De Francis, J., compiled by. A Chinese-English Glossary of the Mathematical Sciences. 286p. (Chinese & Eng.). 1964. $42.20 (ISBN 0-8218-0018-3, UMI-2004670); pap. $37.20 members. Am Math.

Diaz Velazquiz, Mariano. Diccionario basico de matematicas. 3rd ed. 224p. (Span.). 1981. pap. 500.00 ptas (ISBN 84-207-1434-8). Anaya.

Diccionario Monografico de Matematicas. 288p. (Span.). 750.00 ptas (ISBN 84-7153-388-X). Biblograf SP.

Diccionario Monografico de Matematicas. 288p. (Span.). 1981. pap. write for info. (ISBN 84-7153-388-X). Biblo SP.

Dictionary of Mathematical Terms. (Hebrew & Eng.). IL.15.00. Massada Pr.

Dictionary of Mathematics. 252p. (Eng. & Chinese.). 1974. pap. $4.95 (ISBN 0-686-92280-8, M-9575). French & Eur.

Dizionario delle scienze fisiche e matematiche. 178p. (Ital.). L.2500.00. Zanichelli.

Dovnar-Zapolskaia, N. M. Nemetsko-Russkii Mekhaniko-Matematicheskii Slovar. 236p. (Ger. & Rus.). 1960. $2.25 (Pub. by MGU). Four Continent.

Dragnev, M. V. & Rosov, Victor. Dictionnaire Francais-Russe de Mathematique. (Fr. & Rus.). 8.50 F. MIR.

Eisenreich & Sube. Woerterbuch der Mathmetik, 2 vols. 1458p. (Eng., Fr., Rus. & Ger.). 1982. DM.198.00 (ISBN 3-87144-445-6). Verlag Harri Deutsch.

Eisenreich, G. & Sube, R. Dictionary of Mathematics, 2 vols. (Eng., Fr., Ger. & Rus.). 1982. Set. 159.75 (ISBN 0-444-99706-7). Elsevier.

English-Chinese Dictionary of Mathematical Terms. 252p. (Eng. & Chinese.). 1980. $25.00 (ISBN 0-686-92416-9, M-9293). French & Eur.

Fachlexikon ABC Mathematik. 624p. (Ger.). 1978. $30.95 (ISBN 3-87144-030-2, M-7381, Pub. by Verlag Harri Deutsch). French & Eur.

Fachlexikon ABC Mathematik. (Ger.). 1977. $30.95 (ISBN 3-87144-336-0, M-7382, Pub. by Harri Deutsch). French & Eur.

Fachwortschatz Mathematik. LC 77-552687. 96p. (Eng. & Ger.). 1976. M.5.00. VEB Verlag Enzyklopadie.

Gellert, W., et al, eds. Lexikon der Mathematik. (Illus.). 624p. (Ger.). 1981. M.28.00. Bibl Inst Leipzig.

Gheorghita, Stefan. Dictionar Poliglot de Matematica, Mecanica si Astronomie. LC 78-387413. xvi, 664p. (Eng., Rus., Ger., Fr. & Romanian.). 1978. 67.00 lei. Editura Stiintifica.

Grignon, Jean. Lexique Mathematique. 2nd ed. (Illus.). 195p. (Fr.). 1977. 5.75 F. F. I. C.

--Lexique Mathematique, Symboles, Vocabulaire, Tables. (Fr.). Can.$3.30. Centre Psych.

Herland, Leo. Dictionary of Mathematical Sciences, 2 vols. Incl. Vol. 1. German-English. 2nd ed. xii, 320p (ISBN 0-8044-4393-9); Vol. 2. English-German. 320p (ISBN 0-8044-4394-7). LC 65-16622. (Eng. & Ger.). $22.00 ea. Ungar.

James, Glenn. Mathematics Dictionary. 4th ed. LC 76-233. vii, 509p. (Eng., Fr., Ger., Rus. & Span.). 1976. write for info. (ISBN 0-442-24091-0). Van Nos Reinhold.

Kaluzhnin, L. A., et al. Nemetsko-Russkii Matematicheskii Slovar. 182p. (Ger. & Rus.). 1960. $2.70 (Pub. by Fizmatgiz). Four Continent.

Klaften, Berthold. Mathematisches Vokabular. 4th ed. (Eng. & Ger., Vocabulary of Mathematics). 1971. $13.50 (ISBN 0-686-56630-0, M-7551, Pub. by Wila). French & Eur.

Klaften, E. B. German-English, English-German Mathematical Dictionary. (Ger. & Eng.). pap. 15.00 (ISBN 0-686-77978-9). Heinman.

Knerr, Richard. Lexikon der Mathematik. LC 79-368679. 484p. (Ger.). 1978. DM.12.80 (ISBN 3-596-26376-X). Fischer Taschen.

Lohwater, A. J. Russian-English Dictionary of the Mathematical Sciences. LC 61-15685. 267p. (Eng. & Rus.). 1979. Repr. of 1974 ed. $17.00 (ISBN 0-8218-0036-1, RED). Am Math.

Lopatnikov, L. I. Populiarnyi Ekonomiko-Matematicheskii Slovar. 165p. (Rus.). 1973. $1.95 (Pub. by Znanie). Four Continent.

Maravall Casesnovas, Dario. Diccionario de Matematica Moderna. LC 75-513298. 333p. (Span.). 1975. 300.00 ptas (ISBN 8-4276-1235-4). Nacional Editora.

Maravall Casesnoves, Dario. Diccionario De Matematica Moderna. 332p. (Span.). 1975. pap. $9.95 (ISBN 0-686-57333-1, S-50009). French & Eur.

--Diccionario de matematica moderna. 2nd ed. 412p. (Span.). 1982. pap. 1300.00 ptas (ISBN 84-276-1235-4). Nacional Editora.

Marks, Robert W. Diccionario & Manual de las Nuevas Matematicas. (Illus.). 270p. (Span.). 1968. Mex.$3.50. Editors Pr Serv.

--Diccionario y manual de las nuevas matematicas. 2nd, rev. ed. (Illus.). 288p. (Span.). $1.50. Edit Pr Serv.

Millington, William & Millington, T. Alaric. Dictionary of Mathematics. 1971. pap. $3.95 (ISBN 0-06-463311-X, EH 311, EH). B&N NY.

Milne-Thomson, L. M. Russian-English Mathematical Dictionary. (Mathematical Research Center Pubns., No. 7). 206p. (Rus. & Eng.). 1962. $40.00x (ISBN 0-299-02600-0). U of Wis Pr.

Ministry of Education. Scientific Terms Mathematics: Japanese-English, English-Japanese. 146p. (Japanese & Eng.). 1954. Leatherette $14.95 (ISBN 0-686-92202-6, M__9346). French & Eur.

Miranda, Hernany. Diccionario Popular Matematico. LC 79-126000. 313p. (Span.). 1978. write for info. Direc Pubns.

Rack, Guenter. Mathematisch-Naturwissenschaftliches Woerterbuch Deutsch-Dari. 652p. (Ger. & Dari.). 1977. DM.78.00 (ISBN 3-87276-178-1). Groos Verlag.

Reck, J. Herder-Lexikon Mathematik. 238p. (Ger.). 1974. $15.95 (ISBN 3-451-16458-2, M-7445, Pub. by Herder). French & Eur.

--Herder-Lexikon Mathematik. 238p. (Ger.). 1974. $15.95 (ISBN 3-451-16458-2). Herder.

Reck, Jurgen. Diccionario Rioduero Matematica. 224p. (Span.). 1977. leatherette $12.50 (ISBN 84-220-0832-7, S-50162). French & Eur.

--Diccionarios Rioduero: Matematicas. 2nd ed. Strobl, Walter, tr. 224p. (Span.). 1982. pap. 600.00 ptas (ISBN 84-220-0832-7). Catolica Edit.

Roubakine. Dictionnaire Francais-Russe de Mathematique. (Fr. & Rus.). 1978. 47.45 F. MIR.

Saverien, Alexandre. Dictionnaire Universel de Mathematique & de Physique, 1. (Fr.). DM.138.00. Olms.

--Dictionnaire Universel de Mathematique & de Physique, 2. (Fr.). DM.138.00. Olms.

Sharov, V., et al. Nemetsko-Russkii Slovar Po Vychislitelnoi Tekhnike. 400p. (Ger. & Rus.). 1976. $6.50 (Pub. by Russkii Iazyk). Four Continent.

Sube, Ralf. Woerterbuch der Mathematik. 800p. (Eng., Ger., Fr. & Rus., Dictionary of Mathematics). 1979. $80.00 (ISBN 3-87144-445-6, M-6983). French & Eur.

Sube, Ralf & Eisenreich, Gunther. Mathematik Englisch-Deutsch-Franzoesisch-Russisch. 1440p. (Eng., Ger., Fr. & Ger.). 1982. M.info. 140.00for. VEB Technik.

Vera, Francisco. Lexicon Kapelusz: Matematica. 2nd ed. (Illus.). 744p. (Span.). Mex.$12.86. Kapelusz.

Vox, ed. Diccionario Monografico de Matematicas. 287p. (Span.). 1981. $20.25 (ISBN 84-7153-388-X). French & Eur.

Warusfel, Andre. Diccionario razonado de matematicas: De las matematicas clasicas a la matematica moderna. 500p. (Span.). 700.00 ptas. Tecnos SA.

--Dictionnaire Raisonne De Mathematiques. (Fr.). 1966. pap. $27.95 (ISBN 0-686-57257-2, M-6567). French & Eur.

--Dictionnaire Raisonne de Mathematiques. (Fr.). 1966. 69.00 F. Seuil.

MATHEMATICS-FORMULAE

Hernandez, Juan D. Diccionario de Formularios Generales, Vol. 5. 800p. (Span.). 1981. pap. 3000.00 ptas (ISBN 84-85565-06-1). Nereo.

MATRIMONY
see Marriage

MAURITANIA

Gerteiny, Alfred G. Historical Dictionary of Mauritania. LC 81-5291. (African Historical Dictionaries Ser.: No. 31). 116p. 1981. $13.00 (ISBN 0-8108-1433-1). Scarecrow.

MAURITIUS-HISTORY

Riviere, Lindsay. Historical Dictionary of Mauritius. LC 81-16557. (African Historical Dictionaries Ser.: No. 34). 206p. 1982. $13.50 (ISBN 0-8108-1479-X). Scarecrow.

MAXIMS
see also Aphorisms and Apothegms; Proverbs

Maloux, M. Dictionnaire des proverbes, sentences et maximes. (Fr., Fr). 23.50 (ISBN 2-03-020291-6, 3618). Larousse.

MAYA LANGUAGE
see also Tzeltal Language

Andrews Heath de Zapata, Dorothy. Vocabulario de Mayathan. LC 79-351468. 607p. (Maya & Span.). 1978. write for info. Dorothy Andrews Heath de Zapata.

Blair, Robert W., et al. Mayan Language Dictionary. LC 81-43356. 491p. 1982. lib. bdg. $83.00 (ISBN 0-8240-9277-5). Garland Pub.

Collard, Howard & Collard, Elizabeth. Vocabulario Mayo, Vol. 6. rev. ed. 225p. (Span.). 1974. pap. $4.00x (ISBN 0-88312-657-5); microfiche $3.00 (ISBN 0-88312-318-5). Summer Inst Ling.

Michelon, Oscar. Diccionario de San Francisco. LC 78-370238. xvi, 770p. (Eng., Maya & Span.). 1976. S.1600.00 (ISBN 3-201-00972-5). Akademische Druck Verlagt.

MAYAN LANGUAGES
see also Maya Language; Tzeltal Language

Barrera Vasquez, Alfredo. Diccionario Maya Cordemex Maya-Espanol. 69th ed. 360p. (Maya & Span.). 1980. Mex.$pap. 3000.00. Porrua.

Gates, William. An Outline Dictionary of Maya Glyphs. LC 77-92481. (Illus.). 1978. pap. $3.50 (ISBN 0-486-23618-8). Dover.

MAYORS

Holli, Melvin G. & Jones, Peter d'A, eds. Biographical Dictionary of American Mayors, 1820 to 1980. LC 80-1796. (Illus.). Feb. 1981. lib. bdg. 69.50 (ISBN 0-313-21134-5, HDA/). Greenwood.

MAZDAISM
see Zoroastrianism

MBALA LANGUAGE
see Congo Language

MBOCHI LANGUAGE
see Congo Language

MBOMA LANGUAGE
see Congo Language

MEASURABLE SETS
see Measure Theory

MEASURE THEORY

Scientific Apparatus Makers Association. Process Instrumentation Reliability Terminology: 32.1-1976. $2.00; bulk prices avail. Sci Apparatus.

--Process Measurement & Control Terminology: 20.1-1973. $2.00; bulk prices avail. Sci Apparatus.

MEASUREMENTS, OPTICAL
see Optical Measurements

MEASURING
see Mensuration

MEAT
see also Beef

Kulier, Ignac. Englesko-Hrvatska ili Srpska Tehnicko-Tehnoloska. LC 77-459563. 145p. (Eng. & Serbo-Croation., Zagreb). 1976. write for info. Prehrambeno-Tehnoloski.

MEAT CONSUMPTION
see Meat Industry and Trade

MEAT INDUSTRY AND TRADE

Kinsman, Donald M. International Meat Science Dictionary. (Illus.). 282p. 1979. pap. $10.95x (ISBN 0-89641-029-3). American Pr.

MEAT PACKING INDUSTRY
see Meat Industry and Trade

MECHANICAL ANALOGIES IN ELECTRICITY
see Electromechanical Analogies

MECHANICAL BRAINS
see Cybernetics

MECHANICAL DRAWING
see also Engineering Graphics; Graphic Methods

Dictionary of Technical Drawing. (Hebrew, Eng. , Fr. & Ger.). IL.7.00. Massada Pr.

Lexikon der Graphischen Technik. 4th ed. (Ger.). 1977. $29.95 (ISBN 3-7940-4078-3, M-7253). French & Eur.

MECHANICAL ENGINEERING-DICTIONARIES

American Society of Mechanical Engineers. Dictionary of Terms for Computer-Aided Preparation of Product Definition Data (Including Engineering Drawings) Y14.26.3-1975. $3.50 (N00012); members $2.80. ASME.

--Glossary of Mechanical Press Terms: B5.49-1977. $3.50 (M00090); members 2.80. ASME.

--Glossary of Terms Concerning Letter Symbols: Y10.1-1972. $2.25 (K00003); members $1.80. ASME.

--Glossary of Terms for Mechanical Fasteners: B18.12-1962 (R1975) $9.50 (M00046); members $7.60. ASME.

--Pallet Definitions & Terminology: MH1.1.2-1978. $4.00 (M00073); members $3.20. ASME.

European Committee of Associations of Gear & Transmission Element Manufacturers (EUROTRANS), ed. Glossary of Transmission Elements: Gears. (Illus., In 8 languages). 1978. lib. bdg. 30.00x (ISBN 3-7830-0104-8). Marlin.

Freeman, Henry G. Dictionary of Mechanical Engineering. 8th rev. ed. LC 72-347328. (Eng. Ger.). 1971. $45.00x (ISBN 3-7736-5031-0). Intl Pubns Serv.

--Spezialwoerterbuch Maschinenwesen. 207p. (Ger. - Eng., Dictionary of Mechanical Engineering). 1971. write for info (M-7625, Pub. by Verlag W. Girardet). French & Eur.

--Spezialwoerterbuch Maschinenwesen. 207p. (Ger. & Eng.). 1971. write for info. Girardet.

Horner, J. G. Dictionary of Mechanical Engineering Terms. 9th rev. & enl. ed. Grahame-White, G. K., ed. 30.00 (ISBN 0-685-29250-9). Heinman.

Lexikon der Graphischen Technik. 4th ed. (Ger.). 1977. $29.95 (ISBN 3-7940-4078-3, M-7253). French & Eur.

Nayler, J. L. & Nayler, G. H. Dictionary of Mechanical Engineering. 2nd ed. 1978. Repr. of 1975 ed. $29.95 (ISBN 0-408-00175-5). Butterworth.

Schulz, E. Woerterbuch der Optik und Feinmechanik: English-French-German Dictionary of Optics & Mechanical Engineering. (Eng., Fr. & Ger.). 1961. write for info. (M-90925). French & Eur.

Schulz, Ernst. Woerterbuch der Optik und Feinmechanik, Vol. 1. (Fr., Ger. & Eng., Dictionary of Optics & Mechanical Engineering). 1961. pap. $12.00 (ISBN 3-87097-036-7, M-6978). French & Eur.

--Woerterbuch der Optik und Feinmechanik, Vol. 2. (Fr., Ger. & Eng., Dictionary of Optics & Mechanical Engineering). 1961. pap. $12.00 (ISBN 3-87097-037-5, M-6977). French & Eur.

Shvarts, V. V. The Concise Illustrated Russian-English Dictionary of Mechanical Engineering. (Illus.). 224p. (Rus. & Eng.). 1981. pap. 30.00 (ISBN 0-08-027574-5). Pergamon.

--Kratkii Illiustrirovannyi Russko-Angliiskii Slovar Po Mashinostroeniu. 224p. (Rus. & Eng.). 1979. $5.75 (Pub. by Russkii Iazyk). Four Continent.

Shvarts, Vladimir. The Concise Illustrated Russian-English Dictionary of Mechanical Engineering. 224p. (Rus. & Eng.). 1980. $35.00x (ISBN 0-686-44774-3, Pub. by Collets). State Mutual Bk.

Stellhorn, Kurt. Woerterbuch Werkzeuge und Werkzeugmaschinen. (Ger. & Fr.). 1969. leatherette $56.00 (ISBN 3-7736-5260-7, M-6907). French & Eur.

MECHANICAL HANDLING
see Materials Handling
MECHANICAL MOVEMENTS
Bucksch, H. Dictionary of Mechanisms. (Ger. & Eng.). 1976. leatherette $133.00 (ISBN 3-7625-0707-4, M-7111). French & Eur.

--Getriebe-Woerterbuch. 286p. (Eng. & Ger.). 1976. DM.165.00 (ISBN 3-7625-0707-4). Bauverlag.

MECHANICAL PAINTING
see Painting, Industrial
MECHANICS
see also Electromechanical Analogies; Engineering; Force and Energy; Hydraulics; Mechanical Movements; Power (Mechanics); Soil Mechanics; Strength of Materials; Thermodynamics; Vibration

Bossier, Rene. Dictionnaire Technique des Fabrications Mecaniques. 200p. (Fr.). 1975. 28.00 F. Desforges.

Diccionario de mecanica. (Span.). $6.50. Minerva.

Diccionario de mecanica I y II. (Span.). $2.20 ea. Minerva.

Dictionary of Physics: No. 1, Mechanics. (Hebrew, Eng. , Fr. & Ger.). IL.8.00. Massada Pr.

Dovnar-Zapolskaia, N. M. Nemetsko-Russkii Mekhaniko-Matematicheskii Slovar. 236p. (Ger. & Rus.). 1960. $2.25 (Pub. by MGU). Four Continent.

Gluzman, I. S. Anglo-Russkii Slovar Zheleznodorozhnoi Automatike, Telemekhanike & Sviazi. 427p. (Rus. & Eng.). 1958. $5.25 (Pub. by Gosizdat Fizmat. Lit.). Four Continent.

Heller, C. Dictionary of Engineering Mechanics. (Eng. & Rus.). 1965. $14.75 (ISBN 0-444-40274-8). Elsevier.

Hoefling, Oskar, ed. Lexikon der Schulphysik: Bd 1, Mechanik & Akustik. (Ger.). 1978. DM.54.00 (ISBN 3-7614-0107-8). Aulis Verlag.

Mertz De Mertzenteld, R., et al. Dictionnaire Technologique Feutry: Mecanique-Metallurgie-Hydraulique, Vol. 1. 750p. (Eng., Fr. & Ger.). 1976. 250.00 F. Maison Dictionnaire.

Normandeau, Lucien. Lexique de Mecanique d'ajustage. 2nd ed. 256p. (Fr.). 1957. Can.$3.50. Quebec Off.

Saiz, M. Diccionario de Mecanica Ingles-Espanola. 336p. (Eng. & Span.). pap. $5.95. Lectorum Pubns.

Schulz. Woerterbuch der Optik & Feinmechanik: Band II, Englisch-Franzoesisch-Deutsch. 124p. (Eng., Fr. & Ger.). 1982. DM.16.00. Brandstetter.

--Woerterbuch der Optik & Feinmechanik: Band III, Franzoesisch-Deutsch-Englisch. 109p. (Fr., Ger. & Eng.). 1982. DM.16.00. Brandstetter.

Zita, K. Lexikon der Schulphysik: Mechanik und Akustik, Vol. 1. (Ger.). $44.00 (ISBN 3-7614-0107-8, M-7222). French & Eur.

MECHANICS–ELECTRIC ANALOGIES
see Electromechanical Analogies
MECHANISMS (MACHINERY)
see Mechanical Movements
MECHANIZATION
see also Automation
Calbet Sequi, Juan. Terminos & Conceptos Mas Usuales en Mecanizacion Administrativa. 249p. (Span.). $4.80; Mex.$60.00. Limusa.

MECHANIZED INFORMATION STORAGE AND RETRIEVAL SYSTEMS
see Information Storage and Retrieval Systems
MEDICAL BOTANY
see Botany, Medical
MEDICAL CARE, COST OF
American Medical Record Association. Glossary of Hospital Terms. 2nd rev. ed. 128p. 1974. $5.75 (ISBN 0-686-68577-6, 14911). Healthcare Fin Man Assn.

MEDICAL CHEMISTRY
see Chemistry, Medical and Pharmaceutical
MEDICAL CLINICS
see Clinics
MEDICAL COMMUNICATION
see Communication in Medicine
MEDICAL COOPERATION
see Group Medical Practice
MEDICAL COSTS
see Medical Care, Cost of
MEDICAL DIAGNOSIS
see Diagnosis
MEDICAL EMERGENCIES
see also Emergency Medical Services
Diccionario de medicina de urgencia. 210p. (Span.). 1971. 120.00 ptas. Cedel.

MEDICAL ENGINEERING
see Biomedical Engineering
MEDICAL ETHICS
Duncan, A. S., et al, eds. Dictionary of Medical Ethics. 496p. 1981. $24.50 (ISBN 0-8245-0038-5). Crossroad NY.

Scremin. Diccionario de moral profesional medica. (Span.). pap. 200.00 ptas. Garriga.

Thomson. Dictionary of Medical Ethics & Practice. 272p. 1977. $27.95 (ISBN 0-7236-0454-1). Wright-PSG.

MEDICAL EXAMINATIONS
see Diagnosis
MEDICAL FOLK-LORE
see Folk Medicine
MEDICAL GENETICS
Witkowski, Regine. Genetik Erblicher Syndrome & Missbildungen. LC 76-675817. 1071p. (Eng. & Ger.). 1976. write for info. (ISBN 3-437-10409-8). Fischer Verlag.

MEDICAL GROUP MEDICAL PRACTICE
see Group Medical Practice
MEDICAL GYMNASTICS
see Exercise Therapy
MEDICAL LAWS AND LEGISLATION
Hamline Huniversity. Long Term Care & the Law. LC 83-135890. (Illus.). 300p. Date not set. price not set. Hamline Law.

Sloane, Sheila B. & Dusseau, John L. The Legal Speller with Useful Medical Terms. 2nd ed. 380p. 1982. pap. text ed. $7.95 (ISBN 0-314-69679-2). West Pub.

MEDICAL LIBRARIES
see also Information Storage and Retrieval Systems–Medicine
Lea, J. Terminology & Communication Skills in the Health Sciences. 1975. pap. $12.95 (ISBN 0-87909-821-X). Reston.

MEDICAL LITERATURE SEARCHING
see Information Storage and Retrieval Systems–Medicine
MEDICAL PROFESSION
see Medicine; Physicians
MEDICAL RADIOLOGY
see Radiology, Medical
MEDICAL REGISTRATION AND EXAMINATION
see Medical Laws and Legislation
MEDICAL RESEARCH ETHICS
see Medical Ethics
MEDICAL ULTRASONICS
see Ultrasonics in Medicine
MEDICATION, ANTISEPTIC
see Antiseptic Medication
MEDICINAL PLANTS
see Botany, Medical
MEDICINE
see also Aviation Medicine; Biomedical Engineering; Botany, Medical; Chemistry, Medical and Pharmaceutical; Dentistry; Family Medicine; Folk Medicine; Health; Histology; Homeopathy; Hospitals; Hypnotism; Materia Medica; Mind and Body; Nosology; Nurses and Nursing; Osteopathy; Pathology; Pharmacy; Physiology; Surgery also headings beginning with the word Medical

Aeschilimann, Werner-Heinrich. Dictionnaire des Sciences Medicales, 1821-1822. 89p. (Fr.). 1975. 20.00 F. Juris Druck.

Albert, Roald & Hahnewald, Harry. Medizintechnik-Englisch-Deutsch-Franzoesisch-Russisch-Spanisch-Polnisch-Ungarisch-Slowakisch. 596p. (Eng., Ger., Fr., Rus., Span., Pol., Hungarian & Slavic). 1980. M.55.00. VEB Technik.

Gladstone, W. J. Vocabulaire de Medecine & des Sciences Connexes: Francais-Anglais. 298p. (Fr. & Eng.). 1971. 85.00 F. Masson & Cie.

Touati, Maurice A. Lexique Francais des Abreviations: Formules Medico-Chirugicales Courantes. 142p. (Fr.). 1969. 24.00 F. Maloine.

MEDICINE–ABBREVIATIONS
Babecki, Jerzy & Maksys, Anna. Slownik Skrotow w Medycynie i Naukach Pokrewnych. LC 76-526887. 239p. (Pol.). 1976. 100.00 Zl. Panstwowe Zaklad W.

Hughes, Harold H. Dictionary of Abbreviations in Medicine & the Health Sciences. LC 76-8749. 336p. (Eng.). 1977. $26.95 (ISBN 0-669-00688-2). Lexington Bks.

Kerr, Avice H. Medical Hieroglyphs. LC 75-131216. 1970. $14.75 (ISBN 0-918558-01-8). Enterprise Calif.

--Medical Hieroglyphs. LC 75-131216. 1970. $14.75 (ISBN 0-918558-01-8). Enterprise Calif.

MEDICINE–COST OF MEDICAL CARE
see Medical Care, Cost Of
MEDICINE–DICTIONARIES
Aite, M. C. Dizionario di medicina. (Illus.). 1966p. (Ital.). 1966. L.2500.00. Zanichelli.

Alheim, Karl-Heinz, ed. Duden Woerterbuch Medizinischer Fachausdruecke, 3 vols. LC 79-384676. 751p. (Ger.). 1979. write for info. (ISBN 3-41101-747-3). Thieme Verlag.

Armengol, Joseph, et al, eds. English-Spanish Guide for Medical Personnel. (Eng. & Span.). 1966. pap. $7.00 (ISBN 0-87488-721-6). Med Exam.

Arslanian, G. T., et al. Russko-Arabskii Meditsinskii Slovar. 608p. (Rus. & Arabic). 1977. $12.50 (Pub. by Russkii Iazyk). Four Continent.

Babecki, Jerzy. Slownik Lekarski Lacinsko-Polski. LC 80-468620. 855p. (Lat. & Pol.). 1979. 350.00 Zl (ISBN 8-3200-0184-6). Panstwowe Zaklad W.

--Slownik Tekarski Polsko-Lacinksi. LC 79-361211. (Pol. & Lat.). 1978. 250.00 Zl. Panstwowe Zaklad W.

Bailliere, et al. Dizionario medico. 771p. (Ital.). 1977. L.10000.00 (ISBN 88-85019-16-1). Edi Ermes.

Bissanti, Andrea, et al. Diccionario medico. 3rd ed. Blanco, Catala J., tr. 364p. (Span.). 1981. pap. 3195.00 ptas (ISBN 84-85146-93-X). Mas Ivars.

Blacque-Belair, Alain. Dictionnaire Medicine, Clinique, Pharmacologique et Therapeutique. 2nd ed. 1938p. (Fr.). 1978. $115.00 (ISBN 0-686-56920-2, M-6036). French & Eur.

Bolander, B. O. Instant Medical Dictionary. (Career Institute Instant Reference Library). 1970. $3.95 (ISBN 0-531-02009-6). Watts.

Bolander, Donald O., et al. Instant Medical Spelling Dictionary. LC 77-124400. 1970. $3.95 (ISBN 0-911744-10-X). Career Inst.

Bongiovanni, Gail. Medical Spanish. (Span.). 1977. pap. text ed. $12.95 (ISBN 0-07-006470-9, HP). McGraw.

Bonvalot, Marie. Le Vocabulaire Medical De Base, 2 vols. 447p. (Fr.). 1972. Set. pap. $45.00 (ISBN 0-686-56925-3, M-6043). French & Eur.

Bouckaert, J. J. Nieuwe Medische Winkler Prins, 2 vols. LC 76-676261. (Eng. & Dutch). 1976. fl.4.75 (ISBN 9-0100-1653-6). Elsevier Nederland.

Braier, Leon. Diccionario Enciclopedico de Medicino Jims. 1184p. (Span.). 1980. 3.500 ptas. Jims.

Bratescu, Gheorghe. Dictionar Cronologie de Medicina si Farmacie. LC 75-405051. 366p. (Romanian). 1975. 18.50 lei. Editura Stiintifica.

Brenesan, Janos. Orvosi Szotar. LC 80-491065. 464p. (Hungarian). 1979. 85.00 Ft (ISBN 9-6320-5084-3). Terra.

Bunjes, Werner E. Woerterbuch der Medizin und Pharmazeutik: Medical & Pharmaceutical Dictionary, 2 vols. Rev. ed. (Eng. & Ger.). 1981. DM.75.00 ea. Thieme Verlag.

Byers, Edward E. Ten Thousand Medical Words, Spelled & Divided for Quick Reference. 128p. 1972. text ed. $6.40 (ISBN 0-07-009503-5, G). McGraw.

Carpovich, Eugene A. Russian-English Biological & Medical Dictionary. 2nd ed. LC 58-7915. (Rus. & Eng.). 1960. $25.00 (ISBN 0-911484-01-9). Tech Dict.

Carrasco, Castulo. Diccionario de Medicina Farmacia Veterinaria & Quimica. LC 78-392328. 1027p. (Span.). 1977. 2500.00 ptas (ISBN 8-4739-1013-3). Garsi Edit.

Chapman. Medical Dictionary for the Lay Person. 1983. pap. $5.95 (ISBN 0-8120-2247-5). Barron.

Chaumuzeau, P., et al. Dictionnaire de Medecine. LC 75-595740. (Eng. & Fr.). 1975. 0.195 F (ISBN 2-257-10399-8). Flammarion.

Chevallier, J. Precis De Terminologie Medicale. 2nd ed. 208p. (Fr.). 1977. 19.95 (ISBN 0-686-56948-2, M-6070). French & Eur.

Cohen, Andre. Dictionnaire Medical Illustre de Semiologie Patronymique. LC 79-129051. 213p. (Fr.). 1979. write for info. (ISBN 2-224-00513-X). Maloine.

Combs, C. Murphy, ed. Illustrated Medical Dictionary. (Medical Adviser Ser.). (Illus.). 1979. pap. $3.95 (ISBN 0-8326-2237-0, 7455). Delair.

Cortada, Francisco J. Diccionario medico Labor, 3 vols. 2608p. (Span.). 1970. Arg.$500.00. Labor SA.

Critchley, Macdonald, ed. Butterworths Medical Dictionary. 2nd ed. LC 77-30154. 1978. $59.95 (ISBN 0-407-00061-5). Butterworth.

--Butterworths Medical Dictionary. 2nd, unabridged ed. 1980. pap. text ed. $39.95 (ISBN 0-407-00193-X). Butterworth.
Dabout, E., ed. Diccionario de Medicina. (Span.). write for info. (S-37586). French & Eur.
Delamare, J. & Delamare, Th. Dictionnaire Francais-Anglais et Anglais-Francais des Termes Techniques de Medecine. 714p. (Eng. & Fr.). 1970. $39.95 (ISBN 0-686-56980-6, M-6107). French & Eur.
Delamarre. Dictionnaire Francais-Anglais et Anglais-Francais des Termes Techniques De Medecine. (Fr. & Eng.). $49.95 (ISBN 0-685-36680-4). French & Eur.
Di Aichelburg, Ulrico. Dizionario di medicina: Enciclopedia degli alimenti, 3 vols. xvi, 1396p. (Ital.). L.58000.00. UTET.
--Dizionario di medicina per le famiglie, 2 vols. (Illus.). viii, 1124p. (Ital.). 1974. L.48000.00 (ISBN 88-02-01495-7). UTET.
Diccionario de Ciencias Medicas Dorland. (Illus.). 1800p. (Span.). 1974. write for info. Ateneo Edit.
Diccionario de Medicina de Urgencia. 2nd ed. 208p. (Span.). 1977. $6.95 (ISBN 84-352-0174-0, S-13672). French & Eur.
Diccionario Manual de Medicina & Salud. 288p. (Span.). 1979. 595.00 ptas. Biblograf.
Diccionario Medico. 638p. (Span.). 1974. 375.00 ptas. Salvat Editores.
Diccionario Medico. 2nd ed. 640p. (Span.). 1974. write for info. Salvat Editores.
Diccionario medico de bolsillo. 2nd ed. 640p. (Span.). 1981. pap. 875.00 ptas (ISBN 84-345-1017-0). Salvat Editores.
Diccionario Medico: De Bosillo. 2nd ed. 632p. (Span.). 1974. leatherette $18.50 (ISBN 84-345-1017-0, S-13673). French & Eur.
Diccionario Medico Familiar II. 2nd ed. 800p. (Span.). 1981. 2975.00 ptas (ISBN 84-7142-239-5). Sel Rdrs Digest.
Diccionario medico para la familia moderna, 4 vols. 1500p. (Span.). write for info. Gaisa.
Diccionario Monografico de Medicina & Salud. 380p. (Span.). 750.00 ptas (ISBN 84-7153-380-4). Biblograf SP.
Diccionario Terminologico De Ciencias Medicas. 11th ed. 1088p. (Span.). 1978. $52.50 (ISBN 84-345-1206-8, S-13674). French & Eur.
Dictionnaire de Medecine Flammarion. 930p. (Fr.). 1975. $75.00 (ISBN 0-686-57099-5, M-6123). French & Eur.
Dictionnaire de Medecine Flammarion. (Illus.). 930p. (Fr.). 1975. 195.00 F. Flammarion.
Dizionario medico. (Illus.). 1208p. (Ital.). 1971. L.35000.00. Edizioni Paoline.
Domart, Andre. Petit Larousse de la Medecine. LC 77-454005. 842p. (Eng. & Fr.). 1976. 90.00 F (ISBN 2-03-020140-5). Larousse.
Domart, Andre & Bourneuf, Jacques. Larousse de la Medecine, 3 vols. 1728p. 1971. Set. $225.00 (ISBN 0-686-57120-7, M-6166). French & Eur.
Dorland Newman, W. A. Dizionario medico. (Illus.). viii, 686p. (Ital.). 1970. L.10000.00. CEA.
Dorland's Illustrated Medical Dictionary. 26th ed. (Illus.). 1800p. 1981. text ed. $34.50 (ISBN 0-7216-3150-9); indexed $39.50 (ISBN 0-7216-3151-7); deluxe ed. $59.00 indexed (ISBN 0-7216-3145-2). Saunders.
Dorland's Medical Dictionary: Shorter Edition. LC 79-67113. (Illus.). 768p. 1980. $16.95 (ISBN 0-7216-3142-8). Saunders.
Dornette, William H. L. Stedman's Medical Dictionary: Fifth Unabridged Lawyers' Edition. write for info. Anderson Pub Co.
Dox, Ida, et al. Melloni's Illustrated Medical Dictionary. (Illus.). 1979. $21.50 (ISBN 0-683-02642-9). Williams & Wilkins.
Duden-Woerterbuch Medizinischer Fachausdrucke. 2nd ed. (Ger.). DM.25.95 (ISBN 3-411-00943-8). Biblio Inst.
Duncan, A. S., et al, eds. Dictionary of Medical Ethics. 496p. 1981. $24.50 (ISBN 0-8245-0038-5). Crossroad NY.
Duncan, Helen A. Duncan's Dictionary for Nurses. LC 74-121974. (Illus.). 1971. Springer Pub.
Duranteau. Dizionario medico. (Ital.). L.8000.00. Newton Compton.
Eloy, N. F. Dictionnaire Historique de la Medecine Ancienne & Moderne. (Fr.). 1978. DM.138.00 F. Olms.
English-Chinese Dictionary of Medicine. 1675p. (Eng. & Chinese.). 1979. text ed. $24.95 (ISBN 0-8351-1048-6). China Bks.
English-Chinese Medical Dictionary. 1665p. (Eng. & Chinese.). 1980. $95.00 (ISBN 0-686-97366-6, M-9264). French & Eur.
English-Chinese Medical Dictionary. 292p. (Eng. & Chinese.). 1977. pap. $6.95 (ISBN 0-686-92358-8, M-9253). French & Eur.
Fachredaktion. Woerterbuch Medizinischer Fachausdruecke. 2nd ed. (Ger.). 1973. $25.00 (ISBN 3-13-437802-7, M-6913). French & Eur.
Finnegan, Edward G., ed. New Webster's Medical Dictionary: Vest Pocket Edition. 1980. pap. $1.95 (ISBN 0-8326-0048-2, 6453). Delair.
Fishbein, Morris. Modern Home Dictionary of Medical Words: With Descriptions, Uses & Standards of Commonly Used Tests. LC 74-18845. 240p. 1976. pap. $1.95 (ISBN 0-385-01105-9, Dolp). Doubleday.
Franks. Simplified Medical Dictionary. (Medical Economics Books). 1977. $12.50x (ISBN 0-442-84028-4). Van Nos Reinhold.
Garnier, M., et al. Dizionario dei termini tecnici di medicina. 1400p. (Ital.). 1978. L.15000.00. DEMI.
Garnier, Marcel & Delamare, Jean. Dictionnaire des Termes Techniques De Medecine. 19th ed. 1340p. (Fr.). 1978. $35.00 (ISBN 0-686-57190-8, M-6262). French & Eur.
Garrido, J. A. Diccionario Ingles-Espanol para Medicos y Estudiantes de Medicina. 525p. (Eng. & Span.). 1979. $35.95 (ISBN 84-7193-011-0, S-34967). French & Eur.
Garrido, Juan A. Diccionario ingles-espanol para medicos y estudiantes de medicina. 524p. (Eng. & Span.). 1972. 500.00 ptas. Pediatrica.
Gelis, D. N., ed. Greek-English, English-Greek Medical Dictionary. 4th rev. ed. (Illus., Gr. & Eng.). 1978. 75.00 (ISBN 0-686-91764-2). Heinman.
Gladstone. Vocabulaire De Medecine & Des Sciences Connexes Anglais-Francais-Anglais. (Eng. & Fr.). $21.95 (ISBN 0-685-36682-0). French & Eur.
Gladstone, W. J. Dictionnaire Anglais-Francais des Sciences Medicales & Paramedicales. (Eng. & Fr.). 1978. 250.00 F. Edisem.
--Dictionnaire Anglais-Francais des Sciences Medicales et Paramedicales. (Eng. & Fr.). 1978. $99.95 (ISBN 0-686-57303-X, M-6277). French & Eur.
--Dictionnaire Anglais-Francais des Sciences Medicales et Paramedicales. 1154p. (Fr.). 1978. 95.00 F. Maloine.
Gladstone, William J. Dictionnaire Anglais-Francais des Sciences Medicales & Paramedicales. LC 79-118626. 1153p. (Eng. & Fr.). 1978. 55.00 F. Maloine.
Goldhahn, Irmgard. Kleines Medizinisches Fremdworterbuch. LC 76-477700. 122p. (Ger.). 1976. M.9.50. Thieme Verlag.
Governa, Mario. Dizionario di termini medici di uso comune. (Ital.). L.1500.00. ERI.
Guidos, Barbara & Hamilton, Betty. MASA: Medical Acronyms, Symbols & Abbreviations. 200p. 1983. lib. bdg. $39.95 (ISBN 0-918212-72-3). Neal-Schuman.
Habibi, B. Deutsch-Persisches Fachwoerterbuch Fuer Naturwissenschaft, Medezin und Landwirtschaft. 240p. (Ger. & Persian.). 1964. pap. $17.50 (ISBN 3-447-00354-5, M-7331, Pub. by Harrassowitz). French & Eur.
Herbert, W. J. & Wilkinson, P. C. Diccionario De Inmunologia. 256p. (Span.). 1974. leather $28.50 (ISBN 84-7092-106-1, S-50055). French & Eur.
Hitti, Jusuf. Medical English-Arabic Dictionary. (Illus.). 1973. $35.00x (ISBN 0-86685-067-8). Intl Bk Ctr.
Hitti, Yusuf K. English-Arabic Medical Dictionary. (Illus.). 913p. (Eng. & Arabic.). $35.00 (067-8). Intl Bk Ctr.
--Hitti's English-Arabic Medical Dictionary. (Eng. & Arabic.). 1967. $35.00x (ISBN 0-8156-6004-9, Am U Beirut). Syracuse U Pr.
Howell, G. & Perez Y Sabido, J. Spanish-English Handbook. 1977. pap. 11.95 (ISBN 0-87489-073-X). Med Economics.
Iribarren Reta, Mercedes. Diccionario Humano. 2nd ed. 552p. (Span.). 1975. pap. $9.95 (ISBN 84-85000-33-1, S-50088). French & Eur.
Japanese-Latin-English-German-French Medical Terminology. 1259p. (Japanese , Lat. , Eng. , Ger. & Fr.). 1958. leatherette $95.00 (ISBN 0-686-92476-2, M-9350). French & Eur.
Jedraszko, Sabian. Slownik Lekarski Polsko-Angielski. LC 76-511367. 410p. (Eng. & Pol.). 1975. 150.00 Zl. Panstwowy Zaklad W.
Jeharned. Medical Terminology Made Easy. 2nd ed. 352p. 1968. text ed. 9.00 (ISBN 0-917036-06-9). Physicians Rec.
Kamenetz, Herman L. Dictionary of Rehabilitation Medicine. 384p. 1983. text ed. $23.95 (ISBN 0-8261-3320-7). Springer Pub.
Kamenetz, Herman L. & Kamenetz, Georgette. Dictionnaire de Medecine Physique de Reeducation et Readaptation Fonctionelles. 208p. (Fr.). 1972. $19.95 (ISBN 0-686-56986-5, M-6324). French & Eur.
--Dictionnaire Francais-Anglais de Medecine Physique de Reeducation & de Readaptation Fonctionhelles. 192p. (Fr. & Eng.). 1972. 48.00 F. $40.00. Maloine.
Kamenetz, Herman L. & Kamentz, Georgette. Dictionnaire de Medecine Physique de Reeducation & Readaptation. 208p. (Fr.). 1972. 48.00 F. Maloine.
Kaps, Urban. Medizinisches Woerterbuch. (Ger.). pap. $7.50 (ISBN 0-686-56632-7, M-7555, Pub. by Bruno Wilkens). French & Eur.
Kay, Margarita. Southwestern Medical Dictionary: Spanish-English & English-Spanish. LC 76-54591. (Span. & Eng.). 1977. pap. text ed. $4.50 (ISBN 0-8165-0529-2). U of Ariz Pr.
Keller, Sally. English-Khmer Medical Dictionary. (Workpapers of North Dakota: Vol. XX, Suppl. 2). 190p. (Eng. & Khmer.). 1976. pap. $4.50x (ISBN 0-88312-744-X); microfiche $3.00x (ISBN 0-88312-341-X). Summer Inst Ling.
Kobylkova, Andela. Anglicko-Cesky Lekarsky Slovnik. LC 76-509268. 227p. (Eng. & Czech.). 1975. 10.50 Kcs. SNTC.
Lancombe, Michel & Monceaux, Jean-Pierre. Lexique Etymologique des Termes Medicaux. 20p. (Fr.). 1971. 25.00 F. Lamarre Poinot.
Larrauri, A. Dictionary of Oto-Rhino-Laryngology in Five Languages. LC 71-501781. 1008p. (Eng., Fr., Span., Ger. & Ital.). 1971. $65.00x (ISBN 0-8002-0197-3). Intl Pubns Serv.
Lauricella, Emanuele. Dizionario medico, 2 vols. viii, 1654p. (Ital.). 1976. L.48000.00 (ISBN 88-03-00071-2). USES.
Lee-Delisle, Dora. English-Hungarian, Hungarian-English Medical Dictionary. (Eng. & Hungarian.). $18.50 (ISBN 0-87557-040-2, 042-2X). Saphrograph.
Lejeune & Bunjes. Woerterbuch fuer Aerzte. 2nd ed. (Ger., Dictionary for Physicians). 1968. pap. $55.00 (ISBN 3-13-370502-4, M-6924). French & Eur.
Lejeune, F. & Bunjes, W. E. Dictionary for Physicians. 2nd ed. 459p. (Eng. -Ger.). 1968. $55.00 (ISBN 3-13-370502-4, M-7106). French & Eur.
Lepine, Pierre. Dictionnaire Francais-Anglais des Termes Medicaux & Biologiques. 2nd ed. 896p. (Fr. & Eng.). 1974. 160.00 F. Flammarion.
--Dictionnaire Francais-Anglais et Anglais-Francais des Termes Medicaux et Biologiques. 2nd ed. 896p. (Fr. & Eng.). 1974. $65.00 (ISBN 0-686-57292-0, M-4665). French & Eur.
Lexikon-Institut Bertelsmann. Lexikon der Medizin & Gesundheit. 850p. (Ger.). 1975. DM.39.00 (ISBN 3-570-04598-6). C Bertelsmann.
Lexique des Termes Medicaux. (Fr.). 25.00 F. Lamarre Poinot.
Lexis Veinte-dos: Medicina y Salud. 7th ed. 288p. (Span.). 1982. pap. 600.00 ptas. Circulo Lect.
Lichtenstern, Hermann. Duden-Das Woerterbuch Medizinischer Fachausdruecke. 751p. (Ger.). DM.39.00 (ISBN 3-411-01747-3). Biblio Inst.
Lucchesi, M. Dizionario Medico Ragionato Inglese-Italiano. 1489p. (Eng. & Ital.). 1978. $95.00 (ISBN 0-686-92622-6, M-9353). French & Eur.
Lucchesi, Mario. Dizionario Medico Ragionato Inglese-Italiano: Termini, Abbreviazioni, Sigle, Eponimi e Sinonimi Medici, Medico-Biologici e Delle Specializzazioni Mediche. 1490p. (Eng. & Ital.). 1978. $98.00x (ISBN 0-913298-52-2). S F Vanni.
Lucchesi, U. M. Dizionario medico ragionato per le scienze mediche inglese-italiano. 1500p. (Eng. & Ital.). 1978. L.38000.00. Cortina M.
Magalini, Sergio. Dizionario delle sindromi mediche. 800p. (Ital.). 1976. L.25000.00. DEMI.
Manuila, A & Nicole, M. Dictionnaire Francais de Medicine el de Biologie, Vol. 2. (Fr.). 1971. $175.00 (ISBN 0-686-57033-2, M-6393). French & Eur.
Manuila, A. & Nicole, M. Dictionnaire Francais de Medicine et de Biologie, Vol. 1. 866p. (Fr.). 1970. $175.00 (ISBN 0-686-57032-4, M-6392). French & Eur.
Manuila, A., et al. Dictionnaire Francais de Medicine el de Biologie, Vol. 4. 580p. (Fr.). 1975. $130.00 (ISBN 0-686-57035-9, M-6395). French & Eur.
Manuila, L., et al. Petit Dictionnaire Medical. 566p. (Fr.). 1978. pap. $29.95 (ISBN 0-686-57036-7, M-6396). French & Eur.
Manuila, Nicole A. Dictionnaire Francais de Medecine & de Biologie, 1 A-D. 866p. (Fr.). 1970. 500.00 F. Masson.
--Le Dictionnaire Francais de Medecine & de Biologie, 2. (Fr.). 1971. 500.00 F. Masson.
--Dictionnaire Francais de Medecine & de Biologie, 3 N-Z. 1200p. (Fr.). 1972. 600.00 F. Masson.
--Dictionnaire Francais de Medecine & de Biologie, 4. 580p. (Fr.). 1975. 380.00 F. Masson.
Marconi, R. & Zino, E. Dizionario inglese-italiano per le scienze mediche. 572p. (Eng. & Ital.). 1975. L.15000.00. Minerva Medica.
Marcovecchio, E. Dizionario tedesco-italiano per le scienze mediche. 762p. (Ger. & Ital.). 1967. L.16000.00. Minerva Medica.
Martin, M. W. A Concise Dictionary of Medicine. LC 74-23215. (Illus.). 1975. 8.95 (ISBN 0-8246-0193-9). Jonathan David.
Mauila, A., et al. Dictionnaire Francais de Medicine el de Biologie, Vol. 3. 1200p. (Fr.). 1972. $195.00 (ISBN 0-686-57034-0, M-6394). French & Eur.

Maury, E. A. Diccionario familiar de homeopatia. Santos, Domingo, tr. 208p. (Span.). 1980. pap. 350.00 ptas (ISBN 84-286-0578-5). Pomaire.

--Diccionario familiar de las medicinas naturales. Andrue Aznar, Rafael, tr. 448p. (Span.). 1981. pap. 600.00 ptas (ISBN 84-270-0692-6). Martinez Roca.

Maury, E. A. & Rudder, C. Diccionario Familiar de Mediciana Natural. 441p. (Span.). 1981. pap. $17.50 (ISBN 0-686-92544-0, S-3785). French & Eur.

The Medical & Health Sciences Word Book. 2nd ed. 1982. $6.95 (ISBN 0-395-25409-4). HM.

Medical Dictionary. pap. $1.99 (ISBN 0-686-00474-4). Dennison.

Melloni, B., et al. Diccionario de Medicina Ilustrado. (Illus.). 650p. (Span.). 1982. 2750.00 ptas (ISBN 8-42915-548-1). Reverte SA.

Meyer-Camberg, Ernst. Das Praktische Lexikon der Naturheilkunde. (Ger.). 1977. pap. $15.95 (ISBN 3-570-06579-0, M-7594, Pub. by Mosaik/VVA). French & Eur.

Mills, Dorothy H., et al. Spanish Vocabulary & Structure for the Health Professional, Bk. 1. 2nd ed. LC 80-54900. (Illus.). 157p. (Eng. & Span.). 1981. pap. text ed. $15.00 (ISBN 0-935356-02-9). Mills Pub Co.

Mommsen. Diccionario Medico Labor Para la Familia. (Span.). 1979. write for info. (ISBN 84-335-6007-7, S-50063). French & Eur.

--Diccionario medico Labor para la familia. (Span.). 990.00 ptas. Labor SA.

Mommsen, H. Diccionario Medico Labor para la Familia. 5th ed. 816p. (Span.). 1976. $45.00 (ISBN 84-335-6000-X, S-12337). French & Eur.

Mommsen, H., et al. Diccionario Medico Labor para la Familia. 6th ed. Massor Gimeno, Juan & Vilahur Pedrals, J., trs. 880p. (Span.). 1982. pap. 3580.00 ptas (ISBN 84-335-6007-7). Labor SA.

Montagnet, Desgoses. Dictionnaire de Medecine Amusante. 66p. (Fr.). 1971. 130.00 F. De Rache.

Nelson's New Compact Medical Dictionary. 1978. 2.45 (ISBN 0-8407-5635-6). Nelson.

Neuman, Maurice. Dictionnaire des Medicaments. 432p. (Fr.). 1971. pap. $27.50 (ISBN 0-686-56745-5, M-6424). French & Eur.

The New American Medical Dictionary & Health Manual. 1982. pap. $4.50x (ISBN 0-451-12027-2, Pub. by NAL). Formur Intl.

Noehring. Woerterbuch Medizin. 640p. (Eng. & Ger.). 1983. DM.89.00 (ISBN 3-87144-725-0). Verlag Harri Deutsch.

Oeter, D. Herder - Lexikon Medizin. 2nd ed. 240p. (Ger.). pap. $15.95 (ISBN 0-686-56479-0, M-7446, Pub. by Herder). French & Eur.

--Herder-Lexikon Medizin. 2nd ed. 240p. (Ger.). pap. $15.95. Herder.

Ordang, Laurence. The Bantam Medical Dictionary. 464p. 1982. pap. $4.95 (ISBN 0-553-22673-8). Bantam.

Oweida, A. M. The New Medical-Pharmaceutical Dictionary. 2404p. (Eng. & Arabic.). 1970. Leatherette $150.00 (ISBN 0-686-92192-5, M-9766). French & Eur.

Palmieri, G. Giuseppe. Dizionario di terminologia medica. (Ital.). 1974. L.11000.00. Vallardi F.

Parks, Anton. Anglicko-slovensk y lekarsky slovnik. LC 80-466637. 211p. (Slovenian & Eng., Bratislava). 1978. 14.50 Kcs. Univerzita Komenskeho.

Pearce, Evelyn. Pearce's Medical & Nursing Dictionary & Encyclopedia. 15th ed. 500p. (Orig.). 1983. pap. $14.95 (ISBN 0-571-18080-9). Faber & Faber.

Perlemuter, L. Dictionnaire Pratique De Therapeutique Medicale, 3. 2nd ed. Obraska, P., ed. 1032p. (Fr.). 1978. $79.95 (ISBN 0-686-57067-7, M-6439). French & Eur.

Perlemuter, Leon & Cenac, Arnaud. Dictionnaire Pratique De Medecine Clinique. 1830p. (Fr.). 1977. $99.50 (ISBN 0-686-57068-5, M-6440). French & Eur.

Pesonen, Niilo. Laaketieteen Sanairja. LC 76-486173. 559p. (Eng. & Finnish.). 1976. Fmk.100.00 (ISBN 9-5100-7479-9). Werner Soderstrom.

Playfair, A. S. The Pocket Medical Dictionary. (Illus.). 256p. (Eng.). Epap. 1.25 (ISBN 0-600-36311-2). Newnes Bks.

Poinsotte, J. P. Dictionnaire des Sigles Medicaux. 146p. (Fr.). 1982. pap. text ed. $17.95 (ISBN 2-252-02355-4, M-9772). French & Eur.

Poitevin, F. Beer. Diccionario Medico. 352p. (Span.). 1979. $51.95 (ISBN 0-686-92232-8). French & Eur.

Pollak, Kurt. Knaurs Lexikon der Modernen Medizin. (Ger.). 1972. $17.50 (ISBN 3-426-03329-1, M-7519, Pub. by Druckenmueller). French & Eur.

Pompili, G. Glossario di medicina nucleare. 288p. (Ital.). 1961. L.7000.00. Minerva Medica.

Poujol, F. A. Dictionnaire de Medecine Pratique. Migne, J. P., ed. (Nouvelle Encyclopedie Theologique Ser.: Vol. 17). 552p. (Fr.). Date not set. Repr. of 1862 ed. lib. bdg. $71.00x (ISBN 0-89241-264-X). Caratzas Pub Co.

Pouletti, J., et al. Dictionnaire Pratique de Droit Medicale. 424p. (Fr.). 1982. $85.00 (ISBN 2-225-71115-1, M-9773). French & Eur.

Prada Becares, Juan. Diccionario Terminologia Medica Explicada. 128p. (Span.). 1977. pap. $9.95 (ISBN 84-400-3894-1, S-50111). French & Eur.

--Diccionario Terminologia Medica Explicada. LC 79-346078. 125p. (Span.). 1977. write for info. (ISBN 8-4400-3894-1). Autores-Editores.

Pschyrembel, Willibald. Klinisches Woerterbuch Mit Klinischen Syndromen. 253 rev. ed. (Illus., Ger.). 1977. $26.50x (ISBN 3-11-007018-9). De Gruyter.

Rigal, Waldo A. The Inverted Medical Dictionary. LC 73-84126. 1976. $20.00x (ISBN 0-87762-203-5); pap. $14.50x (ISBN 0-87762-170-5). Technomic.

Riley, P. A. & Cunningham, P. J. The Faber Pocket Medical Dictionary. 3rd ed. Forsythe, Elizabeth, ed. (Illus.). 408p. 1979. pap. $4.95 (ISBN 0-571-04999-0). Faber & Faber.

Roper, Nancy. The New American Pocket Medical Dictionary. LC 78-3857. (Illus.). 1978. pap. text ed. $6.25 (ISBN 0-443-08013-5). Churchill.

--New American Pocket Medical Dictionary. 1978. pap. $7.95 (ISBN 0-684-15923-6, SL820, ScribT). Scribner.

Rothenberg, Robert. New American Medical Dictionary & Health Manual. rev. ed. pap. 4.50 (ISBN 0-451-12027-2, AE2027, Sig). NAL.

Roubakine. Dictionnaire Francais-Russe de Medecine. (Fr. & Rus.). 1978. 47.45 F. MIR.

Ruiz, Torres. Diccionario de terminos medicos. (Span. & Eng.). pap. $32.00. Iaconi.

Ruiz Torres, F. Diccionario aleman-espanol de medicina. 560p. (Ger. & Span.). 1960. write for info. MMW Verlag.

--Diccionario aleman-espanol de medicina. 560p. (Ger. & Span.). 1960. write for info. Alhambra.

--Diccionario aleman-espanol y espanol-aleman de medicina. 860p. (Ger. & Span.). 1971. 700.00 ptas. Alhambra.

--Diccionario de terminos medicos Ingles-Espanol & Espanol-Ingles. 596p. (Span. & Eng.). 1980. pap. write for info. (ISBN 84-205-0654-0). Fed Gremios.

--Diccionario de terminos medicos ingles-espanol espanol-ingles. 594p. (Eng. & Span.). 1981. pap. $60.95 (ISBN 84-205-0654-0). Larousse.

--Diccionario Ingles-Espanol de Medicina. 3rd ed. 714p. (Eng. & Span.). 1968. Arg.$600.00. Alhambra.

Ruiz Torres, Francisco. Diccionario Aleman-Espanol, Espanol-Aleman de Medicina. 2nd ed. 860p. (Ger. & Span.). 1971. pap. $41.25 (ISBN 84-205-0010-0, S-50089). French & Eur.

--Vocabulario Ingles-Espanol, Espanol-Ingles de Medicina. 300p. (Eng. & Span.). 1979. pap. $10.75 (ISBN 84-205-0625-7, S-50091). French & Eur.

Russian-English Medical Dictionary. LC 78-40146. (Rus. & Eng.). 1978. $75.00 (ISBN 0-08-023164-0); E37.50. Pergamon.

Schmidt, J. E. English Word Power for Physicians & Other Professionals: A Vigorous & Cultured Vocabulary. 240p. 1971. $19.75x (ISBN 0-398-01666-6). C C Thomas.

--Police Medical Dictionary. 256p. 1968. $19.75x (ISBN 0-398-01673-9). C C Thomas.

Segatore, L. & Poli, G. A. Dizionario medico. (Illus.). 1368p. (Ital.). L.20000.00. Ist Geog Agostini.

Segatore, Luigi & Poli, Gianangelo. Diccionario Medico. 5th ed. 1282p. (Span.). 1975. $44.95 (ISBN 84-307-8013-0, S-12357). French & Eur.

--Diccionario Medico. 1288p. (Span.). 1974. 750.00 ptas. Teide.

Seidler, Eduard. Woerterbuch Medizinischer Grundbegriffe. LC 80-470172. 367p. (Ger.). 1979. DM.12.90 (ISBN 3-451-07706-X). Herder.

Seleccione Reader's Digest. Diccionario Medico Familiar. 756p. (Span.). Date not set. price not set (S-34982). French & Eur.

Sliosberg, A. Elsevier's Medical Dictionary in Five Languages. rev. 2nd ed. LC 72-97436. 1452p. (Eng., Fr., Ital., Span. & Ger.). 1975. $181.00 (ISBN 0-444-41103-8). Elsevier.

Smiddy, F. G. Dictionary of General Pathology. 336p. 1980. $29.00x (ISBN 0-272-79585-2, Pub. by Pitman Bks England). State Mutual Bk.

Smith, Genevieve L. & Davis, Phyllis E. Quick Medical Terminology. LC 72-4193. (Wiley Self-Teaching Guides Ser). 248p. 1972. $8.95x (ISBN 0-471-80198-4, Pub. by Wiley Pr); cassettes $8.95 (ISBN 0-471-80201-8). Wiley.

Stedman. Stedman's Medical Dictionary. 22nd ed. LC 78-176294. 1585p. 1972. 9.95 (ISBN 0-683-07919-0, Pub. by Williams & Wilkins). Krieger.

Stedman's Medical Dictionary. 24th ed. (Illus.). 1750p. 1981. lib. bdg. $33.50 (ISBN 0-683-07915-8). Williams & Wilkins.

Stedman's Medical Dictionary. 23rd ed. (Illus.). 1678p. 1976. $32.00 (ISBN 0-683-07924-7). Williams & Wilkins.

Strauss, Eduard. Medizinische Fachsprache Verstandlich Gemacht. LC 77-562960. 92p. (Ger.). 1975. DM.5.70 (ISBN 3-87240-041-X). Froehlich Verlag.

Terminologia cientifica medica en euskera. (Span.). 1982. write for info. (ISBN 84-300-7123-7). Autor.

Terminologie et Lexicographie Medicales. 60p. (Fr.). 1967. pap. $17.50 (ISBN 0-686-57229-7, M-6530). French & Eur.

Thomas, Clayton L., ed. Taber's Cyclopedic Medical Dictionary. 14th ed. LC 80-16588. (Illus.). 1818p. 1981. $15.95x (ISBN 0-8036-8307-3); Thumb-indexed Edition. text ed. $18.95x (ISBN 0-8036-8306-5). Davis Co.

Thomson, William A., ed. Black's Medical Dictionary. 33rd ed. LC 79-167. (Illus.). 992p. 1982. text ed. $24.50x (ISBN 0-389-20246-0, 07045). B&N Imports.

Touati, Maurice A. Lexique Francais Des Abreviations et Formules Medico-Chirurgicales Courantes. 142p. (Fr.). 1969. $12.50 (ISBN 0-686-57234-3, M-6535). French & Eur.

Tutsch, D. Lexikon der Medizinischen Fachsprache, 2 vols. 388p. (Ger.). 1970. Set. pap. $9.95 (ISBN 3-499-16126-5, M-7249). French & Eur.

Tutsch, Dagobert. Lexikon der Medizin. (Ger.). 1975. $19.95 (ISBN 3-541-07081-1, M-7250). French & Eur.

--Taschenlexikon Medizin. LC 75-508090. 581p. (Eng. & Ger.). 1975. DM.14.80 (ISBN 3-541-03012-7). Urban & Schwarzen.

Tutsch, Dagobert, ed. Lexikon der Medizinischen Fachsprache: Bd 1, A-L. (Ger.). 1978. DM.5.80 (ISBN 3-499-16126-5). Rowohlt.

--Lexikon der Medizinischen Fachsprache: Bd 2, M-Z. (Ger.). 1978. DM.5.80 (ISBN 3-499-16129-X). Rowohlt.

Ullstein Lexikon der Medizin. (Ger.). 1970. $22.50 (ISBN 3-550-06017-3, M-7674, Pub. by Ullstein Verlag/VVA). French & Eur.

Unseld, D. Medizinisches Woerterbuch der Deutschen und Englischen Sprache. 6th rev. ed. 519p. (Eng. & Ger., Medical Dictionary of the German and English Language). 1971. $33.50 (ISBN 3-8047-0415-8, M-7556, Pub. by Wissenschaftlicher Vlg.). French & Eur.

Unseld, D. W. German-English, English-German Medical Dictionary. rev. & enl. 8th ed. (Ger. & Eng.). 35.00 (ISBN 3-8047-0661-4). Heinman.

--Medical Dictionary. (Ger. & Eng.). 1982. $39.50 (ISBN 3-8047-0661-4). Adler.

Unseld, Dieter. Medical Dictionary of the English & German Languages: Medizinisches Worterbuch der Deutschen und Englischen Sprache. 8th ed. 593p. (Eng. & Ger.). 1982. 30.00x (ISBN 0-686-43337-8). Intl Pubns Serv.

Unseld, Dieter W. Medical Dictionary of the English & German Languages. LC 80-465175. 520p. (Eng. & Ger.). 1978. DM.42.00 (ISBN 3-8047-0567-7). Wissenschaftliche.

Urdang. Urdang Dictionary of Current Medical Terms. LC 80-22916. 455p. 1981. $22.95 (ISBN 0-471-05853-X, Pub. by Wiley Med). Wiley.

Veillon & Nobel. Dizionario Medico Poliglotta. (Ital., Span., Eng., Fr., & Ger.). Leatherette $190.00 (ISBN 0-686-92503-3, M-9636). French & Eur.

--Dizionario medico poliglotta: Inglese-tedesco-francese. 1330p. (Eng., Ger. & Fr.). 1969. L.20000.00. Piccin.

Veillon, E. & Nobel, A. Medizinisches Woerterbuch. 5th rev. ed. 1330p. (Ger., Fr. & Eng., Medical Dictionary). 1969. $105.00 (ISBN 3-456-00200-9, M-7554, Pub. by H. Huber). French & Eur.

--Medizinisches Woerterbuch. 5th & rev. ed. 1330p. (Ger., Fr. & Eng.). 1969. $105.00 (ISBN 3-456-00200-9). Huber.

--Spanisches Supplement Zu Medizinisches Woerterbuch. (Ger.). 1971. $48.00 (ISBN 3-456-00271-8, M-7623, Pub. by H. Huber Vlg.). French & Eur.

--Spanisches Supplement Zu Medizinisches Woerterbuch. (Ger.). 1971. $48.00 (ISBN 3-456-00271-8). Huber.

Veillon, Emile & Noble, Albert. Dictionnaire Medical. 1337p. (Eng., Ger. & Fr.). 1977. 400.00 F. Masson.

Veillon, Emmanuel & Nobel, Albert. Dictionnaire Medical. (Fr.). 1969. 132.00 F. Hans.

Veillon-Nobel. Diccionario Medico & su Suplemento Espanol. 1341p. (Span.). 1974. write for info. Cientifico Med.

Vocabulaire De Medecine et Des Sciences Connexes: Francais-Anglais, Anglais-Francais. 298p. (Fr.-Eng.). 1971. $37.50 (ISBN 0-686-57281-5). French & Eur.

Von Schaldach, Herbert. DTV Woerterbuch der Medizin, Vol. 1. 5th ed. (Ger.). 1973. pap. 7.95 (ISBN 3-423-03028-3, M-7342, Pub. by DTV Deutscher Taschenbuch Vlg.). French & Eur.
--DTV Woerterbuch der Medizin, Vol. 1. 5th ed. (Ger.). 1973. DM.pap. 7.95 (ISBN 3-423-03028-3). Deutscher Taschenbuch Verlag.
--DTV Woerterbuch der Medizin, Vol. 2. 5th ed. (Ger.). 1973. pap. 7.95 (ISBN 3-423-03029-1, M-7343, Pub. by DTV Deutscher Taschenbuch Vlg.). French & Eur.
--DTV Woerterbuch der Medizin, Vol. 2. 5th ed. (Ger.). 1973. DM.pap. 7.95 (ISBN 3-423-03029-1). Deutscher Taschenbuch Verlag.
--DTV Woerterbuch der Medizin, Vol. 3. 5th ed. (Ger.). 1973. pap. 7.95 (ISBN 3-423-03030-5, M-7344, Pub. by DTV Deutscher Taschenbuch Vlg.). French & Eur.
--DTV Woerterbuch der Medizin, Vol. 3. 5th ed. (Ger.). 1973. DM.pap. 7.95 (ISBN 3-423-03030-5). Deutscher Taschenbuch Verlag.
Vox, ed. Diccionario Monografico de Medicina y Salud. (Span.). 1979. leatherette $17.50 (ISBN 84-7153-380-4, S-36145). French & Eur.
Woerterbuch Medizinischer Fachausdruecke. (Ger.). 1973. DM.32.00 (ISBN 3-13-437802-7). Thieme Verlag.
Wrete, Martin. Kortfattad Medicinsk Ordbok. Dahlgren, Sven, ed. 254p. (Swedish.). 1980. Kr.110.00 (ISBN 91-24-26515-2). Esselte Studium.
Zlotnicki, B. Lexicon Medicum: Medizinisches Woerterbuch in 6 Sprachen; Englisch, Russisch, Franzoesisch, Deutsch, Latein, Polnisch. 1603p. (Eng., Rus., Fr., Ger., Lat. & Pol.). 1973. DM.116.00 (ISBN 3-7945-0324-4). Langenscheidt.
--Lexikon Medicum. (Eng., Rus., Fr., Ger., Lat. & Pol., Medical Dictionary). 1973. $92.00 (ISBN 3-7945-0324-4, M-7194). French & Eur.
Zlotnicki, Boleslaw. Slownik Lekarski Polsko-Niemiecki. LC 79-389560. 674p. (Ger. & Pol.). 1979. 350.00 Zl (ISBN 8-3200-0152-8). Panstwowe Zaklad W.
Zlotnickiego, Boleslaw. Lexicon Medicum. 1604p. (Eng., Rus., Fr., Ger., Lat. & Pol.). 1976. $95.00 (ISBN 0-686-57263-7, M-6576). French & Eur.
Zoltnicki, B. Medical Dictionary. (Eng., Rus., Fr., Ger., Lat. & Pol.). 1973. $92.50 (ISBN 3-7945-0324-4, M-7552, Pub. by Schattauer). French & Eur.

MEDICINE–HANDBOOKS, MANUALS, ETC.
American Medical Association. Current Medical Information & Terminology. 5th ed. 800p. $20.00 (OP 337); bulk rates avail. AMA.

MEDICINE–LAWS AND LEGISLATION
see Medical Laws and Legislation

MEDICINE–MORAL AND RELIGIOUS ASPECTS
see Medical Ethics

MEDICINE–TERMINOLOGY
American Medical Association. Current Medical Information & Terminology. 5th ed. 800p. $20.00 (OP 337); bulk rates avail. AMA.
American Medical Record Association. Glossary of Hospital Terms. 111p. $7.75 (1001P); members $6.75. Am Med Record Assn.
--Introduction to Medical Terminology for Nursing Home Personnel. 24p. $2.00 (1013P). Am Med Record Assn.
Angela. Daffy Definitions of Medical Terms. 1981. $5.95 (ISBN 0-533-04834-6). Vantage.
Beitler, L. & McDonald, B. English for the Medical Professions. 1982. $6.96 (ISBN 0-07-004521-6). McGraw.
Bonvalot, Marie. Le Vocabulaire Medical de Base, 2 vols. 447p. (Fr.). 1972. 52.00 F. Organisation Instruction Proger.
--Le Vocabulaire Medical de Base, 2 vols. new ed. (Illus.). 447p. (Fr.). 1974. 52.00 F. Soc Etudes Tech.
Coudereau, Henri. Vocabulaires Methodiques Ouayana, Apari, Oyampal, Emerillon. (Fr.). 24.00 F. Kraus.
Delamare, Jean & Delamareriche, Marie-Therese. Dictionnaire Francais-Anglais des Termes Techniques de Medecine. 714p. (Fr. & Eng.). 1970. 100.00 F. Maloine.
Diccionario terminlogico de ciencias medicas. 10th ed. (Illus.). 1200p. (Span.). $19.00; 1200.00 ptas. Salvat Editores.
Diccionario terminoligico de Ciencias Medicas II. 11th ed. 1084p. (Span.). 1981. pap. 2250.00 ptas (ISBN 84-345-1206-8). Salvat Editores.
Diccionario Terminologico de Ciencias Medicas. 11th ed. 1084p. (Span.). 1980. pap. 2250.00 ptas (ISBN 84-345-1206-8). Salvat Editores.
Dumortier, J. Le Vocabulaire Medical d'Eschyle & les Ecrits Hippocratiques. (Fr.). 1975. 42.00 F. Belles Lettres.
Dunmore, Charles W. & Fleischer, Rita M. Medical Terminology: Exercise in Etymology. 327p. 1977. pap. text ed. $13.95x (ISBN 0-8036-2945-1). Davis Co.
Fisher, J. Patrick. Basic Medical Terminology. LC 74-77820. (Allied Health Ser). 1975. pap. text ed. $14.95 (ISBN 0-672-61385-9); tchr's manual o.p. $6.67 (ISBN 0-672-61386-7); tape cassette $115.50 (ISBN 0-672-61387-5). Bobbs.
--Basic Medical Terminology. 2nd ed. 288p. 1983. pap. text ed. $12.95 (ISBN 0-672-61573-8); cassettes $240.00 (ISBN 0-672-61575-4); instr's guide $6.67 (ISBN 0-672-61574-6). Bobbs.
Frenay, Agnes C. Understanding Medical Terminology. 6th ed. LC 77-73986. 1977. pap. text ed. $9.00 (ISBN 0-87125-038-1). Cath Health.
Garcia, W. Joseph. Medical Sign Language: Easily Understood Definitions of Commonly Used Medical, Dental & First Aid Terms. (Illus.). 726p. 1983. $54.50x (ISBN 0-398-04805-3); pap. $43.75x spiral (ISBN 0-398-04806-1). C C Thomas.
Garnier, Marcel & Delamare, Jean. Dictionnaire des Termes Techniques de Medecine. 19th ed. 1340p. (Fr.). 1978. 78.00 F. Maloine.
Garnier, Marcel, et al. Diccionario de los terminos tecnicos de Medicina. Llido Blasco, Julio, tr. 1114p. (Span.). 1981. 2000.00 ptas (ISBN 84-7487-011-9). Norma.
Gylys, Barbara A. & Wedding, Mary E. Medical Terminology: A Systems Approach. LC 82-12927. (Illus.). 421p. 1983. pap. text ed. $14.95 (ISBN 0-8036-4492-2). Davis Co.
Harrington, Arnoldo. Diccionario de terminos medicos: Ingles-espanol, espanol-ingles. 320p. (Span. & Eng.). 1968. write for info. Gnosis Edit.
Jeharned. Medical Terminology Made Easy. 2nd ed. 352p. 1968. text ed. 9.00 (ISBN 0-917036-06-9). Physicians Rec.
Latinsko-Russko-Latyshskii Slovar Meditsinskikh Terminov, 2 vols. (Lat. & Rus.). 1977. $33.50 set (Pub. by Liesma). Four Continent.
Lewis, Carolyn D. Medical Latin. (Lat.). (YA) (gr. 12). $6.00x (ISBN 0-8338-0040-X). M Jones.
Lexique des Termes Medicaux. (Fr.). pap. $14.95 (ISBN 0-686-56722-6, M-6362). French & Eur.
Liu, F. & L. Yan Mau. Chinese Medical Terminology: English to Chinese. 262p. (Chinese & Eng.). 1980. $24.95 (ISBN 962-07-3000-3). French & Eur.
Loechel, William E. Pictorial Medical Terminology. 126p. 1981. pap. $14.75x spiral (ISBN 0-398-04581-X). C C Thomas.
Medical & Health Sciences Word Book. 2nd ed. 1982. $8.95 (ISBN 0-395-32941-8). HM.
National Shorthand Reporters Association. A Systematic Guide to Medical Terminology. 60p. $3.50 (145). Natl Shorthand Rptr.
Parke, Davis & Company. Medical Word Building. (Medical Economics Books). 1970. $6.50 (ISBN 0-442-84015-2). Van Nos Reinhold.
Prendergast, Alice. Medical Terminology: A Text-Workbook. LC 76-62907. 1977. pap. text ed. $13.95 (ISBN 0-201-05966-5, Med-Nurse); instr's man. $9.95 (ISBN 0-201-05967-3). A-W.
Prichard, Robert W. & Robinson, Robert E. Twenty Thousand Medical Words. 288p. 1972. (HP); pap. $11.95 (ISBN 0-07-050874-7). McGraw.
Radcliff, Ruth K. & Ogden, Shelia J. Nursing & Medical Terminology: A Workbook. LC 76-17597. (Illus.). 204p. 1977. pap. text ed. 14.50 (ISBN 0-8016-3714-7). Mosby.
Rickards, Ralph. Understanding Medical Terms: A Self-Instructional Course. (Illus.). 112p. 1980. pap. text ed. $8.25 (ISBN 0-443-02029-9). Churchill.
Ruiz Torres, F. Diccionario de Terminos Medicos Ingles-Espanol. 594p. (Eng. & Span.). 1981. 60.95 ptas (ISBN 84-205-0654-0). Alhambra.
Ruiz Torres, Francisco. Diccionario de terminos medicos: Ingles-Espanol, espanol-ingles. 600p. (Span. & Eng.). 1981. pap. 2100.00 ptas (ISBN 84-205-0654-0). Alhambra.
Schmidt, J. E. Index of Paramedical Vocabulary. (Illus.). 324p. 1974. pap. $10.75x spiral (ISBN 0-398-02833-8). C C Thomas.
Smith, G. L. & Davis, P. E. Medical Terminology. 4th ed. LC 80-17970. 325p. 1981. pap. $16.95 (ISBN 0-471-05827-0, Pub. by Wiley Med); material $1.95 supplementary (ISBN 0-471-09071-9). Wiley.
Smith-Davis. Terminologia Medica: Texto Programado. 280p. (Span.). 1974. Mex.$3.84. Limusa.
Steen, Edwin B. Abbreviations in Medicine. 4th ed. 1978. pap. $12.95 (ISBN 0-7216-0766-7, Pub. by Bailliere-Tindall). Saunders.
Stegeman, Wilson. Medical Terms Simplified. LC 75-12977. (Illus.). 305p. 1975. pap. text ed. $13.95 (ISBN 0-8299-0062-4). West Pub.
Stein, Harold A., et al. Manual of Opthalmic Terminology. LC 81-14136. (Illus.). 269p. 1982. pap. text ed. 18.95 (ISBN 0-8016-4769-X). Mosby.
Tebben, Joseph. Medical & Technical Terminology. 1975. pap. text ed. $4.50 (ISBN 0-88429-013-1). Collegiate Pub.
Teitelbaum & Johnson. Mangled Medicine Definitions We Doubt You Learned in School. (Medical Economics Books). 1972. $4.50 (ISBN 0-442-84017-9). Van Nos Reinhold.
Torres, F. R. Diccionario de Terminos Medicos Ingles-Espanol & Espanol-Ingles. 596p. (Eng. & Span.). 1980. pap. write for info. Edit Alhambra.
Tyrrell, William B. Medical Terminology for Medical Students. (Illus.). 176p. 1979. $16.00x (ISBN 0-398-03810-4). C C Thomas.
Urdang. Urdang Dictionary of Current Medical Terms. LC 80-22916. 455p. 1981. $22.95 (ISBN 0-471-05853-X, Pub. by Wiley Med). Wiley.
Veillon, E. & Nobel, A. Medizinisches Woerterbuch. 5th rev. ed. 1330p. (Ger., Fr. & Eng., Medical Dictionary). 1969. $105.00 (ISBN 3-456-00200-9, M-7554, Pub. by H. Huber). French & Eur.
--Medizinisches Woerterbuch. 5th & rev. ed. 1330p. (Ger., Fr. & Eng.). 1969. $105.00 (ISBN 3-456-00200-9). Huber.
Wain, Harry. The Story Behind the Word: Some Interesting Origins of Medical Terms. 352p. 1958. photocopy ed. spiral $34.75x (ISBN 0-398-02001-9). C C Thomas.
Woolley, LeGrand H. Medical-Dental Terminology: Syllabus. 2nd ed. 1974. pap. text ed. 6.10 (ISBN 0-89420-003-8, 217705); cassette recordings 177.70 (ISBN 0-89420-162-X, 196700). Natl Book.

MEDICINE–TERMINOLOGY–PROGRAMMED INSTRUCTION
Byers, Edward E. Ten Thousand Medical Words, Spelled & Divided for Quick Reference. 128p. 1972. text ed. $6.40 (ISBN 0-07-009503-5, G). McGraw.
Lea, J. Terminology & Communication Skills in the Health Sciences. 1975. pap. $12.95 (ISBN 0-87909-821-X). Reston.

MEDICINE–CHINA
Liu, F. & L. Yan Mau. Chinese Medical Terminology: English to Chinese. 262p. (Chinese & Eng.). 1980. $24.95 (ISBN 962-07-3000-3). French & Eur.

MEDICINE, ANCIENT
Eloy, N. F. Dictionnaire Historique de la Medecine Ancienne & Moderne. (Fr.). 1978. DM.138.00 F. Olms.

MEDICINE, CLINICAL
see also Diagnosis; Pathology
Perlemuter, Leon & Cenac, Arnaud. Dictionnaire Pratique de Medecine Clinique. 1830p. (Fr.). 1977. 250.00 F. Masson.

MEDICINE, COMMUNICATION IN
see Communication in Medicine

MEDICINE, DENTAL
see Teeth–Diseases

MEDICINE, INTERNAL
see Internal Medicine

MEDICINE, VETERINARY
see Veterinary Medicine

MEDICINE AND SPORTS
see Sports Medicine

MEDIEVAL ARCHAEOLOGY
see Archaeology, Medieval

MEDIEVAL HISTORY
see Middle Ages–History

MEDITATIONS
Here are entered works containing thoughts or reflections on spiritual truths. Works on the nature of meditation are entered under the heading Meditation.
see also Devotional Literature also subdivisions Meditations under Bible, Jesus Christ, Lord's Supper, and similar headings
Arcane Order. Encyclopedia of Arcane Wisdom. $50.00. (1790900891). Arcane Order.

MEDIUMS
see Spiritualism

MEETINGS
Herbert, J. Conference Terminology in English, Spanish, Russian, Italian, German & Hungarian. (Eng., Span., Rus., Ital., Ger. & Hungarian.). 1976. $25.00 (ISBN 0-444-41354-5). Elsevier.

MELANESIAN LANGUAGES
see also Austronesian Languages; Fijian Language; Motu Language; Papuan Languages
Fox, Charles E. Arosi Dictionary. LC 78-321214. iii, 598p. (Eng.). 1978. write for info. (ISBN 0-85883-170-8). Linguistic Circle.
Heath, Jeffrey. Basic Material in Ritarungu. LC 81-455870. (Illus.). viii, 249p. (Ritaru.). 1980. Aus.$pap. 9.50 (ISBN 0-85883-204-6). Linguistic Circle.
King, Copland. A Grammar & Dictionary of the Binandere Language, Mamba River...Papua. Bd. with A Grammar & Dictionary of the Wedau Language. LC 75-35129. (Binandere & Wedau.). Repr. of 1927 ed. $15.50 (ISBN 0-404-14145-5). AMS Pr.
Linguistic Society of America & Hall, Robert A., Jr. Melanesian Pidgin Phase-Book & Vocabulary. (Melanesian.). $2.00. Linguistic Soc Am.
Muhlhausler, Peter. Growth & Structure of the Lexicon of New Guinea Pidgin. LC 80-495609. (Illus.). xx, 498p. (Neo-Melanesian.). 1979. Aus.$16.00 (ISBN 0-85883-191-0). Linguistic Circle.
Ray, Sidney H. & Riley, E. B. A Grammar of the Kiwai Language, Fly Delta, Papua, with a Kiwai Vocabulary. LC 75-35152. (Kiwai.). Repr. of 1933 ed. $15.00 (ISBN 0-404-14167-6). AMS Pr.

Z'graggen, J. A. A Comparative Word List of the Mabuso Languages, Madang Province, Papua New Guinea. LC 82-106653. xv, 184p. (Mabuso.). 1980. pap. write for info. (ISBN 0-85883-228-3). Linguistic Circle.

MELVILLE, HERMAN, 1819-1891

Gidmark, Jill B. Melville Sea Dictionary: A Glossed Concordance & Analysis of the Sea Language in Melville's Nautical Novels. LC 82-6122. xiii, 534p. 1982. lib. bdg. 45.00 (ISBN 0-313-23330-6, GMD). Greenwood.

Irey, Eugene F. A Concordance to Melville's Moby Dick. LC 82-9387. 2031p. 1982. lib. bdg. $275.00 (ISBN 0-8240-9398-4). Garland Pub.

Nechas, James W. Synonomy, Repitition & Restatement in the Vocabulary of Herman Melville's Moby Dick. 286p. 1980. Repr. of 1978 ed. lib. bdg. $30.00 (ISBN 0-8414-6311-5). Folcroft.

MEMOIRS

see Autobiography

also subdivision Correspondence, Reminiscences, etc. under classes of people, e.g. Actors–Correspondence, reminiscences, etc.; subdivision History–Sources under names of countries; subdivision Personal Narratives under names of wars, diseases, etc. e.g. World War, 1939-1945–Personal Narratives

MEN

see also Masculinity (Psychology)

Carriere, Anne-Marie. Le Dictionnaire des Hommes. (Fr.). 1962. 20.00 F. Pensee Moderne.

MENDING

see Repairing; Sewing

MENSURATION

see also Geodesy; Surveying

also subdivision Measurement under special subjects, e.g. Altitudes–Measurement

Dictionary of Engineering Metrology Terms. (Hebrew, EnG. , Fr. & Ger.). IL.7.00. Massada Pr.

Hoffman, Peter. Fertigungsmesstechnik-Russischer-Deutsch: Deutsch-Russicherr. LC 76-454994. 140p. (Ger. & Rus.). 1973. M.15.00. VEB Verlag Technik.

Hoffmann, Peter D. Fertigungsmesstechnik. 140p. (Rus. & Ger.). 1975. M.15.00. VEB Verlag Technik.

MENTAL DEFICIENCY

Davitz, Joel R., et al. Terminology & Concepts in Mental Retardation. LC 62-61261. (Orig.). 1964. pap. text ed. $5.50x (ISBN 0-8077-1233-7). Tchrs Coll.

Grossman, Herbert J., ed. Manual on Terminology & Classification in Mental Retardation. 3rd ed. LC 77-87576. 1977. $14.85x (ISBN 0-686-23878-8). Am Assn Mental.

Moore, Byron C., et al. Introduction to Mental Retardation Syndromes & Terminology. 184p. 1978. $14.50x (ISBN 0-398-03718-3). C C Thomas.

Tymchuk, Alexander J. The Mental Retardation Dictionary. LC 73-80058. 149p. 1980. pap. $11.80x (ISBN 0-87424-125-1). Western Psych.

MENTAL DISEASES

see Mental Illness; Psychology, Pathological

MENTAL ILLNESS

Here are entered popular works and works on regional or social aspects of mental disorders. Works on the legal aspects of mental illness are entered under Insanity. Systematic descriptions of mental disorders are entered under Psychology, Pathological. Works on clinical aspects of mental disorders, including therapy, are entered under Psychiatry.

see also Mental Deficiency; Psychiatry; Psychology, Pathological

Glossary of Mental Disorders & Guide to Their Classification - for Use in Conjunction with the International Classification of Diseases. 8th rev. ed. (Also avail. in French & Spanish). 1974. pap. $4.80 (ISBN 92-4-154036-2). World Health.

MENTAL RETARDATION

see Mental Deficiency

MENTAL TESTS

see Intelligence Tests

MENUS

Ellison, Al. Ellison's Latin American Menu Reader. (Lat.). 1978. pap. $2.95 (ISBN 0-930580-06-0). Ellison Ent.

MERCANTILE LAW

see Commercial Law

MERCANTILE SYSTEM

see also Balance of Trade

Codera Martin, Jose M. Diccionario de Calculo Mercantil. 192p. (Span.). 1981. 800.00 ptas (ISBN 84-368-0168-7). Piramide.

MERCHANDISING

Fischer, Rossi K. Glosario de mercadeo. 143p. (Span.). Mex.$3.20; $40.00. Limusa.

MERCHANT MARINE

see also Insurance, Marine; Merchant Ships; Shipping

Dictionnaire Francais-Anglais, Anglais-Francais des Termes et Locutions de la Marine Marchande. (Fr. & Eng.). $25.00 (ISBN 0-686-57108-8, M-6140). French & Eur.

Dictionnaire Francais-Anglais des Termes & Locutions de la Marine Marchande. (Fr. & Eng.). 53.00 F. Maritimes Outremer.

MERCHANT MARINE–LAW

see Maritime Law

MERCHANT MARKS

see Trade-Marks

MERCHANT SHIPS

Rinke, Hans. Woerterbuch der Seeschiffahrt, Vol. 1. 2nd ed. (Eng. & Ger., Dictionary of Merchant Shipping). 1975. $25.00 (ISBN 3-19-006294-3, M-6958). French & Eur.

--Woerterbuch der Seeschiffahrt, Vol. 2. 2nd ed. (Ger. & Eng., Dictionary of Merchant Shipping). $27.50 (ISBN 3-19-006295-1, M-6957). French & Eur.

MERCHANTMEN

see Merchant Ships

MERCHANTS

Grossmann, T. & Friedmann, G. Kaufmaenisches Grundwoerterbuch fuer Schule & Praxis: Part I, Deutsch-Englisch. 280p. (Ger. & Eng.). 1983. pap. $9.40. M. Rosenberg.

MERCURY

Lange-Koval, Ernst E. & Wilhelm, Kurt. Dictionnaire Pratique Mercure: Francais-Allemand, Allemand-Francais. (Fr. & Ger.). 1964. $24.95 (ISBN 0-686-56992-X, M-6332). French & Eur.

Pay-Costa, M. Dictionnaire Pratique Mercure: Francais-Espagnol, Espagnol-Francais. 2nd ed. 1024p. (Fr. & Span.). 1966. $24.95 (ISBN 0-686-57200-9, M-6471). French & Eur.

Urwin, Kenneth. Dictionnaire Pratique Mercure: Francais-Anglais, Anglais-Francais. 1216p. (Fr. & Eng.). 1968. $24.90 (ISBN 0-686-57239-4, M-6540). French & Eur.

METAL CASTINGS

American Foundrymen Society. Metalcasting Dictionary. 1st ed. 203p. $32.00 (GM6805); members $16.00. Am Foundrymen.

METAL CORROSION

see Corrosion and Anti-Corrosives

METAL-CUTTING TOOLS

Freeman, Henry G. Dictionary of Metal-Cutting Machine Tools, 2 vols. (Eng. & Ger.). 1965. $61.75 ea. (ISBN 3-7736-5095-7). Adler.

--Dictionary of Metal-Cutting Machine Tools. 561p. (Eng. & Ger.). 1965. leatherette $72.00 (ISBN 3-7736-5095-7, M-7110). French & Eur.

Heiler, Toni. Dictionnaire Technique Illustre Des Outils Coupants Pour L'usinage Des Metaux. 474p. (Fr., Ger., Eng., Ital. & Span.). 1965. $69.95 (ISBN 0-686-57326-9, M-6313). French & Eur.

Schuurmang, G., ed. Elseviers Dictionary of Metal Cutting Tools. (Eng., Ger., Fr., Dutch, Span., & Rus.). 1970. $106.50 (ISBN 0-444-40856-8). Elsevier.

METAL ENGRAVERS

see Engravers

METAL INDUSTRIES

see Mineral Industries

METAL-WORK–DICTIONARIES

Abd-El-Wahed, A. M. Metal Forming Dictionary. 386p. (Eng., Fr., Ger. & Arabic.). 1978. $45.00 (ISBN 0-686-92426-6, M-9755). French & Eur.

Clason, W. E. Elsevier's Dictionary of Metallurgy & Metal Working. (Eng., Fr., Span., Ital., Dutch & Ger.). 1978. $136.25 (ISBN 0-444-41695-1). Elsevier.

METALLURGY

see also Chemical Engineering; Chemistry, Technical; Metals; Metals–Heat Treatment; Physical Metallurgy

also names of metals, with or without the subdivision Metallurgy

American Society for Metals. Thesaurus of Metallurgical Terms. 4th ed. $35.00. ASM.

Taylor, James L. Dicionario Metalurgico Ingles-Portugues, Portugues-Ingles. 620p. (Port. & Eng.). pap. $41.00. Imported Bks.

--English-Portuguese Metallurgical Dictionary. 300p. (Eng. & Port.). pap. $9.50. Imported Bks.

METALLURGY–DICTIONARIES

Bader, Oliver & Theret, Michel. Diccionario enciclopedico de metalurgia: Espanol-frances, frances-espanol y espanol-engles, engles-espanol. 960p. (Span., Fr. & Eng.). 1969. 980.00 ptas. ETA.

--Diccionario Enciclopedico de Metalurgia. 960p. (Span., Fr. & Eng.). 1975. $44.95 (ISBN 84-7146-054-8, S-50132). French & Eur.

Breaban, M. Dictionar de Metalurgie Englez-Roman. LC 76-511139. 314p. (Eng. & Romanian.). 1975. 20.50 lei. Editura Stiintifica.

Breaban, M. L. Dictionar de Metalurgie Francez-Roman. LC 77-573734. 375p. (Fr. & Romanian.). 1977. 24.50 lei. Editura Stiintifica.

Cagnacci-Schwicker, A. Woerterbuch fuer Metallurgie, Mineralogie, Geologie, Bergbau & die Oelindustrie. 1530p. (Eng., Fr., Ger. & Ital.). 1970. DM.110.00 (ISBN 3-7625-0751-1). Bauverlag.

Cagnacci-Schwicker, Angelo. Dictionnaire International de Metallurgie, Mineralogie, Geologie et Industries Extractives, 2 vols. 1530p. (Fr.). 1969. Set. $95.00 (ISBN 0-686-56933-4, M-6054). French & Eur.

--Woerterbuch fuer Metallurgie, Mineralogie, Geologie, Bergbau & die Oelindustrie Englische-Franzosisch-Deutsch-Italienisch. 1530p. (Eng., Fr., Ger. & Ital.). 1970. DM.110.00 (ISBN 3-7625-0751-1). Bauverlag.

Chekhranov, V. D. Russko-Ukrainskii Metallurgicheskii Slovar. (Rus. & Ukrainian.). 1970. $1.50 (Pub. by Naukova Dumka). Four Continent.

Clason, W. E. Dizionario di metallurgia. (Ital.). 1966. L.16000.00. Etas Libri.

--Elsevier's Dictionary of Metallurgy & Metal Working. (Eng., Fr., Span., Ital., Dutch & Ger.). 1978. $136.25 (ISBN 0-444-41695-1). Elsevier.

Deputatova, N. F., et al. Nemetsko-Russkii Slovar Po Metalloobrabotke. 465p. (Rus. & Ger.). 1957. $6.00 (Pub. by Gosizdat Tekhnich Teoretich. Lit.). Four Continent.

Dollinger, A., ed. Dictionary of Metallurgy. 767p. (Eng., Fr., Ger., Rus., Pol. & Slovene.). 1974. $150.00 (ISBN 0-686-92409-6, M-9893). French & Eur.

Gagnacci-Schwicker, A. & Schwicker. International Dictionary of Metallurgy, Mineralogy, Geology & the Mining & Oil Industries. 1530p. (Eng., Fr., Ger. & Ital.). 1970. $88.00 (ISBN 3-7625-0751-1, M-7482, Pub. by Bauverlag). French & Eur.

--International Dictionary of Metallurgey, Mineralogy, Geology & the Mining & Oil Industries. 1530p. (Eng., Fr., Ger. & Ital.). 1970. $88.00 (ISBN 3-7625-0751-1). Bauverlag.

Mertz De Mertzenteld, R., et al. Dictionnaire Technologique Feutry: Mecanique-Metallurgie-Hydraulique, Vol. 1. 750p. (Eng., Fr. & Ger.). 1976. 250.00 F. Maison Dictionnaire.

Metallurgisk Ordbok. LC 77-468526. 347p. (Eng. & Ger., Norsk Verks). 1976. write for info. (ISBN 8-2902-0400-0). Norsk Verkstedsindustris Standardiseringssentral.

Woerterbuch fuer Metallurgie, Mineralogie, Geologie, Bergbau und die Oelindustrie. (Eng. , Fr. , Ger. & Ital., Dictionary of Metallurgy, Mineralogy, Geology, Mining and Oil Industry). 1970. $88.00 (ISBN 3-7625-0751-1, M-6912). French & Eur.

METALLURGY, PHYSICAL

see Physical Metallurgy

METALS

see also Mineralogy

also particular metals and metal groups, e.g. Iron

Carpovich, Eugene A. Russian-English Metals & Machines Dictionary. LC 60-12013. (Rus. & Eng.). 1960. $15.00x (ISBN 0-911484-02-7). Tech Dict.

Heiler, T. Diccionario tecnico ilustrado de herramientas de corte para el trabajo de metales: Espanol-aleman-ingles-frances-italiano. (Illus.). 474p. (Span., Ger., Eng., Fr. & Ital.). write for info. G Gili.

METALS–CORROSION

see Corrosion and Anti-Corrosives

METALS–DICTIONARIES

Dettner, H. Fachwoerterbuch fuer der Metalloberflaechenveredelung. 391p. (Ger. & Eng.). 1969. DM.20.95 (ISBN 3-87749-011-5). Siemens AG.

Heiler, Toni. Dictionnaire Technique Illustre des Outlis Coupants: L'usinage des Metaux; Francais-Allemand-Anglais-Italien-Espagnol. (Illus.). 474p. (Fr., Ger., Eng., Ital. & Span.). 1965. 156.00 F. Eyrolles.

Longan, Tang & Zenglian, Ni. English-Chinese Dictionary of Metals & Their Heat Treatment. LC 81-1279. iii, 266p. 1981. pap. $27.50 (ISBN 0-8311-1081-3). Indus Pr.

Warren Spring Laboratory, ed. Thesaurus of Terms for Indexing the Literature of Minerals Processing & Metals Extraction, 1974. 1981. $75.00x (ISBN 0-686-97151-5, Pub. by W Spring England). State Mutual Bk.

METALS–HEAT TREATMENT

Association Technique de Traitement Thermique. Glossaire du Traitement Thermique. LC 77-570276. 142p. (Fr.). 1976. 33.00 F (ISBN 2-85330-022-6). Pyc.

METALS, TRANSMUTATION OF

see Alchemy

METAPSYCHOLOGY

see Psychical Research; Spiritualism

METEOROLOGY

see also Atmosphere; Climatology; Humidity; Weather

also headings beginning with the word Meteorological

American Meteorological Society. Glossary of Meteorology. 1959. $25.00. Am Meteorological.

Brazol, D. Diccionario de terminos meterologicos: Ingles-espanol espanol-ingles. (Eng. & Span.). Arg.$25.00. Hachette.

Chassany, Jean-Philippe. Dictionnaire de Meteorologie Populaire. 416p. (Fr.). 1970. $35.00 (ISBN 0-686-56945-8, M-6067). French & Eur.

--Dictionnaire de Meteorologie Populaire. (Illus.). 416p. (Fr.). 1970. 85.00 F. Maison & Larose.

C.I.L.F. Vocabulaire de l'Hydrologie et de la meteorologie. 239p. (Fr.). 1978. 80.00 F. Maison Dictionnaire.

Desruisseaux, Pierre. Dictionnaire de Meteorologie Populaire au Quebec. LC 76-471846. 215p. (Fr.). 1976. Can.$6.95 (ISBN 0-88532-103-0). Edns Laurore.

Des Ruisseaux, Pierre. Dictionnaire de Meteorologie Populaire au Quebec. (Illus.). 215p. (Fr.). 1976. 6.95 F. Aurore.

Dictionary of Meteorological Terms. (Hebrew, Eng. , Fr. & Ger.). IL.10.00. Massada Pr.

Dictionary of Meteorology. 207p. (Eng. & Chinese.). 1974. pap. $4.95 (ISBN 0-686-92293-X, M-9567). French & Eur.
Khromov, S. P. Meteorologicheskii Slovar. 620p. (Rus.). 1963. $7.25 (Pub. by Gidrometeoizdat). Four Continent.
Ministry of Education. Scientific Terms Meteorology: Japanese-English, English-Japanese. 140p. (Japanese & Eng.). 1975. Leatherette $19.95 (ISBN 0-686-92205-0, M-9338). French & Eur.
Silvestrov, P. V. Dictionnaire Meteorologique: Francais-Russe. 191p. (Fr. & Rus.). 1978. leatherette $9.95 (ISBN 0-686-92563-7, M-9122). French & Eur.
Villeneuve, G. O. & Ferland, M. G. Glossaire De Meteorologie et De Climatologie. LC 75-501061. 560p. (Fr.). 1974. $29.95 (ISBN 0-686-57246-7, M-6552). French & Eur.
Villeneuve, Georges O. & Ferland, Michel G. Glossaire de Meteorologie & de Climatologie. 550p. (Fr.). 1974. DM.20.00. Laval P. U.
Vocabulaire Meteorologique International: Quadrilingue (Anglais-Francais-Espagnol-Russe) (Eng. , Fr. , Span. & Rus.). 40.00 F. O. M. M.

METER (STANDARD OF LENGTH)
see Metric System

METERS, ELECTRIC
see Electric Meters

METERS, FLOW
see Flow Meters

METHOD OF WORK
see Work

METRIC SYSTEM
Ferraro, Alfredo. Dizionario di metrologia generale. (Illus.). xvi, 270p. (Ital.). 1965. L.2500.00. Zanichelli.
Zupko, Ronald E. French Weights & Measures before the Revolution: A Dictionary of Provincial & Local Units. LC 78-3249. 256p. 1979. $22.50x (ISBN 0-253-32480-7). Ind U Pr.

METROLOGY
see Mensuration

METROPOLITAN TRANSPORTATION
see Urban Transportation

MEXICAN AMERICANS
Here are entered works on American citizens of Mexican descent or works concerned with Mexican American minority groups. Works on immigration from Mexico, braceros, etc. are entered under Mexicans in the United States.
Meier, Matt S. & Rivera, Feliciano, eds. Dictionary of Mexican American History. LC 80-24750. (Illus.). 472p. 1981. lib. bdg. 35.00 (ISBN 0-313-21203-1, NMD/). Greenwood.
Vasquez, Librado K. & Vasquez, Maria E. Regional Dictionary of Chicano Slang. 111p. 1975. 13.50 (ISBN 0-8363-0083-1). Jenkins.

MEXICAN LANGUAGE
see Aztec Language

MEXICO–BIOGRAPHY
Diccionario Porrua de Historia, Biografia y Geografia de Mexico, 2 vols. (Span.). $150.00 set (ISBN 0-686-56692-0, S-12279). French & Eur.
Suplemento a la Segunda Edicion Del Diccionario Pornua De Historia, Biografia y Geografia de Mexico. 496p. (Span.). $17.50 (ISBN 0-686-56693-9, S-12280). French & Eur.

MEXICO–HISTORY
Briggs, Donald C. & Alisky, Marvin. Historical Dictionary of Mexico. LC 80-27320. (Latin American Historical Dictionaries Ser.: No. 21). 275p. 1981. lib. bdg. $15.00 (ISBN 0-8108-1391-2). Scarecrow.
Diccionario Porrua de Historia, Biografia y Geografia de Mexico, 2 vols. (Span.). $150.00 set (ISBN 0-686-56692-0, S-12279). French & Eur.

MEXICO–HISTORY–1910-1946
Langle, Arturo. Vocabulario, Apodos, Seudonimos, Sobrenombres & Hemerografia de la Revolucion. 151p. (Span.). 1966. Mex.$20.00. UNAM.

MEXICO–POLITICS AND GOVERNMENT
Franco Arias, Froilan. El Vocabulario Politico de Alguno Periodicos de Mexico D. F. 50p. (Span.). 1981. write for info. (ISBN 84-7075-197-2). Fundacion J March.

MEXICO–RELIGION
Penalosa, Joaquin Antonio. Vocabulario & Refranero Religioso de Mexico. (Span.). Mex.$25.00. Jus.

MEXICO–SOCIAL LIFE AND CUSTOMS
Santamaria, Francisco. Diccionario de Mejicanismos. 1197p. (Span.). 1959. Mex.$24.00. Porrua.

MICHIGAN STATE UNIVERSITY
Michigan State University,(East Lansing) Dictionary Catalog of the G. Robert Vincent Library. 1975. $75.00 (ISBN 0-8161-1149-9, Hall Library). G K Hall.

MICKIEWICZ, ADAM, 1798-1855
A Dictionary of Adam Mickiewicz's Language: Vol. 1, A-C. 656p. (Pol. & Eng.). $41.75 (Pub. by Ossolineum). Four Continent.
A Dictionary of Adam Mickiewicz's Language: Vol. 2, D-6. 582p. (Pol. & Eng.). 1977. $41.70 (535-B, Pub. by Ossolineum). Four Continent.
A Dictionary of Adam Mickiewicz's Language: Vol. 8, S. 626p. (Pol. & Eng.). 1977. $38.35 (Pub. by Ossolineum). Four Continent.
A Dictionary of Adam Mickiewicz's Language: Vol. 9, T-W. 728p. (Pol. & Eng.). 1977. $55.00 (Pub. by Ossolineum). Four Continent.

MICRO COMPUTERS
see Microcomputers

MICROBIOLOGY–CLASSIFICATION
Cowan, S. T. A Dictionary of Microbial Taxonomy. Hill, L. R., ed. LC 77-85705. (Illus.). 1978. $45.00 (ISBN 0-521-21890-X). Cambridge U Pr.

MICROBIOLOGY–DICTIONARIES
Cowan, S. T. A Dictionary of Microbial Taxonomic Usage. 1968. 7.50 (ISBN 0-934454-28-0). Lubrecht & Cramer.
English-Chinese Microbiological Dictionary. 138p. (Eng. & Chinese.). 1979. pap. $3.95 (ISBN 0-686-97368-2, M-9573). French & Eur.
Singleton, Paul & Sainsbury, Diana. Dictionary of Microbiology. LC 78-4532. 481p. 1978. $71.95 (ISBN 0-471-99658-0, Pub. by Wiley-Interscience). Wiley.
Sinsoilliez, Robert. Lexique des Termes Parodontologie de Microbiologie: Parodontale & Buccale & de Sciences Fondamentales. (Illus.). 112p. (Fr.). 1973. 38.00 F. Prelat.

MICROCOMPUTERS
Chandor, Anthony. The Facts on File Dictionary of Micro Computers. 1981. 14.95 (ISBN 0-87196-597-6). Facts on File.
--The Facts on File Dictionary of Microcomputers. (Eng.). 1981. $14.95 (ISBN 0-87196-597-6). Facts on File.
Hordeski, Michael. Illustrated Dictionary of Microcomputer Terminology. (Illus.). 1978. pap. $8.95 (ISBN 0-8306-1088-X, 1088). TAB Bks.
The Personal Computer Glossary. 1982. $2.95 (ISBN 0-88284-233-1). Alfred Pub.
Sippl, Charles. Microcomputer Dictionary. LC 81-50565. 1981. pap. 15.95 (ISBN 0-672-21696-5). Sams.
Spencer, Donald D. Microcomputers at a Glance. LC 77-11920. (gr. 9-12). 1977. pap. $3.50x (ISBN 0-89218-021-8). Camelot Pub.
Sybex Staff & Zaks, Rodnay. International Microcomputer Dictionary. rev. ed. LC 81-51133. Orig. Title: Microprocessor Lexicon-Acronyms & Definitions. 120p. (Eng., Ger., Span., Ital. & Pol.). 1981. pap. $3.95x (ISBN 0-89588-067-9). Sybex.

MICROELECTRONICS
IWT Verlag Editors. Microelectronics Dictionary. (Eng. & Ger.). 1980. $23.00 (ISBN 0-9961073-2-0, Pub. by VDI W Germany). Heyden.
Kovacs, Magdolna. Angol-Magyar Mikroelektronikai. LC 79-349423. 367p. (Hungarian.). 1977. 39.00 Ft (ISBN 9-6354-2077-3). KG Informatik.
Worterbuch der Mikroelktronik, Dictionary Microelectronics: English-German, German-English. 218p. (Eng. & Ger.). 1980. pap. $39.95 (ISBN 3-88322-001-9, M-9219). French & Eur.

MICROGRAPHIC ANALYSIS
see Microscope and Microscopy

MICROMINIATURIZATION (ELECTRONICS)
see Microelectronics

MICRONESIAN LANGUAGES
see also Chamorro Language; Malayan Languages; Marshall Language; Melanesian Languages
Jensen, John T., et al. Yapese-English Dictionary. LC 76-47495. (Pali Language Texts: Micronesia). 202p. (Orig., Yapese & Eng.). 1977. pap. text ed. $10.00x (ISBN 0-8248-0517-8). UH Pr.

MICROPROCESSORS
Chandor, Anthony. The Penguin Book of Microprocessors. (Eng.). 1981. pap. $5.95. Penguin.
--The Penguin Dictionary of Microprocessors. 192p. 1981. pap. 5.95 (ISBN 0-14-051100-8). Penguin.

MICROSCOPE AND MICROSCOPY
see also Histology
Glossary of Micrographics. (TR2-1980). 1980. 9.00 (ISBN 0-89258-065-8). Assn Inform Image.

MICROSCOPIC ANALYSIS
see Microscope and Microscopy

MICROSCOPIC ANATOMY
see Histology

MICROWAVE COOKERY
Society of the Plastics Industry. Recommendations for Labeling Plastics Microwave Cookware & Glossary. first copy free (1200); add. copies $0.20. Soc Plastic Ind.

MIDDLE AGES
see also Geography, Medieval; Renaissance
Gay, Victor. Glossaire Archeologique du Moyen-Age & de la Renaissance, 2 vols. (Illus., Fr.). 1928. 243.00 F. Kraus.
Lexikon des Mittelalters. (Ger.). 1977. pap. $25.00 (ISBN 3-7608-8801-1, M-7206). French & Eur.
Lexikon des Mittelalters. 112p. (Ger.). 1977. DM.32.00 (ISBN 3-7608-8801-1). Artemis Verlag.
Strayer, Joseph R., ed. Dictionary of the Middle Ages, Vol. 1. LC 82-5904. 1982. lib. bdg. $70.00 (ISBN 0-684-16760-3, ScribR). Scribner.
--Dictionary of the Middle Ages, Vol. 2. LC 82-5904. 1983. lib. bdg. $70.00 (ISBN 0-684-17022-1, ScribR). Scribner.

MIDDLE AGES–BIBLIOGRAPHY
Pontifical Institute of Mediaeval Studies, Toronto. Dictionary Catalog of the Library of the Pontifical Institute of Mediaeval Studies: First Supplement. 1979. lib. bdg. $125.00 (ISBN 0-8161-1061-1, Hall Library). G K Hall.

MIDDLE AGES–HISTORY
Glossar zur Fruehmittelalterlichen Geschichte im Oestlichen Europa: Lfg 2, Quellensiglenverzeichnis, Aba-Alania. 64p. (Ger.). 1974. DM.32.00 (ISBN 3-515-01786-0). Buch Vertrieb.
Glossar zur Fruehmittelalterlichen Geschichte im Oestlichen Europa: Lfg 3, Alanorum Montes-Antes. 64p. (Ger.). 1974. DM.32.00 (ISBN 3-515-01950-2). Buch Vertrieb.
Glossar zur Fruehmittelalterlichen Geschichte im Oestlichen Europa: Lfg 5, Atto-Avari. 64p. (Ger.). 1975. DM.32.00 (ISBN 3-515-02026-8). Buch Vertrieb.
Glossar zur Fruehmittelalterlichen Geschichte im Oestlichen Europa: Lfg 6, Avari (Arabes)-Baioaria. 64p. (Ger.). 1976. DM.32.00 (ISBN 3-515-02346-1). Buch Vertrieb.
Glossar zur Fruehmittelalterlichen Geschichte im Oestlichen Europa: Lfg 1, Einleitung, Abkuerzungen & Literatursiglenverzeichnis. 64p. (Ger.). 1974. DM.32.00 (ISBN 3-515-01982-0). Buch Vertrieb.
Otto, Norbert & Wojtecki, Dieter. Glossar zur Fruehmittelalterlichen Geschichte im Oestlichen Europa. 64p. (Ger.). 1975. DM.32.00 (ISBN 3-515-01977-4). Buch Vertrieb.
--Glossar zur Fruehmittelalterlichen Geschichte im Oestlichen Europa: Lfg 7, Baioariae Marcha-Behin Redaktion. 64p. (Ger.). 1976. DM.32.00 (ISBN 3-515-02479-4). Buch Vertrieb.

MIDWIFERY
see Obstetrics

MILITARISM
see also Disarmament
Bulgakov. Diccionario militar espanol-ruso. (Span. & Rus.). $1.20. Pueblos Unidos.

MILITARY ART AND SCIENCE
see also Battles; Disarmament; Drill and Minor Tactics; Logistics; Naval Art and Science; Signals and Signaling; Strategy
also headings beginning with the word Military
Gamber, Ortwin, et al, eds. Glossarium Armorum: Bd 6 Texthefte in Deutsch, Englisch, Franzoesisch, Italienisch, Daenisch, Tschechisch. (Ger., Eng., Fr., Ital., Danish & Czech.). DM.420.00. Verlag der Buchhaendler-Vereinigung GmbH.
Lizarraga, Francisco. Diccionario tecnico militar ingles-espanol y espanol-ingles para uso de los ejercitos de tierra, mar y aire. (Eng. & Span.). 125.00 ptas. Bibliografica.
Schneider, Hugo, et al, eds. Glossarium Amorum: Lfg 1, Schutzwaffen. (Ger.). DM.420.00 (ISBN 3-201-00262-3). Verlag der Buchhaendler-Vereinigung GmbH.

MILITARY ART AND SCIENCE–DICTIONARIES
A Szotarszerk Bizottsag Vezetoje Toth Lajos. Magyar-Orosz Katonai Szotar. LC 78-377454. 1177p. (Hungarian & Rus.). 1977. 355.00 Ft (ISBN 9-6305-1022-7). Akademiai Kiado.
Abbreviated Military Dictionary. 334p. (Persian & Rus.). 1954. leatherette $4.50 (ISBN 0-686-97382-8, M-9106). French & Eur.
Aguirre de Carcer. Diccionario militar bilingue. (Span.). write for info. Dossat.
Aliev, G. G. Persidsko-Russkii & Russko-Persidskii Voennyi Slovar. 656p. (Rus. & Persian.). 1972. $6.50 (Pub. by Voenizdat). Four Continent.
Artiukhov, M. G., et al. Bolgarsko-Russkii Voennyi Slovar. 527p. (Rus. & Bulgarian.). 1966. $3.90 (Pub. bu Voenizdat). Four Continent.
Centre De Documentation De L'Armement. Lexique Thematique des Descripteurs et Identificateurs. 151p. (Fr.). 1976. pap. $35.00 (ISBN 0-686-56742-0, M-6371). French & Eur.
Chinese-English Dictionary of Military Terms. 366p. (Chinese & Eng.). 1977. $25.00 (ISBN 0-686-97446-8, M-9275). French & Eur.
Diccionario Militar Espanol-Ruso, Ruso-Espanol. 632p. (Eng. , Rus. & Span.). 1965. Leatherette $10.95 (ISBN 0-686-92245-X, S-31871). French & Eur.
Dictionary of U. S. Military Terms. 1963. 4.50 (ISBN 0-8183-0163-5). Pub Aff Pr.
Eitzen, K. Military Eitzen. (Ger. & Eng.). 1957. pap. $15.95 (ISBN 3-87599-035-8, M-7563, Pub. by Vlg. Offene Worte). French & Eur.
Gaynor, Frank, ed. New Military & Naval Dictionary. Repr. of 1951 ed. lib. bdg. 15.75x (ISBN 0-8371-2129-9, GAMN). Greenwood.
Guglielmotti, Alberto. Vocabolario marino e militare. 1008p. (Ital.). 1967. L.30000.00. Mursia.
Hanrieder, Wolfram F. & Buel, Larry V., eds. Words & Arms: A Dictionary of Security & Defense Terms with Supplementary Data. 1979. lib. bdg. $35.00x (ISBN 0-89158-383-1). Westview.
Heinl, Robert D., Jr., ed. Dictionary of Military & Naval Quotations. LC 66-22342. 1966. 18.95 (ISBN 0-87021-149-8). Naval Inst Pr.

--Dictionary of Military & Naval Quotations. (Illus.). 395p. 1978. $18.95 (ISBN 0-87021-149-8); bulk rates avail. US Naval Inst.

Laprusa, Mariana. Leksykon Wiedzy Wojskowej. 541p. (Pol., Warsaw, Poland). 1979. 180.00 Zl (ISBN 8-3110-6229-3). Wydaw Min. Obrony Narodowej.

Li, P. K., ed. A Text of Chinese Military Terms. 390p. (Chinese & Eng.). 1972. pap. $12.95 (ISBN 0-686-92268-9, M-9577). French & Eur.

Nagy, Istvan G. Haditechnikai Kislexikon. LC 78-343185. 417p. (Hungarian.). 1976. 60.00 Ft (ISBN 9-633-26511-8). Zrinyikatunai.

Neliubin, L. D. Illiustrirovannyi Voenno-Tekhnicheskii Slovar. 482p. (Eng., Ger., Span., Rus. & Fr.). 1968. $17.50 (Pub. by Voenizdat). Four Continent.

Ostapenko. Dictionnaire Francais-Russe Militaire. (Fr. & Rus.). 1976. 45.75 F. Mir.

Peisikov, L. S., et al. Kratkii Voennyi Persidsko-Russkii Slovar. 334p. (Rus.). 1954. $1.50 (Pub. by Voenizdat Inostr & Natsional' Slovarei). Four Continent.

Pooch, H. Fachwoerterbuch des Nachrichtenwesens. 280p. (Ger.). 1976. pap. 22.50 (ISBN 3-7949-0234-3, M-7390, Pub. by Fachvlg. Schiele & Schoen). French & Eur.

Pretz, Bernhard. Dictionary of Military Technological Abbreviations & Acronyms. 450p. 1983. 45.00 (ISBN 0-7100-9274-1). Routledge & Kegan.

Quick, John. Dictionary of Weapons & Military Terms. (Illus.). 515p. 1973. 34.95 (ISBN 0-07-051057-1, P&RB). McGraw.

Ruiz Jodar, Carlos. Diccionario Espanol-Aleman, Aleman-Espanol Militar. 375p. (Span. & Ger.). 1975. pap. $13.95 (ISBN 84-400-8515-X, S-50101). French & Eur.

Russian-Rumanian Military Dictionary. 335p. (Rus. & Rumanian.). 1964. leatherette $6.95 (ISBN 0-686-92131-3, M-9079). French & Eur.

Scott, Henry L. Military Dictionary. Repr. of 1861 ed. lib. bdg. 25.00 (ISBN 0-8371-0648-6, SCMD). Greenwood.

Slovar Osnovnykh Voennykh Terminov. 248p. (Rus.). 1965. $2.85 (Pub. by Voenizdat). Four Continent.

Smith, George. A Universal Military Dictionary. (Eng.). 1969. Can.$37.50 (ISBN 0-919316-57-3). U of Toronto Pr.

Spazhev, Iu. A., et al. Russko-Rumynskii Voennyi Slovar. 335p. (Rus. & Rumanian.). 1964. $3.00 (Pub. by Voenizdat). Four Continent.

Stanway, ed. Dictionary of Operations. Epap. 2.50. Paladin.

Taube, A. M. Frantsuzsko-Russkii Voennyi Slovar. (Fr. & Rus.). 1960. $6.60 (Pub. by Voenizdat). Four Continent.

Toth, Lajos. Orosz-Magyar Katonai Szotar. LC 79-354764. 1147p. (Rus. & Hungarian.). 1976. 245.00 Ft. Akademiai Kiado.

Toth, Lajos, et al. Katonai Ertelmezo Szotar. LC 77-575154. 454p. (Eng. & Hungarian.). 1976. 62.00 Ft (ISBN 9-6332-6510-X). Zrinyi Katonai.

MILITARY ART AND SCIENCE–TERMINOLOGY

Chinese-English Dictionary of Military Technical Terms. LC 80-112476. 206p. (Eng. & Chinese.). 1979. write for info. S.N.

Dictionary of U. S. Military Terms. 1963. 4.50 (ISBN 0-8183-0163-5). Pub Aff Pr.

Garber, Max B. & Bond, P. S. A Modern Military Dictionary: Ten Thousand Technical & Slang Terms of Military Usage. 2nd ed. LC 74-31354. 1975. Repr. of 1942 ed. $34.00x (ISBN 0-8103-4208-1). Gale.

Graves, Donald E. French Military Terminology, 1670-1815. LC 80-510476. 54p. (Fr.). 1979. write for info. (ISBN 0-919326-38-2). New Bruns Mus.

MILITARY-CIVIL RELATIONS
see Militarism; Military Policy

MILITARY DRILL
see Drill and Minor Tactics

MILITARY ENGINEERING

Volodin, N. V. Anglo-Russkii Voenno-Inzhenernyi Slovar. 783p. (Eng. & Rus.). 1962. $8.35 (Pub. by Voenizdat). Four Continent.

MILITARY EXPLOSIVES
see Explosives

MILITARY HISTORY
see also Battles; Military Policy
also subdivisions History, or History, military under names of countries, e.g. United States–History, Military; particular wars, battles, sieges, etc.; also France–Army; United States–Army, and similar headings

Young, Brigadier P. Dictionary of Battles, Vol. 1. (Illus.). 1978. $15.00 (ISBN 0-8317-2260-6, Mayflower Bks). Smith Pubs.

Young, Brigadier P. & Calvert, Brigadier M. Dictionary of Battles, Vol. 2. LC 78-23518. (Illus.). 1979. $15.00 (ISBN 0-8317-2261-4, Mayflower Bks). Smith Pubs.

MILITARY LAW

Dahl, Richard C. & Whelan, John F., eds. The Military Law Dictionary. LC 60-10208. 200p. 1960. 15.00 (ISBN 0-379-00042-3). Oceana.

MILITARY POLICY
see also Militarism
also subdivision Military Policy under names of countries, e.g. United States–Military Policy

De Bordeje Morencos, Fernando. Diccionario militar estrategico y politico. 288p. (Span.). 1981. pap. 500.00 ptas (ISBN 84-7140-202-5). San Martin.

MILITARY POWER
see Disarmament; Military Art and Science

MILITARY SCIENCE
see Military Art and Science

MILITARY SIGNALING
see Signals and Signaling

MILITARY STRATEGY
see Military Art and Science; Strategy

De Bordeje Morencos, Fernando. Diccionario militar estrategico y politico. 288p. (Span.). 1981. pap. 500.00 ptas (ISBN 84-7140-202-5). San Martin.

MILITARY TERMS
see Military Art and Science–Terminology

MILITARY TOPOGRAPHY

Sil'ianov, V. V., et al. Anglo-Russkaia Terminologiia Po Organizatsii & Bezopasnosti Dorozhnogo Divizheniia. 199p. (Rus.). 1977. $2.75 (Pub. by Viniti). Four Continent.

MILK
see also Cheese; Cookery (Dairy Products)

Casalis, Jacques. Dictionnaire Laitier: Francais-Allemand-Anglais. (Fr., Ger. & Eng.). 132.00 F. Litec.

MILK–MARKETING
see Milk Trade

MILK TRADE

Casalis, Jacques. Dictionnaire Laitier: Francais, Allemand, Anglais. (Fr., Ger. & Eng.). 1963. $49.95 (ISBN 0-686-56941-5, M-6063). French & Eur.

MILLS (BUILDINGS)
see Factories

MILTON, JOHN, 1608-1674–CONCORDANCES

Cleveland, Charles D. Complete Concordance to the Poetical Works of John Milton. LC 76-57784. 1867. lib. bdg. $25.00 (ISBN 0-8414-3459-X). Folcroft.

MILTON, JOHN, 1608-1674–DICTIONARIES, INDEXES, ETC.

Gilbert, Allan H. A Geographical Dictionary of Milton. 1979. Repr. of 1919 ed. lib. bdg. $35.00 (ISBN 0-8495-2014-2). Arden Lib.

--Geographical Dictionary of Milton. LC 68-10922. 1968. Repr. of 1919 ed. 9.50x (ISBN 0-8462-1105-X). Russell.

Le Comte, Edward. Dictionary of Puns in Milton's English Poetry. 240p. 1981. $27.00x (ISBN 0-231-05102-6). Columbia U Pr.

Le Comte, Edward S. Milton Dictionary. LC 76-86175. Repr. of 1961 ed. $19.50 (ISBN 0-404-03917-0). AMS Pr.

Lockwood, Laura E. Lexicon to the English Poetical Works of John Milton. LC 72-193205. 1972. lib. bdg. $27.45 (ISBN 0-8414-5878-2). Folcroft.

MIME

Pinedo Peydro, Felix-Jesus. Diccionario mimico espanol. 576p. (Span.). 1981. pap. 1200.00 ptas (ISBN 84-500-5005-7). Organ Ofic Adm.

MIND
see Intellect; Psychology

MIND AND BODY
see also Body, Human; Dreams; Hypnotism; Psychoanalysis; Psychology, Pathological; Psychology, Physiological

Pyles, Donald W. Dictionary of Synergetics. (Illus.). 84p. (Orig.). 1983. pap. $2.00 (ISBN 0-910217-01-7). Synergetics WV.

MIND-CURE
see Christian Science; Mind and Body

MINERAL INDUSTRIES
see also Ceramics; Metallurgy; Mines and Mineral Resources; Mining Engineering
also specific types of mines and mining, e.g. Coal Mines and Mining

Congres International de la Preparation des Minerais. Lexique Quadrilingue de la Preparation des Minerals: Allemand-Anglais-Francais-Russe. 260p. (Ger., Eng., Fr. & Rus.). 1963. 45.00 F. Ste. Industrie Minerale.

Glossaire Anglais-Francais des Termes Miniers & du Vocabulaire Connexe. (Eng & Fr.). Can.$1.50. Centre D'edition.

Polsko-Russkii Gornyi Slovar. 815p. (Rus. & Pol.). 1975. $12.00 (Pub. by Russkii Iazyk). Four Continent.

Schmidt, Helmut. Bergbautechnik & Aufbereitung Deutsch-Englisch. 692p. (Ger. & Eng.). 1981. M.70.00. VEB Technik.

Warren Spring Laboratory, ed. Thesaurus of Terms for Indexing the Literature of Minerals Processing & Metals Extraction, 1974. 1981. $75.00x (ISBN 0-686-97151-5, Pub. by W Spring England). State Mutual Bk.

MINERAL LANDS
see Mines and Mineral Resources

MINERAL RESOURCES
see Mines and Mineral Resources

MINERALOGY
see also Crystallography; Gems; Petrology; Precious Stones; Rocks
also names of minerals, e.g. Feldspar, Quartz

Tezaurus Po Mineralam, Vol. 2. 336p. (Rus.). 1977. $9.95 (Pub. by Viniti). Four Continent.

Tezaurus Po Mineralm, Vol. 1. 300p. (Rus.). 1976. $4.10 (Pub. by Viniti). Four Continent.

MINERALOGY–DICTIONARIES

Armanet, J. & Becquer, A. Annales des Mines: Lexique Technique Allemand-Francais. 344p. (Ger. & Fr.). 1951. $8.95 (ISBN 0-686-56901-6, M-6011). French & Eur.

Cagnacci-Schwicker, A. Woerterbuch fuer Metallurgie, Mineralogie, Geologie, Bergbau & die Oelindustrie. 1530p. (Eng., Fr., Ger. & Ital.). 1970. DM.110.00 (ISBN 3-7625-0751-1). Bauverlag.

Cagnacci-Schwicker, Angelo. Dictionnaire International de Metallurgie, Mineralogie, Geologie et Industries Extractives, 2 vols. 1530p. (Fr.). 1969. Set. $95.00 (ISBN 0-686-56933-4, M-6054). French & Eur.

--Woerterbuch fuer Metallurgie, Mineralogie, Geologie, Bergbau & die Oelindustrie Englische-Franzosisch-Deutsch-Italienisch. 1530p. (Eng., Fr., Ger. & Ital.). 1970. DM.110.00 (ISBN 3-7625-0751-1). Bauverlag.

Congres International de la Preparation des Minerais, ed. Lexique Quadrilinque de la Preparation des Minerais. 260p. (Ger., Eng., Fr & Rus., Four-Language Lexicon of Ore Preparation). 1963. pap. $25.00 (ISBN 0-686-56795-1). French & Eur.

De Michele, Vincenzo. Diccionario: Atlas De Mineralogia. 2nd ed. 216p. (Span.). 1978. $11.50 (ISBN 84-307-8288-5, S-50260). French & Eur.

Diccionario Monografico de Reino Mineral 'Vox' 288p. (Span.). 1981. write for info. (ISBN 84-7153-387-1). Biblo SP.

Diccionario Monografico del Reino Mineral. 288p. (Span.). 750.00 ptas (ISBN 84-7153-386-3). Biblograf SP.

Diccionario Monografico del Reino Mineral. (Span.). 750.00 ptas (ISBN 84-7153-387-1). Biblograf.

Diccionario Rioduero: Geologia y Mineralogia. 2nd ed. (Span.). 1978. leatherette $9.95 (ISBN 0-686-57363-3). French & Eur.

Dictionnaire de Minerologie. (Illus., Fr.). 1978. 21.00 F. Atlas.

Gagnacci-Schwicker, A. & Schwicker. International Dictionary of Metallurgy, Mineralogy, Geology & the Mining & Oil Industries. 1530p. (Eng., Fr., Ger. & Ital.). 1970. $88.00 (ISBN 3-7625-0751-1, M-7482, Pub. by Bauverlag). French & Eur.

--International Dictionary of Metallurgey, Mineralogy, Geology & the Mining & Oil Industries. 1530p. (Eng., Fr., Ger. & Ital.). 1970. $88.00 (ISBN 3-7625-0751-1). Bauverlag.

Harder, Herrmann. Lexikon Fuer Mineralien - und Gesteins Freunde. (Ger.). 1977. $25.00 (ISBN 3-7658-0253-0, M-7198). French & Eur.

Jehan, L. F. Dictionnaire de Chimie et de Mineralogie. Migne, J. P., ed. (Encyclopedie Theologique Ser.: Vol. 46). 830p. (Fr.). Repr. of 1851 ed. lib. bdg. $105.00x (ISBN 0-89241-250-X). Caratzas Pub Co.

Mineralogy Dictionary, German-Russian, 2 Vols. 633p. (Ger. & Rus.). 1976. $19.95 (ISBN 0-686-87191-X, M-9112). French & Eur.

O'Donoghue, Michael. Van Nostrand Reinhold Color Dictionary of Minerals & Gemstones. 160p. 1982. pap. $12.95 (ISBN 0-442-27431-9). Van Nos Reinhold.

Saltikoff, Boris. Mineraalinimisanasto. LC 78-339110. 82p. (Eng. & Finnish.). 1976. write for info. (ISBN 9-516-90044-5). Geo Tutkim.

Von Harder, Hermann, et al. Lexikon fuer Mineralien & Gesteinfreunde. 256p. (Ger.). 1977. DM.29.80 (ISBN 3-7658-0253-0). Bucher Verlag.

Woerterbuch fuer Metallurgie, Mineralogie, Geologie, Bergbau und die Oelindustrie. (Eng. , Fr. , Ger. & Ital., Dictionary of Metallurgy, Mineralogy, Geology, Mining and Oil Industry). 1970. $88.00 (ISBN 3-7625-0751-1, M-6912). French & Eur.

MINERALS
see Mineralogy; Mines and Mineral Resources

MINES AND MINERAL RESOURCES
see also Ceramic Materials; Mineralogy; Mining Engineering; Mining Geology; Prospecting
also specific types of mines and mining, e.g. Coal Mines and Mining, Gold Mines and Mining

Dictionnaire Minier Russe-Francais. (Fr. & Rus.). 1973. pap. $25.00 (ISBN 0-686-56770-6, M-6150). French & Eur.

Woerterbuch fuer Metallurgie, Mineralogie, Geologie, Bergbau und die Oelindustrie. (Eng. , Fr. , Ger. & Ital., Dictionary of Metallurgy, Mineralogy, Geology, Mining and Oil Industry). 1970. $88.00 (ISBN 3-7625-0751-1, M-6912). French & Eur.

MINES AND MINERAL RESOURCES–DICTIONARIES

Auger, Pierre & Rousseau, Louis-Jean. Lexique Anglais-Francais De L'industrie Miniere, 1. 91p. (Eng. & Fr.). 1973. pap. $6.95 (ISBN 0-686-56905-9, M-6016). French & Eur.

Cagnacci-Schwicker, Angelo. Dictionnaire International de Metallurgie, Mineralogie, Geologie et Industries Extractives, 2 vols. 1530p. (Fr.). 1969. Set. $95.00 (ISBN 0-686-56933-4, M-6054). French & Eur.

Ersov, N. N. & Komarov, A. N., eds. Projet de Lexique Minier Russe-Francais. 183p. (Fr. & Rus.). 1972. pap. $22.50 (ISBN 0-686-56769-2, M-6468). French & Eur.

Fueyo Cuesta, Laureano. Diccionario Terminologico De Minas, Canteras y Mineralurgia. 272p. (Span.). 1973. leather $17.95 (ISBN 84-400-6971-5, S-50112). French & Eur.

Gagnacci-Schwicker, A. & Schwicker. International Dictionary of Metallurgy, Mineralogy, Geology & the Mining & Oil Industries. 1530p. (Eng., Fr., Ger. & Ital.). 1970. $88.00 (ISBN 3-7625-0751-1, M-7482, Pub. by Bauverlag). French & Eur.

--International Dictionary of Metallurgey, Mineralogy, Geology & the Mining & Oil Industries. 1530p. (Eng., Fr., Ger. & Ital.). 1970. $88.00 (ISBN 3-7625-0751-1). Bauverlag.

Glossary of Stock Exchange, Mining & Oil Terms. LC 82-126128. 108p. 1981. pap. $6.00 (ISBN 0-9594011-0-5). Fin Analysis.

Hooson, William. The Miners Dictionary. 1979. Repr. of 1747 ed. text ed. 40.25x (ISBN 0-686-32514-1). IMM North Am.

Todd, A. H. Lexicon of Terms Relating to the Assessment & Classification of Coal Resources. 140p. 1982. $99.00x (ISBN 0-86010-403-6, Pub. by Graham & Trotman England). State Mutual Bk.

Verbic, Ing S. English-Serbocroat & Serbocroat-English Geological & Mining Dictionary. 528p. (Eng. & Serbocroatian.). 1981. $90.00x (ISBN 0-686-44714-X, Pub. by Collets). State Mutual Bk.

Verbic, S. Yugoslavian Mining Dictionary: English-Serbo-English. 527p. (Serbocroatian & Eng.). 1981. pap. text ed. $25.00x (ISBN 0-89918-783-8). Vanous.

Wyllie, R. J. & Argall, George O., Jr., eds. World Mining Glossary of Mining, Processing & Geological Terms. LC 74-20169. (A World Mining Book). 432p. 1975. 47.50 (ISBN 0-87930-031-0). Miller Freeman.

MINES AND MINING
see Mineral Industries; Mines and Mineral Resources; Mining Engineering

MINIATURE PAINTING
Foster, Joshua J. A Dictionary of Painters of Miniatures, 1525-1850 with Some Account of Exhibitions, Collections, Sales, Etc. Foster, Ethel M., ed. 1967. Repr. of 1926 ed. $29.50 (ISBN 0-8337-1218-7). B Franklin.

MINIATURES (PORTRAITS)
see Miniature Painting

MINING
see also Mineral Industries; Mines and Mineral Resources; Mining Engineering

MINING ENGINEERING
Bischoff, Walter. Das Kleine Bergbaulexikon. LC 76-487997. 203p. (Ger.). 1976. DM.48.00 (ISBN 3-7739-0185-2). Verlag Glockauf.

--Das Kleine Bergbaulexikon. LC 79-395530. 254p. (Ger.). 1979. write for info. (ISBN 3-7739-0248-4). Verlag Gluckauf.

Dictionnaire Minier Russe-Francais. (Rus. & Fr.). 1973. 45.00 F. France, Centre Et. Charbonnage.

MINING GEOLOGY
Amstutz, G. Glossary of Mining Geology. 196p. (Eng., Span., Fr. & Ger.). 1971. $36.50 (ISBN 3-432-01667-0, M-7428, Pub. by F. Enke). French & Eur.

--Glossary of Mining Geology. 196p. (Span., Fr, & Ger.). 1971. $36.50 (ISBN 3-432-01667-0). Enke.

Amstutz, G. C., et al. Glossary of Mining Geology. Esser, F. & Park, Won C., eds. 196p. (Eng., Span., Fr. & Ger.). 1971. DM.46.00. Enke.

MINOAN WRITING
see Inscriptions–Crete; Inscriptions, Linear B

MINOR TACTICS
see Drill and Minor Tactics

MIRACLES
Brewer, E. Cobham. A Dictionary of Miracles, Imitative, Realistic, & Dogmatic. LC 66-29783. 1966. Repr. of 1885 ed. $42.00 (ISBN 0-8103-3000-8). Gale.

Brewer, Ebenezer. A Dictionary of Miracles. 75.00 (ISBN 0-8490-0040-8). Gordon Pr.

Findeisen, Barbara. A Course in Miracles Concordance. 457p. $15.00 (ISBN 0-942494-45-8). Coleman Graphics.

Wapnick, Ken. Glossary Index for a Course in Miracles. 255p. 1982. $15.00 (ISBN 0-942494-26-1). Coleman Graphics.

MISDEMEANORS (LAW)
see Criminal Law

MISSIONS–BIBLIOGRAPHY
Missionary Research Library. New York Dictionary Catalog of the Missionary Research Library, 17 vols. 1968. Set. $1615.00 (ISBN 0-8161-0778-5, Hall Library). G K Hall.

MIXED LANGUAGES
see Languages, Mixed

MOCHA LANGUAGE
Harrison, Sheldon P. & Albert, Salich. Mokilese-English Dictionary. LC 76-41796. (PALI Language Tests Ser.: Micronesia). 182p. (Orig., Mokilese & Eng.). 1976. pap. text ed $9.50x (ISBN 0-8248-0512-7). UH Pr.

MODEL AIRPLANES
see Airplanes–Models

MODEL CITIES
see City Planning

MODERN ARCHITECTURE
see Architecture, Modern

MODERN ART
see Art, Modern–20th Century; Modernism (Art)

MODERN DANCE
Love, P. Terminologia de la Danza Moderna. (Span.). write for info. EUDEBA.

MODERN LANGUAGES
see Languages, Modern

MODERN MUSIC
see Music–History and Criticism–20th Century

MODERNISM (ART)
see also Art, Modern–20th Century; Expressionism (Art); Impressionism (Art); Surrealism
Aguilera Cerni, Vincente, ed. Diccionario del Arte Moderno: Conceptos, Ideas, Tendencias. LC 80-110365. 569p. (Ital.). 1979. 2800.00 ptas (ISBN 8-473-66108-7). Toreres.

MODERNISM IN ART
see Modernism (Art)

MODES, MUSICAL
see Musical Intervals and Scales

MODOC INDIANS
see Indians of North America–Northwest, Pacific

MODULATION (ELECTRONICS)
see also Carrier Control Systems
Anglo-Russkii Slovar Po Radioelektronike i Sviazi. 548p. (Eng. & Rus.). 1959. $5.75 (Pub. by Soviete Ministrov). Four Continent.

Diccionario tecnico, radio, antenas, video, radar: Espanol-ingles. (Span. & Eng.). Arg.$3.00. Cosmopolita.

Dozorov, N. I. Dopolnenie K Anglo-Russkomu Slovariu Po Radioelektrike & Sviazi. 68p. (Rus. & Eng.). 1960. $0.80 (Pub. by Izd. Glav. upravl. Po Ispol'z. Atomn. Energii). Four Continent.

Semiiazychnyi Slovar Po Elektrosviazi. 708p. (Eng. , Fr. , Rus. , Ger. , Span. , Ital. & Dutch.). 1966. $7.95 (Pub. by Sov. Entsiklopediia). Four Continent.

Verzhikovskii, A. P., et al. Kratkii Slovar Po Radioelektronike. 256p. (Rus.). 1964. $2.50 (Pub. by Voenizdat). Four Continent.

MOGOLLON INDIANS
see Indians of North America–Southwest, New

MOHAMMEDAN
see headings beginning with the word Islamic or Muslim

MOHAMMEDANISM
see Islam

MOHAVE INDIANS
see Indians of North America–Southwest, New

MOHAWK LANGUAGE
University of the State of New York, State Education Department. Iontenwennaweienstahkhwa. LC 77-624515. xi, 93p. (Eng. & Mohawk.). 1977. write for info. State U NY Pr.

MOLD, VEGETABLE
see Soils

MOLIERE, JEAN BAPTISTE POQUELIN, 1622-1673
Desfeuilles, Arthur. Lexique de la Langue de Moliere, 2 vols. (Fr.). 1970. $55.00. Lenox.

--Lexique de la Langue de Moliere avec une, Vol. 1-2. (Fr.). 1900. Set. $64.00 (ISBN 0-8337-4744-4). B Franklin.

Livet, Charles L. Lexique de la Langue de Moliere, 1. 532p. (Fr.). 1970. DM.298.00. Olms.

--Lexique de la Langue de Moliere, 2. 666p. (Fr.). 1970. DM.298.00. Olms.

--Lexique de la Langue de Moliere, 3. 824p. (Fr.). 1970. DM.298.00. Olms.

MOLLUSKS
Arnold, Winifred H. Glossary of a Thousand & One Terms Used in Conchology. 1965. $4.50 (ISBN 0-913792-05-5). Shell Cab.

MONETARY POLICY
see also Credit
Lambert, Denis-Clair. Dictionnaire Francais-Anglais de l'economie Monetaire. 264p. (Fr. & Eng.). 1975. 34.00 F. Ouvrieres.

MONETARY QUESTION
see Money

MONEY
see also Banks and Banking; Coins; Credit; Finance; Finance, Public; Paper Money
also names of coins, e.g. Dollar
Achterberg, E. & Lanz, K. Enzyklopadisches Lexikon Fur des Geld, Bank und Borsen Wesen, 2 vols. (Ger.). 1967. $240.00 set (ISBN 3-7819-0030-4, M-7364, Pub. by Fritz Knapp Verlag). French & Eur.

Ricour, Pierre. Lexique Anglais-Francais De la Banque et De la Monnaie. 87p. (Eng. & Fr.). 1973. pap. $2.95 (ISBN 0-686-57208-4, M-6486). French & Eur.

MONEY–HISTORY
Donati, G. Dizionario dei motti e leggende delle monete italiane. (Ital.). L.2500.00. La Vela.

MONEY SUPPLY
see Money

MONGOLIAN LANGUAGE
Buck, Frederick H. Glossary of Mongolian Technical Terms. LC 58-59834. (American Council of Learned Societies Publications). 79p. (Orig., Mongolian). 1958. pap. $3.00x (ISBN 0-87950-257-6). Spoken Lang Serv.

Krueger, John R. The Kalmyk-Mongolian Vocabulary in Stralenberg's Geography of 1730. LC 76-507500. (Kalmyck.). 1975. Kr.64.75 (ISBN 91-7192-217-2). Almqvist.

--Materials for an Oirat-Mongolian to English Citation Dictionary, Pt. 1. (Eng. & Oirat-Mongolian.). 1978. pap. 10.00 (ISBN 0-910980-42-X). Mongolia.

Lessing, F. D. Mongolian-English Dictionary. LC 60-14517. 1220p. (Mongolian & Eng.). 1982. Repr. of 1960 ed. 55.00x (ISBN 0-910980-40-3). Mongolia.

MONGOLIAN LANGUAGE–DICTIONARIES–RUSSIAN
Russko-Mongol'Skii Razgovornik. 111p. (Rus. & Mongolian.). 1976. $00.60 (Pub. by Russkii Iazyk). Four Continent.

MONOGRAMS
see also Anagrams; Initials
Christ, Jean-Frederic. Dictionnaire des Monogrammes. 484p. (Fr.). 1972. 150.00 F. Minkoff Repr.

MONTAIGNE, MICHEL EYQUEM DE, 1533-1592
Villey-Desmeserets, Pierre L. Lexique de la Langue des Essais de Michel de Montaigne. (Fr.). 1973. $32.50. Lenox.

MOORISH LANGUAGE (INDIA)
see Urdu Language

MORAL THEOLOGY
see Christian Ethics

MOROCCO
Tedjini, Abulgacim. Dictionnaire Francais-Marocain. 394p. (Fr.). 1949. 22.00 F. Maritimes Outre-Mer.

MOROCCO–HISTORY
Spencer, William. Historical Dictionary of Morocco. LC 80-21328. (African Historical Dictionaries Ser.: No. 24). 195p. 1980. $14.00 (ISBN 0-8108-1361-0). Scarecrow.

MORPHOLOGY
Kiefer, Ferenc, ed. Morphologie & Generative Grammatik. LC 76-450339. (Illus.). xix, 289p. (Ger.). 1975. DM.44.00 (ISBN 3-799-70628-3). Akad Verl Ath.

MORTGAGES
Mortgage Bankers Association of America. Mortgage Banking Terms: A Working Glossary. 3rd ed. 115p. $5.00. Mortgage Bankers.

MOSLEM
see headings beginning with the word Islamic or Muslim

MOTHERS
Cloutier, Francois. Dictionnaire des Parents. 250p. (Fr.). 1969. 3.00 F. Edns Du Jour.

MOTION PICTURES
see Moving-Pictures

MOTOR-CARS
see Automobiles

MOTOR CYCLES
see Motorcycles

MOTOR VEHICLE OPERATORS
see Automobile Drivers

MOTOR VEHICLES
see also Automobiles; Motorcycles
Blok, Czeslaw. Ilustrowany Slownik Samochodowy. LC 76-526304. 867p. (Eng., Pol., Rus. & Fr.). 1976. 250.00 Zl. Wydawnictwa.

Saarikoski, Lea. Englantilais-Suomalainen Moottorialan Sanasto. LC 77-473434. 194p. (Eng. & Finnish.). 1976. Fmk.21.70 (ISBN 9-5110-4011-1). Otava.

Schnitzlein, Gerhard. Lexikon Kraftfahrzeugtechnik. LC 77-458501. 263p. (Eng. & Ger.). 1976. M.13.80. VEB Verlag Technik.

MOTORCYCLES
Kosbab, William H. Motorcycle Dictionary. Greenslade-Moore, Dianne & Lamont, Daveta, eds. LC 82-71155. 300p. 1983. lib. bdg. $19.95x (ISBN 0-89262-058-7); pap. text ed. $14.95x (ISBN 0-89262-044-7). Career Pub.

MOTORS
see also Automobiles–Motors; Gas and Oil Engines
also subdivision Motors under subjects, e.g. Automobiles–Motors
General Motor Terminology. 1979. $10.00; members $3.00. Small Motor Mfrs.

MOTTOES
see also Devices
Pine, L. G. A Dictionary of Mottoes. 150p. 1983. 12.95 (ISBN 0-7100-9339-X). Routledge & Kegan.

MOTU LANGUAGE
see also Melanesian Languages
Lawes, William G. Grammar & Vocabulary of Language Spoken by Motu Tribe (New Guinea) 3rd enl. ed. LC 75-35132. 1976. Repr. of 1896 ed. $17.50 (ISBN 0-404-14148-X). AMS Pr.

MOUNTAINS
see also Geology, Structural
Faus, Agustin. Diccionario de la montana. 592p. (Span.). 1963. pap. 340.00 ptas. Juventud.

Gautrat, Jacques. Dictionnaire de la Montagne. 256p. (Fr.). 1970. pap. $8.95 (ISBN 0-686-56820-6, M-6598). French & Eur.

MOVEMENT, ECUMENICAL
see Ecumenical Movement

MOVING-PICTURE DIRECTION
see Moving-Pictures–Production and Direction

MOVING-PICTURE INDUSTRY
see also Moving-Pictures–Production and Direction

Delson, Donn. The Dictionary of Marketing & Related Terms in the Motion Picture Industry. LC 79-67865. (Entertainment Communication Ser.: Vol. 1). 70p. (Orig.). 1979. pap. text ed. $7.95 (ISBN 0-9603574-0-8). Bradson.

MOVING-PICTURE PRODUCERS AND DIRECTORS

Sadoul, Georges. Dictionnaire des Cineastes. 256p. (Fr.). 1974. pap. $9.95 (ISBN 0-686-56798-6, F-79852). French & Eur.

MOVING-PICTURE PRODUCTION

see Moving-Pictures–Production and Direction

MOVING-PICTURES

Here are entered general works on moving-pictures. Works on organization and management in the motion picture field are entered under Moving-Picture Industry. Works on photographic processes are entered under Cinematography.

see also Cinematography; Horror Films; Western Films

Cluny, Claude-Michel. Dictionnaire des Nouveaux Cinemas Arabes. (Illus., Fr. & Arabic.). 1978. 120.00 F. Sindbad.

MOVING-PICTURES–COSTUME

see Costume

MOVING-PICTURES–DICTIONARIES

Arnau, Frank. Universal Film Lexicon. 69.95 (ISBN 0-8490-1246-5). Gordon Pr.

Clason, W. E. Elsevier's Dictionary of Cinema, Sound & Music. (Eng., Fr., Span., Ital., Dutch, & Ger., Polyglot). 1956. $117.00 (ISBN 0-444-40117-2). Elsevier.

Delson, Donn. The Dictionary of Marketing & Related Terms in the Motion Picture Industry. LC 79-67865. (Entertainment Communication Ser.: Vol. 1). 70p. (Orig.). 1979. pap. text ed. $7.95 (ISBN 0-9603574-0-8). Bradson.

Diccionario de fotografia y cine. (Serie Tecnios Especialistas Koel 51). 358p. (Span.). 75.00 ptas. Tesoro.

Fuzellier, Etienne. Dictionnaire des Oeuvres & des Themes du Cinema Mondial. LC 77-454527. 288p. (Fr.). 1976. 21.00 F (ISBN 2-01-003332-9). Hachette-Jeunesse.

Graham, Peter. El Diccionario del cine. (Span.). $1.60; Mex.$20.00. Novaro.

Grau, Wolfgang. Woerterbuch der Photo, Film und Kinotechnik. (Ger., Eng. & Fr., Dictionary of Photo, Film & Cinematechniques). 1958. pap. $28.00 (ISBN 3-8101-0021-8, M-6968). French & Eur.

Houle, Michel & Julien, Alain. Dictionnaire du Cinema Quebecois. LC 79-361413. xxx, 366p. (Eng. & Fr.). 1978. write for info. (ISBN 0-7755-0699-0). Fides.

Jeanne, Pierre-Charles. Dictionnaire du Cinema Universal, 6. 720p. (Fr.). 1970. write for info. Laffont.

Krusche, Dieter & Labenskt, Jurgen. Reclams Filmfuhrer. LC 77-578502. 760p. (Ger.). 1977. DM.36.80 (ISBN 3-15-010205-7). Reclam.

Kurowski, Ulrich. Lexikon des Internationalen Films. LC 79-383266. (Ger.). 1975. DM.12.80 (ISBN 3-446-11945-0). Hanser.

Lexique Photo-Cinema. 104p. (Fr.). 1972. 31.20 F. C. I. L. F.

Mitry, Jean. Diccionario del cine. (Span.). 100.00 ptas. Plaza Janes.

Oakey, Virginia. Dictionary of Film & Television Terms. 206p. (Orig.). 1982. pap. $6.68i (ISBN 0-06-463566-X, EH 566). B&N NY.

Porro, Maurizio & Turroni, Giuseppe. Il Cinema Vuol Dire. LC 79-372048. 219p. (Ital.). 1979. L.2500.00. Garzanti Edit.

Romero Gualda, Maria V. Vocabulario De Cine y Television En Espana. 400p. (Span.). 1976. pap. $23.95 (ISBN 84-313-0234-8, S-50002). French & Eur.

Sadoul, George. Dicccionario del Cine, 2 vols. 800p. (Span.). 1977. Set. pap. $29.95 (ISBN 84-7090-082-X, S-50057). French & Eur.

Sadoul, Georges. Dictionnaire des Films. 288p. (Fr.). 1969. pap. $8.95 (ISBN 0-686-56797-8, F-79854). French & Eur.

--Dictionnaire des Films. (Illus.). 288p. (Fr.). 1969. 20.00 F. Seuil.

MOVING-PICTURES–DIRECTION

see Moving-Pictures–Production and Direction

MOVING-PICTURES–PRODUCTION AND DIRECTION

see also Moving-Picture Producers and Directors

Gibbs, C. R. Dictionnaire Technique du Cinema: Anglais-Francais. 228p. (Eng. & Fr.). 1959. 18.90 F. Film Et Technique.

MOVING-PICTURES–CANADA

Dictionnaire du Cinema Quebecois. (Fr.). 1979. $32.50 (ISBN 0-686-57105-3, M-6132). French & Eur.

MOVING-PICTURES–EUROPE

Diccionario Del Cine Espanol, 1896-1968. 359p. (Span.). 1970. pap. $15.75 (ISBN 84-276-0249-9, S-50008). French & Eur.

MOVING-PICTURES, AMATEUR

see Amateur Moving-Pictures

MOZAMBIQUE

Cabral, Antonio C. Emprestimos Linguisticos nas Linguas Mocambicanas. LC 76-464647. 78p. (Mozambique.). 1975. write for info. Lourenco Marques.

MUHAMMADANISM

see Islam

MULES

Donkey & Mule Terms & Their Definitons. 1p. $0.15. Am Donkey.

MUNICIPAL ADMINISTRATION

see Municipal Government

MUNICIPAL ENGINEERING

see also City Planning; Drainage; Housing; Refuse and Refuse Disposal; Sanitary Engineering; Sewerage; Streets; Water-Supply

Tekniska Nomenklaturcentralen. Komunalteknisk Ordlista. LC 77-454090. 214p. (Eng. Danish, Finnish & Norwegian.). 1976. Kr.50.00 (ISBN 9-1719-6061-9). Tek Nomen.

MUNICIPAL GOVERNMENT

see also Local Government; Mayors; Public Administration

also subdivision Politics and Government under names of cities, e.g. San Francisco–Politics and Government

Dictionnaires des Communes. 36th ed. 1100p. (Fr.). 1976. write for info. Berger Levrault.

MUNICIPAL SERVICES WITHIN CORPORATE LIMITS

see Municipal Government

MUNICIPAL TRANSIT

see Local Transit

MUNICIPAL TRANSPORTATION

see Urban Transportation

MUNICIPALITIES

see Cities and Towns; Municipal Government

MUSEUMS

Benes, Josef & Puba, Vaclay. Muzeologicky slovnik. LC 79-367213. 169p. (Czech.). 1978. write for info. SNTC.

Migne, J. P., ed. Dictionnaire des Muses ou Description des Principaux Musees d'Europe... Suivi Notions sur la Photographie par X. (Troisieme et Derniere Encyclopedie Theologique Ser.: Vol. 4). 740p. (Fr.). Repr. of 1855 ed. lib. bdg. $95.00x (ISBN 0-89241-291-7). Caratzas Pub Co.

MUSHROOMS

see also Fungi

Bels-Koning, H. C. & Van Kuijk, W. M. Mushroom Terms. LC 81-466342. xxii, 312p. 1980. write for info. (ISBN 9-02-200673-5). Centre for Agricultural Pub. & Documentation.

Dickinson, Colin & Lucas, John. Van Nostrand Reinhold Color Dictionary of Mushrooms. 160p. 1982. pap. $12.95 (ISBN 0-442-21998-9). Van Nos Reinhold.

MUSHROOMS, EDIBLE

Mushroom Terms: Polyglot on Research & Cultivation of Edible Fungi. 312p. 1981. pap. $83.00 (ISBN 90-220-0673-5, PDC 211, Pudoc). Unipub.

MUSIC

see also Electronic Music; Instrumental Music; Instrumentation and Orchestration; Sound; Vocal Music

also subdivision Songs and Music under specific subjects, classes of persons, names of individuals, institutions, societies, etc; also other headings beginning with the words Music and Musical

Allorto, Lily, et al. Nuovo dizionario Ricordi della musica e dei musicisti. (Illus.). 730p. (Ital.). 1976. L.15000.00. Ricordi.

Kwiatkowski, Gerhard. Die Musik: Ein Sachlexikon. (Illus.). 464p. (Ger.). DM.19.80 (ISBN 3-411-01748-1). Biblio Inst.

Der Musik-Brockhaus. 686p. (Ger.). DM.68.00 (ISBN 3-7653-0338-0). F A Brockhaus.

MUSIC–ANALYTICAL GUIDES

Muller-Reuter, Theodor. Lexikon der Deutschen Konzertliteratur, 2 Vols. LC 70-171079. (Music Ser). (Ger.). 1972. Repr. of 1921 ed. Set. lib. bdg. $95.00 (ISBN 0-306-70274-6). Da Capo.

MUSIC–BIBLIOGRAPHY

see also Music–Discography; Music Libraries

Boston Public Library. Dictionary Catalog of the Music Collection, Boston Public Library, 20 vols. 15617p. 1972. Set. lib. bdg. $1900.00 (ISBN 0-8161-0956-7, Hall Library); lib. bdg. $420.00 1st suppl., 4 vols. 1977 (ISBN 0-8161-1014-X). G K Hall.

--Dictionary Catalog of the Music Collection, Boston Public Library, 20 vols. 15617p. 1972. Set. lib. bdg. $1900.00 (ISBN 0-8161-0956-7, Hall Library); lib. bdg. $420.00 1st suppl., 4 vols. 1977 (ISBN 0-8161-1014-X). G K Hall.

Research Libraries of the New York Public Library. Second Edition of the Dictionary Catalog of the Music Collection. 1983. lib. bdg. $6000.00 (ISBN 0-8161-0374-7, Hall Library). G K Hall.

MUSIC–BIO-BIBLIOGRAPHY

Young, Percy M. A Critical Dictionary of Composers & Their Music. LC 78-66927. (Encore Music Editions Ser.). 1981. Repr. of 1954 ed. 27.50 (ISBN 0-88355-771-1). Hyperion Conn.

MUSIC–BIOGRAPHY

see Composers; Music–Bio-Bibliography; Musicians; Pianists; Singers

MUSIC–CATALOGING

see Cataloging of Music

MUSIC–DICTIONARIES

see also Music–Terminology

Ammer, Christine. Harper's Dictionary of Music. LC 77-134280. (Illus.). 1972. 20.14i (ISBN 0-06-010113-X, HarpT). Har-Row.

--Harper's Dictionary of Music. LC 77-134280. (Illus.). 1972. 20.14i (ISBN 0-06-010113-X, HarpT). Har-Row.

--Harper's Dictionary of Music. (Illus.). 414p. 1973. pap. $5.50 (ISBN 0-06-463347-0, EH 347). B&N NY.

Apel & Daniel. Harvard Brief Dictionary of Music. pap. 3.95 (ISBN 0-671-43475-6). PB.

Apel, Willi. Harvard Dictionary of Music. rev., enl. ed. LC 68-21970. (Illus.). 1969. 25.00 (ISBN 0-674-37501-7, Belknap Pr). Harvard U Pr.

Apel, Willi & Daniel, Ralph T., eds. The Harvard Brief Dictionary of Music. 348p. 1968. pap. $3.95 (ISBN 0-671-43475-6). WSP.

Baker, Th. Dictionary of Musical Terms: Containing an English-Italian Vocabulary for Composers & Students. (Eng. & Ital.). 24.50 (ISBN 0-87557-053-4, 053-4). Saphrograph.

Baker, Theodore. Dictionary of Musical Terms. LC 75-124595. (BCL Ser.: No. 1). 1970. Repr. of 1923 ed. $8.00 (ISBN 0-404-00468-7). AMS Pr.

Blom, Eric. Diccionario de la musica. 1040p. (Span.). Arg.$pap. 15.00. Claridad.

--Everyman's Dictionary of Music. 816p. (RL 10). 1973. pap. 5.95 (ISBN 0-452-25193-1, 25193, Plume). NAL.

Bonaccorsi, Alfredo. Nuovo dizionario musicale Curci. 556p. (Ital.). 1952. L.5000.00. Curci.

Bozzano, Lily A., et al, eds. Nuovo Dizionario Ricordi Della Musica & dei Musicisti. LC 76-46292. (Illus.). 730p. (Ital.). 1976. write for info. G Ricordi.

Brauner, Rudolf. Von Bach zur Elektronik. LC 78-347055. 96p. (Ger.). 1977. S.60.00 (ISBN 3-853-85001-4). Prugg.

Brenet, Michel. Diccionario de la musica. Rev. ed. (Span.). 1000.00 ptas. Iberia SA.

--Diccionario De la Musica: Historico y Tecnico. 3rd ed. 566p. (Span.). 1976. $50.00 (ISBN 84-7082-139-3, S-16685). French & Eur.

Brossard. Dictionary of Music. Gruber, Albion, ed. (Musical Theorists in Translation Ser.: No. 12). 280p. lib. bdg. $55.00 (ISBN 0-931902-15-0). Inst Mediaeval Mus.

Buck, Dudley. Musical Pronouncing Dictionary. Repr. lib. bdg. $19.00 (ISBN 0-403-03787-5). Scholarly.

--Pronouncing Musical Dictionary. 1976. lib. bdg. $19.00 (ISBN 0-403-03787-5). Scholarly.

Carter, Henry H. Dictionary of Middle English Musical Terms. Gerhard, George B., et al, eds. LC 61-63413. (Indiana University Humanities Ser: No. 45). 1961. 39.00 (ISBN 0-527-15150-5). Kraus Repr.

Clarke, Hugh A. Pronouncing Dictionary of Musical Terms, Giving the Meaning Derivation & Pronunciation of Italian, German, French & Other Words. 1977. Repr. $15.00 (ISBN 0-403-07492-4). Scholarly.

Clason, W. E. Elsevier's Dictionary of Cinema, Sound & Music. (Eng., Fr., Span., Ital., Dutch, & Ger., Polyglot). 1956. $117.00 (ISBN 0-444-40117-2). Elsevier.

Corte, Della & Gatti, trs. Diccionario de la musica. 2nd, rev. ed. (Span.). Arg.$26.00. Ricordi.

Dahlhaus, Carl & Eggebrecht, Hans H. Brockhaus Riemann Musiklexikon, Vol. 1, A-K. (Ger.). 1978. write for info. (ISBN 3-7653-0303-8). Eur-Am Music.

--Brockhaus-Riemann-Musiklexikon in Zwei Baenden: Band 1, A-K. 699p. (Ger.). DM.148.00 (ISBN 3-7653-0303-8). F A Brockhaus.

--Brockhaus-Riemann-Musiklexikon in Zwei Baenden: Band 2, L-Z. 732p. (Ger.). DM.148.00. F A Brockhaus.

Darvas, Gabor. Zenei Zseblexikon. LC 79-380372. 341p. (Hungarian.). 1978. 26.00 Ft (ISBN 9-633-30265-X). Zenemukiado.

De Cande, Roland. Diccionare de la musica. (Span.). 375.00 ptas. EDNS Sesenti Dos.

--Dizionario dei musicisti. 486p. (Ital.). 1978. L.3000.00. Bompiani.

--Dizionario della musica. 288p. (Ital.). 1978. L.2500.00. Bompiani.

Diccionario De Celebridades Musicales. 600p. (Span.). $19.95 (ISBN 0-686-57361-7, S-50141). French & Eur.

Eaglefield-Hull, A., ed. Dictionary of Modern Music & Musicians. LC 78-139192. (Music Ser). 1971. Repr. of 1924 ed. lib. bdg. $55.00 (ISBN 0-306-70086-7). Da Capo.

Elson, Louis C. Elson's Music Dictionary. LC 70-173097. xii, 306p. 1972. Repr. of 1905 ed. $37.00x (ISBN 0-8103-3268-X). Gale.

Engstroem, Ake & Toernblom, H. Bonniers Musiklexikon. LC 75-407960. 446p. (Swedish.). 1975. Kr.215.00. Bonnier Forlag.

Gatti, Guido. Dizionario di musica, 2 vols. (Illus.). xxiv, 2752p. (Ital.). 1971. L.70000.00 (ISBN 88-02-03178-9). UTET.

Grigg, Carolyn D., compiled by. Music Translation Dictionary: An English, Czech, Danish, Dutch, French, German, Hungarian, Italian, Polish, Portuguese, Russian, Spanish, Swedish Vocabulary of Music. LC 78-60526. (Eng., Czech., Danish, Dutch, Fr., Ger., Hungarian, Ital., Pol., Port., Rus., Span. & Swedish.). 1978. lib. bdg. 35.00 (ISBN 0-313-20559-0, GMT/). Greenwood.

Gurlitt, W. & Eggebrecht, H. Riemann Musiklexikon. 108p. (Ger.). 1967. $135.00 (ISBN 3-7957-0031-0, M-7602, Pub. by Schatt's Soehne). French & Eur.
Honegger, M. Dictionnaire de la Musique: Science de la Musique, 2 vols. 1216p. (Fr.). 1976. Set. $125.00 (ISBN 2-04-005140-6, M-6318). French & Eur.
Honegger, Marc. Dictionnaire de la Musique. (Illus.). 1232p. (Fr.). 1970. 165.00 F. Bordas-Dunod.
Honegger, Marc, ed. Dictionnaire de la Musique, Vol. 1. 1232p. (Fr.). 1970. $65.00 (ISBN 0-686-56821-4, M-6599). French & Eur.
Hoyle, John. Dictionarium Musica, Being a Complete Dictionary, or, Treasury of Music. (Monuments of Music & Music Literature in Facsimile: Series II, Vol. 83). 1977. Repr. of 1770 ed. $27.50x (ISBN 0-8450-2283-0). Broude.
Hull, Arthur E., ed. Dictionary of Modern Music & Musicians. LC 72-1619. Repr. of 1924 ed. $27.50 (ISBN 0-404-08315-3). AMS Pr.
--A Dictionary of Modern Music & Musicians. LC 77-166238. 543p. 1924. Repr. $35.00 (ISBN 0-403-01365-8). Scholarly.
Isaacs, Alan, ed. Dictionary of Music. 432p. (Eng.). E6.95 (ISBN 0-600-33211-X). Newnes Bks.
Isaacs, Alan & Martin, Elizabeth, eds. Dictionary of Music. (Illus.). 428p. 1983. $17.95 (ISBN 0-87196-752-9). Facts on File.
Jacobs, Arthur. Diccionario de Musica. 392p. (Span.). 1966. $15.95 (ISBN 0-686-56715-3, S-33050). French & Eur.
--New Dictionary of Music. (Reference Ser.). (Orig.). (YA) (gr. 9 up). 1958. pap. 4.95 (ISBN 0-14-051012-5). Penguin.
Jacobs, Arthur, tr. Diccionario de musica. 392p. (Span.). 1966. Arg.$1.80. Leru.
Kennedy, Michael, ed. The Concise Oxford Dictionary of Music. 3rd ed. (Illus.). 1980. 22.50 (ISBN 0-19-311315-5); pap. 9.95 (ISBN 0-19-311320-1). Oxford U Pr.
Leuchtmann, Horst. Dictionary of Terms in Music. 3rd ed. xvi, 500p. 1981. $38.00 (ISBN 3-598-10338-7, Pub. by K G Saur). Shoe String.
--Woerterbuch Musik. (Ger. & Eng., Dictionary of Terms in Music). 1977. $38.00 (ISBN 3-7940-3186-5, M-6911). French & Eur.
Lindlar, H. Rororo Musikhandbuch, 2 vols. (Ger.). 1976. pap. $12.95 (ISBN 3-499-16167-2, M-7605, Pub. by Rowohlt). French & Eur.
--Rororo Musikhandbuch, 2 vols. (Ger.). 1976. pap. $12.95 (ISBN 3-499-16167-2). Rowohlt.
Mariconda, Barbara & Puccio, Denise. Muppet Music Dictionary. (Illus.). 210p. (gr. 3-7). 1983. $14.95 (ISBN 0-89524-153-6, 8603); pap. $9.95 (ISBN 0-89524-164-1, 8608). Cherry Lane.
Mathews, William S. & Liebling, Emil. Pronouncing & Defining Dictionary of Music. LC 78-173059. Repr. of 1896 ed. $20.50 (ISBN 0-404-07210-0). AMS Pr.
Michelsen, Kari, et al, eds. Cappelens Musikkeleksikon. LC 78-386996. (Illus., Norwegian.). 1978. Kr.330.00 (ISBN 8-202-03690-9). J W Cappelens.
Moore, John W. A Dictionary of Musical Information. LC 72-1714. Repr. of 1876 ed. $15.00 (ISBN 0-404-09915-7). AMS Pr.
--Dictionary of Musical Information. LC 76-143644. (Bibliography & Reference Ser.: No. 418). 1971. Repr. of 1876 ed. lib. bdg. $21.50 (ISBN 0-8337-2449-5). B Franklin.
Moritz, R. E., ed. Knaurs Musiklexikon. 768p. (Ger.). 1982. $27.00. M Rosenberg.
Nicol, Karl Ludwig, ed. Herder-Lexikon Musik: Sachwoerterbuch. LC 79-338562. (Illus.). 222p. (Ger.). 1977. DM.19.80 (ISBN 3-451-17372-7). Herder.
Poblete, Carlos. Diccionario de la Musica. 2nd ed. 379p. (Span.). 1979. write for info. U. de Valparaiso.
Poblete Varas, Carlos. Diccionario de la musica. 320p. (Span.). 1972. write for info. Universitarias Valparaiso.
Polyglot Dictionary of Musical Terms. 798p. 1978. $135.00 (ISBN 0-686-92096-1, M-9436). French & Eur.
Potlog, Alexe. S. Dictionar Practic de Agronomie. LC 79-381952. 308p. (Romanian.). 1979. 24.50 lei. Editura Stiintifica.
Pulver, Jeffrey. A Dictionary of Old English Music & Musical Instruments. 75.00 (ISBN 0-8490-0042-4). Gordon Pr.
Queval, Jean. Lexique de la Musique. 130p. (Fr.). 1968. $5.95 (ISBN 0-686-57289-0, F-11890). French & Eur.
--Lexique de la Musique. 130p. (Fr.). 1968. 12.00 F. Delpire.
Randel, Don M. Harvard Concise Dictionary of Music. LC 78-5948. (Illus.). 1978. 15.00 (ISBN 0-674-37471-1, Belknap Pr); pap. 6.95 (ISBN 0-674-37470-3, Belknap Pr). Harvard U Pr.
Research Libraries of the New York Public Library. Dictionary Catalog of the Music Collection, Supplement 1974. 1976. lib. bdg. $80.00 (ISBN 0-8161-0059-4, Hall Library). G K Hall.
Ricart Matas, Jose. Diccionario de la Musica, Historico & Tecnico. 4th ed. 566p. (Span.). 1981. 3000.00 ptas (ISBN 84-7082-139-3). Iberia SA.
Ricart Matas, Juan. Diccionario Biografico de la Musica. 2nd ed. 1144p. (Span.). 1966. $60.00 (ISBN 84-7082-140-7, S-12347). French & Eur.
Riemann, Hugo. Dictionary of Music. LC 75-125060. (Music Ser). 1970. Repr. of 1908 ed. lib. bdg. $65.00 (ISBN 0-306-70025-5). Da Capo.
--Dictionary of Music. LC 74-166256. 925p. 1893. Repr. $79.00 (ISBN 0-403-01383-6). Scholarly.
Roche, Jerome & Roche, Elizabeth. A Dictionary of Early Music. (Illus.). 1981. 17.95x (ISBN 0-19-520255-4). Oxford U Pr.
Rousseau, Jean J. A Complete Dictionary of Music. LC 72-1664. Repr. of 1779 ed. $30.00 (ISBN 0-404-08335-8). AMS Pr.
--Dictionnaire De Musique. (Fr). Repr. of 1768 ed. 50.00 (ISBN 0-384-52200-9). Johnson Repr.
Rousseau, Jean Jacques. Dictionnaire de Musique. 548p. (Fr.). 1978. 24.50 F. Johnson.
Rousseau, Jean-Jacques. Dictionnaire de Musique. 548p. (Fr.). 1978. 108.00 F. Olms.
Sadie, Stanley, ed. The New Grove Dictionary of Music & Musicians, 20 vols. 1980. Set. 1900.00x (ISBN 0-333-23111-2). Groves Dict Music.
Sava, Iosif & Vartolomei, Luminita. Dictionar de Muzica. LC 79-388120. 225p. (Romanian.). 1979. 18.50 lei. Editura Stiintifica.
Scholes, P. A. Diccionario Oxford de la musica. 2nd ed. (Span.). write for info. Sudamer.
Slagmolen, Gerrit. Muzieklexicon, 2 vols. LC 74-336503. (Dutch.). 1974. fl.15.00 (ISBN 9-022-91367-8). Bruna.
Stainer, J. & Barrett, W. A. A Dictionary of Musical Terms. 35.00 (ISBN 0-8490-0041-6). Gordon Pr.
Stainer, John & Barrett, W. A. Dictionary of Musical Terms. LC 71-166266. 464p. 1898. Repr. $69.00 (ISBN 0-403-01690-8). Scholarly.
Vacchi, G. Dizionario di musica. (Illus.). 278p. (Ital.). L.3600.00. Zanichelli.
Valla Gorina, Manuel. Diccionario de la Musica. 3rd ed. 256p. (Span.). 1981. 300.00 ptas (ISBN 84-206-1334-7). Alianza.
Valls Gorina, Manual. Diccionario de la Musica. 256p. (Span.). 1982. 300.00 ptas (ISBN 8-42061-334-7). Alianza Ed.
Valls Gorina, Manuel. Diccionario de la musica. 244p. (Span.). 1971. 60.00 ptas. Alianza Ed.
Walther, Johann. Musikalisches Lexikon. 3rd ed. (Ger.). 1967. pap. $48.00 (ISBN 3-7618-0229-3, M-7565, Pub. by Baerenreiter). French & Eur.
Willemze, Theo. Spectrum Muzieklexicon, 4 vols. LC 76-500562. (Illus., Dutch.). 1975. fl.40.00 (ISBN 9-027-48298-5). Spectrum NL.
Woerterbuch Musik. xvi, 493p. (Ger. & Eng.). 1977. DM.48.00 (ISBN 3-7940-3186-5). Saur Verlag.
Young, Percy M. A Critical Dictionary of Composers & Their Music. LC 78-66927. (Encore Music Editions Ser.). 1981. Repr. of 1954 ed. 27.50 (ISBN 0-88355-771-1). Hyperion Conn.

MUSIC–DISCOGRAPHY
see also Phonorecord Libraries
New York Public Library, Research Libraries. Dictionary Catalog of the Music Collection, Supplement II, 10 vols. 1973. Set. lib. bdg. $1300.00 (ISBN 0-8161-0760-2, Hall Library). G K Hall.

MUSIC–HISTORY AND CRITICISM
Pulver, Jeffrey. A Dictionary of Old English Music & Musical Instruments. 75.00 (ISBN 0-8490-0042-4). Gordon Pr.
Ricart Matas, Jose. Diccionario de la Musica, Historico & Tecnico. 4th ed. 566p. (Span.). 1981. 3000.00 ptas (ISBN 84-7082-139-3). Iberia SA.

MUSIC–HISTORY AND CRITICISM–METHODS
see Musical Criticism

MUSIC–HISTORY AND CRITICISM–THEORY, ETC.
see Musical Criticism

MUSIC–HISTORY AND CRITICISM–TO 400
Coeuroy, Andre. Dictionnaire Critique de la Musique Ancienne & Moderne. 416p. (Fr.). 1956. write for info. Payot.

MUSIC–HISTORY AND CRITICISM–20TH CENTURY
Coeuroy, Andre. Dictionnaire Critique de la Musique Ancienne & Moderne. 416p. (Fr.). 1956. write for info. Payot.

MUSIC–MANUALS, TEXT-BOOKS, ETC.
De Vito, Albert. Pocket Dictionary of Music Terms. LC 65-8450. 1965. 1.50 (ISBN 0-934286-09-4). Kenyon.

MUSIC–MODES
see Musical Intervals and Scales

MUSIC–NOTATION
see Musical Notation

MUSIC–TERMINOLOGY
Ammer, Christine. Musician's Handbook of Foreign Terms. 1971. pap. $7.95 (ISBN 0-02-870100-3). Assoc-Mus.
Baker, Theodore. Dictionary of Musical Terms. 1923. $10.95 (ISBN 0-02-870200-X). Assoc-Mus.
--Schirmer Pronouncing Pocket Manual of Musical Terms. 4th ed. LC 77-5236. 1978. pap. $3.95 (ISBN 0-02-870250-6). Assoc-Mus.
Berkman, Al. Singers Glossary of Show Business Jargon. 1961. 3.00 (ISBN 0-934972-06-0). Melrose Pub Co.
Buck, Dudley. Musical Pronouncing Dictionary. Repr. lib. bdg. $19.00 (ISBN 0-403-03787-5). Scholarly.
Camilleri, Charles. Camilleri's Dictionary of Musical Terms. (Eng.). 1980. Can.$pap. 4.95 (ISBN 0-88909-039-4). Waterloo.
Fracass, E. A. Terminologia Musical: Texto del Conservatorio "Fracassi". (Span.). write for info. Ricordi.
Grant, W. Parks. Handbook of Music Terms. LC 67-10187. 1967. $27.50 (ISBN 0-8108-0054-3). Scarecrow.
Grigg, Carolyn D., compiled by. Music Translation Dictionary: An English, Czech, Danish, Dutch, French, German, Hungarian, Italian, Polish, Portuguese, Russian, Spanish, Swedish Vocabulary of Music. LC 78-60526. (Eng., Czech., Danish, Dutch, Fr., Ger., Hungarian, Ital., Pol., Port., Rus., Span. & Swedish.). 1978. lib. bdg. 35.00 (ISBN 0-313-20559-0, GMT/). Greenwood.
Leach, R. Musical Thesaurus: A Dictionary of Musical Language. LC 78-51565. 1978. $10.00 (ISBN 0-912728-21-3). Newbury Bks.
Leach, Robert. Musical Thesaurus: A Dictionary of Musical Language. LC 77-370602. 47p. (Eng., Fr., Ger. & Ital.). 1976. E1.00. J Hannon.
Leuchtmann, H., ed. Dictionary of Musical Terms in Seven Languages. 2nd ed. (Illus., Eng., Ger., Fr., Ital., Span., Rus. & Hungarian.). 1980. $120.00 (ISBN 0-686-77981-9). Heinman.
Leuchtmann, Horst. Woerterbuch Musik. (Ger. & Eng., Dictionary of Terms in Music). 1977. $38.00 (ISBN 3-7940-3186-5, M-6911). French & Eur.
Levarie, Siegmund & Levy, Ernst. A Dictionary of Musical Morphology. (Wissenschaftliche Abhandlungen-Musicological Studies: Vol. 29). viii, 400p. 1980. lib. bdg. $132.00 (ISBN 0-912024-32-1). Inst Mediaeval Mus.
--Musical Morphology: A Discourse & a Dictionary. LC 82-21274. (Illus.). 376p. 1983. $29.50X (ISBN 0-87338-286-2). Kent St U Pr.
Padelford, Frederick M. Old English Musical Terms. LC 76-22346. 1976. Repr. of 1899 ed. lib. bdg. $15.00 (ISBN 0-89341-012-8). Longwood Pr.
Picerno, Vincent J. Dictionary of Musical Terms. LC 76-14903. (Studies in Music: N0. 42). 1976. lib. bdg. 49.95x (ISBN 0-8383-2119-4). Haskell.
Reid, Cornelius L. A Dictionary of Vocal Terminology: An Analysis. LC 81-86074. xxi, 457p. 1983. 39.95 (ISBN 0-915282-07-0). J Patelson Music.
Stainer, John & Barrett, W. A. Dictionary of Musical Terms. LC 71-166266. 464p. 1898. Repr. $69.00 (ISBN 0-403-01690-8). Scholarly.
Tinctoris, Johannes. Dictionary of Musical Terms. Parrish, Carl, tr. (Music Reprint Ser.). 1978. Repr. of 1963 ed. lib. bdg. $17.50 (ISBN 0-306-77560-3). Da Capo.
Wotton, Tom S. A Dictionary of Foreign Musical Terms & Handbook of Orchestral Instruments. LC 79-166268. 226p. 1907. Repr. $29.00 (ISBN 0-403-01389-5). Scholarly.

MUSIC, ANCIENT
see Music–History and Criticism–To 400

MUSIC, ARABIC
Al Faruqi, Lois I., ed. An Annotated Glossary of Arabic Musical Terms. LC 81-4129. 536p. (Arabic & Eng.). 1981. lib. bdg. 45.00x (ISBN 0-313-20554-X, AFM/). Greenwood.

MUSIC, BRITISH–HISTORY AND CRITICISM
Padelford, Frederick M. Old English Musical Terms. LC 76-22346. 1976. Repr. of 1899 ed. lib. bdg. $15.00 (ISBN 0-89341-012-8). Longwood Pr.

MUSIC, ELECTRONIC
see Electronic Music

MUSIC, FRENCH
Meude-Monpas, Jean J. de. Dictionnaire de Musique dans Lequel on Simplifie les Expressions et Les Definitions Mathematiques et Physiques qui ont Rapport a cet Art. LC 76-43927. (Music & Theatre in France in the 17th & 18th Centuries). (Fr.). Repr. of 1787 ed. $22.50 (ISBN 0-404-60175-8). AMS Pr.

MUSIC, GERMAN
Muller-Reuter, Theodor. Lexikon der Deutschen Konzertliteratur, 2 Vols. LC 70-171079. (Music Ser). (Ger.). 1972. Repr. of 1921 ed. Set. lib. bdg. $95.00 (ISBN 0-306-70274-6). Da Capo.

MUSIC, INSTRUMENTAL
see Instrumental Music

MUSIC, POPULAR (SONGS, ETC.)
see also Rock Music
Gammond, Peter & Clayton, Peter. Dictionary of Popular Music. LC 73-166229. 274p. 1961. Repr. $29.00 (ISBN 0-403-01563-4). Scholarly.

MUSIC, POPULAR (SONGS, ETC.)–WRITING AND PUBLISHING
Cahn, Sammy. The Songwriter's Rhyming Dictionary. (Illus.). 224p. 1983. $17.95 (ISBN 0-87196-765-0). Facts on File.

Whitfield, Jane. Songwriters Rhyming Dictionary. 1974. pap. $5.00 (ISBN 0-87980-293-6). Wilshire.

MUSIC, VOCAL
see Vocal Music

MUSIC LIBRARIES
New York Public Library, Research Libraries. Dictionary Catalog of the Music Collection, 33 Vols. 1964. Set. lib. bdg. $3135.00 (ISBN 0-8161-0709-2, Hall Library). G K Hall.

MUSIC PUBLISHERS
see Publishers and Publishing

MUSICAL CRITICISM
Slonimsky, Nicolas. Lexicon of Musical Invective: Critical Assaults on Composers Since Beethoven's Time. 2nd ed. LC 65-26270. 331p. 1969. pap. $7.95 (ISBN 0-295-78579-9, WP52). U of Wash Pr.

MUSICAL INSTRUMENTS
see also Instrumentation and Orchestration
also groups of instruments, e.g. Stringed Instruments; also names of individual musical instruments, e.g. Piano, Violin
Read, Gardner. Thesaurus of Orchestral Devices. Repr. of 1953 ed. lib. bdg. $45.00x (ISBN 0-8371-1884-0, REOD). Greenwood.

MUSICAL INTERVALS AND SCALES
Slonimsky, Nicholas. Thesaurus of Scales & Melodic Patterns. 1947. $27.50 (ISBN 0-684-10551-9, ScribT). Scribner.

MUSICAL MODES
see Musical Intervals and Scales

MUSICAL NOTATION
Risatti, Howard. New Music Vocabulary: A Guide to Notational Signs for Contemporary Music. LC 73-81565. (Illus.). 144p. 1975. pap. $7.45 (ISBN 0-252-00406-X). U of Ill Pr.

MUSICIANS
see also Composers; Music–Bio-Bibliography; Pianists; Singers
Cande, Roland de. Dictionnaire Des Musiciens. 288p. (Fr.). 1974. pap. $8.95 (ISBN 0-686-56882-6, F-17742). French & Eur.

Eaglefield-Hull, A., ed. Dictionary of Modern Music & Musicians. LC 78-139192. (Music Ser). 1971. Repr. of 1924 ed. lib. bdg. $55.00 (ISBN 0-306-70086-7). Da Capo.

Hull, Arthur E., ed. Dictionary of Modern Music & Musicians. LC 72-1619. Repr. of 1924 ed. $27.50 (ISBN 0-404-08315-3). AMS Pr.

––A Dictionary of Modern Music & Musicians. LC 77-166238. 543p. 1924. Repr. $35.00 (ISBN 0-403-01365-8). Scholarly.

Sadie, Stanley, ed. The New Grove Dictionary of Music & Musicians, 20 vols. 1980. Set. 1900.00x (ISBN 0-333-23111-2). Groves Dict Music.

Sainsbury, John S., ed. A Dictionary of Musicians: From the Earliest Times. LC 65-23396. (Music Reprint Ser.). 963p. 1966. Repr. of 1825 ed. $55.00 (ISBN 0-306-70931-7). Da Capo.

MUSLIM LITERATURE
see Islamic Literature

MUSLIM PHILOSOPHY
see Philosophy, Islamic

MUSLIMISM
see Islam

MUSSULMANISM
see Islam

MUTSUN LANGUAGE
Arroyo De La Cuesta, Felipe. Vocabulary or Phrase Book of the Mutsun Language of Alta California. (Library of American Linguistics: Vol. 8). (Catalan.). Repr. of 1862 ed. $17.50 (ISBN 0-404-50988-6). AMS Pr.

MUTUAL FUNDS
see Investment Trusts

MUTUAL INSURANCE
see Insurance

MYCENAEAN INSCRIPTIONS
see Inscriptions, Linear B

MYCOLOGY
see also Fungi

Berger, Karl. Mycological Dictionary. 432p. 1980. $99.00x (ISBN 0-686-44735-2, Pub. by Collets). State Mutual Bk.

Snell, Walter & Dick, Esther A. Glossary of Mycology. 2nd ed. LC 77-134946. 1971. 14.00x (ISBN 0-674-35451-6). Harvard U Pr.

Von Berger, Karl. Mykologisches Worterbuch. LC 80-479189. 432p. (Eng., Fr., Span., Lat., Czech., Pol., & Rus.). 1980. write for info. (ISBN 3-437-20220-0). Fischer Verlag.

MYSTICAL THEOLOGY
see Mysticism

MYSTICISM
see also Christian Art and Symbolism
Gaynor, Frank. Dictionary of Mysticism. 211p. 1973. pap. $2.45 (ISBN 0-8065-0172-3). Citadel Pr.

L'Heureux, Mother Aloysius G. Mystical Vocabulary of Venerable Mere Marie De L'Incarnation & Its Problems. LC 72-94190. (Catholic University of America Studies in Romance Languages & Literatures Ser: No. 53). Repr. of 1956 ed. $18.75 (ISBN 0-404-50353-5). AMS Pr.

MYTH
Pernety, Antoine J. Dictionnaire Mythohermetique. (Illus.). 392p. (Fr.). 1972. 49.00 F. Denoel.

MYTHICAL ANIMALS
see Animals, Mythical

MYTHOLOGY–DICTIONARIES
Aubert, Henri. Diccionario de Mitologia. 238p. (Span.). 1961. $14.95 (ISBN 0-686-56710-2, S-33055). French & Eur.

Bayard, Jean P. Dictionnaire Mytho-hermetique: La Symbolique du Feu. 232p. (Fr.). 1973. 39.00 F. Payot.

Bell, Robert E. Dictionary of Classical Mythology: Symbols, Attributes, & Associations. LC 81-19141. 390p. 1982. text ed. $26.50 (ISBN 0-87436-305-5); pap. $19.95 (ISBN 0-87436-023-4). ABC Clio.

Cooper, William R. Archaic Dictionary. LC 73-76018. 1969. Repr. of 1876 ed. $66.00x (ISBN 0-8103-3885-8). Gale.

Diccionario de la Mitologia Mundial. 383p. (Span.). 1971. $12.25 (ISBN 84-7166-165-9, S-12258). French & Eur.

Diccionario de la Mitologia Mundial. 387p. (Span.). 1981. 400.00 ptas (ISBN 84-7166-165-9). Edaf.

Falcon, C., et al. Diccionario de la Mitologia Clasica. 633p. (Span.). 1980. pap. $25.00 (ISBN 84-206-1961-2, S-32723). French & Eur.

Gaytan, C. Diccionario Mitologico. (Span.). $3.75 (ISBN 0-686-56651-3, S-25775). French & Eur.

Gottschalk, Herbert. Lexikon der Mythologie der Eurpaeischen Voelker. (Ger.). $42.00 (ISBN 3-7934-1184-2, M-7246). French & Eur.

Lelama, Homero. Diccionario de Mitologia. 364p. (Span.). 1974. $44.95 (ISBN 0-686-56670-X, S-33075). French & Eur.

Perez Rioja, Jose A. Diccionario de Simbolos y Mitos: Las Ciencias y las Artes en Su Expresion Figurada. 2nd ed. 434p. (Span.). 1971. $15.50 (ISBN 84-309-0310-0, S-12344). French & Eur.

Pernety, Antoine J. Le Dictionnaire Mytho-Hermetique. (Fr.). pap. $25.00 (ISBN 0-686-57069-3, M-6441). French & Eur.

––Le Dictionnaire Mytho-Hermetique. (Fr.). 51.50 F. Retz.

Robelo, Cecilio A. Diccionario de mitologia Nahuatl. (Illus.). 880p. (Span.). 1980. Mex.$pap. 24.40. Innovacion.

Room, Adrian. Room's Classical Dictionary. 320p. 1983. $18.95 (ISBN 0-7100-9262-8). Routledge & Kegan.

Schmidt, J. Dictionnaire mythologie grecque et romaine. (Illus., Fr.). pap. $8.50 (ISBN 2-03-075408-0, 3728). Larousse.

Stephanus, Charles. Dictionarium Historicum, Geographicum, Poeticum. LC 75-27859. (Renaissance & the Gods Ser.: Vol. 16). (Illus.). 1976. Repr. of 1596 ed. lib. bdg. 80.00 (ISBN 0-8240-2065-0). Garland Pub.

Sykes, Egerton. Everyman's Dictionary of Non-Classical Mythology. x ed. (Everyman Reference Library). (Illus.). 298p. 1977. Repr. of 1968 ed. $13.50 (ISBN 0-460-03010-8, Pub. by J. M. Dent England). Biblio Dist.

Thomas, Joseph. Universal Pronouncing Dictionary of Biography & Mythology, 2 Vols. 5th ed. LC 76-137298. Repr. of 1930 ed. Set. $225.00 (ISBN 0-404-06386-1). AMS Pr.

Zimmerman, John E. Dictionary of Classical Mythology. (YA) 1964. 17.26i (ISBN 0-06-007740-9, HarpT). Har-Row.

MYTHOLOGY–JUVENILE LITERATURE
see also subdivision Juvenile Literature under Mythology, Classical, Mythology, Greek, and similar headings
Zimmerman. Dictionary of Classical Mythology. (gr. 9 up). pap. $2.75 (ISBN 0-553-14483-9). Bantam.

MYTHOLOGY, CLASSICAL
see also Gods; Mythology, Greek; Mythology, Roman
also names of mythological persons and objects
Falcon Martinez, Constantino, et al. Diccionario de la mitologia clasica: A-H, Tomo 1. 2nd ed. 368p. (Span.). 1981. pap. 360.00 ptas (ISBN 84-206-1791-1). Alianza Ed.

––Diccionario de la mitologia clasica: I-Z, Tomo 2. 2nd ed. 304p. (Span.). 1981. pap. 360.00 ptas (ISBN 84-206-1792-X). Alianza Ed.

Schmidt, J. Dictionnaire mythologie grecque et romaine. (Illus., Fr.). pap. $8.50 (ISBN 2-03-075408-0, 3728). Larousse.

Starnes, DeWitt T. & Talbert, Ernest W. Classical Myth & Legend in Renaissance Dictionaries. LC 73-11753. 517p. 1973. Repr. of 1955 ed. lib. bdg. 39.75x (ISBN 0-8371-7086-9, STCM). Greenwood.

Zimmerman. Dictionary of Classical Mythology. (gr. 9 up). pap. $2.75 (ISBN 0-553-14483-9). Bantam.

Zimmerman, John E. Dictionary of Classical Mythology. (YA) 1964. 17.26i (ISBN 0-06-007740-9, HarpT). Har-Row.

MYTHOLOGY, CLASSICAL–DICTIONARIES
see Mythology–Dictionaries

MYTHOLOGY, EGYPTIAN
Lanzone, R. V. Dizionario Di Mitologia Egizia, 3 vols. 1312p. (Ital.). 1974. $350.00 (ISBN 90-272-0931-6, 0932-4, 0933-2). Benjamins North Am.

MYTHOLOGY, GREEK
Grimal, Pierre. Dictionnaire de la Mythologie Grecque et Romaine. 5th ed. 612p. (Fr.). 1969. $59.95 (ISBN 0-686-57316-1, M-6299). French & Eur.

Grimal, Pierre & Payarois, Francisco. Diccionario de Mitologia Griega & Romana. Rev. ed. 672p. (Gr. & Romanian.). 1981. write for info. ptas (ISBN 84-7509-053-2). Paidos Iberica.

Hunger, H. Lexikon der Griechischen und Roemischen Mythologie. 452p. (Ger.). 1974. pap. $7.95 (ISBN 3-499-16178-8, M-7252). French & Eur.

MYTHOLOGY, NEAR EASTERN
see Mythology, Oriental

MYTHOLOGY, ORIENTAL
Kremnitz, Walter A. Lexikon der Mythologie Aegyptens, Persiens & des Orients. LC 76-460759. (Illus.). 140p. (Ger.). 1975. write for info. Ambro Lacus.

MYTHOLOGY, ROMAN
Grimal, Pierre. Dictionnaire de la Mythologie Grecque et Romaine. 5th ed. 612p. (Fr.). 1969. $59.95 (ISBN 0-686-57316-1, M-6299). French & Eur.

Grimal, Pierre & Payarois, Francisco. Diccionario de Mitologia Griega & Romana. Rev. ed. 672p. (Gr. & Romanian.). 1981. write for info. ptas (ISBN 84-7509-053-2). Paidos Iberica.

MYTHOLOGY IN LITERATURE
Hunger, H. Lexikon der Griechischen und Roemischen Mythologie. 452p. (Ger.). 1974. pap. $7.95 (ISBN 3-499-16178-8, M-7252). French & Eur.

N

NABOKOV, VLADIMIR VLADIMIROVICH, 1899-1977
Nakhimovsky, A. D. & Paperno, V. A. An English-Russian Dictionary of Nabokov's "Lolita". (Rus. & Eng.). 1982. $17.95x (ISBN 0-88233-443-3); pap. $8.95x (ISBN 0-88233-444-1). Ardis Pubs.

NAHUATL LANGUAGE
see Aztec Language

NAIPALI LANGUAGE
see Nepali Language

NAMES
see also Code Names; Names, Geographical; Names, Personal; Terms and Phrases
Slovar Gidronimov Ukrainy. 784p. (Ukrainian.). 1978. $12.95 (Pub. by Naukova Dumka). Four Continent.

NAMES–DICTIONARIES
Amerlinck, Teodoro. Diccionario poligloto de nombres. 7th ed. 111p. (Span.). 1961. Mex.$20.00. UNAM.

Dictionnaire des Changements de Noms. (Fr.). write for info. Lib.

Haydn, Joseph T. Dictionary of Names & Universal Information. Repr. 89.00 (ISBN 0-403-00083-1). Scholarly.

Pierrard, Pierre. Dictionnaire des Prenoms & des Saints. 224p. (Fr.). 1975. 17.60 F. Larousse.

NAMES, CHRISTIAN
see Names, Personal

NAMES, CODE
see Code Names

NAMES, FICTICIOUS
see Anonyms and Pseudonyms

NAMES, GEOGRAPHICAL
Dorion, Henri & Poirier, Jean. Lexique Des Termes Utiles a L'etude Des Noms De Lieux. 162p. (Fr.). 1975. pap. $12.95 (ISBN 0-686-57121-5, M-6168). French & Eur.

––Lexique des Termes Utiles a l'etude des Noms de Lieux. 162p. (Fr.). 1975. Can.$7.75. Laval P. U.

Gavray-Baty, P. Le Vocabulaire Toponymique du Ban de Fronville. 164p. (Fr.). 1944. 30.00 F. Liege, Fac Lettres.

Gilbert, Allan H. A Geographical Dictionary of Milton. 1979. Repr. of 1919 ed. lib. bdg. $35.00 (ISBN 0-8495-2014-2). Arden Lib.

––Geographical Dictionary of Milton. LC 68-10922. 1968. Repr. of 1919 ed. 9.50x (ISBN 0-8462-1105-X). Russell.

Knox, Alexander. Glossary of Geographical & Topographical Terms. LC 68-30592. 1968. Repr. of 1904 ed. $27.00 (ISBN 0-8103-3236-1). Gale.

Losique, Serge. Dictionnaire Etymologique des Noms de Pays & de Peuples. 243p. (Fr.). 1971. 48.00 F. Klincksieck.

Periaux. Dictionnaire Indicateur des Rues & Places. (Illus.). 454p. (Fr.). 1977. write for info. Lafitte Repr.

Santano. Diccionario de Gentilicios & Toponimos. (Span.). 1981. 1300.00 ptas (ISBN 8-42831-069-6). Paraninfo.

Santano y Leon, Daniel. Diccionario de gentilicios y toponimos. 488p. (Span.). 1980. pap. 1200.00 ptas (ISBN 84-283-1069-6). Paraninfo.

Tischler, Johann. Kleinasiatische Hydronymie: Semantik & Morphologie Analyse der Geichicher Gewaessernamen. LC 78-394985. ix, 191p. (Ger.). 1977. write for info (ISBN 3-882-26001-7). Reichert.

NAMES, GEOGRAPHICAL–GREAT BRITAIN
Hope, Robert C. Glossary of Dialectal Place-Nomenclature. LC 68-58761. 1968. Repr. of 1883 ed. $30.00x (ISBN 0-8103-3530-1). Gale.

NAMES, GEOGRAPHICAL–UNITED STATES

Coulet du Gard, Rene. Dictionary of Spanish Place Names of the Northwest Coast of America: California, Vol. I. 190p. (Span. & Eng.). 1982. $24.00 (ISBN 0-939586-01-0). Edns Des Deux Mondes.

--Dictionary of Spanish Place Names of the Northwest Coast of America: Oregon, Washington State, British Columbia, Alaska, Vol. II. 190p. (Span. & Eng.). 1983. $24.00 (ISBN 0-939586-02-9). Edns Des Deux Mondes.

Finnie, W. Bruce. Topographic Terms in the Ohio Valley 1748-1800. (Publications of the American Dialect Society: No. 53). 144p. 1970. pap. $8.00 (ISBN 0-8173-0653-6). U of Ala Pr.

NAMES, PERSONAL

see also Anonyms and Pseudonyms; Nicknames
also Name under names of persons, Jesus Christ–Name

Bardsley, C. W. A Dictionary of English & Welsh Surnames with Special American Instances. 837p. 1980. 50.00x (ISBN 0-686-79058-8, Pub.by Heraldry Today England). State Mutual Bk.

Kolatch, Alfred J. The Dictionary of First Names. 540p. 1981. pap. 6.95 (ISBN 0-399-50570-9, Perigee). Putnam Pub Group.

Losique, Serge. Dictionnaire Etymologique des Noms de Pays & de Peuples. 243p. (Fr.). 1971. 48.00 F. Klincksieck.

Loughead, Flora H. Dictionary of Given Names. 1966. $12.50 (ISBN 0-87062-048-7). A H Clark.

NAMES, PERSONAL–ENGLISH

Bardsley, Charles W. A Dictionary of English & Welsh Surnames with Special American Instances. LC 67-25404. 837p. 1980. Repr. of 1901 ed. 30.00 (ISBN 0-8063-0022-1). Genealog Pub.

Reaney, P. H. A Dictionary of British Surnames. 2nd ed. 1976. 42.00 (ISBN 0-7100-8106-5). Routledge & Kegan.

NAMES, PERSONAL–FRENCH

Dauzat, Albert. Dictionnaire des noms de famille et prenoms de France. (Fr.). 23.50 (ISBN 2-03-020260-6, 3615). Larousse.

NAMES, PERSONAL–RUSSIAN

Benson, Morton, ed. Dictionary of Russian Personal Names. LC 64-19386. 1964. 15.00x (ISBN 0-8122-7452-0). U of Pa Pr.

NAMES, PERSONAL–WELSH

Bardsley, Charles W. A Dictionary of English & Welsh Surnames with Special American Instances. LC 67-25404. 837p. 1980. Repr. of 1901 ed. 30.00 (ISBN 0-8063-0022-1). Genealog Pub.

NATH LANGUAGE

see Nuer Language

NATIONAL PLANNING

see Economic Policy; Social Policy

NATIONS, LAW OF

see International Law

NATURAL GAS

see Gas, Natural

NATURAL HISTORY–DICTIONARIES

Brockhaus der Naturwissenschaften und der Technik. 832p. (Ger.). $35.00 (ISBN 3-7653-0019-5, M-7314, Pub. by Wiesbaden). French & Eur.

Dizionario della Natura. LC 77-461886. (Ital.). 1976. write for info. A Mondadori.

Habibi, B. Deutsch-Persisches Fachwoerterbuch Fuer Naturwissenschaft, Medezin und Landwirtschaft. 240p. (Ger. & Persian.). 1964. pap. $17.50 (ISBN 3-447-00354-5, M-7331, Pub. by Harrassowitz). French & Eur.

Jehan, L. F. Dictionnaire d'Anthropologie ou Histoire Naturelle del'Homme et des Races Humaines. Migne, J. P., ed. (Nouvelle Encyclopedie Theologique Ser.: Vol. 42). 800p. (Fr.). Repr. of 1853 ed. lib. bdg. $101.50x (ISBN 0-89241-281-X). Caratzas Pub Co.

--Dictionnaire Historique des Sciences Physiques et Naturelles. Migne, J. P., ed. (Troisieme et Derniere Encyclopedie Theologique Ser.: Vol. 30). 654p. (Fr.). Repr. of 1857 ed. lib. bdg. $85.00x (ISBN 0-89241-309-3). Caratzas Pub Co.

Khatib, Ahmad. Dictionary of the Natural Environment: English-Arabic. 1979. pap. $7.95x (ISBN 0-86685-073-2). Intl Bk Ctr.

Lewis, Walter H. Ecology Field Glossary: A Naturalist's Vocabulary. LC 77-71856. 1977. lib. bdg. 25.00 (ISBN 0-8371-9547-0, LEF/). Greenwood.

Natur Zientziak. LC 77-459840. liv, 483p. (Basque.). 1976. write for info. (ISBN 8-4724-0064-6). Aranzazu.

NATURAL SCENERY

see Landscape

NATURAL SCIENCE

see Science

NATURE, EFFECT OF MAN ON

see Man–Influence on Nature

NATUROPATHY

Maury, Emmerick A. Dictionnaire Familial des Medecines Naturelies. LC 79-350663. 568p. (Fr.). 1978. 125.00 F (ISBN 2-7113-0102-8). Delarge.

NAUTICAL TERMS

see Naval Art and Science–Dictionaries; Naval Art and Science–Terminology

NAVAHO INDIANS

see Indians of North America–Southwest, New

NAVAHO LANGUAGE

Franciscan Fathers. Ethnologic Dictionary of the Navaho Language. (Navaho). 1968. $14.50 (ISBN 0-686-32647-4); pap. $12.00 (ISBN 0-686-32648-2). St Michaels.

Franciscans, Saint Michaels, Arizona. An Ethnologic Dictionary of the Navaho Language. LC 76-43710. 536p. (Navaho). 1976. Repr. of 1910 ed. $49.50 (ISBN 0-404-15766-1). AMS Pr.

Haile, Berard. A Stem Vocabulary of the Navaho Language, 2 vols. LC 73-15403. (Navaho). Repr. of 1951 ed. Set. $49.50 (ISBN 0-404-11241-2). AMS Pr.

NAVAL ADMINISTRATION

see Naval Art and Science

NAVAL ART AND SCIENCE

see also Logistics; Marine Engineering; Military Art and Science; Navigation; Seamanship; Seamen; Ship-Building; Signals and Signaling

Berna, Henri. Dictionnaire Technique & Administratif de la Navigation Interieure. (Illus.). 393p. (Fr.). 1977. 175.00 F. Berger-Levrault.

Leal, L. Diccionario naval: Ingles-espanol y espanol-ingles. (Eng. & Span.). 1972. 70.00 ptas. Paraninfo.

NAVAL ART AND SCIENCE–DICTIONARIES

Blackburn, Graham. The Overlook Illustrated Dictionary of Nautical Terms. LC 80-39640. (Illus.). 368p. 1982. 17.95 (ISBN 0-87951-124-9). Overlook Pr.

Cazzaroli, Gianni. Dictionnaire de la Navication. 392p. (Fr.). 1973. $23.50 (ISBN 0-686-56803-6, M-4650). French & Eur.

De Bonnefoux, Pierre M. & Paris, Edmund. Le Dictionnaire de la Marine a Voile. 775p. (Fr.). 1971. 150.00 F. Courtille.

De Pando y Villarroya, Jose L. Diccionario de Marina. 244p. (Span.). 1982. pap. 1000.00 ptas (ISBN 84-300-7801-0). Autores-Editores.

Dizionarietto marinaro. (Ital.). L.1000.00. Bianco.

Falconer, William. Universal Dictionary of the Marine. LC 72-87321. (Illus.). Repr. of 1780 ed. lib. bdg. 37.50x (ISBN 0-678-05655-2). Kelley.

Gaynor, Frank, ed. New Military & Naval Dictionary. Repr. of 1951 ed. lib. bdg. 15.75x (ISBN 0-8371-2129-9, GAMN). Greenwood.

Grzywaczewski, Zbigniew. Okrety i Zegluga. LC 78-354722. 514p. (Pol.). 1977. 190.00 Zl. Wydawnictwa Naukowo.

Heinl, Robert D., Jr., ed. Dictionary of Military & Naval Quotations. (Illus.). 395p. 1978. $18.95 (ISBN 0-87021-149-8); bulk rates avail. US Naval Inst.

Jal, Augustin. Nouveau Glossaire Nautique, 2 lettre. 1848 ed. (Fr.). Lettre A, 1970. pap. $16.00 (ISBN 90-279-442-4); Lettre B,1972. pap. $16.00x (ISBN 90-2797-028-9). Mouton.

--Nouveau Glossaire Nautique, Lettre C: Revision De L'edition Publiee En 1848. (Fr.). 1978. pap. $48.00x (ISBN 90-279-7538-8). Mouton.

Layton, C. W. Dictionary of Nautical Words & Terms. 2nd, rev. ed. 395p. 1982. text ed. $32.50x (ISBN 0-85174-422-2). Sheridan.

Leal. Diccionario Naval. (Span.). 700.00 ptas (ISBN 8-42831-089-0). Paraninfo.

Leal, Luis. Diccionario Naval Ingles-Espanol. 3rd ed. 232p. (Span.). 1980. 650.00 ptas (ISBN 84-283-1089-0). Paraninfo.

Leal y Leal, Luis. Diccionario naval ingles-espanol espanol-ingles. 3rd ed. 232p. (Span. & Eng.). 1980. 650.00 ptas (ISBN 84-283-1089-0). Paraninfo.

Lukianenkov, K. F. Chastotnyi Anglo-Russkii Slovar Minimum Po Sudovozhdeniiu. 200p. (Rus. & Eng.). 1977. $3.95 (Pub. by Voenizdat). Four Continent.

Nobel, John V. Naval Terms Dictionary. 1977. lib. bdg. 75.00 (ISBN 0-8490-2332-7). Gordon Pr.

Noel, John V., Jr. The VNR Dictionary of Ships & the Sea. 400p. 1980. text ed. $19.95 (ISBN 0-442-25631-0). Van Nos Reinhold.

Noel, John V., Jr. & Beach, Edward L. Naval Terms Dictionary. 4th Ed. ed. 352p. 1978. $12.95 (ISBN 0-87021-482-9); bulk rates avail. US Naval Inst.

Palmer, Joseph, compiled by. Jane's Dictionary of Naval Terms. 1976. 11.95 (ISBN 0-356-08258-X). Hippocrene Bks.

Ragazzini, Giuseppe. Dizionario inglese-italiano e italiano-inglese con glossario bilingue di tecnica navale. xxx, 2020p. (Ital. & Eng.). L.24000.00. Zanichelli.

Ratcliff, Ronald E. & Peck, Michael A. Dictionary of Naval Terminology-Dictionnaire de Terminologie Navale: English-French; Anglais-Francais. (Illus.). 160p. (Orig.). 1983. pap. text ed. $39.00x (ISBN 2-85206-200-3, Pub. by Technique Doc France). Sheridan.

Rosamani, Enrico. Vocabolario Marinaresco Giuliano-Dalmata. LC 76-512031. xxiv, 200p. (Ital.). 1975. write for info. Olschki.

--Vocabolario marinaresco giuliano-dalmata. (Illus.). 200p. (Ital.). 1976. L.18000.00 (ISBN 88-222-2222-9). Olschki.

Scharnow, Ulrich. Transpress Lexikon Seefahrt. LC 77-471655. 608p. (Eng., Rus. & Ger., Berlin, East Germany). 1976. M.32.00. Transpress Verlag fur Verkehrswesen.

Segditsas, P., ed. Elseviers Nautical Dictionary, 3 Vols. (Eng., Fr., Ital., Span. & Ger.). 1965-66. Set. $134.25 (ISBN 0-444-40727-8); Vol. 1: Maritime Terminology. $58.75 (ISBN 0-444-40522-4); Marine Engineering. $51.25 (ISBN 0-444-40524-0). Elsevier.

Standard Marine Navigational Vocabulary. 44p. 1977. pap. $8.25 (ISBN 0-686-64013-6, IMCO 38, IMCO). Unipub.

Suariz Gil, L. Diccionario tecnico maritimo: Ingles-espanol espanol-ingles. 706p. (Eng. & Span.). 1980. pap. 980.00 ptas (ISBN 84-205-0772-5). Alhambra.

Telegin, A. I., et al. Frantsuzsko-Russkii Slovar Po Sudostroeniiu i Sudokhodstvu. 295p. (Fr. & Rus.). 1961. $3.75 (Pub. by Glav. Red. Nauchn. Tekhn. Slovarei Fizmatgiza). Four Continent.

Tver, David F. Ocean & Marine Dictionary. LC 79-1529. 1979. $18.50 (ISBN 0-87033-246-5). Cornell Maritime.

Vandenberghe, J. P., compiled by. Elsevier's Nautical Dictionary. 2nd ed. 1971. $181.00 (ISBN 0-444-41694-3). Elsevier.

Vandenberghe, J. P. & Chaballe, L. Y., eds. Elsevier's Nautical Dictionary in Six Languages. 2nd, rev. ed. LC 78-9069. x, 949p. (Eng., Fr., Span., Ital., Dutch & Ger.). 1978. write for info. (ISBN 0-444-41694-3). Elsevier.

Wedertz, Bill, ed. Dictionary of Naval Abbreviations. 2nd ed. LC 77-77336. 352p. 1977. 12.95x (ISBN 0-87021-154-4). Naval Inst Pr.

--Dictionary of Naval Abbreviations. 2nd ed. (Illus.). 352p. 1977. $12.95 (ISBN 0-87021-154-4); bulk rates avail. US Naval Inst.

NAVAL ART AND SCIENCE–TERMINOLOGY

Blackburn, Graham. The Overlook Illustrated Dictionary of Nautical Terms. LC 80-39640. (Illus.). 368p. 1982. 17.95 (ISBN 0-87951-124-9). Overlook Pr.

Colcord, Joanna C. Sea Language Comes Ashore. Dorsen, Richard M., ed. (International Folklore Ser.). 1977. Repr. of 1945 ed. lib. bdg. $12.00x (ISBN 0-405-10089-2). Ayer Co.

Dictionary of Maritime Terms. (Hebrew, Eng. , Fr. & Ger.). IL.15.00. Massada Pr.

Layton, C. W. Dictionary of Nautical Words & Terms. 1981. 60.00x (ISBN 0-85174-324-2, Pub. by Nautical England). State Mutual Bk.

--Dictionary of Nautical Words & Terms. 2nd, rev. ed. 395p. 1982. text ed. $32.50x (ISBN 0-85174-422-2). Sheridan.

NAVAL BATTLES

see also Battles
also subdivision History, Naval under names of countries, e.g. Great Britain–History, Naval; also names of naval battles

Afronin, N. P., et al. Russko-Angliiskii Voenno-Morskoi Slovar. 782p. (Rus. & Eng.). 1976. $11.50 (Pub. by Voenizdat). Four Continent.

NAVAL BIOGRAPHY

see Seamen
also subdivision Biography under Navies e.g. United States–Navy–Biography

NAVAL CONSTRUCTION

see Ship-Building

NAVAL ENGINEERING

see Marine Engineering

NAVAL LOGISTICS

see Logistics

NAVAL SCIENCE

see Naval Art and Science

NAVAL SIGNALING

see Signals and Signaling

NAVAL WARFARE

see Naval Art and Science; Naval Battles

NAVIGATION

see also Inland Navigation; Naval Art and Science; Ocean Currents; Pilots and Pilotage; Seamanship; Ship-Building; Signals and Signaling; Yachts and Yachting
also names of nautical instruments, e.g. Compass, Gyroscope

Cazzaroli, Gianni. Dictionnaire de la Mer & de la Navigation. (Illus.). 392p. (Fr.). 1973. 58.00 F. Denoel.

Layton, C. W. Harbord's Glossary of Navigation. 1981. $50.00x (ISBN 0-85174-277-7, Pub. by Nautical England). State Mutual Bk.

NAVIGATION–DICTIONARIES

see Naval Art and Science–Dictionaries

NAVIGATION, INLAND

see Inland Navigation

NAVIGATION LAWS

see Inland Navigation; Maritime Law

NAVIGATORS

see Discoveries (In Geography); Seamen

NAVY

see Naval Art and Science

also subdivision Navy under names of countries, e.g. United States–Navy

NEAR EAST–BIBLIOGRAPHY
B. D'Herbelot de Molainville, et al. Bibliotheque Orientale, ou Dictionnaire universel, contenant generalment tout ce qui regarde la connaissance des peuples de 'orient, 4 vols. 2864p. (Fr.). Repr. of 1782 ed. lib. bdg. $525.00x (ISBN 0-89241-342-5). Caratzas Pub Co.

NEAR EAST–POLITICS AND GOVERNMENT
Ziring, Lawrence. The Middle East Political Dictionary. LC 82-22673. (Clio Dictionaries in Political Science Ser.: No. 5). (Illus.). 400p. 1983. lib. bdg. $20.75 (ISBN 0-87436-044-7); pap. $10.75 (ISBN 0-87436-045-5). ABC-Clio.

NEAR EASTERN ARCHITECTURE
see Architecture–Near East

NECROMANCY
see Magic

NEEDLEWORK
see also Dressmaking; Lace and Lace Making; Quilting; Sewing
Caulfield, Sophia F. & Saward, Blanche C. Dictionary of Needlework. LC 75-172439. (Illus.). 1971. Repr. of 1882 ed. $85.00x (ISBN 0-8103-3404-6). Gale.

NEGRO LITERATURE
This heading discontinued January 1976. See American Literature–Afro-American Authors for later materials.
Howard University Library, Washington, D.C. Dictionary Catalog of the Arthur B. Spingarn Collection of Negro Authors, 2 vols. 1970. lib. bdg. $190.00 (ISBN 0-8161-0872-2, Hall Library). G K Hall.

NEGRO MUSIC
This heading discontinued January 1976. See Afro-American Music for later materials.
Howard University Library, Washington, D.C. Dictionary Catalog of the Arthur B. Spingarn Collection of Negro Authors, 2 vols. 1970. lib. bdg. $190.00 (ISBN 0-8161-0872-2, Hall Library). G K Hall.

NEGROES–BIBLIOGRAPHY
This heading discontinued January 1976. See Afro-Americans and Blacks for later materials.
Fisk University Library (Nashville) Dictionary Catalog of the Negro Collection of the Fisk University Library, 6 vols. 1974. Set. lib. bdg. $490.00 (ISBN 0-8161-1055-7, Hall Library). G K Hall.
Howard University Library, Washington, D.C. Dictionary Catalog of the Jesse E. Moorland Collection of Negro Life & History, 9 vols. 1970. Set. lib. bdg. $855.00 (ISBN 0-8161-0871-4, Hall Library). G K Hall.

NEO-DADAISM
see Pop Art

NEO-IMPRESSIONISM (ART)
see Impressionism (Art)

NEO-LATIN LANGUAGES
see Romance Languages

NEOLOGISMS
see Words, New

NEO-MELANESIAN LANGUAGE
see Pidgin English

NEOPLASMS
see Tumors

NEPAL
Senior, H. W., ed. A Vocabulary of the Limbu Language of Eastern Nepal. LC 78-908311. 86p. (Eng. & Limbu.). 1977. Repr. of 1908 ed. Rs.65.00. Radha.

NEPALI LANGUAGE
Rabinovich, I. S. Nepal'Sko-Russkii Slovar. 1328p. (Rus. & Nepalese.). 1968. $9.35 (Pub. by Sov Entsiklopediia). Four Continent.

NERVES–ANATOMY
see Neuroanatomy

NERVES–SURGERY
see Nervous System–Surgery

NERVOUS SYSTEM–SURGERY
Gurdjian, E. S., et al, eds. Glossary of Neurotraumatology. LC 78-15626. (Acta Neurochirurgica: Supplementum 25). 63p. (Eng., Ger., Fr. & Span.). 1978. pap. $11.70 (ISBN 0-387-81481-7). Springer-Verlag.

NETHERLANDIC LANGUAGE
see Dutch Language

NETHERLANDS
see also names of cities, towns, geographic areas, etc. in the Netherlands
Van Hee, Marijke. Woordenboek Welzijn. LC 79-391588. 266p. (Dutch.). 1979. fl.37.50 (ISBN 9-060-95489-0). VUGA.

NETWORK THEORY
see System Analysis

NETWORKS, INFORMATION
see Information Networks

NEUROANATOMY
Lockard, L. Desk Reference for Neuroanatomy: A Guide to Essential Terms. LC 77-21707. 1977. $18.00 (ISBN 0-387-90278-3). Springer-Verlag.

NEUROSURGERY
see Nervous System–Surgery

NEW ENGLAND–EMIGRATION AND IMMIGRATION
Banks, Charles E. Topographical Dictionary of Two Thousand Eighty-Five English Emigrants to New England, 1620-1650. LC 63-4154. 295p. 1981. Repr. of 1937 ed. 17.50 (ISBN 0-8063-0019-1). Genealog Pub.

NEW ENGLAND–GENEALOGY
Savage, James. A Genealogical Dictionary of the First Settlers of New England, 4 vols. LC 65-18541. 2541p. 1981. Repr. of 1860 ed. 95.00 (ISBN 0-8063-0309-3). Genealog Pub.
––A Genealogical Dictionary of the First Settlers of New England, 4 vols. 450.00 (ISBN 0-8490-0213-3). Gordon Pr.

NEW HAMPSHIRE–GENEALOGY
Noyes, Sybil, et al. Genealogical Dictionary of Maine & New Hampshire. LC 79-88099. 795p. 1983. Repr. of 1939 ed. 30.00 (ISBN 0-8063-0502-9). Genealog Pub.

NEW JERSEY–GENEALOGY
Gannett, Henry. A Geographic Dictionary of New Jersey. LC 78-59122. 131p. 1978. Repr. of 1894 ed. 12.00 (ISBN 0-8063-0819-2). Genealog Pub.

NEW SUPER-REALISM
see Pop Art

NEW THOUGHT
Bullock, Alan & Stallybrass, Oliver, eds. The Harper Dictionary of Modern Thought. LC 74-15814. 1977. 25.96i (ISBN 0-06-010578-X, HarpT). Har-Row.

NEW WORDS
see Words, New

NEW YORK (CITY)
Research Libraries of the New York Public Library. Dictionary Catalog of Materials on New York City. 1977. lib. bdg. $285.00 (ISBN 0-8161-0079-9, Hall Library). G K Hall.

NEW YORK (STATE)
see also names of cities, counties, and geographic areas in New York (State), e.g. Rochester; Dutchess County; Mohawk River and Valley
New York Public Library, Research Libraries. Dictionary Catalog of the Local History & Genealogy Division, 20 vols. 1974. Set. lib. bdg. $1540.00 (ISBN 0-8161-0784-X, Hall Library). G K Hall.

NEW YORK PUBLIC LIBRARY
New York Public Library, Research Libraries. The Dictionary Catalog of the Prints Division, 5 vols. 1975. Set. lib. bdg. $475.00 (ISBN 0-8161-1148-0, Hall Library). G K Hall.
––Dictionary Catalog of the Rare Book Division: First Supplement. 1973. $110.00 (ISBN 0-8161-1089-1, Hall Library). G K Hall.

NEW ZEALAND
Leland, Louis S., Jr. A Personal Kiwi-Yankee Dictionary. 10/1983 ed. 115p. pap. $5.95 (ISBN 0-88289-414-5). Pelican.

NEW ZEALAND–ECONOMIC CONDITIONS
Dale, D. A. The New Zealand Commercial Dictionary. 2nd ed. 338p. 1967. 11.00x (ISBN 0-8002-0077-2). Intl Pubns Serv.

NEWFOUNDLAND
Story, G. M., ed. Dictionary of Newfoundland English. Kirwin, W. J & Widdowson, J. D. 700p. 1982. $45.00 (ISBN 0-8020-5570-2). U of Toronto Pr.

NEWS AGENCIES
News Dictionary. 1977. $14.95 (ISBN 0-87196-105-9). Facts on File.

NEWS SERVICES
see News Agencies

NEWSPAPER STYLE
see Journalism–Handbooks, Manuals, Etc.

NEWSPAPERS
see also News Agencies
also names of individual newspapers, e.g. New York Times; Washington Post; American Newspapers, English, etc.
Kikuoka, Tadashi, ed. Japanese Newspaper Compounds: The One Thousand Most Important in Order of Frequency. LC 76-125560. (Japanese.). 1970. pap. $4.25 (ISBN 0-8048-0919-4). C E Tuttle.
News Dictionary, Vol. 9: 1972. annual 1973. $14.95 (ISBN 0-87196-095-8). Facts on File.

NEWSPAPERS–INDEXES
Paneth, Donald, ed. News Dictionary Nineteen Seventy-Eight. (Illus.). 1979. $14.95x (ISBN 0-87196-107-5); pap. $6.95 (ISBN 0-87196-108-3). Facts on File.

NEZ PERCE INDIANS
see Indians of North America–The West

NGALA LANGUAGE
see Bangala Language

NICKNAMES
Langle, Arturo. Vocabulario, Apodos, Seudonimos, Sobrenombres & Hemerografia de la Revolucion. 151p. (Span.). 1966. Mex.$20.00. UNAM.
Latham, Edward. Dictionary of Names, Nicknames, & Surnames. LC 66-22674. 1966. Repr. of 1904 ed. $37.00x (ISBN 0-8103-0157-1). Gale.
Mossman, Jennifer, ed. Pseudonyms & Nicknames Dictionary. rev. 2nd ed. LC 80-13274. 980p. 1982. $160.00x (ISBN 0-8103-0547-X). Gale.
Ruffner, Frederick G., Jr. & Thomas, Robert C., eds. Code Names Dictionary: A Guide to Code Names, Slang, Nicknames, Journalese, & Similar Terms. LC 63-21847. 1963. $38.00x (ISBN 0-8103-0685-9). Gale.

NIGERIA–LANGUAGES
Waddell, Hope M. A Vocabulary of the Efik or Old Calabar Language. 2nd ed. 94p. 1972. Repr. of 1849 ed. 7.00x (ISBN 0-8002-1353-X). Intl Pubns Serv.

NISQUALLI LANGUAGE
Gibbs, George. Dictionary of the Nisqually Indian Language of Western Washington. (Shorey Indian Ser.). 82p. Repr. of 1877 ed. pap. $9.95 (ISBN 0-8466-4022-8, 122). Shorey.

NOBILITY
see also Aristocracy; Heraldry; Titles of Honor and Nobility
also subdivision Nobility under names of countries, e.g. France–Nobility
Champreal, J. B. Dictionnaire des Familles Nobles & Notables de la Correze. (Fr.). 1976. 425.00 F. Lafitte Repr.

NOMENCLATURE
see Names

NOMS DE PLUME
see Anonyms and Pseudonyms

NONCONFORMISTS
see Dissenters

NONVIOLENCE
Del Vasto, Lanza. Definitions of Nonviolence. Sidgwick, Jean, tr. Orig. Title: Fr. 27p. (Orig.). 1972. pap. 1.00 (ISBN 0-934676-06-2). Greenlf Bks.

NORMAL SCHOOLS
see Teachers Colleges

NORMANS
Arundel De Conde, Gerard. Dictionnaire des Anoblis Normands. (Illus.). 330p. (Fr.). 1976. 275.00 F. G. Arundel De Conde.

NORSE LANGUAGES
see Icelandic and Old Norse Languages; Scandinavian Languages

NORTH AMERICAN INDIANS
see Indians of North America

NORTHWEST, NEW
see Northwestern States

NORTHWEST, PACIFIC–BIBLIOGRAPHY
University of Washington at Seattle. The Dictionary Catalog of the Pacific Northwest Collection of the University of Washington Libraries, 6 vols. 1972. Set. lib. bdg. $640.00 (ISBN 0-8161-0985-0, Hall Library). G K Hall.

NORWEGIAN LANGUAGE
see also Danish Language
Learn Norwegian for English Speakers. (Norwegian & Eng.). pap. 9.50 (ISBN 0-87557-055-0, 055-0). Saphrograph.
Lyse, Peter. Attved Tyrifjorden. LC 77-452595. (Illus.). 270p. (Norwegian.). 1976. Kr.39.50 (ISBN 8-20009-423-5). Universitetsforlaget.

NORWEGIAN LANGUAGE–DICTIONARIES
Ansteinsson, J. & Andreassen, A. T. Norwegian-English, English-Norwegian Technical Dictionary, 2 Vols. (Norwegian & Eng.). Set. 60.00 (ISBN 8-2702-8007-0). Heinman.
Arakin, V. D. Norvezhsko-Russkii Slovar. 1113p. (Rus. & Norwegian.). 1963. $13.25 (Pub. by GINS). Four Continent.
Beckman, Nat. Norsk-Svensk Ordbok. Maehle, Leif & Sigurd, Bengt, eds. 210p. (Norwegian & Swedish.). 1978. Kr.71.00 (ISBN 91-24-14535-1). Esselte Studium.
Beckman, Natanael. Norsk-Svensk Ordbok. Maehle, Lief & Sigurd, Bengt, eds. 210p. (Swedish & Norwegian.). write for info. (ISBN 91-24-14535-1). Esselte Studium.
Berlitz Editors. Berlitz Pocket Dictionaries: Norwegian-English. 300p. (Eng. & Norwegian.). 1982. pap. $4.95 (ISBN 0-686-92987-X, Berlitz). Macmillan.
Berulfsen, B. English-Norsk Dictionary: Gyldendals. new ed. (Eng. & Norwegian.). 1978. $20.00x (ISBN 8-2573-0007-1, N481); Norsk-English. $22.00x (ISBN 8-2573-0006-3, N-482). Vanous.
Berulfsen, B. & Berulfsen, T. Norwegian Dictionary: Engelsk-Norwegina. rev. ed. 433p. (Norwegian & Eng.). 1981. $22.00x (ISBN 82-573-0161-2, N481). Vanous.
Berulfsen, B. & Svenkerud, A. Norwegian Deluxe Dictionary: English-Norse. (Norwegian & Eng.). 1968. $100.00x (ISBN 82-02-09060-1, N461). Vanous.
Berulfsen, B. & Scavenius, H., eds. McKay's Modern Norwegian-English & English-Norwegian Dictionary. (Modern Dictionaries Ser.). (Norwegian & Eng.). 1953. 14.95 (ISBN 0-679-10076-8). McKay.
Bjerke, L. & Soraas, H., eds. Norwegian Dictionary: English-Norwegian. (Norwegian & Eng.). 1963. $30.00x (ISBN 0-686-31692-4, N434). Vanous.
Christophensen, Scavenius. Norwegian Dictionary: Norsk-English, Vol. 2. Kirkeby, Willie, ed. (Norwegian & Eng.). 1981. $22.00x (ISBN 8-2573-0006-3, N482). Vanous.
Daae, E. English-Norwegian, Norwegian-English, Lommeordbok. 568p. (Eng. & Norwegian.). 1980. pap. $8.95 (ISBN 82-573-0152-3, M-9462). French & Eur.
––Francais-Norvegien-Francais Lommerorbok. 455p. (Fr. & Norwegian.). 1981. pap. $12.95 (ISBN 82-573-0162-0, M-9461). French & Eur.
Dedichen, L. Fransk-Norsk Ordbok. 373p. (Fr.). 1979. $29.95 (ISBN 82-573-0068-3, M-9457). French & Eur.

Diccionario Lexicon Noruego-Espanol, Espanol-Noruego. 400p. (Norwegian & Span.). leatherette $4.95 (ISBN 84-303-0165-8, S-50418); pap. $4.50 (ISBN 84-303-0164-X, S-50417). French & Eur.

English-Norwegian Norwegian-English Pocket Dictionary. (Eng. & Norwegian.). 1981. 6.95 (ISBN 0-88254-584-1). Hippocrene Bks.

Falk, H. S. & Torp, Alf. Norwegisch-Daenisches Etymologisches Woerterbuch, Vol. 1. 2nd ed. (Norwegian & Danish.). 1960. $55.00 (ISBN 3-533-00505-4, M-7570, Pub. by Carl Winter). French & Eur.

--Norwegisch-Daenisches Etymologisches Woerterbuch, Vol. 1. 2nd ed. (Norwegian & Danish.). 1960. $55.00 (ISBN 3-533-00505-4). Winter Univ.

--Norwegisch-Daenisches Etymologisches Woerterbuch, Vol. 2. 2nd ed. (Norwegian & Danish.). 1960. $55.00 (ISBN 3-533-00506-2, M-7571, Pub. by Carl Winter). French & Eur.

--Norwegisch-Daenisches Etymologisches Woerterbuch, Vol. 2. 2nd ed. (Norwegian & Danish.). 1960. $55.00 (ISBN 3-533-00506-2). Winter Univ.

--Norwegisch Daenisches Etymologisches Woerterbuch: Mit Literatur-Nachweisen Strittiger Etymologien Sowie Deutschem und Altnordischen Woerterverzeichnis, 2 Vols. 2nd ed. 1722p. (Norwegian & Danish.). 1960. Set. $80.00x (ISBN 8-200-00085-0, Dist. by Columbia U Pr). Universitet.

Farbregd & Kamarainen. Finnish-Norwegian Norwegian-Finnish Pocket Dictionary. (Finnish & Norwegian.). 1978. write for info. (ISBN 82-573-0116-7). Kunnskapsforlaget.

Farbregd, T., et al. Finnish-Norwegian-Finnish Dictionary (Suomi-Noria-Suomi) 636p. (Finnish & Norwegian.). 1981. pap. $18.95 (ISBN 951-0-10498-1, M-9644). French & Eur.

Farbregd, Turid & Kamarainen, Aili. Suomi-Norja-Suomi: Taskusanakirja. LC 79-350054. 636p. (Finnish & Nor.). 1978. write for info. (ISBN 9-51008-527-8). Soderstrom.

Gresk-Norsk-Gresk Lommeordbok. 381p. (Gr. & Norwegian.). 1981. pap. $14.95 (ISBN 82-573-0163-9, M-9460). French & Eur.

Gribanova, E. P. Karmannyi Russko-Norvezhskii Slovar. 688p. (Rus. & Norwegian.). 1962. $1.95 (Pub. by GINS). Four Continent.

Guha, Elisabeta S. Norsk-Rumensk Lommeordbok med Liten Parloer. LC 77-570195. 48p. (Norwegian & Roman.). 1976. Kr.15.00 (ISBN 8-200-05001-7). Universitetsforlaget.

Gutu, T. Riksmalsordboken: Norwegian Dictionary. (Norwegian.). 1977. write for info. (ISBN 82-573-0004-7). Kunnskapsforlaget.

Guy, W. & Messell, J. Norsk-Engelsk Ordbok Praktisk. 324p. (Norwegian & Eng.). 1979. $29.95 (ISBN 0-686-92442-8, M-9467). French & Eur.

Gyldendals. Norwegian Pocket Dictionary: English-Norwegian, Norwegian-English. rev. 2nd ed. (Norwegian & Eng.). 1980. $9.00x (ISBN 82-573-0152-3, N-407). Vanous.

Kirkeby, Willy. Bil-og Trafikkteknisk Ordbok. LC 79-374320. (Eng. & Norwegian.). 1979. Kr.98.00 (ISBN 8-2573-0079-9). Kunnskapsforlaget.

Langenscheidts Universal-Woerterbuch Norwegisch. 560p. (Norwegian & Ger.). DM.6.80 (18241). Langenscheidt.

Loland, Stale & Thorsen, Arnold. Norsk Forkortingsbok. LC 77-463699. 68p. (Norwegian.). 1976. Kr.35.00 (ISBN 8-20200-892-1). J W Cappelens.

Nilsson, Kare. Norsk-Portugisisk Ordbok. vii, 398p. (Norwegian & Port.). 1979. Kr.95.00 (ISBN 8-20002-437-7). Universitetsforlaget.

Norsk-Nederlansk-Norsk. 379p. (Norwegian & Dutch.). 1981. $14.95 (ISBN 82-573-0164-7, M-9459). French & Eur.

Norwegian Pocket Dictionary. (Norwegian & Eng.). 10.00 (ISBN 82-517-8010-1). Heinman.

Sandvei, Marius. Svensk-Norsk Ordbok. LC 80-457703. 174p. (Swedish & Norse.). 1979. Kr.59.00 (ISBN 8-20700-369-3). Fabritius.

Schoell, K. Dutch-Norwegian & Norwegian-Dutch Pocket Dictionary. (Dutch & Norwegian.). 1981. write for info. (ISBN 82-573-0164-7). Kunnskapsforlaget.

Slette, T. Norwegian-English Dictionary. 1326p. (Norwegian & Eng.). 1977. $100.00x (ISBN 82-521-0692-7, N-537). Vanous.

Theophilakis, E. Greek-Norwegian Norwegian-Greek Pocket Dictionary. (Gr. & Norwegian.). 1981. write for info. (ISBN 82-573-0005-5). Kunnskapsforlaget.

Vogt, J. & Eikeland, I. Swedish-Norwegian Dictionary. (Swedish-Norwegian.). 1982. write for info. (ISBN 82-573-0120-5). Kunnskapsforlaget.

Von Trygue Alsos. Deutsch-Norwegisch-Deutsch. 553p. (Ger. & Norwegian.). 1981. pap. $7.95 (ISBN 82-573-0082-9, M-9438). French & Eur.

NOSOLOGY

Current Procedural Terminology. 4th ed. 1970. pap. $12.00 (ISBN 0-89970-029-2, OP-041). AMA.

NOTARIES

Rothman, Raymond C. Notary Public Practices & Glossary. 3rd ed. LC 77-93911. 1980. text ed. 15.95 (ISBN 0-933134-03-7). Natl Notary.

NOTATION, MUSICAL

see Musical Notation

NOVELISTS

see Authors

NUBIAN LANGUAGE

Armbruster, C. H. Dongolese Nubian: A Grammar. 1965. text ed. $170.00 (ISBN 0-521-04050-7). Cambridge U Pr.

--Dongolese Nubian, a Lexicon. 1965. text ed. $145.00 (ISBN 0-521-04051-5). Cambridge U Pr.

NUCLEAR ENERGY

see Atomic Energy

NUCLEAR ENGINEERING

see also Atomic Power

Freyberger, G. Abkurzungen der Kernkraftwerkstechnik. LC 79-376298. 199p. (Eng. & Ger.). 1979. write for info. (ISBN 3-521-06120-5). Thiemeg.

NUCLEAR ENGINEERING–DICTIONARIES

American Nuclear Society. Glossary of Terms in Nuclear Science & Technology: ANS-9, N1.1-1976. rev. ed. $18.50. Am Nuclear Soc.

Carpovich, Eugene A. Russian-English Atomic Dictionary: Physics, Mathematics, Nucleonics. rev. ed. 2nd ed. LC 57-8256. (Rus. & Eng.). 1959. $15.00 (ISBN 0-911484-00-0). Tech Dict.

Clason, W. E. Elsevier's Dictionary of Nuclear Science & Technology. 2nd rev. ed. (Eng., Fr., Span., Ital., Dutch & Ger.). 1970. $121.50 (ISBN 0-444-40810-X). Elsevier.

Freyberger, G. H. Abbreviations of Nuclear Power Plant Engineering. 280p. (Eng. & Ger.). 1979. $28.95 (ISBN 0-686-56591-6, M-7288, Pub. by Verlag Karl Thiemig). French & Eur.

Stattmann, F. Dictionary of Power Plant Engineering: Nuclear Power Plants, Pt. II. 316p. (Ger. & Fr.). 1973. $15.95 (ISBN 3-521-06081-0, M-7102). French & Eur.

NUCLEAR MEDICINE

Etter, Lewis E. Glossary of Words & Phrases Used in Radiology, Nuclear Medicine & Ultrasound. 2nd ed. 384p. 1970. ed. spiral $32.50xphotocopy (ISBN 0-398-00526-5). C C Thomas.

NUCLEAR PARTICLES

see Particles (Nuclear Physics)

NUCLEAR PHYSICS

see also Atomic Energy; Nuclear Engineering; Particles (Nuclear Physics); Radioactivity

Commissariat a l'Energie Atomique. Dictionnaire des Sciences & Techniques Nucleaires. 492p. (Fr.). DM.135.00. Brandstetter.

Markus, John. Vocabulario Ingles-Espanol de Electronica & Tecnica Nuclear. 196p. (Eng. & Span.). write for info. (ISBN 84-267-0247-3). Marcombo.

NUCLEAR PHYSICS–DICTIONARIES

American Nuclear Society. Glossary of Terms in Nuclear Science & Technology: ANS-9, N1.1-1976. rev. ed. $18.50. Am Nuclear Soc.

Anglo-Russkii Slovar Po Fizike Vysokikh Energii. 520p. (Eng. & Fr.). 1976. $5.75 (Pub. by Russkii Iazyk). Four Continent.

Clason, W. E. Elsevier's Dictionary of Nuclear Science & Technology. 2nd rev. ed. (Eng., Fr., Span., Ital., Dutch & Ger.). 1970. $121.50 (ISBN 0-444-40810-X). Elsevier.

Commissariat a L'energie Atomique. Dictionnaire des Sciences & Techniques Nucleaires. 3rd ed. 492p. (Fr.). 1975. 175.00 F. Eyrolles.

Del Vecchio, Alfred, ed. Concise Dictionary of Atomics. LC 64-13328. 1964. 6.00 (ISBN 0-8022-1771-0). Philos Lib.

Dictionnaire des Sciences & Techniques Nucleaires. 2nd ed. 426p. (Fr.). 1967. 29.85 F. PUF.

English-Russian Dictionary of Nuclear Explosions. 304p. (Eng. & Rus.). 1977. $40.00x (ISBN 0-686-44703-4, Pub. by Collets). State Mutual Bk.

Ghelfi, R. A., et al. Glosario de terminos nucleares. 160p. (Span.). write for info. EUDEBA.

INIS: Thesaurus. (INIS Ser.: No. 13, Rev. 19). 748p. 1980. pap. $45.00 (ISBN 92-0-178480-5, IN13/R19, IAEA). Unipub.

INIS: Thesaurus. (IAEA-INIS Ser.: No. 13, Rev. 21). 759p. 1982. pap. $42.50 (ISBN 92-0-178082-6, IN13/R21, IAEA). Unipub.

Kratkii Nemetsko-Russkii Slovar Po Iadernoi Fizike i Iadernoi Tekhnike. 303p. (Ger. & Eng.). 1958. $3.00. Four Continent.

Lexico De Terminos Nucleares: Diccionario Vocabulario Triligue. 848p. (Span., Eng. & Fr.). 1974. $44.95 (ISBN 84-500-6295-0, S-50124). French & Eur.

Markus, John. Diccionario de Electronica & Tecnica Nuclear. (Illus.). 1052p. (Span.). write for info. (ISBN 84-267-0003-9). Marcombo.

--Vocabulario Ingles-Espanol de Electronica y Tecnica Nuclear. 2nd ed. 196p. (Span. & Eng.). pap. $16.75 (ISBN 84-267-0247-3, S-30684). French & Eur.

Markus, John, tr. Diccionario de electronica y tecnica nuclear. 1052p. (Span.). 1972. 2400.00 ptas. Marcombo.

Petrenko, O. Anglo-Russkii Slovar Po Iadernym Vzryvam. 304p. (Rus. & Eng.). 1978. $4.95 (Pub. by Voenizdat). Four Continent.

Santos, Agustin A. Diccionarior Nuclear. LC 80-109250. xxiv, 708p. (Fr., & Span.). 1979. write for info. (ISBN 8-4500-3077-3). Organ Ofic Adm.

NUCLEAR POWER

see Atomic Power

NUCLEONS

see Particles (Nuclear Physics)

NUCLEUS OF THE ATOM

see Nuclear Physics

NUER LANGUAGE

Huffman, Ray. Nuer English Dictionary. $21.00 (ISBN 0-87559-060-8). Shalom.

NUMBER RHYMES

see Counting-Out Rhymes

NUMERALS

Pecorella, Giusto. Vocabolario numerico siciliano-italiano. 480p. (Ital.). L.4500.00. Bietti.

NUMISMATICS

see also Seals (Numismatics)

American Numismatic Society. Dictionary & Auction Catalogues of the Library of the American Numismatic Society, New York, 7 Vols. 1962. Set. lib. bdg. write for info. (ISBN 0-685-11673-5, Hall Library); lib. bdg. $530.00 dictionary catalog, 6 vols. (ISBN 0-8161-0630-4); lib. bdg. $90.00 auction catalog, 1 vol. (ISBN 0-8161-0102-7). G K Hall.

American Numismatic Society, New York. Dictionary & Auction Catalogues of the Library of the American Numismatic Society, Second Supplement. 1973. lib. bdg. $105.00 (ISBN 0-8161-1058-1, Hall Library). G K Hall.

Dictionary & Auction Catalogues of the Library of the American Numismatic Society: Third Supplement. 1978. lib. bdg. $195.00 (ISBN 0-8161-0247-3, Hall Library). G K Hall.

Doty, Richard G. The Macmillan Encyclopedic Dictionary of Numismatics. LC 81-18632. (Illus.). 416p. 1982. 34.95 (ISBN 0-02-532270-2). Macmillan.

Frey, A. R. Dictionary of Numismatic Names. 1973. 20.00 (ISBN 0-685-51559-1, Pub by Spink & Son England). S J Durst.

Kroha, Tyll. Lexikon der Numismatik. (Ger.). 1977. $48.00 (ISBN 3-570-01588-2, M-7241). French & Eur.

Lexikon der Numismatik. 450p. (Ger.). 1976. DM.39.80 (ISBN 3-524-00598-5). Umschau Verlag.

Rittmann, Herbert. Deutsches Munzsammler-Lexikon. LC 79-34554. (Illus.). 447p. (Ger.). 1977. write for info. (ISBN 3-87045-116-5). Battenberg.

Schroetter, Friedrich Von, ed. Woerterbuch der Muenzkunde. 2nd ed. (Ger.). 1970. $75.00x (ISBN 3-11-001227-8). De Gruyter.

Zvarich, V. V. Numizmaticheskii Slovar. 292p. (Rus.). 1978. $5.95 (Pub. by Izd. L'Vovsk. Unta.). Four Continent.

NUMISMATICS–BIBLIOGRAPHY

American Numismatic Society, New York. Dictionary & Auction Catalogues of the Library of the American Numismatic Society, Second Supplement. 1973. lib. bdg. $105.00 (ISBN 0-8161-1058-1, Hall Library). G K Hall.

NUMISMATICS–COLLECTORS AND COLLECTING

Stevenson. Dictionary Roman Coins. 1982. Repr. of 1892 ed. lib. bdg. 40.00 (ISBN 0-686-45266-6, Pub. by B A Seaby England). S J Durst.

NURSERY RHYMES

see also Counting-Out Rhymes

Opie, Iona & Opie, Peter, eds. Oxford Dictionary of Nursery Rhymes. (Illus.). (ps-3). 1951. 45.00x (ISBN 0-19-869111-4). Oxford U Pr.

NURSES AND NURSING

see also Children–Care and Hygiene; Diet in Disease; Hospitals; Sick also subdivisions Hospitals, Charities, etc. and Medical and Sanitary Affairs under names of wars, e.g. United States–History–Civil War, 1861-1865–Hospitals, Charities, etc.; World War, 1939-1945–Medical and Sanitary Affairs

Espinosa, Aurelio M. & Gambetta, Leon. Spanish for Doctors & Nurses. (Span.). $6.85. Camino Real.

Radcliff, Ruth K. & Ogden, Shelia J. Nursing & Medical Terminology: A Workbook. LC 76-17597. (Illus.). 204p. 1977. pap. text ed. 14.50 (ISBN 0-8016-3714-7). Mosby.

NURSES AND NURSING–ADMINISTRATION

see Nursing Service Administration

NURSES AND NURSING–DICTIONARIES

Albanese, Joseph. The Nurses' Drug Reference. 2nd ed. (Illus.). 1184p. 1981. 28.50x (ISBN 0-07-000767-5); pap. 21.50 (ISBN 0-07-000768-3). McGraw.

Bottero, A. Dizionario dell'infermiera. 664p. (Ital.). 1974. L.3500.00. EIPS.

Duncan, Helen A. Duncan's Dictionary for Nurses. LC 74-121974. (Illus.). 1971. Springer Pub.

Martin, Joan M. The Nurse's Dictionary. 29th ed. 1980. pap. text ed. $3.95 (ISBN 0-571-18007-8). Faber & Faber.

Pearce, Evelyn. Pearce's Medical & Nursing Dictionary & Encyclopedia. 15th ed. 500p. (Orig.). 1983. pap. $14.95 (ISBN 0-571-18080-9). Faber & Faber.

Vega, V. Diccionario ilustrado de efemerides, 2 vols. 1902p. (Span.). write for info. G Gili.

NURSING ADMINISTRATION
see Nursing Service Administration

NURSING HOMES
American Medical Record Association. Introduction to Medical Terminology for Nursing Home Personnel. 24p. $2.00 (1013P). Am Med Record Assn.

NURSING SERVICE ADMINISTRATION
American Medical Record Association. Introduction to Medical Terminology for Nursing Home Personnel. 24p. $2.00 (1013P). Am Med Record Assn.

NUTRITION
see also Animal Nutrition; Diet; Vitamins
also subdivision Nutrition under subjects, e.g. Children–Nutrition

Adrian, J. & Legrand, G. Dictionnaire de Biochimie Alimentaire et de Nutruition. 233p. (Fr.). 1981. $85.00 (ISBN 2-85206-094-9, M-9626). French & Eur.

Ashley, Richard & Duggal, Heidi. Dictionary of Nutrition. 1976. pap. 3.50 (ISBN 0-671-49407-4). PB.

Bender. Dictionary of Nutrition. 5th ed. 1983. text ed. write for info. Butterworth.

Bender, Arnold E. Dictionary of Nutrition & Food Technology. 4th ed. 1975. text ed. $29.95 (ISBN 0-408-00143-7). Butterworth.

Mathieu, Gustave. La Sante Grace a la Dietetique. LC 77-477672. 271p. (Fr.). 1975. 38.00 F (ISBN 2-85256-021-6). Doc Scient.

Porter, J. W. & Rolls, B. A., eds. Proteins in Human Nutrition. 1973. $89.00 (ISBN 0-12-562950-8). Acad Pr.

Ravitsemusalan Sanastro. LC 78-345971. 122p. (Finnish.). 1977. Fmk.15.00 (ISBN 9-511-04160-6). Otava.

Shalhoub, Judy & Murray, Carol. Clinical Spanish for Dietitians. (Illus.). 161p. 1977. text ed. $6.95x (ISBN 0-916434-30-3). Plycon Pr.

Tver, David & Russell, Percy. The Nutrition Dictionary. Date not set. price not set (ISBN 0-442-24843-1). Van Nos Reinhold.

NZOMBO LANGUAGE
see Congo Language

O

OBSCENE WORDS
see Words, Obscene

OBSOLESCENCE (ACCOUNTING)
see Depreciation

OBSTETRICS
Hughes, Edward C. Obsteric-Gynecological Terminology. 1972. text ed. $14.00x (ISBN 0-8036-4725-5). Davis Co.

OBSTETRICS–DICTIONARIES
Brigato, Giovanni & Pisano, Giorgio. Dizionario eponimico ostetrico-ginecologico. xi, 562p. (Ital.). 1977. L.15000.00. Piccin.

OCCIDENTAL ART
see Art

OCCIDENTAL LANGUAGES
see Languages, Modern

OCCITANE LANGUAGE
see Provencal Language

OCCULT SCIENCES
see also Alchemy; Fortune-Telling; Magic; Palmistry; Satanism; Spiritualism; Superstition

Bersez, Jacques. Dictionnaire pratique & explicatif des produits magiques & articles usuels. LC 77-569424. (Illus.). 125p. (Fr.). 1977. 63.00 F (ISBN 2-900272-18-1). Jacques Bersez.

Biedermann, Hans. Handlexikon der magischen Kunste. LC 76-466579. (Illus.). 374p. (Ger.). 1976. DM.9.80 (ISBN 3-426-00421-6). Droemersche Knaur.

Boutet, Frederic. Dictionnaire des sciences occultes suivi d'un dictionnaire des songes. LC 76-486140. (Illus.). 412p. (Fr.). 1976. 42.00 F (ISBN 2-85704-027-X). Pygmalion.

Chaplin, J. P. The Dictionary of the Occult & Paranormal. 1976. pap. $1.95 (ISBN 0-440-31927-7, LE). Dell.

Day, Harvey. Occult Illustrated Dictionary. LC 75-21673. (Illus.). iv, 156p. (Eng.). 1975. $8.50 (ISBN 0-19-519830-1). Oxford U Pr.

Franklyn, Julian; ed. A Dictionary of the Occult. Repr. of 1935 ed. $34.00x (ISBN 0-685-32596-2). Gale.

Gettings, Fred. Dictionary of Occult, Hermetic & Alchemical Sigils. 1981. $40.00 (ISBN 0-7100-0095-2). Routledge & Kegan.

Martin, B. W. The Dictionary of the Occult. LC 79-314043. 139p. (Eng.). 1979. E6.50 (ISBN 0-09-136880-4). Hutch Pub Co.

Miers, Horst E. Lexikon des Geheimwissens. LC 77-466751. (Illus.). 453p. (Ger.). 1976. DM.10.00 (ISBN 3-442-11142-0). Goldmann.

Noordzij, Nel. Woordenboek van magic, okkultisme & parapsychologi. LC 76-456275. 110p. (Dutch.). 1976. fl.12.50 (ISBN 9-02613-015-5). Fontein.

Pappalardo, Armando. Dizionario di scienze occulte. viii, 366p. (Ital.). 1975. L.3600.00 (ISBN 88-205-0023-X). Cisalpino.

Riland, George. The New Steinerbooks Dictionary of the Paranormal. LC 79-93353. (Steinerbks Spiritual Science Library). 370p. 1980. lib. bdg. 20.00 (ISBN 0-89345-028-6). Garber Comm.

Underwood, Peter. Dictionary of the Supernatural: An A to Z of Hauntings, Possession, Witchcraft, Demonology & Other Occult Phenomena. LC 79-303952. (Illus.). 389p. (Eng.). 1978. E5.50 (ISBN 0-245-52784-2). Harrap.

OCCULTISM
see Occult Sciences

OCCUPATION, CHOICE OF
see Vocational Guidance

OCCUPATION THERAPY
see Occupational Therapy

OCCUPATIONAL HEALTH AND SAFETY
see Industrial Safety

OCCUPATIONAL THERAPY
see also Handicraft

American Occupational Therapy Association. Occupational Therapy Product Output Reporting Systems & Uniform Terminology for Reporting Occupational Therapy Services. 1979. $10.00 (C-27); members $5.00. Am Occup Therapy.

--Uniform Terminology System for Reporting Occupational Therapy Services. 1979. $12.00 (C-26); members $10.00. Am Occup Therapy.

OCCUPATIONS
see also Handicraft; Professions; Vocational Guidance
also individual occupations and industries; also subdivision Vocational Guidance under appropriate subjects, e.g. Agriculture–Vocational Guidance

Gautier, T. F. Dictionnaire des Confreries & Corporations d'Arts & Metiers. Migne, J. P., ed. (Nouvelle Encyclopedie Theologique Ser.: Vol. 50). 562p. (Fr.). Repr. of 1854 ed. lib. bdg. $72.00x (ISBN 0-89241-288-7). Caratzas Pub Co.

Ornato, Monique. Dictionnaire des Charges, Emplois & Metiers Relevant des Institutions. LC 76-465640. 206p. (Fr.). 1975. write for info (ISBN 2-222-01896-X). CNRS.

--Dictionnaires des Charges, Emplois & Metiers XIVe. & XVe. Siecles: Relevant des Institutions Monarchiques en France. 208p. (Fr.). 1976. 45.00 F. CNRS.

OCCUPATIONS– CLASSIFICATION
Gottfredson, Gary D. & Holland, John L. Dictionary of Holland Occupational Codes. 520p. (Orig.). 1982. pap. $17.75 (ISBN 0-89106-020-0, 7889). Consulting Psychol.

OCEAN
see also Oceanography
also names of oceans, e.g. Pacific Ocean

Cazzaroli, Gianni. Dictionnaire de la Mer & de la Navigation. (Illus.). 392p. (Fr.). 1973. 58.00 F. Denoel.

Gran Diccionario Infantil Marin, 4 vols. 840p. (Espn.). 1979. Set. $128.00 (ISBN 84-7102-150-1, S-50032). French & Eur.

Navarro Dagnino, Juan. Vocabulario Maritimo Ingles-Espanol y Espanol-Ingles. 5th ed. 151p. (Span. & Eng.). 1976. pap. $8.50 (ISBN 84-252-0225-6, S-12239). French & Eur.

OCEAN–ECONOMIC ASPECTS
see Shipping

OCEAN CURRENTS
Dictionary of Sea Waves & Currents Terms. (Hebrew, Eng. , Fr. & Ger.). IL.7.00. Massada Pr.

OCEAN LIFE
see Marine Biology

OCEAN TRANSPORTATION
see Shipping

OCEAN WAVES
Dictionary of Sea Waves & Currents Terms. (Hebrew, Eng. , Fr. & Ger.). IL.7.00. Massada Pr.

OCEANIC LANGUAGES
Vanoverbergh, Morice. Isneg-English Vocabulary. (Oceanic Linguistics Special Publications: No. 11). 618p. (Isneg & Eng.). 1972. pap. $12.00x (ISBN 0-8248-0235-7). UH Pr.

OCEANICA–HISTORY
Craig, Robert D. & King, Frank P., eds. Historical Dictionary of Oceania. LC 80-24779. (Illus.). 416p. 1981. lib. bdg. 55.00 (ISBN 0-313-21060-8, KHD/). Greenwood.

OCEANOGRAPHY
see also Diving; Marine Biology; Navigation; Ocean; Ocean Currents; Ocean Waves

Agence de Cooperation Culturelle & Technique. Vocabulaire de l'oceanologie. 431p. (Fr.). 1976. 88.70 F. C. I. L. F.

Bernabo, M. & Picchi, F. Grande Dizionario di Marina: Inglese-Italiano, Italiano-Inglese. 963p. (Eng. & Ital.). 1970. $95.00 (ISBN 0-686-92551-3, M-9298). French & Eur.

Gorskii, N. N., et al. Nemetsko-Russkii Okeanograficheskii Slovar. 240p. (Ger. & Rus.). 1957. $2.75 (Pub. by GINS). Four Continent.

Hunt, Lee M. & Groves, Donald G. Glossary of Ocean Science & Undersea Technology Terms. (Illus., Orig.). pap. $6.95 (ISBN 0-685-08544-9). Compass Va.

Pan American Institute of Geography & History. Glosario de Terminos Mareograficos. LC 79-105522. 98p. (Span.). 1977. write for info. Instituto Panamericano.

OCEANOGRAPHY, PHYSICAL
see Oceanography

OCEANOLOGY
see Oceanography

OCKHAM, WILLIAM, d. ca. 1349
Ockham, William. Ockham's Theory of Terms. Loux, Michael J., tr. 234p. 1975. $20.00x (ISBN 0-268-00550-8); pap. $4.95x (ISBN 0-268-00551-6). U of Notre Dame Pr.

ODSCHI LANGUAGE
see Twi Language

OFFICE, TENURE OF
see Civil Service

OFFICE ADMINISTRATION
see Office Management

OFFICE EQUIPMENT AND SUPPLIES
see also Electronic Office Machines

Bueromaschinen Lexikon. 18th ed. (Ger.). 1975. pap. $21.50 (ISBN 3-87264-001-1, M-7316, Pub. by Goeller Verlag). French & Eur.

Edwards, Nancy M., et al, eds. Office Automation: A Glossary and Guide. LC 82-4714. 275p. (Eng.). 1982. $59.50 (ISBN 0-86729-012-9). Knowledge Indus.

OFFICE MACHINES
see Electronic Office Machines; Office Equipment and Supplies

OFFICE MANAGEMENT
see also Office Equipment and Supplies; Personnel Management; Secretaries

Glossaire Europeen de Terminologie Juridique et Administrative. Office Terminology Procedure. German-Italina, No. 24. 79p. (Ger. & Ital.). 1979. pap. $14.95 (ISBN 3-468-49074-7, M-9491). French & Eur.

OFFICE PRACTICE– AUTOMATION
Field, R. M. A Glossary of Office Automation Terms. 32p. 1982. pap. text ed. $15.00 (ISBN 0-914548-42-5). Soc Tech Comm.

OFFICE SUPPLIES
see Office Equipment and Supplies

OGLALA INDIANS
see Indians of North America–The West

OIL
see Petroleum

OIL ENGINES
see Gas and Oil Engines

OIL FIELDS
see also Petroleum

Chaballe, L. Y. & Masuy, L. Elsevier's Oil & Gas Field Dictionary. (in 6 languages plus Arabic suppl.). 1980. $127.75 (ISBN 0-444-41833-4). Elsevier.

OIL INDUSTRIES
see also Petroleum Industry and Trade

Commisssion of the European Communities. Oil & Gas Multilingual Glossary. 500p. 1979. $44.00x (ISBN 0-86010-170-3, Pub. by Graham & Trotman England). State Mutual Bk.

Gagnacci-Schwicker, A. & Schwicker. International Dictionary of Metallurgy, Mineralogy, Geology & the Mining & Oil Industries. 1530p. (Eng., Fr., Ger. & Ital.). 1970. $88.00 (ISBN 3-7625-0751-1, M-7482, Pub. by Bauverlag). French & Eur.

--International Dictionary of Metallurgey, Mineralogy, Geology & the Mining & Oil Industries. 1530p. (Eng., Fr., Ger. & Ital.). 1970. $88.00 (ISBN 3-7625-0751-1). Bauverlag.

Kramer, K. Erdoel-Lexikon (Crude Oil Dictionary) 5th rev. ed. LC 72-313250. 1972. 20.00x (ISBN 3-7785-0233-6). Intl Pubns Serv.

Moureau, Magdeleine & Rouge, Janine. Dictionnaire Technique des Termes Utilises Dans l'Industrie du Petrole, Anglais-Francais, Francais-Anglais. 914p. (Eng. & Fr., Dictionary of Technical Terms Used in the Oil Industry, English-French, French-English). 1977. $95.00 (ISBN 0-686-56757-9, M-6419). French & Eur.

Woerterbuch fuer Metallurgie, Mineralogie, Geologie, Bergbau und die Oelindustrie. (Eng. , Fr. , Ger. & Ital., Dictionary of Metallurgy, Mineralogy, Geology, Mining and Oil Industry). 1970. $88.00 (ISBN 3-7625-0751-1, M-6912). French & Eur.

OIL LANDS
see Oil Fields

OILSEED INDUSTRY
see Oil Industries

OJI LANGUAGE
see Twi Language

OLD AGE, SURVIVORS AND DISABILITY INSURANCE
see Social Security

OLD AGE, SURVIVORS AND DISABILITY INSURANCE
see Social Security

OLD BULGARIAN LANGUAGE
see Church Slavic Language

OLD CHURCH SLAVIC LANGUAGE
see Church Slavic Language

OLD EAST SLAVIC LANGUAGE
see Russian Language–To 1700
OLD FRENCH LANGUAGE
see French Language–To 1500
**OLD HIGH GERMAN
LANGUAGE**
*see German Language–Old High
German, 750-1050*
OLD ICELANDIC LANGUAGE
*see Icelandic and Old Norse
Languages*
OLD NORSE LANGUAGE
*see Icelandic and Old Norse
Languages*
OLD PERSIAN LANGUAGE
see also Indo-Aryan Languages
Kent, Roland G. Old Persian
Grammar Texts Lexicon. 2nd rev.
ed. (American Oriental Ser.: Vol.
33). (Persian). 1953. $17.00
(ISBN 0-940490-33-1). Am Orient
Soc.
OLD RUSSIAN LANGUAGE
see Russian Language–To 1700
OLD SLOVENIAN LANGUAGE
see Church Slavic Language
OLIGOPHRENIA
see Mental Deficiency
OMAHA INDIANS
*see Indians of North America–The
West*
OMAN
Anthony, John D. Historical &
Cultural Dictionary of the
Sultanate of Oman & the Emirates
of Eastern Arabia. LC 76-42216.
(Historical & Cultural Dictionaries
of Asia Ser.: No. 9). 1976. $13.00
(ISBN 0-8108-0975-3). Scarecrow.
OMAR KHAYYAM
Tutin, John R. Concordance to
FitzGerald's Translation of the
Rubaiyat of Omar Khayyam. LC
68-54871. (Bibliography &
Reference Ser.: No. 256). 1969.
Repr. of 1900 ed. $12.50 (ISBN 0-
8337-3581-0). B Franklin.
ONEIROMANCY
see Dreams
ONOMATOPOEIA
Kloe, Donald R. A Dictionary of
Onomatopoeic Sounds, Tones, &
Noises in English & Spanish. LC
77-2627. (Eng. & Span.). 1977.
$25.50 (ISBN 0-87917-059-X).
Ethridge.
ONONDAGA LANGUAGE
Shea, John D. French-Onondaga
Dictionary, from a Manuscript of
the Seventeenth Century. LC 10-
30203. (Library of American
Linguistics: No. 1). (Fr.). Repr. of
1860 ed. $12.50 (ISBN 0-404-
50981-9). AMS Pr.
OPERA–DICTIONARIES
Clement, Felix & Larousse, Pierre.
Dictionnaire Des Operas, 2 Vols.
LC 69-15617. (Music Reprint Ser.)
(Fr.). 1969. Repr. of 1905 ed. Set.
$110.00 (ISBN 0-306-71197-4).
Da Capo.
Osborne, Charles. The Dictionary of
the Opera. 1983. $22.95 (ISBN 0-
671-49218-7). S&S.
Rosenthal, Harold & Warrack, John.
Dictionnaire de L'opera. 420p.
(Fr.). 1974. pap. $36.00 (ISBN 0-
686-56799-4, M-416). French &
Eur.
--Dictionnaire de l'opera. (Illus.).
420p. (Fr. & Eng.). 1974. 90.00 F.
Fayard.
Rosenthal, Harold & Warrack, John,
eds. The Concise Oxford
Dictionary of Opera. 2nd ed. 1979.
29.95 (ISBN 0-19-311318-X).
Oxford U Pr.
--The Concise Oxford Dictionary of
Opera. 2nd ed. (Out-of-Ser.
Paperback). 1979. pap. 12.95
(ISBN 0-19-311321-X). Oxford U
Pr.
Towers, John. Dictionary-Catalogue
of Operas & Operettas, 2 Vols. LC
67-25996. (Music Reprint Ser.).
1967. Repr. of 1910 ed. lib. bdg.
$59.50 (ISBN 0-306-70962-7). Da
Capo.
Varnai, Peter. Operalexikon. LC 77-
564359. 533p. (Hungarian.). 1975.
84.00 Ft (ISBN 9-633-30107-6).
Zenemukiado.
OPERATIONAL ANALYSIS
see Operations Research
OPERATIONAL RESEARCH
see Operations Research

OPERATIONS RESEARCH
Sezepesi, G & Szekely, B. Systems
Analysis & Operations Research
Dictionary. 154p. (Hungarian,
Eng., Fr., Ger., & Rus.). 1980.
$30.00x (ISBN 0-569-08617-5,
Pub. by Collets). State Mutual Bk.
OPHTHALMOLOGY
see also Eye
International Council of
Opthalmology, ed. Perimetric
Standards & Perimetric Glossary.
1979. lib. bdg. 29.00 (ISBN 90-
6193-600-4, Pub. by Junk Pubs
Netherlands). Kluwer Academic.
Stein, Harold A., et al. Manual of
Opthalmic Terminology. LC 81-
14136. (Illus.). 269p. 1982. pap.
text ed. 18.95 (ISBN 0-8016-4769-
X). Mosby.
**OPPOSITES (IN RELIGION,
FOLK-LORE, ETC.)**
*see Polarity (In Religion, Folk-Lore,
etc.)*
OPTICAL INSTRUMENTS
*see also Microscope and Microscopy
also names of specific instruments,
e.g. Spectroscope*
Bindmann, W. Fachwoerterbuch
Optik und Optischer Geraetebau.
408p. (Eng. & Ger., Dictionary of
Optics and Optical Devices). 1974.
$75.00 (ISBN 3-7684-6411-3, M-
7402, Pub. by Dausien). French &
Eur.
OPTICAL MEASUREMENTS
Terminology of Optical
Measurements. 1969. $12.00 (017-
2); members $8.00. TAPPI.
OPTICS
*see also Color; Electron Optics;
Optical Measurements; Spectrum
Analysis
also headings beginning with the
word Optical; also Optics,
Geometrical; Optics, Physiological;
and similar headings*
Bindmann, W. Fachwoerterbuch
Optik und Optischer Geraetebau.
408p. (Eng. & Ger., Dictionary of
Optics and Optical Devices). 1974.
$75.00 (ISBN 3-7684-6411-3, M-
7402, Pub. by Dausien). French &
Eur.
Bindmann, Werner. Fachwoerterbuch
Optik & Optischer Geratebau:
Deutsch-Englisch. 408p. (Ger. &
Eng.). DM.45.00 (ISBN 3-7684-
6512-8). W Dausien.
--Fachwoerterbuch Optik &
Optischer Geratebau: Englisch-
Deutsch. 408p. (Eng. & Ger.).
DM.45.00 (ISBN 3-7684-6512-8).
W Dausien.
--Optik & Optischer Geratebau
Deutsch-Englisch. 432p. (Ger. &
Eng.). 1975. M.45.00. VEB
Technik.
Dictionary of Physics: No. 3, Optics.
(Hebrew, Eng. , Fr. & Ger.).
IL.8.00. Massada Pr.
Hoefling, Oskar, ed. Lexikon der
Schulphysik: Bd 4, Optik &
Relativitaet. (Ger.). 1978.
DM.52.00 (ISBN 3-7614-0109-4).
Aulis Verlag.
Ibeas, Franco. Diccionario
Tecnologico Ingles-Espanol:
Electricidad, Electronica,
Telecomunicacion, & Materias
Afinas con la Fisica, Optica &
Quimica. 452p. (Eng. & Span.).
1974. E950.00 (ISBN 84-205-
0492-0). Alhambra.
Mugler, Charles. Dictionnaire
Historique de la Terminologie
Optique des Grecs. 460p. (Fr.).
1964. pap. $110.00 (ISBN 0-686-
57055-3, M-6421). French & Eur.
Richter, G., ed. Dictionary of Optics
Photography & Photogrammetry:
German-English & English-
German. (Eng. & Ger.). 1966.
$44.00 (ISBN 0-444-40478-3).
Elsevier.
Ruth, W. Lexikon der Schulphysik:
Optik und Relativitaet, Vol. 4.
(Ger.). $42.00 (ISBN 3-7614-0109-
4, M-7226). French & Eur.
Schulz. Woerterbuch der Optik &
Feinmechanik: Band II, Englisch-
Franzoesisch-Deutsch. 124p. (Eng.,
Fr. & Ger.). 1982. DM.16.00.
Brandstetter.
--Woerterbuch der Optik &
Feinmechanik: Band III,
Franzoesisch-Deutsch-Englisch.
109p. (Fr., Ger. & Eng.). 1982.
DM.16.00. Brandstetter.

Schulz, E. Woerterbuch der Optik
und Feinmechanik: English-
French-German Dictionary of
Optics & Mechanical Engineering.
(Eng., Fr. & Ger.). 1961. write for
info. (M-90925). French & Eur.
Schulz, Ernst. Woerterbuch der
Optik und Feinmechanik, Vol. 1.
(Fr., Ger. & Eng., Dictionary of
Optics & Mechanical Engineering).
1961. pap. $12.00 (ISBN 3-87097-
036-7, M-6978). French & Eur.
--Woerterbuch der Optik und
Feinmechanik, Vol. 2. (Fr., Ger. &
Eng., Dictionary of Optics &
Mechanical Engineering). 1961.
pap. $12.00 (ISBN 3-87097-037-5,
M-6977). French & Eur.
Terminology of Optical
Measurements. 1969. $12.00 (017-
2); members $8.00. TAPPI.
Weik, Martin H. Fiber Optics &
Lightwave Communications
Standard Dictionary. 320p. 1980.
text ed. $18.50 (ISBN 0-442-
25658-2). Van Nos Reinhold.
OPTICS, ELECTRONIC
see Electron Optics
OPTICS, FIBER
see Fiber Optics
OPTOMETRY
COPT - Current Optometric
Information & Terminology. $6.00
(ODE 4); members $3.00; students
$2.00. Am Optometric.
COPT Current Optometric
Procedural Terminology. $4.00
(O D E10); members $2.00;
students $1.00. Am Optometric.
ORATORY
see also Debates and Debating
Tesoro del Declamador Universal.
(Span). Mex.$18.00; Mex.$38.00.
EDIMEX.
ORCHESTRATION
*see Instrumentation and
Orchestration*
ORDOS LANGUAGE
Mostaert, Antoine. Dictionnaire
Ordos, 3 Vols in 1. 2nd ed. 1968.
Repr. of 1944 ed. 160.00 (ISBN 0-
384-40225-9). Johnson Repr.
OREGON–HISTORY
Corning, Howard M., ed. Dictionary
of Oregon History. $16.50 (ISBN
0-8323-0099-3). Binford.
ORGAN
see also Electronic Organ
Irwin, Stevens. Dictionary of Pipe
Organ Stops. 2nd ed. 1983. $19.95
(ISBN 0-02-871150-5). Assoc-Mus.
**ORGAN–INSTRUCTION AND
STUDY**
DeVito, Albert. Chord Dictionary.
LC 75-40685. 1980. 4.95 (ISBN 0-
934286-01-9). Kenyon.
ORGAN, ELECTRONIC
see Electronic Organ
ORGAN MUSIC
Irwin, Stevens. Dictionary of
Hammond Organ Stops. 4th rev.
ed. 1970. pap. $8.95 (ISBN 0-02-
871110-6). Assoc-Mus.
Organ Chord Dictionary. 1981. $2.50
(ISBN 0-88284-156-4). Alfred Pub.
ORGANIC CHEMISTRY
see Chemistry, Organic
ORGANIZATION
*see also Industrial Management;
Management; Planning*
Nieuwerth, Hans. Lexikon der Planun
und Organisation. (Ger.). 1968.
$37.00 (ISBN 3-87715-051-9, M-
7235). French & Eur.
Niewwwerth, Hans, et al, eds.
Lexikon der Planung &
Organisation. 220p. (Ger.). 1968.
DM.46.00 (ISBN 3-87715-051-9).
Quickborner Team.
Seone, Joaquin R. Diccionario de
contabilidad, organizacion,
administracion, control & ciencia
afines, 7 vols. 3400p. (Span.).
1972. $45.00. Difusion.
ORGANIZATIONS
see Associations, Institutions, etc.
**ORGANIZATIONS,
INTERNATIONAL**
see International Agencies
ORGANS
see Organ

ORIENTAL LANGUAGES
*see also particular languages or
groups of languages, e.g. Afghan
language; Indo-Aryan languages;
Iranian Languages*
Dalgado, Sebastiao R. Glossario
Luso-Asiatico, 2 Vol. (Romanistik
in Geschicte und Geggenwart 11).
580p. (Ger.). 1982. Repr. of 1921
ed. lib. bdg. $160.00 (ISBN 3-
87118-479-9, Pub. by Helmut
Buske Verlag Hamburg).
Benjamins North Am.
Egerod, Soren. Atayal-English
Dictionary, 2 vols. (Scandinavian
Institute of Asian Studies
Monograph: No. 35). 830p.
(Atayal & Eng.). 1981. Set. pap.
text ed. 41.25x (ISBN 0-7007-
0117-6, Pub. by Curzon Pr
England); Vol. 1. pap. text ed.
(ISBN 0-7007-0118-4); Vol. 2. pap.
text ed. (ISBN 0-7007-0119-2).
Humanities.
Lyman, Thomas A. Dictionary of
Mong Njua: A Miao (Meo)
Language of Southeast Asia. LC
72-94484. (Janua Linguarum, Ser.
Practica: No. 123). (Illus.). 403p.
(Orig., Mongolian.). 1974. pap.
text ed. 94.00x (ISBN 90-2792-
696-4). Mouton.
**ORIENTAL LITERATURE–
BIBLIOGRAPHY**
New York Public Library, Research
Libraries. Dictionary Catalog of
the Oriental Collection: First
Supplement, 8 vols. 1976. Set. lib.
bdg. $955.00 (ISBN 0-8161-0775-
0, Hall Library). G K Hall.
--Dictionary Catalog of the Oriental
Collection, 16 Vols. 1960. Set. lib.
bdg. $1400.00 (ISBN 0-8161-0410-
7, Hall Library). G K Hall.
ORIENTAL MYTHOLOGY
see Mythology, Oriental
ORIENTAL RUGS
see Rugs, Oriental
ORIENTATION (STUDENTS)
see Students
ORIGIN, MARKS OF
see Marks of Origin
ORIGIN OF SPECIES
Barrett, Paul, et al, eds. Concordance
to Darwin's "Origin of Species".
864p. 1981. $42.50x (ISBN 0-
8014-1319-2). Cornell U Pr.
OROGRAPHY
see Mountains
ORTHOEPY
see Phonetics
ORTHOGRAPHY
*see Spelling Reform;
also subdivision Orthography and
spelling under names of languages,
e.g. English Language–Orthography–
Spelling*
ORTHOPEDIA
*see also Locomotion, Disordered
also special conditions to which
orthopedic methods are applicable,
e.g. Hip Joints–Diseases; Spine–
Abnormities and Deformities*
Blauvelt, Carolyn T. & Nelson, Fred.
A Manual of Orthopaedic
Terminology. 2nd ed. LC 81-4029.
(Illus.). 257p. 1981. pap. text ed.
23.95 (ISBN 0-8016-0752-3).
Mosby.
Dizionario di terminologia ortopedica
e traumatologica. 300p. (Ital.).
1975. L.15000.00. Gaggi.
Fusari, Alberto. Dizionario di
Terminologia Ortopedica &
Traumatologia. LC 77-675054.
285p. (Ital.). 1975. L.1500.00.
Gaggi.
ORTHOPEDIC APPARATUS
Feijoo, Guillermo M. Ortografia
Functional: Atlas de la
Aparatologia Ortopedica. 222p.
(Span.). 1980. write for info.
Mundi.
OSAGE INDIANS
*see Indians of North America–The
West*
OSMANIC LANGUAGE
see Turkish Language
OSMANLI LANGUAGE
see Turkish Language
OSSETIC LANGUAGE
Abaev, V. I. Istoriko-Etimologicheskii
Slovar Osetinskogo. 36p. (Rus.).
1979. $8.25 (Pub. by Nauka). Four
Continent.
OSTEOPATHY
American Osteopathic Association.
Osteopathic Terminology. free.
Am Osteopathic.

OTJI LANGUAGE
see Twi Language
OTO INDIANS
see Indians of North America–The West
OTOLARYNGOLOGY
Dictionnaire d'oto-rhino-laryngologie: Francais-Anglais-Espagnol-Allemand-Italien, 5 vols. (Fr. , Eng. , Span. , Ger. & Ital.). 1971. write for info. Maloine.
OTORHINOLARYNGOLOGY
see Otolaryngology
OUTDOOR RELIEF
see Charities; Public Welfare
OUTER SPACE
see also Space Environment
Tver, David F., et al. Dictionary of Astronomy, Space & Atmospheric Phenomena. 288p. 1982. pap. text ed. $12.95 (ISBN 0-442-28422-5). Van Nos Reinhold.
OUTPUT EQUIPMENT (COMPUTERS)
see Computer Input-Output Equipment
OVENS
see Stoves
OXYGEN–INDUSTRIAL APPLICATIONS
see also Metallurgy
Lexique des Termes Techniques Concernant le Material d'une Usine d'oxygene. (Illus.). 99p. (Fr.). 1971. 70.00 F. Soudure Autogene.
OXYGENATION, HYPERBARIC
see Hyperbaric Oxygenation

P

PACIFIC AREA–BIBLIOGRAPHY
Bernice P. Bishop Museum - Honolulu. Dictionary Catalog of the Library of the Bernice P. Bishop Museum, 9 Vols. 1964. Set. lib. bdg. $660.00 (ISBN 0-8161-0679-7, Hall Library); lib. bdg. $115.00 1st suppl. 1967 (ISBN 0-8161-0722-X); lib. bdg. $40.00 2nd suppl. 1969 (ISBN 0-8161-0834-X). G K Hall.
PACIFIC SETTLEMENT OF INTERNATIONAL DISPUTES
see Arbitration, International
PACKAGING
see also Packing for Shipment
Hoffman, Johannes P. Dictionary of Packaging: German-English-French. 2nd, rev. ed. LC 72-352784. 353p. (Ger., Eng. & Fr.). 1971. 62.50 (ISBN 0-8002-0745-9). Intl Pubns Serv.
PACKING (TRANSPORTATION)
see Backpacking
PACKING FOR SHIPMENT
see also Packaging
Illustrated Glossary of Packagings for the Transports of Dangerous Goods. (Illus.). pap. $5.00 (ISBN 0-686-94575-1, UN74/13/1, UN). Unipub.
Vocabulaire Illustre des Emballages: Destines au Transport des Marchandises Dangereuses. (Illus.). 133p. (Fr.). 1974. $4.00. O. N. U.
PACKING INDUSTRY
see Meat Industry and Trade
PADDY FIELD CULTURE
see Irrigation
PAINT
see also Corrosion and Anti-Corrosives
Federation of Societies on Coatings Technology. Paint-Coatings Dictionary. 632p. $50.00; members $30.00. Fed Soc Coat Tech.
PAINTERS
see also Portrait Painters
Aeschlimann, E. & Ancono, Paolo. Dictionnaire des Miniaturistes du Moyan Age: La Renaissance dans les Differentes Contrees de l'Europa. 2nd ed. (Fr.). 1949. 202.50 F. Kraus.
Archibald, E. H. Dictionary of Sea Painters. (Illus.). 1979. $79.50 (ISBN 0-902028-84-7). Apollo.
Benezit, E. Dictionnaire des Peintres, Sculpteurs, Dessinateurs & Graveurs, 10 vols. new, rev. ed. (Illus., Fr.). 1976. $495.00 set (ISBN 2-7000-0149-4). Hacker.

De Fontenay, Louis-Abel. Dictionnaire des Artistes ou Notice Historique: Raisonnee des Architectes, Peintres & Graveurs, 2 vols. (Fr.). 1972. 240.00 F. Minkoff.
Diccionario Universal del Arte y De los Artistas: Pintores, 3 vols. 934p. (Span.). 1970. Set. leatherette $76.50 (ISBN 84-252-0374-0, S-50287). French & Eur.
Laclotte, Michel & Smith, Alistair, eds. Larousse Dictionary of Painters. LC 81-81046. (Illus.). 480p. 1981. $50.00 (ISBN 0-88332-265-X, 8191). Larousse.
Muller, Jean. Dictionnaire Abrege des Imprimeurs-Editeurs du 16 Siecle. 150p. (Fr.). 1970. DM.80.00. Koerner.
PAINTERS–FRANCE
Camard, Jean Pierre & Belfort, Anne Marie. Dictionnaire des Peintres et Sculpteurs Provencaux. 444p. (Fr.). 1974. pap. $19.95 (ISBN 0-686-56858-3). French & Eur.
Fondation Paul Richard & Camard, Jean-Pierre. Dictionnaire des Peintres & Sculpteurs Provencaux: 1880-1950. 444p. (Fr.). 1974. 40.00 F. Bendor.
PAINTERS–GREAT BRITAIN
Grant, Maurice. A Dictionary of British Landscape Painters: From the 16th Century to the Early 20th Century. 236p. 1976. Repr. of 1952 ed. text ed. $30.00x (ISBN 0-85317-250-1, Pub. by A & C Black England). Humanities.
Lewis, Frank. A Dictionary of British Historical Painters. 70p. 1979. text ed. 30.00x (ISBN 0-85317-052-5, Pub. by A & C Black England). Humanities.
Paviere, Sydney. A Dictionary of British Sporting Painters. (Illus.). 1980. Repr. of 1965 ed. text ed. 40.00x (ISBN 0-85317-940-9, Pub. by A & C Black England). Humanities.
Waterhouse, Ellis. The Dictionary of British Eighteenth Century Painters. (Illus.). 415p. 1981. $79.50 (ISBN 0-902028-93-6). Antique Collect.
Wilson, Arnold. A Dictionary of British Marine Painters. (Illus.). 1980. Repr. of 1967 ed. text ed. 40.00x (ISBN 0-85317-051-7, Pub. by A & C Black England). Humanities.
Wood, Christopher. Dictionary of Victorian Painters. (Illus.). 1979. $74.50 (ISBN 0-902028-72-3). Apollo.
PAINTERS–ITALY
Zampetti, Pietro. Dictionary of Venetian Painters, 5 vols. Incl. Vol. 1. Fourteenth to Fifteenth Centuries. 1969. 57.50x (ISBN 0-85317-131-9); Vol. 2. Sixteenth Century. 1970. 57.50x (ISBN 0-85317-171-8); Vol. 3. Seventeenth Century. 1971. 57.50x (ISBN 0-85317-181-5); Vol. 4. Eighteenth Century. 1971. 57.50x (ISBN 0-85317-006-1); Vol. 5. 19th & 20th Centuries. 1979. 57.50x (ISBN 0-85317-035-5). LC 71-484121. Intl Pubns Serv.
PAINTERS–SCOTLAND
Harris, Paul. A Concise Dictionary of Scottish Painters. LC 76-364800. 1976. 6.50x (ISBN 0-904505-08-1). Intl Pubns Serv.
PAINTERS–UNITED STATES
Fielding, Mantle. Dictionary of American Painters, Sculptors & Engravers: Enlarged. 1974. $17.50 (ISBN 0-685-47043-1). Assoc Bk.
PAINTING–DICTIONARIES
Alexandrian, Sarane. Dictionnaire de la Peinture Surrealiste. 58p. (Fr.). 1973. $32.50 (ISBN 0-686-56823-0, M-6601). French & Eur.
––Dictionnaire de la Peinture Surrealiste. 58p. (Fr.). 1973. 50.00 F (Pub. by Filipacchi). Hippocrene Bks.
Benezit, Emmanuel. Dictionnaire Critique & Documentaire: Peintres, Sculptres, Dessinateurs de Tous les Temps & de Tous les Pays. (Fr.). 1976. write for info. Grund.
De Marsy, Francois-Marie. Dictionnaire Abrege de Peinture & d'Architecture, 2 vols. (Fr.). Kr.100.00. Minkoff.

Diccionario de Pintura, 4 vols, Tomo 1. 320p. (Span.). 1982. pap. 2500.00 ptas (ISBN 84-85753-69-0). Fasciculos Planeta.
Diccionario de pintura y dibujo. (Span.). 150.00 ptas. Tesoro.
Diccionario Universal del Arte y De los Artistas: Pintores, 3 vols. 934p. (Span.). 1970. Set. leatherette $76.50 (ISBN 84-252-0374-0, S-50287). French & Eur.
Dizionario delle tecniche pittoriche. (Illus.). 270p. (Ital.). 1977. L.14000.00. Castel Caltan.
Fielding, Mantle. Dictionary of American Painters, Sculptors & Engravers: Enlarged. 1974. $17.50 (ISBN 0-685-47043-1). Assoc Bk.
Maillard, Robert & Legrand, Gerard. Dictionnaire Universel de la Peinture, 6 vols. (Illus.). 3000p. (Fr.). 1976. 1800.00 F. Ste. Nouv. Littre.
Maillard, Robert, ed. Dictionnaire Universal de la Peinture, 6 vols. LC 76-479300. (Illus., Fr.). 1976. 1700.00 F (ISBN 2-850-36002-3). Soc Nouveau.
Pernety, Antoine Joseph. Dictionnaire Portatif de Peinture, Sculpture & Gravure. (Fr.). 1972. 140.00 F. Minkoff Repr.
Taubes, Frederic. Painter's Dictionary of Materials & Methods. (Illus.). 256p. 1979. pap. $7.95 (ISBN 0-8230-1336-7). Watson-Guptill.
Watelet, Claude-Henre & Levesque, Pierre-Charles. Dictionnaire des Arts de Peinture, Sculpture & Gravure, Vol. 1. (Fr.). 1972. 118.00 F. Olms Verlag.
Watelet, Claude-Henri & Levesque, Pierre-Charles. Dictionnaire des Arts de Peinture & Gravure, 5 vols. (Fr.). 1972. Kr.500.00. Minkoff Repr.
––Dictionnaire des Arts de Peinture, Sculpture & Gravure, Vol. 3. (Fr.). 1972. 118.00 F. Olms Verlag.
––Dictionnaire des Arts de Peinture, Sculpture & Gravure, Vol. 4. (Fr.). 1972. 118.00 F. Olms Verlag.
––Dictionnaire des Arts de Peinture, Sculpture & Gravure, Vol. 5. (Fr.). 1972. 118.00 F. Olms Verlag.
PAINTING–HISTORY
see also Painting, French; Painting, Italian; and similar headings
Krichbaum, Jorg & Zondergeld, Rein. Dictionary of Fantastic Art. (Pocket Art Ser.). (Illus.). 1984. pap. $5.95 (ISBN 0-8120-2110-X). Barron.
PAINTING–TECHNIQUE
Brasholz, Anton, et al. Lexikon der Anstrichtechnik: Bd 2. (Ger.). 1975. DM.58.00 (ISBN 3-7667-0338-2). Callwey.
Sponzel, Kurt & Wallenfang, Wilhelm. Lexikon der Anstrichtechnik: Bd 1. (Ger.). 1970. DM.38.00 (ISBN 3-7667-0169-X). Callwey.
PAINTING, CHINESE
March, Benjamin. Some Technical Terms of Chinese Painting. (Illus.). 1969. Repr. of 1935 ed. 8.00 (ISBN 0-8188-0068-2). Paragon.
PAINTING, DECORATIVE
see Art, Decorative
PAINTING, INDUSTRIAL
see House Painting; Paint also subdivision Painting under particular subjects, e.g. Automobiles–Painting
Federation of Societies on Coatings Technology. Paint-Coatings Dictionary. 632p. $50.00; members $30.00. Fed Soc Coat Tech.
National Association of Corrosion Engineers. Glossary of Terms Used in Maintenance Painting. $2.00 (6D165). Natl Corrosion Eng.
Sponzel, Kurt. Lexikon der Anstrichtechnik, Vol. 1. 3rd ed. (Ger.). 1970. $30.00 (ISBN 3-7667-0169-X, M-7279). French & Eur.
PAINTING, ITALIAN
Dictionnaire de la Peinture Italienne. 320p. (Fr.). 1964. $36.00 (ISBN 0-686-56822-2, M-6600). French & Eur.
Zampetti, Pietro. A Dictionary of Venetian Painters: Vol. 1, 14th & 15th Centuries. (Illus.). 1969. text ed. 36.00x (ISBN 0-85317-121-1, Pub. by A & C Black England). Humanities.

––A Dictionary of Venetian Painters: Vol. 2, 16th Century. (Illus.). 1970. text ed. 36.00x (ISBN 0-85317-171-8, Pub. by A & C Black England). Humanities.
––A Dictionary of Venetian Painters: Vol. 4, 18th Century. (Illus.). 1971. text ed. 36.00x (ISBN 0-85317-006-1, Pub. by A & C Black England). Humanities.
––A Dictionary of Venetian Painters: Vol. 5, 19th & First Decade of the 20th Century. (Illus.). 1979. text ed. 36.00x (ISBN 0-85317-035-5, Pub. by A & C Black England). Humanities.
PAINTING, MECHANICAL
see Painting, Industrial
PAINTING, MODERN–20TH CENTURY
Krichbaum, Jorg. Dumonts Kleines Lexikon der Phantastischen Malerei. LC 77-579484. (Illus.). 329p. (Ger.). 1977. write for info. (ISBN 3-770-10908-2). DuMont Buchverlag.
Nouveau Dictionnaire de la Peinture Moderne. 416p. (Fr.). 1963. $47.50 (ISBN 0-686-57270-X, F-10800). French & Eur.
PAINTING, RELIGIOUS
see Christian Art and Symbolism
PAINTINGS, ABSTRACT
see Art, Modern–20th Century
PAINTINGS, ITALIAN
Dictionnaire de la Peinture Italie. (Illus.). 320p. (Ital.). 1964. 90.00 F. Hazan.
PAINTINGS, MODERN
see Art, Modern–20th Century
PAINTS
see Paint
PAIUTE INDIANS
see Indians of North America–Southwest, New
PAKHTO LANGUAGE
see Pushto Language
PALEOASIATIC LANGUAGES
see Hyperborean Languages
PALEOBIOLOGY
see Paleontology
PALEOETHNOGRAPHY
see Archaeology
PALEOGRAPHY
Chassant, Alphonse A. Dictionnaire des Abbreviations Latines et Francaises Usitees dans les Inscriptions Lapidaires et Metalliques, les Manuscrits et les Chartes de Moyen Age. 5th ed. LC 73-3365. (Illus., Fr.). 1973. Repr. of 1884 ed. lib. bdg. $22.50 (ISBN 0-8337-0547-4). B Franklin.
Migne, J. P., ed. Dictionnaire de Paleographie, de Cryptographie, de Dactylologie. (Nouvelle Encyclopedie Theologique Ser.: Vol. 47). 668p. (Fr.). Repr. of 1854 ed. lib. bdg. $85.00x (ISBN 0-89241-285-2). Caratzas Pub Co.
Walther, Johann L. Lexicon Diplomaticum Abbreviationes Syllabarum et Vocum in Diplomatibus et Codicibus a Seculo Octo a Sextum-Decimum Usque Occurentes Exponens, 2 vols. in 1. folio ed. (Lat.). 1967. Repr. of 1756 ed. $87.00 (ISBN 0-8337-3680-9). B Franklin.
PALEONTOLOGY
Jehan, L. F. Dictionnaire De Cosmogonie et De Paleontologie. Migne, J. P., ed. (Nouvelle Encyclopedie Theologique Ser.: Vol. 48). 732p. (Fr.). Repr. of 1854 ed. lib. bdg. $93.00x (ISBN 0-89241-286-0). Caratzas Pub Co.
Lehmann, Ulrich. Palaeontologisches Woerterbuch. (Ger.). 1977. pap. $15.95 (ISBN 3-423-03039-9, M-7577, Pub. by Dtv). French & Eur.
––Palaeontologisches Woerterbuch. 324p. (Ger.). 1977. $46.50 (ISBN 3-432-83572-8, M-7578, Pub. by F. Enke); pap. $15.95. French & Eur.
––Palaeontologisches Woerterbuch. 324p. (Ger.). 1977. $46.50 (ISBN 3-432-83572-8); pap. $15.95 (ISBN 0-686-56636-X). Enke.
––Palaontologisches Woerterbuch. LC 77-560773. viii, 439p. (Ger.). 1977. DM.18.80 (ISBN 3-432-83572-8). Enke.
PALEONTOLOGY, ZOOLOGICAL
see Paleontology
PALEOZOOLOGY
see Paleontology

PALESTINE–ANTIQUITIES
Young, Robert. Young's Analytical Concordance to the Bible. 1955. $19.95 (ISBN 0-8028-8084-3); deluxe ed. $22.95 (ISBN 0-8028-8085-1). Eerdmans.

PALI LANGUAGE
Budd Hadatta Mahathera, A. Pali-English Dictionary. (Pali & Eng.). 22.50 (ISBN 0-87557-056-9, 056-9). Saphrograph.

Carroll, Vern & Soulik, Tobias. Nukuoro Lexicon. LC 73-78975. (PALI Language Texts: Polynesia). 859p. (Orig., Pali.). 1973. pap. text ed. $17.50x (ISBN 0-8248-0250-0). UH Pr.

Childers, Robert. A Dictionary of the Pali language. LC 80-402603. xii, 624p. (Pali & Eng.). 1979. Rs.240.00. Orient Bk Dist.

Davids, T. Rhys. The Pali Text Society's Pali-English Dictionary. 753p. (Pali & Eng.). 1966. Repr. of 1925 ed. 67.50x (ISBN 0-86013-059-2). Intl Pubns Serv.

Lieber, Michael D. & Dikepa, Kalio H. Kapingamarangi Lexicon. LC 73-90855. (Pali Language Texts: Polynesia). 434p. (Orig., Pali.). 1974. pap. text ed. $15.00x (ISBN 0-8248-0304-3). UH Pr.

Sohn, Ho-Min & Tawerilmang, Anthony F. Woleaian-English Dictionary. (Pali Language Texts: Micronesia). 382p. (Pali & Eng.). 1976. pap. text ed. $14.00x (ISBN 0-8248-0415-5). UH Pr.

PALLET SYSTEMS
see Pallets (Shipping, Storage, etc.)

PALLETIZED UNIT LOADS
see Pallets (Shipping, Storage, Etc.)

PALLETS (SHIPPING, STORAGE, ETC.)
American Society of Mechanical Engineers. Pallet Definitions & Terminology: MH1.1.2-1978. $4.00 (M00073); members $3.20. ASME.

PALMISTRY
St. Germain. The Palmistic Dictionary. (Illus.). 118p. 1980. Repr. deluxe ed. $69.85 (ISBN 0-89901-017-2). Found Class Reprints.

PAN-HISPANISM
Clemente, Zamora & Juan-Guitart, Jorge. Dialectologia Hispanoamericana. 160p. (Span.). 1982. pap. 500.00 ptas (ISBN 8-47455-040-8). Almar Edns.

PANJABI LANGUAGE
Pradeeps Standard Oxford Dictionary: English to English, Panjabi & Hindi, with Pronunciations & Idioms. 1983. $15.00x (ISBN 0-8364-0991-4, Pub. by Pradeep Co). South Asia Bks.

Rabinovich, I. S. Pandzhabsko-Russkii Slovar. 1039p. (Rus.). 1961. $6.95 (Pub. by GINS). Four Continent.

PAPACY–HISTORY
Poussin, J. C. & Garnier, J. C. Dictionnaire de la Tradition Pontificale, Patristique et Conciliaire, 2 vols. Migne, J. P., ed. (Troisieme et Derniere Encyclopedie Theologique Ser.: Vol. 12-13). 1464p. (Fr.). Repr. of 1855 ed. lib. bdg. $186.00x (ISBN 0-89241-296-8). Caratzas Pub Co.

PAPAGO INDIANS
see Indians of North America–Southwest, New

PAPAGO LANGUAGE
Mathiot, Madeleine. A Dictionary of Papago Usage: Vol. I, B-K. (Language Science Monographs: No. 8-1). 504p. (Papago.). 1974. pap. text ed. 55.00x (ISBN 0-686-27742-2). Mouton.

Saxton, Dean & Saxton, Lucille. Papago & Pima to English, English to Papago & Pima Dictionary. 2nd ed. Cherry, R. L., ed. (Papago, Pima & Eng.). 1983. text ed. $19.95x (ISBN 0-8165-0826-7). U of Ariz Pr.

PAPER
see also Paper Coatings
Bogdan, Istvan. Papirkeszltoink Mestersegszavai. LC 80-482778. 38p. (Hungarian.). 1979. write for info. (ISBN 9-638-27102-7). MTESZ.

--Papirkeszltoink Mestersegszavai. LC 80-482778. (Papers). 38p. (Hungarian.). 1979. write for info. (ISBN 9-638-27102-7). MTESZ.

PAPER BOX INDUSTRY
Rosa, Manuel A., ed. Corrugating Defect Terminology: Fabrication Manuel for Corrugated Box Plants. 4th, rev. ed. (Illus.). 236p. 1982. pap. $49.95 (ISBN 0-89852-403-2, 01 01R 103). TAPPI.

PAPER COATINGS
Canadian Pulp & Paper Association. Paper Defect Terminology - Coated Papers & Boards. 10p. $2.00; members $1.00. CN Pulp & Paper.

Heiser, Edward J. & Allswede, Jerry L., eds. Blade Coating Defect Terminology. (Illus.). 53p. 1982. pap. $24.95 (ISBN 0-686-43234-7, 01 01 R094). TAPPI.

PAPER FINISHING
see also Paper Coatings
A Glossary of Terms Used in Refining. 1980. $2.00 (012-3); members $1.33. TAPPI.

Surface Strength Terminology. 1965. $13.00 (399-3); members $8.67. TAPPI.

PAPER INDUSTRY
see Paper Making and Trade

PAPER MAKING AND TRADE
see also Book Industries and Trade; Wood Pulp Industry
Bibliography of Papermaking Terminology. 1970. $2.00 (019-1); members $1.33. TAPPI.

Bruno, Michael H., ed. Glossary of Paper Terms for Web & Sheet-Fed Offset Printing. (TAPPI PRESS Reports). 48p. 1971. $4.95 (01-01-R041). TAPPI.

Canadian Pulp & Paper Association. Glossary of Printing Terms for the Papermaker. 103p. 1980. $10.00; members $8.00. CN Pulp & Paper.

Definitions of Graphic Arts Terms. 1964. $4.00 (399-2); members $2.67. TAPPI.

Evanoff, Philip C. & Gerlach, Werner, eds. Surface Strength Terminology. (Illus.). 65p. 1983. pap. price not set (ISBN 0-89852-411-3). TAPPI.

Finney, Frederick M. Dictionary of Syngraphics & Associated Terms. 96p. 1983. $8.95 (ISBN 0-89421-031-9). Challenge Pr.

Garlock, Trisha. Glossary of Papermaking Terms. 30p. 1983. pap. $5.00. World Print Coun.

Glaister, Geoffrey. Glaister's Glossary of the Book: Terms Used in Paper-Making, Printing, Bookbinding, & Publishing. LC 76-47975. 1979. $75.00 (ISBN 0-520-03364-7). U of Cal Pr.

Graphic & Paper Industry. (Eng. & Swedish.). 1982. Kr.159.00 (ISBN 91-86236-06-7). EC Print AB.

Heiser, Edward J. & Allswede, Jerry L., eds. Blade Coating Defect Terminology. (Illus.). 53p. 1982. pap. $24.95 (ISBN 0-686-43234-7, 01 01 R094). TAPPI.

Moisture Content of Paper Terminology & Conversion. 1966. $1.00 (017-7); members $0.67. TAPPI.

Regulating Systems Definitions & Standardizations of Terms. 1965. $6.00 (403-9); members $4.00. TAPPI.

Rosa, Manuel A., ed. Corrugating Defect Terminology: Fabrication Manuel for Corrugated Box Plants. 4th, rev. ed. (Illus.). 236p. 1982. pap. $49.95 (ISBN 0-89852-403-2, 01 01R 103). TAPPI.

Screening Symbols, Terminology & Equations. 1974. $4.00 (003-4); members $2.67. TAPPI.

Seaburg, S. L., et al, eds. Paper Oriented Glossary Covering Advanced Process Control Terminology. 351p. 1970. $14.95 (01-01-R031). TAPPI.

Surface Strength Terminology. 1965. $13.00 (399-3); members $8.67. TAPPI.

Technical Association of the Pulp & Paper Industry Winding Committee. Roll Defect Terminology: Paper Finishing & Converting. Gilmore, William, ed. 55p. 1977. $34.95 (01-08-T016). TAPPI.

Van Derveer, Paul D. & Haas, Leonard E., eds. International Glossary of Technical Terms for the Pulp & Paper Industry. LC 74-20168. (A Pulp & Paper Book). 238p. 1976. 35.00 (ISBN 0-87930-037-X). Miller Freeman.

Weitzel, Wolfgang. Technical Dictionary Pulp & Paper, 2 vols. 2nd ed. Incl. Vol. 1. English-German. 351p (ISBN 0-8002-2073-0); Vol. 2. German-English (ISBN 0-8002-2074-9). (Ger. & Eng.). 1971-1972. 45.00x ea. Intl Pubns Serv.

PAPER MONEY
Finney, Frederick M. Dictionary of Syngraphics & Associated Terms. 96p. 1983. $8.95 (ISBN 0-89421-031-9). Challenge Pr.

Pick, Albert. Papiergeld-Lexikon. LC 79-359190. (Illus.). 416p. (Ger.). 1978. DM.68.00 (ISBN 3-570-05022-X). Mosaik Verlag.

PAPUAN LANGUAGES
see also Melanesian Languages
Franklin, K. J., et al. A Kewa Dictionary with Supplemental Grammatical & Anthropological Materials. LC 81-453278. (Illus.). 514p. (Kewa & Eng.). 1978. Aus.$16.00 (ISBN 0-85883-182-1). Linguistic Circle.

Z'graggen, J. A. A Comparative Word List of the Rai Coast Languages, Madang Province, Papua New Guinea. LC 82-106696. (Illus.). xv, 181p. (Papuan & Madang.). 1980. pap. write for info. (ISBN 0-85883-232-1). Linguistic Circle.

--A Comparative Word List of the Southern Adelbert Range Languages, Madang Province, Papua New Guinea. LC 82-106836. (Illus.). xvi, 97p. (Papuan & Madang.). 1980. pap. write for info. (ISBN 0-85883-234-8). Linguistic Circle.

Z'graggon, J. A. A Comparative Word List of the Northern Adelbert Range Languages, Madang Province, Papua New Guinea. LC 82-106653. xvii, 178p. (Papuan & Madang.). 1980. pap. write for info. (ISBN 0-85883-228-3). Linguistic Circle.

PARABOLE
see Simile

PARAPSYCHOLOGY
see Psychical Research

PARASITIC WORMS
see Worms, Intestinal and Parasitic

PARASITOLOGY
see also Veterinary Medicine
Lombardero, O. J. Glosario de terminos parasitologicos. 59p. (Span.). write for info. EUDEBA.

PARBATE LANGUAGE
see Nepali Language

PARENT-TEACHER RELATIONSHIPS
Groothoff, Hans H., et al, eds. Lexikon fuer Eltern & Erzieher. 306p. (Ger.). 1977. DM.9.80 (ISBN 3-579-03640-8). Gutersloher V.

--Lexikon fuer Eltern & Erzieher. (Ger.). 1973. DM.24.00 (ISBN 3-7831-0410-6). Kreuz Verlag.

PARENTS AND TEACHERS
see Parent-Teacher Relationships

PARIS
Franklin, Afred L. Dictionnaire Historique Des Arts, Metiers & Professions Exerces Dans Paris Depuis Le Treizieme Siecle. (Biblio. & Ref. Ser.: No. 198). (Fr.). 1968. Repr. of 1906 ed. $49.00 (ISBN 0-8337-1231-4); $40.00 (ISBN 0-685-06747-5). B Franklin.

PARIS–HISTORY
Hurtaut, Magny. Dictionnaire Historique de la Ville de Paris & de ses Environs, 4 vols. 3084p. (Fr.). 1977. 560.00 F. Minkoff Repr.

PARISHES
Poulbriere, Jean-Baptiste. Dictionnaire des Paroisses de la Correze, 3. (Fr.). 60.00 F. Correze, Ste Scientifique.

PARK, MUNGO, 1771-1806
Tames, R. Mungo Park. (Clarendon Biography Ser.). (Illus.). 1973. pap. 3.50 (ISBN 0-912728-69-8). Newbury Bks.

PARONYMS
see also Puns and Punning

Fonda Publicaciones U. P. T. C., ed. Diccionario de paronimos. 112p. (Span.). 1972. Col.$12.00. U. Pedagogica y Tec.

PARTICLES (NUCLEAR PHYSICS)
Leschonski, K. & Carter, F. T., eds. Elsevier's Dictionary of Particle Technology. (Ger. & Eng.). 1978. $68.00 (ISBN 0-444-41746-X). Elsevier.

PASCAL, BLAISE, 1623-1662
Davidson, Hugh M. & Dube, Pierre H., eds. A Concordance to the Pascal's Pensees. LC 75-16808. (Cornell Concordances Ser.). 1488p. 1975. $65.00x (ISBN 0-8014-0972-1). Cornell U Pr.

PASSIONS
see Emotions

PASTIMES
see Games; Sports

PASTORAL COUNSELING
Here are entered works on the clergyman as the counselor.
see also Counseling
Adams, Jay E. Christian Counselor's Wordbook. 1981. pap. $1.95 (ISBN 0-8010-0172-2). Baker Bk.

PASTURES
see also Grasses
Glossary of Terms Used in Pasture & Range Survey Research, Ecology, Management. 153p. 1976. pap. $14.00 (ISBN 0-685-68955-7, F925, FAO). Unipub.

PATENT LAWS AND LEGISLATION–JAPAN
Wilds, Thomas. Glossary of Japanese Patent Law Terms: Japanese-English-Japanese. LC 76-372712. 1979. pap. 30.00x (ISBN 0-930624-01-7). Marlin.

PATENT PRACTICE
Vuexkull, J. & Reich, H. J. Dictionary of Patent Practice. 258p. (Ger. & Eng.). 1977. $57.00 (ISBN 3-452-18239-8, M-7107). French & Eur.

PATENTS
see also Inventions; Trade-Marks
Klaften, B. & Allison, F. C. Woerterbuch der Patentfachsprache. 4th ed. (Eng. & Ger., Dictionary of Technical Terms of Patents). 1971. $54.00 (ISBN 3-87910-105-1, M-6974). French & Eur.

Klaften, Berthold. Woerterbuch der Patentfachsprache-Patent Terminological Dictionary: English-German & German-English. 4th ed. LC 76-866071. 568p. (Eng. & Ger.). 1971. 32.50x (ISBN 3-87910-105-1). Intl Pubns Serv.

Szendy, Gyorgy L. Woerterbuch des Pantentwesens in 5 Sprachen. (Ger., Eng., Fr., Span. & Rus., Dictionary of Patents in Five Languages). 1974. $76.00 (ISBN 3-18-400269-1, M-6935). French & Eur.

V. Uexkuell, Detlev. Woerterbuch der Patentpraxis. (Ger. & Eng., Dictionary of Patent Practice). 1976. $57.00 (ISBN 3-452-18239-8, M-6973). French & Eur.

PATHOLOGICAL BOTANY
see Plant Diseases

PATHOLOGICAL CHEMISTRY
see Chemistry, Medical and Pharmaceutical

PATHOLOGICAL HISTOLOGY
see Histology, Pathological

PATHOLOGICAL PSYCHOLOGY
see Psychology, Pathological

PATHOLOGY
see also Chemistry, Clinical; Diagnosis; Histology, Pathological; Medicine; Therapeutics
Smiddy, F. G. Dictionary of General Pathology. 384p. 1980. pap. text ed. $15.95x (ISBN 0-8464-1247-0). Beekman Pubs.

--Dictionary of General Pathology. 336p. 1980. $29.00x (ISBN 0-272-79585-2, Pub. by Pitman Bks England). State Mutual Bk.

PATHOLOGY, DENTAL
see Teeth–Diseases

PATHOLOGY, VEGETABLE
see Plant Diseases

PATIENTS
see Sick

PATRIARCHS AND PATRIARCHATE

Poussin, J. C. & Garnier, J. C. Dictionnaire de la Tradition Pontificale, Patristique et Conciliaire, 2 vols. Migne, J. P., ed. (Troisieme et Derniere Encyclopedie Theologique Ser.: Vol. 12-13). 1464p. (Fr.). Repr. of 1855 ed. lib. bdg. $186.00x (ISBN 0-89241-296-8). Caratzas Pub Co.

PATRIARCHY
see Family

PAWNEE INDIANS
see Indians of North America–The West

PEBBLES
see Rocks

PEDAGOGY
see Education; Teaching

PEDIATRIC DERMATOLOGY
Verbov, Julian & Morley, Neil. Color Atlas of Pediatric Dermatology. (Illus.). 157p. 1983. text ed. 47.50 (ISBN 0-397-58287-0, Lippincott Medical). Lippincott.

PEDIATRIC PSYCHIATRY
see Child Psychiatry

PEDIGREES
see Genealogy; Heraldry

PEDOLOGY (CHILD STUDY)
see Children

PEDOLOGY (SOIL SCIENCE)
see Soil Science

PENAL CODES
see Criminal Law

PENAL INSTITUTIONS
see Prisons

PENAL LAW
see Criminal Law

PENALTIES (CRIMINALS LAW)
see Punishment

PENITENTIARIES
see Prisons

PENNSYLVANIA GERMAN DIALECT
Lambert, Marcus. Pennsylvania German Dictionary. (Illus.). 188p. (Ger.). pap. $15.00 (ISBN 0-916838-07-2). Schiffer.

Lambert, Marcus B. A Dictionary of Non-English Words of the Pennsylvania German Dialect. 1977. 15.00 (ISBN 0-686-79892-9). Penn German Soc.

PENOLOGY
see Prisons; Punishment

PEOPLE'S REPUBLIC OF BENIN
see Benin

PERFORMING ARTS
Giteau, Cecile. Dictionnaire des Arts du Spectacle: Theatre, Cinema, Cirque, Danse, Radio... 456p. (Fr., Eng. & Ger.). 1970. $52.50 (ISBN 0-686-57302-1, M-6276). French & Eur.

Wilmeth, Don B. The Language of American Popular Entertainment: A Glossary of Argot, Slang, & Terminology. LC 80-14795. xxi, 305p. 1981. lib. bdg. 29.95 (ISBN 0-313-22497-8, WEN/). Greenwood.

PERFUMES
Dictionnaires des Parfums de France & de Lignes pour Hommes. 4th ed. 158p. (Fr.). 1972. 25.00 F. Ed.

PERIGORD–DESCRIPTION AND TRAVEL
Miremont, Pierre. Glossaire del Perigord Negre. (Fr.). 1974. 55.00 F. P. Miremont.

PERIMETRY
International Council of Ophthalmology, ed. Perimetric Standards & Perimetric Glossary. 135p. 45.00 (ISBN 90-6193-161-4, Pub. by Junk Pubs Netherlands). Kluwer Academic.

International Council of Opthalmology, ed. Perimetric Standards & Perimetric Glossary. 1979. lib. bdg. 29.00 (ISBN 90-6193-600-4, Pub. by Junk Pubs Netherlands). Kluwer Academic.

PERIODONTIA
Sinsoilliez, Robert. Lexique des Termes de Parodontologie de Microbiologie Parodontale et Buccale et de Sciences Fondamentales. 112p. (Fr.). 1973. pap. $15.95 (ISBN 0-686-56751-X, M-6518). French & Eur.

PERSIAN GULF STATES
Anthony, John D. Historical & Cultural Dictionary of the Sultanate of Oman & the Emirates of Eastern Arabia. LC 76-42216. (Historical & Cultural Dictionaries of Asia Ser.: No. 9). 1976. $13.00 (ISBN 0-8108-0975-3). Scarecrow.

PERSIAN LANGUAGE
Learn Persian for English Speakers. (Persian.). pap. 10.50 (ISBN 0-87557-059-3, 059-3). Saphrograph.

Wood. Two Hundred One Persian Verbs - Arabic Script. (Arabic & Persian.). 1984. $9.95 (ISBN 0-8120-2562-8). Barron.

––Two Hundred One Persian Verbs - Romanization. (Persian.). 1984. $9.95 (ISBN 0-8120-2563-6). Barron.

PERSIAN LANGUAGE–DICTIONARIES
Addi, Al-Sayyid. Dictionary of Persian Loan Words in the Arabic Language. (Persian & Arabic.). 1980. $21.00x (ISBN 0-86685-128-3). Intl Bk Ctr.

Al-Sayyid'Addi Shir. A Dictionary of Persian Loan Words in the Arabic Language. 194p. (Arabic & Persian.). $21.00 (128-3). Intl Bk Ctr.

Bodrogligeti. The Persian Vocabulary of the Codex Cumanicus. (Persian & Eng.). 1971. 15.00 (ISBN 0-9960008-4-4, Pub. by Kaido Hungary). Heyden.

Coletti Gruenbaum, Hanne. Dizionario persiano-italiano classico, moderno, familiare. xvi, 960p. (Persian & Ital.). 1978. L.25000.00. Coletti.

Field, Claud. Dictionary of Arabic-Persian Quotes. (Arabic, Persian & Eng.). $18.00x (ISBN 0-86685-168-2). Intl Bk Ctr.

Lambton, Ann K. Persian Vocabulary. (Persian.). 1954-1962. pap. $24.95x (ISBN 0-521-09154-3). Cambridge U Pr.

Persidsko-Russkii & Russko-Persidskii Obshche-Ekonomicheskii & Vneshnetorgovyi Slovar. 596p. (Persian & Rus.). 1957. $2.95 (Pub. by Vneshtorgizdat). Four Continent.

PERSIAN LANGUAGE–DICTIONARIES–ENGLISH
Boyle, John A. Persian-English Dictionary, Romanized. (Persian & Eng.). 19.50 (ISBN 0-87557-057-7, 057-7). Saphrograph.

Fazl-i-Ali. Dictionary of Persian & English Languages. 668p. (Persian & Eng.). 1979. Repr. of 1885 ed. 39.00 (ISBN 0-89684-266-5, Pub. by Cosmo Pubns India). Orient Bk Dist.

Haim, S. Persian-English, English-Persian Shorter Dictionary, 2 vols. rev., enl. ed. (Persian & Eng.). Set. 50.00 (ISBN 0-686-77974-6). Heinman.

Steingass, F. Comprehensive Persian-English Dictionary. 1540p. (Persian & Eng.). 1975. $65.00x (ISBN 0-86685-130-5). Intl Bk Ctr.

––A Comprehensive Persian-English Dictionary. (Persian & Eng.). 1973. $35.00x (ISBN 0-88386-187-9). South Asia Bks.

PERSIAN LANGUAGE–OLD PERSIAN
see Old Persian Language

PERSONAL BEAUTY
see Beauty, Personal

PERSONAL CLEANLINESS
see Hygiene

PERSONAL COMBAT
see Hand-To-Hand Fighting

PERSONAL COMPUTERS
see Microcomputers

PERSONAL FILMS
see Amateur Moving-Pictures

PERSONAL HEALTH
see Health

PERSONAL INJURIES
see also Sports–Accidents and Injuries
Touati, Maurice A. Lexique Francais de la Reparation Juridique du Dommage Corporel. LC 76-677444. 265p. (Fr.). 1976. 68.00 F (ISBN 2-224-00307-2). Maloine.

PERSONAL NAMES
see Names, Personal

PERSONAL RADIOTELEPHONE
see Citizens Band Radio

PERSONNEL MANAGEMENT
see also Job Satisfaction
also specific subjects with or without the subdivisions Administration or Personnel Management, e.g. Hospitals–Administration; School Personnel Management
Becker, Esther, ed. Dictionary of Personnel & Industrial Relations. 1958. $10.00 (ISBN 0-8022-0088-5). Philos Lib.

Gaugler, Eduard, ed. Handwoerterbuch des Personalwesens. LC 76-483335. (Illus., Ger.). 1975. DM.220.00 (ISBN 3-791-08009-1). Poeschel Verlag.

Schafritz, Jay M. Dictionary of Personnel Management & Labor Relations. LC 79-24632. (Orig.). 1980. 29.00 (ISBN 0-935610-09-X). Moore Pub IL.

PERU
Bendezu Neyra, Guillermo E. Argo Limeno. LC 78-101067. 339p. (Span., Lima). 1977. write for info. Libreria.

Caceres Freire, Julian. Diccionario de Regionalismos de la Provincia de la Rioja. (Span.). $42.50 (ISBN 0-686-56673-4, S-33066). French & Eur.

Diccionario Esedal de la legislacion peruana. 552p. (Span.). 1972. S/.200.00. Esedal.

Landerman, Peter. Vocabulario Quechua del Pastaza. (Peruvian Linguistic Ser.: No. 8). 165p. (Span.). 1973. pap. $2.50x (ISBN 0-88312-664-8); microfiche $2.25 (ISBN 0-88312-366-5). Summer Inst Ling.

Paz Soldan Y Unanue, Pedro & Nunez, Estuardo. Diccionario de Peruanismos, 2 vols. LC 76-460366. xxx, 399p. (Span.). 1975. write for info. Edns Peisa.

Quesada Castillo, Felix. Lexico Quechua de Cajamarca. LC 77-554130. (Eng., Quechua & Span., Lima, Peru). 1976. write for info. Centro Invest.

PERU–HISTORY
Alisky, Marvin. Historical Dictionary of Peru. LC 79-16488. (Latin American Historical Dictionaries Ser.: No. 20). 163p. 1979. $13.00 (ISBN 0-8108-1235-5). Scarecrow.

PETROCHEMICAL INDUSTRY
see Petroleum Chemicals Industry

PETROGRAPHY
see Petrology

PETROLEUM
see also Oil Fields
Al-Khatib, Ahmad S. A New Dictionary of Petroleum & the Oil Industry. LC 75-968070. xv, 577p. (Eng. & Arabic.). 1975. Le.12.50. Lib Liban.

Association of Desk & Derrick Clubs of America. D & D Standard Oil Abbreviator. 2nd ed. LC 72-96172. 230p. 9.50x (ISBN 0-87814-017-4). Pennwell Pub.

Kedrinskii, Vsevolod V. Anglo-Russkii Slovar po Khimii i Pererabotke Nefti. LC 80-467970. 767p. (Eng. & Rus.). 1979. 8.36 Rub. Russkii Iazyk.

Moureau, Magdeleine. Dictionnaire Technique du Petrole. 2nd ed. LC 79-122883. xv, 946p. (Eng. & Fr.). 1979. write for info. (ISBN 2-7108-0361-5). Technip.

Papok, K. K. & Ragozin, N. A. Tekhnicheskii Slovar Spravochnik Po Toplivu & Maslam. 766p. (Rus.). 1963. $6.50 (Pub. by Gostoptekhizdat). Four Continent.

––Tekhnicheskii Slovar Spravochnik po Toplivu i Maslam. 766p. (Rus.). 1963. $6.50 (Pub. by Gostoptekhizda r). Four Continent.

PETROLEUM–REFINING
Pinkevich, A. A., et al. Ispansko-Russkii Slovar Po Dobyche i Pererabotke Nefti. 424p. (Span. & Rus.). 1966. $6.20 (Pub. by Lenizdat). Four Continent.

PETROLEUM CHEMICALS
Applied Technical Dictionary: Oil Processing & Petrochemistry. (Eng. , Ger. , Fr. , Rus. & Slovak.). 1981. $50.00x (ISBN 0-569-08533-0, Pub. by Collets). State Mutual Bk.

Leipnitz. Erdoelverarbeitung-Petrolchemie. 268p. (Eng., Ger., Fr. & Rus.). 1982. DM.60.00. Brandstetter.

Leipnitz, W. Technical Dictionary of Petrochemistry. 240p. (Ger., Eng., Fr. & Rus.). 1976. $48.00 (ISBN 0-686-56469-3, M-7640, Pub. by Vlg. Technik). French & Eur.

PETROLEUM CHEMICALS INDUSTRY
Applied Technical Dictionary: Oil Processing & Petrochemistry. (Eng. , Ger. , Fr. , Rus. & Slovak.). 1981. $50.00x (ISBN 0-569-08533-0, Pub. by Collets). State Mutual Bk.

PETROLEUM ENGINES
see Gas and Oil Engines

PETROLEUM GAS, LIQUEFIED
see Liquefied Petroleum Gas

PETROLEUM INDUSTRY AND TRADE
see also Oil Industries; Petroleum–Refining; Petroleum Chemicals Industry
American Petroleum Institute. Thesaurus. 17th ed. 1980. $150.00; nonprofit institutions $50.00. Am Petroleum.

Langenkamp, R. D. Handbook of Oil Industry Terms & Phrases. 3rd ed. 250p. 1981. 23.95x (ISBN 0-87814-171-5). Pennwell Pub.

Vocabulary. (Manual of Petroleum Measurement Standards: Chap. 1). 1977. $5.00 (85225239). Am Petroleum.

PETROLEUM INDUSTRY AND TRADE–DICTIONARIES
Applied Technical Dictionary: Oil Processing & Petrochemistry. (Eng. , Ger. , Fr. , Rus. & Slovak.). 1981. $50.00x (ISBN 0-569-08533-0, Pub. by Collets). State Mutual Bk.

Arnould, M. & Zubini, F. English-French Petroleum Dictionary. 267p. (Eng. & Fr.). 1982. $75.00x (ISBN 0-86010-374-9, Pub. by Graham & Trotman England). State Mutual Bk.

Arnould, Michel & Zubini, Fabio. English-French Petroleum Dictionary. 267p. (Eng. & Fr.). 1983. pap. $37.00x (ISBN 0-8448-1432-6). Crane-Russak Co.

Bolo, Helene & Cavrois, Philippe. Dictionnaire de l'offshore Petrole Gaz. (Illus.). 360p. (Fr.). 1977. 321.00 F. S. C. M.

A Dictionary of Petroleum Terms. (Eng., Austin). 1979. $7.00 (1-30020). U of TX.

Editions Technip. Glossary of Onshore & Offshore Pipelines. 320p. (Eng. & Fr.). 1979. E28.00. Graham & Trotman.

Glossaire Anglais-Francais de l'industrie petroliere. 36p. (Fr. & Eng.). 1981. pap. 6.50. Imported Bks.

Glossary of Stock Exchange, Mining & Oil Terms. LC 82-126128. 108p. 1981. pap. $6.00 (ISBN 0-9594011-0-5). Fin Analysis.

Heroux, M., et al. Lexique de l'Industrie Petroliere Ra Finage: Anglais-Francais. 163p. (Eng. & Fr.). 1979. pap. $9.95 (ISBN 0-7754-2382-3, M-9235). French & Eur.

Ketchian, S. & Desbrandes, R. Technical Petroleum Dictionary of Well-Logging, Drilling & Production Terms. 366p. 1965. $99.00x (ISBN 2-7108-0046-2, Pub. by Graham & Trotman England). State Mutual Bk.

Ketchian, S., et al, eds. Technical Petroleum Dictionary of Well-Logging, Drilling, & Production Terms. 366p. 1965. 92.00x (ISBN 0-677-61140-4). Gordon.

Ketchian, Sonia. Dictionnaire Petrolier des Techniques de Diagraphie, Forage & Production: Russe-Francais-Anglais-Allemand. (Illus.). 376p. (Rus., Fr., Eng. & Ger.). 1965. 160.00 F. Technip.

Ketchian, Sonia, ed. Technical Petroleum Dictionary of Well-Logging, Drilling & Production Terms. LC 65-74805. (Illus.). 366p. (Rus., Fr., Eng. & Ger.). 1965. 75.00x (ISBN 0-8002-2076-5). Intl Pubns Serv.

Khatib, Ahmad. A Dictionary of Petroleum & the Oil Industry. (Illus.). 550p. (Eng. & Arabic.). $40.00 (074-0). Intl Bk Ctr.

Khatib, Ahmed. English-Arabic Dictionary of Petroleum Terms & the Oil Industry. 1975. $40.00x (ISBN 0-86685-074-0). Intl Bk Ctr.

Kramer, Karlheinz. Erdoel Lexicon. 5th ed. (Eng. & Ger., Lexicon of Petroleum). 1972. $48.00 (ISBN 3-7785-0233-6, M-7366, Pub. by Heuthig). French & Eur.

Langenkamp, Robert D., ed. Illustrated Petroleum: Reference Dictionary. 2nd ed. (Illus.). 584p. 1982. 45.95x (ISBN 0-87814-160-X, P-4263). Pennwell Pub.

Leecraft, Jodie, ed. A Dictionary of Petroleum Terms. 3rd ed. LC 83-61652. (Illus.). 177p. 1983. text ed. $16.00 (ISBN 0-88698-000-3); pap. text ed. $9.00 (ISBN 0-88698-001-1). PETEX.

Leipnitz, E. Dictionary of Petroleum-Industry & Petroleum Chemistry. (Polyglot.). 1979. $40.80 (ISBN 3-87097-073-1). Adler.

Leipnitz, W. Woerterbuch Erdoelverarbeitung-Petrolchemie. (Eng., Ger., Fr. & Rus., Dictionary of Petroleum-processing). 1977. $48.00 (ISBN 0-686-56609-2, M-6925). French & Eur.

Leipnitz, Walter. Erdolverarbeitung und Petrolchemie: A Dictionary of Crude Oil Processing & Petroleum Chemistry English-German-French-Russian. (Eng., Ger., Fr. & Rus.). 1976. 60.00x (ISBN 3-87097-073-1). Intl Learn Syst.

Mendez. Diccionario Basico de la Industria del Petroleo & Derivados. (Eng. & Span. & Fr.). 1981. 1500.00 ptas (ISBN 8-42831-097-1). Paraninfo.

Mendez, ed. Diccionario Tecnico de la Industria del Petroleo y Derivados. 588p. (Span.). 1980. $44.95 (ISBN 84-283-1097-1, S-37582). French & Eur.

Mendez Manzano, Augustin. Basic Dictionary of the Petroleum Industry. 588p. (Eng., Fr. & Span.). 1980. $25.00. Imported Bks.

--Diccionario basico de la industria del petroleo. 592p. (Span.). 1981. pap. 1500.00 ptas (ISBN 84-283-1097-1). Paraninfo.

Moureau, M. & Brace, G. Dictionary of Petroleum Technology: English-French, French-English. Rev. ed. 946p. (Fr. & Eng.). 1979. $115.00. Imported Bks.

Moureau, Madeleine & Rouge, Janine. Dictionnaire Technique des Termes Utilises dans l'industrie du Petrole: Anglais-Francais. (Illus.). 914p. (Eng. & Fr.). 1977. 202.00 F. Technip.

Moureau, Magdaleine & Brace, Gerald, eds. Dictionary of Petroleum Technology-Dictionnaire Technique Du Petrol: English-French - French-English. rev. ed. LC 79-122883. (Collection Des Dictionnaires Techniques: No. 1). 975p. (Eng. & Fr.). 1979. 130.00x (ISBN 2-7108-0361-5). Intl Pubns Serv.

Palmer, Susan R., ed. Petroleum Industry Glossary. 1982. $32.00 (ISBN 0-89931-032-X). Inst Energy.

Pinkevich, A. & Amelin, B. Diccionario Espanol-Ruso de le Prospeccion y Refinacion del Petroleo. Dobriansky, A. F., ed. 424p. (Span. & Rus.). 1966. $12.50 (ISBN 0-686-92531-9, S-37368). French & Eur.

Stoliarov, D. E., ed. Russian-English Oil-Field Dictionary. 432p. (Rus. & Eng.). 1983. 27.00 (ISBN 0-08-028169-9). Pergamon.

Thesaurus Petrole. 288p. (Fr.). 1971. 154.00 F. Technip.

Tver, David F. & Berry, Richard W. The Petroleum Dictionary. 379p. 1980. text ed. $22.50 (ISBN 0-686-65585-0). Van Nos Reinhold.

--Petroleum Dictionary. 384p. 1982. pap. text ed. $16.95 (ISBN 0-442-28529-9). Van Nos Reinhold.

PETROLEUM REFINING
see Petroleum–Refining

PETROLOGY
see also Crystallography; Geology; Mineralogy; Rocks
also varieties of rock, e.g. Quartz

San Miguel de la Camara, Maximino. Diccionario petrografico: Vol 1, Rocas eruptivas. 174p. (Span.). 1944. $60.00 (CSIC). Inst. Jose Acosta y Lucas Mallada.

PEUL LANGUAGE
see Fulah Language

PEWTER

Mory, Ludwig, et al. Brukmanns' Zinn-Lexikon. LC 79-351818. (Illus.). 324p. (Ger.). 1977. DM.58.00 (ISBN 3-765-41361-5). Bruckmann KG.

PHARMACEUTICAL CHEMISTRY
see Chemistry, Medical and Pharmaceutical

PHARMACOLOGY–DICTIONARIES

Blacque-Belair, Alain. Dictionnaire de Medecine Clinique Pharmacologique & Therapeutique. 2nd ed. (Illus.). 1914p. (Fr.). 1978. 196.00 F. Maloine.

Fatturosso, V. & Ritter, O. Dizionario di farmacologia clinica. Branca Ciocetti, M. A., tr. viii, 656p. (Ital.). 1976. L.185000.00. Edipem.

Kazachenok, T. G. Farmakologicheskii Slovar: Latinsko-Russkii & Russko-Latinskii. 464p. (Rus. & Lat.). 1977. $6.70 (Pub. by Vysheishaia). Four Continent.

Marler, E. E., compiled by. Pharmacological & Chemical Synonyms: A Collection of Names of Drugs, Pesticides & Other Compounds Drawn from the Medical Literature of the World. 7th ed. 1983. $76.75 (ISBN 0-444-90227-9). Elsevier.

Mason, David & Dyller, Fran. Pharmaceutical Dictionary & Reference for Prescriptions Drugs. Rev. ed. (Illus.). 270p. 1982. pap. 3.50 (ISBN 0-87216-998-7, Playboy). Putnam Pub Group.

--Pharmaceutical Dictionary & Reference 1982. LC 81-82969. 280p. (Orig.). 1982. pap. 3.50 (ISBN 0-87216-998-7). Berkley Pub.

Oweida, A. M. The New Medical-Pharmaceutical Dictionary. 2404p. (Eng. & Arabic.). 1970. Leatherette $150.00 (ISBN 0-686-92192-5, M-9766). French & Eur.

Pharmacological Dictionary. Latin-Russian, Russian-Latin. 463p. (Lat. & Rus.). 1977. $12.95 (ISBN 0-686-92090-2, M-9078). French & Eur.

Sliosberg, A. Elsevier's Dictionary of Pharmaceutical Science & Techniques, 2 vols. Incl. Vol. 1: Pharmaceutical Technology. 1968. 132.00 (ISBN 0-444-40544-5); Vol. 2: Materia Medica. 1980. $123.50 (ISBN 0-444-41664-1). Set. $255.50 (ISBN 0-686-85925-1). Elsevier.

Touitou, Yvan & Perlemuter, Leon. Dictionnaire Pratique de Pharmacologie: Clinique. 1204p. (Fr.). 1976. $99.50 (ISBN 0-686-57235-1, M-6536). French & Eur.

--Dictionnaire Pratique de Pharmacologie Clinique. 1204p. (Fr.). 1976. 209.00 F. Masson.

Verbeke, Ronald. Un Dictionnaire Critique des Drogues. 160p. (Fr.). write for info. Bourgois.

Vieillefosse, Roger. Dictionnaire de Pharmacologie Dentaire. 228p. (Fr.). 1970. 58.00 F. Maloine.

PHARMACOPOEIAS
see also Drugs; Materia Medica

US Pharmacoepial Convention. USAN & the USP Dictionary. annual $19.50. US Pharmacopeia.

PHARMACY
see also Botany, Medical; Chemistry, Medical and Pharmaceutical; Drugs; Hospitals; Materia Medica; Pharmacopoeias

Gladstone, W. J. Dictionnaire Anglais-Francais des Sciences Medicales et Paramedicales. (Eng. & Fr.). 1978. $99.95 (ISBN 0-686-57303-X, M-6277). French & Eur.

Rosenstein, E., ed. Diccionario De Especialidades Farmaceuticas. 28th Mexican ed. (Span.). 1982. pap. $52.00x (ISBN 968-460-017-8). Drug Intl Pubns.

Sliosberg, A. Elsevier's Dictionary of Pharmaceutical Science & Techniques, 2 vols. Incl. Vol. 1: Pharmaceutical Technology. 1968. 132.00 (ISBN 0-444-40544-5); Vol. 2: Materia Medica. 1980. $123.50 (ISBN 0-444-41664-1). Set. $255.50 (ISBN 0-686-85925-1). Elsevier.

PHENICIAN LANGUAGE

Fuentes Estanol, Maria J. Vocabulario fenicio. 400p. (Span.). 1980. pap. 2000.00 ptas (ISBN 84-00-04757-5). Consejo Superior.

PHILANTHROPY
see Charities; Social Service

PHILATELY AND PHILATELISTS
see Postage-Stamps–Collectors and Collecting

PHILIPPINE LANGUAGES
see also Cebu Dialect; Tagalog Language

Fabri, M. A Bibliography of Hispanic Dictionaries: Catalan, Galician, Spanish, Spanish in Latin America & the Philippines. 1979. pap. 45.00 (ISBN 0-686-77969-X). Heinman.

PHILOLOGY
see also Archaeology; Grammar, Comparative and General; Language and Languages
also specific branches of philology and literature, e.g. Classical Philology, English Philology, German Literature, Greek Literature

Baried, Baroroh, ed. Kamus Istilah Filologi. LC 78-942676. iv, 124p. (Indonesian., Jakarta). 1977. write for info. Universitas Gadjah Mada.

Compendios de Divulgacion Filologica, 11 vols. Incl. Vol. 1. Ortografia Practica Espanola. Gili Gaya, S. 104p. pap. 195.00 ptas (ISBN 84-7153-255-7); Vol. 2. Resumen Practico de Gramatica Espanola. Gili Gaya, S. 112p ptas (ISBN 84-7153-256-5); Vol. 3. Nociones de Gramatica Historica Espanola. Gili Gaya, S. 104p. pap. 195.00 ptas (ISBN 84-7153-257-3); Vol. 5. Resumen Practico de Gramatica Francesa. 132p. pap. 195.00 ptas (ISBN 84-7153-263-8); Vol. 7. Ortografia Practica Francesa. 240p. pap. 250.00 ptas (ISBN 84-7153-264-6); Vol. 8. Ortografia Practica Catalana. 126p. pap. 225.00 ptas (ISBN 84-7153-266-2); Vol. 9. Vocabulario Basico Infantil. 64p. pap. 195.00 ptas (ISBN 84-7153-369-3). (Span.). Biblograf.

Conrad, R., ed. Kleines Woerterbuch Sprachwissenschaftlicher Termini. 3rd ed. 306p. (Ger.). 1981. M.9.80. Bibl Inst Leipzig.

Jehan, L. F. Dictionnaire de Linguistique et de Philologie Comparee. Migne, J. P., ed. (Troisieme et Derniere Encyclopedie Theologique Ser.: Vol. 34). 724p. (Fr.). Repr. of 1864 ed. lib. bdg. $92.50x (ISBN 0-89241-313-1). Caratzas Pub Co.

Nash, Rose. Multilingual Lexicon of Linguistics & Philology: English, Russian, German, French. LC 68-31044. (Miami Linguistics Ser: No. 3). (Eng., Rus., Ger. & Fr.). 1968. $19.95x (ISBN 0-87024-095-1). U of Miami Pr.

Scheler, Auguste. Glossaire Philologique de la Geste de Liege. 319p. (Fr.). 100.00 F. Slatkine.

Springhetti, Emilio. Lexicon linguisticae et philologiae. xi, 687p. (Lat.). 1962. L.13000.00. Univ Gregoriana.

PHILOSOPHERS

Brugger, Walter & Baker, Kenneth. Philosophical Dictionary. rev. ed. LC 72-82135. Orig. Title: Philosophisches Worterbuch. xxiv, 460p. (Orig.). 1973. 15.95 (ISBN 0-685-30124-9); pap. 12.95 (ISBN 0-685-30125-7). Guild Bks.

PHILOSOPHERS–BIBLIOGRAPHY

The Philosopher's Index Thesaurus. 65p. 1979. pap. 10.00 (ISBN 0-686-98025-5). Philos Document.

PHILOSOPHERS' STONE
see Alchemy

PHILOSOPHY
see also Esthetics; Logic; Mind and Body; Mysticism; Psychology; Scholasticism

David. Definitions & Divisions of Philosophy. Kendall, Bridget & Thomson, Robert W., trs. LC 83-3308. (Armenian Texts & Studies). 216p. 1983. $17.50 (ISBN 0-89130-616-1, 21 02 05); pap. $13.00. Scholars Pr CA.

Marti Ballester, Jesus. Diccionario del pensamiento de Santa Teresa de Jesus. 2nd ed. 575p. (Span.). 1982. pap. 1400.00 ptas (ISBN 84-7050-075-9). Edicep.

PHILOSOPHY–BIOGRAPHY
see Philosophers

PHILOSOPHY–DICTIONARIES

Apel, Max & Luds, Peter. Philosophiches Woerterbuch. 6th ed. (Sammlung Goeschen: 2202). (Ger.). 1980. pap. $6.40x (ISBN 3-11-006729-3). De Gruyter.

Aurobindo. Glossary of Terms in Sri Aurobindo's Writings. 1979. $9.50 (ISBN 0-89744-980-0, Pub. by Sri Aurobindo Ashram Trust India); pap. $7.50 (ISBN 0-89744-981-9, Pub. by Sri Aurobindo Ashram Trust India). Auromere.

Aurox, Sylvain & Weil, Yvonne. Nouveau vocabulaire des etudes philosophiques. LC 78-390296. 255p. (Fr.). 1975. 19.00 F (ISBN 2-01-002450-8). Hachette-Jeunesse.

Austeda, Franz. Lexikon der Philosophie. LC 79-380526. ix, 340p. (Ger.). 1979. S.380.00 (ISBN 3-85119-156-0). Hollinek.

Baldwin, James M. Dictionary of Philosophy & Psychology, 3 vols. bound in 4. Incl. Vols. 1 & 2. 27.00 ea.; Vol. 1. (ISBN 0-8446-1047-X); Vol. 2. (ISBN 0-8446-1048-8); Vol. 3., 2 Pts. Bibliography of Philosophy, Psychology and Cognate Subjects. 24.00 ea.; Pt. 1. (ISBN 0-8446-1049-6); Pt. 2. (ISBN 0-8446-1050-X). Set. 102.00 (ISBN 0-8446-1046-1). Peter Smith.

Baldwin, James M., et al. Dictionary of Philosophy & Psychology. 1977. lib. bdg. 395.00 (ISBN 0-8490-1721-1). Gordon Pr.

Breugger, Walter. Diccionario de Filosofia. 9th ed. 684p. (Span.). 1978. $29.95 (ISBN 84-254-0722-2, S-12715, French & Eur); pap. $23.95 (ISBN 84-254-0146-1, S-50197). French & Eur.

Breve Diccionario de Filosofia. 464p. (Span.). 1977. $20.95 (ISBN 84-254-0631-5, S-50199). French & Eur.

Brugger, Walter & Baker, Kenneth. Philosophical Dictionary. rev. ed. LC 72-82135. Orig. Title: Philosophisches Worterbuch. xxiv, 460p. (Orig.). 1973. 15.95 (ISBN 0-685-30124-9); pap. 12.95 (ISBN 0-685-30125-7). Guild Bks.

Carreter, Fernando L. Diccionario de Terminos Filologicos. 5th ed. 444p. (Span.). 1977. pap. $17.95 (ISBN 84-249-1111-3, S-12048, French & Eur). French & Eur.

--Diccionario de Terminos Filologicos. 3rd ed. 444p. (Span.). 1977. $22.25 (ISBN 84-249-1112-1, S-50129, French & Eur). French & Eur.

Centro Studi Filosofici di Gallarate. Dizionario delle idee. (Ital.). L.30000.00. Sansoni.

Costanzo, Maurizio. Dizionario delle idee correnti. 144p. (Ital.). 1975. L.2500.00. Bompiani.

Cuvillier, Armand. Diccionario de Filosofia. 228p. (Span.). 1961. $14.95 (ISBN 0-686-56713-7, S-33052). French & Eur.

Ferrater, Mora. Diccionario de Filosofia, 2 vols. (Span.). $95.00 set (ISBN 0-686-56658-0, S-31443). French & Eur.

Ferrater Mora, Jose. Diccionario de Filosofia, 4 vols. 3630p. (Span.). 1979. Set. pap. $200.00 (ISBN 84-206-5998-3, S-50051); $240.00 set (ISBN 84-206-5299-7). French & Eur.

--Diccionario de Filosofia Abreviado. 2nd ed. 478p. (Span.). 1978. pap. $9.50 (ISBN 84-350-0141-5, S-50081). French & Eur.

Fiedler, F. & Gurst, G., eds. Jugendlexikon Philosophie. (Illus.). 228p. (Ger.). 1981. M.9.80. Bibl Inst Leipzig.

Flew, Antony. A Dictionary of Philosophy. 1980. pap. $8.95 (ISBN 0-312-20922-3). St Martin.

Flew, Antony, ed. Dictionary of Philosophy. LC 78-68699. 1979. $20.00 (ISBN 0-312-20921-5). St Martin.

Foulquie, Paul. Diccionario Del Lenguaje Filosofico. 1100p. (Span.). 1966. $50.00 (ISBN 84-335-1000-2, S-50065). French & Eur.

Frolov, Ivant, ed. Dictionary of Philosophy. 467p. 1983. $8.95 (ISBN 0-7178-0604-9). Intl Pub Co.

Klaus, G. & Buhr, M. Marxistisch-Leninistisches Woerterbuch der Philosophie, 3 vols. 1280p. (Ger.). 1972. $21.50 (ISBN 3-499-16155-9, M-7550, Pub. by Rowohlt). French & Eur.

--Marxistisch-Leninistisches Woerterbuch der Philosophie, 3 vols. 1280p. (Ger.). 1972. $21.50 (ISBN 3-499-16155-9). Rowohlt.

Klaus, G. & Buhr, M., eds. Philosophisches Woerterbuch, 2 vols. (Illus.). 1394p. (Ger.). M.32.00. Bibl Inst Leipzig.

Klaus, Georg & Buhr, Manfred. Philosophisches Worterbuch, 2 vols. LC 78-351881. 1394p. (Ger.). 1975. M.22.00. Bibl Inst Leipzig.

Lacey, A. R. A Dictionary of Philosophy. 1976. 18.00x (ISBN 0-7100-8361-0). Routledge & Kegan.

--A Dictionary of Philosophy. 1977. pap. text ed. $8.95x (ISBN 0-684-14932-X, ScribC). Scribner.

Lamanna, Paolo E. & Adorno, Francesco. Dizionario di termini filosofici. 104p. (Ital.). L.2300.00. Monnier.

Morris, John, ed. Descartes Dictionary. LC 73-137789. 1971. 10.00 (ISBN 0-8022-2046-0). Philos Lib.

Mueller & Halder. Kleines Philosophisches Woerterbuch. 5th ed. 344p. (Ger.). 1976. pap. $7.95 (ISBN 0-686-56623-8, M-7506, Pub. by Herder). French & Eur.

--Kleines Philosophisches Woerterbuch. 5th ed. 344p. (Ger.). 1976. pap. $7.95. Herder.

Pallares, Eduardo. Dixcionario de Filosofia. 652p. (Span.). $17.50 (ISBN 0-686-56706-4, S-21915). French & Eur.

Ranzoli, Cesare & Pigatti Ranzoli, M. Dizionario di scienze filosofiche. xii, 1348p. (Ital.). 1963. L.7000.00 (ISBN 88-203-0222-5). Hoepli.

Reeb, Georg. Thesaurus Philosophorum Seu Distinctiones et Axiomata Philosophica. 377p. (Lat.). 1981. Repr. of 1891 ed. $150.00 (ISBN 0-8287-1490-8). Clearwater Pub.

Reese, William L. Dictionary of Philosophy & Religion: Eastern & Western Thought. iv, 644p. 1980. write for info. (ISBN 0-391-00688-6). Humanities.

Rosenthal, M. & Ioudine, P. Petit Dictionnaire Philosophique. 638p. (Fr.). 1977. pap. $19.95 (ISBN 0-686-56721-8, M-6446). French & Eur.

Runes, Dagobert D. Diccionario De Filosofia. 2nd ed. 400p. (Span.). 1977. $15.75 (ISBN 84-253-0127-0, S-13007). French & Eur.

Runes, Dagobert D., ed. Dictionary of Philosophy. rev., enl. ed. LC 81-80240. 364p. 1983. Repr. 24.95 (ISBN 0-8022-2388-5). Philos Lib.

St. Elmo Naumann, Jr. Dictionary of Asian Philosophies. 1978. pap. $5.95 (ISBN 0-8065-0617-2). Citadel Pr.

Schmidt, Heinrich. Philosophisches Woerterbuch. LC 79-347124. viii, 765p. (Ger.). 1978. write for info. (ISBN 3-520-01320-7). Kroener.

Sri Aurobindo. Glossary of Terms in Sri Aurobindo's Writings. 1978. 10.00 (ISBN 0-89071-271-9). Matagiri.

Voltaire. Diccionario Filosofico, 2 vols. 616p. (Span.). 1978. Set. $17.50 (ISBN 84-7250-634-7, S-50012). French & Eur.

--Diccionario Filosofico, 3 vols. 1000p. (Span.). 1977. Set. $58.50 (ISBN 0-686-57339-0, S-50109). French & Eur.

--Diccionario Filosofico. 378p. (Span.). 1976. pap. $15.75 (ISBN 84-7339-136-5, S-50148). French & Eur.

PHILOSOPHY–HISTORY
Wiener, Philip P., ed. Dictionary of the History of Ideas. 1980. pap. $100.00 5-volume boxed edition (ISBN 0-684-16418-3, ScribR). Scribner.

PHILOSOPHY, CHINESE
Gilkey, Robert, ed. & intro. by. The Chinese Unicorn & Other Conceits from a Chinese Dictionary. (Eng. & Chinese.). 1973. pap. 3.95 (ISBN 0-686-02625-X). Noname Pr.

PHILOSOPHY, EAST INDIAN
see Philosophy, Indic

PHILOSOPHY, INDIC
Aurobindo. Glossary of Terms in Sri Aurobindo's Writings. 1979. $9.50 (ISBN 0-89744-980-0, Pub. by Sri Aurobindo Ashram Trust India); pap. $7.50 (ISBN 0-89744-981-9, Pub. by Sri Aurobindo Ashram Trust India). Auromere.

Sri Aurobindo. Glossary of Terms in Sri Aurobindo's Writings. 1978. 10.00 (ISBN 0-89071-271-9). Matagiri.

PHILOSOPHY, ISLAMIC
Saeeed, M. A Dictionary of Muslim Philosophy. 5.95 (ISBN 0-686-18370-3). Kazi Pubns.

PHILOSOPHY, MUSLIM
see Philosophy, Islamic

PHILOSOPHY AND RELIGION
see also Faith and Reason
Morin, F. Dictionnaire de Philosophie et de Theologie Scolastiques, 2 vols. Migne, J. P., ed. (Troisieme et Derniere Encyclopedie Theologique Ser.: Vols. 21-22). 1496p. (Fr.). Date not set. Repr. of 1865 ed. lib. bdg. $190.00x (ISBN 0-89241-304-2). Caratzas Pub Co.

PHILOSOPHY OF LANGUAGE
see Languages–Philosophy

PHOBIAS
Venturoli, Marcello & Zangrandi, Ruggero. Dizionario della paura. (Illus.). 393p. (Ital.). 1951. L.5000.00. Nistri-Lischi.

PHONETIC TRANSCRIPTIONS
see Language and Languages–Phonetic Transcriptions

PHONETICS
see also Language and Languages–Phonetic Transcriptions; Speech
also subdivision Phonetics, Phonology, and Pronunciation under names of languages, e.g. English Language–Phonetics
Crystal, David. A First Dictionary of Linguistics & Phonetics. (Language Library Ser.). 404p. 1980. lib. bdg. $34.00 (ISBN 0-86531-051-3, Pub. by Andre Deutsch). Westview.

Rockey, D. Phonetic Lexicon of Monosyllabic & Some Disyllabic Words, with Homophones, Arranged According to Their Phonetic Structure. 1973. $47.95 (ISBN 0-471-26113-0, Wiley Heyden). Wiley.

PHONOGRAPHY
see Shorthand

PHONOLOGY
see Grammar, Comparative and General–Phonology; Phonetics; also subdivisions Phonetics, Phonology, and Pronunciation under names of languages, e.g. French Language–Phonetics; English Language–Phonology; Italian Language–Pronunciation

PHONORECORD LIBRARIES
Dictionary Catalog of the Rodgers & Hammerstein Archives of Recorded Sound, 15 vols. 1981. Set. lib. bdg. $1475.00 (ISBN 0-8161-0359-3, Hall Library). G K Hall.

PHOTOCOPYING PROCESSES
see also Electrophotography
Deutsches Kommitee Fur Reprographie, ed. Dictionary of Reprography: Terms & Definitions. 273p. (Ger. & Fr.). 1976. pap. text ed. $34.00 (ISBN 3-7940-3186-5, Pub. by K G Saur). Gale.

PHOTOGRAMMETRY
Multilingual Dictionary of Remote Sensing & Photogrammetry. 1983. $25.00 (ISBN 0-937294-46-2). ASP.

Richter, G., ed. Dictionary of Optics Photography & Photogrammetry: German-English & English-German. (Eng. & Ger.). 1966. $44.00 (ISBN 0-444-40478-3). Elsevier.

PHOTOGRAPHIC APPARATUS AND SUPPLIES
see Photography–Apparatus and Supplies

PHOTOGRAPHIC MEASUREMENTS
see Photogrammetry

PHOTOGRAPHIC REPRODUCTION PROCESSES
see Photocopying Processes

PHOTOGRAPHIC SUPPLIES
see Photography–Apparatus and Supplies

PHOTOGRAPHS–EXHIBITIONS
see Photography–Exhibitions

PHOTOGRAPHY–ANIMATED PICTURES
see Cinematography; Moving-Pictures

PHOTOGRAPHY–APPARATUS AND SUPPLIES
Snelling, Henry H. & Anthony, E. A Dictionary of the Photographic & a Comprehensive & Systematic Catalogue of Photographic Apparatus Material: Manufactured, Imported & Sold by E. Anthony, 2 vols. in 1. Bunnell, Peter & Sobieszek, Robert A., eds. LC 76-23059. (Sources of Modern Photo. Ser.). (Illus.). 1979. Repr. of 1854 ed. lib. bdg. $25.00x (ISBN 0-405-09623-2). Ayer Co.

PHOTOGRAPHY–DICTIONARIES
Craeybeckx, A. S. Elsevier's Dictionary of Photography. (Eng., Fr., & Ger.). 1965. $113.00 (ISBN 0-444-40146-6). Elsevier.

Desilets, Antoine. La Photo de A & Z. LC 79-356697. 331p. (Eng. & Fr.). 1978. Can.27.95 (ISBN 0-7759-0614-X). Edns Homme.

Diccionario de fotografia y cine. (Serie Tecnios Especialistas Koel 51). 358p. (Span.). 75.00 ptas. Tesoro.

Diccionario Ilustrado De Fotografia. 212p. (Span.). 1974. pap. $22.50 (ISBN 84-342-0117-8, S-50014). French & Eur.

Dictionary of Photograhy. (Hebrew, Eng. , Fr. & Ger.). IL.8.00. Massada Pr.

Guerronnan, Anthony. Dictionnaire Synonymique. Bunnell, Peter C. & Sobieszek, Robert A., eds. LC 76-23055. (Sources of Modern Photography Ser.). (Fr.). 1979. Repr. of 1895 ed. lib. bdg. $15.00x (ISBN 0-405-09620-8). Ayer Co.

Harwood, Mary. Photography Language. LC 77-12760. 1978. lib. bdg. 12.90 (ISBN 0-89471-025-7); pap. 2.95 (ISBN 0-89471-024-9). Running Pr.

Lapauri, A. A., et al, eds. Kratkii Fotograficheskii Slovar. 386p. (Rus.). 1956. $2.50 (Pub. by Iskusstvo). Four Continent.

Page, A. A Dictionary of Photographic Terms. (Illus.). 1966. 17.50 (ISBN 0-685-58545-X). Heinman.

Pollet, R. Lexique de la photographie d'Amateur: Anglais-Francais Francais-Anglais. 111p. (Eng. & Fr.). 1970. 50.00 F. Maison Dictionnaire.

Pollet, Ray J. Lexique de la Photographie d'amateur: Francais-Anglais. 112p. (Fr. & Eng.). 1970. 3.50 F. Lemeac.

Snelling, Henry H. & Anthony, E. A Dictionary of the Photographic & a Comprehensive & Systematic Catalogue of Photographic Apparatus Material: Manufactured, Imported & Sold by E. Anthony, 2 vols. in 1. Bunnell, Peter & Sobieszek, Robert A., eds. LC 76-23059. (Sources of Modern Photo. Ser.). (Illus.). 1979. Repr. of 1854 ed. lib. bdg. $25.00x (ISBN 0-405-09623-2). Ayer Co.

Spencer, D. A. Focal Dictionary of Photographic Technologics. (Illus.). 1973. $49.95 (ISBN 0-240-50747-9). Focal Pr.

Stroebel, Leslie & Todd, Hollis. Dictionary of Contemporary Photography. LC 73-93536. (Illus.). 1974. 20.00 (ISBN 0-87100-065-2); pap. $9.95 (ISBN 0-87100-103-9). Morgan.

Stroebel, Leslie & Todd, Hollis N. Dictionary of Contemporary Photography. LC 73-93536. 1976. pap. $9.95 (ISBN 0-87100-103-9, 397). Morgan.

PHOTOGRAPHY–EXHIBITIONS
Migne, J. P., ed. Dictionnaire des Muses ou Description des Principaux Musees d'Europe... Suivi Notions sur la Photographie par X. (Troisieme et Derniere Encyclopedie Theologique Ser.: Vol. 4). 740p. (Fr.). Repr. of 1855 ed. lib. bdg. $95.00x (ISBN 0-89241-291-7). Caratzas Pub Co.

PHOTOGRAPHY–MOVING-PICTURES
see Cinematography; Moving-Pictures

PHOTOGRAPHY–SUPPLIES
see Photography–Apparatus and Supplies

PHOTOGRAPHY, LENSLESS
see Holography

PHOTOGRAPHY OF DOCUMENTS
see Photocopying Processes

PHOTOGRAPHY OF MANUSCRIPTS
see Photocopying Processes

PHOTO-REALISM
see Pop Art

PHYSICAL CULTURE
see Physical Education and Training

PHYSICAL EDUCATION AND TRAINING
see also Games; Gymnastics; Sports
also names of sports or exercises, e.g. Football; also apparatus used in gymnasiums
Rouet, Marcel. Dictionnaire de la Culture Physique. 304p. (Fr.). 1975. $27.50 (ISBN 0-686-57212-2, M-6494). French & Eur.

Thiess, Gunter, et al, eds. Training von A bis Z: Kleines Worterbuch fuer der Theorie & Praxis der Sportl Trainings. LC 78-395459. 279p. (Ger.). 1978. DM.13.50. Sportverlag.

PHYSICAL EDUCATION AND TRAINING–MEDICAL ASPECTS
see Sports Medicine

PHYSICAL GEOGRAPHY–DICTIONARIES
Bennett, Roger G. Naturgeografisk ordbok: Engelsk-Norsk. LC 78-398859. 84p. (Eng. & Norwegian.). 1976. write for info. Berg Inst Sociol.

Moore, W. G. Dictionary of Geography. rev. ed. (Reference Ser.). (Orig.). 1963. pap. 5.95 (ISBN 0-14-051002-8). Penguin.

Shchukin, M. Chetyrekhiazychnyi Entsiklopedicheskii Slovar Terminov Po Fizicheskoi Geografii. 368p. (Rus.). 1978. $6.50 (Pub. by Russkii Iaxyknt Bk). Four Continent.

Soto Mora, Consuelo. Vocabulario Geomortologico. (Illus.). 202p. (Span.). 1965. Mex.$45.00. UNAM.

PHYSICAL METALLURGY
Tyrkiel, E. F. Dictionary of Physical Metallurgy. (Eng., Ger., Fr., Pol. & Rus.). 1978. $85.00 (ISBN 0-444-99810-1). Elsevier.

PHYSICAL OCEANOGRAPHY
see Oceanography

PHYSICAL TRAINING
see Physical Education and Training

PHYSICIANS
see also Women Physicians
American Medical Association. Physician's Current Procedural Terminology. 4th ed. 501p. $19.95 (OP 041; bulk rates avail. AMA.

Espinosa, Aurelio M. & Gambetta, Leon. Spanish for Doctors & Nurses. (Span.). $6.85. Camino Real.

PHYSICIANS–BIOGRAPHY
Diccionario de Medicos Puertorriquenos Que Se Man Distinguico Fuera de la Medicina. (Span.). $17.50 (ISBN 0-686-56650-5). French & Eur.

PHYSICIANS–LEGAL STATUS, LAWS, ETC.
see Medical Laws and Legislation

PHYSICIANS, WOMEN
see Women Physicians

PHYSICS–BIBLIOGRAPHY
Princeton University. Dictionary Catalog of the Princeton University Plasma Physics Laboratory Library, First Supplement. 1973. lib. bdg. $150.00 (ISBN 0-8161-1032-8, Hall Library). G K Hall.

PHYSICS–DICTIONARIES

Alekseev, P. M. English-Russian Glossary of Physics Terms. 288p. (Eng. & Rus.). 1980. $35.00x (ISBN 0-686-44696-8, Pub. by Collets). State Mutual Bk.

Ballentyne, D. W. & Walker, L. E. Diccionario de Leyes y Efectos Cientificos En Quimica-Fisica Matematicas. 216p. (Span.). $14.95 (ISBN 0-686-56711-0, S-33054). French & Eur.

Becker, U. Herder-Lexikon Weltaumphysik. 240p. (Ger.). 1975. pap. $17.95 (ISBN 3-451-16463-9, M-7461, Pub. by Herder). French & Eur.

--Herder-Lexikon Weltaumphysik. 240p. (Ger.). 1975. pap. $17.95 (ISBN 3-451-16463-9). Herder.

Becker, Udo. Diccionario Rioduero: Fisica Del Espacio. 264p. (Span.). 1978. leatherette $13.25 (ISBN 84-220-0846-7, S-50163). French & Eur.

Birdmann, G. English-German, German, English Solid State Physics & Electronics Dictionary. 1103p. (Eng. & Ger.). 1980. $100.00x (ISBN 0-569-07204-2, Pub. by Collet's). State Mutual Bk.

Borucki, Hans, et al. Die Physik: Ein Lexikon der Gesamten Schulphysik. (Illus.). 490p. (Ger.). DM.19.80 (ISBN 3-411-01122-X). Biblio Inst.

Brazhdzhiunas, P. Litovsko-Russko-Anglo-Nemetskii Slovar Fizicheskikh Terminov. (Rus., Eng., Ger. & Lithuanian.). 1979. $15.95 (Pub. by Mokslas). Four Continent.

Chang, S. Chinese-English Dictionary of Physical Terms. 405p. (Eng. & Ger.). 1969. pap. $75.00 (ISBN 0-686-56601-7, M-7322, Pub. by Harrassowitz). French & Eur.

Clason, W. E. Elsevier's Dictionary of General Physics. (Eng., Fr., Span., Ital., Dutch & Ger., Polyglot). 1962. $110.75 (ISBN 0-444-40122-9). Elsevier.

Daintith, John, ed. Dictionary of Physics. 1982. pap. 5.72i (ISBN 0-06-463560-0, EH-560). Har-Row.

--The Facts on File Dictionary of Physics. 248p. 1981. $14.95 (ISBN 0-87196-511-9). Facts on File.

De Vries, L. Woerterbuch der Reinen und Angewandten Physik, Vol. 1. (Ger. & Eng., Dictionary of Physics & Applied Physics). 1964. $38.00 (ISBN 3-486-30942-0, M-6954). French & Eur.

--Woerterbuch der Reinen und Angewandten Physik, Vol. 2. (Eng. & Ger., Dictionary of Physics & Applied Physics). 1964. $38.00 (ISBN 0-686-56615-7, M-6962). French & Eur.

De Vries, L. & Clason, W. E. Dictionary of Pure & Applied Physics, 2 vols. Set. $65.25 (ISBN 0-686-85922-7); Vol. I, Ger.-Eng. $42.00 (ISBN 0-444-41068-6); Vol. II, Eng.-Ger. $42.00 (ISBN 0-685-05581-7). Elsevier.

Diccionario de unidades, efectos y constantes. 224p. (Span.). 50.00 ptas. Tesoro.

Dicionario de Eisica-Illustrado. (Illus., Port.). Cr.$770.00. Edit Atica.

Dictionary of Physics. 1689p. (Eng. & Chinese.). 1978. $19.95 (ISBN 0-686-92341-3, M-9287). French & Eur.

Dictionary of Physics: English-Chinese. 388p. (Eng. & Chinese.). 1980. $25.00 (ISBN 0-686-97645-2, M-9276). French & Eur.

Dictionary of Physics: No. 1, Mechanics. (Hebrew, Eng. , Fr. & Ger.). IL.8.00. Massada Pr.

Dictionary of Physics: No. 2, Electricity & Magnetism. (Hebrew, Eng. , Fr. & Ger.). IL.8.00. Massada Pr.

Dictionary of Physics: No. 3, Optics. (Hebrew, Eng. , Fr. & Ger.). IL.8.00. Massada Pr.

Dizionario delle scienze fisiche e matematiche. 178p. (Ital.). L.2500.00. Zanichelli.

Eisenreich & Sube. Woerterbuch Physik, 3 vols. 2895p. (Eng., Fr., Rus. & Ger.). 1983. DM.390.00 (ISBN 3-87144-143-0). Verlag Harri Deutsch.

English-Russian Dictionary of Minimum Physics. 287p. (Eng. & Rus.). 1980. leatherette $7.95 (ISBN 0-686-97372-0, M-9123). French & Eur.

Franke, tr. Diccionario de fisica. (Span.). 3630.00 ptas. Labor SA.

Glazebrook, Richard, ed. A Dictionary of Applied Physics, 5 vols. 24.00 ea. (ISBN 0-8446-1199-9). Peter Smith.

Gray, H. J. & Isaacs, A., eds. A New Dictionary of Physics. rev. ed. LC 75-307635. Orig. Title: Dictionary of Physics. (Illus.). 640p. 1975. 40.00 (ISBN 0-582-32242-1). Longman.

Hoefling, O. Lexikon der Schulphysik: Atomphysik, Vol. 5. (Ger.). $47.00 (ISBN 3-7614-0110-8, M-7227). French & Eur.

Hoefling, Oskar, ed. Lexikon der Schulphysik: Bd 1, Mechanik & Akustik. (Ger.). 1978. DM.54.00 (ISBN 3-7614-0107-8). Aulis Verlag.

--Lexikon der Schulphysik: Bd 3, Elektrizitaet & Magnetismus-1.Tlbd, A-K. vi, 201p. (Ger.). 1978. DM.46.00 (ISBN 3-7614-0168-X). Aulis Verlag.

--Lexikon der Schulphysik: Bd 3, Elektrizitaet & Magnetismus-2.Tlbd, L-Z. vi, 201p. (Ger.). 1978. DM.46.00 (ISBN 3-7614-0169-8). Aulis Verlag.

--Lexikon der Schulphysik: Bd 4, Optik & Relativitaet. (Ger.). 1978. DM.52.00 (ISBN 3-7614-0109-4). Aulis Verlag.

--Lexikon der Schulphysik: Bd 5, Atomphysik. (Ger.). 1978. DM.58.00 (ISBN 3-7614-0110-8). Aulis Verlag.

--Lexikon der Schulphysik: Waerme & Wetter. (Ger.). 1978. DM.46.00 (ISBN 3-7614-0108-6). Aulis Verlag.

Hyman, Charles J., ed. Dictionary of Physics & Allied Sciences: German-English. LC 77-6949. (Ger. & Eng.). 1978. $30.00 (ISBN 0-8044-4433-1). Ungar.

Ibeas, Franco. Diccionario Tecnologico Ingles-Espanol: Electricidad, Electronica, Telecomunicacion, & Materias Afinas con la Fisica, Optica & Quimica. 452p. (Eng. & Span.). 1974. E950.00 (ISBN 84-205-0492-0). Alhambra.

Idlin, Ralph, ed. Dictionary of Physics & Allied Sciences: English-German. LC 77-6950. (Eng. & Ger.). 1978. $30.00 (ISBN 0-8044-4435-8). Ungar.

Jehan, L. F. Dictionnaire Historique des Sciences Physiques et Naturelles. Migne, J. P., ed. (Troisieme et Derniere Encyclopedie Theologique Ser.: Vol. 30). 654p. (Fr.). Repr. of 1857 ed. lib. bdg. $85.00x (ISBN 0-89241-309-3). Caratzas Pub Co.

Jesse, A. Physics Terminology. 129p. (Fr. Ger. & Eng.). 1980. pap. $24.95 (ISBN 3-7625-0963-8, M-9310). French & Eur.

--Physik-Fachsprache Englisch-Franzosisch-Deutsch. 129p. (Fr., Ger. & Eng.). 1980. DM.28.00 (ISBN 3-7625-0963-8). Bauverlag.

--Terminologie de la physique: Anglais-Allemand-Francais. (Illus.). 129p. (Eng., Ger., & Fr.). 1980. 85.00 F. Maison Dictionnaire.

Laitier, Gabriel. Dictionnaire de Physique. 276p. (Fr.). 1968. pap. $35.00 (ISBN 0-686-56988-1, M-6328). French & Eur.

--Dictionnaire de Physique. (Illus.). 276p. (Fr.). 1968. 80.00 F. Maloine.

Marks, Robert W. Diccionario y manual de la nueva fisica y quimica. (Illus.). 262p. (Span.). $1.50. Edit Pr Serv.

Meyers Physik-Lexikon. (Ger.). 1973. $46.00 (ISBN 3-411-00921-7, M-7561, Pub. by Bibliographisches Institut). French & Eur.

Meyers Physik-Lexikon. (Ger.). 1973. $46.00 (ISBN 3-411-00921-7). Biblio Inst.

Ministry of Education. Scientific Terms Physics: Japanese-English, English-Japanese. 221p. (Japanese & Eng.). 1954. $14.95 (ISBN 0-686-92514-9, M-9343). French & Eur.

Pitt, Valerie H., ed. The Penguin Dictionary of Physics. (Reference Ser.). 1977. pap. 5.95 (ISBN 0-14-051071-0). Penguin.

Precis Thesaurus: Physics. 1981. $55.00x (ISBN 0-686-99804-9, Pub. by Brit Lib England). State Mutual Bk.

Sauermost, R. Herder-Lexikon Physik. (Ger.). 1975. $15.95 (ISBN 0-686-56480-4, M-7449, Pub. by Herder). French & Eur.

--Herder-Lexikon Physik. (Ger.). 1975. $15.95. Herder.

Sauermost, Rolf. Diccionario Rioduero: Fisica. 256p. (Span.). 1976. leatherette $9.95 (ISBN 84-220-0763-0, S-50167). French & Eur.

Saverien, Alexandre. Dictionnaire Universel de Mathematique & de Physique, 1. (Fr.). DM.138.00. Olms.

--Dictionnaire Universel de Mathematique & de Physique, 2. (Fr.). DM.138.00. Olms.

Smirnova, L. A. Russko-Angliiskii Razgovornik Dlia Fizikov. 336p. (Rus. & Eng.). 1968. $2.25 (Pub. by Sov Entsiklopediia). Four Continent.

--Russko-Angliiskii Razgovornik Dlia Fizikov. 312p. (Rus. & Eng.). 1977. $2.95 (Pub. by Russkii Iazyk). Four Continent.

Sube, R. & Eisenreich, G. Physics Dictionary, 3 vols. 2895p. 1980. $185.00x (ISBN 0-569-07879-2, Pub. by Collet's). State Mutual Bk.

Sube, R. & Eisenreich, G., eds. Physics Dictionary, 3 vols. (Eng., Ger., Fr. & Rus.). 1974. $260.00 (ISBN 3-87144-143-0). Adler.

Sube, Ralf & Eisenreich, Gunther. Woerterbuch Physik, 3 vols. (Eng., Ger., Fr. & Rus., Dictionary of Physics). 1970. Set. $312.00 (ISBN 3-87144-143-0, M-6909). French & Eur.

Thewlis, J. Concise Dictionary of Physics: And Related Subjects. 2nd ed. LC 79-40209. 1979. 65.00 (ISBN 0-08-023048-2). Pergamon.

Tolstoi, D. M. English-Russian Physics Dictionary. 848p. (Eng. & Rus.). 1978. $75.00x (ISBN 0-686-44700-X, Pub. by Collets). State Mutual Bk.

Tolstoi, D. M., ed. Anglo-Russkii Fizicheskii Slovar. 848p. (Eng. & Rus.). 1978. $15.95 (Pub. by Russkii Iazyk). Four Continent.

--English-Russian Physics Dictionary. LC 78-40718. (Eng. & Rus.). 1979. 81.00 (ISBN 0-08-023057-1). Pergamon.

PHYSICS–DIRECTORIES

Alekseev, P. M., et al. Chastotnyi Anglo-Russkii Fizicheskii Slovar Minimum. 288p. (Rus. & Eng.). 1980. $4.75 (Pub. by Voenizdat). Four Continent.

Fachlexikon ABC Physik, 2 vols. 1784p. (Ger.). 1974. Set. $95.00 (ISBN 3-87144-003-5, M-7383, Pub. by Verlag Harri Deutsch). French & Eur.

PHYSICS–HISTORY

Hermann, A. Lexikon der Schulphysik: Geschichte der Physik, Vol. 6. (Ger.). $35.00 (ISBN 3-7614-0131-0, M-7228). French & Eur.

--Lexikon der Schulphysik: Geschichte der Physik, Vol. 7. (Ger.). $45.00 (ISBN 3-7614-0153-1, M-7229). French & Eur.

Hoefling, Oskar, ed. Lexikon der Schulphysik: Bd 6, Geschichte der Physik. (Ger.). 1978. DM.44.00 (ISBN 3-7614-0131-0). Aulis Verlag.

--Lexikon der Schulphysik: Bd 7, Geschichte der Physik. viii, 239p. (Ger.). 1972. DM.28.00 (ISBN 3-7614-0153-1). Aulis Verlag.

PHYSICS, ASTRONOMICAL
see Astrophysics

PHYSICS, NUCLEAR
see Nuclear Physics

PHYSICS, TERRESTRIAL
see Geophysics

PHYSIOGRAPHY
see Geology; Geomorphology

PHYSIOLOGICAL PSYCHOLOGY
see Psychology, Physiological

PHYSIOLOGY
see also Health; Nutrition; Psychology, Physiological; Respiration also names of organs and secretions, e.g. Heart, Kidneys, Bile, Gastric Juice

American Physiological Society. Glossary of Terms for Thermal Physiology. (Standards & Glossaries). 1973. Repr. $1.00. Am Physiological.

Boyer, A. L. Dictionnaire de Physiologie. Migne, J. P., ed. (Troisieme et Derniere Encyclopedie Theologique Ser.: Vol. 58). 776p. (Fr.). Date not set. Repr. of 1861 ed. lib. bdg. $98.50x (ISBN 0-89241-324-7). Caratzas Pub Co.

Glossary of Physiological Terms. 116p. (Rus. , Eng. , Fr. & Ger.). 1980. $30.00x (ISBN 0-686-44718-2, Pub. by Collets). State Mutual Bk.

Layman, Dale P. The Terminology of Anatomy & Physiology: A Programmed Approach. LC 82-13448. 293p. 1983. pap. $10.95 (ISBN 0-471-86262-2, Pub. by Wiley Med). Wiley.

PHYTOPATHOLOGY
see Plant Diseases

PIANISTS

Daae, E. English-Norwegian, Norwegian-English, Lommeordbok. 568p. (Eng. & Norwegian.). 1980. pap. $8.95 (ISBN 82-573-0152-3, M-9462). French & Eur.

PIANO MUSIC

Piano Chord Dictionary. 1981. $2.50 (ISBN 0-88284-155-6). Alfred Pub.

PICTORIAL DICTIONARIES
see Picture Dictionaries

PICTURE-BOOKS FOR CHILDREN

Bambi's First Picture Dictionary. (Pic-a-Story Bks.). (Illus.). 24p. (Orig.). (gr. k-1). 1981. $4.95 (ISBN 0-89531-107-0); pap. $1.95 (ISBN 0-686-79397-8). Sharon Pubns.

PICTURE DICTIONARIES
see also English Language–Dictionaries, Juvenile; French Language–Dictionaries, Juvenile

Ettinger, David. Hebrew-English Pictorial Dictionary. (Hebrew & Eng.). $27.50 (ISBN 0-87559-018-7). Shalom.

First Picture Dictionary - English-Arabic. (Illus., Eng. & Arabic.). $2.50x (ISBN 0-86685-202-6). Intl Bk Ctr.

French Duden, Pictorial Dictionary. (Illus.). $20.50 (ISBN 3-4110-0972-1). Adler.

Goldberg, Nathan. New Illustrated Hebrew-English Dictionary for Young Readers. (Illus., Hebrew & Eng.). (gr. 4-7). 1958. pap. 6.95x (ISBN 0-87068-370-5). Ktav.

Herbert. Dictionnaire Pittoresque & Historique: Ou Description d'architecture, Peinture, Sculpture, Gravure, 2 vols. (Fr.). 1972. 150.00 F. Minkoff Repr.

Matthews, B. English-Chinese Picture Dictionary. (Illus.). 48p. (Chinese & Eng.). 1983. pap. $4.50 (ISBN 9971-947-00-5). Hippocrene Bks.

Moore, Lillian. A Child's First Picture Dictionary. (Illus.). 48p. 1970. 1.95 (ISBN 0-448-02248-6, G&D). Putnam Pub Group.

Oxford-Duden Bildwoerterbuch Englisch. 822p. (Ger.). DM.29.80 (ISBN 3-411-01914-X). Biblio Inst.

The Oxford-Duden Pictorial English-Japanese Dictionary. (Illus.). 848p. (Eng. & Japanese.). 1983. $29.95 (ISBN 0-19-864149-4). Oxford U Pr.

The Oxford-Duden Pictorial French-English Dictionary. (Illus.). 880p. (Fr. & Eng.). 1983. $29.95 (ISBN 0-19-864153-2). Oxford U Pr.

Parnwell, E. C. Oxford Picture Dictionary of American English. (Illus.). 1978. pap. 3.95 ea.; pap. monolingual ed. (ISBN 0-19-502332-3); pap. English-Spanish ed. (ISBN 0-19-502333-1); pap. french indexed ed. (ISBN 0-19-502334-X). Oxford U Pr.

Scarry, Huck, illus. My First Picture Dictionary. LC 76-24174. (Pictureback Ser.). (ps-2). 1978. PLB 4.99 (ISBN 0-394-93486-5, BYR); pap. 1.50 (ISBN 0-394-83486-0). Random.

PICTURES
see also Portraits

also engravings, Etchings, Paintings,
and similar headings; and subdivision
Pictorial works under various
subjects, e.g. Natural history–
Pictorial works
Le Boeuf, Christine. Vocabulaire en
Images, 1. (Fr.). 65.00 F. Ecole.
--Vocabulaire en Images, 2. (Fr.).
65.00 F. Ecole.

PIDGIN ENGLISH
Murphy, John J. The Book of Pidgin
English. 3rd ed. LC 75-35144.
(Pidgin Eng.). Repr. of 1949 ed.
$14.50 (ISBN 0-404-14160-9).
AMS Pr.

PIDGIN LANGUAGES
see Languages, Mixed

PIGEON ENGLISH
see Pidgin English

PILGRIMS AND PILGRIMAGES
see also Saints
De Sivry, L. Dictionnaire
Geographique, Historique,
Descriptif, Archeologique des
Pelegrinages, 2 vols. Migne, J. P.,
ed. (Encyclopedie Theologique
Ser.: Vols. 43-44). 1328p. (Fr.).
Repr. of 1851 ed. lib. bdg.
$169.00x (ISBN 0-89241-248-8).
Caratzas Pub Co.

PILIPINO LANGUAGE
see Tagalog Language

PILOTS AND PILOTAGE
see also Navigation
Dizionario dei piloti. (Ital.).
L.12000.00. Mondadori.

PIMA INDIANS
see Indians of North America–
Southwest, New

PIMA LANGUAGE
Saxton, Dean & Saxton, Lucille.
Papago & Pima to English, English
to Papago & Pima Dictionary. 2nd
ed. Cherry, R. L., ed. (Papago,
Pima & Eng.). 1983. text ed.
$19.95x (ISBN 0-8165-0826-7). U
of Ariz Pr.

PINDAR, 522-443 B.C.
Slater, William J., ed. Lexicon to
Pindar. 1969. $131.00x (ISBN 3-
11-002562-0). De Gruyter.

PIPE
see also Pipe Lines
American Society of Mechanical
Engineers. Glossary of Terms Used
in the Measurement of Fluid Flow
in Pipes: ANSI-ASME MFC-1M-
1979. $4.50 (J00065); members
$3.60. ASME.

PIPE LINES
see also Pipe;
also subdivision Pipe Lines under
special subjects, e.g. Petroleum–Pipe
Lines
Bucksch, H. & Altemeyer, A.
Dictionnaire des Canalisations a
Grande Distance: Anglais-
Francais-Allemand. 288p. (Eng.,
Fr. & Ger.). 1969. $120.00 (ISBN
0-686-56931-8, M-6052). French &
Eur.
Bucksch, H. & Altmeyer, A. P.
Pipeline Dictionary. 288p. (Eng.,
Ger. & Fr.). 1969. $99.50 (ISBN 3-
7625-1166-7, M-7588, Pub. by
Bauverlag). French & Eur.
--Pipeline Dictionary. 288p. (Eng.,
Ger. & Fr.). 1969. $70.00x (ISBN
3-7625-1166-7). Intl Pubns Serv.
--Pipeline Dictionary. 288p. (Eng.,
Ger. & Fr.). 1969. DM.125.00
(ISBN 3-7625-1166-7). Bauverlag.
Editions Technip. Glossary of
Onshore & Offshore Pipelines.
320p. (Eng. & Fr.). 1979. E28.00.
Graham & Trotman.
Lexique des Pipelines a Terre et en
Mer. LC 80-472459. xii, 302p.
(Eng. & Fr.). 1979. write for info.
(ISBN 2-7108-0356-9). Technip.
Shann, C. D., ed. The Pipeline
Glossary & Directory. LC 80-
480912. 123p. (Eng.). 1978. write
for info. Scientific Surveys.

PIPE-ORGAN
see Organ

PIPES, TOBACCO
see Tobacco-Pipes

PLACE-NAMES
see Names, Geographical

PLAIN CHANT
see Chants (Plain, Gregorian, etc.)

PLAINSONG
see Chants (Plain, Gregorian, etc.)

PLANNED PARENTHOOD
see Birth Control

PLANNING
see also Economic Policy; Social
Policy

Niewerth, Hans. Lexikon der Planun
und Organisation. (Ger.). 1968.
$37.00 (ISBN 3-87715-051-9, M-
7235). French & Eur.
Niewwwerth, Hans, et al, eds.
Lexikon der Planung &
Organisation. 220p. (Ger.). 1968.
DM.46.00 (ISBN 3-87715-051-9).
Quickborner Team.

PLANNING, CITY
see City Planning

PLANS
see Mechanical Drawing

PLANT CLASSIFICATION
see Botany–Classification

PLANT DISEASES
see also Fungi in Agriculture
also subdivision Disease and Pests
under particular subjects, e.g. Trees–
Diseases and Pests
Cesky a Sovensky Terminologicky
Slovnik z Fytopatologie a Ochrany
Rostlin. LC 79-356902. 392p.
(Czech. & Slovak.). 1977. write for
info. SNTC.
Diakova, G. A. Fitopatologicheskii
Slovar Spravochnik. 478p. (Rus.,
Eng., Ger. & Fr.). 1969. $12.75
(Pub. by Nauka). Four Continent.
Frohlich, Gerd, et al.
Phytopathologie & Pflanzenschutz.
LC 79-377360. 295p. (Eng. &
Ger.). 1979. DM.19.80 (ISBN 3-
437-20207-3). Fischer Verlag.
A Guide to the Use of Terms in
Plant Pathology: Terminology Sub-
Committee of the Federation of
British Plant Pathologists. 55p.
1973. pap. $30.00x (ISBN 0-
85198-290-5, Pub. by CAB Bks
England). State Mutual Bk.
Kwizda, R. Vocabularium Nocentium
Florae. 4th ed. (Lat.). 1963. pap.
$23.50 (ISBN 0-387-80646-6).
Springer-Verlag.
Merino-Rodriguez, Manuel, ed.
Lexicon of Plant Pests & Diseases.
(Eng., Lat., Fr., Span., Ital. & Ger.,
Polyglot). 1966. $70.25 (ISBN 0-
444-40393-0). Elsevier.
Miller, P. R. & Pollard, H. L.
Multilingual Compendium of Plant
Diseases. LC 75-46932.
(Compendia Ser.: Vol. 2). (Illus.).
446p. 1977. $40.00 (ISBN 0-
89054-020-9); member $35.00. Am
Phytopathol Soc.

PLANT GENETICS
Terminologia Fitogenetica &
Citogenetica. (Span.). $3.20;
Mex.$40.00. Herrero.

PLANT NAMES, POPULAR
Carnoy, Albert. Dictionnaire
Etymologique des noms Grecs de
Plantes. 277p. (Gr. & Fr.). 1959.
1000.00 F. Peeters.

PLANT NAMES, SCIENTIFIC
see Botany–Nomenclature

PLANT PATHOLOGY
see Plant Diseases

PLANT TAXONOMY
see Botany–Classification

PLANTING
see Agriculture; Landscape
Gardening; Trees

PLANTS
see also Flowers; House Plants;
Plants, Useful; Poisonous Plants;
Succulent Plants; Weeds
also names of individual plants, and
headings beginning with the word
Plant
Cook, J. Gordon. ABC of Plant
Terms. 293p. 1968. $39.00x (ISBN
0-900541-56-3, Pub. by
Meadowfield Pr England). State
Mutual Bk.
Coon, ed. Dictionary of Useful
Plants: The Use, History &
Folklore of More Than 500 Plant
Species. (Illus.). Epap. 4.50.
Rodale Pr Eng.
Debuigne, Gerard. Dictionnaire des
Plantes qui Guerissent. (Illus.).
250p. (Fr.). 1972. 17.60 F.
Larousse.
Hay, Roy & Synge, Patrick M. The
Color Dictionary of Flowers &
Plants for Home & Garden. (Illus.).
584p. 1982. pap. $11.95 (ISBN 0-
517-52456-2). Crown.
Mensier, Paul H. Dictionnaire des
Hulles Vegetales. (Fr.). 1957.
160.00 F. Lechevalier.
Synge, P. & Hay, R. Dictionary of
Garden Plants & Flowers in
Colour: May 1981. 1981. $60.00x
(ISBN 0-686-78769-2, Pub. by
RHS Ent England). State Mutual
Bk.

PLANTS–CLASSIFICATION
see Botany–Classification

PLANTS–DISEASES
see Plant Diseases

PLANTS–GENETICS
see Plant Genetics

PLANTS–NOMENCLATURE
see Botany–Nomenclature

**PLANTS–NOMENCLATURE
(POPULAR)**
see Plant Names, Popular

PLANTS–PATHOLOGY
see Plant Diseases

PLANTS, CULTIVATED
see also Flowers
Dictionary of Cultivated Plants &
Their Regions of Diversity. 263p.
1983. $49.75 (ISBN 90-220-0785-
5, PDC 241, Pudoc). Unipub.

PLANTS, INDUSTRIAL
see Factories

PLANTS, MEDICINAL
see Botany, Medical

PLANTS, POISONOUS
see Poisonous Plants

PLANTS, USEFUL
see also Botany, Economic; Botany,
Medical; Plants, Cultivated
Danger, Eric P. Dicionario de
Plantas Oteis do Brasil. (Port.).
Cr.$2.300.00. Difel Difusao.

PLASMA (IONIZED GASES)
Princeton University. Dictionary
Catalog of the Princeton
University Plasma Physics
Laboratory Library, 4 vols. 1970.
Set. lib. bdg. $380.00 (ISBN 0-
8161-0881-1, Hall Library). G K
Hall.

PLASTER
see also Cement; Concrete
Volkart, K. Gips - Woerterbuch.
176p. (Ger.). 1971. 68.00 (ISBN 3-
7625-0460-1, M-7426, Pub. by
Bauverlag). French & Eur.
Volkart, K. H. Gypsum & Plaster
Dictionary. 176p. (Ger., Eng. &
Fr.). 1971. $68.00 (ISBN 3-7625-
0460-1, M-7437, Pub. by
Bauverlag). French & Eur.
--Gypsum & Plaster Dictionary.
176p. (Ger., Eng. & Fr.). 1971.
$68.00 (ISBN 3-7625-0460-1).
Bauverlag.

PLASTIC INDUSTRIES
see Plastics Industry and Trade

PLASTIC MATERIALS
see Plastics

PLASTIC PRODUCTS
see Plastics

PLASTICS
Kaliske, Gisbert. Plasttechnik-
Englisch-Deutsch-Franzoesisch-
Russisch. 390p. (Eng., Ger., Fr. &
Rus.). 1982. M.60.00. VEB
Technik.
Society of the Plastics Industry.
Plastic Bottle Glossary. $2.50
(1271). Soc Plastic Ind.
--Recommendations for Labeling
Plastics Microwave Cookware &
Glossary. first copy free (1200);
add. copies $0.20. Soc Plastic Ind.

PLASTICS–DICTIONARIES
Crespi, Irene & Ferrario, Jorge.
Lexico tecnico de las artes
plasticas. (Illus.). 208p. (Span.).
write for info. EUDEBA.
Diccionario Tecnologico Del
Plasticos. 160p. (Span.). 1978.
$9.95 (ISBN 84-85011-02-3, S-
50059). French & Eur.
Domininghaus, Hans. Lexikon der
Kunststoffe, 2 vols. LC 78-364503.
576p. (Ger.). 1978. write for info.
(ISBN 3-453-49070-3). Heyne W
Verlag.
El-Desouti, H. Y. Plastic Technology
Dictionary. 331p. (Eng., Fr., Ger.
& Arabic). 1980. $45.00 (ISBN 0-
686-92400-2, M-9754). French &
Eur.
Ferraris, E. Dictionnaire de
l'Industrie des matieres plastiques.
1977 ed. 320p. (Fr., Eng., & Ger.).
150.00 F. Maison Dictionnaire.
Ferraris, Enrico & Istituto Italiano
dei Plastici. Dizionario per
l'industria delle materie plastiche:
Definizioni italiane e termini
corrispondenti in francese, inglese
e tedesco. vii, 320p. (Ital., Fr.,
Eng. & Ger.). 1977. L.22000.00.
SAPIL.

Josselson, Harry H., ed. Russian-
English Plastics Dictionary:
Reversed from an English-Russian
Dictionary by Computer
Processing. LC 76-99790. (Rus. &
Eng.). 1970. text ed. $14.95x
(ISBN 0-8143-1396-5). Wayne St
U Pr.
Kaliske, G. Dictionary of Plastics
Technology in English, German,
French & Russian. 384p. (Eng.,
Ger., Fr. & Rus.). $74.50 (ISBN 0-
444-99687-7). Elsevier.
Stoeckhert, Klaus & Beck.
Kunststofflexikon. LC 76-452156.
225p. (Ger.). 1975. write for info.
Hanser.
Whittington, Lloyd R. Whittington's
Dictionary of Plastics. 2nd rev. ed.
LC 78-73776. 1978. $29.95 (ISBN
0-87762-267-1). Technomic.
Wittfoht. Dictionnaire des Matieres
Plastiques. 325p. (Fr. & Eng.,
Dictionary of Plastic Materials).
1976. pap. $52.50 (ISBN 0-686-
56774-9, M-6574). French & Eur.
--Dictionnaires des Matieres
Plastiques. 325p. (Fr.). 1976.
135.00 F. Francaise, Compagnie
Edition.
Wittfoht, A. Kunststofftechnik
Woerterbuch. 962p. (Ger. & Eng.,
Dictionary of Plastics). 1975.
$55.00 (ISBN 3-446-12137-4,
M7524, Pub. by C. Hanser).
French & Eur.
--Kunststofftechnik Woerterbuch.
962p. (Ger. & Eng.). 1975. $55.00
(ISBN 3-446-12137-4). Hanser.
--Kunststofftechnisches
Woerterbuch, Vol. 4. (Ger. & Fr.).
1962. $69.50 (ISBN 3-446-10363-
5, M-7526, Pub. by C. Hanser).
French & Eur.
--Kunststofftechnisches
Woerterbuch, Vol. 4. (Ger. & Fr.).
1962. $69.50 (ISBN 3-446-10363-
5). Hanser.
--Kunststofftechnisches
Woerterbuch, Vol. 5. (Ger. &
Span.). 1962. write for info. (ISBN
3-446-10364-3, M-7527, Pub. by
C. Hanser). French & Eur.
--Kunststofftechnisches
Woerterbuch, Vol. 5. (Ger. &
Span.). 1962. write for info. (ISBN
3-446-10364-3). Hanser.
--Kunststofftechnisches
Woerterbuch, Vol. 6. 544p. (Ger. &
Span.). 1962. $68.00 (ISBN 3-446-
10365-1, M-7528). French & Eur.
Wittfoht, A. & Achon, M. A.
Diccionario Tecnico De la
Plasticos Aleman-Espanol. 544p.
(Ger. & Span.). 1970. leatherette
$70.00 (ISBN 0-686-57332-3, S-
50005). French & Eur.
Wittfoht, A & Achon, M. A.
Diccionario tecnico de plasticos
aleman-espanol. (Illus.). 544p.
(Ger. & Span.). 1970. 1500.00 ptas.
Urmo.
Wittfoht, A. & Rubin, A. Diccionario
tecnico de plasticos: Espanol-
aleman. (Illus., Span. & Ger.).
1980. write for info. (Dist. Elcano,
Mexico). Urmo.
Wittfoht, A. M. The Technical Terms
in Plastics Engineering. 1976.
$64.00 (ISBN 0-444-99846-2).
Elsevier.
Wittfoht, A. M., ed. Plastics
Technical Dictionary, 3 vols.
(Illus.). 1700p. 1983. text ed.
135.00x (ISBN 0-02-949940-2,
Pub. by Hanser International).
Macmillan.
--Plastics Technical Dictionary: Part
1: English-German. (Illus.). 600p.
(Eng. & Ger.). 1982. text ed.
59.00x (ISBN 0-02-949980-1, Pub.
by Hanser International).
Macmillan.
--Plastics Technical Dictionary: Part
2: German-English. (Illus.). 600p.
(Ger. & Eng.). 1983. text ed.
59.00x (ISBN 0-02-949960-7, Pub.
by Hanser International).
Macmillan.
--Plastics Technical Dictionary: Part
3: Reference Volume. (Illus.).
508p. 1982. text ed. 49.00x (ISBN
0-02-949970-4, Pub. by Hanser
International). Macmillan.
Wordingham, J. A. & Reboul, P.
Diccionario del Plastico. 208p.
(Span.). $14.95 (ISBN 0-686-
56714-5, S-33051). French & Eur.

--Dictionary of Plastics. (Quality Paperback: No. 174). 1967. pap. 2.95 (ISBN 0-8226-0174-5). Littlefield.
Wordingham, J. A. & Reboul, P., trs. Diccionario plastico. 208p. (Span.). 1966. Arg.$1.80. Leru.

PLASTICS INDUSTRY AND TRADE
Welling, Manfred S. German-English Glossary of Plastics Machiney Terms. 280p. (Ger. & Eng.). 1981. text ed. 14.00x (ISBN 0-02-949800-7, Pub. by Hanser International). Macmillan.

PLATE TECTONICS
Dennis, J. G., ed. International tectonic lexicon. LC 81-47196. (Illus.). v, 153p. (Eng.). 1979. pap. write for info. (ISBN 3-510-65092-1). Schweizerbart.

PLATO, 427?-347 B.C.
Ast, Friedrich. Lexicon Platonicum, 3 vols. (Lat.). 1969. Set. $89.00 (ISBN 0-8337-0105-3). B Franklin.

PLATTDEUTSCH
see Low German Language

PLAYING-CARDS
see Cards

PLECTRAL INSTRUMENTS
see Stringed Instruments

PLOTINUS, d. 270 A.D.
Sleeman, J. H. & Pollet, Gilbert. Lexicon Plotinianum. LC 80-505958. (Gr. & Eng.). 1980. write for info. (ISBN 9-06-186083-0). Leuven U Pr.

PNEUMATIC MACHINERY
Lexique Francais-Anglais: Termes d'usage Courant en Hydraulique & Pneumatique. 42p. (Fr. & Eng.). 14.00 F. Ste. Publications Mecaniques.

PNEUMATICS
see also Aerodynamics; Pneumatic Machinery; Sound
Institute for Power System. Pneumatic Power Glossary. 80p. 1979. $30.00x (ISBN 0-686-65626-1). State Mutual Bk.
Neubert, G. Dictionary of Hydraulics & Pneumatics: English-German-Russian-Slovene. 226p. (Eng., Ger., Rus. & Slovene.). 1973. $75.00 (ISBN 0-686-92602-1, M-9896). French & Eur.
Neubert, Gunter. Dictionary of Hydraulics & Pneumatics. 226p. 1980. $40.00x (ISBN 0-569-08523-3, Pub. by Collet's). State Mutual Bk.

POCKET COMPANIONS
see Handbooks, Vade-Mecums, etc.

POETICS
Here are entered treatises on the art of poetry (technique and philosophy) Works limited to the philosophy of poetry are entered under the heading Poetry.
see also English Language–Rime–Dictionaries; Rime
Morier, Henri. Dictionnaire de Poetique & de Rhetorique. LC 76-473521. 1210p. (Fr.). 1975. 350.00 F. Pr Univ Fr.
Wood, Clement, ed. Complete Rhyming Dictionary. 1936. $10.95 (ISBN 0-385-00046-4). Doubleday.

POETRY–DICTIONARIES, INDEXES, ETC.
Campos, Geir. Pequeno Dicionario de Arte Poetica. LC 79-114787. 181p. (Port.). 1978. Cr.$80.00. Editora Cultrix.
Dictionnaire Imaginaire de Queiques Poetes Reels. (Fr.). write for info. De Feu.
Rodriguez Monino, Antonio. Diccionario Bibliografico De Liegos Sueltos Poeticos, Siglo XVI. 740p. (Span.). 1970. $59.95 (ISBN 84-7039-075-9, S-7006). French & Eur.

POETRY–STUDY AND TEACHING
Deutsch, Babette. Poetry Handbook: A Dictionary of Terms. 4th ed. 224p. 1982. pap. $5.05i (ISBN 0-06-463548-1, EH 548, EH). B&N NY.

POETRY–TECHNIQUE
see Poetics

POETRY FOR CHILDREN
see Nursery Rhymes

POISONOUS PLANTS
Guell, Francisco. Malas Hierbas, Diccionario Clasificatorio Ilustrado. 224p. (Span. & Lat.). 1970. pap. $18.75 (ISBN 84-281-0132-9, S-50018). French & Eur.

POLAR FLIGHTS
see Polar Regions

POLAR REGIONS
Here are entered works dealing with both the Antarctic and Arctic regions.
Dartmouth College Library, Hanover, N. H. Dictionary Catalog of the Stefansson Collection on the Polar Regions, 8 Vols. 1967. Set. lib. bdg. $690.00 (ISBN 0-8161-0676-2, Hall Library). G K Hall.

POLARITY (IN RELIGION, FOLK-LORE, ETC.)
Jehan, L. F. Dictionnaire des Controverses Historiques. Migne, J. P., ed. (Troisieme et Derniere Encyclopedie Theologique Ser.: Vol. 66). 698p. (Fr.). Repr. of 1866 ed. lib. bdg. $90.00x (ISBN 0-89241-329-8). Caratzas Pub Co.

POLEMICS (THEOLOGY)
see Apologetics

POLICE
see also Police Communication Systems
also subdivision Police under names of cities, e.g. Boston–Police
Arnal, Jacques. L Argot de Police. LC 75-513721. (Illus.). 186p. (Fr.). 1975. 9.90 F (ISBN 2-716-70310-8). Euredif.
Ismat, Shafiq. The Police Dictionary. 2nd rev. & enl. ed. (Illus.). 264p. (Eng. & Arabic.). $25.00 (068-6). Intl Bk Ctr.

POLICE–HANDBOOKS, MANUALS, ETC.
Schmidt, J. E. Police Medical Dictionary. 256p. 1968. $19.75x (ISBN 0-398-01673-9). C C Thomas.

POLICE COMMUNICATION SYSTEMS
see also Police; Radio; Telecommunication
Arnal, Jacques. L Argot de Police. LC 75-513721. (Illus.). 186p. (Fr.). 1975. 9.90 F (ISBN 2-716-70310-8). Euredif.

POLICE RADIO
see Police Communication Systems

POLICY SCIENCES
Policy Instruments to Define the Pattern of Demand for Technology. (Science & Technology for Development Ser.: STPI Module 7). 88p. 1981. pap. $5.00 (ISBN 0-88936-265-3, IDRC TS-27, IDRC). Unipub.

POLISH LANGUAGE
Bartminska, Izabela. Nazwiska Obce w Jezyku Polskim. LC 79-349806. (Illus.). 210p. (Eng. & Pol.). 1978. 34.00 Zl. Panstwowe Zaklad W.
Bartminska, Izabela, et al. Narwiska Obce w Jezyku Polskim. LC 79-349806. 210p. (Pol.). 1978. 34.00 Zl. Panstwowe Zaklad W.
Jedraszko, Sabian. Slownik Lekarski Polsko-Angielski. LC 76-511367. 410p. (Eng. & Pol.). 1975. 150.00 Zl. Panstwowy Zaklad W.
Kaczmarski, Stanisaw P. A Glossary of Polish & English Verb Forms. LC 79-345099. 199p. (Pol. & Eng.). 1978. 20.00 Zl. Panstwowy Zaklad W.
Matuschek, Herbert. Einwortlexeme & Wortgruppenlexeme in der Technischen Terminologie des Polnscheni. LC 78-352590. viii, 417p. (Pol.). 1977. write for info. (ISBN 3-87690-135-9). Sagner.
Ostrowski, Roza & Trojanwska, Izabella. Bedekr Kaszubski. LC 80-466240. (Illus.). 513p. (Pol., Gdansk). 1978. 180.00 Zl. Wydawn.
Sambor, Jadwiga. O Slownictwie Statystycznie Rzadkim. LC 75-406998. 113p. (Eng. & Pol.). 1975. 30.00 Zl. Panstwowe Zaklad W.
Wypych, Konrad. Deutsche Lehnworter in der Polnischen Bergbausprache. LC 77-463784. 267p. (Pol. & Ger.). 1976. DM.38.00. MG Schmitz.

POLISH LANGUAGE–CONVERSATION AND PHRASE BOOKS
Polsko-Russkii Razgovornik Dlia Turistov. 240p. (Pol. & Rus.). 1979. $2.95 (Pub. by Russkii Iazyk). Four Continent.

POLISH LANGUAGE–DICTIONARIES
Bartnicka, Barbara & Sinielnikoff, Roxana. Slownik Podstawowy Jezyka Polskiego dia Cudzoziemcow. LC 79-361030. (Illus.). 342p. (Pol., Warsaw). 1978. 100.00 Zl. Wydaw-a U. W.
Bartnicka, Barbara, et al. Slownik Podstawowy Jezyka Polskiego dia Cudzoziemcow. LC 79-361030. 342p. (Pol., Warsaw, Poland). 1978. 100.00 Zl. Wydaw-a UW.
Bielas, Leon. Slownik Minimum Francusko-Polski. LC 77-502306. 558p. (Pol. & Fr.). 1976. 30.00 Zl. Wiedza Powszechna.
Bogusiawski, Andrzej. Illustrowany Slownik Rosyjsko-Polski. LC 79-352771. 1179p. (Rus. & Pol.). 1978. 200.00 Zl. Wiedza Powszechna.
Boguslawski, Andrzej. Illustrowany Slownik Rosyjsko-Polski, Polsko-Rosyjski. LC 79-352771. (Illus.). 1179p. (Pol. & Rus.). 1978. 200.00 Zl. Wiedza Poswzechna.
Bolshoi Polsko-Russkii Slovar, 2 vols. (Rus. & Pol.). 1979. $28.95 (Pub. by Russkii Iazyk). Four Continent.
Borkowski, Piotr. English-Polish Dictionary of Idioms & Phrases. 206p. (Orig., Eng. & Pol.). 1982. pap. $6.95 (ISBN 0-903705-46-X). Hippocrene Bks.
Bulas, Kazimierz, et al. The Kosciuszko Foundation English-Polish, Polish-English Dictionary, 2 vols. (Poland's Millennium Ser.). (Eng. & Pol.). 1973. English-Polish. text ed. 12.50 (ISBN 0-917004-00-0); Polish-English. text ed. 12.50 (ISBN 0-917004-16-7). Kosciuszko.
Bullas, K. & Whitfield, F. J. Dictionary English-Polish, Polish-English, 2 vols. (Eng. & Pol.). 1969. Set. $38.50 (ISBN 0-685-05192-7). Adler.
Bzdega, A., et al. Podreczny Slownik Polsko-Niemiecki (Manual Dictionary Polish-German) 1018p. (Pol. & Ger.). 1977. leatherette $19.95 (ISBN 0-686-87194-4, M-0129). French & Eur.
Dictionary of Polish Pronunciation: Slownik Wymomwy Polskiej PWN. (Pol.). 1980. 25.00x (ISBN 0-686-61083-0). Hippocrene Bks.
Dictionnaire Francais-Polonais. 1004p. (Fr. & Pol.). 1978. 55.80 F. Vander.
Dictionnaire Polonais-Francais. 1076p. (Pol. & Fr.). 1978. 55.80 F. Vander.
Doroszewski, W., ed. Slownik Poprawnej Polszczyzny. 1055p. (Pol.). 1977. $22.50 (Pub. by Panstwowe Wydawnictwo Naukowe). Four Continent.
English-Polish-English Dictionary. (Eng. & Pol.). 15.00 (ISBN 0-87557-060-7). Saphrograph.
Grzebieniowski, T. Concise English-Polish & Polish-English Dictionary. 688p. (Pol. & Eng.). $10.95. Barron.
Grzebieniowski, Tadeusz, ed. Illustrated English-Polish Polish-English Dictionary. rev. & enl. ed. (Illus.). 908p. (Eng. & Pol.). 1978. 13.50x (ISBN 0-8002-2262-8). Intl Pubns Serv.
Grzebienowski, Tadeus Z. Polish-English, English-Polish Dictionary. (Illus., Pol. & Eng.). 1980. 16.95 (ISBN 0-88254-477-2). Hippocrene Bks.
Hamel, Bernard. Dictionnaire de Poche, 1: Francais-Polonais. 490p. (Fr. & Pol.). 1971. 24.00 F. Polonaises.
--Dictionnaire de Poche, 2: Polonais-Francais. 514p. (Pol. & Fr.). 1971. 24.00 F. Polonaises.
A Handy English-Polish Dictionary. 914p. (Eng. & Pol.). 1980. $20.00x (ISBN 0-569-07422-3, Pub. by Collet's). State Mutual Bk.
Hrabcowa, Stanislawa, et al. Slownik Jezyka Polskiego dia Cudzoziemcow. LC 80-485792. viii, 445p. (Pol., Warsaw, Poland). 1979. 50.00 Zl. Wydaw-a UW.
Jozwicki, J. Minimum-Worterbuch: Deutsch-Polnisch, Polnisch-Deutsch. 557p. (Ger. & Pol.). 1980. pap. $4.95 (ISBN 83-214-0099-X). French & Eur.
Kania, Stanislaw & Gora, Zielona. Polska Gwara Konspiracyjno-Partyzancka Czasu Okupacji Hitlerowskiej. LC 77-562382. 295p. (Pol.). 1976. 70.00 Zl. Wyzsza Szkola.
Karmannyi Polsko-Russkii i Russko-Polskii Slovar. 472p. (Pol. & Rus.). 1960. $1.25. Four Continent.
Kierst. Polish-English - English-Polish Dictionary. (Pol. & Eng.). 29.50 (ISBN 0-87557-060-7, 060-7). Saphrograph.
Kierst, W. English-Polish, Polish-English Dictionary. (Eng. & Pol.). 29.50 (ISBN 0-87557-060-7, 060-7). Saphrograph.
Koch, Z. J. Polnisch-Deutsches Wissenschaftlich-Technishes Worterbuch. 598p. (Pol. & Ger.). 1980. $75.00 (ISBN 83-204-0021-X, M-9217). French & Eur.
Kozaklewicz, Stefana. Slownik Terminologiczny Sztuk Pieknych. 2d ed. LC 76-529202. (Illus.). 522p. (Pol.). 1976. 120.00 Zl. Panstwowe Wydawnicto Iskry.
Krawczykiewicz, A. Suomi-Poula Suomi Dictionary: Finnish-Polish-Finnish. 687p. (Finnish & Pol.). 1979. pap. $18.95 (ISBN 951-0-08000-4, M-9638). French & Eur.
Kupisz, Kazimierz, et al. Podreczny Slownik Polsko-Francuski. LC 77-557604. 1150p. (Pol. & Fr.). 1977. 190.00 Zl. Wiedza Powszechna.
Lana, Italo. Vocabolario Della Lingua Latina: Italiano-Latino, Latino-Italiano. LC 80-457571. xvi, 1870p. (Lat. & Ital.). 1978. write for info. Paravia.
Langenscheidts Universal-Woerterbuch Polnisch. 560p. (Pol. & Ger.). DM.6.80 (18260). Langenscheidt.
Marti, A. & Marti, J. Pequeno Diccionario Espanol-Polaco, Polaco-Espanol. 707p. (Span. & Pol.). 1976. $12.95 (ISBN 0-686-92083-X, S-32367). French & Eur.
Marti Marca, Antonio, et al. Maly Slownik Hispansko-Polski & Polsko-Hiszpanski. 3rd. ed. LC 77-502213. 289p. (Pol. & Span.). 1977. 100.00 Zl. Wiedza Powszechna.
Mazzucchi, P. Dizionario polesano-italiano. 308p. (Pol. & Ital.). L.10800.00. Forni.
Mironova, Inessa N. Slownik Kieszonkowy Polsko-Rosyjski. LC 80-450178. 575p. (Pol. & Rus.). 1978. 1.00 Rub. Russkii Iazyk.
Mirowicz. Wielki Slownik Polsko-Rosyski (Polish-Russian Dictionary) 1331p. (Pol. & Rus.). 1980. $70.00 (ISBN 0-686-87195-2, M-9131). French & Eur.
Mitronova, I. N., et al. Karmannyi Pol'Sko-Russkii & Russko-Polskii Slovar. 560p. (Rus. & Pol.). 1976. $2.25 (Pub. by Russkii Iazyk). Four Continent.
Nitronowa, I., et al. Polish-Russian, Russian-Polish Dictionary. 575p. (Pol. & Rus.). 1980. leatherette $4.95 (ISBN 0-686-97442-5, M-9102). French & Eur.
Piprek, J. & Ippoldt, J. Grobworterbuch Polnisch-Deutsch. 2121p. (Ger. & Pol.). 1979. leatherette $75.00 (ISBN 83-214-0011-6, M-9128). French & Eur.
Pisarek, W. Slownik Jezyka Niby-Polskiego, Czyli Bledy Jezykowe. 176p. (Pol.). 1978. $3.95 (Pub. by Ossolineum). Four Continent.
Pognowski, Iwo. The New Polish-English Dictionary. rev. ed. (Pol. & Eng.). 1982. 19.95 (ISBN 0-88254-463-2); pap. 11.95 (ISBN 0-88254-464-0). Hippocrene Bks.
Pogonowski, Iwo. Dictionary, Polish-English, English-Polish: Contemporary Usage American & Polish. (Illus.). v, 647p. (Pol. & Eng.). 1979. write for info. (ISBN 0-88254-463-2); pap. text ed. write for info (ISBN 0-88254-464-0). Hippocrene Bks.
--Practical Polish-English Dictionary: Polish-English; English-Polish. LC 78-64764. (Pol. & Eng.). 1981. pap. 6.95 (ISBN 0-88254-494-2). Hippocrene Bks.
Polish Pocket Dictionary. (Pol. & Eng.). pap. 6.50 (ISBN 0-686-77983-5). Heinman.

Salamaa, Elsa. Maly Slownik Finsko-Polski & Polski-Finski. LC 76-503222. 106p. (Finnish & Pol.). 1975. Fmk.26.00 (ISBN 9-51261-007-8). Kirjayhtyma.

Schimitzek, S., et al. Kleinworterbuch Deutsch-Polnisch (Handy German-Polish Dictionary) 652p. (Ger. & Pol.). 1977. $12.95 (ISBN 0-686-87188-X, M-9133). French & Eur.

Sikorski, Lech. Maly Slownik Polsko-Swedzki. 322p. (Pol. & Swedish.). 1976. 55.00 Zl. Plastik.

--Maly Slownik Szwedzko-Polski. LC 76-525326. xxvi, 300p. (Swedish & Pol.). 1976. write for info. Wiedza Powszechna.

Sinitsyna, G. V. & Mitronova, I. N. Karmannyi Polsko-Russkii & Russko-Polskii Slovar. LC 80-450178. 575p. (Pol. & Rus.). 1978. 1.00 Rub. Russkii Iazyk.

Slopek, Stefan. Slownik Immunologiczny Ilustrowany. LC 77-567783. 339p. (Pol.). 1977. 120.00 Zl. Panstowy Zaklad W.

Soja, Stanislaw, et al. Maly Slownik Wlosko-Polski, 2 vols. LC 77-562532. (Ital. & Pol.). 1977. 130.00 Zl. Wiedza Powszechna.

--Maly Slownik Wlosko-Polski & Polsko-Wloski, 2 vols. 3rd ed. LC 77-562532. (Pol. & Ital.). 1977. 130.00 Zl. Wiedza Powszechna.

Stanislawski, J. The Great English-Polish Dictionary. 1405p. (Eng. & Pol.). 1979. leatherette $75.00 (ISBN 0-686-97431-X, M-9329). French & Eur.

--The Great Polish-English Dictionary. 1728p. (Pol. & Eng.). 1980. leatherette $75.00 (ISBN 83-214-0107-4, M-9368). French & Eur.

--Polish-English & English-Polish Dictionary. (New Pronouncing Dictionaries). (Pol. & Eng.). (YA) (gr. 9 up). 12.95 (ISBN 0-679-10082-2). McKay.

--Polish-English, English-Polish Dictionary (1975, 4 vols. (Pol. & Eng.). 1978. Set. 120.00 (ISBN 0-685-85757-3). Heinman.

--Polish-English, English-Polish Practical Dictionary, 2 vols. (Pol. & Eng.). Set. 50.00 (ISBN 0-685-79114-9). Heinman.

Stanislawski, J. & Billip, K. Polish Practical Dictionary (English-Polish) (Pol. & Eng.). 1981. $20.00x (ISBN 0-89918-533-9, P-533). Vanous.

Stanislawski, J., ed. The Great English-Polish Dictionary, 2 vols. 607p. (Eng. & Pol.). 1980. vinyl $99.00x (ISBN 0-569-00671-6, Pub. by Collet's). State Mutual Bk.

--The Great Polish-English Dictionary, 2 vols. (Pol. & Eng.). 1980. vinyl $60.00x (ISBN 0-569-02649-0, Pub. by Collet's). State Mutual Bk.

Stanislawski, Jan. Polish Great Dictionary, Vol. 1: English-Polish, 2 vols. rev. 6th ed. (Eng. & Pol.). 1982. $55.00x (ISBN 0-89918-502-9, P-502). Vanous.

--A Practical Polish-English Dictionary. LC 77-578742. 1036p. (Pol.). 1981. $17.50x (ISBN 83-214-0124-4). Intl Pubns Serv.

--Wielki Slownik Polsko-Angielski, 2 vols. LC 79-338334. (Pol. & Eng.). 1978. 1600.00 Zl. Wiedza Powszechna.

Stanislowski, J. Polish Great Dictionary, Vol. 2: Polish-English, 2 vols. 4th ed. (Pol. & Eng.). 1978. text ed. $42.00x (ISBN 0-89918-521-5, P-521). Vanous.

Stano, Mikulas. Polsko -Slovensky a Slovensko-Polsky Slovnik. LC 75-590519. 861p. (Pol. & Slovak.). 1975. 55.00 Kcs. SNTC.

Stano, Mikulas, et al. Pol'sko-Slovensky a Slovensko-Polsky Slovnik. LC 75-590519. 861p. (Pol. & Slovak.). 1975. 55.00 Kcs. SNTC.

Stypula, Ryszard, et al. Slownik Polsko-Rosyjski. LC 76-531554. 840p. (Pol. & Rus.). 1976. 2.58 Rub. Wiedza Powszechna.

--Podreczny Slownik Polsko-Rosyjski. LC 77-502170. 840p. (Pol. & Rus.). 1976. 80.00 Zl. Wiedza Powszechna.

Szwykowski, Ludwik, et al. Maly Slownik Francusko-Polski. LC 77-578114. xxviii, 326p. (Fr. & Pol.). 1977. 110.00 Zl. Wiedza Powszechna.

Vaitkiavichiute, V. A. Polsko-Litovskii Slovar. 1024p. (Pol. & Lithuanian.). 1979. $9.95 (Pub. by Mokslas). Four Continent.

Varsanyi, Istvan. Lengyel-Magyar Szotar. LC 76-533514. xvi, 784p. (Pol. & Hungarian.). 1976. 35.00 Ft (ISBN 963-205-048-7). Terra.

--Magyar-Lengyel Szotar. LC 77-457358. 928p. (Hungarian & Pol.). 1976. 35.00 Ft (ISBN 9-6320-5049-5). Terra.

--Magyar-Lengyel Szotar. LC 77-457358. 928p. (Hungarian & Pol.). 1976. 35.00 Ft (ISBN 9-63205-049-5). Terra.

Vocabularios Aleman-Espanol-Polaco. (Ger. , Span. & Pol.). $0.80; Mex.$10.00. Novaro.

Walega, Stanislaw. Slownik Finsko-Polski. LC 78-376750. 658p. (Finnish & Pol.). 1978. Fmk.135.00. Wiedza Powszechna.

Walewski, Stanislaw. Langenscheidts Taschenwoerterbuch Polnisch, 2 vols. in 1. (Pol. & Ger.). DM.29.80 (11260). Langenscheidt.

--Langenscheidts Taschenwoerterbuch Polnisch: Teil II, Deutsch-Polnisch. 591p. (Ger. & Pol.). DM.19.80 (10265). Langenscheidt.

Wysinska, E. Slownik Wspolczesnego T Atru: Tworcy, Teatry, Teorie. 424p. (Pol.). 1979. $12.95 (Pub. by Wydaw. Artystyczne & Filmowe). Four Continent.

POLITENESS
see Courtesy; Etiquette

POLITICAL ECONOMY
see Economics

POLITICAL MURDER
see Assassination

POLITICAL PARTIES–UNITED STATES

Bone, Hugh A. Party Committees & National Politics. rev. ed. LC 58-10481. (Illus.). 272p. 1968. $12.50x (ISBN 0-295-78559-4). U of Wash Pr.

POLITICAL SCIENCE
see also Administrative Law; Aristocracy; Authority; Civics; Civil Rights; Civil Service; Civilization; Constitutional Law; Democracy; Jurisprudence; Legislation; Local Government; Municipal Government; Politics, Practical; Public Administration; Public Law; Revolutions; Socialism; State Governments; Taxation
also subheading Constitution and subdivision Politics and Government under names of countries, states, etc. e.g. United States–Constitution; Massachusetts–Politics and Government

Connolly, William E. The Terms of Political Discourse. LC 83-42928. 240p. 1984. $30.00x (ISBN 0-691-07664-2); pap. $9.95x (ISBN 0-691-02223-2). Princeton U Pr.

Guyard, Marie-Renee. Le Vocabulaire Politique de Paul Eluard. 286p. (Fr.). 68.00 F. Klincksieck.

Kollnig, Karl Rudolf. Politisch-Soziologisches Woerterbuch. LC 75-516317. 254p. (Ger.). 1975. DM.9.80. Kamp Verlag.

Plano, Jack C., et al. Political Science Directory. LC 77-186296. 400p. 1976. 15.00 (ISBN 0-03-016736-1, HIS). HR&W.

Prehl, Hede, et al. Politik & Gesellschaft: Ein Lexikon zur Politischen Bildung. 463p. (Ger.). DM.19.80 (ISBN 3-411-01729-5). Biblio Inst.

Rabotin, Maurice. Le Vocabulaire Politique & Socio-Ethnique a Montreal de 1839 a 1842. (Illus.). 122p. (Fr.). 1975. Can.$4.00. Didier-Canada.

POLITICAL SCIENCE–DICTIONARIES

Akoun, A., et al. Dictionnaire de Politique. LC 79-352686. 351p. (Fr.). 1978. 75.00 F (ISBN 2-03-070104-1). Larousse FR.

Andrianov, B. A., et al. Rumynsko-Russkii Politekhnicheskii. 715p. (Rus. & Romanian.). 1956. $4.50 (Pub. by Gostekhteorizdat). Four Continent.

Aquistapace, Jean N. Diccionario de la politica. 2nd ed. (Span.). 100.00 ptas. Magisterio Esp.

Aquistapace, Jean-Noel. Diccionario De la Politica. 2nd ed. 344p. (Span.). 1969. pap. $7.95 (ISBN 84-265-7047-X, S-21237). French & Eur.

Artobolevskii, I. I., ed. Politekhnicheskii Slovar. 608p. (Rus.). 1977. $19.95 (Pub. by Sov Entsiklopediia). Four Continent.

Ashkharumov, R. T., et al. Russko-Armianskii Politekhnicheskii Slovar. 436p. (Rus. & Armenian.). 1957. $4.95 (Pub. by An Arm SSR). Four Continent.

Back, H., et al. Dictionary of Politics & Economics. 1037p. (Eng., Fr. & Ger., Dictionnaire de Politique et d'Economie - Lexikon fur Politik und Wirschaft). 1967. $37.00 (ISBN 3-11-000892-0, M-7104). French & Eur.

Beck, Carl, et al, eds. Political Science Thesaurus. 1975. $20.00 (ISBN 0-915654-02-4); to institutions $30.00 (ISBN 0-685-53465-0); pap. $15.00, to institutions 25.00 (ISBN 0-685-53466-9). Am Political.

Berardi, Roberto. Dizionario di termini storici, politici ed economici moderni. 182p. (Ital.). L.3300.00. Monnier.

Biard, Roland. Dictionnaire de l'Extreme-Gauche: De 1945 a Nos Jours. 384p. (Fr.). 1978. pap. $22.50 (ISBN 0-686-56917-2, M-6033). French & Eur.

Bierfelder, W. Handwoerterbuch des Oeffentlichen Dienster: Das Personalwesen. 1800p. (Ger.). 1976. $250.00 (ISBN 3-503-01424-1, M-7440, Pub. by E. Schmidt). French & Eur.

--Handwoerterbuch des Oeffentlichen Dienster: Das Personalwesen. 1800p. (Ger.). 1976. $250.00 (ISBN 3-503-01424-1). Schmidt Verlag.

Bobbio, Norberto & Matteuci, Nicola. Dizionario di politica. xii, 1098p. (Ital.). 1977. L.35000.00 (ISBN 88-02-02623-8). UTET.

Bobbio, Norberto & Matteuci, Nicola, eds. Dizionario di Politica. LC 77-467442. xi, 1097p. (Ital.). 1976. L.3200.00. UTET.

Borisov, et al. Diccionario De Economia Politica. 2nd ed. 256p. (Span.). 1977. pap. $6.95 (ISBN 84-253-0610-8, S-50074). French & Eur.

--Diccionario de Economia Politica. 264p. (Span.). 1975. pap. $6.95 (ISBN 84-7339-060-1, S-50150). French & Eur.

Cherukhina, A. E. Anglo-russki i politekhnicheski. LC 80-471023. 687p. (Eng. & Rus.). 1979. pap. 9.70 Rub. Russky Yazyk.

Chinese Language Division of Home Affairs Department. An English-Chinese Glossary of Terms Commonly Used in Government. LC 81-185069. (Chinese & Eng.). 1981. HK.$pap. 5.00. Govt Printer.

Coloma, Jose M. Leico De Politica. 6th ed. 200p. (Span.). 1976. pap. $8.75 (ISBN 84-7222-752-9, S-50039). French & Eur.

--Lexico de Politica. 5th ed. LC 76-450510. 198p. (Span.). 1975. write for info. ptas (ISBN 8-472-22752-9). Laia.

Coston, Henry. Dictionnaire de la Politique Francaise. (Illus.). 1088p. (Fr.). 120.00 F. Francaise Lib.

Davis, Robert R., Jr. Lexicon of Historical & Political Terms. pap. 1.95 (ISBN 0-671-18706-6, 18706). Monarch Pr.

--Lexicon of Historical & Political Terms. Reed, R., ed. LC 81-83626. (Illus.). 125p. 1982. pap. 7.95 (ISBN 0-88247-612-2). R & E Res Assoc.

Debbasch, Charles & Daudet, Yves. Lexique des Termes Politiques. 280p. (Fr.). 1978. pap. $14.95 (ISBN 0-686-57285-8, M-4652). French & Eur.

--Lexique des Termes Politiques. 280p. (Fr.). 1978. 34.00 F. Dalloz.

De Bourbon Parma, Cecilia. Diccionario del Carlismo. LC 77-553587. (Illus.). 93p. (Span.). 1977. 50.00 ptas (ISBN 8-472-35307-9). Dopesa.

Dictionnaire de Politique: Coll. le Present en Question. 350p. (Fr.). 1979. $29.95 (ISBN 0-686-57100-2, M-6124). French & Eur.

Dictionnaire de Politique: Collection le Present en Question. (Fr.). 1978. $25.50 (Dist. by Continental Bk Co). Larousse.

Dietl, Clara E. & Lorenz, Egon. Woerterbuch fuer Recht, Wirtschaft & Politik: Teil II, Deutsch-Englisch. (Ger. & Eng.). 1983. write for info. Recht & Wirtschaft.

Dizionario dei comuni e delle circoscrizioni amminstrative, delle frazioni e delle localita. 640p. (Ital.). 1978. L.8000.00. La Tribuna.

Dreschler, Hanno, et al. Gesellschaft & Staat: Lexikon der Politik. LC 79-388088. (Illus.). xx, 604p. (Ger.). 1979. DM.38.00 (ISBN 3-797-10078-7). Signal-Verlag.

Dreuihe. Dictionnaire Anglais-Francais et Lexique Francais-Anglais des termes Politiques Juridiques et Economiques. (Eng. & Fr.). 1981. pap. $22.95 (ISBN 0-686-92584-X, M-9628). French & Eur.

Dudavskii, V. I., et al. Russko-Pol'skii Politekhnicheskii Slovar. 726p. (Rus. & Pol.). 1955. $4.35 (Pub. by Gosizdat Tekhn. Teoretich. Lit.). Four Continent.

Dudawaki, B., et al. Russian-Polish Political Dictionary. 726p. (Rus. & Pol.). 1955. leatherette $9.95 (ISBN 0-686-92134-8, M-9114). French & Eur.

Duelo, Gerardo. Diccionario De Grupos, Fuerzas, y Partidos Politicos Espanoles. 128p. (Span.). 1977. pap. $5.25 (ISBN 84-7080-940-7, S-50175). French & Eur.

Elliot. Diccionario de politica. (Span.). 290.00 ptas. Labor SA.

Emde, Heiner. Das Lexikon der Politik. LC 76-461039. 170p. (Ger.). 1975. DM.4.80 (ISBN 3-453-41123-4). Heyne W Verlag.

Eynern, Gert V. Woerterbuch zur Politischen Oekonomie. 2nd ed. (Ger.). 1977. pap. $19.95 (ISBN 3-531-21148-X, M-6902). French & Eur.

Foldes, Istvan & Makai, Gyoergy. Politikai Kissotar: A Szocikkek Szerzoi. LC 75-547485. 289p. (Hungarian.). 1974. 40.00 Ft. Kos Kony.

Fuster Ortells, Joan. Diccionari Pera Ociosos. 208p. (Catalan.). 1978. pap. $6.75 (ISBN 84-297-1431-6, S-50213). French & Eur.

Gerescher, Konrad. Politik Aufgespiesst: Heiteres Lexikon der Politischen Missbildung. LC 77-481880. 58p. (Ger.). 1976. write for info. (ISBN 3-87998-010-1). Gauke.

Gil-Robles, Jose M. Diccionario De Terminos Electorales y Parlamentarios. 268p. (Span.). 1977. pap. $15.25 (ISBN 84-306-3039-2, S-50001). French & Eur.

Gil-Robles y Quinones, Jose M. Diccionario de Terminos Electorales & Parlamentarios. LC 77-556193. 267p. (Span.). 1977. write for info. ptas (ISBN 8-430-63039-2). Taurus Ediciones SA.

Goerlitz. Handlexikon Zur Politikwissenschaft, 2 vols. 530p. (Ger.). 1973. pap. $9.50 (ISBN 3-499-16169-9, M-7438, Pub. by Rowohlt). French & Eur.

--Handlexikon zur Politikwissenschaft, 2 vols. 530p. (Ger.). 1973. pap. $9.50 (ISBN 3-499-16169-9). Rowohlt.

Gorlitz, Axel. Diccionario de Ciencia Politica. (Span.). 1979. pap. pns (S-50085). French & Eur.

--Diccionario de Ciencia Politica. 632p. (Span.). 1980. 1.800 ptas. Alianza Ed.

Haensch, Guenther. Woerterbuch der Internationalen Beziehungen und der Politik. 2nd ed. (Ger., Eng., Fr. & Span., Dictionary of International Relations & Politics). pap. $40.00 (ISBN 3-19-006211-0, M-6993). French & Eur.

Haro Tecglen, Eduardo. Diccionario Politico. 6th ed. 288p. (Span.). 1977. pap. $7.50 (ISBN 84-320-0259-3, S-50024). French & Eur.

--Diccionario Politico. 288p. (Span.). 1974. 160.00 ptas (ISBN 84-320-0259-3). Planeta SA.
Heimanson, Rudolph. Dictionary of Political Science & Law. LC 67-14401. 188p. 1967. 12.00 (ISBN 0-379-00325-2). Oceana.
Hellegouarc'H, Jean. Le Vocabulaire Latin Des Relations et Des Partis Politiques Sous la Republique. (Fr.). $39.95 (ISBN 0-686-57327-7, M-6314). French & Eur.
Khopkar, M. B., compiled by. Dictionary of Political Terminology. 1970. pap. $2.75 (ISBN 0-88253-149-2). Ind-US Inc.
Kratkii Politicheskii Slovar. 295p. (Rus.). 1971. $2.30 (Pub. by Politizdat). Four Continent.
Kratkii Politicheskii Slovar. 416p. (Rus.). 1977. $3.95 (Pub. by Politizdat). Four Continent.
Kuznetsova. Russko-Angliiskii Politekhnicheskii Slovar. 728p. (Rus. & Eng.). 1980. $19.95 (Pub. by Russkii Iazyk). Four Continent.
Langenbucher, W. R., ed. Kulturpolitisches Woerterbuch. (Ger.). 1982. $24.00. M Rosenberg.
Laqueur, Walter. Dictionary of Politics. rev. ed. LC 74-9232. 1974. $17.95 (ISBN 0-02-917950-5). Free Pr.
Launay, Michel. Le Vocabulaire Politique de J. J. Rousseau. (Fr.). 35.00 F. Slatkine.
Lexique de Termes Politiques. (Fr.). 1981. 370.00 F. Bruylant.
Lowe, Joseph D. Dictionary of Political Terms: Chinese-English, English-Chinese. (Illus.). xvii, 950p. (Chinese & Eng.). 1983. 75.00 (ISBN 0-9605506-0-7). Lowe Pub.
Malignon, Jean. Dictionnaire de Politique. 460p. (Fr.). 1967. $17.50 (ISBN 0-686-56800-1, F-77270). French & Eur.
--Dictionnaire de Politique. 460p. (Fr.). 1967. 40.00 F. Cujas.
Marquez Bessa, Antonio. Diccionario Politico Para Occidente. 288p. (Span.). 1978. pap. $9.95 (ISBN 84-7335-024-3, S-50003). French & Eur.
Mascitelli. Diccionario De Terminos Marxistos. 416p. (Span.). 1979. pap. $15.75 (ISBN 84-253-1166-7, S-50073). French & Eur.
Modica, Enzo & Triva, Rubes. Dizionario delle autonomie locali. 852p. (Ital.). L.12000.00. Editori Riuniti.
Montgomery, Hugh. A Dictionary of Political Phrases & Allusions. 75.00 (ISBN 0-8490-0044-0). Gordon Pr.
--Dictionary of Political Phrases & Allusions with a Short Bibliography. LC 68-28333. 1968. Repr. of 1906 ed. $34.00x (ISBN 0-8103-3092-X). Gale.
Moreno, Daniel. Diccionario de politica. 256p. (Span.). 1981. Mex.$pap. 150.00. Porrua.
Ott, A. Dictionnaire des Sciences Politiques et Sociales, 3 vols. Migne, J. P., ed. (Troisieme et Derniere Encyclopedie Theologique Ser.: Vols. 1-3). 2014p. (Fr.). Repr. of 1855 ed. lib. bdg. $256.00x (ISBN 0-89241-290-9). Caratzas Pub Co.
Pallotta, Gino. Dizionario politico e parlamentare. (Ital.). L.2500.00. Newton Compton.
--Dizionario Politico e Parlamentare Italiano. LC 77-454206. 302p. (Ital.). 1976. L.2500.00. Newton Compton.
Pfahlberg, B. Herder - Lexikon Politik. 2nd ed. 240p. (Ger.). 1976. pap. $15.95 (ISBN 3-451-16456-6, M-7450, Pub. by Herder). French & Eur.
--Herder-Lexikon Politik. 2nd ed. 240p. (Ger.). 1976. pap. $15.95 (ISBN 3-451-16456-6). Herder.
Pfahlberg, Bernard, ed. Politik: Mit 1800 Stichwoertern. LC 77-377171. (Illus.). 238p. (Ger.). 1979. DM.22.00 (ISBN 3-451-16456-6). Herder.
Phillips, Claude S. The African Political Dictionary. (Clio Dictionaries in Political Science: No. 5). (Illus.). 300p. 1983. lib. bdg. $20.75 (ISBN 0-87436-036-6); pap. $10.75 (ISBN 0-87436-040-4). ABC-Clio.
Plano, Jack C. Political Science Dictionary. LC 73-10501. 1973. pap. text ed. 10.95 (ISBN 0-03-086191-8, HoltC). HR&W.
Plano, Jack C. & Greenberg, Milton. The American Political Dictionary. 6th ed. 1982. 12.50 (ISBN 0-03-060127-4). HR&W.
Plano, Jack C., et al. The Dictionary of Political Analysis. 2nd ed. LC 82-4032. (Clio Dictionaries in Political Science Ser.: No. 3). 197p. 1982. text ed. $19.75 (ISBN 0-87436-331-4); pap. $9.75 (ISBN 0-87436-339-X). ABC-Clio.
Ponomareva, B. N., ed. Politicheskii Slovar. 702p. (Rus.). 1958. $3.95 (Pub. by Politizdat). Four Continent.
Pont Mestres, Magin. Politica & Politiqueria: Diccionario Para el Hombre de la Calle. LC 79-127325. 165p. (Span.). 1979. 500.00 ptas (ISBN 8-470-02275-X). Edns Acervo.
Raymond, Walter J. Dictionary of Politics. LC 78-50189. (Illus.). deluxe ed. $25.95x (ISBN 0-931494-00-1). Brunswick Pub.
Rebollo Torio, Miguel A. Vocabulario Politico Republicano y Franquista, 1931-1971. 184p. (Span.). 1978. $13.95 (ISBN 84-7366-072-2, S-50122). French & Eur.
Rico y Amat, Juan. Diccionario de los Politicos. (Span.). 350.00 ptas. Narcea SA.
Roberts, G. K. Dictionary of Political Analysis. LC 70-151309. 1971. $22.50 (ISBN 0-312-20930-4). St Martin.
Royuela, Alberto. Diccionario de la Ultra Derecha. LC 77-564609. (Illus.). 112p. (Span.). 1977. 50.00 ptas (ISBN 8-472-35311-7). Dopesa.
Safire, William. Safire's Political Dictionary. 1980. pap. $9.95 (ISBN 0-345-28393-7). Ballantine.
--Safire's Political Dictionary: The New Language of Politics. 1978. 17.95 (ISBN 0-394-50261-2). Random.
Samuel, Albert. Petit Vocabulire Politique. LC 79-354581. 143p. (Fr.). 1978. write for info. Chronique Sociale.
Sanchez Carrate, Juan A. Diccionario de la Izquierda Comunista. LC 77-551842. (Illus.). 91p. (Span.). 1977. 50.00 ptas (ISBN 8-472-35308-7). Dopesa.
Sandahl, P. & De Bea, L. Dictionnaire Politique & Diplomatique. 3rd ed. (Fr.). 1976. 340.00 F. Bruylant.
Sandahl, Pierre & Bea, Louise de. Dictionnaire Politique et Diplomatique. 194p. (Fr.). 1976. pap. $14.95 (ISBN 0-686-57214-9, M-6503). French & Eur.
Sandahl, Pierre & De Bea, Louise. Dictionnaire Politique & Diplomatique. 194p. (Fr.). 1976. 28.00 F. Litec.
Sanquiao, O. J. Diccionario Politico: Los Ministros Nacionales. (Span., Buenos Aires, Argentina). 1980. Arg.$16000.00. Platero.
Scruton, Robert. A Dictionary of Political Thought. LC 82-47532. 352p. 1982. 19.18i (ISBN 0-06-015044-0, HarpT). Har-Row.
Theimer, Walter. Lexikon der Politik: Politik Grundbegriffe & Grundgedanken. 8th ed. LC 75-509661. 315p. (Ger.). 1975. DM.17.80 (ISBN 3-772-01037-7). Francke.
Theimer, Walter, tr. Diccionario de poltica mundial. 592p. (Span.). pap. 225.00 ptas. Ariel.
Titone, Virgilio. Dizionario delle idee comuni, 2 vols. (Ital.). 1975. L.6000.00. Pan Italy.
Tokarev, S. A., et al, eds. Frantsuzsko-Russkii Obshchestvenno-Politisheskii Slovar. 283p. (Fr. & Rus.). 1961. $3.00 (Pub. by Izd. In-ta Mezhdunarod. Otnoshenii). Four Continent.
Vajda, Georges. Le Dictionnaire des Autorites. 226p. (Fr.). 1963. pap. $17.50 (ISBN 0-686-56833-8, M-6611). French & Eur.
Wahba, Magdi & Ghali, Wagdi R. A Dictionary of Modern Political Idiom: English-French-Arabic. LC 79-960201. ix, 747p. (Eng., Fr., & Arabic.). 1978. E25.00. Lib Liban.
Whisker, James B. Dictionary of Concepts on American Politics. LC 80-15591. 285p. 1980. pap. $11.95 (ISBN 0-471-07716-X). Wiley.
Zahn, H. Dictionary of Politics & Economic Policy. 384p. (Ger., Eng. & Fr.). 1975. $49.50 (ISBN 0-7121-5514-7, M-7105). French & Eur.
Zahn, Hans E. Woerterbuch zur Politik und Wirtschaftpolitik. (Ger., Eng. & Fr.). 1976. $76.00 (ISBN 3-7819-2011-9, M-6904). French & Eur.

POLITICAL SCIENCE–TERMINOLOGY

Lewis, George C. Remarks on the Use & Abuse of Some Political Terms. LC 72-113816. 370p. 1970. $16.00x (ISBN 0-8262-0089-3). U of Mo Pr.
Scruton, ROger. A Dictionary of Political Thought. 512p. (Eng.). 1982. E12.00 (ISBN 0-333-33439-6). Macmillan London.
Scruton, Roger, ed. Dictionary of Political Thought. 356p. (Orig., Eng.). 1982. E8.95. Macmillan London.
Wahba, Magdi. English-French-Arabic Dictionary of Political Idioms. $35.00x (ISBN 0-86685-118-6). Intl Bk Ctr.
Wahba, Magdi & Ghali, Magdi, eds. A Dictionary of Political Idioms. 747p. (Arabic, Fr & Eng., With index of Fr. & Arabic key words). 1978. $35.00 (118-6). Intl Bk Ctr.

POLITICS, PRACTICAL

Here are entered works dealing with practical political methods in general political machines, electioneering, etc.
see also Agriculture and Politics; Voting
also subdivision Politics and Government under names of countries, states, etc., e.g. Massachusetts–Politics and Government; headings beginning with the word Political

Bobbio, Norberto. Diccionario de politica: Obra completa, 2 vols. Crisafio, Raul, tr. 1800p. (Span.). 1982. write for info. (ISBN 84-323-0429-8). Siglo XXI.
--Diccionario de politica: Tomo 1: A-J. Crisafio, Raul, tr. 896p. (Span.). 1982. 4000.00 ptas (ISBN 84-323-0430-1). Siglo XXI.
Landshut, Siegfried. Politisches Woerterbuch. (Ger.). 1958. pap. $10.95 (ISBN 3-16-811742-0, M-7589, Pub. by Hochschule Fuer Wirtschaft U. Politik). French & Eur.

POLITICS AND AGRICULTURE

see Agriculture and Politics

POLLS

see Voting

POLLUTION

see also Air–Pollution; Environmental Engineering; Refuse and Refuse Disposal; Water–Pollution
also subdivision Pollution under subjects, e.g. Air–Pollution; Water–Pollution

Tver, David F. Dictionary of Dangerous Pollutants, Ecology & Environment. LC 81-1881. (Illus.). 360p. 1981. $27.95 (ISBN 0-8311-1060-0). Indus Pr.

POLLUTION–CONTROL

see Pollution

POLLUTION–DICTIONARIES

Aymard Lapalu, Nicole. Safety at Work & Pollution Control. LC 76-376744. 320p. (Eng., Fr., Ger. & Span.). 1975. write for info. (ISBN 2-7213-0051-2). Elp.

POLLUTION–PREVENTION

see Pollution

POLLUTION OF WATER

see Water–Pollution

POLYGLOT DICTIONARIES

see Dictionaries, Polyglot

POLYGLOT GLOSSARIES, PHRASE BOOKS, ETC.

see also Dictionaries, Polyglot

Glossaire Europeen en Quatre Langues: Francais-Italien-Allemand-Anglais. (Fr. , Ital. , Ger. & Eng.). 1971. 44.00 F. L. G. D. J.
Johannsen, H. Management Glossary: (English-Arabic) 238p. (Eng. & Arabic.). 1972. $16.00x (ISBN 0-86685-069-4). Intl Bk Ctr.
Jones, Hugh P., ed. Dictionary of Foreign Phrases & Classical Quotations. 552p. 1983. pap. $12.75 (ISBN 0-88072-017-4). Tanager Bks.
Muller, Hanns. Pocket Dictionary of Horseman's Terms in English, German, French & Spanish. (Fr.). 1971. $5.25 (ISBN 0-685-00343-4). Transatlantic.
O'Sullivan, James N., ed. Lexicon to Achilles Tatius. (Unter Suchungen Zur Antiken Literatur und Gesschichte: No. 18). 442p. (Ger.). 1980. text ed. $124.00x (ISBN 3-11-007844-9). De Gruyter.
Slovar Inostrannykh Slov. (Rus.). 1979. $8.95. Russki Iazyk.
Vocabularios Ocho Idiomas (Coleccion, 4 vols. (Span.). $0.80 ea.; Mex.$10.00 ea. Novaro.

POLYGRAPH

see Lie Detectors and Detection

POLYMERIZATION

see Polymers and Polymerization

POLYMERS AND POLYMERIZATION

see also Plastics

Dawydoff, W. Technical Dictionary of High Polymers: English, French, German, Russian. 1969. 130.00 (ISBN 0-08-013112-3). Pergamon.
Dictionary of High Polymer Macromolecule. 54p. (Eng. & Chinese.). 1974. pap. $1.95 (ISBN 0-686-92619-6). French & Eur.

POLYNESIAN LANGUAGES

see also Austronesian Languages; Hawaiian Language; Maori Language; Samoan Language; Tahitian Language

Elbert, Samuel H. Dictionary of the Language of Rennell & Bellona: Part One: Rennellese & Bellonese to English. 364p. 1975. $35.00x (ISBN 0-8248-0490-2). UH Pr.
Ivens, Walter G. A Dictionary of the Language of Bugotu, Santa Isabel Island, Solomon Islands. LC 75-35125. Repr. of 1940 ed. $14.50 (ISBN 0-404-14141-2). AMS Pr.
--A Vocabulary of the Lau Language, Big Mala, Solomon Islands. LC 75-35127. (Lao.). Repr. of 1935 ed. $12.00 (ISBN 0-404-14143-9). AMS Pr.
Ranby, Peter. Nanumea Lexicon. LC 81-180454. (Illus.). x, 243p. (Eng. & Tuvalu.). 1980. write for info. (ISBN 0-85883-227-5). Linguistic Circle.
Shumway, Eric B. Intensive Course in Tongan. (PALI Language Texts: Polynesia). 1971. pap. text ed. $15.00x (ISBN 0-87022-757-2). UH Pr.

POLYNESIAN LEGENDS

see Legends, Polynesian

POMO INDIANS

see Indians of North America–Southwest, New

POMOLOGY

see Fruit

POND LIFE

see Fresh-Water Biology

POOR RELIEF

see Charities; Public Welfare

POP ART

Lexikon der Kunststile: Bd 2, Vom Barock bis zur Pop-art. (Ger.). 1974. DM.8.80 (ISBN 3-499-16137-0). Rowohlt.
Pierre, Jose. An Illustrated Dictionary of Pop Art. LC 78-50723. (Pocket Art Ser.). (Illus.). (gr. 10-12). 1978. pap. $3.95 (ISBN 0-8120-0984-3). Barron.

POPES

Kuhner, Hans. Dictionnaire des Papes. (Fr.). pap. $6.95 (ISBN 0-686-56856-7, M-6634). French & Eur.
--Dictionnaire des Papes. (Fr.). 16.50 F. Buchet Chastel.

POPES–HISTORY

see Papacy–History

POPOLUCA LANGUAGE (VERA CRUZ)

Aschmann, Herman P. Vocabulario Totonaco de la Sierra. (Vocabularios Indigenas Ser.: No. 7). 171p. (Span.). 1962. pap. $3.00x (ISBN 0-88312-666-4); $2.25 (ISBN 0-88312-568-4). Summer Inst Ling.

POPULAR MUSIC

see Music, Popular (Songs, etc.)

POPULATION

see also Birth Control; Demography also subdivision Population under names of countries, cities, etc., e.g. United States–Population

Logie, G. Glossary of Populations & Housing. (International Planning Glossaries: Vol. 1). (Eng., Fr., Ital., Dutch, Ger. & Swedish.). 1978. $53.25 (ISBN 0-444-41730-3). Elsevier.

Lucas, Caroline & Turner, Carann. Population-Family Planning Thesaurus: An Alphabetical & Hierarchical Display of Terms Drawn from Population-Related Literature in the Social Sciences. 2nd ed. Long, Karen & Turner, Carann, eds. 286p. 1978. pap. $20.00 spiral bdg., incl. 1981 suppl. (ISBN 0-89055-049-2). Carolina Pop Ctr.

PORCELAIN

Charles, Bernard H. Pottery & Porcelain: A Glossary of Terms. (Illus.). 320p. 1983. pap. $8.95 (ISBN 0-88254-278-8). Hippocrene Bks.

Savage, George & Newman, Harold. Illustrated Dictionary of Ceramics. 1974. $24.95 (ISBN 0-442-27364-9). Van Nos Reinhold.

PORCELAIN–MARKS

see Pottery–Marks

PORTFOLIO

see Investments

PORTO RICO

see Puerto Rico

PORTRAIT PAINTERS

Foster, Joshua J. A Dictionary of Painters of Miniatures, 1525-1850 with Some Account of Exhibitions, Collections, Sales, Etc. Foster, Ethel M., ed. 1967. Repr. of 1926 ed. $29.50 (ISBN 0-8337-1218-7). B Franklin.

PORTRAITS

see also Miniature Painting also subdivision Portraits under local biography, names of wars, and classes of persons, and names of prominent persons

Darlington, C. D. & Heider, Karl G. Bild der Voelker. 280p. (Ger.). DM.49.00 (ISBN 3-7653-0273-2). F A Brockhaus.

Ormond, Richard & Rogers, Malcolm, eds. Dictionary of British Portraiture. 1981. Vol. 3: The Victorians: Historical Figures Born Between 1800-1860. $62.50x (ISBN 0-19-520182-5); Vol. 4: The Twentieth Century: Historical Figures Born Before 1900. $62.50x (ISBN 0-19-520183-3). Oxford U Pr.

PORTRAITS–CATALOGS

Ormond, Richard & Rogers, Malcolm. Dictionary of British Portraiture: Vol. 1, the Middle Ages to the Early Georgian; Historical Figures Born Before 1700. Davies, Adriana, ed. 1979. text ed. $47.50x (ISBN 0-19-520180-9). Oxford U Pr.

--Dictionary of British Portraiture: Vol. 2, the Later Georgians to the Early Victorians; Historical Figures Born Between 1700 & 1800. Kilmurray, Elaine, ed. 1979. text ed. 49.50x (ISBN 0-19-520181-7). Oxford U Pr.

PORTUGUESE LANGUAGE

Jota, Zelio dos Santos. Dicionarios de Linguistica. 3rd ed. LC 76-461651. 353p. (Port.). 1976. Cr.$90.00. Prensa Acad.

Rodriguez Lapa, M. Vocabulario Galego-Portugues. (Galego & Port.). write for info. Galaxia.

Tertulia Edipica. Dicionario de Sinonimos. LC 80-114023. 1125p. (Port.). 1977. write for info. Porto Editora.

PORTUGUESE LANGUAGE–DICTIONARIES

Almeida, Dauster C. Dicionario de Expressoes Idiomaticas Ingles-Portugues. LC 80-109558. 198p. (Eng. & Port.). 1979. Cr.$230.00. Auer.

Almeida Costa, J. & Sampaio de Melo. Dicionario da Lingua Portuguesa. 1556p. (Port.). $18.00. Imported Bks.

Amendola, Joao. Dictionario Italiano Portugues. Behar, Macim & Moretti, Mario, eds. LC 76-464505. 1037p. (Ital. & Port.). 1976. Cr.$150.00. Hemus-Livraria.

Beau, A. E. Langenscheidts Taschenwoerterbuch Portugiesisch: Teil II, Deutsch-Portugiesisch. 607p. (Ger. & Port.). DM.19.80 (10275). Langenscheidt.

Beau, A. E. & Irmen, F. Langenscheidts Taschenwoerterbuch Portugiesisch, 2 vols. in 1. (Ger. & Port.). DM.29.80 (11271). Langenscheidt.

Becker, Idel. Dicionario Espanhol-Portugues & Portugues-Espanhol, 2 vols. 5th ed. LC 76-480630. 471p. (Port. & Span.). 1976. Cr.$70.00. Liv Nobel.

Biava. Dizionario italiano-portoghese. 292p. (Ital. & Port.). 1976. L.2300.00. Vallardi A.

Biava, A. Dizionario Italiano-Portoghese, Portoghese-Italiano. 318p. (Ital. & Port.). 1980. leatherette $5.95 (ISBN 0-686-97345-3, M-9172). French & Eur.

Buarque de Holanda Ferreira, Aurelio. Minidicionario da Lingua Portuguesa. (Port.). Cr.$670.00. Edit Atica.

Chalaguina, I. Dicionario de Bolso Portugues-Russo. 343p. (Rus. & Port.). 1976. $4.95 (ISBN 0-686-92579-3, M-9103). French & Eur.

Conceicao Fernandes, Julio Da. Diccionario Manual Espanol-Portugues, Portugues-Espanol. 3rd ed. 1974p. (Span. & Port.). 1978. $12.25 (ISBN 84-7183-001-9, S-50428). French & Eur.

--Diccionario Portugues-Espanol. 2nd ed. 916p. (Port. & Span.). 1978. $6.95 (ISBN 0-686-57351-X, S-31570). French & Eur.

De Figueiredo, Candido. Grande Dicionario da Lingua Portuguesa. (Port.). Cr.$3000.00. Difel Difusao.

Diccionario Brevis duplex: Portugues-catellano y castellano-portugues. (Port. & Span.). Arg.$15.00. Sopena.

Diccionario Lexicon Portugues-Espanol, Espanol-Portugues. 400p. (Port. & Span.). leatherette $3.95 (ISBN 84-303-0144-5, S-50429); pap. $3.50 (ISBN 84-303-0143-7, S-50430). French & Eur.

Diccionario Parvus duplex: Portugues-castellano y castellano-portugues. (Port. & Span.). Arg.$8.40. Sopena.

Dicionario pratico ilustrado. (Illus.). 2026p. (Port.). Esc.46.00. Lello & Irmao.

Dizionario Completo Italiano-Portoghese (Brasiliano), Portoghese (Brasiliano)-Italiano: Con L'etimologia Delle Voci Italiane e Portoghesi (Brasiliane), la Loro Esatta Traduzione, Frasi e Modi Di Dire, 2 vols. (Ital. & Port.). 1978. Set. $82.00x (ISBN 0-686-70496-7); (ISBN 88-203-1010-4). S F Vanni.

Fernandes. Diccionario de Verbos e Regimes. 606p. (Port.). Date not set. price not set (M-9212). French & Eur.

Fernandes, F. Diccionario Brasileiro Contemporaneo. (Port.). Date not set. price not set (M-9322). French & Eur.

--Dicionario da Lingua Portuguesa. (Port.). Date not set. price not set. French & Eur.

Fernandes, F. & Luft, C. P. Dicionario de Sinonimos e Antonimos da Lingua Portuguesa. 870p. (Port.). 1980. $39.95 (ISBN 0-686-92539-4, M-9321). French & Eur.

Hampl, Zdenek. Portugalsko-Cesky Slovnik. LC 76-508331. 883p. (Czech. & Port.). 1975. 45.00 Kcs. SNTC.

Hampl, Zdenek & Holsan, Jiri. Portugalsko-Cesko-Portugalsky Kapesni Slovnik. LC 77-551645. 497p. (Czech. & Port.). 1976. 29.00 Kcs. SNTC.

Houaiss, Antonio. Dicionario Basico Escolar Koogan-Larousse. (Port.). Cr.$670.00. Edit Atica.

Houaiss, Antonio, ed. Pequeno Dicionario Enciclopedico Koogan Larouse. LC 79-114441. (Illus.). xi, 1643p. (Port.). 1979. write for info. Larousse.

Kiraly, R. Portuguese-Hungarian Concise Dictionary. 728p. (Port. & Hungarian.). 1978. $39.95 (ISBN 963-05-1382-X, M-9326). French & Eur.

Kiraly, Rudolf. Portugal-Magyar Szotar. LC 78-396058. 728p. (Port. & Hungarian.). 1978. 108.00 Ft (ISBN 9-6305-1382-X). Akademiai Kiado.

Langenscheidts Taschenwoerterbuecher Portugiesisch. (Port.). 1978. DM.23.80 (ISBN 3-468-11270-X). Langenscheidt.

Langenscheidts Universal-Woerterbuch Portugiesisch. 560p. (Port. & Ger.). DM.6.80 (18271). Langenscheidt.

Lello Popular: Novo Dicionario Ilustrado Luso-Brasileiro. (Illus.). 1434p. (Port.). Esc.13.50. Lello & Irmao.

Machado, Antonio N. Dicionario Conciso da Lingua Portuguesa. (Port.). write for info. Difel Editorial, S. A.

Machado, Antonio N., ed. Dicionario Conciso da Lingua Portuguesa. LC 77-563116. 768p. (Port.). 1977. Cr.$95.00. Didel Difusao.

Martinez Almoyna, Julio. Dicionario de Portugues-Espanol. 1332p. (Port. & Span.). $18.00. Porto Editora.

Michaelis. Portuguese Pocket Dictionary. (Port.). Date not set. pap. text ed. $15.00 (ISBN 0-686-46535-0). Heinman.

Nilsson, Kare. Norsk-Portugisisk Ordbok. vii, 398p. (Norwegian & Port.). 1979. Kr.95.00 (ISBN 8-20002-437-7). Universitetsforlaget.

Nunes, C. Dicionario de Bolso Russo-Portuguese. 376p. (Rus. & Port.). 1976. $4.95 (ISBN 0-686-92577-7, M-9062). French & Eur.

Ortega Cavero, David. Diccionario Portugues-Espanol, Espanol-Portugues. 1856p. (Port. & Span.). 1975. $50.95 (ISBN 84-303-0166-6, S-12405). French & Eur.

Ortega Cavero, David & Da Conceica, Julio. Diccionario portugues-espanol, espanol-portugues. 1856p. (Port. & Span.). 1977. 31.00 ptas. Sopena.

Ortencio, B. W. Dicionario do Brasil Central. (Port.). Cr.$5000.00. Edit Atica.

Parlagreco. Dizionario portoghese-italiano. 434p. (Port. & Ital.). 1974. L.14000.00. Vallardi A.

Parlagreco, C. Dizionario Portoghese-Italiano, Italiano-Portoghese. 1138p. (Port. & Ital.). 1979. $35.00 (ISBN 0-686-97354-2, M-9183). French & Eur.

Quadros, Janio. Novo Dicionario Pratico da Lingua Portuguesa. LC 77-477029. 1212p. (Port.). 1976. Cr.$280.00. Editora Rideet.

Rahinantti, Kristina, et al. Suomi-Portugali-Suomi. LC 75-546478. xvi, 359p. (Port. & Finnish.). 1975. Fmk.20.00 (ISBN 951-0-06884-5). Werner Soderstrom.

Spinelli, Vincenzo & Casasanta, Mario. Dizionario completo italiano-portoghese (brasiliano) e portoghese (brasiliano)-italiano. xxiv, 896p. (Ital. & Port.). 1978. L.15000.00 (ISBN 88-203-1010-4). Hoepli.

--Dizionario completo italiano-portoghese (brasiliano) e portoghese (brasiliano)-italiano. xii, 1040p. (Ital. & Port.). 1976. L.12000.00 (ISBN 88-203-0216-0). Hoepli.

Toledo, F. & Milioni, B. Dicionario de Administracao de Recursos Humanos com Termos: Ingles-Portugues, Portugues-Ingles. 156p. (Eng. & Port.). 1979. pap. $14.95 (ISBN 0-686-92535-1, M-9356). French & Eur.

Universal Portuguese Dictionary. 560p. (Port.). $2.95 (095). Langenscheidt.

Vocabularios Portugues-Espanol-Italiano. (Port. , Span. & Ital.). $0.80; Mex.$10.00. Novaro.

Voinova, N. & Starets, S. Diccionario Pratico Russo-Portugues. 643p. (Rus. & Port.). 1964. leatherette $4.95 (ISBN 0-686-92576-9, M-9098). French & Eur.

PORTUGUESE LANGUAGE–DICTIONARIES–ENGLISH

Aliandro, H. Dicionario Portugues-Ingles. 311p. (Port. & Eng.). 1980. pap. $8.95 (ISBN 0-686-97641-X, M-9216). French & Eur.

Berlitz Editors. Berlitz Portuguese for Travellers. 192p. (Port.). 1982. pap. 4.95 (ISBN 0-02-963960-3, Berlitz). Macmillan.

--Portuguese-English Dictionary. (Port. & Eng.). 1982. 4.95 (ISBN 0-02-964440-2, Berlitz). Macmillan.

De Morais, Armando. Dicionario De Ingles-Portugues. 1966. $16.00x (ISBN 0-686-19950-2). Intl Learn Syst.

--Dicionario de Ingles-Portugues "Editora". 1490p. (Port. & Eng.). $17.50. Porto Editora.

De Pina, Araujo A. Portuguese-English, English-Portuguese Technical Dictionary, 2 vols. (Port. & Eng.). Set. 115.00 (ISBN 0-685-79115-7). Heinman.

Dicionario Basico Michaelis. 856p. (Eng. & Port.). 1978. $40.00. Imported Bks.

Dicionario de Ingles-Portugues. (Colecca "Escolares"). (Port. & Eng.). Esc.350.00. Porto Ed.

Dicionario de Ingles-Portugues. (Colecca "Estudantes"). (Port. & Eng.). Esc.200.00. Porto Ed.

Dicionario de Ingles-Portugues "Escolares". 976p. (Port. & Eng.). 1976. $16.00. Porto Editora.

Dicionario de Portugues-Ingles. (Colecca "Escolares"). (Port. & Eng.). Esc.500.00. Porto Ed.

Dicionario de Portugues-Ingles. (Port. & Eng.). Esc.200.00. Porto Ed.

Dicionario Portugues-Ingles. (Dicionarios Escolares). (Port. & Eng.). 1973. 19.50x (ISBN 0-686-19953-7). Intl Learn Syst.

Edicoes Melhoramentos. Dicionario Basico do Ingles Moderno. LC 79-345010. xiv, 856p. (Port.). 1978. Cr.$250.00. Edicoes Melhoramentos.

Ferreira, J. A. Portuguese-English, English-Portuguese Dictionary. (Port. & Eng.). 30.00 (ISBN 0-685-12039-2). Heinman.

Ferreira, J. Albino. Portuguese-English Dictionary. rev. ed. De Morais, A., ed. (Port. & Eng.). $32.50 (ISBN 0-87559-029-2); thumb indexed $37.50 (ISBN 0-87559-030-6). Shalom.

Fraenkel, B. Dicionario de termos tecnicos Ingles-Portugues, Portugues-Ingles. 195p. (Port. & Eng.). 1970. pap. $11.00. Imported Bks.

Fraenkel, B. B. Dicionario de Expressoes Idiomaticas da Lingua Inglesa. 136p. (Port. & Eng.). $5.00. Imported Bks.

Galvan, Roberto A. & Teschner, Richard V. El Diccionario del Espanol de Tejas. LC 79-345010. xiv, 856p. (Eng. & Span.). 1978. Cr.$250.00. Edicoes Melhoramentos.

Langenscheidt English-Portuguese Lilliput Dictionary. 640p. (Eng. & Port.). plastic $1.50 (ISBN 3-468-96463-3). Langenscheidt.

Langenscheidt Portuguese-English Lilliput Dictionary. 640p. (Eng. & Port.). plastic $1.50 (ISBN 3-468-96462-5). Langenscheidt.

Martins, M. J. Portuguese-English, English-Portuguese Dictionary, 2 vols. (Port. & Eng.). Set. 45.00 (ISBN 0-685-58543-3). Heinman.

Michaelis. Portuguese-English, English-Portuguese Basic Dictionary. (Eng. & Port.). Date not set. text ed. $35.00 (ISBN 0-686-46534-2). Heinman.

Pequeno diccionario Michaelis Ingles-Portuguese. (Port. & Eng.). $12.50. Iaconi.

Pietzschke, F., ed. Portuguese-English, English-Portuguese Illustrated Dictionary: The New Michaelis, 2 vols. (Port. & Eng.). Set. 125.00 (ISBN 0-685-58551-4). Portuguese-english, 28th Ed (ISBN 3-7653-0050-0). English-portuguese, 30th Ed (ISBN 3-7653-0051-9). Heinman.

Pietzschke, Fritz. Novo Michaelis, Dicionario Ilustrado. 23rd ed. Mariotti, Wilson, ed. LC 79-112996. (Eng. & Port.). 1978. Cr.$2000.00. Edicoes Melhoramentos.

Richardson, Elbert L., et al, eds. McKay's Modern Portuguese-English & English-Portuguese Dictionary. (Modern Dictionaries). (Port. & Eng.). 1943. 10.95 (ISBN 0-679-10077-6). McKay.

Taylor, James L. A Portuguese-English Dictionary. rev. ed. (Port. & Eng.). 1970. $25.00x (ISBN 0-8047-0480-5). Stanford U Pr.

PORTUGUESE LANGUAGE-DICTIONARIES-FRENCH

Da Fonseca, F. Peixoto. Dictionnaire Bilingue Larousse, Francais-Portugais et Portugais-Francais. (Apollo). (Fr. & Port.). $10.50 (ISBN 2-03-020909-0, 3791). Larousse.

De Azevedo, Domingos. Grande Dicionario Portugues-Frances. (Port. & Fr., Sao Paulo, Brazil). Cr.$25.74. Difel Difusao.

De Sousa Vieira, Jose. Dicionario de Frances-Portugues: Com Transcicao Fonetica. 3rd ed. (Port. & Fr.). Esc.65.00. Porto Ed.

Dicionario de Bolso Portugues-Frances. (Port. & Fr.). Cr.$1.92. Difel Difusao.

Dicionario de Frances-Portugues. (Colecca "Escolares"). (Port. & Fr.). Esc.350.00. Porto Ed.

Dicionario de Frances-Portugues. (Collecca "Estudantes"). (Port. & Fr.). Esc.370.00. Porto Ed.

Fournier, J. & Laborde, G. Le Mot et L'idee, Francais-Portugais, Portugais-Francais. 120p. (Fr.-Port.). $6.95 (ISBN 0-686-57185-1, M-6256). French & Eur.

PORTUGUESE LANGUAGE-DICTIONARIES-GERMAN

Dicionario de Alemao-Portugues. (Coleccao "Estudantes"). (Port. & Ger.). Esc.200.00. Porto Ed.

Dicionario de Bolso Portugues-Alemao. (Port. & Ger.). Cr.$pap. 2.21. Difel Difusao.

Dicionario de Portugues-Alemao. (Colecca "Estudantes"). (Port. & Ger.). Esc.200.00. Porto Ed.

Portugiesisch, 2 vols. rev. ed. Incl. Teil I. Portugiesisch-Deutsch. Irmen, F. 632p. DM.18.80 (10270); Teil II. Deutsch-Portugiesisch. Beau, A. E. 607p. DM.18.80 (10275). (Langenscheidts Taschenworterbucher Ser.). (Port. & Ger., Unter Berusichtigung der Brasilianismen). 1982. DM.beide Teile in einem Band 29.80 (11270). Langenscheidt.

PORTUGUESE LANGUAGE-DICTIONARIES-LATIN

Torrinha, Francisco. Dicionario Latino-Portugues. (Port. & Lat.). Esc.230.00. Porto Ed.

PORTUGUESE LANGUAGE-STUDY AND TEACHING

Learn Portugese for English Speakers. (Port. & Eng.). 1974. pap. 9.50 (ISBN 0-87557-108-5, 108-5). Saphrograph.

POSITION ANALYSIS
see Topology

POST-OFFICE
see Postal Service

POSTAGE-STAMP COLLECTIONS
see Postage-Stamps-Collectors and Collecting

POSTAGE-STAMPS

Bailey, Eric V. A Glossary of Spanish Philatelic Terms. (Span. & Eng.). 1974. $2.50 ea. Intl Guatemala.

Bennett, Russell & Watson, James, eds. Stanley Gibbons Philatelic Terms Illustrated. 1972. $6.50 (ISBN 0-85259-895-5). StanGib Ltd.

POSTAGE-STAMPS-COLLECTORS AND COLLECTING

Bailey, Eric V. A Glossary of Spanish Philatelic Terms. (Span. & Eng.). 1974. $2.50 ea. Intl Guatemala.

Basin, O. I. Filatelisticheskii Slovar. 128p. (Rus.). 1976. $1.50 (Pub. by Sviaz). Four Continent.

Grallert, V., et al, eds. Filatelisticheskii Slovar. 272p. (Rus.). 1977. $7.50 (Pub. by Sviaz). Four Continent.

Philatelic Foundation. Philatelic Vocabulary in Five Languages. (Confederate States of America Ser.). (English, French, German, Italian, Spanish.). $3.00 (ISBN 0-911989-04-8). Philatelic Found.

POSTAL LIFE INSURANCE
see Insurance, Life

POSTAL SERVICE

Pothion, Jean. Dictionnaire des Bureaux de Poste Francais. (Fr.). write for info. Poste Aux Lettres.

POTTERS' MARKS
see Pottery-Marks

POTTERY-DICTIONARIES

Barber, Edward A. & Lockwood, Luke V. The Ceramic Furniture & Silver Collectors' Glossary. (Architecture & Decorative Art Ser.). 1976. pap. $6.95 (ISBN 0-306-80049-7). Da Capo.

Barber, Edwin A. The Ceramic Collectors' Glossary. LC 76-8172. (Architecture & Decorative Art Ser.). 1967. Repr. of 1914 ed. $16.50 (ISBN 0-306-70521-4). Da Capo.

Charles, Bernard H. Pottery & Porcelain: A Glossary of Terms. (Illus.). 320p. 1983. pap. $8.95 (ISBN 0-88254-278-8). Hippocrene Bks.

Coysh, A. W. The Dictionary of Blue & White Pottery. (Illus.). 1981. $44.50 (ISBN 0-907462-06-5). Antique Collect.

Fournier, Robert. Diccionario ilustrado de alfareria practica. Torres, Elena, tr. (Illus.). 320p. (Span.). 1981. 2100.00 ptas (ISBN 84-282-0643-0). Omega SA.

--Illustrated Dictionary of Pottery Form. 1981. $24.95 (ISBN 0-442-26112-8) (ISBN 0-686-71500-4). Van Nos Reinhold.

--Illustrated Dictionary of Practical Pottery. rev. ed. 256p. 1980. pap. $9.95 (ISBN 0-442-30181-2). Van Nos Reinhold.

Savage, George & Newman, Harold. Illustrated Dictionary of Ceramics. 1974. $24.95 (ISBN 0-442-27364-9). Van Nos Reinhold.

POTTERY-MARKS

Kovel, Ralph M. & Kovel, Terry H. Dictionary of Marks: Pottery & Porcelain. 1953. $8.95 (ISBN 0-517-00141-1). Crown.

MacDonald-Taylor, Margaret. Dictionary of Marks. (Illus.). 1962. pap. $6.25 (ISBN 0-8015-2089-4, 0607-180, Hawthorn). Dutton.

POTTERY CRAFT

Hamer, Frank. Potter's Dictionary of Materials & Techniques. (Illus.). 400p. 1975. $30.00 (ISBN 0-8230-4210-3). Watson-Guptill.

POTTERY MAKING (HANDICRAFT)
see Pottery Craft

POUL LANGUAGE
see Fulah Language

POWER (MECHANICS)
see also Force and Energy; Power Resources; Power Transmission; Water-Power

Counihan, Martin. A Dictionary of Energy. (Illus.). 200p. 1981. 14.95 (ISBN 0-7100-0847-3). Routledge & Kegan.

Hunt, V. Daniel. Energy Dictionary. 1979. text ed. $24.50x (ISBN 0-442-27395-9). Van Nos Reinhold.

Isaacs, Alan, ed. The Multilingual Energy Dictionary. 288p. 1981. $22.50 (ISBN 0-87196-430-9). Facts on File.

Slesser, Malcolm. The Dictionary of Energy. LC 82-10252. 1983. $29.95 (ISBN 0-8052-3816-6). Schocken.

World Energy Conference. Standard Terms of the Energy Economy. LC 78-40304. xi, 134p. (Eng.). 1978. $50.00 (ISBN 0-08-022445-8); E25.00. Pergamon.

POWER-PLANTS, ATOMIC
see Atomic Power Plants

POWER-PLANTS, ELECTRIC
see Electric Power-Plants

POWER-PLANTS, STEAM
see Steam Power-Plants

POWER PRESSES

Slesser, Malcolm. The Dictionary of Energy. LC 82-10252. 1983. $29.95 (ISBN 0-8052-3816-6). Schocken.

POWER RESOURCES

Here are entered works on the available sources of mechanical power in general. Works on the physics and engineering aspects of power are entered under Power (Mechanics).
see also Energy Conservation; Solar Energy; Water-Power
also specific legal headings related to individual sources of power, e.g. Gas-Law and Legislation; Petroleum Law and Legislation

Counihan, Martin. A Dictionary of Energy. (Illus.). 200p. 1981. 14.95 (ISBN 0-7100-0847-3). Routledge & Kegan.

Hall. Dictionary of Energy. (Energy, Power & Environment Ser.). 360p. 1983. write for info. (ISBN 0-8247-1793-7). Dekker.

Hunt, V. Daniel. Energy Dictionary. 1979. text ed. $24.50x (ISBN 0-442-27395-9). Van Nos Reinhold.

Isaacs, Alan, ed. The Multilingual Energy Dictionary. 288p. 1981. $22.50 (ISBN 0-87196-430-9). Facts on File.

Nelson, Robert V. Understanding Basic Energy Terms. LC 81-2888. 1981. lib. bdg. $10.00 (ISBN 0-86663-806-7); pap. text ed. $5.25 (ISBN 0-86663-807-5). Ide Hse.

World Energy Conference, ed. Energy Terminology: A Multi-Lingual Glossary. 275p. 1983. 100.00 (ISBN 0-08-029314-X, B110); pap. 40.00 (ISBN 0-08-029315-8). Pergamon.

POWER SUPPLY
see Power Resources

POWER TRANSMISSION

Woerterbuch der Kraftuebertragungselemente. (Ger., Eng., Fr., Span., Dutch, Swed., Ital. & Finnish., Dictionary of Power Transmission Elements). 1976. $32.00 (ISBN 3-7830-0104-8, M-6985). French & Eur.

PRACTICE (LAW)
see Procedure (Law)

PRACTICAL POLITICS
see Politics, Practical

PRECIOUS STONES

Here are entered works of mineralogical or technological interest. Works on engraved stones and jewels from the point of view of antiquities or art are entered under Gems.
see also names of precious stones, e.g. Diamonds, Emeralds

O'Donoghue, Michael. Van Nostrand Reinhold Color Dictionary of Minerals & Gemstones. 160p. 1982. pap. $12.95 (ISBN 0-442-27431-9). Van Nos Reinhold.

Shipley, Robert M. Dictionary of Gems & Gemology. 6th ed. 1974. 7.50 (ISBN 0-87311-007-2). Gemological.

PRECISIANS
see Puritans

PRE-EMPTIVE RIGHTS, STOCKHOLDERS'
see Stockholders' Pre-Emptive Rights

PREHISTORIC ANIMALS
see Paleontology

PREHISTORIC ANTIQUITIES
see Archaeology

PREHISTORIC ART
see Art, Primitive

PREHISTORIC FAUNA
see Paleontology

PRESCHOOL EDUCATION
see Education, Preschool

PRESCHOOL READERS
see Readers

PRESERVATION OF HISTORICAL RECORDS
see Archives

PRESERVATION OF MANUSCRIPTS
see Manuscripts-Conservation and Restoration

PRESSES, POWER
see Power Presses

PRESSURE-MEASUREMENT

American Society of Mechanical Engineers. Terminology for Pressure Relief Devices: B95.1-1977. $3.50 (N00088); members $4.00. ASME.

PRESSURE-GAGES

American Society of Mechanical Engineers. Terminology for Pressure Relief Devices: B95.1-1977. $3.50 (N00088); members $4.00. ASME.

PRESTIDIGITATION
see Magic

PRESTRESSED CONCRETE

Gerwick, Ben C., Jr. & Peters, V. P., eds. Russian-English Dictionary of Prestressed Concrete & Concrete Construction. 120p. (Rus. & Eng.). 1966. 33.00x (ISBN 0-677-00260-2). Gordon.

PRESTRESSED CONCRETE CONSTRUCTION

Gerwick, Ben C., Jr. & Peters, V. P., eds. Russian-English Dictionary of Prestressed Concrete & Concrete Construction. 120p. (Rus. & Eng.). 1966. 33.00x (ISBN 0-677-00260-2). Gordon.

PREVENTION OF ACCIDENTS
see Accidents-Prevention

PREVENTION OF CRUELTY TO ANIMALS
see Animals, Treatment Of

PREVENTION OF FIRES
see Fire Prevention

PRIDE AND VANITY

Dictionnaire des Vanites, 1. 212p. (Fr.). 1971. 49.00 F. Contrepoint.

Dictionnaire des Vanites, 2. 192p. (Fr.). 1972. 49.00 F. Contrepoint.

PRIMARY BATTERIES
see Electric Batteries

PRIME FACTORS
see Factor Tables

PRIMERS, SPANISH
see Spanish Language-Textbooks for Children

PRIMITIVE ART
see Art, Primitive

PRINT MAKERS
see Printmakers

PRINTERS

De Fontenay, Louis-Abel. Dictionnaire des Artistes ou Notice Historique: Raisonee des Architectes, Peintres & Graveurs, 2 vols. (Fr.). 1972. 240.00 F. Minkoff.

PRINTING-BIBLIOGRAPHY

Newberry Library - Chicago. Dictionary Catalogue of the History of Printing from the John M. Wing Foundation, 6 Vols. 1961. Set. lib. bdg. $570.00 (ISBN 0-8161-0587-1, Hall Library). G K Hall.

--Dictionary Catalogue of the History of Printing from the John M. Wing Foundation, First Supplement, 3 vols. 1970. Set. lib. bdg. $315.00 (ISBN 0-8161-0809-9, Hall Library). G K Hall.

PRINTING-DICTIONARIES

American Dictionary of Printing & Bookmaking. LC 70-135172. 1971. Repr. of 1894 ed. lib. bdg. $29.00 (ISBN 0-8337-0059-6). B Franklin.

American Dictionary of Printing & Bookmaking. LC 66-27215. 1967. Repr. of 1894 ed. $42.00x (ISBN 0-8103-3345-7). Gale.

Bories, J. & Bonassies, F. Dictionnaire Pratique de la Presse, de l'imprimerie & de la Librairie, 2 vols. 1238p. (Fr.). 1972. $70.00. Gregg.

Dodin, Lucien. Dictionnaire du Petit Offset. 2nd ed. 220p. (Fr.). 1970. 48.90 F. Prismes.

Glaister, Geoffrey. Glaister's Glossary of the Book: Terms Used in Paper-Making, Printing, Bookbinding, & Publishing. LC 76-47975. 1979. $75.00 (ISBN 0-520-03364-7). U of Cal Pr.

Graafinen Sanakirja. 308p. (Finnish, Rus. & Ger.). 1979. write for info. (ISBN 9-5100-90986-7). Soderstrom.

Hostettler, R. Printer's Terms Dictionary. (Illus., Eng., Fr., Ger., Ital. & Dutch). 1983. price not set (ISBN 0-685-12041-4). Heinman.

Institut fur Grafische Technik. Lexikon der Grafischen Technik. LC 78-341716. 656p. (Ger.). 1977. write for info. (ISBN 3-7940-4078-3). Saur Verlag.

Isaacs, Alan, ed. The Multilingual Dictionary of Printing & Publishing. 336p. 1981. $22.50 (ISBN 0-87196-444-9). Facts on File.

Jacobi, Charles T. The Printers' Vocabulary. LC 68-30613. 1975. Repr. of 1888 ed. $30.00x (ISBN 0-8103-3309-0). Gale.

Kent, Ruth. Language of Journalism: A Glossary of Print-Communications Terms. LC 71-100624. (Illus.). 1970. $8.00x (ISBN 0-87338-091-6); pap. $4.00x (ISBN 0-87338-092-4). Kent St U Pr.

Klein, Heijo. DuMont's Kleines Sachworterbuch der Druektechnik & Grafischen Kunst. LC 75-505939. 193p. (Eng. & Ger.). 1975. write for info. (ISBN 3-7701-0760-8). DuMont Buch.

Martinez de Sousa, J. Diccionario de Tipografia & del Libro. (Span.). 1981. 1300.00 ptas (ISBN 8-42831-132-3). Paraninfo.

Martinez de Sousa, Jose. Diccionario de Tipografia & del Libro. 570p. (Span.). 1974. 1070.00 ptas (ISBN 84-335-0300-6). Labor SA.

--Diccionario de tipografia y del libro. 564p. (Span.). 1981. pap. 1100.00 ptas (ISBN 84-283-1132-3). Paraninfo.

Mintz, Patricia. Dictionary of Graphic Arts Terms: A Communication Tool for People Who Buy Type & Printing. 328p. 1981. text ed. $17.95 (ISBN 0-442-26711-8). Van Nos Reinhold.

Pernety, Antoine Joseph. Dictionnaire Portatif de Peinture, Sculpture & Gravure. (Fr.). 1972. 140.00 F. Minkoff Repr.

Reilly, Elizabeth C. Dictionary of Colonial American Printers' Ornaments & Illustrations. LC 75-5023. (Illus.). xxxvi, 514p. 1975. $45.00x (ISBN 0-912296-06-2, Dist. by U Pr of Va). Am Antiquarian.

Rouzet, Anne. Dictionnaire des Imprimeurs. 287p. (Fr.). 1975. fl.21.00. De Graaf.

Savage, William. Dictionary of the Art of Printing. 1965. Repr. of 1841 ed. $32.00 (ISBN 0-8337-3128-9). B Franklin.

--A Dictionary of the Art of Printing. (Printers' Manual Ser.). 1977. Repr. of 1841 ed. lib. bdg. 20.00x (ISBN 0-576-52390-9). Intl Pubns Serv.

Watelet, Claude-Henre & Levesque, Pierre-Charles. Dictionnaire des Arts de Peinture, Sculpture & Gravure, Vol. 1. (Fr.). 1972. 118.00 F. Olms Verlag.

Watelet, Claude-Henri & Levesque, Pierre-Charles. Dictionnaire des Arts de Peinture, Sculpture & Gravure, Vol. 3. (Fr.). 1972. 118.00 F. Olms Verlag.

--Dictionnaire des Arts de Peinture, Sculpture & Gravure, Vol. 4. (Fr.). 1972. 118.00 F. Olms Verlag.

--Dictionnaire des Arts de Peinture, Sculpture & Gravure, Vol. 5. (Fr.). 1972. 118.00 F. Olms Verlag.

Woerterbuch der Reprographie. 273p. (Ger.). 1976. write for info. (ISBN 3-7940-3259-4). Saur Verlag.

PRINTING–HISTORY

American Dictionary of Printing & Bookmaking. LC 66-27215. 1967. Repr. of 1894 ed. $42.00x (ISBN 0-8103-3345-7). Gale.

John M. Wing Foundation, Newberry Library. Dictionary Catalogue of the History of Printing from the John M. Wing Foundation, Second Supplement. 1981. lib. bdg. $435.00 (ISBN 0-8161-0326-7, Hall Library). G K Hall.

Newberry Library - Chicago. Dictionary Catalogue of the History of Printing from the John M. Wing Foundation, 6 Vols. 1961. Set. lib. bdg. $570.00 (ISBN 0-8161-0587-1, Hall Library). G K Hall.

--Dictionary Catalogue of the History of Printing from the John M. Wing Foundation, First Supplement, 3 vols. 1970. Set. lib. bdg. $315.00 (ISBN 0-8161-0809-9, Hall Library). G K Hall.

PRINTING–LAYOUT AND TYPOGRAPHY

see also Printing As a Graphic Art

Kleper, Michael L. Illustrated Dictionary of Typographic Communication. (Illus.). 208p. (Orig.). 1983. pap. text ed. $19.00 (ISBN 0-89938-008-5). Tech & Ed Ctr Graph Arts RIT.

--The Illustrated Dictionary of Typographic Communication. (Illus.). 200p. 1983. pap. $19.00 (ISBN 0-930904-03-6). Graphic Dimensions.

PRINTING–STYLE MANUALS

see also Authorship–Handbooks, Manuals, etc.

Deaton, Donald B., ed. Glossary of Printing Terms. 58p. 1973. $27.00; members $16.00. AATCC.

PRINTING AS A GRAPHIC ART

Collet, K., ed. Polygraph Dictionary for the Graphic Industries in Six Languages. 38th ed. LC 68-117537. (Ger., Eng., Fr., Span. & Ital.). 1967. $65.00x (ISBN 3-87641-150-5). Intl Pubns Serv.

PRINTING OF FOREIGN LANGUAGES

see Printing–Style Manuals

PRINTMAKERS

see also Engravers

Engen, Rodney K. Dictionary of Victorian Engravers, Print Publishers & Their Works. (Illus.). 1979. 60.00x (ISBN 0-914146-86-6). Somerset Hse.

PRINTS

Gordon, Bonnie. The Anatomy of the Image Maps According to Merriam-Webster's Third International Dictionary of the English Language: Unabridged. LC 82-50789. (Artists' Book Ser.). 48p. (Orig.). 1983. pap. $10.00 (ISBN 0-89822-028-9). Visual Studies.

New York Public Library, Research Libraries. The Dictionary Catalog of the Prints Division, 5 vols. 1975. Set. lib. bdg. $475.00 (ISBN 0-8161-1148-0, Hall Library). G K Hall.

PRISONERS, RUSSIAN

Galler, Meyer & Marquess, Harlan E., eds. Soviet Prison Camp Speech: A Survivor's Glossary. LC 75-176411. 216p. 1972. $25.00 (ISBN 0-299-06080-2). U of Wis Pr.

PRISONS

Williams, Vergil L. Dictionary of American Penology: An Introductory Guide. LC 77-94751. 1979. lib. bdg. 45.00x (ISBN 0-313-20327-X, WAP/). Greenwood.

PRISONS–RUSSIA

Galler, Meyer. Soviet Prison Camp Speech: Supplement. LC 77-89596. (Rus.). 1977. $15.00x (ISBN 0-930232-01-1). Soviet Studies.

PRIVACY, RIGHT OF

Casso-Cervera. Diccionario de derecho privado. (Span.). 715.00 ptas. Labor.

PRIVATE LAW

see Civil Law

PRIVATE RADIOTELEPHONE

see Citizens Band Radio

PROCEDURE (LAW)

see also Judicial Process

Barbaud, Roger. Dictionnaire des Delais de Procedure. (Fr.). 1974. write for info. Dalloz.

Leite, Yara Muller. Dicionario de Acoes & de Procedimentos Judiciais. LC 79-115699. vii, 692p. (Port.). 1979. Cr.$590.00. Saraiva SA.

Schaefer, Michael. Die Adjektive auf Isch in der Deutschen Gegenwartssprache. LC 78-355176. (Illus.). 208p. (Ger.). 1977. write for info. (ISBN 3-53302-656-6). Winter Univ.

PROCESS CONTROL

Scientific Apparatus Makers Association. Process Instrumentation Reliability Terminology: 32.1-1976. $2.00; bulk prices avail. Sci Apparatus.

--Process Measurement & Control Terminology: 20.1-1973. $2.00; bulk prices avail. Sci Apparatus.

PROCESS CONTROL–DATA PROCESSING

Schaefer, Peter & Wiczorke, Martin. Lexikon der Prozessrechnertechnik. LC 79-372726. (Illus.). 327p. (Ger.). 1979. write for info. (ISBN 3-800-91278-3). Siemens AG.

PROCESS ENGINEERING

see Production Engineering

PROCESS ENGINEERING (MANUFACTURES)

see Manufacturing Processes

PROCESSING, INDUSTRIAL

see Manufacturing Processes

PRODUCER GAS

see Gas and Oil Engines; Gas Manufacture and Works

PRODUCTION ENGINEERING

see also Manufacturing Processes; Materials Handling

International Institution for Production Engineering Research. Dictionary of Production Engineering: German-English-French, 8 vols. Incl. Vol. 1. Forging & Drop Forging. 108p. 1962. 30.00x (ISBN 3-7736-5920-2); Vol. 2. Grinding - Surface Roughness. 140p. 1963. 30.00x (ISBN 3-7736-5930-X); Vol. 3. Sheet Metal Forming. 136p. 1965. 30.00x (ISBN 3-7736-5940-7); Vol. 4. Fundamental Terms of Cutting. 124p. 1969. 30.00x (ISBN 3-7736-5946-6); Vol. 5. Cold Extrusion & Upsetting. 157p. 1969. 30.00x (ISBN 3-7736-5945-8); Vol. 6. Planing, Slotting, Broaching, Turning. 1972. 30.00x (ISBN 3-7736-5946-6); Vol. 7. 30.00x (ISBN 3-7736-5947-4); Milling, Sawing, Gear Manufacturing. 359p. 1979. 42.50x (ISBN 3-7736-5948-2). (Ger., Eng & Fr.). Intl Pubns Serv.

Paruit, Bernard. Illustrated Glossary of Process Equipment: English-French-Spanish Edition. (Illus.). 324p. 1982. $39.95x (ISBN 0-87201-691-9). Gulf Pub.

Ramalingom, T. Dictionary of Instrument Science. LC 81-14724. 588p. 1982. $24.95x (ISBN 0-471-86396-3, Pub. by Wiley-Interscience). Wiley.

Walther, R. Technical Dictionary of Production Engineering: Vol. 2, German-English. (Ger. & Eng.). $49.00 (ISBN 0-08-016960-0). Pergamon.

Walther, Rudolph. Technical Dictionary of Production Engineering (English-German) 1973. text ed. 49.00 (ISBN 0-08-016959-7). Pergamon.

PRODUCTS, WASTE

see Waste Products

PROFESSIONALISM IN SPORTS

Franklin, Alfred. Dictionnaire Historique des Arts, Metlers & Professions Exerces dans Paris Depuis le Treizieme Siecle. 882p. (Fr.). $40.00. Lenox.

PROFESSIONS

see also Intellectuals; Occupations; Vocational Guidance

also subdivision Vocational Guidance under specific professions

Dion, Gerard. Vocabulaire Francais-Anglais des Relations Professionnelles. 2nd ed. 350p. (Fr.). 16.00 F. Laval P. U.

Franklin, Alfred L. Dictionnaire Historique des Arts, Metiers & Professions: Exercees dans Paris Depuis le 13 Siecle. 856p. (Fr.). 1906. DM.138.00. Olms Verlag.

Ministere du Travail Et du la Main-D'oeuvre. Vocabulaire Francais-Anglais des Relations Professionnelles. 302p. (Fr. & Eng.). 1972. 2.50 F. Quebec Off.

PROFESSORS

see College Teachers

PROFIT-SHARING TRUSTS

see Investment Trusts

PROGRAMMING (ELECTRONIC COMPUTERS)

see also Electronic Digital Computers; Programming Languages (Electronic Computers)

also names of specific computers, e.g. IBM 1620

Amglo-Russko-Nemetsko-Frantsuzskii Tolkovyi Slovar Po Vychislitel Noi Tekhnike & Obrabotke Dannykh. 416p. (Eng., Rus., Ger. & Fr.). 1978. $7.95 (Pub. by Russkii Iazyk). Four Continent.

Buerger. Woerterbuch Datenerfassung: Programmierung. 386p. (Eng., Fr., Rus. & Ger.). 1976. DM.78.00 (ISBN 3-87144-264-X). Verlag Harri Deutsch.

Buerger, E. Woerterbuch Datenerfassung-Programmierung. (Eng., Ger., Fr. & Rus., Dictionary of Data Processing & Programming). 1976. $56.00 (ISBN 3-87144-265-8, M-6967). French & Eur.

Burger, Erich. Datenerfassung Programmierung-Englisch-Deutsch-Franzoesisch-Russisch. 386p. (Eng., Ger., Fr. & Rus.). 1981. M.48.00. VEB Technik.

Dictionary of Computer Programming & Data Processing. 386p. 1976. $90.00x (ISBN 0-686-44722-0, Pub. by Collets). State Mutual Bk.

Theilman, K. Dictionary of Biochemistry. 742p. 1980. $90.00x (ISBN 0-686-44721-2, Pub. by Collets). State Mutual Bk.

Woerterbuch Programmierter Unterricht. (Ger.). 1964. DM.4.80 (ISBN 3-7863-0015-1). Manz.

PROGRAMMING (MATHEMATICS)

Buerger. Woerterbuch Datenerfassung: Programmierung. 386p. (Eng., Fr., Rus. & Ger.). 1976. DM.78.00 (ISBN 3-87144-264-X). Verlag Harri Deutsch.

Burger, Erich. Datenerfassung Programmierung-Englisch-Deutsch-Franzoesisch-Russisch. 386p. (Eng., Ger., Fr. & Rus.). 1981. M.48.00. VEB Technik.

PROGRAMMING LANGUAGES (ELECTRONIC COMPUTERS)

see also specific languages, e.g. FORTRAN (Computer Program Language)

Frederick Muller, Ltd., ed. Multilingual Computer Dictionary. 1981. $30.00x (ISBN 0-584-95567-7, Pub. by Muller Ltd). State Mutual Bk.

Stultz, Russell A. The Illustrated CPM-Wordstar Dictionary with Mailmerge & Spellstar Operations. (Illus.). 272p. 1983. pap. text ed. 14.95 (ISBN 0-13-450528-X). P-H.

PROGRAMS, CONCERT

see Concerts–Programs

PROPER NAMES

see Names

PROPERTY, LITERARY

see Copyright

PROPERTY, REAL

see Real Property

PROPERTY RIGHTS

see Industrial Property

PROPRIETARY RIGHTS

see Industrial Property

PROSPECTING

Kratkii Terminologicheskii Spravochnik po Ekonomike Geologorazvedochnykh Rabot. LC 79-398743. 203p. (Eng., Rus. & Bulgarian.). 1979. 100.00 Zl. Wydawnictwa.

PROSTHODONTICS

Batarec, Evelyn. Lexique des Termes de Prothese Dentaire. 90p. (Fr.). 1973. pap. $19.95 (ISBN 0-686-56749-8, M-6024). French & Eur.

--Lexique des Termes de Prothese Dentaire. 90p. (Fr.). 1973. 30.00 F. Prelat.

PROTECTION OF ANIMALS

see Animals, Treatment of

PROTECTION OF ENVIRONMENT

see Environmental Protection

PROTEIDS

see Proteins

PROTEINS

Kraus, Barbara. Barbara Kraus Dictionary of Protein. 1976. pap. 2.50 (ISBN 0-451-08791-7, E8791, Sig). NAL.

PROTESTANTISM, EVANGELICAL

see Evangelicalism

PROTESTANTS IN ENGLAND

Scott, Thomas. The Interpreter, Wherein Three Principal Terms of State Are Clearly Unfolded. LC 74-80194. (English Experience Ser.: No. 673). 1974. Repr. of 1624 ed. $3.50 (ISBN 90-221-0281-5). Walter J Johnson.

PROTESTS, DIPLOMATIC

see Diplomacy

PROTOZOA

Barrett, A. J. Mammalian Proteases: A Glossary & Bibliography: Vol. 2, Exopeptidases. McDonald, J. K., ed. 1982. write for info. (ISBN 0-12-079502-7). Acad Pr.

PROUST, MARCEL, 1871-1922

Newman-Gordon, Pauline, ed. Dictionnaire Des Idees Dans L'oeuvre De Marcel Proust: Collection Dictionnaires Des Idees Dans les Litteratures Occidentales, Litterature Francaise. (Dictionnaires D'auteurs: No. 3). (Fr.). 1968. 20.50 (ISBN 0-686-21818-3). Mouton.

Vogely, Maxine A. A Proust Dictionary. LC 80-53035. 765p. 1981. $50.00x (ISBN 0-87875-205-6). Whitston Pub.

PROVENCAL LANGUAGE

see also Gascon Dialect

Castellana, Georges. Dictionnaire Francais-Nicois. LC 78-380119. 421p. (Fr.). 1978. 60.00 F. Serre.

Gonfroy, Gerard. Dictionnaire Normatif Limousin-Francais. LC 77-479648. 229p. (Fr.). 1976. write for info. Lemouzi.

Nauton, P., ed. Vocabulaire du Cantal du Nord & de la Margeride Auvergnate d'Apres l'ALMC. LC 76-451549. 73p. (Fr.). 1975. write for info. Cercle Occitan.

PROVENCAL LANGUAGE–DICTIONARIES

Barthe, Roger. Lexique Francais-Occitan. 202p. (Fr.). 1971. 23.00 F. Amis Langue.

--Lexique Francais-Occitan. 240p. (Fr.). 1974. 30.00 F. R. Barthe.

--Lexique Occitan-Francais. rev. ed. (Fr.). 1975. 23.00 F. Amis Langue.

--Lexique Occitan-Francais. 240p. (Fr.). 1973. 32.00 F. Lemouzi.

Mistral, Frederic. Le Tresor de Felibridge: Dictionnaire Provencal-Francais, 2 vols. 2375p. (Fr.). Set. $195.00 (ISBN 0-686-56736-6, M-6414). French & Eur.

Vocabulaire Occitan. rev. ed. (Fr.). 1977. 30.00 F. Lagarde.

PROVERBS

see also Aphorisms and Apothegms; Devices; Epigrams; Maxims; Mottoes

Barella Campos, Juana & Barella Campos, Ana G. Diccionario De Refranes. 534p. (Span.). 1975. pap. $44.95 (ISBN 84-600-6609-6, S-50116). French & Eur.

Collins, John. A Dictionary of Spanish Proverbs. LC 77-25483. (Span.). 1977. Repr. of 1823 ed. lib. bdg. $45.00 (ISBN 0-8414-1101-8). Folcroft.

Felitsyna, V. P. & Prokhorov, Iu. E. Russkie Poslovitsy, Pogovorki i Krylatye Vyrazheniia. 240p. (Rus.). 1979. $5.50 (Pub. by Russkii Iazyk). Four Continent.

Felitsyna, Vera P. Russkie Poslovitsy, Pogovorki & Krylatye Vyrazheniia. LC 80-460368. 238p. (Rus.). 1979. 2.10 Rub. Russkii Iazyk.

Freyha, Anis. Dictionary of Modern Lebanese Proverbs. (Arabic & Eng.). 1974. $25.00x (ISBN 0-86685-086-4). Intl Bk Ctr.

Ilg, G. Proverbes Francais: In French with Equivalents in English, German, Dutch, Italian, Spanish, Latin. (Glossarium Interpretum: No. 4). (Fr., Eng., Ger., Dutch, Ital., Span. & Lat., Polyglot). 1960. $17.00 (ISBN 0-444-40312-4). Elsevier.

Knowles, James H. A Dictionary of Kashmiri Proverbs & Sayings. 59.95 (ISBN 0-8490-0036-X). Gordon Pr.

Laurence Urdang Associates, Ltd. The Penguin Dictionary of Proverbs. 256p. 1983. pap. 5.95 (ISBN 0-14-051118-0). Penguin.

Mackay, Charles. Dictionary of Lowland Scotch. LC 68-17998. (Scottish.). 1968. Repr. of 1888 ed. $45.00x (ISBN 0-8103-3284-1). Gale.

Maloux, M. Dictionnaire des proverbes, sentences et maximes. (Fr., Fr). 23.50 (ISBN 2-03-020291-6, 3618). Larousse.

Sintes Pros, Jorge, ed. Diccionario de maximas, pensamientos y sentencias. 8th ed. 744p. (Span.). 1980. 1200.00 ptas (ISBN 84-302-0439-3). Sintes.

PROVERBS–BIBLIOGRAPHY

Sintes. Diccionario de Aforismos, Proverbios & Refranes. (Span.). $19.50 (SOP). Lectorum Pubns.

PROVIDENT LOAN ASSOCIATIONS

see Building and Loan Associations

PSEUDONYMS

see Anonyms and Pseudonyms

PSYCHIATRY

Here are entered works on the clinical and therapeutic aspects of psychology. Works on abnormal psychology in general are entered under the heading Psychology, Pathological.

see also Child Psychiatry; Clinical Psychology; Mental Illness; Psychology, Pathological; Social Psychiatry

Fann, William E. & Goshen, Charles E. The Language of Mental Health. 2nd ed. LC 76-40210. 165p. 1977. pap. 12.00 (ISBN 0-8016-1548-8). Mosby.

Moor, Lise. Glossaire de Psychiatrie. 196p. (Fr.). 1966. 76.00 F. Masson.

PSYCHIATRY–DICTIONARIES

American Psychiatric Assn., ed. A Psychiatric Glossary. 5th ed. 1980. text ed. 10.95 (ISBN 0-316-03656-0). Little.

American Psychiatric Association. A Psychiatric Glossary. 5th ed. LC 79-55869. 152p. 1980. pap. $6.50x (ISBN 0-89042-005-X, 42-005-X). Am Psychiatric.

Bierens de Haan, Barthhold. Dictionnaire Critique de Psychiatrie. LC 79-124731. 301p. (Fr.). 1979. write for info. (ISBN 2-7203-0057-8). Hameau.

Brussel, James A. & Cantzlaar, George L. Diccionario de Psiquiatria. 306p. (Span.). pap. $25.50 (ISBN 0-686-57366-8, S-50209). French & Eur.

Brussel, James A. & Cantzlaar, Geroge L., trs. Diccionario de psiquiatria. 310p. (Span.). 1972. $6.15. CECSA.

Campbell, Robert J., ed. Psychiatric Dictionary. 5th ed. 1981. 35.00x (ISBN 0-19-502817-1). Oxford U Pr.

--Psychiatric Dictionary. 5th ed. 1981. 35.00x (ISBN 0-19-502817-1). Oxford U Pr.

Carrere, Jean & Dessaigne, Jacques. Lexique des Termes Usuels de Psychiatrie. 114p. (Fr.). 1976. pap. $17.50 (ISBN 0-686-56939-3, M-6061). French & Eur.

--Lexique des Termes Usuels de Psychiatrie. LC 77-464918. 114p. (Fr.). 1976. 35.00 F (ISBN 2-7013-0101-7). Berger-Levrault.

Dizionario di psichiatria. (Ital.). L.2500.00. Newton-Compton.

Dizionario di psichiatria clinica & terapeutica. x, 852p. (Ital.). 1970. L.28000.00. Edizioni Paoline.

Egidius, Henry. Uppslagsbok i Psykoterapi och Medicinsk Psykologi. LC 76-488253. 198p. (Swedish.). 1976. Kr.50.00 (ISBN 9-1270-0680-8). Natur & Kultur.

Fann, William E. & Goshen, Charles E. The Language of Mental Health. 2nd ed. LC 76-40210. 165p. 1977. pap. 12.00 (ISBN 0-8016-1548-8). Mosby.

Haas, Roland. Dictionary of Psychology & Psychiatry. (Eng. & Ger.). 1979. Can.$64.00 (ISBN 0-88937-000-1). Hogrefe.

Haas, Roland, ed. Dictionary of Psychology & Psychiatry: English-German. 453p. (Eng. & Ger.). text ed. $49.00 (ISBN 0-88937-000-1). C J Hogrefe.

Kamenetz, Herman L. Physiatric Dictionary: Glossary of Physical Medicine & Rehabilitation. 180p. 1965. photocopy ed. spiral $16.75x (ISBN 0-398-00964-3). C C Thomas.

Lexique de Psychologie & de Psychiatrie. 155p. (Fr.). 1978. 22.00 F. Medicales Univ.

Lexique de Psychologie & de Psychiatrie. 155p. (Fr.). 22.00 F. Medicales Univ.

Marchais, Pierre. Glossaire De Psychiatrie. 238p. (Fr.). 1970. $37.50 (ISBN 0-686-57038-3, M-6398). French & Eur.

Moor, Lise. English-French-German Glossary for Psychiatry, Child Psychiatry & Abnormal Psychology. 2nd ed. LC 75-450548. (Eng., Fr. & Ger.). 1969. 8.75x (ISBN 0-8002-0766-1). Intl Pubns Serv.

--Glossaire De Psychiatrie. 196p. (Fr.). 1966. pap. $35.00 (ISBN 0-686-57053-7, M-6417). French & Eur.

Mueller, C. Lexikon der Psychiatrie. xii, 592p. (Ger.). 1973. DM.40.00 (ISBN 3-540-06277-7). Springer-Verlag.

Peters, Uwe H. Woerterbuch der Psychiatrie und Medizinischen Psychologie. 2nd ed. (Ger., Eng. & Fr., Dictionary of Psychiatry & Medical Psychology). 1977. pap. $28.00 (ISBN 3-541-06552-4, M-6972). French & Eur.

Porat. Diccionario de psiquiatria. (Span.). write for info. Labor SA.

Porot, Antoine. Diccionario De Psiquiatria, 2 vols. 3rd ed. 650p. (Span.). 1977. Set. $58.00 (ISBN 84-335-6668-7, S-50071). French & Eur.

Porot, Antoine, ed. Manuel Alphabetique De Psychiatrie Clinique et Therapeutique. 5th ed. 679p. (Fr.). 1975. $65.00 (ISBN 0-686-57031-6, M-6391). French & Eur.

Procedural Terminology for Psychiatrists. 16p. 1981. pap. $3.00x (ISBN 0-89042-128-5, 42-128-5). Am Psychiatric.

Rycroft, Charles. A Critical Dictionary of Psychoanalysis. (Quality Paperback: No. 270). 189p. 1973. pap. 3.95 (ISBN 0-8226-0270-9). Littlefield.

Tuke, Daniel H. A Dictionary of Psychological Medicine, 2 vols. LC 75-16737. (Classics in Psychiatry Ser.). 1976. Repr. of 1892 ed. Set. $84.00x (ISBN 0-405-07457-3); $42.00x ea. Vol. 1 (ISBN 0-405-07458-1). Vol. 2 (ISBN 0-405-07459-X). Ayer Co.

PSYCHIATRY, CHILD

see Child Psychiatry

PSYCHIATRY, SOCIAL

see Social Psychiatry

PSYCHICAL RESEARCH

see also Dreams; Hypnotism; Mind and Body; Spiritualism

Bonin, Werner F. Lexikon der Parapsychologie & ihrer Grenzgebiete. LC 77-452317. vii, 587p. (Ger.). 1976. 48.00 F. Scherz AG.

Morel, Hector & Dale Moral, Jose. Diccionario de parapsicologia. 2nd, rev. ed. 240p. (Span.). 1980. pap. write for info. Kier.

Riland, George. New Steinerbooks Dictionary of the Paranormal. LC 79-93353. (Spiritual Science Library). 370p. 1980. cancelled (ISBN 0-8334-0719-8). Garber Comm.

Roca Muntanola, Julio. Diccionario de Parapsicologia. 272p. (Span.). 1979. $17.50 (ISBN 84-203-0086-1, S-50093). French & Eur.

--Diccionario de Parapsicologia. 272p. (Span.). 1979. 500.00 ptas. Alas.

San Martin Unamuno, Jose M. Diccionario de parapsicologia. 64p. (Span.). 1980. pap. 150.00 ptas (ISBN 84-85714-02-4). Don Bosco Ed.

Schreiber, Hermann. Woerterbuch der Parapsychologie. (Ger.). 1974. pap. $12.00 (ISBN 3-463-00660-X, M-6969). French & Eur.

Thalbourne, Michael A. A Glossary of Terms Used in Parapsychology. 128p. 1983. $8.50 (ISBN 0-434-75720-9, Pub. by W Heinemann). David & Charles.

PSYCHOANALYSIS

see also Dianetics; Dreams; Hypnotism; Mind and Body; Psychology; Psychology, Pathological; Psychology, Physiological

Fodor, N. & Gaynor, F. Dizionario di psicoanalisi tratto dalle opere di Sigmund Freud. 208p. (Ital.). 1967. L.600.00. Feltrinelli.

Laplanche, Jean. Vocabulaire de la Psychanalyse. 5th ed. (Fr.). 1976. 145.60 F. PUF.

PSYCHOANALYSIS–DICTIONARIES

Doucet, Friedrich W. Diccionario De Psicoanalisis Clasico. 232p. (Span.). 1974. pap. $15.75 (ISBN 0-686-57337-4, S-50069). French & Eur.

--Diccionario de Psicoanalisis Clasico. 232p. (Span.). 1974. E240.00 (ISBN 84-335-1517-9). Labor.

Fedida, P. Diccionario de Psicoanalisis. (Span.). pap. $6.95 (ISBN 84-206-1730-X, S-32981). French & European.

Fedida, Pierre. Diccionario de Psicoanalisis. 176p. (Span.). 1979. 200.00 ptas. Alianza Ed.

--Dictionnaire de la Psychanalyse. 250p. (Fr.). 1978. 17.60 F. Larousse.

Glanze, Walter D. Longman Dictionary of Psychology & Psychoanalysis. 800p. 1983. $29.95 (ISBN 0-582-28257-8). Longman.

Jung, C. Gustav. Dizionario di psicologia analitica. Musatti, C. L. & Aurigemma, L., trs. 126p. (Ital.). 1978. L.1500.00. Boringhieri.

Laplanche, Jean & Pontalis, Jean-Bertrand. Diccionario Del Psicoanalisis. 3rd ed. Cervantes Gimeno, Fernando, ed. 558p. (Span.). 1977. leatherette $65.50 (ISBN 84-335-1516-0, S-31445). French & Eur.

Laplanche, Jean, ed. Vocabulaire de la Psychanalyse. 5th ed. Pontalis, Jean-Baptiste. (Fr.). 1976. $55.00 (ISBN 0-686-57250-5, M-6558). French & Eur.

Laplanche, Jean, et al. Diccionario de psicoanalisis. 3rd ed. Cervantes Gimeno, Fernando, tr. 560p. (Span.). 1981. 3000.00 ptas (ISBN 84-335-1518-7). Labor SA.

Laplanche Pontalis. Diccionario del psicoanalisis. (Span.). write for info. Labor SA.

Moore, Burness E. & Fine, Bernard D., eds. A Glossary of Psychoanalytic Terms & Concepts. 2nd ed. 120p. 1968. $5.50. Am Psychoanalytic.

Mousseau, Jacques & Moreau, Pierre F. L'Inconscient. LC 77-466781. 538p. (Eng. & Fr.). 1976. 72.50 F (ISBN 2-7256-0109-6). Retz.

Peters, Uwe H. Woerterbuch der Tiefenpsychologie. 2nd ed. LC 80-490459. 182p. (Eng. & Ger.). 1978. DM.18.00 (ISBN 3-463-00734-7). Kindler.

Rycroft, Charles. A Critical Dictionary of Psychoanalysis. (Quality Paperback: No. 270). 189p. 1973. pap. 3.95 (ISBN 0-8226-0270-9). Littlefield.

--Dizionario critico di psicoanalisi. xxxii, 256p. (Ital.). L.4000.00. Astrolabio.

Trempe, Jean-Pierre. Lexique de la Psychanalyse. 146p. (Fr.). 1978. 39.60 F. Quebec P. U.

PSYCHOLINGUISTICS

see also Children–Language; Speech, Disorders of

Elgin, Suzette H. More on the Gentle Art of Verbal Self-Defense. 284p. 1983. 12.95 (ISBN 0-13-601138-1); pap. 6.95 (ISBN 0-13-601120-9). P-H.

PSYCHOLOGY

see also Body, Human; Child Psychology; Cognition; Concepts; Emotions; Human Behavior; Intellect; Logic; New Thought; Psychical Research; Psychoanalysis; Social Psychology

also subdivision Psychology under specific subjects, e.g. Aeronautics–Psychology

Ahlheim, Karl H. Die Psychologie: Ein Sachlexikon fuer die Schule. (Illus.). 408p. (Ger.). DM.19.80 (ISBN 3-411-01795-3). Biblio Inst.

Berger. Dictionary of Psychology. 133p. (Eng.). 1982. DM.45.00. Brandstetter.

Huart, Pierre. Vocabulaire de l'analyse Psychologique dans l'oeuvre de Thucydide. 546p. (Fr.). 1969. 88.00 F. Klincksieck.

Pieron, Henri. Vocabulaire de la Psychologie. 5th ed. (Fr.). 1973. 145.60 F. PUF.

Pinoche, Jacqueline. Le Vocabulaire Psychologique dans les Chroniques de Froissart, 1. (Fr.). 1976. 92.00 F. Klincksieck.

Smith, Stevenson & Guthrie, Edwin R. General Psychology in Terms of Behavior. LC 22-444. (Psychology Ser). 1970. Repr. of 1921 ed. $18.00 (ISBN 0-384-56175-6). Johnson Repr.

PSYCHOLOGY–DICTIONARIES
Alcantud, Adela. Diccionario Bilingue De Psicologia. LC 78-50649. (Senda Lexicografica Ser.). (Span.). 1978. pap. $7.95 (ISBN 0-918454-05-0). Senda Nueva.
Arnold, Wilhelm, et al, eds. Lexikon der Psychologie. 1328p. (Ger.). 1976. DM.85.00 (ISBN 3-451-17680-7). Herder.
--Lexikon der Psychologie: Bd 2, Graphologie-Prompling. 432p. (Ger.). 1971. DM.98.00 (ISBN 3-451-16112-5). Herder.
--Lexikon der Psychologie: Bd 3, Propaganda-Zz. 422p. (Ger.). 1972. DM.98.00 (ISBN 3-451-16113-3). Herder.
--Lexikon der Psychologie: Bd 1, A-Gewissen. 421p. (Ger.). 1971. DM.98.00 (ISBN 3-451-16111-7). Herder.
Baldwin, James M. Dictionary of Philosophy & Psychology, 3 vols. bound in 4. Incl. Vols. 1 & 2. 27.00 ea.; Vol. 1. (ISBN 0-8446-1047-X); Vol. 2. (ISBN 0-8446-1048-8); Vol. 3., 2 Pts. Bibliography of Philosophy, Psychology and Cognate Subjects. 24.00 ea.; Pt. 1. (ISBN 0-8446-1049-6); Pt. 2. (ISBN 0-8446-1050-X). Set. 102.00 (ISBN 0-8446-1046-1). Peter Smith.
Baldwin, James M., et al. Dictionary of Philosophy & Psychology. 1977. lib. bdg. 395.00 (ISBN 0-8490-1721-1). Gordon Pr.
Bastin, G. Diccionario De Psicologia Sexual. 2nd ed. 412p. (Span.). 1976. $19.95 (ISBN 84-254-0585-8, S-13099). French & Eur.
Beigel. Dictionary of Psychology & Related Fields. 256p. (Eng.). 1982. DM.55.00. Brandstetter.
Beigel, Hugo G. Dictionary of Psychology & Related Fields. LC 74-115063. (Ger. & Eng.). $15.00 (ISBN 0-8044-0042-3). Ungar.
Berger. Dictionary of Psychology. 133p. (Eng.). 1982. DM.45.00. Brandstetter.
Berger, Alfred H., ed. Dictionary of Psychology: English-German. LC 76-15645. (Eng. & Ger.). 1977. $14.50 (ISBN 0-8044-0043-1). Ungar.
Blumenberg, Franz-Jurgen. Herder-Lexikon: Psychologie Sachwoerterbuch. LC 77-477664. (Illus.). 238p. (Ger.). 1975. DM.19.80 (ISBN 3-451-16467-1). Herder.
Blumenbrg & Kury. Herder - Lexikon Psychologie. 2nd ed. 239p. (Ger.). 1976. pap. $25.95 (ISBN 3-451-16467-1, M-7451, Pub. by Herder). French & Eur.
--Herder-Lexikon Psychologie. 2nd ed. 239p. (Ger.). 1976. pap. $25.95 (ISBN 3-451-16467-1). Herder.
Castonguay, Jacques. Dictionnaire Francais-Anglais de la Psychologie & des Sciences Connexes. 316p. (Fr.). 1973. 88.00 F. Maloine.
Chaplin, J. P. Dictionary of Psychology. 608p. 1975. pap. $3.50 (ISBN 0-440-31926-9, LE). Dell.
Clauss, G., et al, eds. Woerterbuch der Psychologie. (Illus.). 704p. (Ger.). 1981. write for info. Bibl Inst Leipzig.
Clauss, Guenter. Woerterbuch der Psychologie. 596p. (Ger.). 1976. write for info. (ISBN 3-7609-0256-1). Pahl-Rugenstein.
Clauss, Gunter. Woerterbuch der Psychologie. LC 77-458138. (Illus.). 596p. (Ger.). 1976. M.18.00. Biblio Inst.
Concordance to the Science of Mind. 312p. 1980. pap. $17.95 (ISBN 0-911336-82-6). Sci of Mind.
Dalla Volta, Amedeo. Dizionario di psicologia. (Illus.). 998p. (Ital.). L.18000.00. Giunti-Barbera.
Diccionario de Psicologia. 342p. (Span.). 1982. pap. 375.00 ptas (ISBN 84-271-1272-6). Mensajero Edns.
Dizionario di psicologia. (Ital.). 1975. L.15000.00. Edizioni Paoline.
Dorin, E. Diccionario de psicologia abrangendo terminologia de ciencias correlatas. LC 79-342055. (Illus.). 300p. (Span.). 1978. Cr.$320.00. Edicoes Melhoramentos.
Dorsch, F. Psychologisches Woerterbuch. 9th ed. 784p. (Ger.). 1976. $75.00 (ISBN 3-456-80320-6, M-7595, Pub. by H. Huber). French & Eur.
--Psychologisches Woerterbuch. 9th ed. 784p. (Ger.). 1976. $75.00 (ISBN 3-456-80320-6). Huber.
Dorsch, Friedrich. Diccionario De Psicologia. 3rd ed. 756p. (Span.). 1978. $59.95 (ISBN 84-254-1026-6). French & Eur.
--Psychologisches Woerterbuch. LC 76-472620. (Illus.). 774p. (Ger.). 1976. write for info. (ISBN 3-456-80320-6). H Huber.
Drever, James. A Dictionary of Psychology. rev. ed. lib. bdg. 11.50x (ISBN 0-88307-338-2). Gannon.
--Dictionary of Psychology. rev. ed. (Reference Ser.). (Orig.). (YA) (gr. 11 up). 1964. pap. 4.95 (ISBN 0-14-051005-2). Penguin.
Duijker, Hubert C. & Van Rijswijk, Maria J. Dictionnaire de Psychologie en Trois Langues, 3: Allemand-Anglais-Francais. (Ger., Eng. & Fr.). 897.00 F. Editest.
Duijker, Hubert C. Dictionnaire de Psychologie en Trois Langues, Vol. 2. (Fr., Ger. & Eng.). 1978. pap. $39.95 (ISBN 0-686-57264-5, M-4660). French & Eur.
Duijker, Hubert C. & Van Rijswijk, Maria J. Dictionnaire de Psychologie en Trois Langues: Anglais-Francais-Allemand. (Eng., Fr. & Ger.). 1978. 897.00 F. Editest.
--Dictionnaire de Psychologie en Trois Langues, 2: Francais-Allemand-Anglais. (Fr., Ger. & Eng.). 849.00 F. Editest.
Duijker, Hubert C. & Van Sijswijk, Maria. Dictionnaire de Psychologie en 3 Langues, 3 vols. (Eng., Fr. & Ger., Dictionary of Psychology in 3 Languages). pap. $40.00 (ISBN 0-686-56801-X, M-4661). French & Eur.
Evans, Christopher R. Psychology: ADictionary of the Mind, Brain & Behavior. LC 79-305603. (Illus.). 416p. (Eng.). 1978. E2.50 (ISBN 0-09-918610-1). Arrow Bks.
Froehlich, Werner D. & Drever, James. Woerterbuch zur Psychologie. (Ger.). DM.16.80. Deutscher Taschenbuch.
Genovard. Diccionario de Psicologia. 284p. (Span.). 1980. 1.450 ptas. Jims.
Genovard Rossello, Candid. Vocabulario basico trilingue de psicologia cientifica: Ingles-castellano. 192p. (Eng. & Span.). 1980. pap. 500.00 ptas (ISBN 84-244-0490-4). Fontanella.
Glanze, Walter D. Longman Dictionary of Psychology & Psychoanalysis. 800p. 1983. $29.95 (ISBN 0-582-28257-8). Longman.
Haas, Roland. Dictionary of Psychology & Psychiatry. (Eng. & Ger.). 1979. Can.$64.00 (ISBN 0-88937-000-1). Hogrefe.
Haas, Roland, ed. Dictionary of Psychology & Psychiatry: English-German. 453p. (Eng. & Ger.). text ed. $49.00 (ISBN 0-88937-000-1). C J Hogrefe.
Hanson, D. P. & Penrod, D. A. A Desk Reference of Legal Terms for School Psychologists & Special Educators. 224p. 1980. $19.75x (ISBN 0-398-04015-X). C C Thomas.
Harriman, Philip L. Dictionary of Psychology. 1971. pap. $3.95 (ISBN 0-8065-0252-5). Citadel Pr.
--Handbook of Psychological Terms. (Quality Paperback: No. 35). (Orig.). 1977. pap. 3.95 (ISBN 0-8226-0035-8). Littlefield.
Hehlmann, Wilhelm. Woerterbuch der Psychologie. 11th ed. (Ger.). 1974. pap. $17.50 (ISBN 3-520-26911-2, M-6964). French & Eur.
Heidenreich, Charles A. Dictionary of General Psychology: Basic Terminology & Key Concepts. rev. ed. 1970. pap. text ed. 7.95 (ISBN 0-8403-0171-5). Heidenreich.
Hermann, E. R., et al, eds. Piaget: Dictionary of Terms. 1973. text ed. 28.00 (ISBN 0-08-017039-0). Pergamon.
Knoll, Ludwig. Lexikon der praktischen Psychologie. LC 79-398496. 488p. (Ger.). 1979. DM.36.00 (ISBN 3-7857-0231-0). Luebbe.
Laplanche, Jean. Das Vokabular der Psychoanalyse, 2 vols. (Ger.). 1973. pap. $15.95 (ISBN 3-518-07607-8, M-7680, Pub. by Suhrkamp). French & Eur.
Lexique Psycholologique. (Fr.). 12.00 F. Vie et Action.
Merani, Alberto L. Diccionario de psicologia. LC 77-484135. vii, 258p. (Span.). 1977. 400.00 ptas (ISBN 8-42530-736-8). Grijalbo.
Merrani, Alberto L. Diccionario De Psicologia. 272p. (Span.). 1977. $17.50 (ISBN 84-253-0736-8, S-50072). French & Eur.
Michel, Christian & Novak, Felix. Kleines Psychologisches Woerterbuch. LC 75-506617. (Illus.). 378p. (Ger.). 1975. DM.12.90 (ISBN 3-451-07514-8). Herder.
Parenti, Francesco. Dizionario ragionato di psicologia individuale. 273p. (Ital.). 1975. L.10000.00. Cortina M.
Peters, Uwe H. Woerterbuch der Psychiatrie und Medizinischen Psychologie. 2nd ed. (Ger., Eng. & Fr., Dictionary of Psychiatry & Medical Psychology). 1977. pap. $28.00 (ISBN 3-541-06552-4, M-6972). French & Eur.
Pieron, Henri. Dizionario di psicologia. Canestrari, R., tr. xviii, 664p. (Ital.). 1972. L.14000.00. La Nuova Italia.
--Vocabulaire De la Psychologie. 5th ed. 570p. (Fr.). 1973. $55.00 (ISBN 0-686-57078-2, M-6453). French & Eur.
--Vocabulaire de la psychologie. 6th ed. LC 79-382007. xii, 587p. (Fr.). 1979. 165.00 F (ISBN 2-13-035971-X). Pr Univ Fr.
Pieron, Henri, et al, trs. Lexicon Kapelusz: Psicologia. 768p. (Span.). Mex.$11.17. Kapelusz.
Poinso, Yves. Diccionario Practico De Psicopatologia. 324p. (Span.). 1976. $23.95 (ISBN 84-254-0618-8, S-50194); pap. $19.95 (ISBN 0-686-77261-X, S-50186). French & Eur.
Popescu-Neveanu, Paul. Dictionar de psihologie. LC 78-396355. 783p. (Romanian.). 1978. 30.00 lei. Albatros.
Schutzsenberger, Anne A. Diccionario De la Tecnicas De Grupo. 260p. (Span.). 1974. pap. $10.75 (ISBN 84-301-0603-0, S-50365). French & Eur.
Sillamy, N. Dictionnaire psychologie. (Illus., Fr.). pap. $8.50 (ISBN 0-685-13883-6). Larousse.
Sillamy, Norbert. Diccionario de la psicologia. (Span.). 100.00 ptas. Plaza Janes.
--Dictionnaire de la Psychologie. 4th ed. (Illus.). 250p. (Fr.). 1971. 17.60 F. Larousse.
--Dictionnaire de Psychologie. 220p. (Fr.). 1969. 3.00 F. Larousse.
Sillamy, Norberth. Diccionario de la Psicologia. 4th ed. 344p. (Span.). 1974. $5.25 (ISBN 0-686-57338-2, S-12360). French & Eur.
Statt, David. Dictionary of Psychology. 1982. pap. 4.76i (ISBN 0-06-463553-8, EH-553). Har-Row.
Tewes, U. Lexikon der Medizinischen Psychologie. (Ger.). 1977. $12.95 (ISBN 3-17-004011-1, M-7248). French & Eur.
Thesaurus of Psychological Index Terms. 3rd ed. 336p. (Orig.). 1982. $40.00x (ISBN 0-912704-67-5). Am Psychol.
V. Clauss, Guenther. Woerterbuch der Psychologie. (Ger.). 1976. $22.50 (ISBN 3-7609-0256-1, M-6963). French & Eur.
Vels, Augusto. Diccionario de Grafologia y Terminos Psicologicos Afines. 474p. (Span.). 1972. $17.95 (ISBN 84-352-0114-7, S-13272). French & Eur.
Verplanck, William. Dictionary of Psychology: With Thesaurus. 45.00x (ISBN 0-89197-729-5). Irvington.
Warren, H. C. Diccionario de psicologia. 384p. (Span.). pap. $5.45. Fondo Cult.
Woerterbuch der Paedagogischen Psychologie. 3rd ed. (Ger.). 1976. $7.95 (ISBN 0-686-56617-3, M-6970). French & Eur.
Wolman, Benjamin B. Dictionary of Behavioral Science. 1973. $24.50x (ISBN 0-442-29566-9). Van Nos Reinhold.
Wolman, Benjamin B., ed. Dictionary of Behavorial Science. 1979. pap. text ed. $12.95 (ISBN 0-442-29581-2). Van Nos Reinhold.

PSYCHOLOGY–EARLY WORKS TO 1850
Lexique de Psychologie & de Psychiatrie. 155p. (Fr.). 1978. 22.00 F. Medicales Univ.
Lexique de Psychologie & de Psychiatrie. 155p. (Fr.). 22.00 F. Medicales Univ.

PSYCHOLOGY, ABNORMAL
see Psychology, Pathological

PSYCHOLOGY, CHILD
see Child Psychology

PSYCHOLOGY, CLINICAL
see Clinical Psychology

PSYCHOLOGY, EDUCATIONAL
see Educational Psychology

PSYCHOLOGY, FORENSIC
see also Lie Detectors and Detection
Spirolazzi, Giancarlo. Dizionario di psicologia forense. 376p. (Ital.). 1969. L.3800.00. Giuffre.

PSYCHOLOGY, JURISTIC
see Psychology, Forensic

PSYCHOLOGY, LEGAL
see Psychology, Forensic

PSYCHOLOGY, PATHOLOGICAL
see also Clinical Psychology; Fantasy; Mental Illness; Psychiatry; Psychoanalysis; Psychology, Forensic
Gori, Roland-Claude & Poinso, Yves. Dictionnaire Pratique de Psychopathologie. 208p. (Fr.). 1972. 50.00 F. Delarge.
Moor, Lise. English-French-German Glossary for Psychiatry, Child Psychiatry & Abnormal Psychology. 2nd ed. LC 75-450548. (Eng., Fr & Ger.). 1969. 8.75x (ISBN 0-8002-0766-1). Intl Pubns Serv.
Virel, Andre. Vocabulaire des Psychotherapies. LC 77-573406. 373p. (Fr.). 1977. 59.00 F (ISBN 2-213-00419-6). Fayard.

PSYCHOLOGY, PHYSIOLOGICAL
see also Conditioned Response; Emotions; Human Engineering; Hypnotism; Mind and Body; Psychoanalysis
Tembrock, Gunter. Verhaltensbiologie. LC 80-464719. 224p. (Eng. & Ger.). 1978. DM.19.80 (ISBN 3-437-20175-1). Fischer Verlag.

PSYCHOLOGY, SEXUAL
see Sex (Psychology)

PSYCHOLOGY, SOCIAL
see Social Psychology

PSYCHOLOGY OF LANGUAGE
see Psycholinguistics

PSYCHOLOGY OF LEARNING
see Learning, Psychology Of

PSYCHOPATHOLOGY
see Psychology, Pathological

PSYCHOPHYSICS
see Psychology, Physiological

PSYCHOPHYSIOLOGY
see Psychology, Physiological

PUBLIC ADMINISTRATION
Here are entered works on the principles and techniques involved in the conduct of public business. Works descriptive of governmental machinery are entered under the area concerned, with the subdivision Politics and Government.
see also Administrative Law; Civil Service; Personnel Management also subdivision Politics and Government under names of countries, cities, etc.
Dizionario dei comuni con le circoscrizioni guidiziarie. (Ital.). 1964. L.1000.00. Giuffre.
Preisigke, Friedrich. Fachwoerter des Oeffentlichen Verwaltungsdienstes Aegyptens in den Griechischen Papyrusurkunden der Ptolemaeisch-Romischen Zeit. LC 78-347087. x, 186p. (Ger. & Gr.). 1975. DM.33.80 (ISBN 3-487-05896-0). Olms Verlag.
Rampini, Gino. Dizionario della sicurezza sociale. (Illus.). 230p. (Ital.). 1966. L.1800.00. Giuffre.

Vetrini, Trentino. Dizionario della pubblica istruzione: Legislazione e pratica amministrativa sulla istruzione primaria. vii, 796p. (Ital.). 1967. L.8000.00. Giuffre.

Zanobini, L. & Vetrini, T. Dizionario della publica istruzione, 2 vols. xii, 2270p. (Ital.). 1972. L.28000.00. Giuffre.

--Dizionario della publica istruzione, 2 vols. xii, 1872p. (Ital.). 1975. L.30000.00. Giuffre.

PUBLIC ASSISTANCE
see Public Welfare

PUBLIC CORPORATIONS
see Corporations

PUBLIC FINANCE
see Finance, Public

PUBLIC HEALTH
see also Environmental Health; Hospitals; Pollution; Refuse and Refuse Disposal; Sanitary Engineering; Sewage Disposal; Water-Supply

Deblock, Nick J. Elsevier's Dictionary of Public Health. LC 76-676387. 204p. (Eng., Fr., Span., Ital., Dutch & Ger.). 1976. $47.00 (ISBN 0-444-41395-2). Elsevier.

PUBLIC HEALTH- BIBLIOGRAPHY
University of London. Dictionary Catalogue of the London School of Hygiene & Tropical Medicine, 7 Vols. 1965. Set. lib. bdg. $590.00 (ISBN 0-8161-0703-3, Hall Library); serials catalogue. $35.00 (ISBN 0-8161-0182-5); 1st suppl. (1971) $105.00 (ISBN 0-8161-0821-8). G K Hall.

PUBLIC HEALTH, RURAL
see Health, Rural

PUBLIC HEALTH SERVICES
see Public Health

PUBLIC HYGIENE
see Public Health

PUBLIC LAW
see also Administrative Law; Constitutional Law; Criminal Law; International Law; Military Law also subdivision Constitutional Law under names of countries

Wilkin, Robert. Dictionnaire du Droit Public. (Fr.). write for info. Bruylant.

PUBLIC LAW (CANON LAW)
see Canon Law

PUBLIC POLICY
see Economic Policy; Environmental Policy; Military Policy; Social Policy

PUBLIC RELATIONS
see also Advertising; Publicity

Andrade, Candido T. Dicionario Professional de Relacoes Publicas & Comunicacao & Glossario. LC 79-341351. 134p. (Port.). 1978. Cr.$95.00. Saraiva SA.

PUBLIC RELATIONS--BUSINESS
see Public Relations

PUBLIC RELATIONS- INDUSTRY
see Public Relations

PUBLIC RELIEF
see Public Welfare

PUBLIC WELFARE
Here are entered works on tax-supported welfare activities.
see also Charities; Hospitals; Social Service
also subdivision Charities under names of cities, e.g. New York (City)-Charities; also subdivision Civilian Relief under names of wars, e.g. World War, 1939-1945-Civilian Relief

Sournia, Jean-Charles. Dictionnaire des Assurances Sociales. 112p. (Fr.). 1973. $22.50 (ISBN 0-686-57224-6, M-6522). French & Eur.

PUBLIC WORKS
see also Municipal Engineering
also subdivision Public Works under names of countries, cities, etc., e.g. United States-Public Works

Barbier, et al. Diccionario tecnico ilustrado de edificacion y obras publicas. (Illus.). 177p. (Span.). write for info. G Gili.

Barbier, Maurice. Diccionario Tecnico Ilustrado De Edificacion y Obras Publicas. 177p. (Span.). 1976. pap. $11.50 (ISBN 84-252-0327-9, S-50273). French & Eur.

Barbier, Maurice & Cadiergues, Roger. Dictionnaire Technique du Batiment & des Travaux Publics. 6th ed. (Illus.). 148p. (Fr.). 1978. 60.00 F. Eyrolles.

Benito Bacho, Jose. Diccionario de la Construccion y Obras Publicas Ingles-Espanol, 2 vols. 268p. (Span. & Eng.). 1975. Set. $38.95 (ISBN 84-85198-10-7, S-50117). French & Eur.

--Diccionario de la Construccion y Obras Publicas, Tomo 2: Span. 110p. (Span.). 1975. $18.95 (ISBN 84-85198-09-3, S-50119). French & Eur.

--Diccionario de la Construcion y de Obras Publicas, Tomo I: Ingles. 168p. (Span.). 1975. $18.95 (ISBN 84-85198-00-X, S-50118). French & Eur.

Bucksch. Diccionario Para Obras Publica, Edificacion y Maquinaria En Obra. 1116p. (Ger. & Span.). 1976. $60.00 (ISBN 84-254-0105-4, S-50187). French & Eur.

--Diccionario para obras publicas, edificacion y maquinaria en obra: Aleman-espanol, espanol-aleman. 1116p. (Ger. & Span.). $20.46; 1320.00 ptas. Herder SA.

Bucksch, Hector. Dictionnaire Allemand-Francais pour les Travaux Publics: Le Batiment & l'equipement des Chantiers des Chantiers de Constuction. 2nd ed. 878p. (Ger. & Fr.). 1972. 372.00 F. Eyrolles.

--Dictionnaire Anglais-Francais pour les Travaux Publics: Le Batiment & L'equipement des Chantiers de Construction. 6th ed. 420p. (Eng. & Fr.). 1977. 103.00 F. Eyrolles.

--Dictionnaire Francais-Allemand pour le Travaux Publics le Batiment & l'equipement des Chantiers de Construction. (Illus.). 912p. (Fr. & Ger.). 1970. 375.00 F. Eyrolles.

--Dictionnaire Francais-Anglais pour les Travaux Publics: Le Batiment & l'equipement des Chantiers de Construction. 6th ed. (Illus.). 550p. (Fr. & Eng.). 1977. 130.00 F. Eyrolles.

--Dictionnaire pour les Travaux Publics, le Batiment & l'Equipement des Chantiers de Construction. 7th ed. 420p. (Eng. & Fr.). 1979. $42.50 (ISBN 0-686-56930-X, M-6051). French & Eur.

Bucksch, Herbert & Galan e Hidalgo, Arturo. Diccionario frances-espanol de la construccion y obras publicas. 564p. (Fr. & Span.). 1969. 700.00 ptas. ETA.

Diccionario Para Obras Publicas, Edificacion y Maquinaria en Obra. (Ger. & Span.). 1962. $86.00 (ISBN 3-7625-1160-8, M-7132). French & Eur.

Dictionnaire Pour les Travaux Publics et l'Equipement des Chartiers de Construction, 2 vols. 875p. (Ger. & Fr.). 1976. leatherette, band I $112.00 (ISBN 3-7625-0379-6, M-7097). French & Eur.

Dictionnaire Pour les Travaux Publics et l'Equipement des Chartiers de Construction, 2 vols. 911p. (Ger. & Fr.). 1978. leatherette, band II $112.00 (ISBN 3-7625-0999-9, M-7098). French & Eur.

Machado. Diccionario Tecnico de la Construccion, Edificacion & Obras Publicas. (Fr. & Span.). 1969. 00.1400.00 ptas (ISBN 8-42830-245-6). Paraninfo.

Machado, M. Diccionario tecnico de la construccion: Edificacion y obras publicas; francesa-espanol y espanol-frances. 578p. (Fr. & Span.). 1969. 500.00 ptas. Paraninfo.

Piraux, Henri. Dictionnaire Anglais-Francis des Termes Relatifs a L'electrotechnique: l'ectrotechnique & aux Applications Connexes. 10th ed. (Illus.). 416p. (Eng. & Fr.). 1978. 100.00 F. Eyrolles.

PUBLICITY
see also Advertising; Journalism; Public Relations

Conseil International De la Langue Francaise, ed. Vocabulaire De la Publicite. (Fr.). 1976. pap. $14.50 (ISBN 0-686-57251-3, M-6559). French & Eur.

Giomot, Sylvain. Dictionnaire de la Publicite et du Marketing: Anglais-Francais Francais-Anglais. 500p. (Eng. & Fr.). 1979. 110.00 F. Maison Dictionnaire.

PUBLISHERS AND PUBLISHING
see also Book Industries and Trade; Books; Booksellers and Bookselling; Copyright

Brownstone, David M. & Franck, Irene M. Dictionary of Publishing. 304p. 1982. text ed. $18.95 (ISBN 0-442-25874-7). Van Nos Reinhold.

Dizionario delle forniture grafiche, editoriale e cartotecniche. (Ital.). 1972. L.10600.00. L'Ufficio Moderno.

Frederick Muller, Ltd., ed. Multilingual Dictionary of Printing & Publishing. 1981. $30.00x (ISBN 0-584-95569-3, Pub. by Muller Ltd). State Mutual Bk.

Glaister, Geoffrey. Glaister's Glossary of the Book: Terms Used in Paper-Making, Printing, Bookbinding, & Publishing. LC 76-47975. 1979. $75.00 (ISBN 0-520-03364-7). U of Cal Pr.

Isaacs, Alan, ed. The Multilingual Dictionary of Printing & Publishing. 336p. 1981. $22.50 (ISBN 0-87196-444-9). Facts on File.

Jacob, Henry. Pocket Dictionary of Publishing Terms. (Illus.). 1976. pap. text ed. $5.95x (ISBN 0-8464-0727-2). Beekman Pubs.

Mora, Imra. The Publishers Practical Dictionary. 2nd ed. 389p. 1977. $64.50 (ISBN 3-7940-4112-7, Pub. by K G Saur). Shoe String.

Mora, Imre. Woerterbuch des Verlagswesens in 20 Sprachen. 2nd ed. (Ger., The Publisher's Practical Dictionary in 20 Languages). 1977. $96.00 (ISBN 3-7940-4112-7, M-6933). French & Eur.

--Woerterbuch des Verlagswesens in 20 Sprachen. 389p. (Ger.). 1977. write for info. (ISBN 3-7940-4112-7). Saur Verlag.

Schuwer, Philippe. Dictionnaire de l'Edition: Francais-Anglais, Anglais-Francais. (Fr.-Eng.). 1977. $55.00 (ISBN 0-686-57216-5, M-6508). French & Eur.

PUBLISHERS AND PUBLISHING-DIRECTORIES
Stiehl, Ulrich. Dictionary of Book Publishing. 538p. (Eng. & Ger.). 1977. text ed. $55.00x (ISBN 3-7940-4147-X, Pub. by K G Saur). Gale.

PUEBLO INDIANS
see Indians of North America-Southwest, New

PUERTO RICAN LITERATURE
Arana Soto, Salvador. Diccionario de Temas Regionalistas En la Poesia Puertorriquena. (Span.). $12.50 (ISBN 0-686-56649-1, S-5220). French & Eur.

PUERTO RICO
Farr, Kenneth R. Historical Dictionary of Puerto Rico & the U.S. Virgin Islands. LC 73-7603. (Latin American Historical Dictionaries Ser.: No. 9). 1973. $13.00 (ISBN 0-8108-0670-3). Scarecrow.

PUERTO RICO-BIOGRAPHY
Diccionario de Medicos Puertorriquenos Que Se Man Distinguico Fuera de la Medicina. (Span.). $17.50 (ISBN 0-686-56650-5). French & Eur.

PUERTO RICO-SOCIAL CONDITIONS
Altieri de Barreto, Carmen G. El Lexico De la Delincuencia En Puerto Rico. (UPREX, C. Sociales: No. 18). (Span.). pap. $1.85 (ISBN 0-8477-0018-6). U of PR Pr.

PUKHTU LANGUAGE
see Pushto Language

PULLMAN CARS
see Railroads-Cars

PULPWOOD
Definitions of Terms in the Sulfite Pulping Process. 1972. $4.00 (1201); members $2.67. TAPPI.

PULSE TECHNIQUES (ELECTRONICS)
Diccionario tecnico, radio, antenas, video, radar: Espanol-ingles. (Span. & Eng.). Arg.$3.00. Cosmopolita.

PUMPING MACHINERY
Dictionary of Pump Terms. (Hebrew, Eng. , Fr. & Ger.). IL.7.00. Massada Pr.

Europump Terminology -- Glossary of Pump Applications in English, German, French, Italian, & Spanish. (Illus.). 1979. $150.00x (ISBN 0-85461-071-5). Intl Ideas.

Institute for Power System. Europump Terminology: Pump Applications. 900p. 1982. $210.00x (ISBN 0-85461-071-5). State Mutual Bk.

Trade & Technical Pr.Ltd., ed. Europump Terminology: Pump Applications. 750p. 1981. $120.00x (ISBN 0-686-79319-6, Pub. by Trade & Tech). State Mutual Bk.

PUMPS
see Pumping Machinery

PUNISHMENT
see also Criminal Law; Prisons
also particular forms of punishment

Goehler, Erich, et al. Lexikon des Nebenstrafrechts. 558p. (Ger.). 1977. DM.54.80 (ISBN 3-406-01806-8). Beck Verlag.

PUNJABI LANGUAGE
see Panjabi Language

PUNS AND PUNNING
Crosbie, John S. Crosbie's Dictionary of Puns. 1977. $12.95 (ISBN 0-517-53124-0, Harmony); pap. $6.95 (ISBN 0-517-53125-9). Crown.

PURBUTTI LANGUAGE
see Nepali Language

PURITANS
Scott, Thomas. The Interpreter, Wherein Three Principal Terms of State Are Clearly Unfolded. LC 74-80194. (English Experience Ser.: No. 673). 1974. Repr. of 1624 ed. $3.50 (ISBN 90-221-0281-5). Walter J Johnson.

PUSHKIN, ALEKSANDR SERGEEVICH, 1799-1837
Slovar Iazyka Pushkina, 4 vols. (Rus.). 1961. $40.00 set (Pub. by GINS). Four Continent.

PUSHTO LANGUAGE
Lebedev, K. A. Karmannyi Afgansko-Russkii Slovar. 587p. (Rus. & Afghan.). 1962. $1.95 (Pub. by Gosizdat Natsional Slovarei). Four Continent.

Lebedev, K. A., et al. Russko-Afganskii Slovar. 872p. (Rus. & Afghani.). 1973. $10.95 (Pub. by Sov Entsiklopediia). Four Continent.

Zudin, P. B. Russko-Afganskii Slovar. 1176p. (Rus. & Afghani.). 1955. $4.25 (Pub. by GINS). Four Continent.

PUZZLES
see also Anagrams; Crossword Puzzles; Rebuses; Riddles

Baus, Herbert M. The Master Crossword Puzzle Dictionary. LC 79-7681. 1981. $24.95 (ISBN 0-385-15118-7). Doubleday.

Boni, Luigi. Dizionario dell'enigmista. 176p. (Ital.). 1971. L.1300.00. Mazziana.

Kahn, Gilbert & Mulkerne, Donald J. The Wordbook. 1975. pap. text ed. 6.95x (ISBN 0-02-474780-7, 47478). Glencoe.

Schimpff, Jill W. Oxford Picture Dictionary of American English Workbook. (Illus.). 1981. 3.75x (ISBN 0-19-502819-8). Oxford U Pr.

Q

QUALITY CONTROL
see also Process Control;
also names of specific industries, e.g. Food Industry

American Society for Quality Control. Glossary & Tables for Statistical Quality Control. 100p. $9.20 (66); members $7.75. Am Soc QC.

EOQC Glossary. $30.00 (T2003); $30.00. Am Soc Qc.

Jakosci, Slownik. Glossary of Terms Used in Quality Control. 54p. (Pol., Eng. & Rus.). 1980. $30.00x (ISBN 0-686-44719-0, Pub. by Collets). State Mutual Bk.

QUANTUM ELECTRONICS
Anglo-Russkii Slovar Po Kvantovoi Elektronike i Golografii. 504p. (Eng. & Rus.). 1977. $6.75 (Pub. by Russkii Iazyk). Four Continent.
Voropaev, N. Anglo-Russkii Slovar po Kvantovoi Elektronike i Golografii. LC 79-392952. 501p. (Eng. & Rus.). 1977. 2.80 Rub. Russkii Iazyk.
QUEBEC (PROVINCE)
see also cities, regions, etc. in Quebec (Province)
Houle, Michel & Julien, Alain. Dictionnaire du Cinema Quebecois. LC 79-361413. xxx, 366p. (Eng. & Fr.). 1978. write for info. (ISBN 0-7755-0699-0). Fides.
Laframbois, Yves. L' Architecture Traditionnelle au Quebec: Glossaire Illustre de la Maison aux 17e & 18e Siecles. LC 75-517455. (Illus.). 319p. (Fr.). 1975. write for info. (ISBN 0-7759-0457-0). Edns Homme.
QUECHUA LANGUAGE
Cerron-Palomino, Rodolfo. Diccionario Quechua Junin-Huanca. LC 77-465008. 274p. (Span. & Quechua.). 1976. write for info. Minist Ed Caracas.
Cusihuaman, Antonio G. Diccionario Quechua Cuzco-Collao. LC 77-465799. 303p. (Quechua & Span.). 1976. write for info. Minist Ed Caracas.
Hornberger, Esteban S. & Hornberger, H. N. Diccionario Tri-lingue, 3 vols. LC 79-102496. (Eng., Quechua, & Span.). 1978. write for info. LCA.
Park, Marinell & Weber, Nancy. Diccionario Quechua San Martin. LC 77-465805. 188p. (Span. & Quechua.). 1976. write for info. Ministerio de Educacion.
Parker, Gary J. Diccionario Polilectal del Quechua de Ancash. LC 76-469538. (Span. & Quechua.). 1975. write for info. Centro Invest.
Quesada Castillo, Felix. Diccionario Quechua Cajamarca-Canaris. LC 77-465796. 193p. (Span. & Quechua.). 1976. write for info. Minist Ed Caracas.
--Lexico Quechua de Cajamarca. LC 77-554130. (Eng., Quechua & Span., Lima, Peru). 1976. write for info. Centro Invest.
Soto Ruiz, Clodoaldo. Diccionario Quechua Ayacucho-Chanca. LC 77-465011. 183p. (Quechua & Span.). 1976. write for info. Minist Ed Caracas.
Weber, David J. Los Sufijos Posesivos en el Quechua del Huallaga. LC 77-579192. 61p. (Quechua & Span.). 1976. write for info. Inst Ling Ver.
QUICHES
see Indians of Central America
QUICHUA LANGUAGE
see Quechua Language
QUICKSILVER
see Mercury
QUILEUTE LANGUAGE
Powell, J. Quileute Dictionary, 10 vols. LC 79-307128. xvii, 519p. (Eng. & Quileute.). 1976. write for info. Univ Idaho.
QUILTING
Khin, Yvonne M. The Collector's Dicionary of Quilt Names & Patterns. LC 80-14246. (Illus.). 512p. 1980. $24.95 (ISBN 0-87491-408-6); pap. $18.95 (ISBN 0-87491-409-4). Acropolis.
QUOTATIONS
see also Aphorisms and Apothegms; Maxims; Proverbs
Battista, O. A. Quotoons: A Speakers Dictionary. 472p. 1981. (Perigee); 5.95 (ISBN 0-399-50514-8). Putnam Pub Group.
Bolander, B. O. The Instant Quotation Dictionary. (Career Institute Instant Reference Library). 314p. 1969. $3.95 (ISBN 0-531-02006-1). Watts.
Bolander, Donald O., et al. Instant Quotation Dictionary. LC 74-104786. 1969. $3.95 (ISBN 0-911744-05-3). Career Inst.
Collison, Robert & Collison, Mary. Dictionary of Foreign Quotations. 416p. 1980. $29.95 (ISBN 0-87196-428-7). Facts on File.
The Concise Oxford Dictionary of Quotations. new ed. 1982. pap. 8.95 (ISBN 0-19-281324-2). Oxford U Pr.
Cree, A. Cree's Dictionary of Latin Quotations. LC 78-51482. (Eng. & Lat.). 1979. $16.00 (ISBN 0-912728-12-4). Newbury Bks.
Dictionnaire des Citations Francaises. 664p. (Fr.). 1978. pap. $8.95 (ISBN 0-686-56838-9, M-6616). French & Eur.
Edwards, Tryon, ed. New Dictionary of Thoughts. rev. ed. 1955. $15.95 (ISBN 0-385-00127-4). Doubleday.
Field, Claud. A Dictionary of Oriental Quotations. 75.00 (ISBN 0-8490-0043-2). Gordon Pr.
Field, Claud H. Dictionary of Oriental Quotations. LC 68-23157. 1969. Repr. of 1911 ed. $38.00x (ISBN 0-8103-3183-7). Gale.
Germa, Pierre. Depuis Quand? Les Origines des Choses de la Vie Quotidienne. 376p. (Fr.). 1979. $43.50 (Dist. by Continental Bk Co). Berger-Levrault.
Goldstein-Jackson, Kevin, compiled by. The Dictionary of Essential Quotations. LC 83-2815. 256p. 1983. text ed. $23.50x (ISBN 0-389-20393-9). B&N Imports.
Jones, Hugh P., ed. Dictionary of Foreign Phrases & Classical Quotations. LC 77-13088. 1977. Repr. of 1929 ed. lib. bdg. 35.00 (ISBN 0-89341-457-3). Longwood Pr.
--Dictionary of Foreign Phrases & Classical Quotations. 552p. 1983. pap. $12.75 (ISBN 0-88072-017-4). Tanager Bks.
McKenna, Michael. Stein & Day Dictionary of Definitive Quotations. LC 81-48453. 192p. 1982. $18.95 (ISBN 0-8128-2864-X). Stein & Day.
Mencken, Henry L., ed. New Dictionary of Quotations on Historical Principles from Ancient & Modern Sources. 1942. 30.00 (ISBN 0-394-40079-8). Knopf.
Norton-Kyshe, James W. Dictionary of Legal Quotations. LC 68-30648. 1968. Repr. of 1904 ed. $34.00x (ISBN 0-8103-3189-6). Gale.
The Oxford Dictionary of Quotations. 3rd ed. 1979. 35.00 (ISBN 0-19-211560-X). Oxford U Pr.
Tripp, Rhoda T., ed. International Thesaurus of Quotations. LC 73-106587. 1970. $14.37i (ISBN 0-690-44584-9); $15.34i (ISBN 0-690-44585-7). T Y Crowell.

R

RADIO
see also Electro-Acoustics; Modulation (Electronics); Police Communication Systems
also subdivision Radio Equipment under subjects, e.g. Automobiles–Radio Equipment; and headings beginning with the word Radio, e.g. Radio Frequency Modulation; Radio In Navigation
Cormier, France-Pauline. Vocabulaire de la Radio & de la Television. 17p. (Fr.). 1973. Can.$0.50. Quebec Off.
RADIO–BROADCASTING
see Radio Broadcasting
RADIO–DICTIONARIES
Abd-El-Wahed. Radio & Television Dictionary. 320p. (Eng., Fr., Ger., Arabic.). 1980. $45.00 (ISBN 0-686-92395-2, M-9762). French & Eur.
Anglo-Russkii Slovar Po Radioelektronike i Sviazi. 548p. (Eng. & Rus.). 1959. $5.75 (Pub. by Soviete Ministrov). Four Continent.
Cebrian, Llerrero J. Diccionario de Radio & Television (II) 384p. (Span.). 1981. pap. 620.00 ptas (ISBN 84-205-0789-X). Alhambra.
Cebrian Herreros, Mariano. Diccionario Internacional de Radio & Television. 304p. (Span.). 1981. 500.00 ptas (ISBN 84-500-4295-X). Organ Ofic Adm.
Conrad, W. BI-Taschenlexikon Elektronik-Funktechnik. (Illus.). 400p. (Ger.). 1982. M.15.00. Biblio Inst.
Delson, Donn & Hurst, Walter E. Delson's Dictionary of Radio & Records Industry Terms. Posner, Neil, ed. LC 80-24486. (Entertainment Communication Ser.: Vol. 2). 112p. (Orig.). 1981. pap. $7.95 (ISBN 0-9603574-2-4). Bradson.
Diccionario de Electronica Radio & TV. (Illus.). 199p. (Span.). 1966. $2.50. Minerva Bks.
Diccionario de electronica, radio y TV. (Span.). 135.00 ptas. Afha Intl.
Diccionario De Radio. 104p. (Span.). 1979. $8.75 (ISBN 84-201-0368-3, S-50147). French & Eur.
Dictionary of Radio & Television Terms. BBC & ZDF. (Ger. & Eng.). 1973. $29.95 (ISBN 0-471-25586-6, Pub. by Wiley Heyden). Wiley.
Gaudilat, Louis. Lexique Officiel des lampes Radios. 21st ed. 96p. (Fr.). 1963. pap. $12.50 (ISBN 0-686-56766-8, M-6263). French & Eur.
Gaudillat, Louis. Lexique Officiel des Lampes Radio. 21st ed. 96p. (Fr.). 1963. 20.00 F. Radio.
German-Prozorova, L. P., et al, eds. Anglo-Russkii Radiotekhnicheskii Slovar. 524p. (Rus. & Eng.). 1960. $6.30 (Pub. by Gosizdat. Inostr. Slovarei). Four Continent.
Gorokhov, P. K. Russko-Nemetskii Radiotekhnicheskii Slovar. 390p. (Rus. & Ger.). 1961. $3.60 (Pub. by Glav. Red. Inostr. Nauchno-Tekhn. Slovarei Fizmata). Glav. Red. Inostr. Nauchno-Tekhn. Slovarei Fizmata.
Iakovlev, B. E. Cheshsko-Russkii Radiotekhnicheskii Slovar. 364p. (Rus. & Czech.). 1960. $2.95 (Pub. by Glav. Red. Inostr. Nauchn. Tekhn. Slovarei Fizmata). Four Continent.
Japanese-English-Chinese Radio Technology Dictionary. 1628p. (Japanese, Eng. & Chinese.). 1974. $14.95 (ISBN 0-686-92197-6, M-9590). French & Eur.
Multilingual Vocabulary of Educational Radio & Television Terms. 189p. (Orig., Eng. , Fr. , Ger. , Ital. , Dutch, Span. & Swedish.). 1971. pap. $11.25x (ISBN 3-19-006291-9). Intl Pubns Serv.
Saiz, M. Diccionario de Electronica, Radio & TV: Ingles-Espanol. 144p. (Eng. & Span.). pap. $4.50. Lectorum Pubns.
Stancin, Nicolae. Dictionar Tehnic de Radio si Televiziune. LC 76-506602. 480p. (Eng. & Romanian.). 1976. 28.00 lei. Editura Stiintifica.
Vocabulaire de la Radio & de la Television. 30p. (Fr.). 1977. pap. text ed. $4.95 (ISBN 0-7754-2273-8, M-9022). French & Eur.
RADIO–TRANSMITTERS AND TRANSMISSION
Glossaire d'organes de Transmission, 1: Les Engrenages Allemand-Espagnol-Francais-Anglais-Italien-Neerlandais-Suedois-Finnois. 116p. (Ger. , Span. , Fr. , Eng. , Ital. , Dutch, Swedish & Finnish.). 100.00 F. Maison Dictionnaire.
RADIO, CITIZENS BAND
see Citizens Band Radio
RADIO AS A PROFESSION
see also Television As a Profession
Rosenthal. Dictionnaire d'accentuation pour les Travailleurs de la Radio & de la Television. (Fr.). write for info. MIR.
RADIO BROADCASTING
see also Radio–Transmitters and Transmission; Television Broadcasting
Diamant, Lincoln, ed. The Broadcast Communications Dictionary. 2nd, rev., enl. ed. 1978. 10.95 (ISBN 0-8038-0788-0). Hastings.
RADIO JOURNALISTS
see Journalists
RADIO MODULATION
see Modulation (Electronics)
RADIO TRANSMISSION
see Radio–Transmitters and Transmission
RADIOACTIVITY
see also Nuclear Physics; Radiochemistry; Radiography
Leonhardt, J. BI-Taschenlexikon Radioaktivitaet. (Illus.). 350p. (Ger.). M.15.00. Bibl Inst Leipzig.
RADIOCHEMISTRY
Here are entered works on the chemical properties of radioactive substances and their use in chemical studies. Works on the chemical effects of high energy radiation on matter are entered under Radiation Chemistry. Works on the application of chemical techniques to the study of the structure and properties of atomic nuclei, their transformations and reactions are entered under Nuclear Chemistry.
Haissinsky, M. Radiochemisches Lexikon der Elemente und Ihrer Isotope. (Ger.). 1968. pap. $15.95 (ISBN 3-427-41651-8, M-7596, Pub. by Duemmler). French & Eur.
RADIOGRAPHY
C.I.L.F. Vocabulaire de la radiographie. 92p. (Fr., Eng. & Ger.). 1979. 85.00 F. Maison Dictionnaire.
RADIOISOTOPES IN MEDICINE
see Nuclear Medicine
RADIOLOGICAL PHYSICS
see Radiology
RADIOLOGY
see also Radiography
Angerstein, Wilfried. Lexikon der Radiologischen Technik in der Mediazin. LC 80-471099. 576p. (Ger.). 1979. write for info. (ISBN 3-13-484603-9). Thieme Verlag.
Etter, Lewis E. Glossary of Words & Phrases Used in Radiology, Nuclear Medicine & Ultrasound. 2nd ed. 384p. 1970. ed. spiral $32.50xphotocopy (ISBN 0-398-00526-5). C C Thomas.
Jacob, Alphons & Jackson, Herbert L. Dictionary of Radiologic Terminology. 107p. 1982. 27.50 (ISBN 0-87527-216-9). Green.
Myers, Patricia A. A Glossary for Radiologic Technologists. LC 80-20917. 206p. 1981. 28.50 (ISBN 0-03-057584-2). Praeger.
Neuder, Gustav F. & Ullrich, Heinz M. Dictionary of Radiological Engineering. 1979. pap. text ed. $36.50 (ISBN 3-11-007807-4). De Gruyter.
RADIOLOGY, MEDICAL
see also Nuclear Medicine
Angerstein, Winifred. Lexikon der Radiologischen Technik in der Medizin. LC 75-595971. 480p. (Eng. & Ger.). 1975. DM.44.00 (ISBN 3-13-484602-0). Thieme Verlag.
RAIL TRANSPORTATION
see Railroads
RAILROAD CONSTRUCTION
see Railroad Engineering
RAILROAD ENGINEERING
Schlomann, A. Illustrierte Technische Woerterbucher: Eisenbahnmaschinenwesen, Vol. 6. (Ger., Eng., Fr., Rus., Span. & Ital., Dictionary of Railway Engineering). 1909. pap. $9.95 (ISBN 0-686-56486-3, M-7473, Pub. by R. Oldenbourg). French & Eur.
--Illustrierte Technische Woerterbucher: Eisenbahnmaschinenwesen, Vol. 6. (Ger., Eng., Fr., Rus., Span. & Ital.). 1909. pap. $9.95. Oldenbourg Verlag.
--Illustrierte Technische Woerterbucher: Eisenbahnbau und Betrieb, Vol. 5. (Ger., Eng., Fr., Rus., Span. & Ital., Dictionary of Railway engineering). 1909. pap. $9.95 (ISBN 0-686-56485-5, M-7472, Pub. by R. Oldenbourg). French & Eur.
--Illustrierte Technische Woerterbucher: Eisenbahnbau und Betrieb, Vol. 5. (Ger., Eng., Fr., Rus., Span. & Ital.). 1909. pap. $9.95. Oldenbourg Verlag.
RAILROADS
see also Locomotives
also names of individual railroads
Adams, Ramon F. The Language of the Railroader. 1977. $12.95 (ISBN 0-8061-1435-5). U of Okla Pr.

Albrecht, Gunter E. & Reichardt, Hans D. Modellbahnlexikon. LC 75-519566. 232p. (Eng. & Ger.). 1975. DM.26.00 (ISBN 3-87094-406-4). Alba Buchverlag.

Born, Erhard. Lexikon Fuer Eisenbahnfreunde. (Ger.). 1977. pap. $39.95 (ISBN 3-7658-0238-7, M-7200). French & Eur.

RAILROADS–AUTOMATION

Gluzman, I. S. Anglo-Russkii Slovar Zheleznodorozhnoi Automatike, Telemekhanike & Sviazi. 427p. (Rus. & Eng.). 1958. $5.25 (Pub. by Gosizdat Fizmat. Lit.). Four Continent.

RAILROADS–CARS

Forney, Matthias, ed. The Car Builder's Dictionary. (Illus.). 544p. 1971. Repr. of 1879 ed. lib. bdg. 14.95 buckram (ISBN 0-912318-16-3). N K Gregg.

Forney, Matthias N. The Railroad Car Builders Pictorial Dictionary. (Illus.). 12.00 (ISBN 0-8446-5187-7). Peter Smith.

Wait, John C., ed. Freight & Passenger Cars from the 1898 Car Builder's Dictionary: Part 1, No. 55. (Train Shed Ser.). (Illus.). 1977. pap. 4.50 (ISBN 0-912318-90-2). N K Gregg.

--Freight & Passenger Cars from the 1898 Car Builder's Dictionary: Part 2, No. 57. (Train Shed Ser.). (Illus.). 1977. pap. 4.50 (ISBN 0-912318-92-9). N K Gregg.

--Freight & Passenger Cars from the 1898 Car Builder's Dictionary: Part 3, No. 59. (Train Shed Ser.). (Illus.). 1977. pap. 4.50 (ISBN 0-912318-94-5). N K Gregg.

Wright, Roy V., ed. Freight Cars from the 1919 Car Builder's Dictionary, Pt. 1. (Train Shed Cyclopedia Ser: No. 35). (Illus.). 80p. 1975. pap. 5.50 (ISBN 0-912318-66-X). N K Gregg.

--Freight Cars from the 1919 Car Builder's Dictionary, Pt. 2. (Train Shed Cyclodedia Ser: No. 36). (Illus.). 80p. 1975. pap. 5.50 (ISBN 0-912318-67-8). N K Gregg.

--Passenger Cars from the 1999 Car Builder's Dictionary. (Train Shed Cyclopedia Ser: No. 42). (Illus.). 1976. pap. 3.00 (ISBN 0-912318-73-2). N K Gregg.

RAILROADS–DICTIONARIES

Bunin, D. A. Nemetsko-Russkii Zheleznodorozhnyi Slovar. 531p. (Rus. & Ger.). 1957. $4.95 (Pub. by Gosizdat Tekhn.-Teoret. Lit.). Four Continent.

Bussy, J. H. Diccionario tecnico de terminos ferroviarios: Espanol-frances-aleman-ingles-italiano-holandes. 2nd ed. 1358p. (Span., Fr., Ger., Eng., Ital. & Dutch.). write for info. G Gili.

The Dictionary of Railway Terms. 1033p. (Polyglot.). 1978. $47.50x (ISBN 0-8002-2264-4). Intl Pubns Serv.

English-Chinese Dictionary of Railway Terms. 1025p. (Eng. & Chinese.). 1977. $17.95 (ISBN 0-686-92493-2, M-9559). French & Eur.

Forney, Matthias, ed. The Car Builder's Dictionary. (Illus.). 544p. 1971. Repr. of 1879 ed. lib. bdg. 14.95 buckram (ISBN 0-912318-16-3). N K Gregg.

Forney, Matthias N. The Railroad Car Builders Pictorial Dictionary. (Illus.). 12.00 (ISBN 0-8446-5187-7). Peter Smith.

Kruger, Sabine. Zum Fachwortschatz. LC 80-467779. vii, 523p. (Ger.). 1979. DM.90.00 (ISBN 3-18-150037-2). VDI Verlag.

Railsearch Publishing, Inc., ed. The New Dictionary of Railroad Working Terminology. (Railsearch Railroad Management Ser.). (Illus.). 400p. 1980. 28.00 (ISBN 0-686-27634-5); lib. bdg. 29.25 (ISBN 0-686-27635-3). Railsearch.

Von Born, Erhard, et al. Lexikon fuer Eisenbahnfreunde. 256p. (Ger.). 1977. DM.29.80 (ISBN 3-7658-0238-7). Bucher Verlag.

Wait, John C., ed. Freight & Passenger Cars from the 1898 Car Builder's Dictionary: Part 1, No. 55. (Train Shed Ser.). (Illus.). 1977. pap. 4.50 (ISBN 0-912318-90-2). N K Gregg.

--Freight & Passenger Cars from the 1898 Car Builder's Dictionary: Part 2, No. 57. (Train Shed Ser.). (Illus.). 1977. pap. 4.50 (ISBN 0-912318-92-9). N K Gregg.

Wright, Roy V., ed. Freight Cars from the 1919 Car Builder's Dictionary, Pt. 2. (Train Shed Cyclodedia Ser: No. 36). (Illus.). 80p. 1975. pap. 5.50 (ISBN 0-912318-67-8). N K Gregg.

--Passenger Cars from the 1999 Car Builder's Dictionary. (Train Shed Cyclopedia Ser: No. 42). (Illus.). 1976. pap. 3.00 (ISBN 0-912318-73-2). N K Gregg.

RAILROADS–ENGINEERING

see Railroad Engineering

RAILROADS–FREIGHT CARS

see Railroads–Cars

RAILROADS–SIGNALING

see also Signals and Signaling

Arnold, Hans J. Stellwerksdienst. LC 76-472929. 119p. (Ger., Berlin, East Germany). 1976. M.4.80. Transpress Verlag fur Verkehrswesen.

RAILWAYS

see Railroads

RANGE MANAGEMENT

see also Livestock

Society for Range Management Glossary Committee. A Glossary of Terms Used in Range Management. 36p. $1.50. Soc Range Mgmt.

RAPANUI LANGUAGE

Englert, Sebastian. Diccionario Rapanui-Espanol, Redactado en la Isla de Pascua. LC 75-35191. (Span. & Rapanui.). Repr. of 1938 ed. $15.00 (ISBN 0-404-14219-2). AMS Pr.

RAPID TRANSIT

see Local Transit

RARE BOOKS

see Bibliography–Rare Books

RATIONALIZATION OF INDUSTRY

see Industrial Management

READERS

see also English Language–Dictionaries, Juvenile

Sullivan Assoc. Reading Vocabulary, 5 bks. pap. text ed. 2.75 ea. (ISBN 0-8449-4105-0); tchr's guide for bks. 1-4 avail. Learning Line.

READING

see also Readers

Levine, Harold. Vocabulary & Composition Through Pleasurable Reading, Bk. 3. (Orig.). (gr. 10-12). 1976. wkbk. $8.17 (ISBN 0-87720-306-7); pap. text ed. $7.17 (ISBN 0-87720-377-6). AMSCO Sch.

--Vocabulary & Composition Through Pleasurable Reading, Bk. 6. (gr. 11-12). 1979. pap. text ed. $8.17 (ISBN 0-87720-388-1); wkbk. $7.17 (ISBN 0-87720-387-3). AMSCO Sch.

--Vocabulary Through Pleasurable Reading, Bk. 2. (gr. 7-12). 1974. wkbk $8.17 (ISBN 0-87720-369-5); pap. text ed. $7.17 (ISBN 0-87720-374-1). AMSCO Sch.

Schubert, Delwyn G. A Dictionary of Terms & Concepts in Reading. 2nd ed. 392p. 1969. photocopy ed. spiral $36.75x (ISBN 0-398-01688-7). C C Thomas.

READING–STUDY AND TEACHING

see Reading; Reading (Elementary)

READING (ELEMENTARY)

see also English Language–Phonetics; Initial Teaching Alphabet

Richey, Jim. Drugstore Language. (Survival Vocabulary Ser.). (Illus.). 48p. (gr. 7-12). 1978. pap. 2.95 (ISBN 0-915510-28-6). Janus Bks.

--Supermarket Language. (Survival Vocabulary Ser.). (Illus.). 48p. (gr. 7-12). 1978. pap. 2.95 (ISBN 0-915510-27-8). Janus Bks.

Thorndike, Edward L. A Teacher's Word Book of the Twenty Thousand Words Found Most Frequently & Widely in General Reading for Children & Young People. rev. ed. LC 73-5527. 182p. 1975. Repr. of 1932 ed. $40.00x (ISBN 0-8103-4108-5). Gale.

READING COMPREHENSION

Pearson, P. D. & Johnson, D. D. Teaching Reading Vocabulary & Teaching Reading Comprehension. 1978. Set. boxed 15.95 (ISBN 0-03-042916-1, HoltC). HR&W.

READING DISABILITY

Bush, Clifford L. & Andrews, Robert C. Dictionary of Reading & Learning Disabilities. LC 79-57293. 179p. 1978. pap. $13.40x (ISBN 0-87424-153-7). Western Psych.

READING RETARDATION

see Reading Disability

REAL ESTATE

see Real Property

REAL ESTATE BUSINESS

see also Real Estate Investment

Abraham, Samuel V. Real Estate Dictionary & Reference Guide. McFadden, S. Michele & Wilson-Fulkerson, Roberta, eds. LC 79-9761. 1983. pap. text ed. $6.95x (ISBN 0-89262-059-5). Career Pub.

Boyce, Byrl N., ed. Real Estate Appraisal Terminology. 2nd ed. 384p. 1981. $18.00 (ISBN 0-88410-597-0). Ballinger Pub.

Brownstone, David M. & Franck, Irene M. The VNR Real Estate Dictionary. 352p. 1981. $18.95 (ISBN 0-442-25856-9). Van Nos Reinhold.

Johnsich, John R., intro. By. Real Estate Securities & Title Insurance Terminology. (Orig.). 1980. pap. $3.95 (ISBN 0-914256-12-2). Real Estate Pub.

Marcus, Irving. The Portable Dictionary of Real Estate Terminology. 120p. 1983. pap. $6.95 (ISBN 0-8283-1739-9). Branden.

Plans Sanz De Bremond, Jose M. Diccionario Practico: Asesor De la Propiedad & Copropiedad Inmobiliaria. 392p. (Span.). 1975. pap. $17.95 (ISBN 84-290-1229-X, S-50138). French & Eur.

Real Estate Dictionary, No. 510. rev. ed. 192p. 1980. pap. $5.00 (ISBN 0-695-81526-1). Finan Pub.

Talamo. The Real Estate Dictionary. rev. ed. 192p. 1981. pap. $3.95 (ISBN 0-89803-091-9). Caroline Hse.

Talamo, John. The Real Estate Dictionary. 1982. pap. $3.95 (ISBN 0-8092-5696-7). Contemp Bks.

REAL ESTATE BUSINESS–LAW AND LEGISLATION

Freshman, Samuel K. Real Estate Finance & Syndication Glossary. 3rd., rev. ed. LC 79-2801. 109p. 1979. 5.95 (ISBN 0-9600708-3-4). Law & Cap Dynamics.

REAL ESTATE INVESTMENT

see also Real Estate Business

Johnsich, John R., intro. by. Title Insurance & Real Estate Securities Terminology. (Orig.). 1980. pap. $3.95 (ISBN 0-914256-11-4). Real Estate Pub.

REAL PROPERTY

Here are entered treatises on real property in the legal sense, i.e. the law of immovable property, and works on real estate in general, or real estate conditions in any particular place. Works on the buying, selling, and management of real estate are entered under the heading Real Estate Business. For land laws use Land Tenure–(country subdivision) e.g. Land Tenure–Sweden.

see also Assessment; Mortgages; Real Estate Business–Law and Legislation

Allen, Robert D. & Wolfe, Thomas E. The Allen & Wolfe Illustrated Dictionary of Real Estate. LC 82-13445. (Real Estate for Professional Practitioners). 266p. 1983. $24.95 (ISBN 0-471-09415-3, Pub. by Wiley-Interscience). Wiley.

O'Donnell. Dictionary Real Estate Terms. 1975. $3.00 (ISBN 0-7216-6915-8). Dryden Pr.

REAL PROPERTY–VALUATION

Here are entered works on the general theory and methodology of real property valuation. Works on the valuation of real property for tax purposes are entered under the heading Real Property Tax.

American Institute of Real Estate Appraisers. Real Estate Appraisal Terminology. Boyce, Byrl N., ed. 320p. $12.50 (21-1018). Natl Assoc Realtors.

REALTY

see Real Property

REASON AND FAITH

see Faith and Reason

REBELLIONS

see Insurgency; Revolutions

REBELS (SOCIAL PSYCHOLOGY)

see Dissenters

REBUSES

Clark, Charlotte & Davies, Cornelia Oakes. Standard Rebus Glossary. 95p. 1974. pap. text ed. $6.50 (ISBN 0-913476-41-2). Am Guidance.

RECREATIONS

see Games; Hobbies; Sports

REDEVELOPMENT, URBAN

see City Planning

REFERENCE BOOKS

see also Encyclopedias and Dictionaries

Roget, Peter M. Roget's University Thesaurus. Mawson, C. Sylvester, ed. LC 81-47081. 768p. 1981. pap. $6.68i (ISBN 0-06-463537-6, EH 537, EH). B&N NY.

Smolenskaia Oblast: Slovar Spravochnik Kraeveda. 240p. (Rus.). 1978. $3.50 (Pub. by Rabochii). Four Continent.

Tayyeb, R. & Chandna, K., eds. Dictionary of Acronyms & Abbreviations in Library & Information Science. 146p. pap. $7.00 (ISBN 0-88802-129-1). CLA.

REFERENCE BOOKS, ENGLISH

see Reference Books

REFORM, SOCIAL

see Social Problems

REFRAIN

Sintes. Diccionario de Aforismos, Proverbios & Refranes. (Span.). $19.50 (SOP). Lectorum Pubns.

REFRIGERATION AND REFRIGERATING MACHINERY

see also Air Conditioning

Abd-El-Wahed. Refrigeration & Conditioning Dictionary. 395p. (Eng., Fr., Ger. & Arabic.). 1979. $45.00 (ISBN 0-686-97399-2, M-9756). French & Eur.

American Society of Heating, Refrigerating & Air-Conditioning Engineers. Automatic Control Terminology for Heating, Ventilating, Air Conditioning & Refrigeration Equipment. (Illus.). $14.00 (ST8578); members $7.00. Am Heat Ref & Air Eng.

American Society of Heating, Refrigeration & Air Conditioning Engineers. Refrigeration Terms & Definitions. (Illus.). 1974. $12.00 (ST1275); members $6.00. Am Heat Ref & Air Eng.

Applied Technical Dictionary: Air Conditioning & Refrigeration. (Eng. , Ger. , Fr. , Rus. & Slovak.). $69.00x (ISBN 0-569-08534-9, Pub. by Collets). State Mutual Bk.

Booth, K. M. Dictionary of Refrigeration & Air Conditioning. 1970. $29.90x (ISBN 0-444-20069-X, Pub. by Applied Science). Burgess-Intl Ideas.

Booth, K. M., ed. Dictionary of Refrigeration & Air Conditioning. 1971. $30.75 (ISBN 0-444-20069-X). Elsevier.

Doring, G. & Rudolphi. Tiefkuhl Lexikon. 239p. (Ger.). $10.95 (ISBN 3-87150-020-8, M-7666, Pub. by Deutscher Fachverlag). French & Eur.

Dupuis, H., et al. Lexique de la Fabrication du Refrigerateur: Francais-Anglais. 66p. (Fr. & Eng.). 1975. pap. $5.95 (ISBN 0-686-92434-7, M-9240). French & Eur.

International Institute of Refrigeration. New International Dictionary of Refrigeration. LC 76-373634. xxxvii, 560p. (Eng., Danish, Fr., Ger., Ital., Rus. & Span.). 1976. 3000.00 F (IIR). Unipub.

New International Dictionary of Refrigeration. 1977. $82.50 (ISBN 0-685-99158-X, IIR5, IIR). Unipub.

Nouveau Dictionnaire International du Froid. 300p. (Fr. , Eng. , Ger. , Rus. , Span. & It., New International Dictionary of Refrigeration). 1970. $135.00 (ISBN 0-686-56738-2, M-6432). French & Eur.

Rosenberg, M. B. English-Russian Dictionary of Refrigerating & Cryogenic Engineering. 467p. (Eng. & Rus.). 1978. Leatherette $15.95 (ISBN 0-686-92382-0, M-9063). French & Eur.

Rosenberg, M. B. English-Russian Dictionary of Refrigeration & Low Temperature Technology. 2nd, rev. ed. $73.00 (ISBN 0-08-024737-7). Pergamon.

Technical Dictionary: Refrigeration & Air Conditioning. (Eng. , Fr. , Ger. & Arabic.). 1979. $35.00x (ISBN 0-686-44746-8, Pub. by Collets). State Mutual Bk.

REFUSE AND REFUSE DISPOSAL
see also Pollution; Sewage Disposal; Water–Pollution

Avfallsordlista. LC 78-361963. xxvii, 210p. (Eng. , Fr. & Swedish.). 1977. Kr.40.00 (ISBN 9-1719-6062-7). Tek Nomen.

REGISTRATION OF TRADE-MARKS
see Trade-Marks

REGULATORS
see Governors (Machinery)

REHABILITATION, VOCATIONAL
see Vocational Rehabilitation

REKHTA LANGUAGE
see Urdu Language

RELATIVITY
Ruth, W. Lexikon der Schulphysik: Optik und Relativitaet, Vol. 4. (Ger.). $42.00 (ISBN 3-7614-0109-4, M-7226). French & Eur.

RELATIVITY (PHYSICS)
Hoefling, Oskar, ed. Lexikon der Schulphysik: Bd 4, Optik & Relativitaet. (Ger.). 1978. DM.52.00 (ISBN 3-7614-0109-4). Aulis Verlag.

RELAYS, ELECTRIC
see Electric Relays

RELIEF (AID)
see Charities; Public Welfare

RELIGION–DICTIONARIES
Aubert, Roger & Van Cauwenberg. Dictionnaire d'Histoire et du Geographie Ecclesiastiques, 16 vols. (Fr.). Set. pap. $1795.00 (ISBN 0-686-56903-2, M-6014). French & Eur.

Bertholet, Alfred. Woerterbuch der Religionen. LC 76-483576. x, 659p. (Ger.). 1976. DM.25.00 (ISBN 3-520-12503-X). Kroener.

Blazquez, Jose M. Diccionario de las religiones perromanas de Hispania. LC 76-450345. (Illus.). 191p. (Span.). 1975. 300.00 ptas (ISBN 8-47090-071-4). Istmo.

Brandon, S. G. F. Diccionario de Religiones Comparadas, 2 vols. 1553p. (Span.). 1975. Set. $49.95 (ISBN 8-4705-7188-5). French & Eur.

Bumpus, John S. Dictionary of Ecclesiastical Terms: Being a History & Explanation of Certain Terms Used in Architecture, Ecclesiology, Liturgiology, Music, Ritual, Cathedral, Constitution, Etc. LC 68-30653. 1969. Repr. of 1910 ed. $30.00x (ISBN 0-8103-3321-X). Gale.

Cattell, Ann. Dictionary of Esoteric Words. (Orig.). 1967. pap. $1.75 (ISBN 0-8065-0175-8, C205). Citadel Pr.

Crim, Keith, et al, eds. Abingdon Dictionary of Living Religions. LC 81-1465. 864p. 1981. prepub. $39.95 (ISBN 0-687-00409-8). Abingdon.

Dacio, Juan. Diccionario de los Papas. (Span.). $37.50 (ISBN 84-233-0112-5, S-50110). French & Eur.

Diccionario del Hogar Catolico. 1180p. (Span.). 1962. $17.95 (ISBN 84-261-0075-9, S-12259). French & Eur.

Hoermann, Karl. Diccionario De Moral Cristiana. 2nd ed. 704p. (Span.). 1978. pap. $35.95 (ISBN 84-254-0966-7, S-50192). French & Eur.

--Diccionario De Moral Cristiana. 2nd ed. 704p. (Span.). 1978 $41.95 (ISBN 84-254-0967-5, S-50193). French & Eur.

Kauffman, Donald T., ed. Baker's Pocket Dictionary of Religious Terms. (Direction Books). Orig. Title: The Dictionary of Religious Terms. 446p. 1975. pap. $5.95 (ISBN 0-8010-5361-7). Baker Bk.

Konig. Diccionario De las Religiones. 816p. (Span.). 1977. $37.50 (ISBN 84-254-0358-8, S-50201). French & Eur.

Koning, Frederick. Diccionario de Demonologia. 3rd ed. (Span.). 1978. pap. $2.95 (ISBN 0-686-57362-5, S-50155). French & Eur.

Mathews, Shailer & Smith, Gerald B., eds. Dictionary of Religion & Ethics. LC 70-145713. 1971. Repr. of 1921 ed. $45.00x (ISBN 0-8103-3196-9). Gale.

Neggers, Gladys. Vocabulario Culto. 2nd ed. 168p. (Span.). 1977. pap. $8.75 (ISBN 84-359-0034-7, S-50023). French & Eur.

Neill, S. E. Lexikon Zur Weltmission. (Ger.). $48.00 (ISBN 3-7974-0054-3, M-7190). French & Eur.

Obermayer, H. Kleines Stuttgarter-Bibellexikon. 3rd ed. 344p. (Ger.). 1976. $9.95 (ISBN 3-460-30053-1, M-7507, Pub. by Vlg. Katholisches Bibelwerk). French & Eur.

Reese, William L. Dictionary of Philosophy & Religion: Eastern & Western Thought. iv, 644p. 1980. write for info. (ISBN 0-391-00688-6). Humanities.

Rouillard, Dom P. Diccionario De los Santos De Cada Dia. 472p. (Span.). 1966. $15.75 (ISBN 84-281-0062-4, S-50020). French & Eur.

Vilaro, Josep, et al. Diccionario Religioso Para los Hombres De Hoy. 260p. (Span.). 1976. pap. $7.50 (ISBN 84-320-0273-9, S-50025). French & Eur.

Warshaw, Thayer S. Abingdon Glossary of Religious Terms. LC 80-13121. (Festival Ser.). 96p. (Orig.). 1980. pap. $1.50 (ISBN 0-687-00472-1). Abingdon.

RELIGION AND PHILOSOPHY
see Philosophy and Religion

RELIGIONS–DICTIONARIES
Des Mas-Latrie, L. Dictionnaire de Statistique Religieuse. Migne, J. P., ed. (Nouvelle Encyclopedie Theologique Ser.: Vol. 9). 538p. (Fr.). Date not set. Repr. of 1851 ed. lib. bdg. $69.00x (ISBN 0-89241-259-3). Caratzas Pub Co.

Masson, Herve. Dictionnaire Initiatique. (Fr.). 1970. write for info. Belfond.

RELIGIOUS ART
see Cathedrals; Christian Art and Symbolism; Idols and Images
also Art, Buddhist; Art, Gothic; Art, Medieval, and similar headings

RELIGIOUS BELIEF
see Faith

RELIGIOUS BIOGRAPHY
Missionary Research Library. New York Dictionary Catalog of the Missionary Research Library, 17 vols. 1968. Set. $1615.00 (ISBN 0-8161-0778-5, Hall Library). G K Hall.

RELIGIOUS PAINTING
see Christian Art and Symbolism

RELIGIOUS SCULPTURE
see Christian Art and Symbolism

REMOTE SENSING
Multilingual Dictionary of Remote Sensing & Photogrammetry. 1983. $25.00 (ISBN 0-937294-46-2). ASP.

REMOTE TERRAIN SENSING
see Remote Sensing

RENAISSANCE
see also Middle Ages
Gay, Victor. Glossaire Archeologique du Moyen-Age & de la Renaissance, 2 vols. (Illus., Fr.). 1928. 243.00 F. Kraus.

RENAISSANCE–EUROPE
see Renaissance

RENAISSANCE ART
see Art, Renaissance

REPAIRING
Genette, Francis. Dictionnaire du Bricolage & du Depannage. (Illus.). 450p. (Fr.). 1972. write for info. Sequoia.

REPRODUCTION PROCESSES
see Copying Processes

REPRODUCTIVE ORGANS
see Generative Organs

REPUBLIQUE POPULAIRE DU BENIN
see Benin

RESIDENCES
see Architecture, Domestic

RESIDENTIAL CONSTRUCTION
see House Construction

RESISTANCE OF MATERIALS
see Strength of Materials

RESOURCE MANAGEMENT
see Conservation of Natural Resources

RESPIRATION
American Physiological Society. Glossary of Respiratory & Gas Exchange. (Standards & Glossaries). 1973. Repr. $1.00. Am Physiological.

Krasowski, J. Owen. Dictionary & Reference Guide for Respiratory Therapy. 1977. pap. $15.50 (ISBN 0-8151-5169-1). Year Bk Med.

RESTORATION OF MANUSCRIPTS
see Manuscripts–Conservation and Restoration

RESTRAINT OF ANIMALS
see Animals, Treatment Of

RETAIL ADVERTISING
see Advertising

RETALIATION (ECONOMICS)
see Tariff

RETARDED CHILDREN
see Slow Learning Children

RETARDED READERS
see Reading Disability

RETRIBUTION
see Hell

REVENUE LAW
see Taxation–Law

REVIVAL OF LETTERS
see Renaissance

REVOLUTIONS
see also Insurgency
also France–History–Revolution, 1789-1799; United States–History–Revolution, 1775-1783, and similar headings
Buhler, Alain & Didier, J. Dictionnaire de la revolution Etudiante. (Fr.). 1968. 4.50 F. Controverses.

Fejto, Francois. Dictionnaire des Partis Communistes & des Mouvements Revolutionnaires. 236p. (Fr.). 1971. 31.00 F. Casterman.

RHETORIC
see also Criticism; Debates and Debating; Description (Rhetoric); English Language–Rhetoric; Figures of Speech; Oratory
also subdivisions Composition and Exercises, and Rhetoric under names of languages; also figures of speech, e.g. Metaphor
Marchese, Angelo. Dizionario di Retorica & di Stilistica. LC 78-391880. 309p. (Ital.). 1978. L.4000.00. Mondadori.

RHODE ISLAND–GENEALOGY
Gannett, Henry. A Geographic Dictionary of Connecticut & Rhode Island, 2 vols. in 1. LC 78-59123. 98p. 1978. Repr. of 1894 ed. 9.50 (ISBN 0-8063-0820-6). Genealog Pub.

RHODESIA–HISTORY
Rasmussen, R. Kent. Historical Dictionary of Rhodesia-Zimbabwe. LC 78-23671. (African Historical Dictionaries Ser.: No. 18). 1979. lib. bdg. $24.50 (ISBN 0-8108-1187-1). Scarecrow.

RHYME
see Rime
Buydens, John. Groot Systematisch en Klankalfabetisch Rijmwoordenboek. LC 78-362599. 363p. (Dutch.). 1977. fl.520.00 (ISBN 9-02890-291-0). Nederlandse Boek.

RHYMING DICTIONARIES
see English Language–Rime–Dictionaries

RICE
Rice Terminology. (Terminology Bulletin Ser.: No. 26). 82p. 1975. pap. $7.50 (ISBN 0-685-54197-5, F1197, FAO). Unipub.

RICE TRADE
Illustrated Glossary of Rice Processing Machines. (Agricultural Services Bulletin: No. 37). (Illus.). 104p. 1980. pap. $7.50 (ISBN 92-5-000784-1, F1854, FAO). Unipub.

RIDDLES
see also Puzzles; Rebuses

Crosbie, John S. Crosbie's Dictionary of Riddles. (Illus.). 224p. 1980. $12.95 (ISBN 0-517-54038-X, Harmony); pap. $6.95 (ISBN 0-517-54039-8). Crown.

RIDDLES–JUVENILE LITERATURE
Bennett, A. Y. Picture Dictionary, ABCs, Telling Time, Counting Rhymes, Riddles & Finger Plays. (Illus.). (gr. k-3). 1970. 5.95 (ISBN 0-448-02813-1, G&D). Putnam Pub Group.

RIDICULOUS, THE
see Wit and Humor

RIGHT OF PRIVACY
see Privacy, Right Of

RIGHTS, CIVIL
see Civil Rights

RIGHTS, STOCK
see Stockholders' Pre-Emptive Rights

RIMBAUD, JEAN NICOLAS ARTHUR, 1854-1891
Warnant, Leon. Dictionnaire des Rimes Orales & Ecrites. 554p. (Fr.). 1973. 49.00 F. Larousse.

RIME
Desfeuilles, Paul. Dictionnaire de Rimes. 400p. (Fr.). 1955. 14.00 F. Garnier.

Ferrer Pastor, Francesc. Diccionari de la Rima, 2 vols. 2nd ed. 768p. (Span.). 1981. pap. 3500.00 ptas (ISBN 84-300-4433-7). Piquenas Edit.

Horta. Diccionario de Sinonimos & Ideas Afines & de la Rima. (Span.). 1981. 500.00 ptas (ISBN 8-42830-317-7). Paraninfo.

Horta Massanes, Joaquin. Diccionario de sinonimos e ideas afines y de la rima. 364p. (Span.). 1970. 240.00 ptas. Paraninfo.

Horta Massanet, Joaquin. Diccionario de Sinonimos e Ideas Afines & de la Rima. 3rd ed. 364p. (Span.). 1981. 500.00 ptas (ISBN 84-283-0317-7). Paraninfo.

--Diccionario De Sinonimos E Ideas Afines y De la Rima. 3rd ed. 364p. (Span.). 1978. pap. $13.95 (ISBN 84-283-0317-7, S-50243). French & Eur.

Massanes, Joaquin H. Diccionario de Sinonimos e Ideas Afines y de la Rima. 364p. (Span.). 1981. pap. write for info. Paraninfo.

RIVERS
see also Dams; Hydraulic Engineering; Water–Pollution; Water-Power
also names of specific Rivers, or Rivers and Valleys, e.g. Mississippi River, Rhine River and Valley
Slovar Gidronimov Ukrainy. 784p. (Ukrainian.). 1978. $12.95 (Pub. by Naukova Dumka). Four Continent.

RIVERS–POLLUTION
see Water–Pollution

ROAD CONSTRUCTION
Morilla Abad, I. Diccionario de Ingenieria de Caminos. 360p. (Span.). write for info. (ISBN 8-43680-119-9, 260012). Piramide.

ROAD RESEARCH
see Highway Research

ROAD TRAFFIC
see Traffic Engineering

ROADS
see also Highway Research; Streets
Calamante, Mario. Dizionario illustrato e commentato delle norme di circolazione previste dal nuovo codice della strada. (Illus.). 384p. (Ital.). 1960. L.7000.00. Ateneo & Bizzarri.

ROADS–CONSTRUCTION
see Road Construction

ROADS–RESEARCH
see Highway Research

ROBOTS
see Automation

ROCK MUSIC
Hibbert, Tom. Delilah's International Dictionary of Rock Terms. (Illus.). 176p. (Orig.). 1983. pap. $6.95 (ISBN 0-933328-84-2). Delilah Bks.

Shaw, Arnold. A Dictionary of American Pop-Rock. LC 82-50382. 440p. 1983. $19.95 (ISBN 0-02-872350-3); pap. $12.95 (ISBN 0-02-872360-0). Assoc-Mus.

ROCKETRY–DICTIONARIES
Konarski, M. M. Russian-English Dictionary of Modern Terms in Aeronautics & Rocketry. (Rus. & Eng.). 1962. $88.00 (ISBN 0-08-009658-1). Pergamon.

Murashkevich, A. M. Anglo-Russkii Slovar Po Raketnoi Tekhnike. 231p. (Rus. & Eng.). 1958. $2.75 (Pub. by Gosizdat. Literatury). Four Continent.

ROCKS
see also Crystallography; Geology; Mineralogy; Petrology
also varieties of rock, e.g. Granite, Limestone
Harder, Herrmann. Lexikon Fuer Mineralien - und Gesteins Freunde. (Ger.). 1977. $25.00 (ISBN 3-7658-0253-0, M-7198). French & Eur.
Schmidt-Joos, S. & Graves, B. Rock Lexikon. 7th ed. 448p. (Ger.). 1973. $7.95 (ISBN 3-499-16177-X, M-7603, Pub. by Rowohlt). French & Eur.
--Rock Lexikon. 7th ed. 448p. (Ger.). 1973. $7.95 (ISBN 3-499-16177-X). Rowohlt.

ROCKS–AGE
see Geology, Stratigraphic
ROCKS, SEDIMENTARY
Pettijohn, F. J. & Potter, P. E. Atlas & Glossary of Primary Sedimentary Structures. (Illus., Eng., Span., Fr. & Ger.). 1964. $34.00 (ISBN 0-387-03194-4). Springer-Verlag.

ROLLER-SKATING
Dictionary of Artistic Roller Skating Terms. $1.00. Roller Rink Ops.

ROLLING-MILLS
Herscu, G. F., ed. Elsevier's Dictionary of Rolling Mill Terminology. (Eng., Fr., Span. & Ger.). 1965. $39.75 (ISBN 0-444-40280-2). Elsevier.

ROLLING-STOCK
see Locomotives
ROMAIC LANGUAGE
see Greek Language, Modern
ROMAN ALPHABET
see Alphabet
ROMAN ANTIQUITIES
see Rome–Antiquities
ROMAN EMPERORS
Menge, R. & Preuss, S. Lexicon Caesarianum. (Ger.). 1972. $99.50 (ISBN 3-8067-0094-X, M-7284). French & Eur.
ROMAN LAW
see also Civil Law
also legal headings with subdivision Roman Law in parentheses, e.g. Sales (Roman Law)
De Leon, G. F. Diccionario de derecho romano. (Span.). Arg.$60.00. Plus Ultra.
ROMAN MYTHOLOGY
see Mythology, Roman
ROMANCE LANGUAGES
see also languages belonging to the Romance group, e.g. French Language, Italian Language
Nuessel, Frank H., Jr., ed. Linguistic Approaches to the Romance Lexicon. LC 78-12654. 123p. 1978. pap. text ed. 5.50 (ISBN 0-87840-046-X). Georgetown U Pr.
Tilander, Gunnar. Lexique du Roman de Renart. 163p. (Fr.). 1971. 35.00 F. Champion.
ROMANCES
see also names of specific romances, e.g. Perceval
De Nebrija, Antonio. Vocabulario de Romance: El Latin. 202p. (Span.). 1982. pap. write for info. (ISBN 84-7039-143-7). Castalia Edit.
De Nebruja, Elio de. Vocabulario de romance en latin. 2nd ed. Macdonald, Gerald J., tr. 214p. (Span.). 1981. pap. 1000.00 ptas (ISBN 84-7039-143-7). Castalia Edit.
ROMANIAN LANGUAGE–DICTIONARIES
Andronescu, Serban. Rumanian-English Dictionary. $19.50 (ISBN 0-685-20189-9, 063-01). Saphrograph.
Bagonova-Sidlova, Milota. Dictionar Portrativ Roman-Slovac, Slovac-Roman. 2nd ed. LC 77-456239. 1016p. (Romanian & Slovak.). 1976. 32.50 Kcs. SNTC.
Baubec, A., et al. Dictionar Turc-Roman. LC 80-480771. 377p. (Turkish, & Romanian.). 1979. write for info. lei. Editura Stiintifica.
Buca, M., ed. Dictionar Analogic si de Sinonime al Limbii Romane. LC 79-339807. 479p. (Romanian.). 1978. 27.00 lei. Editura Stiintifica.

Condrea-Derer, Doina. Dictionar Roman-Italian: Pentru uzul Elevilor. LC 79-353106. 364p. (Romanian & Ital.). 1978. 17.50 lei. Editura Stiintifica.
Condruc, Mihai. Dictionar de Electrotehnica. LC 80-490952. 868p. (Fr. & Romanian.). 1979. 49.00 lei. Editura Stiintifica.
Conea, Ana. Dictionar de Stinta Solului. LC 78-362360. 671p. (Romanian.). 1977. 34.00 lei. Editura Stiintifica.
Constantinescu, Silviu. Mic Dictionar de Cuvinte Perechi. LC 77-460405. 169p. (Romanian.). 1976. 7.50 lei. Albatros.
Constantinescu-Dobridor, G. Mic Dictionar de Terminologie Lingvistica. LC 80-471399. 463p. (Romanian.). 1980. 6.50 lei. Albatros.
Cotolulis, Socratis. Dictionar Roman-Grec. LC 76-515769. 534p. (Romanian & Gr.). 1975. 22.50 lei. Editura Stiintifica.
Dictionar Frazeologic German-Roman. LC 75-540143. 538p. (Ger. & Romanian.). 1975. 18.00 lei. Editura Stiintifica.
Eminescu, Mihail. Dictionar de Rime. Bucur, Marin & Tausan, Victoria A., eds. LC 76-485403. 709p. (Romanian.). 1976. 19.00 lei. Albatros.
Ercolani, Libero. Vocabolario romagnolo-italiano, italiano-romagnolo. 920p. (Ital. & Rumanian.). 1971. L.20000.00. Edn Girasole.
Felix, Jiri. Cesko-Rumunsky & Rumunsko-Cesky Slovnik na Cesty. LC 80-451473. 328p. (Czech. & Romanian.). 1979. 18.00 Kcs. SNTC.
Feoktistov, A. P. Russko-Mordovskii Slovar. 370p. (Rus.). 1971. $4.25 (Pub. by Nauka). Four Continent.
Ghitescu, Micaela. Dictionar Roman-Spaniol: Pentru uzul Elevilor. LC 76-481301. 414p. (Romanian & Span.). 1976. 18.00 lei. Editura Stiintifica.
--Dictionar Spaniol-Roman: Pentru uzul Elevilor. LC 76-468723. 391p. (Romanian & Span.). 1976. 17.00 lei. Editura Stiintifica.
Gould, S. H. & Obreanu, P. E., eds. Romanian-English Dictionary & Grammar for the Mathematical Sciences. 60p. (Eng. & Romanian.). 1979. Repr. of 1969 ed. $11.00 (ISBN 0-8218-0038-8, ROMA). Am Math.
Graur, Alexandru. Dictionar de Cuvinte Calatoare. LC 79-376455. 232p. (Romanian.). 1978. 8.75 lei. Albatros.
Grecu, Mitica, et al. Dictionar Roman-Turc. LC 77-574063. 353p. (Romanian & Turkish.). 1977. 16.00 lei. Editura Stiintifica.
Guha, Elisabeta S. Norsk-Rumensk Lommeordbok med Liten Parloer. LC 77-570195. 48p. (Norwegian & Roman.). 1976. Kr.15.00 (ISBN 8-200-05001-7). Universitetsforlaget.
Hincu, Dumitru. Dictionar Scolar, 4 vols. LC 77-454213. 638p. (Romanian.). 1976. 20.40 lei. Editura Didactica.
Karmannyi Rumynsko-Russkii Slovar. 360p. (Romanian & Rus.). 1960. $1.25. Four Continent.
Langenscheidts Universal-Woerterbuch Rumaenisch. 560p. (Romanian & Ger.). DM.6.80 (18280). Langenscheidt.
Langenscheidts Universal-Woerterbuecher Rumaenisch-Deutsch. (Romanian & Ger.). 1978. DM.5.80 (ISBN 3-468-18280-5). Langenscheidt.
Levitchi, V. & Bantas, T. English-Romanian Dictionary. 1068p. (Eng. & Rumanian.). 1980. $55.00x (ISBN 0-569-07472-X, Pub. by Collet's). State Mutual Bk.
Livescu, Jean & Savin, Emilia. Dictionar Roman-German: Pentru uzul Elevilor. LC 77-464118. 493p. (Ger. & Romanian.). 1976. 19.00 lei. Editura Stiintifica.
Marcu, Marinca. Dictionar Elementar de Stiinte. LC 79-367925. 334p. (Romanian.). 1978. 16.00 lei. Editura Stiintifica.

Meyer-Luebke, Wilhelm. Romanisches Etymologisches Woerterbuch. 5th ed. (Ital. & Ger.). 1972. $125.00 (ISBN 3-533-01394-4, M-7604, Pub. by Carl Winter). French & Eur.
--Romanishes Etymologisches Woerterbuch. 5th ed. (Ital. & Ger.). 1972. $125.00 (ISBN 3-533-01394-4). Winter Univ.
Missir, Emile. Dictionnaire Francais-Romaneique. 1060p. (Fr. & Romanian.). 1955. 110.00 F. Klincksieck.
Noveannu, Eugen P. Dictionar-Rus-Roman: Pentru uzal Elevilor. LC 77-479078. 498p. (Romanian & Rus.). 1976. 20.00 lei. Editura Stiintifica.
Petinis, Lambros. Dictionar Grec-Roman. LC 77-481194. 439p. (Gr. & Romanian.). 1976. 19.00 lei. Editura Stiintifica.
Saras, Marcel. Dictionar Francez-Roman: Pentru uzul Elevilor. 2nd ed. LC 77-457298. 413p. (Romanian & Fr.). 1976. 17.00 lei. Editura Stiintifica.
Sava, Iosif & Vartolomei, Luminita. Dictionar de Muzica. LC 79-388120. 225p. (Romanian.). 1979. 18.50 lei. Editura Stiintifica.
Schonkron, M., ed. Rumanian-English, English-Rumanian Dictionary, with Supplement. (Rumanian & Eng.). $25.00 (ISBN 0-8044-0546-8). Ungar.
Solov'ev, V. Moldavsko-Russkii Frazeologicheskii Slovar. 224p. (Rus. Moldavian.). 1976. $2.00 (Pub. by Lumina). Four Continent.
Stanciulescu-Cuza, Mariana. Dictionar Frazeologic Italian-Roman. LC 75-406132. 363p. (Romanian & Ital.). 1975. 13.50 lei. Editura Stiintifica.
Stoicovici, Elena, et al. Dictionar Roman-Vietnamez. LC 77-483746. iv, 344p. (Romanian & Vietnamese.). 1976. 10.00 lei. Tipografia.
Tolkovyi Slovar Moldavskogo Iazyka: A-M, Vol. 1. 848p. (Rus.). 1977. $10.50 (Pub. by Kartia Moldoveniaske). Four Continent.
Vascenco, Victor. Dictionar de Buzunar Roman-Rus. 2nd ed. LC 75-410353. 443p. (Romanian & Rus.). 1975. write for info. Editura Stiintifica.

ROME–ANTIQUITIES
Blumner, Hugo. Technologie und Terminologie der Gewerbe und Kunste bei Griechen und Romern, 4 vols. Finley, Moses, ed. LC 79-4963. (Ancient Economic History Ser.). (Illus., Ger.). 1980. Repr. of 1875 ed. Set. lib. bdg. $128.00x (ISBN 0-405-12350-7); $32.00x ea. Vol. 1 (ISBN 0-405-12351-5). Vol. 2 (ISBN 0-405-12352-3). Vol. 3 (ISBN 0-405-12484-8). Vol. 4 (ISBN 0-405-12485-6). Ayer Co.
Cagnat, Rene & Goyau, G. Lexique des Antiquites Romaines. (Fr.). 1896. 56.00 F. Boccard.
Pelletier, Andre. Lexique d'antiquites Romaines. (Fr.). 1972. 20.60 F. Colin.
Smith, William. Dictionary of Greek & Roman Antiquities, 2 vols. LC 77-6173. 1977. Repr. of 1890 ed. lib. bdg. 65.00 (ISBN 0-89341-166-3). Longwood Pr.
ROME–BIOGRAPHY
see also Roman Emperors
Smith, William, ed. Dictionary of Greek & Roman Biography & Mythology, 3 Vols. LC 11-24983. (Gr. & Lat.). Repr. of 1890 ed. Set. $210.00 (ISBN 0-404-06130-3). AMS Pr.
--Dictionary of Greek & Roman Geography, 2 Vols. LC 4-14843. (Gr.). Repr. of 1873 ed. Set. $125.00 (ISBN 0-404-06134-6).
ROME–CIVILIZATION
Fredoville, Jean C. Dictionnaire civilisation Romaine. (Dictionnaires de l'homme du vingtieme siecle). (Illus., Fr.). 1968. $8.50 (ISBN 0-685-13862-3, 3716). Larousse.

ROME–ECONOMIC CONDITIONS
Korver, Jan. De Terminologie van het Crediet-Wezen in het Grieksch. Finley, Moses, ed. LC 79-4987. (Ancient Economic History Ser.). (Dutch.). 1980. Repr. of 1934 ed. lib. bdg. $14.00x (ISBN 0-405-12372-8). Ayer Co.
ROME–HISTORY–KINGS, 753-510 B.C.
Veh, Otto, ed. Lexikon der Roemischen Kaiser. 96p. (Ger.). 1976. DM.9.80 (ISBN 3-7608-4056-6). Artemis Verlag.
ROME–HISTORY–REPUBLIC, 510-30 B.C.
Hellegouarch, Jean. Le Vocabulaire Latin des Relations & des Partis Politiques sous la Republique. (Lat.). 109.00 F. Belles Lettres.
RONG LANGUAGE
see Lepcha Language
RONSARD, PIERRE DE, 1524-1585
Mellerio, Louis. Lexique de Ronsard. (Fr.). 54.00 F. Kraus.
--Lexique de Ronsard. 250p. (Fr.). 1974. DM.54.00. Olms.
ROTUMANS
Churchward, Clerk M. Rotuman Grammar & Dictionary. LC 75-32808. Repr. of 1940 ed. $30.75 (ISBN 0-404-14112-9). AMS Pr.
ROYAL ACADEMY OF ARTS, LONDON
see London–Royal Academy of Arts
RUBBER
Elseviers Rubber Dictionary. (Eng., Fr., Span., Ital., Port., Ger., Dutch, Swedish, Indonesian & Japanese.). 1959. $170.25 (ISBN 0-444-40499-6). Elsevier.
Glossary of Terms Relating to Rubber & Rubber Technology. 122p. 1972. pap. $10.00 (ISBN 0-8031-0101-5, STP184A). ASTM.
Heinisch, Kurt F. Kautschuk-Lexikon. 2nd ed. LC 79-361675. (Illus.). 572p. (Ger.). 1978. DM.75.00. Gentner.
Plast & Gummilexikon. (Eng., Swedish & Ger.). 1982. Kr.149.00 (ISBN 91-86236-00-8). EC Print AB.
RUBBER-SHEET GEOMETRY
see Topology
RUGS, ORIENTAL
Neff, Ivan C. & Maggs, Carol V. Dictionary of Oriental Rugs: With a Monograph on Identification by Weave. 1979. $29.95 (ISBN 0-442-20617-8). Van Nos Reinhold.
RUINS
see Antiquities; Archaeology
also subdivision Antiquities under names of countries, cities, etc. e.g. Rome–Antiquities
RULE OF LAW
Gosudarstvennye Standarty SSSR, 3 vols. (Rus.). 1980. $14.25 set (Pub. by Izd Standartov). Four Continent.
RULES OF THE ROAD
see Inland Navigation
RURAL ARCHITECTURE
see Architecture, Domestic
RURAL HEALTH
see Health, Rural
RURAL HOSPITALS
see Hospitals
RURAL LIFE
see Country Life
RUSKIN, JOHN, 1819-1900
Royal-Dawson, Warren, compiled by. Miscellaneous Papers by or Concerning John Ruskin, 2 Vols. 80p. 1982. Repr. of 1918 ed. Set. lib. bdg. $200.00 (ISBN 0-89987-722-2). Darby Bks.
RUSSIA
see also names of specific cities, areas, etc. in Russia
Gosudarstvennye Standarty SSSR, 3 vols. (Rus.). 1980. $14.25 set (Pub. by Izd Standartov). Four Continent.
RUSSIA–DEFENSES
Vasmer, Max. Woerterbuch der Russischen Gewaessernamen: Bd 1, A-E. (Ger.). 1961. DM.168.00 (ISBN 3-447-00971-3). Harrassowitz.
Woerterbuch der Russichen Gewaessernamen: Lfg 1. (Ger.). 1961. DM.46.00 (ISBN 3-447-00976-4). Harrassowitz.

Woerterbuch der Russichen Gewaessernamen: Lfg 2. (Ger.). DM.46.00 (ISBN 3-447-00977-2). Harrassowitz.

Woerterbuch der Russichen Gewaessernamen: Bd 2, Z-K. (Ger. & Rus.). DM.154.00 (ISBN 3-447-00972-1). Harrassowitz.

Woerterbuch der Russichen Gewaessernamen: Lfg 4. (Ger. & Rus.). DM.46.00 (ISBN 3-447-00979-9). Harrassowitz.

Woerterbuch der Russischen Gewaessernamen: Bd 3, L-P. (Ger. & Rus.). DM.166.00 (ISBN 3-447-00973-X). Harrassowitz.

Woerterbuch der Russischen Gewaessernamen: Bd 4, R-U. (Ger. & Rus.). 1968. DM.132.00 (ISBN 3-447-00974-8). Harrassowitz.

Woerterbuch der Russischen Gewaessernamen: Bd 5, F-Ja. (Ger. & Rus.). 1969. DM.74.00 (ISBN 3-447-00975-6). Harrassowitz.

Woerterbuch der Russischen Gewaessernamen: Lfg 3. (Ger. & Rus.). DM.46.00 (ISBN 3-447-00978-0). Harrassowitz.

Woerterbuch der Russischen Gewaessernamen: Lfg 5. (Ger.). DM.46.00 (ISBN 3-447-00980-2). Harrassowitz.

Woerterbuch der Russischen Gewaessernamen: Lfg 6. (Ger. & Rus.). DM.32.00 (ISBN 3-447-00981-0). Harrassowitz.

Woerterbuch der Russischen Gewaessernamen: Lfg 7. (Ger. & Rus.). DM.46.00 (ISBN 3-447-00982-9). Harrassowitz.

Woerterbuch der Russischen Gewaessernamen: Lfg 8. (Ger. & Rus.). DM.46.00 (ISBN 3-447-00983-7). Harrassowitz.

Woerterbuch der Russischen Gewaessernamen: Lfg 9. (Ger. & Rus.). DM.74.00 (ISBN 3-447-00984-5). Harrassowitz.

Woerterbuch der Russischen Gewaessernamen: Lfg 10. (Ger. & Rus.). DM.44.00 (ISBN 3-447-00985-3). Harrassowitz.

WOerterbuch der Russischen Gewaessernamen: Lfg 11. (Ger. & Rus.). DM.44.00 (ISBN 3-447-00986-1). Harrassowitz.

Woerterbuch der Russischen Gewaessernamen: Lfg 12. (Ger. & Rus.). DM.44.00 (ISBN 3-447-00987-X). Harrassowitz.

Woerterbuch der Russischen Gewaessernamen: Lfg 13. (Ger. & Rus.). DM.44.00 (ISBN 3-447-00988-8). Harrassowitz.

Woerterbuch der Russischen Gewaessernamen: Lfg 14. (Ger. & Rus.). DM.30.00 (ISBN 3-447-00989-6). Harrassowitz.

Woerterbuch der Russischen Gewaessernamen: Lfg 15. iv, 190p. (Ger. & Rus.). DM.50.00 (ISBN 3-447-01494-6). Harrassowitz.

RUSSIA–POLITICS AND GOVERNMENT

McCrea, Barbara P. & Plano, Jack C. The Soviet & East European Political Dictionary. (Clio Dictionaries in Political Science Ser.: No. 4). 350p. (gr. 10-12). 1983. lib. bdg. $20.75 (ISBN 0-87436-333-0); pap. $10.75 (ISBN 0-87436-347-0). ABC-Clio.

RUSSIAN AUTHORS

see Authors, Russian

RUSSIAN LANGUAGE

Felitsyna, V. P. & Prokhorov, Iu. E. Russkie Poslovitsy, Pogovorki i Krylatye Vyrazheniia. 240p. (Rus.). 1979. $5.50 (Pub. by Russkii Iazyk). Four Continent.

Gribble, Charles E. Russian Root List with a Sketch of Russian Word Formation. 2nd ed. 62p. (Rus.). 1982. soft cover $3.95 (ISBN 0-89357-052-4). Slavica.

RUSSIAN LANGUAGE–TO 1700

Slovar Russkogo Iazyka XI-XVII: E-zinutie, Vol. 5. (Rus.). $8.95 (Pub. by Nauka). Four Continent.

Slovar Russkogo Iazyka XI-XVII: G-diatchiti, Vol. 4. (Rus.). $10.95 (Pub. by Nauka). Four Continent.

Slovar Russkogo Iazyka XI-XVII: Zipun-iianuarii, Vol.6. (Rus.). $7.95 (Pub. by Nauka). Four Continent.

RUSSIAN LANGUAGE–ACCENTS AND ACCENTUATION

Benson, Morton, ed. Dictionary of Russian Personal Names. LC 64-19386. 1964. 15.00x (ISBN 0-8122-7452-0). U of Pa Pr.

RUSSIAN LANGUAGE–CONVERSATION AND PHRASE-BOOKS

Gamrekeli, N., et al. Nemetsko-Gruzinsko-Russkii Frazeologicheskii Slovar. 566p. (Ger., Gr. & Rus.). 1973. $4.35 (Pub. by Ganatleba). Four Continent.

Gavrilovets, A. V. Russko-Angliiskii Slovar-Razgovornik: Letnie Olimpiiskie Vidy Sporta. 352p. (Rus.). 1979. $3.50 (Pub. by Russkii Iazyk). Four Continent.

Kratkii Iaponsko-Russkii Razgovornik. 240p. (Rus. & Japanese.). 1957. $1.95 (Pub. by Iskra Revoliutsii). Four Continent.

Molotkova, A. I. Frazeologicheskii Slovar Russkogo Iazyka. 544p. (Rus. & Fr.). 1978. $11.95 (Pub. by Russkii Iazyk). Four Continent.

Neverov, S. Ispansko-Russkii Razgovornik. 190p. (Rus. & Span.). 1953. $1.25 (Pub. by Izd. Lit. Na Inostr. Iaz.). Four Continent.

Orudzhev, A. Azerbaidzhansko-Russkii Frazeogicheskii (Idiomaticheskii) Slovar. 278p. (Rus.). 1976. $3.95 (Pub. by Elm). Four Continent.

Polsko-Russkii Razgovornik Dlia Turistov. 240p. (Pol. & Rus.). 1979. $2.95 (Pub. by Russkii Iazyk). Four Continent.

Russko-Armianskii Frazeologicheskii Slovar. 616p. (Rus. & Armenian.). 1975. $7.25 (Pub. by Gos. Un-Tet). Four Continent.

Ushakova, L. I., et al. Indioneziisko-Russkii Uchebnyi Razgovornik. 541p. (Rus. & Indonesian.). 1963. $1.75 (Pub. by Gosizdat Inostr Natsional Slovarei). Four Continent.

RUSSIAN LANGUAGE–DIALECTS

Eliasov, L. E. Slovar Russkikh Govorov Zabaikalia. 477p. (Rus.). 1980. $16.75 (Pub. by Nauka). Four Continent.

Rastorguev, P. A. Slovar Narodnykh Govorov Zapadnoi Brianshchiny. 293p. (Rus.). 1973. $2.35 (Pub. by Nauka). Four Continent.

Slovar Russkikh Govorov Novosibirskoi Oblasti. 604p. (Rus.). 1979. $15.95 (Pub. by Nauka). Four Continent.

Slovar Russkikh Narodnykh Govorov, Vol. 4. 355p. (Rus.). 1969. $4.25 (Pub. by Nauka). Four Continent.

Slovar Russkikh Narodnykh Govorov, Vol. 5. 358p. (Rus.). 1970. $3.95 (Pub. by Nauka). Four Continent.

Slovar Russkikh Narodnykh Govorov, Vol. 6. 358p. (Rus.). 1970. $3.95 (Pub. by Nauka). Four Continent.

Slovar Russkikh Narodnykh Govorov, Vol. 7. 355p. (Rus.). 1972. $3.95 (Pub. by Nauka). Four Continent.

Slovar Russkikh Narodnykh Govorov, Vol. 8. 369p. (Rus.). 1972. $5.25 (Pub. by Nauka). Four Continent.

Slovar Russkikh Narodnykh Govorov, Vol. 9. 362p. (Rus.). 1972. $4.75 (Pub. by Nauka). Four Continent.

Slovar Russkikh Narodnykh Govorov, Vol. 10. 388p. (Rus.). 1974. $4.75 (Pub. by Nauka). Four Continent.

Slovar Russkikh Narodnykh Govorov, Vol. 11. 364p. (Rus.). 1975. $4.00 (Pub. by Nauka). Four Continent.

Slovar Russkikh Narodnykh Govorov, Vol. 12. 368p. (Rus.). 1977. $6.25 (Pub. by Nauka). Four Continent.

Slovar Russkikh Narodnykh Govorov, Vol. 14. 372p. (Rus.). 1978. $7.25 (Pub. by Nauka). Four Continent.

Slovar Russkikh Narodnykh Govorov, Vol. 15. 440p. (Rus.). 1979. $7.50 (Pub. by Nauka). Four Continent.

Slovar Russkikh Narodnykh Govorov, Vol. 16. 376p. (Rus.). 1980. $7.25 (Pub. by Nauka). Four Continent.

RUSSIAN LANGUAGE–DICTIONARIES

Abbreviated Russian-Korean Dictionary. 648p. (Rus. & Korean.). $4.95 (ISBN 0-686-97385-2, M-9055). French & Eur.

Abramov, L. Ia., ed. Shakhmatnyi Slovar. 618p. (Rus.). 1964. $5.00 (Pub. by Fiz. & Sport). Four Continent.

Akhmanova, O. S. Slovar Omonimov Russkogo Iazyka. 448p. (Rus.). 1974. $3.25 (Pub. by Sov. Entsiklopediia). Four Continent.

Akhmanova, O. S., ed. Russko-Angliiskii Slovar (Kratkii) 520p. (Rus. & Eng.). 1979. $3.50 (Pub. by Russkii Iazyk). Four Continent.

Aleksandrova, Z. E. Slovar Sinonimov Russkogo Iazyka. 600p. (Rus.). 1968. $3.75 (Pub. by Sov. Entsiklopediia). Four Continent.

Alekseev, M. P. Slovari Inostrannykh Iazykov v Russkom Azbukovnikeveka. 156p. (Rus.). 1968. $3.50 (Pub. by Nauka). Four Continent.

Alexandrova. Dictionnaire des Synonymes de la Langue Russe. (Rus.). 1960. 19.10 F. MIR.

Andronov, M. S. Russko-Tamil'Skii Slovar. 1175p. (Rus. & Tamil.). 1965. $7.95 (Pub. by Sov. Entsiklopediia). Four Continent.

Anglo-Latyshsko-Russkii Frazeologicheskii Slovar. 718p. (Eng. & Rus.). 1977. $3.25 (Pub. by Liesma). Four Continent.

Antelava, H. G. Abbreviated Turkish-Russian Dictionary of New Words. 95p. (Turkish & Rus.). 1978. pap. $7.95 (ISBN 0-686-97387-9, M-9054). French & Eur.

Arakin, V. D. Norvezhsko-Russkii Slovar. 1113p. (Rus. & Norwegian.). 1963. $13.25 (Pub. by GINS). Four Continent.

Araushkin, N. S., et al. Karmannyi Kitaisko-Russkii Slovar. 210p. (Rus.). 1975. $1.95 (Pub. by Russkii Iazyk). Four Continent.

Arumaa, P., et al. Russko-Estonskii Slovar, 2 vols. (Rus. & Estonian.). 1975. $14.95 set (Pub. by Valgus). Four Continent.

Baar, A. Russisch Woordenboek. LC 79-385386. xii, 502p. (Dutch & Rus.). 1979. fl.39.50 (ISBN 9-06283-523-6). Coutinho.

Bekmukhametov, E. Russko-Kazakhskii Terminologicheskii Slovar, 4 Vols. (Rus.). 1959. $7.00 set (Pub. by Izd. An Kaz. SSR). Four Continent.

Belkina, E. S. Russko-Indoneziiskii Slovar. 624p. (Rus. & Indonesian.). 1972. $7.85 (Pub. by Sov. Entsiklopediia). Four Continent.

Beniukh, O. P., et al. Karmannyi Russko-Angliiskii Slovar. 782p. (Rus. & Eng.). 1971. $2.00 (Pub. by Sov Entsiklopediia). Four Continent.

Berger, Marshall D. Vest Pocket Russian. LC 60-9758. (Illus.). 182p. (Rus.). 1961. pap. $2.45 (ISBN 0-06-464905-9, BN4905, BN). B&N NY.

Blattner, Karl. Langenscheidts Taschenwoerterbuecher Russisch. (Rus.). 1978. DM.23.80 (ISBN 3-468-11290-4). Langenscheidt.

Bogusiawski, Andrzej. Illustrowany Slownik Rosyjsko-Polski. LC 79-352771. 1179p. (Rus. & Pol.). 1978. 200.00 Zl. Wiedza Powszechna.

Boguslawski, Andrzej. Illustrowany Slownik Rosyjsko-Polski, Polsko-Rosyjski. LC 79-352771. (Illus.). 1179p. (Pol. & Rus.). 1978. 200.00 Zl. Wiedza Poswzechna.

Borshch, A. T., et al, eds. Russko-Moldavskii Slovar. 835p. (Rus. & Moldavian.). 1954. $6.85 (Pub. by Izd. Inostr. & Natsional Slovarei). Four Continent.

Bulgarian-Russian Dictionary (M-9095) 519p. (Bulgarian & Rus.). 1977. $4.95 (ISBN 0-686-87184-7). French & Eur.

Bulygin, N. F. Karmannyi Indoneziisko-Russkii Slovar. 310p. (Rus. & Indonesian.). 1959. $1.25 (Pub. by GINS). Four Continent.

Bulygin, N. F., et al. Karmannyi Russko-Indoneziiskii Slovar. 576p. (Rus. & Indonesian.). 1958. $1.75 (Pub. by GINS). Four Continent.

Bykova, E. M., et al. Bengal'sko-Russkii Slovar. 908p. (Rus. & Bengali.). 1957. $5.50 (Pub. by Gosizdat Inostr. Natsion. Slovarei). Four Continent.

Chastonyi Slovar' Russkogo Iazyka. 936p. (Rus.). 1976. $7.50 (D-97A). Four Continent.

Chastotnyi Slovar Russkogo Iazyka. 936p. (Rus.). 1977. $7.50 (Pub. by Russkii Iazyk). Four Continent.

Cheshko. Slovar' Sinonimov Russkogo Iazyka. Aleksandrova, Z. E., ed. 600p. (Rus.). 1968. $3.75 (90, 93, 94, 95). Four Continent.

Chukalov, S. K. Russko-Bolgarskii Slovar. 911p. (Rus. & Bulgarian.). 1972. $7.95 (Pub. by Sov. Entsiklopediia). Four Continent.

Cruz, M. & Ignashev, S. P. Tagalog-Russian Dictionary. 388p. (Tagalog & Rus.). 1959. leatherette $4.75 (ISBN 0-686-92479-7, M-9052). French & Eur.

Dal', V. Tolkovyi Slovar' Zhivogo Velikorusskogo Iazyka, 4 vols. (Russkii iazyk Ser.). (Rus.). 1978. $64.50 set. Four Continent.

Daum, Edmund & Schenk, W. Deutsch-Russisches Woerterbuch. 15th ed. (Ger. & Rus.). 1976. $13.50 (ISBN 0-686-56602-5, M-7333, Pub. by Max Hueber). French & Eur.

--Russich-Deutsches Woerterbuch. 7th ed. (Rus. & Ger.). 1976. $17.50 (ISBN 3-19-006219-6, M-7606, Pub. by Max Hueber). French & Eur.

--Russich-Deutsches Woerterbuch. 7th ed. (Ger. & Rus.). 1976. $17.50 (ISBN 3-19-006219-6). Hueber.

Davidova, A. A., et al. Karmannyi Russko-Urdu Slovar. 739p. (Urdu & Rus.). 1958. $1.50 (Pub. by GINS). Four Continent.

Davidson, K., ed. Russko-Shvedskii Slovar. 960p. (Rus.). 1976. $10.95 (C-91, Pub. by Russkii Iazyk). Four Continent.

Denisov, P. N., et al. Uchebnyi Slovar' Sochetaenosti Slov Russkogo Iazyka. (Russkii iazyk Ser.). 688p. (Rus.). 1978. $22.75. Four Continent.

Denisova, M. A. Lingvostranovedcheskii Slovar' (Russkii iazyk Ser.). 277p. (Rus.). 1978. $4.90 (O-119). Four Continent.

Diccionario espanol-ruso. (Span. & Rus.). write for info. Cultura Popular.

Diccionario espanol-ruso. (Span. & Rus.). Arg.$12.00. (Mir) D'lppolito.

Diccionario ilustrado de la lengua rusa. (Illus., Span. & Rus.). Mex.$15.00. Cultura Popular.

Diccionario ilustrado del idioma ruso. (Illus., Span. & Rus.). $1.00. Pueblos Unidos.

Diccionario ruso-espanol. (Span. & Rus.). $0.80. Pueblos Unidos.

Diccionario ruso-espanol, espanol-ruso. 1448p. (Rus. & Span.). 850.00 ptas. Danae.

A Dictionary of Russian Obscenities. 24p. (Rus.). 1971. pap. $2.50x (ISBN 0-685-47489-5). Schoenhof.

Dictionnaire de la Langue Russe. (Rus.). 1978. 45.75 F. Mir.

Dictionnaire des Frequences de Mots dans le Russe. (Rus. & Fr.). 10.55 F. Steinfeld.

Dictionnaire Inverse de la Langue Russe. (Fr. & Rus.). write for info. Mir.

Dlugi, D. A., et al. Karmannyi Cheshsko-Russkii i Russko-Cheshskii Slovar. 476p. (Rus. & Czech.). 1970. $2.50 (Pub. by Sov Entsiklopediia). Four Continent.

Dobrovolskaia, I. A. Karmannyi Ital'iansko-Russkii Slovar. 408p. (Rus. & Ital.). 1959. $1.10 (Pub. by GINS). Four Continent.

Dobrovolskaia, I. A., et al. Karmannyi Russko-Ital'ianskii Slovar. (Ital. & Rus.). $1.85 (Pub. by Sov Entsiklopediia). Four Continent.

Dreniasova, T. N. Karmannyi Niderlandsko-Russkii Slovar. 392p. (Rus. & Dutch.). 1977. $1.80 (Pub. by Russkii Iazyk). Four Continent.
Drummond, David A. & Perkins, G. Dictionary of Russian Obscenities. rev. ed. 79p. (Rus. & Eng.). 1980. pap. text ed. $3.50 (ISBN 0-933884-17-6). Berkeley Slavic.
Dymshits, Z. M., et al. Karmannyi Russko-Khindi Slovar. 867p. (Rus.). 1958. $1.85 (Pub. by GINS). Four Continent.
Dzenit, S. I. Telugu-Russkii Slovar. 744p. (Rus.). 1972. $8.50 (Pub. by Sov. Entsiklopediia). Four Continent.
Eliseev, I. S. Karmannyi Russko-Finskii Slovar. 304p. (Rus. & Finnish.). 1978. $2.85 (Pub. by Russkii Iazyk). Four Continent.
Evgueniev. Dictionnaire des Synonymes de la Langue Russe, 2 vols. (Rus.). 110.90 F. MIR.
Fadanelli. Dizionario italiano-russo. 138p. (Ital. & Rus.). 1976. L.2300.00. Vallardi A.
Fadanelli, R. Dizionario Italiano-Russo, Russo-Italiane. 286p. (Ital. & Rus.). leatherette $5.95 (ISBN 0-686-92582-3). French & Eur.
Farizov, I. O. Russko-Kurdskii Slovar. 781p. (Rus.). 1957. $3.95 (Pub. by GINS). Four Continent.
Feoktistov, A. P. Russko-Mordovskii Slovar. 370p. (Rus.). 1971. $4.25 (Pub. by Nauka). Four Continent.
Filin, F. P., ed. Russkii Iazyk: Entsiklopediia. (Sov. Entsiklopediia Ser.). 432p. (Rus.). 1979. $7.95 (O-33). Four Continent.
Four Languages Dictionary of Geological Terms. 703p. (Eng. , Fr. , Ger. & Rus.). 1980. $19.95 (ISBN 0-686-97380-1). French & Eur.
Galdi, Laszlo. Orosz-Magyar Szotar. 3rd ed. LC 80-467905. 1120p. (Hungarian & Rus.). 1978. 135.00 Ft (ISBN 9-63051-821-X). Akademiai Kiado.
Galler, Meyer & Marquess, Harlan E., eds. Soviet Prison Camp Speech: A Survivor's Glossary. LC 75-176411. 216p. 1972. $25.00 (ISBN 0-299-06080-2). U of Wis Pr.
Ganich, D. I., et al. Russko-Ukrainskii Slovar. 1012p. (Rus. & Ukrainian.). 1978. $8.95 (Pub. by Sov. Entsiklopediia). Four Continent.
Gankin, E. B. Akhmarsko-Russkii Slovar. 968p. (Rus.). 1969. $7.95 (Pub. by Sov Entsiklopediia). Four Continent.
--Russko-Amkharskii Slovar. 1013p. (Rus. & Eng.). 1965. $8.25 (Pub. by Sov. Entsiklopediia). Four Continent.
Garibian, A. Russko-Armianskii Slovar. 1340p. (Rus. & Armenian.). 1977. $16.75 (Pub. by Hayastan). Four Continent.
Garibian, A. S. Russko-Armianskii Slovar. 1421p. (Rus. & Armenian.). 1968. $14.25 (Pub. by Hayastan). Four Continent.
Gere, S. V., et al. Italiansko-Russkii Slovar. 744p. (Rus. & Ital.). 1947. $5.20 (Pub. by Gosizdat Inostr. Natsional Slovarei). Four Continent.
Gisbert. Diccionario manual espanol-ruso. (Span. & Rus.). $0.80. Pueblos Unidos.
Gluskina, A. E., et al. Kratkii Russko-Iaponskii Slovar. 1000p. (Rus. & Japanese.). 1950. $5.75 (Pub. by GINS). Four Continent.
Gorochow, P. K. Russich-Deutsches Worterbuch der Funkechnik. 390p. (Rus. & Ger.). 1961. leatherette $6.95 (ISBN 0-686-92169-0). French & Eur.
Gribanova, E. P. Karmannyi Russko-Norvezhskii Slovar. 688p. (Rus. & Norwegian.). 1962. $1.95 (Pub. by GINS). Four Continent.
Grigorian, V. Z., et al. Russko-Armianskii Tolkovyi Slovar. 339p. (Rus. & Armenian.). 1979. $7.50 (Pub. by An Arm SSR). Four Continent.
Grischen, N. Deutsch-Russische Wirtschaftssprache. 480p. (Ger. & Rus.). 1969. $27.50 (ISBN 3-19-006207-2, M-7332, Pub. by M. Hueber). French & Eur.
Gross, Helmut. Kleines Woerterbuch der Chemie & Chemischen Technik. LC 79-393988. 108p. (Rus. & Ger.). 1979. M.7.00. VEB Verlag Technik.
Gross, Helmut & Hildebrand, Helmut. Chemie & Chemische Technik. 2nd ed. LC 77-550181. (Rus. & Ger.). 1976. M.48.00. VEB Verlag Technik.
Hadrovics, Laszlo. Orosz-Magyar Szotar, 2 vols. 5th ed. LC 78-377287. (Hungarian & Rus.). 1977. 450.00 Ft (ISBN 9-63051-231-9). Akademiai Kiado.
Hadrovics, Laszlo & Hadrovics, Galdi. Magyar-Orosz Keziszotar. 4th ed. LC 79-339814. 712p. (Hungarian & Rus.). 1978. 100.00 Ft (ISBN 9-63051-532-6). Akademiai Kiado.
Hadrovics, Laszlo, et al. Magyar-Orosz Kez Iszotar. LC 79-339814. 712p. (Hungarian & Rus.). 1978. 100.00 Ft (ISBN 9-6305-1532-6). Akademiai Kiado.
Hiltunen, A. Finnish-Russian-Finnish Dictionary (Suomi-Venaja-Suomi) 543p. (Finnish & Rus.). 1981. pap. $19.95 (ISBN 951-0-09631-8, M-9643). French & Eur.
Hoffmann, Peter D. Fertigungsmesstechnik. 140p. (Rus. & Ger.). 1975. M.15.00. VEB Verlag Technik.
Horalek, Karel. Skolni Rusko-Cesky Slovnik. LC 79-389285. 1263p. (Rus. & Czech.). 1977. 54.00 Kcs. SNTC.
Iliev, A., et al. Russko-Uigurskii Slovar. 1473p. (Rus.). 1956. $5.25 (Pub. by Gosizdat Natsional Inostr Slovarei). Four Continent.
Ioannidia, A. A. Russko-Novogrecheskii Slovar. 819p. (Rus & Gr.). 1966. $7.95 (Pub. by Sov. Entsiklopediia). Four Continent.
Isambaev, M. Russko-Latino-Kazakhskii Terminologicheskii Slovar. 506p. (Rus. & Lat.). 1960. $2.40 (Pub. by Izd. An Kaz. SSR). Four Continent.
Iudakhin, K. K., ed. Russko-Kirgizskii Slovar. 990p. (Rus.). 1957. $9.90 (Pub. by GINS). Four Continent.
Karaulov, Iu. N., ed. Chastotnyi Slovar Semanticheskikh Mnozhitelei Russkogo Iazyka. 208p. (Orig., Rus.). 1980. $3.25 (Pub. by Nauka). Four Continent.
Karimova, G. R. Russko-Bashkirskii Slovar. 600p. (Rus. & Bashkirsh.). 1954. $2.70 (Pub. by GINS). Four Continent.
Karmannyi Italiansko-Russkii Slovar. 408p. (Ital. & Rus.). 1959. $1.10. Four Continent.
Karmannyi Polsko-Russkii i Russko-Polskii Slovar. 472p. (Pol. & Rus.). 1960. $1.25. Four Continent.
Karmannyi Rumynsko-Russkii Slovar. 360p. (Romanian & Rus.). 1960. $1.25. Four Continent.
Karmannyi Russko-Bolgarskii Slovar. 464p. (Rus. & Bulgarian.). 1978. $1.95 (Pub. by Russkii Iazyk). Four Continent.
Karmannyi Slovatsko-Russkii i Russko-Slovatskii Slovar. 528p. (Rus. & Slovenian.). 1975. $2.10 (Pub. by Russkii Iazyk). Four Continent.
Kelin, F. V., ed. Ispansko-Russkii Slovar. 944p. (Rus. & Span.). 1961. $4.95 (Pub. by Gosizdat Inostr Natsional Slovarei). Four Continent.
Kelina. Diccionario espanol-ruso. (Span. & Rus.). $0.90. Pueblos Unidos.
Khorikov, I. P. Novogrechesko-Russkii Slovar. 854p. (Rus. & Gr.). 1979. $22.95 (Pub. by Russkii Iazyk). Four Continent.
Kibirkshtis, L. B., et al. Karmannyi Urdu-Russkii Slovar. 551p. (Rus. & Urdu.). 1958. $1.65 (Pub. by GINS). Four Continent.
The Kodansha Japanese-Russian Dictionary. 1154p. (Japanese & Rus.). 1983. 5800.00 Yen. Kodansha.
Kolesnikov, N. P. Slovar' Omonimov Russkogo Iazyka. (Izd. Un-ta Ser.). 632p. (Rus.). 1978. $6.50 (O-112). Four Continent.
Koliadenkov, M. N., et al. Erziansko-Russkii Slovar. 292p. (Rus.). 1949. $2.95 (Pub. by Gosizdat Inostr Natsional Slovarei). Four Continent.
Koliadenkov, M. N., et al, eds. Russko-Erzianskii Slovar. 413p. (Rus.). 1948. $3.95 (Pub. by GINS). Four Continent.
Kopeckeho, L. V., ed. Skolni Rusko-Cesky Slovnik, 2 vols. 6th ed. LC 77-551653. xvi, 1134p. (Rus. & Czech.). 1976. 54.00 Kcs. SNTC.
Kopetskov, L. V., et al. Russko-Cheshskii Slovar, 2 vols. (Rus.). 1977. $23.50 set (Pub. by Russkii Iazyk). Four Continent.
Korigodskii, V. N., et al. Indoneziisko-Russkii Slovar. 1171p. (Rus. & Indonesian.). 1961. $5.75 (Pub. by Gosizdat Inostr Natsional Slovarei). Four Continent.
Korigodsky, R. N., et al. Indonesian-Russian Dictionary. 1171p. (Indonesian & Rus.). 1961. leatherette $14.25 (ISBN 0-686-87187-1, M-9098). French & Eur.
Korneev, L. A. Russko-Malagasiiskii Slovar. 543p. (Rus.). 1970. $4.60 (Pub. bu Sov. Entsiklopediia). Four Continent.
Kostallari, A. Karmannyi Russko-Albanskii Slovar. 428p. (Rus. & Albanian.). 1959. $1.50. Four Continent.
Kotov, A. V. Kitaisko-Russkii Slovar-Minimum. 432p. (Rus.). 1974. $2.95 (Pub. by Russkii Iazyk). Four Continent.
Kratkii Russko-Finskii Slovar. 384p. (Rus. & Finnish.). 1946. $3.20 (Pub. by GINS). Four Continent.
Kratkii Tolkovyi Slovar Russkogo Iazyka. 228p. (Rus.). 1978. $7.50 (Pub. by Russkii Iazyk). Four Continent.
Krus, M. Tagal'sko-Russkii Slovar. 387p. (Rus. & Tagalog.). 1959. $1.95 (Pub. by GINS). Four Continent.
Krus, M., et al. Russko-Tagal'skii Slovar. 760p. (Rus. & Tagalog.). 1965. $4.95 (Pub. by Sov. Entsiklopediia). Four Continent.
--Tagal sko Russkii Slovar. 387p. (Rus. & Tagalog.). 1959. $1.95. Four Continent.
Krymova, N. I., et al. Russko-Datskii Slovar. 906p. (Rus.). 1956. $4.75 (Pub. by GINS). Four Continent.
Kutuzov, A. I. Kratkii Suakhili-Russkii & Russko-Suakhili Slovar. 442p. (Rus. & Swahili.). 1965. $3.50 (Pub. by Sov Entsiklopediia). Four Continent.
--Russian-Swahili, Swahili-Russian Dictionary. 442p. (Rus. & Swahili.). 1965. $4.95 (ISBN 0-686-92156-9, M-9119). French & Eur.
Kuusiena, M. E., et al, eds. Russko-Finskii Slovar. 1000p. (Rus. & Finnish.). 1963. $10.95 (Pub. by GINS). Four Continent.
Langenscheidt Russian Pocket Dictionary. 512p. (Rus.). plastic $5.95 (ISBN 0-340-10708-1). Langenscheidt.
Langenscheidts Universal-Woerterbuch Russisch. 560p. (Rus. & Ger.). DM.6.80 (18291). Langenscheidt.
Laptukhin, V. V. Russko-Khausa Slovar. 409p. (Rus.). 1967. $4.50 (Pub. by Sov. Entsiklopediia). Four Continent.
Lebedev, K. A. Karmannyi Afgansko-Russkii Slovar. 587p. (Rus. & Afghan.). 1962. $1.95 (Pub. by Gosizdat Natsional Slovarei). Four Continent.
Lebedev, K. A., et al. Russko-Afganskii Slovar. 872p. (Rus. & Afghani.). 1973. $10.95 (Pub. by Sov Entsiklopediia). Four Continent.
Lekhin, I. V., et al. Slovar' Inostrannykh Slov. (Russkii iazyk Ser.). 622p. (Rus.). 1980. $8.95 (O-133). Four Continent.
Leonidova. Russian-Bulgarian Dictionary. 463p. (Rus. & Bulgarian.). 1978. leatherette $4.95 (ISBN 0-686-92105-4, M-9101). French & Eur.
Leonidova, M. A. Karmannyi Bolgarsko-Russkii Slovar. 534p. (Rus. & Bulgarian.). 1961. $1.75 (Pub. by Gosizdat Inostr. & Natsional). Four Continent.
--Karmannyi Russko-Bolgarskii Slovar. 474p. (Rus. & Bulgarian.). 1960. $1.25. Four Continent.
Leping, A. A., ed. Russko-Nemetskii Slovar. 568p. (Rus.). 1957. $1.70 (Pub. by GINS). Four Continent.
Leping, E. I., ed. Russko-Nemetskii Slovar. 848p. (Rus. & Ger.). 1978. $15.95 (Pub. by Russkii Iazyk). Four Continent.
Lexico basico espanol-ruso. (Span. & Rus.). Mex.$10.00. Cultura Popular.
Lexico basico espanol-ruso. (Span. & Rus.). Arg.$12.00. D'Ippolito.
Litton. Russko-Bengal'skii Slovar. 760p. (Rus. & Bengali.). 1972. $6.30 (Pub. by Sov. Entsiklopediia). Four Continent.
Litton, D. Karmannyi Bengal'sko-Russkii Slovar. 532p. (Rus. & Bengali.). 1960. $1.95 (Pub. by Gosizdat Natsional Slovarei). Four Continent.
Lordkipanidze, A. G., et al. Russko-Indoneziiskii Uchebnyi Slovar. 707p. (Rus. & Indonesian.). 1963. $2.95 (Pub. by GINS). Four Continent.
L'Vov, M. R. Slovar' Antonimov Russkogo Iazyka. (Russkii iazyk Ser.). 400p. (Rus.). 1978. $4.75. Four Continent.
Martinez Calvo, L. Diccionario Espanol-Ruso. LC 76-456144. 1915p. (Rus. & Span.). 1975. 1000.00 Rub (ISBN 8-43030-133-X). Sopena.
Martinez Calvo, Lorenzo. Diccionario Ruso-Espanol. 2000p. (Rus. & Span.). $44.95 (ISBN 84-303-0131-3, S-50410). French & Eur.
Mazur, I. N. Kratkii Russko-Koreiskii Slovar. 648p. (Rus. & Korean.). 1959. $2.95 (Pub. by GINS). Four Continent.
Messinger, Heinz & Ruedenberg, Werner, eds. Langenscheidts Handwoerterbuecher Russisch. (Rus.). DM.28.00 (ISBN 3-468-80029-0). Langenscheidt.
Miklosich, Franz. Dictionnaire Abrege de Six Langues Slaves. LC 75-506978. 955p. (Fr. & Rus.). 1975. write for info. Philo Pr.
Mirowicz. Wielki Slownik Polsko-Rosyski (Polish-Russian Dictionary) 1331p. (Pol. & Rus.). 1980. $70.00 (ISBN 0-686-87195-2, M-9131). French & Eur.
Mitronova, I. N., et al. Karmannyi Pol'Sko-Russkii & Russko-Polskii Slovar. 560p. (Rus. & Pol.). 1976. $2.25 (Pub. by Russkii Iazyk). Four Continent.
Morev, L. N. Taisko-Ruskii Slovar. 985p. (Rus. & Tai.). 1964. $6.50 (Pub. by Sov. Entsiklopediia). Four Continent.
Mudrov, B. G., ed. Kitaisko-Russkii Slovar. 528p. (Rus.). 1979. $16.95 (Pub. by Russkii Iazyk). Four Continent.
Mudrov, V. G. Karmannyi Russko-Kitaiskii Slovar. 216p. (Rus.). 1977. $3.20 (Pub. by Russkii Iazyk). Four Continent.
Mukhel, V. Kratkii Estonsko-Russkii Slovar. 681p. (Rus. & Estonian.). 1973. $2.75 (Pub. by Tallinn). Four Continent.
--Russko-Estonskii Slovar. 708p. (Rus. & Estonian.). 1955. $3.30 (Pub. by Estonsk. Gos. Izd.). Four Continent.
Nitronowa, I., et al. Polish-Russian, Russian-Polish Dictionary. 575p. (Pol. & Rus.). 1980. leatherette $4.95 (ISBN 0-686-97442-5, M-9102). French & Eur.
Nosova, O. P. Kratkii Lugunda-Russkii & Russko-Lugunda Slovar. 520p. (Rus. & Luganda.). 1969. $3.95 (Pub. by Sov Entsiklopediia). Four Continent.
Noveannu, Eugen P. Dictionar-Rus-Roman: Pentru uzual Elevilor. LC 77-479078. 498p. (Romanian & Rus.). 1976. 20.00 lei. Editura Stiintifica.

Novikov, N. N., et al. Russko-Birmanskii Slovar. 880p. (Rus. & Burmese.). 1966. $7.50 (Pub. by Sov. Entsiklopediia). Four Continent.

Ol'dal, G. I. Russko-Vengerskii Slovar. 368p. (Rus.). 1961. $00.95 (Pub. by Gosizdat Inostr Natsional Slovarei). Four Continent.

Ol'Dal, G. I., et al. Karmannyi Vengersko-Russkii Slovar. 405p. (Rus.). 1969. $1.50 (Pub. by GINS). Four Continent.

Osipov, M. I. Kratkii Taisko-Russkii Slovar. 332p. (Rus.). 1964. $2.50 (Pub. by LGU). Four Continent.

Ozhegov. Diccionario de lengua rusa. (Span. & Rus.). $4.00. Pueblos Unidos.

Ozhegov, S. I. Slovar Russkogo Iazyka. 848p. (Rus.). 1977. $10.50 (Pub. by Russkii Iazyk). Four Continent.

Pallas, Peter S. Linguarum Totius Orbis Vocabularia Comparativa. LC 78-380313. (Lat. & Rus.). 1977. DM.100.00 (ISBN 3-87118-285-0). Buske.

Parsons, Charles. Russian-English Dictionary of...(a,e,i,ya) tel' Words. 32p. (Orig., Rus. & Eng.). 1980. pap. $6.00x (ISBN 0-917564-08-1). Translation Research.

Persidsko-Russkii & Russko-Persidskii Obshche-Ekonomicheskii & Vneshnetorgovyi Slovar. 596p. (Persian & Rus.). 1957. $2.95 (Pub. by Vneshtorgizdat). Four Continent.

Pirog, Zh. I., et al. Karmannyi Russko-Niderlandskii Slovar. 496p. (Rus. & Dutch.). 1977. $2.50 (Pub. by Russkii Iazyk). Four Continent.

Pirot, Z. I. Russko-Gollandskii Slovar. 1225p. (Rus.). 1961. $5.25 (Pub. by GINS). Four Continent.

Podiko, M. V. Russko-Moldavskii Slovar. 1060p. (Rus. & Moldavian.). 1973. $6.50 (Pub. by Kartia Moldoveniaske). Four Continent.

Potikha, Z. A. Shkol' Nyi Slovoobrazovatel Nyi' Slovar' (Prosveshchenie Ser.). 390p. (Rus.). 1964. $1.95. Four Continent.

Prano, A. V. Russko-Litovskii Sel'Skokhoziaistvennyi Slovar. 362p. (Rus.). 1971. $3.50 (Pub. by Mintis). Four Continent.

Prokhorov, I. G., et al, eds. Russkie Poslovitsy, Pogovorki i Krylatye Slovar: Lingvostranovedcheskii Slovar. (Russkii iazyk Ser.). 240p. (Rus.). 1979. $5.50 (C-104). Four Continent.

Rabinovich, I. S. Nepal'Sko-Russkii Slovar. 1328p. (Rus. & Nepalese.). 1968. $9.35 (Pub. by Sov Entsiklopediia). Four Continent.

--Pandzhabsko-Russkii Slovar. 1039p. (Rus.). 1961. $6.95 (Pub. by GINS). Four Continent.

Rankin, N. A. The Pocket Oxford English-Russian Dictionary. (Eng. & Rus.). 1981. text ed. 11.95x (ISBN 0-19-864127-3). Oxford U Pr.

Raskevics, J., et al. English-Latvian-Russian Dictionary. 718p. (Eng., Latvian & Rus.). 1977. $50.00x (ISBN 0-686-82324-9, Pub. by Collets). State Mutual Bk.

Reitsak, A. Russko-Estonskii Razgovornik. 256p. (Rus. & Estonian.). 1976. $1.00 (Pub. by Valgus). Four Continent.

Rott, N. V., ed. Malaiziisko-Russko-Angliiskii Slovar. 400p. (Malay, Rus. & Eng.). 1977. $7.75 (Pub. by Russkii Iazyk). Four Continent.

Rozanova, V. V., ed. Kratkii Tolkovyi Slovar' Russkogo Iazyka: Dlia Inostransev. (Russkii iazyk Ser.). 228p. (Rus.). 1977. $7.50 (O-111). Four Continent.

--Kratkii Tolkovyi Slovar Russkogo Iazyka. (Rus.). 1979. $5.95 (Pub. by Russkii Iazyk). Four Continent.

Rozental, D. E. Russko-Ital'ianskii Ucxhebnyi Slovar. 712p. (Rus. & Ital.). 1966. $2.75 (Pub. by Sov. Entsiklopediia). Four Continent.

Rozental, D. E., et al. Slovar Trudnostei Russkogo Iazyka. (Russkii iazyk Ser.). 694p. (Rus.). 1981. $5.95. Four Continent.

Rozkovcova, L. Z. & Hanusova, S. Stary. Rustina pro Vedecke a Odborne Pracovniky, 2 vols. 208p. (Rus. & Czech.). 1977. 27.00 Kcs. Academia.

Russian-Arabic Dictionary. 1056p. (Rus. & Arabic.). 1979. Leatherette $26.95 (ISBN 0-686-97414-X, M-9073). French & Eur.

Russian-Chinese Dictionary of Export & Economics. 708p. (Rus. & Chinese.). 1961. leatherette $6.95 (ISBN 0-686-92108-9, M-9068). French & Eur.

Russian-German Dictionary. 919p. (Rus. & Ger.). 1960. leatherette $17.50 (ISBN 0-686-92130-5, M-9075). French & Eur.

Russko-Azerbaidzhanskii Slovar, 3 vols. (Rus. & Azerbaijani.). 1971. $28.95 set (Pub. by Elm). Four Continent.

Russko-Chechenskii Slovar. 728p. (Rus.). 1978. $10.95 (Dist. by Four Continent Bk). Russkii Iazyk.

Russko-Latinsko-Uzbekskii Slovar. 188p. (Rus. , Lat. & Uzbek.). 1978. $3.95 (Pub. by Meditsina). Four Continent.

Russko-Litovskii Slovar, 2 vols. (Rus.). 1967. $11.95 set (Pub. by Mintis). Four Continent.

Russko-Moldavskii & Moldavsko-Ruskii Shkolnyi Slovar. 336p. (Rus. & Moldavian.). 1969. $1.75 (Pub. by Lumina). Four Continent.

Russko-V'Etnamskii Slovar, 2 vols. (Rus. & Vietnamese.). 1977. $16.25 set (Pub. by Russkii Iazyk). Four Continent.

Sal'nov, N. Al. Russko-Novogrecheskii Karmannyi Slovar. 352p. (Rus. & Ger.). 1965. $1.60 (Pub. by Sov. Entsiklopediia). Four Continent.

Scanlan, George. Harrap's Russian Vocabulary. viii, 103p. (Rus.). E2.95; pap. $2.00. Harrap Co.

Shanskii, N. M. Chetyre Tys Acha Naibolee Upotrebitel Nykh Slov Russkogo Iazyka. 368p. (Rus.). 1978. $6.50 (O-36). Four Continent.

Sharbatov, G. Sh. Russko-Arabskii Uchebnyi Slovar. 1196p. (Rus. & Arabic.). 1979. $16.95 (Pub. by Russki Iazyk). Four Continent.

Shevchenkovskii Slovar: Na Ukrainskom Iazyke, 2 vols. (Rus.). $16.75 (Pub. by Poligrafkniga). Four Continent.

Sinitsyna, G. V. & Mitronova, I. N. Karmannyi Polsko-Russkii & Russko-Polskii Slovar. LC 80-450178. 575p. (Pol. & Rus.). 1978. 1.00 Rub. Russkii Iazyk.

Skvorzova & Maizel. Dizionario italiano-russo. 954p. (Ital. & Rus.). 1963. L.4000.00. Editori Riuniti.

Slovar Antonimov Russkogo Iazyka. 400p. (Rus.). 1978. $4.75 (Pub. by Russkii Iazyk). Four Continent.

Slovar Russkogo Iazyka XVIII Veka. 165p. (Orig., Rus.). 1977. $2.50 (Pub. by Nauka). Four Continent.

Slovar Simonimov Russkogo Iazyka, Vol. 2. 854p. (Rus.). 1971. $5.95 (Pub. by Nauka). Four Continent.

Slovar' Spravochnik po Russkomu Iazyku Dlia Inostrantsev. (MGU Ser.). 128p. (Rus.). 1976. $0.85. Four Continent.

Slovnik Ukrainskoi: T-F, Vol. 10. (Ukrainian.). 1979. $15.95 (Pub. by Naukova Dumka). Four Continent.

Slovosochetaniia Russkogo Iazyka. 368p. (Rus.). 1979. $5.95 (Pub. by Russkii Iazyk). Four Continent.

Solov'ev, V. Moldavsko-Russkii Frazeologicheskii Slovar. 224p. (Rus. Moldavian.). 1976. $2.00 (Pub. by Lumina). Four Continent.

Strumilin, S. G., ed. Slovar Semiletki. 397p. (Rus.). 1960. $1.95 (Pub. by Politizdat). Four Continent.

Stypula, Ryszard, et al. Slownik Polsko-Rosyjski. LC 76-531554. 840p. (Pol. & Rus.). 1976. 2.58 Rub. Wiedza Powszechna.

--Podreczny Slownik Polsko-Rosyjski. LC 77-502170. 840p. (Pol. & Rus.). 1976. 80.00 Zl. Wiedza Powszechna.

Szabo, Miklos. Orosz-Magyar Szotar Iskolak Szamara, 2 vols. LC 80-467907. (Eng., Rus. & Hungarian.). 1978. 21.50 Ft (ISBN 9-6305-1611-X). Akademiai Kiado.

Tamm, J. Estonsko-Russkii Slovar. 757p. (Estonian & Rus.). 1977. $8.50 (Pub. by Valgus). Four Continent.

Teselkin, A. S., et al. Indoneziisko-Russkii Uchebnyi Slovar. 577p. (Rus. & Indonesian.). 1974. $2.35 (Pub. by Sov Entsiklopediia). Four Continent.

Tikhonov, A. N. Shkol' Nyi Slovoobrazovatel Nyi' Slovar' Russkogo Iazyka: Posobie dlia Uchaschikhsia. (Prosveshchenie Ser.). 728p. (Rus.). 1977. $3.95. Four Continent.

Tolkovyi Slovar Belorusskogo Iazyka, 3 vols. (Rus.). 1977. $14.95 ea. (Pub. by Glav. Red. Bel. Entsiklopedii). Vol. 1, 1977, 608p. Vol. 2, 1978, 768p. Vol. 3, 1979, 672p. Four Continent.

Tolkovyi Slovar Zhivogo Velikorusskogo Iazyka, 4 vols, Vol. 4. (Rus.). 1980. $16.95 (Pub. by Russkii Iazyk). Four Continent.

Tsintsius, V. I. Russko-Evenskii Slovar. 778p. (Rus.). 1952. $4.50 (Pub. by GINS). Four Continent.

U Chin Vei, et al. Karmannyi Russko-Birmanskii Slovar. (Rus. & Burmese.). 1962. $2.50 (Pub. by GINS). Four Continent.

Ul'Tsiferov, O. G. Khindi-Russkii Uchebnyi Slovar. 744p. (Rus.). 1962. $2.75 (Pub. by GINS). Four Continent.

Universal Russian Dictionary. 560p. (Rus.). $2.95 (096). Langenscheidt.

Ushakov, D. N., ed. Tolkovyi Slovar Russkogo Iazyka, 4 vols. 0 ed. (Rus.). 1940. Set $95.00. Four Continent.

Ushakov, D. N., et al. Orfograficheskii Slovar' (Proveshchenie Ser.). 224p. (Rus.). 1977. $1.20 (O-29). Four Continent.

Vakharos, I., et al. Finsko-Russkii Slovar. 815p. (Finnish & Rus.). 1977. $25.50 (Pub. by Russkii Iazyk). Four Continent.

Valenius, A. P. Kratkii Russko-Shvedskii Slovar. 400p. (Rus.). 1948. $2.50 (Pub. by GINS). Four Continent.

Vandelli, Canzio. Dizionario fraseologico di russo-italiano e viceversa. (Rus. & Ital.). 1977. L.24000.00. Mondini Siccardi.

Vangmark, Helge. Dansk-Russik Ordbog. LC 79-396749. 238p. (Rus. & Danish.). 1979. Kr.112.50 (ISBN 8-74297-608-1). Grafisk Forlag.

Vascenco, Victor. Dictionar de Buzunar Roman-Rus. 2nd ed. LC 75-410353. 443p. (Romanian & Rus.). 1975. write for info. Editura Stiintifica.

Vencovska, Marta. Cesko-Rusky Slovnik na Cesty, 2 vols. LC 77-563463. (Illus., Czech. & Rus.). 1976. 20.00 Kcs. SNTC.

Vlchek. Russian-Czechoslovakian Dictionary. 896p. (Rus. & Czech.). 1974. $17.95 (ISBN 0-686-92111-9, M-9116). French & Eur.

Yaselman. Diccionario ruso-espanol. (Rus. & Span.). 160.00 ptas. Aguilar SP.

Zarubin, S. F. Russko-Iaponskii Slovar. 818p. (Rus. & Japanese.). 1964. $16.50 (Pub. by Sov. Entsiklopediia). Four Continent.

Zingitis, A. Russko-Latyshskii Politekhnicheskii Slovar. 568p. (Rus.). 1977. $10.75 (Pub. by Liesma). Four Continent.

Zudin, P. B. Russko-Afganskii Slovar. 1176p. (Rus. & Afghani.). 1955. $4.25 (Pub. by GINS). Four Continent.

RUSSIAN LANGUAGE–DICTIONARIES–ENGLISH

Akhmanova, O. S. Russko-Angliiskii Slovar. 766p. (Rus. & Eng.). 1977. $14.25 (Pub. by Russkii Iazyk). Four Continent.

Akhmanova, O. S. & Wilson, E. English-Russian Dictionary. 639p. (Rus. & Eng.). 1979. $9.95 (ISBN 0-686-97370-4, M-9115). French & Eur.

Akhmanova, O. S., ed. Anglo-Russkii Slovar. 640p. (Eng. & Rus.). 1979. $3.85 (Pub. by Russkii Iazyk). Four Continent.

Akhmanova, Ol'ga S. Russko-Angliiskii. LC 80-490199. 520p. (Eng. & Rus.). 1979. Rs.1.20. Russkii Iazyk.

Akhmanova, Olga S. & Wilson, Elizabeth A. Russko-Angliisku Slovar-Russian-English Dictionary. LC 80-490199. 520p. (Rus.). 1979. write for info. Russkii Iazyk.

Akmanova, A. English-Russian Dictionary. 590p. (Eng. & Rus.). 1980. $25.00x (ISBN 0-569-00012-2, Pub. by Collet's). State Mutual Bk.

Alekseev, P. M. English-Russian Glossary of Physics Terms. 288p. (Eng. & Rus.). 1980. $35.00x (ISBN 0-686-44696-8, Pub. by Collets). State Mutual Bk.

Anglo-Russkii Razgovornik Dlia Turistov. 272p. (Eng. & Rus.). 1978. $8.25 (Pub. by Russkii Iazyk). Four Continent.

Anglo-Russkii Razgovornik Dlia Turistov. 272p. (Eng. & Rus.). 1979. $2.95 (Pub. by Russkii Iazyk). Four Continent.

Anosova, N. N., et al. Bolsho i anglo-russki i slovar, 2 vols. LC 80-482048. (Eng. & Rus.). 1979. vol. 1 16.20 Rub. vol. 2 17.20 Rub. Russkii Iazyk.

Anpilogova, B. G., et al. Foundation Dictionary of Russian: Three Thousand High Semantic Frequency Words. Orig. Title: Essential Russian-English Dictionary. (Rus. & Eng.). (YA) (gr. 9-12). 1967. pap. $3.00 (ISBN 0-486-21860-0). Dover.

Arakin, T. English-Russian Dictionary. 988p. (Eng. & Rus.). 1980. $35.00x (ISBN 0-569-00013-0, Pub. by Collets). State Mutual Bk.

Arakin, V. D. English-Russian Dictionary. (Eng. & Rus.). 1980. leatherette $19.95 (ISBN 0-686-97371-2, M-9107). French & Eur.

Arakin, V. D., et al, eds. Anglo-Russkii Slovar. 808p. (Eng. & Rus.). 1980. $8.95 (Pub. by Russkii Iazyk). Four Continent.

Basic Dictionary Russian-English. 185p. (Rus. & Eng.). write for info. Esselte Studium.

Basic Russian-English Dictionary. (Rus. & Eng.). 1973. pap. $5.95 (ISBN 0-88436-063-6, 65254). EMC.

Carpovich, Eugene A. Russian-English Biological & Medical Dictionary. 2nd ed. LC 58-7915. (Rus. & Eng.). 1960. $25.00 (ISBN 0-911484-01-9). Tech Dict.

Congrat-Butlar, Stefan, ed. Russian Vest Pocket Dictionary. (Rus.). 1974. $2.95 (ISBN 0-394-40068-2). Random.

Coulson, J., ed. The Pocket Oxford Russian-English Dictionary. (Rus. & Eng.). 1975. $12.95x (ISBN 0-19-864113-3). Oxford U Pr.

Coulson, Jessie, et al, eds. The Pocket Oxford Russian Dictionary: Russian-English - English-Russian. (Rus. & Eng.). 1981. pap. $10.95x (ISBN 0-19-864122-2). Oxford U Pr.

Coulson, Jessie S. The Pocket Oxford Russian-English Dictionary. LC 75-316760. vii, 397p. (Eng. & Rus.). 1975. E2.50 (ISBN 0-19-864113-3). Imprint of Oxford U Pr.

Daum, V. & Schenk. Dictionary of Russian Verbs (Russian-English) 750p. (Rus. & Eng.). 1980. $75.00x (ISBN 0-569-08093-2, Pub. by Collet's). State Mutual Bk.

Folomkina, V. & Weiser, T. Learner's English-Russian Dictionary. 655p. (Eng. & Rus.). 1980. $15.00x (ISBN 0-569-05869-4, Pub. by Collet's). State Mutual Bk.

Galperin, I. R., ed. Bolshoi Anglo-Russkii Slovar, 2 vols. (Rus. & Eng.). 1977. $35.00 set (Pub. by Russkii Iazyk). Four Continent.

Garfield, E. Transliterated Dictionary of the Russian Language. LC 79-14068. (Rus.). 1979. lib. bdg. $25.00 (ISBN 0-89495-003-7); pap. $14.95 (ISBN 0-89495-011-8). ISI Pr.

Gerwick, Ben C., Jr. & Peters, V. P., eds. Russian-English Dictionary of Prestressed Concrete & Concrete Construction. 120p. (Rus. & Eng.). 1966. 33.00x (ISBN 0-677-00260-2). Gordon.

Gribble, Charles E. Short Dictionary of Eighteenth Century Russian. (Rus.). 1976. soft cover $8.95 (ISBN 0-89357-039-7). Slavica.

Harrison, W. & LeFlemming, Svetlana. Russian-English & English-Russian Dictionary. (Routledge Pocket Dictionaries Ser.). 580p. (Orig.). 1981. pap. $8.95 (ISBN 0-7100-0800-7). Routledge & Kegan.

Harrison, William & Le Fleming, Svetlana. Russian-English, English-Russian Dictionary. 1973. $14.00 (ISBN 0-7100-6960-X). Routledge & Kegan.

Heron, Patricia A. Russian-English Integrated Dictionary, 2 vols. LC 76-369716. xv, 583p. (Eng. & Rus.). 1975. write for info. Univ Aston.

Hugo Pocket Dictionary: Russian-English, English-Russian. 658p. (Rus. & Eng.). 1975. $3.50 (ISBN 0-8226-0506-6, 506). Littlefield.

Karasaev, Aisash T., et al. Russko-Chechenskii Slovar. LC 79-370228. 728p. (Rus. & Chechen.). 1978. 3.80 Rub. Russkii Iazyk.

Khaikin, Ia. B. Anglo-Russkii Slovar Dorozhnika. 319p. (Eng. & Rus.). 1956. $3.35 (Pub. by Izd. Avtotrnsport. Lit.). Four Continent.

Konarski, M. M. Russian-English Space Technology Dictionary. LC 72-99990. (Rus. & Eng.). 1970. $77.00 (ISBN 0-08-015617-7). Pergamon.

Lapidus, B. A. & Shevisova, S. V. Learner's Russian-English Dictionary for Foreign Students of Russian. 2nd ed. LC 78-342111. 552p. (Rus. & Eng.). 1977. 141.00 Kop. Russica.

Lapidus, B. A. & Shevtsova, S. V. Learner's Russian-English Dictionary. (Rus. & Eng.). 1963. pap. $9.95 (ISBN 0-262-62002-2). MIT Pr.

Leontev, A. A. Slovar Assotsiativnykh Norm Russkogo Iazyka. 192p. (Rus.). 1977. $2.25 (Pub. by MGU). Four Continent.

Mironova, Inessa N. Slownik Kieszonkowy Polsko-Rosyjski. LC 80-450178. 575p. (Pol. & Rus.). 1978. 1.00 Rub. Russkii Iazyk.

Muller, V. English-Russian Dictionary. 888p. (Eng. & Rus.). 1980. vinyl $42.00x (ISBN 0-569-08362-1, Pub. by Collet's). State Mutual Bk.

Muller, V. K., ed. English-Russian Dictionary. rev. ed. (Eng. & Rus.). 1973. $24.75 (ISBN 0-525-09881-X, 02403-720). Dutton.

New English-Russian Dictionary, 2 vols. 1685p. (Eng. & Rus.). 1980. Set. $80.00x (ISBN 0-569-07330-8, Pub. by Collet's). State Mutual Bk.

Parsons, Charles. Russian-English Dictionary of irovat' Verbs. 34p. (Orig., Rus. & Eng.). 1983. $10.00x (ISBN 0-917564-14-6). Translation Research.

Pocket-Shorter Dictionary. 600p. (Rus. & Eng.). $5.95 (090). Langenscheidt.

Rainich, Gabrielle & Kuipers, A. H., eds. Russian-English Vocabulary with Grammatical Sketch. 66p. (Rus. & Eng.). 1980. Repr. of 1972 ed. with corrections $9.00 (ISBN 0-8218-0037-X, REV). Am Math.

Razgovornik Dlia Avtoturistov: Anglo-Russkii. 280p. (Rus. & Eng.). 1979. $4.25 (Pub. by Russkii Iazyk). Four Continent.

Rozenberg, M. B. English-Russian Dictionary of Refrigeration & Low Temperature Technology. 2nd, rev. ed. $73.00 (ISBN 0-08-024737-7). Pergamon.

Russian-English Monograph Series: Skorost' 52p. (Orig., Rus. & Eng.). 1979. pap. $5.00x (ISBN 0-917564-07-3). Translation Research.

Shipp, James F. Russian-English Dictionary of Abbreviations & Initialisms. viii, 637p. (Orig., Rus. & Eng.). 1982. flexi $60.00x (ISBN 0-917564-12-X). Translation Research.

Shvarts, Vladimir. The Concise Illustrated Russian-English Dictionary of Mechanical Engineering. 224p. (Rus. & Eng.). 1980. $35.00x (ISBN 0-686-44774-3, Pub. by Collets). State Mutual Bk.

Smirnitskii, T. Russian-English Dictionary. 766p. (Rus. & Eng.). 1980. $42.00x (ISBN 0-569-00006-8, Pub. by Collet's). State Mutual Bk.

Smirnitsky, A. I. Russian English Dictionary. rev. ed. (Rus. & Eng.). 1973. $24.75 (ISBN 0-525-19520-3, 02403-720). Dutton.

--Russian-English Dictionary. 3rd ed. large ed. $27.50 (ISBN 0-87557-066-6, 066-6). Saphrograph.

Taube, A. M. Russian-English Dictionary. 832p. (Rus. & Eng.). 1980. vinyl bds. $25.00x (ISBN 0-569-06453-8, Pub. by Collet's). State Mutual Bk.

--Russko-Angliiskii Slovar. 832p. (Rus. & Eng.). 1979. $8.95 (Pub. by Russkii Iazyk). Four Continent.

Taube, A. M., et al. Russian-English Dictionary. Daglish, R. C., ed. 831p. (Rus. & Eng.). 1978. leatherette $17.95 (ISBN 0-686-92120-8, M-9108). French & Eur.

U. S. War Department. Dictionary of Spoken Russian: Russian-English: English-Russian. (Rus. & Eng.). 1959. pap. $8.95 (ISBN 0-486-20496-0). Dover.

Wedel, E. & Romanov, A., eds. Langenscheidt's Pocket Russian Dictionary: Russian-English, English-Russian. (Langenscheidt Pocket Dictionaries Ser.). 592p. (Eng. & Rus.). 1969. $5.95 (ISBN 0-685-31322-0). Am Map.

Wheeler, Marcus & Unbegaun, B. O., eds. The Oxford Russian-English Dictionary. (Rus. & Eng.). 1972. $55.00 (ISBN 0-19-864111-7). Oxford U Pr.

Zaimovskii, S. G. Concise English-Russian, Russian-English Dictionary. 464p. (Eng. & Rus.). 1980. $20.00x (ISBN 0-569-06089-3, Pub. by Collet's). State Mutual Bk.

Zaimovsky, S. G. Kratkii Anglo-Russkii i Russko-Angliiskii. 464p. (Rus. & Eng.). 1978. $2.75 (Pub. by Russkii Iazyk). Four Continent.

--Russian-English, English-Russian Dictionary. pap. $8.50 (ISBN 0-685-20192-9, 069-0). Saphrograph.

RUSSIAN LANGUAGE–DICTIONARIES–FRENCH

Dictionnaire Bilingue Francais-Russe et Russe-Francais. (Fr. & Rus.). $10.50 (ISBN 2-03-020904-X, 2715, Apollo). Larousse.

Karmannyi Russko-Frantsuzskii Slovar. 620p. (Rus. & Fr.). 1960. $1.50. Four Continent.

Korina, N. B., et al. Frantsuzsko-Russkii Uchebnyi Slovar. 668p. (Fr. & Rus.). 1977. $8.50 (Pub. by Russkii Iazyk). Four Continent.

Kratkii Russko-Frantsuzskii Uchebnyi Slovar. 688p. (Rus. & Fr.). 1969. $2.75 (Pub. by Sov Entsiklopediia). Four Continent.

Pauliat, P. Dictionnaire russe-francais. (Rus. & Fr.). $11.95 (ISBN 0-685-13884-4, 3790). Larousse.

Pototskaia, V. V., et al. Russko-Frantsuzskii Slovar. 677p. (Rus. & Fr.). 1971. $2.25 (Pub. by Sov. Entsiklopediia). Four Continent.

Vygodskaia, K. S. Karmannyi Frantsuzsko-Russkii Slovar. 648p. (Fr. & Rus.). 1960. $1.75 (Pub. by GINS). Four Continent.

Vygodskaia, K. S., et al. Kratkii Frantsuzsko-Russkii i Russko-Frantsuzskii Slovar. 655p. (Fr. & Rus.). 1968. $2.00 (Pub. by Sov Entsiklopediia). Four Continent.

Zandreitere, I. Frantsuzsko-Russkii Illiustrirovannyi Slovar. (Illus.). 772p. (Fr. & Rus.). 1957. $3.50 (Pub. by Latv Valstsnent Bk). Four Continent.

RUSSIAN LANGUAGE–ETYMOLOGY

Chanski, N. Dictionnaire Etymologique de la Langue Russe, 1, A-J, 5 vols. 400p. (Rus.). 1961. 45.80 F. MIR.

--Dictionnaire Etymologique de la Langue Russe, 3 vols. (Rus.). 1975. 15.85 F. MIR.

Shanskii, N. M. Etimologicheskii Slovar Russkogo Iazyka: Tom. 1, Vyp. 4 (G) 215p. (Rus.). 1972. $2.70 (Pub. by MGU). Four Continent.

--Etimologicheskii Slovar Russkogo Iazyka: Tom. 1, Vyp. 5 (D, E, Zh) 304p. (Rus.). 1973. $3.60 (Pub. by MGU). Four Continent.

--Etimologicheskii Slovar Russkogo Iazyka: Tom. 2, Vyp. 6 (Z) 124p. (Rus.). 1975. $1.00 (Pub. by MGU). Four Continent.

--Etimologichesskii Slovar Russkogo Iazyka: Tom. 2, Vyp. 7 (I) 152p. (Rus.). 1978. $2.50 (Pub. by MGU). Four Continent.

Shanskii, N. M., ed. Etimologicheskii Slovar Russkogo Iazyka: Tom. 1, Vyp. 3 (V) 284p. (Rus.). 1968. $3.25 (Pub. by MGU). Four Continent.

Shanskii, N. M., et al. Kratkii Etimologicheskii Slovar Russkogo Iazyka. 542p. (Rus.). 1975. $3.65 (Pub. by Proveschchenie). Four Continent.

Tsyganenko. Dictionnaire Etymologique de la Langue Russe. (Rus.). 8.60 F. MIR.

Vasmer, Max. Russich Elymologisches Woerterbuch, Vol. 1. (Rus. & Ger.). 1953. $68.00 (ISBN 3-533-00665-4, M-7608, Pub. by Carl Winter). French & Eur.

--Russich Etymologishes Woerterbuch, Vol. 1. (Rus. & Ger.). 1953. $68.00 (ISBN 3-533-00665-4). Winter Univ.

--Russisch Etymologisches Woerterbuch, Vol. 2. (Rus. & Ger.). 1955. $68.00 (ISBN 3-533-00666-2, M-7609, Pub. by Carl Winter). French & Eur.

--Russisch Etymologisches Woerterbuch, Vol. 2. (Rus. & Ger.). 1955. $68.00 (ISBN 3-533-00666-2). Winter Univ.

--Russisch Etymologisches Woerterbuch, Vol. 3. (Rus. & Ger.). 1958. $68.00 (ISBN 3-533-00667-0, M-7610, Pub. by Carl Winter). French & Eur.

--Russisch Etymologisches Woerterbuch, Vol. 3. (Rus. & Ger.). 1958. $68.00 (ISBN 3-533-00667-0). Winter Univ.

Wolkonsky, Catherine & Poltoratzky, Marianna. Handbook of Russian Roots. LC 61-1403. (Columbia Slavic Studies). (Rus.). 1961. $32.50x (ISBN 0-231-02117-8). Columbia U Pr.

RUSSIAN LANGUAGE–GLOSSARIES, VOCABULARIES, ETC.

Buchkina, B. Z., et al. Slitno Ili Razdelno. 480p. (Rus.). 1976. $2.40 (Pub. by Russkii Iazyk). Four Continent.

Daum, E. & Schenk, W. A Directory of Russian Verbs. 748p. (Eng. & Rus.). 1974. $17.50. Hippocrene Bks.

Kotoleva, N. Z., ed. Novoe V Russkoi Leksike. 176p. (Rus.). 1980. $2.85 (Pub. by Russkii Iazyk). Four Continent.

Naibolee Upotrebitel'Nykh Slov Russkogo. 368p. (Rus.). 1978. $6.50 (Pub. by Russkii Iazyk). Four Continent.

Palevskaia, M. F. Materialy Frazeologicheskogo Slovaria Russkogo Iazka XVIII Veka. 368p. (Rus.). 1980. $9.25 (Pub. by Shtiintsa). Four Continent.

Potikha, Z. A. Shkol'nyi Slovoobrazovatel'Nyi Slovar. Barkhudarov, S. G., ed. 390p. (Rus.). 1964. pap. text ed. 1.65 Rub (Pub. by Proveschchenie). Four Continent.

Pronin, Alex. Russian Vocabulary Builder, Seven Verbs a Day. (Rus.). $5.50 (ISBN 0-87505-314-9, Pub. by Lawrence). Borden.

Ruzicka, Rudolf. A Dictionary of Russian Verbs. 748p. (Rus.). 1974. $17.50 (Dist. by Four Continent). Hippocrene Bks.

Slaovosochetaniia Russkogo Iazyka. 368p. (Rus.). 1979. $5.95 (Pub. by Russkii Iazyk). Four Continent.

Tikhonov, A. N. Shkolnyi Slovo-Obrazovatel'Nyislovar Russkogo Iazyka. 728p. (Rus.). 1978. $3.95 (Pub. by Prosveschchenie). Four Continent.

Vocabularios Japones-Espanol-Ruso. (Japanese, Span. & Rus.). $0.80; Mex.$10.00. Novaro.

RUSSIAN LANGUAGE–GRAMMAR

see also Russian Language–Technical Russian

Parsons, Charles. Russian-English Dictionary of...(a,e,i,ya) tel' Words. 32p. (Orig., Rus. & Eng.). 1980. pap. $6.00x (ISBN 0-917564-08-1). Translation Research.

Potapova, N. Learn Russian, Bks. 1-4. (Rus.). pap. $5.50 ea.; Set. pap. $22.00 (ISBN 0-87557-073-9). Saphrograph.

RUSSIAN LANGUAGE–IDIOMS, CORRECTIONS, ERRORS

Dubrovin, M. Russkie Frazeologizmy v Kartinkakh. 352p. (Rus.). 1980. $4.25 (Pub. by Russkii Iazyk). Four Continent.

Dubrovin, M. I. A Book of Russian Idioms. (Illus.). 350p. (Rus. & Eng.). 1980. $4.25 (K-32). Four Continent.

Orudzhev, A. Azerbaidzhansko-Russkii Frazeogicheskii (Idiomaticheskii) Slovar. 278p. (Rus.). 1976. $3.95 (Pub. by Elm). Four Continent.

Shansky, N. & Bystrova, E. Seven Hundred Russian Idioms & Set Phrases. (Russkii iazyk Ser.). 120p. (Rus. & Eng.). 1980. $1.50. Four Continent.

RUSSIAN LANGUAGE–LEXICOGRAPHY

Anisimova, T. I. Posobie Po Leksicheskoi Sochetaemosti Slov Russkogo Iazyka. 303p. (Rus.). 1975. $3.25 (Pub. by Vysheishaia Shkola). Four Continent.

RUSSIAN LANGUAGE–ORTHOGRAPHY AND SPELLING

Barkhudarova. Dictionnaire Orthographique de la Langue Russe. 1040p. (Rus.). 1963. 15.30 F. Mir.

Orfograficheskii Slovar Russkogo Iazyka. 480p. (Rus.). 1977. $4.50 (Pub. by Russkii Iazyk). Four Continent.

Poretskaia, R. E. Orfograficheskii Morskoi Slovar. 293p. (Rus.). 1974. $2.50 (Pub. by Voenizdat). Four Continent.

Ushakov, D. N., et al. Orfograficheskii Slovar. 224p. (Rus.). 1973. $1.00 (Pub. by Prosveschchenie). Four Continent.

RUSSIAN LANGUAGE–READERS

Kent, Rosalind. Reading the Russian Language: A Guide for Librarians & Other Professionals. (Books in Library & Information Science Ser., Vol. 9). (Rus.). 1974. $30.75 (ISBN 0-8247-6236-3). Dekker.

Kotz, Samuel. Russian-English Dictionary & Reader in the Cybernetical Sciences. 1966. $49.00 (ISBN 0-12-422450-4). Acad Pr.

RUSSIAN LANGUAGE–READERS (SCIENCE)

Kompleksnyi Chastotnyi Slovar Russko Nauchnoi & Tekhnicheskoi Leksiki. 408p. (Rus.). 1978. $6.35 (Pub. by Russkii Iazyk). Four Continent.

RUSSIAN LANGUAGE–SPOKEN RUSSIAN

Four Thousand Naibolee Upotrebitel'nykh Slov Russkogo Iazyka. 368p. (Rus.). 1978. $6.50 (Pub. by Russkii Iazyk). Four Continent.

U.S. War Dept., ed. A Phrase & Sentence Dictionary of Spoken Russian. (Eng. & Rus.). pap. $7.50. Imported bks.

RUSSIAN LANGUAGE–TECHNICAL RUSSIAN

see also Russian Language–Readers (Science)

Desov. Concise English-Russian
Technical Dictionary. (Eng. &
Rus.). $5.50. Imported Bks.
Kompleksnyi Chastotnyi Slovar
Russko Nauchnoi & Tekhnicheskoi
Leksiki. 408p. (Rus.). 1978. $6.35
(Pub. by Russkii Iazyk). Four
Continent.

RUSSIAN LANGUAGE, OLD
see Russian Language–To 1700
**RUSSIAN LITERATURE–
BIBLIOGRAPHY**
Harkins, William E. Dictionary of
Russian Literature. LC 75-139135.
1971. Repr. of 1956 ed. lib. bdg.
$22.25x (ISBN 0-8371-5751-X,
HARL). Greenwood.
Oesterby, M., ed. Dictionary of the
Russian Academy, 7 vols. (Rus.).
1981. Repr. of 1822 ed. Set.
$650.00 (ISBN 0-915346-75-3). A
Wofsy Fine Arts.

RUSSIAN PRISONERS
see Prisoners, Russian
RUST
see Corrosion and Anti-Corrosives
RUSTLESS COATINGS
see Corrosion and Anti-Corrosives
RUTHENIAN LANGUAGE
see Ukrainian Language

S

SAAM LANGUAGE
see Lapp Language
**SABAEN LANGUAGE–
GRAMMAR**
Biella, Joan C. Dictionary of Old
South Arabic: Sabaen Dialect. LC
81-8946. (Harvard Semitic
Studies). (Arabic). 1982. $33.00
(ISBN 0-89130-455-X, 04-04-25).
Scholars Pr CA.
SACRED ART
see Christian Art and Symbolism
SAFETY, INDUSTRIAL
see Industrial Safety
SAFETY APPLIANCES
see also Accidents–Prevention
Miller, B. D. Local Warning System
Definition. LC 70-141214. 147p.
1970. $19.50 (ISBN 0-686-01960-
1). Mgmt Info Serv.
SAFETY ENGINEERING
see Industrial Safety
SAFETY MEASURES
see Industrial Safety
SAHARA
Capot-Rey, Robert & Blaudin De
The, Bernard. Glossaire des
Principaux Termes Geographiques
& Logiques Sahariens. (Illus.). 84p.
(Fr.). 1963. 10.00 F. Sahariennes
Inst. Rech.
Hodges, Tony. Historical Dictionary
of Western Sahara. LC 81-21251.
(African Historical Dictionaries
Ser.: No. 35). 473p. 1982. $28.50
(ISBN 0-8108-1497-8). Scarecrow.
SAILING
*see also Boats and Boating;
Navigation; Yachts and Yachting*
Alfaro Perez, Juan. Diccionario
Maritimo y De Construccion
Naval. 478p. (Span. & Eng.). 1976.
leather $53.95 (ISBN 84-7079-081-
1, S-50094). French & Eur.
Barberousse, Michel. Dizionario della
vela, 2 vols. 640p. (Ital.). 1978.
L.14800.00. Mursia S.
Barberousse, Michel, ed. Dictionnaire
de la Voile. 256p. (Fr.). 1970. pap.
$14.95 (ISBN 0-686-56828-1, M-
6606). French & Eur.
Bathe, Basel & Villiers, Alan. The
Visual Encyclopedia of Nautical
Terms Under Sail. (Illus.). 1978.
$15.95 (ISBN 0-517-53317-0).
Crown.
Garmendia y Berasategui, Ignacio de.
Diccionario Maritimo Ilustrado
Vasco-Castellano, Castellano-
Vasco. (Vasco & Span.). $49.50
(ISBN 84-248-0047-8, S-50054).
French & Eur.
Kahane, Henry, et al. Glossario degli
antichi portolani italiani. (Illus.).
134p. (Ital.). 1968. L.8000.00.
Olschki.
Martinez Hidalgo Teran, Jose M.
Diccionario Nautico. 540p. (Span.,
Eng. & Fr.). 1977. leather $56.00
(ISBN 84-7079-058-7, S-50095).
French & Eur.

Rousmaniere, John. A Glossary of
Modern Sailing Terms. LC 75-
31504. (Illus.). 254p. 1976. $6.95
(ISBN 0-396-07006-X). Dodd.
SAILORS
see Seamen
SAINTS
*see also Hagiography; Martyrs
also names of Saints, e.g. Teresa,
Saint*
Petin, L. M. Dictionnaire
Hagiographique, 2 vols. Migne, J.
P., ed. (Encyclopedie Theologique
Ser.: Vols. 40-41). 1580p. (Fr.).
Repr. of 1850 ed. lib. bdg.
$240.00x (ISBN 0-89241-246-1).
Caratzas Pub Co.
Pierrard, Pierre. Dictionnaire des
Prenoms & des Saints. 224p. (Fr.).
1975. 17.60 F. Larousse.
SALES
Mireur, H. Dictionnaire des Ventes
d'art Faites en France & a
l'etranger, 1. (Illus., Fr.). 1912.
DM.118.00. Olms Verlag.
––Dictionnaire des Ventes d'art
Faites en France & a l'etranger, 2.
(Illus., Fr.). 1912. DM.118.00.
Olms Verlag.
––Dictionnaire des Ventes d'art
Faites en France & a l'etranger, 3.
(Illus., Fr.). 1912. DM.118.00.
Olms Verlag.
––Dictionnaire des Ventes d'art
Faites en France & a l'etranger, 4.
(Illus., Fr.). 1912. DM.118.00.
Olms Verlag.
––Dictionnaire des Ventes d'art
Faites en France & a l'etranger, 5.
(Illus., Fr.). 1912. DM.118.00.
Olms Verlag.
––Dictionnaire des Ventes d'art
Faites en France & a l'etranger, 6.
(Illus., Fr.). 1912. DM.118.00.
Olms Verlag.
SALISH INDIANS
*see Indians of North America–
Northwest, Pacific*
SALISH LANGUAGE
Hess, Thom. A Dictionary of Puget
Salish. LC 75-42197. (Illus.). 766p.
1976. $21.50x (ISBN 0-295-95436-
1). U of Wash Pr.
SALISHAN INDIANS
*see Indians of North America–
Northwest, Pacific*
SALVADOR
Flemion, Philip F. Historical
Dictionary of El Salvador. LC 78-
189546. (Latin American
Historical Dictionaries Ser.: No.
5). 1972. $13.00 (ISBN 0-8108-
0471-9). Scarecrow.
––Historical Dictionary of El
Salvador. 1972. $7.50 ea. Intl
Guatemala.
Geoffroy Rivas, Pedro. La Lengua
Salvadorena. LC 79-121608. 131p.
(Span., San Salvador). 1978. write
for info. Direccion de
Publicaciones.
SAMOAN LANGUAGE
Neffgen, H. Grammar & Vocabulary
of the Samoan Language. Stock,
Arnold B., tr. from Ger. LC 75-
35206. (Samoan). Repr. of 1918
ed. $18.00 (ISBN 0-404-14229-X).
AMS Pr.
Violette, Louis. Dictionnaire Samoa-
Francais-Anglais et Francais-
Samoa-Anglais. LC 75-35215. (Fr.
& Eng.). Repr. of 1879 ed. $44.50
(ISBN 0-404-14238-9). AMS Pr.
SAMPLING (STATISTICS)
see also Quality Control
American Society for Quality
Control. Terms, Symbols &
Definitions for Acceptance
Sampling: ANSI-ASQC Standard
a2-1978. $8.50; members $7.00.
Am Soc QC.
SAN FRANCISCO
Michelon, Oscar. Diccionario de San
Francisco. LC 78-370238. xvi,
770p. (Eng., Maya, & Span.). 1976.
S.1600.00 (ISBN 3-201-00972-5).
Akademische Druck Verlagt.
SANITARY AFFAIRS
see Public Health
SANITARY ENGINEERING
*see also Drainage; Municipal
Engineering; Pollution; Refuse and
Refuse Disposal; Sewage; Water-
Supply*
Dictionary of Sewage & Sanitary
Installation Terms. (Hebrew, Eng.,
Fr. & Ger.). IL.6.00. Massada Pr.

SANSKRIT LANGUAGE
Koelver, Bernhard. Verschiffene
Praefixe im Altindischen. LC 78-
391285. 53p (Sanskrit.). 1976.
DM.18.00 (ISBN 3-51502-357-7).
Steiner Verlag.
Kolver, Bernhard. Verschliffene
Prafixe im Altindischen. LC 78-
391285. 53p. (Sanskrit.). 1976.
DM.18.00. Steiner Verlag.
Wezler, Albrecht. Bestimmung &
Angabe der Funktion von
Sekundar-Suffixen Durch Panini.
LC 76-450174. xiii, 155p.
(Sanskrit.). 1975. DM.44.00 (ISBN
3-515-02105-1). Steiner Verlag.
**SANSKRIT LANGUAGE–
DICTIONARIES**
Apte, V. S. Practical Sanskrit-English
Dictionary. rev. ed. (Sanskrit &
Eng.). 1978. Repr. $28.00 (ISBN
0-89684-294-0). Orient Bk Dist.
––Sanskrit-English, English-Sanskrit
Student's Dictionary, 2 vols.
(Sanskrit & Eng.). $40.00 (ISBN 0-
685-36176-4). Heinman.
––The Student's English-Sanskrit
Dictionary, 2 vols. (Sanskrit &
Eng.). 1974. Repr. 9.95 (ISBN 0-8426-
0507-X). Orient Bk Dist.
Banerji, Sures C. Glossary of Smrti
Literature. $6.50x (ISBN 0-8426-
1139-8). Verry.
Edgerton, F. Buddhist Hybrid
Sanskrit Dictionary & Grammar, 2
vols. 864p. (Sanskrit & Eng.).
1972. $65.00x (ISBN 0-87902-218-
3). Orientalia.
––Buddhist Hybrid Sanskrit
Grammer & Dictionary, 2 vols.
(Sanskrit.). 1978. Repr. $56.00 set
(ISBN 0-89684-182-0). Orient Bk
Dist.
Edgerton, Franklin. Buddhist Hybrid
Sanskrit Grammar & Dictionary, 2
vols. Incl. Vol. 1. Grammar; Vol.
2. Dictionary. 896p. (Sanskrit.).
1973. Repr. of 1953 ed. Set.
$45.00x (ISBN 0-8002-0719-X).
Intl Pubns Serv.
––Buddhist Hybrid Sanskrit
Grammar & Dictionary, 2 Vols.
1975. Repr. Set. $60.00x (ISBN 0-
8426-0133-3). Verry.
MacDonnell, Arthur A. Practical
Sanskrit Dictionary: With
Transliteration Accentuation &
Etymological Analysis Throughout.
(Sanskrit). 1924. $37.50x (ISBN
0-19-864303-9). Oxford U Pr.
Monier-Williams. Sanskrit-English
Dictionary. (Sanskrit & Eng.).
1973. $37.00x (ISBN 0-8364-0464-
5). South Asia Bks.
Monier-Williams, Monier, et al.
Sanskrit-English Dictionary. rev.
ed. (Sanskrit & Eng.). 1899.
$105.00x (ISBN 0-19-864308-X).
Oxford U Pr.
Mylius, Klaus. Woerterbuch Sanskrit-
Deutsch. LC 76-506569. 583p.
(Ger. & Sanskrit). 1975. M.86.00.
VEB Verlag Enzyklopadie.
Patkar, Madhukar M. History of
Sanskrit Lexicography. 199p. 1981.
text ed. $14.25x (ISBN 0-391-
02418-3, Pub. by Munshiram
Manoharlal India). Humanities.
Sanskrit-Thai-English Dictionary.
1339p. (Sanskrit, Thai & Eng.).
10.00x (ISBN 0-8002-1951-1). Intl
Pubns Serv.
Scherath, Bernfried. Sanskrit
vocabulary. LC 80-506334. ix,
216p. (Sanskrit.). 1980. fl.pap.
48.00 (ISBN 9-00-406108-8). Brill.
Schlerath, B. Sanskrit Vocabulary
Arranged According to Word
Families with Meanings in English,
German & Spanish. 1980. $35.00
(ISBN 0-686-78392-1). Heinman.
Suryakanta. Sanskrit-Hindi-English
Dictionary. (Sanskrit, Hindi &
Eng.). 1976. $47.50x (ISBN 0-
8002-1950-3). Intl Pubns Serv.
Williams, M. Sanskrit-English
Dictionary. (Sanskrit & Eng.).
1979. $55.00 (ISBN 0-89684-314-
9). Orient Bk Dist.
Williams, M. Monier. Dictionary of
English & Sanskrit. LC 73-495007.
(Eng. & Sanskrit). 1971. Repr. of
1851 ed. 17.50x (ISBN 0-8002-
0172-8). Intl Pubns Serv.
Williams, Monier, et al. Sanskrit-
English Dictionary. 1367p.
(Sanskrit & Eng.). 1981. Repr.
$45.00 (ISBN 0-89581-173-1).
Lancaster-Miller.

WIlliams, Monier. A Dictionary,
English & Sanskrit. 4th ed. (Eng. &
Sanskrit.). 1976. 35.00 (ISBN 0-
89684-193-6). Orient Bk Dist.
**SANSKRIT LANGUAGE–
GRAMMAR**
Abhyankar, Kashinath V. & Shukla,
J. M. A Dictionary of Sanskrit
Grammar. 2nd rev. ed. LC 78-
903053. xv, 448p. (Eng. &
Sanskrit.). 1977. Rs.58.00. Oriental
Institute.
Edgerton, F. Buddhist Hybrid
Sanskrit Dictionary & Grammar, 2
vols. 864p. (Sanskrit & Eng.).
1972. $65.00x (ISBN 0-87902-218-
3). Orientalia.
––Buddhist Hybrid Sanskrit
Grammer & Dictionary, 2 vols.
(Sanskrit.). 1978. Repr. $56.00 set
(ISBN 0-89684-182-0). Orient Bk
Dist.
Edgerton, Franklin. Buddhist Hybrid
Sanskrit Grammar & Dictionary, 2
vols. Incl. Vol. 1. Grammar; Vol.
2. Dictionary. 896p. (Sanskrit.).
1973. Repr. of 1953 ed. Set.
$45.00x (ISBN 0-8002-0719-X).
Intl Pubns Serv.
––Buddhist Hybrid Sanskrit
Grammar & Dictionary, 2 Vols.
1975. Repr. Set. $60.00x (ISBN 0-
8426-0133-3). Verry.
Williams, Monier. Sanskrit Manual
(Enlarged) with a Vocabulary
(English & Sanskrit) (Sanskrit &
Eng.). 1977. text ed. $14.00x
(ISBN 0-8426-1061-8). Verry.
SARCOMA
see Tumors
SATANISM
Baskin, Wade. Dictionary of
Satanism. 1972. pap. $3.95 (ISBN
0-8065-0292-4). Citadel Pr.
SAVING AND INVESTMENT
see also Investments
Beer, Edith L. Monarch's Dictionary
of Investment Terms. 192p.
(Orig.). 1982. pap. $6.95 (ISBN 0-
671-45497-8). Monarch Pr.
**SAVING AND LOAN
ASSOCIATIONS**
see Building and Loan Associations
SAXONS
Berr, Samuel. An Etymological
Glossary to the Old Saxon
Heliand. LC 76-572157. 477p.
1971. pap. $57.50x (ISBN 0-8002-
1269-X). Intl Pubns Serv.
SAYINGS
*see Aphorisms and Apothegms;
Epigrams; Maxims; Proverbs;
Quotations*
SCALES (MUSIC)
see Musical Intervals and Scales
SCANDINAVIAN LANGUAGES
*see also Danish Language; Icelandic
and Old Norse Languages;
Norwegian Language; Swedish
Language*
Hughes, Charles A. Ace's
Scandinavian Phrase Book &
Dictionary. (Ace's Foreign
Phrase). 256p. 1981. pap. $1.95
(ISBN 0-441-75386-8). Ace Bks.
SCARRON, PAUL, 1610-1660
Richardson, Leonard T. Lexique de
la Langue des Oeuvres Burlesques
de Scarron. 286p. (Fr.). 1976.
DM.56.00. Olms.
SCENERY
see Landscape
SCHISM
Pluquet, F. A. Dictionnaire des
Heresies des Erreurs et des
Schismes, 2 vols. Migne, J. P., ed.
(Encyclopedie Theologique Ser.:
Vols. 11-12). 1374p. (Fr.). Repr. of
1847 ed. lib. bdg. $175.00x (ISBN
0-89241-235-6). Caratzas Pub Co.
SCHOLASTICISM
Morin, F. Dictionnaire de
Philosophie et de Theologie
Scolastiques, 2 vols. Migne, J. P.,
ed. (Troisieme et Derniere
Encyclopedie Theologique Ser.:
Vols. 21-22). 1496p. (Fr.). Date
not set. Repr. of 1865 ed. lib. bdg.
$190.00x (ISBN 0-89241-304-2).
Caratzas Pub Co.
SCHOOL ADMINISTRATION
*see School Management and
Organization*
SCHOOL INSPECTION
*see School Management and
Organization*

SCHOOL LIBRARIES

Hayes, Sherman, ed. Primer of Business Terms & Phrases Related to Libraries. 81p. 1978. $1.50. Library Admin.

University Of Chicago - Graduate Library School - 24th Conference. New Definitions of School-Library Service: Proceedings. Fenwick, Sara I., ed. LC 60-2341. (University of Chicago Studies in Library Science). 1960. lib. bdg. $6.00x (ISBN 0-226-24163-7). U of Chicago Pr.

SCHOOL LIFE

see Students

SCHOOL MANAGEMENT AND ORGANIZATION

Here are entered works dealing with the management, organization, supervision, etc. of schools in general, and in the United States as a whole.

see also Teaching

Dejnozka, Edward L. Educational Administration Glossary. LC 83-5719. 224p. 1983. lib. bdg. $35.00 (ISBN 0-313-23301-2, DEA/). Greenwood.

SCHOOL OPERATION POLICIES

see School Management and Organization

SCHOOL ORGANIZATION

see School Management and Organization

SCHOOL TEACHING

see Teaching

SCHOOLS

see also Education; Teachers Colleges; Technical Education; Universities and Colleges

also headings beginning with the word School; and subdivision Study and Teaching under subjects, e.g. Mathematics–Study and Teaching

Diccionario Escuela. 340p. (Span.). Mex.$4.50. Fernandez.

Witty, F. R. Nelson Canadian Elementary School Dictionary. (Eng.). 1975. Can.$pap. 3.30 (ISBN 0-17-600410-6); pap. $3.95 (ISBN 0-17-600411-4). Nelson & Sons Group.

SCHOOLS–INSPECTION

see School Management and Organization

SCHOOLS–MANAGEMENT AND ORGANIZATION

see School Management and Organization

SCHOOLS, COMMERCIAL

see Business Education

SCIENCE

see also Astronomy; Chemistry; Crystallography; Geology; Life Sciences; Mathematics; Meteorology; Mineralogy; Paleontology; Petrology; Physiology; Space Sciences

also headings beginning with the word Scientific

Abkeurzungen & Kurzwoerter aus Technik & Naturwissenschaften: E-D. 859p. (Ger. & Eng.). DM.50.00. Brandstetter.

Abkurzungen & Kurzwoerter aus Technik & Naturwissenschaften. 859p. (Ger.). 1982. DM.50.00. Brandstetter.

Brockhaus der Naturwissenschaften & der Technik. 832p. (Ger.). DM.45.00 (ISBN 3-7653-0019-5). F A Brockhaus.

Diccionario ilustrado de las ciencias pura y aplicades. (Span.). Arg.$35.00; $250.00. Mundi.

Herland. Dictionary of Mathematical Sciences: Band I, German-English. 323p. (Ger. & Eng.). 1982. DM.60.00. Brandstetter.

Kucera. The Compact Dictionary of Exact Science & Technology: Band I, English-German. xix, 571p. (Eng. & Ger.). 1982. DM.55.00. Brandstetter.

--The Compact Dictionary of Exact Science & Technology: Band II, German-English. xiv, 826p. (Ger. & Eng.). 1982. DM.70.00. Brandstetter.

Shemakin, Iu. I., ed. Tezaurus Nauchno-Tekhnicheskikh Terminov. 671p. (Rus.). 1972. $15.00 (Pub. by Voenizdat). Four Continent.

Vocabulaire General d'orientation Scientifique. (Fr.). 17.00 F. Didier.

SCIENCE–ABBREVIATIONS

Murashkevich, A. M. & Vladimirov, O. N. English-Russian Aviation & Space Abbreviations Dictionary. 622p. (Eng. & Rus.). 1981. $45.00x (ISBN 0-686-44706-9, Pub. by Collets). State Mutual Bk.

Wennrich, Peter. Anglo-American & German Abbreviations in Science & Technology. LC 76-151935. (Eng. & Ger.). 1976. write for info. (ISBN 3-7940-1024-8). Bowker.

Zalucki, H. Dictionary of Russian Technical & Scientific Abbreviations. (Rus. & Ger.). 1968. $70.25 (ISBN 0-444-40657-3). Elsevier.

SCIENCE–COLLECTED WORKS

Chambers. Dictionary of Science & Technology. 1328p. 1982. DM.100.00; DM.pap. 40.00. Brandstetter.

SCIENCE–DICTIONARIES

Alford, M. H. & Alford, V. L. Russian-English Scientific & Technical Dictionary, 2 vols. LC 73-88348. (Rus. & Eng.). 1970. Set. $94.00 (ISBN 0-08-012227-2). Pergamon.

Alford, M. H. & Alford, V. L., eds. Russian-English, English-Russian Scientific & Technical Dictionary, 2 vols. 1405p. (Rus. & Eng.). 1970. $32.00; E12.80. Pergamon.

Ballentyne, D. W. & Lovett, D. R. Dictionary of Named Effects: Laws in Chemistry, Physics & Mathematics. 4th ed. 1982. $19.95x (ISBN 0-412-22390-2, NO. 6780, Pub. by Chapman & Hall England). Methuen Inc.

Biddle, Wayne. Coming to Terms: From Alpha to X-Ray, a Lexicon for the Science-Watcher. 128p. 1982. $4.95 (ISBN 0-380-61093-0, 61093-0). Avon.

Brain, James L. A Short Dictionary of Science Terms for Swahili Speakers. (Foreign & Comparative Studies Program, African Special Publications: No. 4). 70p. (Orig., Swahili.). 1969. pap. text ed. $4.50x (ISBN 0-686-74011-4). Syracuse U Foreign Comp.

Braun, Edmund. Wissenschaftstheoretisches Lexikon. (Ger.). 1977. $79.95 (ISBN 3-222-10953-2, M-7688, Pub. by Styria). French & Eur.

Breuer, Karl. Pocket Dictionary of Technology & Science: Technischwissenschaftliches Taschenwoerte'buch: German-English & English-German. 6th ed. LC 75-597125. 413p. (Ger. & Eng.). 1971. 27.50x (ISBN 3-87749-014-X). Intl Pubns Serv.

Brockhaus. Diccionario popular de las ciencias y de la tecnica. 2nd ed. (Illus.). 658p. (Span.). write for info. Gill Gustavo.

Bynum, William F., et al, eds. Dictionary of the History of Science. LC 81-47116. (Illus.). 822p. 1981. 45.00x (ISBN 0-691-08287-1). Princeton U Pr.

Carpovich, Eugene A. Russian-English Atomic Dictionary: Physics, Mathematics, Nucleonics. rev. ed. 2nd ed. LC 57-8256. (Rus. & Eng.). 1959. $15.00 (ISBN 0-911484-00-0). Tech Dict.

Chambers. Dictionary of Science & Technology. 1296p. (Ger.). 1982. DM.pap. 40.00. Brandstetter.

Chambers Dictionary of Science & Technology. (Illus.). 1978. $25.00 (ISBN 0-8467-0520-6, Pub. by Two Continents); pap. $10.95 (ISBN 0-8467-0530-3). Am Map.

Chu-Chi, W. English-Chinese Dictionary of Physical Terms. 218p. (Eng. & Chinese.). 1973. leatherette $25.00 (ISBN 0-686-92350-2, M-9258). French & Eur.

Coudray, Leandre. Lexique des Sciences de l'education. 144p. (Fr.). 1973. 43.00 F. E. S. F.

Czerni & Skrzynka. Polish-English Dictionary of Science & Technology. 754p. (Pol. & Eng.). 1976. $95.00x (ISBN 0-686-44737-9, Pub. by Collets). State Mutual Bk.

Czerni, S. & Skrzynska, M. Polish Science & Technology Dictionary: English-Polish. 5th ed. (Pol. & Eng.). 1976. $35.00x (ISBN 0-89918-536-3, P536). Vanous.

--Polish Science & Technology Dictionary: Polish-English. 3rd rev. ed. (Pol. & Eng.). 1976. $35.00x (ISBN 0-89918-537-1, P-537). Vanous.

Czerni, Sergiusz & Skrzynska, Maria, eds. Polish-English Dictionary of Science & Technology. 3rd ed. (Pol. & Eng.). 1976. 30.00x (ISBN 0-686-19981-2). Intl Learn Syst.

Daintith, John. A Dictionary of Physical Sciences. LC 76-41039. (Illus.). 1977. $20.00x (ISBN 0-87663-723-3, Pica Pr). Universe.

Daintith, John, ed. A Dictionary of Physical Sciences. (A Helix Bk.: No. 379). (Illus.). 333p. 1983. pap. $9.95 (ISBN 0-8226-0379-9). Rowman & Allanheld.

De Benedetti, Rinaldo. Dizionario rapido di scienze pure ed applicate. (Illus.). viii, 1336p. (Ital.). 1966. L.25000.00 (ISBN 88-02-01497-3). UTET.

De Galiana, Thomas. Diccionario de los descubrimientos cientificos. (Span.). 100.00 ptas. Plaza Janes.

De la Cierva, Patronato J. Diccionario Ruso-Espanol de la Ciencia y la Tecnica. 2nd ed. 700p. (Span.). 1972. $50.00 (ISBN 84-237-0407-6, S-50249). French & Eur.

De Vries, Louis. French-English Science Dictionary. LC 75-45091. xii, 683p. (Eng. & Fr.). 1976. $13.50 (ISBN 0-07-016629-3). McGraw.

--German-English Science Dictionary. 4th ed. LC 78-6465. xxxviii, 628p. (Eng. & Ger.). 1978. $14.50 (ISBN 0-07-016602-1). McGraw.

DeVries, Louis & Jacolev, Leon. German-English Science Dictionary. 4th ed. (Ger. & Eng.). 1978. 26.95 (ISBN 0-07-016602-1, P&RB). McGraw.

De Vries, louis & Jacolev, Leon. German-English Science Dictionary. rev. ed. 666p. (Ger. & Eng.). 1978. $28.00. McGraw.

Dictionary of Science & Technology. 469p. (Eng. & Chinese.). 1973. $14.95 (ISBN 0-686-92348-0, M-9261). French & Eur.

Dictionary of Science & Technology. 1689p. (Eng & Chinese.). 1978. $9.95 (ISBN 0-686-92375-8, M-9560). French & Eur.

Dictionary of Science & Technology: Eng. & Chinese. 713p. (Chinese.). 1979. pap. $5.95 (ISBN 0-686-92552-1, M-9587). French & Eur.

Dictionnaire International de Science. (Fr.). 1971. write for info. E. M. E.

Dizionario delle tecniche e delle scienze, 8 vols. 5200p. (Ital.). 1973. L.195000.00. Edizioni Paoline.

Dobrovolny, Bohumil. Piirucni Slovnik Vedy a Techniky. LC 80-488092. 253p. (Czech.). 1979. 25.00 Kcs. Prace.

Dorian, A. F., compiled by. Dictionary of Science & Technology, 2 vols. 2nd, rev. ed. (Ger. & Eng.). 1982. Set. $242.75 (ISBN 0-686-85923-5). Elsevier.

Dorian, A. F., ed. Dictionary of Science & Technology, 2 Vols. 1400p. 1979. Set. $255.50 (ISBN 0-686-85924-3); Vol. I: Fr.- Eng. $127.75 (ISBN 0-444-41911-X); Vol. II: Eng. & Fr. $127.75 (ISBN 0-444-41829-6). Elsevier.

Dorian, Angelo F. Dictionary of Science & Technology. LC 79-18507. 1586p. (Eng. & Fr.). 1979. write for info. (ISBN 0-444-41829-6). Elsevier.

English-Chinese Dictionary of Scientific & Technology Abreviations. 587p. (Eng. & Chinese.). 1979. pap. $9.95 (ISBN 0-686-97363-1, M-9250). French & Eur.

English-Polish Dictionary of Science & Technology. 4th ed. 892p. (Eng. & Pol.). $90.00x (ISBN 0-569-08263-3, Pub. by Collets). State Mutual Bk.

English-Polish Dictionary of Science & Technology. 892p. (Eng. & Pol.). 1976. $19.95 (Pub. by Wydaw. Naukowo-Techniczne). Four Continent.

Fachlexikon ABC Technik und Naturwissenschaft, Vols. 1 & 2. (Ger.). 1970. Set. leatherette $55.00 (ISBN 3-87144-004-3, M-7384). French & Eur.

Garcia Hoz, Victor. Vocabulario General de Orientacion Cientifica y Sus Estratos. 432p. (Span.). 1976. pap. $29.95 (ISBN 84-00-04273-5, S-50108). French & Eur.

Ghaleb, Edouard. Dictionnaire des Sciences de la Nature (Dictionary of the Natural Sciences, 3 vols. (Illus.). 1643p. (Arabic, Lat., Fr., Eng., Ger. & Ital.). 1966. Set. 172.50x (ISBN 0-8002-1208-8). Intl Pubns Serv.

--Dictionnaire des Sciences de la Nature, 1. (Illus.). 589p. (Fr.). 1966. 45.00 F. Dar El-Machreq.

--Dictionnaire des Sciences de la Nature, 2. (Illus.). 670p. (Fr.). 1966. 45.00 F. Dar El-Machreq.

--Dictionnaire des Sciences de la Nature, 3. (Illus.). 384p. (Fr.). 1966. 45.00 F. Dar El-Machreq.

Halbauer, S. Russisch-Deutsches Woerterbuch Fuer Naturwissenschaftler und Ingenieure. 170p. (Ger. & Rus.). 1971. $9.95 (ISBN 0-686-56466-9, M-7607, Pub. by M. Hueber). French & Eur.

--Russisch-Deutsches Woerterbuch Fuer Naturwissenschaftler und Ingenieure. 170p. (Ger. & Rus.). 1971. $9.95. Hueber.

Hyman, Charles J., ed. Dictionary of Physics & Allied Sciences: German-English. LC 77-6949. (Ger. & Eng.). 1978. $30.00 (ISBN 0-8044-4433-1). Ungar.

Idlin, Ralph, ed. Dictionary of Physics & Allied Sciences: English-German. LC 77-6950. (Eng. & Ger.). 1978. $30.00 (ISBN 0-8044-4435-8). Ungar.

Japanese-Chinese Science & Technology Dictionary. 175p. (Japanese & Chinese.). 1976. $19.95 (ISBN 0-686-92480-0, M-9260). French & Eur.

Jerrard, G. & Neill, D. B. Diccionario de Unidades Cientificas. 206p. (Span.). write for info. Bellaterra.

Jerrard, H. G. & McNeill, D. B. Diccionario de Unidades Cientificas. 3rd ed. 216p. (Span.). 1974. pap. $11.95 (ISBN 0-686-57367-6, S-50215). French & Eur.

Jouffroy, A. Dictionnaire des Inventions et Decouvertes Anciennes et Modernes, 2 vols. Migne, J. P., ed. (Nouvelle Encyclopedie Theologique Ser.: Vols. 35-36). 1424p. (Fr.). Repr. of 1860 ed. lib. bdg. $181.00x (ISBN 0-89241-277-1). Caratzas Pub Co.

Kobo Orts Kh., et al. Kratkii Ispansko-Russkii & Russko-Ispanskii Nauchno-Tekhnicheskii Slovar. 438p. (Span. & Rus.). 1960. $3.75 (Pub. by An Arm SSR). Four Continent.

Konarski, M. M. Russian-English Space Technology Dictionary. LC 72-99990. (Rus. & Eng.). 1970. $77.00 (ISBN 0-08-015617-7). Pergamon.

Kucera, A. The Compact Dictionary of Exact Science & Technology, Vol. 1. 590p. E16.50 (ISBN 0-245-53605-1). Harrap.

Lapedes, D. Dizionario Enciclopedico Scientifico e Tecnico: Inglese-Italiano, Italiano-Inglese. 2122p. (Eng. & Ital.). 1980. Leatherette $175.00 (ISBN 0-686-92540-8, M-9201). French & Eur.

Lucas, D. J., et al. A First Science Dictionary: College Edition. LC 76-53302. 206p. 1977. $12.50x (ISBN 0-8448-1056-8). Crane-Russak Co.

Lucas, David. A First Science Dictionary. (Eng.). pap. $9.95 (076-5). Intl Bk Ctr.

McGraw Hill. McGraw Hill Dictionary of Scientific & Technical Terms. 3rd ed. Parker, Sybil P., ed. 1860p. 1983. 70.00 (ISBN 0-07-045269-5, Pub by P & RB). McGraw.

Marcu, Marinca. Dictionar Elementar de Stiinte. LC 79-367925. 334p. (Romanian.). 1978. 16.00 lei. Editura Stiintifica.

Mazzaglia, E. & Castellini, A. Dizionario delle nuove scienze: Astronautica, electronica, fiscia nucleare. 830p. (Ital.). 1968. L.19000.00. Edizioni Paoline.

Mingot, Tomas De Galiana. Pequeno Larousse de ciencias y tecnicas. new ed. 1056p. (Span.). 1975. 26.95 (ISBN 0-685-55467-8, 21115). Larousse.

Mullen, William B. Dictionary of Scientific Word Elements. LC 69-20141. (Quality Paperback: No. 102). (Orig.). 1969. pap. 2.95 (ISBN 0-8226-0102-8). Littlefield.

O'Bannon, Loran. Dictionary of Ceramic Science & Engineering. 330p. 1983. $45.00 (ISBN 0-306-41324-8, Plenum Pr). Plenum Pub.

Patronato Juan de la Cierva. Diccionario ruso-espanol de la ciencia y de la tecnica. 700p. (Rus. & Span.). write for info. Dossat.

Rack, Guenter. Mathematisch-Naturwissenschaftliches Woerterbuch Deutsch-Dari. 652p. (Ger. & Dari.). 1977. DM.78.00 (ISBN 3-87276-178-1). Groos Verlag.

Speck, E. G. Diccionario cientifico ilustrado. (Illus.). 386p. (Span.). $1.50. Editors Pr Serv.

Technisch Wissenschaftliches Taschenwoerterbuch. 408p. (Ger., Technical Scientific Dictionary). $32.00 (ISBN 3-87749-014-X, M-7643, Pub. by Georg Siemens Verlagsbuchhandlung). French & Eur.

Thines, Georges & Lempereur, Agnes. Dictionnaire General des Sciences Humaines. 1000p. (Fr.). 1975. $135.00 (ISBN 0-686-57231-9, M-6532). French & Eur.

Ubanou. Diccionario de eiencias. (Span.). write for info. Dossat.

Ubarov, Chapman. Diccionario de Ciencias. 226p. (Span.). 1970. $12.25 (ISBN 84-237-0299-5, S-50245). French & Eur.

Uvarov, E. B., et al. Dicionario de ciencia. (Port.). Esc.250.00. Pub Euro Am.

Zimmerman, M. G. Russian-English Scientific & Technical Dictionary of Useful Combinations & Expressions. (Rus. & Eng.). $22.00 (ISBN 0-87559-119-1); thumb indexed $29.50 (ISBN 0-87559-140-X). Shalom.

Zimmerman, Mikhail G. Russian-English Translators Dictionary: A Guide to Scientific & Technical Usage. LC 67-19391. 295p. (Rus. & Eng.). 1967. $29.50x (ISBN 0-306-30300-0, Plenum Pr). Plenum Pub.

Zykina, M. I., et al. Chastotnyi Slovar Obschenauchnoi Leksiki. 85p. (Rus.). 1970. $1.00 (Pub. by MGU). Four Continent.

SCIENCE–DICTIONARIES–JUVENILE LITERATURE
Young People's Science Encyclopedia Editors. Young People's Science Dictionary, 2 vols. LC 67-17925. (Illus.). (gr. 4 up). 1979. lib. bdg. $17.25 (ISBN 0-516-00274-0). Childrens.

SCIENCE–HISTORY
Bynum, W. F., et al. Dictionary of the History of Science. 494p. (Eng.). 1981. E19.50 (ISBN 0-333-29316-9); pap. $6.95 (ISBN 0-333-34901-6). Macmillan London.

Bynum, William F., et al, eds. Dictionary of the History of Science. LC 81-47116. (Illus.). 822p. 1981. 45.00x (ISBN 0-691-08287-1). Princeton U Pr.

SCIENCE–INFORMATION SERVICES
Informatsionno-Poiskovyi Tezariius Po Informatike. 206p. (Rus.). 1974. $6.75 (Pub. by Vsesoiuz). Four Continent.

SCIENCE–TERMINOLOGY
Asimov, Isaac. Words of Science. (Illus.). (gr. 7 up). 1959. 10.95 (ISBN 0-395-06571-2). HM.

--Words of Science & the History Behind Them. (Illus.). (RL 7). 1969. pap. 1.95 (ISBN 0-451-61799-1, MJ1799, Ment). NAL.

Biddle, Wayne. Coming to Terms: Lexicon for the Science Watcher. LC 80-54198. (Illus.). 128p. 1981. $8.95 (ISBN 0-670-33092-2). Viking Pr.

Diccionario de Terminos Cientificos & Tecnicos, 5 vols. (Span.). write for info. (ISBN 8-42670-417-4). McGraw.

Diccionario de Terminos Cientificos & Tecnicos, Vol. 2. 600p. (Span.). 1981. pap. write for info. ptas (ISBN 84-267-0419-0). Marcombo.

Diccionario de terminos cientificos y tecnicos: Obra completa, 5 vols. 2900p. (Span.). 1981. pap. 25000.00 ptas (ISBN 84-267-0417-4). Marcombo.

Diccionario de terminos cientificos y tecnicos: Tomo 1 II. 600p. (Span.). 1981. pap. write for info. (ISBN 84-267-0418-2). Marcombo.

Diccionario de terminos cientificos y tecnicos: Tomo 3 II. 600p. (Span.). 1981. pap. write for info. (ISBN 84-267-0420-4). Marcombo.

Diccionario de terminos cientificos y tecnicos: Tomo 4 II. 600p. (Span.). 1981. pap. write for info. (ISBN 84-267-0421-2). Marcombo.

Diccionario espanol-ruso de terminos cientificos y tecnicos. (Span. & Rus.). write for info. Cultura Popular.

Drozd & Seibicke. Deutsche Fach & Wissenschaftssprache. 207p. (Ger.). E27.00. Brandstetter.

Godman, Arthur. Barnes & Noble Thesaurus of Science. (Illus.). 256p. (gr. 11-12). 1983. $13.41i (ISBN 0-06-015176-5, EH 580); pap. $6.68i (ISBN 0-06-463580-5, EH 580). B&N NY.

Hogben, Lancelot. Vocabulary of Science. LC 77-108314. 1971. pap. $3.95 (ISBN 0-8128-1394-4). Stein & Day.

Khatib, Ahmad. A New Dictionary of Scientific & Technical Terms. 768p. (Eng. & Arabic.). 1980. $45.00 (075-9). Intl Bk Ctr.

McGraw-Hill & Boixareu. Diccionario de Terminos Cientificos & Tecnicos, 5 vols. (Illus.). 2952p. (Span.). 1981. write for info. (ISBN 84-267-0417-4). Marcombo.

Malczewski, J. Szkolny Slownik Terminow Nauki i Jezyku. 244p. (Pol.). 1979. $2.75 (Pub. by Wydaw. Szkolne & Pedagogiczne). Four Continent.

Mikhailov, A. I., et al, eds. Terminologicheskii Slovar Po Nauchnoi Informatsii. 192p. (Rus.). 1969. $2.75 (Pub. by Vsesoiuznyi in-tut Nauchin & Tekhn. Imformatsii). Four Continent.

Orts, J. C., et al. Breve Diccionario Espanol-Ruso: Ruso-Espanol de Terminos Cientificos & Tecnicos. 438p. (Span. & Rus.). 1960. leatherette $6.95 (ISBN 0-686-97394-1, S-31835). French & Eur.

Sahai, Hardeo & Berrios, Jose. A Dictionary of Statistical, Scientific & Technical Terms: English-Spanish, Spanish-English. Smith, Richard A. & Heise, Jeanne, eds. (Spanish Ser.). 143p. (Eng. & Span.). 1981. $13.95 (ISBN 8-4534-0004-0, Pub. by Wadsworth Internacional Iberoamerica). Wadsworth Pub.

Steffanides, George F. The Scientist's Thesaurus. 4th ed. 156p. 1978. pap. $3.00 (ISBN 0-9600114-0-4, TX-7-128). Steffanides.

Varios, tr. Diccionario de terminos cientificos y tecnicos: Tomo 5 II. 500p. (Span.). 1981. pap. write for info. (ISBN 84-267-0422-0). Marcombo.

Wennrich, Peter, compiled by. Anglo-American & German Abbreviations in Science & Technology: Part 4, Supplement. 618p. (Eng. & Ger.). 1981. $52.50 (ISBN 3-598-20512-0). Bowker.

SCIENCE, APPLIED
see Technology
SCIENCE, MENTAL
see Psychology
SCIENCE, POLITICAL
see Political Science
SCIENCE, SOCIAL
see Sociology
SCIENCE AND LAW
Bailentyne, D. W. & Walker, L. E., trs. Diccionario de leyes y efectos cientificos. 216p. (Span.). 1963. Arg.$1.80. Leru.
SCIENCE AND SPACE
see Space Sciences

SCIENCE FICTION–ENCYCLOPEDIAS AND DICTIONARIES
Dictionary Catalog of the J. Lloyd Eaton Collection of Science Fiction & Fantasy Literature, 3 vols. 1982. Set. lib. bdg. $290.00 (ISBN 0-8161-0379-8, Hall Library). G K Hall.
SCIENCE OF LANGUAGE
see Linguistics
SCIENCE OF SCIENCE
see Science
SCIENCES, OCCULT
see Occult Sciences
SCIENCES, SOCIAL
see Social Sciences
SCIENTIFIC APPARATUS AND INSTRUMENTS
see also Chemical Apparatus; Engineering Instruments; Optical Instruments
also names of particular instruments, e.g. Spectroscope
Shipp, James F. Russian-English Index to Scientific Apparatus Nomenclature. LC 77-362864. viii, 66p. (Eng. & Rus.). 1977. write for info. (ISBN 0-917564-03-0). Trans Res Inst.
SCIENTIFIC FRENCH
see French Language–Technical French
SCIENTIFIC INSTRUMENTS
see Scientific Apparatus and Instruments
SCIENTIFIC MANAGEMENT
see Industrial Management
SCIENTIFIC RUSSIAN
see Russian Language–Technical Russian
SCIENTISTS
see also Botanists
Shipp, James F. Russian-English Dictionary of Surnames: Important Names from Science & Technology. xvi, 317p. (Orig., Rus. & Eng.). 1981. pap. 30.00x (ISBN 0-917564-10-3). Translation Research.
SCIENTOLOGY
see Dianetics
SCOTT, WALTER, SIR, BART., 1771-1832
Rogers, May. Waverly Dictionary. 2nd ed. LC 66-27850. 1967. Repr. of 1885 ed. $37.00x (ISBN 0-8103-3222-1). Gale.
Scott, Sir Walter. Complete Glossary for Sir Walter Scott's Novels & Romances. Repr. of 1833 ed. $18.50 (ISBN 0-8337-4743-6). B Franklin.
SCOTTISH LANGUAGE
see Gaelic Language
SCRABBLE (GAME)
Carillon, Annie & Goutel, Beatrice. Dictionnaire du Scrabble. 215p. (Fr.). 1976. 30.00 F. Hachette.
The Official Scrabble Player's Dictionary. (gr. 10 up). 1979. pap. 5.95 (ISBN 0-671-49517-8). PB.
The Official Scrabble Players Dictionary. (Eng.). 1978. $9.95 (ISBN 0-87779-020-5, 72440). Merriam.
SCULPTORS
Benezit. Dictionnaire Critique et Documentaire des Peintres, Sculpteurs, Dessinateurs, et Graveurs de Tous les Temps et de Tons les Pays, 10 tomes. (Fr.). 1976. Set. $395.00 (ISBN 0-685-35921-2). French & Eur.
Benezit, E. Dictionnaire des Peintres, Sculpteurs, Dessinateurs et Graveurs, 10 vols. new, rev. ed. (Illus., Fr.). 1976. $495.00 set (ISBN 2-7000-0149-4). Hacker.
Camard, Jean Pierre & Belfort, Anne Marie. Dictionnaire des Peintres et Sculpteurs Provencaux. 444p. (Fr.). 1974. pap. $19.95 (ISBN 0-686-56858-3). French & Eur.
Diccionario Universal del Arte y De los Artistas: Escultores. 301p. (Span.). 1970. leatherette $25.50 (ISBN 84-252-0383-X, S-50281). French & Eur.
SCULPTURE
see also Bronzes; Expressionism (Art)
Benezit, Emmanuel. Dictionnaire Critique & Documentaire: Peintres, Sculptres, Dessinateurs de Tous les Temps & de Tous les Pays. (Fr.). 1976. write for info. Grund.

Diccionario Universal del Arte y De los Artistas: Escultores. 301p. (Span.). 1970. leatherette $25.50 (ISBN 84-252-0383-X, S-50281). French & Eur.
Pernety, Antoine Joseph. Dictionnaire Portatif de Peinture, Sculpture & Gravure. (Fr.). 1972. 140.00 F. Minkoff Repr.
Watelet, Claude-Henre & Levesque, Pierre-Charles. Dictionnaire des Arts de Peinture, Sculpture & Gravure, Vol. 1. (Fr.). 1972. 118.00 F. Olms Verlag.
Watelet, Claude-Henri & Levesque, Pierre-Charles. Dictionnaire des Arts de Peinture, Sculpture & Gravure, Vol. 3. (Fr.). 1972. 118.00 F. Olms Verlag.
--Dictionnaire des Arts de Peinture, Sculpture & Gravure, Vol. 4. (Fr.). 1972. 118.00 F. Olms Verlag.
--Dictionnaire des Arts de Peinture, Sculpture & Gravure, Vol. 5. (Fr.). 1972. 118.00 F. Olms Verlag.
SCULPTURE–FRANCE
Fondation Paul Richard & Camard, Jean-Pierre. Dictionnaire des Peintres & Sculpteurs Provencaux: 1880-1950. 444p. (Fr.). 1974. 40.00 F. Bendor.
SCULPTURE, MODERN–20TH CENTURY
Nouveau Dictionnaire de la Sculpture Moderne. 328p. (Fr.). 1970. $47.50 (ISBN 0-686-57061-8, M-6431). French & Eur.
SCULPTURE, RELIGIOUS
see Christian Art and Symbolism
SEA
see Ocean
SEA, DOMINION OF THE
see Maritime Law
SEA ANIMALS
see Marine Fauna
SEA-FISHERIES
see Fisheries
SEA FOOD
Lindberg, G. U. Multilingual Dictionary of Names of Marine Food-Dishes of World Fauna. 562p. 1980. 79.00x (ISBN 0-686-44732-8, Pub. by Collets). State Mutual Bk.
SEA LAWS
see Maritime Law
SEA LIFE
see Seamen
SEA SCOUTS
see Boy Scouts
SEA TRANSPORTATION
see Shipping
SEA WAVES
see Ocean Waves
SEAFOOD
see Sea Food
SEALING (TECHNOLOGY)
see also Plastics; Welding
American Society of Lubrication Engineers. Glossary of Seal Terms. $4.00; members $3.00. Am Lubrication Engs.
SEALS (NUMISMATICS)
Chassant, Louis A. & Delbarre, P. J. Dictionnaire de Sigillographie Pratique. 264p. (Fr.). DM.39.80. Olms Verlag.
SEAMANSHIP
see also Navigation
Paasch, Henri. Dictionnaire Anglais-Francais et Francais-Anglais des Termes et Locutions Maritimes. 2nd ed. 320p. (Fr. & Eng.). 1974. pap. $23.50 (ISBN 0-686-57065-0, M-6437). French & Eur.
SEAMEN
Here are entered works on naval seamen in general. Works on members of the Armed Forces, including naval seamen, are entered under the heading Soldiers.
see also Merchant Marine; Pilots and Pilotage
also United States–Navy, and similar headings
Gruss, Robert. Dictionnaire de Marine. (Illus.). 368p. (Fr.). 1978. 120.00 F. Maritimes Outre mer.
Pando, J. L. Diccionario maritimo. 245p. (Span.). write for info. Dossat.
SEATS
see Chairs
SECRET SOCIETIES
Mariel, Pierre. Dictionnaire des Societes Secretes En Occident. (Fr.). 1971. pap. $21.50 (ISBN 0-686-56864-8, M-6642). French & Eur.

SECRETARIAL TRAINING
see Business Education; shorthand; Typewriting and allied subjects
SECRETARIES
see also Office Management
Corson, Betty M., ed. The New Secretary's Deskbook. LC 74-34544. 844p. (Eng.). 1975. write for info. (ISBN 0-03-923299-9). HR&W Canada.
SECURITIES EXCHANGE
see Stock-Exchange
SECURITY OFFENSES
see Subversive Activities
SEDIMENTARY ROCKS
see Rocks, Sedimentary
SEDIMENTATION AND DEPOSITION
see also Rocks, Sedimentary
Gonzalez Bonorino. Lexico sedimentologico. 1952p. (Span.). $4.00. Museo Arg. Ciencias Nat.
SEE, HOLY
see Popes
SELF-DEFENSE
see also Hand-To-Hand Fighting; Judo; Martial Arts
Shapiro, Amy. Martial Arts Language. LC 77-12635. 1978. lib. bdg. 12.90 (ISBN 0-89471-015-X); pap. 2.95 (ISBN 0-89471-014-1). Running Pr.
SEMANTICS
see also Words, New
also subdivisions Semantics and Words–History under names of languages, e.g. English Language–Words–History
Dansel, Michel. Dictionnaire des Inconnus aux Noms Communs. LC 79-123074. 247p. (Fr.). 1979. write for info. (ISBN 2-86418-033-2). Encre.
Urdang, Laurance, ed. Allusions, Cultural, Literary, Biblical, & Historical: A Thematic Dictionary. 1982. $52.00x (ISBN 0-8103-1124-0). Gale.
Zwanenburg, Wiecher. Ambiguite Dans le Lexique. (PDR Press Publication in Lexical Ambiguityl Ser.: No. 1). (Fr.). 1977. pap. text ed. 1.00x (ISBN 9-0316-0037-7). Humanities.
SEMASIOLOGY
see Semantics
SEMEIOLOGY
see Symptomatology
SEMEIOTICS
see Semiotics; Signs and Symbols
SEMICONDUCTORS
see also Microelectronics
also particular semiconducting substances, e.g. Germanium, Silicon; and headings beginning with the word Semiconductor
Wiegelmann, Alfred. Dizionario dei semiconduttori. Cascianni, L. & Boscarol, M., trs. (Illus.). 164p. (Ital.). 1978. L.4400.00 (ISBN 88-7021-072-3). Muzzio.
SEMIOLOGY
see Symptomatology
SEMIOLOGY (LINGUISTICS)
see Semiotics
SEMIOLOGY (SEMANTICS)
see Semantics
SEMIOTICS
see also Signs and Symbols
Greimas, Algirdas J. & Courtes, Joseph. Seminotique: Dictionnaire Raisonne de la Theorie du Language. LC 80-462606. vi, 422p. (Fr.). 1979. 90.00 F (ISBN 2-010-05221-8). Hachette-Jeunesse.
SEMI-PRECIOUS STONES
see Precious Stones
SEMITES
see also names of individual Semitic People, e.g. Arabs, Jews
Cohen, David. Dictionnaire des Racines Semitiques. (Fr.). 1974. 58.00 F. Mouton De Gruyter.
SEMITIC LANGUAGES
see also Oriental Languages
also names of languages belonging to the Semitic group, e.g. Arabic Language, Hebrew Language
Cohen, David. Dictionnaire Des Racines Semitiques Ou Attestes Dans les Langues Semitiques: Comprenant un Fichier Comparatif De Jean Cantineau. 36p. (Fr.). 1970. pap. text ed. 20.00x (ISBN 0-686-27743-0). Mouton.

SEMITIC PHILOLOGY
Cohen, David. Dictionnaire Des Racines Semitiques: Ou Attestees Dans les Langues Semitiques. (Fr.). 1976. pap. text ed. 26.25x (ISBN 90-2796-441-6). Mouton.
SENEGAL
Colvin, Lucie G. Historical Dictionary of Senegal. LC 80-25466. (African Historical Dictionaries Ser.: No. 23). 355p. 1981. $17.50 (ISBN 0-8108-1369-6). Scarecrow.
SENSING, REMOTE
see Remote Sensing
SERBIAN LANGUAGE
see Serbo-Croatian Language
SERBO-CROATIAN LANGUAGE
Benson, M. English-Serbocroatian Dictionary. 669p. (Eng. & Serbocroatian). 1981. $75.00 (ISBN 0-686-97376-3, M-9635). French & Eur.
--Serbocroatian-English Dictionary. 770p. (Serbocroatian & Eng.). 1980. $75.00 (ISBN 0-686-97438-7, M-9630). French & Eur.
Benson, Morton. Englesko-srpskohrvatski Recnik. LC 79-343879. xiv, 669p. (Serbo-Croation & Eng.). 1978. write for info. Beogradski.
Benson, Morton, ed. Serbocroatian-English Dictionary. LC 79-146959. (Eng. & Serbocroatian.). 1971. text ed. $37.50x (ISBN 0-8122-7636-1). U of Pa Pr.
Bogadek, Francis A. New English-Croatian, Croatian-English Dictionary. 3rd ed. (Eng. & Croatian.). 1971. Repr. of 1944 ed. 25.95x (ISBN 0-02-841580-9). Hafner.
Brkic, S. Serbocroatian-English Dictionary. 416p. (Serbocroatian & Eng.). 1980. pap. $14.95 (ISBN 0-686-97436-0, M-9631). French & Eur.
Brozovic, Blanka & Gercan, Oktavija. English-Serbocroatian & Serbocroatian-English Dictionary. 7th ed. (Eng. & Serbocroatian.). 1980. pap. 8.00x (ISBN 0-686-31617-7). Intl Learn Syst.
Croatian-English, English-Croatian Pocket Dictionary. (Croation & Eng.). 10.00 (ISBN 0-685-58554-9). Heinman.
Cvetanovic, Ratimir J. English-Serbocroatian, Serbocroatian-English Dictionary. (Eng. & Serbocroatian.). 19.50 (ISBN 0-87557-074-7, 074-7). Saphrograph.
Dictionnaire Francais-Serbo-Croate. 632p. (Fr. , Serbo & Croatian.). pap. $19.95 (ISBN 0-686-57109-6, M-6142). French & Eur.
Dizionario italiano-serbocroato sloveno. 304p. (Ital. & Serbo-Croation.). L.3000.00. Malipiero.
Dizionario serbocroato-italiano e sloveno-italiano. 304p. (Serbo-Croation, Slovenian & Ital.). L.3000.00. Malipiero.
Drvodelic, M. Serbocroatian-English Dictionary. 847p. (Serbocroatian & Eng.). 1978. $49.95 (ISBN 0-686-92510-6, M-9707). French & Eur.
Filipovic, R. Croatian-English, English-Croatian Small Pocket Dictionary. (Croatian & Eng.). 1981. pap. $10.00x (ISBN 0-89918-727-7, Y-727). Vanous.
Filipovic, Rudolf. English-Croatian or Serbian Dictionary. 1436p. (Eng. & Serbocroatian.). 1980. $150.00x (ISBN 0-569-08646-9, Pub. by Collets). State Mutual Bk.
Filipovic, Rudolf, et al. English-Serbocroatian Dictionary. 10th ed. (Eng. & Serbocroatian.). 1975. 80.00x (ISBN 0-686-19960-X). Intl Learn Syst.
Filipuvic, R., et al. Yugoslavic Deluxe Dictionary: English-Croation or Serbian. 11th ed. 1436p. (Eng. & Serbocroatian.). 1980. 95.00x (ISBN 0-89918-779-X, Y-779). Vanous.
--Yugoslavic Pocket Dictionary: English-Croation. 564p. (Eng. & Croatian.). 1979. $20.00x (ISBN 0-89918-780-3, Y-780). Vanous.
Grad, A., et al. Yugoslavic Dictionary: English-Slovene. 3rd ed. 1124p. (Eng. & Slovenian.). 1979. $35.00x (ISBN 0-89918-704-8, Y-704). Vanous.

Grujic, B. Serbocroatian-English, English-Serbocroatian Dictionary. Rev. & enl. ed. (Serbocroatian & Eng.). 25.00 (ISBN 0-685-65374-9). Heinman.
--Serbocroatian-English-Serbocroatian Dictionary: Short Grammar. 33rd ed. 624p. (Serbocroatian & Eng.). 1982. text ed. $18.00x (ISBN 0-89918-647-5, Y-647). Vanous.
Grujic, J. English-Serbo-Croat & Serbo-Croat-English Dictionary. 620p. (Eng. & Serbocroatian.). 1980. $40.00x (ISBN 0-569-03165-6, Pub. by Collet's). State Mutual Bk.
Grujic, V. C. English-Serbocroat & Serbocroat-English Dictionary. 620p. (Eng. & Serbocroatian.). 1971. $65.00x (ISBN 0-686-44712-3, Pub. by Collets). State Mutual Bk.
Hadrovics, Laszlo. Magyar-Szerbhorvat Szotar. LC 76-533581. 655p. (Hungarian & Serbo-Croatian.). 1976. 26.00 Ft (ISBN 9-63205-042-8). Terra.
--Szerbhorvat-Magyar Szotar. 4th ed. LC 77-501008. lxiv, 688p. (Serbo-Croatian & Hungarian.). 1976. 26.00 Ft (ISBN 9-63205-041-X). Terra.
Hadrovics, Laszlo, et al. Magyar-Szerbhorvat Szotar. LC 76-533581. 655p. (Hungarian & Serbo-Croatian.). 1976. 26.00 Ft (ISBN 963-205-042-8). Terra.
--Szerbhorvat-Magyar Szotar. LC 77-501008. lxiv, 688p. (Hungarian & Serbo-Croatian.). 1976. 26.00 Ft (ISBN 9-6320-5041-X). Terra.
Jurancic. Dictionary Slovene-Serbocroatian-Slovene. 566p. (Slovene & Serbocroation.). 1978. leatherette $14.95 (ISBN 0-686-92610-2, M-9703). French & Eur.
Jurancic, J. Serbocroatian-Slovene Dictionary. 1320p. (Serbocroatian & Slovene.). 1972. $49.95 (ISBN 0-686-92509-2, M-9698). French & Eur.
Kadic, Ante. Croation Reader with Vocabulary. (Croatian.). 1960. text ed. 23.00x (ISBN 90-2791-005-7). Mouton.
Kostic. Medicinski Leksikon. 917p. (Serbocroatian.). 1981. leatherette $95.00 (ISBN 0-686-92458-4, M-9706). French & Eur.
Koszinowski, Klaus. Die Von Praefigierten Verben Abgeleiteten Substantive in der Modernen Serbokroatischen Standartsprache. LC 77-463046. 271p. (Serbo-Croatian.). 1976. DM.29.00 (ISBN 3-87690-112-X). Sagner.
Kotnik, J. Yugoslavic Dictionary: Slovene-English. 7th ed. (Eng. & Serbocroatian.). 1978. $40.00x (ISBN 0-89918-708-0, Y-708). Vanous.
Langenscheidts Universal-Woerterbuch Serbokroatisch. 560p. (Serbo-Croatian & Ger.). DM.6.80 (18311). Langenscheidt.
Langenscheidts Universal-Woerterbuecher Serbokroatisch-Deutsch. (Serbo-Croatian & Ger.). 1978. DM.5.80 (ISBN 3-468-18311-9). Langenscheidt.
Learn Serbocroatian for English Speakers. (Serbocroatian & Eng.). pap. 9.50 (ISBN 0-87557-075-5, 075-5). Saphrograph.
Livadic. Dizionario Italiano-Serbo Croato. 554p. (Ital. & Serbo-Croation.). L.2300.00. Vallardi A.
Nichea, Niccolo. Vocabolario croato serbo-italiano de M. Deanovic e J. Jerej. 48p. (Serbo-Croatian & Ital.). 1967. L.3000.00. Del Bianco.
Ristic, Svetomir & Simic, Zivojin. English-Serbocroatian Dictionary. (Eng. & Serbocroatian.). 1975. 29.95x (ISBN 0-686-19961-8). Intl Learn Syst.
Ristic, Syetomir & Simic, Zivojin, eds. Englesko-srpskohrvatski Recnik. LC 76-523250. xxx, 807p. (Serbo-Croatian & Eng.). 1975. write for info. Prosveta.
Rjecnik Stranih Rijeci: Tudice & Posudenice. LC 78-389713. xiii, 1456p. (Serbo-Croatian.). 1978. write for info. Nakladni Zavod.

Simic, Z. English-Serbocroatian Dictionary. 446p. (Eng. & Serbocroatian.). 1979. pap. text ed. $14.95 (ISBN 0-686-97375-5, M-9634). French & Eur.
SERMONS
Nadal, J. C. Dictionnaire d'Eloquence Sacree, Vol. 6. Migne, J. P., ed. (Nouvelle Encyclopedie Theologique Ser.). 650p. (Fr.). Repr. of 1851 ed. lib. bdg. $83.00x (ISBN 0-89241-256-9). Caratzas Pub Co.
SESUTO LANGUAGE
see Sotho Language
SET THEORY
see also Measure Theory
Hocquenghem, Alexis. Vocabulaire Elementaire des Ensembles. (Illus.). 54p. (Fr.). 1969. 14.00 F. Masson & Cie.
SETS (MATHEMATICS)
see Set Theory
SEVIGNE, MARIE (DE RABUTIN CHANTAL) MARQUISE DE, 1626-1696
Fitzgerald, Edward. Dictionary of Madame De Sevigne, 2 Vols. Kerrich, Mary E., ed. LC 74-130598. 1971. Repr. of 1914 ed. lib. bdg. $43.00 (ISBN 0-8337-1140-7). B Franklin.
Sommer, Jean E. Lexique de la Langue de Mme de Sevigne. (Fr.). 1970. $22.50. Lenox.
--Lexique de la Langue de Mme de Sevigne, 1. (Fr.). 1973. DM.97.00. Olms.
--Lexique de la Langue de Mme de Sevigne, 2. (Fr.). 1973. DM.97.00. Olms.
SEVILLE
Gonzalez Salas, Manual. Vocabulario Popular Sevillano. 2nd ed. 182p. (Span.). 1982. pap. 550.00 ptas (ISBN 8-42870-515-1). Prensa Espanola.
SEWAGE
American Society of Civil Engineers & American Water Works Association, eds. Glossary: Water & Wastewater Control Engineering. LC 80-70933. 456p. 1981. text ed. $25.00 (ISBN 0-87262-262-2). Am Soc Civil Eng.
Dictionary of Sewage & Sanitary Installation Terms. (Hebrew, Eng. , Fr. & Ger.). IL.6.00. Massada Pr.
Glossary: Water & Wastewater Control Engineering. 1981. members $25.00; $17.50. Water Pollution.
Meinck, F. & Mohle, K. Dictionary of Water & Sewage Engineering. 2nd ed. (Ger., Eng., Fr., & Ital.). 1977. $127.75 (ISBN 0-444-99811-X). Elsevier.
SEWAGE DISPOSAL
see also Refuse and Refuse Disposal; Water–Pollution
American Water Works Association. Glossary: Water & Wastewater Control Engineering. 2nd ed. (General References Ser.). (Illus.). 456p. 1981. text ed. $25.00 (ISBN 0-89867-263-5). Am Water Wks Assn.
Meinck, Fritz. Woerterbuch fuer das Wasser und Abwasserfach. 2nd ed. (Ger., Eng., Fr. & Ital., Dictionary of Water and Sewage Disposal Plants). 1977. $128.00 (ISBN 3-486-35352-7, M-6920). French & Eur.
Scott & Smith. Dictionary of Waste & Water Treatment. 1981. text ed. write for info. (ISBN 0-408-00495-9). Butterworth.
SEWERAGE
see also Drainage; Sewage
Meinck, Fritz. Woerterbuch fuer das Wasser und Abwasserfach. 2nd ed. (Ger., Eng., Fr. & Ital., Dictionary of Water and Sewage Disposal Plants). 1977. $128.00 (ISBN 3-486-35352-7, M-6920). French & Eur.
SEWERS
see Sewerage
SEWING
see also Dressmaking; Needlework; Quilting
Ladbury, Ann. The Dressmaker's Dictionary. LC 82-8725. (Illus.). 360p. 1983. $19.95 (ISBN 0-668-05653-3, 5653). Arco.
SEX–DICTIONARIES
Bertrand, P., et al. Dizionario di informazione sessuale. 284p. (Ital.). L.2800.00. Gribaudi.

Bertrand, Paul. Diccionario de informacion sexual. (Span.). write for info. Granica.

Borra, Edoardo. Dizionario di sessuologia o dell'armonia coniugale. (Ital.). L.6000.00. Edizioni Paoline.

--Dizionario di sessuologia o dell'armonia coniugale. (Ital.). L.4000.00. Edizioni Paoline.

Capdevila Font, Juan. Diccionario de la Vida Sexual. 200p. (Span.). 1976. $9.95 (ISBN 84-85117-21-2, S-50262). French & Eur.

Cohen, Jean & Dourlen-Rollier, Anne Marie. Dictionnaire de la Vie Affective et Sexuelle. 272p. (Fr.). 1974. $15.95 (ISBN 0-686-56827-3, M-6605). French & Eur.

Diccionario Erotico De El y Ella. 640p. (Span.). 1977. pap. $37.50 (ISBN 84-85265-17-3, S-50128). French & Eur.

Diccionario Visual Del Sexo. 328p. (Span.). 1979. $53.95 (ISBN 84-278-0556-X, S-50031). French & Eur.

Diccionario visual del sexo. 2nd ed. 328p. (Span.). 1980. 1200.00 ptas (ISBN 84-278-0556-X). Nauta SA.

Goldstein, et al. Lexico de la Sexualidad. 224p. (Span.). 1981. 700.00 ptas (ISBN 84-85334-13-2). Loguez Edns.

Guiraud, Pierre. Dictionnaire Erotique. 648p. (Fr.). 1978. pap. $39.95 (ISBN 0-686-57322-6, M-6306). French & Eur.

Indiana University, Institute for Sex Research. Sexual Nomenclature: A Thesaurus. 1976. lib. bdg. $95.00 (ISBN 0-8161-0044-6, Hall Library). G K Hall.

Noguer More, Jesus. Diccionario Enciclopedico De la Vida Sexual, 5 vols. 792p. (Span.). 1974. Set. $160.00 (ISBN 84-278-0331-1, S-50029). French & Eur.

Onega, Pedro L., ed. Diccionario de la Vida Sexual. LC 76-462317. (Illus.). 187p. (Span.). 1976. write for info. (ISBN 8-485-11721-2). Distein.

Reissner, Albert & Wade, Carlson. Dictionary of Sexual Terms. 1968. $3.00 (ISBN 0-685-06550-2). Assoc Bk.

Robinson, Wm. J. Medical Sex Dictionary. 160p. pap. $0.25. Truth Seeker.

Rome, Franca. Atlante Della Sessualita. LC 78-393255. (Illus.). 237p. (Ital.). 1978. L.4500.00. A Mondadi.

Sanchez y Pascual, Enrique. Diccionario de la Vida Sexual. LC 77-550679. (Illus.). 340p. (Span.). 1976. 300.00 ptas. Prod Edit.

Stiller, Richard. Illustrated Sex Dictionary. pap. $2.00 (ISBN 0-685-06563-4). Assoc Bk.

Trimmer, Eric. Diccionario visual del sexo. 2nd ed. Jorda, Ernest, tr. 320p. (Span.). 1980. 900.00 ptas (ISBN 84-226-1056-6). Circulo Lect.

Trimmer, Eric J. The Visual Dictionary of Sex. LC 77-73126. (Illus.). 1977. $25.00 (ISBN 0-89479-006-4); deluxe ed. $35.00 slipcased (ISBN 0-89479-011-0). A & W Pubs.

Trimmer, Eric J., ed. The Visual Dictionary of Sex. (Illus.). 320p. 1981. pap. $12.95 (ISBN 0-89104-275-X, A & W Visual Library). A & W Pubs.

Valensin, Georges. Dictionnaire de la Sexualite. 392p. (Fr.). 1967. $10.95 (ISBN 0-686-56826-5, M-6604). French & Eur.

Volcher, R. Dizionario di sessuologia. 700p. (Ital.). 1975. L.14000.00. Cittadella.

Volker, R. Dizionario si sessuologia. 720p. (Ital.). 1976. L.17000.00. Cittadella.

SEX–PHYSIOLOGICAL ASPECTS
see Sex (Biology)
SEX–PSYCHOLOGICAL ASPECTS
see Sex (Psychology)
SEX (BIOLOGY)
see also Generative Organs
Bastin. Diccionario de psicologia sexual. 412p. (Span.). pap. 280.00 ptas. Herder SA.
SEX (PHYSIOLOGY)
see Sex (Biology)

SEX (PSYCHOLOGY)
see also Masculinity (Psychology)
Bastin, G. Diccionario De Psicologia Sexual. 2nd ed. 412p. (Span.). 1976. $19.95 (ISBN 84-254-0585-8, S-13099). French & Eur.
Bastin, Georges. Dizionario di psicologia sessuale. 472p. (Ital.). 1975. L.8000.00. La Scuola.
SEX EDUCATION
see Sex Instruction
SEX INSTRUCTION
Woerterbuch zur Sexualpolitik und ihren Grenzgebieten. (Ger.). pap. $22.50 (ISBN 3-7615-0016-5, M-6900). French & Eur.
SEX ORGANS
see Generative Organs
SEXUAL BEHAVIOR, PSYCHOLOGY OF
see Sex (Psychology)
SEXUAL ORGANS
see Generative Organs
SEXUAL PSYCHOLOGY
see Sex (Psychology)
SHAKESPEARE, WILLIAM, 1564-1616–CONCORDANCES
Cowden-Clark, Mary. Complete Concordance to Shakespeare. 1973. lib. bdg. $65.00 (ISBN 0-8414-2398-9). Folcroft.
Cunliffe, Richard J. New Shakespearean Dictionary. LC 72-194980. 1922. lib. bdg. $30.00 (ISBN 0-8414-2431-4). Folcroft.
Furness, Mrs. Horace H. Concordance to Shakespeare's Poems: An Index to Every Word Therein Contained. LC 75-109647. (Select Bibliographies Reprint Ser.) 1874. $29.00 (ISBN 0-8369-5256-1). Ayer Co.
SHAKESPEARE, WILLIAM, 1564-1616–CRITICISM, TEXTUAL
Partridge, A. C. Orthography in Shakespeare & Elizabethan Drama: A Study of Colloquial Contractions, Elision, Prosody, & Punctuation. LC 64-17222. viii, 200p. 1964. $14.50x (ISBN 0-8032-0143-5). U of Nebr Pr.
SHAKESPEARE, WILLIAM, 1564-1616–DICTIONARIES, INDEXES, ETC.
Schmidt, Alexander. Shakespeare - Lexicon: A Complete Dictionary of All the English Words, Phrases & Constructions in the Works of the Poet, 2 vols. rev., enl. 6th ed. Sarrazin, Gregor, ed. 1971. $98.50x (ISBN 3-11-002203-6). De Gruyter.
--Shakespeare Lexicon: A Complete Dictionary of All the English Words, Phrases & Constructions in the Work of the Poet, 2 Vols. Sarrazin, Gregor, ed. LC 67-30463. 1968. Repr. of 1901 ed. Set. $86.00 (ISBN 0-405-08935-X); $43.00 ea. Vol. 1 (ISBN 0-405-08936-8). Vol. 2 (ISBN 0-405-08937-6). Ayer Co.
SHAKESPEARE, WILLIAM, 1564-1616–LANGUAGE
Cunliffe, Richard J. A New Shakespearean Dictionary. LC 76-39872. Repr. of 1910 ed. $24.00 (ISBN 0-404-01377-5). AMS Pr.
--New Shakespearean Dictionary. LC 72-194980. 1922. lib. bdg. $30.00 (ISBN 0-8414-2431-4). Folcroft.
Ekwall, Eilert. Shakespeare's Vocabulary: Its Etymological Elements. LC 78-166013. Repr. of 1903 ed. $14.75 (ISBN 0-404-02269-3). AMS Pr.
SHAMANISM
Manzhigeev, I. A. Buriatskie Shamanisticheskie i Doshamanisticheskie Terminy. 128p. (Rus.). 1978. $2.85 (Pub. by Nauka). Four Continent.
SHARK FISHING
Pope, Patricia. Dictionary of Sharks. LC 73-7913. (Illus., Orig.). 1973. pap. 3.95 (ISBN 0-8200-0115-5). Great Outdoors.
SHARKS
see also Shark Fishing
Pope, Patricia. Dictionary of Sharks. LC 73-7913. (Illus., Orig.). 1973. pap. 3.95 (ISBN 0-8200-0115-5). Great Outdoors.

SHAW, GEORGE BERNARD, 1856-1950
Broad, Lewis C. & Broad, Violet M. Dictionary to the Plays & Novels of Bernard Shaw. LC 72-191671. 1929. lib. bdg. $9.75 (ISBN 0-8414-2543-4). Folcroft.
Kozelka, Paul. A Glossary to the Plays of Bernard Shaw. LC 76-28964. 1976. lib. bdg. $12.50 (ISBN 0-8414-5526-0). Folcroft.
SHEEP
Debrie, Rene. Lexique Picard du Berger. LC 78-376584. 23p. (Fr.). 1977. 10.00 F. Eklitra.
SHELLEY, PERCY BYSSHE, 1792-1822
Ellis, Frederick S. Lexical Concordance to the Poetical Works of Percy Bysshe Shelley. LC 67-57904. (Bibliography & Reference Ser: No. 237). 1968. Repr. of 1892 ed. $33.50 (ISBN 0-8337-1053-2). B Franklin.
SHEOL
see Hell
SHEPHERDS
De Armas Chitty, Jose A. Vocabulario del Hato, 9 vols. 209p. (Span.). 1966. $1.40. U. Central Ven.
SHIP-BUILDING
Bensch, Erhard. Schiffbau, Schiffahrt, Fischereitechnik-Russisch-Englisch-Deutsch. 784p. (Rus., Eng. & Ger.). 1981. M.98.00. VEB Technk.
SHIP-BUILDING-DICTIONARIES
Alfaro Perez, Juan. Diccionario Maritimo y De Construccion Naval. 478p. (Span. & Eng.). 1976. leather $53.95 (ISBN 84-7079-081-1, S-50094). French & Eur.
Crespo Rodriguez, Rafael. Vocabulario de Construccion Naval. LC 76-456677. 179p. (Eng. & Span.). 1975. 300.00 ptas (ISBN 8-4060-6612-6). Universidades & Acad.
Dipl-Ling, V. & Bensch, Erhard. Dictionary of Shipbuilding, Shipping & Fisheries. 784p. 1980. vinyl $150.00x (ISBN 0-686-30016-5, Pub. by Collet's). State Mutual Bk.
Dluhy, Robert, ed. Dictionary for Marine Technology, 2 vols. (Ger. & Eng.). 1974. $89.75 ea.; Vol. 1. (ISBN 3-7788-1220-3); Vol. 2. (ISBN 3-7788-1221-1). Adler.
Falconer, William. Universal Dictionary of the Marine. LC 72-87321. (Illus.). Repr. of 1780 ed. lib. bdg. 37.50x (ISBN 0-678-05655-2). Kelley.
Iasulovich, N. I. Tolkovyi Slovar Terminov, Primeniaemykh & Sudovom Mashinostroenii. 432p. (Rus.). 1966. $4.50 (Pub. by Sudostroenie). Four Continent.
Telegin, A. I., et al. Frantsuzsko-Russkii Slovar Po Sudostroeniiu i Sudokhodstvu. 295p. (Fr. & Rus.). 1961. $3.75 (Pub. by Glav. Red. Nauchn. Tekhn. Slovarei Fizmatgiza). Four Continent.
Wiebeck, E. Bi-Taschenlexikon Schiffbau-Schiffahrt. (Illus.). 388p. (Ger.). 1982. M.18.00. Bibl Inst Leipzig.
Yamaguchi, M. Illustratred New Shipbuilding Dictionary: English-Japanese, Japanese-English. 387p. (Eng. & Japanese.). 1960. leatherette $39.95 (ISBN 0-686-92490-8, M-9352). French & Eur.
SHIP HANDLING
see Boats and Boating; Yachts and Yachting
SHIP PILOTS
see Pilots and Pilotage
SHIPPING
see also Inland Navigation; Insurance, Marine; Maritime Law; Merchant Marine
Bensch, Erhard. Schiffbau, Schiffahrt, Fischereitechnik-Russisch-Englisch-Deutsch. 784p. (Rus., Eng. & Ger.). 1981. M.98.00. VEB Technk.
Bes, J. Chartering & Shipping Terms: Time-Sheet Supplements, Vols. 2 & 3. Set. $70.00 (ISBN 0-685-11999-8). Heinman.

SHIPPING–BIBLIOGRAPHY
Mariners Museum Library - Newport News - Virginia. Dictionary Catalog of the Library of the Mariners Museum, 9 Vols. 1964. Set. lib. bdg. $855.00 (ISBN 0-8161-0674-6, Hall Library). G K Hall.
SHIPPING–DICTIONARIES
Branch, Alan E. Dictionary of Shipping-International Trade Terms & Abbreviations. LC 77-361617. ix, 129p. (Eng.). 1976. E3.00 (ISBN 0-900886-16-1). Witherby UK.
Dictionary of Shipping Terms. 591p. (Japanese & Eng.). 1977. $45.00 (ISBN 0-686-92612-9, M-9333). French & Eur.
Dipl-Ling, V. & Bensch, Erhard. Dictionary of Shipbuilding, Shipping & Fisheries. 784p. 1980. vinyl $150.00x (ISBN 0-686-30016-5, Pub. by Collet's). State Mutual Bk.
Olev, Kulno. Maritime Dictionary. 560p. (Eng., Estonian & Rus.). 1981. $39.00x (ISBN 0-686-44731-X, Pub. by Collets). State Mutual Bk.
Practical Dictionary of Shipping Business: Japanese-English; English-Japanese. 236p. (Japanese & Eng.). 1978. $35.00 (ISBN 0-686-92099-6, M-9340). French & Eur.
SHIPPING–LAW
see Maritime Law
SHIPS
see also Boats and Boating; Merchant Marine; Merchant Ships; Navigation; Sailing; Seamanship; Yachts and Yachting
also names of ships, and headings beginning with the word Ship
Society of Naval Architects & Marine Engineers. Glossary for High Speed Surface Craft. 16p. 1974. $9.00 (R-17); members $6.00. Soc Naval Arch.
SHIPS–CONSTRUCTION
see Ship-Building
SHOE INDUSTRY AND TRADE
see Boots and Shoes–Trade and Manufacture
SHOES
see Boots and Shoes
SHORTHAND
see also Abbreviations
Yerian, et al. Personal Shorthand Student Dictionary. 1969. pap. text ed. 5.55 (ISBN 0-89420-025-9, 216711). Natl Book.
SHORTHAND–DICTIONARIES
Brousse, Guy. Dictionnaire Foucher de Stenographie. 346p. (Fr.). 1977. 28.00 F. Foucher.
--Dictionnaire Foucher de Stenographie Prevost-Delauney. (Fr.). 14.40 F. Foucher.
Brown, Frances A. Comprehensive Forkner Shorthand Dictionary. rev. ed. LC 81-66122. 297p. (gr. 10-12). 1982. text ed $11.84x (ISBN 0-912036-37-0). Forkner.
Fleury, Paul & Roy, E. Dictionnaire de Stenographie. 320p. (Fr.). 1978. 40.00 F. Estoup.
Gregg, J. R. & Leslie, L. A. Gregg Shorthand Dictionary. (Gregg Sharthand Ser.: No. 90). 416p. 1983. $15.95 (ISBN 0-07-024599-1). Mcgraw.
Pitman, Isaac. Pitman Dictionary of English & Shorthand. (New Era Edition). 1974. 32.00 (ISBN 0-8224-0024-3). Pitman Learning.
Pommier, Agatha-Marguerite & Guaspare, Blanche. Dictionnaire de Stenographie Duploye. 296p. (Fr.). 1955. 14.00 F. Foucher.
Speedwriting Dictionary: College Edition. LC 76-41047. (Landmark Ser.). 1977. text ed. $14.50 (ISBN 0-672-98095-9). Bobbs.
SHOSHONI INDIANS
see Indians of North America–The West
SHOW BUSINESS
see Performing Arts
SHRUBS
see also specific shrubs, e.g. Rhododendron
Hillier, H. G. The Hillier Color Dictionary of Trees & Shrubs. 323p. 1982. $19.95 (ISBN 0-442-23653-0). Van Nos Reinhold.

Millar Gauult, S. Diccionario Ilustrado En Color De Arbustos. 213p. (Span.). 1978. $48.00 (ISBN 84-252-0695-2, S-50274). French & Eur.

SI
see Metric System

SIAMESE LANGUAGE
Haas, Mary R. Thai Vocabulary. LC 79-92827. 373p. (Thai.). 1980. pap. $10.00x0747121xx (ISBN 0-87950-265-7). Spoken Lang Serv.
Haas, Mary R., ed. Thai-English Student's Dictionary. (Thai & Eng.). 1964. $20.00x (ISBN 0-8047-0567-4). Stanford U Pr.
McFarland, George B. Thai-English Dictionary. (Thai & Eng.). 1944. $32.00x (ISBN 0-8047-0383-3). Stanford U Pr.
Michell, Edward B. Siamese-English Dictionary. (Siamese & Eng.). 1976. Repr. of 1958 ed. $39.50 (ISBN 0-518-19004-8). Ayer Co.

SICILY–BIOBIBLIOGRAPHY
Mira, Giuseppe M. Bibliografia Siciliana, Ovvero Gran Dizionario Bibliografico Delle Opere Editi E Inedite, Antiche E Moderne Di Autori Siciliani O Di Argomento Siciliano Stampate in Sicilia, 3 vols. (Ital.). 1873-1881. $82.50 (ISBN 0-8337-2400-2); inc. supplement by giuseppe salvo-cozzo (ISBN 0-685-06732-7). B Franklin.

SICK
see also Diet in Disease; Hospitals; Nurses and Nursing
Barbier, Jean-Philippe & Hugues, Francois-Claude. Dictionnaire des Maladies. 528p. (Fr.). 1973. 88.00 F. Heures de France.

SIDEROGRAPHY
see Engraving

SIDNEY, PHILIP, SIR, 1554-1586
Donow, Herbert S., ed. A Concordance to the Poems of Sir Philip Sidney. LC 73-20816. (The Concordances Ser.). 1975. $45.00x (ISBN 0-8014-0805-9). Cornell U Pr.

SIERRA LEONE
Foray, Cyril P. Historical Dictionary of Sierra Leone. LC 77-3645. (African Historical Dictionaries Ser.: No. 12). 1977. $17.50 (ISBN 0-8108-1035-2). Scarecrow.

SIERRA POPOLUCA LANGUAGE (VERA CRUZ)
see Popoluca Language (Vera Cruz)

SIGHT
see Vision

SIGHT-SAVING BOOKS
see Large Type Books

SIGILLOGRAPHY
see Seals (Numismatics)

SIGN LANGUAGE
see also Deaf–Means of Communication; Signs and Symbols
Bornstein, Harry. The Signed English Dictionary. LC 75-24685. (Signed English Ser.). (Illus.). 306p. 1975. $17.50 (ISBN 0-913580-46-5). Gallaudet Coll.
Butterworth, Rod & Flodin, Mickey. The Perigee Visual Dictionary of Signing. (Illus.). 416p. (Orig.). 1983. $16.95 (ISBN 0-399-50925-9, G&D); pap. $8.95 (ISBN 0-399-50863-5). Putnam Pub Group.
Garcia, W. Joseph. Medical Sign Language: Easily Understood Definitions of Commonly Used Medical, Dental & First Aid Terms. (Illus.). 726p. 1983. $54.50x (ISBN 0-398-04805-3); pap. $43.75x spiral (ISBN 0-398-04806-1). C C Thomas.
Gustason, Gerilee, et al. Signing Exact English. 1980 ed. LC 80-80571. (Illus.). 460p. (gr. k-12). 1980. text ed. 24.00x (ISBN 0-916708-02-0); pap. text ed. 18.00x (ISBN 0-916708-03-9). Modern Signs.

SIGNALS AND SIGNALING
see also Railroads–Signaling
Dozorov, N. I. Dopolnenie K Anglo-Russkomu Slovariu Po Radioelektrike & Sviazi. 68p. (Rus. & Eng.). 1960. $0.80 (Pub. by Izd. Glav. upravl. Po Ispol'z. Atomn. Energii). Four Continent.
Gluzman, I. S. Anglo-Russkii Slovar Zheleznodorozhnoi Automatike, Telemekhanike & Sviazi. 427p. (Rus. & Eng.). 1958. $5.25 (Pub. by Gosizdat Fizmat. Lit.). Four Continent.

SIGNATURES (WRITING)
see Seals (Numismatics)

SIGNETS
see Seals (Numismatics)

SIGNS
see Signs and Symbols

SIGNS AND SYMBOLS
see also Abbreviations; Cryptography; Devices; Heraldry; Semiotics; Signals and Signaling; Symbolism
Beigbeder, Olivier. Lexique des Symboles. 436p. (Fr.). 1969. 88.00 F. Zodiaque.
Chevalier, Jean & Gheerbrant, Alain. Dictionnaire des Symboles, 4 vols. 416p. (Fr.). 1973. Set. pap. $22.50 (ISBN 0-686-56946-6, M-6068). French & Eur.
--Dictionnaire des Symboles, 4 vols. (Illus.). 416p. (Fr.). 1973. 56.00 F. Seghers.
Cirlot. Diccionario de simbolos. (Span.). 970.00 ptas. Labor SA.
Cirlot, Juan E. Diccionario de Simbolos, 1 vol. 480p. (Span.). 1981. pap. write for info. (ISBN 84-335-7016-1). Editorial Labor SA.
--Diccionario de simbolos. 5th ed. 480p. (Span.). 1982. pap. 1500.00 ptas (ISBN 84-335-7016-1). Labor.
Urech, Edouard. Dictionnaire des Symboles Chretiens. (Illus.). 190p. (Fr.). 1972. 63.00 F. Delachaux.

SIKSIKA INDIANS
see Indians of North America–The West

SILICATES
Applied Technical Dictionary: Silicate Technology. (Eng. , Ger. , Fr. & Slovak.). $50.00x (ISBN 0-569-08557-8, Pub. by Collets). State Mutual Bk.
Petzold, Armin. Silikatova Technika. LC 80-490689. 271p. (Eng., Rus. & Slovak.). 1977. 47.00 Kcs. Alfa-Vydavatel.

SILT
see Sedimentation and Deposition

SILVER-PLATE
see Silverware

SILVERSMITHS
Barber, Edward A. & Lockwood, Luke V. The Ceramic Furniture & Silver Collectors' Glossary. (Architecture & Decorative Art Ser.). 1976. pap. $6.95 (ISBN 0-306-80049-7). Da Capo.
French, Hollis. Silver Collector's Glossary & a List of Early American Silversmiths & Their Marks. LC 67-27454. (Architecture & Decorative Art Ser). 1967. lib. bdg. $19.50 (ISBN 0-306-70969-4). Da Capo.

SILVERWARE
Barber, Edward A. & Lockwood, Luke V. The Ceramic Furniture & Silver Collectors' Glossary. (Architecture & Decorative Art Ser.). 1976. pap. $6.95 (ISBN 0-306-80049-7). Da Capo.
Osterberg, Richard F. & Smith, Betty. Silver Flatware Dictionary. LC 78-75323. (Illus.). 288p. 1979. $12.00 (ISBN 0-498-02327-3). A S Barnes.

SIMILE
Castillo, Gonzalo. Diccionario de Similes & Analogias. (Span.). pap. $2.50 (BCA). Lectorum Pubns.
--Diccionario de similes y analogias. (Span.). Mex.$12.00. EDIMEX.
Wilstach, Frank J., ed. Dictionary of Similes. 2nd ed. 578p. 1981. Repr. of 1924 ed. $45.00x (ISBN 0-8103-4370-3). Gale.

SIMPLIFIED SPELLING
see Spelling Reform

SIN
Vallieres, P., et al. Lexique des Produits de la Peche: Anglais-Francais. 35p. (Eng. & Fr.). 1980. pap. $3.95 (ISBN 2-551-03722-0, M-9223). French & Eur.

SINGERS
Sanchez Sivori, Amalia. Diccionario de Payadores. 163p. (Span.). 1979. write for info. Plus Ultra S. A.

SINHALESE LANGUAGE
Wijewardena, Hema. Kalamanakarana Paribhasika Sabda Sangrahaya. LC 79-904454. viii, 496p. (Eng. & Sinhalese.). 1978. Rs.27.00. Dewan Bahasa.

SINN FEIN REBELLION, 1916
see Ireland–History

SIOUX INDIANS
see Indians of North America–The West

SIOUX LANGUAGE
see Dakota Language

SKEES AND SKEE-RUNNING
see Skis and Skiing

SKETCHING
see Drawing

SKIAGRAPHY
see Radiography

SKIING
see Skis and Skiing

SKIS AND SKIING
Fetz, Friedrich, ed. Lexikon des Alpinen Schifahrens. LC 77-457896. 156p. (Ger.). 1975. S.150.00 (ISBN 3-85123-028-0). Inn Verlag.
Gautrat, Jacques. Dictionnaire du Ski. 256p. (Fr.). 1969. pap. $8.95 (ISBN 0-686-56873-7, M-6651). French & Eur.
--Dictionnaire du Ski. (Illus.). 256p. (Fr.). 1969. 20.00 F. Seuil.
Lund, Morten. The Real Skiers' Dictionary. Date not set. price not set. S&S.

SKIS AND SKIING–JUVENILE LITERATURE
Walter, Claire. Illustrated Skiing Dictionary for Young People. 119p. (gr. 4 up). 1980. pap. $2.50 (ISBN 0-13-450858-0). P-H.

SKITTAGETAN LANGUAGES
see Haida Language

SKWAMISH LANGUAGE
see Squawmish Language

SKY
see Atmosphere

SLANG
see also Words, New; Words, Obscene
also subdivision Slang under names of languages, e.g. English Language–Slang; and subdivision Language (new words, slang, etc.) under classes of persons, names of schools and colleges, names of wars, etc
Barczi, Geza. A Pesti Nyelv. LC 78-374048. 37p. (Hungarian.). 1977. 24.00 Ft (ISBN 9-63750-112-6). Magyar Tarsasag.
Diccionario Malcriado-Naughtical Dictionary. 1980. pap. $6.00 (ISBN 0-915808-38-2). Editorial Justa.
Grose, Frances. Dictionary of Vulgar Tongue, 1811. 236p. (Eng.). 1981. Epap. 1.95 (ISBN 0-333-31502-2). Macmillan London.
Hall, Benjamin H. Collection of College Words & Customs. LC 68-17995. 1968. Repr. of 1856 ed. $42.00x (ISBN 0-8103-3282-5). Gale.
Kania, Stanislaw & Gora, Zielona. Polska Gwara Konspiracyjno-Partyzancka Czasu Okupacji Hitlerowskiej. LC 77-562382. 295p. (Pol.). 1976. 70.00 Zl. Wyzsza Szkola.
Karttunen, Kaarina. Nykyslangin Sanakirja. LC 79-398529. 333p. (Finnish.). 1979. write for info. (ISBN 9-51009-050-6). Soderstrom.
Marks, Joseph & Marks, Georgette A. Harrap's French & English Dictionary of Slang & Colloquialisms. Marks, Georgette A., rev. by. 556p. (Fr. & Eng.). 1980. E10.00. Harrap.
Sanna, Carlo. Il Gergo della Camorra. LC 78-370722. (Illus.). 128p. (Ital.). 1978. L.2400.00. Il Vespro.
Thompson, George J. Verbal Judo: Words for Street Survival. (Illus.). 176p. 1983. text ed. $19.75 (ISBN 0-398-04879-7). C C Thomas.
Wilmeth, Don B. The Language of American Popular Entertainment: A Glossary of Argot, Slang, & Terminology. LC 80-14795. xxi, 305p. 1981. lib. bdg. 29.95 (ISBN 0-313-22497-8, WEN/). Greenwood.

SLAVIC LANGUAGES
Etimologicheskii Slovar Slavianskikh Iazykov: Vyp. 4. 236p. (Rus.). 1977. $4.65 (Pub. by Nauka). Four Continent.
Etimologicheskii Slovar Slavianskikh Iazykov: Vyp. 7. 224p. (Rus.). 1980. $3.95 (Pub. by Nauka). Four Continent.
Herman, Louis J. A Dictionary of Slavic Word Families. LC 74-13341. xv, 667p. (Rus., Pol., Czech & Serbo-Croatian.). 1975. write for info. (ISBN 0-231-03927-1). Columbia U Pr.
Jedlicka, Alois. Dictionary of Slavic Linquistic Terminology, Vol. 2. 480p. (Slovak.). 1979. lib. bdg. $40.00x (ISBN 3-87118-272-9, Pub. by Helmut Buske Verlag Hamburg). Benjamins North Am.
--Dictionary of Slavonic Linquistc Terminology, Vol. 1. 549p. (Orig., Slovak.). 1977. lib. bdg. $45.00x (ISBN 3-87118-271-0, Pub. by Helmut Buske Verlag Hamburg). Benjamins North am.
Langenscheidts Universal-Woerterbuch Slowakisch. 560p. (Slavic & Ger.). DM.6.80 (18320). Langenscheidt.
Langenscheidts Universal-Woerterbuecher Slowakisch-Deutsch. (Slavic & Ger.). 1978. DM.5.80 (ISBN 3-468-18320-8). Langenscheidt.

SLAVIC LITERATURE
see also names of literatures belonging to the Slavic Group, e.g. Russian Literature
New York Public Library, the Research Libraries. Dictionary Catalog of the Slavonic Collection, 44 vols. 2nd, rev. ed. 1974. Set. lib. bdg. $3800.00 (ISBN 0-8161-0777-7, Hall Library). G K Hall.

SLAVIC LITERATURE–BIBLIOGRAPHY
New York Public Library, the Research Libraries. Dictionary Catalog of the Slavonic Collection, 44 vols. 2nd, rev. ed. 1974. Set. lib. bdg. $3800.00 (ISBN 0-8161-0777-7, Hall Library). G K Hall.

SLAVIC PHILOLOGY
see also names of languages and literatures belonging to the Slavic group
Samilov, Michael. A Lexicon to the Glory of God Greek-Russian (18th Century) Facsimile Edition Paris Ms. Suppl. grec 1117. 200p. 1972. $40.00x (ISBN 0-902089-31-5, Pub. by Variorum). State Mutual Bk.

SLEIGHT OF HAND
see Magic

SLOVAK LANGUAGE
Bagonova-Sidlova, Milota. Dictionar Portrativ Roman-Slovac, Slovac-Roman. 2nd ed. LC 77-456239. 1016p. (Romanian & Slovak.). 1976. 32.50 Kcs. SNTC.
Benacka, S. English-Slovak Technical Dictionary. 1358p. (Eng. & Slovak.). 1980. $79.00x (ISBN 0-569-08529-2, Pub. by Collet's). State Mutual Bk.
Gobel, Marianne T. Szlovak-Magyar Szotar. 3rd ed. LC 78-347303. 480p. (Hungarian & Slovak.). 1976. 35.00 Ft (ISBN 9-63205-043-6). Terra.
Karmannyi Slovatsko-Russkii i Russko-Slovatskii Slovar. 528p. (Rus. & Slovenian.). 1975. $2.10 (Pub. by Russkii Iazyk). Four Continent.
Kollar, D., et al. Slovak-Russian Dictionary. 768p. (Slovak & Rus.). 1976. $22.75 (ISBN 0-686-92504-1, M-9076). French & Eur.
Simko, P. English-Slovak Dictionary. 1442p. (Eng. & Slovak.). 1980. $70.00x (ISBN 0-569-03737-9, Pub. by Collet's). State Mutual Bk.
Smejkalova, J., et al. Czechoslovakian Dictionary: English-Slovak & Slovak-English. 5th ed. 793p. (Czech. & Eng.). 1979. $9.50x (ISBN 0-89918-170-8, C-170). Vanous.
--Slovak-English-Slovak Pocket Dictionary. (Slovak & Eng.). 1979. text ed. $9.50x (ISBN 0-89918-170-8, C170). Vanous.
Stano, Mikulas. Polsko -Slovensky a Slovensko-Polsky Slovnik. LC 75-590519. 861p. (Pol. & Slovak.). 1975. 55.00 Kcs. SNTC.
Stano, Mikulas, et al. Pol'sko-Slovensky a Slovensko-Polsky Slovnik. LC 75-590519. 861p. (Pol. & Slovak.). 1975. 55.00 Kcs. SNTC.
Vilikovska, J. & Vilikovsky, P. Slovak-English Dictionary. 522p. (Slovak & Eng.). 1980. $39.50x (ISBN 0-569-08530-6, Pub. by Collet's). State Mutual Bk.
Vilikovska, J. & Vilkovsky, Jan. Slovak-English Dictionary. (Slovak & Eng.). $24.50 (ISBN 0-87559-041-1); thumb indexed $29.50 (ISBN 0-87559-042-X). Shalom.

SLOVENIAN LANGUAGE
Bajec, A. & Kalan, P. Dizionario Italian-Slovar. 843p. (Ital. & Slovene.). 1980. $49.95 (ISBN 0-686-97337-2, M-9692). French & Eur.
Debenjak, D. Modern Dictionary Slovene-German-Slovene. 608p. (Slovene & Ger.). 1981. leatherette $14.95 (ISBN 0-686-97402-6, M-9702). French & Eur.
Dizionario italiano-serbocroato sloveno. 304p. (Ital. & Serbo-Croation.). L.3000.00. Malipiero.
Dizionario serbocroato-italiano e sloveno-italiano. 304p. (Serbo-Croation, Slovenian & Ital.). L.3000.00. Malipiero.
Grad, A. Dizionario Moderno Slovene-Italian-Slovene. 445p. (Ital. & Slovene.). 1979. leatherette $14.95 (ISBN 0-686-97353-4, M9704). French & Eur.
Grad, A., et al. English-Slovene Dictionary. 1120p. (Eng. & Slovene.). 1979. $49.95 (ISBN 0-686-97378-X, M-9695). French & Eur.
Jurancic. Dictionary Slovene-Serbocroatian-Slovene. 566p. (Slovene & Serbocroation.). 1978. leatherette $14.95 (ISBN 0-686-92610-2, M-9703). French & Eur.
Komac & Skeri, J. Modern Dictionary Slovene-English, English-Slovene. 787p. (Eng. & Slovene.). 1981. leatherette $17.50 (ISBN 0-686-97403-4, M-9701). French & Eur.
Kotnick, J. Slovene-English Dictionary. 5th ed. (Slovenian & Eng.). $37.50 (ISBN 0-87559-035-7); thumb indexed $42.00 (ISBN 0-87559-036-5). Shalom.
Kotnik, J. Slovene-English Dictionary. 831p. (Slovene & Eng.). 1978. $35.00 (ISBN 0-686-92508-4, M-9694). French & Eur.
Kotnik, J. & Grad, A. Slovene-English, English-Slovene Dictionary, 2 vols. new ed. (Slovene & Eng.). Set. 75.00 (ISBN 0-685-55016-8). Heinman.
Langenscheidts Universal-Woerterbuch Slowenisch. 560p. (Slovenian.). DM.6.80 (18330). Langenscheidt.
Skerlj, R., et al. Yugoslavian-English Slovene Dictionary. 1122p. (Eng. & Slovenian.). 1979. text ed. $35.00x (ISBN 0-89918-704-8, Y704). Vanous.
Tomsic, F. German-Slovene Dictionary. 989p. (Ger. & Slovene.). 1980. $49.95 (ISBN 0-686-97384-4, M-9696). French & Eur.
--Slovene-German Dictionary. 768p. (Slovene & Ger.). 1977. $35.00 (ISBN 0-686-92505-X, M-9697). French & Eur.
SLOVENIAN LANGUAGE (OLD)
see Church Slavic Language
SLOVO O POLKU IGOREVE
Cizevska, Tatjana. Glossary of the Igor Tale. (S P R Ser: No. 53). 1966. text ed. 72.00x (ISBN 90-2790-198-8). Mouton.
SLOW LEARNING CHILDREN
see also Learning Disabilities
Pope, Lillie. Learning Disabilities Glossary. 64p. 1976. pap. text ed. $3.95 (ISBN 0-87594-144-3). Book-Lab.
SLUM CLEARANCE
see City Planning; Housing
SMALL ARMS
see Firearms
SMALL BUSINESS
Hertz, Leah. In Search of a Small Business Definition: An Exploration of the Small-Business Definitions of the U. S., the U.K., Israel, & the People's Republic of China. LC 81-40926. 482p. 1982. lib. bdg. $29.75 (ISBN 0-8191-2308-0); pap. text ed. $17.25 (ISBN 0-8191-2309-9). U Pr of Amer.
SMALL BUSINESS–ACCOUNTING
see Accounting
SMITH, JOSEPH, 1805-1844
Bluth, John V. Concordance to the Doctrine & Covenants. $8.95 (ISBN 0-87747-048-0). Deseret Bk.
SOAP AND SOAP TRADE
see also Cleaning Compounds
International Fabricare Institute. Terms Related to Soap & Detergents. (Fabric Care Ser.). $0.25 (FC-20). Intl Fabricare Inst.
Soap & Detergent Association. A Handbook of Industry Terms. 2nd ed. 62p. 1981. free. Soap & Detergent.
SOBRIQUETS
see Nicknames
SOCCER
Arias Llamas, Inocencio F., et al. Diccionario periodistico de Futbol. 256p. (Span.). 1982. pap. write for info. (ISBN 84-500-7621-8). Organ Ofic Adm.
Cramer, Dettmar. Lexikon fuer Fussballfreunde: Fachliche Beratung. LC 79-351323. (Illus.). 160p. (Ger.). 1978. 19.80 F (ISBN 3-7658-0260-3). Bucher.
Gardner, James. Illustrated Soccer Dictionary for Young People. LC 76-10044. (Illustrated Dictionary Ser.). (Illus.). (gr. 5 up). 1976. PLB 7.29 (ISBN 0-8178-5482-7). Harvey.
--Illustrated Soccer Dictionary for Young People. (Illus.). 125p. (gr. 4 up). 1978. pap. 2.50 (ISBN 0-13-451146-8, Pub. by Treehouse). P-H.
Siekmann, Rob. Prisma Voetbalwoordenboek. LC 79-398681. 159p. (Dutch.). 1978. write for info. (ISBN 9-027-40962-5). Spectrum NL.
SOCIAL ASPECTS
see subdivision Social Aspects under subjects
SOCIAL CHANGE
Here are entered works on the theory of social change.
Filler, Louis. Dictionary of American Social Change. LC 82-10036. 266p. (Orig.). 1982. 16.50 (ISBN 0-89874-242-0); pap. 10.50 (ISBN 0-89874-564-0). Krieger.
SOCIAL CUSTOMS
see Manners and Customs; also subdivision Social Life and Customs under ethnic groups, e.g. Indians, Jews and under names of countries, cities, etc.
SOCIAL DEMOCRACY
see Socialism
SOCIAL ETHICS
see also Christian Ethics; Civics; Crime and Criminals; Social Problems
Rabotin, Maurice. Le Vocabulaire Politique & Socio-Ethnique a Montreal de 1839 a 1842. (Illus.). 122p. (Fr.). 1975. Can.$4.00. Didier-Canada.
SOCIAL HYGIENE
see Public Health
also related subjects referred to under these headings
SOCIAL INSURANCE
see Social Security
SOCIAL PLANNING
see Social Policy
SOCIAL POLICY
see also Christian Democracy; Economic Policy
also subdivision Social Policy under names of countries, states, cities, etc.
Zorin, I. N. Russko-Kitaiskii Obshcheekonomicheskii i Vneshnetorgovyi Slovar. 708p. (Rus.). 1961. $4.25 (Pub. by Vneshtorgizdat). Four Continent.
SOCIAL PROBLEMS
see also Charities; Civilization; Crime and Criminals; Housing; Juvenile Delinquency; Public Health; Public Welfare; Social Ethics
Filler, Louis. Dictionary of American Social Reform. LC 74-90505. Repr. of 1963 ed. lib. bdg. 26.25x (ISBN 0-8371-2137-X, FIAS). Greenwood.
SOCIAL PSYCHIATRY
Bleandonu, Gerard. Dictionnaire de Psychiatrie Sociale. 288p. (Fr.). 1976. 18.60 F. Payot.
Bleaudonu, Gerard. Dictionnaire de Psychiatrie Sociale. LC 77-454398. 284p. (Eng. & Fr.). 1976. 16.70 F (ISBN 2-228-32910-X). Payot.
SOCIAL PSYCHOLOGY
see also Psychology, Forensic; Social Psychiatry
Stang, David J. & Wrightman, Lawrence S. Dictionary of Social Behavior & Social Research Methods. LC 80-21511. 250p. 1980. pap. text ed. $8.95 (ISBN 0-8185-0243-6). Brooks-Cole.
SOCIAL REFORM
see Social Problems
SOCIAL SCIENCE
see Social Sciences; Sociology
SOCIAL SCIENCES
Here are entered general and comprehensive works dealing with sociology, political science, and economics.
see also Civics; Human Behavior; Social Change
Biron, Alain. Vocabulaire Pratique des Sciences Sociales. 384p. (Fr.). 35.50 F. Ouvrieres.
Lazarsfeld, Paul. Vocabulaire des Sciences Sociales. 2nd ed. (Fr.). 1971. 52.00 F. Mouton De Gruyter.
Schmieder, Christian & Fleischmann, Gunther. Schuelerlexikon fuer Arbeitslehre & Sozialkunde. 2nd ed. 304p. (Ger.). 1980. DM.24.80 (ISBN 3-40300-646-8). Auer.
SOCIAL SCIENCES–DICTIONARIES
Badawi, Zaki, compiled by. A Dictionary of the Social Sciences. 591p. (Arabic, Fr. & Eng.). $25.00 (115-1). Intl Bk Ctr.
An English-Chinese Glossary of Social Sciences & Education. 238p. (Eng. & Chinese.). 1975. Leatherette $9.95 (ISBN 0-686-92309-X, M-9562). French & Eur.
Filler, Louis. Dictionary of American Social Reform. LC 74-90505. Repr. of 1963 ed. lib. bdg. 26.25x (ISBN 0-8371-2137-X, FIAS). Greenwood.
Gould, Julius & Kolb, W. J. UNESCO Dictionary of the Social Sciences. LC 64-20307. 1964. $40.00 (ISBN 0-02-917490-2). Free Pr.
Grossman, Paul & Lang, Viktor, eds. Kleines Lexikon zur Politischen Bildung. LC 75-516868. 181p. (Ger.). 1975. DM.5.80 (ISBN 3-87364-033-3). Hornung-Verlag.
Lexique des Sciences Sociales. (Fr.). 1981. 490.00 F. Bruylant.
Mitchell, G. Duncan, ed. A New Dictionary of the Social Sciences. 2nd ed. 1980. text ed. $24.95x (ISBN 0-202-30285-7). Aldine Pub.
Reading, Hugo F. A Dictionary of the Social Sciences. 1977. 18.00 (ISBN 0-7100-8642-3); pap. 6.95 (ISBN 0-7100-8650-4). Routledge & Kegan.
Roth, Reiner A. & Selzer, Helmut M. Lexikon zur Arbeits & Soziallehre. Schmidt, Jurgen, ed. LC 76-468804. (Illus.). 383p. (Ger.). 1976. DM.32.80 (ISBN 3-403-00593-3). Auer.
Serrano, Miguel G. Diccionario de Terminos Socio-politicos. LC 77-570836. 210p. (Span.). 1977. write for info. (ISBN 8-424-11500-7). Everest.
Thines, Georges & Lempereur, Agnes. Diccionario General de Ciencias Humanas. 976p. (Span.). 1978. $45.00 (ISBN 84-376-0133-9, S-50146). French & Eur.
--Dictionnaire General des Sciences Humaines. 1000p. (Fr.). 1975. 350.00 F. Delarge.
UNESCO. Diccionario De Ciencias Sociales, 2 vols. 2370p. (Span.). 1975. Set. pap. $60.00 (ISBN 84-259-0434-X, S-50061). French & Eur.
Weber, Erich, et al. Kleines Sozial Wissenschaftliches Woerterbuch fuer Paedagogen. 2nd ed. 120p. (Ger.). 1976. DM.9.80. Auer.
SOCIAL SCIENCES–STATISTICS
Pinty, Jean-Jacques & Gaultier, Claude. Dictionnaire Pratique de Statistiques en Sciences Humaines. 300p. (Fr.). 1972. 65.00 F. Delarge.
SOCIAL SCIENCES–TERMINOLOGY
Badawi, A. A Dictionary of the Social Sciences. LC 79-120007. xvi, 591p. (Eng., Fr. & Arabic.). 1978. write for info. Lib Liban.
Birou, Alain. Vocabulaire Pratique des Sciences Sociales. 384p. (Fr.). $29.95 (ISBN 0-686-57277-7, F-136960). French & Eur.
Boudon, Raymond & Lazarsfeld, Paul. Vocabulaire Des Sciences Sociales: Concepts et Indices. (Methodes De la Sociologie: No. 1). (Fr.). 1971. pap. text ed. 17.50x (ISBN 90-2796-891-8). Mouton.
SOCIAL SECURITY
Dictionnaire des Assurances Sociales. 112p. (Fr.). 1973. write for info. Masson.
SOCIAL SERVICE
see also Charities; Public Welfare
Ander Egg, Ezequiel. Diccionario Del Trabajo Social. 424p. (Span.). 1977. pap. $12.25 (ISBN 84-280-0606-7, S-50011). French & Eur.
--Diccionario del Trabajo Social. 7th ed. 355p. (Span.). 1981. pap. 400.00 ptas (ISBN 84-500-4997-0). Organ Ofic Adm.
Deutscher, Ruth, et al, eds. Lexikon der Sozialen Arbeit. 260p. (Ger.). 1978. DM.19.00 (ISBN 3-17-002487-6). Kohlhammer.
Pfeffer, M. Kleines Woerterbuch Zur Arbeits und Sozialpolitik. 396p. (Ger.). 1972. pap. $7.50 (ISBN 0-686-56626-2, M-7516, Pub. by Herder). French & Eur.
--Kleines Woerterbuch Zur Arbeits und Sozialpolitik. 396p. (Ger.). 1972. pap. $7.50. Herder.
School of Social Work, Columbia University. Dictionary Catalog of the Whitney M. Young, Jr., Memorial Library of Social Work. 1980. lib. bdg. $1275.00 (ISBN 0-8161-0307-0, Hall Library). G K Hall.
Schwendtke, Arnold. Woerterbuch der Sozialarbeit & Sozialpaedagogik. 312p. (Ger.). 1977. DM.18.80 (ISBN 3-494-02072-8). Quelle & Meyer.
Timms, Noel & Timms, Rita. Dictionary of Social Welfare. 228p. 1982. 19.95 (ISBN 0-7100-9084-6). Routledge & Kegan.
Van Hee, Marijke. Woordenboek Welzijn. LC 79-391588. 266p. (Dutch.). 1979. fl.37.50 (ISBN 9-060-95489-0). VUGA.
SOCIAL SERVICE–BIBLIOGRAPHY
Clegg, Joan. Dictionary of Social Services: Policy & Practice. 3rd ed. 148p. 1980. 15.00x (ISBN 0-7199-1039-0). Intl Pubns Serv.
SOCIAL STUDIES
see Social Sciences
SOCIAL WELFARE
see Charities; Public Welfare; Social Problems; Social Service
SOCIAL WORK
see Social Service
SOCIAL WORK WITH YOUTH
Deutsch-Franz Jugendwerk. Glossar der Jugendarbeit: Deutsch Jugend & Ihr Soziales Umfeld. LC 80-469662. (Illus.). 147p. (Ger. & Fr.). 1979. DM.15.80 (ISBN 3-472-52033-7). H Luchterhand.
SOCIALISM
see also Labor and Laboring Classes; Marxian Economics
Fetscher, Iring. Lexikon des Marxismus. (Ger.). 1976. $20.00 (ISBN 3-455-09179-2, M-7207). French & Eur.
Mujica Herzog, Enrique. Diccionario del Socialismo. LC 77-568716. (Illus.). 90p. (Span.). 1977. 50.00 ptas (ISBN 8-472-35315-X). Dopesa.
Rappoport, Angelo S. Dictionary of Socialism. 1976. lib. bdg. 44.00 (ISBN 0-8490-1723-8). Gordon Pr.
Suavet, Thomas. Dictionnaire Economique & Social. 526p. (Fr.). 1973. 42.00 F. Ouvrieres.
SOCIETY AND EDUCATION
see Educational Sociology
SOCIETY AND LANGUAGE
see Sociolinguistics
SOCIOLINGUISTICS
William, Raymond. Keywords: A Vocabulary of Culture & Society. 1976. pap. 8.95 (ISBN 0-19-519855-7, GB). Oxford U Pr.
SOCIOLOGY
see also Aristocracy; Charities; Cities and Towns; Civilization; Communication; Crime and Criminals; Educational Sociology; Family; Labor and Laboring Classes; Population; Public Welfare; Secret Societies; Social Change; Social Ethics; Social Problems; Social Psychology; Socialism; Sociolinguistics; Women

Cohen, David. Dictionnaire des Racines Semitiques, 2. 76p. (Fr.). 1976. 60.00 F. Mouton De Gruyter.

Mann, Michael, ed. The International Dictionary of Sociology. 600p. 1983. $34.50 (ISBN 0-8264-0238-0). Continuum.

SOCIOLOGY-DICTIONARIES

Bernsdorf, Wilhelm, ed. Woerterbuch der Soziologie. (Ger.). 1969. DM.78.00 (ISBN 3-432-80392-3). Enke.

--Woerterbuch der Soziologie: Bd 1, 5 Aufl. (Ger.). 1976. DM.6.80 (ISBN 3-596-26131-7). Fischer Taschen.

--Woerterbuch der Soziologie: Bd 2, 4 Aufl. (Ger.). 1975. DM.6.80 (ISBN 3-596-26132-5). Fischer Taschen.

--Woerterbuch der Soziologie: Bd 3, 4 Aufl. (Ger.). 1976. DM.6.80 (ISBN 3-596-26133-3). Fischer Taschen.

Bibliography of Mono- & Multilingual Vocabularies, Thesauri, Subject Headings & Classification Schemes in the Social Sciences. (Reports & Papers in the Social Sciences: No. 54). 101p. 1983. pap. text ed. $7.00 (ISBN 92-3-102072-2, U1272, UNESCO). Unipub.

Birou, Alain. Lexico De Sociologia. 5th ed. 114p. (Span.). 1975. pap. $8.75 (ISBN 84-7222-753-7, S-50041). French & Eur.

Blinkert, B. Herder-Lexikon Soziologie. 240p. (Ger.). $23.95 (ISBN 3-451-16468-X, M-7452, Pub. by Herder). French & Eur.

--Herder-Lexikon Soziologie. 240p. (Ger.). $23.95 (ISBN 3-451-16468-X). Herder.

Claessens, Dieter. Jugendlexikon Gesellschaft: Einfache Antworten afu Schwierige Fragen. LC 76-469431. (Illus.). 184p. (Ger.). 1976. DM.5.80 (ISBN 3-499-16195-8). Rowohlt.

Dictionnaire Marabout Universite: La Sociologie, Vol. 1. (Fr.). 11.50 F. Marabout.

Dictionnaire Marabout Universite: La Sociologie, Vol. 2. (Fr.). 11.50 F. Marabout.

Dictionnaire Marabout Universite: La Sociologie, Vol. 3. (Fr.). 11.50 F. Marabout.

Dictionnaires Marabout Universite: La Sociologie, 3 vols. (Fr.). 34.50 F. Marabout.

Dreisprachiges Woerterbuch der Soziologie. 93p. (Ger. , Eng. & Fr., Trilingual Dictionary of Sociology). 1975. $9.95 (ISBN 3-445-01164-8, M-7353, Pub. by A. Hain). French & Eur.

Echanova, Carlos T. Diccionario de sociologia. (Span.). write for info. Calica.

Fairchild, H. P., et al. Diccionario de sociologia. 336p. (Span.). $5.00. Fondo Cult.

Fairchild, Henry P. Dictionary of Sociology & Related Sciences. LC 76-110377. Repr. of 1955 ed. lib. bdg. 22.75x (ISBN 0-8371-4581-3, FADS). Greenwood.

--Dictionary of Sociology & Related Sciences. (Quality Paperback: No. 120). 1977. pap. 4.50 (ISBN 0-8226-0120-6). Littlefield.

Filler, Louis. Dictionary of American Social Change. LC 82-10036. 266p. (Orig.). 1982. 16.50 (ISBN 0-89874-242-0); pap. 10.50 (ISBN 0-89874-564-0). Krieger.

Frankl, F. Dictionnaire de Droit Social Francais-Allemand. 258p. (Fr. & Ger.). 1970. write for info. (ISBN 3-19-006279-X, M-7099). French & Eur.

Fuchs, W. Lexikon Zur Soziologie, 2 vols. 800p. (Ger.). 1975. $12.95 (ISBN 3-499-16191-5, M-7191). French & Eur.

Fuchs, Werner, et al, eds. Lexikon zur Soziologie: Bd 1. (Ger.). 1975. DM.7.80 (ISBN 3-499-16191-5). Rowohlt.

--Lexikon zur Soziologie: Bd 2. (Ger.). 1975. DM.7.80 (ISBN 3-499-16192-3). Rowohlt.

Galliano, Luciano. Dizionario di sociologia. xii, 840p. (Ital.). 1978. L.34000.00 (ISBN 88-02-03165-7). UTET.

Hartfiel, Guenter. Woerterbuch der Soziologie. LC 77-458366. vi, 715p. (Ger.). 1976. DM.22.00 (ISBN 3-520-41002-8). Kroener.

Hoult, Thomas F. Dictionary of Modern Sociology. 448p. 1969. 11.50x (ISBN 0-87471-225-4). Rowman.

Mitchell, G. Duncan. Dizionario di sociologia. (Ital.). L.2800.00. Newton-Compton.

Ott, A. Dictionnaire des Sciences Politiques et Sociales, 3 vols. Migne, J. P., ed. (Troisieme et Derniere Encyclopedie Theologique Ser.: Vols. 1-3). 2014p. (Fr.). Repr. of 1855 ed. lib. bdg. $256.00x (ISBN 0-89241-290-9). Caratzas Pub Co.

Schoeck. Diccionario de Sociologia. 392p. (Span.). 1974. E480.00 (ISBN 84-254-0853-9). Herder SA.

Schoeck, H. Soziologisches Woerterbuch. 400p. (Ger.). 1975. $7.95 (ISBN 0-686-56468-5, M-7622, Pub. by Herder). French & Eur.

--Soziologisches Woerterbuch. 400p. (Ger.). 1975. $7.95. Herder.

Schoeck, Helmut. Diccionario De Sociologia. 2nd ed. 392p. (Span.). 1977. $19.95 (ISBN 84-254-0853-9, S-50191); pap. $17.50 (ISBN 84-254-0854-7, S-50188). French & Eur.

--Diccionario de sociologia. 3rd ed. Herder, tr. 312p. (Span.). 1981. pap. 600.00 ptas (ISBN 84-254-0854-7). Herder SA.

--Diccionario de sociologia. 3rd ed. Herder, tr. 392p. (Span.). 1981. 800.00 ptas (ISBN 84-254-0853-9). Herder AS.

Schwendtke, Arnold. Woerterbuch der Sozialarbeit und der Sozialpaedagogik. (Ger.). 1977. pap. write for info (ISBN 3-494-02072-8, M-6955). French & Eur.

Suarvet, Thomas H. Dictionnaire Economique et Social. 526p. (Fr.). 1973. $19.95 (ISBN 0-686-57227-0, M-6526). French & Eur.

Sumpf, Joseph & Hugues, Michel. Dictionnaire de Sociologie. 256p. (Fr.). 1973. pap. $7.95 (ISBN 0-686-57228-9, M-6527). French & Eur.

--Dictionnaire de Sociologie. 256p. (Fr.). 1973. 17.60 F. Larousse.

Theodorson, George A. & Theodorson, Achilles A. A Modern Dictionary of Sociology. (Everyday Handbooks). 469p. pap. $5.95 (ISBN 0-06-463483-3). B&N NY.

Tubella, Imma. Diccionari del Nacionalisme. 144p. (Catalan.). 1978. pap. pns (ISBN 84-7410-034-8, S-50125). French & Eur.

Viet, Jean. Thesaurus pour le Traitement de l'information en Sociologie. 355p. (Fr.). 1971. 59.00 F. Mouton de Gruyter.

Willems, Emilio. Dictionnaire de Sociologie. 314p. (Fr.). 1970. pap. $14.95 (ISBN 0-686-57261-0, M-6573). French & Eur.

--Dictionnaire de Sociologie. 314p. (Fr.). 1970. 30.00 F. Riviere.

SOCIOLOGY-METHODOLOGY

Viet, Jean. Thesaurus for Information Processing in Sociology. 1971. pap. text ed. 20.00x (ISBN 90-2796-941-8). Mouton.

SOCIOLOGY, EDUCATIONAL
see Educational Sociology
SOCIOLOGY OF LANGUAGE
see Sociolinguistics
SODA INDUSTRY
Standard Terms Used in the Soda Pulping Process. 1961. $1.00 (1202); members $0.67. TAPPI.
Standard Terms Used in the Sulfate Pulping Process. 1961. $1.00 (1203); members $0.67. TAPPI.
SODIUM
Kraus, Barbara. The Dictionary of Sodium, Fats, & Cholesterol. (Illus.). 384p. Date not set. pap. 6.95 (ISBN 0-399-50945-3, Perigee). Putnam Pub Group.
SOFISM
see Sufism
SOFT DRINKS
see Beverages
SOFTWARE, COMPUTER
see Programming (Electronic Computers); Programming Languages (Electronic Computers)

also similiar headings
SOIL (ENGINEERING)
see Soil Mechanics
SOIL CONSERVATION
Pritchard, H. Wayne, pref. by. Resource Conservation Glossary. 3rd ed. LC 82-5830. 193p. 1982. pap. $7.00 (ISBN 0-935734-09-0). Soil Conservation.
Torrent Control Terminology. (FAO Conservation Guides: No. 6). 156p. (Eng. , Span. , Ital. & Ger.). 1982. pap. $12.00 (ISBN 92-5-001091-5, F2224, FAO). Unipub.
SOIL ENGINEERING
see Soil Mechanics
SOIL MECHANICS
see also Foundations
Barker, John. Dictionary of Soil Mechanics & Foundation Engineering. 1981. pap. text ed. 30.00x (ISBN 0-86095-885-X). Longman.
Dictionary of Soil Science & Soil Engineering Terms. (Hebrew, Eng. , Ger. & Fr.). IL.8.00. Massada Pr.
Schneider, M. E. Semiiazychnyi Slovar Po Mekhanike Gruntov & Fundamentostroeniiu. 139p. (Rus. & Span. & Eng. & Fr., Ger. & Swedish.). 1958. $3.30 (Pub. by Gosizdat Fizmat. Lit.). Four Continent.
Visser, A., ed. Dictionary of Soil Mechanics. (Eng., Fr., Dutch, & Ger.). 1965. $89.50 (ISBN 0-444-40613-1). Elsevier.
SOIL SCIENCE
see also Agriculture
Boleslaw, Adamczyk. Pieciojezyczny Slownik Gleboznawczy. LC 76-532466. 264p. (Eng., Fr., Ger., Pol. & Rus.). 1976. 120.00 Zl. Panstwowe Zaklad W.
Conea, Ana. Dictionar de Stinta Solului. LC 78-362360. 671p. (Romanian.). 1977. 34.00 lei. Editura Stiintifica.
Jongerius, A. & Rutherford, G. K., eds. Glossary of Soil Micromorphology. LC 79-321392. xiii, 138p. (Eng., Fr., Ger., Rus. & Span.). 1979. write for info. (ISBN 9-02-200637-9). Pudoc.
Plaisance, Georges. Lexique Pedologique Trilingue. 355p. (Fr.). 1958. 44.00 F. CDU.
SOILS
see also Clay; Drainage; Irrigation
also headings beginning with the word Soil
Glossary of Soil & Water Terms. 62p. 1967. $6.00 (SP0467); members $4.50. Am Soc Ag Eng.
Plaisance, George. Lexique Pedologique Trilingue. 355p. (Fr.). 1958. pap. $22.50 (ISBN 0-686-57082-0, M-6458). French & Eur.
SOILS-MECHANICS
see Soil Mechanics
SOILS (ENGINEERING)
see Soil Mechanics
SOLAR ENERGY
Aguilar, Peris & Jose-Aguilar Civera, J. Diccionario de Energia Solar. 232p. (Span.). 1982. 410.00 ptas (ISBN 8-42050-923-X). Alhambra.
Dictionnaire Contextuel Anglais-Francais de l'energie Solaire. 67p. (Eng. & Fr.). 1979. pap. $7.95 (ISBN 0-9690950-0-7, M-9032). French & Eur.
Hunt, Daniel V. Conservation & Solar Energy Dictionary. Date not set. $39.50 (ISBN 0-442-20056-0). Van Nos Reinhold.
Hunt, V. Daniel. The Solar Energy Dictionary. (Illus.). 450p. 1982. $29.95 (ISBN 0-8311-1139-9). Indus Pr.
Serre, Robert. Dictionnaire Contextuel Anglais-Francais de l'energie Solaire. LC 80-481480. 67p. (Eng. & Fr.). 1979. Can.$pap. 4.00 (ISBN 0-9690950-0-7). Serre.
SOLAR POWER
see Solar Energy
SOLDIERS-DRILL
see Drill and Minor Tactics
SOLDIERS' LIFE
Elting, John R. & Cragg, Dan. A Dictionary of Soldier Talk. 480p. 1983. $24.95 (ISBN 0-684-17862-1, ScribT). Scribner.
SOLID WASTE MANAGEMENT
see Refuse and Refuse Disposal

SOLOMON ISLANDS
Ivens, Walter G. A Dictionary of the Language of Bugotu, Santa Isabel Island, Solomon Islands. LC 75-35125. Repr. of 1940 ed. $14.50 (ISBN 0-404-14141-2). AMS Pr.
SOLS
see Colloids
SOLUBLE FERMENTS
see Enzymes
SOLZHENITSYN, ALEKSANDR ISAEVICH, 1918-
Carpovich, Vera V. Solzhenitsyn's Peculiar Vocabulary, Russian-English Glossary. LC 76-3932. (Rus. & Eng.). 1976. $15.00 (ISBN 0-911484-04-3). Tech Dict.
SOMALI LANGUAGE
Philbert, Christophe. Petit Lexique Somali-Francais. LC 77-477705. 57p. (Somali & Fr.). 1976. 40.00 F (ISBN 2-25201-849-6). Klincksieck.
SOMALIA
Castagno, Margaret F. Historical Dictionary of Somalia. LC 75-25681. (African Historical Dictionary Ser.: No. 6). 1975. $14.00 (ISBN 0-8108-0830-7). Scarecrow.
SONGS, POPULAR
see Music, Popular (Songs, etc.)
SONIC ENGINEERING
see Acoustical Engineering
SOPHISTRY (LOGIC)
see Fallacies (Logic)
SORCERY
see Magic
SOTHO LANGUAGE
English Sotho-Sotho English Dictionary. (Eng. & Sotho.). $21.00 (ISBN 0-87559-031-4); thumb indexed $27.00 (ISBN 0-87559-032-2). Shalom.
SOUBRIQUETS
see Nicknames
SOUND
see also Acoustical Engineering; Architectural Acoustics; Electro-Acoustics; Phonetics; Vibration
Applied Technical Dictionary: Acoustics. $50.00x (ISBN 0-569-08535-7, Pub. by Collets). State Mutual Bk.
Hoefling, Oskar, ed. Lexikon der Schulphysik: Bd 1, Mechanik & Akustik. (Ger.). 1978. DM.54.00 (ISBN 3-7614-0107-8). Aulis Verlag.
Reichardt, L. Dictionary of Technical Acoustics. (Ger., Fr., Rus., Span., Pol. & Hungarian.). 1978. $20.40 (ISBN 0-685-92166-2). Adler.
Reichardt, W. Dictionary of Acoustics: English-German-French-Russian-Spanish-Polish-Madarsko-Slovene. 267p. (Eng., Ger., Fr., Rus., Span., Pol., Madarsko & Slovene.). 1978. $95.00 (ISBN 0-686-92601-3, M-9897). French & Eur.
Stephens, R. W., ed. Sound: In Eight Languages. LC 74-16209. (International Dictionaries of Science & Technology Ser.). 853p. 1974. 69.95 (ISBN 0-470-82200-7). Halsted Pr.
SOUND ENGINEERING
see Acoustical Engineering
SOUND-WAVES
Peraux, Henry. Diccionario general de acustica y electroacustica. 376p. (Span.). 1967. 300.00 ptas. Paraninfo.
Piraux. Diccionario General de Acustica & Electroacustica. (Span.). 1967. 550.00 ptas (ISBN 8-42830-799-7). Paraninfo.
SOUND-WAVES-INDUSTRIAL APPLICATIONS
see Acoustical Engineering
SOUTH AMERICA
see also names of countries, regions, etc. in South America, e.g. Amazon River and Valley
Diccionario Escolar Hispanoamericano. 4th ed. 600p. (Span.). 1975. pap. $3.95 (ISBN 84-319-0027-X, S-27088). French & Eur.
SOUTHERN SOTHO LANGUAGE
see Sotho Language
SOUTHERN STATES-HISTORY-CIVIL WAR, 1861-1865
see United States-History-Civil War, 1861-1865

SOUTHWEST, NEW–ANTIQUITIES
Barnett, Franklin. Dictionary of Prehistoric Indian Artifacts of the American Southwest. LC 73-82865. (Illus.). 288p. 1973. pap. $8.95 (ISBN 0-87358-120-2). Northland.

SOVEREIGNS
see Roman Emperors
also subdivision Kings and Rulers under names of countries

SPACE, OUTER
see Outer Space

SPACE ENVIRONMENT
Tver, David F. Dictionary of Astronomy, Space & Atmospheric Phenomena. 1979. text ed. $19.95 (ISBN 0-442-24045-7). Van Nos Reinhold.

SPACE MEDICINE
see also Aviation Medicine
Giurdzhian, A. A., et al, eds. Anglo-Russkii Slovar Po Aviatsionno-Kosmicheskoi Meditsine. 388p. (Rus. & Eng.). 1972. $5.60 (Pub. by Voenizdat). Four Continent.

SPACE RESEARCH
see Space Sciences

SPACE SCIENCES
see also Astronomy; Geophysics; Outer Space; Space Medicine
Angelo, Joseph. The Dictionary of Space Technology. 384p. 1982. $70.00x (ISBN 0-584-95011-X, Pub. by Muller Ltd). State Mutual Bk.
Angelo, Joseph A., Jr. The Dictionary of Space Technology. (Illus.). 400p. 1983. pap. $15.50 (ISBN 0-442-20936-3). Van Nos Reinhold.
Murashkevich, A. M. & Vladimirov, O. N. English-Russian Aviation & Space Abbreviations Dictionary. 622p. (Eng. & Rus.). 1981. $45.00x (ISBN 0-686-44706-9, Pub. by Collets). State Mutual Bk.

SPACE VEHICLES–INSTRUMENTS
see Astronautical Instruments

SPACE WEATHER
see Space Environment

SPAIN
see also names of regions, cities, etc. in Spain
Blazquez, Jose M. Diccionario de las religiones perromanas de Hispania. LC 76-450345. (Illus.). 191p. (Span.). 1975. 300.00 ptas (ISBN 8-47090-071-4). Istmo.
Ferrer-Pastor, Francesc. Vocabulari Castella-Valencia & Valencia-Castella. LC 80-117607. 1075p. (Span. & Catalan.). 1979. write for info. (ISBN 8-485-10436-6). Estel Edit.
Otero, Anibal. Vocabulario de San Jorge de Piquin. LC 77-566102. 225p. (Span.). 1977. 500.00 ptas (ISBN 8-47191-009-8). Univers Santiago.

SPAIN–BIBLIOGRAPHY
Hidalgo, Dionisio. Diccionario De Bibliografia Espanola, 7 Vols. LC 68-57908. (Bibliography & Reference Ser.: No. 122). (Span.). 1970. Repr. of 1881 ed. text ed. $215.00 (ISBN 0-8337-1699-9). B Franklin.

SPAIN–ECONOMIC CONDITIONS
Arnal Cavero, Pedro. Vocabulario del Alto-Aragones de Alquezar & Pueblos Proximos. 32p. (Span.). 1944. 50.00 ptas (CSIC). Inst. Antonio de Nebrija.

SPAIN–HISTORY
Here are entered general works on Spanish history, and works on all periods of Spanish history except the Civil War, 1936-1939, which are entered below under Spain–History–Civil War, 1936-1939.
Abos Santabarbara, Angel L. & Marco Martinez, Antonio. Diccionario de terminos basicos para la historia. 636p. (Span.). 1982. pap. 890.00 ptas (ISBN 84-205-0931-0). Alhambra.
Amalric, Jacques, et al. Lexico historico de Espana. Lajo, Rosina & Frigola, Victoria, trs. 224p. (Span.). 1982. pap. 575.00 ptas (ISBN 84-306-5703-7). Taurus Ediciones SA.
Bleiber, German. Diccionario de historia de Espana. 2nd ed. 3861p. (Span.). 1969. 2400.00 ptas. Alianza Ed.
Bleiberg, German. Diccionario de Historia de Espana, 3 vols. 3776p. (Span.). 1979. Set. pap. $70.00 (ISBN 84-206-5997-5, S-50374). French & Eur.
--Diccionario de Historia de Espana, 3 vols. 3776p. (Span.). 1979. Set. $100.00 (ISBN 84-206-5298-9, S-10785). French & Eur.
--Diccionario de Historia de Espana, 3 vols. 2nd ed. 3776p. (Span.). 1981. 6000.00 ptas (ISBN 84-206-5298-9). Alianza Ed.
--Diccionario de Historia de Espana, Vol. 2. 2nd ed. 1192p. (Span.). 1981. 2000.00 ptas (ISBN 84-206-5206-7). Alianza Ed.
--Diccionario de Historia de Espana, Vol. 3. 2nd ed. 1216p. (Span.). 1981. 2000.00 ptas (ISBN 84-206-5207-5). Alianza Ed.
Diccionario de Historia de Espana, Vol. 1. 2nd ed. 1368p. (Span.). 1981. 2000.00 ptas (ISBN 84-206-5205-9). Alianza Ed.
Lexique Historique de l'Espagne XVIe. & XXe. Siecle. (Illus.). 232p. (Fr.). 1976. 26.00 F. Colin.

SPAIN–HISTORY–CIVIL WAR, 1936-1939
Cortada, James W., ed. Historical Dictionary of the Spanish Civil War, 1936-1939. LC 81-13424. (Illus.). xxviii, 571p. 1982. lib. bdg. 67.50 (ISBN 0-313-22054-9, CSP/). Greenwood.

SPAIN–POLITICS AND GOVERNMENT
Rico y Amat, Juan. Diccionario de los Politicos, 1855. 358p. (Span.). 1976. write for info. Narcea SA.

SPAIN–SOCIAL LIFE AND CUSTOMS
Ruiz Fernandez, Ciriaco. El Lexico del Teatro de Valle Inclan. 313p. (Span.). 1981. 600.00 ptas (ISBN 84-7481-152-X). Univ Salamanca.
Vizcaino Casas, Fernando. Diccionario del cine espanol 1896-1968. 3rd ed. (Span.). 450.00 ptas. Nacional Editora.

SPANISH AMERICA
see Latin America

SPANISH-AMERICAN LITERATURE
see also Puerto Rican Literature
Boyd-Bowman, Peter. Lexico hispanoamericano del siglo XVIII. (Spanish Ser.: No. 5). (Span.). 1982. 10.00 (ISBN 0-942260-21-X). Hispanic Seminary.

SPANISH GUITAR
see Guitar

SPANISH LANGUAGE
see also Catalan Language
Aschiero, Hipolito R. Diccionario de Homofonos Castellans: Repertorio Alfabetico de Adjetivos, Verbos & su Correcta Ortografia. LC 77-454249. 120p. (Span.). 1975. write for info. Edit Victor Leru.
Cejador & Frauca, Julio. Vocabulario Medieval Castellano. (Span.). Mex.$12.50. Las Americas.
Clark, Lawrence & Clark, Nancy. Vocabulario Popoluca de Sayula. (Vocabularios Indigenas Ser.: No. 4). 165p. (Span.). 1960. pap. $3.00x (ISBN 0-88312-663-X); microfiche $2.25 (ISBN 0-88312-365-7). Summer Inst Ling.
De Rosario. Vocabulario Puertorriqueno. (Span.). 1966. $10.95 (ISBN 0-87751-010-5, Pub by Troutman Press). E Torres & Sons.
Espinosa, Aurelio M. & Gambetta, Leon. Spanish for Doctors & Nurses. (Span.). $6.85. Camino Real.
Flynn & Montoto. Spanish for Urban Workers. (Span.). $9.95; pap. $7.75. Camino Real.
Silverstein, et al. Spanish Now. (Span.). $5.95. Camino Real.
Tescher & Bills. Spanish & English of the United States Hispanos. (Span. & Eng.). $9.55. Camino Real.

SPANISH LANGUAGE–TO 1500
Aedos. Diccionario Espanol de Sinonimos, Equivalencias & Ideas Alfines. 8th ed. LC 80-100011. 443p. (Span.). 1979. write for info. (ISBN 8-470-03072-8). Aedos.
Gomez de Cadiz, Javier. Diccionario de Siglas. LC 77-471470. 62p. (Span.). 1976. 50.00 ptas (ISBN 8-420-30051-9). Alas.
Mackenzie, David. A Manual of Manuscript Transcription for the Dictionary of the Old Spanish Language. 2nd ed. (Illus.). 128p. (Span.). 1981. pap. $15.00 (ISBN 0-942260-15-5). Hispanic Seminary.
Navarrete Luft, Anita. Diccionario de Terminos Anticuados & en Desuso. (Span.). pap. $9.95. PLY.

SPANISH LANGUAGE–BUSINESS SPANISH
De Renty, Ivan. Lexique Quadrilingue des Affaires: Anglais-Francais-Allemand-Espagnol. 702p. (Eng., Fr., Ger. & Span.). 1977. 72.00 F. Hachette.

SPANISH LANGUAGE–CONVERSATION AND PHRASE BOOKS
see also Spanish Language–Self-Instruction; Spanish Language–Textbooks for Children
Bomse, Marguerite D. Practical Spanish Dictionary & Phrasebook. new ed. (Span.). 1978. pap. text ed. 7.50 (ISBN 0-08-023020-2). Pergamon.
Ellison, Al. Ellison's Latin American Menu Reader. (Lat.). 1978. pap. $2.95 (ISBN 0-930580-06-0). Ellison Ent.
Howell, G. & Perez Y Sabido, J. Spanish-English Handbook. 1977. pap. 11.95 (ISBN 0-87489-073-X). Med Economics.
Neverov, S. Ispansko-Russkii Razgovornik. 190p. (Rus. & Span.). 1953. $1.25 (Pub. by Izd. Lit. Na Inostr. Iaz.). Four Continent.
Patterson, William R. Learn Spanish for English Speakers. rev. ed. MacAndrew, Ronald, ed. (Span. & Eng.). 9.50 (ISBN 0-87557-078-X, 078-X). Saphrograph.
Sanchez Benedito, Francisco. Diccionario Conciso de Modismos Ingles-Espanol, Espanol-Ingles. 270p. (Eng. & Span.). 1977. pap. $17.95 (ISBN 0-686-56890-7, S-50582). French & Eur.
U. S. War Department. A Phrase & Sentence Dictionary of Spoken Spanish. LC 58-14487. (Span. & Eng.). 1958. lib. bdg. 13.50x (ISBN 0-88307-580-6). Gannon.

SPANISH LANGUAGE–DIALECTS
Alcala, A. Vocabulario Andaluz. 676p. (Span.). 1980. $47.95 (ISBN 84-249-1364-7, S-32726). French & Eur.
Arbelaiz, Juan J. Diccionario Vasco-Castellano & Castellano-Vasco. 2nd. ed. 370p. (Span.). 1982. pap. 442.00 ptas (ISBN 8-42480-758-8). Encicl Vasca.
Arbelaiz, Juan Jose. Diccionario Vasco-Castellano & Castellano-Vasco de Voces Comunes. 370p. (Span.). 1982. 370.00 ptas (ISBN 8-42480-758-8). Encicl Vasca.
Ballarin Cornel, Angel. Vocabulario de Benasque. 224p. (Span.). 1972. 200.00 ptas. Fernando el Catolico.
Cano Gonzalez, Ana M. Vocabulario del Bable de Somiedo. 480p. (Span.). 1982. pap. 300.00 ptas (ISBN 8-40005-173-4). Consejo Superior.
Cela, Camilo J. & Margarit, Badia A. M. Diccionari Manual Castella-Catala Catala-Castella. 680p. (Catalan.). 850.00 ptas (ISBN 84-7153-392-8). Bibliograf SP.
Delgaty, Alfa & Sanchez, Augustin R. Diccionario Tzotzil De San Andres Con Variaciones Dialectales. (Vocabularios Indigenas: No. 22). (Illus.). 481p. (Orig., Tzotzil & Span.). 1978. pap. $10.00x (ISBN 0-88312-674-5); microfiche $4.50x (ISBN 0-88312-372-X). Summer Inst Ling.
Diccionari catala general. 1418p. (Span.). 1971. 550.00 ptas. M. Arimany.
Diccionari practic catala general. 400p. (Span.). 1969. write for info. M. Arimany.
Diccionario Castella-Catala Catala-Castella. 4th ed. 680p. (Span.). 1981. 625.00 ptas (ISBN 84-7153-198-4). Biblo SP.
Diccionario Saber miniatura. 414p. (Span.). Mex.$3.75. Fernandez.
Fernandez Armesto, Fermin. Vocabulario castelan-galego. 764p. (Span.). 1981. pap. 950.00 ptas (ISBN 84-7492-075-2). Castro Edns.
Fernandez de la Vega & Hernandez Miyares. Ortografia Activa: Letras & Acentos. (Span.). 1980. write for info. Gale.
Fernandez del Riego, Francisco. Vocabulario Castellano-Gallego. 3rd ed. 366p. (Span.). 1981. 325.00 ptas (ISBN 84-7154-324-9). Galaxia.
Fernandez Naranjo, Nicolas. Diccionario de Bolivianismos. 247p. (Span.). 1980. write for info. Cochabamba.
Ferrer Pastor, Francesc. Vocabulari Valencia-Castella. 566p. (Span.). 1970. write for info. Fermar.
Franco Grande, X. L. Diccionario galego-castelan. 2nd ed. (Span.). 300.00 ptas. Galaxia.
Franco Grande, Xose L. Diccionario galego-castelan. 7th ed. 970p. (Span.). 1982. pap. 1200.00 ptas (ISBN 84-7154-024-X). Galaxia.
--Vocabulario Galego-Castelan. (Span.). 90.00 ptas. Galaxia.
Franco Grande, Xose L. & Fernandez del Riego, Francisco. Vocabulario Galego-Castelan Castellano-Gallego. 584p. (Span.). 1982. pap. 775.00 ptas (ISBN 84-7154-413-X). Galaxia.
Galvan, Roberto A. & Teschner, Richard V. El Diccionario Del Espano! Chicano. 1977. pap. text ed. $6.95 ea. (ISBN 0-88499-146-6). Inst Mod Lang.
Garcia Soriano, Justo. Vocabulario del dialecto murciano. 316p. (Span.). 1980. pap. 500.00 ptas (ISBN 84-500-4063-9). Organ Ofic Adm.
Garriga, Teresa. Lexica (II) 190p. (Span.). 1981. 850.00 ptas (ISBN 84-7091-190-2). Jaimes Libros.
Guasch, Antonio. Diccionario castellano-guarani, guarani-castellano. 788p. (Span.). 1961. $6.80. Dist. Comuneros.
Ibanez, Esteban. Diccionario espanol-senhayi: Dialecto bereber de Senhay de Serair. 382p. (Span.). 1959. 150.00 ptas. Inst. de Estudios Africanos CSIC.
Instituto da Lingua Galega. Dicionario Basico da Lingua Galega. 2nd ed. 288p. (Span.). 1982. 315.00 ptas (ISBN 8-47507-003-5). Xerais de Galicia.
Jover Peralta, A & Ozuna, T. Diccionario guarani-espanol, espanol-guarani. 508p. (Span. & Guarani.). 1951. $4.50. Dist. Comuneros.
Larreula, Frederic. Diccionari Catala-Castella-Castellano-Catalan. 544p. (Span.). 1980. 250.00 ptas. Bruguera.
Munte Vila, Josep. Diccionari Catala-Castella: Vocabulari Basic. 216p. (Span.). 1981. write for info. ptas (ISBN 84-7031-275-8). Blume Edit.
Rodriguez Lapa, M. Vocabulario Galego-Portugues. (Galego & Port.). write for info. Galaxia.
Roncalla, P. Ortografia Practica: Ejercicios & Ensayos Sobre Ortografia Castellano. 162p. (Span.). 1979. $3.00. Gale.
Vocabulari Castella-Valencia. 8th ed. 1076p. (Span.). 1981. 350.00 ptas (ISBN 84-85104-36-6). Estel Edit.

SPANISH LANGUAGE–DICTIONARIES
ABC Dictionary I, Arabic-Spanish. (Arabic & Span.). $7.99 (ISBN 0-86685-308-1). Intl Bk Ctr.
Abd Al-Monem, Mufid Al-Guindi. Diccionario Espanol-Arabe de Verbos, Gramatica y Temas de Conversacion. 2nd ed. 368p. (Span. & Arabic.). 1974. pap. $13.95 (ISBN 84-7074-021-0, S-50423). French & Eur.
Aberlaitz & Buenaventura de Oreyegui, P. Diccionario Vasco-Castellano, Castellano-Vasco De Voces Comunes a Dos O Mas Dialectos Del Euskera. (Span.). $25.50 (ISBN 84-248-0014-1, S-21917). French & Eur.
Aguilera, F. Lexico Espanol-Kawesqar. LC 77-567778. (Alacaluf & Span., Santiago, Chile). 1976. write for info. Centro Invest.

Alberti, Santiago. Diccionari Castella-Catala, Catala-Castella, Mitja. 2nd ed. 584p. (Catalan & Castel.). 1978. $19.95 (ISBN 84-400-0761-2, S-31551). French & Eur.

Alcala Zamora. Diccionario bilingue frances-espanol-aleman. Rev. ed. (Illus.). 960p. (Fr., Span. & Ger.). 100.00 ptas. 75.00 ptas ptas. Sopena.

Alcover, Antoni M. & Moll, Francesc de B. Diccionari I Catala-Valencia-Balear, 10 vols. 2nd ed. 9850p. (Catalan.). 1975. Set. $200.00 (ISBN 84-273-0025-5, S-31549). French & Eur.

Alcover Sureda, Antoni M. & Casasnoves, Moll. Diccionari catala-valencia-balear, 10 vols. (Illus., Span.). 1200.00 ea. ptas. 11000.00 set. Moll Edit.

Alfaro, Ricardo J. Diccionario de Anglicismos. 2nd ed. 520p. (Span.). $29.95 (ISBN 84-249-1342-6, S-11836). French & Eur.

Alfaya, Javier, ed. Diccionario Santillana. LC 76-460370. xii, 1021p. (Span.). 1975. write for info. (ISBN 8-439-94544-2). Santillana.

Alhambra. Diccionario Arabe-Espanol, Espanol-Arabe. 1252p. (Arabic & Span.). $17.95 (ISBN 84-303-0163-1, S-50424). French & Eur.

Alonso, Martin. Diccionario del Espanol Moderno. 5th ed. 1100p. (Span.). 1978. $66.00 (ISBN 84-03-27061-5, S-12229). French & Eur.

--Diccionario espanol moderno. (Span.). 1974. 1000.00 ptas. Aguilar SP.

Andres, F. Diccionario espanol de sinonimos y equivalencias. 6th ed. 386p. (Span.). 1972. 250.00 ptas. Aedos.

Andres, M. F. Diccionario Espanol de Sinonimos y Equivalencias. 8th ed. 444p. (Span.). 1979. $17.50 (ISBN 84-7003-072-8, S-12233). French & Eur.

Andrews Heath de Zapata, Dorothy. Vocabulario de Mayathan. LC 79-351468. 607p. (Maya & Span.). 1978. write for info. Dorothy Andrews Heath de Zapata.

Andujar, Julio I. Mastering Spanish Verbs. (Span.). $2.25. Camino Real.

Aquino-Bermudez, et al. Mi Diccionario Ilustrado: Edicion Bilingue. LC 73-181891. (Illus.). 96p. (Span.). (ps-3). 1972. PLB $7.92 (ISBN 0-688-50994-0); pap. $3.95 (ISBN 0-688-45007-5). Lothrop.

Arana, Evangelina & Swadesh, Mauricio. Diccionario analitico de Mampruli. (Span.). 1967. Mex.$40.00. INAH.

Argentina, ed. Diccionario indice analitico, 3 vols. (Span.). write for info. Ediar.

Arimany Coma, Miguel. Diccionari Catala General Usual. 4th ed. 1418p. (Catalan.). 1976. $35.95 (ISBN 84-7211-097-4, S-50049). French & Eur.

--Diccionari Manual Castella-Catala. 2nd ed. 413p. (Castella & Catalan.). 1975. $8.75 (ISBN 84-7211-084-2, S-50358). French & Eur.

--Diccionari Manual Catala-Castella. 2nd ed. 535p. (Catalan & Castella.). 1975. $8.75 (ISBN 84-7211-078-8, S-50357). French & Eur.

--Diccionari Manual Catala-Castella i Castella-Catala. 9th ed. 956p. (Catalan & Castella.). 1976. $16.50 (ISBN 84-7211-088-5, S-50360). French & Eur.

--Diccionari Practic Castella-Catala, Catala-Castella. 3rd ed. 456p. (Castella & Catalan.). 1976. $9.95 (ISBN 84-7211-087-7, S-50356). French & Eur.

--Diccionari Usual Catala-Castella i Castella-Catala. 7th ed. 958p. (Catalan & Castella.). 1976. $23.95 (ISBN 84-7211-080-X, S-50361). French & Eur.

Arimany Coma, Miquel. Diccionari Basic Catala-Castella, Castella-Catala. 9th ed. 390p. (Catala & Span.). 1975. pap. $3.95 (ISBN 84-7211-085-0, S-50359). French & Eur.

Aristos. Diccionario Ilustrado De la Lengua Espanola. 640p. (Span.). $10.95 (ISBN 84-303-0048-1, S-12234). French & Eur.

Arogones, Pablo. Diccionario basico. (Illus., Span.). 150.00 ptas. Mayfe.

Artella, Eduard. Vocabulari Catala-Castella. 468p. (Span.). 1961. 150.00 ptas. Barcino Edit.

Artells, Eduard. Vocabulari Castella-Catala. 3rd ed. 224p. (Catalan & Span.). 1958. $5.95 (ISBN 84-7226-344-4, S-50355). French & Eur.

--Vocabulari Castella-Catala. 290p. (Span.). 1961. 100.00 ptas. Barcino Edit.

--Vocabulari Catala-Castella. 3rd ed. 465p. (Catalan & Span.). 1961. $5.25 (ISBN 84-7226-345-2, S-50354). French & Eur.

Aschiero, Hipolito F. Diccionario de Homofonos Castellaros. 120p. (Span.). 1975. $15.95 (ISBN 0-686-56712-9, S-33053). French & Eur.

Aulie, H. W. & De Aulie, Evelyn W. Diccionario Ch'ol-Espanol. LC 79-116730. 215p. (Span. & Chold.). 1978. write for info. Inst Ling Ver.

Austridan, Y., ed. Diccionario Hebreo-Castellano: Castellano-Hebreo. 390p. (Hebrew & Span.). 1979. pap. $40.00 (ISBN 0-686-92419-3, S-37819). French & Eur.

Balagur, Miguel. Diccionario griego-espanol. (Gr. & Span.). 300.00 ptas. Bibliografica.

Barcia, Roque. Diccionario de Sinonimos. 160p. (Span., Mexico). 1980. Mex.$275.00. Oasis SA.

--Sinonimus Castellanos. 17th ed. 590p. (Span.). 1978. $27.50 (ISBN 0-686-56660-2, S-11889). French & Eur.

Barrera Vasquez, Alfredo. Diccionario Maya Cordemex Maya-Espanol. 69th ed. 360p. (Maya & Span.). 1980. Mex.$pap. 3000.00. Porrua.

Becker, Idel. Dicionario Espanhol-Portugues & Portugues-Espanhol, 2 vols. 5th ed. LC 76-480630. 471p. (Port. & Span.). 1976. Cr.$70.00. Liv Nobel.

Bildwoerterbuch Spanisch: Diccionario por la Imagen. (Illus.). 912p. (Span. & Ger.). DM.29.80 (ISBN 3-411-00971-3). Biblio Inst.

Blanco Garcia, Vicente. Diccionario latino-espanol y espanol-latino. (Span.). 175.00 ptas. Aguilar SP.

Blanquez. Diccionario Latino-Espanol, Espanol-Latino, 3 vols. 2703p. (Lat. & Span.). Set. leatherette $75.00 (ISBN 84-303-0151-8, S-50419). French & Eur.

Blanquez Fraile, Agustin. Diccionario manual latino-espanol y espanol-latino. 672p. (Lat. & Span.). 150.00 ptas. Sopena.

Blazquez, Jose M. Diccionario de las religiones perromanas de Hispania. LC 76-450345. (Illus.). 191p. (Span.). 1975. 300.00 ptas (ISBN 8-47090-071-4). Istmo.

Bonnin Valls, Ignacio, et al. Lexico Dos. 3rd ed. 336p. (Span.). 1982. pap. 443.00 ptas (ISBN 84-316-1647-4). Vicens-Vives.

--Lexico Uno. 5th ed. 336p. (Span.). 1982. pap. 426.00 ptas (ISBN 84-316-0624-X). Vicens-Vives.

Breve diccionario Porrua de la lengua espanola. (Span.). (gr. 4-9). pap. $3.50. Iaconi.

Brevis Diccionario Practico Castellano. (Span.). $5.95 (ISBN 0-686-56707-2, S-33058). French & Eur.

Canigo Diccionari Castella-Catala, Catala-Castella. 878p. (Span. & Catala.). pap. $17.95 (ISBN 84-303-0089-9, S-31565). French & Eur.

Capdevila Font, Juan. Diccionario Actualizado de la Lengua Espanola. 3rd ed. 392p. (Span.). 1976. $10.50 (ISBN 84-85117-06-9, S-50266); pap. $9.25 (ISBN 84-85117-28-X, S-50265). French & Eur.

--Diccionario Actualizado De Sinonimos y Contrarios De la Lengua Espanola. 2nd ed. 513p. (Span.). 1978. pap. $13.95 (ISBN 84-7176-301-X, S-50267). French & Eur.

--Diccionario de Citas. 132p. (Span.). 1977. pap. $13.95 (ISBN 84-85117-43-3, S-50580). French & Eur.

--Diccionario de la Lengua Espanola y Enciclopedia Escolar. 2nd ed. 407p. (Span.). 1975. pap. $7.95 (ISBN 84-85117-32-8, S-50451). French & Eur.

--Diccionario de la Lengua Espanola y Enciclopedia Escolar Distein. 2nd ed. 407p. (Span.). 1975. $8.95 (ISBN 84-85117-09-3, S-50459). French & Eur.

--Diccionario Escolar De Sinonimos y Contrarios De la Lengua Espanola. 499p. (Span.). 1978. $12.25 (ISBN 84-7176-302-8, S-50268). French & Eur.

--Diccionario Ideologico Manual de la Lengua Espanola. 900p. (Span.). 1976. $18.75 (ISBN 84-85117-22-0, S-50264). French & Eur.

--Diccionario Practico Escolar de la Lengua Espanola. 500p. (Span.). 1976. pap. $3.25 (ISBN 84-85117-38-7, S-50256). French & Eur.

Capdevilla Font, Juan. Diccionario Basico Escolar de la Lengua Espanola. 2nd ed. 398p. (Span.). 1975. $6.75 (ISBN 84-85117-17-4, S-50254). French & Eur.

--Diccionario Basico Escolar de la Lengua Espanola. 2nd ed. 398p. (Span.). 1975. pap. $4.75 (ISBN 84-85117-29-8, S-50255). French & Eur.

--Diccionario De la Lengua Espanola y Enciclopedia Escolar. 6th ed. 437p. (Span.). 1978. $7.50 (ISBN 84-7176-273-0, S-50252); pap. $5.953 (ISBN 84-85117-33-6, S-50253). French & Eur.

Cardenas, Eduardo, ed. Diccionario Moderno. LC 76-465983. (Illus.). iv, 606p. (Span.). 1975. write for info. Edit Norma.

Cardenas Nannetti, Jorge. Diccionario Mininorma. 224p. (Span.). 1981. $2.00 (ISBN 84-8276-251-6). Norma Edit.

--Diccionario Norma: El Lexico de Nuestro Tiempo. 643p. (Span.). 1981. Col.$180.00. Norma.

Casares, Julio. Diccionario ideologico de la lengua espanola. 2nd ed. 1446p. (Span.). write for info. (ISBN 84-252-0126-8). G Gili.

--Diccionario Ideologico de la Lengua Espanola. (Span.). pap. $43.95 (GIL). Lectorum Pubns.

--Novedades en el Diccionario Academico. (Span.). $7.25 (AGL). Lectorum Pubns.

Casares Sanchez, Julio. Diccionario Ideologico de la Lengua Espanola. 2nd ed. 1446p. (Span.). 1982. 3400.00 ptas (ISBN 8-42520-126-8). G Gili.

Cassells. Spanish Concise Dictionary. 1977. 9.95 (ISBN 0-02-052266-5). Macmillan.

Castillo, Carlos & Bond, Otto F. University of Chicago Dictionary. (Span.). $2.95. Camino Real.

Cela, Camilo J. Diccionario Secreto, Vol. 1. (Span.). $12.75 (ALFA). Lectorum Pubns.

Cela, Camilo J. & Margarit, Badia A. M. Diccionari Manual Castella-Catala Catala-Castella. 680p. (Catalan.). 850.00 ptas (ISBN 84-7153-392-8). Biblograf SP.

Cela Trulock, Camilo J. Diccionario Secreto, 3 vols. 2nd ed. 1184p. (Span.). 1975. Set. pap. $20.95 (ISBN 84-206-1997-3, S-29231). French & Eur.

Cerron-Palomino, Rodolfo. Diccionario Quechua Junin-Huanca. LC 77-465008. 274p. (Span. & Quechua.). 1976. write for info. Minist Ed Caracas.

Cesarman, Carlos. Diccionario de sinonimos OMNIA. (Span.). $1.30; Mex.$16.00. Pax.

Clave, Margara. Diccionario de Sinonimos & Antonimos. 597p. (Span.). 1979. Mex.$200.00. Porrua.

Cobos, Ruben. A Dictionary of New Mexico & Southern Colorado Spanish. 200p. (Mexican & Span.). 1983. 14.95 (ISBN 0-89013-141-4); pap. text ed. 7.95 (ISBN 0-686-46179-7). Museum NM Pr.

Coll Garcia, Jose L. El Diccionario de Coll. 27th ed. 224p. (Span.). 1982. pap. 350.00 ptas (ISBN 84-320-4119-X). Planeta SA.

Compacto Diccionario de la Lengua Espanola. 440p. (Span.). 9250.00 ptas. Biblograf SP.

Compacto Diccionario de la Lengua Espanola "Vox". 440p. (Span.). 1982. pap. 195.00 ptas (ISBN 8-47153-203-4). Biblograf.

Compendios de Divulgacion Filologica, 11 vols. Incl. Vol. 1. Ortografia Practica Espanola. Gili Gaya, S. 104p. pap. 195.00 ptas (ISBN 84-7153-255-7); Vol. 2. Resumen Practico de Gramatica Espanola. Gili Gaya, S. 112p ptas (ISBN 84-7153-256-5); Vol. 3. Nociones de Gramatica Historica Espanola. Gili Gaya, S. 104p. pap. 195.00 ptas (ISBN 84-7153-257-3); Vol. 5. Resumen Practico de Gramatica Francesa. 132p. pap. 195.00 ptas (ISBN 84-7153-263-8); Vol. 7. Ortografia Practica Francesa. 240p. pap. 250.00 ptas (ISBN 84-7153-264-6); Vol. 8. Ortografia Practica Catalana. 126p. pap. 225.00 ptas (ISBN 84-7153-266-2); Vol. 9. Vocabulario Basico Infantil. 64p. pap. 195.00 ptas (ISBN 84-7153-369-3). (Span.). Biblograf.

Conceicao Fernandes, Julio Da. Diccionario Manual Espanol-Portugues, Portugues-Espanol. 3rd ed. 1974p. (Span. & Port.). 1978. $12.25 (ISBN 84-7183-001-9, S-50428). French & Eur.

--Diccionario Portugues-Espanol. 2nd ed. 916p. (Port. & Span.). 1978. $6.95 (ISBN 0-686-57351-X, S-31570). French & Eur.

Conciso Diccionario de la Lengua Espanola. 304p. (Span.). 250.00 ptas (ISBN 84-7153-236-0); pap. 150.00 ptas (ISBN 84-7153-234-4). Biblograf SP.

Conciso Diccionario de la Lengua Espanola "Vox". 304p. (Span.). 1982. pap. 125.00 ptas (ISBN 8-47153-234-4). Biblograf.

Coripio Perez, Fernando. Diccionario Etimologico Abreviado. 2nd ed. 320p. (Span.). 1976. pap. $3.50 (ISBN 84-02-03901-4, S-50161). French & Eur.

Corominas, Joan. Breve Diccionario Etimologico de la Lengua Espanola. 3rd ed. 628p. (Span.). 1976. $35.95 (ISBN 84-249-1332-9, S-11936). French & Eur.

--Diccionario Critico Etimologico De la Lengua Espanola, 6 vols. 4418p. (Span.). 1976. Set. $200.00 (ISBN 84-249-1322-1, S-11937). French & Eur.

Corominas, Joan & Pascual, J. A. Diccionario Critico Etimologico Castellano & Hispanico, 2 vols. (Span.). 1979. 3.25 ptas. $3.500. Gredos.

Coromines i Vigneaux, Joan & Pascual, J. A. Diccionario critico etimologico castellano & hispanico, Tomo 3. 904p. (Span.). 1980. write for info. (ISBN 84-249-1365-5). Gredos.

Corriente Cordoba, Federico. Diccionario Espanol-Arabe. 480p. (Span. & Arabic.). 1970. $18.95 (ISBN 0-686-57345-5, S-50343). French & Eur.

--Diccionario espanol-arabe. 2nd ed. 480p. (Span. & Arabic.). 1980. 800.00 ptas (ISBN 84-7472-023-0). Inst Hispano-Arabe.

Corripio Perez, Fernando. Diccionario Abreviado de Sinonimos. 480p. (Span.). 1976. pap. $5.75 (ISBN 84-02-04681-9, S-50157). French & Eur.

--Diccionario Etimologico General de la Lengua Espanola. 2nd ed. (Span.). $18.95 (ISBN 84-02-03344-X, S-50158, French & Eur). French & Eur.

Criado de Val, Manuel. Diccionario de espanol equivoco. 124p. (Span.). 1981. pap. 300.00 ptas (ISBN 84-85786-10-6). Edi-Seis.

Cuervo. Diccionario de construccion y regimen de la lengue castellano. 2270p. (Span.). $18.45 set; Fasciculo 1. $4.33; Fasciculo 2. $3.25. Herder SA.

Cuervo, R. J. Diccionario de construccion y regimen de la lengua castellana. 344p. (Span.). 1961. write for info. Fasciculo 1: ea-empeorar. Faciculo 2: emperezar-emulo. Inst Caro y Cuervo.

Cuervo, Rufino J. Diccionario de Construccion & Regimen de la Lengua Castellana. (Span.). 1974. Col.$3.00. Inst Caro y Cuervo.

Cusihuaman, Antonio G. Diccionario Quechua Cuzco-Collao. LC 77-465799. 303p. (Quechua & Span.). 1976. write for info. Minist Ed Caracas.

De Andrea. Diccionario manual latino-castellano y castellano-latino. (Lat. & Span.). Arg.$21.60. Sopena.

De Covarrubias Horozco, Sebastian. Tesoro De la Lengua Castellana, O Espanola. (Span., Microphoto Reprod). 1927. 7.50 (ISBN 0-87535-020-8). Hispanic Soc.

De La Canal, Julio. Diccionario Ortografico. (Span.). pap. $2.50. MEX.

Delvalle, Juan. Diccionario bilinque para la juventud. 78p. (Span.). 1961. $1.50. Dist. Comuneros.

Diaz-Retg, E. Diccionario de Dificultades de la Lengua Espanola. 344p. (Span.). 1963. $18.95 (ISBN 0-686-92537-8, S-37576). French & Eur.

Diccionari basic castella-catala i catala-castela. 202p. (Span.). 1969. 50.00 ptas. M. Arimany.

Diccionari catala-castella, castella-catala. 683p. (Span.). 1969. 60.00 ptas. Mateu.

Diccionari popular catala-castella. 230p. (Span.). 1970. 75.00 ptas. Milla Lib.

Diccionario. 96p. (Span.). 1982. pap. 275.00 ptas (ISBN 84-305-1297-7). Susaeta.

Diccionario Abreviado de la Lengua Espanola. 512p. (Span.). 295.00 ptas (ISBN 84-7153-201-8). Biblograf SP.

Diccionario abreviado de la Lengua Espanola Vox. 12th ed. 512p. (Span.). 1982. 265.00 ptas (ISBN 84-7153-201-8). Biblo SP.

Diccionario Abreviado Espanol-Chino. 1244p. (Span. & Chinese.). 1979. leatherette $14.95 (ISBN 0-686-92546-7, S-33189). French & Eur.

Diccionario Abreviado Latino-Espanol Espanol-Latino. 316p. (Lat. & Span.). 350.00 ptas (ISBN 84-7153-221-2). Biblograf SP.

Diccionario Abreviado Latino-Espanol Espanol-Latino 'Spes' 9th ed. 316p. (Lat. & Span.). 1980. write for info. (ISBN 84-7153-221-2). Biblo SP.

Diccionario abreviado Latino-Espanol Espanol-Latino Vox. 11th ed. 316p. (Lat. & Span.). 1982. 325.00 ptas (ISBN 84-7153-221-2). Biblo SP.

Diccionario Abreviado Ortografico de la Lengua Espanola. 416p. (Span.). 1980. 325.00 ptas (ISBN 84-7153-227-1). Biblograf SP.

Diccionario Academia. 250p. (Span.). Mex.$9.50. Fernandez.

Diccionario Academico de la Lengua. 848p. (Span.). 1980. 700.00 ptas. pap. $625.00. Albir.

Diccionario Alevin Sopena Escolar de Iniciacion a la Lengua Espanola. (Span.). $3.95. Lectorum Pubns.

Diccionario Anaya de la Lengua. 720p. (Span.). 1978. leatherette $22.50 (ISBN 84-207-1373-2, S-50251). French & Eur.

Diccionario Anaya de la Lengua. 4th ed. 752p. (Span.). 1981. 1100.00 ptas (ISBN 84-207-1373-2). Anaya.

Diccionario Anaya de la Lengua. 752p. (Span.). 1980. 990.00 ptas (ISBN 84-207-1497-6). Anaya.

Diccionario Arabe-Espanol. 876p. (Arabic & Span.). 1977. $22.95 (ISBN 84-600-0842-8, S-50292). French & Eur.

Diccionario Aristos. (Illus.). 640p. (Span.). 125.00 ptas. pap. 80.00 ptas. Sopena.

Diccionario Aristos con perdanismos. (Span.). S 75.00. Bruno.

Diccionario Basico Anaya de la Lengua. 728p. (Span.). 1982. 600.00 ptas (ISBN 8-42072-195-6). Anaya.

Diccionario basico escolar. 416p. (Span.). 1982. Col.$pap. 95.00 (ISBN 84-8279-070-6). Educar.

Diccionario basico escolar de la lengua castellana. 2nd ed. 320p. (Span.). 1980. pap. 110.00 ptas (ISBN 84-391-1003-0). Edit Nebrija.

Diccionario basico Espasa: Tomo 3. 2nd ed. 1000p. (Span.). 1981. 3000.00 ptas (ISBN 84-239-4796-3). Espasa Calpe.

Diccionario Basico Latino-Espanol. 9th ed. 830p. (Lat. & Span.). 1981. 385.00 ptas (ISBN 84-7153-223-9). Biblo SP.

Diccionario Basico Latino-Espanol Espanol-Latino. 830p. (Lat. & Span.). 625.00 ptas (ISBN 84-7153-223-9). Biblograf SP.

Diccionario basico Latino-Espanol Espanol-Latino. 10th ed. 830p. (Lat. & Span.). 1982. 550.00 ptas (ISBN 84-7153-223-9). Biblo SP.

Diccionario Bilingue Maya Mopan & Espanol. LC 77-560678. 393p. (Mopan & Span.). 1976. write for info. Inst Ling Ver.

Diccionario Brevis. (Span.). S/18.00. Bruno.

Diccionario Brevis duplex: Portugues-catellano y castellano-portugues. (Port. & Span.). Arg.$15.00. Sopena.

Diccionario Castella-Catala Catala-Castella. 4th ed. 680p. (Span.). 1981. 625.00 ptas (ISBN 84-7153-198-4). Biblo SP.

Diccionario castellano discolar. 10th ed. 786p. (Span.). 1982. pap. 200.00 ptas (ISBN 84-05-00592-7). Castellana.

Diccionario Castellano Ilustrado. (Span.). pap. $12.50 (ISBN 0-686-56704-8, S-31405). French & Eur.

Diccionario Compendiado de la Lengua Espanola. 638p. (Span.). 250.00 ptas (ISBN 84-7153-232-8). Biblograf SP.

Diccionario Compendiado de la Lengua Espanola 'Vox' 3rd ed. 638p. (Span.). 1980. 165.00 ptas (ISBN 84-7153-232-8). Biblo SP.

Diccionario De Bolsillo De la Lengua Espanola: Mini Sopena. 304p. (Span.). 1975. pap. $1.75 (ISBN 84-303-0062-7, S-12252). French & Eur.

Diccionario de la Lengua, 3 vols. 2nd ed. 2000p. (Span.). 1977. Set. $120.00 (ISBN 84-7017-407-X, S-50097). French & Eur.

Diccionario de la Lengua: A-B, Vol. 1. 2nd ed. 308p. (Span.). 1981. pap. 1458.00 ptas (ISBN 84-7017-633-1). Argos-Vergara.

Diccionario de la Lengua: C-CH, Vol. 2. 2nd ed. 308p. (Span.). 1981. pap. 1458.00 ptas (ISBN 84-7017-634-X). Argos-Vergara.

Diccionario de la Lengua: D-F, Vol. 3. 2nd ed. 312p. (Span.). 1981. pap. 1458.00 ptas (ISBN 84-7017-635-8). Argos-Vergara.

Diccionario de la Lengua Espanola. 228p. (Span.). $3.50 (ISBN 0-686-56676-9, S-25231). French & Eur.

Diccionario De la Lengua Espanola, 2 vols. 704p. (Span.). 1978. Set. leather $50.95 (ISBN 84-278-0536-5, S-50030). French & Eur.

Diccionario de la Lengua Espanola, 2 vols. 696p. (Span.). 1982. Set 2350.00 ptas (ISBN 8-47505-566-4). Oceano.

Diccionario de la lengua espanola. 288p. (Span.). Mex.$0.80; $10.00. Diana.

Diccionario de la lengua espanola. 19th, rev. ed. 1426p. (Span.). 1971. 1100.00 ptas. pap. 700.00 ptas. Real Academia Espasa.

Diccionario de la lengua espanola. 472p. (Span.). 1982. pap. 600.00 ptas (ISBN 84-278-0775-9). Nauta SA.

Diccionario de la Lengua Espanola. 778p. (Span.). 1981. pap. 1600.00 ptas (ISBN 84-7505-214-2). Oceano.

Diccionario de la Lengua Espanola Novus. 778p. (Span.). 1981. 1600.00 ptas (ISBN 84-7505-214-2). Oceano.

Diccionario de la Lengua Espanola: Obra Completa, 2 vols. 696p. (Span.). 1982. 2350.00 set ptas (ISBN 8-47505-566-4). Oceano.

Diccionario de la Lengua Espanola Real Academia Espanola. 1424p. (Span.). $125.00. Lectorum Pubns.

Diccionario de la Lengua: G-M, Vol. 4. 2nd ed. 388p. (Span.). 1981. pap. 1458.00 ptas (ISBN 84-7017-636-6). Argos-Vergar.

Diccionario de la Lengua: N-Q, Vol. 5. 2nd ed. 304p. (Span.). 1981. pap. 1458.00 ptas (ISBN 84-7017-637-4). Argos-Vergara.

Diccionario de la Lengua (Obra Completa, 6 vols. 2nd ed. 2012p. (Span.). 1981. pap. 8750.00 ptas (ISBN 84-7017-632-3). Argos-Vergara.

Diccionario de la Lengua: R-Z, Vol. 6. 2nd ed. 392p. (Span.). 1981. pap. 1460.00 ptas (ISBN 84-7017-638-2). Argos-Vergara.

Diccionario de Sinonimos & Ideas Afines. (Span.). pap. $10.95. CEC.

Diccionario de Sinonimos, Antonimcs y Paronimos. 378p. (Span.). 1979. $22.50 (ISBN 0-686-56667-X, S-33073). French & Eur.

Diccionario de Sinonimos, Antonimos & Ideas Afines. 213p. (Span.). write for info. Andina.

Diccionario de sinonimos, antonimos e ideas afines. (Span.). write for info. Orbe Edns.

Diccionario de sinonimos e ideas afines. (Span.). $1.80. Andina.

Diccionario de Sinonimos Espanoles. (Span.). $7.95 (ISBN 0-686-56686-6, S-12253). French & Eur.

Diccionario de sinonimos y antonimos. 328p. (Span.). 1982. pap. 600.00 ptas (ISBN 84-278-0782-1). Nauta SA.

Diccionario del Lenguaje Usual. 758p. (Span.). 1969. Mex.$2.10. Santillana.

Diccionario Durvan de la Lengua Espanola. 1312p. (Span.). 1977. $44.95 (ISBN 84-85001-40-0, S-11956). French & Eur.

Diccionario Enciclopedico, 6 vols. (Illus., Span.). deluxe ed. $175.00 (7869-6). Natl Textbk.

Diccionario Enciclopedico Abreviado, 9 vols. 7th ed. 11678p. (Span.). 1977. Set. $300.00 (ISBN 84-239-4710-6, S-12263). French & Eur.

Diccionario Enciclopedico Bruguera, 5 vols. 6240p. (Span.). 1976. Set. leather $120.00 (ISBN 84-02-04687-8, S-50525). French & Eur.

Diccionario Enciclopedico Danae, 12 vols. 7220p. (Span.). 1977. Set. leather $600.00 (ISBN 84-7060-457-0, S-50521). French & Eur.

Diccionario Enciclopedico Escolar Basico. (Span.). 1974. 450.00 ptas (ISBN 84-01-60131-2). PlazaJanes.

Diccionario Enciclopedico Espasa, 12 vols. 10800p. (Span.). 1978. Set. leatherette $600.00 (ISBN 84-239-4780-7, S-27954). French & Eur.

Diccionario Enciclopedico Espasa. (Span.). 1980. write for info. (S-37369). French & Eur.

Diccionario Escolar. (Span.). pap. $3.95. Lectorum Pubns.

Diccionario Escolar Billiken Ilustrado. 1226p. (Span.). write for info. Atlantida.

Diccionario escolar de la Lengua Espanola Vox. 7th ed. 872p. (Span.). 1982. 595.00 ptas (ISBN 84-7153-172-0). Biblo SP.

Diccionario escolar hispanoamericano. (Span.). 600.00 ptas. EVA.

El Diccionario Escolar: La/Escuela Alegro. 184p. (Span.). write for info. (ISBN 84-399-4674-0). Escuela Nueva.

Diccionario Escolar Sopena Color De la Lengua Espanola. 928p. (Span.). 1976. pap. $13.25 (ISBN 84-303-0085-6, S-50144). French & Eur.

Diccionario Escolar Sopena Color De la Lengua Espanola. 928p. (Span.). 1976. $15.75 (ISBN 84-303-0084-8, S-50145). French & Eur.

Diccionario Escolar, 2. 4th ed. 1040p. (Span.). 1981. 750.00 ptas (ISBN 84-294-1215-8). Santillana SA.

Diccionario Espanol-Ruso. 944p. (Span. & Rus.). 1961. $9.95 (ISBN 0-686-92536-X, S-31679). French & Eur.

Diccionario espanol-ruso. (Span. & Rus.). write for info. Cultura Popular.

Diccionario espanol-ruso. (Span. & Rus.). Arg.$12.00. (Mir) D'lppolito.

Diccionario espanol Sol. (Span.). 30.00 ptas. pap. 25.00 ptas. Mayfe.

Diccionario Estudiantil. 3rd ed. 326p. (Span.). 1972. pap. $3.50 (ISBN 84-7165-051-7, S-27086). French & Eur.

Diccionario estudiantil J. 326p. (Span.). write for info. C y P.

Diccionario Euskera-Castellano. 432p. (Span.). 1982. 600.00 ptas (ISBN 8-48584-625-7). Sendoa.

Diccionario Everest "Cima". (Illus.). 1088p. (Span.). pap. $9.95. Lectorum Pubns.

Diccionario Everest Cima. (Span.). 110.00 ptas. 100.00 ptas. 90.00 ptas. pap. 80.00 ptas. Everest.

Diccionario Everest Cima: Espanol II. 20th ed. 1088p. (Span.). 1982. pap. 360.00 ptas (ISBN 84-241-1040-4). Everest.

Diccionario Everest Cima Latin-Espanol. 5th ed. 756p. (Lat. & Span.). 1981. 390.00 ptas (ISBN 84-241-1442-6). Everest.

Diccionario Everest Cima latino-espanol, espanol-latino. (Span.). 125.00 ptas. Everest.

Diccionario Everest Corona. (Span.). 500.00 ptas. 400.00 ptas. pap. 300.00 ptas. Everest.

Diccionario Everest 'Corona' Espanol II. 11th ed. 1568p. (Span.). 1982. pap. 1150.00 ptas (ISBN 84-241-1073-0). Everest.

Diccionario Everest Cuarenta Lexico. 2nd ed. 684p. (Span.). 1981. 975.00 ptas (ISBN 84-241-1140-0). Everest.

Diccionario Everest "Cumbre". 680p. (Span.). pap. $4.75. Lectorum Pubns.

Diccionario Everest Cumbre. (Span.). 80.00 ptas. 70.00 ptas. 60.00 ptas. pap. 55.00 ptas. Everest.

Diccionario Everest Cumbre: Espanol II. 24th ed. 672p. (Span.). 1982. pap. 165.00 ptas (ISBN 84-241-1030-7). Everest.

Diccionario Everest Cupula. (Span.). 250.00 ptas. Everest.

Diccionario Everest Cupula: Espanol II. 10th ed. 1536p. (Span.). 1982. 1000.00 ptas (ISBN 84-241-1062-5). Everest.

Diccionario Everest 'Cuspide' Espanol II. 14th ed. 1088p. (Span.). 1980. pap. 475.00 ptas (ISBN 84-241-1052-8). Everest.

Diccionario 'Everest Diez II. 6th ed. 272p. (Span.). 1981. pap. 100.00 ptas (ISBN 84-241-1110-9). Everest.

Diccionario Everest "Punto". 384p. (Span.). pap. $2.50. Lectorum Pubns.

Diccionario Everest Punto. (Illus., Span.). 22.00 ptas. pap. 18.00 ptas. Everest.

Diccionario Everest Punto: Espanol II. 24th ed. 384p. (Span.). 1981. pap. 62.00 ptas (ISBN 84-241-1010-2). Everest.

Diccionario Everest Punto' Espanol II. 23rd ed. 384p. (Span.). 1981. pap. 56.00 ptas (ISBN 84-241-1010-2). Everest.

Diccionario Everest "Vertice". (Illus.). 608p. (Span.). pap. $3.50. Lectorum Pubns.

Diccionario Everest Vertice. (Span.). 55.00 ptas. 35.00 ptas. pap. 30.00 ptas. Everest.

Diccionario Everest Vertice: Espanol II. 30th ed. 606p. (Span.). 1982. pap. 96.00 ptas (ISBN 84-241-1020-X). Everest.

Diccionario Everest 10. 269p. (Fr.). 1975. $2.95 (ISBN 84-241-1110-9, 21466). Larousse.

Diccionario Fundamental de la Lengua Espanola'Vox' 2nd ed. 552p. (Span.). 1980. 275.00 ptas (ISBN 84-7153-229-8). Biblo SP.

Diccionario General Ilustrado de la Lengua Espanol. 1752p. (Span.). 1976. $47.50 (ISBN 0-686-57111-8, M-6144). French & Eur.

Diccionario general ilustrado. 576p. (Span.). 1982. 1500.00 ptas (ISBN 84-7102-196-X). Marin.

Diccionario General Ilustrado de la Lengua. (Illus.). 991p. (Span.). 1980. 24.00 ptas. 20.00 ptas. Albir.

Diccionario general ilustrado de la Lengua Espanola Vox. 5th ed. (Illus.). 1780p. (Span.). 1982. pap. 2650.00 ptas (ISBN 84-7153-109-7). Biblo SP.

Diccionario Gramatical y de Dudas del Idioma. 1500p. (Span.). $29.95 (ISBN 84-303-0061-9, S-12275). French & Eur.
Diccionario Griego-Espanol. 1544p. (Gr. & Span.). leatherette $50.95 (ISBN 84-303-0158-5, S-50425). French & Eur.
Diccionario hebreo-espanol. (Hebrew & Span.). 100.00 ptas. Perpetuo.
Diccionario historico do la lengua espanola, 9 vols. (Span.). 400.00 ea. ptas. (Real Academia) Espasa.
Diccionario Ilustrado Basico. 790p. (Span.). $9.75. Cruzada Span Pubns.
Diccionario ilustrado Daimon. (Illus., Span.). 150.00 ptas. Daimon.
Diccionario Ilustrado Danae de la Lengua Espanola. (Span.). pns leatherette (ISBN 84-7060-397-3, S-50207). French & Eur.
Diccionario Ilustrado de la Lengua Espanola. 375p. (Span.). pap. $3.00. Cruzada Span Pubns.
Diccionario Ilustrado Latino-Espanol Espanol-Latino. (Illus.). 800p. (Lat. & Span.). 1981. 825.00 ptas (ISBN 84-7153-197-6). Biblograf SP.
Diccionario Ilustrado Latino-Espanol Espanol-Latino. 14th ed. (Illus.). 800p. (Span. & Lat.). 1982. pap. 725.00 ptas (ISBN 84-7153-197-6). Biblo SP.
El Diccionario Infantil de Palabras & Figuras. 116p. (Span.). write for info. (ISBN 84-365-0083-0). Escuela Nueva.
Diccionario Infantil Ilustrado. 190p. (Span.). 1975. $20.50 (ISBN 84-271-0968-7, S-50006); pap. $17.95 (ISBN 84-271-0969-5, S-50007). French & Eur.
Diccionario Infantil Ilustrado, 7 vols. 968p. (Span.). 1977. Set. $140.00 (ISBN 84-01-70210-0, S-50043). French & Eur.
Diccionario Infantil Ilustrado. (Illus., Span.). $9.95. Lectorum Pubns.
Diccionario infantil ilustrado. (Illus.). 192p. (Span.). 290.00 ptas. Mensajero Edns.
Diccionario infantil ilustrado. 3200p. (Span.). write for info. Plaza Janes.
Diccionario Infantil Ilustrado. (Illus.). 36p. (Span.). 1981. 85.00 ptas (ISBN 84-7500-081-9). Interediciones.
Diccionario Infantil Ilustrado, Vol. 1. 256p. (Span.). 1981. 2466.00 ptas (ISBN 84-01-70237-2). Plaza Janes.
Diccionario Infantil Ilustrado, Vol.2. 256p. (Span.). 1981. 2466.00 ptas (ISBN 84-01-70238-0). Plaza Janes.
Diccionario Infantil Ilustrado, Vol. 3. (Illus.). 256p. (Span.). 1981. 2466.00 ptas (ISBN 84-01-70239-9). Plaza Janes.
Diccionario Infantil Ilustrado: Obra completa II, 6 vols. 1232p. (Span.). 1981. 14800.00 ptas (ISBN 84-01-70236-4). Plaza Janes.
Diccionario Inicial de la Lengua Espanol. (Illus.). 340p. (Span.). 495.00 ptas (ISBN 84-7153-199-2). Biblograf SP.
Diccionario Inicial de la Lengua Espanola. (Illus., Span.). $7.95. Lectorum Pubns.
Diccionario Inicial de la Lengua Espanola. 2nd ed. 326p. (Span.). 1981. 300.00 ptas (ISBN 84-7153-199-2). Biblo SP.
Diccionario Kapeluse de la Langua Espanola. 1552p. (Span.). 1979. $46.95 (ISBN 0-686-56682-3, S-33044). French & Eur.
Diccionario Kapelusz de la Lengua Espanola. (Span.). 1981. Arg.$55000.00. Kapelusz.
Diccionario Karten Ilustrado. 1680p. (Span.). 1977. $95.00 (ISBN 0-686-56679-3, S-33047). French & Eur.
Diccionario Larousse De la Lengua Espanola-Nuevo Larousse Basico. (Span.). 1980. pap. $7.50 (ISBN 0-686-59502-5). Larousse.
Diccionario Larousse usual. (Illus.). 848p. (Span.). 1974. pap. 11.95 (ISBN 2-03-020543-5, 22800). Larousse.
Diccionario latino-espanol, espanol-latino: Serie Bachillerato Koel. (No. 44). (Lat. & Span.). 75.00 ptas. Tesoro.
Diccionario lengua espanola. (Span.). 50.00 ptas. pap. 35.00 ptas. Mayfe.
Diccionario lexico basico espanol. (Span.). write for info. Cultura Popular.
Diccionario Lexicon Esperanto-Espanol, Espanol-Esperanto. 400p. (Esperanto & Span.). leatherette $4.95 (ISBN 84-303-0148-8, S-50403); pap. $4.50 (ISBN 84-303-0147-X, S-50402). French & Eur.
Diccionario Lexicon Portugues-Espanol, Espanol-Portugues. 400p. (Port. & Span.). leatherette $3.95 (ISBN 84-303-0144-5, S-50429); pap. $3.50 (ISBN 84-303-0143-7, S-50430). French & Eur.
Diccionario Manual Auxiliar Basico. 2nd ed. 524p. (Span.). 1976. $6.95 (ISBN 84-01-60144-4, S-50045). French & Eur.
Diccionario Manual de la Lengua Espanol: Real Academia Espanola. 1572p. (Span.). write for info. (ESP). Lectorum Pubns.
Diccionario manual de la lengua espanola: Real Academia Espanol. 1572p. (Span.). $39.95 (ESP). Lectorum Pub.
Diccionario Manual de Sinonimos, Antonimos e Ideas Afines. 512p. (Span.). pap. $5.25 (ISBN 84-303-0066-X, S-12277). French & Eur.
Diccionario manual de sinonimos y antonimos. 4th ed. 369p. (Span.). 1982. write for info. (ISBN 84-7153-389-8). Biblograf.
Diccionario manual e ilustrado de la lengua espanola. 2nd ed. (Illus.). 1572p. (Span.). 1958. 250.00 ptas. (Real Academia) Espasa.
Diccionario Manual Griego-Espanol Vox. 16th ed. 724p. (Gr. & Span.). 1982. 795.00 ptas (ISBN 84-7153-192-5). Biblo SP.
Diccionario Manual Ilustrado de la Lengua Espanola. (Illus.). 1170p. (Span.). 850.00 ptas (ISBN 84-7153-166-6). Biblograf SP.
Diccionario Manual Ilustrado de la Lengua Espanola Vox. 7th ed. (Illus.). 1174p. (Span.). 1982. 775.00 ptas (ISBN 84-7153-166-6). Biblo SP.
Diccionario manual ilustrado espanol A-Z. (Illus.). 720p. (Span.). $2.50. Universal Medinacelli.
Diccionario Marin de la Lengua Espanola: Obra Completa, 2 vols. 1736p. (Span.). 1982. 4500.00 set ptas (ISBN 8-47102-700-3); $2225.00 ea. Marin.
Diccionario Marin de la Lengua Espanola, 2 vols. 1728p. (Span.). 1982. 5600.00 ptas (ISBN 84-7102-700-3). Marin.
Diccionario Mundo hispano. 426p. (Span.). Mex.$6.00. Fernandez.
Diccionario Oceano de la Lengua Espanola. 778p. (Span.). 1981. pap. 1600.00 ptas (ISBN 84-7505-162-6). Oceano.
Diccionario "Oriente", 4 vols. (Span.). $195.00 set (ISBN 0-686-56661-0, S-33078). French & Eur.
Diccionario: Oriente, 2 vols. (Eng. & Span.). $75.00 (ISBN 0-686-56684-X, S-33042). French & Eur.
Diccionario Ortografico Iter. 640p. (Span.). 1978. leatherette $6.75 (ISBN 84-303-0752-4, S-50143); pap. $5.95 (ISBN 84-303-0751-6, S-50142). French & Eur.
Diccionario para especialistas. (Span.). $6.95. Minerva.
Diccionario Parvus duplex: Portugues-castellano y castellano-portugues. (Port. & Span.). Arg.$8.40. Sopena.
Diccionario Pequeno Nebrija de la lengua castellana. 352p. (Span.). 1982. pap. 90.00 ptas (ISBN 84-391-1001-4). Edit Nebrija.
Diccionario Planeta Abreviado de la Lengua Espanola Usual. (Illus.). 768p. (Span.). 1982. 900.00 ptas (ISBN 8-43206-527-7). Planeta SA.
Diccionario Plaza y Janes: Obra completa II, 2 vols. 1536p. (Span.). 1981. 802.00 ptas (ISBN 84-01-60175-4). Plaza Janes.
Diccionario Plaza y Janes, S.A. Tomo 2 II. 768p. (Span.). 1981. 401.00 ptas (ISBN 84-01-60177-0). Plaza Janes.
Diccionario Plaza y Janes: Tomo 1 II. 768p. (Span.). 1981. 401.00 ptas (ISBN 84-01-60176-2). Plaza Janes.
Diccionario popular castellano-catalan. 230p. (Span.). 1967. 75.00 ptas. Milla Lib.
Diccionario portugues-espanol y espanol-portugues. (Port. & Span.). 60.00 ptas. Mayfe.
Diccionario Rances. (Illus.). 784p. (Span.). 90.00 ptas. 55.00 ptas. pap. 50.00 ptas. Sopena.
Diccionario Real de la Lengua Espanola, 2 vols. 776p. (Span.). 1981. pap. 2100.00 ptas (ISBN 84-7505-178-2). Oceano.
Diccionario Real de la Lengua Espanola. 778p. (Span.). 1981. pap. 1600.00 ptas (ISBN 84-7505-215-0). Oceano.
Diccionario Real de la Lengua Espanola, Vol. 1. 392p. (Span.). 1981. pap. write for info. (ISBN 84-7505-179-0). Oceano.
Diccionario Real de la Lengua Espanola, Vol. 2. 384p. (Span.). 1981. pap. write for info. (ISBN 84-7505-180-4). Oceano.
Diccionario ruso-espanol. (Span. & Rus.). $0.80. Pueblos Unidos.
Diccionario ruso-espanol, espanol-ruso. 1448p. (Rus. & Span.). 850.00 ptas. Danae.
Diccionario Sopena de Dudas & Dificultades del Idioma. 624p. (Span.). 1981. 200.00 ptas (ISBN 84-303-0838-5); pap. 230.00 ptas (ISBN 84-303-0839-3). Sopena.
Diccionario Tematico de la Lengua Espanola. 496p. (Span.). 1980. 1350.00 ptas (ISBN 84-7153-116-X). Biblograf SP.
Diccionario Tematico de la Lengua Espanola 'Vox' 500p. (Span.). 1980. write for info. (ISBN 84-7153-053-8). Biblo SP.
Diccionario Universal Herder De la Lengua Espanola. 460p. (Span.). 1975. pap. $4.50 (ISBN 84-254-0968-3, S-50195). French & Eur.
Diccionario universal Langenscheidt. (Span.). Mex.$1.35; $15.25. Buena Prensa.
Diccionarios mundiales. 600p. (Span.). $5.95; pap. $2.95. Follett.
Diccionaris catala-castella i castella-catala: Tipus breu. 450p. (Span.). 75.00 ptas. M Arimany.
Diccionaris catala-castella i castella-catala: Tipus basic. 400p. (Span.). 48.00 ptas. M Arimany.
Diccionaris catala-castella i castella-catala: Tipus especial. 958p. (Span.). 1971. 350.00 ptas. M Arimany.
Diccionaris catala-castella i castella-catala: Tipus manual. 958p. (Span.). 250.00 ptas. M Arimany.
Diccionaris catala-castella i castella-catala: Tipus practic. 450p. (Span.). 150.00 ptas. M Arimany.
Diccionrio De Sinonimos. (Span.). leatherette $10.95 (ISBN 84-346-0311-X, S-37349). French & Eur.
Diez Mateo, Felix. Diccionario castellano ilustrado. (Illus.). 416p. (Span.). 1980. 275.00 ptas (ISBN 84-85085-26-4). Neguri.
--Diccionario Espanol Etimologico. 396p. (Span.). 1972. $6.95 (ISBN 84-300-5794-3, S-12291). French & Eur.
Distein. Diccionario de la Lengua Espanola. LC 75-513898. 407p. (Span.). 1975. write for info. (ISBN 8-485-11709-3) (ISBN 8-485-11710-7). Distein.
Ducach, Juan. Nuevo Diccionario Castellano-Hebreo, 2 vols. 720p. (Castilian & Hebrew.). 1971. IL.16.50 (36-0000). Massada Pr.
Echauri Martinez, Eustaquio. Diccionario Basico Latino-Espanol, Espanol-Latino. 8th ed. LC 80-100210. 829p. (Lat. & Span.). 1978. 235.00 ptas (ISBN 8-471-53223-9). Biblo Sp.
Echuari, Eustaquio. Vox-Diccionario Basico Latino-Espanol, Espanol-Latino. 8th ed. 830p. (Lat. & Span.). 1978. leatherette $9.95 (ISBN 84-7153-223-9, S-12396). French & Eur.
Eduardo, H. Diccionario Estudios de Castellano sec. Castagnino. 194p. (Span.). 1930. Arg.$1.00. Leru.
E.G.B., ed. Diccionario del lenguaje usual. 758p. (Span.). 175.00 ptas. Santilana SA.
Elies I Busqueta, Pere. Canigo: Dicionario Catalan-Castellano, Castellano-Catalan. LC 75-508636. (Illus.). 877p. (Catalan & Span.). 1975. write for info. (ISBN 8-430-30089-9). Sopena.
Espiru, Salvador. Diccionari Manual de Sinonims. 319p. (Catalan.). 575.00 ptas (ISBN 84-7153-325-1). Biblograf SP.
Everyday Dictionary. LC 84-13528. (Span.). 1982. $12.95; pap. $7.95. Times Bks.
Fabra Poch, Pompeu. Diccionario General de la Lengua Catalana. 9th ed. 1778p. (Catalan.). 1978. $52.50 (ISBN 84-350-0120-2, S-50080). French & Eur.
--Diccionario general de llengua catalana. 15th ed. 1768p. (Span.). 1981. 2500.00 ptas (ISBN 84-350-0120-2). Edhasa.
Fabri, M. A Bibliography of Hispanic Dictionaries: Catalan, Galician, Spanish, Spanish in Latin America & the Philippines. 1979. pap. 45.00 (ISBN 0-686-77969-X). Heinman.
Feijoo Zollern, Inocencio. Diccionario infantil: La lupa magica. 50p. (Span.). 1982. 500.00 ptas (ISBN 84-85825-01-2). Lopez Paco.
Fernandez De La Torriente, Gaston. Vocabulario Superior. 176p. (Span.). 1975. pap. $8.75 (ISBN 84-359-0124-6). French & Eur.
Fernandez de Miranda, Maria T. Diccionario ixcateco. (Span.). 1961. Mex.$60.00. INAH.
Fernandez Gandia, J. M. Diccionario escolar ilustrado. 302p. (Span.). $0.70. CECSA.
Fernandez Pareja, Francisco. Vocabulario de Priego de Cordoba & su Comarca. 83p. (Span.). 1982. 250.00 ptas (ISBN 8-43007-537-2). Autores-Editores.
Flores de Vega. Diccionario ortografico hispanoamericano. 288p. (Span.). $1.25. Peisa.
Fonda Publicaciones U. P. T. C., ed. Diccionario de paronimos. 112p. (Span.). 1972. Col.$12.00. U. Pedagogica y Tec.
Franco Grande, X. L. Diccionario galego-castelan. 2nd ed. (Span.). 300.00 ptas. Galaxia.
Franco Grande, Xose L. Diccionario galego-castelan. 7th ed. 970p. (Span.). 1982. pap. 1200.00 ptas (ISBN 84-7154-024-X). Galaxia.
--Diccionario Galego-Castelan e Vocabulario Castelan-Galego. 4th ed. 970p. (Span.). 1978. $23.95 (ISBN 84-7154-024-X, S-50436). French & Eur.
--Vocabulario Galego-Castelan. 336p. (Gallic & Span.). 1972. pap. $9.50 (ISBN 84-7154-283-8, S-50437). French & Eur.
Franquesa, Miquel. Diccionari de sinonims. 1232p. (Span.). 1971. write for info. Portic.
Fuentes, D. & Lopez, J. A. Barrio Language Dictionary. (Span.). 1976. pap. $5.25 (ISBN 0-87505-143-X). Borden.
Fuentes, Dagaberto & Lopez, Jose A. Barrio Language Dictionary. (Span.). $4.25. Camino Real.
Gallego Tribaldos, Juan J. Ortografia Practica del Espanol. 190p. (Span.). 1982. pap. 450.00 ptas (ISBN 8-48576-413-7). Ave Maria.
Galvan, Roberto A. & Teschner, Richard V. El Diccionario Del Espanol Chicano. 1977. pap. text ed. $6.95 ea. (ISBN 0-88499-146-6). Inst Mod Lang.
Garcia, Mercadel. Diccionario ilustrado de lengua espanola. (Illus., Span.). 90.00 ptas. Mayfe.
Garcia de Diego. Diccionario de voces naturales. (Span.). 600.00 ptas. Aguilar SP.
Garcia de Diego, Vicenete. Diccionario de Voces Naturales. 724p. (Span.). 1968. $20.95 (ISBN 84-03-12031-1, S-11993). French & Eur.
Garcia Hoz, Victor. Diccionario escolar etimologica. (Span.). 160.00 ptas. Magisterio Esp.
--Diccionario Escolar Etimologico. 7th ed. 740p. (Span.). 1977. pap. $13.95 (ISBN 84-265-0123-0, S-11999). French & Eur.

--Diccionario Escolar Etimologico. 9th ed. 740p. (Span.). 1981. 800.00 ptas (ISBN 84-265-0123-0). Magisterio Esp.

Garcia Mercadal, Jose. Diccionario Espanol Ilustrado. 7th ed. (Illus.). 592p. (Span.). 1982. 350.00 ptas (ISBN 8-47105-107-9). Mayfe.

Garcia Patier, Carlos. Diccionario Taurino Ilustrado. (Illus.). 72p. (Span.). 1981. 250.00 ptas (ISBN 84-85951-00-X). Cometa SA.

Garcia-Pelayo, Ramon. Diccionario Larousse Del Espanol Moderno. (Span.). 1983. pap. $4.95 (ISBN 0-451-12352-2, Sig). NAL.

Ghitescu, Micaela. Dictionar Roman-Spaniol: Pentru uzul Elevilor. LC 76-481301. 414p. (Romanian & Span.). 1976. 18.00 lei. Editura Stiintifica.

--Dictionar Spaniol-Roman: Pentru uzul Elevilor. LC 76-468723. 391p. (Romanian & Span.). 1976. 17.00 lei. Editura Stiintifica.

Gili Gaya, S. D. Diccionario De Sinonimos. (Span.). 1958. $8.50x (ISBN 0-686-00854-5). Colton Bk.

Gili Gaya, Samuel. Diccionario Abreviado de Sinonimos. 352p. (Span.). 295.00 ptas (ISBN 84-7153-207-7). Biblograf SP.

--Diccionario de Sinonimos. 376p. (Span.). 250.00 ptas (ISBN 84-7153-178-X). Biblograf SP.

--Diccionario Escolar de la Lengua Espanola. 872p. (Span.). 695.00 ptas (ISBN 84-7153-172-0). Biblograf SP.

--Vox--Diccionario de Sinonimos. 376p. (Span.). 1979. leatherette $10.95 (ISBN 84-7153-178-X, S-12324). French & Eur.

Gili Gaya, Samuel, rev. by. Diccionario Fundamental de la Lengua Espanola. 592p. (Span.). write for info. Biblograf SP.

Ginguay. Diccionario de informatica. 184p. (Span.). write for info. Toray-Masson.

Gisbert. Diccionario manual espanol-ruso. (Span. & Rus.). $0.80. Pueblos Unidos.

Gomez de Segura Beaumont, Angel J. Diccionario Infantil Fher. 24p. (Span.). 1978. pap. $5.25 (ISBN 84-243-1456-5, S-50076). French & Eur.

Good, Claude. Diccionario Triqui de Chicahuaxtla. LC 79-106554. 104p. (Span. & Trique.). 1978. write for info. Inst Ling Ver.

Gordo-Guarinos, Francisco. Diccionario De Sinonimos y Antonimos. 300p. (Span.). 1979. pap. $4.50 (ISBN 84-346-0311-X, S-29130). French & Eur.

Gordo Guarinos, Francisco. Diccionario Escolar Roble. 5th ed. 712p. (Span.). 1975. pap. $4.50 (ISBN 84-346-0191-5, S-50046). French & Eur.

Gordo-Guarinos, Francisco. Diccionario Manual De la Lengua Espanol a-Z. 3rd ed. 688p. (Span.). 1979. pap. $5.25 (ISBN 84-346-0083-8, S-27485). French & Eur.

--Diccionario Manual De la Lengua Espanol A-Z. 3rd ed. 688p. (Span.). 1979. $6.95 (ISBN 84-346-0084-6, S-27486). French & Eur.

Grad, A., ed. Diccionario Esloveno-Espanol. 747p. (Span.). 1979. $49.95 (ISBN 0-686-92391-X, S-37817). French & Eur.

Gran Diccionario & Gramatica Ingles-Espanol, Espanol-Ingles, 2 vols, Vol. 1. 3rd. ed. 464p. (Span. & Eng.). 1982. 2500.00 ptas (ISBN 8-42780-596-9). Nauta SA.

Gran Diccionario Infantil Marin, 4 vols. 800p. (Span.). 1978. 7800.00 ptas (ISBN 84-7102-150-1). Marin.

Gran Diccionario Sopena. 1632p. (Span.). 1982. 3000.00 ptas (ISBN 84-303-0881-4). Sopena.

Gran diccionario y gramatica de la lengua espanola: Obra completa, 2 vols. 2nd ed. 896p. (Span.). 1982. pap. 3200.00 ptas (ISBN 84-278-0568-3). Nauta SA.

Grates. Diccionario de sinonimos castellanos. (Span.). Arg.$14.40. Sopena.

--Diccionario de Sinonimos Castellanos. 21st ed. (Span.). Arg.$5900.00. Sopena.

Guardia Mayarga, Cesar. Diccionario Kechwa-Castellano. 219p. (Kechwa & Castellan.). 1980. S/2.00. Studium.

Guardia Mayorga, Cesar. Diccionario kechua-castellano, castellano-kechua. 4th ed. 217p. (Span.). $1.25. Peisa.

Guisset Poch, Consuelo & Castellanos Alentorn, Prado. Diccionario Infantil Ilustrado Bruguera. 96p. (Span.). 1977. pap. $9.50 (ISBN 84-02-05211-8, S-50160). French & Eur.

Gulsoy, Joseph. El Diccionario valenciano-castellano de Manuel Josquin Savelo. 552p. (Span.). 1964. 550.00 ptas. Soc. Castellonenca de Cultura.

Hamlyn Spanish-English Dictionary. (Span. & Eng.). 1977. pap. 4.95 (ISBN 0-600-36565-4, 8087). Larousse.

Harvey, Herbert. Terminos del Parentesco en el Otomangue. (Span.). 1963. Mex.$35.00. INAH.

Hernandez Aquino, Luis. Diccionario de Voces Indigenas de Puerto Rico. (Span.). $17.95 (ISBN 0-686-56700-5, S-27651). French & Eur.

Herrero, V. J. Diccionario de Expresiones y Frases Latinas. 253p. (Span. & Lat.). 1980. Leatherette $29.95 (ISBN 0-686-92545-9, S-32727). French & Eur.

Hinojosa, Ida, ed. Vest Pocket Spanish Dictionary. rev. & enl. ed. 320p. (Span.). pap. $2.95 (ISBN 0-8329-1534-3). New Century.

Huertas Garcia, Alfredo. Ortografia metodica de la lengua espanola. 19th ed. 360p. (Span.). 1981. M.pap. 65.00. Porrua.

IML-Institute of Modern Languages. Dictionary of the Spanish in Texas. (Span.). $8.35. Camino Real.

Isaacs, Alan, ed. Multilingual Commercial Dictionary. 496p. 1980. $22.50 (ISBN 0-87196-425-2). Facts on File.

Jane, Albert. Diccionari calala de simonims. (Span.). 1972. write for info. Aedos.

Joan-Pascual, J. A. Diccionario Critico Etimologico Castellano & Hispanico, Tomo 4. 960p. (Span.). 1981. write for info. ptas (ISBN 84-249-0066-9). Gredos.

Jover Peralta, A & Ozuna, T. Diccionario guarani-espanol, espanol-guarani. 508p. (Span. & Guarani.). 1951. $4.50. Dist. Comuneros.

Juilland, Alphonse & Chang-Rodriquez, E. Frequency Dictionary of Spanish Words. (R. L. T. S. First Ser: No. S1). (Span.). 1964. text ed. 81.00x (ISBN 90-2790-159-7). Mouton.

Kelin, F. V., ed. Ispansko-Russkii Slovar. 944p. (Rus. & Span.). 1961. $4.95 (Pub. by Gosizdat Inostr Natsional Slovarei). Four Continent.

Kelina. Diccionario espanol-ruso. (Span. & Rus.). $0.90. Pueblos Unidos.

Kendris, Christopher. Dictionary of Five Hundred One Spanish Verbs. (Span.). $3.75. Camino Real.

--Dictionnaire de Docientos Uno Verboes Espagnols Conjugues a Toutes les Personnes. LC 68-8678. (Span.). 1969. pap. text ed. $3.95 (ISBN 0-8120-0394-2). Barron.

Kintana, Xabier. Euskal Histegi Modernoa. LC 77-564729. xxiv, 731p. (Basque, & Span.). 1977. write for info. (ISBN 8-472-77058-3). Cinsa Coord.

Kintana, Xabier, et al, eds. Euskal Histegi Modernoa. LC 77-564729. xxiv, 731p. (Basque.). 1977. write for info. (ISBN 8-47277-058-3). Coord Iniciat.

Ladero Sanchez, Lazaro. Basico Sopena: Diccionario Ilustrado de la Lengua Espanla. (Illus.). 792p. (Span.). $9.95 (SOP). Lectorum Pubns.

Langenscheidts Handwoerterbuecher: Spanisch, 2 Teile in 1. (Span.). 1978. DM.55.00 (ISBN 3-468-05340-1). Langenscheidt.

Langenscheidts Taschenwoerterbuecher Spanisch. (Span.). 1978. DM.21.80 (ISBN 3-468-11340-4). Langenscheidt.

Langenscheidts Universal-Woerterbuch Spanisch. 560p. (Span. & Ger.). DM.6.80 (18342). Langenscheidt.

Lara, Jesus. Diccionario de Ro de Qheshwa-Espanol, Espanol-Qheshwa. (Span. & Qheshwa.). $39.95 (ISBN 0-686-56703-X, S-12399). French & Eur.

--Diccionario Qheshwa-Castellano. 2nd ed. 468p. (Span.). 1971. write for info. Amigos del Libro.

--Diccionaro de Qheshwa-Espanol, Espanol-Qheshwa. (Span. & Qheshwa.). pap. $29.95 (ISBN 0-686-56702-1, S-12398). French & Eur.

Lazzati. Diccionario de paronimos castellanos. (Span.). Arg.$22.80. Sopena.

--Diccionario del verbo castellano. (Span.). Arg.$24.00. Sopena.

Lazzati, Santiago. Diccionario del Verbo Castellano. (Span.). pap. $9.50 (SPA). Lectorum Pubns.

Ledesma, S. Diccionario ortografico: Libro del maestro. 2nd ed. 454p. (Span.). 1906. Urg.$285.00. Barreiro Ramos.

LeFort, Emilio, ed. World-Wide Spanish Dictionary. (Span.). 1978. pap. $2.95 (ISBN 0-449-30851-0, Prem). Fawcett.

Leon, V. Diccionario del Argot Espanol. (Span.). pap. $5.25 (ISBN 84-206-1766-0, S-33020). French & Eur.

Leon, Victor. Diccionario de Argot Espanol. (Illus.). 160p. (Span.). 1980. pap. 180.00 ptas. Alianza Ed.

Leon Nunez, Victor. Diccionario de argot espanol. 2nd ed. 160p. (Span.). 1981. pap. 180.00 ptas (ISBN 84-206-1766-0). Alianza Ed.

Lexico basico espanol-ruso. (Span. & Rus.). Mex.$10.00. Cultura Popular.

Lexico basico espanol-ruso. (Span. & Rus.). Arg.$12.00. D'Ippolito.

Lexicon Sopena: Diccionario de bolsillo, catalan-espanol y espanol-catalan. (Span.). 60.00 ptas. 35.00 ptas. pap. 30.00 ptas. Sopena.

Lexicon Sopena: Diccionario de bolsillo, esperanto-espanol y espanol-esperanto. 384p. (Esperanto & Span.). 60.00 ptas. 35.00 ptas. pap. 30.00 ptas. Sopena.

Lexicon Sopena: Diccionario de bolsillo, lengua espanol. 384p. (Span.). 30.00 ptas. pap. 25.00 ptas. Sopena.

Lexicon sopena diccionario espanola. (Span.). pap. $3.95 (7864-5). Natl Textbk.

Liban, Libr d. ABC Dictionary I: Arabic & Span. (Arabic & Span.). 1983. $7.95x. Intl Bk Ctr.

Libr du Liban. ABC Dictionary Tamhidi: Arabic-Spanish. (Arabic & Span.). 1983. $7.95x (ISBN 0-86685-312-X). Intl Bk Ctr.

--My Illustrated Dictionary: Arabic & Span. (Arabic & Span.). 1983. $9.00x (ISBN 0-86685-320-0). Intl Bk Ctr.

Llauro Padrosa, J. Diccionario latino-espanol. 2nd ed. (Lat. & Span.). 150.00 ptas. SAETA.

Llauro Padrose, J. & Marques Casanovas, J. Diccionario espanol-latino. (Span. & Lat.). 200.00 ptas. SAETA.

Lluis. Diccionario Terminologico. 456p. (Span.). 1980. write for info. Fondo Educativo.

Lopez, Issac M. Basque-Spanish Dictionary. (Basque & Span.). 1974. lib. bdg. $69.95 (ISBN 0-685-51638-5). Revisionist Pr.

Lopez Mendizabal, Isaac. La Lengua Vasca. LC 77-571017. 351p. (Basque & Span.). 1977. write for info. (ISBN 8-470-25126-0). Aunamendi Edit.

Lopez Mendizabal, Isaak. Diccionario Vasco-Castellano. 6th ed. 452p. (Castella.). 1976. $25.50 (ISBN 84-7025-026-4, S-50439). French & Eur.

Luft, Anita. Diccionario de Palabras Anticuadas y en Desuso. 2nd ed. 308p. (Span.). 1974. pap. $17.50 (ISBN 84-359-0071-1, S-12060). French & Eur.

Macazaga Ordono, Cesar. Diccionario de la Lengua Nahuatl. LC 80-106467. 122p. (Eng., Aztec, & Span.). 1979. write for info. Innovacion.

Malczewski, J. Szkolny Slownik Terminow Nauki i Jezyku. 244p. (Pol.). 1979. $2.75 (Pub. by Wydaw. Szkolne & Pedagogiczne). Four Continent.

Manzano, M. Orta. Diccionario de Sinonimos y Antonimos. 368p. (Span.). 1980. $23.50 (ISBN 84-261-1704-X, S-37650). French & Eur.

Marquez Villegas, Luis. Vocabulario Del Espanol Hablado. 128p. (Span.). 1975. pap. $5.95 (ISBN 84-7143-048-7, S-50027). French & Eur.

Marti Marca, Antonio, et al. Maly Slownik Hispansko-Polski & Polsko-Hiszpanski. 3rd. ed. LC 77-502213. 289p. (Pol. & Span.). 1977. 100.00 Zl. Wiedza Powszechna.

Martin, Jaime. Diccionario De Expresiones Malsonantes Del Espanol. 2nd ed. 370p. (Span.). 1974. pap. $13.95 (ISBN 84-7090-058-7, S-31400). French & Eur.

Martinez Almoyna, Julio. Dicionario de Portugues-Espanol. 1332p. (Port. & Span.). $18.00. Porto Editora.

Martinez Burgos, Matias & Ayala Lopez, Manuel. Diccionario escolar latino-espanol y espanol-latino. (Span.). 200.00 ptas. Bibliografica.

Martinez Calvo, L. Diccionario Espanol-Ruso. LC 76-456144. 1915p. (Rus. & Span.). 1975. 1000.00 Rub (ISBN 8-43030-133-X). Sopena.

Martinez Calvo, Lorenzo. Diccionario Espanol-Ruso. 1920p. (Span. & Rus.). 1975. $44.95 (ISBN 84-303-0132-1, S-50411). French & Eur.

--Diccionario Ruso-Espanol. 2000p. (Rus. & Span.). $44.95 (ISBN 84-303-0131-3, S-50410). French & Eur.

Martinez De Sousa, Jose. Diccionario Internacional de Siglas. 472p. (Span.). 1978. leatherette $28.50 (ISBN 84-368-0083-4, S-50372). French & Eur.

Martinez Duenas, Luis M. & Kato Yda, Manuel M. Diccionario espanol-japones. 1160p. (Span. & Japanese.). 1982. 450.00 ptas (ISBN 84-85786-53-X). Edi-Seis.

Mateos, Fernando, et al. Diccionario Espanol de la Lengua China. 1381p. (Span. & Chinese.). 1977. leather $95.00 (ISBN 84-239-4771-8, S-31804). French & Eur.

Menendez Pidal, Ramon D. Diccionario General Ilustrado de la Lengua Espanola. Gili Gaya, Samuel D., ed. 1752p. (Span.). 1980. write for info (ISBN 84-7153-109-7). Biblograf SP.

Merino, Jose. Diccionario de Dudas Ingles-Espanol. 332p. (Eng. & Span.). 1978. pap. write for info. (ISBN 84-283-0425-4). Paraninfo.

Merino Bustamante, Jose. Diccionario De Dudas Ingles-Espanol. 2nd ed. 332p. (Span.). 1978. pap. $17.50 (ISBN 84-283-0425-4, S-50240). French & Eur.

Merino Bustamente, Jose. Diccionario de dudas: Ingles-espanol. (Span.). 1971. 250.00 ptas. Paraninfo.

Messinger, Heinz & Ruedenberg, Werner, eds. Langenscheidts Handwoerterbuecher Spanisch. (Span.). DM.28.00 (ISBN 3-468-80034-7). Langenscheidt.

Mi primer diccionario Sigmar. (Span.). write for info. (608-19). Pan Amer Pub.

Mi Primer Sopena. 128p. (Span.). $11.75. Cruzada Span Pubns.

Mi primer Sopena. (Illus., Span.). $10.50. Iaconi.

Mi Primer Sopena: Diccionario Infantil Ilustrado. (Illus.). 138p. (Span.). $14.95. Lectorum Pubns.

Michelon, Oscar. Diccionario de San Francisco. LC 78-370238. xvi, 770p. (Eng., Maya, & Span.). 1976. S.1600.00 (ISBN 3-201-00972-5). Akademische Druck Verlagt.

Millan Contreras, Donato. Diccionario Internacional Abreviado De Siglas Contracciones y Abreviaturas. 224p. (Span.). 1974. pap. $9.95 (ISBN 0-686-57355-2, S-50239). French & Eur.
Millar. Diccionario en Color de Arbustos. 213p. (Span.). 1977. $60.00 (ISBN 84-252-0695-2, S-50274). French & Eur.
Miracle, Josep. Diccionari Catala-Castella, Castella-Catala. 2nd ed. LC 77-458925. xi, 1122p. (Span. & Catalan.). 1976. write for info. (ISBN 8-485-08300-8). Poseidon SA.
--Diccionari catala-castella, castella-catala. 1084p. (Span.). 1969. 675.00 ptas. Edhasa.
Miracle Montserrat, Josep. Diccionari Manual de la Llengua Catalana. 1401p. (Catalan.). 1975. $19.95 (ISBN 84-298-0594-X, S-31550). French & Eur.
Miri, Hector F. Diccionario Bachiller. 720p. (Span.). Arg.$15.00. Claridad.
Moliner, Maria. Diccionario de uso de espanol: Tomo 1. 1495p. (Span.). 1981. write for info. (ISBN 84-249-1346-9). Gredos.
--Diccionario de uso de espanol: Tomo 2. 1593p. (Span.). 1981. write for info. (ISBN 84-249-1348-5). Gredos.
--Diccionario de uso del espanol, 2 vol. (Span.). 2300.00 ptas. pap. 2000.00 ptas. Gredos.
--Diccionario de uso del espanol: Obra completa, 2 vols. 3088p. (Span.). 1981. write for info. (ISBN 84-249-1344-2). Gredos.
--Diccionario de uso del espanol: Tomo 1. 1495p. (Span.). 1981. write for info. (ISBN 84-249-1346-9). Gredos.
--Diccionario de uso del espanol: Tomo 2. 1593p. (Span.). 1981. write for info. (ISBN 84-249-1348-5). Gredos.
--Diccionario Del Uso Del Espanol, 2 vols. 4th ed. 3036p. (Span.). 1977. Set. $90.00 (ISBN 84-249-1344-2, S-12260). French & Eur.
--Diccionario del Uso del Espanol, 2 vols. (Span.). $125.00. GRD.
Moll Casanovas, Fransesc de B. Diccionari Catala-Castella I Castella-Catala. 816p. (Catala & Span.). 1978. $46.00 (ISBN 84-273-0257-6, S-50362). French & Eur.
Moll Y Cassanovas, Francisco de. Diccionari Catala-Castella. LC 78-351223. 395p. (Span. & Catalan.). 1977. 1100.00 ptas (ISBN 8-427-30238-X). Moll Edit.
Moreno, Alvaro J., compiled by. Voces Homofonas, Homografas & Homonimas Castellanas. LC 77-457746. xxxiii, 315p. (Span.). 1975. write for info. Moreno Ed.
Mugica. Diccionario manual latino-espanol y espanol-latino. 7th ed. 640p. (Lat. & Span.). 230.00 ptas. Razon y Fe.
Mugica Berrondo, Placido. Diccionario Vasco-Castellano: Tomo 1. 1096p. (Span.). 1981. 2800.00 ptas (ISBN 84-271-1267-X). Mensajero Edns.
--Diccionario Vasco-Castellano: Tomo 2. 1000p. (Span.). 1981. pap. 2800.00 ptas (ISBN 84-271-1268-8). Mensajero Edns.
Mugica Betrondo, Placido. Diccionario Vasco-Castellano: Obra completa, 2 vols. 2096p. (Span.). 1981. 5600.00 ptas (ISBN 84-271-1269-6). Mensajero Edns.
Mugika, Placido. Diccionario Castellano-Vasco. 2nd ed. 1027p. (Castella & Vasco.). 1973. $41.95 (ISBN 84-271-0800-1, S-50441). French & Eur.
Munso, J. Diccionario Turistico de Cataluna, Baleares y Andora. 693p. (Span.). 1975. Leatherette $95.00 (ISBN 84-85186-00-1, S-32722). French & Eur.
Nogueira, J. & Turover, G. Diccionario Ruso-Espanol. 956p. (Rus. & Span.). 1979. Leatherette $25.95 (ISBN 0-686-92344-8, S-33593). French & Eur.
Onieva. Diccionario Multiple: Nueve Diccionarios en un Solo Volumen. 3rd ed. (Span.). 1981. 425.00 ptas (ISBN 8-42830-400-9). Paraninfo.
Onieva, Antonio J. Diccionario multiple: Nueve diccionarios en un volumen. 504p. (Span.). 1971. 190.00 ptas. Paraninfo.
Onieva, J. A. Diccionario Multiple. 502p. (Span.). 1976. pap. write for info. (ISBN 84-283-0400-9). Paraninfo.
Ortega Cavero, David. Diccionario Portugues-Espanol, Espanol-Portugues. 1856p. (Port. & Span.). 1975. $50.95 (ISBN 84-303-0166-6, S-12405). French & Eur.
Ortega Cavero, David & Da Conceica, Julio. Diccionario portugues-espanol, espanol-portugues. 1856p. (Port. & Span.). 1977. 31.00 ptas. Sopena.
Oyeregui, Buenaventura de. Diccionario Vasco-Castellano, Castellano-Vasco De Voces Comunes a Dos O Mas Dialectos Del Euskera. 2nd ed. 372p. (Castella.). 1978. pap. $7.50 (ISBN 0-686-57354-4, S-50454). French & Eur.
Pabon, Jose M. Vox-Diccionario Manual Griego-Espanol. 11th ed. 724p. (Gr. & Span.). 1979. leatherette $17.25 (ISBN 84-7153-192-5, S-12136). French & Eur.
Pabon, Jose M. & Fernandez Galiano, M. Diccionario Manual Griego-Espanol. 724p. (Gr. & Span.). 925.00 ptas (ISBN 84-7153-192-5). Biblograf SP.
Paniagua, J. R. Vocabulario Basico de la Arquitectura. 375p. (Span.). 1978. pap. $17.95 (ISBN 84-376-0134-7, S-37345). French & Eur.
Park, Marinell & Weber, Nancy. Diccionario Quechua San Martin. LC 77-465805. 188p. (Span. & Quechua.). 1976. write for info. Ministerio de Educacion.
Parker, Gary J. Diccionario Polilectal del Quechua de Ancash. LC 76-469538. (Span. & Quechua.). 1975. write for info. Centro Invest.
--Diccionario Quechua. LC 77-464932. 311p. (Quechua & Span.). 1976. write for info. Minist Ed Caracas.
Pascual, Recuero. Diccionario Basico Latino-Espanol. LC 78-347492. xviii, 151p. (Span. & Ladino.). 1977. write for info. (ISBN 8-472-13088-6). Ameller Edic.
Pay Estrany, S. Diccionari de sinomins i antonims. 824p. (Span.). 1970. 700.00 ptas. Teide.
Pequeno Diccionara Kapelusz de la Lenguna Espanola. 612p. (Span.). 1980. pap. $6.95 (ISBN 84-499-3146-0, S-32728). French & Eur.
Pequeno Diccionario de Sinonimos. (Span.). $4.50. Camino Real.
Pequeno diccionario Kapelusz de la lengua espanola. (Span.). 1981. Arg.$12500.00. Kapelusz.
Pey, Santiago & Calonja, Juan R. Pequeno Diccionario de Sinonimos, Ideas Afines & Contrarios. 241p. (Span.). E2.95 (ISBN 0-245-59455-8, Pub. by Biblograf S. A., Barcelona). Harrap.
Pey Estrany, Santiago. Diccionari de sinonims i antonims: Edicio economica. 5th ed. (Span.). 1981. pap. 600.00 ptas (ISBN 84-307-7329-0). Teide.
--Diccionario de Sinonimos Ideas Afines & Contrarios. 10th ed. 635p. (Span.). 1981. 750.00 ptas (ISBN 84-307-7070-4). Teide.
Pey Estrany, Santiago & Ruiz Calonja, J. Diccionario De Sinonimos Ideas Afines y Contrarios. 7th ed. 535p. (Span.). 1978. $13.95 (ISBN 84-307-7070-4, S-12142). French & Eur.
Plaja, Aurora D., prologue by. Diccionario Inicial de la Lengua Espanola. LC 75-517454. (Illus.). 310p. (Span.). 1975. write for info. (ISBN 8-471-53199-2). Biblo Sp.
Plans y De Gabriel Sanz De Bremond, Fructuoso. Diccionario Ortografico Mikron. 51st ed. 640p. (Span.). 1978. leatherette $2.75 (ISBN 84-7105-091-9, S-50033). French & Eur.
Putman's Contemporary Spanish Dictionary. (Span.). $1.75. Camino Real.
Quesada Castillo, Felix. Diccionario Quechua Cajamarca-Canaris. LC 77-465596. 193p. (Span. & Quechua.). 1976. write for info. Minist Ed Caracas.
Quiroga Flores, Miguel Angel. Diccionario Kollasuyo, Espanol-Quechua. 150p. (Span. & Quechua.). 1979. write for info. Cochabamba.
R. Diccionario Escolar de la Lengua Espanola. LC 76-466553. (Illus.). 200p. (Span.). 1975. write for info. (ISBN 8-430-30082-1). Sopena.
Rafael, G. Diccionario para un macuto. 2nd ed. (Span.). 350.00 ptas. Nacional Editora.
Raluy Pondevida, Antonio. Diccionario Porrua de la lengua espanola: Contiene las palabras basicas del idioma, con abundantes exicanismos & americanismos, tecnicismos, verbos & notas ortograficas. 9th ed. Monterde, Francisco, ed. 868p. (Eng. & Span.). 1981. Mex.$pap. 90.00. Porrua.
Raluy Poudevida, Antonio. Breve Diccionario Porrua de la Lengua Espanola. 461p. (Span.). pap. $3.25. Lectorum Pubns.
--Breve diccionario Porrua de la lengua espanola. 14th, rev. ed. Monterde, Francisco, rev. by. 462p. (Span.). 1980. Mex.$pap. 50.00. Porrua.
--Diccionario Porrua de la Espanola. 19th ed. 850p. (Span.). 1981. Mex.$90.00; $140.00. Porrua.
--Diccionario Porrua de la lengua espanola. (Span.). Mex.$pap. 15.00. Porrua.
--Diccionario Porrua de la lengua espanola. 19th, rev. ed. Monterde, Francisco, rev. by. 850p. (Span.). 1981. Mex.$140.00; Mex.$pap. 90.00. Porrua.
Raluy Poudevila, Antonio. Diccionario Forrua de la Lengua Espanola. Monterde, Francisco, ed. (Span.). pap. $6.95 (ISBN 0-686-56694-7, S-12281). French & Eur.
--Diccionario Porrua de la Lengua Espanola Para Escuelas Primarias. Monterde, Francisco, ed. 461p. (Span.). pap. $4.95 (ISBN 0-686-56695-5, S-12282). French & Eur.
Raspall de Cauhe, Joana, et al. Diccionari Usual de Sinonims Catalans: Mots i Frases. 572p. (Catalan.). 1975. $17.50 (ISBN 84-7211-111-3, S-50048). French & Eur.
Raventos, M. H. Spanish Dictionary. (Teach Yourself Ser.). (Span.). 1974. pap. 8.95 (ISBN 0-679-10230-2). McKay.
Real Academia de la Lengua Espanol. Diccionario de la Lengua Espanol. 19th ed. 1456p. (Span.). 1979. leatherette $75.00 (ISBN 84-239-4722-X, S-12257). French & Eur.
Real Academia Espanola. Diccionario De la Lengua Espanola. 19th ed. (Span.). 1971. $65.00x (ISBN 0-686-00852-9). Colton Bk.
--Diccionario Manual y Illustrado De La Lengua Espanola. (Span.). $35.00x (ISBN 0-686-00855-3). Colton Bk.
Real Academie de la Lengua Espanol. Diccionario Manual e Ilustrado de la Lengua Espanol. 2nd ed. 1584p. (Span.). 1979. $35.95 (ISBN 84-239-4724-6). French & Eur.
Roman de Bera, P. Diccionario Castellano-Vasco. 4th ed. 524p. (Span. & Vasco.). 1975. $25.50 (ISBN 84-7025-178-3, S-50440). French & Eur.
Roman del Cerro, Juan L. El Lexico base del castellano: Analisis estadistico y de contenido. 110p. (Span.). 1981. pap. write for info. (ISBN 84-7231-596-7). Confed Espanola.
Romeu, Xavier. Vocabulari Ideologic Catala. (Span.). write for info. Teide.
Ruiz Calonja, J. & Pey, Santiago. Diccionario de sininimos, ideas afines y contrarios. 536p. (Span.). pap. 200.00 ptas. Teide.
Sainz de Robles, F. C. Diccionario espanol de sinonimos y antonimos. (Span.). 700.00 ptas. Aguilar SP.
Sainz de Robles, Federico C. Diccionario Espanol de Sinonimos y Antonimos. 8th ed. Arturo del Hoyo, Asesor, ed. 1152p. (Span.). 1977. $50.00 (ISBN 84-03-27029-1, S-12352). French & Eur.
Salto Dolla, Angel. Diccionario De Terminos De Proceso De Datos: Con Vocabulario Espanol-Ingles, Ingles-Espanol. 2nd ed. 446p. (Span. & Eng.). 1979. $20.95 (ISBN 84-283-0830-6, S-50371). French & Eur.
Sanchez Benedito, Francisco. Diccionario consico de modiamos. 3rd ed. 272p. (Span.). 1982. pap. 820.00 ptas (ISBN 84-205-0358-4). Alhambra.
Sanchez-Boudy, Jose. Diccionario De Cubanismos Mas Usuales. LC 76-45322. (Span.). 1978. pap. $9.00 (ISBN 0-89729-199-9). Ediciones.
Sanguinetti, C. S., ed. Mi primer diccionario Larousse en colores. (Illus., Span.). (gr. 3). 1976. PLB 9.95 (ISBN 0-88332-025-8, 21116). Larousse.
Santamaria, A. Diccionario de sinonimos y antonimos. (Span.). 100.00 ptas. 70.00 ptas. pap. 65.00 ptas. Sopena.
Santamaria, Francisco J. Diccionario De Mejicanismos. (Span.). $49.50x (ISBN 0-686-00853-7). Colton Bk.
Santamarie, Andres & Cuartas, Augusto. Diccionario de Incorreciones y Particularidades del Lenguaje. 3rd ed. 531p. (Span.). 1975. leatherette $15.75 (ISBN 84-283-0112-3). French & Eur.
Sebastian Yarza, Florencio I. Diccionario griego-espanol. 1644p. (Gr. & Span.). 1974. 1000.00 ptas. Sopena.
Seco, Manuel. Diccionario de Dudas de la Lengua Espanol. 7th ed. 556p. (Span.). 1976. $44.95 (ISBN 84-03-27064-X, S-12356). French & Eur.
--Diccionario de Dudas de la Lengua Espanola. (Span.). $34.50 (AGL). Lectorum Pubns.
--Diccionario de dudas de la lengua espanola. (Span.). $25.00. Iaconi.
Serrano Laktaw, Pedro, ed. Diccionario hispano-tagalog y tagalog-hispano, 3 vols. 2024p. (Span. & Tagalog.). 1000.00 ptas. Cultura Hispan.
Sese, Bernard. Vocabulaire de la Langue Espagnole Classique: XVIe. & XVIIe. Siecles. 314p. (Span.). 1976. 59.60 F. CDU.
Simeon, Remi. Diccionario de la Lengua Nahuatl o Mexicana. LC 79-116666. xcvi, 782p. (Aztec & Span.). 1977. write for info. Siglo Veintiuno.
Simonet, Francisco J. Glosario de voces Ibericas y Latinas. 628p. (Span. & Arabic.). $18.00 (113-5). Intl Bk Ctr.
--Glosario de voces ibericas y latinas: Tomo 1. 424p. (Span. & Lat.). 1982. pap. 1500.00 ptas (ISBN 84-363-0545-0). Atlas Edns.
--Glosario de voces ibericas y latinas: Obras completa. 849p. (Span. & Lat.). 1982. pap. 3000.00 ptas (ISBN 84-363-0547-7). Atlas Edns.
Sintas, J. Diccionario De Maximas Pensamientos y Sentacias. 742p. 1981. $53.95 (ISBN 84-302-0439-3, S-37665). French & Eur.
Sintes, J. Diccionario de Aforismos: Proverbios Refranes. 894p. (Span.). $60.00 (ISBN 0-686-92530-0, S-37667). French & Eur.
--Diccionario de la Felicidad. 1046p. (Span.). Date not set. $35.95 (ISBN 0-686-92548-3, S-37670). French & Eur.
Sota Aburto, Manuel de. Diccionario Retana De Autoridades De la Lengua Vasca, 4 vols. (Span.). 1976. Set. leather $200.00 (ISBN 84-248-0248-9, S-50053). French & Eur.
Sotelo, Joaquin C., prologue by. Vox-Diccionario Abreviado Ortografico de la Lengua Espanola. 2nd ed. 416p. (Span.). 1978. leatherette $5.75 (ISBN 84-7153-227-1, S-12372). French & Eur.

Soto Ruiz, Clodoaldo. Diccionario Quechua Ayacucho-Chanca. LC 77-465011. 183p. (Quechua & Span.). 1976. write for info. Minist Ed Caracas.
Spanish Dictionary. 320p. (Span.). Epap. 1.25 (ISBN 0-600-36565-4). Newnes Bks.
Spanish Duden, Pictorial Dictionary. (Illus.). $20.50 (ISBN 3-4110-0971-3). Adler.
Spes--Diccionario Abreviado Latino-Espanol, Espanol-Latino. 9th ed. 316p. (Lat. & Span.). 1978. leatherette $7.25 (ISBN 84-7153-221-2, S-12409). French & Eur.
Stahl, Fred A. & Scavnicky, Gary E. Reverse Dictionary of the Spanish Language. LC 68-24625. (Span.). 1973. $18.50 (ISBN 0-252-72540-9). U of Ill Pr.
Standard Spanish Dictionary. 1200p. (Span. & Eng.). $11.95 (321). Langenscheidt.
Torres, Rosa E. Terminologia de la Education. LC 78-111426. 210p. (Span.). 1978. write for info. Minist Ed La Paz.
The Trictionary. 432p. (Chinese , Span. & Eng.). softcover $12.95. Bilingual Pubns.
Turner, Paul & Turner, Shirley. Dictionary of Chontal to Spanish-English, & Spanish to Chontal. LC 78-164366. (Span., Eng. & Chontal.). 1971. pap. $3.95x (ISBN 0-8165-0338-9). U of Ariz Pr.
Umbral Perez, Francisco. Diccionario Para Pobres. 240p. (Span.). 1977. $9.95 (ISBN 84-7454-002-X, S-50099). French & Eur.
U. S. War Department. A Phrase & Sentence Dictionary of Spoken Spanish. LC 58-14487. (Span. & Eng.). 1958. lib. bdg. 13.50x (ISBN 0-88307-580-6). Gannon.
Universal Spanish Dictionary. 560p. (Span.). $2.95 (097). Langenscheidt.
Varios, tr. Diccionario A R V E: Obra completa, 2 vols. 2nd ed. 704p. (Span.). 1982. pap. 1850.00 ptas (ISBN 84-7017-706-0). Argos-Vergara.
--Diccionario A R V E: Tomo 1; Ingles-Espanol. 2nd ed. 432p. (Eng. & Span.). 1982. pap. 925.00 ptas (ISBN 84-7017-707-9). Argos-Vergara.
--Diccionario A R V E: Tomo 2; Espanol-Ingles. 2nd ed. 272p. (Span. & Eng.). 1982. pap. 925.00 ptas (ISBN 84-7017-708-7). Argos-Vergara.
Vest-Pocket Spanish. (Span.). pap. 2.95 (ISBN 0-8329-1534-3). New Century.
Victorica, Ricardo. Nueva Epanortosis al Diccionario de Anonimos Seudonimos de J. T. Medina. LC 73-78357. 207p. (Span.). 1973. Repr. of 1929 ed. $16.00x (ISBN 0-87917-028-X). Ethridge.
Vinoly, A. J., et al. Pequeno Diccionario De Sinonimos y Sus Contrarios. 6th ed. 242p. (Span.). 1976. pap. $5.95 (ISBN 84-307-7052-6, S-12220). French & Eur.
Vinoly, Alberto, ed. Pequeno diccionario de sinonimos, ideas afines y contrarios. (Span.). 1979. pap. $7.95 (ISBN 8-4307-7052-6). Larousse.
Vox. Diccionari Manual Castella-Catala, Catala-Castella, 2 vols. 3rd ed. LC 79-112856. 614p. (Span. & Catalan.). 1977. 425.00 ptas (ISBN 8-471-53198-4). Biblo Sp.
--Diccionario de Sinonimos. 376p. (Span.). 1982. DM.18.00. Brandstetter.
--Diccionario General-Ilustrado la Lengau Espanola. (Illus.). 1752p. (Span.). 1982. DM.80.00. Brandstetter.
--Diccionario Manual Ilustrado de la Lengua Espanola. (Illus.). 1173p. (Span.). 1982. DM.30.00. Brandstetter.
Vox--Diccionari Manual Ortografic. 552p. (Catalan.). 1975. leather $16.75 (ISBN 84-7153-327-8, S-31579). French & Eur.
Vox--Diccionario Conciso de la Lengua Espanola. 2nd ed. 464p. (Span.). 1977. pap. $3.25 (ISBN 84-7153-233-6, S-26963). French & Eur.
Vox--Diccionario Fundamental de la Lengua Espanola. 604p. (Span.). 1975. leatherette $10.50 (ISBN 84-7153-229-8, S-26961). French & Eur.
Vox--Diccionario Fundamental de la Lengua Espanola. 604p. (Span.). 1977. pap. $8.95 (ISBN 84-7153-230-1, S-50220). French & Eur.
Vox--Diccionario General Ilustrado de la Lengua Espanola. 3rd ed. 1752p. (Span.). 1978. leatherette $34.95 (ISBN 84-7153-109-7, S-12378). French & Eur.
Vox--Vocabulari Basic Infantil i d'Adults. 112p. (Catalan.). 1977. pap. $5.50 (ISBN 84-7153-265-4, S-50216). French & Eur.
Vox-Diccionari Manual de Sinonims. 2nd ed. 318p. (Catalan.). 1979. leatherette $12.95 (ISBN 84-7153-325-1, S-50217). French & Eur.
Vox-Diccionario Abreviado de la Lengua Espanola. 9th ed. 512p. (Span.). 1979. leatherette $4.75 (ISBN 84-7153-201-8, S-12371). French & Eur.
Vox-Diccionario Abreviado de Sinonimos. 3rd ed. 352p. (Span.). 1978. leatherette $5.75 (ISBN 84-7153-207-7, S-12370). French & Eur.
Vox-Diccionario Compendiado de la Lengua Espanola. 2nd ed. 646p. (Span.). 1979. leatherette $4.95 (ISBN 84-7153-232-8, S-12373). French & Eur.
Vox-Diccionario Escolar de la Lengua Espanola. 5th ed. 884p. (Span.). 1978. leatherette $13.50 (ISBN 84-7153-172-0, S-12376). French & Eur.
Vox-Diccionario Inicial de la Lengua Espanola. 340p. (Span.). 1975. leatherette $6.95 (ISBN 0-686-57340-4, S-26962). French & Eur.
Vox-Diccionario Manual Ilustrado de la Lengua Espanola. 4th ed. 1170p. (Span.). 1978. leatherette $13.95 (ISBN 84-7153-166-6, S-12379). French & Eur.
Vox-Diccionario Tematico de la Lengua Espanola. 496p. (Span.). 1975. leatherette $26.25 (ISBN 84-7153-116-X, S-50219). French & Eur.
Warman, Adolfo I. Vaughan. Diccionario trilingue miskito-ingles-espanol. 790p. (Eng., Span. & Miskito.). 1959. $10.00. Imp. Nac. Manugua EDUCA.
Williams, Edwin B. Diccionario Del Idioma Espanol. 530p. (Span. & Eng.). pap. $2.95. Lectorum Pubns.
Yaselman. Diccionario ruso-espanol. (Rus. & Span.). 160.00 ptas. Aguilar SP.
Zainqui, Jose M. Diccionario Razonado de Sinonimos y Contrarios. 2nd ed. 1080p. (Span.). 1977. $35.95 (ISBN 84-315-0931-7, S-31379). French & Eur.
Zamora Vicente, Alfonso. Diccionario Moderno del Espanol Usual. LC 75-511707. viii, 1063p. (Span.). 1975. write for info. (ISBN 8-485-09309-7). Sader SA.
Zaniah. Diccionario Esoterico. (Span.). $29.95 (ISBN 0-686-56653-X, S-15045). French & Eur.

SPANISH LANGUAGE–DICTIONARIES–DANISH

Diccionario Lexicon Espanol-Danes & Espanol-Danes. 384p. (Span. & Danish.). 1974. leatherette $4.95 (ISBN 84-303-0160-7, S-50407); pap. $4.50 (ISBN 84-303-0159-3, S-50406). French & Eur.
Lexicon Sopena: Diccionario de bolsillo, danes-espanol y espanol-danes. (Danish & Span.). 60.00 ptas. 35.00 ptas. pap. 30.00 ptas. Sopena.

SPANISH LANGUAGE–DICTIONARIES–DUTCH

Athenum Woordenboek: Espanol-Holandes, Holandes-Espanol. 382p. (Span. & Dutch.). 1979. pap. $5.25 (ISBN 84-303-0801-6, S-35068). French & Eur.
Diccionario Lexicon Holandes-Espanol y Espanol-Holandes. 384p. (Dutch & Span.). 1974. pap. $4.50 (ISBN 84-303-0161-5, S-50408); pap. $4.95 leatherette (ISBN 84-303-0162-3, S-50409). French & Eur.
Diccionario Universal Herder Holandes-Espanol, Espanol-Holandes. 264p. (Dutch & Span.). 1977. leatherette $4.50 (ISBN 84-254-0779-6, S-50412). French & Eur.
Lexicon Sopena: Diccionario de bolsillo, holandes-espanol y espanol-holandes. 384p. (Dutch & Span.). 60.00 ptas. 35.00 ptas. pap. 30.00 ptas. Sopena.

SPANISH LANGUAGE–DICTIONARIES–ENGLISH

Amador, E. M. Martinez. Diccionario Ingles-Espanol, Espanol-Ingles. 1504p. (Span. & Eng.). $47.95 (ISBN 84-303-0105-4, S-2789). French & Eur.
Anorga, J. Nuevo diccionario bilingue Minerva. (Span. & Eng.). write for info. (608-86). Pan Amer Pub.
Benedetto, U. Spanish-English, English-Spanish Dictionary, 2 Vols. (Span. & Eng.). Set. 100.00 (ISBN 8-4716-6211-6). Heinman.
Berlitz Editors. Berlitz Latin-American Spanish for Travellers. 192p. (Span.). 1982. 8.95 (ISBN 0-02-965510-2, Berlitz); pap. 4.95 (ISBN 0-02-963950-6). Macmillan.
--Berlitz Pocket Dictionaries: Spanish-English. 300p. (Eng. & Span.). 1982. pap. $4.95 (ISBN 0-686-92998-5, Berlitz). Macmillan.
--Berlitz Spanish for Travellers. 192p. (Span.). 1982. 8.95 (ISBN 0-02-965190-5, Berlitz); pap. 4.95 (ISBN 0-02-963970-0). Macmillan.
--Spanish-English Dictionary. (Span. & Eng.). 1979. 4.95 (ISBN 0-02-964510-7, Berlitz). Macmillan.
Biblograf. Vox Concise Spanish & English Dictionary. xxvi, 981p. (Span. & Eng.). E6.95 (ISBN 0-245-50989-5, Pub. by Biblograf S. A., Barcelona). Harrap.
--Vox New Compact Spanish & English Dictionary. 796p. (Span. & Eng.). E3.95 (ISBN 0-245-50990-9, Pub. by Biblograf, Barcelona). Harrap.
--Vox Shorter Spanish & English Dictionary. 1448p. (Span. & Eng.). E20.00 (ISBN 0-245-50988-7, Pub. by Biblograf S. A., Barcelona). Harrap.
Bohigas Rosell, Mauricio. Diccionario Ingles-Espanol, Spanish-English. 1370p. (Eng. & Span.). 1974. $7.95 (ISBN 84-7183-007-8, S-12385). French & Eur.
Brown, R. F. Diccionario Collins Contemporary English-Spanish Ingles-Espanol. 7th ed. 480p. (Eng. & Span.). 1982. pap. 450.00 ptas (ISBN 84-253-1179-9). Grijalbo.
Brown, R. F., ed. Spanish-English, English-Spanish Gem Dictionary. (Gem Foreign Language Ser.). (Span. & Eng.). 1957. $2.95 (ISBN 0-00-458653-0, G4). Collins Pubs.
Bruguera Grane, Francisco. Diccionario Ingles-Espanol, Espanol-Ingles. 3rd ed. 680p. (Eng. & Span.). 1979. pap. $4.95 (ISBN 84-02-00835-6, S-50345). French & Eur.
Butterfield, Arthur. Practical Spanish-English, English-Spanish Dictionary. (Hippocrene Practical Language Dictionaries Ser.). 400p. (Orig., Eng. & Span.). 1983. pap. $6.95 (ISBN 0-88254-814-X). Hippocrene Bks.
Caldwell, Pablo. Diccionario de Modismos Ingleses. 496p. (Eng. & Span.). 1973. $17.50 (ISBN 0-686-56672-6, S-33065). French & Eur.
Calvert, G. H. Cortina Handy Spanish-English, English-Spanish Dictionary. LC 81-47221. 546p. (Span. & Eng.). 1982. $7.95 (ISBN 0-06-464800-1, BN-4800). B&N NY.
Calvert, G. H., ed. Cortina Handy Spanish-English Dictionary. LC 78-100109. xxv, 544p. (Eng. & Span.). 1976. write for info. (ISBN 0-8327-0701-5). Cortina.
Cassell. Cassell's Spanish Dictionary: Concise Spanish-English English-Spanish. (Span. & Eng.). $9.95 (ISBN 0-02-522660-6). Macmillan.
--Cassell's Spanish Dictionary: Thumb-indexed Spanish-English English-Spanish. (Span. & Eng.). $19.95 (ISBN 0-02-522910-9). Macmillan.
Cassells. Spanish-English Dictionary. (Span. & Eng.). 1978. standard 17.95; index 19.95 (ISBN 0-02-052291-6). Macmillan.
Cassell's Compact Spanish-English Dictionary. 444p. (Span. & Eng.). 1981. pap. $2.95 (ISBN 0-440-31129-2, LE). Dell.
Cassell's Concise Spanish-English English-Spanish Dictionary. (Span. & Eng.). 1977. 9.95 (ISBN 0-02-522660-6). Macmillan.
Cassell's Spanish Dictionary. (Span. & Eng.). $16.95 (7744-4). Natl Textbk.
Castillo, Carlos & Bond, Otto F. Spanish-English Dictionary. (Span. & Eng.). 1981. pap. 3.50 (ISBN 0-671-47762-5). PB.
--University of Chicago Spanish Dictionary. 3rd rev. & enl. ed. Lincoln Canfield, D., rev. by. (Span. & Eng.). s.p. $12.50 (7815-7); pap. $4.95 s.p. (7855-6). Natl Textbk.
Castillo, Carlos & Garcia, Barbara M. The University of Chicago Spanish Dictionary. 3rd, rev. & enl. ed. LC 76-449. vi, 488p. (Eng. & Span.). 1977. $7.95 (ISBN 0-226-09673-4); $2.95 (ISBN 0-226-09674-2). U of Chicago Pr.
Channazaroff-Waganoff. Diccionario basico de fudicion ingles-castellano. 219p. (Span. & Eng.). Arg.$7.00. Mitre.
Colomer del Castillo, Jordi. Diccionari Angles-Catala. 6th ed. 253p. (Eng. & Span.). 1981. 400.00 ptas (ISBN 84-7306-091-1). Portic.
--Diccionari Ingles-Catala, Catala-Ingles. 3rd ed. 253p. (Eng. & Catalan.). 1978. pap. $8.75 (ISBN 84-7306-091-1, S-50414). French & Eur.
Compacto Diccionario Ingles-Espanol Espanol-Ingles. 608p. (Eng. & Span.). 9295.00 ptas. Biblograf SP.
Compacto Diccionario Ingles-Espanol, Espanol-Ingles Vox. 608p. (Span. & Eng.). 1982. 195.00 ptas (ISBN 8-47153-204-2). Biblograf.
Conciso Diccionario Ingles-Espanol, Espanol-Ingles Vox. 316p. (Eng. & Span.). 1982. 125.00 ptas (ISBN 8-47153-235-2). Biblograf.
Conciso Diccionario Ingles-Espanol Espanol-Ingles. 316p. (Eng. & Span.). 250.00 ptas (ISBN 84-7153-237-9); pap. 165.00 ptas (ISBN 84-7153-235-2). Biblograf SP.
Constantinou, P., ed. Spanish-English Dictionary. (Span. & Eng.). $14.50 (ISBN 0-87559-033-0). Shalom.
Cortina. Cortina-Ace Basic Spanish Dictionary. (Foreign Language Dictionary Ser.). 384p. (Span. & Eng.). 1982. pap. $2.95 (ISBN 0-441-05004-2). Ace Bks.
Coveney & Amey, eds. Glossary of Spanish & English Management Terms. (Span. & Eng.). E3.50. Longman.
Craig, Ruth P. Diccionario de Dos Cientos Uno Verbos Ingleses. LC 77-184894. (Span. & Eng.). 1972. pap. text ed. $7.95 (ISBN 0-8120-0417-5). Barron.
Crowell. Diccionario espanol-ingles, ingles-espanol. (Span. & Eng.). write for info. Hachette.
Cuyas, A., ed. New Appleton's Cuyas English-Spanish & Spanish-English Dictionary. 5th ed. (Eng. & Span.). 1972. 18.95 (ISBN 0-13-611749-X); thumb-indexed 19.95 (ISBN 0-13-611756-2). P-H.
Cuyas, Arturo. English-Spanish to Spanish-English Dictionary. rev. ed. 548p. (Span. & Eng.). 1982. pap. 2.50 (ISBN 0-13-615559-6). P-H.
Cuyas Armengol, Arturo. Diccionario Manual Ingles-Espanol, Spanish-English. 2nd ed. 768p. (Eng. & Span.). 1975. $5.95 (ISBN 84-7183-044-2, S-12389). French & Eur.
--Diccionario Manual Ingles-Espanol, Spanish-English. 35th ed. 768p. (Eng. & Span.). 1978. pap. $4.50 (ISBN 84-7183-005-1, S-12389). French & Eur.
--Gran Diccionario Cuyas Ingles-Espanol, Spanish-English. 6th ed. 1640p. (Eng. & Span.). 1977. $26.95 (ISBN 84-7183-008-6, S-12386). French & Eur.

De Gamez, Tana, ed. Simon & Schuster's Concise International Dictionary. LC 74-33235. xvii, 1379p. (Eng. & Span.). 1975. $12.95 (ISBN 0-671-22020-9). S & S.

De Renty, Ivan. The Businessman's Everyday English to Spanish Dictionary: El Mundo De Negocios. (Eng. & Span.). 1978. pap. $9.95 (ISBN 84-7143-118-1, 8138). Larousse.

Di Benedetto, Ubaldo, ed. New Comprehensive English-Spanish, Spanish-English Dictionary, 2 Vols. 3100p. (Eng. & Span.). 1977. Set. 60.00x (ISBN 84-7166-211-6). Intl Pubns Serv.

Diccionario abreviado Ingles-Espanol Vox. 6th ed. 792p. (Span. & Eng.). 1982. 325.00 ptas (ISBN 84-7153-214-X). Biblo SP.

Diccionario Abreviado Ingles-Espanol Espanol-Ingles. 792p. (Eng. & Span.). 350.00 ptas (ISBN 84-7153-214-X). Biblograf SP.

Diccionario Alianza. 96p. (Span. & Eng.). write for info. (796). Fernandez.

Diccionario Alienza ingles-espanol, espanol-ingles. 392p. (Eng. & Span.). Mex.$10.00. Fernandez.

Diccionario Basico Ilustrado Espanol-Ingles, 4 vols. (Illus.). 1200p. (Span. & Eng.). 1982. 9600.00 set ptas (ISBN 8-48585-616-3); $2400.00 ea. Mediterraneo.

Diccionario Basico Ilustrado Espanol Ingles, Vol. 4. (Illus.). 300p. (Span. & Eng.). 1982. 2400.00 ptas (ISBN 8-48585-620-1). Mediterraneo.

Diccionario Basico Ilustrado Espanol-Ingles-Euskera: Obra Complete, 4 vols. (Illus.). 1200p. (Span. & Eng.). 1982. 9000.00 set ptas (ISBN 8-48585-626-0). Mediterraneo.

Diccionario Basico Ilustrado Espanol Ingles-Gallego, 4 vols. 1200p. (Span.). 1982. 9000.00 set ptas (ISBN 8-48585-621-X); $2400.00 ea. Mediterraneo.

Diccionario Basico Ilustrado Espanol Ingles-Gallego, Vol. 1. (Illus.). 300p. (Span. & Eng.). 1982. 2400.00 ptas (ISBN 8-48585-622-8). Mediterraneo.

Diccionario Basico Ilustrado Espanol-Ingles: Obra Completa. 1200p. (Eng. & Span.). 1982. 9600.00 set ptas (ISBN 8-48585-616-3). Mediterraneo.

Diccionario Basico Ingles-Espanol Espanol-Ingles Vox. 3rd ed. 662p. (Eng. & Span.). 1982. 495.00 ptas (ISBN 84-7153-155-0). Biblo SP.

Diccionario Basico Ingles-Espanol Espanol-Ingles. 672p. (Eng. & Span.). 495.00 ptas (ISBN 84-7153-155-0). Biblograf SP.

Diccionario Bilingue. 95p. (Span. & Eng.). $3.75. Cruzada Span Pubns.

Diccionario bilingue ilustrado, 3 bks. (Illus., Span. & Eng.). (gr. k-8). Vol. 1, gr. k-2. s.p. $4.95 (0052-6); Vol. 2, gr. 2-4. s.p. $5.95 (0053-4); Vol. 3, gr. 4-8. s.p. $8.95 (0054-2). Natl Textbk.

Diccionario Brevis duplex: ingles-castellano y castellano-ingles. (Eng. & Span.). Arg.$15.00. Sopena.

Diccionario Compendiado Ingles-Espanol Espanol-Ingles. 547p. (Eng. & Span.). write for info. Biblograf SP.

Diccionario compendiado Ingles-Espanol, Espanol-Ingles. 547p. (Span. & Eng.). 1979. write for info. (ISBN 84-7153-157-7). Fed Gremios.

Diccionario Compendiado Ingles-Espanol. 2nd ed. 534p. (Eng. & Span.). 1981. 225.00 ptas (ISBN 84-7153-157-7). Biblo SP.

Diccionario Cuyas: Ingles-Espanol-Espanol-Ingles. (Eng. & Span.). $2.50. Camino Real.

Diccionario De Bolsillo, Ingles-Espanol y Spanish-English. 640p. (Eng. & Span.). 1978. pap. $3.50 (ISBN 84-7183-080-9, S-50350). French & Eur.

Diccionario de bolsillo: Spanish-English English-Spanish. (Span. & Eng.). $1.25. Follett.

Diccionario de ingles-espanol, espanol-ingles. (Span.). 75.00 ptas. Bruguera.

Diccionario el internacional. 200p. (Span. & Eng.). write for info. (797). Fernandez.

Diccionario Espanol-Ingles, 2 vols. in 1. 1088p. (Span. & Eng.). write for info. Edns Nauta.

Diccionario Espanol-Ingles. 560p. (Span. & Eng.). 1974. M.18.00; $1.45. Diana.

Diccionario espanol-ingles. (Span. & Eng.). 25.00 ptas. Mayfe.

Diccionario espanol-ingles. (Span. & Eng.). 45.00 ptas. Zeus.

Diccionario Espanol-Ingles-Espanol. 1008p. (Eng. & Span.). 1981. pap. write for info. ptas (ISBN 84-7505-232-0). Oceano.

Diccionario Espanol-Ingles, Ingles-Espanol. 800p. (Eng. & Span.). 1979. pap. $6.95 (ISBN 84-346-0310-1, S-29129). French & Eur.

Diccionario Everest Corona ingles-espanol, espanol-ingles. (Eng. & Span.). 200.00 ptas. Everest.

Diccionario Everest Cumbre, ingles-espanol, espanol-ingles. (Eng. & Span.). 100.00 ptas. 80.00 ptas. 75.00 ptas. pap. 70.00 ptas. Everest.

Diccionario Everest 'Cumbre' Ingles-espanol y espanol-ingles. 11th ed. 704p. (Eng. & Span.). 1981. pap. 175.00 ptas (ISBN 84-241-1230-X). Everest.

Diccionario Everest Cupula, ingles-espanol, espanol-ingles. (Eng. & Span.). 140.00 ptas. pap. 120.00 ptas. Everest.

Diccionario Everest Punto English-Spanish Spanish-English. (Eng. & Span.). 2.95 (ISBN 84-241-1211-3, 22882). Larousse.

Diccionario Everest Punto. Ingles-Espanol. 10th ed. 448p. (Eng. & Span.). 1981. 80.00 ptas (ISBN 84-241-1210-5). Everest.

Diccionario Everest 'Vertice' 14th ed. 700p. (Span.). 1982. 170.00 ptas (ISBN 8-42411-220-2). Everest.

Diccionario Everest Vertice ingles-espanol, espanol-ingles. (Span. & Eng.). 65.00 ptas. 50.00 ptas. pap. 45.00 ptas. Everest.

Diccionario Everest Vertice: Ingles-Espanol. 13th ed. 700p. (Eng. & Span.). 1981. 150.00 ptas (ISBN 84-241-1220-2). Everest.

Diccionario Ingles-Espanol, 2 vols. in 1. 1088p. (Eng. & Span.). write for info. Edns Nauta.

Diccionario Ingles-Espanol. 36th ed. 640p. (Eng. & Span.). 1982. 150.00 ptas (ISBN 8-47105-092-7). Mayfe.

Diccionario ingles-espanol. (Eng. & Span.). 25.00 ptas. Mayfe.

Diccionario ingles-espanol. (Eng. & Span.). 45.00 ptas. Zeus.

Diccionario Ingles-Espanol. 1008p. (Eng. & Span.). 1981. pap. 1600.00 ptas (ISBN 84-7505-234-7). Oceano.

Diccionario Ingles-Espanol & Espanol Ingles: Col. Forja de Idiomas. (Span. & Eng.). 50.00 ptas. pap. 35.00 ptas. Mayfe.

Diccionario Ingles-Espanol & Espanol-Ingles. (Span. & Eng.). 60.00 ptas. Mayfe.

Diccionario Ingles-Espanol Espanol-Ingles. 1450p. (Eng. & Span.). 2100.00 ptas (ISBN 84-7153-151-8). Biblograf SP.

Diccionario Ingles-Espanol, Espanol-Ingles. (Serie Bachillerato Koel: No. 14). 373p. (Eng. & Span.). 75.00 ptas. Tesoro.

Diccionario Ingles-Espanol Espanol-Ingles. (Eng. & Span.). 75.00 ptas. Zeus.

Diccionario Ingles-Espanol, Espanol-Ingles Novus. 1008p. (Eng. & Span.). 1981. 1600.00 ptas (ISBN 84-7505-234-7). Oceano.

Diccionario Ingles-Espanol Espanol-Ingles. 550p. (Eng. & Span.). 1981. pap. write for info. (ISBN 84-7291-330-9). Sarpe.

Diccionario Ingles-Espanol-Ingles. 472p. (Eng. & Span.). 1982. pap. 600.00 ptas (ISBN 84-278-0779-1). Nauta SA.

Diccionario Ingles-Espanol y Espanol-Ingles, 2 vols. 6th ed. 3000p. (Eng. & Span.). 1977. Set. $75.00 (ISBN 84-7166-211-6, S-12391). French & Eur.

Diccionario Ingles: For Spanish Speakers. (Eng. & Span.). s.p. $7.95 (0323-1). Natl Textbk.

Diccionario internacional Simon & Schuster: Ingles-espanol y espanol-ingles. 1632p. (Eng. & Span.). $12.95; pap. $10.95. S & S.

Diccionario Larousse moderno espanol-ingles. (Illus., Span. & Eng.). $29.95. Iaconi.

Diccionario Larousse Moderno Espanol-Ingles, English-Spanish. (Span. & Eng.). 29.95 (ISBN 2-03-020605-9, 21914). Larousse.

Diccionario Larousse usual. (Span.). pap. $11.95. Iaconi.

Diccionario Manual Amador Ingles-Espanol, Espanol-Ingles. 944p. (Span. & Eng.). $17.95 (ISBN 84-303-0116-X, S-50395). French & Eur.

Diccionario Manual Ingles-Espanol Espanol-Ingles Vox. 11th ed. 1008p. (Eng. & Span.). 1982. 725.00 ptas (ISBN 84-7153-184-4). Biblo SP.

Diccionario Manual Ingles-Espanol Espanol-Ingles. 1008p. (Eng. & Span.). 750.00 ptas (ISBN 84-7153-184-4). Biblograf SP.

Diccionario Mini Sopena Ingles-Espanol. 320p. (Eng. & Span.). 1975. pap. $1.75 (ISBN 84-303-0115-1, S-50398). French & Eur.

Diccionario Oceano Espanol-Ingles. 1008p. (Span. & Eng.). 1981. pap. 1600.00 ptas (ISBN 84-7505-232-0). Oceano.

Diccionario Parvus duplex: Ingles-castellano y castellano-ingles. (Eng & Span.). Arg.$8.40. Sopena.

Diccionario Porrua de la lengua espanola. (Span.). (gr. 7-9). pap. $6.00. Iaconi.

Diccionario Real Espanol-Ingles. 1008p. (Span. & Eng.). 1981. pap. 1600.00 ptas (ISBN 84-7505-233-9). Oceano.

Diccionario Real Espanol-Ingles, 2 vols. 1012p. (Span. & Eng.). 1981. pap. 2100.00 ptas (ISBN 84-7505-235-5). Oceano.

Diccionario Real Espanol-Ingles, Vol. 1. 528p. (Span. & Eng.). 1981. pap. 1050.00 ptas (ISBN 84-7505-236-3). Oceano.

Diccionario Real Espanol-Ingles, Vol. 2. 484p. (Span. & Eng.). 1981. pap. 1050.00 ptas (ISBN 84-7505-237-1). Oceano.

Diccionario Real Espanol-Ingles Ingles-Espanol. 1008p. (Span. & Eng.). 1981. pap. 1600.00 ptas (ISBN 84-7505-233-9). Oceano.

Diccionario Universal Herder Ingles-Espanol, Espanol-Ingles. 4th ed. 340p. (Eng. & Span.). 1977. leatherette $4.50 (ISBN 84-254-0781-8, S-12395). French & Eur.

Diccionario universal: Ingles-espanol, espanol-ingles. 340p. (Eng. & Span.). $0.77; 50.00 ptas. Herder SA.

Dictionario Basico: Primary Dictionary. 96p. 1983. pap. $2.25 (ISBN 0-515-07390-3). Jove Pubns.

Diez Mateo, Felix & Hochleitner, Frida. Diccionario Manual Ingles-Espanol, Espanol-Ingles. 1008p. (Eng. & Span.). 1971. $9.95 (ISBN 84-239-4720-3, S-50351). French & Eur.

--Diccionario manual ingles-espanol, espanol-ingles. 1000p. (Eng. & Span.). 150.00 ptas. Espasa Calpe.

Divry, D. C. Divry's Spanish English Dictionary. (Span. & Eng.). $2.70. Camino Real.

Douglas, J. M. & Lomo, A., eds. Divry's New Spanish-English & English-Spanish Handy Dictionary. (Span. & Eng.). 1965. pocket size, flexible $3.50 (ISBN 0-685-09033-7); thumb indexed $5.00 (ISBN 0-685-09034-5). Divry.

Dutton, Brian, et al. Diccionario esencial Ingles-espanol, Espanol-Ingles. 464p. (Eng. & Span.). 1981. pap. 600.00 ptas (ISBN 84-85205-93-6). Diafora.

Editions Berlitz. Spanish-English, English-Spanish Dictionary. Rev. ed. LC 78-78079. 355p. (Eng. & Span.). 1979. $2.95 (ISBN 0-02-964510-7). Macmillan.

English-Spanish Dictionary. (Eng. & Span.). 14.50 (ISBN 0-87557-077-1, 077-1). Saphrograph.

Folley, T. Spanish Aide-Memoire: English-Spanish Vocabulary. pap. $6.50x (ISBN 0-392-08443-0, SpS). Sportshelf.

Fuentes Franco, Jordi. Diccionario y gramatica de la lengua de la isla de Pascua: Pascuense-castellano, castellano-pascuense, pascuense-ingles, ingles-pascuense. 1802p. (Span. & Eng.). 1960. $5.00. Juridica-Andres Bello.

Garcia Merayo, F. Glosario De Informatica: Terminologia Ordenada Segun el Vocablo Ingles y Su Acepcion En Espanol. 290p. (Eng. & Span.). 1971. pap. $28.50 (ISBN 84-314-0001-3, S-50368). French & Eur.

Garcia-Pelayo, Ramon. Diccionario Moderno Espanol-Ingles, English-Spanish. 1992p. (Span. & Eng.). 1976. $25.00 (ISBN 0-686-57189-4, M-6261). French & Eur.

Gomez de Parada, Alejandro. Diccionario Porrua Ingles-Espanol. 400p. (Eng. & Span.). 1974. M.11.00. Porrua.

--Diccionario Porrua Ingles-Espanol. 6th ed. 397p. (Eng. & Span.). 1980. Mex.$45.00. Porrua.

--Diccionario Porrua ingles-espanol, espanol-ingles. 6th ed. 397p. (Eng. & Span.). 1980. Mex.$pap. 45.00. Porrua.

Gooch, Anthony & Garcia de Paredes, Angel. Diccionario Major Ingles-Espanol, Espanol-Ingles. 1132p. (Eng. & Span.). 1981. pap. 2000.00 ptas (ISBN 84-85205-92-8). Diafora.

Gran Diccionario Cuyas Ingles-Espanol. (Eng. & Span.). 1977. $21.00. Camino Real.

Harkovy, A. Spanish-English Technical Dictionary. $37.50 (ISBN 0-87559-187-6). Shalom.

Hinojosa, Ida N., ed. New Century World-Wide Spanish Dictionary: Spanish: Spanish-English, English-Spanish. rev. ed. (Span., Eng). 1965. $7.95 (ISBN 0-8329-9711-0); pap. $3.95 (ISBN 0-8329-9712-9). New Century.

Huerta, Fernando, et al. Diccionario ingles-espanol espanol-ingles. 1012p. (Eng. & Span.). 1981. 1100.00 ptas (ISBN 84-226-1237-2). Circulo Lect.

Hughes, Charles A. Ace's Spanish Phrase Book & Dictionary. (Ace's Foreign Phrase Bk). 192p. 1981. pap. $2.25 (ISBN 0-441-77773-2). Ace Bks.

Hugo Pocket Dictionary: Spanish-English, English-Spanish. 610p. (Span. & Eng.). 1975. 3.50 (ISBN 0-8226-0507-4, 507). Littlefield.

Institute for Language Study. Vest Pocket Spanish. (Illus.). 128p. (Span.). 1979. pap. $2.45 (ISBN 0-06-464900-8, BN 4900, BN). B&N NY.

International Dictionary of Spanish & English. (Span. & Eng.). $34.95. Iaconi.

Interpretes de Bolsillo Espanol-Ingles. 280p. (Span. & Eng.). pap. 150.00 ptas (ISBN 84-7153-252-2). Biblograf SP.

Interpretes de Bolsillo Ingles-Espanol. 320p. (Eng. & Span.). 275.00 ptas (ISBN 84-7153-372-3). Biblograf SP.

Jean's Pocket Dictionaries: Spanish-English. 224p. (Orig., Span. & Eng.). 1981. pap. 2.25 (ISBN 0-8437-1728-9). Hammond Inc.

Jorda, L. Diccionario Ingles-Espanol. 2nd ed. 888p. (Eng. & Span.). 1974. Arg.$110.00. Omega SA.

Jordana, Ricard. Mi Primer Diccionario Ingles-Espanol. 160p. (Eng. & Span.). 1980. write for info. (ISBN 84-278-0591-8). Edns Nauta.

--Mi primer diccionario Ingles-Espanol. 160p. (Span. & Eng.). 1980. write for info. (ISBN 84-278-0591-8). Fed Gremios.

Jordana, Ricard & Chamberlain, Paul. Diccionario Ingles-Espanol, Espanol-Ingles, 2 vols. 1072p. (Eng. & Span.). 1981. write for info. (ISBN 84-278-0592-6). Edns Nauta.

--Diccionario Ingles-Espanol, Espanol-Ingles, 2 vols. 1072p. (Span. & Eng.). 1981. write for info. vol. 1 (ISBN 84-278-0593-4); write for info. vol. 2 (ISBN 84-278-0594-2). Fed Gremios.

Jordana, Ricardo & Chamberlain, Paul. Diccionario ingles-espanol espanol-ingles, 2 vols. 2nd ed. 1104p. (Eng. & Span.). 1981. 2750.00 ptas (ISBN 84-278-0592-6). Nauta SA.

Kloe, Donald R. A Dictionary of Onomatopoeic Sounds, Tones, & Noises in English & Spanish. LC 77-2627. (Eng. & Span.). 1977. $25.50 (ISBN 0-87917-059-X). Ethridge.

--A Dictionary of Onomatopoeic Sounds, Tones, & Noises in English & Spanish. LC 77-2627. (Eng. & Span.). 1977. $25.50 (ISBN 0-87917-059-X). Ethridge.

Laita, Luis M. Cortina-Grosset Basic Spanish Dictionary. Berberi, Dilaver & Berberi, Edel A., eds. LC 73-18525. 384p. (Span.). 1975. $3.95 (ISBN 0-448-11559-X, G&D). Putnam Pub Group.

Laita, Luis M., ed. Cortina-Grosset Basic Spanish Dictionary. (Span.). 1977. pap. 3.50 (ISBN 0-448-14032-2, G&D). Putnam Pub Group.

Langenscheidt English-Spanish Lilliput Dictionary. 640p. (Eng. & Span.). plastic $1.50 (ISBN 3-468-96423-4). Langenscheidt.

Langenscheidt Spanish-English Lilliput Dictionary. 640p. (Eng. & Span.). plastic $1.50 (ISBN 3-468-96424-2). Langenscheidt.

Langenssheidt. Diccionario moderno: Ingles-espanol, espanol-ingles. 2nd ed. 1072p. (Eng. & Span.). 3.86 ptas. 250.00 ptas. Herder SA.

Lazzati, Santiago. Diccionario del Verbo Castellano: Como Se Conjugan los Verbos Americanos. 438p. (Span.). 1977. pap. $13.50 (ISBN 0-686-56657-2, S-12049). French & Eur.

Lexicon Sopena: Diccionario de bolsillo, ingles-espanol y espanol-ingles. (Eng. & Span.). 60.00 ptas. 35.00 ptas. pap. 30.00 ptas. Sopena.

Lipton, G. & Munoz, O. Spanish Bilingual Dictionary: Diccionario Espanol-Ingles-Ingles-Espanol. 2nd ed. (Eng. & Span.). 1982. $3.95 (ISBN 0-8120-2540-7). Barron.

Lipton, Gladys & Munoz, Olivia. Spanish Bilingual Dictionary: Compact Guide. rev. ed. LC 78-27770. (Illus., Span. & Eng.). (gr. 7-12). 1979. pap. $3.95 (ISBN 0-8120-2540-7). Barron.

Lipton, Munoz. Spanish Bilingual Dictionary. (Illus., Span. & Eng.). $3.95. Camino Real.

Macarulla, D. Diccionario Lexicon Ingles-Espanol, Espanol-Ingles. 384p. (Eng. & Span.). 1974. pap. $3.25 (ISBN 84-303-0110-0, S-31391). French & Eur.

Mac Cragh, Esteban. Nuevo Diccionario Ingles-Espanol y Espanol-Ingles. 3rd ed. 376p. (Eng. & Span.). 1979. $9.50 (ISBN 84-261-0079-1, S-12401). French & Eur.

Maurino, Ferdinando D. Modern Language Dictionary. LC 75-10051. xvii, 436p. (Eng. & Span.). 1975. $4.95 (ISBN 0-671-18725-2). S & S.

Merino. Diccionario de Dudas Ingles-Espanol. (Eng. & Span.). 1978. 625.00 ptas (ISBN 8-42830-425-4). Paraninfo.

--Diccionario Tematico Ingles-Espanol & Espanol-Ingles. (Eng. & Span.). 1978. 750.00 ptas (ISBN 8-42830-918-3). Paraninfo.

Merino, Jose. Diccionario de dudas Ingles-Espanol. 332p. (Span. & Eng.). 1978. pap. write for info. (ISBN 84-283-0425-4). Fed Gremios.

--Diccionario Tematico Ingles-Espanol & Espanol-Ingles. 600p. (Eng. & Span.). 1978. write for info. (ISBN 84-283-0918-3). Paraninfo.

--Diccionario tematico Ingles-Espanol & Espanol-Ingles. 600p. (Span. & Eng.). 1978. write for info. (ISBN 84-283-0918-3). Fed Gremios.

--Diccionario Tematico Ingles-Espanol, Espanol-Ingles. 604p. (Eng. & Span.). 1978. pap. $17.95 (ISBN 84-283-0918-3, S-31559). French & Eur.

Merino Bustamante, Jose. Diccionario Auxiliar del Traductor Espanol-Ingles. 144p. (Span. & Eng.). 1978. pap. $8.50 (ISBN 84-85439-00-7, S-50583). French & Eur.

--Vocabulario Ingles-Espanol, Espanol-Ingles. 186p. (Eng. & Span.). 1977. pap. $3.50 (ISBN 84-205-0565-X, S-50346). French & Eur.

Mi Diccionario Ilustrado: Edicion Bilingue. (Illus., Span. & Eng.). pap. $3.95. Lectorum Pubns.

Mini-Sopena Ingles-Espanol. 320p. (Eng. & Span.). $1.45. Cruzada Span Pubns.

New Century Velazquez Spanish-English Dictionary. rev. ed. (Span. & Eng.). 1977. 16.95 (ISBN 0-8329-0472-4). New Century.

New Mayer's Dictionary: English-Spanish, Spanish-English. 438p. (Span. & Eng.). write for info. (798). Fernandez.

New Revised Velazquez Spanish & English Dictionary. (Span. & Eng.). $16.95 (7728-2). Natl Textbk.

New Webster's Quick Reference English-Spanish Dictionary. (Quick Reference Ser.). (Orig.). 1981. pap. $1.95 (ISBN 0-8326-0054-7, 6607). Delair.

Olivetti. Diccionario de Informatica Ingles-Espanol: Edicion Corregida. 3rd ed. 272p. (Eng. & Span.). 1982. 650.00 ptas (ISBN 8-42831-230-3). Paraninfo.

--Diccionario de Informatica Ingles-Espanol. 2nd ed. (Eng. & Span.). 1982. 700.00 ptas (ISBN 8-42831-230-3). Paraninfo.

Padilla, Francisco. Bilingual Dictionary of Anglicismos, Barbarismos, Pachuquismos y Otras Locuciones En el Barrio. LC 80-83981. 214p. (Orig., Span. & Eng.). pap. $7.00 (ISBN 0-9605292-0-9). Padilla.

Peers, E. A. & Jose, V. Diccionario Cassell Espanol-Ingles, Ingles-Espanol, Vol. 2. 3rd ed. 120p. (Span. & Eng.). 1982. 300.00 ptas (ISBN 8-43454-172-6). Salvat Editores.

--Diccionario Cassell Espanol-Ingles, Ingles-Espanol, Vol. 4. 3rd ed. 160p. (Span. & Eng.). 1982. 300.00 ptas (ISBN 8-43454-174-2). Salvat Editores.

--Diccionario Cassell Espanol-Ingles, Ingles-Espanol, Vol. 5. 3rd ed. 128p. (Span. & Eng.). 1982. 300.00 ptas (ISBN 8-43454-175-0). Salvat Editores.

--Diccionario Cassell Espanol-Ingles,Ingles-Espanol, Vol. 6. 3rd ed. 152p. (Span. & Eng.). 1982. 300.00 ptas. Salvat Editores.

Peers, E. A. & Jose, V., eds. Diccionario Cassell Espanol-Ingles, Ingles Espanol, Vol. 1. 3rd ed. 128p. (Span. & Eng.). 1982. 300.00 ptas (ISBN 8-43454-171-8). Salvat Editores.

Peers, Edgar A. Diccionario Cassell espanol-ingles, ingles-espanol: Tomo 1. 3rd ed. 128p. (Span. & Eng.). 1980. pap. write for info. (ISBN 84-345-4171-8). Salvat Editores.

--Diccionario Cassell espanol-ingles, ingles-espanol: Tomo 2. 3rd ed. 120p. (Span. & Eng.). 1980. pap. write for info. (ISBN 84-345-4172-6). Salvat Editores.

--Diccionario Cassell espanol-ingles, ingles-espanol: Tomo 3. 3rd ed. 128p. (Span. & Eng.). 1980. pap. write for info. (ISBN 84-345-4173-4). Salvat Editores.

--Diccionario Cassell espanol-ingles, ingles-espanol: Tomo 4. 3rd ed. 160p. (Span. & Eng.). 1980. pap. write for info. (ISBN 84-345-4174-2). Salvat Editores.

--Diccionario Cassell espanol-ingles, ingles-espanol: Tomo 5. 3rd ed. 128p. (Span. & Eng.). 1980. pap. write for info. (ISBN 84-345-4175-0). Salvat Editores.

--Diccionario Cassell espanol-ingles, ingles-espanol: Tomo 6. 3rd ed. 152p. (Span. & Eng.). 1980. pap. write for info. (ISBN 84-345-4176-9). Salvat Editores.

Peers, Edgar A. & Jose, Victor. Diccionario Cassell Espanol-Ingles, Ingles-Espanol, Vol. 3. 3rd ed. 128p. (Span. & Eng.). 1982. 300.00 ptas (ISBN 8-43454-173-4). Salvat Editores.

Peers, Edgar A., ed. Cassell's Spanish Dictionary: Spanish-English, English-Spanish. LC 77-7403. (Span. & Eng.). 1977. 18.95 (ISBN 0-02-522910-9); plain 16.95 (ISBN 0-02-522900-1). Macmillan.

Peers, Edgar Allison. Diccionario Cassell espanol-ingles, ingles-espanol: Obra completa, 6 vols. 3rd ed. 816p. (Span.). 1980. pap. write for info. (ISBN 84-345-4170-X). Salvat Editores.

Pena, Aurelio. Diccionario ingles-espanol y espanol-ingles. (Eng. & Span.). 150.00 ptas. Bibliografica.

Pineiro, Jaime. Compendio de dificultades de la lengua inglesa. 276p. (Span. & Eng.). 1978. pap. write for info. (ISBN 84-7153-227-1). Fed Gremios.

Plans Sanz de Bremond, Fructuoso. Diccionario Ingles-Espanol. 36th ed. 640p. (Eng. & Span.). 1982. pap. 150.00 ptas (ISBN 84-7105-092-7). Mayfe.

Prats, Alfonso T. Diccionario De Dificultades Del Ingles: Difficulties of English Idioms for Spanish Speaking People. (Eng. & Span.). 17.50 (ISBN 84-261-5814-5). Heinman.

Ramondino, Salvatore, ed. New World Spanish-English & English-Spanish Dictionary. LC 67-17418. (Illus., Span. & Eng.). (YA) (gr. 9up). 1973. thumb-indexed $7.95 (ISBN 0-529-04719-5, 2677N-I). pap. $5.95 (ISBN 0-529-05181-8, 2677P). Collins Pubs.

--New World Spanish-English, English-Spanish Dictionary. (Span. & Eng.). pap. 3.50 (ISBN 0-451-11312-8, E9043, Sig). NAL.

Reventos, Margaret H. Diccionario moderno espanol-ingles, ingles-espanol. 1236p. (Eng. & Span.). $2.20. CECSA.

Revised-Velasquez Spanish English Dictionary. (Span. & Eng.). $12.95. Camino Real.

Roberston, Ricardo. Diccionario bilingue ingles-espanol y espanol-ingles. Rev. ed. (Eng. & Span.). 100.00 ptas. 75.00 ptas. pap. 70.00 ptas. Sopena.

Robertson. Diccionario Ingles-Espanol, Espanol-Ingles. 894p. (Eng. & Span.). $12.25 (ISBN 84-303-0107-0, S-50396); pap. $9.95 (ISBN 84-303-0108-9, S-50397). French & Eur.

Ross, Peter. Practical Italian-English, English-Italian Dictionary. (Hippocrene Practical Language Dictionaries Ser.). 400p. (Orig., Eng. & Ital.). 1983. pap. $6.95 (ISBN 0-88254-816-6). Hippocrene Bks.

Ruiz Torres, Francisco. Diccionario Espanol-Ingles, Ingles-Espanol. 3rd ed. 714p. (Span. & Eng.). 1978. pap. $41.95 (ISBN 84-205-0455-6, S-12408). French & Eur.

Serrano Mesa, Eleesbaan. Diccionario espanol-ingles ingles-espanol. 3rd ed. 448p. (Span. & Eng.). 1982. pap. write for info. (ISBN 84-7105-102-8). Mayfe.

--Diccionario Ingles-Espanol, Espanol-Ingles. 9th ed. 640p. (Eng. & Span.). 1977. leatherette $5.25 (ISBN 84-7105-019-6, S-50353). French & Eur.

Simon & Schuster. Diccionario Espanol-Ingles Pocket Dictionary. (Span. & Eng.). $1.95. Camino Real.

Simon & Schuster International Dictionary: English-Spanish, Spanish-English. (Eng. & Span.). 1973. thumb-indexed 15.95 (ISBN 0-671-21267-2). S&S.

Smith, C. C., et al, eds. Langenscheidt's Standard Spanish Dictionary: Spanish-English, English-Spanish. (Langenscheidt Standard Dictionaries Ser.). 1072p. (Eng. & Span.). 1966. $11.95 (ISBN 0-685-31319-0). Am Map.

Smith, Colin. Diccionario Collins Ingles-Espanol, 2 vols. 3rd ed. 1284p. (Eng. & Span.). 1981. 2500.00 ptas (ISBN 84-253-1199-3). Grijalbo.

Smith Colinbermego, Manuel. Diccionario Collins Spanish-English Ingles-Espanol. 6th ed. 1280p. (Span. & Eng.). 1982. 2250.00 ptas (ISBN 84-253-1184-5). Grijalbo.

Sola, Donald F. & Agard, Frederick B. Spanish Pocket Dictionary. (Span.). 1954. 2.95 (ISBN 0-394-40064-X). Random.

Sola, Donald P., ed. The Random House Basic Dictionary Spanish. (Span. & Eng.). 1981. pap. $1.50 (ISBN 0-345-29620-6). Ballantine.

Spanish-English & English-Spanish Dictionary. (Span. & Eng.). pap. $1.99 (ISBN 0-686-00482-5). Dennison.

Spanish-English, English-Spanish. (Span. & Eng.). $8.95 (522660-6). Inst Mod Lang.

Spanish-English, English-Spanish Dictionary. (Span. & Eng.). pap. $2.50 (ISBN 0-06-465027-8, DI 3, BN). B&N NY.

Torrens dels Prats, Alfonso. Diccionario de dificultades del Ingles. 496p. (Span.). 1976. write for info. (ISBN 84-261-1223-4). Fed Gremios.

--Diccionario de modismos ingleses y norteamericanos. 368p. (Span.). 1979. write for info. (ISBN 84-261-0838-5). Fed Gremios.

Torrents dels Prats, Alfonso. Diccionario De Dificultades Del Ingles. 500p. (Eng. & Span.). 1976. $18.75 (ISBN 84-261-5814-5, S-31568). French & Eur.

--Diccionario de Dificultades del Ingles. 494p. (Eng. & Span.). $17.95. Lectorum Pubns.

--Diccionario de dificultades del ingles. 494p. (Eng. & Span.). $17.95 (JUV). Lectorum Pubns.

--Diccionario de Modismos Inglese y Norteamericanos. 2nd ed. 304p. (Eng. & Span.). 1979. $16.25 (ISBN 84-261-0838-5, S-12364). French & Eur.

U. S. War Department. Dictionary of Spoken Spanish: Spanish-English, English-Spanish. (Span. & Eng.). pap. $5.95 (ISBN 0-486-20495-2). Dover.

Universidad de Chicago. Diccionario ingles-espanol y espanol-ingles. (Eng. & Span.). 125.00 ptas. Aguilar SP.

The University of Chicago Spanish-English Dictionary. 3rd ed. (Span. & Eng.). 1981. pap. 2.95 (ISBN 0-671-83685-4). PB.

Velazquez, et al, eds. The Spanish & English, English & Spanish Dictionary - Self Pronouncing. rev. ed. LC 72-94281. (Span. & Eng.). 1973. thumb-indexed 20.95 (ISBN 0-13-615534-0). P-H.

Velazquez, Mariano. Diccionario Velazquez: Espanol e ingles. (Span. & Eng.). index $8.95; $7.95. Follett.

Velazquez Spanish-English Dictionary: Indexed. (Span. & Eng.). 16.95 (ISBN 0-8329-0472-4). New Century.

Vest-Pocket Spanish. (Span. & Eng.). pap. $2.95 (7723-1). Natl Textbk.

Vox-Diccionario Ingles-Espanol, Espanol-Ingles. 4th ed. 1450p. (Eng. & Span.). 1978. leatherette $24.95 (ISBN 84-7153-151-8, S-12417). French & Eur.

Vox-Diccionario Manual Ingles-Espanol, Espanol-Ingles. 8th ed. 1008p. (Eng. & Span.). 1979. leatherette $15.95 (ISBN 84-7153-181-X, S-12491). French & Eur.

Wiezell, Richard. Ingles Al Dedillo: English at Your Fingertips. (Vest-Pocket Ser.). (Illus.). 1978. pap. 2.95 (ISBN 0-8329-1537-8). New Century.

Williams, Edwin B. New College Spanish & English Dictionary. (Span. & Eng.). (gr. 7-12). 1968. pap. text ed. $8.58 (ISBN 0-87720-511-6). AMSCO Sch.

Williams, Edwin B., ed. Bantam New College Spanish & English Dictionary. (Language Library). (Orig., Span. & Eng.). 1970. pap. $2.75 (ISBN 0-553-20085-2, C13718-2). Bantam.

World-Wide Spanish. (Span. & Eng.). thumb index $7.95 (7736-3); pap. $3.95 (7735-5). Natl Textbk.

Younger, Maria. Diccionario Espanol-Ingles. 41st ed. 640p. (Span. & Eng.). 1982. pap. 150.00 ptas (ISBN 84-7105-093-5). Mayfe.

SPANISH LANGUAGE–DICTIONARIES–FINNISH

Diccionario Lexicon Finlandes-Espanol, Espanol-Finlandes. 400p. (Finnish & Span.). leatherette $4.95 (ISBN 84-303-0150-X, S-50405); pap. $4.50 (ISBN 84-303-0149-6, S-50404). French & Eur.
Lexicon Sopena: Diccionario de bolsillo, finlandes-espanol y espanol-finlandes. 384p. (Finnish & Span.). 60.00 ptas. 35.00 ptas. pap. 30.00 ptas. Sopena.
Neuvonen, E. K. Finnish-Spanish-Finnish Dictionary. 452p. (Finnish & Span.). 1980. pap. $14.95 (ISBN 951-0-07202-8, S-37816). French & Eur.

SPANISH LANGUAGE–DICTIONARIES–FRENCH

Alcala-Zamora. Alcala-Zamora, Diccionario Frances-Espanol, Espanol-Frances. 960p. (Span. & Fr.). pap. $9.95 (ISBN 84-303-0094-5, S-50399). French & Eur.
--Alcala-Zamora, Diccionario Frances-Espanol, Espanol-Frances. 960p. (Span. & Fr.). $12.25 (ISBN 84-303-0093-7, S-50400). French & Eur.
Alcala-Zamora & Antignac, T. Diccionario frances-espanol y espanol-frances. (Span. & Fr.). $7.50. Imported Bks.
Amador, E. M. Martinez. Diccionario Frances-Espanol, Espanol-Frances. 1568p. (Span. & Fr.). 1974. $47.95 (ISBN 84-303-0091-0, S-13282). French & Eur.
--Diccionario Manual Amador Frances-Espanol y Espanol-Frances. 944p. (Span. & Fr.). 1975. $17.95 (ISBN 84-303-0100-3, S-50401). French & Eur.
Azkue, Resurreccion M. Diccionario Vasco-Espanol-Frances, 2 vols. (Span. & Fr.). Set. leatherette $68.00 (ISBN 84-248-0015-X, S-12384). French & Eur.
Cuyas Armengol, Arturo. Diccionario De Bolsillo Frances-Espanol, Espagnol-Francais. 670p. (Span. & Fr.). 1971. pap. $3.50 (ISBN 84-7183-048-5, S-50391). French & Eur.
--Diccionario Manual Frances-Espanol, Espagnol-Francais. 36th ed. 830p. (Span. & Fr.). 1977. $5.95 (ISBN 84-7183-047-7, S-50390). French & Eur.
Denis, S. & Maraval, M. Diccionario espanol-frances. (Span. & Fr.). write for info. Hachette.
--Diccionario frances-espanol. (Fr. & Span.). write for info. Hachette.
Denis, Serge & Maraval, Marcel. Dictionnaire Espagnol-Francais. 1774p. (Fr. & Eng.). 1968. pap. $26.50 (ISBN 0-686-56983-0, M-6110). French & Eur.
Denis, Serge, et al. Le Dictionnaire Espagnol-Francais et Francais-Espagnol. new ed. 904p. (Span. & Fr.). 1976. $36.95 (ISBN 0-686-56984-9, M-6111). French & Eur.
De Toro, M. & Gisbert. Dictionnaire Bilingue Larousse, Francais-Espagnol, Espanol-Frances. (Apollo). (Fr. & Span.). $10.50 (ISBN 0-685-13857-7, 3774). Larousse.
De Toro Gisbert, M. Dictionnaire Bilingue: Francais-Espagnol, Espagnol-Francais. 546p. (Fr. & Span.). 1968. pap. text ed. $7.95 (ISBN 0-686-97445-X, S-36345). French & Eur.
Diaz Mateo, Felix & Hochleitner, Frida. Diccionario manual frances-espanol, espanol-frances. 1000p. (Fr. & Span.). 150.00 ptas. Espasa Calpe.
Diccionari practic catala-frances. 224p. (Span. & Fr.). 1968. 80.00 ptas. M. Arimany.
Diccionari practic frances-catala. 324p. (Fr. & Span.). 1968. 125.00 ptas. M. Arimany.
Diccionari practic frances-catala, catala-frances. 450p. (Fr. & Span.). 1968. 200.00 ptas. M. Arimany.
Diccionario Abreviado Frances-Espanol Espanol-Frances. 672p. (Fr. & Span.). 350.00 ptas (ISBN 84-7153-216-6). Biblograf SP.
Diccionario Basico Frances-Espanol Espanol-Frances. 928p. (Fr. & Span.). 575.00 ptas (ISBN 84-7153-188-7). Biblograf SP.
Diccionario Brevis duplex: frances-castellano y castellano-frances. (Fr. & Span.). Arg.$15.00. Sopena.
Diccionario Compendiado, Frances-Espanol, Espanol-Frances. 647p. (Fr. & Span.). 275.00 ptas (ISBN 84-7153-189-5). Biblograf SP.
Diccionario Cuyas: Spanish-French, French-Spanish. (Span. & Fr.). $6.00x (ISBN 0-686-00850-2). Colton Bk.
Diccionario espanol-frances. (Span. & Fr.). 25.00 ptas. Mayfe.
Diccionario espanol-frances. (Span. & Fr.). 45.00 ptas. Zeus.
Diccionario Everest Cuspide frances-espanol, espanol-frances. (Fr. & Span.). 125.00 ptas. Everest.
Diccionario Everest Cuspide: Frances-Espanol y espanol-frances. 6th ed. 990p. (Fr. & Span.). 1982. pap. 400.00 ptas (ISBN 84-241-1350-0). Everest.
Diccionario Everest 'Cuspide' frances-espanol y espanol-frances: Anonimas y colectivas. 5th ed. 990p. (Fr. & Span.). 1980. pap. 345.00 ptas (ISBN 84-241-1350-0). Everest.
Diccionario Everest Vertice Frances-Espanol, Espano-Frances. 519p. (Fr. & Span.). 1979. pap. $2.50 pocket size. Imported Bks.
Diccionario frances-espanol. (Fr. & Span.). 25.00 ptas. Mayfe.
Diccionario frances-espanol. (Fr. & Span.). 45.00 ptas. Zeus.
Diccionario frances-espanol, espanol-frances. (Serie Bachilarato Koel: No. 43). 527p. (Fr. & Span.). 75.00 ptas. Tesoro.
Diccionario frances-espanol espanol-frances. (Fr. & Span.). 75.00 ptas. Zeus.
Diccionario frances-espanol y espanol-frances. (Fr. & Span.). 60.00 ptas. Mayfe.
Diccionario frances-espanol y espanol-frances. (Fr. & Span.). 50.00 ptas. pap. 35.00 ptas. Mayfe.
Diccionario Manual Frances-Espanol Espanol-Frances. 922p. (Fr. & Span.). write for info. Bibliograf SP.
Diccionario moderno: Frances-espanol, espanol-frances. 1024p. (Fr. & Span.). $3.86; 250.00 ptas. Herder SA.
Diccionario Modernos Herder Frances-Espanol. 644p. (Fr. & Span.). 1981. write for info. (ISBN 84-254-1049-5). Herder SA.
Diccionario Parvus duplex: Frances-castellano y castellano-frances. (Fr. & Span.). Arg.$8.40. Sopena.
Diccionario Superior Frances-Espanol Espanol-Frances. 1224p. (Fr. & Span.). write for info. Biblograf SP.
Diccionario superior Frances-Espanol Espanol-Frances 'Vox' 2nd ed. 710p. (Fr. & Span.). 1981. 825.00 ptas (ISBN 84-7153-187-9). Biblo SP.
Diccionario tecnico espanol-frances; frances-espanol. 610p. (Fr. & Span.). 550.00 ea. ptas. EDAF.
Diccionario universal: Frances-espanol, espanol-frances. 368p. (Fr. & Span.). $0.77; 50.00 ptas. Herder SA.
Diccionario Universal Herder Frances-Espanol, Espanol-Frances. 5th ed. 368p. (Fr. & Span.). 1977. leatherette $4.50 (ISBN 84-254-0780-X, S-12394). French & Eur.
Diez Mateo, Felix & Hochleitner, Frida. Diccionario Manual Frances-Espanol, Espanol-Frances. 992p. (Span. & Fr.). 1971. $9.95 (ISBN 84-239-4721-1, S-50389). French & Eur.
Everest. Diccionario Vertice Everest: Frances-Espanol, Espanol-Frances. LC 76-458632. 519p. (Fr. & Span.). 1975. write for info. (ISBN 8-424-11320-9). Everest.
Fabrega, P. Diccionario moderno frances-espanol y espanol-frances. (Span. & Fr.). 1970. 100.00 ptas. Bosch Casa.
Galant, Armando. Diccionario Espanol-Frances. 31st ed. 640p. (Span. & Fr.). 1982. 150.00 ptas (ISBN 8-47105-094-3). Mayfe.
--Diccionario Espanol-Frances. 31st ed. 640p. (Span. & Fr.). 1982. pap. 160.00 ptas (ISBN 84-7105-094-3). Mayfe.
--Diccionario Frances-Espanol. 26th ed. 640p. (Fr. & Span.). 1982. pap. 150.00 ptas (ISBN 84-7105-095-1). Mayfe.
Garcia-Pelayo, R. & Testas, J. Dictionnaire moderne Larousse, francais-espagnol et espagnol-francais. (Span. & Fr.). $39.95 (ISBN 2-03-020601-6, 3773). Larousse.
Gimenez Sales, Miguel. Diccionario Espanol-Frances, Espagnol-Francais. 736p. (Span. & Fr.). 1975. pap. $3.95 (ISBN 84-02-04265-1, S-50394). French & Eur.
Gimeno, E. Diccionario Lexicon Frances-Espanol, Espanol-Frances. 384p. (Fr. & Span.). 1975. leatherette $3.75 (ISBN 84-303-0099-6, S-31393). French & Eur.
Gonzalez Marimon, Blanca. Diccionario de falsos amigos, frances-espanol. 64p. (Fr. & Span.). 1982. pap. 200.00 ptas (ISBN 84-205-0873-X). Alhambra.
Haensch, Gunther. Diccionario Manual Herder Frances-Espanol, Espanol-Frances. 644p. (Span. & Fr.). 1976. $16.75 (ISBN 84-254-1049-5, S-50392). French & Eur.
Hochleitner, Frida & Mateo, Felix D. Diccionario Manual Frances-Espanol. 100p. (Fr. & Span.). write for info. Espasa Calpe.
Interpretes de Bolsillo Espanol-Frances. 280p. (Span. & Fr.). pap. 150.00 ptas (ISBN 84-7153-253-0). Biblograf SP.
Interpretes de Bolsillo Frances-Espanol. 320p. (Fr. & Span.). 275.00 ptas. Biblograf SP.
Larousse And Co. Petit Dictionnaire bilingue Larousse, francais-espagnol, espanol-frances. (Adonis). (Fr. & Span., Fr & Span). plastic bdg. 6.95 (ISBN 0-685-14033-4, 3775). Larousse.
Larrieu, Roberto & Garcia Morente, Manuel. Diccionario Major Frances-Espanol, Espanol-Frances. 1392p. (Fr. & Span.). 1981. pap. 1800.00 ptas (ISBN 84-85205-91-X). Diafora.
Lexicon Sopena: Diccionario de bolsillo, frances-espanol y espanol-frances. 384p. (Fr. & Span.). 60.00 ptas. 35.00 ptas. pap. 30.00 ptas. Sopena.
Malgorn. Diccionario Tecnico Frances-Espanol. (Fr. & Span.). 1973. 1000.00 ptas (ISBN 8-42830-334-7). Paraninfo.
Malgorn, Guy. Diccionario tecnico frances-espanol y espanol-frances. (Fr. & Span.). 1972. write for info. Paraninfo.
Salva, Vicente & Larrieu, Robert, eds. Dictionnaire Espagnol-Francais et Francais-Espagnol. 1580p. (Fr.-Span.). 1951. $22.50 (ISBN 0-686-57295-5, F-140811). French & Eur.
Sese, Bernard. Vocabulaire de la Langue Espagnole Classique: XVIe & XVIIe Siecles. 4th ed. LC 76-475557. v, 306p. (Span. & Fr.). 1975. 59.50 ptas (ISBN 2-718-15546-9). Doc Univers.
Vidal, Jean P. Diccionario esencial frances-espanol, espanol-frances. 598p. (Fr. & Span.). 1981. pap. 600.00 ptas (ISBN 84-85205-90-1). Diafora.
Vox. Diccionario Superior Frances-Espanol, Espanol-Frances, 2 vols. LC 78-347426. 1136p. (Fr. & Span.). 1977. 475.00 ptas (ISBN 8-471-53187-9). Biblo Sp.
Vox-Diccionario Abreviado Frances-Espanol, Espanol-Frances. 8th ed. 672p. (Fr. & Span.). 1978. leatherette $7.25 (ISBN 84-7153-216-6, S-12414). French & Eur.
VOX-Diccionario basico frances-espanol, espanol-frances. 660p. (Fr. & Span.). $8.90. Imported Bks.

SPANISH LANGUAGE–DICTIONARIES–GERMAN

Amador, E. F. Martinez. Diccionario Aleman-Espanol, Espanol-Aleman. 1616p. (Ger. & Span.). $50.95 (ISBN 84-303-0117-8, S-12381). French & Eur.
Amador, E. M. Martinez. Diccionario Manual Aleman-Espanol, Spanisch-Deutsch. 17th ed. 936p. (Ger. & Span.). 1977. $5.95 (ISBN 84-7183-002-7, S-50382). French & Eur.
--Diccionario Manual Amador Aleman-Espanol, Espanol-Aleman. 1400p. (Ger. & Span.). $17.95 (ISBN 84-303-0118-6, S-50385). French & Eur.
Beinhauer, Werner. Stilistisch-Phraseologisches Woerterbuch Spanisch-Deutsch. LC 78-392750. 1043p. (Ger. & Span.). 1978. DM.120.00 (ISBN 3-190-04016-8). Hueber.
Brandau, Carlos. Diccionario Aleman-Espanol. 16th ed. 640p. (Ger. & Span.). 1982. pap. 150.00 ptas (ISBN 84-7105-090-0). Mayfe.
--Diccionario Espanol-Aleman. 21st ed. 640p. (Span. & Ger.). 1982. pap. 150.00 ptas (ISBN 84-7105-089-7). Mayfe.
Diccionario Abreviado Aleman-Espagnol. 848p. (Ger. & Span.). 1981. write for info. ptas (ISBN 84-7153-217-4). Biblo SP.
Diccionario aleman-espanol. (Ger. & Span.). 25.00 ptas. Mayfe.
Diccionario Aleman-Espanol Espanol-Aleman 'Vox' 848p. (Span. & Ger.). 1981. write for info. (ISBN 84-7153-218-2). Biblo SP.
Diccionario basico. (Illus.). 700p. (Span.). 150.00 ptas. Sopena.
Diccionario Brevis duplex: aleman-castellano y castellano-aleman. (Ger. & Span.). Arg.$15.00. Sopena.
Diccionario Cuyas: Spanish-German, German-Spanish. (Span. & Ger.). $6.00x (ISBN 0-686-00851-0). Colton Bk.
Diccionario espanol-aleman. (Span. & Ger.). 25.00 ptas. Mayfe.
Diccionario Everest Vertice Aleman-Espanol, Spanisch-Deutsch. 582p. (Ger. & Span.). 1978. pap. $3.50. Imported bks.
Diccionario Everest 'Vertice' aleman-espanol y espanol-aleman. 2nd ed. 592p. (Ger. & Span.). 1980. pap. 152.00 ptas (ISBN 84-241-1444-2). Everest.
Diccionario Iter Aleman-Espanol, Espanol-Aleman. 512p. (Ger. & Span.). 1977. leatherette $6.75 (ISBN 84-303-0127-5, S-50377); pap. $5.95 (ISBN 84-303-0126-7, S-50376). French & Eur.
Diccionario Lexicon, Aleman-Espanol, Espanol-Aleman. 400p. (Ale. -Espn.). $5.75 (ISBN 0-686-57343-9, S-31392). French & Eur.
Diccionario Modernos Herder Aleman-Espanol. 684p. (Ger. & Span.). 1981. 560.00 ptas (ISBN 84-254-0652-8). Herder SA.
Diccionario pervus duplex: Aleman-castellano y castellano-aleman. (Ger. & Span.). Arg.$8.40. Sopena.
Diccionario universal: Aleman-espanol, espanol-aleman. 3rd ed. 388p. (Ger. & Span.). 0.77 ptas. 50.00 ptas. Herder SA.
Diccionario Universal Herder Aleman-Espanol, Espanol-Aleman. 4th ed. 388p. (Ger. & Span.). 1977. leatherette $4.50 (ISBN 84-254-0782-6, S-50378). French & Eur.
Haensch, Guenther. Woerterbuch der Spanischen & Deutschen Sprache. LC 77-579293. 684p. (Span. & Ger.). 1977. M.22.80 (ISBN 3-125-17400-7). Klett.
Haensch, Gunther. Diccionario Moderno Herder Aleman-Espanol, Espanol-Aleman. 684p. (Ger. & Span.). 1977. $16.75 (ISBN 84-254-0652-8, S-50379). French & Eur.
--Diccionario moderno Herder Aleman-Espanol. 2nd ed. 684p. (Ger. & Span.). 1982. 650.00 ptas (ISBN 84-254-0652-8). Herder SA.
Interpretes de Bolsillo Aleman-Espanols. 320p. (Ger. & Span.). 275.00 ptas (ISBN 84-7153-371-5). Biblograf SP.
Interpretes de Bolsillo Espanol-Aleman. 280p. (Span. & Ger.). pap. 150.00 ptas (ISBN 84-7153-251-4). Biblograf SP.

Langenscheidt. Diccionario moderno: Aleman-espanol, espanol-aleman. 1092p. (Span. & Ger.). $4.33; 280.00 ptas. Herder SA.
Lerche, Mario R. Deutsch-Spanisches Glossarium. 460p. (Ger. & Span.). 1967. $17.50 (ISBN 3-7819-2012-7, S-7347, Pub. by Fritz Knapp Verlag). French & Eur.
Lexicon Sopena: Diccionario de bolsillo, aleman-espanol y espanol-aleman. 384p. (Ger. & Span.). 60.00 ptas. 35.00 ptas. pap. 30.00 ptas. Sopena.
Mateo, Felix D. & Hochleitner, Frida, eds. Diccionario Manual Aleman-Espanol, Espanol-Aleman. 952p. (Ger. & Span.). 1978. write for info. Espasa Calpe.
Mink, tr. Diccionario tecnico espanol-aleman. (Span. & Ger.). 1970. 1500.00 ptas. Bluma.
Mink, H. Diccionario Tecnico Aleman-Espanol, Espanol-Aleman, 2 vols. 3rd ed. 2530p. (Span. & Ger.). 1978. Set. $120.00 (ISBN 84-254-0704-4, S-50189). French & Eur.
Muller. Diccionario Aleman-Espanol, Espanol-Aleman. 900p. (Ger. & Span.). leatherette $12.25 (ISBN 84-303-0119-4, S-50384). French & Eur.
Muller, F. Atheneum Worterbuch: Aleman-Espanol, Espanol-Aleman. 383p. (Ger. & Span.). 1979. pap. $5.25 (ISBN 84-303-0800-8, S-35066). French & Eur.
Muller, Franz. Diccionario Aleman-Espanol-Aleman. 1195p. (Ger. & Span.). $7.50. Imported Bks.
--Diccionario bilingue aleman-espanol y espanol-aleman. 1200p. (Span. & Ger.). 100.00 ptas. Sopena.
Muller, Hans. Diccionario Lexicon Aleman-Espanol, Espanol-Aleman. 384p. (Ger. & Span.). 1977. pap. $4.50 (ISBN 84-303-0124-0, S-31392). French & Eur.
Ruiz Torres, Francisco. Diccionario Aleman-Espanol, Espanol-Aleman de Medicina. 2nd ed. 860p. (Ger. & Span.). 1971. pap. $41.25 (ISBN 84-205-0010-0, S-50089). French & Eur.
Schmidt, Michael, ed. Diccionario Aleman-Espanol Espanol-Aleman. 814p. (Ger. & Span.). 495.00 ptas. Biblograf SP.
Slaby, R. J. & Grossman, R., eds. Spanish & German Dictionary, 2 vols. Incl. Vol. 1. Spanish-German. 17.00 (ISBN 0-8044-0581-6); Vol. 2. German-Spanish. 28.00 (ISBN 0-8044-0582-4). 2172p. (Span. & Ger.). Set. $45.00 (ISBN 0-8044-0580-8). Ungar.
Slaby, Rudolf. Diccionario De las Lenguas Espanola y Alemana, 2 vols. 3rd ed. 2422p. (Ger. & Span.). 1977. Set. $110.00 (ISBN 84-254-0694-3, S-50380). French & Eur.
--Woerterbuch der Deutschen und Spanischen Sprache, Vol. 1. 3rd ed. (Ger. & Span.). 1975. $76.00 (ISBN 3-87097-067-7, M-7024). French & Eur.
--Woerterbuch der Deutschen und Spanischen Sprache, Vol. 2. 2nd ed. (Ger. & Span.). 1973. $66.00 (ISBN 3-87097-040-5, M-7023). French & Eur.
Slaby, Rudolf, et al. Diccionario de la lengua espanola y alemana: Tomo 1, 2 vols. 4th ed. 1139p. (Span. & Ger.). 1981. pap. 3500.00 ptas (ISBN 84-254-0835-0). Herder SA.
--Diccionario de las lenguas espanola alemana, 2 vols. 5th ed. 969p. (Span. & Ger.). 1980. 5200.00 ptas (ISBN 84-254-0694-3). Herder SA.
Slaby-Grossmann. Diccionario de las lenguas espanola y alemana: Aleman-espanol, 2 vols. 10th ed. (Span. & Ger.). Vol. 1, Espanol-Aleman. $10.07; Vol. 2. 650.00 ptas. Vol. 2, Aleman-Espanol. $12.40; Vol. 2. 800.00 ptas. Herder.

SPANISH LANGUAGE–DICTIONARIES–ITALIAN

Amador, E. M. Martinez. Diccionario Italiano-Espanol, Espanol-Italiano. 1440p. (Span. & Ital.). $50.95 (ISBN 84-303-0133-X, S-12383). French & Eur.
Ambruzzi, Lucio. Nuovo dizionario spagnolo-italiano. xviii, 1128p. (Span. & Ital.). 1978. L.16000.00. Paravia.
Diccionario Abreviado Italiano,-Espanol Espanol-Italiano. 735p. (Ital. & Span.). 1980. $9.95 (ISBN 84-7153-523-8, S-31760). French & Eur.
Diccionario Brevis duplex: Italiano-castellano y castellano-italiano. (Ital. & Span.). Arg.$15.00. Sopena.
Diccionario Cuyas: Spanish-Italian, Italian-Spanish. (Span. & Ital.). $6.00x (ISBN 0-686-00857-X). Colton Bk.
Diccionario Everest Vertice Italian-Espanol, Spagnolo-Italiano. 883p. (Span. & Ital.). pap. $4.50. Imported Bks.
Diccionario Italiano-Espanol Espanol-Italiano Vox. 848p. (Ital. & Span.). 1982. write for info. (ISBN 84-7153-390-1). Biblo SP.
Diccionario Iter Italiano-Espanol, Espanol-Italiano. 712p. (Ital. & Span.). leatherette $6.95 (ISBN 84-303-0139-9, S-50434); pap. $5.95 (ISBN 84-303-0138-0, S-50435). French & Eur.
Diccionario Lexicon Italiano-Espanol, Espanol-Italiano. 400p. (Span. & Ital.). pap. $3.50 (ISBN 84-303-0136-4, S-31394). French & Eur.
Diccionario Parvus duplex: Italiano-castellano y castellano-ingles. (Ital. & Span.). Arg.$8.40. Sopena.
Diccionario Universal Herder Italiano-Espanol, Espanol-Italiano. 5th ed. 364p. (Span. & Ital.). 1977. pap. $4.50 (ISBN 84-254-0558-0, S-50433). French & Eur.
Fornas Prat, Jordi. Diccionari Italia-Catala Catala-Italia. 616p. (Span.). 1982. 1500.00 ptas (ISBN 84-7306-183-7). Portic.
Frisoni, Gaetano. Dizionario Moderno Spagnuolo-Italiano, Italiano-Spagnuolo, 2 vols. 1865p. (Span. & Ital.). Set. $44.00x (ISBN 0-913298-51-4). S F Vanni.
Garcia, A. Dizionario Italiano-Spagnolo, Spagnolo-Italiano. 437p. (Span. & Ital.). 1980. leatherette $5.95 (ISBN 0-686-97347-X, S-31237). French & Eur.
Interpretes de Bolsillo Espanol-Italiano. 280p. (Span. & Ital.). pap. 150.00 ptas (ISBN 84-7153-254-9). Biblograf SP.
Interpretes de Bolsillo Italiano-Espanol. 320p. (Ital. & Span.). 275.00 ptas. Biblograf SP.
Lexicon Sopena: Diccionario de bolsillo, italiano-espanol y espanol-italiano. (Ital. & Span.). 60.00 ptas. 35.00 ptas. pap. 30.00 ptas. Sopena.
Moll, Francisco de B. Diccionario manual italiano-espanol. (Ital. & Span.). 20.00 ptas. Moll Edit.
Ortiz De Burgos, Jose. Diccionario Manual Italiano-Espanol, Spagnuolo-Italiano. 16th ed. 960p. (Span. & Ital.). 1977. $5.95 (ISBN 84-7183-045-0, S-50432). French & Eur.
Schepisi, Givanna, ed. Diccionario Abreviado Italiano-Espanol Espanol-Italiano. 782p. (Ital. & Span.). 460.00 ptas (ISBN 84-7153-523-8). Biblograf SP.

SPANISH LANGUAGE–DICTIONARIES–NORWEGIAN

Blom-Dahl, C. Norwegian-Spanish Dictionary. (Norwegian & Span.). 1983. write for info. (ISBN 82-573-0169-8). Kunnskapsforlaget.
Diccionario Lexicon Noruego-Espanol, Espanol-Noruego. 400p. (Norwegian & Span.). leatherette $4.95 (ISBN 84-303-0165-8, S-50418); pap. $4.50 (ISBN 84-303-0164-X, S-50417). French & Eur.
Evjen, H. Norwegian-Spanish Dictionary of Commerce. (Norwegian & Span.). 1974. write for info. (ISBN 82-573-0107-8). Kunnskapsforlaget.
Lexicon Sopena: Diccionario de bolsillo, noruego-espanol y noruego-espanol. 384p. (Span. & Norwegian.). 60.00 ptas. 35.00 ptas. pap. 30.00 ptas. Sopena.
Loennecken, S. Spanish-Norwegian Dictionary. (Span. & Norwegian.). 1980. write for info. (ISBN 82-573-0148-5). Kunnskapsforlaget.
--Spansk-Norsk Ordbok. 411p. (Span. & Norwegian.). 1980. $39.95 (ISBN 0-686-92543-2, S-37620). French & Eur.

SPANISH LANGUAGE–DICTIONARIES–POLYGLOT

Chtchoukine, Anatoll. Dictionnaire Illustre de la Langue Russe: Francais-Espagnol-Russe. (Fr., Span. & Rus.). write for info. Mir.
Collocott, T. C. Diccionario Cientifico y Tecnologico Espanol, Ingles, Frances, Aleman, 2 vols. (Span., Eng., Fr. & Ger., Definitions in Spanish). Vol. 1, 1793p. $110.00; Vol. 2, 1007p. $80.00. Imported Bks.
Diccionario espanol, ingles, frances, italiano, aleman y holandes. (Eng. , Fr. , Ital. , Ger. & Dutch.). write for info. Rev. Mex. de Seguros.

SPANISH LANGUAGE–DICTIONARIES–SWEDISH

Diccionario Lexicon Sueco-Espanol, Espanol-Sueco. 400p. (Sueco & Span.). leatherette $4.95 (ISBN 84-303-0146-1, S-50416); pap. $4.50 (ISBN 84-303-0145-3, S-50415). French & Eur.
Lexicon Sopena: Diccionario de bolsillo, sueco-espanol y espanol-sueco. 384p. (Swedish & Span.). 60.00 ptas. 35.00 ptas. pap. 30.00 ptas. Sopena.
Spanish-Swedish-Spanish Dictionary. 340p. (Span. & Swedish.). 1968. pap. $9.95 (ISBN 0-686-92501-7, S-37811). French & Eur.

SPANISH LANGUAGE–GLOSSARIES, VOCABULARIES, ETC.

Ajvarado, Lisandro. Glosario de voces indigenas de Venezuela, 4 vols. (Span.). Bs.0.90. Minist Ed Caracas.
Alvarado, Lisandro. Glosario de bajo espanol en Venezuela, 4 vols. (Span.). Bs.0.90 ea. Minist Ed Caracas.
Ballarin Cornel, Angel. Vocabulario de Benasque. 224p. (Span.). 1972. 200.00 ptas. Fernando el Catolico.
Brown, Lawrence K. A Thesaurus of Spanish Idioms & Everyday Language. 165p. (Span.). 1975. pap. $4.95 (ISBN 0-8044-6059-0). Ungar.
Chayne, G. J. Classified Spanish Vocabulary. LC 78-670001. 1964. text ed. $16.95x (ISBN 0-245-55575-7). Intl Ideas.
Consejo Superior de Esenanza. Vocabulario Ortografico: Sugerencias para su Enserianza. 266p. (Span.). 1965. $3.50. U. Puerto Rico.
Cortiella Martret, Aureli. Vocabulari de Barbarismes & Castellanismes. 350p. (Span.). 1981. 350.00 ptas (ISBN 84-500-4509-6). Organ Ofic Adm.
De Casasnovas, F. Vocabulari Mallorqui-Castella. 328p. (Span.). 1965. 250.00 ptas. Moll Edit.
Diccionario de sinonimos e ideas afines y de la rima. (Span.). $14.95 (7986-6). Natl Textbk.
Diccionario Escolar de Sinonimos y Antonimas "Vox". 3rd ed. 370p. (Span.). 1982. write for info. (ISBN 84-7153-379-0). Biblograf.
Diccionario Ortografico. 51st ed. 640p. (Span.). 1982. 150.00 ptas (ISBN 8-47105-091-9). Mayfe.
Diccionario ortografico. (Span.). 25.00 ptas. Mayfe.
Dozy, R. Glossaire des Mots Espagnols et Portugais Derives de L'arabe. (Span., Port. & Arabic.). 1974. $20.00x (ISBN 0-86685-105-4). Intl Bk Ctr.
D'Rovira, Eugenio. Glosari. 352p. (Span.). 1982. pap. 375.00 ptas (ISBN 84-297-1826-5). Ediciones Sesent Dos.
Escarpanter, Jose A. Ortografia Moderna. 6th ed. 200p. (Span.). 1980. pap. 280.00 ptas (ISBN 84-359-0103-3). Playor.
Essential Spanish Vocabulary. (Span.). $3.25. Longman.
Fernandez de la Torriente, Gaston. Vocabulario superior. 7th ed. 176p. (Span.). 1982. pap. 350.00 ptas (ISBN 84-359-0124-6). Playor.
Fernandez del Riego, Francisco. Vocabulario Castellano-Gallego. 3rd ed. 366p. (Span.). 1981. 325.00 ptas (ISBN 84-7154-324-9). Galaxia.
Ferrer Mir, Jaime, et al. Ortografia Castellano. 200p. (Span.). 1982. pap. write for info. (ISBN 84-348-0996-6). S M Edns.
Ferrer Pastor, Francesc. Vocabulari Castella-Valencia. 477p. (Span.). 1967. 200.00 ptas. Sicania.
--Vocabulari Castella-Valencia. 1039p. (Span.). 1967. 500.00 ptas. Sicania.
Flores de Vega. Diccionario ortografico hispanoamericano. 288p. (Span.). $1.25. Peisa.
Franco Grande, Xose L. Vocabulario Galego-Castelan. (Span.). 90.00 ptas. Galaxia.
Franco Grande, Xose L. & Fernandez del Riego, Francisco. Vocabulario Galego-Castelan Castellano-Gallego. 584p. (Span.). 1982. pap. 775.00 ptas (ISBN 84-7154-413-X). Galaxia.
Garcia Merayo, F. Glosario de informatica. 290p. (Span.). 425.00 ptas. Urmo.
Gili Gaya, Samuel. Diccionario de sinonimos. 376p. (Span.). $9.95 (7865-3). Natl Textbk.
--Ortografia Practica Espanola Vox. 8th ed. 104p. (Span.). 1981. 140.00 ptas (ISBN 84-7153-255-7). Biblo SP.
Hernandez De Prieto, Muriel. Vocabulary Made Easy for Spanish Speakers. LC 76-3732. 96p. (Orig., Prog. Bk.). 1976. pap. text ed. $3.75 (ISBN 0-8477-2622-3). U of PR Pr.
Kendris, Christopher. Two Thousand & One Words You Need to Know to Pass Any Spanish Test. (Span.). 1984. pap. $2.95 (ISBN 0-8120-2537-7). Barron.
Luna de la Fuente. Vocabulario de Terminos: Criollos Tipicos Relacionados con el Caballo de Paso. 53p. (Span.). 1966. S/0.75; $15.00. U. Agraria.
Malaret, Augusto. Vocabulario de Puerto Rico. (Span.). Mex.$8.00. Las Americas.
Neggers, Gladys. Vocabulario culto. 8th ed. 168p. (Span.). 1982. pap. 350.00 ptas (ISBN 84-359-0034-7). Playor.
Orellana, Marina. Glosario internacional: Ingles-espanol. 102p. (Eng. & Span.). 1967. $2.00. Universitaria.
Paufique, Robert. Vocabulaire Espagnol par l'image. 96p. (Span.). 1970. 15.00 F. Bordas-Dunod.
Perona Sanchez, Jose D. El Vocabulario vital e irracional en Azorin. 110p. (Span.). 1981. pap. write for info. (ISBN 84-00-04957-8). Consejo Superior.
Plans Sanz de Bremond, Fructuoso. Diccionario ortografico. 51st ed. 640p. (Span.). 1982. pap. 150.00 ptas (ISBN 84-7105-091-9). Mayfe.
Ramirez, Hector. Ortografia Practica: Acentuacion, Consonantes, Vocabulario. 202p. (Span.). 1979. $3.50 (Dist. Lib. Studium). Gale.
Robson, Leonard V. Vocabulario consultivo por secciones: Espanol-ingles. 206p. (Span. & Eng.). 1980. pap. 600.00 ptas (ISBN 84-7231-571-1). Confed Espanola.
Russo. Vocabulario Logico, Historico & Positivo. (Span.). Arg.$3.00. Coop. Der.
Russo, Eduardo Angel. Vocabulario Logico. 51p. (Span.). 1972. write for info. Coop. Der.
Sainz de Robles, F. Diccionario espanol de sinonimos y antonimos. (Span.). $30.00. Iaconi.
Sopena. Diccionario Iter Ortografico. (Span.). pap. $3.95. Lectorum Pubns.
Tovar, Enrique D. Vocabulario del Oriente Peruano. 214p. (Span.). 1966. $3.35. U. San Marcos.
U. S. Armed Forces. Dictionary of Spoken Spanish Words, Phrases, Sentences. LC 30-900. (Span. & Eng.). pap. $7.95 (ISBN 0-385-00976-3). Doubleday.
Valderrama Martinez, Fernando. Glosario Espanol-Arabe y Arabe-Espanol. 333p. (Span. & Arabic.). 1980. pap. 6.00 ptas. pap. 300.00 ptas. Albir.
Villarroel, Raul. Vocabulario Griego-Argentino. (Gr. & Span.). write for info. Castellvi.

Vocabulari Basic Infantil & d'Adults. 114p. (Span.). write for info. Biblograf S. A.
Vocabulari basic infantil i d'Adults 'Vox' 6th ed. 112p. (Span.). 1982. pap. 225.00 ptas (ISBN 84-7153-265-4). Biblo SP.
Vocabulari basic infantil i d'Adults 'Vox' 4th ed. 112p. (Span.). 1980. pap. 200.00 ptas. Biblo SP.
Vocabulari Castella-Catala. (Span.). $2.50; 180.00 ptas. Salvat Editores.
Vocabulario Basico por Areas. 126p. (Span.). 1981. 550.00 ptas (ISBN 8-48583-909-9). Socusa Edit.
Vocabulario con Ilustraciones. (Illus.). 18p. (Span.). $0.20; Mex.$0.50. Novaro.
Vocabularios Aleman-Espanol-Polaco. (Ger. , Span. & Pol.). $0.80; Mex.$10.00. Novaro.
Vocabularios Frances-Espanol-Ingles. (Fr. , Span. & Eng.). $0.80; Mex.$10.00. Novaro.
Vocabularios Japones-Espanol-Ruso. (Japanese, Span. & Rus.). $0.80; Mex.$10.00. Novaro.
Vocabularios Portugues-Espanol-Italiano. (Port. , Span. & Ital.). $0.80; Mex.$10.00. Novaro.
Vox. Diccionario Tematico de la Lengua Espanola. LC 76-452992. 461p. (Span.). 1975. write for info. (ISBN 8-471-53116-X). Biblo Sp.
Zainqui Erro, Jose M. Ortografia Practica. 112p. (Span.). 1982. 390.00 ptas (ISBN 8-43150-566-4). Edit Vecchi.
--Ortografia Practica. 3rd ed. Devecchi, ed. 112p. (Span.). 1982. pap. 390.00 ptas (ISBN 8-43150-566-4). Edit Vecchi.

SPANISH LANGUAGE–GRAMMAR

Canal, Julio de la. Diccionario de sinonimos e ideas afines. 346p. (Span.). 1970. $4.40. CECSA.
Castillo, Gonzalo. Diccionario de similes y analogias. (Span.). Mex.$12.00. Costa Amic.
Corripio, Fernando. Diccionario Abreviado de Sinonimos. (Span.). pap. $4.95 (BRG). Lectorum Pubns.
Craig, Ruth P. Diccionario de Dos Cientos Uno Verbos Ingleses. LC 77-184894. (Span. & Eng.). 1972. pap. text ed. $7.95 (ISBN 0-8120-0417-5). Barron.
Diccionario abreviado de sinonimos 'Vox' 5th ed. 352p. (Span.). 1982. write for info. (ISBN 84-7153-207-7). Biblo SP.
Diccionario de Incorreciones, Dudas y Normas Gramaticales. 655p. (Span.). 1975. pap. $17.50 (ISBN 84-02-04591-X, S-50156). French & Eur.
Diccionario de Paronimos & Antonimos Castellanos. (Span.). pap. $11.50 (SPA). Lectorum Pubns.
Diccionario de Sinonimos-Antonimos. 510p. (Span.). $3.75. Cruzada Span Pubns.
Diccionario de sinonimos y antonimos. 500p. (Span.). 1982. Col.$pap. 250.00 (ISBN 84-8279-072-2). Educar.
Diccionario Escolar de Sinonimos & Antonimos Vox. 2nd ed. 370p. (Span.). 1981. 500.00 ptas (ISBN 84-7153-379-0). Biblo SP.
Diccionario Tematico de Sinonimos & Antonimos. 2nd ed. 640p. (Span.). 1981. 500.00 ptas (ISBN 84-241-1501-5). Everest.
Franquesa Lluelles, Manuel. Diccionario de Sinonimos. 2nd ed. 1234p. (Span.). 1981. 1750.00 ptas (ISBN 84-7306-015-6). Portic.
Fuentes Franco, Jordi. Diccionario y gramatica de la lengua de la isla de Pascua: Pascuense-castellano, castellano-pascuense, pascuense-ingles, ingles-pascuense. 1802p. (Span. & Eng.). 1960. $5.00. Juridica-Andres Bello.
Gran Diccionario & Gramatica Ingles-Espanol, Espanol-Ingles, 2 vols, Vol. 1. 3rd. ed. 464p. (Span. & Eng.). 1982. 2500.00 ptas (ISBN 8-42780-596-9). Nauta SA.
Gran diccionario y gramatica de la lengua espanola: Obra completa, 2 vols. 2nd ed. 896p. (Span.). 1982. pap. 3200.00 ptas (ISBN 84-278-0568-3). Nauta SA.
Grates. Diccionario de Sinonimos Castellanos. (Span.). pap. $7.25 (SPA). Lectorum Pubns.
Hollander, N., et al. Lexico Marinero: Six Idiomas. 128p. (Span.). pap. $22.50 (ISBN 84-261-1668-X, S-37657). French & Eur.
Horta Massanes, Joaquin. Diccionario de Sinonimos e Ideas Afines & de la Rima. (Span.). $13.25 (PAR). Lectorum Pubns.
Lexis-Veinte-Dos: Gramatica, Lengua & Estilo. 288p. (Span.). 1980. 960.00 ptas. Biblograf.
Lexis Veinte-dos: Sinonimos y Antonimos. 9th ed. 370p. (Span.). 1982. pap. 600.00 ptas (ISBN 84-226-1080-9). Circulo Lect.
Lexis Veinte-dos: Sinonimos y Antonimos. 7th ed. 370p. (Span.). 1981. pap. 550.00 ptas (ISBN 84-226-1080-9). Circulo Lect.
Paredes, Luis. Diccionario de Sinonimos, Antonimos & Ideas Afines. 302p. (Span.). 1974. write for info. Gabriela Mistral.
Perez Cuadrado, Cosme. Diccionario General de Sinonimos & Antonimos. 396p. (Span.). 1981. 2100.00 ptas (ISBN 84-7215-363-0). Coculsa.
Pey. Pequeno Diccionario de Sinonimos. 248p. (Span.). 1981. pap. write for info. Edit Teide.
Pey, Santiago. Diccionario de Sinonimos, Ideas Afines & Contrarios. (Span.). $13.50 (TEI). Lectorum Pubns.
Ramirez, Hector. Ortografia Practica: Acentuacion, Consonantes, Vocabulario. 202p. (Span.). 1979. $3.50 (Dist. Lib. Studium). Gale.
Rofer, F. Diccionario de sinonimos espanoles. (Span.). Mex.$40.00. EDIMEX.
Rofer, Francisco. Diccionario de Sinonimos Espanoles. 371p. (Span.). 1971. write for info. Edit Mex U.
Santamaria, Antonio. Diccionario de Sinonimos, Antonimos & Ideas Afines. (Span.). $4.25 (SOP). Lectorum Pubns.
Saubidet, Tito. Vocabulario y Refranero Criollo. (Span.). $85.00 (ISBN 0-686-56666-1, S-33072). French & Eur.
Zamora, Antonio. Diccionario de sininimos espanoles. 6th ed. 328p. (Span.). Arg.$pap. 12.00. Claridad.
Ziegler. Grammatisches Worterbuch der Gebrauchlichsten Spanischer Verben. 160p. (Ger.). $10.50 (ISBN 3-87217-009-0, M-7432, Pub. by Fachverlag Th. Grossman). French & Eur.

SPANISH LANGUAGE–GRAMMAR, COMPARATIVE

Penalosa, Joaquin Antonio. Vocabulario & Refranero Religioso de Mexico. (Span.). Mex.$25.00. Jus.
Raluy Pondevida, Antonio. Diccionario Porrua de la lengua espanola: Contiene las palabras basicas del idioma, con abundantes exicanismos & americanismos, tecnicismos, verbos & notas ortograficas. 9th ed. Monterde, Francisco, ed. 868p. (Eng. & Span.). 1981. Mex.$pap. 90.00. Porrua.

SPANISH LANGUAGE–IDIOMS, CORRECTIONS, ERRORS

Alonso, Martin. Diccionario escolar del idioma espanol. (Span.). 150.00 ptas. Aguilar SP.
--Diccionario ortografico del idioma espanol. (Span.). 100.00 ptas. Aguilar SP.
Boggs, R. S. & Dixon, J. I. Everyday Spanish Idioms. (Span.). (gr. 9-12). 1978. pap. text ed. 5.25 (ISBN 0-88345-326-6). Regents Pub.
Cassell. Cassell's Colloquial Spanish. 304p. (Span.). pap. $4.95 (ISBN 0-02-079430-4). Macmillan.
Corripio, Fernando. Diccionario de Incorrecciones, Dudas & Normas Gramaticales. LC 76-457468. 655p. (Span.). 1975. write for info. (ISBN 8-402-04591-X). Edit Bruguera.
Diccionario del Idioma Espanol Moderno. (Span.). $55.00. AGL.
Diccionario Ortografico del Idioma Espanol Moderno. (Span.). $3.95. AGL.
Diccionario simultaneo en 21 idiomas. (Span.). write for info. (608-80). Pan Amer Pub.
Guasp, Ignacio. Diccionario de la Lengua Mechada. (Span.). $12.50 (ISBN 0-686-56701-3, S-5248). French & Eur.
Miravitlles Serradell, Joan. Diccionari general de barbarismes i altres incorreccions. 224p. (Span.). 1982. pap. 350.00 ptas (ISBN 84-7263-240-7). Claret Edit.
Pierson, Raymond H. Guia de modismos espanoles. (Span.). s.p. $4.46 (7235-2). Natl Textbk.
Salas, Rodrigo. Los Mil Quinientos. 2nd ed. LC 79-126779. 247p. (Span.). 1978. write for info. (ISBN 8-431-54055-9). Edit Vecchi.
Santamaria, Antonio & Cuartas, Augusto. Diccionario de Incorrecciones & Particularidades & Curiosidades del Lenguaje. (Span.). pap. $14.95 (PAR). Lectorum Pubns.
Santamaria, Cuartas & Mangada, J. Diccionario de Incorreciones & Particularidades del Lenguaje. 4th ed. (Span.). 1983. write for info. ptas. Paraninfo.
Santillan, Diego Abad de. Diccionario de Argentinismos de Ayer y de Hoy. 1000p. (Span.). 1978. $195.00 (ISBN 0-686-56685-8, S-33041). French & Eur.
Savaiano, E. & Wing, L. Spanish & English Idioms: 2001 Modismos Espanoles & Ingleses. (Span. & Eng.). 1977. $6.95 (ISBN 0-8120-0438-8). Barron.
Savaiano, E. & Winget, L. Modismos en Ingles. (Span. Eng.). 1981. $3.95 (ISBN 0-8120-2314-5). Barron.
--Spanish-English Idioms: 2001 Modisomos Espanoles & Ingleses (Pocket Size) (Span. & Eng.). 1976. $3.95 (ISBN 0-8120-0711-5). Barron.
Seco, Manuel. Diccionario de Dudas & Dificultades de la Lengua Espanola. 516p. (Span., Mexico). 1966. Mex.$6.40. Aguilar SP.
--Diccionario de dudas de la lengua espanola. (Span.). 375.00 ptas. Aguilar.

SPANISH LANGUAGE–OLD SPANISH

see Spanish Language–To 1500

SPANISH LANGUAGE–PROVINCIALISMS

Bendezu Neyra, Guillermo E. Argo Limeno. LC 78-101067. 339p. (Span., Lima). 1977. write for info. Libreria.
Brache, Jose A. Cinco Mil Seiscientos Refranes & Frases de Uso Comun Entre los Dominicanos. Pichardo, Nicolas, ed. LC 80-100004. xiv, 311p. (Span.). 1978. write for info. Galaxia.
Casullo, Fernando H. Diccionario de Voces Lunfardas & Vulgares. LC 76-151616. 219p. (Span.). 1976. write for info. Plus Ultra SA.
Cobos, Ruben. A Dictionary of New Mexico & Southern Colorado Spanish. 200p. (Mexican & Span.). 1983. 14.95 (ISBN 0-89013-141-4); pap. text ed. 7.95 (ISBN 0-686-46179-7). Museum NM Pr.
Florez, Luis. Del Espanol Hablado en Colombia: Seis Muestras de Lexico. LC 76-460227. 198p. (Span.). 1975. write for info. Instituto Caro & Cuervo.
Gagini, Carlos & Soto, Victor M. Diccionario de Costarriquenismos. 3rd ed. Cuervo, Rufino J., prologue by. LC 77-459051. 243p. (Span.). 1975. write for info. Costa Rica.
Garro, Joaquin. Habla Que el Tiempo se Lleva? LC 79-126852. 129p. (Span., Costa Rica). 1978. write for info. Costa Rica.
Geoffroy Rivas, Pedro. La Lengua Salvadorena. LC 79-121608. 131p. (Span., San Salvador). 1978. write for info. Direccion de Publicaciones.
Gobello, Jose. Diccionario Lunfardo & de Otros Terminos Antiguos & Modernos Usuales. LC 76-460668. 234p. (Span.). 1975. write for info. Pena Lillo.
Kay, Margarita. Southwestern Medical Dictionary: Spanish-English & English-Spanish. LC 76-54591. (Span. & Eng.). 1977. pap. text ed. $4.50 (ISBN 0-8165-0529-2). U of Ariz Pr.
Paz Soldan Y Unanue, Pedro & Nunez, Estuardo. Diccionario de Peruanismos, 2 vols. LC 76-460366. xxx, 399p. (Span.). 1975. write for info. Edns Peisa.
Rodriguez, Zorobabel. Diccionario de Chilenismos. LC 79-124394. xii, 487p. (Span.). 1979. write for info. Universidad & Acad.
Santamaria, Francisco J. Diccionario De Mejicanismos. (Span.). $49.50x (ISBN 0-686-00853-7). Colton Bk.
Schwauss, Maria. Woerterbuch der Regionalen Umgangssprache in Lateinamerika. LC 77-562131. 692p. (Ger. & Span.). 1977. M.52.00. VEB Verlag Enzyklopadie.

SPANISH LANGUAGE–SELF-INSTRUCTION

see also Spanish Language–Conversation and Phrase Books

Ibarra, Francisco. Look & Learn Spanish. (Span.). $1.50. Camino Real.
Madrigal, Margarita. See it-Say it in Spanish. (Span.). $1.50. Camino Real.

SPANISH LANGUAGE–SLANG

Casullo, Fernando. Diccionario de voces lunfardas y vulgares. (Span.). Arg.$15.00. Freeland.
Cortiella Martret, Aureli. Vocabulari de Barbarismes & Castellanismes. 350p. (Span.). 1981. 350.00 ptas (ISBN 84-500-4509-6). Organ Ofic Adm.
Espina Perez, Dario. Diccionario de cubanismos. (Span.). $3.50. Dist. Universal.
Miravitlles Serradell, Joan. Diccionari general de barbarismes i altres incorreccions. 224p. (Span.). 1982. pap. 350.00 ptas (ISBN 84-7263-240-7). Claret Edit.
Navarro Garcia, Felipe. Diccionario del Pasota. LC 79-121713. (Illus.). 204p. (Span.). 1979. 300.00 ptas (ISBN 8-432-04139-4). Planeta SA.
Trejo, Arnulfo D. Diccionario etimologica latinoamericano de lexico de la delincuencia. 272p. (Span.). $1.44. UTEHA.
Vasquez, Librado & Vasquez, Maria E. Regional Dictionary of Chicano Slang. (Span.). $8.95. Camino Real.

SPANISH LANGUAGE–SPOKEN SPANISH

Coluccio, Felix. Diccionario de Voces & Expresiones Argentinas. 223p. (Span.). 1979. write for info. Plus Ultra S. A.
Dictionary of Spoken Spanish. (Span. & Eng.). write for info. (608-19). Pan Amer Pub.
Dictionary of Spoken Spanish Words & Sentences. (Span.). $3.95. Camino Real.
Dictionary of Spoken Spanish Words, Phrases, Sentences. LC 30-900. (Span.). pap. $7.95. Doubleday.
Gallo, Cristine. Language of the Puerto Rican Street. LC 80-66269. ix, 214p. (Span. & Eng.). 1980. write for info. (ISBN 0-9604174-0-0). C Gallo.
Kerchuville, F. M. Practical Spoken Spanish. 7th ed. (Span.). $3.45. Camino Real.

SPANISH LANGUAGE–STUDY AND TEACHING

Rivero Wood, Maria. Vocabulary for the Spanish-Speaking Student of Shorthand. 58p. (Span.). 1966. $0.85. U. Puerto Rico.

SPANISH LANGUAGE–SYNTAX

Sobrrzo, Horacio. Vocabulario Sonorense. (Span.). $25.95 (ISBN 0-686-56691-2, S-12361). French & Eur.

SPANISH LANGUAGE–TEXTBOOKS FOR CHILDREN

see also Spanish Language–Conversation and Phrase Books

Boggs, R. S. & Dixon, J. I. Everyday Spanish Idioms. (Span.). (gr. 9-12). 1978. pap. text ed. 5.25 (ISBN 0-88345-326-6). Regents Pub.

Tireman, Loyd S. Spanish Vocabulary of Four Native Spanish-Speaking Pre-First-Grade Children. LC 48-45159. 64p. (Span.). 1982. lib. bdg. $22.95x (ISBN 0-89370-737-6). Borgo Pr.

SPANISH LITERATURE–BIBLIOGRAPHY
Hidalgo, Dionisio. Diccionario De Bibliografia Espanola, 7 Vols. LC 68-57908. (Bibliography & Reference Ser.: No. 122). (Span.). 1970. Repr. of 1881 ed. text ed. $215.00 (ISBN 0-8337-1699-9). B Franklin.

SPANISH LITERATURE–DICTIONARIES
Richardson, Henry B. Etymological Vocabulary to the Libro De Buen Amor of Juan Ruiz, Arcipreste De Hita. LC 72-1684. (Yale Romanic Studies: No. 2). (Span.). Repr. of 1930 ed. $14.50 (ISBN 0-404-53202-0). AMS Pr.

SPANISH LITERATURE–OUTLINES, SYLLABI, ETC.
Nitti, John & Kasten, Lloyd. Complete Concordances & Texts of the Fourteenth-Century Aragonese Manuscripts of Juan Fernandez de Heredia. (Dialect Ser.: No. 2). 1982. 125.00 (ISBN 0-942260-18-X). Hispanic Seminary.

SPANISH MISSIONS OF CALIFORNIA
Here is entered literature dealing chiefly with the old Spanish mission buildings. Material treating of organized missionary activities is entered under Missions–United States.
Sitjar, Buenaventura. Vocabulary of the Language of San Antonio Mission, California. LC 10-26367. (Library of American Linguistics: No. 7). (Span.). Repr. of 1861 ed. $15.00 (ISBN 0-404-50987-8). AMS Pr.

SPANISH POETRY (COLLECTIONS)
Here are entered collections in Spanish. For English translations see subdivision Translations into English.
Horta Massanes, Joaquin. Diccionario de Sinonimos e Ideas Afines & de la Rima. (Span.). $13.25 (PAR). Lectorum Pubns.

SPANISH POETRY–HISTORY AND CRITICISM
Richards, Ruth M. Concordance to the Sonnets of Gongora. (Spanish Ser.: No. 6). 1982. 15.00 (ISBN 0-942260-20-1). Hispanic Seminary.

SPANISH WIT AND HUMOR
Sintes, J. Diccionario Humoristico. 900p. (Span.). $41.95 (ISBN 0-686-97940-0, S-37666). French & Eur.

SPEAKING
see Debates and Debating; Oratory; Rhetoric

SPECIAL LIBRARIES
see Libraries, Special

SPECIALIZED AGENCIES OF THE UNITED NATIONS
see International Agencies

SPECIE
see Money

SPECIE PAYMENTS
see Finance, Public

SPECIES, ORIGIN OF
see Origin of Species

SPECTATOR, LONDON, 1711-1712
Wheeler, William. Concordance to the Spectator. LC 74-32004. lib. bdg. $15.00 (ISBN 0-8414-9575-0). Folcroft.

SPECTRA
see Spectrum Analysis

SPECTROCHEMICAL ANALYSIS
see Spectrum Analysis

SPECTROSCOPY
see Spectrum Analysis

SPECTRUM ANALYSIS
Denney, R. C. Dictionary of Spectroscopy. 2nd ed. 205p. 1982. $39.95x (ISBN 0-471-87478-7, Pub. by Wiley-Interscience). Wiley.
--A Dictionary of Spectroscopy. 224p. (Eng.). 1982. E15.00 (ISBN 0-333-31670-3). Macmillan London.

Ministry of Education. Scientific Terms Spectroscopy: Japanese-English, English-Japanese. 165p. (Japanese & Eng.). 1974. leatherette $14.95 (ISBN 0-686-92512-2, M-9341). French & Eur.

Moritz, H. & Torok, T. Technical Dictionary of Spectroscopy & Spectral Analysis: English, German, French, Russian. 1971. 65.00 (ISBN 0-08-015864-1). Pergamon.

SPECULATION
see also Investments; Real Estate Investment; Stock-Exchange
Flumiani, C. M. The New Dictionary of Strange & Ingenious Stock Market Tricks the Experts Follow in Their Search for Wealth. 215p. 1976. $57.50 (ISBN 0-89266-002-3). Am Classical Coll Pr.

SPEECH
Here are entered works on the oral production of meaningful sounds in language. Works on speaking as a means of communication are entered under Oral communication or more specific headings, e.g. Public speaking.
see also Children–Language; Language and Languages; Phonetics; Speech Therapy; Verbal Behavior
Dahl, Hartvig. Word Frequencies of Spoken American English. LC 80-116646. xii, 348p. 1980. $60.00 (ISBN 0-930454-07-3). Verbatim.

SPEECH–PSYCHOLOGY
see Psycholinguistics

SPEECH, DISORDERS OF
see also Communicative Disorders
Ogilvie, Mardel. Terminology & Definitions of Speech Defects. LC 70-177132. (Columbia University. Teachers College. Contributions to Education: No. 859). Repr. of 1942 ed. $17.50 (ISBN 0-404-55859-3). AMS Pr.
Perello, Jorge. Lexicon de Comunicologia. LC 78-393509. (Eng. & Span.). 1977. 3000.00 ptas. Augusta SA.

SPEECH, FIGURES OF
see Figures of Speech

SPEECH CORRECTION
see Speech Therapy

SPEECH DEFECTS
see Speech, Disorders Of

SPEECH-READING
see Deaf–Means of Communication

SPEECH THERAPY
Nicolosi, Lucille, et al. Terminology of Communication Disorders: Speech, Language, Hearing. (Illus.). 288p. 1978. pap. $17.50 (ISBN 0-683-06500-9). Williams & Wilkins.

SPELLERS
Botel, Morton. Primary Multi-Level Speller & First Dictionary. (gr. k-2). 1959. pap. 3.10 (ISBN 0-931992-14-1). Penns Valley.
Dougherty, Margaret M., et al. Instant Spelling Dictionary. LC 67-11788. 1967. 3.95 (ISBN 0-911744-01-0). Career Inst.
Kreivsky, Joseph & Linfield, Jordon L. The Bad Spellers Dictionary. 1967. 2.95 (ISBN 0-394-49199-8). Random.
Merriam-Webster Reference Editor, ed. Webster's Instant Word Guide. 384p. 1980. 3.95 (ISBN 0-87779-273-9). Merriam-Webster Inc.
Prichard, Robert W. & Robinson, Robert E. Twenty Thousand Medical Words. 288p. 1972. (HP); pap. $11.95 (ISBN 0-07-050874-7). McGraw.

SPELLING
see English Language–Orthography and Spelling

SPELLING REFORM
Bailly, Victor. Dictionnaire Orthographique. 56p. (Fr.). 1968. 46.00 F. Plantyn Edns.
De La Canal, J. Diccionario ortografico. (Span.). Mex.$9.00. EDIMEX.
Diccionario Abreviado Ortografico de la Lengua Espanola. 416p. (Span.). 1980. 325.00 ptas (ISBN 84-7153-227-1). Biblograf SP.
Ebner, Jakob. Rechtschreibung & Wortkunde: Ein Woerterbuch fur die Schule. 328p. (Ger.). DM.10.80 (ISBN 3-411-01911-5). Biblio Inst.

Henderson, L. Orthography & Word Recognition in Reading. LC 81-68587. 1982. $51.50 (ISBN 0-12-340520-3). Acad Pr.
Lopez, Jesus. Ortografia programada. 5th ed. 120p. (Span.). 1982. pap. 295.00 ptas (ISBN 84-219-0270-9). Del Castillo.
Napalis, I., et al. Orfograficheskii Slovar Litovskogo Iazyka Dlia Shkol. 244p. (Rus.). 1958. $1.35 (Pub. by Izd Pedag Lit). Four Continent.
Partridge, A. C. Orthography in Shakespeare & Elizabethan Drama: A Study of Colloquial Contractions, Elision, Prosody, & Punctuation. LC 64-17222. viii, 200p. 1964. $14.50x (ISBN 0-8032-0143-5). U of Nebr Pr.
Triadu, Joan. Diccionari Ortografic. 552p. (Catalan.). write for info. ptas (ISBN 84-7153-327-8). Biblograf SP.

SPELLS
see Magic

SPHRAGISTICS
see Seals (Numismatics)

SPICES
American Spice Trade Association. Glossary of Spices. minimum order 50. Am Spice Trade.
Clair, Colin. Dictionnaire des Herbes & des Epices. 259p. (Fr.). 1963. 14.00 F. Denoel.
--Dictionnaire des Herbes et des Epices. 259p. (Fr.). 1963. pap. $6.95 (ISBN 0-686-56842-7, M-6621). French & Eur.
Dictionary of Spice Technology. 172p. (Eng. & Chinese.). 1978. pap. $4.95 (ISBN 0-686-92609-9, M-9568). French & Eur.

SPIRITISM
see Spiritualism

SPIRITUAL LIFE–VEDANTA AUTHORS
see Vedanta

SPIRITUAL-MINDEDNESS
see Spirituality

SPIRITUALISM
see also Occult Sciences; Psychical Research
Wedeck, Harry E & Baskin, Wade, eds. Dictionary of Spiritualism. LC 73-104365. 1971. 10.00 (ISBN 0-8022-2338-9). Philos Lib.

SPIRITUALITY
Ancilli, Ermanno. Diccionario de espiritualidad: Obra Completa, 3 vols. Llopis, Joan, tr. 2224p. (Span.). 1982. 9000.00 ptas (ISBN 84-254-1265-X). Herder SA.
--Diccionario de espiritualidad: Tomo 1. Llopis, Joan, tr. 742p. (Span.). 1982. 3000.00 ptas (ISBN 84-254-1264-1). Herder SA.

SPOKEN ENGLISH
see English Language–Conversation and Phrase Books; English Language–Spoken English

SPORTING PRINTS
see also Sports in Art
Der Sport-Brockhaus. 576p. (Ger.). DM.34.00 (ISBN 3-7653-0038-1). F A Brockhaus.

SPORTS
see also Games; Gymnastics; Physical Education and Training; Professionalism in Sports; Track-Athletics
also names of sports, e.g. Golf
Wehlen, Rainer. Regeln & Sprache des Sports 1. 377p. (Ger.). DM.12.80 (ISBN 3-411-01361-3). Biblio Inst.
--Regeln & Sprache des Sports 2. 412p. (Ger.). DM.12.80 (ISBN 3-411-01362-1). Biblio Inst.

SPORTS–ACCIDENTS AND INJURIES
see also Sports Medicine
Subcommittee on Classification of Sports in Injuries & Committee on the Medical Aspects of Sports, eds. Standard Nomenclature of Athletic Injuries. (Orig.). 1968. pap. $2.00 (ISBN 0-89970-079-9, OP-43). AMA.

SPORTS–DICTIONARIES
Considine, Tim. The Language of Sport. Doering, Henry & Fisher, Patricia, eds. 352p. 1982. pap. $8.95 (ISBN 0-911818-24-3). World Almanac.
Cuddon, J. A. The International Dictionary of Sports & Games. LC 79-20983. (Illus.). 898p. 1980. $29.95 (ISBN 0-8052-3733-X). Schocken.

Dizionario dei giochi e degli sport. 206p. (Ital.). L.1800.00. Zanichelli.
English-Russian Dictionary of Sports Terms & Phrases: Summer Olympic Games & Sports. (Russkii iazyk Ser.). (Rus. & Eng.). pap. $4.95 (2533 B). Four Continent.
Enrile, E. Dizionario dello sport. (Illus.). 1312p. (Ital.). 1977. L.18000.00. Edizioni Paoline.
Frommer, Harvey. Sports Lingo: A Dictionary of the Language of Sports. LC 82-12130. 312p. 1983. $9.95 (ISBN 0-689-10939-3, 289); pap. $7.95. Atheneum.
Garilovets, A. V. English-Russian Dictionary of Sports Terms & Phrases. 420p. (Eng. & Rus.). 1980. $35.00x (ISBN 0-569-08602-7, Pub. by Collets). State Mutual Bk.
Gavrilovets, A. V. Russian-English Dictionary of Sports Terms & Phrases. (Rus. & Eng.). $32.00x (ISBN 0-569-08607-8, Pub. by Collets). State Mutual Bk.
Langenscheidts Sportwoerterbuch Deutsch-Englisch-Franzoesisch-Spanisch. (Ger. , Eng. , Fr. & Span.). 1978. DM.12.80 (ISBN 3-468-21400-6). Langenscheidt.
Lembke, R. Langenscheidts Sportwoerterbuch. 319p. (Ger., Eng., Fr. & Span., Dictionary of Sports). 1971. $9.95 (ISBN 0-686-56629-7, M-7538, Pub. by Langenscheidt). French & Eur.
Merriam-Webster Editorial Staff, ed. Webster's Sports Dictionary. 1976. 8.95 (ISBN 0-87779-067-1). Merriam-Webster Inc.
Racquet & Tennis Club New York. Dictionary Catalogue of the Library of Sports in the Racquet & Tennis Club with Special Collections on Tennis, Lawn Tennis, & Early American Sports, 2 vols. 1970. Set. lib. bdg. $190.00 (ISBN 0-8161-0916-8, Hall Library). G K Hall.
Rollin, Jack. The Guinness Book of Soccer Facts & Feats. 3rd ed. LC 80-142758. (Illus.). 255p. (Eng.). 1980. E6.95 (ISBN 0-85112-213-2). Guinness Super.
--The Guinness Book of Soccer Facts & Feats. 2nd ed. LC 80-465139. (Illus.). 251p. 1979. E5.95 (ISBN 0-85112-203-5). Guinness Super.
Russko-Angliiskii Slovar'-Razgovornik. Russian-English Dictionary of Sports Terms & Phrases - Olympic Summer. (Russkii iazyk Ser.). 352p. (Rus. & Eng.). 1979. $3.50 (C-56). Four Continent.
Sport Brockhaus. 576p. (Ger.). $27.50 (ISBN 3-7653-0021-7, M-7626, Pub. by Brockhaus). French & Eur.
Sullivan, George. The Complete Sports Dictionary. (YA) (gr. 7-12). 1979. pap. $1.95 (ISBN 0-590-05731-6). Scholastic Inc.
Wright, Graeme. Illustrated Dictionary of Sports. LC 78-61515. (Illus.). 192p. 1979. 14.95 (ISBN 0-528-81078-2). Rand.
Yazyk, Russkii. Russian-English Dictionary of Sports Terms & Phrases. 352p. (Rus. & Eng.). 1980. pap. $15.00x (ISBN 0-686-72092-X, Pub. by Collet's). State Mutual Bk.

SPORTS–JUVENILE LITERATURE
Emert, Phyllis R. Illustrated Track & Field Dictionary for Young People. (Illus.). (gr. 4 up). 1981. pap. 2.50 (ISBN 0-13-451310-X). P-H.

SPORTS–MEDICAL ASPECTS
see Sports Medicine

SPORTS, INJURIES FROM
see Sports–Accidents and Injuries

SPORTS IN ART
see also Sporting Prints
Paviere, Sydney. A Dictionary of British Sporting Painters. (Illus.). 1980. Repr. of 1965 ed. text ed. 40.00x (ISBN 0-85317-940-9, Pub. by A & C Black England). Humanities.

SPORTS MEDICINE
see also Sports–Accidents and Injuries

SPRINGS (MECHANISM)
Subcommittee on Classification of
Sports in Injuries & Committee on
the Medical Aspects of Sports,
eds. Standard Nomenclature of
Athletic Injuries. (Orig.). 1968.
pap. $2.00 (ISBN 0-89970-079-9,
OP-43). AMA.

SPRINGS (MECHANISM)
S.N.F.R. Les Ressorts: Francais-
Allemand-Anglais-Espagnol, Vol.
2. 110p. (Fr., Ger., Eng. & Span.).
1978. 100.00 F. Maison
Dictionnaire.

SPYING
see Espionage

SQUAWMISH LANGUAGE
Kuipers, Aert H. Squamish Language,
Pt. 1, Grammar, Text, Dictionary.
(Janua Linguarum, Ser. Practica:
No. 732). (Squawmish.). 1967. text
ed. 67.00x (ISBN 90-2790-672-6).
Mouton.

STAGE COSTUME
see Costume

**STAMP-COLLECTING AND
STAMP-COLLECTORS**
*see Postage-Stamps–Collectors and
Collecting*

STAMPS, POSTAGE
see Postage-Stamps

STANDARD OF VALUE
see Money

STANDARDS
*see subdivision Standards under
subjects, e.g. Engineering Instruments*

STATE AND ENVIRONMENT
see Environmental Policy

STATE AND INSURANCE
see Social Security

STATE GOVERNMENTS
*Here are entered works on state
governments in general and in the
United States. See also geographic
subdivisions which follow.*
see also Local Government
Press, Charles & VerBerg, Kenneth.
State & Community Governments
in the Federal System. LC 78-
22064. 1979. text ed. $21.95x
(ISBN 0-471-02725-1); tchrs.'
manual $6.00 (ISBN 0-471-04909-
3). Wiley.

STATE PLANNING
see Economic Policy; Social Policy

STATESMEN–GREAT BRITAIN
Ormond, Richard & Rogers,
Malcolm. Dictionary of British
Portraiture: Vol. 1, the Middle
Ages to the Early Georgian;
Historical Figures Born Before
1700. Davies, Adriana, ed. 1979.
text ed. $47.50x (ISBN 0-19-
520180-9). Oxford U Pr.
--Dictionary of British Portraiture:
Vol. 2, the Later Georgians to the
Early Victorians; Historical Figures
Born Between 1700 & 1800.
Kilmurray, Elaine, ed. 1979. text
ed. 49.50x (ISBN 0-19-520181-7).
Oxford U Pr.

STATISTICAL DIAGRAMS
see Statistics–Graphic Methods

STATISTICS-DICTIONARIES
Barcelo, J. L. Vocabulario de
Estadistica. 292p. (Span.). 1965.
300.00 ptas. Hispano Europa.
Broster, E. J. Glossary of Applied
Management & Financial Statistics.
243p. 1974. $29.50x (ISBN 0-
8448-0608-0). Crane-Russak Co.
Buckland, William R. & Kendall,
Maurice G. Diccionario de
Estadistica. 384p. (Span.). 1980.
1.200 ptas (ISBN 8-43680-141-5).
Piramide.
Davis, Hunter. Book of British Lists.
LC 81-138947. xvii, 222p. 1980.
Epap. 1.25 (ISBN 0-600-20267-4).
Hamlyn Pub.
Dictionnaire Historique, Literaire &
Statistique, 2 vols. 1620p. (Fr.).
1973. write for info. Lafitte Repr.
Gonsalvo Mainar, Gonzalo.
Diccionario De Metologia
Estadistica. 184p. (Span.). 1978.
pap. $19.95 (ISBN 84-7112-096-8,
S-50010). French & Eur.
Kendall, Maurice G. & Buckland,
William K. Dictionary of Statistical
Terms. 4th ed. 1982. 27.95 (ISBN
0-582-47008-0). Longman.
Morice, E. Diccionario de
Estadistica. 220p. (Span.). 1975.
pap. $18.50 (ISBN 84-7051-037-1,
S-50210). French & Eur.
Morice, Eugene. Dizionario di
statistica. Cossarini, M. G., tr.
xxxviii, 260p. (Ital.). 1971.
L.14000.00. ISEDI.

Mulhall, Michael G. Dictionary of
Statistics. 75.00 (ISBN 0-8490-
0046-7). Gordon Pr.
Paenson, Isaac. Systematic Glossary
of the Terminology of Statistical
Methods: English, French,
Spanish, Russian. (Eng., Fr., Span.
& Rus.). 1971. 130.00 (ISBN 0-08-
012285-X). Pergamon.
Rousset, A. Dictionnaire
Geographique, Historique &
Statistique des Communes:
Franche-Comte & des Hameaux
qui en Dependent, 6 vols. 3602p.
(Fr.). 1970. 600.00 F. Guenegaud.
Sahai, Hardeo & Berrios, Jose. A
Dictionary of Statistical, Scientific
& Technical Terms: English-
Spanish, Spanish-English. Smith,
Richard A. & Heise, Jeanne, eds.
(Spanish Ser.). 143p. (Eng. &
Span.). 1981. $13.95 (ISBN 8-
4534-0004-0, Pub. by Wadsworth
Internacional Iberoamerica).
Wadsworth Pub.
Webb, Augustus D. New Dictionary
of Statistics: A Complement to the
Fourth Edition of Mulhall's
Dictionary of Statistics. LC 68-
18017. 1971. Repr. of 1911 ed.
$56.00x (ISBN 0-8103-3988-9).
Gale.

**STATISTICS–GRAPHIC
METHODS**
Williams, C. B. Style & Vocabulary:
Numerical Studies. 162p. 1972.
pap. text ed. 8.75x (ISBN 0-85264-
164-8). Lubrecht & Cramer.

STATISTICS OF SAMPLING
see Sampling (Statistics)

STATUETTES
see Bronzes; Idols and Images

STEAM-BOILERS
see also Furnaces; Pressure-Gages
Babcock, Deutsche, et al, eds.
Woerterbuch der
Dampferzeugungstechnik-
Dictionary of Steam Generator
Engineering. 512p. (Ger., Eng.,
Span. Fr.). 1972. 29.50x (ISBN 3-
8027-2471-2). Intl Pubns Serv.

STEAM GENERATORS
see Steam-Boilers

STEAM POWER-PLANTS
Stattmann, F. Dictionary of Power
Plant Engineering: Conventional
Steam Power Plants, Pt. 1. 252p.
(Ger. & Fr.). 1971. $13.50 (ISBN
3-521-06059-4, M-7103). French &
Eur.

STEAM-PUMPS
see Pumping Machinery

STEEL
Abd-El-Wahed, A. M. Iron & Steel
Industry Dictionary. 441p. (Eng.,
Fr., Ger. & Arabic.). 1974. $45.00
(ISBN 0-686-92487-8, M-9760).
French & Eur.
Freeman, H. Taschenwoerterbuch
Eisen und Stahl. 600p. (Ger. &
Eng., Dictionary of Iron and
Steel). 1966. $12.50 (ISBN 3-19-
006215-3, M-7634, Pub. by M.
Hueber). French & Eur.
--Taschenwoerterbuch Eisen und
Stahl. 600p. (Ger. & Eng.). 1966.
$12.50 (ISBN 3-19-006215-3).
Hueber.

STEEL-ENGRAVING
see Engraving

STEGANOGRAPHY
see Cryptography

STENOGRAPHY
see Shorthand

STEREOMETRY
see Mensuration

STEREOPHOTOGRAMMETRY
see Photogrammetry

STEVEDORING
see Cargo Handling

STILL-LIFE PAINTING
Burbidge, R. A Dictionary of British
Flower, Fruit & Still Life Painters:
Vol. 2, 1850-1950. (Illus.). 1974.
text ed. 30.00x (ISBN 0-85317-
024-X, Pub. by A & C Black
England). Humanities.

STOCK (ANIMALS)
see Livestock

STOCK CONTROL
see Inventory Control

STOCK CORPORATIONS
see Corporations

STOCK-EXCHANGE
*Here are entered works on stock
trading and speculation and on stock
exchanges in general.*
see also Speculation

*also names of specific exchanges, e.g.
New York Stock Exchange*
Achterberg, E. & Lanz, K.
Enzyklopadisches Lexikon Fur des
Geld, Bank und Borsen Wesen, 2
vols. (Ger.). 1967. $240.00 set
(ISBN 3-7819-0030-4, M-7364,
Pub. by Fritz Knapp Verlag).
French & Eur.
De Garmendia Miangolarra, J.
Ignacio. Diccionario de bolsa. 3rd
ed. 208p. (Span.). 1982. pap.
620.00 ptas (ISBN 84-368-0057-5).
Piramide.
Dorfman, John R. Stock Market
Dictionary. LC 81-43558. (DI.).
1982. $9.95 (ISBN 0-385-17286-
9). Doubleday.
Flumiana, Carlo M. The New
Expanded Dictionary of Stock
Market Charts. (Illus.). 189p.
1980. deluxe ed. $67.35 (ISBN 0-
918968-64-X). Inst Econ Finan.
Flumiani, C. M. The New Expanded
Dictionary of Stock Market
Charts. new ed. (Illus.). 1977.
$65.25 (ISBN 0-89266-050-3). Am
Classical Coll Pr.
Flumiani, Carlo M. The New
Expanded Dictionary of Stock
Market Charts. (Illus.). 179p.
1983. $81.75 (ISBN 0-86654-091-
1). Inst Econ Finan.
Garmendia Miangolarra, I.
Diccionario de Bolsa. 2nd ed.
208p. (Span.). write for info.
(ISBN 8-43680-057-5, 250020).
Piramide.
Glossary of Stock Exchange, Mining
& Oil Terms. LC 82-126128. 108p.
1981. pap. $6.00 (ISBN 0-
9594011-0-5). Fin Analysis.
Rudman, Jack. Handbook of the
Stock Market (HOS) (Admission
Test Ser.: ATS-2). 300p. (Cloth
bdg. avail. on request). pap. 7.50
(ISBN 0-8373-5005-0). Natl
Learning.
Sarnoff, Paul. Wall Street Theasuris.
1963. $12.95 (ISBN 0-8392-1127-
9). Astor-Honor.

STOCK MARKET
see Stock-Exchange

STOCK RIGHTS
see Stockholders' Pre-Emptive Rights

**STOCKHOLDERS' PRE-
EMPTIVE RIGHTS**
Dictionnaire du Droit des Societes
Anonymes. (Fr.). 1978. write for
info. Joly.

STOMATOLOGY
see Teeth–Diseases

STONE, PHILOSOPHERS'
see Alchemy

STONE-CARVING
see Sculpture

STONEWORK, DECORATIVE
see Sculpture

STONY INDIANS
*see Indians of North America–The
West*

STOVES
see also Heating
Mercier, Jean. Lexique Anglais-
Francais Du Programmateur De
Cuisiniere: Fonctionnement et
Pieces Composantes. 29p. (Eng. &
Fr.). 1973. pap. $1.95 (ISBN 0-
686-57045-6, M-6406). French &
Eur.

STRATEGY
see also Military Art and Science
Schwarz, Urs & Hadik, Laszlo.
Strategic Terminology. 160p.
(Ger., Eng. & Fr.). $12.50 (ISBN
0-686-57217-3, M-6509). French &
Eur.

STRATIGRAPHIC GEOLOGY
see Geology, Stratigraphic

STREAM POLLUTION
see Water–Pollution

STREAMLINING
see Aerodynamics

STREET TRAFFIC
see Traffic Engineering

STREETS
see also Roads
Foort, Jean. Glossaire des Rues de
Dunkerque. (Illus.). 66p. (Fr.).
1976. 40.00 F. Foort.
Periaux. Dictionnaire Indicateur des
Rues & Places. (Illus.). 454p. (Fr.).
1977. write for info. Lafitte Repr.

STRENGTH OF MATERIALS
Dictionary of Strength of Materials.
(Hebrew, Eng., Fr. & Ger.).
IL.7.00. Massada Pr.

STRINGED INSTRUMENTS
*Here is entered material on
instruments employing strings,
whether bowed, hammered or
plucked.*
Woodcock, C. Dictionary of
Contemporary Violin & Bow
Makers. (Illus.). 1965. 40.00
(ISBN 0-685-12006-6). Heinman.

**STRINGED INSTRUMENTS,
BOWED–MAKERS**
see Violin Makers

STRUCTURAL GEOLOGY
see Geology, Structural

STRUCTURAL MATERIALS
see Building Materials

STUDENT GUIDANCE
see Vocational Guidance

STUDENT LIFE AND CUSTOMS
see Students

STUDENTS
see also College Students
*also headings beginning with College
or School, e.g. College, Choice of;
School Sports; Transfer Students*
Buhler, Alain & Didier, J.
Dictionnaire de la revolution
Etudiante. (Fr.). 1968. 4.50 F.
Controverses.

STUDY WORK PLAN
see Education, Cooperative

STYLE (PRACTICAL PRINTING)
see Printing–Style Manuals

STYLE, LEGAL
see Law–Language

STYLE IN DRESS
see Costume; Fashion

**STYLE MANUALS
(AUTHORSHIP)**
*see Authorship–Handbooks, Manuals,
Etc.*

**STYLE MANUALS
(JOURNALISM)**
*see Journalism–Handbooks, Manuals,
Etc.*

STYLE MANUALS (PRINTING)
see Printing–Style Manuals

SUAHELI LANGUAGE
see Swahili Language

SUBJECT DICTIONARIES
see Encyclopedias and Dictionaries

SUBJECT HEADINGS
Bureau de l'Information Scientifique
& Technique. Thesaurus Genie
Chimique. LC 78-374404. vi,
199p. (Fr.). 1977. 350.00 F (ISBN
2-222-02176-6). Doc Scient.
INIS: Thesaurus. (IAEA-INIS Ser.:
No. 13, Rev. 21). 759p. 1982. pap.
$42.50 (ISBN 92-0-178082-6,
IN13/R21, IAEA). Unipub.
Laureilhe, Marie T. Le Thesaurus:
Son Role, sa Structure, son
Elaboration. LC 77-575129.
(Illus.). 48p. (Fr.). 1977. 20.00 F
(ISBN 2-901-11904-2). Assoc
Biblio.
Rosenberg, Paul, ed. The Urban
Information Thesaurus: A
Vocabulary for Social
Documentation. LC 76-52604.
1977. lib. bdg. 35.00x (ISBN 0-
8371-9483-0, UTH). Greenwood.

SUBSONIC AERODYNAMICS
see Aerodynamics

SUBTERRANEAN WATER
see Water, Underground

SUBVERSIVE ACTIVITIES
see also Espionage
Speroni, Miguel Angel. Diccionario
Subversivo. 238p. (Span.). 1974.
write for info. Hachette Jeunesse.

SUCCULENT PLANTS
see also Cactus
Jacobsen, Hermann. The Lexicon of
Succulent Plants. (Illus.). 1974.
$37.50 (ISBN 0-7137-0652-X, Pub
by Blandford Pr England). Sterling.

SUDAN–HISTORY
Voll, John. Historical Dictionary of
the Sudan. LC 77-28798. (African
Historical Dictionaries Ser.: No.
17). 1978. $13.00 (ISBN 0-8108-
1115-4). Scarecrow.

SUFISM
Razzaqi, Abd A. Dictionary of Sufi
Technical Terms. Safwat, Nabil, tr.
(Eng. & Arabic.). 1983. $38.95
(ISBN 0-86304-032-2, Pub. by
Octagon Pr England). Ins Study
Human.

SUMERIAN LANGUAGE
Gostony, Colman D. Dictionnaire
d'Etymologie Sumerienne et
Grammaire Comparee. 204p. (Fr.).
1975. pap. $52.50 (ISBN 0-686-
57306-4, M-6283). French & Eur.

SUPERREALISM
see Surrealism

SUPERSTITION
see also Alchemy; Animal Lore; Dreams; Fortune-Telling; Magic; Occult Sciences
Canavaggio, Pierre. Dictionnaire Raisonne Des Superstitions et Des Croyances Populaires. 247p. (Fr.). 1977. pap. $19.95 (ISBN 0-686-56937-7, M-6059). French & Eur.
SUPERVISORY NURSING
see Nursing Service Administration
SUPREMACY OF LAW
see Rule of Law
SURF
see Ocean Waves
SURFACE ACTIVE AGENTS
Cariere, G., ed. Dictionary of Surface-Active Agents, Cosmetics & Toiletries. (Eng., Fr., Ger., Span., Ital., Dutch & Pol.). 1978. $36.25 (ISBN 0-444-99809-8). Elsevier.
SURFACTANTS
see Surface Active Agents
SURGERY
see also Orthopedia
also subdivisions Surgery and Wounds and Injuries under names of organs and regions of the body, e.g. Abdomen–Surgery; Chest–Wounds and Injuries
Coleman, F. Guide to Surgical Terminology. 3rd ed. 1978. pap. 16.95 (ISBN 0-87489-191-4). Med Economics.
Coleman, Francis. Guide to Surgical Terminology. (Medical Economics Books). 1978. pap. $12.95x (ISBN 0-442-84003-9). Van Nos Reinhold.
Touati, Maurice A. Lexique Francais des Abreviations: Formules Medico-Chirugicales Courantes. 142p. (Fr.). 1969. 24.00 F. Maloine.
SURGERY, DENTAL
see Dentistry
SURNAMES
see Names, Personal
SURREALISM
see also Pop Art
Alexandrian, Sarane. Dictionnaire de la Peinture Surrealiste. 58p. (Fr.). 1973. $32.50 (ISBN 0-686-56823-0, M-6601). French & Eur.
--Dictionnaire de la Peinture Surrealiste. 58p. (Fr.). 1973. 50.00 F (Pub. by Filipacchi). Hippocrene Bks.
Dobbs, Annie C. Dictionnaire Abrege du Surrealisme. (Fr.). pap. $23.95 (ISBN 0-686-57119-3, M-6165). French & Eur.
--Dictionnaire Abrege du Surrealisme. (Fr.). 1978. 55.00 F. Corti.
Passeron, Rene. Lexikon des Surrealismus. (Ger.). 1975. $25.00 (ISBN 3-8046-0012-3, M-7220). French & Eur.
Passeron, Rene, ed. Lexikon des Surrealismus. 288p. (Ger.). 1975. DM.29.50 (ISBN 3-8046-0012-3). Wissenschaftliche.
Pierre, Jose. An Illustrated Dictionary of Surrealism. (Pocket Art Ser.). (Illus.). (gr. 10-12). 1978. pap. $3.95 (ISBN 0-8120-0987-8). Barron.
SURVEYING
see also Cartography; Geodesy; Topographical Drawing
American Congress on Surveying & Mapping. Definitions of Surveying & Associated Terms. rev. ed. 210p. 1978. $12.00 (S180); members $7.00. Am Congrs Survey.
International Federation of Surveyors. Multilingual Dictionary of the International Federation of Surveyors. Date not set. $78.75 (ISBN 0-444-40795-2). Elsevier.
SURVEYORS
Eden, P., ed. Dictionary of Land Surveyors & Local Cartographers of Great Britain & Ireland. 528p. 1981. $14.00x (ISBN 0-7129-0900-1, Pub. by Dawson). State Mutual Bk.
SURVEYS, CADASTRAL
see Real Property
SUTO LANGUAGE
see Sotho Language
SUTU LANGUAGE
see Sotho Language
SWAHILI LANGUAGE
Brain, James L. A Social Science Vocabulary of Swahili. (Foreign & Comparative Studies Program, African Special Publications: No. 3). (Orig., Swahili.). 1968. pap. text ed. $3.50x (ISBN 0-686-74012-2). Syracuse U Foreign Comp.
Farsi, S. Kamusi Vocabulaire. LC 79-105083. 428p. (Fr. & Swahili.). 1978. write for info. Edns St Paul.
Haddon, Ernest B. Learn Swahili for English Speakers. (Swahili & Eng.). 10.50 (ISBN 0-87557-081-X, 080-1). Saphrograph.
Hoftmann, HIldegard, et al. Woerterbuch Swahili-Deutsch. LC 79-384471. 402p. (Ger. & Swahili.). 1979. DM.42.00. VEB Verlag Enzyklopadie.
Johnson, F. Swahili-English Dictionary. (Swahili & Eng.). $19.50 (ISBN 0-685-20193-7, 079-8). Saphrograph.
Johnson, Frederick, ed. Standard Swahili-English Dictionary. (Swahili & Eng.). 1939. 27.50x (ISBN 0-19-864403-5). Oxford U Pr.
Krapf, Ludwig, ed. Dictionary of the Suahili Language. LC 72-77205. (Illus., Swahili & Eng.). Repr. 30.00x (ISBN 0-8371-1276-1, Pub. by Negro U Pr). Greenwood.
Kutuzov, A. I. Kratkii Suakhili-Russkii & Russko-Suakhili Slovar. 442p. (Rus. & Swahili.). 1965. $3.50 (Pub. by Sov Entsiklopediia). Four Continent.
Lodhi, Abdulaziz, et al. Korfattad Svensk-Swahili Ordbok. LC 79-370772. 114p. (Swahili & Swedish.). 1978. write for info. Nord Afrik.
Merlo Pick, Vittorio. Vocabolario italiano-kiswahili. (Ital. & Swahili.). 1978. L.25000.00. EMI.
--Vocabolario kiswahili-italiano. 496p. (Swahili & Ital.). 1978. L.12000.00. EMI.
--Vocabolario swahili-italiano e italiano-swahili. (Swahili & Ital.). L.7000.00. EMI.
Perrot, D. V. Swahili Dictionary. (Teach Yourself Ser.). (Swahili.). 1974. pap. 3.95 (ISBN 0-679-10015-6). McKay.
Rechenbach, Charles W. Swahili-English Dictionary. (Publications in the Languages of Africa Ser.: No. 1). (Swahili & Eng.). 1968. $36.95 (ISBN 0-8132-0406-2). Cath U Pr.
Sacleux, Charles. Dictionnaire Francais-Swahili. 2nd ed. 755p. (Fr. & Swahili.). 1959. 53.00 F. Institut Ethnologie.
--Dictionnaire Swahili-Francais. 2nd ed. 1594p. (Swahili & Fr.). 1960. 86.10 F. Inst Ethnol.
Shaaban, Robert. Adili Na Nduguze. 66p. (Swahili.). write for info. Macmillan London.
SWAZILAND
Grotpeter, John J. Historical Dictionary of Swaziland. LC 75-4734. (African Historical Dictionaries Ser.: No. 3). 265p. 1975. $15.00 (ISBN 0-8108-0805-6). Scarecrow.
SWEDISH LANGUAGE
Berg, Sture. Olika Lika Ord: Svenskt Homograflexikon. LC 79-366660. xxiv, 228p. (Swedish.). 1978. write for info. (ISBN 9-12200-179-4). Almqvist.
Bildwoerterbuch Schwedisch: Bildlexikon. (Illus.). 872p. (Swedish & Ger.). DM.29.80 (ISBN 3-411-00974-8). Biblio Inst.
Boije af Gennas, Fredrik C. Prinsessans ABC Bok. LC 78-392178. (Illus.). 82p. (Swedish.). 1977. write for info. Rediviva.
Bonniers Trebandlexikon, 3 vols. (Swedish.). 1979. $175.00 (ISBN 0-8277-3004-7). Pergamon.
Cannelin, Aulis, et al. Suomalais-Ruotsalainen Suursanakirja. 3rd. ed. LC 77-471720. xv, 1140p. (Finnish & Swedish.). 1976. Fmk.write for info. (ISBN 9-51007-012-2). Werner Soderstrom.
Collinder, Bjorn. Ordhandboken. LC 75-592135. 361p. (Swedish.). 1975. Kr.45.00 (ISBN 9-18535-600-X). Fyris.
Davidson, K., ed. Russko-Shvedskii Slovar. 960p. (Rus.). 1976. $10.95 (C-91, Pub. by Russkii Iazyk). Four Continent.
Egidius, Henry. Uppslagsbok i Psykoterapi och Medicinsk Psykologi. LC 76-488253. 198p. (Swedish.). 1976. Kr.50.00 (ISBN 9-1270-0680-8). Natur & Kultur.
Eriksson, Erick R. & Baeckbom, Roy. Modernt Foertagsekonomiskt Lexikon. LC 78-349746. (Illus.). 350p. (Swedish.). 1977. Kr.94.00 (ISBN 9-15-180888-9). Prisma.
Guner, Musa. Svensk-Turkisk Ordbok. LC 77-571011. 133p. (Swedish & Turkish.). 1977. Kr.47.00 (ISBN 9-1441-4001-0). Studentlitt.
Hammar, Thekla. Svensk-Fransk Ordbok. 1095p. (Fr. & Swedish.). 1979. Kr.155.00. Esselte Studium.
Hamori, Laszlo. Varldspolitiskt lexikon. LC 77-476973. (Illus.). 200p. (Swedish.). 1976. Kr.68.00 (ISBN 9-12700-182-2). Natur & kultur.
Kalquist, Eskil, et al. Ordlistan Fran Natur & Kultur. LC 79-353437. (Illus.). 192p. (Swedish.). 1978. Kr.28.00 (ISBN 9-12750-000-4). Natur & Kultur.
Lampeu, Lea. Ruotsalais-Suomalaines. LC 79-361738. 547p. (Swedish & Finnish., Helsinki, Finland). 1978. write for info. WSOY.
Langenscheidts Universal-Woerterbuch Schwedisch. 560p. (Swedish & Ger.). DM.6.80 (18300). Langenscheidt.
Larsson, Lars G. & Lorveberg, Sven. Karnkraft Fran A til O. LC 80-468740. 136p. (Swedish.). 1979. write for info. (ISBN 9-1728-4108-7). Ingenjorsforlaget.
Lodhi, Abdulaziz, et al. Korfattad Svensk-Swahili Ordbok. LC 79-370772. 114p. (Swahili & Swedish.). 1978. write for info. Nord Afrik.
Milanova, D. Swedish-Russian Dictionary. 760p. (Swedish & Rus.). 1973. $19.95 (ISBN 0-686-92499-1, M-9077). French & Eur.
Odhner, Einer. Svenskt Rimlexikon. 3rd ed. LC 80-491211. 319p. (Swedish.). 1979. write for info. (ISBN 9-13707-206-4). Forum Bok.
Palm, Goran. Konsten Att Veta Bast Fran ABBA til Ovre Slummen. LC 78-384438. (Illus.). 258p. (Swedish.). 1978. write for info. (ISBN 9-11781-112-0). Norstedt Soner.
Sandvei, Marius. Svensk-Norsk Ordbok. LC 80-457703. 174p. (Swedish & Norse.). 1979. Kr.59.00 (ISBN 8-20700-369-3). Fabritius.
Sikorski, Lech. Maly Slownik Polsko-Swedzki. 322p. (Pol. & Swedish.). 1976. 55.00 Zl. Plastik.
--Maly Slownik Szwedzko-Polski. LC 76-525326. xxvi, 300p. (Swedish & Pol.). 1976. write for info. Wiedza Powszechna.
Strmberg, Alva. Stora Synonymordboken. LC 76-474101. 725p. (Swedish.). 1975. Kr.160.00 (ISBN 9-17148-302-0). Strombergs.
Tekniska Nomenklaturcentralen. Byggordsamling. LC 77-464415. 164p. (Eng. & Swedish.). 1976. Kr.57.00 (ISBN 9-1719-6063-5). Tek Nomen.
--Skogsordlista. LC 80-485348. 676p. (Eng. & Swedish.). 1978. write for info. (ISBN 9-1719-6071-6). Tek Nomen.
Valenius, A. P. Kratkii Russko-Shvedskii Slovar. 400p. (Rus.). 1948. $2.50 (Pub. by GINS). Four Continent.
Wieselgren, Per. Svensk-Estnisk Ordbok. LC 77-458507. xxx, 630p. (Swedish & Estonian.). 1976. Kr.170.00. Fyris.
SWEDISH LANGUAGE–DICTIONARIES–ENGLISH
Berlitz Editors. Berlitz Pocket Dictionaries: Swedish-English. 300p. (Eng. & Swedish.). 1982. pap. $4.95 (ISBN 0-686-92996-9, Berlitz). Macmillan.
--Swedish-English, English-Swedish Pocket Dictionary. LC 74-1987. (Swedish & Eng.). 1974. pap. 2.95 (ISBN 0-02-964410-0, Berlitz). Macmillan.
Christensen, Sven. Engelskt-Svenskt Flyglexikon. 89p. (Eng. & Swedish.). write for info. (ISBN 91-24-13861-4). Esselte Studium.
Danielsson, B. Modern English-Swedish Dictionary. 394p. (Eng. & Swedish.). 1980. $19.95 (ISBN 91-518-1296-7, M-9451). French & Eur.
Danielsson, Bror. Engelsk-Svensk Ordbok (Prisma Modern) 5th ed. 396p. 1980. text ed. $17.50x (ISBN 91-518-0550-2, SW205); Svensk-engelsk, 4th Ed. 1982. text ed. $20.00x (ISBN 9-1518-1297-5, SW-204). Vanous.
Engelsk-Svensk Ordbok. 775p. (Eng. & Swedish.). 1983. write for info. (ISBN 91-24-32208-3). Esselte Studium.
Engelska Ordboksguiden. 30p. (Swedish & Eng.). 1978. Kr.22.00 (ISBN 91-24-27682-0). Esselte Studium.
English-Swedish-English Dictionary. 275p. (Eng. & Swedish.). 1981. pap. $9.95 (ISBN 91-518-1438-2, M-9449). French & Eur.
Engstroem, E. Swedish-English, English-Swedish Technical Dictionary, 2 vols. rev. enl ed. (Swedish & Eng.). Set. 115.00 (ISBN 0-685-42614-9). Heinman.
Gomer, E. Swedish Modern Pocket Dictionary: Svensk-Engelsk, Engelsk-Svensk Grammatik Parlor. (Swedish & Eng.). 1981. text ed. $11.00x (ISBN 91-518-1148-0, SW-208). Vanous.
Gullberg, Ingvar E. Swedish-English Fact Ordbok (Technical Terms) 2nd ed. (Swedish & Eng.). 1977. $200.00x (ISBN 91-1-775052-0, SW-207). Vanous.
Hills, A. Swedish-English-Swedish Pocket Dictionary. (Swedish & Eng.). 1978. $7.50x (ISBN 0-89918-134-1, SW134). Vanous.
Hill's English-Swedish, Swedish-English Pocket Dictionary. 244p. (Eng. & Swedish.). 1981. $15.00x (ISBN 0-561-00191-X, Pub. by Bailey & Swinfen South Africa). State Mutual Bk.
Karre, K. Swedish Karre Dictionary, Vol. 1: Svensk-Engelsk. (Swedish & Eng.). 1976. $50.00x (ISBN 91-24-14308-1, SW132). Vanous.
--Swedish Karre Dictionary, Vol. 2: Engelsk-Svensk. 3rd ed. (Swedish & Eng.). 1981. text ed. $60.00x (ISBN 91-24-29824-7, SW133). Vanous.
Noejd, Rubin. Engelsk-Svensk Ordbok. 248p. (Eng. & Swedish.). write for info. (ISBN 91-24-19951-6). Esselte Studium.
Pretorius, Stanley H. Svensk-Engelsk Affarsordlists. 128p. (Swedish & Eng.). write for info. (ISBN 91-24-15066-5). Esselte Studium.
Prisma-Lagersson, R. Swedish-English Modern Dictionary, Vol. 1. 4th ed. (Swedish & Eng.). 1982. $20.00x (ISBN 91-518-1297-5, SW204). Vanous.
Prisma-Lagersson, Rolf. Svensk-Engelsk Modern Ordbok. 4th ed. (Swedish & Eng.). 1982. $20.00x (ISBN 91-518-1297-5, SW-204). Vanous.
Ruben & Angstrom, M. Swedish-English Dictionary. (Swedish & Eng.). $16.00 (ISBN 0-87557-082-8, 082-8). Saphrograph.
Santesson, R. & Kaerre, Karl K. Swedish-English, English-Swedish Dictionary, 2 vols. (Swedish & Eng.). Set. 120.00 (ISBN 0-686-77012-9). Vol. 1 (ISBN 9-1242-9824-7). Vol. 2 (ISBN 9-1241-4308-1). Heinman.
Stora Engelsk-Svenska Ordboken: A Comprehensive English-Swedish Dictionary. 1071p. (Eng. & Swedish.). 1981. Kr.280.00 (ISBN 91-24-29824-7). Esselte Studium.
Svensk-Engelsk Ordbok. 979p. (Swedish-Eng.). Kr.170.00 (ISBN 91-24-14308-1). Esselte Studium.
Svensk-Engelsk Pocketordbok. 480p. (Swedish & Eng.). 1980. Kr.71.00 (ISBN 91-24-20291-6). Esselte Studium.

Swedish Pocket Dictionary. (Swedish & Eng.). 7.50 (ISBN 8-4399-8784-6). Heinman.

Tornberg, et al. Svensk-Engelsk & Engelsk-Svensk Ordbok. 468p. (Eng. & Swedish.). write for info. Esselte Studium.

Tornberg, Astrid, et al. McKay's Modern Swedish-English & English-Swedish Dictionary. (Modern Dictionaries Ser.). (Swedish & Eng.). 1954. 9.95 (ISBN 0-679-10079-2). McKay.

SWEDISH LANGUAGE–DICTIONARIES–FINNISH

Cannelin, Knut, et al. Finsk-Swensk Storordbok. 1140p. (Swedish & Finnish.). 1976. Kr.360.00 (ISBN 91-24-26676-0). Esselte Studium.

Lampen, Av Lea. Finsk-Svensk & Svensk-Finsk Fickordbok. 564p. (Swedish & Finnish.). write for info. Esselte Studium.

Lampen, L. Finnish-Swedish Dictionary. 571p. (Finnish & Swedish.). 1980. leatherette $24.95 (ISBN 951-0-08620-7, M-9655). French & Eur.

--Finnish-Swedish-Finnish Dictionary (Suomi-Ruotsi-Suomi) 623p. (Finnish & Swedish.). 1980. pap. $15.95 (ISBN 951-0-07771-2, M-09647). French & Eur.

--Swedish-Finnish Dictionary. 548p. (Swedish & Finnish.). 1980. Leatherette $24.95 (ISBN 951-0-08621-5, M-9656). French & Eur.

Lampen, Lea. Finsk-Svensk Skolordbok. 570p. (Finnish & Swedish.). write for info. (ISBN 91-24-27856-4). Esselte Studium.

--Svensk-Finsk Storordbok. 856p. (Swedish & Finnish.). 1977. Kr.300.00. Esselte Studium.

Linnapuomi, Kalervo. Ruotsin Kielen Perus ja Taydennyssanasto. LC 80-465197. 349p. (Finnish & Swedish.). 1979. write for info. (ISBN 9-5110-5181-4). Otava.

SWEDISH LANGUAGE–DICTIONARIES–FRENCH

French-Swedish-French Dictionary. 370p. (Fr. & Swedish.). 1980. pap. $9.95 (ISBN 0-686-97383-6, M-9445). French & Eur.

Maupoix, Edy. Svensk-Fransk Affaersordlista. 144p. (Swedish & Fr.). write for info. Esselte Studium.

Noid, Ruben. Svensk-Fransk & Fransk-Svensk Ordbok. 450p. (Swedish & Fr.). write for info. Esselte Studium.

Nojd, Ruben. Fransk-Svensk Ordbok. 181p. (Fr. & Swedish.). write for info. (ISBN 91-24-20278-9). Esselte Studium.

Svensk-Fransk Ordbok. 269p. (Swedish & Fr.). write for info. (ISBN 91-24-19396-8). Esselte Studium.

Vising, Johan. Fransk-Svensk Ordbok. 779p. (Fr. & Swedish.). 1979. Kr.155.00 (ISBN 91-24-20108-1). Esselte Studium.

SWEDISH LANGUAGE–DICTIONARIES–GERMAN

Birgersson, Helge. Svensk-Tysk Affarsordlista. 128p. (Swedish & Ger.). write for info. (ISBN 91-24-15571-3). Esselte Studium.

Svensk-Tysk & Tysk-Svensk Standardlexikon. 744p. (Ger. & Swedish.). write for info. Esselte Studium.

Svensk-Tysk Ordbok. 783p. (Swedish & Ger.). 1980. Kr.170.00 (ISBN 91-24-27622-7). Esselte Studium.

Svensk-Tysk Ordbok: Supplement 78. 32p. (Swedish & Ger.). 1978. Kr.42.00 (ISBN 91-24-27683-9). Esselte Studium.

Svensk-Tysk Standardlexikon. 351p. (Ger. & Swedish.). write for info. (ISBN 91-24-14301-4). Esselte Studium.

Svensk-Tyskt-Tyskt-Svensk Standardlexikon. 744p. (Swedish & Ger.). write for info. (ISBN 91-24-14305-7). Esselte Studium.

Svenska Duden Bildlexikon. (Illus.). 869p. (Swedish & Ger.). $31.00. Imported Bks.

Tysk-Svensk Ordbok. 894p. (Ger. & Swedish.). 1980. Kr.170.00 (ISBN 91-24-14305-7). Esselte Studium.

Tysk-Svensk Ordbok: Supplement 80. 32p. (Ger. & Swedish.). 1980. Kr.42.00 (ISBN 91-24-29770-4). Esselte Studium.

SWEDISH LANGUAGE–DICTIONARIES–ITALIAN

Italiensk-Svensk Ordbok. 586p. (Ital. & Swedish.). 1981. Kr.135.00 (ISBN 91-24-20219-3). Esselte Studium.

Tomba, Silvia. Svensk-Italiensk Ordbok. 430p. (Swedish & Ital.). 1980. Kr.90.00 (ISBN 91-24-14338-3). Esselte Studium.

SWEDISH LANGUAGE–DICTIONARIES–SPANISH

Akerlung, Alfred. Svensk-Spansk Ordbok. Casa Novas, M. J. & Gronbarj, M., eds. 389p. (Swedish & Span.). 1979. Kr.75.00 (ISBN 91-24-14379-0). Esselte Studium.

Peralta & Cederholm. Svensk-Spansk Affaersordlista. 164p. (Swedish & Span.). write for info. Esselte Studium.

Spansk-Svensk Ordbok. 329p. (Span. & Swedish.). 1980. Kr.84.00 (ISBN 91-24-21080-3). Esselte Studium.

SWEDISH LANGUAGE–GLOSSARIES, VOCABULARIES, ETC.

Ahlberg, Axel W., et al. Latinsk-Svensk Ordbok. 430p. (Lat. & Swedish.). 1968. Kr.200.00 (ISBN 91-24-62108-0). Esselte Studium.

Allen, Sture. Svenska Ordlista. 264p. (Swedish.). write for info. (ISBN 91-24-27572-7); pap. write for info. (ISBN 91-24-27571-9). Esselte Studium.

--Vara Viktiga Ord: Basordlista Med Utbytesord. LC 78-398662. (Illus.). 237p. (Swedish.). 1977. Kr.41.00 (ISBN 9-12426-834-8). Esselte Studium.

Allen, Sture, et al. Svensk Baklaengesordbok. 483p. (Swedish.). 1981. Kr.155.00 (ISBN 91-24-30634-7). Esselte Studium.

Beckman, Nat. Norsk-Svensk Ordbok. Maehle, Lief & Sigurd, Bengt, eds. 210p. (Norwegian & Swedish.). 1978. Kr.71.00 (ISBN 91-24-14535-1). Esselte Studium.

Beckman, Natanael. Norsk-Svensk Ordbok. Maehle, Lief & Sigurd, Bengt, eds. 210p. (Swedish & Norwegian.). write for info. (ISBN 91-24-14535-1). Esselte Studium.

Bra Bockers Lexikon, 25 vols. (Swedish.). 1973-1981. $1250.00 (ISBN 0-8277-3063-2). Pergamon.

Ekbo, Sven & Loman, Bengt. Vaegledning till Svenska Akademiens Ordbok. 124p. (Swedish.). 1971. Kr.22.00 (ISBN 91-24-21113-3). Esselte Studium.

Gibson, Haldo. Svensk Slangordbok. 243p. (Swedish.). 1980. Kr.88.00 (ISBN 91-24-30634-7). Esselte Studium.

Hitta Ratt & Stora Ordlistan. (Swedish.). write for info. (ISBN 91-24-30630-4). Esselte Studium.

Johannisson, Ture & Ljunggren, K. G., eds. Svensk Handordbok: Kronstruktioner & Fraseologi. 891p. (Swedish.). 1980. Kr.145.00 (ISBN 91-24-14309-X). Esselte Studium.

Kornitzky, H. Langenscheidts Taschenwoerterbuecher Schwedisch. (Swedish.). 1978. DM.23.80 (ISBN 3-468-11300-5). Langenscheidt.

Molde, Bertil. Dansk-Svensk Ordbok. Ferlov, Niels, ed. 726p. (Danish & Swedish.). 1980. Kr.170.00 (ISBN 91-24-29601-5). Esselte Studium.

Mystakidis, Antonis. Nygrekisk-Svensk Ordbok. Frangos, Eftychia, ed. 234p. (Gr. & Swedish.). 1980. Kr.115.00 (ISBN 91-24-20176-6). Esselte Studium.

Simoneau, Francois N. Vocabulaire Suedois. 80p. (Swedish.). 13.30 F. Ophrys.

Skolordlista. 353p. (Swedish.). 1980. write for info. (ISBN 91-24-30599-5). Esselte Studium.

Svenska Akademiens Ordlista Oever Svenska Spraket. 616p. (Swedish.). 1981. Kr.105.00 (ISBN 91-24-23222-X). Esselte Studium.

Valmin, Natan & Frangos, Eftychia. Svensk-Nygrekisk Ordbok. 279p. (Swedish & Gr.). 1980. Kr.115.00 (ISBN 91-24-20265-7). Esselte Studium.

Vogt, J. & Eikeland, I. Swedish-Norwegian Dictionary. (Swedish-Norwegian.). 1982. write for info. (ISBN 82-573-0120-5). Kunnskapsforlaget.

Wessen, Elias. Vara Ord: Kortfattad Etymologisk Ordbok. 530p. (Swedish.). write for info. (ISBN 91-24-19975-3). Esselte Studium.

Widman, Karen. Dansk-Svensk Ordbok. 309p. (Danish & Swedish.). write for info. (ISBN 91-24-14367-7). Esselte Studium.

SWELL
see Ocean Waves

SWIFT, JONATHAN, 1667-1745
Shinagel, Michael, ed. A Concordance to the Poems of Jonathan Swift. LC 72-4870. (Concordances Ser.). 1008p. 1973. $55.00x (ISBN 0-8014-0747-8). Cornell U Pr.

SWIMMING
see also Diving
Gleasner, Diana C. Illustrated Swimming, Diving & Surfing Dictionary for Young People. LC 79-93358. (Illustrated Dictionary Ser.). (Illus.). 128p. (gr. 4 up). 1980. PLB 7.29 (ISBN 0-8178-0001-8). Harvey.

SWITCHES, ELECTRIC
see Electric Relays

SWITZERLAND–ECONOMIC CONDITIONS
Lexique de l'economie Suisse. (Fr.). 1965. 100.00 F. Baconniere.

SYLVICULTURE
see Forests and Forestry

SYMBOLIC AND MATHEMATICAL LOGIC
see Logic, Symbolic and Mathematical

SYMBOLIC LANGUAGE
see ALGOL (Computer Program Language)

SYMBOLISM
see also Christian Art and Symbolism; Cryptography; Devices; Figures of Speech; Heraldry; Idols and Images; Jewish Art and Symbolism; Signs and Symbols also references under Religion, Primitive
Cairo, G. Dizionario ragionato dei simboli. (Illus.). xvi, 366p. (Ital.). L.18000.00. Forni.

Cirlot, J. Diccionario de Simbolos. (Span.). pap. $32.95 (ISBN 84-335-7016-1, S-12244). French & Eur.

--Diccionario de simbolos. 2nd ed. LC 79-340125. (Illus.). 473p. (Span.). 1978. write for info. (ISBN 8-43357-016-1). Labor SA.

De Vries, A. Dictionary of Symbols & Imagery. 2nd. rev. ed. 1976. $66.00 (ISBN 0-444-10607-3, North-Holland). Elsevier.

Lurker, Manfred, ed. Woerterbuch der Symbolik. LC 80-464096. xvi, 686p. (Ger.). 1979. write for info. (ISBN 3-520-46401-2). Kroener.

Perez Rioja, Jose A. Diccionario de Simbolos y Mitos: Las Ciencias y las Artes en Su Expresion Figurada. 2nd ed. 434p. (Span.). 1971. $15.50 (ISBN 84-309-0310-0, S-12344). French & Eur.

SYMBOLISM IN LITERATURE
Bell, Robert E. Dictionary of Classical Mythology: Symbols, Attributes, & Associations. LC 81-19141. 390p. 1982. text ed. $26.50 (ISBN 0-87436-305-5); pap. $19.95 (ISBN 0-87436-023-4). ABC Clio.

SYMBOLS
see Signs and Symbols

SYMBOLS (IN SCIENCE TECHNOLOGY, ETC.)
see Technology–Abbreviations; see subdivision Notation under names of sciences, e.g. Chemistry–Notation

SYMPTOMATOLOGY
see also Diagnosis
Dictionnaire Medical Illustre De Semiologie Patronymique. (Fr.). 1979. $35.00 (ISBN 0-686-57113-4, M-6149). French & Eur.

SYMPTOMS
see Diagnosis; Symptomatology

SYNDROMES
Kerdel-Vegas, F. & Adamicska, O. Diccionario de sindromes. 466p. (Span.). write for info. Cientifico Med.

Magalini, Sergio I. & Scrascia, Euclide. Dictionary of Medical Syndromes. 2nd ed. 896p. 1981. text ed. 52.00 (ISBN 0-397-50503-5, Lippincott Medical). Lippincott.

SYNODS
see Councils and Synods

SYNTHESIZER MUSIC
see Electronic Music

SYNTHETIC PERFUMES
see Perfumes

SYRIAC LANGUAGE
see also Aramaic Language
Goshen-Gottstein, Moshe H. A Syriac-English Glossary: With Etymological Notes, Based on Brockelmann's Syriac Chrestomathy. LC 70-559416. 105p. (Syrian & Eng.). 1970. 20.00x (ISBN 3-447-00345-6). Intl Pubns Serv.

Smith, R. Payne. Compendious Syriac Dictionary Founded Upon the Thesaurus Syriacus of R. Payne Smith. Payne Smith, J., ed. (Syriac.). 1903. 85.00x (ISBN 0-19-864307-1). Oxford U Pr.

Stowasser, Karl & Ani, Moukhtar, eds. A Dictionary of Syrian Arabic: English-Arabic. (Richard Slade Harrell Arabic Ser.). 202p. (Eng. & Arabic.). 1964. pap. $9.95 (ISBN 0-87840-010-9). Georgetown U Pr.

SYSTEM ANALYSIS
see also Control Theory
Sezepesi, G & Szekely, B. Systems Analysis & Operations Research Dictionary. 154p. (Hungarian, Eng., Fr., Ger., & Rus.). 1980. $30.00x (ISBN 0-569-08617-5, Pub. by Collets). State Mutual Bk.

SYSTEM INTERCONNECTION, ELECTRIC POWER
see Electric Utilities

SYSTEM THEORY
see System Analysis

SYSTEMATIC BOTANY
see Botany–Classification

SYSTEMATIC THEOLOGY
see Theology, Doctrinal

SYSTEMS, THEORY OF
see System Analysis

SYSTEMS ANALYSIS
see System Analysis

T

TAAL
see Afrikaans Language

TABLES, MATHEMATICAL
see Factor Tables

TABLEWARE
see Cutlery

TABLEWARE, SILVER
see Silverware

TACHYGRAPHY
see Shorthand

TAE KWON DO
see Karate

TAGALOG LANGUAGE
Enriquez & Guzman. English-Tagalog, Tagalog-English Pocket Dictionary. (Eng. & Tagalog.). $3.50x (ISBN 0-686-00861-8). Colton Bk.

Krus, M. Tagal'sko-Russkii Slovar. 387p. (Rus. & Tagalog.). 1959. $1.95 (Pub. by GINS). Four Continent.

Krus, M., et al. Russko-Tagal'skii Slovar. 760p. (Rus. & Tagalog.). 1965. $4.95 (Pub. by Sov. Entsiklopediia). Four Continent.

--Tagal sko Russkii Slovar. 387p. (Rus. & Tagalog.). 1959. $1.95. Four Continent.

Ramos, Teresita V. Tagalog Dictionary. LC 71-152471. (PALI Language Texts: Philippines). 373p. (Orig., Tagalog.). 1971. pap. text ed. $8.50x (ISBN 0-87022-676-2). UH Pr.

Serrano Laktaw, Pedro, ed. Diccionario hispano-tagalog y tagalog-hispano, 3 vols. 2024p. (Span. & Tagalog.). 1000.00 ptas. Cultura Hispan.

TAHITIAN LANGUAGE
Andrews, Edmund & Andrews, Irene D. A Comparative Dictionary of the Tahitian Language: Tahitian-English with an English-Tahitian Finding List. LC 75-35171. (Eng. & Tahitian.). Repr. of 1944 ed. $23.00 (ISBN 0-404-14201-X). AMS Pr.

Clairmont, Leonard. Tahitian-English, English Tahitian Dictionary. (Tahitian & Eng.). $17.50 (ISBN 0-87559-053-5). Shalom.

Davies, John. A Tahitian & English Dictionary. LC 75-35188. (Eng. & Tahitian.). Repr. of 1851 ed. $31.50 (ISBN 0-404-14217-6). AMS Pr.

Lemaitre, Yves. Lexique du Tahitien Contemporain: Tahitien-Francais. 201p. (Tahitian & Fr.). 1973. 27.00 F. Orstom.

Mai-Aru & Anisson du Perron, J. Dictionnaire Francais-Tahitien et Tahitien-Francais. 380p. (Fr. & Tahitian.). 1973. $17.50 (ISBN 0-686-57025-1, M-6383). French & Eur.

Mai-Aru, Mai-Arii & Anisson du Perron, J. Dictionnaire Francais-Tahitien. 380p. (Fr. & Tahitian.). 1973. 40.00 F. Pensee Moderne.

TAHLTAN INDIANS
see Indians of North America–Northwest, Pacific

TAI LANGUAGES
see also Lao Language; Siamese Language

Morev, L. N. Taisko-Ruskii Slovar. 985p. (Rus. & Tai.). 1964. $6.50 (Pub. by Sov. Entsiklopediia). Four Continent.

Osipov, M. I. Kratkii Taisko-Russkii Slovar. 332p. (Rus.). 1964. $2.50 (Pub. by LGU). Four Continent.

TAMIL LANGUAGE
see also Malayalam Language

Andronov, M. S. Russko-Tamil'Skii Slovar. 1175p. (Rus. & Tamil.). 1965. $7.95 (Pub. by Sov. Entsiklopediia). Four Continent.

Arunabharathi, N. Glossary of Linguistics. LC 77-900957. xi, 82p. (Eng. & Tamil.). 1976. Rs.6.00. Tamil Nuulagam.

Dhamotharau, A. Tamil dictionaries. LC 80-471418. 185p. (Tamil.). 1978. pap. write for info. (ISBN 3-515-03005-0). Steiner Verlag.

Winslow, M. Tamil-English, English-Tamil Dictionary, Vol. 1-2. 3rd, rev. ed. (Eng. & Tamil.). Date not set. Set. text ed. $100.00 (ISBN 0-686-46542-3). Heinman.

TANK GAS
see Liquefied Petroleum Gas

TANKS

Truck Trailer Manufacturers Association. Nomenclature & Terminology of Tank Trailers & Containers. (Recommended Practices: RP No. 36-75). 1975. $3.00. Truck Trailer Mfrs.

TANZANIA–HISTORY

Kurtz, Laura S. Historical Dictionary of Tanzania. LC 77-25962. (African Historical Dictionaries Ser.: No. 15). 1978. $19.50 (ISBN 0-8108-1101-4). Scarecrow.

TAOS INDIANS
see Indians of North America–Southwest, New

TAPE-RECORDER MUSIC
see Electronic Music

TARIFF
see also Balance of Trade
also names of special tariffs

Settimj, L. Dizionario merceologico per la pratica applicazione della nuova tariffa doganale italiana. xii, 496p. (Ital.). 1951. L.1250.00 (ISBN 88-203-0226-8). Hoepli.

TARIFF–LAW

Updated Concordance for the Tariff Schedule of the United States (TSUS) with the Brussels Tariff Nomenclature (BTN) (Eng. & Span.). 1977. pap. text ed. $10.00 (ISBN 0-8270-3320-6). OAS.

TARIFF ON RAW MATERIALS
see Tariff

TARIFF SCHEDULES
see Tariff–Law

TAROT

Butler, Bill. Dictionary of the Tarot. LC 74-9230. (Illus.). 1977. $7.95 (ISBN 0-8052-3557-4); pap. $6.50 (ISBN 0-8052-0559-4). Schocken.

TASTE (ESTHETICS)
see Esthetics

TAX ASSESSMENT
see Assessment

TAX LAW
see Taxation–Law

TAXATION
see also Assessment; Tariff
also subdivision Taxation under specific subjects, e.g. Corporations–Taxation; Land–Taxation

Hart, Gerry V. A Dictionary of Tax Definitions. LC 77-363222. iv, 135p. E4.75 (ISBN 0-905753-00-3). Marchmont Pub.

Hart, Gerry V., ed. Dictionary of Taxation. Epap. 10.00. Butterworth.

Ivamy, ed. Dictionary of Taxation. Epap. 4.95. Butterworth.

Wacker, Wilhelm H., ed. Steuerlexikon. LC 75-514753. xii, 486p. (Ger.). 1975. DM.45.80 (ISBN 3-800-60472-8). Vahlen.

TAXATION–LAW

Lexikon des Steuer & Wirtschaftsrechts. (Ger., Munich, Germany). 1973. DM.29.80 (ISBN 3-8092-0000-X). WRS Verlag.

Roessler, Rudolf, et al. Woerterbuch des Steuerrechts. (Ger.). 1973. write for info. (ISBN 3-448-00204-6). Haufe.

TAXATION–FRANCE

Rassat, Patrick & Le Bars, Alain, eds. La Fiscalite. LC 75-510630. (Illus.). 508p. (Fr.). 1975. 56.50 F (ISBN 2-010-01083-3). Hachette L.

TAXATION, INCIDENCE OF
see Taxation

TAXES
see Taxation

TAXONOMY
see Botany–Classification

TEACHER-PARENT RELATIONSHIPS
see Parent-Teacher Relationships

TEACHERS
see also College Teachers; Teaching

Harrison, Francis. English & Low-Dutch Schoolmaster. LC 72-1876. (Eng. & Dutch.). Repr. of 1730 ed. $12.00 (ISBN 0-404-03137-4). AMS Pr.

TEACHERS AND PARENTS
see Parent-Teacher Relationships

TEACHERS COLLEGES

Columbia University. Dictionary Catalog of the Teachers College Library, First Supplement, 5 vols. 1971. Set. lib. bdg. $525.00 (ISBN 0-8161-0958-3, Hall Library). G K Hall.

TEACHING
see also Education; Educational Psychology; School Management and Organization
also subdivision Instruction and Study or Study and Teaching under various subjects, e.g. Music–Instruction and Study; Science–Study and Teaching

Diccionario Didactikon. 392p. (Span.). Mex.$7.50. Fernandez.

Koeck, Peter & Ott, Hans. Woerterbuch fuer Erziehung & Unterricht. 2nd ed. 656p. (Ger.). 1979. DM.44.80. Auer.

Zoepfl, Herbert. Kleines Lexikon der Paedagogik und Didatik. 7th ed. (Ger.). 1976. $22.95 (ISBN 3-403-00472-4, M-7502, Pub. by Auer). French & Eur.

--Kleines Lexikon der Paedagogik und Didatik. 7th ed. (Ger.). 1976. $22.95 (ISBN 3-403-00472-4). Auer.

TEACHING–AIDS AND DEVICES
see also Handicraft

Dictionary Studies Duplicating Masters, 4 vols. (Spice Duplicating Masters Ser). 1974. Vol. 1, Grades K-2, Single Letters. $5.95 (ISBN 0-89273-527-9); Vol. 2, Grades K-2, Letter Combinations. $5.95 (ISBN 0-89273-528-7); Vol. 3, Grades 3-6. $5.95 (ISBN 0-89273-529-5); Vol. 4, Grades 7-9. $5.95 (ISBN 0-89273-530-9). Educ Serv.

TEACHING MATERIALS
see Teaching–Aids and Devices

TECHNICAL CHEMISTRY
see Chemistry, Technical

TECHNICAL DICTIONARIES
see Technology–Dictionaries

TECHNICAL DRAWING
see Mechanical Drawing

TECHNICAL EDUCATION
see also Agricultural Education; Vocational Education

Garcia, Hoz, tr. Diccionario de pedagogia Labor. (Span.). 970.00 ptas. Labor SA.

Glosario de Tecnologia Educativa. 84p. (Span.). 1980. $3.00 (ISBN 0-8270-1060-5). Organize Am States.

Terminology of Technical & Vocational Education. 1979. pap. $5.00 (ISBN 92-3-001593-8, U884, UNESCO). Unipub.

TECHNICAL FRENCH
see French Language–Technical French

TECHNICAL INSTITUTES
see Technical Education

TECHNICAL RUSSIAN
see Russian Language–Technical Russian

TECHNICAL SCHOOLS
see Technical Education

TECHNICAL TERMS
see Technology–Dictionaries; Technology–Terminology

TECHNICAL VOCABULARY
see Technology–Language

TECHNOLOGY
see also Building; Chemistry, Technical; Electric Engineering; Engineering; Factories; Industrial Management; Inventions; Mineral Industries; Railroad Engineering; Technical Education
also names of specific industries, arts trades, etc., e.g. Clock and Watch Making, Printing, Tailoring

Abkeurzungen & Kurzwoerter aus Technik & Naturwissenschaften: E-D. 859p. (Ger. & Eng.). DM.50.00. Brandstetter.

Abkurzungen & Kurzwoerter aus Technik & Naturwissenschaften. 859p. (Ger.). 1982. DM.50.00. Brandstetter.

Ancelin-Schutzenberger, Anne. Vocabulaire des Techniques de Groupe. 194p. (Fr.). 1971. 25.00 F. Epi.

Brockhaus der Naturwissenschaften & der Technik. 832p. (Ger.). DM.45.00 (ISBN 3-7653-0019-5). F A Brockhaus.

Delorme, Jean. Vocabulaire Technique Bilingue. 2nd ed. 32p. (Fr.). 1954. 0.40 F. Quebec Off.

Ergo, A. B., et al. Thesaurus des Symboles Agrobioclimatiques, Geographiques & Techniques, 4. 531p. (Fr.). 1974. 535.00 F. Centre Informatique Develop.

Glossaire des Termes d'usage Courant en Commande Numerique. 28p. (Fr.). 16.00 F. Ste. Publications Mecaniques.

Henry, J. M. & Ergo, A. B. Thesaurus des Symboles Agrobioclimatiques, Geographiques & Techniques, 3. 270p. (Fr.). 1973. 450.00 F. Centre Informatique Develop.

Lagrenade, Marcel. Vocabulaire Technique. 5th ed. LC 80-463753. viii, 584p. (Eng. & Fr.). 1978. write for info. (ISBN 0-88905-004-X). Dotmar.

Petit, J. L., et al. Thesaurus des Symboles Agrobioclimatiques, Geographiques & Techniques, 2 vols. (Illus.). 686p. (Fr.). 1971. 2240.00 F. Centre Informatique Develop.

Policy Instruments to Define the Pattern of Demand for Technology. (Science & Technology for Development Ser.: STPI Module 7). 88p. 1981. pap. $5.00 (ISBN 0-88936-265-3, IDRC TS-27, IDRC). Unipub.

Radde, Karl H. Woerterbuch der Technik. LC 77-464498. 716p. (Span. & Ger.). 1977. DM.108.00 (ISBN 3-7736-5530-4). Girardet.

Shemakin, Iu. I., ed. Tezaurus Nauchno-Tekhnicheskikh Terminov. 671p. (Rus.). 1972. $15.00 (Pub. by Voenizdat). Four Continent.

Uhlig, Siegfried. Einfuhrung in das Technische Russisch Maschinenbau: Lehrmaterial fuer den Fremdsprachenunterricht. 382p. (Ger. & Rus.). 1976. M.7.00. VEB Technik.

TECHNOLOGY–ABBREVIATIONS

Azzaretti, Michel. Dictionnaire International D'abreviations Scientigiques & Techniques. LC 79-345548. iv, 290p. (Eng. & Fr.). 1978. 120.00 F (ISBN 2-85608-003-0). Maison Dictionnaire.

Pugh, Eric, compiled by. Pugh's Dictionary of Acronyms & Abbreviations. LC 81-14029. 348p. 1982. $87.50x (ISBN 0-89774-012-2). Oryx Pr.

Screening Symbols, Terminology & Equations. 1974. $4.00 (003-4); members $2.67. TAPPI.

Zalucki, H. Dictionary of Russian Technical & Scientific Abbreviations. (Rus. & Ger.). 1968. $70.25 (ISBN 0-444-40657-3). Elsevier.

TECHNOLOGY–DICTIONARIES
see also Technology–Terminology; also names of specific industries, with or without the subdivision Dictionaries

Abbreviated Russian-Persian Technical Dictionary. 477p. (Rus. & Persian.). 1974. $13.50 (ISBN 0-686-97386-0, M-9053). French & Eur.

Alford, M. H. & Alford, V. L., eds. Russian-English, English-Russian Scientific & Technical Dictionary, 2 vols. 1405p. (Rus. & Eng.). 1970. $32.00; E12.80. Pergamon.

Altman, M. Dicionario Tecnico Contabil: Portugues-Ingles, Ingles-Portugues. 126p. (Port. & Eng.). 1980. pap. $14.95 (ISBN 0-686-97637-1, M-9355). French & Eur.

Alzugaray, J. J. Voces Extranjeras en el Lengua Technologico. (Span. & Eng.). 1980. pap. $9.95 (ISBN 0-686-92477-0, S-33100). French & Eur.

Angelo, Joseph. The Dictionary of Space Technology. 384p. 1982. $70.00x (ISBN 0-584-95011-X, Pub. by Muller Ltd). State Mutual Bk.

Ansteinsson, J. Norwegian Technical Dictionary: English-Norwegian, Vol. 1. 4th ed. (Norwegian & Eng.). 1979. $42.00x (ISBN 8-2702-8007-0, N433). Vanous.

Ansteinsson, J. & Andreassen, A. T. Norwegian-English, English-Norwegian Technical Dictionary, 2 Vols. (Norwegian & Eng.). Set. 60.00 (ISBN 8-2702-8007-0). Heinman.

Ansteinsson, J., ed. Norwegian Technical Dictionary: Norwegian-English, Vol. 2. rev. 4th ed. (Norwegian & Eng.). 1980. $38.00x (ISBN 8-2702-8006-2, N432). Vanous.

Applied Technical Dictionary: Acoustics. $50.00x (ISBN 0-569-08535-7, Pub. by Collets). State Mutual Bk.

Applied Technical Dictionary: Air Conditioning & Refrigeration. (Eng. , Ger. , Fr. , Rus. & Slovak.). $69.00x (ISBN 0-569-08534-9, Pub. by Collets). State Mutual Bk.

Applied Technical Dictionary: Oil Processing & Petrochemistry. (Eng. , Ger. , Fr. , Rus. & Slovak.). 1981. $50.00x (ISBN 0-569-08533-0, Pub. by Collets). State Mutual Bk.

Applied Technical Dictionary: Silicate Technology. (Eng. , Ger. , Fr. & Slovak.). $50.00x (ISBN 0-569-08557-8, Pub. by Collets). State Mutual Bk.

Bajic, B., et al. Technical-Economical Dictionary for Business Purposes. 1700p. (Eng., Fr., Ger. & Serbocroation.). 1973. $95.00 (ISBN 0-686-92638-2, M-9689). French & Eur.

Belle-Isle, Gerald J. Dictionnaire Technique General: Anglais-Francais. 2nd ed. 572p. (Eng. & Fr.). 1977. 140.00 F. Bordas-Dunod.

Belle-Isle, J. English-French General Technical Dictionary. LC 79-342847. xii, 552p. (Eng. & Fr.). 1977. E10.00 (ISBN 0-7100-8928-7). Routledge & Kegan.

Belle Isle, J. Gerald. Dictionnaire Technique General: Anglais-Francais. 2nd ed. 555p. (Eng. & Fr.). 1977. $79.95 (ISBN 0-686-56913-X, M-6158). French & Eur.

Benacka, S. English-Slovak Technical Dictionary. 1358p. (Eng. & Slovak.). 1980. $79.00x (ISBN 0-569-08529-2, Pub. by Collet's). State Mutual Bk.

Benacka, Stefan. Anglicko-Slovensky Technicky Slovnik. LC 76-508198. 1357p. (Eng. & Slovak.). 1975. 117.00 Kcs. Alfa-Vydavatel.

Bennett, Harry, ed. Concise Chemical & Technical Dictionary. 3rd ed. 1974. $56.50 (ISBN 0-8206-0026-1). Chem Pub.

Bilginer, Sadettin. Deutsch-Turkisches Worterbuch Fur Technische Berufe. 2nd ed. 448p. (Ger. & Turkish.). 1966. leatherette $55.00 (ISBN 3-7736-5270-4, M-7348, Pub. by Verlag W. Girardet). French & Eur.
Bini, Edson. Dicionario Tecnico Industrial. LC 78-105852. 942p. (Eng. & Portuguese.). 1978. Cr.$360.00. Hemus-Livraria.
Bossier, Rene. Dictionnaire Technique des Fabrications Mecaniques. 200p. (Fr.). 1975. 28.00 F. Desforges.
Breuer, Karl. Pocket Dictionary of Technology & Science: Technischwissenschaftliches Taschenwoerte'buch: German-English & English-German. 6th ed. LC 75-597125. 413p. (Ger. & Eng.). 1971. 27.50x (ISBN 3-87749-014-X). Intl Pubns Serv.
Brockhaus. Diccionario popular de las ciencias y de la tecnica. 2nd ed. (Illus.). 658p. (Span.). write for info. Gill Gustavo.
Bucksch, Herbert. Dictionary of Mechanisms-Getriebeworterbuch: German-English, English-German. (Ger. & Eng.). 1976. 92.50x (ISBN 3-7625-0707-4). Intl Pubns Serv.
Burger, E., ed. Technical Reference Dictionary. 571p. 1979. $95.00 (ISBN 0-686-92324-3, M-9890). French & Eur.
Busto, M. Pequeno Diccionario Tecnologico: Farmacia, Quimica, Fisica, Medicina y Ciencias Naturales. 226p. (Span.). 1964. $13.50 (ISBN 0-686-57357-9, S-50248). French & Eur.
Callaham, Ludmilla I. Russian-English Chemical & Polytechnical Dictionary. 3rd ed. LC 75-5982. 852p. (Rus. & Eng.). 1975. $58.50x (ISBN 0-471-12998-4, Pub. by Wiley-Interscience). Wiley.
Camarao, P. C. & Serra, M. A. Great Technical Dictionary: Dicionario Tecnico English-Portuguese. 462p. (Eng. & Portuguese.). 1979. pap. $39.95 (ISBN 0-686-97435-2, M-9214). French & Eur.
Carboni, Paolo. Dizionario tecnico-scientifico: Italiano-tedesco. 752p. (Ital. & Ger.). 1969. L.5000.00. Patron.
--Dizionario tecnico-scientifico: Tedesco-italiano. 708p. (Ger. & Ital.). 1965. L.5000.00. Patron.
Carcamo, L. Dictionnaire pour Ingenieurs et Techniciens: Francais-Espagnol, Espagnol-Francais. 1106p. (Fr. & Span.). 1981. $95.00 (ISBN 0-686-92423-1, M-7669). French & Eur.
Chambers. Dictionary of Science & Technology. 1328p. 1982. DM.100.00; DM.pap. 40.00. Brandstetter.
--Dictionary of Science & Technology. 1296p. (Ger.). 1982. DM.pap. 40.00. Brandstetter.
Chambers Dictionary of Science & Technology. (Illus.). 1978. $25.00 (ISBN 0-8467-0520-6, Pub. by Two Continents); pap. $10.95 (ISBN 0-8467-0530-3). Am Map.
Chambers Dictionary of Science & Technology. 1983. $39.95 (ISBN 0-686-40769-5, Pub by Salem Hse Ltd); pap. $22.95 (ISBN 0-686-40770-9). Merrimack Pub Cir.
Chernukhin, A. E. English-Russian Polytechnical Dictionary. (Eng. & Rus.). $88.00 (ISBN 0-08-021936-5). Pergamon.
Chernukhin, A. E., ed. English-Russian Polytechnical Dictionary. 688p. (Eng. & Rus.). 1979. $70.00x (ISBN 0-569-08580-2, Pub. by Collets). State Mutual Bk.
Chesnel De la Charbouclais, L. P. Dictionnaire de Technologie, 2 vols. Migne, J. P., ed. (Troisieme et Derniere Encyclopedie Theologique Ser.: Vols. 28-29). 1306p. (Fr.). Repr. of 1858 ed. lib. bdg. $166.50x (ISBN 0-89241-308-5). Caratzas Pub Co.
Colas, Rene. Dictionnaire Technique de l'eau & des Questions Connexes. 264p. (Fr.). 1968. 45.00 F. Le Prat.
Collazo, Javier L. English-Spanish Spanish-English Encyclopedic Dictionary of Technical Terms, 3 vols. LC 79-16074. (Eng. & Span.). 1980. Set, English Edition. 154.00 (ISBN 0-07-079172-4); Set, Spanish Edition. 154.00 (ISBN 0-07-079162-7). McGraw.
--English-Spanish, Spanish-English Encyclopedic Dictionary of Technical Terms, 3 vols. 1500p. (Span. & Eng.). write for info. (English cover) (ISBN 0-07-079172-4); write for info. (Spanish cover) (ISBN 0-07-079162-7). McGraw.
Compilation of ASTM Standard Definitions. 1976. $24.75 (ISBN 0-686-52047-5, 03-508076-42). ASTM.
Cusset, Francis. English-French & French-English Technical Dictionary. rev. ed. (Eng. & Fr.). 1967. $28.50 (ISBN 0-8206-0043-1). Chem Pub.
--Vocabulaire Technique Allemand-Francais, Francais-Allemand. 8th ed. 474p. (Fr. & Ger.). 1977. $29.95 (ISBN 0-686-56970-9, M-6097). French & Eur.
--Vocabulaire Technique Anglais-Francais, Francais-Anglais. 9th ed. 434p. (Fr. & Ger.). 1977. $47.50 (ISBN 0-686-56971-7, M-6098). French & Eur.
Czech-English Technical Dictionary. 946p. (Czech. & Eng.). 1972. $23.75 (Pub. by SNTL). Four Continent.
Czerni & Skrzynka. Polish-English Dictionary of Science & Technology. 754p. (Pol. & Eng.). 1976. $95.00x (ISBN 0-686-44737-9, Pub. by Collets). State Mutual Bk.
Czerni, S. & Skrzynska, M. Polish Science & Technology Dictionary: English-Polish. 5th ed. (Pol. & Eng.). 1976. $35.00x (ISBN 0-89918-536-3, P536). Vanous.
--Polish Science & Technology Dictionary: Polish-English. 3rd rev. ed. (Pol. & Eng.). 1976. $35.00x (ISBN 0-89918-537-1, P-537). Vanous.
Czerni, Sergiusz & Skrzynska, Maria, eds. Polish-English Dictionary of Science & Technology. 3rd ed. (Pol. & Eng.). 1976. 30.00x (ISBN 0-686-19981-2). Intl Learn Syst.
Dabac, Ulatko. Technisches Woerterbuch, 2 vols. (Serbocroation & Ger.). 1969. $112.00 (ISBN 3-7625-0550-0, M-7653, Pub. by Bauverlag). French & Eur.
--Technisches Woerterbuch, 2 vols. (Serbo-Croation & Ger.). 1969. $112.00 (ISBN 3-7625-0550-0). Bauverlag.
Daykin, Vernon. Technical Arabic. 132p. (Arabic.). 1980. $15.00x (ISBN 0-686-94054-7, Pub. by Lund Humphries England). State Mutual Bk.
De la Cierva, Patronato J. Diccionario Ruso-Espanol de la Ciencia y la Tecnica. 2nd ed. 700p. (Span.). 1972. $50.00 (ISBN 84-237-0407-6, S-50249). French & Eur.
Denti, Renzo. Dizionario Tecnico Francese-Italiano. LC 79-352645. xx, 1182p. (Fr. & Ital.). 1977. L.15000.00. Hoepli.
--Dizionario Tecnico Italiano-Inglese. LC 76-470277. 1799p. (Eng. & Ital.). 1976. write for info. Hoepli.
--Dizionario Tecnico Italiano-Inglese, Inglese-Italiano. 9th rev. ed. 1811p. (Eng. & Ital.). 1979. $78.00x (ISBN 88-203-1052-X). S F Vanni.
De Pina Araujo, Avelino. De Pina's Technical Dictionary, 2 vols. LC 76-452901. (Eng. & Port.). 1975. Cr.$280.00. McGraw.
De Vogue, Melchior & Oousel, Raymond. Glossaire de Termes Techniques: L'usage des Lecteurs de la Nuit des Temps. rev. ed. (Illus.). 478p. (Fr.). 1971. 88.00 F. Zodiaque.
De Vries & Herrmann. Technical & Engineering Dictionary: Band II, English-German. 1154p. (Eng. & Ger.). 1982. DM.120.00. Brandstetter.
--Technical & Engineering Dictionary: Band I, German-English. 1178p. (Ger. & Eng.). 1982. DM.120.00. Brandstetter.
De Vries, Louis. French-English Science & Technology Dictionary. rev. ed. Hochman, Stanley, rev. by. 683p. (Fr. & Eng.). 1976. $20.00. McGraw.
DeVries, Louis. German-English Technical & Engineering Dictionary. 2nd ed. (Ger. & Eng.). 1966. 63.95 (ISBN 0-07-016631-5, P&RB). McGraw.
De Vries, Louis & Hermann, Theo M. German-English Technical & Engineering Dictionary. (Ger. & Eng.). 1966. $66.00. McGraw.
De Vries, Louis & Hochman, Stanley. French-English Science & Technology Dictionary. 4th ed. 704p. (Fr. & Eng.). write for info. (ISBN 0-07-016629-3). McGraw.
De Vries, Louis & Jacolev, Leon. German-English Science Dictionary. 4th ed. 628p. (Ger. & Eng.). write for info. (ISBN 0-07-016602-1). McGraw.
Deweerdt, Jacques. Vocabulaire Fondamental de Technologie. 272p. (Fr.). 1974. pap. $19.95 (ISBN 0-686-57280-7, M-4654). French & Eur.
--Vocabulaire Fondamental de Technologie. (Illus.). 272p. (Fr.). 1974. 42.00 F. Gamma.
Diccionario de tecnologia. 3rd ed. 320p. (Span.). 1982. pap. 600.00 ptas (ISBN 84-226-1156-2). Circulo Lect.
Diccionario ilustrado de las ciencias pura y aplicades. (Span.). Arg.$35.00; $250.00. Mundi.
Diccionario Monografico de Tecnologia. 320p. (Span.). 750.00 ptas (ISBN 84-7153-383-9). Biblograf SP.
Diccionario Monografico de Tecnologia. 328p. (Span.). 1980. write for info. Biblograf.
Diccionario Tecnico & Industrial Italiano-Espanol. 678p. (Ital. & Span.). 1974. 750.00 ptas. L Carcamo.
Diccionario Tecnico Frances-Espanol. 544p. (Fr. & Span.). 1973. leatherette $20.95 (ISBN 84-283-0334-7, S-31563). French & Eur.
Diccionario Tecnologico Ingles-Espanol. 454p. (Eng. & Span.). 1974. $41.95 (ISBN 84-205-0492-0, S-31501). French & Eur.
Dictionar Tecnic Rus-Roman. xii, 1267p. (Romanian & Rus.). 1975. 135.00 lei. Editura Stiintifica.
Dictionary of Science & Technology. 469p. (Eng. & Chinese.). 1973. $14.95 (ISBN 0-686-92348-0, M-9261). French & Eur.
Dictionary of Science & Technology. 1689p. (Eng. & Chinese.). 1978. $9.95 (ISBN 0-686-92375-8, M-9560). French & Eur.
Dictionary of Science & Technology: Eng. & Chinese. 713p. (Chinese.). 1979. pap. $5.95 (ISBN 0-686-92552-1, M-9587). French & Eur.
Dictionary of Technical Information. 182p. 1980. $20.00x (ISBN 0-569-08388-5, Pub. by Collet's). State Mutual Bk.
Dictionnaire des Sciences & Techniques Nucleaires. 2nd ed. 426p. (Fr.). 1967. 29.85 F. PUF.
Dictionnaire International Electrotechnique: Francais-Russe-Anglais-Allemand-Italien-Suedois-Hollandais-Polonais. (Fr. , Rus. , Eng. , Ger. , Ital. , Swedish, Dutch & Pol.). write for info. Mir.
Dictionnaire International Electrotechnique: Francais-Russe-Anglais-Allemand-Espagnol-Suedois-Hollandais-Polonais. (Fr. , Rus. , Eng. , Ger. , Span. , Swedish, Dutch & Pol.). write for info. Mir.
Dictionnaire Technique de l'eau. (Fr.). 45.00 F. Grund.
Dictionnaire Technique du Bois: Texte en Allemand-Anglais-Francais-Russe. 640p. (Ger. , Eng. , Fr. & Rus.). 1969. 154.00 F. Eyrolles.
Dictionnaire Technique: Francais-Neerlandais. 480p. (Fr. & Dutch.). 1972. 92.00 F. Voutquenne, C.
Dictionnaire Technique Generale Anglais-Francais. new ed. 664p. (Fr. & Eng.). 1979. $39.95 (ISBN 0-686-57117-7, M-6158). French & Eur.
Dictionnaire Technique Russe-Francais: La Preparation Mecanique des Charbons. 129p. (Rus. & Fr.). 1973. 36.00 F. France, Centre Et Charbonnage.
Din Standards: Two-Thousand Six-Hundred Definitions of Technical Terms According to Din. $53.00 (ISBN 0-686-28197-7, 10804-1). Heyden.
Dizionario della tecnica. 188p. (Ital.). 1964. L.2500.00. Zanichelli.
Dorian, A. F., compiled by. Dictionary of Science & Technology, 2 vols. 2nd, rev. ed. (Ger. & Eng.). 1982. Set. $242.75 (ISBN 0-686-85923-5). Elsevier.
Dorian, A. F., ed. Dictionary of Science & Technology, 2 Vols. 1400p. 1979. Set. $255.50 (ISBN 0-686-85924-3); Vol. I: Fr.- Eng. $127.75 (ISBN 0-444-41911-X); Vol. II: Eng. & Fr. $127.75 (ISBN 0-444-41829-6). Elsevier.
Duy-Tu, Tran, et al. Polytechnisches Woerterbuch Deutsch-Vietnamesisch. 502p. (Ger. & Vietnamese.). 1982. M.32.00. VEB Technik.
Editura Tehnica. Dictionar Tehnic Poliglot. 1233p. 1983. Repr. of 1967 ed. text ed. 98.50x (ISBN 0-8290-0987-6). Irvington.
Engelsk-Svensk Teknisk Ordbok. 141p. (Eng. & Swedish.). 1979. Kr.73.00 (ISBN 91-24-20833-7). Esselte Studium.
English-Chinese Dictionary of Scientific & Technology Abreviations. 587p. (Eng. & Chinese.). 1979. pap. $9.95 (ISBN 0-686-97363-1, M-9250). French & Eur.
An English-Chinese Dictionary of Technology. 1098p. (Eng. & Chinese.). 1978. leatherette $19.95 (ISBN 0-686-92474-6, M-9578). French & Eur.
English-Czech Technical Dictionary. 1026p. (Eng. & Czech.). 1971. $22.25 (Pub. by SNTL). Four Continent.
English-Polish Dictionary of Science & Technology. 4th ed. 892p. (Eng. & Pol.). $90.00x (ISBN 0-569-08263-3, Pub. by Collets). State Mutual Bk.
English-Polish Dictionary of Science & Technology. 892p. (Eng. & Pol.). 1976. $19.95 (Pub. by Wydaw. Naukowo-Techniczne). Four Continent.
English-Spanish Technical Dictionary. (Span. & Eng.). $37.50 (ISBN 0-87559-188-4). Shalom.
Engstroem, E. Swedish-English, English-Swedish Technical Dictionary, 2 vols. rev. enl ed. (Swedish & Eng.). Set. 115.00 (ISBN 0-685-42614-9). Heinman.
Ernst. Woerterbuch der Industriellen Technik: Band III, Deutsch-Franzoesisch. 1233p. (Ger. & Fr.). 1982. DM.130.00. Brandstetter.
--Woerterbuch der Industriellen Technik: Band IV, Franzoesisch-Deutsch. 1182p. (Fr. & Ger.). 1982. DM.130.00. Brandstetter.
--Woerterbuch der Industriellen Technik: Band IX, Franzoesisch-Englisch. 1085p. (Fr. & Eng.). 1982. DM.140.00. Brandstetter.
--Woerterbuch der Industriellen Technik: Band VII, Deutsch-Portugiesisch. 450p. (Ger. & Port.). 1983. DM.100.00. Brandstetter.
--Woerterbuch der Industriellen Technik: Band V, Deutsch-Spanisch. 1035p. (Ger. & Span.). 1982. DM.80.00. Brandstetter.
--Woerterbuch der Industriellen Technik: Band VIII, Portugiesch-Deutsch. 587p. (Port. & Ger.). 1982. DM.60.00. Brandstetter.
--Woerterbuch der Industriellen Technik: Band VI, Spanisch-Deutschg) 1073p. (Span. & Ger.). 1982. DM.80.00. Brandstetter.
Ernst, R. Dictionnaire de la Technique Industrielle: Allemand-Francais. 3rd ed. 1233p. (Ger. & Fr.). 1979. 430.00 F. Maison Dictionnaire.

Ernst, Richard. Dictionary of Engineering & Technology, 2 vols. Rev. ed. (Ger. & Eng.). 1980. Vol 1: German-English, 1092p. $69.00; Vol. 2: English-German, 1170p. $69.00. Oxford U Pr.
--Dictionary of Engineering & Technology: With Extensive Treatment of the Most Modern Techniques & Processes, Vol. 2, English-German. 4th, rev. & enl. ed. 1178p. (Eng. & Ger.). 1975. text ed. 69.00x (ISBN 0-19-520109-4). Oxford U Pr.
--Dictionnaire General de la Technique Industrielle: Francais-Anglais. 1080p. (Fr. & Eng.). 1982. 465.00 F. Maison Dictionnaire.
Ernst, Richard, ed. Dictionary of Engineering & Technology, Vol. 1. 4th ed. 1981. 69.00x (ISBN 0-19-520269-4). Oxford U Pr.
European Society for Opinion & Marketing Research. Glossary of Technical Terms for Market Researchers: English-German-Spanish-French-Italian-Dutch. LC 74-520067. (Eng., Ger., Span., Fr., Ital. & Dutch.). 1969. 10.00x (ISBN 0-8002-1461-7). Intl Pubns Serv.
Feutry, Michel. Dictionnaire Technologique, 1: Anglais-Francais-Allemand. 700p. (Eng., Fr. & Ger.). 1976. 160.00 F. Maison Dictionnaire.
--Technological Dictionary. LC 78-346108. (Fr. & Ger.). 1976. 160.00 F (ISBN 2-85608-000-6). Maison Dictionnaire.
Feutry, Michel, et al. Dictionnaire Technologique, 1: Anglais-Francais-Allemand. 736p. (Eng., Fr. & Ger.). 1976. 160.00 F. Maison Dictionnaire.
Feutry, Michel, et al, eds. Technological Dictionary: Mechanics, Metalurgy, Hydraulics & Related Industries. (In 4 languages). 1976. lib. bdg. 55.00x (ISBN 2-85608-000-6). Marlin.
Freeman, H. A Glossary of Technical Concepts Containing 4300 Din Definitions. 703p. 1983. pap. $87.00 (ISBN 0-686-40807-1, Pub. by Din Verlag). Heyden.
--Technisches Taschenwoerterbuch. 3rd ed. 584p. (Ger. & Eng., German-English Technical Dictionary). 1972. $12.50 (ISBN 3-19-006212-9, M-7648, Pub. by M. Hueber). French & Eur.
--Technisches Taschenwoerterbuch. 3rd ed. 584p. (Ger. & Eng.). 1972. $12.50 (ISBN 3-19-006212-9). Heuber.
Freeman, Henry G. Technical Pocket Dictionary-Technisches Taschenwoerterbuch. 2nd ed. (Eng. & Ger.). 1969. German-English 7.50x (ISBN 3-1900-6212-9); English-German 7.50x (ISBN 3-19-006213-7). Intl Pubns Serv.
--Technisches Englisch. 7th ed. (Ger. -Eng.). 1975. $48.00 (ISBN 3-7736-5011-6, M-7647, Pub. by Girardet). French & Eur.
--Technishes Englisch. 7th ed. (Ger. & Eng.). 1975. $48.00 (ISBN 3-7736-5011-6). Girardet.
Furstenau, Eugenio. Dicionario de termos tecnicos Ingles-Portugues, 2 vols. rev. ed. (Illus.). 1157p. (Port. & Eng.). 1974. Cr.$48.00. Editora Globo.
Geiler, L. B., et al, eds. Anglo-Russkii Elektrotekhnicheskii Slovar. 704p. (Eng. & Rus.). 1955. $5.95 (Pub. by Gosizdat Tekhn. Teoret.). Four Continent.
German-Prozorova, L. P., et al, eds. Anglo-Russkii Radiotekhnicheskii Slovar. 524p. (Rus. & Eng.). 1960. $6.30 (Pub. by Gosizdat. Inostr. Slovarei). Four Continent.
Gerrish, Howard H. Technical Dictionary. rev. ed. LC 81-20005. 368p. 1982. text ed. 10.00 (ISBN 0-87006-400-2). Goodheart.
Gil, L. Suarez, ed. Diccionario Tecnico Maritimo: Ingles-Espanol, Espanol-Ingles. 708p. (Eng. & Span.). 1980. pap. $75.00 (ISBN 84-205-0772-5, S-32729). French & Eur.
Ginzburg, M. L., et al. Nemetsko-Russkii Elektrotekhnicheskii Slovar. 1066p. (Rus.). 1959. $12.75 (Pub. by Gosizdat Fizmatlit). Four Continent.
Glossary on Educational Technology. 140p. 1973. pap. $7.95 (ISBN 0-686-56478-2, M-7429, Pub. by Vlg. Dokumentation). French & Eur.
Gorner, Horst. Kleines Polytechnisches Woerterbuch Russisch-Deutsch. 372p. (Rus. & Ger.). 1981. M.14.00. VEB Technik.
Gorner, Horst & Fedirko, J. V. Kleines Polytechnisches Woerterbuch. LC 76-463413. 372p. (Rus. & Ger.). 1975. M.12.00. VEB Verlag Technik.
Grenier, Jean Guy. Dictionnaire Anglais-Francais D'electrotechnique. 260p. (Eng. & Fr.). 1976. C.$12.00. Lanaudiere.
Grunwald-Beyer, A. Technisches Taschenwoerterbuch. 533p. (Ger. & Fr.). $25.00 (ISBN 3-87749-013-1, M-7646, Pub. by Georg Siemens Verlagsbuchhandlung). French & Eur.
Guinle, R. L. A Modern Spanish-English & English-Spanish Technical & Engineering Dictionary. (Span. & Eng.). 1969. Repr. of 1938 ed. 25.00 (ISBN 0-7100-1478-3). Routledge & Kegan.
Gullberg, Ingvar E. Swedish-English Dictionary of Technical Terms Used in Business, Industry, Administration, Education & Research. 2nd rev. & enl. ed. (Swedish & Eng.). 150.00 (ISBN 91-1-775052-0). Heinman.
--Swedish-English Fact Ordbok (Technical Terms) 2nd ed. (Swedish & Eng.). 1977. $200.00x (ISBN 91-1-775052-0, SW-207). Vanous.
Heinrich. Woerterbuch Klima & Kaeltetechnik. 404p. (Eng., Fr., Rus. & Ger.). 1978. DM.85.00 (ISBN 3-87144-303-4). Verlag Harri Deutsch.
Hionides, H. T. Greek-English, English-Greek Technical Dictionary, Vol.1-2. rev. ed. (Eng. & Gr.). Date not set. Set. text ed. $50.00 (ISBN 0-686-46533-4). Heinman.
Hoyer-Kreuter. Technological Dictionary in Three Languages, 3 vols. Schlomann, Alfred, ed. Incl. Vol. 1. German-English-French; Vol. 2. English-German-French; Vol. 3. French-German-English. (Ger., Fr. & Eng.). Set. $135.00 (ISBN 0-8044-0202-7). Ungar.
Hueter, Paul & Goerner, Horst. Polytechnisches Woerterbuch Russisch-Deutsch. 1600p. (Rus. & Ger.). 1982. M.60.00. VEB Technik.
Iakovlev, B. E. Cheshsko-Russkii Radiotekhnicheskii Slovar. 364p. (Rus. & Czech.). 1960. $2.95 (Pub. by Glav. Red. Inostr. Nauchn. Tekhn. Slovarei Fizmata). Four Continent.
Ibeas, F. F. Diccionario Tecnologico Ingles-Espanol. 740p. (Eng. & Span.). 1980. pap. write for info. (ISBN 84-205-0707-5). Edit Alhambra.
--English-Spanish Technical Dictionary. 2nd ed. (Eng. & Span.). pap. 45.00 (ISBN 0-686-77977-0). Heinman.
Ibeas, Franco. Diccionario tecnologico Ingles-Espanol. 740p. (Span. & Eng.). 1980. pap. write for info. (ISBN 84-205-0707-5). Fed Gremios.
Japanese-Chinese Science & Technology Dictionary. 175p. (Japanese & Chinese.). 1976. $19.95 (ISBN 0-686-92480-0, M-9260). French & Eur.
Kaliske, Gisbert. Plasttechnik-Englisch-Deutsch-Franzoesisch-Russisch. 390p. (Eng., Ger., Fr. & Rus.). 1982. M.60.00. VEB Technik.
Katona, Lorant. Magyar-Orosz Muszaki Szotar, 2 vols. LC 76-504224. 1513p. (Hungarian & Rus.). 1975. 490.00 Ft (ISBN 963-05-0723-4). Akademiai Kiado.
Kettridge, J. O. Dictionary of Technical Terms, 2 vols. 628p. (Fr. & Eng.). Set. $38.00; Vol. 2: English-French. $38.00; $70.00. Routledge & Kegan.
--French-English & English-French Dictionary of Technical Terms & Phrases, 2 vols. Incl. Vol. 1. French-English. 40.50 (ISBN 0-7100-0144-4); Vol. 2. English-French. 40.00 (ISBN 0-7100-0166-5). (Fr. & Eng.). 1970. Repr. of 1959 ed. Set. 75.00 (ISBN 0-7100-0082-0). Routledge & Kegan.
Kettridge, Julius O. Dictionary of Technical Terms, 2 vols. (Fr. & Eng.). Set. $55.50 (ISBN 0-685-11207-1). French & Eur.
Knutsen, Knut J. Engelsk-Norsk Teknisk Ordliste. LC 77-572102. 93p. (Eng. & Norwegian.). 1977. Kr.32.00 (ISBN 8-251-90218-5). Tapir.
Kobo Orts Kh., et al. Kratkii Ispansko-Russkii & Russko-Ispanskii Nauchno-Tekhnicheskii Slovar. 438p. (Span. & Rus.). 1960. $3.75 (Pub. by An Arm SSR). Four Continent.
Kroeger-Jannetti, A. Technisches Taschenwoerterbuch. 804p. (Ger. & Span.). $32.00 (ISBN 3-87749-012-3, M-7645, Pub. by Georg Siemens Verlagsbuchhandlung). French & Eur.
Kucera. Technisches Woerterbuch: Band I, Russisch-Deutsch. 330p. (Rus. & Ger.). 1982. DM.40.00. Brandstetter.
--Technisches Woerterbuch: Band II, Deutsch-Russisch. 464p. (Ger. & Rus.). 1982. DM.50.00. Brandstetter.
Kucera, A. The Compact Dictionary of Exact Science & Technology, Vol. 1. 590p. E16.50 (ISBN 0-245-53605-1). Harrap.
--The Compact Dictionary of Exact Science & Technology: English-German. 571p. (Eng. & Ger.). 1980. $49.95 (ISBN 3-87097-088-X, M-9027). French & Eur.
Kucera, Antonin. Technisches Woerterbuch, Vol. 1. (Rus. & Ger.). 1966. $25.00 (ISBN 3-87097-025-1, M-7654, Pub. by Brandstetter). French & Eur.
--Technisches Woerterbuch, Vol. 1. (Rus. & Ger.). 1966. $25.00 (ISBN 3-87097-025-1). Brandstetter.
--Technisches Woerterbuch, Vol. 2. (Rus. & Ger.). 1966. $32.00 (ISBN 3-87097-026-X, M-7655, Pub. by Brandstetter). French & Eur.
--Technisches Woerterbuch, Vol. 2. (Rus. & Ger.). 1966. $32.00 (ISBN 3-87097-026-X). Brandstetter.
Kuznetsov, B., ed. Russian-English Polytechnical Dictionary. LC 80-41193. 900p. (Rus. & Eng.). 1981. 110.00 (ISBN 0-08-023609-X). Pergamon.
Lapedes. Dictionary of Scientific & Technical Terms. 2nd ed. (Illus.). 1800p. $50.00. McGraw.
Lapedes, D. Dizionario Enciclopedico Scientifico e Tecnico: Inglese-Italiano, Italiano-Inglese. 2122p. (Eng. & Ital.). 1980. Leatherette $175.00 (ISBN 0-686-92540-8, M-9201). French & Eur.
Leskova, T. & Plisek, V. Czech-English Technical Textile Dictionary. 468p. (Czech. & Eng.). 1980. $60.00x (ISBN 0-686-72090-3, Pub. by Collet's). State Mutual Bk.
McGraw Hill. McGraw Hill Dictionary of Scientific & Technical Terms. 3rd ed. Parker, Sybil P., ed. 1860p. 1983. 70.00 (ISBN 0-07-045269-5, Pub by P & RB). McGraw.
Malgorn. Diccionario Tecnico Espanol-Ingles. (Span. & Eng.). 1977. 1100.00 ptas (ISBN 8-42830-889-6). Paraninfo.
--Diccionario Tecnico Ingles-Espanol. (Eng. & Span.). 1978. 1100.00 ptas (ISBN 8-42830-923-X). Paraninfo.
Malgorn, G. Dictionnaire Technique Anglais-Francais. 495p. (Eng. & Fr.). 1976. $37.50 (ISBN 0-686-57027-8, M-6385). French & Eur.
--Dictionnaire Technique Francais-Anglais. 475p. (Fr. & Eng.). 1956. $37.50 (ISBN 2-04-002947-8, M-6386). French & Eur.
Malgorn, Guy. Diccionario Tecnico Espanol-Frances. (Span. & Fr.). 1979. write for info. leatherette (S-50241). French & Eur.
--Diccionario Tecnico Espanol-Ingles. 594p. (Span. & Eng.). 1977. $26.95 (ISBN 84-283-0889-6, S-31442). French & Eur.
--Diccionario Tecnico Espanol-Ingles. 576p. (Span. & Eng.). 1978. write for info. (ISBN 84-283-0889-6). Paraninfo.
--Diccionario tecnico Espa n13ol-Ingl e01s. 576p. (Span. & Eng.). 1978. write for info. (ISBN 84-283-0889-6). Fed Gremios.
--Diccionario Tecnico Ingles-Espanol. 632p. (Eng. & Span.). 1978. pap. $26.95 (ISBN 84-283-0923-X, S-31490). French & Eur.
--Dictionaire Technique Francais-Espagnol. 2nd ed. 544p. (Fr.-Eng.). 1974. $42.50 (ISBN 0-686-57028-6, M-6387). French & Eur.
--Dictionnaire Technique Francais-Anglais. 475p. (Fr. & Eng.). 1956. 88.00 F. Gauthier-Villars.
--Dictionnaire Technique Francais-Espagnol. 544p. (Fr. & Span.). 1974. 99.00 F. Gauthier-Villars.
Malgorn, Guy M. Dictionnaire Technique Francais-Anglai. LC 77-450053. xxx, 471p. (Fr.). 1975. 80.00 F (ISBN 2-04-002947-8). Bordas.
Marei, H. Basic Technical Dictionary: French-English-German-Arabic. 363p. (Fr., Eng., Ger. & Arabic.). 1973. lib. bdg. $45.00 (ISBN 0-686-92506-8, M-9752). French & Eur.
Marolli, G. Dizionario Tecnico Italiano-Inglese, Inglese-Italiano. 2048p. (Ital. & Eng.). 1978. write for info. (M-9197). French & Eur.
--Italian-English, English-Italian Technical Dictionary. 11th, enl. ed. (Illus., Ital. & Eng.). 1980. $100.00 (ISBN 8-8005-1040-X). Heinman.
Marolli, Giorgio. Dizionario tecnico inglese-italiano e italiano-inglese. (Illus.). xxiv, 2048p. (Eng. & Ital.). L.35000.00. Monnier.
Marolli, Giorgio & Guarnieri, Orazio. Dizionario Tecnico Tedesco-Italiano. LC 77-466767. 2032p. (Ital. & Ger.). 1976. L.24000.00. Garzanti Edit.
--Dizionario tecnico tedesco-italiano italiano-tedesco. 2044p. (Ger. & Ital.). 1976. L.28000.00. Garzanti Edit.
Martins, Joaquim A. Dicionario Tecnico Ingles-Portugues. (Eng. & Port.). Esc.570.00. Pub Euro Am.
Mastropasqua, V. Dizionario Tecnico Nautico: Italiano-Inglese, Inglese-Italiano. 879p. (Ital. & Eng.). 1967. pap. $49.95 (ISBN 0-686-92533-5, M-9297). French & Eur.
Matveev, Vladimir S. & Asrhants, Konstantin G. Portuagalsko-Russkil Politekhnicheskil Slovar. LC 75-546852. 568p. (Rus. & Portuguese.). 1975. 2.42 Rub. Russkii Iazyk.
Meadows, A. J., et al. Dictionary of New Information Technology. 256p. 1982. $29.00x (ISBN 0-7126-0019-1, Pub. by Century Pub Co). State Mutual Bk.
Mertz De Mertzenteld, R., et al. Dictionnaire Technologique Feutry: Supplement Espagnol, Vol. 1-E. 400p. (Span.). 1976. 180.00 F. Maison Dictionnaire.
--Dictionnaire Technologique: Supplement Portugais. 380p. (Port.). 1981. 160.00 F. Maison Dictionnaire.
Meyer & Orlando. Technisches Woerterbuch: Band I, Italienisch-Deutsch. xii, 1345p. (Ital. & Ger.). 1982. DM.120.00. Brandstetter.
--Technisches Woerterbuch: Band II, Deutsch-Italienisch. 1567p. (Ger. & Ital.). 1982. DM.120.00. Brandstetter.
Meyer, Alice. Dizionario Tecnico Italiano-Tedesco, 2 vols. 5th ed. LC 79-362362. (Eng., Ital. & Ger.). 1977. L.25000.00. Brandstetter.
Mezhdunarodnyi Elektrotekhnicheskii Slovar: Gruppa 07 (Elektronika) 335p. (Rus.). 1959. $3.50 (Pub. by Gosizdat Fiziko-Matematich. Literatury). Four Continent.

Mezhdunarodnyi Elektrotekhnicheskii Slovar: Gruppa 10 (Mashiny & Transformatory) (Rus.). $2.25 (Pub. by Gosizdat Fiziko Matematich. Literatury). Four Continent.

Mezhdunarodnyi Elektrotekhnicheskii Slovar: Gruppa 65 (Radiologiia & Radiologicheskaia Fizika) 252p. (Rus.). 1966. $3.50 (Pub. by Sov Entsiklopediia). Four Continent.

Mezzera, Umberto. Glossario di tecnologia meccanica. 90p. (Ital.). 1967. L.2500.00. Etas Libri.

Mingot, Tomas De Galiana. Pequeno Larousse de ciencias y tecnicas. new ed. 1056p. (Span.). 1975. 26.95 (ISBN 0-685-55467-8, 21115). Larousse.

Mink, tr. Diccionario tecnico espanol-aleman. (Span. & Ger.). 1970. 1500.00 ptas. Bluma.

Mink, Auteur H. Dictionnaire Technique Francais-Espagnol. 1120p. (Fr.). 1979. $75.00 (ISBN 0-686-57049-9, M-6411). French & Eur.

Mink, H. Diccionario Tecnico: Suplemento, Vol. 2. 384p. (Span. & Ger.). 1981. Leatherette $49.50 (ISBN 0-686-92524-6, S-50270). French & Eur.

--Diccionario Tecnico: Suplemento al Tomo II, Espanol-Aleman. 384p. (Span. & Ger.). 1980. 1650.00 ptas. Herder SA.

--Diccionario Tecnico, Tomo 1: Aleman-Espanol. 2nd ed. 1376p. (Span.). 1978. $60.00 (ISBN 84-254-0994-2, S-50190, French & Eur). French & Eur.

--Diccionario Tecnico, Tomo 2: Espanol-Aleman. 3rd ed. 1154p. (Span. & Ger.). 1978. $60.00 (ISBN 84-254-0705-2, S-12404, French & Eur). French & Eur.

Mink, Hermann. Diccionario Tecnico. LC 78-398803. (Fr. & Span.). 1978. write for info. (ISBN 8-4703-1087-9). Blume Edit.

--Technisches Fachwoerterbuch. 3rd ed. LC 76-477060. (Span. & Ital.). 1975. 2000.00 ptas (ISBN 8-4254-0994-2). Gustavo Gili.

Moureau, Magdeleine & Rouge, Janine. Dictionnaire Technique des Termes Utilises Dans l'Industrie du Petrole, Anglais-Francais, Francais-Anglais. 914p. (Eng. & Fr., Dictionary of Technical Terms Used in the Oil Industry, English-French, French-English). 1977. $95.00 (ISBN 0-686-56757-9, M-6419). French & Eur.

Nagy, E. & Klar, J., eds. English-Hungarian Technical Dictionary. 792p. (Eng. & Hungarian.). 1980. $70.00x (ISBN 0-686-72096-2, Pub. by Collet's). State Mutual Bk.

Nagy, Erno & Klar, Janos. Magyar-Angol Muszaki Szotar. LC 77-467592. 752p. (Eng. & Hungarian.). 1975. 300.00 Ft (ISBN 9-6305-0607-6). Akademiai Kiado.

Nagy, T. Hungarian-English Technical Dictionary. 752p. (Hungarian & Eng.). 1980. $70.00x (ISBN 0-569-00731-3, Pub. by Collet's). State Mutual Bk.

Naxerova. Technisches Woerterbuch: Band I, Tschechisch-Deutsch. 1096p. (Czech. & Ger.). 1982. DM.50.00. Brandstetter.

Naxerova, A. Technisches Woerterbuch, Vol. 1. (Czech. & Ger.). 1970. $40.00 (ISBN 3-87097-049-9, M-7649, Pub. by Brandstetter). French & Eur.

--Technisches Woerterbuch, Vol. 1. (Czech. & Ger.). 1970. $40.00 (ISBN 3-87097-049-9). Brandstetter.

Neliubin, L. D. Illiustrirovannyi Voenno-Tekhnicheskii Slovar. 482p. (Eng., Ger., Span., Rus. & Fr.). 1968. $17.50 (Pub. by Voenizdat). Four Continent.

Novak, J. & Binder, R. A Concise English-Slovak & Slovak-English Technical Dictionary. 610p. (Eng. & Slovak.). 1980. 45.00x (ISBN 0-569-07469-X, Pub. by Collet's). State Mutual Bk.

--A Concise English-Slovak & Slovak-English Technical Dictionary. 3rd ed. 610p. (Eng. & Slovak.). 1971. $39.00x (ISBN 0-569-07469-X, Pub. by Collets). State Mutual Bk.

Pahlitzsch, G. Woerterbucher der Fertigungstechnik: Bd 1, Schmieden-Freiformschmieden & Gesenkschmieden. 108p. (Ger.). 1962. DM.45.00 (ISBN 3-7736-5920-2). Girardet.

--Woerterbucher der Fertigungstechnik Deutsch-Englisch-Franzoesisch: Bd 2, Schleifen Oberflaechenrauheit. 139p. (Ger., Eng. & Fr.). 1963. DM.45.00 (ISBN 3-7736-5930-X). Girardet.

--Woerterbucher der Fertigungstechnik Deutsch-Englisch-Franzoesisch: Bd 3, Blechbearbeitung. 136p. (Ger., Eng. & Fr.). 1965. DM.45.00 (ISBN 3-7736-5940-7). Girardet.

--Woerterbucher der Fertigungstechnik Deutsch-Englisch-Franzoesisch: Bd 4, Grundbegriffe des Spanens. 123p. (Ger., Eng. & Fr.). 1969. DM.45.00 (ISBN 3-7736-5941-5). Girardet.

--Woerterbucher der Fertigungstechnik Deutsch-Englisch-Franzoesisch: Bd 5, Kaltfliesspressen & Kaltstauchen. 157p. (Ger., Eng. & Fr.). 1969. DM.45.00 (ISBN 3-7736-5945-8). Girardet.

--Woerterbucher der Fertigungstechnik Deutsch-Englisch-Franzoesisch: Bd 6, Hobeln, Stassen, Raeumen, Drehen. 194p. (Ger., Eng. & Fr.). 1972. DM.45.00 (ISBN 3-7736-5946-6). Girardet.

--Woerterbucher der Fertigungstechnik Deutsch-Englisch-Franzoesisch: Bd 7, Bohren, Senken, Reiben, Gewindeschneiden. 220p. (Ger., Eng. & Fr.). 1977. DM.45.00 (ISBN 3-7736-5947-4). Girardet.

--Woerterbucher der Fertigungstechnik Daenisch-Norwegisch-Schwedisch-Finnisch: Bd 1N, Schmieden-Freiformschmeiden & Gesenkschmieden. 148p. (Danish, Norwegian, Swedish & Finnish.). 1972. DM.45.00 (ISBN 3-7736-5851-6). Girardet.

--Woerterbucher der Fertigungstechnik Deutsch-Spanisch-Italienisch-Portugiesisch: Bd 1R, Schmieden-Freiformschmieden & Gesenkschmieden. 114p. (Ger., Span., Ital. & Port.). 1967. DM.45.00 (ISBN 3-7736-5801-X). Girardet.

Pasquali, Maurizio. Dizionario tascabile delle tecniche ambientale: Italiano, francese, inglese, tedesco. 296p. (Ital., Fr., Eng. & Ger.). 1976. L.8000.00. SAPIL.

Patockova, Vlasta. Technickoekonomicky Rusko-Cesky Slovnik. LC 80-452727. 269p. (Rus. & Czech., Praha, Czechoslovakia). 1979. write for info. SNTL.

Patronato Juan de la Cierva. Diccionario ruso-espanol de la ciencia y de la tecnica. 700p. (Rus. & Span.). write for info. Dossat.

Peek, H. Standaard Nederlands-Engels Technisch Woordenboek. LC 75-539819. 388p. (Eng. & Dutch.). 1975. fl.35.00 (ISBN 90-02-12737-5). Standaard Uitgeverij.

Pihkala, Liisa & Pihkala, Juhani. Englandtilais-Suomalainen Laboratorio- ja Prosessialan Sanasto. LC 78-398796. 184p. (Eng. & Finnish.). 1978. write for info. (ISBN 9-5110-4645-4). Otava.

Piraux, Henri. Dictionnaire Allemand-Francais des Termes Relatifs a l'electrotechnique: L'electrotechnique & aux Applications Connexes. 4th ed. (Illus.). 254p. (Ger. & Fr.). 1976. 72.00 F. Eyrolles.

Pollet, R. J. Lexique de termes techniques: Anglais-Francais & index Francais. 233p. (Eng. & Fr.). 1976. 75.00 F. Maison Dictionnaire.

Pollet, Ray J. Lexique de Termes Techniques: Un Lexique Anglais-Francais. 233p. (Eng. Fr.). 1976. pap. $25.00 (ISBN 0-686-57084-7, M-6460). French & Eur.

Polytechnisches Woerterbuch Deutsch-Franzoesisch. 832p. (Ger. & Fr.). 1982. M.50.00. Veb Technik.

Polytechnisches Woerterbuch Franzoesisch-Deutsch. 724p. (Fr. & Ger.). 1982. M.50.00. VEB Technik.

Polytechnisches Woerterbuch Spanisch-Deutsch. 716p. (Span. & Ger.). 1981. M.50.00. VEB Technik.

Popic, R., et al. Scientific Technological Dictionary. 1140p. (Eng. & Serbocroatian.). 1980. $95.00 (ISBN 0-686-97432-8, M-9688). French & Eur.

Pretz, Bernhard. Dictionary of Military Technological Abbreviations & Acronyms. 450p. 1983. 45.00 (ISBN 0-7100-9274-1). Routledge & Kegan.

Pugh, Eric. Third Dictionary of Acronyms & Abbreviations: More Abbreviations in Management, Technology, & Information Science. 1977. $17.50 (ISBN 0-208-01535-3, Linnet). Shoe String.

Radde, Karl H. Polytechnisches Woerterbuch Deutsch-Spanisch. 812p. (Ger. & Span.). 1982. M.50.00. VEB Technik.

--Woerterbuch der Technik, Vol. 1. (Span. & Ger.). 1977. $86.00 (ISBN 3-7736-5530-4, M-6949). French & Eur.

--Woerterbuch der Technik, Vol. 2. (Span. & Ger.). 1977. $86.00 (ISBN 3-7736-5531-2, M-6950). French & Eur.

Radde, Karl H. & Laguna de la Vera, Francisco. Polytechnisches Woerterbuch. LC 77-562408. 716p. (Eng., Span. & Ger.). 1976. M.50.00. VEB Technik.

Razso, Imre. English-Hungarian Technical Dictionary-Angol-Magyar Muszaki Szotar. (Eng. & Hungarian.). $29.50 (ISBN 0-87557-041-0, 041-0). Saphrograph.

Richling, Drewitz. Woerterbuch der Kabeltechnik: Deutsch-Englisch-Franzoesisch. 610p. (Ger., Eng. & Fr.). 1982. DM.60.00. Brandstetter.

Rohr, B. & Wiele, H., eds. Lexikon der Technik. (Illus.). 700p. (Ger.). 1982. M.28.00. Bibl Inst Leipzig.

Rubin, B. Dictionnaire Technique Hongrois-Francais. 1260p. (Hungarian & Fr.). 1965. 75.00 F. Terra.

Ruhland, Jean. Dictionnaire Technique Bilingue. 154p. (Fr.). 1973. 55.00 F. Ruhland.

Schattner, Friedrich. Dictionar Tehnic Polon-Roman si Roman-Polon. LC 77-465384. 271p. (Pol. & Romanian.). 1976. 53.00 lei. Wydawnictwa Naukowo.

Schildt, Bengt. Rysk-Svensk Teknisk Ordbok. 293p. (Rus. & Swedish.). 1965. Kr.145.00 (ISBN 91-24-62667-8). Esselte Studium.

Schlegelmich, A. Worterbuch der Technik: Italienisch-Deutsch. 630p. (Ital. & Ger.). 1981. $95.00 (ISBN 3-7736-5110-4, M-122653). French & Eur.

Schlegelmilch, Alibert. Polytechnisches Woerterbuch, Vol. 1. 2nd ed. (Fr. & Ger.). 1976. $36.00 (ISBN 0-686-56638-6, M-7590, Pub. by Veb Verlag Technik). French & Eur.

--Polytechnisches Woerterbuch, Vol. 2. 2nd ed. (Fr. & Ger.). 1977. $36.00 (ISBN 0-686-56639-4, M-7591, Pub. by Veb Verlag Technik). French & Eur.

Schlegelmilch, Aribert. Polytechnisches Woerterbuch. LC 77-462031. 723p. (Fr. & Ger.). 1976. M.45.00. VEB Verlag Technik.

--Polytechnisches Woerterbuch Italienisch-Deutsch. 632p. (Ital. & Ger.). 1981. M.50.00. VEB Technik.

--Polytechnisches Worterbuch. LC 77-568103. 831p. (Ger. & Fr.). 1976. DM.58.00 (ISBN 3-19-006298-6). Hueber.

Schlomann, Alfred, ed. Illustrated Technical Dictionaries-Illustrierte Technische Woerterbuechen: In Six Languages. Incl. Vol. 1. Machinenelemante-Elements of Machinery & Tools. 1968. Repr. of 1938 ed; Vol. 2. Elektrotechnik & Elektrochemie-Electrical Engineering, Incl. Telegraphy & Telephony. 1963. Repr. of 1928 ed. 50.00x (ISBN 3-4863-1943-4); Vol. 5. Eisenbahnbau und Betreib-Railway Construction & Operation. 1909; Vol. 14. Faserrohnstoffe - Raw Materials of the Textile Industry. 1958. Repr. of 1923 ed. 20.00 (ISBN 3-4863-1981-7); Vol. 16. Webereiund Gewelbe - Weaving & Woven Fabrics. 1958. Repr. of 1925 ed; Vol. 17. Luftfahrt-Aeronautics. 1956. Repr. of 1932 ed. 52.50x (ISBN 3-4863-2011-4). LC 33-6884. (Ger., Eng., Fr., Rus., Span., Ital.). Intl Pubns Serv.

Schmidt, J. J. Vocabulaire Francais-Arabe de l'ingenieur & du Technicien, 1. 136p. (Fr. & Arabic.). 1973. 45.00 F. Maisonneuve & Larose.

Schuermans-Stekhoven, G. Dictionnaire Technique Universel Kluwer: Francais-Neerlandais. 636p. (Fr. & Dutch.). 1978. 186.00 F. Kluwer-Deventer.

Schuermans Stekhoven, G. Dictionnaire Technique Universel Kluwer: Neerlandais-Francais. 656p. (Dutch & Fr.). 1978. 207.00 F. Kluwer-Deventer.

Schutzenberg. Diccionario de Tecnicas de Grupo. 260p. (Span.). 1974. 240.00 ptas. Soc Ed Atenas.

Schuurmans, G. Kluwer's Universeel Technisch Woordenboek: Duits-Nederlands. 433p. (Ger.). 1980. $75.00 (ISBN 90-201-0606-6, M-9471). French & Eur.

--Kluwer's Universeel Technisch Woordenboek, Nederlands-Engels. 775p. (Dutch & Eng.). 1977. $75.00 (ISBN 90-2010-605-8, M-9468). French & Eur.

--Kluwer's Universeel Technisch Woordenboek: Nederlands-Frans. 643p. (Dutch & Fr.). 1977. $75.00 (ISBN 90-201-0609-0, M-9472). French & Eur.

--Kluwer's Universeel Technish Woordenboek: Frans-Nederlands. 622p. (Fr. & Dutch.). 1975. $75.00 (ISBN 90-201-0608-2, M-9473). French & Eur.

--Kluwer's Universel Technisch Woordenboek: Nederlands-Duits. 428p. (Ger. & Dutch.). 1980. $75.00 (ISBN 90-201-0607-4, M-9470). French & Eur.

Schuurmans, Stekhoven G. & Piriou-Vandamme, M. Kluwer's Universeel Technisch Woordenboek Frans-Nederlands. LC 75-406354. xiv, 622p. (Fr. & Dutch.). 1975. fl.73.75 (ISBN 90-201-0608-2). Kluwer Technische.

Schuurmans, Stekhovenn G. Kluwer's Universeel Technisch Woorenboek Nederlands Frans. LC 77-568049. xii, 643p. (Fr. & Dutch.). 1977. write for info. (ISBN 9-0201-0609-0). Kluwer Technische.

Schuurmans-Stekhoven, G. Dictionnaire Technique Universal Kluwer, Francais-Neerlandais. 636p. (Fr. & Dutch.). 1978. $75.00 (ISBN 0-686-56776-5, M-6506). French & Eur.

--Dictionnaire Technique Universal Kluwer Neerlandais-Francais. 656p. (Dutch & Fr.). 1978. $79.95 (ISBN 0-686-56775-7, M-6507). French & Eur.

Shipp, James F. Russian-English Dictionary of Surnames: Important Names from Science & Technology. xvi, 317p. (Orig., Rus. & Eng.). 1981. pap. 30.00x (ISBN 0-917564-10-3). Translation Research.

Shuurmans, G. Kluwer's Universeel Technisch Woordenboek: Engels-Nederlands. 571p. (Eng. & Dutch.). 1981. $75.00 (ISBN 90-2010-771-2). French & Eur.

Sokolowska, M. & Szarski, J. Maly Slownik Techniczny Niemiecko i Polski-Niemiecki. LC 75-410285. 155p. (Ger. & Pol.). 1975. write for info. Wydawnictwa Naukowo.

Solomon, Boris. Dictionnaire de la Technologie des Corps Gras. (Fr., Eng., Ger., Span. & Ital.). 1971. 25.00 F. Inst Corps Gras.

Strasak, Jaroslav. Technisches Deutschfuer Auslaender. (Ger., Technical German for Foreigners). 1969. $12.95 (ISBN 3-87097-041-3, M-7644). French & Eur.

Suarez Gil, L. Diccionario tecnico-maritimo Ingles-Espanol & Espanol-Ingles. 708p. (Span. & Eng.). 1980. pap. write for info. (ISBN 84-205-0707-5). Fed Gremios.

Talvitie, Jyrki K. Ranskalais-Suomalainen Tekniikan ja Kaupan Sanakirja. LC 79-338502. 296p. (Fr. & Finnish.). 1978. write for info. (ISBN 9-5190-3536-2). Tietoteos.

Taspinar. Technisches Woerterbuch. xii, 1563p. (Ger. & Turkish.). 1982. DM.110.00. Brandstetter.

Taspinar, Adnan H. Taspinar's Technical Dictionary. LC 79-338815. 1316p. (Eng. & Turkish.). 1978. TL.500.00. Taspinar's Technical Publications.

Technical Dictionary English-Slovene. 1137p. (Eng. & Slovene.). 1975. $125.00 (ISBN 0-686-92318-9, M-9891). French & Eur.

Technical Dictionary of Crystallography. 132p. 1980. $40.00x (ISBN 0-686-72093-8, Pub. by Collet's). State Mutual Bk.

Technik-Worterbuch: Optik & Optischer Geratebau. 432p. 1980. vinyl $90.00x (ISBN 0-686-72097-0, Pub. by Collet's). State Mutual Bk.

Technisches Woerterbuch Fuer Die Schuhindustrie: German-English & English-German. LC 67-73812. 304p. (Ger. & Eng.). 1966. 17.50x (ISBN 3-7785-0040-6). Intl Pubns Serv.

Terblanche, H. Engels-Afrikaanse Tegniese Woordeboek. LC 78-348473. 599p. (Eng. & Afrikaan.). 1976. write for info. (ISBN 0-625-01281-X). Nasou.

Tver, David F., compiled by. Dictionary of Business & Science. 3rd ed. 632p. 1974. $22.50x (ISBN 0-87201-172-0). Gulf Pub.

Tweney, C. F. & Hughes, L. E. Diccionario tecnologico Chambers: Espanol-ingles-frances-aleman, 2 vols. 2nd ed. 2006p. (Span., Eng., Fr., & Ger.). 1900.00 ptas. Omega SA.

Vandelli, Canzio. Dizionario fraseologico di Inglese Tecnico. (Ital. & Eng.). 1977. L.4900.00. Mondini Siccardi.

Vassilieva. Dictionnaire Russe-Francais Polytechnique. (Rus. & Fr.). 93.20 F. Mir.

Vomackova, Libuse. Cesko-Francouzsky Technicky Slovnik. LC 80-458243. 907p. (Czech. & Fr.). 1978. $95.00. SNTC.
—–Francouzsko-Cesky Technicky Slovnik. 935p. (Eng., Fr. & Czech.). 1978. 99.00 Kcs. SNTC.

Vox, ed. Diccionario Monografico de Technologia. (Span.). 1979. leatherette $17.50 (ISBN 84-7153-383-9, S-36146). French & Eur.

Walther, Rudolf. Polytechnic Dictionary: German-English, English-German, 2 vols. 4th ed. (Ger. & Eng.). $87.50 ea. (ISBN 3-7736-5100-7). Adler.
—–Polytechnisches Woerterbuch. LC 77-463186. 1248p. (Ger.). 1976. M.50.00. VEB Verlag Technik.
—–Polytechnisches Woerterbuch, Vol. 1. 7th ed. (Eng. & Ger., Dictionary of Polytechnics). 1978. $40.00 (ISBN 0-686-56640-8, M-7592, Pub. by Veb Verlag Technik). French & Eur.
—–Polytechnisches Woerterbuch, Vol. 2. 3rd ed. (Eng. & Ger., Dictionary of Polytechnics). 1977. $40.00 (ISBN 0-686-56641-6, M-7593, Pub. by Veb Verlag Technik). French & Eur.
—–Polytechnisches Woerterbuch Deutsch-Englisch. 1046p. (Ger. & Eng.). 1973. $47.00. VEB Technik.
—–Woerterbuch der Technik. (Eng. & Ger., Dictionary of Technology). 1974. $88.00 (ISBN 3-7736-5100-7, M-6952). French & Eur.

Webel, A. A German-English Dictionary of Technical, Scientific & General Terms. 3rd ed. (Ger. & Eng.). 1969. Repr. of 1952 ed. $37.50 (ISBN 0-7100-2258-1). Routledge & Kegan.

Weroniecki, T., ed. Diccionario Tecnico Espanol-Polaco. 545p. (Span. & Pol.). 1981. $49.95 (ISBN 83-204-0287-5, S-37602). French & Eur.

Wittfoht, A. Kunststofftechnisches Woerterbuch, Vol. 3. 768p. (Fr. & Ger.). 1966. $105.00 (ISBN 3-446-10362-7, M-7525, Pub. by C. Hanser). French & Eur.
—–Kunststofftechnisches Woerterbuch, Vol. 3. 768p. (Fr. & Ger.). 1966. $105.00 (ISBN 3-446-10362-7). Hanser.

Woerterbuch der Industriellen Technik: Band I, Deutsch-Englisch. ix, 1092p. (Ger. & Eng.). 1983. DM.130.00. Brandstetter.

Woerterbuch der Industriellen Technik: Band II, Englisch-Deutsch. ix, 1092p. (Eng. & Ger.). 1983. DM.140.00. Brandstetter.

Zhong Wai Publishing Company. An English-Chinese Dictionary of Engineering & Technology. 1036p. (Eng. & Chinese.). 1981. $69.95x (ISBN 0-471-09371-8). Wiley.

Ziefle, Helmut W. Dictionary of Modern Theological German. LC 82-70464. 360p. (Orig., Ger.). 1982. pap. $9.95 (ISBN 0-8010-9929-3). Baker Bk.

Zimmermann, Ralf. Dictionary of Lighting. 362p. 1980. $70.00x (ISBN 0-569-08526-8, Pub. by Collet's). State Mutual Bk.

TECHNOLOGY–LANGUAGE
see also French Language–Technical French; Russian Language–Technical Russian

Alzugaray, J. J. Voces Extranjeras en el Lenguaje Tecnologico. 126p. (Span.). 1979. pap. write for info. (ISBN 84-205-0647-8). Edit Alhambra.

Killer, W. K. Illustrated Technical German for Builders. 4th ed. 183p. (Eng. & Ger.). 1977. $15.95 (ISBN 3-7625-0898-4, M-7468, Pub. by Bauverlag). French & Eur.
—–Illustrated Technical German for Builders. 4th ed. 183p. (Eng. & Ger.). 1977. $15.95 (ISBN 3-7625-0898-4). Bauverlag.

Smolin, Ronald P., ed. High Technology Glossary: Nineteen Eighty-Three. 1983. pap. $10.00 (ISBN 0-686-46678-0). Intl Ideas.

TECHNOLOGY–TERMINOLOGY

Agnew, Irene, ed. Glossary of English & Russian Computer & Automated Control Systems Terminology. (Eng. & Rus.). 1978. soft covers $15.00 (ISBN 0-686-31723-8). Agnew Tech-Tran.

Buck, Frederick H. Glossary of Mongolian Technical Terms. LC 58-59834. (American Council of Learned Societies Publications). 79p. (Orig., Mongolian.). 1958. pap. $3.00x (ISBN 0-87950-257-6). Spoken Lang Serv.

Diccionario de Terminos Cientificos & Tecnicos, 5 vols. (Span.). write for info. (ISBN 8-42670-417-4). McGraw.

Diccionario de Terminos Cientificos & Tecnicos, Vol. 2. 600p. (Span.). 1981. pap. write for info. ptas (ISBN 84-267-0419-0). Marcombo.

Diccionario de terminos cientificos y tecnicos: Obra completa, 5 vols. 2900p. (Span.). 1981. pap. 25000.00 ptas (ISBN 84-267-0417-4). Marcombo.

Diccionario de terminos cientificos y tecnicos: Tomo 1 II. 600p. (Span.). 1981. pap. write for info. (ISBN 84-267-0418-2). Marcombo.

Diccionario de terminos cientificos y tecnicos: Tomo 3 II. 600p. (Span.). 1981. pap. write for info. (ISBN 84-267-0420-4). Marcombo.

Diccionario de terminos cientificos y tecnicos: Tomo 4 II. 600p. (Span.). 1981. pap. write for info. (ISBN 84-267-0421-2). Marcombo.

Diccionario espanol-ruso de terminos cientificos y tecnicos. (Span. & Rus.). write for info. Cultura Popular.

Gullberg, Ingvar E. Swedish-English Fact Ordbok (Technical Terms) 2nd ed. (Swedish & Eng.). 1977. $200.00x (ISBN 91-1-775052-0, SW-207). Vanous.

Khatib, Ahmad. A New Dictionary of Scientific & Technical Terms. 768p. (Eng. & Arabic.). 1980. $45.00 (075-9). Intl Bk Ctr.

McGraw-Hill & Boixareu. Diccionario de Terminos Cientificos & Tecnicos, 5 vols. (Illus.). 2952p. (Span.). 1981. write for info. (ISBN 84-267-0417-4). Marcombo.

Orts, J. C., et al. Breve Diccionario Espanol-Ruso: Ruso-Espanol de Terminos Cientificos & Tecnicos. 438p. (Span. & Rus.). 1960. leatherette $6.95 (ISBN 0-686-97394-1, S-31835). French & Eur.

Pollet, Ray J. Lexique de Termes Techniques: Un Lexique Anglais-Francais. 233p. (Eng. & Fr.). 1976. 58.15 F. Lemeac.

Sahai, Hardeo & Berrios, Jose. A Dictionary of Statistical, Scientific & Technical Terms: English-Spanish, Spanish-English. Smith, Richard A. & Heise, Jeanne, eds. (Spanish Ser.). 143p. (Eng. & Span.). 1981. $13.95 (ISBN 8-4534-0004-0, Pub. by Wadsworth Internacional Iberoamerica). Wadsworth Pub.

Smolin, Ronald P., ed. High Technology Glossary: Nineteen Eighty-Three. 1983. pap. $10.00 (ISBN 0-686-46678-0). Intl Ideas.

Society for Technical Communication. Glossary of Automated Text Processing Terms. 18p. $8.00; members $5.00. Soc Tech Comm.
—–Glossary of Graphics & Technical Art Terms. 24p. $8.00; members $5.00. Soc Tech Comm.

Standard Notations of Technical Terms. $1.50; members $1.00. US Comm Irrigation.

Strom, D. & Strom, J. A. German-Norwegian Dictionary of Technical Terms. (Ger. & Norwegian.). 1983. write for info. (ISBN 82-573-0170-1). Kunnskapsforlaget.
—–Norwegian-German Dictionary of Technical Terms. (Norwegian & Ger.). 1979. write for info. (ISBN 82-573-0136-1). Kunnskapsforlaget.

Tebben, Joseph. Medical & Technical Terminology. 1975. pap. text ed. $4.50 (ISBN 0-88429-013-1). Collegiate Pub.

Technisch Wissenschaftliches Taschenwoerterbuch. 408p. (Ger., Technical Scientific Dictionary). $32.00 (ISBN 3-87749-014-X, M-7643, Pub. by Georg Siemens Verlagsbuchhandlung). French & Eur.

Tekhnicheskaia Terminologiia. 520p. (Rus.). 1977. $14.75 (Pub. by Metsniereba). Four Continent.

Terminology of Technical & Vocational Education. 1979. pap. $5.00 (ISBN 92-3-001593-8, U884, UNESCO). Unipub.

Varios, tr. Diccionario de terminos cientificos y tecnicos: Tomo 5 II. 500p. (Span.). 1981. pap. write for info. (ISBN 84-267-0422-0). Marcombo.

Wennrich, Peter, compiled by. Anglo-American & German Abbreviations in Science & Technology: Part 4, Supplement. 618p. (Eng. & Ger.). 1981. $52.50 (ISBN 3-598-20512-0). Bowker.

World Energy Conference, ed. Energy Terminology: A Multi-Lingual Glossary. 275p. 1983. 100.00 (ISBN 0-08-029314-X, B110); pap. 40.00 (ISBN 0-08-029315-8). Pergamon.

TECHNOLOGY, EDUCATIONAL
see Educational Technology

TECTONICS, PLATE
see Plate Tectonics

TEEN-AGE
see Adolescence

TEETH–DISEASES

Courtois, Jean. Lexiques de Termes de Pathologie Dentaire. 74p. (Fr.). 1974. 30.00 F. Prelat.

TEETH, ARTIFICIAL
see Prosthodontics

TEILHARD DE CHARDIN, PIERRE, 1881-1955

Baudry, Gerard H. Dictionnaire des Correspondants de Tellhard. 200p. (Fr.). 1974. write for info. G. Baudry.

TELECINE FILM
see Television Film

TELECOMMUNICATION
see also Broadcasting; Data Transmission Systems; Police Communication Systems; Pulse Techniques (Electronics); Radio; Television

Glossary of Fiber Optics Terms. (Eng. , Fr , Span. & Ger.). $35.00 (ISBN 0-686-32959-7). Info Gatekeepers.

Ibeas, Franco. Diccionario Tecnologico Ingles-Espanol: Electricidad, Electronica, Telecomunicacion, & Materias Afinas con la Fisica, Optica & Quimica. 452p. (Eng. & Span.). 1974. E950.00 (ISBN 84-205-0492-0). Alhambra.

Interconnection Glossary. $25.00 (ISBN 0-686-32974-0). Info Gatekeepers.

TELECOMMUNICATION–DICTIONARIES

Bones, R. A., ed. Dictionary of Telecommunications. (Illus.). 1970. 15.00 (ISBN 0-8022-2309-5). Philos Lib.

Clason, W. E. Elsevier's Telecommunication Dictionary. 2nd rev. ed. (Eng., Fr., Ital., Span., Dutch & Ger.). 1976. $113.75 (ISBN 0-444-41394-4). Elsevier.

Diccionario de telecomunicaciones en siete idiomas. (Span.). write for info. Cultura Popular.

Dictionary of Telecommunications & Electronics. (Hebrew & Eng.). IL.7.00. Massada Pr.

Dictionary of Telecommunications: English-Chinese. 721p. (Eng. & Chinese.). 1961. pap. $12.95 (ISBN 0-686-92554-8, M-9589). French & Eur.

Freeman, Roger L. English-Spanish, Spanish-English Dictionary of Communications & Electronic Terms. (Eng. & Span.). 1972. $39.50 (ISBN 0-521-08080-0). Cambridge U Pr.

Goedecke, W. Woerterbuch der Elektrotechnik, Fernmeldetechnik und Elektonik, Vol. 1. (Ger., Eng. & Fr., Dictionary of Electrical Engineering, Telecommunication Engineering & Electronics). 1966-68. $56.00 (ISBN 3-87097-013-8, M-7018). French & Eur.

Graham, John. Facts on File Dictionary of Telecommunications. (Illus.). 224p. 1983. $15.95 (ISBN 0-87196-120-2). Facts on File.

Langenscheidts Fachwoerterbuch Fernmeldewesen. 769p. (Ger. & Span.). $32.00 (ISBN 0-686-56628-9, M-7537, Pub. by Langenscheidt). French & Eur.

Proulx, G. J. Dictionnaire d'Electronique et Tele-Communication: Anglais-Francais. 582p. (Fr. & Eng.). 1979. $15.95 (ISBN 0-686-57089-8, M-6469). French & Eur.

Terminologia Usual de la Ciencia & en la Tecnica de la Telecomunicacion. 3rd ed. 384p. (Span.). 1966. 300.00 ptas. Paraninfo.

Wernicke, H. Dictionary of Electronics, Communications & Electrical Engineering, 2 vols. 1300p. Vol. 1. $32.50 ea. (ISBN 0-685-05199-4); Vol. 2. $36.00 ea. (ISBN 0-685-05200-1). Adler.

TELEGU LANGUAGE
see Telugu Language

TELEPHONE, WIRELESS
see Radio

TELEVISION

Cormier, France-Pauline. Vocabulaire de la Radio & de la Television. 17p. (Fr.). 1973. Can.$0.50. Quebec Off.

Miller, Carolyn H. Illustrated T.V. Dictionary. LC 78-73761. (Illustrated Dictionaries Ser.). (Illus.). (gr. 4 up). 1980. PLB 7.29 (ISBN 0-8178-6220-X). Harvey.

TELEVISION–BROADCASTING
see Television Broadcasting

TELEVISION–DICTIONARIES

Abd-El-Wahed. Radio & Television Dictionary. 320p. (Eng., Fr., Ger., Arabic.). 1980. $45.00 (ISBN 0-686-92395-2, M-9762). French & Eur.

Cebrian, Llerrero J. Diccionario de Radio & Television (II) 384p. (Span.). 1981. pap. 620.00 ptas (ISBN 84-205-0789-X). Alhambra.

Cebrian Herreros, Mariano. Diccionario Internacional de Radio & Television. 304p. (Span.). 1981. 500.00 ptas (ISBN 84-500-4295-X). Organ Ofic Adm.

Clason, W. Elsevier's Dictionary of Television, & Video Recording. LC 74-77577. 608p. (Eng., Ger., Fr., Span., Ital. & Dutch.). 1975. $113.00 (ISBN 0-444-41224-7). Elsevier.

Diamant, Lincoln, ed. The Broadcast Communications Dictionary. 2nd, rev., enl. ed. 1978. 10.95 (ISBN 0-8038-0788-0). Hastings.

Diccionario de Electronica Radio & TV. (Illus.). 199p. (Span.). 1966. $2.50. Minerva Bks.

Diccionario de electronica, radio y TV. (Span.). 135.00 ptas. Afha Intl.

Diccionario tecnico, television: Espanol-Ingles. (Span. & Eng.). Arg.$3.00. Cosmopolita.

Diccionario tecnico, television: Ingles-Espanol. (Eng. & Span.). Arg.$3.00. Cosmopolita.

Dictionary of Radio & Television Terms. BBC & ZDF. (Ger. & Eng.). 1973. $29.95 (ISBN 0-471-25586-6, Pub. by Wiley Heyden). Wiley.

German-Prozorova, L. P., et al. Anglo-Russkii Slovar Po Televideniiu. (Rus. & Eng.). 1960. $3.90 (Pub. by Glav. Red. Fizmatgiza). Four Continent.

Levinsky, Otto. Francouzsko-Cesky a Cesko-Francouzsky Slovnik pro Televizni Pracovniky a Prekladatele. LC 76-523695. 80p. (Fr. & Czech.). 1976. write for info. SNTC.

Multilingual Vocabulary of Educational Radio & Television Terms. 189p. (Orig., Eng. , Fr. , Ger. , Ital. , Dutch, Span. & Swedish.). 1971. pap. $11.25x (ISBN 3-19-006291-9). Intl Pubns Serv.

Oakey, Virginia. Dictionary of Film & Television Terms. 206p. (Orig.). 1982. pap. $6.68i (ISBN 0-06-463566-X, EH 566). B&N NY.

Prosorova, L. P. & Kreizer, V. L. English-Russian Televisions Dictionary. 429p. (Eng. & Rus.). 1960. Leatherette $6.95 (ISBN 0-686-92377-4, M-9065). French & Eur.

Romero Gualda, Maria V. Vocabulario De Cine y Television En Espana. 400p. (Span.). 1976. pap. $23.95 (ISBN 84-313-0234-8, S-50002). French & Eur.

Saiz, M. Diccionario de Electronica, Radio & TV: Ingles-Espanol. 144p. (Eng. & Span.). pap. $4.50. Lectorum Pubns.

TELEVISION AS A PROFESSION

see also Radio As a Profession

Rosenthal. Dictionnaire d'accentuation pour les Travailleurs de la Radio & de la Television. (Fr.). write for info. MIR.

TELEVISION BROADCASTING

see also Video Tape Recorders and Recording

Diamant, Lincoln, ed. The Broadcast Communications Dictionary. 2nd, rev., enl. ed. 1978. 10.95 (ISBN 0-8038-0788-0). Hastings.

Feigl, Josef. Anglicko-Cesky a Cesko-Anglicky Slovnik por Televizni Pracovniky a Prekladatele. LC 77-482571. 122p. (Czech.). 1976. write for info. SNTC.

TELEVISION FILM

Mercer. Glossary of Film Terms. rev. 1979 ed. (UFVA Monograph Ser.: No. 2). 92p. 1978. $5.00. Univ Film & Video.

TELEVISION GAMES

see Video Games

TELINGA LANGUAGE

see Telugu Language

TELOMERIZATION

see Polymers and Polymerization

TELUGU LANGUAGE

see also Dravidian Languages

Brown, Charles P. Dictionary of Telugu & English: Explaining English Idioms & Phrases in Telugu, 2 vols. (Eng. & Telugu.). 1976. Repr. of 1958 ed. $195.00 (ISBN 0-518-19008-0). Ayer Co.

Dzenit, S. I. Telugu-Russkii Slovar. 744p. (Rus.). 1972. $8.50 (Pub. by Sov. Entsiklopediia). Four Continent.

TEMPERANCE

see also Alcoholism

National Woman's Christian Temperance Union. Key Terms & Phrases. for 25 copies $0.40 (2204); bulk rates avail. WCTU.

TEMPERATURES, LOW

see Low Temperatures

TENNIS

Appel, Reinhold. Lexikon fur Tennisfreunde. Baumann, Ernst, ed. LC 78-363843. (Illus.). 256p. (Ger.). 1977. 29.80 F (ISBN 3-7658-0254-9). Bucher.

Kaiser, Ulrich. Lexikon Fuer Tennisfreunde. (Ger.). 1977. $25.00 (ISBN 3-7658-0254-9, M-7195). French & Eur.

Kaiser, Ulrich, et al. Lexikon fuer Tennisfreunde. 256p. (Ger.). 1977. DM.29.80 (ISBN 3-7658-0254-9). Bucher Verlag.

Rebourgeon, P., et al, eds. Dictionnaire de Tennis. 160p. (Fr.). 1981. $69.95 (ISBN 0-686-92396-0, M-9769). French & Eur.

Sweeney, Karen. Illustrated Tennis Dictionary for Young People. LC 78-73758. (Illustrated Sports Dictionary). (Illus.). (gr. 4 up). 1979. PLB 7.29 (ISBN 0-8178-6230-7). Harvey.

TENNYSON, ALFRED TENNYSON, BARON, 1809-1892

Baker, A. E. & Tennyson, Alfred. Concordance to the Devil & the Lady. Tennyson, Charles, ed. Repr. of 1931 ed. 15.00 (ISBN 0-527-04550-0). Kraus Repr.

TENURE OF OFFICE

see Civil Service

TERMINALS, DATA (COMPUTERS)

see Computer Input-Output Equipment

TERMINOLOGY

see Names; Terms and Phrases

TERMS, LITERARY

see Literature–Terminology

TERMS AND PHRASES

see also Allusions; Proverbs; Quotations

also Allusions under names of languages, e.g. English Language–Terms and Phrases

Dubois, M. M. Dictionnaire de Locutions. (Fr. & Eng.). 1973. $22.25 (Dist. by Continental Bk Co). Larousse.

Galisson. La Banalisation Lexicale. (Fr.). $20.00 (Dist. by Continental Bk Co). Lib. Fernand Nathan.

Glossary of Conference Terms: English, French, Arabic, 3 vols. in 1. 91p. (Eng. , Fr. & Arabic.). 1980. pap. $22.50 (ISBN 92-3-001567-9, U-993, UNESCO). Unipub.

Hernadi, Miklos. Koezhelyszotar. LC 78-346072. (Illus.). 363p. (Hungarian.). 1976. 30.00 Ft (ISBN 9-63280-426-0). Gondolat.

--Kozhelyszotar. LC 78-346072. 363p. (Hungarian.). 1976. 30.00 Ft (ISBN 9-632-80426-0). Gondolat.

International Cooperation in Terminology. (Infoterm Ser.: Vol. 3). 333p. 1975. pap. text ed. $35.00x (ISBN 3-7940-5503-9, Pub. by K G Saur). Gale.

Lopez de Haro, Carlos. Diccionario de Reglas, Alforismos & Principios de Derecho. LC 77-452232. 254p. (Span.). 1975. 450.00 ptas (ISBN 8-429-00609-5). Reus SA.

Melnikov, N. V., et al. Gornoe Delo: Terminologicheskii Slovar. 527p. (Rus.). 1974. $12.00 (Pub. by Nedra). Four Continent.

Podolskaia, N. V. Slovar Russkoi Onomasticheskoi Terminologii. 200p. (Rus.). 1978. $2.40 (Pub. by Nauka). Four Continent.

Robb. Diccionario de terminos legales. (Span.). write for info. Rev. Mex. de Seguros.

Terminologia Gramatical para su Empleo en la E. G. B. 44p. (Span.). 1981. write for info. (ISBN 84-369-0852-X). Serv Pub Minist.

Theoretical & Methodical Problems of Terminology: Proceedings, Moscow, 1979. (Infoterm Ser.: Vol. 6). 608p. pap. $65.00 (ISBN 3-598-21366-2, Pub. by K G Saur). Gale.

TERRAIN SENSING, REMOTE

see Remote Sensing

TERRESTRIAL PHYSICS

see Geophysics

TESTACEA

see Mollusks

TEUTONIC LANGUAGES

see Germanic Languages

TEWA INDIANS

see Indians of North America–Southwest, New

TEXAS–SOCIAL LIFE AND CUSTOMS

Atwood, E. Bagby. The Regional Vocabulary of Texas. LC 62-9784. (Illus.). 286p. 1969. pap. $6.95 (ISBN 0-292-77008-1). U of Tex Pr.

TEXTILE CHEMISTRY

Winkler, Werner. Technical Dictionary of Textile Chemistry - Fachwoerterbuch Chemiefasern: German-English-French, English-German-French, French-German-English. LC 67-72234. 276p. (Ger., Eng. & Fr.). 1966. $13.00x (ISBN 0-8002-2072-2). Intl Pubns Serv.

TEXTILE FABRICS

see also Textile Industry

Hohenadel, P. & Relton, V. A Modern Textile Dictionary. 375p. (Ger. & Eng.). 1979. $62.50 (ISBN 3-87097-085-5, M-9023). French & Eur.

International Fabricare Institute. Terms-Mill Defects, II. (Fabric Care Ser.). $0.25 (FC-62); 10 or more $0.20, ea. Intl Fabricare Inst.

--Terms-Mill Defects, III. (Fabric Care Ser.). $0.25, ea. (FC-63); 10 or more $0.20, ea. Intl Fabricare Inst.

TEXTILE FABRICS–ANALYSIS

see Textile Chemistry

TEXTILE FABRICS–DICTIONARIES

Burnham, Dorothy K. Warp & Weft: A Dictionary of Textile Terms. (Illus.). 240p. 1982. $35.00 (ISBN 0-684-17332-8, ScribT). Scribner.

English-Chinese Textile Dictionary. 532p. (Eng. & Chinese.). 1977. leatherette $29.95 (ISBN 0-686-92346-4, M-9269). French & Eur.

Hofer, Alfons. Illustriertes Textil und Mode - Lexikon. (Illus.). 342p. (Ger.). $19.95 (ISBN 3-87150-081-X, M-7476, Pub. by Deutscher Fachverlag). French & Eur.

Hohenadel & Relton. Textilwoerterbuch: Band II, Deutsch-English. 375p. (Ger. & Eng.). 1982. DM.70.00. Brandstetter.

Hohenadel, P. & Relton, J. A Modern Textile Dictionary: English-German. 484p. (Ger. & Eng.). 1977. $62.50 (ISBN 3-87097-077-4, M-9024). French & Eur.

Hohenadel, Relton & Relton. Textilwoerterbuch: Band I, English-Deutsch. 486p. (Eng. & Ger.). 1982. DM.70.00. Brandstetter.

Klapper, Marvin. Textile Glossary. LC 72-88888. 120p. 1973. pap. $1.95 (ISBN 0-87005-116-4). Fairchild.

Leskova, T. & Plisek, V. Czech-English Technical Textile Dictionary. 468p. (Czech. & Eng.). 1980. $60.00x (ISBN 0-686-72090-3, Pub. by Collet's). State Mutual Bk.

Linton, George E. The Modern Textile & Apparel Dictionary. rev. 4th ed. Orig. Title: The Modern Textile Dictionary. 1973. $20.00x (ISBN 0-87245-500-9). Textile Bk.

--The Modern Textile & Apparel Dictionary. 4th, rev. enlarged ed. $89.00x (ISBN 0-686-97037-3, Pub. by Meadowfield Pr England). State Mutual Bk.

Michelson, Derrick O. Fachworterbuch Textil. 136p. (Ger. & Eng., Dictionary of Textiles). $13.50 (ISBN 3-87150-106-9, M-7404, Pub. by Deutscher Fachuerlag). French & Eur.

--Textile Terminology: German-English & English-German. LC 72-402367. 136p. (Ger. & Eng.). 1967. 10.00x (ISBN 3-87150-106-9). Intl Pubns Serv.

Rabinowitch, Z. E. & Lupandin, K. K. English-Russian Textile Dictionary. 640p. (Eng. & Rus.). 1961. Leatherette $14.95 (ISBN 0-686-92372-3, M-9111). French & Eur.

Rodriguez, Joaquin O. Diccionario textil panamericano: English-Spanish Dictionary of Textile Terms. 2nd ed. (Span.). 1971. $35.00 (ISBN 0-912476-04-4). W R C Smith.

Scheengluth, Carlos. Diccionario Ilustrado De Terminologia Textil Aleman-Espanol, Espanol-Aleman. 700p. (Ger. & Span.). 1975. $66.00 (ISBN 84-335-6220-7, S-50056). French & Eur.

Schock, Sarina & Gebert, Erika. Fachworterbuch Textil. 136p. (Ger. & Fr.). $9.95 (ISBN 3-87150-039-9, M-7405, Pub. by Deutscher Fachverlag). French & Eur.

Textile Dictionary. 536p. (Eng. , Fr. , Ger. , & Span.). 1979. $106.50 (ISBN 0-444-41772-9). Elsevier.

Wingate, Isabel B., ed. Fairchild's Dictionary of Textiles. 6th ed. LC 78-73964. 1979. $40.00 (ISBN 0-87005-198-9). Fairchild.

TEXTILE INDUSTRY

see also Dyes and Dyeing; Lace and Lace Making; Textile Chemistry; Wool Trade and Industry

Casa Aruta. Diccionario de la industria textil. (Span.). 2100.00 ptas. Labor SA.

Habert, R., et al. Lexique de l'Industrie Textile: Francais-Anglais. 240p. (Fr. & Eng.). 1974. pap. $9.95 (ISBN 0-686-92180-1, M-9222). French & Eur.

Hohenadel, Paul & Relton, Jonathan. Textil-Worterbuch. LC 78-339373. (Eng. & Ger.). 1977. write for info. (ISBN 3-87097-077-4). Brandstetter.

International Fabricare Institute. Knit Terms. (Selling Sense ser.). $0.25 (SS-81); 10 or more $0.20, ea. Intl Fabricare Inst.

Matthes, Max. Textil-Fachwoerterbuch. 3rd ed. LC 79-385003. 204p. (Ger.). 1979. DM.write for info. (ISBN 3-794-90314-5). Schiele & Schon.

Michelson, Derrick O. Textile Terminology: German-English & English-German. LC 72-402367. 136p. (Ger. & Eng.). 1967. 10.00x (ISBN 3-87150-106-9). Intl Pubns Serv.

Saarikoski, Lea. Englantilais-Suomalainen Tekstiili-ja Vaatetusalan Sanasto. LC 79-394177. 156p. (Finnish.). 1979. Fmk.27.50 (ISBN 9-511-04908-9). Otava Kust.

Sabrie, A. M. & Scharaf, R. S., eds. Textile Industry Dictionary. 394p. (Eng., Fr., Ger. & Arabic.). 1975. $45.00 (ISBN 0-686-92311-1, M-9763). French & Eur.

Shearer, Howard E., ed. Glossary of Textile Terminology for the Paper Manufacturer. (TAPPI PRESS Reports). 38p. 1965. $3.95 (01-01-R003). TAPPI.

Suppa, Giuseppe. Glossario italiano tessile in cinque lingue. (Illus.). 900p. (Ital.). 1975. L.15000.00. Tec Tessile.

Technical Dictionary: The Textile Industry. (Eng. , Fr. , Ger. & Arabic.). 1975. $30.00x (ISBN 0-686-44748-4, Pub. by Collets). State Mutual Bk.

Textile Terms & Definitions. 228p. 1981. $95.00x (ISBN 0-900739-17-7, Pub. by Textile Inst England). State Mutual Bk.

Velco, G. Textile Dictionary. (Eng., Fr., Ger., Rus. & Bulgarian.). 1977. $70.00x (ISBN 0-686-44749-2, Pub. by Collets). State Mutual Bk.

Vries, Louis de. Woerterbuch der Textilindustrie, Vol. 2. (Eng. & Ger., Dictionary of Textile Industry). pap. $25.00 (ISBN 0-686-56612-2, M-6948). French & Eur.

TEXTILE INDUSTRY–DIRECTORIES
Farnfield, Carolyn A. & Alvey, P. J. Textile Terms & Definitions. 228p. 1975. $90.00x (ISBN 0-686-63806-9). State Mutual Bk.

TEXTILES
see Textile Fabrics

THAI LANGUAGE
see Siamese Language

THAI LANGUAGE–DICTIONARIES–ENGLISH
Allison, G. Mini English-Thai-English Dictionary. 460p. (Eng. & Thai.). 1979. pap. $9.95 (ISBN 0-686-92176-3, M-9900). French & Eur.

Sanskrit-Thai-English Dictionary. 1339p. (Sanskrit, Thai & Eng.). 10.00x (ISBN 0-8002-1951-1). Intl Pubns Serv.

So Sethaputra, compiled by. New Model Thai-English Dictionary, 2 vols. 3rd ed. LC 81-915704. 1072p. (Eng. & Thai.). 1978. B.450.00 set. Thai Watana.

Thai-English & English-Thai Dictionary, 1 vol. 1974. $14.00 (ISBN 0-87557-087-9, 087-9). Saphrograph.

THAI LANGUAGES
see Tai Languages

THEATER–COSTUME
see Costume

THEATER–DICTIONARIES
Band-Kuzmany, K. R. Glossary of the Theatre. (Eng., Fr., Ital. & Ger.). 1970. $30.00 (ISBN 0-444-40716-2). Elsevier.

Bowman, Walter P. & Ball, Robert H. Theatre Language, a Dictionary. LC 60-10495. 1976. pap. $6.95 (ISBN 0-87830-551-3). Theatre Arts.

Brunius, Niklas. Teaterord. LC 77-578501. 179p. (Eng., Danish, Finnish, Icelandic, Norwegian & Swedish.). 1975. write for info. Nord Teater.

Dieterich, Genoveva. Pequeno Diccionario De Teatro Mundial. 294p. (Span.). 1976. pap. $5.25 (ISBN 84-7090-028-5, S-31395). French & Eur.

Dubuc, R. Vocabulaire bilingue du theatre: Anglais-Francais Francais Anglais. 174p. (Eng. & Fr.). 1979. 70.00 F. Maison Dictionnaire.

Giteau, Cecile. Dictionnaire des Arts du Spectacle. 456p. (Fr., Eng. & Ger.). 1970. 135.00 F. Bordas-Dunod.

Granville, Wilfred. Theater Dictionary: British & American Terms in the Drama, Opera, and Ballet. Repr. of 1952 ed. lib. bdg. 15.00x (ISBN 0-8371-4428-0, GRTD). Greenwood.

Muller, Vaclav. Maly Divadelni Slovnik. LC 77-553272. 132p. (Czech.). 1977. write for info. Kultura.

Rhae, Kenneth & Southern, Richard. Lexique International Des Termes Techniques De Theatre, en 8 Langues. 144p. (Fr.). $125.00 (ISBN 0-686-57206-8, M-6484). French & Eur.

--Lexique International des Termes Techniques de Theatre en 8 Langues. (Illus.). 144p. (Fr.). 330.00 F. Meddens.

Salazar Lopez, Jose M. Diccionario legislativo de cinematografia y teatro. (Span.). 300.00 ptas. Nacional Editora.

Simon, Alfred. Dictionnaire theatre francais contemporain. (Dict. de l'Homme du Vingtieme Siecle). (Illus., Fr.). 1970. $8.50 (ISBN 0-685-13885-2, 3740). Larousse.

THEATER–FRANCE
Parfaict, Claude. Dictionnaire des Theatres de Paris, 7 vols. 2nd ed. (Fr.). 1967. 500.00 F. Slatkine.

Simon, Alfred. Dictionnaire Du Theatre Francais Contemporain. 250p. (Fr.). 1970. pap. $6.95 (ISBN 0-686-56878-8, M-675). French & Eur.

--Dictionnaire du Theatre Francais Contemporain. (Illus.). 250p. (Fr.). 17.60 F. Larousse.

THEATRICAL COSTUME
see Costume

THEMATIC CATALOGS (MUSIC)
see Vocal Music–Thematic Catalogs

THEOLOGICAL BELIEF
see Faith

THEOLOGICAL VIRTUES
see Faith

THEOLOGY–DICTIONARIES
Alvarez, J. Mateos. Vocabulario Teologico del Evangelio de Saint Juan. 310p. (Span.). 1980. pap. $13.95 (ISBN 84-7057-270-9, S-33107). French & Eur.

Bauer. Diccionario De Teologia Biblica. 2nd ed. 582p. (Span.). 1976. $38.95 (ISBN 84-254-0360-X, S-50203). French & Eur.

Bouyer, Louis. Diccionario De Teologia. 4th ed. 672p. (Span.). 1977. $25.50 (ISBN 84-254-0377-4, S-14671). French & Eur.

Dizionario teologico interdisciplinare, 3 vols. LC 79-384605. (Ital.). 1977. write for info. Marietti.

Harrison, Everett F., ed. Baker's Dictionary of Theology. $17.95 (ISBN 0-8010-4042-6). Baker Bk.

Leon-Dufour, Xavier, ed. Dictionary of Biblical Theology. new ed. Cahill, P. Joseph, tr. from Fr. LC 73-6437. 710p. 1973. Repr. $27.50 (ISBN 0-8164-1146-8). Seabury.

Livingstone, E. A., ed. The Concise Oxford Dictionary of the Christian Church. 1978. 19.95 (ISBN 0-19-211549-9); pap. 9.95 (ISBN 0-19-283014-7). Oxford U Pr.

Mosse, Walter M. Theological German Vocabulary. (Ger.). 1968. lib. bdg. 14.50x (ISBN 0-374-95966-8). Octagon.

Rahner, K. Herders Theologisches Taschenlexikon. 3180p. (Ger.). 1976. pap. $99.50 (ISBN 0-686-56481-2, M-7463, Pub. by Herder). French & Eur.

--Herders Theologisches Taschenlexikon. 3180p. (Ger.). 1976. pap. $99.50. Herder.

Rahner, Karl & Vorgrimler, Herbert. Dictionary of Theology. 2nd ed. 500p. 1981. $17.50 (ISBN 0-8245-0040-7). Crossroad NY.

Taylor, Richard S., ed. Beacon Dictionary of Theology. 648p. 1983. $29.95 (ISBN 0-8341-0811-9). Beacon Hill.

Wright, Charles & Neil, Charles, eds. The Protestant Dictionary: Containing Articles on the History, Doctrines, & Practices of the Christian Church. LC 73-155436. 1971. Repr. of 1933 ed. $56.00x (ISBN 0-8103-3388-0). Gale.

THEOLOGY, BIBLICAL
see Bible–Theology

THEOLOGY, DEVOTIONAL
see Devotional Literature; Meditations

THEOLOGY, DOCTRINAL
see also Apologetics; Bible–Theology; Christian Ethics; Conversion; Faith; Heresies and Heretics; Miracles; Mysticism; Sin
also subdivision Doctrinal and Controversial Works under names of Christian denominations, e.g. Baptism–Doctrinal and Controversial Works
Humphreys, Fisher & Wise, Philip. A Dictionary of Doctrinal Terms. LC 81-86635. (Orig.). 1983. pap. $4.95 (ISBN 0-8054-1141-0). Broadman.

THEOLOGY, DOGMATIC
see Theology, Doctrinal

THEOLOGY, ETHICAL
see Christian Ethics

THEOLOGY, FUNDAMENTAL
see Apologetics

THEOLOGY, MORAL
see Christian Ethics

THEOLOGY, MYSTICAL
see Mysticism

THEOLOGY, SCHOLASTIC
see Scholasticism

THEOLOGY, SYSTEMATIC
see Theology, Doctrinal

THEORY OF SETS
see Set Theory

THERAPEUTIC EXERCISE
see Exercise Therapy

THERAPEUTICS
see also Antiseptic Medication; Chemistry, Medical and Pharmaceutical; Diet in Disease; Drugs; Materia Medica; Nurses and Nursing; Nutrition
also names of individual drugs, and names of diseases and groups of diseases, e.g. Bronchitis, Fever, Nervous System–Diseases; also subdivision Therapeutic Use under specific subjects, e.g. Poetry–Therapeutic Use; X-Rays–Therapeutic Use
Blacque-Belair, Alain. Dictionnaire de Medecine Clinique Pharmacologique & Therapeutique. 2nd ed. (Illus.). 1914p. (Fr.). 1978. 196.00 F. Maloine.

Perlemuter, Leon & Obraska, Paul. Dictionnaire Pratique de Therapeutique Medicale. 2nd ed. 1232p. (Fr.). 1978. 190.00 F. Masson.

THERMAL EQUILIBRIUM
see Heat; Thermodynamics

THERMAL TRANSFER
see Heat–Transmission

THERMODYNAMICS
see also Heat
James, Arthur M. A Dictionary of Thermodynamics. LC 76-5472. 262p. 1976. 29.95x (ISBN 0-470-15035-1). Halsted Pr.

THERMOELECTRICITY
Glossaire des Termes & Symboles en Matiere de Conversion Thermoelectronique. 90p. (Fr.). 1971. 23.00 F. O. C. D. E.

THESAURI, SUBJECT
see Subject Headings

THIERS, ADOLPHE, 1797-1877
Martinez de Sousa, Jose. Diccionario de Tipografia & del Libro. 570p. (Span.). 1974. 1070.00 ptas (ISBN 84-335-03006). Labor SA.

THIN LAYER CHROMATOGRAPHY
Angele, H. Four-Language Technical Dictionary of Chromatography: English, German, French, Russian. LC 76-103000. (Eng., Ger., Fr. & Rus.). 1971. text ed. 45.00 (ISBN 0-08-015865-X). Pergamon.

THOROUGHFARES
see Roads; Streets

THOUGHT, NEW
see New Thought

THUCYDIDES
Huart, Pierre. Vocabulaire de l'analyse Psychologique dans l'oeuvre de Thucydide. 546p. (Fr.). 1969. 88.00 F. Klincksieck.

THULE EXPEDITION, 5TH, 1921-1924
Mathiassen, Therkel. Report on the Expedition. LC 76-21664. (Thule Expedition. 5th. 1921-1924: Vol. 1, No. 1). Repr. of 1945 ed. $32.50 (ISBN 0-404-58301-6). AMS Pr.

TIBETAN LANGUAGE
Buck, Stuart H., ed. Tibetan-English Dictionary with Supplement. (Publications in the Languages of Asia: No. 1). (Tibetan & Eng.). 1969. $36.95 (ISBN 0-8132-0269-8). Cath U Pr.

Chandra Das, S. Tibetan-English Dictionary: With Sanskrit Synonyms. Sanberg, Graham & Heyde, A. William, eds. 1389p. (Tibetan & Eng.). 1976. Repr. 35.00 (ISBN 0-89581-177-4). Lancaster-Miller.

Csoma de Koros, Alexander. A Dictionary of Tibetan & English. 351p. (Tibetan & Eng.). 1978. Repr. of 1834 ed. 39.00 (ISBN 0-89684-107-3, Pub. by Cosmo Pubns India). Orient Bk Dist.

Das, S. C. Tibetan-English Dictionary. (Tibetan & Eng.). Repr. of 1970 ed. 35.00x (ISBN 0-87902-125-X). Orientalia.

Das, S. C. & Kazi, I. D. Tibetan-English, English-Tibetan Dictionary, 2 vols. (Tibetan & Eng.). Set. 70.00 (ISBN 0-686-77964-9). Heinman.

Das, Sarat C. Tibetan-English Dictionary, with Sanskrit Synonyms. Sandberg, G. & Heyde, A. W., eds. 1384p. (Tibetan, Sanskrit & Eng.). 1970. Repr. of 1902 ed. 30.00x (ISBN 0-8002-2086-2). Intl Pubns Serv.

Dass, S. C. Tibetan-English Dictionary. (Tibetan & Eng.). 1979. 42.00 (ISBN 0-89684-329-7). Orient Bk Dist.

Giraudeau & Gore, Francis. Dictionnaire Francais-Tibetain. 310p. (Fr. & Tibetan). 1956. 120.00 F. Maisonneuve, A.

Giraudeau, A. & Gore, Francis. Dictionnaire Francais-Tibetain (Tibet Oriental) 310p. (Fr. & Tibetian). 1956. $49.95 (ISBN 0-686-57301-3, M-6275). French & Eur.

Goldstein, Melvyn C. Tibetan-English Dictionary of Modern Tibetan. (Tibetan & Eng.). 1975. 27.95x (ISBN 0-685-89505-X). Himalaya Hse.

Jaschke, H. A. Tibetan-English Dictionary. (Tibetan & Eng.). 1980. 22.50 (ISBN 0-8426-0962-8). Orient Bk Dist.

TIDAL CURRENTS
see Ocean Currents

TILES
Cerda, et al. Vocabulario Espanol de Tejas. (Eng. & Span.). $15.00. Camino Real.

TIMEX-SINCLAIR (COMPUTER)
Giarratano, Joseph C. Timex-Sinclair One Thousand Pocket Dictionary. 1983. pap. 4.95 (ISBN 0-88022-028-7). Que Corp.

TINCTORIAL SUBSTANCES
see Dyes and Dyeing

TITLES OF ADDRESS
see Titles of Honor and Nobility

TITLES OF HONOR AND NOBILITY
see also Heraldry; Nobility
Hucker, Charles O. A Dictionary of Official Titles in Imperial China: Governmental Nomenclature from Antiquity to 1850. Date not set. price not set. Stanford U Pr.

TOADSTOOLS
see Mushrooms

TOBA LANGUAGE (INDIAN)
Warneck, Johannes G. Toba-Batak-Deutsches Worterbuch. LC 79-353140. xii, 332p. (Ger. & Toba-Batak.). 1977. fl.98.80 (ISBN 9-0247-2018-4). Nyhoff.

TOBACCO-PIPES
Hochrain, Helmut. Das ABC des Pfeifenrauchers. Haisch, Heinrich, ed. LC 78-389542. (Illus.). 204p. (Ger.). 1977. DM.5.80 (ISBN 3-453-41223-0). Heyne W Verlag.

TOGO
Decalo, Samuel. Historical Dictionary of Togo. LC 76-14926. (African Historical Dictionaries Ser.: No. 9). 261p. 1976. $15.00 (ISBN 0-8108-0942-7). Scarecrow.

TOILET (GROOMING)
see Beauty, Personal

TOILET PREPARATIONS
see also Cosmetics; Perfumes; Soap and Soap Trade
Cariere, G., ed. Dictionary of Surface-Active Agents, Cosmetics & Toiletries. (Eng., Fr., Ger., Span., Ital., Dutch & Ger.). 1978. $36.25 (ISBN 0-444-99809-8). Elsevier.

European Directories, ed. The Dictionary of Toiletry & Cosmetic Manufacturers in Western Europe. 1981. $100.00x (ISBN 0-686-78875-3, Pub. by European Directories England). State Mutual Bk.

TOOLS
see also Carpentry–Tools; Cutlery
also specific tools
Clason, ed. Elsevier's Dictionary of Tools & Ironware. (Eng., Fr., Span., Ital., Dutch & Ger.). 1982. $74.50 (ISBN 0-444-42085-1). Elsevier.

Freeman, Henry G. Tool Dictionary. 2nd ed. (Ger. & Eng.). 1960. $78.00 (ISBN 3-7736-5052-3). Adler.

--Woerterbuch Werkzeuge. 2nd ed. (Ger. & Eng., Dictionary of Tools). 1960. leatherette $92.00 (ISBN 3-7736-5052-3, M-6908). French & Eur.

Salaman. Dictionary of Tools. 1974. s.p. $49.50 (ISBN 0-87002-912-6). Bennett IL.

Schlomann, A. Illustrierte Technische Woerterbucher: Maschinenelemente, Vol. 1. (Illus., Ger., Eng., Fr., Rus., Span. & It., Illustrated dictionary elements of machinery & tools). 1968. $59.95 (ISBN 0-686-56482-0, M-7469, Pub. by R. Oldenbourg). French & Eur.

--Illustrierte Technische Woerterbucher: Maschinenelemente, Vol. 1. (Illus., Ger., Eng., Fr., Rus., Span. & Ital.). 1968. $59.95. Oldenbourg Verlag.

TOPOGRAPHICAL DRAWING
see also Map Drawing
Dictionnaire Topographique de la France. 562p. (Fr.). 1881. 30.00 F. Biblio Nationale.
Longnon, Auguste. Dictionnaire Topographique de la France. 468p. (Fr.). 1891. 25.00 F. Biblio Nationale.
Roman, J. Dictionnaire Topographique de la France. 272p. (Fr.). 1884. 20.00 F. Biblio Nationale.
Stein, Henri & Hubert, J. Dictionnaire Topographique de la France. 738p. (Fr.). 1954. 50.00 F. Biblio Nationale.
Vallee, Eugene & Latouche, Robert. Dictionnaire Topographique de la France, 1. 486p. (Fr.). 1954. 40.00 F. Biblio Nationale.

TOPOLOGY
see also Knot Theory
C.I.L.F. Vocabulaire de la topographie. 92p. (Fr.). 1980. 80.00 F. Maison Dictionnaire.

TOPONYMY
see also Names, Geographical
Koichubaev, E. Kratkii Tolkovyi Slovar Toponimov Kazakhstana. 274p. (Rus.). 1974. $3.40 (Pub. by Nauka). Four Continent.
Zhuchkevich, V. A. Kratkii Toponimicheskii Slovar Belorussii. 447p. (Rus.). 1974. $4.25 (Pub. by MGU). Four Continent.

TOTAL ABSTINENCE
see Temperance

TOULOUSE
Doujat, Jean. Dictionnaire de la Langue Toulousaine. 254p. (Fr.). 1974. 110.00 F. Lafitte Repr.

TOUR GUIDES (MANUALS)
see subdivisions Description and Travel as appropriate under names of countries, regions, cities, etc.

TOURISM
see Tourist Trade

TOURIST TRADE
Academie International du Tourisme. Diccionario Turistico Internacional: Edition Espagnole. (Span.). 80.00 F. Acad Intl Tour.
Academie Internationale du Tourisme. Dictionar Turistic International: Edition Roumaine. (Romanian.). 80.00 F. Acad Intl Tour.
--Dictionnaire touristique international: Edition francaise. (Fr.). 80.00 F. Acad Intl Tour.
--International Toeristisch Woordenboek: Edition Neerlandais. (Dutch.). 80.00 F. Acad Intl Tour.
Dictionnaire International du Tourisme: Allemand-Anglais-Espagnol-Italien-Neerlandai. 3rd ed. 325p. (Ger. , Eng. , Span. , Ital. & Dutch.). 1968. write for info. Acad Intl Tour.
Friedreich, W. Taschenwoerterbuch des Fremdenverkehrs. 187p. (Ger. & Eng., Dictionary of Tourism). 1970. $7.95 (ISBN 3-19-006281-1). Hueber.
Friedrich, W. Taschenwoerterbuch des Fremdenverkehrs. 187p. (Ger. & Eng., Dictionary of Tourism). 1970. $7.95 (ISBN 3-19-006281-1, M-7632, Pub. by M. Hueber). French & Eur.
Havas, L. Dictionnaire de Tourisme Francais-Hongrois. 600p. (Fr. & Hungarian.). 1966. 16.20 F. Terra.
Metelka, Charles J., ed. The Dictionary of Tourism. LC 80-83526. 91p. 1981. 12.00 (ISBN 0-916032-10-8). Merton Hse.
Neiger, Elisabetta. Terminologia turistico alberghiera: L'albergatore poliglotta. 3rd ed. (Illus.). vi, 178p. (Ital., Eng., Ger. & Fr.). $L5000.00 (C/980). Ed Calderini.
Novo, G. Diccionario General de Turismo. (Span.). write for info. (S-28710). French & Eur.

TOURISTS
see Tourist Trade

TOURS
see subdivisions Description and Travel as appropriate under names of countries, regions, cities, etc.

TOWN LIFE
see City and Town Life

TOWN MEETING
see Local Government

TOWN PLANNING
see City Planning

TOWNS
see Cities and Towns

TOWNSHIP GOVERNMENT
see Local Government

TRACK-ATHLETICS
see also Cycling
Emert, Phyllis R. Illustrated Track & Field Dictionary for Young People. LC 80-84812. (Illustrated Dictionary Ser.). (Illus.). 128p. (gr. 4 up). 1981. PLB 7.29 (ISBN 0-8178-0028-X). Harvey.

TRACTORS
Jetikov. Dictionnaire Russe-Francais de l'automobile & du Tracteur. (Rus. & Fr.). 34.10 F. Mir.

TRADE
see Business; Commerce

TRADE, BALANCE OF
see Balance of Trade

TRADE-MARKS
see also Marks of Origin
Dubois, Michel. Dictionnaire de Sigles Nationaux et Internationaux. 479p. (Fr.). 1977. pap. $50.00 (ISBN 0-686-56831-1, M-6609). French & Eur.
Room, Adrian. Dictionary of Trade Name Origins. 208p. 1982. 12.95 (ISBN 0-7100-0839-2). Routledge & Kegan.
Wood, Donna, ed. Trade Names Dictionary: Company Index. 3rd ed. 1000p. 1982. $225.00x (ISBN 0-8103-0697-2). Gale.

TRADE NAMES
see Trade-Marks

TRADES
see Building Trades; Occupations

TRADITIONS
see Superstition

TRAFFIC
see Communication and Traffic

TRAFFIC CONTROL
see Traffic Engineering

TRAFFIC ENGINEERING
Bein, Gerhard. Woerterbuch Des Internationalen Verkehrs (Dictionary of International Traffic) 233p. (Ger. & Eng.). 1968. 9.00x (ISBN 0-8002-1306-8). Intl Pubns Serv.

TRAFFIC REGULATION
see Traffic Engineering

TRAGEDY
Mandel, Oscar. A Definition of Tragedy. LC 82-8505. 184p. 1982. pap. text ed. $9.25 (ISBN 0-8191-2530-X). U Pr of Amer.

TRAILERS
Truck Trailer Manufacturers Association. Nomenclature & Terminology of Tank Trailers & Containers. (Recommended Practices: RP No. 36-75). 1975. $3.00. Truck Trailer Mfrs.

TRAINED NURSES
see Nurses and Nursing

TRAINING, PHYSICAL
see Physical Education and Training

TRAINING COLLEGES FOR TEACHERS
see Teachers Colleges

TRAMPING
see Hiking

TRANSCRIPTION (SHORTHAND)
see Shorthand

TRANSCRIPTIONS, PHONETIC
see Language and Languages-Phonetic Transcriptions

TRANSIT SYSTEMS
see Local Transit

TRANSLATING AGENCIES
see Translating Services

TRANSLATING SERVICES
Merino Bustamante, Jose. Diccionario auxiliar de traductor: Espanol-Ingles. 144p. (Span. & Eng.). 1982. pap. 300.00 ptas (ISBN 84-85439-00-7). CEEI.
--Diccionario Auxiliar del Traductor Espanol-Ingles. 144p. (Span. & Eng.). 1981. 300.00 ptas (ISBN 84-85439-00-7). CEEI.

TRANSMISSION, POWER
see Power Transmission

TRANSMISSION OF DATA
see Data Transmission Systems

TRANSMISSION OF HEAT
see Heat-Transmission

TRANSMITTING SETS, RADIO
see Radio-Transmitters and Transmission

TRANSMUTATION OF METALS
see Alchemy

TRANSPORTATION-DICTIONARIES
Bein, G. German-English Dictionary of International Transport. 232p. (Ger. & Eng.). 1980. $15.00x (ISBN 0-569-05117-7, Pub. by Collet's). State Mutual Bk.
Bein, Gerhard. Woerterbuch Des Internationalen Verkehrs (Dictionary of International Traffic) 233p. (Ger. & Eng.). 1968. 9.00x (ISBN 0-8002-1306-8). Intl Pubns Serv.
Cavinato, Joseph L., ed. Transportation-Logistics Dictionary. 2nd ed. 323p. 1982. $14.00 (ISBN 0-87408-022-3). Traffic Serv.
Cvrcek, Jarom. Slovnik Zakladnich Odbornych Rusko-Ceskych Vyrazu ze Silnicni a Mestske Dopravy. LC 77-484205. 260p. (Rus. & Czech.). 1976. write for info. SNTC.
Heinze, S. Fachwoerterbuch des Transportwesens. (Ger. & Eng., Dictionary of Transportation Systems). 1961. 17.50 (ISBN 3-87097-018-9, M-7391, Pub. by Brandstetter). French & Eur.
--Fachwoerterbuch des Transportwesens. (Ger. & Eng.). 1961. DM.17.50 (ISBN 3-87097-018-9). Brandstetter.
Heinze, Siegfried. Dictionary of Transport Terms & Phrases. LC 62-5007. 420p. (Ger. & Eng.). 1961. 11.25x (ISBN 3-87097-018-9). Intl Pubns Serv.
Logie, G. Glossary of Transport. (International Planning Glossaries Ser.: Vol. 2). (in 6 languages). 1980. $53.25 (ISBN 0-444-41888-1). Elsevier.
Mrazek, Jindrich. Slovnik Zakladnich Odbornych Cesko-Nemeckych Vyrazu ze Silnicni a Mestske Dopravy. LC 75-545516. 215p. (Czech. & Ger., Praha, Czechoslovakia). 1975. write for info. SNTL.
Probst, Lester A. & DeGross, Katherine. Transportation Dictionary. LC 79-91885. 127p. (Eng.). 1979. write for info. (ISBN 0-9603760-0-3). Data Tactics.

TRANSPORTATION INSURANCE
see Insurance, Marine

TRASH
see Refuse and Refuse Disposal

TRAVEL BOOKS
see Voyages and Travels
also subdivision Description and Travel under names of countries, regions, etc.

TRAVELS
see Voyages and Travels

TREES
see also Forests and Forestry; Landscape Gardening; Shrubs; Wood
also classes, orders, species, etc. of trees, e.g. Elm, Pine, Spruce
Hillier, H. G. The Hillier Color Dictionary of Trees & Shrubs. 323p. 1982. $19.95 (ISBN 0-442-23653-0). Van Nos Reinhold.

TRENCH LANGUAGE (EUROPEAN WAR)
see European War, 1914-1918-Language (New Words, Slang, etc.)

TRICKS
see also Magic
Chardana, J. L. & Vega, V. Diccionario ilustrado de trucos. 2nd ed. (Illus.). 700p. (Span.). write for info. G Gili.
Vani, Paule. Diccionario de trucos. Giordano, Eduardo, tr. 336p. (Span.). 1982. pap. 740.00 ptas (ISBN 84-85979-25-7). Granica.

TROPES
see Figures of Speech

TROPICAL MEDICINE-BIBLIOGRAPHY
University of London. Dictionary Catalogue of the London School of Hygiene & Tropical Medicine, 7 Vols. 1965. Set. lib. bdg. $590.00 (ISBN 0-8161-0703-3, Hall Library); serials catalogue. $35.00 (ISBN 0-8161-0182-5); 1st suppl. (1971) $105.00 (ISBN 0-8161-0821-8). G K Hall.

TRS-80 (COMPUTER)
Noonan, Larry. Basic BASIC-English Dictionary for the Apple, PET & TRS-80. (Illus.). 154p. $17.95 (ISBN 0-686-88421-3, 1521). TAB Bks.

TSCHI LANGUAGE
see Twi Language

TSHI LANGUAGE
see Twi Language

TSIMSHIAN INDIANS
see Indians of North America-Northwest, Pacific

TSIMSHIAN LANGUAGE
Dunn, John A. A Practical Dictionary of the Coast Tsimshian Language. LC 79-321726. x, 155p. (Eng. & Tsimshian.). 1978. write for info. Natl Mus Can.

TSWI LANGUAGE
see Twi Language

TULLE EMBROIDERY
see Lace and Lace Making

TUMORS
Gerard-Marchant, Remi. Glossaire d'histopathologia des Tumeurs Humaines. (Illus.). 144p. (Fr.). 1971. 70.00 F. Masson & Cie.

TUNGUSIC LANGUAGES
see also Manchu Language
Sravnitelnyi Slovar Tunguso-Manchzhurskikh Iazykov: Materialy & Etimologicheskomu Slovariu, 2 vols. (Rus.). 1975. $37.50 set (Pub. by Nauka). Four Continent.
Tsintsius, V. I. Russko-Evenskii Slovar. 778p. (Rus.). 1952. $4.50 (Pub. by GINS). Four Continent.

TURF MANAGEMENT
Dictionary of Turfgrass Terms. $1.00 (2003). Pro Golfers.

TURKISH LANGUAGE
Alderson, A. D. & Iz, Fahir, eds. Concise Oxford Turkish Dictionary. (Turkish.). 1959. 29.00x (ISBN 0-19-864109-5). Oxford U Pr.
Antelava, H. G. Abbreviated Turkish-Russian Dictionary of New Words. 95p. (Turkish & Rus.). 1978. pap. $7.95 (ISBN 0-686-97387-9, M-9054). French & Eur.
Avery, Robert, et al, eds. Turkish, English-English, Turkish Dictionary (the Redhouse Portable Dictionary) (Turkish & Eng.). 15.00 (ISBN 0-685-80306-6). Heinman.
Baubec, A., et al. Dictionar Turc-Roman. LC 80-480771. 377p. (Turkish & Romanian.). 1979. write for info. lei. Editura Stiintifica.
Budgay. Dizionario turco-italiano. 194p. (Turkish & Ital.). 1976. L.2300.00. Vallardi A.
Bugday, M. Celalettin. Dizionario Italiano-Turco, Turco-Italiano. 410p. (Ital. & Turkish.). 1979. leatherette $5.95 (ISBN 0-686-97351-8, M-9178). French & Eur.
Clauson, Gerard. An Etymological Dictionary of Pre-Thirteenth Century Turkish. (Turkish.). 1972. 160.00x (ISBN 0-19-864112-5). Oxford U Pr.
Goodenough, Ward H. & Sugita, Hiroshi. Trukese-English Dictionary. LC 79-54277. (Memoir Ser.: Vol. 141). (Turkish.). 1980. $10.00 (ISBN 0-87169-141-8). Am Philos.
Grecu, Mitica, et al. Dictionar Roman-Turc. LC 77-574063. 353p. (Romanian & Turkish.). 1977. 16.00 lei. Editura Stiintifica.
Guner, Musa. Svensk-Turkisk Ordbok. LC 77-571011. 133p. (Swedish & Turkish.). 1977. Kr.47.00 (ISBN 9-1441-4001-0). Studentlitt.
Henning, W. B. Fragment of a Khwarezmian Dictionary. MacKenzie, D. N., ed. 1971. 12.50x (ISBN 0-85331-292-3). Intl Pubns Serv.
Hony, H. C. Turkish-English Dictionary. 2nd ed. (Turkish & Eng.). 1957. 39.95x (ISBN 0-19-864108-7). Oxford U Pr.
Karaalioglu, Seyit K. Cagdas Ozturce Sozlugu. LC 77-970026. 398p. (Turkish.). 1975. TL.20.00. Inkilap ve Aka Kitabevleri.
Kornrumpf, H. J. Dictionnaire Europa Francais-Turc. 384p. (Fr. & Turkish.). 1966. 11.00 F. Larousse.

Langenscheidt English-Turkish Lilliput Dictionary. 670p. (Eng. & Turkish.). plastic $1.50 (ISBN 3-468-96532-X). Langenscheidt.

Langenscheidt Turkish-English Lilliput Dictionary. 608p. (Eng. & Turkish.). plastic $1.50 (ISBN 3-468-96533-8). Langenscheidt.

Langenscheidt's Lilliput Turkish-English Dictionary. 640p. (Eng. & Turkish.). 1972. $1.50 (ISBN 0-685-31364-6). Am Map.

Langenscheidts Universal-Woerterbuch Tuerkisch. 560p. (Turkish & Ger.). DM.6.80 (18371). Langenscheidt.

Langenscheidts Universal-Woerterbuecher Tuerkisch-Deutsch. (Turkish & Ger.). 1978. DM.5.80 (ISBN 3-468-18371-2). Langenscheidt.

Learn Turkish, for English Speaker. 224p. (Turkish & Eng.). pap. 9.50 (ISBN 0-87557-086-0, 086-0). Saphrograph.

Meydan-Larousse, 13 vols. (Turkish). 1970-76. $1050.00 (ISBN 0-8277-3069-1). Pergamon.

Portable Redhouse Turkish-English, English-Turkish Dictionary. (Turkish & Eng.). 1975. 9.00x (ISBN 0-686-16857-7). Intl Learn Syst.

Redhouse Cagdas Turkee-Ingilizee Sozlugii. (Turkish & Eng.). $30.00. Redhouse Pr.

Redhouse English-Turkish Dictionary. (Eng. & Turkish.). 1974. 33.00x (ISBN 0-686-16859-3). Intl Learn Syst.

Redhouse Ingilizee-Turkee-Ingilizee Elsozlugu. (Eng. & Turkish.). $8.00. Redhouse Pr.

Redhouse Ingilizee-Turkee Sozlugu. (Eng. & Turkish.). $30.00. Redhouse Pr.

Redhouse, James W. Turkish-English Dictionary, 3 pts. (Turkish & Eng.). 1976. Repr. of 1958 ed. Set. $250.00 (ISBN 0-518-19005-6). Ayer Co.

Redhouse Turkish-English Dictionary. (Turkish & Eng.). 1968. 41.00x (ISBN 0-686-16860-7). Intl Learn Syst.

Redhouse Yeni Turkee-Ingilizee Sozlugu. (Turkish & Eng.). $35.00. Redhouse Pr.

Sak, Ziya. English-Turkish, Turkish-English Dictionary. (Eng. & Turkish.). 19.50 (ISBN 0-87557-085-2, 085-2). Saphrograph.

Sevortian, E. V. Etimologicheskii Slovar Tiurkskikh Iazykov. 767p. (Turkish & Rus.). 1974. $15.95 (Pub. by Nauka). Four Continent.

--Etimologicheskii Slovar Tiurkskikh Iazykov. 352p. (Rus. & Turkish.). 1978. $9.75 (Pub. by Nauka). Four Continent.

Shorter Redhouse Turkish-English Dictionary. (Turkish & Eng.). 1971. 11.50x (ISBN 0-686-16858-5). Intl Learn Syst.

Steuerwald, K. Langenscheidts Taschenwoerterbuch Tuerkisch: Teil I, Tuerkisch-Deutsch. 552p. (Turkish & Ger.). DM.19.80 (10370). Langenscheidt.

Steuerwald, K. & Koprulu, Cemal. Langenscheidts Taschenwoerterbuch Tuerkisch-Deutsch, 2 vols. in 1. (Turkish & Ger.). DM.29.80 (11370). Langenscheidt.

--Langenscheidts Taschenwoerterbuch Tuerkisch: Teil II, Deutsch-Tuerkisch. 616p. (Ger. & Turkish.). DM.19.80 (10375). Langenscheidt.

Steuerwald, Karl. Langenscheidts Taschenwoerterbuecher Tuerkisch. (Turkish.). 1978. DM.23.80 (ISBN 3-468-11370-6). Langenscheidt.

--Langenscheidts Taschenwoerterbuecher Tuerkisch-Deutsch. (Turkish & Ger.). 1978. DM.14.80 (ISBN 3-468-10370-0). Langenscheidt.

Turkish-English, English-Turkish Dictionary: New Red House, 2 Vols. (Turkish & Eng.). Set. 75.00 (ISBN 0-685-12051-1). Heinman.

TWAIN, MARK
see Clemens, Samuel Langhorne, 1835-1910

TWANA INDIANS
see Indians of North America-Northwest, Pacific

TWI LANGUAGE
Here are entered works limited to dialects of the Akuapem, Ashanti, and related peoples who accept the name Twi. Works dealing collectively with the above dialects and the dialect of the Fanti people are entered under Akan Language.
Kgasa, Morulaganyi. Thanodi ya Setswana ya Dikole. LC 79-386132. x, 126p. (Tswana). 1976. write for info. (ISBN 0-582-61708-1). Longman S Africa.

TYPEWRITING
Mackay, E. & Williams, G. M. Typewriting Dictionary. 1980. NT.$12.95. Pitman Bks.

Mackay, Edith. Typewriting Dictionary. (Illus.). 1977. text ed. $15.95x (ISBN 0-8464-0940-2). Beekman Pubs.

TYPEWRITING–COPYING PROCESSES
see Copying Processes

TYPOGRAPHY
see Printing–Layout and Typography

TZELTAL LANGUAGE
Delgaty, Alfa & Sanchez, Augustin R. Diccionario Tzotzil De San Andres Con Variaciones Dialectales. (Vocabularios Indigenas: No. 22). (Illus). 481p. (Orig., Tzotzil & Span.). 1978. pap. $10.00x (ISBN 0-88312-674-5); microfiche $4.50x (ISBN 0-88312-372-X). Summer Inst Ling.

TZENTAL LANGUAGE
see Tzeltal Language

U

UGARITIC LANGUAGE
Young, Douglas. Concordance of Ugaritic. vii, 73p. (Ugaritic & Eng.). 1956. L.5300.00. Pont Ist Biblico.

UGRO-FINNISH LANGUAGES
see Finno-Ugrian Languages

UIGUR LANGUAGE
Iliev, A., et al. Russko-Uigurskii Slovar. 1473p. (Rus.). 1956. $5.25 (Pub. by Gosizdat Natsional Inostr Slovarei). Four Continent.

UKRAINIAN LANGUAGE
Andrusyshen, C. H., ed. Ukrainian-English Dictionary. 1200p. (Ukrainian & Eng.). 1981. pap. $19.50 (ISBN 0-8020-6421-3). U of Toronto Pr.

Ganich, D. I., et al. Russko-Ukrainskii Slovar. 1012p. (Rus. & Ukrainian.). 1978. $8.95 (Pub. by Sov. Entsiklopediia). Four Continent.

Onatskyj, E. Vocabolario ucraino-italiano. 1736p. (Ukranian & Ital.). 1941. L.4000.00. Ist Univers Orient.

Podveska, M. L. & Balla, M. J. English-Ukrainian Dictionary. 664p. (Eng. & Ukrainian.). 1980. $30.00x (ISBN 0-569-08127-0, Pub. by Collet's). State Mutual Bk.

Podvesko, M. L., ed. Ukrainian-English Dictionary. 2nd ed. $22.50 (ISBN 0-87557-088-7, 088-7). Saphrograph.

Podvesko, M. L., compiled by. Ukrainian-English, English-Ukrainian Dictionary, 2 vols. (Ukranian & Eng.). 45.00 set (ISBN 0-686-91769-3). Heinman.

Rudnyckyj, J. B. An Etymological Dictionary of the Ukrainian Language, 10 vols. 2nd ed. (Ukrainian.). 1962-66. $15.00. Ukrainian Acad.

Slovnik Staroukrainskoi Movi XVI-XV, 2 vols. (Ukrainian.). 1978. $29.95 (Pub. by Naukova Dumka). Four Continent.

Slovnik Ukrainskoi Movi: I-M, Vol. 6. (Ukrainian.). 1973. $11.75 (Pub. by Naukova Dumka). Four Continent.

Slovnik Ukrainskoi Movi: N-O, Vol. 5. (Ukrainian.). 1974. $11.75 (Pub. by Naukova Dumka). Four Continent.

Slovnik Ukrainskoi Movi: P-Poiti. (Ukrainian.). 1975. $11.75 (Pub. by Naukova Dumka). Four Continent.

Slovnik Ukrainskoi Movi: Poikhati-Prirobliati, Vol. 7. (Ukrainian.). 1976. $15.75 (Pub. by Naukova Dumka). Four Continent.

Slovnik Ukrainskoi Movi: Priroda-Riakhtlivii, Vol. 8. (Ukrainian.). 1977. $15.75 (Pub. by Naukova Dumka). Four Continent.

Slovnik Ukrainskoi Movi: S, Vol. 9. (Ukrainian.). 1978. $18.95 (Pub. by Naukova Dumka). Four Continent.

Slovnik Ukrainskoi Movi: Z, Vol. 3. (Ukrainian.). 1972. $11.75 (Pub. by Naukova). Four Continent.

Ukrainian-English, English-Ukrainian Pocket Dictionary. (Ukranian & Eng.). 12.50 (ISBN 0-685-58556-5). Heinman.

ULTRASONICS IN MEDICINE
Etter, Lewis E. Glossary of Words & Phrases Used in Radiology, Nuclear Medicine & Ultrasound. 2nd ed. 384p. 1970. ed. spiral $32.50xphotocopy (ISBN 0-398-00526-5). C C Thomas.

UNCONVENTIONAL WARFARE
see Subversive Activities

UNDERGRADUATES
see College Students

UNDERGROUND WATER
see Water, Underground

UNDERWRITING
see Insurance

UNEMPLOYMENT
see Labor Supply

UNESCO
see United Nations Educational, Scientific and Cultural Organization

UNIT TRUSTS
see Investment Trusts

UNITED NATIONS
Here are entered works about the United Nations and about its relations with other countries, either as a group or individualy.
Broad Terms for United Nations Programmes & Activities, 1979. 186p. 1980. pap. $13.00 (ISBN 0-686-68945-3, UN79/0/1, UN). Unipub.

Unbis Thesaurus. 369p. 1982. pap. $25.00 (ISBN 0-686-81419-3, UN81/1/17, UN). Unipub.

UNITED NATIONS–SPECIALIZED AGENCIES
see International Agencies

UNITED NATIONS EDUCATIONAL, SCIENTIFIC AND CULTURAL ORGANIZATION
Glossary of Conference Terms: Arabic, French, English. 117p. (Arabic, Fr. , Span. & Eng.). 1974. pap. $22.50 (ISBN 92-3-601150-0, U993, UNESCO). Unipub.

UNITED STATES–ALIENS
see Aliens

UNITED STATES–ARCHIVES
see Archives

UNITED STATES–ARMED FORCES
see also United States–Army
Heitman, Francis B. Historical Register & Dictionary of the U. S. Army 1789-1903, 2 vols. 200.00 (ISBN 0-8490-0311-3). Gordon Pr.

UNITED STATES–ARMY
Heitman, Francis B. Historical Register & Dictionary of the United States Army, from Its Organization, September 29, 1789, to March 2, 1903, 2 vols. LC 65-15975. 1965. $55.00 (ISBN 0-252-72456-9). U of Ill Pr.

UNITED STATES–COMMERCIAL LAW
see Commercial Law

UNITED STATES–DEPARTMENT OF DEFENSE
Electrical Generating Systems Marketing Association. Glossary of Department of Defense Configuration Management Terminology & Definitions. 1972. $3.00 (CMTD1); members $1.25. Elec Gen Syst.

UNITED STATES–DEPARTMENT OF HOUSING AND URBAN DEVELOPMENT
U. S. Department of Housing and Urban Development, Washington, D. C. Dictionary Catalog of the United States Department of Housing & Urban Development Library & Information Division, First Supplement, 2 vols. 1974. Set. lib. bdg. $210.00 (ISBN 0-8161-1135-9, Hall Library). G K Hall.

U.S. Department of Housing & Urban Development, Washington, D.C. Dictionary Catalog of the United States Department of Housing & Urban Development, Library & Information Division Second Suppl, 2 vols. 1975. Set. lib. bdg. $210.00 (ISBN 0-8161-0012-8, Hall Library). G K Hall.

UNITED STATES–DEPARTMENT OF THE INTERIOR
U. S. Department of the Interior Washington D.C. Dictionary Catalog of the Department Library, Fourth Suppl, 8 vols. 1975. Set. lib. bdg. $790.00 (ISBN 0-8161-0016-0, Hall Library). G K Hall.

U.S. Department of the Interior, Washington D.C. Dictionary Catalog of the Department Library, Third Sup, 8 Vols., 4th Supp. 1973. Set. lib. bdg. $420.00 (ISBN 0-8161-1054-9, Hall Library); lib. bdg. $790.00 1975 (ISBN 0-8161-0016-0). G K Hall.

UNITED STATES–ECONOMIC CONDITIONS
Auld, Douglas & Bannock, Graham. The American Dictionary of Economics. 352p. 1983. $15.95x (ISBN 0-87196-532-1). Facts on File.

UNITED STATES–FOREIGN RELATIONS
This heading is subdivided in three ways: First by subject, according to the nature of the materials, e.g. United States–Foreign Relations–Treaties; second chronologically, e.g. United States–Foreign Relations–1783-1865; Third geographically, e.g. United States–Foreign Relations–Great Britain.
Findling, John E. Dictionary of American Diplomatic History. LC 79-7730. (Illus.). 1980. lib. bdg. 45.00 (ISBN 0-313-22039-5, FDD/). Greenwood.

UNITED STATES–GOVERNMENT
see United States–Politics and Government

UNITED STATES–HISTORY
see also subdivision History under names of states, e.g. Pennsylvania–History; also under various geographic subdivisions of the United States e.g. New England States–History
American Heritage. Exercises to Accompany American Heritage Dictionary. 1977. 0.60 (ISBN 0-395-26171-6). HM.

UNITED STATES–HISTORY–DICTIONARIES
Adams Dictionary of American History, 8 vols. rev. ed. LC 76-6735. 1976. Set. text ed. $430.00 (ISBN 0-684-13856-5, ScribR). Scribner.

Jameson, J. Franklin. Dictionary of United States History: Alphabetical, Chronological, Statistical. rev. ed. McKinley, Albert E., ed. LC 68-30658. (Illus.). 1971. Repr. of 1931 ed. $55.00x (ISBN 0-8103-3332-5). Gale.

Martin, Michael & Gelber, Leonard. Dictionary of American History. rev. & enl. ed. Lieberman, Leo, ed. 714p. 1978. 15.00x (ISBN 0-8476-6104-0). Rowman.

Voorhees, David W. Concise Dictionary of American History. LC 82-43721. 1140p. 1983. lib. bdg. $60.00 (ISBN 0-684-17321-2, ScribR). Scribner.

UNITED STATES–HISTORY–CIVIL WAR, 1861-1865
Here are entered general works about the Civil War. Titles concerning the Civil War in specific states are listed under the names of individual states with the subdivision History.
Boatner, Mark M., 3rd. The Civil War Dictionary. (Illus., Maps & diagrams). 25.00 (ISBN 0-679-50013-8). McKay.

UNITED STATES–HISTORY–1945-
Hochman, Stanley. Yesterday & Today: A Dictionary of Recent American History. LC 79-12265. (Illus.). 407p. 1979. 29.95 (ISBN 0-07-029103-9). McGraw.

UNITED STATES–HISTORY, POLITICAL
see United States–Politics and Government

UNITED STATES–LAW
see Law–United States

UNITED STATES–MAIL
see Postal Service

UNITED STATES–MERCHANT MARINE
see Merchant Marine

UNITED STATES–OCCUPATIONS
see Occupations

UNITED STATES–PATENTS
see Patents

UNITED STATES–POLITICS AND GOVERNMENT
Smith, Edward C. & Zurcher, Arnold J. Dictionary of American Politics. 2nd ed. LC 67-28530. (Orig., Maps). 1968. pap. $5.72i (ISBN 0-06-463261-X, EH 261, EH). B&N NY.

UNITED STATES–POLITICS AND GOVERNMENT–DICTIONARIES
Smith, Edward C. & Zurcher, Arnold J. Dictionary of American Politics. 2nd ed. (Illus.). 434p. 1968. $17.50x (ISBN 0-06-480803-3). B&N Imports.

Sperber, Hans & Trittschuh, Travis. American Political Terms: An Historical Dictionary. LC 62-11233. 1962. $17.95x (ISBN 0-8143-1187-3). Wayne St U Pr.

UNITED STATES–POSTAL SERVICE
see Postal Service

UNITED STATES–REVENUE
see Taxation

UNITED STATES–SOCIAL CONDITIONS
Filler, Louis. Dictionary of American Social Change. LC 82-10036. 266p. (Orig). 1982. 16.50 (ISBN 0-89874-242-0); pap. 10.50 (ISBN 0-89874-564-0). Krieger.

Fogarty, Robert S. Dictionary of American Communal & Utopian History. LC 79-7476. 320p. 1980. lib. bdg. 35.00 (ISBN 0-313-21347-X, FDA/). Greenwood.

UNITED STATES–SOCIAL LIFE AND CUSTOMS
Fogarty, Robert S. Dictionary of American Communal & Utopian History. LC 79-7476. 320p. 1980. lib. bdg. 35.00 (ISBN 0-313-21347-X, FDA/). Greenwood.

UNITED STATES–TAXATION
see Taxation

UNITS
see also Metric System
Jerrard, H. G. & McNeill, D. B. Dictionary of Scientific Units. 3rd ed. 1972. $11.00 (ISBN 0-470-44230-1). Halsted Pr.

UNIVERSAL HISTORY
see World History

UNIVERSE
see Cosmogony

UNIVERSITIES AND COLLEGES
see also Libraries, University and College; Students; Teachers Colleges also headings beginning with the word College, and names of universities and colleges, e.g. Yale University; California, University of
Maldonado, Tomas. Universita la Sperimentazione Dipartimentale. LC 80-499795. 147p. (Ital.). 1978. L.3.500. Guaraldi.

UNIVERSITIES AND COLLEGES–DIRECTORIES
The American College Dictionary. tan buckram bdg., with index o.s.i. 7.95 (ISBN 0-394-40001-1); tan buckram bdg., without index 6.95 (ISBN 0-394-40002-X). Random.

UNIVERSITIES AND COLLEGES–EMPLOYEES
Abel, Emily K. Terminal Degree: The Job Crisis in Higher Education. 250p. 1984. $24.95 (ISBN 0-686-89487-1). Praeger.

UNIVERSITIES AND COLLEGES–STUDENTS
see College Students

UNIVERSITY EMPLOYEES
see Universities and Colleges–Employees

UNIVERSITY LIBRARIES
see Libraries, University and College

UNIVERSITY OF IOWA
see Iowa, University Of

UNIVERSITY STUDENTS
see College Students

UNIVERSITY TEACHERS
see College Teachers

UPPER VOLTA
McFarland, Daniel M. Historical Dictionary of Upper Volta. LC 77-14987. (African Historical Dictionaries Ser.: No. 14). (Illus.). 1978. $14.50 (ISBN 0-8108-1088-3). Scarecrow.

URALIAN LANGUAGES
see Finno-Ugrian Languages; Hyperborean Languages

URBAN AREAS
see Cities and Towns

URBAN DESIGN
see City Planning

URBAN DEVELOPMENT
see City Planning

URBAN LIFE
see City and Town Life

URBAN PLANNING
see City Planning

URBAN POLICY
see City Planning

URBAN TRAFFIC
see Traffic Engineering

URBAN TRANSIT
see Local Transit

URBAN TRANSPORTATION
Here are entered works on general transportation in urban areas, including local transit, private transportation, streets, roads, etc. Works on the transit systems of urban areas are entered under Local Transit.
National Research Council. Glossary of Urban Public Transportation Terms. LC 78-86000. 39p. (Eng.). write for info. (ISBN 0-309-02666-0). Natl Acad Pr.

Transportation Research Board. Glossary of Urban Public Transportation Terms. (Special Report). 39p. 1978. $3.00 (ISBN 0-309-02666-0). Transport Res Bd.

URBANISM
see Cities and Towns

URDU LANGUAGE
see also Hindi Language
Becker, Donald. Reverse Dictionary of Urdu. (Urdu). 1980. $38.00x (ISBN 0-8364-0656-7, Pub. by Manohaar India). South Asia Bks.

Davidova, A. A., et al. Karmannyi Russko-Urdu Slovar. 739p. (Urdu & Rus.). 1958. $1.50 (Pub. by GINS). Four Continent.

English URDV Dictionary. 24.50 (ISBN 0-686-36513-5). Saphrograph.

Kibirkshtis, L. B., et al. Karmannyi Urdu-Russkii Slovar. 551p. (Rus. & Urdu). 1958. $1.65 (Pub. by GINS). Four Continent.

Pakistani. English-Urdu Dictionary. (Eng. & Urdu). 29.00 (ISBN 0-686-18359-2). Kazi Pubns.

Platts, John T. A Dictionary of Urdu Classical Hindi & English. LC 78-670100. (Hindi & Eng.). 1977. Repr. of 1884 ed. 50.00x (ISBN 0-8002-0243-0). Intl Pubns Serv.

––Dictionary of Urdu, Classical Hindi, & English. (Urdu., Hindu & Eng.). 1930. $82.00x (ISBN 0-19-864309-8). Oxford U Pr.

Urdu-English Dictionary. (Urdu & Eng.). 22.00 (ISBN 0-686-18358-4). Kazi Pubns.

Urdu-English Dictionary, Romanized. (Urdu & Eng.). 24.50 (ISBN 0-87557-090-9, 090-7). Saphrograph.

URUGUAY–HISTORY
Willis, Jean. Historical Dictionary of Uruguay. LC 74-14630. (Latin American Historical Dictionaries Ser.: No. 11). 1974. $15.00 (ISBN 0-8108-0766-1). Scarecrow.

USAGE AND CUSTOM (LAW)
see Customary Law

USAGES
see Etiquette; Manners and Customs

USE OF LAND
see Land Use

USEFUL ARTS
see Technology

USEFUL PLANTS
see Plants, Useful

UTE INDIANS
see Indians of North America–Southwest, New

UTILIZATION OF LAND
see Land Use

UTILIZATION OF WASTE
see Waste Products

UZBEK LANGUAGE
Russko-Latinsko-Uzbekskii Slovar. 188p. (Rus. , Lat. & Uzbek.). 1978. $3.95 (Pub. by Meditsina). Four Continent.

Waterson, Natalie. Uzbeck-English Dictionary. (Uzbeck & Eng.). 1980. 55.00x (ISBN 0-19-713597-8). Oxford U Pr.

V

VACUUM IN INDUSTRY
see Vacuum Technology

VACUUM TECHNOLOGY
Dictionary of Terms for Vacuum Science & Technology, Surface Science, Thin Film Technology, Vacuum Metallurgy, Electronic Materials. 1980. $5.00. Am Vacuum Soc.

Dictionary of Terms for Vacuum Science & Technology, Surface Science, Thin Film Technology, Vacuum Metallurgy, Electronic Materials. 1980. $5.00. Am Vacuum Soc.

Hurrle, Karl, et al. Technical Dictionary of Vacuum Physics & Vacuum Technology (English, French, German, Russian) 1973. text ed. 40.00 (ISBN 0-08-016957-0). Pergamon.

Weber, Fritz W. Elsevier's Dictionary of High Vacuum Science & Technology. (Eng., Ger., Fr., Ital., Span. & Rus.). 1968. $106.50 (ISBN 0-444-40625-5). Elsevier.

VADE-MECUMS
see Handbooks, Vade-Mecums, etc.

VAGABONDS
see Gipsies

VALENCE (THEORETICAL CHEMISTRY)
Sommerfeldt, K. & Schreiber, H. Woerter zur Valenz & Distribution der Substantive. 2nd ed. 434p. (Ger.). 1980. M.22.00. Bibl Inst Leipzig.

VALUATION OF LAND
see Real Property–Valuation

VALVES
American Society of Mechanical Engineers. Diaphragm Actuated Control Valve Terminology: 1961-No.112. $2.25 (L00036); members $1.80. ASME.

VANITY
see Pride and Vanity

VARNISH PAINTS
see Paint

VASCULAR PLANTS
see Plants

VEDANTA
Usha, Brahmacharini, ed. Ramakrishna-Vedanta Wordbook: A Brief Dictionary of Hinduism. (Orig.). pap. $3.25 (ISBN 0-87481-017-5). Vedanta Pr.

VEGETABLE MOLD
see Soils

VEGETABLE OILS
see Oil Industries

VEGETABLE PATHOLOGY
see Plant Diseases

VEGETABLES
Appel, L. Lexique des Fruits et Legumes. 133p. (Fr. & Eng.). Date not set. pap. $9.95 (ISBN 0-686-97410-7, M-9238). French & Eur.

Appel, Louise. Lexique Anglais-Francais Des Fruits et Legumes. rev. ed. 128p. (Eng. & Fr.). 1974. pap. $9.95 (ISBN 0-686-56897-4, M-6007). French & Eur.

VEILS
Barberousse, Michel. Dictionnaire de la Voile. (Illus.). 256p. (Fr.). 1970. 20.00 F. Seuil.

VENTILATION
see also Air Conditioning; Heating also subdivision Heating and Ventilation or Ventilation under special subjects
Doring, G. & Rudolphi. Tiefkuhl Lexikon. 239p. (Ger.). $10.95 (ISBN 3-87150-020-8, M-7666, Pub. by Deutscher Fachverlag). French & Eur.

Drying & Related Ventilating Terminology. 1972. $3.00 (014-16); members $2.00. TAPPI.

European Heating & Ventilating Associations, ed. The International Dictionary of Heating, Ventilating, & Air Conditioning. LC 79-41714. 416p. 1982. $79.95x (ISBN 0-419-11650-8, NO. 6553, E&FN Spon England). Methuen Inc.

Lindeke, Wolfgang. Dictionary of Ventilation & Health. 186p. 1980. $25.00x (ISBN 0-569-08522-5, Pub. by Collet's). State Mutual Bk.

VERBAL BEHAVIOR
Elgin, Suzette H. More on the Gentle Art of Verbal Self-Defense. 284p. 1983. 12.95 (ISBN 0-13-601138-1); pap. 6.95 (ISBN 0-13-601120-9). P-H.

VERTEBRATES
see also Birds; Fishes; Mammals
Jacobs, George J. Dictionary of Vertebrate Zoology, Russian-English: English-Russian. LC 78-16321. 1978. pap. text ed. $4.25x (ISBN 0-87474-551-9). Smithsonian.

VESSELS (SHIPS)
see Ships

VETERINARY MEDICINE
see also Parasitology
also subdivision Diseases under classes of animals, e.g. Cattle–Diseases; Horses–Diseases; names of particular diseases, e.g. Foot-and-Mouth disease; and headings beginning with the word veterinary
Commission of the European Communities, ed. Veterinary Multilingual Thesaurus, 4 vols. 1122p. 1979. 4 vols. & index $400.00x (ISBN 3-598-07082-9, Pub. by K G Saur). Gale.

VETERINARY MEDICINE–DICTIONARIES
Beker, T. E. Diccionario de primeros auxilios medico-veterinarios. (Span.). Arg.$5.00. Lib. del Colegio.

Carrasco Martinez, Castulo. Diccionario De Medicina, Farmacia Veterinaria y Quimica. 1040p. (Span.). 1978. pap. $49.95 (ISBN 84-7391-013-3, S-50123). French & Eur.

Lindeke, Wolfgang. Technical Veterinary Dictionary. 185p. (Eng., Ger., Slovene & Rus.). 1972. $75.00 (ISBN 0-686-92494-0, M-9894). French & Eur.

Mack, R. Russian-English Veterinary Dictionary. 104p. (Rus. & Eng.). 1972. $40.00x (ISBN 0-85198-255-7, Pub. by CAB Bks England). State Mutual Bk.

––Veterinary Dictionary: Russian-English. 104p. (Rus. & Eng.). 1972. pap. $25.00 (ISBN 0-686-92151-8, M-9710). French & Eur.

Orlov, F. M. Kratkii Veterinarnyi Slovar Klinicheskikh Terminov. 320p. (Rus.). 1979. $2.95 (Pub. by Khozizdat). Four Continent.

Piccioni, M. Diccionario de alimentacion animal. 820p. (Span.). 1970. 1000.00 ptas. Acribia.

Piccioni, Marcello. DIzionario degli alimenti per il bestiame. 636p. (Ital.). L.9000.00 (ISBN 88-206-0329-2). Edagricole.

Villemin, Martial. Dictionnaire des Termes Veterinaires & Zootechniques. (Fr.). 1963. 130.00 F. Vigot.

West, Geoffrey, ed. Black's Veterinary Dictionary. rev., 14th ed. LC 82-22783. (Illus.). 912p. 1983. text ed. $28.50x (ISBN 0-389-20330-0, 07170). B&N Imports.

VETERINARY SCIENCE
see Veterinary Medicine

VIBRATION
see also Sound-Waves
Vibrating Equipment Terms & Definitions. 7p. 1981. $1.00. Conveyor Equip Mfrs.

VIDEO FILMS
see Television Film

VIDEO GAMES
Reuters Ltd. Reuters Glossary of International Economic & Financial Terms. 224p. 1983. 13.95 (ISBN 0-698-11205-9, Coward). Putnam Pub Group.

VIDEO TAPE RECORDERS AND RECORDING

Clason, W. Elsevier's Dictionary of Television, & Video Recording. LC 74-77577. 608p. (Eng., Ger., Fr., Span., Ital. & Dutch.). 1975. $113.00 (ISBN 0-444-41224-7). Elsevier.

Society of Motion Picture & Television Engineers. Magnetic Video Tape Recording Glossary. 1p. free. Soc Motion Pic & TV Engrs.

VIETNAMESE LANGUAGE

Anh-Viet, Tu Dien. English-Vietnamese Dictionary. 1560p. (Eng. & Vietnamese.). 1975. $99.00x (ISBN 0-686-44716-6, Pub. by Collets). State Mutual Bk.

Boscher, Winfried, et al. Woerterbuch Vietnamesisch-Deutsch. LC 78-375203. 738p. (Ger. & Vietnamese.). 1978. M.48.00. VEB Verlag Enzyklopadie.

Dictionnaire Francais-Vietnamien. 1276p. (Fr. & Vietnamese.). 1981. 260.00 F. Maison Dictionnaire.

English-Vietnamese Pocket Dictionary. (Vietnamese & Eng.). pap. $5.00. Iaconi.

Gage, William & Duong Thanh Binh. Vietnamese-English Phrasebook with Useful Word List: For English Speakers. LC 75-24857. (Vietnamese Refugee Education Ser.: No. 2). 142p. (Vietnamese & Eng.). 1975. pap. $4.00x (ISBN 0-87281-044-5). Ctr Appl Ling.

Hoa. Essential English-Vietnamese Dictionary. (Vietnamese & Eng.). $22.50. Iaconi.

Le-Ba-Kong & Le-Ba-Khanh, eds. Vietnamese-English, English Vietnamese Dictionary. (Vietnamese & Eng.). $30.00 (ISBN 0-8044-0310-4). Ungar.

Nguyen-Dinh-Hoa. Vietnamese Phrase Book. LC 75-34841. 120p. (Vietnamese.). 1976. pap. $4.25 (ISBN 0-8048-1196-2). C E Tuttle.

Nguyen-Dinh-Hoa, ed. Vietnamese-English Dictionary. LC 66-17773. (Eng. & Vietnamese.). 1966. $16.95 (ISBN 0-8048-0618-7). C E Tuttle.

--Vietnamese-English Dictionary. LC 66-17773. (Eng. & Vietnamese.). 1966. $16.95 (ISBN 0-8048-0618-7). C E Tuttle.

Russko-V'Etnamskii Slovar, 2 vols. (Rus. & Vietnamese.). 1977. $16.25 set (Pub. by Russkii Iazyk). Four Continent.

Stoicovici, Elena, et al. Dictionar Roman-Vietnamez. LC 77-483746. iv, 344p. (Romanian & Vietnamese.). 1976. 10.00 lei. Tipografia.

Thanh Nghi. Dictionnaire Vietnamien-Francais, 2 vols. LC 79-343898. (Vietnamese & Fr.). 1977. 186.00 F. Asiatheque.

Vietnamese Dictionaries. (Vietnamese.). handout free. Georgetown U Bil Ed Serv.

Vietnamese-English Dictionary Romanized. (Vietnamese & Eng.). $17.50 (ISBN 0-87559-014-4). Shalom.

Vietnamese-English Pocket Dictionary. (Vietnamese & Eng.). pap. $7.50 (ISBN 0-87559-165-5). Shalom.

VILLAGES–INDIA

Matthews, C. M. Health & Culture in a South Indian village. LC 80-900413. (Illus.). 498p. (Eng. & Tamil.). 1979. Rs.125.00. Orient Bk Dist.

VIOLIN MAKERS

Poidras, Henri. Critical & Documentary Dictionary of Violin Makers Old & Modern, 2 vols. in 1. LC 70-166252. 1928-1930. Repr. $59.00 (ISBN 0-403-01381-X). Scholarly.

Stainer, Cecie. Dictionary of Violin Makers. LC 77-75207. 1977. Repr. of 1896 ed. lib. bdg. 12.50 (ISBN 0-89341-070-5). Longwood Pr.

Woodcock, C. Dictionary of Contemporary Violin & Bow Makers. (Illus.). 1965. 40.00 (ISBN 0-685-12006-6). Heinman.

VIRGIN ISLANDS

Farr, Kenneth R. Historical Dictionary of Puerto Rico & the U.S. Virgin Islands. LC 73-7603. (Latin American Historical Dictionaries Ser.: No. 9). 1973. $13.00 (ISBN 0-8108-0670-3). Scarecrow.

VIROLOGY

Rowson, K., et al. A Dictionary of Virology. 240p. 1981. text ed. 43.25 (ISBN 0-632-00784-2, B 4184-5); pap. text ed. 19.95 (ISBN 0-632-00697-8, B 4192-6). Mosby.

VISIBLE SPEECH

see Deaf–Means of Communication

VISION

see also Eye

Cline, David, et al. Dictionary of Visual Science. 3rd ed. LC 78-14640. 736p. 1980. $35.00 (ISBN 0-8019-6778-3). Chilton.

VISUAL ARTS

see Art

VISUALIZATION

Thompson, Philip & Davenport, Peter, eds. The Dictionary of Graphic Images. 288p. 1980. $30.00 (ISBN 0-312-20108-7). St Martin.

VITAMINS

Diccionario de los alimentos. 830p. (Span.). 1971. 380.00 ptas. Cedel.

VITUPERATION

see Invective

VOCABULARY

Here are entered general works and works on English vocabulary. Works dealing with the vocabularies of other languages are entered under names of specific languages, with subdivision Vocabulary, e.g. French Language–Vocabulary.

see also Children–Language; Vocabulary Tests; Words, New; also subdivisions Dictionaries and Glossaries, Vocabularies, Etc. under names of languages.

Barnard, Helen. Advanced English Vocabulary. 1971. tchrs' bk 2.95 (ISBN 0-912066-19-9); wkbk 1 6.95 (ISBN 0-686-96805-0). Newbury Hse.

--Advanced English Vocabulary. 1975. pap. 6.95 wkbk 3B (ISBN 0-912066-44-X). Newbury Hse.

--Advanced English Vocabulary. 1975. pap. 6.95 wkbk 3A (ISBN 0-912066-43-1). Newbury Hse.

--Advanced English Vocabulary. 1972. wkbk 2A 6.95 (ISBN 0-88377-037-7); pap. 6.50 wkbk 2b (ISBN 0-88377-038-5). Newbury Hse.

Beck, Isabel L., et al. The Rationale & Design of a Program to Teach Vocabulary to Fourth-Grade Students. 49p. 1980. $1.00. Learn Res Dev.

Bellegarde, Ida. Easy Steps to a Large Vocabulary. LC 77-79111. 1977. $4.45x (ISBN 0-918340-04-7). Bell Ent.

Berbrich, Joan D. One Hundred One Ways to Learn Vocabulary. (Orig.). (gr. 10-12). 1971. wkbk. $7.58 (ISBN 0-87720-343-1). AMSCO Sch.

Block, Karen K. & McCaslin, Ellen S. A Plan for Using CAI to Teach Vocabulary Concepts. (Illus.). 36p. 1978. $1.00. Learn Res Dev.

Brown, James I. Programmed Vocabulary. 3rd ed. (The CPD Approach). 1980. pap. text ed. 12.95 (ISBN 0-13-729707-6). P-H.

Cronin, Morton J. Vocabulary One Thousand: With Words in Context. 2nd ed. 180p. 1981. pap. text ed. 9.95 (ISBN 0-15-594987-X, HC); instr's. manual 1.50 (ISBN 0-15-594988-8). HarBraceJ.

Dale, Edgar & O'Rourke, Joseph. The Living Word Vocabulary. LC 81-50682. 704p. 1981. lib. bdg. $49.95 (ISBN 0-7166-3115-6). World Bk.

Davis, Nancy. Vocabulary Improvement. 3rd ed. 1978. pap. text ed. 14.50x (ISBN 0-07-015543-7, C). McGraw.

Davis, Nancy B. Vocabulary Improvement. (Eng.). Epap. 8.25. McGraw.

Dunn-Rankin, Patricia. Vocabulary. (Illus.). 1978. pap. text ed. 13.95 (ISBN 0-07-018268-X, C). McGraw.

--Vocabulary. 2nd ed. (Illus.). 224p. Date not set. pap. text ed. $13.95 (ISBN 0-07-018278-7, Pub. by C.); instr's. manual $12.50 (ISBN 0-07-018279-5). Mcgraw.

Ehrlich, Ida L. Instant Vocabulary. pap. 3.95 (ISBN 0-671-47722-6). PB.

English Language Services. Key to English Vocabulary. (Key to English Ser). pap. 1.60 (ISBN 0-02-971750-7). Macmillan.

Evarts, Prescott. Essential Words for a Perfect Vocabulary. 160p. (Orig.). 1983. pap. $4.95 (ISBN 0-668-05657-6, 5657-6). Arco.

Feinstein, George W. Programmed College Vocabulary Three Thousand Six Hundred. 2nd ed. 1979. pap. text ed. 12.95 (ISBN 0-13-729806-4). P-H.

Felber, Helmut, compiled by. International Bibliography of Standardized Vocabularies. (International Bibliography of Infoterm Ser., Vol. 2). 1978. $95.00x (ISBN 0-89664-075-2, Pub. by K G Saur). Gale.

Funk, Wilfred & Lewis, Norman. Thirty Days to a More Powerful Vocabulary. LC 72-94340. (Funk & W Bk.). (gr. 9-12). 1970. text ed. $12.45 (ISBN 0-308-40079-8, 430180). T Y Crowell.

Greenman, Robert. Captive Vocabulary. (Illus.). 187p. 1980. pap. text ed. $4.50 (ISBN 0-912853-01-8). NY Times.

Gregorich, Barbara. Expanding Your Vocabulary. LC 78-730053. (Illus.). 1978. pap. text ed. $135.00 (ISBN 0-89290-126-8, 327-SATC). Soc for Visual.

Haller, Margaret A. Essential Vocabulary for College-Bound Students. LC 82-1732. 208p. (Orig.). (YA) (gr. 10 up). 1982. pap. $5.95 (ISBN 0-668-05417-4, 5417). Arco.

Hansen, Merrily P. & Hansen, Jeffrey N. High Action Reading for Vocabulary: Level B. (Skillbooster Ser.). 64p. (gr. 2). 1980. write for info. wkbk. (ISBN 0-87895-234-9). Modern Curr.

Henley, Elton P. Vocabulary Building at the College Level. 2nd ed. 1978. pap. text ed. 11.95 (ISBN 0-8403-1088-9). Kendall-Hunt.

Hillerich, Robert L. A Writing Vocabulary of Elementary Children. 316p. 1978. $15.25x (ISBN 0-398-03814-7). C C Thomas.

Holmes, Keith D. Seventy Steps to Vocabulary Power. rev., 2nd ed. (Illus.). 100p. (Orig.). 1983. pap. text ed. $4.95 per box (ISBN 0-9608250-1-0). Educ Serv Pub.

Janicot, Aime. Vocabulaire Anglais par l'image. 100p. (Eng.). 1965. 16.00 F. Bordas-Dunod.

Justus, Fred. Jumbo Vocabulary Development Yearbook: Grade 1. (Jumbo Vocabulary Ser.). 96p. (gr. 1). 1979. $14.00 (ISBN 0-8209-0050-8, JVDY 1). ESP.

--Jumbo Vocabulary Development Yearbook: Grade 2. (Jumbo Vocabulary Ser.). 96p. (gr. 2). 1980. $14.00 (ISBN 0-8209-0051-6, JVDY 2). ESP.

--Jumbo Vocabulary Fun Yearbook. (Jumbo Vocabulary Ser.). 96p. (gr. 3). 1980. $14.00 (ISBN 0-8209-0058-3, JVFY 3). ESP.

Kennon, L. H. Tests of Literary Vocabulary for Teachers of English. LC 70-176966. (Columbia University. Teachers College. Contributions to Education: No. 223). Repr. of 1926 ed. $17.50 (ISBN 0-404-55223-4). AMS Pr.

Kesselman-Turkel, Judi & Peterson, Franklynn. The Vocabulary Builder: The Practically Painless Way to a Larger Vocabulary. 192p. (Orig.). 1982. pap. $4.95 (ISBN 0-8092-5650-9). Contemp Bks.

Koch, Harry W. An Easy Guide to English Grammar & Vocabulary. rev. ed. 119p. 1980. pap. 5.00 (ISBN 0-913164-84-4). Ken-Bks.

Larson, Mildred L. Vocabulario Aguaruna de Amazonas. (Peruvian Linguistic Ser: No. 3). 211p. (Span.). 1966. pap. $3.00x (ISBN 0-88312-653-2). Summer Inst Ling.

Lenier, Minnette & Maker, Janet. Keys to a Powerful Vocabulary: Level I. (Illus.). 240p. 1982. 12.95 (ISBN 0-13-514968-1). P-H.

Levine, Harold. Vocabulary & Composition Through Pleasurable Reading, Bk. 3. (Orig.). (gr. 10-12). 1976. wkbk. $8.17 (ISBN 0-87720-306-7); pap. text ed. $7.17 (ISBN 0-87720-377-6). AMSCO Sch.

--Vocabulary & Composition: Through Pleasurable Reading, Book 4. (gr. 11-12). 1978. wkbk $8.17 (ISBN 0-87720-376-8); pap. text ed. $7.17 (ISBN 0-87720-378-4). AMSCO Sch.

--Vocabulary for the College-Bound Student. (Orig.). (gr. 9-12). 1964. text ed. $11.50 (ISBN 0-87720-367-9); pap. text ed. $6.17 (ISBN 0-87720-366-0); wkbk. o.p. $6.58 (ISBN 0-87720-312-1); with answers o.p. $4.20 (ISBN 0-87720-313-X). AMSCO Sch.

--Vocabulary for the College-Bound Student. 2nd ed. (Orig.). (gr. 11-12). 1982. text ed. $7.00 (ISBN 0-87720-442-X). AMSCO Sch.

--Vocabulary for the High School Student. 224p. (Orig.). (gr. 9-12). 1967. text ed. $11.50 (ISBN 0-87720-365-2); pap. text ed. $6.17 (ISBN 0-87720-364-4); wkbk. o.p. $6.58 (ISBN 0-87720-310-5); with answers o.p. $4.20 (ISBN 0-87720-311-3). AMSCO Sch.

Levine, Harold & Levine, Robert. Vocabulary Resources for the College Student. (Orig.). 1980. pap. $8.92 (ISBN 0-87720-961-8). AMSCO Sch.

Levine, Harold & Levine, Robert T. Vocabulary Foundations for the College Student. (Orig.). 1980. pap. text ed. $8.92 (ISBN 0-87720-962-6). AMSCO Sch.

Lewick-Wallace, Mary. Vocabulary Building & Word Study. Raygor, Alton, ed. (Communication Skills Ser.). 240p. (Orig.). 1981. pap. text ed. 11.95 (ISBN 0-07-067902-9, C). McGraw.

Lewis, Norman & Funk, Wilfred. Thirty Days to a More Powerful Vocabulary. 1981. pap. 2.95 (ISBN 0-671-45675-X). PB.

Licklider, Patricia. Building a College Vocabulary. 256p. (Orig.). 1981. pap. text ed. 8.95 (ISBN 0-316-52424-7); tchrs'. manual avail. (ISBN 0-316-52425-5). Little.

Lieberman, J. E. Enriching Vocabulary Concept in The Classroom. $0.35. Assn Child & Adult Learn.

McMaster, Dale. Vocabulary Development. (Language Arts Ser.). 24p. (gr. 6-9). 1976. wkbk. $5.00 (ISBN 0-8209-0312-4, VD-4). ESP.

McMasters, Dale. Beginning Vocabulary. (Language Arts Ser.). 24p. (gr. 3-5). 1976. wkbk. $5.00 (ISBN 0-8209-0309-4, VD-1). ESP.

--Everyday Vocabulary. (Language Arts Ser.). 24p. (gr. 4-6). 1976. wkbk. $5.00 (ISBN 0-8209-0310-8, VD-2). ESP.

--Vocabulary Study. (Language Arts Ser.). 24p. (gr. 5-7). 1976. wkbk. $5.00 (ISBN 0-8209-0311-6, VD-3). ESP.

Mansat, Andre. Vocabulaire d'anglais Commercial. (Fr. & Eng.). 1966. 14.80 F. Didier.

Miller, Walter J. & Morsecluley, Elizabeth. Vocabulary, Spelling & Grammar. 10th ed. 256p. 1983. pap. $5.95 (ISBN 0-668-05806-4). Arco.

Minor, Eugene E. & Minor, Dorothy. Vocabulario Huitoto Muinane. (Peruvian Linguistic Ser: No. 5). 139p. (Span.). 1970. pap. $3.00x (ISBN 0-88312-656-7); microfiche $2.25x (ISBN 0-88312-362-2). Summer Inst Ling.

Morris, William. It's Easy to Increase Your Vocabulary. rev ed. 256p. (Orig.). 1975. pap. 2.25 (ISBN 0-14-004086-2). Penguin.

Norback, Craig & Norback, Peter. The Must Words: The Six Thousand Most Important Words for a Successful & Profitable Vocabulary. 1979. 12.95 (ISBN 0-07-047136-3). McGraw.

OAS General Secretariat. Vocabulario Vial. 368p. (Eng., Span., Fr. & Port.). 1979. text ed. $15.00 (ISBN 0-8270-1332-9). OAS.

O'Harra, Kristbjorg E. Vocabulary Development Through Language Awareness. (Illus.). 192p. 1984. pap. text ed. $11.95 (ISBN 0-13-150078-3). P-H.

Paternoster, Lewis M. & Frager, Ruth L. Three Dimensions of Vocabulary Growth. (Orig.). (gr. 10-12). 1971. pap. text ed. $6.58 (ISBN 0-87720-345-8). AMSCO Sch.

Pauk, Walter. Vocabulary in Context: Getting the Precise Meaning. (A Skill at a Time Ser). 64p. (gr. 9 up). 1975. pap. text ed. 3.20x (ISBN 0-89061-021-5, ST-1). Jamestown Pubs.

Pearson, P. D. & Johnson, D. D. Teaching Reading Vocabulary & Teaching Reading Comprehension. 1978. Set. boxed 15.95 (ISBN 0-03-042916-1, HoltC). HR&W.

Price, A. Rae. Developing Your Vocabulary. 268p. 1973. pap. text ed. write for info. (ISBN 0-697-03805-X). Wm C Brown.

Pride, Leslie & Pride, Kitty. Vocabulario Chatino de Tataltepec. (Vocabularios Indigenas Ser.: No. 15). 103p. (Span.). 1970. App. $3.00x (ISBN 0-88312-655-9); microfiche $2.25 (ISBN 0-88312-317-7). Summer Inst Ling.

Prieto, Muriel H. Vocabulary Made Easy for Spanish Speakers: Teacher's Guide. LC 76-3732. 1978. pap. text ed. $3.00 (ISBN 0-8477-2635-5). U of PR Pr.

Roloff-Stoddard, Joan, et al. Vocabulary: The Words Used to Express Ideas & Feelings. 1980. pap. text ed. 11.95x (ISBN 0-02-477440-5). Macmillan.

Romine, Jack S. Vocabulary for Adults. LC 75-17660. (Self-Teaching Guides). 221p. 1975. pap. text ed. $5.95 (ISBN 0-471-73285-0, Pub. by Wiley Pr). Wiley.

Rubin, Dorothy. Vocabulary Expansion I. 416p. 1982. pap. text ed. 9.95 (ISBN 0-02-404220-X). Macmillan.

––Vocabulary Expansion II. 288p. 1982. pap. text ed. 9.95 (ISBN 0-02-404240-4). Macmillan.

Schwesinger, Gladys C. The Social-Ethical Significance of Vocabulary. LC 70-177806. (Columbia University. Teachers College. Contributions to Education: No. 211). Repr. of 1926 ed. $17.50 (ISBN 0-404-55211-0). AMS Pr.

Shaw, Marie-Jose. Jumbo Vocabulary Development Yearbook: Grade 3. (Jumbo Vocabulary Ser.). 96p. (gr. 3). 1980. $14.00 (ISBN 0-8209-0052-4, JVDY 3). ESP.

––Jumbo Vocabulary Development Yearbook: Grade 4. (Jumbo Vocabulary Ser.). 96p. (gr. 4). 1980. $14.00 (ISBN 0-8209-0053-2, JVDY 4). ESP.

––Jumbo Vocabulary Development Yearbook: Grade 5. (Jumbo Vocabulary Ser.). 96p. (gr. 5). 1981. $14.00 (ISBN 0-8209-0054-0, JVDY 5). ESP.

Shepherd, James F. College Vocabulary Skills. 2d ed. 1983. pap. text ed. 11.50 (ISBN 0-395-32811-X); instr's. manual 2.00 (ISBN 0-395-32812-8). HM.

Smith, Elliott. Contemporary Vocabulary. LC 78-65215. 1979. pap. text ed. $10.95x (ISBN 0-312-16847-0); inst. manual avail. (ISBN 0-312-16848-9). St Martin.

Stanford, G. McGraw-Hill Vocabulary, Bk. 6. 2nd ed. 1981. 5.28 (ISBN 0-07-060776-1). McGraw.

Stanford, Gene. McGraw-Hill Vocabulary, Bk. 1. 2nd ed. Weeden, Hester E., ed. (Illus.). 128p. (gr. 7-12). 1981. pap. text ed. 5.28 (ISBN 0-07-060771-0). McGraw.

––McGraw-Hill Vocabulary, Bk. 2. 2nd ed. (Illus.). 128p. 1981. pap. text ed. 5.28 (ISBN 0-07-060772-9). McGraw.

Stanford, W. J. McGraw-Hill Vocabulary, Bk. 5. 2nd ed. (McGraw-Hill Vocabulary Ser.). 1982. 5.28 (ISBN 0-07-060775-3). McGraw.

Strong, William. Basic Usage & Vocabulary. 1983. pap. text ed. $4.95 (ISBN 0-394-33615-1, RanC). Random.

Sullivan Assoc. Reading Vocabulary, 5 bks. pap. text ed. 2.75 ea. (ISBN 0-8449-4105-0); tchr's guide for bks. 1-4 avail. Learning Line.

Turner, David R. Vocabulary Builder & Guide to Verbal Tests. 5th ed. LC 73-77242. 1973. pap. $7.95 (ISBN 0-668-00535-1). Arco.

Vaughn, Jim. Jumbo Vocabulary Development Yearbook: Grade 7. (Jumbo Vocabulary Ser.). 96p. (gr. 7-9). 1981. $14.00 (ISBN 0-8209-0056-7, JVDY J). ESP.

––Jumbo Vocabulary Development Yearbook: Grade 10. (Jumbo Vocabulary Ser.). 96p. (gr. 10-12). 1981. $14.00 (ISBN 0-8209-0057-5, JVDY S). ESP.

Visual Education Corporation. Vocabulary Made Easy. LC 83-9882. (Illus.). 136p. (gr. 9 up). 1983. wkbk. $6.00b (ISBN 0-07-039665-5, Pub. by G). McGraw.

Vocabulaire Anglais. (Eng.). 11.00 F. Ligel.

Vocabularios Frances-Espanol-Ingles. (Fr., Span. & Eng.). $0.80; Mex.$10.00. Novaro.

Watson, Diana C. & Watson, Malcom. Vocabulary Building: Syllabus, Level IV. 1975. pap. text ed. 5.35 (ISBN 0-89420-039-9, 270053); cassette recordings 68.90 (ISBN 0-89420-195-6, 270200). Natl Book.

Wesker, Arnold & Appignanesi, Richard. Words As Definitions of Experience. (Education Ser.). 48p. (Orig.). 1980. pap. 1.25 (ISBN 0-904613-26-7). Writers & Readers.

Yorkey, Richard. Checklists for Vocabulary Study. (English As a Second Language Bk.). (Illus.). 1981. pap. text ed. 4.65x (ISBN 0-582-79767-5). Longman.

VOCABULARY–JUVENILE LITERATURE

Daly, Kathleen N. The Macmillan Picture Wordbook. LC 82-6619. (Illus.). 80p. (ps-1). 1982. 7.95 (ISBN 0-02-725600-6). Macmillan.

Forte, Imogene & Pangle, Mary A. Vocabulary Magic. LC 77-89526. (The Magic & Mastery Language Ser.). (Illus.). 112p. (gr. 2-6). 1977. pap. $5.95 (ISBN 0-913916-49-8, IP 49-8). Incentive Pubns.

––Vocabulary Mastery. (Magic & Mastery Language Ser.). (Illus.). 1971. $3.95 (ISBN 0-913916-40-4, IP40-4). Incentive Pubns.

Levine, Harold. Vocabulary Through Pleasurable Reading, Bk. 1. (Orig.). (gr. 7-10). 1974. pap. text ed. $7.17 (ISBN 0-87720-373-3); wkbk. $8.17 (ISBN 0-87720-368-7). AMSCO Sch.

VOCABULARY–PROGRAMMED INSTRUCTION

Payne, Lynette R. Created Fables for Vocabulary Growth: A Classroom Project. (Illus.). 1982. $6.95 (ISBN 0-533-05065-0). Vantage.

Stanford, Gene. McGraw-Hill Vocabulary, Bk. 3. 2nd ed. (Illus.). 128p. 1981. pap. text ed. 5.28 (ISBN 0-07-060773-7). McGraw.

Vocabulary Skills, 3 Bks. Bks. D-F. pap. 1.59 ea.; Tchr's eds. 1.59 ea. Bk. D (ISBN 0-8372-3476-X); Tchr's ed (ISBN 0-8372-9210-7). Bk. E (ISBN 0-8372-3477-8). Tchr's ed (ISBN 0-8372-9211-5). Tchr's ed (ISBN 0-8372-3478-6) (ISBN 0-8372-9212-3). Bowmar-Noble.

Watson, Diana C. & Hurtado, Hernan. Vocabulary Building: Syllabus, Level III. 1973. pap. text ed. 5.25 (ISBN 0-89420-007-0, 270043); cassette recordings 69.20 (ISBN 0-89420-194-8, 270000). Natl Book.

VOCABULARY TESTS

Kahn, Gilbert & Mulkerne, Donald J. The Wordbook. 1975. pap. text ed. 6.95x (ISBN 0-02-474780-7, 47478). Glencoe.

Turner, David R. Vocabulary Builder & Guide to Verbal Tests. 5th ed. LC 73-77242. 1973. pap. $7.95 (ISBN 0-668-00535-1). Arco.

VOCAL MUSIC
see also Music, Popular (Songs, etc.)

Reid, Cornelius L. A Dictionary of Vocal Terminology: An Analysis. LC 81-86074. xxi, 457p. 1983. 39.95 (ISBN 0-915282-07-0). J Patelson Music.

VOCAL MUSIC–THEMATIC CATALOGS

Barlow, Harold & Morgenstern, Sam, eds. Dictionary of Opera & Song Themes. rev. ed. 1976. $15.95 (ISBN 0-517-52503-8). Crown.

VOCALISTS
see Singers

VOCATION, CHOICE OF
see Vocational Guidance

VOCATIONAL EDUCATION
Here are entered works on vocational instruction within the standard educational system. Works on the vocationally oriented process of endowing people with a skill after either completion or termination of their formal education are entered under Occupational Training. Works on retraining persons with obsolete vocational skills are entered under Occupational Retraining. Works on the training of employees on the job are entered under Employees, Training Of.
see also Agricultural Education; Deaf–Education; Education, Cooperative

American Occupational Therapy Association. Occupational Therapy Product Output Reporting Systems & Uniform Terminology for Reporting Occupational Therapy Services. 1979. $10.00 (C-27); members $5.00. Am Occup Therapy.

Rosenthal, Hans J. Schluesselwoerter zur Berufsbildung. Gerds, Peter, ed. LC 77-483344. 431p. (Ger.). 1977. DM.21.00 (ISBN 3-407-50058-0). Beltz & Co.

Terminology of Technical & Vocational Education. 1979. pap. $5.00 (ISBN 92-3-001593-8, U884, UNESCO). Unipub.

VOCATIONAL GUIDANCE
see also Counseling; Deaf–Education; Occupations; Professions; Vocational Rehabilitation

Hopke, William E., ed. Encyclopedia of Career & Vocational Guidance, 2 vols. 5th ed. LC 81-4362. 808p. 1982. 49.95 (ISBN 0-385-18058-6, Anch). Doubleday.

VOCATIONAL OPPORTUNITIES
see Vocational Guidance

VOCATIONAL REHABILITATION
see also Handicapped–Employment; Vocational Guidance

Vocational Rehabilitation & the Employment of the Disabled. 182p. pap. 8.75 (ISBN 92-2-002571-X, ILO177, ILO). Unipub.

VOLTAIC CELL
see Electric Batteries

VOLTAIRE, FRANCOIS MARIE AROUET DE, 1694-1778

Trapnell, William. Voltaire & His Portable Dictionary. 75p. 1972. 15.00x (ISBN 3-465-00905-3). Intl Pubns Serv.

VOLUME FEEDING
see Food Service

VOLUNTARY ORGANIZATIONS
see Associations, Institutions, etc.

VOTING

Prost, Antoine. Vocabulaire des Proclamations Electorales de 1881, 1885. 200p. (Fr.). 1974. 156.00 F. PUF.

VOYAGES AND TRAVELS
see also Discoveries (In Geography); Pilgrims and Pilgrimages; Seamen; Yachts and Yachting
also subdivision Description and Travel (or Description, Geography) and Discovery and Exploration under names of countries, regions, etc., names of regions, e.g. Antarctic Regions; and names of ships

Embacher, F. Lexikon der Reisen und Entdeckungen. (Ger.). 1883. pap. text ed. $18.75x (ISBN 90-6041-016-5). Humanities.

Yapp, Peter, ed. The Travellers' Dictionary of Quotation: Who Said What, about Where. 1022p. 1983. 29.95 (ISBN 0-7100-0992-5). Routledge & Kegan.

VOYAGES AND TRAVELS–BIBLIOGRAPHY

Mariners Museum Library - Newport News - Virginia. Dictionary Catalog of the Library of the Mariners Museum, 9 Vols. 1964. Set. lib. bdg. $855.00 (ISBN 0-8161-0674-6, Hall Library). G K Hall.

VULCANITE
see Rubber

W

WAGNER, RICHARD, 1813-1883

Terry, Edward M. A Richard Wagner Dictionary. LC 79-109865. 186p. Repr. of 1939 ed. lib. bdg. 15.00x (ISBN 0-8371-4356-X, TERW). Greenwood.

WALAPAI INDIANS
see Indians of North America–Southwest, New

WALBIRI TRIBE

Reece, Laurie. Dictionary of the Walbiri (Walpiri) Language of Central Australia. LC 76-370309. (Eng. & Walbiri.). 1975. Aus.$3.50. Univ Syd Aust Lang.

WALL BOARD

Gypsum Board Products Glossary of Terminology. write for info. (GA-505-80). Gypsum Assn.

WAR, ARTICLES OF
see Military Law

WAR, MARITIME
see Naval Art and Science; Naval Battles

WAR MAPS
see Classical Geography

WAR OF SECESSION (U. S.)
see United States–History–Civil War, 1861-1865

WARS
see Military History

WASHING
see Laundry and Laundry Industry

WASHO INDIANS
see Indians of North America–Southwest, New

WASTE, DISPOSAL OF
see Refuse and Refuse Disposal; Sewage Disposal

WASTE PRODUCTS
see also Refuse and Refuse Disposal

Kaupert, W., ed. Dictionary of Waste Disposal & Public Cleansing. (Eng., Ger., & Fr.). 1966. $29.50 (ISBN 0-444-40330-2). Elsevier.

WASTE WATERS
see Sewage

WATCH REPAIRING
see Clocks and Watches–Repairing and Adjusting

WATCHES
see Clocks and Watches

WATER
see also Hydraulic Engineering; Lakes; Ocean; Oceanography; Rivers also headings beginning with the word Water

American Society of Civil Engineers & American Water Works Association, eds. Glossary: Water & Wastewater Control Engineering. LC 80-70933. 456p. 1981. text ed. $25.00 (ISBN 0-87262-262-2). Am Soc Civil Eng.

Catalan Lafuente, Jose. Diccionario Tecnico Del Agua. 301p. (Span.). 1977. pap. $29.95 (ISBN 84-400-2913-6, S-50098). French & Eur.

Colas, Rene. Dictionnaire Technique de l'eau & des Questions Connexes. 264p. (Fr.). 1968. 45.00 F. Le Prat.

Dictionnaire Technique de L'Eau. (Fr.). pap. $19.95 (ISBN 0-686-57115-0, M-6156). French & Eur.

Dictionnaire Technique de l'eau. (Fr.). 45.00 F. Grund.

Glossary of Soil & Water Terms. 62p. 1967. $6.00 (SP0467); members $4.50. Am Soc Ag Eng.

WATER–FLOW
see Hydraulics

WATER–POLLUTION
see also Sewage Disposal; Water-Supply

Water Pollution Control Federation, et al. Glossary: Water & Wastewater Control Engineering. 440p. 1981. $25.00 (ISBN 0-686-36997-1, M0022). Water Pollution.

WATER, UNDERGROUND
see also Hydrogeology
Gavande, S. A. & Bornemisza, Elemer. Terminologia Moderna de Energia de Agua en el Sistema Suelo-Planta Atmosfera. 6p. (Span.). 1969. write for info. IICA.

WATER-COLOR PAINTING
Mallalieu, H. L. The Dictionary of Watercolour Artists up to 1920: Vol. 1, The Text. 298p. 1978. $44.50 (ISBN 0-902028-48-0). Antique Collect.
--The Dictionary of Watercolour Artists up to 1920: Vol. 2, The Plates. (Illus.). 268p. 1980. $44.50 (ISBN 0-902028-63-4). Antique Collect.

WATER CONTAMINATION
see Water-Pollution

WATER POLLUTION
see Water-Pollution

WATER-POWER
see also Dams; Hydraulic Engineering; Hydraulic Machinery
Gavande, S. A. & Bornemisza, Elemer. Terminologia Moderna de Energia de Agua en el Sistema Suelo-Planta Atmosfera. 6p. (Span.). 1969. write for info. IICA.

WATER RESOURCES DEVELOPMENT
see also Inland Navigation; Irrigation; Water-Power; Water-Supply
American Society of Civil Engineers, compiled by. Prospects for Metropolitan Water Management. 256p. 1971. pap. text ed. $5.25 (ISBN 0-87262-026-3). Am Soc Civil Eng.
University Of California - Berkeley. Dictionary Catalog of the Water Resources Center Archives, 5 vols. 1970. lib. bdg. $475.00 (ISBN 0-8161-0884-6, Hall Library); first suppl. (1971) $110.00 (ISBN 0-8161-0895-1); second suppl. (1972 $110.00 (ISBN 0-8161-0983-4). G K Hall.
University of California, Berkeley. Dictionary Catalog of the Water Resources Center Archives, Fourth Suppl. 942p. 1975. lib. bdg. $110.00 (ISBN 0-8161-0002-0, Hall Library). G K Hall.
University of California, Berkeley, Water Resources Center. Dictionary Catalog of the Water Resources Center Archives: Sixth Supplement, 2 vols. 1978. Set. lib. bdg. $250.00 (ISBN 0-8161-0244-9, Hall Library). G K Hall.

WATER-SUPPLY
see also Dams; Forests and Forestry; Irrigation; Water-Pollution
Dictionnaire Technique de L'Eau. (Fr.). pap. $19.95 (ISBN 0-686-57115-0, M-6156). French & Eur.
Meinck, Fritz. Woerterbuch fur das Wasser & Abwasserfach. LC 78-337966. 737p. (Eng., Fr. & Ital.). 1977. write for info. (ISBN 3-486-35352-7). Oldenbourg Verlag.

WATER-SUPPLY ENGINEERING
see also Hydraulic Engineering
American Water Works Association. Glossary: Water & Wastewater Control Engineering. 2nd ed. (General References Ser.). (Illus.). 456p. 1981. text ed. $25.00 (ISBN 0-89867-263-5). Am Water Wks Assn.
Glossary: Water & Wastewater Control Engineering. 1981. members $25.00; $17.50. Water Pollution.
Meinck, F. & Mohle, K. Dictionary of Water & Sewage Engineering. 2nd ed. (Ger., Eng., Fr., & Ital.). 1977. $127.75 (ISBN 0-444-99811-X). Elsevier.

WATER TANKS
see Tanks

WATER TRANSPORTATION
see Shipping

WATERWORKS
see Water-Supply

WAVEFRONT RECONSTRUCTION IMAGING
see Holography

WEAPONS
see Firearms

WEATHER
see also Climatology; Humidity; Meteorology

also names of countries, cities, etc., with or without the subdivision Climate
Hein, W. Lexikon der Schulphysik: Waerme und Wetter, Vol. 2. (Ger.). $37.00 (ISBN 3-7614-0108-6, M-7223). French & Eur.
Hoefling, Oskar, ed. Lexikon der Schulphysik: Waerme & Wetter. (Ger.). 1978. DM.46.00 (ISBN 3-7614-0108-6). Aulis Verlag.

WEBSTER, JOHN, 1580?-1625?
Corballis, R. & Harding, J. M. John Webster Concordance, Vol. 2, Pt. 3. (Jacobean Drama Studies: No. 70). 1979. pap. text ed. 25.00x (ISBN 0-391-01761-6). Humanities.

WEDGWOOD WARE
Reilly, Robin & Savage, George. The Dictionary of Wedgwood. (Illus.). 414p. 1980. $62.50 (ISBN 0-902028-85-5). Antique Collect.
Rielly & Savage. Dictionary of Wedgwood. (Illus.). 1980. $62.50 (ISBN 0-902028-85-5). Apollo.

WEEDS
Kosik, Vaclav. Cesko, Slovensko, Latinsko, Anglicko, Nemecko, Rusky, Slovnik Plevelu. LC 76-507633. 149p. (Czech., Slovak, Lat., Eng., Ger. & Rus.). 1975. write for info. SNTC.
Williams, G. H. Dictionary of Weeds of Western Europe: Their Common Names & Importance. 1982. $74.50 (ISBN 0-444-41978-0). Elsevier.

WEEVILS
see Beetles

WEIGHING MACHINES
Scale Manufacturers Association. Terms & Definitions for the Weighing Industry. 4th ed. 75p. 1981. $5.00 (S*M-2). Scale Mfrs.

WEIGHTS AND MEASURES-DICTIONARIES
Drazil. Dictionary of Quantities & Units of Measurement. 450p. (Eng., Ger. & Fr.). 1983. DM.65.00. Brandstetter.

WEIGHTS AND MEASURES-HISTORY
Zupko, Ronald E. French Weights & Measures before the Revolution: A Dictionary of Provincial & Local Units. LC 78-3249. 256p. 1979. $22.50x (ISBN 0-253-32480-7). Ind U Pr.

WELDING
American Welding Society. Welding Terms & Definitions. $15.00. Am Welding.
Dictionary of Welding. 762p. 1980. $60.00x (ISBN 0-569-08525-X, Pub. by Collet's). State Mutual Bk.
Din Standards for Welding Practice One: Standards for Filler Metals: Manufacture, Quality, Testing. 549.00 (ISBN 0-686-28164-0, 10047-7/08). Heyden.
Dollinger, Alfred. Six Language Dictionary of Welding Technique. LC 75-591161. 1974. 45.00x (ISBN 0-8002-0400-X). Intl Pubns Serv.
English-German -- German-English Welding Engineering Dictionary. 396p. (Eng. & Fr.). 1980. $75.00x (ISBN 0-569-05715-9, Pub. by Collet's). State Mutual Bk.
Kleiber, A. Dictionary of Welding. 396p. (Eng. & Ger.). 1970. $24.00 (ISBN 0-8417-1026-0). Adler.
--English-German, German-English Welding Engineering Dictionary. 396p. (Eng. & Ger.). 1970. $90.00x (ISBN 0-686-44709-3, Pub. by Collets). State Mutual Bk.
--Woerterbuch der Schweisstechnik. (Eng. & Ger., Dictionary of Welding). 1970. $38.00 (ISBN 3-87097-024-3, M-6959). French & Eur.
Recueil de Terminologie Multilinque du Soudage et des Techniques Connexes, 18p. (Fr. & Eng., Multilinqual Collection of Welding Terminology and Terminology of Related Techniques). pap. $24.95 (ISBN 0-686-56760-9, M-6480). French & Eur.

Recueil Terminologique Multilingue du Soudage et des Techniques Connexes, Soudage Electrique a l'Arc, Vol. 2. 144p. (Fr. & Eng., A Collection of Multilingual Welding Terminology & Related Technique: Electrical Arc Welding). pap. $12.50 (ISBN 0-686-56765-X, M-6475). French & Eur.
Recueil Terminologique Multilingue de Soudage et des Techniques Connexes: Soudage Electrique a l'Arc, Vol. 3. 52p. (Fr. & Eng., A Collection of Multilingual Welding Terminology and Related Techniques: Electrical Arc Welding). pap. $12.50 (ISBN 0-686-56764-1, M-6476). French & Eur.
Recueil Terminologique Multilingue du Soudage et des Techniques Connexes. 52p. (Fr., Pol., Rus., Czech., Slovene & Turkish). pap. $12.50 (ISBN 0-686-56743-9, M-6474). French & Eur.
Recueil Terminologique Multilingue du Soudage et des Techniques Connexes. Soudage Electrique Par Resistance, Vol. 4. 254p. (Fr. & Eng., A Collection of Multilingual Welding Terms & Related Techniques: Electrical Welding by Resistance). pap. $17.50 (ISBN 0-686-56763-3, M-6477). French & Eur.
Recueil Terminologique Multilinque du Soudage et des Techniques Connexes: Coupage Thermique, Vol. 5. (Fr. & Eng., A Collection of Multilingual Welding Terms & Related Techniques: Thermal Cutting). pap. $17.50 (ISBN 0-686-56762-5, M-6478). French & Eur.
Recueil Terminologique Multilinque de Soudage et des Techniques Connexes. Projection a Chaud, Vol. 6. (Fr. & Eng., A Collection of Multilingual Welding Terms & Related Techniques: Heat Projection). pap. $19.95 (ISBN 0-686-56761-7, M-6479). French & Eur.
Roemer, Theo. Dictionary of Welding - Fachwoerterbuch der Schweisstechnik: German-English & English-German. LC 74-534541. (Illus.). 340p. (Ger. & Eng.). 1970. 25.00x (ISBN 3-87155-704-8). Intl Pubns Serv.

WELFARE WORK
see Charities; Public Welfare

WELSH LANGUAGE
see also Celtic Languages
Learn Welsh for English Speakers. 180p. (Welsh & Eng.). pap. 9.50 (ISBN 0-87557-092-5, 092-5). Saphrograph.
Wales University. Dictionary of the Welsh Language, Vol. 1. A-ffysvr. (Welsh.). 1950. Pts. 1-21. $90.00 (ISBN 0-7083-0504-0); Pts. 22-31. pap. $8.00x ea. Verry.

WELSH LANGUAGE-DICTIONARIES
Evans, H. Meurig & Thomas, W. O. The Complete Welsh-English, English-Welsh Dictionary. Y Geiriadur Mawr. 8th ed. (Welsh & Eng.). 1979. text ed. 30.50x (ISBN 0-391-01734-9). Humanities.
--Welsh-English, English-Welsh Dictionary. (Welsh & Eng.). 20.50 (ISBN 0-87557-091-7, 091-7). Saphrograph.
Evans, Meurig & Thomas, W. O. Y geiriadur mawr. 8th ed. LC 79-337696. (Eng. & Welsh.). 1978. E4.95. Davies Dewi.
Meurig, H. & Thomas, W. O. Y Geiriadur Mawr: The Complete Welsh-English, English-Welsh Dictionary. Williams, S. J., ed. 859p. (Welsh & Eng.). 1981. $35.00 (ISBN 0-686-97426-3, M-9434). French & Eur.
Stephens, Roy. Yr Odliadur. LC 79-359298. 204p. (Welsh.). 1978. E2.00 (ISBN 0-85088-710-0). Lewis Ltd.
University of Wales Press. A Dictionary of the Welsh Language: Part 31. Bevan, G. A., ed. 63p. (Welsh.). 1982. pap. text ed. $8.00 (ISBN 0-686-81869-5). Verry.

WEST-SOCIAL LIFE AND CUSTOMS
Watts, Peter. A Dictionary of the Old West. 1977. $12.95 (ISBN 0-394-49013-4). Knopf.

WEST ARMENIAN LANGUAGE
see Armenian Language

WEST GERMANY
see Germany, West

WEST INDIES
see also Caribbean Area
Dubois, J. & Giacomo, M. Dictionnaire de Linguistique. 516p. (Fr.). 1974. $27.50 (ISBN 2-03-020299-1, 1002). Larousse.

WEST INDIES-HISTORY
De Alcedo, Antonio. Geographical & Historical Dictionary of America & the West Indies, 5 Vols. Thompson, George A., tr. LC 70-146788. (Research & Source Works Ser: No. 627). 1971. Repr. of 1812 ed. Set. lib. bdg. $220.00 (ISBN 0-8337-3525-X). B Franklin.

WESTERN ART
see Art

WESTERN FILMS
Hembus, Joe. Western Lexikon. LC 79-396669. 816p. (Ger.). 1978. DM.12.80 (ISBN 3-453-00767-0). Heyne W Verlag.

WESTERN GERMANY
see Germany, West

WILD ANIMALS
see Animals; Mammals

WILDFIRES
see Fires

WINDIC DIALECT (SLOVENIAN)
see Slovenian Language

WINE AND WINE MAKING
see also Cookery (Wine)
Debuigne, Gerard. Dictionnaire des Vins. 3rd ed. (Illus.). 250p. (Fr.). 1970. 17.60 F. Larousse.
Jakob, Ludwig. Lexikon der Onologie. LC 79-386617. 415p. (Eng. & Ger.). 1979. write for info. Meininger.

WINE AND WINE-MAKING-DICTIONARIES
Debuigne, Gerard. Dictionnaire vins. (Illus., Fr.). pap. $8.50 (ISBN 0-03-075459-3, 3742). Larousse.
Hamlyn Pocket Dictionary of Wines. 1980. pap. 3.95 (ISBN 0-600-39498-0). Larousse.
Jaffs, Julian. Dictionary of World Wines, Liqueurs, & Other Drinks. 144p. 6.95 (ISBN 0-919364-73-X, ADON 3537). Pagurian.
Paterson, John. The Pocket Dictionary of Wines. 256p. (Eng.). Epap. 1.25 (ISBN 0-600-39498-0); Epap. 12.50 shrink-wrap pack of 10 copies (ISBN 0-600-04876-4). Newnes Bks.
Perez, J. & Alsina, R. Diccionario de vinos espanoles. 238p. (Span.). 125.00 ptas. Teide.
Price, Pamela V. Dictionary of Wines & Spirits. 408p. 1981. $10.00x (ISBN 0-7198-2744-2, Pub. by Northwood Bks). State Mutual Bk.
Renouil, Yves & De Traversay, Yves. Dictionnaire du Vin. (Fr.). 95.00 F. Feret.
Renouil, Yves & Traversay, Yves de. Dictionnaire du Vin. (Fr.). 1962. $39.95 (ISBN 0-686-56731-5, M-6482). French & Eur.

WINE AND WINE-MAKING-EUROPE
Permartin, Julio, ed. Diccionario del vino de Jerez. (Illus.). 246p. (Span.). 400.00 ptas. Jerez Industrial.

WINE AND WINE MAKING-GERMANY
Panwolf, Wilhelm. Kleines Weinlexikon. LC 77-471829. 196p. (Ger.). 1976. DM.5.00 (ISBN 3-442-10541-2). Goldmann.

WIT AND HUMOR
see also Anecdotes; Comedy; Epigrams; Puns and Punning; Riddles
also American Wit and Humor; English Wit and Humor; and similar headings
Claraso, Noel. Diccionario humoristico. 4th ed. 298p. (Span.). 1966. 300.00 ptas. Sintes.
Claraso, V. Diccionario Humoristico. 297p. (Span.). 1966. $26.95 (ISBN 0-686-92238-7, S-37662). French & Eur.
Delacour, Jean. Dictionnaire des Mots d'esprit. 352p. (Fr.). 1976. 39.00 F. Albin Michel.
Diccionario humoristico. (Span.). 20.00 ptas. Sanchez Rodrigo.
Diccionario humoristico. 2nd ed. 552p. (Span.). 1962. 400.00 ptas. Sintes.

Malcoux, M. Diccionario humoristico. (Span.). 140.00 ptas. Grijalbo.
Maloux, Maurice. Dictionnaire Humoristique. (Fr.). write for info. Albin-Michel.
Negre, Herve. Dictionnaire des Histoires Droles. (Fr.). 1970. 59.00 F. Fayard.
--Dictionnaire des Histoires Droles, 1. (Fr.). 1974. pap. 10.50 F. L. G. F.
--Dictionnaire des Histoires Droles, 2. (Fr.). 1974. 10.50 F. L. G. F.
Provenzal, Dino. Dizionario umoristico. iv, 553p. (Ital.). 1976. L.6000.00 (ISBN 88-205-0097-3). Cisalpino-La Goliardica.
Rosenbloom, Joseph. Doctor Knock-Knock's Official Knock-Knock Dictionary. LC 76-19796. (Illus.). (gr. 3 up). 1976. $7.95 (ISBN 0-8069-4536-2); PLB $9.99 (ISBN 0-8069-4537-0). Sterling.
Sintes Pros, Jorge, ed. Diccionario humoristico. 3rd ed. 552p. (Span.). 1982. pap. 1400.00 ptas (ISBN 84-302-0445-8). Sintes.

WIT AND HUMOR–JUVENILE LITERATURE
see Wit and Humor, Juvenile

WIT AND HUMOR, JUVENILE
Phillips, Louis. The Official Funnybones Flaky Dictionary. (Funnybones Ser.). (Illus.). 64p. (Orig.). (gr. 3-7). 1981. pap. $1.95 (ISBN 0-671-43362-8). Wanderer Bks.
Rosenbloom, Joseph. Doctor Knock-Knock's Official Knock-Knock Dictionary. LC 76-19796. (Illus.). 128p. (gr. 3 up). 1980. pap. $2.95 (ISBN 0-8069-8936-X). Sterling.

WOMAN
see Women

WOMEN
see also Feminism; Mothers
also subdivision Women under names of ethnic groups, e.g. Indians of North America–Women; and headings beginning with the word Women
Ardener, Shirley, ed. Defining Females: The Nature of Women in Society. LC 78-16867. 227p. 1978. 24.95x (ISBN 0-470-26465-9). Halsted Pr.
Diccionario de la mujer. (Span.). 150.00 ptas. Daimon.
Le Dictionnaire des Femmes. (Fr.). 20.00 F. Pensee Moderne.
Jourcin, Albert. Dictionnaire des Femmes Celebres. (Illus.). 256p. (Fr.). 1969. 17.60 F. Larousse.
Roux, Genevieve. Dictionnaire Intime de la Femme. 348p. (Fr.). write for info. Privat.

WOMEN–CLOTHING
see Costume

WOMEN–COSTUME
see Costume

WOMEN–DRESS
see Costume

WOMEN–SOCIAL CONDITIONS
Here are entered works which deal specifically with the social conditions and status of women, including historical discussions of the same. Comprehensive works on the history of women, including works which deal collectively with their socio-economic, political and legal position, participation in historical events, contribution to society, etc. are entered under Women–History.
Ardener, Shirley, ed. Defining Females: The Nature of Women in Society. LC 78-16867. 227p. 1978. 24.95x (ISBN 0-470-26465-9). Halsted Pr.
Bart, Pauline. Social Structure & Vocabularies of Discomfort: What Happened to Female Hysteria. (Reprinted from Journal of Health & Social Behavior, sept, 1968). $0.50. Know Inc.

WOMEN ARTISTS
Here are entered works on the attainments of women as artists. Works dealing with women as represented in art are entered under Women in Art.
Prather-Moses, Alice I. The International Dictionary of Women Workers in the Decorative Arts: A Historical Survey from the Distant Past to the Early Decades of the Twentieth Century. LC 81-8947. 218p. 1981. $13.50 (ISBN 0-8108-1450-1). Scarecrow.

WOMEN PHYSICIANS
Diccionario de Ciencias Medicas Dorland (II) 6th ed. 1728p. (Span.). 1981. 4200.00 ptas (ISBN 84-7021-045-9). Ateneo Edit.
Terminologia cientifica medica en euskera: Obra completa. (Span.). 1982. write for info. (ISBN 84-300-7123-7). Autor.
Terminologia cientifica medica en euskera. 192p. (Span.). 1982. write for info. (ISBN 84-300-7124-5). Autor.

WOMEN'S CLOTHING
see Costume

WOMEN'S LIB
see Feminism

WOMEN'S LIBERATION MOVEMENT
see Feminism

WONDERS
see Curiosities and Wonders

WOOD
see also Forests and Forestry; Pulpwood; Woodwork
also kinds of woods, e.g. Mahogany, Walnut
Boerhave Beekman, W., ed. Elsevier's Wood Dictionary, 3 Vols. (Eng., Fr., Span., Ital., Swedish, Dutch & Ger.). 1964-68. Set. $259.75 (ISBN 0-686-43878-7); Vol. 1. $85.00 (ISBN 0-444-40063-X); Vol. 2. $89.50 (ISBN 0-444-40053-2); Vol. 3. $85.00 (ISBN 0-444-40713-8). Elsevier.
Bucksch, Herbert. Holz Woerterbuch, Vol. 1. (Ger. & Eng., Dictionary of wood & woodworking practice). 1966. $59.95 (ISBN 3-7625-1168-3, M-7465, Pub. by Bauverlag). French & Eur.
--Holz Woerterbuch, Vol. 1. (Ger.). 1966. $59.95 (ISBN 3-7625-1168-3). Bauverlag.
--Holz Woerterbuch, Vol. 2. (Ger. & Eng., Dictionary of wood & woodworking practice). 1966. $67.50 (ISBN 3-7625-1170-5, M-7466, Pub. by Bauverlag). French & Eur.
--Holz Woerterbuch, Vol. 2. (Ger.). 1966. $67.50 (ISBN 3-7625-1170-5). Bauverlag.
Corkhill, Thomas. The Complete Dictionary of Wood. LC 79-10183. (Illus.). 664p. 1980. $19.95 (ISBN 0-8128-2708-2). Stein & Day.
Dictionnaire Technique du Bois en 4 Langues. 640p. (Ger., Rus., Eng. & Fr.). $37.50 (ISBN 0-686-57116-9, M-6157). French & Eur.
Dictionnaire Technique du Bois: Texte en Allemand-Anglais-Francais-Russe. 640p. (Ger. , Eng. , Fr. & Rus.). 1969. 154.00 F. Eyrolles.
Forest Products Research Society. Glossary of Terms Related to the Drying of Wood. 81p. $7.00 (607-61); members $5.00. Forest Prod.
Linnard, W. Russian-English Forestry & Wood Dictionary. 109p. (Rus. & Eng.). 1966. $30.00x (ISBN 0-686-45635-1, Pub. by CAB Bks England). State Mutual Bk.
Wallnig, G. & Evered, H. Dictionnaire Technique du Bois, en Quatre Langues. 640p. (Ger., Fr., Eng. & Rus.). 1973. $65.00 (ISBN 0-686-57254-8, M-6563). French & Eur.

WOOD-CARVING–TECHNIQUE
Dictionnaire Technique du Bois en Quatre Langues: Allemand-Russe-Anglais-Francais. 640p. (Ger. , Rus. , Eng. & Fr.). 96.60 F. Vander.

WOOD PULP INDUSTRY
see also Paper Making and Trade
Van Derveer & Haas. International Glossary of Technical Terms for the Pulp & Paper Industry. 234p. (Eng., Ger., Fr., Span. & Swedish.). 1976. $55.00. Imported Bks.

WOODWORK
see also Furniture Making; Joinery
Bucksch, Herbert. Dictionary of Wood & Woodworking Practice, Vol. II. (Eng. & Ger.). 1966. 47.50x (ISBN 3-7625-1169-1). Intl Pubns Serv.
--Dictionary of Wood & Woodworking Practice, Vol. I. (Ger. & Eng.). 1978. 42.50x (ISBN 3-7625-1201-9). Intl Pubns Serv.
--Holz Woerterbuch, Vol. 1. (Ger. & Eng., Dictionary of wood & woodworking practice). 1966. $59.95 (ISBN 3-7625-1168-3, M-7465, Pub. by Bauverlag). French & Eur.
--Holz Woerterbuch, Vol. 1. (Ger.). 1966. $59.95 (ISBN 3-7625-1168-3). Bauverlag.
--Holz Woerterbuch, Vol. 2. (Ger. & Eng., Dictionary of wood & woodworking practice). 1966. $67.50 (ISBN 3-7625-1170-5, M-7466, Pub. by Bauverlag). French & Eur.
--Holz Woerterbuch, Vol. 2. (Ger.). 1966. $67.50 (ISBN 3-7625-1170-5). Bauverlag.
Corkhill, Thomas. The Complete Dictionary of Wood. LC 79-10183. (Illus.). 672p. 1982. pap. $14.95 (ISBN 0-8128-6142-6). Stein & Day.
Vocabulario de Artes de la Madera, Arquitectura y Decoracion. 152p. (Span.). 1975. pap. $15.75 (ISBN 84-236-1246-5, S-50084). French & Eur.

WOODWORKING INDUSTRIES
see also names of specific industries, e.g. Furniture Industry and Trade
Bucksch, H. Holz-Woerterbuch: Band I, Deutsch-Englisch. 461p. (Ger. & Eng.). 1978. DM.75.00 (ISBN 3-7625-1201-9). Bauverlag.
Holz-Woerterbuch: Band II, Englisch-Deutsch. 536p. (Eng. & Ger.). 1966. DM.84.00 (ISBN 3-7625-1170-5). Bauverlag.

WOOL TRADE AND INDUSTRY
Caccianotti, Luigi. Dizionario metodico del commercio laniero. (Illus.). 348p. (Ital.). L.3200.00. Edit Laniera.

WORD GAMES
see also Crossword Puzzles; Scrabble (Game)
Halikas, Coraline E. Just Words. (Word Game & Crossword Puzzle Aid Ser.). 274p. (Orig.). 1982. pap. $14.95x (ISBN 0-686-35739-6). Ili-Cor Pubns.
Moore, Thurston. The Original Word Game Dictionary. LC 83-42631. 272p. 1983. $16.95 (ISBN 0-8128-2926-3); pap. $7.95 (ISBN 0-8128-6191-4). Stein & Day.
Wetterau, Bruce, ed. The Word Game Winning Dictionary. (Orig.). 1980. pap. 2.95 (ISBN 0-451-09214-7, E9214, Sig). NAL.

WORD PROCESSING (COMPUTER PROGRAM)
Stultz, Russell A. The Illustrated Word Processing Dictionary. (Illus.). 176p. 1983. 17.95 (ISBN 0-13-450726-6); pap. 10.95 (ISBN 0-13-450718-5). P-H.

WORD PROCESSING (OFFICE PRACTICE)
Glossary. $5.00; members free. Word Processing.
Stultz, Russell A. The Illustrated Word Processing Dictionary. (Illus.). 176p. 1983. 17.95 (ISBN 0-13-450726-6); pap. 10.95 (ISBN 0-13-450718-5). P-H.

WORDS–HISTORY
Hook, J. N. The Grand Panjandrum: And 1999 Other Rare & Delightful Words & Expressions. 392p. 1980. 15.95 (ISBN 0-02-553620-6). Macmillan.

WORDS, NEW
Antelava, G. I. Kratkii Turetsko-Russkii Slovar "Novykh Slov". 96p. (Rus. & Turkish.). 1978. $1.75 (Pub. by Metsniereba). Four Continent.
Kielitoimisto. Udissanasto Kahdeksankymmenta. LC 80-463931. 194p. (Finnish.). 1979. write for info. (ISBN 9-51009-287-8). Soderstorm.
Kotimaisten Kielten Tutkimuskekus. Uudissanasto Kahdeksankymmenta. LC 80-463931. 194p. (Finnish.). 1979. write for info. (ISBN 9-51009-287-8). Soderstrom.
Mager, N. H. & Mager, S. K. The Morrow Book of New Words: 8500 Terms Not Yet in Standard Dictionaries. LC 81-14205. 256p. 1982. 13.50 (ISBN 0-688-00685-X); pap. 6.50 (ISBN 0-688-00927-1). Morrow.
Steele, Guy L. The Hacker's Dictionary. LC 83-47573. 96p. (Orig.). 1983. pap. $4.76I (ISBN 0-06-091082-8, CN 1082, CN). Har-Row.
Uudissanasto. LC 80-463931. 194p. (Finnish.). 1979. write for info. (ISBN 9-5100-9287-8). Soderstrom.
Van Nierop, Maarten. Nieuwe Woorden. LC 76-504980. 327p. (Dutch.). 1975. fl.22.75 (ISBN 9-06158-054-4). Scheltens.

WORDS, OBSCENE
Kunitskaya-Peterson, Christina. International Dictionary of Obscenities: A Guide to Dirty Words & Indecent Expressions in Spanish, Italian, French, German, & Russian. 93p. (Orig., Span., Ital., Fr., Ger. & Rus.). 1981. pap. $5.95 (ISBN 0-933884-18-4). Berkeley Slavic.

WORDS, STOCK OF
see Vocabulary

WORDSWORTH, WILLIAM, 1770-1850
Miles, Josephine. Wordsworth & the Vocabulary of Emotion. 1965. lib. bdg. 18.00x (ISBN 0-374-95681-2). Octagon.

WORK
see also Job Satisfaction; Labor and Laboring Classes
Jarnier, R. & Fournier, J. Dictionnaire Bordas: Cahier de Travaux Diriges. (Illus.). 64p. (Fr.). E0.70. Harrap.

WORK–PSYCHOLOGICAL ASPECTS
Spaltro, Enzo. Dizionario di psicologia del lavoro. LC 79-378075. 205p. (Ital.). 1976. L.5000.00. Ghisoni.

WORK, PSYCHOLOGY OF
see Work–Psychological Aspects

WORK, THERAPEUTIC EFFECT OF
see Occupational Therapy

WORK EXPERIENCE
see Education, Cooperative; Vocational Education

WORK-STUDY PLAN
see Education, Cooperative

WORKERS
see Labor and Laboring Classes

WORKING-CLASSES
see Labor and Laboring Classes

WORKING MEN
see Labor and Laboring Classes

WORKINGMEN
see Labor and Laboring Classes

WORKSHOPS FOR THE HANDICAPPED
see Vocational Rehabilitation

WORLD ECONOMICS
see Economic Policy

WORLD HISTORY
see also Geography; Middle Ages–History
Andresen, Karl. Lexikon der Alten Welt. (Ger.). 1965. $395.00 (ISBN 3-7608-0137-4, M-7281). French & Eur.
Clifford, Mary E., et al, eds. News Dictionary 1976. LC 65-17649. 1977. lib. bdg. $14.95 (ISBN 0-87196-103-2). Facts on File.
Lexikon der Weltgeschichte. (Ger.). 1977. $20.00 (ISBN 3-88140-000-1, M-7215). French & Eur.
Meyers Illustrierte Weltgeschichte in 20 Banden: Band I, Die Vorgeschichte. (Illus.). 160p. (Ger.). write for info. (ISBN 3-411-01808-9). Biblio Inst.
Pevsner, Nikolaus, et al, eds. Lexikon der Weltgeschichte. 608p. (Ger.). 1977. DM.24.80 (ISBN 3-88140-000-1). Englisch Verlag.
Trotsky, Judith, ed. News Dictionary 1975, Vol. 12. annual LC 65-17649. 1976. lib. bdg. $14.95 (ISBN 0-87196-101-6). Facts on File.

WORLD HISTORY–CHRONOLOGY
see Chronology, Historical

WORLD HISTORY–JUVENILE LITERATURE
Unstead, R. J. Dictionary of History. (Illus.). (gr. 4-8). 1977. 12.95 (ISBN 0-8467-0230-4, Pub. by Two Continents). Hippocrene Bks.

WORLD POLITICS–DICTIONARIES
Ivens, H., et al, eds. Jugendlexikon Weltpolitik. (Illus.). 192p. (Ger.). 1982. M.9.80. Bibl Inst Leipzig.

WORLD POLITICS–20TH CENTURY
Hamori, Laszlo. Varldspolitiskt lexikon. LC 77-476973. (Illus.). 200p. (Swedish). 1976. Kr.68.00 (ISBN 9-12700-182-2). Natur & kultur.

WORLD WAR, 1939-1945
Masson, Philippe. Dictionnaire de la Seconde Guerre mondiale. LC 79-127046. (Illus., Fr.). 1979. write for info. Larousse.
Zentner, Christian, ed. Lexikon des II. Weltkriegs. (Ger.). 1977. DM.29.80 (ISBN 3-517-00639-4). Suedwest.
Zentner, Cristian. Lexikon Des II Weltkriegs. (Ger.). 1977. pap. $25.00 (ISBN 3-517-00639-4, M-7213). French & Eur.

WORLD WAR, 1939-1945– LANGUAGE (NEW WORDS, SLANG, ETC.)
Ruffner, Frederick G., Jr. & Thomas, Robert C., eds. Code Names Dictionary: A Guide to Code Names, Slang, Nicknames, Journalese, & Similar Terms. LC 63-21847. 1963. $38.00x (ISBN 0-8103-0685-9). Gale.

WORMS, INTESTINAL AND PARASITIC
Pozniak, G. J. Russian-English Dictionary of Helminthology & Plant Nematology. 108p. (Rus. & Eng.). 1979. $60.00x (ISBN 0-85198-447-9, Pub. by CAB Bks England). State Mutual Bk.

WORSHIP
see also Idols and Images; Liturgics
Podhradsky, Gerhard. New Dictionary of the Liturgy. 1967. $6.95 (ISBN 0-8189-0101-2). Alba.

WRITERS
see Authors

WRITING–COPYING PROCESSES
see Copying Processes

WRITING, ARABIC
Kraemer, Joerg, et al. Woerterbuch der Klassischen Arabischen Sprache: Bd 1, Lfg 2. (Ger. & Arabic). 1960. DM.9.00 (ISBN 3-447-01046-0). Harrassowitz.
Kroemer, Joerg, et al. Woerterbuch der Klassischen Arabischen: Bd 1. Ullman, Manfred, et al. (Ger. & Arabic.). 1970. DM.178.00 (ISBN 3-447-01276-5). Harrassowitz.
Spitaler, Anton, et al. Woerterbuch der Klassischen Arabischen Sprache: Bd 1, Lfg 1. (Ger. & Arabic.). 1957. DM.9.00 (ISBN 3-447-01045-2). Harrassowitz.
Ullmann, Manfred. Woerterbuch der Klassischen Arabischen Sprache: Bd 2, Lfg 1. 64p. (Ger. & Arabic). 1972. DM.28.00 (ISBN 3-447-01473-3). Harrassowitz.
––Woerterbuch der Klassischen Arabischen Sprache: Bd 2, Lfg 4. 64p. (Ger. & Arabic). 1976. DM.39.80 (ISBN 3-447-01789-9). Harrassowitz.
Ullmann, Manfred & Spitaler, Anton. Woerterbuch der Klassischen Arabischen: Bd 1, Lfg 7. (Ger. & Arabic.). 1965. DM.18.00 (ISBN 3-447-01051-7). Harrassowitz.
––Woerterbuch der Klassischen Arabischen Sprache: Bd 1, Lfg 3. (Ger. & Arabic). 1962. DM.9.00 (ISBN 3-447-01047-9). Harrassowitz.
––Woerterbuch der Klassischen Arabischen Sprache: Bd 1, Lfg 4. (Ger. & Arabic.). 1962. DM.9.00 (ISBN 3-447-01048-7). Harrassowitz.
––Woerterbuch der Klassischen Arabischen Sprache: Bd 1, Lfg 5. (Ger. & Arabic.). 1964. DM.9.00 (ISBN 3-447-01049-5). Harrassowitz.
––Woerterbuch der Klassischen Arabischen Sprache: Bd 1, Lfg 6. (Ger. & Arabic.). 1964. DM.9.00 (ISBN 3-447-01050-9). Harrassowitz.
––Woerterbuch der Klassischen Arabischen Sprache: Bd 1, Lfg 8. (Ger. & Arabic.). 1966. DM.18.00 (ISBN 3-447-01052-5). Harrassowitz.
––Woerterbuch der Klassischen Arabischen Sprache: Bd 1, Lfg 9-10. (Ger. & Arabic.). 1970. DM.56.00 (ISBN 3-447-01053-3). Harrassowitz.

Ullmann, Manfred & Wojtowytsch-Wielandt, Rotraud. Woerterbuch der Klassischen Arabischen Sprache: Bd 2, Lfg 2. 64p. (Ger. & Arabic.). 1973. DM.28.00 (ISBN 3-447-01526-8). Harrassowitz.
Wehr, Hans. A Dictionary of Modern Written Arabic. Cowan, Milton J., ed. 1300p. (Arabic & Eng.). 1979. $115.00 (ISBN 0-87950-002-6). Spoken Lang Serv.
Wehr, Hans, compiled by. A Dictionary of Modern Written Arabic. 1110p. (Arabic & Eng.). 1980. pap. $12.00 pocket-bk. ed. (001-8); library ed. $85.00. Intl Bk Ctr.

X

X-RAY PHOTOGRAPHY
see Radiography

XEROGRAPHY
Morris. Xerox Dictionary Thumb Index. 10.95 (ISBN 0-448-02905-7, G&D). Putnam Pub Group.

XOSA LANGUAGE
Fischer, A. Lumko English-Xhosa Dictionary. (Eng. & Khosa.). 1982. $39.95x (ISBN 0-19-570290-5). Oxford U Pr.
McLaren, J. Xhosa-English Dictionary. Bennie, W. G. & Jolobe, J. J., eds. (Xhosa & Eng.). $22.50 (ISBN 0-87559-069-1). Shalom.

Y

YACHTS AND YACHTING
see also Sailing
Burgess, Francis H. A Dictionary for Yachtsmen. LC 80-85494. (Illus.). 256p. 1981. $11.95 (ISBN 0-7153-6344-1). David & Charles.
Chesnokov, L. A., et al. Parusny i sport. LC 80-479938. 95p. (Eng., Fr., Ger., Rus. & Span.). 1979. 0.45 Rub. Russkii Iazyk.
Tetsmann, A. & Lind, H. Yachting Dictionary. 192p. 1980. $50.00x (ISBN 0-686-82331-1, Pub. by Collets). State Mutual Bk.
Webb, Barbara. Dizionario dello yachting in otto lingue. 160p. (Ital.). L.7500.00. Mursia S.
––Yachtman's Eight Language Dictionary. 3rd ed. 1983. $8.95 (ISBN 0-8286-0092-9). De Graff.
––Yachtsman's Eight Language Dictionary. (Illus.). 160p. 1973. $12.00x (ISBN 0-8464-0983-6). Beekman Pubs.

YAKIMA INDIANS
see Indians of North America– Northwest, Pacific

YAKIMA LANGUAGE
Pandosy, Marie C. Grammar & Dictionary of the Yakama Language. LC 10-30204. (Library of American Linguistics: Vol. 6). (Yakama.). Repr. of 1862 ed. $15.00 (ISBN 0-404-50986-X). AMS Pr.

YANA INDIANS
see Indians of North America– Southwest, New

YANA LANGUAGE
Sapir, Edward & Swadesh, Morris. Yana Dictionary. (U. C. Publ. in Linguistics: Vol. 22). 1960. pap. $14.00x (ISBN 0-520-09219-8). U of Cal Pr.

YEARBOOKS
see also Almanacs; Calendars
also subdivision Yearbooks under special subjects, e.g. Literature– Yearbooks; Medicine–Yearbooks
News Dictionary, 1979: Annual. 1980. $14.95 (ISBN 0-87196-109-1); pap. $9.95 (ISBN 0-87196-110-5). Facts on File.

YEATS, WILLIAM BUTLER, 1865-1939
Domville, Eric, ed. A Concordance to the Plays of W. B. Yeats, 2 vols. LC 71-162547. (Concordances Ser) 2330p. 1972. Set. $75.00x (ISBN 0-8014-0663-3). Cornell U Pr.

Parrish, Stephen M. & Painter, James A., eds. Concordance to the Poems of W. B. Yeats. 1963. $52.50x (ISBN 0-8014-0328-6). Cornell U Pr.

YIDDISH LANGUAGE
Copeland, Robert M. & Susskind, Nathan, eds. The Language of Herz's "Esther". A Study in Judeo-German Dialectology. LC 75-34184. (Judaic Studies: No. 6). 560p. 1976. $29.50 (ISBN 0-8173-6902-3). U of Ala Pr.
Hoffman, Paul & Freedman, Matt. Dictionary, Schmictionary. LC 83-3050. (Illus.). 160p. (Orig.). 1983. pap. write for info. (ISBN 0-688-02162-X). Quill NY.
Jacobs, Sidney J. The Jewish Word Book. 356p. (Eng. & Hebrew.). 1982. $12.50 (ISBN 0-8246-0249-8). Jonathan David.
Kogos, Fred. Dictionary of Yiddish Slang. 176p. (Yiddish.). 1983. pap. 4.95 (ISBN 0-8065-0347-5). Lyle Stuart.
Postman, Frederica. The Yiddish Alphabet Book. LC 78-78188. (Illus., Yiddish & Eng.). 1979. $8.95x (ISBN 0-9602402-0-9). PNye Pr.
Rosenbaum, Samuel. A Yiddish Word Book for English Speaking People. 199p. (Yiddish & Eng.). 1980. pap. text ed. $6.95 (ISBN 0-442-21932-6). Van Nos Reinhold.
––A Yiddish Word Book for English-Speaking People. (Yiddish & Eng.). 1978. $9.95 (ISBN 0-442-27015-1). Van Nos Reinhold.
Rosten, Leo. Joys of Yiddish. 1968. $19.95 (ISBN 0-07-053975-8, GB). McGraw.
Weinreich, Uriel. Modern English-Yiddish, Yiddish-English Dictionary. (Eng. & Yiddish.). 1968. 44.95 (ISBN 0-07-069038-3, P&RB). McGraw.
––Modern English-Yiddish Yiddish-English Dictionary. LC 77-76038. (Eng. & Yiddish.). 1978. pap. $18.95 (ISBN 0-8052-0575-6). Schocken.
––Modern English-Yiddish, Yiddish-English Dictionary. LC 67-23848. 789p. (Eng. & Yiddish.). 1968. write for info (ISBN 0-914512-25-0). Yivo Inst.
Yiddish-English Dictionary. $22.50 (ISBN 0-87559-193-0). Shalom.

YOGA
Aurobindo, Sri. Dictionary of Sri Aurobindo's Yoga. Pandit, Sri M., ed. 1979. Repr. of 1966 ed. 7.50 (ISBN 0-941524-04-3). Lotus Light.
Day, Harvey. Yoga Illustrated Dictionary. (Illus.). 1970. $9.95 (ISBN 0-87523-177-2). Emerson.

YOLA LANGUAGE
see Diola Language

YOUNG ADULTS
Bastian, Hans D., ed. Lexikon fuer Junge Erwachsene. 462p. (Ger.). 1970. DM.19.80 (ISBN 3-7831-0320-7). Kreuz Verlag.

YUGOSLAV LANGUAGE
see Serbo-Croatian Language

Z

ZAMBIA
Grotpeter, John J. Historical Dictionary of Zambia. LC 79-342. (African Historical Dictionaries Ser.: No. 19). 1979. $22.50 (ISBN 0-8108-1207-X). Scarecrow.

ZEBU DIALECT
see Cebu Dialect

ZEN BUDDHISM
Wood, E. Diccionario Zen. 190p. (Span.). pap. 400.00 ptas (ISBN 8-47509-010-9). Paido.
Wood, Ernest. Zen Dictionary. LC 72-77518. 1972. pap. $5.25 (ISBN 0-8048-1060-5). C E Tuttle.

ZEN BUDDHIST LITERATURE
see Zen Literature

ZEN LITERATURE
Wood, E., ed. Diccionario Zen. 190p. (Span.). 1980. pap. $13.95 (ISBN 84-7509-010-9, S-32724). French & Eur.

ZENDAL LANGUAGE
see Tzeltal Language

ZIMSHIAN LANGUAGE
see Tsimshian Language

ZOLA, EMILE, 1840-1902
Patterson, J. G. Zola Dictionary. LC 68-27179. 1969. Repr. of 1912 ed. $34.00x (ISBN 0-8103-3173-X). Gale.
––A Zola Dictionary. 75.00 (ISBN 0-8490-1350-X). Gordon Pr.

ZOMBO LANGUAGE
see Congo Language

ZONING
see also Zoning Law
A Glossary of Zoning Definitions. (PAS Reports: No. 233). 27p. 1968. photocopy $6.00. Am Plan Assn.

ZONING LAW
A Glossary of Zoning Definitions. (PAS Reports: No. 233). 27p. 1968. photocopy $6.00. Am Plan Assn.

ZOOLOGY–DICTIONARIES
Bastian, Hartmut. Ullstein Lexikon der Tierwelt. (Ger.). 1967. $27.50 (ISBN 3-550-06014-9, M-7676, Pub. by Ullstein Verlag/VVA). French & Eur.
Diccionario Axon de zoologia y botanica. (Span.). Arg.$11.00. Plus Ultra.
Diccionario Monografico del Reino Animal. 288p. (Span.). 750.00 ptas (ISBN 84-7153-385-5). Biblograf SP.
Diccionario Rioduero: Zoologia. 432p. (Span.). 1979. $17.95 (ISBN 0-686-57364-1, S-50171). French & Eur.
Dictionary of Zoology: English-Chinese. 52p. (Eng. & Chinese.). 1975. pap. $1.95 (ISBN 0-686-92583-1, M-9571). French & Eur.
Hentschel, Erwin. Tiernamen & Zoologische Fachworter. LC 77-451749. 528p. (Eng. & Ger.). 1976. DM.19.80 (ISBN 3-437-20130-1). Fischer Verlag.
Jacobs, George J. Dictionary of Vertebrate Zoology, Russian-English: English-Russian. LC 78-16321. 1978. pap. text ed. $4.25x (ISBN 0-87474-551-9). Smithsonian.
Jaeger, Edmund C. A Dictionary of Greek & Latin Combining Forms Used in Zoological Names. 2nd ed. 176p. (Gr., Lat. & Eng.). 1930. photocopy ed. spiral $17.50x (ISBN 0-398-04294-2). C C Thomas.
Jehan, L. F. Dictionnaire de Zoologie, 3 vols. Migne, J. P., ed. (Nouvelle Encyclopedie Theologique Ser.: Vols. 14-16). 2666p. (Fr.). Repr. of 1853 ed. lib. bdg. $336.50x (ISBN 0-89241-263-1). Caratzas Pub Co.
Klemm, Michael. Zoologisches Woerterbuch - Palaearktische Tiere. 850p. (Ger., Lat. & Rus.). 1973. 160.00x (ISBN 3-489-71734-1). Intl Pubns Serv.
––Zoologisches Woerterbuch Palaearktische Tiere. (Lat., Ger. & Rus.). 1973. $220.00 (ISBN 0-686-56474-X, M-7692, Pub. by Parey Berlin). French & Eur.
––Zoologisches Woerterbuch Palaearktische Tiere. (Lat., Ger. & Rus.). 1973. $220.00. Parey.
Kowalski, Kazimierz. Maly Slownik Zoologiczny. LC 76-521216. 454p. (Pol.). 1975. write for info. Wiedza Powszechna.
Leftwich, A. W. A Dictionary of Zoology. 3rd ed. 487p. 1973. $27.50x (ISBN 0-8448-0845-8). Crane-Russak Co.
––Dizionario di zoologia. (Ital.). L.4000.00. Newton-Compton.
Parenti, U. Dizionario di zoologia: A-L. (Illus.). 128p. (Ital.). L.3000.00. Ist Geo Agostini.
––Dizionario di zoologia: M-Z. (Illus.). 128p. (Ital.). L.3000.00. Ist Geo Agostini.
Parenti, Umberto. Diccionario De Zoologia. 255p. (Span.). 1973. leatherette $11.50 (ISBN 84-307-8256-7, S-50257). French & Eur.
––Dictionnaire de Zoologie: Vol. 1, A-J. (Fr.). 1972. 21.00 F. Atlas.
––Dictionnaire de Zoologie: Vol. 2, K-Z. (Fr.). 1972. 21.00 F. Atlas.
Pennak, Robert W. Collegiate Dictionary of Zoology. 1964. $29.95x (ISBN 0-471-06790-3, Pub. by Wiley-Interscience). Wiley.

Smolik, H. Tierlexikon, 5 vols.
(Ger.). 1968. pap. $32.00 (ISBN 3-
499-16059-5, M-7667, Pub. by
Rowohlt). French & Eur.

--Tierlexikon, 5 vols. (Ger.). 1968.
pap. $32.00 (ISBN 3-499-16059-5).
Rowohlt.

Villemin, Martial. Dictionnaire des
Termes Veterinaires &
Zootechniques. (Fr.). 1963. 130.00
F. Vigot.

ZOOMBO LANGUAGE
see Congo Language

ZOROASTRIANISM

Mills, Lawrence H. Dictionary of the
Gathic Language. (Gaelic.). $57.50
(ISBN 0-404-12804-1). AMS Pr.
ZULU LANGUAGE
Doke, C. M. English & Zulu
Dictionary. (Zulu & Eng.). 1958.
pap. 14.25x (ISBN 0-85494-010-3).
Intl Learn Syst.

Doke, C. M., ed. Zulu-English,
English-Zulu Dictionary. rev. ed.
(Zulu & Eng.). pap. 20.00 (ISBN
0-85494-010-3). Heinman.
Zulu-English & Zulu Dictionary.
(Zulu & Eng.). 19.50 (ISBN 0-685-
77569-0, 096-8). Saphrograph.

Title Index

A

A-Z of Clinical Chemistry. W. Hood. LC 80-23908. 386p. 1980. 24.95x (ISBN 0-470-27029-2). Halsted Pr.

Abair faclan. I.A.R.R. LC 80-508491. viii, 162p. (Gaelic & Eng.). 1979. pap. write for info. (ISBN 0-906675-00-6). Mingulay.

Abbreviated Military Dictionary. 334p. (Persian & Rus.). 1954. leatherette 4.50 (ISBN 0-686-97382-8, M-9106). French & Eur.

Abbreviated Russian-Korean Dictionary. 648p. (Rus. & Korean.). 4.95 (ISBN 0-686-97385-2, M-9055). French & Eur.

Abbreviated Russian-Persian Technical Dictionary. 477p. (Rus. & Persian.). 1974. 13.50 (ISBN 0-686-97386-0, M-9053). French & Eur.

Abbreviated Turkish-Russian Dictionary of New Words. H. G. Antelava. 95p. (Turkish & Rus.). 1978. pap. 7.95 (ISBN 0-686-97387-9, M-9054). French & Eur.

Abbreviations: A Reverse Guide to Standard & Generally Accepted Abbreviated Forms. Ed. by Stephen A. Rybicki. LC 74-143239. (Reverse Dictionary Ser.: No. 1). 1971. 17.50 (ISBN 0-87650-010-6). Pierian.

Abbreviations & Symbols for Terms Used in Electronics. Standards Council, Society for Technical Communication. 1975. pap. 8.00 (ISBN 0-914548-19-0). Soc Tech Comm.

Abbreviations & Technical Terms Used in Book Catalogues & in Bibliographies. Frank K. Walter. LC 77-6174. 1977. Repr. of 1917 ed. lib. bdg. 12.50 (ISBN 0-89341-152-3). Longwood Pr.

Abbreviations Dictionary. 6th ed. R. De Sola. 1981. 38.00 (ISBN 0-444-00380-0). Elsevier.

Abbreviations in Medicine. 4th ed. Edwin B. Steen. 1978. pap. 12.95 (ISBN 0-7216-0766-7, Pub. by Bailliere-Tindall). Saunders.

Abbreviations of Nuclear Power Plant Engineering. G. H. Freyberger. 280p. (Eng. & Ger.). 1979. 28.95 (ISBN 0-686-56591-6, M-7288, Pub. by Verlag Karl Thiemig). French & Eur.

Abbreviations Used by FAO for International Congresses, Commissions, Etc. (Terminology Bulletin Ser.: No. 27, R. 2). 144p. 1979. pap. 9.75 (ISBN 0-686-72305-8, F2056, FAO). Unipub.

ABC des Pfeifenrauchers. Helmut Hochrain. Ed. by Heinrich Haisch. LC 78-389542. (Illus.). 204p. (Ger.). 1977. DM.5.80 (ISBN 3-453-41223-0). Heyne W Verlag.

ABC Dictionary I: Arabic & Fr. Libr. du Liban. (Arabic & Fr.). 1983. 7.95x (ISBN 0-86685-310-3). Intl Bk Ctr.

ABC Dictionary I: Arabic & Ger. libr. du Liban. (Arabic & Ger.). 1983. 7.95x (ISBN 0-86685-309-X). Intl Bk Ctr.

ABC Dictionary I: Arabic & Span. Libr d. Liban. (Arabic & Span.). 1983. 7.95x. Intl Bk Ctr.

ABC Dictionary I, Arabic Italian. (Arabic & Ital.). 7.99. Intl Bk Ctr.

ABC Dictionary I, Arabic-Spanish. (Arabic & Span.). 7.99 (ISBN 0-86685-308-1). Intl Bk Ctr.

ABC Dictionary Tamhidi: Arabic & Eng. Libr du Liban. (Arabic & Eng.). 1983. 7.95x (ISBN 0-86685-314-6). Intl Bk Ctr.

ABC Dictionary Tamhidi: Arabic & Fr. Libr du Liban. (Arabic & Fr.). 1983. 7.95x (ISBN 0-86685-315-4). Intl Bk Ctr.

ABC Dictionary Tamhidi: Arabic & Ital. Libr du Liban. (Arabic & Ital.). 1983. 7.95x (ISBN 0-86685-316-2). Intl Bk Ctr.

ABC Dictionary Tamhidi: Arabic Ger. Libr du Liban. (Arabic & Ger.). 1983. 7.95x (ISBN 0-86685-313-8). Intl Bk Ctr.

ABC Dictionary Tamhidi: Arabic-Spanish. Libr du Liban. (Arabic & Span.). 1983. 7.95x (ISBN 0-86685-312-X). Intl Bk Ctr.

ABC-Komiker bis Zwitschergemuese. Heinz Kuepper. LC 79-366187. xxiii, 229p. (Ger.). 1978. DM.24.80 (ISBN 3-88228-001-8). Deutsche Sprache.

ABC of Plant Terms. J. Gordon Cook. 293p. 1968. 39.00x (ISBN 0-900541-56-3, Pub. by Meadowfield Pr England). State Mutual Bk.

ABC's Dictionary. Daughters of St. Paul. write for info. Dghtrs St Paul.

Abdallah Dictionary of International Relations & Conference Terminology in English-Arabic. Abdallah. (Eng. & Arabic.). 1982. 40.00x (ISBN 0-86685-289-1). Intl Bk Ctr.

Abhinava Malayala Nikhantu: New Malayalam Dictionary, 2 vols. C. Madhavan Pillai. (Malayalam.). 1980. write for info. DC Bks.

Abingdon Dictionary of Living Religions. Ed. by Keith Crim et al. LC 81-1465. 864p. 1981. prepub. 39.95 (ISBN 0-687-00409-8). Abingdon.

Abingdon Glossary of Religious Terms. Thayer S. Warshaw. LC 80-13121. (Festival Ser.). 96p. (Orig.). 1980. pap. 1.50 (ISBN 0-687-00472-1). Abingdon.

Abkeurzungen & Kurzwoerter aus Technik & Naturwissenschaften: E-D. 859p. (Ger. & Eng.). DM.50.00. Brandstetter.

Abkurzungen & Kurzwoerter aus Technik & Naturwissenschaften. 859p. (Ger.). 1982. DM.50.00. Brandstetter.

Abkurzungen der Kernkraftwerkstechnik. G. Freyberger. LC 79-376298. 199p. (Eng. & Ger.). 1979. write for info. (ISBN 3-521-06120-5). Thiemeg.

Ablak-Zsir Kepes Gyermeklexikon. Ferenc Morei & Agnes V. Binet. (Illus.). 160p. (Hungarian.). (gr. 1 up). 6.00 (3002). Adler Bks.

ABN-Uitspraakgids. Petrus C. Paardekooper. LC 80-499677. xvii, 250p. (Dutch.). 1978. write for info. (ISBN 9-02912-020-7). Heideland-Orbis.

Abreviation du traitement de l'informatique. 2nd ed. Carl Amkreutz. 210p. (Eng., Ger., & Fr.). 1982. 160.00 F. Maison Dictionnaire.

Abridged Greek-English Lexicon. Ed. by H. G. Liddell & Robert Scott. (Gr. & Eng.). 1957. 24.95x (ISBN 0-19-910207-4). Oxford U Pr.

Accounting Dictionary - U.E.C. Lexicon: American-French-German-Spanish-Dutch. 2nd ed. Union Europeenne Des Experts Compatables, Economiques et Financiers. LC 63-31440. (Eng., Fr., Ger., Span. & Dutch.). 1974. 107.50x (ISBN 3-8021-0073-5). Intl Pubns Serv.

Accounting Language. Robert T. March. LC 77-12041. 1978. lib. bdg. 12.90 (ISBN 0-89471-017-6); pap. 2.95 (ISBN 0-89471-016-8). Running Pr.

Ace's French Phrase Book & Dictionary. Charles A. Hughes. (Ace's Foreign Phrase Bk.) 192p. (Eng. & Fr.). 1981. pap. 1.95 (ISBN 0-441-25208-7). Ace Bks.

Ace's Italian Phrase Book & Dictionary. Charles A. Hughes. (Ace's Foreign Phrase Bk.) 192p. 1981. pap. 1.95 (ISBN 0-441-37488-3). Ace Bks.

Ace's Scandinavian Phrase Book & Dictionary. Charles A. Hughes. (Ace's Foreign Phrase). 256p. 1981. pap. 1.95 (ISBN 0-441-75386-8). Ace Bks.

Ace's Spanish Phrase Book & Dictionary. Charles A. Hughes. (Ace's Foreign Phrase Bk). 192p. 1981. pap. 2.25 (ISBN 0-441-77773-2). Ace Bks.

Aces's Italian Phrase Book & Dictionary. Charles A. Hughes. 1982. pap. 2.25 (ISBN 0-441-37490-5). Ace Bks.

Acoustics Dictionary. W. Reichardt. Date not set. lib. bdg. 28.50 (ISBN 90-247-2707-3, Pub. by Martinus Nijhoff Netherlands). Kluwer Academic.

Acronyms, Initialisms & Abbreviations Dictionary, 2 pts, Vol. 1. 8th ed. Ed. by Ellen Crowley. 1701p. 1982. 110.00x (ISBN 0-8103-0505-4). Gale.

Active German Idioms. Conrad Borovski. 64p. (Ger. & Eng.). 1974. DM.pap. 8.00. Hueber.

Actors' Analects. Ed. by Charles W. Dunn. LC 79-8837. (Studies in Oriental Culture Ser.). (Illus.). 306p. 1970. 24.00x (ISBN 0-231-03391-5). Columbia U Pr.

Adams Dictionary of American History, 8 vols. rev. ed. LC 76-6735. 1976. Set. text ed. 430.00 (ISBN 0-684-13856-5, ScribR). Scribner.

Additions Aux Dictionnaires Arabes (Arabic-French) E. Fagnan. 194p. (Arabic & Fr.). 1969. 20.00x (ISBN 0-86685-107-0). Intl Bk Ctr.

Adili Na Nduguze. Robert Shaaban. 66p. (Swahili.). write for info. Macmillan London.

Adjektive auf Isch in der Deutschen Gegenwartssprache. Michael Schaefer. LC 78-355176. (Illus.). 208p. (Ger.). 1977. write for info. (ISBN 3-53302-656-6). Winter Univ.

Administrative & Financial Terms. (FAO Terminology Bulletin: No. 23, Rev. 1). 169p. 1982. pap. 12.75 (ISBN 92-5-001120-2, F2212, FAO). Unipub.

ADS Dictionary - How Soon? Frederic G. Cassidy. Bd. with Linguistic Atlas of New England Revisited. (Publications of the American Dialect Society: No. 39). 27p. 1963. pap. 1.25 (ISBN 0-8173-0639-0). U of Ala Pr.

Adult Approach to Vocabulary Building. Nurnberg & Rosenblum. Epap. 1.40. Mentor Bks.

Advanced English Vocabulary. Helen Barnard. 1971. tchrs' bk 2.95 (ISBN 0-912066-19-9); wkbk 1 6.95 (ISBN 0-686-96805-0). Newbury Hse.

Advanced English Vocabulary. Helen Barnard. 1975. pap. 6.95 wkbk 3B (ISBN 0-912066-44-X). Newbury Hse.

Advanced English Vocabulary. Helen Barnard. 1975. pap. 6.95 wkbk 3A (ISBN 0-912066-43-1). Newbury Hse.

Advanced English Vocabulary. Helen Barnard. 1972. wkbk 2A 6.95 (ISBN 0-88377-037-7); pap. 6.50 wkbk 2b (ISBN 0-88377-038-5). Newbury Hse.

Advanced Learner's Arabic-English Dictionary. Anthony Salmone. 1461p. (Arabic & Eng.). 30.00 (089-9). Intl Bk Ctr.

Advanced Learner's Dictionary of Current English with Chinese Translation. Hornby. (Chinese & Eng.). 16.95. Iaconi.

Advanced Learner's Dictionary of Current English with Chinese Translation. A. S. Hornby et al. (Illus.). 1354p. (Eng. & Chinese.). 25.00. Imported Bks.

Advanced Modern German Vocabulary. Victor Johnson. 63p. (Ger.). 1980. Epap. 1.65. Harrap Co.

Aeronautic Engineering Dictionary: English-French-German-Arabic. M. A. Zimaity. Ed. by Abd-el-Washed. 369p. (Eng., Fr., Ger. & Arabic.). 1976. 45.00 (ISBN 0-686-92564-5, M-9764). French & Eur.

Aerospace Technical Dictionary see Dictionnaire Des Techniques Aeronautiques et Spatiales.

African Countries & Cultures. Hornburger. 1981. 13.95 (ISBN 0-679-20507-1). McKay.

African-English, English-African Dictionary. A. Coetzee. (African & Eng.). 22.50 (ISBN 0-87559-000-4); thumb indexed 27.50 (ISBN 0-87559-001-2). Shalom.

African Political Dictionary. Claude S. Phillips. (Clio Dictionaries in Political Science: No. 5). (Illus.). 300p. 1983. lib. bdg. 20.75 (ISBN 0-87436-036-6); pap. 10.75 (ISBN 0-87436-040-4). ABC-Clio.

Africanderisms. Charles Pettman. LC 68-18007. 1968. Repr. of 1913 ed. 47.00x (ISBN 0-8103-3289-2). Gale.

Afrikaans-English, English-Afrikaans Dictionary. 12th, rev., enl. ed. M. S. Kritzinger. (Afrikaans & Eng.). 60.00 (ISBN 0-627-01082-2). Heinman.

Afrikaanse Verklarende Woordeboek vir Biologie. Eulalie Munnik. LC 80-451787. 152p. (Afrikaan.). 1979. R.3.80 (ISBN 0-620-03588-9). Knaggs Assoc.

Agrarian Landscape Terms: A Glossary for Historical Geography. I. H. Adams. (Special Publication of the Institute of British Geographers: No. 9). 1980. 23.00 (ISBN 0-12-044180-2). Acad Pr.

Agricultural Economics & Rural Sociology: Multilingual Thesaurus. 2nd ed. Ed. by Commission of the European Communities, Directorate-General for Research, Science & Education. Incl. Vol. 1. German. 80p. (Ger.); Vol. 2. English. 84p. pap. 68.00 (ISBN 0-686-81238-7); Vol. 3. French. 84p. (Fr.); Vol. 4. Italian. 78p. (Italian.); Vol. 5. Quadrilingual Index. 130p. (Eng., Fr., Ger. & Ital.). 1979. Set. pap. 200.00x (ISBN 3-598-10097-3, Pub. by K G Saur); 16 microfiches incl. Gale.

Agricultural Engineering Dictionary: English-French-German-Arabic. Abd El Wahed. 446p. (Eng., Fr., Ger. & Arabic.). 1977. 45.00 (ISBN 0-686-92251-4, M-9761). French & Eur.

Agriculture, Forestry, & Allied Terminology Dictionary: English-Arabic with Arabic Glossary. Chihabi. Ed. by A. Khatib. (Eng. & Arabic.). 1978. 40.00x (ISBN 0-86685-072-4). Intl Bk Ctr.

Agypten, die 21: Dynastie. M. Heerma Van Voss. (Iconography of Religions Ser.: XVI/9). (Illus.). viii, 18p. (Ger.). 1982. pap. write for info. (ISBN 90-04-06826-0). E J Brill.

Ainsworth & Bisby's Dictionary of the Fungi, Including the Lichens. 6th ed. G. C. Ainsworth. LC 74-883641. (Illus.). 673p. 1971. 27.50x (ISBN 0-85198-075-9). Intl Pubns Serv.

Aircraft Technical Dictionary. 2nd ed. Dale Crane et al. (Aviation Maintenance Training Course Ser.). pap. write for info. (ISBN 0-89100-124-7). Aviation Maintenance.

Akademiewoerterbuch von 1694: Das Woerterubch des Honnete Homme? Inge Popelar. LC 77-456424. vii, 235p. (Fr.). 1976. write for info. (ISBN 3-484-52057-4). Niemeyer.

Akhmarsko-Russkii Slovar. E. B. Gankin. 968p. (Rus.). 1969. 7.95 (Pub. by Sov Entsiklopediia). Four Continent.

Al-Faraid: Arabic-English Dictionary. J. Hava. 915p. (Arabic & Eng.). 25.00 (2106-9). Intl Bk Ctr.

Al-Faraid Arabic-English Dictionary. 3rd ed. J. G. Hava. 915p. (Arabic & Eng.). 1970. 30.00x (ISBN 2-7214-2106-9). Intl Pubns Serv.

Al-Hadiyati 'I-Hamidiyah. M. Mokri. 400p. (Arabic & Kurdish.). 28.00 (126-7). Intl Bk Ctr.

Al-Kamil Dictionnaire Arabe-Francais-Anglais. M. Chouemi & C. H. Pellat. 64p. (Arabic, Fr. & Eng.). 1981. write for info. (M-9286). French & Eur.

Al Manar: English-Arabic Dictionary. Hassan Karmi. 904p. (Eng. & Arabic.). 25.00 (070-8); student ed. 12.00 (071-6). Intl Bk Ctr.

Al-Wafi. Abdullah Al-Bustani. (Arabic.). 40.00 (095-3). Intl Bk Ctr.

A.L.A. Glossary of Library & Information Science. Hartsill Young. 1983. text ed. 50.00 (ISBN 0-8389-0371-1). ALA.

Alan Leo's Dictionary of Astrology. Alan Leo & Robson. 6.50 (Pub. by Sun Pub). Am Fed Astrologers.

Alan Leo's Dictionary of Astrology. Alan Leo & Vivian E. Robson. 205p. 1981. pap. 10.50 (ISBN 0-89540-101-0, SB-101). Sun Pub.

Albanian-English & English Albanian Dictionary. (Albanian & Eng.). 27.50 (ISBN 0-87557-001-1, 001-1). Saphrograph.

Albanian-English Dictionary. Gasper Kici. (Albanian & Eng.). 1976. 15.00 (ISBN 0-686-17904-8). G Kici.

Albanian-English, English-Albanian Dictionary. Nelo Drizari. LC 57-9330. (Albanian & Eng.). 20.00 (ISBN 0-8044-0130-6). Ungar.

Alcala-Zamora, Diccionario Frances-Espanol, Espanol-Frances. Alcala-Zamora. 960p. (Span. & Fr.). pap. 9.95 (ISBN 84-303-0094-5, S-50399). French & Eur.

Alcala-Zamora, Diccionario Frances-Espanol, Espanol-Frances. Alcala-Zamora. 960p. (Span. & Fr.). 12.25 (ISBN 84-303-0093-7, S-50400). French & Eur.

Alef Bet Picture Dictionary. Melvin Alexenberg & Miriam Alexenberg. (Illus.). (gr. 1-3). 1963. 5.00 (ISBN 0-914080-06-7). Shulsinger Sales.

Aleutian Indian & English Dictionary. facsimile ed. Charles A. Lee. 23p. (Aleut.). Repr. of 1896 ed. pap. 9.95 (ISBN 0-8466-0101-X, SJS101). Shorey.

Alevin sopena color. (Span.). (gr. 4-6). pap. 2.75. Iaconi.

All About the Dictionary. Alan W. Riese & Herbert J. LaSalle. (Orig.). (gr. 8-11). 1976. pap. text ed. 6.58 (ISBN 0-87720-330-X). AMSCO Sch.

All Romanized English-Japanese Dictionary. Kai. (Japanese & Eng.). 6.95. Iaconi.

All-Romanized English-Japanese Dictionary. Hyojun R. Kai. LC 73-90232. 732p. (Eng. & Japanese.). 1973. pap. 6.95 (ISBN 0-8048-1118-0). C E Tuttle.

Allegemeines Lexikon der Bildenden Kunstler von der Antike bis zur Gegenwart, 37 vols. Ed. by Ulrich Thieme & Felix Becker. (Ger.). 1906-50. Repr. 2750.00 set (ISBN 0-403-07236-0). Somerset Pub.

Allen & Wolfe Illustrated Dictionary of Real Estate. Robert D. Allen & Thomas E. Wolfe. LC 82-13445. (Real Estate for Professional Practitioners). 266p. 1983. 24.95 (ISBN 0-471-09415-3, Pub. by Wiley-Interscience). Wiley.

Allen's Synonyms & Antonyms. F. Sturges Allen. pap. 3.95 (ISBN 0-06-463328-4, EH 328, EH). B&N NY.

Allied Health Reading Vocabulary Workbook. Frances McMurtray. 122p. 1978. pap. text ed. 5.95x (ISBN 0-89641-008-0). American Pr.

Allusions, Cultural, Literary, Biblical, & Historical: A Thematic Dictionary. Ed. by Laurance Urdang. 1982. 52.00x (ISBN 0-8103-1124-0). Gale.

Alphabetical Vocabularies of the Clallam & Lumni. George Gibbs. LC 75-168115. (Library of American Linguistics: No. 11). Repr. of 1863 ed. 10.00 (ISBN 0-404-50991-6). AMS Pr.

Alphabetical Vocabulary of the Chinook Language. George Gibbs. LC 72-168141. (Library of American Linguistics: No. 13). (Chinook.). Repr. of 1863 ed. 10.00 (ISBN 0-404-50993-2). AMS Pr.

Altenglisches Elementarbuch Einfuehrung, Grammatik, Texte Mit Uebersetzung und Woerterbuch. rev. 9th ed. Martin Lehnert. (Sammlung Goeschen). (Ger.). 1978. 7.15x (ISBN 3-11-007643-8). De Gruyter.

Altgriechisch, 2 Vols. Incl. Teil I. Altgriechisch-Deutsch. H. Menge. 528p. DM.16.80 (10030); Teil II. Deutsch-Altgriechisch. O. Guthling. 551p. DM.16.80 (10035). (Langenscheidts Taschenwoerterbucher Ser.). (Gr. & Ger.). DM.beide Teile in einem Band 23.80 (11030). Langenscheidt.

Altkirchenslavisch-Griechisches Woerterbuch Des Codex Supraliensis. Karl H. Meyer. (Gr.). 25.00 (ISBN 0-685-71713-5). J J Augustin.

Ambiguite Dans le Lexique. Wiecher Zwanenburg. (PDR Press Publication in Lexical Ambiguityl Ser.: No. 1). (Fr.). 1977. pap. text ed. 1.00x (ISBN 9-0316-0037-7). Humanities.

American College Dictionary. tan buckram bdg., with index o.s.i. 7.95 (ISBN 0-394-40001-1); tan buckram bdg., without index 6.95 (ISBN 0-394-40002-X). Random.

American Dictionaries of the English Language Before 1861. Eva M. Burkett. LC 78-11677. 1979. lib. bdg. 18.00 (ISBN 0-8108-1179-0). Scarecrow.

American Dictionary of Economics. Douglas Auld & Graham Bannock. 352p. 1983. 15.95x (ISBN 0-87196-532-1). Facts on File.

American Dictionary of Printing & Bookmaking. LC 70-135172. 1971. Repr. of 1894 ed. lib. bdg. 29.00 (ISBN 0-8337-0059-6). B Franklin.

American Dictionary of Printing & Bookmaking. LC 66-27215. 1967. Repr. of 1894 ed. 42.00x (ISBN 0-8103-3345-7). Gale.

American Dictionary of the English Language. facsimile ed. Noah Webster. (Facsimile Reprint). 1967. Repr. of 1828 ed. lib. bdg. 30.00 (ISBN 0-912498-03-X). Found Am Christ.

American Dictionary of the English Language: To Which Are Prefixed, an Introductory Dissertation of the Origin, History & Connection of the Language of Western Asia & Europe & A...Grammar of the English Language, 2 Vols. Noah Webster. LC 77-117409. Repr. of 1828 ed. Set. 80.00 (ISBN 0-384-66333-8); Set. deluxe ed. 190.00 deluxe ed. (ISBN 0-384-66336-2). Johnson Repr.

American Heritage Desk Dictionary. 1981. 9.95 (ISBN 0-395-31256-6). HM.

American Heritage Dictionary. rev. ed. 1983. pap. 4.95 (ISBN 0-440-10068-2). Dell.

American Heritage Dictionary. rev. ed. 1983. pap. 9.95 (ISBN 0-440-50079-6, Dell Trade Pbks). Dell.

American Heritage Dictionary. Ed. by Geoffrey Nunberg. 1982. 13.95 (ISBN 0-686-81876-8). HM.

American Heritage Dictionary: College Edition. (Eng.). write for info. HM.

American Heritage Dictionary of the English Language: New College Edition. LC 76-86995. (gr. 9 up). 1981. 12.95 (ISBN 0-395-20359-7); thumb-indexed 13.95 (ISBN 0-395-20360-0); large format ed. thumb-indexed 17.95 (ISBN 0-395-09066-0); pap. text ed. 1.20 user's guide (ISBN 0-395-20515-8). HM.

American Heritage School Dictionary. Ed. by American Heritage Editors. LC 72-75557. 1977. 9.95 (ISBN 0-395-24792-6). HM.

American Political Dictionary. 6th ed. Jack C. Plano & Milton Greenberg. 1982. 12.50 (ISBN 0-03-060127-4). HR&W.

American Political Terms: An Historical Dictionary. Hans Sperber & Travis Trittschuh. LC 62-11233. 1962. 17.95x (ISBN 0-8143-1187-3). Wayne St U Pr.

Americanisms: A Dictionary of Selected Americanisms on Historical Principles. Ed. by Mitford M. Mathews. LC 69-19279. (Orig.). 1966. pap. 1.95 (ISBN 0-226-51012-3, P229, Phoen). U of Chicago Pr.

Amglo-Russko-Nemetsko-Frantsuzskii Tolkovyi Slovar Po Vychislitel Noi Tekhnike & Obrabotke Dannykh. 416p. (Eng., Rus., Ger. & Fr.). 1978. 7.95 (Pub. by Russkii Iazyk). Four Continent.

Anagram Dictionary. Michael Curl. 288p. 1982. 30.00x (ISBN 0-7091-9674-1, Pub. by Robert Hale England). State Mutual Bk.

Analytic Dictionary of Chinese & Sino-Japanese. Bernhard Karlgren. (Chinese & Japanese.). 12.00 (ISBN 0-8446-5208-3). Peter Smith.

Analytical Dictionary of Chinese & Sino-Jepenese. Bernhard Karlgren. LC 74-75625. 448p. (Chinese, Sino-Japanese & Eng.). 1974. pap. 7.00 (ISBN 0-486-21887-2). Dover.

Analytical Dictionary of Nahuatl. Frances Karttunen. (Texas Linguistics Ser.). 385p. 1983. text ed. 35.00x (ISBN 0-292-70365-1). U of Tex Pr.

Analytical Greek Lexicon Revised. rev. ed. Ed. by Harold K. Moulton. (Gr.). 1978. 15.95 (ISBN 0-310-20280-9). Zondervan.

Analytical Hebrew & Chaldee Lexicon. Benjamin Davidson. (Hebrew.). 24.95 (ISBN 0-310-20290-6, Pub. by Bagster). Zondervan.

Analytical Linguistic Concordance to the Book of Isaiah. Yehuda T. Radday. (Computer Bible Ser: Vol. II). 1975. pap. 20.00 (ISBN 0-935106-15-4). Biblical Res Assocs.

Analytical, Linguistic, Key-Word-in-Context Concordance to Esther, Ruth, Canticles, Ecclesiastes & Lamentations. Yehuda T. Radday & G. M. Leb. Ed. by J. Arthur Baird & David Noel Freedman. (The Computer Bible Ser.: Vol. XVI). 1978. pap. 25.00 (ISBN 0-935106-04-9). Biblical Res Assocs.

Analytical, Linguistic Key-Word-in-Context Concordance to the Book of Judges. Yehuda T. Radday. (Computer Bible Ser.: Vol. XI). 1977. pap. 20.00 (ISBN 0-935106-10-3). Biblical Res Assocs.

Anatomy of the Image Maps According to Merriam-Webster's Third International Dictionary of the English Language: Unabridged. Bonnie Gordon. LC 82-50789. (Artists' Book Ser.). 48p. (Orig.). 1983. pap. 10.00 (ISBN 0-89822-028-9). Visual Studies.

Anchor Dictionary of Astronomy. Valerie Illingworth. LC 79-6538. (Illus.). 448p. (Orig.). 1980. pap. 7.50 (ISBN 0-385-15936-6, Anch). Doubleday.

Anglais Dans le Batiment: Text En Anglais Avec un Glossaire Illustre. G. Wallnig & H. Evered. 100p. (Eng., Fr. & Ger.). 1970. pap. 19.95 (ISBN 0-686-57255-6, M-6564). French & Eur.

Anglais Dans le Batiment: Texte En Anglais Avec un Glossaire Illustre, 2. Gunter Wallnig & H. Evered. 192p. (Eng., Fr. & Ger.). 1976. pap. 37.50 (ISBN 0-686-57256-4, M-6565). French & Eur.

Anglicismes au Quebec. Gilles Colpron. 247p. (Fr. & Eng.). 1979. 17.50 (ISBN 0-686-56957-1, M-6080). French & Eur.

Anglicko-Cesky a Cesko-Anglicky Slovnik por Televizni Pracovniky a Prekladatele. Josef Feigl. LC 77-482571. 122p. (Czech.). 1976. write for info. SNTC.

Anglicko-Cesky Lekarsky Slovnik. Andela Kobylkova. LC 76-509268. 227p. (Eng. & Czech.). 1975. 10.50 Kcs. SNTC.

Anglicko-slovensk y lekarsky slovnik. Anton Parks. LC 80-466637. 211p. (Slovenian & Eng., Bratislava). 1978. 14.50 Kcs. Univerzita Komenskeho.

Anglicko-Slovensky Technicky Slovnik. Stefan Benacka. LC 76-508198. 1357p. (Eng. & Slovak.). 1975. 117.00 Kcs. Alfa-Vydavatel.

Anglico-Cesko a Cesko-Anglico Kapesni-Slovnik: English-Czech, Czech-English Dictionary. Karel Hais. 570p. (Eng. & Czech.). 1974. 13.50. Imported Bks.

Anglo-American & German Abbreviations in Environmental Protection. Peter Wennrich. 624p. (Eng. & Ger.). 1979. 60.00x (ISBN 0-89664-096-5, Pub. by K G Saur). Gale.

Anglo-American & German Abbreviations in Science & Technology. Peter Wennrich. LC 76-151935. (Eng. & Ger.). 1976. write for info. (ISBN 3-7940-1024-8). Bowker.

Anglo-American & German Abbreviations in Science & Technology: Part 4, Supplement. Compiled by Peter Wennrich. 618p. (Eng. & Ger.). 1981. 52.50 (ISBN 3-598-20512-0). Bowker.

Anglo-American Interpreter: A Vocabulary & Phrase Book. H. W. Horwill. LC 72-169624. 1939. lib. bdg. 10.00 (ISBN 0-8414-5130-3). Folcroft.

Anglo-Amerikanische Abkuerzungen und Kurzwoerter der Elektrotechnik. P. Wennrich. 307p. (Ger. & Eng., Anglo-American Abbreviations and Acronyms of Electrical Engineering). 1973. pap. 25.00 (ISBN 3-7940-3100-8, M-7296, Pub. by Vlg. Dokumentation). French & Eur.

Anglo-Armianskii Shkolnyi Slovar. Yerevan. 204p. (Eng. & Armenian.). 1968. 1.75 (Pub. by Luys). Four Continent.

Anglo-Ispano-Russko-Frantsuzskii Slovar Nauchnykh & Tekhnicheskikh Terminov Po Atomnoi Energii. 216p. (Eng. , Span. , Rus. & Fr.). 1958. 5.50 (Pub. by United Nations Publications). Four Continent.

Anglo-Latyshsko-Russkii Frazeologicheskii Slovar. 718p. (Eng. & Rus.). 1977. 3.25 (Pub. by Liesma). Four Continent.

Anglo-Litovskii Politekhnicheskii Slovar. A. I. Novodvorkis. 172p. (Eng. & Lith.). 1958. 1.65 (Pub. by Gospolitnauchizdat). Four Continent.

Anglo-Norman Dictionary. Ed. by Louise W. Stone et al. (Publications of the Modern Humanities Research Association: Vol. 8). avail. Modern Humanities Res.

Anglo-Russkaia Terminologiia Po Organizatsii & Bezopasnosti Dorozhnogo Divizheniia. V. V. Sil'ianov et al. 199p. (Rus.). 1977. 2.75 (Pub. by Viniti). Four Continent.

Anglo-russki i biologicheski i slovar. I. N. Afanaseva et al. LC 80-461323. 732p. (Eng. & Rus.). 1979. 8.00 Rub. Russkii Iazyk.

Anglo-russki i politekhnicheski. A. E. Cherukhina. LC 80-471023. 687p. (Eng. & Rus.). 1979. pap. 9.70 Rub. Russky Yazyk.

Anglo-russki i slovar po okhrane okruzha i ushche i sredy. E. L. Milovanov et al. LC 81-473924. 366p. (Eng. & Rus.). 1980. write for info. Russki Iazyk.

Anglo-Russkii Astronomicheskii Slovar. Ed. by O. A. Melnikov et al. 504p. (Eng. & Rus.). 1971. 4.75 (Pub. by Sov Entsiklopediia). Four Continent.

Anglo-Russkii Biologicheskii Slovar. LC 80-461323. 732p. (Eng. & Rus.). 1979. 8.00 Rub. Russkii Iazyk.

Anglo-Russkii Biologischeskii Slovar. 736p. (Eng. & Rus.). 1979. 15.95 (Pub. by Russkii Iazyk). Four Continent.

Anglo-Russkii Eknomicheskii Slovar. Ed. by A. V. Anikin. 728p. (Rus.). 1977. 14.50 (Pub. by Russkii Iazyk). Four Continent.

Anglo-Russkii Elektrotekhnicheskii Slovar. Ed. by L. B. Geiler et al. 704p. (Eng. & Rus.). 1955. 5.95 (Pub. by Gosizdat Tekhn. Teoret.). Four Continent.

Anglo-Russkii Fizicheskii Slovar. Ed. by D. M. Tolstoi. 848p. (Eng. & Rus.). 1978. 15.95 (Pub. by Russkii Iazyk). Four Continent.

Anglo-Russkii Frazeologicheskii Slovar. A. V. Kunin et al. 1456p. (Eng. & Rus.). 1956. 5.25 (294). Four Continent.

Anglo-Russkii Iadernyi Slovar. Ed. by D. I. Doskoboinik et al. 400p. (Eng. & Rus.). 1960. 4.80 (Pub. by Glav. Red. Inostr. Nauchn. Tekhn. Slovarei Fizmatgiza). Four Continent.

Anglo-Russkii Politekhnicheskii Slovar. (Rus.). 19.95. Russki Iazyk.

Anglo-Russkii Radiotekhnicheskii Slovar. Ed. by L. P. German-Prozorova et al. 524p. (Rus. & Eng.). 1960. 6.30 (Pub. by Gosizdat. Inostr. Slovarei). Four Continent.

Anglo-Russkii Razgovornik Dlia Turistov. 272p. (Eng. & Rus.). 1978. 8.25 (Pub. by Russkii Iazyk). Four Continent.

Anglo-Russkii Razgovornik Dlia Turistov. 272p. (Eng. & Rus.). 1979. 2.95 (Pub. by Russkii Iazyk). Four Continent.

Anglo-Russkii Slovar. Ed. by O. S. Akhmanova. 640p. (Eng. & Rus.). 1979. 3.85 (Pub. by Russkii Iazyk). Four Continent.

Anglo-Russkii Slovar. Ol'ga Sergeevna Akhmanova. LC 80-465947. 639p. (Eng. & Rus.). 1978. write for info. Russkii Iazyk.

Anglo-Russkii Slovar. Ed. by V. D. Arakin et al. 808p. (Eng. & Rus.). 1980. 8.95 (Pub. by Russkii Iazyk). Four Continent.

Anglo-Russkii Slovar. Ed. by V. K. Miuller. 888p. (Eng. & Rus.). 1977. 14.25. Four Continent.

Anglo-Russkii Slovar Dorozhnika. Ia. B. Khaikin. 319p. (Eng. & Rus.). 1956. 3.35 (Pub. by Izd. Avtotrnsport. Lit.). Four Continent.

Anglo-Russkii Slovar Po Aerogidrodinamike. 710p. (Eng. & Rus.). 1970. 5.50 (Pub. by Sov Entsiklopediia). Four Continent.

Anglo-Russkii Slovar Po Aerogidrodinamike. M. G. Kotik. 422p. (Eng. & Rus.). 1960. 3.65 (Pub. by Glav. Red. Inostr. Tekhn. Slovrei Fizmatgiza). Four Continent.

Anglo-Russkii Slovar Po Aviatsionno-Kosmicheskoi Meditsine. Ed. by A. A. Giurdzhian et al. 388p. (Rus. & Eng.). 1972. 5.60 (Pub. by Voenizdat). Four Continent.

Anglo-Russkii Slovar Po Avtomatike & Kontrol'noizmeritel'nym Priboram. 380p. (Eng. & Rus.). 1957. 3.25 (Pub. by Gosizdat Tekhnikoteoretich. Lit.). Four Continent.

Anglo-Russkii Slovar Po Elektrokhimii i Korrozii. Ed. by M. M. Melnikova et al. (Eng. & Rus.). 1976. 5.50 (Pub. by Russkii Iazyk). Four Continent.

Anglo-Russkii Slovar Po Fizike Vysokikh Energii. 520p. (Eng. & Fr.). 1976. 5.75 (Pub. by Russkii Iazyk). Four Continent.

Anglo-Russkii Slovar Po Iadernym Vzryvam. O. Petrenko. 304p. (Rus. & Eng.). 1978. 4.95 (Pub. by Voenizdat). Four Continent.

Anglo-Russkii Slovar Po Kauchuku, Rezine & Khimicheskim Voloknam. Ed. by F. I. Iashunskaia et al. 260p. (Rus. & Eng.). 1962. 3.75 (Pub. by Glav. Red. Inostr. Nauchn. Tekhn. Slovrei Fizmatgiza). Four Continent.

Anglo-Russkii Slovar Po Khimii & Tekhnologii Polimerov: Okolo 30000 Terminov. 536p. (Eng. & Rus.). 1977. 9.95 (Pub. by Russkii Iazyk). Four Continent.

Anglo-Russkii Slovar po Khimii i Pererabotke Nefti. Vsevolod V. Kedrinskii. LC 80-467970. 767p. (Eng. & Rus.). 1979. 8.36 Rub. Russkii Iazyk.

Anglo-Russkii Slovar Po Kholodil Noi i Kriogennoi Tekhnike. 468p. (Rus. & Eng.). 1978. 8.95 (Pub. by Russkii Iazyk). Four Continent.

Anglo-Russkii Slovar Po Kvantovoi Elektronike i Golografii. 504p. (Eng. & Rus.). 1977. 6.75 (Pub. by Russkii Iazyk). Four Continent.

Anglo-Russkii Slovar po Kvantovoi Elektronike i Golografii. N. Voropaev. LC 79-392952. 501p. (Eng. & Rus.). 1977. 2.80 Rub. Russkii Iazyk.

Anglo-Russkii Slovar Po Okhrane Okruzhaiushchei Sredy. 368p. (Rus. & Eng.). 1980. 5.95 (Pub. by Russkii Iazyk). Four Continent.

Anglo-Russkii Slovar Po Radioelektronike i Sviazi. 548p. (Eng. & Rus.). 1959. 5.75 (Pub. by Soviete Ministrov). Four Continent.

Anglo-Russkii Slovar Po Raketnoi Tekhnike. A. M. Murashkevich. 231p. (Rus. & Eng.). 1958. 2.75 (Pub. by Gosizdat. Literatury). Four Continent.

Anglo-Russkii Slovar Po Televideniiu. L. P. German-Prozorova et al. (Rus. & Eng.). 1960. 3.90 (Pub. by Glav. Red. Fizmatgiza). Four Continent.

Anglo-Russkii Slovar Zheleznodorozhnoi Automatike, Telemekhanike & Sviazi. I. S. Gluzman. 427p. (Rus. & Eng.). 1958. 5.25 (Pub. by Gosizdat Fizmat. Lit.). Four Continent.

Anglo-Russkii Uchebnyi Slovar' S. K. Folomkina et al. 655p. (Eng. & Rus.). 1970. 3.25. Four Continent.

Anglo-Russkii Voenno-Inzhenernyi Slovar. N. V. Volodin. 783p. (Eng. & Rus.). 1962. 8.35 (Pub. by Voenizdat). Four Continent.

Anglo-Saxon & English Vocabularies, 2 vols. T. Wright. Set. 95.20 (ISBN 3-534-04078-3). Adler.

Anglo-Saxon & Old English Vocabularies, 2 vols. Thomas Wright. Set. lib. bdg. 300.00 (ISBN 0-87968-432-1). Gordon Pr.

Anglo-Saxon Dictionary. Compiled by Joseph Bosworth et al. (Anglo-Saxon & Eng.). 1972. Repr. of 1898 ed. 110.00x (ISBN 0-19-863101-4); 1921 supplement & addenda 85.00x (ISBN 0-19-863112-X). Oxford U Pr.

Anglo-Scandinavian Law Dictionary. R. Anderson. 1977. pap. 15.00x (ISBN 82-00-02365-6, Dist. by Columbia U Pr). Universitet.

Anglo-Scandinavian Law Dictionary of Legal Terms. Ralph J. Anderson. LC 77-481598. 137p. (Eng. & Scandinavian.). 1977. Kr.59.00 (ISBN 8-20002-365-6). Universitets.

Anglo-Ukrainskii Frazeologicheskii Slovar. K. T. Barantsev. 1052p. (Eng. & Ukranian.). 1969. 9.00 (Pub. by Radianska Shkola). Four Continent.

Anglo-Ukrainskii Slovar. 448p. (Eng. & Ukrainian.). 1978. 3.95 (Pub. by Radianska Shkola). Four Continent.

Angol-Magyar Mikroelektronikai. Magdolna Kovacs. LC 79-349423. 367p. (Hungarian.). 1977. 39.00 Ft (ISBN 9-6354-2077-3). KG Informatik.

Angol-Magyar Szotar English-Hungarian Dictionary. L. Orszagn. 791p. (Eng. & Hungarian.). 22.50 (ISBN 0-87557-043-7, 043-7). Saphrograph.

Angol Nyelvkonyv: English Language Book for Self-Learners & Student with Teachers. Latzko Hugo. 180p. (Eng. & Hungarian.). pap. 7.50 (ISBN 0-87557-093-3, 093-3). Saphrograph.

Annales des Mines: Lexique Technique Allemand-Francais. J. Armanet & A. Becquer. 344p. (Ger. & Fr.). 1951. 8.95 (ISBN 0-686-56901-6, M-6011). French & Eur.

Annotated Bibliography of Technical & Specialized Dictionaries. Marisa Luz E. Elerick. Tr. by Charles Elerick & Richard V. Teschner. LC 82-50416. Orig. Title: Span. 109p. 20.00 (ISBN 0-87875-234-X). Whitston Pub.

Annotated Glossary of Arabic Musical Terms. Ed. by Lois I. Al Faruqi. LC 81-4129. 536p. (Arabic & Eng.). 1981. lib. bdg. 45.00x (ISBN 0-313-20554-X, AFM/). Greenwood.

Anzeigenwerbung: Ein Reader fuer Studenten & Lehrer der Deutscher Sprache & Literatur. Ed. by Peter Nusser. LC 77-460308. 274p. (Ger.). 1975. DM.19.80 (ISBN 3-77051-224-3). Fink Verlag.

Apollo Crossword Puzzle Dictionary. Andrew Swanfeldt. (Apollo Eds.). 1971. pap. 6.95i (ISBN 0-8152-0303-9, A303G). T y Crowell.

Appleton-Cuyas Dictionary: English-Spanish, Spanish-English. (Span. & Eng.). write for info. (608-11). Pan Amer Pub.

Applied Technical Dictionary: Acoustics. 50.00x (ISBN 0-569-08535-7, Pub. by Collets). State Mutual Bk.

Applied Technical Dictionary: Air Conditioning & Refrigeration. (Eng. , Ger. , Fr. , Rus. & Slovak.). 69.00x (ISBN 0-569-08534-9, Pub. by Collets). State Mutual Bk.

Applied Technical Dictionary: Oil Processing & Petrochemistry. (Eng. , Ger. , Fr. , Rus. & Slovak.). 1981. 50.00x (ISBN 0-569-08533-0, Pub. by Collets). State Mutual Bk.

Applied Technical Dictionary: Silicate Technology. (Eng. , Ger. , Fr. & Slovak.). 50.00x (ISBN 0-569-08557-8, Pub. by Collets). State Mutual Bk.

Ar-Rafed. Amin Al-Amir Al-Nasiruddin. 200p. (Arabic.). 1971. 18.00 (101-1). Intl Bk Ctr.

Arabe Francais Dictionnaire, 2 vols. A. Kazirmski. (Arabic & Fr.). Repr. of 1860 ed. 80.00x (ISBN 0-86685-110-0). Intl Bk Ctr.

Arabic-Arabic Dictionary Muhit Al Muhit. Butrus Al-Bustani. (Arabic.). 50.00x (ISBN 0-86685-096-1). Intl Bk Ctr.

Arabic-Arabic Dictionary of the Names of Towns & Villages in Lebanon. Annis Freyha. 1974. 16.00x (ISBN 0-86685-099-6). Intl Bk Ctr.

Arabic Dictionary: Al Munjid fi al-Lugha Wal 'Alam. Dar El Mashreq. (Arabic.). 48.00x (ISBN 2-7214-2124-7). Intl Bk Ctr.

Arabic-English Advanced Learners Dictionary. Anthony Salmone. (Arabic & Eng.). 30.00x (ISBN 0-86685-089-9). Intl Bk Ctr.

Arabic-English Collegiate Dictionary. Elias. (Arabic & Eng.). 12.50 (ISBN 0-686-27676-0). Colton Bk.

Arabic-English Dictionary. (Arabic & Eng.). 19.50 (ISBN 0-87557-002-X, 002-X). Saphrograph.

Arabic-English Dictionary. D. Cameron. (Arabic & Eng.). 1979. 16.00x (ISBN 0-86685-084-8). Intl Bk Ctr.

Arabic-English Dictionary. simplified ed. Dar el Mashreq. (Illus.). 747p. (Arabic & Eng.). 1974. student dict. 12.00 (310-7). Intl Bk Ctr.

Arabic-English Dictionary. H. Wehr. (Arabic & Eng.). 12.50. Iaconi.

Arabic-English Dictionary. rev. 3rd ed. Hans Wehr. Ed. by J Milton Cowan. LC 75-24236. (Arabic & Eng.). 1976. pap. 12.00x (ISBN 0-87950-001-8). Spoken Lang Serv.

Arabic-English Dictionary. Hans Wehr & J. M. Cowan. 1110p. (Eng. & Arabic.). pap. 19.00. Imported Bks.

Arabic-English Dictionary. William Wortabet. (Arabic & Eng.). 1968. 18.00x (ISBN 0-86685-092-9). Intl Bk Ctr.

Arabic-English Dictionary. Compiled by William Wortabet & Harvey Porter. 800p. (Arabic & Eng.). 18.00 (092-9); pocket dict. (431 p 5.50 (093-7). Intl Bk Ctr.

Arabic-English Dictionary: Colloquial Arabic of Egypt. Socrates Spiro. (Arabic & Eng.). 1973. 30.00x (ISBN 0-86685-090-2). Intl Bk Ctr.

Arabic-English Dictionary: Hava's Al: Faraid. (Arabic & Eng.). 1974. 35.00x (ISBN 2-7214-2106-9). Intl Bk Ctr.

Arabic-English Dictionary of Agricultural Terms & Allied Terminology. Ahmad Khatib. (Arabic & Eng.). pap. 10.00x (ISBN 0-86685-274-3). Intl Bk Ctr.

Arabic-English Dictionary of Basic Scientific & Technical Terms: "Al Mustalah". Hassan Assaran. 1967. 20.00x (ISBN 0-86685-299-9). Intl Bk Ctr.

Arabic-English Dictionary of the Colloquial Arabic of Egypt. Socrates Spiro. 680p. (Arabic & Eng.). 1973. 30.00 (090-2). Intl Bk Ctr.

Arabic-English, English-Arabic Collegiate Dictionary, Vol. 1-2. Ed. by E. A. Elias. (Illus., Arabic & Eng.). Date not set. Set. text ed. 35.00 (ISBN 0-686-46526-1). Heinman.

Arabic-English, English-Arabic Dictionary, 2 vols. rev. & enl. ed. E. A. Elias. (Arabic & Eng.). Set. 70.00 (ISBN 0-685-55017-6). Heinman.

Arabic-English, English-Arabic School Dictionary. Ed. by E. A. Elias. (Illus., Arabic & Eng.). Date not set. text ed. 20.00 (ISBN 0-686-46527-X). Heinman.

Arabic-English, English-Arabic Student's Dictionary, 2 vols. (Illus., Arabic & Eng.). Set. 50.00 (ISBN 2-7214-2879-9). Heinman.

Arabic-English Learners Dictionary. F. Steingass. (Arabic & Eng.). 1972. 35.00x (ISBN 0-86685-087-2). Intl Bk Ctr.

Arabic-English Lexicon, 8 Vols. Ed. by Edward W. Lane. (Arabic & Eng.). Set. 360.00 (ISBN 0-8044-0272-8). Ungar.

Arabic-English Lexicon, 8 vols. Madd A. Qamus & Wm. Edward. (Arabic & Eng.). Set. 295.00x. Intl Bk Ctr.

Arabic-English Lexicon: Madd al Qamus, 8 vols. Compiled by Edward W. Lane. 3064p. (Arabic & Eng.). 295.00 (087-2). Intl Bk Ctr.

Arabic-English Modern Dictionary. Elias Elias. (Arabic & Eng.). 1981. 30.00x (ISBN 0-86685-287-5). Intl Bk Ctr.

Arabic-English Pocket Dictionary. John Wortabet. 1980. pap. 5.50x (ISBN 0-86685-093-7). Intl Bk Ctr.

Arabic-English Students Dictionary. Dar El Mashreq. (Arabic & Eng.). 1974. 15.00x (ISBN 2-7214-2107-7). Intl Bk Ctr.

Arabic-French Dictionary, 2 vols. Auguste Cherbonneau. (Arabic & Fr.). Set. 30.00x (ISBN 0-86685-103-8). Intl Bk Ctr.

Arabic Pocket Dictionary. (Arabic & Eng.). 10.00 (ISBN 0-685-11992-0). Heinman.

Arabic Student Dictionary. Munjid al Tulab & Dar el Mashreq. (Arabic.). 1979. 15.00x (ISBN 2-7214-2118-2). Intl Bk Ctr.

Arabisch, 2 vols. Incl. Teil I. Arabisch-Deutsch. G. Krotkoff. 624p. DM.18.80 (10060); Teil II. Deutsch-Arabisch. K. Schukry & R. Humberdrotz. 456p. DM.18.80 (10065). (Langenscheidts Taschenwoerterbucher Ser.). (Arabic & Ger.). DM.beide Teile in einem Band 29.80 (11060). Langenscheidt.

Arabsko-Cesky Cesko-Arabsky Slovnik. Lubos Kropacek. LC 75-585137. 529p. (Czech. & Arabic.). 1975. 22.50 Kcs. SNTC.

Arbeitsschutzlexikon. Walter Klost. LC 80-465045. (Illus.). 186p. (Ger.). 1979. write for info. Verlag Moderne.

Archaic Dictionary. W. R. Cooper. 59.95 (ISBN 0-87968-653-7). Gordon Pr.

Archaic Dictionary. William R. Cooper. LC 73-76018. 1969. Repr. of 1876 ed. 66.00x (ISBN 0-8103-3885-8). Gale.

Architectural & Building Trades Dictionary. 3rd ed. R. E. Putnam & G. E. Carlson. 512p. 1983. 17.95 (ISBN 0-442-27461-0). Van Nos Reinhold.

Architectural & Building Trades Dictionary. 3rd ed. Robert Putnam & G. E. Carlson. (Illus.). 1974. 15.50 (ISBN 0-8269-0402-5). Am Technical.

Architectural, Construction, Manufacturing & Engineering Glossary of Terms. Ed. by W. R. Barry. 519p. 1979. pap. 40.00 (ISBN 0-930284-05-4). Am Assn Cost Engineers.

Architecture & Building Dictionary: English-French-German-Arabic. Abd El Gaward. 465p. (Eng., Fr., Ger. & Arabic.). 1976. Leatherette 45.00 (ISBN 0-686-92255-7, M-9753). French & Eur.

Architecture Traditionnelle au Quebec: Glossaire Illustre de la Maison aux 17e & 18e Siecles. Yves Laframbois. LC 75-517455. (Illus.). 319p. (Fr.). 1975. write for info. (ISBN 0-7759-0457-0). Edns Homme.

Architektura & Budownictwo. Witold Szolginia. LC 76-515661. (Illus.). vii, 478p. (Pol.). 1975. 160.00 Zl. Wydawnictwa Naukowo.

Arco Motor Vehicle Dictionary: English & Spanish. Ed. by Robert F. Lima. LC 76-77605. 368p. (Eng. & Span.). 1980. pap. 7.95 (ISBN 0-668-04982-0, 4982-0). Arco.

Argo Limeno. Guillermo E. Bendezu Neyra. LC 78-101067. 339p. (Span., Lima). 1977. write for info. Libreria.

Argot Chez les Vrais de Vrais. Auguste LeBreton. LC 76-454371. (Illus.). 510p. (Fr.). 1975. 45.00 F. Presses Cite.

Argot de Police. Jacques Arnal. LC 75-513721. (Illus.). 186p. (Fr.). 1975. 9.90 F (ISBN 2-716-70310-8). Euredif.

Aristoteles-Lexikon, 2 vols. Matthias Kappes. LC 75-172191. (Bibliography & Reference Ser.: No. 82). 78p. (Philosophy Monographs, No. 437). 1971. Repr. of 1894 ed. Set. lib. bdg. 19.00 (ISBN 0-8337-1893-2). B Franklin.

Arlington Dictionary of Electronics. Ed. by Harold R. Rodgers et al. (Illus.). 1971. text ed. 16.95x (ISBN 0-8464-0146-0). Beekman Pubs.

Armenian-English - English-Armenian Dictionary. 2nd, rev. ed. M. Koushakdjian. (Armenian & Eng.). 45.00 (ISBN 0-686-68934-8). Heinman.

Armenian-English Dictionary. Mathias Bedrossian. (Armenian & Eng.). 35.00x (ISBN 0-86685-122-4). Intl Bk Ctr.

Armenisch-Deutsches Woerterbuch. Froundiian-Dirair. (Armenian & Ger.). 1952. 45.00 (ISBN 3-486-41021-0, Pub. by Oldenbourg). French & Eur.

Armenisch-Deutsches Woerterbuch. Froundiian-Dirair. (Armenian & Ger.). 1952. DM.45.00 (ISBN 3-486-41021-0). Oldenbourg Verlag.

Armorial General Precede d'un Dictionnaire des Termes du Blason, Pt. 1. Johannes B. Rietstap. (Fr.). 1934. 135.00 (ISBN 0-686-56594-0, M-7298, Pub. by Olms). French & Eur.

Armorial general precede d'un dictionnaire des termes du Blason, Pt. 1. Johannes B. Rietstap. (Fr.). 1934. DM.135.00 (M-7298). Olms Verlag.

Armorial General Precede d'un Dictionnaire des Termes du Blason, Pt. 2. Johannes B. Rietstap. (Fr.). 1934. 135.00 (ISBN 0-686-56595-9, M-7299, Pub. by Olms). French & Eur.

Armorial general precede d'un dictionnaire des termes du Blason, Pt. 2. Johannes B. Rietstap. (Fr.). 1934. DM.135.00 (M-7299). Olms Verlag.

Arosi Dictionary. Charles E. Fox. LC 78-321214. iii, 598p. (Eng.). 1978. write for info. (ISBN 0-85883-170-8). Linguistic Circle.

Arzneimttel-Verzeichnis. Klaus Gerecke. LC 79-344736. (Ger.). 1977. M.5.80. VEB Verlag Technik.

Assyrian Dictionary of the Oriental Institute of the University of Chicago. Ed. by A. Leo Oppenheim & Erica Reiner. Incl. Vol. 1, A, Pt. 2. 1976. Repr. of 1968 ed. 42.00x (ISBN 0-918986-07-9); Vol. 3, D. 1977. Repr. of 1959 ed. 17.00x (ISBN 0-918986-09-5); Vol. 4, E. 1974. Repr. of 1958 ed. 31.00x (ISBN 0-918986-10-9); Vol. 7, I-J. 1974. Repr. of 1960 ed. 25.00x (ISBN 0-918986-13-3); Vol. 9, L. 1978. Repr. of 1973 ed. 35.00x (ISBN 0-918986-15-X); Vol. 10, M, Pts 1 & 2. LC 56-58292. 1978. 110.00x (ISBN 0-918986-16-8); Vol. 16, S. 1977. Repr. of 1962 ed. 22.00x (ISBN 0-918986-18-4). LC 56-58292. (Assyrian.). Oriental Inst.

Assyrian Dictionary of the Oriental Institute of the University of Chicago, Vol. 1, A, Pt. 1. Ed. by A. Leo Oppenheim & Erica Reiner. LC 56-58292. (Assyrian.). 1964. lib. bdg. 29.00x (ISBN 0-918986-06-0). Oriental Inst.

Assyrian Dictionary of the Oriental Institute of the University of Chicago, Vol. 2, B. Ed. by A. Leo Oppenheim et al. LC 56-58292. (Assyrian.). 1966. lib. bdg. 28.00x (ISBN 0-918986-08-7). Oriental Inst.

Assyrian Dictionary of the Oriental Institute of the University of Chicago, Vol. 5, G. Ed. by A. Leo Oppenheim. LC 56-58292. (Assyrian & Eng.). 1956. lib. bdg. 14.50x (ISBN 0-918986-11-7). Oriental Inst.

Assyrian Dictionary of the Oriental Institute of the University of Chicago, Vol. 6, H. Ed. by A. Leo Oppenheim. LC 56-58292. (Assyrian & Eng.). 1956. lib. bdg. 21.00x (ISBN 0-918986-12-5). Oriental Inst.

Astrological Dictionary. Johndro. 2.00. Am Fed Astrologers.

Astrology Terms. Leslie Fleming-Mitchell. LC 77-597. (Orig.). 1977. lib. bdg. 12.90 (ISBN 0-914294-69-5); pap. 2.95 (ISBN 0-914294-70-9). Running Pr.

Astronautical Multilingual Dictionary: International Academy of Astronautics. (Eng. , Ger. , Fr. , Ital. , Span. , Rus. & Czech.). 1970. 149.00 (ISBN 0-444-40830-4). Elsevier.

Astronomical Dictionary: In Six Languages. Josip Kleczek. (Eng., Fr., Ger., Ital., Rus. & Czech.). 1962. 109.00 (ISBN 0-12-411950-6). Acad Pr.

Atayal-English Dictionary, 2 vols. Soren Egerod. (Scandinavian Institute of Asian Studies Monograph: No. 35). 830p. (Atayal & Eng.). 1981. Set. pap. text ed. 41.25x (ISBN 0-7007-0117-6, Pub. by Curzon Pr England); Vol. 1. pap. text ed. (ISBN 0-7007-0118-4); Vol. 2. pap. text ed. (ISBN 0-7007-0119-2). Humanities.

Atheneum Worterbuch: Aleman-Espanol, Espanol-Aleman. F. Muller. 383p. (Ger. & Span.). 1979. pap. 5.25 (ISBN 84-303-0800-8, S-35066). French & Eur.

Athenum Woordenboek: Espanol-Holandes, Holandes-Espanol. 382p. (Span. & Dutch.). 1979. pap. 5.25 (ISBN 84-303-0801-6, S-35068). French & Eur.

Atk-Sanakirja. Gustav Tollet. LC 77-568115. ix, 140p. (Eng. & Finnish.). 1975. write for info. (ISBN 9-1576-2112-8). Tietojen.

Atlante Della Sessualita. Franca Rome. LC 78-393255. (Illus.). 237p. (Ital.). 1978. L.4500.00. A Mondadi.

Atlas & Glossary of Primary Sedimentary Structures. F. J. Pettijohn & P. E. Potter. (Illus., Eng., Span., Fr & Ger.). 1964. 34.00 (ISBN 0-387-03194-4). Springer-Verlag.

Attved Tyrifjorden. Peter Lyse. LC 77-452595. (Illus.). 270p. (Norwegian.). 1976. Kr.39.50 (ISBN 8-20009-423-5). Universitetsforlaget.

Austral English. Edward E. Morris. LC 68-18003. 1968. Repr. of 1898 ed. 58.00x (ISBN 0-8103-3287-6). Gale.

Australian Commercial Dictionary. Keith Yorston. LC 73-163182. 340p. 1972. 12.50x (ISBN 0-455-16550-5). Intl Pubns Serv.

Australian Dictionary of Acronyms & Abbreviations. Ed. by David J. Jones. LC 78-312706. 156p. 1977. write for info. (ISBN 0-909325-08-1). Second Back Row.

Australian Dictionary of Acronyms & Abbreviations. 2nd, rev. ed. Ed. by David J. Jones. LC 82-126656. 220p. 1981. write for info. (ISBN 0-909325-24-3). Second Back Row.

Australian Economic Terms. C. E. Noble. LC 78-320336. x, 200p. (Eng.). 1977. Aus.$4.95 (ISBN 0-582-68442-0). Longman.

Australian Pocket Oxford Dictionary. Ed. by Grahame Johnston. (Australian.). 1977. 16.95x (ISBN 0-19-550537-9). Oxford U Pr.

Automatic Control Terminology for Heating, Ventilating, Air Conditioning & Refrigeration Equipment. American Society of Heating, Refrigerating & Air-Conditioning Engineers. (Illus.). 14.00 (ST8578); members 7.00. Am Heat Ref & Air Eng.

Automation in Housing & Systems Building News: Dictionary of Industrialized Manufactured Housing. Ed. by Don Carlson. (Illus.). 1981. 15.00 (ISBN 0-9607408-0-5). Automation in Housing Mag.

Automation Terms in Cartography. American Congress on Surveying & Mapping. 23p. 1973. 3.00 (C120). Am Congrs Survey.
Automatizacna Technika. Jiri Sykora. LC 76-511586. 1023p. (Eng., Fr., Rus., Pol. & Slovak.). 1975. 140.00 Kcs. Alfa-Vydavatel.
Automatizovany Zber Dat Programovanie. Erich Burger. LC 78-373214. 479p. (Eng., Fr. & Rus.). 1976. 80.00 Kcs. Alfa-Vydavatel.
Automobily. Czesaw Blok & Wiesaw Jezewski. (Illus.). 502p. (Rus., Eng., Fr., Ital., & Ger.). 1979. 70.00 Kcs (ISBN 8-320-60049-9). Wydawnictwa.
Automotive Engineering Dictionary: English-German-French-Arabic. Abd-El-Wahed. 436p. (Eng., Fr., Ger. & Arabic.). 1978. 45.00 (ISBN 0-686-92337-5). French & Eur.
Avfallsordlista. LC 78-361963. xxvii, 210p. (Eng., Fr. & Swedish.). 1977. Kr.40.00 (ISBN 9-1719-6062-7). Tek Nomen.
Aviation-Space Dictionary. 6th ed. E. J. Gentle & L. W. Reithmaier. LC 80-67567. (Illus.). 1980. 18.95 (ISBN 0-8168-3002-9). Aero.
Aviation Technical Dictionary. James Foye & Dale Crane. 1978. pap. 3.95 (ISBN 0-89100-089-5). Aviation Maint.
Avviamento All'etimologia Inglese e Tedesca: Dizionario Comparativo dell'Elemento Germanico Commune ad Entrabe le Lingue. Piergiuseppe Scardigli & Teresa Gervasi. LC 79-361495. xv, 406p. (Eng. & Ger.). 1978. L.9500.00. Monnier.
Avviamento All'Etimologia Italiana: Dizionario Etimologico. Devoto. (Ital.). L.10.00. Oscar.
Awa Dictionary. Dick Loving. LC 76-382715. xliv, 203p. (Awa & Eng.). 1975. write for info. (ISBN 0-85883-137-6). Linguistic Circle.
Ayer Glossary of Advertising & Related Terms: 1977. rev. ed. LC 72-185383. 1977. 11.95x (ISBN 0-910190-10-0). Ayer Pr.
Az Inyesmester Nagy Szakacsko-Nyve: The Art of Hungarian Cooking. 19.50 (ISBN 0-87557-097-6, 097-6). Saphrograph.
Azerbaidzhansko-Russkii Frazeogicheskii (Idiomaticheskii) Slovar. A. Orudzhev. 278p. (Rus.). 1976. 3.95 (Pub. by Elm). Four Continent.

B

Bad Spellers Dictionary. Joseph Kreivsky & Jordon L. Linfield. 1967. 2.95 (ISBN 0-394-49199-8). Random.
Bagster's Keyword Concordance. Samuel Bagster. 96p. 1983. Repr. 5.95 (ISBN 0-8007-1335-4). Revell.
Bahnar Dictionary. John Banker et al. 202p. (Orig., Bahnar.). 1979. pap. 9.00x (ISBN 0-88312-997-3); microfiche (3) 3.00 (ISBN 0-686-96898-0). Summer Inst Ling.
Bahri's Law Dictionary. Hardev Bahri. LC 78-912999. x, 290p. (Eng. & Hindi.). 1978. 5.00. Haredeva Bahari.
Bairische Fibel. Josef Ilmberger. LC 77-573555. 223p. (Ger., Munich). 1977. DM.28.00 (ISBN 3-405-11719-4). B. L. V.
Baker's Dictionary. 2nd ed. A. R. Daniel. 1971. 18.50 (ISBN 0-444-20121-1). Elsevier.
Baker's Dictionary of Theology. Ed. by Everett F. Harrison. 17.95 (ISBN 0-8010-4042-6). Baker Bk.
Baker's Pocket Bible Concordance. (Direction Bks.). 1973. pap. 5.95 (ISBN 0-8010-0616-3). Baker Bk.
Baker's Pocket Dictionary of Religious Terms. Ed. by Donald T. Kauffman. (Direction Books). Orig. Title: Dictionary of Religious Terms. 446p. 1975. pap. 5.95 (ISBN 0-8010-5361-7). Baker Bk.
Baktrisch: Ein Woerterbuch. Gholam D. Davary. 308p. (Ger.). 1982. DM.56.00 (ISBN 3-87276-270-2). Groos Verlag.
Ballentine's Law Dictionary with Pronunciations. 3rd ed. Ed. by William Anderson. LC 68-30931. 1429p. write for info. Lawyers Co-Op.
Bambi's First Picture Dictionary. (Pic-a-Story Bks.). (Illus.). 24p. (Orig.). (gr. k-1). 1981. 4.95 (ISBN 0-89531-107-0); pap. 1.95 (ISBN 0-686-79397-8). Sharon Pubns.
Banalisation Lexicale. Galisson. (Fr.). 20.00 (Dist. by Continental Bk Co). Lib. Fernand Nathan.
Banjo Chord Dictionary. 1981. 2.50. Alfred Pub.
Bank Card Standards Manual Glossary. American Bankers Association. 1980. 6.50 (207224); members 5.00. Am Bankers.
Banking & Financial Dictionary: English-French-Arabic. E. Assiouly. 338p. (Eng., Fr. & Arabic.). 1980. pap. 75.00 (ISBN 0-686-92351-0, M-9767). French & Eur.
Banking Dictionary: German-English & English-German. Friedrich K. Feldbausch. 388p. (Ger. & Eng.). 1972. 22.50x (ISBN 3-258-02439-1). Intl Pubns Serv.
Banking Dictionary of English-American & German Terms. 5th ed. Hans Klaus. 234p. (Eng. & Ger.). 1980. pap. 34.95x (ISBN 3-258-02983-0). Intl Ideas.
Banking Language. Laila Batz. LC 77-610. (Orig.). 1977. lib. bdg. 12.90 (ISBN 0-914294-67-9); pap. 2.95 (ISBN 0-914294-68-7). Running Pr.
Banking Terminology. 1-4 copies 33.75 ea. (626600); members 22.50; bulk price avail. Am Bankers.
Bankwoerterbuch Englisch-Deutsch, Deutsch-Englisch. F. Feldbausch. 400p. (Eng. & Ger., Dictionary of Banking). 38.50 (ISBN 3-478-51240-9, M-7304, Pub. by Vlg. Moderne Industrie). French & Eur.
Bantam Crossword Dictionary. Compiled by Jerome Fried. 1979. pap. 2.75 (ISBN 0-553-14828-1). Bantam.
Bantam Hebrew-English, English-Hebrew Dictionary. (Hebrew & Eng.). 2.95 (235-5). Bantam.
Bantam Medical Dictionary. Laurence Ordang. 464p. 1982. pap. 4.95 (ISBN 0-553-22673-8). Bantam.
Bantam New College Dictionary: English-Spanish, Spanish-English. (Span. & Eng.). write for info. (608-39). Pan Amer Pub.
Bantam New College French & English Dictionary. Ed. by Roger Steiner. 736p. (Orig., Fr. & Eng.). 1972. pap. 2.75 (ISBN 0-553-14890-7). Bantam.
Bantam New College French & English Dictionary. Roger J. Steiner. 736p. (Fr. & Eng.). pap. 2.75 (ISBN 0-553-14890-7). Bantam.
Bantam New College German & English Dictionary. Ed. by John C. Traupman. 768p. (Orig., Ger. & Eng.). (gr. 7-12). 1981. pap. 2.50 (ISBN 0-553-14155-4). Bantam.
Bantam New College Italian & English Dictionary. Robert C. Melzi. 736p. (Orig., Ital. & Eng.). 1976. pap. 2.75 (ISBN 0-553-20267-7). Bantam.
Bantam New College Spanish & English Dictionary. Ed. by Edwin B. Williams. (Language Library). (Orig., Span. & Eng.). 1970. pap. 2.75 (ISBN 0-553-20085-2, C13718-2). Bantam.
Barbara Kraus Dictionary of Protein. Barbara Kraus. 1976. pap. 2.50 (ISBN 0-451-08791-7, E8791, Sig). NAL.
Barnes & Noble Thesaurus of Chemistry. Arthur Godman. (Illus.). 256p. (gr. 11-12). 1983. 13.41i (ISBN 0-06-015175-7); pap. 6.68i (ISBN 0-06-463578-3, EH 578). B&N NY.
Barnes & Noble Thesaurus of Geology. Alec Watt. (Illus.). 192p. (gr. 11-12). 1983. 13.41i (ISBN 0-06-015177-3, EH 579); pap. 6.68i (ISBN 0-06-463579-1, EH 579). B&N NY.
Barnes & Noble Thesaurus of Science. Arthur Godman. (Illus.). 256p. (gr. 11-12). 1983. 13.41i (ISBN 0-06-015176-5, EH 580); pap. 6.68i (ISBN 0-06-463580-5, EH 580). B&N NY.
Barrio Language Dictionary. D. Fuentes & J. A. Lopez. (Span.). 1976. pap. 5.25 (ISBN 0-87505-143-X). Borden.
Barrio Language Dictionary. Dagaberto Fuentes & Jose A. Lopez. (Span.). 4.25. Camino Real.
Basic-BASIC English Dictionary. Larry Noonan. 150p. 1982. pap. 10.95 (ISBN 0-918398-54-1). Dilithium Pr.
Basic BASIC-English Dictionary for the Apple, PET & TRS-80. Larry Noonan. (Illus.). 154p. 17.95 (ISBN 0-686-88421-3, 1521). TAB Bks.
Basic Book of Synonyms & Antonyms. Laurence Urdang. 1978. pap. 2.75 (ISBN 0-451-11688-7, AE1688, Sig). NAL.
Basic Chinese-Korean Character Dictionary. Hyogmyou Kwon. LC 79-322885. xxvi, 556p. (Chinese & Korean.). 1978. write for info. (ISBN 3-447-01884-4). Harrassowitz.
Basic Dictionary of Home Economics. Philomena Brown. 64p. 1982. 25.00x (ISBN 0-7135-1317-9, Pub. by Bell & Hyman England). State Mutual Bk.
Basic Dictionary of Synonyms & Antonyms. Laurence Urdang. 1979. 9.95 (ISBN 0-525-66604-4). Lodestar Bks.
Basic Dictionary of Synonyms & Antonyms. Laurence Urdang. LC 79-4064. 1979. 9.95 (ISBN 0-525-66604-4). Lodestar Bks.
Basic Dictionary of the Petroleum Industry. Augustin Mendez Manzano. 588p. (Eng., Fr. & Span.). 1980. 25.00. Imported Bks.
Basic Dictionary Russian-English. 185p. (Rus. & Eng.). write for info. Esselte Studium.
Basic English-Chinese, Chinese-English Dictionary with PINYIN Transliteration. Ed. by Peter Bergman. (Eng. & Chinese.). 1979. text ed. 12.00x (ISBN 0-391-01287-8). Humanities.
Basic English-Chinese, Chinese-English Dictionary. Peter Bergman. 135p. (Eng. & Chinese.). 1980. 16.00. Imported Bks.
Basic English-Chinese, Chinese-English Dictionary. Compiled by Peter M. Bergman. (Chinese & Eng.). (YA) 1980. pap. 2.25 (ISBN 0-451-11688-7, AE1688, Sig). NAL.
Basic English: Writer's Japanese-English Word Book. F. J. Daniels. (Eng. & Japanese.). 1969. 35.00 (ISBN 0-89346-100-8, Pub. by Hokuseido Pr). Heian Intl.
Basic German-English Dictionary & Grammar. 176p. (Ger.). 1976. pap. text ed. 5.95 (ISBN 0-88436-183-7, 45258). EMC.
Basic Glossary for Archivists, Manuscript Curators, & Records Managers. Frank B. Evans et al. 19p. 1974. pap. 2.00 (ISBN 0-931828-02-3). Soc Am Archivists.
Basic Greek Vocabulary. John R. Cheadle. (Gr.). 1969. text ed. 6.95 (ISBN 0-312-06790-9). St Martin.
Basic Japanese Conversation Dictionary: English-Japanese & Japanese-English. Samuel Martin. LC 57-8797. (Eng. & Japanese.). 3.95 (ISBN 0-8048-0057-X). C E Tuttle.
Basic Japanese Conversation Dictionary. S. Martin. (Japanese.). 3.95. Iaconi.
Basic Latin Vocabulary. John Wilson & C. Parsons. (Lat.). 1969. text ed. 7.95 (ISBN 0-312-06825-5). St Martin.
Basic Latin Vocabulary Along Etymological Lines. Gerald F. Else. 15p. (Lat. & Eng.). 0.90 (NO. B14). Am Classical.
Basic Material in Ritarungu. Jeffrey Heath. LC 81-455870. (Illus.). viii, 249p. (Ritaru.). 1980. Aus.$pap. 9.50 (ISBN 0-85883-204-6). Linguistic Circle.
Basic Medical Terminology. J. Patrick Fisher. LC 74-77820. (Allied Health Ser). 1975. pap. text ed. 14.95 (ISBN 0-672-61385-9); tchr's manual o.p. 6.67 (ISBN 0-672-61386-7); tape cassette 115.50 (ISBN 0-672-61387-5). Bobbs.
Basic Medical Terminology. 2nd ed. J. Patrick Fisher. 288p. 1983. pap. text ed. 12.95 (ISBN 0-672-61573-8); cassettes 240.00 (ISBN 0-672-61575-4); instr's guide 6.67 (ISBN 0-672-61574-6). Bobbs.
Basic Russian-English Dictionary. (Rus. & Eng.). 1973. pap. 5.95 (ISBN 0-88436-063-6, 65254). EMC.
Basic Spanish Dictionary: English-Spanish, Spanish-English. Cortina & Grosset. (Eng. & Span.). write for info. (608-63). Pan Amer Pub.
Basic Technical Dictionary: French-English-German-Arabic. H. Marei. 363p. (Fr., Eng., Ger. & Arabic.). 1973. lib. bdg. 45.00 (ISBN 0-686-92506-8, M-9752). French & Eur.
Basic Usage & Vocabulary. William Strong. 1983. pap. text ed. 4.95 (ISBN 0-394-33615-1, RanC). Random.
Basic Vocabulary & Language Thesaurus for Hearing-Impaired Children. Daniel Ling & Agnes H. Ling. LC 76-52826. 1977. 6.00 (ISBN 0-88200-078-0, C1437). Alexander Graham.
Basic Vocabulary Builder. Eugene Ehrlich & Daniel Murphy. (McGraw-Hill Paperbacks). 192p. (Orig.). 1979. pap. 3.95 (ISBN 0-07-019105-0, SP). McGraw.
Basic Vocabulary of American Sign Language for Parents & Children. Terrence J. O'Rourke. (Illus.). 240p. 1978. 12.95 (SL040); pap. 8.95. Natl Assn Deaf.
Basic Words in Japanese. (Eng. & Japanese.). write for info. (454-6). Pan Am Bk Co.
Basic Words in Korean. (Eng. & Korean.). write for info. (454-4). Pan Amer Pub.
Basic Words in Portuguese. (Eng. & Port.). write for info. (454-8). Pan Am Bk Co.
Basic Words in Spanish. (Eng. & Span.). write for info. (454-3). Pan Amer Pub.
Basic words in Vietnamese. (Eng. & Vietnamese.). write for info. (454-7). Pan Am Bk Co.
Basico Sopena: Diccionario Ilustrado de la Lengua Espanla. Lazaro Ladero Sanchez. (Illus.). 792p. (Span.). 9.95 (SOP). Lectorum Pubns.
Basiswoordenlijst Latijn. J. K. Babeliowsky. LC 76-526797. 273p. (Dutch & Lat.). 1975. write for info. (ISBN 9-012-00872-7). Staatsdruk.
Basque-Spanish Dictionary. Issac M. Lopez. (Basque & Span.). 1974. lib. bdg. 69.95 (ISBN 0-685-51638-5). Revisionist Pr.
Batad Ifugao Vocabulary. Leonard E. Newell. (Language & Literature Ser.). 1968. 15.00. HRAFP.
Bauherren-Lexikon. Hans J. Grabbe. LC 76-488016. 251p. (Eng. & Ger.). 1976. DM.29.50 (ISBN 3-528-08657-2). Vieweg.
Bautechnik. Eduard Steiger & Karl F. Busch. LC 78-340416. 375p. (Ger.). 1976. M.15.00. Bibl Inst Leipzig.
Bautechnisches Englisch im Bild: Illustrated Technical German for Builders. 5th ed. W. K. Killer. (Illus.). 183p. (Eng. & Ger.). 1981. DM.24.00 (ISBN 3-7625-1477-1). Bauverlag.
Bauworterbuch. Hanns Frommhold. LC 79-358361. viii, 299p. (Ger.). 1978. DM.75.00 (ISBN 3-8041-1529-2). Werner Verlag.
Beacon Dictionary of Theology. Ed. by Richard S. Taylor. 648p. 1983. 29.95 (ISBN 0-8341-0811-9). Beacon Hill.
Bedekr Kaszubski. Roza Ostrowski & Izabella Trojanwska. LC 80-466240. (Illus.). 513p. (Pol., Gdansk). 1978. 180.00 Zl. Wydawn.
Bedeutungswoerterbuch: Bedeutung & Gebrauch der Woerter. Paul Grebe. 447p. (Ger.). DM.19.80 (ISBN 3-411-01125-4). Biblio Inst.

Beginner's Chinese English Dictionary of the National Language (Gwpyeu) W. Simon. 1200p. (Chinese & Eng.). 1980. 55.00x (ISBN 0-85331-013-0, Pub. by Lund Humphries England). State Mutual Bk.

Beginners Dictionary of Chinese-Japanese Characters. Arthur Rose-Innes. (Chinese & Japanese.). 15.00 (ISBN 0-8446-5657-7). Peter Smith.

Beginner's Dictionary of Chinese-Japanese Characters. Arthur Rose-Innes. 510p. (Chinese, Japanese & Eng.). 1959. pap. 7.95. Dover.

Beginners' Dictionary of Chinese-Japanese Characters & Compounds. Arthur Rose-Innes. (Chinese & Japanese.). 1977. pap. 7.95 (ISBN 0-486-23467-3). Dover.

Beginner's Spanish-English Dictionary. (Span. & Eng., Large format). 12.95; pap. 10.95; in 2 vols. 15.95. Iaconi.

Beginner's Translation Handbook: English-Chinese. F. Lo-Tien. 364p. 1974. pap. 3.95 (ISBN 0-686-92139-9, M-9581). French & Eur.

Beginning Dictionary. LC 78-27760. (Illus.). (gr. 3-6). 1979. text ed. 7.98 (ISBN 0-395-27400-1). HM.

Beginning Dictionary. George Ulrich. Ed. by David R. Hamilton. (Illus., Eng.). 1979. 9.75 (ISBN 0-395-28977-7). HM.

Beginning Vocabulary. Dale McMasters. (Language Arts Ser.). 24p. (gr. 3-5). 1976. wkbk. 5.00 (ISBN 0-8209-0309-4, VD-1). ESP.

Beginnings of a Ngukurr-Bamyili Creole Dictionary: Work Papers of SIL-AAB, Series B; vol. 4. Ed. by John R. Sandefur & Joy L. Sandefur. LC 80-509176. v, 136p. (Creole & Eng.). 1979. write for info. (ISBN 0-86892-190-4). Summer Inst Abor.

Begriffe des Managements. Richard Kerler. LC 75-517995. (Illus.). 126p. (Ger.). 1975. DM.3.80 (ISBN 3-581-66261-2). Humboldt Taschen.

Begriffslexikon der Bildenden Kuenste, 2 vols. B. Bilzer. 320p. (Ger.). 1971. Set. pap. 25.50 (ISBN 3-499-16142-7, M-7305). French & Eur.

Begriffswoerterbuch zur Betriebswirtschafts & Managementlehre. Emil Weinzierl. LC 77-567493. 187p. (Ger.). 1976. S.135.00 (ISBN 3-85122-063-3). Industrieverlag.

Behind the Headlines. Leslie G. Rofe. LC 77-568757. 207p. (Fr.). 1975. 24.00 F. Belin.

Bekleidungslexikon. Ed. by Wilfried Schierbaum. LC 78-381510. (Illus.). 338p. (Ger.). 1978. DM.58.00 (ISBN 3-7949-0305-6). Schiele & Schoen.

Beknopt Juridisch Woordenboek Frans-Nederlands. F. J. Velden. LC 78-349929. viii, 140p. (Dutch & Fr.). 1977. write for info. (ISBN 9-026-80975-1). Kluwer Group.

Bell's Acrostic Dictionary. W. M. Baker. LC 77-141772. 1971. Repr. of 1927 ed. 30.00x (ISBN 0-8103-3379-1). Gale.

Benelux Abbreviations & Symbols: Law & Related Subjects. Adolf Sprudzs. LC 74-140620. 129p. 1971. lib. bdg. 20.00 (ISBN 0-379-00120-9). Oceana.

Benezit Dictionary of Artists, 10 Vols. Grund. 1976. 500.00 (ISBN 0-686-43137-5). Apollo.

Bengali-English Dictionary. (Bengali.). 22.50 (ISBN 0-87557-109-3, 109-3). Saphrograph.

Bengal'sko-Russkii Slovar. E. M. Bykova et al. 908p. (Rus. & Bengali.). 1957. 5.50 (Pub. by Gosizdat Inostr. Natsion. Slovarei). Four Continent.

Bergbautechnik & Aufbereitung Deutsch-Englisch. Helmut Schmidt. 692p. (Ger. & Eng.). 1981. M.70.00. VEB Technik.

Berlitz Arabic for Travellers. Berlitz Editors. 192p. (Arabic.). 1982. 4.95 (ISBN 0-02-964180-2, Berlitz). Macmillan.

Berlitz French for Travellers. Berlitz Editors. 192p. (Fr.). 1982. pap. 4.95 (ISBN 0-686-92978-0, Berlitz). Macmillan.

Berlitz Greek for Travellers. Berlitz Editors. 192p. (Gr.). 1982. pap. 4.95 (ISBN 0-686-92956-X, Berlitz); pap. 4.95 (ISBN 0-02-964040-7). Macmillan.

Berlitz Hebrew for Travellers. Berlitz Editors. 192p. (Hebrew.). 1982. pap. 4.95 (ISBN 0-02-964050-4, Berlitz). Macmillan.

Berlitz Italian for Travellers. Berlitz Editors. 192p. (Ital.). 1982. 8.95 (ISBN 0-02-965180-8, Berlitz); pap. 4.95 (ISBN 0-02-963940-9). Macmillan.

Berlitz Japanese for Travellers. Berlitz Editors. 192p. (Japanese.). 1982. pap. 4.95 (ISBN 0-02-964070-9, Berlitz). Macmillan.

Berlitz Latin-American Spanish for Travellers. Berlitz Editors. 192p. (Span.). 1982. 8.95 (ISBN 0-02-965510-2, Berlitz); pap. 4.95 (ISBN 0-02-963950-6). Macmillan.

Berlitz Pocket Dictionaries: Danish-English-Danish. Berlitz. (Eng. & Danish.). pap. 4.95 (ISBN 0-02-964550-6). Macmillan.

Berlitz Pocket Dictionaries: Danish-English. Berlitz Editors. 300p. (Danish & Eng.). 1982. pap. 4.95 (ISBN 0-686-92980-2, Berlitz). Macmillan.

Berlitz Pocket Dictionaries: Dutch-English-Dutch. Berlitz. (Eng. & Dutch.). pap. 4.95 (ISBN 0-02-964540-9). Macmillan.

Berlitz Pocket Dictionaries: Dutch-English. Berlitz Editors. 300p. (Eng. & Dutch.). 1982. pap. 4.95 (ISBN 0-686-92990-X, Berlitz). Macmillan.

Berlitz Pocket Dictionaries: Finnish-English-Finnish. Berlitz. (Eng. & Finnish.). pap. 4.95 (ISBN 0-02-964580-8). Macmillan.

Berlitz Pocket Dictionaries: Finnish-English. Berlitz Editors. 300p. (Eng. & Finnish.). 1982. pap. 4.95 (ISBN 0-686-92984-5, Berlitz). Macmillan.

Berlitz Pocket Dictionaries: French-English-French. Berlitz. (Fr. & Eng.). pap. 4.95 (ISBN 0-02-964500-X). Macmillan.

Berlitz Pocket Dictionaries: French-English. Berlitz Editors. 300p. (Eng. & Fr.). 1982. pap. 4.95 (ISBN 0-686-93004-5, Berlitz). Macmillan.

Berlitz Pocket Dictionaries: German-English-German. Berlitz. (Ger. & Eng.). pap. 4.95 (ISBN 0-02-964530-1). Macmillan.

Berlitz Pocket Dictionaries: German-English. Berlitz Editors. 300p. (Eng. & Ger.). 1982. pap. 4.95 (ISBN 0-686-93007-X, Berlitz). Macmillan.

Berlitz Pocket Dictionaries: Italian-English-Italian. Berlitz. (Eng. & Ital.). pap. 4.95 (ISBN 0-02-964520-4). Macmillan.

Berlitz Pocket Dictionaries: Italian-English. Berlitz Editors. 300p. (Eng. & Ital.). 1982. pap. 4.95 (ISBN 0-686-93001-0, Berlitz). Macmillan.

Berlitz Pocket Dictionaries: Norwegian-English-Norwegian. Berlitz. (Eng. & Norwegian.). pap. 4.95 (ISBN 0-02-964560-3). Macmillan.

Berlitz Pocket Dictionaries: Norwegian-English. Berlitz Editors. 300p. (Eng. & Norwegian.). 1982. pap. 4.95 (ISBN 0-686-92987-X, Berlitz). Macmillan.

Berlitz Pocket Dictionaries: Portuguese-English-Portuguese. Berlitz. (Port. & Eng.). pap. 4.95 (ISBN 0-02-964440-2). Macmillan.

Berlitz Pocket Dictionaries: Spanish-English. Berlitz Editors. 300p. (Eng. & Span.). 1982. pap. 4.95 (ISBN 0-686-92998-5, Berlitz). Macmillan.

Berlitz Pocket Dictionaries: Spanish-English-Spanish. Berlitz. (Span. & Eng.). pap. 4.95 (ISBN 0-02-964510-7). Macmillan.

Berlitz Pocket Dictionaries: Swedish-English. Berlitz Editors. 300p. (Eng. & Swedish.). 1982. pap. 4.95 (ISBN 0-686-92996-9, Berlitz). Macmillan.

Berlitz Pocket Dictionaries: Swedish-English-Swedish. Berlitz. (Swedish & Eng.). pap. 4.95 (ISBN 0-02-964570-0). Macmillan.

Berlitz Portuguese for Travellers. Berlitz Editors. 192p. (Port.). 1982. pap. 4.95 (ISBN 0-02-963960-3, Berlitz). Macmillan.

Berlitz Spanish for Travellers. Berlitz Editors. 192p. (Span.). 1982. 8.95 (ISBN 0-02-965190-5, Berlitz); pap. 4.95 (ISBN 0-02-963970-0). Macmillan.

Bernstein's Reverse Dictionary. Theodore M. Bernstein. LC 75-8283. 384p. 1975. 16.95 (ISBN 0-8129-0566-0). Times Bks.

Berry's Greek-English New Testament Lexicon with Synonyms: Numerically Coded to Strong's Exhaustive Concordance. George R. Berry. 208p. (Orig., Gr. & Eng.). 1980. pap. 5.95 (ISBN 0-8010-0791-7). Baker Bk.

Bertelsmann Dictionary English-German, German-English. (Ger. & Eng.). 1975. 29.95 (ISBN 3-570-01438-X, M-7444, Pub. by Bertelsmann Lexikon/VVA). French & Eur.

Bertelsmann Dictionary: English-German, German-English. (Ger.). 1975. DM.29.95 (ISBN 3-570-01438-X). C Bertelsmann.

Bertelsmann Lexikon, 10 vols. (Ger.). 1972-74. Set. 1225.00 (ISBN 0-686-56596-7, M-7306, Pub. by Bertelsmann). French & Eur.

Bertelsmann Lexikon, 10 vols. (Ger.). 1980-1981. Set. 720.00 (ISBN 0-8277-3001-2). Pergamon.

Bertelsmann Lexikon, 10 vols. (Ger.). 1972-74. Set. DM.1225.00. C Bertelsmann.

Bertelsmann Woerterbuch Deutsch-Franzoesisch, Franzoesisch-Deutsch. Karl Knauer. 640p. (Ger. & Fr.). 1974. 17.50 (ISBN 3-570-01486-X, M-7307, Pub. by Bertelsmann Lexikon VVA). French & Eur.

Bertelsmann Woerterbuch Deutsch-Franzoesisch, Franzoesisch-Deutsch. Karl Knauer. 640p. (Fr. & Ger.). 1974. DM.17.50 (ISBN 3-570-01486-X). C Bertelsmann.

Bestimmung & Angabe der Funktion von Sekundar-Suffixen Durch Panini. Albrecht Wezler. LC 76-450174. xiii, 155p. (Sanskrit.). 1975. DM.44.00 (ISBN 3-515-02105-1). Steiner Verlag.

BI-Handlexikon, 2 vols, Vol. 1. Lexikonredaktion. (Illus.). 704p. (Ger.). 1982. M.32.00. Bibl Inst Leipzig.

BI-Handlexikon, 2 vols, Vol. 2. Ed. by Lexikonredaktion. (Illus.). 688p. (Ger.). 1982. M.32.00. Bibl Inst Leipzig.

Bi-Lexikon A-Z. Veb. Inst. Leipzig. 1072p. (Ger.). 1982. M.18.00 (5772135). Bibl Inst Leipzig.

BI-Taschenlexikon Elektronik-Funktechnik. W. Conrad. (Illus.). 400p. (Ger.). 1982. M.15.00. Biblio Inst.

BI-Taschenlexikon Energie. W. Conrad et al. (Illus.). 346p. (Ger.). 1981. M.15.00. Bibl Inst Leipzig.

BI-Taschenlexikon Fremdsprachige Schriftsteller. 4th ed. Ed. by G. Steiner & H. Greiner-Mai. 736p. (Ger.). 1982. M.25.00. Bibl Inst Leipzig.

BI-Taschenlexikon Heimtiere. U. Jacob & G. T. Petersein. (Illus.). 352p. (Ger.). 1982. M.15.00. Bibl Inst Leipzig.

BI-Taschenlexikon Orden, Preise & Medaillen Staatliche Auszeichnungen der DDR. G. Tautz. 199p. (Ger.). 1980. M.16.00. Bibl Inst Leipzig.

BI-Taschenlexikon Radioaktivitaet. J. Leonhardt. (Illus.). 350p. (Ger.). M.15.00. Bibl Inst Leipzig.

Bi-Taschenlexikon Schiffbau-Schiffahrt. E. Wiebeck. (Illus.). 388p. (Ger.). 1982. M.18.00. Bibl Inst Leipzig.

Bibeltheologisches Woerterbuch, 2 vols. 3rd ed. Johannes B. Bauer. (Ger.). 1967. Set. 150.00 (ISBN 3-222-10240-6, M-7308, Pub. by Styria). French & Eur.

Bible Dictionary for Young Readers. William N. McElrath. LC 65-15604. (Illus.). (gr. 4-11). 1965. 8.95 (ISBN 0-8054-4404-1). Broadman.

Bibliografia Siciliana, Ovvero Gran Dizionario Bibliografico Delle Opere Editi E Inedite, Antiche E Moderne Di Autori Siciliani O Di Argomento Siciliano Stampate in Sicilia, 3 vols. Giuseppe M. Mira. (Ital.). 1873-1881. 82.50 (ISBN 0-8337-2400-2); inc. supplement by giuseppe salvo-cozzo (ISBN 0-685-06732-7). B Franklin.

Bibliographisches Handbuch der Sprachworterbucher: Ein Internationales Verzeichnis Von 5600 Worterbuchern der Jahre 1460-1958 Fur Mehr Als 500 Sprachen und Dialekte. Wolfram Zaunmuller. LC 59-1510. 264p. (Ger.). 1958. 50.00x (ISBN 3-7772-5812-1). Intl Pubns Serv.

Bibliography of Hispanic Dictionaries: Catalan, Galician, Spanish, Spanish in Latin America & the Philippines. M. Fabri. 1979. pap. 45.00 (ISBN 0-686-77969-X). Heinman.

Bibliography of Mono- & Multilingual Vocabularies, Thesauri, Subject Headings & Classification Schemes in the Social Sciences. (Reports & Papers in the Social Sciences: No. 54). 101p. 1983. pap. text ed. 7.00 (ISBN 92-3-102072-2, U1272, UNESCO). Unipub.

Bibliography of Papermaking Terminology. 1970. 2.00 (019-1); members 1.33. TAPPI.

Bibliotekskoder. Rigsbibliotekareembedet. LC 76-476911. 16p. (Eng. & Danish.). 1975. write for info. Bibliotekscentralen.

Bibliotheca Indosinica. Dictionnaire bibliographique des ouvrages relatifs a la peninsule indo-chinoise, 5 vols. in 3. Henri Cordier. (Span. & Indonesian.). 1912-32. Set. 197.00 (ISBN 0-8337-0676-4). B Franklin.

Bibliotheca Sinica, dictionnaire bibliographique des ouvrages relatifs a l'Empire chinois, 6 vols. in 5. 2nd ed. Henri Cordier. LC 68-58196. (Bibliography & Research Ser.: No. 250). (Span., Chinese & Fr.). 1969. Repr. of 1922 ed. 200.00 (ISBN 0-8337-0671-3). B Franklin.

Bibliotheque Orientale, ou Dictionnaire universel, contenant generalment tout ce qui regarde la connaissance des peuples de 'orient, 4 vols. B. D'Herbelot de Molainville et al. 2864p. (Fr.). Repr. of 1782 ed. lib. bdg. 525.00x (ISBN 0-89241-342-5). Caratzas Pub Co.

Bien Manger dans Quinze Pays. Evelyne Wilhelm. LC 79-390204. 205p. (Eng. & Fr.). 1979. 39.00 F (ISBN 2-86418-029-4). Encre.

Bil-og Trafikkteknisk Ordbok. Willy Kirkeby. LC 79-374320. (Eng. & Norwegian.). 1979. Kr.98.00 (ISBN 8-2573-0079-9). Kunnskapsforlaget.

Bild der Voelker. C. D. Darlington & Karl G. Heider. 280p. (Ger.). DM.49.00 (ISBN 3-7653-0273-2). F A Brockhaus.

Bilder-Conversations-Lexikon fur das Deutsche Volk, 4 vols. LC 79-363849. (Illus., Ger.). 1977. DM.234.00. F A Brockhaus.

Bildwoerterbuch der Kunst. 2nd ed. H. Leutzeler. 404p. (Ger.). 1962. 22.50 (ISBN 3-427-85012-9, M-7310, Pub. by F. Duemmlers). French & Eur.

Bildwoerterbuch Deutsch-Englisch. 864p. (Ger. & Eng.). 1983. 18.00. M Rosenberg.

Bildwoerterbuch Deutsch-Englisch-Franzosisch. 941p. (Ger. , Eng. & Fr.). write for info. (ISBN 3-411-01830-5). Biblio Inst.

Bildwoerterbuch Italienisch: Dizionario Figurato. (Illus.). 896p. (Ital. & Ger.). DM.29.80 (ISBN 3-411-00973-X). Biblio Inst.

Bildwoerterbuch Schwedisch: Bildlexikon. (Illus.). 872p. (Swedish & Ger.). DM.29.80 (ISBN 3-411-00974-8). Biblio Inst.

Bildwoerterbuch Spanisch: Diccionario por la Imagen. (Illus.). 912p. (Span. & Ger.). DM.29.80 (ISBN 3-411-00971-3). Biblio Inst.

Bilingual Dictionary of Anglicismos, Barbarismos, Pachuquismos y Otras Locuciones En el Barrio. Francisco Padilla. LC 80-83981. 214p. (Orig., Span. & Eng.). pap. 7.00 (ISBN 0-9605292-0-9). Padilla.

Bilingualism Among American Slovaks: Analysis of Loans see Use of the Dictionary of American English & the Dictionary of Americanisms.

Biographical Dictionary of American Mayors, 1820 to 1980. Ed. by Melvin G. Holli & Peter d'A Jones. LC 80-1796. (Illus.). 576p. 1981. lib. bdg. 69.50 (ISBN 0-313-21134-5, HDA/). Greenwood.

Biologiai Lexikon. Ferene B. Straub & Gyorgy Adam. LC 76-506702. (Hungarian.). 1975. 165.00 Ft (ISBN 963-05-0529-0). Akademiai Kiado.

Biological Nomenclature. 2nd ed. Charles Jeffrey. LC 77-90821. 72p. 1978. 13.00x (ISBN 0-8448-1264-1). Crane-Russak Co.

Biologie: Ein Lexikon der Gesamten Schulbiologie. Karl H. Ahlheim. 464p. (Ger.). DM.19.80 (ISBN 3-411-01366-4). Biblio Inst.

Bioscientific Terminology. Donald M. Ayers. LC 74-163010. 336p. 1972. pap. 5.95x (ISBN 0-8165-0305-2). U of Ariz Pr.

Birdicide of Cock Robin, & Other Murderous Words Ending in Cide. Sam Goldstein. (Weirdictionaries Ser.). (Illus.). 68p. (Orig.). 1982. pap. 3.95 cancelled (ISBN 0-938338-04-8). Winds World Pr.

Birds: Their Latin Names Explained. A. F. Gotch. (Illus.). 228p. 1981. 22.50 (ISBN 0-7137-1175-2, Pub. by Blandford Pr England). Sterling.

Birdwatcher's Dictionary. Peter Weaver. (Illus.). 160p. (YA) 1981. 17.50 (ISBN 0-85661-028-3, Pub. by T & A D Poyser England). Buteo.

Bituminous Coal Mining Vocabulary of the Eastern United States. Dennis Preston. (Publication of the American Dialect Society: No. 59). (Illus.). 96p. (Orig.). 1973. pap. 7.70 (ISBN 0-8173-0659-5). U of Ala Pr.

Black Vernacular Vocabulary: A Study of Intra-Inter-Cultural Concerns & Usage. Edith A. Folb. (CAAS Monographs: No. V). 53p. (Orig.). 1972. pap. 3.00x (ISBN 0-934934-14-2). Ctr Afro-Am Stud.

Blackfoot-English Vocabulary. Christianus C. Uhlenbeck & R. H. Van Gulik. LC 76-44086. (Verhardelingen der Koninklijke Akademie Van Wetenschappen Te Amsterdam. Afdeeling Letterkunde. Nieuwe Reeks: 33, No. 2). (Blackfoot & Eng.). Repr. of 1934 ed. 35.50 (ISBN 0-404-15795-5). AMS Pr.

Black's Agricultural Dictionary. Ed. by D. B. Dalal-Clayton. (Illus.). 512p. 1981. 28.50x (ISBN 0-389-20261-4, 07079). B&N Imports.

Black's Law Dictionary. 5th ed. Henry C. Black. Ed. by Joseph R. Nolan & Michael J. Connolly. LC 79-12547. 1511p. 1979. text ed. 18.95 (ISBN 0-8299-2041-2); deluxe ed. 37.50 (ISBN 0-8299-2045-5). West Pub.

Black's Law Dictionary: Abridged Fifth Edition. Henry C. Black. Ed. by Joseph R. Nolan et al. 854p. pap. text ed. 11.95 (ISBN 0-314-77135-2). West Pub.

Black's Medical Dictionary. 33rd ed. Ed. by William A. Thomson. LC 79-167. (Illus.). 992p. 1982. text ed. 24.50x (ISBN 0-389-20246-0, 07045). B&N Imports.

Black's Veterinary Dictionary. rev., 14th ed. Ed. by Geoffrey West. LC 82-22783. (Illus.). 912p. 1983. text ed. 28.50x (ISBN 0-389-20330-0, 07170). B&N Imports.

Blade Coating Defect Terminology. Ed. by Edward J. Heiser & Jerry L. Allswede. (Illus.). 53p. 1982. pap. 24.95 (ISBN 0-686-43234-7, 01 01 R094). TAPPI.

Boating Dictionary: Sail & Power. John V. Noel. 304p. 1981. text ed. 16.95 (ISBN 0-442-26048-2). Van Nos Reinhold.

Bokabulario Papiamentu-Ulandes. Mario Dijkhoff. LC 79-340768. 56p. (Eng. & Dutch.). 1978. fl.12.50 (ISBN 9-0601-1085-4). Walburg Pers.

Bola Glossary of Civil Procedural Law: Spanish-English & English-Spanish. Bola Publications. LC 82-72320. (Bola Glossary Ser.: Vol. 2). 100p. (Orig., Span. & Eng.). pap. 19.95 (ISBN 0-943118-01-8). Bola Pubns.

Bola Glossary of Electronic Data Processing & Computer Terms: English-Spanish & Spanish-English. (Span. & Eng.). 29.95. Iaconi.

Bola Glossary of Electronic Data Processing & Computer Terms English-Spanish & Spanish-English. Bola Publications. LC 82-71113. (Glossary Ser.: Vol. 1). 200p. (Orig., Span. & Eng.). 1982. pap. 29.95 (ISBN 0-943118-00-X). Bola Pubns.

Bolgarsko-Russkii Voennyi Slovar. M. G. Artiukhov et al. 527p. (Rus. & Bulgarian.). 1966. 3.90 (Pub. bu Voenizdat). Four Continent.

Bolsho i anglo-russki i slovar, 2 vols. N. N. Anosova et al. LC 80-482048. (Eng. & Rus.). 1979. vol. 1 16.20 Rub. vol. 2 17.20 Rub. Russkii Iazyk.

Bolshoi Anglo-Russkii Slovar, 2 vols. Ed. by I. R. Galperin. (Rus. & Eng.). 1977. 35.00 set (Pub. by Russkii Iazyk). Four Continent.

Bol'Shoi Anglo-Russkii Slovar, 2 vols. Ed. by I. R. Galperin. (Rus. & Eng.). 1977. 35.00 set. Four Continent.

Bolshoi Polsko-Russkii Slovar, 2 vols. (Rus. & Pol.). 1979. 28.95 (Pub. by Russkii Iazyk). Four Continent.

Bonniers Musiklexikon. Ake Engstroem & H. Toernblom. LC 75-407960. 446p. (Swedish.). 1975. Kr.215.00. Bonnier Forlag.

Bonniers Trebandlexikon, 3 vols. (Swedish.). 1979. 175.00 (ISBN 0-8277-3004-7). Pergamon.

Boobytraps of the German Language. Alex Sandri-White. (Ger.). 5.95 (ISBN 0-685-22759-6). Aurea.

Book Illustrators of the Twentieth Century. rev. ed. Brigid Peppin. (Illus.). 544p. 1982. cancelled (ISBN 0-668-04366-0). Arco.

Book of British Lists. Hunter Davis. LC 81-138947. xvii, 222p. 1980. Epap. 1.25 (ISBN 0-600-20267-4). Hamlyn Pub.

Book of Pidgin English. 3rd ed. John J. Murphy. LC 75-35144. (Pidgin Eng.). Repr. of 1949 ed. 14.50 (ISBN 0-404-14160-9). AMS Pr.

Book of Russian Idioms. M. I. Dubrovin. (Illus.). 350p. (Rus. & Eng.). 1980. 4.25 (K-32). Four Continent.

Bookman's Glossary. 6th ed. Ed. by Jean Peters. 200p. 1983. 21.95 (ISBN 0-8352-1686-1). Bowker.

Bornholmsk Ordbog. Johan C. Espersen. LC 75-400668. xxi, 683p. (Danish.). 1975. write for info. Rosenkilde.

Botanical Latin: History, Grammar, Syntax, Terminology & Vocabulary. William T. Stearn. (Illus., Lat.). 1966. 18.95x (ISBN 0-02-852900-6). Hafner.

Boucher's Clinical Dental Terminology: A Glossary of Accepted Terms in All Disciplines of Dentistry. 3rd ed. Thomas J. Zwemer et al. LC 81-18843. (Illus.). 378p. 1982. text ed. 27.95 (ISBN 0-8016-0712-4). Mosby.

Boys & Girls First Dictionary. 2nd ed. John Trevaskis & Robin Hyman. (Illus.). 1979. Can.$pap. 4.95 (ISBN 0-7730-1071-8); pap. 1.50 (ISBN 0-7730-1073-4). U of Toronto Pr.

Bra Bockers Lexikon, 25 vols. (Swedish.). 1973-1981. 1250.00 (ISBN 0-8277-3063-2). Pergamon.

Brei Diccionari Ideologic: Amb Vocabulari Catala-Castella & Castella-Catala. Xavier Romeu. LC 76-465853. (Illus.). 267p. (Catalan.). 1976. write for info. (ISBN 8-430-77321-5). Edit Teide.

Breve Diccionario de Filosofia. 464p. (Span.). 1977. 20.95 (ISBN 84-254-0631-5, S-50199). French & Eur.

Breve Diccionario del Argentino Exquisito. Adolfo Bioy Casares. 162p. (Span.). 1978. 10.50 (ISBN 0-686-56668-8, S-33074). French & Eur.

Breve Diccionario Espanol-Ruso: Ruso-Espanol de Terminos Cientificos & Tecnicos. J. C. Orts et al. 438p. (Span. & Rus.). 1960. leatherette 6.95 (ISBN 0-686-97394-1, S-31835). French & Eur.

Breve Diccionario Etimologico de la Lengua Castellana. Joan Corominas. (Span.). pap. 32.00 (GRD). Lectorum Pubns.

Breve Diccionario Etimologico de la Lengua Espanola. 3rd ed. Joan Corominas. 628p. (Span.). 1976. 35.95 (ISBN 84-249-1332-9, S-11936). French & Eur.

Breve Diccionario Philosofia. Muller-Halder. 464p. (Span.). 1977. pap. 17.95 (ISBN 84-254-0632-3, S-50198). French & Eur.

Breve diccionario Porrua de la lengua espanola. (Span.). (gr. 4-9). pap. 3.50. Iaconi.

Breve Diccionario Porrua de la Lengua Espanola. Antonio Raluy Poudevida. 461p. (Span.). pap. 3.25. Lectorum Pubns.

Breve diccionario Porrua de la lengua espanola. 14th, rev. ed. Antonio Raluy Poudevida. Rev. by Francisco Monterde. 462p. (Span.). 1980. Mex.$pap. 50.00. Porrua.

Brevis Diccionario Practico Castellano. (Span.). 5.95 (ISBN 0-686-56707-2, S-33058). French & Eur.

Brew Vocabulari Catala-Castella-Angles de Comerc Exterior. 43p. (Span., Catalan & Eng.). write for info. (S-37580). French & Eur.

Brewer's Dictionary of Phrase & Fable: Centenary Edition. rev. ed. E. Cobham Brewer. Pref. by Ivor Evans. LC 81-47407. 1248p. 1981. 24.95i (ISBN 0-06-014903-5, HarpT). Har-Row.

Brewer's Dictionary of Phrase & Fable. Ed. by Ivor H. Evans. 1248p. 1982. 50.00x (ISBN 0-304-30706-8, Pub. by Cassell England). State Mutual Bk.

Britannica Book of English Usage. Ed. by Christine Timmons & Frank Gibney. LC 79-7706. (Encyclopedia Britannica Ser.). (Illus.). 672p. 1980. 17.95 (ISBN 0-385-14193-9). Doubleday.

British & American Business in Key Words. Rudolf Sachs. 186p. (Eng. & Ger.). 1975. 25.00 (ISBN 3-7819-2010-0, M-7313, Pub. by Fritz Knapp Verlag). French & Eur.

British & American Business in Keywords. Rudolf Sachs. LC 76-450966. vi, 186p. (Eng. & Ger.). 1975. DM.32.00 (ISBN 3-7819-2010-0). Knapp Verlag.

British & American Business in Keywords. Rudolf Sachs. LC 81-117456. 186p. 1980. pap. write for info. (ISBN 3-7819-2016-X). Knapp Verlag.

British & American Business Terms. Rudolf Sachs. 144p. (Orig.). 1975. pap. text ed. 12.95x (ISBN 0-7121-0242-6, Pub. by Macdonald & Evans England). Intl Ideas.

British Ships & Seamen. Richard Cooper & Grant Uden. (Illus.). 591p. 1981. lib. bdg. 40.00x (ISBN 0-312-20028-5). St Martin.

Britten's Watch & Clock Maker's Handbook, Dictionary & Guide. 16th rev. ed. F. J. Britten. Ed. by Richard Good. LC 78-3539. (Illus.). 1978. 69.95 (ISBN 0-668-04638-4). Arco.

Broad Terms for United Nations Programmes & Activities, 1979. 186p. 1980. pap. 13.00 (ISBN 0-686-68945-3, UN79/0/1, UN). Unipub.

Broadcast Communications Dictionary. 2nd, rev., enl. ed. Ed. by Lincoln Diamant. 1978. 10.95 (ISBN 0-8038-0788-0). Hastings.

Brockhaus ABC Elektronik. Hans D. Junge. LC 79-391270. 751p. (Ger.). 1978. M.18.60. R Brockhaus.

Brockhaus ABC Elektrotechnik. Hans D. Junge. LC 78-399295. 667p. (Ger.). 1978. M.17.30. F A Brockhaus.

Brockhaus Bildwoerterbuch Englisch-Deutsch. (Eng. & Ger.). 1983. pap. 24.00. M Rosenberg.

Brockhaus Bildwoerterbuecher. (Ger.). write for info. F A Brockhaus.

Brockhaus Bildwoerterbuecher in vier Sprachen. (Eng., Fr., Ital. & Ger.). DM.48.00; 28.00. F A Brockhaus.

Brockhaus der Naturwissenschaften & der Technik. 832p. (Ger.). DM.45.00 (ISBN 3-7653-0019-5). F A Brockhaus.

Brockhaus der Naturwissenschaften und der Technik. 832p. (Ger.). 35.00 (ISBN 3-7653-0019-5, M-7314, Pub. by Wiesbaden). French & Eur.

Brockhaus Illustrated Dictionary: English-German, German-English. Rev. ed. (Illus.). 1450p. (Ger. & Eng.). 1976. 39.00. Imported Bks.

Brockhaus in Zwei Baenden. 1440p. (Ger.). DM.89.00 F (ISBN 3-7653-0037-3). F A Brockhaus.

Brockhaus Riemann Musiklexikon, Vol. 1, A-K. Carl Dahlhaus & Hans H. Eggebrecht. (Ger.). 1978. write for info. (ISBN 3-7653-0303-8). Eur-Am Music.

Brockhaus-Riemann-Musiklexikon in Zwei Baenden: Band 1, A-K. Carl Dahlhaus & Hans H. Eggebrecht. 699p. (Ger.). DM.148.00 (ISBN 3-7653-0303-8). F A Brockhaus.

Brockhaus-Riemann-Musiklexikon in Zwei Baenden: Band 2, L-Z. Carl Dahlhaus & Hans H. Eggebrecht. 732p. (Ger.). DM.148.00. F A Brockhaus.

Brockhaus-Wahrig Deutsches Woerterbuch in Sechs Baenden: Band 1-3. Gerhard Wahrig et al. 800p. (Ger.). DM.128.00 (ISBN 3-7653-0312-7). F A Brockhaus.

Browser's Dictionary. John Ciardi. LC 79-1658. 464p. 1980. 17.26i (ISBN 0-06-010766-9, HarpT). Har-Row.

Brukmanns' Zinn-Lexikon. Ludwig Mory et al. LC 79-351818. (Illus.). 324p. (Ger.). 1977. DM.58.00 (ISBN 3-765-41361-5). Bruckmann KG.

Buddhist Dictionary. Nyanatiloka. LC 77-87508. Repr. of 1950 ed. 20.00 (ISBN 0-404-16846-9). AMS Pr.

Buddhist Hybrid Sanskrit Dictionary & Grammar, 2 vols. F. Edgerton. 864p. (Sanskrit & Eng.). 1972. 65.00x (ISBN 0-87902-218-3). Orientalia.

Buddhist Hybrid Sanskrit Grammar & Dictionary, 2 vols. Franklin Edgerton. Incl. Vol. 1. Grammar; Vol. 2. Dictionary. 896p. (Sanskrit.). 1973. Repr. of 1953 ed. Set. 45.00x (ISBN 0-8002-0719-X). Intl Pubns Serv.

Buddhist Hybrid Sanskrit Grammar & Dictionary, 2 Vols. Franklin Edgerton. 1975. Repr. Set. 60.00x (ISBN 0-8426-0133-3). Verry.

Buddhist Hybrid Sanskrit Grammer & Dictionary, 2 vols. F. Edgerton. (Sanskrit.). 1978. Repr. 56.00 set (ISBN 0-89684-182-0). Orient Bk Dist.

Budo-Lexikon: 1500 Fachausdruecke Fernoestl. Herbert Velte. LC 77-475498. (Illus.). 137p. (Ger.). 1976. DM.9.80 (ISBN 3-8068-0383-8). Falken Verlag.

Bueromaschinen Lexikon. 18th ed. (Ger.). 1975. pap. 21.50 (ISBN 3-87264-001-1, M-7316, Pub. by Goeller Verlag). French & Eur.

Building a College Vocabulary. Patricia Licklider. 256p. (Orig.). 1981. pap. text ed. 8.95 (ISBN 0-316-52424-7); tchrs'. manual avail. (ISBN 0-316-52425-5). Little.

Bulgarialais-Suomalainen Sanakirja. Boris Parashkevov et al. LC 76-501852. 91p. (Bulgarian & Swedish.). 1975. write for info. (ISBN 951-662-159-7). Gaudeamus.

Bulgarian-English Dictionary. 2nd ed. T. Atanassova et al. 1050p. (Bulgarian & Eng.). 1980. 55.00x (ISBN 0-569-08665-5, Pub. by Collets). State Mutual Bk.

Bulgarian-English Dictionary. T. Atnassova et al. 1050p. (Bulgarian & Eng.). 1980. 65.00 (ISBN 0-686-97393-3, M-9829). French & Eur.
Bulgarian-English Dictionary. R. Russev. (Bulgarian & Eng.). pap. text ed. 27.50 (ISBN 0-685-20185-6, 006-2). Saphrograph.
Bulgarian-English Dictionary. Ed. by Rusi Russev. (Bulgarian & Eng.). 1953. 12.00 (ISBN 0-8044-0506-9). Ungar.
Bulgarian-Hindi Dictionary. B. Kanti Varma. 706p. (Bulgarian & Hindi.). 1978. leatherette 50.00 (ISBN 0-686-92526-2, M-9836). French & Eur.
Bulgarian-Russian Dictionary (M-9095) 519p. (Bulgarian & Rus.). 1977. 4.95 (ISBN 0-686-87184-7). French & Eur.
Buriatskie Shamanisticheskie i Doshamanisticheskie Terminy. I. A. Manzhigeev. 128p. (Rus.). 1978. 2.85 (Pub. by Nauka). Four Continent.
Bushman Dictionary. Dorothea F. Bleek. (American Oriental Society: Vol. 41). 1956. pap. 11.00x (ISBN 0-940490-41-2). Am Orient Soc.
Business Dictionary: English-French, French-English. 2nd ed. Georges Anderla & Georgette Schmidt-Anderla. 524p. (Eng. & Fr.). 1979. 62.50x (ISBN 2-7034-0153-1). Intl Pubns Serv.
Business English Vocabulary. Jean-Pierre Attal. LC 80-460081. 269p. (Fr. & Eng.). 1979. write for info. (ISBN 2-7081-0409-8). Edns Organisation.
Businessman's Everyday English to Spanish Dictionary: El Mundo De Negocios. Ivan De Renty. (Eng. & Span.). 1978. pap. 9.95 (ISBN 84-7143-118-1, 8138). Larousse.
Butterworths Medical Dictionary. 2nd ed. Ed. by Macdonald Critchley. LC 77-30154. 1978. 59.95 (ISBN 0-407-00061-5). Butterworth.
Butterworths Medical Dictionary. 2nd, unabridged ed. Ed. by Macdonald Critchley. 1980. pap. text ed. 39.95 (ISBN 0-407-00193-X). Butterworth.
Byggordsamling. Tekniska Nomenklaturcentralen. LC 77-464415. 164p. (Eng. & Swedish.). 1976. Kr.57.00 (ISBN 9-1719-6063-5). Tek Nomen.

C

Cactus Lexicon. Curt Backeberg. 1981. 60.00x (ISBN 0-686-78783-8, Pub. by RHS Ent England). State Mutual Bk.
CAD-CAM Glossary. 19.25 (ISBN 0-686-40545-5). Prod Intl.
Caesar Vocabularies. Paul E. Kunzer. (Bk. I- Iv). 1.00 ea (NO. 9). Am Classical.
Cagdas Ozturce Sozlugu. Seyit K. Karaalioglu. LC 77-970026. 398p. (Turkish.). 1975. TL.20.00. Inkilap ve Aka Kitabevleri.
Cahuilla Dictionary. Hansjakob Seiler & Kojiro Hioki. 1979. pap. 15.00 (ISBN 0-939046-04-0). Malki Mus Pr.
Cambodian English. Franklin E. Huffman. 152p. (Eng. & Cambodian.). 1977. 5.95 (ISBN 0-300-02070-8). Yale U Pr.
Cambodian-English Dictionary, 2 vols. R. Headley. (Cambodian & Eng.). 25.00. Iaconi.
Cambodian-English Dictionary, 2 vols. Robert K. Headley. (Publications in the Languages of Asia Ser.: No. 3). (Cambodian & Eng.). 1977. Set. 51.95 (ISBN 0-8132-0509-3). Cath U Pr.
Cambodian-English, English-Cambodian Dictionary. (Cambodian & Eng.). 22.00. Iaconi.
Cambodian-English Glossary. Franklin E. Huffman & Im Proum. (Linguistic Ser.). 160p. (Eng. & Khmerz.). 1981. pap. 7.95x. Yale U Pr.
Cambridge Italian Dictionary, 2 vols. Barbara Reynolds. LC 74-77384. (Ital.). 1962. Vol. 1. Italian-English 1962. 175.00 (ISBN 0-521-06059-1); Vol. 2, English-italian 1981. 225.00 (ISBN 0-521-08708-2). Cambridge U Pr.
Camilleri's Dictionary of Musical Terms. Charles Camilleri. (Eng.). 1980. Can.$pap. 4.95 (ISBN 0-88909-039-4). Waterloo.
Canadian Dictionary-French-English. Jean-Paul Vinay et al. (Fr. & Eng.). 1962. Can.$8.95 (ISBN 0-7710-8715-2); 5.95 (ISBN 0-7710-8715-2). McClelland.
Canadian Intermediate Dictionary. Walter S. Avis. (Illus.). 1980. Can.$12.95 (ISBN 0-7715-1982-6). U of Toronto Pr.
Canadian Junior Dictionary. 2nd ed. Walter S. Avis et al. 1976. Can.$14.95 (ISBN 0-7715-1989-3); 10.50 (ISBN 0-7715-1988-5). U of Toronto Pr.
Canigo Diccionari Castella-Catala, Catala-Castella. 878p. (Span. & Catala.). pap. 17.95 (ISBN 84-303-0089-9, S-31565). French & Eur.
Canigo: Dicionario Catalan-Castellano, Castellano-Catalan. Pere Elies I Busqueta. LC 75-508636. (Illus.). 877p. (Catalan & Span.). 1975. write for info. (ISBN 8-430-30089-9). Sopena.
Canine Terminology. Harold R. Spira. (Illus.). 147p. 1983. 29.95 (ISBN 0-06-312047-X). Howell Bk.
Cantonese Dictionary: Cantonese-English, English-Cantonese. Parker P. Huang. LC 72-110727. (Illus., Chinese & Eng.). 1970. text ed. 50.00x (ISBN 0-300-01293-4). Yale U Pr.
Cantonese Dictionary: Cantonese-English, English-Cantonese. Parker Po-fei Huang. 489p. (Chinese.). 1970. 45.00 (ISBN 0-300-01293-4). Yale U Pr.
Cantonese Speaker's Dictionary. Roy T. Cowles. 1600p. (Chinese.). 1965. text ed. 27.50x (ISBN 0-8188-0139-5). Paragon.
Capire l'Economiea: Dizionario Critico del Capitalismo Contemporaneo. Renzo Stefanelli. LC 78-337064. (Ital.). 1977. L.5500.00. De Donato.
Capitol's Concise Dictionary. 1416p. (Eng. , Swedish , Dutch , Ger. , Ital. & Span.). 1972. 35.95 (ISBN 84-7183-079-5, S-50438). French & Eur.
Capitol's Concise Dictionary of Seven Languages. (gr. 9-12). 1978. 29.95 (ISBN 0-8120-5333-8). Barron.
Cappelens Musikkeleksikon. Ed. by Kari Michelsen et al. LC 78-386996. (Illus., Norwegian.). 1978. Kr.330.00 (ISBN 8-202-03690-9). J W Cappelens.
Captive Vocabulary. Robert Greenman. (Illus.). 187p. 1980. pap. text ed. 4.50 (ISBN 0-912853-01-8). NY Times.
Car Builder's Dictionary. Ed. by Matthias Forney. (Illus.). 544p. 1971. Repr. of 1879 ed. lib. bdg. 14.95 buckram (ISBN 0-912318-16-3). N K Gregg.
Caribbean Cookery. P. De Brissiere. (Chinese & Eng.). pap. 3.95 (ISBN 0-87557-100-X, 100-X). Saphrograph.
Carriage Terminology: An Historical Dictionary. Don H. Berkebile. LC 77-118. (Illus.). 487p. 1979. 35.00x (ISBN 0-87474-166-1). Smithsonian.
Cassell's Colloquial French. Cassell. 160p. (Fr.). pap. 3.95 (ISBN 0-02-079420-7). Macmillan.
Cassell's Colloquial German. Cassell. 176p. (Ger.). pap. 3.95 (ISBN 0-02-079410-X). Macmillan.
Cassell's Colloquial Italian. Cassell. 192p. (Ital.). pap. 3.95 (ISBN 0-02-079440-1). Macmillan.
Cassell's Colloquial Spanish. Cassell. 304p. (Span.). pap. 4.95 (ISBN 0-02-079430-4). Macmillan.
Cassell's Compact French-English, English-French Dictionary. 672p. (Fr. & Eng.). 1981. pap. 3.95 (ISBN 0-440-31128-4, LE). Dell.
Cassell's Compact Spanish-English Dictionary. 444p. (Span. & Eng.). 1981. pap. 2.95 (ISBN 0-440-31129-2, LE). Dell.
Cassell's Concise French-English, English-French Dictionary. abr. ed. Ed. by J. H. Douglas et al. LC 77-7667. 658p. (Fr. & Eng.). 1977. 9.95 (ISBN 0-02-522670-3). Macmillan.
Cassell's Concise Latin-English, English-Latin Dictionary. abr. ed. Compiled by D. P. Simpson. LC 77-7660. (Lat. & Ger.). 1977. 9.95 (ISBN 0-02-522630-4). Macmillan.
Cassell's Concise Spanish-English English-Spanish Dictionary. (Span. & Eng.). 1977. 9.95 (ISBN 0-02-522660-6). Macmillan.
Cassell's Dutch Dictionary: English-Dutch Dutch-English. Cassell. 1364p. (Eng. & Dutch.). 34.95 (ISBN 0-02-522940-0). Macmillan.
Cassell's Dutch Dictionary: English-Dutch, Dutch-English. F. P. Van Wely. LC 77-81889. (Eng. & Dutch.). 1978. 19.95 (ISBN 0-02-522890-0). Macmillan.
Cassell's French Dictionary. Ed. by Denis Girard et al. LC 77-7669. (Fr.). 1977. indexed 18.95 (ISBN 0-02-522620-7); plain 16.50 (ISBN 0-02-522610-X). Macmillan.
Cassell's French Dictionary: Concise French-English English-French. Cassell. (Fr. & Eng.). 9.95 (ISBN 0-02-522670-3). Macmillan.
Cassell's French Dictionary: French-English, English-French. (Fr. & Eng.). standard 17.95 (ISBN 0-02-522610-X); thumb-indexed 19.95 (ISBN 0-02-522620-7); concise 9.95 (ISBN 0-02-522670-3). Macmillan.
Cassell's French Dictionary: French-English, English-French. Rev. ed. Denis Girard et al. 1436p. (Eng. & Fr.). 1977. 16.95; indexed 18.95. Imported Bks.
Cassell's French Dictionary: Standard French-English English-French. Cassell. (Fr. & Eng.). 17.95 (ISBN 0-02-522610-X). Macmillan.
Cassell's French Dictionary: Thumb-indexed French-English English-French. Cassell. (Fr. & Eng.). 19.95 (ISBN 0-02-522620-7). Macmillan.
Cassell's German Dictionary: German-English, English-German. (Ger. & Eng.). standard 17.95 (ISBN 0-02-522920-6); thumb-indexed 19.95 (ISBN 0-02-522930-3); concise 9.95 (ISBN 0-02-522650-9). Macmillan.
Cassell's German-English, English-German Dictionary. H. T. Betteridge. (Eng. & Ger.). 1978. 16.95; indexed 18.95. Imported bks.
Cassell's Italian Dictionary: Italian-English, English-Italian. Cassells et al. LC 77-7405. (Ital. & Eng.). 1977. index 23.95 (ISBN 0-02-522540-5); plain 19.95 (ISBN 0-02-522530-8). Macmillan.
Cassell's Italian Dictionary: Italian-English, English-Italian. Rev. ed. Piero Rebora et al. 1150p. (Eng. & Ital.). 1979. 16.95; indexed 18.95. Imported bks.
Cassell's Italian Dictionary: Standard Italian-English English-Italian. Cassell. (Ital. & Eng.). 17.95 (ISBN 0-02-522530-8). Macmillan.
Cassell's Italian Dictionary: Thumb-indexed Italian-English English-Italian. Cassell. (Ital. & Eng.). 19.95 (ISBN 0-02-522540-5). Macmillan.
Cassell's Latin Dictionary: Concise Latin-English English-Latin. Cassell. (Lat. & Eng.). 9.95 (ISBN 0-02-522630-4). Macmillan.
Cassell's Latin Dictionary: Latin-English, English Latin. Cassell. Ed. by D. P. Simpson. (Lat. & Eng.). standard 17.95 (ISBN 0-02-522570-7); thumb-indexed 19.95 (ISBN 0-02-522580-4); concise 9.95 (ISBN 0-02-522630-4). Macmillan.
Cassell's Latin Dictionary: Latin-English, English-Latin. D. P. Simpson. 883p. (Eng. & Lat.). 1979. indexed 18.95. Imported Bks.
Cassell's Latin Dictionary: Latin-English, English-Latin. Ed. by D. P. Simpson. (Lat. & Eng.). 1977. indexed 18.95 (ISBN 0-02-522580-4); plain 16.95 (ISBN 0-02-522570-7). Macmillan.
Cassell's Latin Dictionary: Standard Latin-English English-Latin. Cassell. (Lat. & Eng.). 17.95 (ISBN 0-02-522570-7). Macmillan.
Cassell's New Compact German Dictionary. 560p. (Ger.). 1981. pap. 3.95 (ISBN 0-440-31100-4, LE). Dell.
Cassell's New Compact German-English, English-German Dictionary. 542p. (Eng. & Ger.). pap. 3.00. Dell.
Cassell's New Compact Latin Dictionary. 384p. (Lat.). 1981. pap. 3.95 (ISBN 0-440-31101-2, LE). Dell.
Cassell's New Dutch Dictionary: English-Dutch, Dutch-English. Cassell. 729p. (Eng. & Dutch.). 1982. 34.95 (ISBN 0-02-522940-0). Macmillan.
Cassell's New Latin-English, English-Latin Dictionary. (Eng. & Lat.). pap. 3.00. Dell.
Cassell's Spanish Dictionary. (Span. & Eng.). 16.95 (7744-4). Natl Textbk.
Cassell's Spanish Dictionary: Concise Spanish-English English-Spanish. Cassell. (Span. & Eng.). 9.95 (ISBN 0-02-522660-6). Macmillan.
Cassell's Spanish Dictionary: English-Spanish, Spanish-English. (Span. & Eng.). write for info. (608-35). Pan Amer Pub.
Cassell's Spanish Dictionary: Spanish-English, English-Spanish. Cassell. Ed. by Edqan A. Peers. (Span. & Eng.). standard 17.95 (ISBN 0-02-522900-1); thumb-indexed 19.95 (ISBN 0-02-522910-9); concise 9.95 (ISBN 0-02-522660-6). Macmillan.
Cassell's Spanish Dictionary: Spanish-English, English-Spanish. Ed. by Edgar A. Peers. LC 77-7403. (Span. & Eng.). 1977. 18.95 (ISBN 0-02-522910-9); plain 16.95 (ISBN 0-02-522900-1). Macmillan.
Cassell's Spanish Dictionary: Thumb-indexed Spanish-English English-Spanish. Cassell. (Span. & Eng.). 19.95 (ISBN 0-02-522910-9). Macmillan.
Cat in the Hat Beginner Book Dictionary. P. D. Eastman. LC 64-1157. (Illus.). (gr. k-6). 1964. 5.95 (ISBN 0-394-81009-0). Beginner.
Cat in the Hat Beginner Book Dictionary in English & Spanish. P. D. Eastman. LC 66-10688. (Illus., Span. & Eng.). (gr. k-3). 1966. 8.95 (ISBN 0-394-81542-4); PLB 8.99 (ISBN 0-394-91542-9). Beginner.
Cat in the Hat Beginner Book Dictionary in French & English. P. D. Eastman. LC 65-22650. (Illus., Fr. & Eng.). (gr. 2-3). 1965. 8.95 (ISBN 0-394-81063-5). Beginner.
Cat in the Hat Beginner Book Dictionary in Spanish & English. (Span. & Eng.). 8.95. Lectorum Pubns.
Cavity Classification & Related Terminology. Ann Ehrlich. (Illus.). 1978. 4.25 (ISBN 0-940012-04-9). Colwell Co.
CB Fact Book & Language Dictionary. William J. Bradley. (Illus.). pap. 1.95 (ISBN 0-89552-011-7). DMR Pubns.
CB Picture Dictionary. Joan Murray. LC 80-1725. (Illus.). 64p. (gr. 5 up). PLB 8.95a (ISBN 0-385-14783-X). Doubleday.
Cebuano-Visayan Dictionary. Elsa P. Yap & Maria V. Bunye. Ed. by Howard P. McKaughan. LC 74-152461. (PALI Language Texts: Philippines). 576p. (Orig.). 1971. pap. text ed. 14.00x (ISBN 0-87022-093-4). UH Pr.
Cement & Concrete Terminology. ACI Committee 116. 1978. pap. 12.95 (ISBN 0-685-85102-8, SP-19). ACI.
Cement & Concrete Thesaurus. 1969. pap. 14.95 (ISBN 0-685-85158-3, CCT). ACI.

Census of French & Provencal Dialect Dictionaries in American Libraries. Linguistic Society of America & C. M. Woodard. 2.00. Linguistic Soc Am.
Central European Geneological Terminology. Jared H. Suess. LC 80-112612. xi, 168p. (Eng.). 1978. write for info. Everton Pubs.
Ceramic Collectors' Glossary. Edwin A. Barber. LC 76-8172. (Architecture & Decorative Art Ser). 1967. Repr. of 1914 ed. 16.50 (ISBN 0-306-70521-4). Da Capo.
Ceramic Furniture & Silver Collectors' Glossary. Edward A. Barber & Luke V. Lockwood. (Architecture & Decorative Art Ser.). 1976. pap. 6.95 (ISBN 0-306-80049-7). Da Capo.
Cesko-Francouzsky Technicky Slovnik. Libuse Vomackova. LC 80-458243. 907p. (Czech. & Fr.). 1978. 95.00. SNTC.
Cesko-Italsky Slovnik na Cesty. Hana Benesova. LC 76-532562. (Illus.). 288p. (Czech. & Ital.). 1976. 17.00 Kcs. SNTC.
Cesko-Rumunsky & Rumunsko-Cesky Slovnik na Cesty. Jiri Felix. LC 80-451473. 328p. (Czech. & Romanian.). 1979. 18.00 Kcs. SNTC.
Cesko-Rusky Slovnik na Cesty, 2 vols. Marta Vencovska. LC 77-563463. (Illus., Czech. & Rus.). 1976. 20.00 Kcs. SNTC.
Cesko, Slovensko, Latinsko, Anglicko, Nemecko, Rusky, Slovnik Plevelu. Vaclav Kosik. LC 76-507633. 149p. (Czech., Slovak, Lat., Eng., Ger. & Rus.). 1975. write for info. SNTC.
Cesky a Sovensky Terminologicky Slovnik z Fytopatologie a Ochrany Rostlin. LC 79-356902. 392p. (Czech. & Slovak.). 1977. write for info. SNTC.
Chaldean Arabic, English Picture Dictionary. (Arabic & Eng.). pap. 4.95x (ISBN 0-86685-132-1). Intl Bk Ctr.
Chambers Biographical Dictionary. Ed. by J. O. Thorne & T. C. Collocott. LC 78-56110. 1974. 25.00 (ISBN 0-8467-0510-9, Pub. by Two Continents). Am Map.
Chambers Compact Dictionary. LC 77-83851. 1978. 3.95 (ISBN 0-8467-0394-7, Pub. by Two Continents). Am Map.
Chambers Dictionary of Science & Technology. (Illus.). 1978. 25.00 (ISBN 0-8467-0520-6, Pub. by Two Continents); pap. 10.95 (ISBN 0-8467-0530-3). Am Map.
Chambers Dictionary of Science & Technology. 1983. 39.95 (ISBN 0-686-40769-5, Pub by Salem Hse Ltd); pap. 22.95 (ISBN 0-686-40770-9). Merrimack Pub Cir.
Chambers' English Dictionary. Ed. by T. C. Collocott. (Quality Paperback: No. 166). 380p. 1965. pap. 2.95 (ISBN 0-8226-0166-4). Littlefield.
Chambers Everyday Dictionary. LC 77-84354. 1978. 6.95 (ISBN 0-8467-0395-5, Pub. by Two Continents); pap. text ed. 3.95 (ISBN 0-8467-0396-3). Am Map.
Chambers Mini Dictionary. 1983. pap. 3.95 (ISBN 0-686-40772-5, Pub by Salem Hse Ltd). Merrimack Pub Cir.
Chambers Mini Dictionary. Ed. by E. M. Fitzgerald. 1980. pap. 2.95 (ISBN 0-550-10701-0, Pub. by W. R. Chambers). Hippocrene Bks.
Chambers Murray Latin-English Dictionary. 3rd ed. Ed. by William Smith & J. L. Lockwood. (Lat. & Eng., Totally Recast Version). 1976. Repr. of 1934 ed. 15.75x (ISBN 0-06-496367-5). B&N Imports.
Chambers Scots Dictionary. Alexander Warrack. (Gaelic.). Repr. of 1911 ed. 14.95 (ISBN 0-550-11801-2, Pub. by Two Continents). Am Map.
Chambers Second Learners' Dictionary. Ed. by E. M. Kirkpatrick et al. LC 78-325064. viii, 376p. (Eng.). 1978. E1.50 (ISBN 0-550-10631-6). W & R Chambers.
Chambers Twentieth Century Dictionary. LC 77-83852. 1978. 10.95 (ISBN 0-8467-0393-9, Pub. by Two Continents). Am Map.
Chambers Twentieth Century Dictionary. 1983. 19.95 (ISBN 0-686-40766-0, Pub. by Michael Joseph). Merrimack Pub Cir.
Chambers Universal Learners' Dictionary. Ed. by E. M. Kirkpatrick. 928p. 1980. 25.00x (ISBN 0-550-10632-4, Pub. by W & R Chambers Scotland). State Mutual Bk.
Chamorro-English Dictionary. Donald M. Topping et al. LC 74-16907. (PALI Language Texts: Micronesian). 365p. (Orig., Chamorro & Eng.). 1975. pap. text ed. 10.00x (ISBN 0-8248-0353-1). UH Pr.
Charlie Brown Dictionary. Charles M. Schulz. (gr. 1 up). 1977. pap. 5.95 (ISBN 0-590-09898-5). Scholastic Inc.
Chartering & Shipping Terms: Time-Sheet Supplements, Vols. 2 & 3. J. Bes. Set. 70.00 (ISBN 0-685-11999-8). Heinman.
Chastonyi Slovar' Russkogo Iazyka. 936p. (Rus.). 1976. 7.50 (D-97A). Four Continent.
Chastotnyi Anglo-Russkii Fizicheskii Slovar Minimum. P. M. Alekseev et al. 288p. (Rus. & Eng.). 1980. 4.75 (Pub. by Voenizdat). Four Continent.
Chastotnyi Anglo-Russkii Slovar Minimum Po Sudovozhdeniiu. K. F. Lukianenkov. 200p. (Rus. & Eng.). 1977. 3.95 (Pub. by Voenizdat). Four Continent.
Chastotnyi Slovar Obschenauchnoi Leksiki. M. I. Zykina et al. 85p. (Rus.). 1970. 1.00 (Pub. by MGU). Four Continent.
Chastotnyi Slovar Russkogo Iazyka. 936p. (Rus.). 1977. 7.50 (Pub. by Russkii Iazyk). Four Continent.
Chastotnyi Slovar Semanticheskikh Mnozhitelei Russkogo Iazyka. Ed. by Iu. N. Karaulov. 208p. (Orig., Rus.). 1980. 3.25 (Pub. by Nauka). Four Continent.
Checklists for Vocabulary Study. Richard Yorkey. (English As a Second Language Bk.). (Illus.). 1981. pap. text ed. 4.65x (ISBN 0-582-79767-5). Longman.
Chemehuevi: A Grammar & Lexicon. Margaret L. Press. (U. C. Publications in Linguistics Ser.: Vol. 92). 1980. pap. 16.50x (ISBN 0-520-09600-2). U of Cal Pr.
Chemical Control Legislation Glossary. OECD. 170p. 1982. pap. 13.50x (ISBN 92-64-12364-4). OECD.
Chemical Dictionary. 3rd ed. J. Fouchier & F. Billet. (Fr., Ger. & Eng.). 1972. 106.50 (ISBN 0-444-41090-2). Elsevier.
Chemical Technology Dictionary: English, French-German-Arabic. A. M. Abd-El-Wahed. 383p. (Eng., Fr., Ger. & Arabic.). 1974. 45.00 (ISBN 0-686-92502-5, M-9759). French & Eur.
Chemical Terms for Washroom Procedures. International Fabricare Institute. (Special Reporter-Laundry Library). 1.00. Intl Fabricare Inst.
Chemie & Chemische Technik. 2nd ed. Helmut Gross & Helmut Hildebrand. LC 77-550181. (Rus. & Ger.). 1976. M.48.00. VEB Verlag Technik.
Chemie & Chemische Technik Englisch-Deutsch. 720p. (Eng. & Ger.). 1978. M.70.00. VEB Technik.
Chemie & Chemische Technik Russisch-Deutsch. Helmut Gross. 832p. (Rus. & Ger.). 1980. M.48.00. VEB Technik.
Chemie: Ein Lexikon der Gesamten Schulchemie. Hans Borucki et al. 424p. (Ger.). DM.19.80 (ISBN 3-411-01367-2). Biblio Inst.
Chemins de Fer Glossary. Bureau International de Documentation de Chemin de Fer. (Fr., Ger., Ital., Span. & Swedish.). 1960. 13.50 (ISBN 0-444-40751-0). Elsevier.
Chemisch-Technisches Lexikon. Dieter Osteroth & Walter G. Von Baeckmann. LC 79-385912. xi, 304p. (Eng. & Ger.). 1979. write for info. (ISBN 0-387-08891-1). Springer-Verlag.
Chemistry. William L. Masterton et al. 1980. text ed. write for info. (ISBN 0-03-056214-7, CBS C). SCP.
Cheshsko-Russkii Radiotekhnicheskii Slovar. B. E. Iakovlev. 364p. (Rus. & Czech.). 1960. 2.95 (Pub. by Glav. Red. Inostr. Nauchn. Tekhn. Slovarei Fizmata). Four Continent.
Chetyre Tys Acha Naibolee Upotrebitel Nykh Slov Russkogo Iazyka. N. M. Shanskii. 368p. (Rus.). 1978. 6.50 (O-36). Four Continent.
Chetyrekhiazychnyi Entsiklopedicheskii Slovar Terminov Po Fizicheskoi Geografii. M. Shchukin. 368p. (Rus.). 1978. 6.50 (Pub. by Russkii Iaxyknt Bk). Four Continent.
Chihabi's Dictionary of Agricultural & Forestry Terms. Ahmed Khatib. (Illus.). 300p. (Eng. & Arabic.). 1978. 40.00 (072-4). Intl Bk Ctr.
Children's Dictionary. LC 78-27636. (Illus.). (gr. 3-6). 1979. 11.95 (ISBN 0-395-27512-1). HM.
Children's Dictionary. Christine Maxwell. 480p. write for info. Wheaton.
Children's Dictionary. George Ulrich. (Illus., Eng.). 1979. 12.95 (ISBN 0-395-28978-5). HM.
Child's Dictionary of Jewish Symbols. Alex J. Goldman. (Illus.). (gr. 1-4). 5.00 (ISBN 0-685-09470-7). Feldheim.
Child's First Picture Dictionary. Lillian Moore. (Illus.). 48p. 1970. 1.95 (ISBN 0-448-02248-6, G&D). Putnam Pub Group.
China Beginner's Traveler's Dictionary. Richard L. Kimball. (Chinese.). 1980. pap. 6.95 (ISBN 0-8351-0732-9). China Bks.
China Beginner's Traveler's Dictionary. Richard L. Kimball. 154p. 6.95 (ISBN 0-8351-0732-9). Eurasia Pr NY.
China Traveler's Phrasebook. Bennett Lee & Geremie Barme. (Chinese.). 1980. pap. 5.95 (ISBN 0-8351-0729-9). China Bks.
Chinese Characters. 2nd ed. Leon Wieger. Tr. by L. Davrout. (Chinese.). 1965. 22.50 (ISBN 0-8188-0094-1). Paragon.
Chinese Characters, Their Origin, Etymology, History, Classification & Signification. 2nd ed. L. Wieger. Tr. by L. Davrout. (Chinese.). 1927. pap. 12.50 (ISBN 0-486-21321-8). Dover.
Chinese Dictionaries: An Extensive Bibliography of Dictionaries in Chinese & Other Languages. Ed. by Chinese-English Translation Assistance Group. LC 82-923. xvi, 448p. (Chinese & Eng.). 1982. lib. bdg. 49.95 (ISBN 0-313-23505-8, MDC/). Greenwood.
Chinese Dictionary: Cantonese Dialect, 3 pts. Ernes J. Eitel. (Chinese.). 1976. Repr. of 1958 ed. 140.00 (ISBN 0-518-19009-9). Ayer Co.
Chinese-English & English-Chinese Astronomical Dictionary. Ed. by Hong-Yee Chiu. LC 65-10966. 173p. (Chinese & Eng.). 1966. 30.00x (ISBN 0-306-10739-2, Consultants). Plenum Pub.
Chinese-English Dictionary. 12.00 (ISBN 0-685-00818-5, 007-0). Saphrograph.
Chinese-English Dictionary. 976p. (Chinese & Eng.). 1981. 49.95 (ISBN 962-07-0005-8, M-9400). French & Eur.
Chinese-English Dictionary. 976p. (Chinese & Eng.). 1982. 30.00x (ISBN 0-8044-0097-0). Ungar.
Chinese-English Dictionary. 976p. (Chinese & Eng.). 1979. pap. 60.00x (ISBN 0-686-44768-9, Pub. by Collets). State Mutual Bk.
Chinese-English Dictionary. Samuel W. Williams. (Eng. & Chinese.). 1976. Repr. of 1958 ed. 65.00 (ISBN 0-518-19007-2). Ayer Co.
Chinese-English Dictionary: A Chinese-English Dictionary Compiled for the China Inland Mission. rev. ed. Robert H. Mathews. (Harvard-Yenching Institute Publications Ser.). 1250p. 1943. text ed. 32.50x (ISBN 0-674-12350-6). Harvard U Pr.
Chinese-English Dictionary: Hakka-Dialect. D. MacIver. (Chinese & Eng.). 1982. Repr. of 1926 ed. 35.00 (ISBN 0-89986-344-2). Oriental Bk Store.
Chinese-English Dictionary of China's Rural Economy. (Chinese & Eng.). 1979. 70.00 (ISBN 0-85198-381-2, CAB 6, CAB). Unipub.
Chinese-English Dictionary of Communist Chinese Terminology. Dennis Doolin & Charles Ridley. LC 70-170210. (Publications Ser.: No. 124). 569p. (Chinese & Eng.). 1973. 30.00x (ISBN 0-8179-6241-7). Hoover Inst Pr.
Chinese-English Dictionary of Contemporary Usage. Ed. by Chi Wen-Shun. (Chinese & Eng.). 1977. 27.50x (ISBN 0-520-02655-1). U of Cal Pr.
Chinese-English Dictionary of Currenct Affairs. 594p. (Chinese & Eng.). 1977. leatherette 25.00 (ISBN 0-686-92562-9, M-9247). French & Eur.
Chinese-English Dictionary of Military Terms. 366p. (Chinese & Eng.). 1977. 25.00 (ISBN 0-686-97446-8, M-9275). French & Eur.
Chinese-English Dictionary of Military Technical Terms. LC 80-112476. 206p. (Eng. & Chinese.). 1979. write for info. S.N.
Chinese-English Dictionary of Physical Terms. S. Chang. 405p. (Eng. & Ger.). 1969. pap. 75.00 (ISBN 0-686-56601-7, M-7322, Pub. by Harrassowitz). French & Eur.
Chinese-English Dictionary: Taiwan Dialect. K. T. Tan. (Chinese & Eng.). 1978. 50.00 (ISBN 0-89986-342-6). Oriental Bk Store.
Chinese-English, English-Chinese Dictionary, 2 vols. (Chinese & Eng.). Set. 40.00 (ISBN 0-685-79110-6). Heinman.
Chinese-English Expressions for Travellers. 90p. (Chinese & Eng.). 1983. pap. 3.95 (ISBN 0-8044-6993-8). Ungar.
Chinese-English Glossary of the Mathematical Sciences. Compiled by J. De Francis. 286p. (Chinese & Eng.). 1964. 42.20 (ISBN 0-8218-0018-3, UMI-2004670); pap. 37.20 members. Am Math.
Chinese-English Idioms & Phrases. S. M. Season. 311p. (Chinese & Eng.). 1978. leatherette 14.95 (ISBN 0-686-92616-1, M-9246). French & Eur.
Chinese-English-Japanese Glossary of Chemical Terms. T. Shiratori. (Chinese, Eng. & Japanese.). write for info. (M-9351). French & Eur.
Chinese-English-Japanese Glossary of Chemical Terms. S. Tamura & F. Shiratori. 661p. (Chinese, Eng. & Japanese.). 1977. 49.95 (ISBN 962-04-0028-3, M-9263). French & Eur.
Chinese-English Phrase Book for Travellers. John S. Montanaro. 304p. (Chinese & Eng.). 1981. pap. 8.95 (ISBN 0-471-08298-8, Pub. by Wiley Pr). Wiley.
Chinese Idioms, English Idioms, English Synonyms Practical Dictionary. S. S. Wei. (Chinese & Eng.). 17.50 (ISBN 0-686-31874-9). Heinman.
Chinese Medical Terminology: English to Chinese. F. Liu & L. Yan Mau. 262p. (Chinese & Eng.). 1980. 24.95 (ISBN 962-07-3000-3). French & Eur.
Chinese Pocket Dictionary. (Chinese & Eng.). 15.00 (ISBN 0-686-77962-2). Heinman.
Chinese-Russian Phonetic Dictionary. 319p. (Chinese & Rus.). 1957. leatherette 4.95 (ISBN 0-686-92615-3, M-9126). French & Eur.
Chinese Unicorn & Other Conceits from a Chinese Dictionary. Ed. & intro. by Robert Gilkey. (Eng. & Chinese.). 1973. pap. 3.95 (ISBN 0-686-02625-X). Noname Pr.

Chinesisch-Deutsches Woerterbuch. 3rd ed. Martin Piasek. (Chinese & Ger.). 1975. 28.95 (ISBN 0-686-56599-1, 7320, Pub. by Max Heuber). French & Eur.

Chinesisch-Deutsches Woerterbuch. 3rd ed. Martin Piasek. (Chinese & Ger.). 1975. DM.28.95. Hueber.

Chinesisch-Deutsches Woerterbuch. 3rd ed. Werner Rudenberg. 821p. (Chinese & Ger.). 1963. 196.00x (ISBN 0-686-56600-9, M-7321). De Gruyter.

Chinesisch-Koreanisch-Deutsch Woerterbuch. Andre Eckardt. 224p. (Chinese, Ger. & Korean.). 1966. write for info. (ISBN 3-87276-115-3). Groos Verlag.

Chord Dictionary. Albert DeVito. LC 75-40685. 1980. 4.95 (ISBN 0-934286-01-9). Kenyon.

Christian Counselor's Wordbook. Jay E. Adams. 1981. pap. 1.95 (ISBN 0-8010-0172-2). Baker Bk.

Christian Student Dictionary. (Illus.). 862p. 1982. text ed. 12.95 (ISBN 0-89084-172-1). Bob Jones Univ Pr.

Chronological English Dictionary. Listing 80,000 Words in Order of Their Earliest Known Occurrence. Thomas Finkenstaedt. 1412p. 1970. 120.00x (ISBN 3-533-02076-2). Intl Pubns Serv.

Cibernetical Dictionary: E-G-F-R-Slovene. A. Sydow. 171p. (Eng., Ger., Fr., Rus. & Slovene.). 1974. 75.00 (ISBN 0-686-92219-0, M-9895). French & Eur.

Cicero Vocabularies. Paul E. Kunzer. (Bk. I Iv). 1.00 ea. (NO. B10). Am Classical.

Cinco Mil Seiscientos Refranes & Frases de Uso Comun Entre los Dominicanos. Jose A. Brache. Ed. by Nicolas Pichardo. LC 80-100004. xiv, 311p. (Span.). 1978. write for info. Galaxia.

Cinema Vuol Dire. Maurizio Porro & Giuseppe Turroni. LC 79-372048. 219p. (Ital.). 1979. L.2500.00. Garzanti Edit.

CIS Online User Guide & Thesaurus. Ed. by Congressional Information Service, Inc. Staff. 400p. 1982. loose-leaf 75.00 (ISBN 0-686-43131-6). Cong Info.

City & Country Purchaser & Builder's Dictionary. Richard Neve. LC 69-16762. Repr. of 1726 ed. 19.50x (ISBN 0-678-05616-1). Kelley.

Civic & Corporate Heraldry: A Dictionary of Impersonal Arms of England, Wales, & Northern Ireland. Ed. by Geoffrey Briggs. (Illus.). 432p. 1971. 32.00x (ISBN 0-685-29194-4). Gale.

Civil Service Arithmetic & Vocabulary. Barbara Erdsneker & Margaret Haller. LC 81-7988. 256p. 1981. lib. bdg. 12.00 (ISBN 0-668-05116-7, 4872-7); pap. 8.00 (ISBN 0-668-04872-7). Arco.

Civil Service Vocabulary. Jack Rudman. (Career Examination Ser.: C-S 10). (Cloth bdg. avail. on request). pap. 6.00 (ISBN 0-8373-3760-7). Natl Learning.

Civil War Dictionary. Mark M. Boatner, 3rd. (Illus., Maps & diagrams). 25.00 (ISBN 0-679-50013-8). McKay.

Classical Dictionary, 2 vols. J. A. Lempriere. Set. lib. bdg. 250.00 (ISBN 0-87968-878-5). Gordon Pr.

Classical Dictionary of India, 2 vols. in 1. John Garrett. 1973. Repr. of 1873 ed. 51.50 (ISBN 0-8337-1289-6). B Franklin.

Classical Dictionary of the Vulgar Tongue. facsimile ed. Francis Grose. Ed. by E. Partridge. LC 70-179523. (Select Bibliographies Reprint Ser). Repr. of 1963 ed. 21.00 (ISBN 0-8369-6652-X). Ayer Co.

Classical Myth & Legend in Renaissance Dictionaries. DeWitt T. Starnes & Ernest W. Talbert. LC 73-11753. (Illus.). 517p. 1973. Repr. of 1955 ed. lib. bdg. 39.75x (ISBN 0-8371-7086-9, STCM). Greenwood.

Classified Concordance, 4 vols. Eliezer Katz. Incl. Vol. 1. Torah. 415p. 1964. 25.00x (ISBN 0-8197-0382-6); Vol. 2. Early Prophets. 702p. 1967. 20.00x (ISBN 0-8197-0383-4); Vol. 3. Later Prophets. 683p. 1970. 20.00x (ISBN 0-8197-0384-2). Bloch.

Classified Concordance: To the Bible & Its Various Subjects, Vol. 4. Ed. by Eliezer Katz. 1000p. (Hebrew & Eng.). 1974. 30.00x (ISBN 0-8197-0385-0). Bloch.

Classified French Vocabulary. H. H. Baker. 96p. (Fr.). Epap. 1.75. Harrap.

Classified Spanish Vocabulary. G. J. Chayne. LC 78-670001. 1964. text ed. 16.95x (ISBN 0-245-55575-7). Intl Ideas.

Claves de la Masoneria. Emilio Castell Blanch. LC 78-391684. (Illus.). 576p. (Span.). 1978. 300.00 ptas (ISBN 8-472-35344-3). Dopesa.

Cleburne County, Arkansas Word List see Use of the Dictionary of American English & the Dictionary of Americanisms.

Clinical Spanish for Dietitians. Judy Shalhoub & Carol Murray. (Illus.). 161p. 1977. text ed. 6.95x (ISBN 0-916434-30-3). Plycon Pr.

Co-operator's Dictionary: Basic List of Co-operative & Commercial Terms for Use at Primary Level in Developing Countries. Compiled by Anne Lamming. LC 77-3716170. 59p. (Eng.). 1977. E1.00 (ISBN 0-904380-26-2). Intl Coop All.

Cochran's Law Lexicon. 5th ed. Wesley Gilmer. LC 72-95860. 429p. 1973. Repr. text ed. 9.00 (ISBN 0-87084-148-3). Anderson Pub Co.

Code Names Dictionary: A Guide to Code Names, Slang, Nicknames, Journalese, & Similar Terms. Ed. by Frederick G. Ruffner, Jr. & Robert C. Thomas. LC 63-21847. 1963. 38.00x (ISBN 0-8103-0685-9). Gale.

Cold Extrusion & Upsetting see Dictionary of Production Engineering: German-English-French.

Collection of College Words & Customs. Benjamin H. Hall. LC 68-17995. 1968. Repr. of 1856 ed. 42.00x (ISBN 0-8103-3282-5). Gale.

Collection of Vocabularies of Central African Languages, 2 vols. Ed. by Heinrich Barth. 1971. Repr. of 1862 ed. Set. 120.00x (ISBN 0-7146-1914-0, F Cass Co). Biblio Dist.

Collector's Dicionary of Quilt Names & Patterns. Yvonne M. Khin. LC 80-14246. (Illus.). 512p. 1980. 24.95 (ISBN 0-87491-408-6); pap. 18.95 (ISBN 0-87491-409-4). Acropolis.

Collector's Glossary. 3rd ed. John R. Bernasconi. 24.50 (ISBN 0-900361-34-4). Transatlantic.

Collector's Glossary of Antiques & Fine Arts. J. R. Bernasconi. (Illus.). 1971. 17.50x (ISBN 0-900361-34-4). Intl Pubns Serv.

College Vocabulary Skills. 2d ed. James F. Shepherd. 1983. pap. text ed. 11.50 (ISBN 0-395-32811-X); instr's. manual 2.00 (ISBN 0-395-32812-8). HM.

Collegiate Dictionary of Zoology. Robert W. Pennak. 1964. 29.95x (ISBN 0-471-06790-3, Pub. by Wiley-Interscience). Wiley.

Collins Contemporary Dictionary: English-Spanish, Spanish-English. (Span & Eng.). write for info. (608-64). Pan Am Bk Co.

Collins English Learner's Dictionary. Ed. by D. J. Carver et al. 640p. 1974. 13.95x (ISBN 0-00-433111-7, Pub. by Collins ELT Scotland). State Mutual Bk.

Collins English Learner's Dictionary. 622p. (Eng.). write for info. (ISBN 91-24-25707-9). Esselte Studium.

Collins English-Spanish & Spanish-English Dictionary. 1242p. (Eng. & Span.). write for info. (ISBN 0-671-41939-0); write for info. thumb-indexed (ISBN 0-671-41938-2). S&S.

Collins French-English English-French Dictionary. 512p. (Orig., Fr. & Eng.). 1982. pap. 2.95 (ISBN 0-425-05449-7). Berkley Pub.

Collins GEM Dictionary: Portuguese-English, English-Portuguese. 768p. (Port. & Eng.). 3.95. Imported Bks.

Collins German Dictionary: German-English, English-Ger. Peter Terrell et al. 1600p. (Ger. & Eng.). 1980. 20.00. Imported Bks.

Collins German-English & English-German Dictionary. 1582p. (Ger. & Eng.). write for info. (ISBN 0-671-42046-1); write for info. thumb-indexed (ISBN 0-671-42045-3). S&S.

Collins German-English English-German Dictionary. 416p. (Orig., Ger. & Eng.). 1983. pap. 2.95 (ISBN 0-425-05450-0). Berkley Pub.

Collins German-English, English-German Dictionary. P. Terrel et al. 790p. (Ger. & Eng.). 19.95 (ISBN 0-671-42045-3); pap. 8.95 (ISBN 0-671-42046-1, M-9309). French & Eur.

Collins Italian-English English-Italian Dictionary. 416p. (Orig., Ital. & Eng.). 1983. pap. 2.95 (ISBN 0-425-05451-9). Berkley Pub.

Collins Pocket French Dictionary. 528p. 1983. 7.95 (ISBN 0-671-49220-9). S&S.

Collins Pocket German Dictionary. 448p. 1983. 7.95 (ISBN 0-671-49222-5). S&S.

Collins Pocket Spanish Dictionary. 448p. 1983. 7.95 (ISBN 0-671-49221-7). S&S.

Collins-Robert Concise French-English & English-French Dictionary. 960p. (Fr. & Eng.). 10.95 (ISBN 0-671-44958-3). S&S.

Collins Robert Dictionary: French-English-English-French. Ed. by B. T. Atkins et al. A. Duval & R. C. Milnet. (Fr. & Eng.). 16.95 (ISBN 0-686-28358-9, CFD1); thumb index avail. (ISBN 0-00-433479-5). Collins Pubs.

Collins Robert French-English & English-French Dictionary. 1498p. (Fr. & Eng.). write for info. (ISBN 0-671-41935-8); write for info. thumb-indexed (ISBN 0-671-41936-6). S&S.

Collins-Robert French-English Dictionary. Beryl T. Atkins et al. LC 79-359393. xxix, 717p. (Eng. & Fr.). 1978. write for info. (ISBN 0-00-433478-7). W Collins Pubs.

Collins-Robert French-English, English-French dictionary. Beryl T. Atkins et al. LC 79-359393. xxix, 781p. (Fr. & Eng.). 1978. E9.95 (ISBN 0-00-433479-5). W Collins Sons.

Collins Robert French-English, English-French Dictionary. 1490p. (Fr. & Eng.). 1978. 19.00; indexed 20.00. Imported Bks.

Collins Spanish Dictionary: English-Spanish, Spanish-English. (Span. & Eng.). write for info. indexed (608-23). Pan Amer Pub.

Colloquial Arabic: An Oral Approach. Raja Nasr. (Arabic.). 1968. 11.00x (ISBN 0-86685-044-9). Intl Bk Ctr.

Color Atlas of Pediatric Dermatology. Julian Verbov & Neil Morley. (Illus.). 157p. 1983. text ed. 47.50 (ISBN 0-397-58287-0, Lippincott Medical). Lippincott.

Color Dictionary of Flowers & Plants for Home & Garden. Roy Hay & Patrick M. Synge. (Illus.). 584p. 1982. pap. 11.95 (ISBN 0-517-52456-2). Crown.

Columbia Dictionary of Modern European Literature. 2nd ed. Ed. by Jean-Albert Bede & William Edgerton. 800p. 1980. 55.00x (ISBN 0-231-03717-1). Columbia U Pr.

Coming to Terms. Josephine Miles. LC 79-18235. 1979. 10.00 (ISBN 0-252-00767-0); pap. 5.95 (ISBN 0-252-00768-9). U of Ill Pr.

Coming to Terms: From Alpha to X-Ray, a Lexicon for the Science-Watcher. Wayne Biddle. 128p. 1982. 4.95 (ISBN 0-380-61093-0, 61093-0). Avon.

Coming to Terms: Lexicon for the Science Watcher. Wayne Biddle. LC 80-54198. (Illus.). 128p. 1981. 8.95 (ISBN 0-670-33092-2). Viking Pr.

Commercial & Financial Dictionary in Four Languages. rev. 4th ed. Jozef V. Servotte. Orig. Title: Dictionnaire Commercial et Financier en 4 Langues. 968p. (Fr., Dutch, Eng. & Ger.). 1972. 52.50x (ISBN 90-02-11109-6). Intl Pubns Serv.

Common English Words & Idioms with Their Equivalents in Bahasa Indonesia. A. Karim. (Indonesian.). 1978. pap. 8.50 (ISBN 0-8048-1283-7). C E Tuttle.

Communications Standard Dictionary. Martin H. Weik. 928p. 1982. text ed. 29.50 (ISBN 0-442-21933-4). Van Nos Reinhold.

Communism-English Dictionary. Roy Colby. 123p. 1973. pap. 1.00 pocketsize (ISBN 0-88279-030-7). Western Islands.

Compact Dictionary of Canadian English. Thomas Paikeday. 1976. pap. 4.25 (ISBN 0-03-923309-X). HRW.

Compact Dictionary of Exact Science & Technology, Vol. 1. A. Kucera. 590p. E16.50 (ISBN 0-245-53605-1). Harrap.

Compact Dictionary of Exact Science & Technology: Band I, English-German. Kucera. xix, 571p. (Eng. & Ger.). 1982. DM.55.00. Brandstetter.

Compact Dictionary of Exact Science & Technology: Band II, German-English. Kucera. xiv, 826p. (Ger. & Eng.). 1982. DM.70.00. Brandstetter.

Compact Dictionary of Exact Science & Technology: English-German. A. Kucera. 571p. (Eng. & Ger.). 1980. 49.95 (ISBN 3-87097-088-X, M-9027). French & Eur.

Compacto Diccionario de la Lengua Espanola. 440p. (Span.). 9250.00 ptas. Biblograf SP.

Compacto Diccionario de la Lengua Espanola "Vox". 440p. (Span.). 1982. pap. 195.00 ptas (ISBN 8-47153-203-4). Biblograf.

Compacto Diccionario Ingles-Espanol Espanol-Ingles. 608p. (Eng. & Span.). 9295.00 ptas. Biblograf SP.

Compacto Diccionario Ingles-Espanol, Espanol-Ingles Vox. 608p. (Span. & Eng.). 1982. 195.00 ptas (ISBN 8-47153-204-2). Biblograf.

Companion Volume to R. H. Mathews' Chinese-English Dictionary. 2nd ed. Olov B. Anderson. LC 78-320299. 335p. (Chinese & Eng.). 1978. E7.50 (ISBN 9-144-15221-3) (ISBN 0-7007-0081-1). Curzon Pr.

Comparative Dictionary of the Finno-Ugric Elements in the Hungarian Vocabulary. Jozsef Budenz. LC 66-64927. (Uralic & Altaic Ser: Vol. 78). (Finnish & Hungarian., Repr. of 1881 ed). 1966. pap. text ed. 22.00x (ISBN 0-87750-029-0). Res Ctr Lang Semiotic.

Comparative Dictionary of the Indo-Aryan Languages. Sir Ralph Turner. (Indo-Aryan.). 1966. text ed. 74.00x (ISBN 0-19-713550-1). Oxford U Pr.

Comparative Dictionary of the Languages of India & High Asia. W. W. Hunter. 218p. 1978. Repr. of 1868 ed. 26.00x (ISBN 0-89684-144-8). Orient Bk Dist.

Comparative Dictionary of the Tahitian Language: Tahitian-English with an English-Tahitian Finding List. Edmund Andrews & Irene D. Andrews. LC 75-35171. (Eng. & Tahitian.). Repr. of 1944 ed. 23.00 (ISBN 0-404-14201-X). AMS Pr.

Comparative Glossary of Accounting Terms in Canada, the United Kingdom & the United States. Accountants International Study Group. 1975. 3.50 (333). Can Inst Chart Accts.

Comparative Trilby Glossary, French-English. James Schonberg. 60p. (Fr. & Eng.). 1983. Repr. of 1895 ed. lib. bdg. 30.00 (ISBN 0-89984-614-9). Century Bookbindery.

Comparative Vocabulary of Aubuan Dialects. Hans Wolff. 293p. 1969. 5.95x (ISBN 0-89771-003-7). State Mutual Bk.

Comparative Word List of the Mabuso Languages, Madang Province, Papua New Guinea. J. A. Z'graggen. LC 82-106653. xv, 184p. (Mabuso.). 1980. pap. write for info. (ISBN 0-85883-228-3). Linguistic Circle.

Comparative Word List of the Northern Adelbert Range Languages, Madang Province, Papua New Guinea. J. A. Z'graggon. LC 82-106653. xvii, 178p. (Papuan & Madang.). 1980. pap. write for info. (ISBN 0-85883-228-3). Linguistic Circle.

Comparative Word List of the Rai Coast Languages, Madang Province, Papua New Guinea. J. A. Z'graggen. LC 82-106696. (Illus.). xv, 181p. (Papuan & Madang.). 1980. pap. write for info. (ISBN 0-85883-232-1). Linguistic Circle.

Comparative Word List of the Southern Adelbert Range Languages, Madang Province, Papua New Guinea. J. A. Z'graggen. LC 82-106836. (Illus.). xvi, 97p. (Papuan & Madang.). 1980. pap. write for info. (ISBN 0-85883-234-8). Linguistic Circle.

Compendio de Dificultades de la Lengua Inglesa. J. Pineiro. 276p. (Eng. & Span.). 1978. 9695.00 ptas (ISBN 84-7153-367-7). Biblograf SP.

Compendio de dificultades de la lengua inglesa. Jaime Pineiro. 276p. (Span. & Eng.). 1978. pap. write for info. (ISBN 84-7153-227-1). Fed Gremios.

Compendios de Divulgacion Filologica, 11 vols. Incl. Vol. 1. Ortografia Practica Espanola. S. Gili Gaya. 104p. pap. 195.00 ptas (ISBN 84-7153-255-7); Vol. 2. Resumen Practico de Gramatica Espanola. S. Gili Gaya. 112p ptas (ISBN 84-7153-256-5); Vol. 3. Nociones de Gramatica Historica Espanola. S. Gili Gaya. 104p. pap. 195.00 ptas (ISBN 84-7153-257-3); Vol. 5. Resumen Practico de Gramatica Francesa. 132p. pap. 195.00 ptas (ISBN 84-7153-263-8); Vol. 7. Ortografia Practica Francesa. 240p. pap. 250.00 ptas (ISBN 84-7153-264-6); Vol. 8. Ortografia Practica Catalana. 126p. pap. 225.00 ptas (ISBN 84-7153-266-2); Vol. 9. Vocabulario Basico Infantil. 64p. pap. 195.00 ptas (ISBN 84-7153-369-3). (Span.). Biblograf.

Compendious Anglo-Saxon & English Dictionary. Joseph Bosworth. 1979. Repr. of 1860 ed. lib. bdg. 30.00 (ISBN 0-89341-478-6). Longwood Pr.

Compendious Syriac Dictionary Founded Upon the Thesaurus Syriacus of R. Payne Smith. R. Payne Smith. Ed. by J. Payne Smith. (Syriac.). 1903. 85.00x (ISBN 0-19-864307-1). Oxford U Pr.

Compilation of ASTM Standard Definitions. 1976. 24.75 (ISBN 0-686-52047-5, 03-508076-42). ASTM.

Compilation of Chinese Dictionaries. J. Mathias & Sandra Hixson. (Chinese.). 1975. 4.50 (ISBN 0-88710-020-1). Far Eastern Pubns.

Complete Categorized Greek-English New Testament Vocabulary. David Holly. 141p. (Eng. & Gr.). 1978. 12.50 (ISBN 0-85150-119-2). Attic Pr.

Complete Categorized Greek-English New Testament Vocabulary. David Holly. (Gr. & Eng.). 1980. pap. 6.95 (ISBN 0-8010-4224-0). Baker Bk.

Complete CB Dictionary. Ed. by APR Industries Division of Aero Products Research, Inc. 1977. pap. 2.98 (ISBN 0-912682-17-5). Aero Products.

Complete CB Slang Dictionary. 3rd ed. Michael Jacobs. 1977. pap. 1.50 (ISBN 0-89596-208-X, Success). Merit Pubns.

Complete Concordance to Shakespeare. Mary Cowden-Clark. 1973. lib. bdg. 65.00 (ISBN 0-8414-2398-9). Folcroft.

Complete Concordance to the Poetical Works of John Milton. Charles D. Cleveland. LC 76-57784. 1867. lib. bdg. 25.00 (ISBN 0-8414-3459-X). Folcroft.

Complete Concordance to the Writings of Mary B. Eddy. 27.00 (ISBN 0-87952-092-2). First Church.

Complete Concordances & Texts of the Fourteenth-Century Aragonese Manuscripts of Juan Fernandez de Heredia. John Nitti & Lloyd Kasten. (Dialect Ser.: No. 2). 1982. 125.00 (ISBN 0-942260-18-X). Hispanic Seminary.

Complete Dictionary of Abbreviations. Robert J. Schwartz. 9.95i (ISBN 0-690-20620-8). T Y Crowell.

Complete Dictionary of Astrology. Leo. 7.95 (Inner Traditions). Am Fed Astrologers.

Complete Dictionary of Music. Jean J. Rousseau. LC 72-1664. Repr. of 1779 ed. 30.00 (ISBN 0-404-08335-8). AMS Pr.

Complete Dictionary of Wood. Thomas Corkhill. LC 79-10183. (Illus.). 672p. 1982. pap. 14.95 (ISBN 0-8128-6142-6). Stein & Day.

Complete Dictionary of Wood. Thomas Corkhill. LC 79-10183. (Illus.). 664p. 1980. 19.95 (ISBN 0-8128-2708-2). Stein & Day.

Complete English-Hebrew Dictionary, 2 vols. Rueben Alcalay. 2150p. (Eng. & Hebrew.). 1981. IL.60.00 set; Vol. I, A-L. (35-2093); Vol. II, M-Z. (35-2094). Massada Pr.

Complete English-Hebrew, Hebrew-English Dictionary, 3 vols. Reuben Alcalay. 7180p. (Eng. & Hebrew.). 1980. Repr. of 1965 ed. 69.00 set (ISBN 0-89961-017-X). Vol. 1 (ISBN 0-89961-003-X). Vol. 2 (ISBN 0-89961-007-2). Vol. 3 (ISBN 0-89961-008-0). SBS Pub.

Complete English-Maori Dictionary. Ed. by Bruce Biggs. (Eng. & Maori.). 1981. 29.95x (ISBN 0-19-647989-4). Oxford U Pr.

Complete Enochian Dictionary. Donald C. Laycock. LC 80-476863. 272p. (Eng. & Enochian.). 1978. write for info. (ISBN 0-905919-01-7). Askin Pub.

Complete Glossary for Sir Walter Scott's Novels & Romances. Sir Walter Scott. Repr. of 1833 ed. 18.50 (ISBN 0-8337-4743-6). B Franklin.

Complete Glossary to the Poetry & Prose of Robert Burns. John Cuthbertson. 1886. 22.50 (ISBN 0-8337-0747-7). B Franklin.

Complete Guide to Country Living. Suzanne Beedell & Barbara Hargreaves. 19.95 (ISBN 0-7153-7665-9). David & Charles.

Complete Hebrew Dictionary in Seven Volumes. Ed. by Abraham Even-Shoshan. (Illus.). 3236p. (Eng. & Hebrew.). text ed. 140.00 (ISBN 965-17-0083-1). K Sefer.

Complete Hebrew Dictionary in Three Volumes. Ed. by Abraham Even-Shoshan. (Illus.). 1664p. (Eng. & Hebrew.). text ed. 80.00 (ISBN 965-17-0084-X). K Sefer.

Complete Hebrew Dictionary Supplement to the 3 Volume Set. Ed. by Abraham E. Shoshan. (Illus.). 352p. (Hebrew.). 1983. 25.00 (ISBN 9-651-7015-60). K Sefer.

Complete Hebrew Dictionary Supplement Volume to Seven Volume Set. Ed. by Abraham E. Shoshan. (Illus.). 352p. (Hebrew.). 1983. 30.00 (ISBN 9-651-7015-52). K Sefer.

Complete Hebrew-English Dictionary. Rueben Alcalay. 1456p. (Hebrew & Eng.). 1981. IL.43.00 (35-2091). Massada Pr.

Complete Manual of Maori Grammar & Conversation, with Vocabulary. 5th rev. enl. ed. Apirana N. Ngata. LC 75-35261. (Maori.). Repr. of 1939 ed. 19.00 (ISBN 0-404-14433-0). AMS Pr.

Complete Rhyming Dictionary. Ed. by Clement Wood. 1936. 10.95 (ISBN 0-385-00046-4). Doubleday.

Complete Sports Dictionary. George Sullivan. (YA) (gr. 7-12). 1979. pap. 1.95 (ISBN 0-590-05731-6). Scholastic Inc.

Complete Welsh-English, English-Welsh Dictionary. Y Geiriadur Mawr. 8th ed. H. Meurig Evans & W. O. Thomas. (Welsh & Eng.). 1979. text ed. 30.50x (ISBN 0-391-01734-9). Humanities.

Complete Word & Phrase Concordance to the Poems & Songs of Robert Burns. J. B. Reid. LC 68-58477. (Bibliography & Reference Ser.: No. 252). 1969. Repr. of 1889 ed. 30.50 (ISBN 0-8337-2932-2). B Franklin.

Complete Word-Finder Crossword Dictionary. Bruce Weeterau. 1981. pap. 3.95 (ISBN 0-451-09910-9, E9910, Sig). NAL.

Comprehensive English-Hindi Dictionary of Governmental & Educational Words & Phrases. Raghu Vira. 1761p. (Eng. & Hindi.). 1976. 40.00x (ISBN 0-8002-0664-9). Intl Pubns Serv.

Comprehensive English-Hindi Dictionary, 2 vols. rev. 2nd ed. Hardev Bahri. 2200p. (Eng. & Hindi.). 1969. 40.00x (ISBN 0-8002-0533-2). Intl Pubns Serv.

Comprehensive Etymological Dictionary of the English Language. Ernest Klein. 1971. 85.00 (ISBN 0-444-40930-0). Elsevier.

Comprehensive Forkner Shorthand Dictionary. rev. ed. Frances A. Brown. LC 81-66122. 297p. (gr. 10-12). 1982. text ed. 11.84x (ISBN 0-912036-37-0). Forkner.

Comprehensive German Dictionary. 1104p. (Ger. & Eng.). 42.50 (02120). Langenscheidt.

Comprehensive Lao-English Dictionary, 2 vols. Allen Kerr. (Lao & Eng.). 42.00. Iaconi.

Comprehensive Old-English Dictionary. Arthur R. Borden, Jr. LC 81-40837. 1612p. 1982. lib. bdg. 101.75 (ISBN 0-8191-2254-8). U Pr of Amer.

Comprehensive Persian-English Dictionary. F. Steingass. 1540p. (Persian & Eng.). 1975. 65.00x (ISBN 0-86685-130-5). Intl Bk Ctr.

Comprehensive Persian-English Dictionary. F. Steingass. (Persian & Eng.). 1973. 35.00x (ISBN 0-88386-187-9). South Asia Bks.

Comprehensive Signed English Dictionary. Ed. by Harry Bornstein & Karen L. Saulnier. LC 82-21044. (Illus.). x, 454p. 1983. 24.95 (ISBN 0-913580-81-3). Gallaudet Coll.

Computer Dictionary. 3rd ed. Charles J. Sippl & Roger J. Sippl. LC 79-91696. 1980. pap. 15.95 (ISBN 0-672-21652-3, 21652). Sams.

Computer Dictionary. 2nd ed. Donald D. Spencer. LC 78-31738. 1979. pap. 6.95 (ISBN 0-89218-038-2). Camelot Pub.

Computer Dictionary: A User-Friendly Guide to Language, Terms, & Jargon. Ed. by John Prenis. (Illus.). 128p. 1983. lib. bdg. 12.90 (ISBN 0-89471-232-2); pap. 4.95 (ISBN 0-89471-231-4). Running Pr.

Computer Dictionary for Everyone. Donald Spencer. 1981. pap. 5.95 (ISBN 0-684-16946-0, ScribT). Scribner.

Computer Dictionary for Everyone. rev. ed. Donald D. Spencer. 1980. 11.95 (ISBN 0-684-16305-5, ScribT). Scribner.

Computer Glossary for Students & Teachers. Larry C. Schmalz & Charles J. Sippl. (Apollo Eds.). pap. 3.25i (ISBN 0-8152-0411-6, A-411). T Y Crowell.

Computer Glossary: It's Not Just a Glossary. 3rd ed. Alan Freedman. (Illus.). 324p. 1983. 14.95 (ISBN 0-941878-02-3). Computer Lang.

Computer Glossary: It's Not Just a Glossary. Alan Freedman & Irma L. Morrison. 320p. 1983. pap. 14.95 (ISBN 0-13-164483-1). P-H.

Computer Graphics Glossary. Stuart W. Hubbard. LC 82-42918. 96p. 1983. pap. 18.50 (ISBN 0-89774-072-6). Oryx Pr.

Computer Networks Terminology. J. Maronski & M. Rupinska. 73p. 1980. pap. 7.50 (ISBN 83-01-01179-3, M-9061). French & Eur.

Computer Terms. John Prenis. LC 77-343. (Orig.). 1977. lib. bdg. 12.90 (ISBN 0-914294-75-X); pap. 2.95 (ISBN 0-914294-76-8). Running Pr.

Computerized Lexicon of Tamazight: Berber Dialect of Ayt Seghrouchen. Ernest T. Abdel-Massih. LC 77-32220. (Berber.). 1971. pap. text ed. 9.00x (ISBN 0-932098-06-1). Ctr for NE & North African Stud.

COMVOC, the Louis A. Allen Common Vocabulary of Professional Management. 5th ed. Louis A. Allen. LC 79-110056. vii, 108p. (Eng.). 1978. write for info. Palo Alto, Ca.

Concept Dictionary of English. Julius Laffal. LC 72-97927. 1973. text ed. 16.95 (ISBN 0-686-77072-2). Gallery Pr.

Concise American Heritage Dictionary. American Heritage Staff. LC 76-4047. 1980. 6.95 (ISBN 0-395-24522-2). HM.

Concise Amharic Dictionary. Wolf Leslau. LC 73-90668. (Amharic.). 1976. 69.50x (ISBN 0-520-02660-8). U of Cal Pr.

Concise Anglo-Saxon Dictionary. 4th ed. John R. Hall & Herbert D. Meritt. 1961. 59.95 (ISBN 0-521-05179-7). Cambridge U Pr.

Concise Arabic Dictionary. Al Wafi & Butros Bustani. (Arabic.). 1980. 40.00x (ISBN 0-86685-095-3). Intl Bk Ctr.

Concise Cambodian-English Dictionary. J. Jacob. (Cambodian & Eng.). 59.00. Iaconi.

Concise Cambodian-English Dictionary. Judith Jacob. (Eng. & Khmerz.). 1974. 59.00x (ISBN 0-19-713574-9). Oxford U Pr.

Concise Cambridge Italian Dictionary. Barbara Reynolds. (Ital.). 1974. 44.50 (ISBN 0-521-07273-5). Cambridge U Pr.

Concise Cambridge Italian Dictionary. Barbara Reynolds. 792p. (Ital.). 1975. pap. 8.95 (ISBN 0-14-051064-8). Penguin.

Concise Chemical & Technical Dictionary. 3rd ed. Ed. by Harry Bennett. 1974. 56.50 (ISBN 0-8206-0026-1). Chem Pub.

Concise Chinese - English Dictionary Romanized. James C. Quo. LC 60-14372. (Chinese & Eng.). 1961. 4.95 (ISBN 0-8048-0116-9). C E Tuttle.

Concise Chinese-English Dictionary Romanized. James Quo. (Chinese & Eng.). 4.95. Iaconi.

Concise Chinese-English Dictionary, Romanized. James C. Quo. 225p. (Chinese & Eng.). pap. 7.75 pocket size. C E Tuttle.

Concise Coptic-English Lexicon. Richard H. Smith. 81p. 1983. 10.95x (ISBN 0-8028-3581-3). Eerdmans.

Concise Dictionary of American History. David W. Voorhees. LC 82-43721. 1140p. 1983. lib. bdg. 60.00 (ISBN 0-684-17321-2, ScribR). Scribner.

Concise Dictionary of American Language. Ed. by Arthur Waldhorn. 1956. 4.50 (ISBN 0-8022-1793-1). Philos Lib.

Concise Dictionary of Atomics. Ed. by Alfred Del Vecchio. LC 64-13328. 1964. 6.00 (ISBN 0-8022-1771-0). Philos Lib.

Concise Dictionary of Business Terminology. Albert G. Giordano. 464p. 1981. text ed. 14.95 (ISBN 0-13-166553-7, Spec); pap. text ed. 5.95 (ISBN 0-13-166546-4). P-H.

Concise Dictionary of Chemistry & Chemical Technology. 128p. 1975. 30.00x (ISBN 0-686-44771-9, Pub. by Collets). State Mutual Bk.

Concise Dictionary of Christian Ethics. Ed. by Bernard Stoeckle. 1979. 19.50 (ISBN 0-8245-0300-7). Crossroad NY.
Concise Dictionary of Correct English. Ed. by B. A. Phythian. (Littlefield, Adams Quality Paperback Ser.: No. 349). 1979. pap. 5.50 (ISBN 0-8226-0349-7). Littlefield.
Concise Dictionary of Correct English. Ed. by B. A. Phythian. 166p. 1979. 12.50x (ISBN 0-8476-6212-8). Rowman.
Concise Dictionary of Education. Gene R. Hawes & Lynne S. Hawes. (Hudson Group Bk.). 256p. 1982. text ed. 18.95 (ISBN 0-442-26298-1). Van Nos Reinhold.
Concise Dictionary of English Idioms. rev ed. William Freeman. 1976. pap. 5.95 (ISBN 0-87116-094-3). Writer.
Concise Dictionary of English-Swahili Idioms. Abdilahi Nassir. LC 76-980032. (Eng. & Swahili.). 1975. write for info. Shungways Publishers.
Concise Dictionary of Foreign Expressions. Ed. by B. A. Phythian. LC 82-13895. 158p. 1982. text ed. 15.50x (ISBN 0-389-20327-0). B&N Imports.
Concise Dictionary of Indian Tribes of North America. Barbara A. Leitch. Ed. by Kendall LePoer. LC 78-21347. 1980. 59.95 (ISBN 0-917256-09-3). Ref Pubns.
Concise Dictionary of Islamic Terms. M. A. Qazi. (Eng. & Arabic.). pap. 6.95 (276-X). Intl Bk Ctr.
Concise Dictionary of Islamic Terms: English-Arabic. 1979. 6.95x (ISBN 0-86685-276-X). Intl Bk Ctr.
Concise Dictionary of Judaism. Ed. by Dagobert D. Runes. LC 77-88933. 124p. Repr. of 1966 ed. lib. bdg. 65.00 (ISBN 0-8371-2109-4, RUDJ). Greenwood.
Concise Dictionary of Literary Terms. Harry Shaw. (McGraw-Hill Paperbacks). Orig. Title: Dictionary of Literary Terms. 224p. 1976. pap. 4.95 (ISBN 0-07-056483-3, SP). McGraw.
Concise Dictionary of Medicine. M. W. Martin. LC 74-23215. (Illus.). 1975. 8.95 (ISBN 0-8246-0193-9). Jonathan David.
Concise Dictionary of Middle Egyptian. R. O. Faulkner. 348p. (Egyptian.). 1976. 37.00x (ISBN 0-900416-32-7, Pub. by Griffith Inst). State Mutual Bk.
Concise Dictionary of Middle English from A. D. 1150-1580. A. L. Mayhew & W. W. Skeat. LC 77-20783. (Middle English.). 1888. lib. bdg. 25.00 (ISBN 0-8414-6220-8). Folcroft.
Concise Dictionary of Middle English from A.D. 1150 to 1580. A. I. Mayhew & Walter W. Skeat. LC 78-3583. xv, 272p. (Eng.). 1978. 35.00 (ISBN 0-8482-4963-1). Norwood Edns.
Concise Dictionary of Old Icelandic. Geir T. Zoega. (Icelandic.). 1910. 39.00x (ISBN 0-19-863108-1). Oxford U Pr.
Concise Dictionary of Physics: And Related Subjects. 2nd ed. J. Thewlis. LC 79-40209. 1979. 65.00 (ISBN 0-08-023048-2). Pergamon.
Concise Dictionary of Scottish Painters. Paul Harris. LC 76-364800. 1976. 6.50x (ISBN 0-904505-08-1). Intl Pubns Serv.
Concise Dictionary of Spoken Chinese. Yuen R. Chao & Lien-Sheng Yang. LC 47-5464. (Harvard-Yenching Institute Publications Ser). 1947. 17.50x (ISBN 0-674-15800-8). Harvard U Pr.
Concise Dictionary of the Assyrian Languages, 2 vols. William Muss-Arnolt. LC 78-72752. (Ancient Mesopotamian Texts & Studies). (Assyrian.). Repr. of 1905 ed. 97.50 set (ISBN 0-404-18195-3). AMS Pr.
Concise Dictionary of the English & Modern Greek Languages. A. N. Jannaris. xvi, 436p. (Eng. & Gr.). 1981. lib. bdg. 35.00x (ISBN 0-89241-333-6); pap. text ed. 20.00x (ISBN 0-89241-339-5). Caratzas Pub Co.
Concise Dictionary of Twenty-Six Languages. Peter M. Bergman. 408p. (Eng.). pap. 2.50 indexed. Imported Bks.
Concise Dictionary of Twenty-Six Languages in Simultaneous Translation. P. H. Bergman. pap. 2.95 (ISBN 0-451-11478-7, AE1478, Sig). NAL.
Concise Dictionary Portuguese-English. Michaelis. (Port. & Eng.). 25.00. Iaconi.
Concise Electronics Dictionary. Georg Moellerke. LC 75-332199. 149p. (Eng. & Ger.). 1975. 16.00 F. A T Fachverlag.
Concise Encyclopedia of Computer Terminology. Adrian V. Stokes. 289p. 1980. text ed. 37.50x (ISBN 0-905897-32-3). Gower Pub Ltd.
Concise English-Chinese Dictionary. rev. ed. Shau Wing Chan. (Eng. & Chinese.). 1955. pap. 6.95x (ISBN 0-8047-0384-1). Stanford U Pr.
Concise English-Chinese Dictionary. 1211p. (Eng. & Chinese.). 1962. 9.95 (ISBN 0-686-92460-6, M-9563). French & Eur.
Concise English-Chinese Dictionary. James C. Quo. LC 55-11585. (Eng. & Chinese.). 1960. 4.95 (ISBN 0-8048-0117-7). C E Tuttle.
Concise English-Chinese Dictionary Romanized. James Quo. (Chinese & Eng.). 4.95. Iaconi.
Concise English-Chinese Dictionary, Romanized. James C. Quo. 324p. (Eng. & Chinese., Avail. in Chinese characters). pap. 7.75. Imported Bks.
Concise English Hindi Dictionary. R. C. Pathak. (Eng. & Hindi.). 1979. 6.50 (ISBN 0-89744-972-X). Auromere.
Concise English-Hungarian Dictionary, 2 vols. Orszagh Laszlo. 1052p. (Eng. & Hungarian.). 1981. Vol. 1: Eng.-Hunagarian. 24.00 Ft. Vol. 2: Hungarian-Eng. 31.00. Akademiai Kiado.
Concise English-Hungarian Dictionary. V. Orszagh. 1091p. (Eng. & Hungarian.). 1980. 50.00 (ISBN 0-569-00407-1, Pub. by Collet's). State Mutual Bk.
Concise English-Italian Italian-English Dictionary. Ed. by Giuseppe Ragazzini & Adele Biagi. LC 73-17088. 1214p. (Eng. & Ital.). 1973. pap. text ed. 12.95x (ISBN 0-582-55505-1). Longman.
Concise English-Korean Dictionary Romanized. Underwood. (Korean & Eng.). 3.95. Iaconi.
Concise English-Korean Dictionary Romanized. Joan V. Underwood. LC 55-5891. (Eng. & Korean.). 1960. 3.95 (ISBN 0-8048-0118-5). C E Tuttle.
Concise English-Mongolian Dictionary. John G. Hangin. (Uralic & Altaic Ser: Vol. 89). (Eng. & Mongolian.). 1970. pap. text ed. 11.50x (ISBN 0-87750-079-7). Res Ctr Lang Semiotic.
Concise English-Polish & Polish-English Dictionary. T. Grzebieniowski. 688p. (Pol. & Eng.). 10.95. Barron.
Concise English-Russian, Russian-English Dictionary. S. G. Zaimovskii. 464p. (Eng. & Rus.). 1980. 20.00x (ISBN 0-569-06089-3, Pub. by Collet's). State Mutual Bk.
Concise English-Russian Technical Dictionary. Desov. (Eng. & Rus.). 5.50. Imported Bks.
Concise English-Slovak & Slovak-English Technical Dictionary. J. Novak & R. Binder. 610p. (Eng. & Slovak.). 1980. 45.00x (ISBN 0-569-07469-X, Pub. by Collet's). State Mutual Bk.
Concise English-Slovak & Slovak-English Technical Dictionary. 3rd ed. J. Novak & R. Binder. 610p. (Eng. & Slovak.). 1971. 39.00x (ISBN 0-569-07469-X, Pub. by Collets). State Mutual Bk.
Concise English-Swedish Dictionary of Legal Terms. Ed. by Andre Bruzelius et al. 175p. (Eng. & Swedish.). 39.95 (ISBN 0-686-80959-9). French & Eur.
Concise English-Tagalog Dictionary. Panganiban. (Tagalog & Eng.). 9.50. Iaconi.
Concise English-Tagalog Dictionary. J. Villar Panganiban. LC 69-13501. (Eng. & Tagalog.). 1969. bds. 9.50 (ISBN 0-8048-0119-3). C E Tuttle.
Concise English-Tagalog Dictionary. Jose Villa Panganiban. 170p. (Eng. & Tagalog.). 1969. 10.75. Imported Bks.
Concise Etymological Dictionary of Chemistry. Stanley C. Bevan et al. ix, 140p. 1976. 18.50 (ISBN 0-85334-653-4, Pub. by Applied Sci England). Elsevier.
Concise Etymological Dictionary of the English Language. Ed. by Walter W. Skeat. 1911. 26.50x (ISBN 0-19-863105-7). Oxford U Pr.
Concise French-American Dictionary of Figurative & Idiomatic Language. Perreau & Langford. (Fr. & Eng.). 17.95 (ISBN 0-685-36686-3). French & Eur.
Concise Glossary of Terms Used in Grecian, Roman, Italian, & Gothic Architecture. John Henry Parker. 1980. Repr. of 1896 ed. lib. bdg. 35.00 (ISBN 0-89341-372-0). Longwood Pr.
Concise Handbook of Linguistics. Ed. by Daniel J. Steible. LC 67-11578. 1967. 6.00 (ISBN 0-8022-1635-8). Philos Lib.
Concise Hebrew & Aramaic Lexicon of the Old Testament. William L. Holladay. (Hebrew & Aramaic.). 1971. 20.00 (ISBN 0-8028-3413-2). Eerdmans.
Concise Hindi-English Dictionary. R. C. Pathak. (Eng. & Hindi.). 1979. 6.50 (ISBN 0-89744-971-1). Auromere.
Concise Hungarian-English Dictionary. V. Orszagh. 1180p. (Hungarian & Eng.). 1980. 50.00x (ISBN 0-569-00343-1, Pub. by Collet's). State Mutual Bk.
Concise Illustrated Russian-English Dictionary of Mechanical Engineering. V. V. Shvarts. (Illus.). 224p. (Rus. & Eng.). 1981. pap. 30.00 (ISBN 0-08-027574-5). Pergamon.
Concise Illustrated Russian-English Dictionary of Mechanical Engineering. Vladimir Shvarts. 224p. (Rus. & Eng.). 1980. 35.00x (ISBN 0-686-44774-3, Pub. by Collets). State Mutual Bk.
Concise Manchu-English Lexicon. Jerry Norman. LC 77-14307. (Publications on Asia of the School for International Studies: No. 32). 336p. (Manchu & Eng.). 1979. 25.00x (ISBN 0-295-95574-0). U of Wash Pr.
Concise Maori Dictionary. (Eng., Auckland, New Zealand). 1980. NT.$3.95. Reed Ltd.
Concise Maori Handbook. Ed. by A. W. Reed & A. E. Brougham. LC 80-497775. (Illus.). 587p. (Eng. & Maori.). 1978. pap. write for info. (ISBN 0-589-01111-1). Reed Ltd.
Concise Oxford Dictionary of Ballet. 2nd ed. Horst Koegler. (Illus.). 1982. pap. 14.95 (ISBN 0-19-311330-9). Oxford U Pr.
Concise Oxford Dictionary of Current English. 7th ed. Ed. by J. B. Sykes. 1982. 19.95 (ISBN 0-19-861131-5); Thumb-Indexed 24.95 (ISBN 0-19-861132-3). Oxford U Pr.
Concise Oxford Dictionary of Music. 3rd ed. Ed. by Michael Kennedy. (Illus.). 1980. 22.50 (ISBN 0-19-311315-5); pap. 9.95 (ISBN 0-19-311320-1). Oxford U Pr.
Concise Oxford Dictionary of Opera. 2nd ed. Ed. by Harold Rosenthal & John Warrack. 1979. 29.95 (ISBN 0-19-311318-X). Oxford U Pr.
Concise Oxford Dictionary of Opera. 2nd ed. Ed. by Harold Rosenthal & John Warrack. (Out-of-Ser. Paperback). 1979. pap. 12.95 (ISBN 0-19-311321-X). Oxford U Pr.
Concise Oxford Dictionary of Quotations. new ed. 1982. pap. 8.95 (ISBN 0-19-281324-2). Oxford U Pr.
Concise Oxford Dictionary of the Christian Church. Ed. by E. A. Livingstone. 1978. 19.95 (ISBN 0-19-211549-9); pap. 9.95 (ISBN 0-19-283014-7). Oxford U Pr.
Concise Oxford French Dictionary. Ed. by H. Ferrar et al. (Fr.). 1980. 27.50 (ISBN 0-19-864126-5). Oxford U Pr.
Concise Oxford French Dictionary: French-English, English-French. H. Ferrar et al. 863p. (Eng. & Fr.). 24.00. Imported Bks.
Concise Oxford Turkish Dictionary. Ed. by A. D. Alderson & Fahir Iz. (Turkish.). 1959. 29.00x (ISBN 0-19-864109-5). Oxford U Pr.
Concise Polish-English-English-Polish Dictionary. Iwo Pogonowski. 436p. (Orig., Pol. & Eng.). 1983. pap. 3.95 (ISBN 0-88254-799-2). Hippocrene Bks.
Concise Swedish-English Glossary of Legal Terms. Torild Backe et al. 164p. (Swedish & Eng.). 1973. text ed. 13.50x (ISBN 0-8377-0305-0). Rothman.
Conciso Diccionario de la Lengua Espanola. 304p. (Span.). 250.00 ptas (ISBN 84-7153-236-0); pap. 150.00 ptas (ISBN 84-7153-234-4). Biblograf SP.
Conciso Diccionario de la Lengua Espanola "Vox". 304p. (Span.). 1982. pap. 125.00 ptas (ISBN 8-47153-234-4). Biblograf.
Conciso Diccionario Ingles-Espanol, Espanol-Ingles Vox. 316p. (Eng. & Span.). 1982. 125.00 ptas (ISBN 8-47153-235-2). Biblograf.
Conciso Diccionario Ingles-Espanol Espanol-Ingles. 316p. (Eng. & Span.). 250.00 ptas (ISBN 84-7153-237-9); pap. 165.00 ptas (ISBN 84-7153-235-2). Biblograf SP.
Concordance of the Bible. Solomon Mendelkern. (Hebrew & Lat.). 1977. Repr. of 1896 ed. 14.50 (ISBN 0-685-81426-2). Feldheim.
Concordance of Ugaritic. Douglas Young. vii, 73p. (Ugaritic & Eng.). 1956. L.5300.00. Pont Ist Biblico.
Concordance to Beowulf. Ed. by J. B. Bessinger, Jr. (Concordances Series). 407p. (Prog. Bk.). 1969. 34.50x (ISBN 0-8014-0480-0). Cornell U Pr.
Concordance to Beowulf. Albert S. Cook. LC 74-46. 1911. lib. bdg. 30.00 (ISBN 0-8414-3456-5). Folcroft.
Concordance to Byron's Don Juan. Ed. by Charles W. Hagelman, Jr. & Robert J. Barnes. (Concordances Ser.). 981p. 1967. 52.50x (ISBN 0-8014-0169-0). Cornell U Pr.
Concordance to Calvin's Institutio. Ford L. Battles & Charles Miller. LC 73-206014. (Bibliographia Tripotamopolitana Ser.: No. 8). 1974. 80.00x (ISBN 0-931222-07-9). C E Barbour.
Concordance to Christian Science Hymnal & Hymnal Notes. 1961. 8.50 (ISBN 0-87510-023-6). Chr Science.
Concordance to Conrad's the Mirror of the Sea & the Inheritors. Todd K. Bender. 340p. 1983. lib. bdg. 45.00 (ISBN 0-8240-9110-8). Garland Pub.
Concordance to Conrad's Under Western Eyes. David Higdon & Todd K. Bender. LC 82-48434. (Conrad Concordances Ser.). 283p. 1982. lib. bdg. 50.00 (ISBN 0-8240-9234-1). Garland Pub.
Concordance to Darwin's "Origin of Species". Ed. by Paul Barrett et al. 864p. 1981. 42.50x (ISBN 0-8014-1319-2). Cornell U Pr.
Concordance to English Poems of Thomas Gray. Albert S. Cook. LC 74-8062. Repr. of 1908 ed. lib. bdg. 20.00 (ISBN 0-8414-3355-0). Folcroft.
Concordance to Finnegans Wake. rev. ed. Clive Hart. 1963. 35.00x (ISBN 0-911858-27-X). Appel.
Concordance to FitzGerald's Translation of the Rubaiyat of Omar Khayyam. John R. Tutin. LC 68-58471. (Bibliography & Reference Ser.: No. 256). 1969. Repr. of 1900 ed. 12.50 (ISBN 0-8337-3581-0). B Franklin.
Concordance to Five Systems of Transcription for Standard Chinese. Olov B. Anderson. 230p. (Chinese.). 1982. pap. text ed. 22.50 (ISBN 0-7007-0080-3, Pub. by Curzon Pr England). Apt Bks.

Concordance to Flaubert's Bouvard et Pecuchet. Charles Carlut. LC 79-7915. 1021p. 1980. lib. bdg. 110.00 (ISBN 0-8240-9518-9). Garland Pub.

Concordance to Melville's Moby Dick. Eugene F. Irey. LC 82-9387. 2031p. 1982. lib. bdg. 275.00 (ISBN 0-8240-9398-4). Garland Pub.

Concordance to Shakespeare's Poems: An Index to Every Word Therein Contained. Mrs. Horace H. Furness. LC 75-109647. (Select Bibliographies Reprint Ser). 1874. 29.00 (ISBN 0-8369-5256-1). Ayer Co.

Concordance to the "Anglo-Saxon Poetic Records". Ed. by J. B. Bessinger, Jr. LC 77-6186. (Concordances Ser.). 1978. 65.00x (ISBN 0-8014-1146-7). Cornell U Pr.

Concordance to the Celestina (1499) Lloyd Kasten & Jean Anderson. (Spanish Ser.: No. 1). 338p. 1976. 12.50 (ISBN 0-942260-10-4). Hispanic Seminary.

Concordance to The Complete Poetry of Stephen Crane. Andrew Crosland. 72.00 (ISBN 0-685-77427-9). Bruccoli.

Concordance to the Complete Writings of George Herbert. Ed. by Mario A. Di Cesare & Rigo Mignani. LC 76-56642. (Cornell Concordances Ser.). 1977. 59.50x (ISBN 0-8014-1106-8). Cornell U Pr.

Concordance to the Devil & the Lady. A. E. Baker & Alfred Tennyson. Ed. by Charles Tennyson. Repr. of 1931 ed. 15.00 (ISBN 0-527-04550-0). Kraus Repr.

Concordance to the Doctrine & Covenants. John V. Bluth. 8.95 (ISBN 0-87747-048-0). Deseret Bk.

Concordance to the English Poems of George Herbert. Cameron Mann. LC 77-4939. 1927. lib. bdg. 19.00 (ISBN 0-8414-6186-4). Folcroft.

Concordance to the Fables & Tales of Jean De la Fontaine. Ed. by J. Allen Tyler & Stephen M. Parrish. LC 73-8388. (Concordances Ser.). 1104p. (Fr. & Eng.). 1974. 55.00x (ISBN 0-8014-0811-3). Cornell U Pr.

Concordance to the Five Novels of Nathaniel Hawthorne. John R. Byers, Jr. & James J. Owen. LC 79-7910. 951p. 1979. lib. bdg. 138.00 (ISBN 0-8240-9545-6). Garland Pub.

Concordance to the Hidden Words of Baha'u'llah. Jalil Mahmoudi. (Orig.). 1980. pap. 6.95 (ISBN 0-87743-148-5, 368-052). Baha'i.

Concordance to the Pascal's Pensees. Ed. by Hugh M. Davidson & Pierre H. Dube. LC 75-16808. (Cornell Concordances Ser.). 1488p. 1975. 65.00x (ISBN 0-8014-0972-1). Cornell U Pr.

Concordance to the Plays & Poems Federico Garcia Lorca. Ed. by Alice M. Pollin & Philip H. Smith. LC 73-20817. (Concordances Ser.). 1216p. 1975. 59.50x (ISBN 0-8014-0808-3). Cornell U Pr.

Concordance to the Plays of W. B. Yeats, 2 vols. Ed. by Eric Domville. LC 71-162547. (Concordances Ser). 2330p. 1972. Set. 75.00x (ISBN 0-8014-0663-3). Cornell U Pr.

Concordance to the Plays of William Congreve. Ed. by David D. Mann. LC 72-13384. (Concordances Ser.). 888p. 1973. 49.50x (ISBN 0-8014-0767-2). Cornell U Pr.

Concordance to the Plays, Poems, & Translations of Christopher Marlowe. Ed. by Robert J. Fehrenbach et al. LC 81-67175. (A Cornell Concordance). 1710p. 75.00x (ISBN 0-8014-1420-2). Cornell U Pr.

Concordance to the Poems of Ben Jonson. Ed. by Mario A. Di Cesare & Ephim Fogel. LC 78-59630. (Concordances Ser). 1978. 57.00x (ISBN 0-8014-1217-X). Cornell U Pr.

Concordance to the Poems of Emily Dickinson. Ed. by Stanford P. Rosenbaum. LC 64-25335. (Concordances Ser.). 921p. 1964. 55.00x (ISBN 0-8014-0362-6). Cornell U Pr.

Concordance to the Poems of Jonathan Swift. Ed. by Michael Shinagel. LC 72-4870. (Concordances Ser.). 1008p. 1973. 55.00x (ISBN 0-8014-0747-8). Cornell U Pr.

Concordance to the Poems of Osip Mandelstam. Ed. by Demetrius J. Koubourlis & Stephen M. Parrish. LC 73-8387. (Concordances Ser.). 704p. (Rus. & Eng.). 1974. 42.50x (ISBN 0-8014-0806-7). Cornell U pr.

Concordance to the Poems of Robert Herrick. Malcolm L. MacLeod. LC 77-13605. 1977. Repr. lib. bdg. 35.00 (ISBN 0-8414-6219-4). Folcroft.

Concordance to the Poems of Samuel Johnson. Ed. by Helen H. Naugle. LC 72-13383. (Concordances Ser). 578p. 1973. 39.50x (ISBN 0-8014-0769-9). Cornell U Pr.

Concordance to the Poems of Sir Philip Sidney. Ed. by Herbert S. Donow. LC 73-20816. (Concordances Ser.). 1975. 45.00x (ISBN 0-8014-0805-9). Cornell U Pr.

Concordance to the Poems of W. B. Yeats. Ed. by Stephen M. Parrish & James A. Painter. 1963. 52.50x (ISBN 0-8014-0328-6). Cornell U Pr.

Concordance to the Poetical Works of William Cowper. John Neve. 1967. Repr. of 1887 ed. 21.00 (ISBN 0-8337-2519-X). B Franklin.

Concordance to the Science of Mind. 312p. 1980. pap. 17.95 (ISBN 0-911336-82-6). Sci of Mind.

Concordance to the Sonnets of Gongora. Ruth M. Richards. (Spanish Ser.: No. 6). 1982. 15.00 (ISBN 0-942260-20-1). Hispanic Seminary.

Concordance to the Spectator. William Wheeler. LC 74-32004. lib. bdg. 15.00 (ISBN 0-8414-9575-0). Folcroft.

Concordance to the Writings of William Blake, 2 Vols. Ed. by David V. Erdman. (Concordances Ser.). 3463p. 1968. 85.00x (ISBN 0-8014-0120-8). Cornell U Pr.

Concordances & Texts of the Royal Scriptorium Manuscripts of Alfonso X, el Sabio, 2 vols. Lloyd Kasten & John Nitti. (Spanish Ser.: No. 2). 1978. 150.00x (ISBN 0-942260-11-2). Hispanic Seminary.

Concordant Literal New Testament with Keyword Concordance. Ed. by A. E. Knoch. 1983. text ed. 15.00 (ISBN 0-910424-14-4). Concordant.

Concordantiae verbales opuscolorum S. Francisci et S. Clarae Assisiensium. Boccali Giovanni. 960p. (Lat.). 1976. L.30000.00. LIEF.

Concordanze dei dialetti di Puglia, 2 vols. Michelle Melillo. 916p. (Ital.). 1975. L.50000.00. Atlantica.

Concordanze verghiane. Marchi G. Paolo. 318p. (Ital.). 1972. L.4300.00. Fiorini.

Concordia Bible Dictionary. 176p. 1963. text ed. 4.75 (ISBN 0-570-03186-9, 12-2213). Concordia.

Condensed Chemical Dictionary. 10th ed. Gessner Hawley. 1472p. 1981. pap. 42.50 (ISBN 0-442-23244-6). Van Nos Reinhold.

Condensed Hebrew Dictionary. Ed. by Abraham Even-Shoshan. (Illus.). 824p. (Hebrew.). 1982. text ed. 35.00 (ISBN 965-17-0103-X). K Sefer.

Condensed Muret-Sanders German-English Dictionary. 1st ed. Ed. by Heinz Messinger. 1296p. (Eng. & Ger.). 1983. 70.00x (ISBN 3-468-02125-9). Gale.

Conference Terminology in English, Spanish, Russian, Italian, German & Hungarian. J. Herbert. (Eng., Span., Rus., Ital., Ger. & Hungarian.). 1976. 25.00 (ISBN 0-444-41354-5). Elsevier.

Congress Ideology & Programme. P. D. Kaushik. 1964. 7.50x (ISBN 0-8188-1064-5). Paragon.

Connoisseur Dictionary of Country Furniture. new ed. Marjorie Filbee. (Illus.). 1977. 12.95 (ISBN 0-900305-17-7). Hearst Bks.

Conservation & Solar Energy Dictionary. Daniel V. Hunt. Date not set. 39.50 (ISBN 0-442-20056-0). Van Nos Reinhold.

Construction Contract Dictionary. Leonard Fletcher et al. LC 81-16935. 128p. 1981. 25.00x (ISBN 0-902132-65-2, 6632, Pub. by E & Fn. Spon England). Methuen Inc.

Consumer's Dictionary of Cosmetic Ingredients. rev. ed. Ruth Winter. 1976. pap. 4.95 (ISBN 0-517-52737-5). Crown.

Consumer's Dictionary of Food Additives. Ruth Winter. 1978. pap. 4.95 (ISBN 0-517-53161-5). Crown.

Contemporary Indonesian-English Dictionary. A. Ed. Schmidgall-Tellings & Alan Stevens. LC 80-20994. xvi, 388p. (Indonesian & Eng.). 1981. 28.95x (ISBN 0-8214-0424-5, 82-83152); pap. 14.95x (ISBN 0-8214-0435-0, 82-83160). Ohio U Pr.

Contemporary Vocabulary. Elliott Smith. LC 78-65215. 1979. pap. text ed. 10.95x (ISBN 0-312-16847-0); inst. manual avail. (ISBN 0-312-16848-9). St Martin.

Control Terminology (A Glossary of Common Control Terms, No. 13. (Tech Tip). 100 copies 6.50. NA Heating & AC Wholesalers.

Conveyor Terms & Definitions. 4th ed. Conveyor Equipment Manufacturers Association & American National Standards Institute. (CEMA Standards: No. 102). (Illus.). 93p. 1982. 7.00. Conveyor Equip Mfrs.

Cookbook Dictionary. Vera Servi. LC 79-15334. 1982. 10.95 (ISBN 0-913290-21-1). Camaro Pub.

COPT - Current Optometric Information & Terminology. 6.00 (ODE 4); members 3.00; students 2.00. Am Optometric.

COPT Current Optometric Procedural Terminology. 4.00 (O*D*E10); members 2.00; students 1.00. Am Optometric.

Coptic Dictionary. Ed. by Walter E. Crum. 1939. 98.00x (ISBN 0-19-864404-3). Oxford U Pr.

Coptic Etymological Dictionary. Jaroslav Cerny. LC 69-10192. 350p. 1976. 175.00 (ISBN 0-521-07228-X). Cambridge U Pr.

Cornish-English Dictionary. (Cornish & Eng.). 10.95 (ISBN 0-686-10840-X). British Am Bks.

Cornish-English Dictionary. 1974. 22.50 (ISBN 0-87557-011-9, 001-9). Saphrograph.

Corrugating Defect Terminology: Fabrication Manuel for Corrugated Box Plants. 4th, rev. ed. Ed. by Manuel A. Rosa. (Illus.). 236p. 1982. pap. 49.95 (ISBN 0-89852-403-2, 01 01R 103). TAPPI.

Cortina-Ace Basic French Dictionary. Cortina. (Foreign Language Dictionary Ser.). 384p. (Fr.). 1983. pap. 3.50 (ISBN 0-441-04999-0). Ace Bks.

Cortina-Ace Basic German Dictionary. Cortina. (Foreign Language Dictionary Ser.). 384p. 1982. pap. 2.95 (ISBN 0-441-05002-6). Ace Bks.

Cortina-Ace Basic Italian Dictionary. Cortina. (Foreign Language Dictionary Ser.). 384p. 1982. pap. 2.95 (ISBN 0-441-05003-4). Ace Bks.

Cortina-Ace Basic Spanish Dictionary. Cortina. (Foreign Language Dictionary Ser.). 384p. (Span. & Eng.). 1982. pap. 2.95 (ISBN 0-441-05004-2). Ace Bks.

Cortina-Grosset Basic Dictionary: Italian. Ed. by Dilaver Berberi & Edel A. Berberi. (Ital.). 1977. pap. 2.95 (ISBN 0-448-14030-6, G&D). Putnam Pub Group.

Cortina-Grosset Basic French Dictionary. Teresa Marcy & Michel Marcy. Ed. by Dilaver Berberi & Edel A. Berberi. LC 73-18522. 384p. (Fr.). 1975. pap. 3.50 (ISBN 0-448-14031-4, G&D). Putnam Pub Group.

Cortina-Grosset Basic French Dictionary. Teresa Nutting & Michel Marcy. LC 73-18522. xi, 368p. (Eng. & Fr.). 1975. 3.95. G&D.

Cortina-Grosset Basic German Dictionary. Ed. by Josefa J. Smith et al. LC 73-18523. 384p. (Ger.). 1975. pap. 3.50 (ISBN 0-686-96722-4, G&D). Putnam Pub Group.

Cortina-Grosset Basic German Dictionary. Josefa Zotter. LC 73-18523. xiii, 366p. (Eng. & Ger.). 1975. 3.95 (ISBN 0-448-11557-3). G&D.

Cortina-Grosset Basic German Dictionary. Ed. by Josefa Zotter. (Ger.). 1977. pap. 2.95 (ISBN 0-448-14029-2, G&D). Putnam Pub Group.

Cortina-Grosset Basic Spanish Dictionary. Luis M. Laita. Ed. by Dilaver Berberi & Edel A. Berberi. LC 73-18525. 384p. (Span.). 1975. 3.95 (ISBN 0-448-11559-X, G&D). Putnam Pub Group.

Cortina-Grosset Basic Spanish Dictionary. Ed. by Luis M. Laita. (Span.). 1977. pap. 3.50 (ISBN 0-448-14032-2, G&D). Putnam Pub Group.

Cortina Handy Spanish-English Dictionary. Ed. by G. H. Calvert. LC 78-100109. xxv, 544p. (Eng. & Span.). 1976. write for info. (ISBN 0-8327-0701-5). Cortina.

Cortina Handy Spanish-English, English-Spanish Dictionary. G. H. Calvert. LC 81-47221. 546p. (Span. & Eng.). 1982. 7.95 (ISBN 0-06-464800-1, BN-4800). B&N NY.

Cosmetics-Perfumery Thesaurus. H. Feinberg. 1972. 17.95 (ISBN 0-02-469030-9). Macmillan Info.

Costume of the Western World. Doreen Yarwood. (Illus.). 192p. 1981. 18.50x (ISBN 0-312-17013-0). St Martin.

Counting Out Rhymes: A Dictionary. Ed. by Roger D. Abrahams & Lois Rankin. (AFS Bibliographical & Special Ser.: Vol. 33). 263p. 1980. text ed. 19.95x (ISBN 0-292-71057-7). U of Tex Pr.

Course in Miracles Concordance. Barbara Findeisen. 457p. 15.00 (ISBN 0-942494-45-8). Coleman Graphics.

Cowboy-English, English-Cowboy Dictionary. Bill Dana. 96p. (Orig.). 1982. pap. 1.95 (ISBN 0-345-30155-2). Ballantine.

Created Fables for Vocabulary Growth: A Classroom Project. Lynette R. Payne. (Illus.). 1982. 6.95 (ISBN 0-533-05065-0). Vantage.

Creativite lexicale. Louis Guilbert. (Collection langue et langage). 285p. (Fr.). 1975. pap. 23.95 (ISBN 2-03-070340-0). Larousse.

Creature Features Movie Guide or An A to Z Encyclopedia to Fantastic Films or Is There a Mad Doctor in the House? John Stanley. LC 81-67664. (Illus.). 208p. (Orig.). (gr. 8 up). 1981. pap. 8.95 (ISBN 0-940064-00-6). Creatures at Large.

Cree's Dictionary of Latin Quotations. A. Cree. LC 78-51482. (Eng. & Lat.). 1979. 16.00 (ISBN 0-912728-12-4). Newbury Bks.

Crime Dictionary. Ralph De Sola. 240p. 1982. 22.50 (ISBN 0-87196-443-0). Facts on File.

Criminal Justice Dictionary. 2nd, rev. ed. Erik Beckman. LC 78-72049. 1983. 22.95 (ISBN 0-87650-153-6); pap. 16.95 (ISBN 0-87650-152-8). Pierian.

Criminal Justice Vocabulary. Julian A. Martin & Nicholas A. Astone. 312p. 1980. lexotone 29.50x (ISBN 0-398-03987-9). C C Thomas.

Critical & Documentary Dictionary of Violin Makers Old & Modern, 2 vols. in 1. Henri Poidras. LC 70-166252. 1928-1930. Repr. 59.00 (ISBN 0-403-01381-X). Scholarly.
Critical Concordance to Catullus. Ed. by V. P. McCarren. (Lat. & Eng.). 1977. text ed. 66.00x (ISBN 90-04-05224-0). Humanities.
Critical Concordance to I & II Corinthians. A. Q. Morton et al. (Computer Bible Ser.: Vol. XIX). 1979. pap. 30.00 (ISBN 0-935106-01-4). Biblical Res Assocs.
Critical Concordance to the Acts of the Apostles. A. Q. Morton & Sidney Michaelson. (Computer Bible Ser.: Vol. VII). 1976. pap. 15.00 (ISBN 0-935106-14-6). Biblical Res Assocs.
Critical Concordance to the Epistle of Paul to the Galatians. A. Q. Morton et al. Ed. by J. Arthur Baird & David Freedman. (Computer Bible Ser.: Vol. XXI). (Orig.). 1980. pap. text ed. 20.00 (ISBN 0-935106-16-2). Biblical Res Assocs.
Critical Concordance to the Letter of Paul to the Colossians. A. Q. Morton et al. Ed. by J. Arthur Baird & David Freedman. (Computer Bible Ser.: Vol. 24). (Orig.). 1981. pap. text ed. 20.00 (ISBN 0-935106-19-7). Biblical Res Assocs.
Critical Concordance to the Letter of Paul to the Ephesians. A. Q. Morton et al. Ed. by J. Arthur Baird & David Freedman. (Computer Bible Ser.: Vol. XXII). (Orig.). 1980. pap. text ed. 20.00 (ISBN 0-935106-17-0). Biblical Res Assocs.
Critical Concordance to the Letter of Paul to the Philippians. A. Q. Morton et al. Ed. by J. Arthur Baird & David Freedman. (Computer Bible Ser.: Vol. 23). (Orig.). 1980. pap. text ed. 20.00 (ISBN 0-935106-18-9). Biblical Res Assocs.
Critical Concordance to the Letter of Paul to the Romans. A. Q. Morton & Sidney Michaelson. Ed. by J. Arthur Baird & David Noel Freedman. (Computer Bible Ser: Vol. XIII). 1977. pap. 27.50 (ISBN 0-935106-08-1). Biblical Res Assocs.
Critical Dictionary of Composers & Their Music. Percy M. Young. LC 78-66927. (Encore Music Editions Ser.). 1981. Repr. of 1954 ed. 27.50 (ISBN 0-88355-771-1). Hyperion Conn.
Critical Dictionary of Psychoanalysis. Charles Rycroft. (Quality Paperback: No. 270). 189p. 1973. pap. 3.95 (ISBN 0-8226-0270-9). Littlefield.
Croatian-English, English-Croatian Pocket Dictionary. (Croation & Eng.). 10.00 (ISBN 0-685-58554-9). Heinman.
Croatian-English, English-Croatian Small Pocket Dictionary. R. Filipovic. (Croatian & Eng.). 1981. pap. 10.00x (ISBN 0-89918-727-7, Y-727). Vanous.
Croation Reader with Vocabulary. Ante Kadic. (Croatian.). 1960. text ed. 23.00x (ISBN 90-2791-005-7). Mouton.
Crosbie's Dictionary of Puns. John S. Crosbie. 1977. 12.95 (ISBN 0-517-53124-0, Harmony); pap. 6.95 (ISBN 0-517-53125-9). Crown.
Crosbie's Dictionary of Riddles. John S. Crosbie. (Illus.). 224p. 1980. 12.95 (ISBN 0-517-54038-X, Harmony); pap. 6.95 (ISBN 0-517-54039-8). Crown.
Cross Word Dictionary. 5th ed. Steve Kowit. 1977. pap. 1.50 (ISBN 0-89596-212-8, Success). Merit Pubns.
Crossword Anagram Dictionary. Compiled by R. J. Edwards. (Illus.). 1979. 6.95 (ISBN 0-8317-1882-X, Mayflower Bks). Smith Pubs.
Crossword Dictionary. Ed. by John Bailie. 304p. (Eng.). E3.95 (ISBN 0-600-31923-7). Newnes Bks.
Crossword Dictionary. (Purse Books). 1964. pap. 0.69 (ISBN 0-440-61529-1). Dell.
Crossword Puzzle Dictionary. pap. 1.99 (ISBN 0-686-00469-8). Dennison.
Crossword Puzzle Dictionary. Betty F. Melnicove. pap. 2.50 (ISBN 0-06-461007-1, D-7). B&N NY.
Crossword Puzzle Dictionary. 4th, rev, new ed. Andrew Swanfeldt. LC 76-57994. 1977. 14.37i (ISBN 0-690-00426-5); thumb-indexed 15.34i (ISBN 0-690-01198-9). T y Crowell.
Crossworder's List Book. John E. Brown & Margaret H. Brown. LC 77-14662. 1978. pap. 4.95 (ISBN 0-312-17690-2). St Martin.
Cruden's Concordance: Handy Reference Edition. Alexander Cruden. (Baker's Paperback Reference Library). 344p. 1982. pap. 6.95 (ISBN 0-8010-2478-1). Baker Bk.
Cruden's Pocket Dictionary of Bible Terms. Alexander Cruden. (Direction Bks). 1976. pap. 5.95 (ISBN 0-8010-2380-7). Baker Bk.
Cruden's Unabridged Concordance. Alexander Cruden. 17.95 (ISBN 0-8010-2316-5). Baker Bk.
Cruden's Unabridged Concordance. Alexander Cruden. LC 54-11084. 17.95 (ISBN 0-8054-1123-2). Broadman.
Current Literary Terms. Ed. by A. F. Scott. 324p. Repr. of 1980 ed. lib. bdg. 16.95x (ISBN 0-312-17956-1). St Martin.
Current Literary Terms: A Concise Dictionary of Their Origin & Use. A. F. Scott. 334p. (Eng.). 1979. E10.00 (ISBN 0-333-03566-6); pap. 3.50 (ISBN 0-333-26101-1). Macmillan London.
Current Medical Information & Terminology. 5th ed. American Medical Association. 800p. 20.00 (OP 337); bulk rates avail. AMA.
Current Procedural Terminology. 4th ed. 1970. pap. 12.00 (ISBN 0-89970-029-2, OP-041). AMA.
Customs Dictionary: German-English-French-Italian. Wilhelm Muller. LC 72-311634. 277p. (Ger., Eng., Fr. & Ital.). 1971. 17.50x (ISBN 3-8029-8565-6). Intl Pubns Serv.
Czech-English-Czech Dictionary. V. Kolafova & D. Slaba. (For Travel Ser.). 394p. (Czech. & Eng.). 1979. text ed. 6.00x (ISBN 0-89918-302-6, C302). Vanous.
Czech-English-Czech Dictionary. 4th ed. J. Poldauf. (Czech. & Eng.). 1980. text ed. 20.00x (ISBN 0-89918-253-4, C253). Vanous.
Czech-English Dictionary. Ed. by I. Poldauf. 1235p. (Czech. & Eng.). 1980. 50.00x (ISBN 0-569-00404-7, Pub. by Collet's). State Mutual Bk.
Czech-English, English-Czech Dictionary. A. Chermak. (Czech. & Eng.). 27.50 (ISBN 0-87557-012-7, 012-7). Saphrograph.
Czech-English, English Czech Dictionary. 9th ed. Ed. by I. Poldauf. (Czech. & Eng.). 25.00 (ISBN 0-686-77982-7). Heinman.
Czech-English, English-Czech Pocket Dictionary. (Czech. & Eng.). 11.00 (ISBN 0-685-68787-2). Heinman.
Czech-English, English-Czech Pocket Dictionary. 1223p. (Czech. & Eng.). 1980. 16.95 (ISBN 0-88254-542-6, Pub. by Artia Czechoslovakia). Hippocrene Bks.
Czech-English, English-Czech Pocket Dictionary. 1223p. (Czech. & Eng.). 1980. 16.95 (ISBN 0-88254-542-6). Artia.
Czech-English Technical Dictionary. 946p. (Czech. & Eng.). 1972. 23.75 (Pub. by SNTL). Four Continent.
Czech-English Technical Textile Dictionary. T. Leskova & V. Plisek. 468p. (Czech. & Eng.). 1980. 60.00x (ISBN 0-686-72090-3, Pub. by Collet's). State Mutual Bk.
Czechoslovakian Dictionary: English-Slovak & Slovak-English. 5th ed. J. Smejkalova et al. 793p. (Czech. & Eng.). 1979. 9.50x (ISBN 0-89918-170-8, C-170). Vanous.
Czechoslovakian Pocket Dictionary: Czech-English-Czech. 3rd ed. K. Hais. (Czech. & Eng.). 1974. text ed. 11.00x (ISBN 0-89918-148-1, C148). Vanous.
Czechoslovakian-Russian Dictionary of Geology. N. A. Pascenkova et al. 248p. (Czech. & Rus.). 1960. 41.95 (ISBN 0-686-92454-1, M-9067). French & Eur.

D

D & D Standard Oil Abbreviator. 2nd ed. Association of Desk & Derrick Clubs of America. LC 72-96172. 230p. 9.50x (ISBN 0-87814-017-4). Pennwell Pub.
Daffy Definitions of Medical Terms. Angela. 1981. 5.95 (ISBN 0-533-04834-6). Vantage.
Dafoar islilah pertanian, 2 vols. Achmad Baihaki et al. LC 81-941728. (Eng. & Indonesian.). 1979. write for info. Pustaka Antara.
Dakota-English Dictionary. facsimile ed. Stephen R. Riggs. (Dakota & Eng.). 1968. Repr. of 1882 ed. buckram bdg. 20.00 (ISBN 0-87018-050-9). Ross.
Danisch, 2 vols. H. Hennigsen. (Langenscheidts Taschenworterbucher). (Ger. & Danish.). Teil 1: Danisch-Deutsch (557p.) DM.mit Lautschrift 18.80 (10100); Teil 2: Deutsch-Danisch (548p.) DM.18.80 (10105); DM.beide Teile in einem Band 29.80 (11100). Langenscheidt.
Danish Dictionary Deluxe. H. Vinterberg & Sen A. Bodel. (Danish & Eng.). 1976. Vol. 1. text ed. 120.00x Danish-English (ISBN 0-89918-726-9, D726); Vol. 2. text ed. 120.00x english-danish (ISBN 0-89918-756-0, D756). Vanous.
Danish Dictionary: Rode Ordbog-Gyldendals, Danish-English. 11th ed. H. Vinterberg et al. (Danish & Eng.). 1981. text ed. 20.00x (ISBN 8-7001-1282-8, D705). Vanous.
Danish Dictionary: Rode Ordbog-Gyldendals, English-Danish. 9th ed. H. Vinterberg et al. (Danish & Eng.). 1979. text ed. 20.00x (ISBN 8-7008-0381-2, D704). Vanous.
Danish-English-Danish Ser. (Berlitz Pocket Dictionaries). (Danish & Eng.). 4.95 (ISBN 0-02-964550-6). Macmillan.
Danish-English Dictionary. rev. ed. K. Schibsbye & H. Kossmann. Ed. by G. Rona & R. Raylor. (Danish & Eng.). 32.50 (ISBN 0-87559-006-3); thumb indexed 37.50 (ISBN 0-87559-007-1). Shalom.
Danish-English, English-Danish Dictionary, 2 vols. 8th & 10th ed. Ed. by H. Vinterberg & J. Axelsen. (Danish & Eng.). Set. 50.00 (ISBN 0-685-36173-X). Vol. 1, Danish-English (ISBN 8-7001-1282-8). Vol. 2, English-Danish (ISBN 8-7013-3451-4). Heinman.
Danish-English, English-Danish Technical Dictionary, 2 vols. new, rev. ed. A. Warrern. (Danish & Eng.). Set. 80.00 (ISBN 8-7110-3767-9). Danish-Eng (ISBN 87-11-03767-9). Eng.-Danish (ISBN 87-11-03867-5). Heinman.
Danish Pocket Dictionary. (Danish & Eng.). 7.50 (ISBN 8-7146-1178-3). Heinman.
Danish Pocket Dictionary. 6th ed. Host. (Eng. & Danish.). 1978. pap. text ed. 7.00x (ISBN 87-146-1178-3, D711). Vanous.
Dansk-Engelsk Handels-og Fagordbog. I. E. Bailey. 514p. (Danish & Eng.). 1973. 75.00 (ISBN 87-570-0533-8, M-8411). French & Eur.
Dansk-Engelsk Ordbog. H. Vinterberg & C. A. Bodelsen. 1846p. (Danish & Eng.). 1981. 95.00 (ISBN 87-00-67161-4, M-1281). French & Eur.
Dansk-Engelsk Ordboger. H. Vinterberg et al. 538p. (Danish & Eng.). 1981. 24.95 (ISBN 0-686-92581-5, M-1272). French & Eur.
Dansk-Engelsk Teknisk Ordbog. 393p. (Dansih, English.). 1981. 49.95 (ISBN 87-11-04027-0, M-1289). French & Eur.
Dansk-Fransk Ordbog. A. Blinkenberg & P. Hoybye. 2058p. (Danish & Fr.). 1975. leatherette 175.00 (ISBN 0-686-92500-9, M-1278). French & Eur.
Dansk-Fransk Ordbog. 3rd ed. A. P. Blinkenberg & Poul Hoybye. Ed. by Margrethe Thiele. LC 77-467208. (Fr. & Dan.). 1975. Kr.180.00 (ISBN 8-71703-231-8). Erhvervso.
Dansk-Fransk Ordbog. N. C. Sorensen. 484p. (Danish & Fr.). 1980. 24.95 (ISBN 87-01-33721-1, M-1284). French & Eur.
Dansk-Fransk Ordbog. Niels C. Sorensen. LC 76-511464. 515p. (Danish & Fr.). 1975. Kr.60.00 (ISBN 8-70049-461-5). Gyldendal Norsk.
Dansk-Italiensk Ordborg. J. Mengel. 660p. (Danish & Ital.). 1979. 39.95 (ISBN 0-686-92569-6, M-1292). French & Eur.
Dansk-Latinsk: Ordbog. L. Ove Kjaer. 580p. (Danish & Lat.). 1979. 29.95 (ISBN 0-686-92574-2, M-1277). French & Eur.
Dansk Retrogradordbog. Henrik Holmboe. LC 78-363861. 259p. (Danish.). 1978. Kr.106.20 (ISBN 8-75001-793-4). Akademisk Forlag.
Dansk-Russik Ordbog. Helge Vangmark. LC 79-396749. 238p. (Rus. & Danish.). 1979. Kr.112.50 (ISBN 8-74297-608-1). Grafisk Forlag.
Dansk-Russik Ordborg. H. Vangmark. 238p. (Danish & Rus.). 1979. 39.95 (ISBN 87-429-7608-1). French & Eur.
Dansk-Spansk Ordborg. 489p. (Danish & Span.). 1980. 29.95 (ISBN 87-01-71901-7, S-39031). French & Eur.
Dansk Sprogbrug. Erik Bruun. LC 79-389408. 588p. (Danish.). 1978. Kr.110.00 (ISBN 8-70130-201-9). Gyldendal Norsk.
Dansk-Svensk Ordbok. Bertil Molde. Ed. by Niels Ferlov. 726p. (Danish & Swedish.). 1980. Kr.170.00 (ISBN 91-24-29601-5). Esselte Studium.
Dansk-Svensk Ordbok. Karen Widman. 309p. (Danish & Swedish.). write for info. (ISBN 91-24-14367-7). Esselte Studium.
Dansk-Tysk Ordbog. E. Bork & E. Kaper. 626p. (Danish & Ger.). 1981. 24.95 (ISBN 87-01-93141-5, M-1283). French & Eur.
Dansk-Tysk Ordbog. Egon Bork & Egon Kaper. LC 76-458154. 531p. (Danish & Ger.). 1975. Kr.55.00 (ISBN 8-70009-141-3). Gyldendal Norsk.
Dansk-Tysk Ordbog. Borge Dissing & Rud Lave. LC 79-383402. (Illus.). 347p. (Ger. & Danish.). 1978. write for info. Gyldendal Norsk.
Dansk-Tysk Ordbog for Korrespondenter. O. Poulsen. 415p. (Danish & Ger.). 1980. 39.95 (ISBN 87-87697-10-6, M-1273). French & Eur.
Dansk-Tysk Teknisk Ordborg. A. Warren. 279p. (Danish & Ger.). 1977. 49.95 (ISBN 87-11-03797-0, M-1290). French & Eur.
Daoud's Aviation Dictionary. Hesham O. Daoud. 1972. pap. 8.00 (ISBN 0-911720-55-3, Pub. by Daouds). Aviation.
Darai-English, English-Darai Glossary. Carl Kotapish & Sharon Kotapish. LC 76-904757. xi, 152p. (Eng. & Darai.). 1975. Rs.20.00. Summer Inst Abor.
Das Grosse Lexikon der Aquaristik. Hans Frey. LC 77-551968. 859p. (Ger.). 1976. write for info. (ISBN 3-7888-0243-X). Neumann-Neudamm.
Data Communications Dictionary. Charles J. Sippl. 533p. 1980. pap. text ed. 12.95 (ISBN 0-442-21931-8). Van Nos Reinhold.
Data Dictionaries & Data Administration: Concepts & Practices for Data Resource Management. Ronald G. Ross. 384p. 1981. 25.95 (ISBN 0-8144-5596-4). Am Mgmt.
Data Dictionary-Directory Systems: Administration Implementation & Usage. Belkis W. Leong-Hong & Bernard K. Plagman. LC 81-21875. 328p. 1982. 31.95x (ISBN 0-471-05164-0, Pub. by Wiley-Interscience). Wiley.

Data Dictionary-Directory Systems: Administration Implementation & Usage. Belkis W. Leong-Hong & Bernard K. Plagman. members 25.95; (W1) 27.95. Data Process Mgmt.

Data Dictionary-Directory Systems: Aministration, Implementation & Usage. Belkis W. Leong-Hong & Bernard K. Plagman. members 25.95; (W7) 27.95. Data Process Mgmt.

Data Dictionary Systems. J. D. Lomax. (Illus.). 1977. pap. 45.00x (ISBN 0-85012-191-4). Intl Pubns Serv.

Data Systems Dictionary. 2nd, rev. & enl. ed. Karl-Heinz Brinkmann et al. LC 80-470062. 399p. (Ger. & Eng.). 1979. DM.55.00 (ISBN 3-87097-095-2). Brandstetter.

Data Systems Dictionary. Joachim Schulz. (Eng., Rus., Ger.). 1978. DM.pap. 39.95 (ISBN 3-87097-075-8). Brandstetter.

Data Systems Dictionary: English-Russian-German. Joachim Schulz. (Eng., Rus. & Ger.). 1978. pap. 39.95 (ISBN 3-87097-075-8, M-7325, Pub. by Brandstetter Verlag). French & Eur.

Dataordbok. Lena Frid. LC 81-451744. 144p. (Eng. & Swedish.). 1980. write for info. (ISBN 9-1970-3442-8). EC Print AB.

Dataordbok: Computers, Automatic, Control & Data Processing. (Eng. & Swedish.). 1983. Kr.195.00 (ISBN 91-86236-16-4). EC Print AB.

Dataordboken. Sveriges Standardiseringskommission. LC 78-393289. 476p. (Eng., Fr., Ger., & Swedish.). 1977. Kr.114.60 (ISBN 9-1716-2052-4). Standard Sver.

Datenerfassung Programmierung. Erich Burger. LC 77-484881. 388p. (Eng., Ger., Fr. & Rus.). 1976. M.38.00. VEB Verlag Technik.

Datenerfassung Programmierung-Englisch-Deutsch-Franzoesisch-Russisch. Erich Burger. 386p. (Eng., Ger., Fr. & Rus.). 1981. M.48.00. VEB Technik.

Davis Dictionary of the Bible. Davis. 21.95 (ISBN 0-8054-1124-0). Broadman.

Davis Dictionary of the Bible. John D. Davis. 1954. 18.95 (ISBN 0-8010-2805-1). Baker Bk.

De la Toponymie Bretonne, Dictionnaire Etymologique. W. B. Smith. (Fr.). Repr. of 1940 ed. 9.00 (ISBN 0-527-00824-9). Kraus Repr.

De Pina's Technical Dictionary, 2 vols. Avelino De Pina Araujo. LC 76-452901. (Eng. & Port.). 1975. Cr.$280.00. McGraw.

Defining a Linquistic Area: South Asia. Colin P. Masica. LC 74-16677. 256p. 1976. lib. bdg. 16.00x (ISBN 0-226-50944-3). U of Chicago Pr.

Defining Child Abuse. Jeanne M. Giovannoni & Rosina Becerra. LC 79-7180. (Illus.). 1979. 24.95 (ISBN 0-02-911750-X). Free Pr.

Defining Family Health Needs, Standards of Care & Priorities: With Particular Reference to Family Planning. Ed. by International Planned Parenthood Federation. (Occasional Essay Ser.: No. 4). 1977. 10.00x (ISBN 0-686-87089-1, Pub. by Intl Planned Parent). State Mutual Bk.

Defining Females: The Nature of Women in Society. Ed. by Shirley Ardener. LC 78-16867. 227p. 1978. 24.95x (ISBN 0-470-26465-9). Halsted Pr.

Definition of Tragedy. Oscar Mandel. LC 82-8505. 184p. 1982. pap. text ed. 9.25 (ISBN 0-8191-2530-X). U Pr of Amer.

Definitions & Criteria. Marcella M. DuPont. LC 65-16526. 1965. 3.50 (ISBN 0-8040-0065-4, 82-70431). Swallow.

Definitions & Divisions of Philosophy. David. Tr. by Bridget Kendall & Robert W. Thomson. LC 83-3308. (Armenian Texts & Studies). 216p. 1983. 17.50 (ISBN 0-89130-616-1, 21 02 05); pap. 13.00. Scholars Pr CA.

Definitions in Political Economy. Thomas R. Malthus. LC 70-21333. Repr. of 1827 ed. 25.00x (ISBN 0-678-00018-2). Kelley.

Definitions of Graphic Arts Terms. 1964. 4.00 (399-2); members 2.67. TAPPI.

Definitions of Nonviolence. Lanza Del Vasto. Tr. by Jean Sidgwick. Orig. Title: Fr. 27p. (Orig.). 1972. pap. 1.00 (ISBN 0-934676-06-2). Greenlf Bks.

Definitions of Surveying & Associated Terms. rev. ed. American Congress on Surveying & Mapping. 210p. 1978. 12.00 (S180); members 7.00. Am Congrs Survey.

Definitions of Surveying & Associated Terms. Compiled By American Society of Civil Engineers. (Manual & Report on Engineering Practice Ser.: No. 34). 216p. 1978. pap. 8.00 (ISBN 0-87262-211-8). Am Soc Civil Eng.

Definitions of Terms in the Sulfite Pulping Process. 1972. 4.00 (1201); members 2.67. TAPPI.

Del Espanol Hablado en Colombia: Seis Muestras de Lexico. Luis Florez. LC 76-460227. 198p. (Span.). 1975. write for info. Instituto Caro & Cuervo.

Delaware Verbal Morphology: A Descriptive & Comparative Study. Ives Goddard. Ed. by Jorge Hankamer. LC 78-66556. (Outstanding Dissertations in Linguistics Ser.). 1979. lib. bdg. 29.00 (ISBN 0-8240-9685-1). Garland Pub.

Delilah's International Dictionary of Rock Terms. Tom Hibbert. (Illus.). 176p. (Orig.). 1983. pap. 6.95 (ISBN 0-933328-84-2). Delilah Bks.

Dell Crossword Dictionary. Ed. by Kathleen Rafferty. 384p. 1983. pap. 5.95 (ISBN 0-440-56314-3, Dell Trade Pbks). Dell.

Dell Crossword Puzzle Dictionary. Ed. by Kathleen Rafferty. 384p. 1983. pap. 2.95 (ISBN 0-440-16314-5). Dell.

Delson's Dictionary of Cable, Video & Satellite Terms. Donn Delson & Ed Michalove. Ed. by Neil Posner. LC 82-17767. (Entertainment Communications Ser.: Vol. 3). (Orig.). 1982. pap. 6.95 (ISBN 0-9603574-3-2, A-4). Bradson.

Delson's Dictionary of Radio & Records Industry Terms. Donn Delson & Walter E. Hurst. Ed. by Neil Posner. LC 80-24486. (Entertainment Communication Ser.: Vol. 2). 112p. (Orig.). 1981. pap. 7.95 (ISBN 0-9603574-2-4). Bradson.

DEMO: Dictionnaire Elementaire de Mathematiques Modernes. Jean-Louis Boursin. 320p. (Fr.). 1972. 21.95 (ISBN 0-686-56927-X, M-6045). French & Eur.

Dental dictionary. Herbert Bucksch. LC 79-315800. 846p. (Eng. & Ger.). 1978. write for info. (ISBN 3-921280-24-9). Verlag Neuer.

Dent's Primary Dictionary. (Eng.). 1970. 4.95 (ISBN 0-460-90925-8); 2.65 (ISBN 0-460-90925-8). Dent.

Dent's Primary Dictionary. Joyce L. Morgan & Beverley Wilbur. (Eng.). 1959. pap. 1.75 (ISBN 0-460-90923-1). Dent.

Depuis Quand? Les Origines des Choses de la Vie Quotidienne. Pierre Germa. 376p. (Fr.). 1979. 43.50 (Dist. by Continental Bk Co). Berger-Levrault.

Der Duden in 10 Baenden das Standardwerk zur Deutschen Sprache, 10 vols. Incl. Vol. 1. Die Rechtschreibung. 792p. 1983. DM.29.80 (ISBN 3-411-00901-2); Vol. 2. Das Stilwoerterbuch. Guenther Drosdowski. 846p. 1983. DM.29.80 (ISBN 3-411-00902-0); Vol. 3. Das Bildwoerterbuch. 784p. 1983. DM.29.80 (ISBN 3-411-00913-6); Vol. 4. Die Grammtik. Paul Grebe et al. 763p. 1983. DM.29.80 (ISBN 3-411-00914-4); Vol. 5. Das Fremdwoerterbuch. Wolfgang Mueller et al. 816p. 1983. DM.29.80 (ISBN 3-411-20905-4); Vol. 6. Das Aussprachewoerterbuch. Max Mangold. 791p. 1983. DM.29.80 (ISBN 3-411-00916-0); Vol. 7. Das Herkunftswoerterbuch. Guenther Drosdowski & Paul Grebe. 816p. 1983. DM.29.80 (ISBN 3-411-00907-1); Vol. 8. Die Sinn & Sachverwandten Woerter & Wendungen. Wolfgang Mueller. 797p. 1983. DM.29.80 (ISBN 3-411-00918-7); Vol. 9. Die Zweifelsfaelle der Deutschen Sprache. Dieter Berger et al. 784p. 1983. DM.29.80 (ISBN 3-411-00919-5); Vol. 10. Das Bedeutungswoerterbuch. Wolfgang Mueller et al. 815p. 1983. DM.29.80 (ISBN 3-411-00910-1). (Ger.). Bibliographisches Institut.

Der Horror-Film. Fernand Jung & Georg Weil. LC 77-474725. 527p. (Eng. & Ger.). 1977. DM.54.00 (ISBN 3-88144-122-0); write for info. Roloff.

Descartes Dictionary. Ed. by John Morris. LC 73-137789. 1971. 10.00 (ISBN 0-8022-2046-0). Philos Lib.

Descriptive Dictionary: Bislama to English. William G. Camden. LC 79-304384. xviii, 138p. (Eng. & Bislama.). 1977. write for info. (ISBN 0-9596774-0-2). Camden Aus.

Designer's Dictionary Two. Bruce T. Barber. (Illus.). 407p. 1981. 28.00 (ISBN 0-911380-54-X). Signs of Times.

Designing & Building Your Own Home. Kay Crowdis & David Crowdis. (Illus.). 240p. 1980. text ed. 14.95 (ISBN 0-8359-1272-8). Reston.

Desk-Book of Errors in English. Frank H. Vizetelly. LC 74-3021. 1974. Repr. of 1920 ed. 34.00x (ISBN 0-8103-3637-5). Gale.

Desk Reference for Neuroanatomy: A Guide to Essential Terms. L. Lockard. LC 77-21707. 1977. 18.00 (ISBN 0-387-90278-3). Springer-Verlag.

Desk Reference of Legal Terms for School Psychologists & Special Educators. D. P. Hanson & D. A. Penrod. 224p. 1980. 19.75x (ISBN 0-398-04015-X). C C Thomas.

Deskbook of Business Management Terms. Leon A. Wortman. LC 78-23257. 1979. 24.95 (ISBN 0-8144-5470-4). Am Mgmt.

Deskbook of Business Management Terms. Leon A. Wortman. 1982. 14.95 (ISBN 0-8144-7571-X). Am Mgmt.

Deutsch-Arabisches Worterbuch. Gotz Schregle. LC 79-366306. xii, 1472p. (Ger. & Arabic.). 1977. write for info. Lib Liban.

Deutsch-Chinesisches Handworterbuch. 1197p. (Ger. & Chinese.). 1980. 54.00 (ISBN 0-686-92250-6, M-9270). French & Eur.

Deutsch-Chinesisches Standard Handworterbuch. 1364p. (Ger. & Chinese.). 1979. 49.95 (ISBN 0-686-92450-9, M-9265). French & Eur.

Deutsch-Englisch, Englisch-Deutsch. (Langenscheidts Schulworterbucher Ser.). 576p. (Ger. & Eng.). DM.12.80 (13120). Langenscheidt.

Deutsch-Englishes Glossarium. C. A. Gunston. 1292p. (Ger. & Eng., German-English Glossary of Financial and Economic Terms). 1977. 69.50 (ISBN 3-7819-2014-3, 7328, Pub. by Fritz Knapp Verlag). French & Eur.

Deutsch-Finnisches Schulworterbuch. A. Rosentahl et al. 673p. (Ger. & Finnish.). 1976. 24.95 (ISBN 951-0-05140-3, M-9637). French & Eur.

Deutsch-Franzoesisches Glossarium: Finanzieller und Wirtschaftlicher Fachausdrueke. 6th ed. Roepke & Haefner. 475p. (Ger. & Fr.). 1982. 325.00 F. Maison Dictionnaire.

Deutsch-Franzosisches Glossarium. F. Roepke. 588p. (Ger. & Fr.). 1966. 35.00 (ISBN 3-7819-2006-2, M-7329, Pub. by Fritz Knapp Verlag). French & Eur.

Deutsch fuer Baufachleute. G. Wallnig & H. Evered. (Illus.). 102p. (Eng. & Ger., Fr. & Span.). 1979. DM.16.00 (ISBN 3-7625-0462-8). Bauverlag.

Deutsch fur Baufachleute fuer Daenen, Norweger & Sshweden. G. Wallnig & H. Evered. (Illus.). 110p. (Danish, Ger., Norwegian & Swedish.). 1982. DM.20.00 (ISBN 3-7625-1467-4). Bauverlag.

Deutsch-Hebraeisches Woerterbuch. David Herstig. (Ger. & Hebrew.). 1971. 17.50 (ISBN 3-19-006285-4, M-7330, Pub. by Max Hueber). French & Eur.

Deutsch-Hebraeisches Woerterbuch. David Herstig. (Ger. & Hebrew.). 1971. DM.17.50 (ISBN 3-447-00354-5). Hueber.

Deutsch-Japanisches Woerterbuch. Eusebius Breitung. LC 79-349548. 1277p. (Ger. & Japanese.). 1977. write for info. Buske.

Deutsch-Koreanisches Woerterbuch. 2nd ed. Andre Eckardt. 332p. (Korean & Ger.). 1976. DM.58.00 (ISBN 3-87276-149-8). Groos Verlag.

Deutsch Lehnwoerter in der Polnischen Bergbausprache. Konrad Wypych. LC 77-463784. 267p. (Pol. & Ger.). 1976. DM.38.00. MG Schmitz.

Deutsch-Norwegisch-Deutsch. Von Trygue Alsos. 553p. (Ger. & Norwegian.). 1981. pap. 7.95 (ISBN 82-573-0082-9, M-9438). French & Eur.

Deutsch-Persisches Fachwoerterbuch Fuer Naturwissenschaft, Medezin und Landwirtschaft. B. Habibi. 240p. (Ger. & Persian.). 1964. pap. 17.50 (ISBN 3-447-00354-5, M-7331, Pub. by Harrassowitz). French & Eur.

Deutsch-Russiches Woerterbuch: S-Z, 3 vols, Vol. 3. Hans H. Bielfeldt. Ed. by Ronald Loetzsch. (Ger. & Rus.). 1984. M.38.00. Akad Verl Ath.

Deutsch-Russische Wirtschaftssprache. N. Grischen. 480p. (Ger. & Rus.). 1969. 27.50 (ISBN 3-19-006207-2, M-7332, Pub. by M. Hueber). French & Eur.

Deutsch-Russische Wirtschaftssprache. N. Grischen. 480p. (Ger. & Rus.). 1969. DM.27.50 (ISBN 3-19-006207-2). Hueber.

Deutsch-Russisches Meteorologisches Worterbuch. W. G. Martschenko. 392p. (Ger. & Rus.). 1973. leatherette 12.95 (ISBN 0-686-92387-1, M-9092). French & Eur.

Deutsch-Russisches Oekonomisches Woerterbuch. Bljach & Bagma. (Rus. & Ger.). M.43.50. Wissenschaftliche.

Deutsch-Russisches Okonomisches Worterbuch: Dictionary German-Russian of Economics. I. S. Bljach & B. T. Bagma. 664p. (Ger. & Rus.). 1977. leatherette 24.75 (ISBN 0-686-92495-9, M-9056). French & Eur.

Deutsch-Russisches Woerterbuch. 15th ed. Edmund Daum & W. Schenk. (Ger. & Rus.). 1976. 13.50 (ISBN 0-686-56602-5, M-7333, Pub. by Max Hueber). French & Eur.

Deutsch-Russisches Woerterbuch. 15th ed. Edmund Daum & W. Schenk. (Ger. & Rus.). 1976. DM.13.50. Hueber.

Deutsch-Russisches Woerterbuch: A-G. Hans H. Bielfeldt. Ed. by R. Loetzsch et al. 1250p. (Ger. & Rus.). 1983. M.38.00 (LSV 0875). Akad Verl Ath.

Deutsch-Russisches Woerterbuch: H-R, 3 vols, Vol. 2. Hans H. Bielfeldt. Ed. by Ronald Loetzsch. 1150p. (Ger. & Rus.). 1983. M.38.00. Akad Verl Ath.
Deutsch-Russisches Worterbuch der Forstund Holzwirtschaft. E. A. Pawlow & O. I. Semjonowa. 477p. (Ger. & Rus.). 1978. 9.95 (ISBN 0-686-92498-3, M-9058). French & Eur.
Deutsch-Russisches Worterbuch der Rechentechnik und Datenverarbeitung. W. A. Scharow & A. L. Nowitschkowa. 400p. (Ger. & Rus.). 1976. leatherette 12.50 (ISBN 0-686-92365-0, M-9057). French & Eur.
Deutsch-Russisches Worterbuch fur Eisenbahnwessen. D. A. Bunin et al. 531p. (Ger. & Rus.). 1957. 7.95 (ISBN 0-686-92383-9, M-9060). French & Eur.
Deutsch-Russisches Worterbuch fur Eisenbahnwesen. A. P. Sulima-Samujillo et al. 536p. (German & Rus.). 1960. write for info. (M-9069). French & Eur.
Deutsch-Russisches Worterbuch fur Ozeanographie. N. N. Gorski et al. 240p. (Ger. & Rus.). 1957. leatherette 4.95 (ISBN 0-686-92378-2, M-9104). French & Eur.
Deutsch-Russisches Worterbuch fur Wasserbau. L. B. Bernstein. 579p. (Rus. & Ger.). 1961. leatherette 19.95 (ISBN 0-686-92359-6, M-9100). French & Eur.
Deutsch-Spanisches Glossarium. Mario R. Lerche. 460p. (Ger. & Span.). 1967. 17.50 (ISBN 3-7819-2012-7, S-7347, Pub. by Fritz Knapp Verlag). French & Eur.
Deutsch-Spanisches Glossarium Finanzieller & Wirtschaftlicher Fachausdrueck. Mario R. Lerche. LC 77-574052. 460p. (Ger. & Span.). 1970. DM.22.00 (ISBN 3-7819-2012-7). Knapp Verlag.
Deutsch-Turkisches Woerterbuch fur Technische Berufe. 2nd ed. Sadettin Bilginer. 448p. (Ger. & Turkish.). 1966. DM.leatherette 55.00 (ISBN 3-7736-5270-4). Girardet.
Deutsch-Turkisches Worterbuch Fur Technische Berufe. 2nd ed. Sadettin Bilginer. 448p. (Ger. & Turkish.). 1966. leatherette 55.00 (ISBN 3-7736-5270-4, M-7348, Pub. by Verlag W. Girardet). French & Eur.
Deutsch-Ungarisches Woerterbuch. 376p. (Ger. & Hungarian.). 1955. 2.50 Ft. Akademiai Kiado.
Deutsche Fach & Wissenschaftssprache. Drozd & Seibicke. 207p. (Ger.). E27.00. Brandstetter.
Deutsche Lehnworter in der Polnischen Bergbausprache. Konrad Wypych. LC 77-463784. 267p. (Pol. & Ger.). 1976. DM.38.00. MG Schmitz.
Deutsche Woerterbuch, 3 vols. 2nd ed. Moritz Heyne. (Ger.). 1970. Set. DM.195.00 (ISBN 3-7776-0053-9). Hirzel Verlag.
Deutsche Woerterbucher. Peter Kuhn. LC 79-369972. viii, 266p. (Ger.). 1978. write for info. (ISBN 3-484-10323-X). Niemeyer.
Deutsches Munzsammler-Lexikon. Herbert Rittmann. LC 79-34554. (Illus.). 447p. (Ger.). 1977. write for info. (ISBN 3-87045-116-5). Battenberg.
Deutsches Woerterbuch. (Ger.). 1977. 7.50 (ISBN 3-411-01702-3, M-7338, Bibliogr. Institut). French & Eur.
Deutsches Woerterbuch, 3 vols. (Ger.). 1977. DM.7.50 (ISBN 3-411-01702-3). Biblio Inst.
Deutsches Woerterbuch. J. Grimm & W. Grimm. (Ger.). 1965. DM.18.00 (7983059). Herzel Verlag.
Deutsches Woerterbuch, 33 vols. Jacob Grimm & Wilhelm Grimm. (Ger.). 1973. Repr. Set. 3150.00 (ISBN 0-685-30396-9). Adler.
Deutsches Woerterbuch, 3 vols. 2nd ed. Moritz Heyne. (Ger.). 1970. Set. 195.00 (ISBN 3-7776-0053-9, M-7334, Pub. by Hirzel). French & Eur.
Deutsches Woerterbuch. Lutz Mackensen. (Ger.). 1977. 38.50 (ISBN 3-517-00637-8, M-7339, Pub. by Suedwest). French & Eur.
Deutsches Woerterbuch. Lutz Mackensen. (Ger.). 1977. DM.38.50 (ISBN 3-517-00637-8). Suedwest.
Deutsches Woerterbuch. 7th ed. Hermann Paul. (Ger.). 1976. 29.95 (ISBN 3-484-10057-5, M-7335, Pub. by Max Niemeyer). French & Eur.
Deutsches Woerterbuch. 7th ed. Hermann Paul. (Ger.). 1976. fl.29.95 (ISBN 3-484-10057-5). Niemeyer.
Deutsches Woerterbuch. 2nd ed. Gerhard Wahrig. (Ger.). 1975. 30.95 (ISBN 3-570-01631-5, M-7336, Pub. by Bertelsmann Lexikon VVA). French & Eur.
Deutsches Woerterbuch. Gerhard Wahrig. 1434p. (Ger.). 1970. 35.00. Imported Bks.
Deutsches Woerterbuch. 2nd ed. Gerhard Wahrig. (Ger.). 1975. DM.30.95 (ISBN 3-570-01631-5). C Bertelsmann.
Deutsches Woerterbuch, 2 vols. 6th ed. Karl Weigand. (Ger.). 1968. Set. 252.00x (ISBN 3-11-000383-X, M-7337). De Gruyter.
Deutsches Woerterbuch in 3 Banden: Band I, Deutsches Woerterbuch, A-F. (Ger.). write for info. (ISBN 3-411-01831-3). Biblio Inst.
Deutsches Woerterbuch in 3 Banden: Band 2, Deutsches Woerterbuch. (Ger.). write for info. (ISBN 3-411-01832-1). Biblio Inst.
Deutsches Woerterbuch in 3 Banden: Band 3, Deutsches Woerterbuch, O-Z. (Ger.). write for info. (ISBN 3-411-01833-X). Biblio Inst.
Deutsches Woerterbuch Tuebingen. H. Paul. 841p. (Ger.). 1983. pap. 24.00. M Rosenberg.
Deutsches Woerterbuch und Lexicon der deutsches Sprachlehre. G. Wahrig. 1500p. (Ger.). simulated leather 24.00. M Rosenberg.
Developing Dictionary Skills. Janice Moldenhauer. (gr. 3-8). 1979. 5.95 (ISBN 0-916456-48-X, GA120). Good Apple.
Developing Your Vocabulary. A. Rae Price. 268p. 1973. pap. text ed. write for info. (ISBN 0-697-03805-X). Wm C Brown.
Devil's Dictionary. Ambrose Bierce. 1911. pap. 2.25 (ISBN 0-486-20487-1). Dover.
Devil's Dictionary. Ambrose Bierce. LC 78-13294. (Illus.). 1978. 14.95 (ISBN 0-916144-34-8); pap. 7.95 (ISBN 0-916144-35-6). Stemmer Hse.
Devil's Dictionary. Jean-Claude Suares. LC 78-3318. (Illus.). 1979. 12.95i (ISBN 0-690-01764-2); pap. 5.95i (ISBN 0-690-01765-0, TYC-T). T Y Crowell.
Devil's DP Dictionary. Stan Kelly-Bootle. (Illus.). 160p. 1981. pap. 8.50 (ISBN 0-07-034022-6, P&RB). McGraw.
Diabetes Dictionary & Guide. Joseph F. Brown. LC 77-92938. (Illus.). 1978. 14.95 (ISBN 0-9601484-1-8). Press West.
Dialectes Romans de France a la Lumiere des Atlas Regionaux. (Fr.). 1973. 201.00 F (ISBN 2-22201-540-5). CNRS.
Dialectologia Hispanoamericana. Zamora Clemente & Jorge Juan-Guitart. 160p. (Span.). 1982. pap. 500.00 ptas (ISBN 8-47455-040-8). Almar Edns.
Dialetti della Liguria Orientale Odierna, 2 vols. Hugo Plomteux. LC 76-514874. (Illus.). 1174p. (Ital.). 1975. L.24000.00. Patron.
Diamond Dictionary. 2nd ed. Robert A. Gaal. (Illus.). 1977. 16.95 (ISBN 0-87311-008-0). Gemological.
Dianetics & Scientology Technical Dictionary. L. Ron Hubbard. 32.00 (ISBN 0-686-30803-4). Church Scient NY.
Dianetics & Scientology Technical Dictionary. L. Ron Hubbard. 1975. 37.00 (ISBN 0-88404-037-2). Bridge Pubns Inc.
Diaphragm Actuated Control Valve Terminology: 1961-No.112. American Society of Mechanical Engineers. 2.25 (L00036); members 1.80. ASME.
Dicccionario del Cine, 2 vols. George Sadoul. 800p. (Span.). 1977. Set. pap. 29.95 (ISBN 84-7090-082-X, S-50057). French & Eur.
Diccionare de la musica. Roland De Cande. (Span.). 375.00 ptas. EDNS Sesenti Dos.
Diccionari Angles-Catala. 6th ed. Jordi Colomer del Castillo. 253p. (Eng. & Span.). 1981. 400.00 ptas (ISBN 84-7306-091-1). Portic.
Diccionari basic castella-catala i catala-castela. 202p. (Span.). 1969. 50.00 ptas. M. Arimany.
Diccionari Basic Catala-Castella, Castella-Catala. 9th ed. Miquel Arimany Coma. 390p. (Catala & Span.). 1975. pap. 3.95 (ISBN 84-7211-085-0, S-50359). French & Eur.
Diccionari calala de simonims. Albert Jane. (Span.). 1972. write for info. Aedos.
Diccionari castella-catala, catala-castella. 4th ed. Alberti & Gubern Santiago. 1183p. (Span.). 1969. 500.00 ptas. Alberti.
Diccionari Castella-Catala, Catala-Castella, Mitja. 2nd ed. Santiago Alberti. 584p. (Catalan & Castel.). 1978. 19.95 (ISBN 84-400-0761-2, S-31551). French & Eur.
Diccionari Castella-Catala, Catala-Castella Petit. Santiago Alberti. LC 75-512211. 338p. (Span. & Catalan.). 1975. write for info. (ISBN 8-472-46057-6). Alberti.
Diccionari Catala-Castella. Francisco de Moll Y Cassanovas. LC 78-351223. 395p. (Span. & Catalan.). 1977. 1100.00 ptas (ISBN 8-427-30238-X). Moll Edit.
Diccionari catala-castella, castella-catala. 683p. (Span.). 1969. 60.00 ptas. Mateu.
Diccionari Catala-Castella, Castella-Catala. 2nd ed. Josep Miracle. LC 77-458925. xi, 1122p. (Span. & Catalan.). 1976. write for info. (ISBN 8-485-08300-8). Poseidon SA.
Diccionari catala-castella, castella-catala. Josep Miracle. 1084p. (Span.). 1969. 675.00 ptas. Edhasa.
Diccionari Catala-Castella-Castellano-Catalan. Frederic Larreula. 544p. (Span.). 1980. 250.00 ptas. Bruguera.
Diccionari Catala-Castella I Castella-Catala. Fransesc de B. Moll Casanovas. 816p. (Catala & Span.). 1978. 46.00 (ISBN 84-273-0257-6, S-50362). French & Eur.
Diccionari Catala-Castella: Vocabulari Basic. Josep Munte Vila. 216p. (Span.). 1981. write for info. ptas (ISBN 84-7031-275-8). Blume Edit.
Diccionari Catala de Sinonims. Albert Jane. 606p. (Catalan.). 1972. 15.75 (ISBN 84-7003-146-5, S-50214). French & Eur.
Diccionari Catala-Frances, Frances-Catala. Carlos Castellanos i Llorenc. LC 79-125113. 1095p. (Fr. & Catalan.). 1979. 1000.00 ptas (ISBN 8-485-19409-8). Encic Catalan.
Diccionari catala general. 1418p. (Span.). 1971. 550.00 ptas. M. Arimany.
Diccionari Catala General Usual. 4th ed. Miguel Arimany Coma. 1418p. (Catalan.). 1976. 35.95 (ISBN 84-7211-097-4, S-50049). French & Eur.
Diccionari catala-valencia-balear, 10 vols. Antoni M. Alcover Sureda & Moll Casasnoves. (Illus., Span.). 1200.00 ea. ptas. 11000.00 set. Moll Edit.
Diccionari de agriculatura ruso-espanol. (Rus. & Span.). Mex.$30.00. Cultura Popular.
Diccionari De la Llengua Catalan. 3rd ed. Santiago Alberti. 412p. (Catalan.). 1978. pap. 13.95 (ISBN 84-7246-058-4, S-50208). French & Eur.
Diccionari de la Llengua Catalana. Santiago Alberti. LC 75-406972. 411p. (Span.). 1975. 350.00 ptas (ISBN 8-472-46058-4). Alberti.
Diccionari de la Rima, 2 vols. 2nd ed. Francesc Ferrer Pastor. 768p. (Span.). 1981. pap. 3500.00 ptas (ISBN 84-300-4433-7). Piquenas Edit.
Diccionari de metjes catalans. Josep Maria Calbet Corbella. 224p. (Span.). 1981. pap. 1000.00 ptas (ISBN 84-232-0186-4). Dalmau.
Diccionari de sinomins i antonims. S. Pay Estrany. 824p. (Span.). 1970. 700.00 ptas. Teide.
Diccionari De Sinonimos I Antonimos. 4th ed. Santiago Pey Estrany. 840p. (Catalan.). 1977. pap. 13.95 (ISBN 84-307-7329-0, S-50235). French & Eur.
Diccionari De Sinonims. Manuel Franquesa. 1248p. (Catalan.). 1970. 40.50 (ISBN 0-686-57365-X, S-50185). French & Eur.
Diccionari de sinonims. Miquel Franquesa. 1232p. (Span.). 1971. write for info. Portic.
Diccionari de sinonims i antonims: Edicio economica. 5th ed. Santiago Pey Estrany. (Span.). 1981. pap. 600.00 ptas (ISBN 84-307-7329-0). Teide.
Diccionari del Nacionalisme. Imma Tubella. 144p. (Catalan.). 1978. pap. pns (ISBN 84-7410-034-8, S-50125). French & Eur.
Diccionari d'electrionica. Lluis Marquet. 177p. (Span.). 1971. 90.00 ptas. Portic.
Diccionari d'Electronica. Luis Marquet. 208p. (Catalan.). 1977. pap. 4.50 (ISBN 84-7306-116-0, S-50184). French & Eur.
Diccionari d'Informatica. 2nd ed. Carmara Oficial de Comercio, Industria y Navegacion Barcelona. 214p. (Span.). 1982. pap. 500.00 ptas (ISBN 84-500-7912-8). Organ Ofic Adm.
Diccionari Escolar Catala Arimany. 4th ed. Miguel Arimany Coma. 310p. (Catalan.). 1978. pap. 7.95 (ISBN 84-7211-117-2, S-50050). French & Eur.
Diccionari escolar de la llengua catalana 'Vox' 510p. (Span.). 1981. 450.00 ptas (ISBN 84-7153-334-0). Biblo SP.
Diccionari Escolarde la Llengua Catalana. 512p. (Span.). write for info. Bibliograf SP.
Diccionari etimologic i complementari de la llengua catalana, Tomo 2. 2nd ed. Joan Coromines i Vigneaux. 1120p. (Span.). 1981. 4500.00 ptas (ISBN 84-7256-191-7). Curial.
Diccionari etimologie i complementari de la llengua catalana, Tomo 3. Joan Coromines i Vegneaux. 1056p. (Span.). 1982. write for info. (ISBN 84-7256-204-2). Curial.
Diccionari Fondamental de la Llengua Catalana. 448p. (Catalan.). 495.00 ptas (ISBN 84-7153-333-2). Bibliograf SP.
Diccionari Fondamental de la Llengua Catalana. Vox. Prologue by Jordi Gali I Herrera. LC 79-110126. (Illus.). 430p. (Catalan.). 1979. write for info. (ISBN 8-471-53333-2). Biblo Sp.
Diccionari general de barbarismes i altres incorreccions. Joan Miravitlles Serradell. 224p. (Span.). 1982. pap. 350.00 ptas (ISBN 84-7263-240-7). Claret Edit.
Diccionari General de la Llengua Catalana. Pompeu Fabra. LC 79-349036. xxxi, 1779p. (Catalan.). 1978. write for info. (ISBN 8-435-00120-2). Edhasa.
Diccionari I Catala-Valencia-Balear, 10 vols. 2nd ed. Antoni M. Alcover & Francesc de B. Moll. 9850p. (Catalan.). 1975. Set. 200.00 (ISBN 84-273-0025-5, S-31549). French & Eur.
Diccionari Ingles-Catala, Catala-Ingles. 3rd ed. Jordi Colomer del Castillo. 253p. (Eng. & Catalan.). 1978. pap. 8.75 (ISBN 84-7306-091-1, S-50414). French & Eur.
Diccionari Italia-Catala Catala-Italia. Jordi Fornas Prat. 616p. (Span.). 1982. 1500.00 ptas (ISBN 84-7306-183-7). Portic.
Diccionari Manual Castella-Catala. 2nd ed. Miguel Arimany Coma. 413p. (Castella & Catalan.). 1975. 8.75 (ISBN 84-7211-084-2, S-50358). French & Eur.

Diccionari Manual Castella-Catala Catala-Castella. Camilo J. Cela & Badia A. M. Margarit. 680p. (Catalan.). 850.00 ptas (ISBN 84-7153-392-8). Biblograf SP.
Diccionari Manual Castella-Catala, Catala-Castella, 2 vols. 3rd ed. Vox. LC 79-112856. 614p. (Span. & Catalan.). 1977. 425.00 ptas (ISBN 8-471-53198-4). Biblo Sp.
Diccionari Manual Catala-Castella. 2nd ed. Miguel Arimany Coma. 535p. (Catalan & Castella.). 1975. 8.75 (ISBN 84-7211-078-8, S-50357). French & Eur.
Diccionari Manual Catala-Castella i Castella-Catala. 9th ed. Miguel Arimany Coma. 956p. (Catalan & Castella.). 1976. 16.50 (ISBN 84-7211-088-5, S-50360). French & Eur.
Diccionari Manual de la Llengua Catalana. Josep Miracle Montserrat. 1401p. (Catalan.). 1975. 19.95 (ISBN 84-298-0594-X, S-31550). French & Eur.
Diccionari Manual de Sinonims. Salvador Espiru. 319p. (Catalan.). 575.00 ptas (ISBN 84-7153-325-1). Biblograf SP.
Diccionari Ortografic. Joan Triadu. 552p. (Catalan.). write for info. ptas (ISBN 84-7153-327-8). Biblograf SP.
Diccionari Pera Ociosos. Joan Fuster Ortells. 208p. (Catalan.). 1978. pap. 6.75 (ISBN 84-297-1431-6, S-50213). French & Eur.
Diccionari Politic De Catalunya. Victor Lluelles Cardona. 344p. (Catalan.). 1977. pap. 18.95 (ISBN 84-7306-086-5, S-50183). French & Eur.
Diccionari popular catala-castella. 230p. (Span.). 1970. 75.00 ptas. Milla Lib.
Diccionari Practic Castella-Catala, Catala-Castella. 3rd ed. Miguel Arimany Coma. 456p. (Castella & Catalan.). 1976. 9.95 (ISBN 84-7211-087-7, S-50356). French & Eur.
Diccionari Practic Catala-Frances. 2nd ed. Miguel Arimany Coma. 256p. (Catalan & Span.). 1977. pap. 5.25 (ISBN 84-7211-048-6, S-50413). French & Eur.
Diccionari practic catala-frances. 224p. (Span. & Fr.). 1968. 80.00 ptas. M. Arimany.
Diccionari practic catala general. 400p. (Span.). 1969. write for info. M. Arimany.
Diccionari practic de comerc exterior Catala-Angles Angles-Catala. Joan Ferrer Santalo. 192p. (Eng. & Span.). 1982. pap. 600.00 ptas (ISBN 84-500-7960-8). Organ Ofic Adm.
Diccionari Practic de Sinonims Catalans: Mots i Frases. 2nd ed. 640p. (Catalan.). 1972. 9.95 (ISBN 84-7211-075-3, S-50047). French & Eur.
Diccionari practic frances-catala. 324p. (Fr. & Span.). 1968. 125.00 ptas. M. Arimany.
Diccionari practic frances-catala, catala-frances. 450p. (Fr. & Span.). 1968. 200.00 ptas. M. Arimany.
Diccionari tecnic de l'automovil. Balbastre & Josep Ferrer. 151p. (Span.). 1972. 90.00 ptas. Portic.
Diccionari Usual Catala-Castella i Castella-Catala. 7th ed. Miguel Arimany Coma. 958p. (Catalan & Castella.). 1976. 23.95 (ISBN 84-7211-080-X, S-50361). French & Eur.
Diccionari Usual de Sinonims Catalans: Mots i Frases. Joana Raspall de Cauhe et al. 572p. (Catalan.). 1975. 17.50 (ISBN 84-7211-111-3, S-50048). French & Eur.
Diccionario. 96p. (Span.). 1982. pap. 275.00 ptas (ISBN 84-305-1297-7). Susaeta.
Diccionario A R V E: Obra completa, 2 vols. 2nd ed. Tr. by Varios. 704p. (Span.). 1982. pap. 1850.00 ptas (ISBN 84-7017-706-0). Argos-Vergara.
Diccionario A R V E: Tomo 1; Ingles-Espanol. 2nd ed. Tr. by Varios. 432p. (Eng. & Span.). 1982. pap. 925.00 ptas (ISBN 84-7017-707-9). Argos-Vergara.
Diccionario A R V E: Tomo 2; Espanol-Ingles. 2nd ed. Tr. by Varios. 272p. (Span. & Eng.). 1982. pap. 925.00 ptas (ISBN 84-7017-708-7). Argos-Vergara.
Diccionario Abreviado Aleman-Espagnol. 848p. (Ger. & Span.). 1981. write for info. ptas (ISBN 84-7153-217-4). Biblo SP.
Diccionario Abreviado de la Lengua Espanola. 512p. (Span.). 295.00 ptas (ISBN 84-7153-201-8). Biblograf SP.
Diccionario abreviado de la Lengua Espanola Vox. 12th ed. 512p. (Span.). 1982. 265.00 ptas (ISBN 84-7153-201-8). Biblo SP.
Diccionario Abreviado de Sinonimos. Fernando Corripio. (Span.). pap. 4.95 (BRG). Lectorum Pubns.
Diccionario Abreviado de Sinonimos. Fernando Corripio Perez. 480p. (Span.). 1976. pap. 5.75 (ISBN 84-02-04681-9, S-50157). French & Eur.
Diccionario Abreviado de Sinonimos. Samuel Gili Gaya. 352p. (Span.). 295.00 ptas (ISBN 84-7153-207-7). Biblograf SP.
Diccionario abreviado de sinonimos 'Vox' 5th ed. 352p. (Span.). 1982. write for info. (ISBN 84-7153-207-7). Biblo SP.
Diccionario Abreviado Espanol-Chino. 1244p. (Span. & Chinese.). 1979. leatherette 14.95 (ISBN 0-686-92546-7, S-33189). French & Eur.
Diccionario Abreviado Frances-Espanol Espanol-Frances. 672p. (Fr. & Span.). 350.00 ptas (ISBN 84-7153-216-6). Biblograf SP.
Diccionario abreviado Ingles-Espanol Vox. 6th ed. 792p. (Span. & Eng.). 1982. 325.00 ptas (ISBN 84-7153-214-X). Biblo SP.
Diccionario Abreviado Ingles-Espanol Espanol-Ingles. 792p. (Eng. & Span.). 350.00 ptas (ISBN 84-7153-214-X). Biblograf SP.
Diccionario Abreviado Italiano,-Espanol Espanol-Italiano. 735p. (Ital. & Span.). 1980. 9.95 (ISBN 84-7153-523-8, S-31760). French & Eur.
Diccionario Abreviado Italiano-Espanol Espanol-Italiano. Ed. by Givanna Schepisi. 782p. (Ital. & Span.). 460.00 ptas (ISBN 84-7153-523-8). Biblograf SP.
Diccionario Abreviado Latino-Espanol Espanol-Latino. 316p. (Lat. & Span.). 350.00 ptas (ISBN 84-7153-221-2). Biblograf SP.
Diccionario Abreviado Latino-Espanol Espanol-Latino 'Spes' 9th ed. 316p. (Lat. & Span.). 1980. write for info. (ISBN 84-7153-221-2). Biblo SP.
Diccionario abreviado Latino-Espanol Espanol-Latino Vox. 11th ed. 316p. (Lat. & Span.). 1982. 325.00 ptas (ISBN 84-7153-221-2). Biblo SP.
Diccionario Abreviado Ortografico de la Lengua Espanola. 416p. (Span.). 1980. 325.00 ptas (ISBN 84-7153-227-1). Biblograf SP.
Diccionario Academia. 250p. (Span.). Mex.$9.50. Fernandez.
Diccionario academia dos. 240p. (Span.). write for info. (705). Fernandez.
Diccionario Academico de la Lengua. 848p. (Span.). 1980. 700.00 ptas. pap. 625.00. Albir.
Diccionario Actualizado de la Lengua Espanola. 3rd ed. Juan Capdevila Font. 392p. (Span.). 1976. 10.50 (ISBN 84-85117-06-9, S-50266); pap. 9.25 (ISBN 84-85117-28-X, S-50265). French & Eur.
Diccionario Actualizado De Sinonimos y Contrarios De la Lengua Espanola. 2nd ed. Juan Capdevila Font. 513p. (Span.). 1978. pap. 13.95 (ISBN 84-7176-301-X, S-50267). French & Eur.
Diccionario Aleman-Espanol. 16th ed. Carlos Brandau. 640p. (Ger. & Span.). 1982. pap. 150.00 ptas (ISBN 84-7105-090-0). Mayfe.
Diccionario aleman-espanol. (Ger. & Span.). 25.00 ptas. Mayfe.
Diccionario Aleman-Espanol-Aleman. Franz Muller. 1195p. (Ger. & Span.). 7.50. Imported Bks.
Diccionario aleman-espanol de medicina. F. Ruiz Torres. 560p. (Ger. & Span.). 1960. write for info. MMW Verlag.
Diccionario aleman-espanol de medicina. F. Ruiz Torres. 560p. (Ger. & Span.). 1960. write for info. Alhambra.
Diccionario Aleman-Espanol, Espanol-Aleman de Medicina. 2nd ed. Francisco Ruiz Torres. 860p. (Ger. & Span.). 1971. pap. 41.25 (ISBN 84-205-0010-0, S-50089). French & Eur.
Diccionario Aleman-Espanol, Espanol-Aleman. E. F. Martinez Amador. 1616p. (Ger. & Span.). 50.95 (ISBN 84-303-0117-8, S-12381). French & Eur.
Diccionario Aleman-Espanol Espanol-Aleman 'Vox' 848p. (Span. & Ger.). 1981. write for info. (ISBN 84-7153-218-2). Biblo SP.
Diccionario Aleman-Espanol, Espanol-Aleman. Muller. 900p. (Ger. & Span.). leatherette 12.25 (ISBN 84-303-0119-4, S-50384). French & Eur.
Diccionario Aleman-Espanol Espanol-Aleman. Ed. by Michael Schmidt. 814p. (Ger. & Span.). 495.00 ptas. Biblograf SP.
Diccionario aleman-espanol y espanol-aleman de medicina. F. Ruiz Torres. 860p. (Ger. & Span.). 1971. 700.00 ptas. Alhambra.
Diccionario Alevin Sopena Escolar de Iniciacion a la Lengua Espanola. (Span.). 3.95. Lectorum Pubns.
Diccionario Alianza. 96p. (Span. & Eng.). write for info. (796). Fernandez.
Diccionario Alienza ingles-espanol, espanol-ingles. 392p. (Eng. & Span.). Mex.$10.00. Fernandez.
Diccionario analitico de Mampruli. Evangelina Arana & Mauricio Swadesh. (Span.). 1967. Mex.$40.00. INAH.
Diccionario Anaya de la Lengua. 720p. (Span.). 1978. leatherette 22.50 (ISBN 84-207-1373-2, S-50251). French & Eur.
Diccionario Anaya de la Lengua. 4th ed. 752p. (Span.). 1981. 1100.00 ptas (ISBN 84-207-1373-2). Anaya.
Diccionario Anaya de la Lengua. 752p. (Span.). 1980. 990.00 ptas (ISBN 84-207-1497-6). Anaya.
Diccionario & Manual de las Nuevas Matematicas. Robert W. Marks. (Illus.). 270p. (Span.). 1968. Mex.$3.50. Editors Pr Serv.
Diccionario Arabe-Espanol. 876p. (Arabic & Span.). 1977. 22.95 (ISBN 84-600-0842-8, S-50292). French & Eur.
Diccionario Arabe-Espanol, Espanol-Arabe. Alhambra. 1252p. (Arabic & Span.). 17.95 (ISBN 84-303-0163-1, S-50424). French & Eur.
Diccionario Aristos. (Illus.). 640p. (Span.). 125.00 ptas. pap. 80.00 ptas. Sopena.
Diccionario Aristos con perdanismos. (Span.). S/75.00. Bruno.
Diccionario Atlas De Anatomia Humana. Nicola Piscitelli. 256p. (Span.). 1974. pap. 13.25 (ISBN 84-307-8290-7, S-50259). French & Eur.
Diccionario: Atlas De Mineralogia. 2nd ed. Vincenzo De Michele. 216p. (Span.). 1978. 11.50 (ISBN 84-307-8288-5, S-50260). French & Eur.
Diccionario Atomico. Victorin Charles. 296p. (Span.). 1962. 14.95 (ISBN 0-686-56708-0, S-33057). French & Eur.
Diccionario atomico. Tr. by Victorin Charles. 296p. (Span.). 1962. Arg.$2.00. Leru.
Diccionario Aunamendi Espanol-Vasco: Tomo 7, Conch-Corr. Bernardo Estornes Lasa et al. 196p. (Span.). 1982. pap. 550.00 ptas (ISBN 84-7025-213-5). Aunamendi Edit.
Diccionario auxiliar de traductor: Espanol-Ingles. Jose Merino Bustamante. 144p. (Span. & Eng.). 1982. pap. 300.00 ptas (ISBN 84-85439-00-7). CEEI.
Diccionario auxiliar del crucigramista. (Span.). 60.00 ptas. Bruguera.
Diccionario Auxiliar del Crucigramista. Baldovi F. Turell. 671p. (Span.). 1970. Mex.$0.86. Bruguera MX.
Diccionario Auxiliar del Crucigramista. 3rd ed. Fausto Turell Baldovi. (Span.). 1978. pap. 8.75 (ISBN 84-02-00817-8, S-50154). French & Eur.
Diccionario auxiliar del crucigramista II. Fausto Turell Baldovi. 256p. (Span.). 1982. pap. write for info. (ISBN 84-02-09116-4). Bruguera.
Diccionario Auxiliar del Traductor Espanol-Ingles. Jose Merino Bustamante. 144p. (Span. & Eng.). 1978. pap. 8.50 (ISBN 84-85439-00-7, S-50583). French & Eur.
Diccionario Auxiliar del Traductor Espanol-Ingles. Jose Merino Bustamante. 144p. (Span. & Eng.). 1981. 300.00 ptas (ISBN 84-85439-00-7). CEEI.
Diccionario Axon de zoologia y botanica. (Span.). Arg.$11.00. Plus Ultra.
Diccionario Bachiller. Hector F. Miri. 720p. (Span.). Arg.$15.00. Claridad.
Diccionario basico. Pablo Arogones. (Illus., Span.). 150.00 ptas. Mayfe.
Diccionario basico. (Illus.). 700p. (Span.). 150.00 ptas. Sopena.
Diccionario Basico Anaya de la Lengua. 728p. (Span.). 1982. 600.00 ptas (ISBN 8-42072-195-6). Anaya.
Diccionario basico de fudicion ingles-castellano. Channazaroff-Waganoff. 219p. (Span. & Eng.). Arg.$7.00. Mitre.
Diccionario Basico de la Construccion. 16th ed. Jose Zurita Ruiz. 248p. (Span.). 1976. pap. 8.95 (ISBN 84-329-2905-0, S-50223). French & Eur.
Diccionario basico de la construccion. Jose Zurita Ruiz. 246p. (Span.). 1982. 390.00 ptas (ISBN 84-329-2805-4). Ceac.
Diccionario basico de la construccion II. Jose Zurita Ruiz. 246p. (Span.). 1982. pap. 340.00 ptas (ISBN 84-329-2905-0). Ceac.
Diccionario basico de la industria del petroleo. Augustin Mendez Manzano. 592p. (Span.). 1981. pap. 1500.00 ptas (ISBN 84-283-1097-1). Paraninfo.
Diccionario Basico de la Industria del Petroleo & Derivados. Mendez. (Eng. & Span. & Fr.). 1981. 1500.00 ptas (ISBN 8-42831-097-1). Paraninfo.
Diccionario basico de matematicas. 3rd ed. Mariano Diaz Velazquiz. 224p. (Span.). 1981. pap. 500.00 ptas (ISBN 84-207-1434-8). Anaya.
Diccionario Basico De Seguros. Julio Castelo Matran. 312p. (Span.). 1978. pap. 18.50 (ISBN 84-7100-049-0, S-50036). French & Eur.
Diccionario Basico de Seguros. 4th ed. Julio Castelo Matran. 312p. (Span.). 1981. 700.00 ptas (ISBN 84-7100-049-0). Mapfre.
Diccionario basico de seguros. rev. ed. (Span.). write for info. Mex. de Seguros.
Diccionario basico escolar. 416p. (Span.). 1982. Col.$pap. 95.00 (ISBN 84-8279-070-6). Educar.
Diccionario basico escolar de la lengua castellana. 2nd ed. 320p. (Span.). 1980. pap. 110.00 ptas (ISBN 84-391-1003-0). Edit Nebrija.
Diccionario Basico Escolar de la Lengua Espanola. 2nd ed. Juan Capdevilla Font. 398p. (Span.). 1975. 6.75 (ISBN 84-85117-17-4, S-50254). French & Eur.
Diccionario Basico Escolar de la Lengua Espanola. 2nd ed. Juan Capdevilla Font. 398p. (Span.). 1975. pap. 4.75 (ISBN 84-85117-29-8, S-50255). French & Eur.
Diccionario basico Espasa: Tomo 3. 2nd ed. 1000p. (Span.). 1981. 3000.00 ptas (ISBN 84-239-4796-3). Espasa Calpe.
Diccionario Basico Frances-Espanol Espanol-Frances. 928p. (Fr. & Span.). 575.00 ptas (ISBN 84-7153-188-7). Biblograf SP.

Diccionario Basico Ilustrado
Espanol-Ingles, 4 vols. (Illus.).
1200p. (Span. & Eng.). 1982.
9600.00 set ptas (ISBN 8-48585-
616-3); 2400.00 ea. Mediterraneo.

Diccionario Basico Ilustrado Espanol
Ingles, Vol. 4. (Illus.). 300p. (Span.
& Eng.). 1982. 2400.00 ptas (ISBN
8-48585-620-1). Mediterraneo.

Diccionario Basico Ilustrado
Espanol-Ingles-Euskera: Obra
Complete, 4 vols. (Illus.). 1200p.
(Span. & Eng.). 1982. 9000.00 set
ptas (ISBN 8-48585-626-0).
Mediterraneo.

Diccionario Basico Ilustrado Espanol
Ingles-Gallego, 4 vols. 1200p.
(Span.). 1982. 9000.00 set ptas
(ISBN 8-48585-621-X); 2400.00
ea. Mediterraneo.

Diccionario Basico Ilustrado Espanol
Ingles-Gallego, Vol. 1. (Illus.).
300p. (Span. & Eng.). 1982.
2400.00 ptas (ISBN 8-48585-622-
8). Mediterraneo.

Diccionario Basico Ilustrado
Espanol-Ingles: Obra Completa.
1200p. (Eng. & Span.). 1982.
9600.00 set ptas (ISBN 8-48585-
616-3). Mediterraneo.

Diccionario Basico Ingles-Espanol
Espanol-Ingles Vox. 3rd ed. 662p.
(Eng. & Span.). 1982. 495.00 ptas
(ISBN 84-7153-155-0). Biblo SP.

Diccionario Basico Ingles-Espanol
Espanol-Ingles. 672p. (Eng. &
Span.). 495.00 ptas (ISBN 84-
7153-155-0). Biblograf SP.

Diccionario Basico Latino-Espanol.
9th ed. 830p. (Lat. & Span.). 1981.
385.00 ptas (ISBN 84-7153-223-9).
Biblo SP.

Diccionario Basico Latino-Espanol.
Recuero Pascual. LC 78-347492.
xviii, 151p. (Span. & Ladino.).
1977. write for info. (ISBN 8-472-
13088-6). Ameller Edic.

Diccionario Basico Latino-Espanol
Espanol-Latino. 830p. (Lat. &
Span.). 625.00 ptas (ISBN 84-
7153-223-9). Biblograf SP.

Diccionario basico latino-espanol,
espanol-latino. (Span. & Lat.).
8.60. Imported Bks.

Diccionario basico Latino-Espanol
Espanol-Latino. 10th ed. 830p.
(Lat. & Span.). 1982. 550.00 ptas
(ISBN 84-7153-223-9). Biblo SP.

Diccionario Basico Latino-Espanol,
Espanol-Latino. 8th ed. Eustaquio
Echauri Martinez. LC 80-100210.
829p. (Lat. & Span.). 1978. 235.00
ptas (ISBN 8-471-53223-9). Biblo
Sp.

Diccionario b a01sico universal.
(Illus.). 104p. (Span.). (gr. 4 up).
write for info. (708). Fernandez.

Diccionario Biblico: Broch. A. R.
Buckland. (Port.). 1981. pap. 4.50
(ISBN 0-8297-1172-4). Life Pubs
Intl.

Diccionario Biblico: Enc. A. R.
Buckland. (Port.). 1981. pap. 6.50
(ISBN 0-8297-0836-7). Life Pubs
Intl.

Diccionario Biblico Manual. Heinz
Obermayer. 352p. (Span.). 1975.
pap. 7.95 (ISBN 84-7263-094-3, S-
50212). French & Eur.

Diccionario Bibliografico De Liegos
Sueltos Poeticos, Siglo XVI.
Antonio Rodriguez Monino. 740p.
(Span.). 1970. 59.95 (ISBN 84-
7039-075-9, S-7006). French &
Eur.

Diccionario Bilingue. 95p. (Span. &
Eng.). 3.75. Cruzada Span Pubns.

Diccionario bilingue aleman-espanol
y espanol-aleman. Franz Muller.
1200p. (Span. & Ger.). 100.00 ptas.
Sopena.

Diccionario Bilingue De Psicologia.
Adela Alcantud. LC 78-50649.
(Senda Lexicografica Ser.). (Span.).
1978. pap. 7.95 (ISBN 0-918454-
05-0). Senda Nueva.

Diccionario bilingue frances-espanol-
aleman. Rev. ed. Alcala Zamora.
(Illus.). 960p. (Fr., Span. & Ger.).
100.00 ptas. 75.00 ptas ptas.
Sopena.

Diccionario bilingue ilustrado, 3 bks.
(Illus., Span. & Eng.). (gr. k-8).
Vol. 1, gr. k-2. s.p. 4.95 (0052-6);
Vol. 2, gr. 2-4. s.p. 5.95 (0053-4);
Vol. 3, gr. 4-8. s.p. 8.95 (0054-2).
Natl Textbk.

Diccionario bilingue ilustrado, 3 vols.
(Illus., Span. & Eng.). Vol. 1. 5.90
(TB6); Vol. 2. 5.90 (TB7); Vol. 3.
8.95 (TB8). Bilingual Ed Serv.

Diccionario bilingue ilustrado, 3 vols.
(Illus., Span. & Eng.). Vol. I. 4.95;
Vol. II. 5.95; Vol. III. 8.95. Iaconi.

Diccionario bilingue ingles-espanol y
espanol-ingles. Rev. ed. Ricardo
Roberston. (Eng. & Span.). 100.00
ptas. 75.00 ptas. pap. 70.00 ptas.
Sopena.

Diccionario Bilingue Maya Mopan &
Espanol. LC 77-560678. 393p.
(Mopan & Span.). 1976. write for
info. Inst Ling Ver.

Diccionario bilinque para la
juventud. Juan Delvalle. 78p.
(Span.). 1961. 1.50. Dist.
Comuneros.

Diccionario Biografico de la Musica.
2nd ed. Juan Ricart Matas. 1144p.
(Span.). 1966. 60.00 (ISBN 84-
7082-140-7, S-12347). French &
Eur.

Diccionario Brasileiro
Contemporaneo. F. Fernandes.
(Port.). Date not set. price not set
(M-9322). French & Eur.

Diccionario Brevis. (Span.). S/18.00.
Bruno.

Diccionario Brevis duplex: aleman-
castellano y castellano-aleman.
(Ger. & Span.). Arg.$15.00.
Sopena.

Diccionario Brevis duplex: frances-
castellano y castellano-frances.
(Fr. & Span.). Arg.$15.00. Sopena.

Diccionario Brevis duplex: ingles-
castellano y castellano-ingles.
(Eng. & Span.). Arg.$15.00.
Sopena.

Diccionario Brevis duplex: Italiano-
castellano y castellano-italiano.
(Ital. & Span.). Arg.$15.00.
Sopena.

Diccionario Brevis duplex:
Portugues-catellano y castellano-
portugues. (Port. & Span.).
Arg.$15.00. Sopena.

Diccionario Bursatil. 195p. (Span.).
1977. pap. 17.50 (ISBN 84-85307-
01-1, S-50126). French & Eur.

Diccionario Cassell espanol-ingles,
ingles-espanol: Obra completa, 6
vols. 3rd ed. Edgar Allison Peers.
816p. (Span.). 1980. pap. write for
info. (ISBN 84-345-4170-X).
Salvat Editores.

Diccionario Cassell espanol-ingles,
ingles-espanol: Tomo 1. 3rd ed.
Edgar A. Peers. 128p. (Span. &
Eng.). 1980. pap. write for info.
(ISBN 84-345-4171-8). Salvat
Editores.

Diccionario Cassell espanol-ingles,
ingles-espanol: Tomo 2. 3rd ed.
Edgar A. Peers. 120p. (Span. &
Eng.). 1980. pap. write for info.
(ISBN 84-345-4172-6). Salvat
Editores.

Diccionario Cassell espanol-ingles,
ingles-espanol: Tomo 3. 3rd ed.
Edgar A. Peers. 128p. (Span. &
Eng.). 1980. pap. write for info.
(ISBN 84-345-4173-4). Salvat
Editores.

Diccionario Cassell espanol-ingles,
ingles-espanol: Tomo 4. 3rd ed.
Edgar A. Peers. 160p. (Span. &
Eng.). 1980. pap. write for info.
(ISBN 84-345-4174-2). Salvat
Editores.

Diccionario Cassell espanol-ingles,
ingles-espanol: Tomo 5. 3rd ed.
Edgar A. Peers. 128p. (Span. &
Eng.). 1980. pap. write for info.
(ISBN 84-345-4175-0). Salvat
Editores.

Diccionario Cassell espanol-ingles,
ingles-espanol: Tomo 6. 3rd ed.
Edgar A. Peers. 152p. (Span. &
Eng.). 1980. pap. write for info.
(ISBN 84-345-4176-9). Salvat
Editores.

Diccionario Cassell Espanol-Ingles,
Ingles-Espanol, Vol. 1. 3rd ed. Ed.
by E. A. Peers & V. Jose. 128p.
(Span. & Eng.). 1982. 300.00 ptas
(ISBN 8-43454-171-8). Salvat
Editores.

Diccionario Cassell Espanol-Ingles,
Ingles-Espanol, Vol. 2. 3rd ed. E.
A. Peers & V. Jose. 120p. (Span. &
Eng.). 1982. 300.00 ptas (ISBN 8-
43454-172-6). Salvat Editores.

Diccionario Cassell Espanol-Ingles,
Ingles-Espanol, Vol. 3. 3rd ed.
Edgar A. Peers & Victor Jose.
128p. (Span. & Eng.). 1982. 300.00
ptas (ISBN 8-43454-173-4). Salvat
Editores.

Diccionario Cassell Espanol-Ingles,
Ingles-Espanol, Vol. 4. 3rd ed. E.
A. Peers & V. Jose. 160p. (Span. &
Eng.). 1982. 300.00 ptas (ISBN 8-
43454-174-2). Salvat Editores.

Diccionario Cassell Espanol-Ingles,
Ingles-Espanol, Vol. 5. 3rd ed. E.
A. Peers & V. Jose. 128p. (Span. &
Eng.). 1982. 300.00 ptas (ISBN 8-
43454-175-0). Salvat Editores.

Diccionario Cassell Espanol-
Ingles,Ingles-Espanol, Vol. 6. 3rd
ed. E. A. Peers & V. Jose. 152p.
(Span. & Eng.). 1982. 300.00 ptas.
Salvat Editores.

Diccionario Castella-Catala, Catala-
Castella Petit. 2nd ed. Santiago
Alberti. 340p. (Castella &
Catalan.). 1977. pap. 13.95 (ISBN
84-7246-057-6, S-50289). French &
Eur.

Diccionario Castella-Catala, Catala-
Castella Gran. 9th ed. Santiago
Alberti. 1182p. (Castella &
Catalan.). 1978. 44.95 (ISBN 84-
7246-056-8, S-50294). French &
Eur.

Diccionario Castella-Catala Catala-
Castella. 4th ed. 680p. (Span.).
1981. 625.00 ptas (ISBN 84-7153-
198-4). Biblo SP.

Diccionario castellano discolar. 10th
ed. 786p. (Span.). 1982. pap.
200.00 ptas (ISBN 84-05-00592-7).
Castellana.

Diccionario castellano-guarani,
guarani-castellano. Antonio
Guasch. 788p. (Span.). 1961. 6.80.
Dist. Comuneros.

Diccionario castellano illustrado.
(Illus.). 368p. (Span.). (gr. 4 up).
write for info. (707). Fernandez.

Diccionario Castellano Ilustrado.
(Span.). pap. 12.50 (ISBN 0-686-
56704-8, S-31405). French & Eur.

Diccionario castellano ilustrado.
Felix Diez Mateo. (Illus.). 416p.
(Span.). 1980. 275.00 ptas (ISBN
84-85085-26-4). Neguri.

Diccionario castellano ilustrado
(Lexicon) (Illus.). 368p. (Span.).
pap. 8.95 (T13). Bilingual Ed Serv.

Diccionario castellano-ingles.
Collins. (Span. & Eng.). Arg.$9.00.
Albatros.

Diccionario Castellano-Vasco. 2nd
ed. Placido Mugika. 1027p.
(Castella & Vasco.). 1973. 41.95
(ISBN 84-271-0800-1, S-50441).
French & Eur.

Diccionario Castellano-Vasco. 4th ed.
P. Roman de Bera. 524p. (Span. &
Vasco.). 1975. 25.50 (ISBN 84-
7025-178-3, S-50440). French &
Eur.

Diccionario Catala-Frances, Frances-
Catala. Carles Castellanos Llorenc
& Rafael Castellanos Llorenc.
1096p. (Catalan & Fr.). 1979.
44.95 (ISBN 0-686-57353-6, S-
50453). French & Eur.

Diccionario Ch'ol-Espanol. H. W.
Aulie & Evelyn W. De Aulie. LC
79-116730. 215p. (Span. & Chold.).
1978. write for info. Inst Ling Ver.

Diccionario cientifico ilustrado. E.
G. Speck. (Illus.). 386p. (Span.).
1.50. Editors Pr Serv.

Diccionario Cientifico y Tecnologico
Espanol, Ingles, Frances, Aleman,
2 vols. T. C. Collocott. (Span.,
Eng., Fr. & Ger., Definitions in
Spanish). Vol. 1, 1793p. 110.00;
Vol. 2, 1007p. 80.00. Imported
Bks.

Diccionario Collins Contemporary
English-Spanish Ingles-Espanol.
7th ed. R. F. Brown. 480p. (Eng. &
Span.). 1982. pap. 450.00 ptas
(ISBN 84-253-1179-9). Grijalbo.

Diccionario Collins Ingles-Espanol, 2
vols. 3rd ed. Colin Smith. 1284p.
(Eng. & Span.). 1981. 2500.00 ptas
(ISBN 84-253-1199-3). Grijalbo.

Diccionario Collins Spanish-English
Ingles-Espanol. 6th ed. Manuel
Smith Colinbermego. 1280p.
(Span. & Eng.). 1982. 2250.00 ptas
(ISBN 84-253-1184-5). Grijalbo.

Diccionario comercial: Espanol-
ingles e ingles-espanol. 2nd ed. A.
Frias. 304p. (Span. & Eng.). 1965.
120.00 ptas. Juventud.

Diccionario Comercial Espanol-
Ingles: El Secretario. 4th ed.
Alejandro Frias-Sucre Giraud.
144p. (Span. & Eng.). 1981.
1200.00 ptas (ISBN 84-261-1223-
4). Juventud.

Diccionario Comercial Espanol-
Ingles y Ingles-Espanol. 3rd ed.
Alejandro Frias-Sucre Giraud.
145p. (Span. & Eng.). 1977. 10.75
(ISBN 84-261-1223-4, S-14158).
French & Eur.

Diccionario Comercial Ingles-
Espanol. Alejandro Frias-Sucre
Girard. 137p. (Eng. & Span.). 9.50.
Lectorum Pubns.

Diccionario comercial Ingles-
Espanol, Espanol-Ingles.
Alejandro Frias-Sucre. 304p.
(Span.). 1981. write for info.
(ISBN 84-261-1223-4). Fed
Gremios.

Diccionario Comercial Ingles-
Espanol, Espanol-Ingles.
Alejandro F. S. Giraud. 304p.
(Eng. & Span.). 1981. write for
info. (ISBN 84-261-1223-4).
Editorial Juventud.

Diccionario comercial y economico
moderno: Ingles-espanol. G.
Varela Colmeiro. 256p. (Eng. &
Span.). 1964. 300.00 ptas. Inter-
Ciencia.

Diccionario Compendiado de la
Lengua Espanola. 638p. (Span.).
250.00 ptas (ISBN 84-7153-232-8).
Biblograf SP.

Diccionario Compendiado de la
Lengua Espanola 'Vox' 3rd ed.
638p. (Span.). 1980. 165.00 ptas
(ISBN 84-7153-232-8). Biblo SP.

Diccionario Compendiado, Frances-
Espanol, Espanol-Frances. 647p.
(Fr. & Span.). 275.00 ptas (ISBN
84-7153-189-5). Biblograf SP.

Diccionario Compendiado Ingles-
Espanol Espanol-Ingles. 547p.
(Eng. & Span.). write for info.
Biblograf SP.

Diccionario compendiado Ingles-
Espanol, Espanol-Ingles. 547p.
(Span. & Eng.). 1979. write for
info. (ISBN 84-7153-157-7). Fed
Gremios.

Diccionario Compendiado Ingles-
Espanol. 2nd ed. 534p. (Eng. &
Span.). 1981. 225.00 ptas (ISBN
84-7153-157-7). Biblo SP.

Diccionario Conciso de Modismos
Ingles-Espanol, Espanol-Ingles.
Francisco Sanchez Benedito. 270p.
(Eng. & Span.). 1977. pap. 17.95
(ISBN 0-686-56890-7, S-50582).
French & Eur.

Diccionario consico de modiamos.
3rd ed. Francisco Sanchez
Benedito. 272p. (Span.). 1982. pap.
820.00 ptas (ISBN 84-205-0358-4).
Alhambra.

Diccionario Cordillera ingles-espanol,
espanol-ingles. (Span.
& Eng.). pap. 3.95 (TH02).
Bilingual Ed Serv.

Diccionario Corona Ingles. 9th ed.
720p. (Span.). 1982. 625.00 ptas
(ISBN 84-241-1272-5). Everest.

Diccionario Critico Etimologico
Castellano & Hispanico, 2 vols.
Joan Corominas & J. A. Pascual.
(Span.). 1979. 3.25 ptas. 3.500.
Gredos.

Diccionario critico etimologico
castellano & hispanico, Tomo 3.
Joan Coromines i Vigneaux & J. A.
Pascual. 904p. (Span.). 1980. write
for info. (ISBN 84-249-1365-5).
Gredos.

Diccionario Critico Etimologico
Castellano & Hispanico, Tomo 4.
J. A. Joan-Pascual. 960p. (Span.).
1981. write for info. ptas (ISBN
84-249-0066-9). Gredos.

Diccionario Critico Etimologico De
la Lengua Espanola, 6 vols. Joan
Corominas. 4418p. (Span.). 1976.
Set. 200.00 (ISBN 84-249-1322-1,
S-11937). French & Eur.

Diccionario Cuyas: Ingles-Espanol-
Espanol-Ingles. (Eng. & Span.).
2.50. Camino Real.

Diccionario Cuyas: Spanish-French,
French-Spanish. (Span. & Fr.).
6.00x (ISBN 0-686-00850-2).
Colton Bk.

Diccionario Cuyas: Spanish-German,
German-Spanish. (Span. & Ger.).
6.00x (ISBN 0-686-00851-0).
Colton Bk.

Diccionario Cuyas: Spanish-Italian, Italian-Spanish. (Span. & Ital.). 6.00x (ISBN 0-686-00857-X). Colton Bk.

Diccionario cuy a01s. (Span. & Eng.). 2.50. Camino Real.

Diccionario d Teoria Folklorica. Paulo de Carvalho Neto. (Span.). 1977. 13.50. Intl Guatemala.

Diccionario de Aforismos, Proverbios & Refranes. Sintes. (Span.). 19.50 (SOP). Lectorum Pubns.

Diccionario de Aforismos: Proverbios Refranes. J. Sintes. 894p. (Span.). 60.00 (ISBN 0-686-92530-0, S-37667). French & Eur.

Diccionario de aforismos, proverbios y refrances. 4th ed. Sintes. 894p. (Span.). 1968. 500.00 ptas. Sintes.

Diccionario de aforismos, proverbios y refrances. 5th ed. Jorge Sintes Pros. 896p. (Span.). 1982. 2200.00 ptas (ISBN 84-302-0440-7). Sintes.

Diccionario de agricultura. Soroa. (Span.). 1375.00 ptas. Labor.

Diccionario de agricultura ruso-espanol. (Rus. & Span.). 1.00. Pueblos Unidos.

Diccionario de Ajedrez. Ramon Ibero. 192p. (Span.). 1977. pap. 8.75 (ISBN 84-270-0413-3, S-30996). French & Eur.

Diccionario de alimentacion animal. M. Piccioni. 820p. (Span.). 1970. 1000.00 ptas. Acribia.

Diccionario de Alimentacion Animal. Ed. by M. Picciony. 820p. (Span.). 1970. write for info. (S-36852). French & Eur.

Diccionario de americanismos. (Eng. & Span.). write for info. Tres Americas.

Diccionario de Americanismos. 576p. (Span.). 1980. 675.00 ptas (ISBN 84-241-1504-X). Everest.

Diccionario De Americanismos. Augusto Malaret. 1977. lib. bdg. 75.00 (ISBN 0-8490-1717-3). Gordon Pr.

Diccionario de Americanismos. Marcos A. Morinigo. (Span.). 35.00 (ISBN 0-686-56690-4, S-12121). French & Eur.

Diccionario de americanismos. Marcos A. Morinigo. 738p. (Span. & Eng.). 800.00 ptas. Teide.

Diccionario de Americanismos. Marcos A. Morinigo. (Span.). 20.00. SEI.

Diccionario de Americanismos. Alfredo N. Neves. (Span. & Eng.). 12.50. SPA.

Diccionario de Anglicismos. 2nd ed. Ricardo J. Alfaro. 520p. (Span.). 29.95 (ISBN 84-249-1342-6, S-11836). French & Eur.

Diccionario de anglicismos, barbaricismos, pachuquismos & otras locuci o01nes. Padill Francisco. (Span. & Eng.). 7.00. Iaconi.

Diccionario de Anonimos y Seudonimos Hispanoamericanos, 2 vols. in 1. Jose T. Medina. LC 73-78355. (Span.). 1973. Repr. of 1925 ed. 38.50x (ISBN 0-87917-026-3). Ethridge.

Diccionario de Antropologia. 200p. (Span.). 1980. 450.00 ptas. Bellaterra.

Diccionario de antropologia. Tr. by Charles Winick. 660p. (Span.). 1969. 7.00. Troquel.

Diccionario de Argentinismos de Ayer y de Hoy. Diego Abad de Santillan. 1000p. (Span.). 1978. 195.00 (ISBN 0-686-56685-8, S-33041). French & Eur.

Diccionario de Argot Espanol. Victor Leon. (Illus.). 160p. (Span.). 1980. pap. 180.00 ptas. Alianza Ed.

Diccionario de argot espanol. 2nd ed. Victor Leon Nunez. 160p. (Span.). 1981. pap. 180.00 ptas (ISBN 84-206-1766-0). Alianza Ed.

Diccionario De Arqueologia. Warwick Bray & David Trump. 276p. (Span.). 1976. pap. 17.95 (ISBN 84-335-9301-3, S-50363). French & Eur.

Diccionario de Arquitectos de la Antiguedad a Nuestros Dias. (Span.). 1981. pap. write for info. G Gili.

Diccionario de Arquitectura. 460p. (Span.). 1974. 75.00 ptas. Tesoro Edit.

Diccionario de Arquitectura. Nikolaus Pevesner. 651p. (Span.). 1981. write for info. Alianza Ed.

Diccionario de arquitectura. Nikolaus Pevsner et al. Tr. by Agustin Bustamente. 651p. (Span. & Eng.). 1981. write for info. Alianza Ed.

Diccionario de Arquitectura. Nikolaus Pevsner et al. (Span.). 1979. pap. pns (S-50087). French & Eur.

Diccionario de Arquitectura. 4th ed. D. Ware & B. Beatty. (Illus.). 204p. (Span.). 1974. write for info. G Gili.

Diccionario de Arte & Artistas. 600p. (Span.). 1979. write for info. Parramon Edns.

Diccionario de Arte & Artistas. (Span.). 1980. 7.00; 600.00 ptas. Parramon Edns.

Diccionario De Artes y Artistas. Peter Murray & Linda Murray. 600p. (Span.). 1978. 17.25 (ISBN 84-342-0144-5, S-50013). French & Eur.

Diccionario De Atres Adivinatorias. Scouezec. 226p. (Span.). 1973. pap. 7.95 (ISBN 84-270-0220-3, S-50042). French & Eur.

Diccionario de Autoridades, 3 vols. 2104p. (Span.). Set. 120.00 (ISBN 84-249-1334-5, S-12251). French & Eur.

Diccionario de Banca. 4th ed. A. Martinez Cerezo. 208p. (Span.). write for info. (ISBN 8-43680-028-1, 250013). Piramide.

Diccionario De Banca. 3rd ed. Antonio Martinez Cerezo. 208p. (Span.). 1976. leatherette 13.95 (ISBN 84-368-0028-1, S-50179). French & Eur.

Diccionario de banca. 5th ed. Antonio Martinez Cerezo. 208p. (Span.). 1980. 500.00 ptas (Dist. Grupo Editorial). Piramide.

Diccionario de Banca & Borsa: Catala-Castella-Diccionario de Banca & Bolsa. Banca Mas Sarda, Servicio de Estudios. LC 76-454176. 69p. (Catalan & Span.). 1975. write for info. (ISBN 8-438-30008-1). Alba.

Diccionario de banca y bolsa. Beltran. (Span.). write for info. Labor.

Diccionario de Banca y Bolsa, Tomo I: Ingles-Espanol. Manuel Bellisco Hernandez. 170p. (Eng. & Span.). 1977. pap. 15.75 (ISBN 84-85198-02-6, S-50120). French & Eur.

Diccionario De Bibliografia Espanola, 7 Vols. Dionisio Hidalgo. LC 68-57908. (Bibliography & Reference Ser.: No. 122). (Span.). 1970. Repr. of 1881 ed. text ed. 215.00 (ISBN 0-8337-1699-9). B Franklin.

Diccionario de Bibliotecologia. 2nd ed. 458p. (Span.). 1976. 44.95 (ISBN 0-686-56656-4, S-12239). French & Eur.

Diccionario De Biologia. M. Abercrombie et al. 242p. (Span.). 1978. pap. 16.75 (ISBN 0-686-57336-6, S-50068). French & Eur.

Diccionario de Biologia. Javier Jimenez Ortega. 322p. (Span.). 1979. Mex.$140.00. Porrua.

Diccionario de Biologia. T. Lender et al. Tr. by Merce Serrano & Ferran Vallespinos. 208p. (Span.). 1982. pap. 1000.00 ptas (ISBN 84-253-1372-4). Grijalbo.

Diccionario De Biologia Animal. Carlos A. Aguayo & Virgilio Biaggi. LC 76-41882. (Span.). 1977. 15.00 (ISBN 0-8477-2318-6). U of PR Pr.

Diccionario de Biologia en Quatre Lenguas: Aleman, Ingles, Frances y Espanol. Gunther Haensch & Gisela Haberkamp. 496p. (Span., Eng., Fr. & Ger.). 1976. 70.00 (ISBN 84-7214-090-3, S-50222). French & Eur.

Diccionario de Bolivianismos. Nicolas Fernandez Naranjo. 247p. (Span.). 1980. write for info. Cochabamba.

Diccionario De bolsa. 3rd ed. J. Ignacio De Garmendia Miangolarra. 208p. (Span.). 1982. pap. 620.00 ptas (ISBN 84-368-0057-5). Piramide.

Diccionario de Bolsa. 2nd ed. I. Garmendia Miangolarra. 208p. (Span.). write for info. (ISBN 8-43680-057-5, 250020). Piramide.

Diccionario De Bolsa. J. Ignacio de Garmendia Miangolarra. 208p. (Span.). 1977. leatherette 14.95 (ISBN 84-368-0057-5, S-50182). French & Eur.

Diccionario De Bolsillo De la Lengua Espanola: Mini Sopena. 304p. (Span.). 1975. pap. 1.75 (ISBN 84-303-0062-7, S-12252). French & Eur.

Diccionario De Bolsillo Frances-Espanol, Espagnol-Francais. Arturo Cuyas Armengol. 670p. (Span. & Fr.). 1971. pap. 3.50 (ISBN 84-7183-048-5, S-50391). French & Eur.

Diccionario De Bolsillo, Ingles-Espanol y Spanish-English. 640p. (Eng. & Span.). 1978. pap. 3.50 (ISBN 84-7183-080-9, S-50350). French & Eur.

Diccionario de bolsillo latino-espanol & espanol-latino. Vives. (Span. & Lat.). write for info. Coculsa.

Diccionario de bolsillo: Spanish-English English-Spanish. (Span. & Eng.). 1.25. Follett.

Diccionario De Botanica. 256p. (Span.). 1973. leatherette 11.50 (ISBN 84-307-8268-0, S-50258). French & Eur.

Diccionario de botanica. Font Quer. (Span.). 990.00 ptas. Labor.

Diccionario De Botanica. Pio Pont Quer. 1244p. (Span.). 1977. 59.95 (ISBN 84-335-5804-8, S-50066). French & Eur.

Diccionario de botanica. 2nd ed. Uberto Tosco. Tr. by Francisco Gil. 255p. (Span.). 1980. pap. 500.00 ptas (ISBN 84-307-8268-0). Teide.

Diccionario de Botanico. Pio Font Quer. 1264p. (Span.). 1979. 2.200 ptas. Labor SA.

Diccionario de Calculo Mercantil. Jose M. Codera Martin. 192p. (Span.). 1981. 800.00 ptas (ISBN 84-368-0168-7). Piramide.

Diccionario de caza. Jose M. Rodero. 512p. (Span.). 1955. 290.00 ptas. Juventud.

Diccionario De Celebridades Musicales. 600p. (Span.). 19.95 (ISBN 0-686-57361-7, S-50141). French & Eur.

Diccionario de Chilenismos. Zorobabel Rodriguez. LC 79-124394. xii, 487p. (Span.). 1979. write for info. Universidad & Acad.

Diccionario de Ciencia Politica. Axel Gorlitz. (Span.). 1979. pap. pns (S-50085). French & Eur.

Diccionario de Ciencia Politica. Axel Gorlitz. 632p. (Span.). 1980. 1.800 ptas. Alianza Ed.

Diccionario de Ciencias. Chapman Ubarov. 226p. (Span.). 1970. 12.25 (ISBN 84-237-0299-5, S-50245). French & Eur.

Diccionario de Ciencias Medicas Dorland. (Illus.). 1800p. (Span.). 1974. write for info. Ateneo Edit.

Diccionario de Ciencias Medicas Dorland (II) 6th ed. 1728p. (Span.). 1981. 4200.00 ptas (ISBN 84-7021-045-9). Ateneo Edit.

Diccionario De Ciencias Sociales, 2 vols. UNESCO. 2370p. (Span.). 1975. Set. pap. 60.00 (ISBN 84-259-0434-X, S-50061). French & Eur.

Diccionario de Citas. Juan Capdevila Font. 132p. (Span.). 1977. pap. 13.95 (ISBN 84-85117-43-3, S-50580). French & Eur.

Diccionario de cocina. (Span.). 250.00 ptas. Bruguera.

Diccionario de Coll. 27th ed. Jose L. Coll Garcia. 224p. (Span.). 1982. pap. 350.00 ptas (ISBN 84-320-4119-X). Planeta SA.

Diccionario de Computadores. Anthony Chandor. 402p. (Span.). 1975. leather 28.50 (ISBN 84-335-6411-0, S-31859). French & Eur.

Diccionario de Construccion & Regimen de la Lengua Castellana. Rufino J. Cuervo. (Span.). 1974. Col.$3.00. Inst Caro y Cuervo.

Diccionario de construccion y regimen de la lengue castellano. Cuervo. 2270p. (Span.). 18.45 set; Fasciculo 1. 4.33; Fasciculo 2. 3.25. Herder SA.

Diccionario de construccion y regimen de la lengua castellana. R. J. Cuervo. 344p. (Span.). 1961. write for info. Fasciculo 1: ea-empeorar. Faciculo 2: emperezar-emulo. Inst Caro y Cuervo.

Diccionario de Contabilidad. F. Cholvis. 469p. (Span.). 1977. 65.00 (ISBN 0-686-92515-7, S-33738). French & Eur.

Diccionario de Contabilidad, 2 vols. 3rd ed. F. Cholvis. 778p. (Span.). 1974. write for info. Ateneo Edit.

Diccionario de contabilidad. Francisco Cholvis. 760p. (Span.). Arg.$760.00. Contabilidad Moderna.

Diccionario De Contabilidad. 2nd ed. Jose M. Codera Martin. (Span.). leatherette 16.50 (ISBN 84-368-0061-3, S-50180). French & Eur.

Diccionario de Contabilidad. 3rd ed. Jose M. Codera Martin. 272p. (Span.). 1980. 700.00 ptas. Piramide.

Diccionario de contabilidad. 4th ed. Jose M. Codera Martin. 272p. (Span.). 1982. pap. 800.00 ptas (ISBN 84-368-0061-3). Piramide.

Diccionario de contabilidad, organizacion, administracion, control & ciencia afines, 7 vols. Joaquin R. Seone. 3400p. (Span.). 1972. 45.00. Difusion.

Diccionario de Costarriquenismos. 3rd ed. Carlos Gagini & Victor M. Soto. Prologue by Rufino J. Cuervo. LC 77-459051. 243p. (Span.). 1975. write for info. Costa Rica.

Diccionario de Crucigramas. 448p. (Span.). 1974. write for info. (ISBN 84-252-0783-5). G Gili.

Diccionario De Crucigramas. Litero. 435p. (Span.). 1974. pap. 7.50 (ISBN 84-252-0783-5, S-50276). French & Eur.

Diccionario de cubanismos. Dario Espina Perez. (Span.). 3.50. Dist. Universal.

Diccionario De Cubanismos Mas Usuales. Jose Sanchez-Boudy. LC 76-45322. (Span.). 1978. pap. 9.00 (ISBN 0-89729-199-9). Ediciones.

Diccionario de Demonologia. 3rd ed. Frederick Koning. (Span.). 1978. pap. 2.95 (ISBN 0-686-57362-5, S-50155). French & Eur.

Diccionario de Derecho. 4th ed. Rafael De Pina. 392p. (Span.). 1975. write for info. Porrua.

Diccionario de Derecho. Rafael de Pina. 355p. (Span.). 25.95 (ISBN 0-686-56688-2, S-12345). French & Eur.

Diccionario de Derecho Mercantil. J. M. Codera Martin. 288p. (Span.). write for info. (ISBN 8-43680-115-6, #230018). Piramide.

Diccionario De Derecho Mercantil. Jose Codera Martin. 286p. (Span.). 1979. leatherette 22.50 (ISBN 84-368-0115-6, S-50178). French & Eur.

Diccionario de derecho privado. Casso-Cervera. (Span.). 715.00 ptas. Labor.

Diccionario de Derecho Procesal Civil. Eduardo Pallares. 877p. (Span.). 37.50 (ISBN 0-686-56687-4, S-12340). French & Eur.

Diccionario de Derecho Procesal Civil. 13th ed. Eduardo Pallares. 880p. (Span.). 1981. Mex.$500.00. Porrua.

Diccionario de derecho romano. G. F. De Leon. (Span.). Arg.$60.00. Plus Ultra.

Diccionario de Dificultades de la Lengua Espanola. E. Diaz-Retg. 344p. (Span.). 1963. 18.95 (ISBN 0-686-92537-8, S-37576). French & Eur.

Diccionario De Dificultades Del Ingles: Difficulties of English Idioms for Spanish Speaking People. Alfonso T. Prats. (Eng. & Span.). 17.50 (ISBN 84-261-5814-5). Heinman.

Diccionario de Dificultades del Ingles. Alfonso T. Dels Prats. 368p. (Span. & Eng.). 1976. write for info. (ISBN 84-261-5814-5). Editorial Juventud.

Diccionario de dificultades del Ingles. Alfonso Torrens dels Prats. 496p. (Span.). 1976. write for info. (ISBN 84-261-1223-4). Fed Gremios.

Diccionario De Dificultades Del Ingles. Alfonso Torrents dels Prats. 500p. (Eng. & Span.). 1976. 18.75 (ISBN 84-261-5814-5, S-31568). French & Eur.
Diccionario de Dificultades del Ingles. Alfonso Torrents dels Prats. 494p. (Eng. & Span.). 17.95. Lectorum Pubns.
Diccionario de dificultades del ingles. Alfonso Torrents dels Prats. 494p. (Eng. & Span.). 17.95 (JUV). Lectorum Pubns.
Diccionario De Dos Cientos Uno Verbos Franceses Conjugados en Todos sus Tiempos & Personas. Christopher Kendris. LC 68-8677. (Orig., Span. & Fr.). 1972. pap. 3.95 (ISBN 0-8120-0393-4). Barron.
Diccionario de Dos Cientos Uno Verbos Ingleses. Ruth P. Craig. LC 77-184894. (Span. & Eng.). 1972. pap. text ed. 7.95 (ISBN 0-8120-0417-5). Barron.
Diccionario de Dudas & Dificultades de la Lengua Espanola. Manuel Seco. 516p. (Span., Mexico). 1966. Mex.$6.40. Aguilar SP.
Diccionario de Dudas de la Lengua Espanol. 7th ed. Manuel Seco. 556p. (Span.). 1976. 44.95 (ISBN 84-03-27064-X, S-12356). French & Eur.
Diccionario de dudas de la lengua espanola. Manuel Seco. (Span.). 375.00 ptas. Aguilar.
Diccionario de Dudas de la Lengua Espanola. Manuel Seco. (Span.). 34.50 (AGL). Lectorum Pubns.
Diccionario de dudas de la lengua espanola. Manuel Seco. (Span.). 25.00. Iaconi.
Diccionario de Dudas Ingles-Espanol. Merino. (Eng. & Span.). 1978. 625.00 ptas (ISBN 8-42830-425-4). Paraninfo.
Diccionario de Dudas Ingles-Espanol. Jose Merino. 332p. (Eng. & Span.). 1978. pap. write for info. (ISBN 84-283-0425-4). Paraninfo.
Diccionario de dudas Ingles-Espanol. Jose Merino. 332p. (Span. & Eng.). 1978. pap. write for info. (ISBN 84-283-0425-4). Fed Gremios.
Diccionario De Dudas Ingles-Espanol. 2nd ed. Jose Merino Bustamante. 332p. (Span.). 1978. pap. 17.50 (ISBN 84-283-0425-4, S-50240). French & Eur.
Diccionario de dudas: Ingles-espanol. Jose Merino Bustamente. (Span.). 1971. 250.00 ptas. Paraninfo.
Diccionario de economia. Tlm Congdon et al. Tr. by Antonio Menduina. 323p. (Span.). 1982. 800.00 ptas (ISBN 84-253-1375-9). Grijalbo.
Diccionario De Economia. 2nd ed. Arthur Seldon & F. G. Pennance. 560p. (Span.). 1975. pap. 26.25 (ISBN 84-281-0294-5, S-50019). French & Eur.
Diccionario de Economia. 2nd ed. Arthur Seldon & F. G. Pennance. 554p. (Span.). 1975. 35.95 (ISBN 84-281-0034-9, S-12358). French & Eur.
Diccionario de economia. Tr. by Arthur Seldon & F. G. Pennanee. 560p. (Span.). 1968. 750.00 ptas. Oikos Tau.
Diccionario de economia. 2nd ed. J. B. Terceiro. 208p. (Span.). 1970. 150.00 ptas. Zyx.
Diccionario De Economia Politica. 2nd ed. Borisov et al. 256p. (Span.). 1977. pap. 6.95 (ISBN 84-253-0610-8, S-50074). French & Eur.
Diccionario de Economia Politica. Borisov et al. 264p. (Span.). 1975. pap. 6.95 (ISBN 84-7339-060-1, S-50150). French & Eur.
Diccionario de Economia Politica. 1650p. (Span.). 1982. 2500.00 ptas (ISBN 8-43007-463-5). Autores-Editores.
Diccionario de economia politica. Heller. (Span.). 500.00 ptas. Labor.
Diccionario de Economia Politica, 2 vols. Claudio Napoleoni. 1668p. (Span.). 1982. 4850.00 ptas (ISBN 8-4718-9163-8). Ortells Ferriz.
Diccionario de economia politicia. Claudio Napoleoni. (Span.). 925.00 ptas. Castilla.
Diccionario de economia y cooperativismo. Olivera. 254p. (Span.). 1970. 40.00 ptas. Albatros.
Diccionario de economia y cooperativismo. J. Olivera. (Span.). Arg.$25.00. Hachette-Jeunesse.
Diccionario de economia y dissiplinas a fines, aleman-espanol. Roca De Togore. 500p. (Span.). 1965. 500.00 ptas. InterCiencia.
Diccionario de educacion infantil. Tr. by H. Joubrel & P. Bertrand. 224p. (Span.). 1968. Arg.$1.40. Leru.
Diccionario de Educacion Infantil. H. Jourbel & P. Bertrand. 224p. (Span.). 1968. 22.50 (ISBN 0-686-56709-9, S-33056). French & Eur.
Diccionario de eiencias. Ubanou. (Span.). write for info. Dossat.
Diccionario de Electronica. Harley Carter. 416p. (Span.). 1962. 19.95 (ISBN 0-686-56716-1, S-33049). French & Eur.
Diccionario de electronica. Tr. by Harley Carter. 416p. (Span.). 1962. Arg.$2.60. Leru.
Diccionario De Electronica. S. Handel. 470p. (Span.). 1976. 39.75 (ISBN 84-335-6408-0, S-50070). French & Eur.
Diccionario de Electronica. Santano. (Span.). 1983. write for info. Paraninfo.
Diccionario de Electronica & Tecnica Nuclear. John Markus. (Illus.). 1052p. (Span.). write for info. (ISBN 84-267-0003-9). Marcombo.
Diccionario de Electronica, Informatica & Centrales Nucleares. Mariano Mataix. 660p. (Span.). 1978. 2400.00 ptas (ISBN 8-42670-350-X). Marcombo.
Diccionario De Electronica, Informatica y Centrales Nucleares. Mariano Mataix Lord. 660p. (Fr. & Eng.). 1978. leather 59.95 (ISBN 84-267-0350-X, S-30687). French & Eur.
Diccionario de electronica, proceso de datos. Averbach. (Span.). 1970. 200.00 ptas. Iber Euro Edns.
Diccionario de Electronica Radio & TV. (Illus.). 199p. (Span.). 1966. 2.50. Minerva Bks.
Diccionario de Electronica, Radio & TV: Ingles-Espanol. M. Saiz. 144p. (Eng. & Span.). pap. 4.50. Lectorum Pubns.
Diccionario de electronica, radio y TV. (Span.). 135.00 ptas. Afha Intl.
Diccionario de Electronica y Tecnica Nuclear. John Markus. 1052p. (Span. & Eng.). 75.95 (ISBN 84-267-0003-9, S-14264). French & Eur.
Diccionario de electronica y tecnica nuclear. Tr. by John Markus. 1052p. (Span.). 1972. 2400.00 ptas. Marcombo.
Diccionario de eletronica y energia nuclear ingles-espanol. M. Mataix. 772p. (Eng. & Span.). 620.00 ptas. Danae.
Diccionario de emociones. Bernardo Arias Truillo. (Span.). 0.60. Berout.
Diccionario de Energia Solar. Peris Aguilar & J. Jose-Aguilar Civera. 232p. (Span.). 1982. 410.00 ptas (ISBN 8-42050-923-X). Alhambra.
Diccionario de Escritores Mexicanos. Aurora Ocampo de Gomez & Ernesto Prado Velazquez. (Span.). 69.95 (ISBN 0-686-56696-3, S-6745). French & Eur.
Diccionario de espanol equivoco. Manuel Criado de Val. 124p. (Span.). 1981. pap. 300.00 ptas (ISBN 84-85786-10-6). Edi-Seis.
Diccionario De Especialidades Farmaceuticas. 28th Mexican ed. Ed. by E. Rosenstein. (Span.). 1982. pap. 52.00x (ISBN 968-460-017-8). Drug Intl Pubns.
Diccionario de espiritualidad: Obra Completa, 3 vols. Ermanno Ancilli. Tr. by Joan Llopis. 2224p. (Span.). 1982. 9000.00 ptas (ISBN 84-254-1265-X). Herder SA.
Diccionario de espiritualidad: Tomo 1. Ermanno Ancilli. Tr. by Joan Llopis. 742p. (Span.). 1982. 3000.00 ptas (ISBN 84-254-1264-1). Herder SA.
Diccionario de Estadistica. William R. Buckland & Maurice G. Kendall. 384p. (Span.). 1980. 1.200 ptas (ISBN 8-43680-141-5). Piramide.
Diccionario de Estadistica. E. Morice. 220p. (Span.). 1975. pap. 18.50 (ISBN 84-7051-037-1, S-50210). French & Eur.
Diccionario de Etologia. A. Heymer. Tr. by Andres De Haro Vera. 284p. (Span.). 1981. 1500.00 ptas (ISBN 84-282-0668-6). Omega SA.
Diccionario de expresiones idiomaticas y modismos ingleses. O. Gonzalez Gutierrez. 328p. (Span. & Span.). write for info. EUDEBA.
Diccionario de Expresiones Idiomaticas y Modismo Ingleses. 2nd ed. Orlando Gonzalez Gutierrez. 328p. (Span. & Eng.). 1976. 35.00 (ISBN 0-686-56683-1, S-33043). French & Eur.
Diccionario De Expresiones Malsonantes Del Espanol. 2nd ed. Jaime Martin. 370p. (Span.). 1974. pap. 13.95 (ISBN 84-7090-058-7, S-31400). French & Eur.
Diccionario de Expresiones y Frases Latinas. V. J. Herrero. 253p. (Span. & Lat.). 1980. Leatherette 29.95 (ISBN 0-686-92545-9, S-32727). French & Eur.
Diccionario de falsos amigos, frances-espanol. Blanca Gonzalez Marimon. 64p. (Fr. & Span.). 1982. pap. 200.00 ptas (ISBN 84-205-0873-X). Alhambra.
Diccionario de Filosofia. 9th ed. Walter Breugger. 684p. (Span.). 1978. 29.95 (ISBN 84-254-0722-2, S-12715, French & Eur); pap. 23.95 (ISBN 84-254-0146-1, S-50197). French & Eur.
Diccionario de Filosofia. Armand Cuvillier. 228p. (Span.). 1961. 14.95 (ISBN 0-686-56713-7, S-33052). French & Eur.
Diccionario de Filosofia, 2 vols. Mora Ferrater. (Span.). 95.00 set (ISBN 0-686-56658-0, S-31443). French & Eur.
Diccionario de Filosofia, 4 vols. Jose Ferrater Mora. 3630p. (Span.). 1979. Set. pap. 200.00 (ISBN 84-206-5998-3, S-50051); 240.00 set (ISBN 84-206-5299-7). French & Eur.
Diccionario De Filosofia. 2nd ed. Dagobert D. Runes. 400p. (Span.). 1977. 15.75 (ISBN 84-253-0127-0, S-13007). French & Eur.
Diccionario de Filosofia Abreviado. 2nd ed. Jose Ferrater Mora. 478p. (Span.). 1978. pap. 9.50 (ISBN 84-350-0141-5, S-50081). French & Eur.
Diccionario de fisica. Tr. by Franke. (Span.). 3630.00 ptas. Labor SA.
Diccionario de Formularios Generales, 6 vols. Juan Diego Hernandez. 700p. (Span.). 1981. pap. 3000.00 ptas. Coleccion Nereo.
Diccionario de Formularios Generales, 4 vols. Juan Diego Hernandez & Alejandro Rodriguez Segui. 800p. (Span.). 1980. 3000.00 ptas (ISBN 84-85565-05-3). Coleccion Nereo.
Diccionario de Formularios Generales, Vol. 5. Juan D. Hernandez. 800p. (Span.). 1981. pap. 3000.00 ptas (ISBN 84-85565-06-1). Nereo.
Diccionario de Formularios Generales: Tomo 7, 7 vols. Juan Diego Hernandez. 756p. (Span.). 1981. pap. 3000.00 ptas (ISBN 84-85565-08-8). Coleccion Nereo.
Diccionario de fotografia y cine. (Serie Tecnios Especialistas Koel 51). 358p. (Span.). 75.00 ptas. Tesoro.
Diccionario de gemologia. (Span.). 480.00 ptas. Jover.
Diccionario de Gentilicios & Toponimos. Santano. (Span.). 1981. 1300.00 ptas (ISBN 8-42831-069-6). Paraninfo.
Diccionario de gentilicios y toponimos. Daniel Santano y Leon. 488p. (Span.). 1980. pap. 1200.00 ptas (ISBN 84-283-1069-6). Paraninfo.
Diccionario de geografia. Moore. (Span.). write for info. Dossat.
Diccionario de Geografia. W. C. Moore. 158p. (Span.). 1972. 11.95 (ISBN 84-237-0340-1, S-50246). French & Eur.
Diccionario de grafologia. Vels. 450p. (Span.). 1972. 320.00 ptas. Cedel.
Diccionario de Grafologia y Terminos Psicologicos Afines. Augusto Vels. 474p. (Span.). 1972. 17.95 (ISBN 84-352-0114-7, S-13272). French & Eur.
Diccionario De Grupos, Fuerzas, y Partidos Politicos Espanoles. Gerardo Duelo. 128p. (Span.). 1977. pap. 5.25 (ISBN 84-7080-940-7, S-50175). French & Eur.
Diccionario de habla inglesa: Ingles-espanol, espanol-ingles. 536p. (Eng. & Span.). 1.50. Edit Pr Serv.
Diccionario de Hacienda & Derecho Fiscal. Luis A. Martinez Cachero. LC 75-521721. 205p. (Span.). 1976. write for info. (ISBN 8-436-80035-4). Piramide.
Diccionario de historia de Espana. 2nd ed. German Bleiber. 3861p. (Span.). 1969. 2400.00 ptas. Alianza Ed.
Diccionario de Historia de Espana, 3 vols. German Bleiberg. 3776p. (Span.). 1979. Set. pap. 70.00 (ISBN 84-206-5997-5, S-50374). French & Eur.
Diccionario de Historia de Espana, 3 vols. German Bleiberg. 3776p. (Span.). 1979. Set. 100.00 (ISBN 84-206-5298-9, S-10785). French & Eur.
Diccionario de Historia de Espana, 3 vols. 2nd ed. German Bleiberg. 3776p. (Span.). 1981. 6000.00 ptas (ISBN 84-206-5298-9). Alianza Ed.
Diccionario de Historia de Espana, Vol. 1. 2nd ed. 1368p. (Span.). 1981. 2000.00 ptas (ISBN 84-206-5205-9). Alianza Ed.
Diccionario de Historia de Espana, Vol. 2. 2nd ed. German Bleiberg. 1192p. (Span.). 1981. 2000.00 ptas (ISBN 84-206-5206-7). Alianza Ed.
Diccionario de Historia de Espana, Vol. 3. 2nd ed. German Bleiberg. 1216p. (Span.). 1981. 2000.00 ptas (ISBN 84-206-5207-5). Alianza Ed.
Diccionario de historia moderna. Palmer. (Span.). 265.00 ptas. Labor SA.
Diccionario de historia natural de las Islas Canarias. Jose Viera Clavijo. 586p. (Span.). 1982. 3500.00 ptas (ISBN 84-7133-434-8). Muralla.
Diccionario de historia universal. J. L. Romero. (Span.). Arg.$22.00. Atlantida.
Diccionario de Homofonos Castellans: Repertorio Alfabetico de Adjetivos, Verbos & su Correcta Ortografia. Hipolito R. Aschiero. LC 77-454249. 120p. (Span.). 1975. write for info. Edit Victor Leru.
Diccionario de Homofonos Castellaros. Hipolito F. Aschiero. 120p. (Span.). 1975. 15.95 (ISBN 0-686-56712-9, S-33053). French & Eur.
Diccionario de Incorrecciones & Particularidades & Curiosidades del Lenguaje. Antonio Santamaria & Augusto Cuartas. (Span.). pap. 14.95 (PAR). Lectorum Pubns.
Diccionario de Incorrecciones, Dudas & Normas Gramaticales. Fernando Corripio. LC 76-457468. 655p. (Span.). 1975. write for info. (ISBN 8-402-04591-X). Edit Bruguera.
Diccionario de Incorreciones & Particularidades del Lenguaje. 4th ed. Cuartas Santamaria & J. Mangada. (Span.). 1983. write for info. ptas. Paraninfo.
Diccionario de Incorreciones, Dudas y Normas Gramaticales. 655p. (Span.). 1975. pap. 17.50 (ISBN 84-02-04591-X, S-50156). French & Eur.
Diccionario de Incorreciones y Particularidades del Lenguaje. 3rd ed. Andres Santamarie & Augusto Cuartas. 531p. (Span.). 1975. leatherette 15.75 (ISBN 84-283-0112-3). French & Eur.
Diccionario de informacion sexual. Paul Bertrand. (Span.). write for info. Granica.
Diccionario de informatica. Ginguay. 184p. (Span.). write for info. Toray-Masson.
Diccionario De Informatica. Michael Ginguay. 184p. (Span.). 1972. pap. 23.50 (ISBN 84-311-0004-4, S-50130). French & Eur.

Diccionario de Informatica Ingles-Espanol: Edicion Corregida. 3rd ed. Olivetti. 272p. (Eng. & Span.). 1982. 650.00 ptas (ISBN 8-42831-230-3). Paraninfo.
Diccionario de Informatica Ingles-Espanol. 2nd ed. Olivetti. (Eng. & Span.). 1982. 700.00 ptas (ISBN 8-42831-230-3). Paraninfo.
Diccionario De Ingenieria Ambiental y Ciencias Afines see Dictionary of Environmental Engineering & Related Sciences.
Diccionario de Ingenieria de Caminos. Abad I. Morilla. LC 79-117965. 358p. (Span.). 1979. write for info. (ISBN 8-4368-0119-9). Piramide.
Diccionario de Ingenieria de Caminos. I. Morilla Abad. 360p. (Span.). write for info. (ISBN 8-43680-119-9, 260012). Piramide.
Diccionario de ingles-americano. Alfonso Torrents dels Prats. 336p. 1983. pap. 950.00 ptas (ISBN 84-261-1948-4). Juventud.
Diccionario de ingles-espanol, espanol-ingles. (Span.). 75.00 ptas. Bruguera.
Diccionario De Inmunologia. W. J. Herbert & P. C. Wilkinson. 256p. (Span.). 1974. leather 28.50 (ISBN 84-7092-106-1, S-50055). French & Eur.
Diccionario de Inmunologia. W. J. Herbert & P. C. Wilkinson. 256p. (Span.). 1974. E750.00 (ISBN 84-7092-106-1). Jims.
Diccionario de Insurgentes. 2nd ed. Jose Maria Miguel i Verges. 628p. (Span.). 1980. Mex.$750.00. Porrua.
Diccionario de Insurgentes. Jose Maria Miquel I Verges. (Span.). 55.00 (ISBN 0-686-56698-X, S-12335). French & Eur.
Diccionario de jurisprudencia chilena: Recopilacionde conceptos y definiciones. Elena Caffarena de Jiles. 346p. (Span.). 1959. 2.00. Juridica-Andres Belio.
Diccionario de la astronautica. Thomas De Galiana. (Span.). 100.00 ptas. Plaza Janes.
Diccionario de la astronomia y astronautica. Pedro Mateu Sancho. (Illus.). 346p. (Span.). 400.00 ptas. Destino.
Diccionario de la Astronomica y Astronautica. Pedro Mateu Sancho. 350p. (Span.). 1962. 37.50 (ISBN 84-233-0114-1, S-12334). French & Eur.
Diccionario De la Biblia. 7th ed. Herbert Haag. 1080p. (Span.). 1977. 50.00 (ISBN 84-254-0077-5, S-50196). French & Eur.
Diccionario de la Civilizacion Griega. Pierre Devambez. 482p. (Span.). 1972. 37.50 (ISBN 84-233-0645-3, S-50367). French & Eur.
Diccionario de la cocina clasica americana y europea, Tomo 1. 234p. (Span.). 1981. pap. 3000.00 ptas (ISBN 84-248-0729-4). Encicl Vasca.
Diccionario de la cocina clasica americana y europea, Tomo 2. 230p. (Span.). 1981. pap. 3000.00 ptas (ISBN 84-248-0730-8). Encicl Vasca.
Diccionario de la cocina clasica american y europea, Tomo 3. 230p. (Span.). 1981. pap. 3000.00 ptas (ISBN 84-248-0731-6). Encicl Vasca.
Diccionario de la cocina clasica americana y europea, Tomo 4. 230p. (Span.). 1981. pap. 3000.00 ptas (ISBN 84-248-0732-4). Encicl Vasca.
Diccionario de la cocina clasica americana y europea, Tomo 5. 230p. (Span.). 1981. pap. 3000.00 ptas (ISBN 84-248-0733-2). Encicl Vasca.
Diccionario de la cocina clasica americana y europea: Obra completa, 5 vols. (Span.). 1981. pap. 15000.00 ptas (ISBN 84-248-0728-6). Encicl Vasca.
Diccionario de la cocina clasica mejicana y europea: Obra completa, 5 vols. 1154p. (Span.). 1981. pap. 15000.00 ptas (ISBN 84-248-0722-7). Encicl Vasca.
Diccionario de la cocina clasica mejicano y europea: Tomo 1. 234p. (Span.). 1981. pap. 3000.00 ptas (ISBN 84-248-0723-5). Encicl Vasca.
Diccionario de la cocina clasica mejicano y europea: Tomo 2. 230p. (Span.). 1981. pap. 3000.00 ptas (ISBN 84-248-0724-3). Encicl Vasca.
Diccionario de la cocina clasica mejicano y europea: Tomo 3. 230p. (Span.). 1981. pap. 3000.00 ptas (ISBN 84-248-0725-1). Encicl Vasca.
Diccionario de la cocina clasica mejicana y europea: Tomo 4. 230p. (Span.). 1981. pap. 3000.00 ptas (ISBN 84-248-0726-X). Encicl Vasca.
Diccionario de la cocina clasica mejicana y europea: Tomo 5. 230p. (Span.). 1981. pap. 3000.00 ptas (ISBN 84-248-0727-8). Encicl Vasca.
Diccionario de la construccion. 246p. (Span.). pap. 90.00 ptas. CEAC.
Diccionario de la Construccion. Equipo Reactor de Ceac. 650p. (Span.). 1978. pap. 26.50 (ISBN 84-329-2608-6, S-50225). French & Eur.
Diccionario de la Construccion y Obras Publicas Ingles-Espanol, 2 vols. Jose Benito Bacho. 268p. (Span. & Eng.). 1975. Set. 38.95 (ISBN 84-85198-10-7, S-50117). French & Eur.
Diccionario de la Construccion y Obras Publicas, Tomo 2: Span. Jose Benito Bacho. 110p. (Span.). 1975. 18.95 (ISBN 84-85198-09-3, S-50119). French & Eur.
Diccionario de la Construcion (II) 2nd ed. 642p. (Span.). 1981. 1115.00 ptas (ISBN 84-329-2608-6). Ceac.
Diccionario de la Construcion y de Obras Publicas, Tomo I: Ingles. Jose Benito Bacho. 168p. (Span.). 1975. 18.95 (ISBN 84-85198-00-X, S-50118). French & Eur.
Diccionario de la Constuccion & Obras Publicas, 2 vols. Jose de Benito y Bacho & Manuel B. Hernandez. LC 76-453130. (Eng. & Span.). write for info. (ISBN 8-4851-9800-X). Lib Tec Bell.
Diccionario de la Decoracion. Equipo Reactor De Ceac. 792p. (Span., Fr., Eng., Ger. & Ital.). 1973. 44.25 (ISBN 84-329-5010-6, S-12256). French & Eur.
Diccionario De la Electronica. 3rd ed. Jean F. Arnaud. 368p. (Span.). 1976. pap. 5.25 (ISBN 84-01-90304-1, S-14211). French & Eur.
Diccionario de la electronica. Jean-Francois Arnaud. (Span.). 100.00 ptas. Plaza Janes.
Diccionario de la Felicidad. J. Sintes. 1046p. (Span.). Date not set. 35.95 (ISBN 0-686-92548-3, S-37670). French & Eur.
Diccionario de la industria textil. Casa Aruta. (Span.). 2100.00 ptas. Labor SA.
Diccionario de la Izquierda Comunista. Juan A. Sanchez Carrate. LC 77-551842. (Illus.). 91p. (Span.). 1977. 50.00 ptas (ISBN 8-472-35308-7). Dopesa.
Diccionario de la legislacion de seguros. Palacios. (Span.). write for info. Rev. Mex. de Seguros.
Diccionario de la Lengua, 3 vols. 2nd ed. 2000p. (Span.). 1977. Set. 120.00 (ISBN 84-7017-407-X, S-50097). French & Eur.
Diccionario de la Lengua: A-B, Vol. 1. 2nd ed. 308p. (Span.). 1981. pap. 1458.00 ptas (ISBN 84-7017-633-1). Argos-Vergara.
Diccionario de la Lengua: C-CH, Vol. 2. 2nd ed. 308p. (Span.). 1981. pap. 1458.00 ptas (ISBN 84-7017-634-X). Argos-Vergara.
Diccionario de la Lengua: D-F, Vol. 3. 2nd ed. 312p. (Span.). 1981. pap. 1458.00 ptas (ISBN 84-7017-635-8). Argos-Vergara.
Diccionario de la Lengua Espanol. 19th ed. Real Academia de la Lengua Espanol. 1456p. (Span.). 1979. leatherette 75.00 (ISBN 84-239-4722-X, S-12257). French & Eur.
Diccionario de la Lengua Espanola. 228p. (Span.). 3.50 (ISBN 0-686-56676-9, S-25231). French & Eur.
Diccionario De la Lengua Espanola, 2 vols. 704p. (Span.). 1978. Set. leather 50.95 (ISBN 84-278-0536-5, S-50030). French & Eur.
Diccionario De la Lengua Espanola. (Span.). 1979. 70.00 (ISBN 0-8277-3007-1). Pergamon.
Diccionario de la Lengua Espanola, 2 vols. 696p. (Span.). 1982. Set 2350.00 ptas (ISBN 8-47505-566-4). Oceano.
Diccionario de la lengua espanola. 288p. (Span.). Mex.$0.80; 10.00. Diana.
Diccionario de la lengua espanola. 19th, rev. ed. 1426p. (Span.). 1971. 1100.00 ptas. pap. 700.00 ptas. Real Academia Espasa.
Diccionario de la lengua espanola. 472p. (Span.). 1982. pap. 600.00 ptas (ISBN 84-278-0775-9). Nauta SA.
Diccionario de la Lengua Espanola. 778p. (Span.). 1981. pap. 1600.00 ptas (ISBN 84-7505-214-2). Oceano.
Diccionario de la Lengua Espanola. Distein. LC 75-513898. 407p. (Span.). 1975. write for info. (ISBN 8-485-11709-3) (ISBN 8-485-11710-7). Distein.
Diccionario De la Lengua Espanola. 19th ed. Real Academia Espanola. (Span.). 1971. 65.00x (ISBN 0-686-00852-9). Colton Bk.
Diccionario de la Lengua Espanola Novus. 778p. (Span.). 1981. 1600.00 ptas (ISBN 84-7505-214-2). Oceano.
Diccionario de la Lengua Espanola: Obra Completa, 2 vols. 696p. (Span.). 1982. 2350.00 set ptas (ISBN 8-47505-566-4). Oceano.
Diccionario de la Lengua Espanola Real Academia Espanola. 1424p. (Span.). 125.00. Lectorum Pubns.
Diccionario de la lengua espanola y alemana: Tomo 1, 2 vols. 4th ed. Rudolf Slaby et al. 1139p. (Span. & Ger.). 1981. pap. 3500.00 ptas (ISBN 84-254-0835-0). Herder SA.
Diccionario de la Lengua Espanola y Enciclopedia Escolar. 2nd ed. Juan Capdevila Font. 407p. (Span.). 1975. pap. 7.95 (ISBN 84-85117-32-8, S-50451). French & Eur.
Diccionario De la Lengua Espanola y Enciclopedia Escolar. 6th ed. Juan Capdevilla Font. 437p. (Span.). 1978. 7.50 (ISBN 84-7176-273-0, S-50252); pap. 5.953 (ISBN 84-85117-33-6, S-50253). French & Eur.
Diccionario de la Lengua Espanola y Enciclopedia Escolar Distein. 2nd ed. Juan Capdevila Font. 407p. (Span.). 1975. 8.95 (ISBN 84-85117-09-3, S-50459). French & Eur.
Diccionario de la Lengua: G-M, Vol. 4. 2nd ed. 388p. (Span.). 1981. pap. 1458.00 ptas (ISBN 84-7017-636-6). Argos-Vergar.
Diccionario de la Lengua Mechada. Ignacio Guasp. (Span.). 12.50 (ISBN 0-686-56701-3, S-5248). French & Eur.
Diccionario de la Lengua: N-Q, Vol. 5. 2nd ed. 304p. (Span.). 1981. pap. 1458.00 ptas (ISBN 84-7017-637-4). Argos-Vergara.
Diccionario de la Lengua Nahuatl. Cesar Macazaga Ordono. LC 80-106467. 122p. (Eng., Aztec, & Span.). 1979. write for info. Innovacion.
Diccionario de la Lengua Nahuatl. Cesar Macazaga Ordono. (Illus.). 128p. (Span.). 1979. Mex.$pap. 3.95. Innovacion.
Diccionario de la Lengua Nahuatl o Mexicana. Remi Simeon. LC 79-116666. xcvi, 782p. (Aztec & Span.). 1977. write for info. Siglo Veintiuno.
Diccionario de la Lengua (Obra Completa, 6 vols. 2nd ed. 2012p. (Span.). 1981. pap. 8750.00 ptas (ISBN 84-7017-632-3). Argos-Vergara.
Diccionario de la Lengua: R-Z, Vol. 6. 2nd ed. 392p. (Span.). 1981. pap. 1460.00 ptas (ISBN 84-7017-638-2). Argos-Vergara.
Diccionario de la Limpieza. Djenane Chappat. 234p. (Span.). 1970. pap. 3.50 (ISBN 84-206-1282-0, S-12249). French & Eur.
Diccionario de la Literatura Mundial. 2nd ed. Joseph T. Shipley. 564p. (Span.). 1974. 37.50 (ISBN 84-233-0781-6, S-12359). French & Eur.
Diccionario de la Literatura Universal. Juan Capdevila Font. 536p. (Span.). 1977. 22.50 (ISBN 84-85117-41-7, S-50261). French & Eur.
Diccionario de la Mitologia Clasica. C. Falcon et al. 633p. (Span.). 1980. pap. 25.00 (ISBN 84-206-1961-2, S-32723). French & Eur.
Diccionario de la mitologia clasica: A-H, Tomo 1. 2nd ed. Constantino Falcon Martinez et al. 368p. (Span.). 1981. pap. 360.00 ptas (ISBN 84-206-1791-1). Alianza Ed.
Diccionario de la mitologia clasica: I-Z, Tomo 2. 2nd ed. Constantino Falcon Martinez et al. 304p. (Span.). 1981. pap. 360.00 ptas (ISBN 84-206-1792-X). Alianza Ed.
Diccionario de la Mitologia Mundial. 383p. (Span.). 1971. 12.25 (ISBN 84-7166-165-9, S-12258). French & Eur.
Diccionario de la Mitologia Mundial. 387p. (Span.). 1981. 400.00 ptas (ISBN 84-7166-165-9). Edaf.
Diccionario de la montana. Agustin Faus. 592p. (Span.). 1963. pap. 340.00 ptas. Juventud.
Diccionario de la mujer. (Span.). 150.00 ptas. Daimon.
Diccionario de la musica. Eric Blom. 1040p. (Span.). Arg.$pap. 15.00. Claridad.
Diccionario de la musica. Rev. ed. Michel Brenet. (Span.). 1000.00 ptas. Iberia SA.
Diccionario de la musica. 2nd, rev. ed. Tr. by Della Corte & Gatti. (Span.). Arg.$26.00. Ricordi.
Diccionario de la Musica. 2nd ed. Carlos Poblete. 379p. (Span.). 1979. write for info. U. de Valparaiso.
Diccionario de la musica. Carlos Poblete Varas. 320p. (Span.). 1972. write for info. Universitarias Valparaiso.
Diccionario de la Musica. 3rd ed. Manuel Valla Gorina. 256p. (Span.). 1981. 300.00 ptas (ISBN 84-206-1334-7). Alianza.
Diccionario de la Musica. Manual Valls Gorina. 256p. (Span.). 1982. 300.00 ptas (ISBN 8-42061-334-7). Alianza Ed.
Diccionario de la musica. Manuel Valls Gorina. 244p. (Span.). 1971. 60.00 ptas. Alianza Ed.
Diccionario de la Musica, Historico & Tecnico. 4th ed. Jose Ricart Matas. 566p. (Span.). 1981. 3000.00 ptas (ISBN 84-7082-139-3). Iberia SA.
Diccionario De la Musica: Historico y Tecnico. 3rd ed. Michel Brenet. 566p. (Span.). 1976. 50.00 (ISBN 84-7082-139-3, S-16685). French & Eur.
Diccionario de la politica. 2nd ed. Jean N. Aquistapace. (Span.). 100.00 ptas. Magisterio Esp.
Diccionario De la Politica. 2nd ed. Jean-Noel Aquistapace. 344p. (Span.). 1969. pap. 7.95 (ISBN 84-265-7047-X, S-21237). French & Eur.
Diccionario de la psicologia. Norbert Sillamy. (Span.). 100.00 ptas. Plaza Janes.
Diccionario de la Psicologia. 4th ed. Norberth Sillamy. 344p. (Span.). 1974. 5.25 (ISBN 0-686-57338-2, S-12360). French & Eur.
Diccionario De la Santa Biblia. W. W. Rand. (Illus.). 768p. (Span.). 1969. pap. 12.95 (ISBN 0-89922-003-7). Edit Caribe.
Diccionario De la Tecnicas De Grupo. Anne A. Schutzsenberger. 260p. (Span.). 1974. pap. 10.75 (ISBN 84-301-0603-0, S-50365). French & Eur.
Diccionario de la Ultra Derecha. Alberto Royuela. LC 77-564609. (Illus.). 112p. (Span.). 1977. 50.00 ptas (ISBN 8-472-35311-7). Dopesa.
Diccionario de la Vida Sexual. Juan Capdevila Font. 200p. (Span.). 1976. 9.95 (ISBN 84-85117-21-2, S-50262). French & Eur.

Diccionario de la Vida Sexual. Ed. by Pedro L. Onega. LC 76-462317. (Illus.). 187p. (Span.). 1976. write for info. (ISBN 8-485-11721-2). Distein.
Diccionario de la Vida Sexual. Enrique Sanchez y Pascual. LC 77-550679. (Illus.). 340p. (Span.). 1976. 300.00 ptas. Prod Edit.
Diccionario De L'art I Els Oficis De la Construccion. Miguel Fullana Llompart. 440p. (Catalan.). 1974. 35.95 (ISBN 84-273-0372-6, S-50000). French & Eur.
Diccionario de las Artes Marciales. Mario Lopez Dominguez. 250p. (Span.). 1981. 250.00 ptas (ISBN 84-7494-032-X). Ramos-Majos.
Diccionario de las lenguas espanola alemana, 2 vols. 5th ed. Rudolf Slaby et al. 969p. (Span. & Ger.). 1980. 5200.00 ptas (ISBN 84-254-0694-3). Herder SA.
Diccionario De las Lenguas Espanola y Alemana, 2 vols. 3rd ed. Rudolf Slaby. 2422p. (Ger. & Span.). 1977. Set. 110.00 (ISBN 84-254-0694-3, S-50380). French & Eur.
Diccionario de las lenguas espanola y alemana: Aleman-espanol, 2 vols. 10th ed. Slaby-Grossmann. (Span. & Ger.). Vol. 1, Espanol-Aleman. 10.07; Vol. 2. 650.00 ptas. Vol. 2, Aleman-Espanol. 12.40; Vol. 2. 800.00 ptas. Herder.
Diccionario De las Matematicas Modernas. 2nd ed. Lucien Chambadal. 264p. (Span.). 1976. pap. 5.25 (ISBN 84-01-90307-6, S-12248). French & Eur.
Diccionario de las matematicas modernas. Lucien Chambadal. (Span.). 100.00. Plaza Janes.
Diccionario De las Religiones. Konig. 816p. (Span.). 1977. 37.50 (ISBN 84-254-0358-8, S-50201). French & Eur.
Diccionario de las religiones perromanas de Hispania. Jose M. Blazquez. LC 76-450345. (Illus.). 191p. (Span.). 1975. 300.00 ptas (ISBN 8-47090-071-4). Istmo.
Diccionario de legislacion. (Span.). 8750.00 ptas. pap. 8000.00 ptas. Apendice 1951-66. 13140.00 ptas. pap. 11520.00 ptas. Aranzadi Edit.
Diccionario de legislacion admisistrativa y fiscal de Navarra. 1912p. (Span.). 1969. 1600.00 ptas. Apendice 1969-70. 200.00 ptas. Apendice 1970-71. 180.00 ptas. Aranzadi Edit.
Diccionario de Legislacion de Navarra, Vol. 2. (Span.). 1981. pap. 2800.00 ptas (ISBN 84-235-0514-6). Diput Foral.
Diccionario de lengua rusa. Ozhegov. (Span. & Rus.). 4.00. Pueblos Unidos.
Diccionario de Leyes y Efectos Cientificos En Quimica-Fisica Matematicas. D. W. Ballentyne & L. E. Walker. 216p. (Span.). 14.95 (ISBN 0-686-56711-0, S-33054). French & Eur.
Diccionario de leyes y efectos cientificos. Tr. by D. W. Bailentyne & L. E. Walker. 216p. (Span.). 1963. Arg.$1.80. Leru.
Diccionario de limpieza. Tr. by Djenane Chappat. 240p. (Span.). 1970. 60.00 ptas. Alianza Ed.
Diccionario de Linguistica. Jean Dubois. (Span.). 1979. pap. pns (S-50086). French & Eur.
Diccionario de linguistica. Theodor Lewandowski et al. Tr. by Enrique Bernardez & M. Luz Garcia. 464p. (Span.). 1982. pap. 2000.00 ptas (ISBN 84-376-0363-3). Edns Catedra.
Diccionario de linguistica. Georges Mounin. Tr. by Ricardo Pochtar. 288p. (Span.). 1982. pap. 1500.00 ptas (ISBN 84-335-4005-X). Labor SA.
Diccionario de los alimentos. 830p. (Span.). 1971. 380.00 ptas. Cedel.
Diccionario de los Alimentos: Vitaminas, Calories, Coccion, Conservacion, Etc. 2nd ed. 758p. (Span.). 1979. pap. 41.95 (ISBN 84-352-0338-7, S-13671). French & Eur.
Diccionario de los Asesinos. Rene Reouven. 386p. (Span.). 1976. pap. 13.95 (ISBN 84-7235-262-5, S-50083). French & Eur.
Diccionario de los descubrimientos cientificos. Thomas De Galiana. (Span.). 100.00 ptas. Plaza Janes.
Diccionario de los fueros & leyes de Navarra. Yanguas & Jose Miranda. 377p. (Span.). 300.00 ptas. pap. 230.00 ptas. Aranzadi Edit.
Diccionario de los infiernos. Santiago Collin de Pianci. (Span.). Arg.$7.00. Rueda.
Diccionario de los ingenios. Oscar Gaimaro. (Span.). write for info. Alonso Edns.
Diccionario de los Ismos. Juan E. Cirlot. (Span.). 18.00 (ARG). Lectorum Pubns.
Diccionario de los Medios de Comunicacion: Tecnica, Semiologia, Linguistica. Jean-Baptiste Fages. 288p. (Span.). 1978. pap. 18.95 (ISBN 84-7366-022-6, S-50121). French & Eur.
Diccionario de los Papas. Juan Dacio. (Span.). 37.50 (ISBN 84-233-0112-5, S-50110). French & Eur.
Diccionario de los Politicos. Juan Rico y Amat. (Span.). 350.00 ptas. Narcea SA.
Diccionario de los Politicos, 1855. Juan Rico y Amat. 358p. (Span.). 1976. write for info. Narcea SA.
Diccionario De los Santos De Cada Dia. Dom P. Rouillard. 472p. (Span.). 1966. 15.75 (ISBN 84-281-0062-4, S-50020). French & Eur.
Diccionario de los Sintomas: Los Testa de su Salud. A. Saponaro. 333p. (Span.). 1973. 29.95 (ISBN 0-686-92559-9, S-35094). French & Eur.
Diccionario de los suenos. Hanns Kurth. Tr. by Carmen Rada. 296p. (Span.). 1982. 525.00 ptas (ISBN 84-226-1484-7). Circulo Lect.
Diccionario de los terminos tecnicos de Medicina. Marcel Garnier et al. Tr. by Julio Llido Blasco. 1114p. (Span.). 1981. 2000.00 ptas (ISBN 84-7487-011-9). Norma.
Diccionario de management. Tr. by Hano & Andrew B. Robertson. 240p. (Span.). 1972. 350.00 ptas. Oikos Tau.
Diccionario de Management. H. Johannsen et al. 244p. (Span.). 1972. 23.95 (ISBN 84-281-0220-1, S-31465). French & Eur.
Diccionario de Marina. Jose L. De Pando y Villarroya. 244p. (Span.). 1982. pap. 1000.00 ptas (ISBN 84-300-7801-0). Autores-Editores.
Diccionario de Marketing. B. Rabassa Asenjo & M. R. Garcia Tous. 168p. (Span.). write for info. (ISBN 8-43680-075-3, 250027). Piramide.
Diccionario de Marketing. Bernardo Rabassa Asenjo & M. R. Garcia Tous. 168p. (Span.). 1978. 14.95 (ISBN 84-368-0075-3, S-50176). French & Eur.
Diccionario de Matematica Moderna. Dario Maravall Casesnovas. LC 75-513298. 333p. (Span.). 1975. 300.00 ptas (ISBN 8-4276-1235-4). Nacional Editora.
Diccionario De Matematica Moderna. Dario Maravall Casesnoves. 332p. (Span.). 1975. pap. 9.95 (ISBN 0-686-57333-1, S-50009). French & Eur.
Diccionario de matematica moderna. 2nd ed. Dario Maravall Casesnoves. 412p. (Span.). 1982. pap. 1300.00 ptas (ISBN 84-276-1235-4). Nacional Editora.
Diccionario De Matematicas. Juan Capdevila Font. 160p. (Span.). 1976. 9.75 (ISBN 84-85117-39-5, S-50263). French & Eur.
Diccionario de materiales y procesos de ingenieria. Clauser. (Span.). 2310.00 ptas. Labor SA.
Diccionario De Materiales y Procesos De Ingenieria. H. R. Clauser. 820p. (Span.). 1970. 98.00 (ISBN 84-335-6404-8, S-50067). French & Eur.
Diccionario De Maximas Pensamientos y Sentacias. J. Sintas. 742p. 1981. 53.95 (ISBN 84-302-0439-3, S-37665). French & Eur.
Diccionario de maximas, pensamientos y sentencias. 8th ed. Ed. by Jorge Sintes Pros. 744p. (Span.). 1980. 1200.00 ptas (ISBN 84-302-0439-3). Sintes.
Diccionario de mecanica. (Span.). 6.50. Minerva.
Diccionario de mecanica I y II. (Span.). 2.20 ea. Minerva.
Diccionario de Mecanica Ingles-Espanola. M. Saiz. 336p. (Eng. & Span.). pap. 5.95. Lectorum Pubns.
Diccionario de Medicina. Ed. by E. Dabout. (Span.). write for info. (S-37586). French & Eur.
Diccionario de Medicina de Urgencia. 2nd ed. 208p. (Span.). 1977. 6.95 (ISBN 84-352-0174-0, S-13672). French & Eur.
Diccionario de medicina de urgencia. 210p. (Span.). 1971. 120.00 ptas. Cedel.
Diccionario de Medicina Farmacia Veterinaria & Quimica. Castulo Carrasco. LC 78-392328. 1027p. (Span.). 1977. 2500.00 ptas (ISBN 8-4739-1013-3). Garsi Edit.
Diccionario De Medicina, Farmacia Veterinaria y Quimica. Castulo Carrasco Martinez. 1040p. (Span.). 1978. pap. 49.95 (ISBN 84-7391-013-3, S-50123). French & Eur.
Diccionario de Medicina Ilustrado. B. Melloni et al. (Illus.). 650p. (Span.). 1982. 2750.00 ptas (ISBN 8-42915-548-1). Reverte SA.
Diccionario de Medicos Puertorriquenos Que Se Man Distinguico Fuera de la Medicina. (Span.). 17.50 (ISBN 0-686-56650-5). French & Eur.
Diccionario de Mejicanismos. Francisco Santamaria. 1197p. (Span.). 1959. Mex.$24.00. Porrua.
Diccionario De Mejicanismos. Francisco J. Santamaria. (Span.). 49.50x (ISBN 0-686-00853-7). Colton Bk.
Diccionario de Mejicanismos. Francisco J. Santamaria. (Span.). 39.50 (ISBN 0-686-56689-0, S-12355). French & Eur.
Diccionario De Metologia Estadistica. Gonzalo Gonsalvo Mainar. 184p. (Span.). 1978. pap. 19.95 (ISBN 84-7112-096-8, S-50010). French & Eur.
Diccionario de Mitologia. Henri Aubert. 238p. (Span.). 1961. 14.95 (ISBN 0-686-56710-2, S-33055). French & Eur.
Diccionario de Mitologia. Homero Lelama. 364p. (Span.). 1974. 44.95 (ISBN 0-686-56670-X, S-33075). French & Eur.
Diccionario de Mitologia Griega & Romana. Rev. ed. Pierre Grimal & Francisco Payarois. 672p. (Gr. & Romanian.). 1981. write for info. ptas (ISBN 84-7509-053-2). Paidos Iberica.
Diccionario de mitologia Nahuatl. Cecilio A. Robelo. (Illus.). 880p. (Span.). 1980. Mex.$pap. 24.40. Innovacion.
Diccionario de Modismos Inglese y Norteamericanos. 2nd ed. Alfonso Torrents del Prats. 304p. (Eng. & Span.). 1979. 16.25 (ISBN 84-261-0838-5, S-12364). French & Eur.
Diccionario de Modismos Ingleses. Pablo Caldwell. 496p. (Eng. & Span.). 1973. 17.50 (ISBN 0-686-56672-6, S-33065). French & Eur.
Diccionario de Modismos Ingleses. 2nd ed. Basset D. Carbonell. LC 77-475058. 223p. (Eng. & Span.). 1976. write for info. (ISBN 8-4850-6508-5). Dos Continentes.
Diccionario de modismos ingleses. (Span.). Arg.$27.60. Sopena.
Diccionario de Modismos Ingleses & Norteamericanos. Alfonso T. Dels Prats. 368p. (Span. & Eng.). 1979. write for info. (ISBN 84-261-0838-5). Editorial Juventud.
Diccionario de modismos ingleses y norteamericanos. 294p. (Eng. & Span.). 1975. 19.95 (ISBN 0-685-55464-3, 21048). Larousse.
Diccionario de modismos ingleses y norteamericanos. A. Torrens dels Prats. 296p. (Span. & Eng.). 1969. pap. 290.00 ptas. Juventud.
Diccionario de modismos ingleses y norteamericanos. Alfonso Torrens dels Prats. 368p. (Span.). 1979. write for info. (ISBN 84-261-0838-5). Fed Gremios.
Diccionario De Moral Cristiana. 2nd ed. Karl Hoermann. 704p. (Span.). 1978. pap. 35.95 (ISBN 84-254-0966-7, S-50192). French & Eur.
Diccionario De Moral Cristiana. 2nd ed. Karl Hoermann. 704p. (Span.). 1978. 41.95 (ISBN 84-254-0967-5, S-50193). French & Eur.
Diccionario de moral profesional medica. Scremin. (Span.). pap. 200.00 ptas. Garriga.
Diccionario de Musica. Arthur Jacobs. 392p. (Span.). 1966. 15.95 (ISBN 0-686-56715-3, S-33050). French & Eur.
Diccionario de musica. Tr. by Arthur Jacobs. 392p. (Span.). 1966. Arg.$1.80. Leru.
Diccionario de Palabras Anticuadas y en Desuso. 2nd ed. Anita Luft. 308p. (Span.). 1974. pap. 17.50 (ISBN 84-359-0071-1, S-12060). French & Eur.
Diccionario de parapsicologia. 2nd, rev. ed. Hector Morel & Jose Dale Moral. 240p. (Span.). 1980. pap. write for info. Kier.
Diccionario de Parapsicologia. Julio Roca Muntanola. 272p. (Span.). 1979. 17.50 (ISBN 84-203-0086-1, S-50093). French & Eur.
Diccionario de Parapsicologia. Julio Roca Muntanola. 272p. (Span.). 1979. 500.00 ptas. Alas.
Diccionario de parapsicologia. Jose M. San Martin Unamuno. 64p. (Span.). 1980. pap. 150.00 ptas (ISBN 84-85714-02-4). Don Bosco Ed.
Diccionario de paronimos. Ed. by Fonda Publicaciones U. P. T. C. 112p. (Span.). 1972. Col.$12.00. U. Pedagogica y Tec.
Diccionario de Paronimos & Antonimos Castellanos. (Span.). pap. 11.50 (SPA). Lectorum Pubns.
Diccionario de paronimos castellanos. Lazzati. (Span.). Arg.$22.80. Sopena.
Diccionario de Payadores. Amalia Sanchez Sivori. 163p. (Span.). 1979. write for info. Plus Ultra S. A.
Diccionario de pedagogia. 2nd ed. Baumgartel. 238p. (Span.). Col.$12.00. Paulinas.
Diccionario De Pedagogia. Paul Foulquie. 464p. (Span.). 1976. 44.95 (ISBN 84-281-0328-3, S-50016). French & Eur.
Diccionario de pedagogia. Lorenzo Luzuriaga. (Span.). write for info. Losada.
Diccionario de pedagogia Labor. Tr. by Hoz Garcia. (Span.). 970.00 ptas. Labor SA.
Diccionario de Pedagogia Labor, 2 vols. 3rd ed. Victor Garcia Hoz. 444p. (Span.). 1974. Set. 44.00 (ISBN 84-335-3715-6, S-12488). French & Eur.
Diccionario De Pedogogia. Paul Foulquie. 464p. (Span.). 1976. pap. 37.50 (ISBN 0-686-57334-X, S-50015). French & Eur.
Diccionario de Peruanismos, 2 vols. Pedro Paz Soldan Y Unanue & Estuardo Nunez. LC 76-460366. xxx, 399p. (Span.). 1975. write for info. Edns Peisa.
Diccionario De Philosofia. 2nd ed. M. Rosental. (Span.). 1977. pap. 9.95 (ISBN 84-7339-107-1, S-50149). French & Eur.
Diccionario de Pintura, 4 vols, Tomo 1. 320p. (Span.). 1982. pap. 2500.00 ptas (ISBN 84-85753-69-0). Fasciculos Planeta.
Diccionario de pintura y dibujo. (Span.). 150.00 ptas. Tesoro.
Diccionario de Plantas Agricolas. Enrique Sanchez Monge y Parellada. 468p. (Span.). 1981. 2250.00 ptas (ISBN 84-7479-098-0). Minist Agricultura.
Diccionario de politica. Elliot. (Span.). 290.00 ptas. Labor SA.
Diccionario de politica. Daniel Moreno. 256p. (Span.). 1981. Mex.$pap. 150.00. Porrua.
Diccionario de politica: Obra completa, 2 vols. Norberto Bobbio. Tr. by Raul Crisafio. 1800p. (Span.). 1982. write for info. (ISBN 84-323-0429-8). Siglo XXI.

Diccionario de politica: Tomo 1: A-J. Norberto Bobbio. Tr. by Raul Crisafio. 896p. (Span.). 1982. 4000.00 ptas (ISBN 84-323-0430-1). Siglo XXI.

Diccionario de poltica mundial. Tr. by Walter Theimer. 592p. (Span.). pap. 225.00 ptas. Ariel.

Diccionario de primeros auxilios medico-veterinarios. T. E. Beker. (Span.). Arg.$5.00. Lib. del Colegio.

Diccionario de Psicoanalisis. P. Fedida. (Span.). pap. 6.95 (ISBN 84-206-1730-X, S-32981). French & European.

Diccionario de Psicoanalisis. Pierre Fedida. 176p. (Span.). 1979. 200.00 ptas. Alianza Ed.

Diccionario de psicoanalisis. 3rd ed. Jean Laplanche et al. Tr. by Fernando Cervantes Gimeno. 560p. (Span.). 1981. 3000.00 ptas (ISBN 84-335-1518-7). Labor SA.

Diccionario De Psicoanalisis Clasico. Friedrich W. Doucet. 232p. (Span.). 1974. pap. 15.75 (ISBN 0-686-57337-4, S-50069). French & Eur.

Diccionario de Psicoanalisis Clasico. Friedrich W. Doucet. 232p. (Span.). 1974. E240.00 (ISBN 84-335-1517-9). Labor.

Diccionario de Psicologia. 342p. (Span.). 1982. pap. 375.00 ptas (ISBN 84-271-1272-6). Mensajero Edns.

Diccionario De Psicologia. 3rd ed. Friedrich Dorsch. 756p. (Span.). 1978. 59.95 (ISBN 84-254-1026-6). French & Eur.

Diccionario de Psicologia. Genovard. 284p. (Span.). 1980. 1.450 ptas. Jims.

Diccionario de psicologia. Alberto L. Merani. LC 77-484135. vii, 258p. (Span.). 1977. 400.00 ptas (ISBN 8-42530-736-8). Grijalbo.

Diccionario De Psicologia. Alberto L. Merrani. 272p. (Span.). 1977. 17.50 (ISBN 84-253-0736-8, S-50072). French & Eur.

Diccionario de psicologia. H. C. Warren. 384p. (Span.). pap. 5.45. Fondo Cult.

Diccionario de psicologia abrangendo terminologia de ciencias correlatas. E. Dorin. LC 79-342055. (Illus.). 300p. (Span.). 1978. Cr.$320.00. Edicoes Melhoramentos.

Diccionario de psicologia sexual. Bastin. 412p. (Span.). pap. 280.00 ptas. Herder SA.

Diccionario De Psicologia Sexual. 2nd ed. G. Bastin. 412p. (Span.). 1976. 19.95 (ISBN 84-254-0585-8, S-13099). French & Eur.

Diccionario de Psiquiatria. James A. Brussel & George L. Cantzlaar. 306p. (Span.). pap. 25.50 (ISBN 0-686-57366-8, S-50209). French & Eur.

Diccionario de psiquiatria. Tr. by James A. Brussel & Geroge L. Cantzlaar. 310p. (Span.). 1972. 6.15. CECSA.

Diccionario de psiquiatria. Porat. (Span.). write for info. Labor SA.

Diccionario De Psiquiatria, 2 vols. 3rd ed. Antoine Porot. 650p. (Span.). 1977. Set. 58.00 (ISBN 84-335-6668-7, S-50071). French & Eur.

Diccionario de quimica y de productos quimicos. 2nd, Rev. ed. Gessner G. Haley. (Span.). pap. write for info. Omega SA.

Diccionario De Radio. 104p. (Span.). 1979. 8.75 (ISBN 84-201-0368-3, S-50147). French & Eur.

Diccionario de Radio & Television (II) Llerrero J. Cebrian. 384p. (Span.). 1981. pap. 620.00 ptas (ISBN 84-205-0789-X). Alhambra.

Diccionario De Refranes. Juana Barella Campos & Ana G. Barella Campos. 534p. (Span.). 1975. pap. 44.95 (ISBN 84-600-6609-6, S-50116). French & Eur.

Diccionario de Regionalismos de la Provincia de la Rioja. Julian Caceres Freire. (Span.). 42.50 (ISBN 0-686-56673-4, S-33066). French & Eur.

Diccionario de Reglas, Alforismos & Principios de Derecho. Carlos Lopez de Haro. LC 77-452232. 254p. (Span.). 1975. 450.00 ptas (ISBN 8-429-00609-5). Reus SA.

Diccionario de relaciones internacionales. Plano & Othon. 465p. (Span.). 2.80; Mex.$35.00. Limusa.

Diccionario de Religiones Comparadas, 2 vols. S. G. F. Brandon. 1553p. (Span.). 1975. Set. 49.95 (ISBN 8-4705-7188-5). French & Eur.

Diccionario de Ro de Qheshwa-Espanol, Espanol-Qheshwa. Jesus Lara. (Span. & Qheshwa.). 39.95 (ISBN 0-686-56703-X, S-12399). French & Eur.

Diccionario de San Francisco. Oscar Michelon. LC 78-370238. xvi, 770p. (Eng., Maya, & Span.). 1976. S.1600.00 (ISBN 3-201-00972-5). Akademische Druck Verlagt.

Diccionario de secretos de Ibiza. Mariano Planells Cardona. 320p. (Span.). 1982. pap. 700.00 ptas (ISBN 84-86000-07-6). Obelisco.

Diccionario de seguros. Molnar. (Span.). write for info. Rev. Mex. de Seguros.

Diccionario de Seguros. 3rd ed. H. Mueller Lutz & Julio Castelo Matran. 282p. (Span.). 1981. 600.00 ptas (ISBN 84-7100-004-0). Mapfre.

Diccionario De Seguros. H. L. Mueller-Lutz. 282p. (Span., Ger., Eng. & Fr.). 1977. pap. 15.75 (ISBN 84-7100-004-0, S-50035). French & Eur.

Diccionario De Seudonimos Literarios Espanoles, Con Algunas Iniciales. P. P. Rogers & F. A. Lapuente. 610p. (Span.). 1977. 38.95 (ISBN 84-249-1352-3, S-50152); pap. 32.95 (ISBN 84-249-1351-5, S-31444). French & Eur.

Diccionario de Siglas. Javier Gomez de Cadiz. LC 77-471470. 62p. (Span.). 1976. 50.00 ptas (ISBN 8-420-30051-9). Alas.

Diccionario de Siglas en Comercio Exterior. Victor Brunner. LC 77-566386. (Illus.). 125p. (Span.). 1977. Arg.$70.00. Liv Nobel.

Diccionario De Siglas Relacionadas Con la Informatica. IBM. 200p. (Span.). 1974. pap. 9.95 (ISBN 84-360-2250-5, S-50370). French & Eur.

Diccionario de Sigles de Organismos Nacionales e Internacionales. Javier Gomez de Cadiz. 64p. (Span.). 1976. pap. 1.75 (ISBN 84-203-0051-9, S-50584). French & Eur.

Diccionario de Simbolismos. 2nd ed. Juan E. Cirlot. 484p. (Span.). 1979. 950.00 ptas. Labor SA.

Diccionario de simbolos. Cirlot. (Span.). 970.00 ptas. Labor SA.

Diccionario de Simbolos. J. Cirlot. (Span.). pap. 32.95 (ISBN 84-335-7016-1, S-12244). French & Eur.

Diccionario de simbolos. 2nd ed. Juan E. Cirlot. LC 79-340125. (Illus.). 473p. (Span.). 1978. write for info. (ISBN 8-43357-016-1). Labor SA.

Diccionario de Simbolos, 1 vol. Juan E. Cirlot. 480p. (Span.). 1981. pap. write for info. (ISBN 84-335-7016-1). Editorial Labor SA.

Diccionario de simbolos. 5th ed. Juan E. Cirlot. 480p. (Span.). 1982. pap. 1500.00 ptas (ISBN 84-335-7016-1). Labor.

Diccionario de simbolos y mitos: Las ciencias y las artes en su expresion figurada. 2nd ed. J. A. Perez Rioja. (Illus.). 434p. (Span.). 320.00 ptas. Tecnos SA.

Diccionario de Simbolos y Mitos: Las Ciencias y las Artes en Su Expresion Figurada. 2nd ed. Jose A. Perez Rioja. 434p. (Span.). 1971. 15.50 (ISBN 84-309-0310-0, S-12344). French & Eur.

Diccionario de Similes & Analogias. Gonzalo Castillo. (Span.). pap. 2.50 (BCA). Lectorum Pubns.

Diccionario de similes y analogias. Gonzalo Castillo. (Span.). Mex.$12.00. Costa Amic.

Diccionario de similes y analogias. Gonzalo Castillo. (Span.). Mex.$12.00. EDIMEX.

Diccionario de sindromes. F. Kerdel-Vegas & O. Adamicska. 466p. (Span.). write for info. Cientifico Med.

Diccionario de sininimos espanoles. 6th ed. Antonio Zamora. 328p. (Span.). Arg.$pap. 12.00. Claridad.

Diccionario de sininimos, ideas afines y contrarios. J. Ruiz Calonja & Santiago Pey. 536p. (Span.). pap. 200.00 ptas. Teide.

Diccionario de Sinonimos. Roque Barcia. 160p. (Span., Mexico). 1980. Mex.$275.00. Oasis SA.

Diccionario de Sinonimos. 2nd ed. Manuel Franquesa Lluelles. 1234p. (Span.). 1981. 1750.00 ptas (ISBN 84-7306-015-6). Portic.

Diccionario De Sinonimos. S. D. Gili Gaya. (Span.). 1958. 8.50x (ISBN 0-686-00854-5). Colton Bk.

Diccionario de Sinonimos. Samuel Gili Gaya. 376p. (Span.). 250.00 ptas (ISBN 84-7153-178-X). Biblograf SP.

Diccionario de sinonimos. Samuel Gili Gaya. 376p. (Span.). 9.95 (7865-3). Natl Textbk.

Diccionario de Sinonimos. Vox. 376p. (Span.). 1982. DM.18.00. Brandstetter.

Diccionario de Sinonimos & Antonimos. Margara Clave. 597p. (Span.). 1979. Mex.$200.00. Porrua.

Diccionario de Sinonimos & Ideas Afines & de la Rima. Horta. (Span.). 1981. 500.00 ptas (ISBN 8-42830-317-7). Paraninfo.

Diccionario de Sinonimos & Ideas Afines. (Span.). pap. 10.95. CEC.

Diccionario de Sinonimos, Antonimcs y Paronimos. 378p. (Span.). 1979. 22.50 (ISBN 0-686-56667-X, S-33073). French & Eur.

Diccionario de Sinonimos-Antonimos. 510p. (Span.). 3.75. Cruzada Span Pubns.

Diccionario de Sinonimos, Antonimos & Ideas Afines. 213p. (Span.). write for info. Andina.

Diccionario de Sinonimos, Antonimos & Ideas Afines. Luis Paredes. 302p. (Span.). 1974. write for info. Gabriela Mistral.

Diccionario de Sinonimos, Antonimos & Ideas Afines. Antonio Santamaria. (Span.). 4.25 (SOP). Lectorum Pubns.

Diccionario de sinonimos, antonimos e ideas afines. (Span.). write for info. Orbe Edns.

Diccionario de sinonimos castellanos. Grates. (Span.). Arg.$14.40. Sopena.

Diccionario de Sinonimos Castellanos. 21st ed. Grates. (Span.). Arg.$5900.00. Sopena.

Diccionario de Sinonimos Castellanos. Grates. (Span.). pap. 7.25 (SPA). Lectorum Pubns.

Diccionario de Sinonimos e Ideas Afines & de la Rima. Joaquin Horta Massanes. (Span.). 13.25 (PAR). Lectorum Pubns.

Diccionario de Sinonimos e Ideas Afines & de la Rima. 3rd ed. Joaquin Horta Massanet. 364p. (Span.). 1981. 500.00 ptas (ISBN 84-283-0317-7). Paraninfo.

Diccionario de sinonimos e ideas afines. Julio de la Canal. 346p. (Span.). 1970. 4.40. CECSA.

Diccionario de sinonimos e ideas afines. (Span.). 1.80. Andina.

Diccionario de sinonimos e ideas afines y de la rima. (Span.). 14.95 (7986-6). Natl Textbk.

Diccionario de sinonimos e ideas afines y de la rima. Joaquin Horta Massanes. 364p. (Span.). 1970. 240.00 ptas. Paraninfo.

Diccionario De Sinonimos E Ideas Afines y De la Rima. 3rd ed. Joaquin Horta Massanet. 364p. (Span.). 1978. pap. 13.95 (ISBN 84-283-0317-7, S-50243). French & Eur.

Diccionario de Sinonimos e Ideas Afines y de la Rima. Joaquin H. Massanes. 364p. (Span.). 1981. pap. write for info. Paraninfo.

Diccionario de Sinonimos Espanoles. (Span.). 7.95 (ISBN 0-686-56686-6, S-12253). French & Eur.

Diccionario de sinonimos espanoles. F. Rofer. (Span.). Mex.$40.00. EDIMEX.

Diccionario de Sinonimos Espanoles. Francisco Rofer. 371p. (Span.). 1971. write for info. Edit Mex U.

Diccionario de Sinonimos, Ideas Afines & Contrarios. Santiago Pey. (Span.). 13.50 (TEI). Lectorum Pubns.

Diccionario de Sinonimos Ideas Afines & Contrarios. 10th ed. Santiago Pey Estrany. 635p. (Span.). 1981. 750.00 ptas (ISBN 84-307-7070-4). Teide.

Diccionario De Sinonimos Ideas Afines y Contrarios. 7th ed. Santiago Pey Estrany & J. Ruiz Calonja. 535p. (Span.). 1978. 13.95 (ISBN 84-307-7070-4, S-12142). French & Eur.

Diccionario de sinonimos OMNIA. Carlos Cesarman. (Span.). 1.30; Mex.$16.00. Pax.

Diccionario de sinonimos y antonimos. 500p. (Span.). 1982. Col.$pap. 250.00 (ISBN 84-8279-072-2). Educar.

Diccionario de sinonimos y antonimos. 328p. (Span.). 1982. pap. 600.00 ptas (ISBN 84-278-0782-1). Nauta SA.

Diccionario De Sinonimos y Antonimos. Francisco Gordo-Guarinos. 300p. (Span.). 1979. pap. 4.50 (ISBN 84-346-0311-X, S-29130). French & Eur.

Diccionario de Sinonimos y Antonimos. M. Orta Manzano. 368p. (Span.). 1980. 23.50 (ISBN 84-261-1704-X, S-37650). French & Eur.

Diccionario de sinonimos y antonimos. A Santamaria. (Span.). 100.00 ptas. 70.00 ptas. pap. 65.00 ptas. Sopena.

Diccionario de Sintomas. Joan Gomez. 625p. (Span.). 1976. 20.95 (ISBN 84-7002-207-5, S-31421). French & Eur.

Diccionario de Sintomas. Joan Gomez. 681p. (Span.). 1980. 800.00 ptas. Acervo.

Diccionario de sociologia. Carlos T. Echanova. (Span.). write for info. Calica.

Diccionario de sociologia. H. P. Fairchild et al. 336p. (Span.). 5.00. Fondo Cult.

Diccionario de Sociologia. Schoeck. 392p. (Span.). 1974. E480.00 (ISBN 84-254-0853-9). Herder SA.

Diccionario De Sociologia. 2nd ed. Helmut Schoeck. 392p. (Span.). 1977. 19.95 (ISBN 84-254-0853-9, S-50191); pap. 17.50 (ISBN 84-254-0854-7, S-50188). French & Eur.

Diccionario de sociologia. 3rd ed. Helmut Schoeck. Tr. by Herder. 312p. (Span.). 1981. pap. 600.00 ptas (ISBN 84-254-0854-7). Herder SA.

Diccionario de sociologia. 3rd ed. Helmut Schoeck. Tr. by Herder. 392p. (Span.). 1981. 800.00 ptas (ISBN 84-254-0853-9). Herder AS.

Diccionario de Tecnicas de Grupo. Schutzenberg. 260p. (Span.). 1974. 240.00 ptas. Soc Ed Atenas.

Diccionario de tecnologia. 3rd ed. 320p. (Span.). 1982. pap. 600.00 ptas (ISBN 84-226-1156-2). Circulo Lect.

Diccionario de telecomunicaciones en siete idiomas. (Span.). write for info. Cultura Popular.

Diccionario de Temas Regionalistas En la Poesia Puertorriquena. Salvador Arana Soto. (Span.). 12.50 (ISBN 0-686-56649-1, S-5220). French & Eur.

Diccionario De Teologia. 4th ed. Louis Bouyer. 672p. (Span.). 1977. 25.50 (ISBN 84-254-0377-4, S-14671). French & Eur.

Diccionario De Teologia Biblica. 2nd ed. Bauer. 582p. (Span.). 1976. 38.95 (ISBN 84-254-0360-X, S-50203). French & Eur.

Diccionario de Terminologia Linguistica Actual. Werner Abraham & Francisco Meno Blanco. 510p. (Span.). 1981. write for info. (ISBN 84-249-0079-0); pap. write for info. (ISBN 84-249-0080-4). Gredos.

Diccionario de terminos administrativos. (Span. & Eng.). write for info. (608-105). Pan Amer Pub.

Diccionario de Terminos Aerauticos. Rosario. (Eng. & Span.). write for info. (A-37343). French & Eur.

Diccionario de Terminos Aeronauticos: Ingles-Espanol & Espanol-Ingles. Rosario et al. (Eng. & Span.). 1983. write for info. ptas. Paraninfo.

Diccionario de Terminos Anticuados & en Desuso. Anita Navarrete Luft. (Span.). pap. 9.95. PLY.
Diccionario de terminos artisticos. Jose L. Morales Marin. 400p. (Span.). 1982. pap. 1800.00 ptas (ISBN 84-85656-36-9). Unali.
Diccionario de terminos basicos para la historia. Angel L. Abos Santabarbara & Antonio Marco Martinez. 636p. (Span.). 1982. pap. 890.00 ptas (ISBN 84-205-0931-0). Alhambra.
Diccionario de Terminos Cientificos & Tecnicos, 5 vols. (Span.). write for info. (ISBN 8-42670-417-4). McGraw.
Diccionario de Terminos Cientificos & Tecnicos, 5 vols. McGraw-Hill & Boixareu. (Illus.). 2952p. (Span.). 1981. write for info. (ISBN 84-267-0417-4). Marcombo.
Diccionario de Terminos Cientificos & Tecnicos, Vol. 2. 600p. (Span.). 1981. pap. write for info. ptas (ISBN 84-267-0419-0). Marcombo.
Diccionario de terminos cientificos y tecnicos: Obra completa, 5 vols. 2900p. (Span.). 1981. pap. 25000.00 ptas (ISBN 84-267-0417-4). Marcombo.
Diccionario de terminos cientificos y tecnicos: Tomo 1 II. 600p. (Span.). 1981. pap. write for info. (ISBN 84-267-0418-2). Marcombo.
Diccionario de terminos cientificos y tecnicos: Tomo 3 II. 600p. (Span.). 1981. pap. write for info. (ISBN 84-267-0420-4). Marcombo.
Diccionario de terminos cientificos y tecnicos: Tomo 4 II. 600p. (Span.). 1981. pap. write for info. (ISBN 84-267-0421-2). Marcombo.
Diccionario de terminos cientificos y tecnicos: Tomo 5 II. Tr. by Varios. 500p. (Span.). 1981. pap. write for info. (ISBN 84-267-0422-0). Marcombo.
Diccionario de terminos comerciales. 623p. (Span.). 1963. 500.00 ptas. Hispano Europa.
Diccionario De Terminos Comerciales. P. Gaballi Prat. 634p. (Eng. & Span.). 1963. 32.95 (ISBN 84-255-0295-0, S-31618). French & Eur.
Diccionario de Terminos Contables. 2nd ed. Joaquin Blanes Prieto. 388p. (Eng. & Span.). 1972. pap. 21.95 (ISBN 0-686-57342-0, S-28549). French & Eur.
Diccionario de terminos contables. Joaquin Blanes Prieto. 118p. (Span.). 1970. 5.30. CECSA.
Diccionario De Terminos De Proceso De Datos: Con Vocabulario Espanol-Ingles, Ingles-Espanol. 2nd ed. Angel Salto Dolla. 446p. (Span. & Eng.). 1979. 20.95 (ISBN 84-283-0830-6, S-50371). French & Eur.
Diccionario de terminos de proceso de datos: Definicion de 2500 terminos de informatica y vocabulario completo espanol-ingles e ingles-espanol. Angel Salto Dolla. 350p. (Span. & Eng.). 1971. 320.00 ptas. Paraninfo.
Diccionario de Terminos Electorales & Parlamentarios. Jose M. Gil-Robles y Quinones. LC 77-556193. 267p. (Span.). 1977. write for info. ptas (ISBN 8-430-63039-2). Taurus Ediciones SA.
Diccionario De Terminos Electrorales y Parlamentarios. Jose M. Gil-Robles. 268p. (Span.). 1977. pap. 15.25 (ISBN 84-306-3039-2, S-50001). French & Eur.
Diccionario de Terminos Filologicos. 5th ed. Fernando L. Carreter. 444p. (Span.). 1977. pap. 17.95 (ISBN 84-249-1111-3, S-12048, French & Eur). French & Eur.
Diccionario de Terminos Filologicos. 3rd ed. Fernando L. Carreter. 444p. (Span.). 1977. 22.25 (ISBN 84-249-1112-1, S-50129, French & Eur). French & Eur.
Diccionario De Terminos Geograficos. F. J. Monkhouse. 560p. (Span.). 1978. 48.00 (ISBN 84-281-0386-0, S-50017). French & Eur.
Diccionario de terminos legales. Robb. (Span.). write for info. Rev. Mex. de Seguros.
Diccionario de terminos legales. Louis Rodd. (Span. & Eng.). 7.95. Iaconi.
Diccionario de Terminos Legales Espanol-Ingles e Ingles-Espanol: Spanish-English, English-Spanish Dictionary of Legal Terms. Louis A. Robb. (Span. & Eng.). pap. 14.95 (ISBN 0-88332-134-3). Larousse.
Diccionario de terminos legales espanol-ingles e ingles-espanol. Louis A. Robb. 228p. (Span. & Eng.). Mex.$3.20; 40.00. Limusa.
Diccionario de Terminos Legales, Espanol-Ingles. Louis A. Robb. 228p. (Span. & Eng.). 1967. Mex.$4.50. Limusa.
Diccionario de Terminos Legales Espanol-Ingles. Louis A. Robb. 228p. (Span. & Eng.). pap. 8.95 (LIM). Lectorum Pubns.
Diccionario de Terminos Legales Espanol-Ingles. Louis A. Ross. (Span. & Eng.). 7.30. Camino Real.
Diccionario de terminos maritimos en seguros. R. H. Brown. Tr. by Raul Gonzalez Hevia. 552p. (Span.). 1980. 2600.00 ptas (ISBN 84-7100-095-4). Mapfre.
Diccionario De Terminos Marxistos. Mascitelli. 416p. (Span.). 1979. pap. 15.75 (ISBN 84-253-1166-7, S-50073). French & Eur.
Diccionario de terminos medicos. Torres Ruiz. (Span. & Eng.). pap. 32.00. Iaconi.
Diccionario de terminos medicos Ingles-Espanol & Espanol-Ingles. F. Ruiz Torres. 596p. (Span. & Eng.). 1980. pap. write for info. (ISBN 84-205-0654-0). Fed Gremios.
Diccionario de Terminos Medicos Ingles-Espanol & Espanol-Ingles. F. R. Torres. 596p. (Eng. & Span.). 1980. pap. write for info. Edit Alhambra.
Diccionario de terminos medicos: Ingles-espanol, espanol-ingles. Arnoldo Harrington. 320p. (Span. & Eng.). 1968. write for info. Gnosis Edit.
Diccionario de terminos medicos ingles-espanol espanol-ingles. F. Ruiz Torres. 594p. (Eng. & Span.). 1981. pap. 60.95 (ISBN 84-205-0654-0). Larousse.
Diccionario de terminos medicos: Ingles-Espanol, espanol-ingles. Francisco Ruiz Torres. 600p. (Span. & Eng.). 1981. pap. 2100.00 ptas (ISBN 84-205-0654-0). Alhambra.
Diccionario de Terminos Medicos Ingles-Espanol. F. Ruiz Torres. 594p. (Eng. & Span.). 1981. 60.95 ptas (ISBN 84-205-0654-0). Alhambra.
Diccionario de terminos meterologicos: Ingles-espanol espanol-ingles. D. Brazol. (Eng. & Span.). Arg.$25.00. Hachette.
Diccionario de terminos periodisticos y graficos. W. H. Pepper. (Span.). Arg.$14.00. Sudamer.
Diccionario de Terminos Socio-politicos. Miguel G. Serrano. LC 77-570836. 210p. (Span.). 1977. write for info. (ISBN 8-424-11500-7). Everest.
Diccionario de textos sociales pontificios. Angel Torres Calvo. (Span.). 600.00 ptas. Bibliografica.
Diccionario de t e01rminos legalese. Louis A. Ross. (Span. & Eng.). 7.30. Camino Real.
Diccionario de Tipografia & del Libro. J. Martinez de Sousa. (Span.). 1981. 1300.00 ptas (ISBN 8-42831-132-3). Paraninfo.
Diccionario de Tipografia & del Libro. Jose Martinez de Sousa. 570p. (Span.). 1974. 1070.00 ptas (ISBN 84-335-0300-6). Labor SA.
Diccionario de tipografia y del libro. Jose Martinez de Sousa. 564p. (Span.). 1981. pap. 1100.00 ptas (ISBN 84-283-1132-3). Paraninfo.
Diccionario de Toponimos Indigenas de Catamarca. Carlos Villafuerte. 93p. (Span.). 1979. write for info. Plus Ultra S. A.
Diccionario de trucos. Paule Vani. Tr. by Eduardo Giordano. 336p. (Span.). 1982. pap. 740.00 ptas (ISBN 84-85979-25-7). Granica.
Diccionario De Unidadaes y Tablas De Conversion. 3rd ed. Vasco Costa & Osvald Frances. 168p. (Span.). 1977. pap. 8.75 (ISBN 84-252-0214-0, S-50579). French & Eur.
Diccionario de Unidades Cientificas. G. Jerrard & D. B. Neill. 206p. (Span.). write for info. Bellaterra.
Diccionario de Unidades Cientificas. 3rd ed. H. G. Jerrard & D. B. McNeill. 216p. (Span.). 1974. pap. 11.95 (ISBN 0-686-57367-6, S-50215). French & Eur.
Diccionario de unidades, efectos y constantes. 224p. (Span.). 50.00 ptas. Tesoro.
Diccionario de unidades y tablas de conversion. 2nd ed. Vasco Costa & Osvaldo Frances. 168p. (Span.). write for info. G Gili.
Diccionario de urbanismo. Petroni & Kenigsberg. (Span.). Arg.$9.00. Cesarini.
Diccionario de uso de espanol: Tomo 1. Maria Moliner. 1495p. (Span.). 1981. write for info. (ISBN 84-249-1346-9). Gredos.
Diccionario de uso de espanol: Tomo 2. Maria Moliner. 1593p. (Span.). 1981. write for info. (ISBN 84-249-1348-5). Gredos.
Diccionario de uso del espanol, 2 vol. Maria Moliner. (Span.). 2300.00 ptas. pap. 2000.00 ptas. Gredos.
Diccionario de uso del espanol: Obra completa, 2 vols. Maria Moliner. 3088p. (Span.). 1981. write for info. (ISBN 84-249-1344-2). Gredos.
Diccionario de uso del espanol: Tomo 1. Maria Moliner. 1495p. (Span.). 1981. write for info. (ISBN 84-249-1346-9). Gredos.
Diccionario de uso del espanol: Tomo 2. Maria Moliner. 1593p. (Span.). 1981. write for info. (ISBN 84-249-1348-5). Gredos.
Diccionario de Valencias Verbales. Aleman-Espanol. Dietrich Rall et al. (Tuebinger Beitraege zur Linguistik: No. 134). 292p. (Orig., Span. & Ger.). 1980. pap. 18.00x (ISBN 3-87808-134-0). Benjamins North Am.
Diccionario de Verbos e Regimes. Fernandes. 606p. (Port.). Date not set. price not set (M-9212). French & Eur.
Diccionario de vinos espanoles. J. Perez & R. Alsina. 238p. (Span.). 125.00 ptas. Teide.
Diccionario de Voces & Expresiones Argentinas. Felix Coluccio. 223p. (Span.). 1979. write for info. Plus Ultra S. A.
Diccionario de Voces Indigenas de Puerto Rico. Luis Hernandez Aquino. (Span.). 17.95 (ISBN 0-686-56700-5, S-27651). French & Eur.
Diccionario de Voces Lunfardas & Vulgares. Fernando H. Casullo. LC 76-151616. 219p. (Span.). 1976. write for info. Plus Ultra SA.
Diccionario de voces lunfardas y vulgares. Fernando Casullo. (Span.). Arg.$15.00. Freeland.
Diccionario de voces naturales. Garcia de Diego. (Span.). 600.00 ptas. Aguilar SP.
Diccionario de Voces Naturales. Vicenete Garcia de Diego. 724p. (Span.). 1968. 20.95 (ISBN 84-03-12031-1, S-11993). French & Eur.
Diccionario De Zoologia. Umberto Parenti. 255p. (Span.). 1973. leatherette 11.50 (ISBN 84-307-8256-7, S-50257). French & Eur.
Diccionario Del Amor. Aline de Nanxe. 122p. (Span.). 1969. pap. 3.50 (ISBN 84-290-1061-0, S-50136). French & Eur.
Diccionario del Argot Espanol. V. Leon. (Span.). pap. 5.25 (ISBN 84-206-1766-0, S-33020). French & Eur.
Diccionario del Arte Actual. Thomas Karin. 224p. (Span.). 1978. pap. 16.50 (ISBN 84-335-7561-9, S-50064). French & Eur.
Diccionario del Arte Moderno: Conceptos, Ideas, Tendencias. Ed. by Vincente Aguilera Cerni. LC 80-110365. 569p. (Ital.). 1979. 2800.00 ptas (ISBN 8-473-66108-7). Toreres.
Diccionario del automovil. 1158p. (Span.). 800.00 ptas. CEAC.
Diccionario del Automovil. Ed. by Equipo Reactor de CEAC. 916p. (Span.). 1978. 37.50 (ISBN 84-329-1010-4, S-14232). French & Eur.
Diccionario del automovil. 3rd ed. R. Guerber. (Illus.). 238p. (Span.). write for info. G Gili.
Diccionario del Automovil. 4th ed. Roger Guerber. 237p. (Span., Eng., Fr. & Ger.). 1972. pap. 16.75 (ISBN 84-252-0065-2, S-14249). French & Eur.
Diccionario del automovil II. 7th ed. 920p. (Span.). 1982. 1820.00 ptas (ISBN 84-329-1010-4). Ceac.
Diccionario del Budo: Artes Marciales. Raymond Thomas. 128p. (Span., Japanese, Chinese, Korean, & Other Oriental Languages.). 1978. pap. 4.50 (ISBN 84-203-0069-1, S-50092). French & Eur.
Diccionario del Carlismo. Cecilia De Bourbon Parma. LC 77-553587. (Illus.). 93p. (Span.). 1977. 50.00 ptas (ISBN 8-472-35307-9). Dopesa.
Diccionario del cine. Peter Graham. (Span.). 1.60; Mex.$20.00. Novaro.
Diccionario del cine. Jean Mitry. (Span.). 100.00 ptas. Plaza Janes.
Diccionario Del Cine Espanol, 1896-1968. 359p. (Span.). 1970. pap. 15.75 (ISBN 84-276-0249-9, S-50008). French & Eur.
Diccionario del cine espanol 1896-1968. 3rd ed. Fernando Vizcaino Casas. (Span.). 450.00 ptas. Nacional Editora.
Diccionario del comercia exterior. D. W. Budic. (Span.). Arg.$15.00. Ergon.
Diccionario del Comunismo. Jorge Sole Tura. 96p. (Espn.). 1977. pap. 2.25 (ISBN 84-7235-299-4, S-50082). French & Eur.
Diccionario del Cristianismo. La. Brosse. 1104p. (Span.). 1976. 53.95 (ISBN 84-254-0777-X, S-50202). French & Eur.
Diccionario del Cristianismo. Olivier Brosse. 1101p. (Span.). 1974. 1500.00 ptas (ISBN 84-254-0777-X). Herder SA.
Diccionario del Democrata. Eduardo Haro Tecglen. LC 77-569550. (Illus.). 92p. (Span.). 1977. 70.00 ptas (ISBN 8-472-35313-3). Dopesa.
Diccionario Del Espanol Chicano. Roberto A. Galvan & Richard V. Teschner. 1977. pap. text ed. 6.95 ea. (ISBN 0-88499-146-6). Inst Mod Lang.
Diccionario del Espanol de Tejas. Roberto A. Galvan & Richard V. Teschner. LC 79-345010. xiv, 856p. (Eng. & Span.). 1978. Cr.$250.00. Edicoes Melhoramentos.
Diccionario del Espanol Moderno. 5th ed. Martin Alonso. 1100p. (Span.). 1978. 66.00 (ISBN 84-03-27061-5, S-12229). French & Eur.
Diccionario del espionaje. Domingo Pastor Petit. (Span.). 100.00 ptas. Plaza Janes.
Diccionario del Hogar Catolico. 1180p. (Span.). 1962. 17.95 (ISBN 84-261-0075-9, S-12259). French & Eur.
Diccionario del Hombre Contemporaneo. Bertrand Russell. (Span.). pap. 17.50 (ISBN 0-686-56655-6). French & Eur.
Diccionario del hombre contemporaneo. Bertrand Russell. (Span.). Arg.$23.00. Rueda.
Diccionario Del Idioma Espanol. Edwin B. Williams. 530p. (Span. & Eng.). pap. 2.95. Lectorum Pubns.
Diccionario del Idioma Espanol Moderno. (Span.). 55.00. AGL.
Diccionario del jazz. Ortiz Oderigo. (Span.). Arg.$30.00. Ricordi.
Diccionario del Jefe de Empresa. Jean Romeuf & Jean P. Guinot. 644p. (Span.). 1966. 44.95 (ISBN 84-335-6524-9, S-14191). French & Eur.
Diccionario Del Lenguaje Filosofico. Paul Foulquie. 1100p. (Span.). 1966. 50.00 (ISBN 84-335-1000-2, S-50065). French & Eur.
Diccionario del Lenguaje Usual. 758p. (Span.). 1969. Mex.$2.10. Santillana.
Diccionario del lenguaje usual. Ed. by E.G.B. 758p. (Span.). 175.00 ptas. Santilana SA.

Diccionario del Nuevo Testamento. Xavier Leon-Dufour. 480p. (Span.). 1977. 20.95 (ISBN 84-7057-213-X, S-50103). French & Eur.

Diccionario del Pasota. Felipe Navarro Garcia. LC 79-121713. (Illus.). 204p. (Span.). 1979. 300.00 ptas (ISBN 8-432-04139-4). Planeta SA.

Diccionario del pensamiento de Santa Teresa de Jesus. 2nd ed. Jesus Marti Ballester. 575p. (Span.). 1982. pap. 1400.00 ptas (ISBN 84-7050-075-9). Edicep.

Diccionario del perfecto automobilista. C. Vebel. (Span.). 120.00 ptas. Grijalbo.

Diccionario del Periodismo. 2nd ed. A. Lopez de Zuazo. 244p. (Span.). write for info. (ISBN 8-43680-053-2, 270003). Piramide.

Diccionario del Periodismo. 2nd ed. Antonio Lopez De Zuazo Algar. 256p. (Span.). 1978. leatherette 16.75 (ISBN 84-368-0053-2, S-50177). French & Eur.

Diccionario del periodismo. 3rd ed. Antonio Lopez de Zuazo Algar. 256p. (Span.). 1981. pap. 800.00 ptas (ISBN 84-368-0053-2). Piramide.

Diccionario del Plastico. J. A. Wordingham & P. Reboul. 208p. (Span.). 14.95 (ISBN 0-686-56714-5, S-33051). French & Eur.

Diccionario Del Psicoanalisis. 3rd ed. Jean Laplanche & Jean-Bertrand Pontalis. Ed. by Fernando Cervantes Gimeno. 558p. (Span.). 1977. leatherette 65.50 (ISBN 84-335-1516-0, S-31445). French & Eur.

Diccionario del psicoanalisis. Laplanche Pontalis. (Span.). write for info. Labor SA.

Diccionario del Socialismo. Enrique Mujica Herzog. LC 77-568716. (Illus.). 90p. (Span.). 1977. 50.00 ptas (ISBN 8-472-35315-X). Dopesa.

Diccionario Del Trabajo Social. Ezequiel Ander Egg. 424p. (Span.). 1977. pap. 12.25 (ISBN 84-280-0606-7, S-50011). French & Eur.

Diccionario del Trabajo Social. 7th ed. Ezequiel Ander Egg. 355p. (Span.). 1981. pap. 400.00 ptas (ISBN 84-500-4997-0). Organ Ofic Adm.

Diccionario Del Uso Del Espanol, 2 vols. 4th ed. Maria Moliner. 3036p. (Span.). 1977. Set. 90.00 (ISBN 84-249-1344-2, S-12260). French & Eur.

Diccionario del Uso del Espanol, 2 vols. Maria Moliner. (Span.). 125.00. GRD.

Diccionario del verbo castellano. Lazzati. (Span.). Arg.$24.00. Sopena.

Diccionario del Verbo Castellano. Santiago Lazzati. (Span.). pap. 9.50 (SPA). Lectorum Pubns.

Diccionario del Verbo Castellano: Como Se Conjugan los Verbos Americanos. Santiago Lazzati. 438p. (Span.). 1977. pap. 13.50 (ISBN 0-686-56657-2, S-12049). French & Eur.

Diccionario del vino de Jerez. Ed. by Julio Permartin. (Illus.). 246p. (Span.). 400.00 ptas. Jerez Industrial.

Diccionario demografico plurilingue. 115p. (Span.). 1958. 1.00. ONU.

Diccionario Didactikon. 392p. (Span.). Mex.$7.50. Fernandez.

Diccionario Disney. Walt Disney. 112p. (Span.). 1973. pap. 5.95 (ISBN 84-305-0601-2, S-24118). French & Eur.

Diccionario Durango: Enciclop e01dia regional. 320p. (Span.). write for info. (730). Fernandez.

Diccionario Durvan de la Lengua Espanola. 1312p. (Span.). 1977. 44.95 (ISBN 84-85001-40-0, S-11956). French & Eur.

Diccionario Economico & Financiero. Yves Bernard. LC 80-9262. xi, 1274p. (Span.). 1975. write for info. (ISBN 8-470-19071-7). Assn Prog Direc.

Diccionario Economico De la Empresa. Andres Santiago Suarez. 384p. (Span.). 1977. leatherette 19.95 (ISBN 84-368-0067-2, S-50181). French & Eur.

Diccionario Economico de la Empresa. 2nd. ed. A. S. Suarez Suarez et al. 384p. (Span.). write for info. (ISBN 8-43680-067-2, 250022). Piramide.

Diccionario Edo. de M e xico: Enciclopedia regional. 320p. (Span.). write for info. (735). Fernandez.

Diccionario el internacional. 200p. (Span. & Eng.). write for info. (797). Fernandez.

Diccionario Electromecanico Ingles-Espanol. 298p. (Eng. & Span.). 1969. pap. 18.95 (ISBN 84-7087-002-5, S-12420). French & Eur.

Diccionario en Color de Arbustos. Millar. 213p. (Span.). 1977. 60.00 (ISBN 84-252-0695-2, S-50274). French & Eur.

Diccionario Enciclopedia Salvat Universal, 20 vols. 10080p. (Span.). 1969. Set. 780.00 (ISBN 84-345-3221-2, S-12270). French & Eur.

Diccionario Enciclopedia Universal, 10 vols. 5036p. (Span. , Ger. , Fr. , Ital. & Eng.). Set. 270.00 (ISBN 0-686-57349-8, S-12271). French & Eur.

Diccionario Enciclopedias Labor, 9 vols. 7th ed. Ed. by Javier Lasso de La Vega & Jose M. Rubert Candau. 6500p. (Span.. Fr., Port., Eng. & Ger.). 1978. Set. leatherette 550.00 (ISBN 84-335-0322-7, S-12269). French & Eur.

Diccionario Enciclopedico, 6 vols. (Illus., Span.). deluxe ed. 175.00 (7869-6). Natl Textbk.

Diccionario Enciclopedico Abreviado, 9 vols. 7th ed. 11678p. (Span.). 1977. Set. 300.00 (ISBN 84-239-4710-6, S-12263). French & Eur.

Diccionario enciclope edico Aguascalientes. 320p. (Span.). write for info. (721). Fernandez.

Diccionario enciclopedico baja California norte. 320p. (Span.). write for info. (722). Fernandez.

Diccionario enciclope dico baja California sur. 320p. (Span.). write for info. (723). Fernandez.

Diccionario Enciclopedico Bruguera, 5 vols. 6240p. (Span.). 1976. Set. leather 120.00 (ISBN 84-02-04687-8, S-50525). French & Eur.

Diccionario enciclope dico Campeche. 320p. (Span.). write for info. (724). Fernandez.

Diccionario enciclope dico Chiapas. 320p. (Span.). write for info. (727). Fernandez.

Diccionario enciclope dico Chihuahua: D. 320p. (Span.). write for info. (728). Fernandez.

Diccionario enciclope dico Colima. (Span.). write for info. Fernandez.

Diccionario Enciclopedico Danae, 12 vols. 7220p. (Span.). 1977. Set. leather 600.00 (ISBN 84-7060-457-0, S-50521). French & Eur.

Diccionario Enciclopedico de la Masoneria. (Span.). 40.95 (ISBN 0-686-56654-8, S-14860). French & Eur.

Diccionario Enciclopedico De la Vida Sexual, 5 vols. Jesus Noguer More. 792p. (Span.). 1974. Set. 160.00 (ISBN 84-278-0331-1, S-50029). French & Eur.

Diccionario Enciclopedico De las Ciencias Del Lenquaje. Varios. (Span.). 32.95 (ISBN 0-686-56652-1, S-30990). French & Eur.

Diccionario Enciclopedico de Medicino Jims. Leon Braier. 1184p. (Span.). 1980. 3.500 ptas. Jims.

Diccionario enciclopedico de metalurgia: Espanol-frances, frances-espanol y espanol-engles, engles-espanol. Oliver Bader & Michel Theret. 960p. (Span., Fr. & Eng.). 1969. 980.00 ptas. ETA.

Diccionario Enciclopedico de Metalurgia. Oliver Bader & Michel Theret. 960p. (Span., Fr. & Eng.). 1975. 44.95 (ISBN 84-7146-054-8, S-50132). French & Eur.

Diccionario enciclop edico Distrito Federal ilustrado. 320p. (Span.). write for info. (729). Fernandez.

Diccionario Enciclopedico Escolar Basico. 808p. (Span.). 1974. pap. 26.95 (ISBN 84-01-60131-2, S-50044). French & Eur.

Diccionario Enciclopedico Escolar Basico. (Span.). 1974. 450.00 ptas (ISBN 84-01-60131-2). PlazaJanes.

Diccionario Enciclopedico Espasa, 12 vols. 10800p. (Span.). 1978. Set. leatherette 600.00 (ISBN 84-239-4780-7, S-27954). French & Eur.

Diccionario Enciclopedico Espasa. (Span.). 1980. write for info. (S-37369). French & Eur.

Diccionario Enciclopedico: Gran Omeba, 12 vols. (Span.). 325.00 (ISBN 0-686-56680-7, S-33046). French & Eur.

Diccionario enciclopedico Hidalgo. 320p. (Span.). write for info. (733). Fernandez.

Diccionario enciclopedico Michoac a01n. 320p. (Span.). write for info. (736). Fernandez.

Diccionario enciclopedico Morelos. 320p. (Span.). write for info. (737). Fernandez.

Diccionario enciclopedico Nayarit. 320p. (Span.). write for info. (738). Fernandez.

Diccionario enciclopedico Nuevo-Le o01n. 320p. (Span.). write for info. (739). Fernandez.

Diccionario enciclopedico Oaxaca. 320p. (Span.). write for info. (740). Fernandez.

Diccionario enciclopedico Puebla. 320p. (Span.). write for info. (741). Fernandez.

Diccionario enciclopedico Quer e01taro. 320p. (Span.). write for info. (742). Fernandez.

Diccionario enciclopedico Quintana Roo. 320p. (Span.). write for info. (743). FErnandez.

Diccionario enciclopedico Sinaloa. 320p. (Span.). write for info. (745). Fernandez.

Diccionario enciclopedico Tlaxcala. 320p. (Span.). write for info. (749). Fernandez.

Diccionario Enciclopedico Tomo IX: Suplemento A-Z. 2nd ed. 808p. (Span.). 1979. 3600.00 ptas. Labor SA.

Diccionario enciclopedico Zacatecas. 320p. (Span.). write for info. (752). Fernandez.

Diccionario Erotico De El y Ella. 640p. (Span.). 1977. pap. 37.50 (ISBN 84-85265-17-3, S-50128). French & Eur.

Diccionario Escolar. (Span.). pap. 3.95. Lectorum Pubns.

Diccionario escolar americano. Manuel Garcia Becerra. (Span.). Mex.$6.00. Iztaccihuatl.

Diccionario Escolar Billiken Ilustrado. 1226p. (Span.). write for info. Atlantida.

Diccionario escolar de la Lengua Espanola Vox. 7th ed. 872p. (Span.). 1982. 595.00 ptas (ISBN 84-7153-172-0). Biblo SP.

Diccionario Escolar de la Lengua Espanola. Samuel Gili Gaya. 872p. (Span.). 695.00 ptas (ISBN 84-7153-172-0). Biblograf SP.

Diccionario Escolar de la Lengua Espanola. Sopena R. LC 76-466553. (Illus.). 200p. (Span.). 1975. write for info. (ISBN 8-430-30082-1). Sopena.

Diccionario Escolar de la llengua Catalana 'Vox' 2nd ed. 512p. (Span.). 1982. write for info. (ISBN 84-7153-334-0). Bibliograf.

Diccionario Escolar de Sinonimos & Antonimos Vox. 2nd ed. 370p. (Span.). 1981. 500.00 ptas (ISBN 84-7153-379-0). Biblo SP.

Diccionario Escolar de Sinonimos y Antonimas "Vox". 3rd ed. 370p. (Span.). 1982. write for info. (ISBN 84-7153-379-0). Bibliograf.

Diccionario Escolar De Sinonimos y Contrarios De la Lengua Espanola. Juan Capdevila Font. 499p. (Span.). 1978. 12.25 (ISBN 84-7176-302-8, S-50268). French & Eur.

Diccionario escolar del idioma espanol. Martin Alonso. (Span.). 150.00 ptas. Aguilar SP.

Diccionario escolar etimologica. Victor Garcia Hoz. (Span.). 160.00 ptas. Magisterio Esp.

Diccionario Escolar Etimologico. 7th ed. Victor Garcia Hoz. 740p. (Span.). 1977. pap. 13.95 (ISBN 84-265-0123-0, S-11999). French & Eur.

Diccionario Escolar Etimologico. 9th ed. Victor Garcia Hoz. 740p. (Span.). 1981. 800.00 ptas (ISBN 84-265-0123-0). Magisterio Esp.

Diccionario Escolar Hispanoamericano. 4th ed. 600p. (Span.). 1975. pap. 3.95 (ISBN 84-319-0027-X, S-27088). French & Eur.

Diccionario escolar hispanoamericano. (Span.). 600.00 ptas. EVA.

Diccionario escolar ilustrado. J. M. Fernandez Gandia. 302p. (Span.). 0.70. CECSA.

Diccionario Escolar: La/Escuela Alegro. 184p. (Span.). write for info. (ISBN 84-399-4674-0). Escuela Nueva.

Diccionario escolar latino-espanol y espanol-latino. Matias Martinez Burgos & Manuel Ayala Lopez. (Span.). 200.00 ptas. Bibliografica.

Diccionario Escolar Roble. 5th ed. Francisco Gordo Guarinos. 712p. (Span.). 1975. pap. 4.50 (ISBN 84-346-0191-5, S-50046). French & Eur.

Diccionario Escolar Sopena Color De la Lengua Espanola. 928p. (Span.). 1976. pap. 13.25 (ISBN 84-303-0085-6, S-50144). French & Eur.

Diccionario Escolar Sopena Color De la Lengua Espanola. 928p. (Span.). 1976. 15.75 (ISBN 84-303-0084-8, S-50145). French & Eur.

Diccionario Escolar, 2. 4th ed. 1040p. (Span.). 1981. 750.00 ptas (ISBN 84-294-1215-8). Santillana SA.

Diccionario Escuela. 340p. (Span.). Mex.$4.50. Fernandez.

Diccionario Esedal de la legislacion peruana. 552p. (Span.). 1972. S/200.00. Esedal.

Diccionario esencial frances-espanol, espanol-frances. Jean P. Vidal. 598p. (Fr. & Span.). 1981. pap. 600.00 ptas (ISBN 84-85205-90-1). Diafora.

Diccionario esencial Ingles-espanol, Espanol-Ingles. Brian Dutton et al. 464p. (Eng. & Span.). 1981. pap. 600.00 ptas (ISBN 84-85205-93-6). Diafora.

Diccionario Esloveno-Espanol. Ed. by A. Grad. 747p. (Span.). 1979. 49.95 (ISBN 0-686-92391-X, S-37817). French & Eur.

Diccionario Esoterico. Zaniah. (Span.). 29.95 (ISBN 0-686-56653-X, S-15045). French & Eur.

Diccionario Espanol-Aleman. 21st ed. Carlos Brandau. 640p. (Span. & Ger.). 1982. pap. 150.00 ptas (ISBN 84-7105-089-7). Mayfe.

Diccionario espanol-aleman. (Span. & Ger.). 25.00 ptas. Mayfe.

Diccionario Espanol-Aleman, Aleman-Espanol Militar. Carlos Ruiz Jodar. 375p. (Span. & Ger.). 1975. pap. 13.95 (ISBN 84-400-8515-X, S-50101). French & Eur.

Diccionario Espanol-Arabe. Federico Corriente Cordoba. 480p. (Span. & Arabic.). 1970. 18.95 (ISBN 0-686-57345-5, S-50343). French & Eur.

Diccionario espanol-arabe. 2nd ed. Federico Corriente Cordoba. 480p. (Span. & Arabic.). 1980. 800.00 ptas (ISBN 84-7472-023-0). Inst Hispano-Arabe.

Diccionario Espanol-Arabe de Verbos, Gramatica y Temas de Conversacion. 2nd ed. Mufid Al-Guindi Abd Al-Monem. 368p. (Span. & Arabic.). 1974. pap. 13.95 (ISBN 84-7074-021-0, S-50423). French & Eur.

Diccionario Espanol de la Lengua China. Fernando Mateos et al. 1381p. (Span. & Chinese.). 1977. leather 95.00 (ISBN 84-239-4771-8, S-31804). French & Eur.

Diccionario Espanol de Sinonimos, Equivalencias & Ideas Alfines. 8th ed. Aedos. LC 80-100011. 443p. (Span.). 1979. write for info. (ISBN 8-470-03072-8). Aedos.

Diccionario espanol de sinonimos y antonimos. F. Sainz de Robles. (Span.). 30.00. Iaconi.

Diccionario espanol de sinonimos y antonimos. F. C. Sainz de Robles. (Span.). 700.00 ptas. Aguilar SP.

Diccionario Espanol de Sinonimos y Antonimos. 8th ed. Federico C. Sainz de Robles. Ed. by Asesor Arturo del Hoyo. 1152p. (Span.). 1977. 50.00 (ISBN 84-03-27029-1, S-12352). French & Eur.

Diccionario espanol de sinonimos y equivalencias. 6th ed. F. Andres. 386p. (Span.). 1972. 250.00 ptas. Aedos.
Diccionario Espanol de Sinonimos y Equivalencias. 8th ed. M. F. Andres. 444p. (Span.). 1979. 17.50 (ISBN 84-7003-072-8, S-12233). French & Eur.
Diccionario Espanol Etimologico. Felix Diez Mateo. 396p. (Span.). 1972. 6.95 (ISBN 84-300-5794-3, S-12291). French & Eur.
Diccionario Espanol Etimologico. Felix Diez Mateo. (Span.). 3.50 (CANT). Lectorum Pubns.
Diccionario espanol etimologico: El pequeno academico. Felix Diez Mateo. (Span.). 1972. write for info. Cantabrica.
Diccionario espanol-frances. S. Denis & M. Maraval. (Span. & Fr.). write for info. Hachette.
Diccionario espanol-frances. (Span. & Fr.). 25.00 ptas. Mayfe.
Diccionario espanol-frances. (Span. & Fr.). 45.00 ptas. Zeus.
Diccionario Espanol-Frances. 31st ed. Armando Galant. 640p. (Span. & Fr.). 1982. 150.00 ptas (ISBN 8-47105-094-3). Mayfe.
Diccionario Espanol-Frances. 31st ed. Armando Galant. 640p. (Span. & Fr.). 1982. pap. 160.00 ptas (ISBN 84-7105-094-3). Mayfe.
Diccionario Espanol-Frances, Espagnol-Francais. Miguel Gimenez Sales. 736p. (Span. & Fr.). 1975. pap. 3.95 (ISBN 84-02-04265-1, S-50394). French & Eur.
Diccionario Espanol Ilustrado. 7th ed. Jose Garcia Mercadal. (Illus.). 592p. (Span.). 1982. 350.00 ptas (ISBN 8-47105-107-9). Mayfe.
Diccionario Espanol-Ingles, 2 vols. in 1. 1088p. (Span. & Eng.). write for info. Edns Nauta.
Diccionario Espanol-Ingles. 560p. (Span. & Eng.). 1974. M.18.00; 1.45. Diana.
Diccionario espanol-ingles. (Span. & Eng.). 25.00 ptas. Mayfe.
Diccionario espanol-ingles. (Span. & Eng.). 45.00 ptas. Zeus.
Diccionario Espanol-Ingles. 41st ed. Maria Younger. 640p. (Span. & Eng.). 1982. pap. 150.00 ptas (ISBN 84-7105-093-5). Mayfe.
Diccionario Espanol-Ingles-Espanol. 1008p. (Eng. & Span.). 1981. pap. write for info. ptas (ISBN 84-7505-232-0). Oceano.
Diccionario espanol, ingles, frances, italiano, aleman y holandes. (Eng. , Fr. , Ital. , Ger. & Dutch.). write for info. Rev. Mex. de Seguros.
Diccionario espanol-ingles, ingles-espanol. Crowell. (Span. & Eng.). write for info. Hachette.
Diccionario Espanol-Ingles, Ingles-Espanol. 800p. (Eng. & Span.). 1979. pap. 6.95 (ISBN 84-346-0310-1, S-29129). French & Eur.
Diccionario Espanol-Ingles, Ingles-Espanol. 3rd ed. Francisco Ruiz Torres. 714p. (Span. & Eng.). 1978. pap. 41.95 (ISBN 84-205-0455-6, S-12408). French & Eur.
Diccionario espanol-ingles ingles-espanol. 3rd ed. Eleesbaan Serrano Mesa. 448p. (Span. & Eng.). 1982. pap. write for info. (ISBN 84-7105-102-8). Mayfe.
Diccionario Espanol-Ingles Pocket Dictionary. Simon & Schuster. (Span. & Eng.). 1.95. Camino Real.
Diccionario espanol-japones. Luis M. Martinez Duenas & Manuel M. Kato Yda. 1160p. (Span. & Japanese.). 1982. 450.00 ptas (ISBN 84-85786-53-X). Edi-Seis.
Diccionario espanol-latino. J. Llauro Padrose & J. Marques Casanovas. (Span. & Lat.). 200.00 ptas. SAETA.
Diccionario espanol moderno. Martin Alonso. (Span.). 1974. 1000.00 ptas. Aguilar SP.
Diccionario Espanol-Ruso. 944p. (Span. & Rus.). 1961. 9.95 (ISBN 0-686-92536-X, S-31679). French & Eur.
Diccionario espanol-ruso. (Span. & Rus.). write for info. Cultura Popular.
Diccionario espanol-ruso. (Span. & Rus.). Arg.$12.00. (Mir) D'lppolito.
Diccionario espanol-ruso. Kelina. (Span. & Rus.). 0.90. Pueblos Unidos.
Diccionario Espanol-Ruso. L. Martinez Calvo. LC 76-456144. 1915p. (Rus. & Span.). 1975. 1000.00 Rub (ISBN 8-43030-133-X). Sopena.
Diccionario Espanol-Ruso. Lorenzo Martinez Calvo. 1920p. (Span. & Rus.). 1975. 44.95 (ISBN 84-303-0132-1, S-50411). French & Eur.
Diccionario Espanol-Ruso de le Prospeccion y Refinacion del Petroleo. A. Pinkevich & B. Amelin. Ed. by A. F. Dobriansky. 424p. (Span. & Rus.). 1966. 12.50 (ISBN 0-686-92531-9, S-37368). French & Eur.
Diccionario espanol-ruso de terminos cientificos y tecnicos. (Span. & Rus.). write for info. Cultura Popular.
Diccionario espanol-senhayi: Dialecto bereber de Senhay de Serair. Esteban Ibanez. 382p. (Span.). 1959. 150.00 ptas. Inst. de Estudios Africanos CSIC.
Diccionario espanol Sol. (Span.). 30.00 ptas. pap. 25.00 ptas. Mayfe.
Diccionario Espa n13ol -- Ingl e01s Pocket Dictionary. Simon & Schuster. (Span. & Eng.). 1.95. Camino Real.
Diccionario Estudiantil. 3rd ed. 326p. (Span.). 1972. pap. 3.50 (ISBN 84-7165-051-7, S-27086). French & Eur.
Diccionario estudiantil J. 326p. (Span.). write for info. C y P.
Diccionario Estudios de Castellano sec. Castagnino. H. Eduardo. 194p. (Span.). 1930. Arg.$1.00. Leru.
Diccionario Estudios de geografia. Armando Zavala Cubillos. 200p. (Span.). 1961. Arg.$1.10. Leru.
Diccionario etimologico espanol e hispanico. Vicente Garcia de Diego. (Span.). 500.00 ptas. SAETA.
Diccionario etimologica latinoamericano de lexico de la delincuencia. Arnulfo D. Trejo. 272p. (Span.). 1.44. UTEHA.
Diccionario Etimologico Abreviado. 2nd ed. Fernando Coripio Perez. 320p. (Span.). 1976. pap. 3.50 (ISBN 84-02-03901-4, S-50161). French & Eur.
Diccionario Etimologico Abreviado. Fernando Corripio. 320p. (Span.). 1974. 80.00 ptas. Bruguera.
Diccionario Etimologico Abreviado. Fernando Corripio. (Span.). pap. 2.95 (BRG). Lectorum Pubns.
Diccionario Etimologico General de la Lengua Castellana. Fernando Corripio. 512p. (Span.). 1974. 425.00 ptas. Bruguera.
Diccionario Etimologico General de la Lengua Espanola. 2nd ed. Fernando Corripio Perez. (Span.). 18.95 (ISBN 84-02-03344-X, S-50158, French & Eur). French & Eur.
Diccionario Euskera-Castellano. 432p. (Span.). 1982. 600.00 ptas (ISBN 8-48584-625-7). Sendoa.
Diccionario Everest "Cima". (Illus.). 1088p. (Span.). pap. 9.95. Lectorum Pubns.
Diccionario Everest Cima. (Span.). 110.00 ptas. 100.00 ptas. 90.00 ptas. pap. 80.00 ptas. Everest.
Diccionario Everest Cima: Espanol II. 20th ed. 1088p. (Span.). 1982. pap. 360.00 ptas (ISBN 84-241-1040-4). Everest.
Diccionario Everest Cima Latin. 6th ed. (Illus.). 756p. (Lat.). 1982. 475.00 ptas (ISBN 8-42411-442-6). Everest.
Diccionario Everest Cima Latin-Espanol. 5th ed. 756p. (Lat. & Span.). 1981. 390.00 ptas (ISBN 84-241-1442-6). Everest.
Diccionario Everest Cima Latin (II) 756p. (Lat.). 1982. 475.00 ptas (ISBN 8-42411-442-6). Everest.
Diccionario Everest Cima latino-espanol, espanol-latino. (Span.). 125.00 ptas. Everest.
Diccionario Everest Corona. (Span.). 500.00 ptas. 400.00 ptas. pap. 300.00 ptas. Everest.
Diccionario Everest 'Corona' Espanol II. 11th ed. 1568p. (Span.). 1982. pap. 1150.00 ptas (ISBN 84-241-1073-0). Everest.
Diccionario Everest Corona ingles-espanol, espanol-ingles. (Eng. & Span.). 200.00 ptas. Everest.
Diccionario Everest Cuarenta Lexico. 2nd ed. 684p. (Span.). 1981. 975.00 ptas (ISBN 84-241-1140-0). Everest.
Diccionario Everest "Cumbre". 680p. (Span.). pap. 4.75. Lectorum Pubns.
Diccionario Everest Cumbre. (Span.). 80.00 ptas. 70.00 ptas. 60.00 ptas. pap. 55.00 ptas. Everest.
Diccionario Everest Cumbre: Espanol II. 24th ed. 672p. (Span.). 1982. pap. 165.00 ptas (ISBN 84-241-1030-7). Everest.
Diccionario Everest Cumbre, ingles-espanol, espanol-ingles. (Eng. & Span.). 100.00 ptas. 80.00 ptas. 75.00 ptas. pap. 70.00 ptas. Everest.
Diccionario Everest 'Cumbre' Ingles-espanol y espanol-ingles. 11th ed. 704p. (Eng. & Span.). 1981. pap. 175.00 ptas (ISBN 84-241-1230-X). Everest.
Diccionario Everest Cupula. (Span.). 250.00 ptas. Everest.
Diccionario Everest Cupula: Espanol II. 10th ed. 1536p. (Span.). 1982. 1000.00 ptas (ISBN 84-241-1062-5). Everest.
Diccionario Everest Cupula, ingles-espanol, espanol-ingles. (Eng. & Span.). 140.00 ptas. pap. 120.00 ptas. Everest.
Diccionario Everest 'Cuspide' Espanol II. 14th ed. 1088p. (Span.). 1980. pap. 475.00 ptas (ISBN 84-241-1052-8). Everest.
Diccionario Everest Cuspide frances-espanol, espanol-frances. (Fr. & Span.). 125.00 ptas. Everest.
Diccionario Everest Cuspide: Frances-Espanol y espanol-frances. 6th ed. 990p. (Fr. & Span.). 1982. pap. 400.00 ptas (ISBN 84-241-1350-0). Everest.
Diccionario Everest 'Cuspide' frances-espanol y espanol-frances: Anonimas y colectivas. 5th ed. 990p. (Fr. & Span.). 1980. pap. 345.00 ptas (ISBN 84-241-1350-0). Everest.
Diccionario 'Everest Diez II. 6th ed. 272p. (Span.). 1981. pap. 100.00 ptas (ISBN 84-241-1110-9). Everest.
Diccionario Everest "Punto". 384p. (Span.). pap. 2.50. Lectorum Pubns.
Diccionario Everest Punto. (Illus., Span.). 22.00 ptas. pap. 18.00 ptas. Everest.
Diccionario Everest Punto English-Spanish Spanish-English. (Eng. & Span.). 2.95 (ISBN 84-241-1211-3, 22882). Larousse.
Diccionario Everest Punto: Espanol II. 24th ed. 384p. (Span.). 1981. pap. 62.00 ptas (ISBN 84-241-1010-2). Everest.
Diccionario Everest Punto' Espanol II. 23rd ed. 384p. (Span.). 1981. pap. 56.00 ptas (ISBN 84-241-1010-2). Everest.
Diccionario Everest Punto. Ingles-Espanol. 10th ed. 448p. (Eng. & Span.). 1981. 80.00 ptas (ISBN 84-241-1210-5). Everest.
Diccionario Everest 'Vertice' 14th ed. 700p. (Span.). 1982. 170.00 ptas (ISBN 8-42411-220-2). Everest.
Diccionario Everest "Vertice". (Illus.). 608p. (Span.). pap. 3.50. Lectorum Pubns.
Diccionario Everest Vertice. (Span.). 55.00 ptas. 35.00 ptas. pap. 30.00 ptas. Everest.
Diccionario Everest Vertice Aleman-Espanol, Spanisch-Deutsch. 582p. (Ger. & Span.). 1978. pap. 3.50. Imported bks.
Diccionario Everest 'Vertice' aleman-espanol y espanol-aleman. 2nd ed. 592p. (Ger. & Span.). 1980. pap. 152.00 ptas (ISBN 84-241-1444-2). Everest.
Diccionario Everest-Vertice: English-Spanish, Spanish-English. (Span. & Eng.). write for info. (608-25). Pan Amer Pub.
Diccionario Everest Vertice: Espanol II. 30th ed. 606p. (Span.). 1982. pap. 96.00 ptas (ISBN 84-241-1020-X). Everest.
Diccionario Everest Vertice Frances-Espanol, Espano-Frances. 519p. (Fr. & Span.). 1979. pap. 2.50 pocket size. Imported Bks.
Diccionario Everest Vertice ingles-espanol, espanol-ingles. (Span. & Eng.). 65.00 ptas. 50.00 ptas. pap. 45.00 ptas. Everest.
Diccionario Everest Vertice: Ingles-Espanol. 13th ed. 700p. (Eng. & Span.). 1981. 150.00 ptas (ISBN 84-241-1220-2). Everest.
Diccionario Everest Vertice Italian-Espanol, Spagnolo-Italiano. 883p. (Span. & Ital.). pap. 4.50. Imported Bks.
Diccionario Everest 10. 269p. (Fr.). 1975. 2.95 (ISBN 84-241-1110-9, 21466). Larousse.
Diccionario familiar de homeopatia. E. A. Maury. Tr. by Domingo Santos. 208p. (Span.). 1980. pap. 350.00 ptas (ISBN 84-286-0578-5). Pomaire.
Diccionario familiar de las medicinas naturales. E. A. Maury. Tr. by Rafael Andrue Aznar. 448p. (Span.). 1981. pap. 600.00 ptas (ISBN 84-270-0692-6). Martinez Roca.
Diccionario Familiar de Mediciana Natural. E. A. Maury & C. Rudder. 441p. (Span.). 1981. pap. 17.50 (ISBN 0-686-92544-0, S-3785). French & Eur.
Diccionario Filosofico, 2 vols. Voltaire. 616p. (Span.). 1978. Set. 17.50 (ISBN 84-7250-634-7, S-50012). French & Eur.
Diccionario Filosofico, 3 vols. Voltaire. 1000p. (Span.). 1977. Set. 58.50 (ISBN 0-686-57339-0, S-50109). French & Eur.
Diccionario Filosofico. Voltaire. 378p. (Span.). 1976. pap. 15.75 (ISBN 84-7339-136-5, S-50148). French & Eur.
Diccionario Forrua de la Lengua Espanola. Antonio Raluy Poudevila. Ed. by Francisco Monterde. (Span.). pap. 6.95 (ISBN 0-686-56694-7, S-12281). French & Eur.
Diccionario frances-espanol. S. Denis & M. Maraval. (Fr. & Span.). write for info. Hachette.
Diccionario frances-espanol. (Fr. & Span.). 25.00 ptas. Mayfe.
Diccionario frances-espanol. (Fr. & Span.). 45.00 ptas. Zeus.
Diccionario Frances-Espanol. 26th ed. Armando Galant. 640p. (Fr. & Span.). 1982. pap. 150.00 ptas (ISBN 84-7105-095-1). Mayfe.
Diccionario frances-espanol de la construccion y obras publicas. Herbert Bucksch & Arturo Galan e Hidalgo. 564p. (Fr. & Span.). 1969. 700.00 ptas. ETA.
Diccionario Frances-Espanol de la Construccion y Obras Publicas. Herbert Bucksch & Arturo Galan e Hildalgo. 564p. (Fr. & Span.). 1975. 35.95 (ISBN 84-7146-047-5, S-50133). French & Eur.
Diccionario Frances-Espanol, Espanol-Frances. E. M. Martinez Amador. 1568p. (Span. & Fr.). 1974. 47.95 (ISBN 84-303-0091-0, S-13282). French & Eur.
Diccionario frances-espanol, espanol-frances. (Serie Bachilarato Koel: No. 43). 527p. (Fr. & Span.). 75.00 ptas. Tesoro.
Diccionario frances-espanol espanol-frances. (Fr. & Span.). 75.00 ptas. Zeus.
Diccionario frances-espanol y espanol-frances. Alcala-Zamora & T. Antignac. (Span. & Fr.). 7.50. Imported Bks.
Diccionario frances-espanol y espanol-frances. (Fr. & Span.). 60.00 ptas. Mayfe.
Diccionario frances-espanol y espanol-frances. (Fr. & Span.). 50.00 ptas. pap. 35.00 ptas. Mayfe.
Diccionario Fraseologico Comercial. Zavada & Eberle. 435p. (Ger. & Port.). 1978. 27.50 (ISBN 0-686-92497-5, M-9026). French & Eur.
Diccionario Fundamental de la Lengua Espanola'Vox' 2nd ed. 552p. (Span.). 1980. 275.00 ptas (ISBN 84-7153-229-8). Biblo SP.
Diccionario Fundamental de la Lengua Espanola. Rev. by Samuel Gili Gaya. 592p. (Span.). write for info. Biblograf SP.

Diccionario Fundamental de la Llengua Catalana 'Vox' 443p. (Span.). 1980. 425.00 ptas (ISBN 84-7153-333-2). Biblo SP.
Diccionario galego-castelan. 2nd ed. X. L. Franco Grande. (Span.). 300.00 ptas. Galaxia.
Diccionario galego-castelan. 7th ed. Xose L. Franco Grande. 970p. (Span.). 1982. pap. 1200.00 ptas (ISBN 84-7154-024-X). Galaxia.
Diccionario Galego-Castelan e Vocabulario Castelan-Galego. 4th ed. Xose L. Franco Grande. 970p. (Span.). 1978. 23.95 (ISBN 84-7154-024-X, S-50436). French & Eur.
Diccionario General de Acustica & Electroacustica. Piraux. (Span.). 1967. 550.00 ptas (ISBN 8-42830-799-7). Paraninfo.
Diccionario General De Acustica y Electro Acustica. Henri Piraux. 374p. (Espn.). 1967. 14.95 (ISBN 84-283-0153-0, S-50237). French & Eur.
Diccionario general de acustica y electroacustica. Henry Peraux. 376p. (Span.). 1967. 300.00 ptas. Paraninfo.
Diccionario General de Ciencias Humanas. Georges Thines & Agnes Lempereur. 976p. (Span.). 1978. 45.00 (ISBN 84-376-0133-9, S-50146). French & Eur.
Diccionario General de la Lengua Catalana. Pompeu Fabra. 1779p. (Span.). 1981. 850.00 ptas (ISBN 84-350-0120-2). Edhasa.
Diccionario General de la Lengua Catalana. 9th ed. Pompeu Fabra Poch. 1778p. (Catalan.). 1978. 52.50 (ISBN 84-350-0120-2, S-50080). French & Eur.
Diccionario general de llengua catalana. 15th ed. Pompeu Fabra Poch. 1768p. (Span.). 1981. 2500.00 ptas (ISBN 84-350-0120-2). Edhasa.
Diccionario General de Periodismo. J. Martinez de Sousa. (Span.). 1981. 2000.00 ptas (ISBN 8-42831-117-X). Paraninfo.
Diccionario General de Sinonimos & Antonimos. Cosme Perez Cuadrado. 396p. (Span.). 1981. 2100.00 ptas (ISBN 84-7215-363-0). Coculsa.
Diccionario General de Turismo. G. Novo. (Span.). write for info. (S-28710). French & Eur.
Diccionario General del Periodismo. Jose Martinez de Sousa. 596p. (Span.). 1980. 1200.00 ptas (ISBN 84-283-1117-X). Paraninfo.
Diccionario General Illustrado de la Lengua Espanol. 1752p. (Span.). 1976. 47.50 (ISBN 0-686-57111-8, M-6144). French & Eur.
Diccionario general ilustrado. 576p. (Span.). 1982. 1500.00 ptas (ISBN 84-7102-196-X). Marin.
Diccionario General Ilustrado de la Lengua Espanola. Ramon D. Menendez Pidal. Ed. by Samuel D. Gili Gaya. 1752p. (Span.). 1980. write for info (ISBN 84-7153-109-7). Biblograf SP.
Diccionario General Ilustrado de la Lengua. (Illus.). 991p. (Span.). 1980. 24.00 ptas. 20.00 ptas. Albir.
Diccionario general ilustrado de la Lengua Espanola Vox. 5th ed. (Illus.). 1780p. (Span.). 1982. pap. 2650.00 ptas (ISBN 84-7153-109-7). Biblo SP.
Diccionario General-Ilustrado la Lengau Espanola. Vox. (Illus.). 1752p. (Span.). 1982. DM.80.00. Brandstetter.
Diccionario General y Tecnico: Hiztegi Orokor-Teknikoa, 2 vols. Luis M. Mugica Urdangarin. #1220p. (Span. & Vasco.). 1977. Set. 80.00 (ISBN 84-85288-07-6, S-50100). French & Eur.
Diccionario Geografico de Guatemala. V. Aquilar Pelaez. (Span.). 1930. 40.00 ea.; pap. 27.50 ea. Intl Guatemala.
Diccionario Gitano. Pablo-Carrillo Moreno Castro & Juan R. Reyes. 82p. (Span.). 1981. 900.00 ptas (ISBN 84-300-4410-8). Piquenas Edit.
Diccionario Grafico de Arte y Oficios Artisticos, 4 vols. J. Lapoulide. 1600p. (Span.). 1963. Set. 125.00 (ISBN 84-7186-037-6, S-12333). French & Eur.
Diccionario Gramatical y de Dudas del Idioma. 1500p. (Span.). 29.95 (ISBN 84-303-0061-9, S-12275). French & Eur.
Diccionario. Grandes Temas de la fe Cristiana. 400p. (Span.). 1981. 1200.00 ptas (ISBN 84-236-1511-1). Don Bosco Ed.
Diccionario Griego-Espanol. 2nd ed. Miguel Balaguer. 940p. (Span. & Gr.). 1977. 17.95 (ISBN 84-216-0362-0, S-50344). French & Eur.
Diccionario griego-espanol. Miguel Balagur. (Gr. & Span.). 300.00 ptas. Bibliografica.
Diccionario Griego-Espanol. 1544p. (Gr. & Span.). leatherette 50.95 (ISBN 84-303-0158-5, S-50425). French & Eur.
Diccionario griego-espanol. Florencio I. Sebastian Yarza. 1644p. (Gr. & Span.). 1974. 1000.00 ptas. Sopena.
Diccionario Guanajuato: Encilopedia regional. 320p. (Span.). write for info. (731). Fernandez.
Diccionario guarani-espanol, espanol-guarani. A Jover Peralta & T. Ozuna. 508p. (Span. & Guarani.). 1951. 4.50. Dist. Comuneros.
Diccionario Guerrero: Enciclopedia regional. 320p. (Span.). write for info. (732). Fernandez.
Diccionario-guia de redaccion. A. Vinoly & J. Vinoly. 200p. (Span.). 70.00 ptas. Teide.
Diccionario-Guia de Redaccion. 3rd ed. A. J. Vinoly. 200p. (Span.). 1976. pap. 5.50 (ISBN 84-307-7091-7, S-12219). French & Eur.
Diccionario Hebreo-Castallano: Castellano-Hebreo. Ed. by Y. Austridan. 390p. (Hebrew & Span.). 1979. pap. 40.00 (ISBN 0-686-92419-3, S-37819). French & Eur.
Diccionario hebreo-espanol. (Hebrew & Span.). 100.00 ptas. Perpetuo.
Diccionario heraldico. 2nd ed. Vicente de Cadenas y Vicent. LC 78-362955. (Illus.). 295p. (Span.). 1976. 1000.00 ptas (ISBN 8-40004-294-8). Consejo Superior.
Diccionario hispano-tagalog y tagalog-hispano, 3 vols. Ed. by Pedro Serrano Laktaw. 2024p. (Span. & Tagalog.). 1000.00 ptas. Cultura Hispan.
Diccionario Historico del Libro. Emili Eroles. 336p. (Span.). 1981. 1500.00 ptas (ISBN 84-7304-062-7). Milla Lib.
Diccionario historico do la lengua espanola, 9 vols. (Span.). 400.00 ea. ptas. (Real Academia) Espasa.
Diccionario Historico Geografico Ilustrado Del Pais Vasco, 3 vols. Real Academia de la Historia. 1400p. (Span.). Set. 102.00 (ISBN 0-686-57346-3, S-10997). French & Eur.
Diccionario Humano. 2nd ed. Mercedes Iribarren Reta. 552p. (Span.). 1975. pap. 9.95 (ISBN 84-85000-33-1, S-50088). French & Eur.
Diccionario humoristico. 4th ed. Noel Claraso. 298p. (Span.). 1966. 300.00 ptas. Sintes.
Diccionario Humoristico. V. Claraso. 297p. (Span.). 1966. 26.95 (ISBN 0-686-92238-7, S-37662). French & Eur.
Diccionario humoristico. (Span.). 20.00 ptas. Sanchez Rodrigo.
Diccionario humoristico. 2nd ed. 552p. (Span.). 1962. 400.00 ptas. Sintes.
Diccionario humoristico. M. Malcoux. (Span.). 140.00 ptas. Grijalbo.
Diccionario Humoristico. J. Sintes. 900p. (Span.). 41.95 (ISBN 0-686-97940-0, S-37666). French & Eur.
Diccionario humoristico. 3rd ed. Ed. by Jorge Sintes Pros. 552p. (Span.). 1982. pap. 1400.00 ptas (ISBN 84-302-0445-8). Sintes.
Diccionario ideografico poligloto. G. Medina. (Span.). 250.00 ptas. Aguilar SP.
Diccionario ideoligico feminista. Victoria Sau Sanchez. 280p. (Span.). 1981. pap. 580.00 ptas (ISBN 84-7426-072-8). Icaria Edit.
Diccionario ideologico de la lengua espanola. 2nd ed. Julio Casares. 1446p. (Span.). write for info. (ISBN 84-252-0126-8). G Gili.
Diccionario Ideologico de la Lengua Espanola. Julio Casares. (Span.). pap. 43.95 (GIL). Lectorum Pubns.
Diccionario Ideologico de la Lengua Espanola. 2nd ed. Julio Casares Sanchez. 1446p. (Span.). 1982. 3400.00 ptas (ISBN 8-42520-126-8). G Gili.
Diccionario Ideologico Feminista. Victoria Sau Sanchez. 280p. (Span.). 580.00 ptas (ISBN 8-47426-072-8). Icaria Edit.
Diccionario Ideologico Manual de la Lengua Espanola. Juan Capdevila Font. 900p. (Span.). 1976. 18.75 (ISBN 84-85117-22-0, S-50264). French & Eur.
Diccionario Ilustrado Basico. 790p. (Span.). 9.75. Cruzada Span Pubns.
Diccionario ilustrado Daimon. (Illus., Span.). 150.00 ptas. Daimon.
Diccionario Ilustrado Danae de la Lengua Espanola. (Span.). pns leatherette (ISBN 84-7060-397-3, S-50207). French & Eur.
Diccionario ilustrado de alfareria practica. Robert Fournier. Tr. by Elena Torres. (Illus.). 320p. (Span.). 1981. 2100.00 ptas (ISBN 84-282-0643-0). Omega SA.
Diccionario ilustrado de anecdotas. 3rd ed. V. Vega. (Illus.). 900p. (Span.). write for info. G Gili.
Diccionario Ilustrado de Arquitectura. Carlos E. Perez Calvo. LC 79-122250. (Illus.). 231p. (Span.). 1979. write for info. Plaza Janes.
Diccionario ilustrado de efemerides, 2 vols. V. Vega. 1902p. (Span.). write for info. G Gili.
Diccionario Ilustrado de Efemerides, 2 vols. Vincente Vega. 1901p. (Span.). 1968. Set. leatherette 47.95 (ISBN 84-252-0600-6, S-12366); pap. 38.95 (ISBN 84-252-0600-6, S-50279). French & Eur.
Diccionario Ilustrado de Electronica. Humberto Ramirez Villareal. 192p. (Span.). 12.95 (ISBN 0-686-56678-5, S-25248). French & Eur.
Diccionario ilustrado de electronica: Espanol-ingles e ingles-espanol. Humberto Ramirez Villarreal. (Illus.). 192p. (Span. & Eng.). 3.60; Mex.$45.00. Diana.
Diccionario Ilustrado De Fotografia. 212p. (Span.). 1974. pap. 22.50 (ISBN 84-342-0117-8, S-50014). French & Eur.
Diccionario ilustrado de la arquitectura contemporanes. 3rd ed. G. Hatje. (Span.). 1980. pap. 700.00 ptas. G Gili.
Diccionario Ilustrado De la Arquitectura Contemporanea. 3rd ed. Gerd Hatje. Ed. by Gerd Sabater. 358p. (Span.). 1975. pap. 29.25 (ISBN 84-252-0860-2, S-50278). French & Eur.
Diccionario ilustrado de la arquitectura contemporanea. 4th ed. Gerd Hatje. Tr. by Jose M. Mantero. (Illus.). 360p. (Span.). 1982. pap. 860.00 ptas (ISBN 84-252-0860-2). G Gili.
Diccionario Ilustrado de la Biblia. Ed. by Wilton M. Nelson. (Illus.). 735p. (Span.). 1974. 27.95 (ISBN 0-89922-033-9); pap. 18.95 (ISBN 0-89922-099-1). Edit Caribe.
Diccionario Ilustrado De la Lengua Espanola. Aristos. 640p. (Span.). 10.95 (ISBN 84-303-0048-1, S-12234). French & Eur.
Diccionario Ilustrado de la Lengua Espanola. 375p. (Span.). pap. 3.00. Cruzada Span Pubns.
Diccionario Ilustrado De la Lengua Espanola. Atilano Rances. 640p. (Span.). 1974. 9.95 (ISBN 84-303-0051-1, S-12346). French & Eur.
Diccionario ilustrado de la lengua rusa. (Illus., Span. & Rus.). Mex.$15.00. Cultura Popular.
Diccionario Ilustrado de la Muerte. Robert Sabatier. 612p. (Span.). 1970. pap. 24.75 (ISBN 84-252-0351-1, S-50581). French & Eur.
Diccionario ilustrado de las ciencias pura y aplicades. (Span.). Arg.$35.00; 250.00. Mundi.
Diccionario ilustrado de lengua espanola. Mercadel Garcia. (Illus., Span.). 90.00 ptas. Mayfe.
Diccionario Ilustrado de Rarezas, Inverosimilitudes y Curiosidades. 4th ed. Vicente Vega. 622p. (Span.). 1971. leatherette 24.75 (ISBN 84-252-0203-5, S-12368). French & Eur.
Diccionario Ilustrado De Terminologia Textil Aleman-Espanol, Espanol-Aleman. Carlos Scheengluth. 700p. (Ger. & Span.). 1975. 66.00 (ISBN 84-335-6220-7, S-50056). French & Eur.
Diccionario ilustrado de trucos. 2nd ed. J. L. Chardana & V. Vega. (Illus.). 700p. (Span.). write for info. G Gili.
Diccionario Ilustrado de Trucos. J. L. Chardans & Vicente Vega. 700p. (Span.). 1970. leatherette 24.75 (ISBN 84-252-0206-X, S-14532). French & Eur.
Diccionario ilustrado del idioma ruso. (Illus., Span. & Rus.). 1.00. Pueblos Unidos.
Diccionario Ilustrado En Color De Arbustos. S. Millar Gauult. 213p. (Span.). 1978. 48.00 (ISBN 84-252-0695-2, S-50274). French & Eur.
Diccionario Ilustrado en Color De Plantas De Interior. Roy Hay et al. 231p. (Span.). 1976. 60.00 (ISBN 84-252-0892-0, S-50277). French & Eur.
Diccionario Ilustrado en Color de Plantas de Jardin con Plantas de Interior y de Invernadero. R. Har & P. M. Synge. 364p. (Span.). 1977. 60.00 (ISBN 84-252-0376-7, S-12330). French & Eur.
Diccionario Ilustrado Latino-Espanol Espanol-Latino. (Illus.). 800p. (Lat. & Span.). 1981. 825.00 ptas (ISBN 84-7153-197-6). Biblograf SP.
Diccionario Ilustrado Latino-Espanol Espanol-Latino. 14th ed. (Illus.). 800p. (Span. & Lat.). 1982. pap. 725.00 ptas (ISBN 84-7153-197-6). Biblo SP.
Diccionario indice analitico, 3 vols. Ed. by Argentina. (Span.). write for info. Ediar.
Diccionario indice de jurisprudencia civil 1947-1956. (Span.). 1958. 400.00 ptas. Bosch Casa.
Diccionario Infantil de Palabras & Figuras. 116p. (Span.). write for info. (ISBN 84-365-0083-0). Escuela Nueva.
Diccionario Infantil Fher. Angel J. Gomez de Segura Beaumont. 24p. (Span.). 1978. pap. 5.25 (ISBN 84-243-1456-5, S-50076). French & Eur.
Diccionario Infantil Ilustrado. 190p. (Span.). 1975. 20.50 (ISBN 84-271-0968-7, S-50006); pap. 17.95 (ISBN 84-271-0969-5, S-50007). French & Eur.
Diccionario Infantil Ilustrado, 7 vols. 968p. (Span.). 1977. Set. 140.00 (ISBN 84-01-70210-0, S-50043). French & Eur.
Diccionario Infantil Ilustrado. (Illus., Span.). 9.95. Lectorum Pubns.
Diccionario infantil ilustrado. (Illus.). 192p. (Span.). 290.00 ptas. Mensajero Edns.
Diccionario infantil ilustrado. 3200p. (Span.). write for info. Plaza Janes.
Diccionario Infantil Ilustrado. (Illus.). 36p. (Span.). 1981. 85.00 ptas (ISBN 84-7500-081-9). Interediciones.
Diccionario Infantil Ilustrado, Vol. 1. 256p. (Span.). 1981. 2466.00 ptas (ISBN 84-01-70237-2). Plaza Janes.
Diccionario Infantil Ilustrado, Vol.2. 256p. (Span.). 1981. 2466.00 ptas (ISBN 84-01-70238-0). Plaza Janes.
Diccionario Infantil Ilustrado, Vol. 3. (Illus.). 256p. (Span.). 1981. 2466.00 ptas (ISBN 84-01-70239-9). Plaza Janes.
Diccionario Infantil Ilustrado Bruguera. Consuelo Guisset Poch & Prado Castellanos Alentorn. 96p. (Span.). 1977. pap. 9.50 (ISBN 84-02-05211-8, S-50160). French & Eur.
Diccionario Infantil Ilustrado: Obra completa II, 6 vols. 1232p. (Span.). 1981. 14800.00 ptas (ISBN 84-01-70236-4). Plaza Janes.

Diccionario infantil: La lupa magica. Inocencio Feijoo Zollern. 50p. (Span.). 1982. 500.00 ptas (ISBN 84-85825-01-2). Lopez Paco.
Diccionario Ingles. American Heritage. 1981. 9.95 (ISBN 0-395-31254-X); pap. 7.95 (ISBN 0-395-31255-8). HM.
Diccionario Ingles. Guenther Haensch. 1012p. (Eng. & Span.). 1981. 950.00 ptas (ISBN 84-254-1156-4). Herder SA.
Diccionario Ingles-Espanol, 2 vols. in 1. 1088p. (Eng. & Span.). write for info. Edns Nauta.
Diccionario Ingles-Espanol. 36th ed. 640p. (Eng. & Span.). 1982. 150.00 ptas (ISBN 8-47105-092-7). Mayfe.
Diccionario ingles-espanol. (Eng. & Span.). 25.00 ptas. Mayfe.
Diccionario ingles-espanol. (Eng. & Span.). 45.00 ptas. Zeus.
Diccionario Ingles-Espanol. 1008p. (Eng. & Span.). 1981. pap. 1600.00 ptas (ISBN 84-7505-234-7). Oceano.
Diccionario Ingles-Espanol. 2nd ed. L. Jorda. 888p. (Eng. & Span.). 1974. Arg.$110.00. Omega SA.
Diccionario Ingles-Espanol. 36th ed. Fructuoso Plans Sanz de Bremond. 640p. (Eng. & Span.). 1982. pap. 150.00 ptas (ISBN 84-7105-092-7). Mayfe.
Diccionario Ingles-Espanol & Espanol Ingles: Col. Forja de Idiomas. (Span. & Eng.). 50.00 ptas. pap. 35.00 ptas. Mayfe.
Diccionario Ingles-Espanol & Espanol-Ingles. (Span. & Eng.). 60.00 ptas. Mayfe.
Diccionario ingles-espanol de electrotecnia y electronica. H. Piraux et al. 534p. (Span. & Eng.). 1966. 600.00 ptas. ETA.
Diccionario ingles-espanol de las ciencias de la tierra. E Orellana. 325p. (Eng. & Span.). 1967. 600.00 ptas. Interciencia.
Diccionario Ingles-Espanol de Medicina. 3rd ed. F. Ruiz Torres. 714p. (Eng. & Span.). 1968. Arg.$600.00. Alhambra.
Diccionario Ingles-Espanol, Espanol-Ingles. E. M. Martinez Amador. 1504p. (Span. & Eng.). 47.95 (ISBN 84-303-0105-4, S-2789). French & Eur.
Diccionario Ingles-Espanol, Espanol-Ingles. 3rd ed. Francisco Bruguera Grane. 680p. (Eng. & Span.). 1979. pap. 4.95 (ISBN 84-02-00835-6, S-50345). French & Eur.
Diccionario Ingles-Espanol Espanol-Ingles. 1450p. (Eng. & Span.). 2100.00 ptas (ISBN 84-7153-151-8). Biblograf SP.
Diccionario Ingles-Espanol, Espanol-Ingles. (Serie Bachillerato Koel: No. 14). 373p. (Eng. & Span.). 75.00 ptas. Tesoro.
Diccionario Ingles-Espanol Espanol-Ingles. (Eng. & Span.). 75.00 ptas. Zeus.
Diccionario Ingles-Espanol, Espanol-Ingles Novus. 1008p. (Eng. & Span.). 1981. 1600.00 ptas (ISBN 84-7505-234-7). Oceano.
Diccionario Ingles-Espanol Espanol-Ingles. 550p. (Eng. & Span.). 1981. pap. write for info. (ISBN 84-7291-330-9). Sarpe.
Diccionario ingles-espanol espanol-ingles. Fernando Huerta et al. 1012p. (Eng. & Span.). 1981. 1100.00 ptas (ISBN 84-226-1237-2). Circulo Lect.
Diccionario Ingles-Espanol, Espanol-Ingles, 2 vols. Ricard Jordana & Paul Chamberlain. 1072p. (Eng. & Span.). 1981. write for info. (ISBN 84-278-0592-6). Edns Nauta.
Diccionario Ingles-Espanol, Espanol-Ingles, 2 vols. Ricard Jordana & Paul Chamberlain. 1072p. (Span. & Eng.). 1981. write for info. vol. 1 (ISBN 84-278-0593-4); write for info. vol. 2 (ISBN 84-278-0594-2). Fed Gremios.
Diccionario ingles-espanol espanol-ingles, 2 vols. 2nd ed. Ricardo Jordana & Paul Chamberlain. 1104p. (Eng. & Span.). 1981. 2750.00 ptas (ISBN 84-278-0592-6). Nauta SA.
Diccionario Ingles-Espanol, Espanol-Ingles. Robertson. 894p. (Eng. & Span.). 12.25 (ISBN 84-303-0107-0, S-50396); pap. 9.95 (ISBN 84-303-0108-9, S-50397). French & Eur.
Diccionario Ingles-Espanol, Espanol-Ingles Forja. 17th ed. Eleesbaan Serrano Mesa. 488p. (Eng. & Span.). 1977. 4.50 (ISBN 84-7105-098-6, S-50352). French & Eur.
Diccionario Ingles-Espanol, Espanol-Ingles. 9th ed. Eleesbaan Serrano Mesa. 640p. (Eng. & Span.). 1977. leatherette 5.25 (ISBN 84-7105-019-6, S-50353). French & Eur.
Diccionario Ingles-Espanol-Ingles. 472p. (Eng. & Span.). 1982. pap. 600.00 ptas (ISBN 84-278-0779-1). Nauta SA.
Diccionario Ingles-Espanol para Medicos y Estudiantes de Medicina. J. A. Garrido. 525p. (Eng. & Span.). 1979. 35.95 (ISBN 84-7193-011-0, S-34967). French & Eur.
Diccionario ingles-espanol para medicos y estudiantes de medicina. Juan A. Garrido. 524p. (Eng. & Span.). 1972. 500.00 ptas. Pediatrica.
Diccionario Ingles-Espanol, Spanish-English. Mauricio Bohigas Rosell. 1370p. (Eng. & Span.). 1974. 7.95 (ISBN 84-7183-007-8, S-12385). French & Eur.
Diccionario ingles-espanol, tecnico-electromecanico. Weiss-Ballesteros. (Eng. & Span.). 340.00 ptas. Index.
Diccionario Ingles-Espanol y Espanol-Ingles, 2 vols. 6th ed. 3000p. (Eng. & Span.). 1977. Set. 75.00 (ISBN 84-7166-211-6, S-12391). French & Eur.
Diccionario ingles-espanol y espanol-ingles. Aurelio Pena. (Eng. & Span.). 150.00 ptas. Bibliografica.
Diccionario ingles-espanol y espanol-ingles. Universidad de Chicago. (Eng. & Span.). 125.00 ptas. Aguilar SP.
Diccionario Ingles: For Spanish Speakers. (Eng. & Span.). s.p. 7.95 (0323-1). Natl Textbk.
Diccionario ingl e01s. (Span. & Eng.). 7.95. Iaconi.
Diccionario Inicial de la Lengua Espanol. (Illus.). 340p. (Span.). 495.00 ptas (ISBN 84-7153-199-2). Biblograf SP.
Diccionario Inicial de la Lengua Espanola. (Illus., Span.). 7.95. Lectorum Pubns.
Diccionario Inicial de la Lengua Espanola. 2nd ed. 326p. (Span.). 1981. 300.00 ptas (ISBN 84-7153-199-2). Biblo SP.
Diccionario Inicial de la Lengua Espanola. Prologue by Aurora D. Plaja. LC 75-517454. (Illus.). 310p. (Span.). 1975. write for info. (ISBN 8-471-53199-2). Biblo Sp.
Diccionario Internacional Abreviado de Siglas, Contracciones & Abreviaturas. Millan Contreras. (Span.). 1974. 350.00 ptas (ISBN 8-42830-539-0). Paraninfo.
Diccionario Internacional Abreviado De Siglas Contracciones y Abreviaturas. Donato Millan Contreras. 224p. (Span.). 1974. pap. 9.95 (ISBN 0-686-57355-2, S-50239). French & Eur.
Diccionario internacional de electronica. (Span.). write for info. Cultura Popular.
Diccionario Internacional de Radio & Television. Mariano Cebrian Herreros. 304p. (Span.). 1981. 500.00 ptas (ISBN 84-500-4295-X). Organ Ofic Adm.
Diccionario Internacional de Siglas. J. Martinez de Sousa. 472p. (Span.). write for info. (ISBN 8-43680-083-4, 270009). Piramide.
Diccionario Internacional de Siglas. Jose Martinez De Sousa. 472p. (Span.). 1978. leatherette 28.50 (ISBN 84-368-0083-4, S-50372). French & Eur.
Diccionario Internacional de Siglas, Contracciones & Abreviaturas. Donato Millan Contreras. 240p. (Span.). 1974. 200.00 ptas (ISBN 84-283-0539-0). Paraninfo.
Diccionario internacional Simon & Schuster: Ingles-espanol y espanol-ingles. 1632p. (Eng. & Span.). 12.95; pap. 10.95. S & S.
Diccionario Italiano-Espanol, Espanol-Italiano. E. M. Martinez Amador. 1440p. (Span. & Ital.). 50.95 (ISBN 84-303-0133-X, S-12383). French & Eur.
Diccionario Italiano-Espanol Espanol-Italiano Vox. 848p. (Ital. & Span.). 1982. write for info. (ISBN 84-7153-390-1). Biblo SP.
Diccionario Iter Aleman-Espanol, Espanol-Aleman. 512p. (Ger. & Span.). 1977. leatherette 6.75 (ISBN 84-303-0127-5, S-50377); pap. 5.95 (ISBN 84-303-0126-7, S-50376). French & Eur.
Diccionario Iter Espanol-Ingles. 700p. (Span. & Eng.). (gr. 7-12). 3.75 ptas (DI52). Cruzada.
Diccionario Iter Italiano-Espanol, Espanol-Italiano. 712p. (Ital. & Span.). leatherette 6.95 (ISBN 84-303-0139-9, S-50434); pap. 5.95 (ISBN 84-303-0138-0, S-50435). French & Eur.
Diccionario Iter Ortografico. Sopena. (Span.). pap. 3.95. Lectorum Pubns.
Diccionario ixcateco. Maria T. Fernandez de Miranda. (Span.). 1961. Mex.$60.00. INAH.
Diccionario Jalisco ilustrado. 320p. (Span.). write for info. (734). Fernandez.
Diccionario juridico. 6th ed. J. D. Ramirez Gronda. 328p. (Span.). Arg.$12.00. Claridad.
Diccionario juridico aleman-espanol de derecho comparado: Con vocabulario juridico espanol-aleman. Quintano Heilpern. (Ger. & Span.). 525.00 ptas. Rev Derecho Pri.
Diccionario juridico peruano. Arelio Perez Caballero. 190p. (Span.). 1972. S/2.40. Mejia.
Diccionario Kapeluse de la Langua Espanola. 1552p. (Span.). 1979. 46.95 (ISBN 0-686-56682-3, S-33044). French & Eur.
Diccionario Kapelusz de la Lengua Espanola. (Span.). 1981. Arg.$55000.00. Kapelusz.
Diccionario Karten Ilustrado. 1680p. (Span.). 1977. 95.00 (ISBN 0-686-56679-3, S-33047). French & Eur.
Diccionario kechua-castellano, castellano-kechua. 4th ed. Cesar Guardia Mayorga. 217p. (Span.). 1.25. Peisa.
Diccionario Kechwa-Castellano. Cesar Guardia Mayarga. 219p. (Kechwa & Castellan.). 1980. S/2.00. Studium.
Diccionario Kollasuyo, Espanol-Quechua. Miguel Angel Quiroga Flores. 150p. (Span. & Quechua.). 1979. write for info. Cochabamba.
Diccionario Laboral. Ramon Bayod Serrat. 546p. (Span.). 1969. pap. 6.95 (ISBN 84-290-0937-X, S-50139). French & Eur.
Diccionario Larousse De la Lengua Espanola-Nuevo Larousse Basico. (Span.). 1980. pap. 7.50 (ISBN 0-686-59502-5). Larousse.
Diccionario Larousse Del Espanol Moderno. Ramon Garcia-Pelayo. (Span.). 1983. pap. 4.95 (ISBN 0-451-12352-2, Sig). NAL.
Diccionario Larousse moderno espanol-ingles. (Illus., Span. & Eng.). 29.95. Iaconi.
Diccionario Larousse Moderno Espanol-Ingles, English-Spanish. (Span. & Eng.). 29.95 (ISBN 2-03-020605-9, 21914). Larousse.
Diccionario Larousse usual. (Illus.). 848p. (Span.). 1974. pap. 11.95 (ISBN 2-03-020543-5, 22800). Larousse.
Diccionario Larousse usual. (Span.). pap. 11.95. Iaconi.
Diccionario latino. L. Macchi. (Lat.). Arg.$40.00. Don Bosco Ed.
Diccionario latino-espanol. 2nd ed. J. Llauro Padrosa. (Lat. & Span.). 150.00 ptas. SAETA.
Diccionario Latino-Espanol, Espanol-Latino, 3 vols. Blanquez. 2703p. (Lat. & Span.). Set. leatherette 75.00 (ISBN 84-303-0151-8, S-50419). French & Eur.
Diccionario latino-espanol, espanol-latino: Serie Bachillerato Koel. (No. 44). (Lat. & Span.). 75.00 ptas. Tesoro.
Diccionario latino-espanol y espanol-latino. Vicente Blanco Garcia. (Span.). 175.00 ptas. Aguilar SP.
Diccionario legislativo de cinematografia y teatro. Jose M. Salazar Lopez. (Span.). 300.00 ptas. Nacional Editora.
Diccionario lengua espanola. (Span.). 50.00 ptas. pap. 35.00 ptas. Mayfe.
Diccionario Lengua Espanola Forja. 24th ed. Jose Garcia Mercadal. 488p. (Span.). 1977. 4.50 (ISBN 84-7105-026-9, S-50034). French & Eur.
Diccionario lexico basico espanol. (Span.). write for info. Cultura Popular.
Diccionario Lexicon, Aleman-Espanol, Espanol-Aleman. 400p. (Ale. -Espn.). 5.75 (ISBN 0-686-57343-9, S-31392). French & Eur.
Diccionario Lexicon Aleman-Espanol, Espanol-Aleman. Hans Muller. 384p. (Ger. & Span.). 1977. pap. 4.50 (ISBN 84-303-0124-0, S-31392). French & Eur.
Diccionario Lexicon Espanol-Danes & Espanol-Danes. 384p. (Span. & Danish.). 1974. leatherette 4.95 (ISBN 84-303-0160-7, S-50407); pap. 4.50 (ISBN 84-303-0159-3, S-50406). French & Eur.
Diccionario Lexicon Esperanto-Espanol, Espanol-Esperanto. 400p. (Esperanto & Span.). leatherette 4.95 (ISBN 84-303-0148-8, S-50403); pap. 4.50 (ISBN 84-303-0147-X, S-50402). French & Eur.
Diccionario Lexicon Finlandes-Espanol, Espanol-Finlandes. 400p. (Finnish & Span.). leatherette 4.95 (ISBN 84-303-0150-X, S-50405); pap. 4.50 (ISBN 84-303-0149-6, S-50404). French & Eur.
Diccionario Lexicon Frances-Espanol, Espanol-Frances. E. Gimeno. 384p. (Fr. & Span.). 1975. leatherette 3.75 (ISBN 84-303-0099-6, S-31393). French & Eur.
Diccionario Lexicon Holandes-Espanol y Espanol-Holandes. 384p. (Dutch & Span.). 1974. pap. 4.50 (ISBN 84-303-0161-5, S-50408); pap. 4.95 leatherette (ISBN 84-303-0162-3, S-50409). French & Eur.
Diccionario Lexicon Ingles-Espanol, Espanol-Ingles. D. Macarulla. 384p. (Eng. & Span.). 1974. pap. 3.25 (ISBN 84-303-0110-0, S-31391). French & Eur.
Diccionario Lexicon Italiano-Espanol, Espanol-Italiano. 400p. (Span. & Ital.). pap. 3.50 (ISBN 84-303-0136-4, S-31394). French & Eur.
Diccionario Lexicon Noruego-Espanol, Espanol-Noruego. 400p. (Norwegian & Span.). leatherette 4.95 (ISBN 84-303-0165-8, S-50418); pap. 4.50 (ISBN 84-303-0164-X, S-50417). French & Eur.
Diccionario Lexicon Portugues-Espanol, Espanol-Portugues. 400p. (Port. & Span.). leatherette 3.95 (ISBN 84-303-0144-5, S-50429); pap. 3.50 (ISBN 84-303-0143-7, S-50430). French & Eur.
Diccionario Lexicon Sueco-Espanol, Espanol-Sueco. 400p. (Sueco & Span.). leatherette 4.95 (ISBN 84-303-0146-1, S-50416); pap. 4.50 (ISBN 84-303-0145-3, S-50415). French & Eur.
Diccionario Lexikon. 368p. (Span.). 1974. Mex.$17.50. Fernandez.
Diccionario Literario Universal. Jose A. Perez-Rioja. LC 77-466197. 989p. (Span.). 1977. write for info. (ISBN 8-4309-0690-8). Tecnos SA.
Diccionario Lunfardo & de Otros Terminos Antiguos & Modernos Usuales. Jose Gobello. LC 76-460668. 234p. (Span.). 1975. write for info. Pena Lillo.
Diccionario Lunfardo Ilustrado. Jose Gobello. (Span.). 55.00 (ISBN 0-686-56669-6, S-33076). French & Eur.
Diccionario Magico Infantil. 7th ed. Eulalia Goma. 50p. (Span.). 1978. 10.75 (ISBN 84-324-0190-0, S-26065). French & Eur.
Diccionario Magico Infantil. 10th ed. Eulalia Goma. 50p. (Span.). 1982. 500.00 ptas (ISBN 84-324-0190-0). Vilamala.
Diccionario Magico Infantil. 9th ed. Eulalia Goma. 50p. (Span.). 1981. 430.00 ptas (ISBN 84-324-0190-0). Vilamala.

Diccionario Magico Infantil En Seis Lenguas. 2nd ed. Eulalia Goma. 96p. (Span., Catalan, Vasco, Gallic, Fr. & Eng.). 1978. 20.25 (ISBN 84-324-0249-4, S-50028). French & Eur.

Diccionario Major Frances-Espanol, Espanol-Frances. Roberto Larrieu & Manuel Garcia Morente. 1392p. (Fr. & Span.). 1981. pap. 1800.00 ptas (ISBN 84-85205-91-X). Diafora.

Diccionario Major Ingles-Espanol, Espanol-Ingles. Anthony Gooch & Angel Garcia de Paredes. 1132p. (Eng. & Span.). 1981. pap. 2000.00 ptas (ISBN 84-85205-92-8). Diafora.

Diccionario Malcriado-Naughtical Dictionary. 1980. pap. 6.00 (ISBN 0-915808-38-2). Editorial Justa.

Diccionario Manual Aleman-Espanol, Espanol-Aleman. Felix Diez Mateo. 952p. (Ger. & Span.). 1978. pap. 12.95 (ISBN 84-239-4766-1, S-50383). French & Eur.

Diccionario Manual Aleman-Espanol, Espanol-Aleman. Ed. by Felix D. Mateo & Frida Hochleitner. 952p. (Ger. & Span.). 1978. write for info. Espasa Calpe.

Diccionario Manual Aleman-Espanol, Spanisch-Deutsch. 17th ed. E. M. Martinez Amador. 936p. (Ger. & Span.). 1977. 5.95 (ISBN 84-7183-002-7, S-50382). French & Eur.

Diccionario Manual Amador Aleman-Espanol, Espanol-Aleman. E. M. Martinez Amador. 1400p. (Ger. & Span.). 17.95 (ISBN 84-303-0118-6, S-50385). French & Eur.

Diccionario Manual Amador Frances-Espanol y Espanol-Frances. E. M. Martinez Amador. 944p. (Span. & Fr.). 1975. 17.95 (ISBN 84-303-0100-3, S-50401). French & Eur.

Diccionario Manual Amador Ingles-Espanol, Espanol-Ingles. 944p. (Span. & Eng.). 17.95 (ISBN 84-303-0116-X, S-50395). French & Eur.

Diccionario Manual Auxiliar Basico. 2nd ed. 524p. (Span.). 1976. 6.95 (ISBN 84-01-60144-4, S-50045). French & Eur.

Diccionario Manual de Bellas Artes. 320p. (Span.). 1979. write for info. Biblograf.

Diccionario Manual De la Lengua Espanol a-Z. 3rd ed. Francisco Gordo-Guarinos. 688p. (Span.). 1979. pap. 5.25 (ISBN 84-346-0083-8, S-27485). French & Eur.

Diccionario Manual De la Lengua Espanol A-Z. 3rd ed. Francisco Gordo-Guarinos. 688p. (Span.). 1979. 6.95 (ISBN 84-346-0084-6, S-27486). French & Eur.

Diccionario Manual de la Lengua Espanol: Real Academia Espanola. 1572p. (Span.). write for info. (ESP). Lectorum Pubns.

Diccionario manual de la lengua espanola: Real Academia Espanol. 1572p. (Span.). 39.95 (ESP). Lectorum Pub.

Diccionario Manual de Medicina & Salud. 288p. (Span.). 1979. 595.00 ptas. Biblograf.

Diccionario Manual de Sinonimos, Antonimos e Ideas Afines. 512p. (Span.). pap. 5.25 (ISBN 84-303-0066-X, S-12277). French & Eur.

Diccionario manual de sinonimos y antonimos. 4th ed. 369p. (Span.). 1982. write for info. (ISBN 84-7153-389-8). Biblograf.

Diccionario manual e ilustrado de la lengua espanola. 2nd ed. (Illus.). 1572p. (Span.). 1958. 250.00 ptas. (Real Academia) Espasa.

Diccionario Manual e Ilustrado de la Lengua Espanol. 2nd ed. Real Academie de la Lengua Espanol. 1584p. (Span.). 1979. 35.95 (ISBN 84-239-4724-6). French & Eur.

Diccionario Manual Espanol-Portugues, Portugues-Espanol. 3rd ed. Julio Da Conceicao Fernandes. 1974p. (Span. & Port.). 1978. 12.25 (ISBN 84-7183-001-9, S-50428). French & Eur.

Diccionario manual espanol-ruso. Gisbert. (Span. & Rus.). 0.80. Pueblos Unidos.

Diccionario Manual Frances-Espanol. Frida Hochleitner & Felix D. Mateo. 100p. (Fr. & Span.). write for info. Espasa Calpe.

Diccionario Manual Frances-Espanol, Espagnol-Francais. 36th ed. Arturo Cuyas Armengol. 830p. (Span. & Fr.). 1977. 5.95 (ISBN 84-7183-047-7, S-50390). French & Eur.

Diccionario manual frances-espanol, espanol-frances. Felix Diaz Mateo & Frida Hochleitner. 1000p. (Fr. & Span.). 150.00 ptas. Espasa Calpe.

Diccionario Manual Frances-Espanol Espanol-Frances. 922p. (Fr. & Span.). write for info. Bibliograf SP.

Diccionario Manual Frances-Espanol, Espanol-Frances. Felix Diez Mateo & Frida Hochleitner. 992p. (Span. & Fr.). 1971. 9.95 (ISBN 84-239-4721-1, S-50389). French & Eur.

Diccionario Manual Frances-Espanol Espanol-Frances Vox. 10th ed. 922p. (Fr. & Span.). 1982. 725.00 ptas (ISBN 84-7153-186-0). Biblo SP.

Diccionario Manual Griego-Espanol. Jose M. Pabon & M. Fernandez Galiano. 724p. (Gr. & Span.). 925.00 ptas (ISBN 84-7153-192-5). Biblograf SP.

Diccionario Manual Griego-Espanol Vox. 16th ed. 724p. (Gr. & Span.). 1982. 795.00 ptas (ISBN 84-7153-192-5). Biblo SP.

Diccionario Manual Herder Frances-Espanol, Espanol-Frances. Gunther Haensch. 644p. (Span. & Fr.). 1976. 16.75 (ISBN 84-254-1049-5, S-50392). French & Eur.

Diccionario Manual Ilustrado de la Lengua Espanola. (Illus.). 1170p. (Span.). 850.00 ptas (ISBN 84-7153-166-6). Biblograf SP.

Diccionario Manual Ilustrado de la Lengua Espanola. Vox. (Illus.). 1173p. (Span.). 1982. DM.30.00. Brandstetter.

Diccionario Manual Ilustrado de la Lengua Espanola Vox. 7th ed. (Illus.). 1174p. (Span.). 1982. 775.00 ptas (ISBN 84-7153-166-6). Biblo SP.

Diccionario manual ilustrado espanol A-Z. (Illus.). 720p. (Span.). 2.50. Universal Medinacelli.

Diccionario Manual Ingles-Espanol Espanol-Ingles Vox. 11th ed. 1008p. (Eng. & Span.). 1982. 725.00 ptas (ISBN 84-7153-184-4). Biblo SP.

Diccionario Manual Ingles-Espanol Espanol-Ingles. 1008p. (Eng. & Span.). 750.00 ptas (ISBN 84-7153-184-4). Biblograf SP.

Diccionario Manual Ingles-Espanol, Espanol-Ingles. Felix Diez Mateo & Frida Hochleitner. 1008p. (Eng. & Span.). 1971. 9.95 (ISBN 84-239-4720-3, S-50351). French & Eur.

Diccionario manual ingles-espanol, espanol-ingles. Felix Diez Mateo & Frida Hochleitner. 1000p. (Eng. & Span.). 150.00 ptas. Espasa Calpe.

Diccionario Manual Ingles-Espanol, Spanish-English. 2nd ed. Arturo Cuyas Armengol. 768p. (Eng. & Span.). 1975. 5.95 (ISBN 84-7183-044-2, S-12389). French & Eur.

Diccionario Manual Ingles-Espanol, Spanish-English. 35th ed. Arturo Cuyas Armengol. 768p. (Eng. & Span.). 1978. pap. 4.50 (ISBN 84-7183-005-1, S-12389). French & Eur.

Diccionario manual italiano-espanol. Francisco de B. Moll. (Ital. & Span.). 20.00 ptas. Moll Edit.

Diccionario Manual Italiano-Espanol, Spagnuolo-Italiano. 16th ed. Jose Ortiz De Burgos. 960p. (Span. & Ital.). 1977. 5.95 (ISBN 84-7183-045-0, S-50432). French & Eur.

Diccionario manual latino-castellano y castellano-latino. De Andrea. (Lat. & Span.). Arg.$21.60. Sopena.

Diccionario manual latino-espanol y espanol-latino. Agustin Blanquez Fraile. 672p. (Lat. & Span.). 150.00 ptas. Sopena.

Diccionario manual latino-espanol y espanol-latino. 7th ed. Mugica. 640p. (Lat. & Span.). 230.00 ptas. Razon y Fe.

Diccionario Manual y Illustrado De La Lengua Espanola. Real Academia Espanola. (Span.). 35.00x (ISBN 0-686-00855-3). Colton Bk.

Diccionario Marin de la Lengua Espanola: Obra Completa, 2 vols. 1736p. (Span.). 1982. 4500.00 set ptas (ISBN 8-47102-700-3); 2225.00 ea. Marin.

Diccionario Marin de la Lengua Espanola, 2 vols. 1728p. (Span.). 1982. 5600.00 ptas (ISBN 84-7102-700-3). Marin.

Diccionario maritimo. 2nd ed. Julian Amich. 427p. (Span.). 1971. 380.00 ptas. Juventud.

Diccionario maritimo. J. L. Pando. 245p. (Span.). write for info. Dossat.

Diccionario Maritimo Ilustrado Vasco-Castellano, Castellano-Vasco. Ignacio de Garmendia y Berasategui. (Vasco & Span.). 49.50 (ISBN 84-248-0047-8, S-50054). French & Eur.

Diccionario maritimo ingles-espanol y espanol-ingles. Jose Garcia de Paredes y Castro & Enrique Barbudo Duarte. 256p. (Eng. & Span.). 1965. 340.00 ptas. Fragata.

Diccionario Maritimo y De Construccion Naval. Juan Alfaro Perez. 478p. (Span. & Eng.). 1976. leather 53.95 (ISBN 84-7079-081-1, S-50094). French & Eur.

Diccionario Maya Cordemex Maya-Espanol. 69th ed. Alfredo Barrera Vasquez. 360p. (Maya & Span.). 1980. Mex.$pap. 3000.00. Porrua.

Diccionario medico. 3rd ed. Andrea Bissanti et al. Tr. by Catala J. Blanco. 364p. (Span.). 1981. pap. 3195.00 ptas (ISBN 84-85146-93-X). Mas Ivars.

Diccionario Medico. 638p. (Span.). 1974. 375.00 ptas. Salvat Editores.

Diccionario Medico. 2nd ed. 640p. (Span.). 1974. write for info. Salvat Editores.

Diccionario Medico. F. Beer Poitevin. 352p. (Span.). 1979. 51.95 (ISBN 0-686-92232-8). French & Eur.

Diccionario Medico. 5th ed. Luigi Segatore & Gianangelo Poli. 1282p. (Span.). 1975. 44.95 (ISBN 84-307-8013-0, S-12357). French & Eur.

Diccionario Medico. Luigi Segatore & Gianangelo Poli. 1288p. (Span.). 1974. 750.00 ptas. Teide.

Diccionario Medico & su Suplemento Espanol. Veillon-Nobel. 1341p. (Span.). 1974. write for info. Cientifico Med.

Diccionario medico de bolsillo. 2nd ed. 1400p. (Span.). 1981. pap. 875.00 ptas (ISBN 84-345-1017-0). Salvat Editores.

Diccionario Medico: De Bosillo. 2nd ed. 632p. (Span.). 1974. leatherette 18.50 (ISBN 84-345-1017-0, S-13673). French & Eur.

Diccionario Medico Familiar. Seleccione Reader's Digest. 756p. (Span.). Date not set. price not set (S-34982). French & Eur.

Diccionario Medico Familiar II. 2nd ed. 800p. (Span.). 1981. 2975.00 ptas (ISBN 84-7142-239-5). Sel Rdrs Digest.

Diccionario medico Labor, 3 vols. Francisco J. Cortada. 2608p. (Span.). 1970. Arg.$500.00. Labor SA.

Diccionario Medico Labor Para la Familia. Mommsen. (Span.). 1979. write for info. (ISBN 84-335-6007-7, S-50063). French & Eur.

Diccionario medico Labor para la familia. Mommsen. (Span.). 990.00 ptas. Labor SA.

Diccionario Medico Labor para la Familia. 5th ed. H. Mommsen. 816p. (Span.). 1976. 45.00 (ISBN 84-335-6000-X, S-12337). French & Eur.

Diccionario Medico Labor para la Familia. 6th ed. H. Mommsen et al. Tr. by Juan Massor Gimeno & J. Vilahur Pedrals. 880p. (Span.). 1982. pap. 3580.00 ptas (ISBN 84-335-6007-7). Labor SA.

Diccionario medico para la familia moderna, 4 vols. 1500p. (Span.). write for info. Gaisa.

Diccionario mi amigo: Diccionario escolar de bosillo, 4 bks. (Illus., Span.). (gr. 3-6). write for info. (713/716). Fernandez.

Diccionario militar bilingue. Aguirre de Carcer. (Span.). write for info. Dossat.

Diccionario militar espanol-ruso. Bulgakov. (Span. & Rus.). 1.20. Pueblos Unidos.

Diccionario Militar Espanol-Ruso, Ruso-Espanol. 632p. (Eng. , Rus. & Span.). 1965. Leatherette 10.95 (ISBN 0-686-92245-X, S-31871). French & Eur.

Diccionario militar estrategico y politico. Fernando De Bordeje Morencos. 288p. (Span.). 1981. pap. 500.00 ptas (ISBN 84-7140-202-5). San Martin.

Diccionario mimico espanol. Felix-Jesus Pinedo Peydro. 576p. (Span.). 1981. pap. 1200.00 ptas (ISBN 84-500-5005-7). Organ Ofic Adm.

Diccionario Mini Sopena Ingles-Espanol. 320p. (Eng. & Span.). 1975. pap. 1.75 (ISBN 84-303-0115-1, S-50398). French & Eur.

Diccionario Mininorma. Jorge Cardenas Nannetti. 224p. (Span.). 1981. 2.00 (ISBN 84-8276-251-6). Norma Edit.

Diccionario Mitologico. C. Gaytan. (Span.). 3.75 (ISBN 0-686-56651-3, S-25775). French & Eur.

Diccionario Mixteco del Este De Jamiltepec. Brenda Pensinger. (Vocabularios Indigenas Ser.: No. 18). 156p. (Span.). 1974. 7.00 (ISBN 0-88312-751-2); microfiche 2.25x (ISBN 0-88312-586-2). Summer Inst Ling.

Diccionario Moderno. Ed. by Eduardo Cardenas. LC 76-465983. (Illus.). iv, 606p. (Span.). 1975. write for info. Edit Norma.

Diccionario moderno: Aleman-espanol, espanol-aleman. Langenscheidt. 1092p. (Span. & Ger.). 4.33; 280.00 ptas. Herder SA.

Diccionario Moderno del Espanol Usual. Alfonso Zamora Vicente. LC 75-511707. viii, 1063p. (Span.). 1975. write for info. (ISBN 8-485-09309-7). Sader SA.

Diccionario Moderno Espanol-Ingles, English-Spanish. Ramon Garcia-Pelayo. 1992p. (Span. & Eng.). 1976. 25.00 (ISBN 0-686-57189-4, M-6261). French & Eur.

Diccionario moderno espanol-ingles, ingles-espanol. Margaret H. Reventos. 1236p. (Eng. & Span.). 2.20. CECSA.

Diccionario moderno: Frances-espanol, espanol-frances. 1024p. (Fr. & Span.). 3.86; 250.00 ptas. Herder SA.

Diccionario moderno frances-espanol y espanol-frances. P. Fabrega. (Span. & Fr.). 1970. 100.00 ptas. Bosch Casa.

Diccionario Moderno Herder Aleman-Espanol, Espanol-Aleman. Gunther Haensch. 684p. (Ger. & Span.). 1977. 16.75 (ISBN 84-254-0652-8, S-50379). French & Eur.

Diccionario moderno Herder Aleman-Espanol. 2nd ed. Gunther Haensch. 684p. (Ger. & Span.). 1982. 650.00 ptas (ISBN 84-254-0652-8). Herder SA.

Diccionario moderno: Ingles-espanol, espanol-ingles. 2nd ed. Langenssheidt. 1072p. (Eng. & Span.). 3.86 ptas. 250.00 ptas. Herder SA.

Diccionario moderno Larousse. (Eng. & Span.). write for info. (608-63). Pan Am Bk co.

Diccionario Modernos Herder Aleman-Espanol. 684p. (Ger. & Span.). 1981. 560.00 ptas (ISBN 84-254-0652-8). Herder SA.

Diccionario Modernos Herder Frances-Espanol. 644p. (Fr. & Span.). 1981. write for info. (ISBN 84-254-1049-5). Herder SA.

Diccionario Monografico de Bellas Artes. 288p. (Span.). 750.00 ptas (ISBN 84-7153-381-2). Biblograf SP.

Diccionario Monografico de Bellas Artes. Vox. (Span.). 1979. leatherette 17.50 (ISBN 84-7153-381-2, S-36147). French & Eur.

Diccionario Monografico de Matematicas. 288p. (Span.). 750.00 ptas (ISBN 84-7153-388-X). Biblograf SP.
Diccionario Monografico de Matematicas. 288p. (Span.). 1981. pap. write for info. ptas (ISBN 84-7153-388-X). Biblo SP.
Diccionario Monografico de Matematicas. Ed. by Vox. 287p. (Span.). 1981. 20.25 (ISBN 84-7153-388-X). French & Eur.
Diccionario Monografico de Medicina & Salud. 380p. (Span.). 750.00 ptas (ISBN 84-7153-380-4). Biblograf SP.
Diccionario Monografico de Medicina y Salud. Ed. by Vox. (Span.). 1979. leatherette 17.50 (ISBN 84-7153-380-4, S-36145). French & Eur.
Diccionario Monografico de Reino Mineral 'Vox' 288p. (Span.). 1981. write for info. (ISBN 84-7153-387-1). Biblo SP.
Diccionario Monografico de Technologia. Ed. by Vox. (Span.). 1979. leatherette 17.50 (ISBN 84-7153-383-9, S-36146). French & Eur.
Diccionario Monografico de Tecnologia. 320p. (Span.). 750.00 ptas (ISBN 84-7153-383-9). Biblograf SP.
Diccionario Monografico de Tecnologia. 328p. (Span.). 1980. write for info. Biblograf.
Diccionario Monografico del Reino Animal. 286p. (Span.). 1980. 19.95 (ISBN 84-7153-385-5, S-32725). French & Eur.
Diccionario Monografico del Reino Animal. 288p. (Span.). 750.00 ptas (ISBN 84-7153-385-5). Biblograf SP.
Diccionario Monografico del Reino Mineral. 288p. (Span.). 750.00 ptas (ISBN 84-7153-386-3). Biblograf SP.
Diccionario Monografico del Reino Mineral. (Span.). 750.00 ptas (ISBN 84-7153-387-1). Biblograf.
Diccionario Monografico del Reino Vegetal. 288p. (Span.). 750.00 ptas (ISBN 84-7153-387-1). Biblograf SP.
Diccionario Monografico del Reino Vegetal. (Span.). 750.00 ptas (ISBN 84-7153-386-3). Biblograf.
Diccionario Monografico del Reino Vegetal 'Vox' 288p. (Span.). 1980. write for info. (ISBN 84-7153-386-3). Biblo SP.
Diccionario Morfologico del Nuevo Testamento. Manuel Guerra y Gomez. LC 79-108693. 443p. (Span.). 1978. 1500.00 ptas (ISBN 8-470-09048-8). Aldecoa.
Diccionario multilingue. Edwin B. Williams & Alfred Senn. 304p. (Span.). 1.50. Edit Pr Serv.
Diccionario Multiple. J. A. Onieva. 502p. (Span.). 1976. pap. write for info. (ISBN 84-283-0400-9). Paraninfo.
Diccionario Multiple: Nueve Diccionarios en un Solo Volumen. 3rd ed. Onieva. (Span.). 1981. 425.00 ptas (ISBN 8-42830-400-9). Paraninfo.
Diccionario multiple: Nueve diccionarios en un volumen. Antonio J. Onieva. 504p. (Span.). 1971. 190.00 ptas. Paraninfo.
Diccionario Mundo hispano. 426p. (Span.). Mex.$6.00. Fernandez.
Diccionario Nautico. Jose M. Martinez Hidalgo Teran. 540p. (Span., Eng. & Fr.). 1977. leather 56.00 (ISBN 84-7079-058-7, S-50095). French & Eur.
Diccionario Naval. Leal. (Span.). 700.00 ptas (ISBN 8-42831-089-0). Paraninfo.
Diccionario Naval Ingles-Espanol. 3rd ed. Luis Leal. 232p. (Span.). 1980. 650.00 ptas (ISBN 84-283-1089-0). Paraninfo.
Diccionario naval ingles-espanol espanol-ingles. 3rd ed. Luis Leal y Leal. 232p. (Span. & Eng.). 1980. 650.00 ptas (ISBN 84-283-1089-0). Paraninfo.
Diccionario naval: Ingles-espanol y espanol-ingles. L. Leal. (Eng. & Span.). 1972. 70.00 ptas. Paraninfo.
Diccionario Norma: El Lexico de Nuestro Tiempo. Jorge Cardenas Nannetti. 643p. (Span.). 1981. Col.$180.00. Norma.
Diccionario nuevo Larousse manual ilustrado. (Span.). (gr. 9). 1977. Repr. 19.95 (ISBN 2-03-020546-X, 21121). Larousse.
Diccionario Oceano de la Lengua Espanola. 778p. (Span.). 1981. pap. 1600.00 ptas (ISBN 84-7505-162-6). Oceano.
Diccionario Oceano Espanol-Ingles. 1008p. (Span. & Eng.). 1981. pap. 1600.00 ptas (ISBN 84-7505-232-0). Oceano.
Diccionario odontologico. Ciro Durante Avellanal. (Span.). 23.00; Arg.$120.00. Mundi.
Diccionario onomastico y heraldico vasco: Tomo 7. Domingo Lizaso. 592p. (Span.). 1982. pap. 2390.00 ptas (ISBN 84-248-0741-3). Encicl Vasca.
Diccionario Onomastico y Heraldico Vasco, 6 vols. Jaime Querexeta Gallostequi. (Span.). 1974. Set. leather 205.00 (ISBN 84-248-0011-7, S-50375). French & Eur.
Diccionario "Oriente", 4 vols. (Span.). 195.00 set (ISBN 0-686-56661-0, S-33078). French & Eur.
Diccionario: Oriente, 2 vols. (Eng. & Span.). 75.00 (ISBN 0-686-56684-X, S-33042). French & Eur.
Diccionario ortografico. J. De La Canal. (Span.). Mex.$9.00. EDIMEX.
Diccionario Ortografico. Julio De La Canal. (Span.). pap. 2.50. MEX.
Diccionario Ortografico. 51st ed. 640p. (Span.). 1982. 150.00 ptas (ISBN 8-47105-091-9). Mayfe.
Diccionario ortografico. (Span.). 25.00 ptas. Mayfe.
Diccionario ortografico. 51st ed. Fructuoso Plans Sanz de Bremond. 640p. (Span.). 1982. pap. 150.00 ptas (ISBN 84-7105-091-9). Mayfe.
Diccionario Ortografico del Idioma Espanol Moderno. (Span.). 3.95. AGL.
Diccionario ortografico del idioma espanol. Martin Alonso. (Span.). 100.00 ptas. Aguilar SP.
Diccionario ortografico hispanoamericano. Flores de Vega. 288p. (Span.). 1.25. Peisa.
Diccionario Ortografico Iter. 640p. (Span.). 1978. leatherette 6.75 (ISBN 84-303-0752-4, S-50143); pap. 5.95 (ISBN 84-303-0751-6, S-50142). French & Eur.
Diccionario ortografico: Libro del maestro. 2nd ed. S. Ledesma. 454p. (Span.). 1906. Urg.$285.00. Barreiro Ramos.
Diccionario Ortografico Mikron. 51st ed. Plans y De Gabriel Sanz De Bremond, Fructuoso. 640p. (Span.). 1978. leatherette 2.75 (ISBN 84-7105-091-9, S-50033). French & Eur.
Diccionario Oxford de la musica. 2nd ed. P. A. Scholes. (Span.). write for info. Sudamer.
Diccionario para especialistas. (Span.). 6.95. Minerva.
Diccionario para especialistas de seguros. Sell. (Span.). write for info. Rev. Mex. de Seguros.
Diccionario para Ingenieros Espanol-Ingles, Ingles-Espanol. Louis A. Robb. 664p. (Span. & Eng.). 1977. 42.75 (ISBN 84-7051-048-7, S-31339). French & Eur.
Diccionario para ingenieros: Ingles-espanol, espanol-ingles. Louis A. Robb. 664p. (Eng. & Span.). 10.15. CECSA.
Diccionario Para Obras Publica, Edificacion y Maquinaria En Obra. Bucksch. 1116p. (Ger. & Span.). 1976. 60.00 (ISBN 84-254-0105-4, S-50187). French & Eur.
Diccionario para Obras Publicas, Edificacion & Maquinaria en Obra. 1114p. (Ger. & Span.). 1962. DM.108.00 (ISBN 3-7625-1160-8). Bauverlag.
Diccionario para obras publicas, edificacion y maquinaria en obra: Aleman-espanol, espanol-aleman. Bucksch. 1116p. (Ger. & Span.). 20.46; 1320.00 ptas. Herder SA.
Diccionario Para Obras Publicas, Edificacion y Maquinaria en Obra. (Ger. & Span.). 1962. 86.00 (ISBN 3-7625-1160-8, M-7132). French & Eur.
Diccionario Para Pobres. Francisco Umbral Perez. 240p. (Span.). 1977. 9.95 (ISBN 84-7454-002-X, S-50099). French & Eur.
Diccionario para resolver palabras cruzadas. (Span.). Arg.$3.00. Cosmopolita.
Diccionario para un macuto. 2nd ed. G. Rafael. (Span.). 350.00 ptas. Nacional Editora.
Diccionario Parvus duplex: Frances-castellano y castellano-frances. (Fr. & Span.). Arg.$8.40. Sopena.
Diccionario Parvus duplex: Ingles-castellano y castellano-ingles. (Eng. & Span.). Arg.$8.40. Sopena.
Diccionario Parvus duplex: Italiano-castellano y castellano-ingles. (Ital. & Span.). Arg.$8.40. Sopena.
Diccionario Parvus duplex: Portugues-castellano y castellano-portugues. (Port. & Span.). Arg.$8.40. Sopena.
Diccionario pedagogico, 4 vols. 2nd ed. Rafael. (Span.). Bs.0.90. Min. Educ.
Diccionario Penal: Libro del Opositor C. G. P. Angel Sanchez Ordonez. LC 76-461919. (Illus.). 304p. (Span.). 1975. write for info. (ISBN 8-485-03319-1). Lemos.
Diccionario Pequeno Nebrija de la lengua castellana. 352p. (Span.). 1982. pap. 90.00 ptas (ISBN 84-391-1001-4). Edit Nebrija.
Diccionario periodistico de Futbol. Inocencio F. Arias Llamas et al. 256p. (Span.). 1982. pap. write for info. (ISBN 84-500-7621-8). Organ Ofic Adm.
Diccionario pervus duplex: Aleman-castellano y castellano-aleman. (Ger. & Span.). Arg.$8.40. Sopena.
Diccionario petrografico: Vol 1, Rocas eruptivas. Maximino San Miguel de la Camara. 174p. (Span.). 1944. 60.00 (CSIC). Inst. Jose Acosta y Lucas Mallada.
Diccionario Planeta Abreviado de la Lengua Espanola Usual. (Illus.). 768p. (Span.). 1982. 900.00 ptas (ISBN 8-43206-527-7). Planeta SA.
Diccionario plastico. Tr. by J. A. Wordingham & P. Reboul. 208p. (Span.). 1966. Arg.$1.80. Leru.
Diccionario Plaza y Janes: Obra completa II, 2 vols. 1536p. (Span.). 1981. 802.00 ptas (ISBN 84-01-60175-4). Plaza Janes.
Diccionario Plaza y Janes, S.A. Tomo 2 II. 768p. (Span.). 1981. 401.00 ptas (ISBN 84-01-60177-0). Plaza Janes.
Diccionario Plaza y Janes: Tomo 1 II. 768p. (Span.). 1981. 401.00 ptas (ISBN 84-01-60176-2). Plaza Janes.
Diccionario poliglota de la arquitectura. B. Bassegoda Muste. 366p. (Span., Ger., Fr., Eng. & Ital.). 1976. pap. 35.00. Imported Bks.
Diccionario poliglota de nombres. 7th ed. Teodoro Amerlinck. 111p. (Span.). 1961. Mex.$20.00. UNAM.
Diccionario poliglota de terminos de Arte y Arquitectura. L. Reau. (Span.). write for info. Fondo Cult.
Diccionario Polilectal del Quechua de Ancash. Gary J. Parker. LC 76-469538. (Span. & Quechua.). 1975. write for info. Centro Invest.
Diccionario politecnico de las lenguas espanola e inglesa, 2 vols. 3rd ed. (Span. & Eng.). 3000.00 ptas. Castilla.
Diccionario Politico. 6th ed. Eduardo Haro Tecglen. 288p. (Span.). 1977. pap. 7.50 (ISBN 84-320-0259-3, S-50024). French & Eur.
Diccionario Politico. Eduardo Haro Tecglen. 288p. (Span.). 1974. 160.00 ptas (ISBN 84-320-0259-3). Planeta SA.
Diccionario politico de Chile. Jordi Fuentes & Lia Cortes. 532p. (Span.). write for info. Orbe Edns.
Diccionario Politico: Los Ministros Nacionales. O. J. Sanquiao. (Span., Buenos Aires, Argentina). 1980. Arg.$16000.00. Platero.
Diccionario Politico Para Occidente. Antonio Marquez Bessa. 288p. (Span.). 1978. pap. 9.95 (ISBN 84-7335-024-3, S-50003). French & Eur.
Diccionario popular castellano-catalan. 230p. (Span.). 1967. 75.00 ptas. Milla Lib.
Diccionario popular de las ciencias y de la tecnica. 2nd ed. Brockhaus. (Illus.). 658p. (Span.). write for info. Gill Gustavo.
Diccionario Popular Matematico. Hernany Miranda. LC 79-126000. 313p. (Span.). 1978. write for info. Direc Pubns.
Diccionario por Fechas de Historia Universal. 2nd ed. Christfried Coler. 480p. (Span.). 1977. 50.95 (ISBN 84-261-5799-8, S-50366). French & Eur.
Diccionario Porrua de Historia, Biografia y Geografia de Mexico, 2 vols. (Span.). 150.00 set (ISBN 0-686-56692-0, S-12279). French & Eur.
Diccionario Porrua de la Espanola. 19th ed. Antonio Raluy Poudevida. 850p. (Span.). 1981. Mex.$90.00; 140.00. Porrua.
Diccionario Porrua de la lengua espanola: Contiene las palabras basicas del idioma, con abundantes exicanismos & americanismos, tecnicismos, verbos & notas ortograficas. 9th ed. Antonio Raluy Pondevida. Ed. by Francisco Monterde. 868p. (Eng. & Span.). 1981. Mex.$pap. 90.00. Porrua.
Diccionario Porrua de la lengua espanola. (Span.). (gr. 7-9). pap. 6.00. Iaconi.
Diccionario Porrua de la lengua espanola. Antonio Raluy Poudevida. (Span.). Mex.$pap. 15.00. Porrua.
Diccionario Porrua de la lengua espanola. 19th, rev. ed. Antonio Raluy Poudevida. Rev. by Francisco Monterde. 850p. (Span.). 1981. Mex.$140.00; Mex.$pap. 90.00. Porrua.
Diccionario Porrua de la Lengua Espanola Para Escuelas Primarias. Antonio Raluy Poudevila. Ed. by Francisco Monterde. 461p. (Span.). pap. 4.95 (ISBN 0-686-56695-5, S-12282). French & Eur.
Diccionario Porrua Ingles-Espanol. Alejandro Gomez de Parada. 400p. (Eng. & Span.). 1974. M.11.00. Porrua.
Diccionario Porrua Ingles-Espanol. 6th ed. Alejandro Gomez de Parada. 397p. (Eng. & Span.). 1980. Mex.$45.00. Porrua.
Diccionario Porrua ingles-espanol, espanol-ingles. 6th ed. Alejandro Gomez de Parada. 397p. (Eng. & Span.). 1980. Mex.$pap. 45.00. Porrua.
Diccionario Portugues-Espanol. 2nd ed. Julio da Conceicao Fernandes. 916p. (Port. & Span.). 1978. 6.95 (ISBN 0-686-57351-X, S-31570). French & Eur.
Diccionario Portugues-Espanol, Espanol-Portugues. David Ortega Cavero. 1856p. (Port. & Span.). 1975. 50.95 (ISBN 84-303-0166-6, S-12405). French & Eur.
Diccionario portugues-espanol, espanol-portugues. David Ortega Cavero & Julio Da Conceica. 1856p. (Port. & Span.). 1977. 31.00 ptas. Sopena.
Diccionario portugues-espanol y espanol-portugues. (Port. & Span.). 60.00 ptas. Mayfe.
Diccionario Practico: Asesor De la Propiedad & Copropiedad Inmobiliaria. Jose M. Plans Sanz De Bremond. 392p. (Span.). 1975. pap. 17.95 (ISBN 84-290-1229-X, S-50138). French & Eur.
Diccionario Practico De Psicopatologia. Yves Poinso. 324p. (Span.). 1976. 23.95 (ISBN 84-254-0618-8, S-50194); pap. 19.95 (ISBN 0-686-77261-X, S-50186). French & Eur.
Diccionario practico de seguros. Garrido y Comas. (Span.). write for info. Rev. Mex. de Seguros.
Diccionario practico de seguros. Juan J. Garrido y Comas. 216p. (Span.). 130.00 ptas. Ariel.

Diccionario Practico Escolar de la Lengua Espanola. Juan Capdevila Font. 500p. (Span.). 1976. pap. 3.25 (ISBN 84-85117-38-7, S-50256). French & Eur.

Diccionario Pratico Russo-Portugues. N. Voinova & S. Starets. 643p. (Rus. & Port.). 1964. leatherette 4.95 (ISBN 0-686-92576-9, M-9098). French & Eur.

Diccionario Punto. (Span.). pap. 2.95 (ISBN 84-241-1211-3). Larousse.

Diccionario Qheshwa-Castellano. 2nd ed. Jesus Lara. 468p. (Span.). 1971. write for info. Amigos del Libro.

Diccionario Quechua. Gary J. Parker. LC 77-464932. 311p. (Quechua & Span.). 1976. write for info. Minist Ed Caracas.

Diccionario Quechua Ayacucho-Chanca. Clodoaldo Soto Ruiz. LC 77-465011. 183p. (Quechua & Span.). 1976. write for info. Minist Ed Caracas.

Diccionario Quechua Cajamarca-Canaris. Felix Quesada Castillo. LC 77-465596. 193p. (Span. & Quechua.). 1976. write for info. Minist Ed Caracas.

Diccionario Quechua Cuzco-Collao. Antonio G. Cusihuaman. LC 77-465799. 303p. (Quechua & Span.). 1976. write for info. Minist Ed Caracas.

Diccionario Quechua Junin-Huanca. Rodolfo Cerron-Palomino. LC 77-465008. 274p. (Span. & Quechua.). 1976. write for info. Minist Ed Caracas.

Diccionario Quechua San Martin. Marinell Park & Nancy Weber. LC 77-465805. 188p. (Span. & Quechua.). 1976. write for info. Ministerio de Educacion.

Diccionario Rances. (Illus.). 784p. (Span.). 90.00 ptas. 55.00 ptas. pap. 50.00 ptas. Sopena.

Diccionario Rapanui-Espanol, Redactado en la Isla de Pascua. Sebastian Englert. LC 75-35191. (Span. & Rapanui.). Repr. of 1938 ed. 15.00 (ISBN 0-404-14219-2). AMS Pr.

Diccionario razonado de matematicas: De las matematicas clasicas a la matematica moderna. Andre Warusfel. 500p. (Span.). 700.00 ptas. Tecnos SA.

Diccionario Razonado de Sinonimos y Contrarios. 2nd ed. Jose M. Zainqui. 1080p. (Span.). 1977. 35.95 (ISBN 84-315-0931-7, S-31379). French & Eur.

Diccionario Real de la Lengua Espanola, 2 vols. 776p. (Span.). 1981. pap. 2100.00 ptas (ISBN 84-7505-178-2). Oceano.

Diccionario Real de la Lengua Espanola. 778p. (Span.). 1981. pap. 1600.00 ptas (ISBN 84-7505-215-0). Oceano.

Diccionario Real de la Lengua Espanola, Vol. 1. 392p. (Span.). 1981. pap. write for info. (ISBN 84-7505-179-0). Oceano.

Diccionario Real de la Lengua Espanola, Vol. 2. 384p. (Span.). 1981. pap. write for info. (ISBN 84-7505-180-4). Oceano.

Diccionario Real Espanol-Ingles. 1008p. (Span. & Eng.). 1981. pap. 1600.00 ptas (ISBN 84-7505-233-9). Oceano.

Diccionario Real Espanol-Ingles, 2 vols. 1012p. (Span. & Eng.). 1981. pap. 2100.00 ptas (ISBN 84-7505-235-5). Oceano.

Diccionario Real Espanol-Ingles, Vol. 1. 528p. (Span. & Eng.). 1981. pap. 1050.00 ptas (ISBN 84-7505-236-3). Oceano.

Diccionario Real Espanol-Ingles, Vol. 2. 484p. (Span. & Eng.). 1981. pap. 1050.00 ptas (ISBN 84-7505-237-1). Oceano.

Diccionario Real Espanol-Ingles Ingles-Espanol. 1008p. (Span. & Eng.). 1981. pap. 1600.00 ptas (ISBN 84-7505-233-9). Oceano.

Diccionario Religioso Para los Hombres De Hoy. Josep Vilaro et al. 260p. (Span.). 1976. pap. 7.50 (ISBN 84-320-0273-9, S-50025). French & Eur.

Diccionario Retana De Autoridades De la Lengua Vasca, 4 vols. Manuel de Sota Aburto. (Span.). 1976. Set. leather 200.00 (ISBN 84-248-0248-9, S-50053). French & Eur.

Diccionario Rioduero: Arte. Ursula Boeing-Haeusgen. 620p. (Span.). 1978. leatherette 26.95 (ISBN 84-220-0873-4, S-50170). French & Eur.

Diccionario Rioduero: Biologia. 2nd ed. Rainer Bergfeld. 244p. (Span.). 1977. 9.95 (ISBN 84-220-0683-9, S-50169). French & Eur.

Diccionario Rioduero: Ecologia. Udo Becker. 216p. (Span.). 1975. leatherette 7.50 (ISBN 84-220-0714-2, S-50165). French & Eur.

Diccionario Rioduero: Fisica. Rolf Sauermost. 256p. (Span.). 1976. leatherette 9.95 (ISBN 84-220-0763-0, S-50167). French & Eur.

Diccionario Rioduero: Fisica Del Espacio. Udo Becker. 264p. (Span.). 1978. leatherette 13.25 (ISBN 84-220-0846-7, S-50163). French & Eur.

Diccionario Rioduero: Geografia. 2nd ed. Margit Klein & Johannes Klein. (Span.). 1977. leatherette 15.75 (ISBN 84-220-0670-7, S-50173). French & Eur.

Diccionario Rioduero: Geologia y Mineralogia. 2nd ed. (Span.). 1978. leatherette 9.95 (ISBN 0-686-57363-3). French & Eur.

Diccionario Rioduero Matematica. Jurgen Reck. 224p. (Span.). 1977. leatherette 12.50 (ISBN 84-220-0832-7, S-50162). French & Eur.

Diccionario Rioduero: Paises De la Tierra. Johannes Klein. 296p. (Span.). 1978. leatherette 15.75 (ISBN 84-220-0876-9, S-50165). French & Eur.

Diccionario Rioduero: Quimica. 2nd ed. Peter Ottokar. 272p. (Span.). 1977. leatherette 11.95 (ISBN 84-220-0726-6, S-50172). French & Eur.

Diccionario Rioduero: Quimica. 3rd ed. Peter Ottokar. Tr. by Gloria Arroyo Marcos. 272p. (Span.). 1981. pap. 600.00 ptas (ISBN 84-220-0726-6). Catolica Edit.

Diccionario Rioduero: Zoologia. 432p. (Span.). 1979. 17.95 (ISBN 0-686-57364-1, S-50171). French & Eur.

Diccionario ruso-espanol. (Span. & Rus.). 0.80. Pueblos Unidos.

Diccionario Ruso-Espanol. Lorenzo Martinez Calvo. 2000p. (Rus. & Span.). 44.95 (ISBN 84-303-0131-3, S-50410). French & Eur.

Diccionario Ruso-Espanol. J. Nogueira & G. Turover. 956p. (Rus. & Span.). 1979. Leatherette 25.95 (ISBN 0-686-92344-8, S-33593). French & Eur.

Diccionario ruso-espanol. Yaselman. (Rus. & Span.). 160.00 ptas. Aguilar SP.

Diccionario ruso-espanol de la ciencia y de la tecnica. Patronato Juan de la Cierva. 700p. (Rus. & Span.). write for info. Dossat.

Diccionario Ruso-Espanol de la Ciencia y la Tecnica. 2nd ed. Patronato J. De la Cierva. 700p. (Span.). 1972. 50.00 (ISBN 84-237-0407-6, S-50249). French & Eur.

Diccionario ruso-espanol, espanol-ruso. 1448p. (Rus. & Span.). 850.00 ptas. Danae.

Diccionario Saber miniatura. 414p. (Span.). Mex.$3.75. Fernandez.

Diccionario San Luis Potosi: Enciclopedia regional. 320p. (Span.). write for info. (744). Fernandez.

Diccionario Santillana. Ed. by Javier Alfaya. LC 76-460370. xii, 1021p. (Span.). 1975. write for info. (ISBN 8-439-94544-2). Santillana.

Diccionario Secreto, 3 vols. 2nd ed. Camilo J. Cela Trulock. 1184p. (Span.). 1975. Set. pap. 20.95 (ISBN 84-206-1997-3, S-29231). French & Eur.

Diccionario Secreto, Vol. 1. Camilo J. Cela. (Span.). 12.75 (ALFA). Lectorum Pubns.

Diccionario Simultaneo en 21 Idiomas. Juan Capdevilla Font. 416p. (Span., Eng., Fr., Ger., Ital., Port., Catalan, Czech, Danish, Esparanto, Finnish, Gr., Dutch, Hungarian, Malaysian, Pol., Rumanian, Rus., Swedish & Turkish.). 1977. pap. 18.75 (ISBN 0-686-57350-1, S-31466). French & Eur.

Diccionario simultaneo en 21 idiomas. (Span.). write for info. (608-80). Pan Amer Pub.

Diccionario Simultaneo en 6 Idiomas. Juan Capdevila Font. 192p. (Span., Eng., Fr., Ital., Ger. & Port.). 1975. pap. 6.75 (ISBN 84-85117-14-X, S-31467). French & Eur.

Diccionario Sopena de Dudas & Dificultades del Idioma. 624p. (Span.). 1981. 200.00 ptas (ISBN 84-303-0838-5); pap. 230.00 ptas (ISBN 84-303-0839-3). Sopena.

Diccionario Sopena De Literatura. Parnaso. 1820p. (Span.). 54.00 (ISBN 84-303-0247-6, S-50140). French & Eur.

Diccionario Subversivo. Miguel Angel Speroni. 238p. (Span.). 1974. write for info. Hachette Jeunesse.

Diccionario Superior Frances-Espanol Espanol-Frances. 1224p. (Fr. & Span.). write for info. Biblograf SP.

Diccionario Superior Frances-Espanol, Espanol-Frances, 2 vols. Vox. LC 78-347426. 1136p. (Fr. & Span.). 1977. 475.00 ptas (ISBN 8-471-53187-9). Biblo Sp.

Diccionario superior Frances-Espanol Espanol-Frances 'Vox' 2nd ed. 710p. (Fr. & Span.). 1981. 825.00 ptas (ISBN 84-7153-187-9). Biblo SP.

Diccionario Tabasco: Enciclopedia regional. 320p. (Span.). write for info. (747). Fernandez.

Diccionario Taurino Ilustrado. Carlos Garcia Patier. (Illus.). 72p. (Span.). 1981. 250.00 ptas (ISBN 84-85951-00-X). Cometa SA.

Diccionario Tecnic Aeronautico Espanol-Ingles: Tomo 2. 106p. (Span. & Eng.). 1980. pap. write for info. (ISBN 84-300-3349-1). Autor.

Diccionario Tecnico. Hermann Mink. LC 78-398803. (Fr. & Span.). 1978. write for info. (ISBN 8-4703-1087-9). Blume Edit.

Diccionario Tecnico Aeronautico Espanol-Ingles-Espanol, 6 vols. 1628p. (Span. & Eng.). 1980. pap. write for info. (ISBN 84-300-3345-9). Autor.

Diccionario Tecnico Aeronautico Espanol-Ingles, Tomo 1. 227p. (Span. & Eng.). 1980. pap. write for info. (ISBN 84-300-3347-5). Autor.

Diccionario Tecnico Aeronautico Espanol-Ingles, Tomo 3. 459p. (Span. & Eng.). 1980. pap. write for info. (ISBN 84-300-3351-3). Autor.

Diccionario Tecnico Aeronautico Ingles-Espanol, Tomo 1. 247p. (Eng. & Span.). 1980. pap. write for info. (ISBN 84-300-3346-7). Autor.

Diccionario Tecnico Aeronautico Ingles-Espanol, Tomo 3. 479p. (Eng. & Span.). 1980. pap. write for info. (ISBN 84-300-3350-5). Autor.

Diccionario Tecnico Aeronautico Ingles-Espanol, Tomo 2. 110p. (Eng. & Span.). 1980. pap. write for info. (ISBN 84-300-3348-3). Autor.

Diccionario Tecnico Aleman-Espanol, Espanol-Aleman, 2 vols. 3rd ed. H. Mink. 2530p. (Span. & Ger.). 1978. Set. 120.00 (ISBN 84-254-0704-4, S-50189). French & Eur.

Diccionario Tecnico & Industrial Italiano-Espanol. 678p. (Ital. & Span.). 1974. 750.00 ptas. L Carcamo.

Diccionario tecnico automovilismo, mecanica automotriz: Espanol-Ingles. (Span. & Eng.). Arg.$3.00. Cosmopolita.

Diccionario tecnico, automovilismo, mecanica automotriz: Ingles-espanol. (Eng. & Span.). Arg.$3.00. Cosmopolita.

Diccionario Tecnico-Comercial y Profesional de Automocion. Luiz Miguel Ortega Garcia. 214p. (Span.). 1982. 1500.00 ptas (ISBN 84-86104-00-9). Tecnipublicaciones.

Diccionario Tecnico de Aeronautica. F. Fernandez-Martinez. (Span.). 1983. write for info. Paraninfo.

Diccionario tecnico de biblioteconomia espanol-ingles, ingles-espanol. 3rd ed. Beatriz Massa de Gil et al. 390p. (Span. & Eng.). 1964. 9.60; Mex.$120.00. Trillas.

Diccionario Tecnico de Biblioteconomia. Beatriz Massa De Gil. 387p. (Span.). 1965. Mex.$10.75. Trillas.

Diccionario Tecnico De Electromecanica: Ingles-Espanol. Luis W. Ballesteros. 1976. pap. 13.50x (ISBN 968-18-0522-4). Intl Learn Syst.

Diccionario Tecnico de electromecanica: Ingles-espanol. L. Ballesteros Weis. 298p. (Eng. & Span.). Mex.$4.00; 50.00. Limusa.

Diccionario Tecnico de la Construccion, Edificacion & Obras Publicas. Machado. (Fr. & Span.). 1969. 00.1400.00 ptas (ISBN 8-42830-245-6). Paraninfo.

Diccionario Tecnico De la Construccion, Edificacion y Obras Publicas Frances-Espanol y Espanol-Frances. M. Machado. 576p. (Fr. & Span.). 1969. leatherette 35.95 (ISBN 84-283-0245-6, S-50242). French & Eur.

Diccionario tecnico de la construccion: Edificacion y obras publicas; francesa-espanol y espanol-frances. M. Machado. 578p. (Fr. & Span.). 1969. 500.00 ptas. Paraninfo.

Diccionario Tecnico de la Industria del Petroleo y Derivados. Ed. by Mendez. 588p. (Span.). 1980. 44.95 (ISBN 84-283-1097-1, S-37582). French & Eur.

Diccionario Tecnico De la Plasticos Aleman-Espanol. A. Wittfoht & M. A. Achon. 544p. (Ger. & Span.). 1970. leatherette 70.00 (ISBN 0-686-57332-3, S-50005). French & Eur.

Diccionario tecnico de plasticos aleman-espanol. A Wittfoht & M. A. Achon. (Illus.). 544p. (Ger. & Span.). 1970. 1500.00 ptas. Urmo.

Diccionario tecnico de plasticos: Espanol-aleman. A. Wittfoht & A. Rubin. (Illus., Span. & Ger.). 1980. write for info. (Dist. Elcano, Mexico). Urmo.

Diccionario Tecnico de Terminologia Comercial Cantable y Bancaria. Jaime Garza Bores. (Span.). 6.95 (ISBN 0-686-56677-7, S-25235). French & Eur.

Diccionario tecnico de terminologia comercial, contable y bancaria: Espanol-Ingles, Ingles-Espanol. Jaime Garza Bores. (Span. & Eng.). 1.60; Mex.$20.00. Diana.

Diccionario tecnico de terminos ferroviarios: Espanol-frances-aleman-ingles-italiano-holandes. 2nd ed. J. H. Bussy. 1358p. (Span., Fr., Ger., Eng., Ital. & Dutch.). write for info. G Gili.

Diccionario Tecnico Del Agua. Jose Catalan Lafuente. 301p. (Span.). 1977. pap. 29.95 (ISBN 84-400-2913-6, S-50098). French & Eur.

Diccionario tecnico del seguro de vida. Karlsruhe. (Span.). write for info. Rev. Mex. de Seguros.

Diccionario tecnico electrotecnia; luminotecnia; espanol-ingles. (Span. & Eng.). Arg.$3.00. Cosmopolita.

Diccionario tecnico, electrotecnia, luminotecnia: Ingles-espanol. (Eng. & Span.). Arg.$3.00. Cosmopolita.

Diccionario tecnico espanol-aleman. Tr. by Mink. (Span. & Ger.). 1970. 1500.00 ptas. Bluma.

Diccionario Tecnico Espanol-Frances. Guy Malgorn. (Span. & Fr.). 1979. write for info. leatherette (S-50241). French & Eur.

Diccionario tecnico espanol-frances; frances-espanol. 610p. (Fr. & Span.). 550.00 ea. ptas. EDAF.

Diccionario Tecnico Espanol-Ingles. Malgorn. (Span. & Eng.). 1977. 1100.00 ptas (ISBN 8-42830-889-6). Paraninfo.

Diccionario Tecnico Espanol-Ingles. Guy Malgorn. 594p. (Span. & Eng.). 1977. 26.95 (ISBN 84-283-0889-6, S-31442). French & Eur.

Diccionario Tecnico Espanol-Ingles. Guy Malgorn. 576p. (Span. & Eng.). 1978. write for info. (ISBN 84-283-0889-6). Paraninfo.

Diccionario Tecnico Espanol-Polaco. Ed. by T. Weroniecki. 545p. (Span. & Pol.). 1981. 49.95 (ISBN 83-204-0287-5, S-37602). French & Eur.

Diccionario tecnico Espa n13ol-Ingl e01s. Guy Malgorn. 576p. (Span. & Eng.). 1978. write for info. (ISBN 84-283-0889-6). Fed Gremios.

Diccionario Tecnico Frances-Espanol. 544p. (Fr. & Span.). 1973. leatherette 20.95 (ISBN 84-283-0334-7, S-31563). French & Eur.

Diccionario Tecnico Frances-Espanol. Malgorn. (Fr. & Span.). 1973. 1000.00 ptas (ISBN 8-42830-334-7). Paraninfo.

Diccionario Tecnico Frances-Espanol. Hermann Mink. 1120p. (Fr. & Span.). 1978. 64.00 (ISBN 84-7031-087-9, S-50221). French & Eur.

Diccionario tecnico frances-espanol y espanol-frances. Guy Malgorn. (Fr. & Span.). 1972. write for info. Paraninfo.

Diccionario tecnico-grafico del automovil. (Span.). 1967. 200.00 ptas. Bluma.

Diccionario Tecnico Hostelero. Fernando Molina Aranda. 245p. (Span.). 1972. pap. 12.25 (ISBN 84-85087-02-X, S-50021). French & Eur.

Diccionario tecnico ilustrado de edificacion y obras publicas. Barbier et al. (Illus.). 177p. (Span.). write for info. G Gili.

Diccionario Tecnico Ilustrado De Edificacion y Obras Publicas. Maurice Barbier. 177p. (Span.). 1976. pap. 11.50 (ISBN 84-252-0327-9, S-50273). French & Eur.

Diccionario tecnico ilustrado de herramientas de corte para el trabajo de metales: Espanol-aleman-ingles-frances-italiano. T. Heiler. (Illus.). 474p. (Span., Ger., Eng., Fr. & Ital.). write for info. G Gili.

Diccionario tecnico ilustrado del automovil. Jezewski Blok. Tr. by Diorki. 500p. (Span.). 1981. 6000.00 ptas (ISBN 84-85647-06-8). Aneto Edns.

Diccionario tecnico industrial: Vol. 1, Espanol-aleman. R. Ernst. 480p. (Span. & Ger.). write for info. G Gili.

Diccionario tecnico industrial: Vol. 2, Aleman-espanol. 584p. (Ger. & Span.). write for info. G Gili.

Diccionario Tecnico Ingles-Espanol. Malgorn. (Eng. & Span.). 1978. 1100.00 ptas (ISBN 8-42830-923-X). Paraninfo.

Diccionario Tecnico Ingles-Espanol. Guy Malgorn. 632p. (Eng. & Span.). 1978. pap. 26.95 (ISBN 84-283-0923-X, S-31490). French & Eur.

Diccionario Tecnico-Maritimo Ingles-Espanol & Espanol-Ingles. L. S. Gil. 708p. (Eng. & Span.). 1980. pap. write for info. (ISBN 84-205-0772-5). Edit Alhambra.

Diccionario tecnico-maritimo Ingles-Espanol & Espanol-Ingles. L. Suarez Gil. 708p. (Span. & Eng.). 1980. pap. write for info. (ISBN 84-205-0707-5). Fed Gremios.

Diccionario Tecnico Maritimo: Ingles-Espanol, Espanol-Ingles. Ed. by L. Suarez Gil. 708p. (Eng. & Span.). 1980. pap. 75.00 (ISBN 84-205-0772-5, S-32729). French & Eur.

Diccionario tecnico maritimo: Ingles-espanol espanol-ingles. L. Suariz Gil. 706p. (Eng. & Span.). 1980. pap. 980.00 ptas (ISBN 84-205-0772-5). Alhambra.

Diccionario tecnico militar ingles-espanol y espanol-ingles para uso de los ejercitos de tierra, mar y aire. Francisco Lizarraga. (Eng. & Span.). 125.00 ptas. Bibliografica.

Diccionario tecnico, radio, antenas, video, radar: Espanol-ingles. (Span. & Eng.). Arg.$3.00. Cosmopolita.

Diccionario Tecnico: Suplemento, Vol. 2. H. Mink. 384p. (Span. & Ger.). 1981. Leatherette 49.50 (ISBN 0-686-92524-6, S-50270). French & Eur.

Diccionario Tecnico: Suplemento al Tomo II, Espanol-Aleman. H. Mink. 384p. (Span. & Ger.). 1980. 1650.00 ptas. Herder SA.

Diccionario tecnico, television: Espanol-Ingles. (Span. & Eng.). Arg.$3.00. Cosmopolita.

Diccionario tecnico, television: Ingles-Espanol. (Eng. & Span.). Arg.$3.00. Cosmopolita.

Diccionario Tecnico, Tomo 1: Aleman-Espanol. 2nd ed. H. Mink. 1376p. (Span.). 1978. 60.00 (ISBN 84-254-0994-2, S-50190, French & Eur). French & Eur.

Diccionario Tecnico, Tomo 2: Espanol-Aleman. 3rd ed. H. Mink. 1154p. (Span. & Ger.). 1978. 60.00 (ISBN 84-254-0705-2, S-12404, French & Eur). French & Eur.

Diccionario tecnologico Chambers: Espanol-ingles-frances-aleman, 2 vols. 2nd ed. C. F. Tweney & L. E. Hughes. 2006p. (Span., Eng., Fr., & Ger.). 1900.00 ptas. Omega SA.

Diccionario Tecnologico Del Plasticos. 160p. (Span.). 1978. 9.95 (ISBN 84-85011-02-3, S-50059). French & Eur.

Diccionario Tecnologico Ingles-Espanol: Electricidad, Electronica, Telecomunicacion, & Materias Afinas con la Fisica, Optica & Quimica. Franco Ibeas. 452p. (Eng. & Span.). 1974. E950.00 (ISBN 84-205-0492-0). Alhambra.

Diccionario Tecnologico Ingles-Espanol. 454p. (Eng. & Span.). 1974. 41.95 (ISBN 84-205-0492-0, S-31501). French & Eur.

Diccionario Tecnologico Ingles-Espanol. F. F. Ibeas. 740p. (Eng. & Span.). 1980. pap. write for info. (ISBN 84-205-0707-5). Edit Alhambra.

Diccionario tecnologico Ingle s-Espa n ol. Franco Ibeas. 740p. (Span. & Eng.). 1980. pap. write for info. (ISBN 84-205-0707-5). Fed Gremios.

Diccionario Tematico de la Lengua Espanola. 496p. (Span.). 1980. 1350.00 ptas (ISBN 84-7153-116-X). Biblograf SP.

Diccionario Tematico de la Lengua Espanola 'Vox' 500p. (Span.). 1980. write for info. (ISBN 84-7153-053-8). Biblo SP.

Diccionario Tematico de la Lengua Espanola. Vox. LC 76-452992. 461p. (Span.). 1975. write for info. (ISBN 8-471-53116-X). Biblo Sp.

Diccionario Tematico de Sinonimos & Antonimos. 2nd ed. 640p. (Span.). 1981. 500.00 ptas (ISBN 84-241-1501-5). Everest.

Diccionario Tematico Ingles-Espanol & Espanol-Ingles. Merino. (Eng. & Span.). 1978. 750.00 ptas (ISBN 8-42830-918-3). Paraninfo.

Diccionario Tematico Ingles-Espanol & Espanol-Ingles. Jose Merino. 600p. (Eng. & Span.). 1978. write for info. (ISBN 84-283-0918-3). Paraninfo.

Diccionario tematico Ingles-Espanol & Espanol-Ingles. Jose Merino. 600p. (Span. & Eng.). 1978. write for info. (ISBN 84-283-0918-3). Fed Gremios.

Diccionario Tematico Ingles-Espanol, Espanol-Ingles. Jose Merino. 604p. (Eng. & Span.). 1978. pap. 17.95 (ISBN 84-283-0918-3, S-31559). French & Eur.

Diccionario Teorico y Practico del Juicio de Amparo. Eduardo Pallares. 321p. (Span.). 17.50 (ISBN 0-686-56705-6, S-21916). French & Eur.

Diccionario terminlogico de ciencias medicas. 10th ed. (Illus.). 1200p. (Span.). 19.00; 1200.00 ptas. Salvat Editores.

Diccionario terminoligico de Ciencias Medicas II. 11th ed. 1084p. (Span.). 1981. pap. 2250.00 ptas (ISBN 84-345-1206-8). Salvat Editores.

Diccionario terminoligico de la Comunidades Europeas. Daniel Busturia. 680p. (Span.). 1982. 3200.00 ptas (ISBN 84-7019-084-9). Assn Prog Direc.

Diccionario Terminologia Medica Explicada. Juan Prada Becares. 128p. (Span.). 1977. pap. 9.95 (ISBN 84-400-3894-1, S-50111). French & Eur.

Diccionario Terminologia Medica Explicada. Juan Prada Becares. LC 79-346078. 125p. (Span.). 1977. write for info. (ISBN 8-4400-3894-1). Autores-Editores.

Diccionario Terminologico. Lluis. 456p. (Span.). 1980. write for info. Fondo Educativo.

Diccionario Terminologico De Ciencias Medicas. 11th ed. 1088p. (Span.). 1978. 52.50 (ISBN 84-345-1206-8, S-13674). French & Eur.

Diccionario Terminologico de Ciencias Medicas. 11th ed. 1084p. (Span.). 1980. pap. 2250.00 ptas (ISBN 84-345-1206-8). Salvat Editores.

Diccionario Terminologico De Minas, Canteras y Mineralurgia. Laureano Fueyo Cuesta. 272p. (Span.). 1973. leather 17.95 (ISBN 84-400-6971-5, S-50112). French & Eur.

Diccionario terminologico de Quimaca. 2nd ed. Jose Barcelo Matutano. 788p. (Span.). 1982. pap. 3160.00 ptas (ISBN 84-205-0521-8). Alhambra.

Diccionario Terminologico de Quimica. J. R. Barcelo. 1100p. (Span.). 1974. write for info. Alhambra.

Diccionario Terminologico de Quimica. Jose R. Barcelo. LC 76-480438. xi, 774p. (Eng. & Span.). 1976. write for info. (ISBN 8-4205-0521-8). Edit Alhambra.

Diccionario Terminologico de Quimica. 2nd ed. Jose R. Barcelo Matutano. 1100p. (Span., Ger. & Eng.). 1976. pap. 46.00 (ISBN 84-205-0521-8, S-50090). French & Eur.

Diccionario Terminos. Thierrey Maulmier. 340p. (Span.). 1977. pap. 13.95 (ISBN 84-321-1924-5, S-50250). French & Eur.

Diccionario textil panamericano: English-Spanish Dictionary of Textile Terms. 2nd ed. Joaquin O. Rodriguez. (Span.). 1971. 35.00 (ISBN 0-912476-04-4). W R C Smith.

Diccionario Totonaco De Papantla. Herman Aschmann & Bessie Aschmann. (Vocabularios Indigenas Ser.: No. 16). 268p. (Span.). 1973. pap. 5.00x (ISBN 0-88312-750-4); microfiche 3.00x (ISBN 0-88312-585-4). Summer Inst Ling.

Diccionario Totonaco de Xicotepec de Juarez. Reid et al. (Vocabularios Indigenas Ser.: No. 17). (Span.). 1974. pap. 12.00x (ISBN 0-88312-752-0); microfiche 4.50 (ISBN 0-88312-552-8). Summer Inst Ling.

Diccionario Tri-lingue, 3 vols. Esteban S. Hornberger & H. N. Hornberger. LC 79-102496. (Eng., Quechua, & Span.). 1978. write for info. LCA.

Diccionario trilingue miskito-ingles-espanol. Adolfo I. Vaughan Warman. 790p. (Eng., Span. & Miskito.). 1959. 10.00. Imp. Nac. Manugua EDUCA.

Diccionario Triqui de Chicahuaxtla. Claude Good. LC 79-106554. 104p. (Span. & Trique.). 1978. write for info. Inst Ling Ver.

Diccionario Turistico de Cataluna, Baleares y Andora. J. Munso. 693p. (Span.). 1975. Leatherette 95.00 (ISBN 84-85186-00-1, S-32722). French & Eur.

Diccionario Turistico Internacional: Edition Espagnole. Academie International du Tourisme. (Span.). 80.00 F. Acad Intl Tour.

Diccionario Tzotzil De San Andres Con Variaciones Dialectales. Alfa Delgaty & Augustin R. Sanchez. (Vocabularios Indigenas: No. 22). (Illus.). 481p. (Orig., Tzotzil & Span.). 1978. pap. 10.00x (ISBN 0-88312-674-5); microfiche 4.50x (ISBN 0-88312-372-X). Summer Inst Ling.

Diccionario universal: Aleman-espanol, espanol-aleman. 3rd ed. 388p. (Ger. & Span.). 0.77 ptas. 50.00 ptas. Herder SA.

Diccionario Universal del Arte, 5 vols. 2nd ed. 1808p. (Span.). 1981. pap. 13450.00 ptas (ISBN 84-7017-621-8). Argos-Vergara.

Diccionario Universal del Arte: A-CH, Vol. 1. 2nd ed. 376p. (Span.). 1981. pap. 2690.00 ptas (ISBN 84-7017-622-6). Argos-Vergara.

Diccionario Universal del Arte: D-H, Vol. 2. 2nd ed. 352p. (Span.). 1981. pap. 2690.00 ptas (ISBN 84-7017-623-4). Argos-Vergara.

Diccionario Universal del Arte: I-M, Vol. 3. 2nd ed. 368p. (Span.). 1981. pap. 2690.00 ptas (ISBN 84-7017-624-2). Argos-Vergara.

Diccionario Universal del Arte: N-R, Vol. 4. 2nd ed. 344p. (Span.). 1981. pap. 2690.00 ptas (ISBN 84-7017-625-0). Argos-Vergara.

Diccionario Universal del Arte: S-Z, Vol. 5. 2nd ed. 368p. (Span.). 1981. pap. 2690.00 ptas (ISBN 84-7017-626-9). Argos-Vergara.

Diccionario Universal del Arte y De los Artistas: Arquitectos. 323p. (Span.). 1970. leatherette 25.50 (ISBN 84-252-0381-3, S-50282). French & Eur.

Diccionario Universal del Arte y De los Artistas: Arte Occidental y del Proximo Oriente, II. 300p. (Span.). 1969. leatherette 25.50 (ISBN 0-686-77260-1, S-50284). French & Eur.

Diccionario Universal del Arte y De los Artistas: Arte Occidental y del Proximo Oriente, I. 300p. (Span.). 1969. leatherette 25.50 (ISBN 84-252-0578-6, S-50285). French & Eur.

Diccionario Universal del Arte y De los Artistas: Arte Oriental, Precolombino y De los Pueblos Primitivos. 315p. (Span.). 1969. leatherette 25.50 (ISBN 84-252-0598-0, S-50286). French & Eur.

Diccionario Universal del Arte y De los Artistas: Escultores. 301p. (Span.). 1970. leatherette 25.50 (ISBN 84-252-0383-X, S-50281). French & Eur.

Diccionario Universal del Arte y De los Artistas: Estilos y Tendencias En el Arte Occidental. 320p. (Span.). 1969. leatherette 25.50 (ISBN 0-686-57358-7, S-50283). French & Eur.

Diccionario Universal del Arte y De los Artistas: Pintores, 3 vols. 934p. (Span.). 1970. Set. leatherette 76.50 (ISBN 84-252-0374-0, S-50287). French & Eur.

Diccionario Universal del Arte y los Artistas, 9 vols. Juan-Eduardo Cirlot. 2794p. (Span.). 1969. Set. leatherette 229.50 (ISBN 0-686-57347-1, S-12283). French & Eur.

Diccionario universal: Frances-espanol, espanol-frances. 368p. (Fr. & Span.). 0.77; 50.00 ptas. Herder SA.

Diccionario Universal Herder Aleman-Espanol, Espanol-Aleman. 4th ed. 388p. (Ger. & Span.). 1977. leatherette 4.50 (ISBN 84-254-0782-6, S-50378). French & Eur.

Diccionario Universal Herder De la Lengua Espanola. 460p. (Span.). 1975. pap. 4.50 (ISBN 84-254-0968-3, S-50195). French & Eur.

Diccionario Universal Herder Frances-Espanol, Espanol-Frances. 5th ed. 368p. (Fr. & Span.). 1977. leatherette 4.50 (ISBN 84-254-0780-X, S-12394). French & Eur.

Diccionario Universal Herder Holandes-Espanol, Espanol-Holandes. 264p. (Dutch & Span.). 1977. leatherette 4.50 (ISBN 84-254-0779-6, S-50412). French & Eur.

Diccionario Universal Herder Ingles-Espanol, Espanol-Ingles. 4th ed. 340p. (Eng. & Span.). 1977. leatherette 4.50 (ISBN 84-254-0781-8, S-12395). French & Eur.

Diccionario Universal Herder Italiano-Espanol, Espanol-Italiano. 5th ed. 364p. (Span. & Ital.). 1977. pap. 4.50 (ISBN 84-254-0558-0, S-50433). French & Eur.

Diccionario universal: Ingles-espanol, espanol-ingles. 340p. (Eng. & Span.). 0.77; 50.00 ptas. Herder SA.

Diccionario universal: Italiano-espanol, espanol-italiano. 364p. (Ital. & Span.). 0.77; 50.00 ptas. Herder SA.

Diccionario universal Langenscheidt. (Span.). Mex.$1.35; 15.25. Buena Prensa.

Diccionario valenciano-castellano de Manuel Josquin Savelo. Joseph Gulsoy. 552p. (Span.). 1964. 550.00 ptas. Soc. Castellonenca de Cultura.

Diccionario Vasco-Castellano. 6th ed. Isaak Lopez Mendizabal. 452p. (Castella.). 1976. 25.50 (ISBN 84-7025-026-4, S-50439). French & Eur.

Diccionario Vasco-Castellano & Castellano-Vasco. 2nd. ed. Juan J. Arbelaiz. 370p. (Span.). 1982. pap. 442.00 ptas (ISBN 8-42480-758-8). Encicl Vasca.

Diccionario Vasco-Castellano & Castellano-Vasco de Voces Comunes. Juan Jose Arbelaiz. 370p. (Span.). 1982. 370.00 ptas (ISBN 8-42480-758-8). Encicl Vasca.

Diccionario Vasco-Castellano, Castellano-Vasco De Voces Comunes a Dos O Mas Dialectos Del Euskera. Aberlaitz & P. Buenaventura de Oreyegui. (Span.). 25.50 (ISBN 84-248-0014-1, S-21917). French & Eur.

Diccionario Vasco-Castellano, Castellano-Vasco De Voces Comunes a Dos O Mas Dialectos Del Euskera. 2nd ed. Buenaventura de Oyeregui. 372p. (Castella.). 1978. pap. 7.50 (ISBN 0-686-57354-4, S-50454). French & Eur.

Diccionario Vasco-Castellano: Obra completa, 2 vols. Placido Mugica Betrondo. 2096p. (Span.). 1981. 5600.00 ptas (ISBN 84-271-1269-6). Mensajero Edns.

Diccionario Vasco-Castellano: Tomo 1. Placido Mugica Berrondo. 1096p. (Span.). 1981. 2800.00 ptas (ISBN 84-271-1267-X). Mensajero Edns.

Diccionario Vasco-Castellano: Tomo 2. Placido Mugica Berrondo. 1000p. (Span.). 1981. pap. 2800.00 ptas (ISBN 84-271-1268-8). Mensajero Edns.

Diccionario Vasco-Espanol-Frances, 2 vols. Resurreccion M. Azkue. (Span. & Fr.). Set. leatherette 68.00 (ISBN 84-248-0015-X, S-12384). French & Eur.

Diccionario Velazquez: Espanol e ingles. Mariano Velazquez. (Span. & Eng.). index 8.95; 7.95. Follett.

Diccionario Veracruz ilustrado. 320p. (Span.). write for info. (750). Fernandez.

Diccionario Vertice Everest: Frances-Espanol, Espanol-Frances. Everest. LC 76-458632. 519p. (Fr. & Span.). 1975. write for info. (ISBN 8-424-11320-9). Everest.

Diccionario Visual Del Sexo. 328p. (Span.). 1979. 53.95 (ISBN 84-278-0556-X, S-50031). French & Eur.

Diccionario visual del sexo. 2nd ed. 328p. (Span.). 1980. 1200.00 ptas (ISBN 84-278-0556-X). Nauta SA.

Diccionario visual del sexo. 2nd ed. Eric Trimmer. Tr. by Ernest Jorda. 320p. (Span.). 1980. 900.00 ptas (ISBN 84-226-1056-6). Circulo Lect.

Diccionario y gramatica de la lengua de la isla de Pascua: Pascuense-castellano, castellano-pascuense, pascuense-ingles, ingles-pascuense. Jordi Fuentes Franco. 1802p. (Span. & Eng.). 1960. 5.00. Juridica-Andres Bello.

Diccionario y manual de la nueva fisica y quimica. Robert W. Marks. (Illus.). 262p. (Span.). 1.50. Edit Pr Serv.

Diccionario y manual de las nuevas matematicas. 2nd, rev. ed. Robert W. Marks. (Illus.). 288p. (Span.). 1.50. Edit Pr Serv.

Diccionario y tablas electronicas. (Span.). 6.50. Minerva.

Diccionario Yucat a01n: Enciclopedia regional. 320p. (Span.). write for info. (751). Fernandez.

Diccionario Zen. E. Wood. 190p. (Span.). pap. 400.00 ptas (ISBN 8-47509-010-9). Paido.

Diccionario Zen. Ed. by E. Wood. 190p. (Span.). 1980. pap. 13.95 (ISBN 84-7509-010-9, S-32724). French & Eur.

Diccionarior Nuclear. Agustin A. Santos. LC 80-109250. xxiv, 708p. (Fr., & Span.). 1979. write for info. (ISBN 8-4500-3077-3). Organ Ofic Adm.

Diccionarios mundiales. 600p. (Span.). 5.95; pap. 2.95. Follett.

Diccionarios Rioduero: Biologia. 3rd ed. Rainer Bergfeld. Tr. by Gloria Arroyo Marcos. 244p. (Span.). 1981. pap. 600.00 ptas (ISBN 84-220-0683-9). Catolica Edit.

Diccionarios Rioduero: Matematicas. 2nd ed. Jurgen Reck. Tr. by Walter Strobl. 224p. (Span.). 1982. pap. 600.00 ptas (ISBN 84-220-0832-7). Catolica Edit.

Diccionaris catala-castella i castella-catala: Tipus breu. 450p. (Span.). 75.00 ptas. M Arimany.

Diccionaris catala-castella i castella-catala: Tipus basic. 400p. (Span.). 48.00 ptas. M Arimany.

Diccionaris catala-castella i castella-catala: Tipus especial. 958p. (Span.). 1971. 350.00 ptas. M Arimany.

Diccionaris catala-castella i castella-catala: Tipus manual. 958p. (Span.). 250.00 ptas. M Arimany.

Diccionaris catala-castella i castella-catala: Tipus practic. 450p. (Span.). 150.00 ptas. M Arimany.

Diccionaro de Qheshwa-Espanol, Espanol-Qheshwa. Jesus Lara. (Span. & Qheshwa.). pap. 29.95 (ISBN 0-686-56702-1, S-12398). French & Eur.

Diccionrio De Sinonimos. (Span.). leatherette 10.95 (ISBN 84-346-0311-X, S-37349). French & Eur.

Dicionario Basico da Lingua Galega. 2nd ed. Instituto da Lingua Galega. 288p. (Span.). 1982. 315.00 ptas (ISBN 8-47507-003-5). Xerais de Galicia.

Dicionario Basico do Ingles Moderno. Edicoes Melhoramentos. LC 79-345010. xiv, 856p. (Port.). 1978. Cr.$250.00. Edicoes Melhoramentos.

Dicionario Basico Escolar Koogan-Larousse. Antonio Houaiss. (Port.). Cr.$670.00. Edit Atica.

Dicionario Basico Michaelis. 856p. (Eng. & Port.). 1978. 40.00. Imported Bks.

Dicionario Conciso da Lingua Portuguesa. Antonio N. Machado. (Port.). write for info. Difel Editorial, S. A.

Dicionario Conciso da Lingua Portuguesa. Ed. by Antonio N. Machado. LC 77-563116. 768p. (Port.). 1977. Cr.$95.00. Didel Difusao.

Dicionario da Lingua Portuguesa. J. Almeida Costa & Sampaio de Melo. 1556p. (Port.). 18.00. Imported Bks.

Dicionario da Lingua Portuguesa. F. Fernandes. (Port.). Date not set. price not set. French & Eur.

Dicionario de Acoes & de Procedimentos Judiciais. Yara Muller Leite. LC 79-115699. vii, 692p. (Port.). 1979. Cr.$590.00. Saraiva SA.

Dicionario de Administracao de Recursos Humanos com Termos: Ingles-Portugues, Portugues-Ingles. F. Toledo & B. Milioni. 156p. (Eng. & Port.). 1979. pap. 14.95 (ISBN 0-686-92535-1, M-9356). French & Eur.

Dicionario de Alemao-Portugues. (Coleccao "Estudantes"). (Port. & Ger.). Esc.200.00. Porto Ed.

Dicionario de Biologia. M. Abercrombie et al. (Port.). Esc.495.00. Pub Euro Am.

Dicionario de Bolso Portugues-Alemao. (Port. & Ger.). Cr.$pap. 2.21. Difel Difusao.

Dicionario de Bolso Portugues-Frances. (Port. & Fr.). Cr.$1.92. Difel Difusao.

Dicionario de Bolso Portugues-Russo. I. Chalaguina. 343p. (Rus. & Port.). 1976. 4.95 (ISBN 0-686-92579-3, M-9103). French & Eur.

Dicionario de Bolso Russo-Portuguese. C. Nunes. 376p. (Rus. & Port.). 1976. 4.95 (ISBN 0-686-92577-7, M-9062). French & Eur.

Dicionario de ciencia. E. B. Uvarov et al. (Port.). Esc.250.00. Pub Euro Am.

Dicionario de Direito do Trabalho. Christovao P. Malta. LC 76-452001. 535p. (Port.). 1975. Cr.$115.00. Rio Grafica.

Dicionario de Eisica-Illustrado. (Illus., Port.). Cr.$770.00. Edit Atica.

Dicionario de Expressoes Idiomaticas da Lingua Inglesa. B. B. Fraenkel. 136p. (Port. & Eng.). 5.00. Imported Bks.

Dicionario de Expressoes Idiomaticas Ingles-Portugues. Dauster C. Almeida. LC 80-109558. 198p. (Eng. & Port.). 1979. Cr.$230.00. Auer.

Dicionario de Frances-Portugues. (Colecca "Escolares"). (Port. & Fr.). Esc.350.00. Porto Ed.

Dicionario de Frances-Portugues. (Collecca "Estudantes"). (Port. & Fr.). Esc.370.00. Porto Ed.

Dicionario de Frances-Portugues: Com Transcicao Fonetica. 3rd ed. Jose De Sousa Vieira. (Port. & Fr.). Esc.65.00. Porto Ed.

Dicionario de Geografia do Brasil. 544p. (Port.). 23.00. Imported Bks.

Dicionario de Historia do Brasil. 618p. (Port.). 1973. 25.00. Imported Bks.

Dicionario de Ingles Coloquial. Roy H. Copperud. (Eng.). write for info. Difel Editorial, S. A.

Dicionario De Ingles-Portugues. Armando De Morais. 1966. 16.00x (ISBN 0-686-19950-2). Intl Learn Syst.

Dicionario de Ingles-Portugues. (Colecca "Escolares"). (Port. & Eng.). Esc.350.00. Porto Ed.

Dicionario de Ingles-Portugues. (Colecca "Estudantes"). (Port. & Eng.). Esc.200.00. Porto Ed.

Dicionario de Ingles-Portugues "Editora". Armando De Morais. 1490p. (Port. & Eng.). 17.50. Porto Editora.

Dicionario de Ingles-Portugues "Escolares". 976p. (Port. & Eng.). 1976. 16.00. Porto Editora.

Dicionario de Plantas Oteis do Brasil. Eric P. Danger. (Port.). Cr.$2.300.00. Difel Difusao.

Dicionario de Portugues-Alemao. (Colecca "Estudantes"). (Port. & Ger.). Esc.200.00. Porto Ed.

Dicionario de Portugues-Espanol. Julio Martinez Almoyna. 1332p. (Port. & Span.). 18.00. Porto Editora.

Dicionario de Portugues-Ingles. (Colecca "Escolares"). (Port. & Eng.). Esc.500.00. Porto Ed.

Dicionario de Portugues-Ingles. (Port. & Eng.). Esc.200.00. Porto Ed.

Dicionario de Sinonimos. Tertulia Edipica. LC 80-114023. 1125p. (Port.). 1977. write for info. Porto Editora.

Dicionario de Sinonimos e Antonimos da Lingua Portuguesa. F. Fernandes & C. P. Luft. 870p. (Port.). 1980. 39.95 (ISBN 0-686-92539-4, M-9321). French & Eur.

Dicionario de termos tecnicos Ingles-Portugues, 2 vols. rev. ed. Eugenio Furstenau. (Illus.). 1157p. (Port. & Eng.). 1974. Cr.$48.00. Editora Globo.

Dicionario de termos tecnicos Ingles-Portugues, Portugues-Ingles. B. Fraenkel. 195p. (Port. & Eng.). 1970. pap. 11.00. Imported Bks.

Dicionario do Brasil Central. B. W. Ortencio. (Port.). Cr.$5000.00. Edit Atica.

Dicionario Escolar de Quimica. Horacio Macedo. (Port.). Cr.$1450.00. Edit Atica.

Dicionario Espanhol-Portugues & Portugues-Espanhol, 2 vols. 5th ed. Idel Becker. LC 76-480630. 471p. (Port. & Span.). 1976. Cr.$70.00. Liv Nobel.

Dicionario Frances-Portugues de Locucoes. Aluizio Mendes Campos. (Fr. & Port.). Cr.$2000.00. Edit Atica.

Dicionario Frances-Portugues, Portugues-Frances. 27th ed. S. Burtin Vinholes et al. LC 78-379871. 836p. (Fr. & Port.). 1975. write for info. Editora Globo.

Dicionario Frances-Portuques. Difel. (Fr. & Port.). write for info. Difel Editorial, S. A.

Dicionario Ingles-Portugues. H. Aliandro. 402p. (Eng. & Port.). 1980. pap. 8.95 (ISBN 0-686-97638-X, M-9215). French & Eur.

Dicionario Ingles-Portugues. (Dicionarios Academicos). 1974. 6.50x (ISBN 0-686-19951-0). Intl Learn Syst.

Dicionario Ingles-Portugues de Economia. F. N. Santos. (Eng. & Port.). Esc.450.00. Pub Euro Am.

Dicionario Juridico Brasileiro: Contendo Termos, Expressoes Idiomaticas & Brocardos Usuais em Direito. 3rd ed. Yara M. Leite. LC 77-570484. 223p. (Port.). 1976. Cr.$70.00. Saraiva SA.

Dicionario Latino-Portugues. Francisco Torrinha. (Port. & Lat.). Esc.230.00. Porto Ed.

Dicionario Melhoramentos da lingua Portuguesa. 2nd ed. 1035p. (Port.). 1977. 22.00. Imported Bks.

Dicionario Metalurgico Ingles-Portugues, Portugues-Ingles. James L. Taylor. 620p. (Port. & Eng.). pap. 41.00. Imported Bks.

Dicionario Portuges-Ingles. (Dicionarios Academicos). 1975. 6.50x (ISBN 0-686-19952-9). Intl Learn Syst.

Dicionario Portugues-Ingles. H. Aliandro. 311p. (Port. & Eng.). 1980. pap. 8.95 (ISBN 0-686-97641-X, M-9216). French & Eur.

Dicionario Portugues-Ingles. (Dicionarios Escolares). (Port. & Eng.). 1973. 19.50x (ISBN 0-686-19953-7). Intl Learn Syst.

Dicionario pratico ilustrado. (Illus.). 2026p. (Port.). Esc.46.00. Lello & Irmao.

Dicionario Professional de Relacoes Publicas & Comunicacao & Glossario. Candido T. Andrade. LC 79-341351. 134p. (Port.). 1978. Cr.$95.00. Saraiva SA.

Dicionario Tecnico Contabil: Portugues-Ingles, Ingles-Portugues. M. Altman. 126p. (Port. & Eng.). 1980. pap. 14.95 (ISBN 0-686-97637-1, M-9355). French & Eur.

Dicionario Tecnico Industrial. Edson Bini. LC 78-105852. 942p. (Eng. & Portuguese.). 1978. Cr.$360.00. Hemus-Livraria.

Dicionario Tecnico Ingles-Portugues. Joaquim A. Martins. (Eng. & Port.). Esc.570.00. Pub Euro Am.

Dicionarios de Linguistica. 3rd ed. Zelio dos Santos Jota. LC 76-461651. 353p. (Port.). 1976. Cr.$90.00. Prensa Acad.

Dickens Concordance. Mary Williams. LC 74-31478. 1907. lib. bdg. 12.50 (ISBN 0-8414-9373-1). Folcroft.

Dictamenes Juridicos. Luis Diez-Picazo. 480p. (Span.). 2000.00 ptas (ISBN 8-47398-126-X). Civitas.

Diction Harry's Magical, Marvelous, Motivational Dictionary Kit. Elaine Prizzi & Jeanne Hoffman. (gr. 3-6). 1982. pap. 9.95 (ISBN 0-8224-2252-2). Pitman Learning.

Dictionaire Des Termes Economiques et Commerciaux: Francais-Arabe. Mustapha Henni. (Fr. & Arabic.). 18.00x (ISBN 0-86685-109-7). Intl Bk Ctr.

Dictionaire Detaille des Noms de Vetements Chez Les Arabes. R. Dozy. (Arabic & Fr.). 20.00x. Intl Bk Ctr.

Dictionaire Francais-Anglais d'electro-technique et d'electronique. Piraux. (Fr.). 32.50 (ISBN 0-685-36687-1). French & Eur.

Dictionaire Francais-Arabe. Louis Saisse. (Fr. & Arabic.). 1980. pap. 8.95x (ISBN 0-86685-112-7). Intl Bk Ctr.

Dictionaire Juridique Francais-Anglais, Anglais-Francais, 2 vols. in 1. Quemner. (Fr. & Eng.). 75.00 (ISBN 0-685-36688-X). French & Eur.

Dictionaire Technique Francais-Espagnol. 2nd ed. Guy Malgorn. 544p. (Fr.-Eng.). 1974. 42.50 (ISBN 0-686-57028-6, M-6387). French & Eur.

Dictionanaire Francais-Breton. (Fr. - Bret.). 1979. 15.00 (ISBN 0-686-56718-8, M-6141). French & Eur.

Dictionar Analogic si de Sinonime al Limbii Romane. Ed. by M. Buca. LC 79-339807. 479p. (Romanian.). 1978. 27.00 lei. Editura Stiintifica.

Dictionar Cronologie de Medicina si Farmacie. Gheorghe Bratescu. LC 75-405051. 366p. (Romanian.). 1975. 18.50 lei. Editura Stiintifica.

Dictionar de Astronomie Astronautica. Calin Popovici. LC 77-567521. 439p. (Romanian.). 1977. 28.00 lei. Editura Stiintifica.

Dictionar de Buzunar Roman-Rus. 2nd ed. Victor Vascenco. LC 75-410353. 443p. (Romanian & Rus.). 1975. write for info. Editura Stiintifica.

Dictionar de Chimie si Inginerie Chimica Rus-Roman. Dumitru Turtoi et al. LC 79-363446. 654p. (Rus. & Romanian.). 1978. 36.00 lei. Editura Stiintifica.

Dictionar de Cuvinte Calatoare. Alexandru Graur. LC 79-376455. 232p. (Romanian.). 1978. 8.75 lei. Albatros.

Dictionar de Electrotehnica. Mihai Condruc. LC 80-490952. 868p. (Fr. & Romanian.). 1979. 49.00 lei. Editura Stiintifica.

Dictionar de Electrotehnica. Friedrich Schattner. LC 75-407648. 700p. (Ger. & Romanian.). 1975. 39.00 lei. Editura Stiintifica.

Dictionar de Electrotehnica. Friedrich Schattner. LC 79-386549. 815p. (Ger. & Romanian.). 1979. 48.00 lei. Editura Stiintifica.

Dictionar de Electrotehnik. Mihai Condruc. LC 76-467628. 841p. (Fr., & Romanian.). 1976. 48.00 lei. Editura Stiintifica.

Dictionar de Etnologie. Romulus Vulcanescu. LC 80-475520. 436p. (Romanian.). 1979. 19.50 lei. Albatros.

Dictionar de Jazz. Mihai Berindei. LC 78-353033. (Illus.). 298p. (Romanian.). 1976. 23.50 lei. Editura Stiintifica.

Dictionar de Metalurgie Englez-Roman. M. Breaban. LC 76-511139. 314p. (Eng. & Romanian.). 1975. 20.50 lei. Editura Stiintifica.

Dictionar de Metalurgie Francez-Roman. M. L. Breaban. LC 77-573734. 375p. (Fr. & Romanian.). 1977. 24.50 lei. Editura Stiintifica.

Dictionar de Muzica. Iosif Sava & Luminita Vartolomei. LC 79-388120. 225p. (Romanian.). 1979. 18.50 lei. Editura Stiintifica.

Dictionar de psihologie. Paul Popescu-Neveanu. LC 78-396355. 783p. (Romanian.). 1978. 30.00 lei. Albatros.

Dictionar de Rime. Mihail Eminescu. Ed. by Marin Bucur & Victoria A. Tausan. LC 76-485403. 709p. (Romanian.). 1976. 19.00 lei. Albatros.

Dictionar de Stinta Solului. Ana Conea. LC 78-362360. 671p. (Romanian.). 1977. 34.00 lei. Editura Stiintifica.

Dictionar Elementar de Stiinte. Marinca Marcu. LC 79-367925. 334p. (Romanian.). 1978. 16.00 lei. Editura Stiintifica.

Dictionar englez-roman. Irina Panovf. LC 79-344523. 422p. (Eng. & Romanian.). 1978. 16.50 lei. Editura Stiintificia.

Dictionar Francez-Roman: Pentru uzul Elevilor. 2nd ed. Marcel Saras. LC 77-457298. 413p. (Romanian & Fr.). 1976. 17.00 lei. Editura Stiintifica.

Dictionar Frazeologic German-Roman. LC 75-540143. 538p. (Ger. & Romanian.). 1975. 18.00 lei. Editura Stiintifica.

Dictionar Frazeologic Italian-Roman. Mariana Stanciulescu-Cuza. LC 75-406132. 363p. (Romanian & Ital.). 1975. 13.50 lei. Editura Stiintifica.

Dictionar Grec-Roman. Lambros Petinis. LC 77-481194. 439p. (Gr. & Romanian.). 1976. 19.00 lei. Editura Stiintifica.

Dictionar Juridic Penal. George Antoniu et al. LC 76-471534. 286p. (Romanian.). 1976. 21.00 lei. Editura Stiintifica.

Dictionar Poliglot. Ernest M. Lates et al. LC 79-393899. xviii, 827p. (Eng., Romanian, Ger., Fr. & Rus.). 1979. 91.00 lei. Editura Stiintifica.

Dictionar Poliglot de Geodezie: Fotogrammetrie si Cartografie. Mihail Albota. LC 76-477531. xv, 325p. (Eng., Ger., Fr., Rus. & Romanian.). 1976. 41.00 lei. Editura Stiintifica.

Dictionar Poliglot de Industrie Alimentara. Mihai Papa-Sotir. LC 78-344895. xiv, 619p. (Eng., Romanian, Ger., Fr. & Rus.). 1977. 56.00 lei. Editura Stiintifica.

Dictionar Poliglot de Matematica, Mecanica si Astronomie. Stefan Gheorghita. LC 78-387413. xvi, 664p. (Eng., Rus., Ger., Fr. & Romanian.). 1978. 67.00 lei. Editura Stiintifica.

Dictionar Portrativ Roman-Slovac, Slovac-Roman. 2nd ed. Milota Bagonova-Sidlova. LC 77-456239. 1016p. (Romanian & Slovak.). 1976. 32.50 Kcs. SNTC.

Dictionar Practic de Agronomie. Alexe. S. Potlog. LC 79-381952. 308p. (Romanian.). 1979. 24.50 lei. Editura Stiintifica.

Dictionar Roman-German: Pentru uzul Elevilor. Jean Livescu & Emilia Savin. LC 77-464118. 493p. (Ger. & Romanian.). 1976. 19.00 lei. Editura Stiintifica.

Dictionar Roman-Grec. Socratis Cotolulis. LC 76-515769. 534p. (Romanian & Gr.). 1975. 22.50 lei. Editura Stiintifica.

Dictionar Roman-Italian: Pentru uzul Elevilor. Doina Condrea-Derer. LC 79-353106. 364p. (Romanian & Ital.). 1978. 17.50 lei. Editura Stiintifica.

Dictionar Roman-Spaniol: Pentru uzul Elevilor. Micaela Ghitescu. LC 76-481301. 414p. (Romanian & Span.). 1976. 18.00 lei. Editura Stiintifica.

Dictionar Roman-Turc. Mitica Grecu et al. LC 77-574063. 353p. (Romanian & Turkish.). 1977. 16.00 lei. Editura Stiintifica.

Dictionar Roman-Vietnamez. Elena Stoicovici et al. LC 77-483746. iv, 344p. (Romanian & Vietnamese.). 1976. 10.00 lei. Tipografia.

Dictionar-Rus-Roman: Pentru uzual Elevilor. Eugen P. Noveannu. LC 77-479078. 498p. (Romanian & Rus.). 1976. 20.00 lei. Editura Stiintifica.

Dictionar Scolar, 4 vols. Dumitru Hincu. LC 77-454213. 638p. (Romanian.). 1976. 20.40 lei. Editura Didactica.

Dictionar Spaniol-Roman: Pentru uzul Elevilor. Micaela Ghitescu. LC 76-468723. 391p. (Romanian & Span.). 1976. 17.00 lei. Editura Stiintifica.

Dictionar Tecnic Rus-Roman. xii, 1267p. (Romanian & Rus.). 1975. 135.00 lei. Editura Stiintifica.

Dictionar Tehnic Auto de Buzunar in Sapte Limbi. Petre Cristea. LC 76-503037. 441p. (Eng., Romanian, Ger., Fr., Ital., Span. & Rus.). 1975. 21.00 lei. Editura Stiintifica.

Dictionar Tehnic de Radio si Televiziune. Nicolae Stancin. LC 76-506602. 480p. (Eng. & Romanian.). 1976. 28.00 lei. Editura Stiintifica.

Dictionar Tehnic Poliglot. Editura Tehnica. 1233p. 1983. Repr. of 1967 ed. text ed. 98.50x (ISBN 0-8290-0987-6). Irvington.

Dictionar Tehnic Polon-Roman si Roman-Polon. Friedrich Schattner. LC 77-465384. 271p. (Pol. & Romanian.). 1976. 53.00 lei. Wydawnictwa Naukowo.

Dictionar Turc-Roman. A. Baubec et al. LC 80-480771. 377p. (Turkish, & Romanian.). 1979. write for info. lei. Editura Stiintifica.

Dictionar Turistic International: Edition Roumaine. Academie Internationale du Tourisme. (Romanian.). 80.00 F. Acad Intl Tour.

Dictionarie of the French & English Tongues. Randle Cotgrave. LC 77-171741. (English Experience Ser.: No. 367). 992p. (Fr. & Eng.). 1971. Repr. of 1611 ed. 105.00 (ISBN 90-221-0367-6). Walter J Johnson.

Dictionaries, Vols. II-III. (J). 1980-81. 14.00. Dict Soc NA.

Dictionaries, Vol. 1. 164p. (J). 1979. 9.00. Dict Soc NA.

Dictionaries & Their Users. Ed. by R. R. Hartmann. (Papers from the 1978 Seminar on Lexicography). 1979. pap. 20.00 (ISBN 0-686-46740-X). Heinman.

Dictionaries & Vocabularies Nineteen Sixty-Six to Nineteen Seventy-Seven. 170p. 1978. pap. 12.50 (ISBN 0-686-79528-8, F2185, FAO). Unipub.

Dictionaries, Encyclopedias, & Other Word-Related Books, 3 vols. 3rd ed. Ed. by Annie M. Brewer. LC 81-20247. 1982. Vol. 1: English. 110.00x (ISBN 0-8103-1191-7); Vol. 2: Polyglot. 160.00x (ISBN 0-8103-1192-5); Vol. 3: Foreign. 160.00x (ISBN 0-8103-1193-3). Gale.

Dictionaries of English & Foreign Languages. 2nd ed. R. L. Collison. 1971. 20.50x (ISBN 0-02-843110-3). Hafner.

Dictionaries of John de Garlande. Tr. by Barbara B. Rubin from Latin. 98p. 1981. 8.50x (ISBN 0-87291-155-1). Coronado Pr.

Dictionario Basico: Primary Dictionary. 96p. 1983. pap. 2.25 (ISBN 0-515-07390-3). Jove Pubns.

Dictionario de Portugues-Frances. (Coleccaao "Estudantes"). (Port. & Fr.). Esc.200.00. Porto Ed.

Dictionario Italiano Portugues. Joao Amendola. Ed. by Macim Behar & Mario Moretti. LC 76-464505. 1037p. (Ital. & Port.). 1976. Cr.$150.00. Hemus-Livraria.

Dictionariolum Puerorum Tribus Linguis: Lat., Ang. & Gall. Conscriptum. Robert Estienne. LC 72-194. (English Experience Ser.: No. 351). 616p. (Lat., Eng. & Fr.). 1971. Repr. of 1552 ed. 76.00 (ISBN 90-221-0351-X). Walter J Johnson.

Dictionarium Historicum, Geographicum, Poeticum. Charles Stephanus. LC 75-27859. (Renaissance & the Gods Ser.: Vol. 16). (Illus.). 1976. Repr. of 1596 ed. lib. bdg. 80.00 (ISBN 0-8240-2065-0). Garland Pub.

Dictionarium Linguae Thai Slve Slamensis Interpretatione Latina, Gallica & Anglica. Jean-Baptiste Pallegoix. 902p. (Lat., Fr. & Eng.). 1972. 24.00. Gregg.

Dictionarium Musica, Being a Complete Dictionary, or, Treasury of Music. John Hoyle. (Monuments of Music & Music Literature in Facsimile: Series II, Vol. 83). 1977. Repr. of 1770 ed. 27.50x (ISBN 0-8450-2283-0). Broude.

Dictionarium Tetraglotten Seu Voces Latinae Omnes, et Graecae Eis Respondentes, Cum Gallica & Teutonica (Quam Passim Flandricam Vocant) Earum Interpretatione: Dictionarum Tetraglotten A.D. MDLXII Ed, 2 vols. (Monumenta Lexicographica Neerlandica Ser.: No. 2). (Fr. , Lat. & Ger.). 1972. 120.00x (ISBN 90-2797-063-7). Mouton.

Dictionarium Teutonicolatinum. Cornelis Kiel. LC 76-459868. xii, 246p. (Lat.). 1975. DM.68.00 (ISBN 3-487-05227-X). Olms Verlag.

Dictionary. Brooke M. Beebe & Ruth Y. Rosenblatt. LC 77-730283. (Illus.). (gr. 3-5). 1977. pap. text ed. 125.00 (ISBN 0-89290-121-7, A151-SAR). Soc for Visual.

Dictionary. Dale McMasters. (Language Arts Ser.). 24p. (gr. 6 up). 1980. wkbk. 5.00 (ISBN 0-8209-0308-6, D-1). ESP.

Dictionary. Marie-Jose Shaw. (Sound Filmstrip Kits Ser.). (gr. 3-6). 1981. tchrs ed. 24.00 (ISBN 0-8209-0441-4, FCW-18). ESP.

Dictionary. 4th ed. Tom Wallace. LC 79-90362. 30p. 1980. pap. 7.50 ref. (ISBN 0-935406-00-X). Am Prod & Inventory.

Dictionary & Auction Catalogues of the Library of the American Numismatic Society, New York, 7 Vols. American Numismatic Society. 1962. Set. lib. bdg. write for info. (ISBN 0-685-11673-5, Hall Library); lib. bdg. 530.00 dictionary catalog, 6 vols. (ISBN 0-8161-0630-4); lib. bdg. 90.00 auction catalog, 1 vol. (ISBN 0-8161-0102-7). G K Hall.

Dictionary & Auction Catalogues of the Library of the American Numismatic Society: First Supplement 1962-67. American Numismatic Society, New York. 1967. lib. bdg. 105.00 (ISBN 0-8161-0788-2, Hall Library). G K Hall.

Dictionary & Auction Catalogues of the Library of the American Numismatic Society, Second Supplement. American Numismatic Society, New York. 1973. lib. bdg. 105.00 (ISBN 0-8161-1058-1, Hall Library). G K Hall.

Dictionary & Auction Catalogues of the Library of the American Numismatic Society: Third Supplement. 1978. lib. bdg. 195.00 (ISBN 0-8161-0247-3, Hall Library). G K Hall.

Dictionary & Glossary of the Koran. John Penrice. (Arabic.). 1982. text ed. 18.95x (ISBN 0-7007-0001-3, Pub. by Curzon Pr England). Apt Bks.

Dictionary & Glossary of the Koran. John Penrice. (Arabic & Eng.). 20.00x (ISBN 0-86685-088-0). Intl Bk Ctr.

Dictionary & Glossary of the Koran. John Penrice. 166p. (Arabic & Eng.). 1968. 20.00 (088-0). Intl Bk Ctr.

Dictionary & Glossary of the Koran, with Copious Grammatical References & Explanations. John Penrice. LC 70-90039. (Arabic.). 1969. Repr. of 1873 ed. 17.00x (ISBN 0-8196-0252-3). Biblo.

Dictionary & Glossary of the Koran with Grammatical References & Explanations. John Penrice. 1980. lib. bdg. 55.00 (ISBN 0-8490-3123-0). Gordon Pr.

Dictionary & Price Guide to Kitchenware Collectibles. Louise K. Lantz. (Illus.). 160p. 1981. pap. 6.95 (ISBN 0-686-32593-1). Everybodys Pr.

Dictionary & Reference Guide for Respiratory Therapy. J. Owen Krasowski. 1977. pap. 15.50 (ISBN 0-8151-5169-1). Year Bk Med.

Dictionary & Thesaurus of the Hebrew Language, 8 Vols. Ed. by Eliezer Ben-Yehuda. Set. 150.00 (ISBN 0-498-07038-7, Yoseloff); lea. bd. set o.p. 250.00 (ISBN 0-498-08915-0). A S Barnes.

Dictionary Arabic-Chinese. 1505p. (Arabic & Chinese.). 1978. 45.00 (ISBN 0-686-92338-3, M-9288). French & Eur.

Dictionary Catalog & Shelf List of the Spencer Collection of Illustrated Books & Manuscripts & Fine Bindings, 2 vols. New York Public Library, Research Libraries. 1970. Set. lib. bdg. 190.00 (ISBN 0-8161-0862-5, Hall Library). G K Hall.

Dictionary Catalog of Jewish Collection, 14 Vols. New York Public Library, Research Libraries. 1960. Set. 1190.00 (ISBN 0-8161-0409-3, Pub. by Hall Library). G K Hall.

Dictionary Catalog of Materials on New York City. Research Libraries of the New York Public Library. 1977. lib. bdg. 285.00 (ISBN 0-8161-0079-9, Hall Library). G K Hall.

Dictionary Catalog of Printed Books, 38 Vols. Mitchell Library, the Library of New South Wales. (Sydney, Australia) 1968. Set. lib. bdg. 3590.00 (ISBN 0-8161-0790-4, Hall Library); lib. bdg. 130.00 1st suppl. (ISBN 0-8161-0848-X). G K Hall.

Dictionary Catalog of the Albert A. & Henry W. Berg Collection of English & American Literature, First Supplement. New York Public Library, Research Libraries. 1975. lib. bdg. 105.00 (ISBN 0-8161-0014-4, Hall Library). G K Hall.

Dictionary Catalog of the American Indian Collection. Huntington Free Library & Reading Room. 1977. lib. bdg. 380.00 (ISBN 0-8161-0065-9, Hall Library). G K Hall.

Dictionary Catalog of the Applied Life Studies Library, First Supplement, 2 vols. 1982. Set. lib. bdg. 235.00 (ISBN 0-8161-0390-9, Hall Library). G K Hall.

Dictionary Catalog of the Art & Architecture Division, Supplement 1974. Research Libraries of the New York Public Library. 1976. lib. bdg. 80.00 (ISBN 0-8161-0061-6, Hall Library). G K Hall.

Dictionary Catalog of the Art & Architecture Division, The Research Libraries of The New York Public Library, 30 vols. New York Public Library Research Libraries. 1975. Set. lib. bdg. 2950.00 (ISBN 0-8161-1157-X, Hall Library). G K Hall.

Dictionary Catalog of the Arthur B. Spingarn Collection of Negro Authors, 2 vols. Howard University Library, Washington, D.C. 1970. lib. bdg. 190.00 (ISBN 0-8161-0872-2, Hall Library). G K Hall.

Dictionary Catalog of the Columbia University Law Library, 28 Vols. Columbia University Law Library, New York. 1969. Set. lib. bdg. 2750.00 (ISBN 0-8161-0800-5, Hall Library). G K Hall.

Dictionary Catalog of the Columbia University Law Library, First Supplement, 7 vols. Columbia University Law Library, New York. 1973. Set. lib. bdg. 900.00 (ISBN 0-8161-0802-1, Hall Library). G K Hall.

Dictionary Catalog of the Dance Collection, Performing Arts Research Center, 10 vols. New York Public Library, Research Libraries. 1974. Set. lib. bdg. 820.00 (ISBN 0-8161-1124-3, Hall Library). G K Hall.

Dictionary Catalog of the Department Library, 37 Vols. U. S. Department of the Interior, Washington, D. C. 1967. Set. 3515.00 (ISBN 0-8161-0715-7, Hall Library). G K Hall.

Dictionary Catalog of the Department Library, Fourth Suppl. 8 vols. U. S. Department of the Interior Washington D.C. 1975. Set. lib. bdg. 790.00 (ISBN 0-8161-0016-0, Hall Library). G K Hall.

Dictionary Catalog of the Department Library, Third Sup, 8 Vols., 4th Supp. U.S. Department of the Interior, Washington D.C. 1973. Set. lib. bdg. 420.00 (ISBN 0-8161-1054-9, Hall Library); lib. bdg. 790.00 1975 (ISBN 0-8161-0016-0). G K Hall.

Dictionary Catalog of the Edward E. Ayer Collection of Americana & American Indians, First Supplement, 3 vol. Newberry Library - Chicago. 1970. Set. lib. bdg. 315.00 (ISBN 0-8161-0810-2, Hall Library). G K Hall.

Dictionary Catalog of the Edward E. Ayer Collection of Americana & American Indians, 16 Vols. Newberry Library - Chicago. 1961. Set. 1120.00 (ISBN 0-8161-0586-3, Hall Library). G K Hall.

Dictionary Catalog of the G. Robert Vincent Library. Michigan State University,(East Lansing) 1975. 75.00 (ISBN 0-8161-1149-9, Hall Library). G K Hall.

Dictionary Catalog of the Giannini Foundation of Agricultural Economics Library, 12 vols. University of California - Berkeley. 1971. 1140.00 (ISBN 0-8161-0908-7, Hall Library). G K Hall.

Dictionary Catalog of the Harris Collection of American Poetry & Plays, Brown University, 13 vols. Brown University. 1972. Set. lib. bdg. 1620.00 (ISBN 0-8161-0974-5, Hall Library). G K Hall.

Dictionary Catalog of the Henry W. & Albert A. Berg Collection of English & American Literature, 5 Vols. New York Public Library, Research Libraries. 1969. Set. lib. bdg. 465.00 (ISBN 0-8161-0870-6, Hall Library). G K Hall.

Dictionary Catalog of the History of the Americas Collection, 28 Vols. New York Public Library, Research Libraries. 1961. Set. lib. bdg. 2200.00 (ISBN 0-8161-0540-5, Hall Library). G K Hall.

Dictionary Catalog of the History of the Americas Collection, First Supplement, 9 vols. New York Public Library, Research Libraries. 1974. Set. lib. bdg. 945.00 (ISBN 0-8161-0771-8, Hall Library). G K Hall.

Dictionary Catalog of the J. Lloyd Eaton Collection of Science Fiction & Fantasy Literature, 3 vols. 1982. Set. lib. bdg. 290.00 (ISBN 0-8161-0379-8, Hall Library). G K Hall.

Dictionary Catalog of the Jesse E. Moorland Collection of Negro Life & History, 9 vols. Howard University Library, Washington, D.C. 1970. Set. lib. bdg. 855.00 (ISBN 0-8161-0871-4, Hall Library). G K Hall.

Dictionary Catalog of the Jesse E. Moorland Collection of Negro Life & History, First Supplement, 3 vols. Howard University Library, Washington, D.C. 1976. lib. bdg. 350.00 (ISBN 0-8161-0944-3, Hall Library). G K Hall.

Dictionary Catalog of the Jewish Collection, First Supplement, 8 vols. New York Public Library, Research Libraries. 5424p. 1975. Set. lib. bdg. 840.00 (ISBN 0-8161-0773-4, Hall Library). G K Hall.

Dictionary Catalog of the Library of the Bernice P. Bishop Museum, 9 Vols. Bernice P. Bishop Museum - Honolulu. 1964. Set. lib. bdg. 660.00 (ISBN 0-8161-0679-7, Hall Library); lib. bdg. 115.00 1st suppl. 1967 (ISBN 0-8161-0722-X); lib. bdg. 40.00 2nd suppl. 1969 (ISBN 0-8161-0834-X). G K Hall.

Dictionary Catalog of the Library of the Center for Applied Linguistics, Washington, D. C, 4 vols. Center for Applied Linguistics, Washington D.C. 1974. Set. lib. bdg. 355.00 (ISBN 0-8161-1114-6, Hall Library). G K Hall.

Dictionary Catalog of the Library of the Freer Gallery of Art, 6 Vols. Smithsonian Institution, Washington, D. C. 1967. Set. lib. bdg. 530.00 (ISBN 0-8161-0799-8, Hall Library). G K Hall.

Dictionary Catalog of the Library of the Massachusetts Horticultural Society, 3 Vols. Massachusetts Horticultural Society, Boston. 1963. Set. lib. bdg. 250.00 (ISBN 0-8161-0648-7, Hall Library). G K Hall.

Dictionary Catalog of the Library of the Massachusetts Horticultural Society, First Supplement. Massachusetts Horticultural Society, Boston. 1972. lib. bdg. 105.00 (ISBN 0-8161-1038-7, Hall Library). G K Hall.

Dictionary Catalog of the Library of the Mariners Museum, 9 Vols. Mariners Museum Library - Newport News - Virginia. 1964. Set. lib. bdg. 855.00 (ISBN 0-8161-0674-6, Hall Library). G K Hall.

Dictionary Catalog of the Library of the Pontifical Institute of Mediaeval Studies: First Supplement. Pontifical Institute of Mediaeval Studies, Toronto. 1979. lib. bdg. 125.00 (ISBN 0-8161-1061-1, Hall Library). G K Hall.

Dictionary Catalog of the Library of the School of Library Service, 7 Vols. Columbia University. 1962. Set. lib. bdg. 665.00 (ISBN 0-8161-0634-7, Hall Library). G K Hall.

Dictionary Catalog of the Library of the School of Library Service, 1st Suppl, 4 vols. Columbia University. 1976. Set. lib. bdg. 460.00 (ISBN 0-8161-1166-9, Hall Library). G K Hall.

Dictionary Catalog of the Local History & Genealogy Division, 20 vols. New York Public Library, Research Libraries. 1974. Set. lib. bdg. 1540.00 (ISBN 0-8161-0784-X, Hall Library). G K Hall.

Dictionary Catalog of the M. C. Migel Memorial Library, 2 Vols. American Foundation for the Blind (New York) 1966. Set. lib. bdg. 150.00 (ISBN 0-8161-0705-X, Hall Library). G K Hall.

Dictionary Catalog of the Manuscript Division, 2 Vols. New York Public Library, Research Libraries. 1967. Set. lib. bdg. 150.00 (ISBN 0-8161-0750-5, Hall Library). G K Hall.

Dictionary Catalog of the Map Division, 10 vols. New York Public Library, Research Libraries. 1971. Set. lib. bdg. 950.00 (ISBN 0-8161-0783-1, Hall Library). G K Hall.

Dictionary Catalog of the Music Collection, Boston Public Library, 20 vols. Boston Public Library. 15617p. 1972. Set. lib. bdg. 1900.00 (ISBN 0-8161-0956-7, Hall Library); lib. bdg. 420.00 1st suppl., 4 vols. 1977 (ISBN 0-8161-1014-X). G K Hall.

Dictionary Catalog of the Music Collection, 33 Vols. New York Public Library, Research Libraries. 1964. Set. lib. bdg. 3135.00 (ISBN 0-8161-0709-2, Hall Library). G K Hall.

Dictionary Catalog of the Music Collection, Supplement II, 10 vols. New York Public Library, Research Libraries. 1973. Set. lib. bdg. 1300.00 (ISBN 0-8161-0760-2, Hall Library). G K Hall.

Dictionary Catalog of the Music Collection, Supplement 1974. The Research Libraries of the New York Public Library. 1976. lib. bdg. 80.00 (ISBN 0-8161-0059-4, Hall Library). G K Hall.

Dictionary Catalog of the National Agricultural Library, 1862-1965, 73 Vols. 56500p. Set. 1460.00x (ISBN 0-87471-001-4). Rowman.

Dictionary Catalog of the Negro Collection of the Fisk University Library, 6 vols. Fisk University Library (Nashville) 1974. Set. lib. bdg. 490.00 (ISBN 0-8161-1055-7, Hall Library). G K Hall.

Dictionary Catalog of the Oriental Collection: First Supplement, 8 vols. New York Public Library, Research Libraries. 1976. Set. lib. bdg. 955.00 (ISBN 0-8161-0775-0, Hall Library). G K Hall.

Dictionary Catalog of the Oriental Collection, 16 Vols. New York Public Library, Research Libraries. 1960. Set. lib. bdg. 1400.00 (ISBN 0-8161-0410-7, Hall Library). G K Hall.

Dictionary Catalog of the P. K. Yonge Library of Florida History, the University of Florida, Gainesville. 1977. lib. bdg. 380.00 (ISBN 0-8161-0019-5, Hall Library). G K Hall.

Dictionary Catalog of the Pacific Northwest Collection of the University of Washington Libraries, 6 vols. University of Washington at Seattle. 1972. Set. lib. bdg. 640.00 (ISBN 0-8161-0985-0, Hall Library). G K Hall.

Dictionary Catalog of the Princeton University Plasma Physics Laboratory Library, 4 vols. Princeton University. 1970. Set. lib. bdg. 380.00 (ISBN 0-8161-0881-1, Hall Library). G K Hall.

Dictionary Catalog of the Princeton University Plasma Physics Laboratory Library, First Supplement. Princeton University. 1973. lib. bdg. 150.00 (ISBN 0-8161-1032-8, Hall Library). G K Hall.

Dictionary Catalog of the Prints Division, 5 vols. New York Public Library, Research Libraries. 1975. Set. lib. bdg. 475.00 (ISBN 0-8161-1148-0, Hall Library). G K Hall.

Dictionary Catalog of the Rare Book Division: First Supplement. New York Public Library, Research Libraries. 1973. 110.00 (ISBN 0-8161-1089-1, Hall Library). G K Hall.

Dictionary Catalog of the Rare Book Division, 21 vols. New York Public Library, Research Libraries. 1971. Set. 1996.00 (ISBN 0-8161-0782-3, Hall Library). G K Hall.

Dictionary Catalog of the Rodgers & Hammerstein Archives of Recorded Sound, 15 vols. 1981. Set. lib. bdg. 1475.00 (ISBN 0-8161-0359-3, Hall Library). G K Hall.

Dictionary Catalog of the Schomburg Collection of Negro Literature & History, Supplement 1974. New York Public Library. 1976. lib. bdg. 105.00 (ISBN 0-8161-0062-4, Hall Library). G K Hall.

Dictionary Catalog of the Slavonic Collection, 44 vols. 2nd, rev. ed. New York Public Library, the Research Libraries. 1974. Set. lib. bdg. 3800.00 (ISBN 0-8161-0777-7, Hall Library). G K Hall.

Dictionary Catalog of the Stefansson Collection on the Polar Regions, 8 Vols. Dartmouth College Library, Hanover, N. H. 1967. Set. lib. bdg. 690.00 (ISBN 0-8161-0676-2, Hall Library). G K Hall.

Dictionary Catalog of the Teachers College Library, 36 vols. Columbia University. 1970. Set. lib. bdg. 3750.00 (ISBN 0-8161-0855-2, Hall Library). G K Hall.

Dictionary Catalog of the Teachers College Library, Columbia University, Third Supplement. Columbia University, Teachers College Library. 1977. lib. bdg. 1050.00 (ISBN 0-8161-0017-9, Hall Library). G K Hall.

Dictionary Catalog of the Teachers College Library, First Supplement, 5 vols. Columbia University. 1971. Set. lib. bdg. 525.00 (ISBN 0-8161-0958-3, Hall Library). G K Hall.

Dictionary Catalog of the Teachers College Library, Second Supplement, 2 vols. Columbia University. 1973. Set. lib. bdg. 260.00 (ISBN 0-8161-1039-5, Hall Library). G K Hall.

Dictionary Catalog of the United States Department of Housing & Urban Development Library & Information Division, 19 vols. U. S. Department of Housing & Urban Development, Washington, D. C. 1972. Set. lib. bdg. 1805.00 (ISBN 0-8161-1007-7, Hall Library). G K Hall.

Dictionary Catalog of the United States Department of Housing & Urban Development Library & Information Division, First Supplement, 2 vols. U. S. Department of Housing and Urban Development, Washington, D. C. 1974. Set. lib. bdg. 210.00 (ISBN 0-8161-1135-9, Hall Library). G K Hall.

Dictionary Catalog of the United States Department of Housing & Urban Development, Library & Information Division Second Suppl, 2 vols. U.S.Department of Housing & Urban Development, Washington, D.C. 1975. Set. lib. bdg. 210.00 (ISBN 0-8161-0012-8, Hall Library). G K Hall.

Dictionary Catalog of the Vivian G. Harsh Collection of Afro-American History & Literature: Chicago Public Library, 4 vols. 1978. Set. lib. bdg. 352.00 (ISBN 0-8161-0252-X, Hall Library). G K Hall.

Dictionary Catalog of the Water Resources Center Archives, 5 vols. University Of California - Berkeley. 1970. lib. bdg. 475.00 (ISBN 0-8161-0884-6, Hall Library); first suppl. (1971) 110.00 (ISBN 0-8161-0895-1); second suppl. (1972 110.00 (ISBN 0-8161-0983-4). G K Hall.

Dictionary Catalog of the Water Resources Center Archives, Fourth Suppl. University of California, Berkeley. 942p. 1975. lib. bdg. 110.00 (ISBN 0-8161-0002-0, Hall Library). G K Hall.

Dictionary Catalog of the Water Resources Center Archives: Sixth Supplement, 2 vols. University of California, Berkeley, Water Resources Center. 1978. Set. lib. bdg. 250.00 (ISBN 0-8161-0244-9, Hall Library). G K Hall.

Dictionary Catalog of the Whitney M. Young, Jr., Memorial Library of Social Work. School of Social Work, Columbia University. 1980. lib. bdg. 1275.00 (ISBN 0-8161-0307-0, Hall Library). G K Hall.

Dictionary Catalog on Deafness & the Deaf, 2 vols. Gallaudet College Library, Washington, D. C. 1970. Set. lib. bdg. 190.00 (ISBN 0-8161-0877-3, Hall Library). G K Hall.

Dictionary Catalogue. Emanuel Molho. LC 80-67876. 196p. 4.95 (ISBN 0-8288-0150-9). French & Eur.

Dictionary-Catalogue of Operas & Operettas, 2 Vols. John Towers. LC 67-25996. (Music Reprint Ser.). 1967. Repr. of 1910 ed. lib. bdg. 59.50 (ISBN 0-306-70962-7). Da Capo.

Dictionary Catalogue of the Blacker - Wood Library of Zoology & Ornithology, 9 vols. McGill University, Blacker - Wood Library of Zoology & Ornithology. 6300p. 1966. Set. lib. bdg. 810.00 (ISBN 0-8161-0719-X, Hall Library). G K Hall.

Dictionary Catalogue of the Byzantine Collection of the Dumbarton Oaks Research Library, 12 vols. Harvard University Dumbarton Oaks Research Library. 1975. Set. lib. bdg. 1335.00 (ISBN 0-8161-1150-2, Hall Library). G K Hall.

Dictionary Catalogue of the History of Printing from the John M. Wing Foundation, Second Supplement. John M. Wing Foundation, Newberry Library. 1981. lib. bdg. 435.00 (ISBN 0-8161-0326-7, Hall Library). G K Hall.

Dictionary Catalogue of the History of Printing from the John M. Wing Foundation, 6 Vols. Newberry Library - Chicago. 1961. Set. lib. bdg. 570.00 (ISBN 0-8161-0587-1, Hall Library). G K Hall.

Dictionary Catalogue of the History of Printing from the John M. Wing Foundation, First Supplement, 3 vols. Newberry Library - Chicago. 1970. Set. lib. bdg. 315.00 (ISBN 0-8161-0809-9, Hall Library). G K Hall.

Dictionary Catalogue of the Library of Sports in the Racquet & Tennis Club with Special Collections on Tennis, Lawn Tennis, & Early American Sports, 2 vols. Racquet & Tennis Club New York. 1970. Set. lib. bdg. 190.00 (ISBN 0-8161-0916-8, Hall Library). G K Hall.

Dictionary Catalogue of the Library of the Provincial Archives of British Columbia, 8 vols. Provincial Archives & Victoria, British Columbia. 1971. Set. lib. bdg. 760.00 (ISBN 0-8161-0912-5, Hall Library). G K Hall.

Dictionary Catalogue of the Library of the Pontifical Institute of Medieval Studies, 5 vols. Pontifical Institute of Medieval Studies, Ontario. 1972. Set. lib. bdg. 485.00 (ISBN 0-8161-0970-2, Hall Library). G K Hall.

Dictionary Catalogue of the London School of Hygiene & Tropical Medicine, 7 Vols. University of London. 1965. Set. lib. bdg. 590.00 (ISBN 0-8161-0703-3, Hall Library); serials catalogue. 35.00 (ISBN 0-8161-0182-5); 1st suppl. (1971) 105.00 (ISBN 0-8161-0821-8). G K Hall.

Dictionary Catalogue of the Yale Forestry Library, 12 Vols. Yale University. Henry S. Graves Memorial Library. 1962. Set. lib. bdg. 1140.00 (ISBN 0-8161-0631-2, Hall Library). G K Hall.

Dictionary Chart. 1.30 (P4). Am Classical.

Dictionary Des Terms Economiques et Commerciaux (French-English-Arabic) Mustapha Henni. (Fr., Eng. & Arabic). 25.00x (ISBN 0-86685-111-9). Intl Bk Ctr.

Dictionary Dictionary. (Eng.). 1967. 13.95 (ISBN 0-7715-1977-X). Gage.

Dictionary Dynamite. Imogene Forte & Joy MacKenzie. (Choose-A-Card Ser.). (gr. 2-6). 1979. pap. text ed. 5.95 (ISBN 0-913916-85-4, IP85-4). Incentive Pubns.

Dictionary, English & Sanskrit. 4th ed. Monier Williams. (Eng. & Sanskrit). 1976. 35.00 (ISBN 0-89684-193-6). Orient Bk Dist.

Dictionary English-Polish, Polish-English, 2 vols. K. Bullas & F. J. Whitfield. (Eng. & Pol.). 1969. Set. 38.50 (ISBN 0-685-05192-7). Adler.

Dictionary for Automotive Engineering. Jean DeCoster. 280p. 1983. 38.00 (ISBN 3-598-10430-8, Pub. by K G Saur). Shoe String.

Dictionary for Computer Languages. Hans Breuer. (Automatic Programming Information Centre Studies in Data Processing: Vol. 6). 1966. 65.00 (ISBN 0-12-132950-X). Acad Pr.

Dictionary for Marine Technology, 2 vols. Ed. by Robert Dluhy. (Ger. & Eng.). 1974. 89.75 ea.; Vol. 1. (ISBN 3-7788-1220-3); Vol. 2. (ISBN 3-7788-1221-1). Adler.

Dictionary for Physicians. 2nd ed. F. Lejeune & W. E. Bunjes. 459p. (Eng. -Ger.). 1968. 55.00 (ISBN 3-13-370502-4, M-7106). French & Eur.

Dictionary for the Glass Industry: Fachwoerterbuch fuer die Glasindustrie, 2 Pts. E. Hoffmann. (Pt, 1, Ger-Eng, Pt, 2, Eng-Ger). 1963. 26.60 (ISBN 0-387-03007-7). Springer-Verlag.

Dictionary for the Graphic Arts: German-English, English-German. (Ger. & Eng.). 1979. plastic bdg. 26.25 (ISBN 3-87641-158-0). Perfect Graphic.

Dictionary for the Graphic Arts in Eight Languages: German-English-French-Spanish-Russian-Hungarian-Polish-Slowak. (Ger. , Eng. , Fr. , Span. , Rus. , Pol. , Hungarian & Slovak). 1979. plastic bdg. 109.00 (ISBN 3-87641-192-0). Perfect Graphic.

Dictionary for Yachtsmen. Francis H. Burgess. LC 80-85494. (Illus.). 256p. 1981. 11.95 (ISBN 0-7153-6344-1). David & Charles.

Dictionary French-Slovene. A. Grad. 1402p. (Fr. & Slovene.). 1975. 35.00 (ISBN 0-686-92263-8, M-9693). French & Eur.

Dictionary Hebrew Verbs. M. Debahy. 1974. 15.00x (ISBN 0-86685-123-2). Intl Bk Ctr.

Dictionary Industrial Chemistry: English-Chinese. 81p. (Eng. & Chinese.). 1977. pap. 1.95 (ISBN 0-686-92273-5, M-9585). French & Eur.

Dictionary Johnson. James L. Clifford. 384p. 1981. pap. 6.95 (ISBN 0-07-011379-3, GB). McGraw.

Dictionary Johnson: The Middle Years of Samuel Johnson. James L. Clifford. (Illus.). 1979. 17.95 (ISBN 0-07-011378-5, GB). McGraw.

Dictionary Korean-Chinese. 1274p. (Korean & Chinese.). 1978. 30.00 (ISBN 0-686-92316-2, M-9289). French & Eur.

Dictionary-Marathi & English. 2nd ed. James T. Molesworth. (Marathi & Eng.). 1973. Repr. of 1857 ed. 295.00x (ISBN 0-8002-0173-6). Intl Pubns Serv.

Dictionary, Material Towards the Compilation of a Concise Old Church Slavonic English. T. Lysaght. 25.00. VicUni.

Dictionary of Abbreviations. Ed. by John Paxton. 384p. 1973. 15.00x (ISBN 0-87471-188-6). Rowman.

Dictionary of Abbreviations. Walter T. Rogers. LC 68-30662. 1969. Repr. of 1913 ed. 37.00x (ISBN 0-8103-3338-4). Gale.

Dictionary of Abbreviations & Symbols. E. F. Allen. 18.50 (ISBN 0-87559-167-1). Shalom.

Dictionary of Abbreviations in Information Science. 406p. 1976. 50.00x (ISBN 0-686-44776-X, Pub. by Collets). State Mutual Bk.

Dictionary of Abbreviations in Medicine & the Health Sciences. Harold H. Hughes. LC 76-8749. 336p. (Eng.). 1977. 26.95 (ISBN 0-669-00688-2). Lexington Bks.

Dictionary of Accounting. Ralph W. Estes. 176p. 1981. text ed. 16.50x (ISBN 0-262-05024-2); pap. 4.95 (ISBN 0-262-55009-1). MIT Pr.

Dictionary of Accounting & Finance. Adnan Abdeen. (Arabic & Eng.). 1980. 30.00 (275-1). Intl Bk Ctr.

Dictionary of Acoustics: English-German-French-Russian-Spanish-Polish-Madarsko-Slovene. W. Reichardt. 267p. (Eng., Ger., Fr., Rus., Span., Pol., Madarsko & Slovene.). 1978. 95.00 (ISBN 0-686-92601-3, M-9897). French & Eur.

Dictionary of Acronyms & Abbreviations in Library & Information Science. Compiled by R. Tayyeb & K. Chandna. 146p. pap. 7.00 (ISBN 0-88802-129-1). CLA.

Dictionary of Adam Mickiewicz's Language: Vol. 1, A-C. 656p. (Pol. & Eng.). 41.75 (Pub. by Ossolineum). Four Continent.

Dictionary of Adam Mickiewicz's Language: Vol. 2, D-6. 582p. (Pol. & Eng.). 1977. 41.70 (535-B, Pub. by Ossolineum). Four Continent.

Dictionary of Adam Mickiewicz's Language: Vol. 3, H-K. (Pol. & Eng.). 1977. 38.38 (Pub. by Ossolineum). Four Continent.

Dictionary of Adam Mickiewicz's Language: Vol. 5, N-O. 678p. (Pol. & Eng.). 1977. 41.70 (Pub. by Ossolineum). Four Continent.

Dictionary of Adam Mickiewicz's Language: Vol. 6, P. 620p. (Pol. & Eng.). 1977. 39.15 (Pub. by Ossolineum). Four Continent.

Dictionary of Adam Mickiewicz's Language: Vol. 7, P-R. 578p. (Pol. & Eng.). 1977. 38.35 (Pub. by Ossolineum). Four Continent.

Dictionary of Adam Mickiewicz's Language: Vol. 8, S. 626p. (Pol. & Eng.). 1977. 38.35 (Pub. by Ossolineum). Four Continent.

Dictionary of Adam Mickiewicz's Language: Vol. 9, T-W. 728p. (Pol. & Eng.). 1977. 55.00 (Pub. by Ossolineum). Four Continent.

Dictionary of Adam Mickiewicz's Language: Vol. 4, L-M, Vol. 4. 506p. (Pol. & Eng.). 1977. 41.70 (Pub. by Ossolineum). Four Continent.

Dictionary of Administration & Management. Systems Research Institute Staff. LC 78-56093. 752p. 1981. 24.95 (ISBN 0-912352-04-3). Systems Res.

Dictionary of Advertising & Marketing. Clemens Gruber. (Eng. & Ger.). 1977. pap. 15.75 (ISBN 3-1900-6312-5). Adler.

Dictionary of Advertising & Marketing Terms in Six Languages: English-Spanish-French-German-Italian-Japanese. International Chain of Industrial & Technical Advertising Agencies. Ed. by George Black. 300p. 1982. lib. bdg. cancelled (ISBN 0-930624-03-3). Marlin.

Dictionary of Advertising Terms. Ed. by Laurence Urdang. LC 76-45506. (Orig.). 1979. pap. text ed. 15.95 (ISBN 0-87251-042-5). Crain Bks.

Dictionary of Aerodynamics. 250p. (Eng. & Chinese.). 1974. pap. 5.95 (ISBN 0-686-92380-4, M-9595). French & Eur.

Dictionary of Africanisms: Contributions of Sub-Saharan Africa to the English Language. Gerard M. Dalgish. LC 82-9366. xviii, 203p. 1982. lib. bdg. 35.00 (ISBN 0-313-23585-6, DDA/). Greenwood.

Dictionary of Afro-American Slang. Clarence Major. LC 74-130863. 128p. 1970. pap. 1.95 (ISBN 0-7178-0269-8). Intl Pub Co.

Dictionary of Afro-Latin American Civilization. Benjamin Nunez. LC 79-7731. (Illus.). xxxv, 525p. 1980. lib. bdg. 45.00 (ISBN 0-313-21138-8, NAL/). Greenwood.

Dictionary of Agricultural & Allied Terminology. Ahmad Khatib. 88p. (Arabic & Eng.). pap. 10.00 (274-3). Intl Bk Ctr.

Dictionary of Agricultural & Allied Terminology. Ed. by John N. Winburne et al. 906p. 1962. 24.95x (ISBN 0-87013-067-6). Mich St U Pr.

Dictionary of Agricultural & Food Engineering. Arthur W. Farrall & James A. Basselman. LC 78-71856. 1979. 17.50 (ISBN 0-8134-2023-7, 2023). Interstate.

Dictionary of Agriculture. 3rd ed. G. Haensch. 1963. 29.80 (ISBN 0-444-40266-7). Elsevier.

Dictionary of Agriculture in German, French, Spanish, & Russian. 4th ed. G. Haensch. Ed. by Haberkamp G. De Anton. 1000p. (Ger., Fr., Span. & Rus.). 1976. 110.75 (ISBN 0-444-99849-7). Elsevier.

Dictionary of American Communal & Utopian History. Robert S. Fogarty. LC 79-7476. 320p. 1980. lib. bdg. 35.00 (ISBN 0-313-21347-X, FDA/). Greenwood.

Dictionary of American Composers. Neil Butterworth. LC 81-43331. 600p. 1983. lib. bdg. 75.00 (ISBN 0-8240-9311-9). Garland Pub.

Dictionary of American Diplomatic History. John E. Findling. LC 79-7730. (Illus.). 1980. lib. bdg. 45.00 (ISBN 0-313-22039-5, FDD/). Greenwood.

Dictionary of American English. (Gem Reference Ser.). 1980. 2.95 (ISBN 0-529-05687-9, GR 13). Collins Pubs.

Dictionary of American English on Historical Principles, 4 Vols. Ed. by William A. Craigie & James R. Hulbert. LC 36-21500. 1938-1944. Set. 250.00x (ISBN 0-226-11741-3); Vol. 1. o.s.i. (ISBN 0-226-11737-5). U of Chicago Pr.

Dictionary of American Food & Drink. John F. Mariani. 352p. 1983. 17.95 (ISBN 0-89919-199-1). Ticknor & Fields.

Dictionary of American History. rev. & enl. ed. Michael Martin & Leonard Gelber. Ed. by Leo Lieberman. 714p. 1978. 15.00x (ISBN 0-8476-6104-0). Rowman.

Dictionary of American Idioms. Ed. by M. T. Boatner et al. 1976. 14.95. Barron.

Dictionary of American Idioms. rev. ed. Maxine Boetner & John E. Gates. Ed. by Adam Makkai. LC 75-42110. 1984. 14.95 (ISBN 0-8120-5102-5); pap. 9.95 (ISBN 0-8120-0612-7). Barron.

Dictionary of American Idioms for Deaf. Ed. by M. Boatner et al. 1976. 9.95 (ISBN 0-8120-0612-7). Barron.

Dictionary of American Idioms for the Deaf. Ed. by M. T. Boatner et al. 1976. 14.95 (ISBN 0-8120-5103-3). Barron.

Dictionary of American Idioms in Chinese. Adam Makkai. Ed. by Gates & Boatner. 396p. (Chinese & Eng.). Date not set. pap. 14.95 (ISBN 0-8120-2386-2). Barron.

Dictionary of American Idioms Workbook, Vol. 2. 1984. pap. price not set (ISBN 0-8120-2515-6). Barron.

Dictionary of American Painters, Sculptors & Engravers: Enlarged. Mantle Fielding. 1974. 17.50 (ISBN 0-685-47043-1). Assoc Bk.

Dictionary of American Penology: An Introductory Guide. Vergil L. Williams. LC 77-94751. 1979. lib. bdg. 45.00x (ISBN 0-313-20327-X, WAP/). Greenwood.

Dictionary of American Politics. 2nd ed. Edward C. Smith & Arnold J. Zurcher. (Illus.). 434p. 1968. 17.50x (ISBN 0-06-480803-3). B&N Imports.

Dictionary of American Politics. 2nd ed. Edward C. Smith & Arnold J. Zurcher. LC 67-28530. (Orig., Maps). 1968. pap. 5.72i (ISBN 0-06-463261-X, EH 261, EH). B&N NY.

Dictionary of American Pop-Rock. Arnold Shaw. LC 82-50382. 440p. 1983. 19.95 (ISBN 0-02-872350-3); pap. 12.95 (ISBN 0-02-872360-0). Assoc-Mus.

Dictionary of American Slang. 2nd ed. Harold Wentworth & Stuart B. Flexner. LC 75-8644. 766p. 1975. 15.34i (ISBN 0-690-00670-5). T Y Crowell.

Dictionary of American Slang. Harold Wentworth & Stuart B. Flexner. 766p. DM.48.00 (49016). Langenscheidt.

Dictionary of American Social Change. Louis Filler. LC 82-10036. 266p. (Orig.). 1982. 16.50 (ISBN 0-89874-242-0); pap. 10.50 (ISBN 0-89874-564-0). Krieger.

Dictionary of American Social Reform. Louis Filler. LC 74-90505. Repr. of 1963 ed. lib. bdg. 26.25x (ISBN 0-8371-2137-X, FIAS). Greenwood.

Dictionary of Americanism: A Glossary of Words & Phrases, Usually Regarded As Peculiar to the United States. John R Bartlett. 1976. Repr. of 1848 ed. 69.00 (ISBN 0-403-06365-5, Regency). Scholarly.

Dictionary of Anagrams. Samuel D. Hunter. 160p. 1982. 12.95 (ISBN 0-7100-9006-4). Routledge & Kegan.

Dictionary of Anonymous & Pseudonymous Publications in the English Language: Vol. 1, 1475-1640. Halkett & Laing. Ed. by John Horden. 1980. 150.00 (ISBN 0-582-55521-3). Longman.

Dictionary of Anthropology. Roger Pearson. (Orig.). 1984. write for info. (ISBN 0-89874-510-1). Krieger.

Dictionary of Anthropology. Charles Winick. Repr. of 1956 ed. lib. bdg. 29.75x (ISBN 0-8371-2094-2, WIDA). Greenwood.

Dictionary of Anthropology. Charles Winick. (Quality Paperback: No. 131). 1977. pap. 5.95 (ISBN 0-8226-0131-1). Littlefield.

Dictionary of Antiques. 2nd ed. George Savage. (Illus.). 1978. 20.00 (ISBN 0-8317-0011-4, Mayflower Bks). Smith Pubs.

Dictionary of Aphrodisiacs. Ed. by Harry E. Wedeck. LC 61-12626. 1961. 10.00 (ISBN 0-8022-1828-8). Philos Lib.

Dictionary of Applied Energy Conservation: An Illustrated Dictionary of Terms. David Kut. (Illus.). 300p. 1983. 32.00 (ISBN 0-89397-131-6). Nichols Pub.

Dictionary of Applied Physics, 5 vols. Ed. by Richard Glazebrook. 24.00 ea. (ISBN 0-8446-1199-9). Peter Smith.

Dictionary of Arab Grammatical Terms: The Monitor. 200p. (Arabic & Eng.). 15.00 (119-4). Intl Bk Ctr.

Dictionary of Arabic Grammar, in Charts & Tables. Antoine Dahdah. (Illus., Arabic.). 1982. 30.00x (ISBN 0-86685-292-1). Intl Bk Ctr.

Dictionary of Arabic-Persian Quotes. Claud Field. (Arabic, Persian & Eng.). 18.00x (ISBN 0-86685-168-2). Intl Bk Ctr.

Dictionary of Arabic-Persian Quotes. Claud Field. 352p. (Arabic, Persian & Eng.). 18.00 (168-2). Intl Bk Ctr.

Dictionary of Arbitration & Its Terms. American Arbitration Association. LC 70-94692. 334p. 1970. lib. bdg. 21.00 (ISBN 0-379-00386-4). Oceana.

Dictionary of Archaeology. rev. ed. Bray & Trump. 1982. pap. 6.95. Penguin.

Dictionary of Archaic & Provincial Words, Obsolete Phrases, Proverbs, & Ancient Customs, from the Fourteenth Century, 2 Vols. 3rd ed. James O. Halliwell-Phillipps. LC 76-168221. Repr. of 1855 ed. Set. 35.00 (ISBN 0-404-03055-6). AMS Pr.

Dictionary of Archaic & Provincial Words, Obsolete Phrases, Proverbs, & Ancient Customs, from the Fourteenth Century, 2 vols. James O. Halliwell-Phillipps. LC 66-27837. 1968. Repr. of 1847 ed. Set. 86.00x (ISBN 0-8103-3283-3). Gale.

Dictionary of Archaic & Provincial Words, Obsolete Phrases, Proverbs, & Ancient Customs from the 14th Century, 2 Vols. 11th ed. Ed. by James O. Halliwell-Phillipps. LC 10-30948. 1971. Repr. of 1889 ed. Set. 90.00 (ISBN 0-384-21083-X). Johnson Repr.

Dictionary of Architectural Science. Henry J. Cowan. LC 73-15839. (Illus.). 354p. 1973. pap. 18.95x (ISBN 0-470-18070-6). Halsted Pr.

Dictionary of Architecture, 3 vols. Robert Meikleham. 1980. Set. lib. bdg. 500.00 (ISBN 0-8490-3122-2). Gordon Pr.

Dictionary of Architecture. Nikolaus Pevsner et al. LC 75-27325. (Illus.). 554p. 1976. 25.00 (ISBN 0-87951-040-4). Overlook Pr.

Dictionary of Architecture. Henry H. Saylor. LC 52-8260. 221p. 1952. pap. 11.95 (ISBN 0-471-75601-6). Wiley.

Dictionary of Architecture & Building, Biographical & Descriptive, 3 Vols. Russell Sturgis. LC 66-26997. (Illus.). 1966. Repr. of 1902 ed. Set. 79.00x (ISBN 0-8103-3075-X). Gale.

Dictionary of Architecture & Building, 3 vols. R. Sturgis. 300.00 (ISBN 0-8490-0032-7). Gordon Pr.

Dictionary of Architecture & Construction. Cyril M. Harris. 1975. 42.50 (ISBN 0-07-026756-1, P&RB). McGraw.

Dictionary of Architecture, Building Construction & Materials, Vol. II. Herbert Bucksch. 1137p. (Eng. & Ger.). 1976. 175.00 (ISBN 3-7625-0714-7, M-7130). French & Eur.

Dictionary of Architecture, Building Construction & Materials, Vol. I. Herbert Bucksch. 942p. (Eng. & Ger.). 1974. 175.00 (ISBN 3-7625-0357-5, M-7131). French & Eur.

Dictionary of Architecture, Building Construction & Materials, 2 vols. Herbert Bucksch. 1974-76. plastic bdg. 120.00x ea. Vol. 1, Ger.-Eng (ISBN 3-7625-0357-5). Vol. 2, Eng.-Ger (ISBN 3-7625-0714-7). Intl Pubns Serv.

Dictionary of Art Terms & Techniques. Ralph Mayer. LC 80-8854. (Illus.). 464p. 1981. pap. 6.95 (ISBN 0-06-463531-7, EH 531, EH). B&N NY.

Dictionary of Art Terms & Techniques. Ralph Mayer. 1981. 25.00x (ISBN 0-7136-1095-6, Pub. by Lewis Pubs). State Mutual Bk.

Dictionary of Art Terms & Techniques. Ralph Mayer. (Illus.). 1969. 14.37i (ISBN 0-690-23673-5). T Y Crowell.

Dictionary of Artistic Roller Skating Terms. 1.00. Roller Rink Ops.

Dictionary of Artists: London Exhibitions 1760-1893. 3rd rev. ed. Algernon Graves. 24.00 (ISBN 0-912729-04-X). Newbury Bks.

Dictionary of Artists of the English School. 2nd rev. ed. Samuel Redgrave. 12.00 (ISBN 0-912728-16-7). Newbury Bks.

Dictionary of Artists of the English School. Samuel Redgrave. 500p. 1970. Repr. of 1878 ed. 20.00 (ISBN 0-87556-249-3). Saifer.

Dictionary of Arts & Crafts. Ed. by John L. Stoutenburgh. 1956. 6.00 (ISBN 0-8022-1661-7). Philos Lib.

Dictionary of Asian Philosophies. St. Elmo Naumann, Jr. 1978. pap. 5.95 (ISBN 0-8065-0617-2). Citadel Pr.

Dictionary of Assyrian Botany. Reginald C. Thompson. LC 78-72767. (Ancient Mesopotamian Texts & Studies). (Assyrian.). Repr. of 1949 ed. 45.00 (ISBN 0-404-18221-6). AMS Pr.

Dictionary of Assyrian Chemistry & Geology. Reginald C. Thompson. LC 78-72768. (Ancient Mesopotamian Texts & Studies). (Assyrian.). Repr. of 1936 ed. 24.50 (ISBN 0-404-18222-4). AMS Pr.

Dictionary of Astrology. H. E. Wedeck. (Illus.). 288p. 1973. pap. 3.95 (ISBN 0-8065-0371-8). Citadel Pr.

Dictionary of Astrology. James Wilson. LC 79-16506. (Illus.). 1970. Repr. 15.00 (ISBN 0-87728-086-X). Weiser.

Dictionary of Astrology. James Wilson. LC 79-16506. 15.00 (Samuel Weiser Inc.). Am Fed Astrologers.

Dictionary of Astronomy. 103p. (Eng. & Chinese.). 1974. pap. 3.95 (ISBN 0-686-92284-0, M-9574). French & Eur.

Dictionary of Astronomy. Robert Maddison. 208p. E5.95 (ISBN 0-600-32996-8). Newnes Bks.

Dictionary of Astronomy. Ed. by Iain Nicolson. (Illus.). 250p. 1980. pap. 4.95 (ISBN 0-06-463524-4, EH 524). B&N NY.

Dictionary of Astronomy, Space & Atmospheric Phenomena. David F. Tver. 1979. text ed. 19.95 (ISBN 0-442-24045-7). Van Nos Reinhold.

Dictionary of Astronomy, Space & Atmospheric Phenomena. David F. Tver et al. 288p. 1982. pap. text ed. 12.95 (ISBN 0-442-28422-5). Van Nos Reinhold.

Dictionary of Audio & Hi-Fi. Howard W. Sams Editorial Staff. LC 74-79354. 1975. pap. 7.50 (ISBN 0-672-21084-3). Sams.

Dictionary of Audio Visual Terms. 1983. text ed. 24.95. Butterworth.

Dictionary of Australian Colloquialisms. G. A. Wilkes. 1978. 28.00x (ISBN 0-424-00034-2, Pub. by Sydney U Pr). Intl Schol Bk Serv.

Dictionary of Australian History. B. Murphy. 340p. 1982. 19.00 (ISBN 0-07-072946-8). McGraw.

Dictionary of Austrialian Education. J. McLaren. 1974. 12.00x (ISBN 0-7022-0956-2). U of Queensland Pr.

Dictionary of Automatic Data Processing. Habil E. Burger. 480p. 1980. 75.00x (Pub. by Collet's). State Mutual Bk.

Dictionary of Automatic Data Processing. Ing H. Burger. 480p. (Eng., Ger., Fr., Rus. & Slovak.). 1976. 80.00x (ISBN 0-569-08521-7, Pub. by Collets). State Mutual Bk.

Dictionary of Automatical Technique. Ed. by Jiri Sykora. 1023p. (Eng., Ger., Fr., Rus., Span., Pol., Madasko & Sloven.). 1975. 150.00 (ISBN 0-686-92413-4, M-9892). French & Eur.

Dictionary of Automation Techniques. Jiri Sykora. 1024p. 1980. 80.00x (Pub. by Collet's). State Mutual Bk.

Dictionary of Automation Techniques. Jiri Sykora. 1024p. 1975. 95.00x (ISBN 0-569-08528-4, Pub. by Collets). State Mutual Bk.

Dictionary of Automobile Terms. (Hebrew, Eng. , Fr. & Ger.). IL.8.00. Massada Pr.

Dictionary of Automotive Engineering. Frank Shaw. LC 78-40918. 1979. E9.00 (ISBN 0-408-00409-6). Newnes Bks.

Dictionary of Aviation. David Wragg. LC 74-75382. 286p. 1974. 9.95 (ISBN 0-8119-0236-6). Fell.

Dictionary of Aviation. David W. Wragg. 286p. 1973. 17.95x (ISBN 0-8464-0331-5). Beekman Pubs.

Dictionary of Bad Manners. London Ganning. 1982. 14.95 (ISBN 0-395-32509-9). HM.

Dictionary of Bahamian English. John A. Holm & Alison W. Shilling. LC 82-83045. 270p. 1982. 42.00 (ISBN 0-936368-03-9). Lexik Hse.

Dictionary of Ballet Terms. Leo Kersley & Janet Sinclair. (Paperbacks Ser.). 1979. pap. 5.95 (ISBN 0-306-80094-2). Da Capo.

Dictionary of Banking. F. E. Perry. 304p. 1979. text ed. 28.50x (ISBN 0-7121-0428-3, Pub. by Macdonald & Evans England). Intl Ideas.

Dictionary of Banking & Finance. Lewis E. Davids. (Littlefield, Adams Quality Paperback: No. 336). 1979. pap. 7.95 (ISBN 0-8226-0336-5). Littlefield.

Dictionary of Banking & Finance. Lewis E. Davids. 229p. 1980. Repr. of 1978 ed. 15.00x (ISBN 0-8476-6132-6). Rowman.

Dictionary of Banking & Finance. Jerry M. Rosenberg. LC 81-21961. 690p. 1982. 24.95 (ISBN 0-471-08096-9, Pub. by Wiley-Interscience). Wiley.

Dictionary of Banking & Finance. Jerry M. Rosenberg. 690p. 1983. pap. 14.95 (ISBN 0-471-88039-6, Pub. by Wiley-Interscience). Wiley.

Dictionary of Basic Words. Ed. by Day Perry & Josephine B. Wolfe. LC 73-86343. (Illus.). 640p. (gr. 2-8). 1969. PLB 19.95 (ISBN 0-516-00810-2). Childrens.

Dictionary of Battles. T. B. Harbottle. 69.95 (ISBN 0-8490-0033-5). Gordon Pr.

Dictionary of Battles. Thomas B. Harbottle. LC 66-22672. 1966. Repr. of 1905 ed. 33.00x (ISBN 0-8103-3004-0). Gale.

Dictionary of Battles, Vol. 1. Brigadier P. Young. (Illus.). 1978. 15.00 (ISBN 0-8317-2260-6, Mayflower Bks). Smith Pubs.

Dictionary of Battles, Vol. 2. Brigadier P. Young & Brigadier M. Calvert. LC 78-23518. (Illus.). 1979. 15.00 (ISBN 0-8317-2261-4, Mayflower Bks). Smith Pubs.

Dictionary of Behavioral Science. Benjamin B. Wolman. 1973. 24.50x (ISBN 0-442-29566-9). Van Nos Reinhold.

Dictionary of Behavorial Science. Ed. by Benjamin B. Wolman. 1979. pap. text ed. 12.95 (ISBN 0-442-29581-2). Van Nos Reinhold.

Dictionary of Bharata Natya. Krishna Rao. (Illus.). 100p. 1980. text ed. 15.95x (ISBN 0-86131-155-8, Pub. by Orient Longman Ltd India). Apt Bks.

Dictionary of Bharatnatya. V. S. Krishan Rao. 1981. 15.00x (ISBN 0-8364-0698-2, Orient Longman). South Asia Bks.

Dictionary of Bible Words. John Eddison. LC 79-302346. 126p. 1977. E1.95 (ISBN 0-85421-539-5). Scripture Union.

Dictionary of Biblical Theology. new ed. Ed. by Xavier Leon-Dufour. Tr. by P. Joseph Cahill from Fr. LC 73-6437. 710p. 1973. Repr. 27.50 (ISBN 0-8164-1146-8). Seabury.

Dictionary of Biochemistry. J. Stenesh. LC 75-23037. 344p. 1975. 42.50 (ISBN 0-471-82105-5, Pub. by Wiley-Interscience). Wiley.

Dictionary of Biochemistry. K. Theilman. 742p. 1980. 90.00x (ISBN 0-686-44721-2, Pub. by Collets). State Mutual Bk.

Dictionary of Biochemistry. K. Thielmann. (Ger., Eng., Fr., Rus. & Span.). 1978. pap. 36.00 (ISBN 3-87144-346-8, M-7129). French & Eur.

Dictionary of Biography. George Kurian. 560p. (Orig.). 1980. pap. 3.50 (ISBN 0-440-31889-0, LE). Dell.

Dictionary of Biology. Guenther Haensch. (Eng., Ger., Fr. & Span.). 1976. pap. 78.00 (ISBN 3-405-10950-7, M-7128). French & Eur.

Dictionary of Biology. Edwin B. Steen. LC 70-156104. (EH); pap. 5.95 (ISBN 0-06-463321-7). B&N NY.

Dictionary of Biology. Edwin B. Steen. LC 70-156104. 630p. 1971. text ed. 17.50x (ISBN 0-686-83546-8). B&N Imports.

Dictionary of Biology. Ed. by Elizabeth Tootil. LC 81-125830. (Illus.). 282p. (Eng.). 1980. E5.95. Intl Bk Ctr.

Dictionary of Biology in English, French, German & Spanish. 2nd, rev. & enl. ed. G. Haensch & G. Haberkamp De Anton. (Eng., Fr., Ger. & Span.). 1981. 106.50 (ISBN 0-444-41968-3). Elsevier.

Dictionary of Blue & White Pottery. A. W. Coysh. (Illus.). 1981. 44.50 (ISBN 0-907462-06-5). Antique Collect.

Dictionary of Book Publishing. Ulrich Stiehl. 538p. (Eng. & Ger.). 1977. text ed. 55.00x (ISBN 3-7940-4147-X, Pub. by K G Saur). Gale.

Dictionary of Botany. R. J. Little & C. E. Jones. 416p. 1980. text ed. 22.50 (ISBN 0-442-24169-0). Van Nos Reinhold.

Dictionary of Botany, 2 vols. P. Macura. 1982. Set. 213.00 (ISBN 0-686-94134-9); Vol. 1. write for info.; Vol. 2: General Terms. 110.75 (ISBN 0-444-41977-2). Elsevier.

Dictionary of Botany. George Usher. 408p. 1979. text ed. 19.00x (ISBN 0-8448-1387-7). Crane-Russak Co.

Dictionary of British & Irish Botanists & Horticulturists. 3rd ed. Ed. by Ray Desmond. 764p. 1977. write for info (ISBN 0-85066-089-0). Taylor & Francis.

Dictionary of British & Irish Botanists & Horticulturists: Including Plant Collectors & Botanical Artists. 3rd ed. Ray Desmond. 747p. 1977. 99.50x (ISBN 0-8476-1392-5). Rowman.

Dictionary of British Artists Eighteen Eighty to Nineteen Forty. Johnson & Greutyner. (Illus.). 1980. 59.50 (ISBN 0-902028-36-7). Apollo.

Dictionary of British Artists: 1880-1940. The Antique Collector's Club. 567p. 1977. 59.50 (ISBN 0-902028-36-7). Antique Collect.

Dictionary of British Book Illustrators & Caricaturists: 1800-1914. Simon Houfe. (Illus.). 520p. 1980. 62.50 (ISBN 0-902028-73-1). Antique Collect.

Dictionary of British Eighteenth Century Painters. Ellis Waterhouse. (Illus.). 415p. 1981. 79.50 (ISBN 0-902028-93-6). Antique Collect.

Dictionary of British Flower, Fruit & Still Life Painters: Vol. 2, 1850-1950. R. Burbidge. (Illus.). 1974. text ed. 30.00x (ISBN 0-85317-024-X, Pub. by A & C Black England). Humanities.

Dictionary of British Historical Painters. Frank Lewis. 70p. 1979. text ed. 30.00x (ISBN 0-85317-052-5, Pub. by A & C Black England). Humanities.

Dictionary of British History. Ed. by J. P. Kenyon. LC 82-42759. 415p. 1983. 20.00 (ISBN 0-8128-2910-7). Stein & Day.

Dictionary of British Landscape Painters: From the 16th Century to the Early 20th Century. Maurice Grant. 236p. 1976. Repr. of 1952 ed. text ed. 30.00x (ISBN 0-85317-250-1, Pub. by A & C Black England). Humanities.

Dictionary of British Landscape Painters: From the 16th to the 20th Century. Maurice H. Grant. (Illus.). 236p. 1970. 40.00x (ISBN 0-85317-250-1). Intl Pubns Serv.

Dictionary of British Marine Painters. Arnold Wilson. (Illus.). 1980. Repr. of 1967 ed. text ed. 40.00x (ISBN 0-85317-051-7, Pub. by A & C Black England). Humanities.

Dictionary of British Portraiture. Ed. by Richard Ormond & Malcolm Rogers. 1981. Vol. 3: The Victorians: Historical Figures Born Between 1800-1860. 62.50x (ISBN 0-19-520182-5); Vol. 4: The Twentieth Century: Historical Figures Born Before 1900. 62.50x (ISBN 0-19-520183-3). Oxford U Pr.

Dictionary of British Portraiture: Vol. 1, the Middle Ages to the Early Georgian; Historical Figures Born Before 1700. Richard Ormond & Malcolm Rogers. Ed. by Adriana Davies. 1979. text ed. 47.50x (ISBN 0-19-520180-9). Oxford U Pr.

Dictionary of British Portraiture: Vol. 2, the Later Georgians to the Early Victorians; Historical Figures Born Between 1700 & 1800. Richard Ormond & Malcolm Rogers. Ed. by Elaine Kilmurray. 1979. text ed. 49.50x (ISBN 0-19-520181-7). Oxford U Pr.

Dictionary of British Sporting Painters. Sydney Paviere. (Illus.). 1980. Repr. of 1965 ed. text ed. 40.00x (ISBN 0-85317-940-9, Pub. by A & C Black England). Humanities.

Dictionary of British Surnames. 2nd ed. P. H. Reaney. 1976. 42.00 (ISBN 0-7100-8106-5). Routledge & Kegan.

Dictionary of Buddhism. T. O. Ling. LC 72-37231. 244p. 1972. 7.95 (ISBN 0-684-12763-6, ScribT). Scribner.

Dictionary of Buddhism: Indian & South-East Asia. Trevor Ling. (Bagchi Indological Ser.: No. 2). 202p. 1981. text ed. 14.00x (ISBN 0-391-02587-2, Pub. by K P Bagchi India). Humanities.

Dictionary of Building. rev. ed. John S. Scott. (Reference Ser.). 392p. 1964. pap. 4.95 (ISBN 0-14-051015-X). Penguin.

Dictionary of Business & Credit Terms. Ben Berman. Ed. by James J. Andover. LC 82-14231. 208p. 1983. 19.95 (ISBN 0-934914-45-1). NACM.

Dictionary of Business & Economics. rev. & expanded ed. Christine Ammer & Dean Ammer. 1983. 29.95 (ISBN 0-02-900790-9). Free Pr.

Dictionary of Business & Economics. Christine Ammer & Dean S. Ammer. LC 76-41625. 1977. 27.95 (ISBN 0-02-900590-6). Free Pr.

Dictionary of Business & Management. Jerry M. Rosenberg. LC 78-7796. 1978. pap. 9.95 (ISBN 0-471-09885-X). Wiley.

Dictionary of Business & Management. 2nd. ed. Jerry M. Rosenberg. LC 82-24743. 631p. 1983. 29.95 (ISBN 0-471-86730-6, Pub. by Wiley-Interscience). Wiley.

Dictionary of Business & Science. 3rd ed. Compiled by David F. Tver. 632p. 1974. 22.50x (ISBN 0-87201-172-0). Gulf Pub.

Dictionary of Business, Finance, & Investment. Norman D. Moore. LC 74-29447. (Illus.). 560p. 1975. lib. bdg. 14.95x (ISBN 0-915610-00-0). Investor's Syst.

Dictionary of Business Terms. Peron. (Fr. & Eng.). 30.95 (ISBN 2-03-020609-1). Larousse.

Dictionary of Canadian Artists, 6 Vols. MacDonald. 1977. 100.00 (ISBN 0-686-43129-4). Apollo.

Dictionary of Canadian Economics. David Crane. (Eng.). 1980. Can.$pap. 18.95 (ISBN 0-88830-174-X); pap. 8.95 (ISBN 0-88830-173-1). Hurtig.

Dictionary of Canadian Economics. David Crane. LC 80-143762. ix, 372p. 1980. Can.$18.95 (ISBN 0-88830-174-X); pap. 8.95 (ISBN 0-88830-173-1). Hurtig.

Dictionary of Canadianisms. Walter S. Avis et al. 1967. Can.$19.95 (ISBN 0-7715-1970-2); 25.00 (ISBN 0-7715-1972-9). U of Toronto Pr.

Dictionary of Catch Phrases. Eric Partridge. LC 77-8750. 1979. pap. 11.95 (ISBN 0-8128-6037-3). Stein & Day.

Dictionary of Cebuano Visayan, Vols 1 & 2. John V. Wolff. 120p. 1972. 8.00 (ISBN 0-87727-087-2, DP 87). Cornell SE Asia.

Dictionary of Cement. C. Van Amerongen. 202p. (Ger. & Eng.). 1967. 44.00 (ISBN 3-7625-1171-3, M-7127). French & Eur.

Dictionary of Ceramic Science & Engineering. Loran O'Bannon. 330p. 1983. 45.00 (ISBN 0-306-41324-8, Plenum Pr). Plenum Pub.

Dictionary of Cereal Processing & Cereal Chemistry. R. Schneeweiss. (Eng., Fr., Ger. & Rus.). 1982. 121.50 (ISBN 0-444-42049-5). Elsevier.

Dictionary of Chemical Terminology. 562p. (Pol. , Ger. , Eng. , Fr. & Rus.). 1974. 16.95 (Pub. by Vyd. Naukowo-Techniczne). Four Continent.

Dictionary of Chemical Terminology. D. Kryt. (Eng., Ger., Fr., Pol. & Rus.). 1980. 83.00 (ISBN 0-444-99788-1). Elsevier.

Dictionary of Chemical Terms, 2 vols. R. Ernst. Vol. 1, Ger-Eng. 33.70 (ISBN 3-8709-7011-1); Vol. 2, Eng-Ger. 41.20 (ISBN 3-8709-7012-X). Adler.

Dictionary of Chemistry. Ed. by John Daintith. 1982. pap. 5.72i (ISBN 0-06-463559-7, EH-559). Har-Row.

Dictionary of Chemistry. Ed. by John Daintith. (Illus.). 240p. 1982. pap. 5.72i (ISBN 0-06-463559-7). B&N NY.

Dictionary of Chemistry, Vol. 1. Richard Ernst. (Eng. & Ger.). 1961. 36.00 (ISBN 3-87097-011-1, M-7124). French & Eur.

Dictionary of Chemistry, Vol. 2. Richard Ernst. (Eng. & Ger.). 1963. 44.00 (ISBN 3-87097-012-X, M-7123). French & Eur.

Dictionary of Chemistry & Chemical Engineering, 2 vols. 2nd ed. Louis DeVries & Helga Kolb. Incl. Vol. 1. German-English. 1978. 150.00x (ISBN 0-686-53141-8); Vol. 2. English-German. LC 77-138815. 150.00x (ISBN 0-89573-025-1). (Ger. & Eng.). 1979. Verlag Chemie.

Dictionary of Chemistry & Chemical Engineering, Vol. 1. Louis de Vries. (Eng. & Ger.). 1970. pap. 125.00 (ISBN 3-527-25303-3, M-7126). French & Eur.

Dictionary of Chemistry & Chemical Engineering, Vol. 2. Louis de Vries. (Eng. & Ger.). 1972. pap. 125.00 (ISBN 3-527-25358-0, M-7125). French & Eur.

Dictionary of Chemistry & Chemical Technology in Six Languages. rev. ed. Ed. by Z. Sobecka et al. 1966. 130.00 (ISBN 0-08-011600-0). Pergamon.

Dictionary of China's Rural Economy. K. Broadbent. 406p. (Chinese & Eng.). 1978. 125.00 (ISBN 0-85198-381-2, M-9712). French & Eur.

Dictionary of Chinese & Japanese Art. Hugo Munsterberg. LC 79-83856. 1981. lib. bdg. 40.00 (ISBN 0-87817-248-3). Hacker.

Dictionary of Chinese Buddhist Terms. W. E. Soothill & L. Hodous. (Chinese & Eng.). 1977. 35.00 (ISBN 0-89684-194-4, Pub. by Motilal Banarsidass India). Orient Bk Dist.

Dictionary of Chinese Buddhist Terms, with Sanskrit & English Equivalents & a Sanskrit-Pali Index. Ed. by William E. Soothill & L. Hodous. (Chinese, Sanskrit & Eng.). 1977. text ed. 50.00x (ISBN 0-8426-1030-8). Verry.

Dictionary of Chinese History. Michael Dillon. 240p. 1979. 27.50x (ISBN 0-7146-3107-8, F Cass Co). Biblio Dist.

Dictionary of Chinese Law & Government. Philip R. Bilancia. LC 73-80618. 832p. (Chinese & Eng.). 1981. 45.00x (ISBN 0-8047-0864-9). Stanford U Pr.

Dictionary of Chinook Jargon. (Shorey Indian Ser.). 42p. Repr. pap. 4.95 (ISBN 0-8466-0005-6, S5). Shorey.

Dictionary of Chontal to Spanish-English, & Spanish to Chontal. Paul Turner & Shirley Turner. LC 78-164366. (Span., Eng. & Chontal.). 1971. pap. 3.95x (ISBN 0-8165-0338-9). U of Ariz Pr.

Dictionary of Chromatography. 2nd ed. R. C. Denney. 224p. 1982. E15.00 (ISBN 0-333-31667-3). Macmillan London.

Dictionary of Chromatography. 2nd ed. Roland C. Denney. 229p. 1982. 43.95 (ISBN 0-471-87477-9, Pub. by Wiley-Interscience). Wiley.

Dictionary of Civil Engineering. 3rd ed. John S. Scott. LC 80-24419. 308p. 1982. 22.95x (ISBN 0-470-27087-X). Halsted Pr.

Dictionary of Civil Engineering & Construction Machinery & Equipment, 2 vols. 7th ed. H. Bucksch. 420p. 1979. Vol. 1, Eng.-Fr. 35.00x (ISBN 0-8002-2313-6); Vol. 2, Fr.-Eng. 45.00x (ISBN 0-8002-2314-4). Intl Pubns Serv.

Dictionary of Civil Engineering & Construction Machinery & Equipment, 2 vols. 4th ed. 1180p. 1978. plastic bdg. 90.00x ea. Vol. 1, Ger-Eng (ISBN 3-7625-0502-0). Vol. 2, Eng.-Ger (ISBN 3-7625-0950-6). Intl Pubns Serv.

Dictionary of Civil Engineering & Construction Machinery & Equipment, Vol. 1. 5th ed. Herbert Bucksch. 420p. (Fr. & Eng.). 1976. 30.00 (ISBN 3-7625-0533-0, M-7120). French & Eur.

Dictionary of Civil Engineering & Construction Machinery & Equipment, Vol. 1. 7th ed. Herbert Bucksch. (Eng. & Ger.). 1978. leatherette 135.00 (ISBN 3-7625-0950-6, M-7122). French & Eur.

Dictionary of Civil Engineering & Construction Machinery & Equipment, Vol. 2. 5th ed. Herbert Bucksch. 548p. (Fr. & Eng.). 1976. 40.00 (ISBN 3-7625-0534-9, M-7119). French & Eur.

Dictionary of Civil Engineering & Construction Machinery & Equipment, Vol. 2. 7th ed. Herbert Bucksch. (Eng. & Ger.). 1978. leatherette 135.00 (ISBN 3-7625-0951-4, M-7121). French & Eur.

Dictionary of Classical Allusion in English Literature. Eric Smith. LC 83-12273. 256p. 1983. 39.50x (ISBN 0-389-20430-7). B&N Imports.

Dictionary of Classical Antiquities. rev. ed. Oskar Seyffert. Ed. by Nettleship. (Illus.). 18.00 (ISBN 0-8446-2910-3). Peter Smith.

Dictionary of Classical Mythology. Zimmerman. (gr. 9 up). pap. 2.75 (ISBN 0-553-14483-9). Bantam.

Dictionary of Classical Mythology. John E. Zimmerman. (YA) 1964. 17.26i (ISBN 0-06-007740-9, HarpT). Har-Row.

Dictionary of Classical Mythology: Symbols, Attributes, & Associations. Robert E. Bell. LC 81-19141. 390p. 1982. text ed. 26.50 (ISBN 0-87436-305-5); pap. 19.95 (ISBN 0-87436-023-4). ABC Clio.

Dictionary of Cliches. 5th ed. Eric Partridge. 1978. pap. 8.95 (ISBN 0-7100-0049-9). Routledge & Kegan.

Dictionary of Coleoptera Collections of North America: Canada Through Panama. Ross H. Annett, Jr. & G. Allen Samuelson. 1969. 6.95 (ISBN 0-916846-05-9). World Natural Hist.

Dictionary of Collective Nouns & Group Terms. Ed. by Ivan G. Sparkes. LC 75-4117. 213p. 1975. 42.00x (ISBN 0-8103-2016-9, Pub. by White Lion Publishers). Gale.

Dictionary of Colonial American Printers' Ornaments & Illustrations. Elizabeth C. Reilly. LC 75-5023. (Illus.). xxxvi, 514p. 1975. 45.00x (ISBN 0-912296-06-2, Dist. by U Pr of Va). Am Antiquarian.

Dictionary of Commerce, Finance & Law. Robert Herbst. (Eng. & Ger.). 1975. 92.00 (ISBN 3-85942-003-8, M-7118). French & Eur.

Dictionary of Commercial, Financial & Legal Terms, 3 vols. R. Herbst. (Eng., Fr. & Ger.). 98.60 ea.; Vol. I. (ISBN 3-85942-000-3); Vol. II. (ISBN 3-85942-006-2); Vol. III. Adler.

Dictionary of Commercial, Financial & Legal Terms, 3 Vols. R. Herbst. (Eng, Fr, & Ger.). Set. 330.00 (ISBN 0-686-76877-9); Vol. 1. 125.00 ea. (ISBN 3-8594-2000-3). Vol. 2 (ISBN 3-8594-2006-2). Vol. 3 (ISBN 3-8594-2002-X). Heinman.

Dictionary of Commericial, Financial & Legal Terms in Two Languages. R. Herbst. (Eng. & Ger.). 78.25 ea. Vol. A, Eng. & Ger. Vol. B, Ger. & Eng (ISBN 3-85942-004-6). Adler.

Dictionary of Common Fallacies. 2nd ed. Philip Ward. (Oleander Reference Bks.: Vols. 3 & 4). 1980. 17.50 ea. Vol. 1 (ISBN 0-900891-63-7). Vol. 2 (ISBN 0-900891-64-5). Set. 35.00 (ISBN 0-900891-65-3). Oleander Pr.

Dictionary of Common Language Errors & their Corrections. Muhammad Al-Adnani. 368p. (Arabic.). 20.00 (894-5). Intl Bk Ctr.

Dictionary of Common Language Errors & Their Corrections: Arabic-Arabic. Muhammad Adnani. (Arabic.). 20.00x (ISBN 0-86685-104-6). Intl Bk Ctr.

Dictionary of Computer Programming & Data Processing. 386p. 1976. 90.00x (ISBN 0-686-44722-0, Pub. by Collets). State Mutual Bk.

Dictionary of Computer Words. Robert W. Bly. (Illus.). 208p. (gr. 7 up). 1983. pap. 3.95 (ISBN 0-440-01920-6, Banbury). Dell.

Dictionary of Computing. Compiled by Ian Pyle & Edward Glazer. 450p. 1983. 34.95 (ISBN 0-19-853905-3). Oxford U Pr.

Dictionary of Computing: Data Communications, Hardware & Software Basics, Digital Electronics. Ed. by Frank J. Galland. 330p. 1982. 34.95x (ISBN 0-471-10468-X, Pub. by Wiley-Interscience); pap. 19.95x (ISBN 0-471-10469-8). Wiley.

Dictionary of Concepts on American Politics. James B. Whisker. LC 80-15591. 285p. 1980. pap. 11.95 (ISBN 0-471-07716-X). Wiley.

Dictionary of Concrete Terms. (Hebrew, Eng. , Fr. & Ger.). IL.8.00. Massada Pr.

Dictionary of Construction Industries. Ed. by B. Vukicevic. 516p. (Eng. & Serbocroation.). 1981. 95.00 (ISBN 0-686-92430-4, M-9686). French & Eur.

Dictionary of Contemporary & Colloquial Usage. 40p. (Eng.). 1978. 15.00 F. Garnier.

Dictionary of Contemporary British Artists, 1929. Bernard Dolman. 551p. 1981. 39.50 (ISBN 0-902028-99-5). Antique Collect.

Dictionary of Contemporary English. Givi Zvidadze. 400p. 1983. text ed. 27.00x (ISBN 0-686-89414-6). Humanities.

Dictionary of Contemporary English (DCE) 1344p. (Eng.). DM.33.50 (50810); DM.Wkbk. 6.80; DM.Cassette 19.00. Langenscheidt.

Dictionary of Contemporary Latin American Authors. Ed. by David W. Foster. LC 75-17988. 250p. 1975. pap. 6.95x (ISBN 0-87918-021-8). ASU Lat Am St.

Dictionary of Contemporary Photography. Leslie Stroebel & Hollis Todd. LC 73-93536. (Illus.). 1974. 20.00 (ISBN 0-87100-065-2); pap. 9.95 (ISBN 0-87100-103-9). Morgan.

Dictionary of Contemporary Photography. Leslie Stroebel & Hollis N. Todd. LC 73-93536. 1976. pap. 9.95 (ISBN 0-87100-103-9, 397). Morgan.

Dictionary of Contemporary Violin & Bow Makers. C. Woodcock. (Illus.). 1965. 40.00 (ISBN 0-685-12006-6). Heinman.

Dictionary of Correct English. M. Alderton Pink. 1977. Repr. of 1928 ed. lib. bdg. 22.50 (ISBN 0-8492-2055-6). R West.

Dictionary of Cosmetology & Related Sciences. Anthony B. Colletti. (Illus.). 1981. 25.00x (ISBN 0-912126-58-2). Sheridan.

Dictionary of Cosmetology & Related Services. Anthony B. Colletti. Ed. by Gary Chiranky. 1981. text ed. 23.57 (ISBN 0-912126-58-2, 1275-00). Keystone Pubns.

Dictionary of Costume. R. Wilcox. 1979. 37.00 (ISBN 0-7134-0856-1, Pub. by Batsford England). David & Charles.

Dictionary of Costume. R. Turner Wilcox. LC 68-12503. (Illus.). 1963. lib. rep. ed. 32.50 (ISBN 0-684-15150-2, ScribT). Scribner.

Dictionary of Counseling Techniques & Terms. Frederick D. Harper. LC 81-82985. 62p. 1981. pap. text ed. 4.95 (ISBN 0-935392-02-5). Douglass Pubs.

Dictionary of Country Furniture. Marjorie Filbee. 208p. 1981. 30.00x (ISBN 0-900305-17-7, Pub. by Ebury Pr England). State Mutual Bk.

Dictionary of Criminal Justice Terms. Gould Editorial Dept. 500p. 1982. text ed. 8.95 looseleaf (ISBN 0-87526-276-7). Gould.

Dictionary of Criminology. Dermot Walsh & Adrian Poole. LC 83-4611. 1983. 20.00 (ISBN 0-7100-9549-X). Routledge & Kegan.

Dictionary of Cryptic Crossword Clues. Adrian Room. 288p. 1983. 16.95 (ISBN 0-7100-9415-9). Routledge & Kegan.

Dictionary of Cuisine French. 2nd ed. Steve Combes. 1973. 12.50x (ISBN 0-214-15569-2). Intl Pubns Serv.

Dictionary of Cultivated Plants & Their Regions of Diversity. 263p. 1983. 49.75 (ISBN 90-220-0785-5, PDC 241, Pudoc). Unipub.

Dictionary of Cybernetics. A. Sydow. 172p. 1980. 35.00x (ISBN 0-569-08527-6, Pub. by Collet's). State Mutual Bk.

Dictionary of Dairy Terminology. (Eng. , Fr. , Ger. & Span.). Date not set. 83.00 (ISBN 0-444-42101-7). Elsevier.

Dictionary of Dams. (Hebrew, Eng. , Fr. & Ger.). IL.5.00. Massada Pr.

Dictionary of Dangerous Pollutants, Ecology & Environment. David F. Tver. LC 81-1881. (Illus.). 360p. 1981. 27.95 (ISBN 0-8311-1060-0). Indus Pr.

Dictionary of Data Processing. 2nd ed. Maynard. 1982. text ed. 29.95 (ISBN 0-408-00591-2). Butterworth.

Dictionary of Data Processing. 3rd. rev. ed. A. Wittman & J. Klos. 1977. 89.50 (ISBN 0-444-99823-3). Elsevier.

Dictionary of Data Processing. Alfred Wittmann. LC 76-28194. (Eng. & Fr.). 1977. write for info. Elsevier.

Dictionary of Data Processing & Computer Terms. R. G. Anderson. 112p. 1982. pap. text ed. 13.95x (ISBN 0-7121-0429-1). Intl Ideas.

Dictionary of Dataprocessing. Karl H. Brinkmann. (Ger. & Eng.). 1974. 59.95 (ISBN 3-87097-059-6, M-7117). French & Eur.

Dictionary of Dataprocessing. 4th ed. Egon Hofmann. (Eng. & Ger.). 1976. 15.95 (ISBN 3-19-006288-9, M-7115). French & Eur.

Dictionary of Dataprocessing. 2nd ed. Alfred Oppermann. (Ger. & Eng.). 1973. pap. 30.00 (ISBN 3-7940-3099-0, M-7116). French & Eur.

Dictionary of Dates. Ed. by Robert L. Collison. LC 77-95116. Repr. of 1961 ed. lib. bdg. 23.00x (ISBN 0-8371-2495-6, CODD). Greenwood.

Dictionary of Dermatologic Therapy. Harry M. Robinson, Jr. & Joseph W. Burnett. LC 78-62796. 1978. text ed. 25.00 (ISBN 0-914316-15-X). Yorke Med.

Dictionary of Development Banking: A Compilation of Terms in English, French, & German with Definitions in English. T. Scharf & M. C. Shetty. LC 72-83212. (Eng., Fr. & Ger.). 1973. 42.00 (ISBN 0-444-41028-7). Elsevier.

Dictionary of Difficult Words. Ed. by Robert Hill. 1959. 5.00 (ISBN 0-8022-0722-7). Philos Lib.

Dictionary of Difficult Words. Robert H. Hill. 1975. pap. 3.95 (ISBN 0-451-11803-0, AE1803, Sig). NAL.

Dictionary of Dinosaurs. Joseph Rosenbloom. LC 80-18525. (Illus.). 96p. (gr. 4 up). 1980. PLB 8.29 (ISBN 0-671-34038-7). Messner.

Dictionary of Diplomacy & International Affairs. Samuhi Fouk al-Ada. 566p. (Arabic, Fr. & Eng.). 30.00 (114-3). Intl Bk Ctr.

Dictionary of Discoveries. Isaac A. Langnas. LC 68-8064. (Illus.). 1968. Repr. of 1959 ed. lib. bdg. 15.00x (ISBN 0-8371-0526-9, LADD). Greenwood.

Dictionary of Doctrinal Terms. Fisher Humphreys & Philip Wise. LC 81-86635. (Orig.). 1983. pap. 4.95 (ISBN 0-8054-1141-0). Broadman.

Dictionary of Drawing. Arthur Zaidenberg. LC 81-65858. (Illus.). 192p. 1982. 15.00 (ISBN 0-8453-4701-2). Cornwall Bks.

Dictionary of Drugs: The Medicines You Use. rev. ed. Richard B. Fisher & George A. Christie. LC 76-12241. 1976. 7.95x (ISBN 0-8052-3638-4). Schocken.

Dictionary of Drying. Hall. 1979. 52.25 (ISBN 0-8247-6652-0). Dekker.

Dictionary of Dyes & Dyeing. Ken Ponting. 216p. 1982. 35.00x (ISBN 0-7135-1311-X, Pub. by Bell & Hyman England). State Mutual Bk.

Dictionary of Early English. Joseph T. Shipley. (Quality Paperback: No. 150). 1977. pap. 5.95 (ISBN 0-8226-0150-8). Littlefield.

Dictionary of Early Music. Jerome Roche & Elizabeth Roche. (Illus.). 1981. 17.95x (ISBN 0-19-520255-4). Oxford U Pr.

Dictionary of Earth Sciences. (Helix Bks.: No. 377). (Illus.). 301p. 1983. pap. text ed. 9.95 (ISBN 0-8226-0377-2). Rowman & Allanheld.

Dictionary of Earth Sciences. Stella E. Stiegeler. LC 76-41042. (Illus.). 1977. 20.00x (ISBN 0-87663-725-X, Pica Pr). Universe.

Dictionary of Ecclesiastical Terms: Being a History & Explanation of Certain Terms Used in Architecture, Ecclesiology, Liturgiology, Music, Ritual, Cathedral, Constitution, Etc. John S. Bumpus. LC 68-30653. 1969. Repr. of 1910 ed. 30.00x (ISBN 0-8103-3321-X). Gale.

Dictionary of Ecology, Evolution & Systematics. R. J. Lincoln & G. A. Boxshall. LC 81-18013. 350p. 1982. 47.50 (ISBN 0-521-23957-5). Cambridge U Pr.

Dictionary of Economic Business & Finance. Nabih Ghattas. 977p. (Eng. & Arabic., With Arabic glossary). 25.00 (271-9). Intl Bk Ctr.

Dictionary of Economic Definitions for the Leaving Certificate. Noel Dowling. LC 77-380100. (Illus.). 45p. (Eng.). 1977. 0.45p. Educ Co Ire.

Dictionary of Economic Plants. 2nd, rev. & enl. ed. J. C. Uphof. 1968. 28.00 (ISBN 3-7682-0001-9). Lubrecht & Cramer.

Dictionary of Economic Quotations. Compiled by Simon James. LC 81-6632. 244p. 1981. 23.50x (ISBN 0-389-20230-4). B&N Imports.

Dictionary of Economic Terms. S. Bubic. 1040p. (Eng. & Serbocroation.). 1975. 95.00 (ISBN 0-686-92261-1, M-9699). French & Eur.

Dictionary of Economics, 2 vols. R. V. Eichborn. Incl. Vol. 1. English & German. 168.00 (ISBN 3-921392-06-3); plastic bdg. 59.95 (ISBN 3-92139-047-8); Vol. 2. German & English. 168.00 (ISBN 3-921392-07-1); plastic bdg. 59.95 (ISBN 3-92139-055-9). (Eng. & Ger.). 1982. Adler.

Dictionary of Economics. 5th ed. Harold S. Sloan & Arnold J. Zurcher. LC 70-118099. text ed. 15.00x (ISBN 0-06-480799-1). B&N Imports.

Dictionary of Economics. Harold S. Sloan & Arnold J. Zurcher. LC 70-118099. pap. text ed. 5.95 (ISBN 0-06-463266-0, EH 266, EH). B&N NY.

Dictionary of Economics & Commerce. Mamdouh Hansen. 496p. (Eng. & Arabic., With Eng. & Arabic Glossary). 20.00 (066-X). Intl Bk Ctr.

Dictionary of Economics & Commerce. 5th ed. J. L. Hanson. 472p. 1981. pap. 17.50x (ISBN 0-7121-0424-0). Intl Ideas.

Dictionary of Economics & Commerce. Ed. by Libr. du Liban. (Eng. & Arabic.). pap. 7.95 (0-76-7). Intl Bk Ctr.

Dictionary of Economics & Commerce. Ed. by Zacharia Nasr. 320p. (Eng., Fr. & Arabic.). 1980. E17.50 (ISBN 0-333-23109-0). Macmillan London.

Dictionary of Economics, Business & Finance: English-Arabic with Arabic Glossary. Nabih Ghattas. (Eng. & Arabic.). 25.00x (ISBN 0-86685-169-0). Intl Bk Ctr.

Dictionary of Education. Derek Rowntree. 362p. 1982. text ed. 18.50x (ISBN 0-389-20263-0). B&N Imports.

Dictionary of Electrical Circuits. 203p. (Eng. & Chinese.). 1975. pap. 3.95 (ISBN 0-686-92288-3, M-9572). French & Eur.

Dictionary of Electronic Organ Stops. Stevens Irwin. 1969. pap. 9.95 (ISBN 0-02-871120-3). Assoc-Mus.

Dictionary of Electronics. Alfred Opperman. 692p. (Eng. & Ger.). 1980. 120.00x (ISBN 0-686-98305-X, K G Saur). Gale.

Dictionary of Electronics, Communications & Electrical Engineering, 2 vols. H. Wernicke. 1300p. Vol. 1. 32.50 ea. (ISBN 0-685-05199-4); Vol. 2. 36.00 ea. (ISBN 0-685-05200-1). Adler.

Dictionary of Electronics Engineering. 785p. (Eng. & Chinese.). 1976. 12.95 (ISBN 0-686-92369-3). French & Eur.

Dictionary of Energy. Martin Counihan. (Illus.). 200p. 1981. 14.95 (ISBN 0-7100-0847-3). Routledge & Kegan.

Dictionary of Energy. Hall. (Energy, Power & Environment Ser.). 360p. 1983. write for info. (ISBN 0-8247-1793-7). Dekker.

Dictionary of Energy. Malcolm Slesser. LC 82-10252. 1983. 29.95 (ISBN 0-8052-3816-6). Schocken.

Dictionary of Energy. Malcolm Slesser. 320p. (Eng.). 1982. E25.00 (ISBN 0-333-31825-0). Macmillan London.

Dictionary of Energy. Ed. by Malcom Slesser et al. 400p. 1982. E15.00 (ISBN 0-333-31825-0). Macmillan London.

Dictionary of Engineering & Technology, 2 vols. Rev. ed. Richard Ernst. (Ger. & Eng.). 1980. Vol 1: German-English, 1092p. 69.00; Vol. 2: English-German, 1170p. 69.00. Oxford U Pr.

Dictionary of Engineering & Technology, Vol. 1. 4th ed. Ed. by Richard Ernst. 1981. 69.00x (ISBN 0-19-520269-4). Oxford U Pr.

Dictionary of Engineering & Technology: With Extensive Treatment of the Most Modern Techniques & Processes, Vol. 2, English-German. 4th, rev. & enl. ed. Richard Ernst. 1178p. (Eng. & Ger.). 1975. text ed. 69.00x (ISBN 0-19-520109-4). Oxford U Pr.

Dictionary of Engineering Mechanics. C. Heller. (Eng. & Rus.). 1965. 14.75 (ISBN 0-444-40274-8). Elsevier.

Dictionary of Engineering Metrology Terms. (Hebrew, EnG. , Fr. & Ger.). IL.7.00. Massada Pr.

Dictionary of English & Sanskrit. M. Monier Williams. LC 73-495007. (Eng. & Sanskrit.). 1971. Repr. of 1851 ed. 17.50x (ISBN 0-8002-0172-8). Intl Pubns Serv.

Dictionary of English & Welsh Surnames with Special American Instances. C. W. Bardsley. 837p. 1980. 50.00x (ISBN 0-686-79058-8, Pub.by Heraldry Today England). State Mutual Bk.

Dictionary of English & Welsh Surnames with Special American Instances. Charles W. Bardsley. LC 67-25404. 837p. 1980. Repr. of 1901 ed. 30.00 (ISBN 0-8063-0022-1). Genealog Pub.

Dictionary of English Bahasa Malaysia Idiomatic Phrases. A. Karim & T. Lucy. LC 78-942330. 145p. (Eng., Bahasa & Malay.). 1978. write for info. Jaya Ciencia.

Dictionary of English Collogulal Idioms. F. T. Wood & Robert Hill. 328p. 1979. Epap. 4.55 (ISBN 0-333-25450-3). Macmillan LOndon.
Dictionary of English Colloquial Idioms. F. T. Wood. Rev. by R. Hill. 304p. 1982. write for info. (ISBN 0-333-27839-9). Macmillan.
Dictionary of English Idioms. Michael J. Wallace. 256p. 1983. 15.00x (ISBN 0-00-370014-3, Pub. by Collins ELT Scotland). State Mutual Bk.
Dictionary of English Phrasal Verbs & Their Idioms. Tom McArthur & Beryl Atkins. 256p. 1982. 15.00x (ISBN 0-00-370200-6, Pub. by Collins ELT Scotland). State Mutual Bk.
Dictionary of English Phrasal Verbs & Their Idioms. Tom McArthur & Beryl Atkins. 160p. (Eng.). 1976. 4.20 (ISBN 9-97163-154-7). Pan Pacific Bk.
Dictionary of English Phrases: Phraseological Allusions, Catchwords, Stereotyped Modes of Speech & Metaphors, Nicknames, Sobriquets, Derivations from Personal Names. Albert M. Hyamson. LC 66-22673. 1970. Repr. of 1922 ed. 37.00x (ISBN 0-8103-3852-1). Gale.
Dictionary of English Phrases with Illustrative Sentences. Kwong Ki Chaou. LC 74-136559. (Illus.). 1971. Repr. of 1881 ed. 63.00 (ISBN 0-8103-3386-4). Gale.
Dictionary of English Synonyms & Synonymous Parallel Expressions. rev. ed. Ed. by Richard Soule & G. Howson. 32.50 (ISBN 0-87559-043-8); thumb indexed 37.50 (ISBN 0-87559-044-6). Shalom.
Dictionary of English Usage in Southern Africa. Douglas R. Beeton & Helene T. Dorner. 1976. 19.95x (ISBN 0-19-570069-4). Oxford U Pr.
Dictionary of English Word-Roots. Robert W. Smith. 373p. 1966. 9.00x (ISBN 0-87471-238-6). Rowman.
Dictionary of English Word-Roots: English-Roots & Roots-English with Examples & Exercises. Robert W. Smith. (Quality Paperback: No. 98). (Orig.). 1980. pap. 4.95 (ISBN 0-8226-0098-6). Littlefield.
Dictionary of English Words in Context. Wolf Von Friederich. LC 80-482234. 379p. 1979. DM.36.00 (ISBN 3-559-22638-4). Lensing Verlag.
Dictionary of Entomology. A. W. Leftwich. LC 75-27143. 364p. 1976. 27.50x (ISBN 0-8448-0820-2). Crane-Russak Co.
Dictionary of Environmental Engineering & Related Sciences. Jose T. Villate. LC 78-67002. (Coleccion Diccionrios). Orig. Title: Diccionario De Ingenieria Ambiental y Ciencias Afines. 445p. (Eng. & Span.). 1979. 25.00 (ISBN 0-89729-209-X). Ediciones.
Dictionary of Environmental Engineering & Related Sciences. Jose T. Villate. LC 78-67002. xvi, 445p. (Span.). 1979. write for info. (ISBN 0-89729-209-X). Edns Universal.
Dictionary of environmental protection, 3 vols. Otto E. Tutzaver & Ingrid M. Tutzaver. LC 80-458477. (Eng., Fr., & Ger.). 1979. DM.70.00 (ISBN 3-452-18481-1). Heymanns Verlag.
Dictionary of Environmental Terms. Alan Gilpin. 191p. 1976. 14.95x (ISBN 0-7022-1010-2); pap. 8.95x (ISBN 0-7022-1011-0). U of Queensland Pr.
Dictionary of Epilepsy: Part I - Definitions. H. Gastaut. (Also avail. in French, Russian & Spanish). 1973. 8.00 (ISBN 92-4-154027-3). World Health.
Dictionary of Eponyms. Cyril L. Beeching. 1979. 13.00 (ISBN 0-85157-283-9, Pub. by Bingley England). Shoe String.
Dictionary of Eponyms. 2nd ed. Cyril L. Beeching. 160p. 1983. 20.00 (ISBN 0-85157-329-0, Pub. by Bingley England). Shoe String.
Dictionary of Esoteric Words. Ann Cattell. (Orig.). 1967. pap. 1.75 (ISBN 0-8065-0175-8, C205). Citadel Pr.
Dictionary of Essential Quotations. Compiled by Kevin Goldstein-Jackson. LC 83-2815. 256p. 1983. text ed. 23.50x (ISBN 0-389-20393-9). B&N Imports.
Dictionary of Euphemisms & Other Double Talk. Hugh Rawson. 320p. 1981. 15.95 (ISBN 0-517-54518-7). Crown.
Dictionary of European Art. Ed. by Emerich Schaffran. 1958. 4.75 (ISBN 0-8022-1497-5). Philos Lib.
Dictionary of Even More Diseased English. Kenneth Hudson. 416p. 1983. E12.95 (ISBN 0-333-34867-2). MacMillan London.
Dictionary of Even More Diseased English. Kenneth Hudson. 320p. (Eng.). 1983. E12.95 (ISBN 0-333-34170-8). Macmillan.
Dictionary of Eye Terminology. Barbara Cassin & Sheila Solomon. (Illus., Orig.). 1983. 14.95 (ISBN 0-937404-07-1). Triad Pub FL.
Dictionary of Fantastic Art. Jorg Krichbaum & Rein Zondergeld. (Pocket Art Ser.). (Illus.). 1984. pap. 5.95 (ISBN 0-8120-2110-X). Barron.
Dictionary of Film & Television Terms. Virginia Oakey. 206p. (Orig.). 1982. pap. 6.68i (ISBN 0-06-463566-X, EH 566). B&N NY.
Dictionary of Film Terms. Frank Beaver. (Illus.). 320p. 1983. text ed. 15.95 (ISBN 0-07-004216-0, C); pap. text ed. 9.95 (ISBN 0-07-004212-8). McGraw.
Dictionary of Fine Arts. Denis Thomas. (Illus.). 208p. E6.95 (ISBN 0-600-32995-X). Newnes Bks.
Dictionary of Fire Technology. 3rd, rev. ed. Institution of Fire Engineers. LC 80-510226. 170p. (Eng.). 1979. 4.00 (ISBN 0-903345-03-X). Inst Fire Eng.
Dictionary of First Names. Alfred J. Kolatch. 540p. 1981. pap. 6.95 (ISBN 0-399-50570-9, Perigee). Putnam Pub Group.
Dictionary of Fishes. Rube Allyn. LC 52-334. (Orig.). pap. 4.95 (ISBN 0-8200-0101-5). Great Outdoors.
Dictionary of Fishing Terms: Japanese-English, English-Japanese. 443p. (Japanese & Eng.). 1980. 39.95 (ISBN 0-686-92534-3, M-9344). French & Eur.
Dictionary of Five-Hundred-One French Verbs Fully Conjugated. C. Kendris. 527p. (Fr. & Eng.). 11.75; pap. 5.00. Barron.
Dictionary of Five Hundred One German Verbs Fully Conjugated. H. Strutz. 523p. (Ger. & Eng.). 1972. pap. 5.00. Barron.
Dictionary of Five Hundred One Spanish Verbs. Christopher Kendris. (Span.). 3.75. Camino Real.
Dictionary of Floor, Wall & Ceiling Covering. (Hebrew, Eng. , Fr. & Ger.). IL.7.00. Massada Pr.
Dictionary of Folklore: English-Arabic. Younis. (Arabic & Eng.). 1983. 30.00 (ISBN 0-86685-307-3). Intl Bk Ctr.
Dictionary of Food & What's in It for You. Barbara L. Gelb. 1979. pap. 3.50 (ISBN 0-345-29479-3). Ballantine.
Dictionary of Food Ingredients. Robert S. Igoe. 192p. 1982. text ed. 17.95 (ISBN 0-442-24002-3). Van Nos Reinhold.
Dictionary of Foods. Gaylord Hauser & Ragnar Berg. 156p. 1971. pap. 2.25 (ISBN 0-87904-008-4). Lust.
Dictionary of Foreign Musical Terms & Handbook of Orchestral Instruments. Tom S. Wotton. LC 79-166268. 226p. 1907. Repr. 29.00 (ISBN 0-403-01389-5). Scholarly.
Dictionary of Foreign Phrases & Abbreviations. 3rd ed. Tr. & compiled by Kevin Guinagh. 288p. 1982. 28.00 (ISBN 0-8242-0675-4). Wilson.
Dictionary of Foreign Phrases & Classical Quotations. R. D. Blackman. Repr. of 1893 ed. 25.00 (ISBN 0-686-20089-6). Quality Lib.
Dictionary of Foreign Phrases & Classical Quotations. Ed. by Hugh P. Jones. LC 77-13088. 1977. Repr. of 1929 ed. lib. bdg. 35.00 (ISBN 0-89341-457-3). Longwood Pr.
Dictionary of Foreign Phrases & Classical Quotations. Ed. by Hugh P. Jones. 552p. 1983. pap. 12.75 (ISBN 0-88072-017-4). Tanager Bks.
Dictionary of Foreign Quotations. Robert Collison & Mary Collison. 416p. 1980. 29.95 (ISBN 0-87196-428-7). Facts on File.
Dictionary of Foreign Terms. 2nd ed. C. O. Mawson. (Everyday Handbooks Ser.). 384p. 1979. pap. 4.95 (ISBN 0-06-463494-9). B&N NY.
Dictionary of Foreign Terms in the English Language. David Carroll. 1979. pap. 4.95 (ISBN 0-8015-2053-3, Hawthorn). Dutton.
Dictionary of Foreign Words & Phrases in Current English. A. J. Bliss. 400p. 1983. 18.00 (ISBN 0-7100-1092-3); pap. 9.95 (ISBN 0-7100-9521-X). Routledge & Kegan.
Dictionary of Foreign Words & Phrases. Maxim Newmark. Repr. of 1957 ed. lib. bdg. 18.50x (ISBN 0-8371-2103-5, NEFW). Greenwood.
Dictionary of Forestry. 274p. (Eng. & Chinese.). 1977. pap. 5.95 (ISBN 0-686-92384-7, M-9594). French & Eur.
Dictionary of Forestry. J. Weck. (Eng., Ger., Fr., Span. & Rus.). 1966. 106.50 (ISBN 0-444-40626-3). Elsevier.
Dictionary of Foundry Terms. (Hebrew, Eng. , Fr. & Ger.). IL.8.00. Massada Pr.
Dictionary of French Slang. Alex Sandir-White. (Fr. & Eng.). 4.95. Aurea.
Dictionary of Freshman Composition. Forrest G. Smith. LC 70-78633. (Quality Paperback: No. 239). (Orig.). 1969. pap. 3.95 (ISBN 0-8226-0239-3). Littlefield.
Dictionary of Garden Plants & Flowers in Colour: May 1981. P. Synge & R. Hay. 1981. 60.00x (ISBN 0-686-78769-2, Pub. by RHS Ent England) . State Mutual Bk.
Dictionary of Gardening - Supplement. Ed. by Patrick M. Synge. 1969. 74.00x (ISBN 0-19-869116-5). Oxford U Pr.
Dictionary of Gas Turbine Installation. 170p. (Eng. & Chinese.). 1973. pap. 3.95 (ISBN 0-686-92296-4, M-9566). French & Eur.
Dictionary of Gastronomy. 2nd ed. Andre L. Simon & Robin Howe. LC 78-16260. (Illus.). 400p. 1979. 37.95 (ISBN 0-87951-081-1). Overlook Pr.
Dictionary of Gemmology. Read. 1982. text ed. 34.95 (ISBN 0-408-00571-8). Butterworth.
Dictionary of Gems & Gemology. 6th ed. Robert M. Shipley. 1974. 7.50 (ISBN 0-87311-007-2). Gemological.
Dictionary of General Pathology. F. G. Smiddy. 384p. 1980. pap. text ed. 15.95x (ISBN 0-8464-1247-0). Beekman Pubs.
Dictionary of General Pathology. F. G. Smiddy. 336p. 1980. 29.00x (ISBN 0-272-79585-2, Pub. by Pitman Bks England). State Mutual Bk.
Dictionary of General Psychology: Basic Terminology & Key Concepts. rev. ed. Charles A. Heidenreich. 1970. pap. text ed. 7.95 (ISBN 0-8403-0171-5). Heidenreich.
Dictionary of Geography. rev. ed. W. G. Moore. (Reference Ser.). (Orig.). 1963. pap. 5.95 (ISBN 0-14-051002-8). Penguin.
Dictionary of Geography: Definitions & Explanations of Terms Used in Physical Geography. W. G. Moore. LC 77-94144. (Illus.). 260p. 1978. text ed. 19.50x (ISBN 0-06-494934-6). B&N Imports.
Dictionary of Geological Terms. 3rd ed. American Geological Institute. LC 82-45315. (Illus.). 480p. 1984. 19.95 (ISBN 0-385-18100-0, Anchor Pr); pap. 7.95 (ISBN 0-385-18101-9, Anch). Doubleday.
Dictionary of Geology. 5th ed. John Challinor. 365p. 1978. text ed. 22.00x (ISBN 0-7083-0675-6). Verry.
Dictionary of Geology. 5th ed. John Challinor. LC 78-4530. xvii, 365p. (Eng.). 1978. 14.95 (ISBN 0-19-520063-2). Oxford U Pr.
Dictionary of Geosciences, 2 vols. A. Watznauer. (Eng. & Ger.). Date not set. English-German. 57.50 (ISBN 0-444-99702-4); German-English. 57.50 (ISBN 0-444-99701-6). Elsevier.
Dictionary of Geotechnics. Paul Sommerville. 1983. text ed. 49.95 (ISBN 0-408-00437-1). Butterworth.
Dictionary of German & English Legal & Economic Terminology, Vol. 1. Alfred Romain. (Eng. & Ger.). 1976. 78.00 (ISBN 3-406-03370-9, M-7101). French & Eur.
Dictionary of German & English Legal & Economic Terminology, Vol. 2. Alfred Romain. (Ger. & Fr.). 1975. 78.00 (ISBN 3-406-03371-7, M-7100). French & Eur.
Dictionary of German History 1806-1945. Wilfried Fest. LC 78-54658. 1979. 27.50x (ISBN 0-312-20103-6). St Martin.
Dictionary of German Synonyms. 3rd ed. R. B. Farrell. LC 75-36175. (Ger.). 1977. 54.50 (ISBN 0-521-21189-1); pap. 14.95 (ISBN 0-521-29068-6). Cambridge U Pr.
Dictionary of German Synonyms. 3rd ed. Ralph B. Farrell. LC 75-36175. ix, 412p. (Eng. & Ger.). 1977. 17.00 (ISBN 0-521-21189-1); 7.50 (ISBN 0-521-29068-6). Cambridge U Pr.
Dictionary of Given Names. Flora H. Loughead. 1966. 12.50 (ISBN 0-87062-048-7). A H Clark.
Dictionary of Glass Making. ICG. 402p. (Eng., Fr. & Ger.). 1983. 106.50 (ISBN 0-444-42048-7). Elsevier.
Dictionary of Good English. S. G. McKaskill. 173p. 1981. Epap. 2.95 (ISBN 0-333-30883-2). Macmillan London.
Dictionary of Graphic Arts Terms: A Communication Tool for People Who Buy Type & Printing. Patricia Mintz. 328p. 1981. text ed. 17.95 (ISBN 0-442-26711-8). Van Nos Reinhold.
Dictionary of Graphic Cliches. Ed. by Philip Thompson & Peter Davenport. LC 79-2094. (Illus.). 1979. 30.00x (ISBN 0-312-20108-7). St Martin.
Dictionary of Graphic Images. Compiled By Philip Thompson & Peter Davenport. 288p. 1980. 30.00 (ISBN 0-312-20108-7). St Martin.
Dictionary of Greek & Latin Combining Forms Used in Zoological Names. 2nd ed. Edmund C. Jaeger. 176p. (Gr., Lat. & Eng.). 1930. photocopy ed. spiral 17.50x (ISBN 0-398-04294-2). C C Thomas.
Dictionary of Greek & Roman Antiquities, 2 vols. William Smith. LC 77-6173. 1977. Repr. of 1890 ed. lib. bdg. 65.00 (ISBN 0-89341-166-3). Longwood Pr.
Dictionary of Greek & Roman Biography & Mythology, 3 Vols. Ed. by William Smith. LC 11-24983. (Gr. & Lat.). Repr. of 1890 ed. Set. 210.00 (ISBN 0-404-06130-3). AMS Pr.
Dictionary of Greek & Roman Geography, 2 Vols. Ed. by William Smith. LC 4-14843. (Gr.). Repr. of 1873 ed. Set. 125.00 (ISBN 0-404-06134-6). AMS Pr.
Dictionary of Greek Coin Inscriptions. S. Icard. (Gr. & Eng.). 1979. 30.00 (ISBN 0-916710-42-4); pap. 20.00 (ISBN 0-916710-43-2). Obol Intl.
Dictionary of Greek Coin Inscriptions. Severin Icard. (Gr. & Eng.). 1979. Repr. of 1920 ed. lib. bdg. 42.50 (ISBN 0-915262-31-2). S J Durst.

Dictionary of Hammond Organ Stops. 4th rev. ed. Stevens Irwin. 1970. pap. 8.95 (ISBN 0-02-871110-6). Assoc-Mus.

Dictionary of Hebrew Verbs. M. Debahy. 96p. (Arabic & Hebrew.). 15.00 (123-2). Intl Bk Ctr.

Dictionary of Helminthology & Plant Nematology. Ed. by G. I. Pozniak. 108p. (Rus. & Eng.). 1979. 35.00 (ISBN 0-85198-447-9). French & EUr.

Dictionary of Heraldry & Related Subjects. A. G. Puttock. LC 76-137421. (Illus.). 256p. 1970. 15.00 (ISBN 0-8063-0449-9). Genealog Pub.

Dictionary of Herpetology: Description of Words & Terms. Peters J. A. (Illus.). 392p. 1981. lib. bdg. 15.00x (ISBN 0-02-850230-2). Lubrecht & Cramer.

Dictionary of High Polymer Macromolecule. 54p. (Eng. & Chinese.). 1974. pap. 1.95 (ISBN 0-686-92619-6). French & Eur.

Dictionary of Hindu Architecture: Treating of Sanskrit Architectural Terms. Prasanna K. Acharya. LC 79-912314. xxi, 861p. (Eng. & Hindu.). 1979. write for info. Bharatiya Publishing House.

Dictionary of Historical Allusions. Thomas B. Harbottle. LC 68-23163. 1968. Repr. of 1904 ed. 34.00x (ISBN 0-8103-3088-1). Gale.

Dictionary of Historical Terms. Chris Cook. 384p. (Eng.). 1983. E12.95 (ISBN 0-333-28470-4); pap. 6.95 (ISBN 0-333-35190-8). Macmillan London.

Dictionary of History. R. J. Unstead. (Illus.). (gr. 4-8). 1977. 12.95 (ISBN 0-8467-0230-4, Pub. by Two Continents). Hippocrene Bks.

Dictionary of Holland Occupational Codes. Gary D. Gottfredson & John L. Holland. 520p. (Orig.). 1982. pap. 17.75 (ISBN 0-89106-020-0, 7889). Consulting Psychol.

Dictionary of Homonyms: New Word Patterns. Louise Ellyson. 166p. 1979. lib. bdg. 8.95x (ISBN 0-88411-136-9). Amereon Ltd.

Dictionary of Human Behavior. D. Statt. 1981. text ed. 15.50 (ISBN 0-686-69149-0, Pub. by Har-Row Ltd England). Har-Row.

Dictionary of Hungarian Slang. Alex Sandri-White. (Hungarian.). 5.95 (ISBN 0-685-22762-6). Aurea.

Dictionary of Hydraulic Machinery. A. T. Troskolanski. (Eng., Ger., Span., Fr & Ital. & Rus.). Date not set. 117.00 (ISBN 0-444-99728-8). Elsevier.

Dictionary of Hydraulics & Pneumatics: English-German-Russian-Slovene. G. Neubert. 226p. (Eng., Ger., Rus. & Slovene.). 1973. 75.00 (ISBN 0-686-92602-1, M-9896). French & Eur.

Dictionary of Hydraulics & Pneumatics. Gunter Neubert. 226p. 1980. 40.00x (ISBN 0-569-08523-3, Pub. by Collet's). State Mutual Bk.

Dictionary of Hydrology Terms. (Hebrew, Eng. , Fr. & Ger.). IL.8.00. Massada Pr.

Dictionary of Hymnology: Origin & History of Christian Hymns, 4 vols. Ed. by J. Julian. 1977. Set. lib. bdg. 600.00 (ISBN 0-8490-1719-X). Gordon Pr.

Dictionary of Idioms. W. S. Fowler. 112p. (Eng.). E1.95 (ISBN 0-17-555381-5). Nelson & Sons Group.

Dictionary of Idioms for the Deaf. Maxine Boatner & John Gates. 1975. pap. 8.95 (E001). Natl Assn Deaf.

Dictionary of Idioms, French & English. W. A. Bellenger. 331p. (Fr. & Eng.). 1983. Repr. of 1830 ed. lib. bdg. 125.00 (ISBN 0-89760-052-5). Telegraph Bks.

Dictionary of Idioms French-English: Dictionnaire des locutions. (Fr. & Eng.). 33.95 (ISBN 2-03-021101-X, 3681). Larousse.

Dictionary of Igbo Names, Culture & Proverbs. John E. Njoku. LC 78-66416. 1978. pap. text ed. 7.00 (ISBN 0-8191-0134-6). U Pr of Amer.

Dictionary of Indian History. Sachchidananda Bhattacharya. LC 77-1105. 1977. Repr. of 1972 ed. lib. bdg. 58.50x (ISBN 0-8371-9515-2, BHDI). Greenwood.

Dictionary of Indians of North America, 3 vols. Ed. by Harry Waldman. 1978. Set. 145.00 (ISBN 0-403-01799-8). Scholarly.

Dictionary of Industrial Chemistry. 24p. (Eng. & Chinese.). 1973. pap. 1.95 (ISBN 0-686-92145-3, M-9570). French & Eur.

Dictionary of Industrial Chemistry. 164p. (Chinese & Eng.). 1979. pap. 3.95 (ISBN 0-686-92529-7, M-9576). French & Eur.

Dictionary of Industrial Organic Chemistry. 56p. (Eng. & Chinese.). 1973. pap. 1.95 (ISBN 0-686-92279-4, M-9584). French & Eur.

Dictionary of Industrial Property, Legal & Related Terms: English, Spanish, French & German. Ed. by Francis J. Kase. 232p. (Eng., Span., Fr. & Ger.). 1980. 50.00x (ISBN 90-286-0619-X). Sijthoff & Noordhoff.

Dictionary of Industrial Technology: English-French-German-Portuguese-Spanish. Ed. by Michel Feutry et al. 90.00 (ISBN 2-85608-000-6). Heinman.

Dictionary of Information Technology. Dennis Longley & Michael Shain. 379p. 1982. 34.95 (ISBN 0-471-89574-1, Pub. by Wiley-Interscience). Wiley.

Dictionary of Information Technology. Dennis Longley & Michael Shain. 400p. (Eng.). 1982. E20.00 (ISBN 0-333-32762-4); pap. 6.95 (ISBN 0-333-34806-0). Macmillan London.

Dictionary of Information Technology. M. Shain & D. Longley. 1982. 75.00x (ISBN 0-686-42940-0, Pub. by Macmillan England). State Mutual Bk.

Dictionary of Information Technology. Michael Shain & David Longley. 450p. (Ger.). 1982. E15.00 (ISBN 0-333-32762-4). Macmillan London.

Dictionary of Instrument Science. T. Ramalingom. LC 81-14724. 588p. 1982. 24.95x (ISBN 0-471-86396-3, Pub. by Wiley-Interscience). Wiley.

Dictionary of Insurance. 5th ed. Lewis E. Davids. (Quality Paperback Ser: No. 62). (Orig.). 1977. pap. 5.95 (ISBN 0-8226-0062-5). Littlefield.

Dictionary of Insurance. 6th Rev. ed. Lewis E. Davids. 1983. pap. 8.95 (ISBN 0-8226-0381-0). Rowman & Allanheld.

Dictionary of Interior Design. Martin M. Pegler. (Illus.). 260p. 1983. 25.00 (ISBN 0-87005-447-3). Fairchild.

Dictionary of International Economics: German, Russian, English, French, Spanish. Ed. by S. Kohls. 620p. (Ger., Rus., Eng., Fr. & Span.). 1976. 32.50x (ISBN 90-286-0505-3). Sijthoff & Noordhoff.

Dictionary of International Finance. Julian Walmsley. LC 79-17753. 270p. 1979. lib. bdg. 27.50 (ISBN 0-313-20974-X, WIF/). Greenwood.

Dictionary of International Finance. Julian Walmsley. 356p. (Eng.). 1979. E12.95 (ISBN 0-333-23109-0). Macmillan London.

Dictionary of International Slurs. A. A. Roback. LC 76-5696. (Maledicta Press Publications Ser.: Vol. 5). 1979. pap. 15.00 (ISBN 0-916500-05-5). Maledicta.

Dictionary of International Trade Fairs, 3 vols. T. Martius. 1267p. 1980. 70.00x set (ISBN 0-569-05140-1, Pub. by Collet's). State Mutual Bk.

Dictionary of Iraqi Arabic. B. Clarity. 202p. (Eng. & Arabic.). 8.00. Intl Bk Ctr.

Dictionary of Iraqi Arabic: Arabic-English. Ed. by Daniel Woodhead & Wayne Beene. (Richard Slade Harrell Arabic Ser). 509p. (Arabic & Eng.). 1967. pap. 9.50 (ISBN 0-87840-003-6). Georgetown U Pr.

Dictionary of Irish Artists, 2 vols. Walter G. Strickland. (Illus.). 1358p. 1969. Repr. of 1913 ed. 90.00x set (ISBN 0-7165-0602-5, Pub. by Irish Academic Pr Ireland). Biblio Dist.

Dictionary of Irish History Since 1800. D. J. Hickey & J. E. Doherty. 615p. 1981. 38.50x (ISBN 0-389-20160-X). B&N Imports.

Dictionary of Irish Myth & Legend. Ronan Coghlan. LC 80-497675. (Gaelic.). 1979. Epap. 1.80 (ISBN 0-9505767-1-9). Donard Pub Co.

Dictionary of Islam. Hughes. 29.00 (ISBN 0-686-18366-5). Kazi Pubns.

Dictionary of Islam, 2 vols. Thomas P. Hughes. 1980. Set. lib. bdg. 199.95 (ISBN 0-8490-3121-4). Gordon Pr.

Dictionary of Islam. Thomas P. Hughes. LC 71-14622. (Illus.). 1976. Repr. of 1885 ed. 30.00x (ISBN 0-8002-0207-4). Intl Pubns Serv.

Dictionary of Islam. Thomas P. Hughes. 1976. Repr. 35.00x (ISBN 0-8364-0395-9). South Asia Bks.

Dictionary of Jamaican English. 2nd ed. Ed. by Frederick G. Cassidy & R. B. Le Page. LC 78-17799. 1980. 82.50 (ISBN 0-521-22165-X). Cambridge U Pr.

Dictionary of Japanese & English Idiomatic Equivalents. Charles Corwin et al. LC 68-11818. 302p. (Japanese & Eng.). 1980. 18.75 (ISBN 0-87011-111-6). Kodansha.

Dictionary of Joinery Terms: Doors, Windows, Shutters. (Hebrew, Eng. , Fr. & Ger.). IL.8.00. Massada Pr.

Dictionary of Judaism. Dagobert D. Runes. 236p. 1981. 5.95 (ISBN 0-8065-0787-X). Citadel Pr.

Dictionary of Kashmiri Proverbs & Sayings. James H. Knowles. 59.95 (ISBN 0-8490-0036-X). Gordon Pr.

Dictionary of Kathakali. K. P. Menon. 1980. 11.00 (ISBN 0-8364-0573-0, Orient Longman). South Asia Bks.

Dictionary of Kathakali. K. P. Menon. LC 80-903797. (Illus.). vi, 80p. (Eng.). 1979. Rs.45.00 (Orient Longman). South Asia Bks.

Dictionary of Khotan Saka. Harold W. Bailey. LC 77-80825. 1979. 210.00 (ISBN 0-521-21737-7). Cambridge U Pr.

Dictionary of Lace. Pat Earnshaw. (Illus.). 240p. (Orig.). 1983. pap. 14.95 (ISBN 0-85263-602-4, 3380389, Pub. by Shire Pubns England). Seven Hills Bks.

Dictionary of Land Surveyors & Local Cartographers of Great Britain & Ireland. Ed. by P. Eden. 528p. 1981. 14.00x (ISBN 0-7129-0900-1, Pub. by Dawson). State Mutual Bk.

Dictionary of Language & Linguistics. Ed. by R. R. Hartmann & F. C. Stork. LC 72-6251. 302p. 1976. pap. 29.95 (ISBN 0-470-15200-1). Halsted Pr.

Dictionary of Late Egyptian, Vol. 1 of 3 Vols. Ed. by Leonard H. Lesko. (Egyptian.). 1982. lib. bdg. 35.00x (ISBN 0-930548-03-5); pap. text ed. 20.00x (ISBN 0-930548-04-3). B C Scribe.

Dictionary of Law. George G. Coughlin. 224p. 1982. pap. 5.72i (ISBN 0-06-463539-2, EH-539). Har-Row.

Dictionary of Law. L. B. Curzon. 384p. 1979. pap. 18.95x (ISBN 0-7121-0380-5, Pub. by Macdonald & Evans England). Intl Ideas.

Dictionary of Law. rev. ed. LC 75-40443. 144p. 1976. lib. bdg. 12.90 (ISBN 0-914294-44-X); pap. 3.95 (ISBN 0-914294-43-1). Running Pr.

Dictionary of Legal Abbreviations Used in American Law Books. Doris M. Bieber. LC 78-60173. 337p. 1979. lib. bdg. 19.50 (ISBN 0-930342-61-5); pap. text ed. 7.95 (ISBN 0-930342-96-8). W S Hein.

Dictionary of Legal Quotations. J. W. Norton-Kyshe. 75.00 (ISBN 0-8490-0037-8). Gordon Pr.

Dictionary of Legal Quotations. James W. Norton-Kyshe. LC 68-30648. 1968. Repr. of 1904 ed. 34.00x (ISBN 0-8103-3189-6). Gale.

Dictionary of Legal Terms. (Eng. & Span.). write for info. Lectorum Pubns.

Dictionary of Legal Terms & Citations. H. Sturgess & A. Hewitt. 75.00 (ISBN 0-87968-408-9). Gordon Pr.

Dictionary of Legal Terms, Spanish-English & English-Spanish. Louis A. Robb. (Span. & Eng.). 1955. 27.95 (ISBN 0-471-72534-X, Pub. by Wiley-Interscience). Wiley.

Dictionary of Legal Terms: Spanish-English,English-Spanish. Louis A. Robb. (Span. & Eng.). 1976. pap. 10.95x (ISBN 968-18-0384-1). Intl Learn Syst.

Dictionary of Library & Educational Technology. 2nd, rev., & enl. ed. Kenyon C. Rosenberg & Paul T. Feinstein. 300p. 1983. lib. bdg. write for info. (ISBN 0-87287-396-X). Libs Unl.

Dictionary of Library Science Information & Documentation. rev. ed. Ed. by W. Clason. (Eng., Fr., Span., Ital., Dutch, Ger., & Arabic.). 1977. 95.75 (ISBN 0-444-41475-4). Elsevier.

Dictionary of Library Terms. (Hebrew, Eng. , Fr. & Ger.). IL.8.00. Massada Pr.

Dictionary of Life Sciences. 2nd ed. E. A. Martin. 416p. (Eng.). 1983. E17.50 (ISBN 0-333-34867-2). Macmillan London.

Dictionary of Lighting. Ralf Zimmermann. 362p. 1980. 70.00x (ISBN 0-569-08526-8, Pub. by Collet's). State Mutual Bk.

Dictionary of Linguistics. Mario Pei & Frank Gaynor. (Quality Paperback: No. 177). 1980. pap. 4.95 (ISBN 0-8226-0177-X). Littlefield.

Dictionary of Linguistics. Ed. by Mario Pei & Frank Gaynor. 1960. 6.00 (ISBN 0-685-77553-4). Philos Lib.

Dictionary of Literary & Linguistic Terms. Magdi Wahba & Kamel Muhandes. 266p. (Arabic., With Arabic-English glossary). 30.00 (131-3). Intl Bk Ctr.

Dictionary of Literary-Rhetorical Conventions of the English Renaissance. Marjorie Donker & George M. Muldrow. LC 81-4266. xvi, 268p. 1982. lib. bdg. 35.00 (ISBN 0-313-23000-5, DER/). Greenwood.

Dictionary of Literary Terms. J. A. Cuddon. LC 76-47853. 1977. 17.95 (ISBN 0-385-12713-8). Doubleday.

Dictionary of Literary Terms. rev. ed. Charles Duffy & Henry Petit. pap. 2.00 (ISBN 0-910294-02-X). Brown Bk.

Dictionary of Literary Terms. Compiled by Magdi Wahba. 616p. (Arabic, Fr. & Eng.). 28.00 (117-8). Intl Bk Ctr.

Dictionary of Literary Terms see Concise Dictionary of Literary Terms.

Dictionary of Literary Terms (English-French-Arabic) Magdi Wahba. 1974. 28.00x (ISBN 0-86685-117-8). Intl Bk Ctr.

Dictionary of Livestock Breeds. I. L. Mason. 268p. 1969. cloth 50.00x (ISBN 0-85198-007-4, Pub. by CAB Bks England). State Mutual Bk.

Dictionary of Locksmithing. Keith Mayers. 1980. pap. 6.50 (ISBN 0-9604860-0-3). Mayers-Joseph.

Dictionary of Logical Terms & Symbols. Carol Greenstein. 1982. pap. text ed. 9.95 (ISBN 0-442-22836-8). Van Nos Reinhold.

Dictionary of Logical Terms & Symbols. Carol Greenstein. 1978. text ed. 13.95 (ISBN 0-442-22834-1). Van Nos Reinhold.

Dictionary of Lowland Scotch. Charles Mackay. LC 68-17998. (Scottish.). 1968. Repr. of 1888 ed. 45.00x (ISBN 0-8103-3284-1). Gale.

Dictionary of Machining. Eric N. Simons. (Illus.). 240p. 1973. 15.00 (ISBN 0-685-27907-3). Philos Lib.

Dictionary of Madame De Sevigne, 2 Vols. Edward Fitzgerald. Ed. by Mary E. Kerrich. LC 74-130598. 1971. Repr. of 1914 ed. lib. bdg. 43.00 (ISBN 0-8337-1140-7). B Franklin.

Dictionary of Man's Foods. William L. Esser. (Illus.). 1983. pap. 3.95 (ISBN 0-914532-06-5). Natural Hygiene.

Dictionary of Marine Engineering Terms: Japanese-English, English-Japanese. Ed. by M. Masuda. 313p. (Japanese & Eng.). 1980. 35.00 (ISBN 0-686-92525-4, M-9339). French & Eur.

Dictionary of Maritime Terms. (Hebrew, Eng. , Fr. & Ger.). IL.15.00. Massada Pr.

Dictionary of Marketing & Communication. Frank Jefkins. 1973. text ed. 19.95x (ISBN 0-7002-0218-8). Intl Ideas.

Dictionary of Marketing & Related Terms in the Motion Picture Industry. Donn Delson. LC 79-67865. (Entertainment Communication Ser.: Vol. 1). 70p. (Orig.). 1979. pap. text ed. 7.95 (ISBN 0-9603574-0-8). Bradson.

Dictionary of Marketing Terms. 4th ed. Irving J. Shapiro. (Littlefield, Adams Quality Paperback Ser.: No. 363). 280p. (Orig.). 1981. pap. 7.95 (ISBN 0-8226-0363-2). Littlefield.

Dictionary of Marketing Terms. 4th ed. Irving J. Shapiro. LC 80-25669. 280p. 1981. 16.50x (ISBN 0-8476-6967-X). Rowman.

Dictionary of Marks. Margaret MacDonald-Taylor. (Illus.). 1962. pap. 6.25 (ISBN 0-8015-2089-4, 0607-180, Hawthorn). Dutton.

Dictionary of Marks. Margaret Macdonald-Taylor. 320p. 1981. 25.00x (ISBN 0-900305-11-8, Pub. by Ebury Pr England). State Mutual Bk.

Dictionary of Marks: Pottery & Porcelain. Ralph M. Kovel & Terry H. Kovel. 1953. 8.95 (ISBN 0-517-00141-1). Crown.

Dictionary of Marxist Thought. Ed. by Tom Bottomore & Laurence Harris. 544p. 1983. 35.00 (ISBN 0-686-47014-1); prepub. 27.50 until 12/31/83. Harvard U Pr.

Dictionary of Materia Medica & Therapeutics. C. Henri Leonard & Thomas Christy. 1980. lib. bdg. 75.00 (ISBN 0-8490-3120-6). Gordon Pr.

Dictionary of Mathematical Sciences, 2 vols. Leo Herland. Incl. Vol. 1. German-English. 2nd ed. xii, 320p (ISBN 0-8044-4393-9); Vol. 2. English-German. 320p (ISBN 0-8044-4394-7). LC 65-16622. (Eng. & Ger.). 22.00 ea. Ungar.

Dictionary of Mathematical Sciences: Band II, Englisch-German. Herland. 349p. (Eng. & Ger.). 1982. DM.65.00. Brandstetter.

Dictionary of Mathematical Sciences: Band I, German-English. Herland. 323p. (Ger. & Eng.). 1982. DM.60.00. Brandstetter.

Dictionary of Mathematical Terms. (Hebrew & Eng.). IL.15.00. Massada Pr.

Dictionary of Mathematics. 252p. (Eng. & Chinese.). 1974. pap. 4.95 (ISBN 0-686-92280-8, M-9575). French & Eur.

Dictionary of Mathematics, 2 vols. G. Eisenreich & R. Sube. (Eng., Fr., Ger. & Rus.). 1982. Set. 159.75 (ISBN 0-444-99706-7). Elsevier.

Dictionary of Mathematics. William Millington & T. Alaric Millington. 1971. pap. 3.95 (ISBN 0-06-463311-X, EH 311, EH). B&N NY.

Dictionary of Measurement Technology for Computers. 161p. (Eng. & Chinese.). 1977. pap. 3.95 (ISBN 0-686-92302-2, M-9565). French & Eur.

Dictionary of Mechanical Engineering. 8th rev. ed. Henry G. Freeman. LC 72-347328. (Eng. Ger.). 1971. 45.00x (ISBN 3-7736-5031-0). Intl Pubns Serv.

Dictionary of Mechanical Engineering. 2nd ed. J. L. Nayler & G. H. Nayler. 1978. Repr. of 1975 ed. 29.95 (ISBN 0-408-00175-5). Butterworth.

Dictionary of Mechanical Engineering Terms. 9th rev. & enl. ed. J. G. Horner. Ed. by G. K. Grahame-White. 30.00 (ISBN 0-685-29250-9). Heinman.

Dictionary of Mechanisms. H. Bucksch. (Ger. & Eng.). 1976. leatherette 133.00 (ISBN 3-7625-0707-4, M-7111). French & Eur.

Dictionary of Mechanisms-Getriebeworterbuch: German-English, English-German. Herbert Bucksch. (Ger. & Eng.). 1976. 92.50x (ISBN 3-7625-0707-4). Intl Pubns Serv.

Dictionary of Medical Ethics. Ed. by A. S. Duncan et al. 496p. 1981. 24.50 (ISBN 0-8245-0038-5). Crossroad NY.

Dictionary of Medical Ethics & Practice. Thomson. 272p. 1977. 27.95 (ISBN 0-7236-0454-1). Wright-PSG.

Dictionary of Medical Folklore. Carol A. Rinzler. LC 78-69518. 1979. 14.37i (ISBN 0-690-01704-9). T Y Crowell.

Dictionary of Medical Syndromes. 2nd ed. Sergio I. Magalini & Euclide Scrascia. 896p. 1981. text ed. 52.00 (ISBN 0-397-50503-5, Lippincott Medical). Lippincott.

Dictionary of Medieval Latin from British Sources: Fascicule I, A-B. Compiled by R. E. Latham. (Medieval Lat.). 1975. pap. 55.00x (ISBN 0-19-725948-0); Fascicule 2 C. pap. 198.00x 1981 (ISBN 0-19-725968-5). Oxford U Pr.

Dictionary of Mesa Grande Dieguено. Ted Couro & Christina Hutcheson. 1973. pap. 5.50 (ISBN 0-939046-14-8). Malki Mus Pr.

Dictionary of Metal-Cutting Machine Tools, 2 vols. Henry G. Freeman. (Eng. & Ger.). 1965. 61.75 ea. (ISBN 3-7736-5095-7). Adler.

Dictionary of Metal-Cutting Machine Tools. Henry G. Freeman. 561p. (Eng. & Ger.). 1965. leatherette 72.00 (ISBN 3-7736-5095-7, M-7110). French & Eur.

Dictionary of Metallurgy. Ed. by A. Dollinger. 767p. (Eng., Fr., Ger., Rus., Pol. & Slovene.). 1974. 150.00 (ISBN 0-686-92409-6, M-9893). French & Eur.

Dictionary of Meteorological Terms. (Hebrew, Eng. , Fr. & Ger.). IL.10.00. Massada Pr.

Dictionary of Meteorology. 207p. (Eng. & Chinese.). 1974. pap. 4.95 (ISBN 0-686-92293-X, M-9567). French & Eur.

Dictionary of Mexican American History. Ed. by Matt S. Meier & Feliciano Rivera. LC 80-24750. (Illus.). 472p. 1981. lib. bdg. 35.00 (ISBN 0-313-21203-1, NMD/). Greenwood.

Dictionary of Microbial Taxonomic Usage. S. T. Cowan. 1968. 7.50 (ISBN 0-934454-28-0). Lubrecht & Cramer.

Dictionary of Microbial Taxonomy. S. T. Cowan. Ed. by L. R. Hill. LC 77-85705. (Illus.). 1978. 45.00 (ISBN 0-521-21890-X). Cambridge U Pr.

Dictionary of Microbiology. Paul Singleton & Diana Sainsbury. LC 78-4532. 481p. 1978. 71.95 (ISBN 0-471-99658-0, Pub. by Wiley-Interscience). Wiley.

Dictionary of Middle English Musical Terms. Henry H. Carter. Ed. by George B. Gerhard et al. LC 61-63413. (Indiana University Humanities Ser: No. 45). 1961. 39.00 (ISBN 0-527-15150-5). Kraus Repr.

Dictionary of Military & Naval Quotations. Ed. by Robert D. Heinl, Jr. LC 66-22342. 1966. 18.95 (ISBN 0-87021-149-8). Naval Inst Pr.

Dictionary of Military & Naval Quotations. Ed. by Robert D. Heinl, Jr. (Illus.). 395p. 1978. 18.95 (ISBN 0-87021-149-8); bulk rates avail. US Naval Inst.

Dictionary of Military Technological Abbreviations & Acronyms. Bernhard Pretz. 450p. 1983. 45.00 (ISBN 0-7100-9274-1). Routledge & Kegan.

Dictionary of Ming Biography, 1364-1644, 2 vols. Ed. by L. Carrington Goodrich & Chaoying Fang. (Illus.). 1976. 140.00x set (ISBN 0-685-62034-4). Vol. 1, 1054pgs (ISBN 0-231-03801-1). Vol. 2, 634pgs (ISBN 0-231-03833-X). Columbia U Pr.

Dictionary of Miniaturists, Illustrators, Calligraphers, & Copyists, with References to Their Works, & Notices of Their Patrons, from the Establishment of Christianity to the 18th Century, 3 vols. John W. Bradley. LC 61-35160. 1973. Repr. of 1887 ed. Set. lib. bdg. 85.00 (ISBN 0-8337-0353-6). B Franklin.

Dictionary of Minicomputing & Microcomputing. Philip E. Burton. 368p. 1983. pap. 17.95 (ISBN 0-8240-7286-3). Garland Pub.

Dictionary of Miracles. Ebenezer Brewer. 75.00 (ISBN 0-8490-0040-8). Gordon Pr.

Dictionary of Miracles, Imitative, Realistic, & Dogmatic. E. Cobham Brewer. LC 66-29783. 1966. Repr. of 1885 ed. 42.00 (ISBN 0-8103-3000-8). Gale.

Dictionary of Modern Business. Louis Robb. (Span. & Eng.). 1960. 30.00 (ISBN 0-910136-00-9). Anderson Kramer.

Dictionary of Modern Critical Terms. Ed. by Roger Fowler. 218p. 1973. 18.00x (ISBN 0-7100-7543-X); pap. 5.95 (ISBN 0-7100-7544-8). Routledge & Kegan.

Dictionary of Modern Economics. 2nd ed. D. W. Pearce. 480p. (Eng.). 1983. E17.95 (ISBN 0-333-36122-9); pap. 5.95 (ISBN 0-333-35173-8). Macmillan London.

Dictionary of Modern Engineering, 2 vols. 3rd ed. Ed. by Alfred Oppermann. Incl. Vol. 1. English-German. 912p. (Eng. & Ger.). 1972. 80.00 (ISBN 3-7940-6001-6); Vol. 2. German-English. 952p. (Ger. & Eng.). 1974. 80.00 (ISBN 3-7940-6002-4). 160.00x set (ISBN 3-7940-6003-2, Pub. by K G Saur). Gale.

Dictionary of Modern Engineering, Vol. 1. 3rd ed. Alfred Oppermann. (Eng. & Ger.). 1971. 113.00 (ISBN 3-7940-6001-6, M-7109). French & Eur.

Dictionary of Modern Engineering, Vol. 2. 3rd ed. Alfred Oppermann. (Ger. & Eng.). 1974. 113.00 (ISBN 3-7940-6002-4, M-7108). French & Eur.

Dictionary of Modern English Usage. 2nd ed. H. W. Fowler. 1983. pap. 8.95 (ISBN 0-19-281389-7, GB 725, GB). Oxford U Pr.

Dictionary of Modern English Usage. 2nd ed. Henry W. Fowler. Ed. by Ernest Gowers. (YA) (gr. 9 up). 1965. 15.95 (ISBN 0-19-500153-2); with thumb index 18.95 (ISBN 0-19-500154-0). Oxford U Pr.

Dictionary of Modern French Idioms, 2 vols. Barbara L. Gerber & Gerald H. Storzer. LC 76-24743. (Reference Library of the Humanities Ser.: Vol. 63). (Fr. & Eng.). 1977. Set. lib. bdg. 110.00 (ISBN 0-8240-9935-4). Garland Pub.

Dictionary of Modern German Prose Usage. H. F. Eggeling. (Ger.). 1961. 34.00x (ISBN 0-19-864110-9). Oxford U Pr.

Dictionary of Modern History. Alan W. Palmer. (Reference Ser.). (Orig.). (YA) (gr. 11 up). 1964. pap. 5.95 (ISBN 0-14-051026-5). Penguin.

Dictionary of Modern Iraqi Arabic. Daniel Woodhead. 509p. (Arabic & Eng.). pap. 10.00 (003-6). Intl Bk Ctr.

Dictionary of Modern Lebanese Proverbs. Anis Freyha. (Arabic & Eng.). 1974. 25.00x (ISBN 0-86685-086-4). Intl Bk Ctr.

Dictionary of Modern Lebanese Proverbs. Anis Freyha. 758p. (Arabic & Eng.). 1974. 25.00 (ISBN 0-86685-086-4, 086-4). Intl Bk Ctr.

Dictionary of Modern Linguistic Terms (English-Arabic) (Eng. & Arabic.). 1975. 20.00 (ISBN 0-86685-304-9). Intl Bk Ctr.

Dictionary of Modern Linguistic Terms: English-Arabic, Arabic-English. Bakalla. (Arabic & Eng.). 1975. 20.00 (ISBN 0-86685-304-9). Intl Bk Ctr.

Dictionary of Modern Music & Musicians. Ed. by A. Eaglefield-Hull. LC 78-139192. (Music Ser). 1971. Repr. of 1924 ed. lib. bdg. 55.00 (ISBN 0-306-70086-7). Da Capo.

Dictionary of Modern Music & Musicians. Ed. by Arthur E. Hull. LC 72-1619. Repr. of 1924 ed. 27.50 (ISBN 0-404-08315-3). AMS Pr.

Dictionary of Modern Music & Musicians. Ed. by Arthur E. Hull. LC 77-166238. 543p. 1924. Repr. 35.00 (ISBN 0-403-01365-8). Scholarly.

Dictionary of Modern Political Idiom. Magdi Wahba. ix, 747p. (Eng., Fr. & Arabic.). 1978. 25.00 (79-960201). Lib Liban.

Dictionary of Modern Political Idiom: English-French-Arabic. Magdi Wahba & Wagdi R. Ghali. LC 79-960201. ix, 747p. (Eng., Fr., & Arabic.). 1978. E25.00. Lib Liban.

Dictionary of Modern Sociology. Thomas F. Hoult. 448p. 1969. 11.50x (ISBN 0-87471-225-4). Rowman.

Dictionary of Modern Theological German. Helmut W. Ziefle. LC 82-70464. 360p. (Orig., Ger.). 1982. pap. 9.95 (ISBN 0-8010-9929-3). Baker Bk.

Dictionary of Modern Written Arabic. 4th, rev. ed. Ed. by J. Milton Cowan. 1300p. (Arabic & Eng.). 1979. 115.00x (ISBN 3-447-02002-4). Intl Pubns Serv.

Dictionary of Modern Written Arabic. 4th rev. ed. Hans Wehr. Ed. by J. M. Cowan. 1300p. (Arabic.). 1980. 115.00x (ISBN 0-87950-002-6). Spoken Lang Serv.

Dictionary of Modern Written Arabic. Hans Wehr. Ed. by Milton J. Cowan. 1300p. (Arabic & Eng.). 1979. 115.00 (ISBN 0-87950-002-6). Spoken Lang Serv.

Dictionary of Modern Written Arabic. Hans Wehr. Ed. by J. M. Cowan. xvii, 1110p. (Arabic & Eng.). E12.00 (ISBN 0-245-53120-3). Harrap.

Dictionary of Modern Written Arabic. 4th & enl. ed. Hans Wehr. Ed. by J. Milton Cowan. LC 80-466867. xviii, 1301p. (Arabic & Eng.). 1979. write for info. (ISBN 3-447-02002-4). Harrassowitz.

Dictionary of Modern Written Arabic. Compiled by Hans Wehr. 1110p. (Arabic & Eng.). 1980. pap. 12.00 pocket-bk. ed. (001-8); library ed. 85.00. Intl Bk Ctr.

Dictionary of Mong Njua: A Miao (Meo) Language of Southeast Asia. Thomas A. Lyman. LC 72-94484. (Janua Linguarum, Ser. Practica: No. 123). (Illus.). 403p. (Orig., Mongolian.). 1974. pap. text ed. 94.00x (ISBN 90-2792-696-4). Mouton.

Dictionary of Moroccan Arabic: Moroccan-Arabic English-Moroccan. Ed. by Richard S. Harrell & Harvey Sobelman. (Richard Slade Harrell Arabic Ser.). 528p. (Moroccan, Arabic & Eng.). 1963. pap. 19.95 (ISBN 0-87840-008-7). Georgetown U Pr.

Dictionary of Mottoes. L. G. Pine. 150p. 1983. 12.95 (ISBN 0-7100-9339-X). Routledge & Kegan.

Dictionary of Music. Brossard. Ed. by Albion Gruber. (Musical Theorists in Translation Ser.: No. 12). 280p. lib. bdg. 55.00 (ISBN 0-931902-15-0). Inst Mediaeval Mus.

Dictionary of Music. Ed. by Alan Isaacs. 432p. (Eng.). E6.95 (ISBN 0-600-33211-X). Newnes Bks.

Dictionary of Music. Ed. by Alan Isaacs & Elizabeth Martin. (Illus.). 428p. 1983. 17.95 (ISBN 0-87196-752-9). Facts on File.
Dictionary of Music. Hugo Riemann. LC 75-125060. (Music Ser). 1970. Repr. of 1908 ed. lib. bdg. 65.00 (ISBN 0-306-70025-5). Da Capo.
Dictionary of Music. Hugo Riemann. LC 74-166256. 925p. 1893. Repr. 79.00 (ISBN 0-403-01383-6). Scholarly.
Dictionary of Musical Information. John W. Moore. LC 72-1714. Repr. of 1876 ed. 15.00 (ISBN 0-404-09915-7). AMS Pr.
Dictionary of Musical Information. John W. Moore. LC 76-143644. (Bibliography & Reference Ser.: No. 418). 1971. Repr. of 1876 ed. lib. bdg. 21.50 (ISBN 0-8337-2449-5). B Franklin.
Dictionary of Musical Morphology. Siegmund Levarie & Ernst Levy. (Wissenschaftliche Abhandlungen-Musicological Studies: Vol. 29). viii, 400p. 1980. lib. bdg. 132.00 (ISBN 0-912024-32-1). Inst Mediaeval Mus.
Dictionary of Musical Terms. Theodore Baker. LC 75-124595. (BCL Ser.: No. 1). 1970. Repr. of 1923 ed. 8.00 (ISBN 0-404-00468-7). AMS Pr.
Dictionary of Musical Terms. Theodore Baker. 1923. 10.95 (ISBN 0-02-870200-X). Assoc-Mus.
Dictionary of Musical Terms. Vincent J. Picerno. LC 76-14903. (Studies in Music: N0. 42). 1976. lib. bdg. 49.95x (ISBN 0-8383-2119-4). Haskell.
Dictionary of Musical Terms. J. Stainer & W. A. Barrett. 35.00 (ISBN 0-8490-0041-6). Gordon Pr.
Dictionary of Musical Terms. John Stainer & W. A. Barrett. LC 71-166266. 464p. 1898. Repr. 69.00 (ISBN 0-403-01690-8). Scholarly.
Dictionary of Musical Terms. Johannes Tinctoris. Tr. by Carl Parrish. (Music Reprint Ser.). 1978. Repr. of 1963 ed. lib. bdg. 17.50 (ISBN 0-306-77560-3). Da Capo.
Dictionary of Musical Terms: Containing an English-Italian Vocabulary for Composers & Students. Th. Baker. (Eng. & Ital.). 24.50 (ISBN 0-87557-053-4, 053-4). Saphrograph.
Dictionary of Musical Terms in Seven Languages. 2nd ed. Ed. by H. Leuchtmann. (Illus., Eng., Ger., Fr., Ital., Span., Rus. & Hungarian.). 1980. 120.00 (ISBN 0-686-77981-9). Heinman.
Dictionary of Musical Themes. rev. ed. Compiled by Harold Barlow & Sam Morgenstern. (Illus.). 1976. 14.95 (ISBN 0-517-52446-5). Crown.
Dictionary of Musicians: From the Earliest Times. Ed. by John S. Sainsbury. LC 65-23396. (Music Reprint Ser.). 963p. 1966. Repr. of 1825 ed. 55.00 (ISBN 0-306-70931-7). Da Capo.
Dictionary of Muslim Philosophy. M. Saeeed. 5.95 (ISBN 0-686-18370-3). Kazi Pubns.
Dictionary of Mysticism. Frank Gaynor. 211p. 1973. pap. 2.45 (ISBN 0-8065-0172-3). Citadel Pr.
Dictionary of Named Effects: Laws in Chemistry, Physics & Mathematics. 4th ed. D. W. Ballentyne & D. R. Lovett. 1982. 19.95x (ISBN 0-412-22390-2, NO. 6780, Pub. by Chapman & Hall England). Methuen Inc.
Dictionary of Names & Universal Information. Joseph T. Haydn. Repr. 89.00 (ISBN 0-403-00083-1). Scholarly.
Dictionary of Names, Nicknames, & Surnames. Edward Latham. LC 66-22674. 1966. Repr. of 1904 ed. 37.00x (ISBN 0-8103-0157-1). Gale.
Dictionary of Natural Environment. Ahmad Khatib. 59p. (Eng. & Arabic.). 1979. pap. 7.95 (073-2). Intl Bk Ctr.
Dictionary of Natural Environment. F. J. Monkhouse & John Small. 326p. 1978. pap. text ed. 9.95 (ISBN 0-7131-5958-8). E Arnold.
Dictionary of Natural Environment with English-Arabic Glossary. F. Monkhouse. 16.00x (ISBN 0-86685-078-3). Intl Bk Ctr.
Dictionary of Natural Foods. William L. Esser. (Illus.). 1983. pap. 4.95 (ISBN 0-914532-30-8). Natural Hygiene.
Dictionary of Nautical Words & Terms. C. W. Layton. 1981. 60.00x (ISBN 0-85174-324-2, Pub. by Nautical England). State Mutual Bk.
Dictionary of Nautical Words & Terms. 2nd, rev. ed. C. W. Layton. 395p. 1982. text ed. 32.50x (ISBN 0-85174-422-2). Sheridan.
Dictionary of Naval Abbreviations. 2nd ed. Ed. by Bill Wedertz. LC 77-77336. 352p. 1977. 12.95x (ISBN 0-87021-154-4). Naval Inst Pr.
Dictionary of Naval Abbreviations. 2nd ed. Ed. by Bill Wedertz. (Illus.). 352p. 1977. 12.95 (ISBN 0-87021-154-4); bulk rates avail. US Naval Inst.
Dictionary of Naval Terminology-Dictionnaire de Terminologie Navale: English-French; Anglais-Francais. Ronald E. Ratcliff & Michael A. Peck. (Illus.). 160p. (Orig.). 1983. pap. text ed. 39.00x (ISBN 2-85206-200-3, Pub. by Technique Doc France). Sheridan.
Dictionary of Needlework. Sophia F. Caulfield & Blanche C. Saward. LC 75-172439. (Illus.). 1971. Repr. of 1882 ed. 85.00x (ISBN 0-8103-3404-6). Gale.
Dictionary of New English. Clarence Barnhart. 572p. (Eng.). 1973. 110.00. Colin.
Dictionary of New Information Technology. A. J. Meadows et al. 256p. 1982. 29.00x (ISBN 0-7126-0019-1, Pub. by Century Pub Co). State Mutual Bk.
Dictionary of New Mexico & Southern Colorado Spanish. Ruben Cobos. 200p. (Mexican & Span.). 1983. 14.95 (ISBN 0-89013-141-4); pap. text ed. 7.95 (ISBN 0-686-46179-7). Museum NM Pr.
Dictionary of New Testament Greek Synonyms. George R. Berry. (Gr.). 1979. 4.95 (ISBN 0-310-21161-1). Zondervan.
Dictionary of Newfoundland English. Ed. by G. M. Story. W. J Kirwin & J. D. Widdowson. 700p. 1982. 45.00 (ISBN 0-8020-5570-2). U of Toronto Pr.
Dictionary of Nggela. Charles El. Fox. 271p. (Nggela.). 1955. 2.50. Anthro AucMus.
Dictionary of Ngizim. Russell G. Schuh. (U.C. Publications in Linguistics: Vol. 99). 256p. 1981. 12.50x (ISBN 0-520-09636-3). U of Cal Pr.
Dictionary of Nigerian Arabic. Alan S. Kaye. LC 81-71736. (Bibliotheca Afroasiatica Ser.: Vol. 1). 104p. (Orig., Nigerian Arabic.). 1982. 26.00x (ISBN 0-89003-100-2); pap. 19.50x (ISBN 0-89003-101-0). Undena Pubns.
Dictionary of Non-Classical Vocables in Spoken Arabic. Anis Freyha. (Arabic.). 1973. 16.00x (ISBN 0-86685-098-8). Intl Bk Ctr.
Dictionary of Non-English Words of the Pennsylvania German Dialect. Marcus B. Lambert. 1977. 15.00 (ISBN 0-686-79892-9). Penn German Soc.
Dictionary of Numismatic Names. A. R. Frey. 1973. 20.00 (ISBN 0-685-51559-1, Pub by Spink & Son England). S J Durst.
Dictionary of Nutrition. Richard Ashley & Heidi Duggal. 1976. pap. 3.50 (ISBN 0-671-49407-4). PB.
Dictionary of Nutrition. 5th ed. Bender. 1983. text ed. write for info. Butterworth.
Dictionary of Nutrition & Food Technology. 4th ed. Arnold E. Bender. 1975. text ed. 29.95 (ISBN 0-408-00143-7). Butterworth.
Dictionary of Occult, Hermetic & Alchemical Sigils. Fred Gettings. 1981. 40.00 (ISBN 0-7100-0095-2). Routledge & Kegan.
Dictionary of Official Titles in Imperial China: Governmental Nomenclature from Antiquity to 1850. Charles O. Hucker. Date not set. price not set. Stanford U Pr.
Dictionary of Old English Music & Musical Instruments. Jeffrey Pulver. 75.00 (ISBN 0-8490-0042-4). Gordon Pr.
Dictionary of Old South Arabic: Sabaen Dialect. Joan C. Biella. LC 81-8946. (Harvard Semitic Studies). (Arabic.). 1982. 33.00 (ISBN 0-89130-455-X, 04-04-25). Scholars Pr CA.
Dictionary of One Thousand Dreams. R. Greer. 1.00 (ISBN 0-685-02610-8, 00545193). Stein Pub.
Dictionary of Onomatopoeic Sounds, Tones, & Noises in English & Spanish. Donald R. Kloe. LC 77-2627. (Eng. & Span.). 1977. 25.50 (ISBN 0-87917-059-X). Ethridge.
Dictionary of Opera & Song Themes. rev. ed. Compiled by Harold Barlow & Sam Morgenstern. 1976. 15.95 (ISBN 0-517-52503-8). Crown.
Dictionary of Operations. Ed. by Stanway. Epap. 2.50. Paladin.
Dictionary of Optics Photography & Photogrammetry: German-English & English-German. Ed. by G. Richter. (Eng. & Ger.). 1966. 44.00 (ISBN 0-444-40478-3). Elsevier.
Dictionary of Oregon History. Ed. by Howard M. Corning. 16.50 (ISBN 0-8323-0099-3). Binford.
Dictionary of Organic Compounds, 7 Vols. 5th ed. Ed. by J. Buckingham et al. 1982. Set. 1950.00x (ISBN 0-412-17000-0, NO.6611, Pub. by Chapman & Hall). Methuen Inc.
Dictionary of Organic Compounds: First Supplement. Ed. by J. B. Buckingham et al. 1983. 175.00 (ISBN 0-412-17010-8, NO. 6798, Pub. by Chapman & Hall). Methuen Inc.
Dictionary of Oriental Quotations. Claud Field. 75.00 (ISBN 0-8490-0043-2). Gordon Pr.
Dictionary of Oriental Quotations. Claud H. Field. LC 68-23157. 1969. Repr. of 1911 ed. 38.00x (ISBN 0-8103-3183-7). Gale.
Dictionary of Oriental Rugs: With a Monograph on Identification by Weave. Ivan C. Neff & Carol V. Maggs. 1979. 29.95 (ISBN 0-442-20617-8). Van Nos Reinhold.
Dictionary of Oto-Rhino-Laryngology in Five Languages. A. Larrauri. LC 71-501781. 1008p. (Eng., Fr., Span., Ger. & Ital.). 1971. 65.00x (ISBN 0-8002-0197-3). Intl Pubns Serv.
Dictionary of Packaging: German-English-French. 2nd, rev. ed. Johannes P. Hoffman. LC 72-352784. 353p. (Ger., Eng. & Fr.). 1971. 62.50 (ISBN 0-8002-0745-9). Intl Pubns Serv.
Dictionary of Painters of Miniatures, 1525-1850 with Some Account of Exhibitions, Collections, Sales, Etc. Joshua J. Foster. Ed. by Ethel M. Foster. 1967. Repr. of 1926 ed. 29.50 (ISBN 0-8337-1218-7). B Franklin.
Dictionary of Painting & Decorating. J. H. Goodier. 308p. 1974. 39.50x (ISBN 0-85264-224-5, Pub. by Griffin England). State Mutual Bk.
Dictionary of Papago Usage: Vol. I, B-K. Madeleine Mathiot. (Language Science Monographs: No. 8-1). 504p. (Papago.). 1974. pap. text ed. 55.00x (ISBN 0-686-27742-2). Mouton.
Dictionary of Patent Practice. J. Vuexkull & H. J. Reich. 258p. (Ger. & Eng.). 1977. 57.00 (ISBN 3-452-18239-8, M-7107). French & Eur.
Dictionary of Persian & English Languages. Fazl-i-Ali. 668p. (Persian & Eng.). 1979. Repr. of 1885 ed. 39.00 (ISBN 0-89684-266-5, Pub. by Cosmo Pubns India). Orient Bk Dist.
Dictionary of Persian Loan Words in the Arabic Language. Al-Sayyid Addi. (Persian & Arabic.). 1980. 21.00x (ISBN 0-86685-128-3). Intl Bk Ctr.
Dictionary of Persian Loan Words in the Arabic Language. Al-Sayyid'Addi Shir. 194p. (Arabic & Persian.). 21.00 (128-3). Intl Bk Ctr.
Dictionary of Personnel & Industrial Relations. Ed. by Esther Becker. 1958. 10.00 (ISBN 0-8022-0088-5). Philos Lib.
Dictionary of Personnel Management & Labor Relations. Jay M. Schafritz. LC 79-24632. (Orig.). 1980. 29.00 (ISBN 0-935610-09-X). Moore Pub IL.
Dictionary of Petroleum & the Oil Industry. Ahmad Khatib. (Illus.). 550p. (Eng. & Arabic.). 40.00 (074-0). Intl Bk Ctr.
Dictionary of Petroleum-Industry & Petroleum Chemistry. E. Leipnitz. (Polyglot.). 1979. 40.80 (ISBN 3-87097-073-1). Adler.
Dictionary of Petroleum Technology-Dictionnaire Technique Du Petrol: English-French - French-English. rev. ed. Ed. by Magdaleine Moureau & Gerald Brace. LC 79-122883. (Collection Des Dictionnaires Techniques: No. 1). 975p. (Eng. & Fr.). 1979. 130.00x (ISBN 2-7108-0361-5). Intl Pubns Serv.
Dictionary of Petroleum Technology: English-French, French-English. Rev. ed. M. Moureau & G. Brace. 946p. (Fr. & Eng.). 1979. 115.00. Imported Bks.
Dictionary of Petroleum Terms. (Eng., Austin). 1979. 7.00 (1-30020). U of TX.
DIctionary of Petroleum Terms. 3rd ed. Ed. by Jodie Leecraft. LC 83-61652. (Illus.). 177p. 1983. text ed. 16.00 (ISBN 0-88698-000-3); pap. text ed. 9.00 (ISBN 0-88698-001-1). PETEX.
Dictionary of Philosophy. Antony Flew. 1980. pap. 8.95 (ISBN 0-312-20922-3). St Martin.
Dictionary of Philosophy. Ed. by Antony Flew. LC 78-68699. 1979. 20.00 (ISBN 0-312-20921-5). St Martin.
Dictionary of Philosophy. Ed. by Ivant Frolov. 467p. 1983. 8.95 (ISBN 0-7178-0604-9). Intl Pub Co.
Dictionary of Philosophy. A. R. Lacey. 1976. 18.00x (ISBN 0-7100-8361-0). Routledge & Kegan.
Dictionary of Philosophy. A. R. Lacey. 1977. pap. text ed. 8.95x (ISBN 0-684-14932-X, ScribC). Scribner.
Dictionary of Philosophy. rev., enl. ed. Ed. by Dagobert D. Runes. LC 81-80240. 364p. 1983. Repr. 24.95 (ISBN 0-8022-2388-5). Philos Lib.
Dictionary of Philosophy & Psychology, 3 vols. bound in 4. James M. Baldwin. Incl. Vols. 1 & 2. 27.00 ea.; Vol. 1. (ISBN 0-8446-1047-X); Vol. 2. (ISBN 0-8446-1048-8); Vol. 3., 2 Pts. Bibliography of Philosophy, Psychology and Cognate Subjects. 24.00 ea.; Pt. 1. (ISBN 0-8446-1049-6); Pt. 2. (ISBN 0-8446-1050-X). Set. 102.00 (ISBN 0-8446-1046-1). Peter Smith.
Dictionary of Philosophy & Psychology. James M. Baldwin et al. 1977. lib. bdg. 395.00 (ISBN 0-8490-1721-1). Gordon Pr.
Dictionary of Philosophy & Religion: Eastern & Western Thought. William L. Reese. iv, 644p. 1980. write for info. (ISBN 0-391-00688-6). Humanities.
Dictionary of Photograhy. (Hebrew, Eng. , Fr & Ger.). IL.8.00. Massada Pr.
Dictionary of Photographic Terms. A. Page. (Illus.). 1966. 17.50 (ISBN 0-685-58545-X). Heinman.
Dictionary of Phrase & Fable. E. C. Brewer. Date not set. 7.98 (ISBN 0-517-25921-4). Outlet Bk Co.
Dictionary of Physical Metallurgy. E. F. Tyrkiel. (Eng., Ger., Fr., Pol. & Rus.). 1978. 85.00 (ISBN 0-444-99810-1). Elsevier.
Dictionary of Physical Sciences. John Daintith. LC 76-41039. (Illus.). 1977. 20.00x (ISBN 0-87663-723-3, Pica Pr). Universe.

Dictionary of Physical Sciences. Ed. by John Daintith. (Helix Bk.: No. 379). (Illus.). 333p. 1983. pap. 9.95 (ISBN 0-8226-0379-9). Rowman & Allanheld.

Dictionary of Physics. Ed. by John Daintith. 1982. pap. 5.72i (ISBN 0-06-463560-0, EH-560). Har-Row.

Dictionary of Physics. 1689p. (Eng. & Chinese.). 1978. 19.95 (ISBN 0-686-92341-3, M-9287). French & Eur.

Dictionary of Physics see New Dictionary of Physics.

Dictionary of Physics & Allied Sciences: English-German. Ed. by Ralph Idlin. LC 77-6950. (Eng. & Ger.). 1978. 30.00 (ISBN 0-8044-4435-8). Ungar.

Dictionary of Physics & Allied Sciences: German-English. Ed. by Charles J. Hyman. LC 77-6949. (Ger. & Eng.). 1978. 30.00 (ISBN 0-8044-4433-1). Ungar.

Dictionary of Physics: English-Chinese. 388p. (Eng. & Chinese.). 1980. 25.00 (ISBN 0-686-97645-2, M-9276). French & Eur.

Dictionary of Physics: No. 1, Mechanics. (Hebrew, Eng. , Fr. & Ger.). IL.8.00. Massada Pr.

Dictionary of Physics: No. 2, Electricity & Magnetism. (Hebrew, Eng. , Fr. & Ger.). IL.8.00. Massada Pr.

Dictionary of Physics: No. 3, Optics. (Hebrew, Eng. , Fr. & Ger.). IL.8.00. Massada Pr.

Dictionary of Pipe Organ Stops. 2nd ed. Stevens Irwin. 1983. 19.95 (ISBN 0-02-871150-5). Assoc-Mus.

Dictionary of Plastics. J. A. Wordingham & P. Reboul. (Quality Paperback: No. 174). 1967. pap. 2.95 (ISBN 0-8226-0174-5). Littlefield.

Dictionary of Plastics Technology in English, German, French & Russian. G. Kaliske. 384p. (Eng., Ger., Fr. & Rus.). 74.50 (ISBN 0-444-99687-7). Elsevier.

Dictionary of Polish Pronunciation: Slownik Wymomwy Polskiej PWN. (Pol.). 1980. 25.00x (ISBN 0-686-61083-0). Hippocrene Bks.

Dictionary of Political Analysis. 2nd ed. Jack C. Plano et al. LC 82-4032. (Clio Dictionaries in Political Science Ser.: No. 3). 197p. 1982. text ed. 19.75 (ISBN 0-87436-331-4); pap. 9.75 (ISBN 0-87436-339-X). ABC-Clio.

Dictionary of Political Analysis. G. K. Roberts. LC 70-151309. 1971. 22.50 (ISBN 0-312-20930-4). St Martin.

Dictionary of Political Economy, 3 vols. Robert H. Palgrave. LC 74-31358. 1976. Repr. of 1910 ed. Set. 191.00x (ISBN 0-8103-4210-3). Gale.

Dictionary of Political Idioms. Compiled by Magdi Wahba & Magdi Ghali. 747p. (Arabic, Fr. & Eng., With index of Fr. & Arabic key words). 1978. 35.00 (118-6). Intl Bk Ctr.

Dictionary of Political Phrases & Allusions. Hugh Montgomery. 75.00 (ISBN 0-8490-0044-0). Gordon Pr.

Dictionary of Political Phrases & Allusions with a Short Bibliography. Hugh Montgomery. LC 68-28333. 1968. Repr. of 1906 ed. 34.00x (ISBN 0-8103-3092-X). Gale.

Dictionary of Political Science & Law. Rudolph Heimanson. LC 67-14401. 188p. 1967. 12.00 (ISBN 0-379-00325-2). Oceana.

Dictionary of Political Terminology. Compiled by M. B. Khopkar. 1970. pap. 2.75 (ISBN 0-88253-149-2). Ind-US Inc.

Dictionary of Political Terms: Chinese-English, English-Chinese. Joseph D. Lowe. (Illus.). xvii, 950p. (Chinese & Eng.). 1983. 75.00 (ISBN 0-9605506-0-7). Lowe Pub.

Dictionary of Political Thought. Robert Scruton. LC 82-47532. 352p. 1982. 19.18i (ISBN 0-06-015044-0, HarpT). Har-Row.

Dictionary of Political Thought. ROger Scruton. 512p. (Eng.). 1982. E12.00 (ISBN 0-333-33439-6). Macmillan London.

Dictionary of Political Thought. Ed. by Roger Scruton. 356p. (Orig., Eng.). 1982. E8.95. Macmillan London.

Dictionary of Politics. rev. ed. Walter Laqueur. LC 74-9232. 1974. 17.95 (ISBN 0-02-917950-5). Free Pr.

Dictionary of Politics. Walter J. Raymond. LC 78-50189. (Illus.). deluxe ed. 25.95x (ISBN 0-931494-00-1). Brunswick Pub.

Dictionary of Politics & Economic Policy. H. Zahn. 384p. (Ger., Eng. & Fr.). 1975. 49.50 (ISBN 0-7121-5514-7, M-7105). French & Eur.

Dictionary of Politics & Economics. H. Back et al. 1037p. (Eng., Fr. & Ger., Dictionnaire de Politique et d'Economie - Lexikon fur Politik und Wirschaft). 1967. 37.00 (ISBN 3-11-000892-0, M-7104). French & Eur.

Dictionary of Popular Music. Peter Gammond & Peter Clayton. LC 73-166229. 274p. 1961. Repr. 29.00 (ISBN 0-403-01563-4). Scholarly.

Dictionary of Power Plant Engineering: Conventional Steam Power Plants, Pt. I. F. Stattmann. 252p. (Ger. & Fr.). 1971. 13.50 (ISBN 3-521-06059-4, M-7103). French & Eur.

Dictionary of Power Plant Engineering: Nuclear Power Plants, Pt. II. F. Stattmann. 316p. (Ger. & Fr.). 1973. 15.95 (ISBN 3-521-06081-0, M-7102). French & Eur.

Dictionary of Practical Law. Charles F. Hemphill, Jr. & Phyllis Hemphill. 1979. text ed. 12.95 (ISBN 0-13-210567-5, Spec); pap. text ed. 4.95 (ISBN 0-13-210559-4). P-H.

Dictionary of Practical Materia Medica. John H. Clarke. 1980. 125.00x (ISBN 0-85032-139-5, Pub. by Daniel Co England). State Mutual Bk.

Dictionary of Practical Materia Medica, 3 vols. 2585p. 1980. text ed. 119.95x (ISBN 0-8464-1004-4). Beekman Pubs.

Dictionary of Prehistoric Indian Artifacts of the American Southwest. Franklin Barnett. LC 73-82865. (Illus.). 288p. 1973. pap. 8.95 (ISBN 0-87358-120-2). Northland.

Dictionary of Problem Words & Expressions. Harry Shaw. 1975. 24.95 (ISBN 0-07-056489-2, P&RB). McGraw.

Dictionary of Production Engineering: German-English-French, 8 vols. International Institution for Production Engineering Research. Incl. Vol. 1. Forging & Drop Forging. 108p. 1962. 30.00x (ISBN 3-7736-5920-2); Vol. 2. Grinding - Surface Roughness. 140p. 1963. 30.00x (ISBN 3-7736-5930-X); Vol. 3. Sheet Metal Forming. 136p. 1965. 30.00x (ISBN 3-7736-5940-7); Vol. 4. Fundamental Terms of Cutting. 124p. 1969. 30.00x (ISBN 3-7736-5946-6); Vol. 5. Cold Extrusion & Upsetting. 157p. 1969. 30.00x (ISBN 3-7736-5945-8); Vol. 6. Planing, Slotting, Broaching, Turning. 1972. 30.00x (ISBN 3-7736-5946-6); Vol. 7. 30.00x (ISBN 3-7736-5947-4); Milling, Sawing, Gear Manufacturing. 359p. 1979. 42.50x (ISBN 3-7736-5948-2). (Ger., Eng. & Fr.). Intl Pubns Serv.

Dictionary of Pronunciation. Abraham Lass & Betty Lass. LC 75-36252. 356p. 1976. 15.95 (ISBN 0-8129-0614-4). Times Bks.

Dictionary of Pronunciation. 4th ed. Samuel Noory. LC 81-66273. 512p. 1981. 19.95 (ISBN 0-8453-4722-5). Cornwall Bks.

Dictionary of Proto-Circassian Roots. A. H. Kuipers. (PDR Press Publication on North Caucasian Languages: No. 1). 1975. pap. text ed. 13.75x (ISBN 90-316-0018-0). Humanities.

Dictionary of Psychological Medicine, 2 vols. Daniel H. Tuke. LC 75-16737. (Classics in Psychiatry Ser.). 1976. Repr. of 1892 ed. Set. 84.00x (ISBN 0-405-07457-3); 42.00x ea. Vol. 1 (ISBN 0-405-07458-1). Vol. 2 (ISBN 0-405-07459-X). Ayer Co.

Dictionary of Psychology. Berger. 133p. (Eng.). 1982. DM.45.00. Brandstetter.

Dictionary of Psychology. J. P. Chaplin. 608p. 1975. pap. 3.50 (ISBN 0-440-31926-9, LE). Dell.

Dictionary of Psychology. rev. ed. James Drever. lib. bdg. 11.50x (ISBN 0-88307-338-2). Gannon.

Dictionary of Psychology. rev. ed. James Drever. (Reference Ser.). (Orig.). (YA) (gr. 11 up). 1964. pap. 4.95 (ISBN 0-14-051005-2). Penguin.

Dictionary of Psychology. Philip L. Harriman. 1971. pap. 3.95 (ISBN 0-8065-0252-5). Citadel Pr.

Dictionary of Psychology. David Statt. 1982. pap. 4.76i (ISBN 0-06-463553-8, EH-553). Har-Row.

Dictionary of Psychology & Psychiatry: English-German. Ed. by Roland Haas. 453p. (Eng. & Ger.). text ed. 49.00 (ISBN 0-88937-000-1). C J Hogrefe.

Dictionary of Psychology & Psychiatry. Roland Haas. (Eng. & Ger.). 1979. Can.$64.00 (ISBN 0-88937-000-1). Hogrefe.

Dictionary of Psychology & Related Fields. Beigel. 256p. (Eng.). 1982. DM.55.00. Brandstetter.

Dictionary of Psychology & Related Fields. Hugo G. Beigel. LC 74-115063. (Ger. & Eng.). 15.00 (ISBN 0-8044-0042-3). Ungar.

Dictionary of Psychology: English-German. Ed. by Alfred H. Berger. LC 76-15645. (Eng. & Ger.). 1977. 14.50 (ISBN 0-8044-0043-1). Ungar.

Dictionary of Psychology: With Thesaurus. William Verplanck. 45.00x (ISBN 0-89197-729-5). Irvington.

Dictionary of Publishing. David M. Brownstone & Irene M. Franck. 304p. 1982. text ed. 18.95 (ISBN 0-442-25874-7). Van Nos Reinhold.

Dictionary of Puget Salish. Thom Hess. LC 75-42197. (Illus.). 766p. 1976. 21.50x (ISBN 0-295-95436-1). U of Wash Pr.

Dictionary of Pump Terms. (Hebrew, Eng. , Fr. & Ger.). IL.7.00. Massada Pr.

Dictionary of Puns in Milton's English Poetry. Edward Le Comte. 240p. 1981. 27.00x (ISBN 0-231-05102-6). Columbia U Pr.

Dictionary of Pure & Applied Physics, 2 vols. L. De Vries & W. E. Clason. Set. 65.25 (ISBN 0-686-85922-7); Vol. I, Ger.-Eng. 42.00 (ISBN 0-444-41068-6); Vol. II, Eng.-Ger. 42.00 (ISBN 0-685-05581-7). Elsevier.

Dictionary of Quantities & Units of Measurement. Drazil. 450p. (Eng., Ger. & Fr.). 1983. DM.65.00. Brandstetter.

Dictionary of Quotoons. O. A. Battista. LC 66-12694. 9.95 (ISBN 0-915074-04-4). Research Servs Corp.

Dictionary of Races or Peoples. D. Folkman & E. Folkman. 75.00 (ISBN 0-8490-0045-9). Gordon Pr.

Dictionary of Radio & Television Terms. BBC & ZDF. (Ger. & Eng.). 1973. 29.95 (ISBN 0-471-25586-6, Pub. by Wiley Heyden). Wiley.

Dictionary of Radiologic Terminology. Alphons Jacob & Herbert L. Jackson. 107p. 1982. 27.50 (ISBN 0-87527-216-9). Green.

Dictionary of Radiological Engineering. Gustav F. Neuder & Heinz M. Ullrich. 1979. pap. text ed. 36.50 (ISBN 3-11-007807-4). De Gruyter.

Dictionary of Railway Terms. 1033p. (Polyglot.). 1978. 47.50x (ISBN 0-8002-2264-4). Intl Pubns Serv.

Dictionary of Reading & Learning Disabilities. Clifford L. Bush & Robert C. Andrews. LC 79-57293. 179p. 1978. pap. 13.40x (ISBN 0-87424-153-7). Western Psych.

Dictionary of Reduplicated Words in the English Language. Henry B. Wheatley. LC 75-22169. 1975. Repr. of 1866 ed. lib. bdg. 15.00 (ISBN 0-8414-9407-X). Folcroft.

Dictionary of Refrigeration & Air Conditioning. K. M. Booth. 1970. 29.90x (ISBN 0-444-20069-X, Pub. by Applied Science). Burgess-Intl Ideas.

Dictionary of Refrigeration & Air Conditioning. Ed. by K. M. Booth. 1971. 30.75 (ISBN 0-444-20069-X). Elsevier.

Dictionary of Rehabilitation Medicine. Herman L. Kamenetz. 384p. 1983. text ed. 23.95 (ISBN 0-8261-3320-7). Springer Pub.

Dictionary of Religion & Ethics. Ed. by Shailer Mathews & Gerald B. Smith. LC 70-145713. 1971. Repr. of 1921 ed. 45.00x (ISBN 0-8103-3196-9). Gale.

Dictionary of Religious Terms see Baker's Pocket Dictionary of Religious Terms.

Dictionary of Reprography: Terms & Definitions. Ed. by Deutsches Kommitee Fur Reprographie. 273p. (Ger. & Fr.). 1976. pap. text ed. 34.00 (ISBN 3-7940-3186-5, Pub. by K G Saur). Gale.

Dictionary of Rhyming Slang. rev ed. Julian Franklyn. 1975. 16.00 (ISBN 0-7100-8051-4); pap. 7.95 (ISBN 0-7100-8052-2). Routledge & Kegan.

Dictionary of Russian Literature. William E. Harkins. LC 75-139135. 1971. Repr. of 1956 ed. lib. bdg. 22.25x (ISBN 0-8371-5751-X, HARL). Greenwood.

Dictionary of Russian Obscenities. 24p. (Rus.). 1971. pap. 2.50x (ISBN 0-685-47489-5). Schoenhof.

Dictionary of Russian Obscenities. rev. ed. David A. Drummond & G. Perkins. 79p. (Rus. & Eng.). 1980. pap. text ed. 3.50 (ISBN 0-933884-17-6). Berkeley Slavic.

Dictionary of Russian Personal Names. Ed. by Morton Benson. LC 64-19386. 1964. 15.00x (ISBN 0-8122-7452-0). U of Pa Pr.

Dictionary of Russian Technical & Scientific Abbreviations. H. Zalucki. (Rus. & Ger.). 1968. 70.25 (ISBN 0-444-40657-3). Elsevier.

Dictionary of Russian Verbs. R. Ruzicka. Compiled by E. Daum & W. Schenk. 752p. (Rus. & Eng.). 1974. 17.50 (O-26). Hippocrene Bks.

Dictionary of Russian Verbs. Rudolf Ruzicka. 748p. (Rus.). 1974. 17.50 (Dist. by Four Continent). Hippocrene Bks.

Dictionary of Russian Verbs (Russian-English) V. Daum & Schenk. 750p. (Rus. & Eng.). 1980. 75.00x (ISBN 0-569-08093-2, Pub. by Collet's). State Mutual Bk.

Dictionary of Sanskrit Grammar. 2nd rev. ed. Kashinath V. Abhyankar & J. M. Shukla. LC 78-903053. xv, 448p. (Eng. & Sanskrit.). 1977. Rs.58.00. Oriental Institute.

Dictionary of Satanism. Wade Baskin. 1972. pap. 3.95 (ISBN 0-8065-0292-4). Citadel Pr.

Dictionary of Science & Technology. Chambers. 1328p. 1982. DM.100.00; DM.pap. 40.00. Brandstetter.

Dictionary of Science & Technology. Chambers. 1296p. (Ger.). 1982. DM.pap. 40.00. Brandstetter.

Dictionary of Science & Technology. 469p. (Eng. & Chinese.). 1973. 14.95 (ISBN 0-686-92348-0, M-9261). French & Eur.

Dictionary of Science & Technology. 1689p. (Eng. & Chinese.). 1978. 9.95 (ISBN 0-686-92375-8, M-9560). French & Eur.

Dictionary of Science & Technology, 2 vols. 2nd, rev. ed. Compiled by A. F. Dorian. (Ger. & Eng.). 1982. Set. 242.75 (ISBN 0-686-85923-5). Elsevier.

Dictionary of Science & Technology, 2 Vols. Ed. by A. F. Dorian. 1400p. 1979. Set. 255.50 (ISBN 0-686-85924-3); Vol. I: Fr.- Eng. 127.75 (ISBN 0-444-41911-X); Vol. II: Eng. & Fr. 127.75 (ISBN 0-444-41829-6). Elsevier.

Dictionary of Science & Technology. Angelo F. Dorian. LC 79-18507. 1586p. (Eng. & Fr.). 1979. write for info. (ISBN 0-444-41829-6). Elsevier.
Dictionary of Science & Technology: Eng. & Chinese. 713p. (Chinese.). 1979. pap. 5.95 (ISBN 0-686-92552-1, M-9587). French & Eur.
Dictionary of Scientific & Technical Terms. 2nd ed. Lapedes. (Illus.). 1800p. 50.00. McGraw.
Dictionary of Scientific Units. 3rd ed. H. G. Jerrard & D. B. McNeill. 1972. 11.00 (ISBN 0-470-44230-1). Halsted Pr.
Dictionary of Scientific Word Elements. William B. Mullen. LC 69-20141. (Quality Paperback: No. 102). (Orig.). 1969. pap. 2.95 (ISBN 0-8226-0102-8). Littlefield.
Dictionary of Sea Painters. E. H. Archibald. (Illus.). 453p. 1980. 79.50 (ISBN 0-902028-84-7). Antique Collect.
Dictionary of Sea Painters. E. H. Archibald. (Illus.). 1979. 79.50 (ISBN 0-902028-84-7). Apollo.
Dictionary of Sea Waves & Currents Terms. (Hebrew, Eng. , Fr. & Ger.). IL.7.00. Massada Pr.
Dictionary of Selected Legal Terms & Maxims, Vol. 58. 2nd ed. Edward J. Bander. LC 79-19266. (Legal Almanac Ser.: No. 58). 140p. 1979. 5.95 (ISBN 0-379-11119-5). Oceana.
Dictionary of Selected Synonyms in the Principal Indo-European Languages. Carl D. Buck. LC 49-11769. 1949. 80.00x (ISBN 0-226-07932-5). U of Chicago Pr.
Dictionary of Sewage & Sanitary Installation Terms. (Hebrew, Eng. , Fr. & Ger.). IL.6.00. Massada Pr.
Dictionary of Sexual Terms. Albert Reissner & Carlson Wade. 1968. 3.00 (ISBN 0-685-06550-2). Assoc Bk.
Dictionary of Sharks. Patricia Pope. LC 73-7913. (Illus., Orig.). 1973. pap. 3.95 (ISBN 0-8200-0115-5). Great Outdoors.
Dictionary of Shipbuilding, Shipping & Fisheries. V. Dipl-Ling & Erhard Bensch. 784p. 1980. vinyl 150.00x (ISBN 0-686-30016-5, Pub. by Collet's). State Mutual Bk.
Dictionary of Shipping-International Trade Terms & Abbreviations. Alan E. Branch. LC 77-361617. ix, 129p. (Eng.). 1976. E3.00 (ISBN 0-900886-16-1). Witherby UK.
Dictionary of Shipping Terms. 591p. (Japanese & Eng.). 1977. 45.00 (ISBN 0-686-92612-9, M-9333). French & Eur.
Dictionary of Sigla & Abbreviations to & in Law Books Before 1607. William H. Bryson. LC 75-5675. (Virginia Legal Studies). 224p. 1975. 20.00x (ISBN 0-8139-0615-6). U Pr of Va.
Dictionary of Similes. 2nd ed. Ed. by Frank J. Wilstach. 578p. 1981. Repr. of 1924 ed. 45.00x (ISBN 0-8103-4370-3). Gale.
Dictionary of Slang & Unconventional English. 7th ed. Eric Partridge. 1970. 45.00 (ISBN 0-02-594970-5). Macmillan.
Dictionary of Slavic Linquistic Terminology, Vol. 2. Alois Jedlicka. 480p. (Slovak.). 1979. lib. bdg. 40.00x (ISBN 3-87118-272-9, Pub. by Helmut Buske Verlag Hamburg). Benjamins North Am.
Dictionary of Slavic Word Families. Louis J. Herman. LC 74-13341. xv, 667p. (Rus., Pol., Czech & Serbo-Croatian.). 1975. write for info. (ISBN 0-231-03927-1). Columbia U Pr.
Dictionary of Slavonic Linquistc Terminology, Vol. 1. Alois Jedlicka. 549p. (Orig., Slovak.). 1977. lib. bdg. 45.00x (ISBN 3-87118-271-0, Pub. by Helmut Buske Verlag Hamburg). Benjamins North am.
Dictionary of Social Behavior & Social Research Methods. David J. Stang & Lawrence S. Wrightman. LC 80-21511. 250p. 1980. pap. text ed. 8.95 (ISBN 0-8185-0243-6). Brooks-Cole.
Dictionary of Social Services: Policy & Practice. 3rd ed. Joan Clegg. 148p. 1980. 15.00x (ISBN 0-7199-1039-0). Intl Pubns Serv.
Dictionary of Social Welfare. Noel Timms & Rita Timms. 228p. 1982. 19.95 (ISBN 0-7100-9084-6). Routledge & Kegan.
Dictionary of Socialism. Angelo S. Rappoport. 1976. lib. bdg. 44.00 (ISBN 0-8490-1723-8). Gordon Pr.
Dictionary of Sociology & Related Sciences. Henry P. Fairchild. LC 76-110377. Repr. of 1955 ed. lib. bdg. 22.75x (ISBN 0-8371-4581-3, FADS). Greenwood.
Dictionary of Sociology & Related Sciences. Henry P. Fairchild. (Quality Paperback: No. 120). 1977. pap. 4.50 (ISBN 0-8226-0120-6). Littlefield.
Dictionary of Sodium, Fats, & Cholesterol. Barbara Kraus. (Illus.). 384p. Date not set. pap. 6.95 (ISBN 0-399-50945-3, Perigee). Putnam Pub Group.
Dictionary of Soil Mechanics. Ed. by A. Visser. (Eng., Fr., Dutch, & Ger.). 1965. 89.50 (ISBN 0-444-40613-1). Elsevier.
Dictionary of Soil Mechanics & Foundation Engineering. John Barker. 1981. pap. text ed. 30.00x (ISBN 0-86095-885-X). Longman.
Dictionary of Soil Science & Soil Engineering Terms. (Hebrew, Eng. , Ger. & Fr.). IL.8.00. Massada Pr.
Dictionary of Soldier Talk. John R. Elting & Dan Cragg. 480p. 1983. 24.95 (ISBN 0-684-17862-1, ScribT). Scribner.
Dictionary of South African English. 2nd ed. Jean Branford. 1980. 22.50x (ISBN 0-19-570177-1). Oxford U Pr.
Dictionary of Space English. 80p. (Eng.). 1978. 18.00 F. Garnier.
Dictionary of Space Technology. Joseph Angelo. 384p. 1982. 70.00x (ISBN 0-584-95011-X, Pub. by Muller Ltd). State Mutual Bk.
Dictionary of Space Technology. Joseph A. Angelo, Jr. LC 81-3144. (Illus.). 392p. 1982. 19.95x (ISBN 0-87196-583-6). Facts on File.
Dictionary of Space Technology. Joseph A. Angelo, Jr. (Illus.). 400p. 1983. pap. 15.50 (ISBN 0-442-20936-3). Van Nos Reinhold.
Dictionary of Spanish Place Names of the Northwest Coast of America: California, Vol. I. Rene Coulet du Gard. 190p. (Span. & Eng.). 1982. 24.00 (ISBN 0-939586-01-0). Edns Des Deux Mondes.
Dictionary of Spanish Place Names of the Northwest Coast of America: Oregon, Washington State, British Columbia, Alaska, Vol. II. Rene Coulet du Gard. 190p. (Span. & Eng.). 1983. 24.00 (ISBN 0-939586-02-9). Edns Des Deux Mondes.
Dictionary of Spanish Proverbs. John Collins. LC 77-25483. (Span.). 1977. Repr. of 1823 ed. lib. bdg. 45.00 (ISBN 0-8414-1101-8). Folcroft.
Dictionary of Spanish Terms in English, with Special Reference to the American Southwest. Harold W. Bentley. LC 73-1936. 243p. (Span. & Eng.). 1973. Repr. of 1932 ed. lib. bdg. 20.00x (ISBN 0-374-90582-7). Octagon.
Dictionary of Special Education Terms. Byron C. Moore et al. 128p. 1980. lexotone 12.75x (ISBN 0-398-04009-5). C C Thomas.
Dictionary of Spectroscopy. 2nd ed. R. C. Denney. 205p. 1982. 39.95x (ISBN 0-471-87478-7, Pub. by Wiley-Interscience). Wiley.
Dictionary of Spectroscopy. R. C. Denney. 224p. (Eng.). 1982. E15.00 (ISBN 0-333-31670-3). Macmillan London.
Dictionary of Spice Technology. 172p. (Eng. & Chinese.). 1978. pap. 4.95 (ISBN 0-686-92609-9, M-9568). French & Eur.
Dictionary of Spiritualism. Ed. by Harry E Wedeck & Wade Baskin. LC 73-104365. 1971. 10.00 (ISBN 0-8022-2338-9). Philos Lib.
Dictionary of Spoken Russian: Russian-English: English-Russian. U. S. War Department. (Rus. & Eng.). 1959. pap. 8.95 (ISBN 0-486-20496-0). Dover.
Dictionary of Spoken Spanish. (Span. & Eng.). write for info. (608-19). Pan Amer Pub.
Dictionary of Spoken Spanish: Spanish-English, English-Spanish. U. S. War Department. (Span. & Eng.). pap. 5.95 (ISBN 0-486-20495-2). Dover.
Dictionary of Spoken Spanish Words & Sentences. (Span.). 3.95. Camino Real.
Dictionary of Spoken Spanish Words & Sentences. (Span. & Eng.). 3.95. Camino Real.
Dictionary of Spoken Spanish Words, Phrases, Sentences. LC 30-900. (Span.). pap. 7.95. Doubleday.
Dictionary of Spoken Spanish Words, Phrases, Sentences. U. S. Armed Forces. LC 30-900. (Span. & Eng.). pap. 7.95 (ISBN 0-385-00976-3). Doubleday.
Dictionary of Sri Aurobindo's Yoga. Sri Aurobindo. Ed. by Sri M. Pandit. 1979. Repr. of 1966 ed. 7.50 (ISBN 0-941524-04-3). Lotus Light.
Dictionary of Statistical, Scientific & Technical Terms: English-Spanish, Spanish-English. Hardeo Sahai & Jose Berrios. Ed. by Richard A. Smith & Jeanne Heise. (Spanish Ser.). 143p. (Eng & Span.). 1981. 13.95 (ISBN 8-4534-0004-0, Pub. by Wadsworth Internacional Iberoamerica). Wadsworth Pub.
Dictionary of Statistical Terms. 4th ed. Maurice G. Kendall & William K. Buckland. 1982. 27.95 (ISBN 0-582-47008-0). Longman.
Dictionary of Statistics. Michael G. Mulhall. 75.00 (ISBN 0-8490-0046-7). Gordon Pr.
Dictionary of Stock Market Terms in Four Languages. B. L. Thole & Theodor Gilissen. (Eng., Fr., Ger. & Dutch.). 18.50 (ISBN 0-87559-068-3). Shalom.
Dictionary of Strength of Materials. (Hebrew, Eng. , Fr. & Ger.). IL.7.00. Massada Pr.
Dictionary of Stroke Structures in Graphoanalysis. International Graphoanalysis Society. 35.25 (G1029). Intl Graphoanalysis.
Dictionary of Subjects & Symbols in Art. 2nd, rev. ed. James Hall. LC 74-6578. (Icon Editions). (Illus.). 1979. o. p. 15.95i (ISBN 0-06-433316-7, HarpT); pap. 8.95i (ISBN 0-06-430100-1, IN-100, HarpT). Har-Row.
Dictionary of Sufi Technical Terms. Abd A. Razzaqi. Tr. by Nabil Safwat. (Eng. & Arabic.). 1983. 38.95 (ISBN 0-86304-032-2, Pub. by Octagon Pr England). Ins Study Human.
Dictionary of Superseded Accentuations in 18th Century English. Thomas A. Reisner. (European University Studies: Series 14, Anglo-Saxon Language & Literature. Vol. 40). 171p. 1976. pap. write for info. (ISBN 3-261-01961-1). P Lang Pubs.
Dictionary of Surface-Active Agents, Cosmetics & Toiletries. Ed. by G. Cariere. (Eng., Fr., Ger., Span., Ital., Dutch & Pol.). 1978. 36.25 (ISBN 0-444-99809-8). Elsevier.
Dictionary of Surface Active Agents, Cosmetics & Toiletries. G. Carriere. LC 77-8552. 198p. (Eng., Fr., Ger., Span., Ital., Pol. & Dutch.). 1978. write for info. (ISBN 0-444-99809-8). Elsevier.
Dictionary of Symbols & Imagery. 2nd. rev. ed. A. De Vries. 1976. 66.00 (ISBN 0-444-10607-3, North-Holland). Elsevier.
Dictionary of Symbols of Mathematical Logic. Ed. by R. Feys & F. Fitch. (Studies in Logic: Vol. 20). 1973. 22.00 (ISBN 0-7204-2250-7, North Holland). Elsevier.
Dictionary of Symptoms. rev. ed. Joan Gomez. LC 82-42525. (Illus.). 324p. 1983. pap. 5.95 (ISBN 0-8128-1949-7). Stein & Day.
Dictionary of Synergetics. Donald W. Pyles. (Illus.). 84p. (Orig.). 1983. pap. 2.00 (ISBN 0-910217-01-7). Synergetics WV.
Dictionary of Syngraphics & Associated Terms. Frederick M. Finney. 96p. 1983. 8.95 (ISBN 0-89421-031-9). Challenge Pr.
Dictionary of Synonyms & Antonyms. Devlin. 384p. 1982. pap. 2.95 (ISBN 0-446-31028-X). Warner Bks.
Dictionary of Synonyms & Antonyms. V. J. Smith. 32.50 (ISBN 0-87559-045-4); thumb indexed 31.00 (ISBN 0-87559-046-2). Shalom.
Dictionary of Synonyms & Antonyms. Ed. by Urdang & Manser. Epap. 1.95. Pan Bks.
Dictionary of Syrian Arabic: English-Arabic. Ed. by Karl Stowasser & Moukhtar Ani. (Richard Slade Harrell Arabic Ser). 202p. (Eng. & Arabic.). 1964. pap. 9.95 (ISBN 0-87840-010-9). Georgetown U Pr.
Dictionary of Tax Definitions. Gerry V. Hart. LC 77-363222. iv, 135p. E4.75 (ISBN 0-905753-00-3). Marchmont Pub.
Dictionary of Taxation. Ed. by Gerry V. Hart. Epap. 10.00. Butterworth.
Dictionary of Taxation. Ed. by Ivamy. Epap. 4.95. Butterworth.
Dictionary of Technical Acoustics. L. Reichardt. (Ger., Fr., Rus., Span., Pol. & Hungarian.). 1978. 20.40 (ISBN 0-685-92166-2). Adler.
Dictionary of Technical Drawing. (Hebrew, Eng. , Fr. & Ger.). IL.7.00. Massada Pr.
Dictionary of Technical Information. 182p. 1980. 20.00x (ISBN 0-569-08388-5, Pub. by Collet's). State Mutual Bk.
Dictionary of Technical Information, Vol. 41. Building Industry & Civil Engineering Society. 210p. 1980. 15.00x (ISBN 0-569-08243-9, Pub. by Collet's). State Mutual Bk.
Dictionary of Technical Terms, 2 vols. J. O. Kettridge. 628p. (Fr. & Eng.). Set. 38.00; Vol. 2: English-French. 38.00; 70.00. Routledge & Kegan.
Dictionary of Technical Terms, 2 vols. Julius O. Kettridge. (Fr. & Eng.). Set. 55.50 (ISBN 0-685-11207-1). French & Eur.
Dictionary of Telecommunications. Ed. by R. A. Bones. (Illus.). 1970. 15.00 (ISBN 0-8022-2309-5). Philos Lib.
Dictionary of Telecommunications & Electronics. (Hebrew & Eng.). IL.7.00. Massada Pr.
Dictionary of Telecommunications: English-Chinese. 721p. (Eng. & Chinese.). 1961. pap. 12.95 (ISBN 0-686-92554-8, M-9589). French & Eur.
Dictionary of Telugu & English: Explaining English Idioms & Phrases in Telugu, 2 vols. Charles P. Brown. (Eng. & Telugu.). 1976. Repr. of 1958 ed. 195.00 (ISBN 0-518-19008-0). Ayer Co.
Dictionary of Terms & Concepts in Reading. 2nd ed. Delwyn G. Schubert. 392p. 1969. photocopy ed. spiral 36.75x (ISBN 0-398-01688-7). C C Thomas.
Dictionary of Terms & Techniques in Archaeology. Sara Champion. (Illus.). 144p. 1982. pap. 7.95 (ISBN 0-89696-162-1, An Everest House Book). Dodd.
Dictionary of Terms & Techniques in Archaeology. Sarah Champion. LC 80-66774. (Illus.). 144p. (Eng.). 1980. 15.95 (ISBN 0-87196-445-7). Facts on File.
Dictionary of Terms for Computer-Aided Preparation of Product Definition Data (Including Engineering Drawings) Y14.26.3-1975. American Society of Mechanical Engineers. 3.50 (N00012); members 2.80. ASME.
Dictionary of Terms for Vacuum Science & Technology, Surface Science, Thin Film Technology, Vacuum Metallurgy, Electronic Materials. 1980. 5.00. Am Vacuum Soc.
Dictionary of Terms in Art. Frederick W. Fairholt. 59.95 (ISBN 0-8490-0047-5). Gordon Pr.
Dictionary of Terms in Art. Ed. by Frederick W. Fairholt. LC 68-30630. (Illus.). 1969. Repr. of 1854 ed. 37.00x (ISBN 0-8103-3071-7). Gale.

Dictionary of Terms in Music. 3rd ed. Horst Leuchtmann. xvi, 500p. 1981. 38.00 (ISBN 3-598-10338-7, Pub. by K G Saur). Shoe String.

Dictionary of Terms Used in the Safety Profession. Ed. by William E. Tarrants. 1980. Repr. of 1971 ed. 25.00 (ISBN 0-939874-41-5). ASSE.

Dictionary of the Art of Printing. William Savage. 1965. Repr. of 1841 ed. 32.00 (ISBN 0-8337-3128-9). B Franklin.

Dictionary of the Art of Printing. William Savage. (Printers' Manual Ser.). 1977. Repr. of 1841 ed. lib. bdg. 20.00x (ISBN 0-576-52390-9). Intl Pubns Serv.

Dictionary of the Biological Sciences. Peter Gray. 1967. 26.95 (ISBN 0-442-15590-5). Van Nos Reinhold.

Dictionary of the Black Theatre: Broadway, Off-Broadway, & Selected Harlem Theatre. Allen Woll. LC 82-21090. (Illus.). 416p. 1983. lib. bdg. 39.95 (ISBN 0-313-22561-3, WDB/). Greenwood.

Dictionary of the Chinese Particles. W. A. DObson. (Chinese.). 1974. Can.$50.00 (ISBN 0-8020-2119-0). U of Toronto Pr.

Dictionary of the Chinese Particles, with a Prolegomenon in Which the Problems of the Particles are Considered & They are Classified by Their Grammaticel Functions. W. A. Dobson. LC 73-91242. (Chinese.). 1974. 75.00x (ISBN 0-8020-2119-0). U of Toronto Pr.

Dictionary of the Chinook Jargon, or Trade Languages of Oregon. George Gibbs. LC 76-168142. (Library of American Linguistics: No. 12). (Chinook.). Repr. of 1863 ed. 10.00 (ISBN 0-404-50992-4). AMS Pr.

Dictionary of the Choctaw Language. Cyrus Byington. (Choctaw.). Repr. of 1915 ed. 49.00 (ISBN 0-403-03579-1). Scholarly.

Dictionary of the Cree Language. R. Faries & E. A. Watkins. (Cree.). 1938. Can.$24.00. Anglican Church.

Dictionary of the Decorative Arts. Hugh Honour & John Fleming. LC 76-50163. (Illus.). 1977. 29.95i (ISBN 0-06-011936-5, HarpT). Har-Row.

Dictionary of the Economic Products of India, 6 vols. in 10. George Watt. 5450p. 1972. Repr. of 1889 ed. Set. 300.00x (ISBN 0-8002-0198-1). Intl Pubns Serv.

Dictionary of the Economic Products of India, 6 vols. George Watt. 1978. Repr. of 1889 ed. Set. 324.00 (ISBN 0-89955-259-5, Pub. by Intl Bk Dist). Intl Schol Bk Serv.

Dictionary of the English Language. (Eng.). 1978. write for info. Belin.

Dictionary of the English Language, 2 Vols. facsimile ed. Samuel Johnson. LC 74-181906. Repr. of 1755 ed. 100.00 (ISBN 0-404-09840-1). AMS Pr.

Dictionary of the English Language. facsimile ed. Samuel Johnson. LC 79-14941. (Illus.). 2320p. 1980. Repr. of 1755 ed. 95.00 (ISBN 0-405-12414-7). Ayer Co.

Dictionary of the English Language, 2 vols. Samuel Johnson. 1978. Set. 220.00x (ISBN 0-86685-125-9). Intl Bk Ctr.

Dictionary of the English Language, 2 vols. facsimile ed. Samuel Johnson. 2285p. (Eng.). Repr. 220.00 set (125-9). Intl Bk Ctr.

Dictionary of the English Language: In Which the Words Are Deduced from Their Originals & Illustrated in Their Different Significations by Examples from the Best Writers, 2 Vols. Samuel Johnson. 1968. Repr. of 1755 ed. Set. 257.50 (ISBN 3-4870-1935-3). Adler.

Dictionary of the Environment. Ed. by Allaby. (Eng.). Epap. 5.95. Macmillan.

Dictionary of the Environment. Michael Allaby. 1977. text ed. 17.95 (ISBN 0-442-20288-1). Van Nos Reinhold.

Dictionary of the European Communities. Ed. by G. Parker & B. Parker. (Eng.). Epap. 3.95. Butterworth.

Dictionary of the European Communities. 2nd ed. John Paxton. LC 82-10375. 290p. 1983. 27.50x (ISBN 0-312-20099-4). St Martin.

Dictionary of the European Communities. 2nd ed. John Paxton. 288p. (Eng.). 1982. E20.00 (ISBN 0-333-33438-8). Macmillan LOndon.

Dictionary of the European Community. Ed. by Paxton. (Eng.). Epap. 4.95. Macmillan.

Dictionary of the European Economic Community. Ed. by John Paxton. LC 77-3595. 304p. 1977. lib. bdg. 20.00x (ISBN 0-87196-370-1). Facts on File.

Dictionary of the Flowering Plants & Ferns Vol. 1: Generic & Family Names. 8th ed. J. C. Willis. LC 72-83581. 1300p. 1973. 99.00 (ISBN 0-521-08699-X). Cambridge U Pr.

Dictionary of the French & English Tongues. Randle Cotgrave. (Fr. & Eng.). 1971. Repr. of 1611 ed. 128.00 (ISBN 0-685-05204-4). Adler.

Dictionary of the Fungi. Ainsworth & Bisby. 663p. 1971. 69.00x (ISBN 0-85198-075-9, Pub. by CAB Bks England). State Mutual Bk.

Dictionary of the Fungi. Ainsworth & Bisby's. 663p. 1978. 75.00 (ISBN 0-85198-075-9, M-9711). French & Eur.

Dictionary of the Gathic Language. Lawrence H. Mills. LC 74-21253. (Gaelic.). Repr. of 1913 ed. 57.50 (ISBN 0-404-12804-1). AMS Pr.

Dictionary of the Graphic Arts Industry. Ed. by W. Muller. (Eng., Ger., Fr., Rus., Span., Pol., Slovak & Hungarian.). 1981. 117.00 (ISBN 0-444-99745-8). Elsevier.

Dictionary of the Hawaiian Language. Andrews. (Hawaiian & Eng.). 17.50. Iaconi.

Dictionary of the Hawaiian Language. Lorrin Andrews. LC 72-89745. (Hawaiian.). 1973. 17.50 (ISBN 0-8048-1087-7). C E Tuttle.

Dictionary of the History of Ideas. Ed. by Philip P. Wiener. 1980. pap. 100.00 5-volume boxed edition (ISBN 0-684-16418-3, ScribR). Scribner.

Dictionary of the History of Ideas, 5 vols. Ed. by Philip P. Wiener. LC 72-7943. 1973. Set. text ed. 275.00 (ISBN 0-684-13293-1, ScribR); pap. 100.00 (ISBN 0-684-16418-3). Scribner.

Dictionary of the History of Science. W. F. Bynum et al. 494p. (Eng.). 1981. E19.50 (ISBN 0-333-29316-9); pap. 6.95 (ISBN 0-333-34901-6). Macmillan London.

Dictionary of the History of Science. Ed. by William F. Bynum et al. LC 81-47116. (Illus.). 822p. 1981. 45.00x (ISBN 0-691-08287-1). Princeton U Pr.

Dictionary of the History of the American Brewing & Distilling Industries. William L. Downard. LC 79-6826. (Illus.). xxv, 268p. 1980. lib. bdg. 45.00 (ISBN 0-313-21330-5, DOD/). Greenwood.

Dictionary of the Irish Language. 2500p. (Gaelic.). 1982. 250.00 (ISBN 0-686-96570-1, Pub by Royal Irish Ireland). State Mutual Bk.

Dictionary of the Isle of Wight Dialect, & of Provincialisms Used in the Island, with Illustrative Anecdotes & Tales. William H. Long. LC 76-9101. 1976. Repr. of 1886 ed. lib. bdg. 20.00 (ISBN 0-8414-5740-9). Folcroft.

Dictionary of the Language of Bugotu, Santa Isabel Island, Solomon Islands. Walter G. Ivens. LC 75-35125. Repr. of 1940 ed. 14.50 (ISBN 0-404-14141-2). AMS Pr.

Dictionary of the Language of Rennell & Bellona: Part One: Rennellese & Bellonese to English. Samuel H. Elbert. 364p. 1975. 35.00x (ISBN 0-8248-0490-2). UH Pr.

Dictionary of the Languages of the Micmac Indians, Who Reside in Nova Scotia, New Brunswick, Prince Edward Island, Cape Breton & Newfoundland. Silas T. Rand. Repr. of 1888 ed. 40.00 (ISBN 0-384-49565-6). Johnson Repr.

Dictionary of the Lepcha language. Compiled by G. B. Mainwaring & Albert Grunwedal. LC 80-905482. xvi, 552p. (Lepcha.). 1979. Rs.130.00. Radha.

Dictionary of the Life Sciences. McGraw-Hill Editors. (Illus.). 1976. 32.50 (ISBN 0-07-045262-8, P&RB). McGraw.

Dictionary of the Life Sciences. Sue Martin. LC 76-41041. 20.00x (ISBN 0-87663-724-1). Universe.

Dictionary of the Maori Language. H. W. Williams. 500p. (Maori.). 1975. 7.50. Govern.

Dictionary of the Middle Ages, Vol. 1. Ed. by Joseph R. Strayer. LC 82-5904. 1982. lib. bdg. 70.00 (ISBN 0-684-16760-3, ScribR). Scribner.

Dictionary of the Middle Ages, Vol. 2. Ed. by Joseph R. Strayer. LC 82-5904. 1983. lib. bdg. 70.00 (ISBN 0-684-17022-1, ScribR). Scribner.

Dictionary of the Names of Towns & Villages in Lebanon. Anis Freyha. 210p. (Arabic.). 16.00 (099-6). Intl Bk Ctr.

Dictionary of the Natural Environment: English-Arabic. Ahmad Khatib. 1979. pap. 7.95x (ISBN 0-86685-073-2). Intl Bk Ctr.

Dictionary of the Natural Environment. Monkhouse & Small. (Eng.). Epap. 3.95. E. Arnold.

Dictionary of the Natural Environment. F. Monkhouse. (Illus.). 381p. (Eng. & Arabic.). 1978. 16.00 (078-3). Intl Bk Ctr.

Dictionary of the Nisqually Indian Language of Western Washington. George Gibbs. (Shorey Indian Ser.). 82p. Repr. of 1877 ed. pap. 9.95 (ISBN 0-8466-4022-8, I22). Shorey.

Dictionary of the Occult. Ed. by Julian Franklyn. Repr. of 1935 ed. 34.00x (ISBN 0-685-32596-2). Gale.

Dictionary of the Occult. B. W. Martin. LC 79-314043. 139p. (Eng.). 1979. E6.50 (ISBN 0-09-136880-4). Hutch Pub Co.

Dictionary of the Occult & Paranormal. J. P. Chaplin. 1976. pap. 1.95 (ISBN 0-440-31927-7, LE). Dell.

Dictionary of the Old English Language: Compiled from Writings of the XII, XIII, XIV, & XV Centuries. Francis H. Stratmann. LC 73-4631. 1973. lib. bdg. 85.00 (ISBN 0-8414-7511-3). Folcroft.

Dictionary of the Old West. Peter Watts. 1977. 12.95 (ISBN 0-394-49013-4). Knopf.

Dictionary of the Opera. Charles Osborne. 1983. 22.95 (ISBN 0-671-49218-7). S&S.

Dictionary of the Osage Language. Francis La Fleche. Repr. of 1932 ed. 49.00 (ISBN 0-403-03580-5). Scholarly.

Dictionary of the Otchipwe Language. R. R. Baraga. (Chippwe.). Repr. 20.00 (ISBN 0-87018-002-9). Ross.

Dictionary of the Pali language. Robert Childers. LC 80-402603. xii, 624p. (Pali & Eng.). 1979. Rs.240.00. Orient Bk Dist.

Dictionary of the Photographic & a Comprehensive & Systematic Catalogue of Photographic Apparatus Material: Manufactured, Imported & Sold by E. Anthony, 2 vols. in 1. Henry H. Snelling & E. Anthony. Ed. by Peter Bunnell & Robert A. Sobieszek. LC 76-23059. (Sources of Modern Photo. Ser.). (Illus.). 1979. Repr. of 1854 ed. lib. bdg. 25.00x (ISBN 0-405-09623-2). Ayer Co.

Dictionary of the Russian Academy, 7 vols. Ed. by M. Oesterby. (Rus.). 1981. Repr. of 1822 ed. Set. 650.00 (ISBN 0-915346-75-3). A Wofsy Fine Arts.

Dictionary of the Social Sciences. A. Badawi. LC 79-120007. xvi, 591p. (Eng., Fr. & Arabic.). 1978. write for info. Lib Liban.

Dictionary of the Social Sciences. Compiled by Zaki Badawi. 591p. (Arabic, Fr. & Eng.). 25.00 (115-1). Intl Bk Ctr.

Dictionary of the Social Sciences. Hugo F. Reading. 1977. 18.00 (ISBN 0-7100-8642-3); pap. 6.95 (ISBN 0-7100-8650-4). Routledge & Kegan.

Dictionary of the Spanish in Texas. IML-Institute of Modern Languages. (Span.). 8.35. Camino Real.

Dictionary of the Spanish in Texas. Institute of Modern Language. (Span. & Eng.). 8.35. Camino Real.

Dictionary of the Suahili Language. Ed. by Ludwig Krapf. LC 72-77205. (Illus., Swahili & Eng.). Repr. 30.00x (ISBN 0-8371-1276-1, Pub. by Negro U Pr). Greenwood.

Dictionary of the Supernatural: An A to Z of Hauntings, Possession, Witchcraft, Demonology & Other Occult Phenomena. Peter Underwood. LC 79-303952. (Illus.). 389p. (Eng.). 1978. E5.50 (ISBN 0-245-52784-2). Harrap.

Dictionary of the Tarot. Bill Butler. LC 74-9230. (Illus.). 1977. 7.95 (ISBN 0-8052-3557-4); pap. 6.50 (ISBN 0-8052-0559-4). Schocken.

Dictionary of the Teenage Revolution & its Aftermath. Kenneth Hudson. 320p. 1983. E12.95 (ISBN 0-333-28517-4). Macmillan London.

Dictionary of the Vedic rituals. Chitrabhanu Sen. LC 78-901425. 172p. (Eng. & Sanskrit.). 1978. 20.00; Rs.100.00. Concept Pub. Co.

Dictionary of the Walbiri (Walpiri) Language of Central Australia. Laurie Reece. LC 76-370309. (Eng. & Walbiri.). 1975. Aus.$3.50. Univ Syd Aust Lang.

Dictionary of the Welsh Language, Vol. 1. A-ffysvr. Wales University. (Welsh.). 1950. Pts. 1-21. 90.00 (ISBN 0-7083-0504-0); Pts. 22-31. pap. 8.00x ea. Verry.

Dictionary of the Welsh Language: Part 31. University of Wales Press. Ed. by G. A. Bevan. 63p. (Welsh.). 1982. pap. text ed. 8.00 (ISBN 0-686-81869-5). Verry.

Dictionary of Theology. 2nd ed. Karl Rahner & Herbert Vorgrimler. 500p. 1981. 17.50 (ISBN 0-8245-0040-7). Crossroad NY.

Dictionary of Theoretical Concepts in Biology. Keith E. Roe & Richard G. Frederick. LC 80-19889. 312p. 1981. 17.50 (ISBN 0-8108-1353-X). Scarecrow.

Dictionary of Theoretical Linguistics (English-Arabic) Arabic-English Glossary. (Eng. & Arabic.). 30.00 (ISBN 0-86685-306-5). Intl Bk Ctr.

Dictionary of Theoretical Linguistics: English-Arabic with Arabic-English Glossary. Muhammad A. Al-Khuli. (Arabic & Eng.). 1983. 30.00 (ISBN 0-86685-306-5). Intl Bk Ctr.

Dictionary of Thermodynamics. Arthur M. James. LC 76-5472. 262p. 1976. 29.95x (ISBN 0-470-15035-1). Halsted Pr.

Dictionary of Things to Draw. Howard Boughner. (gr. 1-7). 1979. PLB 3.99 (ISBN 0-448-13125-0, G&D); pap. 1.50 (ISBN 0-448-14991-5). Putnam Pub Group.

Dictionary of Tibetan & English. Alexander Csoma de Koros. 351p. (Tibetan & Eng.). 1978. Repr. of 1834 ed. 39.00 (ISBN 0-89684-107-3, Pub. by Cosmo Pubns India). Orient Bk Dist.

Dictionary of Toiletry & Cosmetic Manufacturers in Western Europe. Ed. by European Directories. 1981. 100.00x (ISBN 0-686-78875-3, Pub. by European Directories England). State Mutual Bk.

Dictionary of Tools. Salaman. 1974. s.p. 49.50 (ISBN 0-87002-912-6). Bennett IL.

Dictionary of Tools Used in the Woodworking & Allied Trades c. 1700-1970. R. A. Salaman. LC 75-35059. 1976. 49.50 (ISBN 0-684-14535-9, ScribT). Scribner.

Dictionary of Tourism. Ed. by Charles J. Metelka. LC 80-83526. 91p. 1981. 12.00 (ISBN 0-916032-10-8). Merton Hse.

Dictionary of Tourism: German-English & English-German. Wolf Friedrich. LC 71-520026. (Ger. & Eng.). 1970. 5.00x (ISBN 0-8002-1259-2). Intl Pubns Serv.

Dictionary of Trade Name Origins. Adrian Room. 208p. 1982. 12.95 (ISBN 0-7100-0839-2). Routledge & Kegan.

Dictionary of Transport Terms & Phrases. Siegfried Heinze. LC 62-5007. 420p. (Ger. & Eng.). 1961. 11.25x (ISBN 3-87097-018-9). Intl Pubns Serv.

Dictionary of Turfgrass Terms. 1.00 (2003). Pro Golfers.

Dictionary of Turfgrass Terms. United States Golf Association. 0.50 (016). US Golf Assn.

Dictionary of United States History: Alphabetical, Chronological, Statistical. rev. ed. J. Franklin Jameson. Ed. by Albert E. McKinley. LC 68-30658. (Illus.). 1971. Repr. of 1931 ed. 55.00x (ISBN 0-8103-3332-5). Gale.

Dictionary of U. S. Military Terms. 1963. 4.50 (ISBN 0-8183-0163-5). Pub Aff Pr.

Dictionary of Urdu Classical Hindi & English. John T. Platts. LC 78-670100. (Hindi & Eng.). 1977. Repr. of 1884 ed. 50.00x (ISBN 0-8002-0243-0). Intl Pubns Serv.

Dictionary of Urdu, Classical Hindi, & English. John T. Platts. (Urdu-, Hindu & Eng.). 1930. 82.00x (ISBN 0-19-864309-8). Oxford U Pr.

Dictionary of Useful & Everyday Plants & Their Common Names. F. N. Howes. LC 73-91701. 300p. 1974. 34.50 (ISBN 0-521-08520-9). Cambridge U Pr.

Dictionary of Useful Plants: The Use, History & Folklore of More Than 500 Plant Species. Ed. by Coon. (Illus.). Epap. 4.50. Rodale Pr Eng.

Dictionary of Venetian Painters, 5 vols. Pietro Zampetti. Incl. Vol. 1. Fourteenth to Fifteenth Centuries. 1969. 57.50x (ISBN 0-85317-131-9); Vol. 2. Sixteenth Century. 1970. 57.50x (ISBN 0-85317-171-8); Vol. 3. Seventeenth Century. 1971. 57.50x (ISBN 0-85317-181-5); Vol. 4. Eighteenth Century. 1971. 57.50x (ISBN 0-85317-006-1); Vol. 5. 19th & 20th Centuries. 1979. 57.50x (ISBN 0-85317-035-5). LC 71-484121. Intl Pubns Serv.

Dictionary of Venetian Painters: Vol. 1, 14th & 15th Centuries. Pietro Zampetti. (Illus.). 1969. text ed. 36.00x (ISBN 0-85317-121-1, Pub. by A & C Black England). Humanities.

Dictionary of Venetian Painters: Vol. 2, 16th Century. Pietro Zampetti. (Illus.). 1970. text ed. 36.00x (ISBN 0-85317-171-8, Pub. by A & C Black England). Humanities.

Dictionary of Venetian Painters: Vol. 4, 18th Century. Pietro Zampetti. (Illus.). 1971. text ed. 36.00x (ISBN 0-85317-006-1, Pub. by A & C Black England). Humanities.

Dictionary of Venetian Painters: Vol. 5, 19th & First Decade of the 20th Century. Pietro Zampetti. (Illus.). 1979. text ed. 36.00x (ISBN 0-85317-035-5, Pub. by A & C Black England). Humanities.

Dictionary of Ventilation & Health. Wolfgang Lindeke. 186p. 1980. 25.00x (ISBN 0-569-08522-5, Pub. by Collet's). State Mutual Bk.

Dictionary of Vertebrate Zoology, Russian-English: English-Russian. George J. Jacobs. LC 78-16321. 1978. pap. text ed. 4.25x (ISBN 0-87474-551-9). Smithsonian.

Dictionary of Victorian Engravers, Print Publishers & Their Works. Rodney K. Engen. (Illus.). 1979. 60.00x (ISBN 0-914146-86-6). Somerset Hse.

Dictionary of Victorian Painters. Christopher Wood. (Illus.). 764p. 1979. 74.50 (ISBN 0-902028-72-3). Antique Collect.

Dictionary of Victorian Painters. Christopher Wood. (Illus.). 1979. 74.50 (ISBN 0-902028-72-3). Apollo.

Dictionary of Violin Makers. Cecie Stainer. LC 77-75207. 1977. Repr. of 1896 ed. lib. bdg. 12.50 (ISBN 0-89341-070-5). Longwood Pr.

Dictionary of Virology. K. Rowson et al. 240p. 1981. text ed. 43.25 (ISBN 0-632-00784-2, B 4184-5); pap. text ed. 19.95 (ISBN 0-632-00697-8, B 4192-6). Mosby.

Dictionary of Visual Science. 3rd ed. David Cline et al. LC 78-14640. 736p. 1980. 35.00 (ISBN 0-8019-6778-3). Chilton.

Dictionary of Vocal Terminology: An Analysis. Cornelius L. Reid. LC 81-86074. xxi, 457p. 1983. 39.95 (ISBN 0-915282-07-0). J Patelson Music.

Dictionary of Vulgar Tongue, 1811. Frances Grose. 236p. (Eng.). 1981. Epap. 1.95 (ISBN 0-333-31502-2). Macmillan London.

Dictionary of Waste & Water Treatment. Scott & Smith. 1981. text ed. write for info. (ISBN 0-408-00495-9). Butterworth.

Dictionary of Waste Disposal & Public Cleansing. Ed. by W. Kaupert. (Eng., Ger., & Fr.) 1966. 29.50 (ISBN 0-444-40330-2). Elsevier.

Dictionary of Water & Sewage Engineering. 2nd ed. F. Meinck & K. Mohle. (Ger., Eng., Fr., & Ital.). 1977. 127.75 (ISBN 0-444-99811-X). Elsevier.

Dictionary of Watercolors Artists, Vol. I. H. L. Mallalien. (Illus.). 1976. 45.00 (ISBN 0-902028-48-0). Apollo.

Dictionary of Watercolors Artists, Vol. II. H. L. Mallalien. (Illus.). 1979. 45.00 (ISBN 0-902028-63-4). Apollo.

Dictionary of Watercolour Artists up to 1920: Vol. 1, The Text. H. L. Mallalieu. 298p. 1978. 44.50 (ISBN 0-902028-48-0). Antique Collect.

Dictionary of Watercolour Artists up to 1920: Vol. 2, The Plates. H. L. Mallalieu. (Illus.). 268p. 1980. 44.50 (ISBN 0-902028-63-4). Antique Collect.

Dictionary of Weapons & Military Terms. John Quick. (Illus.). 515p. 1973. 34.95 (ISBN 0-07-051057-1, P&RB). McGraw.

Dictionary of Wedgewood. Rielly & Savage. (Illus.). 1980. 62.50 (ISBN 0-902028-85-5). Apollo.

Dictionary of Wedgwood. Robin Reilly & George Savage. (Illus.). 414p. 1980. 62.50 (ISBN 0-902028-85-5). Antique Collect.

Dictionary of Weeds of Western Europe: Their Common Names & Importance. G. H. Williams. 1982. 74.50 (ISBN 0-444-41978-0). Elsevier.

Dictionary of Welding. 762p. 1980. 60.00x (ISBN 0-569-08525-X, Pub. by Collet's). State Mutual Bk.

Dictionary of Welding. A. Kleiber. 396p. (Eng. & Ger.). 1970. 24.00 (ISBN 0-8417-1026-0). Adler.

Dictionary of Welding - Fachwoerterbuch der Schweisstechnik: German-English & English-German. Theo Roemer. LC 74-534541. (Illus.). 340p. (Ger. & Eng.). 1970. 25.00x (ISBN 3-87155-704-8). Intl Pubns Serv.

Dictionary of Western Sculptors in Bronze. James Mackay. 414p. 1977. 49.50 (ISBN 0-902028-55-3). Antique Collect.

Dictionary of Western Sculptors in Bronze. James Mackey. (Illus.). 1977. 49.50 (ISBN 0-902028-55-3). Apollo.

Dictionary of Wines & Spirits. Pamela V. Price. 408p. 1981. 40.00x (ISBN 0-7198-2744-2, Pub. by Northwood Bks). State Mutual Bk.

Dictionary of Wood & Woodworking Practice, Vol. II. Herbert Bucksch. (Eng. & Ger.). 1966. 47.50x (ISBN 3-7625-1169-1). Intl Pubns Serv.

Dictionary of Wood & Woodworking Practice, Vol. I. Herbert Bucksch. (Ger. & Eng.). 1978. 42.50x (ISBN 3-7625-1201-9). Intl Pubns Serv.

Dictionary of Word Makers: Pen Pictures of the People Behind Our Language. Cecil Hunt. LC 72-13203. Repr. of 1949 ed. lib. bdg. 15.00 (ISBN 0-8414-1153-0). Folcroft.

Dictionary of Word Origins. 2nd ed. Joseph T. Shipley. Repr. of 1945 ed. lib. bdg. 32.00 (ISBN 0-8371-1966-9, SHWO). Greenwood.

Dictionary of Word Origins. Joseph T. Shipley. (Quality Paperback: No. 121). 1979. pap. 5.95 (ISBN 0-8226-0121-4). Littlefield.

Dictionary of Word Roots & Combining Forms. Donald J. Borror. LC 60-15564. 134p. 1960. pap. 4.95 (ISBN 0-87484-053-8). Mayfield Pub.

Dictionary of Words About Alcohol. 2nd, Rev. ed. M. Keller et al. LC 81-620046. xxviii, 291p. 1982. 19.50x (ISBN 0-911290-12-5). Rutgers Ctr Al.

Dictionary of Work Study Terms. (Hebrew & Eng.). IL.7.00. Massada Pr.

Dictionary of World Literary Terms. Ed. by Joseph T. Shipley. 15.95 (ISBN 0-87116-012-9). Writer.

Dictionary of World Wines, Liqueurs, & Other Drinks. Julian Jaffs. 144p. 6.95 (ISBN 0-919364-73-X, ADON 3537). Pagurian.

Dictionary of Yiddish Slang. Fred Kogos. 176p. (Yiddish). 1983. pap. 4.95 (ISBN 0-8065-0347-5). Lyle Stuart.

Dictionary of Zoology. 3rd ed. A. W. Leftwich. 487p. 1973. 27.50x (ISBN 0-8448-0845-8). Crane-Russak Co.

Dictionary of Zoology: English-Chinese. 52p. (Eng. & Chinese). 1975. pap. 1.95 (ISBN 0-686-92583-1, M-9571). French & Eur.

Dictionary, Polish-English, English-Polish: Contemporary Usage American & Polish. Iwo Pogonowski. (Illus.). v, 647p. (Pol. & Eng.). 1979. write for info. (ISBN 0-88254-463-2); pap. text ed. write for info (ISBN 0-88254-464-0). Hippocrene Bks.

Dictionary Polish-English, English-Polish Slovnik. Iwo Pogonowski. 648p. (Eng. & Pol.). 16.50. Hippocrene Bks.

Dictionary Real Estate Terms. O'Donnell. 1975. 3.00 (ISBN 0-7216-6915-8). Dryden Pr.

Dictionary Roman Coins. Stevenson. 1982. Repr. of 1892 ed. lib. bdg. 40.00 (ISBN 0-686-45266-6, Pub. by B A Seaby England). S J Durst.

Dictionary, Schmictionary. Paul Hoffman & Matt Freedman. LC 83-3050. (Illus.). 160p. (Orig.). 1983. pap. write for info. (ISBN 0-688-02162-X). Quill NY.

Dictionary Skills. Barbara Gregorich. (Horizons II Ser.). (Illus.). 24p. (gr. 3-4). 1980. wkbk. 2.50 (ISBN 0-89403-605-X). EDC.

Dictionary Slovene-Serbocroatian-Slovene. Jurancic. 566p. (Slovene & Serbocroation). 1978. leatherette 14.95 (ISBN 0-686-92610-2, M-9703). French & Eur.

Dictionary Studies Duplicating Masters, 4 vols. (Spice Duplicating Masters Ser). 1974. Vol. 1, Grades K-2, Single Letters. 5.95 (ISBN 0-89273-527-9); Vol. 2, Grades K-2, Letter Combinations. 5.95 (ISBN 0-89273-528-7); Vol. 3, Grades 3-6. 5.95 (ISBN 0-89273-529-5); Vol. 4, Grades 7-9. 5.95 (ISBN 0-89273-530-9). Educ Serv.

Dictionary to the Plays & Novels of Bernard Shaw. Lewis C. Broad & Violet M. Broad. LC 72-191671. 1929. lib. bdg. 9.75 (ISBN 0-8414-2543-4). Folcroft.

Dictionnaire. Robert Prefontaine & Gisele Cote-Prefont. (Fr.). 1968. write for info. Beauchemin.

Dictionnaire. Abulqacim Tedjini. (Fr.). 1948. 22.00 F. Maritimes Outremer.

Dictionnaire a l'Usage des Plaisanciers. 160p. (Fr. & Eng.). 1969. pap. 15.50 (ISBN 0-686-57258-0, M-6569). French & Eur.

Dictionnaire a l'usage des Plaisanciers. Barbara Webb. 160p. (Fr.). 1969. 33.00 F. Maritimes Outre mer.

Dictionnaire Abrege de Peinture & d'Architecture, 2 vols. Francois-Marie De Marsy. (Fr.). Kr.100.00. Minkoff.

Dictionnaire Abrege de Six Langues Slaves. Franz Miklosich. LC 75-506978. 955p. (Fr. & Rus.). 1975. write for info. Philo Pr.

Dictionnaire Abrege des Imprimeurs-Editeurs du 16 Siecle. Jean Muller. 150p. (Fr.). 1970. DM.80.00. Koerner.

Dictionnaire Abrege du Surrealisme. Annie C. Dobbs. (Fr.). pap. 23.95 (ISBN 0-686-57119-3, M-6165). French & Eur.

Dictionnaire Abrege du Surrealisme. Annie C. Dobbs. (Fr.). 1978. 55.00 F. Corti.

Dictionnaire Abrege Grec-Francais. Anatole Bailly. 1012p. (Gr. & Fr.). 1969. pap. 39.95 (ISBN 0-686-56906-7, M-6019). French & Eur.

Dictionnaire Abrege Grec-Francais. Anatole Bailly. 1012p. (Gr. & Fr.). 1969. 58.00. Hachette-Jeunesse.

Dictionnaire Abrege Latin-Francais. Felix Gaffiot. 1720p. (Lat. & Fr.). 1970. pap. 15.95 (ISBN 0-686-57186-X, M-6258). French & Eur.

Dictionnaire Abrege Latin-Francais. Felix Gaffiot. 1720p. (Lat. & Fr.). 1970. 40.00. Hachette Jeunesse.

Dictionnaire Abrege Latin-Francais Illustre. Felix Gaffiot. (Illus.). 720p. (Lat. & Fr.). 1969. C.$9.35. Renouveau Pedagogique.

Dictionnaire Actif Nathan. (Fr.). 14.55 (Dist. by Continental Bk Co). Lib. Fernand Nathan.

Dictionnaire Actif Nathan. Frank Marchand. (Illus.). 288p. (Fr.). 1976. 36.00 F. Nathan.

Dictionnaire Aerotechnique Anglais-Francais. 3rd ed. Louis Henry. 576p. (Fr.). 51.40 F. Petit.

Dictionnaire Agricole Allemand-Anglais-Francais-Espagnol-Russe. 4th ed. Gunther Haensch. (Illus.). 746p. (Ger., Eng., Fr., Span. & Rus.). 1975. 260.00 F. pap. 170.00. Maison Rustique.

Dictionnaire Agricole Allemand, Anglais, Francais, Espagnol, Russe. 4th ed. Gunther Haensch & Gisela Haberkamp. 746p. (Ger., Eng., Fr., Span. & Rus.). Agriculture Dictionary, German, English, French, Spanish, Russian). 1975. 69.95 (ISBN 0-686-56783-8, M-6579, Pub. by Maison Rust). French & Eur.

Dictionnaire agricole Allemand, Anglais, Francais, Espanol, Russe. 4th ed. Gunther Haensch & Gisela Haberkamp. 746p. (Ger., Fr., Span., Rus.). 1975. 69.95 F. Maison Rustique.

Dictionnaire Aide Memoire de Botanique. Charles Louis Gatin. 867p. (Fr.). 1924. 99.50 (ISBN 0-686-56785-4, M-6581, Pub. by Lechevalier). French & Eur.

Dictionnaire Al-Fara-id Arabe-Francais. 18th ed. P. Belot. (Illus.). 1114p. (Arabic & Fr.). 1964. 15.00 F. Dar El-Machreq.

Dictionnaire Alde-Memoire de Botanique. Charles-Louis Gatin. (Illus.). 867p. (Fr.). 1924. 260.00 F. Lechevalier.

Dictionnaire Allemand-Francais. 640p. (Ger. & Fr.). 1978. 7.50 F. Larousse.

Dictionnaire Allemand-Francais. Denis Eckel & Manfred Hofer. (Illus.). 1324p. (Ger. & Fr.). 1970. 64.00 F. Garnier.

Dictionnaire Allemand-Francais. Rotteck. (Illus.). 980p. (Ger. & Fr.). 1970. 18.00 F. Garnier.

Dictionnaire Allemand-Francais. Siefried P. Villain. 460p. (Ger. & Fr.). 1964. 9.50 F. Garnier-Flammarion.

Dictionnaire Allemand-Francais. Siegfried P. Villain. 612p. (Ger. & Fr.). 1960. 11.00 F. Garnier-Flammarion.

Dictionnaire Allemand-Francais. Erich Weis & Heinrich Mattutat. 570p. (Ger. & Fr.). 1977. 29.95 (ISBN 0-686-57259-9, M-6570). French & Eur.

Dictionnaire Allemand-Francais. Erich Weis & Heinrich Mattutat. 570p. (Ger. & Fr.). 1977. 75.00 F. Bordas-Dunod.
Dictionnaire Allemand-Francais des Termes Relatifs a l'Electrorechnique, l'Electronique, et aux Applications Connexes. 4th ed. Henri Piraux. 254p. (Fr. & Ger.). 1976. pap. 31.95 (ISBN 0-686-57080-4, M-6455). French & Eur.
Dictionnaire Allemand-Francais des Termes Relatifs a l'electrotechnique: L'electrotechnique & aux Applications Connexes. 4th ed. Henri Piraux. (Illus.). 254p. (Ger. & Fr.). 1976. 72.00 F. Eyrolles.
Dictionnaire Allemand-Francais et Francais-Allemand. Denis Eckel & Hofer Manfred. 1324p. (Fr. & Ger.). 1970. 25.95 (ISBN 0-686-57131-2, M-6184). French & Eur.
Dictionnaire Allemand-Francais, Francais-Allemand. Ed. by Rotteck. 980p. (Fr. & Ger.). 1970. pap. 7.50 (ISBN 0-686-57093-6, M-6115). French & Eur.
Dictionnaire Allemand-Francais pour les Travaux Publics: Le Batiement & l'equipement des Chantiers des Chantiers de Constuction. 2nd ed. Hector Bucksch. 878p. (Ger. & Fr.). 1972. 372.00 F. Eyrolles.
Dictionnaire Alphabetique & Analogique de la Langue Francais. Paul Robert. Ed. by A. Ray & J. ReyDebove. LC 77-569782. xxxi, 2171p. (Fr.). 1977. 158.00 F (ISBN 2-850-36030-9). Soc Nouveau.
Dictionnaire Alphabetique & Analogique de la Langue Francais, 7 vols. Paul Robert. 6000p. (Fr.). 1964. 1430.00 F. Ste. Nouv. Littre.
Dictionnaire Alphabetique & Analogique de la Langue Francais, 6 vols. Paul Robert. (Fr.). 1964. 1380.00 F. Ste. Nouv. Littre.
Dictionnaire Alphabetique & Analogique de la Langue Francais, 6 vols. Paul Robert. 534p. (Fr.). 1970. 150.00 F. Ste. Nouv. Littre.
Dictionnaire Alphabetique et Analogique de la Langue Francaise, 7 vols. Robert. (Illus., Fr.). Set. 437.50 (ISBN 0-685-11140-7). French & Eur.
Dictionnaire Analogique. Charles Maquet. 591p. (Fr.). 1971. 16.00 F. Larousse.
Dictionnaire Analogique. 11th ed. Charles Maquet. 600p. (Fr.). 1971. 49.00 F. Larousse.
Dictionnaire Analogique de Poche. Niobey. (Fr.). 1980. pap. 10.25 F (Dist. by Continental Bk Co). Larousse.
Dictionnaire Analogique et de Synonymes Pour la Resolution des Problemes des Mots Croises. 6th ed. Maurice Denis-Papin. (Fr.). 1970. pap. 6.95 (ISBN 0-686-56786-2, M-6582, Pub. by Albin Michel). French & Eur.
Dictionnaire Analoqique & de Synonymes pour la Resolution des Problemes des Mots Croises. 6th ed. Maurice Denis-Papin. (Fr.). 1970. 16.00 F. Albin Michel.
Dictionnaire Anglais Chambers: Essential Dictionary. (Eng.). 10.50 (Dist. by Continental Bk Co). Lib. Fernand Nathan.
Dictionnaire Anglais Chambers: Junior Learners' Dictionary. (Fr.). 7.15 (Dist. by Continental Bk Co). Lib. Fernand Nathan.
Dictionnaire Anglais Chambers: 20th Century Dictionary. (Eng.). 32.25. Lib. Fernand Nathan.
Dictionnaire Anglais-Francais. John Bell. (Illus.). 960p. (Eng. & Fr.). 1959. 18.00 F. Garnier.
Dictionnaire Anglais-Francais. Ebenezer Clifton & Horace J. Mac Laughlin. (Illus.). 1260p. (Eng. & Fr.). 1968. 56.00 F. Garnier.
Dictionnaire Anglais-Francais. 640p. (Eng. & Fr.). 1978. 7.50 F. Larousse.
Dictionnaire Anglais-Francais. Eugene Kuentz. 824p. (Eng. & Fr.). 1973. 23.50 F. Ecole.
Dictionnaire Anglais-Francais. Eugene Kuentz & Emile Saillens. (Eng. & Fr.). 1970. 20.00 F. Licet.
Dictionnaire Anglais-Francais. Eugene Kuentz & Emile Saillens. 872p. (Eng. & Fr.). 1978. 23.50 F. Magnard.
Dictionnaire Anglais-Francais. Jean Vincent. (Eng. & Fr.). 1978. pap. 11.00 F. Garnier-Flammarion.
Dictionnaire Anglais-Francais. Jean Vincent. 394p. (Eng. & Fr.). 1964. 9.50 F. Garnier-Flammarion.
Dictionnaire Anglais-Francais D'electrotechnique. Jean Guy Grenier. 260p. (Eng. & Fr.). 1976. C.$12.00. Lanaudiere.
Dictionnaire Anglais-Francais des Sciences Medicales & Paramedicales. W. J. Gladstone. (Eng. & Fr.). 1978. 250.00 F. Edisem.
Dictionnaire Anglais-Francais des Sciences Medicales & Paramedicales. William J. Gladstone. LC 79-118626. 1153p. (Eng. & Fr.). 1978. 55.00 F. Maloine.
Dictionnaire Anglais-Francais des Sciences Medicales et Paramedicales. W. J. Gladstone. (Eng. & Fr.). 1978. 99.95 (ISBN 0-686-57303-X, M-6277). French & Eur.
Dictionnaire Anglais-Francais des Sciences Medicales et Paramedicales. W. J. Gladstone. 1154p. (Fr.). 1978. 95.00 F. Maloine.
Dictionnaire Anglais-Francais Des Termes & Locutions Maritimes. 2nd ed. Henri Paasch. 320p. (Fr.). 1974. 53.00 F. Maritimes Outre mer.
Dictionnaire Anglais-Francais et Francais-Anglais des Termes et Locutions Maritimes. 2nd ed. Henri Paasch. 320p. (Fr. & Eng.). 1974. pap. 23.50 (ISBN 0-686-57065-0, M-6437). French & Eur.
Dictionnaire Anglais-Francais et Lexique Francais-Anglais des termes Politiques Juridiques et Economiques. Dreuihe. (Eng. & Fr.). 1981. pap. 22.95 (ISBN 0-686-92584-X, M-9628). French & Eur.
Dictionnaire Anglais-Francais pour les Travaux Publics: Le Batiment & L'equipement des Chantiers de Construction. 6th ed. Hector Bucksch. 420p. (Eng. & Fr.). 1977. 103.00 F. Eyrolles.
Dictionnaire Anglais-Francais: Sciences Medicales & Paramedicales. W. J. Gladstone. 1154p. (Eng. & Fr.). 1978. 250.00 F. Maloine.
Dictionnaire Anglais-Francis des Termes Relatifs a L'electrotechnique: l'ectrotechnique & aux Applications Connexes. 10th ed. Henri Piraux. (Illus.). 416p. (Eng. & Fr.). 1978. 100.00 F. Eyrolles.
Dictionnaire Anglo-Francais des Nouveautes Linguistiques. Albert Beaudet. 198p. (Fr.). 1972. 4.95 F. Fides.
Dictionnaire Animaux. Scarry. (Fr.). (gr. 3-8). 14.95 (ISBN 0-685-28442-5). French & Eur.
Dictionnaire-Annuaire de l'agriculture. 152p. (Fr.). 1975. 89.00 F. Faure.
Dictionnaire Arabe-Francais. LC 77-980964. 155p. (Fr. & Arabic.). 1977. write for info. N'Damena Tchad.
Dictionnaire Arabe-Francais, 2 vols. A. B. Kazimirski. (Arabic & Fr.). Repr. of 1860 ed. 80.00 set (110-0). Intl Bk Ctr.
Dictionnaire Arabe-Francais. Ben Sedira. 628p. (Arabic & Fr.). 1980. write for info. (M-9305). French & Eur.
Dictionnaire Arabe-Francais-Anglais, 12 vols. Regis Blachere & Moustafa Chouemi. (Arabic, Fr. & Eng.). 1970. 650.00 F. Maison & Larose.
Dictionnaire Arabe-Francais-Anglais, 1, Pts. 1-12. Regis Blachere & Moustafa Chouemi. (Arabic, Fr. & Eng.). 1967. 350.00 (ISBN 0-686-56918-0, M-6034). French & Eur.
Dictionnaire Arabe-Francais-Anglais, 2, Pts. 13-24. Regis Blachere & Moustafa Chouemi. (Arab., Fr. & Eng.). 1970. 350.00 (ISBN 0-686-56919-9, M-6035). French & Eur.
Dictionnaire Arabe-Francais: Dialectes de Syrie. Adrien Barthelemy. (Illus.). 68p. (Arabic & Fr.). 1969. 15.00 F. Geuthner.
Dictionnaire Arabe-Francais: Langue ecrite, 2 vols. Auguste Cherbonneau. 436p. (Arabic & Fr.). 30.00 (103-8). Intl Bk Ctr.
Dictionnaire Arabe Moderne Larousse. Khalil Georr. (Illus.). 1360p. (Arabic.). 1973. 57.20 F. Larousse.
Dictionnaire Arabe moderne Larousse. Khalil Georr. 1360p. (Arabic.). 1973. 25.00 F. Larousse.
Dictionnaire Archeologique de la Gaul. Emile Cartailhac. 160p. (Fr.). 1923. 10.00 F. Nationale.
Dictionnaire Archeologique de la Gaule. Emile Cartailhac. 472p. (Fr.). 1923. 10.00 F. Biblio Nationale.
Dictionnaire Armenien-Francais, 2 vols. Ambroise Calfa. 1038p. (Armenian & Fr.). 1973. Set. pap. 49.95 (ISBN 0-686-56934-2, M-6056). French & Eur.
Dictionnaire Armenien-Francais, 2 vols. Ambroise Calfa. 1038p. (Armenian & Fr.). 1973. 120.00 F. Klincksieck.
Dictionnaire Astrologique. Henry J. Gouchou. 670p. (Fr.). 1975. 67.50 (ISBN 0-686-57307-2, M-6284). French & Eur.
Dictionnaire Astrologique. Henry J. Gouchou. 670p. (Fr.). 1975. 170.00 F. Dervy Livres.
Dictionnaire Banda-Francais. C. Tisserant. 611p. (Fr & Banda.). 1931. 66.20 F. Institut Ethnologie.
Dictionnaire Banda-Francais. Ch. Tisserant. 611p. (Banda-Fr.). 1931. 32.50 (ISBN 0-686-56789-7, M-6585, Pub. by Institut Ethnologie). French & Eur.
Dictionnaire Basque Francais. Pierre Lhande. 1117p. (Basque & Fr.). 1938. 79.95 (ISBN 0-686-57020-0, M-6377). French & Eur.
Dictionnaire Basque Francais. Pierre Lhande. (Illus.). 1117p. (Fr.). 1938. 200.00 F. Beauchesne.
Dictionnaire Bearnais Ancien & Moderne, 2 vols. Jean-Desire Lespy & Paul Raymond. 878p. (Fr.). 1970. 150.00 F. Slatkine.
Dictionnaire Beauchemin Canadien. Jean-Jacques Lefebvre. (Fr.). 1968. Can.$12.00. Beauchemin.
Dictionnaire Berrichon. Jean Tissier. 117p. (Fr.). 1970. 25.00 F. Slatkine.
Dictionnaire Berrichon avec Citations Litteraires. Jean Tissier. 112p. (Fr.). 1978. 50.00 F. Lafitte Repr.
Dictionnaire Bibliographique du Canada. Victor Barbeau. 246p. (Fr.). 1974. Can.$25.00. Acad Can Fr.
Dictionnaire Biblique. Joseph Dheilly. 1284p. (Fr.). 1964. 22.50 (ISBN 0-686-57092-8, M-6114). French & Eur.
Dictionnaire Bilingue "Apollo". (Fr. & Eng.). 1973. 7.25 (Dist. by Continental Bk Co). Larousse.
Dictionnaire Bilingue Apollo. Paul Pauliat. (Fr.). 1976. 18.00 F. Larousse.
Dictionnaire Bilingue Apollo Francais-Allemand. Jolivet A. Pinoche. (Fr. & Ger.). 18.70 F. Larousse.
Dictionnaire Bilingue Apollo Francais-Anglais. Louis Chaffurin & Jean Mergault. 768p. (Fr. & Eng.). 1971. 18.70 F. Larousse.
Dictionnaire Bilingue Apollo Francais-Espagnol. Miguel De Toro & Gisbert De Toro. 792p. (Fr. & Span.). 1978. 18.70 F. Larousse.
Dictionnaire Bilingue Apollo Francais-Italien. Giuseppe Padovani & Richard Silvestri. 768p. (Fr. & Ital.). 1971. 18.70 F. Larousse.
Dictionnaire Bilingue Apollo Francais-Portugais. Fernando V. Peixoto da Fonseca. 758p. (Fr. & Port.). 1958. 18.70 F. Larousse.
Dictionnaire Bilingue: Francais-Espagnol, Espagnol-Francais. M. De Toro Gisbert. 546p. (Fr. & Span.). 1968. pap. text ed. 7.95 (ISBN 0-686-97445-X, S-36345). French & Eur.
Dictionnaire Bilingue Francais-Russe et Russe-Francais. (Fr. & Rus.). 10.50 (ISBN 2-03-020904-X, 2715, Apollo). Larousse.
Dictionnaire Bilingue Larousse, Francais-Anglais, Anglais-Francais. L. Chaffurin & J. Mergault. (Apollo). (Fr. & Eng.). 10.50 (ISBN 0-685-13856-9, 3767). Larousse.
Dictionnaire Bilingue Larousse, Francais-Alemand et Allemand-Francais. A. Pinloche & A. Jolivet. (Apollo). (Fr. & Ger.). 10.50 (ISBN 0-685-13853-4, 3779). Larousse.
Dictionnaire Bilingue Larousse, Francais-Espagnol, Espanol-Frances. M. De Toro & Gisbert. (Apollo). (Fr. & Span.). 10.50 (ISBN 0-685-13857-7, 3774). Larousse.
Dictionnaire Bilingue Larousse, Francais-Italien et Italien-Francais. G. Padovani & R. Silvestri. (Apollo). (Fr.). 10.50 (ISBN 0-685-13854-2, 3784). Larousse.
Dictionnaire Bilingue Larousse, Francais-Portugais et Portugais-Francais. F. Peixoto Da Fonseca. (Apollo). (Fr. & Port.). 10.50 (ISBN 2-03-020909-0, 3791). Larousse.
Dictionnaire Bordas. Robert Jarnier. 60p. (Fr.). 1974. DM.6.50. Bordas-Dunod.
Dictionnaire Bordas: Cahier de Travaux Diriges. R. Jarnier & J. Fournier. (Illus.). 64p. (Fr.). E0.70. Harrap.
Dictionnaire Bordas: Dictionnaire du Francais Vivant. Ed. by M. R. Davau et al. 1530p. (Fr.). 1980. E12.95 (ISBN 2-45538-828-X). Harrap.
Dictionnaire Breton-Francais, Francais-Breton. (Fr. & Breton.). 1979. 29.95 (ISBN 0-686-56717-X, M-6118). French & Eur.
Dictionnaire Bulgare-Francais. L. Stephanova et al. 978p. (Bulgarian & Fr.). 1973. leatherette 45.00 (ISBN 0-686-92575-0, M-9834). French & Eur.
Dictionnaire Canadien des Relations du Travail: Francais-Anglais. Gerard Dion. 682p. (Eng. & Fr.). 1976. 49.95 (ISBN 0-686-57118-5, M-6163). French & Eur.
Dictionnaire Canadien des Relations du Travall Francais-Anglais. Gerard Dion. (Fr. & Eng.). 1976. write for info. Laval P. U.
Dictionnaire Canadien-Francais. Sylva Clapin. 394p. (Canadian & Fr.). 1974. 17.50 (ISBN 0-686-56809-5, M-6587). French & Eur.
Dictionnaire Canadien-Francais. Sylva Clapin. xlvi, 394p. (Fr.). 1974. Can.$12.00 (ISBN 2-7637-6723-0). Soc Dev Liv.
Dictionnaire Canadien-Francais. Sylva Clapin. (Fr.). 1974. write for info. Laval.
Dictionnaire Chasse. Tony Burnand. (Dictionnaires de l'homme du vingtieme siecle). (Fr., Fr). 1970. 8.50 (ISBN 0-685-13859-3, 3711). Larousse.
Dictionnaire Chimique. 6th ed. Raymond Cornubert. (Eng. & Fr.). 1970. 17.50x (ISBN 2-04-007334-5). Intl Pubns Serv.
Dictionnaire Chinois-Francais. 673p. (Fr. & Chinese.). 1979. 25.00 (ISBN 0-686-97329-1, M-9268). French & Eur.
Dictionnaire Chinois-Francais des Locutions et Proverbes. 565p. (Chinese & Fr.). 1980. 14.95 (ISBN 0-686-92595-5). French & Eur.
Dictionnaire civilisation Grecque. G. Rachet & M. F. Rachet. (Illus., Fr.). pap. 8.50 (ISBN 0-685-13861-5, 3715). Larousse.
Dictionnaire civilisation Romaine. Jean C. Fredoville. (Dictionnaires de l'homme du vingtieme siecle). (Illus., Fr.). 1968. 8.50 (ISBN 0-685-13862-3, 3716). Larousse.
Dictionnaire Classique Anglais-Francais. Charles Patit & William Savage. 686p. (Eng. & Fr.). 1967. write for info. Hac.

Dictionnaire Classique Anglais-Francais et Francais-Anglais. Charles Petit & William Savage. 686p. (Eng. & Fr.). 1967. pap. 27.50 (ISBN 0-686-57072-3, M-6444). French & Eur.

Dictionnaire Classique de la Langue Chinoise. Couvreur. 1080p. (Chinese.). 1966. write for info. Mason & Larose.

Dictionnaire Classique de la Langue Chinoise. F. S. Couvveur. 1080p. (Fr. & Chinese.). 1966. 35.00 (ISBN 0-686-56810-9, M-6588). French & Eur.

Dictionnaire Classique Francais-Allemand. 2nd ed. Bertaux. 1310p. (Fr. & Ger.). 1970. write for info. Hachette.

Dictionnaire Classique Francais-Neerlandais. 22nd ed. Ludovic Grootaers. LC 75-505480. 10019p. (Dutch & Fr.). 1975. write for info. Vander.

Dictionnaire Classique: Francais-Neerlandais, Neerlandais-Francais. 22nd ed. Ludovic Grootaers. 1050p. (Fr. & Dutch.). 1969. 29.95 (ISBN 0-686-57317-X, M-6300). French & Eur.

Dictionnaire Commente de l'oeuvre de General de Gaulle. 880p. (Fr.). 1975. 30.00 (ISBN 0-686-56811-7, M-6589). French & Eur.

Dictionnaire Commercial & Financier en Quatre Langues: Francais-Neerlandais-Anglais-Allemand. 5th ed. Josef V. Servotte. 960p. (Fr., Dutch, Eng. & Ger.). write for info. Erasme.

Dictionnaire Commercial & Financier: Francais-Anglais. Josef V. Servotte. (Fr. & Eng.). 1977. write for info. Marabout.

Dictionnaire Commercial et Financier en 4 Langues see Commercial & Financial Dictionary in Four Languages.

Dictionnaire Commercial: Italien-Francais Francais-Italien. Mario Mormile. 650p. (Ital. & Fr.). 1978. 150.00 F. Maison Dictionnaire.

Dictionnaire Commerciale. 297p. (Fr.). 1979. pap. 49.95 (ISBN 2-85319-069-2, M-9307). French & Eur.

Dictionnaire Complet des Mots Croises. (Fr.). 9.95 (ISBN 0-686-56804-4, F-136830). French & Eur.

Dictionnaire Complet des Mots Croises. Larousse & Co. (Fr., Fr). 27.50 (ISBN 2-03-020294-0, 3617). Larousse.

Dictionnaire Contextuel Anglais-Francais de l'energie Solaire. 67p. (Eng. & Fr.). 1979. pap. 7.95 (ISBN 0-9690950-0-7, M-9032). French & Eur.

Dictionnaire Contextuel Anglais-Francais de l'energie Solaire. Robert Serre. LC 80-481480. 67p. (Eng. & Fr.). 1979. Can.$pap. 4.00 (ISBN 0-9690950-0-7). Serre.

Dictionnaire Correctif du Francais au Canada. Dulong. 256p. (Fr.). 1968. write for info. Laval P. U.

Dictionnaire Corse-Francais, Pierre d'Evisa. Mathieu Ceccald. 464p. (Fr.). 1974. write for info. Klincksieck.

Dictionnaire Corse-Francais (Pierre d'Evisa) Mathieu Ceccald. 98p. (Fr.). 1974. write for info. CNRS.

Dictionnaire Corse-Francais, Pierre d'Evisa. Mathieu Ceccaldi. 464p. (Corsican & Fr.). 1974. pap. 29.95 (ISBN 0-686-56944-X, M-6066). French & Eur.

Dictionnaire Critique & Documentaire: Peintres, Sculptres, Dessinateurs et Graveurs de Tous les Temps & de Tous les Pays. Emmanuel Benezit. (Fr.). 1976. write for info. Grund.

Dictionnaire Critique de la Musique Ancienne & Moderne. Andre Coeuroy. 416p. (Fr.). 1956. write for info. Payot.

Dictionnaire Critique de Psychiatrie. Barthhold Bierens de Haan. LC 79-124731. 301p. (Fr.). 1979. write for info. (ISBN 2-7203-0057-8). Hameau.

Dictionnaire Critique des Drogues. Ronald Verbeke. 160p. (Fr.). 1978. 39.95 (ISBN 0-686-57243-2, M-6548). French & Eur.

Dictionnaire Critique des Drogues. Ronald Verbeke. 160p. (Fr.). write for info. Bourgois.

Dictionnaire Critique et Documentaire des Peintres, Sculpteurs, Dessinateurs, et Graveurs de Tous les Temps et de Tons les Pays, 10 tomes. Benezit. (Fr.). 1976. Set. 395.00 (ISBN 0-685-35921-2). French & Eur.

Dictionnaire d'accentuation pour les Travailleurs de la Radio & de la Television. Rosenthal. (Fr.). write for info. MIR.

Dictionnaire d'Agriculture. (Fr.). 1976. 45.00 (ISBN 0-686-57095-2, M-6119). French & Eur.

Dictionnaire d'agriculture. (Fr.). 1976. write for info. C. I. L. F.

Dictionnaire d'Agriculture. L. N. Mauroy. Ed. by J. P. Migne. (Nouvelle Encyclopedie Theologique Ser.: Vol. 28). 726p. (Fr.). Repr. of 1862 ed. lib. bdg. 92.50x (ISBN 0-89241-271-2). Caratzas Pub Co.

Dictionnaire d'Anecdotes Chretiennes. P. Jouhanneaud. Ed. by J. P. Migne. (Nouvelle Encyclopedie Theologique Ser.: Vol. 10). 610p. (Fr.). Repr. of 1857 ed. lib. bdg. 78.00x (ISBN 0-89241-260-7). Caratzas Pub Co.

Dictionnaire D'anglais. F. Dubois-Charlier. LC 77-559350. xvii, 868p. (Eng. & Fr.). 1975. 29.00 F (ISBN 2-03-040531-0); pap. 11.50 text ed. Larousse FR.

Dictionnaire d'Anglais. F. Dubois-Charlier et al. 868p. (Fr.). 1975. pap. text ed. 11.50 (ISBN 2-03-040531-0). Larousse.

Dictionnaire d'anglais. Francois Dubois-Charlier et al. LC 77-559350. xvii, 868p. (Eng. & Fr.). 1975. write for info. Larousse.

Dictionnaire d'Anglais Niveau 1. Dubois Charlier et al. (Fr.). 1975. write for info. Larousse.

Dictionnaire Danois-Francais. 640p. (Danish & Fr.). write for info. Larousse.

Dictionnaire d'Anthropologie ou Histoire Naturelle del'Homme et des Races Humaines. L. F. Jehan. Ed. by J. P. Migne. (Nouvelle Encyclopedie Theologique Ser.: Vol. 42). 800p. (Fr.). Repr. of 1853 ed. lib. bdg. 101.50x (ISBN 0-89241-281-X). Caratzas Pub Co.

Dictionnaire d'Antiphilosophisme ou Refutation des Erreurs du 18e Siecle. E. Grosse. Ed. by J. P. Migne. (Troisieme et Derniere Encyclopedie Theologique Ser.: Vol. 18). 770p. (Fr.). Repr. of 1856 ed. lib. bdg. 97.50x (ISBN 0-89241-301-8). Caratzas Pub Co.

Dictionnaire d'Apologetique, 2 vols. L. F. Jehan. Ed. by J. P. Migne. (Nouvelle Encyclopedie Theologique Ser.: Vols. 51-52). 1702p. (Fr.). Repr. of 1855 ed. lib. bdg. 215.00x (ISBN 0-89241-289-5). Caratzas Pub Co.

Dictionnaire d'argot. Andre La Rue. (Fr.). write for info. Flammarion.

Dictionnaire d'Argot et des Principales Locutions Populaires. Jean La Rue. 189p. (Fr.). 1975. pap. 5.95 (ISBN 0-686-92571-8, F-136760). French & Eur.

Dictionnaire de Ballet Moderne. (Fr.). 43.25 (ISBN 0-685-35976-X). French & Eur.

Dictionnaire de Biochimie Alimentaire et de Nutruition. J. Adrian & G. Legrand. 233p. (Fr.). 1981. 85.00 (ISBN 2-85206-094-9, M-9626). French & Eur.

Dictionnaire de Biographie des Hommes Celebres: Despuis les Temps les Plus Recules Jusqu'a nos Jours. Edourd Sitzmann. (Fr.). 1973. write for info. Berger Levrault.

Dictionnaire de Biologie Animale. 2nd ed. Roger Husson. 280p. (Fr.). 1970. 44.00 F. Gauthier-Villars.

Dictionnaire de Botanique. Charles Louis Gatin. (Fr.). 1966. write for info. Kraus.

Dictionnaire de Botanique. L. F. Jehan. Ed. by J. P. Migne. (Nouvelle Encyclopedie Theologique Ser.: Vol. 8). 758p. (Fr.). Repr. of 1860 ed. lib. bdg. 105.00x (ISBN 0-89241-258-5). Caratzas Pub Co.

Dictionnaire de Botanique: Vol. 1, A-H. Uberto Tosco. (Fr.). write for info. Atlas.

Dictionnaire de Botanique: Vol. 2, I-Z. Uberto Tosco. (Fr.). write for info. Atlas.

Dictionnaire de Chimie Allemand-Francais. 3rd ed. Raymond Cornubert. 240p. (Fr. & Ger.). 1977. pap. 29.65 (ISBN 0-686-56964-4, M-6088). French & Eur.

Dictionnaire de Chimie et de Mineralogie. L. F. Jehan. Ed. by J. P. Migne. (Encyclopedie Theologique Ser.: Vol. 46). 830p. (Fr.). Repr. of 1851 ed. lib. bdg. 105.00x (ISBN 0-89241-250-X). Caratzas Pub Co.

Dictionnaire De Cosmogonie et De Paleontologie. L. F. Jehan. Ed. by J. P. Migne. (Nouvelle Encyclopedie Theologique Ser.: Vol. 48). 732p. (Fr.). Repr. of 1854 ed. lib. bdg. 93.00x (ISBN 0-89241-286-0). Caratzas Pub Co.

Dictionnaire de Danse. Jacques Baril. 288p. (Fr.). 1964. pap. 14.95 (ISBN 0-686-56812-5, M-6590). French & Eur.

Dictionnaire de Demographie. 1st ed. Roland Pressat. LC 79-123891. vi, 295p. (Fr.). 1979. write for info. (ISBN 2-13-036008-4). Pr Univ Fr.

Dictionnaire De Deux Cent Un Verbes Anglais Conjugues Completement a Tous les Temps & a Toutes les Personnes. Kendris. (Fr.). Date not set. pap. 3.95 (ISBN 0-8120-0550-3). Barron.

Dictionnaire de Deux Cent un Verbes Allemandes. (Fr. & Ger.). Date not set. 6.95 (ISBN 0-8120-2118-5). Barron.

Dictionnaire de Diagnostic Clinique et Topographique. Alain Blacque-Belair & Bernard M. de Fossey. 1250p. (Fr.). 1969. 55.00 (ISBN 0-686-56921-0, M-6037). French & Eur.

Dictionnaire de Didactique des Langues. Ed. by R. Galisson & D. Coste. LC 77-462328. 612p. (Fr.). 1976. write for info. (ISBN 2-010-03576-3). Hachette-Jeunesse.

Dictionnaire de Didactique des Largues. Ed. by R. Galisson & D. Coste. 612p. (Fr.). 1976. 22.50 (ISBN 0-686-56813-3, M-6591). French & Eur.

Dictionnaire de Docientos Uno Verboes Espagnols Conjugues a Toutes les Personnes. Christopher Kendris. LC 68-8678. (Span.). 1969. pap. text ed. 3.95 (ISBN 0-8120-0394-2). Barron.

Dictionnaire de Droit, 2 vols. 2nd ed. (Fr.). 1966. Set. 17.50 (ISBN 0-686-57096-0, M-6120). French & Eur.

Dictionnaire de Droit Canonique, 7 vols. R. Naz. (Fr.). 1965. Set. 695.00 (ISBN 0-686-57057-X, M-6423). French & Eur.

Dictionnaire de Droit Social Francais-Allemand. F. Frankl. 258p. (Fr. & Ger.). 1970. write for info. (ISBN 3-19-006279-X, M-7099). French & Eur.

Dictionnaire de Echecs. E. Maget. 429p. (Fr.). 1974. 67.50 (ISBN 0-686-57023-5, M-6381). French & Eur.

Dictionnaire de Franglais. 175p. (Fr.). 1980. pap. 16.50 (ISBN 0-686-92565-3, M-8980). French & Eur.

Dictionnaire de Genetique. Philippe L'Heritier. LC 79-386405. 259p. (Fr.). 1979. 55.00 F (ISBN 2-225-52657-5). Masson & Cie.

Dictionnaire de Geographie Ancienne et Moderne. 2nd ed. Pierre Deschamps. 1008p. (Fr.). 1965. 85.00 (ISBN 0-686-56814-1, M-6592). French & Eur.

Dictionnaire de Geographie Historique de la Gaule et de la France. Joseph Moreau. 426p. (Fr.). 1972. pap. 37.50 (ISBN 0-686-56815-X, M-6593). French & Eur.

Dictionnaire de Geologie... et Dictionnaire de Chronologie Universelle par M. Champagnac, Vol. 50. L. P. Chesnel De La Charbouclais. Ed. by J. P. Migne. (Encyclopedie Theologique Ser.). 728p. (Fr.). Repr. of 1849 ed. lib. bdg. 192.50x (ISBN 0-89241-253-4). Caratzas Pub Co.

Dictionnaire de Halles. Claude Mallement De Messanges. (Fr.). 1972. 150.00 F. Slatkine.

Dictionnaire de la Beaute Feminine. Floriane Prevot. 268p. (Fr.). 1972. 9.95 (ISBN 0-686-56816-8, M-6594). French & Eur.

Dictionnaire de la Biologie. Gunther Haensch. LC 77-451261. xii, 483p. (Eng., Ger., Fr. & Span.). 1976. DM.98.00 (ISBN 3-405-10933-7). BLV Verlag.

Dictionnaire de la Biologie--B.L.V. 496p. (Eng., Ger., Fr. & Span.). 1976. 95.00 (ISBN 0-686-57097-9, M-6121). French & Eur.

Dictionnaire de la Chasse. Tony Burnand. 250p. (Fr.). 1970. pap. 7.50 (ISBN 0-686-56817-6, M-6595, Pub. by Larousse). French & Eur.

Dictionnaire de la chasse. Tony Burnand. 250p. (Fr.). 1970. pap. 7.50 F. Larousse.

Dictionnaire de la Chimie et de Ses Applications. 3rd ed. C. Duval. 1100p. (Fr.). 1977. 225.00 (ISBN 0-686-56741-2, M-6183). French & Eur.

Dictionnaire de la Civilisation Egytienne. Georges Posener. 326p. (Fr.). 1970. 47.50 (ISBN 0-686-57085-5, M-6462). French & Eur.

Dictionnaire de la Civilisation Grecque. 500p. (Fr.). 1966. 36.95 (ISBN 0-686-57098-7, M-6122). French & Eur.

Dictionnaire de la Commune, Vol. 1. Bernard Noel. (Fr.). 1978. pap. 6.95 (ISBN 0-686-57059-6, M-6428). French & Eur.

Dictionnaire de la comptabilite. Fernand Sylvain. (Fr.). 1977. 17.50 (220). Can Inst Chart Accts.

Dictionnaire de la Constitution: Les Institutions de la Ve Republique. 2nd ed. Raymond Barrillon. xxxiv, 538p. (Fr.). 1978. write for info. Cujas.

Dictionnaire de la Contradiction. Maurice Toesca. 234p. (Fr.). 1969. pap. 10.95 (ISBN 0-686-56825-7, M-6603). French & Eur.

Dictionnaire de la Culture Physique. Marcel Rouet. 304p. (Fr.). 1975. 27.50 (ISBN 0-686-57212-2, M-6494). French & Eur.

Dictionnaire de la Danse, Historique, Theorique, Pratique & Bibliographique. G. Desrat. LC 79-347641. (Illus.). vi, 484p. (Fr.). 1977. DM.68.00 (ISBN 3-487-06327-1). Olms Verlag.

Dictionnaire de la Foi Chretienne, 2 vols. Ed. by Antonir Marie Henry & Olivier De LaBrosse. 792p. (Fr.). 1968. pap. 47.50 (ISBN 0-686-56818-4, M-6596). French & Eur.

Dictionnaire de la Franc-Maconnerie et des Francs-Macons. Allec Mellor. 400p. (Fr.). 1971. 27.50 (ISBN 0-686-57043-X, M-6403). French & Eur.

Dictionnaire de la Geographie. 2nd ed. Pierre George. 460p. (Fr.). 1974. 47.50 (ISBN 0-686-57193-2, M-6267). French & Eur.

Dictionnaire de la Langue des Iles Marquises. Ildefonse Dordillon. 598p. (Fr & Marquise.). 1932. 27.50 (ISBN 0-686-56819-2, M-6597). French & Eur.

Dictionnaire de la Langue Francaise. Littre. Ed. by Beaujean & Geraud-Venzac. (Fr.). 24.95 (ISBN 0-685-36652-9). French & Eur.

Dictionnaire de La Langue Francaise, 7 tomes. Emile Littre. (Fr.). 21.95 (ISBN 0-685-11141-5); Set. 245.00 (ISBN 0-685-11142-3). French & Eur.

Dictionnaire de la Langue Pedagogique. Paul Foulquie. 496p. (Fr.). 124.80 F. PUF.

Dictionnaire de la Langue Quebecoise. L. Bergeron. 574p. (Fr.). 1980. pap. 75.00 (ISBN 0-686-92606-4, M-9360). French & Eur.

Dictionnaire de la Langue Romane ou du Vieux Langue Francois, 2 vols. Francois Lacombe. 1200p. (Fr.). 1978. 250.00 F. Slatkine.

Dictionnaire de la Langue Romano-Casteaise & des Contrees Limitrophes. J. Couzinie. 563p. (Fr.). 1976. 210.00 F. Lafitte Repr.

Dictionnaire de la Langue Russe. (Rus.). 1978. 45.75 F. Mir.

Dictionnaire de la Langue Toulousaine. Jean Doujat. 254p. (Fr.). 1974. 110.00 F. Lafitte Repr.

Dictionnaire de la Langue Verte. Alfred Delvau. 600p. (Fr.). 1972. 120.00 F. Slatkine.
Dictionnaire de la Linguistique. Georges Mounin. (Illus.). 384p. (Fr.). 1974. 130.00 F. PUF.
Dictionnaire de la Loi. Robert Millet. 176p. (Fr.). 1965. 2.50 F. Homme.
Dictionnaire de la Marine a Voile. Pierre M. De Bonnefoux & Edmund Paris. 775p. (Fr.). 1971. 150.00 F. Courtille.
Dictionnaire de la Mer & de la Navigation. Gianni Cazzaroli. (Illus.). 392p. (Fr.). 1973. 58.00 F. Denoel.
Dictionnaire de la Montagne. Jacques Gautrat. 256p. (Fr.). 1970. pap. 8.95 (ISBN 0-686-56820-6, M-6598). French & Eur.
Dictionnaire de la Musique. Marc Honegger. (Illus.). 1232p. (Fr.). 1970. 165.00 F. Bordas-Dunod.
Dictionnaire de la Musique, Vol. 1. Ed. by Marc Honegger. 1232p. (Fr.). 1970. 65.00 (ISBN 0-686-56821-4, M-6599). French & Eur.
Dictionnaire de la Musique: Science de la Musique, 2 vols. M. Honegger. 1216p. (Fr.). 1976. Set. 125.00 (ISBN 2-04-005140-6, M-6318). French & Eur.
Dictionnaire de la Mythologie Grecque et Romaine. 5th ed. Pierre Grimal. 612p. (Fr.). 1969. 59.95 (ISBN 0-686-57316-1, M-6299). French & Eur.
Dictionnaire de la Navication. Gianni Cazzaroli. 392p. (Fr.). 1973. 23.50 (ISBN 0-686-56803-6, M-4650). French & Eur.
Dictionnaire de la Noblesse, 10 vols. Francais Aubert de la Chenaye-Desbois. 9800p. (Fr.). 1978. Set. 155.00 (ISBN 0-686-56904-0, M-6015). French & Eur.
Dictionnaire de la Noblesse Francais. F. Saint-Simon. (Illus.). 1214p. (Fr.). 1975. 240.00 F. Contrepoint.
Dictionnaire de la Noblesse Francais. Etienne De Sereville & F. de Saint-Simon. 1214p. (Fr.). 1975. 95.00 (ISBN 0-686-56753-6, M-6513). French & Eur.
Dictionnaire de la Peinture Italie. (Illus.). 320p. (Ital.). 1964. 90.00 F. Hazan.
Dictionnaire de la Peinture Italienne. 320p. (Fr.). 1964. 36.00 (ISBN 0-686-56822-2, M-6600). French & Eur.
Dictionnaire de la Peinture Surrealiste. Sarane Alexandrian. 58p. (Fr.). 1973. 32.50 (ISBN 0-686-56823-0, M-6601). French & Eur.
Dictionnaire de la Peinture Surrealiste. Sarane Alexandrian. 58p. (Fr.). 1973. 50.00 F (Pub. by Filipacchi). Hippocrene Bks.
Dictionnaire de la Politique Francaise, 2 vols. Henry Coston. (Illus.). 1088p. (Fr.). 1970. 240.00 F. Coston.
Dictionnaire de la Politique Francaise. Henry Coston. (Illus.). 1088p. (Fr.). 120.00 F. Francaise Lib.
Dictionnaire de la Politique Francaise, 3. Henry Coston. (Fr.). 1976. 150.00 F. Coston.
Dictionnaire de la presse ecrite et audiovisuelle. Divers. 580p. (Span., Fr., Ital., Port. & Romanian.). 1981. 160000.00 F. Maison Dictionnaire.
Dictionnaire de la Prononciation. A. Lerond. 589p. (Fr.). 1980. text ed. 20.95 (ISBN 2-03-340101-4, M-9124). French & Eur.
Dictionnaire de la Prononciation. A. Lerond. (Fr.). 1980. 17.75 (Dist. by Continental Bk Co). Larousse.
Dictionnaire de la Prononciation Francaise Dans Son Usage Reel. Andre Martinet & Henriette Walter. 932p. (Fr.). 1973. 95.00 (ISBN 0-686-56802-8, M-4739). French & Eur.
Dictionnaire de la Prononciation Francaise dans son Usage Reel. Andre Martinet & Henriette Walter. 932p. (Fr.). 1973. 236.00 F. France Expansion.
Dictionnaire de la Prononciation Francais. 3rd ed. Leon Warnant. (Fr.). 1968. 750.00 F. Duculot.
Dictionnaire de la Prononciation Francais. Leon Warnant. 236p. (Fr.). 1967. 225.00 F. Duculot.
Dictionnaire de la Prononciation Francais. 3rd ed. Leon Warnant. 654p. (Fr.). 1968. C.$21.00. Renouveau Pedagogique.
Dictionnaire de la Prononciation Francaise, Vol. 1. 3rd ed. Leon Warnant. (Fr.). 1968. pap. 35.00 (ISBN 0-686-56824-9, M-6602). French & Eur.
Dictionnaire de la Provence & du Comte Venaissin, 2 vols. Claude F. Achard. 1162p. (Fr.). 1971. 235.00 F. Slatkine.
Dictionnaire de la Psychanalyse. Pierre Fedida. 250p. (Fr.). 1978. 17.60 F. Larousse.
Dictionnaire de la Psychologie. 4th ed. Norbert Sillamy. (Illus.). 250p. (Fr.). 1971. 17.60 F. Larousse.
Dictionnaire de la Publicite et du Marketing: Anglais-Francais Francais-Anglais. Sylvain Giomot. 500p. (Eng. & Fr.). 1979. 110.00 F. Maison Dictionnaire.
Dictionnaire de la revolution Etudiante. Alain Buhler & J. Didier. (Fr.). 1968. 4.50 F. Controverses.
Dictionnaire de la Revolution Francaise. E. Boursin & Auguste Challamel. (Fr.). 1971. 163.50 F. Kraus.
Dictionnaire de la Science Economique. 3rd ed. Alain Cotta. 448p. (Fr.). pap. 22.50 (ISBN 0-686-56965-2, M-6092). French & Eur.
Dictionnaire de la Science Economique. 3rd ed. Alain Cotta. 448p. (Fr.). 50.00 F. Delarge.
Dictionnaire de la Seconde Guerre mondiale. Philippe Masson. LC 79-127046. (Illus., Fr.). 1979. write for info. Larousse.
Dictionnaire de la Sexualite. Georges Valensin. 392p. (Fr.). 1967. 10.95 (ISBN 0-686-56826-5, M-6604). French & Eur.
Dictionnaire de la Technique Industrielle: Allemand-Francais. 3rd ed. R. Ernst. 1233p. (Ger. & Fr.). 1979. 430.00 F. Maison Dictionnaire.
Dictionnaire de la Technologie des Corps Gras. Boris Solomon. (Fr., Eng., Ger., Span. & Ital.). 1971. 25.00 F. Inst Corps Gras.
Dictionnaire de la Tradition Pontificale, Patristique et Conciliaire, 2 vols. J. C. Poussin & J. C. Garnier. Ed. by J. P. Migne. (Troisieme et Derniere Encyclopedie Theologique Ser.: Vol. 12-13). 1464p. (Fr.). Repr. of 1855 ed. lib. bdg. 186.00x (ISBN 0-89241-296-8). Caratzas Pub Co.
Dictionnaire de la Troisieme Republique. Pierre Pierrard. (Illus.). 250p. (Fr.). 1968. 17.60 F. Larousse.
Dictionnaire de la Vie Affective et Sexuelle. Jean Cohen & Anne Marie Dourlen-Rollier. 272p. (Fr.). 1974. 15.95 (ISBN 0-686-56827-3, M-6605). French & Eur.
Dictionnaire de la Virilite. P. Vincent. 370p. (Fr.). 1973. 12.50 (ISBN 0-686-57247-5, M-6553). French & Eur.
Dictionnaire de la Virilite. Paul Vincent. (Illus.). 370p. (Fr.). 1973. 28.00 F. Maloine.
Dictionnaire de la Voile. Michel Barberousse. (Illus.). 256p. (Fr.). 1970. 20.00 F. Seuil.
Dictionnaire de la Voile. Ed. by Michel Barberousse. 256p. (Fr.). 1970. pap. 14.95 (ISBN 0-686-56828-1, M-6606). French & Eur.
Dictionnaire de l'academie Francois, 2 vols. 878p. (Fr.). 1968. 800.00 F. Slatkine.
Dictionnaire de L'agriculture. 8th ed. Robert Faure. LC 76-469040. 295p. (Fr.). 1976. 98.00 F. Doc Univers.
Dictionnaire de l'Ancien Francais. 4th ed. Julien A. Greimas. (Fr.). 1970. 57.20 F. Larousse.
Dictionnaire de L'ancienne Langue Francaise, 10 vols. Frederic Godefroy. (Fr.). 1961. 2364.00 F. Kraus.
Dictionnaire de l'Arabe Parle Palestinien. Yohanan Elihai. 418p. (Fr. & Arabic.). 1974. pap. 22.50 (ISBN 0-686-57132-0, M-6185). French & Eur.
Dictionnaire de L'arabe Parte Palestinien: Francais-Arabe. Yohanan Elihai. 418p. (Fr. & Arabic.). 1974. 52.00 F. Klincksieck.
Dictionnaire de l'art Contemporain. Raymond Charmet. (Illus.). 250p. (Fr.). 1965. 17.60 F. Larousse.
Dictionnaire de l'art de Verifier les Dates. Benedictines de la Congregation de Saint-Maur. Ed. by J. P. Migne. (Nouvelle Encyclopedie Theologique Ser.: Vol. 49). 680p. (Fr.). Repr. of 1854 ed. lib. bdg. 86.50x (ISBN 0-89241-287-9). Caratzas Pub Co.
Dictionnaire de l'astrologie. Jean-Louis Brau. LC 77-559018. (Illus.). 222p. (Fr.). 1977. 16.90 F (ISBN 2-03-075477-3). Larousse FR.
Dictionnaire de l'astrologie. Jean-Louis Brau. (Illus.). 222p. (Fr.). 1977. 17.60 F. Larousse.
Dictionnaire de l'astrologie. Michele Curcio. LC 77-451302. (Illus.). 290p. (Fr.). 1976. 39.00 F (ISBN 2-203-22107-0). Casterman.
Dictionnaire de l'audio-Visual. Guitta Pessis-Pasternak. 372p. (Fr.). 1976. Can.$10.00. Flammarion.
Dictionnaire de l'audio-Visual: Francais-Anglais. Guitta Pessis-Pasternak. 384p. (Fr. & Eng.). 1976. 38.00 F. Flammarion.
Dictionnaire de l'Audio-Visuel: Francais-Anglais, Anglais-Francais. Guitta Pessis-Pasternak. 384p. (Fr. & Eng.). 1976. pap. 15.95 (ISBN 0-686-57070-7, M-6442). French & Eur.
Dictionnaire de l'automobile. Robert Guerber. 174p. (Fr.). 1967. 28.00 F. Flammarion.
Dictionnaire de l'Edition: Francais-Anglais, Anglais-Francais. Philippe Schuwer. (Fr.-Eng.). 1977. 55.00 (ISBN 0-686-57216-5, M-6508). French & Eur.
Dictionnaire de l'edition: Francais-Anglais. Philippe Schuwer. (Fr. & Eng.). 1977. 130.00 F. Cercle Librairie.
Dictionnaire de l'effusion. Claude Bossicart. (Fr.). 85.00 F. Dryade.
Dictionnaire de l'electricien Praticien. Eugene Marec. (Illus.). 330p. (Fr.). 1955. 16.00 F. Bailliere.
Dictionnaire de l'electronique. 3rd ed. Jean F. Arnaud. (Illus.). 250p. (Fr.). 1971. 17.60 F. Larousse.
Dictionnaire de l'Enfantement. Max Ploquin. 264p. (Fr.). 1974. pap. 22.50 (ISBN 0-686-57083-9, M-6459). French & Eur.
Dictionnaire de l'ethnologie. Michel Panoff & Michel Perrin. 224p. (Fr.). 1973. 20.00 F. Payot.
Dictionnaire de l'Evaluation et de la Recherche en Education. Gilbert De Landsheere. 352p. (Fr.). 1979. 62.50 (ISBN 0-686-56981-4, M-6108). French & Eur.
Dictionnaire de L'Extreme-Gauche. Roland Biard. 384p. (Fr.). 1978. 59.00 F. Belfond.
Dictionnaire de l'Extreme-Gauche: De 1945 a Nos Jours. Roland Biard. 384p. (Fr.). 1978. pap. 22.50 (ISBN 0-686-56917-2, M-6033). French & Eur.
Dictionnaire de l'Extreme-Gauche: De 1945 a Nos Jours. Roland Biard. LC 78-399569. 411p. (Fr.). 1978. 50.00 F (ISBN 2-7144-1131-2). Belfond.
Dictionnaire de L'histoire de Belgique. Eugene De Seyn. (Illus.). 512p. (Fr.). 250.00 F. Halbart Wahle.
Dictionnaire de l'Histoire Universelle de l'Eglise, 6 vols. L. F. Guerin. Ed. by J. P. Migne. (Troisieme et Derniere Encyclopedie Theologique Ser.: Vols. 51-56). 4187p. (Fr.). Repr. of 1873 ed. lib. bdg. 532.50x (ISBN 0-89241-322-0). Caratzas Pub Co.
Dictionnaire de l'Industrie des matieres plastiques. 1977 ed. E. Ferraris. 320p. (Fr., Eng., & Ger.). 150.00 F. Maison Dictionnaire.
Dictionnaire de l'industrie Francaise. (Fr.). 1976. 150.00 F. U. F. A. P.
Dictionnaire de l'Industrie Routiere. Jacques Choppy. LC 77-573401. (Illus.). 143p. (Fr.). 1977. 55.00 F. Eyrolles.
Dictionnaire de l'Informatique. Jacques Bureau. 250p. (Fr.). 1972. pap. 6.95 (ISBN 0-686-56932-6, M-6053). French & Eur.
Dictionnaire de l'informatique. Jacques Bureau. (Illus.). 250p. (Fr.). 1972. 17.60 F. Larousse.
Dictionnaire de l'informatique. Andre Le Garff. 584p. (Fr.). 1975. 202.80 F. PUF.
Dictionnaire de l'Informatique, Francais-Anglais. Cl. Camille & M. Dehaine. 248p. (Fr & Eng.). 1972. 22.50 (ISBN 0-686-56936-9, M-6058). French & Eur.
Dictionnaire de l'informatique: Francais-Anglais. Claude Camille & Michel Dehaine. 248p. (Fr. & Eng.). 1972. 59.00 F. Bordas-Dunod.
Dictionnaire de Linguistique. J. Dubois & M. Giacomo. 516p. (Fr.). 1974. 27.50 (ISBN 2-03-020299-1, 1002). Larousse.
Dictionnaire de Linguistique. J. Dubois et al. (Fr.). 1977. pap. text ed. 21.00 (Dist. by Continental Bk Co). Larousse.
Dictionnaire de Linguistique. Jean Dubois et al. 516p. (Fr.). 1972. 57.20 F. Larousse.
Dictionnaire de Linguistique et de Philologie Comparee. L. F. Jehan. Ed. by J. P. Migne. (Troisieme et Derniere Encyclopedie Theologique Ser.: Vol. 34). 724p. (Fr.). Repr. of 1864 ed. lib. bdg. 92.50x (ISBN 0-89241-313-1). Caratzas Pub Co.
Dictionnaire de l'insolite & du Fantastique. Jean-Louis Bernard. 356p. (Fr.). 1974. 30.00 F. Dauphin.
Dictionnaire de Litterature Francais Contemporaine. Claude Bonnefoy et al. 411p. (Fr.). 1977. 39.95 (ISBN 0-686-56924-5, M-6042). French & Eur.
Dictionnaire de Locutions. M. M. Dubois. (Fr. & Eng.). 1973. 22.25 (Dist. by Continental Bk Co). Larousse.
Dictionnaire de Locutions, Francais-Anglais. Marguerite-Marie Dubois. 392p. (Fr. & Eng.). 1973. 22.50 (ISBN 0-686-57125-8, M-6173). French & Eur.
Dictionnaire de Locutions: Francais-Anglais. Marguerite-Marie Dubois. 392p. (Fr.). 1973. 60.00 F. Larousse.
Dictionnaire de l'offshore Petrole Gaz. Helene Bolo & Philippe Cavrois. (Illus.). 360p. (Fr.). 1977. 321.00 F. S. C. M.
Dictionnaire de L'opera. Harold Rosenthal & John Warrack. 420p. (Fr.). 1974. pap. 36.00 (ISBN 0-686-56799-4, M-416). French & Eur.
Dictionnaire de l'opera. Harold Rosenthal & John Warrack. (Illus.). 420p. (Fr. & Eng.). 1974. 90.00 F. Fayard.
Dictionnaire de L'outillage et de la Machine-Outil. Jean P. Michauz. LC 78-354894. 179p. (Fr.). 1976. 20.00 F (ISBN 2-7080-0444-1). Ophrys.
Dictionnaire de Marine. Robert Gruss. (Illus.). 368p. (Fr.). 1978. 120.00 F. Maritimes Outre mer.
Dictionnaire de Marine, Francais et Anglais. Robert Gruss. 368p. (Fr. & Eng.). 1978. 49.95 (ISBN 0-686-57319-6, M-6302). French & Eur.
Dictionnaire de Maximes & Locutions Latines Utilisees en Droit Quebecois. Albert Mayrand. 235p. (Fr.). 1972. Can.$8.95. Guerin.
Dictionnaire de Medecine. P. Chaumuzeau et al. LC 75-595740. (Eng. & Fr.). 1975. 0.195 F (ISBN 2-257-10399-8). Flammarion.
Dictionnaire de Medecine Amusante. Desgoses Montagnet. 66p. (Fr.). 1971. 130.00 F. De Rache.
Dictionnaire de Medecine Clinique Pharmacologique & Therapeutique. 2nd ed. Alain Blacque-Belair. (Illus.). 1914p. (Fr.). 1978. 196.00 F. Maloine.

Dictionnaire de Medecine Flammarion. 930p. (Fr.). 1975. 75.00 (ISBN 0-686-57099-5, M-6123). French & Eur.

Dictionnaire de Medecine Flammarion. (Illus.). 930p. (Fr.). 1975. 195.00 F. Flammarion.

Dictionnaire de Medecine Physique de Reeducation & Readaptation. Herman L. Kamenetz & Georgette Kamentz. 208p. (Fr.). 1972. 48.00 F. Maloine.

Dictionnaire de Medecine Physique de Reeducation et Readaptation Fonctionelles. Herman L. Kamenetz & Georgette Kamenetz. 208p. (Fr.). 1972. 19.95 (ISBN 0-686-56986-5, M-6324). French & Eur.

Dictionnaire de Medecine Pratique. F. A. Poujol. Ed. by J. P. Migne. (Nouvelle Encyclopedie Theologique Ser.: Vol. 17). 552p. (Fr.). Date not set. Repr. of 1862 ed. lib. bdg. 71.00x (ISBN 0-89241-264-X). Caratzas Pub Co.

Dictionnaire de Meteorologie Populaire. Jean-Philippe Chassany. 416p. (Fr.). 1970. 35.00 (ISBN 0-686-56945-8, M-6067). French & Eur.

Dictionnaire de Meteorologie Populaire. Jean-Philippe Chassany. (Illus.). 416p. (Fr.). 1970. 85.00 F. Maison & Larose.

Dictionnaire de Meteorologie Populaire au Quebec. Pierre Desruisseaux. LC 76-471846. 215p. (Fr.). 1976. Can.$6.95 (ISBN 0-88532-103-0). Edns Laurore.

Dictionnaire de Meteorologie Populaire au Quebec. Pierre Des Ruisseaux. (Illus.). 215p. (Fr.). 1976. 6.95 F. Aurore.

Dictionnaire de Minerologie. (Illus., Fr.). 1978. 21.00 F. Atlas.

Dictionnaire de Moi-Meme. Jean Ethier-Blais. (Fr.). 1976. Can.$6.50. Presse.

Dictionnaire de Mots Croises. (Fr.). 1978. pap. 25.00 F. Larousse.

Dictionnaire De Musique. Jean J. Rousseau. (Fr). Repr. of 1768 ed. 50.00 (ISBN 0-384-52200-9). Johnson Repr.

Dictionnaire de Musique. Jean Jacques Rousseau. 548p. (Fr.). 1978. 24.50 F. Johnson.

Dictionnaire de Musique. Jean-Jacques Rousseau. 548p. (Fr.). 1978. 108.00 F. Olms.

Dictionnaire de Musique dans Lequel on Simplifie les Expressions et Les Definitions Mathematiques et Physiques qui ont Rapport a cet Art. Jean J. de Meude-Monpas. LC 76-43927. (Music & Theatre in France in the 17th & 18th Centuries). (Fr.). Repr. of 1787 ed. 22.50 (ISBN 0-404-60175-8). AMS Pr.

Dictionnaire de Paleographie, de Cryptographie, de Dactylologie. Ed. by J. P. Migne. (Nouvelle Encyclopedie Theologique Ser.: Vol. 47). 668p. (Fr.). Repr. of 1854 ed. lib. bdg. 85.00x (ISBN 0-89241-285-2). Caratzas Pub Co.

Dictionnaire de Patrologie, 4 vols. in 5. A. Sevestre. Ed. by J. P. Migne. (Nouvelle Encyclopedie Theologique Ser.: Vols. 20-23b). 3830p. (Fr.). Repr. of 1859 ed. lib. bdg. 485.00x (ISBN 0-89241-267-4). Caratzas Pub Co.

Dictionnaire de Pharmacologie Dentaire. Roger Vieillefosse. 228p. (Fr.). 1970. 58.00 F. Maloine.

Dictionnaire de Pharmacologie Dentaire. Roger Viellefosse. 228p. (Fr.). 1970. 24.95 (ISBN 0-686-57245-9, M-6550). French & Eur.

Dictionnaire de Philosophie et de Theologie Scolastiques, 2 vols. F. Morin. Ed. by J. P. Migne. (Troisieme et Derniere Encyclopedie Theologique Ser.: Vols. 21-22). 1496p. (Fr.). Date not set. Repr. of 1865 ed. lib. bdg. 190.00x (ISBN 0-89241-304-2). Caratzas Pub Co.

Dictionnaire de Physiologie. A. L. Boyer. Ed. by J. P. Migne. (Troisieme et Derniere Encyclopedie Theologique Ser.: Vol. 58). 776p. (Fr.). Date not set. Repr. of 1861 ed. lib. bdg. 98.50x (ISBN 0-89241-324-7). Caratzas Pub Co.

Dictionnaire de Physique. Gabriel Laitier. 276p. (Fr.). 1968. pap. 35.00 (ISBN 0-686-56988-1, M-6328). French & Eur.

Dictionnaire de Physique. Gabriel Laitier. (Illus.). 276p. (Fr.). 1968. 80.00 F. Maloine.

Dictionnaire de poche du teletraitement des donnees. W. H. Carl. 290p. (Eng., Ger., & Fr.). 1982. 210.00 F. Maison Dictionnaire.

Dictionnaire de Poche Explicatif. J. Froimont. 528p. (Fr.). 65.00 F. Erasme.

Dictionnaire de Poche Francais-Allemand. (Fr. & Ger.). pap. 11.00 F. Berlitz.

Dictionnaire de Poche Francais-Anglais. (Fr. & Eng.). 11.00 F. Berlitz.

Dictionnaire de Poche Francais-Chinois. 558p. (Fr. & Chinese.). 1975. pap. 4.95 (ISBN 0-686-92470-3, M-9579). French & Eur.

Dictionnaire de Poche Francais-Chinois. 560p. (Fr. & Chinese.). 1977. 8.70 F. Pekin.

Dictionnaire de Poche Francais-Danois. (Fr. & Danish.). 11.00 F. Berlitz.

Dictionnaire de Poche Francais-Espagnol. (Fr. & Span.). 11.00 F. Berlitz.

Dictionnaire de Poche Francais-Finnois. (Fr. & Finnish.). pap. 11.00 F. Berlitz.

Dictionnaire de Poche Francais-Hongrois. 6th ed. S. Eckhardt. 480p. (Fr. & Hungarian.). 1977. 10.00 F. Terra.

Dictionnaire de Poche Francais-Italien. (Fr. & Ital.). 11.00 F. Berlitz.

Dictionnaire de Poche Francais-Neerlandais. (Fr. & Dutch.). 11.00 F. Berlitz.

Dictionnaire de Poche: Francais-Neerlandias. 15th ed. 330p. (Fr. & Dutch.). 1977. 30.00 F. Erasme.

Dictionnaire de Poche Francais-Norvegien. (Fr. & Norwegian.). 11.00 F. Berlitz.

Dictionnaire de Poche Francais-Suedois. (Fr. & Swedish.). 11.00 F. Berlitz.

Dictionnaire de Poche Russe-Francais. Dolgopolova. (Rus. & Fr.). 6.00 F. MIR.

Dictionnaire de Poche, 1: Francais-Polonais. Bernard Hamel. 490p. (Fr & Pol.). 1971. 24.00 F. Polonaises.

Dictionnaire de Poche, 2: Polonais-Francais. Bernard Hamel. 514p. (Pol. & Fr.). 1971. 24.00 F. Polonaises.

Dictionnaire de Poetique & de Rhetorique. Henri Morier. LC 76-473521. 1210p. (Fr.). 1975. 350.00 F. Pr Univ Fr.

Dictionnaire de Poitiers, Ville d'art & d'histoire. Hubert Le Roux. (Illus.). 298p. (Fr.). 1976. 59.50 F. H. Le Roux.

Dictionnaire de Politique. A. Akoun et al. LC 79-352686. 351p. (Fr.). 1978. 75.00 F (ISBN 2-03-070104-1). Larousse FR.

Dictionnaire de Politique. Jean Malignon. 460p. (Fr.). 1967. 17.50 (ISBN 0-686-56800-1, F-77270). French & Eur.

Dictionnaire de Politique. Jean Malignon. 460p. (Fr.). 1967. 40.00 F. Cujas.

Dictionnaire de Politique: Coll. le Present en Question. 350p. (Fr.). 1979. 29.95 (ISBN 0-686-57100-2, M-6124). French & Eur.

Dictionnaire de Politique: Collection le Present en Question. (Fr.). 1978. 25.50 (Dist. by Continental Bk Co). Larousse.

Dictionnaire de Prevention, 3 vols. Gustave Capron & Jackie Boisselier. (Illus.). 249p. (Fr.). 1976. 58.00 F. Soc Corp Hygiene.

Dictionnaire de Psychiatrie Sociale. Gerard Bleandonu. 288p. (Fr.). 1976. 18.60 F. Payot.

Dictionnaire de Psychiatrie Sociale. Gerard Bleaudonu. LC 77-454398. 284p. (Eng. & Fr.). 1976. 16.70 F (ISBN 2-228-32910-X). Payot.

Dictionnaire de Psychologie. Norbert Sillamy. 220p. (Fr.). 1969. 3.00 F. Larousse.

Dictionnaire de Psychologie en Trois Langues: Anglais-Francais-Allemand. Hubert C. Duijker & Maria J. Van Rijswijk. (Eng., Fr. & Ger.). 1978. 897.00 F. Editest.

Dictionnaire de Psychologie en Trois Langues, Vol. 2. Hubert C. Duijker. (Fr., Ger. & Eng.). 1978. pap. 39.95 (ISBN 0-686-57264-5, M-4660). French & Eur.

Dictionnaire de Psychologie en Trois Langues, 2: Francais-Allemand-Anglais. Hubert C. Duijker & Maria J. Van Rijswijk. (Fr., Ger. & Eng.). 849.00 F. Editest.

Dictionnaire de Psychologie en Trois Langues, 3: Allemand-Anglais-Francais. Hubert C. Duijker & Maria J. Van Rijswijk. (Ger., Eng & Fr.). 897.00 F. Editest.

Dictionnaire de Psychologie en 3 Langues, 3 vols. Hubert C. Duijker & Maria Van Sijswijk. (Eng., Fr. & Ger., Dictionary of Psychology in 3 Languages). pap. 40.00 (ISBN 0-686-56801-X, M-4661). French & Eur.

Dictionnaire de Rampa. Lobsang T. Rampa (Fr.). 1972. Can.$3.00. Presse.

Dictionnaire de Rimes. Paul Desfeuilles. 400p. (Fr.). 1955. 14.00 F. Garnier.

Dictionnaire de Rimes Francaises. Jean Le Fevre. 562p. (Fr.). 1973. 120.00 F. Slatkine.

Dictionnaire de Sigillographie Pratique. Louis A. Chassant & P. J. Delbarre. 264p. (Fr.). DM.39.80. Olms Verlag.

Dictionnaire de Sigles Nationaux & Internationaux. 2nd ed. Michel Dubois. 479p. (Fr.). 1977. 100.00 F. Maison Dictionnaire.

Dictionnaire de sigles nationaux et internationaux. M. Dubois. 405p. (Fr.). 1977. 130.00 F. Maison Dictionnaire.

Dictionnaire de Sigles Nationaux et Internationaux. Michel Dubois. 479p. (Fr.). 1977. pap. 50.00 (ISBN 0-686-56831-1, M-6609). French & Eur.

Dictionnaire de Sociologie. Joseph Sumpf & Michel Hugues. 256p. (Fr.). 1973. pap. 7.95 (ISBN 0-686-57228-9, M-6527). French & Eur.

Dictionnaire de Sociologie. Joseph Sumpf & Michel Hugues. 256p. (Fr.). 1973. 17.60 F. Larousse.

Dictionnaire de Sociologie. Emilio Willems. 314p. (Fr.). 1970. pap. 14.95 (ISBN 0-686-57261-0, M-6573). French & Eur.

Dictionnaire de Sociologie. Emilio Willems. 314p. (Fr.). 1970. 30.00 F. Riviere.

Dictionnaire De Sociologie Phalansterienne: Guide Des Oeuvres Completes De Charles Fourier. E. Silberling. (Fr.). 1964. Repr. of 1911 ed. 29.50 (ISBN 0-8337-3266-8). B Franklin.

Dictionnaire de Statistique Religieuse. L. Des Mas-Latrie. Ed. by J. P. Migne. (Nouvelle Encyclopedie Theologique Ser.: Vol. 9). 538p. (Fr.). Date not set. Repr. of 1851 ed. lib. bdg. 69.00x (ISBN 0-89241-259-3). Caratzas Pub Co.

Dictionnaire de Stenographie. Paul Fleury & E. Roy. 320p. (Fr.). 1978. 40.00 F. Estoup.

Dictionnaire de Stenographie Duploye. Agatha-Marguerite Pommier & Blanche Guaspare. 296p. (Fr.). 1955. 14.00 F. Foucher.

Dictionnaire de Sylviculture: Francais-Allemand-Anglais-Espagnol-Italien. Alberto Bruttini. (Illus.). 384p. (Fr., Ger., Eng., Span. & Ital.). 1930. 70.00 F. Lechevalier.

Dictionnaire de Technologie, 2 vols. L. P. Chesnel De la Charbouclais. Ed. by J. P. Migne. (Troisieme et Derniere Encyclopedie Theologique Ser.: Vols. 28-29). 1306p. (Fr.). Repr. of 1858 ed. lib. bdg. 166.50x (ISBN 0-89241-308-5). Caratzas Pub Co.

Dictionnaire de Tennis. Ed. by P. Rebourgeon et al. 160p. (Fr.). 1981. 69.95 (ISBN 0-686-92396-0, M-9769). French & Eur.

Dictionnaire de Tourisme Francais-Hongrois. L. Havas. 600p. (Fr. & Hungarian.). 1966. 16.20 F. Terra.

Dictionnaire de Zoologie, 3 vols. L. F. Jehan. Ed. by J. P. Migne. (Nouvelle Encyclopedie Theologique Ser.: Vols. 14-16). 2666p. (Fr.). Repr. of 1853 ed. lib. bdg. 336.50x (ISBN 0-89241-263-1). Caratzas Pub Co.

Dictionnaire de Zoologie: Vol. 1, A-J. Umberto Parenti. (Fr.). 1972. 21.00 F. Atlas.

Dictionnaire de Zoologie: Vol. 2, K-Z. Umberto Parenti. (Fr.). 1972. 21.00 F. Atlas.

Dictionnaire d'Economic Charitable, 4 vols. F. Martin-Doisy. Ed. by J. P. Migne. (Troisieme et Derniere Encyclopedie Theologique Ser.: Vols. 5-8). 3616p. (Fr.). Repr. of 1857 ed. lib. bdg. 456.00x (ISBN 0-89241-292-5). Caratzas Pub Co.

Dictionnaire d'Education. D. Raymond. Ed. by J. P. Migne. (Nouvelle Encyclopedie Theologique Ser.: Vol. 34). 856p. (Fr.). Repr. of 1853 ed. lib. bdg. 108.50x (ISBN 0-89241-276-3). Caratzas Pub Co.

Dictionnaire D'electronique & Tele-Communication: Anglais-Francais. G. J. Proulx. 582p. (Eng & Fr.). 1959. Can.$8.50. Beauchemin.

Dictionnaire d'Electronique et Tele-Communication: Anglais-Francais. G. J. Proulx. 582p. (Fr & Eng.). 1979. 15.95 (ISBN 0-686-57089-8, M-6469). French & Eur.

Dictionnaire d'Eloquence Sacree, Vol. 6. J. C. Nadal. Ed. by J. P. Migne. (Nouvelle Encyclopedie Theologique Ser.). 650p. (Fr.). Repr. of 1851 ed. lib. bdg. 83.00x (ISBN 0-89241-256-9). Caratzas Pub Co.

Dictionnaire d'Epigraphie Chretienne, 2 vols. J. J. Bourasse. Ed. by J. P. Migne. (Nouvelle Encyclopedie Theologique Ser.: Vols. 30-31). 1262p. (Fr.). Repr. of 1852 ed. lib. bdg. 161.00x (ISBN 0-89241-273-9). Caratzas Pub Co.

Dictionnaire d'Epistemologie Genetique. A. M. Battro. 188p. (Fr.). 1966. 29.00 (ISBN 90-277-0002-8, Pub. by Reidel Holland). Kluwer Academic.

Dictionnaire des Abbreviations Latines et Francaises Usitees dans les Inscriptions Lapidaires et Metalliques, les Manuscrits et les Chartes de Moyen Age. 5th ed. Alphonse A. Chassant. LC 73-3365. (Illus., Fr.). 1973. Repr. of 1884 ed. lib. bdg. 22.50 (ISBN 0-8337-0547-4). B Franklin.

Dictionnaire des Abreviations Latines & Francaise: Usitees dans les Inscriptions du Moyen-Age. 5th ed. Louis A. Chassant. (Lat. & Fr.). 28.50. Lenox.

Dictionnaire des Abreviations Latines & Francaises: Usitees dans les Inscriptions du Moyen Age. Louis A. Chassant. (Lat. & Fr.). DM.26.80. Olms Verlag.

Dictionnaire des Affaires. Wilfrid Lebel. (Fr.). 1967. 4.00 F. Homme.

Dictionnaire des Affaires Francais-Anglais, Anglais-Francais. Delmas-Harrap. (Fr. & Eng.). 65.50 (ISBN 0-685-36681-2). French & Eur.

Dictionnaire des Affaires: Francais-Anglais. Michel Peron & William Withnell. 512p. (Fr. & Eng.). 1969. 57.00 F. Larousse.

Dictionnaire des Aliments. Rosie Maurel. (Fr.). 15.50 F. Table Ronde.

Dictionnaire des Aliments pour les Animaux. Marcello Piccioni. (Illus.). 620p. (Fr.). 1965. 110.00 F. Maison Rustique.

Dictionnaire des Aliments pour les Animaux. Marcello Picconi. 620p. (Fr.). 1965. 42.50 (ISBN 0-686-57077-4, M-6452). French & Eur.

Dictionnaire des Amateurs Francais au Dix-Septieme Siecle. Edmond Bonnaffe. (Bibliography & Reference Ser.: No. 138). (Fr.). 1968. Repr. of 1884 ed. 26.50 (ISBN 0-8337-0335-8). B Franklin.

Dictionnaire des Amateurs Francais au 17 Siecle. Edmond Bonaffe. 535p. (Fr.). 1967. 25.00. Lenox.

Dictionnaire des Americanismes. 6th ed. Etienne Deak & Simone Deak. 928p. (Fr.). 1974. 25.00 (ISBN 0-686-56976-8, M-6103). French & Eur.

Dictionnaire des Americanismes. 6th ed. Etienne Deak & Simone Deak. 928p. (Fr. & Eng.). 1974. 65.00 F. Dauphin.

Dictionnaire des Anglicismes. G. Rey-Debove. (Fr.). 1980. 44.95 (ISBN 0-686-92557-2, M-3259). French & Eur.

Dictionnaire des Animaux. (Illus., Fr.). 40.00 F. Deux Coqs.

Dictionnaire des Animaux. Blanc P. Rousselet. 250p. (Fr.). 1981. 12.95 (ISBN 0-686-97634-7, M-9771). French & Eur.

Dictionnaire des Anoblis Normands. Gerard Arundel De Conde. (Illus.). 330p. (Fr.). 1976. 275.00 F. G. Arundel De Conde.

Dictionnaire des Anthropologistes. Paul-Emile Duroux. 336p. (Fr.). 1974. pap. 35.00 (ISBN 0-686-57130-4, M-6182). French & Eur.

Dictionnaire des Anthropologistes. Paul-Emile Duroux. 336p. (Fr.). 1974. 90.00 F. Delarge.

Dictionnaire des Antiquites Grecques. Pierre Paris. (Fr.). 1909. 68.00 F. Boccard.

Dictionnaire des Antiquites Grecques & Romaines, 10 vols. Charles Daremberg & E. Saglio. (Illus.). 8464p. (Fr.). 1962. S.15400.00. Akadem Druck-U Verlagsanstalt.

Dictionnaire des Apocryphes, 2 vols. G. Brunet. Ed. by J. P. Migne. (Troisieme et Derniere Encyclopedie Theologique Ser.: Vols. 23-24). 1310p. (Fr.). Repr. of 1858 ed. lib. bdg. 167.50x (ISBN 0-89241-305-0). Caratzas Pub Co.

Dictionnaire des Apologistes Involontaires, 2 vols. C. F. Cheve. Ed. by J. P. Migne. (Nouvelle Encyclopedie Theologique Ser.: Vols. 38-39). 1494p. (Fr.). Repr. of 1853 ed. lib. bdg. 189.50x (ISBN 0-89241-279-8). Caratzas Pub Co.

Dictionnaire des Argots Francais. Esnault. (Fr.). 16.50 (ISBN 0-685-36663-4). French & Eur.

Dictionnaire Des Artistes, Dont Nous Avons Des Estampes, Avec une Notice Detailee De Leurs Ouvrages Graves, 4 vols. Karl H. Von Heinecken. LC 4-7666. (Fr). 1970. Repr. of 1790 ed. Set. 280.00 (ISBN 0-384-22089-4). Johnson Repr.

Dictionnaire des Artistes ou Notice Historique: Raisonnee des Architectes, Peintres & Graveurs, 2 vols. Louis-Abel De Fontenay. (Fr.). 1972. 240.00 F. Minkoff.

Dictionnaire des Arts de Peinture & Gravure, 5 vols. Claude-Henri Watelet & Pierre-Charles Levesque. (Fr.). 1972. Kr.500.00. Minkoff Repr.

Dictionnaire des Arts de Peinture, Sculpture & Gravure, Vol. 1. Claude-Henre Watelet & Pierre-Charles Levesque. (Fr.). 1972. 118.00 F. Olms Verlag.

Dictionnaire des Arts de Peinture, Sculpture & Gravure, Vol. 2. Claude-Henri Watelet & Pierre-Charles Levesque. (Fr.). 1972. 118.00 F. Olms Verlag.

Dictionnaire des Arts de Peinture, Sculpture & Gravure, Vol. 3. Claude-Henri Watelet & Pierre-Charles Levesque. (Fr.). 1972. 118.00 F. Olms Verlag.

Dictionnaire des Arts de Peinture, Sculpture & Gravure, Vol. 4. Claude-Henri Watelet & Pierre-Charles Levesque. (Fr.). 1972. 118.00 F. Olms Verlag.

Dictionnaire des Arts de Peinture, Sculpture & Gravure, Vol. 5. Claude-Henri Watelet & Pierre-Charles Levesque. (Fr.). 1972. 118.00 F. Olms Verlag.

Dictionnaire des Arts du Spectacle. Cecile Giteau. 456p. (Fr., Eng. & Ger.). 1970. 135.00 F. Bordas-Dunod.

Dictionnaire des Arts du Spectacle: Theatre, Cinema, Cirque, Danse, Radio... Cecile Giteau. 456p. (Fr., Eng. & Ger.). 1970. 52.50 (ISBN 0-686-57302-1, M-6276). French & Eur.

Dictionnaire des Assurances Sociales. 112p. (Fr.). 1973. write for info. Masson.

Dictionnaire des Assurances Sociales. Jean-Charles Sournia. 112p. (Fr.). 1973. 22.50 (ISBN 0-686-57224-6, M-6522). French & Eur.

Dictionnaire des Auteurs de Langue Francais. Yves-Alain A. Favre. (Fr.). 1978. write for info. Flammarion.

Dictionnaire des Autorites. Georges Vajda. 226p. (Fr.). 1963. pap. 17.50 (ISBN 0-686-56833-8, M-6611). French & Eur.

Dictionnaire des Autorites. Georges Vajda. 226p. (Fr.). 1963. pap. 49.00 F (ISBN 2-22200-635-X). CNRS.

Dictionnaire des Bureaux de Poste Francais. Jean Pothion. (Fr.). write for info. Poste Aux Lettres.

Dictionnaire des Canalisations a Grande Distance: Anglais-Francais-Allemand. H. Bucksch & A. Altemeyer. 288p. (Eng., Fr. & Ger.). 1969. 120.00 (ISBN 0-686-56931-8, M-6052). French & Eur.

Dictionnaire des Canalisations: Francais-Allemand. Hector Bucksch. 288p. (Fr. & Ger.). 1969. write for info. Eyrolles.

Dictionnaire des Cardinaux. C. Berton. Ed. by J. P. Migne. (Troisieme et Derniere Encyclopedie Theologique Ser.: Vol. 31). 912p. (Fr.). Repr. of 1857 ed. lib. bdg. 115.00x (ISBN 0-89241-310-7). Caratzas Pub Co.

Dictionnaire des Changements de Noms. (Fr.). write for info. Lib.

Dictionnaire des Charges, Emplois & Metiers Relevant des Institutions. Monique Ornato. LC 76-465640. 206p. (Fr.). 1975. write for info (ISBN 2-222-01896-X). CNRS.

Dictionnaire des Chateaux de France. 2nd ed. (Illus.). 250p. (Fr.). 1970. write for info. Larousse.

Dictionnaire des Cineastes. Georges Sadoul. 256p. (Fr.). 1974. pap. 9.95 (ISBN 0-686-56798-6, F-79852). French & Eur.

Dictionnaire des Citations. Karl Petit. (Fr.). 1960. write for info. Bout.

Dictionnaire des Citations Francaises. 664p. (Fr.). 1978. pap. 8.95 (ISBN 0-686-56838-9, M-6616). French & Eur.

Dictionnaire des Citations Francaises. Pierre Serand & Samuel S. De Sacy. (Fr.). write for info. Larousse.

Dictionnaire des Communes. (Illus.). 862p. (Fr.). write for info. Larousse.

Dictionnaire des Communes (de France) (Fr.). 20.95 (ISBN 0-685-36659-6). French & Eur.

Dictionnaire des Communes de France (Guide to French Townships) Michelin Guides & Maps. (Fr.). 1979. 45.00 (ISBN 2-06-007500-9). Michelin.

Dictionnaire des Communes de la Haute-Saone, 3. 450p. (Fr.). 1971. write for info. M. Bon.

Dictionnaire des Communes de la Haute-Saone, 4. (Fr.). 1972. write for info. M. Bon.

Dictionnaire des Communes de la Haute-Saone, 1. 400p. (Fr.). 1969. write for info. M. Bon.

Dictionnaire des Communes de la Haute-Saone, 2. 416p. (Fr.). 1970. write for info. M. Bon.

Dictionnaire des Communes de la Haute-Saone, 5. (Fr.). 1973. write for info. M. Bon.

Dictionnaire des Communes de la Haute-Saone, 6. (Fr.). 1974. write for info. M. Bon.

Dictionnaire des Confreries & Corporations d'Arts & Metiers. T. F. Gautier. Ed. by J. P. Migne. (Nouvelle Encyclopedie Theologique Ser.: Vol. 50). 562p. (Fr.). Repr. of 1854 ed. lib. bdg. 72.00x (ISBN 0-89241-288-7). Caratzas Pub Co.

Dictionnaire des Controverses Historiques. L. F. Jehan. Ed. by J. P. Migne. (Troisieme et Derniere Encyclopedie Theologique Ser.: Vol. 66). 698p. (Fr.). Repr. of 1866 ed. lib. bdg. 90.00x (ISBN 0-89241-329-8). Caratzas Pub Co.

Dictionnaire des Conventionnels. A. Kuscinski. (Fr.). 1973. 250.00 F. Francais, Ed. Du Vexin.

Dictionnaire des Conversions. C. F. Cheve. Ed. by J. P. Migne. (Nouvelle Encyclopedie Theologique Ser.: Vol. 33). 836p. (Fr.). Repr. of 1852 ed. lib. bdg. 106.00x (ISBN 0-89241-275-5). Caratzas Pub Co.

Dictionnaire des Correspondants de l'academie. Leon-Noel Berthe. (Fr.). 1969. write for info. Eveche D'Arras.

Dictionnaire des Correspondants de Tellhard. Gerard H. Baudry. 200p. (Fr.). 1974. write for info. G. Baudry.

Dictionnaire des Costumes, Croyances & Langages. 131p. (Fr.). 1976. write for info. Reprints.

Dictionnaire des Couleurs. Viviane Cohen. (Illus., Fr.). 1973. write for info. Paris Livre de Odege.

Dictionnaire des Couleurs. Viviane Cohen. (Illus.). 24p. (Fr.). 1973. write for info. Livre de Paris.

Dictionnaire des Critiques Litteraires. Laurent Le Sage. 218p. (Fr.). 1969. write for info. Pa St U Pr.

Dictionnaire des Delais de Procedure. Roger Barbaud. (Fr.). 1974. write for info. Dalloz.

Dictionnaire des Devises Heraldiques. Louis A. Chassant & Henri Tausin. 1624p. (Fr.). write for info. Olms Verlag.

Dictionnaire des Devises Historiques & Heraldiques. A. Chassant & H. Tausin. 1728p. (Fr.). write for info. Slatkine.

Dictionnaire des Difficultes de la Langue Francaise. A. V. Thomas. (Fr., Fr) 23.50 (ISBN 0-685-13865-8, 3611). Larousse.

Dictionnaire des Difficultes de la Langue Francaise. 12th ed. A. V. Thomas. 448p. (Fr.). 1971. pap. 6.00 (Dist. by Continental Bk Co). Larousse.

Dictionnaire des Difficultes Grammaticale & Lexicologiques. 760p. (Fr.). 48.00 F. Scientifiques & Litteraires.

Dictionnaire des Difficultes Grammaticales & Lecicologiques. 760p. (Fr.). 550.00 F. Samson, CED.

Dictionnaire des Droits et de la Raison. C. P. LeNoir. Ed. by J. P. Migne. (Troisieme et Derniere Encyclopedie Theologique Ser.: Vol. 57). 952p. (Fr.). Repr. of 1860 ed. lib. bdg. 120.00x (ISBN 0-89241-323-9). Caratzas Pub Co.

Dictionnaire des Dynasties Bourgeoises & du Monde des Affaires. Henry Coston. (Illus.). 599p. (Fr.). 1975. 120.00 F. A. Moreau.

Dictionnaire des Echecs. Francois Le Lionnais. (Fr.). 1974. 176.80 F. PUF.

Dictionnaire des Ecrivains Francais. J. Malignon. 576p. (Fr.). 1971. 29.95 (ISBN 0-686-57029-4, M-6388). French & Eur.

Dictionnaire des Erreurs Sociales. A. Jouffroy. Ed. by J. P. Migne. (Nouvelle Encyclopedie Theologique Ser.: Vol. 19). 664p. (Fr.). Repr. of 1852 ed. lib. bdg. 84.50x (ISBN 0-89241-266-6). Caratzas Pub Co.

Dictionnaire des Facultes Intellectuelles et Affectives de l'ame ou l'on Traite des Passions, des Vertus, des Vices, Des Defauts. F. A. Poujol. Ed. by J. P. Migne. (Encyclopedie Theologique Ser.: Vol. 39). 560p. (Fr.). Repr. of 1849 ed. lib. bdg. 72.00x (ISBN 0-89241-245-3). Caratzas Pub Co.

Dictionnaire des Familles Nobles & Notables de la Correze. J. B. Champeval. (Fr.). 1976. 425.00 F. Lafitte Repr.

Dictionnaire des Femmes. (Fr.). 20.00 F. Pensee Moderne.

Dictionnaire des Femmes Celebres. Albert Jourcin. (Illus.). 256p. (Fr.). 1969. 17.60 F. Larousse.

Dictionnaire des Filigranes Classes en Groupe Alphabetique. F. Marmol. (Fr.). 1900. DM.31.80. Olms Verlag.

Dictionnaire des Films. Georges Sadoul. 288p. (Fr.). 1969. pap. 8.95 (ISBN 0-686-56797-8, F-79854). French & Eur.

Dictionnaire des Films. Georges Sadoul. (Illus.). 288p. (Fr.). 1969. 20.00 F. Seuil.

Dictionnaire Des Forets. 5th ed. Georges Plaisance. (Fr.). 1975. pap. 22.50 (ISBN 0-686-56725-0, M-6457). French & Eur.

Dictionnaire des Forets. 5th ed. Georges Plaisance. (Fr.). 1975. 54.00 F. G. Plaisance.

Dictionnaire des Frequences de Mots dans le Russe. (Rus. & Fr.). 10.55 F. Steinfeld.

Dictionnaire des Frequences: Vocabulaire Literaire des 19 & 20 Siecles, 1, 4 vols. 2284p. (Fr.). 1976. 280.00 F. Klincksieck.

Dictionnaire des Frequences: Vocabulaire Literaire des 19 & 20 Siecles, 2. 575p. (Fr.). 1976. 74.00 F. Klincksieck.

Dictionnaire des Frequences: Vocabulaire Literaire des 19 & 20 Siecles, 3. 352p. (Fr.). 1976. 60.00 F. Klincksieck.

Dictionnaire des Frequences: Vocabulaire Literaire des 19 & 20 Siecle, 4. 98p. (Fr.). 1976. 12.00 F. Klincksieck.

Dictionnaire des Fromages. Robert H. Courtine. 250p. (Fr.). 1972. pap. 6.95 (ISBN 0-686-56807-9, F-A16). French & Eur.

Dictionnaire des Fromages. Robert H. Courtine. 250p. (Fr.). 1972. 17.60 F. Larousse.

Dictionnaire des Grands Evenements de L'histoire. Georges Masquet. 315p. (Fr.). 1973. pap. 8.95 (ISBN 0-686-56796-X, M-174, Pub. by Hachette). French & Eur.

Dictionnaire des Grands Evenements de l'histoire. Georges Masquet. (Illus.). 315p. (Fr.). 1973. 20.00 F. Hachette.

Dictionnaire des Grands Evenements de l'Historie. Georges Masquet. 315p. (Fr.). 1973. pap. 8.95. Hachette-Jeunesse.

Dictionnaire des Groupes Industriels & Financiers en France. Michel Beaud & Bertrand Bellon. (Illus.). 361p. (Fr.). 1978. 45.00 F. Seuil.

Dictionnaire des Groupes Industriels & Financiers en France. 360p. (Fr.). 1978. 17.95 (ISBN 0-686-57102-9, M-6127). French & Eur.

Dictionnaire des Harmonies de la Raison et de la Foi. C. P. LeNoir. Ed. by J. P. Migne. (Troisieme et Derniere Encyclopedie Theologique Ser.: Vol. 19). 876p. (Fr.). Repr. of 1856 ed. lib. bdg. 110.50x (ISBN 0-89241-302-6). Caratzas Pub Co.

Dictionnaire des Herbes & des Epices. Colin Clair. 259p. (Fr.). 1963. 14.00 F. Denoel.

Dictionnaire des Herbes et des Epices. Colin Clair. 259p. (Fr.). 1963. pap. 6.95 (ISBN 0-686-56842-7, M-6621). French & Eur.

Dictionnaire des Heresies des Erreurs et des Schismes, 2 vols. F. A. Pluquet. Ed. by J. P. Migne. (Encyclopedie Theologique Ser.: Vols. 11-12). 1374p. (Fr.). Repr. of 1847 ed. lib. bdg. 175.00x (ISBN 0-89241-235-6). Caratzas Pub Co.

Dictionnaire Des Heresies Meridionales. Rene Nelli. 384p. (Fr.). 18.50 (ISBN 0-686-56886-9, F-21110). French & Eur.

Dictionnaire des Heresies Meridionales. Rene Nelli. (Illus.). 384p. (Fr.). 44.10 F. Privat.

Dictionnaire des Histoires Droles. Herve Negre. (Fr.). 1970. 59.00 F. Fayard.

Dictionnaire des Histoires Droles, 1. Herve Negre. (Fr.). 1974. pap. 10.50 F. L. G. F.

Dictionnaire des Histoires Droles, 2. Herve Negre. (Fr.). 1974. 10.50 F. L. G. F.

Dictionnaire des Hommes. Anne-Marie Carriere. (Fr.). 1962. 20.00 F. Pensee Moderne.

Dictionnaire des Horlogers Francais. Tardy. (Illus.). 350p. (Fr.). 195.00 F. Tardy-Lengelle.

Dictionnaire des Hulles Vegetales. Paul H. Mensier. (Fr.). 1957. 160.00 F. Lechevalier.

Dictionnaire Des Idees Dans L'oeuvre D'andre Malraux. Ileana Juilland. 325p. (Fr.). 1968. 29.95 (ISBN 0-686-56887-7, F-111080). French & Eur.

Dictionnaire Des Idees Dans L'oeuvre D'Andre Malraux: Collection Dictionaries Des Idees Dans les Litteratures Occidentales, Litterature Francaise: Dictionnnaires D'auteurs. Ileana Julland. (No. 2). (Fr.). 1968. 17.00x (ISBN 0-686-21240-1). Mouton.

Dictionnaire Des Idees Dans L'oeuvre De Marcel Proust: Collection Dictionnaires Des Idees Dans les Litteratures Occidentales, Litterature Francaise. Ed. by Pauline Newman-Gordon. (Dictionnaires D'auteurs: No. 3). (Fr.). 1968. 20.50 (ISBN 0-686-21818-3). Mouton.

Dictionnaire des Idees dans L'oeuvre de Simone de Beauvoir. Christian van den Berghe. (Collection Dictionnaires Des Idees, Litterature Francaise: No. 1). (Fr.). 1966. 16.00x (ISBN 0-686-20917-6). Mouton.

Dictionnaire des Idees Suggerees par les Mots. 32nd ed. Paul Rouaix. 540p. (Fr.). 51.00 F. Colin.

Dictionnaire des Imprimeurs. Anne Rouzet. 287p. (Fr.). 1975. fl.21.00. De Graaf.

Dictionnaire des Inconnus aux Noms Communs. Michel Dansel. LC 79-123074. 247p. (Fr.). 1979. write for info. (ISBN 2-86418-033-2). Encre.

Dictionnaire des Industries Alimentaires. Jean M. Clement. LC 78-366424. (Illus.). xiii, 348p. (Fr.). 1978. 78.00 F (ISBN 2-225-46079-5). Masson & Cie.

Dictionnaire des Industries Alimentaires. Jean-Michel Clement. 361p. (Fr.). 1978. 32.50 (ISBN 0-686-56949-0, M-6071). French & Eur.

Dictionnaire des Infixes de l'esquimau de l'Ungava. Lucien Schneider. 144p. (Fr.). 1972. Can.$2.00. Quebec Off.

Dictionnaire Des Institutions De la France Aux Dix-Septieme et Dix-Huitieme Siecles. Ed. by Marcel Marion. LC 68-6230. (Bibliography & Reference Ser.: No. 214). (Fr.). 1968. Repr. of 1923 ed. 39.00 (ISBN 0-8337-2216-6). B Franklin.

Dictionnaire des Institutions de la France aux XVII & XVIII Siecles. Marcel Marion. 573p. (Fr.). 1968. 27.50. Lenox.

Dictionnaire des Institutions de la France aux 17 & 18 Siecles. Marcel Marion. 564p. (Fr.). 1972. 65.00 F. Picard.

Dictionnaire des Institutions, Moeurs & Costumes du Rouergue. Henri Affre & Rodez. 470p. (Fr.). 150.00 F. Lafitte Repr.

Dictionnaire des Inventions et Decouvertes Anciennes et Modernes, 2 vols. A. Jouffroy. Ed. by J. P. Migne. (Nouvelle Encyclopedie Theologique Ser.: Vols. 35-36). 1424p. (Fr.). Repr. of 1860 ed. lib. bdg. 181.00x (ISBN 0-89241-277-1). Caratzas Pub Co.

Dictionnaire des Journalistes. Jean Sgard. (Illus., Fr.). 1976. 25.00 F. Club Livre Select.

Dictionnaire des Journalistes, 1600-1789. Jean Sgard & Michel Gilot. 391p. (Fr.). 1976. pap. 75.00 (ISBN 0-686-57221-1, M-6516). French & Eur.

Dictionnaire des Locutions Francais-Allemand. Paul Werny & Alexandre Snyckers. LC 77-568508. viii, 636p. (Ger. & Fr.). 1976. 60.00 F (ISBN 2-030-21103-6). Larousse FR.

Dictionnaire des Locutions Francaises. M. Rat. (Fr., Fr). 23.50 (ISBN 0-685-13866-6, 3613). Larousse.

Dictionnaire des Locutions Francaises. 7th ed. Maurice Rat. 464p. (Fr.). 1970. 49.00 F. Larousse.

Dictionnaire des locutions idiomatiques Francaises. Bruno Lafleur. (Fr.). Can.$14.95. Soc Dev Liv.

Dictionnaire des Maladies. Jean-Philippe Barbier & Francois-Claude Hugues. 528p. (Fr.). 1973. 88.00 F. Heures de France.

Dictionnaire des Manuscrits, Ou Recueil De Catalogues De Manuscrits Existants Dans les Pri Cipales Bibliotheques D'europe, 2 vols. G. F. Haenel. Ed. by J. P. Migne. (Nouvelle Encyclopedie Theologique Ser.: Vols. 40-41). 1624p. (Fr.). Repr. of 1853 ed. lib. bdg. 205.50x (ISBN 0-89241-280-1). Caratzas Pub Co.

Dictionnaire des Mathematiques Modernes. rev. ed. Lucien Chambadal. 250p. (Fr.). 1972. pap. 6.95 (ISBN 0-686-56847-8, M-6625). French & Eur.

Dictionnaire des Mathematiques Modernes. Lucien Chambadal. (Illus.). 250p. (Fr.). 1972. 17.60 F. Larousse.

Dictionnaire des Matieres Plastiques. Wittfoht. 325p. (Fr. & Eng., Dictionary of Plastic Materials). 1976. pap. 52.50 (ISBN 0-686-56774-9, M-6574). French & Eur.

Dictionnaire des Media. Jean B. Fages & Christian Pagano. 350p. (Fr.). Can.$12.50. Hurtubise H. M. H.

Dictionnaire des Media. Jean Baptiste Fages & Christian Pagano. 364p. (Fr.). 1971. pap. 22.50 (ISBN 0-686-56848-6, M-6626). French & Eur.

Dictionnaire des Media. Jean Baptiste Fages & Christian Pagano. 364p. (Fr.). 1971. 50.00 F. Delarge.

Dictionnaire des Medicaments. Maur Neuman. 432p. (Fr.). 1971. 66.00 F. Heures de France.

Dictionnaire des Medicaments. Maurice Neuman. 432p. (Fr.). 1971. pap. 27.50 (ISBN 0-686-56745-5, M-6424). French & Eur.

Dictionnaire des Merveilles et Curiosites de Nature et De Art. L. P. Chesnel De la Charbouclais. Ed. by J. P. Migne. (Nouvelle Encycliopedie Theologique Ser.: Vol. 44). 634p. (Fr.). Repr. of 1853 ed. lib. bdg. 81.00x (ISBN 0-89241-283-6). Caratzas Pub Co.

Dictionnaire des Meubles & Objets D'art 1965 & 1966. Enrique Mayer. 112p. (Fr.). 1967. 120.00 F. Mayer.

Dictionnaire des Meubles & Objets d'art, 1963 & 1964. Enrique Mayer. 320p. (Fr.). 1965. 99.00 F. Mayer Ed.

Dictionnaire des Miniaturistes du Moyan Age: La Renaissance dans les Differentes Contrees de l'Europa. 2nd ed. E. Aeschlimann & Paolo Ancono. (Fr.). 1949. 202.50 F. Kraus.

Dictionnaire des Monogrammes. Jean-Frederic Christ. 484p. (Fr.). 1972. 150.00 F. Minkoff Repr.

Dictionnaire des Mots Cles du Dessin de la Peinture, de l'Estampe. Gerard Capou. LC 80-450957. 89p. (Fr.). 1979. 35.00 F. Capou.

Dictionnaire des Mots Contemporains. (Fr.). 1979. pns (M-6128). French & Eur.

Dictionnaire Des Mots Croises. Maurice Denis-Papin. 384p. (Fr.). 1978. pap. 11.95 (ISBN 0-686-56883-4, F-137060). French & Eur.

Dictionnaire des Mots Croises. rev. ed. Maurice Denis-Papin. 384p. (Fr.). 1978. 29.00 F. Albin Michel.

Dictionnaire des Mots Croises. (Fr.). 1978. 25.00 F. Larousse.

Dictionnaire des Mots Croises. Robert Piquette et al. 300p. (Fr.). 1966. 8.00 F. Homme.

Dictionnaire des Mots Croises & Jeux Divers. Maurice Denis-Papin. 384p. (Fr.). 1973. 22.00 F. Albin Michel.

Dictionnaire des Mots Croises: Noms Communs. Paul Lasnier. 317p. (Fr.). 1975. Can.$7.00. Homme.

Dictionnaire des Mots, des Phrases, des Images. Aime Gabillon. (Illus.). 128p. (Fr.). 1963. 36.00 F. RST.

Dictionnaire des Mots d'esprit. Jean Delacour. 352p. (Fr.). 1976. 39.00 F. Albin Michel.

Dictionnaire des Mots Libres d'Apollinaire. Scott Bates. 160p. (Fr.). 1975. 45.00 F. 30.00 F. Filipacchi.

Dictionnaire des Mots Nouveaux. Pierre Gilbert. 572p. (Fr.). 49.00 F. Tchou.

Dictionnaire des Muses ou Description des Principaux Musees d'Europe... Suivi Notions sur la Photographie par X. Ed. by J. P. Migne. (Troisieme et Derniere Encyclopedie Theologique Ser.: Vol. 4). 740p. (Fr.). Repr. of 1855 ed. lib. bdg. 95.00x (ISBN 0-89241-291-7). Caratzas Pub Co.

Dictionnaire Des Musiciens. Roland de Cande. 288p. (Fr.). 1974. pap. 8.95 (ISBN 0-686-56882-6, F-17742). French & Eur.

Dictionnaire des noms de famille et prenoms de France. Albert Dauzat. (Fr). 23.50 (ISBN 2-03-020260-6, 3615). Larousse.

Dictionnaire des Nouveaux Cinemas Arabes. Claude-Michel Cluny. (Illus., Fr. & Arabic.). 1978. 120.00 F. Sindbad.

Dictionnaire des Objections Populaires contre le Dogme, la Morale, la Discipline et L'histoire de Eglise Catholique. C. Pinard. Ed. by J. P. Migne. (Troisieme et Derniere Encyclopedie Theologique Ser.: Vol. 33). 756p. (Fr.). Repr. of 1858 ed. lib. bdg. 96.50x (ISBN 0-89241-312-3). Caratzas Pub Co.

Dictionnaire des Oeuvres & des Themes du Cinema Mondial. Etienne Fuzellier. LC 77-454527. 288p. (Fr.). 1976. 21.00 F (ISBN 2-01-003332-9). Hachette-Jeunesse.

Dictionnaire des Oeuvres: Index. 5th ed. (Fr.). 1969. 295.00 (ISBN 0-686-56851-6, M-6629). French & Eur.

Dictionnaire des Oiseaux. Michel Cuisin. (Illus.). 250p. (Fr.). 1969. 17.60 F. Larousse.

Dictionnaire Des Operas, 2 Vols. Felix Clement & Pierre Larousse. LC 69-15617. (Music Reprint Ser). (Fr.). 1969. Repr. of 1905 ed. Set. 110.00 (ISBN 0-306-71197-4). Da Capo.

Dictionnaire Des Ouvrages Anonymes, 4 Vols. Barbier. (Fr.). Set. 325.00 (ISBN 0-685-11143-1, F-12410). French & Eur.

Dictionnaire des Papes. Hans Kuhner. (Fr.). pap. 6.95 (ISBN 0-686-56856-7, M-6634). French & Eur.

Dictionnaire des Papes. Hans Kuhner. (Fr.). 16.50 F. Buchet Chastel.

Dictionnaire Des Paralleles, Concordances et Analogies Bibliques. 300p. (Fr.). 1981. Repr. of 1856 ed. lib. bdg. 120.00 (ISBN 0-8287-1511-4). Clearwater Pub.

Dictionnaire des Parents. Francois Cloutier. 250p. (Fr.). 1969. 3.00 F. Edns Du Jour.

Dictionnaire des Parlementaires Francais: Vol. 3, 1889-1940. Jean Jolly. 380p. (Fr.). 1962. 41.60 F. PUF.

Dictionnaire des Parlementaires Francais: Vol. 4, 1889-1940. Jean Jolly. 316p. (Fr.). 1968. 48.80 F. PUF.

Dictionnaire des Parlers Arabes de Syrie, Libyan & Palestine. Claude Denizeau. 580p. (Arabic.). 1961. 120.00 F. Maison & Larose.

Dictionnaire des Parlers Arabes de Syrie, Liban et Palestine. Claude Denizeau. 581p. (Fr. & Arabic.). 1961. pap. 49.95 (ISBN 0-686-57090-1, M-6112). French & Eur.

Dictionnaire des Paroisses de la Correze, 3. Jean-Baptiste Poulbriere. (Fr.). 60.00 F. Correze, Ste Scientifique.

Dictionnaire des Partis Communistes & des Mouvements Revolutionnaires. Francois Fejto. 236p. (Fr.). 1971. 31.00 F. Casterman.

Dictionnaire des Patols de l'Yonne. Sophie Jossier. 130p. (Fr.). 1970. 30.00 F. Slatkine.

Dictionnaire des Patols du Dauphine. Nicolas Charbot & Hector Blanchet. 448p. (Fr.). 1973. 150.00 F. Lafitte Repr.

Dictionnaire des Patols du Dauphine, 2 vols. Nicolas Charbot & Hector Blanchet. 457p. (Fr.). 1973. 100.00 F. Slatkine.

Dictionnaire des Patols Romans de la Moselle. Leon Zeliqzon. (Illus.). 735p. (Fr.). 1924. 32.33 F. Strasbourg, U.

Dictionnaire des Peintres & Sculpteurs Provencaux: 1880-1950. Fondation Paul Richard & Jean-Pierre Camard. 444p. (Fr.). 1974. 40.00 F. Bendor.

Dictionnaire des Peintres et Sculpteurs Provencaux. Jean Pierre Camard & Anne Marie Belfort. 444p. (Fr.). 1974. pap. 19.95 (ISBN 0-686-56858-3). French & Eur.

Dictionnaire des Peintres, Sculpteurs, Dessinateurs et Graveurs, 10 vols. new, rev. ed. E. Benezit. (Illus., Fr.). 1976. 495.00 set (ISBN 2-7000-0149-4). Hacker.

Dictionnaire des Personnages. 3rd ed. 776p. (Fr.). 1970. 85.00 (ISBN 0-686-56859-1, M-6637). French & Eur.

Dictionnaire des Personnages de Tous les Temps & de Tous les Pays. (Fr.). 81.50 (ISBN 0-685-36081-4). French & Eur.

Dictionnaire des Plantes Qui Guerissent. Gerard Debuigne. 250p. (Fr.). 1972. pap. 6.95 (ISBN 0-686-56860-5, M-6638). French & Eur.

Dictionnaire des Plantes qui Guerissent. Gerard Debuigne. (Illus.). 250p. (Fr.). 1972. 17.60 F. Larousse.

Dictionnaire des Poincons de l'Orfevrerie Provinciale Francaise. LC 77-565816. (Illus., Fr.). 1976. 240.00 F. Droz.

Dictionnaire des Preccleuses, 2 vols. Antoine B. De Somaize. (Fr.). 75.00 F. Kraus.

Dictionnaire des Prenoms & des Saints. Pierre Pierrard. 224p. (Fr.). 1975. 17.60 F. Larousse.

Dictionnaire des Principaux Sigles Utilises dans le Monde Juridique de A-Z. M. Gendrel. (Fr.). 460.00 F. Bruylant.

Dictionnaire des proverbes, sentences et maximes. M. Maloux. (Fr., Fr). 23.50 (ISBN 2-03-020291-6, 3618). Larousse.

Dictionnaire des Racines Semitiques. David Cohen. (Fr.). 1974. 58.00 F. Mouton De Gruyter.

Dictionnaire des Racines Semitiques. Edmond G. Heylli. 567p. (Fr.). 1971. 100.00 F. Slatkine.

Dictionnaire Des Racines Semitiques Ou Attestees Dans les Langues Semitiques: Comprenant un Fichier Comparatif De Jean Cantineau. David Cohen. 36p. (Fr.). 1970. pap. text ed. 20.00x (ISBN 0-686-27743-0). Mouton.

Dictionnaire Des Racines Semitiques: Ou Attestees Dans les Langues Semitiques. David Cohen. (Fr.). 1976. pap. text ed. 26.25x (ISBN 90-2796-441-6). Mouton.

Dictionnaire des Racines Semitiques, 2. David Cohen. 76p. (Fr.). 1976. 60.00 F. Mouton De Gruyter.

Dictionnaire des Reves. Tom Chetwynd. 315p. (Fr.). 1975. 34.00 F. Seghers.

Dictionnaire des Richesses de la Langue Francoise: Neologisme qui s'y Introduit. Pons Auguste Alletz. 512p. (Fr.). 1968. 90.00 F. Slatkine.

Dictionnaire des Rimes Orales & Ecrites. Leon Warnant. 554p. (Fr.). 1973. 49.00 F. Larousse.

Dictionnaire des rimes orales et ecrites. new ed. Leon Warnant. 553p. (Fr.). 1972. 23.50 (ISBN 2-03-020271-1, 3546). Larousse.

Dictionnaire des Sciences & Techniques Nucleaires. Commissariat a l'Energie Atomique. 492p. (Fr.). DM.135.00. Brandstetter.

Dictionnaire des Sciences & Techniques Nucleaires. 3rd ed. Commissariat a L'energie Atomique. 492p. (Fr.). 1975. 175.00 F. Eyrolles.

Dictionnaire des Sciences & Techniques Nucleaires. 2nd ed. 426p. (Fr.). 1967. 29.85 F. PUF.

Dictionnaire des Sciences de la Gestion. Henri Tezenas Du Montcel. 332p. (Fr.). 1972. 50.00 F. Delarge.

Dictionnaire des Sciences de la Gestion. Henri Tezenas Du Montcel. 368p. (Fr.). 1972. Can.$12.50. Hurtubise H. M. H.

Dictionnaire des Sciences de la Nature (Dictionary of the Natural Sciences, 3 vols. Edouard Ghaleb. (Illus.). 1643p. (Arabic, Lat., Fr., Eng., Ger. & Ital.). 1966. Set. 172.50x (ISBN 0-8002-1208-8). Intl Pubns Serv.

Dictionnaire des Sciences de la Nature, 1. Edouard Ghaleb. (Illus.). 589p. (Fr.). 1966. 45.00 F. Dar El-Machreq.

Dictionnaire des Sciences de la Nature, 2. Edouard Ghaleb. (Illus.). 670p. (Fr.). 1966. 45.00 F. Dar El-Machreq.

Dictionnaire des Sciences de la Nature, 3. Edouard Ghaleb. (Illus.). 384p. (Fr.). 1966. 45.00 F. Dar El-Machreq.

Dictionnaire des Sciences Medicales, 1821-1822. Werner-Heinrich Aeschilimann. 89p. (Fr.). 1975. 20.00 F. Juris Druck.

Dictionnaire des sciences occultes suivi d'un dictionnaire des songes. Frederic Boutet. LC 76-486140. (Illus.). 412p. (Fr.). 1976. 42.00 F (ISBN 2-85704-027-X). Pygmalion.

Dictionnaire des Sciences Politiques et Sociales, 3 vols. A. Ott. Ed. by J. P. Migne. (Troisieme et Derniere Encyclopedie Theologique Ser.: Vols. 1-3). 2014p. (Fr.). Repr. of 1855 ed. lib. bdg. 256.00x (ISBN 0-89241-290-9). Caratzas Pub Co.

Dictionnaire des Sigles Economiques & Sociaux. (Fr.). 25.00 F. Liaisons Sociales.

Dictionnaire des Sigles Medicaux. J. P. Poinsotte. 146p. (Fr.). 1982. pap. text ed. 17.95 (ISBN 2-252-02355-4, M-9772). French & Eur.

Dictionnaire des Societes Secretes En Occident. Pierre Mariel. (Fr.). 1971. pap. 21.50 (ISBN 0-686-56864-8, M-6642). French & Eur.

Dictionnaire des Structures Fondamentales du Francais. P. Celerier & J. P. Maillard. (Fr.). 13.50 (Dist. by Continental Bk Co). Cle International.

Dictionnaire des Symboles, 4 vols. Jean Chevalier & Alain Gheerbrant. 416p. (Fr.). 1973. Set. pap. 22.50 (ISBN 0-686-56946-6, M-6068). French & Eur.

Dictionnaire des Symboles, 4 vols. Jean Chevalier & Alain Gheerbrant. (Illus.). 416p. (Fr.). 1973. 56.00 F. Seghers.

Dictionnaire des Symboles Chretiens. Edouard Urech. (Illus.). 190p. (Fr.). 1972. 63.00 F. Delachaux.

Dictionnaire des Symptomes. 602p. (Fr.). 1978. 88.00 F. Edito Serv.

Dictionnaire des synonymes. R. Bailly. (Fr., Fr) 23.50 (ISBN 0-685-13870-4, 3621). Larousse.

Dictionnaire des Synonymes. E. Bar. 406p. (Fr.). 1968. 14.00 F. Garnier.

Dictionnaire des Synonymes. new ed. Henri Benac. 1026p. (Fr.). 1975. 46.50 F. Hachette.

Dictionnaire des Synonymes. Henri Benac. (Fr.). Can.$13.60. Renouveau Pedagogique.

Dictionnaire des Synonymes. Henri Bertrand Du Chazaud. LC 79-122880. iv, 468p. (Fr.). 1979. 85.00 F (ISBN 2-85036-025-2). Soc Nouveau.

Dictionnaire des Synonymes. R. De Noter & P. Vuillermoz. 284p. (Fr.). 1969. 33.20 F. PUF.

Dictionnaire des Synonymes. 17th ed. 640p. (Fr.). 1971. 51.00 F. Larousse.

Dictionnaire des Synonymes, Analogies & Antonymes. Roger Boussinot. 1031p. (Fr.). 1977. 58.00 F. Bordas-Dunod.

Dictionnaire des Synonymes & Antonymes. Bernard Lamizet. (Fr.). 1978. 6.00 F. Garnier-Flammarion.

Dictionnaire des Synonymes & des Antonymes. Hector Dupuis. 607p. (Fr.). 1975. Can.$8.95. Fides.

Dictionnaire des Synonymes & des Antonymes. Hector Dupuis & Romain Legare. 608p. (Fr.). 1975. 54.00 F. Ecole.

Dictionnaire des Synonymes de la Langue Russe. Alexandrova. (Rus.). 1960. 19.10 F. MIR.

Dictionnaire des Synonymes de la Langue Russe, 2 vols. Evgueniev. (Rus.). 110.90 F. MIR.

Dictionnaire des Synonymes de Poche. E. Genouvrier. (Fr.). 1977. pap. 7.25 (Dist. by Continental Bk Co). Larousse.

Dictionnaire des synonymes et des antonymes. 2nd rev. ed. Hector Dupuis. Rev. by Romain Legare. 608p. (Fr.). 1975. Can.$15.95. Soc Dev Liv.

Dictionnaire des Synonymes: Francais-Neerlandais. J. Froimont. 428p. (Fr. & Dutch.). 195.00 F. Erasme.

Dictionnaire des Techniques Aeronautiques & Spatiales. LC 78-394540. 374p. (Eng. , Fr. & Ger.). 1978. write for info. (ISBN 2-0401-0124-1). Bordas.

Dictionnaire Des Techniques Aeronautiques et Spatiales. 2nd ed. Ed. by Societe Nationale Industrielle Aerospatiale. Orig. Title: Aerospace Technical Dictionary. 1152p. (Eng., Fr. & Ger.). 1978. 165.00x (ISBN 2-04-010124-1). Intl Pubns Serv.

Dictionnaire des Techniques Aeronautiques et Spatiales-- Trilingue: Francais, Anglais, Allemand: 24,000 Entrees Dans Chaque Langue. 1200p. (Fr., Eng. & Ger.). 1978. 175.00 (ISBN 2-04-010124-1, M-6131). French & Eur.

Dictionnaire des Termes Agricoles: Francais-Arabe. 2nd ed. Emir Al-Chihabi. (Arabic & Fr.). 40.00 (ISBN 0-86685-305-7). Intl Bk Ctr.

Dictionnaire des Termes d'anatomie, d'embryologie & d'histologie. Ernest Lovasy & Emmanuel Veillon. 624p. (Fr.). 1954. 40.00 F. Maloine.

Dictionnaire des Termes d'Anatomie, d'Embryologie et d'Histologie. Ernst Lovasy. 624p. (Fr.). 1954. 17.50 (ISBN 0-686-57022-7, M-6380). French & Eur.

Dictionnaire des termes economiques et commerciaux. Mustapha Henni. 412p. (Arabic, Fr. & Eng.). 20.00 (109-7). Intl Bk Ctr.

Dictionnaire des Termes Juridique en Quartre Langues: Francais, Neerlandais, Anglais, Allemand. E. Le Docte. (Fr., Dutch, Eng. & Ger.). 1978. 95.00 (ISBN 0-686-57008-1, M-6349). French & Eur.

Dictionnaire des Termes Juridiques en Quatre Langues: Francais-Neerlandais-Anglais-Allemand. E. Le Docte. (Fr., Dutch, Eng. & Ger.). 1978. 240.00 F. Vander Oyez.

Dictionnaire des termes juridiques et commerciaux. Mamdouh Hakki. (Fr. & Arabic). 1973. 20.00 (108-9). Intl Bk Ctr.

Dictionnaire des termes relatifs a electrotechnique, l'electronique et aux applications connexes, 2 vols. H. Piraux. 387p. (Eng. & Fr.). 1978. Vol. 1: English-French. 49.00 F. Vol. 2: French-English. 49.00. Eyrolles.

Dictionnaire des Termes Techniques d'Entomologies Elementaire. Eugene Seguy. 465p. (Fr.). 1967. 79.95 (ISBN 2-7205-0466-1, M-6512). French & Eur.

Dictionnaire des Termes Techniques d'entomologie Elementaire. Eugene Seguy. (Illus.). 465p. (Fr.). 1967. 200.00 F. Lechevalier.

Dictionnaire des Termes Techniques De Medecine. 19th ed. Marcel Garnier & Jean Delamare. 1340p. (Fr.). 1978. 35.00 (ISBN 0-686-57190-8, M-6262). French & Eur.

Dictionnaire des Termes Techniques de Medecine. 19th ed. Marcel Garnier & Jean Delamare. 1340p. (Fr.). 1978. 78.00 F. Maloine.

Dictionnaire des Termes Techniques et Commerciaux. Compiled by Mustapha Henni. 386p. (Arabic, Fr. & Eng.). 25.00 (11-9). INtl Bk Ctr.

Dictionnaire des Termes Veterinaires & Zootechniques. Martial Villemin. (Fr.). 1963. 130.00 F. Vigot.

Dictionnaire Des Terms Juridiques et Commerciaux (Francais-Arabe) Mamdouh Hakki. 1973. 20.00x (ISBN 0-86685-108-9). Intl Bk Ctr.

Dictionnaire des Theatres de Paris, 7 vols. 2nd ed. Claude Parfaict. (Fr.). 1967. 500.00 F. Slatkine.

Dictionnaire des Valeurs de Meubles & Objets d'art. E. Mayer. (Illus.). 450p. (Fr.). 1973. 99.00 F. Fischbacher.

Dictionnaire des Vanites, 1. 212p. (Fr.). 1971. 49.00 F. Contrepoint.

Dictionnaire des Vanites, 2. 192p. (Fr.). 1972. 49.00 F. Contrepoint.

Dictionnaire des Varietes, A-Z. Frank Lipsik. (Illus.). 188p. (Fr.). 1977. 29.00 F. Menges.

Dictionnaire des Ventes d'art Faites en France & a l'etranger, 1. H. Mireur. (Illus., Fr.). 1912. DM.118.00. Olms Verlag.

Dictionnaire des Ventes d'art Faites en France & a l'etranger, 2. H. Mireur. (Illus., Fr.). 1912. DM.118.00. Olms Verlag.

Dictionnaire des Ventes d'art Faites en France & a l'etranger, 3. H. Mireur. (Illus., Fr.). 1912. DM.118.00. Olms Verlag.

Dictionnaire des Ventes d'art Faites en France & a l'etranger, 4. H. Mireur. (Illus., Fr.). 1912. DM.118.00. Olms Verlag.

Dictionnaire des Ventes d'art Faites en France & a l'etranger, 5. H. Mireur. (Illus., Fr.). 1912. DM.118.00. Olms Verlag.

Dictionnaire des Ventes d'art Faites en France & a l'etranger, 6. H. Mireur. (Illus., Fr.). 1912. DM.118.00. Olms Verlag.

Dictionnaire des Verbe Francais. J. P. Caput & J. Caput. (Fr.). 1979. 13.50 (Dist. by Continental Bk Co). Larousse.

Dictionnaire des verbes francais. J. P. Caput & J. Caput. (Fr., Fr) 27.50 (ISBN 0-685-13871-2, 3622). Larousse.

Dictionnaire des Verbes Francais. 2nd ed. Jean Caput & Josette Caput. (Fr.). 1970. 57.20 F. Larousse.

Dictionnaire des Vins. 3rd ed. Gerard Debuigne. (Illus.). 250p. (Fr.). 1970. 17.60 F. Larousse.

Dictionnaire des 10,000 Dirigeants Politiques Francais. Pierre-Marie Dioudonnat & Sabine Bragadir. 756p. (Fr.). 1978. 69.50 (ISBN 0-686-56727-7, M-6164). French & Eur.

Dictionnaire des 1001 Tournures: La Correspondance Pratique. Jean-Yves Dournon. (Illus.). 434p. (Fr.). 1977. 5.50 F. L. G. F.

Dictionnaire Descriptif & Synonymique des Genres de Plantes Phanerogmes, 7. Albert Lemee. 693p. (Fr.). 1939. 65.00 F. Lechevalier.

Dictionnaire Descriptif & Synonymique des Genres de Plantes Phanerogmes, 8. Albert Lemee. 273p. (Fr.). 1941. 45.00 F. Lechevalier.

Dictionnaire Descriptif & Synonymique des Genres de Plantes Phanerogames, 9. Albert Lemee. 287p. (Fr.). 1951. 65.00 F. Lechevalier.

Dictionnaire Descriptif & Synonymique des Genres de Plantes Phanerogames, 10. Albert Lemee. 219p. (Fr.). 1959. 75.00 F. Lechevalier.

Dictionnaire d'Esthetique Chretienne ou Theorie du Beau dans l'Art Chretien. E. G. Jouve. Ed. by J. P. Migne. (Troisieme et Derniere Encyclopedie Theologique Ser.: Vol. 17). 646p. (Fr.). Repr. of 1856 ed. lib. bdg. 82.50x (ISBN 0-89241-300-X). Caratzas Pub Co.

Dictionnaire detaille des noms des vetements chez les Arabes. R. Dozy. 445p. (Arabic & Fr.). 20.00 (104-5). Intl Bk Ctr.

Dictionnaire d'Ethnographie. Ed. by J. P. Migne. (Nouvelle Encyclopedie Theologique Ser.: Vol. 37). 964p. (Fr.). Repr. of 1853 ed. lib. bdg. 121.50x (ISBN 0-686-82875-5). Caratzas Pub Co.

Dictionnaire d'etymologie Sumerienne & Grammaire Comparee. Colman G. Gostony. 204p. (Fr.). 1975. 130.00 F. Boccard.

Dictionnaire d'Etymologie Sumerienne et Grammaire Comparee. Colman G. Gostony. 204p. (Fr.). 1975. pap. 52.50 (ISBN 0-686-57306-4, M-6283). French & Eur.

Dictionnaire d'histoire & de Geographie Ecclesiastiques, 16 vols. Roger Aubert & Van Cauwenberg. (Fr.). 4464.00 F. Letouzey & Ane.

Dictionnaire d'histoire & de Geographie Ecclesiastiques. Roger Aubert et al. 176p. (Fr.). 88.00 F. Letouzey & Ane.

Dictionnaire d'Histoire & de Geographie Ecclesiastiques. 128p. (Fr.). 1975. 87.00 F. Letouzey & Ane.

Dictionnaire d'Histoire Contemporaine 1776-1969. Jacques De Launay & Emile Lousse. 550p. (Fr.). 1973. 16.00 F. Rencontre.

Dictionnaire d'Histoire et du Geographie Ecclesiastiques, 16 vols. Roger Aubert & Van Cauwenberg. (Fr.). Set. pap. 1795.00 (ISBN 0-686-56903-2, M-6014). French & Eur.

Dictionnaire d'informatique. Georges Nania. 1000p. (Fr., Eng., Ital., Span. & Port.). 1983. 450.00 F. Maison Dictionnaire.

Dictionnaire d'informatique: Anglais-Francais. 3rd ed. 172p. (Eng. & Fr.). 1975. write for info. Masson.

Dictionnaire d'Informatique: Anglais-Francais. M. Ginguay. 172p. (Eng. & Fr.). 1977. pap. 27.50 (ISBN 0-686-57299-8, F-137100). French & Eur.

Dictionnaire D'informatique Anglais-Francais. 5th ed. Michel Ginguay. LC 79-381483. 208p. (Eng. & Fr.). 1979. 68.00 F (ISBN 2-225-63459-9). Masson & Cie.

Dictionnaire d'informatique: Francais-Anglais-Italien-Espagnol-Portugais. G. Nania. 1000p. (Fr., Eng., Ital., Span. & Port.). 1982. 450.00 F. Maison Dictionnaire.

Dictionnaire d'informatique: Francais-Anglais. 152p. (Fr. & Eng.). 1976. write for info. Masson.

Dictionnaire Dogon: Ethnologique & Linguistique. Genevieve Calamegriaule. 296p. (Fr.). 1968. 45.00 F. S. E. L. A. F.

Dictionnaire d'oto-rhino-laryngologie: Francais-Anglais-Espagnol-Allemand-Italien, 5 vols. (Fr. , Eng. , Span. , Ger. & Ital.). 1971. write for info. Maloine.

Dictionnaire Dramatique, 3 vols. Nicolas De Chamfort. (Fr.). 1967. write for info. Slatkine.

Dictionnaire du Batiment: Francais-Anglais. Marcel Lefebvre. 356p. (Fr. & Eng.). 1965. write for info. LEMEAC.

Dictionnaire du Bearnais & du Gascon Modernes. Simon Palay. 1052p. (Fr.). 1980. 290.00 F (ISBN 2-22201-608-8). CNRS.

Dictionnaire du Bearnais & du Gascon Moderne. Simin. 1044p. (Fr.). 1974. write for info. CNRS.

Dictionnaire du Bernais & du Gascon Modernes. Simin Palay. 45p. (Fr.). 1980. pap. 35.00 F (ISBN 2-22202-708-X). CNRS.

Dictionnaire du Blues. Jean-Claude Arnaudon. (Illus., Fr.). write for info. Filipacchi.

Dictionnaire du Bon Francais. J. Girodet. 896p. (Fr.). 1981. lib. bdg. 37.50 (ISBN 2-04-010580-8, M-9362). French & Eur.

Dictionnaire du Bon Langage. 8th ed. E. Blanchard. 318p. (Fr.). write for info. LIDEC.

Dictionnaire du Bricolage & du Depannage. Francis Genette. (Illus.). 450p. (Fr.). 1972. write for info. Sequoia.

Dictionnaire du Bridge. Georges Versini. (Fr.). 1968. write for info. PUF.

Dictionnaire du Cheval et du Chevalier. C. Cassart & R. Moirant. 288p. (Fr.). 1979. 49.95 (ISBN 0-686-56942-3, M-6064). French & Eur.

Dictionnaire du Chien. Pierre Rousselet-Blanc & Josette Rousselet-Blanc. 267p. (Fr.). 1976. 27.50 (ISBN 0-686-56869-9, M-6647). French & Eur.
Dictionnaire du Chien. Pierre Rousselet-Blanc & Josette Rousselet-Blanc. (Illus.). 267p. (Fr.). 1976. write for info. Laffont.
Dictionnaire du Cinema Quebecois. (Fr.). 1979. 32.50 (ISBN 0-686-57105-3, M-6132). French & Eur.
Dictionnaire du Cinema Quebecois. Michel Houle & Alain Julien. LC 79-361413. xxx, 366p. (Eng. & Fr.). 1978. write for info. (ISBN 0-7755-0699-0). Fides.
Dictionnaire du Cinema Universal, 6. Pierre-Charles Jeanne. 720p. (Fr.). 1970. write for info. Laffont.
Dictionnaire du Consommateur. R. Pujol. 288p. (Fr.). write for info. Gonthier.
Dictionnaire du Droit des Societes Anonymes. (Fr.). 1978. write for info. Joly.
Dictionnaire du Droit des Societes a Responsabille, 6 vols. (Fr.). write for info. JolY.
Dictionnaire du Droit des Societes a Responsabille. (Fr.). 1978. write for info. Joly.
Dictionnaire du Droit Public. Robert Wilkin. (Fr.). write for info. Bruylant.
Dictionnaire du Francais Argotique & Populaire. (Illus.). 255p. (Fr.). 1977. write for info. Larousse.
Dictionnaire du Francais Classique. Jean Dubois & Rene Lagane. 608p. (Fr.). 1971. 22.50 (ISBN 0-686-57298-X, F-133960). French & Eur.
Dictionnaire du Francais Classique. Jean Dubois & Rene Lagane. 608p. (Fr.). 1971. write for info. Larousse.
Dictionnaire du francais contemporain: Manuel et travaux pratique. (Fr.). 18.95 (ISBN 0-685-92177-8, 4078). Larousse.
Dictionnaire du Francais Contemporain. J. Dubois. 1263p. (Fr.). 1980. 19.95 (ISBN 2-03-320101-5, M-9357). French & Eur.
Dictionnaire du Francais Contemporain. J. Dubois. (Illus., Fr.). 1980. 17.75 (Dist. by Continental Bk Co). Larousse.
Dictionnaire du Francais Contemporain. Jean Dubois & Rene Lagane. (Fr.). 1971. write for info. Larousse.
Dictionnaire du Francais Contemporain. Ed. by Jean Dubois et al. LC 77-468961. xxii, 1263p. (Fr.). 1975. 34.00 F (ISBN 2-030-29321-0). Larousse FR.
Dictionnaire du Francais Contemporain (DFC) 1119p. (Fr.). DM.29.80 (49005). Larousse-Langenscheidt.
Dictionnaire du Francais Facile. 86p. (Fr.). 1974. write for info. Hachette.
Dictionnaire du Francais Fondamental. G. Gougenheim. (Fr.). 8.75 (Dist. by Continental Bk Co). Didier.
Dictionnaire du Francais Fondamental pour l'Afrique. 440p. (Fr.). 1974. write for info. Didier.
Dictionnaire du Francais Langue Etrangere. J. Dubois. (Fr.). 1977. write for info. Larousse.
Dictionnaire du Francais Langue Etrangere: Niveau I. Dubois & F. Dubois-Charlier. (Fr.). 1977. 15.00 (Dist. by Continental Bk Co). Larousse.
Dictionnaire du Francais Langue Etrangere: Niveau II. J. Dubois & F. Dubois-Charlier. (Fr.). 1979. 15.00 (Dist. by Continental Bk Co). Larousse.
Dictionnaire du Francais Moderne. Maurice Remy. (Fr.). write for info. Hatier.
Dictionnaire du Francais non Conventionnel. J. Cellard & A. Key. 893p. (Fr.). 1980. 65.00 (ISBN 2-01-007382-7). French & eur.
Dictionnaire du Francais Vivant. 1342p. (Fr.). 2500.00 ptas (ISBN 84-7153-150-X). Biblograf SP.
Dictionnaire du Francais Vivant: Collection "Dunod Entreprise". P. Conso et al. 448p. (Fr.). 1979. 45.00 F (Dist. by Continental Bk Co). Bordas.
Dictionnaire du Francais Vivant: Nouvelle Edition. M. Davaux et al. 1360p. (Fr.). 1980. 23.75 F (Dist. by Continental Bk Co). Bordas.
Dictionnaire du Jazz. rev. ed. Hugues Panassie & Gautier. (Illus.). 363p. (Fr.). 1971. write for info. Albin Michel.
Dictionnaire du Jazz. Hugues Panassie & Madeleine Gautier. 363p. (Fr.). 1971. pap. 18.95 (ISBN 0-686-56870-2, M-6648). French & Eur.
Dictionnaire du Marche Commun, 4 vols. (Fr.). 1978. Set. 250.00 (ISBN 0-686-56746-3, M-6135). French & Eur.
Dictionnaire du Marche Commun. (Fr.). 1978. write for info. Joly.
Dictionnaire du Marche de l'Art. Didier Romand & Gerald Schurr. 416p. (Fr.). 1978. pap. 55.00 (ISBN 0-686-56728-5, M-6490). French & Eur.
Dictionnaire du Marche de l'art. new ed. Didier Romand & Gerard Schurr. 420p. (Fr.). 1978. write for info. Amateur.
Dictionnaire du Marche de l'Art: Meubles, Objects, Curiosities. Didier Romand. LC 78-384890. (Illus.). 415p. (Fr.). 1978. 135.00 F (ISBN 2-859-17007-3). Amateur.
Dictionnaire du Mepris. Jacques Sternberg. (Fr.). write for info. Calmann Levy.
Dictionnaire du Parfait Automobiliste. Christian Vebel. 256p. (Fr.). write for info. Pensee Moderne.
Dictionnaire du Patois Normand. Henri Moisy. 864p. (Fr.). 1969. write for info. Slatkine.
Dictionnaire du Patois de la Flandre Francaise. Louis Vermesse & Douai. (Fr.). 1969. write for info. Slatkine.
Dictionnaire du Patols du Bas-Limousin. 375p. (Fr.). 1971. write for info. Slatkine.
Dictionnaire du Patols Forezien. Louis-Pierre Gras. 302p. (Fr.). 1970. write for info. Slatkine.
Dictionnaire du Patols Normand. E. Dumeril. 326p. (Fr.). 1969. write for info. Slatkine.
Dictionnaire du Patols Valdotain. Jean B. Cerlogne. 321p. (Fr.). 1971. 75.00 F. Slatkine.
Dictionnaire du Petit Offset. 2nd ed. Lucien Dodin. 220p. (Fr.). 1970. 48.90 F. Prismes.
Dictionnaire du Savoir-Vivre Moderne. Floriane Prevot. (Fr.). 1970. 27.00 F. Casterman.
Dictionnaire du Scrabble. Annie Carillon & Beatrice Goutel. 215p. (Fr.). 1976. 30.00 F. Hachette.
Dictionnaire du Ski. Jacques Gautrat. 256p. (Fr.). 1969. pap. 8.95 (ISBN 0-686-56873-7, M-6651). French & Eur.
Dictionnaire du Ski. Jacques Gautrat. (Illus.). 256p. (Fr.). 1969. 20.00 F. Seuil.
Dictionnaire du Style & des Usages Administratifs. 484p. (Fr.). 43.50 F. Sodi.
Dictionnaire du Style et des Usages Administratifs. Marcel Spreutels. 484p. (Fr.). 19.95 (ISBN 0-686-57225-4, M-6523). French & Eur.
Dictionnaire du Symbolisme Animal. Jean Paul Clebert. (Illus.). 455p. (Fr.). 75.00 F. Albin-Michel.
Dictionnaire Du Theatre Francais Contemporain. Alfred Simon. 250p. (Fr.). 1970. pap. 6.95 (ISBN 0-686-56878-8, M-675). French & Eur.
Dictionnaire du Theatre Francais Contemporain. Alfred Simon. (Illus.). 250p. (Fr.). 17.60 F. Larousse.
Dictionnaire du Traducteur: Francais-Neerlandais. J. E. Van Grieken. 1760p. (Fr. & Dutch.). 1484.00 F. Administratives.
Dictionnaire du Traitement de l'information: Francais-Allemand. 900p. (Fr. & Ger.). 85.00 F. Pioton.
Dictionnaire du Traitement de l'information: Francais-Allemand-Anglais. Carl Amkreutz. 900p. (Fr., Ger. & Eng.). 1972. 85.00 F. Carl Amkreutz.
Dictionnaire du traitement de l'informatique. 2nd ed. Carl Amkreutz. 1944p. (Eng., Fr., & Ger.). 1981. 600.00 F. Maison Dictionnaire.
Dictionnaire du Vin. Yves Renouil & Yves De Traversay. (Fr.). 95.00 F. Feret.
Dictionnaire du Vin. Yves Renouil & Yves de Traversay. (Fr.). 1962. 39.95 (ISBN 0-686-56731-5, M-6482). French & Eur.
Dictionnaire du vocabulaire essentiel. Larousse & Co. (Illus., Fr.). pap. 12.25 (ISBN 0-685-13873-9, 3753). Larousse.
Dictionnaire du Vocabulaire Essentiel. 5th ed. Georges Matore. 360p. (Fr.). 1970. pap. 10.95 (ISBN 0-686-56874-5, M-6652). French & Eur.
Dictionnaire du Vocabulaire Essentiel. 5th ed. Georges Matore. (Illus.). 360p. (Fr.). 26.00 F. Larousse.
Dictionnaire du Vocabulaire Orthographique. 7th ed. (Fr.). 1971. 8.00 F. Larousse.
Dictionnaire Duala-Francais. Paul Helmlinger. 666p. (Fr.). 1972. 105.00 F. S. E. L. A. F.
Dictionnaire Duden-Larousse: Tout Allemand. (Fr. & Ger.). 38.50 F. Larousse.
Dictionnaire d'un Polygraphe. L. S. Mercier. (Fr.). 1978. 17.70 F. U. G. E.
Dictionnaire Economique & Financier. Yves Bernard et al. 1200p. (Eng., Fr & Ger.). 1975. 250.00 F. Seuil.
Dictionnaire Economique & Financier. 248p. (Fr.). 1972. 4.00 F. Homme.
Dictionnaire Economique & Social. Maurice Bouvier-Ajam et al. LC 75-508274. 765p. (Fr.). 1975. 59.00 F. Edns Sociales.
Dictionnaire Economique & Social. Thomas Suavet. 526p. (Fr.). 1973. 42.00 F. Ouvrieres.
Dictionnaire Economique & Social: Dictionnaire Thomas Suavet. 11th ed. Michel Branciard. LC 79-368728. 582p. (Fr.). 1978. 110.00 F (ISBN 2-7082-0209-X). Ouvrieres.
Dictionnaire Economique et Financier. Yves Bernard et al. Ed. by Dominique Lewandowski. 1200p. (Fr.). 1975. 119.95 (ISBN 0-686-57297-1, M-4643). French & Eur.
Dictionnaire Economique et Social. Thomas H. Suarvet. 526p. (Fr.). 1973. 19.95 (ISBN 0-686-57227-0, M-6526). French & Eur.
Dictionnaire Elementaire Creole Haitien-Francais. Pierre Nougayrol et al. Ed. by Alain Bentolila. 511p. (Haitian & Fr.). 1976. 29.95 (ISBN 0-686-57060-X, M-6430). French & Eur.
Dictionnaire Elementaire Creole Haitien-Francais. Pierre Vernet & Charles Alexandre. (Illus.). 511p. (Fr.). 1976. 75.00 F. Hatier.
Dictionnaire En Couleurs Des Animaux. Maurice Burton. 400p. (Fr.). 1974. 57.00 (ISBN 0-686-56875-3, M-6653). French & Eur.
Dictionnaire en Couleurs des Animaux. Maurice Burton. (Illus.). 400p. (Fr.). 145.00 F. Elsevier Sequoia.
Dictionnaire Erotique. Pierre Guiraud. 648p. (Fr.). 1978. pap. 39.95 (ISBN 0-686-57322-6, M-6306). French & Eur.
Dictionnaire Espagnol-Francais. A. Corbiere & Lautier. 1046p. (Span. & Fr.). 25.20 F. Dessain & Tolra.
Dictionnaire Espagnol-Francais. Serge Denis & M. Maraval. 1774p. (Span. & Fr.). 66.00 F. Hachette.
Dictionnaire Espagnol-Francais. Serge Denis & Marcel Maraval. 1774p. (Fr. & Eng.). 1968. pap. 26.50 (ISBN 0-686-56983-0, M-6110). French & Eur.
Dictionnaire Espagnol-Francais. Serge Denis et al. 904p. (Span. & Fr.). 1976. 90.00. Hachette Jeunesse.
Dictionnaire Espagnol-Francais. 640p. (Span. & Fr.). 7.50 F. Larousse.
Dictionnaire Espagnol-Francais. Robert Larrieu. 512p. (Span. & Fr.). 1961. 11.00. Garnier.
Dictionnaire Espagnol-Francais. Robert Larrieu. (Span. & Fr.). 9.50 F. Garnier-Flammarion.
Dictionnaire Espagnol-Francais. Vicente Salva. (Illus.). 948p. (Span. & Fr.). 1959. 18.00 F. Garnier-Flammarion.
Dictionnaire Espagnol-Francais. Vicente Salva & Robert Larrieu. (Illus.). 1580p. (Span. & Fr.). 1951. 26.00 F. Garnier.
Dictionnaire Espagnol-Francais et Francais-Espagnol. new ed. Serge Denis et al. 904p. (Span. & Fr.). 1976. 36.95 (ISBN 0-686-56984-9, M-6111). French & Eur.
Dictionnaire Espagnol-Francais et Francais-Espagnol. Ed. by Vicente Salva & Robert Larrieu. 1580p. (Fr.-Span.). 1951. 22.50 (ISBN 0-686-57295-5, F-140811). French & Eur.
Dictionnaire Esquimau-Francais du Parler de l'Ungava & Contrees Limitrophes. 2nd ed. Lucien Schneider. 446p. (Fr.). 1970. Can.$15.00. Laval P. U.
Dictionnaire Etymologiqe du Moyen-Breton. 225p. (Fr.). 80.00 F. Slatkine.
Dictionnaire Etymologique. Octave Caillon. (Fr.). 1967. 44.00 F. Ligel.
Dictionnaire Etymologique. Albert Dauzat et al. 805p. (Fr.). 1971. 20.00 F. Larousse.
Dictionnaire Etymologique de la Langue Francaise avec les Origines Francaises, 2 vols. Gilles Menage. 950p. (Fr.). 1973. 750.00 F. Slatkine.
Dictionnaire Etymologique de la Langue Russe, 1, A-J, 5 vols. N. Chanski. 400p. (Rus.). 1961. 45.80 F. MIR.
Dictionnaire Etymologique de la Langue Francaise. 6th ed. Oscar Bloch & Walther Von Wartburg. 684p. (Fr.). 1975. 166.40 F. PUF.
Dictionnaire Etymologique de la Langue Francaise. 6th ed. Oscar Bloch & Walther Von Wartburg. 684p. (Fr.). 1975. 83.95 (ISBN 0-686-57293-9, F-C1016). French & Eur.
Dictionnaire Etymologique de la Langue Grecque. Pierre Chantraine. 609p. (Gr.). 1976. 300.00 F. Klincksieck.
Dictionnaire Etymologique de la Langue Grecque, 2. Pierre Chantraine. (Gr.). 110.00 F. Klincksieck.
Dictionnaire Etymologique de la Langue Grecque, 3. Pierre Chantraine. 360p. (Gr.). 1975. 180.00 F. Klincksieck.
Dictionnaire Etymologique de la Langue Grecque, 4. Pierre Chantraine. 200p. (Gr.). 1977. 140.00 F. Klincksieck.
Dictionnaire Etymologique de la Langue Latine. 4th ed. Alfred Ernout & Antoine Meillet. 946p. (Lat.). 1967. 280.00 F. Klincksieck.
Dictionnaire Etymologique de la Langue Russe, 3 vols. N. Chanski. (Rus.). 1975. 15.85 F. MIR.
Dictionnaire Etymologique de la Langue Russe. Tsyganenko. (Rus.). 8.60 F. MIR.
Dictionnaire Etymologique de la Langue Wallonne, 3 vols. Charles-Marie Grandgagnage. 1275p. (Fr. & Waloon.). 1969. 220.00 F. Slatkine.
Dictionnaire Etymologique de l'ancien Francais. Kurt Baldinger. 144p. (Fr.). 1974. Can.$14.00. Laval P. U.
Dictionnaire Etymologique de l'ancien Francais. Kurt Baldinger. (Fr.). 1974. Can.$14.00. Laval P. U.
Dictionnaire Etymologique de l'ancien Francais, 1. Kurt Baldinger & Georges Straka. 120p. (Fr.). 1971. 92.00 F. Klincksieck.
Dictionnaire Etymologique de l'ancien Francais. Kurt Baldinger et al. 112p. (Fr.). 1974. Can.$14.00. Laval P. U.

Dictionnaire Etymologique des Noms de Pays & de Peuples. Serge Losique. 243p. (Fr.). 1971. 48.00 F. Klincksieck.

Dictionnaire Etymologique des noms Grecs de Plantes. Albert Carnoy. 277p. (Gr. & Fr.). 1959. 1000.00 F. Peeters.

Dictionnaire Etymologique du Patols Lyonnais. Nizier Du Puitspelu. 595p. (Fr.). 1970. 100.00 F. Slatkine.

Dictionnaire Etymologique: Historique & Anecdotique des Proverbes & des Locutions Proverbiales de la Langue Francaise. Pierre-Marie Quitard. 715p. (Fr.). 1968. 130.00 F. Slatkine.

Dictionnaire Europa: Francais-Allemand. 424p. (Fr. & Ger.). 1959. 11.00 F. Larousse.

Dictionnaire Europa Francais-Anglais. 460p. (Fr. & Eng.). 1978. 11.00 F. Larousse.

Dictionnaire Europa Francais-Espagnol. 460p. (Fr. & Span.). 1978. 11.00 F. Larousse.

Dictionnaire Europa Francais-Italien. 352p. (Fr. & Ital.). 1960. 11.00 F. Larousse.

Dictionnaire Europa Francais-Portugais. 460p. (Fr. & Port.). 1978. 11.00 F. Larousse.

Dictionnaire Europa Francais-Turc. H. J. Kornrumpf. 384p. (Fr. & Turkish.). 1966. 11.00 F. Larousse.

Dictionnaire Familial des Medecines Naturelies. Emmerick A. Maury. LC 79-350663. 568p. (Fr.). 1978. 125.00 F (ISBN 2-7113-0102-8). Delarge.

Dictionnaire Familial d'homeopathie. Emmerick A. Maury. 216p. (Fr.). 30.00 F. Delarge.

Dictionnaire Familial D'homoeopathie. Emmerick A. Maury. LC 77-675217. 210p. (Fr.). 1976. 25.00 F. Edns Univers.

Dictionnaire Finnois-Francais. Tauno Nurmela. 694p. (Finnish & Fr.). 1976. 15.00 F. 40.65 F. Soderstrom.

Dictionnaire Finnois-Francais-Finnois. Raila-Maarit Koistinen & Helene Lasslo. 393p. (Finnish & Fr.). 1973. 7.00 F. 20.32 F. Soderstrom.

Dictionnaire Fondamental. Georges Gougenheim. 256p. (Fr.). 1958. 17.10 F. Didier.

Dictionnaire Fondamental Harrap: Francais-Anglais. Colin Henstock. 136p. (Fr. & Eng.). 1973. 15.00 F. Bordas-Dunod.

Dictionnaire Forestier Multilingue. Andre Metro. 434p. (Fr.). 1976. 79.95 (ISBN 0-686-57047-2, M-6409). French & Eur.

Dictionnaire Forestier Multilingue. Andre Metro. 434p. (Fr.). 1976. 200.00 F. C. I. L. F.

Dictionnaire-Formulaire Commercial. Raoul Michel & Humbert Pardel-Lans. 152p. (Fr.). 1953. 7.00 F. Foucher.

Dictionnaire Foucher de Stenographie. Guy Brousse. 346p. (Fr.). 1977. 28.00 F. Foucher.

Dictionnaire Foucher de Stenographie Prevost-Delauney. Guy Brousse. (Fr.). 14.40 F. Foucher.

Dictionnaire Francais-Allemand. Jean Clediere et al. LC 75-512974. (Illus.). 1094p. (Fr. & Ger.). 1975. 45.00 F (ISBN 2-030-20811-6). Larousse FR.

Dictionnaire Francais-Allemand. Erich Weis & Heinrich Mattutat. 480p. (Fr. & Ger.). 1976. 75.00 F. Bordas-Dunod.

Dictionnaire Francais-Allemand. Erich Weis & Heinrich Mattutat. 1022p. (Fr. & Ger.). 1977. 139.00 F. Bordas-Dunod.

Dictionnaire Francais-Allemand-Anglais pour le Commerce Exterieur. Jean Ruhland. (Fr., Ger. & Eng.). 60.00 F. Ruhland.

Dictionnaire Francais-Allemand des Locutions. F. Dubois & P. Werny. (Fr. & Ger.). 1976. 23.95 (ISBN 0-686-57124-X, M-6172). French & Eur.

Dictionnaire Francais-Allemand, Deutsch-Franzosisch. A. Pinloche. 805p. (Fr. & Ger.). Date not set. pap. 6.50 (ISBN 0-686-97409-3, M-9043). French & Eur.

Dictionnaire Francais-Allemand et Allemand-Francais. Erich Weis & Heinrich Mattutat. 1022p. (Fr. & Ger.). 1977. 55.00 (ISBN 0-686-57260-2, M-6571). French & Eur.

Dictionnaire Francais-Allemand pour le Travaux Publics le Batiment & l'equipement des Chantiers de Construction. Hector Bucksch. (Illus.). 912p. (Fr. & Ger.). 1970. 375.00 F. Eyrolles.

Dictionnaire Francais-Anglais. Denis Girard. (Illus.). 1464p. (Fr. & Eng.). 1972. 68.00 F. Garnier.

Dictionnaire Francais-Anglais, Anglais-Francais des affaires. Michel Peron et al. 476p. (Fr. & Eng.). 1968. 29.80 F. Larousse.

Dictionnaire francais-anglais, anglais-francais des affaires: A French-English English-French Dictionary of Business Terms. rev. ed. Michel Peron et al. 512p. (Fr. & Eng.). 1974. 30.95 (ISBN 2-03-020609-1, 3764). Larousse.

Dictionnaire Francais-Anglais, Anglais-Francais des Termes et Locutions de la Marine Marchande. (Fr. & Eng.). 25.00 (ISBN 0-686-57108-8, M-6140). French & Eur.

Dictionnaire Francais-Anglais de la Psychologie & des Sciences Connexes. Jacques Castonguay. 316p. (Fr.). 1973. 88.00 F. Maloine.

Dictionnaire Francais-Anglais de l'economie Monetaire. Denis-Clair Lambert. 264p. (Fr. & Eng.). 1975. 34.00 F. Ouvrieres.

Dictionnaire Francais-Anglais de l'Economie. 264p. (Fr. & Eng.). 1975. pap. 14.95 (ISBN 0-686-56989-X, M-6329). French & Eur.

Dictionnaire Francais-Anglais de l'economie. Denis-Clair Lambert. 264p. (Fr. & Eng.). 1975. 34.00 F. Ouvrieres.

Dictionnaire Francais-Anglais de Medecine Physique de Reeducation & de Readaptation Fonctionhelles. Herman L. Kamenetz & Georgette Kamenetz. 192p. (Fr. & Eng.). 1972. 48.00 F. 40.00. Maloine.

Dictionnaire Francais-Anglais des Debutantes. Charlier F. Dubois. (Fr. & Eng.). 1978. 8.95 (Dist. by Continental Bk Co). Larousse.

Dictionnaire Francais-Anglais des Termes & Locutions de la Marine Marchande. (Fr. & Eng.). 53.00 F. Maritimes Outremer.

Dictionnaire Francais-Anglais des Termes Medicaux & Biologiques. 2nd ed. Pierre Lepine. 896p. (Fr. & Eng.). 1974. 160.00 F. Flammarion.

Dictionnaire Francais-Anglais des Termes Relatifs a l'electronique: L'electronique & aux Applications Connexes. 6th ed. Henri Piraux. (Illus.). 204p. (Fr. & Eng.). 1978. 82.00 F. Eyrolles.

Dictionnaire Francais-Anglais des Termes Techniques de Medecine. Jean Delamare & Marie-Therese Delamarericke. 714p. (Fr. & Eng.). 1970. 100.00 F. Maloine.

Dictionnaire Francais-Anglais et Anglais-Francais des Termes Medicaux et Biologiques. 2nd ed. Pierre Lepine. 896p. (Fr. & Eng.). 1974. 65.00 (ISBN 0-686-57292-0, M-4665). French & Eur.

Dictionnaire Francais-Anglais et Anglais-Francais des Termes Techniques de Medecine. J. Delamare & Th. Delamare. 714p. (Eng. & Fr.). 1970. 39.95 (ISBN 0-686-56980-6, M-6107). French & Eur.

Dictionnaire Francais-Anglais et Anglais-Francais des Termes Techniques De Medecine. Delamarre. (Fr. & Eng.). 49.95 (ISBN 0-685-36680-4). French & Eur.

Dictionnaire Francais-Anglais et Anglais-Francais. Denis Girard. 1464p. (Fr.-Eng.). 1972. 27.50 (ISBN 0-686-57300-5, M-6274). French & Eur.

Dictionnaire Francais-Anglais pour les Travaux Publics: Le Batiment & l'equipement des Chantiers de Construction. 6th ed. Hector Bucksch. (Illus.). 550p. (Fr. & Eng.). 1977. 130.00 F. Eyrolles.

Dictionnaire Francais-Arabe, 6 vols. in 3. M. Naggary-Bey. (Fr. & Arabic.). 1974. 90.00x set (ISBN 0-8426-0756-0). Verry.

Dictionnaire Francais-Arabe. Louis Saisse. 425p. (Fr. & Arabic.). pap. 8.95 student dict. (112-7). Intl Bk Ctr.

Dictionnaire Francais-Arabe. Ben Sedira. 828p. (Fr. & Arabic.). 1980. write for info. (M-9306). French & Eur.

Dictionnaire Francais-Arabe(Arabe Parle-Arabe Grammatical, 2 vols. E. Gasselin. (Fr. & Arabic.). 1974. Repr. of 1880 ed. text ed. 75.00x (ISBN 0-8426-0757-9). Verry.

Dictionnaire Francais Azed. 940p. (Fr.). 1978. 20.60 F. Hatier.

Dictionnaire Francais-Chinois. 1498p. (Fr. & Chinese.). 1979. 49.95 (ISBN 962-04-0090-9, M-9262). French & Eur.

Dictionnaire Francais-Chinois. 956p. (Fr. & Chinese.). 1979. leatherette 19.95 (ISBN 0-686-97330-5, M-9256). French & Eur.

Dictionnaire Francais-Corse. Jean Albertini. 349p. (Fr. & Corse.). 1974. pap. 39.95 (ISBN 0-686-56891-5, M-6001). French & Eur.

Dictionnaire Francais-Corse. Jean Albertini. 349p. (Fr.). 1974. 76.00 F. C. E. R. C.

Dictionnaire Francais-Creole. Faine. 488p. (Fr. & Creole.). 1974. 300.00 F. Maison Dictionnaire.

Dictionnaire Francais-Creole. Jules Faine. 480p. (Fr. Creole.). 1975. pap. 39.95 (ISBN 0-686-57291-2, M-4608). French & Eur.

Dictionnaire Francais-Creole. Jules Faine. 480p. (Fr.). 1975. 27.50 F. Lemeac.

Dictionnaire Francais de Medecine & de Biologie, 1 A-D. Nicole A. Manuila. 866p. (Fr.). 1970. 500.00 F. Masson.

Dictionnaire Francais de Medecine & de Biologie, 2. Nicole A. Manuila. (Fr.). 1971. 500.00 F. Masson.

Dictionnaire Francais de Medecine & de Biologie, 3 N-Z. Nicole A. Manuila. 1200p. (Fr.). 1972. 600.00 F. Masson.

Dictionnaire Francais de Medecine & de Biologie, 4. Nicole A. Manuila. 580p. (Fr.). 1975. 380.00 F. Masson.

Dictionnaire Francais de Medicine el de Biologie, Vol. 2. A Manuila & M. Nicole. (Fr.). 1971. 175.00 (ISBN 0-686-57033-2, M-6393). French & Eur.

Dictionnaire Francais de Medicine el de Biologie, Vol. 3. A. Mauila et al. 1200p. (Fr.). 1972. 195.00 (ISBN 0-686-57034-0, M-6394). French & Eur.

Dictionnaire Francais de Medicine el de Biologie, Vol. 4. A. Manuila et al. 580p. (Fr.). 1975. 130.00 (ISBN 0-686-57035-9, M-6395). French & Eur.

Dictionnaire Francais de Medicine et de Biologie, Vol. 1. A. Manuila & M. Nicole. 866p. (Fr.). 1970. 175.00 (ISBN 0-686-57032-4, M-6392). French & Eur.

Dictionnaire Francais d'Hydrogeologie. G. Castany. LC 78-359598. (Illus.). 249p. (Fr.). 1977. 75.00 F. Bureau Recherches.

Dictionnaire Francais-Dyola. E. Wintz. 280p. (Fr.). 1968. 18.00. Gregg.

Dictionnaire Francais-Espagnol. Lautier Corbiere. 932p. (Fr. & Span.). 1966. 23.10 F. Dessain & Tolra.

Dictionnaire Francais-Esperanto. Albault A. Leger. 736p. (Fr. & Esperanto.). 1961. 21.00 F. Esperanto.

Dictionnaire Francais-Esquimau du Parier: l'Ungava & Contrees Limitrophes, 2. Lucien Schneider. 430p. (Fr. & Eskimo.). 1970. Can.$15.00. Laval P. U.

Dictionnaire Francais-Fang. Samuel Galley. 594p. (Fr.). 1978. 45.00 F. Messeiller.

Dictionnaire Francais-Francais des Mots Rare et Precieux. (Fr.). 8.50 (ISBN 0-685-36677-4). French & Eur.

Dictionnaire francais-hebreu. M. M. Cohn. (Fr. & Hebrew.). 35.95 (ISBN 0-685-13874-7). Larousse.

Dictionnaire Francais-Hebreu. Marc M. Cohn. 760p. (Fr. & Hebrew.). 1966. 27.50 (ISBN 0-686-56955-5, M-6077). French & Eur.

Dictionnaire Francais-Hebreu. Marc M. Cohn. 760p. (Fr. & Hebrew.). 1966. 69.00 F. Larousse.

Dictionnaire Francais-Langue. Piat. 1000p. (Fr.). 1978. 180.00 F. Ramoun.

Dictionnaire Francais-Langue d'Oc. Piat. 1000p. (Fr.). 75.00 (ISBN 0-686-56730-7, M-6451). French & Eur.

Dictionnaire Francais-Latin. Jean-Elie Decahors. 864p. (Fr. & Lat.). 1957. 19.50 F. Hatier.

Dictionnaire Francais-Latin. Georges Edon. (Fr. & Lat.). 37.50 (ISBN 0-686-57201-7, M-6703). French & Eur.

Dictionnaire Francais-Latin. Georges Edon. 1800p. (Fr. & Lat.). 1978. 92.00 F. Belin.

Dictionnaire Francais-Latin. Robert Estienne. 680p. (Fr. & Lat.). 1972. 300.00 F. Slatkine.

Dictionnaire Francais-Latin. Geoffroy. 1200p. (Fr. & Lat.). 1978. 21.40 F. Delalain.

Dictionnaire Francais-Latin. Henri Goelzer. 640p. (Fr. & Lat.). 1966. 11.50 F. Garnier-Flammarion.

Dictionnaire Francais-Latin. Henri Goelzer. 744p. (Fr. & Lat.). 1967. 21.00 F. Garnier.

Dictionnaire Francais-Latin. Louis Quicherat. (Fr. & Lat.). 1967. 86.80. Hachette-Jeinesse.

Dictionnaire Francais-Liegois. Jean Haust. (Fr. & Walloon.). 1974. write for info. Vaillant-Carmanne.

Dictionnaire Francais-Malgache. R. P. Malzac. 861p. (Fr. & Malgache.). 1953. pap. 32.50 (ISBN 0-686-57030-8, M-6390). French & Eur.

Dictionnaire Francais-Malgache. R. P. Malzac. 861p. (Fr.). 1953. 70.00 F. Maritimes Outremer.

Dictionnaire Francais-Marocain. Abulgacim Tedjini. 394p. (Fr.). 1949. 22.00 F. Maritimes Outre-Mer.

Dictionnaire Francais-Nicois. Georges Castellana. LC 78-380119. 421p. (Fr.). 1978. 60.00 F. Serre.

Dictionnaire Francais Nicois. Georges Castellana. 422p. (Fr.). 1977. Can.$90.00. Serre.

Dictionnaire Francais-Occitanien. L. Piat. 1000p. (Fr.). 1978. 250.00 F. Berenguie.

Dictionnaire Francais-Polonais. 1004p. (Fr. & Pol.). 1978. 55.80 F. Vander.

Dictionnaire Francais-Portugais. Domingos De Azevedo. 1506p. (Fr. & Port.). 1955. 100.00 F. Garnier.

Dictionnaire Francais-Romaneique. Emile Missir. 1060p. (Fr. & Romanian.). 1955. 110.00 F. Klincksieck.

Dictionnaire Francais-Russe. K. Gamchina. 911p. (Fr. & Rus.). 1977. 19.95 (ISBN 0-686-92572-6, M-9066). French & Eur.

Dictionnaire Francais-Russe. K. A. Ganchina. (Fr. & Rus.). 1978. 32.85 F. MIR.

Dictionnaire Francais-Russe. Noctuel & Calmann-Levy. (Fr. & Rus.). 1978. 9.15 F. Labiche.

Dictionnaire Francais-Russe. Paul Pauliat. 473p. (Fr. & Rus.). 1976. 27.60 F. Larousse.

Dictionnaire Francais-Russe. Varvara Potozkaia. (Fr. & Rus.). 1978. 10.95 F. MIR.

Dictionnaire Francais-Russe de Mathematique. M. V. Dragnev & Victor Rosov. (Fr. & Rus.). 8.50 F. MIR.

Dictionnaire Francais-Russe de Mathematique. Roubakine. (Fr. & Rus.). 1978. 47.45 F. MIR.

Dictionnaire Francais-Russe de Medecine. Roubakine. (Fr. & Rus.). 1978. 47.45 F. MIR.

Dictionnaire Francais-Russe du Batiment. Sakharov. (Fr. & Rus.). 1976. 280.00 F. MIR.

Dictionnaire Francais-Russe Militaire. Ostapenko. (Fr. & Rus.). 1976. 45.75 F. Mir.

Dictionnaire Francais-Serbo-Croate. 632p. (Fr. , Serbo & Croatian.). pap. 19.95 (ISBN 0-686-57109-6, M-6142). French & Eur.

Dictionnaire Francais-Serbo-Croate. 632p. (Fr. & Serbo-Croatian.). 1978. 39.20 F. Vander.

Dictionnaire Francais-Swahili. 2nd ed. Charles Sacleux. 755p. (Fr. & Swahili.). 1959. 53.00 F. Institut Ethnologie.

Dictionnaire Francais-Tahitien. Mai-Arii Mai-Aru & J. Anisson du Perron. 380p. (Fr. & Tahitian.). 1973. 40.00 F. Pensee Moderne.

Dictionnaire Francais-Tahitien et Tahitien-Francais. Mai-Aru & J. Anisson du Perron. 380p. (Fr. & Tahitian.). 1973. 17.50 (ISBN 0-686-57025-1, M-6383). French & Eur.

Dictionnaire Francais-Tibetain. Giraudeau & Francis Gore. 310p. (Fr. & Tibetan.). 1956. 120.00 F. Maisonneuve, A.

Dictionnaire Francais-Tibetain (Tibet Oriental) A. Giraudeau & Francis Gore. 310p. (Fr. & Tibetian.). 1956. 49.95 (ISBN 0-686-57301-3, M-6275). French & Eur.

Dictionnaire Francais-Vietnamien. 1276p. (Fr. & Vietnamese.). 1981. 260.00 F. Maison Dictionnaire.

Dictionnaire Franco-Hongrois. (Fr. & Hungarian.). 1978. 15.00 F. Voyages.

Dictionnaire Franco-Montcellien. Kiwanis-Club. (Illus.). 117p. (Fr.). 1976. 15.00 F. Kiwanis-Club.

Dictionnaire Francois. Pierre Richelet. 1148p. (Fr.). 1973. DM.356.00 F. Olms.

Dictionnaire Francois, 2 vols. Pierre Richelet. 1040p. (Fr.). 1970. 200.00 F. Slatkine.

Dictionnaire Garzanti Francais-Italien. 2046p. (Fr. & Ital.). 1978. 108.00 F. Bordas-Dunod.

Dictionnaire Garzanti Francais-Italien, Italien-Francais. 2046p. (Fr. & Ital.). 1969. 39.95 (ISBN 0-686-57110-X, M-6143). French & Eur.

Dictionnaire Gascon-Francais du Departement du Gers. Justin E. Cenacmoncaut. 155p. (Fr.). 1971. 30.00 F. Slatkine.

Dictionnaire Gastronomique. 2nd ed. 225p. (Fr.). 1974. 22.00 F. Union Helvi.

Dictionnaire Gemeaux Francais-Allemand. (Fr. & Ger.). 19.50 F. Hatier.

Dictionnaire Gemeaux: Francais-Anglais. (Fr. & Eng.). 19.50 F. Hatier.

Dictionnaire Gemeaux: Francais-Espagnol. (Fr. & Span.). 19.50 F. Hatier.

Dictionnaire Gemeaux: Francais-Italien. (Fr. & Ital.). 30.00 F. Hatier.

Dictionnaire Genealogique des Familles Canadiennes: Depuls la Fondation de la Colonie Jusqu'a nos Jours, 7 vols. Cyprien Tanguay & Senechal. (Fr.). 1975. Can.$210.00. Elysee.

Dictionnaire General, 5 vols. Emile B. De La Chavignerie & Louis Auvray. Ed. by Robert Rosenblum. LC 78-68412. (Dictionnaire General Ser.). 2000p. 1979. Repr. of 1885 ed. lib. bdg. 303.00 (ISBN 0-8240-3539-9). Garland Pub.

Dictionnaire General & Curieux Contenant les Principaux Mots: Les Plus Usitez en la Langue Francoise. Cesar De Rochefort. 850p. (Fr.). 1972. 300.00 F. Slatkine.

Dictionnaire General de la Langue Francaise au Canada. Louis-Alexandre Belisle. (Illus.). 1487p. (Fr.). 1976. Can.$25.00. Beauchemin.

Dictionnaire General de la Langue Francaise: Commencement du 17 Siecle Jusqu'a nos Jours, 2 vols. Adolphe Hatzfeld & Arsene Darmesteter. 1468p. (Fr.). 1964. 230.00 F. Delagrave.

Dictionnaire General de la Langue Francaise du Commencement du 17e Siecle Jusqu' a Nos Jours, 2 vols. Adophe Hatzfeld & Arsene Darmesteter. 1468p. (Fr.). 1964. Set. 89.95 (ISBN 0-686-57290-4, F-134240). French & Eur.

Dictionnaire General de la Technique Industrielle: Francais-Anglais. Richard Ernst. 1080p. (Fr. & Eng.). 1982. 465.00 F. Maison Dictionnaire.

Dictionnaire General des Sciences Humaines. Georges Thines & Agnes Lempereur. 1000p. (Fr.). 1975. 135.00 (ISBN 0-686-57231-9, M-6532). French & Eur.

Dictionnaire General des Sciences Humaines. Georges Thines & Agnes Lempereur. 1000p. (Fr.). 1975. 350.00 F. Delarge.

Dictionnaire Geographique, Historique & Literaire: La Perse & des Contrees Adjacentes, 8 vols. Achille Barbier De Meynard. 640p. (Fr.). 1970. fl.96.00. Philo Pr.

Dictionnaire Geographique, Historique & Statistique des Communes: Franche-Comte & des Hameaux qui en Dependent, 6 vols. A. Rousset. 3602p. (Fr.). 1970. 600.00 F. Guenegaud.

Dictionnaire Geographique, Historique, Descriptif, Archeologique des Pelegrinages, 2 vols. L. De Sivry. Ed. by J. P. Migne. (Encyclopedie Theologique Ser.: Vols. 43-44). 1328p. (Fr.). Repr. of 1851 ed. lib. bdg. 169.00x (ISBN 0-89241-248-8). Caratzas Pub Co.

Dictionnaire Geologique: Francais-Russe. V. Dybovskaia & I. Kirillova. 406p. (Fr. & Rus.). 1958. leatherette 4.95 (ISBN 0-686-92570-X, M-9099). French & Eur.

Dictionnaire Grec-Francais. Anatole Bailly. 2230p. (Gr.-Fr.). 1967. pap. 95.00 (ISBN 0-686-56907-5, M-6020). French & Eur.

Dictionnaire Grec-Francais. Anatole Bailly. 2230p. (Gr. & Fr.). 1967. 123.00 F. Hachette-Jeunesse.

Dictionnaire Grec-Francais. Georgin. (Gr. & Fr.). 1978. 30.00 F. Hatier.

Dictionnaire Grec-Francais. Ch. Georgin. (Gr. & Fr.). pap. 14.95 (ISBN 0-686-57194-0, M-6268). French & Eur.

Dictionnaire Grec-Francais. Victor Magnien & M. Lacroix. 2168p. (Fr. & Gr.). 1969. 57.50 (ISBN 0-686-57024-3, M-6382). French & Eur.

Dictionnaire Grec-Francais. Victor Magnien & M. Lacroix. 2168p. (Gr. & Fr.). 1969. 157.00 F. Belin.

Dictionnaire Grec-Francais. Emile Pessoneaux. 896p. (Fr. & Gr.). 1953. 35.95 (ISBN 0-686-57071-5, M-6443). French & Eur.

Dictionnaire Grec-Francais. Emile Pessonneaux. 896p. (Gr. & Fr.). 1953. 90.00 F. Belin.

Dictionnaire Grec Moderne Francais. Hubert Pernot. 544p. (Gr. & Fr.). 1970. 25.50 F. Garnier.

Dictionnaire Hachette de la Langue Francaise. C. Setton et al. 1813p. (Fr.). 1980. 65.00 (ISBN 0-686-97331-3, M-9373). French & Eur.

Dictionnaire Hagiographique, 2 vols. L. M. Petin. Ed. by J. P. Migne. (Encyclopedie Theologique Ser.: Vols. 40-41). 1580p. (Fr.). Repr. of 1850 ed. lib. bdg. 240.00x (ISBN 0-89241-246-1). Caratzas Pub Co.

Dictionnaire Hatier-Beauchemin: Francais-Latin. Jean E. De Cahors. (Fr. & Lat.). 1957. Can.$2.95. Beauchemin.

Dictionnaire Hatier-Beauchemin: Latin-Francais. A. Gariel. (Lat. & Fr.). 1960. Can.$2.95. Beauchemin.

Dictionnaire Hebrau-Francais, 2 vols. Joseph Hadar. 832p. (Hebrew & Fr.). 1973. IL.18.70 (2114). Massada Pr.

Dictionnaire Hebreu-Francais. Rabbin Marchand-Ennery. 302p. (Hebrew & Fr.). 1976. 18.00 F. Colbo.

Dictionnaire Historique. Prosper Marchand. 702p. (Fr.). DM.228.00. Olms.

Dictionnaire Historique & Artistique de la Rose. Abel Belmont. (Illus.). 207p. (Fr.). 30.00 F. Lechevalier.

Dictionnaire Historique & Critique, 16 vols. Pierre Bayle. 9546p. (Fr.). 1969. 1800.00 F. Slatkine.

Dictionnaire Historique & Critique. Pierre Bayle. (Illus.). 236p. (Fr.). 1974. 15.00 F. Sociales.

Dictionnaire Historique & Geographique de la Province de Bretagne, 2 vols. Jean Ogee et al. 1520p. (Fr.). 1973. 450.00 F. Floch.

Dictionnaire Historique & Heraldique, 2 vols. C. P. Dayre De Mailhol. 2120p. (Fr.). write for info. Slatkine.

Dictionnaire Historique & Heraldique. D. De Mailhol. (Fr.). write for info. Fac.

Dictionnaire Historique & Topographique de la Ancienne & Moderne, 2 vols. E. Garcin. 1232p. (Fr.). write for info. Chantemerle.

Dictionnaire Historique, Archeologique, Philologique, Chronologique Geographique et Literal de la Bible, 4 vols. A. Calmet. Ed. by J. P. Migne. (Encyclopedie Theologique Ser. (First Series): Vols. 1-4). 2602p. (Fr.). Repr. of 1846 ed. lib. bdg. 332.50x (ISBN 0-89241-231-3). Caratzas Pub Co.

Dictionnaire Historique, Chronologique, Geographique, Genealogique, Heraldique, Juridique, Politique & Botanographique du Daup, 2 vols. Guy Allard & Granoble. 754p. (Fr.). 1970. 150.00 F. Slatkine.

Dictionnaire Historique De la France, 2 Vols. 2nd ed. Ludovic Lalanne. (Fr.). 1967. Repr. of 1877 ed. 93.00 (ISBN 0-8337-1985-8). B Franklin.

Dictionnaire Historique de la France. Ludovic Lalanne. 1971p. (Fr.). 1974. 350.00 F. Slatkine.

Dictionnaire Historique de la France, 2 vols. Ludovic Lalanne. 1884p. (Fr.). 1978. 300.00 F. Slatkine.

Dictionnaire Historique de la France Contenant l'histoire Civile, Politique, 2 vols. Ludovic Lalanne. (Fr.). 1967. 65.00. Lenox.

Dictionnaire Historique de la Medecine Ancienne & Moderne. N. F. Eloy. (Fr.). 1978. DM.138.00 F. Olms.

Dictionnaire Historique de la Terminologie Optique des Grecs. Charles Mugler. 460p. (Fr.). 1964. pap. 110.00 (ISBN 0-686-57055-3, M-6421). French & Eur.

Dictionnaire Historique de la Terminologique Optique des Grecs. Charles Mugler. 460p. (Gr.). 1964. 280.00 F. Klincksieck.

Dictionnaire Historique de la Ville de Paris & de ses Environs, 4 vols. Magny Hurtaut. 3084p. (Fr.). 1977. 560.00 F. Minkoff Repr.

Dictionnaire Historique Des Arts, Metiers & Professions Exerces Dans Paris Depuis Le Treizieme Siecle. Afred L. Franklin. (Biblio. & Ref. Ser.: No. 198). (Fr.). 1968. Repr. of 1906 ed. 49.00 (ISBN 0-8337-1231-4); 40.00 (ISBN 0-685-06747-5). B Franklin.

Dictionnaire Historique des Arts, Metlers & Professions Exerces dans Paris Depuis le Treizieme Siecle. Alfred Franklin. 882p. (Fr.). 40.00. Lenox.

Dictionnaire Historique des Arts: Metiers & Professions Exerces dans Paris, Depuis 13 Siecle. Alfred Franklin. 882p. (Fr.). 1977. 230.00 F. Lafitte Repr.

Dictionnaire Historique des Arts, Metiers & Professions: Exercees dans Paris Depuis le 13 Siecle. Alfred L. Franklin. 856p. (Fr.). 1906. DM.138.00. Olms Verlag.

Dictionnaire Historique des Fiefs: Chateilenies & Paroisses de la Haute & de la Basse Auvergne. G. M. Chabrol. 1060p. (Fr.). 1973. 330.00 F. Guenegaud.

Dictionnaire historique des monnoies tant anciennes que modernes. M. De Salzade. LC 79-359296. (Illus.). 187p. (Fr.). 1978. 32.00 F. Thimonier.

Dictionnaire Historique des Sciences Physiques et Naturelles. L. F. Jehan. Ed. by J. P. Migne. (Troisieme et Derniere Encyclopedie Theologique Ser.: Vol. 30). 654p. (Fr.). Repr. of 1857 ed. lib. bdg. 85.00x (ISBN 0-89241-309-3). Caratzas Pub Co.

Dictionnaire Historique, Literaire & Statistique, 2 vols. 1620p. (Fr.). 1973. write for info. Lafitte Repr.

Dictionnaire Historique, Stylistique, Rhetorique, Etomologique, de la Litterature Erotique. Pierre Guiraud. LC 377481. 639p. (Fr.). 1978. 90.00 F (ISBN 2-228-12040-5). Payot.

Dictionnaire Homeopatheque d'Urgerce. 11th ed. 765p. (Fr.). 1978. 35.00 (ISBN 0-686-56732-3, M-6461). French & Eur.

Dictionnaire Homeopathique d'urgence. 11th ed. 765p. (Fr.). 1978. write for info. Ste. Ind. D'imprimere.

Dictionnaire Humoristique. Maurice Maloux. (Fr.). write for info. Albin-Michel.

Dictionnaire Iconologique. (Fr.). 1972. write for info. Minkoff Repr.

Dictionnaire Illustre de la Langue Russe: Francais-Espagnol-Russe. Anatoll Chtchoukine. (Fr., Span. & Rus.). write for info. Mir.

Dictionnaire Illustre de l'Automobile "Kluwer," en 6 Langues. C. Blok & W. Jezewski. 504p. (Fr., Eng., Ger., Ital., Rus. & Dutch.). 1979. 145.00 (ISBN 0-686-56923-7, M-6039). French & Eur.

Dictionnaire Illustre des Merveliles Naturelles. (Illus.). 464p. (Fr.). write for info. Reader's Digest.

Dictionnaire Illustre des Petites Voitures. (Illus.). 1976p. (Fr.). write for info. Rossel Edns.

Dictionnaire Illustre: Francais-Russe. A. Kolesnikova & L. Lulchak. 856p. (Fr. & Rus.). 1977. 17.95 (ISBN 0-686-92566-1, M-9070). French & Eur.

Dictionnaire Illustre Multilingue de l'Architecture du Proche Orient Ancien. Ed. by Oliver Aurenche. LC 78-392938. (Illus.). 391p. (Fr.). 1977. 250.00 F. Boccard.

Dictionnaire Illustre Multilinque De L'architecture du Procher-Orient Ancien. Olivier Aureneche. 392p. (Fr.). 1978. 125.00 (ISBN 0-686-56729-3, M-6017). French & Eur.

Dictionnaire Image d'enfants. (Illus.). 14p. (Fr.). 1974. write for info. Mesure.

Dictionnaire Imaginaire de Queiques Poetes Reels. (Fr.). write for info. De Feu.

Dictionnaire Indicateur des Rues & Places. Periaux. (Illus.). 454p. (Fr.). 1977. write for info. Lafitte Repr.

Dictionnaire Initiatique. (Fr.). write for info. Herve-Masson.

Dictionnaire Initiatique. Herre Masson. 376p. (Fr.). 1970. 25.00 (ISBN 0-686-57040-5, M-6400). French & Eur.

Dictionnaire Initiatique. Herve Masson. (Fr.). 1970. write for info. Belfond.

Dictionnaire Insolite. Jacques Languirand. (Fr.). write for info. Jour, Ed. Du.

Dictionnaire International D'abreviations Scientigiques & Techniques. Michel Azzaretti. LC 79-345548. iv, 290p. (Eng. & Fr.). 1978. 120.00 F (ISBN 2-85608-003-0). Maison Dictionnaire.

Dictionnaire International d'abreviations Scientifiques et Techniques. M. Azzaretti. 300p. (Eng., Fr., Span., Ital. & Ger.). 1978. 120.00 F. Maison Dictionnaire.

Dictionnaire International d'abreviation Scientifiques et Techniques. M. Azzaretti. 300p. (Eng., Fr., Span., Ital., Ger. & Rus.). 1978. 150.00 F. Maison Dictionnaire.

Dictionnaire International de Metallurgie, Mineralogie, Geologie et Industries Extractives, 2 vols. Angelo Cagnacci-Schwicker. 1530p. (Fr.). 1969. Set. 95.00 (ISBN 0-686-56933-4, M-6054). French & Eur.

Dictionnaire International de Science. (Fr.). 1971. write for info. E. M. E.

Dictionnaire International des Arts. Pierre Cabanne. LC 80-106368. (Illus., Fr.). 1979. write for info (ISBN 2-040-10638-3). Bordas.

Dictionnaire International des Arts, 2 vols. Pierre Cabanne. 1456p. (Fr.). 1979. 135.00 set (Dist. by Continental Bk Co). Bordas.
Dictionnaire International des Termes Literaires. Robert Escarpit. 86p. (Fr.). 1973. write for info. Mouton-De.
Dictionnaire International du Tourisme: Allemand-Anglais-Espagnol-Italien-Neerlandai. 3rd ed. 325p. (Ger. , Eng. , Span. , Ital. & Dutch.). 1968. write for info. Acad Intl Tour.
Dictionnaire International Electrotechnique: Francais-Russe-Anglais-Allemand-Italien-Suedois-Hollandais-Polonais. (Fr. , Rus. , Eng. , Ger. , Ital. , Swedish, Dutch & Pol.). write for info. Mir.
Dictionnaire International Electrotechnique: Francais-Russe-Anglais-Allemand-Espagnol-Suedois-Hollandais-Polonais. (Fr. , Rus. , Eng. , Ger. , Span. , Swedish, Dutch & Pol.). write for info. Mir.
Dictionnaire Intime de la Femme. Genevieve Roux. 348p. (Fr.). write for info. Privat.
Dictionnaire Inverse de la Langue Francais. (Illus.). 504p. (Fr.). 1965. write for info. Mouton-De.
Dictionnaire Inverse De la Langue Francaise. Alphonse Juilland. (Janua Linguarum, Ser. Practica: No. 7). (Fr.). 1965. text ed. 81.00x (ISBN 90-2790-626-2). Mouton.
Dictionnaire Inverse de la Langue Russe. (Fr. & Rus.). write for info. Mir.
Dictionnaire inverse de l'ancien francais. Ralph De Gorog. LC 81-18874. (Medieval & Renaissance Texts & Studies: No. 4). 256p. (Fr.). 1981. 13.50 (ISBN 0-86698-010-5). Medieval & Renaissance NY.
Dictionnaire Italien-Francais. 640p. (Ital. & Fr.). write for info. Larousse FR.
Dictionnaire Italien-Francais. Jacqueline Herselin. (Ital. & Fr.). 1969. write for info. Garnier.
Dictionnaire Italien-Francais. Denis Rouede. (Illus.). 1256p. (Ital. & Fr.). 1970. write for info. Garnier.
Dictionnaire Italien-Francais et Francais-Italien. Pierre Rouede & Denise Rouede. 1256p. (Fr. & Ital.). 1970. 25.00 (ISBN 0-686-57211-4, M-6493). French & Eur.
Dictionnaire Italien-Francais, Francais-Italien de la Langue d'Aujourd'hui. Ghiotti et al. (Fr. & Ital.). 1976. 27.50 (ISBN 0-686-57196-7, M-6270). French & Eur.
Dictionnaire Jersias-Francais, 2 tomes. Le Maistre. (Fr.). Set. 86.50 (ISBN 0-685-36662-6). French & Eur.
Dictionnaire Juridique. (Fr. & Arabic.). 40.00 (ISBN 0-86685-303-0). Intl Bk Ctr.
Dictionnaire Juridique. M. Matteucci. (Fr.-It.). 39.95 (ISBN 0-686-57042-1, M-6402). French & Eur.
Dictionnaire Juridique & Economique Francais-Allemand & Allemand Francais, 2 vols. 4th ed. M Doucet. Ed. by E. W. Klaus. (Fr. & Ger.). 8600.00 F. Bruylant.
Dictionnaire Juridique & Economique Francais-Allemand & Allemand-Francais, Vol. 1. 4th ed. M. Doucet. Ed. by K. Fleck. (Fr. & Ger.). 1980. 1800.00 F. Bruylant.
Dictionnaire Juridique & Economique Francias-Allemand & Allemand-Francais, Vol. 2. M. Doucet. Ed. by K. Fleck. (Fr. & Ger.). 1980. 1140.00 F. Bruylant.
Dictionnaire Juridique & Economique, 1: Francais-Allemand. 2nd ed. (Fr. & Ger.). 1967. 81.00 F. Litec.
Dictionnaire Juridique et Economique: Anglais-Francais Francais-Anglais. Doucet. 770p. (Eng. & Fr.). 1979. 350.00 F. Maison Dictionnaire.
Dictionnaire Juridique et Economique, 1: Francais-Allemand. 2nd ed. Michel Douret. (Fr. & Ger.). 1967. 39.95 (ISBN 0-686-57122-3, M-6170). French & Eur.
Dictionnaire Juridique Flammand-Francais. Jules Brassine. (Flemish & Fr.). 252.00 F. Bruylant.
Dictionnaire Juridique Francais-Allemand, Allemand-Francais. Hugo Neumann. Ed. by Thomas A. Quemner. 592p. (Fr.-Ger.). 1964. 59.95 (ISBN 0-686-57058-8, M-6425). French & Eur.
Dictionnaire Juridique, Francais-Espagnol, Espagnol-Francais. Luis Jordana de Pozas & Olivier Merlin. 608p. (Fr. & Span.). 1968. 45.00 (ISBN 0-686-57112-6, M-6148). French & Eur.
Dictionnaire Juridique: Francais-Espagnol. Olivier Merlin. 608p. (Fr. & Span.). 1968. 100.00 F. Navarre.
Dictionnaire Juridique: Francais-Italien. (Fr. & Ital.). 80.00 F. Navarre.
Dictionnaire Juridique: Frances-Allemand. Thomas A. Quemner. 592p. (Fr. & Ger.). 1964. 130.00 F. Navarre.
Dictionnaire Juridique: Italien-Francais Francais-Italien. Giovanni Tortora. 700p. (Ital. & Fr.). 1982. 240.00 F. Maison Dictionnaire.
Dictionnaire Kikongo-Francais. Karl Edward Laman. 1278p. (Fr.). 1936. 24.00. Gregg.
Dictionnaire Kurde-Francais. Auguste Jaba. LC 76-472421. xviii, 463p. (Fr. & Kurdish.). 1975. DM.98.00 (ISBN 3-7648-0409-2). Biblio-Verlag.
Dictionnaire Laitier: Francais, Allemand, Anglais. Jacques Casalis. (Fr., Ger. & Eng.). 1963. 49.95 (ISBN 0-686-56941-5, M-6063). French & Eur.
Dictionnaire Laitier: Francais-Allemand-Anglais. Jacques Casalis. (Fr., Ger & Eng.). 132.00 F. Litec.
Dictionnaire Laitier: French-English-French. J. F. Boudier & F. M. Luquet. 220p. (Fr. & Eng.). 1981. leatherette 69.95 (ISBN 2-85206-092-2, M-9627). French & Eur.
Dictionnaire Languedocien-Francais. Adelin Moulis. (Fr.). 1978. 75.00 F. Moulis, Ad.
Dictionnaire Laotien Francais. Theodore Guignard. 1034p. (Laotian & Fr.). 1971. 28.00. Gregg.
Dictionnaire Laotien-Francais, 2 vols. Marc Reinhorm. (Laotian & Fr.). 215.00 F. C. N. R. S.
Dictionnaire Laotien-Francais, 2 vols. Marc Reinhorn. 2000p. (Fr. & Laotian.). 1970. Set. 85.00 (ISBN 0-686-57204-1, M-6481). French & Eur.
Dictionnaire Laotien-Francais, 2 vols. Marc Reinhorn. 2000p. (Fr. & Laotian.). 1970. 300.00 F (ISBN 2-22201-295-3). CNRS.
Dictionnaire Larousse Bilingue de Poche. (Fr. & Eng.). 1968. 3.95 (Dist. by Continental Bk Co). Larousse.
Dictionnaire Larousse Bilingue de Poche: Francais-Allemand. 500p. (Fr. & Ger.). 11.70 F. Larousse FR.
Dictionnaire Larousse Bilingue de Poche: Francais-Anglais. 500p. (Fr. & Eng.). pap. 11.70 F. Larousse FR.
Dictionnaire Larousse Bilingue de Poche: Francais-Espagnol. 500p. (Fr. & Span.). 11.70 F. Larousse FR.
Dictionnaire Larousse Bilingue de Poche: Francais-Italien. (Fr. & Ital.). pap. 11.70 F. Larousse FR.
Dictionnaire Larousse de Poche. (Fr.). pap. 10.50 F. L. G. F.
Dictionnaire Larousse de Poche. new ed. (Fr.). 1967. pap. 10.00 F. Larousse FR.
Dictionnaire Larousse: Francais-Allemand. (Fr. & Ger.). pap. 10.50 F. L. G. F.
Dictionnaire Larousse: Francais-Anglais. (Fr. & Eng.). pap. 10.50 F. L. G. F.
Dictionnaire Larousse: Francais-Espagnol. (Fr. & Span.). pap. 10.50 F. L. G. F.
Dictionnaire Larousse: Francais-Italien. (Fr. & Ital.). pap. 10.50 F. L. G. F.
Dictionnaire Larousse Moderne Francais-Anglais. (Illus.). 1552p. (Fr. & Eng.). 1968. Can.$7.95. Edns Francaises.
Dictionnaire Latin-Francais. Henri Bornecque & Fernand Cauet. 560p. (Fr. & Lat.). 1953. 39.95 (ISBN 0-686-56926-1, M-6044). French & Eur.
Dictionnaire Latin-Francais. Felix Gaffiot. (Lat. & Fr.). 1967. pap. 32.50 (ISBN 0-686-57187-8, M-6259). French & Eur.
Dictionnaire Latin-Francais. Felix Gaffiot. (Lat. & Fr.). 1967. 83.00 F. Hachette.
Dictionnaire Latin-Francais. Geoffroy. 1200p. (Lat. & Fr.). 21.40 F. Delalain.
Dictionnaire Latin-Francais. Henri Goelzer. 704p. (Lat. & Fr.). 1966. 11.50 F. Garnier.
Dictionnaire Latin-Francais. Henri Goelzer. 792p. (Lat. & Fr.). 1967. pap. 21.00 F. Garnier.
Dictionnaire Latin-Francais. Henri Goelzer. 734p. (Lat. & Fr.). pap. 35.50 F. Garnier.
Dictionnaire Latin-Francais. Charles Lebaigue. 1382p. (Fr. & Lat.). 33.50 (ISBN 0-686-56999-7, M-6340). French & Eur.
Dictionnaire les termes juridiques en quatre langues: Francais-Neerlandais-Anglais-Allemand. 3rd ed. E. LeDocte. 800p. (Fr., Dutch, Eng. & Ger.). 1982. 520.00 F. Maison Dictionnaire.
Dictionnaire Liegeois. Jean Haust. (Illus., Walloon.). 1933. write for info. Vaillant-Carmanne.
Dictionnaire Lilliput Bilingue Francais-Allemand. 640p. (Fr. & Ger.). 1961. 7.50 F. Larousse FR.
Dictionnaire Lilliput Bilingue Francais-Anglais. 640p. (Fr. & Eng.). 7.50 F. Larousse FR.
Dictionnaire Lilliput Bilingue Francais-Danois. 640p. (Fr. & Danish.). 7.50 F. Larousse FR.
Dictionnaire Lilliput Bilingue Francais-Espagnol. 640p. (Fr. & Span.). 7.50 F. Larousse FR.
Dictionnaire Lilliput Bilingue Francais-Italien. 640p. (Fr. & Ital.). 7.50 F. Larousse FR.
Dictionnaire Lilliput Bilingue Francais-Portugais. 640p. (Fr. & Port.). 7.50 F. Larousse FR.
Dictionnaire Lilliput Bilingue Francais-Neerlandais. 640p. (Fr. & Dutch.). 7.50 F. Larousse FR.
Dictionnaire Liturgique, Historique et Theorique de Plainchant et de Musique d'Eglise. M. J. D'Ortigue. LC 79-155353. (Music Ser). (Fr.). 1971. Repr. of 1854 ed. lib. bdg. 75.00 (ISBN 0-306-70165-0). Da Capo.
Dictionnaire Magique. Walt Disney. (Illus., Fr.). 1978. 19.50 F. Nathan.
Dictionnaire Marabout des Mots Croises, 1. L. Noel-Henrard & M. Noel-Henrard. (Fr.). 17.50 F. Marabout.
Dictionnaire Marabout des Mots Croises, 2. L. Noel-Henrard & M. Noel-Henrard. (Fr.). 17.50 F. Marabout.
Dictionnaire Marabout du Bricolage. Francis Genette. (Illus.). 414p. (Fr.). 16.50 F. Marabout.
Dictionnaire Marabout Universite. (Fr.). 19.50 F. Marabout.
Dictionnaire Marabout Universite, 3 vols. (Fr.). 34.50 F. Marabout.
Dictionnaire Marabout Universite: La Sociologie, Vol. 1. (Fr.). 11.50 F. Marabout.
Dictionnaire Marabout Universite: La Sociologie, Vol. 2. (Fr.). 11.50 F. Marabout.
Dictionnaire Marabout Universite: La Sociologie, Vol. 3. (Fr.). 11.50 F. Marabout.
Dictionnaire Medical. Emile Veillon & Albert Noble. 1337p. (Eng., Ger. & Fr.). 1977. 400.00 F. Masson.
Dictionnaire Medical. Emmanuel Veillon & Albert Nobel. (Fr.). 1969. 132.00 F. Hans.
Dictionnaire Medical Illustre de Semiologie Patronymique. Andre Cohen. LC 79-129051. 213p. (Fr.). 1979. write for info. (ISBN 2-224-00513-X). Maloine.
Dictionnaire Medical Illustre De Semiologie Patronymique. (Fr.). 1979. 35.00 (ISBN 0-686-57113-4, M-6149). French & Eur.
Dictionnaire Medicine, Clinique, Pharmacologique et Therapeutique. 2nd ed. Alain Blacque-Belair. 1938p. (Fr.). 1978. 115.00 (ISBN 0-686-56920-2, M-6036). French & Eur.
Dictionnaire Memento D'electronique. 3rd ed. Raymond Brosset & Pierre Fondaneche. 512p. (Fr.). 1969. 39.95 (ISBN 0-686-56929-6, M-6047). French & Eur.
Dictionnaire Memento d'electronique. 3rd ed. Raymond Brosset & Pierre Fondaneche. 512p. (Fr.). 1969. 95.00 F. Bordas-Dunod.
Dictionnaire Meteorologique: Francais-Russe. P. V. Silvestrov. 191p. (Fr. & Rus.). 1978. leatherette 9.95 (ISBN 0-686-92563-7, M-9122). French & Eur.
Dictionnaire Minier Russe-Francais. (Fr. & Rus.). 1973. pap. 25.00 (ISBN 0-686-56770-6, M-6150). French & Eur.
Dictionnaire Minier Russe-Francais. (Rus. & Fr.). 1973. 45.00 F. France, Centre Et. Charbonnage.
Dictionnaire Moderne Francais-Arabe. 868p. (Fr. & Arabic.). 1979. leatherette 29.95 (ISBN 0-686-97332-1, M-9749). French & Eur.
Dictionnaire Moderne: Francaise-Espagnol, Espagnol-Francais. Ed. by R. Garcia-Pelayo. (Fr. & Span.). 35.00 (ISBN 2-03-020601-6, S-32371). French & Eur.
Dictionnaire moderne Larousse francais-anglais et anglais-francais. new rev. ed. M. M. Dubois. (Fr. & Eng.). 29.95 (ISBN 0-88332-003-7, 3769). Larousse.
Dictionnaire moderne Larousse, francais-allemand et allemand-francais. P. Grappin. (Fr. & Ger.). 39.95 (ISBN 2-03-020603-2, 3778). Larousse.
Dictionnaire moderne Larousse, francais-espagnol et espagnol-francais. R. Garcia-Pelayo & J. Testas. (Span. & Fr.). 39.95 (ISBN 2-03-020601-6, 3773). Larousse.
Dictionnaire Moderne "Saturne". M. M. Dubois. (Fr. & Eng.). 1979. 27.00 (Dist. by Continental Bk Co). Larousse.
Dictionnaire Moderne "Saturne". R. Garcia-Pelayo. (Span. & Eng.). 1976. 35.00 (Dist. by Continental Bk Co). Larousse.
Dictionnaire Moderne Saturne: Francais-Anglais, Anglais-Francais. 10th ed. Marie-Marguerite Dubois. 1552p. (Fr. & Eng.). 1972. 29.95 (ISBN 0-686-57126-6, M-6174). French & Eur.
Dictionnaire Moderne Saturne: Francais-Allemand. 9th ed. P. Grappin. 1744p. (Fr. & Ger.). 1971. 70.00 F. Larousse FR.
Dictionnaire Moderne Saturne: Francais-Anglais. 10th ed. Marie M. Dubois. 1552p. (Fr. & Eng.). 1972. 70.00 F. Larousse FR.
Dictionnaire Moderne Saturne: Francais-Espagnol. 3rd ed. Ramon Garcia-Pelayo & Jean Testas. 1758p. (Fr. & Span.). 1971. 70.00 F. Larousse FR.
Dictionnaire Moderne: Slovene-French-Slovene. A. Grad. 745p. (Slovenian & Fr.). 1978. leatherette 14.95 (ISBN 0-686-92561-0, M-9705). French & Eur.
Dictionnaire Montagnais Francais. Antoine Silvy. 192p. (Fr.). 1974. 9.95 F. Quebec P. U.
Dictionnaire Mytho-Hermetique. Antoine J. Pernety. (Fr.). pap. 25.00 (ISBN 0-686-57069-3, M-6441). French & Eur.
Dictionnaire Mytho-Hermetique. Antoine J. Pernety. (Fr.). 51.50 F. Retz.
Dictionnaire Mytho-hermetique: La Symbolique du Feu. Jean P. Bayard. 232p. (Fr.). 1973. 39.00 F. Payot.
Dictionnaire Mythohermetique. Antoine J. Pernety. (Illus.). 392p. (Fr.). 1972. 49.00 F. Denoel.
Dictionnaire mythologie grecque et romaine. J. Schmidt. (Illus., Fr.). pap. 8.50 (ISBN 2-03-075408-0, 3728). Larousse.
Dictionnaire National des Communes de France. 20th ed. Dominique De Fleurian et al. (Illus.). 1150p. (Fr.). 1977. 98.00 F. Albin-Michel.

Dictionnaire National des Communes de France. rev. ed. 1416p. (Fr.). 1977. 98.00 F. Albin-Michel.
Dictionnaire National des Communes de France. 20th ed. Dominique de Fleurian. Ed. by Jacques Simond & Jacques Frenay. 1150p. (Fr.). 1977. 39.95 (ISBN 0-686-57184-3, M-6254). French & Eur.
Dictionnaire Neerlandais-Francais. 640p. (Dutch & Fr.). 7.50 F. Larousse FR.
Dictionnaire Normatif Limousin-Francais. Gerard Gonfroy. LC 77-479648. 229p. (Fr.). 1976. write for info. Lemouzi.
Dictionnaire Normatif Limousin-Francais. Gerard Gonfroy. 300p. (Fr.). 1972. 34.00 F. Lemouzi.
Dictionnaire oiseaux. Michel Cuisin. (Illus., Fr.). pap. 8.50 (ISBN 0-685-13879-8, 3729). Larousse.
Dictionnaire Ordos, 3 Vols in 1. 2nd ed. Antoine Mostaert. 1968. Repr. of 1944 ed. 160.00 (ISBN 0-384-40225-9). Johnson Repr.
Dictionnaire Orthographique. Victor Bailly. 56p. (Fr.). 1968. 46.00 F. Plantyn Edns.
Dictionnaire Orthographique. Bojana Lamizet & Bernard Lamizet. (Fr.). 1974. 11.50 F. Garnier.
Dictionnaire Orthographique de la Langue Russe. Barkhudarova. 1040p. (Rus.). 1963. 15.30 F. Mir.
Dictionnaire Orthographique du Vocabulaire de Base. 324p. (Fr.). 1.20 F. Desoer.
Dictionnaire Orthographique Garnier. new ed. Maurice Rat. 384p. (Fr.). 14.00 F. Garnier.
Dictionnaire Orthographique Suivi d'Une Liste des Verbes Irreguliers. Bojana Lamizet. LC 75-517895. 411p. (Fr.). 1975. 11.50 F. Garnier.
Dictionnaire Patois. Lucien Guillemaut. 351p. (Fr.). 1970. 60.00 F. Slatkine.
Dictionnaire Patois-Francais a l'usage du Departement du Tarn & des Departements Circonvoisins. Leger Gary. (Fr.). 1978. 150.00 F. Lafitte Repr.
Dictionnaire Patois-Francais du Departement de l'Aveyron. Aime R. Vayssier. 704p. (Fr.). 1971. 120.00 F. Slatkine.
Dictionnaire Petrolier des Techniques de Diagraphie, Forage & Production: Russe-Francais-Anglais-Allemand. Sonia Ketchian. (Illus.). 376p. (Rus., Fr., Eng. & Ger.). 1965. 160.00 F. Technip.
Dictionnaire Petrolier des Techniques de Diagraphique, Forage et Production. Sonia Ketchian. 376p. (Rus., Fr., Eng. & Ger., Oil Industry Dictionary of Diagraphy, Sinking, and Production Techniques). 1965. 65.00 (ISBN 0-686-56756-0, M-6326). French & Eur.
Dictionnaire Phonetique d'Orthographe. Francois Gallet. (Fr.). 1978. 67.50 F. PenseeUniv.
Dictionnaire Pittoresque & Historique: Ou Description d'architecture, Peinture, Sculpture, Gravure, 2 vols. Herbert. (Fr.). 1972. 150.00 F. Minkoff Repr.
Dictionnaire Politique & Diplomatique. 3rd ed. P. Sandahl & L. De Bea. (Fr.). 1976. 340.00 F. Bruylant.
Dictionnaire Politique & Diplomatique. Pierre Sandahl & Louise De Bea. 194p. (Fr.). 1976. 28.00 F. Litec.
Dictionnaire Politique et Diplomatique. Pierre Sandahl & Louise de Bea. 194p. (Fr.). 1976. pap. 14.95 (ISBN 0-686-57214-9, M-6503). French & Eur.
Dictionnaire Polonais-Francais. 1076p. (Pol. & Fr.). 1978. 55.80 F. Vander.
Dictionnaire Portatif de Peinture, Sculpture & Gravure. Antoine Joseph Pernety. (Fr.). 1972. 140.00 F. Minkoff Repr.
Dictionnaire Portugais-Francais. Ersilio Cardoso. 544p. (Port. & Fr.). 1978. 11.00 F. Garnier.
Dictionnaire Portugais-Francais. Ersillo Cardoso. 1820p. (Port. & Fr.). 1963. 58.40 F. Garnier.
Dictionnaire Portugais-Francais. Domingos De Azevedo. 1500p. (Port. & Fr.). 1978. 100.00 F. Garnier.
Dictionnaire Portugais-Francais. 640p. (Port. & Fr.). 1978. 7.50 F. Larousse.
Dictionnaire Poucet Allemand-Francais. Ersillo Cardoso. (Ger. & Fr.). 1978. 5.15 F. Hatier.
Dictionnaire Poucet Anglais-Francais. (Eng. & Fr.). 5.15 F. Hatier.
Dictionnaire Poucet Espagnol-Francais. (Span. & Fr.). 1978. pap. 5.15 F. Hatier.
Dictionnaire Poucet Francais-Allemand. (Fr. & Ger.). 1978. pap. 5.15 F. Hatier.
Dictionnaire Poucet Francais-Anglais. (Fr. & Eng.). 1978. pap. 5.15 F. Hatier.
Dictionnaire pour Ingenieurs et Techniciens: Francais-Espagnol, Espagnol-Francais. L. Carcamo. 1106p. (Fr. & Span.). 1981. 95.00 (ISBN 0-686-92423-1, M-7669). French & Eur.
Dictionnaire Pour l'Architecture, le Batiment et les Materiaux de Construction, 2 vols. 820p. (Ger. & Fr.). 1977. band I 236.00 (ISBN 3-7625-0786-4, M-7095). French & Eur.
Dictionnaire Pour l'Architecture, le Batiment et les Materiaux de Construction, 2 vols. 688p. (Ger. & Fr.). 1979. band II 236.00 (ISBN 3-7625-0787-2, M-7096). French & Eur.
Dictionnaire pour L'Architecture, le Batiment et les Mateiaux de Construction: Band I, Deutsch-Franzosisch. 820p. (Ger. & Fr.). 1980. DM.290.00 (ISBN 3-7625-0787-2). Bauverlag.
Dictionnaire pour l'Architecture, le Batiment et les Materiaux de Constrction: Band II, Franzosisch-Deutsch. 688p. (Fr. & Ger.). 1979. DM.290.00 (ISBN 3-7625-0787-2). Bauverlag.
Dictionnaire pour l'Architecture le Batiment et les Materiaux de Construction: Allemand-Francais, Vol. 1. Bucksch. 819p. (Ger. & Fr.). 1977. 930.00 F. Maison Dictionnaire.
Dictionnaire pour l'architecture le Batiment et les Materiaux de Construction: Francais-Allemand, Vol. 2. Bucksch. 675p. (Fr. & Ger.). 1979. 930.00 F. Maison Dictionnaire.
Dictionnaire Pour L'Ecole: Mes 10,000 Mots. M. Didler. (Fr.). 1977. 14.95 (ISBN 0-8120-5207-2). Barron.
Dictionnaire pour les Travaux Publics & l'equipement des Chantiers de Construction. 5th ed. 420p. (Eng. & Fr.). 1976. DM.38.00 (ISBN 3-7625-0533-0). Bauverlag.
Dictionnaire pour les Travaux Publics & l'equipement des Chantiers de Construction. 5th ed. 548p. (Fr. & Eng.). 1976. DM.48.00 (ISBN 3-7625-0534-9). Bauverlag.
Dictionnaire Pour les Travaux Publics et l'Equipement des Chartiers de Construction, 2 vols. 875p. (Ger. & Fr.). 1976. leatherette, band I 112.00 (ISBN 3-7625-0379-6, M-7097). French & Eur.
Dictionnaire Pour les Travaux Publics et l'Equipement des Chartiers de Construction, 2 vols. 911p. (Ger. & Fr.). 1978. leatherette, band II 112.00 (ISBN 3-7625-0999-9, M-7098). French & Eur.
Dictionnaire pour les Travaux Publics, le Batiment et l'Equipement des Chantiers de Construction. 7th ed. Hector Bucksch. 420p. (Eng. & Fr.). 1979. 42.50 (ISBN 0-686-56930-X, M-6051). French & Eur.
Dictionnaire pour l'intelligence des Choses. Andre Wurmser. (Fr.). 6.00 F. Sagittaire.
Dictionnaire pratique & explicatif des produits magiques & articles usuels. Jacques Bersez. LC 77-569424. (Illus.). 125p. (Fr.). 1977. 63.00 F (ISBN 2-900272-18-1). Jacques Bersez.
Dictionnaire Pratique & Explicatif des Produits Magiques & Articles Usuels. Jacques Bersez. (Illus.). 125p. (Fr.). 1977. 63.00 F. Bersez.
Dictionnaire Pratique de Droit Medicale. J. Pouletti et al. 424p. (Fr.). 1982. 85.00 (ISBN 2-225-71115-1, M-9773). French & Eur.
Dictionnaire Pratique de la Presse, de l'imprimerie & de la Librairie, 2 vols. J. Bories & F. Bonassies. 1238p. (Fr.). 1972. 70.00. Gregg.
Dictionnaire Pratique De Medecine Clinique. Leon Perlemuter & Arnaud Cenac. 1830p. (Fr.). 1977. 99.50 (ISBN 0-686-57068-5, M-6440). French & Eur.
Dictionnaire Pratique de Medecine Clinique. Leon Perlemuter & Arnaud Cenac. 1830p. (Fr.). 1977. 250.00 F. Masson.
Dictionnaire Pratique de Pharmacologie: Clinique. Yvan Touitou & Leon Perlemuter. 1204p. (Fr.). 1976. 99.50 (ISBN 0-686-57235-1, M-6536). French & Eur.
Dictionnaire Pratique de Pharmacologie Clinique. Yvan Touitou & Leon Perlemuter. LC 76-675973. vi, 1196p. (Fr.). 1976. 167.00 F (ISBN 2-225-43550-2). Masson & Cie.
Dictionnaire Pratique de Pharmacologie Clinique. Yvan Touitou & Leon Perlemuter. 1204p. (Fr.). 1976. 209.00 F. Masson.
Dictionnaire Pratique de Psychopathologie. Roland-Claude Gori & Yves Poinso. 208p. (Fr.). 1972. 50.00 F. Delarge.
Dictionnaire Pratique de Statistiques en Sciences Humaines. Jean-Jacques Pinty & Claude Gaultier. 300p. (Fr.). 1972. 65.00 F. Delarge.
Dictionnaire Pratique de Theraeutique Medicale. 2nd ed. Leon Perlemuter & Paul Obraska. 1232p. (Fr.). 1978. 190.00 F. Masson.
Dictionnaire Pratique De Therapeutique Medicale, 3. 2nd ed. L. Perlemuter. Ed. by P. Obraska. 1032p. (Fr.). 1978. 79.95 (ISBN 0-686-57067-7, M-6439). French & Eur.
Dictionnaire Pratique des Termes Juridiques: Francais-Arabe. Elle Malka. 88p. (Fr. & Arabic.). 1972. 16.00 F. France Selection.
Dictionnaire Pratique d'orthographe & des Difficultes du Francais. Jean-Yves Dournon. 650p. (Fr.). 1975. 46.50 F. Hachette.
Dictionnaire Pratique Francais-Breton. Jean Le Du & Yves Le Berre. 87p. (Fr.). 1976. 8.00 F. Rennes, C. R. D. P.
Dictionnaire Pratique Francais-Polonais. K. Kupisz & B. Kielski. 1036p. (Fr. & Polish.). 1976. 19.95 (ISBN 0-686-92636-6, M-9327). French & Eur.
Dictionnaire Pratique Mercure: Francais-Allemand, Allemand-Francais. Ernst E. Lange-Koval & Kurt Wilhelm. (Fr. & Ger.). 1964. 24.95 (ISBN 0-686-56992-X, M-6332). French & Eur.
Dictionnaire Pratique Mercure: Francais-Anglais, Anglais-Francais. Kenneth Urwin. 1216p. (Fr. & Eng.). 1968. 24.90 (ISBN 0-686-57239-4, M-6540). French & Eur.
Dictionnaire Pratique Mercure: Francais-Espagnol, Espagnol-Francais. 2nd ed. M. Pay-Costa. 1024p. (Fr. & Span.). 1966. 24.95 (ISBN 0-686-57200-9, M-6471). French & Eur.
Dictionnaire Pratique Mercure Francais-Allemand. 3rd ed. Ernst E. Lange-Koval & Kurt Wilhelm. 1206p. (Fr. & Ger.). 1964. 62.00 F. Larousse.
Dictionnaire Pratique Mercure Francais-Espagnol. 2nd ed. M. Puy-Costa. 1024p. (Fr. & Span.). 1966. 62.00 F. Larousse.
Dictionnaire Pratique Quillet, 4 vols. 2416p. (Fr.). 1978. 875.00 F. Quillet.
Dictionnaire prehistoire. (Illus., Fr.). pap. 8.50 (ISBN 0-685-13882-8). Larousse.
Dictionnaire Provencal-Francais. J. T. Avril. 651p. (Fr.). 1978. 110.00 F. Slatkine.
Dictionnaire Provencal-Francais ou Dictionnaire de la Langue D'oc Ancienne & Moderne, 3 vols. Simon-Jude Honnorat. 2365p. (Fr.). 1971. 500.00 F. Slatkine.
Dictionnaire psychologie. N. Sillamy. (Illus., Fr.). pap. 8.50 (ISBN 0-685-13883-6). Larousse.
Dictionnaire Quillet De la Langue Francais, 4 vols. 2132p. (Fr.). Set. 195.00 (ISBN 0-686-57114-2, M-6153). French & Eur.
Dictionnaire Quillet de la Langue Francaise, 4 vols. 2132p. (Fr.). 1978. 545.00 F. Quillet.
Dictionnaire Quillet de la Langue Francaise, 4 vols. Librairie A. Quillet. LC 76-460437. (Fr.). 1978. write for info. Librairie Aritide.
Dictionnaire Raisonne de Diplomatie Chretienne, Vol. 47. M. Quantin. Ed. by J. P. Migne. (Encyclopedie Theologique Ser.). 578p. (Fr.). Repr. of 1846 ed. lib. bdg. 74.00x (ISBN 0-89241-251-8). Caratzas Pub Co.
Dictionnaire Raisonne de Droit et de Jurisprudence en Matiere Civile Ecclesiastique, 3 vols. J. H. Prompsault. Ed. by J. P. Migne. (Encyclopedie Theologique Ser.: Vols. 36-38). 1948p. (Fr.). Repr. of 1849 ed. lib. bdg. 248.00x (ISBN 0-89241-244-5). Caratzas Pub Co.
Dictionnaire Raisonne de l'Architecture Francaise, du XIe au Siecles, 10 tomes. facsimile ed. Viollet-Le-Duc. (Fr.). Repr. of 1868 ed. Set. 250.00 (ISBN 0-685-36003-2). French & Eur.
Dictionnaire Raisonne De Mathematiques. Andre Warusfel. (Fr.). 1966. pap. 27.95 (ISBN 0-686-57257-2, M-6567). French & Eur.
Dictionnaire Raisonne de Mathematiques. Andre Warusfel. (Fr.). 1966. 69.00 F. Seuil.
Dictionnaire Raisonne des Mots-Croises. Jacqueline Charron. 315p. (Fr.). 1977. Can.$8.00. Homme.
Dictionnaire Raisonne Des Superstitions et Des Croyances Populaires. Pierre Canavaggio. 247p. (Fr.). 1977. pap. 19.95 (ISBN 0-686-56937-7, M-6059). French & Eur.
Dictionnaire Raisonne Du Mobilier Francais De L'epoque Carlovingienne a la Renaissance, 6 Vols. 2nd ed. Eugene E. Viollet-Le-Duc. LC 76-153606. (Illus., Fr.). Repr. of 1875 ed. Set. lib. bdg. 345.00 (ISBN 0-404-09750-2); lib. bdg. 57.50 ea. Vol. 1 (ISBN 0-404-09751-0). Vol. 2 (ISBN 0-404-09752-9). Vol. 3 (ISBN 0-404-09753-7). Vol. 4 (ISBN 0-404-09754-5). Vol. 5 (ISBN 0-404-09755-3). Vol. 6 (ISBN 0-404-09756-1). AMS Pr.
Dictionnaire Redige en Caracteres Latins: Allemand-Francais. Felix Bertaux & Emile Lepointe. (Ger. & Fr.). 1972. 76.00 F. Hachette.
Dictionnaire Redige en Caracteres Latins: Francais-Allemand. Felix Bertaux & Emile Lepointe. 1310p. (Ger. & Fr.). 1967. 68.50 F. Hachette.
Dictionnaire Roman, Wallon, Celtique & Tudesque: Servir a l'intelligence des Anciennes lois & Contrats, des Chartes. Dom Jean Francois. 380p. (Fr.). 100.00 F. Slatkine.
Dictionnaire Russe-Francais. 9th ed. De Chtcherba. (Rus. & Fr.). 31.85 F. Mir.
Dictionnaire russe-francais. P. Pauliat. (Rus. & Fr.). 11.95 (ISBN 0-685-13884-4, 3790). Larousse.
Dictionnaire Russe-Francais. Varvara Potozkaia. (Rus. & Fr.). 7.00 F. Mir.
Dictionnaire Russe-Francais de l'automobile & du Tracteur. Jetikov. (Rus. & Fr.). 34.10 F. Mir.
Dictionnaire Russe-Francais du Batiment. V. V. Voronine et al. Ed. by A. I. Denissov. 462p. (Rus. & Fr.). 1978. leatherette 13.25 (ISBN 0-686-92634-X, M-9064). French & Eur.
Dictionnaire Russe-Francais Polytechnique. Vassilieva. (Rus. & Fr.). 93.20 F. Mir.

Dictionnaire Samoa-Francais-Anglais et Francais-Samoa-Anglais. Louis Violette. LC 75-35215. (Fr. & Eng.). Repr. of 1879 ed. 44.50 (ISBN 0-404-14238-9). AMS Pr.

Dictionnaire Savoyard. Aime Constantin & Joseph Desormaux. (Illus.). 514p. (Fr.). 1973. 100.00 F. Slatkine.

Dictionnaire Savoyard. Aime Constantin & Joseph Desormeaux. 443p. (Fr.). 1973. 160.00 F. Lafitte Repr.

Dictionnaire Scolaire du Francais. 320p. (Fr.). DM.14.80 (46500). Langenscheidt.

Dictionnaire Scolaire Francais-Finnois. Edvin Hagford & Seppo Sundelin. 610p. (Fr. & Finnish.). 1974. 16.00 F. 40.65 F. Soderstrom.

Dictionnaire Selectif & Commente des Difficultes de la Version Anglais. Jean Rey. 288p. (Fr. & Eng.). 1973. 27.00 F. Ophrys.

Dictionnaire Serbocrate-Francais, Francais-Serbocroate, suivi d'une courte grammaire de Langue Francaise. B. Grujic. 631p. (Serbocroatian & Fr.). Date not set. 19.95 (ISBN 0-686-92591-2). French & Eur.

Dictionnaire Swahili-Francais. 2nd ed. Charles Sacleux. 1594p. (Swahili & Fr.). 1960. 86.10 F. Inst Ethnol.

Dictionnaire Synonymique. Anthony Guerronnan. Ed. by Peter C. Bunnell & Robert A. Sobieszek. LC 76-23055. (Sources of Modern Photography Ser.). (Fr.). 1979. Repr. of 1895 ed. lib. bdg. 15.00x (ISBN 0-405-09620-8). Ayer Co.

Dictionnaire Syraique-Francais-Anglais. Louis Costaz. 423p. (Syrian & Eng.). 1963. 25.00 F. Dar El-Machreq.

Dictionnaire Technique & Administratif de la Navigation Interieure. Henri Berna. (Illus.). 393p. (Fr.). 1977. 175.00 F. Berger-Levrault.

Dictionnaire Technique & Critique du Dessin. Andre Beguin. (Fr.). 1978. 247.50 F. Vander Oyez.

Dictionnaire Technique Anglais-Francais. G. Malgorn. 495p. (Eng. & Fr.). 1976. 37.50 (ISBN 0-686-57027-8, M-6385). French & Eur.

Dictionnaire technique Anglais-Francais. 5th ed. Guy Malgorn. (Fr. & Eng.). 1972. 38.00. Imported Bks.

Dictionnaire Technique Anglais-Francais d'electronique. 82p. (Eng. & Fr.). 1967. 45.00 F. Chiron.

Dictionnaire Technique Bilingue. Jean Ruhland. 154p. (Fr.). 1973. 55.00 F. Ruhland.

Dictionnaire Technique De la Construction Electrique. P. Sizaire. 172p. (Fr.). 1968. 29.95 (ISBN 0-686-57222-X, M-6520). French & Eur.

Dictionnaire Technique de la Construction Electrique. Pierre Sizaire. (Illus.). 172p. (Fr.). 1968. 67.00 F. Eyrolles.

Dictionnaire Technique de la Maroquinerie. Louis Rama. (Illus.). xxxviii, 532p. (Fr.). 1975. write for info. Centre Technique.

Dictionnaire Technique de la Mecanisation Agricole. (Fr. , Eng. , Ger. , Span. & Ital., Technical Dictionary of Agricultural Mechanics). 1968-70. pap. 59.95 (ISBN 0-686-56723-4, M-6155). French & Eur.

Dictionnaire Technique de la Mecanisation Agricole: Francais-Anglais-Allemand-Espagnol-Italien, 3 vols. (Fr. , Eng. , Ger. , Span. & Ital.). 125.00 F. Centre Nat. Et. Machin Agricole.

Dictionnaire Technique de l'automobile. Daniel Carnelutti. (Illus.). 580p. (Fr.). 55.00 F. Spes SA.

Dictionnaire Technique de L'Automobile. George Zlatovski. Ed. by P. R. Russek. 184p. (Fr., Eng. & Ger.). 1973. pap. 22.50 (ISBN 0-686-57262-9, M-6575). French & Eur.

Dictionnaire Technique de l'automobile. George Zlatovski & P. R. Russek. 184p. (Fr.). 1973. 50.00 F. Bordas-Dunod.

Dictionnaire Technique de L'Eau. (Fr.). pap. 19.95 (ISBN 0-686-57115-0, M-6156). French & Eur.

Dictionnaire Technique de l'eau. (Fr.). 45.00 F. Grund.

Dictionnaire Technique de l'eau & des Questions Connexes. Rene Colas. 264p. (Fr.). 1968. 45.00 F. Le Prat.

Dictionnaire Technique des Fabrications Mecaniques. Rene Bossier. 200p. (Fr.). 1975. 28.00 F. Desforges.

Dictionnaire Technique des Termes Utilises dans l'industrie du Petrole: Anglais-Francais. Madeleine Moureau & Janine Rouge. (Illus.). 914p. (Eng. & Fr.). 1977. 202.00 F. Technip.

Dictionnaire Technique des Termes Utilises Dans l'Industrie du Petrole, Anglais-Francais, Francais-Anglais. Magdeleine Moureau & Janine Rouge. 914p. (Eng. & Fr., Dictionary of Technical Terms Used in the Oil Industry, English-French, French-English). 1977. 95.00 (ISBN 0-686-56757-9, M-6419). French & Eur.

Dictionnaire Technique du Batiment & des Travaux Publics. Maurice Barbier. LC 76-456147. 150p. (Eng. & Fr.). 1976. 47.00 F. Eyrolles.

Dictionnaire Technique du Batiment & des Travaux Publics. 6th ed. Maurice Barbier & Roger Cadiergues. (Illus.). 148p. (Fr.). 1978. 60.00 F. Eyrolles.

Dictionnaire Technique du Bois, en Quatre Langues. G. Wallnig & H. Evered. 640p. (Ger., Fr., Eng. & Rus.). 1973. 65.00 (ISBN 0-686-57254-8, M-6563). French & Eur.

Dictionnaire Technique du Bois en Quatre Langues: Allemand-Russe-Anglais-Francais. 640p. (Ger. , Rus. , Eng. & Fr.). 96.60 F. Vander.

Dictionnaire Technique du Bois en 4 Langues. 640p. (Ger., Rus., Eng. & Fr.). 37.50 (ISBN 0-686-57116-9, M-6157). French & Eur.

Dictionnaire Technique du Bois: Texte en Allemand-Anglais-Francais-Russe. 640p. (Ger. , Eng. , Fr. & Rus.). 1969. 154.00 F. Eyrolles.

Dictionnaire Technique du Cinema: Anglais-Francais. C. R. Gibbs. 228p. (Eng. & Fr.). 1959. 18.90 F. Film Et Technique.

Dictionnaire Technique du Petrole. 2nd ed. Magdeleine Moureau. LC 79-122883. xv, 946p. (Eng. & Fr.). 1979. write for info. (ISBN 2-7108-0361-5). Technip.

Dictionnaire Technique et Administratif De la Navigation Interieure. Henri Berna. 393p. (Fr.). 1977. 82.50 (ISBN 0-686-56914-8, M-6030). French & Eur.

Dictionnaire Technique et Critique du Dessin. Andre Beguin. (Fr.). 1978. 99.50 (ISBN 0-686-56911-3, M-6027). French & Eur.

Dictionnaire Technique Francais-Anglai. Guy M. Malgorn. LC 77-450053. xxx, 471p. (Fr.). 1975. 80.00 F (ISBN 2-04-002947-8). Bordas.

Dictionnaire Technique Francais-Anglais. G. Malgorn. 475p. (Fr. & Eng.). 1956. 37.50 (ISBN 2-04-002947-8, M-6386). French & Eur.

Dictionnaire Technique Francais-Anglais. Guy Malgorn. 475p. (Fr. & Eng.). 1956. 88.00 F. Gauthier-Villars.

Dictionnaire Technique Francais-Espagnol. Guy Malgorn. 544p. (Fr. & Span.). 1974. 99.00 F. Gauthier-Villars.

Dictionnaire Technique Francais-Espagnol. Auteur H. Mink. 1120p. (Fr.). 1979. 75.00 (ISBN 0-686-57049-9, M-6411). French & Eur.

Dictionnaire Technique: Francais-Neerlandais. 480p. (Fr. & Dutch.). 1972. 92.00 F. Voutquenne, C.

Dictionnaire technique general. 2nd ed. J. G. Belle-Isle. 554p. (Fr. & Eng.). 1977. 45.00. Imported Bks.

Dictionnaire Technique General: Anglais-Francais. 2nd ed. Gerald J. Belle-Isle. 572p. (Eng. & Fr.). 1977. 140.00 F. Bordas-Dunod.

Dictionnaire Technique General Anglais-Francais. 2nd ed. Gerald J. Belle-Isle. 555p. (Eng. & Fr.). 1977. 24.00 F. Beauchemin.

Dictionnaire Technique General: Anglais-Francais. 2nd ed. J. Gerald Belle Isle. 555p. (Eng. & Fr.). 1977. 79.95 (ISBN 0-686-56913-X, M-6158). French & Eur.

Dictionnaire Technique Generale Anglais-Francais. new ed. 664p. (Fr. & Eng.). 1979. 39.95 (ISBN 0-686-57117-7, M-6158). French & Eur.

Dictionnaire Technique Hongrois-Francais. B. Rubin. 1260p. (Hungarian & Fr.). 1965. 75.00 F. Terra.

Dictionnaire Technique Illustre des Outlis Coupants: L'usinage des Metaux; Francais-Allemand-Anglais-Italien-Espagnol. Toni Heiler. (Illus.). 474p. (Fr., Ger., Eng., Ital. & Span.). 1965. 156.00 F. Eyrolles.

Dictionnaire Technique Illustre Des Outils Coupants Pour L'usinage Des Metaux. Toni Heiler. 474p. (Fr., Ger., Eng., Ital. & Span.). 1965. 69.95 (ISBN 0-686-57326-9, M-6313). French & Eur.

Dictionnaire Technique Russe-Francais de la Preparation. 129p. (Fr. & Rus.). 1973. pap. 19.95 (ISBN 0-686-56771-4, M-6160). French & Eur.

Dictionnaire Technique Russe-Francais: La Preparation Mecanique des Charbons. 129p. (Rus. & Fr.). 1973. 36.00 F. France, Centre Et Charbonnage.

Dictionnaire Technique Universal Kluwer, Francais-Neerlandais. G. Schuurmans-Stekhoven. 636p. (Fr. & Dutch.). 1978. 75.00 (ISBN 0-686-56776-5, M-6506). French & Eur.

Dictionnaire Technique Universal Kluwer Neerlandais-Francais. G. Schuurmans-Stekhoven. 656p. (Dutch & Fr.). 1978. 79.95 (ISBN 0-686-56775-7, M-6507). French & Eur.

Dictionnaire Technique Universel Kluwer: Francais-Neerlandais. G. Schuermans-Stekhoven. 636p. (Fr. & Dutch.). 1978. 186.00 F. Kluwer-Deventer.

Dictionnaire Technique Universel Kluwer: Neerlandais-Francais. G. Schuermans Stekhoven. 656p. (Dutch & Fr.). 1978. 207.00 F. Kluwer-Deventer.

Dictionnaire Technologique: Aeronautique, Vol. 3. H. Demaison. 671p. (Eng., Fr., & Span.). 1978. 350.00 F. Maison Dictionnaire.

Dictionnaire Technologique Feutry: Mecanique-Metallurgie-Hydraulique, Vol. 1. R. Mertz De Mertzenteld et al. 750p. (Eng., Fr. & Ger.). 1976. 250.00 F. Maison Dictionnaire.

Dictionnaire Technologique Feutry: Supplement Espagnol, Vol. 1-E. R. Mertz De Mertzenteld et al. 400p. (Span.). 1976. 180.00 F. Maison Dictionnaire.

Dictionnaire Technologique: Supplement Portugais. R. Mertz De Mertzenteld et al. 380p. (Port.). 1981. 160.00 F. Maison Dictionnaire.

Dictionnaire Technologique, 1: Anglais-Francais-Allemand. Michel Feutry. 700p. (Eng., Fr & Ger.). 1976. 160.00 F. Maison Dictionnaire.

Dictionnaire Technologique, 1: Anglais-Francais-Allemand. Michel Feutry et al. 736p. (Eng., Fr. & Ger.). 1976. 160.00 F. Maison Dictionnaire.

Dictionnaire theatre francais contemporain. Alfred Simon. (Dict. de l'Homme du Vingtieme Siecle). (Illus., Fr.). 1970. 8.50 (ISBN 0-685-13885-2, 3740). Larousse.

Dictionnaire Topographique & Historique de la Drome. Justin Brun-Durand. 580p. (Fr.). 1973. 120.00 F. Chantermerle.

Dictionnaire Topographique de la France. 562p. (Fr.). 1881. 30.00 F. Biblio Nationale.

Dictionnaire Topographique de la France. Auguste Longnon. 468p. (Fr.). 1891. 25.00 F. Biblio Nationale.

Dictionnaire Topographique de la France. J. Roman. 272p. (Fr.). 1884. 20.00 F. Biblio Nationale.

Dictionnaire Topographique de la France. Henri Stein. Ed. by J. Hubert. 738p. (Fr.). 1954. pap. 25.00 (ISBN 0-686-57226-2, M-6525). French & Eur.

Dictionnaire Topographique de la France. Henri Stein & J. Hubert. 738p. (Fr.). 1954. 50.00 F. Biblio Nationale.

Dictionnaire Topographique de la France, 1. Eugene Vallee & Robert Latouche. 486p. (Fr.). 1954. 40.00 F. Biblio Nationale.

Dictionnaire Touareg-Francais, 4 vols. Charles De Foucauld. 2040p. (Fr.). 1952. 70.00 F. Imprimerie Nat.

Dictionnaire touristique international: Edition francaise. Academie Internationale du Tourisme. (Fr.). 80.00 F. Acad Intl Tour.

Dictionnaire Trilingue. Jean Ruhland. 220p. (Fr., Ger. & Eng.). 1977. 60.00 F. Ruhland.

Dictionnaire trilingue du Droit des Affaires pour le Commerce & l'industrie: Allemand-Anglais-Francais & index. 2nd ed. H. Becker. 992p. (Ger., Eng. & Fr.). 1980. 420.00 F. Maison Dictionnaire.

Dictionnaire Universal de la Peinture, 6 vols. Ed. by Robert Maillard. LC 76-479300. (Illus., Fr.). 1976. 1700.00 F (ISBN 2-850-36002-3). Soc Nouveau.

Dictionnaire Universal de l'Art et des Artistes, 3 tomes. (Fr.). Set. 341.25 (ISBN 0-685-36013-X). French & Eur.

Dictionnaire Universel, 3 vols. Antoine Furetiere. 1650p. (Fr.). 1970. 1000.00 F. Slatkine.

Dictionnaire Universel: Contenant Generalement tous les Mots Francois, 2. Antoine Furetiere. (Fr.). 1972. DM.298.00. Olms.

Dictionnaire Universel: Contenant Generalement tous les Mots Francois, 3. Antoine Furetiere. (Fr.). 1972. DM.298.00. Olms.

Dictionnaire Universel: Contenant Generalement tous les Mots Francois, 4. Antoine Furetiere. (Fr.). 1972. DM.298.00. Olms.

Dictionnaire Universel: Contenant Generalement tous les Mots Francois, 1. Antoine Furetiere & La Haye. (Fr.). 1972. DM.298.00. Olms.

Dictionnaire Universel d'Antoine Furetiere, 3 vols. Antoine Furetiere. (Illus.). 2504p. (Fr.). 1978. 690.00 F. Ste. Nouv. Littre.

Dictionnaire Universel de la Franc-Maconnerie, 2 vols. Daniel Ligou. 1518p. (Fr.). 1975. 300.00 F. Prisme.

Dictionnaire Universel de la Peinture, 6 vols. Robert Maillard & Gerard Legrand. (Illus.). 3000p. (Fr.). 1976. 1800.00 F. Ste. Nouv. Littre.

Dictionnaire Universel de Mathematique & de Physique, 1. Alexandre Saverien. (Fr.). DM.138.00. Olms.

Dictionnaire Universel de Mathematique & de Physique, 2. Alexandre Saverien. (Fr.). DM.138.00. Olms.

Dictionnaire Universel des Noms Propres see Robert Dictionaries.

Dictionnaire Universel et Complet des Conciles, 2 vols. A. C. Peltier. Ed. by J. P. Migne. (Encyclopedie Theologique Ser.: Vols. 13-14). 1378p. (Fr.). Repr. of 1846 ed. lib. bdg. 175.00x (ISBN 0-89241-236-4). Caratzas Pub Co.

Dictionnaire Usuel Hongrois-Francais. S. Eckhardt. 376p. (Hungarian & Fr.). 1973. 35.00 F. Terra.

Dictionnaire Vidal. (Fr.). 1976. 96.00 F. O. V. P.

Dictionnaire Vidal, 1982. 58th ed. 1168p. (Fr.). 1982. 75.00x (ISBN 2-85091-058-9). Intl Pubns Serv.

Dictionnaire Vietnamien-Francais, 2 vols. Thanh Nghi. LC 79-343898. (Vietnamese & Fr.). 1977. 186.00 F. Asiatheque.
Dictionnaire vins. Gerard Debuigne. (Illus., Fr.). pap. 8.50 (ISBN 0-03-075459-3, 3742). Larousse.
Dictionnaires. (Fr.). 15.00 F. I. P. E. C.
Dictionnaires Bilingues Francais-Anglais. 500p. (Fr. & Eng.). 6.50 (Dist. by Continental Bk Co). Larousse.
Dictionnaires Bilingues Larousse Francais-Anglais. (Fr. & Eng.). 9.95 (Dist. by Continental Bk Co). Larousse.
Dictionnaires des Cathedrales de France. (Illus.). 256p. (Fr.). 1971. write for info. Larousse.
Dictionnaires des Charges, Emplois & Metiers XIVe. & XVe. Siecles: Relevant des Institutions Monarchiques en France. Monique Ornato. 208p. (Fr.). 1976. 45.00 F. CNRS.
Dictionnaires des Comediens Francais, 2 vols. (Fr.). 1969. write for info. Slatkine.
Dictionnaires des Communes. 36th ed. 1100p. (Fr.). 1976. write for info. Berger Levrault.
Dictionnaires des Matieres Plastiques. Wittfoht. 325p. (Fr.). 1976. 135.00 F. Francaise, Compagnie Edition.
Dictionnaires des Parfums de France & de Lignes pour Hommes. 4th ed. 158p. (Fr.). 1972. 25.00 F. Ed.
Dictionnaires des Plantes Medicinales. J. Duquesne. (Illus.). 556p. (Fr.). 1975. 49.00 F. Chiron.
Dictionnaires Marabout Universite: La Sociologie, 3 vols. (Fr.). 34.50 F. Marabout.
Dictionnaires Modernes Larousse Francais-Anglais. 1290p. (Fr. & Eng.). 32.50 (Dist. by Continental Bk Co). Larousse.
Dictonnaire de L'Automobile. Robert Guerber. 174p. (Fr.). 1967. pap. 12.50 (ISBN 0-686-57320-X, M-6303). French & Eur.
Dictonnaire des Synonymes et des Antonymes. Hector Dupuis & Romain Legare. 608p. (Fr.). 1975. 22.50 (ISBN 0-686-57129-0, M-6180). French & Eur.
Dictonnaire Du Francais Argotique et Populaire. Francois Caradec. 255p. (Fr.). 1977. pap. 6.95 (ISBN 0-686-56879-6, M-4968). French & Eur.
Dieter's Dictionary: Chubby Webster's. Sandy Bergeson. (Illus.). 1983. pap. 4.95 (ISBN 0-943084-09-1). Print Mat.
Dietetic Policies & Procedures Manual for Long Term Care Facilities. Jim Rose & Jayne Gilbert. 400p. Date not set. price not set. Aspen Systems.
DIN Definitions: German-English with an English-German Vocabulary. 2nd rev. ed. Compiled by Henry G. Freeman. (Ger. & Eng.). 80.00 (ISBN 3-4101-0804-1). Heinman.
Din Standards for Welding Practice One: Standards for Filler Metals: Manufacture, Quality, Testing. 549.00 (ISBN 0-686-28164-0, 10047-7/08). Heyden.
Din Standards: Two-Thousand Six-Hundred Definitions of Technical Terms According to Din. 53.00 (ISBN 0-686-28197-7, 10804-1). Heyden.
Dinosaur Dictionary. Donald F. Glut. (Illus.). 218p. 1976. pap. 6.95 (ISBN 0-8065-0519-2). Citadel Pr.
Dinosaur Dictionary. Donald F. Glut. 1972. 12.50 (ISBN 0-8065-0283-5). Citadel Pr.
Directory of Russian Verbs. E. Daum & W. Schenk. 748p. (Eng. & Rus.). 1974. 17.50. Hippocrene Bks.
Disarmament Terminology: English, German, French, Spanish, Russian. Ed. by Language Services Division of the Foreign Office of the Federal Republic of Germany. (Terminological Ser.: Vol. 1). 645p. 1982. pap. 45.00 (ISBN 3-11-008858-4). De Gruyter.
Distribuzione della Posposizione nel Lituano Antico. Loredana Serafini Amato. LC 78-401196. 74p. (Eng. & Lithuanian.). 1976. write for info. Ist Univers Orient.
Divorce Dictionary: A Book for You & Your Children. Stuart Glass. (Illus.). 80p. (gr. 7 up). 1980. 7.95 (ISBN 0-316-31581-8). Little.
Divry's Modern English-Greek & Greek-English Desk Dictionary. (Eng. & Gr.). 1982. 9.50 (ISBN 0-685-81638-9); thumb indexed 12.00 (ISBN 0-685-81639-7). Divry.
Divry's New Modern Greek-English & English-Greek Handy Dictionary. rev. ed. Ed. by George C. Divry. (Gr. & Eng.). 1978. pocket ed. 4.20 (ISBN 0-685-09029-9); with thumb indexes 5.50 (ISBN 0-685-09030-2); lea. 8.50 (ISBN 0-685-09031-0). Divry.
Divry's New Spanish-English & English-Spanish Handy Dictionary. Ed. by J. M. Douglas & A. Lomo. (Span. & Eng.). 1965. pocket size, flexible 3.50 (ISBN 0-685-09033-7); thumb indexed 5.00 (ISBN 0-685-09034-5). Divry.
Divry's Spanish English Dictionary. D. C. Divry. (Span. & Eng.). 2.70. Camino Real.
Dixcionario de Filosofia. Eduardo Pallares. 652p. (Span.). 17.50 (ISBN 0-686-56706-4, S-21915). French & Eur.
Dizinario italiano-spagnolo. (Ital. & Span.). L.1500.00. Malipiero.
Dizionari dei Formaggi: Tutte le Notizie le Ricette come & con che Cosa Servirli. Fernanda Gosetti. LC 78-400002. 293p. (Eng. & Ital.). 1977. L.5000.00. Marietti.
Dizionarietto degli uomini illustri della riviera di Sabo. G. Brunati. 184p. (Ital.). L.7800.00. Forni.
Dizionarietto del costume della moda e dell'acconciatura. Coratelli Vincenzo. 112p. (Ital.). L.1000.00. San Marco.
Dizionarietto della lingua italiana lussuosa. Barosso Giampaolo. (Illus.). 216p. (Ital.). 1977. L.5500.00. Rizzoli Edit.
Dizionarietto della malavita napoletana. 47p. (Ital.). L.500.00. Colonnese.
Dizionarietto di informatica. Graziano Frizzi. 112p. (Ital.). 1972. L.1500.00. Bucalo.
Dizionarietto di tecnica bancaria, mercantile con appendice trilingue. Monetti Ugo. (Ital.). L.750.00. RIREA.
Dizionarietto fraseologico commerciale italiano-francese. Cenni Clara & Sandri Clotilde. 152p. (Ital. & Fr.). L.2000.00. Trevisini.
Dizionarietto fraseologico commerciale italiano-inglese. Cenni Clara. 184p. (Ital.). L.2500.00. Trevisini.
Dizionarietto marinaro. (Ital.). L.1000.00. Bianco.
Dizionario abruzzese e molisano: A-E, Vol. 1. Ernesto Giammarco. xl, 750p. (Ital.). 1968. L.25000.00. Ateneo & Bizzarri.
Dizionario abruzzese e molisano: F-M, Vol. 2. Ernesto Giammarco. 496p. (Ital.). 1969. L.25000.00. Ateneo & Bizzarri.
Dizionario abruzzese e molisano: N-R, Vol. 3. Ernesto Giammarco. 560p. (Ital.). 1977. L.25000.00. Ateneo & Bizzarri.
Dizionario Amministrativo. Giuseppe Guarino. LC 78-367131. xvi, 671p. (Ital.). 1978. L.1600.00. Giuffre.
Dizionario amministrativo. Giuseppe Guarino. xvi, 672p. (Ital.). 1978. L.16000.00. Giuffre.
Dizionario araldico. Guelfi C. Piero. (Illus.). vi, 586p. (Ital.). 1966. L.9500.00. Forni.
Dizionario assicurativo: Tedesco-francese-inglese-italiano. (Ger. , Fr. , Eng. & Ital.). L.5000.00. Centro St Assic.
Dizionario astrologico. Federico Capone. 224p. (Ital.). 1978. L.7500.00. Capone C.
Dizionario Avicolo Internazionale. A. Brunoli. (Illus.). viii, 300p. (Ital.). 1983. write for info. Ed Calderini.
Dizionario avicolo internazionale. Alberto Brunoli. 330p. (Ital.). L.4000.00 (ISBN 88-206-0904-5). Edagricole.
Dizionario aziendale. Umberto Arisi Rota. 428p. (Ital.). L.9000.00. Buffetti.
Dizionario biblico. John L. McKenzie & B. Maggioni. 1100p. (Ital.). L.18000.00. Cittadella.
Dizionario borana-italiano. B. Venturino. (Ital.). L.2500.00. EMI.
Dizionario botanico. Alfio Musmarra. 1184p. (Ital.). 1973. L.12000.00 (ISBN 88-206-0730-1). Edagricole.
Dizionario botanico italiano. Ottaviano T. Tozzetti. xiv, 558p. (Ital.). L.26000.00. Forni.
Dizionario ceco-italiano. Jaroslav Rosendorfsky. 820p. (Czech. & Ital.). L.2000.00. Ist Univers Orient.
Dizionario chitarristico italiano. C. Cafagna & M. Gangi. (Ital.). L.5000.00. Berben.
Dizionario Commerciale Francese-Italiano. V. Emolumento. 533p. (Fr. & Ital.). 1978. pap. 37.50 (ISBN 88-7075-024-8, M-9281). French & Eur.
Dizionario commerciale francese-italiano. Vincenzo Emolumento. 536p. (Fr. & Ital.). 1978. L.8000.00 (ISBN 88-7075-024-8). Editrice Bibliografica.
Dizionario commerciale fraseologico italiano-inglese, inglese-italiano. Ada Duse. 736p. (Ital. & Eng.). 1975. L.5000.00. Bignami.
Dizionario Commerciale Inglese-Italiano, Italiano-Inglese: Economia, Legge, Finanza, Banca, Etc. Giuseppe Motta. 1051p. (Eng. & Ital.). 1978. 48.00x (ISBN 0-913298-50-6). S F Vanni.
Dizionario commerciale italiano-francese. Vincenzo Emolumento. 656p. (Ital. & Fr.). 1975. L.8000.00 (ISBN 88-7075-006-X). Bibliografica.
Dizionario commerciale italiano-francese e francese-italiano. Mario Mormile. 622p. (Ital. & Fr.). 1979. L.18000.00. Bulzoni.
Dizionario Commerciale Italiano-Francese, Francese-Italiano. Mario Mormile. LC 79-352644. xxv, 622p. (Fr. & Ital.). 1978. L.18000.00. Maison Dictionnaire.
Dizionario completo italiano-portoghese (brasiliano) e portoghese (brasiliano)-italiano. Vincenzo Spinelli & Mario Casasanta. xxiv, 896p. (Ital. & Port.). 1978. L.15000.00 (ISBN 88-203-1010-4). Hoepli.
Dizionario completo italiano-portoghese (brasiliano) e portoghese (brasiliano)-italiano. Vincenzo Spinelli & Mario Casasanta. xii, 1040p. (Ital. & Port.). 1976. L.12000.00 (ISBN 88-203-0216-0). Hoepli.
Dizionario Completo Italiano-Portoghese (Brasiliano), Portoghese (Brasiliano)-Italiano: Con L'etimologia Delle Voci Italiane e Portoghesi (Brasiliane), la Loro Esatta Traduzione, Frasi e Modi Di Dire, 2 vols. (Ital. & Port.). 1978. Set. 82.00x (ISBN 0-686-70496-7); (ISBN 88-203-1010-4). S F Vanni.
Dizionario critico di psicoanalisi. Charles Rycroft. xxxii, 256p. (Ital.). L.4000.00. Astrolabio.
Dizionario danese-italiano e italiano-danese. 304p. (Danish & Ital.). L.3000.00. Malipiero.
DIzionario degli alimenti per il bestiame. Marcello Piccioni. 636p. (Ital.). L.9000.00 (ISBN 88-206-0329-2). Edagricole.
Dizionario degli animali. (Illus.). 48p. (Ital.). L.3500.00. Dami.
Dizionario degli architetti. Bernard Oudin. (Illus.). 280p. (Ital.). 1971. L.20000.00. ISEDI.
Dizionario degli errori. Mauro Magni. 416p. (Ital.). L.8500.00. Edit Vecchi.
Dizionario dei comuni. E. Nicchi. 800p. (Ital.). 1978. L.8000.00. La Tribuna.
Dizionario dei comuni con le circoscrizioni guidiziarie. (Ital.). 1964. L.1000.00. Giuffre.
Dizionario dei comuni e delle circoscrizioni amminstrative, delle frazioni e delle localita. 640p. (Ital.). 1978. L.8000.00. La Tribuna.
Dizionario dei dubbi linguistici. Dino Provenzal. vii, 380p. (Ital.). 1967. L.2000.00 (ISBN 88-203-0217-9). Hoepli.
Dizionario dei formaggi. Fernanda Gosetti. (Ital.). L.5000.00. Marietti.
Dizionario dei formaggi. Fernanda Gosetti. (Illus.). 296p. (Ital.). 1977. L.5000.00. AMZ.
Dizionario dei Frizzetti Popolari Firoentini. Giuseppe Frizzi. LC 76-488668. vii, 267p. (Ital.). 1975. L.9000.00. Multigrafica.
Dizionario dei giochi e degli sport. 206p. (Ital.). L.1800.00. Zanichelli.
Dizionario dei motti e leggende delle monete italiane. G. Donati. (Ital.). L.2500.00. La Vela.
Dizionario dei musicisti. Roland De Cande. 486p. (Ital.). 1978. L.3000.00. Bompiani.
Dizionario dei patrioti lucani artefici ed oppositori (1700-1870) Vol. 1, A-C. Tommaso Pedio. xxiv, 520p. (Ital.). 1969. L.8000.00. Soc Bari.
Dizionario dei patrioti lucani artefici ed oppositori (1700-1870) Vol. 2, D-I. Tommaso Pedio. 590p. (Ital.). 1972. L.8500.00. Soc Bari.
Dizionario dei piloti. (Ital.). L.12000.00. Mondadori.
Dizionario dei semiconduttori. Alfred Wiegelmann. Tr. by L. Cascianni & M. Boscarol. (Illus.). 164p. (Ital.). 1978. L.4400.00 (ISBN 88-7021-072-3). Muzzio.
Dizionario dei sinonimi della lingua italiana, 4 vols. Niccolo Tommaseo. (Ital.). 1973. L.15000.00. Nuova Vallecchi.
Dizionario dei sinonimi della lingua italiana, 2 vols. Niccolo Tommaseo & G. Rigutini. (Ital.). 1974. L.60000.00. Vallardi F.
Dizionario dei sinonimi e dei contrari. Decio Cinti. 632p. (Ital.). L.5500.00. Ist Geo Agostini.
Dizionario dei sinonimi e dei contrari. Aldo Gabrielli. (Ital.). L.23000.00. Ist Edit Ital.
Dizionario dei sintomi. Joan Gomez. Tr. by E. V. Ferrario. (Illus.). 496p. (Ital.). 1977. L.2800.00. Garzanti Edit.
Dizionario dei sogni e cabala del lotto. (Illus., Ital.). L.2700.00. Malipiero.
Dizionario dei temi della fede. 511p. (Ital.). 1977. L.7000.00. SEI.
Dizionario dei termini cinematografici. Glenn Alvey, Jr. 180p. (Ital.). 1952. L.2000.00. Edizioni Mediterranee.
Dizionario dei termini giuridici. Angelo Favata. 500p. (Ital.). 1978. L.4000.00. La Tribuna.
Dizionario dei termini storiografici. G. Arnaldi. 120p. (Ital.). L.2500.00. Zanichelli.
Dizionario dei termini tecnici di medicina. M. Garnier et al. 1400p. (Ital.). 1978. L.15000.00. DEMI.
Dizionario dei verbi italiani regolari ed irregolari. Aldo Gabrielli. (Ital.). L.10000.00. Ist Edit Ital.
Dizionario del cacciatore italiano. Luigi Ugolini. (Illus.). 336p. (Ital.). L.8500.00. Bietti.
Dizionario del Concilio Ecumenico Vaticano Secondo. 1800p. (Ital.). L.36000.00; L.pap. 30000.00. Scode.
Dizionario del dialetto calabrese, 3 vols. Luigi Accattatis. 1330p. (Ital.). L.48000.00. Brenner.
Dizionario del dialetto cremonese. Comitato Del Folklore Cremonese. (Illus.). xxiii, 389p. (Ital.). L.15000.00. Libreria Convegno.
Dizionario del dialetto di Cortina d'Ampezzo. Vincenzo M. Tamburin. (Illus.). 212p. (Ital.). 1973. L.5000.00. Pozza.
Dizionario del dialetto valdese della Val Germanasca. Teofilo Pons. 280p. (Ital.). L.7000.00. Soc Studi Valdesi.
Dizionario del dialetto valsesiano. F. Tonetti. 334p. (Ital.). L.9800.00. Forni.
Dizionario del dialetto veneziano. Giuseppe Boerio. 976p. (Ital.). L.25000.00. Giunti-Martello.

Dizionario del disegno. Gaspare De Fiore. (Illus.). 616p. (Ital.). 1967. L.6500.00. La Scuola.
Dizionario del feltrino rustico. Bruno Migliorini & G. Pellegrini. (Ital.). L.7000.00. Liviana.
Dizionario del francese fondamentale. Raoul Boch. 248p. (Fr. & Ital.). 1975. L.3600.00. Zanichelli.
Dizionario del gergo milanese e lombardo. Nino Bazzetta de Vemenia. (Illus.). 112p. (Ital.). L.4200.00. Forni.
Dizionario del linguaggio italiano storico e amministrativo. G. Rezasco. xlvii, 128p. (Ital.). L.55000.00. Forni.
Dizionario del pescatore italiano di acqua dolce. Ugo Veronese. (Illus.). 384p. (Ital.). L.8500.00. Bietti.
Dizionario del vernacolo fiorentino. Pirro Giacchi. 123p. (Ital.). 1966. L.3500.00. Multigrafica.
Dizionario della critica d'arte, 2 vols. Luigi Grassi & Mario Pepe. (Illus.). xx, 676p. (Ital.). 1978. L.50000.00 (ISBN 88-02-02578-9). UTET.
Dizionario della geografica: Geografica umana, Vol. 1. G. Cotti-Cometti & P. George. 256p. (Ital.). 1971. L.3000.00. CESVIET.
Dizionario della lingua e della civita italiana contemporanea. Emido De Felice & Aldo Duro. 2250p. (Ital.). 1975. L.18500.00. Palumbo.
Dizionario della lingua italiana. Giuseppe Cantamessa & Giuseppe Messina. 1424p. (Ital.). L.6000.00. Signorelli C.
Dizionario della lingua italiana. Giacomo Devoto & Giancarlo Oli. (Illus.). xvi, 2712p. (Ital.). 1974. L.22800.00. Monnier.
Dizionario della lingua italiana, 2 vols. 2008p. (Ital.). 1977. L.23500.00. Garzanti Edit.
Dizionario della lingua italiana. (Illus.). 2008p. (Ital.). 1971. L.pap. 17500.00. Garzanti Edit.
Dizionario della lingua italiana. (Illus.). 1008p. (Ital.). 1976. L.5000.00. Garzanti Edit.
Dizionario della lingua italiana. (Illus.). 1008p. (Ital.). 1971. L.6800.00. Garzanti Edit.
Dizionario della lingua italiana. (Illus.). 1062p. (Ital.). L.4800.00. Bietti.
Dizionario della lingua italiana. (Illus.). 1032p. (Ital.). 1971. L.13000.00. Garzanti Edit.
Dizionario della lingua italiana. Mario Nuzzo. (Illus.). 1724p. (Ital.). 1977. L.18000.00. Marotta.
Dizionario della lingua italiana, 20 vols. Niccolo Tommaseo & Bernardo Bellini. 14824p. (Ital.). 1977. L.90000.00. Rizzoli Edit.
Dizionario della lingua italiana. Carlo P. Tosi. (Illus.). xii, 1730p. (Ital.). L.16000.00. Principato.
Dizionario della lingua italiano. L. Bellini. (Ital.). L.135000.00. Rizzoli Edit.
Dizionario della Lingua Italiano. Ed. by G. Devoto & G. C. Oli. 2712p. (Ital.). write for info. (M-9196). French & Eur.
Dizionario della lingua latina: Latino-italiano e italiano-latino. Ed. by Calonghi et al. 1329p. (Lat. & Ital.). 1968. L.15000.00 (ISBN 88-7011-006-0). Rosenberg & Sellier.
Dizionario della musica. Roland De Cande. 288p. (Ital.). 1978. L.2500.00. Bompiani.
Dizionario della Natura. LC 77-461886. (Ital.). 1976. write for info. A Mondadi.
Dizionario della paura. Marcello Venturoli & Ruggero Zangrandi. (Illus.). 393p. (Ital.). 1951. L.5000.00. Nistri-Lischi.
Dizionario della pubblica istruzione: Legislazione e pratica amministrativa sulla istruzione primaria. Trentino Vetrini. vii, 796p. (Ital.). 1967. L.8000.00. Giuffre.
Dizionario della publica istruzione, 2 vols. L. Zanobini & T. Vetrini. xii, 2270p. (Ital.). 1972. L.28000.00. Giuffre.
Dizionario della publica istruzione, 2 vols. L. Zanobini & T. Vetrini. xii, 1872p. (Ital.). 1975. L.30000.00. Giuffre.
Dizionario della scuola democratica. Giorgio Pecorini. 160p. (Ital.). 1977. L.3500.00. Emme.
Dizionario della sicurezza sociale. Gino Rampini. (Illus.). 230p. (Ital.). 1966. L.1800.00. Giuffre.
Dizionario della strumentazione nucleare. CEI. 188p. (Ital.). L.1100.00. AEEI.
Dizionario della tecnica. 188p. (Ital.). 1964. L.2500.00. Zanichelli.
Dizionario della vela, 2 vols. Michel Barberousse. 640p. (Ital.). 1978. L.14800.00. Mursia S.
Dizionario dell'antichita classica. Tr. by M. R. Rogger. (Illus.). 352p. (Ital.). L.3300.00. Zanichelli.
Dizionario dell'arte. (Illus., Ital.). L.19800.00. Mondadori.
Dizionario delle arti figurative. B. Garzena. (Illus.). 162p. (Ital.). L.2500.00. Zanichelli.
Dizionario delle Autonomie Locali. Enzo Modica. LC 77-575264. xi, 851p. (Ital.). 1977. L.1200.00. Editori Riuniti.
Dizionario delle autonomie locali. Enzo Modica & Rubes Triva. 852p. (Ital.). L.12000.00. Editori Riuniti.
Dizionario delle buone maniere. Fluffy M. Mazzucato. (Illus.). 304p. (Ital.). L.5000.00; L.pap. 2500.00. Bietti.
Dizionario delle contravvenzioni. Igino Alessandrino. xvi, 640p. (Ital.). L.9000.00. Patron.
Dizionario delle forniture grafiche, editoriale e cartotecniche. (Ital.). 1972. L.10600.00. L'Ufficio Moderno.
Dizionario delle idee. Centro Studi Filosofici di Gallarate. (Ital.). L.30000.00. Sansoni.
Dizionario delle idee comuni, 2 vols. Virgilio Titone. (Ital.). 1975. L.6000.00. Pan Italy.
Dizionario delle idee correnti. Maurizio Costanzo. 144p. (Ital.). 1975. L.2500.00. Bompiani.
Dizionario delle immagini. Dino Provenzal. (Illus.). xxiv, 1064p. (Ital.). 1954. L.3200.00 (ISBN 88-203-0218-7). Hoepli.
Dizionario delle lingue italiana e inglese, 2 vols. Lysle & Gualtieri. 3320p. (Ital.). L.16000.00. Casanova F & C.
Dizionario delle malattie, sindromi e sintori oculari. Vincenzo Marsico. 158p. (Ital.). 1968. L.7000.00. Minerva Medica.
Dizionario delle nuove scienze: Astronautica, electronica, fiscia nucleare. E. Mazzaglia & A. Castellini. 830p. (Ital.). 1968. L.19000.00. Edizioni Paoline.
Dizionario delle parlate corse. G. Bottiglioni. (Ital.). L.10000.00. Stem Mucchi.
Dizionario delle parole nuovissime e dificili. Gennaro Vaccaro. 497p. (Ital.). 1967. L.6000.00. Romana Libri ALfabeto.
Dizionario delle scienze fisiche e matematiche. 178p. (Ital.). L.2500.00. Zanichelli.
Dizionario delle sindromi mediche. Sergio Magalini. 800p. (Ital.). 1976. L.25000.00. DEMI.
Dizionario delle tecniche e delle scienze, 8 vols. 5200p. (Ital.). 1973. L.195000.00. Edizioni Paoline.
Dizionario delle tecniche pittoriche. (Illus.). 270p. (Ital.). 1977. L.14000.00. Castel Caltan.
Dizionario delle voci. Dino Provenzal. xii, 540p. (Ital.). 1957. L.2500.00 (ISBN 88-203-0219-5); L.pap. 1800.00 (ISBN 88-203-0220-9). Hoepli.
Dizionario dell'enigmista. Luigi Boni. 176p. (Ital.). 1971. L.1300.00. Mazziana.
Dizionario dell'epilessia. H. Gastaut. Tr. by E. De Fiore & R. Vizioli. 156p. (Ital.). 1976. L.6000.00. Il Pensiero.
Dizionario dell'infermiera. A. Bottero. 664p. (Ital.). 1974. L.3500.00. EIPS.
Dizionario dell'intellettuale di sinistra. Elias Condal. 119p. (Ital.). 1970. L.1500.00. Savelli.
Dizionario dello sport. E. Enrile. (Illus.). 1312p. (Ital.). 1977. L.18000.00. Edizioni Paoline.
Dizionario dello yachting in otto lingue. Barbara Webb. 160p. (Ital.). L.7500.00. Mursia S.
Dizionario demografico multilingue. xix, 166p. (Ital.). 1959. L.1200.00. Giuffre.
Dizionario di Abbreviature Latine & Italiane. Capelli. (Ital. & Lat.). L.16.00. Hoepli.
Dizionario di abbreviature latine ed italiane. A. Capelli. (Illus.). lxxiv, 536p. (Lat. & Ital.). 1979. L.8000.00 (ISBN 88-203-0221-7). Hoepli.
Dizionario di agricoltura, 2 vols. A. Carena. xii, 1914p. (Ital.). 1956. L.40000.00 (ISBN 88-02-01492-2). UTET.
Dizionario di Agricoltura. F. Favati. (Illus.). x, 990p. (Ital.). 1983. write for info. Ed Calderini.
Dizionario di agricoltura: English-italian e italiano-inglese. Franco Favati. (Illus.). x, 990p. (Eng. & Ital.). 1973. L.20000.00 (ISBN 88-206-0667-4). Edagricole.
Dizionario di alchimia e di chimica antiquaria. Gino Testi. (Illus.). 300p. (Ital.). 1950. L.4000.00. Edizioni Mediterranee.
Dizionario di anatomia e fisiologia umana. N. Piscitelli. (Illus.). 128p. (Ital.). L.3000.00. Ist Geo Agostini.
Dizionario di antichita classiche. Caffarello Nelida. (Illus.). xii, 532p. (Ital.). 1971. L.22000.00. Olschki.
Dizionario di archeologia. Warwick Bray & David Trump. (Ital.). 1974. L.2000.00. Mondadori.
Dizionario di architettura. Giacomo Ravazzini. LC 78-365683. (Illus.). viii, 250p. (Ital.). 1976. L.4200.00 (ISBN 88-205-0092-2). Cisalpino.
Dizionario di balletto. Luigi Rossi. 251p. (Ital.). 1978. L.7000.00. Edizioni Della Danza.
Dizionario di banca e di borsa: Vol. 1, A-D. Istituto per l'Enciclopedia della Banca e della Borsa. 584p. (Ital.). 1979. L.15000.00. Giuffre.
Dizionario di biologia. 352p. (Ital.). L.3600.00. Zanichelli.
Dizionario di botanica: A-L. U. Tosco. (Illus.). 96p. (Ital.). L.3000.00. Ist Geo Agostini.
Dizionario di Botanica: M-Z. U. Tosco. (Illus.). 96p. (Ital.). L.3000.00. Ist Geo Agostini.
Dizionario di cultura universale, 5 vols. (Ital.). 1974. L.100000.00. Vallardi F.
Dizionario di economia. Graham Bannock et al. vii, 154p. (Ital.). 1977. L.3900.00. Laterza.
Dizionario di economia. G. Mayer. (Ital.). L.3000.00. Bulzoni.
Dizionario di economia. Giuseppe U. Papi. iv, 1512p. (Ital.). 1972. L.20000.00 (ISBN 88-02-01493-0). UTET.
Dizionario di elettronica. Saul Handel. Tr. by E. Suriani. (Illus.). 284p. (Ital.). 1966. L.3600.00. Zanichelli.
Dizionario di elettronica. Saul Handel. Tr. by E. Suriani. (Illus.). 286p. (Ital.). 1967. L.13000.00. Zanichelli.
Dizionario di Elettronica Italiano-Inglese, Inglese-Italiano. S. Handel. 284p. (Eng. & Ital.). 1966. 39.95 (ISBN 0-686-92632-3, M-9192). French & Eur.
Dizionario di elettronica: Tedesco-italiano. G. Fiandaca. 408p. (Ger. & Ital.). 1962. L.10000.00. Il Rostro.
Dizionario di estetica & di linguistica generale. Giovanni Giraldi. LC 76-503182. (Illus.). 946p. (Ital.). 1975. L.25000.00. Pergamena.
Dizionario di etnologia. Panoff & Perrin. (Ital.). L.2800.00. Newton-Compton.
Dizionario di farmacologia clinica. V. Fatturosso & O. Ritter. Tr. by M. A. Branca Ciocetti. viii, 656p. (Ital.). 1976. L.185000.00. Edipem.
Dizionario di genetica. Robert C. King. vi, 372p. (Ital.). 1974. L.10000.00. ISEDI.
Dizionario di geografia. F. J. Monkhouse. Tr. by M. Manzoni. (Illus.). 400p. (Ital.). 1974. L.13000.00. Zanichelli.
Dizionario di geografia. Moore. (Ital.). L.3000.00. Newton-Compton.
Dizionario di geologia. Marcello Manzoni. (Illus.). 234p. (Ital.). 1968. L.13000.00. Zanichelli.
Dizionario di geologia. D. G. Whitten & J. R. Brooks. (Ital.). 1978. L.5500.00. Mondadori.
Dizionario di giornalismo. Mario Lenzi. 260p. (Ital.). 1974. L.5000.00. Mursia.
Dizionario di informatica. Anthony Chandor. Tr. by G. Rapelli. xvi, 356p. (Ital.). 1972. L.13000.00. Zanichelli.
Dizionario di informatica e degli elaboratori elettronici. Marcello Morelli. (Illus.). 216p. (Ital.). 1978. L.5000.00 (ISBN 88-204-0203-3). Angeli.
Dizionario di informazione sessuale. P. Bertrand et al. 284p. (Ital.). L.2800.00. Gribaudi.
Dizionario di ipnopsicologia. Marco Marchesan. 230p. (Ital.). 1971. L.5000.00 (ISBN 88-85021-01-8). Ist. Indagini Psicologiche.
Dizionario di linguistica. L. Rosiello & I. Loi. viii, 368p. (Ital.). 1979. L.13000.00. Zanichelli.
Dizionario di matematica moderna. L. L. Chambadal. (Ital.). L.7500.00. Mursia.
Dizionario di medicina. M. C. Aite. (Illus.). 1966p. (Ital.). 1966. L.2500.00. Zanichelli.
Dizionario di medicina: Enciclopedia degli alimenti, 3 vols. Ulrico Di Aichelburg. xvi, 1396p. (Ital.). L.58000.00. UTET.
Dizionario di medicina per le famiglie, 2 vols. Ulrico Di Aichelburg. (Illus.). viii, 1124p. (Ital.). 1974. L.48000.00 (ISBN 88-02-01495-7). UTET.
Dizionario di merceologia e chimica applicata. G. V. Villavecchia et al. vi, 490p. (Ital.). 1976. L.10000.00 (ISBN 88-203-1045-7). Hoepli.
Dizionario di metallurgia. W. E. Clason. (Ital.). 1966. L.16000.00. Etas Libri.
Dizionario di metrologia generale. Alfredo Ferraro. (Illus.). xvi, 270p. (Ital.). 1965. L.2500.00. Zanichelli.
Dizionario Di Mitologia Egizia, 3 vols. R. V. Lanzone. 1312p. (Ital.). 1974. 350.00 (ISBN 90-272-0931-6, 0932-4, 0933-2). Benjamins North Am.
Dizionario di musica, 2 vols. Guido Gatti. (Illus.). xxiv, 2752p. (Ital.). 1971. L.70000.00 (ISBN 88-02-03178-9). UTET.
Dizionario di musica. G. Vacchi. (Illus.). 278p. (Ital.). L.3600.00. Zanichelli.
Dizionario di pedagogia, psicologia, storia dell'educazione. Paolo E. Lamanna & Maria Goretti. 130p. (Ital.). L.2200.00. Monnier.
Dizionario di politica. Norberto Bobbio & Nicola Matteuci. xii, 1098p. (Ital.). 1977. L.35000.00 (ISBN 88-02-02623-8). UTET.
Dizionario di Politica. Ed. by Norberto Bobbio & Nicola Matteuci. LC 77-467442. xi, 1097p. (Ital.). 1976. L.3200.00. UTET.
Dizionario di politica economica. Luciano Barca. 256p. (Ital.). 1979. L.3500.00. Editori Riuniti.
Dizionario di psichiatria. (Ital.). L.2500.00. Newton-Compton.
Dizionario di psichiatria clinica & terapeutica. x, 852p. (Ital.). 1970. L.28000.00. Edizioni Paoline.
Dizionario di psicoanalisi tratto dalle opere di Sigmund Freud. N. Fodor & F. Gaynor. 208p. (Ital.). 1967. L.600.00. Feltrinelli.
Dizionario di psicologia. Amedeo Dalla Volta. (Illus.). 998p. (Ital.). L.18000.00. Giunti-Barbera.
Dizionario di psicologia. (Ital.). 1975. L.15000.00. Edizioni Paoline.
Dizionario di psicologia. Henri Pieron. Tr. by R. Canestrari. xviii, 664p. (Ital.). 1972. L.14000.00. La Nuova Italia.
Dizionario di psicologia analitica. C. Gustav Jung. Tr. by C. L. Musatti & L. Aurigemma. 126p. (Ital.). 1978. L.1500.00. Boringhieri.

Dizionario di psicologia del lavoro. Enzo Spaltro. LC 79-378075. 205p. (Ital.). 1976. L.5000.00. Ghisoni.
Dizionario di psicologia forense. Giancarlo Spirolazzi. 376p. (Ital.). 1969. L.3800.00. Giuffre.
Dizionario di psicologia sessuale. Georges Bastin. 472p. (Ital.). 1975. L.8000.00. La Scuola.
Dizionario di Retorica & di Stilistica. Angelo Marchese. LC 78-391880. 309p. (Ital.). 1978. L.4000.00. Mondadori.
Dizionario di scienze filosofiche. Cesare Ranzoli & M. Pigatti Ranzoli. xii, 1348p. (Ital.). 1963. L.7000.00 (ISBN 88-203-0222-5). Hoepli.
Dizionario di scienze occulte. Armando Pappalardo. viii, 366p. (Ital.). 1975. L.3600.00 (ISBN 88-205-0023-X). Cisalpino.
Dizionario di sessuologia. R. Volcher. 700p. (Ital.). 1975. L.14000.00. Cittadella.
Dizionario di sessuologia o dell'armonia coniugale. Edoardo Borra. (Ital.). L.6000.00. Edizioni Paoline.
Dizionario di sessuologia o dell'armonia coniugale. Edoardo Borra. (Ital.). L.4000.00. Edizioni Paoline.
Dizionario di sociologia. Luciano Galliano. xii, 840p. (Ital.). 1978. L.34000.00 (ISBN 88-02-03165-7). UTET.
Dizionario di sociologia. G. Duncan Mitchell. (Ital.). L.2800.00. Newton-Compton.
Dizionario di statistica. Eugene Morice. Tr. by M. G. Cossarini. xxxviii, 260p. (Ital.). 1971. L.14000.00. ISEDI.
Dizionario di termini artistici. Michelangelo Masciotta. 272p. (Ital.). L.4000.00. Monnier.
Dizionario di termini della critica letteraria. Roberto Berardi. 234p. (Ital.). L.3500.00. Monnier.
Dizionario di termini della geografia umana. Fulvio Fulvi. 150p. (Ital.). 1978. L.3900.00. Patron.
Dizionario di termini filosofici. Paolo E. Lamanna & Francesco Adorno. 104p. (Ital.). L.2300.00. Monnier.
Dizionario di termini medici di uso comune. Mario Governa. (Ital.). L.1500.00. ERI.
Dizionario di termini storici, politici ed economici moderni. Roberto Berardi. 182p. (Ital.). L.3300.00. Monnier.
Dizionario di Terminini Della Geografia Umana. Fulvio Fulvi. LC 80-475625. 149p. (Ital.). 1978. L.3900.00. Patron.
Dizionario di terminologia di storia dell'arte. Rossana Bossaglia. (Illus.). 143p. (Ital.). 1970. L.1000.00. Bignami.
Dizionario di terminologia medica. G. Giuseppe Palmieri. (Ital.). 1974. L.11000.00. Vallardi F.
Dizionario di Terminologia Ortopedica & Traumatologia. Alberto Fusari. LC 77-675054. 285p. (Ital.). 1975. L.1500.00. Gaggi.
Dizionario di terminologia ortopedica e traumatologica. 300p. (Ital.). 1975. L.15000.00. Gaggi.
Dizionario di zoologia. A. W. Leftwich. (Ital.). L.4000.00. Newton-Compton.
Dizionario di zoologia: A-L. U. Parenti. (Illus.). 128p. (Ital.). L.3000.00. Ist Geo Agostini.
Dizionario di zoologia: M-Z. U. Parenti. (Illus.). 128p. (Ital.). L.3000.00. Ist Geo Agostino.
Dizionario Dialettale Vogherese. Alessandro Maragliano. LC 76-457376. xlvi, 794p. (Ital.). 1976. L.14000.00. Patron.
Dizionario d'ingegneria. Eligio Perucca. (Illus.). xx, 976p. (Ital.). 1968. L.55000.00 (ISBN 88-02-01486-8). UTET.
Dizionario d'ingegneria. 2nd ed. Eligio Perucca. (Illus.). xvi, 1028p. (Ital.). 1969. L.55000.00 (ISBN 88-02-01487-6). UTET.
Dizionario d'ingegneria. 3rd ed. Eligio Perucca. (Illus.). xvi, 984p. (Ital.). 1970. L.55000.00 (ISBN 88-02-01488-4). UTET.
Dizionario d'ingegneria. 4th ed. Eligio Perucca. (Illus.). xvi, 1028p. (Ital.). 1972. L.55000.00 (ISBN 88-02-01489-2). UTET.
Dizionario d'ingegneria. 5th ed. Eligio Perucca. (Illus.). xvi, 940p. (Ital.). 1973. L.55000.00 (ISBN 88-02-01490-6). UTET.
Dizionario d'ingegneria. 6th ed. Eligio Perucca. (Illus.). xvi, 976p. (Ital.). 1974. L.55000.00 (ISBN 88-02-01491-4). UTET.
Dizionario d'ingegneria. 7th ed. Eligio Perucca. (Ital.). 1975. L.55000.00 (ISBN 88-02-02396-4). UTET.
Dizionario d'ingegneria. 8th ed. Eligio Perucca. (Illus.). xvi, 1040p. (Ital.). 1976. L.55000.00 (ISBN 88-02-02998-9). UTET.
Dizionario d'ingegneria. 9th ed. Eligio Perucca. (Illus.). xvi, 1024p. (Ital.). 1977. L.55000.00 (ISBN 88-02-02445-6). UTET.
Dizionario d'ingeneria. 10th ed. Eligio Perucca. (Illus.). xvi, 972p. (Ital.). 1978. L.55000.00 (ISBN 88-02-02526-6). UTET.
Dizionario elementare. Giuseppe Pittano. 864p. (Ital.). 1978. L.6500.00. Edipem.
Dizionario elementare: Per la Scuola elementare. Giuseppe Pittano. (Ital.). L.7500.00. Edipem.
Dizionario elementare: Per la Scuola elementare. Giuseppe Pittano. (Ital.). L.6500.00. Edipem.
Dizionario Enciclopedico Scientifico e Tecnico: Inglese-Italiano, Italiano-Inglese. D. Lapedes. 2122p. (Eng. & Ital.). 1980. Leatherette 175.00 (ISBN 0-686-92540-8, M-9201). French & Eur.
Dizionario epigrafico di antichita romane, 3 vols. Ettore De Ruggiero. 4358p. (Ital.). 1961. L.254000.000. L'Erma.
Dizionario eponimico ostetrico-ginecologico. Giovanni Brigato & Giorgio Pisano. xi, 562p. (Ital.). 1977. L.15000.00. Piccin.
Dizionario etimologico della lingua italiana: Vol. 1, A-C. Manlio Cortelazzo & Paolo Zolli. xxviii, 308p. (Ital.). 1979. L.13000.00. Zanichelli.
Dizionario etimologico italiano. Angelico Prati. (Illus.). 1100p. (Ital.). 1969. L.18000.00. Multigrafica.
Dizionario etimologico veneto-italiano. Dino Durante & Gianfranco Turato. xvi, 720p. (Ital.). 1976. L.20000.00. Erredici.
Dizionario Etnologico Africano, 3 vols. Tina Novelli. LC 76-463596. (Illus., Ital.). L.9000.00. Jaca Bk.
Dizionario francese-italiano e italiano-francese. (Fr. & Ital.). 1975. L.18000.00. Garzanti Edit.
Dizionario francese-italiano e italiano-francese, 2 vols. 2048p. (Fr. & Ital.). 1975. L.28000.00. Garzanti Edit.
Dizionario francese-italiano e italiano-francese. 304p. (Fr. & Ital.). L.2000.00. Malipiero.
Dizionario francese-italiano e italiano-francese. Filippi & La Tour. (Fr. & Ital.). L.3500.00. Giunti-Martello.
Dizionario Francese Italiano, Italiano Francese. Raol Boch. LC 79-348264. (Illus.). xxix, 2175p. (Fr. & Ital.). 1978. write for info. Zanichelli.
Dizionario francese-italiano italiano-francese. Raoul Boch. 2208p. (Fr. & Ital.). 1978. L.21600.00. Zanichelli.
Dizionario francese-italiano italiano-francese. (Fr. & Ital.). L.2000.00. La Mondadori.
Dizionario fraseologico commerciale italiano-francese e francese-italiano. Ada Duse. 538p. (Ital. & Fr.). 1973. L.5000.00. Bignami.
Dizionario fraseologico completo italiano-spagnolo e spagnolo-italiano: Parte italiana-spagnola. Sebastiano Carbonell. (Illus.). xvi, 840p. (Ital. & Span.). 1977. L.12000.00 (ISBN 88-203-0225-X). Hoepli.
Dizionario fraseologico completo italiano-spagnolo e spagnolo-italiano: Parte spagnola-italiana. Sebastiano Carbonell. xii, 1524p. (Span. & Ital.). 1979. L.18000.00 (ISBN 88-203-0224-1). Hoepli.
Dizionario fraseologico di Inglese Tecnico. Canzio Vandelli. (Ital. & Eng.). 1977. L.4900.00. Mondini Siccardi.
Dizionario fraseologico di russo-italiano e viceversa. Canzio Vandelli. (Rus. & Ital.). 1977. L.24000.00. Mondini Siccardi.
Dizionario fraseologico e grammaticale della lingua inglese. Francesco Pipitone. 662p. (Ital. & Eng.). L.7000.00. Galeati.
Dizionario fraseologico e grammaticale italiano-francese. Massimo Gatto. 376p. (Ital. & Fr.). L.2200.00. Sandron.
Dizionario fraseologico e grammaticale italiano-inglese. Massimo Gatto. 306p. (Ital. & Eng.). L.2000.00. Sandron.
Dizionario Garzanti della Lingua Italiana. G. Cusatelli. 1008p. (Ital.). 1979. 19.95 (ISBN 0-686-97335-6, M-9189). French & Eur.
Dizionario Garzanti della Lingua Italiana. G Cusatelli. 2008p. (Ital.). 1980. 49.95 (ISBN 0-686-97336-4, M-9190). French & Eur.
Dizionario Garzanti della Lingua Italiana. Ed. by G. Cusatelli. 968p. (Ital.). write for info. (M-9188). French & Eur.
Dizionario Garzanti Della Lingua Italiana. (Orig., Ital.). L.12.00. Speedimpex.
Dizionario Garzanti Della Lingua Italiana. (Ital.). L.17.00. Speedimpex.
Dizionario Garzanti: Francese-Italiano, Italiano-Francese. G. Cusatelli & G. Brunacci. Ed. by U. Salati & F. Dominicis. 2029p. (Fr. & Ital.). 1980. 49.95 (ISBN 0-686-92560-2, M-6143). French & Eur.
Dizionario Garzanti Italiano-Inglese & Inglese-Italiano. (Orig., Eng. & Ital.). L.12.00. Speedimpex.
Dizionario Garzanti Italiano-Inglese & Inglese-Italiano. Hazon. (Ital. & Eng.). L.30.00. Speedimpex.
Dizionario Garzanti Italiano-Inglese & Inglese-Italiano. Hazon. (Eng. & Ital.). L.45.00. Speedimpex.
Dizionario Garzanti: Italiano-Inglese, Inglese-Italiano. M. Hazon. 1024p. (Eng. & Ital.). 1980. 19.95 (ISBN 0-686-97642-8, M-9187). French & Eur.
Dizionario Garzantil Italiano-Francese, Francese-Italiano. 1020p. (Ital. & Fr.). 1979. 19.95 (ISBN 0-686-97334-8, M-9191). French & Eur.
Dizionario gastronomico. Elisabetta Neiger. 139p. (Ital.). L.3000.00. Buffetti.
Dizionario genovese-italiano. G. Casaccia. 871p. (Ital.). L.30000.00. Brenner.
Dizionario geografico. Giovanni Boccaccio. (Ital.). 1978. L.7000.00. Fogola.
Dizionario giuridico del lavoro e delle assicurazioni sociali. Antonio Palermo & Carlo Palermo. 1550p. (Ital.). 1972. L.15000.00. La Tribuna.
Dizionario giuridico-economico: Vol. 1, Italiano-tedesco. Giuseppe Conte. vii, 356p. (Ital. & Ger.). 1971. L.11000.00. Giuffre.
Dizionario giuridico-economico: Vol. 2, Tedesco-italiano. Giuseppe Conte. 458p. (Ger. & Ital.). 1969. L.11000.00. Giuffre.
Dizionario grammaticale. Vincenzo Ceppellini. 650p. (Ital.). 1968. L.5000.00. Ist Geo Agostini.
Dizionario greco-italiano. Benedetto Bonazzi. v, 1232p. (Gr. & Ital.). L.7000.00. Morano.
Dizionario greco moderno-italiano e italiano-greco moderno: Vol. 1, Greco moderno-italiano. Eliseo Brighenti. xvi, 696p. (Gr. & Ital.). 1976. L.6300.00 (ISBN 88-205-0045-0). Cisalpino.
Dizionario greco moderno-italiano e italiano-greco moderno: Vol. 2, Italiano-greco moderno. 672p. (Ital. & Gr.). 1976. L.6000.00 (ISBN 88-205-0046-9). Cisalpino.
Dizionario greco moderno-italiano, italiano-greco moderno. 304p. (Gr. & Ital.). L.3000.00. Malipiero.
Dizionario Hazon Garzanti: Inglese-Italiano, Italiano-Inglese. Ed. by M. Hazon. 1686p. (Eng. & Ital.). write for info. (M-9185). French & Eur.
Dizionario illustrato degli incisori italiani. L. L. Servolini. (Illus., Ital.). L.34500.00. Goerlich.
Dizionario illustrato della lingua italiana. (Illus.). xvi, 1216p. (Ital.). 1978. L.10000.00. Sansoni.
Dizionario illustrato della lingua italiana. (Illus.). 1304p. (Ital.). L.9000.00. Ist Geo Agostini.
Dizionario illustrato della lingua italiana, 2 vols. (Illus.). 1280p. (Ital.). L.15000.00. Curcio.
Dizionario illustrato della lingua latina. E. Bianchi et al. (Illus.). xx, 2582p. (Lat.). 1973. L.2300.00. Monnier.
Dizionario illustrato della lingua latina, 2 vols. E. Bianchi et al. xxxvi, 2482p. (Lat.). 1973. L.19000.00. Monnier.
Dizionario illustrato e commentato delle norme di circolazione previste dal nuovo codice della strada. Mario Calamante. (Illus.). 384p. (Ital.). 1960. L.7000.00. Ateneo & Bizzarri.
Dizionario illustrato greco-italiano. H. G. Liddell et al. (Illus.). xvi, 1568p. (Gr. & Ital.). 1975. L.23800.00. Monnier.
Dizionario illustrato italiano-tedesco. (Illus.). 776p. (Ital. & Ger.). 1974. L.12000.00. Longanesi.
Dizionario illustrato latino-italiano. F. Gaffiot. (Illus.). 1576p. (Lat. & Ital.). 1973. L.15000.00. Piccin.
Dizionario illustrato tedesco-italiano. (Illus.). 828p. (Ger. & Ital.). L.12000.00. Longanesi.
Dizionario inglese. A. Borelli et al. (Eng.). L.18000.00. Ist Geo Agostini.
Dizionario inglese-italiano. Giuseppe Ragazzini & Adele Biagi. 1150p. (Eng. & Ital.). 1972. L.8400.00; L.pap. 6800.00. Zanichelli.
Dizionario inglese-italiano dei termini relativi all'elettrotecnica. Henry Piraux. 544p. (Eng. & Ital.). L.6400.00. Signorelli C.
Dizionario Inglese-Italiano dei Termini Relativi All'Elettronica: All'Elettrotecnica e Alle Applicazioni Connesse. H. Piraux. 534p. (Eng. & Ital.). 1977. pap. 29.95 (ISBN 0-686-92527-0, M-9195). French & Eur.
Dizionario inglese-italiano e italiano-inglese con glossario bilingue di tecnica navale. Giuseppe Ragazzini. xxx, 2020p. (Ital. & Eng.). L.24000.00. Zanichelli.
Dizionario inglese-italiano e italiano-inglese con glossario bilingue di economia e organizzazione aziendale. Gualtiero Rossi. xxxii, 2044p. (Eng. & Ital.). L.24000.00. Zanichelli.
Dizionario inglese-italiano e italiano-inglese: Edizione scholastica. Mario Hazon. (Illus.). 1686p. (Eng. & Ital.). 1975. L.16000.00. Garzanti Edit.
Dizionario inglese-italiano e italiano-inglese. 304p. (Eng. & Ital.). L.2000.00. Malipiero.
Dizionario inglese-italiano e italiano-inglese. (Eng. & Ital.). 1975. L.17500.00. Sansoni.
Dizionario inglese-italiano e italiano-inglese. Giuseppe Ragazzini. xxxii, 1864p. (Ital.). 1967. L.26000.00; L.pap. 21800.00. Zanichelli.
Dizionario inglese-italiano-francese-tedesco. L. Gives et al. 296p. (Eng., Ital., Fr. & Ger.). 1973. L.1600.00. De Bono.
Dizionario inglese-italiano, italiano-inglese: Adattamento e ristrutturazione dell'originale. lxv, 1894p. (Eng. & Ital.). 1977. L.18000.00. SEI.
Dizionario inglese-italiano per le scienze mediche. R. Marconi & E. Zino. 572p. (Eng. & Ital.). 1975. L.15000.00. Minerva Medica.
Dizionario inglese moderno. Franceso M. Gualtieri. (Illus.). 1400p. (Eng.). L.12000.00. Trevisini.
Dizionario inverso italiano. M. Alinei. (Ital.). L.10000.00. Il Mulino.
Dizionario Italian-Slovar. A. Bajec & P. Kalan. 843p. (Ital. & Slovene.). 1980. 49.95 (ISBN 0-686-97337-2, M-9692). French & Eur.
Dizionario Italiano-Albanese. F. Cordignano. xii, 758p. (Ital. & Albanian.). L.26000.00. Forni.

Dizionario italiano-arabo moderno, 2 vols. Elpidio Jannota. (Ital. & Arabic.). 1964. L.31500.00. Ist Poligrafico.

Dizionario Italiano-Bulgaro. M. Cavaletto et al. 967p. (Ital. & Bulgarian.). 1979. leatherette 35.00 (ISBN 0-686-97340-2, M-9835). French & Eur.

Dizionario italiano-ceco. Jaroslav Rosendorfsky. 716p. (Ital. & Czech.). L.2000.00. Ist Univers Orient.

Dizionario italiano-danese. 576p. (Ital. & Danish.). L.1800.00. Malipiero.

Dizionario italiano di vocaboli e modi usati in poesia: Per le Scuole superiori. Vittorio Busa. 68p. (Ital.). L.1910.00. Mori.

Dizionario Italiano-Finlandes, Finlandes-Italiano. Ed. by G. Colussi. (Ital. & Finnish.). leatherette 5.95 (ISBN 0-686-92443-6, M-9170). French & Eur.

Dizionario italiano-finlandese. Colussi. 460p. (Ital. & Finnish.). L.2300.00. Vallardi A.

Dizionario italiano-francese. 576p. (Ital. & Fr.). L.1500.00. Malipiero.

Dizionario italiano-francese. (Ital. & Fr.). L.1500.00. Mondadori.

Dizionario italiano-francese. Claire Laurent. 190p. (Ital. & Fr.). 1975. L.2000.00. Vallardi A.

Dizionario italiano-francese e francese-italiano. Amato Bertet et al. (Illus.). xii, 1824p. (Ital. & Fr.). L.11500.00. Paravia.

Dizionario italiano-francese e francese-italiano. 1024p. (Ital. & Fr.). 1974. L.5000.00. Garzanti Edit.

Dizionario italiano-francese e francese-italiano. 1024p. (Ital. & Fr.). 1975. L.6800.00. Garzanti Edit.

Dizionario italiano-francese e francese-italiano. R. Simone. 640p. (Ital. & Fr.). 1975. L.2500.00. La Nuova Italia.

Dizionario Italiano-Francese e Francese-Italiano di termini in uso in economia, borsa, finanza. Vera Pegna. 512p. (Ital. & Fr.). 1969. L.5000.00. Etas Libri.

Dizionario Italiano-Francese, Francese-Italiano. G. Laurent. 413p. (Fr. & Ital.). 1979. leatherette 5.95 (ISBN 0-686-97341-0, M-9173). French & Eur.

Dizionario italiano-francese francese-italiano della lingua d'oggi. Candido Ghiotto et al. 1230p. (Ital. & Fr.). 1977. L.9500.00. Petrini.

Dizionario italiano-francese-italiano. G. Sbrulli & T. Biffoli. xvi, 1056p. (Ital. & Fr.). L.7000.00. Valmartina.

Dizionario italiano-greco moderno. 304p. (Ital. & Gr.). L.3000.00. Malipiero.

Dizionario italiano illustrato. (Illus.). 866p. (Ital.). L.8500.00. SEI.

Dizionario italiano illustrato. (Illus.). 1472p. (Ital.). 1974. L.14000.00. Ist Geog Agostini.

Dizionario italiano illustrato per l'uso essenziale della lingua. G. Colli. (Illus.). 862p. (Ital.). 1978. L.8500.00 (ISBN 88-05-03624-2). SEI.

Dizionario italiano-inglese. (Ital. & Eng.). L.1500.00. Mondadori.

Dizionario italiano-inglese. 576p. (Ital. & Eng.). L.1500.00. Malipiero.

Dizionario italiano-inglese. Boy Musu. 508p. (Ital. & Eng.). L.2000.00. Vallardi A.

Dizionario italiano-inglese e inglese-italiano. 1100p. (Ital. & Eng.). 1975. L.6800.00. Garzanti Edit.

Dizionario italiano-inglese e inglese-italiano. 1072p. (Ital. & Eng.). 1975. L.5000.00. Garzanti Edit.

Dizionario italiano-inglese e inglese-italiano. F. M. Gualtieri. xii, 680p. (Ital. & Eng.). 1967. L.3200.00. Casanova F & C.

Dizionario italiano-inglese e inglese-italiano. Giuseppe Motta. x, 1052p. (Ital. & Eng.). L.12400.00. Signorelli C.

Dizionario italiano-inglese e inglese-italiano: Edizione minore. Giuseppe Orlandi. xiv, 1184p. (Ital. & Eng.). L.7600.00. Signorelli C.

Dizionario italiano-inglese e inglese-italiano tecnico. Renzo Denti. xvi, 1812p. (Ital. & Eng.). 1979. L.18000.00 (ISBN 88-203-1052-X). Hoepli.

Dizionario italiano-inglese-francese-tedesco. L. Gives et al. 304p. (Ital., Eng., Fr. & Ger.). 1973. L.1600.00. De Bono.

Dizionario italiano-inglese inglese-italiano. (Ital. & Eng.). L.2000.00. Mondadori.

Dizionario Italiano-Inglese, Inglese-Italiano. R. Musu-Boy. 463p. (Ital. & Eng.). 1979. leatherette 4.95 (ISBN 0-686-97343-7, M-9177). French & Eur.

Dizionario italiano-latino. Oreste Badellino. 1480p. (Ital. & Lat.). 1972. L.17500.00 (ISBN 88-7011-007-9). Rosenberg & Sel.

Dizionario italiano-latino. 576p. (Ital. & Lat.). L.1500.00. Malipiero.

Dizionario Italiano-Latino. Angelo Perugini. LC 78-337088. x, 2322p. (Ital. & Lat.). 1976. write for info. Libr Ed Vat.

Dizionario italiano-latino. Angelo Perugini. xii, 2322p. (Ital. & Lat.). 1977. L.35000.00 (ISBN 88-209-1227-9). Libr Ed Vat.

Dizionario italiano-latino. Sacerdoti. 208p. (Ital. & Lat.). 1976. L.2000.00. Vallardi A.

Dizionario italiano-latino: Edizione speciale. Oreste Badellino. 213p. (Ital. & Lat.). 1972. L.25000.00 (ISBN 88-7011-008-7). Rosenberg & Sel.

Dizionario Italiano-Latino, Latino-Italiano. N. Sacerdoti. 391p. (Ital. & Lat.). 1977. leatherette 5.95 (ISBN 0-686-92629-3, M-9175). French & Eur.

Dizionario italiano moderno. A. Rossi. (Ital.). L.4300.00. Malipiero.

Dizionario italiano-olandese. 576p. (Ital. & Dutch.). L.1800.00. Malipiero.

Dizionario italiano-olandese. Van Cappen. 540p. (Ital. & Dutch.). L.2300.00. Vallardi A.

Dizionario Italiano-Olandese, Olandese-Italiano. V. Van Kampen. 486p. (Ital. & Dutch.). 1980. leatherette 5.95 (ISBN 0-686-97344-5, M-9171). French & Eur.

Dizionario italiano-portoghese. Biava. 292p. (Ital. & Port.). 1976. L.2300.00. Vallardi A.

Dizionario Italiano-Portoghese, Portoghese-Italiano. A. Biava. 318p. (Ital. & Port.). 1980. leatherette 5.95 (ISBN 0-686-97345-3, M-9172). French & Eur.

Dizionario italiano-russo. Fadanelli. 138p. (Ital. & Rus.). 1976. L.2300.00. Vallardi A.

Dizionario italiano-russo. Skvorzova & Maizel. 954p. (Ital. & Rus.). 1963. L.4000.00. Editori Riuniti.

Dizionario Italiano-Russo, Russo-Italiane. R. Fadanelli. 286p. (Ital. & Rus.). leatherette 5.95 (ISBN 0-686-92582-3). French & Eur.

Dizionario Italiano-Serbo Croato. Livadic. 554p. (Ital. & Serbo-Croation.). L.2300.00. Vallardi A.

Dizionario Italiano-Serbocroato, Serbocroato-Italiano. Ed. by P. Livadic. 500p. (Ital. & Serbocroatian.). 1980. leatherette 5.95 (ISBN 0-686-92461-4, M-9180). French & Eur.

Dizionario italiano-serbocroato sloveno. 304p. (Ital. & Serbo-Croation.). L.3000.00. Malipiero.

Dizionario italiano-spagnolo. Garcia. 232p. (Ital. & Span.). 1975. L.2000.00. Vallardi A.

Dizionario Italiano-Spagnolo, Spagnolo-Italiano. A. Garcia. 437p. (Span. & Ital.). 1980. leatherette 5.95 (ISBN 0-686-97347-X, S-31237). French & Eur.

Dizionario italiano-svedese. 576p. (Ital. & Swedish.). L.1800.00. Malipiero.

Dizionario italiano-svedese. Gaft & Bassoli. 530p. (Ital. & Swedish.). L.2300.00. Vallardi A.

Dizionario Italiano-Svedese, Svedese-Italiano. G. Gareff & F. Bassoli. 442p. (Ital. & Swedish.). 1973. Leatherette 5.95 (ISBN 0-686-92541-6, M-9174). French & Eur.

Dizionario italiano-tedesco. Altenberg. 246p. (Ital. & Ger.). 1975. L.2300.00. Vallardi A.

Dizionario italiano-tedesco. Guido Cosciani. xxiv, 1096p. (Ital. & Ger.). 1970. L.16000.00. Paravia.

Dizionario italiano-tedesco. 576p. (Ital. & Ger.). L.1500.00. Malipiero.

Dizionario italiano-tedesco. (Ital. & Ger.). L.1500.00. Mondadori.

Dizionario italiano-tedesco e tedesco-italiano. Giovanni Ciardi Dupre & Angelica Escher. x, 1762p. (Ital. & Ger.). 1978. L.21000.00 (ISBN 88-05-04137-8). SEI.

Dizionario italiano-tedesco e tedesco-italiano. Giovannelli. 1224p. (Ital. & Ger.). L.13600.00. Signorelli C.

Dizionario italiano-tedesco e tedesco-italiano. A. Gullino Kuhn. xxii, 950p. (Ital. & Ger.). 1967. L.5400.00. Casanova F & C.

Dizionario italiano-tedesco e tedesco-italiano. Lysle & Pontevideo. 2200p. (Ital. & Ger.). L.12000.00. Casanova F & C.

Dizionario Italiano-Tedesco, Tedesco-Italian. G. A. Altenberg & V. Ubaldi. 395p. (Ger. & Ital.). 1979. leatherette 6.95 (ISBN 0-686-97349-6, M-9176). French & Eur.

Dizionario italiano-tedesco tedesco-italiano. Langenscheidt. 112p. (Ital. & Ger.). L.18000.00. Signorelli C.

Dizionario Italiano-Turco, Turco-Italiano. M. Celalettin Bugday. 410p. (Ital. & Turkish.). 1979. leatherette 5.95 (ISBN 0-686-97351-8, M-9178). French & Eur.

Dizionario italo-indonesiano. L. Lini. 818p. (Ital. & Indonesian.). L.18000.00. EMI.

Dizionario latino. Gino Angelini et al. xii, 1908p. (Lat.). 1975. L.16000.00. Dante Alighieri.

Dizionario latino-italiano. Ferruccio Calonghi. 1480p. (Lat. & Ital.). 1972. L.17500.00 (ISBN 88-7011-009-5). Rosenberg & Sel.

Dizionario latino-italiano e italiano-latino. 304p. (Lat. & Ital.). L.2000.00. Malipiero.

Dizionario latino-italiano e italiano-latino. Giuseppe Pittano. 1696p. (Lat. & Ital.). L.22000.00. Edn Scol Mond.

Dizionario latino-italiano: Stato della Chiesa-Veneto-Abruzzi. Pietro Sella. xxxii, 687p. (Lat. & Ital.). 1965. L.10000.00 (ISBN 88-210-0387-6). Biblioteca Apostolica Vaticana.

Dizionario linguistico moderno. Aldo Gabrielli. 1192p. (Ital.). L.12000.00. Edn Scol Mond.

Dizionario medico. Bailliere et al. 771p. (Ital.). 1977. L.10000.00 (ISBN 88-85019-16-1). Edi Ermes.

Dizionario medico. (Illus.). 1208p. (Ital.). 1971. L.35000.00. Edizioni Paoline.

Dizionario medico. W. A. Dorland Newman. (Illus.). viii, 686p. (Ital.). 1970. L.10000.00. CEA.

Dizionario medico. Duranteau. (Ital.). L.8000.00. Newton Compton.

Dizionario medico, 2 vols. Emanuele Lauricella. viii, 1654p. (Ital.). 1976. L.48000.00 (ISBN 88-03-00071-2). USES.

Dizionario medico. L. Segatore & G. A. Poli. (Illus.). 1368p. (Ital.). L.20000.00. Ist Geog Agostini.

Dizionario Medico Poliglotta. Veillon & Nobel. (Ital., Span., Eng., Fr., & Ger.). Leatherette 190.00 (ISBN 0-686-92503-3, M-9636). French & Eur.

Dizionario medico poliglotta: Inglese-tedesco-francese. Veillon & Nobel. 1330p. (Eng., Ger. & Fr.). 1969. L.20000.00. Piccin.

Dizionario Medico Ragionato Inglese-Italiano. M. Lucchesi. 1489p. (Eng. & Ital.). 1978. 95.00 (ISBN 0-686-92622-6, M-9353). French & Eur.

Dizionario Medico Ragionato Inglese-Italiano: Termini, Abbreviazioni, Sigle, Eponimi e Sinonimi Medici, Medico-Biologici e Delle Specializzazioni Mediche. Mario Lucchesi. 1490p. (Eng. & Ital.). 1978. 98.00x (ISBN 0-913298-52-2). S F Vanni.

Dizionario medico ragionato per le scienze mediche inglese-italiano. U. M. Lucchesi. 1500p. (Eng. & Ital.). 1978. L.38000.00. Cortina M.

Dizionario merceologico per la pratica applicazione della nuova tariffa doganale italiana. L. Settimj. xii, 496p. (Ital.). 1951. L.1250.00 (ISBN 88-203-0226-8). Hoepli.

Dizionario Merli geografico, storico, economico: Vol. 1, Lettera AZ. Marcello G. Compagnol. (Illus.). 176p. (Ital.). 1975. L.25000.00. ERGA.

Dizionario metodico del commercio laniero. Luigi Caccianotti. (Illus.). 348p. (Ital.). L.3200.00. Edit Laniera.

Dizionario milanese-italiano. Cletto Arrighi. xii, 904p. (Ital.). 1978. L.9000.00 (ISBN 88-203-0964-5). Hoepli.

Dizionario moderno. Alfredo Panzini et al. xxiv, 1096p. (Ital.). 1963. L.10000.00 (ISBN 88-203-0228-4). Hoepli.

Dizionario moderno genovese-italiano e italiano-genovese. Giuseppe Frisoni. 538p. (Ital.). L.19500.00. Forni.

Dizionario moderno italiano-francese e francese-italiano. Ernesto Cassiani. xvi, 2238p. (Ital. & Fr.). L.18000.00. SEI.

Dizionario moderno italiano-francese e francese-italiano. Bruno A. Paoli. 1584p. (Ital. & Fr.). L.8000.00. Edn Scol Mond.

Dizionario moderno italiano-spagnolo e spagnolo-italiano: Vol. 1, Italiano-spagnolo. Gaetano Frisoni. xii, 1118p. (Ital. & Span.). 1977. L.7500.00 (ISBN 88-203-0229-2). Hoepli.

Dizionario moderno italiano-spagnolo e spagnolo-italiano: Vol. 2, Spagnolo-italiano. Gaetano Frisoni. xii, 748p. (Span. & Ital.). 1977. L.5000.00 (ISBN 88-203-0230-6). Hoepli.

Dizionario Moderno Slovene-Italian-Slovene. A. Grad. 445p. (Ital. & Slovene.). 1979. leatherette 14.95 (ISBN 0-686-97353-4, M9704). French & Eur.

Dizionario Moderno Spagnuolo-Italiano, Italiano-Spagnuolo, 2 vols. Gaetano Frisoni. 1865p. (Span. & Ital.). Set. 44.00x (ISBN 0-913298-51-4). S F Vanni.

Dizionario Mondadori di storia universale, 2 vols. Michel Mourre. (Ital.). L.30000.00. Mondadori.

Dizionario monferrino. Giuseppe Ferraro. 137p. (Ital.). L.5500.00. Forni.

Dizionario Motta della lingua italiana, 2 vols. E. Bazzarelli. (Illus.). 1800p. (Ital.). L.69600.00. Motta.

Dizionario olandese-italiano e italiano. 304p. (Dutch & Ital.). L.3000.00. Malipiero.

Dizionario per le scuole elementari. Ludwig Wittgenstein. Tr. by D. Antiseri. 284p. (Ital.). 1978. L.8000.00. Armando.

Dizionario per l'industria delle materie plastiche: Definizioni italiane e termini corrispondenti in francese, inglese e tedesco. Enrico Ferraris & Istituto Italiano dei Plastici. vii, 320p. (Ital., Fr., Eng. & Ger.). 1977. L.22000.00. SAPIL.

Dizionario persiano-italiano classico, moderno, familiare. Hanne Coletti Gruenbaum. xvi, 960p. (Persian & Ital.). 1978. L.25000.00. Coletti.

Dizionario polesano-italiano. P. Mazzucchi. 308p. (Pol. & Ital.). L.10800.00. Forni.

Dizionario politico e parlamentare. Gino Pallotta. (Ital.). L.2500.00. Newton Compton.

Dizionario Politico e Parlamentare Italiano. Gino Pallotta. LC 77-454206. 302p. (Ital.). 1976. L.2500.00. Newton Compton.

Dizionario portoghese-italiano. Parlagreco. 434p. (Port. & Ital.). 1974. L.14000.00. Vallardi A.

Dizionario Portoghese-Italiano, Italiano-Portoghese. C. Parlagreco. 1138p. (Port. & Ital.). 1979. 35.00 (ISBN 0-686-97354-2, M-9183). French & Eur.

Dizionario pratico della lingua francese. Enea Balmas. (Illus.). 1950p. (Fr.). 1979. L.16000.00. Ist Geog Agostini.

Dizionario pratico della lingua francese. Enea Balmas. 1936p. (Fr.). 1974. L.15000.00. Ghisetti & Corvi.

Dizionario pratico e frasario per conversazione italiano-amarica. L. Fusella & A. Girace. (Ital.). 1937. L.1500.00. Ist Univers Orient.

Dizionario pratico tedesco-italiano italiano-tedesco. Langenscheidt. 624p. (Ger. & Ital.). L.6800.00. Signorelli C.

Dizionario primierotto. Livio Tissot. (Illus.). 368p. (Ital.). 1976. L.12000.00. Manfrini.

Dizionario ragionato dei simboli. G. Cairo. (Illus.). xvi, 366p. (Ital.). L.18000.00. Forni.

Dizionario ragionato di psicologia individuale. Francesco Parenti. 273p. (Ital.). 1975. L.10000.00. Cortina M.

Dizionario ragionato di sinonimi e dei contrari. Gianni Cesana. 662p. (Ital.). L.7500.00. De Vecchi Italy.

Dizionario rapido di scienze pure ed applicate. Rinaldo De Benedetti. (Illus.). viii, 1336p. (Ital.). 1966. L.25000.00 (ISBN 88-02-01497-3). UTET.

Dizionario Sandron della lingua italiana. (Illus.). xvi, 2160p. (Ital.). 1976. L.18500.00. Sandron.

Dizionario serbocroato-italiano e sloveno-italiano. 304p. (Serbo-Croation, Slovenian & Ital.). L.3000.00. Malipiero.

Dizionario si sessuologia. R. Volker. 720p. (Ital.). 1976. L.17000.00. Cittadella.

Dizionario siciliano-italiano. Giuseppe Biundi. 600p. (Ital.). L.18000.00. Forni.

Dizionario siciliano-italiano. Giuseppe Biundi & A. Rigoli. xvi, 540p. (Ital.). 1978. L.6000.00. Il Vespro.

Dizionario siciliano-italiano. Giovanni Cavallaro. (Ital.). L.1450.00. Bonanno.

Dizionario siciliano-italiano. V. Nicotra. 926p. (Ital.). L.33000.00. Forni.

Dizionario sinottico di iconologia. Norma Cecchini. (Illus.). xxx, 472p. (Ital.). 1976. L.24500.00. Patron.

Dizionario Sinottico di Iconologia. Norma Cecchini & Giuseppe Plessi. LC 77-466702. (Illus.). xxx, 471p. (Ital.). 1976. L.24500.00. Patron.

Dizionario sintattico latino. Bruno Nelli. 280p. (Lat.). 1968. L.6000.00. Giardini Pisa.

Dizionario sintattico latino: Italiano-latino e latino-italiano. Giovanni La Magna. 180p. (Ital. & Lat.). L.2000.00. Signorelli C.

Dizionario sintetico da tavolo. L. Pallini. (Illus.). xvi, 790p. (Ital.). L.11000.00. Vallardi F.

Dizionario spagnolo-italiano e italiano-spagnolo. 304p. (Span. & Ital.). L.2000.00. Malipiero.

Dizionario spagnolo-italiano e italiano-spagnolo. Enrico Migliori. (Span. & Ital.). L.3500.00. Giunti-Martello.

Dizionario storico araldico dell'antico ducato di Ferrara. Frassoni F. Pasini. (Illus.). 793p. (Ital.). L.35000.00. Forni.

Dizionario Storico Della Mafia. Gino Pallotta. LC 77-576985. (Illus.). 134p. (Ital.). 1977. L.2000.00. Newton Compton.

Dizionario svedes-italiano e italiano-svedese. 304p. (Swedish & Ital.). L.3000.00. Malipiero.

Dizionario tascabile delle tecniche ambientale: Italiano, francese, inglese, tedesco. Maurizio Pasquali. 296p. (Ital., Fr., Eng. & Ger.). 1976. L.8000.00. SAPIL.

Dizionario tascabile illustrato. Ernesto Carletti. (Illus.). 104p. (Ital.). 1978. L.2800.00. Citta Nuova.

Dizionario Tecnico Francese-Italiano. Renzo Denti. LC 79-352645. xx, 1182p. (Fr. & Ital.). 1977. L.15000.00. Hoepli.

Dizionario tecnico francese-italiano e italiano-francese. Renzo Denti. xx, 1840p. (Fr. & Ital.). 1977. L.15000.00 (ISBN 88-203-0937-8). Hoepli.

Dizionario tecnico inglese-italiano e italiano-inglese. Giorgio Marolli. (Illus.). xxiv, 2048p. (Eng. & Ital.). L.35000.00. Monnier.

Dizionario Tecnico Italiano-Inglese. Renzo Denti. LC 76-470277. 1799p. (Eng. & Ital.). 1976. write for info. Hoepli.

Dizionario Tecnico Italiano-Inglese, Inglese-Italiano. 9th rev. ed. Renzo Denti. 1811p. (Eng. & Ital.). 1979. 78.00x (ISBN 88-203-1052-X). S F Vanni.

Dizionario Tecnico Italiano-Inglese, Inglese-Italiano. G. Marolli. 2048p. (Ital. & Eng.). 1978. write for info. (M-9197). French & Eur.

Dizionario Tecnico Italiano-Tedesco, 2 vols. 5th ed. Alice Meyer. LC 79-362362. (Eng., Ital. & Ger.). 1977. L.25000.00. Brandstetter.

Dizionario tecnico italiano-tedesco e tedesco-italiano, 2 vols. A. Meyer & S. Orlando. 2860p. (Ital. & Ger.). L.25000.00 (ISBN 88-203-0936-X). Hoepli.

Dizionario Tecnico Nautico: Italiano-Inglese, Inglese-Italiano. V. Mastropasqua. 879p. (Ital. & Eng.). 1967. pap. 49.95 (ISBN 0-686-92533-5, M-9297). French & Eur.

Dizionario tecnico-scientifico: Italiano-tedesco. Paolo Carboni. 752p. (Ital. & Ger.). 1969. L.5000.00. Patron.

Dizionario tecnico-scientifico: Tedesco-italiano. Paolo Carboni. 708p. (Ger. & Ital.). 1965. L.5000.00. Patron.

Dizionario Tecnico Tedesco-Italiano. Giorgio Marolli & Orazio Guarnieri. LC 77-466767. 2032p. (Ital. & Ger.). 1976. L.24000.00. Garzanti Edit.

Dizionario tecnico tedesco-italiano italiano-tedesco. Giorgio Marolli & Orazio Guarnieri. 2044p. (Ger. & Ital.). 1976. L.28000.00. Garzanti Edit.

Dizionario Tecnico Tedesco-Italiano, Italiano-Tedesco Garzanti. M. Guarnieri & O. Guarnieri. 2032p. (Ger. & Ital.). 1979. 75.00 (ISBN 0-686-97355-0, M9184). French & eur.

Dizionario tedesco-italiano. Emilio Bidoli & Guido Cosciani. xxii, 1282p. (Ger. & Ital.). 1970. L.16000.00. Paravia.

Dizionario tedesco-italiano. A. Lanzara. 744p. (Ger. & Ital.). L.34000.00. Forni.

Dizionario tedesco-italiano di biologia e medicina. Valentino Grandis & Mario Donati. xii, 710p. (Ger. & Ital.). 1964. L.7000.00 (ISBN 88-7011-010-9). Rosenberg & Sel.

Dizionario tedesco-italiano e italiano-tedesco. 304p. (Ger. & Ital.). L.2000.00. Malipiero.

Dizionario tedesco-italiano e italiano-tedesco. (Ger. & Ital.). 1975. L.20000.00. Sansoni.

Dizionario tedesco-italiano per le scienze chimiche e affini. Clara Giua Lollini & Michele Giua. viii, 798p. (Ger. & Ital.). 1962. L.6500.00 (ISBN 88-7011-011-7). Rosenberg & Sel.

Dizionario tedesco-italiano per le scienze mediche. E. Marcovecchio. 762p. (Ger. & Ital.). 1967. L.16000.00. Minerva Medica.

Dizionario teologico interdisciplinare, 3 vols. LC 79-384605. (Ital.). 1977. write for info. Marietti.

Dizionario trentino-italiano. Lionello Groff. 206p. (Ital.). L.3500.00. Monauni.

Dizionario turco-italiano. Budgay. 194p. (Turkish & Ital.). 1976. L.2300.00. Vallardi A.

Dizionario umoristico. Dino Provenzal. iv, 553p. (Ital.). 1976. L.6000.00 (ISBN 88-205-0097-3). Cisalpino-La Goliardica.

Dr. Gabler's die Sprache der Chefs. 227p. (Ger.). 1977. 15.95 (ISBN 3-409-90031-4, M-7352, Pub. by Betriebswirtschaftlicher Vlg.). French & Eur.

Dr. Gablers Wirtschafts - Lexikon. R. Sellien. 2565p. (Ger.). 1975. 189.00 (ISBN 3-409-32992-7, M-7351, Pub. by Betriebswirtschaftlicher Vlg.). French & Eur.

Doctor Johnson & His English Dictionary. John E. Wallis. 1978. Repr. of 1945 ed. lib. bdg. 10.00 (ISBN 0-8495-5643-0). Arden Lib.

Doctor Knock-Knock's Official Knock-Knock Dictionary. Joseph Rosenbloom. LC 76-19796. (Illus.). 128p. (gr. 3 up). 1980. pap. 2.95 (ISBN 0-8069-8936-X). Sterling.

Doctor Knock-Knock's Official Knock-Knock Dictionary. Joseph Rosenbloom. LC 76-19796. (Illus.). (gr. 3 up). 1976. 7.95 (ISBN 0-8069-4536-2); PLB 9.99 (ISBN 0-8069-4537-0). Sterling.

Doctrine of Propositions & Terms. Arthur N. Prior. Ed. by P. T. Geach & A. J. Kenny. LC 76-9375. 1976. 9.00x (ISBN 0-87023-214-2). U of Mass Pr.

Doktor Gabler's Wirtschafts-Lexikon, 2 vols. Ed. by R. Sellien & H. Sellien. LC 75-522546. (Illus., Ger.). 1975. DM.224.00 (ISBN 3-409-30932-2). Gabler.

Dongolese Nubian: A Grammar. C. H. Armbruster. 1965. text ed. 170.00 (ISBN 0-521-04050-7). Cambridge U Pr.

Dongolese Nubian, a Lexicon. C. H. Armbruster. 1965. text ed. 145.00 (ISBN 0-521-04051-5). Cambridge U Pr.

Donkey & Mule Terms & Their Definitons. 1p. 0.15. Am Donkey.

Dopolnenie K Anglo-Russkomu Slovariu Po Radioelektrike & Sviazi. N. I. Dozorov. 68p. (Rus. & Eng.). 1960. 0.80 (Pub. by Izd. Glav. upravl. Po Ispol'z. Atomn. Energii). Four Continent.

Dorland's Illustrated Medical Dictionary. 26th ed. (Illus.). 1800p. 1981. text ed. 34.50 (ISBN 0-7216-3150-9); indexed 39.50 (ISBN 0-7216-3151-7); deluxe ed. 59.00 indexed (ISBN 0-7216-3145-2). Saunders.

Dorland's Medical Dictionary: Shorter Edition. LC 79-67113. (Illus.). 768p. 1980. 16.95 (ISBN 0-7216-3142-8). Saunders.

Dostoevsky Dictionary. Richard Chapple. 512p. 1983. 35.00 (ISBN 0-88233-727-0). Ardis Pubs.

Doubleday Dictionary: For Home, School & Office. Ed. by Sidney Landau & Ronald Bogus. LC 74-3543. 936p. 1975. 9.95 (ISBN 0-385-04099-7); thumb-indexed 10.95 (ISBN 0-385-03368-0). Doubleday.

Doubleday Roget's Thesaurus in Dictionary Form. Ed. by Sidney Landau & Ronald Bogus. LC 76-7696. 564p. 1977. 9.95 (ISBN 0-385-01236-5); thumb-indexed 11.95 (ISBN 0-385-12379-5). Doubleday.

Doublespeak Dictionary. William Lambdin. 295p. 1981. pap. 2.95 (ISBN 0-523-41194-4). Pinnacle Bks.

Doubtful Dictionary. Douglas D. Drill. Ed. by Roberta Wilson-Fulkerson. (Illus.). 1979. pap. 6.95 (ISBN 0-89262-023-4). Career Pub.

Dravidian Etymological Dictionary. Thomas Burrow & Murray B. Emeneau. 1961. 69.00x (ISBN 0-19-864310-1). Oxford U Pr.

Dream Dictionary. Wallace Yancy. 1981. 6.95 (ISBN 0-8062-1685-9). Carlton.

Dream Dictionary: The Key to Your Unconscious. Jo J. Boushahla & Virginia Reidel-Geubtner. 192p. 1983. 18.95 (ISBN 0-8298-0695-4); pap. 9.95 (ISBN 0-8298-0696-2). Pilgrim NY.

Dreamer's Dictionary. Stearn Robinson. 1975. pap. 3.96 (ISBN 0-446-30610-X). Warner Bks.

Dreamer's Dictionary: Complete Guide to Interpreting Your Dreams. Stearn Robinson & Tom Corbett. LC 72-6612. 256p. 1974. 9.95 (ISBN 0-8008-2270-6). Taplinger.

Dreisprachiges Woerterbuch der Soziologie. 93p. (Ger. , Eng. & Fr., Trilingual Dictionary of Sociology). 1975. 9.95 (ISBN 3-445-01164-8, M-7353, Pub. by A. Hain). French & Eur.

Drents Woordenboek. H. Hadderingh. LC 79-385034. (Illus.). 344p. (Dutch.). 1979. fl.35.00 (ISBN 9-06397-019-6). Interbk Intl.

Dressmaker's Dictionary. Ann Ladbury. LC 82-8725. (Illus.). 360p. 1983. 19.95 (ISBN 0-668-05653-3, 5653). Arco.

Drietalige Elementere Woordeboek. Petrus J. Wentzel. LC 77-460273. ix, 525p. (Eng. & Afrikaan.). 1976. write for info. (ISBN 0-86981-069-3). U Sth Africa.

Drinks Dictionary. Norman Allison & Sonia Allison. LC 78-317531. (Illus.). 154p. 1978. E2.25 (ISBN 0-00-435220-3); pap. write for info. (ISBN 0-00-435221-1). W Collins Sons.

Droit Administratif. Raymond Barrillon. LC 79-361007. 191p. (Fr.). 1979. 29.00 F (ISBN 2-130-35777-6). Pr Univ Fr.

Drugs from A to Z: A Dictionary. 2nd ed. Richard R. Lingeman. (McGraw-Hill Paperbacks). 320p. (Orig.). 1974. text ed. 9.95 (ISBN 0-07-037913-0, SP); pap. 5.95 (ISBN 0-07-037912-2). McGraw.

Drugstore Language. Jim Richey. (Survival Vocabulary Ser.). (Illus.). 48p. (gr. 7-12). 1978. pap. 2.95 (ISBN 0-915510-28-6). Janus Bks.

Dryer Felt Terminology. 1966. 4.00 (014-14); members 2.67. TAPPI.

Drying & Related Ventilating Terminology. 1972. 3.00 (014-16); members 2.00. TAPPI.

DTV Junior Lexikon, 10 vols. (Ger.). 1974. Set. pap. 62.50 (ISBN 3-423-05951-6, M-7340, Pub. by DTV/KNO). French & Eur.

DTV Junior Lexikon, 10 vols. (Ger.). 1974. Set. DM.pap. 62.50 (ISBN 3-423-05951-6). Deutscher Taschenbuch Verlag.

DTV Woerterbuch der deutschen Sprache. Wahrig. 942p. (Ger.). pap. 17.90. Imported Bks.

DTV-Woerterbuch der deutschen Sprache. Ed. by G. Wahrig. 943p. (Ger.). pap. 9.25. M Rosenberg.

DTV Woerterbuch der Medizin, Vol. 1. 5th ed. Herbert Von Schaldach. (Ger.). 1973. pap. 7.95 (ISBN 3-423-03028-3, M-7342, Pub. by DTV Deutscher Taschenbuch Vlg.). French & Eur.

DTV Woerterbuch der Medizin, Vol. 1. 5th ed. Herbert Von Schaldach. (Ger.). 1973. DM.pap. 7.95 (ISBN 3-423-03028-3). Deutscher Taschenbuch Verlag.

DTV Woerterbuch der Medizin, Vol. 2. 5th ed. Herbert Von Schaldach. (Ger.). 1973. pap. 7.95 (ISBN 3-423-03029-1, M-7343, Pub. by DTV Deutscher Taschenbuch Vlg.). French & Eur.

DTV Woerterbuch der Medizin, Vol. 2. 5th ed. Herbert Von Schaldach. (Ger.). 1973. DM.pap. 7.95 (ISBN 3-423-03029-1). Deutscher Taschenbuch Verlag.

DTV Woerterbuch der Medizin, Vol. 3. 5th ed. Herbert Von Schaldach. (Ger.). 1973. pap. 7.95 (ISBN 3-423-03030-5, M-7344, Pub. by DTV Deutscher Taschenbuch Vlg.). French & Eur.

DTV Woerterbuch der Medizin, Vol. 3. 5th ed. Herbert Von Schaldach. (Ger.). 1973. DM.pap. 7.95 (ISBN 3-423-03030-5). Deutscher Taschenbuch Verlag.

Ductor in Linguas: The Guide into Tongues. John Minsheu. LC 78-14754. xxi, 543p. (Eng. & Span.). 1978. Repr. of 1617 ed. lib. bdg. 120.00x (ISBN 0-8201-1321-2). Schol Facsimiles.

Duden-Das Grosse Woerterbuch der Deutschen Sprache in 6 Baenden, 6 vols. 3000p. (Ger.). DM.64.00 ea. (ISBN 3-411-01354-0). Biblio Inst.

Duden-Das Woerterbuch Medizinischer Fachausdruecke. Hermann Lichtenstern. 751p. (Ger.). DM.39.00 (ISBN 3-411-01747-3). Biblio Inst.
Duden Francais Bildworterbuch Deutsch & Franzoesisch. (Illus.). 872p. (Ger. & Fr.). M.39.00 (ISBN 3-411-01954-9). Biblio Inst.
Duden in 10 Banden Das Standardwerk zur Deutschen Sprache: Duden Band I, Die Rechtschreibung der Deutschen Sprache & der Fremdwoerter. 792p. (Ger.). DM.29.80 (ISBN 3-411-00901-2). Biblio Inst.
Duden-Lexikon in Drei Banden, 3 vols. LC 80-481771. (Illus.). 2016p. (Ger.). 1980. DM.26.00 (ISBN 3-411-01777-5). Biblio Inst.
Duden-Lexikon in Drei Banden, 3 vols. Ed. by Lexikonredaktion des Bibliographischen Instituts. (Illus.). 2016p. (Ger.). DM.32.00 ea. Vol. 1 (ISBN 3-411-01778-3). Vol. 2 (ISBN 3-411-01778-3). Vol. 3 (ISBN 3-411-01779-1). Biblio Inst.
Duden-Rechnen & Mathematik. Ed. by Fachredaktionen des Bibliographischen Instituts. 1056p. (Ger.). DM.39.00 (ISBN 3-411-00920-9). Biblio Inst.
Duden-Stilwoerterbuch. 5th rev. ed. R. Duden. (Grosse Duden: Vol. 2). (Ger.). 15.95 (ISBN 3-411-00902-0). Adler.
Duden-Was Bedeutet Das? Kleines Bedeutungswoerterbuch der Deutschen Sprache. Harrap & Dudenredaktion. (Illus.). 444p. (Ger.). E3.00 (ISBN 0-245-50332-3). Harrap.
Duden Woerterbuch Medizinischer Fachausdruecke, 3 vols. Ed. by Karl-Heinz Alheim. LC 79-384676. 751p. (Ger.). 1979. write for info. (ISBN 3-41101-747-3). Thieme Verlag.
Duden-Woerterbuch Medizinischer Fachausdrucke. 2nd ed. (Ger.). DM.25.95 (ISBN 3-411-00943-8). Biblio Inst.
Duits-Neederland Woordenboek. Ed. by Van Gelderen. 972p. (Ger.). 1980. pap. 24.95 (ISBN 90-01-96814-7, M-9745). French & Eur.
Duits voor Bouwkundigen-Saksaa Rakentajille. H. Evered & G. Wallnig. 102p. (Ger., Dutch & Finnish.). 1978. DM.18.00 (ISBN 3-7625-0916-6). Bauverlag.
Dumas on Food. Alexandre Dumas. Tr. by Alan Davidson & Jane Davidson. (Illus.). 327p. (Fr.). 1982. 14.95x (ISBN 0-7181-1842-1). U Pr of Va.
Dumonts Kleines Lexikon der Phantastischen Malerei. Jorg Krichbaum. LC 77-579484. (Illus.). 329p. (Ger.). 1977. write for info. (ISBN 3-770-10908-2). DuMont Buchverlag.
DuMont's Kleines Sachworterbuch der Druektechnik & Grafischen Kunst. Heijo Klein. LC 75-505939. 193p. (Eng. & Ger.). 1975. write for info. (ISBN 3-7701-0760-8). DuMont Buch.
DuMont's Kleines Sachworterbuch der Drucktechnik & Grafischen Kunst. Heijo Klein. LC 77-564784. 205p. (Eng. & Ger.). 1977. write for info. (ISBN 3-7701-0760-8). DuMont Buchverlag.
Duncan's Dictionary for Nurses. Helen A. Duncan. LC 74-121974. (Illus.). 1971. Springer Pub.
Dutch-English Dictionary. K. T. Bruggencate. Ed. by J. Gerritsen et al. 1048p. (Dutch & Eng.). 1980. 24.95 (ISBN 90-01-96819-8, M-9746). French & Eur.
Dutch-English Dictionary. Fernand Renier. (Dutch & Eng.). 1982. pap. 7.95 (ISBN 0-7100-9352-7). Routledge & Kegan.
Dutch-English-Dutch. (Berlitz Pocket Dictionaries Ser.). (Eng. & Dutch.). 4.95 (ISBN 0-02-964550-6). Macmillan.
Dutch-English, English-Dutch Dictionary, 2 vols. K. Ten Bruggencate. (Dutch & Eng.). Set. 50.00 (ISBN 9-0019-6819-8). Dutch-Eng. Eng.-Dutch (ISBN 90-01-96818-X). Heinman.
Dutch-English, English-Dutch Dictionary, 2 vols. 36th, rev., enl. ed. Kramers. (Dutch & Eng.). 35.00 (ISBN 9-0100-2541-1). Heinman.
Dutch-English, English-Dutch Dictionary. Fernand G. Renier. (Dutch & Eng.). 19.50 (ISBN 0-87557-014-3, 014-3). Saphrograph.
Dutch-English, English-Dutch Engineering Dictionary, 2 vols. G Schuurmans Stekhoven. (Dutch & Eng.). 125.00 set (ISBN 90-2010-602-3). Heinman.
Dutch-English-French-German Engineering Dictionary. 11th ed. Ten Bosch. (Dutch, Eng., Fr. & Ger.). 45.00 (ISBN 90-2010-132-3). Heinman.
Dutch-English (Only) New Great Dictionary, 3 vols. 2nd ed. H. Jansonius. (Dutch & Eng.). Set. 225.00 (ISBN 90-6110-032-1). Heinman.
Dutch-Norwegian & Norwegian-Dutch Pocket Dictionary. K. Schoell. (Dutch & Norwegian.). 1981. write for info. (ISBN 82-573-0164-7). Kunnskapsforlaget.

E

E. M. Forster Glossary. Alfred Borrello. LC 74-188548. 1972. 15.00 (ISBN 0-8108-0475-1). Scarecrow.
Early American Houses & a Glossary of Colonial Architectural Terms, 2 vols. Norman M. Isham. LC 67-27458. (Architecture & Decorative Art Ser). 1967. Repr. of 1939 ed. lib. bdg. 19.50 (ISBN 0-306-70973-2). Da Capo.
Early Blazon: Heraldic Terminology in the Twelfth & Thirteenth Centuries; with Special Reference to Arthurian Literature. Gerard J. Brault. (Illus.). 1972. text ed. 45.00x (ISBN 0-19-822337-4). Oxford U Pr.
Early Hebrew Orthography: A Study of the Epigraphic Evidence. Frank M. Cross, Jr. & David N. Freedman. (American Oriental Ser.: Vol. 36). (Hebrew.). 1952. pap. 9.00x (ISBN 0-940490-36-6). Am Orient Soc.
Early Prophets see Classified Concordance.
Eastern Definitions. Edward Rice. LC 77-19359. (Illus.). 1980. pap. 8.95 (ISBN 0-385-15631-6, Anch). Doubleday.
Easy Guide to English Grammar & Vocabulary. rev. ed. Harry W. Koch. 119p. 1980. pap. 5.00 (ISBN 0-913164-84-4). Ken-Bks.
Easy Steps to a Large Vocabulary. Ida Bellegarde. LC 77-79111. 1977. 4.45x (ISBN 0-918340-04-7). Bell Ent.
Easy Ways to Enlarge Your German Vocabulary. Karl A. Schmidt. LC 73-92020. (Orig., Ger. & Eng.). 1974. 4.50 (ISBN 0-486-23044-9). Dover.
Ecce Homo! A Lexicon of Man. Luigi Romeo. xv, 163p. 1979. 18.00x (ISBN 90-272-2006-9). Benjamins North Am.
Eckankar Dictionary. Paul Twitchell. LC 75-306747. 160p. (Orig.). 1981. pap. 9.00 (ISBN 0-914766-74-0, 0154). IWP Pub.
Ecology Field Glossary: A Naturalist's Vocabulary. Walter H. Lewis. LC 77-71856. 1977. lib. bdg. 25.00 (ISBN 0-8371-9547-0, LEF/). Greenwood.
Economic Terminology. Miguel Moreno Pacheo. (Eng. & Span.). 1967. 30.00 (ISBN 3-1900-6205-6). Adler.
Economic Terminology. Miguel Pacheco Moreno. 480p. (Eng. & Span.). DM.17.50. Hueber.
Economic Terminology: English-Spanish. M. Pacheco. 480p. (Eng. & Span.). 1967. DM.19.95 (ISBN 3-19-006205-6). Hueber.
Economic Terminology German-English. 2nd ed. Renner et al. (Ger. & Eng.). 1970. 27.50 (ISBN 3-1900-6201-3). Adler.
Economics & Foreign Trade Dictionary. V. Kohls. 619p. 1980. 90.00x (ISBN 0-686-72095-4, Pub. by Collet's). State Mutual Bk.
Economics Dictionary. A. Schuler. 784p. 1980. 95.00x (ISBN 0-686-44670-4, Pub. by Collets). State Mutual Bk.
Economisch Woorden Boek: Engels-Frans-Duits-Nederlands. F. J. Jong. 685p. (Eng., Fr., Ger. & Dutch.). 1980. 75.00 (ISBN 90-247-2243-8, M9474). French & Eur.
Economische Begrippen. G. Dijk. LC 78-383140. 144p. (Dutch.). 1978. fl.9.75 (ISBN 9-027-52020-8). NIB.
Education A-Z. Izbicki. LC 78-323295. 196p. (Eng.). 1978. E2.95 (ISBN 0-00-412069-8); pap. write for info. (ISBN 0-00-412070-1). W Collins Sons.
Educational Administration Glossary. Edward L. Dejnozka. LC 83-5719. 224p. 1983. lib. bdg. 35.00 (ISBN 0-313-23301-2, DEA/). Greenwood.
EDV-Abkurzungen. Rolf Kohler & Ernst Mayr. LC 79-342495. 332p. (Ger.). 1978. write for info. (ISBN 3-8009-1262-7). Siemens AG.
EDV-Taschenlexikon: In Zusammenarbeit Mit Guido Lobel. Hans Schmid & Peter Von Muller. LC 76-481702. 227p. (Eng. & Ger.). 1976. DM.19.80. Verlag Moderne Industrie.
Egyptian Hieroglyphic Dictionary, Vols. 1 & 2. E. Wallis Budge. LC 77-86708. 1978. pap. 12.00 ea. Vol. 1 (ISBN 0-486-23615-3). Vol. 2 (ISBN 0-486-23616-1). Dover.
Einfuehrung in die Benutzung der Neufranzoesischen Woerterbucher. Franz J. Hausmann. LC 77-478069. 166p. (Fr. & Ger.). 1977. write for info. (ISBN 3-484-50090-5). Niemeyer Verlag.
Einfuehrung in die Deutsche Wortbildungslehre. Werner Eckert. LC 75-51569. (Illus.). 160p. (Ger.). 1975. DM.14.80 (ISBN 3-50301-210-9). Schmidt Verlag.
Einfuhrung in das Technische Russisch Maschinenbau: Lehrmaterial fuer den Fremdsprachenunterricht. Siegfried Uhlig. 382p. (Ger. & Rus.). 1976. M.7.00. VEB Technik.
Einwortlexeme & Wortgruppenlexeme in der Technischen Terminologie des Polnscheni. Herbert Matuschek. LC 78-352590. viii, 417p. (Pol.). 1977. write for info. (ISBN 3-87690-135-9). Sagner.
Ekonomicheskii Slovar Spravochnik Rabochego. A. V. Moiseev. (Rus.). 1979. 1.50 (Pub. by Politizdat). Four Continent.
Ekonomicheskii Slovar-Spravochnik Rabochego. 4th ed. Anatolii V. Moiseev. LC 79-387742. (Illus.). 231p. (Rus.). 1979. 0.45 Rub. Politizdat.
Eksportno-Importnyi Slovar, 3 vols. (Rus.). 1954. 18.00 set (Pub. by Vneshtorgizdat). Four Continent.
Electrical Machines Dictionary. Heinrich Bezner. LC 80-452859. 544p. (Eng. & Ger.). 1978. DM.80.00 (ISBN 3-87097-087-1). Brandstetter.
Electricity & Electronics Technical Dictionary. 2nd, rev. ed. Ed. by Peter-Klaus Budig. 724p. (Eng. & Ger.). 1979. 62.50x (ISBN 0-8002-2468-X). Intl Pubns Serv.
Electronics Dictionary. 254p. (Pol. , Eng. & Rus.). 59.00x (ISBN 0-686-44676-3, Pub. by Collets). State Mutual Bk.
Electronics Dictionary: Russian Supplement. Ed. by W. Clason. 1963. 32.70 (ISBN 0-444-40127-X). Elsevier.
Electronics Dictionary: Swedish Supplement. Ed. by W. Clason. 1960. 9.60 (ISBN 0-444-40121-0). Elsevier.
Electrophotography Definitions & Standardization of Terms. 1965. 3.00 (399-1); members 2.00. TAPPI.
Elef Millim. Nello Pavoncello. LC 79-367877. 60p. (Hebrew & Ital.). 1979. L.00.2000.00 (ISBN 8-88502-709-1). Carucci.
Elektromaschinen-Woerterbuch. Bezner. 558p. (Ger. & Eng.). 1982. DM.80.00. Brandstetter.
Elektrorazvedka: Spravochnik Geofizika. 520p. (Rus.). 1979. 9.95 (Pub. by Nedra). Four Continent.
Elektrotechnik Elektronik. William Athenstaedt. LC 79-349122. 964p. (Rus. & Ger.). 1978. write for info. VEB Verlag Technik.
Elektrotechnik Elektronik. Peter K. Budig. LC 77-454020. 724p. (Eng. & Ger.). 1975. M.55.00. VEB Verlag Technik.
Elektrotechnik Elektronik Deutsch-Englisch. Peter K. Budig. 770p. (Ger. & Eng.). 1982. M.98.00. VEB Technik.
Elektrotechnik Elektronik Russisch-Deutsch. Helmut Gross. 964p. (Rus. & Ger.). 1982. M.60.00. VEB Technik.
Elementary Dictionary of English. 283p. (Eng.). DM.13.80 (50800). Langenscheidt-Longman.
Elementary Latin Dictionary. Charlton T. Lewis. (Eng & Lat.). 1891. 23.00x (ISBN 0-19-910205-8). Oxford U Pr.
Elements de Geologie En Six Langues. E. Cailleux. 191p. (Fr., Ger., Rus., Span. & Eng., Elements of Geology in Six Languages). 1965. pap. 19.95 (ISBN 0-686-56735-8, M-6055). French & Eur.
Elements of the Structure & Terminology of Agricultural Education in India. 82p. 1982. pap. 11.50 (ISBN 92-3-101866-3, U1170, UNESCO). Unipub.
Elias Arabic-English Modern Dictionary. Elias. (Arabic & Eng.). 29.00 (ISBN 0-686-18362-2); pap. 6.50 pocket size (ISBN 0-686-18363-0). Kazi Pubns.
Elias English-Arabic & Arabic-English Pocket Dictionary. Elias. (Arabic & Eng.). pap. 15.95 (ISBN 0-686-18361-4). Kazi Pubns.
Elias' English-Arabic Dictionary. Elias Elias. (Eng. & Arabic.). 1979. 25.00x (ISBN 0-86685-288-3). Intl Bk Ctr.
Elias English-Arabic Modern Dictionary. Elias. (Arabic & Eng.). 29.00 (ISBN 0-686-18364-9); pap. 6.50 pocket size (ISBN 0-686-18365-7). Kazi Pubns.
Elias English-Arabic Practical Dictionary of the Arabic of the Middle East. (Eng. & Arabic.). 8.95 (ISBN 0-86685-296-4). Intl Bk Ctr.
Elias English-Arabic Practical Dictionary of the Colloquial Arabic of the Middle East. Elias Elias. (Arabic & Eng.). 1971. 8.95x (ISBN 0-86685-296-4). Intl Bk Ctr.
Elias' Pocket Dictionary Arabic-English. M. Elias. 533p. (Eng. & Arabic.). 1981. 12.95 (ISBN 0-686-91623-9, M-9750). French & Eur.
Elias Pocket Dictionary: English, Arabic. E. Elias. (Eng. & Arabic.). leatherette 16.95 (ISBN 0-686-92306-5, M-9365). French & Eur.
Ellison's French Menu Reader. Al Ellison. (Fr.). 1977. 2.95 (ISBN 0-930580-00-1). Ellison Ent.
Ellison's Latin American Menu Reader. Al Ellison. (Lat.). 1978. pap. 2.95 (ISBN 0-930580-06-0). Ellison Ent.
Elseviers Automobile Dictionary. Ed. by G. Schuurmans. (Eng., Fr., Span., Port., Ger., Rus. & Japanese.). 1960. 139.75 (ISBN 0-444-40517-8). Elsevier.
Elsevier's Banking Dictionary. 2nd ed. J. Ricci. (Eng., Fr., Ital., Span., Dutch & Ger.). 1980. 64.00 (ISBN 0-444-41834-2). Elsevier.
Elsevier's Dictionary of Amplification Modulation Reception & Transmission. Ed. by W. Clason. (Eng., Fr & Span.). 1963. 63.50 (ISBN 0-444-40113-X). Elsevier.
Elsevier's Dictionary of Automatic Control. Ed. by W. Clason. (Eng., Fr., Ger. & Rus.). 1961. 37.25 (ISBN 0-444-40752-9). Elsevier.
Elsevier's Dictionary of Automobile Engineering. K. Kondo. 1977. 127.75 (ISBN 0-444-41590-4). Elsevier.

Elsevier's Dictionary of Barley, Malting, & Brewing. Bernard D. Hartong. (Eng., Ger., Fr., Danish, Ital., & Span., Polyglot). 1961. 76.75 (ISBN 0-444-40270-5). Elsevier.

Elsevier's Dictionary of Botany, Vol. 1: Plant Names. P. Macura. LC 79-15558. 580p. 1979. 110.75 (ISBN 0-444-41787-7). Elsevier.

Elsevier's Dictionary of Brewing. European Brewery Convention. 1983. 83.00 (ISBN 0-444-42131-9). Elsevier.

Elsevier's Dictionary of Building Tools & Materials. L. Y. Chaballe & J. P. Vandenberghe. (Eng., Fr., Span., Ger. & Dutch.). 1982. 138.50 (ISBN 0-444-42047-9). Elsevier.

Elsevier's Dictionary of Chemical Engineering, 2 Vols. W. Clason. (Eng., Fr., Span., Ital., Dutch, & Ger.). 1969. Set. 170.25 (ISBN 0-444-40736-7); Vol. 1. 85.00 (ISBN 0-444-40714-6); Vol. 2. 85.00 (ISBN 0-444-40715-4). Elsevier.

Elsevier's Dictionary of Cinema, Sound & Music. W. E. Clason. (Eng., Fr., Span., Ital., Dutch, & Ger., Polyglot). 1956. 117.00 (ISBN 0-444-40117-2). Elsevier.

Elsevier's Dictionary of Computers, Automatic Control & Data Processing. 2nd ed. W. E. Clason. (Eng., Fr., Span., & Ital., Polyglot). 1971. 85.00 (ISBN 0-444-40928-9). Elsevier.

Elsevier's Dictionary of Criminal Science. J. A. Adler. (Eng., Fr., Span., Ital., Port., Dutch, Swedish, & Ger., Polyglot). 1960. 127.75 (ISBN 0-444-40003-6). Elsevier.

Elsevier's Dictionary of Electronics & Waveguides. 2nd ed. W. E. Clason. (Eng., Fr., Span., Ital., Dutch & Ger., Polyglot). 1965. 106.50 (ISBN 0-444-40119-9). Elsevier.

Elsevier's Dictionary of Financial Terms. F. J. Thomson. LC 79-11810. 496p. (Eng., Ger., Span., Fr., Ital., Dutch.). 1980. 113.00 (ISBN 0-444-41775-3). Elsevier.

Elsevier's Dictionary of Food Science & Technology. Ian Morton & C. Morton. 1977. 42.75 (ISBN 0-444-41559-9). Elsevier.

Elsevier's Dictionary of General Physics. W. E. Clason. (Eng., Fr., Span., Ital., Dutch & Ger., Polyglot). 1962. 110.75 (ISBN 0-444-40122-9). Elsevier.

Elsevier's Dictionary of High Vacuum Science & Technology. Fritz W. Weber. (Eng., Ger., Fr., Ital., Span. & Rus.). 1968. 106.50 (ISBN 0-444-40625-5). Elsevier.

Elsevier's Dictionary of Horticulture. Ed. by Ministry of Agriculture & Fisheries-Netherlands & J. Nijdam. (Eng., Fr., Dutch, Ger., Danish, Swedish, Span., Ital., & Lat.). 1970. 89.50 (ISBN 0-444-40812-6). Elsevier.

Elsevier's Dictionary of Hydrogeology. Hans-Olaf Pfannkuch. (Eng., Fr., & Ger.). 1969. 42.75 (ISBN 0-444-40717-0). Elsevier.

Elseviers Dictionary of Metal Cutting Tools. Ed. by G. Schuurmang. (Eng., Ger., Fr., Dutch, Span., & Rus.). 1970. 106.50 (ISBN 0-444-40856-8). Elsevier.

Elsevier's Dictionary of Metallurgy & Metal Working. W. E. Clason. (Eng., Fr., Span., Ital., Dutch & Ger.). 1978. 136.25 (ISBN 0-444-41695-1). Elsevier.

Elsevier's Dictionary of Nuclear Science & Technology. 2nd rev. ed. W. E. Clason. (Eng., Fr., Span., Ital., Dutch & Ger.). 1970. 121.50 (ISBN 0-444-40810-X). Elsevier.

Elsevier's Dictionary of Particle Technology. Ed. by K. Leschonski & F. T. Carter. (Ger. & Eng.). 1978. 68.00 (ISBN 0-444-41746-X). Elsevier.

Elsevier's Dictionary of Pharmaceutical Science & Techniques, 2 vols. A. Sliosberg. Incl. Vol. 1: Pharmaceutical Technology. 1968. 132.00 (ISBN 0-444-40544-5); Vol. 2: Materia Medica. 1980. 123.50 (ISBN 0-444-41664-1). Set. 255.50 (ISBN 0-686-85925-1). Elsevier.

Elsevier's Dictionary of Photography. A. S. Craeybeckx. (Eng., Fr., & Ger.). 1965. 113.00 (ISBN 0-444-40146-6). Elsevier.

Elsevier's Dictionary of Public Health. Nick J. Deblock. LC 76-676387. 204p. (Eng., Fr., Span., Ital., Dutch & Ger.). 1976. 47.00 (ISBN 0-444-41395-2). Elsevier.

Elsevier's Dictionary of Rolling Mill Terminology. Ed. by G. F. Herscu. (Eng., Fr., Span. & Ger.). 1965. 39.75 (ISBN 0-444-40280-2). Elsevier.

Elsevier's Dictionary of Television, & Video Recording. W. Clason. LC 74-77577. 608p. (Eng., Ger., Fr., Span., Ital. & Dutch.). 1975. 113.00 (ISBN 0-444-41224-7). Elsevier.

Elsevier's Dictionary of the Gas Industry, 2 vols. Ed. by International Gas Union. (Polyglot). 1961. Set. 95.75 (ISBN 0-444-40758-8); Incl. suppl. pap. 138.50 (ISBN 0-686-85926-X). Elsevier.

Elsevier's Dictionary of Tools & Ironware. Ed. by Clason. (Eng., Fr., Span., Ital., Dutch & Ger.). 1982. 74.50 (ISBN 0-444-42085-1). Elsevier.

Elsevier's Electrotechnical Dictionary. W. E. Clason. (Eng., Fr., Span., Ital., Dutch & Ger.). 1965. 113.00 (ISBN 0-444-40118-0). Elsevier.

Elsevier's Football Dictionary. H. Sirages. (Eng. & Ger.). 1980. 40.50 (ISBN 0-444-41890-3). Elsevier.

Elsevier's Geneesmiddelengids. LC 75-595997. 399p. (Eng. & Dutch.). 1975. fl.22.50 (ISBN 90-10-01263-8). Elsevier Nederland.

Elsevier's Medical Dictionary in Five Languages. rev. 2nd ed. A. Sliosberg. LC 72-97436. 1452p. (Eng., Fr., Ital., Span. & Ger.). 1975. 181.00 (ISBN 0-444-41103-8). Elsevier.

Elsevier's Multilingual Dictionary of Insurance Technology. W. A. Ruysch. (Eng., Dutch, Fr., Ger., Span. & Ital.). write for info (ISBN 0-685-82355-5). Elsevier.

Elseviers Nautical Dictionary, 3 Vols. Ed. by P. Segditsas. (Eng., Fr., Ital., Span. & Ger.). 1965-66. Set. 134.25 (ISBN 0-444-40727-8); Vol. 1: Maritime Terminology. 58.75 (ISBN 0-444-40522-4); Marine Engineering. 51.25 (ISBN 0-444-40524-0). Elsevier.

Elsevier's Nautical Dictionary. 2nd ed. Compiled by J. P. Vandenberghe. 1971. 181.00 (ISBN 0-444-41694-3). Elsevier.

Elsevier's Nautical Dictionary in Six Languages. 2nd, rev. ed. Compiled by J. P. Vandenberghe & L. Y. Chaballe. LC 78-9069. x, 949p. (Eng., Fr., Span., Ital., Dutch & Ger.). 1978. write for info. (ISBN 0-444-41694-3). Elsevier.

Elsevier's Oil & Gas Field Dictionary. L. Y. Chaballe & L. Masuy. (in 6 languages plus Arabic suppl.). 1980. 127.75 (ISBN 0-444-41833-4). Elsevier.

Elseviers Rubber Dictionary. (Eng. , Fr. , Span. , Ital. , Port. , Ger. , Dutch, Swedish, Indonesian & Japanese.). 1959. 170.25 (ISBN 0-444-40499-6). Elsevier.

Elsevier's Telecommunication Dictionary. 2nd rev. ed. W. E. Clason. (Eng., Fr., Ital., Span., Dutch & Ger.). 1976. 113.75 (ISBN 0-444-41394-4). Elsevier.

Elsevier's Wood Dictionary, 3 Vols. Ed. by W. Boerhave Beekman. (Eng., Fr., Span., Ital., Swedish, Dutch & Ger.). 1964-68. Set. 259.75 (ISBN 0-686-43878-7); Vol. 1. 85.00 (ISBN 0-444-40063-X); Vol. 2. 89.50 (ISBN 0-444-40053-2); Vol. 3. 85.00 (ISBN 0-444-40713-8). Elsevier.

Elson's Music Dictionary. Louis C. Elson. LC 70-173097. xii, 306p. 1972. Repr. of 1905 ed. 37.00x (ISBN 0-8103-3268-X). Gale.

Emerson: A Lecture. Augustine Birrell. 1978. Repr. of 1903 ed. lib. bdg. 8.50 (ISBN 0-8495-0422-8). Arden Lib.

Emprestimos Linguisticos nas Linguas Mocambicanas. Antonio C. Cabral. LC 76-464647. 78p. (Mozambique.). 1975. write for info. Lourenco Marques.

Enciclopedia simultanea de correspondencia comercial en seis idiomas. 495p. (Eng. , Span. , Fr. , Ital. , Ger. & Port.). 1976. Mex.$16.50. Distein.

Encyclopedia of Arcane Wisdom. Arcane Order. 50.00. (1790900891). Arcane Order.

Encyclopedia of Biblical Interpretation, 9 vols. M. M. Kasher. Set. 35.00 ea. (ISBN 0-87068-315-2). Ktav.

Encyclopedia of Biology Terms. 1984. 6.95 (ISBN 0-8120-2511-3). Barron.

Encyclopedia of Building & Construction Terms. Hugh Brooks. LC 82-21565. 416p. 1983. 50.00 (ISBN 0-13-275511-4). P-H.

Encyclopedia of Career & Vocational Guidance, 2 vols. 5th ed. Ed. by William E. Hopke. LC 81-4362. 808p. 1982. 49.95 (ISBN 0-385-18058-6, Anch). Doubleday.

Encyclopedia of Finance & Investment Terms. Peter K. Ewald. 1983. pap. price not set (ISBN 0-8120-2522-9). Barron.

Encyclopedia of Homonyms 'Sound-Alikes' Dora Newhouse. LC 76-27486. 1977. 16.95 (ISBN 0-918050-01-4). Newhouse Pr.

Encyclopedia Yiddishanica. Endel Markowitz. LC 79-114831. (Eng. & Yiddish.). 1979. write for info. (ISBN 0-933910-02-9). Haymark.

Encyclopedic Dictionary of English Usage. Nathan H. Mager & Sylvia K. Mager. 1974. 14.95 (ISBN 0-13-275792-3, Reward). P-H.

Encyclopedic Dictionary of the Sciences of Language. Oswald Ducrot & Tzvetan Todorov. Tr. by Catherine Porter. LC 78-23901. 400p. 1979. pap. 10.95x (ISBN 0-8018-2857-0). Johns Hopkins.

Encyclopedie ou dictionnaire raisonne des sciences, des arts et des metiers, 35 Vols. Ed. by Denis Diderot & D'Alembert. (Illus.). 1967. Repr. of 1751 ed. Set. 4208.75 (ISBN 3-7728-0116-1). Adler.

Encyklopedia Techniki. Henryk Baniecki. LC 79-354168. vii, 928p. (Pol.). 1978. 300.00 Zl. Wydawnictwa Naukowo.

Energy Dictionary. V. Daniel Hunt. 1979. text ed. 24.50x (ISBN 0-442-27395-9). Van Nos Reinhold.

Energy Terminology: A Multi-Lingual Glossary. Ed. by World Energy Conference. 275p. 1983. 100.00 (ISBN 0-08-029314-X, B110); pap. 40.00 (ISBN 0-08-029315-8). Pergamon.

Engels-Afrikaanse Tegniese Woordeboek. H. Terblanche. LC 78-348473. 599p. (Eng. & Afrikaan.). 1976. write for info. (ISBN 0-625-01281-X). Nasou.

Engels-Nederlands Woordenboek. Van Baars & Van der Schoot. 359p. (Eng. & Dutch.). 1969. pap. 5.50. Spectrum Pub.

Engels voor Bouwkundigen-Englantia Rakentajille. G. Wallnig & H. Evered. 95p. (Eng., Ger., Finnish & Dutch.). 1980. DM.18.00 (ISBN 3-7625-1226-4). Bauverlag.

Engelsk-Dansk-Ordbog. B. K. Nielsen et al. (Eng. & Danish.). 1981. 95.00 (ISBN 87-01-44971-0, M-1270). French & Eur.

Engelsk-Dansk Teknisk Ordbog. A. Warren. 393p. (Eng. & Danish.). 1981. 49.95 (ISBN 87-11-04029-7, M-8413). French & Eur.

Engelsk-Norsk Ordbok. B. Berulfsen. 430p. 1978. 24.95 (ISBN 82-573-0007-1, M-9455). French & Eur.

Engelsk-Norsk Teknisk Ordliste. Knut J. Knutsen. LC 77-572102. 93p. (Eng. & Norwegian.). 1977. Kr.32.00 (ISBN 8-251-90218-5). Tapir.

Engelsk-Svensk Elteknisk Forkortningslista. Ake Nyblom. LC 75-547472. 24p. (Eng. & Swedish.). 1975. Kr.19.00 (ISBN 91-7284-026-9). Ingenjorsforlaget.

Engelsk-Svensk Ordbog. Mats Bergstrom & Ingvar Carlson. LC 77-471718. 451p. (Eng. & Swedish.). 1976. Kr.42.00 (ISBN 9-1275-7032-0). Natur & Kultur.

Engelsk-Svensk Ordbok. 775p. (Eng. & Swedish.). 1983. write for info. (ISBN 91-24-32208-3). Esselte Studium.

Engelsk-Svensk Ordbok. Rubin Noejd. 248p. (Eng. & Swedish.). write for info. (ISBN 91-24-19951-6). Esselte Studium.

Engelsk-Svensk Ordbok (Prisma Modern) 5th ed. Bror Danielsson. 396p. 1980. text ed. 17.50x (ISBN 91-518-0550-2, SW205); Svensk-engelsk, 4th Ed. 1982. text ed. 20.00x (ISBN 9-1518-1297-5, SW-204). Vanous.

Engelsk-Svensk Teknisk Ordbok. 141p. (Eng. & Swedish.). 1979. Kr.73.00 (ISBN 91-24-20833-7). Esselte Studium.

Engelska Ordboksguiden. 30p. (Swedish & Eng.). 1978. Kr.22.00 (ISBN 91-24-27682-0). Esselte Studium.

Engelskt-Svenskt Flyglexikon. Sven Christensen. 89p. (Eng. & Swedish.). write for info. (ISBN 91-24-13861-4). Esselte Studium.

Engineering Index Thesaurus. Engineering Index, Inc. LC 72-78325. 1972. 19.50 (ISBN 0-02-468550-X). Macmillan Info.

Engineers' Dictionary, Spanish-English, English-Spanish. 2nd ed. Louis A. Robb. (Span. & Eng.). 1949. 49.50 (ISBN 0-471-72501-3, Pub. by Wiley-Interscience). Wiley.

Englandtilais-Suomalainen Laboratorio- ja Prosessialan Sanasto. Liisa Pihkala & Juhani Pihkala. LC 78-398796. 184p. (Eng. & Finnish.). 1978. write for info. (ISBN 9-5110-4645-4). Otava.

Englantilais-Suomaainen Elektromikka ja Instrumentointisanasto. Lea Saarikoski. LC 77-469166. 123p. (Eng. & Finnish.). 1976. Fmk.18.00 (ISBN 9-5110-2382-9). Otava.

Englantilais-Suomalainen Asunto ja Rakennusalan Sanasto. Irma Lehtipuu. LC 79-392967. 247p. (Eng. & Finnish.). 1978. write for info. (ISBN 9-5110-5150-4). Otava.

Englantilais-Suomalainen Moottorialan Sanasto. Lea Saarikoski. LC 77-473434. 194p. (Eng. & Finnish.). 1976. Fmk.21.70 (ISBN 9-5110-4011-1). Otava.

Englantilais-suomalainen Suursanakirja: English-Finnish General Dictionary. Raija Hurme & Maritta Pesonen. LC 80-461357. xl, 1182p. (Finnish-Eng.). 1978. Fmk.190.00 (ISBN 9-510-0855-45); pap. 173.00 (ISBN 9-510-0855-37). Soderstrom.

Englantilais-Suomalainen Tekstiili-ja Vaatetusalan Sanasto. Lea Saarikoski. LC 79-394177. 156p. (Finnish.). 1979. Fmk.27.50 (ISBN 9-511-04908-9). Otava Kust.

Englesko-Hrvatska ili Srpska Tehnicko-Tehnoloska. Ignac Kulier. LC 77-459563. 145p. (Eng. & Serbo-Croation., Zagreb). 1976. write for info. Prehrambeno-Tehnoloski.

Englesko-srpskohrvatski Recnik. Morton Benson. LC 79-343879. xiv, 669p. (Serbo-Croation & Eng.). 1978. write for info. Beogradski.

Englesko-srpskohrvatski Recnik. Ed. by Syetomir Ristic & Zivojin Simic. LC 76-523250. xxx, 807p. (Serbo-Croatian & Eng.). 1975. write for info. Prosveta.

Englisch, 2 vols. Incl. Englisch-Deutsch. Heinz Messinger & Werner Rudenberg. 1440p (07121); Deutsch-Englisch. Heinz Messinger. 1328p (07126). (Langenscheidts Grosse Schulworterbucher Ser.). (Eng. & Ger.). DM.23.80 ea. Langenscheidt.

Englisch, 2 vols. rev. ed. Incl. Teil I. Englisch-Deutsch. E. Klatt. Rev. by D. Roy. 640p. DM.16.80 (10120); Teil II. Deutsch-Englisch. E. Klatt & G. Klatt. Rev. by Heinz Messinger. 639p. DM.16.80 (10126). (Langenscheidts Taschenworterbucher. Ser.). (Eng. & Ger.). DM.beide Teile in einem Band 23.80 (11121). Langenscheidt.

Englisch, 2 vols. Compiled by Heinz Messinger & Werner Rudenberg. (Langenscheidts Hanworterbucher Ser.). (Eng. & Ger.). Teil 1: Englisch-Deutsch (760p.) DM.32.00 (04121); Teil 2: Deutsch-Englisch. DM.32.00 (04126); DM.beide Teile in einem Band (1471p.) 48.00 (05122). Langenscheidt.

Englisch-Deutsches, Deutsch-Englisches Woerterbuch, Vol. 1. 2nd ed. Wildhagen. (Ger. & Eng.). 1973. DM.52.00 (ISBN 3-87097-046-4). Brandstetter.

Englisch-Deutsches, Deutsch-Englisches Woerterbuch, Vol. 2. 2nd ed. Wildhagen. (Ger. & Eng.). 1972. DM.72.00 (ISBN 3-87097-047-2). Brandstetter.

Englisch-Deutsches Deutsch-Englisches Woerterbuch: Band II, Deutsch-Englisch. Heraucourt Wildhagen. 1524p. (Eng. & Ger.). 1982. DM.90.00. Brandstetter.

Englisch-Deutsches Deutsch-Englisches Woerterbuch: Band I, Englisch-Deutsch. Heraucourt Wildhagen. 1180p. (Eng. & Ger.). 1982. DM.65.00. Brandstetter.

Englisch-Deutsches Glossarium. Hans E. Zahn. 528p. (Eng. & Ger., English - German Glossary). 1977. 78.50 (ISBN 3-7819-2013-5, M-7355, Pub. by Fritz Knapp Verlag). French & Eur.

Englisch fuer Baufachleute: Band 1. 6th ed. G. Wallnig & H. Evered. 101p. (Eng., Ger. & Fr.). 1978. DM.16.00 (ISBN 3-7625-0807-0). Bauverlag.

Englisch fuer die Seewirtschaft Aufbaukurs Stufe IIa. (Eng. & Ger.). M.21.80. Wissenschaftliche.

Englisch fur Baufachleute: Band 2. 2nd ed. G. Wallnig & H. Evered. viii, 192p. (Eng., Ger. & Fr.). 1977. DM.38.00 (ISBN 3-7625-0807-0). Bauverlag.

Englisch in Wirtschaft und Handel, Vol. 2. Dieter Hamblock. (Eng. & Ger.). 1977. DM.15.95 (ISBN 3-7736-3351-3). Girardet.

Englische & Franzoesisch Fachsprache im Auslandsbau. K. Lange et al. 131p. (Fr., Eng. & Ger.). 1980. DM.24.00 (ISBN 3-7625-1235-3). Bauverlag.

Englische in Wirtschaft und Handel, Vol. 1. Dieter Hamblock. (Eng. & Ger.). 1977. DM.pap. 15.95 (ISBN 3-7736-3350-5). Girardet.

Englische Rechtssprache: Mustertexte & Fachausdruecke unter Einbeziehung von Amerikanismen. G. Glass. 80p. (Eng. & Ger.). 1982. DM.24.00 (ISBN 3-7625-1487-9). Bauverlag.

Englisches Handelsvokabularium Nach Sachgebieten. Grossmann. 330p. (Ger. & Eng., English Commercial Vokabulary Subjects). 1950. pap. 15.95 (ISBN 3-87217-001-5, 7360, Pub. by Th. Grossmann). French & Eur.

Englisches Wirtschaftsalphabet. 6th ed. H. Freyd-Wadham. 156p. (Eng. & Ger., English Economic Terms With German Vocabulary). 1975. 9.95 (ISBN 3-87217-006-6, Pub. by Th. Grossmann). French & Eur.

English - SerboCroatian Dictionary. Morton Benson. LC 78-64520. (Eng. & Serbocroatian.). 1979. 35.50x (ISBN 0-8122-7764-3). U of Pa Pr.

English-Albanian Dictionary. Gasper Kici & Hysni Aliko. (Eng. & Albanian.). 1969. 15.00 (ISBN 0-686-04914-4). G Kici.

English & Chinese Dictionary of the Amoy Dialect. J. MacGowan. (Chinese & Eng.). 1978. Repr. of 1883 ed. 25.00 (ISBN 0-89986-343-4). Oriental Bk Store.

English & Low-Dutch School-Master. Francis Harrison. LC 72-1876. 144p. (Eng. & Dutch.). 1976. write for info. (ISBN 0-404-03137-4). AMS Pr.

English & Low-Dutch Schoolmaster. Francis Harrison. LC 72-1876. (Eng. & Dutch.). Repr. of 1730 ed. 12.00 (ISBN 0-404-03137-4). AMS Pr.

English & Zulu Dictionary: English-Zulu, Zulu-English. C. M. Doke. (Zulu & Eng.). 1958. pap. 14.25x (ISBN 0-85494-010-3). Intl Learn Syst.

English Arabic, Arabic-English Dictionary. A. E. Elias. (Arabic & Eng.). student simplified ed. 15.00; pocket ed. 12.00. Intl Bk Ctr.

English-Arabic; Arabic-English Dictionary. E. A. Elias. (Eng. & Arabic.). 12.00x (ISBN 0-86685-173-9). Intl Bk Ctr.

English-Arabic, Arabic-English Dictionary. Ed. by J. Wortabet & H. Porter. 880p. (Eng. & Arabic.). 30.00 (ISBN 0-8044-0875-0). Ungar.

English-Arabic; Arabic-English Dictionary. John Wortabet. (Eng. & Arabic.). 1979. 16.00x (ISBN 0-86685-120-8). Intl Bk Ctr.

English-Arabic, Arabic-English Dictionary. John Wortabet. 900p. (Arabic & Eng.). 1979. 16.00 (120-8); pap. 10.00 pocket size (121-6). Intl Bk Ctr.

English Arabic, Arabic-English Pocket Dictionary. Ed. by Elias. (Eng. & Arabic.). 7.50x (ISBN 0-686-00859-6). Colton Bk.

English-Arabic; Arabic-English Pocket Dictionary. John Wortabet. (Eng. & Arabic.). pap. 10.00x (ISBN 0-86685-121-6). Intl Bk Ctr.

English-Arabic Collegiate Dictionary. Elias. (Eng. & Arabic.). 12.50 (ISBN 0-686-27677-9). Colton Bk.

English Arabic Conversational Dictionary. R. Jaschke. (Arabic & Eng.). 6.95. Iaconi.

English-Arabic Conversational Dictionary. Richard Jaschke. (Eng. & Arabic.). pocket dictionary using phonetic letters 6.95x. Intl Bk Ctr.

English-Arabic Conversational Dictionary, with Supplement. Ed. by Richard Jaschke. LC 54-11491. (Eng. & Arabic.). 1978. pap. 7.95 (ISBN 0-8044-6311-5). Ungar.

English-Arabic Dictionary. (Eng. & Arabic.). 19.50 (ISBN 0-87557-003-8, 003-8). Saphrograph.

English-Arabic Dictionary. F. Steingass. 464p. (Eng. & Arabic.). 1978. Repr. of 1882 ed. 22.00 (ISBN 0-89684-148-0). Orient Bk Dist.

English-Arabic Dictionary: Al-Manar. Hasan Karmi. (Eng. & Arabic.). 1971. lib. bdg. 25.00x (ISBN 0-86685-070-8). Intl Bk Ctr.

English-Arabic Dictionary: Al-Mawrid. Munir Ba'Albaki. 1982. 48.00x (ISBN 0-86685-059-7). Intl Bk Ctr.

English-Arabic Dictionary: Al-Mawrid. Munir Ba'Albaki. (Eng. & Arabic.). 1983. 48.00 (ISBN 0-86685-059-7). Intl Bk Ctr.

English-Arabic Dictionary: Al-Mawrid Al-Waset. Munir Ba'Albaki. (Eng. & Arabic.). 25.00x (ISBN 0-86685-060-0). Intl Bk Ctr.

English-Arabic Dictionary: Colloquial Arabic of Egypt. Socrates Spiro. (Eng. & Arabic.). 1974. 20.00x (ISBN 0-86685-080-5). Intl Bk Ctr.

English-Arabic Dictionary for Accounting & Finance. Adnan Abdeen. LC 79-41213. (Eng. & Arabic.). 1981. 23.95x (ISBN 0-471-27673-1, Pub. by Wiley-Interscience). Wiley.

English-Arabic Dictionary of Accounting & Finance. Adnan Abdeen. 1981. 30.00x (ISBN 0-86685-275-1). Intl Bk Ctr.

English-Arabic Dictionary of Diplomacy & Related Terminology. Gamal Barakat. (Eng. & Arabic.). 1982. 25.00x (ISBN 0-86685-290-5). Intl Bk Ctr.

English-Arabic Dictionary of Petroleum Terms & the Oil Industry. Ahmed Khatib. (Illus.). 1975. 40.00x (ISBN 0-86685-074-0). Intl Bk Ctr.

English-Arabic Dictionary of the Colloquial Arabic of Egypt. Socrates Spiro. 586p. (Eng. & Arabic.). 1975. 20.00 (080-5). Intl Bk Ctr.

English-Arabic Dictionary, Romanized. Edward Elias. (Eng. & Arabic.). 22.50 (ISBN 0-87559-002-0); thumb indexed 27.50 (ISBN 0-87559-003-9). Shalom.

English-Arabic Learner's Dictionary. F. Steingass. (Eng. & Arabic.). 1972. 20.00x (ISBN 0-86685-081-3). Intl Bk Ctr.

English-Arabic Lexicon. George P. Bagder. 80.00x (ISBN 0-86685-064-3). Intl Bk Ctr.

English-Arabic Lexicon. George Percy Badger. 1250p. (Eng. & Arabic.). 80.00 (064-3). Intl Bk Ctr.

English-Arabic Medical Dictionary. Yusuf K. Hitti. (Illus.). 913p. (Eng. & Arabic.). 35.00 (067-8). Intl Bk Ctr.

English-Arabic Pocket Dictionary. (Eng. & Arabic.). 4.00 (ISBN 0-86685-325-1). Intl Bk Ctr.

English-Arabic Pocket Dictionary. John Wortabet. (Eng. & Arabic.). 1980. pap. 5.50x (ISBN 0-86685-083-X). Intl Bk Ctr.

English-Arabic Pocket Dictionary: Al-Mawrid Al Quareb. Munir Ba'Alabaki. (Eng. & Arabic.). 1980. pap. 5.95x (ISBN 0-86685-062-7). Intl Bk Ctr.

English-Arabic Pocket Dictionary: Al Mawrid. Munir Ba'Albaki. (Arabic & Eng.). 1978. 4.00x (ISBN 0-86685-325-1). Intl Bk Ctr.

English-Arabic Reader's Dictionary. J. John Abcarius. 1974. 18.00x (ISBN 0-86685-063-5). Intl Bk Ctr.

English-Arabic Readers' Dictionary. John Abcarius. 700p. (Arabic & Eng.). 18.00 (063-5). Intl Bk. Ctr.

English-Arabic Student Dictionary: Al-Muyassar. Munir Ba'Albaki. (Eng. & Arabic.). 12.00x (ISBN 0-86685-061-9). Intl Bk Ctr.

English-Arabic Student Dictionary: Dar el Mashreq. (Eng. & Arabic.). 12.00x (ISBN 2-7214-2123-9). Intl Bk Ctr.

English-Arabic Vocabulary. Merrill Van Wagoner. 452p. (Eng. & Arabic.). 1980. 10.00x. Intl Bk Ctr.

English-Arabic Vocabulary: Students Pronouncing Dictionary. Merrill Y. Van Wagoner et al. LC 80-81198. 452p. (Orig., Eng. & Arabic.). 1980. pap. text ed. 10.00x (ISBN 0-87950-028-X). Spoken Lang Serv.

English-Armenian, Armenian English Dictionary. A. H. Yacobian. (Eng. & Armenian.). 24.50 (ISBN 0-87559-004-7); thumb indexed 29.50 (ISBN 0-87559-005-5). Shalom.

English-Basque Dictionary. Joe V. Eiguren. (Eng. & Basque.). 5.95. L Fereday Schol.

English-Bengali Dictionary. (Bengali.). 22.50 (ISBN 0-87557-110-7, 110-7). Saphrograph.

English-Blackfoot Vocabulary. Christianus C. Uhlenbeck & R. H. Van Gulik. LC 76-44087. (Verhandelingen der Koninklijke Akademie Van Wetenschappen Te Amsterdam. Afdeeling Letterkunde. Nieuwe Reeks: 29, No. 4). 261p. (Eng. & Blackfoot.). 1979. Repr. of 1930 ed. 26.50 (ISBN 0-404-15796-3). AMS Pr.

English-Bulgarian Concise Technical Dictionary. A. Desov. (Eng. & Bulgarian.). 17.50 (ISBN 0-686-91776-6). Heinman.

English-Bulgarian Dictionary. 2nd ed. Ivanka Harlakova & Elena Stankova. 392p. (Eng. & Bulgarian.). 1978. 30.00x (ISBN 0-686-44692-5, Pub. by Collets). State Mutual Bk.

English-Cheyenne Dictionary: A Dictionary of the Cheyenne Language. (Eng. & Cheyenne.). 1976. 4.95 (ISBN 0-686-26100-3); pap. write for info. MT Coun Indian.

English-Chinese & Chinese-English Dictionary. (Eng. & Chinese.). 1977. 7.95 (ISBN 0-8351-0725-6). China Bks.

English-Chinese Architectural Engineering Dictionary. 441p. (Eng. & Chinese.). 1973. 14.95 (ISBN 0-686-92620-X, M-9254). French & Eur.

English-Chinese Biology Dictionary. Y. Dongwuxue Cihui. 477p. (Eng. & Chinese.). 1975. 25.00 (ISBN 0-686-92343-X, M-9277). French & Eur.

English-Chinese Chinese-English Dictionary of Business Terms. Hsiu-Feng Chu et al. 476p. (Orig.). 1973. pap. 7.95x (ISBN 0-917056-85-X, Pub. by Chih-Wen Pub Co China). Cheng & Tsui.

English-Chinese Dictionary of Abbreviation & Acronyms. Zhou Long Ru. 1290p. (Eng. & Chinese.). 1980. 9.95 (ISBN 0-8351-1106-7). China Bks.

English-Chinese Dictionary of Abreviations & Acronyms. 1162p. (Eng. & Chinese.). 1979. lib. bdg. 9.95 (ISBN 0-686-92171-2, M-9555). French & Eur.

English-Chinese Dictionary of Aeronautical Engineering. 367p. (Eng. & Chinese.). 1975. Leatherette 25.00 (ISBN 0-686-92353-7, M-9257). French & Eur.

English-Chinese Dictionary of Chemistry & Chemical Engineering. 1458p. (Eng. & Chinese.). 1978. leatherette 49.95 (ISBN 0-686-92360-X, M-9248). French & Eur.

English-Chinese Dictionary of Civil & Architectural Engineering Terms. 706p. (Eng. & Chinese.). 1979. 29.95 (ISBN 0-686-97359-3, M-9271). French & Eur.

English-Chinese Dictionary of Construction Engineering. 251p. (Eng. & Chinese.). 1980. leatherette 14.95 (ISBN 0-686-97360-7, M-9279). French & Eur.

English-Chinese Dictionary of Engineering & Technology. Zhong Wai Publishing Company. 1036p. (Eng. & Chinese.). 1981. 69.95x (ISBN 0-471-09371-8). Wiley.

English-Chinese Dictionary of Mathematical Terms. 252p. (Eng. & Chinese.). 1980. 25.00 (ISBN 0-686-92416-9, M-9293). French & Eur.

English-Chinese Dictionary of Medicine. 1675p. (Eng. & Chinese.). 1979. text ed. 24.95 (ISBN 0-8351-1048-6). China Bks.

English-Chinese Dictionary of Metals & Their Heat Treatment. Tang Longan & Ni Zenglian. LC 81-1279. iii, 266p. 1981. pap. 27.50 (ISBN 0-8311-1081-3). Indus Pr.

English-Chinese Dictionary of Physical Geography. 279p. (Eng. & Chinese.). 1980. 25.00 (ISBN 0-686-97362-3, M-9292). French & Eur.

English-Chinese Dictionary of Physical Terms. W. Chu-Chi. 218p. (Eng. & Chinese.). 1973. leatherette 25.00 (ISBN 0-686-92350-2, M-9258). French & Eur.

English-Chinese Dictionary of Railway Terms. 1025p. (Eng. & Chinese.). 1977. 17.95 (ISBN 0-686-92493-2, M-9559). French & Eur.

English-Chinese Dictionary of Scientific & Technology Abreviations. 587p. (Eng. & Chinese.). 1979. pap. 9.95 (ISBN 0-686-97363-1, M-9250). French & Eur.

English-Chinese Dictionary of Technology. 1098p. (Eng. & Chinese.). 1978. leatherette 19.95 (ISBN 0-686-92474-6, M-9578). French & Eur.

English-Chinese Dictionary Romanized. J. C. Quo. 323p. (Eng. & Chinese.). 1964. pap. 6.95 (ISBN 0-686-92269-7, M-9591). French & Eur.

English-Chinese Dictionary, Romanized. James C. Quo. 323p. (Eng. & Chinese.). 15.00 (ISBN 0-87557-008-9, 008-9). Saphrograph.

English-Chinese Dictionary: Standard Chinese, 3 vols. Karl E. Hemeling. (Chinese & Eng.). 1976. Repr. of 1958 ed. 165.00 (ISBN 0-518-19001-3). Ayer Co.

English-Chinese Glossary for Elementary Chinese. Ed. by David J. Daehler. LC 77-83819. (CT Language Ser.). (Eng. & Chinese.). 1977. pap. text ed. 2.50 (ISBN 0-917056-05-1). Cheng & Tsui.

English-Chinese Glossary of Electronic & Electrical Engineering. 636p. (Eng. & Chinese.). 1980. 29.95 (ISBN 0-686-97364-X, M-9255). French & Eur.

English-Chinese Glossary of Social Sciences & Education. 238p. (Eng. & Chinese.). 1975. Leatherette 9.95 (ISBN 0-686-92309-X, M-9562). French & Eur.

English-Chinese Glossary of Terms Commonly Used in Government. Chinese Language Division of Home Affairs Department. LC 81-185069. (Chinese & Eng.). 1981. HK.$pap. 5.00. Govt Printer.

English-Chinese Maritime Dictionary. 678p. (Eng. & Chinese.). 1979. 14.95 (ISBN 0-686-97365-8, M-9251). French & Eur.

English-Chinese Medical Dictionary. 1665p. (Eng. & Chinese.). 1980. 95.00 (ISBN 0-686-97366-6, M-9264). French & Eur.

English-Chinese Medical Dictionary. 292p. (Eng. & Chinese.). 1977. pap. 6.95 (ISBN 0-686-92358-8, M-9253). French & Eur.

English-Chinese Microbiological Dictionary. 138p. (Eng. & Chinese.). 1979. pap. 3.95 (ISBN 0-686-97368-2, M-9573). French & Eur.

English-Chinese Picture Dictionary. B. Mathews. (Illus.). 48p. (Eng. & Chinese.). 2.50. G Brash.

English-Chinese Picture Dictionary. B. Matthews. (Illus.). 48p. (Chinese & Eng.). 1983. pap. 4.50 (ISBN 9971-947-00-5). Hippocrene Bks.

English-Chinese Picture Dictionary. B. Matthews & K. Tan. (Illus., Chinese & Eng.). 5.00. Iaconi.

English-Chinese Textile Dictionary. 532p. (Eng. & Chinese.). 1977. leatherette 29.95 (ISBN 0-686-92346-4, M-9269). French & Eur.

English Colloquial Arabic Dictionary. Raja Nasr. 1972. 18.00x (ISBN 0-86685-079-1). Intl Bk Ctr.

English-Colloquial Arabic Dictionary. Raja Nasr. 382p. (Eng. & Arabic.). 1982. 18.00 (079-1). Intl Bk Ctr.

English Colloquial Arabic Dictionary in Phonetic Script. Raja T. Nasr. 285p. 1974. text ed. 30.00 (ISBN 0-685-50128-0). Transatlantic.

English-Congo & Congo-English Dictionary. facs. ed. Henry Craven & John Barfield. LC 75-157365. (Black Heritage Library Collection). (Eng. & Congo.). 1883. 17.75 (ISBN 0-8369-8803-5). Ayer Co.

English-Cornish Dictionary. Frederick W. Jago. LC 78-72629. (Celtic Language & Literature: Goidelic & Brythonic). (Eng. & Cornish.). Repr. of 1887 ed. 34.50 (ISBN 0-404-17553-8). AMS Pr.

English-Croatian or Serbian Dictionary. 5th ed. Milan Drvodelic. (Eng. & Serbocroatian.). 1978. 30.00x (ISBN 0-686-19962-6). Intl Learn Syst.

English-Croatian or Serbian Dictionary. Rudolf Filipovic. 1436p. (Eng. & Serbocroatian.). 1980. 150.00x (ISBN 0-569-08646-9, Pub. by Collets). State Mutual Bk.

English-Czech & Czech-English Pocket Dictionary. K. Hais. 570p. (Eng. & Czech.). 1974. 5.50 (Pub. by State Pedag. Publ. House). Four Continent.

English-Czech, Czech-English Dictionary. A. Chermak. (Eng. & Czech.). 27.50 (ISBN 0-87557-012-7). Saphrograph.

English-Czech Dictionary. J. Caha & J. Kramsky. 878p. (Eng. & Czech.). 1980. 50.00x (ISBN 0-569-00405-5, Pub. by Collet's). State Mutual Bk.

English-Czech Dictionary. Ed. by J. Caha. 878p. (Eng. & Czech.). 1964. 10.75 (Pub. by State Pedag. Publ. House). Four Continent.

English-Czech Dictionary. Ed. by V. Osicka & I. Poldauf. 636p. (Eng. & Czech.). 1980. 50.00x (ISBN 0-569-06529-1, Pub. by Collet's). State Mutual Bk.

English-Czech Technical Dictionary. 1026p. (Eng. & Czech.). 1971. 22.25 (Pub. by SNTL). Four Continent.

English-Dakota Dictionary. J. P. Williamson. (Eng. & Dakota.). Repr. 15.00 (ISBN 0-87018-061-4). Ross.

English Dialect Dictionary: Being the Complete Vocabulary of All Dialect Words...During the Last Two Hundred Years, 6 vols. Ed. by John Wright. 1970. Repr. of 1905 ed. Set. text ed. 525.00x (ISBN 0-19-580497-X). Oxford U Pr.

English Dictionary. E. Coles. Repr. of 1676 ed. 55.00 (ISBN 3-4870-4748-9). Adler.

English Dictionary. (Eng.). 1980. NT.$3.95. Reed Ltd.

English Dictionary: An Interpreter of Hard English Words. Henry Cockeram. 1970. Repr. of 1626 ed. 39.50 (ISBN 3-4870-2632-5). Adler.

English-Dutch Dictionary. A. Broers & J. Smit. Ed. by R. Born. 674p. (Eng. & Dutch.). 1980. pap. 24.95 (ISBN 90-01-81264-3, M-9748). French & Eur.

English-Dutch Dictionary. K. T. Bruggencate. Ed. by J. Gerritsen et al. 898p. (Eng. & Dutch.). 1980. 24.95 (ISBN 90-01-96818-X, M-9747). French & Eur.

English-Efik Dictionary. R. F. Adams. (Eng. & Efik.). 27.50 (ISBN 0-87559-056-X); thumb indexed 32.50 (ISBN 0-87559-057-8). Shalom.

English English: A Descriptive Dictionary. Norman W. Schur. LC 77-20390. 332p. 1980. 24.95 (ISBN 0-930454-05-7). Verbatim.

English-English Dictionary. 640p. 14.00 (ISBN 0-87557-017-8, 017-8). Saphrograph.

English-English-Malayalam Dictionary. T. Ramalingam Pillai. Rev. by N. V. Krishna. 3333p. (Eng. & Malayalam.). 1976. write for info. DC Bks.

English-English-Malayalam Dictionary. T. Ramalingam Pillai. Ed. by M. S. Octavo. 1200p. (Eng. & Malayalam.). 1983. write for info. DC Bks.

English-Eskimo & Eskimo-English Vocabularies. Compiled by Roger Wells & John W. Kelley. LC 74-5889. (Eng. & Eskimo.). Repr. of 1890 ed. 11.50 (ISBN 0-404-11698-1). AMS Pr.

English-Eskimo & Eskimo-English Vocabularies. Compiled by Roger Wells, Jr. Tr. by John W. Kelly. LC 82-51153. 72p. (Inupiaq & Eng.). 1982. pap. 6.95 (ISBN 0-8048-1403-1). C E Tuttle.

English-Eskimo, Eskimo-English Dictionary. (Eng. & Eskimo.). 22.50 (ISBN 0-87559-061-6); thumb indexed 27.50 (ISBN 0-87559-062-4). Shalom.

English-Estonian Dictionary for Schools. M. Rauk. 444p. (Eng. & Estonian.). 1977. 3.95 (Pub. by Valgus). Four Continent.

English-Estonian-Russian Maritime Dictionary. Kulno Olev. 560p. (Eng., Estonian & Rus.). 1981. 60.00x (ISBN 0-686-82322-2, Pub. by Collets). State Mutual Bk.

English Expositor: Teaching the Interpretation of the Hardest Words Used in Our Language. John Bullokar. 1971. Repr. of 1616 ed. 32.00 (ISBN 3-4870-4070-0). Adler.

English Field-Names: A Dictionary. John Field. LC 76-148407. (Illus.). xxx, 120p. 1973. 25.00 (ISBN 0-8103-2010-X). Gale.

English Finderlist of Reconstructions in Austronesian Languages. Stefan A. Wurm & Basil Wilson. LC 79-342769. xxxii, 246p. (Proto-Austronesian & Eng.). 1975. write for info. (ISBN 0-85883-129-5). Linguistic Circle.

English-Finnish Dictionary. A. Wuolle. 512p. (Eng. & Finnish.). 1980. leatherette 19.95 (ISBN 951-0-08500-6, M-9653). French & Eur.

English-Finnish General Dictionary. R. Hurme et al. 1183p. (Eng. & Finnish.). 1981. 75.00 (ISBN 951-0-08553-7, M-9659). French & Eur.

English for the Medical Professions. L. Beitler & B. McDonald. 1982. 6.96 (ISBN 0-07-004521-6). McGraw.

English-French & French-English Technical Dictionary. rev. ed. Francis Cusset. (Eng. & Fr.). 1967. 28.50 (ISBN 0-8206-0043-1). Chem Pub.

English-French-Arabic Dictionary of Political Idioms. Magdi Wahba. 35.00x (ISBN 0-86685-118-6). Intl Bk Ctr.

English-French-Arabic Trilingual Dictionary. Jerwan Sabek. (Eng., Fr. & Arabic.). 35.00x (ISBN 0-86685-116-X). Intl Bk Ctr.

English-French Dictionary. rev. ed. Editions Berlitz S. A. LC 78-78078. 335p. (Eng. & Fr.). 1979. 2.95 (ISBN 0-02-964500-X, Pub by Berlitz). Macmillan.

English-French Dictionary. (Eng. & Fr.). 14.50 (ISBN 0-87557-022-4, 021-6). Saphrograph.

English-French Dictionary of Computer Science. R. Fisher & P. Krchten. (Eng. & Fr.). Date not set. text ed. 25.00 (ISBN 0-686-46529-6). Heinman.

English-French, French-English Dictionary. (Eng. & Fr.). write for info. (608-70). B&N.

English-French General Technical Dictionary. J. Belle-Isle. LC 79-342847. xii, 552p. (Eng. & Fr.). 1977. E10.00 (ISBN 0-7100-8928-7). Routledge & Kegan.

English-French-German Glossary for Psychiatry, Child Psychiatry & Abnormal Psychology. 2nd ed. Lise Moor. LC 75-450548. (Eng., Fr. & Ger.). 1969. 8.75x (ISBN 0-8002-0766-1). Intl Pubns Serv.

English-French Glossary. Lucienne V. Wolfe. LC 77-601793. 645p. (Eng. & Fr.). 1976. 7.90. Govt Print.

English-French Glossary of Educational Terminology. Robert L. Gieber. LC 80-5652. 212p. (Eng. & Fr.). 1980. lib. bdg. 20.25 (ISBN 0-8191-1344-1); pap. text ed. 10.25 (ISBN 0-8191-1345-X). U Pr of Amer.

English-French Petroleum Dictionary. M. Arnould & F. Zubini. 267p. (Eng. & Fr.). 1982. 75.00x (ISBN 0-86010-374-9, Pub. by Graham & Trotman England). State Mutual Bk.

English-French Petroleum Dictionary. Michel Arnould & Fabio Zubini. 267p. (Eng. & Fr.). 1983. pap. 37.00x (ISBN 0-8448-1432-6). Crane-Russak Co.

English Fuer Elektrotechniker & Elektroniker. Wanke & Havlicek. xv, 368p. (Eng. & Ger.). DM.40.00. Brandstetter.

English-German -- German-English Welding Engineering Dictionary. 396p. (Eng. & Fr.). 1980. 75.00x (ISBN 0-569-05715-9, Pub. by Collet's). State Mutual Bk.

English-German Chemical Terminology: An Introduction to Chemistry in English & German. 5th rev. ed. H. Fromherz & A. King. 588p. (Eng. & Ger.). 1968. 55.00 (ISBN 0-686-56603-3, M-7362, Pub. by Vlg. Chemie). French & Eur.

English-German Chemical Terminology: An Introduction to Chemistry in English & German. 5th, rev. ed. H. Fromherz & A. King. 588p. (Eng. & Ger.). 1968. DM.55.00. Verlag Chemie.

English-German Chemical Terminology: An Introduction to Chemistry in English & German. 5th ed. Hans Fromherz & Alexander King. LC 68-26705. 609p. (Eng. & Ger.). 1968. 46.30x (ISBN 3-527-25093-X). Verlag Chemie.

English-German Dictionary. K. Briese. 624p. (Eng. & Ger.). 1980. 20.00x (ISBN 0-569-06892-4, Pub. by Collet's). State Mutual Bk.

English-German Dictionary. (Eng. & Ger.). 14.50 (ISBN 0-87557-026-7, 026-7X). Saphrograph.

English-German Dictionary of Chemistry & Chemical Technology. 2nd ed. Ed. by Technishe Universitaet, Dresden. LC 76-455777. (Eng. & Ger.). 1978. 47.50x (ISBN 0-8002-0401-8). Intl Pubns Serv.

English-German Dictionary of Idioms. K. Engeroff & C. Lovelace-Kaeufer. (Eng. & Ger.). 22.75 (ISBN 3-1900-6217-X). Adler.

English-German, German-English Dictionary, 2 vols. rev. ed. Wildhagen & Hereaucourt. (Ger. & Eng.). 1972. Vol. 1: English-German, 1148p. 32.50; Vol. 2: German-English, 1524p. 45.00. M Rosenberg.

English-German, German, English Solid State Physics & Electronics Dictionary. G. Birdmann. 1103p. (Eng. & Ger.). 1980. 100.00x (ISBN 0-569-07204-2, Pub. by Collet's). State Mutual Bk.

English-German, German-English Welding Engineering Dictionary. A. Kleiber. 396p. (Eng. & Ger.). 1970. 90.00x (ISBN 0-686-44709-3, Pub. by Collets). State Mutual Bk.

English-German Glossary of Financial & Economic Terms. Hans E. Zahn. (Eng. & Ger.). 1977. 56.00x (ISBN 3-7819-2013-5). Intl Pubns Serv.

English Glossary: A Supplementary. T. Lewis Davies. 736p. 1980. Repr. of 1881 ed. lib. bdg. 125.00 (ISBN 0-8495-1119-4). Arden Lib.

English-Greek Pocket Dictionary. (Eng. & Gr.). pap. 8.50 (ISBN 0-685-77571-2, 030-5). Saphrograph.

English-Hawaiian Dictionary. Hitchcock. (Hawaiian & Eng.). 7.25. Iaconi.

English-Hawaiian Dictionary. Harvey R. Hitchcock. LC 68-13870. (Hawaiian & Eng.). (gr. 7 up). 1968. Repr. 7.25 (ISBN 0-8048-0168-1). C E Tuttle.

English Hindi Dictionary. Bulke. (Eng. & Hindi.). 1979. 15.00 (ISBN 0-89744-967-3). Auromere.

English-Hindi Dictionary. (Eng. & Hindi.). large ed. 27.50 (ISBN 0-87557-034-8); small ed. 19.50 (ISBN 0-686-66962-2, 033-XX). Saphrograph.

English-Hindustani Dictionary. (Eng. & Hindustani.). pap. 17.50 (ISBN 0-87557-036-4, 036-4). Saphrograph.

English-Hittite Glossary. Harry A. Hoffner, Jr. 1967. 10.50x (ISBN 0-8002-1398-X). Intl Pubns Serv.

English-Hungarian Dictionary. L. Orszagh. (Eng. & Hungarian.). 24.50 (ISBN 0-686-65153-7, 043-7). Saphrograph.

English-Hungarian Dictionary. 13th ed. Ed. by Laszlo Orszagh. 608p. (Eng. & Hungarian.). 1982. 6.25x (ISBN 963-05-2975-0). Intl Pubns Serv.

English-Hungarian Dictionary, 2 vols. V. Orszagh. 2336p. (Eng. & Hungarian.). 1980. 99.00x (ISBN 0-569-00359-8, Pub. by Collet's). State Mutual Bk.

English-Hungarian, Hungarian-English Dictionary-Angol-Magyar-Angol Szotar. Biro Willerfest. (Eng. & Hungarian.). 19.50 (ISBN 0-87557-039-9, 042-2). Saphrograph.

English-Hungarian, Hungarian-English Medical Dictionary. Dora Lee-Delisle. (Eng. & Hungarian.). 18.50 (ISBN 0-87557-040-2, 042-2X). Saphrograph.

English-Hungarian Technical Dictionary-Angol-Magyar Muszaki Szotar. Imre Razso. (Eng. & Hungarian.). 29.50 (ISBN 0-87557-041-0, 041-0). Saphrograph.

English-Hungarian Technical Dictionary. Ed. by E. Nagy & J. Klar. 792p. (Eng. & Hungarian.). 1980. 70.00x (ISBN 0-686-72096-2, Pub. by Collet's). State Mutual Bk.

English-Icelandic Dictionary. S. O. Bogason. (Eng. & Icelandic.). 75.00 (ISBN 0-685-29251-7). Heinman.

English-Indonesian Dictionary. John M. Echols & Hassan Shadily. LC 72-5638. 660p. (Eng. & Indonesian.). 1975. 49.50x (ISBN 0-8014-0728-1); softcover 27.50x (ISBN 0-8014-9859-7). Cornell U Pr.

English-Indonesian, Indonesian-English Dictionary. A. L. Kramer, Sr. (Eng. & Indonesian.). 24.50 (ISBN 0-87559-066-7); thumb indexed 29.50 (ISBN 0-87559-067-5). Shalom.

English-Irish Dictionary. Tomas De Bhaldraithe. LC 79-304424. 25p. (Eng. & Gaelic.). 1978. E0.30. Oifig An Tsolathair.

English-Irish Dictionary. T. De Bhardraithe. (Eng. & Irish.). 1959. 12.50x (ISBN 0-686-00860-X). Colton Bk.

English-Irish Dictionary. rev. ed. Patrick S. Dinneen. Ed. by L. O. Murcava. (Eng. & Irish.). 22.50 (ISBN 0-87559-072-1); thumb indexed 27.50 (ISBN 0-87559-040-3). Shalom.

English-Irish Dictionary: Terminological Additions & Corrections. Tomas De Bhaldraithe & Baile A. Claithe. LC 79-304424. 25p. (Eng. & Gaelic.). 1978. E0.30. Govt Publications Sale Office.

English-Italian, Italian-English Dictionary, 1 vol. (Eng. & Ital.). 19.50 (ISBN 0-685-33020-6, 045-3). Saphrograph.

English-Italian, Italian-English Dictionary. 1960p. (Ital. & Eng.). 1981. 62.00. Oxford U Pr.

English-Italian, Italian-English Dictionary. Ed. by Malcolm Skey. (Eng. & Ital.). 1981. 49.95x (ISBN 0-19-431158-9). Oxford U Pr.

English-Japanese Dictionary (Romanized) (Eng. & Japanese.). 19.50 (ISBN 0-87557-047-X, 048-X). Saphrograph.

English-Japanese Marine Terms Dictionary. 542p. (Eng. & Japanese.). 95.00 (ISBN 0-686-92390-1, M-93491). French & Eur.

English-Kham, Kham-English Glossary. David Watters & Nancy Watters. 126p. (Eng. & Kham.). 1973. pap. 2.00x (ISBN 0-88312-756-3); 2.25. Summer Inst Ling.

English-Khmer Dictionary. Franklin E. Huffman & Im Proum. LC 78-7705. (Linguistic Ser.). (Eng. & Khmer.). 1978. text ed. 40.00x (ISBN 0-300-02261-1). Yale U Pr.

English-Khmer Medical Dictionary. Sally Keller. (Workpapers of North Dakota: Vol. XX, Suppl. 2). 190p. (Eng. & Khmer.). 1976. pap. 4.50x (ISBN 0-88312-744-X); microfiche 3.00x (ISBN 0-88312-341-X). Summer Inst Ling.

English-Khmer Phrasebook with Useful Wordlist. (Khmer & Eng.). 4.00; cassettes 18.00. Iaconi.

English-Khmer Phrasebook with Useful Word List: For Cambodians. Tr. by Samnang Soeur. LC 80-66143. 140p. (Eng. & Cambodian.). 1980. pap. text ed. 5.00x (ISBN 0-87281-115-8). Ctr Appl Ling.

English-Kikuyu Dictionary. A. R. Barlow. Tr. by T. G. Benson. 340p. (Eng. & Kikuyu.). 1975. 24.95x (ISBN 0-19-864407-8). Oxford U Pr.

English-Korean Dictionary for Practical Conversation. B. J. Jones. LC 83-81486. (Korean.). 1983. price not set (ISBN 0-930878-22-1). Hollym Corp.

English Korean Dictionary Romanized. M. E. Song. (Eng. & Korean.). 27.50 (ISBN 0-87559-174-4). Shalom.

English-Kotiya Oriya, Kotiya Oriya-English Glossary. Uwe Gustafsson. 1974. pap. 2.00x (ISBN 0-88312-748-2). Summer Inst Ling.

English-Lamba Dictionary. Clement M. Doke. (Eng. & Lamba.). 22.00 (ISBN 0-87559-055-1). Shalom.

English-Lao, Lao-English Dictionary. Russell Marcus. LC 77-116487. (Eng. & Laotian.). 1970. 10.50 (ISBN 0-8048-0909-7). C E Tuttle.

English-Lao, Lao-English Dictionary. Marcus Russell. (Lao & Eng.). 10.50. Iaconi.

English-Lao Phrasebook with Useful Word List: For Laotians. Tr. by Kamchong Luangpraseut. (Eng. & Lao.). 1980. pap. text ed. 5.00x (ISBN 0-87281-117-4). Ctr Appl Ling.

English-Latvian-Russian Dictionary. J. Raskevics et al. 718p. (Eng., Latvian & Rus.). 1977. 50.00x (ISBN 0-686-82324-9, Pub. by Collets). State Mutual Bk.

English-Lingala Manual. John D. Odhner. LC 80-6174. 206p. (Orig., Eng. & Bangala.). 1981. lib. bdg. 19.50 (ISBN 0-8191-1554-1); pap. text ed. 10.00 (ISBN 0-8191-1555-X). U Pr of Amer.

English-Lithuanian Dictionary. A. Laucka et al. 1096p. (Eng. & Lithuanian.). 1978. 11.95 (Pub. by Mokslas). Four Continent.

English-Lithuanian Dictionary of Economic Terms. A. Buracas. 488p. (Eng. & Lithuanian.). 1980. 4.95 (Pub. by Mokslas). Four Continent.

English Loanwords in Japanese: A Selection. Akira Miura. LC 78-65031. (Japanese & Eng.). 1979. 11.50 (ISBN 0-8048-1248-9). C E Tuttle.

English-Malayalam Dictionary. T. R. Pillai. Ed. by M. S. Chandrasekhara. 904p. (Eng. & Malayalam.). 1980. write for info. DC Bks.

English-Mbukusha dictionary. R. C. Wynne. LC 80-487422. xxxii, 615p. (Eng. & Mbukusha.). 1980. E24.00 (ISBN 0-86127-203-X). Avebury Pub Co.

English-Mbukushu Dictionary. R. C. Wynne. 615p. (Eng. & Mbukushu.). 1980. text ed. 45.00x (ISBN 0-86127-203-X, Pub. by Avebury England). Humanities.

English-Mbukushu Dictionary. Ronald C. Wynne. LC 80-487422. xxxii, 615p. (Mbukushu & Eng.). 1980. E24.00 (ISBN 0-86127-203-X). Avebury Pub Co.

English-Norsk Dictionary: Gyldendals. new ed. B. Berulfsen. (Eng. & Norwegian.). 1978. 20.00x (ISBN 8-2573-0007-1, N481); Norsk-English. 22.00x (ISBN 8-2573-0006-3, N-482). Vanous.

English-Norwegian Dictionary. B. Berulfsen & T. Berulfsen. (Eng. & Norwegian.). 1981. write for info. (ISBN 82-573-0161-2). Kunnskapsforlaget.

English-Norwegian, Norwegian-English. 7th ed. Jan W. Dietrichson & Orm Verland. LC 78-387531. 448p. (Eng. & Norwegian.). 1978. Kr.19.50 (ISBN 8-257-30054-3). Kunnskapsforlaget.

English-Norwegian, Norwegian-English Dictionary, Norwegian-English Dictionary. J. Meyer Myklestad & H. Soras. (Eng. & Norwegian.). 19.50 (ISBN 0-87557-054-2, 054-2). Saphrograph.

English-Norwegian, Norwegian-English, Lommeordbok. E. Daae. 568p. (Eng. & Norwegian.). 1980. pap. 8.95 (ISBN 82-573-0152-3, M-9462). French & Eur.

English-Norwegian Norwegian-English Pocket Dictionary. (Eng. & Norwegian.). 1981. 6.95 (ISBN 0-88254-584-1). Hippocrene Bks.

English-Nubian Comparative Dictionary. G. W. Murray. Ed. by E. A. Hooton & Natica I. Bates. (Harvard African Studies: Vol. 4). (Eng. & Nubian.). 1923. 37.00 (ISBN 0-527-01027-8). Kraus Repr.

English-Nyanja Dictionary. Thomas Price. (Eng. & Nyanja.). 22.50 (ISBN 0-87559-114-0). Shalom.

English Persian Dictionary. A. N. Wollaston. 462p. (Eng. & Persian.). 1978. Repr. of 1842 ed. 28.00 (ISBN 0-89684-156-1, Pub. by Cosmo Pubns India). Orient Bk Dist.

English-Persian Dictionary Compiled from Original Sources. 2nd ed. A. N. Wollaston. (Eng. & Persian.). 1904. text ed. 21.00x (ISBN 0-391-01068-9). Humanities.

English-Persian Dictionary: Romanized. (Eng. & Persian.). 19.50 (ISBN 0-87557-058-5, 058-5). Saphrograph.

English-Polish & Polish-English Compact Dictionary. Rev. ed. 542p. (Eng. & Pol.). 1977. 5.50. Imported Bks.

English-Polish & Polish-English Dictionary. J. Stanislawski. 879p. (Eng. & Pol.). E12.95. McKay.

English-Polish & Polish-English Minimum Dictionary. K. Billip. 543p. (Eng. & Pol.). 1979. 2.85. Wiedza Powszechna.

English-Polish Dictionary of Idioms & Phrases. Pioter Borkowski. 244p. (Orig., Eng. & Pol.). 1983. pap. 6.95. Hippocrene Bks.

English-Polish Dictionary of Idioms & Phrases. Piotr Borkowski. 206p. (Orig., Eng. & Pol.). 1982. pap. 6.95 (ISBN 0-903705-46-X). Hippocrene Bks.

English-Polish Dictionary of Science & Technology. 4th ed. 892p. (Eng. & Pol.). 90.00x (ISBN 0-569-08263-3, Pub. by Collets). State Mutual Bk.

English-Polish Dictionary of Science & Technology. 892p. (Eng. & Pol.). 1976. 19.95 (Pub. by Wydaw. Naukowo-Techniczne). Four Continent.

English-Polish-English Dictionary. (Eng. & Pol.). 15.00 (ISBN 0-87557-060-7). Saphrograph.

English-Polish Polish-English Chemical Dictionary. Ed. by Dobromila Kryt & Bazyli Semniuk. LC 79-393179. 912p. (Eng. & Pol.). 1979. 32.50x (ISBN 83-204-0004-X). Intl Pubns Serv.

English-Polish, Polish-English Dictionary. W. Kierst. (Eng. & Pol.). 29.50 (ISBN 0-87557-060-7, 060-7). Saphrograph.

English-Portuguese Dictionary. rev. ed. J. Albino Ferreira. Ed. by O. De Morais. (Eng. & Port.). 32.50 (ISBN 0-87559-027-6); thumb indexed 37.50 (ISBN 0-87559-028-4). Shalom.

English-Portuguese Metallurgical Dictionary. James L. Taylor. 300p. (Eng. & Port.). pap. 9.50. Imported Bks.

English-Reader's Dictionary. 2nd ed. Ed. by Albert S. Hornby & E. C. Parnwell. 1969. pap. 5.95x (ISBN 0-19-431116-3). Oxford U Pr.

English-Romanian Dictionary. Serban C. Andronescu. (Eng. & Romanian.). Date not set. price not set (ISBN 0-917944-03-8). Am Inst Writing Res.

English-Romanian Dictionary. V. Levitchi & T. Bantas. 1068p. (Eng. & Rumanian.). 1980. 55.00x (ISBN 0-569-07472-X, Pub. by Collet's). State Mutual Bk.

English-Russian Astronomical Dictionary. O. Meinikov. 504p. (Eng. & Rus.). 1980. 15.00x (ISBN 0-569-06519-4, Pub. by Collet's). State Mutual Bk.

English-Russian Aviation & Space Abbreviations Dictionary. A. M. Murashkevich & O. N. Vladimirov. 622p. (Eng. & Rus.). 1981. 45.00x (ISBN 0-686-44706-9, Pub. by Collets). State Mutual Bk.

English-Russian Biological Dictionary. 3rd, rev. & enl. ed. LC 78-40145. (Eng. & Rus.). 1978. E100.00 (ISBN 0-08-023163-2); 50.00. Pergamon.

English-Russian Dictionary. O. S. Akhmanova & E. Wilson. 639p. (Rus. & Eng.). 1979. 9.95 (ISBN 0-686-97370-4, M-9115). French & Eur.

English-Russian Dictionary. A. Akmanova. 590p. (Eng. & Rus.). 1980. 25.00x (ISBN 0-569-00012-2, Pub. by Collet's). State Mutual Bk.

English-Russian Dictionary. T. Arakin. 988p. (Eng. & Rus.). 1980. 35.00x (ISBN 0-569-00013-0, Pub. by Collets). State Mutual Bk.

English-Russian Dictionary. V. D. Arakin. (Eng. & Rus.). 1980. leatherette 19.95 (ISBN 0-686-97371-2, M-9107). French & Eur.

English-Russian Dictionary. V. Muller. 888p. (Eng. & Rus.). 1980. vinyl 42.00x (ISBN 0-569-08362-1, Pub. by Collet's). State Mutual Bk.

English-Russian Dictionary. rev. ed. Ed. by V. K. Muller. (Eng. & Rus.). 1973. 24.75 (ISBN 0-525-09881-X, 02403-720). Dutton.

English-Russian Dictionary. 6th ed. Vladimir K. Muller. (Eng. & Rus.). 19.50 (ISBN 0-685-20186-4, 066-6). Saphrograph.

English-Russian Dictionary. 3rd ed. Louis Segal. (Rus. & Eng.). 1958. text ed. 19.95x (ISBN 0-8464-0380-3). Beekman Pubs.

English-Russian Dictionary of Electrochemistry & Corrosion. M. M. Melnikova & I. P. Smirnov. 496p. (Eng. & Rus.). 1976. 9.95 (ISBN 0-686-92367-7, M-9121). French & Eur.

English-Russian Dictionary of Environmental Control. Ed. by E. L. Milovanov & E. A. Veistman. 338p. (Eng. & Rus.). 1981. 29.50 (ISBN 0-08-023576-X). Pergamon.

English-Russian Dictionary of Finance & World Trade. E. E. Israelevich. 544p. (Eng. & Rus.). 10.50. Imported Bks.

English-Russian Dictionary of Minimum Physics. 287p. (Eng. & Rus.). 1980. leatherette 7.95 (ISBN 0-686-97372-0, M-9123). French & Eur.

English-Russian Dictionary of Nabokov's "Lolita". A. D. Nakhimovsky & V. A. Paperno. (Rus. & Eng.). 1982. 17.95x (ISBN 0-88233-443-3); pap. 8.95x (ISBN 0-88233-444-1). Ardis Pubs.

English-Russian Dictionary of Nuclear Explosions. 304p. (Eng. & Rus.). 1977. 40.00x (ISBN 0-686-44703-4, Pub. by Collets). State Mutual Bk.

English-Russian Dictionary of Refrigerating & Cryogenic Engineering. M. B. Rosenberg. 467p. (Eng. & Rus.). 1978. Leatherette 15.95 (ISBN 0-686-92382-0, M-9063). French & Eur.

English-Russian Dictionary of Refrigeration & Low Temperature Technology. 2nd, rev. ed. M. B. Rozenberg. 73.00 (ISBN 0-08-024737-7). Pergamon.

English-Russian Dictionary of Reliability & Quality Control. Y. G. Kovalenko. LC 77-70279. (Eng. & Rus.). 1977. text ed. 72.00 (ISBN 0-08-021933-0). Pergamon.

English-Russian Dictionary of Sports Terms & Phrases. A. V. Garilovets. 420p. (Eng. & Rus.). 1980. 35.00x (ISBN 0-569-08602-7, Pub. by Collets). State Mutual Bk.

English-Russian Dictionary of Sports Terms & Phrases: Summer Olympic Games & Sports. (Russkii iazyk Ser.). 420p. (Rus. & Eng.). pap. 4.95 (2533 B). Four Continent.

English-Russian Glossary of Computer Systems & Networks Terminology. E. A. Yakubaitis. 270p. (Eng. & Rus.). 1981. 40.00x (ISBN 0-686-44705-0, Pub. by Collets). State Mutual Bk.

English-Russian Glossary of Physics Terms. P. M. Alekseev. 288p. (Eng. & Rus.). 1980. 35.00x (ISBN 0-686-44696-8, Pub. by Collets). State Mutual Bk.

English-Russian Phrase Book. Compiled by L. D. Pochertsova et al. (Vyscha shkola Ser.). 335p. (Eng. & Rus.). 1979. 4.95 (C-94). Four Continent.

English-Russian Physics Dictionary. D. M. Tolstoi. 848p. (Eng. & Rus.). 1978. 75.00x (ISBN 0-686-44700-X, Pub. by Collets). State Mutual Bk.

English-Russian Physics Dictionary. Ed. by D. M. Tolstoi. LC 78-40718. (Eng. & Rus.). 1979. 81.00 (ISBN 0-08-023057-1). Pergamon.

English-Russian Polytechnical Dictionary. A. E. Chernukhin. (Eng. & Rus.). 88.00 (ISBN 0-08-021936-5). Pergamon.

English-Russian Polytechnical Dictionary. Ed. by A. E. Chernukhin. 688p. (Eng. & Rus.). 1979. 70.00x (ISBN 0-569-08580-2, Pub. by Collets). State Mutual Bk.

English-Russian, Russian-English Dictionary. 464p. (Eng. & Rus.). 1978. 4.75 (ISBN 0-686-92374-X, M-9094). French & Eur.

English-Russian-Serbocroatian Aviations Dictionary. J. Dragovic. 460p. (Eng., Rus. & Serbocroation.). 1973. Leatherette 35.00 (ISBN 0-686-92266-2, M-9632). French & Eur.

English-Russian Televisions Dictionary. L. P. Prosorova & V. L. Kreizer. 429p. (Eng. & Rus.). 1960. Leatherette 6.95 (ISBN 0-686-92377-4, M-9065). French & Eur.

English-Russian Textile Dictionary. Z. E. Rabinowitch & K. K. Lupandin. 640p. (Eng. & Rus.). 1961. Leatherette 14.95 (ISBN 0-686-92372-3, M-9111). French & Eur.

English Sanskrit Dictionary. Monier Monier-Williams. (Eng. & Sanskrit.). 1979. 30.00x (ISBN 0-89744-966-5). Auromere.

English-Sanskrit Dictionary. Monier Monier-Williams. (Eng. & Sanskrit.). 1976. Repr. of 1851 ed. Set. text ed. 34.00x (ISBN 0-391-01069-7). Humanities.

English-Sanskrit Dictionary. Monier Monier-Williams. (Eng. & Sanskrit.). 1976. Repr. of 1851 ed. 27.50x (ISBN 0-8002-0205-8). Intl Pubns Serv.

English-Serbo-Croat & Serbo-Croat-English Dictionary. J. Grujic. 620p. (Eng. & Serbocroatian.). 1980. 40.00x (ISBN 0-569-03165-6, Pub. by Collet's). State Mutual Bk.

English-Serbocroat & Serbocroat-English Dictionary. V. C. Grujic. 620p. (Eng. & Serbocroatian.). 1971. 65.00x (ISBN 0-686-44712-3, Pub. by Collets). State Mutual Bk.

English-Serbocroat & Serbocroat-English Geological & Mining Dictionary. Ing S. Verbic. 528p. (Eng. & Serbocroatian.). 1981. 90.00x (ISBN 0-686-44714-X, Pub. by Collets). State Mutual Bk.

English-Serbocroatian & Serbocroatian-English Dictionary. 7th ed. Blanka Brozovic & Oktavija Gercan. (Eng. & Serbocroatian.). 1980. pap. 8.00x (ISBN 0-686-31617-7). Intl Learn Syst.

English-Serbocroatian Dictionary. M. Benson. 669p. (Eng. & Serbocroatian.). 1981. 75.00 (ISBN 0-686-97376-3, M-9635). French & Eur.

English-Serbocroatian Dictionary. 10th ed. Rudolf Filipovic et al. (Eng. & Serbocroatian.). 1975. 80.00x (ISBN 0-686-19960-X). Intl Learn Syst.

English-Serbocroatian Dictionary. Svetomir Ristic & Zivojin Simic. (Eng. & Serbocroatian.). 1975. 29.95x (ISBN 0-686-19961-8). Intl Learn Syst.

English-Serbocroatian Dictionary. Z. Simic. 446p. (Eng. & Serbocroatian.). 1979. pap. text ed. 14.95 (ISBN 0-686-97375-5, M-9634). French & Eur.

English-Serbocroatian, Serbocroatian-English Dictionary. Ratimir J. Cvetanovic. (Eng. & Serbocroatian.). 19.50 (ISBN 0-87557-074-7, 074-7). Saphrograph.

English-Slovak Dictionary. P. Simko. 1442p. (Eng. & Slovak.). 1980. 70.00x (ISBN 0-569-03737-9, Pub. by Collet's). State Mutual Bk.

English-Slovak Technical Dictionary. S. Benacka. 1358p. (Eng. & Slovak.). 1980. 79.00x (ISBN 0-569-08529-2, Pub. by Collet's). State Mutual Bk.

English-Slovene Dictionary. A. Grad et al. 1120p. (Eng. & Slovene.). 1979. 49.95 (ISBN 0-686-97378-X, M-9695). French & Eur.

English Sotho-Sotho English Dictionary. (Eng. & Sotho.). 21.00 (ISBN 0-87559-031-4); thumb indexed 27.00 (ISBN 0-87559-032-2). Shalom.

English-Spanish Banking Dictionary. Rafael Gil Esteban. LC 78-323192. 270p. (Eng. & Span.). 1978. write for info. (ISBN 8-440-04115-2). Autores Propias.

English-Spanish Dictionary. P. Constantinon. (Eng. & Span.). 14.50 (ISBN 0-87559-172-8). Shalom.

English-Spanish Dictionary. (Eng. & Span.). 14.50 (ISBN 0-87557-077-1, 077-1). Saphrograph.

English-Spanish Guide for Medical Personnel. Ed. by Joseph Armengol et al. (Eng. & Span.). 1966. pap. 7.00 (ISBN 0-87488-721-6). Med Exam.

English-Spanish picture dictionary. E. C. Parnwell. (Illus.). 96p. (Eng. & Span.). 1980. write for info. Fondo Educativo.

English-Spanish, Spanish-English Dictionary of Communications & Electronic Terms. Roger L. Freeman. (Eng. & Span.). 1972. 39.50 (ISBN 0-521-08080-0). Cambridge U Pr.

English-Spanish Spanish-English Encyclopedic Dictionary of Technical Terms, 3 vols. Javier L. Collazo. LC 79-16074. (Eng. & Span.). 1980. Set, English Edition. 154.00 (ISBN 0-07-079172-4); Set, Spanish Edition. 154.00 (ISBN 0-07-079162-7). McGraw.

English-Spanish, Spanish-English Encyclopedic Dictionary of Technical Terms, 3 vols. Javier L. Collazo. 1500p. (Span. & Eng.). write for info. (English cover) (ISBN 0-07-079172-4); write for info. (Spanish cover) (ISBN 0-07-079162-7). McGraw.

English-Spanish Sports Dictionary for Soccer. Jose A. Sierra. (Eng. & Span.). 1982. 25.00x (ISBN 0-905473-84-1, Pub. by Wolfhound Pr Ireland). State Mutual Bk.

English-Spanish Technical Dictionary. (Span. & Eng.). 37.50 (ISBN 0-87559-188-4). Shalom.

English-Spanish Technical Dictionary. 2nd ed. F. F. Ibeas. (Eng. & Span.). pap. 45.00 (ISBN 0-686-77977-0). Heinman.

English-Spanish to Spanish-English Dictionary. rev. ed. Arturo Cuyas. 548p. (Span. & Eng.). 1982. pap. 2.50 (ISBN 0-13-615559-6). P-H.

English-Swedish Dictionary. Ruben Nojd. (Eng. & Swedish.). 16.00 (ISBN 0-87557-083-6, 083-6). Saphrograph.

English-Swedish-English Dictionary. 275p. (Eng. & Swedish.). 1981. pap. 9.95 (ISBN 91-518-1438-2, M-9449). French & Eur.

English-Tagalog-Ilocano Pocket Dictionary. Enriquez & Quimba. (Eng. & Tagalog.). 4.00x (ISBN 0-686-05264-1). Colton Bk.

English-Tagalog, Tagalog-English Pocket Dictionary. Enriquez & Guzman. (Eng. & Tagalog.). 3.50x (ISBN 0-686-00861-8). Colton Bk.

English-Tagalog-Visayan Pocket Dictionary. Enriquez & Bautista. (Eng. & Tagalog.). 4.00x (ISBN 0-686-05265-X). Colton Bk.

English-Turkish, Turkish-English Dictionary. Ziya Sak. (Eng. & Turkish.). 19.50 (ISBN 0-87557-085-2, 085-2). Saphrograph.

English-Ukrainian Dictionary. M. L. Podveska & M. J. Balla. 664p. (Eng. & Ukrainian.). 1980. 30.00x (ISBN 0-569-08127-0, Pub. by Collet's). State Mutual Bk.

English-Ukrainian Dictionary. 2nd ed. Ed. by M. L. Podvesko. (Eng. & Ukrainian.). 24.50 (ISBN 0-87557-089-5, 089-5). Saphrograph.

English-Ukrainian Dictionary. Ed. by I. O. Zhluktenko. (Rad. Shkola Ser.). 446p. (Eng. & Ukrainian.). 1978. 3.95 (O-38). Four Continent.

English-Urdu Dictionary. Pakistani. (Eng. & Urdu.). 29.00 (ISBN 0-686-18359-2). Kazi Pubns.

English-Urdu Dictionary of Christian Terminology. Liberius Pieterse. Ed. by Jan Slomp. LC 77-930423. xxviii, 108p. (Eng. & Urdu.). 1976. write for info. Christian Study Centre.

English URDV Dictionary. 24.50 (ISBN 0-686-36513-5). Saphrograph.

English-Venda Dictionary. L. T. Marole & F. S. De Goma. (Eng. & Venda.). 22.50 (ISBN 0-87559-185-X); thumb indexed 26.00 (ISBN 0-686-66534-1). Shalom.

English-Vietnamese Dictionary. Tu Dien Anh-Viet. 1560p. (Eng. & Vietnamese.). 1975. 99.00x (ISBN 0-686-44716-6, Pub. by Collets). State Mutual Bk.

English-Vietnamese Dictionary Romanized. (Eng. & Vietnamese.). 17.50 (ISBN 0-87559-012-8); thumb indexed 22.50 (ISBN 0-87559-013-6). Shalom.

English-Vietnamese Phrasebook with Useful Word List: For Vietnamese Speakers. Nguyen Hy Quang. LC 75-24856. (Vietnamese Refugee Education Ser.: No. 1). (Eng. & Vietnamese.). 1975. pap. text ed. 5.00x (ISBN 0-87281-043-7). Ctr Appl Ling.

English-Vietnamese Pocket Dictionary. (Eng. & Vietnamese.). pap. 7.50 (ISBN 0-87559-164-7). Shalom.

English-Vietnamese Pocket Dictionary. (Vietnamese & Eng.). pap. 5.00. Iaconi.

English Without Teacher & Dictionary: English-Arabic. J. R. Mouthany. 7.95x (ISBN 0-86685-058-9). Intl Bk Ctr.

English Word Power for Physicians & Other Professionals: A Vigorous & Cultured Vocabulary. J. E. Schmidt. 240p. 1971. 19.75x (ISBN 0-398-01666-6). C C Thomas.

English-Yiddish Dictionary. A. Harkovy. 22.50 (ISBN 0-87559-192-2). Shalom.

Englishman's Greek Concordance of the New Testament. rev. ed. George V. Vigram. (Gr. & Eng.). 1982. pap. 29.95 (ISBN 0-8054-1388-X). Broadman.

Englishman's Greek Concordance of the New Testament: Numerically Coded to Strong's Exhaustive Concordance. rev. ed. (Gr.). 1980. pap. 23.95 (ISBN 0-8010-3357-8). Baker Bk.

Englishman's Hebrew & Chaldee Concordance of the Old Testament. 1792p. (Hebrew.). 1980. softcover 29.95 (ISBN 0-8010-3360-8). Baker Bk.

Englishman's Hebrew Chaldee Concordance of the Old Testament. (Hebrew & Eng.). 1980. pap. 35.95 (ISBN 0-8054-1387-1). Broadman.

Enriching Vocabulary Concept in The Classroom. J. E. Lieberman. 0.35. Assn Child & Adult Learn.

Environmental Geology: Practical Exercises. Bernard Pipkin & David Cummings. (Illus.). 240p. 1983. pap. 14.95 (ISBN 0-89863-058-4). Star Pub CA.

Environmental Glossary. 2nd ed. G. William Frick. LC 82-83908. 310p. 1982. text ed. 28.00 (ISBN 0-86587-096-9). Gov Insts.

Environmental Impact Statement Glossary: A Reference Source for EIS Writers, Reviewers & Citizens. Ed. by Marc Landy. LC 79-19586. 547p. 1979. 75.00x (ISBN 0-306-65185-8, IFI Plenum). Plenum Pub.

Enzyklopadisches Lexikon Fur des Geld, Bank und Borsen Wesen, 2 vols. E. Achterberg & K. Lanz. (Ger.). 1967. 240.00 set (ISBN 3-7819-0030-4, M-7364, Pub. by Fritz Knapp Verlag). French & Eur.

EOQC Glossary. 30.00 (T2003); 30.00. Am Soc Qc.

Eponyms Dictionaries Index: A Compilation of Terms Based on Names of Actual or Legendary Persons. Ed. by James Ruffner et al. LC 76-20341. 1977. 104.00x (ISBN 0-8103-0688-3). Gale.

Epuletgepeszet. Ivan Fekete. LC 76-504896. 211p. (Eng., Ger. & Rus.). 1975. 48.00 Ft (ISBN 963-05-0560-6). Akademiai Kiado.

Erdoel Lexicon. 5th ed. Karlheinz Kramer. (Eng. & Ger., Lexicon of Petroleum). 1972. 48.00 (ISBN 3-7785-0233-6, M-7366, Pub. by Heuthig). French & Eur.

Erdoel-Lexikon (Crude Oil Dictionary) 5th rev. ed. K. Kramer. LC 72-313250. 1972. 20.00x (ISBN 3-7785-0233-6). Intl Pubns Serv.

Erdoelverarbeitung-Petrolchemie. Leipnitz. 268p. (Eng., Ger., Fr. & Rus.). 1982. DM.60.00. Brandstetter.

Erdolverarbeitung und Petrolchemie: A Dictionary of Crude Oil Processing & Petroleum Chemistry English-German-French-Russian. Walter Leipnitz. (Eng., Ger., Fr. & Rus.). 1976. 60.00x (ISBN 3-87097-073-1). Intl Learn Syst.

Ergemes Izloksnes Vardnica. Elga Kagaine & S. Rage. LC 79-394141. (Illus., Latvian & Riga.). 1977. 3.50 Rub. Zinatne.

Ergonomics Glossary: Terms Commonly Used in Ergonomics. Ed. by European Coal & Steel Community, Luxembourg. 264p. (Eng., Fr. & Ger.). 1982. 47.50x (ISBN 90-313-0500-6). Intl Pubns Serv.

Errores y Omisiones del Diccionario de Anonimos y Seudonimos Hispanoamericanos de Jose Toribio Medina. Ricardo Victorica. LC 73-78356. 338p. (Span.). 1973. Repr. of 1928 ed. 24.50x (ISBN 0-87917-027-1). Ethridge.

Erziansko-Russkii Slovar. M. N. Koliadenkov et al. 292p. (Rus.). 1949. 2.95 (Pub. by Gosizdat Inostr Natsional Slovarei). Four Continent.

Eskimo-English, English-Eskimo Dictionary. rev. ed. A. Thibert. (Eskimo & Eng.). pap. 12.50 (ISBN 0-685-12011-2). Heinman.

Esperanto Dictionary. J. C. Wells. (Teach Yourself Ser.). (Esperanto.). 1974. pap. 6.95 (ISBN 0-679-10205-1). McKay.

Esperanto-English Dictionary. Montagu C. Butler. (Esperanto & Eng.). 1967. 8.95x (ISBN 0-685-71601-5, 1065). Esperanto League North Am.

Esperanto-English Dictionary. Edward A. Millidge. (Esperanto & Eng.). 24.50 (ISBN 0-87557-018-6, 018-6). Saphrograph.

Essai d'un Glossaire des Patois de Lyonnais, Forez & Beaujolais. Jean B. Onofrio. LC 76-467468. (Illus.). lxxxii, 455p. (Fr.). 1975. write for info. (ISBN 2-717-10090-3). Horvath.

Essential Computer Dictionary & Speller for Secretaries, Managers, & Office Personnel. JoAnne C. Mayer & Charles J. Sippl. (Illus.). 256p. 1980. text ed. 14.95 (ISBN 0-13-284364-1, Spec); pap. 6.95 (ISBN 0-13-284356-0). P-H.

Essential English-Vietnamese Dictionary. Hoa. (Vietnamese & Eng.). 22.50. Iaconi.

Essential English-Vietnamese Dictionary. Nguyen-Dinh-Hoa. LC 82-80014. 328p. (Eng. & Vietnamese.). 1983. 22.50 (ISBN 0-8048-1444-9). C E Tuttle.

Essential French Vocabulary. (Fr.). 3.10. Longman.

Essential Russian-English Dictionary. B. G. Anpilogova et al. (Progress Ser.). 180p. (Rus. & Eng.). 1.50 (98 F). Four Continent.

Essential Russian-English Dictionary see Foundation Dictionary of Russian: Three Thousand High Semantic Frequency Words.

Essential Spanish Vocabulary. (Span.). 3.25. Longman.

Essential Vocabulary for College-Bound Students. Margaret A. Haller. LC 82-1732. 208p. (Orig.). (YA) (gr. 10 up). 1982. pap. 5.95 (ISBN 0-668-05417-4, 5417). Arco.

Essential Words for a Perfect Vocabulary. Prescott Evarts. 160p. (Orig.). 1983. pap. 4.95 (ISBN 0-668-05657-6, 5657-6). Arco.

Estonian-English Dictionary. Paul F. Saagpakk. LC 81-43606. (Yale Linguistic Ser.). 1216p. (Estonian & Eng.). 1982. 150.00x (ISBN 0-300-02849-0). Yale U Pr.

Estonian-English Dictionary. J. Silvert. (Estonian & Eng.). 35.00 (ISBN 0-87559-009-8); thumb indexed 40.00 (ISBN 0-87559-186-8). Shalom.
Estonsko-Russkii Slovar. J. Tamm. 757p. (Estonian & Rus.). 1977. 8.50 (Pub. by Valgus). Four Continent.
Estudio Comparativo de Vocabularios Tobas y Pilagas. Elena Bruno Natlis. 107p. (Span.). 1965. pap. 49.95 (ISBN 0-686-56659-9, S-33083). French & Eur.
Ethnography & Philology of the Hidatsa Indians: U. S. Geological & Geographical Survey of the Territories, Miscellaneous Publication, No. 7. Washington Matthews. LC 3-8072. 1971. Repr. of 1877 ed. 25.00 (ISBN 0-384-35892-6). Johnson Repr.
Ethnologic Dictionary of the Navaho Language. Franciscan Fathers. (Navaho.). 1968. 14.50 (ISBN 0-686-32647-4); pap. 12.00 (ISBN 0-686-32648-2). St Michaels.
Ethnologic Dictionary of the Navaho Language. Franciscans, Saint Michaels, Arizona. LC 76-43710. 536p. (Navaho.). Repr. of 1910 ed. 49.50 (ISBN 0-404-15766-1). AMS Pr.
Ethnologisches Woerterbuch. A. Heymer. 256p. (Ger., Eng. & Fr., Ethnological Dictionary). 1977. 22.50 (ISBN 3-489-66366-7, M-7367, Pub. by P. Parey). French & Eur.
Ethnologisches Woerterbuch. A. Heymer. 256p. (Ger., Eng. & Fr.). 1977. DM.22.50 (ISBN 3-489-66366-7). Parey.
Ethological Dictionary: In English, French & German. Armin Heymer. LC 77-78418. (Illus.). 238p. (Eng., Fr. & Ger.). 1979. Repr. of 1977 ed. lib. bdg. 35.00 (ISBN 0-8240-7005-4, Garland STPM Pr). Garland Pub.
Etimologicheskii Slovar Adygskikh (Cherkesskikh) A. K. Shagirov. 224p. (Rus.). 1978. 5.95 (Pub. by Nauka). Four Continent.
Etimologicheskii Slovar Russkogo Iazyka: Tom. 1, Vyp. 3 (V) Ed. by N. M. Shanskii. 284p. (Rus.). 1968. 3.25 (Pub. by MGU). Four Continent.
Etimologicheskii Slovar Russkogo Iazyka: Tom. 1, Vyp. 4 (G) N. M. Shanskii. 215p. (Rus.). 1972. 2.70 (Pub. by MGU). Four Continent.
Etimologicheskii Slovar Russkogo Iazyka: Tom. 1, Vyp. 5 (D, E, Zh) N. M. Shanskii. 304p. (Rus.). 1973. 3.60 (Pub. by MGU). Four Continent.
Etimologicheskii Slovar Russkogo Iazyka: Tom. 2, Vyp. 6 (Z) N. M. Shanskii. 124p. (Rus.). 1975. 1.00 (Pub. by MGU). Four Continent.
Etimologicheskii Slovar Slavianskikh Iazykov: Vyp. 4. 236p. (Rus.). 1977. 4.65 (Pub. by Nauka). Four Continent.
Etimologicheskii Slovar Slavianskikh Iazykov: Vyp. 7. 224p. (Rus.). 1980. 3.95 (Pub. by Nauka). Four Continent.
Etimologicheskii Slovar Tiurkskikh Iazykov. E. V. Sevortian. 767p. (Turkish & Rus.). 1974. 15.95 (Pub. by Nauka). Four Continent.
Etimologicheskii Slovar Tiurkskikh Iazykov. E. V. Sevortian. 352p. (Rus. & Turkish.). 1978. 9.75 (Pub. by Nauka). Four Continent.
Etimologichesskii Slovar Russkogo Iazyka: Tom. 2, Vyp. 7 (I) N. M. Shanskii. 152p. (Rus.). 1978. 2.50 (Pub. by MGU). Four Continent.
Etlapiras. Gyorgy Arva. LC 77-473040. 513p. (Eng., Czech. & Hungarian.). 1975. 71.00 Ft (ISBN 9-6322-0195-7). Kozgazdasagi.
Etnologico africano, 3 vols. Tina Novelli. (Ital.). 1976. L.9000.00. Jaca Bk.
Etymological Dictionaries: A Tentative Typology. Yakov Malkiel. LC 75-11866. 160p. 1976. lib. bdg. 19.00x (ISBN 0-226-50292-9). U of Chicago Pr.
Etymological Dictionary of Family Christian Names. William Arthur. 59.95 (ISBN 0-8490-0135-8). Gordon Pr.
Etymological Dictionary of Latin. T. G. Tucker. (Lat.). 1976. 25.00 (ISBN 0-89005-172-0). Ares.
Etymological Dictionary of Modern English, 2 Vols. E. Weekley. Set. 25.00 (ISBN 0-8446-3142-6). Peter Smith.
Etymological Dictionary of Modern English, 2 Vols. Ernest Weekley. 1967. pap. text ed. 6.50 ea.; Vol. 1. pap. text ed. (ISBN 0-486-21873-2); Vol. 2. pap. text ed. (ISBN 0-486-21874-0). Dover.
Etymological Dictionary of Pre-Thirteenth Century Turkish. Gerard Clauson. (Turkish.). 1972. 160.00x (ISBN 0-19-864112-5). Oxford U Pr.
Etymological Dictionary of the English Language. rev. & enl. ed. Ed. by Walter W. Skeat. 1910. 69.00x (ISBN 0-19-863104-9). Oxford U Pr.
Etymological Dictionary of the Norn Language in Shetland, 2 vols. Jakob Jakobsen. LC 78-72630. (Celtic Language & Literature: Goidelic & Brythonic). (Celtic.). Repr. of 1932 ed. Set. 87.50 (ISBN 0-404-17554-6). AMS Pr.
Etymological Dictionary of the Scottish Language, 5 Vols. rev. ed. John Jamieson. Ed. by John Longmuir & David Donaldson. LC 70-144425. (Gaelic.). Repr. of 1887 ed. Set. 325.00 (ISBN 0-404-59470-0). AMS Pr.
Etymological Dictionary of the Ukrainian Language, 10 vols. 2nd ed. J. B. Rudnyckyj. (Ukrainian.). 1962-66. 15.00. Ukrainian Acad.
Etymological Glossary to the Old Saxon Heliand. Samuel Berr. LC 76-572157. 477p. 1971. pap. 57.50x (ISBN 0-8002-1269-X). Intl Pubns Serv.
Etymological Lexicon of Classical Greek. E. R. Wharton. LC 74-7787. 192p. (Gr.). 1975. Repr. 10.00 (ISBN 0-89005-033-3). Ares.
Etymological Vocabulary to the Libro De Buen Amor of Juan Ruiz, Arcipreste De Hita. Henry B. Richardson. LC 72-1684. (Yale Romanic Studies: No. 2). (Span.). Repr. of 1930 ed. 14.50 (ISBN 0-404-53202-0). AMS Pr.
Etymologisch Geographisches Lexikon. Jakob Egli. (Ger.). 1970. 62.50 (ISBN 3-500-21620-X, M-7371, Pub. by Saendig-Walluf). French & Eur.
Etymologisches Woertenbuch der Botanischen Pflanzennamen. Helmut Genaust. 390p. (Ger.). 1976. 62.50 (ISBN 3-7643-0755-2, M-7368, Pub. by Birkhaeuser). French & Eur.
Etymologisches Woerterbuch der Europaeischen Woerter Orientalischen Ursprungs. 2nd ed. Karl Lokotsch. (Ger.). 1975. pap. 43.50 (ISBN 3-533-02427-X, M-7369, Pub. by Carl Winter). French & Eur.
Etymologisches Woerterbuch der Europaeischen Woerter Orientalischen Ursprungs. 2nd ed. Karl Lokotsch. (Ger.). 1975. pap. 43.50 (ISBN 3-533-02427-X). Winter Univ.
Etymologisches Woerterbuch der Franzoesischen Sprache. 2nd ed. Ernst Gamillscheg. (Fr. & Ger.). 1969. 195.00 (ISBN 0-686-56604-1, M-7370, Pub. by Carl Winter). French & Eur.
Etymologisches Woerterbuch der Franzoesischen Sprache. 2nd ed. Ernst Gamillscheg. (Fr. & Ger.). 1969. DM.195.00. Winter Univ.
Eudised Multilingual Thesaurus for Information Processing in the Field of Education. Ed. by Jean Viet. 391p. (Orig.). 1974. pap. text ed. 17.50x (ISBN 0-686-22571-6). Mouton.
Euro Dictionary of Economics & Business. Hans E. Zahn. xiii, 702p. (Ger., Eng. & Fr.). 1973. 72.50x (ISBN 3-78192-009-7). Rothman.
Euro-Wirtschafts Worterlrich in Drei Sprachen. Hans E. Zahn. 716p. (Ger., Eng. & Fr., Euro-Dictionary of Economics in Three Languages). 1973. 99.50 (ISBN 3-7819-2009-7, M-7372, Pub. by Fritz Knapp Verlag). French & Eur.
Europump Terminology -- Glossary of Pump Applications in English, German, French, Italian, & Spanish. (Illus.). 1979. 150.00x (ISBN 0-85461-071-5). Intl Ideas.
Europump Terminology: Pump Applications. Institute for Power System. 900p. 1982. 210.00x (ISBN 0-85461-071-5). State Mutual Bk.
Europump Terminology: Pump Applications. Ed. by Trade & Technical Pr.Ltd. 750p. 1981. 120.00x (ISBN 0-686-79319-6, Pub. by Trade & Tech). State Mutual Bk.
Euskal Histegi Modernoa. Xabier Kintana. LC 77-564729. xxiv, 731p. (Basque, & Span.). 1977. write for info. (ISBN 8-472-77058-3). Cinsa Coord.
Euskal Histegi Modernoa. Ed. by Xabier Kintana et al. LC 77-564729. xxiv, 731p. (Basque.). 1977. write for info. (ISBN 8-47277-058-3). Coord Iniciat.
Evangelisches Staatslexikon. 2nd rev. ed. H. Kunst. (Ger.). 1975. 125.00 (ISBN 3-7831-0463-7, M-7373, Pub. by Kreuz Vlg.). French & Eur.
Evangelisches Staatslexikon. 2nd, rev. ed. H. Kunst. (Ger.). 1975. DM.125.00 (ISBN 3-7831-0463-7). Kreuz.
Everyday Dictionary. LC 84-13528. (Span.). 1982. 12.95; pap. 7.95. Times Bks.
Everyday Dictionary. (Eng.). 1982. 12.95; pap. 7.95. Times Books.
Everyday Greek: Greek Words in English, Including Scientific Terms. Horace Addison Hoffman. (Midway Reprint). 1976. pap. 8.00x (ISBN 0-226-34787-7). U of Chicago Pr.
Everyday Japanese. Eldora Thorlin & Noah Brannen. LC 69-19854. 180p. (Japanese.). 1969. 3.95 (ISBN 0-8348-0037-3). Weatherhill.
Everyday Spanish Idioms. R. S. Boggs & J. I. Dixon. (Span.). (gr. 9-12). 1978. pap. text ed. 5.25 (ISBN 0-88345-326-6). Regents Pub.
Everyday Vocabulary. Dale McMasters. (Language Arts Ser.). 24p. (gr. 4-6). 1976. wkbk. 5.00 (ISBN 0-8209-0310-8, VD-2). ESP.
Everyman's Classical Dictionary. 3rd rev. ed. John Warrington. (Everyman's Reference Library). 537p. 1978. Repr. of 1969 ed. 11.00 (ISBN 0-460-03004-3, Pub. by J. M. Dent England). Biblio Dist.
Everyman's Dictionary of Abbreviations: With Supplement. rev. ed. Ed. by John Paxton. 408p. 1981. 20.00x (ISBN 0-8476-6973-4). Rowman.
Everyman's Dictionary of Literary Biography. 3rd ed. D. S. Browning. (Everyman's Reference Library). 812p. 1969. 13.50 (ISBN 0-460-03008-6, Pub by J M Dent England). Biblio Dist.
Everyman's Dictionary of Music. Eric Blom. 816p. (RL 10). 1973. pap. 5.95 (ISBN 0-452-25193-1, 25193, Plume). NAL.
Everyman's Dictionary of Non-Classical Mythology. x ed. Egerton Sykes. (Everyman Reference Library). (Illus.). 298p. 1977. Repr. of 1968 ed. 13.50 (ISBN 0-460-03010-8, Pub. by J. M. Dent England). Biblio Dist.
Everyman's English Pronouncing Dictionary: Completely Revised. Ed. by Daniel Jones. (Everyman's Reference Library Ser.). 592p. 1981. Repr. of 1977 ed. 13.50 (ISBN 0-460-03029-9, Pub. by J. M. Dent England). Biblio Dist.
Exercises to Accompany American Heritage Dictionary. American Heritage. 1977. 0.60 (ISBN 0-395-26171-6). HM.
Expanding Your Vocabulary. Barbara Gregorich. LC 78-730053. (Illus.). 1978. pap. text ed. 135.00 (ISBN 0-89290-126-8, 327-SATC). Soc for Visual.
Expense & Payroll Dictionary. American Hotel & Motel Association. 8.50; members 6.00. Am Hotel & Motel Assn.
Experts Crossword Puzzle Dictionary. Herbert M. Baus. LC 72-84960. pap. 6.95 (ISBN 0-385-04788-6, Dolp). Doubleday.
Explanatory Dictionary for Students of English. R. A. Davidenko. 664p. (Eng. & Rus.). 1977. 8.50 (Pub. by Ganatleba). Four Continent.
Explanatory Dictionary for Students of English. R. A. Davidenko. 664p. (Eng.). 1977. 8.50 (Pub by Ganatleba). Four Continent.
Explanatory Dictionary of Computing Machinery & Data Processing. A. I. Shishmarev & A. P. Zamorin. 416p. 1978. 60.00x (ISBN 0-686-44717-4, Pub. by Collets). State Mutual Bk.
Explanatory Dictionary of Computing Machinery & Data Processing. A. I. Shismarev & A. P. Zamorin. 416p. 1978. Leatherette 7.95 (ISBN 0-686-92229-8, M-9080). French & Eur.
Explosives. 2nd ed. Rudolph Meyer. (Illus.). 440p. 1981. 60.00x (ISBN 3-527-25933-3). Verlag Chemie.
Export for Marketing French. A. M. Nuss. 96p. (Fr. & Eng.). 1979. pap. 13.95 (ISBN 0-582-35157-X, M-9208). French & Eur.
Expressoes Idiomaticas Inglesas: English Idioms. W. G. Kennedy & Maria Silva. 132p. (Port. & Eng.). pap. 2.75. Imported Bks.

F

Faber Pocket Medical Dictionary. 3rd ed. P. A. Riley & P. J. Cunningham. Ed. by Elizabeth Forsythe. (Illus.). 408p. 1979. pap. 4.95 (ISBN 0-571-04999-0). Faber & Faber.
Fach Lexikon ABC Automatisierung. 739p. (Ger.). 1976. 22.50 (ISBN 3-87144-243-7, M-7377, Pub. by Verlag Harri Deutsch). French & Eur.
Fachbegriffe der Versicherungwirtschaft. Manfred Lipperheide et al. LC 75-537357. 288p. (Ger.). 1974. write for info. Deutsch Spark.
Fachenglisch Fur Technik und Industrie. Henry G. Freeman. 303p. (Ger. & Eng., English for Engineering and Industry). 1974. 22.50 (ISBN 3-452-17766-1, M-7376, Pub. by Carl Heymanns Verlag KG). French & Eur.
Fachlexikon ABC Biologie. 2nd ed. (Ger.). 1972. leatherette 49.95 (ISBN 3-87144-001-9, M-7378, Pub. by Harri Deutsch). French & Eur.
Fachlexikon ABC Chemie, 2 vols. 1590p. (Ger.). 1976. Set. letherette 79.95 (ISBN 3-87144-002-7, M-7379, Pub. by Verlag Harri Deutsch). French & Eur.
Fachlexikon ABC Mathematik. 624p. (Ger.). 1978. 30.95 (ISBN 3-87144-030-2, M-7381, Pub. by Verlag Harri Deutsch). French & Eur.
Fachlexikon ABC Mathematik. (Ger.). 1977. 30.95 (ISBN 3-87144-336-0, M-7382, Pub. by Harri Deutsch). French & Eur.
Fachlexikon ABC Physik, 2 vols. 1784p. (Ger.). 1974. Set. 95.00 (ISBN 3-87144-003-5, M-7383, Pub. by Verlag Harri Deutsch). French & Eur.
Fachlexikon ABC Technik und Naturwissenschaft, Vols. 1 & 2. (Ger.). 1970. Set. leatherette 55.00 (ISBN 3-87144-004-3, M-7384). French & Eur.
Fachwoerter des Oeffentlichen Verwaltungsdienstes Aegyptens in den Griechischen Papyrusurkunden der Ptolemaeisch-Romischen Zeit. Friedrich Preisigke. LC 78-347087. x, 186p. (Ger. & Gr.). 1975. DM.33.80 (ISBN 3-487-05896-0). Olms Verlag.
Fachwoerterbuch der Datenverarbeitung. 3rd ed. Alfred Wittman. (Eng., Fr. & Ger.). 1977. DM.67.50 (ISBN 3-486-39063-5). Oldenbourg Verlag.

Fachwoerterbuch der Luftfahrt. A. Dorian & J. Osenton. (Eng., Fr., Span., Ital., Port & Ger., Dictionary of Aviation). 1964. 75.00 (ISBN 3-486-30971-4, M-7389, Pub. by R. Oldenbourg). French & Eur.

Fachwoerterbuch der Luftfahrt. J. Osenton. (Eng., Fr., Span., Ital., Portuguese & Ger.). 1964. DM.75.00 (ISBN 3-486-30971-4). Oldenbourg Verlag.

Fachwoerterbuch des Nachrichtenwese. H. Pooch. 280p. (Ger.). 1976. DM.pap. 22.50 (ISBN 3-7949-0234-3). Schiele & Schon.

Fachwoerterbuch des Nachrichtenwesens. H. Pooch. 280p. (Ger.). 1976. pap. 22.50 (ISBN 3-7949-0234-3, M-7390, Pub. by Fachvlg. Schiele & Schoen). French & Eur.

Fachwoerterbuch des Transportwesens. S. Heinze. (Ger. & Eng., Dictionary of Transportation Systems). 1961. 17.50 (ISBN 3-87097-018-9, M-7391, Pub. by Brandstetter). French & Eur.

Fachwoerterbuch des Transportwesens. S. Heinze. (Ger. Eng.). 1961. DM.17.50 (ISBN 3-87097-018-9). Brandstetter.

Fachwoerterbuch des Versicherungswesen. S. Heinze. (Ger. & Eng., Dictionary of Insurance Terms, English-German). 1961. 12.00 (ISBN 3-87097-017-0, M-7393, Pub. by Brandstetter). French & Eur.

Fachwoerterbuch des Versicherungswesen, Vol. 1. Heinze. (Ger. & Eng., Dictionary of Insurance Terms). 1961. 12.50 (ISBN 3-87097-016-2, M-7392, Pub. by Brandstetter). French & Eur.

Fachwoerterbuch des Versicherungswesen, Vol. 1. Heinze. (Ger. & Eng.). 1961. DM.12.50 (ISBN 3-87097-016-2). Brandstetter.

Fachwoerterbuch des Vesicherungswesen, Vol. 2. S. Heinze. (Ger. & Eng.). 1961. DM.12.00 (ISBN 3-87097-017-0). Brandstetter.

Fachwoerterbuch Elektrotechnik, Elektronik. Peter K. Budig. (Eng. & Ger., Dictionary of Electrical Engineering and Electronics). 1976. 86.50 (ISBN 3-7785-0357-X, M-7394, Pub. by Huethig). French & Eur.

Fachwoerterbuch fuer Batterien & Energie-Direktumwandlung. Bogenschuetz. 200p. (Eng. & Ger.). 1982. DM.22.00. Brandstetter.

Fachwoerterbuch fuer Batterien und Energie-Direktumwandlung. A. Bogenschuetz. 200p. (Ger. & Eng.). 1968. DM.29.95 (ISBN 3-87097-002-2). Brandstetter.

Fachwoerterbuch fuer der Metalloberflaechenveredelung. H. Dettner. 391p. (Ger. & Eng.). 1969. DM.20.95 (ISBN 3-87749-011-5). Siemens AG.

Fachwoerterbuch fuer die Glasindustriel. E. Hoffman. 160p. (Ger. & Eng.). 1963. DM.36.00 (ISBN 3-540-03007-7). Springer-Verlag.

Fachwoerterbuch Fuer die Glasindustriel. E. Hoffmann. 160p. (Ger. & Eng., Dictionary doe the Glass Industry). 1963. 36.00 (ISBN 3-540-03007-7, M-7396, Pub. by Springer). French & Eur.

Fachwoerterbuch fuer Wirtschaft, Handel & Finanzen. 3rd ed. Rudolf Thomik. LC 77-562019. 685p. (Ger.). 1977. DM.74.00. Heymanns Verlag.

Fachwoerterbuch Fur Recht und Wirtschaft. Gunther Parsenow. 504p. (Swedish & Ger.). 1975. 68.00 (ISBN 3-452-18010-7, M-7399, Pub. by Carl Heymanns Verlag KG). French & Eur.

Fachwoerterbuch Fur Wirtschaft, Handel und Finanzen. Rudolf Thomik. 685p. (Fr. & Ger.). 1977. 59.95 (ISBN 3-452-18138-3, 7400, Pub. by Carl Heymanns Verlag KG). French & Eur.

Fachwoerterbuch Kraftfahrtechnik, 2 vols, Vol. 1. Bosch. 354p. (Ger. & Eng., Technical Dictionary for Automotive Engineering). 1976. 85.00 (ISBN 3-18-419044-7, M-7638, Pub. by VDI Verlag GMBH). French & Eur.

Fachwoerterbuch Kraftfahrtechnik, 2 vols, Vol. 2. Bosch. 369p. (Ger. & Eng., Technical dictionary of automotive engineering). 1977. 59.95 (ISBN 3-18-419046-3, M-7639, Pub. by VDI Verlag GMBH). French & Eur.

Fachwoerterbuch Optik & Optischer Geratebau: Deutsch-Englisch. Werner Bindmann. 408p. (Ger. & Eng.). DM.45.00 (ISBN 3-7684-6512-8). W Dausien.

Fachwoerterbuch Optik & Optischer Geratebau: Englisch-Deutsch. Werner Bindmann. 408p. (Eng. & Ger.). DM.45.00 (ISBN 3-7684-6512-8). W Dausien.

Fachwoerterbuch Optik und Optischer Geraetebau. W. Bindmann. 408p. (Eng. & Ger., Dictionary of Optics and Optical Devices). 1974. 75.00 (ISBN 3-7684-6411-3, M-7402, Pub. by Dausien). French & Eur.

Fachwoerterbuch Spanende Werkzeugmaschinen. Henry G. Freeman. 527p. (Ger. & Eng., Dictionary of Machine Tools). 1965. leatherette 72.00 (ISBN 3-7736-5090-6, M-7403, Pub. by Verlag W. Gerardet). French & Eur.

Fachwoerterbuch Spanende Werkzeugmaschinen. Henry G. Freeman. 527p. (Ger. & Eng.). 1965. DM.leatherette 72.00 (ISBN 3-7736-5090-6). Girardet.

Fachworter der Elektronik. Georg I. Franz. LC 76-488356. 86p. (Ger.). 1976. DM.4.80 (ISBN 3-7723-0402-8). Franzis Verlag.

Fachworterbuch der Brauerei & Abfullpraxis. Tilman Schmitt. LC 78-344854. viii, 200p. (Eng. & Ger.). 1977. DM.25.00 (ISBN 3-418-00637-X). Carl KG.

Fachworterbuch Fur Recht und Verwaltung. Crescencio Antolinez. (Span. & Ger.). 1970. leatherette 35.00 (ISBN 3-452-17065-9, M-7398, Pub. by Carl Heymanns Verlag KG). French & Eur.

Fachworterbuch Polygrafie: English-Deutsch-French-Russian-Spanish-Polish-Hungarian-Slowakian. 1019p. (Eng. & Deutsch & Fr. & Rus. & Span & Pol. & Hungarian & Slowakian.). 1980. leatherette 125.00 (ISBN 3-87150-141-7, M-11292). French & Eur.

Fachworterbuch Textil. Derrick O. Michelson. 136p. (Ger. & Eng., Dictionary of Textiles). 13.50 (ISBN 3-87150-106-9, M-7404, Pub. by Deutscher Fachuerlag). French & Eur.

Fachworterbuch Textil. Sarina Schock & Erika Gebert. 136p. (Ger. & Fr.). 9.95 (ISBN 3-87150-039-9, M-7405, Pub. by Deutscher Fachverlag). French & Eur.

Fachwortschatz Mathematik. LC 77-552687. 96p. (Eng. & Ger.). 1976. M.5.00. VEB Verlag Enzyklopadie.

Facts on File: Dictionary of Astronomy. Ed. by Valerie Illingworth. (Illus.). 1979. 17.50 (ISBN 0-87196-326-4). Facts on File.

Facts on File Dictionary of Biology. Ed. by Elizabeth Tootill. 288p. 1981. 14.95 (ISBN 0-87196-510-0). Facts on File.

Facts on File Dictionary of Chemistry. Ed. by John Daintith. 224p. 1981. 14.95 (ISBN 0-87196-513-5). Facts on File.

Facts on File Dictionary of European History: 1485-1789. E. N. Williams. 1980. lib. bdg. 22.50 (ISBN 0-87196-327-2). Facts on File.

Facts on File Dictionary of Mathematics. Ed. by Carol Gibson. 224p. 1981. prepub. 14.95 (ISBN 0-87196-512-7). Facts on File.

Facts on File Dictionary of Micro Computers. Anthony Chandor. 1981. 14.95 (ISBN 0-87196-597-6). Facts on File.

Facts on File Dictionary of Microcomputers. Anthony Chandor. (Eng.). 1981. 14.95 (ISBN 0-87196-597-6). Facts on File.

Facts on File Dictionary of Physics. Ed. by John Daintith. 248p. 1981. 14.95 (ISBN 0-87196-511-9). Facts on File.

Facts on File Dictionary of Telecommunications. John Graham. (Illus.). 224p. 1983. 15.95 (ISBN 0-87196-120-2). Facts on File.

Facts on File Dictionary of Twentieth Century History. Alan Palmer. 403p. 1980. 22.50 (ISBN 0-686-60214-5). Facts on File.

Fairchild's Dictionary of Fashion. Charlotte M. Calasibetta. Ed. by Lorraine Davis & Ermina S. Goble. LC 74-84805. (Illus.). 700p. 1975. 50.00 (ISBN 0-87005-133-4). Fairchild.

Fairchild's Dictionary of Textiles. 6th ed. Ed. by Isabel B. Wingate. LC 78-73964. 1979. 40.00 (ISBN 0-87005-198-9). Fairchild.

Family Portrait, from a Mother's Diary. Anne M. Zanzucchi. Tr. by Lenny Szczesniak from It. LC 81-80031. Orig. Title: Giorno per Giorno. 100p. 1981. pap. 2.95 (ISBN 0-911782-19-2). New City.

Family Word Finder. Readers Digest Editors. LC 75-18006. 896p. 1975. 18.45 (ISBN 0-89577-023-7). RD Assn.

Farbige Duden Schuelerlexikon. 768p. (Ger.). 24.50 (1094). Adler Bks.

Fargher's English-Manx Dictionary. Douglas Fargher. 928p. 1979. 90.00x (ISBN 0-904980-23-5, Pub. by Shearwater England). State Mutual Bk.

Fargher's English Manx Dictionary. Douglas C. Fargher. 1979. text ed. 67.75x (ISBN 0-904980-23-5). Humanities.

Farmakologicheskii Slovar: Latinsko-Russkii & Russko-Latinskii. T. G. Kazachenok. 464p. (Rus. & Lat.). 1977. 6.70 (Pub. by Vysheishaia). Four Continent.

Fashion Production Terms. Gioello & Berke. LC 78-62289. (Languages of Fashion Ser.). (Illus.). 1979. lib. bdg. 25.00 (ISBN 0-87005-200-4). Fairchild.

Fashion Vocabulary & Dictation. 1969. pap. 10.95 (ISBN 0-672-96058-3). Bobbs.

Faulkner Glossary. Harry Runyon. 1966. pap. 2.25 (ISBN 0-8065-0152-9, 228). Citadel Pr.

Femmedordbog. 11th ed. Jorgen Bang. LC 77-561717. 480p. (Danish.). 1976. Kr.56.00 (ISBN 8-71940-170-1). Berlingske Forlag.

Fenno-Ugric Vocabulary: An Etymological Dictionary of the Uralic Languages. Bjorn Collinder. 158p. (Finnish & Hungarian.). 1977. pap. text ed. 41.00x (ISBN 3-87118-187-0, Pub. by Helmut Buske Verlag Hamburg). Benjamins North Am.

Fenno-Ugric Vocabulary: An Etymologic Dictionary of the Uralic Languages. 2nd ed. Bjorn Collinder. LC 78-387096. 217p. (Uralic.). 1977. write for info. (ISBN 3-87118-187-0). Buske.

Fern Dictionary. Wilson W. Olson. 4.70. LA Intl Fern.

Feroz-ul-Lughat (Urdu) Dictionary. (Urdu.). 39.50 (ISBN 0-686-83586-7). Kazi Pubns.

Ferozsons Concise Dictionary. Ed. by A. Hameed Khan. LC 78-931279. 647p. (Eng. & Urdu.). 1978. Rs.45.00. Ferozsons.

Fertigungsmesstechnik. Peter D. Hoffmann. 140p. (Rus. & Ger.). 1975. M.15.00. VEB Verlag Technik.

Fertigungsmesstechnik-Russischer-Deutsch: Deutsch-Russicherr. Peter Hoffman. LC 76-454994. 140p. (Ger. & Rus.). 1973. M.15.00. VEB Verlag Technik.

Festkorperelektronik. Helmut Muchow. 212p. (Rus. & Ger.). 1974. M.20.00. VEB Technik.

Fiber Optics & Lightwave Communications Standard Dictionary. Martin H. Weik. 320p. 1980. text ed. 18.50 (ISBN 0-442-25658-2). Van Nos Reinhold.

Fiberoptics & Lightwave Communications Vocabulary. Ed. & frwd. by Dennis Bodson. LC 80-26168. 156p. (Orig.). 1983. pap. text ed. 12.95 (ISBN 0-07-606706-8, R-030). McGraw.

Fifty Chinese Recipes. pap. 3.95 (ISBN 0-87557-105-0, 105-05). Saphrograph.

Fijian & English & an English & Fijian Dictionary. 2nd ed. David Hazlewood. LC 75-35119. (Eng. & Fijian.). Repr. of 1872 ed. 28.00 (ISBN 0-404-14136-6). AMS Pr.

Filatelisticheskii Slovar. O. I. Basin. 128p. (Rus.). 1976. 1.50 (Pub. by Sviaz). Four Continent.

Filatelisticheskii Slovar. Ed. by V. Grallert et al. 272p. (Rus.). 1977. 7.50 (Pub. by Sviaz). Four Continent.

Filmgyartas es Filmtechnika. Gabor Pozsonyi. LC 78-391538. 220p. (Eng., Hungarian, Fr., Ger. & Rus.). 1975. 50.00 Ft (ISBN 9-6305-0592-4). Akademiai Kiado.

Filmlexikon. Wim De Poorter. LC 77-572112. 102p. (Dutch.). 1976. fl.14.50 (ISBN 9-0236-5349-1). Nygh Ditmar.

Financial & Mercantile Dictionary. Julius O. Kettridge. (Fr. & Eng.). 13.95 (ISBN 0-685-11187-3). French & Eur.

Finansovo-Kreditynyi Slovar, 2 vols. (Rus.). 1964. 10.00 set (Pub. by Finansy). Four Continent.

Fine Paper Dictionary, 1982. 6th ed. 512p. 1982. pap. 45.00 (ISBN 0-686-17578-6). Grade Finders.

Finnish-Danish-Finnish Dictionary: Suomi-Tanska-Suomi. A. S. Gersov. 315p. (Finnish & Danish.). 1976. pap. 14.95 (ISBN 951-0-07507-8, M-9648). French & Eur.

Finnish Deluxe Dictionary: English-Finnish. 2nd ed. R. Hurme & M. Pesonen. (Eng. & Finnish.). 1978. 85.00x (ISBN 9-5100-5699-5, F-565). Vanous.

Finnish Dictionary: English-Finnish. 10th ed. E. Riikon & A. Tuomikowski. (Finnish & Eng.). 1979. text ed. 55.00x (ISBN 95-110-4266-1, F560). Vanous.

Finnish Dictionary: Suomalais-Englantilainen, Vol. 1. 3rd ed. V. S. Alanne. (Finnish & Eng.). 1980. 85.00x (ISBN 95-100-1069-3, F563). Vanous.

Finnish-English, English-Finnish Dictionary. A. Wuole. (Finnish & Eng.). 24.50 (ISBN 0-87559-010-1); thumb indexed 29.00 (ISBN 0-87559-011-X). Shalom.

Finnish-English, English-Finnish Dictionary, 2 Vols. 11th ed. A. Wuolle. (Finnish & Eng.). Set. 37.50. Finnish-Eng (ISBN 9-5100-9469-2). Eng.-Finnish (ISBN 951-0-08500-6). Heinman.

Finnish-English, English-Finnish Dictionary. 2nd, rev. ed. A. Wuolle. (Eng. & Finnish.). Date not set. text ed. 30.00 (ISBN 0-686-46544-X). Heinman.

Finnish-English-Finnish. (Berlitz Pocket Dictionaries Ser.). (Eng. & Finnish.). 4.95 (ISBN 0-02-964580-8). Macmillan.

Finnish-English-Finnish Dictionary. Wuolle. 470p. (Finnish & Eng.). 1980. pap. 13.95 (ISBN 0-686-92371-5, M-9639). French & Eur.

Finnish-English General Dictionary. V. S. Alanne. 1111p. (Eng. & Finnish.). 1980. 75.00 (ISBN 951-0-01069-3, M-9658). French & Eur.

Finnish-Esthonian-Finnish Dictionary: Suomi-Eesti-s. H. Laanpere. 499p. (Finnish & Estonian.). 1977. pap. 15.95 (ISBN 951-0-07765-8, M-9641). French & Eur.

Finnish-French Dictionary. T. Nurmela. 683p. (Finnish & Fr.). Date not set. 24.95 (ISBN 951-0-05012-1, M-9651). French & Eur.

Finnish-French-Finnish Dictionary (Suomi-Ranska-Suomi) R. M. Koistinen. 438p. (Fr. & Finnish.). 1981. pap. 14.95 (ISBN 951-0-08071-3). French & Eur.

Finnish-German-Finnish Dictionary (Suomi-Saksa-Suomi) L. Hirvensalo. 610p. (Finnish & Ger.). 1980. pap. 14.95 (ISBN 951-0-08070-5, M-9646). French & Eur.

Finnish-German Great Dictionary. P. Katara et al. 1443p. (Ger. & Finnish.). 1981. 39.95 (ISBN 951-0-10060-9, M-9660). French & Eur.

Finnish-Hungarian-Finnish Dictionary (Suomi-Unkari-Suomi) I. Nyirkos. 712p. (Finnish & Hungarian.). 1979. pap. 19.95 (ISBN 951-0-07860-3). French & Eur.

Finnish-Italian Dictionary. G. Colussi. 302p. (Finnish & Italian.). 1978. 29.95 (ISBN 951-0-08233-3, M-9650). French & Eur.

Finnish-Italian-Finnish Dictionary. G. Colussi. 532p. (Ital. & Finnish.). 1981. pap. 14.95 (ISBN 951-0-07998-7, M-9640). French & Eur.

Finnish-Norwegian-Finnish Dictionary (Suomi-Noria-Suomi) T. Farbregd et al. 636p. (Finnish & Norwegian.). 1981. pap. 18.95 (ISBN 951-0-10498-1, M-9644). French & Eur.

Finnish-Norwegian Norwegian-Finnish Pocket Dictionary. Farbregd & Kamarainen. (Finnish & Norwegian.). 1978. write for info. (ISBN 82-573-0116-7). Kunnskapsforlaget.

Finnish Pocket Dictionary. (Finnish & Eng.). 13.00 (ISBN 9-5100-7468-3). Heinman.

Finnish Pocket Dictionary, Finnish-English - English-Finnish. 465p. (Eng. & Finnish.). 1980. pap. text ed. 13.00x (ISBN 9-5100-7468-3, F559). Vanous.

Finnish-Portuguese-Finnish Dictionary. K. Rahinantti. 359p. (Finnish & Port.). 1975. pap. 16.95 (ISBN 0-686-92218-2, M-9649). French & Eur.

Finnish-Russian-Finnish Dictionary (Suomi-Venaja-Suomi) A. Hiltunen. 543p. (Finnish & Rus.). 1981. pap. 19.95 (ISBN 951-0-09631-8, M-9643). French & Eur.

Finnish Small Dictionary: English-Finnish, Vol. 1. Aino Wuolle. (Finnish & Eng.). 1980. text ed. 20.00x (ISBN 9-5100-8500-6, F557). Vanous.

Finnish Small Dictionary: Finnish-English, Vol. 2. 11th ed. Aino Wuolle. (Finnish & Eng.). 1979. text ed. 20.00x (ISBN 95-100-9469-2, F558). Vanous.

Finnish-Spanish-Finnish Dictionary. E. K. Neuvonen. 452p. (Finnish & Span.). 1980. pap. 14.95 (ISBN 951-0-07202-8, S-37816). French & Eur.

Finnish-Swedish Dictionary. L. Lampen. 571p. (Finnish & Swedish.). 1980. leatherette 24.95 (ISBN 951-0-08620-7, M-9655). French & Eur.

Finnish-Swedish-Finnish Dictionary. 272p. (Finnish & Swedish.). 1981. pap. 9.95 (ISBN 91-518-1442-0, M-9444). French & Eur.

Finnish-Swedish-Finnish Dictionary (Suomi-Ruotsi-Suomi) L. Lampen. 623p. (Finnish & Swedish.). 1980. pap. 15.95 (ISBN 951-0-07771-2, M-09647). French & Eur.

Finsk-Svensk & Svensk-Finsk Fickordbok. Av Lea Lampen. 564p. (Swedish & Finnish.). write for info. Esselte Studium.

Finsk-Svensk Skolordbok. Lea Lampen. 570p. (Finnish & Swedish.). write for info. (ISBN 91-24-27856-4). Esselte Studium.

Finsk-Swensk Storordbok. Knut Cannelin et al. 1140p. (Swedish & Finnish.). 1976. Kr.360.00 (ISBN 91-24-26676-0). Esselte Studium.

Finsko-Russkii Slovar. I. Vakharos et al. 815p. (Finnish & Rus.). 1977. 25.50 (Pub. by Russkii Iazyk). Four Continent.

Fire Sciences Dictionary. Ed. by B. W. Kuvshinoff et al. LC 77-3489. 439p. 1977. 25.00x (ISBN 0-471-51113-7, Pub. by Wiley-Interscience). Wiley.

Fire Terminology. 4th ed. 67p. 1970. 4.00 (ISBN 0-685-46056-8, FSD-3A). Natl Fire Prot.

Fire Terms: A Guide to Their Meaning & Use. National Fire Protection Association. 11.00 (SPP-60). Natl Fire Prot.

Firenze si Parla Cosi: Frasario Moderno del Vernacolo Fiorentino. Renzo Raddi. LC 76-468656. xxvii, 290p. (Ital., Firenze). 1976. L.5000.00. Libreria.

First Dictionary of Linguistics & Phonetics. David Crystal. (Language Library Ser.). 404p. 1980. lib. bdg. 34.00 (ISBN 0-86531-051-3, Pub. by Andre Deutsch). Westview.

First One Thousand Words-English, 4 Bks. Amery & Mila. (First Thousand Words Ser.). (gr. 1-9). 1979. 10.95 ea. (Usborne-Hayes). English ed. EDC.

First Picture Dictionary - English-Arabic. (Illus., Eng. & Arabic.). 2.50x (ISBN 0-86685-202-6). Intl Bk Ctr.

First Science Dictionary. David Lucas. (Eng.). pap. 9.95 (076-5). Intl Bk Ctr.

First Science Dictionary: College Edition. D. J. Lucas et al. LC 76-53302. 206p. 1977. 12.50x (ISBN 0-8448-1056-8). Crane-Russak Co.

First Thousand Words in German. Amery et al. (Illus.). 62p. (Ger.). (gr. 1-4). 7.95 (1095). Adler Bks.

Fiscalite. Ed. by Patrick Rassat & Alain Le Bars. LC 75-510630. (Illus.). 508p. (Fr.). 1975. 56.50 F (ISBN 2-010-01083-3). Hachette L.

Fitopatologicheskii Slovar Spravochnik. G. A. Diakova. 478p. (Rus., Eng., Ger. & Fr.). 1969. 12.75 (Pub. by Nauka). Four Continent.

Five Hundred & Four Absolutely Essential Words. rev. ed. Murray Bromberg et al. LC 74-5052. 1975. pap. 4.95 (ISBN 0-8120-0525-2). Barron.

Five Hundred & One German Verbs: Written in Japanese. Strutz. (Japanese & Ger.). Date not set. pap. 4.25 (ISBN 0-8120-2182-7). Barron.

Five Hundred Terms of Home Economic. (Hebrew & Eng.). IL.7.00. Massada Pr.

Five Thousand Dictionary: A Chinese-English Pocket Dictionary & Index to the Character Cards of the College of Chinese Studies. rev. ed. Ed. by Courtenay H. Fenn. LC 43-754. 1942. 20.00x (ISBN 0-674-30550-7); pap. 8.95 (ISBN 0-674-30551-5, HP35). Harvard U Pr.

Five Thousand French Words. (Fr.). write for info. (ISBN 0-671-41964-1). S&S.

Five Thousand German Words. (Ger.). write for info. (ISBN 0-671-41965-X). S&S.

Flash in New South Wales, 1788-1850. R. Langker. LC 81-205617. 61p. (Eng.). 1980. write for info. Univ Syd Aust Lang.

Fletamentos y Terminos de Embarque. 7th, rev. ed. J. Bes. (Span.). text ed. 60.00 (ISBN 0-686-46539-3). Heineman.

Fletcher's Book of Rhyming Slang. Ronnie Barker. (Illus.). 1982. pap. 10.00x (ISBN 0-330-25980-6, Pub. by Pan Bks). State Mutual Bk.

Focal Dictionary of Photographic Technologies. D. A. Spencer. (Illus.). 1973. 49.95 (ISBN 0-240-50747-9). Focal Pr.

Fockema Andreae's Rechtsgeleerd Handwoordenboek. Andreae Fockman & Johannes Sybrandus. Rev. by N. E. Algra. LC 78-343297. 713p. (Dutch.). 1977. fl.write for info. Tjeenk Willinik.

Foclair Gaeilge Bearla (Irish-English Dictionary) O'Donaill. (Irish & Eng.). 25.00x (ISBN 0-686-28280-9). Colton Bk.

Focloir Modulach. Ireland Department of Education. LC 80-484412. 25p. (Eng. & Gaelic.). 1978. write for info. Le Ceannach Direach on Oifig Dhiolta Foilseachan Rialtais.

Foerkortningslexikon. Sven E. Oestling. LC 76-512672. 32p. (Swedish.). 1975. write for info (ISBN 9-171-82159-7). Utrikespolitiska.

Fogtdals et-binds leksikon i farver. Henning Dehn-Nielsen. Ed. by Gorm Sejersen. LC 80-459104. (Illus.). 656p. (Danish.). 1979. Kr.298.00 (ISBN 8-74270-116-3). Fogtdals Boger.

Folk-Etymology: A Dictionary of Verbal Corruptions or Words Perverted in Form. Abram Palmer. LC 68-26365. (Studies in Language, No. 41). 1969. Repr. of 1882 ed. lib. bdg. 59.95x (ISBN 0-8383-0279-3). Haskell.

Folk-Etymology, a Dictionary of Verbal Corruptions or Words Perverted in Form or Meaning, by False Derivation or Mistaken Analogy. Abram S. Palmer. LC 68-57636. (Illus.). 1969. Repr. of 1882 ed. lib. bdg. 29.25x (ISBN 0-8371-1153-6, PAFE). Greenwood.

Follet World-Wide Dictionary. (Eng. & Span.). write for info. (608-5). Pan Amer Pub.

Follet World Wide Dictionary: Spanish-English, English-Spanish. (Span. & Eng.). write for info. (608-7). Pan Am Bk Co.

Follett-Velazquez Spanish & English Dictionary. 1488p. (Span. & Eng.). 17.95. Cruzada Span Pubns.

Follett World-Wide Spanish-English Dictionary. 640p. (Span. & Eng.). 7.95. Cruzada Span Pubns.

Food Additives Dictionary. Melvin A. Benarde. 96p. 1981. pap. 4.95 (ISBN 0-671-42837-3, Wallaby). S&S.

Food & Menu Dictionary. C. Dahl. LC 77-123002. 160p. 1972. 12.50 (ISBN 0-8436-0556-1). CBI Pub.

Food: Multilingual Thesaurus. Ed. by Commission of the European Communities, Directorate-General for Scientific & Technical Information & Information Management. Incl. Vol. 1. German. 129p. (Ger.); Vol. 2. English. 145p. pap. 95.00 (ISBN 0-686-81239-5); Vol. 3. French. 144p. (Fr.); Italian. 132p. (Ital.); Vol. 5. Quadrilingual Index. 168p. (Eng., Fr., Ger. & Ital.). 1979. pap. 240.00x (ISBN 3-598-10103-1, Pub. by K G Saur). Gale.

Football Language. Bill Shefski. LC 77-12492. 1978. lib. bdg. 12.90 (ISBN 0-89471-021-4); pap. 2.95 (ISBN 0-89471-020-6). Running Pr.

Forging & Drop Forging see Dictionary of Production Engineering: German-English-French.

Formation du Vocabulaire de L'Aviation. Louis Guilbert. 712p. (Fr.). 1966. 37.50 (ISBN 0-686-57276-9, F-135660). French & Eur.

Foundation Dictionary of Russian: Three Thousand High Semantic Frequency Words. B. G. Anpilogova et al. Orig. Title: Essential Russian-English Dictionary. (Rus. & Eng.). (YA) (gr. 9-12). 1967. pap. 3.00 (ISBN 0-486-21860-0). Dover.

Foundry Dictionary: German-English & English-German. Compiled by Wolfgang Standke. (Ger. & Eng.). 1971. 21.50x (ISBN 3-87260-002-8). Intl Pubns Serv.

Four Language Culinary Dictionary: French, Hungarian, English, German. (Fr. , Hungarian, Eng. & Ger.). pap. 9.50 saddle stitched bdg. (ISBN 0-87557-099-2, 099-2). Saphrograph.

Four-Language Technical Dictionary of Chromatography: English, German, French, Russian. H. Angele. LC 76-103000. (Eng., Ger., Fr. & Rus.). 1971. text ed. 45.00 (ISBN 0-08-015865-X). Pergamon.

Four Languages Dictionary of Geological Terms. 703p. (Eng. , Fr. , Ger. & Rus.). 1980. 19.95 (ISBN 0-686-97380-1). French & Eur.

Four Thousand Naibolee Upotrebitel'nykh Slov Russkogo Iazyka. 368p. (Rus.). 1978. 6.50 (Pub. by Russkii Iazyk). Four Continent.

Foursquare Dictionary. J. A. Herring. 605p. 1969. 12.50x (ISBN 0-89955-232-3, Pub. by Mei Ya China). Intl Schol Bk Serv.

Fr. see Definitions of Nonviolence.

Fragment of a Khwarezmian Dictionary. W. B. Henning. Ed. by D. N. MacKenzie. 1971. 12.50x (ISBN 0-85331-292-3). Intl Pubns Serv.

Francais-Norvegien-Francais Lommerorbok. E. Daae. 455p. (Fr. & Norwegian.). 1981. pap. 12.95 (ISBN 82-573-0162-0, M-9461). French & Eur.

Francouzsko-Cesky a Cesko-Francouzsky Slovnik pro Televizni Pracovniky a Prekladatele. Otto Levinsky. LC 76-523695. 80p. (Fr. & Czech.). 1976. write for info. SNTC.

Francouzsko-Cesky Technicky Slovnik. Libuse Vomackova. 935p. (Eng., Fr. & Czech.). 1978. 99.00 Kcs. SNTC.

Franklin's Vocabulary. Lois M. MacLaurin. 1928. 35.00 (ISBN 0-8274-2371-3). R West.

Fransk-Dansk, Dansk-Fransk Specialordbog. Ed. by Ejnar Fryd. LC 78-377405. 199p. (Danish & Fr.). 1977. Kr.175.00. For Stat Rev.

Fransk-Norsk Ordbok. L. Dedichen. 373p. (Fr.). 1979. 29.95 (ISBN 82-573-0068-3, M-9457). French & Eur.

Fransk-Svensk Ordbok. Ruben Nojd. 181p. (Fr. & Swedish.). write for info. (ISBN 91-24-20278-9). Esselte Studium.

Fransk-Svensk Ordbok. Johan Vising. 779p. (Fr. & Swedish.). 1979. Kr.155.00 (ISBN 91-24-20108-1). Esselte Studium.

Frantsuzsko-Latviiskii Slovar. I. Zandreitere et al. 772p. (Fr. & Latvian.). 1957. 3.50 (Pub. by Latv Valsts). Four Continent.

Frantsuzsko-Russkii Frazeologicheskii Slovar. Ed. by I. I. Retsker. 1112p. (Fr. & Rus.). 1963. 8.95 (Pub. by Gosizdat Inostr Natsional Lit). Four Continent.

Frantsuzsko-Russkii Geologicheskii Slovar. I. K. Dobovskaia. 406p. (Fr. & Rus.). 1958. 2.90 (Pub. by Gosfizmat). Four Continent.

Frantsuzsko-Russkii Illiustrirovannyi Slovar. A. D. Kolesnikova et al. (Illus.). 856p. (Fr. & Rus.). 1977. 7.25 (Pub. by Sov Entsiklopediia). Four Continent.

Frantsuzsko-Russkii Illiustrirovannyi Slovar. I. Zandreitere. (Illus.). 772p. (Fr. & Rus.). 1957. 3.50 (Pub. by Latv Valstsnent Bk). Four Continent.

Frantsuzsko-Russkii Obshchestvenno-Politisheskii Slovar. Ed. by S. A. Tokarev et al. 283p. (Fr. & Rus.). 1961. 3.00 (Pub. by Izd. In-ta Mezhdunarod. Otnoshenii). Four Continent.

Frantsuzsko-Russkii Slovar Po Sudostroeniiu i Sudokhodstvu. A. I. Telegin et al. 295p. (Fr. & Rus.). 1961. 3.75 (Pub. by Glav. Red. Nauchn. Tekhn. Slovarei Fizmatgiza). Four Continent.

Frantsuzsko-Russkii Uchebnyi Slovar. N. B. Korina et al. 668p. (Fr. & Rus.). 1977. 8.50 (Pub. by Russkii Iazyk). Four Continent.

Frantsuzsko-Russkii Voennyi Slovar. A. M. Taube. (Fr. & Rus.). 1960. 6.60 (Pub. by Voenizdat). Four Continent.

Franzoesisch, 2 vols. Incl. Teil I. Franz oesisch-Deutsch. Compiled by Ernst E. Lange-Kowal. 640p. DM.34.00 (04151); Teil II. Deutsch-Franzoe sisch. rev. ed. Compiled by Kurt Wilhelm & Ernst E. Lange-Kowal. 700p. 1983. DM.34.00 (04157). (Langenscheidts Handworterbucher Ser.). (Fr. & Ger.). DM.beide Teile in einem Band (1364p.) 49.00 (05153). Langenscheidt.

Franzoesisch-Deutsches-Deutsch-Franzoesisches Woerterbuch: Band II, Deutsch-Franzoesisch. Lepointe Bertraux. 1392p. (Ger. & Eng.). 1982. DM.65.00. Brandstetter.

Franzoesisch-Deutsches Glossarium. F. Roepke. 540p. (Ger. & Fr.). 1964. 36.00 (ISBN 3-7819-2007-0, M-7413, Pub. by Fritz Knapp Verlag). French & Eur.

Franzoesisch Etymologisches Woerterbuch. 2nd ed. Walter von Wartburg. (Fr.). 1948. 38.50 (ISBN 3-16-926772-8, M-7414, Pub. by Francke). French & Eur.

Franzoesische Fachausdruecke im Bankgeschaeft: Franzoesisch-Deutsch, Deutsch-Franzoesisch. Hans A. Klaus. LC 75-513804. 248p. (Fr. & Ger.). 1975. 26.00 F (ISBN 3-258-01279-2). Haupt Verlag.

Franzoesische und Deutsche Chemische Fachuasdruecke. H. Fromherz & A. King. 568p. (Fr. & Ger.). 1968. DM.52.50 (ISBN 3-527-25094-8). Verlag Chemie.

Franzosisch, 2 vols. Incl. Franzoesisch-Deutsch. Ernst E. Lange-Kowal. 1200p (07151); Deutsch-Franzoesisch. rev. ed. Rev. by Ernst E. Lange-Kowal. 1312p. 1982 (07157). (Langenscheidts Grosse Schulworterbucher Ser.). (Fr. & Ger.). DM.23.80 ea. Langenscheidt.

Franzosisch, 2 vols. rev. ed. Incl. Teil I. Franzoesisch-Deutsch. E. E. Lange-Kowal. 576p. DM.16.80 (10151); Teil II. Deutsch-Franzoesisch. E. Weymuth. 640p. DM.16.80 (10156). (Langenscheidts Taschenworterbucher Ser.). (Fr. & Ger.). 1982. DM.beide Teile in einem Band 23.80 (11151). Langenscheidt.

Franzosisch-Deutsch, Deutsch-Franzosisch. (Langenscheidts Schulworterbucher Ser.). 576p. (Ger. & Fr.). DM.12.80 (13150). Langenscheidt.

Franzosisch-Deutsches, Deutsch-Franzosisches Woerterbuch, Vol. 1. Pierre Bertaux. (Ger. & Fr.). 1966. 69.95 (ISBN 3-87097-000-6, M-7411, Pub. by Brandstetter). French & Eur.

Franzosisch-Deutsches, Deutsch-Franzosisches Woerterbuch, Vol. 1. Pierre Bertaux. (Ger. & Fr.). 1966. DM.69.95 (ISBN 3-87097-000-6). Brandstetter.

Franzosisch-Deutsches, Deutsch-Franzosisches Woerterbuch, Vol. 2. Pierre Bertaux. (Ger. & Fr.). 1966. DM.69.95 (ISBN 3-87097-001-4). Brandstetter.

Franzosisch-Deutsches-Deutsch-Franzosisches Woerterbuch: Band I, Franzoesisch-Deutsch. Lepointe Bertraux. 1312p. (Fr. & Ger.). 1982. DM.65.00. Brandstetter.

Frazeologicheskii Slovar Russkogo Iazyka. A. I. Molotkova. 544p. (Rus. & Fr.). 1978. 11.95 (Pub. by Russkii Iazyk). Four Continent.

Frazeologicheskii Slovar' Russkogo Iazyka. Ed. by L. A. Voinova et al. (Russkii iazyk Ser.). 544p. (Rus.). 1978. 11.95 (C-33). Four Continent.

Freight & Passenger Cars from the 1898 Car Builder's Dictionary: Part 1, No. 55. Ed. by John C. Wait. (Train Shed Ser.). (Illus.). 1977. pap. 4.50 (ISBN 0-912318-90-2). N K Gregg.

Freight & Passenger Cars from the 1898 Car Builder's Dictionary: Part 2, No. 57. Ed. by John C. Wait. (Train Shed Ser.). (Illus.). 1977. pap. 4.50 (ISBN 0-912318-92-9). N K Gregg.

Freight & Passenger Cars from the 1898 Car Builder's Dictionary: Part 3, No. 59. Ed. by John C. Wait. (Train Shed Ser.). (Illus.). 1977. pap. 4.50 (ISBN 0-912318-94-5). N K Gregg.

Freight Cars from the 1919 Car Builder's Dictionary, Pt. 1. Ed. by Roy V. Wright. (Train Shed Cyclopedia Ser: No. 35). (Illus.). 80p. 1975. pap. 5.50 (ISBN 0-912318-66-X). N K Gregg.

Freight Cars from the 1919 Car Builder's Dictionary, Pt. 2. Ed. by Roy V. Wright. (Train Shed Cyclodedia Ser: No. 36). (Illus.). 80p. 1975. pap. 5.50 (ISBN 0-912318-67-8). N K Gregg.

Fremdwoerter Lexikon. Wahrig-Gerhard. (Ger.). 1976. DM.15.95 (ISBN 3-570-01631-5). C Bertelsmann.

Fremdwoerterbuch: Herkunft & Bedeutung der Fremdwoerter. Gunther Drosdowski. 466p. (Ger.). DM.19.80 (ISBN 3-411-01121-1). Biblio Inst.

French & English Idioms. F. Denoeu et al. (Fr. & Eng.). 1982. 7.95 (ISBN 0-8120-0435-3). Barron.

French & International Acronyms & Initialisms Dictionary. 2nd ed. 1977. pap. 30.00x (ISBN 0-930624-00-9). Marlin.

French Bilingual Dictionary. Gladys Lipton. (Illus., Fr. & Eng.). 1979. pap. 5.00; Pocket ed., 335p. pap. 3.25. Barron.

French Bilingual Dictionary: A Beginner's Guide in Words & Pictures. G. Lipton. (Fr. & Eng.). 1974. 4.95 (ISBN 0-8120-0470-1). Barron.

French Bilingual Dictionary: A Beginner's Guide in Words & Pictures. rev. ed. Gladys Lipton. LC 72-84411. (Fr. & Eng.). (gr. 4-12). 1984. pap. text ed. 4.50 (ISBN 0-8120-2330-7). Barron.

French Bilingual Dictionary: A Beginner's Guide in Words & Pictures. Gladys C. Lipton. LC 78-20788. ix, 355p. (Eng. & Fr.). 1979. 2.95 (ISBN 0-8120-2007-3). Barron.

French Bilingual Dictionary: Compact Ed. rev. ed. Gladys Lipton. LC 78-20788. (Illus., Fr. & Eng.). (gr. 7-12). 1979. pap. 3.25 (ISBN 0-8120-2007-3). Barron.

French Concise Dictionary. Cassells. 1977. 9.95 (ISBN 0-02-522670-3). Macmillan.

French Dictionary. (Teach Yourself Ser.). (Fr.). 1977. pap. 5.95 (ISBN 0-679-10245-0). McKay.

French Dictionary. Hamlyn. 320p. (Fr. & Eng.). Epap. 1.00 (ISBN 0-600-36563-8). Hamlyn-Amer.

French Dishes, Easy & Delicious. R. Picard. pap. 3.95 (ISBN 0-87557-101-8, 101-8). Saphrograph.

French Duden, Pictorial Dictionary. (Illus.). 20.50 (ISBN 3-4110-0972-1). Adler.

French-Eng., Eng-French Dictionary of Electrotechnic Electronics & Allied Fields, 2 Vols. H. Piraux. (Fr. & Eng.). Set. 90.00 (ISBN 0-685-12017-1). Heinman.

French-English & English-French Dictionary. (Fr. & Eng.). pap. 1.99 (ISBN 0-686-02351-X). Dennison.

French-English & English-French Dictionary of Commercial & Financial Terms, Phrases & Practice. 2nd ed. J. O. Kettridge. (Fr. & Eng.). 1969. Repr. of 1968 ed. 30.00 (ISBN 0-7100-1671-9). Routledge & Kegan.

French-English & English-French Dictionary of Commercial & Financial Terms. J. O. Kettridge. 655p. (Fr. & Eng.). 1978. 32.00. Routledge & Kegan.

French-English & English-French Dictionary of Financial & Mercantile Terms, Phrases & Practice. J. O. Kettridge. 288p. (Fr. & Eng.). 1971. Repr. of 1934 ed. 20.00 (ISBN 0-7100-1667-0). Routledge & Kegan.

French-English & English-French Dictionary of Technical Terms & Phrases, 2 vols. J. O. Kettridge. Incl. Vol. 1. French-English. 40.50 (ISBN 0-7100-0144-4); Vol. 2. English-French. 40.00 (ISBN 0-7100-0166-5). (Fr. & Eng.). 1970. Repr. of 1959 ed. Set. 75.00 (ISBN 0-7100-0082-0). Routledge & Kegan.

French-English Chemical Terminology: An Introduction to Chemistry in French & English. H. Fromherz & A. King. 561p. (Fr. & Ger.). 1968. 52.50 (ISBN 0-686-56475-8, M-7417, Pub. by Vlg. Chemie). French & Eur.

French-English Chemical Terminology: An Introduction to Chemistry in French & English. H. Fromherz & A. King. 561p. (Fr. & Ger.). 1968. DM.52.50. Verlag Chemie.

French-English Chemical Terminology: An Introduction to Chemistry in French & English. Hans Fromherz & Alexander King. 580p. (Fr. & Eng.). 1968. 46.30x (ISBN 3-527-25095-6). Verlag Chemie.

French-English Dictionary. Robert Collins. (Fr. & Eng.). 19.95. Iaconi.

French-English Dictionary. (Fr. & Eng.). 14.50 (ISBN 0-87557-021-6, 021-6). Saphrograph.

French-English Dictionary of Technical Terms Used in Classical Ballet. Cyril W. Beaumont. LC 79-307143. iv, 44p. (Eng. & Fr.). 1977. E0.60. Imp Soc Tchrs Da.

French-English English-French Dictionary. Robert Collins. (Fr. & Eng.). 1978. Can.$pap. 22.95 (ISBN 0-00-216695-X); 24.95 (ISBN 0-00-216696-8). U of Toronto Pr.

French-English, English-French Dictionary of Commercial & Financial Terms. Kettridge. (Fr. & Eng.). 21.50 (ISBN 0-685-36684-7). French & Eur.

French-English, English-French Gem Dictionary. Ed. by G. Rudler & N. C. Anderson. (Gem Foreign Language Ser.). (Fr. & Eng.). 1952. 2.95 (ISBN 0-00-458617-4, G2). Collins Pubs.

French-English, English-French Legal Dictionary. new ed. T. A. Quemner. Ed. by Jean Baleyte & Alexander Kurgansky. (Fr. & Eng.). 75.00 (ISBN 0-685-01106-2). Heinman.

French-English Horticultural Dictionary. D. O. Bourke. 196p. 1974. 59.00x (ISBN 0-85198-308-1, Pub. by CAB Bks England). State Mutual Bk.

French-English Instant Vocabulary. Eleanor P. Cruikshank. 88p. (Fr. & Eng.). 1980. pap. 4.00 (ISBN 0-9605284-0-7). Cruikshank.

French-English Science & Technology Dictionary. rev. ed. Louis De Vries. Rev. by Stanley Hochman. 683p. (Fr. & Eng.). 1976. 20.00. McGraw.

French-English Science & Technology Dictionary. 4th ed. Louis De Vries & Stanley Hochman. 704p. (Fr. & Eng.). write for info. (ISBN 0-07-016629-3). McGraw.

French-English Science Dictionary. Louis De Vries. LC 75-45091. xii, 683p. (Eng. & Fr.). 1976. 13.50 (ISBN 0-07-016629-3). McGraw.

French-Finnish Dictionary. E. Hagfors et al. 599p. (Fr. & Finnish.). 1980. leatherette 24.95 (ISBN 951-0-04682-5, M-9657). French & Eur.

French for Business Studies. M. Rover. 95p. (Fr. & Eng.). 1980. pap. 5.95 (ISBN 0-582-35900-7, M-9207). French & Eur.

French for English Idioms & Figurative Phrases. J. O. Kettridge. (Fr. & Eng.). 1966. Repr. of 1940 ed. 16.00 (ISBN 0-7100-1669-7). Routledge & Kegan.

French for the English-Speaking Tourist see Phrase Dictionaries for the American Tourist.

French-German Chemical Terminology: An Introduction to Chemistry in French & German. Hans Fromherz & Alexander King. LC 68-54575. 587p. (Fr. & Ger.). 1969. 46.30x (ISBN 3-527-25094-8). Verlag Chemie.

French Idioms & Figurative Phrases. J. O. Kettridge. (Fr.). pap. 9.50 (ISBN 0-87557-024-0, 024-0). Saphrograph.

French Idioms on the Way. Barbara Gerber & Gerald Storzer. (Illus., Fr.). 1984. pap. 4.95 (ISBN 0-8120-2108-8). Barron.

French Military Terminology, 1670-1815. Donald E. Graves. LC 80-510476. 54p. (Fr.). 1979. write for info. (ISBN 0-919326-38-2). New Bruns Mus.

French-Norwegian Dictionary. Line Dedichen. (Fr. & Norwegian.). 1973. write for info. (ISBN 82-573-0068-3). Kunnskapsforlaget.

French-Onondaga Dictionary, from a Manuscript of the Seventeenth Century. John D. Shea. LC 10-30203. (Library of American Linguistics: No. 1). (Fr.). Repr. of 1860 ed. 12.50 (ISBN 0-404-50981-9). AMS Pr.

French-Swedish-French Dictionary. 370p. (Fr. & Swedish.). 1980. pap. 9.95 (ISBN 0-686-97383-6, M-9445). French & Eur.

French Vest Pocket Dictionary. Robert A. Hall, Jr. & Francesca V. Langbaum. (Fr.). 1954. pap. 2.95 (ISBN 0-394-40054-2). Random.

French Weights & Measures before the Revolution: A Dictionary of Provincial & Local Units. Ronald E. Zupko. LC 78-3249. 256p. 1979. 22.50x (ISBN 0-253-32480-7). Ind U Pr.

Frequency Dictionary of Chinese Words. Eric S. Liu. (Linguistic Structures, First Ser.). (Chinese.). 1973. pap. text ed. 57.50x (ISBN 90-2792-627-1). Mouton.

Frequency Dictionary of Spanish Words. Alphonse Juilland & E. Chang-Rodriquez. (R. L. T. S. First Ser: No. S1). (Span.). 1964. text ed. 81.00x (ISBN 90-2790-159-7). Mouton.

Fruehneuhochdeutsches Glossar. 7th ed. Alfred Goetze. (Kleine Texte, No. 101). (Ger.). 1971. Repr. of 1967 ed. bds. 9.90x (ISBN 3-11-003527-8). De Gruyter.

Fuchsia Lexicon. Ron Ewart. 280p. 1982. 29.95 (ISBN 0-442-22283-1). Van Nos Reinhold.

Fundamental Terms of Cutting see Dictionary of Production Engineering: German-English-French.

Funk & Wagnalls Modern Guide to Synonyms & Related Words. Ed. by S. I. Hayakawa & Funk And Wagnalls Dictionary Staff. LC 67-26446. (Funk & W Bk.). 1968. 9.95i (ISBN 0-308-40073-9). T Y Crowell.

Funk & Wagnalls Standard College Dictionary. new updated ed. Funk And Wagnalls Editors. LC 72-13007. (Funk & W Bk.). 1632p. 1977. 9.95i (ISBN 0-308-10309-2); thumb indexed 10.95i (ISBN 0-308-10310-6). T Y Crowell.

Funk & Wagnalls Standard College Dictionary. 1978. Can.$12.95 (ISBN 0-88902-440-5); 14.95 (ISBN 0-88902-573-8). Fitzhenry.

Funk & Wagnalls Standard Desk Dictionary. rev. ed. (Illus.). 890p. 1980. 8.95 (ISBN 0-308-10352-1); thumb indexed 9.95 (ISBN 0-308-10353-X). T Y Crowell.

Funk & Wagnall's Standard Handbook of Synonyms, Antonyms & Prepositions. rev. ed. James C. Fernald. LC 47-11924. (Funk & W Bk.). (gr. 9-12). 1947. 13.41i (ISBN 0-308-40024-0, 420140). T y Crowell.

Furniture Collector's Glossary. Luke V. Lockwood. LC 67-27460. (Architecture & Decorative Art Ser.). 1967. Repr. of 1940 ed. lib. bdg. 15.00 (ISBN 0-306-70968-6). Da Capo.

G

Gablers Wirtschaftslexikon. 10th ed. (Ger.). 1979. DM.248.00 (ISBN 3-409-96542-4). Gabler.

Gaelic Dictionary: Gaelic-English English-Gaelic. Malcolm MacLennan. 632p. (Gaelic & Eng.). 1980. 45.00 (ISBN 0-08-025713-5); pap. 22.00 (ISBN 0-08-025712-7). Pergamon.

Gardener's Dictionary. P. Miller. 1969. Repr. of 1754 ed. 64.00 (ISBN 3-7682-0613-0). Lubrecht & Cramer.

Gardner's Chemical Synonyms & Trade Names: A Dictionary & Commercial Handbook Containing Over 35,500 Definitions & Identifications. 8th ed. E. I. Cooke & R. W. Cooke. 776p. 1980. 99.50x (ISBN 0-291-39678-X, Pub. by Tech Pr). State Mutual Bk.

Geillustrrerd Woordenboek Voor de Autombieltechniek en Zes Talen. C. Block et al. 502p. (Dutch, Rus., Eng., Ger. & Ital.). 1978. 145.00 (ISBN 90-201-1070-5, M-9475). French & Eur.

Gem Dictionary of Synonyms. (Gem Reference Ser.). 1964. 2.95 (ISBN 0-529-05651-8, GR12). Collins Pubs.

Gem English Learner's Dictionary. (Eng.). write for info. (ISBN 0-671-42047-X). S&S.

Gem Language Dictionaries: French-English & English-French. (Fr. & Eng.). write for info. (ISBN 0-671-41957-9). S&S.

Gem Language Dictionaries: French-German & German-French. (Fr. & Ger.). write for info. (ISBN 0-671-41943-9). S&S.

Gem Language Dictionaries: German-English & English-German. (Ger. & Eng.). write for info. (ISBN 0-671-41958-7). S&S.

Gem Language Dictionaries: Italian-English & English-Italian. (Ital. & Eng.). write for info. (ISBN 0-671-41956-0). S&S.

Gem Language Dictionaries: Latin-English & English-Latin. (Lat. & Eng.). write for info. (ISBN 0-671-41961-7). S&S.

Gem Language Dictionaries: Portuguese-English & English-Portuguese. (Port. & Eng.). write for info. (ISBN 0-671-41946-3). S&S.

Gem Language Dictionaries: Russian-English & English-Russian. (Rus. & Eng.). write for info. (ISBN 0-671-41960-9). S&S.

Gem Language Dictionaries: Spanish-English & English-Spanish. (Span. & Eng.). write for info (ISBN 0-671-41959-5). S&S.

Genealogical Dictionary of Maine & New Hampshire. Sybil Noyes et al. LC 79-88099. 795p. 1983. Repr. of 1939 ed. 30.00 (ISBN 0-8063-0502-9). Genealog Pub.

Genealogical Dictionary of the First Settlers of New England, 4 vols. James Savage. LC 65-18541. 2541p. 1981. Repr. of 1860 ed. 95.00 (ISBN 0-8063-0309-3). Genealog Pub.

Genealogical Dictionary of the First Settlers of New England, 4 vols. James Savage. 450.00 (ISBN 0-8490-0213-3). Gordon Pr.

Geneesmiddelenzakboekje. G. A. Van Gemert & A. De Maesschalck. LC 76-677126. 144p. (Eng. & Dutch.). 1976. fl.16.50 (ISBN 9-0100-1588-2). Agon Elsevier.

General Basic English Dictionary. Ed. by C. K. Ogden. 438p. 1970. Repr. of 1940 ed. 15.00x (ISBN 0-87471-362-5). Rowman.

General Chinese-English Dictionary. 926p. (Chinese & Eng.). 1979. 9.95 (ISBN 0-686-92471-1, M-9583). French & Eur.

General Motor Terminology. 1979. 10.00; members 3.00. Small Motor Mfrs.

General Psychology in Terms of Behavior. Stevenson Smith & Edwin R. Guthrie. LC 22-444. (Psychology Ser). 1970. Repr. of 1921 ed. 18.00 (ISBN 0-384-56175-6). Johnson Repr.

Genetik Erblicher Syndrome & Missbildungen. Regine Witkowski. LC 76-675817. 1071p. (Eng. & Ger.). 1976. write for info. (ISBN 3-437-10409-8). Fischer Verlag.

Geobotanic Dictionary. O. S. Grebenshchikov. (Rus., Eng., Ger. & Fr.). 1979. lib. bdg. 36.00x (ISBN 3-87429-164-2). Lubrecht & Cramer.

Geographic Dictionary of Connecticut & Rhode Island, 2 vols. in 1. Henry Gannett. LC 78-59123. 98p. 1978. Repr. of 1894 ed. 9.50 (ISBN 0-8063-0820-6). Genealog Pub.

Geographic Dictionary of Massachusetts. Henry Gannett. LC 78-59121. 126p. 1978. Repr. of 1894 ed. 12.00 (ISBN 0-8063-0818-4). Genealog Pub.

Geographic Dictionary of New Jersey. Henry Gannett. LC 78-59122. 131p. 1978. Repr. of 1894 ed. 12.00 (ISBN 0-8063-0819-2). Genealog Pub.

Geographical & Historical Dictionary of America & the West Indies, 5 Vols. Antonio De Alcedo. Tr. by George A. Thompson. LC 70-146788. (Research & Source Works Ser: No. 627). 1971. Repr. of 1812 ed. Set. lib. bdg. 220.00 (ISBN 0-8337-3525-X). B Franklin.

Geographical Dictionary of Ancient & Mediaeval India. Nundo Lal Dey. LC 42-31336. (Illus.). 272p. 1971. Repr. of 1927 ed. 19.50x (ISBN 0-8002-1453-6). Intl Pubns Serv.

Geographical Dictionary of Ancient & Mediaeval India. 3rd ed. Nundo Lal Dey. (Illus.). 262p. 1971. 22.00x (ISBN 0-8426-0332-8). Verry.

Geographical Dictionary of Ancient & Medieval India. Nando Lal Dey. 262p. 1979. Repr. of 1927 ed. 27.50 (ISBN 0-89684-150-2). Orient Bk Dist.

Geographical Dictionary of Milton. Allan H. Gilbert. 1979. Repr. of 1919 ed. lib. bdg. 35.00 (ISBN 0-8495-2014-2). Arden Lib.

Geographical Dictionary of Milton. Allan H. Gilbert. LC 68-10922. 1968. Repr. of 1919 ed. 9.50x (ISBN 0-8462-1105-X). Russell.

Geographical Lexicon of Greek Coin Inscriptions. A. Florance. (Gr.). 1978. pap. 10.00 (ISBN 0-89005-232-8). Ares.

Geographie: Ein Lexikon der Gesamten Schul-Erdkunde. Adolf Hanle. (Illus.). 420p. (Ger.). DM.19.80 (ISBN 3-411-01731-7). Biblio Inst.

Geologicheskii Slovar, 2 vols. (Rus.). 1973. 35.00 set (Pub. by Nedra). Four Continent.

Geologicheskii Slovar, 2 Vols. A. N. Krishtofovich. (Rus.). 1960. 15.00 set (Pub. by Gos. Nauch. Tekhn. Izd. Lit. Po Geologii & Okhrane Nedr.). Four Continent.

Geologisches Woerterbuch. 7th ed. H. Murawski. (Ger.). 1977. DM.pap. 10.95 (ISBN 3-432-84107-8). Deutscher Taschenbuch Verlag.

Geologisches Woerterbuch. H. Murawski. (Ger.). 1972. DM.pap. 10.95. Deutscher Taschenbuch Verlag.

GeoRef Thesaurus & Guide to Indexing. 2nd ed. Ed. by Carol Heckman et al. LC 78-65083. 1978. pap. 35.00 (ISBN 0-913312-07-X) (ISBN 0-913312-40-1). Am Geol.

GeoRef Thesaurus & Guide to Indexing. 3rd ed. Ed. by Sharon J. Riley. 468p. 1981. 45.00 (ISBN 0-913312-53-3). Am Geol.

George Eliot Dictionary. Isadore G. Mudge & Minnie E. Sears. LC 76-27710. 1924. lib. bdg. 21.00 (ISBN 0-8414-6114-7). Folcroft.

Geowissenschaften. LC 77-466982. (Fr. & Ger.). 1975. write for info. Schweizerbart.

Geowissenschaften Deutsch-Englisch. Adolf Watznauer. 372p. (Ger. & Eng.). 1981. M.46.00. VEB Technik.

Geowissenschaften Englisch-Deutsch. Adolf Watznauer. 400p. (Eng. & Ger.). 1981. M.46.00. VEB Technik.

Gergo della Camorra. Carlo Sanna. LC 78-370722. (Illus.). 128p. (Ital.). 1978. L.2400.00. Il Vespro.

German & English Glossary of Geographical Terms. Eric Fischer & Francis E. Elliott. LC 76-20474. (American Geographical Society Library Ser: No. 5). 111p. (Ger. & Eng.). 1976. Repr. of 1950 ed. lib. bdg. 15.00x (ISBN 0-8371-8994-2, ELGG). Greenwood.

German-Chinese Dictionary. Hellmut Wilhelm. (Ger. & Chinese.). 1976. Repr. of 1958 ed. 175.00 (ISBN 0-518-19006-4). Ayer Co.

German Dictionary. 320p. (Ger.). Epap. 1.25 (ISBN 0-600-36564-6). Newnes Bks.

German Dictionary. (Eng. & Ger.). write for info. (608-94). Pan Amer Pub.

German-English & English-German Dictionary. (Ger. & Eng.). pap. 1.99 (ISBN 0-686-00471-X). Dennison.

German-English Dictionary. (Ger. & Eng.). 14.50 (ISBN 0-87557-025-9, 026-7). Saphrograph.

German-English Dictionary. G. Wahrig. 661p. (Ger. & Eng.). 1980. 35.00x (ISBN 0-569-05717-5, Pub. by Collet's). State Mutual Bk.

German-English Dictionary: Art History-Archaeology. M. Apelt. (Eng. & Ger.). Date not set. text ed. 25.00 (ISBN 0-686-46538-5). Heinman.

German-English Dictionary: Art History, Archaeology. M. L. Apelt. 240p. (Ger. & Eng.). 1982. pap. 24.00. M Rosenberg.

German-English Dictionary for Chemists. 3rd ed. A. M. Patterson. (Ger. & Fr.). 1950. 32.50 (ISBN 0-471-66990-3, Pub. by Wiley-Interscience). Wiley.

German-English Dictionary of Chemistry & Chemical Technology-Chemie und Chemische Technik: Deutsch-Englisch. Ed. by Technische Universitat Dresden. 633p. (Ger. & Eng.). 1980. 45.00x (ISBN 0-8002-2765-4). Intl Pubns Serv.

German-English Dictionary of Idioms. Ronald J. Taylor & W. Gottschalk. (Eng. & Ger.). 30.00 (ISBN 3-19-006216-1). Adler.

German-English Dictionary of International Transport. G. Bein. 232p. (Ger. & Eng.). 1980. 15.00x (ISBN 0-569-05117-7, Pub. by Collet's). State Mutual Bk.

German-English Dictionary of Technical, Scientific & General Terms. 3rd ed. A. Webel. (Ger. & Eng.). 1969. Repr. of 1952 ed. 37.50 (ISBN 0-7100-2258-1). Routledge & Kegan.

German-English, English-German: A Dictionary of Professional Terminology of Speech Pathology & Audiology. Peter B. Mueller. 64p. (Ger. & Eng.). 1967. photocopy ed. spiral 6.75x (ISBN 0-398-01368-3). C C Thomas.

German-English, English-German Astronautics Dictionary. Charles J. Hyman. LC 65-20216. 273p. (Ger. & Eng.). 1968. 30.00x (ISBN 0-306-10748-1, Consultants). Plenum Pub.

German-English, English-German Dictionary. Ed. by Ottenheimer. (Ger. & Eng.). pap. 2.50 (ISBN 0-06-465028-6, DI 2, BN). B&N NY.

German-English, English-German Dictionary. Schoffler-Weiss. 1062p. (Ger. & Eng.). 1981. 16.95. M Rosenberg.

German-English, English-German Dictionary of Industrial Technics, 2 vols. 4th, rev., enl. ed. R. Ernst. (Ger. & Eng.). Set. 150.00 (ISBN 0-686-77968-1). German-english (ISBN 3-87097-096-0). English-german (ISBN 3-87097-068-5). Heinman.

German-English, English-German Dictionary: Woerterbuch Deutsch-Englisch, Englisch-Deutsch. Rev ed. Editions Berlitz. LC 78-78082. 359p. (Ger. & Eng.). 1979. E0.95 (ISBN 0-02-964530-1, Pub. by Berlitz). Macmillan.

German-English, English-German Electronics Dictionary. Charles J. Hyman. LC 64-7757. 182p. (Ger. & Eng.). 1965. 35.00x (ISBN 0-306-10710-4, Consultants). Plenum Pub.

German-English, English-German Gem Dictionary. Ed. by J. M. Clark. (Gem Foreign Language Ser.). (Ger. & Eng.). 1953. leatheroid 2.95 (ISBN 0-00-458619-0, G3). Collins Pubs.

German-English, English-German Mathematical Dictionary. E. B. Klaften. (Ger. & Eng.). pap. 15.00 (ISBN 0-686-77978-9). Heinman.

German-English, English-German Medical Dictionary. rev. & enl. 8th ed. D. W. Unseld. (Ger. & Eng.). 35.00 (ISBN 3-8047-0661-4). Heinman.

German-English, English-German Patent Terminological Dictionary. E. B. Klaften & F. C. Allison. (Ger. & Eng.). 50.00 (ISBN 0-685-12020-1). Heinman.

German-English, English-German Technical Pocket Dictionary. 6th. ed. K. Breuer. (Ger. & Eng.). pap. 22.50 (ISBN 0-685-25495-X). Heinman.

German-English-German. (Berlitz Pocket Dictionaries Ser.). (Ger. & Eng.). 4.95 (ISBN 0-02-964530-1). Macmillan.

German-English Glossary of Plastics Machinery Terms. Manfred S. Welling. 280p. (Ger. & Eng.). 1981. text ed. 14.00x (ISBN 0-02-949800-7, Pub. by Hanser International). Macmillan.

German-English Science Dictionary. 4th ed. Louis De Vries. LC 78-6465. xxxviii, 628p. (Eng. & Ger.). 1978. 14.50 (ISBN 0-07-016602-1). McGraw.

German-English Science Dictionary. 4th ed. Louis DeVries & Leon Jacolev. (Ger. & Eng.). 1978. 26.95 (ISBN 0-07-016602-1, P&RB). McGraw.

German-English Science Dictionary. 4th ed. Louis De Vries & Leon Jacolev. 628p. (Ger. & Eng.). write for info. (ISBN 0-07-016602-1). McGraw.

German-English Science Dictionary. rev. ed. louis De Vries & Leon Jacolev. 666p. (Ger. & Eng.). 1978. 28.00. McGraw.

German-English Technical & Engineering Dictionary. 2nd ed. Louis DeVries. (Ger. & Eng.). 1966. 63.95 (ISBN 0-07-016631-5, P&RB). McGraw.

German-English Technical & Engineering Dictionary. Louis De Vries & Theo M. Hermann. (Ger. & Eng.). 1966. 66.00. McGraw.

German for Building Specialists, (L'allemand Dans le Batiment, el Aleman En la Construccion) G. Wallnig & H. Evered. 102p. (Ger. & Eng.). 1979. 12.95 (ISBN 3-7625-0462-8, M-7420, Pub. by Bauverlag). French & Eur.

German for Building Specialists: L'Allemand dans le Batiment, el Aleman en la construccion. G. Wallnig & H. Evered. 102p. (Ger. & Fr.). 1979. DM.12.95 (ISBN 3-7625-0462-8). Bauverlag.

German for Business Studies. F. Kershaw & S. Russon. 203p. (Ger.). pap. 7.95 (ISBN 0-582-36186-9, M-9203). French & Eur.

German for the American Tourist **see Phrase Dictionaries for the American Tourist.**

German-Norwegian Dictionary. Haukoy & Zickfeldt. (Ger. & Norwegian.). 1976. write for info. (ISBN 82-573-0077-2). Kunnskapsforlaget.

German-Norwegian Dictionary of Technical Terms. D. Strom & J. A. Strom. (Ger. & Norwegian.). 1983. write for info. (ISBN 82-573-0170-1). Kunnskapsforlaget.

German Root Lexicon. Howard H. Keller. LC 72-85112. (Miami Linguistics Ser: No. 11). 128p. (Ger.). 1973. 12.95x (ISBN 0-87024-244-X). U of Miami Pr.

German-Russian Dictionary. Rahmanoba. 556p. (Ger. & Rus.). 1957. 4.95 (ISBN 0-686-92465-7, M-9105). French & Eur.

German-Serbocroatian Electrotechnical Dictionary. N. S. Arsenijevic. 150p. (Ger. & Serbocroatian.). 1971. Leatherette 24.95 (ISBN 0-686-92462-2, M-963X3). French & Eur.

German-Slovene Dictionary. F. Tomsic. 989p. (Ger. & Slovene.). 1980. 49.95 (ISBN 0-686-97384-4, M-9696). French & Eur.

German-Swedish-German Dictionary. (Ger. & Swedish.). 9.95 (ISBN 0-686-92401-0, M-9448). French & Eur.

German Word Family Dictionary: Together with English Equivalents. Howard H. Keller. LC 76-19988. (Ger. & Eng.). 1978. 14.95 (ISBN 0-520-03291-8). U of Cal Pr.

Geschichte: Ein Sachlexikon fuer die Schule. Wilfried Forstmann et al. (Illus.). 503p. (Ger.). DM.19.80 (ISBN 3-411-01799-6). Biblio Inst.

Gesellschaft & Staat: Lexikon der Politik. Hanno Dreschler et al. LC 79-388088. (Illus.). xx, 604p. (Ger.). 1979. DM.38.00 (ISBN 3-797-10078-7). Signal-Verlag.

Gesundheits-Brockhaus. 848p. (Ger.). DM.48.00 (ISBN 3-7653-0026-8). F A Brockhaus.

Getriebe-Woerterbuch. H. Bucksch. 286p. (Eng. & Ger.). 1976. DM.165.00 (ISBN 3-7625-0707-4). Bauverlag.

Gidabal Grammar & Dictionary. Brian Geytenbeek & Helen Geytenbeek. (AIAS Linguistics Ser.: No. 17). (Orig.). 1971. pap. text ed. 10.50x (ISBN 0-85575-019-7). Humanities.
Gidrologicheskii Slovar. A. I. Chebotarev. 308p. (Rus.). 1978. 6.50 (Pub. by GIdrometeoizdat). Four Continent.
Gidrologicheskii Slovar. L. Chebotarev. 221p. (Rus.). 1964. 2.40 (Pub. by Gidrometeorologich Izd.). Four Continent.
Gidrologicheskii Slovar na Inostrannykh Iazykakh. O. A. Spenger. 216p. (Rus.). 1959. 2.95 (Pub. by Gidrometeoizdat). Four Continent.
Giesserei - Fachwoerterbuch. E. Brunhuber. 802p. (Ger., Eng., Fr. & Ital., Dictionary of Foundry). 1977. 120.00 (ISBN 3-7949-0283-1, M-7424, Pub. by Fachverlag, Schiele & Schon). French & Eur.
Giesserei - Lexikon 1978. E. Brunhuber. 960p. (Ger.). 1977. 62.50 (ISBN 3-7949-0282-3, M-7425, Pub. by Fachverlag, Schiele & Schon). French & Eur.
Giesserei-Fachwoerterbuch. E. Brunhuber. 802p. (Ger., Eng., Fr. & Ital.). 1977. DM.120.00 (ISBN 3-7949-0283-1). Schiele & Schon.
Giesserei-Fachworterbuch. Ernst Brunhuber. LC 78-350030. 729p. (Eng., Fr., Ger. & Ital.). 1977. DM.148.00 (ISBN 3-7949-0283-1). Schiele & Schon.
Giesserei-Lexikon 1978. E. Brunhuber. 960p. (Ger.). 1977. DM.62.50 (ISBN 3-7949-0282-3). Schiele & Schon.
Gilbert & Sullivan Dictionary. George E. Dunn. LC 72-10177. 1972. Repr. of 1936 ed. lib. bdg. 25.00 (ISBN 0-8414-0683-9). Folcroft.
Ginn Beginning Dictionary. William Morris. (Eng.). 1975. Can.$9.95 (ISBN 0-7702-0000-1). Ginn.
Giorno per Giorno see Family Portrait, from a Mother's Diary.
Gips - Woerterbuch. K. Volkart. 176p. (Ger.). 1971. 68.00 (ISBN 3-7625-0460-1, M-7426, Pub. by Bauverlag). French & Eur.
Gips-Woerterbuch. K. Volkart. 176p. (Ger.). 1971. DM.68.00 (ISBN 3-7625-0460-1). Bauverlag.
Gips-Woerterbuch. K. H. Volkart. 176p. (Ger., Eng. & Fr.). 1971. DM.85.00 (ISBN 3-7625-0460-1). Bauverlag.
Gjellerups Gronne Ordbog. Flemming G. Albertus. LC 78-343138. (Danish.). 1977. Kr.34.50 (ISBN 8-71301-300-9). Gjellerup Forlag.
Glaister's Glossary of the Book: Terms Used in Paper-Making, Printing, Bookbinding, & Publishing. Geoffrey Glaister. LC 76-47975. 1979. 75.00 (ISBN 0-520-03364-7). U of Cal Pr.
Global Woerterbuch: English-German, German-English, 2 vols. Pons. (Ger. & Eng.). 10.90 ea. M Rosenberg.
Glosar der Wichtigsten Saugetiere Chinas. Alfred Hoffman. xi, 103p. (Ger. & Chinese.). 1978. write for info. (ISBN 3-447-02001-6). Harrassowitz.
Glosari. Eugenio D'Rovira. 352p. (Span.). 1982. pap. 375.00 ptas (ISBN 84-297-1826-5). Ediciones Sesent Dos.
Glosario de bajo espanol en Venezuela, 4 vols. Lisandro Alvarado. (Span.). Bs.0.90 ea. Minist Ed Caracas.
Glosario de Genetica y Citogenetica II. R. Rieger et al. Tr. by M. J. Puertas Gallego. 512p. (Span.). 1982. pap. 920.00 ptas (ISBN 84-205-0875-6). Alhambra.
Glosario de informatica. F. Garcia Merayo. 290p. (Span.). 425.00 ptas. Urmo.
Glosario De Informatica: Terminologia Ordenada Segun el Vocablo Ingles y Su Acepcion En Espanol. F. Garcia Merayo. 290p. (Eng. & Span.). 1971. pap. 28.50 (ISBN 84-314-0001-3, S-50368). French & Eur.
Glosario de la farsa urbana. Roberto Gache. 120p. (Span.). Arg.$2.40. Centro Ed.
Glosario de mercadeo. Rossi K. Fischer. 143p. (Span.). Mex.$3.20; 40.00. Limusa.
Glosario de Tecnologia Educativa. 84p. (Span.). 1980. 3.00 (ISBN 0-8270-1060-5). Organize Am States.
Glosario de terminos entomologicos. R. H. Quintanilla & C. P. Fraga. 120p. (Span.). write for info. EUDEBA.
Glosario de terminos geograficos. Consuelo Soto Mora & Luis Fuentes Aguilar. (Illus.). 232p. (Span.). 1966. Mex.$55.00. UNAM.
Glosario de terminos hospitalarios. (Span.). write for info. OPS.
Glosario de terminos linguisticos. 132p. (Span.). 1982. pap. write for info. (ISBN 84-369-0934-8). Serv Pub Minist.
Glosario de Terminos Mareograficos. Pan American Institute of Geography & History. LC 79-105522. 98p. (Span.). 1977. write for info. Instituto Panamericano.
Glosario de terminos nucleares. R. A. Ghelfi et al. 160p. (Span.). write for info. EUDEBA.
Glosario de terminos parasitologicos. O. J. Lombardero. 59p. (Span.). write for info. EUDEBA.
Glosario de voces Ibericas y Latinas. Francisco J. Simonet. 628p. (Span. & Arabic.). 18.00 (113-5). Intl Bk Ctr.
Glosario de voces ibericas y latinas: Tomo 1. Francisco J. Simonet. 424p. (Span. & Lat.). 1982. pap. 1500.00 ptas (ISBN 84-363-0545-0). Atlas Edns.
Glosario de voces ibericas y latinas: Tomo 2. Francisco J. Simonet. 425p. (Span. & Lat.). 1982. pap. 1500.00 ptas (ISBN 84-363-0546-9). Atlas Edns.
Glosario de voces ibericas y latinas: Obras completas. Francisco J. Simonet. 849p. (Span. & Lat.). 1982. pap. 3000.00 ptas (ISBN 84-363-0547-7). Atlas Edns.
Glosario de voces indigenas de Venezuela, 4 vols. Lisandro Ajvarado. (Span.). Bs.0.90. Minist Ed Caracas.
Glosario Espanol-Arabe. Fernando Valderrama Martinez. 333p. (Span. & Arabic.). 1980. 300.00 ptas. Albir.
Glosario Espanol-Arabe y Arabe-Espanol. Fernando Valderrama Martinez. 333p. (Span. & Arabic.). 1980. pap. 6.00 ptas. pap. 300.00 ptas. Albir.
Glosario internacional: Ingles-espanol. Marina Orellana. 102p. (Eng. & Span.). 1967. 2.00. Universitaria.
Glossaire Abrege Patois de la Meuse. Henri A. Labourasse. 570p. (Fr.). 1970. 100.00 F. Slatkine.
Glossaire Anglais-Francais de l'industrie petroliere. 36p. (Fr. & Eng.). 1981. pap. 6.50. Imported Bks.
Glossaire Anglais-Francais des Termes Miniers & du Vocabulaire Connexe. (Eng. & Fr.). Can.$1.50. Centre D'edition.
Glossaire Archeologique du Moyen-Age & de la Renaissance, 2 vols. Victor Gay. (Illus., Fr.). 1928. 243.00 F. Kraus.
Glossaire Archeologique du Moyen-Age & de la Renaissance, 2 vols. Victor Gay. (Illus.). 1290p. (Fr.). 1927. 585.00 F. Picard.
Glossaire archeologique du moyer age et de la Renaissance, 2 tomes. Gay. (Fr.). Set. 167.00 (ISBN 0-685-34006-6). French & Eur.
Glossaire Datinois, 3 vols. C. De Landberg & K. V. Zettersteen. 2976p. (Fr.). 1942. 360.00 F. Brill.
Glossaire de Bale, 2 vols. Menahem Banitt. 670p. (Fr.). 1972. fl.128.00. Brill.
Glossaire de la Finance. 284p. (Fr. & Eng.). 1976. 22.50 (ISBN 0-686-57009-X, M-6350). French & Eur.
Glossaire de la Finance. Marcel Lefebvre. 284p. (Fr.). 1976. Can.$15.95. Lemeac.
Glossaire de la Langue d'Oc. Pierre Malvezin. 285p. (Fr.). 1975. 130.00 F. Laffitte Reprints.
Glossaire de la Langue d'Oc. Pierre Malvezin. 285p. (Fr.). 1976. 70.00 F. Slatkine.
Glossaire de la Langue d'OIl. Alphonse Bos. 495p. (Fr.). 1974. 200.00 F. Laffitte Reprints.
Glossaire de la Langue d'OIl. Aphonse Bos. 495p. (Fr.). 1974. 110.00 F. Slatkine.
Glossaire de la Langue Romane, 3 vols. Jean-Baptiste B. De Roquefort. 1915p. (Fr.). 1978. 400.00 F. Slatkine.
Glossaire de la Vallee d'Yeres, 2 vols. Achille Delboulle. 424p. (Fr.). 1969. 75.00 F. Slatkine.
Glossaire de Meteorologie & de Climatologie. Georges O. Villeneuve & Michel G. Ferland. 550p. (Fr.). 1974. DM.20.00. Laval P. U.
Glossaire De Meteorologie et De Climatologie. G. O. Villeneuve & M. G. Ferland. LC 75-501061. 560p. (Fr.). 1974. 29.95 (ISBN 0-686-57246-7, M-6552). French & Eur.
Glossaire de Patois: Lyonnais, Forez & Beaujolais. Jean B. Onofrio. 550p. (Fr.). 1974. 180.00 F. Horvath.
Glossaire de Pedologie. 173p. (Fr.). 1972. 50.00 F. Biosphere.
Glossaire De Psychiatrie. Pierre Marchais. 238p. (Fr.). 1970. 37.50 (ISBN 0-686-57038-3, M-6398). French & Eur.
Glossaire De Psychiatrie. Lise Moor. 196p. (Fr.). 1966. pap. 35.00 (ISBN 0-686-57053-7, M-6417). French & Eur.
Glossaire de Psychiatrie. Lise Moor. 196p. (Fr.). 1966. 76.00 F. Masson.
Glossaire de Termes Litteraires. Wolfgang V. Ruttkowski & R. E. Blake. 68p. (Fr.). 1969. 9.40 F. Francke.
Glossaire de Termes Relatifs aus Pratiques Commerciales Restrictes. 100p. (Fr.). 1965. 6.00 F. O. C. D. E.
Glossaire de Termes Techniques: L'usage des Lecteurs de la Nuit des Temps. rev. ed. Melchior De Vogue & Raymond Oousel. (Illus.). 478p. (Fr.). 1971. 88.00 F. Zodiaque.
Glossaire del Perigord Negre. Pierre Miremont. (Fr.). 1974. 55.00 F. P. Miremont.
Glossaire des Inscriptions Pehlevies et Parthes. Phillipe Gignoux. (Fr.). 1972. 17.50x (ISBN 0-8002-1459-5). Intl Pubns Serv.
Glossaire des mots Espagnols derives de l'Arabe. R. Dozy. 426p. (Arabic & Fr.). 20.00 (105-4). Intl Bk Ctr.
Glossaire des Mots Espagnols et Portugais Derives de L'arabe. R. Dozy. (Span., Port. & Arabic.). 1974. 20.00x (ISBN 0-86685-105-4). Intl Bk Ctr.
Glossaire des Patois & des Parlers de l'Aunis & de la Saintonge, 5 vols. Georges Musset. 2612p. (Fr.). 1977. 950.00 F. Lafitte Repr.
Glossaire des Patois de la Suisse Romande. (Fr.). 1978. 30.00 F. Droz.
Glossaire des Patois Franco-Provencaux. Antonin Duraffour. (Illus.). 758p. (Fr.). 447.00 F. CNRS.
Glossaire des Patois Franco-Provencaux. Antonin Duraffour. (Illus.). 758p. (Fr.). 1969. 320.40 F. CNRS.
Glossaire des Principaux Termes Geographiques & Logiques Sahariens. Robert Capot-Rey & Bernard Blaudin De The. (Illus.). 84p. (Fr.). 1963. 10.00 F. Sahariennes Inst. Rech.
Glossaire des Rues de Dunkerque. Jean Foort. (Illus.). 66p. (Fr.). 1976. 40.00 F. Foort.
Glossaire des Termes & Symboles en Matiere de Conversion Thermoelectronique. 90p. (Fr.). 1971. 23.00 F. O. C. D. E.
Glossaire des Termes d'usage Courant en Commande Numerique. 28p. (Fr.). 16.00 F. Ste. Publications Mecaniques.
Glossaire des Vieux Parlers du Departement de la Vilenne. Robert Mineau & Lucien Racinoux. (Illus.). 497p. (Fr.). 1975. 165.00 F. Quiniste.
Glossaire d'histopathologia des Tumeurs Humaines. Remi Gerard-Marchant. (Illus.). 144p. (Fr.). 1971. 70.00 F. Masson & Cie.
Glossaire Dictionnaire des Locutions Obscures & des Mots Vieillis: Recontrent dans les Oeuvres de Calvin. Jean Calvin. 45p. (Fr.). 1968. 10.00 F. Slatkine.
Glossaire d'organes de Transmission, 1: Les Engrenages Allemand-Espagnol-Francais-Anglais-Italien-Neerlandais-Suedois-Finnois. 116p. (Ger. , Span. , Fr. , Eng. , Ital. , Dutch, Swedish & Finnish.). 100.00 F. Maison Dictionnaire.
Glossaire du Centre de la France, 2 vols. Le Comte Jaubert. 915p. (Fr.). 1970. 190.00 F. Slatkine.
Glossaire du Centre de la France, 2 vols. Hippolyte-Francois Jaubert. 915p. (Fr.). 1970. 190.00 F. Slatkine.
Glossaire du Droit Francais. Francois Ragueau. 616p. (Fr.). 1969. 150.00 F. Slatkine.
Glossaire du Morvan. Eugene De Chambure. Pref. by Gerard Taverdet. LC 80-463586. xxii, 966p. (Fr.). 1978. 350.00 F. Lafitte Repr.
Glossaire du Parler de Piechatel. Georges Dottin & J. Langouet. 373p. (Fr.). 1970. 70.00 F. Slatkine.
Glossaire du Parler Francais au Canada. Societe du Paler Francais au Canada. LC 68-143461. 710p. (Fr.). 1968. 25.00 (ISBN 0-686-57223-8, M-6521). French & Eur.
Glossaire du Parler Francais au Canada. Societe du Parler Francais au Canada. 710p. (Fr.). 1968. Can.$18.00. Laval P. U.
Glossaire du Patois de Chatenois avec Vocables des Autres: Localites du Territoire de Belfort & des Environs. Auguste Vautherin. 548p. (Fr.). 1970. 95.00 F. Slatkine.
Glossaire du Patois de la Foret de Clairvaux. Alphonse Baudouin. 342p. (Fr.). 1970. 60.00 F. Slatkine.
Glossaire du Patois de la Suisse Romande. Philippe Cyriaque Bridel & Louis Favrat. 565p. (Fr.). 1970. 100.00 F. Slatkine.
Glossaire du Patois Poitavin. Charles C. Lalanne. 303p. (Fr.). 1976. 105.00 F. Lafitte Repr.
Glossaire du Patois Thierachien. Paul Devigne. 240p. (Fr.). 1978. 60.00 F. Ste. Linguistique Picarde.
Glossaire du Pays Biaiaois. Adrien Thibault. 387p. (Fr.). 1970. 65.00 F. Slatkine.
Glossaire du Traitement Thermique. Association Technique de Traitement Thermique. LC 77-570276. 142p. (Fr.). 1976. 33.00 F (ISBN 2-85330-022-6). Pyc.
Glossaire Etymologique & Comparatif du Patois Picard Ancien & Moderne. Jules Corblet. 645p. (Fr.). 140.00 F. Slatkine.
Glossaire Etymologique & Historique des Patois & des Parlers de l'Anjou, 2 vols. A. J. Verrier & Rene Onillon. 1157p. (Fr.). 1970. 200.00 F. Slatkine.
Glossaire Europeen de Terminologe Juridique et Administrative: Local Government, No. 14. (Ger, & Eng.). write for info. (M-9481). French & Eur.
Glossaire Europeen de Terminologie Juridique & Administrative: No. 15 Termes de Droit Anglais des Obligations, Anglais-Francais. 36p. (Eng. & Fr.). Date not set. pap. 9.95 (ISBN 0-686-97408-5, M-9482). French & Eur.
Glossaire Europeen de Terminologie Juridique & Administrative, 1. Institut International de Terminologie Juridique & Administrative. 64p. (Fr.). 1969. 15.00 F. Bordas-Dunod.
Glossaire Europeen de Terminologie Juridique & Administrative, 2. 68p. (Fr.). 1969. 15.00 F. Bordas-Dunod.
Glossaire Europeen de Terminologie Juridique & Administrative, 3. Institut International de Terminologie Juridique & Administrative. 48p. (Fr.). 1969. 15.00 F. Bordas-Dunod.

Glossaire Europeen de Terminologie Juridique & Administrative, 5. Institut International de Terminologie Juridique & Administrative. 72p. (Fr.). 1969. 15.00 F. Bordas-Dunod.

Glossaire Europeen de Terminologie Juridique & Administrative, 6. Institut International de Terminologie Juridique & Administrative. 64p. (Fr.). 1969. 15.00 F. Bordas-Dunod.

Glossaire Europeen de Terminologie Juridique & Administrative, 8. Institut International de Terminologie Juridique & Administrative. 64p. (Fr.). 1969. 15.00 F. Bordas-Dunod.

Glossaire Europeen de Terminologie Juridque et Administrative. 127p. (Ger. & Eng.). 1973. pap. 14.95 (ISBN 3-468-49068-2, M-9485). French & Eur.

Glossaire Europeen de Terminologie Juridique et Administrative, No. 5. (Organization Administrative). (Fr.). write for info. (M-9601). French & Eur.

Glossaire Europeen de Terminologie Juridique et Administrative: Amenagement du Territiore, No 9. (Fr. & Ger.). write for info. (M-9605). French & Eur.

Glossaire Europeen de Terminologie Juridique et Administrative: Budget, No. 7. (Ger. & Fr.). write for info. (M-9603). French & Eur.

Glossaire Europeen de Terminologie Juridique et Administrative. Budgeting & Auditing. German-Italian, No. 26. 144p. (Ger. & Ital.). 1980. pap. 19.95 (ISBN 3-468-49076-3, M-9493). French & Eur.

Glossaire Europeen de Terminologie Juridique et Administrative: Civil Service Organizations, No. 22. 83p. (Ger. & Eng.). 1976. pap. 14.95 (ISBN 0-686-92436-3, M-9489). French & Eur.

Glossaire Europeen de Terminologie Juridique et Administrative: Driot Administratif, No. 4. (Procedure Contentieuses). (Ger. & Fr.). write for info. (M-9499). French & Eur.

Glossaire Europeen de Terminologie Juridiqe et Administrative: Droits des Collectivites Locales, No. 6. (Ger. & Fr.). write for info. (M-96902). French & Eur.

Glossaire Europeen de Terminologie Juridique et Administrative: Driot de al Fonction Publique, No. 8. (Ger. & Fr.). write for info. (M-9604). French & Eur.

Glossaire Europeen de Terminologie Juridique et Administrative: Droit du Mariage, No. 19. 96p. (Ger. & Fr.). 1973. pap. 14.95 (ISBN 0-686-92449-5, M-9486). French & Eur.

Glossaire Europeen de Terminologie Juridique et Administrative: Droits D'Etablissement, No. 21. 146p. (Ger. & Fr.). 1976. pap. 18.95 (ISBN 0-686-92444-4, M-9488). French & Eur.

Glossaire Europeen de Terminologie Juridique et Administrative: Eductions et Enseignment, No. 23. 168p. (Ger. & Fr.). pap. 18.95 (ISBN 0-686-92507-6, M-9490). French & Eur.

Glossaire Europeen de Terminologie Juridique et Administrative: Environment Policy Protection & Management of the Environment, No. 29. 160p. (Ger. & Eng.). pap. 22.50 (ISBN 0-686-92511-4, M-9496). French & Eur.

Glossaire Europeen de Terminologie Juridique et Administrative: Jeunesse, No. 11. (Allemand-Francais Ser.). 109p. (Ger. & Fr.). 1972. pap. 12.95 (ISBN 0-686-92456-8, M-9478). French & Eur.

Glossaire Europeen de Terminologie Juridique et Administrative: Local Government, No. 20. 96p. (Ger. & Ital.). 1975. pap. 14.95 (ISBN 0-686-92446-0). French & Eur.

Glossaire Europeen de Terminologie Juridique et Administrative: Law of Establishment, No. 13. 100p. (Fr.). 1973. pap. 12.95 (ISBN 0-686-92453-3, M-9480). French & Eur.

Glossaire Europeen de Terminologie Juridique et Administrative. Motor, Insurance, German-Italian, No. 27. 152p. (Ger. & Ital.). 1980. pap. 19.95 (ISBN 0-686-97437-9, M-9494). French & Eur.

Glossaire Europeen de Terminologie Juridique et Administrative: Marches Publics, No. 10. 72p. (Ger. & Fr.). 1972. pap. 12.95 (ISBN 0-686-92459-2, M-9479). French & Eur.

Glossaire Europeen de Terminologie Juridique et Administrative. Office Terminology Procedure. German-Italina, No. 24. 79p. (Ger. & Ital.). 1979. pap. 14.95 (ISBN 3-468-49074-7, M-9491). French & Eur.

Glossaire Europeen de Terminologie Juridique et Administrative: Renumeration, No. 3. (Ger. & Fr.). write for info. (M-9498). French & Eur.

Glossaire Europeen de Terminologie Juridique et Administrative: Regional Policy, Ger. & Ital. 111p. (Fr.). write for info. (M-9484). French & Eur.

Glossaire Europeen de Terminologie Juridique et Administrative: Terminologie Administrative et Secretariat, No. 1. (Ger. & Fr.). write for info. (M-9495). French & Eur.

Glossaire Europeen de Terminologie Juridique et Administrative: Terminologie de Reunions, No. 2. (Ger, & Ital.). write for info. (M-9497). French & Eur.

Glossaire Europeen en Quatre Langues: Francais-Italien-Allemand-Anglais. (Fr. , Ital. , Ger. & Eng.). 1971. 44.00 F. L. G. D. J.

Glossaire Francais du Moyen Age: L'usage de l'archeologue & de l'amateur des Arts. Leon De Laborde. 562p. (Fr.). 1975. 110.00 F. Slatkine.

Glossaire Franco-Canadien. Oscar Dunn. LC 77-552917. 196p. (Fr.). 1976. Can.$9.95 (ISBN 0-7746-6779-6). Univ Laval.

Glossaire Franco-Canadien: Vocabulaire de Locutions Vicieuses Usitees au Canada. Oscar Dunn. 198p. (Fr.). 1976. 9.75 F. Laval P. U.

Glossaire Hebreu-Francais. Mayer Lambert & Louis Brandin. 315p. (Hebrew & Fr.). 1975. 75.00 F. Slatkine.

Glossaire Hebreu-Francais du XIIIe. Siecle. Mayer Lambert & Louis Brandin. 315p. (Hebrew & Fr.). 1977. 75.00 F. Slatkine.

Glossaire International d'Hydrologie. 393p. (Fr.). 1974. pap. 29.95 (ISBN 0-686-57304-8, M-6281). French & Eur.

Glossaire International d'hydrologie. 393p. (Fr.). 1974. 64.00 F. Unesco.

Glossaire: Mots sans Memoire. Michel Leirie. 160p. (Fr.). 1969. 22.00 F. Gallimard.

Glossaire Moyen-Breton, 2 vols. Emile Ernault. 870p. (Fr.). 175.00 F. Slatkine.

Glossaire Moyen-Breton, 2 vols. Emile Jean M. Ernault. LC 77-553414. xxviii, 833p. (Fr.). 1976. 290.00 F. Lafitte Repr.

Glossaire Philologique de la Geste de Liege. Auguste Scheler. 319p. (Fr.). 100.00 F. Slatkine.

Glossaire Picard du Parler de Long. J. B. Carton. (Fr.). 15.00 F. Eklitra.

Glossaire sur la T. V. A. Becker. (Fr.). 327.00 F. Office Intern. Librairie.

Glossar & Erlaeuterungen zur Grammatik Deutsch-Englisch. 72p. (Ger. & Eng.). 1983. 3.25. M Rosenberg.

Glossar der Heute Chinesischen Vogelnamen. Alfred Hoffmann. LC 75-516973. xvi, 366p. (Ger. & Chinese.). 1975. DM.52.00 (ISBN 3-447-01693-0). Harrassowitz.

Glossar der Jugendarbeit: Deutsch Jugend & Ihr Soziales Umfeld. Deutsch-Franz Jugendwerk. LC 80-469662. (Illus.). 147p. (Ger. & Fr.). 1979. DM.15.80 (ISBN 3-472-52033-7). H Luchterhand.

Glossar Deutsch-Englisch. 50p. (Ger. & Eng.). 1983. pap. 2.90. M Rosenberg.

Glossar Deutsch-Englisch. 68p. (Ger. & Eng.). pap. 4.10. M Rosenberg.

Glossar Deutsch-Englisch. 46p. (Ger. & Eng.). pap. 3.50. M Rosenberg.

Glossar Englisch. (Eng.). 1983. 2.50. M Rosenberg.

Glossar zur Fruehmittelalterlichen Geschichte im Oestlichen Europa. Norbert Otto & Dieter Wojtecki. 64p. (Ger.). 1975. DM.32.00 (ISBN 3-515-01977-4). Buch Vertrieb.

Glossar zur Fruehmittelalterlichen Geschichte im Oestlichen Europa: Lfg 2, Quellensiglenverzeichnis, Aba-Alania. 64p. (Ger.). 1974. DM.32.00 (ISBN 3-515-01786-0). Buch Vertrieb.

Glossar zur Fruehmittelalterlichen Geschichte im Oestlichen Europa: Lfg 3, Alanorum Montes-Antes. 64p. (Ger.). 1974. DM.32.00 (ISBN 3-515-01950-2). Buch Vertrieb.

Glossar zur Fruehmittelalterlichen Geschichte im Oestlichen Europa: Lfg 5, Atto-Avari. 64p. (Ger.). 1975. DM.32.00 (ISBN 3-515-02026-8). Buch Vertrieb.

Glossar zur Fruehmittelalterlichen Geschichte im Oestlichen Europa: Lfg 6, Avari (Arabes)-Baioaria. 64p. (Ger.). 1976. DM.32.00 (ISBN 3-515-02346-1). Buch Vertrieb.

Glossar zur Fruehmittelalterlichen Geschichte im Oestlichen Europa: Lfg 1, Einleitung, Abkuerzungen & Literatursiglenverzeichnis. 64p. (Ger.). 1974. DM.32.00 (ISBN 3-515-01982-0). Buch Vertrieb.

Glossar zur Fruehmittelalterlichen Geschichte im Oestlichen Europa: Lfg 7, Baioariae Marcha-Behin Redaktion. Norbert Otto & Dieter Wojtecki. 64p. (Ger.). 1976. DM.32.00 (ISBN 3-515-02479-4). Buch Vertrieb.

Glossari Ilustrat. Centre Culturel Occitan Pais Nissart. (Illus.). 16p. (Fr.). 8.00 F. Centre Cult. Pais Nissart.

Glossario al milanese di Bonvesin. Fabio Marri. 220p. (Ital.). 1977. L.6700.00. Patron.

Glossario degli antichi portolani italiani. Henry Kahane et al. (Illus.). 134p. (Ital.). 1968. L.8000.00. Olschki.

Glossario della Elabarione dei Dati: Inglese-Italiano, Italiono-Inglese. IBM. 221p. (Eng. & Ital.). 1978. pap. 35.00 (ISBN 0-686-92478-9, M-9294). French & Eur.

Glossario di immunologia. G. S. Del Giacco. 142p. (Ital.). 1975. L.8000.00. Minerva Medica.

Glossario di medicina nucleare. G. Pompili. 288p. (Ital.). 1961. L.7000.00. Minerva Medica.

Glossario di tecnologia meccanica. Umberto Mezzera. 90p. (Ital.). 1967. L.2500.00. Etas Libri.

Glossario geografico. Mario Riccardi. (Ital.). L.3500.00 (ISBN 88-7006-903-6). Japadre.

Glossario italiano tessile in cinque lingue. Giuseppe Suppa. (Illus.). 900p. (Ital.). 1975. L.15000.00. Tec Tessile.

Glossario latino-emiliano. Pietro Sella. xxiv, 407p. (Ital.). 1973. L.11000.00 (ISBN 88-210-0415-5). Biblio Apost.

Glossario Luso-Asiatico, 2 Vol. Sebastiao R. Dalgado. (Romanistik in Geschicte und Geggenwart 11). 580p. (Ger.). 1982. Repr. of 1921 ed. lib. bdg. 160.00 (ISBN 3-87118-479-9, Pub. by Helmut Buske Verlag Hamburg). Benjamins North Am.

Glossario storico popolare piemontese. U. Rosa. 118p. (Ital.). L.4800.00. Forni.

Glossarium ad Scriptores Mediae & Infimae Graecitatis. Charles D. Du Cange. 1280p. (Lat.). 1958. S.1500.00. Akad Druck.

Glossarium Ad Scriptores Mediae et Infimae Graecitatis. Charles Du Fresne DuCange. LC 60-21441. 1280p. (Lat.). 1958. Repr. of 1688 ed. 135.00x (ISBN 0-8002-1276-2). Intl Pubns Serv.

Glossarium Amorum: Lfg 1, Schutzwaffen. Ed. by Hugo Schneider et al. (Ger.). DM.420.00 (ISBN 3-201-00262-3). Verlag der Buchhaendler-Vereinigung GmbH.

Glossarium Armorum: Bd 6 Texthefte in Deutsch, Englisch, Franzoesisch, Italienisch, Daenisch, Tschechisch. Ed. by Ortwin Gamber et al. (Ger., Eng., Fr., Ital., Danish & Czech.). DM.420.00. Verlag der Buchhaendler-Vereinigung GmbH.

Glossarium Artis: Deutsch-Franzoesisches Woerterbuch zur Kunst. Ed. by Rudolf Huber & Renate Rieth. (Ger. & Fr.). write for info. Max Niemeyer.

Glossarium Artis: Fasz 1, Burgen & Feste Plaetze. Ed. by Rudolf Huber & Renate Rieth. 200p. (Ger.). 1977. DM.35.00 (ISBN 3-484-60053-5). Max Niemeyer.

Glossarium Artis: Fasz 2, Liturgische Geraete-Objets Liturgiques. Ed. by Rudolf Huber & Renate Rieth. 160p. (Ger.). 1972. DM.35.00 (ISBN 3-484-60047-0). Max Niemeyer.

Glossarium Artis: Fasz 3, Bogen & Arkaden-Arcs et Arcades. Ed. by Rudolf Huber & Renate Rieth. 167p. (Ger.). 1973. DM.35.00 (ISBN 3-484-60048-9). Max Niemeyer.

Glossarium Artis: Fasz 4, Paramente & Buecher der Christlichen Kirchen. Ed. by Rudolf Huber & Renate Rieth. 203p. (Ger.). DM.35.00 (ISBN 3-484-60049-7). Max Niemeyer.

Glossarium Artis: Fasz 6, Gewoelbe & Kuppeln-Voutes et Coupoles. Ed. by Rudolf Huber & Renate Rieth. 250p. (Ger.). 1974. DM.35.00 (ISBN 3-484-60051-9). Niemeyer.

Glossarium Harlemense: Circa 1440. (Monumenta Lexicographica Neelandica, Ser. I: Vol. I). 422p. 1973. text ed. 120.00x (ISBN 0-686-27746-5). Mouton.

Glossarium van Zeventiende-Eeuws Nederlands. P. Sterkenburg. LC 76-505834. lix, 152p. (Dutch.). 1975. fl.25.00 (ISBN 9-00181-210-4). Tjeenk Willinik.

Glossary. 5.00; members free. Word Processing.

Glossary. LC 78-107662. (Illus.). iv, 55p. (Eng.). 1978. write for info. (ISBN 0-87588-142-4). United Federation Doll Clubs.

Glossary. Institute of Signage Research. 7.50 (ISR); 5.00, members. Natl Elec Sign.

Glossary & Genetics & Cytogenetics. 4th rev. ed. R. Rieger et al. LC 76-16183. (Illus.). 1976. soft cover 16.00 (ISBN 3-540-07668-9). Springer-Verlag.

Glossary & Tables for Statistical Quality Control. American Society for Quality Control. 100p. 9.20 (66); members 7.75. Am Soc QC.

Glossary for High Speed Surface Craft. Society of Naval Architects & Marine Engineers. 16p. 1974. 9.00 (R-17); members 6.00. Soc Naval Arch.

Glossary for Radiologic Technologists. Patricia A. Myers. LC 80-20917. 206p. 1981. 28.50 (ISBN 0-03-057584-2). Praeger.

Glossary for the Gas Industry. rev. ed. American Gas Association. 83p. 1975. pap. 3.50 (F50000). Am Gas Assn.

Glossary for the Study of English. Lemon. E3.00. Oxford U Pr.

Glossary Index for a Course in Miracles. Ken Wapnick. 255p. 1982. 15.00 (ISBN 0-942494-26-1). Coleman Graphics.

Glossary of a Thousand & One Terms Used in Conchology. Winifred H. Arnold. 1965. 4.50 (ISBN 0-913792-05-5). Shell Cab.

Glossary of Agricultural Terms. H. Miyayama et al. 261p. (Eng. & Japanese.). 1975. 39.95 (ISBN 0-686-92558-0, M-9345). French & Eur.

Glossary of Agricultural Terms, English-Bengali. Jack A. Dabbs. LC 79-626525. (Eng. & Bengali.). 1969. 3.00 (ISBN 0-911494-05-7). Dabbs.

Glossary of American Technical Linguistic Usage, 1925-1950. 3rd ed. Eric L. Hamp. 1966. 10.50x (ISBN 0-8002-1460-9). Intl Pubns Serv.

Glossary of Anesthesia. Sanford L. Klein. 1984. pap. text ed. price not set (ISBN 0-87488-973-1). Med Exam.

Glossary of Applied Management & Financial Statistics. E. J. Broster. 243p. 1974. 29.50x (ISBN 0-8448-0608-0). Crane-Russak Co.

Glossary of Arms Control Terms. Arms Control Association. free. Arms Control.

Glossary of Art, Architecture, & Design Since 1945. 2nd ed. John A. Walker. 1977. 19.50 (ISBN 0-208-01543-4, Linnet). Shoe String.

Glossary of Astronomy & Astrophysics. 2nd, rev. & enl. ed. Ed. by Jeanne Hopkins. LC 80-5226. (Phoenix Ser.). x, 196p. 1982. pap. 10.00 (ISBN 0-226-35169-6). U of Chicago Pr.

Glossary of Astronomy & Astrophysics. rev. ed. Ed. by Jeanne Hopkins. LC 80-5226. 224p. 1980. lib. bdg. 17.50x (ISBN 0-226-35171-8). U of Chicago Pr.

Glossary of Automated Text Processing Terms. Society for Technical Communication. 18p. 8.00; members 5.00. Soc Tech Comm.

Glossary of Automatic Identification Terms. Material Handling Institute. free (V-13). Material Handling.

Glossary of Automotive Electronic Terms. Society of Automotive Engineers. 8p. 5.00 (ISBN 0-89883-392-2, J1213); members 4.00. Soc Auto Engineers.

Glossary of Automotive Terminology: French-English English-French. Chrysler Corporation. 230p. (Fr. & Eng.). 1977. 9.95 (ISBN 0-89883-195-4, SP-423). members 7.95. Soc Auto Engineers.

Glossary of Automotive Terminology: Spanish-English English-Spanish. Chrysler Corporation. 380p. (Span. & Eng.). 1978. 12.50 (ISBN 0-89883-208-X, SP-436); members 9.75. Soc Auto Engineers.

Glossary of Botanic Terms, with Their Derivation & Accent. 4th rev. ed. Benjamin D. Jackson. 1960. Repr. of 1928 ed. 27.50x (ISBN 0-02-847110-5). Hafner.

Glossary of Cargo Handling Terms. A. G. Course & R. B. Oram. 1981. 12.00x (ISBN 0-85174-080-4, Pub. by Nautical England). State Mutual Bk.

Glossary of Cargo Handling Terms. 2nd ed. A. G. Course & R. B. Oram. 96p. 1974. pap. 7.50x (ISBN 0-85174-080-4). Sheridan.

Glossary of Chemical Terms. Clifford Hampel & Gessner Hawley. 300p. 1976. text ed. 17.95x (ISBN 0-442-23238-1); pap. text ed. 9.95x (ISBN 0-442-23243-8). Van Nos Reinhold.

Glossary of Chemical Terms. 2nd ed. Clifford A. Hampel & Gessner G. Hawley. 1982. text ed. 19.95 (ISBN 0-442-23871-1). Van Nos Reinhold.

Glossary of Chinese Archaeology. Zhang Xinglian. Ed. by Zhao Shuhan. 199p. (Orig., Chinese & Eng.). 1983. 4.95 (ISBN 0-8351-1210-1); pap. 3.95 (ISBN 0-8351-1082-6). China Bks.

Glossary of Clinical Chemistry Terms. P. Haisman & B. R. Muller. 133p. 1974. 13.95 (ISBN 0-407-72700-0). Butterworth.

Glossary of Color Terms. Ed. by Federation of Societies for Coatings Technology, Definitions Committee. 96p. 6.00 (ISBN 0-686-95498-X). Fed Soc Coat Tech.

Glossary of Commonly Used Terms. Institute of Industrial Launderers. 12.00 (ILP-TE-01); members 8.00. Inst Indus Launderer.

Glossary of Computer Controlled Environmental Testing Terminology. Institute of Environmental Science. 27p. non-member 3.00 (ISBN 0-915414-53-8); member 2.40; 2.00, for shipping & handling. Inst Environ Sci.

Glossary of Computer Controlled Environmental Testing Terminology. Technical Committee on Computer Controlled Environmental Testing of the Inst. of Environ. Sciences. LC 62-38584. 27p. 1977. pap. text ed. 3.00 (ISBN 0-915414-53-8). Inst Environ Sci.

Glossary of Conference Terms: Arabic, French, English. 117p. (Arabic, Fr. , Span. & Eng.). 1974. pap. 22.50 (ISBN 92-3-601150-0, U993, UNESCO). Unipub.

Glossary of Conference Terms, English, French, Arabic. (Eng. , Fr. & Arabic.). 1978. pap. 6.00 (ISBN 92-3-101566-4, U840, UNESCO). Unipub.

Glossary of Conference Terms: English, French, Arabic, 3 vols. in 1. 91p. (Eng. , Fr. & Arabic.). 1980. pap. 22.50 (ISBN 92-3-001567-9, U-993, UNESCO). Unipub.

Glossary of Construction Industry Terms. The American Institute of Architects. pap. 2.00 (ISBN 0-913962-18-X). Am Inst Arch.

Glossary of Costume in England, Vol. 11. Fredrick W. Fairholt. (Illus.). 1976. Repr. write for info. (ISBN 0-7158-1142-8). Charles River Bks.

Glossary of Current Chinese-English Phrases. 594p. (Chinese & Eng.). 1972. 9.95 (ISBN 0-8351-0600-4). China Bks.

Glossary of Current Terminology. Lawrence Marwick. LC 79-12383. 188p. (Eng. & Hebrew.). 1980. write for info. (ISBN 0-8444-0308-3). Govt Print.

Glossary of Decorating Terminology. Society of Glass Decorations. (Publications). 1982. 50.00; 13.00, members. Soc Glass Decorators.

Glossary of Department of Defense Configuration Management Terminology & Definitions. Electrical Generating Systems Marketing Association. 1972. 3.00 (CMTD1); members 1.25. Elec Gen Syst.

Glossary of Depreciation Terms. 44p. 1980. 3.50. NARUC.

Glossary of Dialectal Place-Nomenclature. Robert C. Hope. LC 68-58761. 1968. Repr. of 1883 ed. 30.00x (ISBN 0-8103-3530-1). Gale.

Glossary of Diving & Hyperbaric Terms. Undersea Medical Society, Inc. 2.50. Undersea Med.

Glossary of Economic Terms. Howard Wilson. 1964. pap. 1.00 (ISBN 0-910022-22-4). ARA.

Glossary of Economics. F. Clifford Vaughn. (Eng., Fr., Ger. & Rus.). 1966. 24.50 (ISBN 0-444-40129-6). Elsevier.

Glossary of Educational Terms: Usage in Five English Speaking Countries. W. G. Walker et al. 1973. 12.00x (ISBN 0-7022-0802-7). U of Queensland Pr.

Glossary of Electric Utility Terms. Edison Electric Institute. 86p. 1970. 1.25 (01704000). Edison Electric.

Glossary of EMG Terms. American Association of Electromyography & Electrodiagnosis. 5.00. Am Assn Electromyography.

Glossary of Employment & Industry. G. Logie. (International Planning Glossaries Ser.: Vol. 3). 1982. 57.50 (ISBN 0-444-42064-9). Elsevier.

Glossary of English & German Management Terms. James Coveney. (English for Special Purposes Bk.). (Eng. & Ger.). 1977. pap. text ed. 6.95x (ISBN 0-582-55525-6). Longman.

Glossary of English & Russian Computer & Automated Control Systems Terminology. Ed. by Irene Agnew. (Eng. & Rus.). 1978. soft covers 15.00 (ISBN 0-686-31723-8). Agnew Tech-Tran.

Glossary of English Equivalents of Terms Commonly Used in French Auctions, Catalogues, & Stamp Trade. R. G. Stone et al. (Fr. & Eng.). 2.00. France & Col Philatelist.

Glossary of Entomology. J. R. dela Torre-Bueno. 1973. 14.00 (ISBN 0-934454-45-0). Lubrecht & Cramer.

Glossary of Environmental Terms (Terrestrial) U. S. Army Natick Laboratories. LC 73-2851. 149p. 1973. Repr. of 1968 ed. 34.00x (ISBN 0-8103-3277-9). Gale.

Glossary of Faulkner's South. Calvin S. Brown. LC 75-43308. (Illus.). 1976. 24.00x (ISBN 0-300-01944-0); pap. 6.95x (ISBN 0-300-02240-9). Yale U Pr.

Glossary of Fiber Optics Terms. (Eng. , Fr , Span. & Ger.). 35.00 (ISBN 0-686-32959-7). Info Gatekeepers.

Glossary of Fiduciary Terms. 1968. 2.00 (ISBN 0-89982-137-5, 360300); 1-24 copies 6.00 ea.; 25-99 copies 5.25 ea.; over 100 copies 4.50 ea. Am Bankers.

Glossary of Film Terms. rev. 1979 ed. Mercer. (UFVA Monograph Ser.: No. 2). 92p. 1978. 5.00. Univ Film & Video.

Glossary of Fish Health Terms. Ed. by G. Post. American Fisheries Society, Fish Health Section. 48p. 1977. 5.00. Am Fisheries Soc.

Glossary of French & English Management Terms. Coveney & Moore. 146p. (Fr. & Eng.). 1972. pap. 8.50 pocket size. Imported Bks.

Glossary of French & English Management Terms. Coveney & Moore. xii, 146p. (Fr. & Eng.). E3.50. Longman.

Glossary of French & English Management Terms. Ed. by James Coveney & Shelia J. Moore. (English for Special Purposes Bk.). 158p. (Fr. & Eng.). 1972. pap. text ed. 6.95x (ISBN 0-582-55502-7). Longman.

Glossary of French & English Management Terms. (Fr. & Eng.). 6.95. Longman.

Glossary of Genetics. Francoise Biass-Ducroux. (Eng., Fr., Span., Ital., Ger. & Rus.). 1970. 72.50 (ISBN 0-444-40712-X). Elsevier.

Glossary of Geographical & Topographical Terms. Alexander Knox. LC 68-30592. 1968. Repr. of 1904 ed. 27.00 (ISBN 0-8103-3236-1). Gale.

Glossary of Geology. 2nd ed. Ed. by Robert L. Bates & Julia A. Jackson. LC 79-57360. 749p. 1980. 60.00 (ISBN 0-913312-15-0). Am Geol.

Glossary of Geology. M. Gary et al. 1717p. (Eng. & Rus.). 1977. 75.00 (ISBN 0-686-92556-4, M-9113). French & Eur.

Glossary of German & English Management Terms. James Coveny & Christina Degens. (Ger. & Eng.). pap. 6.95. Longman.

Glossary of German & English Management Terms. (Ger. & Eng.). pap. 8.50. Imported Bks.

Glossary of Graphics & Technical Art Terms. Society for Technical Communication. 24p. 8.00; members 5.00. Soc Tech Comm.

Glossary of Group & Family Therapy. Edward L. Pinney, Jr. & Samuel Slipp. LC 82-4193. 120p. 1982. 15.00 (ISBN 0-87630-300-9). Brunner-Mazel.

Glossary of Hematological & Seriological Terms. P. Samson. (Illus.). 128p. 1973. text ed. 13.95 (ISBN 0-407-72720-5). Butterworth.

Glossary of Histopathological Terms. J. Law & H. J. Oliver. (Illus.). 128p. 1972. text ed. 13.95 (ISBN 0-407-72730-2). Butterworth.

Glossary of Hospital Terms. 2nd rev. ed. American Medical Record Association. 128p. 1974. 5.75 (ISBN 0-686-68577-6, 14911). Healthcare Fin Man Assn.

Glossary of Hospital Terms. American Medical Record Association. 111p. 7.75 (1001P); members 6.75. Am Med Record Assn.

Glossary of Immunological Terms. W. J. Halliday. 102p. 1971. 13.95 (ISBN 0-407-72740-X). Butterworth.

Glossary of Indexing Terms. Brian W. Buchanan. 144p. 1976. 14.00 (ISBN 0-208-01377-6, Linnet). Shoe String.

Glossary of Indian Figures of Speech. Edwin Gerow. (Publications in Near & Middle East Ser. A: No. 16). 436p. 1971. text ed. 48.00x (ISBN 90-2791-759-0). Mouton.

Glossary of Inland Fishery Terms. (EIFAC Occasional Papers: No. 12). 129p. 1979. pap. 9.50 (ISBN 92-5-000724-8, F1558, FAO). Unipub.

Glossary of Insurance Terms. Thomas E. Green & Robert W. Osler. 240p. 1980. pap. text ed. 11.95 (ISBN 0-930868-06-4). Merritt Co.

Glossary of International Treaties. Y. Renoux & J. Yates. (Eng., Fr., Span., Ital., Dutch & Rus.). 1970. 28.00 (ISBN 0-444-40813-4). Elsevier.

Glossary of Japanese Patent Law Terms: Japanese-English-Japanese. Thomas Wilds. LC 76-372712. 1979. pap. 30.00x (ISBN 0-930624-01-7). Marlin.

Glossary of Legal Terminology: An Aid to Geneologists. American Association for State & Local History. 1.00 (55); members 0.75. AASLH.

Glossary of Linguistic Terminology. Mario A. Pei. LC 66-21013. 299p. 1966. 30.00x (ISBN 0-231-03012-6). Columbia U Pr.

Glossary of Linguistics. N. Arunabharathi. LC 77-900957. xi, 82p. (Eng. & Tamil.). 1976. Rs.6.00. Tamil Nuulagam.

Glossary of Literary Terms. 4th ed. M. H. Abrams. LC 80-26095. 220p. 1981. pap. text ed. 10.95 (ISBN 0-03-054166-2, HoltC). HR&W.

Glossary of Literature & Composition. rev ed. Arnold Lazarus & H. Wendell Smith. 326p. (Orig.). 1983. pap. 13.00 (ISBN 0-8141-1852-6, 18526); pap. 11.50 members. NCTE.

Glossary of Liturgical & Ecclesiastical Terms. Frederick G. Lee. LC 76-174069. (Tower Bks). (Illus.). xl, 452p. 1972. Repr. of 1877 ed. 38.00x (ISBN 0-8103-3949-8). Gale.

Glossary of Marine Technology Terms. Institute of Marine Engineers. 178p. 1980. pap. 15.00x (ISBN 0-434-90840-1). Sheridan.

Glossary of Marine Technology Terms. Institute of Marine Engineers. 256p. 1980. 35.00x (Pub. by Heinemann England). State Mutual Bk.

Glossary of Marketing Terms. 2nd ed. Norman A. Hart & John Stapleton. 156p. 1981. 30.00x (ISBN 0-434-91861-X, Pub. by Heinemann England). State Mutual Bk.

Glossary of Marketing Terms. Norman A. Hart & John Stapleton. 1981. pap. 11.50 (ISBN 0-434-91861-X, Pub. by W Heinemann England). David & Charles.

Glossary of Mechanical Press Terms: B5.49-1977. American Society of Mechanical Engineers. 3.50 (M00090); members 2.80. ASME.

Glossary of Mediaeval Terms of Business, 1200-1600. Florence Edler. 1934. 32.00 (ISBN 0-527-01690-X). Kraus Repr.

Glossary of Mental Disorders & Guide to Their Classification - for Use in Conjunction with the International Classification of Diseases. 8th rev. ed. (Also avail. in French & Spanish). 1974. pap. 4.80 (ISBN 92-4-154036-2). World Health.

Glossary of Meteorology. American Meteorological Society. 1959. 25.00. Am Meteorological.

Glossary of Micrographics. (TR2-1980). 1980. 9.00 (ISBN 0-89258-065-8). Assn Inform Image.

Glossary of Mining Geology. G. Amstutz. 196p. (Eng., Span., Fr. & Ger.). 1971. 36.50 (ISBN 3-432-01667-0, M-7428, Pub. by F. Enke). French & Eur.

Glossary of Mining Geology. G. Amstutz. 196p. (Span., Fr, & Ger.). 1971. 36.50 (ISBN 3-432-01667-0). Enke.

Glossary of Mining Geology. G. C. Amstutz et al. Ed. by F. Esser & Won C. Park. 196p. (Eng., Span., Fr. & Ger.). 1971. DM.46.00. Enke.

Glossary of Modern Art. R. O'Dwyer & R. Le Page. pap. 1.45 (ISBN 0-685-19403-5, 99, WL). Citadel Pr.

Glossary of Modern Sailing Terms. John Rousmaniere. LC 75-31504. (Illus.). 254p. 1976. 6.95 (ISBN 0-396-07006-X). Dodd.

Glossary of Mongolian Technical Terms. Frederick H. Buck. LC 58-59834. (American Council of Learned Societies Publications). 79p. (Orig., Mongolian.). 1958. pap. 3.00x (ISBN 0-87950-257-6). Spoken Lang Serv.

Glossary of Mutual Fund Terms. The Investment Funds Institute of Canada-L' Institut Des Fonds D' Investissement Du Canada. free. Inv Funds Inst CN.

Glossary of Mycology. 2nd ed. Walter Snell & Esther A. Dick. LC 77-134946. 1971. 14.00x (ISBN 0-674-35451-6). Harvard U Pr.

Glossary of Neurotraumatology. Ed. by E. S. Gurdjian et al. LC 78-15626. (Acta Neurochirurgica: Supplementum 25). 63p. (Eng., Ger., Fr. & Span.). 1978. pap. 11.70 (ISBN 0-387-81481-7). Springer-Verlag.

Glossary of Ocean Science & Undersea Technology Terms. Lee M. Hunt & Donald G. Groves. (Illus., Orig.). pap. 6.95 (ISBN 0-685-08544-9). Compass Va.

Glossary of Office Automation Terms. R. M. Field. 32p. 1982. pap. text ed. 15.00 (ISBN 0-914548-42-5). Soc Tech Comm.

Glossary of Old Akkadian. Ignace J. Gelb. (Materials for the Assyrian Dictionary Ser: No. 3). 1957. pap. text ed. 12.00x (ISBN 0-226-62307-6). U of Chicago Pr.

Glossary of Old Lamps & Lighting Devices. American Association for State & Local History. 1.00 (30); members 0.75. AASLH.

Glossary of Onshore & Offshore Pipelines. Editions Technip. 320p. (Eng. & Fr.). 1979. E28.00. Graham & Trotman.

Glossary of Paper Terms for Web & Sheet-Fed Offset Printing. Ed. by Michael H. Bruno. (TAPPI PRESS Reports). 48p. 1971. 4.95 (01-01-R041). TAPPI.

Glossary of Papermaking Terms. Trisha Garlock. 30p. 1983. pap. 5.00. World Print Coun.

Glossary of Physiological Terms. 116p. (Rus. , Eng. , Fr. & Ger.). 1980. 30.00x (ISBN 0-686-44718-2, Pub. by Collets). State Mutual Bk.

Glossary of Polish & English Verb Forms. Stanisaw P. Kaczmarski. LC 79-345099. 199p. (Pol. & Eng.). 1978. 20.00 Zl. Panstwowy Zaklad W.

Glossary of Polish & English Verb Forms. Stanislaw P. Kaczmarski. LC 77-352469. 199p. (Eng. & Pol.). 1976. write for info. Panstwowe Zaklad W.

Glossary of Populations & Housing. G. Logie. (International Planning Glossaries: Vol. 1). (Eng., Fr., Ital., Dutch, Ger. & Swedish.). 1978. 53.25 (ISBN 0-444-41730-3). Elsevier.

Glossary of Printing Terms. Ed. by Donald B. Deaton. 58p. 1973. 27.00; members 16.00. AATCC.

Glossary of Printing Terms for the Papermaker. Canadian Pulp & Paper Association. 103p. 1980. 10.00; members 8.00. CN Pulp & Paper.

Glossary of Psychoanalytic Terms & Concepts. 2nd ed. Ed. by Burness E. Moore & Bernard D. Fine. 120p. 1968. 5.50. Am Psychoanalytic.

Glossary of Reliability, Availability, & Maintainability Terminology for Rail Rapid Transit. American Public Transit Association. 3.00; 1st. copy free, members; add'l 1.50 ea. Am Public Transit.

Glossary of Respiratory & Gas Exchange. American Physiological Society. (Standards & Glossaries). 1973. Repr. 1.00. Am Physiological.

Glossary of Savings Association Terminology. The Institute of Financial Education. 68p. 1983. softcover 4.95. Inst Finan Educ.

Glossary of Seal Terms. American Society of Lubrication Engineers. 4.00; members 3.00. Am Lubrication Engs.

Glossary of Selected Demographic Terms. Eliska Chanlett. LC 77-71130. (Occasional Publications Ser.). 1974. pap. text ed. 3.50 (ISBN 0-89383-060-7). Intl Program Labs.

Glossary of Selected Legal Terms for Juvenile Justice Personnel. 10p. 1978. 2.00 (GLT). Natl Juv & Family Ct Judges.

Glossary of Smrti Literature. Sures C. Banerji. 6.50x (ISBN 0-8426-1139-8). Verry.

Glossary of Soil & Water Terms. 62p. 1967. 6.00 (SP0467); members 4.50. Am Soc Ag Eng.

Glossary of Soil Micromorphology. Ed. by A. Jongerius & G. K. Rutherford. LC 79-321392. xiii, 138p. (Eng., Fr., Ger., Rus. & Span.). 1979. write for info. (ISBN 9-02-200637-9). Pudoc.

Glossary of Spanish & English Management Terms. James Conveney & Julian Amey. 138p. (Span. & Eng.). pap. 6.95 (C-107S). Biling Rev Pr.

Glossary of Spanish & English Management Terms. Ed. by Coveney & Amey. (Span. & Eng.). E3.50. Longman.

Glossary of Spanish & English Management Terms. James Coveney & J. Amey. (English for Special Purposes Bk.). (Span. & Eng.). 1978. pap. text ed. 6.95x (ISBN 0-582-55541-8). Longman.

Glossary of Spanish & English Management Terms. (Span. & Eng.). 6.95. Longman.

Glossary of Spanish Philatelic Terms. Eric V. Bailey. (Span. & Eng.). 1974. 2.50 ea. Intl Guatemala.

Glossary of Spices. American Spice Trade Association. minimum order 50. Am Spice Trade.

Glossary of Standard Industry Terminology & Definitions. Electrical Generating Systems Marketing Association. 1980. 5.00 (GDT4); members 2.00. Elec Gen Syst.

Glossary of Stock Exchange, Mining & Oil Terms. LC 82-126128. 108p. 1981. pap. 6.00 (ISBN 0-9594011-0-5). Fin Analysis.

Glossary of Technical Concepts Containing 4300 Din Definitions. H. Freeman. 703p. 1983. pap. 87.00 (ISBN 0-686-40807-1, Pub. by Din Verlag). Heyden.

Glossary of Technical Terms for Market Researchers: English-German-Spanish-French-Italian-Dutch. European Society for Opinion & Marketing Research. LC 74-520067. (Eng., Ger., Span., Fr., Ital. & Dutch.). 1969. 10.00x (ISBN 0-8002-1461-7). Intl Pubns Serv.

Glossary of Terms & Phrases. Henry P. Smith. LC 79-175746. x, 521p. 1972. Repr. of 1889 ed. 45.00x (ISBN 0-8103-3816-5). Gale.

Glossary of Terms Concerning Letter Symbols: Y10.1-1972. American Society of Mechanical Engineers. 2.25 (K00003); members 1.80. ASME.

Glossary of Terms for Compressed Air Dryers (Included in Supplement to the Glossary of Terms, ANSI-B93.2a-1978) NFPA-T3.27.1. National Fluid Power Association. 1981. 10.50; 7.00, NFPA member. Natl Fluid Power.

Glossary of Terms for Fluid Power (Includes Supplement B93.2a) ANSI-B93.2m. American National Standards Institute & National Fluid Power Association. 1971. 24.00; 16.00, NFPA member. Natl Fluid Power.

Glossary of Terms for Fluid Power Quick Disconnect Couplings (Included in Supplement to the Glossary of Terms) NFPA-T3.20.1. National Fluid Power Association. 1981. 10.50; 7.00, NFPA member. Natl Fluid Power.

Glossary of Terms for Hydraulic Fluid Power Filters & Separator: NFPA-T3.10.3m. rev. ed. National Fluid Power Association. 1980. 10.50; 7.00, NFPA member. Natl Fluid Power.

Glossary of Terms for Mechanical Fasteners: B18.12-1962 (R1975) American Society of Mechanical Engineers. 9.50 (M00046); members 7.60. ASME.

Glossary of Terms for Thermal Physiology. American Physiological Society. (Standards & Glossaries). 1973. Repr. 1.00. Am Physiological.

Glossary of Terms in Computer Assisted Cartography. International Cartographic Association. 166p. 1980. 8.00 (C155). Am Congrs Survey.

Glossary of Terms in Heat Transfer, Fluid Flow & Related Topics. Ed. by William Begell. LC 82-3153. (Hemisphere Engineering Paperback Ser.). 112p. (Eng., Rus., Ger., Fr. & Japanese.). 1983. pap. 29.95 (ISBN 0-89116-261-5). Hemisphere Pub.

Glossary of Terms in Nuclear Science & Technology: ANS-9, N1.1-1976. rev. ed. American Nuclear Society. 18.50. Am Nuclear Soc.

Glossary of Terms in Sri Aurobindo's Writings. Aurobindo. 1979. 9.50 (ISBN 0-89744-980-0, Pub. by Sri Aurobindo Ashram Trust India); pap. 7.50 (ISBN 0-89744-981-9, Pub. by Sri Aurobindo Ashram Trust India). Auromere.

Glossary of Terms in Sri Aurobindo's Writings. Sri Aurobindo. 1978. 10.00 (ISBN 0-89071-271-9). Matagiri.

Glossary of Terms Related to the Drying of Wood. Forest Products Research Society. 81p. 7.00 (607-61); members 5.00. Forest Prod.

Glossary of Terms Relating to Brick Masonry. Rev. ed. (No.2). 1975. 0.50. Brick Inst Amer.

Glossary of Terms Relating to Rubber & Rubber Technology. 122p. 1972. pap. 10.00 (ISBN 0-8031-0101-5, STP184A). ASTM.

Glossary of Terms Used in Heraldry. H. Gough. 59.95 (ISBN 0-8490-0239-7). Gordon Pr.

Glossary of Terms Used in Heraldry. James Parker. LC 77-94021. (Illus.). (gr. 9 up). 1970. 29.50 (ISBN 0-8048-0715-9). C E Tuttle.

Glossary of Terms Used in Industrial Relations. 2nd ed. Gerard Dion. (Eng. & Fr.). 1975. pap. 16.00 (ISBN 0-7746-6733-8). Univ Laval.

Glossary of Terms Used in Maintenance Painting. National Association of Corrosion Engineers. 2.00 (6D165). Natl Corrosion Eng.

Glossary of Terms Used in Parapsychology. Michael A. Thalbourne. 128p. 1983. 8.50 (ISBN 0-434-75720-9, Pub. by W Heinemann). David & Charles.

Glossary of Terms Used in Pasture & Range Survey Research, Ecology, Management. 153p. 1976. pap. 14.00 (ISBN 0-685-68955-7, F925, FAO). Unipub.

Glossary of Terms Used in Quality Control. Slownik Jakosci. 54p. (Pol., Eng. & Rus.). 1980. 30.00x (ISBN 0-686-44719-0, Pub. by Collets). State Mutual Bk.

Glossary of Terms Used in Range Management. Society for Range Management Glossary Committee. 36p. 1.50. Soc Range Mgmt.

Glossary of Terms Used in Refining. 1980. 2.00 (012-3); members 1.33. TAPPI.

Glossary of Terms Used in the Measurement of Fluid Flow in Pipes: ANSI-ASME MFC-1M-1979. American Society of Mechanical Engineers. 4.50 (J00065); members 3.60. ASME.

Glossary of Textile Terminology for the Paper Manufacturer. Ed. by Howard E. Shearer. (TAPPI PRESS Reports). 38p. 1965. 3.95 (01-01-R003). TAPPI.

Glossary of the English Bible Words. J. Eastwood & W. Aldis Wright. 564p. 1981. Repr. of 1866 ed. lib. bdg. 75.00 (ISBN 0-89760-210-2). Telegraph Bks.

Glossary of the Igor Tale. Tatjana Cizevska. (S P R Ser: No. 53). 1966. text ed. 72.00x (ISBN 90-2790-198-8). Mouton.

Glossary of the Theatre. K. R. Band-Kuzmany. (Eng., Fr., Ital. & Ger.). 1970. 30.00 (ISBN 0-444-40716-2). Elsevier.

Glossary of Transmission Elements: Gears. Ed. by European Committee of Associations of Gear & Transmission Element Manufacturers (EUROTRANS) (Illus., In 8 languages). 1976. lib. bdg. 30.00x (ISBN 3-7830-0104-8). Marlin.

Glossary of Transport. G. Logie. (International Planning Glossaries Ser.: Vol. 2). (in 6 languages). 1980. 53.25 (ISBN 0-444-41888-1). Elsevier.

Glossary of UK Fishing Gear Terms. 1980. 39.50x (ISBN 0-686-64737-8, Pub. by Fishing News England). State Mutual Bk.

Glossary of United Kingdom Fishing Gear Terms. 115p. 1982. 47.25 (ISBN 0-85238-119-0, FN95, FNB). Unipub.

Glossary of Urban Public Transportation Terms. National Research Council. LC 78-86000. 39p. (Eng.). write for info. (ISBN 0-309-02666-0). Natl Acad Pr.

Glossary of Urban Public Transportation Terms. Transportation Research Board. (Special Report). 39p. 1978. 3.00 (ISBN 0-309-02666-0). Transport Res Bd.

Glossary of Value Terms. The Institute of Business Appraiser. 5.00; 2.00. Inst Busn Appraisers.

Glossary of Virginia Words. P. J. Nixon. (Publications of the American Dialect Society: No. 5). 46p. 1946. pap. 3.50 (ISBN 0-8173-0605-6). U of Ala Pr.

Glossary of Words & Phrases Used in Radiology, Nuclear Medicine & Ultrasound. 2nd ed. Lewis E. Etter. 384p. 1970. ed. spiral 32.50xphotocopy (ISBN 0-398-00526-5). C C Thomas.

Glossary of Zoning Definitions. (PAS Reports: No. 233). 27p. 1968. photocopy 6.00. Am Plan Assn.

Glossary on Air Pollution. American Lung Association. 8p. avail. (0450). Am Lung Assn.

Glossary on Educational Technology. 140p. 1973. pap. 7.95 (ISBN 0-686-56478-2, M-7429, Pub. by Vlg. Dokumentation). French & Eur.

Glossary on Educational Technology. (Eng. & Ger.). 1973. DM.9.80 (ISBN 3-7940-5134-3). Saur Verlag.

Glossary to the Plays of Bernard Shaw. Paul Kozelka. LC 76-28964. 1976. lib. bdg. 12.50 (ISBN 0-8414-5526-0). Folcroft.

Glossary: Water & Wastewater Control Engineering. Ed. by American Society of Civil Engineers & American Water Works Association. LC 80-70933. 456p. 1981. text ed. 25.00 (ISBN 0-87262-262-2). Am Soc Civil Eng.

Glossary: Water & Wastewater Control Engineering. 2nd ed. American Water Works Association. (General References Ser.). (Illus.). 456p. 1981. text ed. 25.00 (ISBN 0-89867-263-5). Am Water Wks Assn.

Glossary: Water & Wastewater Control Engineering. 1981. members 25.00; 17.50. Water Pollution.

Glossary: Water & Wastewater Control Engineering. Water Pollution Control Federation et al. 440p. 1981. 25.00 (ISBN 0-686-36997-1, M0022). Water Pollution.

Glossay of Clinical Chemistry Terms. Haisman & Muller. (Eng.). E4.95. Butterworth.
Glosses & Glossaires Hebreux-Francais. Arsene Darmesteter. 52p. (Hebrew & Fr.). 1878. 30.00 F. Champion.
Golden Greek Glossary. American Classical League. (Gr.). 1.00 (NO. L3). Am Classical.
Golf Dictionary. Hugh Taylor. 7.50x (ISBN 0-392-12072-0, SpS). Sportshelf.
Gonja-English Dictionary & Spelling Book. Compiled by J. W. Amankwaah & O. Rytz. LC 79-303260. v, 273p. (Gonja & Eng.). 1977. write for info. Inst Afr Stu.
Good Housekeeping Dictionary of Symptoms. A. Ward Gardner. 256p. 1982. pap. 2.95 (ISBN 0-441-29822-2). Ace Bks.
Good Spelling Dictionary. Ed. by John Bailie. 176p. Epap. 75.00p (ISBN 0-600-38293-1); pap. 9.00 (ISBN 0-600-04982-5). Newnes Bks.
Gornoe Delo: Terminologicheskii Slovar. N. V. Melnikov et al. 527p. (Rus.). 1974. 12.00 (Pub. by Nedra). Four Continent.
Gosudarstvennye Standarty SSSR, 3 vols. (Rus.). 1980. 14.25 set (Pub. by Izd Standartov). Four Continent.
Gothic Architecture in England with an Illustrated Glossary of Technical Terms. Roge T. Smith. (Illus.). 164p. 1983. 91.85 (ISBN 0-86650-059-6). Gloucester Art.
Gourmet's Lexicon. Norman Kolpas. 1982. 3.95 (ISBN 0-686-83115-2, Perigee). Putnam Pub Group.
Graafinen Sanakirja. 308p. (Finnish , Rus. & Ger.). 1979. write for info. (ISBN 9-5100-9086-7). Soderstrom.
Grammar & Dictionary of the Binandere Language, Mamba River...Papua. Copland King. Bd. with Grammar & Dictionary of the Wedau Language. LC 75-35129. (Binandere & Wedau.). Repr. of 1927 ed. 15.50 (ISBN 0-404-14145-5). AMS Pr.
Grammar & Dictionary of the Language of the Hidatsa. Washington Matthews. LC 76-44080. (Shea's American Linguistics, Ser. 2: Nos. 1 & 2). Repr. of 1873 ed. 27.50 (ISBN 0-404-15787-4). AMS Pr.
Grammar & Dictionary of the Wedau Language see Grammar & Dictionary of the Binandere Language, Mamba River...Papua.
Grammar & Dictionary of the Yakama Language. Marie C. Pandosy. LC 10-30204. (Library of American Linguistics: Vol. 6). (Yakama.). Repr. of 1862 ed. 15.00 (ISBN 0-404-50986-X). AMS Pr.
Grammar & Orthography, Bks. 1-4. Marjorie K. Lawrence et al. Ed. by William B. Smeeth. (gr. 1-6). 1966. pap. text ed. 1.67 ea. (Pub. by Lawrence); word study supplement 0.80 (ISBN 0-87505-308-4). Borden.
Grammar & Vocabulary of Language Spoken by Motu Tribe (New Guinea) 3rd enl. ed. William G. Lawes. LC 75-35132. 1976. Repr. of 1896 ed. 17.50 (ISBN 0-404-14148-X). AMS Pr.
Grammar & Vocabulary of the Samoan Language. H. Neffgen. Tr. by Arnold B. Stock from Ger. LC 75-35206. (Samoan.). Repr. of 1918 ed. 18.00 (ISBN 0-404-14229-X). AMS Pr.
Grammar of the Dialect of Kendal (Wesmoreland) Descriptive & Historical with Specimens & a Glossary. T. O. Hirst. 175p. 1968. Repr. of 1906 ed. 37.50x (ISBN 0-8002-0880-3). Intl Pubns Serv.
Grammar of the English Language. George O. Curme. 1983. 40.00 set (ISBN 0-930454-03-0). Verbatim.
Grammar of the English Language: Parts of Speech, Vol. 1. George O. Curme. LC 77-87423. 400p. 1983. 20.00 (ISBN 0-930454-02-2). Verbatim.
Grammar of the English Language: Syntax, Vol. 2. George O. Curme. LC 77-87422. 640p. 1983. 20.00 (ISBN 0-930454-01-4). Verbatim.
Grammar of the Kiwai Language, Fly Delta, Papua, with a Kiwai Vocabulary. Sidney H. Ray & E. B. Riley. LC 75-35152. (Kiwai.). Repr. of 1933 ed. 15.00 (ISBN 0-404-14167-6). AMS Pr.
Grammar, Vocabulary, Exercises of the Latvian Language for the Use of Students. Antonia Millers. LC 79-89077. (Latvian & Eng.). 10.00x (ISBN 0-912852-26-7). Echo Pubs.
Grammaticheskii Slovar' Russkogo Iazyka. Ed. by A. A. Zalizniak. (Russkii iazyk Ser.). 892p. (Rus.). 1977. 14.95 (D-207A). Four Continent.
Grammatiken und Woerterbuecher des Schweizer Deutschen. 2nd ed. Albert Weber. 354p. (Ger.). 1968. 14.50 (ISBN 3-85865-029-3, M-7431, Pub. by Hans Rohr). French & Eur.
Grammatisches Worterbuch der Gebrauchlichsten Spanischer Verben. Ziegler. 160p. (Ger.). 10.50 (ISBN 3-87217-009-0, M-7432, Pub. by Fachverlag Th. Grossman). French & Eur.
Gran Diccionario & Gramatica Ingles-Espanol, Espanol-Ingles, 2 vols, Vol. 1. 3rd. ed. 464p. (Span. & Eng.). 1982. 2500.00 ptas (ISBN 8-42780-596-9). Nauta SA.
Gran Diccionario Cuyas Ingles-Espanol. (Eng. & Span.). 1977. 21.00. Camino Real.
Gran Diccionario Cuyas Ingles-Espanol, Spanish-English. 6th ed. Arturo Cuyas Armengol. 1640p. (Eng. & Span.). 1977. 26.95 (ISBN 84-7183-008-6, S-12386). French & Eur.
Gran Diccionario Cuyas Ingl e01s-Espa n13ol. (Span. & Eng.). 1977. 21.00. Camino Real.
Gran Diccionario Infantil Marin, 4 vols. 840p. (Espn.). 1979. Set. 128.00 (ISBN 84-7102-150-1, S-50032). French & Eur.
Gran Diccionario Infantil Marin, 4 vols. 800p. (Span.). 1978. 7800.00 ptas (ISBN 84-7102-150-1). Marin.
Gran Diccionario Sopena. 1632p. (Span.). 1982. 3000.00 ptas (ISBN 84-303-0881-4). Sopena.
Gran diccionario y gramatica de la lengua espanola: Obra completa, 2 vols. 2nd ed. 896p. (Span.). 1982. pap. 3200.00 ptas (ISBN 84-278-0568-3). Nauta SA.
Grand Dictionnaire d'Americanismes: Contenant les Principaux Termes Americains avec Leur Equivalent Exact en Francais. 5th ed. Etienne Deak. 839p. (Fr. & Eng.). 1973. 22.50x (ISBN 0-8002-1466-8). Intl Pubns Serv.
Grand Larousse de la Langue Francaise, 7 vols. Louis Guilbert. (Fr.). 1975. Set. 495.00 (ISBN 0-686-57308-0, M-6287). French & Eur.
Grand Larousse de la Langue Francaise: Tome I, 7 vols. L. Guilbert et al. (Fr.). 1971. 67.80 ea. (Dist. by Continental Bk Co); 450.00 set. Larousse.
Grand Larousse de la Langue Francaise: Tome VII, 7 vols. L. Guilbert et al. (Fr.). 1978. 67.80 ea. (Dist. by Continental Bk Co); 450.00 set. Larousse.
Grand Panjandrum: And 1999 Other Rare & Delightful Words & Expressions. J. N. Hook. 392p. 1980. 15.95 (ISBN 0-02-553620-6). Macmillan.
Grand Robert see Robert Dictionaries.
Grande Dicionario da Lingua Portuguesa. Candido De Figueiredo. (Port.). Cr.$3000.00. Difel Difusao.
Grande Dicionario Frances-Portugues. Ersilio Cardoso. (Fr. & Port.). Cr.$25.74. Difel Difusao.
Grande Dicionario Portugues-Frances. Domingos De Azevedo. (Port. & Fr., Sao Paulo, Brazil). Cr.$25.74. Difel Difusao.
Grande Dizionario di Marina: Inglese-Italiano, Italiano-Inglese. M. Bernabo & F. Picchi. 963p. (Eng. & Ital.). 1970. 95.00 (ISBN 0-686-92551-3, M-9298). French & Eur.
Grande Dizionario Hazon-Garzanti Inglese-Italiano Italiano-Inglese. (Eng. & Ital.). 1976. 45.00x (ISBN 0-686-19963-4). Intl Learn Syst.
Grande Dizionario Hazon Garzanti Inglese-Italiano, Italiano-Inglese. M. Hazon. 2112p. (Eng. & Ital.). 1980. 49.95 (ISBN 0-686-97429-8, M-9186). French & Eur.
Grande Encyclopedie Larousse, 22 vols. (Illus.). 13000p. (Fr.). 1972-1981. incl. suppl. 1250.00 set (ISBN 0-8277-3030-6). Pergamon.
Grandes diccionarios bilingues Amador. (Span. & Eng.). 43.20 ea. (TF4). Bilingual Ed Serv.
Graphic & Paper Industry. (Eng. & Swedish.). 1982. Kr.159.00 (ISBN 91-86236-06-7). EC Print AB.
Great Encyclopedic Dictionary. (Eng.). 1966. Can.$29.95 (ISBN 0-88850-023-8). Reader's Digest.
Great English-Polish Dictionary. J. Stanislawski. 1405p. (Eng. & Pol.). 1979. leatherette 75.00 (ISBN 0-686-97431-X, M-9329). French & Eur.
Great English-Polish Dictionary, 2 vols. Ed. by J. Stanislawski. 607p. (Eng. & Pol.). 1980. vinyl 99.00x (ISBN 0-569-00671-6, Pub. by Collet's). State Mutual Bk.
Great English-Polish Dictionary. Ed. by Jan Stanislawski. 1178p. (Eng. & Pol.). 1977. 40.00x (ISBN 0-8002-1469-2). Intl Pubns Serv.
Great Polish-English Dictionary. J. Stanislawski. 1728p. (Pol. & Eng.). 1980. leatherette 75.00 (ISBN 83-214-0107-4, M-9368). French & Eur.
Great Polish-English Dictionary, 2 vols. Ed. by J. Stanislawski. (Pol. & Eng.). 1980. vinyl 60.00x (ISBN 0-569-02649-0, Pub. by Collet's). State Mutual Bk.
Great technical dictionary. Paulo C. Camarao et al. LC 79-122945. 303p. (Eng. & Port.). 1979. Cr.$250.00. Ao Livro Tecnico.
Great Technical Dictionary: Dicionario Tecnico English-Portuguese. P. C. Camarao & M. A. Serra. 462p. (Eng. & Portuguese.). 1979. pap. 39.95 (ISBN 0-686-97435-2, M-9214). French & Eur.
Greek & English Lexicon. Parkhurst. 680p. (Gr. & Eng.). Repr. of 1769 ed. loose leaf bdg. 29.95 (ISBN 0-89957-549-8). AMG Pubs.
Greek-English Analytical Concordance of the Greek-English New Testament. J. Stegenga. (Gr. & Eng.). 1963. 14.95 (ISBN 0-910710-01-5). Hellenes.
Greek-English Concordance. Ed. by Jacob B. Smith. 430p. (Gr. & Eng.). 1955. 24.95 (ISBN 0-8361-1368-3). Herald Pr.
Greek English Derivative Dictionary. Ed. by Rudolph F. Schaeffer. (Gr. & Eng.). 1.95 (B6). Am Classical.
Greek-English Dictionary "Modern". (Gr. & Eng.). 15.00 (ISBN 0-87557-029-1, 028-3Y). Saphrograph.
Greek-English, English-Greek Dictionary, 2 vols. C. Patsis. (Gr. & Eng.). Set. 50.00 (ISBN 0-685-79111-4). Heinman.
Greek-English, English-Greek Medical Dictionary. 4th rev. ed. Ed. by D. N. Gelis. (Illus., Gr. & Eng.). 1978. 75.00 (ISBN 0-686-91764-2). Heinman.
Greek-English, English-Greek Pocket Dictionary. (Gr. & Eng.). 9.00 (ISBN 0-685-58555-7). Heinman.
Greek-English, English-Greek Technical Dictionary, Vol.1-2. rev. ed. H. T. Hionides. (Eng. & Gr.). Date not set. Set. text ed. 50.00 (ISBN 0-686-46533-4). Heinman.
Greek-English Lexicon. 9th ed. Ed. by Henry G. Liddell & Robert Scott. (Gr. & Eng.). 1940. 79.00x (ISBN 0-19-864214-8). Oxford U Pr.
Greek-English Lexicon of the New Testament: A Dictionary Numerically Coded to Strong's Exhaustive Concordance. Joseph H. Thayer. (Gr. & Eng.). 1977. pap. 14.95 (ISBN 0-8010-8838-0). Baker Bk.
Greek-English Lexicon of the New Testament. W. J. Hickie. (Direction Bks.). (Gr. & Eng.). 1977. pap. 4.95 (ISBN 0-8010-4164-3). Baker Bk.
Greek-English Pocket Dictionary. (Gr. & Eng.). pap. 8.50 (ISBN 0-685-77570-4, 030-5X). Saphrograph.
Greek for the English-Speaking Tourist see Phrase Dictionaries for the American Tourist.
Greek-Norwegian Norwegian-Greek Pocket Dictionary. E. Theophilakis. (Gr. & Norwegian.). 1981. write for info. (ISBN 82-573-0005-5). Kunnskapsforlaget.
Greek Vocabulary. Joint Association of Classical Teachers. (Gr.). 1980. pap. 5.95 (ISBN 0-521-23277-5). Cambridge U Pr.
Greek Word Roots: A Practical List with Greek & English Derivatives. Thomas Rogers. 32p. (Gr. & Eng.). 1981. pap. 1.95 (ISBN 0-8010-7707-9). Baker Bk.
Gregg Shorthand Dictionary. J. R. Gregg & L. A. Leslie. (Gregg Sharthand Ser.: No. 90). 416p. 1983. 15.95 (ISBN 0-07-024599-1). Mcgraw.
Gresk-Norsk-Gresk Lommeordbok. 381p. (Gr. & Norwegian.). 1981. pap. 14.95 (ISBN 82-573-0163-9, M-9460). French & Eur.
Griechiesches Etymologisches Woerterbuch, Vol. 1. Hjalmar Frisk. (Gr. & Ger.). 1960. 95.00 (ISBN 3-533-00652-2). Winter Univ.
Griechisch-Deutsches Taschenwoerterbuch zum Neuen Testament. 6th ed. Erwin Preuschen. LC 77-484567. 197p. (Gr. & Ger.). 1976. DM.19.80 (ISBN 3-110-06960-1). De Gruyter.
Griechisch-Deutsches Woerterbuch zu den Schriften des Neuen Testaments und der uebrigen urchristlichen Literatur. 5th rev. ed. Walter Bauer. (Gr. & Ger.). 1981. Repr. 54.00x (ISBN 3-11-002073-4). De Gruyter.
Griechisches Etymologiches Woerterbuch, Vol. 3. Hjalmar Frisk. (Gr. & Ger.). 1972. 45.00 (ISBN 3-533-02203-X). Winter Univ.
Griechisches Etymologisches Woerterbuch, Vol. 1. Hjalmar Frisk. (Gr. & Ger.). 1960. 95.00 (ISBN 3-533-00652-2, M-7434, Pub. by Carl Winter). French & Eur.
Griechisches Etymologisches Woerterbuch, Vol. 2. Hjalmar Frisk. (Gr. & Ger.). 1960. 132.00 (ISBN 3-533-00653-0, M-7435, Pub. by Carl Winter). French & Eur.
Griechisches Etymologisches Woerterbuch, Vol. 3. Hjalmar Frisk. (Gr. & Ger.). 1972. 45.00 (ISBN 3-533-02203-X, M-7436, Pub. by Carl Winter). French & Eur.
Griechishes Etymologishes Woerterbuch, Vol. 2. Hjalmar Frisk. (Gr. & Ger.). 1960. 132.00 (ISBN 3-533-00653-0). Winter Univ.
Grinding - Surface Roughness see Dictionary of Production Engineering: German-English-French.
Grobworterbuch Polnisch-Deutsch. J. Piprek & J. Ippoldt. 2121p. (Ger. & Pol.). 1979. leatherette 75.00 (ISBN 83-214-0011-6, M-9128). French & Eur.
Groot Noord-Sotho-Woordeboek. D. Ziervogel. LC 76-516085. 1536p. (Sotho.). 1975. write for info. (ISBN 0-627-00366-4). Van Schaik.
Groot Systematisch en Klankalfabetisch Rijmwoordenboek. John Buydens. LC 78-362599. 363p. (Dutch.). 1977. fl.520.00 (ISBN 9-02890-291-0). Nederlandse Boek.
Groot Woordenboek der Nederlandse Taal, 2 vols. 10th ed. Johan H. Van Dale. Ed. by C. Kruyskamp. LC 76-461655. xli, 3230p. (Dutch.). 1976. fl.168.00 (ISBN 9-02471-829-5). Nyhoff.
Grosse Brockhaus, 12 vols. 18th ed. (Ger.). 1977. Set. 995.00 (ISBN 3-7653-0039-X, M-7326, Pub. by Brockhaus). French & Eur.
Grosse Brockhaus, 12 Vols. 18th ed. (Illus., Ger.). 1977-81. 895.00 (ISBN 3-7653-0039-X). Pergamon.

Grosse Brockhaus. 400p. (Ger.). write for info. (ISBN 3-7653-0329-1). F A Brockhaus.
Grosse Brockhaus: Band 14, Ergaenzungen A-Z. (Ger.). 1982. write for info. (ISBN 3-7653-0331-3). F A Brockhaus.
Grosse Brockhaus: Band 15. (Ger.). DM.128.00 (ISBN 3-7653-0332-1). F A Brockhaus.
Grosse Brockhaus: Band 15-20. (Ger.). 1983. write for info. (ISBN 3-7653-0330-5). F A Brockhaus.
Grosse Duden. 23rd ed. 768p. (Ger.). 1982. M.16.80. Bibl Inst Leipzig.
Grosse Duden-Schulerlexikon: Ein Nachschlagewerk fuer Jeden Schueler. Gisela Preuss. (Illus.). 704p. (Ger.). DM.write for info. (ISBN 3-411-01773-2). Biblio Inst.
Grosse Lexikon der Fischwaid. Arnold Bacmeister. (Ger.). 1969. 65.00 (ISBN 3-87372-001-9, M-7324, Pub. by Jfland). French & Eur.
Grosse Muret-Sanders: Teil I, Englisch-Deutsch, 2 vols. Otto Springer. 1843p. (Eng. & Ger.). 1963. DM.178.00 set; Band A-M. (01120); Band N-Z. (01122). Langenscheidt.
Grosse Muret-Sanders: Teil II, Deutsch-Englisch, 2 vols. Otto Springer. 2021p. (Ger. & Eng.). 1975. DM.198.00 set; Band A-K. (01124); Band L-Z. (01126). Langenscheidt.
Grosse Ravensburger Werkkunstbuch. Jutta Lammar. LC 76-470410. (Illus.). 424p. (Ger.). 1975. DM.29.80 (ISBN 3-473-42348-3). Maier Verlag.
Grosse Woerterbuch der Deutschen Sprache, 6 vols. 3000p. (Ger.). 1983. 32.00. M Rosenberg.
Grosse Woerterbuch der Italienischen & Deutschen Sprache: Band I, Italienisch-Deutsch. Sansoni. 1472p. (Ital. & Ger.). 1982. DM.280.00. Brandstetter.
Grosse Woerterbuch der Italienischen & Deutschen Sprache: Band II, Deutsch-Italienisch. Sansoni. 1596p. (Ger. & Ital.). 1982. DM.280.00. Brandstetter.
Grosses Abkuerzungsbuch. 2nd ed. H. Koblischke. 508p. (Ger.). 1980. M.24.00. Bibl Inst Leipzig.
Grosses Fremdwoerterbuch. 4th ed. 832p. (Ger.). 1982. M.24.00. Bibl Inst Leipzig.
Grosses Schulwoerterbuch English-German, 2 vols. 1439p. (Eng. & Ger.). 1983. pap. 10.90 per vol. M Rosenberg.
Grosses Woerterbuck der Deutschen Aussprache. Ed. by U. Stoetzer. (Illus.). 592p. (Ger.). 1982. M.26.00. Bibl Inst Leipzig.
Grosset Webster Dictionary. (Illus.). 672p. 1981. pap. 6.95 (ISBN 0-686-81504-1, G&D). Putnam Pub Group.
Grosset Webster Large-Type Dictionary. Ed. by Charles P. Chadsey & Harold Wentworth. (Illus.). 1978. pap. 5.95 (ISBN 0-448-14636-3, G&D). Putnam Pub Group.
Grosset's Italian Phrase Book & Dictionary for Travelers. Charles A. Hughes. 300p. (Orig., Ital.). 1971. pap. 3.50 (ISBN 0-448-00653-7, G&D). Putnam Pub Group.
Grosswoerterbuch der Englischen & Deutschen Sprache. 1300p. (Eng. & Ger.). 1983. pap. 60.00. M Rosenberg.
Growth & Structure of the Lexicon of New Guinea Pidgin. Peter Muhlhausler. LC 80-495609. (Illus.). xx, 498p. (Neo-Melanesian.). 1979. Aus.$16.00 (ISBN 0-85883-191-0). Linguistic Circle.
Grundbegriffe der Marxistischen Politischen Oekonomie des Kapitalismus. Friedrich Haffner. LC 79-340061. 160p. (Ger.). 1978. DM.9.80 (ISBN 3-7678-0441-7). Colloguium Verlag.
Grundbegriffe der Marxistischen Theorie. 1st ed. Joachim Bischoff. LC 79-397548. 263p. (Ger.). 1978. DM.16.00 (ISBN 3-87975-136-6). VSA Verlag.
Grundwortschatz: Deutsch Essential German-Allemand. (Ger. & Fr.). pap. 13.45. M Rosenberg.
Grundwortschatz wirtschaftswissenshcaftlicher Begriffe: Deutsch- Englisch, Englisch-Deutsch. 2nd ed. U. P. Ritter & K. G. Zinn. 199p. (Ger. & Eng.). 1980. pap. 9.25 (UTB644). M Rosenberg.
Guia de modismos espanoles. Raymond H. Pierson. (Span.). s.p. 4.46 (7235-2). Natl Textbk.
Guide to Foreign Language Courses & Dictionaries. Ed. by Alberto J. Walford & J. E. Screen. LC 77-26283. 1978. lib. bdg. 25.00 (ISBN 0-313-20100-5, WGL/). Greenwood.
Guide to Korean Characters: Reading & Writing Hangul & Hanja. Bruce K. Grant. 400p. (Korean & Eng.). 1979. 21.95 (ISBN 0-930878-13-2). Hollym Intl.
Guide to Korean Characters: Reading & Writing Hangul & Hanja. Bruce K. Grant. 367p. (Korean.). 16.70 (ISBN 0-930878-13-2). Hollym Corp.
Guide to Surgical Terminology. 3rd ed. F. Coleman. 1978. pap. 16.95 (ISBN 0-87489-191-4). Med Economics.
Guide to Surgical Terminology. Francis Coleman. (Medical Economics Books). 1978. pap. 12.95x (ISBN 0-442-84003-9). Van Nos Reinhold.
Guide to the Use of Terms in Plant Pathology: Terminology Sub-Committee of the Federation of British Plant Pathologists. 55p. 1973. pap. 30.00x (ISBN 0-85198-290-5, Pub. by CAB Bks England). State Mutual Bk.
Guides for American-English Pronunciation. Kendall K. Ward & Arthur L. Kaltenborn. (Illus.). 256p. 1971. photocopy ed. spiral 19.75x (ISBN 0-398-02019-1). C C Thomas.
Guilielmi Gesenii Thesaurus Philologicus Linguae Hebraeae, 3 vols. Friedrich H. Gesenius. LC 78-392234. 1522p. (Hebrew & Lat.). 1977. DM.780.00. Biblio-Verlag.
Guinness Book of Soccer Facts & Feats. 3rd ed. Jack Rollin. LC 80-142758. (Illus.). 255p. (Eng.). 1980. E6.95 (ISBN 0-85112-213-2). Guinness Super.
Guinness Book of Soccer Facts & Feats. 2nd ed. Jack Rollin. LC 80-465139. (Illus.). 251p. 1979. E5.95 (ISBN 0-85112-203-5). Guinness Super.
Gurung-Nepali-English Glossary. Deu B. Gurung et al. 223p. (Nepalese & Eng.). 1976. pap. 3.00x (ISBN 0-88312-854-3); 3.00 (ISBN 0-88312-391-6). Summer Inst Ling.
Gyldendals Antikvitetshandbog, 2 vols. Gorm R. Benzon. LC 76-488522. (Illus., Danish.). 1976. Kr.296.00 (ISBN 8-700-09561-3). Gyldendal Norsk.
Gypsum & Plaster Dictionary. K. H. Volkart. 176p. (Ger., Eng & Fr.). 1971. 68.00 (ISBN 3-7625-0460-1, M-7437, Pub. by Bauverlag). French & Eur.
Gypsum & Plaster Dictionary. K. H. Volkart. 176p. (Eng., Ger. & Fr.). 1971. 47.50x (ISBN 3-7625-0460-1). Intl Pubns Serv.
Gypsum & Plaster Dictionary. K. H. Volkart. 176p. (Ger., Eng & Fr.). 1971. 68.00 (ISBN 3-7625-0460-1). Bauverlag.
Gypsum Board Products Glossary of Terminology. write for info. (GA-505-80). Gypsum Assn.

H

Habla Que el Tiempo se Lleva? Joaquin Garro. LC 79-126852. 129p. (Span., Costa Rica). 1978. write for info. Costa Rica.
Hacker's Dictionary. Guy L. Steele. LC 83-47573. 96p. (Orig.). 1983. pap. 4.76I (ISBN 0-06-091082-8, CN 1082, CN). Har-Row.
Hackh's Chemical Dictionary. 4th ed. Julius Grant. 1968. 63.25 (ISBN 0-07-024064-7, P&RB). McGraw.
Haditechnikai Kislexikon. Istvan G. Nagy. LC 78-343185. 417p. (Hungarian.). 1976. 60.00 Ft (ISBN 9-633-26511-8). Zrinyikatunai.
Haida Dictionary. Erma Lawrence. Ed. by Christine Edenso & Robert Cogo. LC 78-101871. 464p. (Eng & Haida.). 1977. write for info. Society for the Preservation of Haida Language & Literature.
Haitian Creole Grammar, Texts, Vocabulary. Ed. by Robert A. Hall et al. LC 53-9364. (Haitian Creole.). Repr. of 1953 ed. 38.00 (ISBN 0-527-01095-2). Kraus Repr.
Hamlyn Crossword dictionary. rev. ed. Ed. by J. M. Bailie. LC 78-324843. 301p. (Eng.). 1978. E2.95 (ISBN 0-600-31923-7). Hamlyn Pub.
Hamlyn French Dictionary. Laurence Urdang Associates. LC 77-377030. 305p. (Eng. & Fr.). 1976. E0.75 (ISBN 0-600-36563-8). Hamlyn-Amer.
Hamlyn French-English Dictionary. (Fr. & Eng.). 1977. pap. 4.95 (ISBN 0-600-36563-8, 8086). Larousse.
Hamlyn German Dictionary: German-English, English-German. Compiled by Laurence Urdang Associates, Ltd. 306p. (Eng. & Ger.). 1976. 0.75p (ISBN 0-600-36564-6). Hamlyn-Amer.
Hamlyn German-English Dictionary. (Ger. & Eng.). 1977. pap. 4.95 (ISBN 0-600-36564-6, 8088). Larousse.
Hamlyn Guide to English Usage. 1980. pap. 3.95 (ISBN 0-600-33189-X). Larousse.
Hamlyn Italian-English Dictionary. (Ital. & Eng.). 1977. pap. 4.95 (ISBN 0-600-36566-2, 8089). Larousse.
Hamlyn Pocket Dictionary of Business Terms. C. F. Horner & L. M. Liebster. LC 81-131528. 317p. 1980. Epap. 1.25 (ISBN 0-600-31599-1). Hamlyn Pub.
Hamlyn Pocket Dictionary of Wines. 1980. pap. 3.95 (ISBN 0-600-39498-0). Larousse.
Hamlyn Pocket Thesaurus of English Words. 1979. pap. 3.95 (ISBN 0-600-38779-8). Larousse.
Hamlyn Spanish-English Dictionary. (Span. & Eng.). 1977. pap. 4.95 (ISBN 0-600-36565-4, 8087). Larousse.
Handbook of American Idioms & Idiomatic Usage. rev. ed. Harold C. Whitford & Robert J. Dixson. 188p. (gr. 9 up). 1973. pap. 4.25 (ISBN 0-88345-196-4, 18014). Regents Pub.
Handbook of Electronic Formulas, Symbols, & Definitions. John R. Brand. 1979. text ed. 15.95 (ISBN 0-442-20999-1). Van Nos Reinhold.
Handbook of English. Clarence Stratton. LC 74-19222. 1975. Repr. of 1940 ed. 45.00x (ISBN 0-8103-4112-3). Gale.
Handbook of Heart Terms. National Heart, Lung & Blood Institute. LC 81-12490. (Illus.). 64p. 1982. 6.95x (ISBN 0-89490-052-8). Enslow Pubs.
Handbook of Homophones. W. C. Townsend. 121p. 1975. pap. 1.50x (ISBN 0-88312-772-5); microfiche 2.25x (ISBN 0-88312-350-9). Summer Inst Ling.
Handbook of Industry Terms. 2nd ed. Soap & Detergent Association. 62p. 1981. free. Soap & Detergent.
Handbook of Insurance Terms & Concepts. Marshall W. Reavis. 208p. 1983. pap. 14.95 (ISBN 0-88462-630-X, 4101-10). Develop Sys Corp.
Handbook of Literary Terms. H. L. Yelland et al. LC 79-14512. 1980. bds. 10.00 laminated (ISBN 0-87116-118-4). Writer.
Handbook of Modern Rhetorical Terms. Linda Woodson. LC 79-17400. (Orig.). 1979. pap. 4.60 (ISBN 0-8141-2019-9); pap. 3.30 members (ISBN 0-686-86419-0). NCTE.
Handbook of Music Terms. W. Parks Grant. LC 67-10187. 1967. 27.50 (ISBN 0-8108-0054-3). Scarecrow.
Handbook of Oil Industry Terms & Phrases. 3rd ed. R. D. Langenkamp. 250p. 1981. 23.95x (ISBN 0-87814-171-5). Pennwell Pub.
Handbook of Psychological Terms. Philip L. Harriman. (Quality Paperback: No. 35). (Orig.). 1977. pap. 3.95 (ISBN 0-8226-0035-8). Littlefield.
Handbook of Russian Roots. Catherine Wolkonsky & Marianna Poltoratzky. LC 61-1403. (Columbia Slavic Studies). (Rus.). 1961. 32.50x (ISBN 0-231-02117-8). Columbia U Pr.
Handbook of Terms Used in Algebra & Analysis. A. G. Howson. LC 71-178281. (Illus.). 260p. 1972. 35.50 (ISBN 0-521-08434-2); pap. 14.95 (ISBN 0-521-09695-2). Cambridge U Pr.
Handbook of the Stock Market (HOS) Jack Rudman. (Admission Test Ser.: ATS-2). 300p. (Cloth bdg. avail. on request). pap. 7.50 (ISBN 0-8373-5005-0). Natl Learning.
Handbook to Literature. W. F. Thrall & A. Hibbard. 582p. 1980. Repr. lib. bdg. 40.00 (ISBN 0-89987-807-5). Darby Bks.
Handbuch der Namensverfahren in der Chemischen Technik. Fritz Rosendahl. LC 78-366424. 335p. (Ger.). 1976. write for info. (ISBN 2-225-46079-5). Vulkan Verlag.
Handelskorrenpondenz in Vier Sprachen. F. Berset. 253p. (Ger., Eng., Fr. & Span.). 1982. pap. 14.00. M Rosenberg.
Handlexikon der magischen Kunste. Hans Biedermann. LC 76-466579. (Illus.). 374p. (Ger.). 1976. DM.9.80 (ISBN 3-426-00421-6). Droemersche Knaur.
Handlexikon der Schulpaedogogik. Karl Aschersleben. LC 80-450953. 255p. (Ger.). 1979. write for info. (ISBN 3-170-05394-9). Kohlhammer.
Handlexikon fuer Handel & Absatz. Bernard Falk & Jakob Wolf. LC 80-469758. (Illus.). 750p. (Ger.). 1979. DM.48.00 (ISBN 3-478-24150-2). Verlag Moderne Industrie.
Handlexikon zur Erziehungswissenschaft. Ed. by Leo Roth. LC 76-465106. (Illus.). 488p. (Ger.). 1976. DM.58.00 (ISBN 3-431-01703-7). Ehrenwirth.
Handlexikon Zur Politikwissenschaft, 2 vols. Goerlitz. 530p. (Ger.). 1973. pap. 9.50 (ISBN 3-499-16169-9, M-7438, Pub. by Rowohlt). French & Eur.
Handlexikon zur Politikwissenschaft, 2 vols. Goerlitz. 530p. (Ger.). 1973. pap. 9.50 (ISBN 3-499-16169-9). Rowohlt.
Handlist of Rhetorical Terms: A Guide for Students of English Literature. Richard A. Lanham. LC 68-31636. 1968. pap. 5.95x (ISBN 0-520-01414-6). U of Cal Pr.
Handwoerterbuch der Finanzwirtschaft. Ed. by Hans E. Bueschgen. LC 77-460396. (Illus., Ger.). 1976. DM.220.00 (ISBN 3-791-08010-5). Poeschel.
Handwoerterbuch der Schulpaedagogik. Ed. by Werner S. Niklis. LC 75-516726. 459p. (Ger.). 1975. write for info. (ISBN 3-781-50267-8). Klinkhardt.
Handwoerterbuch der Volkwirtschaft. LC 80-460492. (Ger.). 1978. write for info. Gabler.
Handwoerterbuch des Oeffentlichen Dienster: Das Personalwesen. W. Bierfelder. 1800p. (Ger.). 1976. 250.00 (ISBN 3-503-01424-1, M-7440, Pub. by E. Schmidt). French & Eur.
Handwoerterbuch des Oeffentlichen Dienster: Das Personalwesen. W. Bierfelder. 1800p. (Ger.). 1976. 250.00 (ISBN 3-503-01424-1). Schmidt Verlag.

Handwoerterbuch des Oeffentlichen Dienstes. Ed. by Wilhelm Bierfelder. LC 77-457292. (Illus., Ger.). DM.228.00 (ISBN 3-503-01424-1). Schmidt Verlag.
Handwoerterbuch des Personalwesens. Ed. by Eduard Gaugler. LC 76-483335. (Illus., Ger.). 1975. DM.220.00 (ISBN 3-791-08009-1). Poeschel Verlag.
Handwoerterbuch Deutsch-Englisch. 699p. (Ger. & Eng.). 1983. pap. 16.00. M Rosenberg.
Handwoerterbuch fur der Bank & Sparkassenwesen. Bank-Lexikon. LC 79-355716. (Illus., Ger.). 1978. DM.96.00 (ISBN 3-409-46105-1). Gabler.
Handwoerterbuch Internationale Politik. Ed. by Wichard Woyke. LC 80-482177. xiv, 412p. (Ger.). 1980. DM.write for info. (ISBN 3-810-00287-9). Leske-Budrich.
Handworterbuch der Neu-Arabischen und Deutschen Sprache, 3 vols. Adolf Wahrmund. (Arabic & Ger.). 1974. Set. text ed. 50.50x (ISBN 0-8426-0776-5). Verry.
Handworterbuch der neu Arabischen und Deutschen Sprache, 3 vols. Adolf Wahrmund. 2826p. (Ger. & Arabic.). Repr. 70.00 set (178-X). Intl Bk Ctr.
Handy English-Polish Dictionary. 914p. (Eng. & Pol.). 1980. 20.00x (ISBN 0-569-07422-3, Pub. by Collet's). State Mutual Bk.
Harbord's Glossary of Navigation. C. W. Layton. 1981. 50.00x (ISBN 0-85174-277-7, Pub. by Nautical England). State Mutual Bk.
Harbottle's Dictionary of Battles. 3rd rev. ed. George Bruce. 304p. 1981. 14.95 (ISBN 0-442-22336-6); pap. 7.95 (ISBN 0-442-22335-8). Van Nos Reinhold.
Harbrace Vocabulary Guide. 2nd ed. Donald W. Lee. 184p. (Orig.). 1970. pap. text ed. 9.95 (ISBN 0-15-534471-4, HC); instr. key avail. (ISBN 0-15-534472-2, HC). HarBraceJ.
Harkavy's Complete Dictionary. Alexander Harkavy. 1123p. 1898. 12.50 (ISBN 0-88482-666-X). Hebrew Pub.
Harley Latin-Old English Glossary. Robert Oliphant. (Janua Linguarum, Ser. Practica: No. 20). (Lat. & Eng.). 1966. pap. text ed. 36.00x (ISBN 90-2790-639-4). Mouton.
Harper Dictionary of Contemporary Usage. William Morris & Mary Morris. LC 73-4112. 672p. 1975. 23.99i (ISBN 0-06-013062-8, HarpT). Har-Row.
Harper Dictionary of Modern Thought. Ed. by Alan Bullock & Oliver Stallybrass. LC 74-15814. 1977. 25.96i (ISBN 0-06-010578-X, HarpT). Har-Row.
Harper English-Spanish, Spanish-English Dictionary. (No. 5027). (Span. & Eng.). write for info. (608-44). Pan Amer Pub.
Harper's Dictionary of Music. Christine Ammer. LC 77-134280. (Illus.). 1972. 20.14i (ISBN 0-06-010113-X, HarpT). Har-Row.
Harper's Dictionary of Music. Christine Ammer. (Illus.). 414p. 1973. pap. 5.50 (ISBN 0-06-463347-0, EH 347). B&N NY.
Harrap Portuguese-English Dictionary. James L. Taylor. xx, 662p. (Port. & Eng.). E17.50 (ISBN 0-245-57228-7). Harrap.
Harrap's Compact Italian & English Dictionary. Annamaria F. Maiocchi & Ada De Bichiacchi. 667p. (Eng. & Ital.). E5.95 (ISBN 0-245-59636-4). Harrap.
Harrap's Concise French & English Dictionary. 2nd ed. Patricia Forbes & Muriel H. Smith. Ed. by P. H. Collin. LC 78-320359. 933p. (Fr. & Eng.). 1978. E4.95 (ISBN 0-245-52829-6). Harrap.
Harrap's Concise German & English Dictionary. Ed. by Robin Sawers. 1120p. (Ger. & Eng.). E6.95 (ISBN 0-245-53869-0). Harrap.
Harrap's Concise Student French & English Dictionary. new ed. J. E. Mansion. Ed. by P. H. Collin et al. (Fr. & Eng.). (gr. 9-12). 1978. Repr. text ed. 9.95 (ISBN 0-8442-1872-3, 1872-4). Natl Textbk.
Harrap's Dictionnaire d'argot: French to English, English to French Slang Dictionary. G. Marks. 555p. (Fr. & Eng.). 1981. pap. 24.50 (ISBN 0-245-53601-9, M-6308). French & Eur.
Harrap's Easy English Dictionary. Ed. by P. H. Collin. (Eng.). write for info. (ISBN 0-245-53660-4); pap. write for info. (ISBN 0-245-53624-8). Harrap.
Harrap's English-Brazilian Portuguese Business Dictionary. Ed. by Terence Lewis et al. 250p. (Port. & Eng.). E35.00. Harrap.
Harrap's English Dictionary. Ed. by P. H. Collin. 608p. (Eng.). write for info. (ISBN 0-245-53660-4); pap. write for info. (ISBN 0-245-53624-8). Harrap.
Harrap's English-French Dictionary of Data Processing. 2nd ed. Claude Camille & Michel Dehaine. LC 78-300149. 137p. (Eng. & Fr.). 1976. E13.00 (ISBN 0-245-52293-X). Harrap.
Harrap's English-French Dictionary of Slang & Colloquialisms. Georgette A. Marks & Charles B. Johnson. LC 75-329804. 299p. (Eng. & Fr.). 1975. E7.25 (ISBN 0-245-52267-0). Harrap.
Harrap's First French Dictionary. Colin Henstock. 133p. (Fr. & Eng.). E2.95 (ISBN 0-245-59978-9). Harrap.
Harrap's French & English Business Dictionary. Francoise Colin et al. 507p. (Fr. & Eng.). 1981. 48.00. Imported Bks.
Harrap's French & English Business Dictionary. Ed. by Francoise Collin et al. 222p. (Fr. & Eng.). 1983. 45.00 (ISBN 0-686-44824-3). Natl Textbk.
Harrap's French & English Business Dictionary. Ed. by F. Laurendeau et al. 514p. (Fr. & Eng.). E20.00 (ISBN 0-245-53594-2). Harrap.
Harrap's French & English Dictionary of Data Processing, 2 vols. in 1. 2nd ed. Claude Camille & Michael Dehaine. ii, 261p. (Fr. & Eng.). 1980. E16.00. Harrap.
Harrap's French & English Dictionary of Slang & Colloquialisms. Joseph Marks & Georgette A. Marks. Rev. by Georgette A. Marks. 556p. (Fr. & Eng.). 1980. E10.00. Harrap.
Harrap's French-English Dictionary of Slang & Colloquialisms. (Fr. & Eng.). 1975. 14.95 (ISBN 0-686-57323-4, M-6308). French & Eur.
Harrap's German & English Glossary of Terms in International Law. G. Gilbertson. xii, 355p. (Eng. & Ger.). E25.00 (ISBN 0-245-53524-1). Harrap.
Harrap's Mini Pocket French & English Dictionary. Abridged by Patricia Forbes & Margaret Ledesert. 544p. (Fr. & Eng.). E1.25 (ISBN 0-245-53135-1). Harrap.
Harrap's Modern Portuguese & English Dictionary, 2 pts. Ed. by Milton S. Pereira & Maria S. Pereira. 347p. (Port. & Eng.). E5.25 (ISBN 0-245-56866-2). Harrap.
Harrap's New Collegiate French & English Dictionary. rev. ed. J. E. Mansion. Ed. by D. H. Ledesert. LC 75-182800. (Fr. & Eng.). (gr. 9-12). 1967. Repr. text ed. 14.95 (ISBN 0-8442-1873-1, 1873-4). Natl Textbk.
Harrap's New Collegiate French Dictionary: English-French, French-English. 1450p. (Fr. & Eng.). 1978. 19.50. Imported Bks.
Harrap's New Pocket French & English Dictionary. Abridged by Patricia Forbes & Margaret Ledesert. 525p. (Fr. & Eng.). 1969. E2.95 (ISBN 0-245-59812-X). Harrap.
Harrap's New Standard Francais-Anglais, 1: A-I. (Fr.-Eng.). 1972. 32.50 (ISBN 0-8442-1876-6, M-6309). French & Eur.
Harrap's New Standard Francais-Anglais, 2: J-Z. 1162p. (Fr.-Eng.). 1972. 32.50 (ISBN 0-8442-1898-7, M-6310). French & Eur.
Harrap's New Standard French & English Dictionary, 4 vols. Rev. ed. J. E. Mansion. (Fr. & Eng.). 1980. Vols. 1-2: Eng.-Fr. 90.00; Vols. 3-4: Fr.-Eng. 90.00; of 4 vols. 169.00 set. Imported Bks.
Harrap's New Standard French & English Dictionary, 2 vols. J. E. Mansion. (Fr. & Eng.). 1973. 35.95 ea. (ISBN 0-7720-0546-X); 35.95 ea. (ISBN 0-7720-0546-X). Clarke Ltd.
Harrap's New Standard French & English Dictionary: A-I, French-English, Vol. 1. J. E. Mansion. Rev. by D. M. Ledesert & R. P. Ledesert. xxx, 567p. (Fr. & Eng.). E20.00 (ISBN 0-245-50972-0). Harrap.
Harrap's New Standard French & English Dictionary: A-K, English-French, Vol. 3. J. E. Mansion. Rev. by D. M. Ledesert & R. L. Ledesert. xxiii, 638p. (Fr. & Eng.). E20.00 (ISBN 0-245-51859-2). Harrap.
Harrap's New Standard French & English Dictionary: J-Z, French-English, Vol. 2. J. E. Mansion. Rev. by D. M. Ledesert & R. P. Ledesert. x, 546p. (Fr. & Eng.). E20.00 (ISBN 0-245-50973-9). Harrap.
Harrap's New Standard French & English Dictionary: L-Z, English-French, Vol. 4. J. E. Mansion. Rev. by D. M. Ledesert & R. P. Ledesert. iv, 727p. (Fr. & Eng.). E20.00 (ISBN 0-245-51860-6). Harrap.
Harrap's New Standard French & English Dictionary, Part One, French-English (A-I) rev. ed. J. E. Mansion. Ed. by D. H. Ledesert & R. P. Ledesert. (Fr. & Eng.). 1972. Repr. text ed. 32.50 (ISBN 0-8442-1876-6, 1874-4). Natl Textbk.
Harrap's New Standard French & English Dictionary, Part One, French-English (J-Z) rev. ed. J. E. Mansion. Ed. by D. H. Ledesert & R. P. Ledesert. (Fr. & Eng.). 1972. Repr. 32.50 (ISBN 0-8442-1884-7, 1875-4). Natl Textbk.
Harrap's Russian Vocabulary. George Scanlan. viii, 103p. (Rus.). E2.95; pap. 2.00. Harrap Co.
Harrap's Schoeffler-Weis German & English Dictionary, 2 PTS. Rev. by Erich Weis & Heinrich Mattutat. 1077p. (Eng. & Ger.). E9.95 (ISBN 0-245-59813-8). Harrap.
Harrap's Shorter French & English Dictionary. P. H. Collin et al. 1781p. (Fr. & Eng.). 1982. E9.95 (ISBN 0-245-53926-3). Harrap.
Harrap's Shorter French & English Dictionary. J. E. Mansion et al. (Fr. & Eng.). 1967. 19.95 (ISBN 0-7720-0142-1); 12.95 (ISBN 0-7720-0143-X). Harrap Co.
Harrap's Standard Anglais-Francais. 1530p. (Fr.-Eng.). 1970. 49.95 (ISBN 0-686-57324-2, M-6311). French & Eur.
Harrap's Standard French & English Dictionary. J. E. Mansion. xii, 1488p. (Fr. & Eng.). E17.00 (ISBN 0-245-57661-4). Harrap.
Harrap's Standard French & English Dictionary, Part 2, English-French (A-Z) rev. ed. J. E. Mansion. (Fr. & Eng.). 1962. Repr. text ed. 49.50 (ISBN 0-8442-1898-7, 1876-4). Natl Textbk.
Harrap's Super-Mini French & English Dictionary. abridged ed. J. E. Mansion. Ed. by Patricia Forbes & Margaret Ledesert. (Fr. & Eng.). (gr. 7-12). 1977. pap. 2.75 (ISBN 0-8442-1871-5, 1871-4). Natl Textbk.
Harrap's Two Thousand Word English Dictionary. Ed. by P. H. Collin. (Illus.). vi, 271p. (Eng.). write for info. (ISBN 0-245-53834-8). Harrap.
Harsusi Lexicon & English-Harsusi Word-list. Thomas M. Johnstone. LC 77-364070. xxviii, 181p. (Harsusi & Eng.). 1977. E13.00 (ISBN 0-19-713580-3). Oxford U Pr.
Harvard Brief Dictionary of Music. Apel & Daniel. pap. 3.95 (ISBN 0-671-43475-6). PB.
Harvard Brief Dictionary of Music. Ed. by Willi Apel & Ralph T. Daniel. 348p. 1968. pap. 3.95 (ISBN 0-671-43475-6). WSP.
Harvard Concise Dictionary of Music. Don M. Randel. LC 78-5948. (Illus.). 1978. 15.00 (ISBN 0-674-37471-1, Belknap Pr); pap. 6.95 (ISBN 0-674-37470-3, Belknap Pr). Harvard U Pr.
Harvard Dictionary of Music. rev., enl. ed. Willi Apel. LC 68-21970. (Illus.). 1969. 25.00 (ISBN 0-674-37501-7, Belknap Pr). Harvard U Pr.
Hawaiian Dictionary. rev. ed. Mary K. Pukui & Samuel H. Elbert. Orig. Title: Hawaiian-English Dictionary English-Hawaiian Dictionary. 639p. (Hawaiian & Eng.). 1971. 20.00 (ISBN 0-87022-662-2). UH Pr.
Hawaiian-English Dictionary English-Hawaiian Dictionary see Hawaiian Dictionary.
Hawaiian Language & Hawaiian-English Dictionary. Henry P. Judd. LC 78-101212. (Eng. & Hawaiian.). 1966. soft bdg. 4.95 (ISBN 0-930492-06-4). Hawaiian Serv.
Hawaiian Phrase Book. Ed. by J. H. Soper. LC 68-13868. (Hawaiian.). 1968. pap. 3.50 (ISBN 0-8048-0241-6). C E Tuttle.
Hawaii's Real Estate Industry & Technical Terminology in English & Japanese. Kazuo Nishiyama & Hiroshi Katayama. 201p. (Japanese & Eng.). 8.32. Honolulu Japanese.
Haydn's Dictionary of Dates & Universal Information Relating to All Ages & Nations. Joseph T. Haydn. 1968. Repr. of 1911 ed. 89.00 (ISBN 0-403-00083-1). Scholarly.
Health & Culture in a South Indian village. C. M. Matthews. LC 80-900413. (Illus.). 498p. (Eng. & Tamil.). 1979. Rs.125.00. Orient Bk Dist.
Hebraeisch-Deutches Woerterbuch. David Herstig. (Hebrew & Ger.). 1971. 17.50 (ISBN 3-19-006289-7). Hueber.
Hebraeisch-Deutsches Woerterbuch. David Herstig. (Hebrew & Ger.). 1971. 17.50 (ISBN 3-19-006289-7, M-7441, Pub. by Max Hueber). French & Eur.
Hebraisch, 2 vols. Jaacov Lavy. (Langenscheidts Handworterbucher Ser.). (Ger. & Hebrew.). Teil 1: Hebraisch-Deutsch (639p.) DM.78.00 (04160); Teil 2: Deutsch-Hebraisch (xxiii, 824p.) DM.88.00 (04165). Langenscheidt.
Hebraisch-Deutsch: Zum Alten Testament. K. Feyerabend. (Langenscheidts Taschenworterbucher Ser.). 306p. (Ger. & Hebrew.). DM.18.80 (10040). Langenscheidt.
Hebrew & Aramaic Dictionary of the Old Testament. Ed. by Georg Fohrer et al. Tr. by W. A. Johnstone from Ger. LC 73-82430. viii, 344p. (Hebrew & Aramaic.). 1973. text ed. 16.00x (ISBN 3-11-004572-9). De Gruyter.
Hebrew & Chaldee Lexicon: Keyed to Strong's Exhaustive Concordance. Wilhelm Gesenius. Tr. by Samuel P. Tregelles. (Hebrew & Chaldee.). kivar 18.95 (ISBN 0-8010-3736-0). Baker Bk.
Hebrew & Chaldee Lexicon, Tregelles Translation. William Gesenius. (Hebrew & Chaldee.). 1949. 12.95 (ISBN 0-8028-8029-0). Eerdmans.
Hebrew & English Lexicon to the Old Testament. 2nd ed. William Gesenius. Ed. by Francis Brown et al. Tr. by Edward Robinson. (Hebrew & Eng.). 1959. 34.95x (ISBN 0-19-864301-2). Oxford U Pr.
Hebrew-Arabic Dictionary of the Bible, Known As Kitab Jami al-Alfaz (Agron, 2 vols. David Ben Abraham. Ed. by Solomon L. Skoss. LC 78-63565. (Yale Oriental Ser. Researches: Nos. 20-21). (Hebrew & Arabic.). Repr. of 1945 ed. Set. 97.50 (ISBN 0-404-60290-8). AMS Pr.

Hebrew-Arabic Dictionary of the Bible Known As Kitab Jami-Al-Alfaz, 2 vols. Ed. by Solomon Skoss. (Yale Oriental Researches Ser.: No. XX, XXI). (Hebrew & Arabic.). 1945. 50.00x ea.; 95.00x set (ISBN 0-686-57837-6). Elliots Bks.

Hebrew-Aramaic-English Dictionary, a Dictionary of Talmud Babli & Talmud Yerushalmi Targum & Midrash, 2 Vols. Marcus Jastrow. (Hebrew, Aramaic & Eng.). 68.50 (ISBN 0-87559-019-5). Shalom.

Hebrew-English Dictionary: Hebrew & Chaldee Lexicon to the Old Testament. rev. ed. Gesenius Furst. Ed. by Edward C. Mitchell. (Hebrew & Eng.). 42.50 (ISBN 0-87559-021-7); thumb indexed 42.50 (ISBN 0-87559-022-5). Shalom.

Hebrew-English, English-Hebrew Dictionary. A. Waldstein. (Hebrew & Eng.). 18.50 (ISBN 0-87559-016-0); thumb indexed 23.50 (ISBN 0-87559-017-9). Shalom.

Hebrew-English Lexicon of the Bible. LC 74-26705. 296p. (Orig., Hebrew & Eng.). 1975. pap. 7.50 (ISBN 0-8052-0481-4). Schocken.

Hebrew-English Pictorial Dictionary. David Ettinger. (Hebrew & Eng.). 27.50 (ISBN 0-87559-018-7). Shalom.

Hebrew Nomenclature of Inorganic Chemistry. (Eng. & Hebrew.). IL.5.00. Massada Pr.

Hebrew Pocket Dictionary. (Hebrew & Eng.). 12.50 (ISBN 0-685-12022-8). Heinman.

Hebrew Vocabularies. J. Barton Payne. (Hebrew.). pap. 3.95 (ISBN 0-8010-6949-1). Baker Bk.

Heimerans Kuchenlexikon. Erhard Gorys. LC 76-453925. 558p. (Ger.). 1975. write for info. (ISBN 3-8063-1093-9). Kochbuch Verlag.

Heinemann Australian Dictionary. Ed. by K. Harber. 1976. text ed. 14.50x (ISBN 0-686-65318-1, 00511). Heinemann Ed.

Heinemann Modern Dictionary for Dental Students. Jennifer Fowler. 184p. (Eng. & Fr.). 1973. 29.95 (ISBN 0-686-56750-1, M-6257). French & Eur.

Heinemann Modern Dictionary for Dental Students. (Illus.). 1973. text ed. 16.95x (ISBN 0-433-10701-4). Intl Ideas.

Heinemann New Zealand Dictionary. Ed. by H. W. Orsman. 1339p. 1981. 13.50x (ISBN 0-86863-373-9, 00564). Heinemann Ed.

Heinemann New Zealand Dictionary. Ed. by H. W. Orsman. LC 80-466872. ix, 1339p. (Eng.). 1979. write for info. (ISBN 0-86863-373-9). Heinemann Ed Bks.

Henderson's Dictionary of Biological Terms. 9th ed. Sandra Holmes. 521p. text ed. 35.00 (ISBN 0-442-24865-2). Van Nos Reinhold.

Herbst Dictionaries of Commercial, Financial & Legal Terms: Deutsch-Englisch. Ed. by Robert Herbst & Alan G. Readett. (Two-Language Ser.: Vol. B). 906p. (Ger. & Eng.). 1976. text ed. 69.95x (ISBN 0-686-92258-1). Birkhauser.

Herbst Dictionaries of Commercial, Financial & Legal Terms: English-German. Robert Herbst & Alan G. Readett. (Two-Language Ser.: Vol. A). 688p. (Eng. & Ger.). 1975. text ed. 69.95 (ISBN 0-686-92254-9). Birkhauser.

Herbst Dictionaries of Commercial, Financial & Legal Terms Vol. I. Robert Herbst & Alan G. Readett. (Herbst Dictionaries; 3-Language Ser.). 1138p. (Eng., Ger. & Fr.). 1979. text ed. 98.95 (ISBN 3-85942-000-3). Birkhauser.

Herbst Dictionaries of Commercial, Financial & Legal Terms Vol. 2. Ed. by Robert Herbst & Alan G. Readett. (Herbst Dictioaries; 3-Language Ser.). 1106p. (Ger., Eng. & Fr.). 1979. text ed. 98.95 (ISBN 3-85942-006-2). Birkhauser.

Herbst Dictionary of Commercial, Financial & Legal Terms. Ed. by Robert Herbst & Alan G. Readett. (Three-Language Ser.: Vol. 3). 980p. (Fr., Eng. & Ger.). 1979. text ed. 98.95 (ISBN 3-85942-002-X). Birkhauser.

Herbst Dictionay of Commercial, Financial & Legal Terms. Ed. by Robert Herbst & Alan G. Readett. (Two-Language Ser.: Vol. A). 688p. (Eng. & Ger.). 1975. text ed. 69.95 (ISBN 0-686-97268-6). Birkhauser.

Herbst-Readett Three-Language Dictionaries of Commerce, Finance & Law, 3 Vols. Birkhauser-Boston Publishing. (Eng., Ger. & Fr.). 1983. Vol. 1 1979 English-German-French. 98.95 (ISBN 0-686-87520-6); Vol. 2 1982 German-English-French. 98.95 (ISBN 0-686-87521-4); Vol. 3 1983 French-English-German. 98.95 (ISBN 0-686-87522-2). Birkhauser.

Herbst-Readett Two-Language Dictionaries of Finance, Commerce & Law, 2 vols. Birkhauser-Boston Publishing. (Eng. & Ger.). 1976. Vol. 1 1975 English-German. 24.95 (ISBN 0-686-87523-0); Vol. 2 1976 German-English. 24.95 (ISBN 3-85942-004-6). Birkhauser.

Herder - Lexikon Gemeinschaftskunde. M. Klein. (Ger.). pap. 15.95 (ISBN 3-451-16465-5, M-7455, Pub. by Herder). French & Eur.

Herder - Lexikon Geographie. M. Klein. 238p. (Ger.). 1975. pap. 15.95 (ISBN 3-451-16451-5, M-7456, Pub. by Herder). French & Eur.

Herder - Lexikon Medizin. 2nd ed. D. Oeter. 240p. (Ger.). pap. 15.95 (ISBN 0-686-56479-0, M-7446, Pub. by Herder). French & Eur.

Herder - Lexikon Paedagogik. B. Kaluza. 216p. (Ger.). 1976. pap. 15.95 (ISBN 3-451-16466-3, M-7447, Pub. by Herder). French & Eur.

Herder - Lexikon Politik. 2nd ed. B. Pfahlberg. 240p. (Ger.). 1976. pap. 15.95 (ISBN 3-451-16456-6, M-7450, Pub. by Herder). French & Eur.

Herder - Lexikon Psychologie. 2nd ed. Blumenbrg & Kury. 239p. (Ger.). 1976. pap. 25.95 (ISBN 3-451-16467-1, M-7451, Pub. by Herder). French & Eur.

Herder - Lexikon Tiere. Gack & Jahn. 342p. (Ger.). 1976. pap. 15.95 (ISBN 3-451-17371-9, M-7459, Pub. by Herder). French & Eur.

Herder - Lexikon Umwelt. U. Becker. 216p. (Ger.). 1976. 17.95 (ISBN 3-451-16457-4, M-7460, Pub. by Herder). French & Eur.

Herder - Lexikon Wirtschaft. 2nd ed. G. Boeing. 256p. (Ger.). 1975. pap. 25.95 (ISBN 3-451-16460-4, M-7462, Pub. by Herder). French & Eur.

Herder-Lexikon. Udo Becker. LC 75-514614. 239p. (Ger.). 1975. DM.19.80 (ISBN 3-451-16463-9). Herder.

Herder Lexikon. Hans Kossel. LC 80-471281. 271p. (Ger.). 1978. write for info. (ISBN 3-451-17378-6). Herder.

Herder-Lexikon Biologie. R. Bergfeld. 238p. (Ger.). 1975. pap. 24.95 (ISBN 3-451-16453-1, M-7453, Pub. by Herder). French & Eur.

Herder-Lexikon Biologie. R. Bergfeld. 238p. (Ger.). 1975. pap. 24.95 (ISBN 3-451-16453-1). Herder.

Herder-Lexikon Chemie. 3rd ed. O. Peter. 256p. (Ger.). 1975. pap. 15.95 (ISBN 3-451-16465-5, M-7454, Pub. by Herder). French & Eur.

Herder-Lexikon Chemie. 3rd ed. O. Peter. 256p. (Ger.). 1975. pap. 15.95 (ISBN 3-451-16465-5). Herder.

Herder-Lexikon Gemeinschaftskunde. M. Klein. (Ger.). pap. 15.95 (ISBN 3-451-16465-5). Herder.

Herder-Lexikon Geographie. M. Klein. 238p. (Ger.). 1975. pap. 15.95 (ISBN 3-451-16451-5). Herder.

Herder-Lexikon Geologie und Mineralogie. J. Klein. 238p. (Ger.). 1975. 15.95 (ISBN 3-451-16452-3, M-7457, Pub. by Herder). French & Eur.

Herder-Lexikon Geologie und Mineralogie. J. Klein. 238p. (Ger.). 1975. 15.95. Herder.

Herder-Lexikon Kunst. Boeing & Haeusgen. 240p. (Ger.). 1974. pap. 25.95 (ISBN 3-451-16459-0, M-7458, Pub. by Herder). French & Eur.

Herder-Lexikon Kunst. Boeing & Haeusgen. 240p. (Ger.). 1974. 15.95 (ISBN 3-451-16458-2). Herder.

Herder-Lexikon Mathematik. J. Reck. 238p. (Ger.). 1974. 15.95 (ISBN 3-451-16458-2, M-7445, Pub. by Herder). French & Eur.

Herder-Lexikon Mathematik. J. Reck. 238p. (Ger.). 1974. 15.95 (ISBN 3-451-16458-2). Herder.

Herder-Lexikon Medizin. 2nd ed. D. Oeter. 240p. (Ger.). pap. 15.95. Herder.

Herder-Lexikon Musik: Sachwoerterbuch. Ed. by Karl Ludwig Nicol. LC 79-338562. (Illus.). 222p. (Ger.). 1977. DM.19.80 (ISBN 3-451-17372-7). Herder.

Herder-Lexikon Paedagogik. B. Kaluza. 216p. (Ger.). 1976. pap. 15.95 (ISBN 3-451-16466-3). Herder.

Herder Lexikon Paedogogik. Ed. by Bjorn Kaluza. LC 76-481667. (Illus.). 209p. (Ger.). 1976. write for info. (ISBN 3-451-16466-3). Herder.

Herder-Lexikon Pflanzen. H. Jahn. 256p. (Ger.). 1975. pap. 15.95 (ISBN 3-451-17370-0, M-7448, Pub. by Herder). French & Eur.

Herder-Lexikon Pflanzen. H. Jahn. 256p. (Ger.). 1975. pap. 15.95 (ISBN 3-451-17370-0). Herder.

Herder-Lexikon Physik. R. Sauermost. (Ger.). 1975. 15.95 (ISBN 0-686-56480-4, M-7449, Pub. by Herder). French & Eur.

Herder-Lexikon Physik. R. Sauermost. (Ger.). 1975. 15.95. Herder.

Herder-Lexikon Politik. 2nd ed. B. Pfahlberg. 240p. (Ger.). 1976. pap. 15.95 (ISBN 3-451-16456-6). Herder.

Herder-Lexikon Psychologie. 2nd ed. Blumenbrg & Kury. 239p. (Ger.). 1976. pap. 25.95 (ISBN 3-451-16467-1). Herder.

Herder-Lexikon: Psychologie Sachwoerterbuch. Franz-Jurgen Blumenberg. LC 77-477664. (Illus.). 238p. (Ger.). 1975. DM.19.80 (ISBN 3-451-16467-1). Herder.

Herder-Lexikon Soziologie. B. Blinkert. 240p. (Ger.). 23.95 (ISBN 3-451-16468-X, M-7452, Pub. by Herder). French & Eur.

Herder-Lexikon Soziologie. B. Blinkert. 240p. (Ger.). 23.95 (ISBN 3-451-16468-X). Herder.

Herder-Lexikon Tiere. Gack & Jahn. 342p. (Ger.). 1976. pap. 15.95 (ISBN 3-451-17371-9). Herder.

Herder-Lexikon Umwelt. U. Becker. 216p. (Ger.). 1976. 17.95 (ISBN 3-451-16457-4). Herder.

Herder-Lexikon Weltaumphysik. U. Becker. 240p. (Ger.). 1975. pap. 17.95 (ISBN 3-451-16463-9, M-7461, Pub. by Herder). French & Eur.

Herder-Lexikon Weltaumphysik. U. Becker. 240p. (Ger.). 1975. pap. 17.95 (ISBN 3-451-16463-9). Herder.

Herder-Lexikon Wirtschaft. 2nd ed. G. Boeing. 256p. (Ger.). 1975. pap. 25.95 (ISBN 3-451-16460-4). Herder.

Herders Theologisches Taschenlexikon. K. Rahner. 3180p. (Ger.). 1976. pap. 99.50 (ISBN 0-686-56481-2, M-7463, Pub. by Herder). French & Eur.

Herders Theologishes Taschenlexikon. K. Rahner. 3180p. (Ger.). 1976. pap. 99.50. Herder.

Hering's Dictionary of Classical & Modern Cookery. 5th ed. Ed. by Walter Bickel. 1974. 27.95 (ISBN 3-8057-0232-9, Pub. by Virtuea Col Ltd. England). CBI Pub.

Hering's Dictionary of Classical & Modern Cookery. rev. ed. R. Hering. 30.00x (ISBN 0-685-47437-2). Corner.

Hering's Dictionary of Classical & Modern Cookery. rev. ed. Richard Hering. Tr. by Walter Bickel from Ger. (Illus.). 1977. text ed. 42.95 (ISBN 0-911202-08-0). Radio City.

Hethitisches Etymologisches Glossar. Johann Tischler. Ed. by Guenther Neumann. LC 79-384968. (Ger.). 1977. S.240.00 (ISBN 3-851-24537-7). Inst Verg Sprach.

Hethitisches Woerterbuch. 2nd ed. Johannes Friedrich & Annelies Kammenhuber. (Ger.). 1975. write for info. Winter Univ.

Hieroglyphic Vocabulary to the Theban Recension of the Book of the Dead. Ernest A. Budge. LC 73-18846. Repr. of 1911 ed. 26.50 (ISBN 0-404-11335-4). AMS Pr.

High Action Reading for Vocabulary: Level B. Merrily P. Hansen & Jeffrey N. Hansen. (Skillbooster Ser.). 64p. (gr. 2). 1980. write for info. wkbk. (ISBN 0-87895-234-9). Modern Curr.

High Technology Glossary: Nineteen Eighty-Three. Ed. by Ronald P. Smolin. 1983. pap. 10.00 (ISBN 0-686-46678-0). Intl Ideas.

Hillier Color Dictionary of Trees & Shrubs. H. G. Hillier. 323p. 1982. 19.95 (ISBN 0-442-23653-0). Van Nos Reinhold.

Hill's English-Swedish, Swedish-English Pocket Dictionary. 244p. (Eng. & Swedish.). 1981. 15.00x (ISBN 0-561-00191-X, Pub. by Bailey & Swinfen South Africa). State Mutual Bk.

Hindi-English - English-Hindi Standard Illustrated Dictionary, 2 vols. Ed. by R. C. Pathak. (Illus., Hindi & Eng.). Set. 40.00 (ISBN 0-686-68936-4). Vol. 1, Hindi-Eng., 1512pp. Vol. 2. Eng.-Hindi, Heinman.

Hindi-English Dictionary. (Hindi & Eng.). 27.50 (ISBN 0-87557-033-X, 034-8); large ed. 24.50 (ISBN 0-685-59369-X). Saphrograph.

Hindi English Dictionary. R. C. Pathak. (Hindi & Eng.). 1979. 11.00 (ISBN 0-89744-969-X). Auromere.

Hindi-English Dictionary: With Pronounciations Romanized. A. T. Shanney. (Hindi & Eng.). 27.50 (ISBN 0-87559-113-2). Shalom.

Hindi Pocket Dictionary, 2 vols. (Hindi & Eng.). 15.00 set (ISBN 0-685-30576-7). Heinman.

Hindu-Kashmiri Common Vocabulary. Jawaharlal Handoo & Lalita Handoo. LC 76-902046. vii, 292p. (Kashmiri & Hindu.). 1975. Rs.20.00. Ctr Inst Ind Lang.

Hiradastechnikai Kislexikon. Miklos Izak. LC 78-399684. 435p. (Hungarian.). 1976. write for info. Mueszaki Konyv.

Histopathological Definition of Burkitt's Tumour. (WHO Bulletin Reprint: Vol. 40, No. 4). (Summary in French & Russian). 1969. pap. 2.00 (ISBN 92-4-056000-9). World Health.

Historical & Cultural Dictionary of Afghanistan. M. Jamil Hanifi. LC 75-40249. (Historical & Cultural Dictionaries of Asia Ser.: No. 5). 1976. 15.00 (ISBN 0-8108-0892-7). Scarecrow.

Historical & Cultural Dictionary of Burma. Joel M. Maring & Ester G. Maring. LC 73-1477. (Historical & Cultural Dictionaries of Asia Ser.: No. 4). 1973. 15.00 (ISBN 0-8108-0596-0). Scarecrow.

Historical & Cultural Dictionary of India. George T. Kurian. LC 76-16186. (Historical & Cultural Dictionaries of Asia Ser.: No. 8). 1976. 17.50 (ISBN 0-8108-0951-6). Scarecrow.

Historical & Cultural Dictionary of the Sultanate of Oman & the Emirates of Eastern Arabia. John D. Anthony. LC 76-42216. (Historical & Cultural Dictionaries of Asia Ser.: No. 9). 1976. 13.00 (ISBN 0-8108-0975-3). Scarecrow.

Historical & Geographical Dictionary of Japan. E. Papinot. LC 71-152116. (Illus.). 1972. pap. 10.50 (ISBN 0-8048-0996-8). C E Tuttle.

Historical Dictionary of Algeria. Alf A. Heggoy & Robert R. Crout. LC 80-24126. (African Historical Dictionaries Ser.: No. 28). x, 247p. 1981. 15.00 (ISBN 0-8108-1376-9). Scarecrow.

Historical Dictionary of Angola. Phyllis M. Martin. LC 80-15662. (African Historical Dictionaries Ser.: No. 26). 196p. 1980. 14.00 (ISBN 0-8108-1322-X). Scarecrow.

Historical Dictionary of Bolivia. Dwight D. Heath. LC 73-172476. (Latin American Historical Dictionaries Ser.: No. 4). 1972. 15.00 (ISBN 0-8108-0451-4). Scarecrow.

Historical Dictionary of Brazil. Robert M. Levine. LC 78-10178. (Latin American Historical Dictionaries Ser.: No. 19). 1979. lib. bdg. 14.50 (ISBN 0-8108-1178-2). Scarecrow.

Historical Dictionary of Burundi. Warren Weinstein. LC 76-13594. (African Historical Dictionaries Ser.: No. 8). 1976. 19.50 (ISBN 0-8108-0962-1). Scarecrow.

Historical Dictionary of Cameroon. Victor T. Le Vine & Roger Nye. LC 74-901. (African Historical Dictionaries Ser.: No. 1). 1974. 13.00 (ISBN 0-8108-0707-6). Scarecrow.

Historical Dictionary of Chad. Samuel Decalo. LC 77-23585. (African Historical Dictionaries Ser.: No. 13). 1977. 21.00 (ISBN 0-8108-1046-8). Scarecrow.

Historical Dictionary of Costa Rica. Theodore S. Creedman. LC 77-6390. (Latin American Historical Dictionaries Ser.: No. 16). 1977. 14.00 (ISBN 0-8108-1040-9). Scarecrow.

Historical Dictionary of Costa Rica. Theodore S. Creedman. 1977. 10.00 ea. Intl Guatemala.

Historical Dictionary of Dahomey. Samuel Decalo. LC 75-42168. (African Historical Dictionaries Ser.: No. 7). 1976. 14.00 (ISBN 0-8108-0833-1). Scarecrow.

Historical Dictionary of El Salvador. Philip F. Flemion. LC 78-189546. (Latin American Historical Dictionaries Ser.: No. 5). 1972. 13.00 (ISBN 0-8108-0471-9). Scarecrow.

Historical Dictionary of El Salvador. Philip F. Flemion. 1972. 7.50 ea. Intl Guatemala.

Historical Dictionary of Equatorial Guinea. Max Liniger-Goumaz. LC 79-15914. (African Historical Dictionaries Ser.: No. 21). 246p. 1979. 14.00 (ISBN 0-8108-1230-4). Scarecrow.

Historical Dictionary of Ethiopia. Chris Prouty & Eugene Rosenfeld. LC 81-8729. (African Historical Dictionaries Ser.: No. 32). 454p. 1981. 25.00 (ISBN 0-8108-1448-X). Scarecrow.

Historical Dictionary of Fascist Italy. Ed. by Philip V. Cannistraro. LC 81-4493. (Illus.). xxix, 657p. 1982. lib. bdg. 49.95 (ISBN 0-313-21317-8, CFA/). Greenwood.

Historical Dictionary of Gabon. David E. Gardinier. LC 81-5290. (African Historical Dictionaries Ser.: No. 30). 284p. 1981. 15.00 (ISBN 0-8108-1435-8). Scarecrow.

Historical Dictionary of Guatemala. rev. ed. Richard A. Moore. 1973. 10.00 ea. Intl Guatemala.

Historical Dictionary of Guinea: Republic of Guinea-Conakry. Thomas E. O'Toole. LC 77-28145. (African Historical Dictionaries Ser.: No. 16). 1978. 13.00 (ISBN 0-8108-1112-X). Scarecrow.

Historical Dictionary of Haiti. Roland I. Perusse. LC 76-30264. (Latin American Historical Dictionaries Ser: No. 15). (Illus.). 1977. 13.00 (ISBN 0-8108-1006-9). Scarecrow.

Historical Dictionary of Honduras. Harvey K. Meyer. (Illus.). 1976. 15.00 ea. Intl Guatemala.

Historical Dictionary of Kenya. Bethwell A. Ogot. LC 81-1815. (African Historical Dictionaries Ser.: No. 29). 299p. 1981. 16.00 (ISBN 0-8108-1419-6). Scarecrow.

Historical Dictionary of Lesotho. Gordon Haliburton. LC 76-49550. (African Historical Dictionaries Ser.: No. 10). (Illus.). 1977. 15.00 (ISBN 0-8108-0993-1). Scarecrow.

Historical Dictionary of Libya. Lorna Hahn. LC 81-5228. (African Historical Dictionaries Ser.: No. 33). 132p. 1981. 13.00 (ISBN 0-8108-1442-0). Scarecrow.

Historical Dictionary of Malawi. Cynthia A. Crosby. LC 80-18. (African Historical Dictionaries Ser.: No. 25). 280p. 1980. lib. bdg. 15.00 (ISBN 0-8108-1287-8). Scarecrow.

Historical Dictionary of Mali. Ed. by Pascal J. Imperato. LC 76-55775. (African Historical Dictionaries Ser.: No. 11). (Illus.). 1977. 15.00 (ISBN 0-8108-1004-2). Scarecrow.

Historical Dictionary of Mauritania. Alfred G. Gerteiny. LC 81-5291. (African Historical Dictionaries Ser.: No. 31). 116p. 1981. 13.00 (ISBN 0-8108-1433-1). Scarecrow.

Historical Dictionary of Mauritius. Lindsay Riviere. LC 81-16557. (African Historical Dictionaries Ser.: No. 34). 206p. 1982. 13.50 (ISBN 0-8108-1479-X). Scarecrow.

Historical Dictionary of Mexico. Donald C. Briggs & Marvin Alisky. LC 80-27320. (Latin American Historical Dictionaries Ser.: No. 21). 275p. 1981. lib. bdg. 15.00 (ISBN 0-8108-1391-2). Scarecrow.

Historical Dictionary of Morocco. William Spencer. LC 80-21328. (African Historical Dictionaries Ser.: No. 24). 195p. 1980. 14.00 (ISBN 0-8108-1361-0). Scarecrow.

Historical Dictionary of Niger. Samuel Decalo. LC 79-15704. (African Historical Dictionaries Ser.: No. 20). 376p. 1979. 20.50 (ISBN 0-8108-1229-0). Scarecrow.

Historical Dictionary of Oceania. Ed. by Robert D. Craig & Frank P. King. LC 80-24779. (Illus.). 416p. 1981. lib. bdg. 55.00 (ISBN 0-313-21060-8, KHD/). Greenwood.

Historical Dictionary of Peru. Marvin Alisky. LC 79-16488. (Latin American Historical Dictionaries Ser.: No. 20). 163p. 1979. 13.00 (ISBN 0-8108-1235-5). Scarecrow.

Historical Dictionary of Puerto Rico & the U.S. Virgin Islands. Kenneth R. Farr. LC 73-7603. (Latin American Historical Dictionaries Ser.: No. 9). 1973. 13.00 (ISBN 0-8108-0670-3). Scarecrow.

Historical Dictionary of Rhodesia-Zimbabwe. R. Kent Rasmussen. LC 78-23671. (African Historical Dictionaries Ser.: No. 18). 1979. lib. bdg. 24.50 (ISBN 0-8108-1187-1). Scarecrow.

Historical Dictionary of Senegal. Lucie G. Colvin. LC 80-25466. (African Historical Dictionaries Ser.: No. 23). 355p. 1981. 17.50 (ISBN 0-8108-1369-6). Scarecrow.

Historical Dictionary of Sierra Leone. Cyril P. Foray. LC 77-3645. (African Historical Dictionaries Ser.: No. 12). 1977. 17.50 (ISBN 0-8108-1035-2). Scarecrow.

Historical Dictionary of Somalia. Margaret F. Castagno. LC 75-25681. (African Historical Dictionary Ser.: No. 6). 1975. 14.00 (ISBN 0-8108-0830-7). Scarecrow.

Historical Dictionary of Swaziland. John J. Grotpeter. LC 75-4734. (African Historical Dictionaries Ser.: No. 3). 265p. 1975. 15.00 (ISBN 0-8108-0805-6). Scarecrow.

Historical Dictionary of Tanzania. Laura S. Kurtz. LC 77-25962. (African Historical Dictionaries Ser.: No. 15). 1978. 19.50 (ISBN 0-8108-1101-4). Scarecrow.

Historical Dictionary of the Central African Republic. Pierre Kalck. Tr. by Thomas O'Toole. LC 80-21199. (African Historical Dictionaries Ser.: No. 27). 194p. 1980. 13.00 (ISBN 0-8108-1360-2). Scarecrow.

Historical Dictionary of the French & Netherlands Antilles. Albert Gastmann. LC 78-19070. (Latin American Historical Dictionaries Ser.: No. 18). 1978. lib. bdg. 13.00 (ISBN 0-8108-1153-7). Scarecrow.

Historical Dictionary of the Gambia. Harry A. Gailey. LC 75-5882. (African Historical Dictionaries Ser.: No. 4). 180p. 1975. 13.00 (ISBN 0-8108-0810-2). Scarecrow.

Historical Dictionary of the People's Republic of the Congo (Congo-Brazzaville) Virginia Thompson & Richard Adloff. LC 74-14975. (African Historical Dictionaries Ser.: No. 2). 1974. 13.00 (ISBN 0-8108-0762-9). Scarecrow.

Historical Dictionary of the Republic of Botswana. Richard P. Stevens. LC 75-16489. (African Historical Dictionaries Ser.: No. 5). 189p. 1975. 13.00 (ISBN 0-8108-0857-9). Scarecrow.

Historical Dictionary of the Republics of Guinea-Bissau & Cape Verde. Richard Lobban. LC 79-18227. (African Historical Dictionaries Ser.: No. 22). 209p. 1979. 14.00 (ISBN 0-8108-1240-1). Scarecrow.

Historical Dictionary of the Spanish Civil War, 1936-1939. Ed. by James W. Cortada. LC 81-13424. (Illus.). xxviii, 571p. 1982. lib. bdg. 67.50 (ISBN 0-313-22054-9, CSP/). Greenwood.

Historical Dictionary of the Sudan. John Voll. LC 77-28798. (African Historical Dictionaries Ser.: No. 17). 1978. 13.00 (ISBN 0-8108-1115-4). Scarecrow.

Historical Dictionary of Togo. Samuel Decalo. LC 76-14926. (African Historical Dictionaries Ser.: No. 9). 261p. 1976. 15.00 (ISBN 0-8108-0942-7). Scarecrow.

Historical Dictionary of Upper Volta. Daniel M. McFarland. LC 77-14987. (African Historical Dictionaries Ser.: No. 14). (Illus.). 1978. 14.50 (ISBN 0-8108-1088-3). Scarecrow.

Historical Dictionary of Uruguay. Jean Willis. LC 74-14630. (Latin American Historical Dictionaries Ser.: No. 11). 1974. 15.00 (ISBN 0-8108-0766-1). Scarecrow.

Historical Dictionary of Western Sahara. Tony Hodges. LC 81-21251. (African Historical Dictionaries Ser.: No. 35). 473p. 1982. 28.50 (ISBN 0-8108-1497-8). Scarecrow.

Historical Dictionary of Zambia. John J. Grotpeter. LC 79-342. (African Historical Dictionaries Ser.: No. 19). 1979. 22.50 (ISBN 0-8108-1207-X). Scarecrow.

Historical Register & Dictionary of the U.S. Army 1789-1903, 2 vols. Francis B. Heitman. 200.00 (ISBN 0-8490-0311-3). Gordon Pr.

Historical Register & Dictionary of the United States Army, from Its Organization, September 29, 1789, to March 2, 1903, 2 vols. Francis B. Heitman. LC 65-15975. 1965. 55.00 (ISBN 0-252-72456-9). U of Ill Pr.

History of English Critical Terms. J. W. Bray. 59.95 (ISBN 0-8490-0325-3). Gordon Pr.

History of English Critical Terms. J. W. Bray. 1977. lib. bdg. 59.95 (ISBN 0-8490-1974-5). Gordon Pr.

History of Foreign-Language Dictionaries. Robert Collison. 216p. 1982. 60.00x (ISBN 0-233-97310-9, Pub. by A Deutsch England). State Mutual Bk.

History of Sanskrit Lexicography. Madhukar M. Patkar. 199p. 1981. text ed. 14.25x (ISBN 0-391-02418-3, Pub. by Munshiram Manoharlal India). Humanities.

Hitta Ratt & Stora Ordlistan. (Swedish). write for info. (ISBN 91-24-30630-4). Esselte Studium.

Hitti's English-Arabic Medical Dictionary. Yusuf K. Hitti. (Eng. & Arabic). 1967. 35.00x (ISBN 0-8156-6004-9, Am U Beirut). Syracuse U Pr.

Hittite Dictionary of the Oriental Institute of the University of Chicago, Vol. 3, Fasc. 1, L. Ed. by Harry A. Hoffner, Jr. & Hans G. Guterbock. LC 79-53554. (Hittite). 1980. pap. 9.00x (ISBN 0-918986-27-3). Oriental Inst.

Hittite Glossary. 2nd ed. Linguistic Society of America & E. H. Sturtevant. (William Dwight Whitney Linguistic Ser.: W2). 2.00. Linguistic Soc Am.

Hoa's Essential English-Vietnamese Dictionary. Tu-Dien Tieu-Chuan Anh-Viet. (Vietnamese & Eng.). pap. 7.50. Iaconi.

Holt Intermediate Dictionary of American English. Holt Staff. (gr. 4-9). 1967. text ed. 7.92 (ISBN 0-03-067320-8); tchrs' manual incl. regional pronunciation record. 2.28 (ISBN 0-03-060406-0). HR&W.

Holz Woerterbuch, Vol. 1. Herbert Bucksch. (Ger. & Eng., Dictionary of wood & woodworking practice). 1966. 59.95 (ISBN 3-7625-1168-3, M-7465, Pub. by Bauverlag). French & Eur.

Holz Woerterbuch, Vol. 1. Herbert Bucksch. (Ger.). 1966. 59.95 (ISBN 3-7625-1168-3). Bauverlag.

Holz Woerterbuch, Vol. 2. Herbert Bucksch. (Ger. & Eng., Dictionary of wood & woodworking practice). 1966. 67.50 (ISBN 3-7625-1170-5, M-7466, Pub. by Bauverlag). French & Eur.

Holz Woerterbuch, Vol. 2. Herbert Bucksch. (Ger.). 1966. 67.50 (ISBN 3-7625-1170-5). Bauverlag.

Holz-Woerterbuch: Band I, Deutsch-Englisch. H. Bucksch. 461p. (Ger. & Eng.). 1978. DM.75.00 (ISBN 3-7625-1201-9). Bauverlag.

Holz-Woerterbuch: Band II, Englisch-Deutsch. 536p. (Eng. & Ger.). 1966. DM.84.00 (ISBN 3-7625-1170-5). Bauverlag.

Homeric Dictionary for Schools & Colleges. Georg Autenrieth. Ed. by Isaac Flagg. Tr. by Robert P. Keep. (Illus.). (YA) (gr. 9 up). 1979. pap. 8.95x (ISBN 0-8061-1289-1). U of Okla Pr.

Homeric Vocabularies: Greek & English Word-Lists for the Study of Homer. William B. Owen & Edgar J. Goodspeed. LC 68-31669. (Gr. & Eng.). (YA) (gr. 9 up). 1969. pap. 3.95x (ISBN 0-8061-0828-2). U of Okla Pr.

Homonyms. Dora Newhouse. LC 77-82190. viii, 247p. (Eng. & Span.). 1978. write for info. Newhouse Pr.

Homonyms-Homonimos: Sound-Alikes. Dora Newhouse. LC 77-82190. (Illus., Eng. & Span.). 1978. pap. 6.95 (ISBN 0-918050-27-8). Newhouse Pr.

Horses' Health A to Z. Peter D. Rossdale & Susan M. Wreford. LC 73-89678. 256p. 1974. 19.95 (ISBN 0-668-03414-9). Arco.

Horticultural Dictionary: French-English. D. O. Bourke. (Fr. & Eng.). 1974. 49.95 (ISBN 0-85198-308-1, M-9713). French & Eur.

Hospital Administration Terminology. 48p. (Orig.). 1982. pap. 10.75 (ISBN 0-87258-367-8, AHA-001110). Am Hospital.

Houghton Mifflin Canadian Dictionary of the English Language. (Eng.). 1980. 13.95 (ISBN 0-395-29653-6); 16.95 (ISBN 0-395-29654-4). HM.

Housing-Planning Glossary. United States League of Savings Associations. 6.00 (15388). US League Savings Assns.

How to Improve Your Spelling & Vocabulary. Jessica Davidson. (gr. 7 up). 1980. PLB 8.90 (ISBN 0-531-04133-6). Watts.

How to Read German Church Records Without Knowing Much German. Arta F. Johnson. LC 80-128394. (Illus.). 48p. (Ger.). 1980. write for info. Johnson.

How to Say It in Hungarian: An English-Hungarian Phrase-Book with Lists of Words. 6th ed. L. T. Andras & M. Murval. (Illus., Eng. & Hungarian). 1979. 6.50 (ISBN 9-6317-4194-X). Heinman.

How to Talk Golf: David Langdon's A-Z of Golfing Terms. David Langdon. LC 76-353017. (Illus.). 80p. (Eng.). 1975. E1.75 (ISBN 0-413-34250-6). Spon Ltd.
How to Use the Thesaurus. Louise Colligan. (gr. 7-12). 1978. pap. 1.50 (ISBN 0-590-11860-9). Scholastic Inc.
Hugo Grotius Drama Concordance. Christian Gellinek. LC 83-70923. (Studies in German Literature, Linguistics, & Culture: Vol. 7). (Illus.). 800p. 1983. 29.50x (ISBN 0-938100-23-8). Camden Hse.
Hugo Pocket Dictionary: Dutch-English, English-Dutch. 624p. 1969. 3.50 (ISBN 0-8226-0502-3, 502). Littlefield.
Hugo Pocket Dictionary: French-English, English-French. (Fr. & Eng.). 1973. 3.50 (ISBN 0-8226-0503-1, 503). Littlefield.
Hugo Pocket Dictionary: German-English, English-German. 622p. (Ger. & Eng.). 1969. 3.50 (ISBN 0-8226-0504-X, 504). Littlefield.
Hugo Pocket Dictionary: Italian-English, English-Italian. 622p. (Ital. & Eng.). 1971. 3.50 (ISBN 0-8226-0505-8, 505). Littlefield.
Hugo Pocket Dictionary: Russian-English, English-Russian. 658p. (Rus. & Eng.). 1975. 3.50 (ISBN 0-8226-0506-6, 506). Littlefield.
Hugo Pocket Dictionary: Russian-English, English-Russian. 657p. (Rus. & Eng.). 1969. 3.95 (ISBN 0-686-92547-5, M-9011). French & Eur.
Hugo Pocket Dictionary: Spanish-English, English-Spanish. 610p. (Span. & Eng.). 1975. 3.50 (ISBN 0-8226-0507-4, 507). Littlefield.
Hungarian Concise Dictionary: English-Hungarian. 9th ed. Laszlo Orszagh. (Hungarian & Eng.). 1981. 25.00x (ISBN 96-305-2464-3, H-269). Vanous.
Hungarian Concise Dictionary: Hungarian-English, Vol. 2. 7th ed. Laszlo Orszagh. (Hungarian & Eng.). 1976. 25.00x (H268). Vanous.
Hungarian Cooking. Elizabeth De Biro. 9.50 (ISBN 0-87557-098-4, 098-4). Saphrograph.
Hungarian Deluxe Dictionary: English-Hungarian, Vol. 1. 6th ed. Orszagh. (Hungarian & Eng.). 1980. 95.00x (ISBN 96-305-0554-1, H-331). Vanous.
Hungarian Deluxe Dictionary: Hungarian-English, Vol. 2. 5th ed. Orszagh. (Hungarian & Eng.). 1977. 75.00x (ISBN 96-305-0067-1, H-330). Vanous.
Hungarian Dictionary for Tourists. 5th ed. Magay Tamas. (Hungarian & Eng.). 1980. 6.00x (ISBN 96-320-5110-6, H300). Vanous.
Hungarian-English Dictionary, 2 vols. L. Orszagh. (Hungarian & Eng.). 29.50 (ISBN 0-87557-042-9, 042-9). Saphrograph.
Hungarian-English Dictionary, 2 vols. V. Orszagh. 2160p. (Hungarian & Eng.). 1980. 125.00x (ISBN 0-569-00409-8, Pub. by Collet's). State Mutual Bk.
Hungarian-English, English-Hungarian Concise Dictionary (1976-79, 2 vols. rev & enl ed. L. Orszagh. (Hungarian & Eng.). 55.00 set (ISBN 0-685-29277-0). Vol. 1, Hungarian-English, 9th ed. Vol. 2, English-Hungarian, 10th ed (ISBN 9-6305-2464-3). Heinman.
Hungarian-English: English Hungarian Dictionary, 2 vols. 13th rev. ed. Laszlo Orszagh. (Hungarian & Eng.). Set. 20.00x (ISBN 963-05-2019-2). Heinman.
Hungarian-English Technical Dictionary. T. Nagy. 752p. (Hungarian & Eng.). 1980. 70.00x (ISBN 0-569-00731-3, Pub. by Collet's). State Mutual Bk.
Hungarian-French Concise Dictionary. S. Eckhardt. 1092p. (Hungarian & Fr.). 1973. leatherette 39.95 (ISBN 0-686-92492-4, M-9324). French & Eur.
Hungarian Kitchen Parade. L. Erdfly-Markovics. pap. 3.95 (ISBN 0-87557-102-6, 102-6). Saphrograph.
Hungarian Pocket Dictionary: Hungarian-English, Vol. 2. 12th ed. Laszlo Orszagh. 462p. (Hungarian & Eng.). 1979. 8.50x (ISBN 96-305-1256-4, H273). Vanous.
Hungarian-Vietnamese Dictionary. I. Kotet. 864p. (Hungarian & Vietnamese.). 1974. 95.00 (ISBN 963-05-0366-2, M-9325). French & Eur.
Husznyelvu Kiadoi Szotar. Imre Mora. LC 77-477898. 389p. (Eng., Ger. & Hungarian.). 1977. 175.00 Ft (ISBN 9-6305-0996-2). Akademiai Kiado.
Hydraulic Standards, Lexicon & Data. Institute for Power System. 200p. 1979. 35.00x (ISBN 0-85461-005-7). State Mutual Bk.
Iaponsko-Russkii Politekhnicheskii Slovar. 496p. (Japanese & Rus.). 1976. 9.95 (Pub. by Russkii Iazyk). Four Continent.

I

Iaponsko-Russkii Uchebnyi Slovar Ieroglifov. N. I. Feldman-Konrad. 683p. (Japanese & Rus.). 1977. 15.50 (Pub. by Russkii Iazyk). Four Continent.
Iban-English Dictionary. Ed. by A. J. Richards. (Illus., Iban & Eng.). 1982. 65.00x (ISBN 0-19-864325-X). Oxford U Pr.
Icelandic-English - English-Icelandic Dictionary, 2 vols. 3rd ed. A. Sigurdsson & S. O. Bogason. (Icelandic & Eng.). Set. 155.00 (ISBN 0-686-68938-0). Heinman.
Icelandic-English Dictionary. 2nd ed. Ed. by Richard Cleasby & Gudbrand Vigfusson. (Icelandic & Eng.). 1957. 125.00x (ISBN 0-19-863103-0). Oxford U Pr.
Icelandic-English Dictionary. 3rd ed. A. Sigurdsson. (Icelandic & Eng.). 80.00 (ISBN 0-686-64772-6). Heinman.
Icelandic-English Dictionary. Arngrimur Sigurdsson. (Icelandic & Eng.). 42.50 (ISBN 0-87559-166-3). Shalom.
Icelandic-English-Icelandic, Pocket Dictionary. A. Taylor. 176p. (Icelandic & Eng.). 1980. pap. 11.00x (ISBN 0-89918-103-1, IC103). Vanous.
Icelandic Grammar, Text & Glossary. 2nd ed. Stefan Einarsson. 538p. 1949. 25.00x (ISBN 0-8018-0187-7). Johns Hopkins.
Icelandic Pocket Dictionary. (Icelandic & Eng.). 12.50 (ISBN 0-685-36175-6). Heinman.
Iconographic Index to Stanislas Lami's Dictionnaire des Sculpteurs de l'Ecole Francaise au Dix-Neuvieme Siecle. H. W. Janson. LC 82-48768. 230p. 1983. lib. bdg. 75.00 (ISBN 0-8240-9399-2). Garland Pub.
Idegen Szavak Szotara. Ferenc Bakos et al. LC 77-554987. 544p. (Hungarian.). 1975. 35.00 Ft (ISBN 9-6320-5037-1). Terra.
Idegen Szavak Szotara. Forenc Bakos & Pal Fabian. LC 77-554987. 544p. (Hungarian.). 1976. 35.00 Ft (ISBN 9-63205-037-1). Terra.
Idiomatic Expressions English-Spanish. (Eng. & Span.). write for info. (608-111). Pan Amer Pub.
Idioms in the Bible Explained. 3rd ed. George M. Lamsa. pap. 1.00 (ISBN 0-686-09905-2). Aramaic Bible.
Idiotismes du Francais Fondamental, Premier Degre. D. K. Pryce. (Illus.). 192p. (Fr.). E2.50 (ISBN 0-245-51978-5). Harrap.
IEEE Standard Dictionary of Electrical & Electronics Terms. 2nd ed. Institute of Electrical & Electronics Engineers, Inc. LC 77-92333. 1977. 37.50x (ISBN 0-471-04264-1, Pub. by Wiley-Interscience). Wiley.
IFIP Fachtworterbuch der Informationsverabeitung. IFIP. (Ger.). 1968. 22.00 (ISBN 0-7204-2027-X, North Holland). Elsevier.
IFIP-Sach Worterbuch der Datenverarbeitung. I. Gould. 170p. (Ger.). 1977. 19.95 (ISBN 3-87144-335-2, M-7467, Pub. by Verlag Harri Deutsch). French & Eur.
IFIP Sachwoerterbuch der Datenverarbeitung. Gould. (Illus.). 170p. (Eng., Rus. & Ger.). 1977. DM.24.80 (ISBN 3-87144-335-2). Verlag Harri Deutsch.
Illiustrirovannyi Aviatsionnyi Slovar Dlia Molodezhi. A. T. Stepanets. 454p. (Rus.). 1964. 4.85 (Pub. by Dosaaf). Four Continent.
Illiustrirovannyi Voenno-Tekhnicheskii Slovar. L. D. Neliubin. 482p. (Eng., Ger., Span., Rus. & Fr.). 1968. 17.50 (Pub. by Voenizdat). Four Continent.
Illustrated Auto Racing Dictionary for Young People. Ross R. Olney. LC 78-59243. (Illustrated Dictionary Ser.). (Illus.). (gr. 4 up). 1978. PLB 7.29 (ISBN 0-8178-5762-1). Harvey.
Illustrated Auto Racing Dictionary for Young People. Ross R. Olney. (Treehouse Bks). (Illus.). (gr. 4 up). 1981. pap. 2.50 (ISBN 0-13-450742-8). P-H.
Illustrated Automobile Dictionary. Czeslaw Blok & Wieslaw Jezewski. (Illus.). 1978. lib. bdg. 89.00 (ISBN 9-0201-1070-5, Pub. by Kluwer Tech Netherlands). Kluwer Academic.
Illustrated Backpacking & Hiking Dictionary for Young People. Randy Larson. (Treehouse Bks). (Illus.). (gr. 4 up). 1981. pap. 2.50 (ISBN 0-13-450759-2). P-H.
Illustrated Ballet Dictionary. Evan Jaffe. LC 78-73753. (Illustrated Culture Dictionary). (Illus.). (gr. 4 up). 1979. PLB 7.29 (ISBN 0-8178-6155-6). Harvey.
Illustrated Baseball Dictionary for Young People. Henry Walker. LC 70-102354. (Illustrated Dictionary Ser.). (Illus.). (gr. 5 up). 1970. PLB 7.29 (ISBN 0-8178-4592-5). Harvey.
Illustrated Basketball Dictionary for Young People. Steve Clark. LC 77-77859. (Illustrated Dictionary Ser.). (Illus.). (gr. 5 up). 1977. PLB 7.29 (ISBN 0-8178-5642-0). Harvey.
Illustrated Computer Dictionary. Rev. ed. Donald D. Spencer. 187p. 1983. pap. 8.95 (ISBN 0-686-46828-7). Merrill.
Illustrated Computer Dictionary for Young People. Donald D. Spencer. LC 81-21795. (Illus.). 1982. 8.95x (ISBN 0-89218-052-8). Camelot Pub.
Illustrated CPM-Wordstar Dictionary with Mailmerge & Spellstar Operations. Russell A. Stultz. (Illus.). 272p. 1983. pap. text ed. 14.95 (ISBN 0-13-450528-X). P-H.
Illustrated Dictionary of Art Terms: A Handbook for the Artist & Art Lover. Kimberley Reynolds & Richard Seddon. 190p. 1981. 35.00x (ISBN 0-85223-207-1, Pub. by Ebury Pr England). State Mutual Bk.
Illustrated Dictionary of Bible Manners & Customs. A. Van Deursen. (Illus.). 1979. pap. 3.95 (ISBN 0-8065-0707-1). Citadel Pr.
Illustrated Dictionary of British History. Ed. by Arthur Marwick et al. (Illus.). 320p. 1981. 19.95 (ISBN 0-500-25072-3). Thames Hudson.
Illustrated Dictionary of Ceramics. George Savage & Harold Newman. 1974. 24.95 (ISBN 0-442-27364-9). Van Nos Reinhold.
Illustrated Dictionary of Chemistry. Arthur Godman. (Illustrated Dictionaries Ser.). (Illus.). 256p. 1982. text ed. 7.95x (ISBN 0-582-55550-7). Longman.
Illustrated Dictionary of Chess. Edward R. Brace. (Illus.). 320p. (Ger.). E4.50 (ISBN 0-600-32920-8). Newnes Bks.
Illustrated Dictionary of Expressionism. Joseph-Emile Muller. LC 78-50723. (Pocket Art Ser.). (Illus.). (gr. 10-12). 1978. pap. 3.95 (ISBN 0-8120-0985-1). Barron.
Illustrated Dictionary of Glass. Harold Newman. (Illus.). 1978. 29.95 (ISBN 0-500-23262-8). Thames Hudson.
Illustrated Dictionary of Impressionism. Raymond Cognia & Frank Elgar. (Pocket Art Ser.). (Illus., Eng.). (gr. 10-12). 1979. pap. 3.95 (ISBN 0-8120-0986-X). Barron.
Illustrated Dictionary of Jewelry. Harold Newman. (Illustrated Dictionary Ser.). (Illus.). 1981. 29.95 (ISBN 0-500-23309-8). Thames Hudson.
Illustrated Dictionary of Lobstering. Kendall A. Merriam. LC 78-61525. (Illus., Orig.). 1978. pap. 6.95 (ISBN 0-87027-192-X). Cumberland Pr.
Illustrated Dictionary of Microcomputer Terminology. Michael Hordeski. (Illus.). 1978. pap. 8.95 (ISBN 0-8306-1088-X, 1088). TAB Bks.
Illustrated Dictionary of Pop Art. Jose Pierre. LC 78-50723. (Pocket Art Ser.). (Illus.). (gr. 10-12). 1978. pap. 3.95 (ISBN 0-8120-0984-3). Barron.
Illustrated Dictionary of Pottery Form. Robert Fournier. 1981. 24.95 (ISBN 0-442-26112-8) (ISBN 0-686-71500-4). Van Nos Reinhold.
Illustrated Dictionary of Practical Pottery. rev. ed. Robert Fournier. 256p. 1980. pap. 9.95 (ISBN 0-442-30181-2). Van Nos Reinhold.
Illustrated Dictionary of Sports. Graeme Wright. LC 78-61515. (Illus.). 192p. 1979. 14.95 (ISBN 0-528-81078-2). Rand.
Illustrated Dictionary of Surrealism. Jose Pierre. (Pocket Art Ser.). (Illus.). (gr. 10-12). 1978. pap. 3.95 (ISBN 0-8120-0987-8). Barron.
Illustrated Dictionary of Typographic Communication. Michael L. Kleper. (Illus.). 208p. (Orig.). 1983. pap. text ed. 19.00 (ISBN 0-89938-008-5). Tech & Ed Ctr Graph Arts RIT.
Illustrated Dictionary of Typographic Communication. Michael L. Kleper. (Illus.). 200p. 1983. pap. 19.00 (ISBN 0-930904-03-6). Graphic Dimensions.
Illustrated Dinosaur Dictionary. Helen R. Sattler. (Illus.). 1983. 17.00 (ISBN 0-686-46202-5). Lothrop.
Illustrated Dinosaur Dictionary. Helen Roney Sattler. LC 82-22947. (Illus.). 316p. 1983. 17.00 (ISBN 0-688-00479-2). Lothrop.
Illustrated Encyclopedic Dictionary of Electronic Circuits. John Douglas-Young. LC 82-23067. 444p. 1983. 27.95 (ISBN 0-13-450734-7). P-H.
Illustrated English-Polish Polish-English Dictionary. T. Grzebieniowski. 908p. (Pol. & Eng.). 1978. 9.95 (Pub. by Wiedza Powszechna). Four Continent.
Illustrated English-Polish Polish-English Dictionary. rev. & enl. ed. Ed. by Tadeusz Grzebieniowski. (Illus.). 908p. (Eng. & Pol.). 1978. 13.50x (ISBN 0-8002-2262-8). Intl Pubns Serv.
Illustrated Football Dictionary for Young People. Joseph Olgin. LC 74-82014. (Illustrated Dictionary Ser.). (Illus.). 128p. (gr. 5 up). 1974. PLB 7.29 (ISBN 0-8178-5182-8). Harvey.
Illustrated Gaelic-English Dictionary. 8th ed. Dwelly. (Illus., Gaelic & Eng.). 35.00x (ISBN 0-686-00868-5). Colton Bk.
Illustrated Glossary of Architecture: Eight Fifty to Eighteen Thirty. John Harris & Jill Lever. (Illus.). 314p. 1979. pap. 9.95 (ISBN 0-571-09074-5). Faber & Faber.
Illustrated Glossary of Packagings for the Transports of Dangerous Goods. (Illus.). pap. 5.00 (ISBN 0-686-94575-1, UN74/13/1, UN). Unipub.
Illustrated Glossary of Process Equipment: Chinese-English-French Edition. Bernard Paruit. (Illus.). 400p. 1983. text ed. 40.00x (ISBN 0-87201-692-7). Gulf Pub.

Illustrated Glossary of Process Equipment: English-French-Spanish Edition. Bernard Paruit. (Illus.). 324p. 1982. 39.95x (ISBN 0-87201-691-9). Gulf Pub.

Illustrated Glossary of Rice Processing Machines. (Agricultural Services Bulletin: No. 37). (Illus.). 104p. 1980. pap. 7.50 (ISBN 92-5-000784-1, F1854, FAO). Unipub.

Illustrated Graphics Glossary. Ken Garland. 192p. 1981. 30.00x (ISBN 0-09-141511-X, Pub. by Barrie & Jenkins England). State Mutual Bk.

Illustrated Gymnastics Dictionary for Young People. Ila Guraedy. LC 79-93357. (Illustrated Dictionary Ser.). (Illus.). 120p. (gr. 4 up). 1980. PLB 7.29 (ISBN 0-8178-0002-6). Harvey.

Illustrated Hawaiian Word Book. Robin Burningham. (Illus.). 104p. (Orig., Hawaiian.). 1982. pap. 5.95 (ISBN 0-935848-12-6). Bess Pr.

Illustrated Heritage Dictionary & Information Book. 1977. 34.95 (ISBN 0-395-25441-8). HM.

Illustrated Horseback Riding Dictionary for Young People. Elizabeth Van Vansteenwyk. 119p. (gr. 4 up). 1980. pap. 2.50 (ISBN 0-13-450908-0). P-H.

Illustrated Magic Dictionary. Geoffrey Lamb. (Illus.). 160p. 1980. 7.95 (ISBN 0-525-66689-3). Lodestar Bks.

Illustrated Medical Dictionary. Ed. by C. Murphy Combs. (Medical Adviser Ser.). (Illus.). 1979. pap. 3.95 (ISBN 0-8326-2237-0, 7455). Delair.

Illustrated Petroleum: Reference Dictionary. 2nd ed. Ed. by Robert D. Langenkamp. (Illus.). 584p. 1982. 45.95x (ISBN 0-87814-160-X, P-4263). Pennwell Pub.

Illustrated Riding Dictionary for Young People. Elizabeth Van Steenwyk. LC 80-81789. (Illustrated Dictionaries Ser.). (Illus.). 128p. (gr. 5 up). 1981. PLB 7.29 (ISBN 0-8178-0015-8). Harvey.

Illustrated Sex Dictionary. Richard Stiller. pap. 2.00 (ISBN 0-685-06563-4). Assoc Bk.

Illustrated Skiing Dictionary for Young People. Claire Walter. 119p. (gr. 4 up). 1980. pap. 2.50 (ISBN 0-13-450858-0). P-H.

Illustrated Soccer Dictionary for Young People. James Gardner. LC 76-10044. (Illustrated Dictionary Ser.). (Illus.). (gr. 5 up). 1976. PLB 7.29 (ISBN 0-8178-5482-7). Harvey.

Illustrated Soccer Dictionary for Young People. James Gardner. (Illus.). 125p. (gr. 4 up). 1978. pap. 2.50 (ISBN 0-13-451146-8, Pub. by Treehouse). P-H.

Illustrated Swimming, Diving & Surfing Dictionary for Young People. Diana C. Gleasner. LC 79-93358. (Illustrated Dictionary Ser.). (Illus.). 128p. (gr. 4 up). 1980. PLB 7.29 (ISBN 0-8178-0001-8). Harvey.

Illustrated Technical Dictionaries-Illustrierte Technische Woerterbuechen: In Six Languages. Ed. by Alfred Schlomann. Incl. Vol. 1. Machinenelemante-Elements of Machinery & Tools. 1968. Repr. of 1938 ed; Vol. 2. Elektrotechnik & Elektrochemie-Electrical Engineering, Incl. Telegraphy & Telephony. 1963. Repr. of 1928 ed. 50.00x (ISBN 3-4863-1943-4); Vol. 5. Eisenbahnbau und Betreib-Railway Construction & Operation. 1909; Vol. 14. Faserrohnstoffe - Raw Materials of the Textile Industry. 1958. Repr. of 1923 ed. 20.00 (ISBN 3-4863-1981-7); Vol. 16. Webereiund Gewelbe - Weaving & Woven Fabrics. 1958. Repr. of 1925 ed; Vol. 17. Luftfahrt-Aeronautics. 1956. Repr. of 1932 ed. 52.50x (ISBN 3-4863-2011-4). LC 33-6884. (Ger., Eng., Fr., Rus., Span., Ital.). Intl Pubns Serv.

Illustrated Technical German for Builders. 4th ed. W. K. Killer. 183p. (Eng. & Ger.). 1977. 15.95 (ISBN 3-7625-0898-4, M-7468, Pub. by Bauverlag). French & Eur.

Illustrated Technical German for Builders. 4th ed. W. K. Killer. 183p. (Eng. & Ger.). 1977. 15.95 (ISBN 3-7625-0898-4). Bauverlag.

Illustrated Tennis Dictionary for Young People. Karen Sweeney. LC 78-73758. (Illustrated Sports Dictionary). (Illus.). (gr. 4 up). 1979. PLB 7.29 (ISBN 0-8178-6230-7). Harvey.

Illustrated Texas Dictionary of the English Language, 5 Vols. Jim Everhart. pap. 2.95 ea.; Vol. 1. (ISBN 0-8220-1477-7); Vol. 2. (ISBN 0-8220-1478-5); Vol. 3. (ISBN 0-8220-1479-3); Vol. 4. (ISBN 0-8220-1480-7); Vol. 5. (ISBN 0-8220-1487-4). Cliffs.

Illustrated Topical Dictionary of the Western Desert Language: 1959. 2nd rev. ed. W. H. Douglas. (AIAS Research Regional Studies: No. 11). 1977. pap. text ed. 3.75x (ISBN 0-85575-061-8). Humanities.

Illustrated Track & Field Dictionary for Young People. Phyllis R. Emert. LC 80-84812. (Illustrated Dictionary Ser.). (Illus.). 128p. (gr. 4 up). 1981. PLB 7.29 (ISBN 0-8178-0028-X). Harvey.

Illustrated Track & Field Dictionary for Young People. Phyllis R. Emert. (Illus.). (gr. 4 up). 1981. pap. 2.50 (ISBN 0-13-451310-X). P-H.

Illustrated T.V. Dictionary. Carolyn H. Miller. LC 78-73761. (Illustrated Dictionaries Ser.). (Illus.). (gr. 4 up). 1980. PLB 7.29 (ISBN 0-8178-6220-X). Harvey.

Illustrated Vocabulary for the Use of the Deaf & Dumb. T. J. Watson. 69.95 (ISBN 0-8490-0383-0). Gordon Pr.

Illustrated Word Processing Dictionary. Russell A. Stultz. (Illus.). 176p. 1983. 17.95 (ISBN 0-13-450726-6); pap. 10.95 (ISBN 0-13-450718-5). P-H.

Illustratred New Shipbuilding Dictionary: English-Japanese, Japanese-English. M. Yamaguchi. 387p. (Eng. & Japanese.). 1960. leatherette 39.95 (ISBN 0-686-92490-8, M-9352). French & Eur.

Illustrierte Technische Woerterbucher: Eisenbahnmaschinenwesen, Vol. 6. A. Schlomann. (Ger., Eng., Fr., Rus., Span. & Ital., Dictionary of Railway Engineering). 1909. pap. 9.95 (ISBN 0-686-56486-3, M-7473, Pub. by R. Oldenbourg). French & Eur.

Illustrierte Technische Woerterbucher: Eisenbahnmaschinenwesen, Vol. 6. A. Schlomann. (Ger., Eng., Fr., Rus., Span. & Ital.). 1909. pap. 9.95. Oldenbourg Verlag.

Illustrierte Technische Woerterbucher: Eisenbahnbau und Betrieb, Vol. 5. A. Schlomann. (Ger., Eng., Fr., Rus., Span. & Ital., Dictionary of Railway engineering). 1909. pap. 9.95 (ISBN 0-686-56485-5, M-7472, Pub. by R. Oldenbourg). French & Eur.

Illustrierte Technische Woerterbucher: Eisenbahnbau und Betrieb, Vol. 5. A. Schlomann. (Ger., Eng., Fr., Rus., Span. & Ital.). 1909. pap. 9.95. Oldenbourg Verlag.

Illustrierte Technische Woerterbucher: Elektrotechnik und Elektrochemie, Vol. 2. A. Schlomann. (Illus., Ger., Eng., Fr., Rus., Span. & Ital., Illustrated Dictionary of Electrical Engineering & Electro-Ehemistry). 1963. 105.00 (ISBN 0-686-56483-9, M-7470, Pub. by R. Oldenbourg). French & Eur.

Illustrierte Technische Woerterbucher: ELektrotechnik und Elektrochemie, Vol. 2. A. Schlomann. (Illus., Ger., Eng., Fr., Rus., Span. & Ital.). 1963. 105.00. Oldenbourg Verlag.

Illustrierte Technische Woerterbucher: Maschinenelemente, Vol. 1. A. Schlomann. (Illus., Ger., Eng., Fr., Rus., Span. & It., Illustrated dictionary elements of machinery & tools). 1968. 59.95 (ISBN 0-686-56482-0, M-7469, Pub. by R. Oldenbourg). French & Eur.

Illustrierte Technische Woerterbucher: Maschinenelemente, Vol. 1. A. Schlomann. (Illus., Ger., Eng., Fr., Rus., Span. & Ital.). 1968. 59.95. Oldenbourg Verlag.

Illustrierter Technische Woerterbucher: Luffahrts, Vol. 17. A. Schlomann. (Illus., Ger., Eng., Fr., Rus., Span. & It., Aeronautics). 1956. 62.50 (ISBN 0-686-56488-X, M-7475, Pub. by R. Oldenbourg). French & Eur.

Illustrierter Technische Woerterbucher: Luffahrts, Vol. 17. A. Schlomann. (Illus., Ger., Eng., Fr., Rus., Span. & Ital.). 1956. 62.50. Oldenbourg Verlag.

Illustriertes Textil und Mode - Lexikon. Alfons Hofer. (Illus.). 342p. (Ger.). 19.95 (ISBN 3-87150-081-X, M-7476, Pub. by Deutscher Fachverlag). French & Eur.

Illustriertes Woerterbuch. 3rd ed. (Illus.). 192p. (Ger. , Eng. , Fr. & Span., Illustrated Dictionary). 1962. 29.95 (ISBN 3-8036-0250-5, M-7477, Pub. by Gebrueder Weiss). French & Eur.

Illustrowany Slownik Rosyjsko-Polski. Andrzej Bogusiawski. LC 79-352771. 1179p. (Rus. & Pol.). 1978. 200.00 Zl. Wiedza Powszechna.

Illustrowany Slownik Rosyjsko-Polski, Polsko-Rosyjski. Andrzej Boguslawski. LC 79-352771. (Illus.). 1179p. (Pol. & Rus.). 1978. 200.00 Zl. Wiedza Poswzechna.

ILO Thesaurus: Labour, Employment & Training Terminology. 2nd ed. 223p. 1980. 13.70 (ISBN 92-2-001982-5). Intl Labour Office.

Ilokano Dictionary. Constantino. (Ilokano.). 10.00. Iaconi.

Ilokano Dictionary. Ernesto Constantino. Ed. by Howard P. McKaughan. (PALI Language Texts: Philippines). 510p. (Orig.). 1971. pap. text ed. 12.00x (ISBN 0-87022-152-3). UH Pr.

Ilustrowany slownik angielsko-polski, polsko-angielski. Takeusz Grzebieniowski. LC 79-361868. (Illus.). 903p. (Eng. & Pol.). 1978. 200.00 Zl. Wiedza Powszechna.

Ilustrowany Slownik Niemiecko-Polski. Wanda Brzeska & Alojzy Brzeski. LC 75-547124. (Illus.). 995p. (Pol.). 1975. 150.00 Zl. Wiedza Powszechna.

Ilustrowany Slownik Niemiecko-Polski. Wanda Brzeska et al. LC 75-547124. 995p. (Ger. & Pol.). 1975. 150.00 Zl. Wiedza Powszechna.

Ilustrowany Slownik Samochodowy. Czeslaw Blok. LC 76-526304. 867p. (Eng., Pol., Rus. & Fr.). 1976. 250.00 Zl. Wydawnictwa.

IMF Glossary: English-French-Spanish. rev. ed. International Monetary Fund, Bureau of Language Services. (Eng., Fr. & Span.). 1980. pap. 5.00 (ISBN 0-939934-04-3). Intl Monetary.

In Search of a Small Business Definition: An Exploration of the Small-Business Definitions of the U. S., the U.K., Israel, & the People's Republic of China. Leah Hertz. LC 81-40926. 482p. 1982. lib. bdg. 29.75 (ISBN 0-8191-2308-0); pap. text ed. 17.25 (ISBN 0-8191-2309-9). U Pr of Amer.

Inbred & Genetically Defined Strains of Laboratory Animals. Ed. by Philip L. Altman & Dorothy D. Katz. Incl. Pt. 1. Mouse & Rat. 65.00 (ISBN 0-913822-12-4); Pt. 2. Hamster, Guinea Pig, Rabbit & Chicken. 50.00 (ISBN 0-913822-13-2). LC 78-73555. (Biological Handbooks: Vol. 3). (Illus.). 1979. Set. 100.00 (ISBN 0-913822-14-0). FASEB.

Increase Your Vocabulary, 2 Bks. Cambridge Book Editors. (Illus.). pap. text ed. 4.00 ea.; Bk. 1. pap. text ed. (ISBN 0-8428-0008-5); Bk. 2. pap. text ed. (ISBN 0-8428-0009-3); Bk. 1. key 1.13 (ISBN 0-8428-0028-X); Bk. 2. key 1.13 (ISBN 0-8428-0029-8). Cambridge Bk.

Index of Paramedical Vocabulary. J. E. Schmidt. (Illus.). 324p. 1974. pap. 10.75x spiral (ISBN 0-398-02833-8). C C Thomas.

Index to Bauer Arndt, Gingrich Greek Lexicon. 2nd ed. John R. Alsop. (Gr.). Date not set. 11.95 (ISBN 0-310-44031-9). Zondervan.

Index to the Brown, Driver & Briggs Hebrew Lexicon. Compiled by Bruce Einspahr. LC 76-25479. (Hebrew.). 1976. 23.95 (ISBN 0-8024-4082-7). Moody.

Index to the Theological Dictionary to the New Testament. Ed. by Pitkin. (Theological Dictionary to the N. T. Ser.). 1976. text ed. 25.00 (ISBN 0-8028-2323-8). Eerdmans.

Indian Epigraphical Glossary. D. C. Sircar. 1966. 13.95 (ISBN 0-89684-222-3). Orient Bk Dist.

Indioneziisko-Russkii Uchebnyi Razgovornik. L. I. Ushakova et al. 541p. (Rus. & Indonesian.). 1963. 1.75 (Pub. by Gosizdat Inostr Natsional Slovarei). Four Continent.

Indo-European Lexicon: Synchronic Theory. R. Beard. (North Holland Linguistic Ser.: Vol. 44). 1981. 47.00 (ISBN 0-444-86214-5). Elsevier.

Indogermanisches Etymologisches Woerterbuch, 2 vols, Vols. 1 & 2. Julius Pokorny. 1648p. (Ger.). 1969. 240.00 set (ISBN 3-7720-0526-8, M-7478, Pub. by Francke). French & Eur.

Indonesian-English Dictionary. 2nd ed. John M. Echols & Hassan Shadily. 431p. (Eng. & Indonesian.). 1963. 30.00x (ISBN 0-8014-0112-7). Cornell U Pr.

Indonesian-Russian Dictionary. R. N. Korigodsky et al. 1171p. (Indonesian & Rus.). 1961. leatherette 14.25 (ISBN 0-686-87187-1, M-9098). French & Eur.

Indoneziisko-Russkii Slovar. V. N. Korigodskii et al. 1171p. (Rus. & Indonesian.). 1961. 5.75 (Pub. by Gosizdat Inostr Natsional Slovarei). Four Continent.

Indoneziisko-Russkii Uchebnyi Slovar. A. S. Teselkin et al. 577p. (Rus. & Indonesian.). 1974. 2.35 (Pub. by Sov Entsiklopediia). Four Continent.

Industrial & Labor Relations Terms: A Glossary. 4th rev. ed. Robert E. Doherty. LC 79-18839. (ILR Bulletin: No. 44). 40p. 1979. pap. 2.50 (ISBN 0-87546-075-5). ILR Pr.

Industrial Engineering Terminology Index. American Institute of Industrial Engineers. (Industrial Engineering Terminology: 663). 11.00; 8.80, with membership. Inst Indus Eng.

Industrial Property Glossary. 1979. pap. 20.00 (ISBN 0-685-96910-X, WIPO58, WIPO). Unipub.

Informationsverarbeitung-Englisch-Deutsch-Franzoesisch-Russisch. Erich Burger. 464p. (Eng., Ger., Fr. & Rus.). 1980. M.48.00. VEB Technik.

Informatsionno-Poiskovyi Tezariius Po Informatike. 206p. (Rus.). 1974. 6.75 (Pub. by Vsesoiuz). Four Continent.

Ingles Al Dedillo: English at Your Fingertips. Richard Wiezell. (Vest-Pocket Ser.). (Illus.). 1978. pap. 2.95 (ISBN 0-8329-1537-8). New Century.

Ingles en la Construccion. Gunter Wallnig & Harry Evered. 104p. (Eng.-Span.). 1975. pap. 26.95 (ISBN 84-7146-082-3, S-50131). French & Eur.

Inglese-italiano, italiano-inglese. Ed. by Vladimiro Macchi. LC 80-500584. xii, 997p. (Ital. & Eng.). 1980. L.2000.00. Sansoni.

INIS: Thesaurus. (INIS Ser.: No. 13, Rev. 19). 748p. 1980. pap. 45.00 (ISBN 92-0-178480-5, IN13/R19, IAEA). Unipub.

INIS: Thesaurus. (IAEA-INIS Ser.: No. 13, Rev. 21). 759p. 1982. pap. 42.50 (ISBN 92-0-178082-6, IN13/R21, IAEA). Unipub.
INIS Thesaurus: Version Francaise. (INIS Reference Ser.: No. 13). 840p. 1979. pap. write for info. (ISBN 92-0-278079-X, IAEA-INIS-13, IAEA). Unipub.
Initials & Pseudonyms: A Dictionary of Literary Disguises, 2 Vols. William Cushing. 936p. 1982. Repr. of 1888 ed. Set. 79.00x (ISBN 0-8103-3962-5). Gale.
Initiation Au Vocabulaire Du Batiment et Des Travaux Publics. Profor. 176p. (Fr.). 1979. 37.50 (ISBN 0-686-57088-X, M-6467). French & Eur.
Inoue's Smaller Japanese-English Dictionary. Jukichi Inoue. LC 81-52936. 968p. (Japanese & Eng.). 1982. 13.95 (ISBN 0-8048-1440-6). C E Tuttle.
Instant Business Dictionary. L. E. Davids. (Career Institute Instant Reference Library). 1971. 3.95 (ISBN 0-531-02012-6). Watts.
Instant Business Dictionary. Lewis E. Davids. LC 78-150232. 1970. 3.95 (ISBN 0-911744-07-X). Career Inst.
Instant Medical Dictionary. B. O. Bolander. (Career Institute Instant Reference Library). 1970. 3.95 (ISBN 0-531-02009-6). Watts.
Instant Medical Spelling Dictionary. Donald O. Bolander et al. LC 77-124400. 1970. 3.95 (ISBN 0-911744-10-X). Career Inst.
Instant Quotation Dictionary. B. O. Bolander. (Career Institute Instant Reference Library). 314p. 1969. 3.95 (ISBN 0-531-02006-1). Watts.
Instant Quotation Dictionary. Donald O. Bolander et al. LC 74-104786. 1969. 3.95 (ISBN 0-911744-05-3). Career Inst.
Instant Spelling Dictionary. Margaret M. Dougherty et al. LC 67-11788. 1967. 3.95 (ISBN 0-911744-01-0). Career Inst.
Instant Spelling Dictionary. Ed. by Margaret M. Dougherty et al. (Career Institute Instant Reference Library). (gr. 9 up). 1967. 3.95 (ISBN 0-531-01697-8). Watts.
Instant Vocabulary. Ida L. Ehrlich. pap. 3.95 (ISBN 0-671-47722-6). PB.
Insult Dictionary: How to Get What You Want in Five Nasty Languages. 1981. pap. 4.95 (ISBN 0-686-29649-4). Natl Textbk.
Insurance Language. Marianne Keim. LC 77-12037. 1978. lib. bdg. 12.90 (ISBN 0-89471-019-2); pap. 2.95 (ISBN 0-89471-018-4). Running Pr.
Intensive Course in Tongan. Eric B. Shumway. (PALI Language Texts: Polynesia). 1971. pap. text ed. 15.00x (ISBN 0-87022-757-2). UH Pr.
Interconnection Glossary. 25.00 (ISBN 0-686-32974-0). Info Gatekeepers.
Intermediate Dictionary. (Eng.). 1972. 12.95 (ISBN 0-7715-1974-5). Gage Ed Pub.
Intermediate Greek-English Lexicon. Liddell & Scott. 910p. (Gr. & Eng.). 1980. 35.00. Oxford U Pr.
Intermediate Greek-English Lexicon. Compiled by H. G. Liddell & Robert Scott. (Gr. & Eng.). 1959. text ed. 30.00x (ISBN 0-19-910206-6). Oxford U Pr.
International Bible Dictionary. 1977. (Pub. by Logos); pap. 6.95 (ISBN 0-88270-235-1). Bridge Pub.
International Bibliography of African Lexicons. Melvin K. Hendrix. LC 81-16533. 370p. 1982. 22.50 (ISBN 0-8108-1478-1). Scarecrow.
International Bibliography of Standardized Vocabularies. Compiled by Helmut Felber. (International Bibliography of Infoterm Ser., Vol. 2). 1978. 95.00x (ISBN 0-89664-075-2, Pub. by K G Saur). Gale.
International Bibliography of Standardized Vocabularies. 2nd & rev. ed. Eugen Wuster et al. Ed. by International Information Centre for Terminology. LC 78-13537. xxiv, 540p. (Eng., Fr. & Ger.). 1979. write for info. (ISBN 0-89664-075-2). K G Saur.
International Business Dictionary in Nine Languages. Ed. by F. Munniksma. 1974. 45.00x (ISBN 90-267-0394-5, 1526). Esperanto League North Am.
International Construction Terminology. K. Lange & L. Ferval. 120p. (Eng. & Fr.). 1979. 14.50 (ISBN 3-7625-1235-3, M-7479, Pub. by Bauverlag). French & Eur.
International Construction Terminology. K. Lange & L. Ferval. 120p. (Eng. & Fr.). 1979. 14.50 (ISBN 3-7625-1235-3). Bauverlag.
International Cooperation in Terminology. (Infoterm Ser.: Vol. 3). 333p. 1975. pap. text ed. 35.00x (ISBN 3-7940-5503-9, Pub. by K G Saur). Gale.
International Dictionary. Otto Jesperson. (Ger., Fr. & Eng.). 1930. 9.95 (ISBN 3-533-01130-5, M-7480, Pub. by Carl Winter). French & Eur.
International Dictionary. Otto Jesperson. (Ger., Fr. & Eng.). 1930. 9.95 (ISBN 3-533-01130-5). Winter Univ.
International Dictionary of Abbreviations of Organizations, 3 vols. 2nd ed. Paul Spillner. (Eng. & Ger.). 1970. 120.00 (ISBN 3-7940-1398-0, M-7481, Pub. by Verlag Dokumentation SVK). French & Eur.
International Dictionary of Building Construction: English-French-German-Italian. Angelo C. Schwicker. 1280p. (Eng., Fr., Ger. & Ital.). 1975. lib. bdg. 60.00x (ISBN 0-87936-004-6). Scholium Intl.
International Dictionary of Business. Hano Johannsen & G. Terry Page. 376p. 1981. 17.95 (ISBN 0-13-470823-7); pap. 7.95 (ISBN 0-13-470815-6). P-H.
International Dictionary of Heating, Ventilating, & Air Conditioning. Ed. by European Heating & Ventilating Associations. LC 79-41714. 416p. 1982. 79.95x (ISBN 0-419-11650-8, NO. 6553, E&FN Spon England). Methuen Inc.
International Dictionary of Management. 2nd ed. Ed. by H. Johannsen & G. T. Page. 1981. pap. 29.95 (ISBN 0-686-86508-1, Pub by Kogan Pg). Nichols Pub.
International Dictionary of Metallurgy, Mineralogy, Geology & the Mining & Oil Industries. A. Gagnacci-Schwicker & Schwicker. 1530p. (Eng., Fr., Ger. & Ital.). 1970. 88.00 (ISBN 3-7625-0751-1, M-7482, Pub. by Bauverlag). French & Eur.
International Dictionary of Metallurgey, Mineralogy, Geology & the Mining & Oil Industries. A. Gagnacci-Schwicker & Schwicker. 1530p. (Eng., Fr., Ger. & Ital.). 1970. 88.00 (ISBN 3-7625-0751-1). Bauverlag.
International Dictionary of Obscenities: A Guide to Dirty Words & Indecent Expressions in Spanish, Italian, French, German, & Russian. Christina Kunitskaya-Peterson. 93p. (Orig., Span., Ital., Fr., Ger. & Rus.). 1981. pap. 5.95 (ISBN 0-933884-18-4). Berkeley Slavic.
International Dictionary of Sociology. Ed. by Michael Mann. 600p. 1983. 34.50 (ISBN 0-8264-0238-0). Continuum.
International Dictionary of Spanish & English. (Span. & Eng.). 34.95. Iaconi.
International Dictionary of Sports & Games. J. A. Cuddon. LC 79-20983. (Illus.). 898p. 1980. 29.95 (ISBN 0-8052-3733-X). Schocken.
International Dictionary of Women Workers in the Decorative Arts: A Historical Survey from the Distant Past to the Early Decades of the Twentieth Century. Alice I. Prather-Moses. LC 81-8947. 218p. 1981. 13.50 (ISBN 0-8108-1450-1). Scarecrow.
International Dictionary Simon & Schuster. (Span. & Eng.). write for info. (608-72). Pan Amer Pub.
International Directory of Acronyms in Library, Information & Computer Sciences. Pauline M. Vaillancourt. LC 80-18352. xi, 518p. 1980. 45.00 (ISBN 0-8352-1152-5). Bowker.
International Electrotechnical Vocabulary: Electronics. 335p. (Eng. , Fr. & Rus.). 1956. leatherette 9.95 (ISBN 0-686-92485-1, M-9071). French & Eur.
International Electrotechnical Vocabulary, Machines & Transformers. 212p. (Eng. , Fr. & Rus.). 1958. leatherette 4.95 (ISBN 0-686-92488-6, M-9072). French & Eur.
International Glossary of Technical Terms for the Pulp & Paper Industry. Van Derveer & Haas. 234p. (Eng., Ger., Fr., Span. & Swedish.). 1976. 55.00. Imported Bks.
International Glossary of Technical Terms for the Pulp & Paper Industry. Ed. by Paul D. Van Derveer & Leonard E. Haas. LC 74-20168. (A Pulp & Paper Book). 238p. 1976. 35.00 (ISBN 0-87930-037-X). Miller Freeman.
International Horseman's Dictionary. Zdzislaw Baranowski. (Illus.). 9.10 (ISBN 0-85131-262-4, Dist. by Sporting Book Center). J A Allen.
International Hospital Vade Mecum & English, French, Spanish Glossary. Paul Aurousseau. LC 78-675029. 340p. (Eng., Fr. & Span.). 1977. 0.257 F. Editions Sedip F.Galula.
International Meat Science Dictionary. Donald M. Kinsman. (Illus.). 282p. 1979. pap. 10.95x (ISBN 0-89641-029-3). American Pr.
International Microcomputer Dictionary. rev. ed. Sybex Staff & Rodnay Zaks. LC 81-51133. Orig. Title: Microprocessor Lexicon-Acronyms & Definitions. 120p. (Eng., Ger., Span., Ital. & Pol.). 1981. pap. 3.95x (ISBN 0-89588-067-9). Sybex.
International Planning Glossary. Ed. by Gordon Logie & Hemel Hemstead. LC 77-367067. (Eng., Fr., Ital., Dutch, Ger., Swedish, Finnish, Dannish & Norwegian.). 1975. E3.00 (ISBN 0-9504753-0-0). Intl Plan Glos.
International Reader's Dictionary. 2nd ed. Michael P. West & Roger Kingdon. LC 79-104746. x, 401p. (Eng.). 1978. write for info. (ISBN 0-582-52566-7). Longman England.
International Relations Dictionary. 3rd ed. Jack C. Plano & Roy Olton. LC 82-3996. (Clio Dictionaries in Political Science Ser.: No. 2). 488p. 1982. text ed. 22.50 (ISBN 0-87436-332-2); pap. 10.75 (ISBN 0-87436-336-5). ABC-Clio.
International tectonic lexicon. Ed. by J. G. Dennis. LC 81-47196. (Illus.). v, 153p. (Eng.). 1979. pap. write for info. (ISBN 3-510-65092-1). Schweizerbart.
International Thesaurus of Quotations. Ed. by Rhoda T. Tripp. LC 73-106587. 1970. 14.37i (ISBN 0-690-44584-9); 15.34i (ISBN 0-690-44585-7). T Y Crowell.
International Toeristisch Woordenboek: Edition Neerlandais. Academie Internationale du Tourisme. (Dutch.). 80.00 F. Acad Intl Tour.
International Vocabulary of Town Planning & Architecture. LC 70-860237. (Illus.). 366p. (Fr. , Ger. & Eng.). 1970. 55.00x (ISBN 0-8002-1582-6). Intl Pubns Serv.
Internationales Woerterbuch der Abkuerzungen Von Organisationen, 3 vols. P. Spillner. 1295p. (Ger. & Eng., International Dictionary of Abbreviations of Organizations). 1972. 120.00 (ISBN 3-7940-1098-1, M-7484, Pub. by Vlg. Dokumentation). French & Eur.
Internationes Kaselexikon. Othmar Hasselfeldt. LC 77-575279. 141p. (Ger.). 1977. DM.5.80 (ISBN 3-436-02465-1). Fischer Taschen.
Interpreter, Wherein Three Principal Terms of State Are Clearly Unfolded. Thomas Scott. LC 74-80194. (English Experience Ser.: No. 673). 1974. Repr. of 1624 ed. 3.50 (ISBN 90-221-0281-5). Walter J Johnson.
Interpreter's Dictionary of the Bible, 5 vols. Ed. by George A. Buttrick & Keith R. Crim. LC 62-9387. 1976. Set. 99.50 (ISBN 0-687-19268-4). Abingdon.
Interpretes de Bolsillo Aleman-Espanols. 320p. (Ger. & Span.). 275.00 ptas (ISBN 84-7153-371-5). Biblograf SP.
Interpretes de Bolsillo Espanol-Aleman. 280p. (Span. & Ger.). pap. 150.00 ptas (ISBN 84-7153-251-4). Biblograf SP.
Interpretes de Bolsillo Espanol-Frances. 280p. (Span. & Fr.). pap. 150.00 ptas (ISBN 84-7153-253-0). Biblograf SP.
Interpretes de Bolsillo Espanol-Ingles. 280p. (Span. & Eng.). pap. 150.00 ptas (ISBN 84-7153-252-2). Biblograf SP.
Interpretes de Bolsillo Espanol-Italiano. 280p. (Span. & Ital.). pap. 150.00 ptas (ISBN 84-7153-254-9). Biblograf SP.
Interpretes de Bolsillo Frances-Espanol. 320p. (Fr. & Span.). 275.00 ptas. Biblograf SP.
Interpretes de Bolsillo Ingles-Espanol. 320p. (Eng. & Span.). 275.00 ptas (ISBN 84-7153-372-3). Biblograf SP.
Interpretes de Bolsillo Italiano-Espanol. 320p. (Ital. & Span.). 275.00 ptas. Biblograf SP.
Introduction, Key to Text, Vocabularies. Mansoor. (Legal & Documentary Ser.). 1965. write for info. E J Brill.
Introduction to Dental Terminology. Ann Ehrlich. (Illus.). 1978. 3.95 (ISBN 0-940012-10-3). Colwell Co.
Introduction to Dental Terminology. Rice. 1982. pap. 12.95 (ISBN 0-8151-7239-7). Year Bk Med.
Introduction to Medical Terminology for Nursing Home Personnel. American Medical Record Association. 24p. 2.00 (1013P). Am Med Record Assn.
Introduction to Mental Retardation Syndromes & Terminology. Byron C. Moore et al. 184p. 1978. 14.50x (ISBN 0-398-03718-3). C C Thomas.
Introduction to Modern Japanese Orthography: Kana. Elizabeth F. Gardner & Samuel E. Martin. (Japanese.). 3.00 (ISBN 0-88710-039-2). Far Eastern Pubns.
Inupiat Dialect of Eskimo see Inupiat Eskimo Dictionary.
Inupiat Eskimo Dictionary. Donald H. Webster & Wilfried Zibell. LC 76-632478. Orig. Title: Inupiat Dialect of Eskimo. (Illus.). 212p. (Eng. & Eskimo.). 1970. pap. 2.20 (ISBN 0-88312-377-0); microfiche 3.00. Summer Inst Ling.
Inverted Medical Dictionary. Waldo A. Rigal. LC 73-84126. 1976. 20.00x (ISBN 0-87762-203-5); pap. 14.50x (ISBN 0-87762-170-5). Technomic.
Investigationslexikon. Wolfgang Luecke. Ed. by Juergen Bloech. LC 75-514621. (Illus.). 403p. (Ger.). 1975. DM.59.80 (ISBN 3-800-60482-5). Vahlen.
Investment Terms & Definitions. Canadian Securities Institute. 56p. first ten copies 1.25; eleven copies & over 1.00. Can Securities Inst.
Iontenwennaweienstahkhwa. University of the State of New York, State Education Department. LC 77-624515. xi, 93p. (Eng. & Mohawk.). 1977. write for info. State U NY Pr.

Irish-English Dictionary. Dinneen. (Irish & Eng.). 25.00x (ISBN 0-686-12048-5). Colton Bk.

Irish-English Dictionary. Rev. by Patrick S. Dinneen. (Irish & Eng.). 22.50 (ISBN 0-87559-070-5); thumb indexed 27.50 (ISBN 0-685-32982-8, 071-3). Shalom.

Irish-English Dictionary. Edward O'Reilly. (Irish & Eng.). 75.00 (ISBN 0-8490-0424-1). Gordon Pr.

Iron & Steel Dictionary: German-English & English-German. 2nd ed. Iron & Steel Institute. 1962. 22.50x (ISBN 3-514-00197-9). Intl Pubns Serv.

Iron & Steel Dictionary: German-French & French-German. Iron & Steel Institute. (Ger. & Fr.). 1962. 22.50x (ISBN 3-514-00209-6). Intl Pubns Serv.

Iron & Steel Dictionary: German-Italian & Italian-German. Iron & Steel Institute. (Ger. & Ital.). 1969. 22.50x (ISBN 3-514-00012-3). Intl Pubns Serv.

Iron & Steel Dictionary: German-Spanish & Spanish-German. 2nd ed. Iron & Steel Institute. (Ger. & Span.). 1966. 22.50x (ISBN 3-514-00011-5). Intl Pubns Serv.

Iron & Steel Industry Dictionary. A. M. Abd-El-Wahed. 441p. (Eng., Fr., Ger. & Arabic.). 1974. 45.00 (ISBN 0-686-92487-8, M-9760). French & Eur.

Islaendisches Etymologisches Woerterbuch. Alex Johannesson. 1406p. (Icelandic & Ger.). 1956. 232.00 (ISBN 3-7720-0429-6, M-7485, Pub. by Francke). French & Eur.

Isler's Pocket Dictionary of Diagnostic Tests, Procedures & Terms. C. Isler. 1980. pap. 8.95 (ISBN 0-87489-189-2). Med Economics.

Isneg-English Vocabulary. Morice Vanoverbergh. (Oceanic Linguistics Special Publications: No. 11). 618p. (Isneg & Eng.). 1972. pap. 12.00x (ISBN 0-8248-0235-7). UH Pr.

Ispansko-Russkii Razgovornik. S. Neverov. 190p. (Rus. & Span.). 1953. 1.25 (Pub. by Izd. Lit. Na Inostr. Iaz.). Four Continent.

Ispansko-Russkii Slovar. Ed. by F. V. Kelin. 944p. (Rus. & Span.). 1961. 4.95 (Pub. by Gosizdat Inostr Natsional Slovarei). Four Continent.

Ispansko-Russkii Slovar Po Dobyche i Pererabotke Nefti. A. A. Pinkevich et al. 424p. (Span. & Rus.). 1966. 6.20 (Pub. by Lenizdat). Four Continent.

Istilah biologi, bahasa Inggeris-bahasa Malaysia, bahasa Malaysia-Bahasa Inggeris. LC 81-941148. xxii, 388p. (Eng. & Malay.). 1980. M.$pap. 6.00. Dewan Bahasa.

Istilah geografi, Inggeris-Malaysia-Inggeris. LC 76-941849. xvi, 511p. (Eng. & Malay.). 1976. M.$6.50. Dewan Bahasa.

Istilah percetakan, penerbitan, dan komunikasi massa, Inggeris-Malaysia-Inggeris. LC 79-102377. xiv, 594p. (Malay & Eng.). 1978. M.$7.00. Dewan Bahasa.

Istilah perpustakaan, Inggeris-Malaysia-Inggeris. LC 79-102563. xvi, 421p. (Eng. & Malay.). 1978. M.$5.50. Dewan Bahasa.

Istilah pertanian, bahasa Ingeris-bahas a Malaysia, bahasa Malaysia-bahasa Inggeris. LC 80-942013. xviii, 276p. (Eng. & Malay.). 1980. M.$pap. 4.00. Dewan Bahasa.

Istilah Senibina, Perancangan dan Ukur Kuantiti. Dewan Bahasa dan Pustaka. LC 79-941288. xv, 217p. (Eng. & Malay.). 1978. M.$3.50. Dewan Bahasa.

Istoriko-Etimologicheskii Slovar Osetinskogo. V. I. Abaev. 360p. (Rus.). 1979. 8.25 (Pub. by Nauka). Four Continent.

Italian Abbreviations & Symbols: Law & Related Subjects. Adolf Sprudzs. LC 70-95307. 124p. 1969. 20.00 (ISBN 0-379-00451-8). Oceana.

Italian & English Idioms. R. Hall & F. Hall. (Eng. & Ital.). 1982. 9.95 (ISBN 0-8120-0467-1). Barron.

Italian Bilingual Dictionary. (Illus.). 436p. (Eng. & Ital.). 1980. pap. 3.50 pocket ed. Barron.

Italian Bilingual Dictionary: A Beginner's Guide in Words & Pictures. (Eng. & Ital.). 1979. 3.50. Barron.

Italian Bilingual Dictionary: A Beginner's Guide in Words & Pictures. Gladys Lipton & John Colinari. LC 79-10831. (Ital. & Eng.). (gr. 9-12). 1980. pap. text ed. 3.50 (ISBN 0-8120-0885-5). Barron.

Italian Dictionary. 320p. (Ital.). Epap. 1.25 (ISBN 0-600-36566-2). Newnes Bks.

Italian Dictionary. John Purves. (Routledge Pocket Dictionaries Ser.). 862p. (Ital.). 1980. pap. 8.95 (ISBN 0-7100-0602-0). Routledge & Kegan.

Italian-English Dictionary. Cassells. (Ital. & Eng.). 1977. standard 23.95 (ISBN 0-02-052254-1); indexed 17.95 (ISBN 0-02-052253-3). Macmillan.

Italian-English Dictionary, 1 vol. (Ital. & Eng.). 19.50 (ISBN 0-685-33019-2, 045-3). Saphrograph.

Italian-English Dictionary. (Eng. & Ital.). 12.95. Longman.

Italian-English, English-Italian Commercial Dictionary. Ragazzini & Gagliardelli. (Ital. & Eng.). 50.00 (ISBN 0-685-25202-7). Heinman.

Italian-English, English-Italian Gem Dictionary. Ed. by May Isopel. (Gem Foreign Language Ser.). (Ital. & Eng.). 1954. 2.95 (ISBN 0-00-458625-5, G1). Collins Pubs.

Italian-English, English-Italian (Grande) Dictionary. 27th, rev. ed. M. Hazon. (Eng. & Ital.). Date not set. text ed. 60.00 (ISBN 0-686-46532-6). Heinman.

Italian-English, English-Italian Pocket Dictionary. J. Purves. 833p. (Ital. & Eng.). 1980. pap. 13.95 (ISBN 0-7100-0602-0, M-9364). French & Eur.

Italian-English, English-Italian Technical Dictionary. 11th, enl. ed. G. Marolli. (Illus., Ital. & Eng.). 1980. 100.00 (ISBN 8-8005-1040-X). Heinman.

Italian-English-Italian. (Berlitz Pocket Dictionaries Ser.). (Ital. & Eng.). 4.95 (ISBN 0-02-964520-4). Macmillan.

Italian for the English-Speaking Tourist see Phrase Dictionaries for the American Tourist.

Italian-Norwegian Dictionary. M. Ulleland. (Norwegian & Ital.). 1981. write for info. (ISBN 82-573-0149-3). Kunnskapsforlaget.

Italian-Swedish-Italian Dictionary. 279p. (Ital. & Swedish.). 1978. pap. 9.95 (ISBN 0-686-92481-9, M-9446). French & Eur.

Italian Vest Pocket Dictionary. Robert A. Hall, Jr. (Ital.). 1957. pap. 3.50 (ISBN 0-394-40060-7). Random.

Ital'iansko-Russkii i Rusko-Ital'ianskii Stroitel'nyi Slovar. Boris I. Avramenko. 480p. (Ital. & Rus.). 1978. 4.20 Rub. Russkii Iazyk.

Italiansko-Russkii Slovar. S. V. Gere et al. 744p. (Rus. & Ital.). 1947. 5.20 (Pub. by Gosizdat Inostr. Natsional Slovarei). Four Continent.

Italic, Latin, Italian. Ernst Pulgram. LC 79-312793. 400p. (Lat. & Ital.). 1978. pap. write for info. (ISBN 3-533-02769-4). C Winter.

Italienisch, 2 vols. Incl. Teil I. Italienish-Deutsch. Compiled by Paolo Giovanelli & Walter Frenzel. 568p. DM.39.80 (04180); Teil II. Deutsch-Italienisch. rev. ed. Compiled by Herbert Frenzel & Walter Frenzel. 656p. 1982. DM.39.80 (04186). (Langenscheidts Handworterbucher Ser.). (Ger. & Ital.). DM.biede Teile in einem Band 72.00 (05181). Langenscheidt.

Italienisch, 2 vols. Incl. Teil I. Italienisch-Deutsch. V. Macchi. 640p. DM.17.80 (10181); Teil II. Deutsch-Italienisch. W. Frenzel. 606p. DM.17.80 (10186). (Langenscheidts Taschenworterbucher Ser.). (Ital. & Ger.). DM.26.80 set (11181). Langenscheidt.

Italiensk-Dansk Ordbog. K. Anderson & G. Mafera. 485p. (Ital. & Danish.). 1980. 29.95 (ISBN 87-01-83431-2, M-1286). French & Eur.

Italiensk-Norsk Ordbok. M. Ulleland. 412p. (Ital. & Norwegian.). 1981. pap. 39.95 (ISBN 82-573-0149-3, M-9464). French & Eur.

Italiensk-Svensk Ordbok. 586p. (Ital. & Swedish.). 1981. Kr.135.00 (ISBN 91-24-20219-3). Esselte Studium.

Iterated Inductive Definitions & Subsystems of Analysis: Recent Proof-Theoretical Studies. W. Buchholz et al. (Lecture Notes in Mathematics Ser.: Vol. 897). 383p. 1982. pap. 20.00 (ISBN 0-387-11170-0). Springer-Verlag.

It's Easy to Increase Your Vocabulary. rev ed. William Morris. 256p. (Orig.). 1975. pap. 2.25 (ISBN 0-14-004086-2). Penguin.

J

Jane Austen Dictionary. G. L. Apperson. LC 73-15997. 1932. lib. bdg. 10.75 (ISBN 0-8414-2922-7). Folcroft.

Jane's Aerospace Dictionary. Bill Gunston. 492p. 1980. 34.95 (ISBN 0-86720-573-3). Jane's Pub Inc.

Jane's Dictionary of Naval Terms. Compiled by Joseph Palmer. 1976. 11.95 (ISBN 0-356-08258-X). Hippocrene Bks.

Japanese & English Dictionary with an English & Japanese Index. James C. Hepburn. LC 81-52935. 704p. (Japanese & Eng.). 1982. Repr. of 1867 ed. 29.50 (ISBN 0-8048-1441-4). C E Tuttle.

Japanese-Chinese Dictionary. 2587p. (Japanese & Chinese.). 1979. leatherette 49.95 (ISBN 0-686-97413-1, M-9267). French & Eur.

Japanese-Chinese Dictionary. 569p. (Japanese & Chinese.). 1980. pap. 7.95 (ISBN 0-686-97415-8, M-9252). French & Eur.

Japanese-Chinese Loanword Dictionary (M-9259) 748p. (Japanese & Chinese.). Date not set. Leatherette 25.00 (ISBN 0-686-97404-2, M-9259). French & Eur.

Japanese-Chinese Science & Technology Dictionary. 175p. (Japanese & Chinese.). 1976. 19.95 (ISBN 0-686-92480-0, M-9260). French & Eur.

Japanese-English-Chinese Radio Technology Dictionary. 1628p. (Japanese, Eng & Chinese.). 1974. 14.95 (ISBN 0-686-92197-6, M-9590). French & Eur.

Japanese-English Dictionary, 2 vols. Eric B. Ceadel. (Japanese & Eng.). romanized 35.00 (ISBN 0-87557-048-8, 048-8). Saphrograph.

Japanese-English Dictionary: Romanized. (Japanese & Eng.). 19.50 (ISBN 0-686-65152-9, 047-X). Saphrograph.

Japanese-Latin-English-German-French Medical Terminology. 1259p. (Japanese , Lat. , Eng. , Ger. & Fr.). 1958. leatherette 95.00 (ISBN 0-686-92476-2, M-9350). French & Eur.

Japanese Newspaper Compounds: The One Thousand Most Important in Order of Frequency. Ed. by Tadashi Kikuoka. LC 76-125560. (Japanese.). 1970. pap. 4.25 (ISBN 0-8048-0919-4). C E Tuttle.

Japanese Word & Phrase Book for Tourists. Eldora S. Thorlin. LC 76-113904. (Japanese & Eng.). 1970. flexible leatherette bdg. 5.95 (ISBN 0-8048-0876-7). C E Tuttle.

Jargon du XVe Siecle: Etude Philologique. Auguste C. Vitu. LC 78-375979. 542p. (Fr.). 1977. 120.00 F. Slatkine.

Javanese-English Dictionary. Elinor C. Horne. (Linguistic Ser). (Javanese & Eng.). 1974. text ed. 55.00x (ISBN 0-300-01689-1). Yale U Pr.

Je Sais Tout Sur le Monde & la Nature. Antoine Icart. LC 77-574200. 115p. (Eng. & Fr.). 1977. write for info. (ISBN 2-01-000928-2). Hachette-Jeunesse.

Jean's Pocket Dictionaries: French-English. 224p. (Orig., Fr. & Eng.). 1981. pap. 2.25 (ISBN 0-8437-1725-4). Hammond Inc.

Jean's Pocket Dictionaries: German-English. 224p. (Orig., Ger. & Eng.). 1981. pap. 2.25 (ISBN 0-8437-1726-2). Hammond Inc.

Jean's Pocket Dictionaries: Italian-English. 224p. (Orig., Ital. & Eng.). 1981. pap. 2.25 (ISBN 0-8437-1727-0). Hammond Inc.

Jean's Pocket Dictionaries: Spanish-English. 224p. (Orig., Span. & Eng.). 1981. pap. 2.25 (ISBN 0-8437-1728-9). Hammond Inc.

Jewelers' Dictionary. 3rd ed. Ed. by Donald S. McNeil. LC 76-26012. 268p. 1979. 39.95x (ISBN 0-931744-01-6). Jewelers Circular.

Jewelers' Dictionary. Compiled by Donald S. McNeil. 1976. 39.95 (ISBN 0-685-84983-X). Jewelers Circular.

Jewish Word Book. Sidney J. Jacobs. 356p. (Eng. & Hebrew.). 1982. 12.50 (ISBN 0-8246-0249-8). Jonathan David.

Job Success Dictionary: A Hutar Guide to Becoming a More Valuable Employee & Earning More. Laddie F. Hutar. (Illus.). pap. 2.00 (ISBN 0-918896-02-9). Hutar.

John Webster Concordance, Vol. 2, Pt. 3. R. Corballis & J. M. Harding. (Jacobean Drama Studies: No. 70). 1979. pap. text ed. 25.00x (ISBN 0-391-01761-6). Humanities.

Johnson's Dictionary: A Modern Selection. Ed. by E. L. McAdam & G. Milne. 480p. (Eng.). 1982. Epap. 3.95 (ISBN 0-333-32984-8). Macmillan London.

Joint Disease. 3rd ed. Huskisson & Hart. 192p. 1982. pap. 21.50 (ISBN 0-7236-0465-7). Wright-PSG.

Jowitt's Dictionary of English Law. 2nd ed. William A. Jowitt. LC 78-302082. vii, 1935p. 1977. write for info. (ISBN 0-421-23090-8). Sweet & Maxwell.

Joys of Yiddish. Leo Rosten. 1968. 19.95 (ISBN 0-07-053975-8, GB). McGraw.

Judo: Encyclopedie in Beeld. Francois M. Haesendock. LC 78-353537. (Illus.). 272p. (Dutch.). 1976. fl.245.00 (ISBN 9-002-13418-5). Standard.

Juedisches Lexikon, 5 vols. Ed. by G. Herlitz. (Illus.). 4482p. (Ger.). 1982. pap. 320.00. M. Rosenberg.

Jugendlexikon A-Z. Ed. by G. Butzmann et al. (Illus.). 752p. (Ger.). 1982. M.42.00. Bibl Inst Leipzig.

Jugendlexikon Astronomie & Raumfahrt. K. Lindner & K. H. Neumann. (Illus.). 256p. (Ger.). 1982. M.12.00. Bibl Inst Leipzig.

Jugendlexikon Biologie. Ed. by G. Dietrich & A. Mueller-Hegemann. (Illus.). 408p. (Ger.). 1981. M.22.00. Bibl Inst Leipzig.

Jugendlexikon Gesellschaft: Einfache Antworten afu Schwierige Fragen. Dieter Claessens. LC 76-469431. (Illus.). 184p. (Ger.). 1976. DM.5.80 (ISBN 3-499-16195-8). Rowohlt.

Jugendlexikon Jugend zu Zweit. 3rd ed. Ed. by L. Areisin & A. Mueller-Hegemann. (Illus.). 243p. (Ger.). 1982. M.9.80. Bibl Inst Leipzig.

Jugendlexikon Junge Ehe. Ed. by L. Aresin & A. Mueller-Hegemann. (Illus.). 192p. (Ger.). 1982. M.9.80. Bibl InstLeipzig.

Jugendlexikon Philosophie. Ed. by F. Fiedler & G. Gurst. (Illus.). 228p. (Ger.). 1981. M.9.80. Bibl Inst Leipzig.

Jugendlexikon Politische Okonomie. Ed. by J. Gottschalg & K. Just. 220p. (Eng.). 1981. M.9.80. Bibl Inst Leipzig.

Jugendlexikon UdSSR. Ed. by G. Butzmann. (Illus.). 352p. (Ger.). 1981. M.14.80. Bibl Inst Leipzig.

Jugendlexikon Weltpolitik. Ed. by H. Ivens et al. (Illus.). 192p. (Ger.). 1982. M.9.80. Bibl Inst Leipzig.
Jugendlexikon Wirtschaft. H. Guenter. 192p. (Ger.). 1976. 5.95 (ISBN 3-499-16189-3, M-7492, Pub. by Rowohlt). French & Eur.
Jugendlexikon Wissenschaftlicher Kommunismus. 2nd ed. Ed. by J. Gottschalg & G. Wolter. (Illus.). 188p. (Ger.). 1981. DM.9.80. Bibl Inst Leipzig.
Jugenlexikon Wirtschaft. H. Guenter. 192p. (Ger.). 1976. 5.95 (ISBN 3-499-16189-3). Rowohlt.
Jumbo Vocabulary Development Yearbook: Grade 1. Fred Justus. (Jumbo Vocabulary Ser.). 96p. (gr. 1). 1979. 14.00 (ISBN 0-8209-0050-8, JVDY 1). ESP.
Jumbo Vocabulary Development Yearbook: Grade 2. Fred Justus. (Jumbo Vocabulary Ser.). 96p. (gr. 2). 1980. 14.00 (ISBN 0-8209-0051-6, JVDY 2). ESP.
Jumbo Vocabulary Development Yearbook: Grade 3. Marie-Jose Shaw. (Jumbo Vocabulary Ser.). 96p. (gr. 3). 1980. 14.00 (ISBN 0-8209-0052-4, JVDY 3). ESP.
Jumbo Vocabulary Development Yearbook: Grade 4. Marie-Jose Shaw. (Jumbo Vocabulary Ser.). 96p. (gr. 4). 1980. 14.00 (ISBN 0-8209-0053-2, JVDY 4). ESP.
Jumbo Vocabulary Development Yearbook: Grade 5. Marie-Jose Shaw. (Jumbo Vocabulary Ser.). 96p. (gr. 5). 1981. 14.00 (ISBN 0-8209-0054-0, JVDY 5). ESP.
Jumbo Vocabulary Development Yearbook: Grade 7. Jim Vaughn. (Jumbo Vocabulary Ser.). 96p. (gr. 7-9). 1981. 14.00 (ISBN 0-8209-0056-7, JVDY J). ESP.
Jumbo Vocabulary Development Yearbook: Grade 10. Jim Vaughn. (Jumbo Vocabulary Ser.). 96p. (gr. 10-12). 1981. 14.00 (ISBN 0-8209-0057-5, JVDY S). ESP.
Jumbo Vocabulary Fun Yearbook. Fred Justus. (Jumbo Vocabulary Ser.). 96p. (gr. 3). 1980. 14.00 (ISBN 0-8209-0058-3, JVFY 3). ESP.
Junckers Worterbuch German-American Slang. Juncker. Ed. by Arthur Seiffhart. (Eng. & Ger.). 1968. 3.00 (ISBN 0-685-06570-7). Assoc Bk.
Junior English-Chinese Dictionary. 1023p. (Eng. & Chinese.). 1977. pap. 5.95 (ISBN 0-686-92475-4, M-9557). French & Eur.
Junior Thesaurus: In Other Words II. rev. ed. Andrew Schiller & William A. Jenkins. LC 77-84159. (Illus.). (gr. 3-6). 1978. PLB 12.68 (ISBN 0-688-51827-3). Lothrop.
Jurdicia Lexikon: Das Kleine Oesterreicher Rechtswoerterbuch. Hans G. Zedtwitz. LC 75-590427. 223p. (Ger.). 1974. S.175.00. Juridica Verlag.
Jurdisk Ordbog. W. Gubba. LC 79-366377. 72p. (Ger. & Danish.). 1978. write for info. Guba.
Juridical Terminology of International Relations in Egyptian Texts Through Dynasty XVIII. David Lorton. LC 73-8114. (Near Eastern Studies). 208p. 1974. 16.00x (ISBN 0-8018-1535-5). Johns Hopkins.
Juridisk Leksikon. Egil Gulbransen. LC 78-376208. 237p. (Norwegian.). 1977. Kr.79.00 (ISBN 8-251-80150-8). Tanum-Norli.
Juridisk Ordbog. Oscar A. Borum & W. E. Von Eyben. LC 77-459744. 254p. (Danish.). 1976. Kr.92.00 (ISBN 8-712-08818-8). Gad Forlag.
Juridisk Ordbog, Dansk-Tysk: Supplement & Forkortelsesliste. W. Gubba. 68p. (Danish & Ger.). 1978. write for info. Guba.
Just Words. Coraline E. Halikas. (Word Game & Crossword Puzzle Aid Ser.). 274p. (Orig.). 1982. pap. 14.95x (ISBN 0-686-35739-6). Ili-Cor Pubns.

K

Kalamanakarana Paribhasika Sabda Sangrahaya. Dharmasena De Silva. LC 79-904454. viii, 496p. (Eng.). 1978. Rs.27.00. Kojamba.
Kalamanakarana Paribhasika Sabda Sangrahaya. Hema Wijewardena. LC 79-904454. viii, 496p. (Eng. & Sinhalese.). 1978. Rs.27.00. Dewan Bahasa.
Kalmyk-Mongolian Vocabulary in Stralenberg's Geography of 1730. John R Krueger. LC 76-507500. (Kalmyck.). 1975. Kr.64.75 (ISBN 91-7192-217-2). Almqvist.
Kamus dwibahasa, bahasa Inggeris-bahasa Malaysia. Dewan Bahasa dan Pustaka. LC 79-941803. xv, 1457p. (Eng. & Malay.). 1979. M.$25.00. Dewan Bahasa.
Kamus Inggeris Indonesia: Dictionary English-Indonesia for School, Office & Home. A. Hamid Siregar. LC 74-940821. 313p. (Indonesian & Eng.). 1974. write for info. Pustaka Antara.
Kamus Istilah Filologi. Ed. by Baroroh Baried. LC 78-942676. iv, 124p. (Indonesian., Jakarta). 1977. write for info. Universitas Gadjah Mada.
Kamus Lengkap: Penyunting. Sudjai H. Awang & Khan Yusoff. LC 77-940970. (Illus.). 1244p. (Maylay & Eng.). 1977. write for info. Pustaka Antara.
Kamus Logika. Liang G. The. LC 75-940899. 209p. (Indonesian.). 1975. write for info. Nur Cahaya.
Kamus pembaca, Inggeris-Malayu. Albert S. Hornby. LC 81-940893. (Illus.). 409p. (Eng. & Malay.). 1980. write for info. (ISBN 0-19-580771-5). Oxford U Pr.
Kamus Umum Bahasa Indonesia. W. Poerwadarminta. LC 76-941594. 1156p. (Eng. & Indonesian.). 1976. write for info. P N Balai Pustaka.
Kamusi Vocabulaire. S. Farsi. LC 79-105083. 428p. (Fr. & Swahili.). 1978. write for info. Edns St Paul.
Kansanperinteen Sanakirja. Toivo Vuorela. LC 79-373974. (Illus.). 542p. (Finnish.). write for info. (ISBN 9-510-08803-X). Soderstrom.
Kant Dictionary. Morris Stockhammer. LC 76-155974. 1971. 10.00 (ISBN 0-8022-1649-8). Philos Lib.
Kapingamarangi Lexicon. Michael D. Lieber & Kalio H. Dikepa. LC 73-90855. (Pali Language Texts: Polynesia). 434p. (Orig., Pali.). 1974. pap. text ed. 15.00x (ISBN 0-8248-0304-3). UH Pr.
Karmannyi Afgansko-Russkii Slovar. K. A. Lebedev. 587p. (Rus. & Afghan.). 1962. 1.95 (Pub. by Gosizdat Natsional Slovarei). Four Continent.
Karmannyi Anglo-Russkii Slovar. O. P. Beniukh. 832p. (Eng. & Rus.). 1973. 2.00 (Pub. by Sov Entsiklopediia). Four Continent.
Karmannyi Anglo-Russkii Slovar. O. P. Beniukh. 832p. (Eng. & Rus.). 1973. 2.00 (Pub. by Russkii Iazyk). Four Continent.
Karmannyi Anglo-Russkii Slovar. O. P. Beniukh et al. 832p. (Eng. & Rus.). 1977. 2.25 (Pub. by Russkii Iazyk). Four Continent.
Karmannyi Anglo-Russkii Slovar' O. P. Beniukh et al. (Russkii iazyk Ser.). 832p. (Rus. & Eng.). 2.00 (C-102). Four Continent.
Karmannyi Bengal'sko-Russkii Slovar. D. Litton. 532p. (Rus. & Bengali.). 1960. 1.95 (Pub. by Gosizdat Natsional Slovarei). Four Continent.
Karmannyi Bolgarsko-Russkii Slovar. M. A. Leonidova. 534p. (Rus. & Bulgarian.). 1961. 1.75 (Pub. by Gosizdat Inostr. & Natsional). Four Continent.
Karmannyi Cheshsko-Russkii i Russko-Cheshskii Slovar. D. A. Dlugi et al. 476p. (Rus. & Czech.). 1970. 2.50 (Pub. by Sov Entsiklopediia). Four Continent.
Karmannyi Frantsuzsko-Russkii Slovar. K. S. Vygodskaia. 648p. (Fr. & Rus.). 1960. 1.75 (Pub. by GINS). Four Continent.
Karmannyi Indoneziisko-Russkii Slovar. N. F. Bulygin. 310p. (Rus. & Indonesian.). 1959. 1.25 (Pub. by GINS). Four Continent.
Karmannyi Ital'iansko-Russkii Slovar. I. A. Dobrovolskaia. 408p. (Rus. & Ital.). 1959. 1.10 (Pub. by GINS). Four Continent.
Karmannyi Italiansko-Russkii Slovar. 408p. (Ital. & Rus.). 1959. 1.10. Four Continent.
Karmannyi Kitaisko-Russkii Slovar. N. S. Araushkin et al. 210p. (Rus.). 1975. 1.95 (Pub. by Russkii Iazyk). Four Continent.
Karmannyi Niderlandsko-Russkii Slovar. T. N. Dreniasova. 392p. (Rus. & Dutch.). 1977. 1.80 (Pub. by Russkii Iazyk). Four Continent.
Karmannyi Pol'Sko-Russkii & Russko-Polskii Slovar. I. N. Mitronova et al. 560p. (Rus. & Pol.). 1976. 2.25 (Pub. by Russkii Iazyk). Four Continent.
Karmannyi Polsko-Russkii & Russko-Polskii Slovar. G. V. Sinitsyna & I. N. Mitronova. LC 80-450178. 575p. (Pol. & Rus.). 1978. 1.00 Rub. Russkii Iazyk.
Karmannyi Polsko-Russkii i Russko-Polskii Slovar. 472p. (Pol. & Rus.). 1960. 1.25. Four Continent.
Karmannyi Rumynsko-Russkii Slovar. 360p. (Romanian & Rus.). 1960. 1.25. Four Continent.
Karmannyi Russko-Albanskii Slovar. A. Kostallari. 428p. (Rus. & Albanian.). 1959. 1.50. Four Continent.
Karmannyi Russko-Angliiskii Slovar. O. P. Beniukh et al. 782p. (Rus. & Eng.). 1971. 2.00 (Pub. by Sov Entsiklopediia). Four Continent.
Karmannyi Russko-Angliiskii Slovar' Ed. by O. P. Beniukh et al. (Sov. Entsiklopediia Ser.). 784p. (Rus. & Eng.). 1977. 2.00. Four Continent.
Karmannyi Russko-Birmanskii Slovar. U Chin Vei et al. (Rus. & Burmese.). 1962. 2.50 (Pub. by GINS). Four Continent.
Karmannyi Russko-Bolgarskii Slovar. 464p. (Rus. & Bulgarian.). 1978. 1.95 (Pub. by Russkii Iazyk). Four Continent.
Karmannyi Russko-Bolgarskii Slovar. M. A. Leonido... (Rus. & Bulgarian.). 196... Four Continent.
Karmannyi Russko-Finskii Slovar. I. S. Eliseev. 304p. (Rus. & Finnish.). 1978. 2.85 (Pub. by Russkii Iazyk). Four Continent.
Karmannyi Russko-Frantsuzskii Slovar. 620p. (Rus. & Fr.). 1960. 1.50. Four Continent.
Karmannyi Russko-Indoneziiskii Slovar. N. F. Bulygin et al. 576p. (Rus. & Indonesian.). 1958. 1.75 (Pub. by GINS). Four Continent.
Karmannyi Russko-Ital'ianskii Slovar. I. A. Dobrovolskaia et al. (Ital. & Rus.). 1.85 (Pub. by Sov Entsiklopediia). Four Continent.
Karmannyi Russko-Khindi Slovar. Z. M. Dymshits et al. 867p. (Rus.). 1958. 1.85 (Pub. by GINS). Four Continent.
Karmannyi Russko-Kitaiskii Slovar. V. G. Mudrov. 216p. (Rus.). 1977. 3.20 (Pub. by Russkii Iazyk). Four Continent.
Karmannyi Russko-Niderlandskii Slovar. Zh. I. Pirog et al. 496p. (Rus. & Dutch.). 1977. 2.50 (Pub. by Russkii Iazyk). Four Continent.
Karmannyi Russko-Norvezhskii Slovar. E. P. Gribanova. 688p. (Rus. & Norwegian.). 1962. 1.95 (Pub. by GINS). Four Continent.
Karmannyi Russko-Urdu Slovar. A. A. Davidova et al. 739p. (Urdu & Rus.). 1958. 1.50 (Pub. by GINS). Four Continent.
Karmannyi Slovar Ateista. 280p. (Rus.). 1979. 2.85 (Pub. by Politizdat). Four Continent.
Karmannyi Slovatsko-Russkii i Russko-Slovatskii Slovar. 528p. (Rus. & Slovenian.). 1975. 2.10 (Pub. by Russkii Iazyk). Four Continent.
Karmannyi Urdu-Russkii Slovar. L. B. Kibirkshtis et al. 551p. (Rus. & Urdu.). 1958. 1.65 (Pub. by GINS). Four Continent.
Karmannyi Vengersko-Russkii Slovar. G. I. Ol'Dal et al. 405p. (Rus.). 1969. 1.50 (Pub. by GINS). Four Continent.
Karnkraft Fran A til O. Lars G. Larsson & Sven Lorveberg. LC 80-468740. 136p. (Swedish.). 1979. write for info. (ISBN 9-1728-4108-7). Ingenjorsforlaget.
Katonai Ertelmezo Szotar. Lajos Toth et al. LC 77-575154. 454p. (Eng. & Hungarian.). 1976. 62.00 Ft (ISBN 9-6332-6510-X). Zrinyi Katonai.
Katu Vocabulary. Nancy A. Costello. 124p. (Katu.). 1971. microfiche 2.25. Summer Inst Ling.
Kaufmaenisches Grundwoerterbuch fuer Schule & Praxis: Part I, Deutsch-Englisch. T. Grossmann & G. Friedmann. 280p. (Ger. & Eng.). 1983. pap. 9.40. M. Rosenberg.
Kaufmannisches Grundwoerterbuch fuer Schule und Praxis: Deutsch-Englisch. T. Grossmann & G. Friedmann. 280p. (Ger. & Eng.). pap. 9.40. M Rosenberg.
Kaufmannisches Grundworte Buch Fur Schule und Praxis. Grossmann & Friedmann. 280p. (Ger. -Eng., Dictionary of Commerce for School and Practice). 14.50 (ISBN 3-87217-300-6, M-7494, Pub by Fachverlag Th. Grossmann). French & Eur.
Kautschuk-Lexikon. 2nd ed. Kurt F. Heinisch. LC 79-361675. (Illus.). 572p. (Ger.). 1978. DM.75.00. Gentner.
Kawi Lexicon. Soewojo Wojowasito. Ed. by Roger F. Mills. LC 78-57221. (Michigan Papers on South & Southeast Asia: No. 17). xv, 629p. (Orig.). 1980. pap. 16.00x (ISBN 0-89148-017-X). Ctr S&SE Asian.
Kazakh-English Dictionary. Boris N. Shnitnikov. (Orig., Kazakh & Eng.). 1966. pap. text ed. 36.00x (ISBN 90-2790-367-0). Mouton.
Kennis Gids tot Moderne Afrikaans. E. DuPlessis. LC 80-468749. 240p. (Afrikaans.). 1979. write for info. (ISBN 0-7981-0916-5). Human & Rousseau.
Kettridge's English-French - French-English Dictionary. Ed. by Hochman. (Eng. & Fr.). 1971. pap. 3.50 (ISBN 0-451-11804-9, AE1804, Sig). NAL.
Kettridge's French-English, English-French Dictionary. 700p. (Fr. & Eng.). pap. 2.50. NAL.
Kewa Dictionary with Supplementary Grammatical & Anthropological Materials. K. J. Franklin et al. LC 81-453278. (Illus.). 514p. (Kewa & Eng.). 1978. Aus.$16.00 (ISBN 0-85883-182-1). Linguistic Circle.
Key Definitions in Astronomy. Jacqueline Mitton. LC 82-183. (Quality Paperback: No. 375). 174p. (Orig.). 1982. pap. text ed. 4.95 (ISBN 0-8226-0375-6). Littlefield.
Key into the Language of America. 5th ed. Roger Williams. LC 70-157500. Repr. of 1643 ed. 43.00x (ISBN 0-8103-3723-1). Gale.
Key Terms & Phrases. National Woman's Christian Temperance Union. for 25 copies 0.40 (2204); bulk rates avail. WCTU.
Key to English Vocabulary. English Language Services. (Key to English Ser). pap. 1.60 (ISBN 0-02-971750-7). Macmillan.
Keyes Encyclopedic Dictionary of Procurement Law: Definitions of Legal Terms & Concepts in Private Procurement & Public Procurement of Federal, State & Local Governments, Their Contractors & Subcontractors. W. Noel Keyes. LC 75-9984. 500p. 1976. text ed. 100.00x looseleaf (ISBN 0-379-00311-2); suppl. 20.00 ea. Oceana.
Keys to a Powerful Vocabulary: Level I. Minnette Lenier & Janet Maker. (Illus.). 240p. 1982. 12.95 (ISBN 0-13-514968-1). P-H.
Keywords: A Vocabulary of Culture & Society. Raymond William. 1976. pap. 8.95 (ISBN 0-19-519855-7, GB). Oxford U Pr.
Khindi-Russkii Uchebnyi Slovar. O. G. Ul'Tsiferov. 744p. (Rus.). 1962. 2.75 (Pub. by GINS). Four Continent.

Kinder Duden: Mein Erster Duden. (Illus.). 160p. (Ger.). 6.40 (1096). Adler Bks.
Kinship Terminology in Jane Austen's Novels. I Schapera. (Royal Anthropological Institute of Great Britain & Ireland Occasional Paper Ser.: No.33). 24p. 1977. pap. text ed. 5.50x (ISBN 0-391-01112-X). Humanities.
Kipling Dictionary. W. A. Younge. 75.00 (ISBN 0-8490-0473-X). Gordon Pr.
Kirjastotermien Sanakirja. Martti Kahla. LC 80-460426. vi, 127p. (Finnish & Rus.). 1979. write for info. (ISBN 9-5170-7031-4). Neuvost.
Kitab al-Ta Rifat (Book of Definitions) Arabic-Arabic Dictionary. Al Sharif Jurjani. (Arabic.). 1969. 16.00x (ISBN 0-86685-100-3). Intl Bk Ctr.
Kitab Al-Ta'rifat: Book of Definitions. Al-Sharif Al-Juriani. 336p. (Arabic.). 16.00 (0-3). Intl Bk Ctr.
Kitaisko-Russkii Slovar. Ed. by B. G. Mudrov. 528p. (Rus.). 1979. 16.95 (Pub. by Russkii Iazyk). Four Continent.
Kitaisko-Russkii Slovar-Minimum. A. V. Kotov. 432p. (Rus.). 1974. 2.95 (Pub. by Russkii Iazyk). Four Continent.
Kiwi: Yankee Dictionary. Louis S. Leland. 115p. 1980. pap. 5.95 (ISBN 0-86868-001-X). Bradt Ent.
Kleinasiatische Hydronymie: Semantik & Morphologie Analyse der Geichicher Gewaessernamen. Johann Tischler. LC 78-394985. ix, 191p. (Ger.). 1977. write for info (ISBN 3-882-26001-7). Reichert.
Kleine Bergbaulexikon. Walter Bischoff. LC 76-487997. 203p. (Ger.). 1976. DM.48.00 (ISBN 3-7739-0185-2). Verlag Glockauf.
Kleine Bergbaulexikon. Walter Bischoff. LC 79-395530. 254p. (Ger.). 1979. write for info. (ISBN 3-7739-0248-4). Verlag Gluckauf.
Kleine Duden: Deutsches Woerterbuch. 445p. (Ger.). DM.10.80 (ISBN 3-411-01961-1). Bibl io Inst.
Kleine Duden, Fremdenwoerterbuch. Dudenredaktion Manheim. LC 78-340908. 448p. (Ger.). 1977. write for info. Biblio Inst.
Kleine Duden: Fremdwoerterbuch. 448p. (Ger.). DM.10.80 (ISBN 3-411-01703-1). Biblio Inst.
Kleine Eichborn, Taschenwoerterbuch der Wirtschaftssprache, Vol. 1. R. Eichborn. (Ger. & Eng., English-German Dictionary of Commercial Terms). 1975. 33.50 (ISBN 3-921392-00-4, M-7495, Pub. by Siebenpunkt Vlg.). French & Eur.
Kleine Eichborn, Taschenwoerterbuch der Wirtschaftssprache, Vol. 2. R. Eichborn. (Ger. & Eng., German-English Dictionary of Economic Terms). 1975. 33.50 (ISBN 3-921392-01-2, M-7496, Pub. by Siebenpunkt Vlg.). French & Eur.
Kleine Muret-Sanders: Deutsch-Englisch. Heinz Messinger. 1296p. (Ger. & Eng.). 1982. DM.148.00 (02125). Langenscheidt.
Kleine Wahrig: Woerterbuch der deutschen Sprache. 943p. (Ger.). 1982. 14.90. M Rosenberg.
Kleiner Wortschatz. 2nd ed. Albert A. Meras & Maud Miller. Rev. by W. R. Ridgeway. 64p. (Ger.). 1956. 0.95p (ISBN 0-245-56653-8). Harrap.
Kleines Abkuerzungsbuch. 3rd ed. H. Koblischke. 144p. (Ger.). 1981. M.9.80. Bibl Inst Leipzig.
Kleines Fachwoerterbuch Geologie. V Rosenfeld. 197p. (Ger.). 1966. 14.50 (ISBN 3-443-39048-X, M-7500, Pub. by Borntaeger). French & Eur.
Kleines Fremdwoerterbuch. 7th ed. Ed. by G. Gurst et al. 400p. (Ger.). 1982. M.9.80. Bibl Inst Leipzig.
Kleines Kriminologisches Woerterbuch. Kaiser. (Ger.). 1974. pap. 7.95 (ISBN 0-686-56620-3, M-7501, Pub. by Herder). French & Eur.
Kleines Kriminologishes Woerterbuch. Kaiser. (Ger.). 1974. pap. 7.95. Herder.
Kleines Lexikon der Paedagogik & Didaktik. 7th ed. Helmut Zoepfl & Gerhard Bittner. Ed. by Herbert Tschamler. 398p. (Ger.). 1976. DM.28.80 (ISBN 3-40300-472-4). Auer.
Kleines Lexikon der Paedagogik & Didaktik. Ed. by Helmut Zoepfl. LC 75-521594. 398p. (Ger.). 1975. DM.28.80 (ISBN 3-403-00472-4). Auer.
Kleines Lexikon der Paedagogik und Didatik. 7th ed. Herbert Zoepfl. (Ger.). 1976. 22.95 (ISBN 3-403-00472-4, M-7502, Pub. by Auer). French & Eur.
Kleines Lexikon der Paedagogik und Didatik. 7th ed. Herbert Zoepfl. (Ger.). 1976. 22.95 (ISBN 3-403-00472-4). Auer.
Kleines Lexikon zur Politischen Bildung. Ed. by Paul Grossman & Viktor Lang. LC 75-516868. 181p. (Ger.). 1975. DM.5.80 (ISBN 3-87364-033-3). Hornung-Verlag.
Kleines Medizinisches Fremdworterbuch. Irmgard Goldhahn. LC 76-477700. 122p. (Ger.). 1976. M.9.50. Thieme Verlag.
Kleines Philosophisches Woerterbuch. 5th ed. Mueller & Halder. 344p. (Ger.). 1976. pap. 7.95 (ISBN 0-686-56623-8, M-7506, Pub. by Herder). French & Eur.
Kleines Philosophisches Woerterbuch. 5th ed. Mueller & Halder. 344p. (Ger.). 1976. pap. 7.95. Herder.
Kleines Polytechnisches Woerterbuch. Horst Gorner & J. V. Fedirko. LC 76-463413. 372p. (Rus. & Ger.). 1975. M.12.00. VEB Verlag Technik.
Kleines Polytechnisches Woerterbuch Russisch-Deutsch. Horst Gorner. 372p. (Rus. & Ger.). 1981. M.14.00. VEB Technik.
Kleines Psychologisches Woerterbuch. Christian Michel & Felix Novak. LC 75-506617. (Illus.). 378p. (Ger.). 1975. DM.12.90 (ISBN 3-451-07514-8). Herder.
Kleines Sozial Wissenschaftliches Woerterbuch fuer Paedagogen. 2nd ed. Erich Weber et al. 120p. (Ger.). 1976. DM.9.80. Auer.
Kleines Stuttgarter-Bibellexikon. 3rd ed. H. Obermayer. 344p. (Ger.). 1976. 9.95 (ISBN 3-460-30053-1, M-7507, Pub. by Vlg. Katholisches Bibelwerk). French & Eur.
Kleines Weinlexikon. Wilhelm Panwolf. LC 77-471829. 196p. (Ger.). 1976. DM.5.00 (ISBN 3-442-10541-2). Goldmann.
Kleines Wirtschafts-Woerterbuch. Wolfgang Mentzel & Helmut Wittlesberger. LC 78-349791. (Illus.). 379p. (Ger.). 1977. DM.12.90 (ISBN 3-451-07629-2). Herder.
Kleines Woerterbuch Chemie & Chemische Technik. Gross & Hildebrand. 128p. (Eng. & Ger.). 1976. DM.14.80 (ISBN 3-87144-218-6). Verlag Harri Deutsch.
Kleines Woerterbuch Chemie & Chemische Technik. Gross & Hildebrand. 96p. (Ger. & Eng.). 1980. DM.14.80 (ISBN 3-87144-219-4). Verlag Harri Deutsch.
Kleines Woerterbuch der Aegyptologie. 2nd ed. Wolfgang Helck & Eberhard Otto. (Ger.). 1970. 35.00 (ISBN 3-447-00064-3, M-7509, Pub. by Harrassowitz). French & Eur.
Kleines Woerterbuch der Chemie & Chemischen Technik. Helmut Gross. LC 79-393988. 108p. (Rus. & Ger.). 1979. M.7.00. VEB Verlag Technik.
Kleines Woerterbuch der Chemie & Chemischen Technik Deutsch-Englisch. 96p. (Ger. & Eng.). 1980. M.11.00. VEB Technik.
Kleines Woerterbuch der Chemie & Chemischen Technik Englisch-Deutsch. 128p. (Eng. & Ger.). 1975. M.11.00. VEB Technik.
Kleines Woerterbuch der Chemie & Chemischen Technik Russisch-Deutsch. Helmut Gross. 108p. (Rus. & Ger.). 1979. M.7.00. VEB Technik.
Kleines Woerterbuch der Elektrotechnik Elektronik Russisch-Deutsch. Helmut Gross. 128p. (Rus. & Ger.). 1980. M.7.00. VEB Technik.
Kleines Woerterbuch der Japanologie. B. Lewin. 596p. (Ger. & Japanese.). 1968. 38.00 (ISBN 3-447-00530-0, M-7512, Pub. by Harrassowitz). French & Eur.
Kleines Woerterbuch der Sonderpaedagogik: Englisch-Deutsche. Erika Reinartz & Friedrich Masendorf. LC 76-454597. 177p. (Eng. & Ger.). 1975. DM.12.80 (ISBN 3-786-43456-5). Marhold.
Kleines Woerterbuch Des Christlichen Orients. 1st ed. Julius Assfalg & P. Krueger. (Ger.). 1975. 52.00 (ISBN 3-447-01707-4, M-7514, Pub. by Harrassowitz). French & Eur.
Kleines Woerterbuch Des Hellenismus. 1st ed. (Ger. & Gr.). 1972. 30.95 (ISBN 0-686-56625-4, M-7515, Pub. by Harrassowitz). French & Eur.
Kleines Woerterbuch Sprachwissenschaftlicher Termini. 3rd ed. Ed. by R. Conrad. 306p. (Ger.). 1981. M.9.80. Bibl Inst Leipzig.
Kleines Woerterbuch Zur Arbeits und Sozialpolitik. M. Pfeffer. 396p. (Ger.). 1972. pap. 7.50 (ISBN 0-686-56626-2, M-7516, Pub. by Herder). French & Eur.
Kleines Woerterbuch Zur Arbeits und Sozialpolitik. M. Pfeffer. 396p. (Ger.). 1972. pap. 7.50. Herder.
Kleines Worterbuch der Chemie und Chem. Technik, Vol. 2. H. Gross & H. Hildebrand. 128p. (Ger. & Eng., Dictionary of Chemistry and Chemical Engineering). 9.95 (ISBN 3-87144-219-4, M-7510, Pub. by Verlag Harri Deutsch). French & Eur.
Kleinnes Lexikon des Judentums. Johann Maier & Peter Schaefer. (Illus.). 300p. (Ger.). DM.24.50 (ISBN 3-76737-616-4). F Bahn.
Kleinworterbuch Deutsch-Polnisch (Handy German-Polish Dictionary) S. Schimitzek et al. 652p. (Ger. & Pol.). 1977. 12.95 (ISBN 0-686-87188-X, M-9133). French & Eur.
Klinisches Woerterbuch Mit Klinischen Syndromen. 253 rev. ed. Willibald Pschyrembel. (Illus., Ger.). 1977. 26.50x (ISBN 3-11-007018-9). De Gruyter.
Klipp & Klar. Karl O. Saur. LC 79-375153. 208p. (Ger.). 1978. DM.17.80 (ISBN 3-411-01711-2). Biblio Inst.
Kluwer's Universeel Technisch Woordenboek: Duits-Nederlands. G. Schuurmans. 433p. (Ger.). 1980. 75.00 (ISBN 90-201-0606-6, M-9471). French & Eur.
Kluwer's Universeel Technisch Woordenboek: Engels-Nederlands. G. Shuurmans. 571p. (Eng. & Dutch.). 1981. 75.00 (ISBN 90-2010-771-2). French & Eur.
Kluwer's Universeel Technisch Woordenboek Frans-Nederlands. Stekhoven G. Schuurmans & M. Piriou-Vandamme. LC 75-406354. xiv, 622p. (Fr. & Dutch.). 1975. fl.73.75 (ISBN 90-201-0608-2). Kluwer Technische.
Kluwer's Universeel Technisch Woordenboek, Nederlands-Engels. G. Schuurmans. 775p. (Dutch & Eng.). 1977. 75.00 (ISBN 90-2010-605-8, M-9468). French & Eur.
Kluwer's Universeel Technisch Woordenboek: Nederlands-Frans. G. Schuurmans. 643p. (Dutch & Fr.). 1977. 75.00 (ISBN 90-201-0609-0, M-9472). French & Eur.
Kluwer's Universeel Technisch Woorenboek Nederlands Frans. Stekhovenn G. Schuurmans. LC 77-568049. xii, 643p. (Fr. & Dutch.). 1977. write for info. (ISBN 9-0201-0609-0). Kluwer Technische.
Kluwer's Universeel Technish Woordenboek: Frans-Nederlands. G. Schuurmans. 622p. (Fr. & Dutch.). 1975. 75.00 (ISBN 90-201-0608-2, M-9473). French & Eur.
Kluwer's Universel Technisch Woordenboek: Nederlands-Duits. G. Schuurmans. 428p. (Ger. & Dutch.). 1980. 75.00 (ISBN 90-201-0607-4, M-9470). French & Eur.
Knaura Lexikon, A-Z. (Ger.). 17.50 (ISBN 0-686-56627-0, M-7518, Pub. by Druckenmuellar). French & Eur.
Knaurs Lexicon A-Z. (Illus.). 1056p. (Ger.). 17.00. M Rosenberg.
Knaurs Lexicon der sinnverwandten Woerter. 560p. (Ger.). 1983. 12.40. M Rosenberg.
Knaurs Lexikon A-Z. (Illus.). 1056p. (Ger.). 1983. pap. 17.00. M Rosenberg.
Knaurs Lexikon der Modernen Medizin. Kurt Pollak. (Ger.). 1972. 17.50 (ISBN 3-426-03329-1, M-7519, Pub. by Druckenmueller). French & Eur.
Knaurs Lexikon der Technik. Hans Heck. (Ger.). 55.00 (ISBN 3-426-04577-X, M-7520, Pub. by Druckenmueller). French & Eur.
Knaurs Lexikon der Weltliteratur. Diether Krywalski. LC 80-462297. 942p. (Ger.). 1979. DM.39.80 (ISBN 3-426-26011-5). Droemersche Knaur.
Knaurs Musiklexikon. Ed. by R. E. Moritz. 768p. (Ger.). 1982. 27.00. M Rosenberg.
Knit Terms. International Fabricare Institute. (Selling Sense ser.). 0.25 (SS-81); 10 or more 0.20, ea. Intl Fabricare Inst.
Knitting Dictionary. rev. ed. National Knitted Outerwear Association. (Illus.). text ed. 10.00. Natl Knit Outwear.
Knowledge Encyclopedia. John Paton. LC 80-471792. (Illus.). 415p. (Eng.). 1979. E7.95 (ISBN 0-7112-0004-1). Windward.
Kodansha English-Japanese Dictionary. Ed. by Shigeo Kawamoto & Junzaburo Nishiwaki. Tr. by Shigehisa Narita & Mamoru Shimizu. 1557p. (Japanese & Eng.). 1980. pap. 22.50 flexible soft-binding (ISBN 0-87011-420-4). Kodansha.
Kodansha English-Japanese Dictionary. 1572p. (Eng. & Japanese.). 1983. 1900.00 Yen. Kodansha.
Kodansha Japanese-English Dictionary. 1250p. (Japanese & Eng.). 1983. 1900.00 Yen. Kodansha.
Kodansha Japanese-Russian Dictionary. 1154p. (Japanese & Rus.). 1983. 5800.00 Yen. Kodansha.
Koezhelyszotar. Miklos Hernadi. LC 78-346072. (Illus.). 363p. (Hungarian.). 1976. 30.00 Ft (ISBN 9-63280-426-0). Gondolat.
Kokugo Daijiten: Comprehensive Dictionary of the Japanese Language. 2640p. (Japanese.). 1981. 8800.00 Yen. Shogakukan.
Kompleksnyi Chastotnyi Slovar Russko Nauchnoi & Tekhnicheskoi Leksiki. 408p. (Rus.). 1978. 6.35 (Pub. by Russkii Iazyk). Four Continent.
Komunalteknisk Ordlista. Tekniska Nomenklaturcentralen. LC 77-454090. 214p. (Eng. Danish, Finnish & Norwegian.). 1976. Kr.50.00 (ISBN 9-1719-6061-9). Tek Nomen.
Konsten Att Veta Bast Fran ABBA til Ovre Slummen. Goran Palm. LC 78-384438. (Illus.). 258p. (Swedish.). 1978. write for info. (ISBN 9-11781-112-0). Norstedt Soner.
Korean Dictionary, 2 vols. 4100p. (Korean.). 80.00 (Dist. by Koryo Bks Importing, Inc). Sam-Sung Pub.
Korean-English Dictionary. Samuel E. Martin et al. (Linguistic Ser.). (Korean & Eng.). 1967. text ed. 75.00x (ISBN 0-300-00753-1). Yale U Pr.

Koreanisch-Deutsches Woerterbuch. 2nd ed. Andre Eckardt. 332p. (Korean & Ger.). 1976. DM.69.99 (ISBN 3-87276-149-8). Groos Verlag.
Korfattad Svensk-Swahili Ordbok. Abdulaziz Lodhi et al. LC 79-370772. 114p. (Swahili & Swedish.). 1978. write for info. Nord Afrik.
Korrosion & Korrosionsschutz Deutsch-Russisch. Helmut Gross. 240p. (Ger. & Rus.). 1982. M.22.00. VEB Technik.
Kortfattad Engelsk-svensk Juridisk Ordbok. Anders Bruzelius et al. LC 81-188653. 16p. (Eng. & Swedish.). 1980. Kr.130.00 (ISBN 9-14-030185-0). Liber Gleerup.
Kortfattad Medicinsk Ordbok. Martin Wrete. Ed. by Sven Dahlgren. 254p. (Swedish.). 1980. Kr.110.00 (ISBN 91-24-26515-2). Esselte Studium.
Koryak Texts. Vladimir G. Bogoraz. LC 73-3540. (American Ethnological Society. Publications: No. 5). Repr. of 1917 ed. 16.75 (ISBN 0-404-58155-2). AMS Pr.
Kosciuszko Foundation English-Polish, Polish-English Dictionary, 2 vols. Kazimierz Bulas et al. (Poland's Millennium Ser.). (Eng. & Pol.). 1973. English-Polish. text ed. 12.50 (ISBN 0-917004-00-0); Polish-English. text ed. 12.50 (ISBN 0-917004-16-7). Kosciuszko.
Kotowaza Daijiten: Comprehensive Dictionary of Japanese Phrase, Fable & Proverb. 2016p. (Japanese.). 1982. 9800.00 Yen. Shogakukan.
Kozhelyszotar. Miklos Hernadi. LC 78-346072. 363p. (Hungarian.). 1976. 30.00 Ft (ISBN 9-632-80426-0). Gondolat.
Kramer's Engels Woordenboek, 2 vols. 1330p. (Dutch & Eng.). Set. fl.35.00. Elsevier.
Kratikii Russko-Angliiskii i Anglo-Russkii Frazeologicheskii Slovar' A. I. Alekhina. (BGU im. V. I. Lenina Ser.). 400p. (Rus. & Eng.). 1980. 4.50 (Q-36). Four Continent.
Kratkii Anglo-Gruzinskii Slovar. 154p. (Rus.). 1975. 2.25 (Pub. by Metsniereba). Four Continent.
Kratkii Anglo-Russkii i Russko-Angliiskii Slovar' S. G. Zaimovskii. (Russkii iazyk Ser.). 464p. (Rus. & Eng.). 1978. 3.10 (O-134). Four Continent.
Kratkii Anglo-Russkii i Russko-Angliiskii. S. G. Zaimovsky. 464p. (Rus. & Eng.). 1978. 2.75 (Pub. by Russkii Iazyk). Four Continent.
Kratkii Cheshsko-Russkii Geofizicheskii Slovar. N. A. Pashchenko et al. 248p. (Rus. & Czech.). 1960. 2.00 (Pub. by Glav. Red. Nauchn. Tekhn. Slovarei Fizmata). Four Continent.
Kratkii Cheshsko-Russkii i Russko-Cheshskii Vneshnetorgovyi Slovar. V. S. Shevchenko et al. (Rus. & Czech.). 1955. 2.50 (Pub. by Vneshtorgizdat). Four Continent.
Kratkii Defektologicheskii Slovar. Ed. by A. I. D'Iachkov et al. 398p. (Rus.). 1964. 3.50 (Pub. by Prosveschchenie). Four Continent.
Kratkii Ekonomicheskii Slovar. Ed. by G. A. Kozlov et al. 390p. (Rus.). 1958. 2.75 (Pub. by Politizdat). Four Continent.
Kratkii Ekonomicheskii Slovar Piatiletki Effektivnosti & Kachestva. 264p. (Rus.). 1978. 2.70 (Pub. by Politizdat Ukrainy). Four Continent.
Kratkii Ekonomicheskii Slovar-Spravochnik Mastera i Nachal'nika Tsekha. V. T. Nikitin. 279p. (Rus.). 1968. 5.25 (Pub. by Ekonomika). Four Continent.
Kratkii Ekonomiko-Matematicheskii Slovar. L. I. Lopatnikov. 360p. (Rus.). 1979. 5.25 (Pub. by Nauka). Four Continent.
Kratkii Estonsko-Russkii Slovar. V. Mukhel. 681p. (Rus. & Estonian.). 1973. 2.75 (Pub. by Tallinn). Four Continent.
Kratkii Etimologicheskii Slovar Russkogo Iazyka. N. M. Shanskii et al. 542p. (Rus.). 1975. 3.65 (Pub. by Proveschchenie). Four Continent.
Kratkii Fotograficheskii Slovar. Ed. by A. A. Lapauri et al. 386p. (Rus.). 1956. 2.50 (Pub. by Iskusstvo). Four Continent.
Kratkii Frantsuzsko-Russkii i Russko-Frantsuzskii Slovar. K. S. Vygodskaia et al. 655p. (Fr. & Rus.). 1968. 2.00 (Pub. by Sov Entsiklopediia). Four Continent.
Kratkii Iaponsko-Russkii Razgovornik. 240p. (Rus. & Japanese.). 1957. 1.95 (Pub. by Iskra Revoliutsii). Four Continent.
Kratkii Illiustrirovannyi Russko-Angliiskii Slovar Po Mashinostroeniu. V. V. Shvarts. 224p. (Rus. & Eng.). 1979. 5.75 (Pub. by Russkii Iazyk). Four Continent.
Kratkii Ispansko-Russkii & Russko-Ispanskii Nauchno-Tekhnicheskii Slovar. Kobo Orts Kh. et al. 438p. (Span. & Rus.). 1960. 3.75 (Pub. by An Arm SSR). Four Continent.
Kratkii Lugunda-Russkii & Russko-Lugunda Slovar. O. P. Nosova. 520p. (Rus. & Luganda.). 1969. 3.95 (Pub. by Sov Entsiklopediia). Four Continent.
Kratkii Nemetsko-Russkii Slovar Po Iadernoi Fizike i Iadernoi Tekhnike. 303p. (Ger. & Eng.). 1958. 3.00. Four Continent.
Kratkii Nemetsko-Russkii Vneshnetorgovyi Slovar. L. T. Bagma. 480p. (Ger. & Rus.). 1954. 2.95 (Pub. by Vneshtorgizdat). Four Continent.
Kratkii Politicheskii Slovar. 295p. (Rus.). 1971. 2.30 (Pub. by Politizdat). Four Continent.
Kratkii Politicheskii Slovar. 416p. (Rus.). 1977. 3.95 (Pub. by Politizdat). Four Continent.
Kratkii Russko-Finskii Slovar. 384p. (Rus. & Finnish.). 1946. 3.20 (Pub. by GINS). Four Continent.
Kratkii Russko-Frantsuzskii Uchebnyi Slovar. 688p. (Rus. & Fr.). 1969. 2.75 (Pub. by Sov Entsiklopediia). Four Continent.
Kratkii Russko-Iaponskii Slovar. A. E. Gluskina et al. 1000p. (Rus. & Japanese.). 1950. 5.75 (Pub. by GINS). Four Continent.
Kratkii Russko-Koreiskii Slovar. I. N. Mazur. 648p. (Rus. & Korean.). 1959. 2.95 (Pub. by GINS). Four Continent.
Kratkii Russko-Nemetskii Frazeologicheskii Slovar. (Rus. & Ger.). 1977. 5.95 (Pub. by Russkii Iazyk). Four Continent.
Kratkii Russko-Shvedskii Slovar. A. P. Valenius. 400p. (Rus.). 1948. 2.50 (Pub. by GINS). Four Continent.
Kratkii Shkol'Nyi Anglo-Litovskii i Litovsko-Angliiskii Slovar. V. Baravikas et al. 329p. (Rus.). 1970. 2.25 (Pub. by Shviesa). Four Continent.
Kratkii Slovar Botanicheskikh Terminov. D. P. Viktorov. 213p. (Rus.). 1957. 00.95 (Pub. by Sov. Nauka). Four Continent.
Kratkii Slovar Botanicheskikh Terminov. D. P. Viktorov. 178p. (Rus.). 1964. 1.40 (Pub. by Nauka). Four Continent.
Kratkii Slovar Gazovika. Iu. M. Belodvorskii. 187p. (Rus.). 1955. 1.65 (Pub. by Ministertvo Kommun Khoz). Four Continent.
Kratkii Slovar Inostrannykh Slov. S. M. Lokshina. 360p. (Rus.). 1.80 (Pub. by Russkii Iazyk). Four Continent.
Kratkii Slovar' Literaturovedcheskikh Terminov. Ed. by L. I. Timofeev et al. (Prosveshchenie Ser.). 224p. (Rus.). 1978. 1.95 ()-21). Four Continent.
Kratkii Slovar Literaturovedcheskikh Terminov. Leonid I. Timofeev & S. V. Turev. LC 79-378589. 233p. (Rus.). 1978. 0.55 (Pub. by Proveschchenie). Four Continent.
Kratkii Slovar Po Radioelektronike. A. P. Verzhikovskii et al. 256p. (Rus.). 1964. 2.50 (Pub. by Voenizdat). Four Continent.
Kratkii Suakhili-Russkii & Russko-Suakhili Slovar. A. I. Kutuzov. 442p. (Rus. & Swahili.). 1965. 3.50 (Pub. by Sov Entsiklopediia). Four Continent.
Kratkii Taisko-Russkii Slovar. M. I. Osipov. 332p. (Rus.). 1964. 2.50 (Pub. by LGU). Four Continent.
Kratkii Terminologicheskii Spravochnik po Ekonomike Geologorazvedochnykh Rabot. LC 79-398743. 203p. (Eng. , Rus. & Bulgarian.). 1979. 100.00 Zl. Wydawnictwa.
Kratkii Tolkovyi Slovar' Russkogo Iazyka: Dlia Inostransev. Ed. by V. V. Rozanova. (Russkii iazyk Ser.). 228p. (Rus.). 1977. 7.50 (O-111). Four Continent.
Kratkii Tolkovyi Slovar Russkogo Iazyka. 228p. (Rus.). 1978. 7.50 (Pub. by Russkii Iazyk). Four Continent.
Kratkii Tolkovyi Slovar Russkogo Iazyka. Ed. by V. V. Rozanova. (Rus.). 1979. 5.95 (Pub. by Russkii Iazyk). Four Continent.
Kratkii Tolkovyi Slovar Toponimov Kazakhstana. E. Koichubaev. 274p. (Rus.). 1974. 3.40 (Pub. by Nauka). Four Continent.
Kratkii Topografo-Geodezicheskii Slovar. Ed. by B. S. Kuzmin. 280p. (Rus.). 1973. 4.75 (Pub. by Nedra). Four Continent.
Kratkii Toponimicheskii Slovar Belorussii. V. A. Zhuchkevich. 447p. (Rus.). 1974. 4.25 (Pub. by MGU). Four Continent.
Kratkii Tsitologicheskii Slovar. A. A. Klishov. 116p. (Rus.). 1968. 1.50 (Pub. by Meditsina). Four Continent.
Kratkii Turetsko-Russkii Slovar "Novykh Slov". G. I. Antelava. 96p. (Rus. & Turkish.). 1978. 1.75 (Pub. by Metsniereba). Four Continent.
Kratkii Veterinarnyi Slovar Klinicheskikh Terminov. F. M. Orlov. 320p. (Rus.). 1979. 2.95 (Pub. by Khozizdat). Four Continent.
Kratkii Vneshnetorgovyi Slovar. Ed. by B. T. Kolpakov. 544p. (Rus.). 1954. 1.50 (Pub. by Vneshtorgizdat). Four Continent.
Kratkii Voennyi Persidsko-Russkii Slovar. L. S. Peisikov et al. 334p. (Rus.). 1954. 1.50 (Pub. by Voenizdat Inostr & Natsional' Slovarei). Four Continent.
Krio-English Dictionary. Compiled by Clifford N. Fyle. (Krio & Eng.). 1980. text ed. 65.00x (ISBN 0-19-864409-4). Oxford U Pr.
Kritische Stichwoerter zur Kinderkultur. Karl W. Bauer & Heinz Hengst. 366p. (Ger.). 1978. write for info. (ISBN 3-770-51634-6). W Fink.
Kritisches Lexikon der Erzeihungswissenschaft und Bildungspolitik. H. Speichert. 400p. (Ger.). 1975. pap. 7.98 (ISBN 3-499-16190-7, M-7522, Pub. by Rowohlt). French & Eur.
Kritisches Lexikon der Erzeihungswissenschaft und Bildungspolitik. H. Speichert. 400p. (Ger.). 1975. pap. 7.98 (ISBN 3-499-16190-7). Rowohlt.
Kritisches Lexikon der Erziehungswissenschaft & Bildungspolitik. 4th ed. Ed. by Horst Speichert. LC 76-454595. (Ger.). 1975. DM.9.80 (ISBN 3-499-16190-7). Verlag.
Kuenstlerlexikon. A. Schenck. 320p. (Ger.). 1973. pap. 12.95 (ISBN 3-499-16165-6, M-7523, Pub. by Rowohlt). French & Eur.
Kuenstlerlexikon. A. Schenck. 320p. (Ger.). 1973. pap. 12.95 (ISBN 3-499-16165-6). Rowohlt.
Kulturpolitisches Woerterbuch. Ed. by W. R. Langenbucher. (Ger.). 1982. 24.00. M Rosenberg.
Kunststofflexikon. Klaus Stoeckhert & Beck. LC 76-452156. 225p. (Ger.). 1975. write for info. Hanser.
Kunststofftechnik Woerterbuch. A. Wittfoht. 962p. (Ger. & Eng., Dictionary of Plastics). 1975. 55.00 (ISBN 3-446-12137-4, M7524, Pub. by C. Hanser). French & Eur.
Kunststofftechnik Woerterbuch. A. Wittfoht. 962p. (Ger. & Eng.). 1975. 55.00 (ISBN 3-446-12137-4). Hanser.
Kunststofftechnisches Woerterbuch, Vol. 3. A. Wittfoht. 768p. (Fr. & Ger.). 1966. 105.00 (ISBN 3-446-10362-7, M-7525, Pub. by C. Hanser). French & Eur.
Kunststofftechnisches Woerterbuch, Vol. 3. A. Wittfoht. 768p. (Fr. & Ger.). 1966. 105.00 (ISBN 3-446-10362-7). Hanser.
Kunststofftechnisches Woerterbuch, Vol. 4. A. Wittfoht. (Ger. & Fr.). 1962. 69.50 (ISBN 3-446-10363-5, M-7526, Pub. by C. Hanser). French & Eur.
Kunststofftechnisches Woerterbuch, Vol. 4. A. Wittfoht. (Ger. & Fr.). 1962. 69.50 (ISBN 3-446-10363-5). Hanser.
Kunststofftechnisches Woerterbuch, Vol. 5. A. Wittfoht. (Ger. & Span.). 1962. write for info. (ISBN 3-446-10364-3, M-7527, Pub. by C. Hanser). French & Eur.
Kunststofftechnisches Woerterbuch, Vol. 5. A. Wittfoht. (Ger. & Span.). 1962. write for info. (ISBN 3-446-10364-3). Hanser.
Kunststofftechnisches Woerterbuch, Vol. 6. A. Wittfoht. 544p. (Ger. & Span.). 1962. 68.00 (ISBN 3-446-10365-1, M-7528). French & Eur.
Kurdish-Arabic Dictionary: Al-Hadiyati 'l-Hamidiyah. M. Mokri. (Arabic.). 1975. 28.00x (ISBN 0-86685-126-7). Intl Bk Ctr.
Kurzgefasstes Etymologisches Des Altindischen, Vol. 3. Manfred Mayrhofer. (Ger. & Sanskrit.). 1976. 130.00 (ISBN 3-533-02466-0). Winter Univ.
Kurzgefasstes Etymologisches Woerterbuch Des Altindischen, Vol. 2. Manfred Mayrhofer. (Ger. & Sanskrit.). 1963. 92.00 (ISBN 3-533-00657-3, M-7530, Pub. by Carl Winter). French & Eur.
Kurzgefasstes Etymologisches Woerterbuch Des Altindischen, Vol. 2. Manfred Mayrhofer. (Ger. & Sanskrit.). 1963. 92.00 (ISBN 3-533-00657-3). Winter Univ.
Kurzgefasstes Etymologisches Woerterbuch Des Altindischen, Vol. 3. Manfred Mayrhofer. (Ger. & Sanskrit.). 1976. 130.00 (ISBN 3-533-02466-0, M-7531, Pub. by Carl Winter). French & Eur.
Kurzlexikon der Elektrotechnik. Gregor D. Haberle & Heinz O. Haberle. LC 79-387542. 104p. (Ger.). 1979. DM.15.00 (ISBN 3-87234-054-9). Frankfurt Fachverlag.
Kurzzeichen-Lexikon fur Kabel & Isoierte Leitungen Nach VDE IEC & CEE. Ewald Retzlaff. LC 76-454451. 65p. (Eng. & Ger.). 1975. DM.12.00 (ISBN 3-8007-1105-2). VDE Verlag.
Kusaiean-English Dictionary. Kee-Dong Lee. (PALI Language Texts-Micronesia). 330p. (Kusaiiean & Eng.). 1976. pap. text ed. 12.00x (ISBN 0-8248-0413-9). UH Pr.
Kwakiutl Grammar - with a Glossary of Suffixes. Franz Boas. LC 74-7939. (Kwankiutl.). Repr. of 1947 ed. 24.50 (ISBN 0-404-11826-7). AMS Pr.
Kwanyama-English Dictionary. Compiled by B. Turvey. LC 78-306064. xvii, 162p. (Kuanyama & Eng.). 1977. write for info. (ISBN 0-85494-315-3). Witwatersrand.
Kybernetik. Achim Sydow. LC 78-387093. 138p. (Eng. & Ger.). 1976. DM.20.00. VEB Verlag Technik.

L

Laaketieteen Sanairja. Niilo Pesonen. LC 76-486173. 559p. (Eng. & Finnish.). 1976. Fmk.100.00 (ISBN 9-5100-7479-9). Werner Soderstrom.
Lace Dictionary: Including Historic & Commercial Terms, Technical Terms, Native & Foreign. Ed. by C. R. Clifford. (Illus.). 156p. 1981. Repr. of 1913 ed. 30.00x (ISBN 0-8103-4311-8). Gale.
Lademanns Leksikon, 20 vols. (Danish.). 1970-1976. 850.00 (ISBN 0-8277-3066-7). Pergamon.

Lademanns Rejseleksikon Danmark. Bernhard Linder & Adam S. Paltorp. LC 76-478984. (Illus., Danish.). 1976. Kr.550.00 (ISBN 8-715-07133-2). Lademann Forlag.

Land Allocation Terminology. British Columbia, Ministry of Lands, Parks & Housing. LC 81-478975. 71p. (Eng.). 1979. write for info. (ISBN 0-7719-8201-1). Minist Prov Sec.

Landwirtschaftliches Woeterbuch in Acht Sprachen, 2 vols. (Ger. , Eng. , Rus. , Bulg. , Hungarian , Czech. & Pol., Dictionary of Agriculture in Eight Languages). 1971. 225.00 (ISBN 3-405-11076-9, M-7532, Pub. by BLV). French & Eur.

Langenscheidt Comprehensive German Dictionary. 1104p. (Ger.). 42.50 (ISBN 0-340-14967-1). Langenscheidt.

Langenscheidt Condensed Muret-Sanders German Dictionary. 1293p. (Ger.). 70.00 (ISBN 3-468-02125-9). Langenscheidt.

Langenscheidt Danish-English Lilliput Dictionary. 615p. (Danish & Eng.). plastic 1.50 (ISBN 3-468-96467-6). Langenscheidt.

Langenscheidt Dutch-English Lilliput Dictionary. 640p. (Dutch & Eng.). plastic 1.50 (ISBN 3-468-96476-5). Langenscheidt.

Langenscheidt English-Danish Lilliput Dictionary. 615p. (Danish & Eng.). plastic 1.50 (ISBN 3-468-96467-6). Langenscheidt.

Langenscheidt English-Dutch Lilliput Dictionary. 637p. (Dutch & Eng.). plastic 1.50 (ISBN 3-468-96477-3). Langenscheidt.

Langenscheidt English-French Lilliput Dictionary. 640p. (Fr. & Eng.). plastic 1.50 (ISBN 3-468-96408-0). Langenscheidt.

Langenscheidt English-German Lilliput Dictionary. 575p. (Eng. & Ger.). plastic 1.50 (ISBN 3-468-96404-8). Langenscheidt.

Langenscheidt English-Italian Lilliput Dictionary. 640p. (Eng. & Ital.). plastic 1.50 (ISBN 3-468-96415-3). Langenscheidt.

Langenscheidt English-Latin Lilliput Dictionary. 640p. (Eng. & Lat.). plastic 1.50 (ISBN 3-468-96484-6). Langenscheidt.

Langenscheidt English-Portuguese Lilliput Dictionary. 640p. (Eng. & Port.). plastic 1.50 (ISBN 3-468-96463-3). Langenscheidt.

Langenscheidt English-Spanish Lilliput Dictionary. 640p. (Eng. & Span.). plastic 1.50 (ISBN 3-468-96423-4). Langenscheidt.

Langenscheidt English-Turkish Lilliput Dictionary. 670p. (Eng. & Turkish.). plastic 1.50 (ISBN 3-468-96532-X). Langenscheidt.

Langenscheidt French-English Lilliput Dictionary. 640p. (Fr. & Eng.). plastic 1.50 (ISBN 3-468-96407-2). Langenscheidt.

Langenscheidt German-English Lilliput Dictionary. 576p. (Eng. & Ger.). plastic 1.50 (ISBN 3-468-96403-X). Langenscheidt.

Langenscheidt Grosswoerterbuch: Englisch-Deutsch. Heinz Messinger. 1104p. (Ger. & Eng.). DM.88.00 (02120). Langenscheidt.

Langenscheidt Grosswoerterbucher Franzosisch, 2 pts. Rev. ed. Incl. Teil I. Franz o06sisch-Deutsch. Compiled by Karl Sachs & C e01saire Villatte. xxxii, 1047p. DM.108.00 (02151); Teil II. Deutsch-Franz o06sisch. Ed. by Walter Gottschalk & Gaston Bentot. xxxii, 1080p. DM.108.00 (02156); DM.nachtrag 1979 7.80 (02159). (Ger. & Fr.). 1979. Langenscheidt.

Langenscheidt Italian-English Lilliput Dictionary. 640p. (Eng. & Ital.). plastic 1.50 (ISBN 3-468-96416-1). Langenscheidt.

Langenscheidt Little Webster Lilliput Dictionary. 640p. plastic 1.50 (ISBN 0-686-40190-5). Langenscheidt.

Langenscheidt Modern Greek-English Lilliput Dictionary. 640p. (Eng. & Ger.). plastic 1.50 (ISBN 3-468-96472-2). Langenscheidt.

Langenscheidt New Muret-Sanders Encyclopedic Dictionary. Incl. Part I, Vol. 1, A-M (English-German) 883p. (Eng. & Ger.). 70.00 (ISBN 3-468-01120-2); Part II, Vol. 2, N-Z (English-German) 960p. (Eng. & Ger.). 70.00 (ISBN 3-468-01122-9); Part II, Vol. 1, A-K (German-English) 973p. (Eng. & Ger.). 80.00 (ISBN 3-468-01124-5); Part II, Vol. 2, L-Z (German-English) 1048p. (Eng. & Ger.). 80.00 (ISBN 3-468-01126-1). Langenscheidt.

Langenscheidt New Muret-Sanders Encyclopedic Dictionary: German-English, 2 vols. 2020p. (Eng. & Ger.). 1974. 180.00 set. Imported Bks.

Langenscheidt Portuguese-English Lilliput Dictionary. 640p. (Eng. & Port.). plastic 1.50 (ISBN 3-468-96462-5). Langenscheidt.

Langenscheidt Russian-English Lilliput Dictionary. 640p. (Eng. & Rus.). plastic 1.50 (ISBN 3-468-96453-6). Langenscheidt.

Langenscheidt Russian Pocket Dictionary. 512p. (Rus.). plastic 5.95 (ISBN 0-340-10708-1). Langenscheidt.

Langenscheidt Spanish-English Lilliput Dictionary. 640p. (Eng. & Span.). plastic 1.50 (ISBN 3-468-96424-2). Langenscheidt.

Langenscheidt Taschenwoerterbuch Englisch komplett. 1278p. (Ger.). 10.95 (ISBN 3-468-10126-0). Langenscheidt.

Langenscheidt Turkish-English Lilliput Dictionary. 608p. (Eng. & Turkish.). plastic 1.50 (ISBN 3-468-96533-8). Langenscheidt.

Langenscheidt's Comprehensive English-German Dictionary. Heinz Messinger. 1134p. (Eng. & Ger.). 36.00. Imported Bks.

Langenscheidts Fachwoerterbuch Fernmeldewesen. 769p. (Ger. & Span.). 32.00 (ISBN 0-686-56628-9, M-7537, Pub. by Langenscheidt). French & Eur.

Langenscheidts Fachwoerterbuecher Deutsch-Spanisch. Arturo E. Von Baumgart. (Ger. & Span.). 1960. DM.39.00 (ISBN 3-468-49150-6). Langenscheidt.

Langenscheidts Grosse Schulwoerterbuch Deutsch-Englisch. Heinz Messinger. 1328p. (Eng. & Ger.). DM.23.80 (07126). Langenscheidt.

Langenscheidts Grosse Schulwoerterbuch Deutsch-Franzoesisch. Ernst E. Lange-Kowal. 1312p. (Ger. & Fr.). DM.23.80 (07157). Langenscheidt.

Langenscheidts Grosse Schulwoerterbuecher Deutsch-Franzoesisch. Kurt Wilhelm. 1400p. (Ger. & Fr.). 1977. DM.19.80 (ISBN 3-468-07156-6). Langenscheidt.

Langenscheidts Grosse Schulwoerterbuecher Englisch-Deutsch. H. Messinger & H. Ruedenberger. 1400p. (Eng. & Ger.). 1977. DM.19.80 (ISBN 3-468-07121-3). Langenscheidt.

Langenscheidts Grosse Schulwoerterbuch Englisch-Deutsch. Heinz Messinger & Werner Rudenberg. 07121p. (Eng. & Ger.). DM.23.80. Langenscheidt.

Langenscheidts Grosse Schulwoerterbuecher Franzoesisch-Deutsch. Ernst E. Lange-Kowal. 1400p. (Fr. & Ger.). 1977. DM.19.80 (ISBN 3-468-07151-5). Langenscheidt.

Langenscheidts Grosse Schulwoerterbuch Franzoesisch-Deutsch. Ernst E. Lange-Kowal & Louis Beaucaire. 1200p. (Fr. & Ger.). DM.23.80 (07151). Langenscheidt.

Langenscheidts Grosses Schulwoerterbuch Lateinisch-Deutsch. Erich Pertsch. 1344p. (Lat. & Ger.). DM.23.80 (07202). Langenscheidt.

Langenscheidts Grosswoerterbuch Altgriechisch: Tl 1, Altgriechisch-Deutsch. (Gr. & Ger.). 1978. DM.58.00 (ISBN 3-468-02030-9). Langenscheidt.

Langenscheidts Grosswoerterbuch Deutsch-Lateinisch. Menge & Guethling. (Ger. & Lat.). 1978. DM.58.00 (ISBN 3-468-02205-0). Langenscheidt.

Langenscheidts Grosswoerterbuch: Englisch-Deutsch. H. Messinger. 1104p. (Eng. & Ger.). DM.88.00 (02120). Langenscheidt.

Langenscheidts Grosswoerterbuch Englisch-Deutsch. Heinz Messinger. (Eng. & Ger.). 1971. DM.78.00 (ISBN 3-468-02120-8). Langenscheidt.

Langenscheidts Grosswoerterbuch Franzoesisch: Tl 1, Franzoesisch-Deutsch. Sachs & Villatte. (Fr. & Ger.). 1978. DM.68.00 (ISBN 3-468-02150-X). Langenscheidt.

Langenscheidts Grosswoerterbuch Franzoesisch: Tl 2, Deutsch-Franzoesisch. (Ger. & Fr.). 1978. DM.78.00 (ISBN 3-468-02155-0). Langenscheidt.

Langenscheidts Grosswoerterbuch Italienisch. Vladimiro Von Macchi. 786p. (Ger. & Ital.). 1977. DM.48.00 (ISBN 3-468-02180-1). Langenscheidt.

Langenscheidts Grosswoerterbuch Italienisch. Vladimiro Von Macchi. 938p. (Ger. & Ital.). 1977. DM.48.00 (ISBN 3-468-02185-2). Langenscheidt.

Langenscheidts Grosswoerterbuch Lateinisch-Deutsch. Menge & Guethling. (Lat. & Ger.). 1978. DM.58.00 (ISBN 3-468-02200-X). Langenscheidt.

Langenscheidts Grosswoerterbuch: Lateinisch-Deutsch, 2 vols. Hermann Menge & Otto Guethling. 1553p. (Lat. & Ger.). DM.78.00; Teil I, Lateinisch-Deutsch. (02200); Teil II, Deutsch-Lateinisch. (02205). Langenscheidt.

Langenscheidts Grosswoerterbuch Lateinisch: Tl 1, Lateinisch-Deutsch. (Lat. & Ger.). 1978. DM.58.00 (ISBN 3-468-02200-X). Langenscheidt.

Langenscheidts Grosswoerterbuch Lateinisch: Tl 2, Deutsch-Lateinisch. (Ger. & Lat.). 1978. DM.58.00 (ISBN 3-468-02205-0). Langenscheidt.

Langenscheidts Grosswoerterbuch: Teil II, Deutsch-Franzoesisch. Karl Sachs & Cesaire Villatte. Ed. by Walter Gottschalk & Gaston Bentot. 1080p. (Ger. & Fr.). 1979. DM.118.00 (02156). Langenscheidt.

Langenscheidts Grosswoerterbuch: Teil II, Deutsch-Italienisch. Ed. by Lexikographischen Institut Sansoni. Vladimiro Macchi. 938p. (Ger. & Ital.). DM.78.00 (02185). Langenscheidt.

Langenscheidts Grosswoerterbuch: Teil I, Franzoesisch-Deutsch. Karl Sachs & Cesaire Villatte. 1047p. (Fr. & Ger.). 1979. DM.118.00 (02151). Langenscheidt.

Langenscheidts Grosswoerterbuch: Teil I, Italienisch-Deutsch. Ed. by Lexikographischen Institut Sansoni. 786p. (Ital. & Ger.). DM.78.00 (02180). Langenscheidt.

Langenscheidts Grosswoerterbuch Altgriechisch-Deutsch. Menge & Guthling. xxiv, 762p. (Gr. & Ger.). DM.68.00 (02030). Langenscheidt.

Langenscheidts Grosswoerterbucher Italienisch, 2 vols. Ed. by Vladimiro Macchi. (Ger. & Ital.). Teil 1: Italienisch-Deutsch (xix, 786p.) DM.68.00 (02180); Teil 2: Deutsch-Italienisch (xvii, 938p.) DM.68.00 (02185). Langenscheidt.

Langenscheidts Handwoerterbuch: Englisch-Deutsch Deutsch-Englisch, 2 vols. in 1. Heinz Messinger & Werner Ruedenberg. 1471p. (Eng. & Ger.). DM.49.00 (05122). Langenscheidt.

Langenscheidts Handwoerterbuch: Franzoesisch-Deutsch Deutsch-Franzoesisch, 2 vols. in 1. Ernst E. Lange-Kowal & Louis Beaucaire. 1320p. (Fr. & Ger.). DM.49.00 (05153). Langenscheidt.

Langenscheidts Handwoerterbuch: Franzoesisch. 4th ed. Ernst Erwin Lange-Kowal. Ed. by Louis Beaucaire. LC 78-373125. (Ger. & Fr.). 1977. write for info. (ISBN 3-468-04151-9). Langenscheidt.

Langenscheidts Handwoerterbuch Hebraisch: Teil II, Deutsch-Hebraisch. Jaacov Lavy. 823p. (Hebrew & Ger.). DM.88.00 (04165). Langenscheidt.

Langenscheidts Handwoerterbuch Hebraisch: Teil I, Hebraisch-Deutsch. Jaacov Lavy. 639p. (Hebrew & Ger.). DM.78.00 (04160). Langenscheidt.

Langenscheidts Handwoerterbuch Italienisch-Deutsch, 2 vols. in 1. Paolo Giovannelli & Walter Frenzel. (Ital. & Ger.). DM.72.00 (05181). Langenscheidt.

Langenscheidts Handwoerterbuch Italienisch: Teil II, Deutsch-Italienisch. Herbert Frenzel & Walter Frenzel. Ed. by Vladimiro Macchi. 656p. (Ital. & Ger.). DM.39.80 (04186). Langenscheidt.

Langenscheidts Handwoerterbuch Italienisch: Teil I, Italienisch-Deutsch. Paolo Giovannelli & Walter Frenzel. 568p. (Ital. & Ger.). DM.39.80 (04180). Langenscheidt.

Langenscheidts Handwoerterbuch Lateinisch-Deutsch. Erich Pertsch. 652p. (Lat. & Ger.). DM.34.00 (04200). Langenscheidt.

Langenscheidts Handwoerterbuch Niederlaendisch Wolters: Teil I, Niederlaendisch-Deutsch. I. Van Gelderen & W. H. Wallis. 976p. (Dutch & Ger.). DM.42.00 (04230). Langenscheidt.

Langenscheidts Handwoerterbuch Schwedisch PRISMA. 640p. (Swedish & Ger.). DM.48.00 (04300). Langenscheidt.

Langenscheidts Handwoerterbuch Spanisch-Deutsch, 2 vols. in 1. Heinz Muller et al. (Span. & Ger.). DM.72.00 (05340). Langenscheidt.

Langenscheidts Handwoerterbuch Spanisch: Teil II, Deutsch-Spanisch. Enrique Alvarez-Prada. 768p. (Span. & Ger.). DM.39.80 (04345). Langenscheidt.

Langenscheidts Handwoerterbuch Spanisch: Teil I, Spanisch-Deutsch. Heinz Muller & Gunther Haensch. 640p. (Span. & Ger.). DM.39.80 (04340). Langenscheidt.

Langenscheidts Handwoerterbuch: Teil II, Deutsch-Englisch. Heinz Messinger. 702p. (Ger. & Eng.). DM.34.00 (04126). Langenscheidt.

Langenscheidts Handwoerterbuch: Teil II, Deutsch-Franzoesisch. Ernst E. Lange-Kowal. 700p. (Ger. & Fr.). DM.34.00 (04157). Langenscheidt.

Langenscheidts Handwoerterbuch: Teil I, Englisch-Deutsch. Heinz Messinger & Werner Ruedenberg. 760p. (Eng. & Ger.). DM.34.00 (04121). Langenscheidt.

Langenscheidts Handwoerterbuch: Teil I, Franzoesisch-Deutsch. Ernst E. Lange-Kowal & Louis Beaucaire. 640p. (Fr. & Ger.). DM.34.00 (04151). Langenscheidt.

Langenscheidts Handwoerterbuch Ungarisch HALASZ: Teil II, Deutsch-Ungarisch. I. Kadar & O. Ratz. 775p. (Ger. & Hungarian.). DM.44.00 (04385). Langenscheidt.

Langenscheidts Handwoerterbuch Ungarisch HALASZ: Teil I, Ungarisch-Deutsch. Ratz S. Skripecz et al. 1064p. (Hungarian & Ger.). DM.48.00 (04381). Langenscheidt.

Langenscheidts Handwoerterbuecher Deutsch-Polnisch. Ed. by Chodera & Kubica. (Ger. & Pol.). 1978. DM.38.00 (ISBN 3-468-04265-5). Langenscheidt.

Langenscheidts Handwoerterbuecher Englisch. Ed. by Heinz Messinger & Werner Ruedenberg. (Eng.). DM.28.00 (ISBN 3-468-80012-6). Langenscheidt.

Langenscheidts Handwoerterbuecher Franzoesisch. Ed. by Heinz Messinger & Werner Ruedenberg. (Fr.). DM.28.00 (ISBN 3-468-80015-0). Langenscheidt.

Langenscheidts Handwoerterbuecher: Franzoesisch, 2 Teile in 1. (Fr.). 1978. DM.44.00 (ISBN 3-468-05151-4). Langenscheidt.

Langenscheidts Handwoerterbuecher Italienisch. Ed. by Heinz Messinger & Werner Ruedenberg. (Ital.). DM.28.00 (ISBN 3-468-80018-5). Langenscheidt.

Langenscheidts Handwoerterbuecher: Italienisch, 2 Teile in 1. (Ital.). 1978. DM.55.00 (ISBN 3-468-05180-8). Langenscheidt.
Langenscheidts Handwoerterbuecher Norwegisch-Deutsch. (Norwegian & Ger.). 1978. DM.38.00 (ISBN 3-468-05240-5). Langenscheidt.
Langenscheidts Handwoerterbuecher Polnisch-Deutsch. (Pol. & Ger.). 1966. DM.38.00 (ISBN 3-468-04261-2). Langenscheidt.
Langenscheidts Handwoerterbuecher Russisch. Ed. by Heinz Messinger & Werner Ruedenberg. (Rus.). DM.28.00 (ISBN 3-468-80029-0). Langenscheidt.
Langenscheidts Handwoerterbuecher Spanisch. Ed. by Heinz Messinger & Werner Ruedenberg. (Span.). DM.28.00 (ISBN 3-468-80034-7). Langenscheidt.
Langenscheidts Handwoerterbuecher: Spanisch, 2 Teile in 1. (Span.). 1978. DM.55.00 (ISBN 3-468-05340-1). Langenscheidt.
Langenscheidts Handwoerterbuecher: Tl 1, Englisch-Deutsch. Heinz Messinger & Werner Ruedenberg. (Eng. & Ger.). 1978. DM.28.00 (ISBN 3-468-04120-9). Langenscheidt.
Langenscheidts Handwoerterbuecher: Tl 1, Franzoesisch-Deutsch. Ed. by Ernst E. Lange-Kowal. (Fr. & Ger.). 1978. DM.28.00 (ISBN 3-468-04151-9). Langenscheidt.
Langenscheidts Handwoerterbuecher: Tl 1, Gelderen, 1 van: Niederlandisch-Deutsch. Ed. by J. H. Van Beckum. (Dutch & Ger.). 1975. DM.38.00 (ISBN 3-468-04230-2). Langenscheidt.
Langenscheidts Handwoerterbuecher: Tl 1, Italienisch-Deutsch. Ed. by Paolo Giovannelli. (Ital. & Ger.). 1978. DM.33.00 (ISBN 3-468-04180-2). Langenscheidt.
Langenscheidts Handwoerterbuecher: Tl 1, Spanisch-Deutsch. Ed. by Heinz Mueller & Guenther Haensch. (Span. & Ger.). 1978. DM.33.00 (ISBN 3-468-04340-6). Langenscheidt.
Langenscheidts Handwoerterbuecher: Tl 2, Deutsch-Englisch. Heinz Messinger. (Ger. & Eng.). 1978. DM.28.00 (ISBN 3-468-04125-X). Langenscheidt.
Langenscheidts Handwoerterbuecher: Tl 2, Deutsch-Franzoesisch. Ed. by Kurt Wilhelm. (Ger. & Fr.). 1978. DM.28.00 (ISBN 3-468-04155-1). Langenscheidt.
Langenscheidts Handwoerterbuecher: Tl 2, Deutsch-Italienisch. Ed. by Herbert Frenzel & Walter Frenzel. (Ger. & Ital.). 1978. DM.33.00 (ISBN 3-468-04185-3). Langenscheidt.
Langenscheidts Handwoerterbuecher: Tl 2, Deutsch-Ungarisch. 1978 ed. Ed. by Halasz. (Ger. & Hungarian.). DM.38.00 (ISBN 3-468-04385-6). Langenscheidt.
Langenscheidts Handwoerterbuecher: Tl 2, Gelderen, 1 van, Deutsch-Niederlandisch. Ed. by J. H. Van Beckum & H. Wallis. (Ger. & Dutch.). 1975. DM.38.00 (ISBN 3-468-04235-3). Langenscheidt.
Langenscheidt's Hebrew-German Dictionary. Jaacom Lavy. 638p. (Ger. & Hebrew.). 1978. 32.00 (ISBN 0-685-64071-X). Am Map.
Langenscheidt's Lilliput Danish-English Dictionary. 640p. (Danish & Eng.). 1972. 1.50 (ISBN 0-685-31350-6). Am Map.
Langenscheidt's Lilliput Dutch-English Dictionary. 640p. (Dutch & Eng.). 1972. 1.50 (ISBN 0-685-31373-5). Am Map.
Langenscheidt's Lilliput English-Danish Dictionary. 640p. (Danish & Eng.). 1972. 1.50 (ISBN 0-685-31374-3). Am Map.
Langenscheidt's Lilliput English-Dutch Dictionary. 640p. (Dutch & Eng.). 1972. 1.50 (ISBN 0-685-31372-7). Am Map.
Langenscheidt's Lilliput English-French Dictionary. 640p. (Eng. & Fr.). 1972. 1.50 (ISBN 0-685-31353-0). Am Map.
Langenscheidt's Lilliput English-German Dictionary. 640p. (Eng. & Ger.). 1972. 1.50 (ISBN 0-685-31336-0). Am Map.
Langenscheidt's Lilliput English-Italian Dictionary. 640p. (Eng. & Ital.). 1972. 1.50 (ISBN 0-685-31370-0). Am Map.
Langenscheidt's Lilliput English-Latin Dictionary. 640p. (Eng. & Lat.). 1972. 1.50 (ISBN 0-685-31355-7). Am Map.
Langenscheidt's Lilliput English-Portuguese Dictionary. 640p. (Eng. & Port.). 1972. 1.50 (ISBN 0-685-31367-0). Am Map.
Langenscheidt's Lilliput English-Russian Dictionary. 640p. (Eng. & Rus.). 1972. 1.50 (ISBN 0-685-31365-4). Am Map.
Langenscheidt's Lilliput English-Spanish Dictionary. 640p. (Eng. & Span.). 1972. 1.50 (ISBN 0-685-31351-4). Am Map.
Langenscheidt's Lilliput English-Turkish Dictionary. 640p. (Eng. & Turkish.). 1972. 1.50 (ISBN 0-685-31363-8). Am Map.
Langenscheidt's Lilliput French-English Dictionary. 640p. (Eng. & Fr.). 1972. 1.50 (ISBN 0-685-31354-9). Am Map.
Langenscheidt's Lilliput German-English Dictionary. 640p. (Eng. & Ger.). 1972. 1.50 (ISBN 0-685-31337-9). Am Map.
Langenscheidt's Lilliput Italian-English Dictionary. 640p. (Eng. & Ital.). 1972. 1.50 (ISBN 0-685-31371-9). Am Map.
Langenscheidt's Lilliput Latin-English Dictionary. 640p. (Eng. & Lat.). 1972. 1.50 (ISBN 0-685-31369-7). Am Map.
Langenscheidt's Lilliput Little Webster Dictionary. 640p. 1972. 1.50 (ISBN 0-685-31362-X). Am Map.
Langenscheidt's Lilliput Modern Greek-English Dictionary. (Eng. & Ger.). 1972. 1.50 (ISBN 0-685-87395-1). Am Map.
Langenscheidt's Lilliput Portuguese-English Dictionary. 640p. (Eng. & Port.). 1972. 1.50 (ISBN 0-685-31368-9). Am Map.
Langenscheidt's Lilliput Russian-English Dictionary. 640p. (Eng. & Rus.). 1972. 1.50 (ISBN 0-685-31366-2). Am Map.
Langenscheidt's Lilliput Spanish-English Dictionary. 640p. (Eng. & Span.). 1972. 1.50 (ISBN 0-685-31352-2). Am Map.
Langenscheidt's Lilliput Turkish-English Dictionary. 640p. (Eng. & Turkish.). 1972. 1.50 (ISBN 0-685-31364-6). Am Map.
Langenscheidts Lilliput-Woerterbuch Deutsch-Englisch. 640p. (Ger. & Eng.). DM.3.00 (20003). Langenscheidt.
Langenscheidts Lilliput-Woerterbuch Deutsch-Franzoesisch. 640p. (Ger. & Fr.). DM.3.00 (20001). Langenscheidt.
Langenscheidts Lilliput-Woerterbuch Deutsch-Italienisch. 640p. (Ger. & Ital.). DM.3.00 (20005). Langenscheidt.
Langenscheidts Lilliput-Woerterbuch Deutsch-Lateinisch. 640p. (Ger. & Lat.). DM.3.00 (20013). Langenscheidt.
Langenscheidts Lilliput-Woerterbuch Deutsch-Spanisch. 640p. (Ger. & Span.). DM.3.00 (20017). Langenscheidt.
Langenscheidts Lilliput-Woerterbuch Englisch-Deutsch. 640p. (Eng. & Ger.). DM.3.00 (20004). Langenscheidt.
Langenscheidts Lilliput-Woerterbuch Franzoesisch-Deutsch. 640p. (Fr. & Ger.). DM.3.00 (20002). Langenscheidt.
Langenscheidts Lilliput-Woerterbuch Italienisch-Deutsch. 640p. (Ital. & Ger.). DM.3.00 (20006). Langenscheidt.
Langenscheidts Lilliput-Woerterbuch Lateinisch-Deutsch. 640p. (Lat. & Ger.). DM.3.00 (20014). Langenscheidt.
Langenscheidts Lilliput-Woerterbuch Spanisch-Deutsch. 640p. (Span. & Ger.). DM.3.00 (20018). Langenscheidt.
Langenscheidts Lilliput-Woerterbucher Franzoesisch-Deutsch. (Fr. & Ger.). 1978. DM.2.20 (ISBN 3-468-20002-1). Langenscheidt.
Langenscheidts Lilliput-Woerterbuecher Altgriechisch-Deutsch. (Gr. & Ger.). 1978. DM.2.20 (ISBN 3-468-20032-3). Langenscheidt.
Langenscheidts Lilliput-Woerterbuecher Deutsch-Englisch. (Ger. & Eng.). 1978. DM.2.20 (ISBN 3-468-20003-X). Langenscheidt.
Langenscheidts Lilliput-Woerterbuecher Deutsch-Franzoesisch. (Ger. & Fr.). 1978. DM.2.20 (ISBN 3-468-20001-3). Langenscheidt.
Langenscheidts Lilliput-Woerterbuecher Deutsch-Italienisch. (Ger. & Ital.). 1978. DM.2.20 (ISBN 3-468-20005-6). Langenscheidt.
Langenscheidts Lilliput-Woerterbuecher Deutsch-Lateinisch. (Ger. & Lat.). 1978. DM.2.20 (ISBN 3-468-20013-7). Langenscheidt.
Langenscheidts Lilliput-Woerterbuecher Deutsch-Spanisch. (Ger. & Span.). 1978. DM.2.20 (ISBN 3-468-20017-X). Langenscheidt.
Langenscheidts Lilliput-Woerterbuecher Englisch-Deutsch. (Eng. & Ger.). 1978. DM.2.20 (ISBN 3-468-20004-8). Langenscheidt.
Langenscheidts Lilliput-Woerterbuecher Italienisch-Deutsch. (Ital. & Ger.). 1978. DM.2.20 (ISBN 3-468-20006-4). Langenscheidt.
Langenscheidts Lilliput-Woerterbuecher Lateinisch-Deutsch. (Lat. & Ger.). 1978. DM.2.20 (ISBN 3-468-20014-5). Langenscheidt.
Langenscheidts Lilliput-Woerterbuecher Spanisch-Deutsch. (Span. & Ger.). 1978. DM.2.20 (ISBN 3-468-20018-8). Langenscheidt.
Langenscheidt's New College German Dictionary: German-English, English-German. Heinz Messinger. 1390p. (Ger. & Eng.). 1973. 16.95. Imported Bks.
Langenscheidt's New College German Dictionary (German-English, English-German) Heinz Messinger & Werner Rudenberg. 1400p. (Eng. & Ger.). 1973. 16.95 (ISBN 0-685-30210-5); thumb indexed 18.95 (ISBN 0-685-30211-3). Am Map.
Langenscheidt's New Muret-Sanders English-German Dictionary, 2 vols, Part I. Ed. by Otto Springer. Incl. Vol. 1. A-M. 924p. 1962. 70.00x (ISBN 3-468-01120-2); Vol. 2. N-Z. 958p. 1963. 70.00x (ISBN 0-685-31317-4). (Eng. & Ger.). Hippocrene Bks.
Langenscheidt's New Muret-Sanders German-English Encyclopedic Dictionary: Part 2, Vol. 2, L-Z. Ed. by Otto Springer. (Eng. & Ger.). 1975. 80.00x (ISBN 3-468-01126-1). Am Map.
Langenscheidt's New Pocket French Dictionary: French-English, English-French. Ed. by Langenscheidt Staff. (Langenscheidt Pocket Dictionaries Ser.). 640p. (Fr. & Eng.). 1970. 5.95 (ISBN 0-685-31331-X). Am Map.
Langenscheidt's New Pocket German Dictionary: German-English, English-German. Ed. by Langenscheidt Staff. (Langenscheidt Pocket Dictionaries Ser.). 702p. (Ger. & Eng.). 1970. 5.95 (ISBN 0-685-31330-1). Am Map.
Langenscheidt's Pocket Greek Dictionary, Classical Greek-English. Ed. by Karl Feyerabend. (Langenscheidt Pocket Dictionaries Ser.). 428p. (Eng. & Gr.). 1969. 5.95 (ISBN 0-685-31349-2). Am Map.
Langenscheidt's Pocket Hebrew Dictionary, Hebrew-English. Ed. by Karl Feyerabend. (Langenscheidt Pocket Dictionaries Ser.). 400p. (Eng. & Hebrew.). 1969. 5.95 (ISBN 0-685-31348-4). Am Map.
Langenscheidt's Pocket Latin Dictionary, Latin-English, English-Latin. Ed. by S. A. Handford & M. Herberg. (Langenscheidt Pocket Dictionaries Ser.). 480p. (Eng. & Lat.). 1969. 5.95 (ISBN 0-685-31347-6). Am Map.
Langenscheidt's Pocket Russian Dictionary: Russian-English, English-Russian. Ed. by E. Wedel & A. Romanov. (Langenscheidt Pocket Dictionaries Ser.). 592p. (Eng. & Rus.). 1969. 5.95 (ISBN 0-685-31322-0). Am Map.
Langenscheidts Reisewoerterbuecher Spanisch-Deutsch. (Span. & Ger.). DM.9.80 (ISBN 3-468-14340-0). Langenscheidt.
Langenscheidts Satz-Lexikon des Englischen Geschaeftsbriefes. (Ger. & Eng.). 1978. DM.19.80 (ISBN 3-468-39150-1). Langenscheidt.
Langenscheidts Satz-Lexikon des Franzoesischen Geschaeftsbriefes. (Ger. & Fr.). 1978. DM.19.80 (ISBN 3-468-39150-1). Langenscheidt.
Langenscheidts Satz-Lexikon des Spanischen Geschaeftsbriefes. H. Burfeindt-Moral & J. A. Moral-Arroyo. (Ger. & Span.). 1978. DM.19.80 (ISBN 3-468-39340-7). Langenscheidt.
Langenscheidts Schulwoerterbuch Englisch-Deutsch. Langenscheidt-Redaktion. 576p. (Eng. & Ger.). DM.13.80 (13120). Langenscheidt.
Langenscheidts Schulwoerterbuch Franzoesisch-Deutsch. Ernst E. Lange-Kowal & Paul Hartig. 576p. (Fr. & Ger.). DM.13.80 (13150). Langenscheidt.
Langenscheidts Schulwoerterbuch Lateinisch-Deutsch. Erich Pertsch & Ernst E. Lange-Kowal. 512p. (Lat. & Ger.). DM.13.80 (13200). Langenscheidt.
Langenscheidts Schulwoerterbuecher Englisch-Deutsch. (Eng. & Ger.). 1978. DM.10.80 (ISBN 3-468-13120-8). Langenscheidt.
Langenscheidts Schulwoerterbuecher Franzoesisch-Deutsch. (Fr. & Ger.). 1978. DM.10.80 (ISBN 3-468-13150-X). Langenscheidt.
Langenscheidts Schulwoerterbuecher Lateinisch-Deutsch. (Lat. & Ger.). 1978. DM.10.80 (ISBN 3-468-13200-X). Langenscheidt.
Langenscheidts Schulwoerterbuecher Lateinisch-Deutsch. Erich Pertsch. 1400p. (Lat. & Ger.). 1977. DM.19.80 (ISBN 3-468-07201-5). Langenscheidt.
Langenscheidts Sportwoerterbuch. R. Lembke. 319p. (Ger., Eng., Fr. & Span., Dictionary of Sports). 1971. 9.95 (ISBN 0-686-56629-7, M-7538, Pub. by Langenscheidt). French & Eur.
Langenscheidts Sportwoerterbuch Deutsch-Englisch-Franzoesisch-Spanisch. (Ger. , Eng. , Fr. & Span.). 1978. DM.12.80 (ISBN 3-468-21400-6). Langenscheidt.
Langenscheidt's Standard Dictionary. Edmund Klatt. 1278p. (Eng. & Ger.). 14.50. Imported Bks.
Langenscheidt's Standard French Dictionary: French-English, English-French. Kenneth Unwin. Orig. Title: Standard French Dictionary. 1216p. (Fr. & Eng.). 1974. 11.95 (ISBN 0-88254-285-0). Am Map.
Langenscheidt's Standard German Dictionary: German-English, English-German. Edmund Klatt et al. Orig. Title: Standard German Dictionary. 1264p. (Ger. & Eng.). 1974. 11.95 (ISBN 0-685-39723-8). Am Map.
Langenscheidt's Standard Spanish Dictionary: Spanish-English, English-Spanish. Ed. by C. C. Smith et al. (Langenscheidt Standard Dictionaries Ser.). 1072p. (Eng. & Span.). 1966. 11.95 (ISBN 0-685-31319-0). Am Map.
Langenscheidts Taschenwoerterbuch Altgriechisch, 2 vols. in 1. H. Menge & O. Guthling. (Gr. & Ger.). DM.24.80 (11030). Langenscheidt.

Langenscheidts Taschenwoerterbuch Altgriechisch: Teil I, Altgriechisch-Deutsch. H. Menge. 528p. (Gr. & Ger.). DM.17.80 (10030). Langenscheidt.

Langenscheidts Taschenwoerterbuch Altgriechisch: Teil II, Deutsch-Altgriechisch. O. Guthling. 547p. (Ger. & Gr.). DM.17.80 (10035). Langenscheidt.

Langenscheidts Taschenwoerterbuch Arabisch, 2 vols. in 1. G. Krotkoff et al. (Arabian & Ger.). DM.29.80 (11060). Langenscheidt.

Langenscheidts Taschenwoerterbuch Arabisch: Teil I, Arabisch-Deutsch. G. Krotkoff. 624p. (Arabian & Ger.). DM.19.80 (10060). Langenscheidt.

Langenscheidts Taschenwoerterbuch Arabisch: Teil II, Deutsch-Arabisch. K. Schukry & R. Humberdrotz. 456p. (Ger. & Arabic.). DM.19.80 (10065). Langenscheidt.

Langenscheidts Taschenwoerterbuch Danisch, 2 vols. in 1. H. Henningsen. (Danish & Ger.). DM.29.80 (11100). Langenscheidt.

Langenscheidt's Taschenwoerterbuch Danisch: Teil I, Danisch-Deutsch. H. Henningsen. 557p. (Danish & Ger.). DM.19.80 (10100). Langenscheidt.

Langenscheidts Taschenwoerterbuch Danisch: Teil II, Deutsch-Danisch. H. Henningsen. 548p. (Ger. & Danish.). DM.19.80 (10105). Langenscheidt.

Langenscheidts Taschenwoerterbuch der Italienischen & Deutschen Sprache. Ed. by W. Frenzel & V. Macchi. LC 79-385348. 1244p. (Ger. & Ital.). 1978. write for info. Langenscheidt.

Langenscheidts Taschenwoerterbuch Englisch, 2 vols. in 1. E. Klatt et al. (Eng. & Ger.). DM.23.80 (11121). Langenscheidt.

Langenscheidts Taschenwoerterbuch Englisch: Teil II, Deutsch-Englisch. E. Klatt & G. Klatt. 639p. (Ger. & Eng.). DM.16.80 (10126). Langenscheidt.

Langenscheidts Taschenwoerterbuch Englisch: Teil I, Englisch-Deutsch. E. Klatt & D. Roy. 640p. (Eng. & Ger.). DM.16.80 (10120). Langenscheidt.

Langenscheidts Taschenwoerterbuch Franzoesisch, 2 vols. in 1. E. E. Lange-Kowal et al. (Fr. & Ger.). DM.23.80 (11151). Langenscheidt.

Langenscheidts Taschenwoerterbuch Franzoesisch: Teil II, Deutsch-Franzoesisch. E. Weymuth. 640p. (Ger. & Fr.). DM.16.80 (10156). Langenscheidt.

Langenscheidts Taschenwoerterbuch Franzoesisch: Teil I, Franzoesisch-Deutsch. E. E. Lange-Kowal. 576p. (Fr. & Ger.). DM.16.80 (10151). Langenscheidt.

Langenscheidts Taschenwoerterbuch Hebraisch. K. Feyerabend. 306p. (Hebrew & Ger.). DM.19.80 (10040). Langenscheidt.

Langenscheidts Taschenwoerterbuch Italienisch-Deutsch, 2 vols. in 1. V. Macchi & W. Frenzel. (Ital. & Ger.). DM.27.80 (11181). Langenscheidt.

Langenscheidts Taschenwoerterbuch Italienisch: Teil II, Deutsch-Italienisch. W. Frenzel. 606p. (Ger. & Ital.). DM.18.80 (10186). Langenscheidt.

Langenscheidts Taschenwoerterbuch Italienisch: Teil I, Italienisch-Deutsch. V. Macchi. 640p. (Ital. & Ger.). DM.19.80 (10181). Langenscheidt.

Langenscheidts Taschenwoerterbuch Lateinisch, 2 vols. in 1. H. Menge & E. Pertsch. (Lat. & Ger.). DM.24.80 (11200). Langenscheidt.

Langenscheidts Taschenwoerterbuch Lateinisch: Teil II, Deutsch-Lateinisch. Hermann Menge. 460p. (Ger. & Lat.). DM.17.80 (10205). Langenscheidt.

Langenscheidts Taschenwoerterbuch Lateinisch: Teil I, Lateinisch-Deutsch. H. Menge & E. Pertsch. 576p. (Lat. & Ger.). DM.17.80 (10200). Langenscheidt.

Langenscheidts Taschenwoerterbuch Neugriechisch: Teil II, Deutsch-Neugriechisch. A. Steinmetz. 487p. (Ger. & Gr.). DM.19.80 (10215). Langenscheidt.

Langenscheidts Taschenwoerterbuch Neugriechisch: Teil I, Neugriechisch-Deutsch. H. F. Wendt. 552p. (Gr. & Ger.). DM.19.80 (10210). Langenscheidt.

Langenscheidts Taschenwoerterbuch Niederlandisch-Deutsch, 2 vols. in 1. F. J. J. Van De Wiele & Frans Beersmans. (Dutch & Ger.). DM.29.80 (11231). Langenscheidt.

Langenscheidts Taschenwoerterbuch Niederlaendisch: Teil II, Deutsch-Niederlaendisch. Frans Beersmans. 542p. (Ger. & Dutch.). DM.19.80 (10236). Langenscheidt.

Langenscheidts Taschenwoerterbuch Niederlaendisch: Teil I, Niederlaendisch-Deutsch. F. J. Van De Wiele. 527p. (Dutch & Ger.). DM.19.80 (10231). Langenscheidt.

Langenscheidts Taschenwoerterbuch Polnisch, 2 vols. in 1. Stanislaw Walewski. (Pol. & Ger.). DM.29.80 (11260). Langenscheidt.

Langenscheidts Taschenwoerterbuch Portugeisisch, 2 vols. in 1. A. E. Beau & F. Irmen. (Ger. & Port.). DM.29.80 (11271). Langenscheidt.

Langenscheidts Taschenwoerterbuch Portugiesisch: Teil II, Deutsch-Portugiesisch. A. E. Beau. 607p. (Ger. & Port.). DM.19.80 (10275). Langenscheidt.

Langenscheidts Taschenwoerterbuch Polnisch: Teil II, Deutsch-Polnisch. Stanislaw Walewski. 591p. (Ger. & Pol.). DM.19.80 (10265). Langenscheidt.

Langenscheidts Taschenwoerterbuch Portugiesisch: Teil I, Portugiesisch-Deutsch. F. Irmen. 640p. (Port. & Ger.). DM.19.80 (10271). Langenscheidt.

Langenscheidts Taschenwoerterbuch Polnisch: Teil I, Polnisch-Deutsch. Stanislaw Walewski. 624p. (Pol. & Ger.). DM.19.80 (10260). Langenscheidt.

Langenscheidts Taschenwoerterbuch Russisch, 2 vols. in 1. Karl Blattner et al. (Rus. & Ger.). DM.29.80 (11290). Langenscheidt.

Langenscheidts Taschenwoerterbuch Russisch: Teil II, Deutsch-Russisch. M. Braun & K. Pollok. 604p. (Ger. & Rus.). DM.19.80 (10295). Langenscheidt.

Langenscheidts Taschenwoerterbuch Russisch: Teil I, Russisch-Deutsch. Karl Blattner & H. Orschel. 568p. (Rus. & Ger.). DM.19.80 (10290). Langenscheidt.

Langenscheidts Taschenwoerterbuch Schwedisch, 2 vols. in 1. H. Kornitzky. (Swedish & Ger.). DM.29.80 (11300). Langenscheidt.

Langenscheidts Taschenwoerterbuch Schwedisch: Teil II, Deutsch-Schwedisch. H. Kornitzky. 510p. (Ger. & Swedish.). DM.19.80 (10305). Langenscheidt.

Langenscheidts Taschenwoerterbuch Schwedisch: Teil I, Schwedisch-Deutsch. H. Kornitzky. 573p. (Swedish & Ger.). DM.19.80 (10300). Langenscheidt.

Langenscheidts Taschenwoerterbuch Spanisch, 2 vols. in 1. G. Haberkamp de Anton & D. H. Willers. (Span. & Ger.). DM.27.80 (11341). Langenscheidt.

Langenscheidts Taschenwoerterbuch Spanisch: Teil II, Deutsch-Spanisch. D. H. Willers. 511p. (Ger. & Span.). DM.18.80 (10345). Langenscheidt.

Langenscheidts Taschenwoerterbuch Spanisch: Teil I, Spanisch-Deutsch. G. Haberkamp de Anton. 544p. (Span. & Ger.). DM.18.80 (10341). Langenscheidt.

Langenscheidts Taschenwoerterbuch Tschechisch-Deutsch, 2 vols. in 1. Rolf Ulbrich & Friedrich Kabesch. (Czech. & Ger.). DM.29.80 (11360). Langenscheidt.

Langenscheidts Taschenwoerterbuch Tschechisch: Teil II, Deutsch-Tschechisch. Friedrich Kabesch. 478p. (Ger. & Czech.). DM.19.80 (10365). Langenscheidt.

Langenscheidts Taschenwoerterbuch Tschechisch: Teil I, Tschechisch-Deutsch. Rolf Ulbrich. 576p. (Czech. & Ger.). DM.19.80 (10360). Langenscheidt.

Langenscheidts Taschenwoerterbuch Tuerkisch-Deutsch, 2 vols. in 1. K. Steuerwald & Cemal Koprulu. (Turkish & Ger.). DM.29.80 (11370). Langenscheidt.

Langenscheidts Taschenwoerterbuch Tuerkisch: Teil II, Deutsch-Tuerkisch. K. Steuerwald & Cemal Koprulu. 616p. (Ger. & Turkish.). DM.19.80 (10375). Langenscheidt.

Langenscheidts Taschenwoerterbuch Tuerkisch: Teil I, Tuerkisch-Deutsch. K. Steuerwald. 552p. (Turkish & Ger.). DM.19.80 (10370). Langenscheidt.

Langenscheidts Taschenwoerterbuecher Daenisch. H. Henningsen. (Danish.). 1978. DM.23.80 (ISBN 3-468-11100-2). Langenscheidt.

Langenscheidts Taschenwoerterbuecher Italienisch. Gustavo Sacerdote. (Ital.). 1978. DM.21.80. Langenscheidt.

Langenscheidts Taschenwoerterbuecher Lateinisch. H. Menge. (Lat.). 1978. DM.21.80 (ISBN 3-468-11200-9). Langenscheidt.

Langenscheidts Taschenwoerterbuecher Russisch. Karl Blattner. (Rus.). 1978. DM.23.80 (ISBN 3-468-11290-4). Langenscheidt.

Langenscheidts Taschenwoerterbuecher Schwedisch. H. Kornitzky. (Swedish.). 1978. DM.23.80 (ISBN 3-468-11300-5). Langenscheidt.

Langenscheidts Taschenwoerterbuecher Spanisch. (Span.). 1978. DM.21.80 (ISBN 3-468-11340-4). Langenscheidt.

Langenscheidts Taschenwoerterbuecher Tschechisch. 1100p. (Czech.). 1977. DM.23.80 (ISBN 3-468-11360-9). Langenscheidt.

Langenscheidts Taschenwoerterbuecher Tuerkisch. Karl Steuerwald. (Turkish.). 1978. DM.23.80 (ISBN 3-468-11370-6). Langenscheidt.

Langenscheidts Taschenwoerterbuecher Arabisch-Deutsch. Georg Krolkoff. (Arabic & Ger.). 1975. DM.14.80 (ISBN 3-468-10060-4). Langenscheidt.

Langenscheidts Taschenwoerterbuecher Altgriechisch-Deutsch. H. Menge. (Gr. & Ger.). DM.13.80 (ISBN 3-468-10030-2). Langenscheidt.

Langenscheidts Taschenwoerterbuecher Deutsch-Arabisch. K. Schukry. (Ger. & Arabic.). 1978. DM.14.80 (ISBN 3-468-10065-5). Langenscheidt.

Langenscheidts Taschenwoerterbuecher Deutsch-Daenisch. (Ger. & Danish.). 1978. DM.14.80 (ISBN 3-468-10105-8). Langenscheidt.

Langenscheidts Taschenwoerterbuecher Deutsch-Lateinisch. (Ger. & Lat.). 1978. DM.13.80 (ISBN 3-468-10205-4). Langenscheidt.

Langenscheidts Taschenwoerterbuecher Deutsch-Tschechisch. Friedrich Kabesch. 500p. (Ger. & Czech.). 1977. DM.14.80 (ISBN 3-468-10365-4). Langenscheidt.

Langenscheidts Taschenwoerterbuecher Englisch-Deutsch. E. Klatt & D. Roy. (Eng. & Ger.). 1970. DM.13.80 (ISBN 3-468-10120-1). Langenscheidt.

Langenscheidts Taschenwoerterbuecher Franzoesisch-Deutsch. Lange-Kowal & E. Ernst. (Fr. & Ger.). 1978. DM.13.80 (ISBN 3-468-10150-3). Langenscheidt.

Langenscheidts Taschenwoerterbuecher Hebraeisch-Deutsch. K. Feierabend. (Hebrew & Ger.). 1978. DM.14.80 (ISBN 3-468-10040-X). Langenscheidt.

Langenscheidts Taschenwoerterbuecher Italienisch-Deutsch. (Ital. & Ger.). 1978. DM.13.80 (ISBN 3-468-10180-5). Langenscheidt.

Langenscheidts Taschenwoerterbuecher Neugriechisch. (Gr.). 1978. DM.23.80 (ISBN 3-468-11210-6). Langenscheidt.

Langenscheidts Taschenwoerterbuecher Niederlaendisch-Deutsch. Ed. by Jan Schneider. (Dutch & Ger.). 1978. DM.14.80 (ISBN 3-468-10230-5). Langenscheidt.

Langenscheidts Taschenwoerterbuecher Neugriechisch-Deutsch. Ed. by H. F. Wendt. (Gr & Ger.). 1978. DM.14.80 (ISBN 3-468-10210-0). Langenscheidt.

Langenscheidts Taschenwoerterbuecher Portugiesisch. (Port.). 1978. DM.23.80 (ISBN 3-468-11270-X). Langenscheidt.

Langenscheidts Taschenwoerterbuecher Portugiesisch-Deutsch. F. Irmen. (Port. & Ger.). 1978. DM.14.80 (ISBN 3-468-10270-4). Langenscheidt.

Langenscheidts Taschenwoerterbuecher Russisch-Deutsch. H. Orschel. (Rus. & Ger.). 1978. DM.14.80 (ISBN 3-468-10290-9). Langenscheidt.

Langenscheidts Taschenwoerterbuecher Schwedisch-Deutsch. (Swedish & Ger.). 1978. DM.14.80 (ISBN 3-468-10300-X). Langenscheidt.

Langenscheidts Taschenwoerterbuecher Spanisch-Deutsch. H. Willers. (Span. & Ger.). 1978. DM.13.80 (ISBN 3-468-10340-9). Langenscheidt.

Langenscheidts Taschenwoerterbuecher Tuerkisch-Deutsch. Karl Steuerwald. (Turkish & Ger.). 1978. DM.14.80 (ISBN 3-468-10370-0). Langenscheidt.

Langenscheidts Taschenwoerterbuecher Tschechisch-Deutsch. Rolf Ulbrich. 600p. (Czech. & Ger.). 1977. DM.14.80 (ISBN 3-468-10360-3). Langenscheidt.

Langenscheidt's Taschenworterbuch. 6th ed. Ed. by Edmund Klatt et al. 1264p. (Ger.). 1970. 10.95 (ISBN 3-468-11121-5). Am Map.

Langenscheidt's Universal French-English, English-French Dictionary. 12th ed. 464p. (Eng. & Fr.). 1972. 2.95x (ISBN 0-685-31346-8). Am Map.

Langenscheidt's Universal German-English, English-German Dictionary. 35th ed. (Universal Dictionaries Ser.). 512p. (Eng. & Ger.). 2.95 (ISBN 3-468-18121-3). Am Map.

Langenscheidt's Universal Italian-English, English-Italian Dictionary. 384p. (Eng. & Ital.). 1972. 2.95 (ISBN 0-685-31344-1). Am Map.

Langenscheidt's Universal Latin-English, English-Latin Dictionary. 456p. (Eng. & Lat.). 1972. 2.95 (ISBN 0-685-31343-3). Am Map.

Langenscheidt's Universal Portuguese-English, English-Portuguese Dictionary. 8th ed. 384p. (Eng. & Port.). 1972. 2.95 (ISBN 0-685-31342-5). Am Map.

Langenscheidt's Universal Russian-English, English-Russian Dictionary. 415p. (Eng. & Rus.). 1972. 2.95 (ISBN 0-685-31341-7). Am Map.

Langenscheidt's Universal Spanish-English, English-Spanish Dictionary. 15th ed. 464p. (Eng. & Span.). 1972. 2.95 (ISBN 0-685-31340-9). Am Map.

Langenscheidt's Universal Turkish-English, English-Turkish Dictionary. 9th ed. 408p. (Eng. & Turkish.). 1972. 2.95 (ISBN 0-685-31339-5). Am Map.

Langenscheidt's Universal Webster Dictionary. 416p. 1972. 2.95 (ISBN 0-685-31338-7). Am Map.

Langenscheidts Universal-Woerterbuch Bulgarisch. 560p. (Bulgarian & Ger.). DM.6.80 (18080). Langenscheidt.

Langenscheidts Universal-Woerterbuch Danisch. 560p. (Danish & Ger.). DM.6.80 (18101). Langenscheidt.
Langenscheidts Universal-Woerterbuch Englisch. 560p. (Eng. & Ger.). DM.6.80 (18121). Langenscheidt.
Langenscheidts Universal-Woerterbuch Finnisch. 560p. (Finnish & Ger.). DM.6.80 (18141). Langenscheidt.
Langenscheidts Universal-Woerterbuch Franzoesisch. 560p. (Fr. & Ger.). DM.6.80 (18151). Langenscheidt.
Langenscheidts Universal-Woerterbuch Islaendisch. 560p. (Icelandic & Ger.). DM.6.80 (18170). Langenscheidt.
Langenscheidts Universal-Woerterbuch Italienisch. 560p. (Ital. & Ger.). DM.6.80 (18181). Langenscheidt.
Langenscheidts Universal-Woerterbuch Japanisch. 560p. (Japanese & Ger.). DM.6.80 (18190). Langenscheidt.
Langenscheidts Universal-Woerterbuch Lateinisch. 560p. (Lat. & Ger.). DM.6.80 (18200). Langenscheidt.
Langenscheidts Universal-Woerterbuch Norwegisch. 560p. (Norwegian & Ger.). DM.6.80 (18241). Langenscheidt.
Langenscheidts Universal-Woerterbuch Polnisch. 560p. (Pol. & Ger.). DM.6.80 (18260). Langenscheidt.
Langenscheidts Universal-Woerterbuch Rumaenisch. 560p. (Romanian & Ger.). DM.6.80 (18280). Langenscheidt.
Langenscheidts Universal-Woerterbuch Russisch. 560p. (Rus. & Ger.). DM.6.80 (18291). Langenscheidt.
Langenscheidts Universal-Woerterbuch Schwedisch. 560p. (Swedish & Ger.). DM.6.80 (18300). Langenscheidt.
Langenscheidts Universal-Woerterbuch Slowakisch. 560p. (Slavic & Ger.). DM.6.80 (18320). Langenscheidt.
Langenscheidts Universal-Woerterbuch Slowenisch. 560p. (Slovenian.). DM.6.80 (18330). Langenscheidt.
Langenscheidts Universal-Woerterbuch Spanisch. 560p. (Span. & Ger.). DM.6.80 (18342). Langenscheidt.
Langenscheidts Universal-Woerterbuch Tschechisch. 560p. (Czech. & Ger.). DM.6.80 (18360). Langenscheidt.
Langenscheidts Universal-Woerterbuch Tuerkisch. 560p. (Turkish & Ger.). DM.6.80 (18371). Langenscheidt.
Langenscheidts Universal-Woerterbuch Ungarisch. 560p. (Hungarian & Ger.). DM.6.80 (18381). Langenscheidt.
Langenscheidts Universal-Woerterbuch Neugriechisch. 560p. (Gr. & Ger.). DM.6.80 (18210). Langenscheidt.
Langenscheidts Universal-Woerterbuch Niederlaendisch. 560p. (Dutch & Ger.). DM.6.80 (18231). Langenscheidt.
Langenscheidts Universal-Woerterbuch Portugiesisch. 560p. (Port. & Ger.). DM.6.80 (18271). Langenscheidt.
Langenscheidts Universal-Woerterbuch Serbokroatisch. 560p. (Serbo-Croatian & Ger.). DM.6.80 (18311). Langenscheidt.
Langenscheidts Universal-Woerterbuecher Bulgarisch-Deutsch. (Bulgarian & Ger.). 1978. DM.5.80 (ISBN 3-468-18080-2). Langenscheidt.
Langenscheidts Universal-Woerterbuecher Daenisch-Deutsch. (Danish & Ger.). 1978. DM.5.80 (ISBN 3-468-18101-9). Langenscheidt.
Langenscheidts Universal-Woerterbuecher Englisch-Deutsch. (Eng. & Ger.). 1978. DM.5.80 (ISBN 3-468-18121-3). Langenscheidt.
Langenscheidts Universal-Woerterbuecher Franzoesisch-Deutsch. (Fr. & Ger.). 1978. DM.5.80 (ISBN 3-468-18151-5). Langenscheidt.
Langenscheidts Universal-Woerterbuecher Islaendisch-Deutsch. (Icelandic & Ger.). 1978. DM.5.80 (ISBN 3-468-18170-1). Langenscheidt.
Langenscheidts Universal-Woerterbuecher Italienisch-Deutsch. (Ital. & Ger.). 1978. DM.5.80 (ISBN 3-468-18181-7). Langenscheidt.
Langenscheidts Universal-Woerterbuecher Lateinisch-Deutsch. (Lat. & Ger.). 1978. DM.5.80 (ISBN 3-468-18200-7). Langenscheidt.
Langenscheidts Universal-Woerterbuecher Neugriechisch-Deutsch. (Gr. & Ger.). 1978. DM.5.80 (ISBN 3-468-18200-7). Langenscheidt.
Langenscheidts Universal-Woerterbuecher Norwegisch-Deutsch. (Norwegian & Ger.). 1978. DM.5.80 (ISBN 3-468-18240-6). Langenscheidt.
Langenscheidts Universal-Woerterbuecher Polnisch-Deutsch. (Pol. & Ger.). 1978. DM.5.80 (ISBN 3-468-18260-0). Langenscheidt.
Langenscheidts Universal-Woerterbuecher Portugiesisch-Deutsch. (Port. & Ger.). 1978. DM.5.80 (ISBN 3-468-18270-8). Langenscheidt.
Langenscheidts Universal-Woerterbuecher Rumaenisch-Deutsch. (Romanian & Ger.). 1978. DM.5.80 (ISBN 3-468-18280-5). Langenscheidt.
Langenscheidts Universal-Woerterbuecher Russisch-Deutsch. (Rus. & Ger.). 1978. DM.5.80 (ISBN 3-468-18290-2). Langenscheidt.
Langenscheidts Universal-Woerterbuecher Serbokroatisch-Deutsch. (Serbo-Croatian & Ger.). 1978. DM.5.80 (ISBN 3-468-18311-9). Langenscheidt.
Langenscheidts Universal-Woerterbuecher Slowakisch-Deutsch. (Slavic & Ger.). 1978. DM.5.80 (ISBN 3-468-18320-8). Langenscheidt.
Langenscheidts Universal-Woerterbuecher Spanisch-Deutsch. (Span. & Ger.). 1978. DM.5.80 (ISBN 3-468-18341-0). Langenscheidt.
Langenscheidts Universal-Woerterbuecher Tschechisch-Deutsch. (Czech. & Ger.). 1978. DM.5.80 (ISBN 3-468-18360-7). Langenscheidt.
Langenscheidts Universal-Woerterbuecher Tuerkisch-Deutsch. (Turkish & Ger.). 1978. DM.5.80 (ISBN 3-468-18371-2). Langenscheidt.
Langenscheidts Universal-Woerterbuecher Ungarisch-Deutsch. (Hungarian & Ger.). 1978. DM.5.80 (ISBN 3-468-18381-X). Langenscheidt.
Language of American Popular Entertainment: A Glossary of Argot, Slang, & Terminology. Don B. Wilmeth. LC 80-14795. xxi, 305p. 1981. lib. bdg. 29.95 (ISBN 0-313-22497-8, WEN/). Greenwood.
Language of Ballet. Thalia Mara. LC 78-181477. (Illus.). 120p. pap. 4.95 (ISBN 0-87127-038-2). Dance Horiz.
Language of British Industry. Peter Wright. 207p. 1974. text ed. 20.00x (ISBN 0-333-15359-6). Verry.
Language of Herz's "Esther" A Study in Judeo-German Dialectology. Ed. by Robert M. Copeland & Nathan Susskind. LC 75-34184. (Judaic Studies: No. 6). 560p. 1976. 29.50 (ISBN 0-8173-6902-3). U of Ala Pr.
Language of Journalism: A Glossary of Print-Communications Terms. Ruth Kent. LC 71-100624. (Illus.). 1970. 8.00x (ISBN 0-87338-091-6); pap. 4.00x (ISBN 0-87338-092-4). Kent St U Pr.
Language of Judaism. rev. ed. Simon Glustrom. 1973. pap. 7.95x (ISBN 0-87068-224-5). Ktav.
Language of Mental Health. 2nd ed. William E. Fann & Charles E. Goshen. LC 76-40210. 165p. 1977. pap. 12.00 (ISBN 0-8016-1548-8). Mosby.
Language of Sport. Tim Considine. Ed. by Henry Doering & Patricia Fisher. 352p. 1982. pap. 8.95 (ISBN 0-911818-24-3). World Almanac.
Language of the Foreign Book Trade: Abbreviations, Terms, Phrases. 3rd ed. Jerrold Orne. 20.00 (ISBN 0-8389-0219-7). ALA.
Language of the Puerto Rican Street. Cristine Gallo. LC 80-66269. ix, 214p. (Span. & Eng.). 1980. write for info. (ISBN 0-9604174-0-0). C Gallo.
Language of the Railroader. Ramon F. Adams. 1977. 12.95 (ISBN 0-8061-1435-5). U of Okla Pr.
Lao-English Dictionary, 2 vols. Allen Kerr. (Publications in the Languages of Asia Ser.: No. 2). (Laotian & Eng.). 1973. Set. 44.95 (ISBN 0-8132-0526-3). Cath U Pr.
Lapp Dictionary, 5 vols. Ed. by Konrad Nielsen & Asbjorn Nesheim. 3221p. 1980. 250.00x set (ISBN 82-00-14201-9). Universitet.
L'argile pour votre Sante. Andre Passebecq. LC 80-471204. 129p. (Fr.). 1978. 27.00 F (ISBN 2-7033-0192-8). Dangles.
Larouse de la Langue Francaise, 2 vols. (Fr.). 1977. 98.50 (ISBN 2-03-020287-8). Pergamon.
Larousse Arab Dictionary. (Illus.). 1400p. (Arabic.). 30.00. Intl Bk Ctr.
Larousse Bi-Lingual French-English, English French Dictionary. (Apollo). (Fr. & Eng.). 10.50 (ISBN 2-03-020903-1, 3767). Larousse.
Larousse de Base: Dictionnaire d'Apprentissage du Francais. Ed. by Jean Dubois & Francoise Duboise-Charlier. LC 78-380974. viii, 1023p. (Fr.). 1977. 30.00 F (ISBN 2-030-20144-8). Larousse FR.
Larousse de la Langue Francaise, 2 vols. (Fr.). 1977. 98.50 set (ISBN 2-03-020287-8). Pergamon.
Larousse de la Langue Francaise Lexis, Illustre. J. Dubois. (Illus., Fr.). 1979. 43.95 (Dist. by Continental Bk Co). Larousse.
Larousse de la Medecine, 3 vols. Andre Domart & Jacques Bourneuf. 1728p. 1971. Set. 225.00 (ISBN 0-686-57120-7, M-6166). French & Eur.
Larousse de poche. Larousse & Co. (Fr.). pap. 6.95 (ISBN 2-03-020166-9, 1008). Larousse.
Larousse De Poche. (Fr.). pap. 4.95 (ISBN 0-671-48896-1). PB.
Larousse de poche, francais-allemand et allemand-francais. Larousse & Co. (Fr. & Ger.). pap. 6.95 (ISBN 0-685-13959-X). Larousse.
Larousse de poche francais-espagnol, & espanol-frances. Larousse And Co. (Fr. & Span.). pap. 6.95 (ISBN 0-685-13961-1, 1010). Larousse.
Larousse de poche, francais-italien et italien-francais. Larousse & Co. (Fr. & It.). pap. 6.95 (ISBN 0-685-13960-3, 1012). Larousse.
Larousse de poche French-English & English-French. Larousse & Co. (Fr. & Eng.). pap. 6.95 (ISBN 2-03-029203-6, 1009). Larousse.
Larousse de Poche: Precis de Grammaire. Librairie Larousse. LC 80-105478. lv, 543p. (Fr.). 1979. write for info. (ISBN 2-253-00344-1). Lib Gen Fr.
Larousse des Citations: Francaises et Etrangeres. Pierre Germa. (Fr.). 1975. 33.00 (Dist. by Continental Bk Co). Larousse.
Larousse des debutants. Larousse & Co. (Illus., Fr.). 16.25 (ISBN 2-03-020151-0, 3752). Larousse.
Larousse des Enfants. L. Lamblin. (Fr.). 1978. 22.75 (Dist. by Continental Bk Co). Larousse.
Larousse Dictionary of Painters. Ed. by Michel Laclotte & Alistair Smith. LC 81-81046. (Illus.). 480p. 1981. 50.00 (ISBN 0-88332-265-X, 8191). Larousse.
Larousse Dictionary of the Fresh-Water Aquarium. Henri Favre. Tr. by Gwynne Vevers. LC 77-11664. 1978. 6.95 (ISBN 0-8120-5192-0). Barron.
Larousse du chat. Ed. by Pierre Rousselet-Blanc. (Larousse des animaux familiers). (Illus.). 240p. (Fr.). 1975. 43.95x (ISBN 2-03-014852-0). Larousse.
Larousse Elementaire a L'usage des Allemand. 672p. (Ger.). DM.18.80 (49009). Langenscheidt.
Larousse French-English Dictionary. (Fr. & Eng.). 1981. pap. 3.95 (ISBN 0-671-47166-X). PB.
Larousse Modern French-English, English-French Dictionary. (Fr. & Eng.). 29.95 (ISBN 2-03-020602-4, 3776). Larousse.
L'aspect Verbal en Francais. Milan Golian. (Hamburger Phonetische Beitrage Ser.: No. 29). 269p. (Orig., Fr.). 1979. pap. text ed. 19.00x (ISBN 3-87118-390-3, Pub. by Helmut Buske Verlag Hamburg). Benjamins North Am.
Lateinisch, 2 vols. rev. ed. Hermann Menge. Rev. by E. Pertsch. (Langenscheidts Taschewoerterbuecher Ser.). (Lat. & Ger.). Teil 1: Lateinisch-Deutsch (576p.) DM.16.80 (10200); Teil 2: Deutsch-Lateinisch (460p.) DM.16.80 (10205); DM.beide Teile in einem Band 23.80 (11200). Langenscheidt.
Lateinisch-Deutsch. rev. & enl. ed. Dietrich Pertsch. (Langenscheidts Grosse Schulwoerbuecher Ser.). 1344p. (Lat. & Ger.). 1983. DM.23.80 (07202). Langenscheidt.
Lateinisch-Deutsch. Compiled by Erich Pertsch. (Langenscheidts Handwoerterbuecher Ser.). 652p. (Lat. & Ger.). DM.32.00 (04200). Langenscheidt.
Lateinisch-Deutsch, Deutsch-Lateinisch. (Langenscheidts Schulwoerterbuecher Ser.). 512p. (Ger. & Lat.). DM.12.80 (13200). Langenscheidt.
Lateinische Wortkunde fuer Anfaenger & Fortgeschrittene. Ruediger Vischer. LC 79-383471. 224p. (Ger. & Lat.). 1977. write for info. (ISBN 3-519-07407-9). Teubner.
Lateinischen Woerter auf -Ura. Ernst Zellmer. LC 78-374219. 293p. (Ger.). 1976. write for info. Selbstverlag Inst.
Later Prophets see Classified Concordance.
Latin American Political Dictionary. Ernest E. Rossi & Jack C. Plano. LC 79-27128. (Clio Dictionaries in Political Science Ser.: No. 1). 261p. 1981. 19.75 (ISBN 0-87436-324-1); pap. 9.75 (ISBN 0-87436-327-6). ABC-Clio.
Latin & Greek for Biologists. Theodore Savory. 42p. (Lat. & Gr.). 1971. 39.00x (ISBN 0-900541-47-4, Pub. by Meadowfield Pr England). State Mutual Bk.
Latin-Bulgarian Dictionary. M. Voinov. 840p. (Lat. & Bulgarian.). 1980. 45.00 (ISBN 0-686-97420-4, M-9831). French & Eur.
Latin Concise Dictionary. Cassells. (Lat.). 1977. 9.95 (ISBN 0-02-052263-0). Macmillan.
Latin-Dansk Ordbog. T. Hastrup. 307p. (Lat. & Danish.). 1981. 24.95 (ISBN 87-01-67511-7, M-1288). French & Eur.
Latin Dictionary. A. Wilson. (Teach Yourself Ser.). (Lat.). 1974. pap. 4.95 (ISBN 0-679-10204-3). McKay.
Latin Dictionary: Founded on Andrews Edition of Freund's Latin Dictionary. Charlton T. Lewis & Charles Short. (Lat.). 1879. 69.00x (ISBN 0-19-864201-6). Oxford U Pr.
Latin-English & English-Latin Dictionary. (Lat. & Eng.). pap. 1.99 (ISBN 0-686-00473-6). Dennison.
Latin-English & English-Latin Dictionary. Ed. by S. C. Woodhouse. (Routledge Pocket Dictionaries Ser.). 496p. (Orig., Lat. & Eng.). 1982. pap. 8.95 (ISBN 0-7100-9267-9). Routledge & Kegan.

Latin English Derivative Dictionary. Ed. by Randolph F. Schaeffer & W. L. Carr. (Lat. & Eng.). 1.95 (B5). Am Classical.

Latin-English Dictionary. Cassells. (Lat. & Eng.). 1977. standard 16.95 (ISBN 0-686-63973-1); index 19.95 (ISBN 0-02-052258-4). Macmillan.

Latin-English, English-Latin. (Cassell's Concise Dictionaries). (Eng. & Lat.). 8.95 (522630-4). Inst Mod Lang.

Latin-English, English-Latin Dictionary. D. A. Kidd. (Lat. & Eng.). 19.50 (ISBN 0-87557-050-X, 052-6). Saphrograph.

Latin-English, English-Latin Dictionary. (Lat. & Eng.). pap. 2.50 (ISBN 0-686-79571-7, DI 6, BN). B&N NY.

Latin Sexual Vocabulary: Three Years of Confrontation. James N. Adams. LC 82-82629. 272p. 1983. 27.50 (ISBN 0-8018-2968-2). Johns Hopkins.

Latinsk-Svensk Ordbok. Axel W. Ahlberg et al. 430p. (Lat. & Swedish.). 1968. Kr.200.00 (ISBN 91-24-62108-0). Esselte Studium.

Latinsko-Cesky Slovnik, 2 vols. 2nd ed. Josef M. Prazak. LC 76-502083. (Lat. & Czech.). 1975. 94.00 Kcs. SNTC.

Latinsko-Russko-Latyshskii Slovar Meditsinskikh Terminov, 2 vols. (Lat. & Rus.). 1977. 33.50 set (Pub. by Liesma). Four Continent.

Latvian-English Dictionary. Phil E. Turkina. (Latvian & Eng.). 19.50 (ISBN 0-87557-052-6, 052-6). Saphrograph.

Law Dictionary. rev. ed. Steven H. Gifis. LC 74-18126. 240p. 1975. pap. 4.95 (ISBN 0-8120-0543-0). Barron.

Law Dictionary. rev. ed. Wesley Gilmer. 1981. pap. 6.95 (ISBN 0-684-17329-8, ScribT). Scribner.

Law Dictionary. 2nd, rev. ed. Ed. by Max Radin & Lawrence G. Greene. LC 74-123997. (Illus.). 1970. 17.50 (ISBN 0-379-00465-8). Oceana.

Law Dictionary (Arabic-English) Harith Faruqi. 288p. (Arabic & Eng.). 1972. 30.00x (ISBN 0-86685-085-6). Intl Bk Ctr.

Law Dictionary (English-Arabic) Ibrahim Al-Wahab. 320p. (Eng. & Arabic.). 1972. 20.00x (ISBN 0-86685-082-1). Intl Bk Ctr.

Law Dictionary (English-Arabic) rev. ed. Harith Faruqi. 1972. 35.00x (ISBN 0-86685-065-1). Intl Bk Ctr.

Law Dictionary: Fachwoerterbuch der anglo-amerikanischen Rechtssprache, Englisch-Deutsch. 3rd. rev. ed. Dora Von Beseler & Barbara Jacobs. (Ger.). 1976. 123.25x (ISBN 3-11-006774-9); pap. 111.00x (ISBN 3-11-001698-2). De Gruyter.

Law Dictionary for Laymen. LC 80-65097. 1980. write for info. (ISBN 0-89648-074-7); pap. write for info. (ISBN 0-89648-075-5). Citizens Law.

Law Dictionary French-Arabic: Dictionnaire Juridique. Najjar. (Arabic & Fr.). 1983. 40.00x (ISBN 0-86685-303-0). Intl Bk Ctr.

Law Dictionary: Technical Dictionary of Anglo-American Legal Terminology, German-English. 3rd rev. ed. Ed. by D. v. Beseler & B. Jacobs. 385p. (Ger. & Eng.). 1971. 56.00x (ISBN 3-11-006775-7); pap. 45.00x (ISBN 3-11-002187-0). De Gruyter.

Law Dictionary: The Canadian Edition. John Yogis. (Barron's Educational Ser.). (Orig.). 1983. pap. text ed. 6.95 (ISBN 0-8120-2116-9). Barron.

Law Enforcement Vocabulary. Julian A. Martin. 262p. 1973. 13.75x (ISBN 0-398-02599-1). C C Thomas.

Law Latin Lexicon. Abdul G. Chaudhary. LC 79-930806. 248p. (Eng. & Lat.). 1979. Rs.35.00. Khyber Law Publishers.

Learn Arabic for English Speakers. (Arabic & Eng.). pap. 10.50 (ISBN 0-87557-004-6, 004-6). Saphrograph.

Learn Bengali: For English Speakers. (Begali.). pap. 9.50 (ISBN 0-87557-005-4, 005-4). Saphrograph.

Learn Chinese: For English Speakers. (Chinese.). pap. 9.50 (ISBN 0-87557-009-7, 092-6). Saphrograph.

Learn Czech for English Speakers. (Czech. & Eng.). pap. 9.50 (ISBN 0-87557-013-5, 013-5). Saphrograph.

Learn Esperanto for English Speakers. (Esperanto & Eng.). pap. 9.50 (ISBN 0-87557-019-4, 019-4). Saphrograph.

Learn Finnish for English Speakers. (Finnish & Eng.). pap. 10.50 (ISBN 0-87557-020-8, 020-8). Saphrograph.

Learn French for English Speakers. W. R. Patterson. 230p. (Fr. & Eng.). pap. 9.50 (ISBN 0-87557-023-2, 023-2). Saphrograph.

Learn Greek for English Speakers. (Gr. & Eng.). pap. 9.50 (ISBN 0-87557-031-3, 031-3). Saphrograph.

Learn Hebrew for English Speakers. (Hebrew & Eng.). pap. 9.50 romanized (ISBN 0-87557-032-1, 032-1). Saphrograph.

Learn Hindustani. (Hindustani.). pap. 9.50 (ISBN 0-87557-037-2, 037-2). Saphrograph.

Learn Hungarian for English Speakers. A. H. Whitney. 264p. (Hungarian.). pap. 9.50 (ISBN 0-87557-044-5, 044-5). Saphrograph.

Learn Italian for English Speakers. Arthur L. Hayward & C. McFarlane. (Ital. & Eng.). 9.50 (ISBN 0-87557-046-1, 046-1). Saphrograph.

Learn Japanese for English Speakers. (Japanese & Eng.). pap. 9.50 (ISBN 0-87557-049-6, 049-6). Saphrograph.

Learn Norwegian for English Speakers. (Norwegian & Eng.). pap. 9.50 (ISBN 0-87557-055-0, 055-0). Saphrograph.

Learn Persian for English Speakers. (Persian.). pap. 10.50 (ISBN 0-87557-059-3, 059-3). Saphrograph.

Learn Portugese for English Speakers. (Port. & Eng.). 1974. pap. 9.50 (ISBN 0-87557-108-5, 108-5). Saphrograph.

Learn Russian, Bks. 1-4. N. Potapova. (Rus.). pap. 5.50 ea.; Set. pap. 22.00 (ISBN 0-87557-073-9). Saphrograph.

Learn Serbocroatian for English Speakers. (Serbocroatian & Eng.). pap. 9.50 (ISBN 0-87557-075-5, 075-5). Saphrograph.

Learn Spanish for English Speakers. rev. ed. William R. Patterson. Ed. by Ronald MacAndrew. (Span. & Eng.). 9.50 (ISBN 0-87557-078-X, 078-X). Saphrograph.

Learn Swahili for English Speakers. Ernest B. Haddon. (Swahili & Eng.). 10.50 (ISBN 0-87557-081-X, 080-1). Saphrograph.

Learn Turkish, for English Speaker. 224p. (Turkish & Eng.). pap. 9.50 (ISBN 0-87557-086-0, 086-0). Saphrograph.

Learn Welsh for English Speakers. 180p. (Welsh & Eng.). pap. 9.50 (ISBN 0-87557-092-5, 092-5). Saphrograph.

Learner's Arabic-English Dictionary. F. Steingass. (Arabic & Eng.). 1978. 24.00x (ISBN 0-8364-0312-6). South Asia Bks.

Learner's Arabic-English Dictionary. F. Steingass. 1243p. (Arabic & Eng.). 35.00 (091-0). Intl Bk Ctr.

Learner's Chinese-English Dictionary. (Chinese & Eng.). 1979. 14.95 (ISBN 0-8351-0641-1). China Bks.

Learner's Chinese-English Dictionary. 666p. (Chinese & Eng.). 1979. pap. 14.95 (ISBN 0-8351-0641-1). China Bks.

Learner's Chinese-English Dictionary. (Chinese & Eng.). pap. 14.95. Iaconi.

Learner's English-Arabic Dictionary. F. Steingass. 466p. (Eng. & Arabic.). 1978. 20.00 (081-3). Intl Bk Ctr.

Learner's English-Russian Dictionary. A. Folomkina & H. Weiser. 472p. (Eng. & Rus.). 1975. 3.00. Russki Iazyk.

Learner's English-Russian Dictionary. S. Folomkina & H. Weiser. (Eng. & Rus.). 1963. pap. 9.95 (ISBN 0-262-56002-X). MIT Pr.

Learner's English-Russian Dictionary. S. Folomkina & H. Weiser. 471p. (Eng. & Rus.). 1975. leatherette 9.95 (ISBN 0-686-92469-X, M-9118). French & Eur.

Learner's English-Russian Dictionary. V. Folomkina & T. Weiser. 655p. (Eng. & Rus.). 1980. 15.00x (ISBN 0-569-05869-4, Pub. by Collet's). State Mutual Bk.

Learner's English-Russian Dictionary: For English Speaking Students. (Russkii iazyk Ser.). 472p. (Eng. & Rus.). 1975. 3.00 (D-202 A). Four Continent.

Learner's First Dictionary. Christopher Scott. 176p. (Orig., Eng.). write for info. Macmillan London.

Learner's Russian-English Dictionary. B. A. Lapidus & S. V. Shevtsoka. 550p. (Eng. & Rus.). 1977. leatherette 9.95 (ISBN 0-686-92466-5, M-9117). French & Eur.

Learner's Russian-English Dictionary. B. A. Lapidus & S. V. Shevtsova. (Rus. & Eng.). 1963. pap. 9.95 (ISBN 0-262-62002-2). MIT Pr.

Learner's Russian-English Dictionary. B. A. Lapidus et al. 552p. (Rus. & Eng.). 1977. 3.95 (Pub. by Russkii Iazyk). Four Continent.

Learner's Russian-English Dictionary: For Foreign Students of Russian. A. Lapidus et al. 552p. (Rus. & Eng.). 4.65. Four Continent.

Learner's Russian-English Dictionary for Foreign Students of Russian. 2nd ed. B. A. Lapidus & S. V. Shevisova. LC 78-342111. 552p. (Rus. & Eng.). 1977. 141.00 Kop. Russica.

Learning Disabilities Glossary. Lillie Pope. 64p. 1976. pap. text ed. 3.95 (ISBN 0-87594-144-3). Book-Lab.

Learning Inc. Dictionary of Learning Handicaps. Manset & Maine. 0.75. Assn Child & Adult Learn.

Learning Incorporated Dictionary of Learning Handicaps. 3rd ed. E. R. Welles. 1970. prepaid 1.00 ea. (ISBN 0-913692-01-8). Learning Inc.

Least You Should Know About Vocabulary. Glazier. (Eng.). Epap. 6.95. HR&W.

Left-Handed Dictionary. Leonard L. Levinson. (Orig.). 1964. pap. 2.50 (ISBN 0-02-040550-2, Collier). Macmillan.

Legal Dictionary. E. A. Geissler & Lise Wolff. 200p. 1980. 45.00x (ISBN 0-686-44720-4, Pub. by Collets). State Mutual Bk.

Legal Dictionary. H. P. Kniepkamp. (Ger. & Eng.). 26.50 (ISBN 3-7678-0013-6). Adler.

Legal Dictionary: French-English & English-French. Thomas A. Quemner. (Fr. & Eng.). 1969. 62.50x (ISBN 0-8002-1647-4). Intl Pubns Serv.

Legal Dictionary in Four Languages. 2nd ed. Ed. by E. Le Docte. 696p. 1978. 75.00x (ISBN 0-8377-0808-7). Oyez.

Legal Dictionary in Four Languages. 2nd ed. Ed. by E. Le Docte. xix, 696p. 1978. lib. bdg. 80.00x. Rothman.

Legal Dictionary: Part 1, Dutch-German. Hans Langendorf. 365p. (Dutch & Ger.). 1977. 26.00 (ISBN 90-26-8070-74). Kluwer Academic.

Legal Secretary's Concise Dictionary. M. Roshton. 1974. 5.50 (ISBN 0-685-42669-6). Claitors.

Legal Speller with Useful Medical Terms. 2nd ed. Sheila B. Sloane & John L. Dusseau. 380p. 1982. pap. text ed. 7.95 (ISBN 0-314-69679-2). West Pub.

Legal Terminology English & German. Ruediger Renner & Jeffery Tooth. (Eng. & Ger.). 1971. 38.50 (ISBN 3-1900-6280-3). Adler.

Legal Terminology English-German. Ruediger Renner & Jeffery Tooth. 526p. (Eng. & Ger.). 1971. 22.50x (ISBN 3-19-006280-3). Intl Pubns Serv.

Legal Terms. 1.30 (P6). Am Classical.

Legal Thesaurus. Trade ed. William C. Burton. 1983. 19.95 (ISBN 0-02-691020-9). Macmillan.

Legal Thesaurus. William C. Burton & Steven E. DeCosta. LC 80-83803. 1980. 35.00 (ISBN 0-02-691000-4). Free Pr.

Legal Word Book. Frank S. Gordon & Thomas Hemnes. 1978. 7.95 (ISBN 0-395-26662-9). HM.

Lehmann's Little Dictionary of Liturgical Terms. Arnold O. Lehmann. 1980. 3.75 (ISBN 0-8100-0127-6, 15N0371). Northwest Pub.

Leico De Politica. 6th ed. Jose M. Coloma. 200p. (Span.). 1976. pap. 8.75 (ISBN 84-7222-752-9, S-50039). French & Eur.

Leksykon Wiedzy Wojskowej. Mariana Laprusa. 541p. (Pol., Warsaw, Poland). 1979. 180.00 Zl (ISBN 8-3110-6229-3). Wydaw Min. Obrony Narodowej.

Lello Popular: Novo Dicionario Ilustrado Luso-Brasileiro. (Illus.). 1434p. (Port.). Esc.13.50. Lello & Irmao.

Lempriere's Classical Dictionary. new rev. ed. Ed. by F. A. Wright. 1969. Repr. of 1788 ed. 22.00 (ISBN 0-7100-1734-0). Routledge & Kegan.

Lenape-English Dictionary. Daniel G. Brinton. LC 77-153000. iii, 77p. (Eng. & Lenape.). 1977. write for info. Waletittin.

Lenape-English Dictionary. Daniel G. Brinton. LC 76-43670. 236p. (Eng. & Lenape.). 1979. write for info. (ISBN 0-404-15764-5). AMS Pr.

Lenape-English Dictionary. Ed. by Daniel G. Brinton & Albert S. Anthony. LC 76-43670. (Eng. & Lenape.). Repr. of 1888 ed. 22.50 (ISBN 0-404-15764-5). AMS Pr.

Lengua Salvadorena. Pedro Geoffroy Rivas. LC 79-121608. 131p. (Span., San Salvador). 1978. write for info. Direccion de Publicaciones.

Lengua Vasca. Isaac Lopez Mendizabal. LC 77-571017. 351p. (Basque & Span.). 1977. write for info. (ISBN 8-470-25126-0). Aunamendi Edit.

Lengua Vasca: Gramatica, Conversacion, Diccionario Vasco-Castellano, Castellano-Vasco. Isaac Lopez Mendizabal. LC 77-571017. 351p. (Basque.). 1977. write for info. (ISBN 8-47025-126-0). Aunamendi Edit.

Lengyel-Magyar Szotar. Istvan Varsanyi. LC 76-533514. xvi, 784p. (Pol. & Hungarian.). 1976. 35.00 Ft (ISBN 963-205-048-7). Terra.

Lessico Vento. Fabio Mutinelli. LC 79-388187. 425p. (Ital., Sala Bolgonese). 1978. write for info. Forni.

Let's Learn a Little Hawaiian. W. Ray Helbig. (Eng. & Hawaiian.). 1970. soft bdg. 2.50 (ISBN 0-930492-07-2). Hawaiian Serv.

Let's Talk D. P. Computer Lexicon. Jean P. Drieux & Alain Jarlaud. 116p. (Eng., Amer. & Fr.). 1977. pap. 11.95 (ISBN 0-686-57123-1, M-6171). French & Eur.

Let's Talk D. P. Lexique D'informatique. Jean-Pierre Drieux & Alain Jarlaud. LC 78-360973. 116p. (Eng. & Fr.). 1977. write for info. (ISBN 2-04-008033-3). Bordas.

Letter to John Pickering on the Subject of His Vocabulary or Collection of Words & Phrases see Vocabulary; or, Collection of Words & Phrases, Which Have Been Supposed to Be Peculiar to the United States of America; to Which Is Prefixed an Essay on the Present State of the English Language in the United States.

L'Europe & ses population. Abel Miroglio & Yvonne D. Miroglio. LC 78-777166. 828p. (Fr.). 1978. write for info. (ISBN 9-02472-082-6). Nyhoff.

Lexers Mittlehochdeutsches Taschenwoerterbuch: Mit Bearbeiteten & Erweiterten Nachtraegen. 36th ed. Ed. by E. Henschel & U. Pretzel. 504p. (Ger.). 1980. M.24.00 (796 739 0). Hirzel Verlag.

Lexica (II) Teresa Garriga. 190p. (Span.). 1981. 850.00 ptas (ISBN 84-7091-190-2). Jaimes Libros.

Lexical Concordance to the Poetical Works of Percy Bysshe Shelley. Frederick S. Ellis. LC 68-57904. (Bibliography & Reference Ser: No. 237). 1968. Repr. of 1892 ed. 33.50 (ISBN 0-8337-1053-2). B Franklin.

Lexico base del castellano: Analisis estadistico y de contenido. Juan L. Roman del Cerro. 110p. (Span.). 1981. pap. write for info. (ISBN 84-7231-596-7). Confed Espanola.

Lexico basico del contador. 2nd ed. R. Enriquez Palomic. 160p. (Span.). 1968. 2.24; Mex.$28.00. Trillas.

Lexico basico espanol-ruso. (Span. & Rus.). Mex.$10.00. Cultura Popular.

Lexico basico espanol-ruso. (Span. & Rus.). Arg.$12.00. D'Ippolito.

Lexico Caribe en el Caribe Negro de Honduras Britanica. Micolas De Castillo Mathieu. LC 77-472040. 70p. (Cariban.). 1975. write for info. Instituto Caro & Cuervo.

Lexico De Antropologia. 3rd ed. Abelardo Martinez Cruz. 184p. (Span.). 1975. pap. 8.75 (ISBN 84-7222-754-5, S-50038). French & Eur.

Lexico de Ceramica & Alfareria Aragonesas. Maria Isabel Alvaro Zamora. 210p. (Fr.). 1981. 750.00 ptas (ISBN 84-85264-40-1). Portico.

Lexico De Economia. 6th ed. Alain Birou. 200p. (Span.). 1977. pap. 8.75 (ISBN 84-7222-751-0, S-50040). French & Eur.

Lexico de la artesania. Luis Marquez Villagas. 144p. (Span.). 1961. 60.00 ptas (CSIC). Univ Granada.

Lexico de la casa popular urbano en Bolivar, Colombia. L. Florez. (Span.). 1962. write for info. Inst Caro y Cuervo.

Lexico De la Delincuencia En Puerto Rico. Carmen G. Altieri de Barreto. (UPREX, C. Sociales: No. 18). (Span.). pap. 1.85 (ISBN 0-8477-0018-6). U of PR Pr.

Lexico de la Sexualidad. Goldstein et al. 224p. (Span.). 1981. 700.00 ptas (ISBN 84-85334-13-2). Loguez Edns.

Lexico de lenguaje figurado. 2nd ed. Ivon P. De Dony. 262p. (Span.). 1951. 15.00. Club de Lectores.

Lexico de Politica. 5th ed. Jose M. Coloma. LC 76-450510. 198p. (Span.). 1975. write for info. ptas (ISBN 8-472-22752-9). Laia.

Lexico De Sociologia. 5th ed. Alain Birou. 114p. (Span.). 1975. pap. 8.75 (ISBN 84-7222-753-7, S-50041). French & Eur.

Lexico De Terminos Nucleares: Diccionario Vocabulario Triligue. 848p. (Span., Eng. & Fr.). 1974. 44.95 (ISBN 84-500-6295-0, S-50124). French & Eur.

Lexico del cuerpo humano en Colombia. L. Florez. (Span.). 1966. write for info. Inst Caro y Cuervo.

Lexico del Teatro de Valle Inclan. Ciriaco Ruiz Fernandez. 313p. (Span.). 1981. 600.00 ptas (ISBN 84-7481-152-X). Univ Salamanca.

Lexico Dos. 3rd ed. Ignacio Bonnin Valls et al. 336p. (Span.). 1982. pap. 443.00 ptas (ISBN 84-316-1647-4). Vicens-Vives.

Lexico Espanol-Kawesqar. F. Aguilera. LC 77-567778. (Alacaluf & Span., Santiago, Chile). 1976. write for info. Centro Invest.

Lexico hispanoamericano del siglo XVIII. Peter Boyd-Bowman. (Spanish Ser.: No. 5). (Span.). 1982. 10.00 (ISBN 0-942260-21-X). Hispanic Seminary.

Lexico historico de Espana. Jacques Amalric et al. Tr. by Rosina Lajo & Victoria Frigola. 224p. (Span.). 1982. pap. 575.00 ptas (ISBN 84-306-5703-7). Taurus Ediciones SA.

Lexico indigena en el espanol de Mexico. J. M. Lope Blanch. 74p. (Span.). Mex.$1.20; 12.00. Col. de Mexico.

Lexico Marinero: Six Idiomas. N. Hollander et al. 128p. (Span.). pap. 22.50 (ISBN 84-261-1668-X, S-37657). French & Eur.

Lexico Quechua de Cajamarca. Felix Quesada Castillo. LC 77-554130. (Eng., Quechua & Span., Lima, Peru). 1976. write for info. Centro Invest.

Lexico rural del noroeste iberico. Tr. by Fritz Kruger. 142p. (Span.). 1947. 60.00 ptas (CSIC). Inst. Antonio de Nebrija.

Lexico sedimentologico. Gonzalez Bonorino. 1952p. (Span.). 4.00. Museo Arg. Ciencias Nat.

Lexico Sucinto del Erotismo. Andre Breton. 110p. (Span.). 1974. pap. 6.75 (ISBN 84-339-0419-1, S-50153). French & Eur.

Lexico tecnico de las artes plasticas. Irene Crespi & Jorge Ferrario. (Illus.). 208p. (Span.). write for info. EUDEBA.

Lexico Uno. 5th ed. Ignacio Bonnin Valls et al. 336p. (Span.). 1982. pap. 426.00 ptas (ISBN 84-316-0624-X). Vicens-Vives.

Lexicography in India. National Conference on Dictionary Making in Indian Languages & Bal G. Misra. LC 81-901003. xv, 253p. (Indic.). 1970. 27.00 Rub. Central Institute of Indian Languages.

Lexicolabor: Diccionario Enciclopedico Ilustrado, 4 vols. 2216p. (Span.). 1977. Set. 295.00 (ISBN 84-335-0344-8, S-50443). French & Eur.

Lexicologie. Picoche. (Fr.). 19.00 (Dist. by Continental Bk Co). Lib. Fernand Nathan.

Lexicologie & Lexicographie Francaises & Romanes. 294p. (Fr. & Ital.). 1959. 42.00 F (ISBN 2-22200-359-8). CNRS.

Lexicon Arabico-Latinum, 4 vols. George W. Freytag. (Arabic & Lat.). 95.00x (ISBN 0-86685-124-0). Intl Bk Ctr.

Lexicon Arabico-Latinum, 4 vols. George W. Freytag. 2257p. (Arabic & Lat.). Repr. of 1830 ed. 95.00 (124-0). Intl Bk Ctr.

Lexicon Caesarianum. R. Menge & S. Preuss. (Ger.). 1972. 99.50 (ISBN 3-8067-0094-X, M-7284). French & Eur.

Lexicon Chaldaicum Talmudicum & Rabbinicum. Johann Buxtorf. LC 78-359320. (Aramaic & Lat.). 1977. write for info. (ISBN 3-487-06386-7). Olms Verlag.

Lexicon comercial internacional: Espanol, frances, ingles, italiano, portugues y aleman. J. Vicens Carrio. (Span., Fr., Eng., Ital., Port. & Ger.). 800.00 ptas. Reverte SA.

Lexicon Creticum: Estudios sobre Escritura & lengua cretense; inscripciones monumentales; faistos, arkolochori, mallia. Benito Gaya Nuno. 84p. (Span.). 1953. 60.00 ptas (CSIC). Inst. Antonio de Nebrija.

Lexicon de Comunicologia. Jorge Perello. LC 78-393509. (Eng. & Span.). 1977. 3000.00 ptas. Augusta SA.

Lexicon de Comunicologia: Diccinario para Audiologos, Audioprotesistas, Foniatras, Logopedas, Profesores De Sordos y Psicolinguistas. Jorge Perello. 856p. (Span., Fr., Eng. & Ger.). 1977. 60.00 (ISBN 84-7024-067-6, S-50096). French & Eur.

Lexicon de fauna y flora. A. Malaret. (Span.). 1961. write for info. Inst Caro y Cuervo.

Lexicon des Buchwesen: Bd 4, Bilderatlas zum Buchwesen Teil 2. Ed. by Joachim Kirchner. xlvii, 343p. (Ger.). 1956. DM.90.00 (ISBN 3-7772-5613-7). Hiersemann.

Lexicon Diplomaticum Abbreviationes Syllabarum et Vocum in Diplomatibus et Codicibus a Seculo Octo a Sextum-Decimum Usque Occurentes Exponens, 2 vols. in 1. folio ed. Johann L. Walther. (Lat.). 1967. Repr. of 1756 ed. 87.00 (ISBN 0-8337-3680-9). B Franklin.

Lexicon etymologicum: Supplemento ai dizionario etimologici latini e romanzi. Giovanni Alessio. 689p. (Lat. & Ital.). 1976. L.60000.00. Licosa.

Lexicon Forestale. Karl-Johan Ahlsved et al. LC 80-487653. xix, 592p. (Eng., Finnish, Ger., Swedish, & Rus.). 1979. Fmk.350.00 (ISBN 9-5100-9174-X). Suomen Standard.

Lexicon Heptaglotton, 2 vols. Edmund Castell. LC 70-870022. 1544p. 1970. Repr. of 1686 ed. Set. 175.00x (ISBN 3-201-00074-4). Intl Pubns Serv.

Lexicon Hesiodeum: Cum Indice Inverso. M. Hofinger. LC 79-345373. xi, 745p. (Gr.). 1978. write for info. Brill Verlag.

Lexicon in Phonological Change. W. Wang. (Monographs on Linguistics Analysis: No. 5). 1977. 62.00 (ISBN 90-279-7814-X). Mouton.

Lexicon in Veteris Testamenti Libros: Hebrew-Aramaic Lexicon, Incl. Supplement. Ludwig Koehler & Walter Baumgartner. (Hebrew & Aramaic.). 1951-53. 49.50x (ISBN 0-8028-2176-6). Eerdmans.

Lexicon Kapelusz: Matematica. 2nd ed. Francisco Vera. (Illus.). 744p. (Span.). Mex.$12.86. Kapelusz.

Lexicon Kapelusz: Psicologia. Tr. by Henri Pieron et al. 768p. (Span.). Mex.$11.17. Kapelusz.

Lexicon Latinitatis Medii Aevi: Praesertim ad res Ecclesiasticas Investigandas Pertinens. 1040p. (Lat.). 1975. 3750.00 F. Brepols.

Lexicon linguisticae et philologiae. Emilio Springhetti. xi, 687p. (Lat.). 1962. L.13000.00. Univ Gregoriana.

Lexicon Medicum. T. Zlotnicki. 1603p. 1980. 150.00x (ISBN 0-569-07372-3, Pub. by Collet's). State Mutual Bk.

Lexicon Medicum. Boleslaw Zlotnickiego. 1604p. (Eng., Rus., Fr., Ger., Lat. & Pol.). 1976. 95.00 (ISBN 0-686-57263-7, M-6576). French & Eur.

Lexicon Medicum: Medizinisches Woerterbuch in 6 Sprachen; Englisch, Russisch, Franzoesisch, Deutsch, Latein, Polnisch. B. Zlotnicki. 1603p. (Eng., Rus., Fr., Ger., Lat. & Pol.). 1973. DM.116.00 (ISBN 3-7945-0324-4). Langenscheidt.

Lexicon of American Business Terms. James H. Filkins & Donald L. Caruth. pap. 1.95 (ISBN 0-671-18705-8). Monarch Pr.

Lexicon of Black English. J. L. Dillard. LC 76-30389. 1977. pap. 6.95 (ISBN 0-8264-0125-2). Continuum.

Lexicon of Canadian Stratigraphy Arctic Archipelago, Vol. 1. Canadian Society of Petroleum Geologists. 1981. 8.00; pap. 6.00. Can Soc Petro Geo.

Lexicon of Canadian Stratigraphy Yukon-MacKenzie, Vol. 2. Canadian Society of Petroleum Geologists. 1981. 22.00; 20.00. Can Soc Petro Geo.

Lexicon of Comicana. Mort Walker. (Illus.). 96p. (Orig.). 1980. pap. 4.95 (ISBN 0-940420-00-7). Comicana.

Lexicon of French Borrowings in the German Vocabulary. William J. Jones. (Studia Linguistica Germanica Ser.: No. 12). (Fr. & Ger.). 1976. 79.50x (ISBN 3-11-004769-1). De Gruyter.

Lexicon of Historical & Political Terms. Robert R. Davis, Jr. pap. 1.95 (ISBN 0-671-18706-6, 18706). Monarch Pr.

Lexicon of Historical & Political Terms. Robert R. Davis, Jr. Ed. by R. Reed. LC 81-83626. (Illus.). 125p. 1982. pap. 7.95 (ISBN 0-88247-612-2). R & E Res Assoc.

Lexicon of International & National Units. Ed. by M. Merino-Rodriguez. (Eng., Ger., Span., Fr., Ital., Dutch, Port., Pol. & Japanese.). 1966. 70.25 (ISBN 0-444-40392-2). Elsevier.

Lexicon of Jewish Cooking. rev. ed. Patti Shosteck. 1981. pap. 6.95 (ISBN 0-8092-5995-8). Contemp Bks.

Lexicon of Literary Terms. Robert Anderson & Ronald Eckhard. 160p. 1975. pap. 3.50 (ISBN 0-671-18749-X). Monarch Pr.

Lexicon of Musical Invective: Critical Assaults on Composers Since Beethoven's Time. 2nd ed. Nicolas Slonimsky. LC 65-26270. 331p. 1969. pap. 7.95 (ISBN 0-295-78579-9, WP52). U of Wash Pr.

Lexicon of Plant Pests & Diseases. Ed. by Manuel Merino-Rodriguez. (Eng., Lat., Fr., Span., Ital. & Ger., Polyglot). 1966. 70.25 (ISBN 0-444-40393-0). Elsevier.

Lexicon of Succulent Plants. Hermann Jacobsen. (Illus.). 1974. 37.50 (ISBN 0-7137-0652-X, Pub by Blandford Pr England). Sterling.

Lexicon of Terms Relating to the Assessment & Classification of Coal Resources. A. H. Todd. 140p. 1982. 99.00x (ISBN 0-86010-403-6, Pub. by Graham & Trotman England). State Mutual Bk.

Lexicon of Terms Relating to the Assessment & Classification of Coal Resources. A. H. Todd. 140p. 1983. 55.00x (ISBN 0-8448-1438-5). Crane-Russak Co.

Lexicon of the Homeric Dialect. Richard J. Cunliffe. 1977. pap. 14.95x (ISBN 0-8061-1430-4). U of Okla Pr.

Lexicon of the Sports & Racing Car Enthusiast. Ann S. Haskell. Bd. with Words Relating to Plants & Animals in the Mammoth Cave Region. Gordon Wilson; Terms of Abuse for Some Chicago Social Groups. Lee A. Pederson. (Publications of the American Dialect Society: No. 42). 48p. 1964. pap. 3.50 (ISBN 0-8173-0642-0). U of Ala Pr.

Lexicon Platonicum, 3 vols. Friedrich Ast. (Lat.). 1969. Set. 89.00 (ISBN 0-8337-0105-3). B Franklin.

Lexicon Plotinianum. J. H. Sleeman & Gilbert Pollet. LC 80-505958. (Gr. & Eng.). 1980. write for info. (ISBN 9-06-186083-0). Leuven U Pr.

Lexicon por una Comision de Trabajo del CIMAC: Conseil International des Machines a Combustion. 96p. (Span.). write for info. (ISBN 84-600-0836-3). Marcombo.

Lexicon Sopena: Diccionario de bolsillo, aleman-espanol y espanol-aleman. 384p. (Ger. & Span.). 60.00 ptas. 35.00 ptas. pap. 30.00 ptas. Sopena.

Lexicon Sopena: Diccionario de bolsillo, catalan-espanol y espanol-catalan. (Span.). 60.00 ptas. 35.00 ptas. pap. 30.00 ptas. Sopena.

Lexicon Sopena: Diccionario de bolsillo, danes-espanol y espanol-danes. (Danish & Span.). 60.00 ptas. 35.00 ptas. pap. 30.00 ptas. Sopena.

Lexicon Sopena: Diccionario de bolsillo, esperanto-espanol y espanol-esperanto. 384p. (Esperanto & Span.). 60.00 ptas. 35.00 ptas. pap. 30.00 ptas. Sopena.

Lexicon Sopena: Diccionario de bolsillo, finlandes-espanol y espanol-finlandes. 384p. (Finnish & Span.). 60.00 ptas. 35.00 ptas. pap. 30.00 ptas. Sopena.

Lexicon Sopena: Diccionario de bolsillo, frances-espanol y espanol-frances. 384p. (Fr. & Span.). 60.00 ptas. 35.00 ptas. pap. 30.00 ptas. Sopena.

Lexicon Sopena: Diccionario de bolsillo, holandes-espanol y espanol-holandes. 384p. (Dutch & Span.). 60.00 ptas. 35.00 ptas. pap. 30.00 ptas. Sopena.

Lexicon Sopena: Diccionario de bolsillo, ingles-espanol y espanol-ingles. (Eng. & Span.). 60.00 ptas. 35.00 ptas. pap. 30.00 ptas. Sopena.

Lexicon Sopena: Diccionario de bolsillo, italiano-espanol y espanol-italiano. (Ital. & Span.). 60.00 ptas. 35.00 ptas. pap. 30.00 ptas. Sopena.

Lexicon Sopena: Diccionario de bolsillo, lengua espanol. 384p. (Span.). 30.00 ptas. pap. 25.00 ptas. Sopena.

Lexicon Sopena: Diccionario de bolsillo, noruego-espanol y noruego-espanol. 384p. (Span. & Norwegian.). 60.00 ptas. 35.00 ptas. pap. 30.00 ptas. Sopena.
Lexicon Sopena: Diccionario de bolsillo, sueco-espanol y espanol-sueco. 384p. (Swedish & Span.). 60.00 ptas. 35.00 ptas. pap. 30.00 ptas. Sopena.
Lexicon sopena diccionario espanola. (Span.). pap. 3.95 (7864-5). Natl Textbk.
Lexicon Techicum, or, a Universal English Dictionary of Arts & Sciences, 2 Vols. John Harris. (Illus.). 1967. Repr. of 1710 ed. Set. 195.00 (ISBN 0-384-21473-8). Johnson Repr.
Lexicon to Achilles Tatius. Ed. by James N. O'Sullivan. (Unter Suchungen Zur Antiken Literatur und Gesschichte: No. 18). 442p. (Ger.). 1980. text ed. 124.00x (ISBN 3-11-007844-9). De Gruyter.
Lexicon to Pindar. Ed. by William J. Slater. 1969. 131.00x (ISBN 3-11-002562-0). De Gruyter.
Lexicon to the English Poetical Works of John Milton. Laura E. Lockwood. LC 72-193205. 1972. lib. bdg. 27.45 (ISBN 0-8414-5878-2). Folcroft.
Lexicon to the Glory of God Greek-Russian (18th Century) Facsimile Edition Paris Ms. Suppl. grec 1117. Michael Samilov. 200p. 1972. 40.00x (ISBN 0-902089-31-5, Pub. by Variorum). State Mutual Bk.
Lexicon totius latinitatus, 6 vols. Egidio Forcellini. 5816p. (Lat.). 1965. L.460000.00. Lib Edit Greg.
Lexicon typographicum Italiae. Giuseppe Fumagalli. (Illus.). xlvii, 587p. (Lat.). 1966. L.65000.00. Olschki.
Lexicon Van de Economie. Marcel A. Van Meerhaeghe. LC 77-557822. 170p. (Dutch.). 1977. write for info. (ISBN 9-020-70684-5). Stenfert Kroese.
Lexicue Trilingue des Termes d'usage Courant En Machines Outils; les Tours, Pt. 1. 74p. (Fr., Trilingual Lexicon of Common Terms in Machine Tools; Wheels). 1961. pap. 12.50 (ISBN 0-686-56791-9, M-6374). French & Eur.
Lexiko tes Mykenaikes Hellenikes. Giannes K. Pomponas. LC 79-121485. (Gr.). 1978. write for info. Ekdoseis Filon.
Lexikon Allergologicum. K. Wilken-Jensen. 1965. 16.25 (ISBN 0-08-011838-0). Pergamon.
Lexikon Angloamerikanischer und Deutscher Managementbegriffe. Peter Linnert. (Ger.). 1972. 75.00 (ISBN 3-921099-00-5, M-7286). French & Eur.
Lexikon Archivwesen der DDR. Elisabeth Brachmann-Teubner. LC 76-478503. 319p. (Ger.). 1976. M.12.00. Staatsdruk.
Lexikon Biochemie. H. D. Jakubke. (Ger.). 1976. 25.00 (ISBN 3-527-25662-8, M-7285). French & Eur.
Lexikon biochemie. Hans D. Jakubke & Hans Jeschkeit. LC 77-460833. 605p. (Ger.). 1976. write for info. (ISBN 3-527-25662-8). Verlag Chemie.
Lexikon Chemischer Kurzbezeichnungen Von Arzneistoffen. (Ger.). 1970. pap. 13.95 (ISBN 3-7741-9909-4, M-7283). French & Eur.
Lexikon Chemischer Kurzbezeichnungen von Arzneistoffen. 104p. (Ger.). 1970. DM.16.50 (ISBN 3-7741-9909-4). Govi Verlag.
Lexikon Christlicher Symbole. Edouard Urech. (Illus.). 256p. (Ger.). DM.12.50 (ISBN 3-76737-609-1). F Bahn.
Lexikon Datens & Datensicherung. Hans Kassel. LC 79-373659. 157p. (Ger.). 1978. write for info. (ISBN 3-8009-1257-0). Siemens AG.
Lexikon der Aegyptologie. Wolfgang Helck & Eberhard Otto. 80p. (Ger.). 1973. DM.38.00 (ISBN 3-447-01521-7). Harrassowitz.
Lexikon der Aegyptologie: Bd II, Lfg 10. Wolfgang Helck & Eberhard Otto. 80p. (Ger.). 1975. DM.46.00 (ISBN 3-447-01728-7). Harrassowitz.
Lexikon der Aegyptologie: Bd II, Lfg 11. Wolfgang Helck & Eberhard Otto. 80p. (Ger.). 1976. DM.46.00 (ISBN 3-447-01746-5). Harrassowitz.
Lexikon der Aegyptologie: Bd II, Lfg 12. Wolfgang Helck & Eberhard Otto. 80p. (Ger.). 1976. DM.46.00 (ISBN 3-447-01749-X). Harrassowitz.
Lexikon der Aegyptologie: Bd II, Lfg 13. Wolfgang Helck & Eberhard Otto. 80p. (Ger.). 1976. DM.46.00 (ISBN 3-447-01819-4). Harrassowitz.
Lexikon der Aegyptologie: Bd II, Lfg 14. Wolfgang Helck & Eberhard Otto. 80p. (Ger.). 1976. DM.46.00 (ISBN 3-447-01825-9). Harrassowitz.
Lexikon der Aegyptologie: Bd II, Lfg 9. Wolfgang Helck & Eberhard Otto. 80p. (Ger.). 1975. DM.46.00 (ISBN 3-447-01708-2). Harrassowitz.
Lexikon der Aegyptologie: Bd 1, Lfg 1. Wolfgang Helck & Eberhard Otto. (Ger.). 1972. DM.38.00 (ISBN 3-447-01441-5). Harrassowitz.
Lexikon der Aegyptologie: Bd 1, Lfg. 2. Wolfgang Helck & Eberhard Otto. 80p. (Ger.). 1973. DM.38.00 (ISBN 3-447-01481-4). Harrassowitz.
Lexikon der Aegyptologie: Bd 1, Lfg. 3. Wolfgang Helck & Eberhard Otto. 80p. (Ger.). 1973. DM.38.00 (ISBN 3-447-01499-7). Harrassowitz.
Lexikon der Aegyptologie: Bd 1, Lfg 4. Wolfgang Helck & Eberhard Otto. 80p. (Ger.). 1973. DM.38.00 (ISBN 3-447-01508-X). Harrassowitz.
Lexikon der Aegyptologie: Bd 1, Lfg 6. Wolfgang Helck & Eberhard Otto. 80p. (Ger.). 1974. DM.38.00 (ISBN 3-447-01557-8). Langenscheidt.
Lexikon der Aegyptologie: Bd 1, Lfg 7. Wolfgang Helck & Eberhard Otto. 80p. (Ger.). 1974. DM.38.00 (ISBN 3-447-01605-1). Harrassowitz.
Lexikon der Aegyptologie: Bd 1, Lfg 8. Wolfgang Helck & Eberhard Otto. xxxvi, 76p. (Ger.). 1975. DM.80.00 (ISBN 3-447-01619-1). Harrassowitz.
Lexikon der Aero & Astronautik Einschliesslich Raketentechnik: Lexikon der Alpen. Toni Hiebeler. (Ger.). 1972. write for info. (ISBN 3-920902-07-6). Sokoll.
Lexikon der Aero und Astronautik Enischliesslich Raketentechnik. (Ger.). 1972. write for info. (ISBN 3-920902-07-6, M-7282). French & Eur.
Lexikon der Alten Welt. Carl Andresen et al. (Ger.). 1965. DM.320.00 (ISBN 3-7608-0137-4). Artemis Verlag.
Lexikon der Alten Welt. Karl Andresen. (Ger.). 1965. 395.00 (ISBN 3-7608-0137-4, M-7281). French & Eur.
Lexikon der Anstrichtechnik, Vol. 1. 3rd ed. Kurt Sponzel. (Ger.). 1970. 30.00 (ISBN 3-7667-0169-X, M-7279). French & Eur.
Lexikon der Anstrichtechnik: Bd 1. Kurt Sponzel & Wilhelm Wallenfang. (Ger.). 1970. DM.38.00 (ISBN 3-7667-0169-X). Callwey.
Lexikon der Anstrichtechnik: Bd 2. Anton Brasholz et al. (Ger.). 1975. DM.58.00 (ISBN 3-7667-0338-2). Callwey.
Lexikon der Antike, 5 vols. Ed. by K. Ziegler & W. Sontheimer. 800p. (Ger.). 1975. pap. 79.00 per vol. M Rosenberg.
Lexikon der Arabischen Welt. Nandy Ronart. (Ger.). 184.00 (ISBN 3-7608-0138-2, M-7277). French & Eur.
Lexikon der Arabischen Welt. Nandy Von Ronart & Stephan Ronart. 1100p. (Ger.). 1978. DM.230.00 (ISBN 3-7608-0138-2). Artemis Verlag.
Lexikon der Arbeits und Soziallere. Rainer Roth. (Ger.). 1976. 26.00 (ISBN 3-403-00593-3, M-7278). French & Eur.
Lexikon der Archaeologie, 2 vols. W. Bray & D. Trump. (Ger.). 1975. Set. pap. 29.95 (ISBN 3-499-16187-7, M-7276). French & Eur.
Lexikon der Audio-Visuellen Bildungsmittel. Heribert Heinrichs. (Ger.). 1971. 28.00 (ISBN 3-466-30097-5, M-7275). French & Eur.
Lexikon der Audio-Visuellen Bildungsmittel. Ed. by Heribert Heinrichs. xvi, 404p. (Ger.). 1971. DM.35.00 (ISBN 3-466-30097-5). Koesel.
Lexikon der Ausbildungspraxis. Helmut Paulik. (Ger.). 1975. pap. 30.00 (ISBN 3-478-11610-4, M-7274). French & Eur.
Lexikon der Ausbildungspraxis. Ed. by Helmut Paulik. 276p. (Ger.). 1975. DM.36.00 (ISBN 3-478-11610-4). Verlag Mod Ind.
Lexikon der Ausbildungspraxis. Ed. by Helmut Paulik et al. LC 80-478372. 253p. (Ger.). 1980. write for info. (ISBN 3-478-11612-0). Verlag Moderne Industrie.
Lexikon der Datenverarbeitung. Loebel & Mueller. 704p. (Ger.). 1975. 62.00 (ISBN 3-478-33206-0, M-7264). French & Eur.
Lexikon der Datenverarbeitung. Peter Mueller. (Ger.). 1968. 55.00 (ISBN 3-478-33205-2, M-7265). French & Eur.
Lexikon der Deutschen Geschichte. Gerhard Taddey. (Ger.). 1977. 99.50 (ISBN 3-520-81301-7, M-7263). French & Eur.
Lexikon der Deutschen Geschichte. Ed. by Gerhard Taddey. 1120p. (Ger.). 1977. DM.125.00 (ISBN 3-520-81301-7). Kroener.
Lexikon der Deutschen Konzertliteratur, 2 Vols. Theodor Muller-Reuter. LC 70-171079. (Music Ser). (Ger.). 1972. Repr. of 1921 ed. Set. lib. bdg. 95.00 (ISBN 0-306-70274-6). Da Capo.
Lexikon der Deutschen Marinegeschichte. Hans Witthoeft. (Ger.). 1977. 35.00 (ISBN 3-7822-0144-2, M-7262). French & Eur.
Lexikon der Deutschen Marinegeschichte. Ed. by Hans J. Witthoeft. 300p. (Ger.). 1977. DM.44.00 (ISBN 3-7822-0144-2). Koehlers Verlag.
Lexikon der Deutschen Staedt und Gemeinden. Fritz Siefert. (Ger.). 1973. 25.00 (ISBN 3-517-00453-7, M-7261). French & Eur.
Lexikon der Deutschen Staedte & Gemeinden. Ed. by Fritz Sieferl. 576p. (Ger.). 1975. DM.29.00 (ISBN 3-87220-336-3). Fackelverlag.
Lexikon der Deutschen Staedte & Gemeinden. Ed. by Fritz Siefert. 584p. (Ger.). 1973. DM.26.00 (ISBN 3-517-00453-7). Suedwest.
Lexikon der Elektronischen Musik. Herbert Eimert. 426p. (Ger.). 1973. 27.50 (ISBN 3-7649-2083-1, M-7260). French & Eur.
Lexikon der Ethik. Otfried Hoffe. LC 77-566300. 287p. (Ger.). 1977. DM.14.80 (ISBN 3-406-06752-2). Beck Verlag.
Lexikon der Gastechnik. Walter G. Von Baeckmann. LC 79-366542. 346p. (Ger.). 1978. DM.38.00 (ISBN 3-8027-2262-0). Vulkan Verlag.
Lexikon der Geldenlage. Werner Schwilling. (Ger.). 1974. 35.00 (ISBN 3-478-51560-2, M-7258). French & Eur.
Lexikon der Genetik der Hundekrankheiten. E. Wiesner & S. Willer. (Illus.). 480p. (Ger.). 1983. 29.50 (ISBN 3-8055-3616-X). S. Karger.
Lexikon der Germanistischen. 2nd rev. ed. Ed. by H. P. Althaus et al. 870p. (Ger.). 1980. pap. 74.00. M Rosenberg.
Lexikon der Germanistischen Linguistik. Ed. by Hans P. Althaus et al. (Ger.). 1973. DM.106.00 (ISBN 3-484-10186-5). Niemeyer.
Lexikon der Geschaeftsbriefe in Vier Sprachen, 3 vols. (Ger , Eng. , Fr. & Ital., Lexicon of Commercial Letters in Four Languages). 1972. Set. 168.00 (ISBN 3-478-52340-0, M-7257). French & Eur.
Lexikon der Geschaeftsbriefe in vier Sprachen. 700p. (Ger.). 1972. DM.210.00 (ISBN 3-478-52340-0). Verlag Moderne.
Lexikon der Geschichte. (Ger.). 1976. DM.29.40 (ISBN 3-453-41149-8). Heyne W Verlag.
Lexikon der Geschicte, 3 vols. (Ger.). 1976. Set. pap. 25.00 (ISBN 3-453-41149-8, M-7255). French & Eur.
Lexikon der Goethe-Zitate. Ed. by Richard Dobel. viii, 654p. (Ger.). 1978. DM.78.00 (ISBN 3-7608-0139-0); 150.00 (ISBN 3-7608-0140-4). Artemis Verlag.
Lexikon der Grafischen Technik. Institut fur Grafische Technik. LC 78-341716. 656p. (Ger.). 1977. write for info. (ISBN 3-7940-4078-3). Saur Verlag.
Lexikon der Grafischen Technik. 656p. (Ger.). 1977. DM.36.00 (ISBN 3-7940-4078-3). Saur Verlag.
Lexikon der Grammatischen Linguistik. Hans Althaus. (Ger.). 1973. 95.00 (ISBN 3-484-10186-5, M-7256). French & Eur.
Lexikon der Grammatischen Terminologie. Otmar Bohusch. (Ger.). 1972. 27.50 (ISBN 3-403-00298-5, M-7254). French & Eur.
Lexikon der Grammatischen Terminologie. Otmar Bohusch. 336p. (Ger.). DM.22.80 (ISBN 3-40300-298-5). Auer.
Lexikon der Graphischen Technik. 4th ed. (Ger.). 1977. 29.95 (ISBN 3-7940-4078-3, M-7253). French & Eur.
Lexikon der Griechischen und Roemischen Mythologie. H. Hunger. 452p. (Ger.). 1974. pap. 7.95 (ISBN 3-499-16178-8, M-7252). French & Eur.
Lexikon der Heizungs, Lueftungs & Klimatechnik. Walter Haeder & Guenther Reichow. (Ger.). 1978. write for info. (ISBN 3-7864-1448-3). Langenscheidt.
Lexikon der Islamischen Welt. Ed. by Klaus Kreiser et al. (Ger.). 1974. DM.36.00 (ISBN 3-17-001802-7). Kohlhammer.
Lexikon der Islamischen Welt: Bd 1, A-Grab. Ed. by Klaus Kreiser et al. 212p. (Ger.). 1974. DM.12.00 (ISBN 3-17-002160-5). Kohlhammer.
Lexikon der Islamischen Welt: Bd 2, Gram-Nom. Ed. by Klaus Kreiser et al. 212p. (Ger.). 1974. DM.12.00 (ISBN 3-17-002161-3). Kohlhammer.
Lexikon der Islamischen Welt: Bd 3, Nor-Z. Ed. by Klaus Kreiser et al. 192p. (Ger.). 1974. DM.12.00 (ISBN 3-17-002162-1). Kohlhammer.
Lexikon der Kostenrechnung. Max Munz & Harald Winkel. LC 77-567449. (Illus.). 234p. (Ger.). 1977. DM.24.00 (ISBN 3-470-58153-3). Kiehl.
Lexikon der Kunstslile: Bd 1, Von der Griechischen Archaik bis zur Renaissance. (Ger. & Ger.). 1978. DM.8.80 (ISBN 3-499-16132-X). Rowohlt.
Lexikon der Kunststile. G. Lindemann. 360p. (Ger.). 1970. pap. 15.95 (ISBN 3-499-16132-X, M-7251). French & Eur.
Lexikon der Kunststile: Bd 2, Vom Barock bis zur Pop-art. (Ger.). 1974. DM.8.80 (ISBN 3-499-16137-0). Rowohlt.
Lexikon der Kunststoffe, 2 vols. Hans Domininghaus. LC 78-364503. 576p. (Ger.). 1978. write for info. (ISBN 3-453-49070-3). Heyne W Verlag.
Lexikon der Kybernetik, 4 vols. 590p. (Ger.). 1980. Set. 395.00x (ISBN 0-686-44730-1, Pub. by Collets). State Mutual Bk.
Lexikon der Kybernetik. Ed. by A. Mueller. 224p. (Ger.). 1964. DM.46.00 (ISBN 3-87715-022-5). Quickborner Team.
Lexikon der Managementbegriffe. Von Linnert et al. (Ger.). 1977. DM.9.80 (ISBN 3-453-49068-1). Heyne W Verlag.
Lexikon der Mathematik. Ed. by W. Gellert et al. (Illus.). 624p. (Ger.). 1981. M.28.00. Bibl Inst Leipzig.

Lexikon der Mathematik. Richard Knerr. LC 79-368679. 484p. (Ger.). 1978. DM.12.80 (ISBN 3-596-26376-X). Fischer Taschen.
Lexikon der Medizin. Dagobert Tutsch. (Ger.). 1975. 19.95 (ISBN 3-541-07081-1, M-7250). French & Eur.
Lexikon der Medizin & Gesundheit. Lexikon-Institut Bertelsmann. 850p. (Ger.). 1975. DM.39.00 (ISBN 3-570-04598-6). C Bertelsmann.
Lexikon der Medizinischen Fachsprache, 2 vols. D. Tutsch. 388p. (Ger.). 1970. Set. pap. 9.95 (ISBN 3-499-16126-5, M-7249). French & Eur.
Lexikon der Medizinischen Fachsprache: Bd 1, A-L. Ed. by Dagobert Tutsch. (Ger.). 1978. DM.5.80 (ISBN 3-499-16126-5). Rowohlt.
Lexikon der Medizinischen Fachsprache: Bd 2, M-Z. Ed. by Dagobert Tutsch. (Ger.). 1978. DM.5.80 (ISBN 3-499-16129-X). Rowohlt.
Lexikon der Medizinischen Psychologie. U. Tewes. (Ger.). 1977. 12.95 (ISBN 3-17-004011-1, M-7248). French & Eur.
Lexikon der Modernen Konservation. Hanns Kurth. (Ger.). 1973. 16.95 (ISBN 3-87718-502-9, M-7247). French & Eur.
Lexikon der Mythologie Aegyptens, Persiens & des Orients. Walter A. Kremnitz. LC 76-460759. (Illus.). 140p. (Ger.). 1975. write for info. Ambro Lacus.
Lexikon der Mythologie der Eurpaeischen Voelker. Herbert Gottschalk. (Ger.). 42.00 (ISBN 3-7934-1184-2, M-7246). French & Eur.
Lexikon der Neuzeitlichen Landwirtschaft, 3 vols. 776p. (Ger.). 1973. DM.75.00 (ISBN 3-7736-8002-3). Girardet.
Lexikon der Neuzeitlichen Landwirtschaft, Vol. 1. 9th ed. (Ger.). 1973. 25.00 (ISBN 3-7736-8003-1, M-7242). French & Eur.
Lexikon der Neuzeitlichen Landwirtschaft, Vol. 2. 9th ed. (Ger.). 1974. 25.00 (ISBN 3-7736-8004-X, M-7243). French & Eur.
Lexikon der Neuzeitlichen Landwirtschaft, Vol. 3. 9th ed. (Ger.). 1974. 25.00 (ISBN 3-7736-8005-8, M-7244). French & Eur.
Lexikon der Neuzeittlichen Landwirtschaft: Bd 1, Tierernaehrung, Tierzucht, Tierhaltung. 257p. (Ger.). 1974. DM.29.00 (ISBN 3-7736-8003-1). Girardet.
Lexikon der Neuzeittlichen Landwirtschaft: Bd 2, Ackerbau, Pflanzenbau, Gruenlandwirtschaft. 252p. (Ger.). 1974. DM.29.00 (ISBN 3-7736-8004-X). Girardet.
Lexikon der Neuzeittlichen Landwirtschaft: Bd 3, Belriebswirtschaft, Markt, Recht. 267p. (Ger.). 1974. DM.29.00 (ISBN 3-7736-8005-8). Girardet.
Lexikon der Numismatik. Tyll Kroha. (Ger.). 1977. 48.00 (ISBN 3-570-01588-2, M-7241). French & Eur.
Lexikon der Numismatik. 450p. (Ger.). 1976. DM.39.80 (ISBN 3-524-00598-5). Umschau Verlag.
Lexikon der Onologie. Ludwig Jakob. LC 79-386617. 415p. (Eng. & Ger.). 1979. write for info. Meininger.
Lexikon der Paedagogik: Bd 1, 3 Aubl. (Ger.). 1971. DM.95.00 (ISBN 3-451-01041-0). Herder.
Lexikon der Paedagogik: Bd 2, 3 Aufl. 512p. (Ger.). 1974. DM.95.00 (ISBN 3-451-01042-9). Herder.
Lexikon der Paedagogik: Bd 3, 3 Aufl. (Ger.). 1974. DM.95.00 (ISBN 3-451-01043-7). Herder.
Lexikon der Paedagogik: Bd 4, 3 Aufl. 496p. (Ger.). 1975. DM.95.00 (ISBN 3-451-01044-5). Herder.
Lexikon der Parapsychologie & ihrer Grenzgebiete. Werner F. Bonin. LC 77-452317. vii, 587p. (Ger.). 1976. 48.00 F. Scherz AG.
Lexikon der Philosophie. Franz Austeda. LC 79-380526. ix, 340p. (Ger.). 1979. S.380.00 (ISBN 3-85119-156-0). Hollinek.
Lexikon der Planun und Organisation. Hans Niewerth. (Ger.). 1968. 37.00 (ISBN 3-87715-051-9, M-7235). French & Eur.
Lexikon der Planung & Organisation. Ed. by Hans Niewwwerth et al. 220p. (Ger.). 1968. DM.46.00 (ISBN 3-87715-051-9). Quickborner Team.
Lexikon der Politik. Heiner Emde. LC 76-461039. 170p. (Ger.). 1975. DM.4.80 (ISBN 3-453-41123-4). Heyne W Verlag.
Lexikon der Politik: Politik Grundbegriffe & Grundgedanken. 8th ed. Walter Theimer. LC 75-509661. 315p. (Ger.). 1975. DM.17.80 (ISBN 3-772-01037-7). Francke.
Lexikon der praktischen Psychologie. Ludwig Knoll. LC 79-398496. 488p. (Ger.). 1979. DM.36.00 (ISBN 3-7857-0231-0). Luebbe.
Lexikon der Prozessrechnertechnik. Peter Schaefer & Martin Wiczorke. LC 79-372726. (Illus.). 327p. (Ger.). 1979. write for info. (ISBN 3-800-91278-3). Siemens AG.
Lexikon der Psychiatrie. C. Mueller. xii, 592p. (Ger.). 1973. DM.40.00 (ISBN 3-540-06277-7). Springer-Verlag.
Lexikon der Psychologie. Ed. by Wilhelm Arnold et al. 1328p. (Ger.). 1976. DM.85.00 (ISBN 3-451-17680-7). Herder.
Lexikon der Psychologie: Bd 1, A-Gewissen. Ed. by Wilhelm Arnold et al. 421p. (Ger.). 1971. DM.98.00 (ISBN 3-451-16111-7). Herder.
Lexikon der Psychologie: Bd 2, Graphologie-Prompling. Ed. by Wilhelm Arnold et al. 432p. (Ger.). 1971. DM.98.00 (ISBN 3-451-16112-5). Herder.
Lexikon der Psychologie: Bd 3, Propaganda-Zz. Ed. by Wilhelm Arnold et al. 422p. (Ger.). 1972. DM.98.00 (ISBN 3-451-16113-3). Herder.
Lexikon der Radiologischen Technik in der Mediazin. Wilfried Angerstein. LC 80-471099. 576p. (Ger.). 1979. write for info. (ISBN 3-13-484603-9). Thieme Verlag.
Lexikon der Radiologischen Technik in der Medizin. Winifred Angerstein. LC 75-595971. 480p. (Eng. & Ger.). 1975. DM.44.00 (ISBN 3-13-484602-0). Thieme Verlag.
Lexikon der Reisen und Entdeckungen. F. Embacher. (Ger.). 1883. pap. text ed. 18.75x (ISBN 90-6041-016-5). Humanities.
Lexikon der Roemischen Kaiser. Ed. by Otto Veh. 96p. (Ger.). 1976. DM.9.80 (ISBN 3-7608-4056-6). Artemis Verlag.
Lexikon der Schulphysik: Atomphysik, Vol. 5. O. Hoefling. (Ger.). 47.00 (ISBN 3-7614-0110-8, M-7227). French & Eur.
Lexikon der Schulphysik: Bd 1, Mechanik & Akustik. Ed. by Oskar Hoefling. (Ger.). 1978. DM.54.00 (ISBN 3-7614-0107-8). Aulis Verlag.
Lexikon der Schulphysik: Bd 3, Elektrizitaet & Magnetismus-1.Tlbd, A-K. Ed. by Oskar Hoefling. vi, 201p. (Ger.). 1978. DM.46.00 (ISBN 3-7614-0168-X). Aulis Verlag.
Lexikon der Schulphysik: Bd 3, Elektrizitaet & Magnetismus-2.Tlbd, L-Z. Ed. by Oskar Hoefling. vi, 201p. (Ger.). 1978. DM.46.00 (ISBN 3-7614-0169-8). Aulis Verlag.
Lexikon der Schulphysik: Bd 4, Optik & Relativitaet. Ed. by Oskar Hoefling. (Ger.). 1978. DM.52.00 (ISBN 3-7614-0109-4). Aulis Verlag.
Lexikon der Schulphysik: Bd 5, Atomphysik. Ed. by Oskar Hoefling. (Ger.). 1978. DM.58.00 (ISBN 3-7614-0110-8). Aulis Verlag.
Lexikon der Schulphysik: Bd 6, Geschichte der Physik. Ed. by Oskar HOefling. (Ger.). 1978. DM.44.00 (ISBN 3-7614-0131-0). Aulis Verlag.
Lexikon der Schulphysik: Bd 7, Geschichte der Physik. Ed. by Oskar Hoefling. viii, 239p. (Ger.). 1972. DM.28.00 (ISBN 3-7614-0153-1). Aulis Verlag.
Lexikon der Schulphysik: Elektrizitaet und Magnetismus A-K, Vol. 3A. Breitsameter. (Ger.). 42.50 (ISBN 3-7614-0168-X, M-7224). French & Eur.
Lexikon der Schulphysik: Elektrizitaet und Magnetismus L-Z, Vol. 3B. Breitsameter. (Ger.). 42.50 (ISBN 3-7614-0169-8, M-7225). French & Eur.
Lexikon der Schulphysik: Geschichte der Physik, Vol. 6. A Hermann. (Ger.). 35.00 (ISBN 3-7614-0131-0, M-7228). French & Eur.
Lexikon der Schulphysik: Geschichte der Physik, Vol. 7. A Hermann. (Ger.). 45.00 (ISBN 3-7614-0153-1, M-7229). French & Eur.
Lexikon der Schulphysik: Mechanik und Akustik, Vol. 1. K. Zita. (Ger.). 44.00 (ISBN 3-7614-0107-8, M-7222). French & Eur.
Lexikon der Schulphysik: Optik und Relativitaet, Vol. 4. W. Ruth. (Ger.). 42.00 (ISBN 3-7614-0109-4, M-7226). French & Eur.
Lexikon der Schulphysik: Waerme & Wetter. Ed. by Oskar Hoefling. (Ger.). 1978. DM.46.00 (ISBN 3-7614-0108-6). Aulis Verlag.
Lexikon der Schulphysik: Waerme und Wetter, Vol. 2. W. Hein. (Ger.). 37.00 (ISBN 3-7614-0108-6, M-7223). French & Eur.
Lexikon der Sozialen Arbeit. Ed. by Ruth Deutscher et al. 260p. (Ger.). 1978. DM.19.00 (ISBN 3-17-002487-6). Kohlhammer.
Lexikon der Sozialerziehung. Tobias Brocher. (Ger.). 1972. 15.95 (ISBN 3-7831-0378-9, M-7221). French & Eur.
Lexikon der Sprichwoertlichen Redensarten, 2 vols. L. Roehrich. (Illus.). 1256p. (Ger.). 130.00 set. M Rosenberg.
Lexikon der Technik. Ed. by B. Rohr & H. Wiele. (Illus.). 700p. (Ger.). 1982. M.28.00. Bibl Inst Leipzig.
Lexikon der Unternehmensfuehrung. Klaus Altfelder. (Ger.). 1973. 65.00 (ISBN 3-470-56191-5, M-7219). French & Eur.
Lexikon der Unternehmensfuehrung. Klaus Altfelder et al. 292p. (Ger.). 1973. DM.58.00 (ISBN 3-470-56191-5). Kiehl.
Lexikon der Voelker & Kulturen: Bd 1. (Ger.). 1972. DM.9.80 (ISBN 3-499-16158-3). Rowohlt.
Lexikon der Voelker & Kulturen: Bd 2. (Ger.). 1978. DM.9.80 (ISBN 3-499-16159-1). Rowohlt.
Lexikon der Voelker & Kulturen: Bd 3. (Ger.). 1978. DM.9.80 (ISBN 3-499-16160-5). Rowohlt.
Lexikon der Voelker und Kulturen, 3 vols. W. Stoehr. (Ger.). 1972. pap. 25.00 (ISBN 3-499-16158-3, M-7218). French & Eur.
Lexikon der Volkswirtschaft. Friedrich Geigant. (Ger.). 1975. 32.00 (ISBN 3-478-37050-7, M-7217). French & Eur.
Lexikon der Volkswirtschaft. Friedrich Geigant et al. LC 75-508655. 580p. (Ger.). 1975. write for info. (ISBN 3-478-37050-7). Verlag Moderne Industrie.
Lexikon der Weltarchitektur, 2 vols. N. Pevsner. (Ger.). 1976. Set. pap. 25.00 (ISBN 3-499-16199-0, M-7216). French & Eur.
Lexikon der Weltarchitektur. Ed. by Nikolaus Pevsner et al. (Ger.). 1971. DM.22.50 (ISBN 3-7913-0319-8); 30.00 (ISBN 3-7913-0318-X). Prestel-Verlag.
Lexikon der Weltgeschichte. (Ger.). 1977. 20.00 (ISBN 3-88140-000-1, M-7215). French & Eur.
Lexikon der Weltgeschichte. Ed. by Nikolaus Pevsner et al. 608p. (Ger.). 1977. DM.24.80 (ISBN 3-88140-000-1). Englisch Verlag.
Lexikon der Weltliteratur: Werke, Vol. 2. 2nd ed. Gero von Wilpert. (Ger.). 1968. 77.00 (ISBN 3-520-80801-3, M-7211). French & Eur.
Lexikon des Alpinen Schifahrens. Ed. by Friedrich Fetz. LC 77-457896. 156p. (Ger.). 1975. S.150.00 (ISBN 3-85123-028-0). Inn Verlag.
Lexikon des Bibliothekswesens, 2 vols. 2nd ed. Ed. by H. Kunze & G. Rueckl. (Ger.). 1975. M.48.00. Bibl Inst Leipzig.
Lexikon des Bibliothekswesens. Ed. by Horst Kunze & Gotthard Rueckl. (Ger.). 1975. DM.102.00 (ISBN 3-7940-4210-7). Saur Verlag.
Lexikon des Bibliothekswesens, 2 vols, Vols. 1 & 2. 2nd ed. Horst Kunze. (Ger.). 1974. 82.00 (ISBN 3-7940-4210-7, M-7209). French & Eur.
Lexikon des Buchwesens. Ed. by Joachim Kirchner. 1688p. (Ger.). 1956. DM.360.00 (ISBN 3-7772-5214-X). Hiersemann.
Lexikon des Buchwesens: Bd 1, Text A-K. Ed. by Joachim Kirchner. viii, 405p. (Ger.). 1952. DM.90.00 (ISBN 3-7772-5215-8). Hiersemann.
Lexikon des Buchwesens: Bd 2, Text L-Z. Ed. by Joachim Kirchner. vii, 519p. (Ger.). 1953. DM.90.00 (ISBN 3-7772-5311-1). Hiersemann.
Lexikon des Buchwesens: Bd 3, Bilderatlas zum Buchwesen Teil 1. Ed. by Joachim Kirchner. xxxix, 320p. (Ger.). 1955. DM.90.00 (ISBN 3-7772-5504-1). Hiersemann.
Lexikon des Fruehgriechischen Epos: Lfg 1. Bruno Snell & Hartmut Erbse. 96p. (Ger. & Gr.). 1955. DM.60.00 (ISBN 3-525-25015-0). Vandenhoeck.
Lexikon des Fruehgriechischen Epos: Lfg 2. Bruno Snell & Hartmut Erbse. 96p. (Ger. & Gr.). 1956. DM.60.00 (ISBN 3-525-25016-9). Vandenhoeck.
Lexikon des Fruehgriechischen Epos: Lfg 3. Bruno Snell & Hartmut Erbse. 96p. (Ger. & Gr.). 1959. DM.60.00 (ISBN 3-525-25017-7). Vandenhoeck.
Lexikon des Fruehgriechischen Epos: Lfg 4. Bruno Snell & Hartmut Erbse. 96p. (Ger. & Gr.). 1965. DM.60.00 (ISBN 3-525-25018-5). Vandenhoeck.
Lexikon des Fruehgriechischen Epos: Lfg 5. Bruno Snell & Hartmut Erbse. 96p. (Ger. & Gr.). 1967. DM.60.00 (ISBN 3-525-25501-2). Vandenhoeck.
Lexikon des Fruehgriechischen Epos: Lfg 6. Bruno Snell & Hartmut Erbse. 97p. (Ger. & Gr.). 1969. DM.60.00 (ISBN 3-525-25502-0). Vandenhoeck.
Lexikon des Fruehgriechischen Epos: Lfg 7. Bruno Snell & Hartmut Erbse. 97p. (Ger. & Gr.). 1973. DM.60.00 (ISBN 3-525-25503-9). Vandenhoeck.
Lexikon des Fruehgriechischen Epos: Lfg 8. Bruno Snell & Hartmut Erbse. 112p. (Ger. & Gr.). 1976. DM.86.00 (ISBN 3-525-25504-7). Vandenhoeck.
Lexikon des Geheimwissens. Horst E. Miers. (Ger.). leatherette 68.00 (ISBN 3-7626-0028-7, M-7214). French & Eur.
Lexikon des Geheimwissens. Horst E. Miers. LC 77-466751. (Illus.). 453p. (Ger.). 1976. DM.10.00 (ISBN 3-442-11142-0). Goldmann.
Lexikon des II. Weltkriegs. Ed. by Christian Zentner. (Ger.). 1977. DM.29.80 (ISBN 3-517-00639-4). Suedwest.
Lexikon Des II Weltkriegs. Cristian Zentner. (Ger.). 1977. pap. 25.00 (ISBN 3-517-00639-4, M-7213). French & Eur.
Lexikon des Impressionismus. Maurice Serullaz. (Ger.). 1975. 25.00 (ISBN 3-8046-0011-5, M-7208). French & Eur.
Lexikon des Internationalen Films. Ulrich Kurowski. LC 79-383266. (Ger.). 1975. DM.12.80 (ISBN 3-446-11945-0). Hanser.
Lexikon des Marxismus. Iring Fetscher. (Ger.). 1976. 20.00 (ISBN 3-455-09179-2, M-7207). French & Eur.
Lexikon des Mittelalters. (Ger.). 1977. pap. 25.00 (ISBN 3-7608-8801-1, M-7206). French & Eur.

Lexikon des Mittelalters. 112p. (Ger.). 1977. DM.32.00 (ISBN 3-7608-8801-1). Artemis Verlag.

Lexikon des Nebenstrafrechts. 2nd ed. Erich Goehler. (Ger.). 1977. pap. 44.00 (ISBN 3-406-01806-8, M-7245). French & Eur.

Lexikon des Nebenstrafrechts. Erich Goehler et al. 558p. (Ger.). 1977. DM.54.80 (ISBN 3-406-01806-8). Beck Verlag.

Lexikon des Rechts. 3706p. (Ger.). 1978. write for info. H Luchterhand.

Lexikon des Rechts. Adolph Reifferscheid & Frank Benseler. 4947p. (Ger.). 1978. DM.80.00. H Luchterhand.

Lexikon des Steuer & Wirtschaftsrechts. (Ger., Munich, Germany). 1973. DM.29.80 (ISBN 3-8092-0000-X). WRS Verlag.

Lexikon des Surrealismus. Rene Passeron. (Ger.). 1975. 25.00 (ISBN 3-8046-0012-3, M-7220). French & Eur.

Lexikon des Surrealismus. Ed. by Rene Passeron. 288p. (Ger.). 1975. DM.29.50 (ISBN 3-8046-0012-3). Wissenschaftliche.

Lexikon des Wirtschaftsrechnens. 2nd ed. Franz Kafitz. (Ger.). 1976. 15.00 (ISBN 3-470-71192-5, M-7210). French & Eur.

Lexikon Deutschsprachiger Schriftsteller: Bd 1. Ed. by Guenther Albrecht et al. 262p. (Ger.). 1974. DM.12.80 (ISBN 3-589-00061-9). Scriptor Verlag.

Lexikon Deutschsprachiger Schriftsteller: Bd 3. Ed. by Guenther Albrecht et al. 248p. (Ger.). 1974. DM.12.80 (ISBN 3-589-00063-5). Scriptor Verlag.

Lexikon Deutschsprachiger Schriftsteller: Bd 4. Ed. by Guenther Albrecht et al. 262p. (Ger.). 1974. DM.12.80 (ISBN 3-589-00064-3). Scriptor Verlag.

Lexikon Deutschsprachiger Schriftsteller: Bd 1. Ed. by Guenther Albrecht et al. 509p. (Ger.). 1974. DM.29.00 (ISBN 3-589-00091-0). Scriptor Verlag.

Lexikon Deutschsprachiger Schriftsteller: Bd 2. Ed. by Guenther Albrecht et al. 254p. (Ger.). 1974. DM.12.80 (ISBN 3-589-00062-7). Scriptor Verlag.

Lexikon Deutschsprachiger Schriftsteller, Vol. 1. Guenther Albrecht. (Ger.). 1974. 45.00 (ISBN 3-589-00091-0, M-7204). French & Eur.

Lexikon Deutschsprachiger Schriftsteller, Vol. 2. Guenther Albrecht. (Ger.). 1974. 45.00 (ISBN 3-589-00092-9, M-7205). French & Eur.

Lexikon EDV und Rechnungswesen. Kurt Nagel. (Ger.). 1977. 28.50 (ISBN 3-470-58181-9, M-7203). French & Eur.

Lexikon Feurden Bauherrn. Ernst Huerlimann. (Ger.). 1975. 28.50 (ISBN 3-478-04250-X, M-7202). French & Eur.

Lexikon Fremdsprachiger Schriftsteller, 3 vols. Ed. by G. Steiner et al. 1828p. (Ger.). 1981. M.60.00. Bibl Inst Leipzig.

Lexikon fuer Bergfreunde. Ed. by Hans Bibelriether et al. LC 77-337290. (Illus.). 256p. (Ger.). 1978. 29.80 F (ISBN 3-7658-0259-X). Bucher.

Lexikon fuer Berufs & Arbeitspaedagogik: Ueber 2400 Haupt- & Hinweisstichworte. Klaus Rischer. LC 77-474241. 162p. (Ger.). 1976. DM.18.60 (ISBN 3-470-71401-0). Kiehl.

Lexikon Fuer Die Graphische Industrie. 2nd ed. Ernst Born. (Ger.). 95.00 (ISBN 3-87641-184-X, M-7201). French & Eur.

Lexikon Fuer Eisenbahnfreunde. Erhard Born. (Ger.). 1977. pap. 39.95 (ISBN 3-7658-0238-7, M-7200). French & Eur.

Lexikon fuer Eisenbahnfreunde. Erhard Von Born et al. 256p. (Ger.). 1977. DM.29.80 (ISBN 3-7658-0238-7). Bucher Verlag.

Lexikon fuer Eltern & Erzieher. Ed. by Hans H. Groothoff et al. 306p. (Ger.). 1977. DM.9.80 (ISBN 3-579-03640-8). Gutersloher V.

Lexikon fuer Eltern & Erzieher. Ed. by Hans H. Groothoff et al. (Ger.). 1973. DM.24.00 (ISBN 3-7831-0410-6). Kreuz Verlag.

Lexikon Fuer Eltern und Erzieher. Hans Groothoff. (Ger.). 1973. 20.00 (ISBN 3-7831-0320-7, M-7199). French & Eur.

Lexikon fuer Fussballfreunde: Fachliche Beratung. Dettmar Cramer. LC 79-351323. (Illus.). 160p. (Ger.). 1978. 19.80 F (ISBN 3-7658-0260-3). Bucher.

Lexikon fuer Junge Erwachsene. Ed. by Hans D. Bastian. 462p. (Ger.). 1970. DM.19.80 (ISBN 3-7831-0320-7). Kreuz Verlag.

Lexikon Fuer Mineralien - und Gesteins Freunde. Herrmann Harder. (Ger.). 1977. 25.00 (ISBN 3-7658-0253-0, M-7198). French & Eur.

Lexikon fuer Mineralien & Gesteinfreunde. Hermann Von Harder et al. 256p. (Ger.). 1977. DM.29.80 (ISBN 3-7658-0253-0). Bucher Verlag.

Lexikon Fuer Pferdefreunde. (Ger.). 1976. 25.00 (ISBN 3-7658-0221-2, M-7197). French & Eur.

Lexikon fuer Pferdefreunde. 256p. (Ger.). 1976. DM.32.80 (ISBN 3-7658-0221-2). Bucher Verlag.

Lexikon Fuer Planetenbilder. Ilse Schnitzler. (Ger.). 1975. 25.00 (ISBN 3-920807-07-3, M-7196). French & Eur.

Lexikon Fuer Tennisfreunde. Ulrich Kaiser. (Ger.). 1977. 25.00 (ISBN 3-7658-0254-9, M-7195). French & Eur.

Lexikon fuer Tennisfreunde. Ulrich Kaiser et al. 256p. (Ger.). 1977. DM.29.80 (ISBN 3-7658-0254-9). Bucher Verlag.

Lexikon fur den Bauherrn. Ernst Hurlimann. LC 76-459881. 224p. (Ger.). 1975. write for info. (ISBN 3-478-04250-X). Verlag Moderne.

Lexikon fur Pferdefreunde. Reiner Klimke & Jorg Savelsberg. LC 76-468179. 255p. (Ger.). 1976. 29.80 F (ISBN 3-7658-0221-2). Bucher.

Lexikon fur Tennisfreunde. Reinhold Appel. Ed. by Ernst Baumann. LC 78-363843. (Illus.). 256p. (Ger.). 1977. 29.80 F (ISBN 3-7658-0254-9). Bucher.

Lexikon Geologie Geografie Mine Petrol. Nicolae Mihailescu. LC 76-506712. (Romanian.). 1975. 88.00 lei. Editura Stiintifica.

Lexikon in Farbe. (Ger.). 1974. DM.725.00 (ISBN 3-85012-018-X). Andreas & Andreas.

Lexikon Kraftfahrzeugtechnik. Gerhard Schnitzlein. LC 77-458501. 263p. (Eng. & Ger.). 1976. M.13.80. VEB Verlag Technik.

Lexikon Medicum. B. Zlotnicki. (Eng., Rus., Fr., Ger., Lat. & Pol., Medical Dictionary). 1973. 92.00 (ISBN 3-7945-0324-4, M-7194). French & Eur.

Lexikon Recht der Landwirtschaft der Deutschen Demokratischen Republik. Ed. by Reiner Arlt et al. LC 76-487653. 397p. (Ger.). 1975. M.10.50. Staatsdruk.

Lexikon RGW. Ed. by M. Engert & H. Stephan. 282p. (Ger.). 1981. M.18.00. Bibl Inst Leipzig.

Lexikon Staedte & Wappen der Deutschen Demokratischen Republik. 1st ed. Karlheinz Blaschke et al. LC 80-460533. (Illus.). 526p. (Ger.). 1979. M.25.00. VEB Verlag Enzyklopadie.

Lexikon tes Hellenikes Glosses Tritomon: Lexicon of the Greek Language in Three Volumes, 3 vols. Ed. by Anthimos Gazes. 2627p. (Gr.). 1980. Repr. of 1835 ed. lib. bdg. 450.00x (ISBN 0-89241-136-8). Caratzas Pub Co.

Lexikon van de Taalwetenschap. G Booij et al. LC 76-502048. (Illus.). 187p. (Dutch.). 1975. fl.9.90. Spectrum NL.

Lexikon Wirtschaft, Gesellschaft, Gewerkschaften. Werner Rittershofer. LC 76-457119. (Illus.). 379p. (Ger.). 1975. DM.18.00 (ISBN 3-7663-0095-4). Bund.

Lexikon zu Lycophron. Maria G. Ciani. LC 79-342190. 359p. (Gr.). 1975. write for info. (ISBN 3-487-05593-7). Olms Verlag.

Lexikon Zur - und Fruehgeschichtlicher Fundstaetten Oesterreichs. L. Franz. (Ger.). 1965. 47.00 (ISBN 3-7749-0255-0, M-7193). French & Eur.

Lexikon Zur & Freuhgeschictlicher Fundstaetten Oesterreichs. Ed. by L. Franz & A. R. Neumann. (Ger.). 1965. DM.58.00 (ISBN 3-7749-0255-0). Habelt.

Lexikon zur Arbeits & Soziallehre. Ed. by Rainer A. Roth & Helmut M. Selzer. 384p. (Ger.). 1976. DM.32.80 (ISBN 3-403-00593-3). Habelt.

Lexikon zur Arbeits & Soziallehre. Reiner A. Roth & Helmut M. Selzer. Ed. by Jurgen Schmidt. LC 76-468804. (Illus.). 383p. (Ger.). 1976. DM.32.80 (ISBN 3-403-00593-3). Auer.

Lexikon Zur Soziologie, 2 vols. W. Fuchs. 800p. (Ger.). 1975. 12.95 (ISBN 3-499-16191-5, M-7191). French & Eur.

Lexikon zur Soziologie: Bd 1. Ed. by Werner Fuchs et al. (Ger.). 1975. DM.7.80 (ISBN 3-499-16191-5). Rowohlt.

Lexikon zur Soziologie: Bd 2. Ed. by Werner Fuchs et al. (Ger.). 1975. DM.7.80 (ISBN 3-499-16192-3). Rowohlt.

Lexikon Zur Weltmission. S. E. Neill. (Ger.). 48.00 (ISBN 3-7974-0054-3, M-7190). French & Eur.

Lexikon zur Wortbildung, 3 vols. Gerhard Augst. LC 76-457738. 1306p. (Ger.). 1975. write for info. (ISBN 3-87808-624-5). Narr.

Lexikon 2000, Vol. 1. (Ger.). 1970. 86.00 (ISBN 3-8075-1001-X, M-7189, Pub. by Wissen). French & Eur.

Lexikon 2000, Vol. 2. (Ger.). 1970. 86.00 (ISBN 3-8075-1002-8, M-7188, Pub. by Wissen). French & Eur.

Lexikon 2000, Vol. 3. (Ger.). 1971. 86.00 (ISBN 3-8075-1003-6, M-7187, Pub. by Wissen). French & Eur.

Lexikon 2000, Vol. 4. (Ger.). 1971. 86.00 (ISBN 3-8075-1004-4, M-7186, Pub. by Wissen). French & Eur.

Lexikon 2000, Vol. 5. (Ger.). 1971. 86.00 (ISBN 3-8075-1005-2, M-7185, Pub. by Wissen). French & Eur.

Lexikon 2000, Vol. 6. (Ger.). 1971. 86.00 (ISBN 3-8075-1006-0, M-7184, Pub. by Wissen). French & Eur.

Lexikon 2000, Vol. 7. (Ger.). 1972. 86.00 (ISBN 3-8075-1007-9, M-7183, Pub. by Wissen). French & Eur.

Lexikon 2000, Vol. 8. (Ger.). 1972. 86.00 (ISBN 3-8075-1008-7, M-7182, Pub. by Wissen). French & Eur.

Lexikon 2000, Vol. 9. (Ger.). 1972. 86.00 (ISBN 3-8075-1009-5, M-7181, Pub. by Wissen). French & Eur.

Lexikon 2000, Vol. 10. (Ger.). 1972. 86.00 (ISBN 3-8075-1010-9, M-7180, Pub. by Wissen). French & Eur.

Lexikon 2000, Vol. 11. (Ger.). 1973. 86.00 (ISBN 3-8075-1011-7, M-7179, Pub. by Wissen). French & Eur.

Lexikon 2000, Vol. 12. (Ger.). 1973. 86.00 (ISBN 3-8075-1012-5, M-7178, Pub. by Wissen). French & Eur.

Lexikon 2000, Vol. 13. (Ger.). 1973. 86.00 (ISBN 3-8075-1013-3, M-7177, Pub. by Wissen). French & Eur.

Lexikothek: Bd 10, Torp-Z. (Ger.). 1978. DM.118.00 (ISBN 3-570-06560-X). C Bertelsmann.

Lexikothek: Bd 2, Bez-Dit. (Ger.). 1978. DM.118.00 (ISBN 3-570-06552-9). C Bertelsmann.

Lexikothek: Bd 3, Diu-Gass. (Ger.). 1978. DM.118.00 (ISBN 3-570-06553-7). C Bertelsmann.

Lexikothek: Bd 4, Gast-Hz. (Ger.). 1978. DM.118.00 (ISBN 3-570-06554-5). C Bertelsmann.

Lexikothek: Bd 5, I-Kreb. (Ger.). 1978. DM.118.00 (ISBN 3-570-06555-3). C Bertelsmann.

Lexikothek: Bd 6, Kred-Mit. (Ger.). 1978. DM.118.00 (ISBN 3-570-06556-1). C Bertelsmann.

Lexikothek: Bd 7, Miv-Phyo. (Ger.). 1978. DM.118.00 (ISBN 3-570-06557-X). C Bertelsmann.

Lexikothek: Bd 8, Phys-Schlo. (Ger.). 1978. DM.118.00 (ISBN 3-570-06558-8). C Bertelsmann.

Lexikothek: Bd 9, Schlu-Toro. (Ger.). 1978. DM.118.00 (ISBN 3-570-06559-6). C Bertelsmann.

Lexikothek: Das Bertelsmann Lexikon in 10 Baenden. (Ger.). 1978. DM.118.00 (ISBN 3-570-06551-0). C Bertelsmann.

Lexique Aborite. Marcel Lagrenade. (Fr.). 1974. Can.$pap. 5.75 (ISBN 0-88905-003-1). Dotmar.

Lexique Analytique du Vocabulaire Inuit Moderne au Quebec-Labrador. Louis J. Dorais. LC 79-363935. 136p. (Fr. & Inupiaq.). 1978. Can.$9.00 (ISBN 0-7746-6850-4, Dist. by Four Continent Bk). Univ Laval.

Lexique Anglais-Francais. J. Vaillancourt. LC 79-347577. 427p. (Eng. & Fr.). 1978. Can.$13.25 (ISBN 0-7766-8004-8). Edns Ottawa.

Lexique Anglais-Francais De la Banque et De la Monnaie. Pierre Ricour. 87p. (Eng. & Fr.). 1973. pap. 2.95 (ISBN 0-686-57208-4, M-6486). French & Eur.

Lexique Anglais-Francais de L'Aciere Electrique. B. Besse et al. 135p. (Eng. & Fr.). 1975. pap. 8.95 (ISBN 0-686-92555-6, M-9239). French & Eur.

Lexique Anglais-Francais De L'industrie Miniere, 1. Pierre Auger & Louis-Jean Rousseau. 91p. (Eng. & Fr.). 1973. pap. 6.95 (ISBN 0-686-56905-9, M-6016). French & Eur.

Lexique Anglais-Francais Des Appareils De Mesures Electriques. Jean Mercier. 44p. (Eng. & Fr.). 1973. pap. 1.95 (ISBN 0-686-57044-8, M-6405). French & Eur.

Lexique Anglais-Francais Des Fruits et Legumes. rev. ed. Louise Appel. 128p. (Eng. & Fr.). 1974. pap. 9.95 (ISBN 0-686-56897-4, M-6007). French & Eur.

Lexique Anglais-Francais des Petits Appareils Electromenagers. French Language Bureau. LC 76-471924. 183p. (Eng. & Fr.). 1975. write for info. (ISBN 0-7754-2280-0). Edit Quebec.

Lexique Anglais-Francais des Termes Appartenant aux Techniques en Usage a I. G. N. Brommer. 122p. (Eng. & Fr.). 1958. 13.00 F. I. G. N.

Lexique Anglais-Francais des Termes Appartenant Aux Technques En Usage I.G.N, 2 vols, Pt. 1. Thuillier. 464p. (Fr. & Eng., English-French Lexicon of Terms Pertaining to Techniques Used at I.G.N.). 1958. pap. 14.95 (ISBN 0-686-56781-1, M-6357). French & Eur.

Lexique Anglais-Francais des Termes Appartenant Aux Techniques En Usage a I.G.N, Pt.2. Ed. by Brommer. 122p. (Fr. & Eng., English-French Lexicon of Terms Pertaining to Techniques Used at I.G.N). 1958. pap. 7.95 (ISBN 0-686-56778-1, M-6356). French & Eur.

Lexique Anglais-Francais du Compteur d'electricite. Jean Mercier. 42p. (Eng. & Fr.). 1973. Can.$1.00. Quebec Off.

Lexique Anglais-Francais du Compteur d'electricite. Office de la Langue Francaise. 56p. (Eng. & Fr.). 1972. Can.$1.00. Quebec Off.

Lexique Anglais-Francais Du Compteur D'electricite: Principes et Pieces Composantes. Jean Mercier. 42p. (Eng. & Fr.). 1973. pap. 3.50 (ISBN 0-686-57046-4, M-6407). French & Eur.

Lexique Anglais-Francais du Programmateur de Cuisiniere. Jean Mercier. 29p. (Eng. & Fr.). 1973. Can.$0.50. Quebec Off.

Lexique Anglais-Francais Du Programmateur De Cuisiniere: Fonctionnement et Pieces Composantes. Jean Mercier. 29p. (Eng. & Fr.). 1973. pap. 1.95 (ISBN 0-686-57045-6, M-6406). French & Eur.

Lexique Anglais-Francais: Termes Appartenant aux Techniques en Usage a I. G. N. Premiere Partie, 2 vols. Thuiluer. 464p. (Eng. & Fr.). 1958. 28.60 F. I. G. N.
Lexique Anglais-Francais: Termes Techniques a l'usage des Biologistes. Jean Vaillancourt. (Eng. & Fr.). 1978. Can.$pap. 12.00 (ISBN 0-7766-8004-8). U of Toronto Pr.
Lexique CN: Anglais-Allemand-Francais. Y. H. Attiyate. (Illus.). 526p. (Eng., Ger. & Fr.). 1977. 65.00 F. Iron Age Metalworking Int.
Lexique Commente de la Douane & du Commerce Exterieur. 307p. (Fr.). 1973. 500.00 F. Editorial Office.
Lexique Commercial: Tout le vocabulaire des affaires. C.I.D.A. 450p. (Eng. & Fr.). 1974. 80.00 F. Maison Dictionnaire.
Lexique Compare de la Langue de Corneille, 2 vols. Frederic Godefroy. (Fr.). 1971. 144.00 F. Kraus.
Lexique Compare des Fabilaux de Jean Bedel. Pierre Nardin. 188p. (Fr.). 1942. 50.00 F. Slatkine.
Lexique Complet de la Langue de Villon. Andre Burger. 110p. (Fr.). 1974. 16.00 F. Droz.
Lexique d'amenagement du Territoire. (Fr.). 1973. 10.70 F. C. N. I. P. E.
Lexique d'antiquites Grecques. Claude Vial. 272p. (Fr.). 1972. 20.60 F. Colin.
Lexique d'antiquites Romaines. Andre Pelletier. (Fr.). 1972. 20.60 F. Colin.
Lexique de base du Latin. J. Michel & Michel Gester. 236p. (Fr. & Lat.). 1967. 236.00 F. Sikkel.
Lexique de Charles d'Orleans dans les Ballades. Daniel Poirion. 160p. (Fr.). 1967. 18.00 F. Droz.
Lexique de Comptabilite & de Gestion. Colasse. (Fr.). 1975. 23.00 F. Ecole Electricite.
Lexique de Comptabilite et de Gestion. Colasse. (Fr.). 1975. pap. 14.95 (ISBN 0-686-56768-4, M-6079). French & Eur.
Lexique de la Banque & de la Monnaie. Pierre Ricour & Rene Cousineau. LC 79-353044. 87p. (Eng. & Fr.). 1978. write for info. (ISBN 0-7754-2667-9). Edit Quebec.
Lexique de la Fabrication du Refrigerateur: Francais-Anglais. H. Dupuis et al. 66p. (Fr. & Eng.). 1975. pap. 5.95 (ISBN 0-686-92434-7, M-9240). French & Eur.
Lexique de la Gestion. Pierre Lauzel. 240p. (Fr.). 1970. 39.00 F. E. M. E.
Lexique de la Langue de Bonaventure Des Periers. Adolphe Cheneviere & Felix Frank. 251p. (Fr.). 1971. 55.00 F. Slatkine.
Lexique de la Langue de Chapelain. Antonin Fabre. 77p. (Fr.). 1971. 20.00 F. Slatkine.
Lexique de la Langue de Jean Chapelain. Alfred C. Hunter. 160p. (Fr.). 1967. 30.00 F. Droz.
Lexique de la Langue de Jean de La Fontaine, 2 vols. Henri De Regnier. (Fr.). 1970. 55.00. Lenox.
Lexique de la Langue de la Bruyere. Adolphe Regnier. 381p. (Fr.). 1970. DM.74.00. Olms.
Lexique de la Langue de La Rochefoucauld. Henri De Regnier. 446p. (Fr.). 1883. DM.98.00. Olms.
Lexique de la Langue de Mme de Sevigne. Jean E. Sommer. (Fr.). 1970. 22.50. Lenox.
Lexique de la Langue de Mme de Sevigne, 1. Jean E. Sommer. (Fr.). 1973. DM.97.00. Olms.
Lexique de la Langue de Mme de Sevigne, 2. Jean E. Sommer. (Fr.). 1973. DM.97.00. Olms.
Lexique de la Langue de Moliere, 2 vols. Arthur Desfeuilles. (Fr.). 1970. 55.00. Lenox.
Lexique de la Langue de Moliere avec une, Vol. 1-2. Arthur Desfeuilles. (Fr.). 1900. Set. 64.00 (ISBN 0-8337-4744-4). B Franklin.
Lexique de la Langue de Moliere, 1. Charles L. Livet. 532p. (Fr.). 1970. DM.298.00. Olms.
Lexique de la Langue de Moliere, 2. Charles L. Livet. 666p. (Fr.). 1970. DM.298.00. Olms.
Lexique de la Langue de Moliere, 3. Charles L. Livet. 824p. (Fr.). 1970. DM.298.00. Olms.
Lexique de la Langue de Pierre Corneille, 2 vols. Charles J. Marty-Lavezux. (Fr.). 1970. 42.50. Lenox.
Lexique de la Langue des Essais de Michel de Montaigne. Pierre L. Villey-Desmeserets. (Fr.). 1973. 32.50. Lenox.
Lexique de la Langue des Oeuvres Burlesques de Scarron. Leonard T. Richardson. 286p. (Fr.). 1976. DM.56.00. Olms.
Lexique de la Langue du Cardinal de Retz. Adolphe Regnier. 439p. (Fr.). 1896. DM.98.00. Olms.
Lexique de la Langue Turen: Parler des Banen du sud-ouest du Cameroun. Idelette Dugast. (Fr.). 1967. 51.00 F. S. E. L. A. F.
Lexique de la Musique. Jean Queval. 130p. (Fr.). 1968. 5.95 (ISBN 0-686-57289-0, F-11890). French & Eur.
Lexique de la Musique. Jean Queval. 130p. (Fr.). 1968. 12.00 F. Delpire.
Lexique de la photographie d'Amateur: Anglais-Francais Francais-Anglais. R. Pollet. 111p. (Eng. & Fr.). 1970. 50.00 F. Maison Dictionnaire.
Lexique de la Photographie d'amateur: Francais-Anglais. Ray J. Pollet. 112p. (Fr. & Eng.). 1970. 3.50 F. Lemeac.
Lexique de la Prevention des Accidents. Maria E. De Villiers-Sidani. (Illus.). 173p. (Fr.). 1973. Can.$2.00. Quebec Off.
Lexique de la Psychanalyse. Jean-Pierre Trempe. 146p. (Fr.). 1978. 39.60 F. Quebec P. U.
Lexique de la Resistance Grecque: Journal de Resistance. Mikis Theodorakis. 324p. (Fr.). 1971. 43.85 F. Flammarion.
Lexique De la Terminologie Linguistique. 3rd ed. Jules Marouzeau. LC 53-5692. 280p. (Fr., Ger., Eng. & Ital.). 1969. Repr. of 1951 ed. 7.50x (ISBN 0-8002-0840-4). Intl Pubns Serv.
Lexique de l'ancien Francais. Frederic Godefroy. 544p. (Fr.). 1976. 39.95 (ISBN 0-686-57305-6, M-6282). French & Eur.
Lexique de l'ancien Francais. Frederic Godefroy. 544p. (Fr.). 1976. 80.00 F. Champion.
Lexique de l'ancien Francais. Frederic Godefroy. 544p. (Fr.). 1901. DM.78.00. Olms.
Lexique de l'Anglais des affaires. Ivan De Renty. 352p. (Fr. & Eng.). pap. 8.00. Imported Bks.
Lexique de l'anglais des Affaires. Ivan De Renty. 320p. (Fr.). 1977. 10.50 F. L. G. F.
Lexique de L'Anglais des Affaires. Ivan de Renty. 352p. (Eng. & Fr.). 1977. pap. 5.95 (ISBN 0-686-57286-6, M-4761). French & Eur.
Lexique de l'economie Suisse. (Fr.). 1965. 100.00 F. Baconniere.
Lexique de L'education au Nouveau-Brunswick. Ministere de L'education. LC 77-550177. 98p. (Fr.). 1976. write for info. Ministere de L'education.
Lexique de l'homme a Cheval. Marc Saint Riquier & Jacques Delporte. (Fr.). 1975. 47.00 F. Amphora.
Lexique de l'homme a Cheval. Marc de Saint-Riquier. (Fr.). 25.00 (ISBN 0-686-57287-4, M-4669). French & Eur.
Lexique de l'Industrie Petroliere Ra Finage: Anglais-Francais. M. Heroux et al. 163p. (Eng. & Fr.). 1979. pap. 9.95 (ISBN 0-7754-2382-3, M-9235). French & Eur.
Lexique de l'Industrie Textile: Francais-Anglais. R. Habert et al. 240p. (Fr. & Eng.). 1974. pap. 9.95 (ISBN 0-686-92180-1, M-9222). French & Eur.
Lexique de l'informatique. 3rd ed. Jean Guilhaumou. 122p. (Fr.). 1976. 36.00 F. E. M. E.
Lexique de Mecanique d'ajustage. 2nd ed. Lucien Normandeau. 256p. (Fr.). 1957. Can.$3.50. Quebec Off.
Lexique de Prevention des Accidents. Maria E. De Villiers-Sidani et al. 137p. (Eng. & Fr.). 1980. pap. 4.95 (ISBN 0-686-97398-4, M-9225). French & Eur.
Lexique de Psychologie & de Psychiatrie. 155p. (Fr.). 1978. 22.00 F. Medicales Univ.
Lexique de Psychologie & de Psychiatrie. 155p. (Fr.). 22.00 F. Medicales Univ.
Lexique de Ronsard. Louis Mellerio. (Fr.). 54.00 F. Kraus.
Lexique de Ronsard. Louis Mellerio. 250p. (Fr.). 1974. DM.54.00. Olms.
Lexique de Sylviculture Allemand-Francais. Martinot Lagarde. (Ger. & Fr.). 5.00 F. Genie Rural.
Lexique de Termes Anglais-Francais de Gestion. James Coveney & Sheila J. Moore. 160p. (Eng. & Fr.). 1972. 23.50 F. Colin.
Lexique De Termes Anglais-Francais De Gestion: Les Cycle Au Superieur, Ecoles Superieures De Gestion. James Conveney & Shiela J. Moore. 160p. (Eng. & Fr.). 1972. pap. 9.95 (ISBN 0-686-56963-6, M-6087). French & Eur.
Lexique de Termes Juridiques. 4th ed. Ed. by Raymond Guillen & Jean Vincent. LC 78-381853. viii, 406p. (Fr.). 1978. 30.00 F (ISBN 2-247-01448-8). Dalloz.
Lexique de Termes Juridiques. 3rd ed. Raymond Guillien & Jean Vincent. 354p. (Fr.). 1978. 30.00 F. Dalloz.
Lexique de Termes Juridiques. (Fr.). 1981. 490.00 F. Bruylant.
Lexique de Termes Politiques. (Fr.). 1981. 370.00 F. Bruylant.
Lexique de termes techniques: Anglais-Francais & index Francais. R. J. Pollet. 233p. (Eng. & Fr.). 1976. 75.00 F. Maison Dictionnaire.
Lexique de Termes Techniques: Un Lexique Anglais-Francais. Ray J. Pollet. 233p. (Eng. Fr.). 1976. pap. 25.00 (ISBN 0-686-57084-7, M-6460). French & Eur.
Lexique de Termes Techniques: Un Lexique Anglais-Francais. Ray J. Pollet. 233p. (Eng. & Fr.). 1976. 58.15 F. Lemeac.
Lexique d'Erquinghem-Lys. Paul Barbier. 70p. (Fr.). 1978. 20.00 F. Ste. Linguistique Picarde.
Lexique Des Antiquites Grecques. Pierre Paris. (Fr.). 1909. pap. 23.50 (ISBN 0-686-57066-9, M-6438). French & Eur.
Lexique des Antiquites Romaines. Rene Cagnat & G. Goyau. (Fr.). 1896. 56.00 F. Boccard.
Lexique des Bons Petits Plats. Jehanne Jean-Charles. 222p. (Fr.). 1970. 19.40 F. Presses Cite.
Lexique des Dieux. Pierre Chastel. 110p. (Fr.). 1968. 12.00 F. Delpire.
Lexique des Epices et Assaisonnements: Anglais-Francais. J. Maurais. 73p. (Eng. & Fr.). 1979. pap. 5.95 (ISBN 0-7754-2593-1, M-9236). French & Eur.
Lexique des Fruits et Legumes. L. Appel. 133p. (Fr & Eng.). Date not set. pap. 9.95 (ISBN 0-686-97410-7, M-9238). French & Eur.
Lexique des Industries Graphiques. R. Comte & A. Pernin. 128p. (Fr.). 1975. pap. 17.50 (ISBN 0-686-56959-8, M-6082). French & Eur.
Lexique des Industries Graphiques. Rene Comte & Andre Pernin. 125p. (Fr.). 1974. 35.00 F. Comp Fr Edns.
Lexique des Lettres Commerciales en Quatre Langues, 3 vols. 735p. (Fr.). 1972. 260.00 F. Multi Ling Verlag A. G.
Lexique des Mots-cles, Descripteurs & Identificateurs, Francais-Anglais: Utiliser pour la Recherche Documentaire, 3 vols. Centre de Documentation de L'armement. 2001p. (Fr. & Eng.). 1976. 200.00 F. Centre Documentation Armement.
Lexique des Parlers Arabes-Tchado-Soudanais. Arlette Roth-Laly. 294p. (Arabic, Chad & Soudanese.). 1969. pap. 50.00 F (ISBN 2-22201-164-7). Editions du CNRS.
Lexique des Parlers Arabes-Tchado-Soudanais: K-Y. Arlette Roth-Laly. 148p. (Arabic & Sudanese.). 1972. pap. 50.00 F (ISBN 2-22201-428-X). CNRS.
Lexique des Parlers Arabes-Tchado-Soudanais. Arlette Roth-Laly. 148p. (Fr., Arabic & Sudanese.). 1972. 35.50 F. CNRS.
Lexique des Parlers Arabes-Tchado-Soudanais. Arlette Roth-Laly. 164p. (Fr., Arabic & Sudanese.). 1969. 35.50 F. CNRS.
Lexique des Parlers Arabes-Tchado-Soudanais, 3. Arlette Roth-Laly. 144p. (Arabic, Sudanese & Fr.). 1971. 34.20 F. CNRS.
Lexique des Pipelines a Terre et en Mer. LC 80-472459. xii, 302p. (Eng. & Fr.). 1979. write for info. (ISBN 2-7108-0356-9). Technip.
Lexique des Produits de la Peche: Anglais-Francais. P. Vallieres et al. 35p. (Eng. & Fr.). 1980. pap. 3.95 (ISBN 2-551-03722-0, M-9223). French & Eur.
Lexique des Sciences de l'education. Leandre Coudray. 144p. (Fr.). 1973. 43.00 F. E. S. F.
Lexique des Sciences Sociales. (Fr.). 1981. 490.00 F. Bruylant.
Lexique des Symboles. Olivier Beigbeder. 436p. (Fr.). 1969. 88.00 F. Zodiaque.
Lexique des Termes de Parodontologie de Microbiologie Parodontale et Buccale et de Sciences Fondamentales. Robert Sinsoilliez. 112p. (Fr.). 1973. pap. 15.95 (ISBN 0-686-56751-X, M-6518). French & Eur.
Lexique des Termes de Prothese Dentaire. Evelyn Batarec. 90p. (Fr.). 1973. pap. 19.95 (ISBN 0-686-56749-8, M-6024). French & Eur.
Lexique des Termes de Prothese Dentaire. Evelyn Batarec. 90p. (Fr.). 1973. 30.00 F. Prelat.
Lexique Des Termes Du Batiment. 212p. (Fr.). 1963. pap. 14.95 (ISBN 0-686-57014-6, M-6361). French & Eur.
Lexique des Termes du Batiment. (Illus.). 212p. (Fr.). 1963. 32.00 F. Massin.
Lexique des Termes Economiques. 2nd ed. Jean F. Phelizon. LC 76-477732. (Illus.). 184p. (Fr.). 1975. 30.00 F. Tech Vulgar.
Lexique des Termes Economiques. new ed. Jean-Francois Phelizon. 192p. (Fr.). 1977. 23.00 F. Tech Vulgar.
Lexique des Termes Juridiques. 3rd ed. Raymond Guillien & Jean Vincent. 354p. (Fr.). 1978. pap. 14.95 (ISBN 0-686-57321-8, M-6304). French & Eur.
Lexique des Termes Medicaux. (Fr.). pap. 14.95 (ISBN 0-686-56722-6, M-6362). French & Eur.
Lexique des Termes Medicaux. (Fr.). 25.00 F. Lamarre Poinot.
Lexique des Termes Parodontologie de Microbiologie: Parodontale & Buccale & de Sciences Fondamentales. Robert Sinsoilliez. (Illus.). 112p. (Fr.). 1973. 38.00 F. Prelat.
Lexique des Termes Politiques. Charles Debbasch & Yves Daudet. 280p. (Fr.). 1978. pap. 14.95 (ISBN 0-686-57285-8, M-4652). French & Eur.
Lexique des Termes Politiques. Charles Debbasch & Yves Daudet. 280p. (Fr.). 1978. 34.00 F. Dalloz.
Lexique des Termes Techniques Concernant le Material d'Une Usine d'Acetylene Dissous. 78p. (Fr., Lexicon of Technical Terms Concerning the Materials of Dissolved Acetylene Manufacturing). 1970. pap. 29.95 (ISBN 0-686-56759-5, M-6363). French & Eur.
Lexique des Termes Techniques Concernant le Material d'une Usine d'oxygene. (Illus.). 99p. (Fr.). 1971. 70.00 F. Soudure Autogene.
Lexique des Termes Usuels de Psychiatrie. Jean Carrere & Jacques Dessaigne. 114p. (Fr.). 1976. pap. 17.50 (ISBN 0-686-56939-3, M-6061). French & Eur.

Lexique des Termes Usuels de Psychiatrie. Jean Carrere & Jacques Dessaigne. LC 77-464918. 114p. (Fr.). 1976. 35.00 F (ISBN 2-7013-0101-7). Berger-Levrault.
Lexique Des Termes Utiles a L'etude Des Noms De Lieux. Henri Dorion & Jean Poirier. 162p. (Fr.). 1975. pap. 12.95 (ISBN 0-686-57121-5, M-6168). French & Eur.
Lexique des Termes Utiles a l'etude des Noms de Lieux. Henri Dorion & Jean Poirier. 162p. (Fr.). 1975. Can.$7.75. Laval P. U.
Lexique d'Informatique. Michel Ginguay & Annette Lauret. 244p. (Fr.). 1973. pap. 32.50 (ISBN 0-686-57198-3, M-6273). French & Eur.
Lexique d'informatique. Michel Ginguay & Annette Lauret. (Illus.). 244p. (Fr.). 1973. 73.00 F. Masson & Cie.
Lexique Du Batiment. (Fr.). 14.95 (ISBN 0-686-57015-4, M-6364). French & Eur.
Lexique du Boeuf. LC 79-356928. 140p. (Eng. & Fr.). 1977. write for info. (ISBN 0-7754-2796-9). Edit Quebec.
Lexique du Calcul Economique & de l'econometrie. Andre Olmi & Fortune July. 192p. (Fr.). 1970. 39.00 F. E. M. E.
Lexique du cinema d'Amateur: Anglais-Francais Francais-Anglais. R. Pollet. 127p. (Eng. & Fr.). 1971. 50.00 F. Maison Dictionnaire.
Lexique du Journal des Debats. 7th ed. Ministere des Communications Assemblee Nationale. (Fr.). 1974. Can.$2.00. Quebec Off.
Lexique du Journal des Debats. 8th ed. Ministere des Communications Assemblee Nationale. 232p. (Fr.). 1976. Can.$3.00. Quebec Off.
Lexique du Journal des Debats. 6th ed. Ministere des Communications Assemblee Nationale. 146p. (Fr.). 1972. Can.$1.50. Quebec Off.
Lexique du Journal des Goncourt. Maximilien Fuchs. 190p. (Fr.). 1972. 45.00 F. Slatkine.
Lexique du Marketing. Hubert Nyssen. 86p. (Fr.). 1971. pap. 7.50 (ISBN 0-686-57064-2, M-6435). French & Eur.
Lexique du Marketing. Hubert Nyssen. (Fr.). 1971. 12.00 F. Delpire.
Lexique du Marketing. 3rd ed. Francois Roche. 108p. (Fr.). 1970. 32.00 F. E. M. E.
Lexique du Parler Creole de la Reunion, 2 vols. Robert Chaudenson. (Illus.). 1252p. (Fr. & Creole.). 1973. 220.00 F. Champion.
Lexique du Parler de Saviese. Christophe Favre & Robert Balet. (Illus.). 1252p. (Fr.). 1973. 220.00 F. Champion.
Lexique du Parler des Marazig. Gilbert Boris & M. Denizeau. 686p. (Fr.). 1958. 66.00 F. Imprimerie Nat.
Lexique du Roman de Renart. Gunnar Tilander. 163p. (Fr.). 1971. 35.00 F. Champion.
Lexique du Secourisme & de la Plongee Autonome. Andre Hourcastagne. (Fr.). 8.00 F. France Selection.
Lexique du Tahitien Contemporain: Tahitien-Francais. Yves Lemaitre. 201p. (Tahitian & Fr.). 1973. 27.00 F. Orstom.
Lexique Etymologique de L'Irlandais Ancien: Fascicule R-S. Joseph Vendryes. 272p. (Fr.). 1975. 70.00 F (ISBN 2-22201-629-0). CNRS.
Lexique Etymologique de L'Irlandais Ancien: Fascicule T-U. Joseph Vendryes. 211p. (Fr.). 1978. 110.00 F (ISBN 2-22202-227-4). CNRS.
Lexique Etymologique de L'Irlandais Ancien: Lettre B. Joseph Vendryes & E. Bachellery. 120p. (Fr.). 1981. 90.00 F (ISBN 2-22202-800-0). CNRS.
Lexique Etymologique de l'Irlandais Ancien. Joseph Vendryes. 272p. (Fr. & Gaelic.). 1975. 70.00 F. CNRS.
Lexique Etymologique de l'Irlandais Ancien, 1. Joseph Vendryes. 106p. (Fr. & Gaelic.). 1959. 20.00 F. CNRS.
Lexique Etymologique des Termes Medicaux. Michel Lancombe & Jean-Pierre Monceaux. 20p. (Fr.). 1971. 25.00 F. Lamarre Poinot.
Lexique EUC Woerterbuch des Rechnungswesens. 1100p. (Ger.). 1974. write for info. (ISBN 3-8021-0073-5). IdW Verlag.
Lexique Forestier: Anglais-Francais. Marcel Lagrenade. (Illus., Eng. & Fr.). 1978. Can.$pap. 19.50 (ISBN 0-88905-005-8). Dotmar.
Lexique Francais-Anglais et Anglais-Francais des Termes d'usage Courant en Machines Outils et Machines Similaires. 56p. (Fr., French-English, English-French Lexicon of Commonly Used Terms in Machine Tools and Similar Machines). 1960. pap. 6.95 (ISBN 0-686-56794-3, M-6365). French & Eur.
Lexique Francais-Anglais et Anglais-Francais des Termes d'usage Courant En Hydraulique et Pneumatique. P. Nichil. 42p. (Fr. & Eng., French-English, English-French Lexicon of Commonly Used Terms in Hydraulics and Pneumatics). 1974. pap. 8.95 (ISBN 0-686-56790-0, M-6426). French & Eur.
Lexique Francais-Anglais: Termes d'usage Courant en Hydraulique & Pneumatique. 42p. (Fr. & Eng.). 14.00 F. Ste. Publications Mecaniques.
Lexique Francais-Anglais: Termes d'usage Courant en Machines-Outlis & Machines Similaires. 56p. (Fr. & Eng.). 1960. 11.00 F. Ste. Publications Mecaniques.
Lexique Francais-Arabe de la Protection Civile & du Secourisme. (Fr. & Arabic.). 14.00 F. France Selection.
Lexique Francais-Corse. Xavier Moreschi. 175p. (Fr.). 1973. 18.00 F. Corses.
Lexique Francais De la Reparation Juridique Du Dommage Corporel. Maurice A. Touati. 268p. (Fr.). 1976. 32.50 (ISBN 0-686-57233-5, M-6534). French & Eur.
Lexique Francais de la Reparation Juridique du Dommage Corporel. Maurice A. Touati. LC 76-677444. 265p. (Fr.). 1976. 68.00 F (ISBN 2-224-00307-2). Maloine.
Lexique Francais Des Abreviations et Formules Medico-Chirurgicales Courantes. Maurice A. Touati. 142p. (Fr.). 1969. 12.50 (ISBN 0-686-57234-3, M-6535). French & Eur.
Lexique Francais des Abreviations: Formules Medico-Chirugicales Courantes. Maurice A. Touati. 142p. (Fr.). 1969. 24.00 F. Maloine.
Lexique Francais-Duala: Dictionnaire Duala-Francais. Paul Helmlinger. 666p. (Fr.). 1972. 105.00 F. S. E. L. A. F.
Lexique Francais-Grec. L. Feuillet. 496p. (Fr. & Gr.). 1976. 35.20 F. Belin.
Lexique Francais: La Reparation Juridique du Dommage Corporel. Maurice A. Touati. 268p. (Fr.). 1976. 68.00 F. Maloine.
Lexique Francais-Latin. Edouard Sommer. 480p. (Fr. & Lat.). 1967. 11.30 F. Hachette-Jeunesse.
Lexique Francais-Latin. Jacques Trenel. 694p. (Fr. & Lat.). 1978. 30.40 F. Belin.
Lexique Francais Moderne - Ancien Francais. Ralph De Gorog. LC 72-91996. 488p. (Fr.). 1973. 25.00x (ISBN 0-8203-0312-7). U of Ga Pr.
Lexique Francais-Occitan. Roger Barthe. 202p. (Fr.). 1971. 23.00 F. Amis Langue.
Lexique Francais-Occitan. Roger Barthe. 240p. (Fr.). 1974. 30.00 F. R. Barthe.
Lexique General. (Eng. , Fr. , Span. & Rus., ST/DCS/1/Rev. 1). pap. 35.00 (ISBN 0-686-94816-5, UN). Unipub.
Lexique Guide D'acoustique Architecturale. Jean Pujolle. (Illus.). 152p. (Fr.). 1971. 92.00 F. Eyrolles.
Lexique Histoire du Moyen-Age. R. Fedou. (Fr.). pap. 16.50 (ISBN 0-686-92260-3, M-8981). French & Eur.
Lexique historique de la France d'Ancien regime. Guy Cabourdin & Georges Viard. LC 79-381603. (Illus.). 324p. (Fr.). 1978. 65.00 F. A Colin.
Lexique Historique de la Grande-Bretagne XVIe. & XXe. Siecle. Roland Marx. (Illus.). 216p. (Fr.). 1976. 26.00 F. Colin.
Lexique Historique de l'Espagne XVIe. & XXe. Siecle. (Illus.). 232p. (Fr.). 1976. 26.00 F. Colin.
Lexique Historique de l'Europa Danublenne, XVIe.-XXe. Siecle. Jean Berenger. (Illus.). 256p. (Fr.). 1976. 26.00 F. Colin.
Lexique Historique de l'Italie XVIe.-XXe. Siecle. Pierre Racine. (Illus.). 384p. (Fr.). 1977. 39.00 F. Colin.
Lexique Index du Kitab de Sibawayhl. Gerard Troupeau. 268p. (Fr.). 1976. 64.00 F. Klincksieck.
Lexique Informatique. Maurice Balay. 128p. (Fr.). 1971. pap. 9.95 (ISBN 0-686-56908-3, M-6021). French & Eur.
Lexique Informatique. Maurice Balay. 128p. (Fr.). 1971. 11.00 F. Bordas-Dunod.
Lexique International De Petrographie Des Charbons. 2nd ed. 160p. (Eng. & Fr.). 1963. 32.50 (ISBN 0-686-57016-2, M-6366). French & Eur.
Lexique International de Petrographie des Charbons. 2nd ed. (Illus.). 160p. (Fr.). 1963. 67.70 F. CNRS.
Lexique International de Petrographie des Charbons. 250p. (Fr.). 1971. 67.40 F. CNRS.
Lexique International De Petrographie Des Charbon: Supplement. 250p. (Fr.). 1971. pap. 32.50 (ISBN 0-686-57017-0, M-6367). French & Eur.
Lexique International Des Termes Techniques De Theatre, en 8 Langues. Kenneth Rhae & Richard Southern. 144p. (Fr.). 125.00 (ISBN 0-686-57206-8, M-6484). French & Eur.
Lexique International des Termes Techniques de Theatre en 8 Langues. Kenneth Rhae & Richard Southern. (Illus.). 144p. (Fr.). 330.00 F. Meddens.
Lexique Latin-Francais. Edouard Sommer. 512p. (Fr.). 1967. 29.00 F. Hachette.
Lexique Latin Medieval-Francais-Anglais. J. F. Niermeyer. (Lat., Fr & Eng.). 20.00 F. Brill.
Lexique Macedonien du XV Siecle. Ciro Giannelli. 71p. (Fr.). 1958. 17.10 F. Inst Etudes Slaves.
Lexique Mathematique. 2nd ed. Jean Grignon. (Illus.). 195p. (Fr.). 1977. 5.75 F. F. I. C.
Lexique Mathematique, Symboles, Vocabulaire, Tables. Jean Grignon. (Fr.). Can.$3.30. Centre Psych.
Lexique Methodique Illustre du Machinisme Agricole, 1. (Illus., Fr.). 36.00 F. Centre Nat. & Machin Agricole.
Lexique Occitan-Francais. rev. ed. Roger Barthe. (Fr.). 1975. 23.00 F. Amis Langue.
Lexique Occitan-Francais. Roger Barthe. 240p. (Fr.). 1973. 32.00 F. Lemouzi.
Lexique Officiel des Lampes Radio. 21st ed. Louis Gaudillat. 96p. (Fr.). 1963. 20.00 F. Radio.
Lexique Officiel des lampes Radios. 21st ed. Louis Gaudilat. 96p. (Fr.). 1963. pap. 12.50 (ISBN 0-686-56766-8, M-6263). French & Eur.
Lexique Patois-Francais du Parler de Vaux-Bugey, 1919-1940, 2 vols. 508p. (Fr.). 1942. 72.00 F. Klincksieck.
Lexique Pedologique Trilingue. George Plaisance. 355p. (Fr.). 1958. pap. 22.50 (ISBN 0-686-57082-0, M-6458). French & Eur.
Lexique Pedologique Trilingue. Georges Plaisance. 355p. (Fr.). 1958. 44.00 F. CDU.
Lexique Photo-Cinema. 104p. (Fr.). 1972. 31.20 F. C. I. L. F.
Lexique Picard des Parlers Ouest-Amienois. Rene Debrie. LC 76-451761. 424p. (Fr.). 1975. write for info. Univers Picardie.
Lexique Picard du Berger. Rene Debrie. LC 78-376584. 23p. (Fr.). 1977. 10.00 F. Eklitra.
Lexique Poular-Francais: Le Poular Dialecte Peul du Fouta Senegalais. Henri Gaden. 280p. (Fr.). 1967. 16.00. Gregg.
Lexique Pratique Commercial. Centre International Du Droit Des Affaires (CIDA) (Fr.). 1973. pap. 25.00x (ISBN 2-85273-001-4). Marlin.
Lexique Pratique Francais-Arabe. Jacques Jomier & Institut Francais D'Archeologie Orientale. 231p. (Fr. & Arabic.). 1976. 35.00 F. Francais, Inst. Archeo. Orient.
Lexique Psycholologique. (Fr.). 12.00 F. Vie et Action.
Lexique Quadrilingue de la Preparation des Minerals: Allemand-Anglais-Francais-Russe. Congres International de la Preparation des Minerais. 260p. (Ger., Eng., Fr. & Rus.). 1963. 45.00 F. Ste. Industrie Minerale.
Lexique Quadrilingue Des Affaires. Ivan de Renty. 702p. (Eng., Fr., Ger. & Span.). 1977. 29.95 (ISBN 0-686-57205-X, M-6483). French & Eur.
Lexique Quadrilingue des Affaires: Anglais-Francais-Allemand-Espagnol. Ivan De Renty. 702p. (Eng., Fr., Ger. & Span.). 1977. 72.00 F. Hachette.
Lexique Quadrilinque de la Preparation des Minerais. Ed. by Congres International de la Preparation des Minerais. 260p. (Ger., Eng., Fr. & Rus., Four-Language Lexicon of Ore Preparation). 1963. pap. 25.00 (ISBN 0-686-56795-1). French & Eur.
Lexique Queze-Amharique. Makonnen Argaw. 432p. (Fr.). 1974. 65.00 F. Publ. Orientalistes France.
Lexique Soncy Francais. Jean M. Ducroz & Marie C. Charles. 282p. (Fr.). 1978. 65.00 F. Harmattan.
Lexique Stratigraphique International. (Fr. & Eng.). pap. 37.50 (ISBN 0-686-57018-9, M-6369). French & Eur.
Lexique Technique des Produits Chimiques, 2 vols. 15th ed. Jean-Claude Donadini & G. Donadini. 2140p. (Fr.). 1976. 350.00 F. Rous.
Lexique Technique des Produits Chimiques, 2 vols. 15th ed. (Fr.). 300.00 F. Officielles, Ed. Vente Publ.
Lexique Thematique des Des Descripteurs & Identificateurs. new ed. Centre de Documentatio de. 151p. (Fr.). 1976. 75.00 F. Centre Documentation.
Lexique Thematique des Descripteurs et Identificateurs. Centre De Documentation De L'Armement. 151p. (Fr.). 1976. pap. 35.00 (ISBN 0-686-56742-0, M-6371). French & Eur.
Lexique Trilingue des Termes d'usage Courant: Electrotechnique, Electronique, Acoustique, Optique, Controle. 340p. (Fr.). 1966. 72.00 F. Ste. Publications Mecaniques.
Lexique Trilingue des Termes D'Usage Courant En Electrotechnique, Electronique, Acoustique, Optique et Controle Par Ultrasons. 340p. (Fr., Trilingual Lexicon of Currently Used Terms in Electrotechnics, Electronics, Acoustics, Optics and Control by Ultra-Sound). 1966. pap. 35.00 (ISBN 0-686-56793-5, M-6373). French & Eur.
Lexique Trilinque des Termes de l'Eau. 224p. (Fr., Trilingual Lexicon of Water Terminology). 1975. pap. 29.95 (ISBN 0-686-56724-2, M-6372). French & Eur.
Lexique Trilingue des Termes d'Usage Courant En Machines Outils, les Perceuses, Pt. 2. 96p. (Fr., Trilingual Lexicon of Commonly Used Terms in Machine Tools; Drilling Tools). pap. 12.50 (ISBN 0-686-56792-7, M-6375). French & Eur.
Lexique Trillingue des Termes d'usage Courant en Machines. (Illus.). 74p. (Fr.). 1961. 21.00 F. Ste. Publications.
Lexique Trillingue des Termes d'usage Courant en Machines: Les Perceuses. 96p. (Fr.). 1963. 21.00 F. Ste. Publications Mecaniques.

Lexique Tumak-Francais Tchad. Jean P. Caprile. LC 76-459019. iv, 137p. (Eng., Tumak, & Fr.). 1975. write for info. Reimer.
Lexique Usuel d'informatique. Serge Valensi. 63p. (Fr.). 1976. 27.50 F. S. C. M.
Lexiques de Termes de Pathologie Dentaire. Jean Courtois. 74p. (Fr.). 1974. 30.00 F. Prelat.
Lexiques des Boissons Gazeuses. J. Maurais & S. Giroux. 63p. (Eng. & Fr.). 1979. pap. 4.95 (ISBN 0-686-92432-0, M-9241). French & Eur.
Lexiques Picards du Cidrier & du Meunier. Rene Debrie. 424p. (Fr.). 1977. 15.00 F. Eklitra.
Lexis: Dictionnaire De la Langue Francaise. Ed. by Jean Dubois. 2032p. (Fr.). 1975. 47.50 (ISBN 0-686-57019-7, M-6376). French & Eur.
Lexis-Dictionnaire de la langue francaise. Ed. by Jean Dubois. 1939p. (Fr.). 1975. 56.25 (ISBN 2-03-020285-1, 3924). Larousse.
Lexis-Dictionnaire de la Langue Francaise. Ed. by Jean Dubois. (Fr.). 1979. 56.25 (ISBN 0-686-60644-2, 2427). Larousse.
Lexis: Dictionnaire de la Langue Frances. Ed. by Jean Dubois. LC 76-455682. lxxix, 1950p. (Fr.). 1975. 139.00 F (ISBN 2-030-20285-1). Larousse.
Lexis Veinte-dos: Apendice Botanica. 7th ed. 280p. (Span.). 1982. pap. 600.00 ptas (ISBN 84-226-1041-8). Circulo Lect.
Lexis Veinte-dos: Apendice Botanica. 2nd ed. 288p. (Span.). 1981. pap. 550.00 ptas (ISBN 84-226-1218-6). Circulo Lect.
Lexis-Veinte-Dos: Gramatica, Lengua & Estilo. 288p. (Span.). 1980. 960.00 ptas. Biblograf.
Lexis Veinte-dos: Medicina y Salud. 7th ed. 288p. (Span.). 1982. pap. 600.00 ptas. Circulo Lect.
Lexis Veinte-dos: Sinonimos y Antonimos. 9th ed. 370p. (Span.). 1982. pap. 600.00 ptas (ISBN 84-226-1080-9). Circulo Lect.
Lexis Veinte-dos: Sinonimos y Antonimos. 7th ed. 370p. (Span.). 1981. pap. 550.00 ptas (ISBN 84-226-1080-9). Circulo Lect.
Lexix Veinte-Dos: Apendice, Botanica. 3rd ed. 288p. (Span.). 1982. pap. 600.00 ptas (ISBN 84-226-1218-6). Circulo Lect.
Librarians' Glossary & Reference Book: Of Terms Used in Librarianship Documentation & the Book Trade. L. M. Harrod. (Grafton Library Ser.). 904p. 1982. Repr. of 1977 ed. 49.95x (ISBN 0-233-96744-3). Lexington Bks.
Librarian's Practical Dictionary in Twenty-Two Languages. Z. Pipics. 386p. 1980. 90.00x (ISBN 0-686-72094-6, Pub. by Collet's). State Mutual Bk.
Librarians Practical Dictionary in 22 Languages (Worterbuch Des Bibliothekars in 22 Sprachen) 6th ed. Zoltan Pipics. LC 73-695. 1974. 64.50 (ISBN 3-7940-4109-7, Pub by Verlag Dokumentation). Bowker.
Life-Writing: A Glossary of Terms in Biography, Autobiography & Related Forms. Donald J. Winslow. (Biography Monographs). 60p. (Orig.). pap. text ed. 5.00x (ISBN 0-8248-0748-0). UH Pr.
Lilliput Dictionary. 640p. (Fr. & Eng., New York). 1.50 (102). Langenscheidt.
Lilliput Dictionary. 640p. (Span. & Eng.). 1.50 (104). Langenscheidt.
Lilliput Dictionary. 640p. (Danish & Eng.). 1.50 (106). Langenscheid-Hachette.
Lilliput Dictionary. 640p. (Dutch & Eng.). 1.50 (108). Langenscheidt.
Lilliput Dictionary. 640p. (Ital. & Eng.). 1.50 (110). Langenscheidt.
Lilliput Dictionary. 640p. (Modern Gr. & Eng.). 1.50 (114). Langenscheidt.
Lilliput Dictionary. 640p. (Port. & Eng.). 1.50 (116). Langenscheidt.
Lilliput Dictionary. 640p. (Rus. & Eng.). 1.50 (118). Langenscheidt.
Lilliput Dictionary. 640p. (Turkish & Eng.). 1.50 (122). Langenscheidt.
Lilliput Dictionary. 640p. (Eng. & Ger.). 1.50 (101). Langenscheidt.
Lilliput Dictionary. 640p. (Eng. & Fr.). 1.50 (103). Langenscheidt.
Lilliput Dictionary. 640p. (Eng. & Span.). 1.50 (105). Langenscheidt.
Lilliput Dictionary. 640p. (Eng. & Danish.). 1.50 (107). Langenscheidt.
Lilliput Dictionary. 640p. (Eng. & Dutch.). 1.50 (109). Langenscheidt.
Lilliput Dictionary. 640p. (Eng. & Ital.). 1.50 (111). Langenscheidt.
Lilliput Dictionary. 640p. (Eng. & Lat.). 1.50 (113). Langenscheidt.
Lilliput Dictionary. 640p. (Eng. & Port.). 1.50 (117). Langenscheidt.
Lilliput Dictionary. 640p. (Eng. & Turkish.). 1.50 (123). Langenscheidt.
Lilliput Dictionary: Little Webster. 640p. (Eng.). 1.50 (124). Langenscheidt.
Lilliput German-English Dictionary. 640p. (Ger. & Eng.). 1.50 (100). Langenscheidt.
Lincoln Dictionary. Abraham Lincoln. Ed. by Ralph Winn. pap. 1.45 (ISBN 0-685-19407-8, 43, WL). Citadel Pr.
L'Inconscient. Jacques Mousseau & Pierre F. Moreau. LC 77-466781. 538p. (Eng. & Fr.). 1976. 72.50 F (ISBN 2-7256-0109-6). Retz.
Linguarum Totius Orbis Vocabularia Comparativa. Peter S. Pallas. LC 78-380313. (Lat. & Rus.). 1977. DM.100.00 (ISBN 3-87118-285-0). Buske.
Linguistic Approaches to the Romance Lexicon. Ed. by Frank H. Nuessel, Jr. LC 78-12654. 123p. 1978. pap. text ed. 5.50 (ISBN 0-87840-046-X). Georgetown U Pr.
Linguistic Atlas of New England Revisited see ADS Dictionary - How Soon?.
Linguistic Concordance of Ruth & Jonah: Hebrew Vocabulary & Idiom. Francis I. Andersen & A. Dean Forbes. (Computer Bible Ser.: Vol. IX). 1976. pap. 15.00 (ISBN 0-935106-12-X). Biblical Res Assocs.
Linguistics & Bilingual Dictionaries. Ali M. Al-Kasimi. 1977. text ed. 20.50x (ISBN 90-04047-87-5). Humanities.
Linguistisches Woerterbuch. Carl Heupel. LC 79-363518. (Illus.). 161p. (Ger.). 1978. DM.12.80 (ISBN 3-423-03040-2). Deutscher Taschenbuch.
Lingvisticheskii Slovar. M. A. Denisova. 276p. (Rus.). 1978. 4.90 (Pub. by Russkii Iazyk). Four Continent.
Lingvostranovedcheskii Slovar' M. A. Denisova. (Russkii iazyk Ser.). 277p. (Rus.). 1978. 4.90 (O-119). Four Continent.
Linquarum Totius Orbis Vocabularia Comparativa, Vol. 1. Peter S. Pallas. 411p. (Rus.). 1977. Repr. of 1786 ed. lib. bdg. 49.00x (ISBN 3-87118-285-0, Pub. by Helmut Buske Verlag Hamburg). Benjamins North Am.
Linquarum Totius Orbis Vocabularia Comparativa, Vol. 2. Peter S. Pallas. 491p. (Rus.). 1978. Repr. of 1789 ed. lib. bdg. 57.00x (ISBN 3-87118-286-9, Pub. by Helmut Buske Verlag Hamburg). Benjamins North Am.
Lists of Words Occurring Frequently in the Hebrew Bible. John D. Watts. (Hebrew & Eng.). 1960. pap. 2.95 (ISBN 0-8028-1214-7). Eerdmans.
Litauisches Etymologisches Woerterbuch, Vol. 1. Ernst Fraenkel. (Lithuanian & Ger.). 1960. 152.00 (ISBN 3-533-00650-6, M-7541, Pub. by Westdeutscher Verlag/VVA). French & Eur.
Litauisches Etymologisches Woerterbuch, Vol. 2. Ernst Fraenkel. (Lithuanian & Ger.). 1965. 195.00 (ISBN 3-533-00651-4, M-7542, Pub. by Westdeutscher Verlag/VVA). French & Eur.
Lithuanian-English Dictionary. Vilius Peteraitis. (Lithuanian & Eng.). 27.50 (ISBN 0-87559-037-3); thumb indexed 31.00 (ISBN 0-87559-038-1). Shalom.
Lithuanian-English Dictionary. B. Piesarskas et al. 912p. (Lithuanian & Eng.). 1979. 8.50 (Pub. by Vilnius). Four Continent.
Lithuanian-English, English-Lithuanian Dictionary, 2 vols. B. Piesarskas & V. Baravykas. (Lithuanian & Eng.). 30.00 set (ISBN 0-685-39857-9). Heinman.
Lithuanian Reverse Dictionary. David F. Robinson. ix, 209p. (Lithuanian.). 1976. soft cover 11.95 (ISBN 0-89357-034-6). Slavica.
Litovsko-Russkii Slovar. 392p. (Rus.). 1956. 1.95 (Pub. by Gosizdat Polit. & Nauchn.Lit. SSR.). Four Continent.
Litovsko-Russkii Slovar. 893p. (Rus.). 1971. 7.95 (Pub. by Mintis). Four Continent.
Litovsko-Russko-Anglo-Nemetskii Slovar Fizicheskikh Terminov. P. Brazhdzhiunas. (Rus., Eng., Ger. & Lithuanian.). 1979. 15.95 (Pub. by Mokslas). Four Continent.
Litteraert Lekxikon. Asbjorn Aarnes. LC 77-555382. 278p. (Norwegian.). 1977. write for info. Tanum-Norli.
Little Beginner's Dictionary. Anne Anderson. 1973. Can.$pap. 5.00. U of Toronto Pr.
Little League Baseball Lingo. rev. ed. Mary Remmers. (Illus.). 64p. (gr. 2 up). 1981. pap. 2.95 (ISBN 0-88319-059-1). Hart Graphics.
Little Oxford Dictionary. 5th ed. Ed. by Julia Swannell. 1980. 8.95 (ISBN 0-19-861128-5). Oxford U Pr.
Liturgical Terms for Music Students: A Dictionary. Compiled by Dom A. Hughes. LC 70-166236. 1972. Repr. of 1940 ed. 14.00 (ISBN 0-403-01363-1). Scholarly.
Living Language Dictionaries & Manuals. (Living Language Course Ser). pap. 3.00 ea. Crown.
Living Word Vocabulary. Edgar Dale & Joseph O'Rourke. LC 81-50682. 704p. 1981. lib. bdg. 49.95 (ISBN 0-7166-3115-6). World Bk.
Load Cell Terminology & Test Procedure Recommendations. 20p. 1979. 2.50 (SM-1). Scale Mfrs.
Local Warning System Definition. B. D. Miller. LC 70-141214. 147p. 1970. 19.50 (ISBN 0-686-01960-1). Mgmt Info Serv.
Locomotive Dictionary. Ed. by George L. Fowler. (Illus.). 684p. 1972. Repr. of 1906 ed. lib. bdg. 24.95 buckram (ISBN 0-912318-20-1). N K Gregg.
Locomotives from the Nineteen Sixteen Locomotive Dictionary. Ed. by Roy V. Wright. (Train Shed Cyclopedia Ser., No. 18). (Illus.). 1974. pap. 4.95 (ISBN 0-912318-47-3). N K Gregg.
Logicheskii Slovar. N. I. Kondakov. Ed. by D. P. Gorskii. 656p. (Rus.). 1971. 11.75 (Pub. by Nauka). Four Continent.
Logos: Grand Dictionnaire de la Langue Francaise, 3 vols. Jean Girodet. LC 78-391601. xv, 3113p. (Fr.). 1978. 510.00 F (ISBN 2-040-07060-5). Bordas.
Logos-Grand Dictionnaire de la Langue Francaise, 3 vols. Ed. by Jean Girodet. 3113p. (Fr.). E110.00 set (ISBN 0-245-53130-0). Harrap.
Long Term Care & the Law. Hamline Huniversity. LC 83-135890. (Illus.). 300p. Date not set. price not set. Hamline Law.
Longman Dictionary of Business English. Ed. by J. H. Adam. 528p. 1982. 15.95 (ISBN 0-582-55558-2). Longman.
Longman Dictionary of Contemporary English. Ed. by Paul Proctor. (Illus.). 1979. text ed. 14.95x (ISBN 0-582-52571-3); pap. text ed. 11.95x (ISBN 0-582-55608-2). Longman.
Longman Dictionary of English Idioms. Laurence Urdang Associates Under the Editorial Supervision of the Longman Dictionary Department. (Illus.). 404p. 1979. 18.95 (ISBN 0-582-55524-8). Longman.
Longman Dictionary of Psychology & Psychoanalysis. Walter D. Glanze. 800p. 1983. 29.95 (ISBN 0-582-28257-8). Longman.
Longman Dictionary of the Mass Media & Communication. Tracy D. Connors. LC 82-92. (Public Communication Ser.). (Illus.). 256p. 1982. text ed. 24.95x (ISBN 0-582-28337-X); pap. text ed. 12.95x (ISBN 0-582-28336-1). Longman.
Longman's Modern English Dictionary. 2nd ed. Ed. by Owen Watson. LC 77-368512. (Illus.). xv, 1286p. (Eng.). 1976. E5.50 (ISBN 0-582-55512-4). Longman England.
Look & Learn Spanish. Francisco Ibarra. (Span.). 1.50. Camino Real.
Los Sufijos Posesivos en el Quechua del Huallaga. David J. Weber. LC 77-579192. 61p. (Quechua & Span.). 1976. write for info. Inst Ling Ver.
Lover's Dictionary: How to Be Amorous in Five Delectable Languages. 1981. pap. 4.95 (ISBN 0-686-29648-6). Natl Textbk.
Low German in Mexico see Use of the Dictionary of American English & the Dictionary of Americanisms.
Low-Income Glossary. 0.15 ea. (SL3638). BSA.
Lucky Number Lottery Guide. (Illus.). 240p. 1982. pap. 2.95 (ISBN 0-87637-370-8). Hse of Collectibles.
Luftartsteknisk Ordbog Engelsk-Dansk. H. Bach & J. Florant. 255p. (Eng. & Danish.). 1968. 35.00 (ISBN 0-686-92484-3, M-1280). French & Eur.
Luftfahrtechisches Worterbuch, Deutsch-English. Ed. by H. L. Darcy. (Dictionary of Aviation Ser.). 312p. (Ger. & Eng.). 1960. 33.50 (ISBN 3-11-000723-1, M-7545, Pub. by Walter de Gruyter, Inc.). French & Eur.
Luganda-English Dictionary. (Luganda & Eng.). 35.00. Iaconi.
Luganda-English Dictionary. John D. Murphy. (Publications in the Languages of Africa Ser.: No. 2). (Luganda & Eng.). 1973. 36.95 (ISBN 0-8132-0525-5). Cath U Pr.
Lumko English-Xhosa Dictionary. A. Fischer. (Eng. & Khosa.). 1982. 39.95x (ISBN 0-19-570290-5). Oxford U Pr.
Lydisches Woerterbuch. Roberto Gusmani. (Ger.). 1964. 49.95 (ISBN 3-533-00655-7, M-7546, Pub. by Carl Winter). French & Eur.
Lydisches Woerterbuch. Roberto Gusmani. (Ger.). 1964. 49.95 (ISBN 3-533-00655-7). Winter Univ.

M

McGraw-Hill Dictionary of Modern Economics. 3rd ed. Douglas Greenwald et al. (Illus.). 656p. 1983. 49.95 (ISBN 0-07-024376-X, P&RB). McGraw.
McGraw Hill Dictionary of Scientific & Technical Terms. 3rd ed. McGraw Hill. Ed. by Sybil P. Parker. 1860p. 1983. 70.00 (ISBN 0-07-045269-5, Pub by P & RB). McGraw.
McGraw-Hill Vocabulary, Bk. 1. 2nd ed. Gene Stanford. Ed. by Hester E. Weeden. (Illus.). 128p. (gr. 7-12). 1981. pap. text ed. 5.28 (ISBN 0-07-060771-0). McGraw.
McGraw-Hill Vocabulary, Bk. 2. 2nd ed. Gene Stanford. (Illus.). 128p. 1981. pap. text ed. 5.28 (ISBN 0-07-060772-9). McGraw.
McGraw-Hill Vocabulary, Bk. 3. 2nd ed. Gene Stanford. (Illus.). 128p. 1981. pap. text ed. 5.28 (ISBN 0-07-060773-7). McGraw.
McGraw-Hill Vocabulary, Bk. 5. 2nd ed. W. J. Stanford. (McGraw-Hill Vocabulary Ser.). 1982. 5.28 (ISBN 0-07-060775-3). McGraw.
McGraw-Hill Vocabulary, Bk. 6. 2nd ed. G. Stanford. 1981. 5.28 (ISBN 0-07-060776-1). McGraw.
Machine Knitter's Dictionary. Linda Gartshore. (Illus.). 192p. 1983. pap. 9.95 (ISBN 0-312-50221-4). St Martin.

Machine Tools Dictionary: English-French-German-Arabic. A. M. Abd-El-Wahed. 334p. (Eng., Fr., Ger. & Arabic.). 1977. 45.00 (ISBN 0-686-92135-6, M-9757). French & Eur.

McKay's Modern English-Swedish, Swedish-English Dictionary. Ruben Nojd & Astrid Tornberg. 470p. (Eng. & Swedish.). 9.95. Imported Bks.

McKay's Modern Norwegian-English & English-Norwegian Dictionary. Ed. by B. Berulfsen & H. Scavenius. (Modern Dictionaries Ser.). (Norwegian & Eng.). 1953. 14.95 (ISBN 0-679-10076-8). McKay.

McKay's Modern Portuguese-English & English-Portuguese Dictionary. Ed. by Elbert L. Richardson et al. (Modern Dictionaries). (Port. & Eng.). 1943. 10.95 (ISBN 0-679-10077-6). McKay.

McKay's Modern Portuguese-English, English-Portuguese Dictionary. Richardson & Pereira. 347p. (Port. & Eng.). 1976. 11.00. Imported Bks.

McKay's Modern Swedish-English & English-Swedish Dictionary. Astrid Tornberg et al. (Modern Dictionaries Ser.). (Swedish & Eng.). 1954. 9.95 (ISBN 0-679-10079-2). McKay.

McMaster Glossary of Fortran Seventy-Seven. Fleming-Redish. 64p. 1983. pap. text ed. 3.95 (ISBN 0-8403-3052-9). Kendall-Hunt.

Macmillan Colour Dictionary. J. Bevington. (Illus.). write for info. (ISBN 0-333-28859-9). Macmillan.

Macmillan Concise Dictionary of World History. Bruce Wetterau. 672p. 1983. 39.95 (ISBN 0-02-626110-3). Macmillan.

Macmillan Contemporary Dictionary. (Illus.). 1979. pap. 6.95 (ISBN 0-686-65754-3). Macmillan.

Macmillan Dictionary. (Illus. & Eng.). write for info. Macmillan London.

Macmillan Dictionary. Macmillan Pub. Co. 1973. 8.40 (ISBN 0-02-195000-8). Macmillan.

Macmillan Dictionary for Children. LC 81-13651. 756p. 1982. 12.95 (ISBN 0-02-578790-X). Macmillan.

Macmillan Dictionary for Children. rev. ed. (Illus.). (gr. 2 up). 1977. 12.95 (ISBN 0-02-578750-0). Macmillan.

Macmillan Dictionary of Archaeology. Ed. by Ruth Whitehouse. 608p. 1983. E19.95 (ISBN 0-333-27190-4). Macmillan.

Macmillan Dictionary of Australian Politics. Dean Jaensch & Max E. Teichmann. LC 81-461270. 264p. 1979. pap. write for info. (ISBN 0-333-29883-7). Macmillan Aust.

Macmillan Dictionary of Modern Economics. D. W. Pearce. 450p. (Eng.). 1981. E14.95 (ISBN 0-333-26962-4). Macmillan London.

Macmillan Encyclopedic Dictionary of Numismatics. Richard G. Doty. LC 81-18632. (Illus.). 416p. 1982. 34.95 (ISBN 0-02-532270-2). Macmillan.

Macmillan Lensing New Basic Dictionary. Friedrich Pollmann. LC 78-302181. (Illus.). viii, 247p. 1976. E1.00 (ISBN 0-333-21213-4). Macmillan London.

Macmillan New Dictionary. (Illus.). 1979. pap. 6.95 (ISBN 0-686-67747-1, Collier). Macmillan.

Macmillan Picture Wordbook. Kathleen N. Daly. LC 82-6619. (Illus.). 80p. (ps-1). 1982. 7.95 (ISBN 0-02-725600-6). Macmillan.

Macmillan School Dictionary. Macmillan Pub. Co. 1974. 7.00 (ISBN 0-02-195050-4). Macmillan.

Macmillan School Dictionary. (Illus., Eng.). 1981. write for info. Macmillan London.

Macmillan School Dictonary. (Illus., Eng.). 1981. write for info. Macmillan London.

Macmillan Very First Dictionary: A Magic World of Words. LC 82-22901. (Illus.). 280p. (ps-2). 1983. 10.95 (ISBN 0-02-761730-0). Macmillan.

Magic World of Words: The New Macmillan Very First Dictionary. 2nd ed. (Illus.). (gr. 4-7). 1980. 8.95 (ISBN 0-02-578980-5). Macmillan.

Magnetic Video Tape Recording Glossary. Society of Motion Picture & Television Engineers. 1p. free. Soc Motion Pic & TV Engrs.

Magyar-Angol Muszaki Szotar. Erno Nagy & Janos Klar. LC 77-467592. 752p. (Eng. & Hungarian.). 1975. 300.00 Ft (ISBN 9-6305-0607-6). Akademiai Kiado.

Magyar-Angol Szotar, Hungarian-English Dictionary. rev. ed. Ed. by L. Orszagh. (Hungarian & Eng.). 29.50 (ISBN 0-87557-042-9, 042-9). Saphrograph.

Magyar-Bolgar Szotar. Jozsef Bodey. LC 77-474283. 584p. (Hungarian & Bulgarian.). 1975. 35.00 Ft (ISBN 9-6320-5050-9). Terra.

Magyar-Bolgar Szotar. Jozsef Bodey. LC 77-474283. 584p. (Hungarian & Bulgarian.). 1975. 35.00 Ft (ISBN 9-6320-5050-9). Terra.

Magyar Ertelmezo Keziszotar. Jozsef Juhasz. LC 76-532553. xv, 1550p. (Hungarian.). 1975. 260.00 Ft (ISBN 963-05-0731-5). Akademiai Kiado.

Magyar Ertelmezo Keziszotar. Ed. by Jozsef Juhasz et al. LC 76-532553. (Illus.). xv, 1550p. (Hungarian.). 1975. 260.00 Ft (ISBN 9-63050-731-5). Akademiai Kiado.

Magyar-Francia Szotar, 2 vols. Sandor Eckhardt. LC 79-337569. xvi, 2558p. (Fr. & Hungarian.). 1978. 500.00 Ft (ISBN 9-6305-1297-1). Akademiai Kiado.

Magyar-Francia Szotar, 2 vols. 2nd ed. Sandor Eckhardt. LC 79-337569. xvi, 2558p. (Hungarian & Fr.). 1978. 500.00 Ft (ISBN 9-63051-297-1). Akademiai Kiado.

Magyar-Lengyel Szotar. Istvan Varsanyi. LC 77-457358. 928p. (Hungarian & Pol.). 1976. 35.00 Ft (ISBN 9-6320-5049-5). Terra.

Magyar-Lengyel Szotar. Istvan Varsanyi. LC 77-457358. 928p. (Hungarian & Pol.). 1976. 35.00 Ft (ISBN 9-63205-049-5). Terra.

Magyar Neprajzi Lexikon. Ed. by Gyula Ortutay. LC 77-569808. (Illus., Hungarian.). 1977. 187.00 Ft (ISBN 9-630-51285-8). Akademiai Kiado.

Magyar-Olasz Szotar. Gyula Herczeg. LC 78-397749. 768p. (Ital. & Hungarian.). 1978. 35.00 Ft (ISBN 9-6320-5072-X). Terra.

Magyar-Olasz Szotar. 5th ed. Gyula Herczeg. LC 78-397749. 768p. (Hungarian & Ital.). 1978. 35.00 Ft (ISBN 9-63205-072-X). Terra.

Magyar-Orosz Katonai Szotar. A Szotarszerk Bizottsag Vezetoje Toth Lajos. LC 78-377454. 1177p. (Hungarian & Rus.). 1977. 355.00 Ft (ISBN 9-6305-1022-7). Akademiai Kiado.

Magyar-Orosz Kez Iszotar. Laszlo Hadrovics et al. LC 79-339814. 712p. (Hungarian & Rus.). 1978. 100.00 Ft (ISBN 9-6305-1532-6). Akademiai Kiado.

Magyar-Orosz Keziszotar. 4th ed. Laszlo Hadrovics & Galdi Hadrovics. LC 79-339814. 712p. (Hungarian & Rus.). 1978. 100.00 Ft (ISBN 9-63051-532-6). Akademiai Kiado.

Magyar-Orosz Muszaki Szotar, 2 vols. Lorant Katona. LC 76-504224. 1513p. (Hungarian & Rus.). 1975. 490.00 Ft (ISBN 963-05-0723-4). Akademiai Kiado.

Magyar-Szerbhorvat Szotar. Laszlo Hadrovics. LC 76-533581. 655p. (Hungarian & Serbo-Croatian.). 1976. 26.00 Ft (ISBN 9-63205-042-8). Terra.

Magyar-Szerbhorvat Szotar. Laszlo Hadrovics et al. LC 76-533581. 655p. (Hungarian & Serbo-Croatian.). 1976. 26.00 Ft (ISBN 963-205-042-8). Terra.

Magyar Szinonimaszotar. Gabor O. Nagy et al. LC 78-397301. 593p. (Hungarian.). 1978. 147.00 Ft (ISBN 9-6305-1607-1). Akademiai Kiado.

Magyar Tajszotar. Magyar Tudomanyos Akademia Nyelvtudomany Intezeteben. Ed. by Eva B. Lorinczy. LC 80-480571. (Hungarian.). 1979. 207.00 Ft (ISBN 9-63051-810-4). Akademiai Kiado.

Malaiziisko-Russko-Angliiskii Slovar. Ed. by N. V. Rott. 400p. (Malay, Rus. & Eng.). 1977. 7.75 (Pub. by Russkii Iazyk). Four Continent.

Malas Hierbas, Diccionario Clasificatorio Ilustrado. Francisco Guell. 224p. (Span. & Lat.). 1970. pap. 18.75 (ISBN 84-281-0132-9, S-50018). French & Eur.

Malay-English Dictionary. William Marsden. (Eng. & Malayian.). 1976. Repr. of 1958 ed. 92.00 (ISBN 0-518-19003-X). Ayer Co.

Maly Divadelni Slovnik. Vaclav Muller. LC 77-553272. 132p. (Czech). 1977. write for info. Kultura.

Maly Slownik Antropologiczny. Ed. by Tadeusz Bielecki. LC 77-500992. (Illus.). 511p. (Pol.). 1976. 100.00 Zl. Wiedza Powszechna.

Maly Slownik Finsko-Polski & Polski-Finski. Elsa Salamaa. LC 76-503222. 106p. (Finnish & Pol.). 1975. Fmk.26.00 (ISBN 9-51261-007-8). Kirjayhtyma.

Maly Slownik Francusko-Polski. Ludwik Szwykowski et al. LC 77-578114. xxviii, 326p. (Fr. & Pol.). 1977. 110.00 Zl. Wiedza Powszechna.

Maly Slownik Hispansko-Polski & Polsko-Hiszpanski. 3rd. ed. Antonio Marti Marca et al. LC 77-502213. 289p. (Pol. & Span.). 1977. 100.00 Zl. Wiedza Powszechna.

Maly Slownik Kultury Antycznej. Lida Winniczuk. LC 76-523030. (Illus.). 674p. (Pol.). 1976. 110.00 Zl. Wiedza Powszechna.

Maly Slownik Polsko-Swedzki. Lech Sikorski. 322p. (Pol. & Swedish.). 1976. 55.00 Zl. Plastik.

Maly Slownik Szwedzko-Polski. Lech Sikorski. LC 76-525326. xxvi, 300p. (Swedish & Pol.). 1976. write for info. Wiedza Powszechna.

Maly Slownik Techniczny Niemiecko i Polski-Niemiecki. M. Sokolowska & J. Szarski. LC 75-410285. 155p. (Ger. & Pol.). 1975. write for info. Wydawnictwa Naukowo.

Maly Slownik Wlosko-Polski, 2 vols. Stanislaw Soja et al. LC 77-562532. (Ital. & Pol.). 1977. 130.00 Zl. Wiedza Powszechna.

Maly Slownik Wlosko-Polski & Polsko-Wloski, 2 vols. 3rd ed. Stanislaw Soja et al. LC 77-562532. (Pol. & Ital.). 1977. 130.00 Zl. Wiedza Powszechna.

Maly Slownik Zoologiczny. Kazlmierz Kowalski. LC 76-521216. 454p. (Pol.). 1975. write for info. Wiedza Powszechna.

Maly Starocesky Slovnik. Jaromir Belic & Adolf Kamis. LC 79-399115. 707p. (Czech., Prague). 1979. 43.00 Kcs. S. P. N.

Mammalian Proteases: a Glossary & Bibliography: Vol. 1: Endopeptidases. Alan Barrett & J. Ken McDonald. 1980. 32.00 (ISBN 0-12-079501-9). Acad Pr.

Mammalian Proteases: A Glossary & Bibliography: Vol. 2, Exopeptidases. A. J. Barrett. Ed. by J. K. McDonald. 1982. write for info. (ISBN 0-12-079502-7). Acad Pr.

Mammals: Their Latin Names Explained. A. F. Gotch. (Illus.). 1979. 18.95 (ISBN 0-7137-0939-1, Pub. by Blandford Pr England). Sterling.

Managalasi Language: Managalasi Dictionary. Jim Parlier & Jaki Parlier. LC 82-130942. viii, 504p. (Eng. & Managalasi.). 1981. pap. write for info (ISBN 0-7263-0761-0). Summer Inst Abor.

Management Dictionary. (Ger. & Eng.). 1978. 4th ed. 26.00 (ISBN 3-11-004863-9); 5th ed. 29.25x (ISBN 3-11-007708-6). De Gruyter.

Management Dictionary. 5th rev. enl. ed. Werner Sommer & Hanns-Martin Schoenfeld. 621p. 1979. text ed. 34.25x (ISBN 0-686-77467-1). De Gruyter.

Management Dictionary: Fachwoerterbuch fuer Betriebswirtschaft, Wirtschafts und Steuerrecht und Datenverarbeitung. 4th ed. Werner Sommer & Hans-Martin Schoenfeld. LC 78-190431. (English-Deutsch). 328p. (Eng. & Ger.). 1972. 17.75x (ISBN 3-11-001981-7). De Gruyter.

Management Glossary: (English-Arabic) H. Johannsen. 238p. (Eng. & Arabic.). 1972. 16.00x (ISBN 0-86685-069-4). Intl Bk Ctr.

Management-Taschenlexikon. Peter Haas. LC 80-477370. (Illus.). 189p. (Ger.). 1978. DM.9.80. Verlag Moderne Industrie.

Management Terminology: English-Spanish & Spanish-English. Victor H. Bolado. 192p. (Eng. & Span.). 1981. 9.95 (ISBN 0-89962-034-5). Todd & Honeywell.

Mangled Medicine Definitions We Doubt You Learned in School. Teitelbaum & Johnson. (Medical Economics Books). 1972. 4.50 (ISBN 0-442-84017-9). Van Nos Reinhold.

Manipulus Vocabulorum. Peter Levens. (Camden Society, London. Publications, First Series: No. 95). Repr. of 1867 ed. 28.00 (ISBN 0-404-50195-8). AMS Pr.

Manobo-English Dictionary. Richard E. Elkins. LC 68-63364. (Oceanic Linguistics Special Publications: No. 3). 376p. (Manobo & Eng.). 1968. pap. text ed. 10.00x (ISBN 0-87022-225-2). UH Pr.

Manual del Automovil en 5 Idiomas: Diccionario Idiomatico del Automovil. Equipo Reactor de Ceac. 240p. (Span., Fr., Eng., It. & Ger.). 1974. 8.50 (ISBN 84-329-1403-7, S-50224). French & Eur.

Manual for Bilingual Dictionaries, 3 vols. Dow F. Robinson. 1969. o. p. 5.00 (ISBN 0-685-40975-9); Set. microfiche 9.00; Vol. I. microfiche 3.00 (ISBN 0-88312-327-4); Vol. II. microfiche 3.00 (ISBN 0-88312-328-2); Vol. III. microfiche 3.00 (ISBN 0-88312-329-0). Summer Inst Ling.

Manual of English Meters. Joseph Malof. LC 78-823. 1978. Repr. of 1970 ed. lib. bdg. 24.25 (ISBN 0-313-20293-1, MAMEM). Greenwood.

Manual of Manuscript Transcription for the Dictionary of the Old Spanish Language. 2nd ed. David Mackenzie. (Illus.). 128p. (Span.). 1981. pap. 15.00 (ISBN 0-942260-15-5). Hispanic Seminary.

Manual of Opthalmic Terminology. Harold A. Stein et al. LC 81-14136. (Illus.). 269p. 1982. pap. text ed. 18.95 (ISBN 0-8016-4769-X). Mosby.

Manual of Orthopaedic Terminology. 2nd ed. Carolyn T. Blauvelt & Fred Nelson. LC 81-4029. (Illus.). 257p. 1981. pap. text ed. 23.95 (ISBN 0-8016-0752-3). Mosby.

Manual of the Terminology of Public International Law & International Organizations. I. Paenson. (Fr. & Span. & Rus. & Eng.). 110.00 (ISBN 90-65-44052-6). Kluwer Academic.

Manual on Terminology & Classification in Mental Retardation. 3rd ed. Ed. by Herbert J. Grossman. LC 77-87576. 1977. 14.85x (ISBN 0-686-23878-8). Am Assn Mental.

Manuel Alphabetique De Psychiatrie Clinique et Therapeutique. 5th ed. Ed. by Antoine Porot. 679p. (Fr.). 1975. 65.00 (ISBN 0-686-57031-6, M-6391). French & Eur.

Manuel De Gramatica Comercial. A. Lugo-Guernelli et al. 204p. (Eng. & Span.). 1976. pap. 9.95 (ISBN 84-7119-018-4, S-50369). French & Eur.

March's Thesaurus & Dictionary of the English Language. 2nd ed. Francis March et al. LC 79-92443. 1324p. 1980. 19.95 (ISBN 0-89659-107-7); pap. 10.95 (ISBN 0-89659-161-1). Abbeville Pr.

Marihuana Dictionary: Words, Terms, Events & Persons Relating to Cannabis. Ernest L. Abel. LC 81-13427. xi, 136p. 1982. lib. bdg. 25.00 (ISBN 0-313-23252-0, ABM/). Greenwood.

Maritime Dictionary. Kulno Olev. 560p. (Eng., Estonian & Rus.). 1981. 39.00x (ISBN 0-686-44731-X, Pub. by Collets). State Mutual Bk.

Mark Twain's Vocabulary. Frances G. Emberson. 1978. Repr. of 1935 ed. lib. bdg. 10.00 (ISBN 0-8495-1316-2). Arden Lib.

Mark Twain's Vocabulary. Frances G. Emberson. 53p. 1980. Repr. of 1935 ed. lib. bdg. 12.50 (ISBN 0-89987-206-9). Darby Bks.

Mark Twain's Vocabulary. Frances G. Emberson. LC 73-16345. 1935. lib. bdg. 15.00 (ISBN 0-8414-3922-2). Folcroft.

Marshallese-English Dictionary. Takaji Abo et al. LC 76-26156. (PALI Language Texts-Micronesia). 624p. (Marshallese & Eng.). 1976. pap. text ed. 12.50x (ISBN 0-8248-0457-0). UH Pr.

Martial Arts Language. Amy Shapiro. LC 77-12635. 1978. lib. bdg. 12.90 (ISBN 0-89471-015-X); pap. 2.95 (ISBN 0-89471-014-1). Running Pr.

Martyrology Pronouncing Dictionary. Anthony I. Russo-Alesi. LC 79-167151. 1973. Repr. of 1939 ed. 30.00x (ISBN 0-8103-3272-8). Gale.

Marx-Engels Dictionary. James Russell. LC 80-786. (Illus.). xxv, 140p. 1981. lib. bdg. 22.50x (ISBN 0-313-22035-2, RME/). Greenwood.

Marxist Glossary. L. Harry Gould. 99p. 1980. pap. text ed. 2.95 (ISBN 0-89380-018-X). Proletarian Pubs.

Marxistisch-Leninistisches Woerterbuch der Philosophie, 3 vols. G. Klaus & M. Buhr. 1280p. (Ger.). 1972. 21.50 (ISBN 3-499-16155-9, M-7550, Pub. by Rowohlt). French & Eur.

Marxistisch-Leninistisches Woerterbuch der Philosophie, 3 vols. G. Klaus & M. Buhr. 1280p. (Ger.). 1972. 21.50 (ISBN 3-499-16155-9). Rowohlt.

MASA: Medical Acronyms, Symbols & Abbreviations. Barbara Guidos & Betty Hamilton. 200p. 1983. lib. bdg. 39.95 (ISBN 0-918212-72-3). Neal-Schuman.

Masarykuv Slovnik Naucny, 7 vols. (Bohemian.). 1925-1933. Set. 435.00 (ISBN 0-8277-3050-0). Pergamon.

Masonry Glossary. International Masonry Institute. 100p. 1981. 12.95 (ISBN 0-8436-0134-5). CBI Pub.

Mass Communications Dictionary. Ed. by Howard B. Jacobson. LC 60-53157. 1961. 6.00 (ISBN 0-8022-0785-5). Philos Lib.

Mass Communications Dictionary: A Reference Work of Common Terminologies for Press, Print, Broadcast, Film, Advertising & Communications Research. Ed. by Howard B. Jacobson. Repr. of 1961 ed. lib. bdg. 25.00x (ISBN 0-8371-2124-8, JAMC). Greenwood.

Massada English-Hebrew Student Dictionary. Reuben Alcalay. 734p. (Eng. & Hebrew). 1980. Repr. 18.95 (ISBN 0-89961-006-4). SBS Pub.

Massada Student Dictionary English-Hebrew. Rueben ALcalay. 736p. (Eng. & Hebrew). 1978. IL.13.00 (002198). Massada Pr.

Master Crossword Puzzle Dictionary. Herbert M. Baus. LC 79-7681. 1981. 24.95 (ISBN 0-385-15118-7). Doubleday.

Master Crossword Puzzle Dictionary: The Unabridged Wordbank. Herbert M. Baus. LC 79-7681. (Eng.). 1981. write for info. (ISBN 0-385-17515-9). Doubleday.

Mastering Spanish Verbs. Julio I. Andujar. (Span.). 2.25. Camino Real.

Material Towards the Compilation of a Concise Old Church Slavonic-English Dictionary. T. Lysaght. LC 79-322674. xiv, 472p. (Eng. & Slavic.). 1978. write for info. (ISBN 0-7055-0668-1). Victoria University Press.

Material Towards the Compilation of a Concise Old Church Slavonic-English Dictionary. T. A. Lysaght. LC 79-322674. xiv, 472p. (Slavic & Eng.). 1978. write for info. (ISBN 0-7055-0668-1). Price Milburn.

Materials for an Oirat-Mongolian to English Citation Dictionary, Pt. 1. John R. Krueger. (Eng. & Oirat-Mongolian.). 1978. pap. 10.00 (ISBN 0-910980-42-X). Mongolia.

Materialy Frazeologicheskogo Slovaria Russkogo Iazka XVIII Veka. M. F. Palevskaia. 368p. (Rus.). 1980. 9.25 (Pub. by Shtiintsa). Four Continent.

Mathematics Dictionary. 4th ed. Glenn James. LC 76-233. vii, 509p. (Eng., Fr., Ger., Rus. & Span.). 1976. write for info. (ISBN 0-442-24091-0). Van Nos Reinhold.

Mathematics Illustrated Dictionary: Facts, Figures & People, Including the New Math. Jeanne Bendick & Marcia Levin. (Illus.). (gr. 7 up). 1972. 8.95 (ISBN 0-07-004460-0, GB). McGraw.

Mathematik Englisch-Deutsch-Franzoesisch-Russisch. Ralf Sube & Gunther Eisenreich. 1440p. (Eng., Ger., Fr. & Ger.). 1982. M.info. 140.00for. VEB Technik.

Mathematik I: Ein Lexikon zur Schulmathematik Sekundarstufe. Harald Scheid et al. (Illus.). 539p. (Ger.). 1981. DM.19.80 (ISBN 3-411-01912-3). Biblio Inst.

Mathematik II: Ein Lexikon zur Schulmathematik Sekundarstufe II. Harald Scheid et al. (Illus.). 468p. (Ger.). 1982. DM.19.80 (ISBN 3-411-01959-X). Biblio Inst.

Mathematisch-Naturwissenschaftliches Woerterbuch Deutsch-Dari. Guenter Rack. 652p. (Ger. & Dari.). 1977. DM.78.00 (ISBN 3-87276-178-1). Groos Verlag.

Mathematisches Vokabular. 4th ed. Berthold Klaften. (Eng. & Ger., Vocabulary of Mathematics). 1971. 13.50 (ISBN 0-686-56630-0, M-7551, Pub. by Wila). French & Eur.

Mayan Language Dictionary. Robert W. Blair et al. LC 81-43356. 491p. 1982. lib. bdg. 83.00 (ISBN 0-8240-9277-5). Garland Pub.

MBA's Dictionary. Daniel Oran & Jay M. Shafritz. LC 83-4524. 448p. 1983. 26.95 (ISBN 0-8359-4146-9); pap. 15.95 (ISBN 0-8359-4145-0). P-H.

Media Law Dictionary. John Murray. LC 78-63257. 1978. pap. text ed. 8.00 (ISBN 0-8191-0616-X). U Pr of Amer.

Medical & Health Sciences Word Book. 2nd ed. 1982. 6.95 (ISBN 0-395-25409-4). HM.

Medical & Health Sciences Word Book. 2nd ed. 1982. 8.95 (ISBN 0-395-32941-8). HM.

Medical & Technical Terminology. Joseph Tebben. 1975. pap. text ed. 4.50 (ISBN 0-88429-013-1). Collegiate Pub.

Medical-Dental Terminology: Syllabus. 2nd ed. LeGrand H. Woolley. 1974. pap. text ed. 6.10 (ISBN 0-89420-003-8, 217705); cassette recordings 177.70 (ISBN 0-89420-162-X, 196700). Natl Book.

Medical Dictionary. pap. 1.99 (ISBN 0-686-00474-4). Dennison.

Medical Dictionary. D. W. Unseld. (Ger. & Eng.). 1982. 39.50 (ISBN 3-8047-0661-4). Adler.

Medical Dictionary. B. Zoltnicki. (Eng., Rus., Fr., Ger., Lat. & Pol.). 1973. 92.50 (ISBN 3-7945-0324-4, M-7552, Pub. by Schattauer). French & Eur.

Medical Dictionary for the Lay Person. Chapman. 1983. pap. 5.95 (ISBN 0-8120-2247-5). Barron.

Medical Dictionary of the English & German Languages. Dieter W. Unseld. LC 80-465175. 520p. (Eng. & Ger.). 1978. DM.42.00 (ISBN 3-8047-0567-7). Wissenschaftliche.

Medical Dictionary of the English & German Languages: Medizinisches Worterbuch der Deutschen und Englischen Sprache. 8th ed. Dieter Unseld. 593p. (Eng. & Ger.). 1982. 30.00x (ISBN 0-686-43337-8). Intl Pubns Serv.

Medical English-Arabic Dictionary. Jusuf Hitti. (Illus.). 1973. 35.00x (ISBN 0-86685-067-8). Intl Bk Ctr.

Medical Group Practice Terminology with Accompanying Definitions. Center for Research in Ambulatory Health Care Administration. LC 81-65571. 58p. (Orig.). 1981. pap. 15.00 three ring binder (ISBN 0-933948-09-3). Med Group Mgmt.

Medical Hieroglyphs. Avice H. Kerr. LC 75-131216. 1970. 14.75 (ISBN 0-918558-01-8). Enterprise Calif.

Medical Latin. Carolyn D. Lewis. (Lat.). (YA) (gr. 12). 6.00x (ISBN 0-8338-0040-X). M Jones.

Medical Sex Dictionary. Wm. J. Robinson. 160p. pap. 0.25. Truth Seeker.

Medical Sign Language: Easily Understood Definitions of Commonly Used Medical, Dental & First Aid Terms. W. Joseph Garcia. (Illus.). 726p. 1983. 54.50x (ISBN 0-398-04805-3); pap. 43.75x spiral (ISBN 0-398-04806-1). C C Thomas.

Medical Spanish. Gail Bongiovanni. (Span.). 1977. pap. text ed. 12.95 (ISBN 0-07-006470-9, HP). McGraw.

Medical Terminology. 4th ed. G. L. Smith & P. E. Davis. LC 80-17970. 325p. 1981. pap. 16.95 (ISBN 0-471-05827-0, Pub. by Wiley Med); material 1.95 supplementary (ISBN 0-471-09071-9). Wiley.

Medical Terminology: A Systems Approach. Barbara A. Gylys & Mary E. Wedding. LC 82-12927. (Illus.). 421p. 1983. pap. text ed. 14.95 (ISBN 0-8036-4492-2). Davis Co.

Medical Terminology: A Text-Workbook. Alice Prendergast. LC 76-62907. 1977. pap. text ed. 13.95 (ISBN 0-201-05966-5, Med-Nurse); instr's man. 9.95 (ISBN 0-201-05967-3). A-W.

Medical Terminology: Exercise in Etymology. Charles W. Dunmore & Rita M. Fleischer. 327p. 1977. pap. text ed. 13.95x (ISBN 0-8036-2945-1). Davis Co.

Medical Terminology for Medical Students. William B. Tyrrell. (Illus.). 176p. 1979. 16.00x (ISBN 0-398-03810-4). C C Thomas.

Medical Terminology Made Easy. 2nd ed. Jeharned. 352p. 1968. text ed. 9.00 (ISBN 0-917036-06-9). Physicians Rec.

Medical Terminology Outline: 1980. American Medical Record Association. 68p. 6.00 (3003A). Am Med Record Assn.

Medical Terms Simplified. Wilson Stegeman. LC 75-12977. (Illus.). 305p. 1975. pap. text ed. 13.95 (ISBN 0-8299-0062-4). West Pub.

Medical Word Building. Parke, Davis & Company. (Medical Economics Books). 1970. 6.50 (ISBN 0-442-84015-2). Van Nos Reinhold.

Medicinski Leksikon. Kostic. 917p. (Serbocroatian.). 1981. leatherette 95.00 (ISBN 0-686-92458-4, M-9706). French & Eur.

Medizinische Fachsprache Verstandlich Gemacht. Eduard Strauss. LC 77-562960. 92p. (Ger.). 1975. DM.5.70 (ISBN 3-87240-041-X). Froehlich Verlag.

Medizinisches Woerterbuch. Urban Kaps. (Ger.). pap. 7.50 (ISBN 0-686-56632-7, M-7555, Pub. by Bruno Wilkens). French & Eur.

Medizinisches Woerterbuch. 5th rev. ed. E. Veillon & A. Nobel. 1330p. (Ger., Fr. & Eng., Medical Dictionary). 1969. 105.00 (ISBN 3-456-00200-9, M-7554, Pub. by H. Huber). French & Eur.

Medizinisches Woerterbuch. 5th & rev. ed. E. Veillon & A. Nobel. 1330p. (Ger., Fr. & Eng.). 1969. 105.00 (ISBN 3-456-00200-9). Huber.

Medizinisches Woerterbuch der Deutschen und Englischen Sprache. 6th rev. ed. D. Unseld. 519p. (Eng. & Ger., Medical Dictionary of the German and English Language). 1971. 33.50 (ISBN 3-8047-0415-8, M-7556, Pub. by Wissenschaftlicher Vlg.). French & Eur.

Medizintechnik. Albert Von Roald & Harry Hahnewald. LC 79-359051. 596p. (Eng., Fr., Rus., Span. & Pol.). 1978. M.55.00. VEB Verlag Technik.

Medizintechnik-Englisch-Deutsch-Franzoesisch-Russisch-Spanisch-Polnisch-Ungarisch-Slowakisch. Roald Albert & Harry Hahnewald. 596p. (Eng., Ger., Fr., Rus., Span., Pol., Hungarian & Slavic.). 1980. M.55.00. VEB Technik.

Meenakshi Hindi-English Dictionary. (Hindi & Eng.). 1981. 13.50x (ISBN 0-8364-0790-3, Pub. by Meenakshi). South Asia Bks.

Megiddo Modern Dictionary: English-Hebrew, Hebrew-English, 3 Vols. Ed. by Edward A. Levenston & Reuban Sivan. (Eng. & Hebrew.). 1983. 75.00 (ISBN 0-686-43009-3, Carta Maps & Guides Pub Israel). Hippocrene Bks.

Megiddo Modern Dictionary: English-Hebrew, Hebrew-English, 3 Vols. Ed. by Edward A. Levenston & Reuban Sivan. (Hebrew & Eng.). 1983. 75.00 (ISBN 0-686-43009-3). Carta Pub Co.

Megiddo Modern Dictionary: English-Hebrew to Hebrew-English, 2 Vols. 2000p. (Eng. & Hebrew.). 1982. lib. bdg. 125.00 (ISBN 0-686-97939-7, M-9904). French & Eur.

Mein Allerschoenstes Woerterbuch. Richard Scarry. (Illus.). 78p. (Ger., Eng. & Fr.). 8.35 (1097). Adler Bks.

Mein Erster Brockhaus. 142p. (Ger.). DM.28.00 (ISBN 3-7653-0335-6). F A Brockhaus.

Melanesian Pidgin Phase-Book & Vocabulary. Linguistic Society of America & Robert A. Hall, Jr. (Melanesian.). 2.00. Linguistic Soc Am.

Melanges: Tables generales (1954-1977, Tomes 1-14. Ed. by Institut Dominicain d'Etudes Orientales du Caire. (Fr. & Arabic.). 1980. Tomes 1-13 (168 p - 13.00 (283-2); Tome 14 (516 p . 40.00 (284-0). Intl Bk Ctr.

Melloni's Illustrated Medical Dictionary. Ida Dox et al. (Illus.). 1979. 21.50 (ISBN 0-683-02642-9). Williams & Wilkins.

Melville Sea Dictionary: A Glossed Concordance & Analysis of the Sea Language in Melville's Nautical Novels. Jill B. Gidmark. LC 82-6122. xiii, 534p. 1982. lib. bdg. 45.00 (ISBN 0-313-23330-6, GMD/). Greenwood.

Mennonite Low-German Dictionary. John Thiessen & Jack Thiessen. LC 79-304075. 70p. (Eng. & Ger.). 1977. write for info. (ISBN 3-7708-0579-8). Elwert.

Mental Retardation Dictionary. Alexander J. Tymchuk. LC 73-80058. 149p. 1980. pap. 11.80x (ISBN 0-87424-125-1). Western Psych.

Menu French. David Atkinson. LC 78-323348. (Illus.). 94p. (Fr.). 1978. E1.00 (ISBN 0-902692-17-8). Oxford Poly Pr.

Merknader til en dell Norrone Tekster. Kare Skadberg & Tor Ulset. LC 75-542801. 255p. (Norse & Icelandic.). 1975. Kr.34.00 (ISBN 8-27000-020-5). Univers Oslo.

Merriam Webster Dictionary. 1981. pap. 8.95 (ISBN 0-671-79073-0). PB.

Merriam-Webster Dictionary. 1978. pap. 8.95 (ISBN 0-671-79073-0, Wallaby). PB.

Merriam-Webster Dictionary for Large Print Users. (General Ser.). 1977. lib. bdg. 29.50 (ISBN 0-8161-6459-2, Large Print Bks). G K Hall.
Merriam Webster Dictionary of Synonyms. 1981. pap. 3.50 (ISBN 0-671-46893-6). PB.
Merriam Webster "Mod" Dictionary. 1981. pap. 3.50 (ISBN 0-671-47344-1). PB.
Merriam-Webster Thesaurus. 1981. 7.95 (ISBN 0-671-79095-1, Wallaby). PB.
Mes Dix Mille Mots. Marcel Dider. (Illus.). 792p. (Fr.). E5.75. Harrap.
Mes dix millet mots. Marcel Didier. (Fr.). (gr. 3-6). 1977. text ed. 14.95 (ISBN 0-8120-5207-2). Barron.
Metal Forming Dictionary. A. M. Abd-El-Wahed. 386p. (Eng., Fr., Ger. & Arabic.). 1978. 45.00 (ISBN 0-686-92426-6, M-9755). French & Eur.
Metalcasting Dictionary. 1st ed. American Foundrymen Society. 203p. 32.00 (GM6805); members 16.00. Am Foundrymen.
Metallurgisk Ordbok. LC 77-468526. 347p. (Eng. & Ger., Norsk Verks). 1976. write for info. (ISBN 8-2902-0400-0). Norsk Verkstedsindustris Standardiseringssentral.
Meteorologicheskii Slovar. S. P. Khromov. 620p. (Rus.). 1963. 7.25 (Pub. by Gidrometeoizdat). Four Continent.
Meu Primeiro Dicionario Ilustrado de Ingles. Dixson & Fox. (Illus.). 67p. (Port. & Eng.). (gr. 2-6). pap. 6.50. Imported Bks.
Mexican-Aryan Comparative Vocabulary. T. S. Denison. (Span.). 1976. lib. bdg. 59.95 (ISBN 0-8490-0613-9). Gordon Pr.
Meydan-Larousse, 13 vols. (Turkish.). 1970-76. 1050.00 (ISBN 0-8277-3069-1). Pergamon.
Meyers Grosses Handlexikon in Farbe. Ed. by Lexikonredaktion. 1147p. (Ger.). M.42.00 (ISBN 3-411-01784-8). Biblio Inst.
Meyers grosses Handlexikon in Farbe. 12th ed. LC 76-450981. (Illus.). 1147p. (Ger.). 1975. DM.34.00 (ISBN 3-411-01344-3). Biblio Inst.
Meyers Grosses Jahreslexikon. Ferdinand Hirschelmann. 328p. (Ger.). 1981. write for info. (ISBN 3-411-01963-8). Biblio Inst.
Meyers Grosses Jahreslexikon. Ferdinand Hirschelmann. 328p. (Ger.). 1982. write for info. (ISBN 3-411-01964-6). Biblio Inst.
Meyers Grosses Jahreslexikon: Berichtszeitraum. Ferdinand Herschelmann. 328p. (Ger.). 1979. write for info. (ISBN 3-411-01946-8). Biblio Inst.
Meyers Grosses Kinderlexikon. Achim Broeger. (Illus.). 323p. (Ger.). DM.29.80 (ISBN 3-411-01797-X). Biblio Inst.
Meyers Grosses Personenlexikon. (Ger.). 46.00 (ISBN 3-411-01152-1, M-7559, Pub. by Bibliographisches Institut). French & Eur.
Meyers Grosses Personenlexikon. (Ger.). 46.00 (ISBN 3-411-01152-1). Biblio Inst.
Meyers Grosses Standardlexikon in 3 Banden, 3 vols. Ed. by Lexikonredaktion des Bibliographischen Instituts. (Illus.). 2200p. (Ger.). M.294.00 set (ISBN 3-411-01970-0); DM.98.00 ea. Bd. 1, A-Gh (ISBN 3-411-01971-9). Bd. 2, Gi-Pd (ISBN 3-411-01972-7). Bd. 3, Pe-Zz (ISBN 3-411-01973-5). Biblio Inst.
Meyers Grosses Sternbuch fur Kinder. Joachim Herrmann. (Illus.). 126p. (Ger.). M.write for info. (ISBN 3-411-01909-3). Biblio Inst.
Meyers Grosses Taschenlexikon in 24 Banden. (Ger.). write for info. (ISBN 3-411-01920-4). Biblio Inst.
Meyers Grosses Universallexikon-Jahrbucher. 328p. (Ger.). 1980. write for info. (ISBN 3-411-01862-3). Biblio Inst.
Meyers Grosses Universallexikon-Jahrbucher. 328p. (Ger.). write for info. (ISBN 3-411-01892-5). Biblio Inst.
Meyers Grosses Universallexikon-Jahrbucher. 328p. (Ger.). 1981. write for info. (ISBN 3-411-01864-X). Biblio Inst.
Meyers Grosses Universallexikon-Jahrbucher: Luxusausgabe. 328p. (Ger.). 1982. write for info. (ISBN 3-411-01894-1). Biblio Inst.
Meyers Illustrierte Weltgeschichte in 20 Banden: Band I, Die Vorgeschichte. (Illus.). 160p. (Ger.). write for info. (ISBN 3-411-01808-9). Biblio Inst.
Meyers Kinderlexikon: Mein Erstes Lexikon. (Illus.). 256p. (Ger.). 10.00 (1098). Adler Bks.
Meyers Kinderlexikon: Mein erstes Lexikon. (Illus.). 259p. (Ger.). DM.16.80 (ISBN 3-411-01774-0). Biblio Inst.
Meyers Lexikon A-Z. Bibliographisches Institut. LC 75-522777. 1060p. (Ger.). 1975. M.14.00. Bibl Inst Leipzig.
Meyers Neues Lexikon, 8 vols. (Ger.). 1978-81. 445.00 (ISBN 3-411-01750-3). Pergamon.
Meyers Neues Lexikon Jahrbucher. 328p. (Ger.). write for info. (ISBN 3-411-01769-4). Biblio Inst.
Meyers Neues Lexikon Jahrbucher. 328p. (Ger.). write for info. (ISBN 3-411-01789-9). Biblio Inst.
Meyers Neues Lexikon Jahrbucher. 328p. (Ger.). write for info. (ISBN 3-411-01948-4). Biblio Inst.
Meyers Neues Lexikon Weltatlas. Adolf Hanle. 354p. (Ger.). write for info. (ISBN 3-411-01759-7). Biblio Inst.
Meyers Physik-Lexikon. (Ger.). 1973. 46.00 (ISBN 3-411-00921-7, M-7561, Pub. by Bibliographisches Institut). French & Eur.
Meyers Physik-Lexikon. (Ger.). 1973. 46.00 (ISBN 3-411-00921-7). Biblio Inst.
Meyers Standardlexikon Des Gesamten Wissens. (Ger.). 1975. 15.95 (ISBN 3-411-01346-X, M-7562, Pub. by Bibliographisches Institut). French & Eur.
Meyers Standardlexikon Des Gesamten Wissens. (Ger.). 1975. 15.95 (ISBN 3-411-01346-X). Biblio Inst.
Meyers Taschenlexikon Bionik. Ed. by E. Forth & E. Schewitzer. 375p. (Ger.). 1976. M.16.00. Bibl Inst Leipzig.
Meyers Taschenlexikon Urheberrecht. A. Glucksmann et al. 556p. (Ger.). 1980. M.22.00. Bibl Inst Leipzig.
Meyers Universal Lexikon, Vol. 1. 3rd ed. Ed. by H. Goeschel & A. Zwahr. 720p. (Ger.). 1980. M.35.00. Bibl Inst Leipzig.
Meyers Universal Lexikon, Vol. 2. 3rd ed. Ed. by H. Goeschel & A. Zwahr. 744p. (Ger.). 1981. M.35.00. Bibl Inst Leipzig.
Meyers Universal Lexikon, Vol. 3. 3rd ed. Ed. by H. Goeschel & A. Zwahr. 704p. (Ger.). 1981. M.35.00. Bibl Inst Leipzig.
Meyers Universal Lexikon, Vol. 4. 3rd ed. Ed. by H. Goeschel & A. Zwahr. (Ger.). M.35.00. Bibl Inst Leipzig.
Meyers Universallexikon. LC 80-451635. (Illus., Ger.). 1978. M.29.80. Bibl Inst Leipzig.
Mezhdunarodnaia Anatomicheskaia Nomenklatura. 224p. (Rus.). 1976. 5.50 (Pub. by Ganatleba). Four Continent.
Mezhdunarodnyi Elektrotekhnicheskii Slovar: Gruppa 07 (Elektronika) 335p. (Rus.). 1959. 3.50 (Pub. by Gosizdat Fiziko-Matematich. Literatury). Four Continent.
Mezhdunarodnyi Elektrotekhnicheskii Slovar: Gruppa 10 (Mashiny & Transformatory) (Rus.). 2.25 (Pub by Gosizdat Fiziko Matematich. Literatury). Four Continent.
Mezhdunarodnyi Elektrotekhnicheskii Slovar: Gruppa 65 (Radiologiia & Radiologicheskaia Fizika) 252p. (Rus.). 1966. 3.50 (Pub. by Sov Entsiklopediia). Four Continent.
Mi Diccionario Ilustrado. 2nd ed. Concepcion Zendrera. 20p. (Span.). 1974. 4.95 (ISBN 84-261-0358-8, S-16498). French & Eur.
Mi Diccionario Ilustrado: Edicion Bilingue. Aquino-Bermudez et al. LC 73-181891. (Illus.). 96p. (Span.). (ps-3). 1972. PLB 7.92 (ISBN 0-688-50994-0); pap. 3.95 (ISBN 0-688-45007-5). Lothrop.
Mi Diccionario Ilustrado: Edicion Bilingue. (Illus., Span. & Eng.). pap. 3.95. Lectorum Pubns.
Mi Primer Diccionario Biblico. William N. McElrath. Tr. by Ruth G. McElrath from Eng. (Illus.). 128p. (Span.). 1980. pap. 2.85 (ISBN 0-311-03656-2). Casa Bautista.
Mi Primer Diccionario Escolar. 4th ed. 480p. (Span.). 1975. pap. 2.95 (ISBN 84-319-0028-8, S-27087). French & Eur.
Mi primer diccionario ilustrado. (Illus.). 95p. (Span. & Eng.). (gr. 2 up). pap. 3.95 (T102). Bilingual Ed Serv.
Mi Primer Diccionario Ingles-Espanol. Ricard Jordana. 160p. (Eng. & Span.). 1980. write for info. (ISBN 84-278-0591-8). Edns Nauta.
Mi primer diccionario Ingles-Espanol. Ricard Jordana. 160p. (Span & Eng.). 1980. write for info. (ISBN 84-278-0591-8). Fed Gremios.
Mi primer diccionario Larousse en colores. Ed. by C. S. Sanguinetti. (Illus., Span.). (gr. 3). 1976. PLB 9.95 (ISBN 0-88332-025-8, 21116). Larousse.
Mi primer diccionario Sigmar. (Span.). write for info. (608-19). Pan Amer Pub.
Mi Primer Gran Diccionario Infantil. 4th ed. Richard Scarry. 90p. (Span.). 1978. leatherette 13.95 (ISBN 84-02-03836-0, S-26637). French & Eur.
Mi Primer Sopena. 128p. (Span.). 11.75. Cruzada Span Pubns.
Mi primer Sopena. (Illus., Span.). 10.50. Iaconi.
Mi Primer Sopena: Diccionario Infantil Ilustrado. (Illus.). 138p. (Span.). 14.95. Lectorum Pubns.
Miall's Dictionary of Chemistry. Ed. by D. W. Sharp. (Illus.). 528p. text ed. 60.00x (ISBN 0-582-35152-9). Longman.
Mianownictwo Histologiczne. Marka Wawrzyniak. LC 80-463674. 209p. (Pol. & Lat.). 1979. 160.00 Zl (ISBN 8-3200-0033-5). Panstowy Zaklad W.
Mic Dictionar de Biologie. Teofil Craciun. LC 77-452607. 414p. (Romanian.). 1976. 16.00 lei. Albatros.
Mic Dictionar de Cuvinte Perechi. Silviu Constantinescu. LC 77-460405. 169p. (Romanian.). 1976. 7.50 lei. Albatros.
Mic Dictionar de Terminologie Lingvistica. G. Constantinescu-Dobridor. LC 80-471399. 463p. (Romanian.). 1980. 6.50 lei. Albatros.
Mic Dictionar Folkloric: Spicuiri Folklorice si Etnografice Comparate. Tache Papahagi. LC 80-478266. xxxiv, 545p. (Romanian.). 1979. 28.00 lei. Minerva Yugo.
Micro Robert see Robert Dictionaries.
Micro-Robert: Dictionnaire Du Francais Primordial. Paul Robert. 1231p. (Fr.). 1971. 14.95 (ISBN 0-686-57209-2, M-6487). French & Eur.
Micro Robert en Poche see Robert Dictionaries.
Microcomputer Dictionary. Charles Sippl. LC 81-50565. 1981. pap. 15.95 (ISBN 0-672-21696-5). Sams.
Microcomputers at a Glance. Donald D. Spencer. LC 77-11920. (gr. 9-12). 1977. pap. 3.50x (ISBN 0-89218-021-8). Camelot Pub.
Microelectronics Dictionary. IWT Verlag Editors. (Eng. & Ger.). 1980. 23.00 (ISBN 0-9961073-2-0, Pub. by VDI W Germany). Heyden.
Microprocessor Lexicon-Acronyms & Definitions see International Microcomputer Dictionary.
Middle East Political Dictionary. Lawrence Ziring. LC 82-22673. (Clio Dictionaries in Political Science Ser.: No. 5). (Illus.). 400p. 1983. lib. bdg. 20.75 (ISBN 0-87436-044-7); pap. 10.75 (ISBN 0-87436-045-5). ABC-Clio.
Mil Quinientos. 2nd ed. Rodrigo Salas. LC 79-126779. 247p. (Span.). 1978. write for info. (ISBN 8-431-54055-9). Edit Vecchi.
Milieuvriendelijk van A tot Z. Greet Buchner. LC 79-365782. 117p. (Dutch.). 1979. fl.12.50 (ISBN 9-0603-0246-X). Driehoek.
Military Dictionary. Henry L. Scott. Repr. of 1861 ed. lib. bdg. 25.00 (ISBN 0-8371-0648-6, SCMD). Greenwood.
Military Eitzen. K. Eitzen. (Ger. & Eng.). 1957. pap. 15.95 (ISBN 3-87599-035-8, M-7563, Pub. by Vlg. Offene Worte). French & Eur.
Military Law Dictionary. Ed. by Richard C. Dahl & John F. Whelan. LC 60-10208. 200p. 1960. 15.00 (ISBN 0-379-00042-3). Oceana.
Miljoleksikon. LC 75-546754. 121p. (Norwegian.). 1975. Kr.32.00. Norges Natur.
Mille Parole Fondamentali. Nello Pavoncello. LC 79-367877. 60p. (Hebrew & Ital.). 1979. L.2000.00 (ISBN 8-8850-2709-1). Carucci.
Milling, Sawing, Gear Manufacturing see Dictionary of Production Engineering: German-English-French.
Milon Kis: A Hebrew Pocket Dictionary. Ed. by A. Even Shoshan & Dov Yarden. (Illus.). 662p. (Hebrew.). 5.00 (11-575). Board Jewish Educ.
Miloni: Illustrated Dictionary for Children. Board of Jewish Education. (Illus.). 206p. (Hebrew.). pap. 9.00 (11-500). Board Jewish Educ.
Milton Dictionary. Edward S. Le Comte. LC 76-86175. Repr. of 1961 ed. 19.50 (ISBN 0-404-03917-0). AMS Pr.
Min Forste Ordbok: English & Norwegian. R. Scarry. (Illus., Eng & Norwegian.). 15.00x (ISBN 0-686-31678-9, N504). Vanous.
Mineraalinimisanasto. Boris Saltikoff. LC 78-339110. 82p. (Eng. & Finnish.). 1976. write for info. (ISBN 9-516-90044-5). Geo Tutkim.
Mineralogy Dictionary, German-Russian, 2 Vols. 633p. (Ger. & Rus.). 1976. 19.95 (ISBN 0-686-87191-X, M-9112). French & Eur.
Miners Dictionary. William Hooson. 1979. Repr. of 1747 ed. text ed. 40.25x (ISBN 0-686-32514-1). IMM North Am.
Mini English-Thai-English Dictionary. G. Allison. 460p. (Eng. & Thai.). 1979. pap. 9.95 (ISBN 0-686-92176-3, M-9900). French & Eur.
Mini-Sopena Ingles-Espanol. 320p. (Eng. & Span.). 1.45. Cruzada Span Pubns.
Minidicionario da Lingua Portuguesa. Aurelio Buarque de Holanda Ferreira. (Port.). Cr.$670.00. Edit Atica.
Minimum Standard German Vocabulary. Walter Wadepuhl & Bayard Morgan. (Ger.). 1982. pap. text ed. 4.95x (ISBN 0-89197-549-7). Irvington.
Minimum Vocabularies of Written Chinese. George A. Kennedy. (Chinese.). 2.50 (ISBN 0-88710-048-1). Far Eastern Pubns.
Minimum-Worterbuch: Deutsch-Polnisch, Polnisch-Deutsch. J. Jozwicki. 557p. (Ger. & Pol.). 1980. pap. 4.95 (ISBN 83-214-0099-X). French & Eur.
Miscellaneous Papers by or Concerning John Ruskin, 2 Vols. Compiled by Warren Royal-Dawson. 80p. 1982. Repr. of 1918 ed. Set. lib. bdg. 200.00 (ISBN 0-89987-722-2). Darby Bks.
Misspeller's Dictionary. New World Dictionary Editors. 1983. write for info. (ISBN 0-671-46864-2). S&S.

Mr. Men Picture Dictionary. Roger Hargreaves. (Mr. Men Bks.). (Illus.). 256p. (ps-1). Date not set. pap. 7.95 (ISBN 0-8431-1300-6). Price Stern.

Model English-Chinese Dictionary with Illustrative Examples. (Illus.). 1674p. (Eng. & Chinese.). 1979. leatherette 19.95 (ISBN 0-686-97401-8). French & Eur.

Modellbahnlexikon. Gunter E. Albrecht & Hans D. Reichardt. LC 75-519566. 232p. (Eng. & Ger.). 1975. DM.26.00 (ISBN 3-87094-406-4). Alba Buchverlag.

Modellflug-Lexikon. Werner Thies. LC 80-470206. 269p. (Ger.). 1977. DM.28.00 (ISBN 3-88180-001-8). Verlag Technik.

Modern American Business Dictionary: Including Reaganomics & an Appendix of Business Slang. John Berenyi. LC 81-22342. 288p. 1982. 22.50 (ISBN 0-688-00986-7). Morrow.

Modern American Business Dictionary: Including Reagonomics & an Appendix of Business Slang. John Berenyi. LC 81-21185. 288p. 1982. pap. 7.50 (ISBN 0-688-00987-5). Quill NY.

Modern American Usage: A Guide. Wilson Follett. Ed. by Jacques Barzun. 443p. 1966. 12.95 (ISBN 0-8090-6950-4); pap. 9.95 (ISBN 0-8090-0139-X). Hill & Wang.

Modern Arab Dictionary. (Arabic.). 29.95 (ISBN 2-03-020540-0, 3680); pap. 14.95 (ISBN 2-03-020540-0). Larousse.

Modern Arab Dictionary. (Eng. & Arabic.). write for info. (608-122). Pan Amer Pub.

Modern Arabic-English Dictionary. Elias Elias. (Illus.). 970p. (Arabic & Eng.). 1981. 30.00. Intl Bk Ctr.

Modern Business Language & Usage in Dictionary Form. J. Harold Janis. LC 80-1656. (Illus.). 504p. 1984. 19.95 (ISBN 0-385-14489-X). Doubleday.

Modern Catholic Dictionary. John A. Hardon. LC 77-82945. 1980. 19.95 (ISBN 0-385-12162-8). Doubleday.

Modern Concordance to the New Testament. Ed. by Michael Darton. LC 75-34831. 1977. 12.95 (ISBN 0-385-07901-X). Doubleday.

Modern Dictionary of Sociology. George A. Theodorson & Achilles A. Theodorson. (Everyday Handbooks). 469p. pap. 5.95 (ISBN 0-06-463483-3). B&N NY.

Modern Dictionary Slovene-English, English-Slovene. Komac & J. Skeri. 787p. (Eng. & Slovene.). 1981. leatherette 17.50 (ISBN 0-686-97403-4, M-9701). French & Eur.

Modern Dictionary Slovene-German-Slovene. D. Debenjak. 608p. (Slovene & Ger.). 1981. leatherette 14.95 (ISBN 0-686-97402-6, M-9702). French & Eur.

Modern English-Arabic Dictionary, 4 eds. Munir Ba'Albaki. (Illus., Eng. & Arabic.). Al-Mawrid. 48.00 (059-7); Al-Mawrid Al-Waset. medium size 25.00 (060-0); Al-Mawrid Al-Muyassar. student dict. (575p) 12.00 (061-9); Al-Mawrid Al-Qareb. pocket dict. (484p) 5.95 (062-7). Intl Bk Ctr.

Modern English-Greek & Greek-English Dictionary. I. Kykkotis. 652p. (Eng. & Gr.). 1980. 40.00x (ISBN 0-85331-046-7, Pub. by Lund Humphries England). State Mutual Bk.

Modern English-Greek Dictionary. C. N. Brown. 420p. (Gr. & Eng.). 1976. 12.50 (ISBN 0-686-92187-9, M-9592). French & Eur.

Modern English-Greek-English Desk Dictionary with Thumb Index. G. C. Divry. 768p. (Gr. & Eng.). 1979. 19.95 (ISBN 0-686-97405-0, M-9443). French & Eur.

Modern English-Gujarati Dictionary. P. G. Deshpande. 820p. (Eng. & Gujarati.). 1983. 29.95 (ISBN 0-19-561140-3). Oxford U Pr.

Modern English-Swedish Dictionary. B. Danielsson. 394p. (Eng. & Swedish.). 1980. 19.95 (ISBN 91-518-1296-7, M-9451). French & Eur.

Modern English-Yiddish, Yiddish-English Dictionary. Uriel Weinreich. (Eng. & Yiddish.). 1968. 44.95 (ISBN 0-07-069038-3, P&RB). McGraw.

Modern English-Yiddish Yiddish-English Dictionary. Uriel Weinreich. LC 77-76038. (Eng. & Yiddish.). 1978. pap. 18.95 (ISBN 0-8052-0575-6). Schocken.

Modern English-Yiddish, Yiddish-English Dictionary. Uriel Weinreich. LC 67-23848. 789p. (Eng. & Yiddish.). 1968. write for info (ISBN 0-914512-25-0). Yivo Inst.

Modern Greek Evidence for the Ancient Greek Vocabulary. G. P. Shipp. LC 80-670068. (Gr.). 1980. 43.00x (ISBN 0-424-00076-8, Pub. by Sydney U Pr). Intl Schol Bk Serv.

Modern Greek Idiom & Phrase Book. Constantine N. Tsirpanlis. 320p. (Orig., Gr. & Eng.). 8.95. Barron.

Modern Home Dictionary of Medical Words: With Descriptions, Uses & Standards of Commonly Used Tests. Morris Fishbein. LC 74-18845. 240p. 1976. pap. 1.95 (ISBN 0-385-01105-9, Dolp). Doubleday.

Modern Language Dictionary. Ferdinando D. Maurino. LC 75-10051. xvii, 436p. (Eng. & Span.). 1975. 4.95 (ISBN 0-671-18725-2). S & S.

Modern Legal Glossary. Kenneth R. Redden & Enid L. Veron. 576p. 1980. 19.00 (ISBN 0-87215-237-5). Michie Co.

Modern Military Dictionary: Ten Thousand Technical & Slang Terms of Military Usage. 2nd ed. Max B. Garber & P. S. Bond. LC 74-31354. 1975. Repr. of 1942 ed. 34.00x (ISBN 0-8103-4208-1). Gale.

Modern Reader's Japanese-English Character Dictionary. Andrew Nelson. LC 61-11973. (Japanese & Eng.). 1962. 35.00 (ISBN 0-8048-0408-7). C E Tuttle.

Modern Reader's Japanese-English Character Dictionary. rev. ed. Andrew N. Nelson. 1109p. (Japanese & Eng.). 1980. 42.00. C E Tuttle.

Modern Rhyming Dictionary. Gene Lees. 360p. (YA) 1981. 14.95 (ISBN 0-89524-129-3, 8601). Cherry Lane.

Modern Russian Dictionary for English Speakers: English-Russian. E. A. Wilson. LC 81-12141. 1200p. (Rus. & Eng.). 1983. 39.50 (ISBN 0-08-020554-2). Pergamon.

Modern Spanish-English & English-Spanish Technical & Engineering Dictionary. R. L. Guinle. (Span. & Eng.). 1969. Repr. of 1938 ed. 25.00 (ISBN 0-7100-1478-3). Routledge & Kegan.

Modern Textile & Apparel Dictionary. rev. 4th ed. George E. Linton. Orig. Title: Modern Textile Dictionary. 1973. 20.00x (ISBN 0-87245-500-9). Textile Bk.

Modern Textile & Apparel Dictionary. 4th, rev. enlarged ed. George E. Linton. 89.00x (ISBN 0-686-97037-3, Pub. by Meadowfield Pr England). State Mutual Bk.

Modern Textile Dictionary. P. Hohenadel & V. Relton. 375p. (Ger. & Eng.). 1979. 62.50 (ISBN 3-87097-085-5, M-9023). French & Eur.

Modern Textile Dictionary see Modern Textile & Apparel Dictionary.

Modern Textile Dictionary: English-German. P. Hohenadel & J. Relton. 484p. (Ger. & Eng.). 1977. 62.50 (ISBN 3-87097-077-4, M-9024). French & Eur.

Modern Usage in Bahasa Indonesia. J. Sarumpaet. LC 80-484867. vii, 264p. (Indonesian & Eng.). 1980. write for info (ISBN 0-85896-484-8). Pitman Ltd.

Modern Word-Finder: A Living Guide to Modern Usage, Spelling, Synonyms, Pronunciation, Grammar, Word Origins, & Authorship. Paul D. Hugon. LC 73-20139. 420p. 1974. Repr. of 1934 ed. 45.00x (ISBN 0-8103-3970-6). Gale.

Moderne Kinder-Lexikon in Farbe.Unsere Welt in Wort Und Bild: Unsere Welt in Wort & Bild. K. Finke & R. Goock. (Illus.). 320p. (Ger.). 20.30 (1099). Adler Bks.

Modernt Foertagsekonomiskt Lexikon. Erick R. Eriksson & Roy Baeckbom. LC 78-349746. (Illus.). 350p. (Swedish.). 1977. Kr.94.00 (ISBN 9-15-180888-9). Prisma.

Modismos en Ingles. E. Savaiano & L. Winget. (Span. Eng.). 1981. 3.95 (ISBN 0-8120-2314-5). Barron.

Moisture Content of Paper Terminology & Conversion. 1966. 1.00 (017-7); members 0.67. TAPPI.

Mokilese-English Dictionary. Sheldon P. Harrison & Salich Albert. LC 76-41796. (PALI Language Tests Ser.: Micronesia). 182p. (Orig., Mokilese & Eng.). 1976. pap. text ed. 9.50x (ISBN 0-8248-0512-7). UH Pr.

Moldavsko-Russkii Frazeologicheskii Slovar. V. Solov'ev. 224p. (Rus. Moldavian.). 1976. 2.00 (Pub. by Lumina). Four Continent.

Mon Dictionnaire Francais-Anglais. M. Fonteneau & S. Theureau. (Fr. & Eng.). 1969. 15.95 (Dist. by Continental Bk Co). Larousse.

Mon Grand Dictionnaire Francais-Anglais. (Fr. & Eng.). 13.50 (ISBN 0-685-11402-3). French & Eur.

Mon Premier Dictionnaire en 2000 mots & 2000 Images. Thoburn et al. (Fr.). 19.50 (Dist. by Continental Bk Co). Casterman.

Mon Premier Larousse francais-anglais, anglais-francais en couleurs. Larousse And Co. (Fr. & Eng.). (gr. 6-9). 23.75 (ISBN 2-03-051431-4, 3794). Larousse.

Monarch's Dictionary of Investment Terms. Edith L. Beer. 192p. (Orig.). 1982. pap. 6.95 (ISBN 0-671-45497-8). Monarch Pr.

Monarch's Dictionary of Legal Terms. Shirley R. Bysiewicz. 192p. (Orig.). 1983. pap. 7.95 (ISBN 0-671-09232-4). Monarch Pr.

Mondadori's Pocket Italian-English, English-Italian Dictionary. 600p. (Eng. & Ital.). pap. 2.50. Imported Bks.

Mongolian-English Dictionary. F. D. Lessing. LC 60-14517. 1220p. (Mongolian & Eng.). 1982. Repr. of 1960 ed. 55.00x (ISBN 0-910980-40-3). Mongolia.

More on the Gentle Art of Verbal Self-Defense. Suzette H. Elgin. 284p. 1983. 12.95 (ISBN 0-13-601138-1); pap. 6.95 (ISBN 0-13-601120-9). P-H.

Morphologie & Generative Grammatik. Ed. by Ferenc Kiefer. LC 76-450339. (Illus.). xix, 289p. (Ger.). 1975. DM.44.00 (ISBN 3-799-70628-3). Akad Verl Ath.

Morris Dictionary of Word & Phrase Origins. William Morris & Mary Morris. LC 77-3763. 1977. bds. 21.10i (ISBN 0-06-013058-X, HarpT). Har-Row.

Morrow Book of New Words: 8500 Terms Not Yet in Standard Dictionaries. N. H. Mager & S. K. Mager. LC 81-14205. 256p. 1982. 13.50 (ISBN 0-688-00685-X); pap. 6.50 (ISBN 0-688-00927-1). Morrow.

Mortgage Banking Terms: A Working Glossary. 3rd ed. Mortgage Bankers Association of America. 115p. 5.00. Mortgage Bankers.

Moselfraenkische Mundart. Edmund Endres. LC 80-471656. 94p. (Ger.). 1979. write for info. (ISBN 3-79270-488-9). Rheinland Verlag.

Moses Maimonides Glossary of Drug Names. Fred Rosner. (Memoirs Ser.: No. 135). 1979. 20.75 (ISBN 0-87169-135-3). Am Philos.

Mot et L'idee, Francais-Portugais, Portugais-Francais. J. Fournier & G. Laborde. 120p. (Fr.-Port.). 6.95 (ISBN 0-686-57185-1, M-6256). French & Eur.

Mot Juste. (Fr.). 3.50. Longman.

Mot Juste: A Dictionary of Classical & Foreign Words & Phrases. Compiled by Kogan Page, Ltd. & John Buchanan-Brown. LC 80-6122. 176p. 1981. pap. 2.95 (ISBN 0-394-74690-2, V-690, Vin). Random.

Mot Juste: A Dictionary of Foreign & Classical Words & Phrases. write for info. (ISBN 0-333-30583-3). Macmillan.

Motorcycle Dictionary. William H. Kosbab. Ed. by Dianne Greenslade-Moore & Daveta Lamont. LC 82-71155. 300p. 1983. lib. bdg. 19.95x (ISBN 0-89262-058-7); pap. text ed. 14.95x (ISBN 0-89262-044-7). Career Pub.

Mots croises. (Fr.). 1978. pap. text ed. 9.75 (ISBN 2-03-029307-5). Larousse.

Mrs. Byrne's Dictionary of Unusual, Obscure, & Preposterous Words. Josefa Heifetz Byrne. Ed. & intro. by Robert Byrne. 1976. pap. 5.95 (ISBN 0-8065-0498-6). Citadel Pr.

Mrs. Byrne's Dictionary of Unusual, Obscure, & Preposterous Words, Gathered from Numerous & Diverse Authoritative Sources. Josefa H. Byrne. Ed. & intro. by Robert Byrne. 1974. 12.50 (ISBN 0-8216-0203-9). Univ Bks.

Muhit al-Muhit. Butros Bustani. 997p. (Arabic.). 50.00 (096-1). Intl Bk Ctr.

Multi-Lingual Dictionary of Concrete. Federation Internationale de la Precontrainte. 1976. 89.50 (ISBN 0-444-41237-9). Elsevier.

Multidiccionario. 544p. (Span.). 1979. 29.95 (ISBN 84-278-0559-4, S-50514). French & Eur.

Multilengua Diccionario de Cartas Comerciales en Cuatro Idiomas, 3 vols. 972p. (Eng., Span., Ger. & Fr.). 1975. Set. 120.00 (ISBN 84-221-0412-1, S-50102). French & Eur.

Multilingual Commercial Dictionary. Alan Isaacs. 485p. 1978. 25.00. Facts on File.

Multilingual Commercial Dictionary. Ed. by Alan Isaacs. 496p. 1980. 22.50 (ISBN 0-87196-425-2). Facts on File.

Multilingual Compendium of Plant Diseases. P. R. Miller & H. L. Pollard. LC 75-46932. (Compendia Ser.: Vol. 2). (Illus.). 446p. 1977. 40.00 (ISBN 0-89054-020-9); member 35.00. Am Phytopathol Soc.

Multilingual Computer Dictionary. Ed. by Frederick Muller, Ltd. 1981. 30.00x (ISBN 0-584-95567-7, Pub. by Muller Ltd). State Mutual Bk.

Multilingual Computer Dictionary. Alan Isaacs. 332p. (Eng., Fr., Ger., Span., Ital. & Port.). 1981. 27.00. Facts on File.

Multilingual Computer Dictionary. Ed. by Alan Isaacs. 336p. 1981. 22.50 (ISBN 0-87196-431-7). Facts on File.

Multilingual Computer Dictionary. Ed. by Alan Isaacs. (Eng., Fr., Span., Ital. & Port.). 1980. 22.50. Facts on File.

Multilingual Dictionary of Fish & Fish Products. 1978. 60.00 (ISBN 0-85238-086-0, FN 64, FNB). Unipub.

Multilingual Dictionary of Fish & Fish Products. OECD. 1978. 59.00 (ISBN 0-685-63442-6). State Mutual Bk.

Multilingual Dictionary of Fish & Fish Products. 2nd ed. Ed. by OECD. 446p. 1978. 42.50x (ISBN 0-85238-086-0). Intl Pubns Serv.

Multilingual Dictionary of Names of Marine Food-Dishes of World Fauna. G. U. Lindberg. 562p. 1980. 79.00x (ISBN 0-686-44732-8, Pub. by Collets). State Mutual Bk.

Multilingual Dictionary of Printing & Publishing. Ed. by Frederick Muller, Ltd. 1981. 30.00x (ISBN 0-584-95569-3, Pub. by Muller Ltd). State Mutual Bk.

Multilingual Dictionary of Printing & Publishing. Ed. by Alan Isaacs. 336p. 1981. 22.50 (ISBN 0-87196-444-9). Facts on File.

Multilingual Dictionary of Remote Sensing & Photogrammetry. 1983. 25.00 (ISBN 0-937294-46-2). ASP.

Multilingual Dictionary of Technical Terms in Cartography. E. Meynen. 572p. (Eng. & Ger.). 1973. pap. 88.00 (ISBN 3-515-00127-1, M-7564, Pub. by F. Steiner). French & Eur.

Multilingual Dictionary of the International Federation of Surveyors. International Federation of Surveyors. Date not set. 78.75 (ISBN 0-444-40795-2). Elsevier.

Multilingual Energy Dictionary. Ed. by Frederick Muller, Ltd. 1981. 30.00x (ISBN 0-584-95568-5, Pub. by Muller Ltd). State Mutual Bk.

Multilingual Energy Dictionary. Ed. by Alan Isaacs. 288p. 1981. 22.50 (ISBN 0-87196-430-9). Facts on File.

Multilingual Glossary of Automatic Control Technology: English-French-German-Russian-Italian-Spanish-Japanese. D. T. Broadbent & M. Masubuchi. 230p. (Eng., Fr., Ger., Rus., Ital., Span. & Japanese.). 1981. 45.00 (ISBN 0-08-027607-5). Pergamon.

Multilingual Law Dictionary: English, French, Spanish, German. Lawrence D. Egbert. LC 77-25072. 551p. (Eng., Fr., Span. & Ger.). 1978. lib. bdg. 50.00 (ISBN 0-379-00589-1). Oceana.

Multilingual Lexicon of Linguistics & Philology: English, Russian, German, French. Rose Nash. LC 68-31044. (Miami Linguistics Ser: No. 3). (Eng., Rus., Ger. & Fr.). 1968. 19.95x (ISBN 0-87024-095-1). U of Miami Pr.

Multilingual Technical Dictionary on Irrigation & Drainage. (Eng. & Turkish.). 1972. 12.00; members 8.00. US Comm Irrigation.

Multilingual Technical Dictionary on Irrigation & Drainage. (Eng. & Ger., French translation of terms only). 1971. 40.00; members 30.00. US Comm Irrigation.

Multilingual Technical Dictionary on Irrigation & Drainage. (Eng. & Fr.). 1967. 15.00; members 7.50. US Comm Irrigation.

Multilingual Technical Dictionary on Irrigation & Drainage, Suppl. 1. 1980. 7.00; members 5.00. US Comm Irrigation.

Multilingual Vocabulary of Educational Radio & Television Terms. 189p. (Orig., Eng. , Fr. , Ger. , Ital. , Dutch, Span. & Swedish.). 1971. pap. 11.25x (ISBN 3-19-006291-9). Intl Pubns Serv.

Multinlingual Lexicon of Linguistics & Philology. Nash. (Miami Linguistic Ser.). (Polyglot.). 52.50 (ISBN 0-685-36678-2). French & Eur.

Mungo Park. R. Tames. (Clarendon Biography Ser.). (Illus.). 1973. pap. 3.50 (ISBN 0-912728-69-8). Newbury Bks.

Munjid al Tulab. Dar el Mashreq. 950p. (Arabic.). student dict. 15.00 (2128-2). Intl Bk Ctr.

Munjid fi al Lugha wal A'Alam. (Illus.). 900p. (Arabic.). 48.00 (2124-7). Intl Bk Ctr.

Muppet Music Dictionary. Barbara Mariconda & Denise Puccio. (Illus.). 210p. (gr. 3-7). 1983. 14.95 (ISBN 0-89524-153-6, 8603); pap. 9.95 (ISBN 0-89524-164-1, 8608). Cherry Lane.

Mushroom Terms. H. C. Bels-Koning & W. M. Van Kuijk. LC 81-466342. xxii, 312p. 1980. write for info. (ISBN 9-02-200673-5). Centre for Agricultural Pub. & Documentation.

Mushroom Terms: Polyglot on Research & Cultivation of Edible Fungi. 312p. 1981. pap. 83.00 (ISBN 90-220-0673-5, PDC 211, Pudoc). Unipub.

Music Translation Dictionary: An English, Czech, Danish, Dutch, French, German, Hungarian, Italian, Polish, Portuguese, Russian, Spanish, Swedish Vocabulary of Music. Compiled by Carolyn D. Grigg. LC 78-60526. (Eng., Czech., Danish, Dutch, Fr., Ger., Hungarian, Ital., Pol., Port., Rus., Span. & Swedish.). 1978. lib. bdg. 35.00 (ISBN 0-313-20559-0, GMT/). Greenwood.

Musical Morphology: A Discourse & a Dictionary. Siegmund Levarie & Ernst Levy. LC 82-21274. (Illus.). 376p. 1983. 29.50X (ISBN 0-87338-286-2). Kent St U Pr.

Musical Pronouncing Dictionary. Dudley Buck. Repr. lib. bdg. 19.00 (ISBN 0-403-03787-5). Scholarly.

Musical Thesaurus: A Dictionary of Musical Language. R. Leach. LC 78-51565. 1978. 10.00 (ISBN 0-912728-21-3). Newbury Bks.

Musical Thesaurus: A Dictionary of Musical Language. Robert Leach. LC 77-370602. 47p. (Eng., Fr., Ger. & Ital.). 1976. E1.00. J Hannon.

Musician's Handbook of Foreign Terms. Christine Ammer. 1971. pap. 7.95 (ISBN 0-02-870100-3). Assoc-Mus.

Musik-Brockhaus. 686p. (Ger.). DM.68.00 (ISBN 3-7653-0338-0). F A Brockhaus.

Musik: Ein Sachlexikon. Gerhard Kwiatkowski. (Illus.). 464p. (Ger.). DM.19.80 (ISBN 3-411-01748-1). Biblio Inst.

Musikalisches Lexikon. 3rd ed. Johann Walther. (Ger.). 1967. pap. 48.00 (ISBN 3-7618-0229-3, M-7565, Pub. by Baerenreiter). French & Eur.

Musisches Lexikon. Willi A. Koch. LC 77-457599. (Illus., Ger.). 1976. DM.48.00 (ISBN 3-520-80303-8). Kroener.

Must Words: The Six Thousand Most Important Words for a Successful & Profitable Vocabulary. C. Norback & P. Norback. 312p. 1983. pap. 5.95 (ISBN 0-07-047141-X, GB). McGraw.

Must Words: The Six Thousand Most Important Words for a Successful & Profitable Vocabulary. Craig Norback & Peter Norback. 1979. 12.95 (ISBN 0-07-047136-3). McGraw.

Muyuw Dictionary. David Lithgow & Daphne Lithgow. (Muyuw.). 1974. pap. 2.50x o. p. (ISBN 0-7263-0205-8); microfiche 2.25 (ISBN 0-88312-332-0). Summer Inst Ling.

Muzeologicky slovnik. Josef Benes & Vaclay Puba. LC 79-367213. 169p. (Czech.). 1978. write for info. SNTC.

Muzieklexicon, 2 vols. Gerrit Slagmolen. LC 74-336503. (Dutch.). 1974. fl.15.00 (ISBN 9-022-91367-8). Bruna.

My First Dictionary. (Illus.). 342p. (gr. k-3). 1980. 9.95 (ISBN 0-395-29210-7). HM.

My First Dictionary. Laura Oftedal & Nina Jacob. (Illus.). (gr. k-3). 1948. 4.50 (ISBN 0-448-02962-6, G&D). Putnam Pub Group.

My First English-Japanese Picture Dictionary. Dixson et al. (Illus., Eng. & Japanese.). (gr. 1-6). 1978. pap. text ed. 4.50 (ISBN 0-88345-260-X). Regents Pub.

My First Picture Dictionary. rev. ed. William A. Jenkins & Andrew Schiller. LC 78-13248. (Illus.). (gr. k-3). 1977. PLB 11.28 (ISBN 0-688-51786-2). Lothrop.

My First Picture Dictionary. Illus. by Huck Scarry. LC 76-24174. (Pictureback Ser.). (ps-2). 1978. PLB 4.99 (ISBN 0-394-93486-5, BYR); pap. 1.50 (ISBN 0-394-83486-0). Random.

My Illustrated Dictionary: Arabic & Fr. Libr du Liban. (Arabic & Fr.). 1983. 9.00x (ISBN 0-86685-321-9). Intl Bk Ctr.

My Illustrated Dictionary: Arabic & Ger. Libr du Liban. (Arabic & Ger.). 1983. 9.00x (ISBN 0-86685-318-9). Intl Bk Ctr.

My Illustrated Dictionary: Arabic & Ital. Libr du Liban. (Arabic & Ital.). 1983. 9.00x (ISBN 0-86685-319-7). Intl Bk Ctr.

My Illustrated Dictionary: Arabic & Span. Libr du Liban. (Arabic & Span.). 1983. 9.00x (ISBN 0-86685-320-0). Intl Bk Ctr.

My Illustrated Dictionary: Arabic Eng. Libr du Liban. (Arabic & Eng.). 1983. 9.00x (ISBN 0-86685-317-0). Intl Bk Ctr.

My Little Dictionary. Board of Jewish Education. (Illus.). 36p. (Hebrew.). 4.50 (11-551). Board Jewish Educ.

My Picture Dictionary. Hale Reid & Helen Crane. (Illus., Eng.). 1963. Can.$2.95 (ISBN 0-7702-0098-2). Ginn.

My Second Picture Dictionary. Hale Reid & Helen Crane. (Illus., Eng.). 1963. Can.$8.95 (ISBN 0-7702-0098-2). Ginn.

My Very Own Dictionary. Charlie Daniel & Becky Daniel. (gr. 1-4). 1978. 5.50 (ISBN 0-916456-17-X, GA81). Good Apple.

Mycological Dictionary. Karl Berger. 432p. 1980. 99.00x (ISBN 0-686-44735-2, Pub. by Collets). State Mutual Bk.

Mykologisches Worterbuch. K. Berger. 432p. (Ger. & Eng. & Fr. & Span. & Lat. & Czech. & Pol. & Rus.). 1980. write for info. (M-9435). French & Eur.

Mykologisches Worterbuch. Karl Von Berger. LC 80-479189. 432p. (Eng., Fr., Span., Lat., Czech., Pol., & Rus.). 1980. write for info. (ISBN 3-437-20220-0). Fischer Verlag.

Mystical Vocabulary of Venerable Mere Marie De L'Incarnation & Its Problems. Mother Aloysius G. L'Heureux. LC 72-94190. (Catholic University of America Studies in Romance Languages & Literatures Ser: No. 53). (Fr.). Repr. of 1956 ed. 18.75 (ISBN 0-404-50353-5). AMS Pr.

N

N. B. C. Handbook of Pronunciation. 3rd, rev. ed. James F. Bender. Ed. by Thomas Crowell, Jr. 1964. 14.37i (ISBN 0-690-57472-X). T Y Crowell.

Nahual-English Dictionary & Concordance to the "Cantares Mexicanos" With an Analytic Transcription & Grammatical Notes. John Bierhorst. write for info. Stanford U Pr.

Naibolee Upotrebitel'Nykh Slov Russkogo. 368p. (Rus.). 1978. 6.50 (Pub. by Russkii Iazyk). Four Continent.

Naj'ati Ur-Ra'id wa-Shar'Atu al-Warid fi al-Mutaradifi wa al-Mu tawarid. Ibrahim Al-Yaziji. 555p. (Arabic.). 30.00 (102-X). Intl Bk Ctr.

Namenforschung im Ostniederlandisch-Westfalischen Grengebiet. Pierre Hessmann. LC 78-375124. 104p. (Ger. & Dutch.). 1978. fl.20.00 (ISBN 9-0620-3380-6). Rodopi.

Names in Gardening see Webster's Third on Non-Standard Usage.

Nanumea Lexicon. Peter Ranby. LC 81-180454. (Illus.). x, 243p. (Eng & Tuvalu.). 1980. write for info. (ISBN 0-85883-227-5). Linguistic Circle.

Narwiska Obce w Jezyku Polskim. Izabela Bartminska et al. LC 79-349806. 210p. (Pol.). 1978. 34.00 Zl. Panstwowe Zaklad W.

National Geographical Dictionary of India. Jagdish S. Sharma. LC 72-929631. 350p. 1972. 11.25x (ISBN 0-8002-0942-7). Intl Pubns Serv.

Natur Zientziak. LC 77-459840. liv, 483p. (Basque.). 1976. write for info. (ISBN 8-4724-0064-6). Aranzazu.

Naturgeografisk ordbok: Engelsk-Norsk. Roger G. Bennett. LC 78-398859. 84p. (Eng. & Norwegian.). 1976. write for info. Berg Inst Sociol.

Naval Terms Dictionary. John V. Nobel. 1977. lib. bdg. 75.00 (ISBN 0-8490-2332-7). Gordon Pr.

Naval Terms Dictionary. 4th Ed. ed. John V. Noel, Jr. & Edward L. Beach. 352p. 1978. 12.95 (ISBN 0-87021-482-9); bulk rates avail. US Naval Inst.

Nazwiska Obce w Jezyku Polskim. Izabela Bartminska. LC 79-349806. (Illus.). 210p. (Eng. & Pol.). 1978. 34.00 Zl. Panstwowe Zaklad W.

Ndonga, Afrikaans, English: Dreitalige Woordeboek. Johannes J. Viljoen. LC 76-479622. 89p. (Ndonga, Afrikaans & Eng.). 1975. write for info. (ISBN 0-627-00328-1). Van Schaik.

Nederlands-Engels Woordenboek. G. J. Visser. 323p. (Dutch & Eng.). 1981. pap. 5.00. Spectrum Pub.

Neederland-Duits: Wolter's Woorden Boek. W. H. Wallis. 956p. (Ger.). 1981. 24.95 (ISBN 90-01-96815-5, M-9744). French & Eur.

Nelson Canadian Elementary School Dictionary. F. R. Witty. (Eng.). 1975. Can.$pap. 3.30 (ISBN 0-17-600410-6); pap. 3.95 (ISBN 0-17-600411-4). Nelson & Sons Group.

Nelson Canadian Elementary School Dictionary. Ed. by F. R. Witty. LC 77-365319. 252p. 1975. Can.$3.00 (ISBN 0-17-600410-6). Nelson & Sons Group.

Nelson ELT Pocket Dictionary. Ed. by Ronald Ridout. 352p. (Eng.). E1.75 (ISBN 0-17-555210-X). Nelson & Sons Group.

Nelson-Webster Vest Pocket Dictionary. 1978. 0.95 (ISBN 0-8407-5637-2). Nelson.

Nelson's New Compact Medical Dictionary. 1978. 2.45 (ISBN 0-8407-5635-6). Nelson.

Nelson's New Compact Roget's Thesaurus. 1978. 2.45 (ISBN 0-8407-5634-8). Nelson.

Nelson's New Compact Webster's Dictionary. 1978. 2.45 (ISBN 0-8407-5633-X). Nelson.

Nemetsko-Gruzinsko-Russkii Frazeologicheskii Slovar. N. Gamrekeli et al. 566p. (Ger., Gr. & Rus.). 1973. 4.35 (Pub. by Ganatleba). Four Continent.

Nemetsko-Russkii Arkhitekturnyi Slovar. M. M. Zhitomirskii. 208p. (Ger. & Rus.). 1957. 1.95 (Pub. by GINS). Four Continent.

Nemetsko-Russkii Elektrotekhnicheskii Slovar. M. L. Ginzburg et al. 1066p. (Rus.). 1959. 12.75 (Pub. by Gosizdat Fizmatlit). Four Continent.

Nemetsko-Russkii Frazeologicheskii Slovar. 904p. (Ger. & Rus.). 1956. 3.30 (Pub. by GINS). Four Continent.

Nemetsko-Russkii Geodezicheskii Slovar. I. A. Piskunova. 210p. (Rus.). 1965. 2.95 (Pub. by Nedra). Four Continent.

Nemetsko-Russkii Gidrotekhnicheskii Slovar. L. B. Bernshtein. 579p. (Ger. & Rus.). 1961. 7.75 (Pub. by Fizmatgiz). Four Continent.

Nemetsko-Russkii Matematicheskii Slovar. L. A. Kaluzhnin et al. 182p. (Ger. & Rus.). 1960. 2.70 (Pub. by Fizmatgiz). Four Continent.

Nemetsko-Russkii Meditsinskii Slovar. E. F. Sommerau. 460p. (Ger. & Rus.). 1958. 4.95 (Pub. by Medgiz). Four Continent.

Nemetsko-Russkii Mekhaniko-Matematicheskii Slovar. N. M. Dovnar-Zapolskaia. 236p. (Ger. & Rus.). 1960. 2.25 (Pub. by MGU). Four Continent.

Nemetsko-Russkii Okeanograficheskii Slovar. N. N. Gorskii et al. 240p. (Ger. & Rus.). 1957. 2.75 (Pub. by GINS). Four Continent.

Nemetsko-Russkii Slovar. Ed. by I. V. Rakhmanov. 557p. (Ger. & Rus.). 1956. 1.95 (Pub. by GINS). Four Continent.

Nemetsko-Russkii Slovar. Ed. by I. V. Rakhmanov. 556p. (Ger. & Rus.). 1958. 1.65 (Pub. by GINS). Four Continent.

Nemetsko-Russkii Slovar po Lesnomu Khoziaistvu. Ernst A. Pavlov & Olga I. Semenova. LC 80-466812. 477p. (Ger. & Rus.). 1978. 4.20 Rub. Russkii Iazyk.

Nemetsko-Russkii Slovar Po Metalloobrabotke. N. F. Deputatova et al. 465p. (Rus. & Ger.). 1957. 6.00 (Pub. by Gosizdat Tekhnich Teoretich. Lit.). Four Continent.
Nemetsko-Russkii Slovar Po Vychislitelnoi Tekhnike. V. Sharov et al. 400p. (Ger. & Rus.). 1976. 6.50 (Pub. by Russkii Iazyk). Four Continent.
Nemetsko-Russkii Zheleznodorozhnyi Slovar. D. A. Bunin. 531p. (Rus. & Ger.). 1957. 4.95 (Pub. by Gosizdat Tekhn.-Teoret. Lit.). Four Continent.
Nemzetkozi Kutya Enciklopedia. Ed. by Pal Sarkany. LC 77-560281. (Illus.). 741p. (Hungarian.). 1976. 210.00 Ft (ISBN 9-632-05052-5). Terra.
Nepal'Sko-Russkii Slovar. I. S. Rabinovich. 1328p. (Rus. & Nepalese.). 1968. 9.35 (Pub. by Sov Entsiklopediia). Four Continent.
Neue Brockhaus. 653p. (Ger.). DM.120.00 (ISBN 3-7653-0310-0). F A Brockhaus.
Neue Brockhaus Lexikon & Woerterbuch in funf Baenden & Einem Atlas: Band 1. 700p. (Ger.). DM.108.00 (ISBN 3-7653-0300-3). F A Brockhaus.
Neue Chinesische Vogelnamen. Alfred Hoffmann. LC 79-361040. x, 113p. (Ger. & Chinese.). 1978. write for info. (ISBN 3-447-01980-8). Harrassowitz.
Neue Herder, 14 vols. Incl. Grossa Atlas. (Ger.). 1973-1975. Set. 955.00 (ISBN 0-685-40123-5). Pergamon.
Neue Herder: Lexikon, 14 vols. (Ger.). 1968-73. Set. 995.00 (ISBN 0-686-56635-1, M-7568, Pub. by Herder). French & Eur.
Neue Herder: Lexikon, 14 vols. (Ger.). 1968-73. Set. 995.00 (ISBN 0-686-56635-1). Herder.
Neue Muret-Sanders, 2 pts. Ed. by Otto Springer. Incl. Teil I. Englisch-Deutsch. 1962-63. Band A-M (883p.) DM.168.00 (0112-0); Band N-Z (viii, 960p.) DM.168.00 (0112-1); Teil II. Deutsch-Englisch. 1974-75. Band A-K (973p.) DM.198.00 (01124); Band N-Z (viii, 1048p.) DM.198.00 (01126). (Ger. & Eng.). Langenscheidt.
Neues Grosses Gartenlexikon. (Ger.). 1973. 32.00 (ISBN 3-517-00442-1, M-7567, Pub. by Suedwest). French & Eur.
Neues Grosses Gartenlexikon. (Ger.). 1973. 32.00 (ISBN 3-517-00442-1). Suedwest.
Neues Taschenlexikon. Roland Goock. LC 75-519004. 192p. (Ger.). 1975. write for info. (ISBN 3-87644-045-9). Prae Heinz.
Neugriechisch, 2 vols. Incl. Teil I. Neugriechisch-Deutsch. H. F. Wendt. 552p. DM.18.80 (10210); Teil II. Deutsch-Neugriechisch. A. Steinmetz. 487p. DM.18.80 (10215). (Langenscheidts Taschenworterbucher Ser.). (Ger. & Gr.). DM.beide Teile in einem Band 29.80 (11210). Langenscheidt.
New American Crossword Puzzle Dictionary. Tom Wilson & Loy Morehead. 1971. pap. 3.50 (ISBN 0-451-12648-3, Sig). NAL.
New American Medical Dictionary & Health Manual. 1982. pap. 4.50x (ISBN 0-451-12027-2, Pub. by NAL). Formur Intl.
New American Medical Dictionary & Health Manual. rev. ed. Robert Rothenberg. pap. 4.50 (ISBN 0-451-12027-2, AE2027, Sig). NAL.
New American Pocket Medical Dictionary. Nancy Roper. LC 78-3857. (Illus.). 1978. pap. text ed. 6.25 (ISBN 0-443-08013-5). Churchill.
New American Pocket Medical Dictionary. Nancy Roper. 1978. pap. 7.95 (ISBN 0-684-15923-6, SL820, ScribT). Scribner.
New American Roget's College Thesaurus in Dictionary Form. Ed. by Albert H. Morehead et al. (gr. 9 up). 1957. 4.95 (ISBN 0-448-01605-2, G&D); thumb-indexed ed. 4.95 (ISBN 0-448-01622-2). Putnam Pub Group.
New American Roget's Thesaurus in Dictionary Form. rev. ed. 1978. pap. 2.95 (ISBN 0-451-12539-8, Sig). NAL.
New American Webster Handy College Dictionary. Philip D. Morehead & Andrew T. Morehead. 1981. pap. 2.50 (ISBN 0-451-12537-1). NAL.
New Appleton's Cuyas English-Spanish & Spanish-English Dictionary. 5th ed. Ed. by A. Cuyas. (Eng. & Span.). 1972. 18.95 (ISBN 0-13-611749-X); thumb-indexed 19.95 (ISBN 0-13-611756-2). P-H.
New Bantam-Meggido Hebrew & English Dictionary. Reuben Sivan & Edward A. Levenston. 736p. (Eng. & Hebrew.). pap. 2.95 (ISBN 0-553-14420-0). Bantam.
New Bantam-Megiddo Hebrew & English Dictionary. Reuven Sivan & Edward A. Levenston. LC 77-75289. (Hebrew & Eng.). 1977. 24.95 (ISBN 0-8052-3666-X). Schocken.
New Bantam-Megiddo Hebrew Dictionary. Edward A. Levenston & Reuven Sivan. 736p. (Hebrew.). 1975. pap. 2.95 (ISBN 0-553-02094-3, G14420-0). Bantam.
New Basic Dictionary. Poolman & Christopher Scott. 256p. write for info. Macmillan London.
New Century Velazquez Spanish-English Dictionary. rev. ed. (Span. & Eng.). 1977. 16.95 (ISBN 0-8329-0472-4). New Century.
New Century Vest Pocket French Dictionary. rev. ed. Ed. by Richard Switzer & Herbert S. Gochberg. (Orig., Fr.). 2.95 (ISBN 0-686-86497-2). New Century.
New Century Vest-Pocket Italian Dictionary. Ed. by Vittore Bocchetta & Ruth E. Young. (Ital.). 1967. 2.95 (ISBN 0-8329-1535-1). New Century.
New Century Vest-Pocket: Webster Dictionary. rev. ed. 304p. 1975. pap. 2.95 (ISBN 0-8329-1536-X). New Century.
New Century World-Wide Italian Dictionary: Italian-English, English-Italian. Ed. by Vittore E. Bocchetta. (Orig., Ital. & Eng.). 7.95 (ISBN 0-8329-9696-3). New Century.
New Century World-Wide Spanish Dictionary: Spanish: Spanish-English, English-Spanish. rev. ed. Ed. by Ida N. Hinojosa. (Span., Eng). 1965. 7.95 (ISBN 0-8329-9711-0); pap. 3.95 (ISBN 0-8329-9712-9). New Century.
New Chinese-English Dictionary. 718p. (Chinese & Eng.). 1979. Leatherette 14.95 (ISBN 0-686-92174-7, M-9554). French & Eur.
New College Dictionary English-German. 1400p. (Eng. & Ger.). 1983. pap. 16.95. M Rosenberg.
New College French & English Dictionary. Roger J. Steiner. (Fr. & Eng.). (gr. 7-12). 1972. pap. text ed. 8.58 (ISBN 0-87720-463-2). AMSCO Sch.
New College German & English Dictionary. John C. Traupman. (Ger. & Eng.). (gr. 9-12). 1981. reference 12.00 (ISBN 0-87720-584-1). AMSCO Sch.
New College German Dictionary (Plain Edition) 1416p. (Ger. & Eng.). 16.95 (074). Langenscheidt.
New College German Dictionary (Thumb-Indexed) 1416p. (Ger. & Eng.). 18.95 (073). Langenscheidt-Hachette.
New College Italian & English Dictionary. Robert C. Melzi. (Orig., Ital. & Eng.). (gr. 7-12). 1976. pap. text ed. 9.92 (ISBN 0-87720-592-2). AMSCO Sch.
New College Latin & English Dictionary. 512p. (Lat. & Eng.). pap. 2.95 (ISBN 0-553-20255-3). Bantam.
New College Latin & English Dictionary. John C. Traupman. (Lat. & Eng.). (gr. 7-12). 1966. pap. text ed. 7.67 (ISBN 0-87720-560-4). AMSCO Sch.
New College Latin & English Dictionary. Ed. by John C. Traupman. (Language Library). (Orig., Lat. & Eng.). 1970. pap. 2.95 (ISBN 0-553-20255-3). Bantam.
New College Spanish & English Dictionary. Edwin B. Williams. (Span. & Eng.). (gr. 7-12). 1968. pap. text ed. 8.58 (ISBN 0-87720-511-6). AMSCO Sch.
New Color Picture Dictionary for Children. Archie Bennett. LC 76-42144. (Illus.). (gr. 1-4). 1978. 8.95 (ISBN 0-8326-2214-1, 6391). Delair.
New Color Picture Dictionary for Children. Archie Bennett. (Illus.). 252p. (Eng.). 1981. 12.95 (ISBN 0-516-00820-X). Childrens.
New Combined Bible Dictionary & Concordance. (Direction Bks). 1973. pap. 3.95 (ISBN 0-8010-6680-8). Baker Bk.
New Compact Bible Dictionary. Al Bryant. 1967. 8.95 (ISBN 0-310-22080-7); pap. 4.95 (ISBN 0-310-22082-3). Zondervan.
New Comprehensive A-Z Crossword Dictionary. Tuazon & Schaffer. 1982. pap. 3.95 (ISBN 0-380-00168-3, 50492-8). Avon.
New Comprehensive A-Z Crossword Dictionary. Redentor M. Tuazon & Schaffer. LC 72-79971. 600p. 1973. 5.95 (ISBN 0-448-01525-0, G&D). Putnam Pub Group.
New Comprehensive English-Spanish, Spanish-English Dictionary, 2 Vols. Ed. by Ubaldo Di Benedetto. 3100p. (Eng. & Span.). 1977. Set. 60.00x (ISBN 84-7166-211-6). Intl Pubns Serv.
New Condensed Muret-Sanders German Dictionary. 1296p. (Ger. & Eng.). 70.00 (33071). Langenscheidt.
New Definitions of School-Library Service: Proceedings. University Of Chicago - Graduate Library School - 24th Conference. Ed. by Sara I. Fenwick. LC 60-2341. (University of Chicago Studies in Library Science). 1960. lib. bdg. 6.00x (ISBN 0-226-24163-7). U of Chicago Pr.
New Dictionary of Americanisms. Sylvia Clapin. LC 68-17985. 1968. Repr. of 1902 ed. 42.00x (ISBN 0-8103-3244-2). Gale.
New Dictionary of Armenian-English. Matthias Bedrossian. 816p. (Eng. & Armenian.). 35.00 (122-4). Intl Bk Ctr.
New Dictionary of Existentialism. St. Elmo Nauman, Jr. 1972. pap. 2.95 (ISBN 0-8065-0281-9). Citadel Pr.
New Dictionary of Foreign Phrases & Classical Quotations. Ed. by Hugh P. Jones. 532p. 1981. Repr. of 1902 ed. lib. bdg. 75.00 (ISBN 0-89984-264-X). Century Bookbindery.
New Dictionary of Kanji Usage. (Kanji.). 1982. 28.95 (ISBN 0-8120-5493-8). Barron.
New Dictionary of Kent Dialect. Alan Major. 1981. 39.00x (ISBN 0-905270-27-4, Pub. by Meresborough England). State Mutual Bk.
New Dictionary of Modern Maori. P. Ryan. (Maori.). 2.65. Hein.
New Dictionary of Modern Maori. Ed. by P. M. Ryan. 104p. (Maori.). 1983. pap. 4.95 (ISBN 0-86863-565-0, Pub. by Heinemann Pub New Zealand). Intl Schol Bk Serv.
New Dictionary of Music. Arthur Jacobs. (Reference Ser.). (Orig.). (YA) (gr. 9 up). 1958. pap. 4.95 (ISBN 0-14-051012-5). Penguin.
New Dictionary of Petroleum & the Oil Industry. Ahmad S. Al-Khatib. LC 75-968070. xv, 577p. (Eng. & Arabic.). 1975. Le.12.50. Lib Liban.
New Dictionary of Physics. rev. ed. Ed. by H. J. Gray & A. Isaacs. LC 75-307635. Orig. Title: Dictionary of Physics. (Illus.). 640p. 1975. 40.00 (ISBN 0-582-32242-1). Longman.
New Dictionary of Quotations on Historical Principles from Ancient & Modern Sources. Ed. by Henry L. Mencken. 1942. 30.00 (ISBN 0-394-40079-8). Knopf.
New Dictionary of Railroad Working Terminology. Ed. by Railsearch Publishing, Inc. (Railsearch Railroad Management Ser.). (Illus.). 400p. 1980. 28.00 (ISBN 0-686-27634-5); lib. bdg. 29.25 (ISBN 0-686-27635-3). Railsearch.
New Dictionary of Scientific & Technical Terms. Ahmad Khatib. 768p. (Eng. & Arabic.). 1980. 45.00 (075-9). Intl Bk Ctr.
New Dictionary of Statistics: A Complement to the Fourth Edition of Mulhall's Dictionary of Statistics. Augustus D. Webb. LC 68-18017. 1971. Repr. of 1911 ed. 56.00x (ISBN 0-8103-3988-9). Gale.
New Dictionary of Strange & Ingenious Stock Market Tricks the Experts Follow in Their Search for Wealth. C. M. Flumiani. 215p. 1976. 57.50 (ISBN 0-89266-002-3). Am Classical Coll Pr.
New Dictionary of the Liturgy. Gerhard Podhradsky. 1967. 6.95 (ISBN 0-8189-0101-2). Alba.
New Dictionary of the Social Sciences. 2nd ed. Ed. by G. Duncan Mitchell. 1980. text ed. 24.95x (ISBN 0-202-30285-7). Aldine Pub.
New Dictionary of Thoughts. rev. ed. Ed. by Tryon Edwards. 1955. 15.95 (ISBN 0-385-00127-4). Doubleday.
New Diesterweg-Larousse: Dictionnaire du Francais Langue Etrangere. Frwd. by F. J. Hausmann. 1104p. (Fr.). DM.29.80. Diesterweg.
New Dinosaur Dictionary. Donald F. Glut. (Illus.). 256p. 1982. 19.95 (ISBN 0-8065-0782-9). Citadel Pr.
New Encyclopedic Dictionary of Business Law: With Forms. 2nd ed. Martin J. Ross & Jeffrey S. Ross. LC 81-78. 349p. 1981. 32.95 (ISBN 0-13-612630-8, Busn). P-H.
New England Farmer; or, Georgical Dictionary. Samuel Deane. LC 72-5043. (Technology & Society Ser.). 543p. 1972. Repr. of 1822 ed. 25.00 (ISBN 0-405-04695-2). Ayer Co.
New English Astrological Thesaurus. James J. Francis. LC 76-47426. 1977. pap. 1.95 (ISBN 0-87707-179-9). CSA Pr.
New English-Chinese Dictionary. 1252p. (Eng. & Chinese.). 1979. 17.95 (ISBN 0-686-97423-9, M-9290). French & Eur.
New English-Chinese Dictionary. 1542p. (Eng. & Chinese.). 1982. 18.50x (ISBN 0-8044-0138-1). Ungar.
New English-Chinese Dictionary. 1688p. (Eng. & Chinese.). 1975. leatherette 24.95 (ISBN 0-686-92166-6, M-9556). French & Eur.
New English-Chinese Dictionary. 1688p. (Eng. & Chinese.). 1976. Leatherette 19.95 (ISBN 0-686-92177-1, M-9553). French & Eur.
New English-Chinese Dictionary. 1702p. (Chinese & Eng.). 1975. 17.50 (ISBN 0-8351-0596-2); PLB 29.95 (ISBN 0-8351-0597-0). China Bks.
New English-Chinese Dictionary. Xin Ying-Han-Cidian Editing Committee. 1648p. 1975. 29.95 (ISBN 0-917056-59-0, Pub. by Joint Pub Co China). Cheng & Tsui.
New English-Chinese Law Dictionary. W. S. Hung. 162p. (Eng. & Chinese.). 1979. 17.50 (ISBN 962-204-001-2, M-9558). French & Eur.
New English-Chinese Law Dictionary. William Hung. LC 80-113867. 162p. (Eng. & Chinese.). 1979. HK.$60.00 (ISBN 9-622-04001-2). M Stevenson.
New English-Croatian & Croatian-English Dictionary. F. A. Bogadek. 531p. (Eng. & Croatian.). 1944. 25.00. Hafner.
New English-Croatian, Croatian-English Dictionary. 3rd ed. Francis A. Bogadek. (Eng. & Croatian.). 1971. Repr. of 1944 ed. 25.95x (ISBN 0-02-841580-9). Hafner.
New English Dictionary. J. Kersey. Repr. of 1702 ed. 38.00 (ISBN 3-4870-5349-7). Adler.

New English-French Dictionary of Slang & Colloquialisms. Georgette A. Marks. LC 74-32524. 299p. (Eng. & Fr.). 1975. 12.95 (ISBN 0-87690-149-6). Dutton.

New English-Greek-English Handy Dictionary. G. C. Divry. 511p. (Eng. & Gr.). 1978. 9.95 (ISBN 0-686-92414-2, M-9439). French & Eur.

New English-Japanese Dictionary. LC 81-101348. (Illus.). xxi, 2477p. (Eng. & Japanese.). 1980. 10000.00 Yen. Kenkyusha.

New English-Russian Dictionary, 2 vols. 1685p. (Eng. & Rus.). 1980. Set. 80.00x (ISBN 0-569-07330-8, Pub. by Collet's). State Mutual Bk.

New Expanded Dictionary of Stock Market Charts. Carlo M. Flumiana. (Illus.). 189p. 1980. deluxe ed. 67.35 (ISBN 0-918968-64-X). Inst Econ Finan.

New Expanded Dictionary of Stock Market Charts. new ed. C. M. Flumiani. (Illus.). 1977. 65.25 (ISBN 0-89266-050-3). Am Classical Coll Pr.

New Expanded Dictionary of Stock Market Charts. Carlo M. Flumiani. (Illus.). 179p. 1983. 81.75 (ISBN 0-86654-091-1). Inst Econ Finan.

New Functional Hebrew-English, English-Hebrew Dictionary. Nathan Goldberg. (Hebrew & Eng.). (gr. 9-12). 1958. 5.00x (ISBN 0-87068-379-9). Ktav.

New General English Dictionary. Thomas Dyche. 1971. Repr. of 1723 ed. 114.25 (ISBN 3-4870-4398-X). Adler.

New Golden Dictionary. Bertha M. Parker. (Illus.). 120p. (ps-3). 1972. 7.95 (ISBN 0-307-16837-9, Golden Pr); lib. bdg. 12.23 (ISBN 0-307-66837-1). Western Pub.

New Grove Dictionary of Music & Musicians, 20 vols. Ed. by Stanley Sadie. 1980. Set. 1900.00x (ISBN 0-333-23111-2). Groves Dict Music.

New Horizon Ladder Dictionary of the English Language for Young Readers. rev. ed. John R. Shaw & Janet Shaw. (Illus.). 686p. 1973. pap. 2.95 (ISBN 0-451-12421-9, Sig). NAL.

New Illustrated Grosset Dictionary. Ed. by Archie Bennett. LC 76-42144. (Illus.). (gr. k-5). 1977. pap. 6.95 (ISBN 0-448-14384-4, G&D). Putnam Pub Group.

New Illustrated Hebrew-English Dictionary for Young Readers. Nathan Goldberg. (Illus., Hebrew & Eng.). (gr. 4-7). 1958. pap. 6.95x (ISBN 0-87068-370-5). Ktav.

New International Dictionary of Refrigeration. International Institute of Refrigeration. LC 76-373634. xxxvii, 560p. (Eng., Danish, Fr., Ger., Ital., Rus. & Span.). 1976. 3000.00 F (IIR). Unipub.

New International Dictionary of Refrigeration. 1977. 82.50 (ISBN 0-685-99158-X, IIR5, IIR). Unipub.

New Japanese-English Dictionary of Economic Terms. 580p. (Japanese & Eng.). 1977. Leatherette 45.00 (ISBN 0-686-92411-8, M-9334). French & Eur.

New Jewish Encyclopedia. rev. ed. Bridger & Wolk. LC 76-15251. (Illus.). 542p. 1976. 14.95 (ISBN 0-87441-120-3). Behrman.

New Mayer's Dictionary: English-Spanish, Spanish-English. 438p. (Span. & Eng.). write for info. (798). Fernandez.

New Medical-Pharmaceutical Dictionary. A. M. Oweida. 2404p. (Eng. & Arabic.). 1970. Leatherette 150.00 (ISBN 0-686-92192-5, M-9766). French & Eur.

New Method Dictionary. M. P. West & J. G. Endicott. 27.50 (ISBN 0-87559-106-X); thumb index 32.00 (ISBN 0-87559-139-6). Shalom.

New Michaelis Illustrated Dictionary: English-Portuguese, Portuguese English, 2 vols. (Illus., Port. & Eng.). 1976. Vol. 1 Eng.-Port. 42.00; Vol. 2 Port.-Eng. 45.00. Imported Bks.

New Military & Naval Dictionary. Ed. by Frank Gaynor. Repr. of 1951 ed. lib. bdg. 15.75x (ISBN 0-8371-2129-9, GAMN). Greenwood.

New Model English - Thai Dictionary. Compiled by So Sethaputra. (Illus.). 879p. (Eng. & Thai.). 1973. 17.50x (ISBN 0-8002-1748-9). Intl Pubns Serv.

New Model Thai-English Dictionary, 2 vols. 3rd ed. Compiled by So Sethaputra. LC 81-915704. 1072p. (Eng. & Thai.). 1978. B.450.00 set. Thai Watana.

New Muret-Sanders Encyclopedic Dictionary: Part I, English-German, 2 vols. Ed. by O. Springer. 958p. (Eng. & Ger.). 1983. pap. 70.00 ea. M Rosenberg.

New Muret-Sanders Encyclopedic Dictionary: Part II, German-English, 2 vols. O. Springer. 1040p. (Ger. & Eng.). 1983. pap. 80.00 ea. M Rosenberg.

New Muret-Sanders Encyclopedic Dictionary: Pt. I, vol. 1, A-M. 1050p. (Eng. & Ger.). 70.00 (01120). Langenscheidt.

New Muret-Sanders Encyclopedic Dictionary: Pt. II, vol. 1, A-K. 1050p. (Ger. & Eng.). 80.00 (01124). Langenscheidt.

New Muret-Sanders Encyclopedic Dictionary: Pt. I, vol. 2, N-Z. 1050p. (Eng. & Ger.). 70.00 (01122). Langenscheidt.

New Muret-Sanders Encyclopedic Dictionary: Pt. II, vol. 2, L-Z. 1050p. (Ger. & Eng.). 80.00 (01126). Langenscheidt.

New Music Vocabulary: A Guide to Notational Signs for Contemporary Music. Howard Risatti. LC 73-81565. (Illus.). 144p. 1975. pap. 7.45 (ISBN 0-252-00406-X). U of Ill Pr.

New Oxford Illustrated Dictionary, 2 vols. (Illus.). 1920p. (Eng.). 1976. Aus.$99.95. Oxford U Pr.

New Polish-English Dictionary. rev. ed. Iwo Pognowski. (Pol. & Eng.). 1982. 19.95 (ISBN 0-88254-463-2); pap. 11.95 (ISBN 0-88254-464-0). Hippocrene Bks.

New Practical Chinese-English Dictionary. Shi-Chiu Liang. 1355p. 1973. 32.00x (ISBN 0-917056-53-1, Pub. by Far East Bk Co China). Cheng & Tsui.

New Practical Chinese-English Dictionary. Shi-Chiu Liang. 1355p. 1973. pap. 16.95x (ISBN 0-917056-54-X, Pub. by Far East Bk Co China). Cheng & Tsui.

New Practical Chinese-English Dictionary. Ed. by Shi-Chiu Liang. 1355p. 1973. 45.00x (ISBN 0-917056-52-3, Pub. by Far East Bk Co China). Cheng & Tsui.

New Practical Dictionary for Crossword Puzzles. Frank E. Newman. LC 74-5608. (Eng.). 1975. 7.95 (ISBN 0-385-14776-7). Doubleday.

New Practical Dictionary for Crossword Puzzles. rev. ed. Frank Eaton Newman. LC 74-5608. 336p. 1975. 7.95 (ISBN 0-385-05280-4). Doubleday.

New Practical English-Chinese Dictionary. Ed. by Shi-Chiu Liang. 2401p. 1980. pap. 25.00x (ISBN 0-917056-56-6, Pub. by Far East Bk Co China). Cheng & Tsui.

New Practical English-Chinese Dictionary. 2410p. (Eng. & Chinese.). 14.95 (ISBN 0-686-92368-5, M-9552). French & Eur.

New Revised Velazquez Spanish & English Dictionary. (Span. & Eng.). 16.95 (7728-2). Natl Textbk.

New Rhyming Dictionary of One & Two Syllable Rhymes. Ottenheimer. pap. 2.50 (ISBN 0-06-461009-8, BN). B&N NY.

New Roget's Thesaurus in Dictionary Form. 512p. 1983. pap. 2.95 (ISBN 0-425-06400-X). Berkley Pub.

New Russian-English & English-Russian Dictionary. O'Brien. 710p. (Rus. & Eng.). 6.00. Imported Bks.

New Secretary's Deskbook. Ed. by Betty M. Corson. LC 74-34544. 844p. (Eng.). 1975. write for info. (ISBN 0-03-923299-9). HR&W Canada.

New Shakespearean Dictionary. Richard J. Cunliffe. LC 76-39872. Repr. of 1910 ed. 24.00 (ISBN 0-404-01377-5). AMS Pr.

New Shakespearean Dictionary. Richard J. Cunliffe. LC 72-194980. 1922. lib. bdg. 30.00 (ISBN 0-8414-2431-4). Folcroft.

New Smith's Bible Dictionary. rev. ed. William Smith. Ed. by Reuel G. Lemmons et al. LC 66-20927. 1966. 9.95 (ISBN 0-385-04869-6); thumb-indexed 10.95 (ISBN 0-385-04872-6). Doubleday.

New Smith's Bible Dictionary. rev. ed. William Smith. LC 78-69668. 1979. pap. 8.95 (ISBN 0-385-14652-3, Galilee). Doubleday.

New Steinerbooks Dictionary of the Paranormal. George Riland. LC 79-93353. (Spiritual Science Library). 370p. 1980. cancelled (ISBN 0-8334-0719-8). Garber Comm.

New Steinerbooks Dictionary of the Paranormal. George Riland. LC 79-93353. (Steinerbks Spiritual Science Library). 370p. 1980. lib. bdg. 20.00 (ISBN 0-89345-028-6). Garber Comm.

New Testament Wordbook for Translators. R. G. Bratcher et al. (Translational Articles Ser.). 1966. pap. 1.00x (ISBN 0-8267-0020-9, 08638). United Bible.

New Webster's Crossword Puzzle Dictionary. Bettye F. Melnicove. 1978. pap. 2.50 (ISBN 0-449-24071-1, Crest). Fawcett.

New Webster's Crossword Puzzle Dictionary: Vest Pocket Edition. Ed. by Edward G. Finnegan. 1978. pap. 1.95 (ISBN 0-8326-2221-4, 6430). Delair.

New Webster's Dictionary. pap. 1.99 (ISBN 0-686-00475-2). Dennison.

New Webster's Dictionary of the English Language (College Edition) Ed. by Edward G. Finnegan. LC 75-18559. (Illus.). 1975. 14.95 (ISBN 0-8326-0035-0, 6602). Delair.

New Webster's Dictionary of the English Language (Handy School & Office Edition) Ed. by Sidney R. Bergquist. LC 75-15424. 1975. 4.95 (ISBN 0-8326-0033-4, 6501). Delair.

New Webster's Dictionary of the English Language (Modern Desk Edition) Ed. by Sidney R. Bergquist. LC 76-3282. (Illus.). 1976. 8.95 (ISBN 0-8326-0040-7, 6603). Delair.

New Webster's Dictionary (Vest Pocket Edition) Ed. by Edward G. Finnegan. LC 75-18560. 1976. pap. 1.75 (ISBN 0-8326-0036-9, 6401). Delair.

New Webster's English-Spanish Dictionary: Vest Pocket Edition. Ed. by Edward G. Finnegan. 1980. pap. 1.75 (ISBN 0-8326-0050-4, 6454). Delair.

New Webster's Law for Everyone: Vest Pocket Edition. Ed. by Edward G. Finnegan. 1980. pap. 1.75 (ISBN 0-8326-0049-0, 6452). Delair.

New Webster's Medical Dictionary: Vest Pocket Edition. Ed. by Edward G. Finnegan. 1980. pap. 1.95 (ISBN 0-8326-0048-2, 6453). Delair.

New Webster's Quick Reference Dictionary. 1981. pap. 1.95 (ISBN 0-8326-0051-2, 6604). Delair.

New Webster's Quick Reference English-Spanish Dictionary. (Quick Reference Ser.). (Orig.). 1981. pap. 1.95 (ISBN 0-8326-0054-7, 6607). Delair.

New Webster's Quick Reference Thesaurus. (Quick Reference Ser.). (Orig.). 1981. pap. 1.95 (ISBN 0-8326-0052-0, 6605). Delair.

New Webster's Vest Pocket Thesaurus. Ed. by Edward G. Finnegan. LC 78-52347. 1978. pap. 1.75 (ISBN 0-8326-0045-8, 6440). Delair.

New Webster's Word Divider: Vest Pocket Edition. Ed. by Edward G. Finnegan. LC 76-6038. 1978. pap. 1.95 (ISBN 0-8326-0041-5, 6450). Delair.

New World English-Spanish, Spanish-English Dictionary. 592p. (Eng. & Span.). write for info. (ISBN 0-671-41836-X); pap. 6.95 (ISBN 0-671-41837-8). S&S.

New World English-Spanish, Spanish-English Dictionary. (Span. & Eng.). 9.95; pap. 6.95. Iaconi.

New World Spanish-English & English-Spanish Dictionary. Ed. by Salvatore Ramondino. LC 67-17418. (Illus., Span. & Eng.). (YA) (gr. 9up). 1973. thumb-indexed 7.95 (ISBN 0-529-04719-5, 2677N-I). pap. 5.95 (ISBN 0-529-05181-8, 2677P). Collins Pubs.

New World Spanish-English, English-Spanish Dictionary. Ed. by Salvatore Ramondino. (Span. & Eng.). pap. 3.50 (ISBN 0-451-11312-8, E9043, Sig). NAL.

New York Dictionary Catalog of the Missionary Research Library, 17 vols. Missionary Research Library. 1968. Set. 1615.00 (ISBN 0-8161-0778-5, Hall Library). G K Hall.

New York Historical Society's Dictionary of Artists in America, 1564-1860. Grocet Wallace. 1979. 65.00 (ISBN 0-686-43145-6). Apollo.

New York Times Crossword Puzzle Dictionary. expanded ed. Pulliam & Grundman. LC 76-50913. 1977. 19.95 (ISBN 0-8129-0668-3). Times Bks.

New York Times Crossword Puzzle Dictionary. Ed. by Tom Pulliam & Claire Grundman. 704p. 1976. pap. 9.95 (ISBN 0-446-37262-5). Warner Bks.

New York Times Everyday Dictionary. The New York Times. Ed. by Thomas M. Paikeday. LC 81-84903. 832p. (Orig.). 1982. 12.95 (ISBN 0-8129-0910-0); pap. 7.95 (ISBN 0-8129-6318-0). Times Bks.

New York Times Everyday Reader's Dictionary of Misunderstood, Misused, Mispronounced Words. Ed. by Laurence Urdang. LC 74-184644. 196p. 1972. pap. 7.95 (1975) (ISBN 0-8129-0232-7); pap. 4.95 (ISBN 0-8129-6244-3). Times Bks.

New Zealand Commercial Dictionary. 2nd ed. D. A. Dale. 338p. 1967. 11.00x (ISBN 0-8002-0077-2). Intl Pubns Serv.

New Zealand Dictionary. Ordman. 1339p. 1983. 9.95 (ISBN 0-86863-373-9, Pub. by Heinemann Pubs New Zealand). Intl Schol Bk Serv.

Newe Natekwinappeh: Shoshoni Stories & Dictionary. Wick R. Miller. (Utah Anthropological Papers: No. 94). (Shoshoni.). Repr. of 1972 ed. 24.00 (ISBN 0-404-60694-6). AMS Pr.

News Dictionary. 1977. 14.95 (ISBN 0-87196-105-9). Facts on File.

News Dictionary Nineteen Seventy-Eight. Ed. by Donald Paneth. (Illus.). 1979. 14.95x (ISBN 0-87196-107-5); pap. 6.95 (ISBN 0-87196-108-3). Facts on File.

News Dictionary: Vol. 1, 1964. annual Lester A. Sobel et al. LC 65-17649. (Orig.). 1965. 14.95 (ISBN 0-87196-079-6). Facts on File.

News Dictionary: Vol. 2, 1965. annual Ed. by Lester A. Sobel et al. LC 65-17649. (Orig.). 1966. 14.95 (ISBN 0-87196-081-8). Facts on File.

News Dictionary: Vol. 3, 1966. annual Ed. by Lester A. Sobel et al. LC 65-17649. (Orig.). 1967. 14.95 (ISBN 0-87196-083-4). Facts on File.

News Dictionary: Vol. 4, 1967. annual Ed. by Lester A. Sobel et al. LC 65-17649. 1968. 14.95 (ISBN 0-87196-085-0). Facts on File.

News Dictionary: Vol. 5, 1968. annual Ed. by Howard M. Epstein & Gerald B. Kanner. LC 65-17649. (Illus.). 1969. 14.95 (ISBN 0-87196-087-7). Facts on File.

News Dictionary: Vol. 7, 1970. annual 1971. 14.95 (ISBN 0-87196-091-5). Facts on File.

News Dictionary: Vol. 8, 1971. annual 1972. 14.95 (ISBN 0-87196-093-1). Facts on File.

News Dictionary, Vol. 9: 1972. annual 1973. 14.95 (ISBN 0-87196-095-8). Facts on File.
News Dictionary: 1973, Vol. 10. annual Ed. by Lester A. Sobel. 500p. 1974. lib. bdg. 14.95 (ISBN 0-87196-097-4). Facts on File.
News Dictionary 1974, Vol. 11. annual Ed. by Judith Trotsky. LC 65-17649. 500p. 1975. lib. bdg. 14.95 (ISBN 0-87196-099-0). Facts on File.
News Dictionary 1975, Vol. 12. annual Ed. by Judith Trotsky. LC 65-17649. 1976. lib. bdg. 14.95 (ISBN 0-87196-101-6). Facts on File.
News Dictionary 1976. Ed. by Mary E. Clifford et al. LC 65-17649. 1977. lib. bdg. 14.95 (ISBN 0-87196-103-2). Facts on File.
News Dictionary, 1979: Annual. 1980. 14.95 (ISBN 0-87196-109-1); pap. 9.95 (ISBN 0-87196-110-5). Facts on File.
News Dictionary 1980. Donald Paneth. 400p. 1981. 14.95 (ISBN 0-87196-111-3). Facts on File.
Newu Diesterweg-Larousse: Dictionnaire du Francais Langue Etrangere. Frwd. by F. J. Hausmann. 928p. (Fr.). DM.26.80. Diesterweg.
NICSEM Special Education Thesaurus. 2nd ed. National Information Center for Educational Media. LC 80-83509. 1980. pap. 16.00 (ISBN 0-89320-048-4). Univ SC Natl Info.
Niederlaendisch, 2 vols. rev. ed. Incl. Teil I. Niederlaendisch-Deutsch. Rev. by F. J. Van de Wiele. 527p. DM.18.80 (10231); Teil II. Deutsch-Niederlaendisch. Rev. by Frans Beermans. 544p. DM.18.80 (10236). (Langenscheidts Taschenworterbucher Ser.). (Ger. & Dutch.). DM.beide Teile in einem Band 29.80 (11231). Langenscheidt.
Niederlassungsrecht. Institut International de Terminologie Juridique & Administrative. 145p. (Ger. & Fr.). 1976. DM.15.80. Langen AG.
Nieuwe Medische Winkler Prins, 2 vols. J. J. Bouckaert. LC 76-676261. (Eng. & Dutch.). 1976. fl.4.75 (ISBN 9-0100-1653-6). Elsevier Nederland.
Nieuwe Woorden. Maarten Van Nierop. LC 76-504980. 327p. (Dutch.). 1975. fl.22.75 (ISBN 9-06158-054-4). Scheltens.
NIV Handy Concordance. Edward W. Goodrick & John R. Kohlenberger, III. 384p. (Orig.). 1982. pap. 4.95 (ISBN 0-310-43662-1). Zondervan.
Nomenclature & Terminology of Tank Trailers & Containers. Truck Trailer Manufacturers Association. (Recommended Practices: RP No. 36-75). 1975. 3.00. Truck Trailer Mfrs.
Nomenclature des Appelations d'emploi dans L' Industrie Papetiere Quebecoise: Anglais-Francais. N. Cote & J. Gaumond. 114p. (Eng. & Fr.). 1977. pap. 6.95 (ISBN 0-7754-2765-9, M-9234). French & Eur.
Norsk Dataordbok. Norsk Sprakrad. LC 77-552785. 184p. (Eng. & Norwegian.). 1976. Kr.49.50 (ISBN 8-2000-2403-2). Universitetsforlaget.
Norsk-Engelsk Ordbok. W. A. Kirkeby & S. Utgabes. 1276p. (Norweigian & Eng.). 1979. 95.00 (ISBN 82-573-0079-9, M-9458). French & Eur.
Norsk-Engelsk Ordbok. 3rd ed. Willy Kirkeby. LC 79-374954. 514p. (Eng. & Norwegian.). 1978. Kr.55.00 (ISBN 8-2573-0006-3). Kunnskapsforlaget.
Norsk-Engelsk Ordbok. 4th ed. Willie Kirkely. 514p. (Norwegian & Eng.). 1981. 22.00x (ISBN 82-573-0006-3, N482). Vanous.
Norsk-Engelsk Ordbok Praktisk. W. Guy & J. Messell. 324p. (Norwegian & Eng.). 1979. 29.95 (ISBN 0-686-92442-8, M-9467). French & Eur.
Norsk Forkortingsbok. Stale Loland & Arnold Thorsen. LC 77-463699. 68p. (Norwegian.). 1976. Kr.35.00 (ISBN 8-20200-892-1). J W Cappelens.
Norsk-Fransk Ordbok. M. Lesoil. 445p. (Fr. & Norse.). 1978. 24.95 (ISBN 82-573-0074-8, M-9463). French & Eur.
Norsk Landbruksordbok, 2 vols. Nikolai Nelvik. LC 79-377494. (Eng. & Norwegian.). 1979. write for info. (ISBN 8-2521-0870-9). Samlaget.
Norsk-Nederlansk-Norsk. 379p. (Norwegian & Dutch.). 1981. 14.95 (ISBN 82-573-0164-7, M-9459). French & Eur.
Norsk-Portugisisk Ordbok. Kare Nilsson. vii, 398p. (Norwegian & Port.). 1979. Kr.95.00 (ISBN 8-20002-437-7). Universitetsforlaget.
Norsk-Rumensk Lommeordbok med Liten Parloer. Elisabeta S. Guha. LC 77-570195. 48p. (Norwegian & Roman.). 1976. Kr.15.00 (ISBN 8-200-05001-7). Universitetsforlaget.
Norsk-Svensk Ordbok. Nat. Beckman. Rev. by Leif Maehle & Bengt Sigurd. 210p. (Norwegian & Swedish.). 1978. Kr.71.00 (ISBN 91-24-14535-1). Esselte Studium.
Norsk-Svensk Ordbok. Natanael Beckman. Rev. by Lief Maehle & Bengt Sigurd. 210p. (Swedish & Norwegian.). write for info. (ISBN 91-24-14535-1). Esselte Studium.
Norsk-Tysk Ordbok. G. Paulsen. 416p. (Norwegian & Ger.). 1973. 34.95 (ISBN 82-573-0121-3, M-9466). French & Eur.
Norvezhsko-Russkii Slovar. V. D. Arakin. 1113p. (Rus. & Norwegian.). 1963. 13.25 (Pub. by GINS). Four Continent.
Norwegian Deluxe Dictionary: English-Norse. B. Berulfsen & A. Svenkerud. (Norwegian & Eng.). 1968. 100.00x (ISBN 82-02-09060-1, N461). Vanous.
Norwegian Dictionary: Engelsk-Norwegina. rev. ed. B. Berulfsen & T. Berulfsen. 433p. (Norwegian & Eng.). 1981. 22.00x (ISBN 82-573-0161-2, N481). Vanous.
Norwegian Dictionary: English-Norwegian. Ed. by L. Bjerke & H. Soraas. (Norwegian & Eng.). 1963. 30.00x (ISBN 0-686-31692-4, N434). Vanous.
Norwegian Dictionary: Norsk-English, Vol. 2. Scavenius Christophensen. Ed. by Willie Kirkeby. (Norwegian & Eng.). 1981. 22.00x (ISBN 8-2573-0006-3, N482). Vanous.
Norwegian Dictionary: Norwegian-English. G. Haugen. (Norwegian & Eng.). 1976. pap. 20.00x (ISBN 0-299-03874-2, N533). Vanous.
Norwegian-English Dictionary. W. A. Kirkeby. (Norwegian & Eng.). 1977. write for info. (ISBN 82-573-0006-3). Kunnskapsforlaget.
Norwegian-English Dictionary. Large ed. W. A. Kirkeby. (Norwegian & Eng.). 1979. write for info. (ISBN 82-573-0135-3). Kunnskapsforlaget.
Norwegian-English Dictionary. T. Slette. 1326p. (Norwegian & Eng.). 1977. 100.00x (ISBN 82-521-0692-7, N-537). Vanous.
Norwegian-English Dictionary of Commerce. Daae Gabrielsen. (Norwegian & Eng.). 1978. write for info. (ISBN 82-573-0108-6). Kunnskapsforlaget.
Norwegian-English, English-Norwegian Dictionary, 2 vols. 4th rev. ed. W. Kirkeby & B. Berulfsen. (Norwegian & Eng.). 45.00 set (ISBN 82-573-0007-1). Norwegian-Eng (ISBN 82-573-0006-3). Eng.-Norwegian (ISBN 82-573-0007-1). Heinman.
Norwegian-English, English-Norwegian Maritime-Technical Dictionary, 2 vols. P. Askim. (Norwegian & Eng.). Set. 45.00 (ISBN 82-504-0031-3). Heinman.
Norwegian-English, English-Norwegian Technical Dictionary, 2 Vols. J. Ansteinsson & A. T. Andreassen. (Norwegian & Eng.). Set. 60.00 (ISBN 8-2702-8007-0). Heinman.
Norwegian-English-Norwegian. (Berlitz Pocket Dictionaries Ser.). (Eng. & Norwegian.). 4.95 (ISBN 0-02-964560-3). Macmillan.
Norwegian-French Dictionary. M. Lesoil. (Norwegian & Fr.). 1970. write for info. (ISBN 82-573-0074-8). Kunnskapsforlaget.
Norwegian-French Dictionary of Commerce. Daae Gabrielsen. (Norwegian & Fr.). 1975. write for info. (ISBN 82-573-0094-2). Kunnskapsforlaget.
Norwegian-German Dictionary. Gerd Paulsen. (Norwegian & Ger.). 1979. write for info. (ISBN 8-25730-121-3). Kunnskapsforlaget.
Norwegian-German Dictionary of Commerce. Daae Gabrielsen. (Norwegian & Ger.). 1971. write for info. (ISBN 82-573-0092-6). Kunnskapsforlaget.
Norwegian-German Dictionary of Technical Terms. D. Strom & J. A. Strom. (Norwegian & Ger.). 1979. write for info. (ISBN 82-573-0136-1). Kunnskapsforlaget.
Norwegian Pocket Dictionary. (Norwegian & Eng.). 10.00 (ISBN 82-517-8010-1). Heinman.
Norwegian Pocket Dictionary: English-Norwegian, Norwegian-English. rev. 2nd ed. Gyldendals. (Norwegian & Eng.). 1980. 9.00x (ISBN 82-573-0152-3, N-407). Vanous.
Norwegian-Spanish Dictionary. C. Blom-Dahl. (Norwegian & Span.). 1983. write for info. (ISBN 82-573-0169-8). Kunnskapsforlaget.
Norwegian-Spanish Dictionary of Commerce. H. Evjen. (Norwegian & Span.). 1974. write for info. (ISBN 82-573-0107-8). Kunnskapsforlaget.
Norwegian Technical Dictionary: English-Norwegian, Vol. 1. 4th ed. J. Ansteinsson. (Norwegian & Eng.). 1979. 42.00x (ISBN 8-2702-8007-0, N433). Vanous.
Norwegian Technical Dictionary: Norwegian-English, Vol. 2. rev. 4th ed. Ed. by J. Ansteinsson. (Norwegian & Eng.). 1980. 38.00x (ISBN 8-2702-8006-2, N432). Vanous.
Norwegisch-Daenisches Etymologisches Woerterbuch, Vol. 1. 2nd ed. H. S. Falk & Alf Torp. (Norwegian & Danish.). 1960. 55.00 (ISBN 3-533-00505-4, M-7570, Pub. by Carl Winter). French & Eur.
Norwegisch-Daenisches Etymologisches Woerterbuch, Vol. 1. 2nd ed. H. S. Falk & Alf Torp. (Norwegian & Danish.). 1960. 55.00 (ISBN 3-533-00505-4). Winter Univ.
Norwegisch-Daenisches Etymologisches Woerterbuch, Vol. 2. 2nd ed. H. S. Falk & Alf Torp. (Norwegian & Danish.). 1960. 55.00 (ISBN 3-533-00506-2, M-7571, Pub. by Carl Winter). French & Eur.
Norwegisch-Daenisches Etymologisches Woerterbuch, Vol. 2. 2nd ed. H. S. Falk & Alf Torp. (Norwegian & Danish.). 1960. 55.00 (ISBN 3-533-00506-2). Winter Univ.
Norwegisch Daenisches Etymologisches Woerterbuch: Mit Literatur-Nachweisen Strittiger Etymologien Sowie Deutschem und Altnordischen Woerterverzeichnis, 2 Vols. 2nd ed. H. S. Falk & Alf Torp. 1722p. (Norwegian & Danish.). 1960. Set. 80.00x (ISBN 8-200-00085-0, Dist. by Columbia U Pr). Universitet.
Notary Public Practices & Glossary. 3rd ed. Raymond C. Rothman. LC 77-93911. 1980. text ed. 15.95 (ISBN 0-933134-03-7). Natl Notary.
Notes on the Sounds & Vocabulary of Gullah. L. D. Turner. (Publications of the American Dialect Society: No. 3). 28p. 1945. pap. 2.50x (ISBN 0-8173-0603-X). U of Ala Pr.
Notes Towards the Definition of Culture. T. S. Eliot. 8.95 (ISBN 0-15-167277-6). HarBraceJ.
Nou Diccionari de la Llengua Catalana. J. B. Xuriguera. 836p. (Catalan.). 1975. 18.95 (ISBN 84-7263-111-7, S-50211). French & Eur.
Nouveau Dictionnaire de Droit et de Sciences Economiques. Raymond Barraine. 540p. (Fr.). 1974. 39.95 (ISBN 0-686-56779-X, M-6023). French & Eur.
Nouveau Dictionnaire de la Peche. Jean Schreiner et al. 384p. (Fr.). 1975. 35.95 (ISBN 0-686-57331-5). French & Eur.
Nouveau Dictionnaire de la Peinture Moderne. 416p. (Fr.). 1963. 47.50 (ISBN 0-686-57270-X, F-10800). French & Eur.
Nouveau Dictionnaire de la Sculpture Moderne. 328p. (Fr.). 1970. 47.50 (ISBN 0-686-57061-8, M-6431). French & Eur.
Nouveau Dictionnaire des Synonymes. Emile Genouvrier et al. (Fr.). 1977. 19.95 (ISBN 0-686-57192-4, M-6266). French & Eur.
Nouveau Dictionnaire Du Batiment. Marcel Lefebvre. 411p. (Fr.). 1971. pap. 25.00 (ISBN 0-686-57010-3, M-6351). French & Eur.
Nouveau Dictionnaire du Batiment: Anglais-Francais Francais-Anglais. 1971 ed. M. Lefebvre. (Illus.). 450p. (Eng. & Fr.). 300.00 F. Maison Dictionnaire.
Nouveau Dictionnaire du Francais Contemporain Illustre. 1290p. (Fr.). 27.00 (Dist. by Continental Bk Co). Larousse.
Nouveau Dictionnaire etymologique. A. Dauzat et al. (Fr., Fr). 27.50 (ISBN 2-03-020210-X, 3612). Larousse.
Nouveau Dictionnaire Etymologique. 6th ed. Albert Dauzat. 856p. (Fr.). 1971. 23.50 (ISBN 0-686-57269-6, F-135950). French & Eur.
Nouveau Dictionnaire: Francais-Chinois. 846p. (Fr. & Chinese.). 1980. leatherette 9.95 (ISBN 0-686-97425-5, M-9278). French & Eur.
Nouveau Dictionnaire Francais-Chinois. 1499p. (Fr. & Chinese.). 1981. 25.95 (ISBN 962-04-0090-9, M-9372). French & Eur.
Nouveau Dictionnaire Francais-Hebreu. (Fr. & Hebrew.). 1973. 35.85 (ISBN 0-685-55772-3). Larousse.
Nouveau Dictionnaire Francais-Neerlandais, Nederlands-Francais. 18th ed. Ludovic Grootaers. 826p. (Fr. & Dutch.). 1969. 65.00 (ISBN 0-686-57318-8, M-6301). French & Eur.
Nouveau Dictionnaire Hebreu-Francais. Marc M. Cohn. 792p. (Fr. & Hebrew.). 1974. 32.50 (ISBN 0-686-56956-3, M-6078). French & Eur.
Nouveau Dictionnaire hebreu-francais. (Hebrew & Fr.). 1973. 39.25 (ISBN 0-685-55771-5). Larousse.
Nouveau Dictionnaire International du Froid. 300p. (Fr., Eng., Ger., Rus., Span. & It., New International Dictionary of Refrigeration). 1970. 135.00 (ISBN 0-686-56738-2, M-6432). French & Eur.
Nouveau Glossaire Nautique, 2 lettre. 1848 ed. Augustin Jal. (Fr.). Lettre A, 1970. pap. 16.00 (ISBN 90-2796-442-4); Lettre B,1972. pap. 16.00x (ISBN 90-2797-028-9). Mouton.
Nouveau Glossaire Nautique, Lettre C: Revision De L'edition Publiee En 1848. Augustin Jal. (Fr.). 1978. pap. 48.00x (ISBN 90-279-7538-8). Mouton.
Nouveau Larousse Eementaire. Larousse & Co. (Illus., Fr.). 23.95 (ISBN 0-685-14003-2). Larousse.
Nouveau Larousse Elementaire. (Fr.). 1967. 18.50 (Dist. by Continental Bk Co). Larousse.
Nouveau Larousse Francais-Anglais, English-French. (Mars). (Eng. & Fr.). 24.50 (ISBN 2-03-020812-4, 4083). Larousse.
Nouveau Larousse "Mars". J. Mergault. (Fr. & Eng.). 1971. 16.75 (Dist. by Continental Bk Co). Larousse.

Nouveau Lexique d'Economie: Economie, Droit, Gestion, Finance. Jacques Vuitton & Philippe Vuitton. LC 79-385411. (Illus.). 185p. (Fr.). 1978. 37.00 F. Doc Univers.
Nouveau Petit Larousse en couleurs. Larousse And Co. (Illus., Fr.). 1974. 75.00 (ISBN 2-03-020111-1, 3676). Larousse.
Nouveau vocabulaire des etudes philosophiques. Sylvain Aurox & Yvonne Weil. LC 78-390296. 255p. (Fr.). 1975. 19.00 F (ISBN 2-01-002450-8). Hachette-Jeunesse.
Novedades en el Diccionario Academico. Julio Casares. (Span.). 7.25 (AGL). Lectorum Pubns.
Novissimo Dizionario della Lingua Italiana. F. Palazzi. Ed. by G. Folena. 1624p. (Ital.). 1981. 75.00 (ISBN 0-686-97427-1, M-9363). French & Eur.
Novo Dicionario Pratico da Lingua Portuguesa. Janio Quadros. LC 77-477029. 1212p. (Port.). 1976. Cr.$280.00. Editora Rideet.
Novo Michaelis, Dicionario Ilustrado. 23rd ed. Fritz Pietzschke. Ed. by Wilson Mariotti. LC 79-112996. (Eng. & Port.). 1978. Cr.$2000.00. Edicoes Melhoramentos.
Novoe V Russkoi Leksike. Ed. by N. Z. Kotoleva. 176p. (Rus.). 1980. 2.85 (Pub. by Russkii Iazyk). Four Continent.
Novogrechesko-Russkii Slovar. I. P. Khorikov. 854p. (Rus. & Gr.). 1979. 22.95 (Pub. by Russkii Iazyk). Four Continent.
Novye Parallel'nye Slovari Iazykov Russkago, Frantsuzskago, Nemetskago i Angliiskago, 4 vols. 4th ed. Filipp Reiff. Incl. Vol. 1. Russkii Slovar. 832p. 1884; Vol. 2. Dictionnaire Francais. 832p. 1885; Vol. 3. Deutsches Woerterbuch. 816p. 1884; Vol. 4. English Dictionary. 848p. 1884. (Rus., Fr., Ger. & Eng.). 100.00 set. Four Continent.
Nuclear Power Dictionary, Vol. 63. E. Brandenberger & F. Stattmann. 456p. (Eng. & Ger.). 1978. pap. 52.50 (ISBN 3-521-06112-4, M-7572, Verlag Karl Thiemig). French & Eur.
Nuer English Dictionary. Ray Huffman. 21.00 (ISBN 0-87559-060-8). Shalom.
Nueva Epanortosis al Diccionario de Anonimos Seudonimos de J. T. Medina. Ricardo Victorica. LC 73-78357. 207p. (Span.). 1973. Repr. of 1929 ed. 16.00x (ISBN 0-87917-028-X). Ethridge.
Nuevo diccionario academia. 240p. (Span.). write for info. (706). Fernandez.
Nuevo diccionario bilingue Minerva. J. Anorga. (Span. & Eng.). write for info. (608-86). Pan Amer Pub.
Nuevo Diccionario Castellano-Hebreo, 2 vols. Juan Ducach. 720p. (Castilian & Hebrew.). 1971. IL.16.50 (36-0000). Massada Pr.
Nuevo Diccionario Ilustrado de la Lengua Espanola. 1232p. (Span.). 20.95 (ISBN 84-303-0047-3, S-12227). French & Eur.
Nuevo Diccionario Ingles-Espanol y Espanol-Ingles. 3rd ed. Esteban Mac Cragh. 376p. (Eng. & Span.). 1979. 9.50 (ISBN 84-261-0079-1, S-12401). French & Eur.
Nuevo diccionario mundo hispano. 368p. (Span.). write for info. (704). Fernandez.
Nuevo Glosario, Diccionario Poliglota de la Arquitectura. Buenaventura Bassegoda Muste. 366p. (Span., Ger., Catalan, Fr., Eng. & Ital.). 1976. pap. 44.95 (ISBN 84-600-0588-7, S-50134). French & Eur.
Nuevo Lexico Griego Espanol. McKibben-Stockwell. 316p. (Span.). 1981. pap. 10.50 (ISBN 0-311-42058-3, Edit Mundo). Casa Bautista.
Nukuoro Lexicon. Vern Carroll & Tobias Soulik. LC 73-78975. (PALI Language Texts: Polynesia). 859p. (Orig., Pali.). 1973. pap. text ed. 17.50x (ISBN 0-8248-0250-0). UH Pr.
Numismatisches Wappen-Lexicon, 2 vols. in 1. Wilhelm Rentzmann. LC 78-380299. (Illus., Ger., Berlin). 1978. M.30.00. Transpress Verlag fur Verkehrswesen.
Numizmaticheskii Slovar. V. V. Zvarich. 292p. (Rus.). 1978. 5.95 (Pub. by Izd. L'Vovsk. Unta.). Four Continent.
Nung Fan Slihng Vocabulary. Nancy Freiberger & Vy Thi Be. 353p. 1976. pap. 9.00x (ISBN 0-88312-793-8); microfiche 3.75 (ISBN 0-88312-337-1). Summer Inst Ling.
Nuovo dizionario del dialetto triestino. Gianni Pinguentini. (Illus.). 574p. (Ital.). L.12000.00. Nuova Cappelli.
Nuovo dizionario della lingua italiana. (Illus.). 1280p. (Ital.). L.12500.00. Curcio.
Nuovo Dizionario di Elettrotecnic e di Elettronica: Italiano-Inglese, Inglese-Italiano. A. Colella. 541p. (Ital. & Eng.). 1977. 95.00 (ISBN 0-686-92200-X, M-9296). French & Eur.
Nuovo Dizionario di Elettrotecnica & di elettronica. 2nd ed. Antonio Colella. LC 79-382317. 541p. (Ital.). 1977. L.30000.00. Il Rostro.
Nuovo dizionario di elettrotecnica e elettronica italiano-inglese, inglese-italiano. Antonio Colella. (Illus.). 540p. (Ital & Eng.). L.30000.00. Il Rostro.
Nuovo dizionario di merceologia e chimica applicata, Vol. 1. G. V. Villavecchia et al. (Illus.). xvi, 516p. (Ital.). 1973. L.10000.00 (ISBN 88-203-0528-3). Hoepli.
Nuovo dizionario di merceologia e chimica applicata, Vol. 2. G. V. Villavecchia et al. (Illus.). vi, 506p. (Ital.). 1973. L.10000.00 (ISBN 88-203-0529-1). Hoepli.
Nuovo dizionario di merceologia e chimica applicata, Vol. 3. G. V. Villavecchia et al. (Illus.). vi, 506p. (Ital.). 1973. L.10000.00 (ISBN 88-203-0530-5). Hoepli.
Nuovo dizionario di merceologia e chimica applicata, Vol. 4. G. V. Villavecchia et al. (Illus.). vi, 506p. (Ital.). 1973. L.10000.00 (ISBN 88-203-0531-3). Hoepli.
Nuovo dizionario di merceologia e chimica applicata, Vol. 5. G. V. Villavecchia et al. (Illus.). vi, 506p. (Ital.). 1974. L.10000.00 (ISBN 88-203-0532-1). Hoepli.
Nuovo dizionario di merceologia e chimia applicata, Vol. 7. G. V. Villavecchia & G. Eigenmann. (Illus.). vii, 372p. (Ital.). 1977. L.10000.00 (ISBN 88-203-0892-4). Hoepli.
Nuovo Dizionario di Terminologia Giuridica. A. Menghi. (Ital.). 1979. pap. 25.00 (ISBN 0-686-92407-X, M-(354). French & Eur.
Nuovo dizionario di terminologia giuridica. A. Menghi. 308p. (Ital.). 1977. L.4500.00. Cortina M.
Nuovo Dizionario Dialettale Della Calabria. Gerhard Rohlfs. LC 77-476371. (Illus.). 945p. (Ital.). 1977. L.30000.00. Longo A.
Nuovo dizionario dialettale della Calabria. Gerhard Rohlfs. 1000p. (Ital.). 1979. L.30000.00. Longo A.
Nuovo Dizionario Inglese-Italiano Delle Science Mediche. Luciano Bussi & Maria Cognazzo. 864p. (Eng. & Ital.). 1980. 78.00 (ISBN 0-913298-55-7). S F Vanni.
Nuovo dizionario italiano-latino. Cosimo Mariano. viii, 1646p. (Ital. & Lat.). 1975. L.10000.00. Dante Alighieri.
Nuovo dizionario italiano-spagnolo. Lucio Ambruzzi. xx, 1332p. (Ital. & Span.). 1978. L.16000.00. Paravia.
Nuovo dizionario latino-italiano. Gino Angelini. xii, 1828p. (Lat. & Ital.). 1975. L.10000.00. Dante Alighieri.
Nuovo dizionario musicale Curci. Alfredo Bonaccorsi. 556p. (Ital.). 1952. L.5000.00. Curci.
Nuovo Dizionario Ricordi Della Musica & dei Musicisti. Ed. by Lily A. Bozzano et al. LC 76-46292. (Illus.). 730p. (Ital.). 1976. write for info. G Ricordi.
Nuovo dizionario Ricordi della musica e dei musicisti. Lily Allorto et al. (Illus.). 730p. (Ital.). 1976. L.15000.00. Ricordi.
Nuovo dizionario siciliano-italiano. Vincenzo Mortillaro. 1200p. (Ital.). L.30000.00. Soc St Catanese.
Nuovo dizionario siciliano-italiano. Vincenzo Mortillaro. 1220p. (Ital.). L.44000.00. Forni.
Nuovo dizionario spagnolo-italiano. Lucio Ambruzzi. xviii, 1128p. (Span. & Ital.). 1978. L.16000.00. Paravia.
Nurse's Dictionary. 29th ed. Joan M. Martin. 1980. pap. text ed. 3.95 (ISBN 0-571-18007-8). Faber & Faber.
Nurses' Drug Reference. 2nd ed. Joseph Albanese. (Illus.). 1184p. 1981. 28.50x (ISBN 0-07-000767-5); pap. 21.50 (ISBN 0-07-000768-3). McGraw.
Nursing & Medical Terminology: A Workbook. Ruth K. Radcliff & Shelia J. Ogden. LC 76-17597. (Illus.). 204p. 1977. pap. text ed. 14.50 (ISBN 0-8016-3714-7). Mosby.
Nutrition Dictionary. David Tver & Percy Russell. Date not set. price not set (ISBN 0-442-24843-1). Van Nos Reinhold.
Nutritional Energetics of Domestic Animals & Glossary of Energy Terms. Committee on Animal Nutrition, National Research Council. 54p. (Orig.). 1981. pap. text ed. 5.25 (ISBN 0-309-03127-3). Natl Acad Pr.
Nye Forkortningsordboken. Ed. by Dag Sundby. LC 76-514223. 87p. (Norweigan.). 1975. Kr.33.00 (ISBN 8-251-60275-0). Schibsted.
Nygrekisk-Svensk Ordbok. Antonis Mystakidis. Ed. by Eftychia Frangos. 234p. (Gr. & Swedish.). 1980. Kr.115.00 (ISBN 91-24-20176-6). Esselte Studium.
Nykvsuomen Saneiston Yleisyystilastoa Sanennloppuisessa Aakkosjarjestykessa. Pauli Saukkonen. LC 78-386714. xxiv, 111p. (Finnish.). 1977. write for info. (ISBN 9-51420-45-81). Oulun Yliopisto.
Nykyslangin Sanakirja. Kaarina Karttunen. LC 79-398529. 333p. (Finnish.). 1979. write for info. (ISBN 9-51009-050-6). Soderstrom.
Nykysuomen Sivistyssankirja: Vierasperaiset Sanat. Nykysuomen Laitos. LC 77-576667. 464p. (Finnish.). 1977. write for info. (ISBN 9-51008-134-5). Suoma Kirja.

O

Obsteric-Gynecological Terminology. Edward C. Hughes. 1972. text ed. 14.00x (ISBN 0-8036-4725-5). Davis Co.
Obtaining a Computer & Computer Terminology. Society of American Registered Architects. 1.50; members 1.00. Soc Am Reg Architects.
Occult Illustrated Dictionary. Harvey Day. LC 75-21673. (Illus.). iv, 156p. (Eng.). 1975. 8.50 (ISBN 0-19-519830-1). Oxford U Pr.
Occupational Therapy Product Output Reporting Systems & Uniform Terminology for Reporting Occupational Therapy Services. American Occupational Therapy Association. 1979. 10.00 (C-27); members 5.00. Am Occup Therapy.
Ocean & Marine Dictionary. David F. Tver. LC 79-1529. 1979. 18.50 (ISBN 0-87033-246-5). Cornell Maritime.
Ockham's Theory of Terms. William Ockham. Tr. by Michael J. Loux. 234p. 1975. 20.00x (ISBN 0-268-00550-8); pap. 4.95x (ISBN 0-268-00551-6). U of Notre Dame Pr.
Odliadur. Roy Stephens. LC 79-359298. 204p. (Welsh.). 1978. E2.00 (ISBN 0-85088-710-0). Lewis Ltd.
Oekonomisches Lexikon: A-G. (Ger.). M.33.00. Wissenschaftliche.
Oekonomisches Lexikon: H-P. (Ger.). M.33.00. Wissenschaftliche.
Oekonomisches Lexikon: Q-Z. (Ger.). M.33.00. Wissenschaftliche.
Oekonomisches Woerterbuch Aussenwirtschaft (Dictionary of External Exonomic Relations & Trade) Ed. by Siegfried Kohls. 619p. (Ger., Rus., Eng., Fr. & Span.). 1972. 25.00x (ISBN 3-87106-018-6). Intl Pubns Serv.
Oekonomisches Woerterbuch Aussenwirtschaft. S. Kohls. 619p. (Ger., Rus., Eng., Fr. & Span., Dictionary of Economics (Foriegn Trade)). 1972. 38.00 (ISBN 3-87106-018-6, M-7574, Pub. by Ruceken Vlg). French & Eur.
Oekonomisches Woerterbuch Aussenwirtschaft. (Ger., Rus. , Span. , Eng. & Fr.). M.48.00. Wissenschaftliche.
Oekonomisches Woerterbuch Englisch-Deutsch. (Eng. & Ger.). M.76.80. Wissenschaftliche.
Oekonomisches Woerterbuch Russisch-Deutsch. 3rd ed. G. Moechel. 692p. (Rus. & Ger.). 1976. 43.50 (ISBN 3-87106-011-9, M-7575, Pub. by Vlg. Die Wirtschaft). French & Eur.
Office Automation: A Glossary and Guide. Ed. by Nancy M. Edwards et al. LC 82-4714. 275p. (Eng.). 1982. 59.50 (ISBN 0-86729-012-9). Knowledge Indus.
Official CB Slanguage Language Dictionary. Lanie Dills. 1981. pap. 3.75 (ISBN 0-930414-00-4). Burrows & Baker.
Official Funnybones Flaky Dictionary. Louis Phillips. (Funnybones Ser.). (Illus.). 64p. (Orig.). (gr. 3-7). 1981. pap. 1.95 (ISBN 0-671-43362-8). Wanderer Bks.
Official Scrabble Player's Dictionary. (gr. 10 up). 1979. pap. 5.95 (ISBN 0-671-49517-8). PB.
Official Scrabble Players Dictionary. (Eng.). 1978. 9.95 (ISBN 0-87779-020-5, 72440). Merriam.
Oil & Gas Multilingual Glossary. Commisssion of the European Communities. 500p. 1979. 44.00x (ISBN 0-86010-170-3, Pub. by Graham & Trotman England). State Mutual Bk.
Oil Refinery Terms in Oklahoma. A. T. King. Bd. with State-Wide Dialect Collecting. E. H. Criswell; Problems Confronting the Investigator of Gullah. L. D. Turner. (Publications of the American Dialect Society: No. 9). 99p. 1948. pap. 5.50 (ISBN 0-8173-0609-9). U of Ala Pr.
Okologie. Wolfgang Tischler. LC 76-457603. 125p. (Ger.). 1975. DM.9.80 (ISBN 3-437-20142-5). Fischer Verlag.
Okrety i Zegluga. Zbigniew Grzywaczewski. LC 78-354722. 514p. (Pol.). 1977. 190.00 Zl. Wydawnictwa Naukowo.
Olasz-Magyar Szotar, 2 vols. Gyula Herczeg. LC 78-399851. (Hungarian, & Ital.). 1978. 510.00 Ft (ISBN 9-6305-1613-6). Akademiai Kiado.
Olasz-Magyar-Szotar. 5th ed. Gyula Herczeg. LC 78-399544. 896p. (Ital. & Hungarian.). 1978. 35.00 Ft (ISBN 9-63205-073-8). Terra.
Olasz-Magyar Szotar: Vocabolario Italiano-Ungherese, 2 vols. 3rd ed. Gyula Herczeg. Ed. by Jeno Kolttay-Kastner. LC 78-399851. xv, 1781p. (Ital. & Hungarian.). 1978. 510.00 Ft (ISBN 9-63051-613-6). Akademiai Kiado.
Old English Musical Terms. Frederick M. Padelford. LC 76-22346. 1976. Repr. of 1899 ed. lib. bdg. 15.00 (ISBN 0-89341-012-8). Longwood Pr.
Old Persian Grammar Texts Lexicon. 2nd rev. ed. Roland G. Kent. (American Oriental Ser.: Vol. 33). (Persian.). 1953. 17.00 (ISBN 0-940490-33-1). Am Orient Soc.
Oldtimer-Lexikon. Halwart Schrader. LC 76-473673. 187p. (Ger.). 1976. DM.18.00 (ISBN 3-405-11397-0). BLV-Verlag.
Olika Lika Ord: Svenskt Homograflexikon. Sture Berg. LC 79-366660. xxiv, 228p. (Swedish.). 1978. write for info. (ISBN 9-12200-179-4). Almqvist.

Ologies & Isms: A Thematic Dictionary. 2nd ed. Ed. by Lawrence Urdang & Charles Hoequist, Jr. 365p. 1981. 72.00x (ISBN 0-8103-1055-4). Gale.
One & Only Wacky Wordbook. Peter Lippman. (Golden Storybk.). (Illus.). (gr. 2-7). 1979. 3.95 (ISBN 0-307-13739-2, Golden Pr); PLB 10.69 (ISBN 0-307-63379-9). Western Pub.
One Hundred Eleven Viennese Dishes. Gertrude A. Ulrich. pap. 3.95 (ISBN 0-87557-103-4, 103-4). Saphrograph.
One Hundred One Ways to Learn Vocabulary. Joan D. Berbrich. (Orig.). (gr. 10-12). 1971. wkbk. 7.58 (ISBN 0-87720-343-1). AMSCO Sch.
One Hundred Simple Chinese Recipes. Lenli Jackson. pap. 3.95 (ISBN 0-87557-104-2, 104-2). Saphrograph.
One of the Keys: The Wampanoag Contribution. Milton A. Travers. LC 75-10246. 64p. (Eng. & Wampanoag.). 1975. 4.95 (ISBN 0-8158-0326-5). Chris Mass.
Onteszet. Arpad Voros. LC 79-244881. 435p. (Eng., Hungarian, Fr., Ger. & Rus.). 1978. 95.00 Ft (ISBN 9-6305-1597-0). Akademiai Kiado.
Op 't Aljemint. 2nd ed. J. K. Dykstra. LC 79-389433. 343p. (Friesian.). 1978. fl.25.00 (ISBN 9-06273-079-5). AFUK-LEARMIDDELFUNS.
Open Sesame Picture Dictionary: Featuring Jim Henson's Sesame Street Muppets, Children's Television Workshop. Jill W. Schimpff. 1982. pap. text ed. 4.95x (ISBN 0-19-503035-4). Oxford U Pr.
Operalexikon. Peter Varnai. LC 77-564359. 533p. (Hungarian.). 1975. 84.00 Ft (ISBN 9-633-30107-6). Zenemukiado.
Optik & Optischer Geratebau Deutsch-Englisch. Werner Bindmann. 432p. (Ger. & Eng.). 1975. M.45.00. VEB Technik.
Oran's Dictionary of the Law. Daniel Oran. 333p. 1980. pap. text ed. 6.95 (ISBN 0-8299-2062-5). West Pub.
Oran's Dictionary of the Law. New ed. Daniel Oran. (Illus.). 512p. 1982. pap. 9.95 (ISBN 0-314-68800-5). West Pub.
Orbis Latinus: Lexikon lateinischer geographischer Namen des Mittelalters und der Neuzeit, 3 vols. new ed. Johann G. Graesse. Ed. by Helmut Plechl. 1800p. (Lat. & Ger.). 1970. 275.00x (ISBN 3-7814-0087-5). Intl Pubns Serv.
Ordbog for Korrespondenter, Dansk-Tysk. Sven-Olaf Poulsen. LC 79-353149. 411p. (Danish & Ger.). 1977. Kr.110.00 (ISBN 8-787-69700-9). Kjaer Bogtryk.
Ordbog for Rensning Vask og Rengoring. H. Asmussen. LC 79-344243. 112p. (Eng. & Dutch.). 1978. Kr.54.10 (ISBN 8-7751-1064-4). Tek Inst.
Ordbok for Automatiseringsteknikk. Radet for Teknisk Terminologi. 143p. (Eng. & Dutch.). 1979. Kr.80.00 (ISBN 8-2002-6067-4). Universitesforlaget.
Ordhandboken. Bjorn Collinder. LC 75-592135. 361p. (Swedish.). 1975. Kr.45.00 (ISBN 9-18535-600-X). Fyris.
Ordlistan Fran Natur & Kultur. Eskil Kalquist et al. LC 79-353437. (Illus.). 192p. (Swedish.). 1978. Kr.28.00 (ISBN 9-12750-000-4). Natur & Kultur.
Orfograficheskii Morskoi Slovar. R. E. Poretskaia. 293p. (Rus.). 1974. 2.50 (Pub. by Voenizdat). Four Continent.
Orfograficheskii Slovar. D. N. Ushakov et al. 224p. (Rus.). 1973. 1.00 (Pub. by Prosveschchenie). Four Continent.
Orfograficheskii Slovar' D. N. Ushakov et al. (Proveshchenie Ser.). 224p. (Rus.). 1977. 1.20 (O-29). Four Continent.
Orfograficheskii Slovar Litovskogo Iazyka Dlia Shkol. I. Napalis et al. 244p. (Rus.). 1958. 1.35 (Pub. by Izd Pedag Lit). Four Continent.
Orfograficheskii Slovar Russkogo Iazyka. 480p. (Rus.). 1977. 4.50 (Pub. by Russkii Iazyk). Four Continent.
Organ Chord Dictionary. 1981. 2.50 (ISBN 0-88284-156-4). Alfred Pub.
Original Word Game Dictionary. Thurston Moore. LC 83-42631. 272p. 1983. 16.95 (ISBN 0-8128-2926-3); pap. 7.95 (ISBN 0-8128-6191-4). Stein & Day.
Orosz-Magyar Katonai Szotar. Lajos Toth. LC 79-354764. 1147p. (Rus. & Hungarian.). 1976. 245.00 Ft. Akademiai Kiado.
Orosz-Magyar Szotar. 3rd ed. Laszlo Galdi. LC 80-467905. 1120p. (Hungarian & Rus.). 1978. 135.00 Ft (ISBN 9-63051-821-X). Akademiai Kiado.
Orosz-Magyar Szotar, 2 vols. 5th ed. Laszlo Hadrovics. LC 78-377287. (Hungarian & Rus.). 1977. 450.00 Ft (ISBN 9-63051-231-9). Akademiai Kiado.
Orosz-Magyar Szotar Iskolak Szamara, 2 vols. Miklos Szabo. LC 80-467907. (Eng., Rus. & Hungarian.). 1978. 21.50 Ft (ISBN 9-6305-1611-X). Akademiai Kiado.
Orthography & Word Recognition in Reading. L. Henderson. LC 81-68587. 1982. 51.50 (ISBN 0-12-340520-3). Acad Pr.
Orthography in Shakespeare & Elizabethan Drama: A Study of Colloquial Contractions, Elision, Prosody, & Punctuation. A. C. Partridge. LC 64-17222. viii, 200p. 1964. 14.50x (ISBN 0-8032-0143-5). U of Nebr Pr.
Orthography Studies. W. A. Smalley et al. 1964. 3.00 (ISBN 0-686-14418-X, 08508). Am Bible.
Orthography Studies. W. A. Smalley et al. 1964. 3.00x (ISBN 0-8267-0027-6, 08508). United Bible.
Ortografia Activa: Letras & Acentos. Fernandez de la Vega & Hernandez Miyares. (Span.). 1980. write for info. Gale.
Ortografia Castellano. Jaime Ferrer Mir et al. 200p. (Span.). 1982. pap. write for info. (ISBN 84-348-0996-6). S M Edns.
Ortografia Functional: Atlas de la Aparatologia Ortopedica. Guillermo M. Feijoo. 222p. (Span.). 1980. write for info. Mundi.
Ortografia metodica de la lengua espanola. 19th ed. Alfredo Huertas Garcia. 360p. (Span.). 1981. M.pap. 65.00. Porrua.
Ortografia Moderna. 6th ed. Jose A. Escarpanter. 200p. (Span.). 1980. pap. 280.00 ptas (ISBN 84-359-0103-3). Playor.
Ortografia Practica. Jose M. Zainqui Erro. 112p. (Span.). 1982. 390.00 ptas (ISBN 8-43150-566-4). Edit Vecchi.
Ortografia Practica. 3rd ed. Jose M. Zainqui Erro. Ed. by Devecchi. 112p. (Span.). 1982. pap. 390.00 ptas (ISBN 8-43150-566-4). Edit Vecchi.
Ortografia Practica: Acentuacion, Consonantes, Vocabulario. Hector Ramirez. 202p. (Span.). 1979. 3.50 (Dist. Lib. Studium). Gale.
Ortografia Practica del Espanol. Juan J. Gallego Tribaldos. 190p. (Span.). 1982. pap. 450.00 ptas (ISBN 8-48576-413-7). Ave Maria.
Ortografia Practica: Ejercicios & Ensayos Sobre Ortografia Castellano. P. Roncalla. 162p. (Span.). 1979. 3.00. Gale.
Ortografia Practica Espanola Vox. 8th ed. Samuel Gili Gaya. 104p. (Span.). 1981. 140.00 ptas (ISBN 84-7153-255-7). Biblo SP.
Ortografia programada. 5th ed. Jesus Lopez. 120p. (Span.). 1982. pap. 295.00 ptas (ISBN 84-219-0270-9). Del Castillo.
Orvosi Szotar. Janos Brenesan. LC 80-491065. 464p. (Hungarian.). 1979. 85.00 Ft (ISBN 9-6320-5084-3). Terra.
Osborne's Concise Law Dictionary. 6th ed. John Burke. LC 77-375736. vii, 396p. (Eng.). E3.25 (ISBN 0-421-20820-1). Sweet Max.
Osteopathic Terminology. American Osteopathic Association. free. Am Osteopathic.
Outline Dictionary of Maya Glyphs. William Gates. LC 77-92481. (Illus.). 1978. pap. 3.50 (ISBN 0-486-23618-8). Dover.
Outline of French Grammar with Vocabularies. rev. ed. Henry B. Richardson. (Fr.). 1950. text ed. 12.50x (ISBN 0-89197-327-3); pap. text ed. 4.95x (ISBN 0-89197-328-1). Irvington.
Overlook Illustrated Dictionary of Nautical Terms. Graham Blackburn. LC 80-39640. (Illus.). 368p. 1982. 17.95 (ISBN 0-87951-124-9). Overlook Pr.
Oxford Advanced Learner's Dictionary of Current English. 3rd ed. A. S. Hornby. (Illus.). 1974. text ed. 14.95x (ISBN 0-19-431101-5). Oxford U Pr.
Oxford Advanced Learner's Dictionary of Current English. Horny. (Eng. & Chinese.). 17.50. Iaconi.
Oxford Advanced Learner's Dictionary of Current English with Chinese Translations. A. S. Hornby et al. (Illus., Chinese & Eng.). 1980. text ed. 17.50x (ISBN 0-19-580003-6). Oxford U Pr.
Oxford American Dictionary. Ed. by Stuart Bergflexner. 1982. pap. 3.95 (ISBN 0-380-60772-7, 60772-7). Avon.
Oxford American Dictionary. Ed. by Stuart Bergflexner et al. 832p. 1980. pap. 5.95 (ISBN 0-380-51052-9, 55897-1). Avon.
Oxford American Dictionary. Compiled by Eugene Ehrlich et al. 1980. 14.95 (ISBN 0-19-502795-7). Oxford U Pr.
Oxford Children's Dictionary in Colour. Compiled by John Weston. (gr. 3-9). 1976. text ed. 11.95x (ISBN 0-19-910209-0). Oxford U Pr.
Oxford Classical Dictionary. 2nd ed. Ed. by N. G. Hammond & H. H. Scullard. 1970. 45.00 (ISBN 0-19-869117-3). Oxford U Pr.
Oxford Companion to Twentieth-Century Art. Ed. by Harold Osborne. (Illus.). 1982. 39.95 (ISBN 0-19-866119-3). Oxford U Pr.
Oxford Concordance: King James Version. write for info. Oxford U Pr.
Oxford Dictionary for Writers & Editors. 1981. 12.95x (ISBN 0-19-212970-8). Oxford U Pr.
Oxford Dictionary of Current Idiomatic English: Verbs with Prepositions & Particles, Vol. 1. A. P. Cowie & Ronald Mackin. 1975. 13.95x (ISBN 0-19-431145-7). Oxford U Pr.
Oxford Dictionary of English Etymology. Ed. by Charles T. Onions et al. 1966. 39.95 (ISBN 0-19-861112-9). Oxford U Pr.
Oxford Dictionary of Modern Greek: English-Greek. Ed. by J. T. Pring. (Gr. Eng.). 1982. 15.95x (ISBN 0-19-864136-2). Oxford U Pr.
Oxford Dictionary of Modern Greek: Greek-English, English-Greek. Ed. by J. T. Pring. (Gr. & Eng.). 1982. 19.95 (ISBN 0-19-864137-0). Oxford U Pr.
Oxford Dictionary of Nursery Rhymes. Ed. by Iona Opie & Peter Opie. (Illus.). (ps-3). 1951. 45.00x (ISBN 0-19-869111-4). Oxford U Pr.
Oxford Dictionary of Quotations. 3rd ed. 1979. 35.00 (ISBN 0-19-211560-X). Oxford U Pr.
Oxford Dictionary of the Christian Church. F. L. Cross & Elizabeth A. Livingstone. 1974. 60.00x (ISBN 0-19-211545-6). Oxford U Pr.
Oxford-Duden Bildwoerterbuch Deutsch & Englisch. 864p. (Ger.). DM.39.00 (ISBN 3-411-01765-1). Biblio Inst.
Oxford-Duden Bildwoerterbuch Englisch. 822p. (Ger.). DM.29.80 (ISBN 3-411-01914-X). Biblio Inst.
Oxford-Duden Pictorial English Dictionary. Ed. by J. A. Pheby. (Illus.). 1981. text ed. 19.95x (ISBN 0-19-864140-0). Oxford U Pr.
Oxford-Duden Pictorial English-Japanese Dictionary. (Illus.). 848p. (Eng. & Japanese.). 1983. 29.95 (ISBN 0-19-864149-4). Oxford U Pr.
Oxford-Duden Pictorial French-English Dictionary. (Illus.). 880p. (Fr. & Eng.). 1983. 29.95 (ISBN 0-19-864153-2). Oxford U Pr.
Oxford Elementary Learner's Dictionary of English. Ed. by Shirley Burridge. (Illus., Orig.). 1981. pap. text ed. 9.95x (ISBN 0-19-431253-4). Oxford U Pr.
Oxford English-Arabic Dictionary of Current Usage. Ed. by N. S. Doniach. (Eng. & Arabic.). 1972. 49.50x (ISBN 0-19-864312-8). Oxford U Pr.
Oxford English Dictionary: Compact Edition, 2 vols. boxed set with magnifying glass 150.00 (ISBN 0-686-75482-4). Oxford U Pr.
Oxford English Dictionary: Compact Edition, 2 vols. compact ed. 16569p. 1971. 100.00 (ISBN 0-918414-08-3). Readex Bks.
Oxford English-Reader's Dictionary. A. S. Hornby & E. C. Parnwell. 638p. (Eng.). DM.18.80 (49003). Langenscheidt.
Oxford English-Turkish Dictionary. 2nd ed. Ed. by A. D. Alderson. Fahir Iz. (Eng. & Turkish.). 1978. text ed. 39.95x (ISBN 0-19-864123-0). Oxford U Pr.
Oxford English-Turkish Dictionary. 2nd ed. Fahir Iz & H. C. Hony. LC 78-40230. xvi, 619p. (Eng. & Turkish.). 1978. E10.00 (ISBN 0-19-864123-0). Oxford U Pr.
Oxford Illustrated Dictionary. 2nd rev. ed. Ed. by J. Coulson et al. 1975. 29.50x (ISBN 0-19-861118-8). Oxford U Pr.
Oxford Latin Dictionary, Fascicle 5. Ed. by P. G. Glare. (Lat.). 1975. pap. 49.50x (ISBN 0-19-864218-0). Oxford U Pr.
Oxford Latin Dictionary: Fascicle 1, a-Calcitro. Ed. by P. G. Glare. (Lat.). 1968. pap. 49.50x (ISBN 0-19-864209-1). Oxford U Pr.
Oxford Latin Dictionary: Fascicle 2, Calcitro-Demitto. Ed. by P. G. Glare. (Lat.). 1969. pap. 49.50x (ISBN 0-19-864215-6). Oxford U Pr.
Oxford Latin Dictionary, Fascicle 3: Demiurgus-Gorgoneus. Ed. by P. G. Glare. (Lat.). 1971. pap. 49.50x (ISBN 0-19-864216-4). Oxford U Pr.
Oxford Latin Dictionary, Fascicle 4. Gorgonia-Libero. Ed. by G. P. Glare. (Lat.). 1973. pap. 49.50x (ISBN 0-19-864217-2). Oxford U Pr.
Oxford Latin Dictionary: Fascicle 6-a-Calcitro. Ed. by P. G. W. Glare. (Lat.). 1978. pap. 49.50x (ISBN 0-19-864219-9). Oxford U Pr.
Oxford Latin Dictionary: Fascicle 7. Ed. by P. G. Glare. (Orig., Lat.). 1980. pap. 49.50x (ISBN 0-19-864220-2). Oxford U Pr.
Oxford Latin Dictionary: Fascicle 8. P. G. Glare. (Lat.). 1982. pap. 48.00x (ISBN 0-19-864221-0). Oxford U Pr.
Oxford Minidictionary. Compiled by Joyce M. Hawkins. 1982. pap. 3.95 (ISBN 0-19-861138-2). Oxford U Pr.
Oxford Paperback Dictionary. Ed. by Hawkins. (Eng.). Epap. 2.25. Oxford U Pr.
Oxford Picture Dictionary. (Illus.). 4.00; charts 30.00; wkbk. 3.75; cassettes 14.95. Iaconi.
Oxford Picture Dictionary of American English & Spanish. E. Parnwell. (Illus., Span. & Eng.). 4.00. Iaconi.
Oxford Picture Dictionary of American English: English-Japanese. (Eng. & Japanese.). write for info. (608-106). Pan Amer Pub.
Oxford Picture Dictionary of American English: English-Japanese Edition. E. C. Parnwell. (Illus., Orig.). 1981. pap. text ed. 6.95x (ISBN 0-19-581877-6). Oxford U Pr.
Oxford Picture Dictionary of American English: English-Japanese Edition. E. C. Parnwell. (Illus., Eng. & Japanese.). 1978. pap. 8.80. Oxford U Pr.
Oxford Picture Dictionary of American English: English-Spanish. (Span. & Eng.). write for info. (608-107). Pan Amer Pub.

Oxford Picture Dictionary of American English: English-Spanish Edition. (Illus.). 95p. (Eng. & Span.). 1978. pap. 5.50. Oxford U Pr.

Oxford Picture Dictionary of American English Workbook. Jill W. Schimpff. (Illus.). 1981. 3.75x (ISBN 0-19-502819-8). Oxford U Pr.

Oxford Picture Dictionary of American English. (Illus.). 95p. (Eng. & Fr.). 1978. pap. 5.50. Oxford U Pr.

Oxford Picture Dictionary of American English. E. C. Parnwell. (Illus.). 1978. pap. 3.95 ea.; pap. monolingual ed. (ISBN 0-19-502332-3); pap. English-Spanish ed. (ISBN 0-19-502333-1); pap. french indexed ed. (ISBN 0-19-502334-X). Oxford U Pr.

Oxford Russian-English Dictionary. Ed. by Marcus Wheeler & B. O. Unbegaun. (Rus. & Eng.). 1972. 55.00 (ISBN 0-19-864111-7). Oxford U Pr.

Oxford Student's Dictionary of American English. A. S. Hornby. (Illus.). 1983. pap. 11.95 (ISBN 0-19-431140-6). Oxford U Pr.

Oxford Student's Dictionary of American English. A. S. Hornby. (Illus.). write for info. Oxford U Pr.

Oxford Student's Dictionary of Current English. A. S. Hornby. Ed. by Christina Ruse. 6.95. Oxford U Pr.

Oxford Student's Dictionary of Current English. Compiled by A. S. Hornby. 1978. pap. text ed. 6.95x (ISBN 0-19-431114-7). Oxford U Pr.

Oxford student's dictionary of Current English. A. S. Hornby et al. LC 78-323797. v, 774p. 1978. write for info. (ISBN 0-19-431114-7). Oxford U Pr.

Pacific College Dictionary. 936p. (Eng.). 1981. 19.00 (ISBN 9-97163-188-1). Pan Pacific Bk.

P

Pacific Junior Dictionary. F. R. Witty. 352p. (Eng.). 1975. 5.40 (ISBN 9-97163-001-X). Pan Pacific Bk.

Pacific School Dictionary. 496p. (Eng.). 1979. 6.00 (ISBN 9-97163-023-0). Pan Pacific Bk.

Paedagogikkens Hvem Hvad Hvor. Ed. by K. Grue-Sorensen & Thyge Winther-Jensen. LC 78-379066. (Illus.). 295p. (Danish.). 1978. Kr.75.00 (ISBN 8-756-72555-8). Politikens Forlag.

Paedagogisches Taschenlexikon. Karl E. Maier. Ed. by Ludwig Eckinger. LC 79-391256. (Illus.). 462p. (Ger.). 1978. DM.29.00 (ISBN 3-523-67002-0). Wolf Verlag.

Paedagogisches Taschenlexikon: A-Z. 8th ed. Alfons O. Schorb. LC 75-518208. 258p. (Ger.). 1975. DM.9.80. Kamp Verlag.

Paedagogisk Opslangsbog: Alfabetisk Ordnet. Ed. by Lars J. Muschinsky & Karsten Schnack. LC 79-371231. (Illus.). 285p. (Danish.). 1977. Kr.74.50 (ISBN 8-772-41417-0). Ejlers Forlag.

Paint-Coatings Dictionary. Federation of Societies on Coatings Technology. 632p. 50.00; members 30.00. Fed Soc Coat Tech.

Painter's Dictionary of Materials & Methods. Frederic Taubes. (Illus.). 256p. 1979. pap. 7.95 (ISBN 0-8230-1336-7). Watson-Guptill.

Palaeontologisches Woerterbuch. Ulrich Lehmann. (Ger.). 1977. pap. 15.95 (ISBN 3-423-03039-9, M-7577, Pub. by Dtv). French & Eur.

Palaeontologisches Woerterbuch. Ulrich Lehmann. 324p. (Ger.). 1977. 46.50 (ISBN 3-432-83572-8, M-7578, Pub. by F. Enke); pap. 15.95. French & Eur.

Palaeontologisches Woerterbuch. Ulrich Lehmann. 324p. (Ger.). 1977. 46.50 (ISBN 3-432-83572-8); pap. 15.95 (ISBN 0-686-56636-X). Enke.

Palaontologisches Woerterbuch. Ulrich Lehmann. LC 77-560773. viii, 439p. (Ger.). 1977. DM.18.80 (ISBN 3-432-83572-8). Enke.

Palauan-English Dictionary. Edwin G. McManus et al. LC 76-9058. (Pali Language Texts: Micronesia). (Palauan & Eng.). 1977. pap. text ed. 16.00x (ISBN 0-8248-0450-3). UH Pr.

Pali-English Dictionary. A Budd Hadatta Mahathera. (Pali & Eng.). 22.50 (ISBN 0-87557-056-9, 056-9). Saphrograph.

Pali Text Society's Pali-English Dictionary. T. Rhys Davids. 753p. (Pali & Eng.). 1966. Repr. of 1925 ed. 67.50x (ISBN 0-86013-059-2). Intl Pubns Serv.

Pallet Definitions & Terminology: MH1.1.2-1978. American Society of Mechanical Engineers. 4.00 (M00073); members 3.20. ASME.

Palmistic Dictionary. St. Germain. (Illus.). 118p. 1980. Repr. deluxe ed. 69.85 (ISBN 0-89901-017-2). Found Class Reprints.

Pandzhabsko-Russkii Slovar. I. S. Rabinovich. 1039p. (Rus.). 1961. 6.95 (Pub. by GINS). Four Continent.

Papago & Pima to English, English to Papago & Pima Dictionary. 2nd ed. Dean Saxton & Lucille Saxton. Ed. by R. L. Cherry. (Papago, Pima & Eng.). 1983. text ed. 19.95x (ISBN 0-8165-0826-7). U of Ariz Pr.

Paper Defect Terminology - Coated Papers & Boards. Canadian Pulp & Paper Association. 10p. 2.00; members 1.00. CN Pulp & Paper.

Paper Oriented Glossary Covering Advanced Process Control Terminology. Ed. by S. L. Seaburg et al. 351p. 1970. 14.95 (01-01-R031). TAPPI.

Papers of the Dictionary Society of North America, 1977. Ed. by Donald Hobar. 93p. members 5.50 (ISBN 0-686-95920-5); members 7.00 (ISBN 0-686-99671-2). Ind St Univ.

Papers of the Dictionary Society of North America 1977. Ed. by Donald Hobar. 93p. 1982. 7.00; members 5.50. Dict Soc NA.

Papers of the Dictionary Society of North America 1979. Ed. by Gillian Michell. 179p. 1982. members 6.50 (ISBN 0-686-95917-5); non-members 8.00 (ISBN 0-686-99669-0). Ind St Univ.

Papers of the Dictionary Society of North America 1979. Ed. by Gillian Michell. 179p. 1981. 8.00; members 6.50. Dict Soc NA.

Papiae Elementarium. Gramarian Papias. Ed. by V. De Angelis. LC 77-578447. (Lat. & Ital.). 1977. write for info. Cisalpino.

Papiergeld-Lexikon. Albert Pick. LC 79-359190. (Illus.). 416p. (Ger.). 1978. DM.68.00 (ISBN 3-570-05022-X). Mosaik Verlag.

Papirkeszltoink Mestersegszavai. Istvan Bogdan. LC 80-482778. 38p. (Hungarian.). 1979. write for info. (ISBN 9-638-27102-7). MTESZ.

Papirkeszltoink Mestersegszavai. Istvan Bogdan. LC 80-482778. (Papers). 38p. (Hungarian.). 1979. write for info. (ISBN 9-638-27102-7). MTESZ.

Paralegal's Encyclopedic Dictionary. Valera Grapp. 1979. 29.50 (ISBN 0-13-648675-4). P-H.

Parole & Storia. Bruno Migliorini. LC 75-545498. 163p. (Ital.). 1975. L.3000.00. Rizzoli Edit.

Part I, Vol. 1, A-M (English-German) see Langenscheidt New Muret-Sanders Encyclopedic Dictionary.

Part II, Vol. 1, A-K (German-English) see Langenscheidt New Muret-Sanders Encyclopedic Dictionary.

Part II, Vol. 2, L-Z (German-English) see Langenscheidt New Muret-Sanders Encyclopedic Dictionary.

Part II, Vol. 2, N-Z (English-German) see Langenscheidt New Muret-Sanders Encyclopedic Dictionary.

Partial Vocabulary of the Ngalooma Aboriginal Tribe. Harold A. Hall. (AIAS Linguistics Ser.: No. 18). 1971. pap. text ed. 6.00x (ISBN 0-85575-020-0). Humanities.

Partially Naturalised French Words in Modern English. Francis D. Dow. LC 76-370523. 65p. (Eng. & Fr.). 1976. E1.00 (ISBN 0-903745-02-X). Dow.

Partially Naturalised French Words in Modern English. Francis D. Dow. LC 76-370523. 65p. (Eng. & Fr.). E1.00 (ISBN 0-903745-02-X). Dow.

Party Committees & National Politics. rev. ed. Hugh A. Bone. LC 58-10481. (Illus.). 272p. 1968. 12.50x (ISBN 0-295-78559-4). U of Wash Pr.

Parusny i sport. L. A. Chesnokov et al. LC 80-479938. 95p. (Eng., Fr., Ger., Rus. & Span.). 1979. 0.45 Rub. Russkii Iazyk.

Passenger Cars from the 1999 Car Builder's Dictionary. Ed. by Roy V. Wright. (Train Shed Cyclopedia Ser: No. 42). (Illus.). 1976. pap. 3.00 (ISBN 0-912318-73-2). N K Gregg.

Patristic Greek Lexicon. Ed. by G. W. Lampe. 1616p. (Gr.). 1976. 5200.00 F. Brepols.

Patristic Greek Lexicon, Fascicle 5. Ed. by G. W. Lampe. (Gr.). 1968. 22.00x (ISBN 0-19-864212-1). Oxford U Pr.

Patristic Greek Lexicon Nineteen Sixty-One to Sixty-Eight. Ed. by G. W. Lampe. (Gr.). 149.00x (ISBN 0-19-864213-X). Oxford U Pr.

Pearce's Medical & Nursing Dictionary & Encyclopedia. 15th ed. Evelyn Pearce. 500p. (Orig.). 1983. pap. 14.95 (ISBN 0-571-18080-9). Faber & Faber.

Pedagogia Moderna. Jose M. Quintana Cabanas. LC 79-126501. 196p. (Span.). 1978. 150.00 ptas (ISBN 8-427-91316-8). Noguer SA.

Pedagogiai Lexikon. Ed. by Sandor Nagy. LC 77-483334. (Illus., Hungarian.). 1976. 124.00 Ft (ISBN 9-630-50851-6). Akademiai Kiado.

Pedagogicheskii Slovar, 2 vols. Ed. by I. A. Kairov. (Rus.). 1960. 10.75 set (980, Pub. by Izd. Akademii Ped. Nauk). Four Continent.

Pekhleviisko-Persidsko-Armiano-Russko-Angliiskii Slovar. R. Abrahamian. 336p. (Rus. & Eng. & Armenian.). 1965. 3.65 (Pub. by Mitk). Four Continent.

Penguin Book of Microprocessors. Anthony Chandor. (Eng.). 1981. pap. 5.95. Penguin.

Penguin Dictionary of Archaeology. rev. ed. David Trump. (Reference Ser.). (Illus.). 1972. pap. 6.95 (ISBN 0-14-051116-4). Penguin.

Penguin Dictionary of Architecture. rev. ed. John Fleming et al. (Reference Ser.). 1973. pap. 5.95 (ISBN 0-14-051013-3). Penguin.

Penguin Dictionary of Art & Artists. Peter Murray & Linda Murray. lib. bdg. 11.50x (ISBN 0-88307-415-X). Gannon.

Penguin Dictionary of Biology. M. Abercrombie et al. 1978. 12.95 (ISBN 0-670-27222-1). Viking Pr.

Penguin Dictionary of Computers. 2nd ed. Anthony Chandor et al. 1977. pap. 4.95. Penguin.

Penguin Dictionary of English & European History 1485-1789. E. N. Williams. (Reference Ser.). 480p. 1980. pap. 6.95 (ISBN 0-14-051084-2). Penguin.

Penguin Dictionary of Microprocessors. Anthony Chandor. 192p. 1981. pap. 5.95 (ISBN 0-14-051100-8). Penguin.

Penguin Dictionary of Physics. Ed. by Valerie H. Pitt. (Reference Ser.). 1977. pap. 5.95 (ISBN 0-14-051071-0). Penguin.

Penguin Dictionary of Proverbs. Laurence Urdang Associates, Ltd. 256p. 1983. pap. 5.95 (ISBN 0-14-051118-0). Penguin.

Penguin Dictionary of Twentieth Century History: Nineteen Hundred to Nineteen Seventy-Eight. Alan Palmer. (Reference Ser.). 1979. pap. 5.95 (ISBN 0-14-051085-0). Penguin.

Penguin-Hellenews English-Greek Dictionary. Ed. by G. Vassiliades. (Eng. & Gr.). 1978. 35.00 (ISBN 0-89241-051-5). Caratzas Pub Co.

Pennsylvania German Dictionary. Marcus Lambert. (Illus.). 188p. (Ger.). pap. 15.00 (ISBN 0-916838-07-2). Schiffer.

Penquin English Dictionary. Ed. by G. N. Garmonsway. LC 80-460939. xiv, 842p. (Eng.). E5.95 (ISBN 0-7139-0199-3). Lane.

Pequeno Diccionara Kapelusz de la Lenguna Espanola. 612p. (Span.). 1980. pap. 6.95 (ISBN 84-499-3146-0, S-32728). French & Eur.

Pequeno Diccionario de Sinonimos. (Span.). 4.50. Camino Real.

Pequeno Diccionario de Sinonimos. Pey. 248p. (Span.). 1981. pap. write for info. Edit Teide.

Pequeno Diccionario de Sinonimos, Ideas Afines & Contrarios. Santiago Pey & Juan R. Calonja. 241p. (Span.). E2.95 (ISBN 0-245-59455-8, Pub. by Biblograf S. A., Barcelona). Harrap.

Pequeno diccionario de sinonimos, ideas afines y contrarios. Ed. by Alberto Vinoly. (Span.). 1979. pap. 7.95 (ISBN 8-4307-7052-6). Larousse.

Pequeno Diccionario De Sinonimos y Sus Contrarios. 6th ed. A. J. Vinoly et al. 242p. (Span.). 1976. pap. 5.95 (ISBN 84-307-7052-6, S-12220). French & Eur.

Pequeno Diccionario De Teatro Mundial. Genoveva Dieterich. 294p. (Span.). 1976. pap. 5.25 (ISBN 84-7090-028-5, S-31395). French & Eur.

Pequeno Diccionario Espanol-Polaco, Polaco-Espanol. A. Marti & J. Marti. 707p. (Span. & Pol.). 1976. 12.95 (ISBN 0-686-92083-X, S-32367). French & Eur.

Pequeno diccionario Kapelusz de la lengua espanola. (Span.). 1981. Arg.$12500.00. Kapelusz.

Pequeno Diccionario Tecnologico: Farmacia, Quimica, Fisica, Medicina y Ciencias Naturales. M. Busto. 226p. (Span.). 1964. 13.50 (ISBN 0-686-57357-9, S-50248). French & Eur.

Pequeno Dicionario de Arte Poetica. Geir Campos. LC 79-114787. 181p. (Port.). 1978. Cr.$80.00. Editora Cultrix.

Pequeno Dicionario Enciclopedico Koogan Larouse. Ed. by Antonio Houaiss. LC 79-114441. (Illus.). xi, 1643p. (Port.). 1979. write for info. Larousse.

Pequeno Dicionario Michaelis: English-Portuguese, Portuguese English. 642p. (Port. & Eng.). 1980. pap. 8.75. Imported Bks.

Peque n o diccionario Michaelis Ingl e s-Portuguese. (Port. & Eng.). 12.50. Iaconi.

Pequeno Larousse de ciencias y tecnicas. new ed. Tomas De Galiana Mingot. 1056p. (Span.). 1975. 26.95 (ISBN 0-685-55467-8, 21115). Larousse.

Peque n o Larousse de ciencias y t ecnicas. (Span.). 23.00. Iaconi.

Peque n o Larousse ilustrado. (Illus., Span.). 29.95. Iaconi.

Perigee Visual Dictionary of Signing. Rod Butterworth & Mickey Flodin. (Illus.). 416p. (Orig.). 1983. 16.95 (ISBN 0-399-50925-9, G&D); pap. 8.95 (ISBN 0-399-50863-5). Putnam Pub Group.

Perimetric Standards & Perimetric Glossary. Ed. by International Council of Ophthalmology. 135p. 45.00 (ISBN 90-6193-161-4, Pub. by Junk Pubs Netherlands). Kluwer Academic.

Perimetric Standards & Perimetric Glossary. Ed. by International Council of Opthalmology. 1979. lib. bdg. 29.00 (ISBN 90-6193-600-4, Pub. by Junk Pubs Netherlands). Kluwer Academic.

Peristilahan Kimia dan Farmasi. LC 78-940182. x, 288p. (Eng. & Indonesian.). 1976. write for info. Penerbit Jaya.

Persian-English Dictionary. Steingass. (Persian & Eng.). 75.00. Iaconi.

Persian-English Dictionary, Romanized. John A. Boyle. (Persian & Eng.). 19.50 (ISBN 0-87557-057-7, 057-7). Saphrograph.

Persian-English, English-Persian Shorter Dictionary, 2 vols. rev., enl. ed. S. Haim. (Persian & Eng.). Set. 50.00 (ISBN 0-686-77974-6). Heinman.

Persian Vocabulary. Ann K. Lambton. (Persian.). 1954-1962. pap. 24.95x (ISBN 0-521-09154-3). Cambridge U Pr.

Persian Vocabulary of the Codex Cumanicus. Bodrogligeti. (Persian & Eng.). 1971. 15.00 (ISBN 0-9960008-4-4, Pub. by Kaido Hungary). Heyden.

Persidsko-Russkii & Russko-Persidskii Obshche-Ekonomicheskii & Vneshnetorgovyi Slovar. 596p. (Persian & Rus.). 1957. 2.95 (Pub. by Vneshtorgizdat). Four Continent.

Persidsko-Russkii & Russko-Persidskii Voennyi Slovar. G. G. Aliev. 656p. (Rus. & Persian.). 1972. 6.50 (Pub. by Voenizdat). Four Continent.

Personal Computer Glossary. 1982. 2.95 (ISBN 0-88284-233-1). Alfred Pub.

Personal Kiwi-Yankee Dictionary. 10/1983 ed. Louis S. Leland, Jr. 115p. pap. 5.95 (ISBN 0-88289-414-5). Pelican.

Personal Shorthand Student Dictionary. Yerian et al. 1969. pap. text ed. 5.55 (ISBN 0-89420-025-9, 216711). Natl Book.

Pesti Nyelv. Geza Barczi. LC 78-374048. 37p. (Hungarian.). 1977. 24.00 Ft (ISBN 9-63750-112-6). Magyar Tarsasag.

Petit Dictionnaire-Bambara-Francais Francais-Bambara. Charles Bailleul. 339p. (Bambara & Fr.). 1981. text ed. 36.00x (ISBN 0-86127-220-X, Pub. by Avebury England). Humanities.

Petit Dictionnaire Bilingue "Adonis". (Fr. & Eng.). 1941. 3.95 (Dist. by Continental Bk Co). Larousse.

Petit Dictionnaire bilingue Larousse, francais-anglais et English-French. L. Chauffurin. (Adonis). (Fr. & Eng.). plastic bdg. 6.25 (ISBN 0-685-14032-6, 3768). Larousse.

Petit Dictionnaire bilingue Larousse, francais-espagnol, espanol-frances. Larousse And Co. (Adonis). (Fr. & Span., Fr & Span). plastic bdg. 6.95 (ISBN 0-685-14033-4, 3775). Larousse.

Petit Dictionnaire de Droit Quebecois & Canadien. Dominique Page. LC 77-476465. 165p. (Fr.). 1975. Can.$write for info. (ISBN 0-7755-0542-0). Fides.

Petit Dictionnaire du Francais gue l'on n'Apprend pas a l'Ecole. Andre Kahlmann. LC 78-396931. 38p. (Fr.). 1977. write for info. (ISBN 9-124-27154-3). Esselte Studium.

Petit Dictionnaire du Francais que l'on n'Apprend Pas a l'Ecole. Andre Kahlmann. 38p. (Fr.). 1977. Kr.42.00 (ISBN 91-24-27154-3). Esselte Studium.

Petit Dictionnaire Francais. (Fr.). 9.50 (Dist. by Continental Bk Co). Larousse.

Petit Dictionnaire Francais-Chinois. 177p. (Fr. & Chinese.). 1978. pap. 3.95 (ISBN 0-686-92073-2, M-9280). French & Eur.

Petit Dictionnaire Francais-Grec Moderne et Grec Moderne-Francais. Andre Mirambel. 486p. (Fr. & Gr.). 1969. 29.95 (ISBN 0-686-57051-0, M-6413). French & Eur.

Petit Dictionnaire francais Larousse. Larousse And Co. (Illus., Fr.). 9.95 (ISBN 0-685-14034-2, 3754). Larousse.

Petit Dictionnaire Francais: Nouvelle Edition. (Fr.). 1978. 7.95 (Dist. by Continental Bk Co). Larousse.

Petit Dictionnaire Medical. L. Manuila et al. 566p. (Fr.). 1978. pap. 29.95 (ISBN 0-686-57036-7, M-6396). French & Eur.

Petit Dictionnaire Moderne: Nouvelle Edition. (Fr.). 1979. 9.95 (Dist. by Continental Bk Co). Larousse.

Petit Dictionnaire Philosophique. M. Rosenthal & P. Ioudine. 638p. (Fr.). 1977. pap. 19.95 (ISBN 0-686-56721-8, M-6446). French & Eur.

Petit Glossaire du Language Erotique aux XVIIe & XVIIIe Siecles. Marie F. Le Pennec. LC 79-379970. 110p. (Fr.). 1979. 35.00 F (ISBN 2-863-80004-3). Borderie.

Petit Larousse de la Medecine. Andre Domart. LC 77-454005. 842p. (Eng. & Fr.). 1976. 90.00 F (ISBN 2-03-020140-5). Larousse.

Petit Larousse en Couleur 1980. M. Claude Dubois. (Fr.). 1980. 56.75 (Dist. by Continental Bk Co). Larousse.

Petit Larousse 1980. M. Claude Dubois. (Fr.). 1980. 31.25 (Dist. by Continental Bk Co). Larousse.

Petit Lexique de la Manutentio n. Anglais-Francais. F. Bacon et al. Ed. by P. Chartrand. 37p. (Eng. & Fr.). 1974. pap. 5.95 (ISBN 0-686-92075-9, M-9226). French & Eur.

Petit Lexique des Termes Judiciares: A l'Usage des Journalistes. Centre de Formation et de Perfectionnement des Journalistes. LC 77-456720. 27p. (Fr.). 1975. write for info. Centre Formation.

Petit Lexique du Soudage. Anglais-Francais. A. Fortin et al. Ed. by P. Chartrand. 47p. (Eng. & Fr.). 1974. pap. 2.95 (ISBN 0-686-92078-3, M-9227). French & Eur.

Petit Lexique Somali-Francais. Christophe Philbert. LC 77-477705. 57p. (Somali & Fr.). 1976. 40.00 F (ISBN 2-25201-849-6). Klincksieck.

Petit Robert see Robert Dictionaries.

Petit Vocabulire Politique. Albert Samuel. LC 79-354581. 143p. (Fr.). 1978. write for info. Chronique Sociale.

Petits Dictionnaires Bilingues Larousse Francais-Anglais. 500p. (Fr. & Eng.). 5.75 (Dist. by Continental Bk Co). Larousse.

Petroleum Dictionary. Lalla P. Boone. 1952. 5.00 (ISBN 0-686-88791-3). U of Okla Pr.

Petroleum Dictionary. David F. Tver & Richard W. Berry. 379p. 1980. text ed. 22.50 (ISBN 0-686-65585-0). Van Nos Reinhold.

Petroleum Dictionary. David F. Tver & Richard W. Berry. 384p. 1982. pap. text ed. 16.95 (ISBN 0-442-28529-9). Van Nos Reinhold.

Petroleum Industry Glossary. Ed. by Susan R. Palmer. 1982. 32.00 (ISBN 0-89931-032-X). Inst Energy.

Petroleum Industry Glossary Handbook. Ed. by Susan Reeves Palmer. pap. 32.00. Inst Energy.

Pharmaceutical Dictionary & Reference for Prescriptions Drugs. Rev. ed. David Mason & Fran Dyller. (Illus.). 270p. 1982. pap. 3.50 (ISBN 0-87216-998-7, Playboy). Putnam Pub Group.

Pharmaceutical Dictionary & Reference 1982. David Mason & Fran Dyller. LC 81-82969. 280p. (Orig.). 1982. pap. 3.50 (ISBN 0-87216-998-7). Berkley Pub.

Pharmacological & Chemical Synonyms: A Collection of Names of Drugs, Pesticides & Other Compounds Drawn from the Medical Literature of the World. 7th ed. Compiled by E. E. Marler. 1983. 76.75 (ISBN 0-444-90227-9). Elsevier.

Pharmacological Dictionary. Latin-Russian, Russian-Latin. 463p. (Lat. & Rus.). 1977. 12.95 (ISBN 0-686-92090-2, M-9078). French & Eur.

Pharmazeutische. Axel Kleemann. LC 80-453717. xv, 555p. (Ger.). 1978. DM.200.00 (ISBN 3-13-558401-1). Thieme Verlag.

Philatelic Vocabulary in Five Languages. Philatelic Foundation. (Confederate States of America Ser.). (English, French, German, Italian, Spanish.). 3.00 (ISBN 0-911989-04-8). Philatelic Found.

Philosopher's Index Thesaurus. 65p. 1979. pap. 10.00 (ISBN 0-686-98025-5). Philos Document.

Philosophical Dictionary. rev. ed. Walter Brugger & Kenneth Baker. LC 72-82135. Orig. Title: Philosophisches Worterbuch. xxiv, 460p. (Orig.). 1973. 15.95 (ISBN 0-685-30124-9); pap. 12.95 (ISBN 0-685-30125-7). Guild Bks.

Philosophiches Woerterbuch. 6th ed. Max Apel & Peter Luds. (Sammlung Goeschen: 2202). (Ger.). 1980. pap. 6.40x (ISBN 3-11-006729-3). De Gruyter.

Philosophisches Woerterbuch, 2 vols. Ed. by G. Klaus & M. Buhr. (Illus.). 1394p. (Ger.). M.32.00. Bibl Inst Leipzig.

Philosophisches Woerterbuch. Heinrich Schmidt. LC 79-347124. viii, 765p. (Ger.). 1978. write for info. (ISBN 3-520-01320-7). Kroener.

Philosophisches Worterbuch, 2 vols. Georg Klaus & Manfred Buhr. LC 78-351881. 1394p. (Ger.). 1975. M.22.00. Bibl Inst Leipzig.

Philosophisches Worterbuch see Philosophical Dictionary.

Phonetic French Dictionary: Contrasting French-English Sounds. Jeanne V. Pleasants. 1959p. (Fr. & Eng.). pap. text ed. 5.95 (ISBN 0-940630-01-X, T-7010). Playette Corp.

Phonetic Lexicon of Monosyllabic & Some Disyllabic Words, with Homophones, Arranged According to Their Phonetic Structure. D. Rockey. 1973. 47.95 (ISBN 0-471-26113-0, Wiley Heyden). Wiley.

Photo de A & Z. Antoine Desilets. LC 79-356697. 331p. (Eng. & Fr.). 1978. Can.$27.95 (ISBN 0-7759-0614-X). Edns Homme.

Photography Language. Mary Harwood. LC 77-12760. 1978. lib. bdg. 12.90 (ISBN 0-89471-025-7); pap. 2.95 (ISBN 0-89471-024-9). Running Pr.

Phrase & Sentence Dictionary of Spoken Spanish. U. S. War Department. LC 58-14487. (Span. & Eng.). 1958. lib. bdg. 13.50x (ISBN 0-88307-580-6). Gannon.

Phrase & Sentence Dictionary of Spoken Russian. Ed. by U.S. War Dept. (Eng. & Rus.). pap. 7.50. Imported bks.

Phrase & Sentence Dictionary Spanish-English. (Span. & Eng.). write for info. (608-109). Pan Amer Pub.

Phrase & Word Origins: A Study of Familiar Expressions. 2nd ed. Alfred H. Holt. Orig. Title: Phrase Origins. 1961. pap. 4.50 (ISBN 0-486-20758-7). Dover.

Phrase Dictionaries for the American Tourist, 6 bks. Frederick Stark. Incl. German for the American Tourist. (Ger. & Eng.). pap. (ISBN 0-8326-2409-8, 6570); Spanish for the English-Speaking Tourist. (Span. & Eng.). pap. (ISBN 0-8326-2410-1, 6571); French for the English-Speaking Tourist. (Fr. & Eng.). pap. (ISBN 0-8326-2411-X, 6572); Italian for the English-Speaking Tourist. (Ital. & Eng.). pap. (ISBN 0-8326-2412-8, 6573); Greek for the English-Speaking Tourist. (Gr. & Eng.). pap. (ISBN 0-8326-2413-6, 6574); Russian for the English-Speaking Tourist. (Rus. & Eng.). pap. (ISBN 0-8326-2414-4, 6575). 128p. (Orig., Ger., Span., Fr., Ital., Gr. & Rus.). 1981. pap. 2.50 ea. Delair.

Phrase Origins see Phrase & Word Origins: A Study of Familiar Expressions.

Physiatric Dictionary: Glossary of Physical Medicine & Rehabilitation. Herman L. Kamenetz. 180p. 1965. photocopy ed. spiral 16.75x (ISBN 0-398-00964-3). C C Thomas.

Physician's Current Procedural Terminology. 4th ed. American Medical Association. 501p. 19.95 (OP 041); bulk rates avail. AMA.

Physics Dictionary, 3 vols. R. Sube & G. Eisenreich. 2895p. 1980. 185.00x (ISBN 0-569-07879-2, Pub. by Collet's). State Mutual Bk.

Physics Dictionary, 3 vols. Ed. by R. Sube & G. Eisenreich. (Eng., Ger., Fr. & Rus.). 1974. 260.00 (ISBN 3-87144-143-0). Adler.

Physics Terminology. A. Jesse. 129p. (Fr. Ger. & Eng.). 1980. pap. 24.95 (ISBN 3-7625-0963-8, M-9310). French & Eur.

Physik: Ein Lexikon der Gesamten Schulphysik. Hans Borucki et al. (Illus.). 490p. (Ger.). DM.19.80 (ISBN 3-411-01122-X). Biblio Inst.

Physik-Fachsprache Englisch-Franzosisch-Deutsch. A. Jesse. 129p. (Fr., Ger. & Eng.). 1980. DM.28.00 (ISBN 3-7625-0963-8). Bauverlag.

Phytopathologie & Pflanzenschutz. Gerd Frohlich et al. LC 79-377360. 295p. (Eng. & Ger.). 1979. DM.19.80 (ISBN 3-437-20207-3). Fischer Verlag.

Piaget: Dictionary of Terms. Ed. by E. R. Hermann et al. 1973. text ed. 28.00 (ISBN 0-08-017039-0). Pergamon.

Piano Chord Dictionary. 1981. 2.50 (ISBN 0-88284-155-6). Alfred Pub.

Piccolo Dizionario Americano Italiano. Friedrich W. Horlacher. LC 78-343989. 111p. (Eng. & Ital.). 1976. L.1800.00. Nuova Vallecchi.

Piccolo Dizionario del Dialetto Bresciano. Stefano Pinelli. LC 77-467177. (Illus.). 109p. (Ital.). 1976. write for info. Grafo.

Piccolo lessico universale. Sergio Rapetti et al. LC 79-342345. 369p. (Ital.). 1976. L.3500.00. Nuova Vallecchi.

Pichon Diccionari Frances-Occitan. Jacme Taupiac. LC 80-454080. (Illus.). 304p. (Fr.). 1977. 75.00 F. Inst Occit Tlse.

Pickwickian Dictionary & Cyclopaedia. Percy H. Fitzgerald. LC 71-148777. Repr. of 1902 ed. 27.50 (ISBN 0-404-08778-7). AMS Pr.

Pickwickian Dictionary & Cyclopedia. Percy Fitzgerald. LC 74-7473. Repr. of 1900 ed. lib. bdg. 50.00 (ISBN 0-8414-4179-0). Folcroft.

Pictorial Dictionary of Ancient Athens. John Travlos. LC 79-91823. (Illus.). 590p. 1980. Repr. of 1971 ed. lib. bdg. 100.00 (ISBN 0-87817-267-X). Hacker.

Pictorial Dictionary of British Nineteenth Century Furniture Design. Antique Collectors' Club. 583p. 1980. 69.50 (ISBN 0-902028-47-2). Antique Collect.

Pictorial Dictionary of British Nineteenth Century Furniture Designs. Edward Joy. (Illus.). 578p. 1980. 59.50 (ISBN 0-686-65051-4). Hacker.

Pictorial Dictionary of Nineteeth Century Furniture Design. E. Jay. (Illus.). 1980. 69.50 (ISBN 0-902028-47-2). Apollo.

Pictorial Medical Terminology. William E. Loechel. 126p. 1981. pap. 14.75x spiral (ISBN 0-398-04581-X). C C Thomas.

Picture Dictionary, ABCs, Telling Time, Counting Rhymes, Riddles & Finger Plays. A. Y. Bennett. (Illus.). (gr. k-3). 1970. 5.95 (ISBN 0-448-02813-1, G&D). Putnam Pub Group.

Picture Dictionary for Children. Garnette Watters & S. A. Courtis. (Illus.). (gr. 1-3). pap. 3.95 (ISBN 0-448-14002-0, G&D). Putnam Pub Group.

Picturesque Expressions: A Thematic Dictionary. Ed. by Nancy LaRoche & Laurence Urdang. LC 80-22705. 300p. 1980. 55.00x (ISBN 0-8103-1122-4). Gale.

Piecewise Linear Concordances & Isotopies. Kenneth C. Millet. LC 74-18328. (Memoirs Ser.: No. 153). 74p. 1974. pap. 9.00 (ISBN 0-8218-1853-8, MEMO-153). Am Math.

Pieciojezyczny Slownik Gleboznawczy. Adamczyk Boleslaw. LC 76-532466. 264p. (Eng., Fr., Ger., Pol. & Rus.). 1976. 120.00 Zl. Panstwowe Zaklad W.

Piers Plowman Glossary, Pt. 4. William Langland. Ed. by W. W. Skeat. (EETS, OS Ser.: No. 81). Repr. of 1884 ed. 29.00 (ISBN 0-527-00060-4). Kraus Repr.
Piirucni Slovnik Vedy a Techniky. Bohumil Dobrovolny. LC 80-488092. 253p. (Czech.). 1979. 25.00 Kcs. Prace.
Pinyin Chinese-English Dictionary. Beijing Foreign Institute. Ed. by Wu Jingrong. LC 79-2477. 976p. (Chinese & Eng.). 1979. 68.95x (ISBN 0-471-27557-3, Pub. by Wiley-Interscience); pap. 16.95 (ISBN 0-471-86796-9). Wiley.
Pinyin Chinese-English Dictionary. (Chinese & Eng.). 61.00. Iaconi.
Pipeline Dictionary. H. Bucksch & A. P. Altmeyer. 288p. (Eng., Ger. & Fr.). 1969. 99.50 (ISBN 3-7625-1166-7, M-7588, Pub. by Bauverlag). French & Eur.
Pipeline Dictionary. H. Bucksch & A. P. Altmeyer. 288p. (Eng., Ger. & Fr.). 1969. 70.00x (ISBN 3-7625-1166-7). Intl Pubns Serv.
Pipeline Dictionary. H. Bucksch & A. P. Altmeyer. 288p. (Eng., Ger. & Fr.). 1969. DM.125.00 (ISBN 3-7625-1166-7). Bauverlag.
Pipeline Glossary & Directory. Ed. by C. D. Shann. LC 80-480912. 123p. (Eng.). 1978. write for info. Scientific Surveys.
Pitman Dictionary of English & Shorthand. Isaac Pitman. (New Era Edition). 1974. 32.00 (ISBN 0-8224-0024-3). Pitman Learning.
Pitman Two Thousand Student Dictionary. 1980. NT.$4.50. Pitman Bks.
Pitman's Dictionary of Industrial Administration: A Comprehensive Encyclopedia of the Organization, Administration, & Management of Modern Industry, 2 vols. Ed. by John Lee & Alfred D. Chandler. LC 79-7552. (History of Management Thought & Practice Ser.). 1980. Repr. of 1928 ed. Set. lib. bdg. 125.00x (ISBN 0-405-12336-1); lib. bdg. 62.50x ea. Vol. 1 (ISBN 0-405-12337-X). Vol. 2 (ISBN 0-405-12338-8). Ayer Co.
Plain-Language Law Dictionary. Robert Rothenberg. (Reference Ser.). 1981. pap. 7.95 (ISBN 0-14-051109-1). Penguin.
Plains Cree Dictionary. 2nd rev. ed. Henry Nanooch et al. (Illus., Cree.). 1976. Can.$22.00 (ISBN 0-919864-19-8). U of Toronto Pr.
Plan for the Dictionary of Old English. Roberta Frank & Angus Cameron. 1973. Can.$25.00 (ISBN 0-8020-3303-2). U of Toronto Pr.
Plan for the Dictionary of Old English. Ed. by Roberta Frank & Angus Cameron. LC 72-97152. (Toronto Old English Ser.). 1973. 35.00x (ISBN 0-8020-3303-2). U of Toronto Pr.
Plan for Using CAI to Teach Vocabulary Concepts. Karen K. Block & Ellen S. McCaslin. (Illus.). 36p. 1978. 1.00. Learn Res Dev.
Plan och Byggtermer. Tekniska Nomenklaturcentralen. LC 76-522778. 198p. (Swedish.). 1975. Kr.50.00 (ISBN 91-7196-058-9). Tek Nomen.
Planing, Slotting, Broaching, Turning see Dictionary of Production Engineering: German-English-French.
Plast & Gummilexikon. (Eng. , Swedish & Ger.). 1982. Kr.149.00 (ISBN 91-86236-00-8). EC Print AB.
Plastic Bottle Glossary. Society of the Plastics Industry. 2.50 (1271). Soc Plastic Ind.
Plastic Technology Dictionary. H. Y. El-Desouti. 331p. (Eng., Fr., Ger. & Arabic.). 1980. 45.00 (ISBN 0-686-92400-2, M-9754). French & Eur.
Plastics Technical Dictionary, 3 vols. Ed. by A. M. Wittfoht. (Illus.). 1700p. 1983. Set. text ed. 135.00x (ISBN 0-02-949940-2, Pub. by Hanser International). Macmillan.
Plastics Technical Dictionary: Part 1: English-German. Ed. by A. M. Wittfoht. (Illus.). 600p. (Eng. & Ger.). 1982. text ed. 59.00x (ISBN 0-02-949980-1, Pub. by Hanser International). Macmillan.
Plastics Technical Dictionary: Part 2: German-English. Ed. by A. M. Wittfoht. (Illus.). 600p. (Ger. & Eng.). 1983. text ed. 59.00x (ISBN 0-02-949960-7, Pub. by Hanser International). Macmillan.
Plastics Technical Dictionary: Part 3: Reference Volume. Ed. by A. M. Wittfoht. (Illus.). 508p. 1982. text ed. 49.00x (ISBN 0-02-949970-4, Pub. by Hanser International). Macmillan.
Plasttechnik-Englisch-Deutsch-Franzoesisch-Russisch. Gisbert Kaliske. 390p. (Eng., Ger., Fr. & Rus.). 1982. M.60.00. VEB Technik.
Plates Illustrative of the Vocabulary for the Deaf & Dumb. Harvey Darton. 69.95 (ISBN 0-8490-0841-7). Gordon Pr.
Pluri Dictionnaire. new ed. C. Dubois. (Illus., Fr.). 1974. 31.50x (ISBN 2-03-020124-3, 3677). Larousse.
Pneumatic Power Glossary. Institute for Power System. 80p. 1979. 30.00x (ISBN 0-686-65626-1). State Mutual Bk.
Pocket Automotive Dictionary, with Metric Conversion Table. new ed. William H. Crouse & Donald L. Anglin. (Automotive Technology Ser). 1976. pap. text ed. 4.95 (ISBN 0-07-014752-3, G). McGraw.
Pocket Chinese-English Dictionary: Zhong Hua Edition. 620p. (Chinese & Eng.). 1978. 8.95 (ISBN 0-8351-0601-2); pap. 5.95 (ISBN 0-8351-0602-0). China Bks.
Pocket Concise Chinese-English Dictionary. 620p. (Chinese , Eng.). 1978. pap. 6.95 (ISBN 0-686-92467-3, M-9182). French & Eur.
Pocket Crossword Dictionary. Ed. by John Bailie. 320p. (Span.). Epap. 1.25 (ISBN 0-600-32145-2). Newnes Bks.
Pocket Dictionary. LC 78-13455. 1978. pap. 1.95 (ISBN 0-395-26661-0). HM.
Pocket Dictionary Iron & Steel. Henry G. Freeman. LC 76-354255. (Eng. & Ger.). 11.25x ea.; Vol. 1. German-English. (ISBN 3-19-006214-5); Vol. 2. English-German. (ISBN 3-19-006215-3). Intl Pubns Serv.
Pocket Dictionary of American Slang. abr. ed. Harold Wentworth & Stuart B. Flexner. 1968. pap. 3.95 (ISBN 0-671-78976-7). PB.
Pocket Dictionary of Art Terms. Ed. by Julia M. Ehresmann. LC 74-143464. (Illus.). 1971. pap. 3.95 (ISBN 0-8212-0748-2, 712019). NYGS.
Pocket Dictionary of Automotive Engineering: Taschenwoerterbuch Kraftfahrzuegtechnik. Henry G. Freeman. LC 71-362034. 380p. (Ger. & Eng.). 1968. 12.50x (ISBN 3-19-006270-6). Intl Pubns Serv.
Pocket Dictionary of Banjo Chords. Neil Lambard. pap. 1.50 (ISBN 0-934286-19-1). Kenyon.
Pocket Dictionary of Business Terms. Leo Liebster & Colin Horner. 320p. E1.25 (ISBN 0-600-31599-1); Epap. 12.50 shrink-wrap pack of 10 copies (ISBN 0-600-04831-4). Newnes Bks.
Pocket Dictionary of Horseman's Terms in English, German, French & Spanish. Hanns Muller. (Fr.). 1971. 5.25 (ISBN 0-685-00343-4). Transatlantic.
Pocket Dictionary of Music Terms. Albert De Vito. LC 65-8450. 1965. 1.50 (ISBN 0-934286-09-4). Kenyon.
Pocket Dictionary of Publishing Terms. Henry Jacob. (Illus.). 1976. pap. text ed. 5.95x (ISBN 0-8464-0727-2). Beekman Pubs.
Pocket Dictionary of Synonyms & Antonyms. 1960. pap. 2.95 (ISBN 0-394-51933-7). Random.
Pocket Dictionary of Technology & Science: Technischwissenschaftliches Taschenwoerte'buch: German-English & English-German. 6th ed. Karl Breuer. LC 75-597125. 413p. (Ger. & Eng.). 1971. 27.50x (ISBN 3-87749-014-X). Intl Pubns Serv.
Pocket Dictionary of Wines. John Paterson. 256p. (Eng.). Epap. 1.25 (ISBN 0-600-39498-0); Epap. 12.50 shrink-wrap pack of 10 copies (ISBN 0-600-04876-4). Newnes Bks.
Pocket English-Chinese Dictionary. (Eng. & Chinese.). 1980. pap. 4.95 (ISBN 0-8351-0727-2). China Bks.
Pocket English-Chinese Dictionary. 451p. (Eng. & Chinese.). 1980. pap. text ed. 4.95 (ISBN 0-686-92473-8, M-9580). French & Eur.
Pocket English-Chinese Dictionary. 451p. (Chinese & Eng.). 1980. 4.95 (ISBN 0-8351-0727-2). China Bks.
Pocket English-Chinese Dictionary. (Chinese & Eng.). pap. 2.25. Iaconi.
Pocket English Dictionary. 320p. (Eng.). Epap. 1.00 . (ISBN 0-600-37091-7). Newnes Bks.
Pocket English-Hungarian Dictionary. I. Orszagh. (Eng. & Hungarian.). 1980. 20.00x (ISBN 0-569-00408-X, Pub. by Collet's). State Mutual Bk.
Pocket Hawaiian Dictionary: With a Concise Hawaiian Grammar. Mary K. Pukui et al. LC 74-78865. 286p. (Hawaiian.). 1975. pap. 2.95 (ISBN 0-8248-0307-8). UH Pr.
Pocket Hungarian-English Dictionary. I. Orszagh. (Hungarian & Eng.). 1980. 20.00x (ISBN 0-569-00344-X, Pub. by Collet's). State Mutual Bk.
Pocket Lexicon of Freemasonry. 1.50 (ISBN 0-685-19495-7). Powner.
Pocket Medical Dictionary. A. S. Playfair. (Illus.). 256p. (Eng.). Epap. 1.25 (ISBN 0-600-36311-2). Newnes Bks.
Pocket Oxford Dictionary of Current English. 6th ed. Ed. by J. B. Sykes. 1978. 12.95 (ISBN 0-19-861129-3). Oxford U Pr.
Pocket Oxford English-Russian Dictionary. N. A. Rankin. (Eng. & Rus.). 1981. text ed. 11.95x (ISBN 0-19-864127-3). Oxford U Pr.
Pocket Oxford German Dictionary, 2 vols. in 1. Compiled by M. L. Barker & H. Homeyer. Incl. Pt. 1. German-English. 3rd ed. (Eng. & Ger.). 1975; Pt. 2. English-German. Compiled by C. T. Carr. (Eng. & Ger.). 1975. (Ger.). pap. 5.95x (ISBN 0-19-864138-9). Oxford U Pr.
Pocket Oxford Russian Dictionary: Russian-English - English-Russian. Ed. by Jessie Coulson et al. (Rus. & Eng.). 1981. pap. 10.95x (ISBN 0-19-864122-2). Oxford U Pr.
Pocket Oxford Russian-English Dictionary. Ed. by J. Coulson. (Rus. & Eng.). 1975. 12.95x (ISBN 0-19-864113-3). Oxford U Pr.
Pocket Oxford Russian-English Dictionary. Jessie S. Coulson. LC 75-316760. vii, 397p. (Eng. & Rus.). 1975. E2.50 (ISBN 0-19-864113-3). Imprint of Oxford U Pr.
Pocket Rhyming Dictionary. 1960. pap. 2.95 (ISBN 0-394-40062-3). Random.
Pocket-Shorter Dictionary. 600p. (Ger. & Eng.). 5.95 (085). Langenscheidt.
Pocket-Shorter Dictionary. 600p. (Hebrew & Eng.). 5.95 (088). Langenscheidt.
Pocket-Shorter Dictionary. 600p. (Fr. & Eng.). 5.95 (086). Langenscheidt.
Pocket-Shorter Dictionary. 600p. (Lat. & Eng.). 5.95 (089). Langenscheidt.
Pocket-Shorter Dictionary. 600p. (Gr. & Eng.). 5.95 (087). Langenscheidt.
Pocket-Shorter Dictionary. 600p. (Rus. & Eng.). 5.95 (090). Langenscheidt.
Pocket Thesaurus of English Words. Ed. by M. H. Manser. 336p. (Eng.). Epap. 1.25 (ISBN 0-600-38779-8). Hamlyn-Amer.
Podreczny Slownik Polsko-Francuski. Kazimierz Kupisz et al. LC 77-557604. 1150p. (Pol. & Fr.). 1977. 190.00 Zl. Wiedza Powszechna.
Podreczny Slownik Polsko-Niemiecki (Manual Dictionary Polish-German) A. Bzdega et al. 1018p. (Pol. & Ger.). 1977. leatherette 19.95 (ISBN 0-686-87194-4, M-0129). French & Eur.
Podreczny Slownik Polsko-Rosyjski. Ryszard Stypula et al. LC 77-502170. 840p. (Pol. & Rus.). 1976. 80.00 Zl. Wiedza Powszechna.
Poetry Handbook: A Dictionary of Terms. 4th ed. Babette Deutsch. 224p. 1982. pap. 5.05i (ISBN 0-06-463548-1, EH 548, EH). B&N NY.
Poet's Manual & Rhyming Dictionary. Frances Stillman & Jane S. Whitfield. LC 65-11650. 1965. 12.45i (ISBN 0-690-64572-4). T Y Crowell.
Police Dictionary. 2nd rev. & enl. ed. Shafiq Ismat. (Illus.). 264p. (Eng. & Arabic.). 25.00 (068-6). Intl Bk Ctr.
Police Dictionary: English-Arabic Dictionary. Shafiq Ismat. (Eng. & Arabic.). 1980. 25.00x (ISBN 0-86685-068-6). Intl Bk Ctr.
Police Medical Dictionary. J. E. Schmidt. 256p. 1968. 19.75x (ISBN 0-398-01673-9). C C Thomas.
Police Terminology: Programmed Manual for Criminal Justice Personnel. Jack M. Seitzinger & Thomas M. Kelley. (Illus.). 152p. 1974. spiral 11.75x (ISBN 0-398-02947-4). C C Thomas.
Policy Instruments to Define the Pattern of Demand for Technology. (Science & Technology for Development Ser.: STPI Module 7). 88p. 1981. pap. 5.00 (ISBN 0-88936-265-3, IDRC TS-27, IDRC). Unipub.
Polish-English - English-Polish Dictionary. Kierst. (Pol. & Eng.). 29.50 (ISBN 0-87557-060-7, 060-7). Saphrograph.
Polish-English & English-Polish Dictionary. J. Stanislawski. (New Pronouncing Dictionaries). (Pol. & Eng.). (YA) (gr. 9 up). 12.95 (ISBN 0-679-10082-2). McKay.
Polish-English Dictionary of Science & Technology. Czerni & Skrzynka. 754p. (Pol. & Eng.). 1976. 95.00x (ISBN 0-686-44737-9, Pub. by Collets). State Mutual Bk.
Polish-English Dictionary of Science & Technology. 3rd ed. Ed. by Sergiusz Czerni & Maria Skrzynska. (Pol. & Eng.). 1976. 30.00x (ISBN 0-686-19981-2). Intl Learn Syst.
Polish-English, English-Polish Dictionary. Tadeus Z. Grzebienowski. (Illus., Pol. & Eng.). 1980. 16.95 (ISBN 0-88254-477-2). Hippocrene Bks.
Polish-English, English-Polish Dictionary (1975, 4 vols. J. Stanislawski. (Pol. & Eng.). 1978. Set. 120.00 (ISBN 0-685-85757-3). Heinman.
Polish-English, English-Polish Practical Dictionary, 2 vols. J. Stanislawski. (Pol. & Eng.). Set. 50.00 (ISBN 0-685-79114-9). Heinman.
Polish-English Practical Dictionary. J. Stanisljawski et al. 1030p. (Pol. & Eng.). 1978. 20.00x (ISBN 0-89918-532-0, P-532). Vanous.
Polish Great Dictionary, Vol. 1: English-Polish, 2 vols. rev. 6th ed. Jan Stanislawski. (Eng. & Pol.). 1982. 55.00x (ISBN 0-89918-502-9, P-502). Vanous.
Polish Great Dictionary, Vol. 2: Polish-English, 2 vols. 4th ed. J. Stanislowski. (Pol. & Eng.). 1978. text ed. 42.00x (ISBN 0-89918-521-5, P-521). Vanous.
Polish Pocket Dictionary. (Pol. & Eng.). pap. 6.50 (ISBN 0-686-77983-5). Heinman.
Polish Practical Dictionary (English-Polish) J. Stanislawski & K. Billip. (Pol. & Eng.). 1981. 20.00x (ISBN 0-89918-533-9, P-533). Vanous.
Polish-Russian Dictionary of Economics. M. N. Osmowej. 494p. (Pol. & Rus.). 1977. leatherette 19.50 (ISBN 0-686-92093-7, M-9121). French & Eur.

Polish-Russian, Russian-Polish Dictionary. I. Nitronowa et al. 575p. (Pol. & Rus.). 1980. leatherette 4.95 (ISBN 0-686-97442-5, M-9102). French & Eur.
Polish Science & Technology Dictionary: English-Polish. 5th ed. S. Czerni & M. Skrzynska. (Pol. & Eng.). 1976. 35.00x (ISBN 0-89918-536-3, P536). Vanous.
Polish Science & Technology Dictionary: Polish-English. 3rd rev. ed. S. Czerni & M. Skrzynska. (Pol. & Eng.). 1976. 35.00x (ISBN 0-89918-537-1, P-537). Vanous.
Politekhnicheskii Slovar. Ed. by I. I. Artobolevskii. 608p. (Rus.). 1977. 19.95 (Pub. by Sov Entsiklopediia). Four Continent.
Politekonomicheskii Slovar. Ed. by E. F. Borisov. 267p. (Rus.). 1972. 3.35 (Pub. by Politizdat). Four Continent.
Politica & Politiqueria: Diccionario Para el Hombre de la Calle. Magin Pont Mestres. LC 79-127325. 165p. (Span.). 1979. 500.00 ptas (ISBN 8-470-02275-X). Edns Acervo.
Political Science Dictionary. Jack C. Plano. LC 73-10501. 1973. pap. text ed. 10.95 (ISBN 0-03-086191-8, HoltC). HR&W.
Political Science Directory. Jack C. Plano et al. LC 77-186296. 400p. 1976. 15.00 (ISBN 0-03-016736-1, HIS). HR&W.
Political Science Thesaurus. Ed. by Carl Beck et al. 1975. 20.00 (ISBN 0-915654-02-4); to institutions 30.00 (ISBN 0-685-53465-0); pap. 15.00, to institutions 25.00 (ISBN 0-685-53466-9). Am Political.
Politicheskaia Ekonomiia Slovar. Ed. by V. A. Zhamin. 464p. (Rus.). 1979. 6.50 (Pub. by Politizdat). Four Continent.
Politicheskii Slovar. Ed. by B. N. Ponomareva. 702p. (Rus.). 1958. 3.95 (Pub. by Politizdat). Four Continent.
Politik & Gesellschaft: Ein Lexikon zur Politischen Bildung. Hede Prehl et al. 463p. (Ger.). DM.19.80 (ISBN 3-411-01729-5). Biblio Inst.
Politik Aufgespiesst: Heiteres Lexikon der Politischen Missbildung. Konrad Gerescher. LC 77-481880. 58p. (Ger.). 1976. write for info. (ISBN 3-87998-010-1). Gauke.
Politik: Mit 1800 Stichwoertern. Ed. by Bernard Pfahlberg. LC 77-377171. (Illus.). 238p. (Ger.). 1979. DM.22.00 (ISBN 3-451-16456-6). Herder.
Politikai Kissotar: A Szocikkek Szerzoi. Istvan Foldes & Gyoergy Makai. LC 75-547485. 289p. (Hungarian.). 1974. 40.00 Ft. Kos Kony.
Politisch-Soziologisches Woerterbuch. Karl Rudolf Kollnig. LC 75-516317. 254p. (Ger.). 1975. DM.9.80. Kamp Verlag.
Politisches Woerterbuch. Siegfried Landshut. (Ger.). 1958. pap. 10.95 (ISBN 3-16-811742-0, M-7589, Pub. by Hochschule Fuer Wirtschaft U. Politik). French & Eur.
Pollock's Dictionary of English Dolls. Mary Hillier. 1983. 19.95 (ISBN 0-517-54922-0). Crown.
Polnisch, 2 vols. Stanislaw Walewski. (Langenscheidts Taschenworterbucher Ser.). (Ger. & Pol.). Teil 1: Polnisch-Deutsch (624p.) DM.18.80 (10260); Teil 2: Deutsch-Polnisch (590p.) DM.18.80 (10265); DM.beide Teile in einem Band 29.80 (11260). Langenscheidt.
Polnisch-Deutsches Wissenschaftlich-Technishes Worterbuch. Z. J. Koch. 598p. (Pol. & Ger.). 1980. 75.00 (ISBN 83-204-0021-X, M-9217). French & Eur.
Polovodicove Soucastky. Adolf Klimek. LC 77-472717. 444p. (Eng. & Czech., Praha, Czechoslovakia). 1977. 30.00 Kcs. SNTL.
Polska Gwara Konspiracyjno-Partyzancka Czasu Okupacji Hitlerowskiej. Stanislaw Kania & Zielona Gora. LC 77-562382. 295p. (Pol.). 1976. 70.00 Zl. Wyzsza Szkola.
Polsko -Slovensky a Slovensko-Polsky Slovnik. Mikulas Stano. LC 75-590519. 861p. (Pol. & Slovak.). 1975. 55.00 Kcs. SNTC.
Polsko-Litovskii Slovar. V. A. Vaitkiavichiute. 1024p. (Pol. & Lithuanian.). 1979. 9.95 (Pub. by Mokslas). Four Continent.
Polsko-Ruskii Khimicheskii Slovar. I. A. Titova. 459p. (Rus. & Pol.). 1970. 6.75 (Pub. by Sov Entsiklopediia). Four Continent.
Polsko-Russkii Ekonomicheskii Slovar. 496p. (Pol. & Rus.). 1977. 9.50 (0-22, Pub. by Russkii Iazyk). Four Continent.
Polsko-Russkii Gornyi Slovar. 815p. (Rus. & Pol.). 1975. 12.00 (Pub. by Russkii Iazyk). Four Continent.
Polsko-Russkii Razgovornik Dlia Turistov. 240p. (Pol. & Rus.). 1979. 2.95 (Pub. by Russkii Iazyk). Four Continent.
Pol'sko-Slovensky a Slovensko-Polsky Slovnik. Mikulas Stano et al. LC 75-590519. 861p. (Pol. & Slovak.). 1975. 55.00 Kcs. SNTC.
Polyglot Dictionary of Musical Terms. 798p. 1978. 135.00 (ISBN 0-686-92096-1, M-9436). French & Eur.
Polyglotta Africana. Sigismund W. Koelle. LC 65-82544. 1963. Repr. of 1854 ed. 42.50x (ISBN 3-201-00766-8). Intl Pubns Serv.
Polyglotta Africana Orientalis. J. T. Last. 251p. 1972. Repr. of 1885 ed. 13.50x (ISBN 0-8002-1333-5). Intl Pubns Serv.
Polygrafie-Englisch-Deutsch-Franzoesisch-Russisch-Spanisch-Polnisch-Ungarisch-Solwakisch. Wolfgang Muller. 1020p. (Eng., Ger., Fr., Rus., Span., Pol., Hungarian & Czech.). 1981. M.110.00. VEB Technik.
Polygraph Dictionary for the Graphic Industries in Six Languages. 38th ed. Ed. by K. Collet. LC 68-117537. (Ger., Eng., Fr., Span. & Ital.). 1967. 65.00x (ISBN 3-87641-150-5). Intl Pubns Serv.
Polytechnic Dictionary: German-English, English-German, 2 vols. 4th ed. Rudolf Walther. (Ger. & Eng.). 87.50 ea. (ISBN 3-7736-5100-7). Adler.
Polytechnisches Woerterbuch. Karl H. Radde & Francisco Laguna de la Vera. LC 77-562408. 716p. (Eng., Span. & Ger.). 1976. M.50.00. VEB Technik.
Polytechnisches Woerterbuch. Aribert Schlegelmilch. LC 77-462031. 723p. (Fr. & Ger.). 1976. M.45.00. VEB Verlag Technik.
Polytechnisches Woerterbuch. Rudolf Walther. LC 77-463186. 1248p. (Ger.). 1976. M.50.00. VEB Verlag Technik.
Polytechnisches Woerterbuch, Vol. 1. 2nd ed. Alibert Schlegelmilch. (Fr. & Ger.). 1976. 36.00 (ISBN 0-686-56638-6, M-7590, Pub. by Veb Verlag Technik). French & Eur.
Polytechnisches Woerterbuch, Vol. 1. 7th ed. Rudolf Walther. (Eng. & Ger., Dictionary of Polytechnics). 1978. 40.00 (ISBN 0-686-56640-8, M-7592, Pub. by Veb Verlag Technik). French & Eur.
Polytechnisches Woerterbuch, Vol. 2. 2nd ed. Alibert Schlegelmilch. (Fr. & Ger.). 1977. 36.00 (ISBN 0-686-56639-4, M-7591, Pub. by Veb Verlag Technik). French & Eur.
Polytechnisches Woerterbuch, Vol. 2. 3rd ed. Rudolf Walther. (Eng. & Ger., Dictionary of Polytechnics). 1977. 40.00 (ISBN 0-686-56641-6, M-7593, Pub. by Veb Verlag Technik). French & Eur.
Polytechnisches Woerterbuch Deutsch-Englisch. Rudolf Walther. 1046p. (Ger. & Eng.). 1973. 47.00. VEB Technik.
Polytechnisches Woerterbuch Deutsch-Franzoesisch. 832p. (Ger. & Fr.). 1982. M.50.00. Veb Technik.
Polytechnisches Woerterbuch Deutsch-Spanisch. Karl H. Radde. 812p. (Ger. & Span.). 1982. M.50.00. VEB Technik.
Polytechnisches Woerterbuch Deutsch-Vietnamesisch. Tran Duy-Tu et al. 502p. (Ger. & Vietnamese.). 1982. M.32.00. VEB Technik.
Polytechnisches Woerterbuch Franzoesisch-Deutsch. 724p. (Fr. & Ger.). 1982. M.50.00. VEB Technik.
Polytechnisches Woerterbuch Italienisch-Deutsch. Aribert Schlegelmilch. 632p. (Ital. & Ger.). 1981. M.50.00. VEB Technik.
Polytechnisches Woerterbuch Russisch-Deutsch. Paul Hueter & Horst Goerner. 1600p. (Rus. & Ger.). 1982. M.60.00. VEB Technik.
Polytechnisches Woerterbuch Spanisch-Deutsch. 716p. (Span. & Ger.). 1981. M.50.00. VEB Technik.
Polytechnisches Worterbuch. Aribert Schlegelmilch. LC 77-568103. 831p. (Ger. & Fr.). 1976. DM.58.00 (ISBN 3-19-006298-6). Hueber.
Ponapean-English Dictionary. Kenneth L. Rehg & Damian G. Sohl. LC 79-19451. (Pali Language Texts: Micronesia). 265p. (Ponapean & Eng.). 1979. pap. text ed. 14.00x (ISBN 0-8248-0562-3). UH Pr.
Pons Globalwoerterbuch Englisch-Deutsch, 2 vols. 1178p. (Eng. & Ger.). pap. 10.90. M Rosenberg.
Pons Globalworterbuch. Schoffler & Weis. LC 78-400567. (Eng. & Ger.). 1978. DM.21.80 (ISBN 3-12-517130-X). Klett.
Pons-Grosswoerterbuch, 2 vols. Erich Weiss. Ed. by Heinrich Mattutat & Christian Nugue. LC 79-337909. (Ger. & Fr.). 1978. DM.56.00 (ISBN 3-125-17220-9). Klett.
Pons Schoffler Weis English-German, German-English Dictionary. E. Weis et al. 1060p. (Eng. & Ger.). 1979. 52.50 (ISBN 3-12-517120-2, M-9361). French & Eur.
Popular Dictionary of Judaism. Hugh J. Schonfield. 1966. pap. 1.75 (ISBN 0-8065-0075-1, 232). Citadel Pr.
Popular Northern Sotho Dictionary. 2nd ed. T. Kriel. LC 77-363921. 342p. (Eng. & Sotho.). 1976. write for info. (ISBN 0-627-00932-8). Van Schaik.
Population-Family Planning Thesaurus: An Alphabetical & Hierarchical Display of Terms Drawn from Population-Related Literature in the Social Sciences. 2nd ed. Caroline Lucas & Carann Turner. Ed. by Karen Long & Carann Turner. 286p. 1978. pap. 20.00 spiral bdg., incl. 1981 suppl. (ISBN 0-89055-049-2). Carolina Pop Ctr.
Populiarnyi Ekonomiko-Matematicheskii Slovar. L. I. Lopatnikov. 165p. (Rus.). 1973. 1.95 (Pub. by Znanie). Four Continent.
Portable Dictionary of Real Estate Terminology. Irving Marcus. 120p. 1983. pap. 6.95 (ISBN 0-8283-1739-9). Branden.
Portable Redhouse Turkish-English, English-Turkish Dictionary. (Turkish & Eng.). 1975. 9.00x (ISBN 0-686-16857-7). Intl Learn Syst.
Portuagalsko-Russkil Politekhnicheskil Slovar. Vladimir S. Matveev & Konstantin G. Asrhants. LC 75-546852. 568p. (Rus. & Portuguese.). 1975. 2.42 Rub. Russkii Iazyk.
Portugal-Magyar Szotar. Rudolf Kiraly. LC 78-396058. 728p. (Port. & Hungarian.). 1978. 108.00 Ft (ISBN 9-6305-1382-X). Akademiai Kiado.
Portugalsko-Cesko-Portugalsky Kapesni Slovnik. Zdenek Hampl & Jiri Holsan. LC 77-551645. 497p. (Czech. & Port.). 1976. 29.00 Kcs. SNTC.
Portugalsko-Cesky Slovnik. Zdenek Hampl. LC 76-508331. 883p. (Czech. & Port.). 1975. 45.00 Kcs. SNTC.
Portugiesisch, 2 vols. rev. ed. Incl. Teil I. Portugiesisch-Deutsch. F. Irmen. 632p. DM.18.80 (10270); Teil II. Deutsch-Portugiesisch. A. E. Beau. 607p. DM.18.80 (10275). (Langenscheidts Taschenworterbucher Ser.). (Port. & Ger., Unter Berusichtigung der Brasilianismen). 1982. DM.beide Teile in einem Band 29.80 (11270). Langenscheidt.
Portuguese-English Dictionary. Hygino Aliandro. 311p. (Port. & Eng.). 1978. pap. 4.80. Imported Bks.
Portuguese-English Dictionary. Berlitz Editors. (Port. & Eng.). 1982. 4.95 (ISBN 0-02-964440-2, Berlitz). Macmillan.
Portuguese-English Dictionary. rev. ed. J. Albino Ferreira. Ed. by A. De Morais. (Port. & Eng.). 32.50 (ISBN 0-87559-029-2); thumb indexed 37.50 (ISBN 0-87559-030-6). Shalom.
Portuguese-English Dictionary. rev. ed. James L. Taylor. (Port. & Eng.). 1970. 25.00x (ISBN 0-8047-0480-5). Stanford U Pr.
Portuguese-English, English-Portuguese Basic Dictionary. Michaelis. (Eng. & Port.). Date not set. text ed. 35.00 (ISBN 0-686-46534-2). Heinman.
Portuguese-English, English-Portuguese Dictionary. J. A. Ferreira. (Port. & Eng.). 30.00 (ISBN 0-685-12039-2). Heinman.
Portuguese-English, English-Portuguese Dictionary, 2 vols. M. J. Martins. (Port. & Eng.). Set. 45.00 (ISBN 0-685-58543-3). Heinman.
Portuguese-English, English-Portuguese Illustrated Dictionary: The New Michaelis, 2 vols. Ed. by F. Pietzschke. (Port. & Eng.). Set. 125.00 (ISBN 0-685-58551-4). Portuguese-english, 28th Ed (ISBN 3-7653-0050-0). English-portuguese, 30th Ed (ISBN 3-7653-0051-9). Heinman.
Portuguese-English, English-Portuguese Technical Dictionary, 2 vols. Araujo A. De Pina. (Port. & Eng.). Set. 115.00 (ISBN 0-685-79115-7). Heinman.
Portuguese-English-Portuguese. (Berlitz Pocket Dictionaries Ser.). (Port. & Eng.). 4.95 (ISBN 0-02-964440-2). Macmillan.
Portuguese-Hungarian Concise Dictionary. R. Kiraly. 728p. (Port. & Hungarian.). 1978. 39.95 (ISBN 963-05-1382-X, M-9326). French & Eur.
Portuguese Pocket Dictionary. Michaelis. (Port.). Date not set. pap. text ed. 15.00 (ISBN 0-686-46535-0). Heinman.
Position of the Charleston Dialect see Vocabulary of Marble Playing.
Posobie Po Leksicheskoi Sochetaemosti Slov Russkogo Iazyka. T. I. Anisimova. 303p. (Rus.). 1975. 3.25 (Pub. by Vysheishaia Shkola). Four Continent.
Potter's Dictionary of Materials & Techniques. Frank Hamer. (Illus.). 400p. 1975. 30.00 (ISBN 0-8230-4210-3). Watson-Guptill.
Pottery & Porcelain: A Glossary of Terms. Bernard H. Charles. (Illus.). 320p. 1983. pap. 8.95 (ISBN 0-88254-278-8). Hippocrene Bks.
Pracovni Heslar Ceskeho Pravnehistorickeho Terminologickeho Slovniku. Bohuslav Roucka. LC 78-366665. ii, 773p. (Czech., Prague). 1975. write for info. Ustav Statu a Prava Ceskoslovenske Akademie Ved.
Practical Dictionary for Press & Advertising. 256p. (Ger. , Eng. & Fr.). 1972. pap. 15.00x (ISBN 0-8002-1334-3). Intl Pubns Serv.
Practical Dictionary of Chinese Idioms, English Idioms, English Synonyms. S. Wei. (Illus., Chinese & Eng.). 16.50. Iaconi.
Practical Dictionary of Crosswords. Mary Menacho. pap. cancelled (ISBN 0-912314-07-9). Academy Pr-Santa.

Practical Dictionary of Shipping Business: Japanese-English; English-Japanese. 236p. (Japanese & Eng.). 1978. 35.00 (ISBN 0-686-92099-6, M-9340). French & Eur.
Practical Dictionary of the Coast Tsimshian Language. John A. Dunn. LC 79-321726. x, 155p. (Eng. & Tsimshian.). 1978. write for info. Natl Mus Can.
Practical English-Cantonese Dictionary. Chiang Ker-Chiu. (Eng. & Cantonese.). 25.00x (ISBN 0-686-00881-2). Colton Bk.
Practical English-Chinese Dictionary. 1674p. (Eng. & Chinese.). 1979. leatherette 19.95 (ISBN 0-686-97443-3, M-9291). French & Eur.
Practical English-Chinese Pronouncing Dictionary. Janet Chen. (Chinese & Eng.). 22.50. Iaconi.
Practical English-Chinese Pronouncing Dictionary. Janey Chen. LC 78-77122. (Eng. & Chinese.). 1970. 22.50 (ISBN 0-8048-0663-2). C E Tuttle.
Practical English-Chinese Pronouncing Dictionary. Janey Chen & Ena Simms. 601p. (Chinese & Eng., Chinese characters, romanized Mandarin & Cantonese). 1980. 29.00. C E Tuttle.
Practical English-German, German-English Dictionary. Stephen Jones. (Hippocrene's Practical Language Dictionary Ser.). 400p. (Orig., Eng. & Ger.). 1983. pap. 6.95 (ISBN 0-88254-813-1). Hippocrene Bks.
Practical English-Polish Dictionary. J. Stanislawski et al. 913p. (Eng. & Pol.). 1976. leatherette 19.95 (ISBN 0-686-92102-X, M-9328). French & Eur.
Practical English-Polish Dictionary. Jan Stanislawski. LC 77-578742. 913p. (Pol.). 1981. 17.50x (ISBN 83-214-0245-3). Intl Pubns Serv.
Practical English-Thai Dictionary. S. Robertson. (Thai & Eng.). 6.25. Iaconi.
Practical English-Vietnamese Idioms for Teachers & Students. Ed. by Nguyen-Trung Hieu. (Eng. & Vietnamese.). 1981. 6.50 (ISBN 0-533-04431-6). Vantage.
Practical French-English, English-French Dictionary. Rosalind Williams. (Hippocrene Practical Language Dictionaries Ser.). 400p. (Orig., Eng. & Fr.). 1983. pap. 6.95 (ISBN 0-88254-815-8). Hippocrene Bks.
Practical Hindi-English Dictionary. Mahendra Chaturvedi & Nath T. Bhola. 700p. (Hindi & Eng.). 1974. 14.00x (ISBN 0-88386-380-4). South Asia Bks.
Practical Italian-English, English-Italian Dictionary. Peter Ross. (Hippocrene Practical Language Dictionaries Ser.). 400p. (Orig., Eng. & Ital.). 1983. pap. 6.95 (ISBN 0-88254-816-6). Hippocrene Bks.
Practical Polish-English Dictionary. J. Stanislawski. 1030p. (Pol. & Eng.). 1978. Leatherette 19.95 (ISBN 0-686-92364-2, M-9134). French & Eur.
Practical Polish-English Dictionary. Jan Stanislawski. LC 77-578742. 1036p. (Pol.). 1981. 17.50x (ISBN 83-214-0124-4). Intl Pubns Serv.
Practical Polish-English Dictionary: Polish-English; English-Polish. Iwo Pogonowski. LC 78-64764. (Pol. & Eng.). 1981. pap. 6.95 (ISBN 0-88254-494-2). Hippocrene Bks.
Practical Sanskrit Dictionary: With Transliteration Accentuation & Etymological Analysis Throughout. Arthur A. MacDonnell. (Sanskrit.). 1924. 37.50x (ISBN 0-19-864303-9). Oxford U Pr.
Practical Sanskrit-English Dictionary. rev. ed. V. S. Apte. (Sanskrit & Eng.). 1978. Repr. 28.00 (ISBN 0-89684-294-0). Orient Bk Dist.
Practical Sanskrit-English Dictionary. new ed. Vaman S. Apte. (Sanskrit & Eng.). 1975. 40.00x (ISBN 0-8426-0996-2). Verry.
Practical Sanskrit-English Dictionary. Rev. & enl. ed. Ed. by P. K. Gode et al. LC 78-911335. (Sanskrit & Eng.). write for info. Prasarnmitr.
Practical Spanish Dictionary & Phrasebook. new ed. Marguerite D. Bomse. (Span.). 1978. pap. text ed. 7.50 (ISBN 0-08-023020-2). Pergamon.
Practical Spanish-English, English-Spanish Dictionary. Arthur Butterfield. (Hippocrene Practical Language Dictionaries Ser.). 400p. (Orig., Eng. & Span.). 1983. pap. 6.95 (ISBN 0-88254-814-X). Hippocrene Bks.
Practical Spoken Spanish. 7th ed. F. M. Kerchuville. (Span.). 3.45. Camino Real.
Pradeeps Standard Oxford Dictionary: English to English, Panjabi & Hindi, with Pronunciations & Idioms. 1983. 15.00x (ISBN 0-8364-0991-4, Pub. by Pradeep Co). South Asia Bks.
Praktische Lexikon der Naturheilkunde. Ernst Meyer-Camberg. (Ger.). 1977. pap. 15.95 (ISBN 3-570-06579-0, M-7594, Pub. by Mosaik/VVA). French & Eur.
Pratique d'un Dictionnaire. B. Planque & N. Chabaud. (Fr.). 1977. 23.75 (Dist. by Continental Bk Co). Larousse.
Precis De Terminologie Medicale. 2nd ed. J. Chevallier. 208p. (Fr.). 1977. 19.95 (ISBN 0-686-56948-2, M-6070). French & Eur.
Precis Thesaurus: Physics. 1981. 55.00x (ISBN 0-686-99804-9, Pub. by Brit Lib England). State Mutual Bk.
Preliminary Glossary of New Mexican Spanish. F. M. Kercheville. LC 34-27896. 102p. (Span.). 1982. lib. bdg. 29.95x (ISBN 0-89370-727-9). Borgo Pr.
Preliminary Survey of the Vocabulary of White Alabamians. Virginia O. Foscue. (Publications of the American Dialect Society Ser., No. 56). 48p. 1971. pap. 2.80 (ISBN 0-8173-0656-0, Am Dialect Soc). U of Ala Pr.
Premier Dictionnaire Nathan. Marchand. (Fr.). 8.95 (Dist. by Continental Bk Co). Lib. Fernand Nathan.
Prentice-Hall Dictionary of Business, Finance & Law. Michael D. Rice. LC 83-3022. 362p. 1983. 39.95 (ISBN 0-13-696583-0). P-H.
Prentice-Hall Students Edition of the Concise Webster's New World Dictionary of the American Language. World Pub. Co. 1971. 7.80 (ISBN 0-13-944561-7). P-H.
Press, Radio & Television. Denise Escarpit. LC 76-472541. 349p. (Eng., Ger., Fr., & Span.). 1975. 28.00 F (ISBN 2-7213-0050-4). Elp.
Primary Aeronautical Language Manual. Deborah J. Balter. 1980. pap. 30.95 (ISBN 0-941456-00-5). Aviation.
Primary Multi-Level Speller & First Dictionary. Morton Botel. (gr. k-2). 1959. pap. 3.10 (ISBN 0-931992-14-1). Penns Valley.
Primer of Business Terms & Phrases Related to Libraries. Ed. by Sherman Hayes. 81p. 1978. 1.50. Library Admin.
Primo Dizionario. Richard Scarry. (Ital.). 1976. 9.00x (ISBN 0-686-16891-7). Intl Learn Syst.
Prinsessans ABC Bok. Fredrik C. Boije af Gennas. LC 78-392178. (Illus.). 82p. (Swedish.). 1977. write for info. Rediviva.
Printer's Terms Dictionary. R. Hostettler. (Illus., Eng., Fr., Ger., Ital. & Dutch.). 1983. price not set (ISBN 0-685-12041-4). Heinman.
Printers' Vocabulary. Charles T. Jacobi. LC 68-30613. 1975. Repr. of 1888 ed. 30.00x (ISBN 0-8103-3309-0). Gale.
Prirucni Slovnik Jazyka Ceskeho, 8 vols. Vydava Treti Trida Ceske Akademie Ved a Umeni. (Czech.). 215.00 set (EG). Vol. 1 A-J. Vol. 2, K-M. Vol. 3, N-O. Vol. 4, Pt. 1, P-Prusvitne. Vol. 4 Pt. 2, Prusvitneti-R. Vol. 5, S-S. Vol. 6, T-Vuzek. Vol. 7, Vy-Zap. Statni.
Prirucni Slovnik Jazyka Ceskeho: Zarabcty-Zzonka, Vol. 8. (Czech.). 215.00 set (EG). Statni.
Prirucni Slovnik Naucny, 4 vols. (Czech.). 1963-1967. 195.00 (ISBN 0-8227-3051-9). Pergamon.
Prisma Voetbalwoordenboek. Rob Siekmann. LC 79-398681. 159p. (Dutch.). 1978. write for info. (ISBN 9-027-40962-5). Spectrum NL.
Problems Confronting the Investigator of Gullah see Oil Refinery Terms in Oklahoma.
Procedural Terminology for Internists. American Society of Internal Medicine. 3.00 (312). Am Soc Intern Med.
Procedural Terminology for Psychiatrists. 16p. 1981. pap. 3.00x (ISBN 0-89042-128-5, 42-128-5). Am Psychiatric.
Process Instrumentation Reliability Terminology: 32.1-1976. Scientific Apparatus Makers Association. 2.00; bulk prices avail. Sci Apparatus.
Process Measurement & Control Terminology: 20.1-1973. Scientific Apparatus Makers Association. 2.00; bulk prices avail. Sci Apparatus.
Programmed College Vocabulary Three Thousand Six Hundred. 2nd ed. George W. Feinstein. 1979. pap. text ed. 12.95 (ISBN 0-13-729806-4). P-H.
Programmed Vocabulary. 3rd ed. James I. Brown. (The CPD Approach). 1980. pap. text ed. 12.95 (ISBN 0-13-729707-6). P-H.
Progressive English Dictionary. 2nd ed. Ed. by A. S. Hornby & E. C. Parnwell. 1972. pap. 2.95x (ISBN 0-19-431120-1). Oxford U Pr.
Projet de Lexique Minier Russe-Francais. Ed. by N. N. Ersov & A. N. Komarov. 183p. (Fr. & Rus.). 1972. pap. 22.50 (ISBN 0-686-56769-2, M-6468). French & Eur.
Promptorium Parvulorum Sive Clericorum, Dictionarius Anglolatinus Princeps, 3 Pts. Galfridus Anglicus. Repr. of 1865 ed. 37.00 ea. Johnson Repr.
Promptorium Parvulorum Sive Clericorum, Lexicon Anglo-Latinum Princeps, 3 Vols. Anglicus Galfridus. LC 70-168091. (Camden Society, London. Publications, First Ser.: Nos. 25, 54, 89). (Lat.). Repr. of 1865 ed. Set. 84.00 (ISBN 0-404-50209-1); 28.00 ea. AMS Pr.
Pronouncing & Defining Dictionary of Music. William S. Mathews & Emil Liebling. LC 78-173059. Repr. of 1896 ed. 20.50 (ISBN 0-404-07210-0). AMS Pr.
Pronouncing & Etymological Dictionary of the Gaelic Language. Malcolm Maclennan. LC 80-494565. xv, 613p. (Eng. & Gaelic.). 1979. E12.00 (ISBN 0-08-025713-5); write for info. (ISBN 0-08-025712-7). Aberdeen U Pr.
Pronouncing Dictionary of American English. 2nd ed. John S. Kenyon & Thomas A. Knott. 1953. 7.95 (ISBN 0-87779-047-7). Merriam-Webster Inc.
Pronouncing Dictionary of American English: No. 47. 7.95 (ISBN 0-87779-047-7). Ency Brit Ed.
Pronouncing Dictionary of English-Place Names. Klaus Forster. 308p. 1981. 30.00 (ISBN 0-7100-0756-6). Routledge & Kegan.
Pronouncing Dictionary of Musical Terms, Giving the Meaning Derivation & Pronunciation of Italian, German, French & Other Words. Hugh A. Clarke. 1977. Repr. 15.00 (ISBN 0-403-07492-4). Scholarly.
Pronouncing Musical Dictionary. Dudley Buck. 1976. lib. bdg. 19.00 (ISBN 0-403-03787-5). Scholarly.
Pronunciation of American English. Arthur J. Bronstein. (Illus.). 1960. 18.95 (ISBN 0-13-730887-6). P-H.
Prospects for Metropolitan Water Management. Compiled by American Society of Civil Engineers. 256p. 1971. pap. text ed. 5.25 (ISBN 0-87262-026-3). Am Soc Civil Eng.
Proteins in Human Nutrition. Ed. by J. W. Porter & B. A. Rolls. 1973. 89.00 (ISBN 0-12-562950-8). Acad Pr.
Protestant Dictionary: Containing Articles on the History, Doctrines, & Practices of the Christian Church. Ed. by Charles Wright & Charles Neil. LC 73-155436. 1971. Repr. of 1933 ed. 56.00x (ISBN 0-8103-3388-0). Gale.
Proust Dictionary. Maxine A. Vogely. LC 80-53035. 765p. 1981. 50.00x (ISBN 0-87875-205-6). Whitston Pub.
Proverbes Francais: In French with Equivalents in English, German, Dutch, Italian, Spanish, Latin. G. Ilg. (Glossarium Interpretum: No. 4). (Fr., Eng., Ger., Dutch, Ital., Span. & Lat., Polyglot). 1960. 17.00 (ISBN 0-444-40312-4). Elsevier.
Prusskii Iazyk Slovar: E-H. V. N. Toporov. 352p. (Ger. & Rus.). 1978. 8.50 (Pub. by Nauka). Four Continent.
Prusskii Iazyk Slovar: I-L. V. N. Toprov. 384p. (Ger. & Rus.). 1979. 7.95 (Pub. by Nauka). Four Continent.
Pseudonyms & Nicknames Dictionary. rev. 2nd ed. Ed. by Jennifer Mossman. LC 80-13274. 980p. 1982. 160.00x (ISBN 0-8103-0547-X). Gale.
Pskovskii Oblastnoi Slovar S Istoricheskimi Dannymi, Vol. 2. 244p. (Rus.). 1973. 4.50 (Pub. by LGU). Four Continent.
Pskovskii Oblastnoi Slovar S Istoricheskimi Dannymi, Vol. 3. 180p. (Rus.). 1976. 3.90 (Pub. by LGU). Four Continent.
Pskovskii Oblastnoi Slovar S Istorischeskmi Dannymi, Vol. 4. 184p. (Rus.). 1979. 3.95 (Pub. by LGU). Four Continent.
Psychiatric Dictionary. 5th ed. Ed. by Robert J. Campbell. 1981. 35.00x (ISBN 0-19-502817-1). Oxford U Pr.
Psychiatric Glossary. 5th ed. Ed. by American Psychiatric Assn. 1980. text ed. 10.95 (ISBN 0-316-03656-0). Little.
Psychiatric Glossary. 5th ed. American Psychiatric Association. LC 79-55869. 152p. 1980. pap. 6.50x (ISBN 0-89042-005-X, 42-005-X). Am Psychiatric.
Psychologie: Ein Sachlexikon fuer die Schule. Karl H. Ahlheim. (Illus.). 408p. (Ger.). DM.19.80 (ISBN 3-411-01795-3). Biblio Inst.
Psychologisches Woerterbuch. 9th ed. F. Dorsch. 784p. (Ger.). 1976. 75.00 (ISBN 3-456-80320-6, M-7595, Pub. by H. Huber). French & Eur.
Psychologisches Woerterbuch. 9th ed. F. Dorsch. 784p. (Ger.). 1976. 75.00 (ISBN 3-456-80320-6). Huber.
Psychologisches Woerterbuch. Friedrich Dorsch. LC 76-472620. (Illus.). 774p. (Ger.). 1976. write for info. (ISBN 3-456-80320-6). H Huber.
Psychology: ADictionary of the Mind, Brain & Behavior. Christopher R. Evans. LC 79-305603. (Illus.). 416p. (Eng.). 1978. E2.50 (ISBN 0-09-918610-1). Arrow Bks.
Public School Word-Book. Johns Farmer. 1900. 30.00 (ISBN 0-8274-3224-0). R West.
Publishers Practical Dictionary. 2nd ed. Imra Mora. 389p. 1977. 64.50 (ISBN 3-7940-4112-7, Pub. by K G Saur). Shoe String.
Pugh's Dictionary of Acronyms & Abbreviations. Compiled by Eric Pugh. LC 81-14029. 348p. 1982. 87.50x (ISBN 0-89774-012-2). Oryx Pr.
Putman's Contemporary Spanish Dictionary. (Span.). 1.75. Camino Real.
Putnam's Contemporary German Dictionary. (Ger. & Eng.). 1980. pap. 2.25 (ISBN 0-425-04362-2). Berkley Pub.
Putnam's Contemporary Italian Dictionary. (Ital. & Eng.). pap. 2.25 (ISBN 0-425-04363-0). Berkley Pub.

Putnam's Contemporary Spanish Dictionary. (Span. & Eng.). 1980. pap. 2.50 (ISBN 0-425-04387-8). Berkley Pub.

Pyramid Primary Dictionary, 2 vols. (Span. & Eng.). Vol. 1: Spanish. write for info. (608-21); Vol. 2: English. write for info. (608-22). Pan Amer Pub.

Quadrilingual Business Dictionary. (Eng. , Fr. , Ger. & Span.). 1981. 60.00x (ISBN 0-686-75659-2, Pub. by European Schoolbks England). State Mutual Bk.

Q

Quadrilingual Economics Dictionary. Ed. by Frits J. De Jong et al. 1981. lib. bdg. 48.00 (ISBN 90-247-2243-8, Pub. by Martinus Nijhoff Netherlands). Kluwer Academic.

Quantities, Formulae, Definitions. Siemens. 1979. 4.95 (ISBN 0-471-26120-3, Wiley Heyden). Wiley.

Que Paso? Martin P. Kantrowitz. (Eng. & Span.). 3.00. Camino Real.

Quebecois Dictionary. Leandre Bergeron. 206p. 1983. 28.00x (ISBN 0-88862-548-0); pap. 17.95x (ISBN 0-88862-547-2). Enslow Pubs.

Qui a dit Quoi? Dictionanaire des Mots & des Phrases qui Ont Une Historire. Bernadette De Castelbajac. LC 80-453759. 277p. (Fr.). 1978. 36.00 F (ISBN 2-235-00575-6). Tallandier.

Quick Legal Terminology. Randolph Z. Volkell. LC 79-13647. (Self-Teaching Guides Ser.). 1979. pap. text ed. 7.50 (ISBN 0-471-03786-9, Pub. by Wiley Pr). Wiley.

Quick Medical Terminology. Genevieve L. Smith & Phyllis E. Davis. LC 72-4193. (Wiley Self-Teaching Guides Ser). 248p. 1972. 8.95x (ISBN 0-471-80198-4, Pub. by Wiley Pr); cassettes 8.95 (ISBN 0-471-80201-8). Wiley.

Quileute Dictionary, 10 vols. J. Powell. LC 79-307128. xvii, 519p. (Eng. & Quileute.). 1976. write for info. Univ Idaho.

Quintessential Dictionary. I. Moyer Hunsberger. 512p. 1978. 15.00 (ISBN 0-89104-247-4). A & W Pubs.

Quotoons: A Speakers Dictionary. O. A. Battista. 472p. 1981. (Perigee); 5.95 (ISBN 0-399-50514-8). Putnam Pub Group.

Qutr Al-Muhit, 2 vols. Butros Al-Bustani. 2452p. (Arabic.). 45.00 (097-X). Intl Bk Ctr.

R

Race & Ethnic Relations in Latin America & the Caribbean: An Historical Dictionary & Bibliography. Robert M. Levine. LC 80-15179. 260p. 1980. 14.50 (ISBN 0-8108-1324-6). Scarecrow.

Radio & Television Dictionary. Abd-El-Wahed. 320p. (Eng., Fr., Ger., Arabic.). 1980. 45.00 (ISBN 0-686-92395-2, M-9762). French & Eur.

Radiochemisches Lexikon der Elemente und Ihrer Isotope. M. Haissinsky. (Ger.). 1968. pap. 15.95 (ISBN 3-427-41651-8, M-7596, Pub. by Duemmler). French & Eur.

Railroad Car Builders Pictorial Dictionary. Matthias N. Forney. (Illus.). 12.00 (ISBN 0-8446-5187-7). Peter Smith.

Rainbow Dictionary for Young Reader. Ed. by Wendell W. Wright. (Illus.). 7.95 (ISBN 0-529-05399-3). Collins Pubs.

Rakennusalan Sanastot ja Sanastohankkeet Suomessa. Ritva Swanljung. LC 77-483474. (Finnish.). 1975. write for info. (ISBN 9-5138-0250-7). Valtion.

Ramakrishna-Vedanta Wordbook: A Brief Dictionary of Hinduism. Ed. by Brahmacharini Usha. (Orig.). pap. 3.25 (ISBN 0-87481-017-5). Vedanta Pr.

Random House Basic Dictionary. (Eng. & Span.). write for info. (608-100). Pan Amer Pub.

Random House Basic Dictionary. (Eng. & Ital.). write for info. (608-103). Pan Amer Pub.

Random House Basic Dictionary French. Ed. by Francesca L. Langbaum. (Fr. & Eng.). 1981. pap. 1.50 (ISBN 0-345-29617-6). Ballantine.

Random House Basic Dictionary German. Ed. by Jenni H. Moulton. (Ger. & Eng.). 1981. pap. 1.50 (ISBN 0-345-29619-2). Ballantine.

Random House Basic Dictionary Italian. Ed. by Robert A. Hall. (Ital. & Eng.). 1981. pap. 1.50 (ISBN 0-345-29618-4). Ballantine.

Random House Basic Dictionary Spanish. Ed. by Donald P. Sola. (Span. & Eng.). 1981. pap. 1.50 (ISBN 0-345-29620-6). Ballantine.

Random House Basic Dictionary-Synonyms & Antonyms. Ed. by Lawrence Urdung. 1981. pap. 1.50 (ISBN 0-345-29712-1). Ballantine.

Random House Basic Speller-Divider. Ed. by Jess Stein. 1981. pap. 1.50 (ISBN 0-345-29255-3). Ballantine.

Random House College Dictionary. rev. ed. Date not set. thumb-indexed ed. incl. Pocket Thesaurus 14.95 (ISBN 0-394-52760-7); thumb-indexed ed. incl. Bad Speller's Dictionary 14.95 (ISBN 0-394-52762-3). Random.

Random House College Dictionary. thumb-indexed ed. incl. pocket thesaurus 14.95 (ISBN 0-394-43600-8); deluxe ed. 14.95 thumb-indexed ed. incl. Bad Speller's Dictionary (ISBN 0-394-52762-3). Random.

Random House Dictionary. Ed. by Jess Stein. (Orig.). 1981. pap. 2.25 (ISBN 0-345-29096-8). Ballantine.

Random House Dictionary: Concise Edition. Random House, Inc. 1980. 4.95 (ISBN 0-394-51200-6). Random.

Random House Dictionary of the English Language. 1966. 49.95 (ISBN 0-394-47176-8). Random.

Ranskalais-Suomalainen-Sanakirja. Pentti Pesonen. LC 79-355820. 746p. (Fr. & Finnish.). 1978. write for info. Otava.

Ranskalais-Suomalainen Tekniikan ja Kaupan Sanakirja. Jyrki K. Talvitie. LC 79-338502. 296p. (Fr. & Finnish.). 1978. write for info. (ISBN 9-5190-3536-2). Tietoteos.

Rationale & Design of a Program to Teach Vocabulary to Fourth-Grade Students. Isabel L. Beck et al. 49p. 1980. 1.00. Learn Res Dev.

Ravitsemusalan Sanastro. LC 78-345971. 122p. (Finnish.). 1977. Fmk.15.00 (ISBN 9-511-04160-6). Otava.

Razgovornik Dlia Avtoturistov: Anglo-Russkii. 280p. (Rus. & Eng.). 1979. 4.25 (Pub. by Russkii Iazyk). Four Continent.

Razoruzhenie: Spravochnik. 160p. (Rus.). 1980. 00.85 (Pub. by Politizdat). Four Continent.

Read & Write Chinese: A Simplified Guide to the Chinese Characters. rev. ed. Rita Mei-Wah Choy. 336p. (Chinese.). 1982. pap. text ed. 9.95 (ISBN 0-941340-09-0). China West.

Reader's Hebrew-English Lexicon of the Old Testament: (Genesis-Deuteronomy, Vol. 1. Ed. by Terry Armstrong et al. (Hebrew & Eng.). 1978. 9.95 (ISBN 0-310-37020-5). Zondervan.

Reading & Writing Chinese: A Guide to the Chinese Writing System. William McNaughton. LC 77-77699. (Chinese.). 1979. 17.50 (ISBN 0-8048-1188-1). C E Tuttle.

Reading the Russian Language: A Guide for Librarians & Other Professionals. Rosalind Kent. (Books in Library & Information Science Ser., Vol. 9). (Rus.). 1974. 30.75 (ISBN 0-8247-6236-3). Dekker.

Reading Vocabulary, 5 bks. Sullivan Assoc. pap. text ed. 2.75 ea. (ISBN 0-8449-4105-0); tchr's guide for bks. 1-4 avail. Learning Line.

Real Estate Appraisal Terminology. American Institute of Real Estate Appraisers. Ed. by Byrl N. Boyce. 320p. 12.50 (21-1018). Natl Assoc Realtors.

Real Estate Appraisal Terminology. 2nd ed. Ed. by Byrl N. Boyce. 384p. 1981. 18.00 (ISBN 0-88410-597-0). Ballinger Pub.

Real Estate Dictionary. rev. ed. Talamo. 192p. 1981. pap. 3.95 (ISBN 0-89803-091-9). Caroline Hse.

Real Estate Dictionary. John Talamo. 1982. pap. 3.95 (ISBN 0-8092-5696-7). Contemp Bks.

Real Estate Dictionary, No. 510. rev. ed. 192p. 1980. pap. 5.00 (ISBN 0-695-81526-1). Finan Pub.

Real Estate Dictionary & Reference Guide. Samuel V. Abraham. Ed. by S. Michele McFadden & Roberta Wilson-Fulkerson. LC 79-9761. 1983. pap. text ed. 6.95x (ISBN 0-89262-059-5). Career Pub.

Real Estate Finance & Syndication Glossary. 3rd., rev. ed. Samuel K. Freshman. LC 79-2801. 109p. 1979. 5.95 (ISBN 0-9600708-3-4). Law & Cap Dynamics.

Real Estate Securities & Title Insurance Terminology. Intro. By John R. Johnsich. (Orig.). 1980. pap. 3.95 (ISBN 0-914256-12-2). Real Estate Pub.

Real Skiers' Dictionary. Morten Lund. Date not set. price not set. S&S.

Recherches sur la Prefixation en Francais Contemporain, 3 vols. Jean Peytard. LC 77-456063. (Illus.). 790p. (Fr.). 1975. write for info. F (ISBN 2-252-01690-6). Klincksieck.

Rechtschreibung & Wortkunde: Ein Woerterbuch fur die Schule. Jakob Ebner. 328p. (Ger.). DM.10.80 (ISBN 3-411-01911-5). Biblio Inst.

Rechtskundig Woerdenboek: Dictionnaire Juridique. J. Brassine. 248p. (Flemmish & Fr.). 1935. 267.00 F. Bruylant.

Rechtssprache Englisch-Deutsch. R. Renner & J. Tooth. 526p. (Ger.). 1971. 35.00 (ISBN 3-19-006280-3, M-7597, Pub. by M. Hueber). French & Eur.

Rechtssprache Englisch-Deutsch. R. Renner & J. Tooth. 526p. (Ger.). 1971. 35.00 (ISBN 3-19-006280-3). Hueber.

Rechtsworterbuch Fur Die Gewerbliche Wirtschaft. Ursula Becker. 600p. (Ger., Eng. & Fr., Dictionary of Industrial Economics). 1978. 145.00 (ISBN 3-7819-2015-1, M-7599, Pub. by Fritz Knapp Verlag). French & Eur.

Reclams Filmfuhrer. Dieter Krusche & Jurgen Labenskt. LC 77-578502. 760p. (Ger.). 1977. DM.36.80 (ISBN 3-15-010205-7). Reclam.

Recommendations for Labeling Plastics Microwave Cookware & Glossary. Society of the Plastics Industry. first copy free (1200); add. copies 0.20. Soc Plastic Ind.

Recueil de Terminologie Multilinque du Soudage et des Techniques Connexes, 18p. (Fr. & Eng., Multilinqual Collection of Welding Terminology and Terminology of Related Techniques). pap. 24.95 (ISBN 0-686-56760-9, M-6480). French & Eur.

Recueil Terminologique Multilingue du Soudage et des Techniques Connexes, Soudage Electrique a l'Arc, Vol. 2. 144p. (Fr. & Eng., A Collection of Multilingual Welding Terminology & Related Technique: Electrical Arc Welding). pap. 12.50 (ISBN 0-686-56765-X, M-6475). French & Eur.

Recueil Terminologique Multilingue de Soudage et des Techniques Connexes: Soudage Electrique a l'Arc, Vol. 3. 52p. (Fr. & Eng., A Collection of Multilingual Welding Terminology and Related Techniques: Electrical Arc Welding). pap. 12.50 (ISBN 0-686-56764-1, M-6476). French & Eur.

Recueil Terminologique Multilinque du Soudage et des Techniques Connexes. 52p. (Fr. , Pol. , Rus. , Czech. , Slovene & Turkish.). pap. 12.50 (ISBN 0-686-56743-9, M-6474). French & Eur.

Recueil Terminologique Multilinque du Soudage et des Techniques Connexes. Soudage Electrique Par Resistance, Vol. 4. 254p. (Fr. & Eng., A Collection of Multilingual Welding Terms & Related Techniques: Electrical Welding by Resistance). pap. 17.50 (ISBN 0-686-56763-3, M-6477). French & Eur.

Recueil Terminologique Multilinque du Soudage et des Techniques Connexes: Coupage Thermique, Vol. 5. (Fr. & Eng., A Collection of Multilingual Welding Terms & Related Techniques: Thermal Cutting). pap. 17.50 (ISBN 0-686-56762-5, M-6478). French & Eur.

Recueil Terminologique Multilinque de Soudage et des Techniques Connexes. Projection a Chaud, Vol. 6. (Fr. & Eng., A Collection of Multilingual Welding Terms & Related Techniques: Heat Projection). pap. 19.95 (ISBN 0-686-56761-7, M-6479). French & Eur.

Redhouse Cagdas Turkce-Ingilizce. 430p. (Turkish & Eng.). 1983. 30.00 (440). Redhouse Pr.

Redhouse Cagdas Turkee-Ingilizee Sozlugii. (Turkish & Eng.). 30.00. Redhouse Pr.

Redhouse English-Turkish Dictionary. (Eng. & Turkish.). 1974. 33.00x (ISBN 0-686-16859-3). Intl Learn Syst.

Redhouse Ingilizce-Turkce Sozlugu. rev. 9th ed. viii, 1152p. (Eng. & Turkish.). 1983. 30.00 (396). Redhouse Pr.

Redhouse Ingilizce-Turkce, Turkce-Ingilizce elsozlugu. 503p. (Eng. & Turkish.). 1982. 8.00 (401). Redhouse Pr.

Redhouse Ingilizee-Turkee-Ingilizee Elsozlugu. (Eng. & Turkish.). 8.00. Redhouse Pr.

Redhouse Ingilizee-Turkee Sozlugu. (Eng. & Turkish.). 30.00. Redhouse Pr.

Redhouse Turkce-Ingilizce sozlugu. 5th ed. xxiii, 1292p. (Turkish & Eng.). 1981. 35.00 (369). Redhouse Pr.

Redhouse Turkish-English Dictionary. (Turkish & Eng.). 1968. 41.00x (ISBN 0-686-16860-7). Intl Learn Syst.

Redhouse Yeni Turkee-Ingilizee Sozlugu. (Turkish & Eng.). 35.00. Redhouse Pr.

Refrigeration & Conditioning Dictionary. Abd-El-Wahed. 395p. (Eng., Fr., Ger. & Arabic.). 1979. 45.00 (ISBN 0-686-97399-2, M-9756). French & Eur.

Refrigeration Terms & Definitions. American Society of Heating, Refrigeration & Air Conditioning Engineers. (Illus.). 1974. 12.00 (ST1275); members 6.00. Am Heat Ref & Air Eng.

Regeln & Sprache des Sports 1. Rainer Wehlen. 377p. (Ger.). DM.12.80 (ISBN 3-411-01361-3). Biblio Inst.

Regeln & Sprache des Sports 2. Rainer Wehlen. 412p. (Ger.). DM.12.80 (ISBN 3-411-01362-1). Biblio Inst.

Regional Dictionary of Chicano Slang. Librado Vasquez & Maria E. Vasquez. (Span.). 8.95. Camino Real.

Regional Dictionary of Chicano Slang. Librado K. Vasquez & Maria E. Vasquez. 111p. 1975. 13.50 (ISBN 0-8363-0083-1). Jenkins.

Regional Vocabulary of Texas. E. Bagby Atwood. LC 62-9784. (Illus.). 286p. 1969. pap. 6.95 (ISBN 0-292-77008-1). U of Tex Pr.

Regulating Systems Definitions & Standardizations of Terms. 1965. 6.00 (403-9); members 4.00. TAPPI.

Reisewoerrterbuch: German-English, English-German. 239p. (Ger. & Eng.). plastic cover 5.90. M Rosenberg.

Reisewoerterbuch Deutsch-Englisch. 239p. (Ger. & Eng.). 5.90. M Rosenberg.

Relais Lexikon. Hans Sauer. LC 76-453351. 242p. (Ger.). 1975. write for info. Vertrieb.

Remarks on the Use & Abuse of Some Political Terms. George C. Lewis. LC 72-113816. 370p. 1970. 16.00x (ISBN 0-8262-0089-3). U of Mo Pr.

Report on the Expedition. Therkel Mathiassen. LC 76-21664. (Thule Expedition. 5th. 1921-1924: Vol. 1, No. 1). Repr. of 1945 ed. 32.50 (ISBN 0-404-58301-6). AMS Pr.

Resource Conservation Glossary. 3rd ed. Pref. by H. Wayne Pritchard. LC 82-5830. 193p. 1982. pap. 7.00 (ISBN 0-935734-09-0). Soil Conservation.

Ressorts: Francais-Allemand-Anglais-Espagnol, Vol. 2. S.N.F.R. 110p. (Fr., Ger., Eng. & Span.). 1978. 100.00 F. Maison Dictionnaire.

Reuters Glossary of International Economic & Financial Terms. Reuters Ltd. 224p. 1983. 13.95 (ISBN 0-698-11205-9, Coward). Putnam Pub Group.

Reverse Acronyms, Initialisms, & Abbreviations Dictionary. 8th ed. Ed. by Ellen Crowley. (Acronyms, Initialisms, & Abbreviations Dictionary Ser.: Vol. 3). 1600p. 1982. 130.00x (ISBN 0-8103-0507-0). Gale.

Reverse Dictionary of Czech. Jiri Marvan. LC 73-11586. (Czech. & Eng.). Date not set. 22.50x (ISBN 0-271-01164-5). Pa St U Pr.

Reverse Dictionary of the Spanish Language. Fred A. Stahl & Gary E. Scavnicky. LC 68-24625. (Span.). 1973. 18.50 (ISBN 0-252-72540-9). U of Ill Pr.

Reverse Dictionary of Urdu. Donald Becker. (Urdu.). 1980. 38.00x (ISBN 0-8364-0656-7, Pub. by Manohaar India). South Asia Bks.

Reverse Lexicon of Greek Proper Names. F. Dornseiff & Bernard Hansen. (Gr.). 1978. Repr. 30.00 (ISBN 0-89005-251-4). Ares.

Reviewing German Grammar & Building Vocabulary. Roselinde Konrad. LC 80-6238. 415p. (Ger.). 1981. pap. text ed. 19.75 (ISBN 0-8191-1605-X). U Pr of Amer.

Revised-Velasquez Spanish English Dictionary. (Span. & Eng.). 12.95. Camino Real.

Rhade-English Dictionary with English-Rhade Finder List. James A. Tharp. LC 81-157706. ix, 271p. (Eng. & Rade.). 1980. write for info. (ISBN 0-85883-217-8). Linguistic Circle.

Rhymer & Other Helps for Poets. Nel Modglin. 147p. 1977. 5.95 (ISBN 0-8059-2421-3). Dorrance.

Rice Terminology. (Terminology Bulletin Ser.: No. 26). 82p. 1975. pap. 7.50 (ISBN 0-685-54197-5, F1197, FAO). Unipub.

Richard Scarry's Storybook Dictionary. Richard Scarry. (Illus.). (gr. k-2). 1966. 7.95 (ISBN 0-307-15548-X, Golden Pr); PLB 12.23 (ISBN 0-307-65548-2). Western Pub.

Richard Wagner Dictionary. Edward M. Terry. LC 79-109865. 186p. Repr. of 1939 ed. lib. bdg. 15.00x (ISBN 0-8371-4356-X, TERW). Greenwood.

Richtige Wortwahl: Ein Vergleichendes Woerterbuch Sinnverwandter Ausdruecke. Wolfgang Muller. 480p. (Ger.). DM.19.80 (ISBN 3-411-01370-2). Biblio Inst.

Riemann Musiklexikon. W. Gurlitt & H. Eggebrecht. 108p. (Ger.). 1967. 135.00 (ISBN 3-7957-0031-0, M-7602, Pub. by Schatt's Soehne). French & Eur.

Right Word: A Concise Thesauras. LC 78-3461. (gr. 9 up). 1978. 3.95 (ISBN 0-395-26672-6). HM.

Right Word II. (Eng.). 3.95. HM.

Riksmalsordboken: Norwegian Dictionary. T. Gutu. (Norwegian.). 1977. write for info. (ISBN 82-573-0004-7). Kunnskapsforlaget.

Rjecnik Stranih Rijeci: Tudice & Posudenice. LC 78-389713. xiii, 1456p. (Serbo-Croatian.). 1978. write for info. Nakladni Zavod.

Ro Ro Ro Woerterbuch: Deutsch-Englisch, Englisch-Deutsch, 2 vols. Friedrich Kohler. (Eng. & Ger.). DM.pap. 3.60 ea. Rowohlt.

Road & Track Illustrated Auto Dictionary. John Dinkel. (Illus.). 96p. 1981. pap. 3.95 (ISBN 0-393-00028-1). Norton.

Robert Dictionaries. Ed. by Paul Robert. Incl. Micro Robert en Poche, 2 vols. 1171p; Micro Robert, 2 vols. in 1. 1230p; Petit Robert. rev. ed. 1972p; Grand Robert, 7 vols. 6530p. Set. 295.00x (ISBN 0-684-14004-7); suppl. only (ISBN 0-684-14085-3); Dictionnaire Universel des Noms Propres, 4 vols. (Illus.). 3200p. (Fr.). 1974. Scribner.

Roberts' Dictionary of Industrial Relations. rev. ed. Harold S. Roberts. LC 78-175029. 616p. 1971. 22.00 (ISBN 0-87179-135-8). BNA.

Robertson's Practical English-Thai Dictionary. Ed. by Richard G. Robertson. LC 79-87787. (Eng. & Thai.). 1969. bds. 6.75 (ISBN 0-8048-0706-X). C E Tuttle.

Robotics Sourcebook & Dictionary. David F. Tver & Roger W. Bolz. 304p. 1983. 29.95 (ISBN 0-8311-1152-6). Indus Pr.

Rock Lexikon. 7th ed. S. Schmidt-Joos & B. Graves. 448p. (Ger.). 1973. 7.95 (ISBN 3-499-16177-X, M-7603, Pub. by Rowohlt). French & Eur.

Rock Lexikon. 7th ed. S. Schmidt-Joos & B. Graves. 448p. (Ger.). 1973. 7.95 (ISBN 3-499-16177-X). Rowohlt.

Roget's II: The New Thesaurus. 1980. Plain-edged. 9.95 (ISBN 0-395-29604-8); Thumb-indexed. 10.95 (ISBN 0-395-29605-6). HM.

Roget's International Thesaurus. 4th ed. Peter M. Roget. LC 62-12806. 1977. 12.50i (ISBN 0-690-00010-3); thumb indexed 13.95i (ISBN 0-690-00011-1). T y Crowell.

Roget's Thesaurus. 1981. pap. 2.95 (ISBN 0-671-43675-9). PB.

Roget's Thesaurus in Dictionary Form. Norman Lewis. 1983. pap. 2.25 (ISBN 0-425-06400-X, Medallion). Berkley Pub.

Roget's Thesaurus of English Words & Phrases. Peter M. Roget. Ed. by R. A. Dutch. 1965. 11.95 (ISBN 0-312-68880-6); thumb indexed 13.50 (ISBN 0-312-68845-8). St Martin.

Roget's Thesaurus of Synonyms & Antonyms. Date not set. pap. 2.95 (ISBN 0-87505-254-1). Borden.

Roget's Thesaurus of Synonyms & Antonyms. pap. 2.95 (ISBN 0-686-17306-6). Dennison.

Roget's Thesaurus of Words & Phrases. Peter M. Roget. 774p. 1960. 6.95 (ISBN 0-448-01607-9, G&D). Putnam Pub Group.

Roget's University Thesaurus. Peter M. Roget. Ed. by C. Sylvester Mawson. LC 81-47081. 768p. 1981. pap. 6.68i (ISBN 0-06-463537-6, EH 537, EH). B&N NY.

Roll Defect Terminology: Paper Finishing & Converting. Technical Association of the Pulp & Paper Industry Winding Committee. Ed. by William Gilmore. 55p. 1977. 34.95 (01-08-T016). TAPPI.

Romanian-English Dictionary & Grammar for the Mathematical Sciences. Ed. by S. H. Gould & P. E. Obreanu. 60p. (Eng. & Romanian.). 1979. Repr. of 1969 ed. 11.00 (ISBN 0-8218-0038-8, ROMA). Am Math.

Romanisches Etymologisches Woerterbuch. 5th ed. Wilhelm Meyer-Luebke. (Ital. & Ger.). 1972. 125.00 (ISBN 3-533-01394-4, M-7604, Pub. by Carl Winter). French & Eur.

Romanishes Etymologisches Woerterbuch. 5th ed. Wilhelm Meyer-Luebke. (Ital. & Ger.). 1972. 125.00 (ISBN 3-533-01394-4). Winter Univ.

Romanov Russian-English Dictionary. A. S. Romanov. (Rus. & Eng.). pap. 4.95 (ISBN 0-671-49619-0). PB.

Romanov's Pocket Russian-English, English-Russian Dictionary. (Rus. & Eng.). pap. 2.75. Imported Bks.

Room's Classical Dictionary. Adrian Room. 320p. 1983. 18.95 (ISBN 0-7100-9262-8). Routledge & Kegan.

Room's Dictionary of Confusibles. Adrian Room. 1979. 16.00 (ISBN 0-7100-0120-7). Routledge & Kegan.

Room's Dictionary of Distinguishables. Adrian Room. 220p. 1981. 12.95 (ISBN 0-7100-0775-2). Routledge & Kegan.

Roots: A Hebrew-English Word List. Ed. by Mordechai Kamrat & Edwin Samuel. (Illus.). 308p. (Eng. & Hebrew.). 1982. pap. text ed. 7.50 (ISBN 965-17-0118-8). K Sefer.

Rororo-Lexikon zur Datenverarbeitung. Hans H. Schulze. LC 80-453504. 258p. (Ger.). 1978. DM.7.80 (ISBN 3-499-16220-2). Rowohlt.

Rororo Musikhandbuch, 2 vols. H. Lindlar. (Ger.). 1976. pap. 12.95 (ISBN 3-499-16167-2, M-7605, Pub. by Rowohlt). French & Eur.

Rororo Musikhandbuch, 2 vols. H. Lindlar. (Ger.). 1976. pap. 12.95 (ISBN 3-499-16167-2). Rowohlt.

Rotuman Grammar & Dictionary. Clerk M. Churchward. LC 75-32808. Repr. of 1940 ed. 30.75 (ISBN 0-404-14112-9). AMS Pr.

Round the World-English. Watson & Folliet. (Round the World Ser.). (gr. 1-9). 1980. 10.95 (ISBN 0-86020-485-5, Usborne-Hayes). French ed (ISBN 0-86020-488-X). Spanish ed (ISBN 0-86020-484-7). EDC.

Royal Academy of Arts, a Complete Dictionary of Contributors & Their Work from Its Foundation in 1769 to 1904, Compiled with the Sanction of the President & Council of the Royal Academy, 8 vols. in 4. Algernon Graves. LC 76-118750. 1972. Repr. of 1905 ed. Set. lib. bdg. 181.00 (ISBN 0-8337-1425-2). B Franklin.

Rumanian-English & Dictionary. M. Schonkron. (Rumanian & Eng.). 25.00. Iaconi.

Rumanian-English Dictionary. Serban Andronescu. 19.50 (ISBN 0-685-20189-9, 063-01). Saphrograph.

Rumanian-English, English-Rumanian Dictionary, with Supplement. Ed. by M. Schonkron. (Rumanian & Eng.). 25.00 (ISBN 0-8044-0546-8). Ungar.

Rumynsko-Russkii Politekhnicheskii. B. A. Andrianov et al. 715p. (Rus. & Romanian.). 1956. 4.50 (Pub. by Gostekhteorizdat). Four Continent.

Running Press Glossary of Accounting Language. LC 77-12041. 78p. (Eng.). 1978. 9.80 (ISBN 0-89471-017-6); pap. 1.95 (ISBN 0-89471-016-8). Running Pr.

Running Press Glossary of Computer Terms: An Insider's Guide to the Language of the Experts. John Prenis. (Eng.). pap. 2.95. Running Pr.

Running Press Glossary of Football Language. Bill Shefski. LC 77-12492. 120p. (Eng.). 1978. 2.50 (ISBN 0-89471-020-6). Running Pr.

Ruotsalais-Suomalaines. Lea Lampeu. LC 79-361738. 547p. (Swedish & Finnish., Helsinki, Finland). 1978. write for info. WSOY.

Ruotsin Kielen Perus ja Taydennyssanasto. Kalervo Linnapuomi. LC 80-465197. 349p. (Finnish & Swedish.). 1979. write for info. (ISBN 9-5110-5181-4). Otava.

Rusko-Sesky Chemicky Slovnik. M. Bubnikova. LC 80-466659. 494p. (Rus. & Czech.). 1978. 57.00 Kcs. Russkii Iazyk.

Russian-Arabic Dictionary. 1056p. (Rus. & Arabic.). 1979. Leatherette 26.95 (ISBN 0-686-97414-X, M-9073). French & Eur.

Russian-Bulgarian Dictionary. Leonidova. 463p. (Rus. & Bulgarian.). 1978. leatherette 4.95 (ISBN 0-686-92105-4, M-9101). French & Eur.

Russian-Bulgarian Phraseological Dictionary. K. Andreichina et al. Ed. by Vlasova. 582p. (Rus. & Bulgarian.). 1980. 65.00 (ISBN 0-686-97416-6, M-9830). French & Eur.

Russian-Chinese Dictionary of Export & Economics. 708p. (Rus. & Chinese.). 1961. leatherette 6.95 (ISBN 0-686-92108-9, M-9068). French & Eur.

Russian-Chinese-English Glossary of Education. C. T. Hu & Beatrice Beach. LC 73-108419. 1970. text ed. 10.95x (ISBN 0-8077-1529-8). Tchrs Coll.

Russian-Czechoslovakian Dictionary. Vlchek. 896p. (Rus. & Czech.). 1974. 17.95 (ISBN 0-686-92111-9, M-9116). French & Eur.

Russian-Czechoslovakian Polytechnical Dictionary. V. S. Petrov & S. A. Tulin. 639p. (Rus. & Czech.). 1962. leatherette 6.95 (ISBN 0-686-92116-X, M-9074). French & Eur.

Russian-English & English-Russian Dictionary. W. Harrison & Svetlana LeFlemming. (Routledge Pocket Dictionaries Ser.). 580p. (Orig.). 1981. pap. 8.95 (ISBN 0-7100-0800-7). Routledge & Kegan.

Russian-English Atomic Dictionary: Physics, Mathematics, Nucleonics. rev. ed. 2nd ed. Eugene A. Carpovich. LC 57-8256. (Rus. & Eng.). 1959. 15.00 (ISBN 0-911484-00-0). Tech Dict.

Russian-English Biological & Medical Dictionary. 2nd ed. Eugene A. Carpovich. LC 58-7915. (Rus. & Eng.). 1960. 25.00 (ISBN 0-911484-01-9). Tech Dict.

Russian-English Botanical Dictionary. Paul Macura. 678p. (Rus. & Eng.). 1982. 49.95 (ISBN 0-89357-092-3). Slavica.

Russian-English Chemical & Polytechnical Dictionary. 3rd ed. Ludmilla I. Callaham. LC 75-5982. 852p. (Rus. & Eng.). 1975. 58.50x (ISBN 0-471-12998-4, Pub. by Wiley-Interscience). Wiley.

Russian-English Chemical & Polytechnical Dictionary. 3rd ed. Ludmilla I. Callaham. LC 75-5982. xxviii, 852p. (Eng. & Rus.). 1975. 58.50 (ISBN 0-471-12998-4). Wiley.

Russian-English Chemical Dictionary. 2nd ed. Eugene A. Carpovich. LC 61-11700. (Rus. & Eng.). 1963. 25.00 (ISBN 0-911484-03-5). Tech Dict.

Russian-English Dictionary. Akhmanova et al. 510p. (Rus. & Eng.). 4.00. Imported Bks.

Russian-English Dictionary. (Russkii iazyk Ser.). 520p. (Rus. & Eng.). 1979. 3.95 (O-50). Four Continent.

Russian-English Dictionary. T. Smirnitskii. 766p. (Rus. & Eng.). 1980. 42.00x (ISBN 0-569-00006-8, Pub. by Collet's). State Mutual Bk.

Russian English Dictionary. rev. ed. A. I. Smirnitsky. (Rus. & Eng.). 1973. 24.75 (ISBN 0-525-19520-3, 02403-720). Dutton.

Russian-English Dictionary. 3rd ed. A. I. Smirnitsky. large ed. 27.50 (ISBN 0-87557-066-6, 066-6). Saphrograph.

Russian-English Dictionary. A. M. Taube. 832p. (Rus. & Eng.). 1980. vinyl bds. 25.00x (ISBN 0-569-06453-8, Pub. by Collet's). State Mutual Bk.

Russian-English Dictionary. A. M. Taube et al. Ed. by R. C. Daglish. 831p. (Rus. & Eng.). 1978. leatherette 17.95 (ISBN 0-686-92120-8, M-9108). French & Eur.

Russian-English Dictionary & Reader in the Cybernetical Sciences. Samuel Kotz. 1966. 49.00 (ISBN 0-12-422450-4). Acad Pr.

Russian-English Dictionary of Abbreviations & Initialisms. James F. Shipp. viii, 637p. (Orig., Rus. & Eng.). 1982. flexi 60.00x (ISBN 0-917564-12-X). Translation Research.

Russian-English Dictionary of...(a,e,i,ya) tel' Words. Charles Parsons. 32p. (Orig., Rus. & Eng.). 1980. pap. 6.00x (ISBN 0-917564-08-1). Translation Research.

Russian-English Dictionary of Data Processing Terminology. 359p. (Rus. & Eng.). 1971. text ed. 6.95 (ISBN 0-686-92123-2, M-9127). French & Eur.

Russian-English Dictionary of Helminthology & Plant Nematology. G. J. Pozniak. 108p. (Rus. & Eng.). 1979. 60.00x (ISBN 0-85198-447-9, Pub. by CAB Bks England). State Mutual Bk.

Russian-English Dictionary of irovat' Verbs. Charles Parsons. 34p. (Orig., Rus. & Eng.). 1983. 10.00x (ISBN 0-917564-14-6). Translation Research.

Russian-English Dictionary of Modern Terms in Aeronautics & Rocketry. M. M. Konarski. (Rus. & Eng.). 1962. 88.00 (ISBN 0-08-009658-1). Pergamon.

Russian-English Dictionary of....ost' Words. Charles Parsons. 64p. (Orig., Rus. & Eng.). 1978. pap. text ed. 10.00x (ISBN 0-917564-05-7). Translation Research.

Russian-English Dictionary of Prestressed Concrete & Concrete Construction. Ed. by Ben C. Gerwick, Jr. & V. P. Peters. 120p. (Rus. & Eng.). 1966. 33.00x (ISBN 0-677-00260-2). Gordon.

Russian-English Dictionary of Sports Terms & Phrases. A. V. Gavrilovets. (Rus. & Eng.). 32.00x (ISBN 0-569-08607-8, Pub. by Collets). State Mutual Bk.

Russian-English Dictionary of Sports Terms & Phrases. Russkii Yazyk. 352p. (Rus. & Eng.). 1980. pap. 15.00x (ISBN 0-686-72092-X, Pub. by Collet's). State Mutual Bk.

Russian-English Dictionary of Surnames: Important Names from Science & Technology. James F. Shipp. xvi, 317p. (Orig., Rus. & Eng.). 1981. pap. 30.00x (ISBN 0-917564-10-3). Translation Research.

Russian-English Dictionary of the Mathematical Sciences. A. J. Lohwater. LC 61-15685. 267p. (Eng. & Rus.). 1979. Repr. of 1974 ed. 17.00 (ISBN 0-8218-0036-1, RED). Am Math.

Russian-English, English-Russian Dictionary. William Harrison & Svetlana Le Fleming. 1973. 14.00 (ISBN 0-7100-6960-X). Routledge & Kegan.

Russian-English, English-Russian Dictionary. S. G. Zaimovsky. pap. 8.50 (ISBN 0-685-20192-9, 069-0). Saphrograph.

Russian-English, English-Russian Scientific & Technical Dictionary, 2 vols. Ed. by M. H. Alford & V. L. Alford. 1405p. (Rus. & Eng.). 1970. 32.00; E12.80. Pergamon.

Russian-English Forestry & Wood Dictionary. W. Linnard. 109p. (Rus. & Eng.). 1966. 30.00x (ISBN 0-686-45635-1, Pub. by CAB Bks England). State Mutual Bk.

Russian-English Glossary of Hydrobiology. 113p. (Rus. & Eng.). 1958. 35.00x (ISBN 0-306-10599-3, Consultants). Plenum Pub.

Russian-English Index to Scientific Apparatus Nomenclature. James F. Shipp. LC 77-362864. viii, 66p. (Eng. & Rus.). 1977. write for info. (ISBN 0-917564-03-0). Trans Res Inst.

Russian-English Integrated Dictionary, 2 vols. Patricia A. Heron. LC 76-369716. xv, 583p. (Eng. & Rus.). 1975. write for info. Univ Aston.

Russian-English Mathematical Dictionary. L. M. Milne-Thomson. (Mathematical Research Center Pubns., No. 7). 206p. (Rus. & Eng.). 1962. 40.00x (ISBN 0-299-02600-0). U of Wis Pr.

Russian-English Medical Dictionary. LC 78-40146. (Rus. & Eng.). 1978. 75.00 (ISBN 0-08-023164-0); E37.50. Pergamon.

Russian-English Metals & Machines Dictionary. Eugene A. Carpovich. LC 60-12013. (Rus. & Eng.). 1960. 15.00x (ISBN 0-911484-02-7). Tech Dict.

Russian-English Monograph Series: Skorost' 52p. (Orig., Rus. & Eng.). 1979. pap. 5.00x (ISBN 0-917564-07-3). Translation Research.

Russian-English Oil-Field Dictionary. Ed. by D. E. Stoliarov. 432p. (Rus. & Eng.). 1983. 27.00 (ISBN 0-08-028169-9). Pergamon.

Russian-English Plastics Dictionary: Reversed from an English-Russian Dictionary by Computer Processing. Ed. by Harry H. Josselson. LC 76-99790. (Rus. & Eng.). 1970. text ed. 14.95x (ISBN 0-8143-1396-5). Wayne St U Pr.

Russian-English Polytechnical Dictionary. Ed. by B. Kuznetsov. LC 80-41193. 900p. (Rus. & Eng.). 1981. 110.00 (ISBN 0-08-023609-X). Pergamon.

Russian-English Scientific & Technical Dictionary, 2 vols. M. H. Alford & V. L. Alford. LC 73-88348. (Rus. & Eng.). 1970. Set. 94.00 (ISBN 0-08-012227-2). Pergamon.

Russian-English Scientific & Technical Dictionary of Useful Combinations & Expressions. M. G. Zimmerman. (Rus. & Eng.). 22.00 (ISBN 0-87559-119-1); thumb indexed 29.50 (ISBN 0-87559-140-X). Shalom.

Russian-English Space Technology Dictionary. M. M. Konarski. LC 72-99990. (Rus. & Eng.). 1970. 77.00 (ISBN 0-08-015617-7). Pergamon.

Russian-English Translators Dictionary: A Guide to Scientific & Technical Usage. Mikhail G. Zimmerman. LC 67-19391. 295p. (Rus. & Eng.). 1967. 29.50x (ISBN 0-306-30300-0, Plenum Pr). Plenum Pub.

Russian-English Veterinary Dictionary. R. Mack. 104p. (Rus. & Eng.). 1972. 40.00x (ISBN 0-85198-255-7, Pub. by CAB Bks England). State Mutual Bk.

Russian-English Vocabulary with Grammatical Sketch. Ed. by Gabrielle Rainich & A. H. Kuipers. 66p. (Rus. & Eng.). 1980. Repr. of 1972 ed. with corrections 9.00 (ISBN 0-8218-0037-X, REV). Am Math.

Russian Fare. R. Gorina. pap. 3.95 (ISBN 0-87557-106-9, 106-9). Saphrograph.

Russian for the English-Speaking Tourist see Phrase Dictionaries for the American Tourist.

Russian-German Dictionary. 919p. (Rus. & Ger.). 1960. leatherette 17.50 (ISBN 0-686-92130-5, M-9075). French & Eur.

Russian-Polish Political Dictionary. B. Dudawaki et al. 726p. (Rus. & Pol.). 1955. leatherette 9.95 (ISBN 0-686-92134-8, M-9114). French & Eur.

Russian Root List with a Sketch of Russian Word Formation. 2nd ed. Charles E. Gribble. 62p. (Rus.). 1982. soft cover 3.95 (ISBN 0-89357-052-4). Slavica.

Russian-Rumanian Military Dictionary. 335p. (Rus. & Rumanian.). 1964. leatherette 6.95 (ISBN 0-686-92131-3, M-9079). French & Eur.

Russian-Swahili, Swahili-Russian Dictionary. A. I. Kutuzov. 442p. (Rus. & Swahili.). 1965. 4.95 (ISBN 0-686-92156-9, M-9119). French & Eur.

Russian Vest Pocket Dictionary. Ed. by Stefan Congrat-Butlar. (Rus.). 1974. 2.95 (ISBN 0-394-40068-2). Random.

Russian Vocabulary Builder, Seven Verbs a Day. Alex Pronin. (Rus.). 5.50 (ISBN 0-87505-314-9, Pub. by Lawrence). Borden.

Russian Word-Collocations: Learner's Dictionary. B. V. Bratus et al. (Russkii iazyk Ser.). 368p. (Rus. & Eng.). 1979. 5.95 (D-205 A). Four Continent.

Russian Word Count. E. Steinfeldt. (Progress Ser.). 228p. (Rus. & Eng.). guide for tchrs. 3.00 (C-35). Four Continent.

Russich-Deutsches Woerterbuch. 7th ed. Edmund Daum & W. Schenk. (Rus. & Ger.). 1976. 17.50 (ISBN 3-19-006219-6, M-7606, Pub. by Max Hueber). French & Eur.

Russich-Deutsches Woerterbuch. 7th ed. Edmund Daum & W. Schenk. (Ger. & Rus.). 1976. 17.50 (ISBN 3-19-006219-6). Hueber.

Russich-Deutsches Worterbuch der Funkechnik. P. K. Gorochow. 390p. (Rus. & Ger.). 1961. leatherette 6.95 (ISBN 0-686-92169-0). French & Eur.

Russich Elymologisches Woerterbuch, Vol. 1. Max Vasmer. (Rus. & Ger.). 1953. 68.00 (ISBN 3-533-00665-4, M-7608, Pub. by Carl Winter). French & Eur.

Russich Etymologishes Woerterbuch, Vol. 1. Max Vasmer. (Rus. & Ger.). 1953. 68.00 (ISBN 3-533-00665-4). Winter Univ.

Russisch, 2 vols. rev. ed. Karl Blattner. Incl. Teil I. Russisch-Deutsch. Rev. by H. Orschel. 568p. DM.18.80 (10290); Teil II. Deutsch-Russisch. Rev. by M. Braun & K. Pollok. 604p. DM.18.80 (10295). (Langenscheidts Taschenworterbucher Ser.). (Ger. & Rus.). DM.biede Teile in einem Band 29.80 (11290). Langenscheidt.

Russisch-Deutsches Woerterbuch der Chemie & Chemischen. 2nd ed. Institut fur Angewandte Sprachwissenschaft. LC 78-382767. 832p. (Rus. & Ger.). 1977. write for info. VEB Verlag Technik.

Russisch-Deutsches Woerterbuch Fuer Naturwissenschaftler und Ingenieure. S. Halbauer. 170p. (Ger. & Rus.). 1971. 9.95 (ISBN 0-686-56466-9, M-7607, Pub. by M. Hueber). French & Eur.

Russisch-Deutsches Woerterbuch Fuer Naturwissenschaftler und Ingenieure. S. Halbauer. 170p. (Ger. & Rus.). 1971. 9.95. Hueber.

Russisch Etymologisches Woerterbuch, Vol. 2. Max Vasmer. (Rus. & Ger.). 1955. 68.00 (ISBN 3-533-00666-2, M-7609, Pub. by Carl Winter). French & Eur.

Russisch Etymologisches Woerterbuch, Vol. 2. Max Vasmer. (Rus. & Ger.). 1955. 68.00 (ISBN 3-533-00666-2). Winter Univ.

Russisch Etymologisches Woerterbuch, Vol. 3. Max Vasmer. (Rus. & Ger.). 1958. 68.00 (ISBN 3-533-00667-0, M-7610, Pub. by Carl Winter). French & Eur.

Russisch Etymologisches Woerterbuch, Vol. 3. Max Vasmer. (Rus. & Ger.). 1958. 68.00 (ISBN 3-533-00667-0). Winter Univ.

Russisch fuer Ingenieur & Fashschulen. (Rus.). M.12.00 (674 947 1). Wissenschaftliche.

Russisch fuer Oekonomen: Lehrbuch fuer die Sprachkundigenausbildung IIb. (Rus.). M.18.00. Wissenschaftliche.

Russisch Woordenboek. A. Baar. LC 79-385386. xii, 502p. (Dutch & Rus.). 1979. fl.39.50 (ISBN 9-06283-523-6). Coutinho.

Russkie Frazeologizmy v Kartinkakh. M. Dubrovin. 352p. (Rus.). 1980. 4.25 (Pub. by Russkii Iazyk). Four Continent.

Russkie Poslovitsy, Pogovorki & Krylatye Vyrazheniia. Vera P. Felitsyna. LC 80-460368. 238p. (Rus.). 1979. 2.10 Rub. Russkii Iazyk.

Russkie Poslovitsy, Pogovorki i Krylatye Slovar: Lingvostranovedcheskii Slovar. Ed. by I. G. Prokhorov et al. (Russkii iazyk Ser.). 240p. (Rus.). 1979. 5.50 (C-104). Four Continent.

Russkie Poslovitsy, Pogovorki i Krylatye Vyrazheniia. V. P. Felitsyna & Iu. E. Prokhorov. 240p. (Rus.). 1979. 5.50 (Pub. by Russkii Iazyk). Four Continent.

Russkii Iazyk: Entsiklopediia. Ed. by F. P. Filin. (Sov. Entsiklopediia Ser.). 432p. (Rus.). 1979. 7.95 (O-33). Four Continent.

Russkikh Glagolov. A. S. Vasil'Eva. (Russkii iazyk Ser.). (Rus., Eng., Fr., Ital. & Span.). 1980. pap. 2.95. Four Continent.

Russko-Afganskii Slovar. K. A. Lebedev et al. 872p. (Rus. & Afghani.). 1973. 10.95 (Pub. by Sov Entsiklopediia). Four Continent.

Russko-Afganskii Slovar. P. B. Zudin. 1176p. (Rus. & Afghani.). 1955. 4.25 (Pub. by GINS). Four Continent.

Russko-Amkharskii Slovar. E. B. Gankin. 1013p. (Rus. & Eng.). 1965. 8.25 (Pub. by Sov. Entsiklopediia). Four Continent.

Russko-Angliiskii. Ol'ga S. Akhmanova. LC 80-490199. 520p. (Eng. & Rus.). 1979. Rs.1.20. Russkii Iazyk.

Russko-Angliiskii Politekhnicheskii Slovar. Kuznetsova. 728p. (Rus. & Eng.). 1980. 19.95 (Pub. by Russkii Iazyk). Four Continent.

Russko-Angliiskii Razgovornik Dlia Fizikov. L. A. Smirnova. 336p. (Rus. & Eng.). 1968. 2.25 (Pub. by Sov Entsiklopediia). Four Continent.

Russko-Angliiskii Razgovornik Dlia Fizikov. L. A. Smirnova. 312p. (Rus. & Eng.). 1977. 2.95 (Pub. by Russkii Iazyk). Four Continent.

Russko-Angliiskii Shkol'No-Pedagogicheskii Slovar. V. V. Botiakova et al. 455p. (Rus. & Eng.). 1959. 3.90 (Pub. by Iaroslavsk. Knizhn. Izd.). Four Continent.

Russko-Angliiskii Slovar. O. S. Akhmanova. 766p. (Rus. & Eng.). 1977. 14.25 (Pub. by Russkii Iazyk). Four Continent.

Russko-Angliiskii Slovar. A. I. Smirnitskii. (Russkii iazyk Ser.). 768p. (Rus. & Eng.). 1977. 14.25 (D-215 A). Four Continent.

Russko-Angliiskii Slovar. A. M. Taube. 832p. (Rus. & Eng.). 1979. 8.95 (Pub. by Russkii Iazyk). Four Continent.

Russko-Angliiskii Slovar' - Razgovornik: Russian-English Dictionary of Sports Terms & Phrases - Olympic Summer. (Russkii iazyk Ser.). 352p. (Rus. & Eng.). 1979. 3.50 (C-56). Four Continent.

Russko-Angliiskii Slovar (Kratkii) Ed. by O. S. Akhmanova. 520p. (Rus. & Eng.). 1979. 3.50 (Pub. by Russkii Iazyk). Four Continent.

Russko-Angliiskii Slovar-Razgovornik: Letnie Olimpiiskie Vidy Sporta. A. V. Gavrilovets. 352p. (Rus.). 1979. 3.50 (Pub. by Russkii Iazyk). Four Continent.

Russko-Angliiskii Voenno-Morskoi Slovar. N. P. Afronin et al. 782p. (Rus. & Eng.). 1976. 11.50 (Pub. by Voenizdat). Four Continent.

Russko-Angliisku Slovar-Russian-English Dictionary. Olga S. Akhmanova & Elizabeth A. Wilson. LC 80-490199. 520p. (Rus.). 1979. write for info. Russkii Iazyk.

Russko-Anglo-Azerbaidzhansko-Kirgozsko-Turkmensko-Uzbekskii Terminologicheskii Slovar Po Avtomati cheskomu Upravleniiu. 642p. (Rus. & Eng.). 1977. 12.50 (Pub. by Elm). Four Continent.

Russko-Anglo-Nemetsko-Frantsuzskii Slovar Terminov Po Avtomaticheskomu Upravleniiu. Ed. by A. V. Khramov. 229p. (Rus., Eng., Fr. & Ger.). 1963. 4.80 (Pub. by An Arm SSR). Four Continent.

Russko-Arabskii Meditsinskii Slovar. G. T. Arslanian et al. 608p. (Rus. & Arabic.). 1977. 12.50 (Pub. by Russkii Iazyk). Four Continent.

Russko-Arabskii Uchebnyi Slovar. G. Sh. Sharbatov. 1196p. (Rus. & Arabic.). 1979. 16.95 (Pub. by Russki Iazyk). Four Continent.

Russko-Armianskii Frazeologicheskii Slovar. 616p. (Rus. & Armenian.). 1975. 7.25 (Pub. by Gos. Un-Tet). Four Continent.

Russko-Armianskii Politekhnicheskii Slovar. R. T. Ashkharumov et al. 436p. (Rus. & Armenian.). 1957. 4.95 (Pub. by An Arm SSR). Four Continent.

Russko-Armianskii Slovar. A. Garibian. 1340p. (Rus. & Armenian.). 1977. 16.75 (Pub. by Hayastan). Four Continent.

Russko-Armianskii Slovar. A. S. Garibian. 1421p. (Rus. & Armenian.). 1968. 14.25 (Pub. by Hayastan). Four Continent.

Russko-Armianskii Tolkovyi Slovar. V. Z. Grigorian et al. 339p. (Rus. & Armenian.). 1979. 7.50 (Pub. by An Arm SSR). Four Continent.

Russko-Azerbaidzhanskii Slovar, 3 vols. (Rus. & Azerbaijani.). 1971. 28.95 set (Pub. by Elm). Four Continent.

Russko-Bashkirskii Slovar. G. R. Karimova. 600p. (Rus. & Bashkirsh.). 1954. 2.70 (Pub. by GINS). Four Continent.

Russko-Bengal'skii Slovar. Litton. 760p. (Rus. & Bengali.). 1972. 6.30 (Pub. by Sov. Entsiklopediia). Four Continent.

Russko-Birmanskii Slovar. N. N. Novikov et al. 880p. (Rus. & Burmese.). 1966. 7.50 (Pub. by Sov. Entsiklopediia). Four Continent.

Russko-Bolgarskii Slovar. S. K. Chukalov. 911p. (Rus. & Bulgarian.). 1972. 7.95 (Pub. by Sov. Entsiklopediia). Four Continent.

Russko-Chechenskii Slovar. Aisash T. Karasaev et al. LC 79-370228. 728p. (Rus. & Chechen.). 1978. 3.80 Rub. Russkii Iazyk.

Russko-Chechenskii Slovar. 728p. (Rus.). 1978. 10.95 (Dist. by Four Continent Bk). Russkii Iazyk.

Russko-Cheshskii Slovar, 2 vols. L. V. Kopetskov et al. (Rus.). 1977. 23.50 set (Pub. by Russkii Iazyk). Four Continent.

Russko-Datskii Slovar. N. I. Krymova et al. 906p. (Rus.). 1956. 4.75 (Pub. by GINS). Four Continent.

Russko-Erzianskii Slovar. Ed. by M. N. Koliadenkov et al. 413p. (Rus.). 1948. 3.95 (Pub. by GINS). Four Continent.

Russko-Estonskii Razgovornik. A. Reitsak. 256p. (Rus. & Estonian.). 1976. 1.00 (Pub. by Valgus). Four Continent.

Russko-Estonskii Slovar, 2 vols. P. Arumaa et al. (Rus. & Estonian.). 1975. 14.95 set (Pub. by Valgus). Four Continent.

Russko-Estonskii Slovar. V. Mukhel. 708p. (Rus. & Estonian.). 1955. 3.30 (Pub. by Estonsk. Gos. Izd.). Four Continent.

Russko-Evenskii Slovar. V. I. Tsintsius. 778p. (Rus.). 1952. 4.50 (Pub. by GINS). Four Continent.

Russko-Finskii Slovar. Ed. by M. E. Kuusiena et al. 1000p. (Rus. & Finnish.). 1963. 10.95 (Pub. by GINS). Four Continent.

Russko-Frantsuzskii Aviatsionno-Tekhnicheskii Slovar. P. E. Turchin. 624p. (Rus. & Fr.). 1968. 7.25 (Pub. by Sov. Entsiklopedia). Four Continent.

Russko-Frantsuzskii Shkol'No-Pedagogicheskii Slovar. N. V. Goliakova et al. 544p. (Fr. & Rus.). 1969. 3.30 (Pub. by Sov. Entsiklopediia). Four Continent.

Russko-Frantsuzskii Slovar. V. V. Pototskaia et al. 677p. (Rus. & Fr.). 1971. 2.25 (Pub. by Sov. Entsiklopediia). Four Continent.

Russko-Frantsuzskii Stroitelnyi Slovar. V. V. Voronin et al. 464p. (Fr. & Rus.). 1978. 7.25 (Pub. by Russkii Iazyk). Four Continent.

Russko-Gollandskii Slovar. Z. I. Pirot. 1225p. (Rus.). 1961. 5.25 (Pub. by GINS). Four Continent.

Russko-Iaponskii Slovar. S. F. Zarubin. 818p. (Rus. & Japanese.). 1964. 16.50 (Pub. by Sov. Entsiklopediia). Four Continent.

Russko-Indoneziiskii Slovar. E. S. Belkina. 624p. (Rus. & Indonesian.). 1972. 7.85 (Pub. by Sov. Entsiklopediia). Four Continent.

Russko-Indoneziiskii Uchebnyi Slovar. A. G. Lordkipanidze et al. 707p. (Rus. & Indonesian.). 1963. 2.95 (Pub. by GINS). Four Continent.

Russko-Ital'ianskii Ucxhebnyi Slovar. D. E. Rozental. 712p. (Rus. & Ital.). 1966. 2.75 (Pub. by Sov. Entsiklopediia). Four Continent.

Russko-Kabardinsko-Cherkesskii Slovar. B. M. Kardanov et al. 1054p. (Rus.). 1955. 5.85 (Pub. by GINS). Four Continent.

Russko-Karachaevo-Balkarskii Slovar. Ed. by Kh. I Siunchev et al. 744p. (Rus.). 1955. 7.50 (Pub. by Sov. Entsiklopediia). Four Continent.

Russko-Kazakhsii Slovar Lingvisticheskikh Terminov. S. Kenesbaev et al. 206p. (Rus.). 1966. 1.85 (Pub. by An Arm SSR). Four Continent.

Russko-Kazakhskii Terminologicheskii Slovar, 4 Vols. E. Bekmukhametov. (Rus.). 1959. 7.00 set (Pub. by Izd. An Kaz. SSR). Four Continent.

Russko-Kazakhskii Tolkovyi Geograficheskii Slovar. Z. Aubakirov et al. 203p. (Rus.). 1966. 2.70 (Pub. by Nauka). Four Continent.

Russko-Khausa Slovar. V. V. Laptukhin. 409p. (Rus.). 1967. 4.50 (Pub. by Sov. Entsiklopediia). Four Continent.

Russko-Kirgizskii Slovar. Ed. by K. K. Iudakhin. 990p. (Rus.). 1957. 9.90 (Pub. by GINS). Four Continent.

Russko-Kitaiskii Obschcheekonomicheskii i Vneshnetorgovyi Slovar. I. N. Zorin. 708p. (Rus.). 1961. 4.25 (Pub. by Vneshtorgizdat). Four Continent.

Russko-Kurdskii Slovar. I. O. Farizov. 781p. (Rus.). 1957. 3.95 (Pub. by GINS). Four Continent.

Russko-Latino-Kazakhskii Terminologicheskii Slovar. M. Isambaev. 506p. (Rus. & Lat.). 1960. 2.40 (Pub. by Izd. An Kaz. SSR). Four Continent.

Russko-Latinsko-Uzbekskii Slovar. 188p. (Rus. , Lat. & Uzbek.). 1978. 3.95 (Pub. by Meditsina). Four Continent.

Russko-Latyshskii Politekhnicheskii Slovar. A. Zingitis. 568p. (Rus.). 1977. 10.75 (Pub. by Liesma). Four Continent.

Russko-Litovskii Sel'Skokhoziaistvennyi Slovar. A. V. Prano. 362p. (Rus.). 1971. 3.50 (Pub. by Mintis). Four Continent.

Russko-Litovskii Slovar, 2 vols. (Rus.). 1967. 11.95 set (Pub. by Mintis). Four Continent.

Russko-Malagasiiskii Slovar. L. A. Korneev. 543p. (Rus.). 1970. 4.60 (Pub. bu Sov. Entsiklopediia). Four Continent.

Russko-Moldavskii & Moldavsko-Ruskii Shkolnyi Slovar. 336p. (Rus. & Moldavian.). 1969. 1.75 (Pub. by Lumina). Four Continent.

Russko-Moldavskii Ekonomicheskii Slovar. V. B. Bortnikov et al. 363p. (Rus. & Moldavian.). 1973. 2.65 (Pub. by Kartia Moldoveniaske). Four Continent.

Russko-Moldavskii Slovar. Ed. by A. T. Borshch et al. 835p. (Rus. & Moldavian.). 1954. 6.85 (Pub. by Izd. Inostr. & Natsional Slovarei). Four Continent.

Russko-Moldavskii Slovar. M. V. Podiko. 1060p. (Rus. & Moldavian.). 1973. 6.50 (Pub. by Kartia Moldoveniaske). Four Continent.

Russko-Mongol'Skii Razgovornik. 111p. (Rus. & Mongolian.). 1976. 00.60 (Pub. by Russkii Iazyk). Four Continent.

Russko-Mordovskii Slovar. A. P. Feoktistov. 370p. (Rus.). 1971. 4.25 (Pub. by Nauka). Four Continent.

Russko-Nemetskii Radiotekhnicheskii Slovar. P. K. Gorokhov. 390p. (Rus. & Ger.). 1961. 3.60 (Pub. by Glav. Red. Inostr. Nauchno-Tekhn. Slovarei Fizmata). Glav. Red. Inostr. Nauchno-Tekhn. Slovarei Fizmata.

Russko-Nemetskii Slovar. Ed. by A. A. Leping. 568p. (Rus.). 1957. 1.70 (Pub. by GINS). Four Continent.

Russko-Nemetskii Slovar. Ed. by E. I. Leping. 848p. (Rus. & Ger.). 1978. 15.95 (Pub. by Russkii Iazyk). Four Continent.

Russko-Nemetskii Slovar. Ed. by A. A. Strakhova et al. 920p. (Rus.). 1960. 7.50 (Pub. by GINS). Four Continent.

Russko-Novogrecheskii Karmannyi Slovar. N. Al. Sal'nov. 352p. (Rus. & Ger.). 1965. 1.60 (Pub. by Sov. Entsiklopediia). Four Continent.

Russko-Novogrecheskii Slovar. A. A. Ioannidia. 819p. (Rus. & Gr.). 1966. 7.95 (Pub. by Sov. Entsiklopediia). Four Continent.

Russko-Pol'skii Politekhnicheskii Slovar. V. I. Dudavskii et al. 726p. (Rus. & Pol.). 1955. 4.35 (Pub. by Gosizdat Tekhn. Teoretich. Lit.). Four Continent.

Russko-Rumynskii Voennyi Slovar. Iu. A. Spazhev et al. 335p. (Rus. & Rumanian.). 1964. 3.00 (Pub. by Voenizdat). Four Continent.

Russko-Shvedskii Slovar. Ed. by K. Davidson. 960p. (Rus.). 1976. 10.95 (C-91, Pub. by Russkii Iazyk). Four Continent.

Russko-Tagal'skii Slovar. M. Krus et al. 760p. (Rus. & Tagalog.). 1965. 4.95 (Pub. by Sov. Entsiklopediia). Four Continent.

Russko-Tamil'Skii Slovar. M. S. Andronov. 1175p. (Rus. & Tamil.). 1965. 7.95 (Pub. by Sov. Entsiklopediia). Four Continent.

Russko-Uigurskii Slovar. A. Iliev et al. 1473p. (Rus.). 1956. 5.25 (Pub. by Gosizdat Natsional Inostr Slovarei). Four Continent.

Russko-Ukrainskii Khimicheskii Slovar. E. F. Nekriach. 204p. (Rus. & Ukrainian.). 1959. 1.50 (Pub. by An Arm SSR). Four Continent.

Russko-Ukrainskii Metallurgicheskii Slovar. V. D. Chekhranov. (Rus. & Ukrainian.). 1970. 1.50 (Pub. by Naukova Dumka). Four Continent.

Russko-Ukrainskii Slovar. D. I. Ganich et al. 1012p. (Rus. & Ukrainian.). 1978. 8.95 (Pub. by Sov. Entsiklopediia). Four Continent.

Russko-Ukrainskii Slovar Sotsial'No-Ekonomicheskoi Terminologii. 412p. (Rus. & Ukrainian.). 1976. 3.95 (Pub. by Ukr. Entsiklopediia). Four Continent.

Russko-Vengerskii Slovar. G. I. Ol'dal. 368p. (Rus.). 1961. 00.95 (Pub. by Gosizdat Inostr Natsional Slovarei). Four Continent.

Russko-V'Etnamskii Slovar, 2 vols. (Rus. & Vietnamese.). 1977. 16.25 set (Pub. by Russkii Iazyk). Four Continent.

Rustina pro Vedecke a Odborne Pracovniky, 2 vols. L. Z. Rozkovcova & S. Stary Hanusova. 208p. (Rus. & Czech.). 1977. 27.00 Kcs. Academia.

Rysk-Svensk Teknisk Ordbok. Bengt Schildt. 293p. (Rus. & Swedish.). 1965. Kr.145.00 (ISBN 91-24-62667-8). Esselte Studium.

S

Sabon Kamus na Hausa Zuwa Turanci. Paul Newman. LC 79-104420. xii, 151p. (Hausa & Eng.). 1977. write for info. (ISBN 0-19-575303-8). Oxford U Pr.

SAE Motor Vehicle, Safety & Environmental Terminology. Society of Automotive Engineers. 179p. pap. 9.50 (ISBN 0-89883-370-1, HS-215); pap. 7.95 members. Soc Auto Engineers.

Safety at Work & Pollution Control. Nicole Aymard Lapalu. LC 76-376744. 320p. (Eng., Fr., Ger. & Span.). 1975. write for info. (ISBN 2-7213-0051-2). Elp.

Safire's Political Dictionary. William Safire. 1980. pap. 9.95 (ISBN 0-345-28393-7). Ballantine.

Safire's Political Dictionary: The New Language of Politics. William Safire. 1978. 17.95 (ISBN 0-394-50261-2). Random.

Saggio di un dizionario del linguaggio archivistico veneto. Bartolomeo Cecchetti. LC 79-353675. 74p. (Ital.). 1978. write for info. Forni.

Sahkotieteellinen Sanasto. Suomen Standardisoimislitto. LC 77-481554. 167p. (Eng., Finnish, Fr., Ger., Rus. & Swedish.). 1976. write for info. Suomen Standard.

Sailee Nihantu: Dictionary of Idioms & Phrases. T. Ramalingam Pilla. 1008p. (Malayalam.). 1975. write for info. DC Bks.

Sammlung Duden: Band I, Vollstaendiges Orthographisches Woerterbuch der Deutschen Sprache. Konrad Duden. 202p. (Ger.). DM.6.80 (ISBN 3-411-01041-X). Biblio Inst.

Sammlung Duden: Band II, Regeln & Woerterverzeichnis fuer die Deutsch Rechtschreibung. 47p. (Ger.). DM.6.80 (ISBN 3-411-01042-8). Biblio Inst.

Sammlung Duden: Band III, Akten zur Geschichte der Deutschen Einheitsschreibung. Paul Grebe. 48p. (Ger.). DM.6.80 (ISBN 3-411-01043-6). Biblio Inst.

Sample Lexicon of Pan-Arabic. Ernest T. Abdel-Massih. LC 75-18985. (Arabic.). 1975. pap. text ed. 7.00x (ISBN 0-932098-10-X). Ctr for NE & North African Stud.

Sana Alimentazione. Edoardo Borra et al. LC 77-456792. xxx, 826p. (Ital.). 1976. L.15.000. Edizioni Paoline.

Sanskrit-English Dictionary. Monier-Williams. (Sanskrit & Eng.). 1973. 37.00x (ISBN 0-8364-0464-5). South Asia Bks.

Sanskrit-English Dictionary. rev. ed. Monier Monier-Williams et al. (Sanskrit & Eng.). 1899. 105.00x (ISBN 0-19-864308-X). Oxford U Pr.

Sanskrit-English Dictionary. M. Williams. (Sanskrit & Eng.). 1979. 55.00 (ISBN 0-89684-314-9). Orient Bk Dist.

Sanskrit-English Dictionary. Monier Williams et al. 1367p. (Sanskrit & Eng.). 1981. Repr. 45.00 (ISBN 0-89581-173-1). Lancaster-Miller.

Sanskrit-English Dictionary: Etymologically & Philologically Arranged with Special Reference to Cognate Indo-European Languages. Ed. by Monier Williams. LC 73-495007. 1333p. (Sanskrit & Eng.). 1981. Repr. of 1899 ed. 50.00x (ISBN 0-8002-0204-X). Intl Pubns serv.

Sanskrit-English, English-Sanskrit Student's Dictionary, 2 vols. V. S. Apte. (Sanskrit & Eng.). 40.00 (ISBN 0-685-36176-4). Heinman.

Sanskrit-Hindi-English Dictionary. Suryakanta. (Sanskrit, Hindi & Eng.). 1976. 47.50x (ISBN 0-8002-1950-3). Intl Pubns Serv.

Sanskrit Manual (Enlarged) with a Vocabulary (English & Sanskrit) Monier Williams. (Sanskrit & Eng.). 1977. text ed. 14.00x (ISBN 0-8426-1061-8). Verry.

Sanskrit-Thai-English Dictionary. 1339p. (Sanskrit, Thai & Eng.). 10.00x (ISBN 0-8002-1951-1). Intl Pubns Serv.

Sanskrit vocabulary. Bernfried Scherath. LC 80-506334. ix, 216p. (Sanskrit.). 1980. fl.pap. 48.00 (ISBN 9-00-406108-8). Brill.

Sanskrit Vocabulary Arranged According to Word Families with Meanings in English, German & Spanish. B. Schlerath. 1980. 35.00 (ISBN 0-686-78392-1). Heinman.

Sante Grace a la Dietetique. Gustave Mathieu. LC 77-477672. 271p. (Fr.). 1975. 38.00 F (ISBN 2-85256-021-6). Doc Scient.

Sanyo's Tri-Lingual Glossary of Chemical Terms. Hiroshi Yamada. 1977. 150.00 (ISBN 0-685-51744-6). Sadtler Res.

Satzlexikon der Handelskorrespondenz. Zavada. 356p. (Ger. & Eng.). 1982. DM.25.00. Brandstetter.

Satzlexikon der Handelskorrespondenz. Zavada & Eberle. 435p. (Ger. & Port.). 1982. DM.30.00. Brandstetter.

Satzlexikon der Handelskorrespondenz. Zavada & Hartgenbush. 430p. (Ger. & Fr.). 1982. DM.30.00. Brandstetter.

Satzlexikon der Handelskorrespondenz. Zavada & Schraffl. 388p. (Ger. & Ital.). 1982. DM.30.00. Brandstetter.

Satzlexikon der Handelskorrespondenz. Zavada & Weis. 405p. (Ger. & Span.). 1982. DM.30.00. Brandstetter.

Say It in Arabic. Farouk El-Baz. LC 67-17506. (Arabic.). 1968. lib. bdg. 8.50x (ISBN 0-88307-557-1). Gannon.

Scandinavian Smorgasbord, Soups, Savouries & Sweets. M. Savonius. pap. 3.95 (ISBN 0-87557-107-7, 107-7). Saphrograph.

Schiffbau, Schiffahrt, Fischereitechnik-Russisch-Englisch-Deutsch. Erhard Bensch. 784p. (Rus., Eng. & Ger.). 1981. M.98.00. VEB Technk.

Schirmer Pronouncing Pocket Manual of Musical Terms. 4th ed. Theodore Baker. LC 77-5236. 1978. pap. 3.95 (ISBN 0-02-870250-6). Assoc-Mus.

Schluesselwoerter zur Berufsbildung. Hans J. Rosenthal. Ed. by Peter Gerds. LC 77-483344. 431p. (Ger.). 1977. DM.21.00 (ISBN 3-407-50058-0). Beltz & Co.

Scholar's Glossary of Sex. Roy Goliard. (Illus., Orig.). 1968. pap. 1.95 (ISBN 0-685-11982-3, 20). Heineman.

Schrift & Sprache der Chinesen. Bernhard Karlgren. LC 74-34031. x, 119p. (Chinese.). 1975. write for info. (ISBN 0-387-07108-3). Springer-Verlag.

Schuelerlexikon fuer Arbeitslehre & Sozialkunde. 2nd ed. Christian Schmieder & Gunther Fleischmann. 304p. (Ger.). 1980. DM.24.80 (ISBN 3-40300-646-8). Auer.

Schwachen Verben des Althochdeutschen, Vol. 2. F. A. Raven. LC 64-23934. 224p. (Ger.). 1967. 24.60 (ISBN 0-8173-0801-6). U of Ala Pr.

Schwedisch, 2 vols. H. Kornitzky. (Langenscheidts Taschenworterbucher Ser.). (Ger. & Swedish.). Teil 1: Schwedisch-Deutsch (xvi, 557p.) DM.18.80 (10300); Teil 2: Deutsch-Schwedisch (xv, 510p.) DM.18.80 (10305); DM.Beide Teile in einem Band 29.80 (11300). Langenscheidt.

Schwierigkeiten des Deutsch-Italienischen Wortschatzes. Bruno Storni. Ed. by Paolo Giovannelli. LC 76-455176. 335p. (Ital. & Ger.). 1975. DM.32.00 (ISBN 3-125-21500-5). Klett.

Science Readings for Students of English As a Second Language, with Exercises for Vocabulary Development. K. Croft. 1968. 2.75 (ISBN 0-07-013883-4, I). McGraw.

Scientific Technological Dictionary. R. Popic et al. 1140p. (Eng. & Serbocroatian.). 1980. 95.00 (ISBN 0-686-97432-8, M-9688). French & Eur.

Scientific Terms, Aeronautics: Japanese-English, English-Japanese. Ministry of Education. 235p. (Japanese & Eng.). 1973. leatherette 19.95 (ISBN 0-686-92173-9, M-9347). French & Eur.

Scientific Terms, Chemistry: Japanese-English, English-Japanese. Ministry of Education. 630p. (Japanese & Eng.). 1974. 25.00 (ISBN 0-686-92209-3, M-9335). French & Eur.

Scientific Terms Electrical Engineering. Ministry of Education Science & Culture. 675p. (Eng. & Japanese.). 1979. 39.95 (ISBN 0-686-97433-6, M-9330). French & Eur.

Scientific Terms Mathematics: Japanese-English, English-Japanese. Ministry of Education. 146p. (Japanese & Eng.). 1954. Leatherette 14.95 (ISBN 0-686-92202-6, M__9346). French & Eur.

Scientific Terms Meteorology: Japanese-English, English-Japanese. Ministry of Education. 140p. (Japanese & Eng.). 1975. Leatherette 19.95 (ISBN 0-686-92205-0, M-9338). French & Eur.

Scientific Terms Physics: Japanese-English, English-Japanese. Ministry of Education. 221p. (Japanese & Eng.). 1954. 14.95 (ISBN 0-686-92514-9, M-9343). French & Eur.

Scientific Terms Spectroscopy: Japanese-English, English-Japanese. Ministry of Education. 165p. (Japanese & Eng.). 1974. leatherette 14.95 (ISBN 0-686-92512-2, M-9341). French & Eur.

Scientist's Thesaurus. 4th ed. George F. Steffanides. 156p. 1978. pap. 3.00 (ISBN 0-9600114-0-4, TX-7-128). Steffanides.

Scots Dictionary. A. Warrack. LC 65-16666. (Alabama Linguistic & Philological Ser: Vol. 6). 717p. 1965. 25.00 (ISBN 0-8173-0400-2). U of Ala Pr.

Scots Word Book. 2nd ed. William Graham. LC 79-301141. 194p. (Eng.). 1978. E4.60 (ISBN 0-902859-47-1). Ramsay Head Pr.

Scots Words from Burns. LC 75-329215. 53p. 1976. 5.75x (ISBN 0-284-98564-3). Intl Pubns Serv.

Scott, Foresman Advanced Dictionary. rev. ed. Ed. by Clarence L. Barnhart. 1978. 19.95 (ISBN 0-385-14852-6). Doubleday.

Scott, Foresman Beginning Dictionary. Ed. by Clarence L. Barnhart. (Illus.). 15.95 (ISBN 0-385-13330-8). Doubleday.

Scott, Foresman Intermediate Dictionary. Ed. by Clarence L. Barnhart. (Illus.). 1978. 19.95 (ISBN 0-385-14853-4). Doubleday.

Scrabble Trade Mark Crossword Games Scorebook. Ed. by Running Press. 128p. (Orig.). 1980. lib. bdg. 12.90 (ISBN 0-89471-104-0); pap. 3.95 (ISBN 0-89471-105-9). Running Pr.

Screening Symbols, Terminology & Equations. 1974. 4.00 (003-4); members 2.67. TAPPI.

Scribner-Bantam English Dictionary. Ed. by Edwin B. Williams. 1979. pap. 2.25 (ISBN 0-553-13217-2, B14408-1). Bantam.

Sea Language Comes Ashore. Joanna C. Colcord. Ed. by Richard M. Dorsen. (International Folklore Ser.). 1977. Repr. of 1945 ed. lib. bdg. 12.00x (ISBN 0-405-10089-2). Ayer Co.

Sea Language Comes Ashore. Joanna C. Colcord. LC 45-966. 1945. pap. 5.00 (ISBN 0-87033-095-0). Cornell Maritime.

Second Barnhart Dictionary of New English. Clarence L. Barnhart et al. LC 79-6815. 1980. 19.95i (ISBN 0-06-010154-7, HarpT). Har-Row.

Second Browser's Dictionary: Native's Guide to the Unknown American Language. John Ciardi. LC 82-48658. 420p. 1983. 16.30i (ISBN 0-06-015125-0, HarpT). Har-Row.

Second Edition of the Dictionary Catalog of the Music Collection. Research Libraries of the New York Public Library. 1983. lib. bdg. 6000.00 (ISBN 0-8161-0374-7, Hall Library). G K Hall.

See it-Say it in Spanish. Margarita Madrigal. (Span.). 1.50. Camino Real.

Seemaennisches Woerterbuch. Wolfram Claviez. (Ger.). 1973. 38.50 (ISBN 3-7688-0166-7, M-7620, Pub. by Delius, Klaving & Co.). French & Eur.

Select Glossary of English Words Used Formerly in Senses Different from Their Present. Richard C. Trench. Ed. by A. Smythe Palmer. 1979. Repr. of 1906 ed. lib. bdg. 25.00 (ISBN 0-8495-5138-2). Arden Lib.

Selective English Old-French Glossary As a Basis for Studies in Old French Onomatology & Synonymics. Joseph P. Murray. LC 77-128932. (Carl Ser.: No. 40). (Fr. & Eng.). Repr. of 1950 ed. 16.00 (ISBN 0-404-50340-3). AMS Pr.

Semantica Guatemala O Diccionario De Guatemaltequisma, 2 vols. Lisandro Sandoval. (Span.). 1941-1942. 85.00ea. Intl Guatemala.

Semantische Struktur Desubstantivischer Bildungen auf Maessig. Goran Inghult. LC 76-458533. 206p. (Ger.). 1975. Kr.50.00. Almqvist.

Semiiazychnyi Slovar Po Elektrosviazi. 708p. (Eng. , Fr. , Rus. , Ger. , Span. , Ital. & Dutch.). 1966. 7.95 (Pub. by Sov. Entsiklopediia). Four Continent.

Semiiazychnyi Slovar Po Mekhanike Gruntov & Fundamentostroeniiu. M. E. Sceneider. 139p. (Rus. & Span. & Eng. & Fr., Ger. & Swedish.). 1958. 3.30 (Pub. by Gosizdat Fizmat. Lit.). Four Continent.

Seminotique: Dictionnaire Raisonne de la Theorie du Language. Algirdas J. Greimas & Joseph Courtes. LC 80-462606. vi, 422p. (Fr.). 1979. 90.00 F (ISBN 2-010-05221-8). Hachette-Jeunesse.

Senarai istilah seni lukis, bahasa Inggeris-bahasa Malaysia. LC 81-940245. xi, 37p. (Eng. & Malay.). 1980. M.$1.20. Dewan Bahasa.

Septemligual Dictionary of the Names of European Animals, 2 vols. Laslo Gozmany. 2188p. 1980. 500.00x (ISBN 0-569-08577-2, Pub. by Collet's). State Mutual Bk.

Septemlingual Dictionary of the Names of European Animal, 2 vols. Ed. by L. Gozmany et al. (Eng., Rus., Span., Ger., Hungarian, Fr., & Lat.). 1979. Set. 230.00 (ISBN 0-9960010-0-X, Pub. by Kiado Hungary). Heyden.

Septemlingual Dictionary of the Names of European Animals, 2 vols. Ed. by Laszlo Gozmany. 2228p. 1979. Set. 200.00x (ISBN 963-05-1381-1). Intl Pubns Serv.

Serbocroatian-English Dictionary. M. Benson. 770p. (Serbocroatian & Eng.). 1980. 75.00 (ISBN 0-686-97438-7, M-9630). French & Eur.

Serbocroatian-English Dictionary. Ed. by Morton Benson. LC 79-146959. (Eng. & Serbocroatian.). 1971. text ed. 37.50x (ISBN 0-8122-7636-1). U of Pa Pr.

Serbocroatian-English Dictionary. S. Brkic. 416p. (Serbocroatian & Eng.). 1980. pap. 14.95 (ISBN 0-686-97436-0, M-9631). French & Eur.

Serbocroatian-English Dictionary. M. Drvodelic. 847p. (Serbocroatian & Eng.). 1978. 49.95 (ISBN 0-686-92510-6, M-9707). French & Eur.

Serbocroatian-English, English-Serbocroatian Dictionary. Rev. & enl. ed. B. Grujic. (Serbocroatian & Eng.). 25.00 (ISBN 0-685-65374-9). Heinman.

Serbocroatian-English-Serbocroatian Dictionary: Short Grammar. 33rd ed. B. Grujic. 624p. (Serbocroatian & Eng.). 1982. text ed. 18.00x (ISBN 0-89918-647-5, Y-647). Vanous.

Serbocroatian-Slovene Dictionary. J. Jurancic. 1320p. (Serbocroatian & Slovene.). 1972. 49.95 (ISBN 0-686-92509-2, M-9698). French & Eur.

Seven Hundred Russian Idioms & Set Phrases. N. Shansky & E. Bystrova. (Russkii iazyk Ser.). 120p. (Rus. & Eng.). 1980. 1.50. Four Continent.

Seven Language Dictionary. Ed. by David Shumaker. LC 78-16509. 828p. (Eng., Fr., Ger., Hebrew, Ital., Port., & Rus.). 1978. write for info. (ISBN 0-517-26296-7). Crown.

Seven Languages Dictionary. 829p. (Fr. , Ger. , Hebrew, Ital. , Port. , Rus. & Span.). 1978. 10.50. Imported Bks.

Seventy Steps to Vocabulary Power. rev., 2nd ed. Keith D. Holmes. (Illus.). 100p. (Orig.). 1983. pap. text ed. 4.95 per box (ISBN 0-9608250-1-0). Educ Serv Pub.

Sexual Nomenclature: A Thesaurus. Indiana University, Institute for Sex Research. 1976. lib. bdg. 95.00 (ISBN 0-8161-0044-6, Hall Library). G K Hall.

Shakespeare - Lexicon: A Complete Dictionary of All the English Words, Phrases & Constructions in the Works of the Poet, 2 vols. rev., enl. 6th ed. Alexander Schmidt. Ed. by Gregor Sarrazin. 1971. 98.50x (ISBN 3-11-002203-6). De Gruyter.

Shakespeare Lexicon: A Complete Dictionary of All the English Words, Phrases & Constructions in the Work of the Poet, 2 Vols. Alexander Schmidt. Ed. by Gregor Sarrazin. LC 67-30463. 1968. Repr. of 1901 ed. Set. 86.00 (ISBN 0-405-08935-X); 43.00 ea. Vol. 1 (ISBN 0-405-08936-8). Vol. 2 (ISBN 0-405-08937-6). Ayer Co.

Shakespeare Word-Book, Being a Glossary of Archaic Forms & Varied Usages of Words Employed by Shakespeare. Compiled by John Foster. LC 68-15123. 1969. Repr. of 1908 ed. 17.50x (ISBN 0-8462-1234-X). Russell.

Shakespeare's Vocabulary: Its Etymological Elements. Eilert Ekwall. LC 78-166013. Repr. of 1903 ed. 14.75 (ISBN 0-404-02269-3). AMS Pr.

Shakhmatnyi Slovar. Ed. by L. Ia. Abramov. 618p. (Rus.). 1964. 5.00 (Pub. by Fiz. & Sport). Four Continent.

Sheet Metal Forming see Dictionary of Production Engineering: German-English-French.

Shevchenkovskii Slovar: Na Ukrainskom Iazyke, 2 vols. (Rus.). 16.75 (Pub. by Poligrafkniga). Four Continent.

Shkol' Nyi Slovoobrazovatel Nyi' Slovar' Z. A. Potikha. (Prosveshchenie Ser.). 390p. (Rus.). 1964. 1.95. Four Continent.

Shkol' Nyi Slovoobrazovatel Nyi' Slovar' Russkogo Iazyka: Posobie dlia Uchaschikhsia. A. N. Tikhonov. (Prosveshchenie Ser.). 728p. (Rus.). 1977. 3.95. Four Continent.

Shkolnyi Slovo-Obrazovatel'Nyislovar Russkogo Iazyka. A. N. Tikhonov. 728p. (Rus.). 1978. 3.95 (Pub. by Prosveschchenie). Four Continent.

Shkol'nyi Slovoobrazovatel'Nyi Slovar. Z. A. Potikha. Ed. by S. G. Barkhudarov. 390p. (Rus.). 1964. pap. text ed. 1.65 Rub (Pub. by Proveschchenie). Four Continent.

Shogakukan Iwa Chujiten: Comprehensive Italian-Japanese Dictionary. 1744p. (Ital. & Japanese.). 1983. 5800.00 Yen. Shogakukan.

Shogakukan Random House Eiwa Daijiten. 3072p. (Eng. & Japanese.). 1979. 9800.00 Yen. Shogakukan.

Short Bengali-English, English-Bengali Dictionary. 3rd ed. Jack A. Dabbs. LC 78-149931. (Bengali & Eng.). Date not set. 4.00 (ISBN 0-911494-01-4). Dabbs.

Short Bengali-English, English-Bengali Dictionary. 3rd ed. Jack A. Dabbs. LC 78-149931. 5.00 (ISBN 0-911494-01-4). Dabbs.

Short Dictionary of Eighteenth Century Russian. Charles E. Gribble. (Rus.). 1976. soft cover 8.95 (ISBN 0-89357-039-7). Slavica.

Short Dictionary of Furniture. John Gloag. 1976. pap. 14.95 (ISBN 0-04-749009-8). Allen Unwin.

Short Dictionary of Science Terms for Swahili Speakers. James L. Brain. (Foreign & Comparative Studies Program, African Special Publications: No. 4). 70p. (Orig., Swahili.). 1969. pap. text ed. 4.50x (ISBN 0-686-74011-4). Syracuse U Foreign Comp.

Short Dictionary of Simplified Chinese Characters. 3rd ed. E. W. Jameson, Jr. (Chinese & Eng.). 1975. pap. 6.95 (ISBN 0-9606576-2-2). E W Jameson Jr.

Short Handbook of Literary Terms. George G. Loane. LC 72-188273. 1972. lib. bdg. 15.00 (ISBN 0-8414-0600-6). Folcroft.

Short Old French Dictionary for Students. Ed. by Kenneth Urwin. 108p. (Fr.). 1972. pap. 7.50x (ISBN 0-631-07970-X, Pub. by Basil Blackwell). Biblio Dist.

Shorter Dictionary of English Furniture. Ralph Edwards. (Illus.). 684p. (Eng.). E50.00 (ISBN 0-600-43082-0). Newnes Bks.

Shorter Lexicon of the Greek New Testament. Ed. by F. Wilbur Gingrich. LC 65-24434. 1965. 10.00x (ISBN 0-226-29520-6). U of Chicago Pr.

Shorter Oxford English Dictionary. 1973. 125.00 (ISBN 0-19-861126-9); 2 vols. indexed ed. 135.00 (ISBN 0-19-861127-7). Oxford U Pr.

Shorter Redhouse Turkish-English Dictionary. (Turkish & Eng.). 1971. 11.50x (ISBN 0-686-16858-5). Intl Learn Syst.

Shorter Technological Dictionary: English-Polish, Polish-English. (Pol. & Eng.). 7.95 (Pub. by Wydaw. Naukowo-Tech.). Four Continent.

Shorthand Guide to Legal Terminology. 1982 ed. 700p. 7.00. Gould.

Shuter's New Basic English Dictionary for Xhosa Speakers. H. L. Nabel et al. LC 81-455769. (Illus.). viii, 246p. 1979. R.pap. 2.85 (ISBN 0-86985-423-2). Shuter & Shooter.

Siamese-English Dictionary. Edward B. Michell. (Siamese & Eng.). 1976. Repr. of 1958 ed. 39.50 (ISBN 0-518-19004-8). Ayer Co.

Siebenbuergisch-Saechsisches Woerterbuch, 3 vols. Incl. Vol. 1 (a-c) 851p. 1924. 61.00x (ISBN 3-11-009500-9); Vol 2 (d-f) 548p. 1911-25. 35.50x (ISBN 3-11-009501-7); Vol 3 (g). 355p. 1971. 42.25x (ISBN 3-11-003707-6). (Ger.). De Gruyter.

Siglas & Abreviaturas Latinas con su Significado por Orden Alfabetico de un Catalogo de las Abreviaturas. Ramon Alvarez de la Brana. LC 78-366525. xi, 215p. (Lat.). 1978. write for info. (ISBN 3-487-06454-5). Olms Verlag.

Signed English Dictionary. Harry Bornstein. LC 75-24685. (Signed English Ser.). (Illus.). 306p. 1975. 17.50 (ISBN 0-913580-46-5). Gallaudet Coll.

Signet Hebrew-English - English-Hebrew Dictionary. Dov Ben Abba. (Orig., Hebrew & Eng.). 1978. pap. 2.95 (ISBN 0-451-09654-1, E9654, Sig). NAL.

Signing Exact English. 1980 ed. Gerilee Gustason et al. LC 80-80571. (Illus.). 460p. (gr. k-12). 1980. text ed. 24.00x (ISBN 0-916708-02-0); pap. text ed. 18.00x (ISBN 0-916708-03-9). Modern Signs.

Silikatova Technika. Armin Petzold. LC 80-490689. 271p. (Eng., Rus. & Slovak.). 1977. 47.00 Kcs. Alfa-Vydavatel.

Silver Collector's Glossary & a List of Early American Silversmiths & Their Marks. Hollis French. LC 67-27454. (Architecture & Decorative Art Ser). 1967. lib. bdg. 19.50 (ISBN 0-306-70969-4). Da Capo.

Silver Flatware Dictionary. Richard F. Osterberg & Betty Smith. LC 78-75323. (Illus.). 288p. 1979. 12.00 (ISBN 0-498-02327-3). A S Barnes.

Simon & Schuster Gem Ben-Yehuda's Hebrew-English & English-Hebrew Dictionary. (Hebrew & Eng.). write for info. vinyl jacket (ISBN 0-671-46098-6). S&S.

Simon & Schuster International Dictionary: English-Spanish, Spanish-English. (Eng. & Span.). 1973. thumb-indexed 15.95 (ISBN 0-671-21267-2). S&S.

Simon & Schuster's Concise International Dictionary. Ed. by Tana De Gamez. LC 74-33235. xvii, 1379p. (Eng. & Span.). 1975. 12.95 (ISBN 0-671-22020-9). S & S.

Simon & Schuster's International Dictionary English-Spanish. 1065p. (Eng. & Span.). 29.95. Lectorum Pubns.

Simon & Schuster's International Dictionary: English-Spanish & Spanish-English. 1632p. (Eng. & Span.). thumb-indexed 39.95 (ISBN 0-671-21267-2). S&S.

Simple Chinese Conversation. Jianyi H. Huihua. (Chinese.). pap. 6.50 (ISBN 0-87557-010-0, 010-0). Saphrograph.

Simplified Medical Dictionary. Franks. (Medical Economics Books). 1977. 12.50x (ISBN 0-442-84028-4). Van Nos Reinhold.

Singers Glossary of Show Business Jargon. Al Berkman. 1961. 3.00 (ISBN 0-934972-06-0). Melrose Pub Co.

Sinonimus Castellanos. 17th ed. Roque Barcia. 590p. (Span.). 1978. 27.50 (ISBN 0-686-56660-2, S-11889). French & Eur.

Six Language Dictionary of Welding Technique. Alfred Dollinger. LC 75-591161. 1974. 45.00x (ISBN 0-8002-0400-X). Intl Pubns Serv.

Six Thousand Words: A Supplement to Webster's Third New International Dictionary. Ed. by Merriam Webster Editorial Staff. 240p. 1976. 8.50 (ISBN 0-87779-007-8). Merriam-Webster Inc.

Six Thousand Words: No. 76. 8.50 (ISBN 0-87779-007-8). Ency Brit Ed.

Six Thousand Words: Supplement to Webster's Third New International Dictionary. (Eng.). 1976. 8.50 (ISBN 0-87779-007-8, 72422). Merriam.

Skogsordlista. Tekniska Nomenklaturcentralen. LC 80-485348. 676p. (Eng. & Swedish.). 1978. write for info. (ISBN 9-1719-6071-6). Tek Nomen.

Skolni Rusko-Cesky Slovnik. Karel Horalek. LC 79-389285. 1263p. (Rus. & Czech.). 1977. 54.00 Kcs. SNTC.

Skolni Rusko-Cesky Slovnik, 2 vols. 6th ed. Ed. by L. V. Kopeckeho. LC 77-551653. xvi, 1134p. (Rus. & Czech.). 1976. 54.00 Kcs. SNTC.

Skolordlista. 353p. (Swedish.). 1980. write for info. (ISBN 91-24-30599-5). Esselte Studium.

Slang & Euphemism: Abridged Edition. Richard A. Spears. 1982. pap. 4.50 (ISBN 0-451-11889-8, AE1889, Sig). NAL.

Slaovosochetaniia Russkogo Iazyka. 368p. (Rus.). 1979. 5.95 (Pub. by Russkii Iazyk). Four Continent.

Slitno Ili Razdelno. B. Z. Buchkina et al. 480p. (Rus.). 1976. 2.40 (Pub. by Russkii Iazyk). Four Continent.

Slovak-English Business Correspondence Dictionary. Dusan Zavada. 560p. (Slovak & Eng.). 1980. 30.00 (ISBN 0-569-08524-1, Pub. by Collet's). State Mutual Bk.

Slovak-English Dictionary. 3rd ed. Vilikovska. (Slovak & Eng.). 1971. text ed. 10.00x (ISBN 0-89918-259-3, C259). Vanous.

Slovak-English Dictionary. J. Vilikovska & P. Vilikovsky. 522p. (Slovak & Eng.). 1980. 39.50x (ISBN 0-569-08530-6, Pub. by Collet's). State Mutual Bk.

Slovak-English Dictionary. J. Vilikovska & Jan Vilkovsky. (Slovak & Eng.). 24.50 (ISBN 0-87559-041-1); thumb indexed 29.50 (ISBN 0-87559-042-X). Shalom.

Slovak-English, English-Slovak Dictionary. 791p. (Slovak & Eng.). 1981. 14.95 (ISBN 0-88254-543-4, Pub. by Slovart Czechoslovakia). Hippocrene Bks.

Slovak-English-Slovak Pocket Dictionary. J. Smejkalova et al. (Slovak & Eng.). 1979. text ed. 9.50x (ISBN 0-89918-170-8, C170). Vanous.

Slovak-Russian Dictionary. D. Kollar et al. 768p. (Slovak & Rus.). 1976. 22.75 (ISBN 0-686-92504-1, M-9076). French & Eur.

Slovar Angliishkikh & Amerikanskikh Sokrashchenii. V. O. Bluvshtein. 767p. (Eng. & Rus.). 1957. 4.50 (Pub. by GINS). Four Continent.

Slovar Angliiskogo Proiznosheniia. D. Dzhouiz. 538p. (Eng.). 1963. 3.85 (Pub. by GINS). Four Continent.

Slovar Anglo-Amerikanskikh Sokrashchenii Po Aviatsionnoi & Raketno-Kosmicheskoi Tekhnike. A. M. Murashkevich. 440p. (Rus. & Eng.). 1969. 5.50 (Pub. by Voenizdat). Four Continent.

Slovar' Antonimov Russkogo Iazyka. M. R. L'Vov. (Russkii iazyk Ser.). 400p. (Rus.). 1978. 4.75. Four Continent.

Slovar Antonimov Russkogo Iazyka. 400p. (Rus.). 1978. 4.75 (Pub. by Russkii Iazyk). Four Continent.

Slovar Assotsiativnykh Norm Russkogo Iazyka. A. A. Leontev. 192p. (Rus.). 1977. 2.25 (Pub. by MGU). Four Continent.

Slovar Ekonomicheskikh Terminov. 598p. (Rus.). 1975. 3.60 (Pub. by Liesma). Four Continent.

Slovar Epitetov Russkogo Literaturnogo Iazyka. S. Gorbachevich et al. 568p. (Rus.). 1979. 7.95 (Pub. by Nauka). Four Continent.

Slovar Gidronimov Ukrainy. 784p. (Ukrainian.). 1978. 12.95 (Pub. by Naukova Dumka). Four Continent.

Slovar Iazyka Pushkina, 4 vols. (Rus.). 1961. 40.00 set (Pub. by GINS). Four Continent.

Slovar' Inostrannykh Slov. I. V. Lekhin et al. (Russkii iazyk Ser.). 622p. (Rus.). 1980. 8.95 (O-133). Four Continent.

Slovar Inostrannykh Slov. (Rus.). 1979. 8.95. Russki Iazyk.

Slovar Naibolee Upotrebitel'Nykh Slov Anglii-Skogo, Nemetskogo & Frantsuzskogo Iazykov. Ed. by I. V. Rakhmanov. 582p. (Rus., Ger. & Fr.). 1960. 2.40 (Pub. by Izd. Inostr. & Natsional'Nal'Nykh Slovarei). Four Continent.

Slovar Narodnykh Govorov Zapadnoi Brianshchiny. P. A. Rastorguev. 293p. (Rus.). 1973. 2.35 (Pub. by Nauka). Four Continent.

Slovar Nemetskikh Sokrashchenii. V. O. Bluvshtein. 442p. (Rus.). 1958. 2.25 (Pub. by GINS). Four Continent.

Slovar Obshchegeo graficheskikh Terminov, 2 vols. L. Stamp & A. S. Perevod. (Rus.). 1974. 14.95 set (Pub. by Progress). Four Continent.

Slovar Omonimov Russkogo Iazyka. O. S. Akhmanova. 448p. (Rus.). 1974. 3.25 (Pub. by Sov. Entsiklopediia). Four Continent.

Slovar' Omonimov Russkogo Iazyka. N. P. Kolesnikov. (Izd. Un-ta Ser.). 632p. (Rus.). 1978. 6.50 (O-112). Four Continent.

Slovar Osnovnykh Voennykh Terminov. 248p. (Rus.). 1965. 2.85 (Pub. by Voenizdat). Four Continent.

Slovar Po Etike. 392p. (Rus.). 1975. 2.90 (Pub. by Politizdat). Four Continent.

Slovar Po Kibernetike. 624p. (Rus.). 1979. 8.95 (Pub. by Sov. Entsiklopediia). Four Continent.

Slovar Po Mineral Nomu Syriu Dlia Promyshlennosti Stroitelnykh Materialov. M. V. Grigorovich et al. 87p. (Rus.). 1976. 1.35 (Pub. by Nedra). Four Continent.

Slovar PsevdonimovRusskikh Pisatelei: Uchenykh & Obshchestvennykh Deiatelei, 4 vols. I. F. Masanov. (Rus.). 1960. 35.00 set (Pub. by Izd. Vsesoiuzn Knizhn Palaty). Four Continent.

Slovar Russkikh Govorov Novosibirskoi Oblasti. 604p. (Rus.). 1979. 15.95 (Pub. by Nauka). Four Continent.

Slovar Russkikh Govorov Zabaikalia. L. E. Eliasov. 477p. (Rus.). 1980. 16.75 (Pub. by Nauka). Four Continent.

Slovar Russkikh Narodnykh Govorov, Vol. 4. 355p. (Rus.). 1969. 4.25 (Pub. by Nauka). Four Continent.

Slovar Russkikh Narodnykh Govorov, Vol. 5. 358p. (Rus.). 1970. 3.95 (Pub. by Nauka). Four Continent.

Slovar Russkikh Narodnykh Govorov, Vol. 6. 358p. (Rus.). 1970. 3.95 (Pub. by Nauka). Four Continent.

Slovar Russkikh Narodnykh Govorov, Vol. 7. 355p. (Rus.). 1972. 3.95 (Pub. by Nauka). Four Continent.

Slovar Russkikh Narodnykh Govorov, Vol. 8. 369p. (Rus.). 1972. 5.25 (Pub. by Nauka). Four Continent.

Slovar Russkikh Narodnykh Govorov, Vol. 9. 362p. (Rus.). 1972. 4.75 (Pub. by Nauka). Four Continent.

Slovar Russkikh Narodnykh Govorov, Vol. 10. 388p. (Rus.). 1974. 4.75 (Pub. by Nauka). Four Continent.

Slovar Russkikh Narodnykh Govorov, Vol. 11. 364p. (Rus.). 1975. 4.00 (Pub. by Nauka). Four Continent.

Slovar Russkikh Narodnykh Govorov, Vol. 12. 368p. (Rus.). 1977. 6.25 (Pub. by Nauka). Four Continent.

Slovar Russkikh Narodnykh Govorov, Vol. 14. 372p. (Rus.). 1978. 7.25 (Pub. by Nauka). Four Continent.

Slovar Russkikh Narodnykh Govorov, Vol. 15. 440p. (Rus.). 1979. 7.50 (Pub. by Nauka). Four Continent.

Slovar Russkikh Narodnykh Govorov, Vol. 16. 376p. (Rus.). 1980. 7.25 (Pub. by Nauka). Four Continent.

Slovar Russko-Suakhili Gazetnoi Leksiki. A. I. Kutuzov. 174p. (Rus. & Swahili.). 1963. 2.10 (Pub. by In-Tut Mezhdunarod. Otnoshenii). Four Continent.

Slovar Russkogo Iazyka. S. I. Ozhegov. 848p. (Rus.). 1977. 10.50 (Pub. by Russkii Iazyk). Four Continent.

Slovar Russkogo Iazyka XI-XVII: E-zinutie, Vol. 5. (Rus.). 8.95 (Pub. by Nauka). Four Continent.

Slovar Russkogo Iazyka XI-XVII: G-diatchiti, Vol. 4. (Rus.). 10.95 (Pub. by Nauka). Four Continent.

Slovar Russkogo Iazyka XI-XVII: Zipun-iianuarii, Vol.6. (Rus.). 7.95 (Pub. by Nauka). Four Continent.

Slovar Russkogo Iazyka XVIII Veka. 165p. (Orig., Rus.). 1977. 2.50 (Pub. by Nauka). Four Continent.

Slovar Russkoi Onomasticheskoi Terminologii. N. V. Podolskaia. 200p. (Rus.). 1978. 2.40 (Pub. by Nauka). Four Continent.

Slovar Semiletki. Ed. by S. G. Strumilin. 397p. (Rus.). 1960. 1.95 (Pub. by Politizdat). Four Continent.

Slovar Simonimov Russkogo Iazyka, Vol. 2. 854p. (Rus.). 1971. 5.95 (Pub. by Nauka). Four Continent.

Slovar Sinonimov Russkogo Iazyka. Z. E. Aleksandrova. 600p. (Rus.). 1968. 3.75 (Pub. by Sov. Entsiklopediia). Four Continent.

Slovar' Sinonimov Russkogo Iazyka. Cheshko. Ed. by Z. E. Aleksandrova. 600p. (Rus.). 1968. 3.75 (90, 93, 94, 95). Four Continent.

Slovar Sokrashchenii Po Informatike. 406p. (Rus.). 1974. 9.75 (Pub. by Izd. Mexdunarod. Tsentral' Nauchin. & Tekhn. Informatsii). Four Continent.

Slovar Sovremennogo Russkogo Literaturnogo Iazyka: I-K, Vol. 5. 1915p. (Rus.). 1956. 15.00 (Pub. by An Arm SSR). Four Continent.

Slovar Sovremennogo Russkogo Literaturnogo Iazyka: O, Vol. 8. 1840p. (Rus.). 1959. 15.00 (Pub. by An Arm SSR). Four Continent.

Slovar Sovremennogo Russkogo Literaturnogo Iazyka: Zh-Z, Vol. 4. 1363p. (Rus.). 1955. 15.00 (Pub. by An Arm SSR). Four Continent.

Slovar-Spravochni k Lingvisticheskikh Terminov. D. E. Rozental et al. 544p. (Rus.). 1976. 3.50 (Pub. by Prosveschchenie). Four Continent.

Slovar Spravochnik Nazvanii Obraztsov Vooruzheniia & Boevoi Tekhniki Kapitalisticheskikh Stran & Osnovnykh Firm Proizvodiashikh Vooruzhenie. V. D. Kurochkin et al. 200p. (Rus.). 1966. 1.50 (Pub. by Voenizdat). Four Continent.

Slovar' Spravochnik po Russkomu Iazyku Dlia Inostrantsev. (MGU Ser.). 128p. (Rus.). 1976. 0.85. Four Continent.

Slovar Terminov Pedagogiki. 472p. (Latvian & Rus.). 1978. 4.50 (Pub. by Liesma). Four Continent.

Slovar Terminov PoElektroprovodu & Avtomatizatsii Promyshlennykh Ustanovo. 154p. (Rus. & Eng. & Azerbaidian.). 1966. 2.70 (Pub. by Izd. An Az. SSR). Four Continent.

Slovar Trudnostei Russkogo Iazyka. D. E. Rozental et al. (Russkii iazyk Ser.). 694p. (Rus.). 1981. 5.95. Four Continent.

Slovari Inostrannykh Iazykov v Russkom Azbukovnikeveka. M. P. Alekseev. 156p. (Rus.). 1968. 3.50 (Pub. by Nauka). Four Continent.

Slovarnyi Ukazatel Po Knigovedeniiu. A. V. Mezer. 927p. (Rus.). 1924. 11.00 (Pub. by Kolos). Four Continent.

Slovene-English Dictionary. 5th ed. J. Kotnick. (Slovenian & Eng.). 37.50 (ISBN 0-87559-035-7); thumb indexed 42.00 (ISBN 0-87559-036-5). Shalom.

Slovene-English Dictionary. J. Kotnik. 831p. (Slovene & Eng.). 1978. 35.00 (ISBN 0-686-92508-4, M-9694). French & Eur.

Slovene-English, English-Slovene Dictionary, 2 vols. new ed. J. Kotnik & A. Grad. (Slovene & Eng.). Set. 75.00 (ISBN 0-685-55016-8). Heinman.

Slovene-German Dictionary. F. Tomsic. 768p. (Slovene & Ger.). 1977. 35.00 (ISBN 0-686-92505-X, M-9697). French & Eur.

Slovnik Staroukrainskoi Movi XVI-XV, 2 vols. (Ukrainian.). 1978. 29.95 (Pub. by Naukova Dumka). Four Continent.

Slovnik Ukrainskoi Movi: I-M, Vol. 6. (Ukrainian.). 1973. 11.75 (Pub. by Naukova Dumka). Four Continent.

Slovnik Ukrainskoi Movi: N-O, Vol. 5. (Ukrainian.). 1974. 11.75 (Pub. by Naukova Dumka). Four Continent.

Slovnik Ukrainskoi Movi: P-Poiti. (Ukrainian.). 1975. 11.75 (Pub. by Naukova Dumka). Four Continent.

Slovnik Ukrainskoi Movi: Poikhati-Prirobliati, Vol. 7. (Ukrainian.). 1976. 15.75 (Pub. by Naukova Dumka). Four Continent.

Slovnik Ukrainskoi Movi: Priroda-Riakhtlivii, Vol. 8. (Ukrainian.). 1977. 15.75 (Pub. by Naukova Dumka). Four Continent.

Slovnik Ukrainskoi Movi: S, Vol. 9. (Ukrainian.). 1978. 18.95 (Pub. by Naukova Dumka). Four Continent.

Slovnik Ukrainskoi Movi: Z, Vol. 3. (Ukranian.). 1972. 11.75 (Pub. by Naukova). Four Continent.

Slovnik Ukrainskoi: T-F, Vol. 10. (Ukrainian.). 1979. 15.95 (Pub. by Naukova Dumka). Four Continent.

Slovnik Zakladnich Odbornych Cesko-Nemeckych Vyrazu ze Silnicni a Mestske Dopravy. Jindrich Mrazek. LC 75-545516. 215p. (Czech. & Ger., Praha, Czechoslovakia). 1975. write for info. SNTL.

Slovnik Zakladnich Odbornych Rusko-Ceskych Vyrazu ze Silnicni a Mestske Dopravy. Jarom Cvrcek. LC 77-484205. 260p. (Rus. & Czech.). 1976. write for info. SNTC.

Slovosochetaniia Russkogo Iazyka. 368p. (Rus.). 1979. 5.95 (Pub. by Russkii Iazyk). Four Continent.

Slownictwie Statystycznie Rzadkim. Jadwiga Sambor. LC 75-406998. 113p. (Eng & Pol.). 1975. 30.00 Zl. Panstwowe Zaklad W.

Slownik Elektroniczny Polsko-Angielsko-Rosyjski. Ewa Sozanskiej. LC 78-384390. vii, 254p. (Eng., Pol. & Rus.). 1977. 100.00 Zl. Wydawnictwa Naukowo.

Slownik Finsko-Polski. Stanislaw Walega. LC 78-376750. 658p. (Finnish & Pol.). 1978. Fmk.135.00. Wiedza Powszechna.

Slownik Immunologiczny Ilustrowany. Stefan Slopek. LC 77-567783. 339p. (Pol.). 1977. 120.00 Zl. Panstowy Zaklad W.

Slownik Informatyki Polsko-Angielsko-Rosyjski. LC 77-469027. 159p. (Eng. , Rus. & Pol.). 1976. 50.00 Zl. Wydawnictwa Naukowo.

Slownik Jezyka Niby-Polskiego, Czyli Bledy Jezykowe. W. Pisarek. 176p. (Pol.). 1978. 3.95 (Pub. by Ossolineum). Four Continent.

Slownik Jezyka Polskiego dia Cudzoziemcow. Stanislawa Hrabcowa et al. LC 80-485792. viii, 445p. (Pol., Warsaw, Poland). 1979. 50.00 Zl. Wydaw-a UW.

Slownik Kieszonkowy Polsko-Rosyjski. Inessa N. Mironova. LC 80-450178. 575p. (Pol. & Rus.). 1978. 1.00 Rub. Russkii Iazyk.

Slownik Lekarski Lacinsko-Polski. Jerzy Babecki. LC 80-468620. 855p. (Lat. & Pol.). 1979. 350.00 Zl (ISBN 8-3200-0184-6). Panstwowe Zaklad W.

Slownik Lekarski Polsko-Angielski. Sabian Jedraszko. LC 76-511367. 410p. (Eng. & Pol.). 1975. 150.00 Zl. Panstwowy Zaklad W.

Slownik Lekarski Polsko-Niemiecki. Boleslaw Zlotnicki. LC 79-389560. 674p. (Ger. & Pol.). 1979. 350.00 Zl (ISBN 8-3200-0152-8). Panstwowe Zaklad W.

Slownik Minimum Francusko-Polski. Leon Bielas. LC 77-502306. 558p. (Pol. & Fr.). 1976. 30.00 Zl. Wiedza Powszechna.

Slownik Podstawowy Jezyka Polskiego dia Cudzoziemcow. Barbara Bartnicka & Roxana Sinielnikoff. LC 79-361030. (Illus.). 342p. (Pol., Warsaw). 1978. 100.00 Zl. Wydaw-a U. W.

Slownik Podstawowy Jezyka Polskiego dia Cudzoziemcow. Barbara Bartnicka et al. LC 79-361030. 342p. (Pol., Warsaw, Poland). 1978. 100.00 Zl. Wydaw-a UW.

Slownik Polskiej Terminologii Chemicznej. Antoni Basinski. LC 75-404572. 278p. (Pol.). 1975. write for info. Wydawnictwa Naukowo.

Slownik Polsko-Rosyjski. Ryszard Stypula et al. LC 76-531554. 840p. (Pol. & Rus.). 1976. 2.58 Rub. Wiedza Powszechna.

Slownik Poprawnej Polszczyzny. Ed. by W. Doroszewski. 1055p. (Pol.). 1977. 22.50 (Pub. by Panstwowe Wydawnictwo Naukowe). Four Continent.

Slownik Skrotow w Medycynie i Naukach Pokrewnych. Jerzy Babecki & Anna Maksys. LC 76-526887. 239p. (Pol.). 1976. 100.00 Zl. Panstwowe Zaklad W.

Slownik Tekarski Polsko-Lacinksi. Jerzy Babecki. LC 79-361211. (Pol. & Lat.). 1978. 250.00 Zl. Panstwowe Zaklad W.

Slownik Terminologiczny Sztuk Pieknych. 2d ed. Stefana Kozaklewicz. LC 76-529202. (Illus.). 522p. (Pol.). 1976. 120.00 Zl. Panstwowe Wydawnicto Iskry.

Slownik Terminow z Zakresu Informatyki. Bronislawa Lenczewska. LC 77-557144. 116p. (Eng & Pol.). 1977. 15.00 Zl. Politekens Forlag.

Slownik Wspolczesnego T Atru: Tworcy, Teatry, Teorie. E. Wysinska. 424p. (Pol.). 1979. 12.95 (Pub. by Wydaw. Artystyczne & Filmowe). Four Continent.

Small Craft Dictionary. R. De Kerchove. Date not set. price not set (ISBN 0-442-21890-7); pap. price not set (ISBN 0-442-25420-2). Van Nos Reinhold.

Smaller Slang Dictionary. Eric Partridge. 1968. 16.95 (ISBN 0-7100-1938-6); pap. 7.95 (ISBN 0-7100-8331-9). Routledge & Kegan.

Smith's Dictionary of the Bible, 4 vols. William Smith. 1981. Repr. 95.00 (ISBN 0-8010-8211-0). Baker Bk.

Smolenskaia Oblast: Slovar Spravochnik Kraeveda. 240p. (Rus.). 1978. 3.50 (Pub. by Rabochii). Four Continent.

Snaak Friisk: Interfriisk Leksikon. V. Tams Jorgensen. LC 78-398618. (Norwegian.). 1977. DM.7.50 (ISBN 3-88007-063-6). Verein Nord.

So Werd bei uns Geredd. Kurt Brautigam. LC 80-491003. 168p. (Ger.). 1979. DM.16.80 (ISBN 3-87804-072-5). SVA Verlag.

Social Aspects of Bilingualism in San Antonio, Texas see Webster's Third on Non-Standard Usage.

Social-Ethical Significance of Vocabulary. Gladys C. Schwesinger. LC 70-177806. (Columbia University. Teachers College. Contributions to Education: No. 211). Repr. of 1926 ed. 17.50 (ISBN 0-404-55211-0). AMS Pr.

Social Science Vocabulary of Swahili. James L. Brain. (Foreign & Comparative Studies Program, African Special Publications: No. 3). (Orig., Swahili.). 1968. pap. text ed. 3.50x (ISBN 0-686-74012-2). Syracuse U Foreign Comp.

Social Structure & Vocabularies of Discomfort: What Happened to Female Hysteria. Pauline Bart. (Reprinted from Journal of Health & Social Behavior, sept, 1968). 0.50. Know Inc.

Socialfoersaekringslexikon. Sigvard Classon. LC 75-577397. 142p. (Swedish.). 1975. Kr.22.00 (ISBN 9-138-01724-5). LiberFoerlag.

Society of Vehicle Safety & Environmental Terminology Handbook. Society of Automotive Engineers. 184p. 1976. 9.50 (ISBN 0-89883-370-1, HS-215); members 7.95. Soc Auto Engineers.

Solar Energy Dictionary. V. Daniel Hunt. (Illus.). 450p. 1982. 29.95 (ISBN 0-8311-1139-9). Indus Pr.

Soldier & Sailor Words & Phrases. Edward Fraser & John Gibbons. LC 68-30635. 1968. Repr. of 1925 ed. 40.00x (ISBN 0-8103-3281-7). Gale.

Solzhenitsyn's Peculiar Vocabulary, Russian-English Glossary. Vera V. Carpovich. LC 76-3932. (Rus. & Eng.). 1976. 15.00 (ISBN 0-911484-04-3). Tech Dict.

Some Royal Arch Terms Examined. Roy A. Wells. LC 79-301402. (Illus.). 64p. (Eng.). 1978. E2.95 (ISBN 0-85318-106-3). Lewis Ltd.

Some Technical Terms of Chinese Painting. Benjamin March. (Illus.). 1969. Repr. of 1935 ed. 8.00 (ISBN 0-8188-0068-2). Paragon.

Sommer-Schoenfeld, Management Dictionary, Deutsch-English: Fachwoerterbuch Fuer Betriebswirtschaft Wirtschafts-und Steuerrecht und Datenverarbeitung. 4th ed. 290p. (Ger. & Eng.). 1978. 24.50x (ISBN 3-11-002663-5). De Gruyter.

Songwriter's Rhyming Dictionary. Sammy Cahn. (Illus.). 224p. 1983. 17.95 (ISBN 0-87196-765-0). Facts on File.

Songwriters Rhyming Dictionary. Jane Whitfield. 1974. pap. 5.00 (ISBN 0-87980-293-6). Wilshire.

Soule's Dictionary of English Synonyms. Richard Soule. (gr. 8-12). pap. 2.95 (ISBN 0-553-14954-7). Bantam.

Sound: In Eight Languages. Ed. by R. W. Stephens. LC 74-16209. (International Dictionaries of Science & Technology Ser). 853p. 1974. 69.95 (ISBN 0-470-82200-7). Halsted Pr.

Southwestern Medical Dictionary: Spanish-English & English-Spanish. Margarita Kay. LC 76-54591. (Span. & Eng.). 1977. pap. text ed. 4.50 (ISBN 0-8165-0529-2). U of Ariz Pr.

Soviet & East European Political Dictionary. Barbara P. McCrea & Jack C. Plano. (Clio Dictionaries in Political Science Ser.: No. 4). 350p. (gr. 10-12). 1983. lib. bdg. 20.75 (ISBN 0-87436-333-0); pap. 10.75 (ISBN 0-87436-347-0). ABC-Clio.

Soviet Prison Camp Speech: A Survivor's Glossary. Ed. by Meyer Galler & Harlan E. Marquess. LC 75-176411. 216p. 1972. 25.00 (ISBN 0-299-06080-2). U of Wis Pr.

Soviet Prison Camp Speech: Supplement. Meyer Galler. LC 77-89596. (Rus.). 1977. 15.00x (ISBN 0-930232-01-1). Soviet Studies.

Soziologisches Woerterbuch. H. Schoeck. 400p. (Ger.). 1975. 7.95 (ISBN 0-686-56468-5, M-7622, Pub. by Herder). French & Eur.

Soziologisches Woerterbuch. H. Schoeck. 400p. (Ger.). 1975. 7.95. Herder.

Space Age Dictionary. 2nd ed. Charles McLaughlin. (Illus.). 1963. 11.95x (ISBN 0-442-05284-7). Van Nos Reinhold.

Span. see Annotated Bibliography of Technical & Specialized Dictionaries.

Spanende Werkzeugmaschinen, Deutsch-Englische Begriffserlauterungen und Kommentare. Henry G. Freeman. 617p. (Ger. & Eng., Machine Tools, German-English Explanations and Comments). 1973. 75.00 (ISBN 3-7736-5082-5, M-7624, Pub. by Verlag W. Girardet). French & Eur.

Spanende Werkzeugmaschinen, Deutsch-Englische Begriffserlauterungen und Kommentare. Henry G. Freeman. 617p. (Ger. & Eng.). 1973. 75.00 (ISBN 3-7736-5082-5). Girardet.

Spanisch, 2 vols. Incl. Teil I. Spanisch-Deutsch. Heinz M u06ller & G u06nther H a06nsch. 640p. DM.39.80 (03340); Teil II. Deutsch-Spanisch. Enrique Alvarez-Prada. 768p. DM.39.80 (04345). (Langenscheidts HandworterbucherSer.). (Span. & Ger.). DM.beide Teile in einem Band 72.00 (05340). Langenscheidt.

Spanisch, 2 vols. Incl. Teil I. Spanisch-Deutsch. rev. ed. Ed. by G. Haberkamp de Anton. 544p. 1980. DM.17.80 (10341); Teil II. Deutsch-Spanisch. D. H. Willers. 511p. DM.17.80 (10345). (Langenscheidts Taschenworterbucher Ser.). (Span. & Ger., Unter Berucksichtigung der Sudamerikanismen). DM.beide Teile in einem Band 26.80 (11341). Langenscheidt.

Spanisches Supplement Zu Medizinisches Woerterbuch. E. Veillon & A. Nobel. (Ger.). 1971. 48.00 (ISBN 3-456-00271-8, M-7623, Pub. by H. Huber Vlg.). French & Eur.

Spanisches Supplement Zu Medizinisches Woerterbuch. E. Veillon & A. Nobel. (Ger.). 1971. 48.00 (ISBN 3-456-00271-8). Huber.

Spanish Aide-Memoire: English-Spanish Vocabulary. T. Folley. pap. 6.50x (ISBN 0-392-08443-0, SpS). Sportshelf.

Spanish & English, English & Spanish Dictionary - Self Pronouncing. rev. ed. Ed. by Velazquez et al. LC 72-94281. (Span. & Eng.). 1973. thumb-indexed 20.95 (ISBN 0-13-615534-0). P-H.

Spanish & English Idioms: 2001 Modismos Espanoles & Ingleses. E. Savaiano & L. Wing. (Span. & Eng.). 1977. 6.95 (ISBN 0-8120-0438-8). Barron.

Spanish & English of the United States Hispanos. Tescher & Bills. (Span. & Eng.). 9.55. Camino Real.

Spanish & German Dictionary, 2 vols. Ed. by R. J. Slaby & R. Grossman. Incl. Vol. 1. Spanish-German. 17.00 (ISBN 0-8044-0581-6); Vol. 2. German-Spanish. 28.00 (ISBN 0-8044-0582-4). 2172p. (Span. & Ger.). Set. 45.00 (ISBN 0-8044-0580-8). Ungar.

Spanish Bilingual Dictionary. Lipton & Munoz. (Illus., Span. & Eng.). 3.95. Camino Real.

Spanish Bilingual Dictionary. Munoz Lipton. (Illus., Span. & Eng.). 3.95. Camino Real.

Spanish Bilingual Dictionary. (Span. & Eng.). (gr. 4-9). 4.95. Iaconi.

Spanish Bilingual Dictionary. (Span. & Eng.). write for info. (608-54). Pan Amer Pub.

Spanish Bilingual Dictionary: A Beginners Guide in Words & Pictures. Gladys Lipton & Olivia Munoz. LC 74-26654. (Span. & Eng.). (gr. 7-12). 1975. pap. text ed. 4.95 (ISBN 0-8120-0468-X). Barron.

Spanish Bilingual Dictionary: Compact Guide. rev. ed. Gladys Lipton & Olivia Munoz. LC 78-27770. (Illus., Span. & Eng.). (gr. 7-12). 1979. pap. 3.95 (ISBN 0-8120-2540-7). Barron.

Spanish Bilingual Dictionary: Diccionario Espanol-Ingles-Ingles-Espanol. 2nd ed. G. Lipton & O. Munoz. (Eng. & Span.). 1982. 3.95 (ISBN 0-8120-2540-7). Barron.

Spanish Concise Dictionary. Cassells. 1977. 9.95 (ISBN 0-02-052266-5). Macmillan.

Spanish Dictionary. G. H. Calvert. (Routledge Pocket Dictionaries Ser.). 560p. 1980. pap. 7.95 (ISBN 0-7100-0558-X). Routledge & Kegan.
Spanish Dictionary. M. H. Raventos. (Teach Yourself Ser.). (Span.). 1974. pap. 8.95 (ISBN 0-679-10230-2). McKay.
Spanish Dictionary. 320p. (Span.). Epap. 1.25 (ISBN 0-600-36565-4). Newnes Bks.
Spanish Duden, Pictorial Dictionary. (Illus.). 20.50 (ISBN 3-4110-0971-3). Adler.
Spanish-English & English-Spanish Dictionary. (Span. & Eng.). pap. 1.99 (ISBN 0-686-00482-5). Dennison.
Spanish-English Dictionary. Berlitz Editors. (Span. & Eng.). 1979. 4.95 (ISBN 0-02-964510-7, Berlitz). Macmillan.
Spanish-English Dictionary. Cassells. (Span. & Eng.). 1978. standard 17.95; index 19.95 (ISBN 0-02-052291-6). Macmillan.
Spanish-English Dictionary. Carlos Castillo & Otto F. Bond. (Span. & Eng.). 1981. pap. 3.50 (ISBN 0-671-47762-5). PB.
Spanish-English Dictionary. Ed. by P. Constantinou. (Span. & Eng.). 14.50 (ISBN 0-87559-033-0). Shalom.
Spanish-English Dictionary. 14.50 (ISBN 0-685-00817-7, 076-3). Saphrograph.
Spanish-English, English-Spanish. (Span. & Eng.). 8.95 (522660-6). Inst Mod Lang.
Spanish-English, English-Spanish Chemical Vocabulary. J. R. Barcelo. (Span. & Eng.). pap. 7.50 (ISBN 84-205-0696-6). Heinman.
Spanish-English, English-Spanish Commercial Dictionary. C. R. Orozco. (Span. & Eng.). 1969. 23.00 (ISBN 0-08-006381-0); pap. 12.00 (ISBN 0-08-006380-2). Pergamon.
Spanish-English, English-Spanish Commercial Dictionary: "the Secretary". rev. & enl. ed. A. Frias-Sucre Giraud. (Eng. & Span.). 17.50 (ISBN 8-4261-1223-4). Heinman.
Spanish-English, English-Spanish Crossword Puzzle Book. Lily Powell-Froissard. (Span. & Eng.). 1979. pap. 2.95 (ISBN 0-8065-0676-8). Citadel Pr.
Spanish-English, English-Spanish Dictionary, 2 Vols. U. Benedetto. (Span. & Eng.). Set. 100.00 (ISBN 8-4716-6211-6). Heinman.
Spanish-English, English-Spanish Dictionary. Rev. ed. Editions Berlitz. LC 78-78079. 355p. (Eng. & Span.). 1979. 2.95 (ISBN 0-02-964510-7). Macmillan.
Spanish-English, English-Spanish Dictionary. (Span. & Eng.). pap. 2.50 (ISBN 0-06-465027-8, DI 3, BN). B&N NY.
Spanish-English, English-Spanish Gem Dictionary. Ed. by R. F. Brown. (Gem Foreign Language Ser.). (Span. & Eng.). 1957. 2.95 (ISBN 0-00-458653-0, G4). Collins Pubs.
Spanish-English, English-Spanish Medical Guide. Howard H. Hirschhorn. (gr. 11 up). 1968. pap. text ed. 2.95 (ISBN 0-88345-157-3, 17429). Regents Pub.
Spanish-English Handbook. G. Howell & J. Perez Y Sabido. 1977. pap. 11.95 (ISBN 0-87489-073-X). Med Economics.
Spanish-English Idioms: 2001 Modisomos Espanoles & Ingleses (Pocket Size) E. Savaiano & L. Winget. (Span. & Eng.). 1976. 3.95 (ISBN 0-8120-0711-5). Barron.
Spanish-English-Spanish. (Berlitz Pocket Dictionaries Ser.). (Span. & Eng.). 4.95 (ISBN 0-02-964510-7). Macmillan.
Spanish-English Technical Dictionary. A. Harkovy. 37.50 (ISBN 0-87559-187-6). Shalom.
Spanish for Doctors & Nurses. Aurelio M. Espinosa & Leon Gambetta. (Span.). 6.85. Camino Real.
Spanish for the English-Speaking Tourist see Phrase Dictionaries for the American Tourist.
Spanish for Urban Workers. Flynn & Montoto. (Span.). 9.95; pap. 7.75. Camino Real.
Spanish-Norwegian Dictionary. S. Loennecken. (Span. & Norwegian.). 1980. write for info. (ISBN 82-573-0148-5). Kunnskapsforlaget.
Spanish Now. Silverstein et al. (Span.). 5.95. Camino Real.
Spanish Pocket Dictionary. Donald F. Sola & Frederick B. Agard. (Span.). 1954. 2.95 (ISBN 0-394-40064-X). Random.
Spanish-Swedish-Spanish Dictionary. 340p. (Span. & Swedish.). 1968. pap. 9.95 (ISBN 0-686-92501-7, S-37811). French & Eur.
Spanish Vocabulary & Structure for the Health Professional, Bk. 1. 2nd ed. Dorothy H. Mills et al. LC 80-54900. (Illus.). 157p. (Eng. & Span.). 1981. pap. text ed. 15.00 (ISBN 0-935356-02-9). Mills Pub Co.
Spanish Vocabulary of Four Native Spanish-Speaking Pre-First-Grade Children. Loyd S. Tireman. LC 48-45159. 64p. (Span.). 1982. lib. bdg. 22.95x (ISBN 0-89370-737-6). Borgo Pr.
Spansk-Norsk Ordbok. S. Loennecken. 411p. (Span. & Norwegian.). 1980. 39.95 (ISBN 0-686-92543-2, S-37620). French & Eur.
Spansk-Svensk Ordbok. 329p. (Span. & Swedish.). 1980. Kr.84.00 (ISBN 91-24-21080-3). Esselte Studium.
Special Dictionary Machinery. 8th ed. H. G. Freeman. 207p. (Eng. & Ger.). 1971. 44.25 (ISBN 3-7736-5031-0). Adler.
Specialized Dictionaries, Bi & Multilingual. (Eng.). 1979. write for info. M Rosenberg.
Spectrum Muzieklexicon, 4 vols. Theo Willemze. LC 76-500562. (Illus., Dutch.). 1975. fl.40.00 (ISBN 9-027-48298-5). Spectrum NL.
Speech Is the Form of Though - With a New Glossary. Dana Densmore. (Reprinted from Cell 16). 1970. 0.50 (015). Know Inc.
Speedwriting Dictionary: College Edition. LC 76-41047. (Landmark Ser.). 1977. text ed. 14.50 (ISBN 0-672-98095-9). Bobbs.
Spell It Fast! The Quick Way to Spell Using Sixty Stimualting Word Lists. Robert C. Gilboy. LC 81-1146. pap. 5.95 (ISBN 0-87491-071-4). Acropolis.
Spelling Helper Dictionary. Dennis A. Olivares. Ed. by Dorothy K. Berdell. 1979. 6.95 (ISBN 0-686-26693-5). Denco Intl.
Spes--Diccionario Abreviado Latino-Espanol, Espanol-Latino. 9th ed. 316p. (Lat. & Span.). 1978. leatherette 7.25 (ISBN 84-7153-221-2, S-12409). French & Eur.
Spezialwoerterbuch Maschinenwesen. Henry G. Freeman. 207p. (Ger. -Eng., Dictionary of Mechanical Engineering). 1971. write for info (M-7625, Pub. by Verlag W. Girardet). French & Eur.
Spezialwoerterbuch Maschinenwesen. Henry G. Freeman. 207p. (Ger. & Eng.). 1971. write for info. Girardet.
Spoken Chamorro: With Gramatical Notes & Glossary. 2nd ed. Donald Topping. LC 80-14596. (PALI Language Texts: Micronesia). 376p. (Orig., Chamorro.). 1980. pap. text ed. 11.00x (ISBN 0-8248-0417-1). UH Pr.
Spoken Marshallese. Byron W. Bender. (PALI Language Texts: Micronesian). (Orig., Marshallese & Eng.). 1969. pap. text ed. 13.00x (ISBN 0-87022-070-5). UH Pr.
Sport Brockhaus. 576p. (Ger.). 27.50 (ISBN 3-7653-0021-7, M-7626, Pub. by Brockhaus). French & Eur.
Sport-Brockhaus. 576p. (Ger.). DM.34.00 (ISBN 3-7653-0038-1). F A Brockhaus.
Sports Lingo: A Dictionary of the Language of Sports. Harvey Frommer. LC 82-12130. 312p. 1983. 9.95 (ISBN 0-689-10939-3, 289); pap. 7.95. Atheneum.
Sprach Brockhaus. (Illus.). 835p. (Ger.). 22.80. Imported Bks.
Sprach-Brockhaus: Deutsches Bildwoerterbuch von A-Z. 835p. (Ger.). DM.30.00 (ISBN 3-7653-0023-3). F A Brockhaus.
Sprechen Sie Rotwelsch. Guenter Puchner. LC 76-456534. 62p. (Ger.). 1975. write for info. (ISBN 3-77650-202-9). Heimeran.
Squamish Language, Pt. 1, Grammar, Text, Dictionary. Aert H. Kuipers. (Janua Linguarum, Ser. Practica: No. 732). (Squawmish.). 1967. text ed. 67.00x (ISBN 90-2790-672-6). Mouton.
SRA Data Processing Glossary. Robert C. Malstrom. 281p. 1979. pap. write for info (ISBN 0-574-21250-7, 13-4250). SRA.
Sravnitelnyi Slovar Tunguso-Manchzhurskikh Iazykov: Materialy & Etimologicheskomu Slovariu, 2 vols. (Rus.). 1975. 37.50 set (Pub. by Nauka). Four Continent.
Standaard Nederlands-Engels Technisch Woordenboek. H. Peek. LC 75-539819. 388p. (Eng. & Dutch.). 1975. fl.35.00 (ISBN 90-02-12737-5). Standaard Uitgeverij.
Standaard Nieuw Engels-Nederlands Woordenboek. Schot E. Verhoeff. LC 76-478704. 1437p. (Eng. & Dutch.). 1975. 450.00 F (ISBN 9-0021-2736-7). Standaard Uitgeverij.
Standard Alphabet for Reducing Unwritten Languages & Foreign Graphic Systems to a Uniform Orthography in European Letters. 2nd ed. Richard Lepsius. Ed. by J. Alan Kemp. (Amsterdam Classics in Linguistics Ser.: Vol. 5). 462p. 1981. 48.00x (ISBN 90-272-0876-X). Benjamins North Am.
Standard Definition of Broadcast Research Terms. National Association of Broadcasters. 2.00. Natl Assn Broadcasters.
Standard Dictionary of Computers & Information Processing. rev., 2nd ed. Martin H. Weik. 1977. 23.95 (ISBN 0-8104-5099-2). Hayden.
Standard Dictionary of Computers & Information Processing. 2nd, rev. ed. Martin H. Welk. 390p. 1977. 23.95 (ISBN 0-686-98126-X). Telecom Lib.
Standard English-Korean Dictionary for Foreigners. B. J. Jones. LC 81-84204. (Illus.). 386p. (Korean & Eng.). 1982. 7.95 (ISBN 0-930878-21-3). Hollym Intl.
Standard English-Korean Dictionary: For Foreigners. Ed. by B. J. Jones. LC 81-84204. 369p. (Korean.). 5.50 (ISBN 0-930878-21-3). Hollym Corp.
Standard English-Korean Dictionary for Foreigners. Pong Kook Lee. Ed. by B. J. Jones. 386p. (Korean & Eng.). 1982. pap. 6.95 (ISBN 0-89346-223-3). Hollym Intl.
Standard French Dictionary. 1200p. (Fr. & Eng.). 11.95 (320). Langenscheidt.
Standard French Dictionary see Langenscheidt's Standard French Dictionary: French-English, English-French.
Standard German Dictionary. 1200p. (Ger. & Eng., New York). 11.95 (319). Langenscheidt.
Standard German Dictionary see Langenscheidt's Standard German Dictionary: German-English, English-German.
Standard Glossary of Terms Relating to Chimneys, Vents & Heat Producing Appliances. (Eighty-Ninety Ser). 1972. pap. 2.00 (ISBN 0-685-58178-0, 97M). Natl Fire Prot.
Standard Marine Navigational Vocabulary. 44p. 1977. pap. 8.25 (ISBN 0-686-64013-6, IMCO 38, IMCO). Unipub.
Standard Niew Engels-Nederlands, Nederlands-Engels Woordenboek. E. Verhoeff-Schot & J. R. Cauberghe. LC 76-478704. 1437p. (Dutch & Eng.). 1975. fl.450.00 (ISBN 9-00212-736-7). Standaard Uitgeverij.
Standard Nomenclature of Athletic Injuries. Ed. by Subcommittee on Classification of Sports in Injuries & Committee on the Medical Aspects of Sports. (Orig.). 1968. pap. 2.00 (ISBN 0-89970-079-9, OP-43). AMA.
Standard Notations of Technical Terms. 1.50; members 1.00. US Comm Irrigation.
Standard Pronouncing English-Vietnamese Dictionary. Tu-Dien Tieu-Chuan Anh-Viet. (Vietnamese & Eng.). pap. 8.75. Iaconi.
Standard Pronouncing Vietnamese English Dictionary. Tu-Dien Tuie-Chuan Viet-Anh. (Vietnamese & Eng.). pap. 7.50. Iaconi.
Standard Rebus Glossary. Charlotte Clark & Cornelia Oakes Davies. 95p. 1974. pap. text ed. 6.50 (ISBN 0-913476-41-2). Am Guidance.
Standard Spanish Dictionary. 1200p. (Span. & Eng.). 11.95 (321). Langenscheidt.
Standard Swahili-English Dictionary. Ed. by Frederick Johnson. (Swahili & Eng.). 1939. 27.50x (ISBN 0-19-864403-5). Oxford U Pr.
Standard Terminology & Definition for Filled Thermal Systems for Remote Sensing Temperature Regulators: FCI 70-1. 2.00. Fluid Controls.
Standard Terminology for Regulators: FCI 71-1. 2.00. Fluid Controls.
Standard Terms of the Energy Economy. The World Energy Conference. LC 78-40304. xi, 134p. (Eng.). 1978. 50.00 (ISBN 0-08-022445-8); E25.00. Pergamon.
Standard Terms Used in the Soda Pulping Process. 1961. 1.00 (1202); members 0.67. TAPPI.
Standard Terms Used in the Sulfate Pulping Process. 1961. 1.00 (1203); members 0.67. TAPPI.
Stanley Gibbons Philatelic Terms Illustrated. Ed. by Russell Bennett & James Watson. 1972. 6.50 (ISBN 0-85259-895-5). StanGib Ltd.
State & Community Governments in the Federal System. Charles Press & Kenneth VerBerg. LC 78-22064. 1979. text ed. 21.95x (ISBN 0-471-02725-1); tchrs.' manual 6.00 (ISBN 0-471-04909-3). Wiley.
State-Wide Dialect Collecting see Oil Refinery Terms in Oklahoma.
Stateville Names: A Prison Vocabulary. Nathan Kantrowitz & Joanne Kantrowitz. (Maledicta Press Publications Ser.: Vol. 12). Date not set. 15.00 (ISBN 0-916500-12-8). Maledicta.
Stedman's Medical Dictionary. 22nd ed. Stedman. LC 78-176294. 1585p. 1972. 9.95 (ISBN 0-683-07919-0, Pub. by Williams & Wilkins). Krieger.
Stedman's Medical Dictionary. 24th ed. (Illus.). 1750p. 1981. lib. bdg. 33.50 (ISBN 0-683-07915-8). Williams & Wilkins.
Stedman's Medical Dictionary. 23rd ed. (Illus.). 1678p. 1976. 32.00 (ISBN 0-683-07924-7). Williams & Wilkins.
Stedman's Medical Dictionary: Fifth Unabridged Lawyers' Edition. William H. L. Dornette. write for info. Anderson Pub Co.
Stein & Day Dictionary of Definitive Quotations. Michael McKenna. LC 81-48453. 192p. 1982. 18.95 (ISBN 0-8128-2864-X). Stein & Day.
Stellwerksdienst. Hans J. Arnold. LC 76-472929. 119p. (Ger., Berlin, East Germany). 1976. M.4.80. Transpress Verlag fur Verkehrswesen.
Stem Dictionary of the English Language. John Kennedy. LC 78-142547. 1971. Repr. of 1870 ed. 45.00x (ISBN 0-8103-3377-5). Gale.
Stem Dictionary of the English Language. John Kennedy. 1890. 30.00 (ISBN 0-8274-3506-1). R West.
Stem Vocabulary of the Navaho Language, 2 vols. Berard Haile. LC 73-15403. (Navaho.). Repr. of 1951 ed. Set. 49.50 (ISBN 0-404-11241-2). AMS Pr.
Steuerlexikon. Ed. by Wilhelm H. Wacker. LC 75-514753. xii, 486p. (Ger.). 1975. DM.45.80 (ISBN 3-800-60472-8). Vahlen.

Stilistisch-Phraseologisches Woerterbuch Spanisch-Deutsch. Werner Beinhauer. LC 78-392750. 1043p. (Ger. & Span.). 1978. DM.120.00 (ISBN 3-190-04016-8). Hueber.
Stock Market Dictionary. John R. Dorfman. LC 81-43558. (DI.). 1982. 29.95 (ISBN 0-385-17286-9). Doubleday.
Stoelenboek. Anton van Oirschot. LC 78-384766. (Illus.). 128p. (Dutch.). 1978. fl.7.90 (ISBN 9-025-26367-4). Helmond.
Stora Engelsk-Svenska Ordboken: A Comprehensive English-Swedish Dictionary. 1071p. (Eng. & Swedish.). 1981. Kr.280.00 (ISBN 91-24-29824-7). Esselte Studium.
Stora Synonymordboken. Alva Strmberg. LC 76-474101. 725p. (Swedish.). 1975. Kr.160.00 (ISBN 9-17148-302-0). Strombergs.
Story Behind the Word: Some Interesting Origins of Medical Terms. Harry Wain. 352p. 1958. photocopy ed. spiral 34.75x (ISBN 0-398-02001-9). C C Thomas.
Strategic Terminology. Urs Schwarz & Laszlo Hadik. 160p. (Ger., Eng. & Fr.). 12.50 (ISBN 0-686-57217-3, M-6509). French & Eur.
Stratigraficheskii Slovar SSSR. (Rus.). 1977. 8.75 (Pub. by Nedra). Four Continent.
Stratigraficheskii Slovar SSSR. 592p. (Rus.). 1979. 10.95 (Pub. by Nedra). Four Continent.
Strong's Exhaustive Concordance. James Strong. 17.95 (ISBN 0-8010-8228-5); pap. 13.95 (ISBN 0-8010-8108-4). Baker Bk.
Strong's Exhaustive Concordance. James Strong. LC 78-73138. 1978. pap. 15.95 (ISBN 0-8054-1134-8). Broadman.
Structure of English Orthography. Richard L. Venezky. (Janua Linguarum, Ser. Minor: No. 82). 1970. pap. text ed. 14.00x (ISBN 90-2790-707-2). Mouton.
Structure of Lelemi Language. Hildegard Hoeftmann. 130p. 1973. 17.50x (ISBN 0-8002-1344-0). Intl Pubns Serv.
Structure of the Noun Phrase in English & Hindi. M. K. Verma. (Eng. & Hindi.). 1971. 8.50 (ISBN 0-89684-322-X). Orient Bk Dist.
Structures in the Subjective Lexicon: An Experimental Approach to the Study of Semantic Fields. Samuel Fillenbaum & Amnon Rapoport. 1971. 46.00 (ISBN 0-12-256250-X). Acad Pr.
Student Arabic-English Dictionary. Dar el Mashreq. (Illus.). 440p. (Engl. & Arabic.). Arabic script 11.00 (2123-9). Intl Bk Ctr.
Student Dictionary of Biology. Ed. by Peter Gray. 1973. pap. 4.95x (ISBN 0-442-22816-3). Van Nos Reinhold.
Student Dictionary with Merriam-Webster Phonetic Key. 1976. pap. 3.00 (ISBN 0-685-22408-2). Youth Ed.
Student English-Chinese Dictionary. (Illus.). 978p. (Orig., Chinese & Eng.). 1983. pap. text ed. 7.95 (ISBN 9971-9060-3-1). Hippocrene Bks.
Students' Accounting Vocabulary. Diane Houghton & Ralph G. Wallace. 278p. 1980. pap. text ed. 15.00x (ISBN 0-566-00330-9). Gower Pub Ltd.
Student's Dictionary. Ed. by Abraham Even-Shoshan. (Illus.). 592p. (Hebrew.). 1982. text ed. 12.00 (ISBN 965-17-0105-6). K Sefer.
Student's Dictionary of Anglo-Saxon. Henry Sweet. (Anglo-Saxon.). 1896. 27.50x (ISBN 0-19-863107-3). Oxford U Pr.
Student's English-Sanskrit Dictionary. V. S. Apte. (Eng. & Sanskrit.). 1974. Repr. 9.95 (ISBN 0-8426-0507-X). Orient Bk Dist.
Student's English-Sanskrit Dictionary. V. S. Apte. 501p. (Sanskrit & Eng.). 1973. text ed. 9.50x (ISBN 0-8426-0507-X). Verry.
Student's Glossary of Finnish. Michael Branch et al. LC 80-14030. (Illus.). 378p. (Finnish.). 1980. Fmk.147.00 (ISBN 9-510-08746-7). Soderstrom.
Student's Webster Dictionary. Ed. by Jess Stein. 48p. 1981. pap. 1.95 (ISBN 0-89531-021-X, 0114-72). Sharon Pubns.
Studies in Greek Colour Terminology, Vol. 1. Maxwell P. Stuart. (Mnemosyne Supplement Ser.: No. 65). 254p. 1981. pap. text ed. 35.50x (ISBN 90-04-06406-0, Pub. by E J Brill Holland). Humanities.
Studies in Greek Colour Terminology, Vol. 2. Stuart P. Maxwell. (Mnemosyne Supplement Ser.: No. 67). 90p. 1981. pap. text ed. 15.25x (ISBN 90-04-06407-9, Pub. by E J Brill Holland). Humanities.
Studies in Legal Terminology. Erwin Hexner. vi, 150p. 1981. Repr. of 1941 ed. lib. bdg. 20.00x (ISBN 0-8377-0635-1). Rothman.
Study Dictionary of Social English. W. R. Lee. Ed. by B. Newson. (Pergamon Institute of English Dictionaries Ser.). 160p. 1983. 14.95 (ISBN 0-08-024561-7); pap. 7.50 (ISBN 0-08-024560-9). Pergamon.
Study of Hindu Art & Architecture with Special Reference to Terminology. Lalit K. Shukla. (Chowkamba Sanskrit Studies Ser.: Vol. 82). (Illus.). 1972. 32.00x (ISBN 0-8426-0382-4). Verry.
Style & Vocabulary: Numerical Studies. C. B. Williams. 162p. 1972. pap. text ed. 8.75x (ISBN 0-85264-164-8). Lubrecht & Cramer.
Subject in the Dictionary Catalog From Cutter to the Present. Frances Miksa. 496p. 1983. 55.00 (ISBN 0-8389-0367-3). ALA.
Suffixes: And Other Word-Final Elements of English. Ed. by Laurence Urdang. 320p. 1982. 60.00x (ISBN 0-8103-1123-2). Gale.
Suomalais-Englantilainen Sanakirja. Aino Vuolle. LC 76-478143. 484p. (Finnish & Eng.). 1975. write for info. (ISBN 9-5164-359-63). Femi Suuri.
Suomalais-Ruotsalainen Suursanakirja. 3rd. ed. Aulis Cannelin et al. LC 77-471720. xv, 1140p. (Finnish & Swedish.). 1976. Fmk.write for info. (ISBN 9-51007-012-2). Werner Soderstrom.
Suomi-Norja-Suomi: Taskusanakirja. Turid Farbregd & Aili Kamarainen. LC 79-350054. 636p. (Finnish & Nor.). 1978. write for info. (ISBN 9-51008-527-8). Soderstrom.
Suomi-Portugali-Suomi. Kristina Rahinantti et al. LC 75-546478. xvi, 359p. (Port. & Finnish.). 1975. Fmk.20.00 (ISBN 951-0-06884-5). Werner Soderstrom.
Suomi-Poula Suomi Dictionary: Finnish-Polish-Finnish. A. Krawczykiewicz. 687p. (Finnish & Pol.). 1979. pap. 18.95 (ISBN 951-0-08000-4, M-9638). French & Eur.
Suomi-Unkari-Suomi: Taskusanakirja. Istvan Nyirkos. LC 78-346065. 712p. (Finnish & Hungarian.). 1977. Fmk.44.00 (ISBN 9-51007-860-3). Soderstrom.
Super Dictionary. Ed. by Warner Educational Services. LC 78-55453. (Illus.). 1978. 9.95 (ISBN 0-03-043756-3). HR&W.
Supermarket Language. Jim Richey. (Survival Vocabulary Ser.). (Illus.). 48p. (gr. 7-12). 1978. pap. 2.95 (ISBN 0-915510-27-8). Janus Bks.
Suplemento a la Segunda Edicion Del Diccionario Pornua De Historia, Biografia y Geografia de Mexico. 496p. (Span.). 17.50 (ISBN 0-686-56693-9, S-12280). French & Eur.
Supplement au Dictionnaire de la Noblesse Francaise. Etienne de Sereville & Fernand de Saint-Simon. 668p. (Fr.). 1977. 65.00 (ISBN 0-686-56752-8, M-6514). French & Eur.
Supplement Aux Dictionnaire Arabe (Arabic-French, 2 vols. R. Dozy. (Arabic & Fr.). 1969. 80.00x (ISBN 0-86685-106-2). Intl Bk Ctr.
Supplement aux dictionnaires Arabes, 2 vols. R. Dozy. 1721p. (Arabic & Fr.). 80.00 set (106-2). Intl Bk Ctr.
Supplement of the Dictionary of the English Language of the XII, XIII, XIV, & XV Centuries. 3rd ed. Franz H. Stratmann. 93p. 1980. Repr. of 1881 ed. lib. bdg. 22.50 (ISBN 0-8492-8111-3). R West.
Supplement to Elsevier's Dictionary of the Gas Industry: Polygot. Compiled by International Gas Union. LC 61-8851. 216p. 1973. 42.75 (ISBN 0-444-40757-X). Elsevier.
Supplement to the Dictionary of the English Language of the 12th, 13th, 14th, & 15th Centuries. 3rd ed. Franz H. Stratmann. LC 76-30620. 1977. Repr. of 1881 ed. lib. bdg. 15.00 (ISBN 0-8414-7554-7). Folcroft.
Supplement to the Glossary of Terms for Fluid Power: ANSI-B93.2a. American National Standards Institute & National Fluid Power Association. 1978. 12.00; 8.00, NFPA member. Natl Fluid Power.
Supplement to the New English-Russian Dictionary. Ed. by I. R. Galperin. (Russkii iazyk Ser.). 432p. (Rus. & Eng.). 1980. 6.95 (D-209A). Four Continent.
Supplement to the Oxford English Dictionary, Vol. 3. Ed. by Robert W. Burchfield. 1982. 110.00x (ISBN 0-19-861124-2). Oxford U Pr.
Supplement to the Oxford English Dictionary Vol. 1: A-G. Ed. by R. W. Burchfield. 1972. 110.00x (ISBN 0-19-861115-3). Oxford U Pr.
Supplement to the Oxford English Dictionary, Volume 2 H-N. R. W. Burchfield. 1976. 110.00x (ISBN 0-19-861123-4). Oxford U Pr.
Supplementary English Glossary. T. L. Davies. 1875. 25.00 (ISBN 0-8274-3557-6). R West.
Supplementary English Glossary. Thomas L. Davies. LC 68-23468. 1968. Repr. of 1881 ed. 47.00x (ISBN 0-8103-3245-0). Gale.
Supplementary Indexes to Lin Yutang's Chinese-English Dictionary of Modern Usage. LC 79-319125. 105p. (Chinese & Eng.). 1978. write for info. (ISBN 9-622-01160-8). Chinese U Pr.
Surface Strength Terminology. Ed. by Philip C. Evanoff & Werner Gerlach. (Illus.). 65p. 1983. pap. price not set (ISBN 0-89852-411-3). TAPPI.
Surface Strength Terminology. 1965. 13.00 (399-3); members 8.67. TAPPI.
Surface Treatment of Aluminum--A Glossary of Technical Terms. Kehler. 1981. 11.50 (ISBN 0-9960034-1-X). Heyden.
Surface Treatment of Aluminum: Glossary of Technical Terms. LC 76-356688. 50p. (Eng. , Fr. & Ger.). 1975. write for info. (ISBN 3-87017-121-9). Aluminum Verlag.
Svensk Baklaengesordbok. Sture Allen et al. 483p. (Swedish.). 1981. Kr.155.00 (ISBN 91-24-30634-7). Esselte Studium.
Svensk-Engelsk Affarsordlists. Stanley H. Pretorius. 128p. (Swedish & Eng.). write for info. (ISBN 91-24-15066-5). Esselte Studium.
Svensk-Engelsk & Engelsk-Svensk Ordbok. Tornberg et al. 468p. (Eng. & Swedish.). write for info. Esselte Studium.
Svensk-Engelsk Modern Ordbok. 4th ed. Rolf Prisma-Lagersson. (Swedish & Eng.). 1982. 20.00x (ISBN 91-518-1297-5, SW-204). Vanous.
Svensk-Engelsk Ordbok. 979p. (Swedish-Eng.). Kr.170.00 (ISBN 91-24-14308-1). Esselte Studium.
Svensk-Engelsk Pocketordbok. 480p. (Swedish & Eng.). 1980. Kr.71.00 (ISBN 91-24-20291-6). Esselte Studium.
Svensk-Estnisk Ordbok. Per Wieselgren. LC 77-458507. xxx, 630p. (Swedish & Estonian.). 1976. Kr.170.00. Fyris.
Svensk-Finsk Storordbok. Lea Lampen. 856p. (Swedish & Finnish.). 1977. Kr.300.00. Esselte Studium.
Svensk-Fransk Affaersordlista. Edy Maupoix. 144p. (Swedish & Fr.). write for info. Esselte Studium.
Svensk-Fransk & Fransk-Svensk Ordbok. Ruben Noid. 450p. (Swedish & Fr.). write for info. Esselte Studium.
Svensk-Fransk Ordbok. Thekla Hammar. 1095p. (Fr. & Swedish.). 1979. Kr.155.00. Esselte Studium.
Svensk-Fransk Ordbok. 269p. (Swedish & Fr.). write for info. (ISBN 91-24-19396-8). Esselte Studium.
Svensk Handordbok: Kronstruktioner & Fraseologi. Ed. by Ture Johannisson & K. G. Ljunggren. 891p. (Swedish.). 1980. Kr.145.00 (ISBN 91-24-14309-X). Esselte Studium.
Svensk-Italiensk Ordbok. Silvia Tomba. 430p. (Swedish & Ital.). 1980. Kr.90.00 (ISBN 91-24-14338-3). Esselte Studium.
Svensk-Norsk Ordbok. Marius Sandvei. LC 80-457703. 174p. (Swedish & Norse.). 1979. Kr.59.00 (ISBN 8-20700-369-3). Fabritius.
Svensk-Nygrekisk Ordbok. Natan Valmin & Eftychia Frangos. 279p. (Swedish & Gr.). 1980. Kr.115.00 (ISBN 91-24-20265-7). Esselte Studium.
Svensk Slangordbok. Haldo Gibson. 243p. (Swedish.). 1980. Kr.88.00 (ISBN 91-24-30634-7). Esselte Studium.
Svensk-Spansk Affaersordlista. Peralta & Cederholm. 164p. (Swedish & Span.). write for info. Esselte Studium.
Svensk-Spansk Ordbok. Alfred Akerlung. Ed. by M. J. Casa Novas & M. Gronbarj. 389p. (Swedish & Span.). 1979. Kr.75.00 (ISBN 91-24-14379-0). Esselte Studium.
Svensk-Turkisk Ordbok. Musa Guner. LC 77-571011. 133p. (Swedish & Turkish.). 1977. Kr.47.00 (ISBN 9-1441-4001-0). Studentlitt.
Svensk-Tysk Affarsordlista. Helge Birgersson. 128p. (Swedish & Ger.). write for info. (ISBN 91-24-15571-3). Esselte Studium.
Svensk-Tysk & Tysk-Svenskt Standardlexikon. 744p. (Ger. & Swedish.). write for info. Esselte Studium.
Svensk-Tysk Ordbok. 783p. (Swedish & Ger.). 1980. Kr.170.00 (ISBN 91-24-27622-7). Esselte Studium.
Svensk-Tysk Ordbok: Supplement 78. 32p. (Swedish & Ger.). 1978. Kr.42.00 (ISBN 91-24-27683-9). Esselte Studium.
Svensk-Tysk Standardlexikon. 351p. (Ger. & Swedish.). write for info. (ISBN 91-24-14301-4). Esselte Studium.
Svensk-Tyskt-Tyskt-Svenskt Standardlexikon. 744p. (Swedish & Ger.). write for info. (ISBN 91-24-14305-7). Esselte Studium.
Svenska Akademiens Ordlista Oever Svenska Spraket. 616p. (Swedish.). 1981. Kr.105.00 (ISBN 91-24-23222-X). Esselte Studium.
Svenska Duden Bildlexikon. (Illus.). 869p. (Swedish & Ger.). 31.00. Imported Bks.
Svenska Ordlista. Sture Allen. 264p. (Swedish.). write for info. (ISBN 91-24-27572-7); pap. write for info. (ISBN 91-24-27571-9). Esselte Studium.
Svenskt Rimlexikon. 3rd ed. Einer Odhner. LC 80-491211. 319p. (Swedish.). 1979. write for info. (ISBN 9-13707-206-4). Forum Bok.
Swahili Dictionary. D. V. Perrot. (Teach Yourself Ser.). (Swahili.). 1974. pap. 3.95 (ISBN 0-679-10015-6). McKay.
Swahili-English Dictionary. F. Johnson. (Swahili & Eng.). 19.50 (ISBN 0-685-20193-7, 079-8). Saphrograph.
Swahili-English Dictionary. Charles W. Rechenbach. (Publications in the Languages of Africa Ser.: No. 1). (Swahili & Eng.). 1968. 36.95 (ISBN 0-8132-0406-2). Cath U Pr.
Swahili-English Dictionary. (Swahili & Eng.). 35.00. Iaconi.

Swanfeldt Famous Crossword Puzzle Dictionary. Andrew Swanfeldt. 736p. 1982. pap. 7.64i (EH 552, EH). B&N NY.

Swedish-English Dictionary. Ruben & M. Angstrom. (Swedish & Eng.). 16.00 (ISBN 0-87557-082-8, 082-8). Saphrograph.

Swedish-English Dictionary of Technical Terms Used in Business, Industry, Administration, Education & Research. 2nd rev. & enl. ed. Ingvar E. Gullberg. (Swedish & Eng.). 150.00 (ISBN 91-1-775052-0). Heinman.

Swedish-English, English-Swedish Dictionary, 2 vols. R. Santesson & Karl K. Kaerre. (Swedish & Eng.). Set. 120.00 (ISBN 0-686-77012-9). Vol. 1 (ISBN 9-1242-9824-7). Vol. 2 (ISBN 9-1241-4308-1). Heinman.

Swedish-English, English-Swedish Pocket Dictionary. Berlitz Editors. LC 74-1987. (Swedish & Eng.). 1974. pap. 2.95 (ISBN 0-02-964410-0, Berlitz). Macmillan.

Swedish-English, English-Swedish Technical Dictionary, 2 vols. rev. enl ed. E. Engstroem. (Swedish & Eng.). Set. 115.00 (ISBN 0-685-42614-9). Heinman.

Swedish-English Fact Ordbok (Technical Terms) 2nd ed. Ingvar E. Gullberg. (Swedish & Eng.). 1977. 200.00x (ISBN 91-1-775052-0, SW-207). Vanous.

Swedish-English Modern Dictionary, Vol. 1. 4th ed. R. Prisma-Lagersson. (Swedish & Eng.). 1982. 20.00x (ISBN 91-518-1297-5, SW204). Vanous.

Swedish-English-Swedish. (Berlitz Pocket Dictionaries Ser.). (Eng. & Swedish.). 4.95 (ISBN 0-02-964570-0). Macmillan.

Swedish-English-Swedish Pocket Dictionary. A. Hills. (Swedish & Eng.). 1978. 7.50x (ISBN 0-89918-134-1, SW134). Vanous.

Swedish-Finnish Dictionary. L. Lampen. 548p. (Swedish & Finnish.). 1980. Leatherette 24.95 (ISBN 951-0-08621-5, M-9656). French & Eur.

Swedish Karre Dictionary, Vol. 1: Svensk-Engelsk. K. Karre. (Swedish & Eng.). 1976. 50.00x (ISBN 91-24-14308-1, SW132). Vanous.

Swedish Karre Dictionary, Vol. 2: Engelsk-Svensk. 3rd ed. K. Karre. (Swedish & Eng.). 1981. text ed. 60.00x (ISBN 91-24-29824-7, SW133). Vanous.

Swedish Modern Pocket Dictionary: Svensk-Engelsk, Engelsk-Svensk Grammatik Parlor. E. Gomer. (Swedish & Eng.). 1981. text ed. 11.00x (ISBN 91-518-1148-0, SW-208). Vanous.

Swedish-Norwegian Dictionary. J. Vogt & I. Eikeland. (Swedish-Norwegian.). 1982. write for info. (ISBN 82-573-0120-5). Kunnskapsforlaget.

Swedish Pocket Dictionary. (Swedish & Eng.). 7.50 (ISBN 8-4399-8784-6). Heinman.

Swedish-Russian Dictionary. D. Milanova. 760p. (Swedish & Rus.). 1973. 19.95 (ISBN 0-686-92499-1, M-9077). French & Eur.

Synonomy, Repitition & Restatement in the Vocabulary of Herman Melville's Moby Dick. James W. Nechas. 286p. 1980. Repr. of 1978 ed. lib. bdg. 30.00 (ISBN 0-8414-6311-5). Folcroft.

Synonym Finder. rev. ed. J. I. Rodale. 1978. 19.95 (ISBN 0-87857-236-8); deluxe ed. 21.95 (ISBN 0-87857-244-9). Rodale Pr Inc.

Synonyms Discriminated. Charles J. Smith. Ed. by Percy H. Smith. LC 78-126007. 1970. Repr. of 1903 ed. 42.00x (ISBN 0-8103-3010-5). Gale.

Synonymwoerterbuch. 7th ed. Ed. by H. Goerner & G. Kempcke. 643p. (Ger.). 1982. M.22.00. Bibl Inst Leipzig.

Synoptic Concordance of Aramaic Inscriptions. Walter E. Aufrecht & John Hurd. (International Concordance Library: Vol. I). 1975. pap. 20.00 (ISBN 0-935106-24-3). Biblical Res Assocs.

Syntactical & Critical Concordance to the Greek Text of Baruch & the Epistle of Jeremiah. R. A. Martin. (Computer Bible Ser.: Vol. XII). (Gr.). 1977. pap. 15.00 (ISBN 0-935106-09-X). Biblical Res Assocs.

Syntax of Urban Hijazi Arabic. Mahmoud Sieny. (Arabic.). 12.00x (ISBN 0-86685-051-1). Intl Bk Ctr.

Syriac-English Glossary: With Etymological Notes, Based on Brockelmann's Syriac Chrestomathy. Moshe H. Goshen-Gottstein. LC 70-559416. 105p. (Syrian & Eng.). 1970. 20.00x (ISBN 3-447-00345-6). Intl Pubns Serv.

Systematic Glossary of the Terminology of Statistical Methods: English, French, Spanish, Russian. Isaac Paenson. (Eng., Fr., Span. & Rus.). 1971. 130.00 (ISBN 0-08-012285-X). Pergamon.

Systematic Guide to Medical Terminology. National Shorthand Reporters Association. 60p. 3.50 (145). Natl Shorthand Rptr.

Systematische Zoologie Insekten. Werner Jacobs. LC 76-483862. 377p. (Ger.). 1975. write for info. (ISBN 3-437-30195-0). Fischer Verlag.

Systems Analysis & Operations Research Dictionary. G Sezepesi & B. Szekely. 154p. (Hungarian, Eng., Fr., Ger., & Rus.). 1980. 30.00x (ISBN 0-569-08617-5, Pub. by Collets). State Mutual Bk.

Szerbhorvat-Magyar Szotar. 4th ed. Laszlo Hadrovics. LC 77-501008. lxiv, 688p. (Serbo-Croatian & Hungarian.). 1976. 26.00 Ft (ISBN 9-63205-041-X). Terra.

Szerbhorvat-Magyar Szotar. Laszlo Hadrovics et al. LC 77-501008. lxiv, 688p. (Hungarian & Serbo-Croatian.). 1976. 26.00 Ft (ISBN 9-6320-5041-X). Terra.

Szkolny Slownik Terminow Nauki i Jezyku. J. Malczewski. 244p. (Pol.). 1979. 2.75 (Pub. by Wydaw. Szkolne & Pedagogiczne). Four Continent.

Szlovak-Magyar Szotar. 3rd ed. Marianne T. Gobel. LC 78-347303. 480p. (Hungarian & Slovak.). 1976. 35.00 Ft (ISBN 9-63205-043-6). Terra.

T

Taber's Cyclopedic Medical Dictionary. 14th ed. Ed. by Clayton L. Thomas. LC 80-16588. (Illus.). 1818p. 1981. 15.95x (ISBN 0-8036-8307-3); Thumb-indexed Edition. text ed. 18.95x (ISBN 0-8036-8306-5). Davis Co.

Table Alphabeticall of English Wordes. Robert Cawdrey. LC 73-25889. (English Experience Ser.: No. 226). 132p. 1970. Repr. of 1604 ed. 11.50 (ISBN 90-221-0226-2). Walter J Johnson.

Tachenlexikon Umweltschultz. Otto E. Ahlhaus et al. LC 80-470211. 288p. (Ger.). 1979. DM.10.00 (ISBN 3-590-14362-2). Pr Univ Fr.

Tagal sko Russkii Slovar. M. Krus et al. 387p. (Rus. & Tagalog.). 1959. 1.95. Four Continent.

Tagalog Dictionary. T. Ramos. (Tagalog.). 7.50. Iaconi.

Tagalog Dictionary. Teresita V. Ramos. LC 71-152471. (PALI Language Texts: Philippines). 373p. (Orig., Tagalog.). 1971. pap. text ed. 8.50x (ISBN 0-87022-676-2). UH Pr.

Tagalog-English - English-Tagalog Dictionary. rev. ed. Maria O. Guzman. (Tagalog & Eng.). pap. 22.50 (ISBN 0-686-68939-9). Heinman.

Tagalog-Russian Dictionary. M. Cruz & S. P. Ignashev. 388p. (Tagalog & Rus.). 1959. leatherette 4.75 (ISBN 0-686-92479-7, M-9052). French & Eur.

Tagal'sko-Russkii Slovar. M. Krus. 387p. (Rus. & Tagalog.). 1959. 1.95 (Pub. by GINS). Four Continent.

Tahitian & English Dictionary. John Davies. LC 75-35188. (Eng. & Tahitian.). Repr. of 1851 ed. 31.50 (ISBN 0-404-14217-6). AMS Pr.

Tahitian-English, English Tahitian Dictionary. Leonard Clairmont. (Tahitian & Eng.). 17.50 (ISBN 0-87559-053-5). Shalom.

Tai-Khamti Phonology & Vocabulary. Alfons Wiedert. LC 77-479800. 92p. (Khamti.). 1977. write for info. (ISBN 3-515-02582-0). Steiner Verlag.

Taisko-Ruskii Slovar. L. N. Morev. 985p. (Rus. & Tai.). 1964. 6.50 (Pub. by Sov. Entsiklopediia). Four Continent.

Talk & Taxonomy. Peter Elgin. LC 81-160082. ix, 125p. (Eng.). 1980. fl.pap. 30.00 (ISBN 9-02-722510-9). Benjamins.

Talking Dictionary. Richard Ballard. (Michigan Learning Modules Ser.: No. 21). 1978. write for info. (ISBN 0-914004-24-7). Ulrich.

Tamil dictionaries. A. Dhamotharau. LC 80-471418. 185p. (Tamil.). 1978. pap. write for info. (ISBN 3-515-03005-0). Steiner Verlag.

Tamil-English, English-Tamil Dictionary, Vol. 1-2. 3rd, rev. ed. M. Winslow. (Eng. & Tamil.). Date not set. Set. text ed. 100.00 (ISBN 0-686-46542-3). Heinman.

T'ang Poetic Vocabulary. Hugh M. Stimson. 8.95 (ISBN 0-88710-121-6). Far Eastern Pubns.

Tanga-English, English-Tanga Dictionary. Francis L. Bell. LC 78-311012. xxx, 156p. (Tanga & Eng.). 1977. Aus.$3.00. Univ Syd Aust Lang.

Taschen-Lexikon Internationale Abkurzungen & Kurzzeichen. Thomas Krist. LC 80-474810. 144p. (Eng. & Ger.). 1979. DM.9.80 (ISBN 3-87807-110-8). Technik Tabel.

Taschenlexikon der Verhaltenskunde. Peter K. Meyer. LC 77-462747. 240p. (Ger.). 1976. DM.12.80 (ISBN 3-506-99191-4). Schoningh.

Taschenlexikon Elektronik, Funktechnik. 320p. (Ger.). 1974. 12.50 (ISBN 3-87144-176-7, M-7630, Pub. by Verlag Harri Deutsch). French & Eur.

Taschenlexikon Medizin. Dagobert Tutsch. LC 75-508090. 581p. (Eng. & Ger.). 1975. DM.14.80 (ISBN 3-541-03012-7). Urban & Schwarzen.

Taschenlexikon Ungarn. Ed. by Akademie Verlages Budapest. (Illus.). 280p. (Hungarian.). 1981. M.12.00. Bibl Inst Leipzig.

Taschenwoerterbuch. 1278p. (Ger.). 10.95 (11121). Langenscheidt.

Taschenwoerterbuch der Botanischen Pflanzennamem. 2nd ed. F. Boerner. 435p. (Ger.). 1966. 39.95 (ISBN 3-489-56322-0, M-7631, Pub. by P. Parey). French & Eur.

Taschenwoerterbuch der Botanischen Pflanzennamem. 2nd ed. F. Boerner. 435p. (Ger.). 1966. 39.95 (ISBN 3-489-56322-0). Parey.

Taschenwoerterbuch des Fremdenverkehrs. W. Friedreich. 187p. (Ger. & Eng., Dictionary of Tourism). 1970. 7.95 (ISBN 3-19-006281-1). Hueber.

Taschenwoerterbuch des Fremdenverkehrs. W. Friedrich. 187p. (Ger. & Eng., Dictionary of Tourism). 1970. 7.95 (ISBN 3-19-006281-1, M-7632, Pub. by M. Hueber). French & Eur.

Taschenwoerterbuch Deutsch-Niederlaendisch. Ed. by Gerhard Worgt. LC 78-349037. xxiv, 359p. (Ger. & Dutch.). 1977. M.5.80. VEB Verlag Enzyklopadie.

Taschenwoerterbuch Deutsch-Ungarisch. Ed. by Heinrich Weissling. LC 76-472365. 272p. (Ger. & Hungarian.). 1975. M.5.80. VEB Verlag Enzyklopaedie.

Taschenwoerterbuch Eisen und Stahl. H. Freeman. 600p. (Ger. & Eng., Dictionary of Iron and Steel). 1966. 12.50 (ISBN 3-19-006215-3, M-7634, Pub. by M. Hueber). French & Eur.

Taschenwoerterbuch Eisen und Stahl. H. Freeman. 600p. (Ger. & Eng.). 1966. 12.50 (ISBN 3-19-006215-3). Hueber.

Taschenwoerterbuch Englisch-Deutsch. Ed. by Walter Schmidt. LC 77-554903. 347p. (Ger.). 1977. DM.5.85. VEB Verlag Enzyklopadie.

Taschenwoerterbuch Kraftfahrzeugtechnik. H. Freeman. 377p. (Ger. & Eng., Dictionary of Automotive Engineering). 1968. 12.50 (ISBN 3-19-006270-6, M-7635, Pub. by M. Hueber). French & Eur.

Taschenwoerterbuch Kraftfahrzeugtechnik. H. Freeman. 377p. (Ger. & Eng.). 1968. 12.50 (ISBN 3-19-006270-6). Hueber.

Taschenworterbuch. Walter Schmidt. LC 77-554903. xiv, 347p. (Eng. & Ger.). 1977. M.5.80. VEB Verlag Enzyklopadie.

Taschenworterbuch Deutsch-Ungarisch. Heinrich Weissling. LC 76-472365. 272p. (Ger. & Hungarian.). 1975. M.5.80. VEB Verlag Enzyklopadie.

Tasmennyssanasto. Jouko Vesikansa. LC 77-480112. 127p. (Finnish.). 1976. Fmk.27.50 (ISBN 9-5100-7425-X); write for info. (ISBN 9-5100-7424-1). Werner Soderstrom.

Taspinar's Technical Dictionary. Adnan H. Taspinar. LC 79-338815. 1316p. (Eng & Turkish.). 1978. TL.500.00. Taspinar's Technical Publications.

Tausug-English Dictionary. Irene Hassan. LC 78-317697. 789p. (Eng. & Tausug.). 1975. write for info. Jolu, Sulu.

Taxonomist's Glossary of Genitalia in Insects. Ed. by S. L. Tuxen. 1970. text ed. 27.50 (ISBN 0-934454-76-0). Lubrecht & Cramer.

Teacher's Word Book of the Twenty Thousand Words Found Most Frequently & Widely in General Reading for Children & Young People. rev. ed. Edward L. Thorndike. LC 73-5527. 182p. 1975. Repr. of 1932 ed. 40.00x (ISBN 0-8103-4108-5). Gale.

Teaching Reading Vocabulary & Teaching Reading Comprehension. P. D. Pearson & D. D Johnson. 1978. Set. boxed 15.95 (ISBN 0-03-042916-1, HoltC). HR&W.

Teaterord. Niklas Brunius. LC 77-578501. 179p. (Eng., Danish, Finnish, Icelandic, Norwegian & Swedish.). 1975. write for info. Nord Teater.

Technical & Engineering Dictionary: Band II, English-German. De Vries & Herrmann. 1154p. (Eng. & Ger.). 1982. DM.120.00. Brandstetter.

Technical & Engineering Dictionary: Band I, German-English. De Vries & Herrmann. 1178p. (Ger. & Eng.). 1982. DM.120.00. Brandstetter.

Technical Arabic. Vernon Daykin. 132p. (Arabic.). 1980. 15.00x (ISBN 0-686-94054-7, Pub. by Lund Humphries England). State Mutual Bk.

Technical Automotive Dictionary: Russian-English-German-French-Bulgarian. G. Sikora. 624p. (Rus., Eng., Ger., Fr & Bulgarian.). 1977. leatherette 95.00 (ISBN 0-686-92472-X, M-9828). French & Eur.

Technical Dictionary. rev. ed. Howard H. Gerrish. LC 81-20005. 368p. 1982. text ed. 10.00 (ISBN 0-87006-400-2). Goodheart.

Technical Dictionary: Archtiecture & Building. Tawfik Abd-El-Gawad. 1319p. (Eng., Fr., Ger. & Arabic.). 1976. 35.00x (ISBN 0-686-44745-X, Pub. by Collets). State Mutual Bk.

Technical Dictionary English-Slovene. 1137p. (Eng. & Slovene.). 1975. 125.00 (ISBN 0-686-92318-9, M-9891). French & Eur.

Technical Dictionary for Automotive Engineering, 2 vols. Ed. by R. Bosch. (Eng. & Ger.). 1976. 68.00 (ISBN 0-9961072-5-8, Pub. by VDI W Germany). Heyden.

Technical Dictionary for Civil Engineers. Research & Education Association. 1408p. 1981. 32.65 (ISBN 0-87891-531-1). Res & Educ.

Technical Dictionary for the Shoe Industry. Gerhard Knebel. (Eng. & Ger.). 1966. pap. 29.95 (ISBN 3-7785-0040-6, M-7641, Pub. by Huethig). French & Eur.
Technical Dictionary for Weaponry. Gustav Sybertz. (Ger. & Eng.). 1969. pap. 120.00 (ISBN 3-7888-0081-X, M-7642, Pub. by Neumann-Neudamm). French & Eur.
Technical Dictionary of Anglo-American Legal Terminology. 3rd ed. D. Beseler & B. Jacobs. 385p. (Ger. & Eng.). 1971. 110.00 (ISBN 3-11-002187-0, M-7636, Pub. by de Gruyter). French & Eur.
Technical Dictionary of Automatization & Programming: English, French, German, Russian,- Slovene. Ed. by E. Burger. 479p. (Eng., Fr., Ger., Rus. & Slovene.). 1976. 95.00 (ISBN 0-686-92330-8, M-9889). French & Eur.
Technical Dictionary of Crystallography. 132p. 1980. 40.00x (ISBN 0-686-72093-8, Pub. by Collet's). State Mutual Bk.
Technical Dictionary of Data Processing, Computers & Office Machines, English, German, French, Russian. E. Burger. (Eng., Ger., Fr. & Rus.). 1970. 130.00 (ISBN 0-08-006425-6). Pergamon.
Technical Dictionary of High Polymers: English, French, German, Russian. W. Dawydoff. 1969. 130.00 (ISBN 0-08-013112-3). Pergamon.
Technical Dictionary of Hydraulics & Pneumatics. Ed. by Gunter Neubert. 1973. text ed. 40.00 (ISBN 0-08-016958-9). Pergamon.
Technical Dictionary of Petrochemistry. W. Leipnitz. 240p. (Ger., Eng., Fr. & Rus.). 1976. 48.00 (ISBN 0-686-56469-3, M-7640, Pub. by Vlg. Technik). French & Eur.
Technical Dictionary of Production Engineering (English-German) Rudolph Walther. 1973. text ed. 49.00 (ISBN 0-08-016959-7). Pergamon.
Technical Dictionary of Production Engineering: Vol. 2, German-English. R. Walther. (Ger. & Eng.). 49.00 (ISBN 0-08-016960-0). Pergamon.
Technical Dictionary of Spectroscopy & Spectral Analysis: English, German, French, Russian. H. Moritz & T. Torok. 1971. 65.00 (ISBN 0-08-015864-1). Pergamon.
Technical Dictionary of Textile Chemistry - Fachwoerterbuch Chemiefasern: German-English-French, English-German-French, French-German-English. Werner Winkler. LC 67-72234. 276p. (Ger., Eng. & Fr.). 1966. 13.00x (ISBN 0-8002-2072-2). Intl Pubns Serv.
Technical Dictionary of Vacuum Physics & Vacuum Technology (English, French, German, Russian) Karl Hurrle et al. 1973. text ed. 40.00 (ISBN 0-08-016957-0). Pergamon.
Technical Dictionary Pulp & Paper, 2 vols. 2nd ed. Wolfgang Weitzel. Incl. Vol. 1. English-German. 351p (ISBN 0-8002-2073-0); Vol. 2. German-English (ISBN 0-8002-2074-9). (Ger. & Eng.). 1971-1972. 45.00x ea. Intl Pubns Serv.
Technical Dictionary: Refrigeration & Air Conditioning. (Eng., Fr., Ger. & Arabic.). 1979. 35.00x (ISBN 0-686-44746-8, Pub. by Collets). State Mutual Bk.
Technical Dictionary: The Textile Industry. (Eng., Fr., Ger. & Arabic.). 1975. 30.00x (ISBN 0-686-44748-4, Pub. by Collets). State Mutual Bk.
Technical-Economical Dictionary for Business Purposes. B. Bajic et al. 1700p. (Eng., Fr., Ger. & Serbocroation.). 1973. 95.00 (ISBN 0-686-92638-2, M-9689). French & Eur.
Technical Glossary of Horticultural & Landscape Terminology. American Association of Nurserymen. 9.95; educators 6.00; 10 or more 5.00. Am Nurserymen.
Technical Glossary of Horticultural & Landscape Terminology. Ed. by Edward B. Ballard et al. LC 78-165521. 1971 (ISBN 0-686-26652-8). text ed. 5.50 (ISBN 0-935336-00-1); tchrs' ed. 4.00 (ISBN 0-935336-00-1). Horticult Research.
Technical Manual & Dictionary of Classical Ballet. 3rd, rev. ed. Gail Grant. (Illus.). 160p. 1982. pap. 2.95 (ISBN 0-486-21843-0). Dover.
Technical Petroleum Dictionary of Well-Logging, Drilling & Production Terms. S. Ketchian & R. Desbrandes. 366p. 1965. 99.00x (ISBN 2-7108-0046-2, Pub. by Graham & Trotman England). State Mutual Bk.
Technical Petroleum Dictionary of Well-Logging Drilling, & Production Terms. Ed. by S. Ketchian et al. 366p. 1965. 92.00x (ISBN 0-677-61140-4). Gordon.
Technical Petroleum Dictionary of Well-Logging, Drilling & Production Terms. Ed. by Sonia Ketchian. LC 65-74805. (Illus.). 366p. (Rus., Fr., Eng. & Ger.). 1965. 75.00x (ISBN 0-8002-2076-5). Intl Pubns Serv.
Technical Pocket Dictionary, English-German, German-English, 2 vols. 2nd ed. Henry G. Freeman. (Eng. & Ger.). 12.00 ea. Ger.-Eng (ISBN 3-1900-6212-9). Eng.-Ger (ISBN 3-1900-6213-7). Adler.
Technical Pocket Dictionary-Technisches Taschenwoerterbuch. 2nd ed. Henry G. Freeman. (Eng. & Ger.). 1969. German-English 7.50x (ISBN 3-1900-6212-9); English-German 7.50x (ISBN 3-19-006213-7). Intl Pubns Serv.
Technical Reference Dictionary. Ed. by E. Burger. 571p. 1979. 95.00 (ISBN 0-686-92324-3, M-9890). French & Eur.
Technical Terms in Plastics Engineering. A. M. Wittfoht. 1976. 64.00 (ISBN 0-444-99846-2). Elsevier.
Technical Veterinary Dictionary. Wolfgang Lindeke. 185p. (Eng., Ger., Slovene & Rus.). 1972. 75.00 (ISBN 0-686-92494-0, M-9894). French & Eur.
Technicka Akustika. Walter Reichardt. LC 80-465612. 268p. (Eng., Rus., Span. & Slovak.). 1978. 50.00 Kcs. VEB Verlat Technik.
Technickoekonomicky Rusko-Cesky Slovnik. Vlasta Patockova. LC 80-452727. 269p. (Rus. & Czech., Praha, Czechoslovakia). 1979. write for info. SNTL.
Technik-Worterbuch: Chemie & Chemische Technik. 720p. (Ger.). 1980. vinyl 90.00x (ISBN 0-569-07861-X, Pub. by Collet's). State Mutual Bk.
Technik-Worterbuch: Elektronik, Elektrotechnik. 1980. 120.00x (ISBN 0-686-72091-1, Pub. by Collet's). State Mutual Bk.
Technik-Worterbuch: Optik & Optischer Geratebau. 432p. 1980. vinyl 90.00x (ISBN 0-686-72097-0, Pub. by Collet's). State Mutual Bk.
Techniques in Teaching Vocabulary. Virginia F. Allen. (Illus., Orig.). 1983. pap. 3.95x (ISBN 0-19-503231-4). Oxford U Pr.
Technisch Wissenschaftliches Taschenwoerterbuch. 408p. (Ger., Technical Scientific Dictionary). 32.00 (ISBN 3-87749-014-X, M-7643, Pub. by Georg Siemens Verlagsbuchhandlung). French & Eur.
Technische Akustik. Walter Reichardt. LC 80-491210. 268p. (Eng., Ger., Fr., Rus., Span., Pol., Hungarian, & Slovak.). 1979. M.30.00. VEB Verlag Technik.
Technische Kybernetik Grundlagen & Anwendungen Deutsch-Englisch. Hans D. Junge. 560p. (Ger. & Eng.). 1982. M.70.00. VEB Technik.
Technisches Deutsch fuer Auslaender. Strasak & Sulek. 156p. (Ger.). DM.16.00. Brandstetter.
Technisches Deutschfuer Auslaender. Jaroslav Strasak. (Ger., Technical German for Foreigners). 1969. 12.95 (ISBN 3-87097-041-3, M-7644). French & Eur.
Technisches Englisch. 7th ed. Henry G. Freeman. (Ger. -Eng.). 1975. 48.00 (ISBN 3-7736-5011-6, M-7647, Pub. by Girardet). French & Eur.
Technisches Fachwoerterbuch. 3rd ed. Hermann Mink. LC 76-477060. (Span. & Ital.). 1975. 2000.00 ptas (ISBN 8-4254-0994-2). Gustavo Gili.
Technisches Taschen Woerterbuch: Deutsch-Englisch, Englisch-Deutsch, 2 vols. Henry Freeman. (Ger. & Eng.). 1978. DM.pap. 17.50 ea. Hueber.
Technisches Taschenwoerterbuch. 3rd ed. H. Freeman. 584p. (Ger. & Eng., German-English Technical Dictionary). 1972. 12.50 (ISBN 3-19-006212-9, M-7648, Pub. by M. Hueber). French & Eur.
Technisches Taschenwoerterbuch. 3rd ed. H. Freeman. 584p. (Ger. & Eng.). 1972. 12.50 (ISBN 3-19-006212-9). Heuber.
Technisches Taschenwoerterbuch. A. Grunwald-Beyer. 533p. (Ger. & Fr.). 25.00 (ISBN 3-87749-013-1, M-7646, Pub. by Georg Siemens Verlagsbuchhandlung). French & Eur.
Technisches Taschenwoerterbuch. A. Kroeger-Jannetti. 804p. (Ger. & Span.). 32.00 (ISBN 3-87749-012-3, M-7645, Pub. by Georg Siemens Verlagsbuchhandlung). French & Eur.
Technisches Woerterbuch, 2 vols. Ulatko Dabac. (Serbocroation & Ger.). 1969. 112.00 (ISBN 3-7625-0550-0, M-7653, Pub. by Bauverlag). French & Eur.
Technisches Woerterbuch, 2 vols. Ulatko Dabac. (Serbo-Croation & Ger.). 1969. 112.00 (ISBN 3-7625-0550-0). Bauverlag.
Technisches Woerterbuch. Taspinar. xii, 1563p. (Ger. & Turkish.). 1982. DM.110.00. Brandstetter.
Technisches Woerterbuch, Vol. 1. Antonin Kucera. (Rus. & Ger.). 1966. 25.00 (ISBN 3-87097-025-1, M-7654, Pub. by Brandstetter). French & Eur.
Technisches Woerterbuch, Vol. 1. Antonin Kucera. (Rus. & Ger.). 1966. 25.00 (ISBN 3-87097-025-1). Brandstetter.
Technisches Woerterbuch, Vol. 1. A. Naxerova. (Czech. & Ger.). 1970. 40.00 (ISBN 3-87097-049-9, M-7649, Pub. by Brandstetter). French & Eur.
Technisches Woerterbuch, Vol. 1. A. Naxerova. (Czech. & Ger.). 1970. 40.00 (ISBN 3-87097-049-9). Brandstetter.
Technisches Woerterbuch, Vol. 1. 2nd ed. Salvatore Orlando-Meyer. (Ital. & Ger.). 1977. 40.00 (ISBN 3-87097-079-0, M-7651, Pub. by Brandstetter). French & Eur.
Technisches Woerterbuch, Vol. 1. 2nd ed. Salvatore Orlando-Meyer. (Ital. & Ger.). 1977. 40.00 (ISBN 3-87097-079-0). Brandstetter.
Technisches Woerterbuch, Vol. 2. Antonin Kucera. (Rus. & Ger.). 1966. 32.00 (ISBN 3-87097-026-X, M-7655, Pub. by Brandstetter). French & Eur.
Technisches Woerterbuch, Vol. 2. Antonin Kucera. (Rus. & Ger.). 1966. 32.00 (ISBN 3-87097-026-X). Brandstetter.
Technisches Woerterbuch, Vol. 2. A. Naxerova. (Czech. & Ger.). 1972. 40.00 (ISBN 3-87097-056-1, M-7650, Pub. by Brandstetter). French & Eur.
Technisches Woerterbuch, Vol. 2. A. Naxerova. (Czech. & Ger.). 1972. 40.00 (ISBN 3-87097-056-1). Brandstetter.
Technisches Woerterbuch, Vol. 2. 2nd ed. Salvatore Orlando-Meyer. (Ital. & Ger.). 1977. 40.00 (ISBN 3-87097-080-4, M-7652, Pub. by Brandstetter). French & Eur.
Technisches Woerterbuch, Vol. 2. 2nd ed. Salvatore Orlando-Meyer. (Ital. & Ger.). 1977. 40.00 (ISBN 3-87097-080-4). Brandstetter.
Technisches Woerterbuch: Band I, Italienisch-Deutsch. Meyer & Orlando. xii, 1345p. (Ital. & Ger.). 1982. DM.120.00. Brandstetter.
Technisches Woerterbuch: Band I, Russisch-Deutsch. Kucera. 330p. (Rus. & Ger.). 1982. DM.40.00. Brandstetter.
Technisches Woerterbuch: Band I, Tschechisch-Deutsch. Naxerova. 1096p. (Czech. & Ger.). 1982. DM.50.00. Brandstetter.
Technisches Woerterbuch: Band II, Deutsch-Italienisch. Meyer & Orlando. 1567p. (Ger. & Ital.). 1982. DM.120.00. Brandstetter.
Technisches Woerterbuch: Band II, Deutsch-Russisch. Kucera. 464p. (Ger. & Rus.). 1982. DM.50.00. Brandstetter.
Technisches Woerterbuch Deutsch-Esperanto. R. Haferkorn. (Ger. & Esperanto.). 1967. Can.$1.80 (ISBN 0-919186-01-7). U of Toronto Pr.
Technisches Woerterbuch Fuer Die Schuhindustrie: German-English & English-German. LC 67-73812. 304p. (Ger. & Eng.). 1966. 17.50x (ISBN 3-7785-0040-6). Intl Pubns Serv.
Technishes Englisch. 7th ed. Henry G. Freeman. (Ger. & Eng.). 1975. 48.00 (ISBN 3-7736-5011-6). Girardet.
Technological Dictionary. Michel Feutry. LC 78-346108. (Fr. & Ger.). 1976. 160.00 F (ISBN 2-85608-000-6). Maison Dictionnaire.
Technological Dictionary in Three Languages, 3 vols. Hoyer-Kreuter. Ed. by Alfred Schlomann. Incl. Vol. 1. German-English-French; Vol. 2. English-German-French; Vol. 3. French-German-English. (Ger., Fr & Eng.). Set. 135.00 (ISBN 0-8044-0202-7). Ungar.
Technological Dictionary: Mechanics, Metalurgy, Hydraulics & Related Industries. Ed. by Michel Feutry et al. (In 4 languages). 1976. lib. bdg. 55.00x (ISBN 2-85608-000-6). Marlin.
Technological Engineering Dictionary German-Serbocroatian. Ed. by S. Radic. 495p. (Ger. & Serbocroation.). 1981. 95.00 (ISBN 0-686-92294-8, M-9687). French & Eur.
Technologie und Terminologie der Gewerbe und Kunste bei Griechen und Romern, 4 vols. Hugo Blumner. Ed. by Moses Finley. LC 79-4963. (Ancient Economic History Ser.). (Illus., Ger.). 1980. Repr. of 1875 ed. Set. lib. bdg. 128.00x (ISBN 0-405-12350-7); 32.00x ea. Vol. 1 (ISBN 0-405-12351-5). Vol. 2 (ISBN 0-405-12352-3). Vol. 3 (ISBN 0-405-12484-8). Vol. 4 (ISBN 0-405-12485-6). Ayer Co.
Technologisches Woerterbuch. Egon Von Bahder. (Rus. & Ger.). 1970. 72.00 (ISBN 3-7736-5280-1, M-7656, Pub. by Girardet). French & Eur.
Technologisches Woerterbuch. Egon Von Bahder. (Rus. & Ger.). 1970. 72.00 (ISBN 3-7736-5280-1). Girardet.
Technologisches Woerterbuch Franzoisisch. Martin Pabst. 550p. (Port. & Ger.). 1971. leatherette 92.00 (ISBN 0-686-56470-7, M-7662, Pub. by Verlag W. Girardet). French & Eur.
Technologisches Woerterbuch Franzoisisch. Martin Pabst. 550p. (Port. & Ger.). 1971. leatherette 92.00. Girardet.
Technologisches Woerterbuch Franzoisisch. 3rd ed. Kurt Stellhorn. (Fr. & Ger.). 1965. leatherette 86.00 (ISBN 3-7736-5221-6, M-7660, Pub. by Verlag W. Girardet). French & Eur.
Technologisches Woerterbuch Franzoisisch. 3rd ed. Kurt Stellhorn. (Fr. & Ger.). 1965. leatherette 86.00 (ISBN 3-7736-5221-6). Girardet.
Technologisches Woerterbuch Spanisch. 564p. (Span. & Ger.). 1967. leatherette 99.50 (ISBN 3-7736-5410-3, M-7664, Pub. by Verlag W. Girardet). French & Eur.
Technologisches Woerterbuch Spanisch. 564p. (Span. & Ger.). 1967. leatherette 99.50 (ISBN 3-7736-5410-3). Girardet.

Tedesco-Italiano, Italiano-Tedesco. Ed. by Vladimiro Macchi. LC 77-579817. xvi, 938p. (Ital. & Ger.). 1976. L.18000.00. Sansoni.

Tekhnicheskaia Terminologiia. 520p. (Rus.). 1977. 14.75 (Pub. by Metsniereba). Four Continent.

Tekhnicheskii Slovar Spravochnik Po Toplivu & Maslam. K. K. Papok & N. A. Ragozin. 766p. (Rus.). 1963. 6.50 (Pub. by Gostoptekhizdat). Four Continent.

Tekhnicheskii Slovar Spravochnik po Toplivu i Maslam. K. K. Papok & N. A. Ragozin. 766p. (Rus.). 1963. 6.50 (Pub. by Gostoptekhizda r). Four Continent.

Telugu-Russkii Slovar. S. I. Dzenit. 744p. (Rus.). 1972. 8.50 (Pub. by Sov. Entsiklopediia). Four Continent.

Ten Bosch's Quadralingual Engineering Dictionary. 692p. (Dutch, Eng. , Fr. & Ger.). 40.00. Imported Bks.

Ten Thousand Legal Words. M. Kurtz et al. 1971. 6.56 (ISBN 0-07-035669-6, G). McGraw.

Ten Thousand Medical Words, Spelled & Divided for Quick Reference. Edward E. Byers. 128p. 1972. text ed. 6.40 (ISBN 0-07-009503-5, G). McGraw.

Term Loan Handbook. Committee on Developments in Business Financing of the Section of Corporation et al. 300p. 1983. 55.00 (ISBN 0-686-89076-0). HarBraceJ.

Terminal Degree: The Job Crisis in Higher Education. Emily K. Abel. 250p. 1984. 24.95 (ISBN 0-686-89487-1). Praeger.

Terminologia Anatomica. Yves Chatain. 316p. (Span.). 1967. 5.00. Norma.

Terminologia cientifica medica en euskera: Obra completa. (Span.). 1982. write for info. (ISBN 84-300-7123-7). Autor.

Terminologia cientifica medica en euskera. 192p. (Span.). 1982. write for info. (ISBN 84-300-7124-5). Autor.

Terminologia cientifica medica en euskera. (Span.). 1982. write for info. (ISBN 84-300-7123-7). Autor.

Terminologia de la Danza Moderna. P. Love. (Span.). write for info. EUDEBA.

Terminologia de la Education. Rosa E. Torres. LC 78-111426. 210p. (Span.). 1978. write for info. Minist Ed La Paz.

Terminologia del Contador. 7th ed. Mancera. 401p. (Span.). Mex.$50.00. Banca Comercio.

Terminologia del Paludismo & de la Erradicacion del Paludismo. 161p. (Span.). 1964. 3.25. OMS.

Terminologia Fitogenetica & Citogenetica. (Span.). 3.20; Mex.$40.00. Herrero.

Terminologia Gramatical para su Empleo en la E. G. B. 44p. (Span.). 1981. write for info. (ISBN 84-369-0852-X). Serv Pub Minist.

Terminologia Medica: Texto Programado. Smith-Davis. 280p. (Span.). 1974. Mex.$3.84. Limusa.

Terminologia Moderna de Energia de Agua en el Sistema Suelo-Planta Atmosfera. S. A. Gavande & Elemer Bornemisza. 6p. (Span.). 1969. write for info. IICA.

Terminologia Musical: Texto del Conservatorio "Fracassi". E. A. Fracass. (Span.). write for info. Ricordi.

Terminologia Turistico Alberghiera. E. Neiger. vi, 788p. (Ital.). 1983. write for info. Ed Calderini.

Terminologia turistico alberghiera: L'albergatore poliglotta. 3rd ed. Elisabetta Neiger. (Illus.). vi, 178p. (Ital., Eng., Ger. & Fr.). L.5000.00 (C/980). Ed Calderini.

Terminologia Usual de la Ciencia & en la Tecnica de la Telecomunicacion. 3rd ed. 384p. (Span.). 1966. 300.00 ptas. Paraninfo.

Terminological Dictionary of Automatic Control. 641p. 1977. Leatherette 19.95 (ISBN 0-686-92164-X, M-9059). French & Eur.

Terminologicheskii Slovar Po Informatike: Na 14-i Iazykakh. 752p. (Rus.). 1975. 29.85. Four Continent.

Terminologicheskii Slovar Po Nauchnoi Informatsii. Ed. by A. I. Mikhailov et al. 192p. (Rus.). 1969. 2.75 (Pub. by Vsesoiuznyi in-tut Nauchin & Tekhn. Imformatsii). Four Continent.

TerminologicheskiiSLovar Po Informatike. 752p. (Rus.). 1975. 29.85 (Pub. by Izd. Mezhdunarod. Tsentra & Tekhn. Informatsii). Four Continent.

Terminologie de la physique: Anglais-Allemand-Francais. A. Jesse. (Illus.). 129p. (Eng., Ger., & Fr.). 1980. 85.00 F. Maison Dictionnaire.

Terminologie et Lexicographie Medicales. 60p. (Fr.). 1967. pap. 17.50 (ISBN 0-686-57229-7, M-6530). French & Eur.

Terminologie Fondamentale En Odonto-Stomatologie et Lexique: Francais-Anglais, Anglais-Francais. 259p. (Fr. & Eng.). 1977. 27.50 (ISBN 0-686-57210-6, M-6492). French & Eur.

Terminologie Fondamentale en Odonto-Stomatologie. Leon Roucoules. LC 77-469099. 259p. (Eng. & Fr.). 1977. write for info. (ISBN 2-224-00328-5). Maloine.

Terminologie van het Crediet-Wezen in het Grieksch. Jan Korver. Ed. by Moses Finley. LC 79-4987. (Ancient Economic History Ser.). (Dutch). 1980. Repr. of 1934 ed. lib. bdg. 14.00x (ISBN 0-405-12372-8). Ayer Co.

Terminology & Communication Skills in the Health Sciences. J. Lea. 1975. pap. 12.95 (ISBN 0-87909-821-X). Reston.

Terminology & Concepts in Mental Retardation. Joel R. Davitz et al. LC 62-61261. (Orig.). 1964. pap. text ed. 5.50x (ISBN 0-8077-1233-7). Tchrs Coll.

Terminology & Definitions of Speech Defects. Mardel Ogilvie. LC 70-177132. (Columbia University. Teachers College. Contributions to Education: No. 859). Repr. of 1942 ed. 17.50 (ISBN 0-404-55859-3). AMS Pr.

Terminology for Accountants. 1976 ed. Canadian Institute of Chartered Accountants. LC 77-370287. 92p. (Eng.). 1976. write for info. (ISBN 0-88800-002-2). Canadian Inst Chart.

Terminology for Accountants. 1976. 8.50 (219). Can Inst Chart Accts.

Terminology for Automatic Control: MC85.1-1963. American Society of Mechanical Engineers. incl. supplements 6.00 (NX0036); members 4.80; Supplement MC85.1a-1966 1.75 (N00052); Supplement MC85.1b-1972 1.75 (N00037). ASME.

Terminology for Pressure Relief Devices: B95.1-1977. American Society of Mechanical Engineers. 3.50 (N00088); members 4.00. ASME.

Terminology of Adult Education. (IBE Data Ser.). 154p. 1980. pap. 10.50 (ISBN 92-3-001683-7, U950, UNESCO). Unipub.

Terminology of Anatomy & Physiology: A Programmed Approach. Dale P. Layman. LC 82-13448. 293p. 1983. pap. 10.95 (ISBN 0-471-86262-2, Pub. by Wiley Med). Wiley.

Terminology of Communication Disorders: Speech, Language, & Hearing. 2nd ed. Lucille Nicolosi. (Illus.). 338p. 1982. 18.50 (ISBN 0-683-06499-1). Williams & Wilkins.

Terminology of Communication Disorders: Speech, Language, Hearing. Lucille Nicolosi et al. (Illus.). 288p. 1978. pap. 17.50 (ISBN 0-683-06500-9). Williams & Wilkins.

Terminology of Documentation: A Selection of 1200 Basic Terms Published in English, French, German, Spanish & Russian. 274p. (Eng., Fr., Ger., Span. & Rus.). 1976. pap. 24.25 (ISBN 92-3-001232-7, U673, UNESCO). Unipub.

Terminology of Environmental Hygiene, 2 vols. European Parliament - Translation Division. 148p. (Eng., Fr., Ital., Ger. & Dutch). 1971-72. 5.00x ea (ISBN 0-8002-1350-5). Intl Pubns Serv.

Terminology of Forest Science, Technology, Practice & Products (with 1978 Addendum) Society of American Foresters. 1971. 21.00 set; Addendum only 3.00. Soc Am Foresters.

Terminology of Malaria & of Malaria Eradication: Report of a Drafting Committee. 127p. (Eng., Fr. , Rus. & Span.). 1963. pap. 6.40 (ISBN 92-4-154014-1). World Health.

Terminology of Optical Measurements. 1969. 12.00 (017-2); members 8.00. TAPPI.

Terminology of Technical & Vocational Education. 1979. pap. 5.00 (ISBN 92-3-001593-8, U884, UNESCO). Unipub.

Terminology: Special Education. 1978. pap. 15.75 (ISBN 92-3-001564-4, U844, UNESCO). Unipub.

Terminology: UNESCO: IBE Education Thesaurus. 1978. pap. 15.75 (ISBN 92-3-101531-1, U842, UNESCO). Unipub.

Terminoloski Komparativni Srpskohrvatsko. Rudolf Toth. LC 77-476859. 224p. (Eng. & Hungarian). 1976. write for info. Ekonomski Fakultet.

Terminos & Conceptos Mas Usuales en Mecanizacion Administrativa. Juan Calbet Sequi. 249p. (Span.). 4.80; Mex.$60.00. Limusa.

Terminos del Parentesco en el Otomangue. Herbert Harvey. (Span.). 1963. Mex.$35.00. INAH.

Terminos Fundamentales en Etica. Robert S. Hartman. 43p. (Span.). 1972. write for info. Univ Aut Nuevo.

Terminos Internacionales en la Gestion de Compras & Ventas. Roman San Juan Rubio. 44p. (Span.). 70.00 ptas. APD.

Terminos Judiciales. Pascual Castan. 184p. (Span.). 1964. 200.00 ptas. Dist. Anfora.

Terminos Judiciales. Pascual Castan. 184p. (Span.). 1964. 200.00 ptas. Dist. Arenzadi.

Terminos Topograficos en la Argentina Colonial, 1516-1810. Benjamin Nunez. 351p. (Span.). 1965. Mex.$2.00. Inst. Pan. Georg.

Terms & Conveyors Definitions: ANSI-CEMA No. 102, ANSI MH4.1. American National Standards Institute. 1975. 5.00 (VI-18). Material Handling.

Terms & Definitions for the Weighing Industry. 4th ed. Scale Manufacturers Association. 75p. 1981. 5.00 (S*M-2). Scale Mfrs.

Terms Defining Humidity of Air. 1978. 4.00 (014-23); members 2.67. TAPPI.

Terms for happiness in Euripides. Marianne McDonald. LC 79-312780. 335p. (Eng.). 1978. write for info. (ISBN 3-525-25149-1). Vandenhoeck.

Terms in Systemic Linguistics. Alex DeJoia & Adrian Stenton. LC 80-5089. 1980. 20.00 (ISBN 0-312-79180-1). St Martin.

Terms-Mill Defects, II. International Fabricare Institute. (Fabric Care Ser.). 0.25 (FC-62); 10 or more 0.20, ea. Intl Fabricare Inst.

Terms-Mill Defects, III. International Fabricare Institute. (Fabric Care Ser.). 0.25, ea. (FC-63); 10 or more 0.20, ea. Intl Fabricare Inst.

Terms of Abuse for Some Chicago Social Groups see Lexicon of the Sports & Racing Car Enthusiast.

Terms of Political Discourse. William E. Connolly. LC 83-42928. 240p. 1984. 30.00x (ISBN 0-691-07664-2); pap. 9.95x (ISBN 0-691-02223-2). Princeton U Pr.

Terms of Trade & Class Relations: An Essay in Political Economy. Ashok Mitra. 208p. 1977. 30.00x (ISBN 0-7146-3083-7, F Cass Co). Biblio Dist.

Terms Related to Soap & Detergents. International Fabricare Institute. (Fabric Care Ser.). 0.25 (FC-20). Intl Fabricare Inst.

Terms, Symbols & Definitions for Acceptance Sampling: ANSI-ASQC Standard a2-1978. American Society for Quality Control. 8.50; members 7.00. Am Soc QC.

Tesoro De la Lengua Castellana, O Espanola. Sebastian De Covarrubias Horozco. (Span., Microphoto Reprod). 1927. 7.50 (ISBN 0-87535-020-8). Hispanic Soc.

Tesoro del Declamador Universal. (Span.). Mex.$18.00; Mex.$38.00. EDIMEX.

Tesoro Della Linqua Greca-Volgare Ed Italiana, cioe Ricchissimo dizzionario greco-volgare et italiano, 2 vols. Alexis De Sommevoire & Tomaso Da Parigi. (Gr. & Ital.). Repr. of 1709 ed. lib. bdg. 175.00x (ISBN 0-686-72425-9). Pt. 1, Italian-Greek, Viii, 513 Pages. Pt. 2, Greek-Italian, Xxviii, 461 Pages. Caratzas Pub Co.

Tesoro Lexicografico 1492-1726. Samuel Gili Gaya. 712p. (Span.). 1974. 240.00 ptas. 260.00. CSIS.

Tests of Literary Vocabulary for Teachers of English. L. H. Kennon. LC 70-176966. (Columbia University. Teachers College. Contributions to Education: No. 223). Repr. of 1926 ed. 17.50 (ISBN 0-404-55223-4). AMS Pr.

Teutscher, & Reussischer, Dictionarium: Dictionarium Vindobonense. Ed. by Gerhard Birkfellner. 960p. (Ger. & Rus.). 1983. M.120.00. Akad Verl Ath.

Text of Chinese Military Terms. Ed. by P. K. Li. 390p. (Chinese & Eng.). 1972. pap. 12.95 (ISBN 0-686-92268-9, M-9577). French & Eur.

Textil-Fachwoerterbuch. 3rd ed. Max Matthes. LC 79-385003. 204p. (Ger.). 1979. DM.write for info. (ISBN 3-794-90314-5). Schiele & Schon.

Textil-Worterbuch. Paul Hohenadel & Jonathan Relton. LC 78-339373. (Eng. & Ger.). 1977. write for info. (ISBN 3-87097-077-4). Brandstetter.

Textile Dictionary. 536p. (Eng. , Fr. , Ger. , & Span.). 1979. 106.50 (ISBN 0-444-41772-9). Elsevier.

Textile Dictionary. G. Velco. (Eng., Fr., Ger., Rus. & Bulgarian). 1977. 70.00x (ISBN 0-686-44749-2, Pub. by Collets). State Mutual Bk.

Textile Glossary. Marvin Klapper. LC 72-88888. 120p. 1973. pap. 1.95 (ISBN 0-87005-116-4). Fairchild.

Textile Industry Dictionary. Ed. by A. M. Sabrie & R. S. Scharaf. 394p. (Eng., Fr., Ger. & Arabic). 1975. 45.00 (ISBN 0-686-92311-1, M-9763). French & Eur.

Textile Terminology: German-English & English-German. Derrick O. Michelson. LC 72-402367. 136p. (Ger. & Eng.). 1967. 10.00x (ISBN 3-87150-106-9). Intl Pubns Serv.

Textile Terms & Definitions. Carolyn A. Farnfield & P. J. Alvey. 228p. 1975. 90.00x (ISBN 0-686-63806-9). State Mutual Bk.

Textile Terms & Definitions. 228p. 1981. 95.00x (ISBN 0-900739-17-7, Pub. by Textile Inst England). State Mutual Bk.

Textilwoerterbuch: Band I, English-Deutsch. Relton Hohenadel & Relton. 486p. (Eng. & Ger.). 1982. DM.70.00. Brandstetter.

Textilwoerterbuch: Band II, Deutsch-English. Hohenadel & Relton. 375p. (Ger. & Eng.). 1982. DM.70.00. Brandstetter.

Tezaurus Nauchno-Tekhnicheskikh Terminov. Ed. by Iu. I. Shemakin. 671p. (Rus.). 1972. 15.00 (Pub. by Voenizdat). Four Continent.

Tezaurus Po Mineralam, Vol. 2. 336p. (Rus.). 1977. 9.95 (Pub. by Viniti). Four Continent.

Tezaurus Po Mineralm, Vol. 1. 300p. (Rus.). 1976. 4.10 (Pub. by Viniti). Four Continent.

Thai-English & English-Thai Dictionary, 1 vol. 1974. 14.00 (ISBN 0-87557-087-9, 087-9). Saphrograph.

Thai-English Dictionary. George B. McFarland. (Thai & Eng.). 1944. 32.00x (ISBN 0-8047-0383-3). Stanford U Pr.

Thai-English Student's Dictionary. Ed. by Mary R. Haas. (Thai & Eng.). 1964. 20.00x (ISBN 0-8047-0567-4). Stanford U Pr.

Thai Vocabulary. Mary R. Haas. LC 79-92827. 373p. (Thai.). 1980. pap. 10.00x0747121xx (ISBN 0-87950-265-7). Spoken Lang Serv.

Thanodi ya Setswana ya Dikole. Morulaganyi Kgasa. LC 79-386132. x, 126p. (Tswana.). 1976. write for info. (ISBN 0-582-61708-1). Longman S Africa.

That's What People Say! A Dictionary of Common Speech Idioms. Martin H. Manser. (Illus,). write for info. (ISBN 0-333-33298-9). Macmillan.

Thayer's Greek-English Lexicon of the New Testament. Joseph H. Thayer. LC 78-67264. (Gr. & Eng.). 1978. pap. 16.95 (ISBN 0-8054-1376-6). Broadman.

The Taste of France: A Dictionary of French Food & Wine. Fay Sharman. Ed. by Brian Chadwick & Klaus Boehm. (Eng.). 1982. 10.95 (ISBN 0-395-32561-7). HM.

Theater Dictionary: British & American Terms in the Drama, Opera, and Ballet. Wilfred Granville. Repr. of 1952 ed. lib. bdg. 15.00x (ISBN 0-8371-4428-0, GRTD). Greenwood.

Theatre Language, a Dictionary. Walter P. Bowman & Robert H. Ball. LC 60-10495. 1976. pap. 6.95 (ISBN 0-87830-551-3). Theatre Arts.

Theological Dictionary of the New Testament, 10 vols. Ed. by Gerhard Kittel & Gerhard Friedrich. Incl. Vol. 1. 1964. 27.50 (ISBN 0-8028-2243-6); Vol. 2. 1965. 27.50 (ISBN 0-8028-2244-4); Vol. 3. 1966. 29.95 (ISBN 0-8028-2245-2); Vol. 4. 1967. 29.95 (ISBN 0-8028-2246-0); Vol. 5. 1968. 29.95 (ISBN 0-8028-2247-9); Vol. 6. 1969. 27.50 (ISBN 0-8028-2248-7); Vol. 7. 1970. 29.95 (ISBN 0-8028-2249-5); Vol. 8. 1972. 25.00 (ISBN 0-8028-2250-9); Vol. 9. 1973. 27.50 (ISBN 0-8028-2322-X); Vol. 10. 1976. 25.00 (ISBN 0-8028-2323-8). 279.80 set (ISBN 0-8028-2324-6). Eerdmans.

Theological Dictionary of the Old Testament, 4 vols. Ed. by G. Johannes Botterweck & Helmer Ringgren. Incl. Vol. I. (ISBN 0-8028-2325-4); Vol. II. (ISBN 0-8028-2326-2); Vol. III. (ISBN 0-8028-2327-0). 1978. 22.50ea (ISBN 0-686-77203-2). Eerdmans.

Theological Dictionary of the Old Testament, Vol. 4. Ed. by G. Johannes Botterweck & Helmer Ringgren. 560p. 1981. 22.50 (ISBN 0-8028-2328-9). Eerdmans.

Theological German Vocabulary. Walter M. Mosse. (Ger.). 1968. lib. bdg. 14.50x (ISBN 0-374-95966-8). Octagon.

Theoretical & Methodical Problems of Terminology: Proceedings, Moscow, 1979. (Infoterm Ser.: Vol. 6). 608p. pap. 65.00 (ISBN 3-598-21366-2, Pub. by K G Saur). Gale.

Thesarus of ERIC Descriptors. 9th ed. LC 80-52477. 512p. 1982. lib. bdg. 35.00x (ISBN 0-89774-019-X). Oryx Pr.

Thesaurus. 17th ed. American Petroleum Institute. 1980. 150.00; nonprofit institutions 50.00. Am Petroleum.

Thesaurus. Marie-Therese Laureilhe. (Illus.). 48p. (Fr.). 1977. 20.00 F. Ecole Biblio.

Thesaurus. (INIS Ser.: Rev. 20). 756p. 1981. pap. 46.50 (ISBN 92-0-178081-8, IN13-R20, IAEA). Unipub.

Thesaurus Ceramique. 2nd ed. Institut de Ceramique Francaise. 163p. (Fr.). 1974. 170.00 F. Francaise, Institut Ceramique.

Thesaurus de l'education de l'Unesco: Francais-Anglais. 264p. (Fr. & Eng.). 1974. 32.00 F. Unesco.

Thesaurus des Symboles Agrobioclimatiques, Geographiques & Techniques, 2 vols. J. L. Petit et al. (Illus.). 686p. (Fr.). 1971. 2240.00 F. Centre Informatique Develop.

Thesaurus des Symboles Agrobioclimatiques, Geographiques & Techniques, 3. J. M. Henry & A. B. Ergo. 270p. (Fr.). 1973. 450.00 F. Centre Informatique Develop.

Thesaurus des Symboles Agrobioclimatiques, Geographiques & Techniques, 4. A. B. Ergo et al. 531p. (Fr.). 1974. 535.00 F. Centre Informatique Develop.

Thesaurus des Termes Geographiques. 96p. (Fr.). 1971. 69.00 F. Technip.

Thesaurus di Scienze della Terra. LC 79-350721. 119p. (Eng. , Fr. , Ger. & Ital.). 1977. L.4000.00. Patron.

Thesaurus Doctrine Catholicae: Documentis Magisteri Eccleslasticae, Ordine Methodico. 812p. (Fr.). 51.00 F. Beauchesne.

Thesaurus du Management & de L'economie, 2 vols. 2nd ed. LC 77-461651. (Eng. & Fr.). 1975. 2025.00 F (ISBN 2-9500-2031-3). Bureau Marcel.

Thesaurus du Management & de l'economie, 2 vols. Marcel Van Dijk & Georges Sandeau. 150p. (Fr.). 1975. 225.00 F. M. Van Dijk.

Thesaurus Economie de l'energie. Institut Francais du Petrole. 232p. (Fr.). 1974. 194.00 F. Technip.

Thesaurus for Informatics. (Illus.). 167p. 1982. pap. 35.00 (ISBN 0-686-87240-1, IB100, Pub. by Intergovernmental Bureau). Unipub.

Thesaurus for Information Processing in Sociology. Jean Viet. 1971. pap. text ed. 20.00x (ISBN 90-2796-941-8). Mouton.

Thesaurus Genie Chimique. Bureau de l'Information Scientifique & Technique. LC 78-374404. vi, 199p. (Fr.). 1977. 350.00 F (ISBN 2-222-02176-6). Doc Scient.

Thesaurus Graecae Linguae, 9 vols. Henri Estienne. 10800p. (Lat. & Gr.). 1954. S.11000.00. Akad Druck.

Thesaurus Hydrologie. Ed. by Joelle Cicchini. LC 76-472957. iv, 134p. (Fr.). 1975. 30.00 F (ISBN 2-901560-00-8). Serv Doc Cart.

Thesaurus I. R. S. I. D. 242p. (Fr.). 1971. 70.00 F. Francais, (Comptor) Siderurg.

Thesaurus-Making: Grow Your Own Word-Stock. Helen M. Townley & Ralph C. Gee. (Grafton Ser.). 208p. 1981. lib. bdg. 32.00 (ISBN 0-86531-107-2). Westview.

Thesaurus Normalisation, 1: Liste Alphabetique Structuree Francais-Anglais. 281p. (Fr, & Eng.). 1976. 705.60 F. A. F. N. O. R.

Thesaurus Normalisation, 2: Index Bilingue Francais-Anglais par Mots Vedettes. 193p. (Fr. & Eng.). 1976. 600.00 F. A. F. N. O. R.

Thesaurus Normalisation, 3: Table de Correspondance Anglais-Francais. 124p. (Eng. & Fr.). 1976. 600.00 F. A. F. N. O. R.

Thesaurus of Agricultural Terms. 2nd ed. LC 78-61381. 1978. lib. bdg. 27.50x (ISBN 0-912700-45-9). Oryx Pr.

Thesaurus of British Archaeology. Lesley Adkins & Roy A. Adkins. LC 81-12898. (Illus.). 320p. 1982. 27.50x (ISBN 0-389-20245-2). B&N Imports.

Thesaurus of Computing Terms. 8th ed. Ed. by National Computing Centre. 1977. pap. 82.50x (ISBN 0-85012-169-8). Intl Pubns Serv.

Thesaurus of Engineering & Scientific Terms. rev. ed. Engineers Joint Council Editors. LC 68-6569. 1967. flexible cover 50.00 (ISBN 0-87615-163-2). AAES.

Thesaurus of English Words. Ed. by M. H. Manser. 224p. (Eng.). E5.00 (ISBN 0-600-33213-6). Hamlyn-Amer.

Thesaurus of English Words & Phrases. rev. ed. Peter M. Roget. Ed. by John L. Roget & Samuel R. Roget. 35.00 (ISBN 0-87559-049-7); thumb indexed 40.00 (ISBN 0-87559-050-0). Shalom.

Thesaurus of Entomology. Ed. by Foote. 1977. 15.00 (ISBN 0-686-22689-5); members 9.00. Entomol Soc.

Thesaurus of Forest Products Terms. Forest Products Research Society. 167p. 30.00 (685T1). Forest Prod.

Thesaurus of Metallurgical Terms. 4th ed. American Society for Metals. 35.00. ASM.

Thesaurus of Orchestral Devices. Gardner Read. Repr. of 1953 ed. lib. bdg. 45.00x (ISBN 0-8371-1884-0, REOD). Greenwood.

Thesaurus of Psychological Index Terms. 3rd ed. 336p. (Orig.). 1982. 40.00x (ISBN 0-912704-67-5). Am Psychol.

Thesaurus of Scales & Melodic Patterns. Nicholas Slonimsky. 1947. 27.50 (ISBN 0-684-10551-9, ScribT). Scribner.

Thesaurus of Slang. Howard N. Rose. LC 72-167144. xii, 120p. Repr. of 1934 ed. 34.00x (ISBN 0-8103-3115-2). Gale.

Thesaurus of Spanish Idioms & Everyday Language. Lawrence K. Brown. 165p. (Span.). 1975. pap. 4.95 (ISBN 0-8044-6059-0). Ungar.

Thesaurus of Terms for Indexing the Literature of Minerals Processing & Metals Extraction, 1974. Ed. by Warren Spring Laboratory. 1981. 75.00x (ISBN 0-686-97151-5, Pub. by W Spring England). State Mutual Bk.

Thesaurus Petrole. 288p. (Fr.). 1971. 154.00 F. Technip.

Thesaurus Philosophicus Linguae Hebraica, 4 pts. in 2 vols. Klatzkin. (Hebrew.). 47.50 (ISBN 0-87306-118-7). Feldheim.

Thesaurus Philosophorum Seu Distinctiones et Axiomata Philosophica. Georg Reeb. 377p. (Lat.). 1981. Repr. of 1891 ed. 150.00 (ISBN 0-8287-1490-8). Clearwater Pub.

Thesaurus Pollution Atmospherique. 158p. (Fr.). 1973. 107.00 F. I. F. C. E.

Thesaurus pour le Traitement de l'information en Sociologie. Jean Viet. 355p. (Fr.). 1971. 59.00 F. Mouton de Gruyter.

Thesaurus: Son Role, sa Structure, son Elaboration. Marie T. Laureilhe. LC 77-575129. (Illus.). 48p. (Fr.). 1977. 20.00 F (ISBN 2-901-11904-2). Assoc Biblio.

Thesaurus Verrier, 2 vols. (Fr.). 1971. 160.00 F. Inst Verre.

Thesaurus, 3: Liste Alphabetique. 2nd ed. 257p. (Fr.). 1975. 100.00 F. E. D. F.

Third Dictionary of Acronyms & Abbreviations: More Abbreviations in Management, Technology, & Information Science. Eric Pugh. 1977. 17.50 (ISBN 0-208-01535-3, Linnet). Shoe String.

Thirty Days to a More Powerful Vocabulary. Wilfred Funk & Norman Lewis. LC 72-94340. (Funk & W Bk.). (gr. 9-12). 1970. text ed. 12.45 (ISBN 0-308-40079-8, 430180). T Y Crowell.

Thirty Days to a More Powerful Vocabulary. Norman Lewis & Wilfred Funk. 1981. pap. 2.95 (ISBN 0-671-45675-X). PB.

Thirty-Thousand Selected Words Organized by Letter, Sound & Syllable. Joan Frazer et al. 1978. text ed. 15.95 (ISBN 0-88450-799-8, 3083-B); pap. text ed. 10.95 (ISBN 0-88450-798-X, 2506-B). Communication Skill.

Thorndike Barnhart Handy Dictionary. Ed. by Clarence L. Barnhart. 1971. pap. 2.25 (ISBN 0-553-20012-7, 12839-6). Bantam.

Thraenen-Samen & Steckdosenschnauze. Hilke Moeller. Ed. by C. R. Von Grieffenberg & Wolfdietrich Schnurres. LC 77-455717. (Ger.). 1975. 26.00 F (ISBN 3-26003-966-X). Jurisdruck.

Three Dimensions of Vocabulary Growth. Lewis M. Paternoster & Ruth L. Frager. (Orig.). (gr. 10-12). 1971. pap. text ed. 6.58 (ISBN 0-87720-345-8). AMSCO Sch.

Tibetan-English Dictionary. S. C. Das. (Tibetan & Eng.). Repr. of 1970 ed. 35.00x (ISBN 0-87902-125-X). Orientalia.

Tibetan-English Dictionary. S. C. Dass. (Tibetan & Eng.). 1979. 42.00 (ISBN 0-89684-329-7). Orient Bk Dist.

Tibetan-English Dictionary. H. A. Jaschke. (Tibetan & Eng.). 1980. 22.50 (ISBN 0-8426-0962-8). Orient Bk Dist.

Tibetan-English Dictionary. (Tibetan & Eng.). 35.00. Iaconi.

Tibetan-English Dictionary of Modern Tibetan. Melvyn C. Goldstein. (Tibetan & Eng.). 1975. 27.95x (ISBN 0-685-89505-X). Himalaya Hse.

Tibetan-English Dictionary: With Sanskrit Synonyms. S. Chandra Das. Ed. by Graham Sanberg & A. William Heyde. 1389p. (Tibetan & Eng.). 1976. Repr. 35.00 (ISBN 0-89581-177-4). Lancaster-Miller.

Tibetan-English Dictionary, with Sanskrit Synonyms. Sarat C. Das. Ed. by G. Sandberg & A. W. Heyde. 1384p. (Tibetan, Sanskrit & Eng.). 1970. Repr. of 1902 ed. 30.00x (ISBN 0-8002-2086-2). Intl Pubns Serv.

Tibetan-English Dictionary with Supplement. Ed. by Stuart H. Buck. (Publications in the Languages of Asia: No. 1). (Tibetan & Eng.). 1969. 36.95 (ISBN 0-8132-0269-8). Cath U Pr.

Tibetan-English, English-Tibetan Dictionary, 2 vols. S. C. Das & I. D. Kazi. (Tibetan & Eng.). Set. 70.00 (ISBN 0-686-77964-9). Heinman.

Tiefkuhl Lexikon. G. Doring & Rudolphi. 239p. (Ger.). 10.95 (ISBN 3-87150-020-8, M-7666, Pub. by Deutscher Fachverlag). French & Eur.

Tierlexikon, 5 vols. H. Smolik. (Ger.). 1968. pap. 32.00 (ISBN 3-499-16059-5, M-7667, Pub. by Rowohlt). French & Eur.

Tierlexikon, 5 vols. H. Smolik. (Ger.). 1968. pap. 32.00 (ISBN 3-499-16059-5). Rowohlt.

Tiernamen & Zoologische Fachworter. Erwin Hentschel. LC 77-451749. 528p. (Eng. & Ger.). 1976. DM.19.80 (ISBN 3-437-20130-1). Fischer Verlag.

Timber Trade Terminology. Hilkka Saario. LC 78-392222. 51p. (Eng. & Finnish.). 1975. write for info. (ISBN 9-5166-2165-1). Gaudeamus.

Timex-Sinclair One Thousand Pocket Dictionary. Joseph C. Giarratano. 1983. pap. 4.95 (ISBN 0-88022-028-7). Que Corp.

Title Insurance & Real Estate Securities Terminology. Intro. by John R. Johnsich. (Orig.). 1980. pap. 3.95 (ISBN 0-914256-11-4). Real Estate Pub.

Toba-Batak-Deutsches Worterbuch. Johannes G. Warneck. LC 79-353140. xii, 332p. (Ger. & Toba-Batak.). 1977. fl.98.80 (ISBN 9-0247-2018-4). Nyhoff.

Today's Dictionary of the Bible. Compiled by T. A. Bryant. 678p. (Orig.). 1982. 15.95 (ISBN 0-87123-569-2, 230569). Bethany Hse.

Toimitustyon Terminologiaa. Liisa Miettinen. LC 77-469600. 39p. (Finnish.). 1975. Fmk.6.50 (ISBN 9-5110-2130-3). Otava.

Tolkovyi Slovar' Angliskikh Geologicheskikh Terminov, 3 vols. Ed. by M. Geri. (Rus. & Eng.). 1977. 37.50 set (Pub. by Prosveshchenie). Four Continent.

Tolkovyi Slovar Belorusskogo Iazyka, 3 vols. (Rus.). 1977. 14.95 ea. (Pub. by Glav. Red. Bel. Entsiklopedii). Vol. 1, 1977, 608p. Vol. 2, 1978, 768p. Vol. 3, 1979, 672p. Four Continent.

Tolkovyi Slovar Moldavskogo Iazyka: A-M, Vol. 1. 848p. (Rus.). 1977. 10.50 (Pub. by Kartia Moldoveniaske). Four Continent.

Tolkovyi Slovar Russkogo Iazyka, 4 vols. 0 ed. Ed. by D. N. Ushakov. (Rus.). 1940. Set 95.00. Four Continent.

Tolkovyi Slovar Terminov, Primeniaemykh & Sudovom Mashinostroenii. N. I. Iasulovich. 432p. (Rus.). 1966. 4.50 (Pub. by Sudostroenie). Four Continent.

Tolkovyi Slovar' Zhivogo Velikorusskogo Iazyka, 4 vols. V. Dal' (Russkii iazyk Ser.). (Rus.). 1978. 64.50 set. Four Continent.

Tolkovyi Slovar Zhivogo Velikorusskogo Iazyka, 4 vols, Vol. 4. (Rus.). 1980. 16.95 (Pub. by Russkii Iazyk). Four Continent.

Tool Dictionary. 2nd ed. Henry G. Freeman. (Ger. & Eng.). 1960. 78.00 (ISBN 3-7736-5052-3). Adler.

Tooley's Dictionary of Mapmakers. R. V. Tooley. LC 79-1936. 696p. (Orig.). 1981. pap. 40.00 (ISBN 0-8451-1702-5). A R Liss.

Tooley's Dictionary of Mapmakers. R. V. Tooley. LC 79-1936. 696p. 1979. 120.00x (ISBN 0-8451-1701-7). A R Liss.

Topical Dictionary of Bible Texts. James Inglis. (Direction Bks.). pap. 3.95 (ISBN 0-8010-5030-8). Baker Bk.

Topics & Terms in Environmental Problems. John R. Holum. LC 77-12805. 1977. 39.95x (ISBN 0-471-01982-8, Pub. by Wiley-Interscience). Wiley.

Topographic Terms in the Ohio Valley 1748-1800. W. Bruce Finnie. (Publications of the American Dialect Society: No. 53). 144p. 1970. pap. 8.00 (ISBN 0-8173-0653-6). U of Ala Pr.

Topographical Dictionary of Ireland, 3 Vols. Samuel Lewis. LC 75-102611. (Irish Culture & History Ser). 1970. Repr. of 1837 ed. Set. 150.00x (ISBN 0-8046-0788-5, Pub by Kennikat). Assoc Faculty Pr.

Topographical Dictionary of Two Thousand Eighty-Five English Emigrants to New England, 1620-1650. Charles E. Banks. LC 63-4154. 295p. 1981. Repr. of 1937 ed. 17.50 (ISBN 0-8063-0019-1). Genealog Pub.

Torah see Classified Concordance.

Torrent Control Terminology. (FAO Conservation Guides: No. 6). 156p. (Eng., Span., Ital. & Ger.). 1982. pap. 12.00 (ISBN 92-5-001091-5, F2224, FAO). Unipub.

Trade Names Dictionary: Company Index. 3rd ed. Ed. by Donna Wood. 1000p. 1982. 225.00x (ISBN 0-8103-0697-2). Gale.

Training von A bis Z: Kleines Worterbuch fuer der Theorie & Praxis der Sportl Trainings. Compiled by Gunter Thiess et al. LC 78-395459. 279p. (Ger.). 1978. DM.13.50. Sportverlag.

Transliterated Dictionary of the Russian Language. E. Garfield. LC 79-14068. (Rus.). 1979. lib. bdg. 25.00 (ISBN 0-89495-003-7); pap. 14.95 (ISBN 0-89495-011-8). ISI Pr.

Transportation Dictionary. Lester A. Probst & Katherine DeGross. LC 79-91885. 127p. (Eng.). 1979. write for info. (ISBN 0-9603760-0-3). Data Tactics.

Transportation-Logistics Dictionary. 2nd ed. Ed. by Joseph L. Cavinato. 323p. 1982. 14.00 (ISBN 0-87408-022-3). Traffic Serv.

Transpress Lexikon Seefahrt. Ulrich Scharnow. LC 77-471655. 608p. (Eng., Rus. & Ger., Berlin, East Germany). 1976. M.32.00. Transpress Verlag fur Verkehrswesen.

Travellers' Dictionary of Quotation: Who Said What, about Where. Ed. by Peter Yapp. 1022p. 1983. 29.95 (ISBN 0-7100-0992-5). Routledge & Kegan.

Tresor de Felibridge: Dictionnaire Provencal-Francais, 2 vols. Frederic Mistral. 2375p. (Fr.). Set. 195.00 (ISBN 0-686-56736-6, M-6414). French & Eur.

Tresor De la Langue Francaise: Dictionnaire De la Langue Du 19th et Du 20th Siecle (1789-1960, 14 vols. Ed. by Centre National De la Recherche Scientifique & Paul Imbs. 2000p. (Fr.). 1972. 55.00x ea. Intl Pubns Serv.

Tresor de la Langue Francaise: Dictionnaire de la langue du 19e & du 20e siecle, Tome 7. 1380p. (Fr.). 1979. 114.00 F (Dist. by Continental Bk Co). Klincksieck.

Trial Use Nuclear Glossary. American Nuclear Society. Incl. ANS-6.5, ANS-19.2, ANS-50 Glossaries. 25.00. Am Nuclear Soc.

Trictionary. 432p. (Chinese, Span. & Eng.). softcover 12.95. Bilingual Pubns.

Trilingual Dictionary. 216p. 1982. pap. 35.00 (ISBN 0-686-87246-0, IB101, Pub. by Intergovernmental Bureau). Unipub.

Trilingual Dictionary of Fisheries Technological Terms-Curing. (FAO Fisheries Ser.: No. 12). 91p. 1980. pap. 11.50 (ISBN 0-686-68188-6, F483, FAO). Unipub.

Trois Cent Cinquante Definitions Biologiques Raisonnees. Mireille Blain. LC 77-472766. 86p. (Fr.). 1976. 28.50 F (ISBN 2-7181-6364-X). Doc Univers.

Trubners Deutsches Woerterbuch, 8 vols. Alfred Gotze. 4851p. (Ger.). 1939. Set. 283.00 (ISBN 3-11-000319-8, M-7671, Pub. by de Gruyter). French & Eur.

Trudovoe Pravo: Entsiklopedicheskii Slovar. Ed. by A. I. Denisov. 576p. (Rus.). 1963. 4.60 (Pub. by Sov. Entsiklopediia). Four Continent.

Truebners Deutsches Woerterbuch, 8 vols. Ed. by Alfred Goetze & Walther Mitzka. (Ger.). 1947-57. Set. 240.00x (ISBN 3-11-000319-8). De Gruyter.

Trukese-English Dictionary. Ward H. Goodenough & Hiroshi Sugita. LC 79-54277. (Memoir Ser.: Vol. 141). (Turkish.). 1980. 10.00 (ISBN 0-87169-141-8). Am Philos.

Tschechisch, 2 vols. Incl. Teil I. Tschechisch-Deutsch. Rolf Ulbrich. 576p. DM.18.80 (10360); Teil II. Deutsch-Tschechisch. Friedrich Kabesch. 478p. DM.18.80 (10365). (Langenscheidts Taschenworterbucher Ser.). (Czech. & Ger.). DM.29.80 (11360). Langenscheidt.

Tu-Dien Dictionary. (Eng. & Vietnamese.). write for info. (608-55). Pan Amer Pub.

Tu Dien Mien Dich Hoc. LC 79-984056. (Eng., Fr. & Vietnamese.). 1976. write for info. Y Hoc.

Turkish-English Dictionary. 2nd ed. H. C. Hony. (Turkish & Eng.). 1957. 39.95x (ISBN 0-19-864108-7). Oxford U Pr.

Turkish-English Dictionary, 3 pts. James W. Redhouse. (Turkish & Eng.). 1976. Repr. of 1958 ed. Set. 250.00 (ISBN 0-518-19005-6). Ayer Co.

Turkish-English, English-Turkish Dictionary: New Red House, 2 Vols. (Turkish & Eng.). Set. 75.00 (ISBN 0-685-12051-1). Heinman.

Turkish, English-English, Turkish Dictionary (the Redhouse Portable Dictionary) Ed. by Robert Avery et al. (Turkish & Eng.). 15.00 (ISBN 0-685-80306-6). Heinman.

Tuttle's Watch-Pocket Dictionary. Eng.-Japanese 2.00 (ISBN 0-8048-0600-4). C E Tuttle.

Twenty-One Language Dictionary: International Dictionary. H. L. Ouseg. write for info. Philos Lib.

Twenty Thousand Medical Words. Robert W. Prichard & Robert E. Robinson. 288p. 1972. (HP); pap. 11.95 (ISBN 0-07-050874-7). McGraw.

Two Hundred One Persian Verbs - Arabic Script. Wood. (Arabic & Persian.). 1984. 9.95 (ISBN 0-8120-2562-8). Barron.

Two Hundred One Persian Verbs - Romanization. Wood. (Persian.). 1984. 9.95 (ISBN 0-8120-2563-6). Barron.

Two Thousand & One German & English Idioms: 2001 Deutsche und Englische Idiome. Bernard Rechtschaffen & Louis Marck. (Ger. & Eng.). 1984. pap. 9.95 (ISBN 0-8120-0474-4). Barron.

Two Thousand & One Italian & English Idioms: 2001 Locuzione Italiane e Inglese. Robert R. Hall, Jr. & Frances A. Hall. LC 81-66403. (Ital. & Eng.). 1981. pap. text ed. 9.95 (ISBN 0-8120-0467-1). Barron.

Two Thousand & One Spanish & English Idioms. (Span. & Eng.). write for info. (608-66). Pan Amer Pub.

Two Thousand & One Words You Need to Know to Pass Any Spanish Test. Christopher Kendris. (Span.). 1984. pap. 2.95 (ISBN 0-8120-2537-7). Barron.

Two Word Verb: A Dictionary of the Verb Preposition Phrases in American English. George A. Meyer. (Janua Linguarum Series Didactica: No. 19). 268p. 1975. text ed. 55.00x (ISBN 90-2793-323-5). Mouton.

Typewriting Dictionary. E. Mackay & G. M. Williams. 1980. NT.$12.95. Pitman Bks.

Typewriting Dictionary. Edith Mackay. (Illus.). 1977. text ed. 15.95x (ISBN 0-8464-0940-2). Beekman Pubs.

Tysiac Slow o Samolocie i Lotnictwie. Jerzy Domanski. LC 79-392676. 422p. (Pol., Warsaw, Poland). 1978. 70.00 Zl. Wydaw. Min. Obrony Narodowej.

Tysk-Dansk: Dansk-Tysk Ordbog. F. Albertus. 532p. (Danish & Ger.). 1982. 19.95 (ISBN 0-686-92489-4, M-1293). French & Eur.

Tysk-Dansk Dansk-Tysk Special Ordbog. E. Fryd. 175p. (Ger. & Danish.). 1974. 35.00 (ISBN 0-686-92491-6, M-1274). French & Eur.

Tysk-Dansk, Dansk-Tysk Specialordbog. Ejnar Fryd. LC 75-582435. 175p. (Ger. & Danish.). 1975. Kr.115.00. For Stat Rev.

Tysk-Dansk Ordbog. E. Bork & E. Kaper. 550p. (Ger. & Danish.). 1981. 24.95 (ISBN 0-686-92483-5, M-1282). French & Eur.

Tysk-Dansk Teknisk Ordbog. A. Warrern. 275p. (Ger. & Danish.). 1974. 49.95 (ISBN 0-686-92486-X, M-1291). French & Eur.

Tysk-Svensk Ordbok. 894p. (Ger. & Swedish.). 1980. Kr.170.00 (ISBN 91-24-14305-7). Esselte Studium.

Tysk-Svensk Ordbok: Supplement 80. 32p. (Ger. & Swedish.). 1980. Kr.42.00 (ISBN 91-24-29770-4). Esselte Studium.

U

Uchebny Slovar Obschetekhnich: Leksiki. I. F. Rudakova. 190p. (Rus., Ger., Fr., & Eng.). 1976. 1.00 (237-B, Pub. by Russkii Iazyk). Four Continent.

Uchebnyi Slovar Obshchetekhnich: Russko-Anglo-Frantsuzsko-Nemetskii. I. F. Rudakova et al. 190p. (Rus., Eng., Fr & Ger.). 1976. 1.00 (Pub. by Russkii Iazyk). Four Continent.

Uchebnyi Slovar' Sochetaenosti Slov Russkogo Iazyka. P. N. Denisov et al. (Russkii iazyk Ser.). 688p. (Rus.). 1978. 22.75. Four Continent.

Udissanasto Kahdeksankymmenta. Kielitoimisto. LC 80-463931. 194p. (Finnish.). 1979. write for info. (ISBN 9-51009-287-8). Soderstorm.

UJ Magyar Lexikon, 7 vols. (Hungarian.). 1960-1972. Set. 350.00 (ISBN 0-8277-3103-5). Pergamon.

Uj Magyar Tajszotar. Eva B. Lorinczy. LC 80-480571. (Hungarian.). 1979. 207.00 Ft (ISBN 9-6305-1810-4). Akademiai Kiado.

Ukrainian-English Dictionary. Ed. by C. H. Andrusyshen. 1200p. (Ukrainian & Eng.). 1981. pap. 19.50 (ISBN 0-8020-6421-3). U of Toronto Pr.

Ukrainian-English Dictionary. 2nd ed. Ed. by M. L. Podvesko. 22.50 (ISBN 0-87557-088-7, 088-7). Saphrograph.

Ukrainian-English, English-Ukrainian Dictionary, 2 vols. Compiled by M. L. Podvesko. (Ukranian & Eng.). 45.00 set (ISBN 0-686-91769-3). Heinman.

Ukrainian-English, English-Ukrainian Pocket Dictionary. (Ukranian & Eng.). 12.50 (ISBN 0-685-58556-5). Heinman.

Ullstein Lexikon der Deutschen Sprache. Rudolf Koester. (Ger.). 1969. 20.00 (ISBN 3-550-06016-5, M-7672, Pub. by Ullstein Verlag/VVA). French & Eur.

Ullstein Lexikon der Kunst und Architektur. Heiner Knell. (Ger.). 1976. 20.00 (ISBN 3-550-06013-0, M-7673, Pub. by Ullstein Verlag/VVA). French & Eur.

Ullstein Lexikon der Medizin. (Ger.). 1970. 22.50 (ISBN 3-550-06017-3, M-7674, Pub. by Ullstein Verlag/VVA). French & Eur.

Ullstein Lexikon der Pflanzenwelt. Hartmut Bastian. (Ger.). 1973. 27.50 (ISBN 0-686-56471-5, M-7675, Pub. by Ullstein Verlag VA). French & Eur.

Ullstein Lexikon der Tierwelt. Hartmut Bastian. (Ger.). 1967. 27.50 (ISBN 3-550-06014-9, M-7676, Pub. by Ullstein Verlag/VVA). French & Eur.

Ullstein Lexikon des Rechts. Otto Gritschneder. (Ger.). 1971. 20.00 (ISBN 3-550-06018-1, M-7677, Pub. by Ullstein Verlag/VVA). French & Eur.

Ultimate Crossword Puzzle Index. Douglas M. Hershey. LC 81-3591. (Illus.). 192p. 1981. pap. 7.95 (ISBN 0-498-02557-8). A S Barnes.

Unabridged Crossword Puzzle Dictionary. A. F. Sisson. 1963. 8.95 (ISBN 0-385-02843-1); thumb-indexed edition 10.95 (ISBN 0-385-01350-7). Doubleday.

Unbis Thesaurus. 369p. 1982. pap. 25.00 (ISBN 0-686-81419-3, UN81/1/17, UN). Unipub.

Understanding Basic Energy Terms. Robert V. Nelson. LC 81-2888. 1981. lib. bdg. 10.00 (ISBN 0-86663-806-7); pap. text ed. 5.25 (ISBN 0-86663-807-5). Ide Hse.

Understanding Electricity & Electrical Terms. 48p. 5.00. Natl Assn Elect Dist.

Understanding French Cookery: A Guide to French Recipes & Cooking Terms. Francoise Bourdet. LC 78-318824. iivi, 58p. (Eng. & Fr.). 1978. E0.95 (ISBN 0-901571-92-X). Kingsmead Pr.

Understanding Medical Terminology. 6th ed. Agnes C. Frenay. LC 77-73986. 1977. pap. text ed. 9.00 (ISBN 0-87125-038-1). Cath Health.

Understanding Medical Terms: A Self-Instructional Course. Ralph Rickards. (Illus.). 112p. 1980. pap. text ed. 8.25 (ISBN 0-443-02029-9). Churchill.

UNESCO Dictionary of the Social Sciences. Julius Gould & W. J. Kolb. LC 64-20307. 1964. 40.00 (ISBN 0-02-917490-2). Free Pr.

UNESCO Thesaurus, Vols. 1 & 2. 1978. 93.50 (ISBN 92-3-101469-2, U816, UNESCO). Unipub.

Ungarisch-Deutsches Woerterbuch der Rechts & Verwaltungssprache: Teil I, Ungarisch-Deutsch. Sandor Karcsay. xix, 487p. (Hungarian & Ger.). 1969. DM.48.00. Recht & Wirtschaft.

Ungarisch-Deutsches Woerterbuch der Rechts & Verwaltungssprache: Teil II, Deutsch-Ungarisch. Sandor Karcsay. xvii, 427p. (Ger. & Hungarian.). 1972. DM.48.00. Recht & Wirtschaft.

Uniform System of Accounts & Expense Dictionary for Small Hotels & Motels. American Hotel & Motel Association. (Illus.). 157p. 1981. Repr. 15.00 (ISBN 0-86612-001-7). Educ Inst Am Hotel.

Uniform Terminology System for Reporting Occupational Therapy Services. American Occupational Therapy Association. 1979. 12.00 (C-26); members 10.00. Am Occup Therapy.

Universal Dictionary of the English Langauge. rev. ed. Ed. by Henry C. Wyld. 1447p. 1978. 45.00 (ISBN 0-7100-2333-2). Routledge & Kegan.
Universal Dictionary of the Marine. William Falconer. LC 72-87321. (Illus.). Repr. of 1780 ed. lib. bdg. 37.50x (ISBN 0-678-05655-2). Kelley.
Universal Dictionary of Trade & Commerce, 2 Vols. 4th ed. Malachy Postlethwayt. LC 67-29516. Repr. of 1774 ed. Set. 250.00x (ISBN 0-678-00551-6). Kelley.
Universal Etymological English Dictionary. Nathan Bailey. 1969. Repr. of 1721 ed. 100.00 (ISBN 3-4870-2625-2). Adler.
Universal Film Lexicon. Frank Arnau. 69.95 (ISBN 0-8490-1246-5). Gordon Pr.
Universal French Dictionary. 560p. (Fr.). 2.95 (091). Langenscheidt.
Universal German Dictionary. 560p. (Ger.). 2.95 (092). Langenscheidt.
Universal Italian Dictionary. 560p. (Ital.). 2.95 (093). Langenscheidt.
Universal Latin Dictionary. 560p. (Lat.). 2.95 (094). Langenscheidt.
Universal Military Dictionary. George Smith. (Eng.). 1969. Can.$37.50 (ISBN 0-919316-57-3). U of Toronto Pr.
Universal Portuguese Dictionary. 560p. (Port.). 2.95 (095). Langenscheidt.
Universal Pronouncing Dictionary of Biography & Mythology, 2 Vols. 5th ed. Joseph Thomas. LC 76-137298. Repr. of 1930 ed. Set. 225.00 (ISBN 0-404-06386-1). AMS Pr.
Universal Russian Dictionary. 560p. (Rus.). 2.95 (096). Langenscheidt.
Universal Spanish Dictionary. 560p. (Span.). 2.95 (097). Langenscheidt.
Universal Turkish Dictionary. 560p. (Turkish.). 2.95 (098). Langenscheidt.
Universal Webster Dictionary. 560p. (Eng.). 2.95 (099). Langenscheidt.
Universal Woerterbuch Englisch-Deutsch. (Eng. & Ger.). 1983. 4.10. M Rosenberg.
Universita la Sperimentazione Dipartimentale. Tomas Maldonado. LC 80-499795. 147p. (Ital.). 1978. L.3.500. Guaraldi.
University Dictionary of Business & Finance. Ed. by Donald T. Clark & Bert A. Gottfried. (Apollo Eds.). 1972. pap. 4.95i (ISBN 0-8152-0143-5, A143). T Y Crowell.
University of Chicago Dictionary. Carlos Castillo & Otto F. Bond. (Span.). 2.95. Camino Real.
University of Chicago Dictionary. (Span. & Eng.). write for info. (608-4). Pan Amer Pub.
University of Chicago Spanish Dictionary. 3rd rev. enl. ed. Carlos Castillo & Otto F. Bond. (Span.). 1977. 12.50 (ISBN 0-226-09673-4, Phoen); pap. 4.95 (ISBN 0-226-09674-2). U of Chicago Pr.
University of Chicago Spanish Dictionary. 3rd rev. & enl. ed. Carlos Castillo & Otto F. Bond. Rev. by D. Lincoln Canfield. (Span. & Eng.). s.p. 12.50 (7815-7); pap. 4.95 s.p. (7855-6). Natl Textbk.
University of Chicago Spanish Dictionary. 3rd, rev. & enl. ed. Carlos Castillo & Barbara M. Garcia. LC 76-449. vi, 488p. (Eng. & Span.). 1977. 7.95 (ISBN 0-226-09673-4); 2.95 (ISBN 0-226-09674-2). U of Chicago Pr.
University of Chicago Spanish-English Dictionary. Bond Castillo. (Span. & Eng.). pap. 2.95. Iaconi.
University of Chicago Spanish-English Dictionary. 3rd ed. (Span. & Eng.). 1981. pap. 2.95 (ISBN 0-671-83685-4). PB.
Unkarilais-Suomalainen Sanakirja. Istvan Nyirkos. LC 78-389367. 392p. (Hungarian & Finnish.). 1977. write for info. (ISBN 9-51717-114-5). Suoma Kirja.
Unraveling the Integral Knot Concordance Group. N. Stoltzfus. LC 77-10133. (Memoirs Ser.: No. 192). 1977. 12.00 (ISBN 0-8218-2192-X, MEMO 192). Am Math.
Updated Concordance for the Tariff Schedule of the United States (TSUS) with the Brussels Tariff Nomenclature (BTN) (Eng. & Span.). 1977. pap. text ed. 10.00 (ISBN 0-8270-3320-6). OAS.
Upper Egypt: Its People & Its Products. Karl B. Klunzinger. LC 76-44747. Repr. of 1878 ed. 31.50 (ISBN 0-404-15866-8). AMS Pr.
Uppslagsbok i Psykoterapi och Medicinsk Psykologi. Henry Egidius. LC 76-488253. 198p. (Swedish.). 1976. Kr.50.00 (ISBN 9-1270-0680-8). Natur & Kultur.
Urban Information Thesaurus: A Vocabulary for Social Documentation. Ed. by Paul Rosenberg. LC 76-52604. 1977. lib. bdg. 35.00x (ISBN 0-8371-9483-0, UTH). Greenwood.
Urdang Dictionary of Current Medical Terms. Urdang. LC 80-22916. 455p. 1981. 22.95 (ISBN 0-471-05853-X, Pub. by Wiley Med). Wiley.
Urdu-English Dictionary. (Urdu & Eng.). 22.00 (ISBN 0-686-18358-4). Kazi Pubns.
Urdu-English Dictionary, Romanized. (Urdu & Eng.). 24.50 (ISBN 0-87557-090-9, 090-7). Saphrograph.
Urdu-English Vocabulary: Student's Dictionary. M. A. Barker et al. LC 79-92847. 382p. (Urdu & Eng.). 1980. pap. text ed. 10.00x (ISBN 0-87950-438-2). Spoken Lang Serv.
Usage in Dictionaries & Dictionaries of Usage. Thomas J. Creswell. 212p. 1975. 10.00 (55774); members 9.25. NCTE.
USAN & the USP Dictionary. annual US Pharmacoepial Convention. 19.50. US Pharmacopeia.
USAN & the USP Dictionary of Drug Names: 1983. 1982. 35.00 (ISBN 0-686-37681-1). USPC.
Use of the Dictionary of American English & the Dictionary of Americanisms. Atcheson L. Hench. Bd. with Bilingualism Among American Slovaks: Analysis of Loans. Goldie P. Meyerstein; Cleburne County, Arkansas Word List. Billy G. Skillman; Low German in Mexico. Wolfgang W. Moelleken. (Publications of the American Dialect Society: No. 46). 41p. 1966. pap. 4.20 (ISBN 0-8173-0646-3). U of Ala Pr.
Using the ICL Data Dictionary: Proceedings of the ICL DDS User Group. Ed. by A. T. Windsor. 160p. 1980. text ed. 29.95 (ISBN 0-906812-06-2). Birkhauser.
Utiszotar, Angol-Magyar. Tamas Magy. LC 79-345136. 313p. (Hungarian & Eng.). 1978. 33.00 Ft (ISBN 9-632-05069-X). Terra.
Uudissanasto. LC 80-463931. 194p. (Finnish.). 1979. write for info. (ISBN 9-5100-9287-8). Soderstrom.
Uudissanasto Kahdeksankymmenta. Kotimaisten Kielten Tutkimuskeskus. LC 80-463931. 194p. (Finnish.). 1979. write for info. (ISBN 9-51009-287-8). Soderstrom.
Uzbeck-English Dictionary. Natalie Waterson. (Uzbeck & Eng.). 1980. 55.00x (ISBN 0-19-713597-8). Oxford U Pr.

V

Vad Betyder Vaxtens Latinska Namn. Ivar Anell. LC 76-470315. 159p. (Eng., Danish, Finnish, Fr., Lat., Norwegian, & Swedish.). 1976. Kr.55.00 (ISBN 9-1370-6121-6). Forum Bok.
Vaegledning till Svenska Akademiens Ordbok. Sven Ekbo & Bengt Loman. 124p. (Swedish.). 1971. Kr.22.00 (ISBN 91-24-21113-3). Esselte Studium.
Van Goor's Concise Indonesian Dictionary. Kramer. (Indonesian.). 8.95. Iaconi.
Van Goor's Concise Indonesian Dictionary: English-Indonesian Indonesian-English. A. L. Kramer, Sr. LC 66-23535. (Indonesian.). 1966. Repr. 8.95 (ISBN 0-8048-0611-X). C E Tuttle.
Van Goor's Deens Woordenboek, 2 vols. Geerte De Vries. LC 76-477773. (Dutch & Danish.). 1976. fl.85.00 (ISBN 9-00002-195-2). Goor.
Van Nostrand Reinhold Color Dictionary of Herbs & Herbalism. Malcolm Stuart. 160p. 1982. pap. 12.95 (ISBN 0-442-28338-5). Van Nos Reinhold.
Van Nostrand Reinhold Color Dictionary of Mushrooms. Colin Dickinson & John Lucas. 160p. 1982. pap. 12.95 (ISBN 0-442-21998-9). Van Nos Reinhold.
Van Nostrand Reinhold Color Dictionary of Minerals & Gemstones. Michael O'Donoghue. 160p. 1982. pap. 12.95 (ISBN 0-442-27431-9). Van Nos Reinhold.
Vara Ord: Kortfattad Etymologisk Ordbok. Elias Wessen. 530p. (Swedish.). write for info. (ISBN 91-24-19975-3). Esselte Studium.
Vara Viktiga Ord: Basordlista Med Utbytesord. Sture Allen. LC 78-398662. (Illus.). 237p. (Swedish.). 1977. Kr.41.00 (ISBN 9-12426-834-8). Esselte Studium.
Variant Spellings in Modern American Dictionaries. rev. ed. Donald W. Emery. LC 73-83843. (Orig.). 1973. pap. 5.70 (ISBN 0-8141-5630-4); pap. 4.00 members (ISBN 0-686-86874-9). NCTE.
Varldspolitiskt lexikon. Laszlo Hamori. LC 77-476973. (Illus.). 200p. (Swedish.). 1976. Kr.68.00 (ISBN 9-12700-182-2). Natur & kultur.
Vehicle Dynamics Terminology. Society of Automotive Engineers. 24p. 1978. 5.00 (ISBN 0-89883-379-5, HS-J670E). Soc Auto Engineers.
Velasquez Dictionary: English-Spanish, Spanish-English. (Span. & Eng.). write for info. (608-6). Pan Am Bk Co.
Velasquez Spanish-English Dictionary. Revised ed. (Span. & Eng.). 12.95. Camino Real.
Velazquez Spanish & English Dictionary. Mariana Velazquez. 1486p. (Span. & Eng.). 16.95 (ISBN 0-8329-0472-4). New Century.
Velazquez Spanish-English Dictionary: Indexed. (Span. & Eng.). 16.95 (ISBN 0-8329-0472-4). New Century.
Velazquez Spanish-English, English-Spanish Dictionary. (Span. & Eng.). 19.95. Iaconi.
Velosipeday i sport. S. N. Novozhilov et al. LC 80-482184. 96p. (Rus., Fr., Eng., Ger. & Span.). 1979. 0.40 Rub. Russky Yazyk.
Verbal Games of Pre-School Children. Susan Iwamura. LC 79-22384. 1979. 25.00x (ISBN 0-312-83877-8). St Martin.
Verbal Judo: Words for Street Survival. George J. Thompson. (Illus.). 176p. 1983. text ed. 19.75 (ISBN 0-398-04879-7). C C Thomas.
Vergil Vocabularies. Paul E. Kunzer. (Bk. I- II). 1.00ea (8). Am Classical.
Vergleichendes und Etymologisches Worterbuch der Germanischen Starken Verben. Elmar Seebold. (Janua Linguarum, Ser. Practica: No. 85). (Ger., Ger.). 1970. pap. text ed. 87.00x (ISBN 0-686-22397-7). Mouton.
Vergleichendes Woerterbuch der Indogermanischen Sprachen, 3 vols. Alois Walde. Ed. by Julius Pokorny. (Ger.). 1973. Repr. of 1932 ed. Set. 224.00x (ISBN 3-11-004556-7). De Gruyter.
Verhaltensbiologie. Gunter Tembrock. LC 80-464719. 224p. (Eng. & Ger.). 1978. DM.19.80 (ISBN 3-437-20175-1). Fischer Verlag.
Verklarend Handwoordenboek der Nederlandse Taal. Matthijs J. Koenen & J. B. Drewes. LC 78-375038. xii, 1696p. (Dutch.). 1977. write for info. (ISBN 0-949964-77-8). Academia Edms.
Verschiffene Praefixe im Altindischen. Bernhard Koelver. LC 78-391285. 53p. (Sanskrit.). 1976. DM.18.00 (ISBN 3-51502-357-7). Steiner Verlag.
Verschliffene Prafixe im Altindischen. Bernhard Kolver. LC 78-391285. 53p. (Sanskrit.). 1976. DM.18.00. Steiner Verlag.
Versicherungsenzykolpaedie. Ed. by Walter G. Grosse et al. LC 77-574020. 3109p. (Ger.). 1976. DM.165.00 (ISBN 3-409-85531-9). Gabler.
Vest Pocket Arabic. Institute for Language Study. LC 74-17006. (Illus.). 252p. (Arabic.). 1979. pap. 3.50 (ISBN 0-06-464907-5, BN 4907, BN). B&N NY.
Vest Pocket English. Institute for Language Study. LC 58-59519. (Illus.). 188p. 1979. pap. 2.95 (ISBN 0-06-464908-3, BN 4908, BN). B&N NY.
Vest Pocket French. Institute for Language Study. (Illus.). 128p. (Fr.). 1979. pap. 1.95 (ISBN 0-06-464901-6, BN 4901, BN). B&N NY.
Vest-Pocket French. (Fr.). pap. 2.95 (ISBN 0-8329-1532-7). New Century.
Vest Pocket French Dictionary. rev. & enl. ed. 288p. (Fr.). pap. 2.95 (ISBN 0-8329-1532-7). New Century.
Vest Pocket German. Institute for Language Study. LC 58-8920. (Illus.). 128p. (Ger.). 1979. pap. 2.45 (ISBN 0-06-464902-4, BN 4902, BN). B&N NY.
Vest Pocket German Dictionary. rev. & enl. ed. 344p. (Ger.). pap. 2.95 (ISBN 0-8329-1533-5). New Century.
Vest Pocket Italian. Institute for Language Study. LC 58-8919. (Illus.). 128p. (Ital.). 1979. pap. 2.45 (ISBN 0-06-464903-2, BN 4903, BN). B&N NY.
Vest Pocket Italian Dictionary. Ed. by V. Bocchetta. 288p. (Ital.). pap. 2.95 (ISBN 0-8329-1535-1). New Century.
Vest Pocket Japanese. Institute for Language Study. (Illus.). 240p. (Japanese.). 1979. pap. 2.95 (ISBN 0-06-464906-7, BN 4906, BN). B&N NY.
Vest Pocket Modern Greek. Institute for Language Study. LC 60-53247. (Illus.). 184p. (Modern Greek.). 1979. pap. 2.95 (ISBN 0-06-464904-0, BN4904, BN). B&N NY.
Vest Pocket Russian. Marshall D. Berger. LC 60-9758. (Illus.). 182p. (Rus.). 1961. pap. 2.45 (ISBN 0-06-464905-9, BN4905, BN). B&N NY.
Vest Pocket Spanish. Institute for Language Study. (Illus.). 128p. (Span.). 1979. pap. 2.45 (ISBN 0-06-464900-8, BN 4900, BN). B&N NY.
Vest-Pocket Spanish. (Span.). pap. 2.95 (ISBN 0-8329-1534-3). New Century.
Vest-Pocket Spanish. (Span. & Eng.). pap. 2.95 (7723-1). Natl Textbk.
Vest Pocket Spanish Dictionary. rev. & enl. ed. Ed. by Ida Hinojosa. 320p. (Span.). pap. 2.95 (ISBN 0-8329-1534-3). New Century.
Vest Pocket Webster Dictionary. rev. ed. 304p. pap. 2.95 (ISBN 0-8329-1536-X). New Century.
Veterinary Dictionary: Russian-English. R. Mack. 104p. (Rus. & Eng.). 1972. pap. 25.00 (ISBN 0-686-92151-8, M-9710). French & Eur.
Veterinary Multilingual Thesaurus, 4 vols. Ed. by Commission of the European Communities. 1122p. 1979. 4 vols. & index 400.00x (ISBN 3-598-07082-9, Pub. by K G Saur). Gale.
Vibrating Equipment Terms & Definitions. 7p. 1981. 1.00. Conveyor Equip Mfrs.
Vietnamese Dictionaries. (Vietnamese.). handout free. Georgetown U Bil Ed Serv.

Vietnamese English Conversational Dictionary. (Vietnamese & Eng.). 4.95. Iaconi.

Vietnamese-English Dictionary. Dinh Nguyen Hoa. (Vietnamese & Eng.). 16.95. Iaconi.

Vietnamese-English Dictionary. Nguyen-Dinh-Hoa. 563p. (Eng. & Vietnamese.). 18.00. C E Tuttle.

Vietnamese-English Dictionary. Ed. by Nguyen-Dinh-Hoa. LC 66-17773. (Eng. & Vietnamese.). 1966. 16.95 (ISBN 0-8048-0618-7). C E Tuttle.

Vietnamese-English Dictionary Romanized. (Vietnamese & Eng.). 17.50 (ISBN 0-87559-014-4). Shalom.

Vietnamese-English, English Vietnamese Dictionary. Ed. by Le-Ba-Kong & Le-Ba-Khanh. (Vietnamese & Eng.). 30.00 (ISBN 0-8044-0310-4). Ungar.

Vietnamese-English Phrasebook with Useful Word List. Duong Thanh Binh & William Cage. 74p. (Eng. & Vietnamese.). pap. 5.00. Ctr Appl Ling.

Vietnamese-English Phrasebook with Useful Word List: For English Speakers. William Gage & Duong Thanh Binh. LC 75-24857. (Vietnamese Refugee Education Ser.: No. 2). 142p. (Vietnamese & Eng.). 1975. pap. 4.00x (ISBN 0-87281-044-5). Ctr Appl Ling.

Vietnamese-English Pocket Dictionary. (Vietnamese & Eng.). pap. 7.50 (ISBN 0-87559-165-5). Shalom.

Vietnamese Phrase Book. Nguyen-Dinh-Hoa. LC 75-34841. 120p. (Vietnamese.). 1976. pap. 4.25 (ISBN 0-8048-1196-2). C E Tuttle.

Virgil Eclogues & a Special Vocabulary to Virgil. Virgil. Ed. by J. B. Greenough & G. L. Kittredge. (College Classical Ser). 1977. lib. bdg. 20.00x (ISBN 0-89241-027-2). Caratzas Pub Co.

Visual Dictionary of Sex. Eric J. Trimmer. LC 77-73126. (Illus.). 1977. 25.00 (ISBN 0-89479-006-4); deluxe ed. 35.00 slipcased (ISBN 0-89479-011-0). A & W Pubs.

Visual Dictionary of Sex. Ed. by Eric J. Trimmer. (Illus.). 320p. 1981. pap. 12.95 (ISBN 0-89104-275-X, A & W Visual Library). A & W Pubs.

Visual Display Terminal: Usability Issues & Health Concerns. Ed. by John Bennett et al. 1983. 32.00 (ISBN 0-13-942482-2). P-H.

Visual Encyclopedia of Nautical Terms Under Sail. Basel Bathe & Alan Villiers. (Illus.). 1978. 15.95 (ISBN 0-517-53317-0). Crown.

VNR Dictionary of Business & Finance. David M. Brownstone et al. 320p. 1980. text ed. 18.95 (ISBN 0-442-20949-5). Van Nos Reinhold.

VNR Dictionary of Ships & the Sea. John V. Noel, Jr. 400p. 1980. text ed. 19.95 (ISBN 0-442-25631-0). Van Nos Reinhold.

VNR Investor's Dictionary. David M. Brownstone & Irene M. Franck. 320p. 1980. 16.95 (ISBN 0-442-21578-9). Van Nos Reinhold.

VNR Real Estate Dictionary. David M. Brownstone & Irene M. Franck. 352p. 1981. 18.95 (ISBN 0-442-25856-9). Van Nos Reinhold.

Vocabolari delle parlate italiante. Angelico Prati. 68p. (Ital.). 1966. L.3500.00. Forni.

Vocabolarietto del dialetto trevigiano 1884. Vincenzo Bindoni & G. Netto. 112p. (Ital.). 1978. L.2500.00. Canova.

Vocabolarietto del vernacolo pisano. Giuseppe Malagoli. (Illus.). 112p. (Ital.). 1937. L.3000.00. Nistri-Lischi.

Vocabolarietto della Lingua Italiana. C. Grassi. (Ital.). write for info. French & Eur.

Vocabolarietto figurato. Giannina Facco & Maria Facco. (Illus.). 380p. (Ital.). 1979. L.3800.00. Edipem.

Vocabolario agronomico nel dialetto della provincia de Lecce. G. Gorgoni. viii, 515p. (Ital.). L.23000.00. Forni.

Vocabolario biblico. J. Von Allmen. 548p. (Ital.). 1975. L.7000.00. AVE.

Vocabolario bresciano-italiano. G. Battista Malchiori. 732p. (Ital.). L.32000.00. Forni.

Vocabolario commerciale italiano-francese e francese-italiano, Caputo Cataldo. A. Jannini Pasquale. xii, 260p. (Ital. & Fr.). 1978. L.8000.00. Monnier.

Vocabolario cremasco-italiano. B. Samarani. 280p. (Ital.). L.9000.00. Forni.

Vocabolario cremonese-italiano. A. Peri. viii, 704p. (Ital.). L.25000.00. Forni.

Vocabolario croato serbo-italiano de M. Deanovic e J. Jerej. Niccolo Nichea. 48p. (Serbo-Croatian & Ital.). 1967. L.3000.00. Del Bianco.

Vocabolario degli accademici della Crusca. 1260p. (Ital.). 1976. L.90000.00. Licosa.

Vocabolario degli accademici della Crusca. 1260p. (Ital.). 1976. L.78000.00. Licosa.

Vocabolario dei dealetti bergamashi. Antonio Tiraboschi. (Ital.). L.13000.00. Forni.

Vocabolario dei deatetti bergamashi, 3 vols. Antonio Tiraboschi. 1676p. (Ital.). L.48000.00. Forni.

Vocabolario dei dialette della citta e diocesi di Como. Pietro Monti. xlviii, 483p. (Ital.). L.21000.00. Forni.

Vocabolario dei dialette salentini, 3 vols. Gerhard Rohlfs. (Illus.). 1300p. (Ital.). 1976. L.60000.00. Congedo.

Vocabolario dei dialetti della Corsica. F. D. Falcucci. 474p. (Ital.). 1972. L.30000.00. Licosa.

Vocabolario dei dialetti della Corsica. F. D. Falcucci. xxiii, 473p. (Ital.). 1972. L.12000.00. Licosa.

Vocabolario dei dialetto antico vicentino. D. Bortolan. 312p. (Ital.). L.13000.00. Forni.

Vocabolario dei piccoli. Guglielmo Valle. (Illus.). 190p. (Ital.). L.3500.00. La Scuola.

Vocabolario del dialetto antico vicentino. D. Bortolan. 312p. (Ital.). L.13000.00. Forni.

Vocabolario del dialetto bolognese. Gaspare Ungarelli. 412p. (Ital.). 1965. L.12000.00. Multigrafica.

Vocabolario del dialetto calabrese. Luigi Accattatis. 1300p. (Ital.). 1978. L.46500.00. Pellegrini.

Vocabolario del dialetto de Magione. Giovanni Moretti. xxxii, 672p. (Ital.). L.20000.00. Univ Perugia.

Vocabolario del dialetto de Vigevano. Giovanni Vidari et al. xii, 444p. (Ital.). 1972. L.18000.00. Olschki.

Vocabolario del dialetto modenese. A. Neri. xvi, 335p. (Ital.). 1973. L.9800.00. Forni.

Vocabolario del dialetto tarantino in corrispondenza della lingua italiana. D. L. De Vincentiis. 320p. (Ital.). L.11500.00. Forni.

Vocabolario del francese moderno. E. Balmas & R. L. Wagner. (Illus.). 2517p. (Fr.). 1979. L.21000.00. Ist Geo Agostini.

Vocabolario del francese moderno. Enea Balmas. 2536p. (Ital. & Fr.). 1979. L.21000.00. Ghisetti & Corvi.

Vocabolario del milanese d'oggi. Spiller. (Illus.). 208p. (Ital.). L.4500.00. Rizzoli Edit.

Vocabolario della lingua italiana. P. Colombo. (Illus.). 544p. (Ital.). L.3500.00 (CEB). Capitol-Dischi.

Vocabolario della lingua italiana. P. Colombo. (Illus.). 912p. (Ital.). L.8000.00 (CEB). Capitol-Dischi.

Vocabolario della lingua italiana. Alessandro Cutolo. (Illus.). 1250p. (Ital.). L.28000.00. Euro Co.

Vocabolario della lingua italiana. Giacomo Devoto & Giancarlo Oli. vi, 1200p. (Ital.). 1979. L.8800.00. Monnier.

Vocabolario della lingua italiana. Grassi. 540p. (Ital.). 1976. L.2000.00. Vallardi A.

Vocabolario della lingua italiana. Bruno Migliorini. (Illus.). xviii, 1638p. (Ital.). 1978. L.16800.00. Paravia.

Vocabolario della lingua italiana. Nicola Zingarelli. (Illus.). xxxii, 2044p. (Ital.). 1970. L.pap. 26000.00. Zanichelli.

Vocabolario della lingua italiana. Nicola Zingarelli. (Illus.). 1248p. (Ital.). L.8400.00; L.pap. 6800.00. Zanichelli.

Vocabolario Della Lingua Latina. 15th ed. Luigi Castiglioni. Ed. by A. Brambilla & G. Campagna. LC 76-485030. xii, 2493p. (Lat. & Ital.). 1976. L.18000.00. Loescher.

Vocabolario Della Lingua Latina: Italiano-Latino, Latino-Italiano. Italo Lana. LC 80-457571. xvi, 1870p. (Lat. & Ital.). 1978. write for info. Paravia.

Vocabolario della lingua latina: Latino-italiano e italiano-latino. Luigi Castiglioni & Scevola Mariotti. 2500p. (Lat. & Ital.). 1966. L.25000.00. Loescher.

Vocabolario della lingua oromonica. E. Viterbo. 241p. (Ital.). L.350.00 (ISBN 88-203-0824-X). Hoepli.

Vocabolario della lingua parlata in Piazza Armerina. Remingio Roccella. 292p. (Ital.). L.11800.00. Forni.

Vocabolario dell'argot. Luigi Alessio. 100p. (Ital.). L.700.00. Petrini.

Vocabolario delle istituzioni indoeuropee: Vol. 1, Economia-parentela-societa. Emile Benveniste. Tr. by M. A. Liborio. xix, 286p. (Ital.). 1976. L.12000.00. Einaudi.

Vocabolario dell'uso abruzzese. G. Finamore. 328p. (Ital.). 1967. L.8500.00. Dante Alighieri.

Vocabolario dell'uso abruzzese. G. Finamore. 322p. (Ital.). L.10800.00. Forni.

Vocabolario dell'uso toscano, 2 vol. Pietro Fanfani. 1036p. (Ital.). L.18000.00. Le Lettere.

Vocabolario dialettale calabro-reggino-italiano. G. Malara. xx, 496p. (Ital.). L.16000.00. Forni.

Vocabolario domestico genovese-italiano. A. Paganini. (Illus.). 297p. (Ital.). L.15500.00. Forni.

Vocabolario Domestico Genovese-Italiano. Angelo Paganini. LC 79-391544. (Illus.). 297p. (Ital.). 1977. write for info. Forni.

Vocabolario domestico sardo-italiano. E. Atzeni. 96p. (Ital.). L.3800.00. Forni.

Vocabolario etimologico italiano. Angelico Prati. 1100p. (Ital.). 1970. L.7800.00. Garzanti Edit.

Vocabolario etimologico italiano. Francesco Zambaldi. xiv, 630p. (Ital.). 1913. L.7500.00. Dante Alighieri.

Vocabolario ferrarese-italiano. L. Ferri. 310p. (Ital.). L.18000.00. Forni.

Vocabolario fondamentale della lingua italiana. Giuseppe Sciarone Abondio. 288p. (Ital.). 1977. L.11000.00. Minerva Italica.

Vocabolario francese-italiano e italiano-francese. Edwin Rostan. 1184p. (Fr. & Ital.). L.12000.00. Malipiero.

Vocabolario fraseologico italiano-latino. L. Luciano & A. Traina. xxiii, 1092p. (Ital & Lat.). 1962. L.10600.00. Patron.

Vocabolario greco-italiano. Alessandro Annaratone & Giovanni La Magna. xii, 1602p. (Gr. & Ital.). L.18400.00. Signorelli C.

Vocabolario greco-italiano. Guglielmo Gemoll. 1202p. (Gr. & Ital.). L.14500.00. Sandron.

Vocabolario greco-italiano. Lorenzo Rocci. xx, 2076p. (Gr. & Ital.). 1976. L.26800.00. Dante Alighieri.

Vocabolario ilustrato della lingua italiana, 2 vols. Giacomo Devoto & Giancarlo Oli. 3104p. (Ital.). 1978. L.42500.00. Sel Rdrs Digest.

Vocabolario inglese-italiano e italiano-inglese. C. G. Cecioni. 1056p. (Ital. & Eng.). L.11000.00. Malipiero.

Vocabolario inglese-italiano e italiano-inglese. Luciano Sani. xlii, 918p. (Eng. & Ital.). 1977. L.8000.00. Dante Alighieri.

Vocabolario inglese-italiano, italiano-inglese. Luciano Sani. xxviii, 2316p. (Eng. & Ital.). L.19000.00. Dante Alighieri.

Vocabolario italiano-francese e francese-italiano. Francesco Grimod & G. Caselli. xii, 2216p. (Ital. & Fr.). 1977. L.15000.00. Dante Alighieri.

Vocabolario italiano-francese-italiano. F. Cassone. 1408p. (Ital. & Fr.). L.14500.00 (CEB); L.pap. 7500.00. Capitol-Dischi.

Vocabolario italiano-inglese, inglese-italiano. J. McAllister. 1232p. (Ital. & Eng.). L.15000.00 (CEB); L.pap. 7500.00. Capitol-Dischi.

Vocabolario italiano-kiswahili. Vittorio Merlo Pick. (Ital. & Swahili.). 1978. L.25000.00. EMI.

Vocabolario italiano-macedone. Giorgio Nurigiani. 752p. (Ital. & Macedonian.). 1969. L.7000.00. Lint.

Vocabolario italiano-piemontese. G. Gavuzzi. viii, 696p. (Ital.). 1971. L.24000.00. Bottega d'Erasmo.

Vocabolario italiano-tedesco. Introito & Porta. x, 112p. (Ital. & Ger.). 1971. L.8500.00. Bottega d'Erasmo.

Vocabolario italiano-tedesco-italiano, 2 vols. S. David. cviii, 2656p. (Ital. & Ger.). L.35000.00 (CEB). Capitol-Dischi.

Vocabolario italiano-tedesco-italiano. S. David. (Illus.). 1406p. (Ital. & Ger.). 1977. L.12500.00 (CEB). Capitol-Dischi.

Vocabolario Italiano-Tedesco, Tedesco-Italiano. Ed. by Sante David. LC 79-354933. liii, 1351p. (Ger. & Ital.). 1977. L.00.12500.00. Capitol Edit.

Vocabolario kiswahili-italiano. Vittorio Merlo Pick. 496p. (Swahili & Ital.). 1978. L.12000.00. EMI.

Vocabolario latino. Italo Lana. xvi, 1870p. (Span.). 1978. L.18500.00. Paravia.

Vocabolario Latino-Italiano & Italiano-Latino. Raffaello Bianchi. LC 77-578107. (Illus.). 619p. (Ital. & Lat.). 1977. L.5000.00. Monnier.

Vocabolario latino-italiano e italiano-latino. Edmondo D'Arbela et al. viii, 2030p. (Lat. & Span.). L.16800.00. Signorelli C.

Vocabolario latino-italiano e italiano-latino. L. Lipparini. 1008p. (Lat. & Ital.). L.10000.00. Malipiero.

Vocabolario Latino-italiano, italiano-latino. Raffaello Bianchi & Onorio Lelli. (Illus.). iv, 620p. (Lat. & Ital.). 1973. L.5000.00. Monnier.

Vocabolario latino-italiano, italiano-latino. Natale Vianello. xii, 884p. (Lat. & Ital.). 1975. L.6000.00. Dante Alighieri.

Vocabolario latino-italiano-latino. Giuseppe Campanini et al. 1506p. (Lat. & Ital.). 1976. L.14500.00. Paravia.

Vocabolario lucchese. I. Nieri. xlviii, 286p. (Ital.). L.14500.00. Forni.

Vocabolario Marinaresco Giuliano-Dalmata. Enrico Rosamani. LC 76-512031. xxiv, 200p. (Ital.). 1975. write for info. Olschki.

Vocabolario marinaresco giuliano-dalmata. Enrico Rosamani. (Illus.). 200p. (Ital.). 1976. L.18000.00 (ISBN 88-222-2222-9). Olschki.

Vocabolario marino e militare. Alberto Guglielmotti. 1008p. (Ital.). 1967. L.30000.00. Mursia.

Vocabolario metaurense. Elio Conti. xv, 362p. (Ital.). L.17500.00. Forni.

Vocabolario milanese-italiano. Francesco Angiloini. xl, 1056p. (Ital.). 1978. L.21000.00. Imago Libri.

Vocabolario milanese-italiano. Francesco Cherubini. 2400p. (Ital.). L.56000.00. Brenner.

Vocabolario milanese-italiano coi segni per la pronuncia. Francesco Angiolini. xxxviii, 1054p. (Ital.). L.28000.00. Forni.

Vocabolario minimo della lingua italiana per stranieri. Ignazio Baldelli & Alberto Mazzetti. iv, 194p. (Ital.). 1974. L.3200.00. Monnier.

Vocabolario minimo della lingua italiana per stranieri con dizionarietto somalo. Ignazio Baldelli et al. vi, 222p. (Ital.). 1978. L.4500.00. Monnier.

Vocabolario mirandolese-italiano. E. Meschiari. (Ital.). L.3000.00. La Vela.

Vocabolario modenese-italiano. Ernesto Maranesi & P. Papini. xxiii, 448p. (Ital.). L.18000.00. Forni.
Vocabolario napolitano-italiano. P. P. Volpe. lv, 438p. (Ital.). L.14500.00. Forni.
Vocabolario napolitano-toscano. R. D'Ambra. xi, 551p. (Ital.). L.25000.00. Forni.
Vocabolario numerico siciliano-italiano. Giusto Pecorella. 480p. (Ital.). L.4500.00. Bietti.
Vocabolario parmigiano-italiano, 4 vols. Carlo Malaspina. 1888p. (Ital.). L.75000.00. Forni.
Vocabolario per le favole de Fedro. Pietro Pettoello. 84p. (Ital.). L.600.00. Loescher.
Vocabolario reggiano-italiano. G. B. Ferrari. 935p. (Ital.). L.29000.00. Forni.
Vocabolario romagnolo-italiano. A. Morri. vi, 926p. (Ital. & Rumanian.). L.36000.00. Forni.
Vocabolario romagnolo-italiano, italiano-romagnolo. Libero Ercolani. 920p. (Ital. & Rumanian.). 1971. L.20000.00. Edn Girasole.
Vocabolario romanesco-belliano e italiano-romanesco. Gennaro Vaccaro. lxii, 819p. (Ital.). 1969. L.13000.00. Romana Libri.
Vocabolario romanesco-trilussiano e italiano-romanesco. Gennaro Vaccaro. 404p. (Ital.). 1971. L.10000.00. Romana Libri.
Vocabolario sallustiano. F. Natta. 206p. (Ital.). 1972. L.26500.00. L'Erma.
Vocabolario sardo-italiano e italiano-sardo, 2 vols. Giovanni Spano. 992p. (Ital.). L.39000.00. Forni.
Vocabolario spagnolo-italiano e italiano-spagnolo. Alvisi & Arce. 928p. (Ital. & Span.). L.16000.00. Malipiero.
Vocabolario swahili-italiano e italiano-swahili. Vittorio Merlo Pick. (Swahili & Ital.). L.7000.00. EMI.
Vocabolario tedesco-italiano e italiano-tedesco. A. Deidda. 2496p. (Ger. & Ital.). L.22000.00. Malipiero.
Vocabolario topografico dei ducati di Parma, Piacenza e Guastalla, 2 vols. L. Molossi. (Illus.). 924p. (Ital.). L.42000.00. Forni.
Vocabolario trentino-italiano. V. Ricci. vi, 522p. (Ital.). L.18000.00. Forni.
Vocabolario ucraino-italiano. E. Onatskyj. 1736p. (Ukranian & Ital.). 1941. L.4000.00. Ist Univers Orient.
Vocabolario vernacolo-italiano pei destrette roveretano e trentino. Giambattista Azzolini. 1156p. (Ital.). 1976. L.30000.00. Manfrini.
Vocabula amatoria. 280p. (Ital.). L.6000.00. Le Lettere.
Vocabulaire. 3rd ed. Arthur Masson. 64p. (Fr.). 1967. 4.90 F. Hachette.
Vocabulaire Allemand. Jean Chassard & Gonthier Weil. (Ger.). 1969. 13.60 F. Hachette.
Vocabulaire Allemand du Bacheller. 3rd ed. Rudolf Zellweger. 80p. (Fr.). 1967. 8.00 F. Payot.
Vocabulaire Allemand par l'image. O. N. Scheid. 80p. (Ger.). 1971. 15.00 F. Bordas-Dunod.
Vocabulaire Allemand Progressif & livret d'exercices. Rene Michea. 40p. (Fr. & Eng.). 1959. 21.70 F. Didier.
Vocabulaire Alphabetique & Analogique Destine aus Ecollers Africains Francophones. Placide-Raphael Lumeka. 229p. (Fr.). 1972. 40.00 F. Lang, H.
Vocabulaire Analogique de la Langue Corse. Jean Costa. 376p. (Fr.). 1972. 35.00 F. C. E. R. C.
Vocabulaire & Elocution les Debutants. Solange Buissonnier. (Illus., Fr.). 1969. 4.70 F. Hachette.
Vocabulaire & Exercices Francais. Adolphe Lelu & Louis Kluber. (Illus.). 96p. (Fr.). 11.00 F. Hatier.
Vocabulaire & Exercices Francais. Adolphe Lelu & Louis Kluber. (Illus.). 302p. (Fr.). 15.25 F. Hatier.
Vocabulaire & Exercices Francais. Adolphe Lelu & Louis Kluber. (Illus.). 366p. (Fr.). 9.00 F. Hatier.
Vocabulaire & Exercises Francais. Adolphe Lelu & Louis Kluber. (Illus.). 256p. (Fr.). 14.95 F. Hatier.
Vocabulaire & Exercises Francais. Adolphe Lelu & Louis Kluber. (Illus.). 256p. (Fr.). 6.20 F. Hatier.
Vocabulaire & Grammaire de la Langue Houailou. Maurice Leenhardt. 414p. (Hawaiian.). 1935. 66.20 F. Inst Ethnol.
Vocabulaire & la Societe Sous Louis Phillippe. Georges Matore & Geneve Matore. 385p. (Fr.). 1967. 70.00 F. Slatkine.
Vocabulaire & Language. 3rd ed. Andree Girolami-Boulinier. (Illus.). 156p. (Fr.). 1976. 41.00 F. Delachaux.
Vocabulaire & Redaction. (Fr.). 7.75 F. Ligel.
Vocabulaire & Redaction. (Fr.). 6.30 F. Ligel.
Vocabulaire & Style. 5th ed. Roger Schmitt & Pierre Filbert. 160p. (Fr.). 20.25 F. Nathan.
Vocabulaire Anglais. Paul Bacquet. 128p. (Fr.). 1974. 9.60 F. PUF.
Vocabulaire Anglais. (Eng.). 11.00 F. Ligel.
Vocabulaire Anglais au Baccalaureat. Christian Bouscaren. 152p. (Fr. & Eng.). 1972. 11.90 F. Ophrys.
Vocabulaire Anglais-Francais de Terminologie, Economique & Juridique. Peter Nichols & Pierre Vibes. 104p. (Eng. & Fr.). 1971. 16.00 F. L. G. D. J.
Vocabulaire Anglais par l'image. Aime Janicot. 100p. (Eng.). 1965. 16.00 F. Bordas-Dunod.
Vocabulaire Architecturale. Jules Auger. 28p. (Fr.). 1975. Can.$2.30. Montreal P. U.
Vocabulaire Barometre Dans le Langage Economique. 3rd ed. J. Delattre & G. DeVernisy. 160p. (Eng. & Fr.). 1967. pap. 9.95 (ISBN 0-686-56982-2, M-6109). French & Eur.
Vocabulaire Barometre dans le Langage Economique. 3rd ed. J. Delattre & G. Vernisy. 160p. (Fr.). 1967. 12.00 F. Georg.
Vocabulaire Bilingue des Assurances sur la Vie. Jean-Paul De Grandpre. 39p. (Fr.). 1969. Can.$1.00. Quebec Off.
Vocabulaire bilinque du theatre: Anglais-Francais Francais Anglais. R. Dubuc. 174p. (Eng. & Fr.). 1979. 70.00 F. Maison Dictionnaire.
Vocabulaire Commercial Francais-Allemand. Erich Weis & Eva Haberfellner. LC 77-576772. 271p. (Fr.). 1976. DM.14.80 (ISBN 3-125-23410-7). Klett.
Vocabulaire Critique des relations culturelles internationales. A. Salon. 175p. (Fr.). 1978. 80.00 F. Maison Dictionnaire.
Vocabulaire d'anglais Commercial. Andre Mansat. (Fr. & Eng.). 1966. 14.80 F. Didier.
Vocabulaire, Dans: Larousse pour Tous. (Illus.). 832p. (Fr.). 23.90 F. Larousse FR.
Vocabulaire d'Arabe Moderne: Economie-Politique-Actualite, Vol. 1. J. Schmidt. 627p. (Fr. & Arabic.). 1979. 100.00 F. Maison Dictionnaire.
Vocabulaire d'Arabe moderne: Economie-Politique-Actualite, Vol. 2. J. Schmidt. 670p. (Arabic & Fr.). 1982. 120.00 F. Maison Dictionnaire.
Vocabulaire d'Astronomie. (Fr., Eng. & Ger.). 1978. pap. 39.95 (ISBN 0-686-57249-1, M-6555). French & Eur.
Vocabulaire d'astronomie: Francais-Anglais-Allemand. (Fr. , Eng. & Ger.). 1978. 85.00 F. C. I. L. F.
Vocabulaire de Base Allemand-Francais. Charles Chatelanat & Theodor Henzi. 214p. (Ger. & Fr.). 1972. 19.00 F. Hachette.
Vocabulaire de Base du Chinois Moderne. Yvonne Andre. 160p. (Chinese.). 1965. 40.00 F. Klincksieck.
Vocabulaire de Fonderie Anglais-Francais. Centre Technique des Industries de la Fonderie. LC 77-577539. 75p. (Eng. & Fr.). 1976. 24.00 F (ISBN 2-7119-0032-0). Ed Tech Ind.
Vocabulaire de Fonderie Francais-Allemand. Centre Technique des Industries de la Fonderie. LC 77-570223. 100p. (Fr. & Ger.). 1976. 36.00 F (ISBN 2-7119-0033-9). Ed Tech Ind.
Vocabulaire de gestion. R. Dubac. 135p. (Eng. & Fr.). 1974. 60.00 F. Maison Dictionnaire.
Vocabulaire de Gestion. Robert Dubuc. 135p. (Fr.). 1974. Can.$3.96. Radio-Canada.
Vocabulaire de Kant, 1. Roger Verneaux. (Fr.). 1973. 36.00 F. Aubier-Montaigne.
Vocabulaire de la Chasse & de la Venerie. Conseil International de la Langue Francaise. (Fr.). 1974. 16.60 F. Hachette.
Vocabulaire de la Fonderie: Anglais-Francais. (Eng. & Fr.). 22.40 F. Techniques Fonderie.
Vocabulaire de la Fonderie: Francais-Anglais. (Fr. & Eng.). 33.38 F. Techniques Fonderie.
Vocabulaire de la geomorphologie. C.I.L.F. 200p. (Fr.). 1979. 100.00 F. Maison Dictionnaire.
Vocabulaire de la Langue Espagnole Classique: XVIe & XVIIe Siecles. 4th ed. Bernard Sese. LC 76-475557. v, 306p. (Span. & Fr.). 1975. 59.50 ptas (ISBN 2-718-15546-9). Doc Univers.
Vocabulaire de la Langue Espagnole Classique: XVIe. & XVIIe. Siecles. Bernard Sese. 314p. (Span.). 1976. 59.60 F. CDU.
Vocabulaire de la Princesse de Cleves. new ed. Jean De Bazin. 56p. (Fr.). 1974. 19.26 F. Nizet.
Vocabulaire de la Psychanalyse. 5th ed. Jean Laplanche. (Fr.). 1976. 145.60 F. PUF.
Vocabulaire de la Psychanalyse. 5th ed. Ed. by Jean Laplanche. Jean-Baptiste Pontalis. (Fr.). 1976. 55.00 (ISBN 0-686-57250-5, M-6558). French & Eur.
Vocabulaire De la Psychologie. 5th ed. Henri Pieron. 570p. (Fr.). 1973. 55.00 (ISBN 0-686-57078-2, M-6453). French & Eur.
Vocabulaire de la psychologie. 6th ed. Henri Pieron. LC 79-382007. xii, 587p. (Fr.). 1979. 165.00 F (ISBN 2-13-035971-X). Pr Univ Fr.
Vocabulaire de la Psychologie. 5th ed. Henri Pieron. (Fr.). 1973. 145.60 F. PUF.
Vocabulaire de la Publicite. Conseil International de la Langue Francaise. (Fr.). 1976. 31.20 F. Hachette.
Vocabulaire De la Publicite. Ed. by Conseil International De la Langue Francaise. (Fr.). 1976. pap. 14.50 (ISBN 0-686-57251-3, M-6559). French & Eur.
Vocabulaire de la Publicite. Pierre Herbin. 148p. (Fr.). 30.00 F. Bourdine.
Vocabulaire de la Radio & de la Television. France-Pauline Cormier. 17p. (Fr.). 1973. Can.$0.50. Quebec Off.
Vocabulaire de la Radio & de la Television. 30p. (Fr.). 1977. pap. text ed. 4.95 (ISBN 0-7754-2273-8, M-9022). French & Eur.
Vocabulaire de la Radiodifussion. Conseil International de la Langue Francaise. (Fr.). 1973. 15.40 F. Hachette.
Vocabulaire de la radiographie. C.I.L.F. 92p. (Fr., Eng. & Ger.). 1979. 85.00 F. Maison Dictionnaire.
Vocabulaire de la topographie. C.I.L.F. 92p. (Fr.). 1980. 80.00 F. Maison Dictionnaire.
Vocabulaire de la Vente Promotionelle: Anglais-Francais. M. Villiers et al. 30p. (Eng. & Fr.). 1975. pap. 3.95 (ISBN 0-7754-3244-X, M-9242). French & Eur.
Vocabulaire de la Vie Amoureuse. Julien Teppe. 224p. (Fr.). 1973. 24.00 F. Pavillon.
Vocabulaire de Lais de Marie de France. MacClelland. 204p. (Fr.). 1978. 58.50 F. Ottawa U.
Vocabulaire de l'analyse Psychologique dans l'oeuvre de Thucydide. Pierre Huart. 546p. (Fr.). 1969. 88.00 F. Klincksieck.
Vocabulaire De L'astronautique. L. Guilbert. 361p. (Fr.). pap. 45.00 (ISBN 0-686-57265-3, F-137130). French & Eur.
Vocabulaire de L'astronautique: Enquete Linguistique a travers la Presse d'information a L'occasion De Cinq Exploits de Cosmonautes. Guilbert. (Publ. de l'Univ. de Rouen Fac. des Lettres et Sc. Hum.). (Fr.). 15.95 (ISBN 0-685-36683-9). French & Eur.
Vocabulaire De L'economie. Gilbert Mathieu. (Fr.). pap. 17.50 (ISBN 0-686-57041-3, M-6401). French & Eur.
Vocabulaire de l'economie. Gilbert Mathieu. (Fr.). 40.00 F. Delarge.
Vocabulaire de L'economie. 3rd ed. LC 79-360009. 62p. (Fr.). 1978. write for info. (ISBN 0-7754-2244-4). Edit Quebec.
Vocabulaire De L'Education. Gaston Mialaret. 488p. (Fr.). 1979. 62.50 (ISBN 0-686-57048-0, M-6410). French & Eur.
Vocabulaire de l'Education. Ed. by Gaston Mialaret. LC 79-385192. xxii, 457p. (Fr.). 1979. 160.00 F (ISBN 2-130-35643-5). Pr Univ Fr.
Vocabulaire de l'electroacoustique de l'acoustique. France-Pauline Cormier. 186p. (Fr.). 1973. Can.$2.50. Quebec Off.
Vocabulaire de l'environnement. new ed. Conseil International de la Langue Francaise. (Fr.). 1976. 37.60 F. Hachette.
Vocabulaire de L'Environnement. Ed. by Conseil International de la Langue Fran c04aise. (Fr.). 1976. pap. 14.95 (ISBN 0-686-57283-1, M-4648). French & Eur.
Vocabulaire de l'Hydrologie et de la meteorologie. C.I.L.F. 239p. (Fr.). 1978. 80.00 F. Maison Dictionnaire.
Vocabulaire de l'Hydrologie et de la Meteorologie. Conseil International de la Language Francaise. LC 79-353461. (Illus.). 239p. (Fr.). 1978. 65.00 F (ISBN 2-85319-048-X). Maison Dictionnaire.
Vocabulaire de l'Informatique de Gestion: Anglais-Francais. M. Villers. 31p. (Eng. & Fr.). 1980. pap. 3.95 (ISBN 2-551-03899-5, M-9228). French & Eur.
Vocabulaire de l'oceanologie. Agence de Cooperation Culturelle & Technique. 431p. (Fr.). 1976. 88.70 F. C. I. L. F.
Vocabulaire de l'oceanologie. LC 77-456565. (Illus.). 431p. (Eng. , Ger. , Rus. & Fr.). 1976. 75.00 F (ISBN 2-85319-028-5). Hachette-Jeunesse.
Vocabulaire de l'urbanisme. 53p. (Fr.). 1971. 16.05 F. C. N. I. P. E.
Vocabulaire De Medecine & Des Sciences Connexes Anglais-Francais-Anglais. Gladstone. (Eng. & Fr.). 21.95 (ISBN 0-685-36682-0). French & Eur.
Vocabulaire de Medecine & des Sciences Connexes: Francais-Anglais. W. J. Gladstone. 298p. (Fr. & Eng.). 1971. 85.00 F. Masson & Cie.
Vocabulaire De Medecine et Des Sciences Connexes: Francais-Anglais, Anglais-Francais. 298p. (Fr.-Eng.). 1971. 37.50 (ISBN 0-686-57281-5). French & Eur.
Vocabulaire de Pedagogie Moderne. Mauro Laeng & Guy Auandani. 256p. (Fr.). 1974. 34.00 F. Centurion.
Vocabulaire de Psychopedagogic et de Psychiatrie de l'Enfant. 4th ed. Robert Lafon. LC 79-381763. xix, 1060p. (Fr.). 1979. 182.00 F. Pr Univ Fr.
Vocabulaire de Psychopedagogie & de Psychiatrie de l'enfant. 3rd ed. 868p. (Fr.). 1973. 145.60 F. PUF.
Vocabulaire De Psychopedagogie et De Psychiatrie De L'enfant. 3rd ed. Robert Lafon. 868p. (Fr.). 1973. 57.50 (ISBN 0-686-57282-3, F-19440). French & Eur.
Vocabulaire de Racine. Jacques-Gabriel Cahen. 252p. (Fr.). 1970. 50.00 F. Slatkine.
Vocabulaire de sciences et techniques spatiales. C.I.L.F. 193p. (Ger. & Eng.). 1978. 125.00 F. Maison Dictionnaire.

Vocabulaire d'ecologie. Conseil International de la Langue Francaise. (Fr.). 1974. 23.70 F. Hachette.

Vocabulaire des Animaux Marins en Latin Classique. 154p. (Fr.). 1947. 32.00 F. Klincksieck.

Vocabulaire des assurances Sociales. G. Desrosiers & J. Boulay. 21p. (Fr.). 1971. pap. 3.95 (ISBN 0-7754-2274-6, M-9231). French & Eur.

Vocabulaire des Assurances Sur la Vie. Jean-Paul Grandpre. 16p. (Fr.). 1973. Can.$0.50. Quebec Off.

Vocabulaire des Conferences: Francais-Anglais-Arabe: Francais-Anglais-Arabe. (Fr. , Eng. & Arabic.). 1974. 12.00 F. Unesco.

Vocabulaire des Finances Locales. 78p. (Fr.). 1973. 16.05 F. C. N. I. P. E.

Vocabulaire des Institutions Indo-Europeennes, 2. Emile Benveniste. 344p. (Fr.). 1969. 45.00 F. Minuit.

Vocabulaire des Moeurs de la Vie Parisienne Sous le Second Empire. J. R. Klein. 342p. (Fr.). 1977. 78.40 F. Vander.

Vocabulaire des Proclamations Electorales de 1881, 1885. Antoine Prost. 200p. (Fr.). 1974. 156.00 F. PUF.

Vocabulaire des Psychotherapies. Andre Virel. LC 77-573406. 373p. (Fr.). 1977. 59.00 F (ISBN 2-213-00419-6). Fayard.

Vocabulaire des Quinze Joles du Mariage. Marcel Pressot. 145p. (Fr.). 1974. 45.00 F. Slatkine.

Vocabulaire des Sciences Sociales. 2nd ed. Paul Lazarsfeld. (Fr.). 1971. 52.00 F. Mouton De Gruyter.

Vocabulaire Des Sciences Sociales: Concepts et Indices. Raymond Boudon & Paul Lazarsfeld. (Methodes De la Sociologie: No. 1). (Fr.). 1971. pap. text ed. 17.50x (ISBN 90-2796-891-8). Mouton.

Vocabulaire des Techniques de Groupe. Anne Ancelin-Schutzenberger. 194p. (Fr.). 1971. 25.00 F. Epi.

Vocabulaire des Termes: Essentiels Utilises pour la Transmissien Ligne; Francais-Espagnol-Russe-Allemand-Italien-Neerlandais-Polonais-Portugais-Suedois. (Fr. , Span. , Rus. , Ger. , Ital. , Dutch, Pol. , Port. & Swedish.). 1959. 11.20 F. U. I. T.

Vocabulaire d'initation aux Etudes Agronomiques. (Fr.). 5.40 F. C. R. E. D. I. F.

Vocabulaire Disponible du Francais en France & en Acadie. William Francis Mackey & J. G. Savard. (Fr.). 134.30 F. Didier.

Vocabulaire Du Beton. Conseil International De la Langue Francais. 192p. (Fr.). 1976. pap. 39.95 (ISBN 0-686-56961-X, M-6084). French & Eur.

Vocabulaire du Beton. Conseil International de la Langue Francaise. 192p. (Fr.). 1976. 98.00 F. Eyrolles.

Vocabulaire du Cantal du Nord & de la Margeride Auvergnate d'Apres l'ALMC. Ed. by P. Nauton. LC 76-451549. 73p. (Fr.). 1975. write for info. Cercle Occitan.

Vocabulaire du Patois Lillois. Louis Vermesse & Lille. 238p. (Fr.). 1977. 85.00 F. Lafitte Repr.

Vocabulaire du Patois Lillois. Louis Vermesse & Lille. 242p. (Fr.). 1978. 50.00 F. Slatkine.

Vocabulaire du Patols de Bettant, 2. Armand Decour. 209p. (Fr.). 1975. 20.00 F. Decour.

Vocabulaire du Vieux Breton. Joseph Loth. 258p. (Fr.). 1970. 36.00 F. Champion.

Vocabulaire Economique & Financier. Yves Bernard & Jean-Claude Colli. 384p. (Fr.). 1976. 17.00 F. Seuil.

Vocabulaire Economique et Financier: Coll. Points Economie. Yves Bernard & Jean-Claude Colli. 384p. (Fr.). 1976. pap. 10.95 (ISBN 0-686-56915-6, M-6031). French & Eur.

Vocabulaire Elementaire des Ensembles. Alexis Hocquenghem. (Illus.). 54p. (Fr.). 1969. 14.00 F. Masson & Cie.

Vocabulaire en Images, 1. Christine Le Boeuf. (Fr.). 65.00 F. Ecole.

Vocabulaire en Images, 2. Christine Le Boeuf. (Fr.). 65.00 F. Ecole.

Vocabulaire Espagnol par l'image. Robert Paufique. 96p. (Span.). 1970. 15.00 F. Bordas-Dunod.

Vocabulaire Esperanto. Michel Duc-Goninaz. 108p. (Fr. & Esperanto.). 1971. 13.30 F. Ophrys.

Vocabulaire Ethnologique. Armin Heymer. 237p. (Ger., Eng. & Fr.). 1977. 37.50 (ISBN 0-686-57329-3, M-6317). French & Eur.

Vocabulaire Ethologique: Allemand-Anglais-Francais. Armin Heymer. (Illus.). 237p. (Ger., Eng. & Fr.). 1977. 92.00 F. PUF.

Vocabulaire Fondamental de Technologie. Jacques Deweerdt. 272p. (Fr.). 1974. pap. 19.95 (ISBN 0-686-57280-7, M-4654). French & Eur.

Vocabulaire Fondamental de Technologie. Jacques Deweerdt. (Illus.). 272p. (Fr.). 1974. 42.00 F. Gamma.

Vocabulaire Fondamentale du Francais. 4th ed. Robert Dottrens & Dino Massarenti. (Illus.). 64p. (Fr.). 1963. 18.00 F. Delachaux.

Vocabulaire Fondamentale du Francais. James D. Haygood. 160p. (Fr.). 1948. 12.00 F. Droz.

Vocabulaire Forestier Francais-Allemand-Danois. C. Jacobi. 207p. (Fr., Ger. & Danish.). 1907. 25.00 F. Picard.

Vocabulaire Francais-Anglais d'archeologie Prehistorique. Roger Marois. 116p. (Fr. & Eng.). 1972. Can.$7.95. Quebec P. U.

Vocabulaire Francais-Anglais De la Machine a Coudre Industrielle. Francois Lanecki & Celine Dupre. 85p. (Fr.-Eng.). 1973. pap. 3.50 (ISBN 0-686-56991-1, M-6331). French & Eur.

Vocabulaire Francais-Anglais de la Machine a Coudre Industrielle. Francois Lanecki & Celine Dupre. 85p. (Fr. & Eng.). 1973. Can.$1.50. Quebec Off.

Vocabulaire Francais-Anglais De L'automobile: Le Moteur. Anne-Marie Baudoin. 174p. (Eng. & Fr.). 1973. pap. 9.95 (ISBN 0-686-56909-1, M-6025). French & Eur.

Vocabulaire Francais-Anglais de l'automobile. Anne-Marie Baudoin. (Illus.). 174p. (Fr. & Eng.). 1973. Can.$2.50. Quebec Off.

Vocabulaire Francais-Anglais des Relations Professionnelles. 2nd ed. Gerard Dion. 350p. (Fr.). 16.00 F. Laval P. U.

Vocabulaire Francais-Anglais des Relations Professionnelles. Ministere du Travail Et du la Main-D'oeuvre. 302p. (Fr. & Eng.). 1972. 2.50 F. Quebec Off.

Vocabulaire Francais-Arabe de l'ingenieur & du Technicien, 1. J. J. Schmidt. 136p. (Fr. & Arabic.). 1973. 45.00 F. Maisonneuve & Larose.

Vocabulaire Francais-Malgache. R. P. Malzac. 446p. (Fr.). 1952. 18.00 F. Maritimes Outremer.

Vocabulaire Francais-Mentonnais. James B. Andrews. 174p. (Fr.). 1977. 75.00 F. Lafitte Repr.

Vocabulaire Francais-Provencal: Dictionnaire Provencal-Francais. J. T. Avril. 651p. (Fr.). 1970. 110.00 F. Slatkine.

Vocabulaire Francais, 1. Rene L. Wagner. 192p. (Fr.). 1967. 19.00 F. Didier Erudition.

Vocabulaire Francais, 2. Rene L. Wagner. (Fr.). 1970. 19.00 F. Didier Erudition.

Vocabulaire Franco-Anglo-Allemand de Geomorphologie. Henri Baulig. 230p. (Fr., Eng. & Ger.). 1970. 26.90 F. Strasbourg, U.

Vocabulaire Francois-Provencal, 2 vols. Claude F. Achard. 1425p. (Fr.). 300.00 F. Slatkine.

Vocabulaire General d'orientation Scientifique. (Fr.). 17.00 F. Didier.

Vocabulaire Grammatical. Robert Dagneaud. 247p. (Fr.). 1965. 32.50 F. CDU.

Vocabulaire Grec. Paul Collin. 328p. (Gr.). 1963. 24.25 F. Dessain & Tolra.

Vocabulaire Grec. 8th ed. Victor Fontoynont. 200p. (Gr.). 1974. 35.00 F. Picard.

Vocabulaire Grec. Joannes Saunier. 220p. (Gr.). 1977. 19.80 F. Gigord.

Vocabulaire Grec de Base. Simon Byl. 132p. (Gr.). 20.00 F. Dessain & Tolra.

Vocabulaire Grec de la Terminologie Rhetorique: Dans; Etudes sur Quintillen. Jean Cousin. 1023p. (Gr.). 1967. fl.160.00 (Pub. by B R Gruner Netherlands). Humanities.

Vocabulaire Illustre des Emballages: Destines au Transport des Marchandises Dangereuses. (Illus.). 133p. (Fr.). 1974. 4.00. O. N. U.

Vocabulaire International des Termes d'urbanisme & d'architecture: Francais-Allemand-Anglais. Jean-Henri Calsat. (Illus.). 350p. (Fr., Ger. & Eng.). 1970. 250.00 F. Eyrolles.

Vocabulaire International des Termes d'urbanisme & d'architecture: Francais-Allemand-Anglais. Jean-Henri Calsat & Jean-Pierre Sydler. 368p. (Fr., Ger. & Eng.). 1970. 139.65 F. Ste. Diff. Tech. Bat. T. P.

Vocabulaire International des Termes d'Urbanisme et d'Architecture. Jean-Henri Calsat & Jean P. Sydler. 350p. (Fr., Ger. & Eng.). 1970. 95.00 (ISBN 0-686-56935-0, M-6057). French & Eur.

Vocabulaire Italien par l'image. Roger H. Durand & Salvatore Greco. 96p. (Ital.). 1969. 15.00 F. Bordas-Dunod.

Vocabulaire Latin. Arthur Bodson. 48p. (Lat.). 1974. 42.00 F. Sciences Lettres.

Vocabulaire Latin des Relations & des Partis Politiques sous la Republique. Jean Hellegouarch. (Lat.). 109.00 F. Belles Lettres.

Vocabulaire Latin Des Relations et Des Partis Politiques Sous la Republique. Jean Hellegouarc'H. (Fr.). 39.95 (ISBN 0-686-57327-7, M-6314). French & Eur.

Vocabulaire Medical De Base, 2 vols. Marie Bonvalot. 447p. (Fr.). 1972. Set. pap. 45.00 (ISBN 0-686-56925-3, M-6043). French & Eur.

Vocabulaire Medical de Base, 2 vols. Marie Bonvalot. 447p. (Fr.). 1972. 52.00 F. Organisation Instruction Proger.

Vocabulaire Medical de Base, 2 vols. new ed. Marie Bonvalot. (Illus.). 447p. (Fr.). 1974. 52.00 F. Soc Etudes Tech.

Vocabulaire Medical d'Eschyle & les Ecrits Hippocratiques. J. Dumortier. (Fr.). 1975. 42.00 F. Belles Lettres.

Vocabulaire Meteorologique International: Quadrilingue (Anglais-Francais-Espagnol-Russe) (Eng. , Fr. , Span. & Rus.). 40.00 F. O. M. M.

Vocabulaire Methodique Chinois-Francais a l'usage des Interpretes. (Chinese & Fr.). 1971. 25.00 F. Asie-Orientale Cent. Pub.

Vocabulaire Multilingue de la Science du Sol: Anglais-Francais-Espagnol-Allemand-Portugais-Italien-Neerlandais-Suedois-Russe. 3rd ed. G. V. Jacks & R. Tavernier. 430p. (Eng., Fr., Span., Ger., Port., Ital., Dutch, Swedish & Rus.). 1968. 22.50 F. F. A. O.

Vocabulaire Occitan. rev. ed. (Fr.). 1977. 30.00 F. Lagarde.

Vocabulaire Oecumenique. Yves Congar & Gerard Siegwalt. 428p. (Fr.). 51.00 F. Cerf.

Vocabulaire, Orthographe, Conjugaison, Analyse. Debleser M. Deneubourg. (Illus.). 210p. (Fr.). 1974. 178.00 F. Wesmael-Charlier.

Vocabulaire, Orthographe, Conjugalson, Analyse. N. Deneubourg. 208p. (Fr.). 1974. 210.00 F. Wesmael-Charlier.

Vocabulaire, Orthographe, Conlugalson, Analyse. N. Deneubourg. (Illus.). 274p. (Fr.). 1976. 243.00 F. Wesmael-Charlier.

Vocabulaire Orthographique de Base. Francois Ters. 228p. (Fr.). 46.00 F. OCDL.

Vocabulaire Orthographique de Base. Francois Ters et al. 304p. (Fr.). 321.00 F. Messeiller.

Vocabulaire par la Vie des Mots. Marc M. Ballot & Fougerouse. 152p. (Fr.). 1958. 10.00 F. Lavauzelle.

Vocabulaire Patois Vellavien-Francais. Jules-Gabriel De Vinols De Montfleury. 227p. (Fr.). 1975. 100.00 F. Lafitte Repr.

Vocabulaire, Phraseologie, Lecture, Informations. Albert Pierret & Basiaux. (Illus.). 144p. (Fr.). 1975. 228.00 F. Wesmael-Charlier.

Vocabulaire, Phraseologie, Lecture, Informations. Albert Pierret et al. (Illus.). 272p. (Fr.). 1975. 192.00 F. Wesmael-Charlier.

Vocabulaire, Phraseologie, Lecture Mentale. Albert Pierret & Basiaux. 132p. (Fr.). 1977. 182.00 F. Wesmael-Charlier.

Vocabulaire Politique & Social en France de 1869 a 1872. Jean Dubois. 460p. (Fr.). 1963. 40.00 F. Larousse FR.

Vocabulaire Politique & Socio-Ethnique a Montreal de 1839 a 1842. Maurice Rabotin. (Illus.). 122p. (Fr.). 1975. Can.$4.00. Didier-Canada.

Vocabulaire Politique de J. J. Rousseau. Michel Launay. (Fr.). 35.00 F. Slatkine.

Vocabulaire Politique de Paul Eluard. Marie-Renee Guyard. 286p. (Fr.). 68.00 F. Klincksieck.

Vocabulaire Pratique des Sciences Sociales. Alain Biron. 384p. (Fr.). 35.50 F. Ouvrieres.

Vocabulaire Pratique des Sciences Sociales. Alain Birou. 384p. (Fr.). 29.95 (ISBN 0-686-57277-7, F-136960). French & Eur.

Vocabulaire Pratique du Grec. P. Leonard. 152p. (Gr.). 1968. 125.00 F. Duculot.

Vocabulaire Professional du Houilleur Borain. Pierre Ruelle. 200p. (Fr.). 1953. 280.00 F. Acad Royale.

Vocabulaire Progressif de l'allemand. Paul Banvard & Pierre Kuhn. (Illus.). 224p. (Ger.). 1976. 47.50 F. CDU.

Vocabulaire Psychologique dans les Chroniques de Froissart, 1. Jacqueline Pinoche. (Fr.). 1976. 92.00 F. Klincksieck.

Vocabulaire Raisonne & Compare du Dialecte & du Patols de la Province de Bourgogne. Thomas Mignard. 335p. (Fr.). 1970. 70.00 F. Slatkine.

Vocabulaire Raisonne Latin-Francais. Gerard Cotton. 332p. (Lat. & Fr.). 19.40 F. Dessain & Tolra.

Vocabulaire Redaction. Pierre Moreau & Andre Masson. 64p. (Fr.). 1969. 4.50 F. Hachette.

Vocabulaire Suedois. Francois N. Simoneau. 80p. (Swedish.). 13.30 F. Ophrys.

Vocabulaire Systematique Francais-Allemand. Pierre Borel. 171p. (Fr. & Ger.). 1959. 9.80 F. Francke.

Vocabulaire Technique. 5th ed. Marcel Lagrenade. LC 80-463753. viii, 584p. (Eng. & Fr.). 1978. write for info. (ISBN 0-88905-004-X). Dotmar.

Vocabulaire Technique Allemand-Francais. 8th ed. Francis Cusset. 474p. (Ger. & Fr.). 1977. 66.50 F. Berger-Levrault.

Vocabulaire Technique Allemand-Francais, Francais-Allemand. 8th ed. Francis Cusset. 474p. (Fr. & Ger.). 1977. 29.95 (ISBN 0-686-56970-9, M-6097). French & Eur.

Vocabulaire Technique Anglais-Francais, Francais-Anglais. 9th ed. Francis Cusset. 434p. (Fr. & Ger.). 1977. 47.50 (ISBN 0-686-56971-7, M-6098). French & Eur.

Vocabulaire Technique Anglais-Francais. 9th ed. Francis Cusset. 434p. (Eng. & Fr.). 1977. 118.50 F. Berger-Levrault.

Vocabulaire Technique Bilingue. 2nd ed. Jean Delorme. 32p. (Fr.). 1954. 0.40 F. Quebec Off.

Vocabulaire Technique de la Bibliotheconomie. Paule Rolland-Thomas & Victor Coulombe. 187p. (Fr.). 1969. Can.$5.00. Assoc. Canad. Biblio. Lang. Fr.

Vocabulaire Technique des Assurances sur la Vie, Vol. 1. L. Beguin et al. 309p. (Eng. & Fr.). 1979. pap. 9.95 (ISBN 0-7754-2396-3, M-9244). French & Eur.

Vocabulaire Technique des Assurances sur la Vie, Vol. 2. J. Beguin et al. 335p. (Eng. & Fr.). 1979. pap. 9.95 (ISBN 2-551-03302-0, M-9245). French & Eur.
Vocabulaire Technique Des Assurances: Anglais-Francais, Francais-Anglais. J. Lesobre & H. Sommer. 255p. (Eng.-Fr.). 1972. 27.50 (ISBN 0-686-57013-8, M-6354). French & Eur.
Vocabulaire Technique des Assurances & Reassurances Anglais-Francais. Henri Sommer. 255p. (Eng. & Fr.). 1972. 54.00 F. Berger-Levrault.
Vocabulaire Toponymique du Ban de Fronville. P. Gavray-Baty. 164p. (Fr.). 1944. 30.00 F. Liege, Fac Lettres.
Vocabulaire Usuel du Chinois Moderne. Helmut Martin et al. LC 78-358753. vvi, 328p. (Chinese.). 1977. write for info. (ISBN 3-468-49025-9). Langen Kommand.
Vocabulaire Usuel du Chinois Moderne. 4th ed. Marcel Midoux. 1141p. (Chinese.). 1971. 88.00 F. Pubns Orient.
Vocabulaire Usuel du Chinois Moderne, 2: Chinois-Francais. Marcel Midoux. (Illus.). 276p. (Chinese & Fr.). 1970. 19.00 F. Geuthner.
Vocabulaire Usuel du Chinois Moderne, 3: Chinois-Francais. Marcel Midoux. (Illus.). 254p. (Chinese & Fr.). 1971. 20.00 F. Geuthner.
Vocabulaire Vivant. Emile Ballereau & Georges Bouquet. (Illus.). 192p. (Fr.). 1961. 9.75 F. SUDEL.
Vocabulaire Vivant. Andre Marthaler. (Illus.). 208p. (Fr.). 1961. 15.00 F. Payot.
Vocabulaire Vivant, 1. Andre Marthaler. (Illus.). 155p. (Fr.). 1970. 9.00 F. Payot.
Vocabulaire Vivant, 3. Andre Marthaler. 240p. (Fr.). 1967. 16.00 F. 13.00 F. Payot.
Vocabulaires Methodiques Ouayana, Apari, Oyampal, Emerillon. Henri Coudereau. (Fr.). 24.00 F. Kraus.
Vocabulaius Teutonico-Latinus. Pref. by Klaus Grabmueller. LC 77-46995. xxxiv, 622p. (Lat.). 1976. write for info. (ISBN 3-487-05883-9). Olms Verlag.
Vocabular Latina. 119p. (Lat. , Eng. , Fr. & Ger.). write for info. Esselte Studium.
Vocabulari Automobilistic. Merenciano & Antoni Frederic i Ricart. (Span.). 1972. write for info. Claret.
Vocabulari Basic Infantil & d'Adults. 114p. (Span.). write for info. Biblograf S. A.
Vocabulari basic infantil i d'Adults 'Vox' 6th ed. 112p. (Span.). 1982. pap. 225.00 ptas (ISBN 84-7153-265-4). Biblo SP.
Vocabulari basic infantil i d'Adults 'Vox' 4th ed. 112p. (Span.). 1980. pap. 200.00 ptas. Biblo SP.
Vocabulari Castella-Catala. 3rd ed. Eduard Artells. 224p. (Catalan & Span.). 1958. 5.95 (ISBN 84-7226-344-4, S-50355). French & Eur.
Vocabulari Castella-Catala. Eduard Artells. 290p. (Span.). 1961. 100.00 ptas. Barcino Edit.
Vocabulari Castella-Catala. (Span.). 2.50; 180.00 ptas. Salvat Editores.
Vocabulari Castella-Valencia. Francesc Ferrer Pastor. 477p. (Span.). 1967. 200.00 ptas. Sicania.
Vocabulari Castella-Valencia. Francesc Ferrer Pastor. 1039p. (Span.). 1967. 500.00 ptas. Sicania.
Vocabulari Castella-Valencia. 8th ed. 1076p. (Span.). 1981. 350.00 ptas (ISBN 84-85104-36-6). Estel Edit.
Vocabulari Castella-Valencia & Valencia-Castella. Francesc Ferrer-Pastor. LC 80-117607. 1075p. (Span. & Catalan.). 1979. write for info. (ISBN 8-485-10436-6). Estel Edit.
Vocabulari Catala-Castella. Eduard Artella. 468p. (Span.). 1961. 150.00 ptas. Barcino Edit.
Vocabulari Catala-Castella. 3rd ed. Eduard Artells. 465p. (Catalan & Span.). 1961. 5.25 (ISBN 84-7226-345-2, S-50354). French & Eur.
Vocabulari Catala De Matematica Basica. Claudi Alsina. 48p. (Catalan.). 1977. pap. 8.75 (ISBN 84-85008-06-5, S-50127). French & Eur.
Vocabulari de Barbarismes. Santiago Estrany. 87p. (Span.). 1982. 220.00 ptas (ISBN 8-43077-431-9). Teide.
Vocabulari de Barbarismes & Castellanismes. Aureli Cortiella Martret. 350p. (Span.). 1981. 350.00 ptas (ISBN 84-500-4509-6). Organ Ofic Adm.
Vocabulari de Fusteria: Generalitat de Catalunya. 58p. (Span.). 1982. pap. 320.00 ptas (ISBN 84-500-5206-8). Organ Ofic Adm.
Vocabulari Ideologic Catala. Xavier Romeu. (Span.). write for info. Teide.
Vocabulari Mallorqui-Castella. F. De Casasnovas. 328p. (Span.). 1965. 250.00 ptas. Moll Edit.
Vocabulari Valencia-Castella. Francesc Ferrer Pastor. 566p. (Span.). 1970. write for info. Fermar.
Vocabulario Aguaruna de Amazonas. Mildred L. Larson. (Peruvian Linguistic Ser: No. 3). 211p. (Span.). 1966. pap. 3.00x (ISBN 0-88312-653-2). Summer Inst Ling.
Vocabulario & Refranero Religioso de Mexico. Joaquin Antonio Penalosa. (Span.). Mex.$25.00. Jus.
Vocabulario Andaluz. A. Alcala. 676p. (Span.). 1980. 47.95 (ISBN 84-249-1364-7, S-32726). French & Eur.
Vocabulario, Apodos, Seudonimos, Sobrenombres & Hemerografia de la Revolucion. Arturo Langle. 151p. (Span.). 1966. Mex.$20.00. UNAM.
Vocabulario Basico de la Arquitectura. J. R. Paniagua. 375p. (Span.). 1978. pap. 17.95 (ISBN 84-376-0134-7, S-37345). French & Eur.
Vocabulario Basico Frances. E. Moreu-Rey. 112p. (Fr.). 40.00 ptas. Teide.
Vocabulario Basico Frances. 5th ed. Enrico Moreu Rey. 112p. (Fr.). 1981. 125.00 ptas (ISBN 84-307-7062-3). Teide.
Vocabulario Basico por Areas. 126p. (Span.). 1981. 550.00 ptas (ISBN 8-48583-909-9). Socusa Edit.
Vocabulario basico trilingue de psicologia cientifica: Ingles-castellano. Candid Genovard Rossello. 192p. (Eng. & Span.). 1980. pap. 500.00 ptas (ISBN 84-244-0490-4). Fontanella.
Vocabulario castelan-galego. Fermin Fernandez Armesto. 764p. (Span.). 1981. pap. 950.00 ptas (ISBN 84-7492-075-2). Castro Edns.
Vocabulario Castellano-Gallego. 3rd ed. Francisco Fernandez del Riego. 366p. (Span.). 1981. 325.00 ptas (ISBN 84-7154-324-9). Galaxia.
Vocabulario Chatino de Tataltepec. Leslie Pride & Kitty Pride. (Vocabularios Indigenas Ser.: No. 15). 103p. (Span.). 1970. pap. 3.00x (ISBN 0-88312-655-9); microfiche 2.25 (ISBN 0-88312-317-7). Summer Inst Ling.
Vocabulario con Ilustraciones. (Illus.). 18p. (Span.). 0.20; Mex.$0.50. Novaro.
Vocabulario consultivo por secciones: Espanol-ingles. Leonard V. Robson. 206p. (Span. & Eng.). 1980. pap. 600.00 ptas (ISBN 84-7231-571-1). Confed Espanola.
Vocabulario Culto. 2nd ed. Gladys Neggers. 168p. (Span.). 1977. pap. 8.75 (ISBN 84-359-0034-7, S-50023). French & Eur.
Vocabulario culto. 8th ed. Gladys Neggers. 168p. (Span.). 1982. pap. 350.00 ptas (ISBN 84-359-0034-7). Playor.
Vocabulario de Artes de la Madera, Arquitectura y Decoracion. 152p. (Span.). 1975. pap. 15.75 (ISBN 84-236-1246-5, S-50084). French & Eur.
Vocabulario de Benasque. Angel Ballarin Cornel. 224p. (Span.). 1972. 200.00 ptas. Fernando el Catolico.
Vocabulario De Cine y Television En Espana. Maria V. Romero Gualda. 400p. (Span.). 1976. pap. 23.95 (ISBN 84-313-0234-8, S-50002). French & Eur.
Vocabulario de Construccion Naval. Rafael Crespo Rodriguez. LC 76-456677. 179p. (Eng. & Span.). 1975. 300.00 ptas (ISBN 8-4600-6612-6). Universidades & Acad.
Vocabulario de Economia. J. Piernas. (Span.). 10.00 ptas. Espasa Calpe.
Vocabulario de Electronica. 56p. (Span.). 1981. 180.00 ptas (ISBN 84-353-0009-9). Inst Amer.
Vocabulario de Estadistica. J. L. Barcelo. 292p. (Span.). 1965. 300.00 ptas. Hispano Europa.
Vocabulario de la Cronica Troyana. K. Parker. 327p. (Span.). 1958. 150.00 ptas. U de Salamanca.
Vocabulario de las lenguas ibericas. Marina Regueiro & Ricardo Goyoaga. 192p. (Span.). 1982. pap. 480.00 ptas (ISBN 84-7465-048-8). Nuestra Cultura.
Vocabulario de Mayathan. Dorothy Andrews Heath de Zapata. LC 79-351468. 607p. (Maya & Span.). 1978. write for info. Dorothy Andrews Heath de Zapata.
Vocabulario de Pedagogia. Laeng. 310p. (Span.). 3.86; 250.00 ptas. Herder SA.
Vocabulario de Pedagogia. 3rd ed. Mauro Laeng. Ed. by C. Genovart Rosello. 308p. (Span.). 1982. pap. 600.00 ptas (ISBN 84-254-0581-5). Herder SA.
Vocabulario de Priego de Cordoba & su Comarca. Francisco Fernandez Pareja. 83p. (Span.). 1982. 250.00 ptas (ISBN 8-43007-537-2). Autores-Editores.
Vocabulario de Puerto Rico. Augusto Malaret. (Span.). Mex.$8.00. Las Americas.
Vocabulario de Romance: El Latin. Antonio De Nebrija. 202p. (Span.). 1982. pap. write for info. (ISBN 84-7039-143-7). Castalia Edit.
Vocabulario de romance en latin. 2nd ed. Elio de De Nebruja. Tr. by Gerald J. Macdonald. 214p. (Span.). 1981. pap. 1000.00 ptas (ISBN 84-7039-143-7). Castalia Edit.
Vocabulario De Romance En Latin: Antonio De Nebrija. Ed. by Gerald MacDonald. LC 72-96003. 214p. (Lat. & Span.). 1973. 19.95 (ISBN 0-87722-018-2). Temple U Pr.
Vocabulario de San Jorge de Piquin. Anibal Otero. LC 77-566102. 225p. (Span.). 1977. 500.00 ptas (ISBN 8-47191-009-8). Univers Santiago.
Vocabulario de Terminos: Criollos Tipicos Relacionados con el Caballo de Paso. Luna de la Fuente. 53p. (Span.). 1966. S/0.75; 15.00. U. Agraria.
Vocabulario del Alto-Aragones de Alquezar & Pueblos Proximos. Pedro Arnal Cavero. 32p. (Span.). 1944. 50.00 ptas (CSIC). Inst. Antonio de Nebrija.
Vocabulario del Bable de Somiedo. Ana M. Cano Gonzalez. 480p. (Span.). 1982. pap. 300.00 ptas (ISBN 8-40005-173-4). Consejo Superior.
Vocabulario del Comercio Medieval. 2nd ed. Miguel Gual Camarena. 532p. (Span.). 1976. leather 59.95 (ISBN 84-7370-017-1, S-50115). French & Eur.
Vocabulario del dialecto murciano. Justo Garcia Soriano. 316p. (Span.). 1980. pap. 500.00 ptas (ISBN 84-500-4063-9). Organ Ofic Adm.
Vocabulario Del Espanol Hablado. Luis Marquez Villegas. 128p. (Span.). 1975. pap. 5.95 (ISBN 84-7143-048-7, S-50027). French & Eur.
Vocabulario del Hato, 9 vols. Jose A. De Armas Chitty. 209p. (Span.). 1966. 1.40. U. Central Ven.
Vocabulario del Oriente Peruano. Enrique D. Tovar. 214p. (Span.). 1966. 3.35. U. San Marcos.
Vocabulario do Cheque. J. Sidou. LC 76-464726. 333p. (Port.). 1975. write for info. Editora Revista.
Vocabulario Economico & Financiero. Yves Bernard & Jose M. Suarez Campos. 488p. (Span.). 1981. 1300.00 ptas (ISBN 84-7019-077-6). Assn Prog Direc.
Vocabulario Electronico Internacional. International Electrotechnical Com. 318p. (Span.). 1975. 14.95 (ISBN 84-237-0148-4, S-50247). French & Eur.
Vocabulario Espanol de Tejas. Cerda et al. (Eng. & Span.). 15.00. Camino Real.
Vocabulario fenicio. Maria J. Fuentes Estanol. 400p. (Span.). 1980. pap. 2000.00 ptas (ISBN 84-00-04757-5). Consejo Superior.
Vocabulario Fundamental de la Lengua Francesa. Henri Hargous. 55p. (Fr.). Mex.$5.00. UNAM.
Vocabulario Galego-Castelan. Xose L. Franco Grande. 336p. (Gallic & Span.). 1972. pap. 9.50 (ISBN 84-7154-283-8, S-50437). French & Eur.
Vocabulario Galego-Castelan. Xose L. Franco Grande. (Span.). 90.00 ptas. Galaxia.
Vocabulario Galego-Castelan Castellano-Gallego. Xose L. Franco Grande & Francisco Fernandez del Riego. 584p. (Span.). 1982. pap. 775.00 ptas (ISBN 84-7154-413-X). Galaxia.
Vocabulario Galego-Portugues. M. Rodriguez Lapa. (Galego & Port.). write for info. Galaxia.
Vocabulario General de Orientacion Cientifica y Sus Estratos. Victor Garcia Hoz. 432p. (Span.). 1976. pap. 29.95 (ISBN 84-00-04273-5, S-50108). French & Eur.
Vocabulario Geomortologico. Consuelo Soto Mora. (Illus.). 202p. (Span.). 1965. Mex.$45.00. UNAM.
Vocabulario Griego. 4th ed. Fontoynont-Ribot. 214p. (Span.). 80.00 ptas. Sal Terrae.
Vocabulario Griego-Argentino. Raul Villarroel. (Gr. & Span.). write for info. Castellvi.
Vocabulario Huitoto Muinane. Eugene E. Minor & Dorothy Minor. (Peruvian Linguistic Ser: No. 5). 139p. (Span.). 1970. pap. 3.00x (ISBN 0-88312-656-7); microfiche 2.25x (ISBN 0-88312-362-2). Summer Inst Ling.
Vocabulario Ingles-Espanol de Electronica & Tecnica Nuclear. John Markus. 196p. (Eng. & Span.). write for info. (ISBN 84-267-0247-3). Marcombo.
Vocabulario Ingles-Espanol de Electronica. Francisco J. D'Agostino. (Eng. & Span.). write for info. ARBO.
Vocabulario Ingles-Espanol de Electronica y Tecnica Nuclear. 2nd ed. John Markus. 196p. (Span. & Eng.). pap. 16.75 (ISBN 84-267-0247-3, S-30684). French & Eur.
Vocabulario Ingles-Espanol, Espanol-Ingles de Medicina. Francisco Ruiz Torres. 300p. (Eng. & Span.). 1979. pap. 10.75 (ISBN 84-205-0625-7, S-50091). French & Eur.
Vocabulario Ingles-Espanol, Espanol-Ingles. Jose Merino Bustamante. 186p. (Eng. & Span.). 1977. pap. 3.50 (ISBN 84-205-0565-X, S-50346). French & Eur.
Vocabulario Ingles-Espanol para Servicio Clinico. Hellen H. Cooper. (Eng. & Span.). 0.80; Mex.$10.00. Pax.
Vocabulario Juridico. H. Capitant. 652p. (Span.). 1972. write for info. Depalma.
Vocabulario Juridico Frances-Espanol. G. Larousse. (Fr. & Span.). 1960. Arg.$5.00. Abeledo Perrot.
Vocabulario Lengua General Quichua. 5th ed. Guillermo Escobar. 221p. (Quichua.). 1951. 3.00; S/95.00. U. San Marcos.
Vocabulario Logico. Eduardo Angel Russo. 51p. (Span.). 1972. write for info. Coop. Der.
Vocabulario Logico, Historico & Positivo. Russo. (Span.). Arg.$3.00. Coop. Der.
Vocabulario Maritimo Ingles-Espanol. 3rd ed. J. Navarro Dagnino. 152p. (Eng. & Span.). write for info. G Gili.
Vocabulario Maritimo Ingles-Espanol y Espanol-Ingles. 5th ed. Juan Navarro Dagnino. 151p. (Span. & Eng.). 1976. pap. 8.50 (ISBN 84-252-0225-6, S-12239). French & Eur.

Vocabulario maritimo ingles-espanol y espanol-ingles. 5th ed. Juan Navarro Dagnino. 152p. (Eng. & Span.). 1980. pap. 280.00 ptas (ISBN 84-252-0225-6). G Gili.

Vocabulario Mayo, Vol. 6. rev. ed. Howard Collard & Elizabeth Collard. 225p. (Span.). 1974. pap. 4.00x (ISBN 0-88312-657-5); microfiche 3.00 (ISBN 0-88312-318-5). Summer Inst Ling.

Vocabulario Medieval Castellano. Cejador & Julio Frauca. (Span.). Mex.$12.50. Las Americas.

Vocabulario Mexicano de Tetelcingo. Forrest Brewer & Jean Brewer. (Vocabularios Indigenas Ser.: No. 8). 274p. (Span.). 1962. pap. 4.00x (ISBN 0-88312-658-3); microfiche 3.00x (ISBN 0-88312-363-0). Summer Inst Ling.

Vocabulario Mexicano Relativo a la Muerte. Juan M. Lope Blanch. 183p. (Span.). 1964. Mex.$20.00. UNAM.

Vocabulario Mixe de Totontepec. Alvin Schoenhals & Louise Schoenhals. (Vocabularios Indigenas Ser.: No. 14). 353p. (Span.). 1965. pap. 5.00x (ISBN 0-88312-659-1); microfiche 3.75 (ISBN 0-88312-319-3). Summer Inst Ling.

Vocabulario Mixteco de San Miguel el Grande. Betty Stoudt. (Vocabularios Indigenas Ser.: No. 12). (Span.). 1965. pap. 3.00 (ISBN 0-88312-660-5); microfiche 1.60x (ISBN 0-88312-580-3). Summer Inst Ling.

Vocabulario Ortografico: Sugerencias para su Enserianza. Consejo Superior de Esenanza. 266p. (Span.). 1965. 3.50. U. Puerto Rico.

Vocabulario Politico de Alguno Periodicos de Mexico D. F. Froilan Franco Arias. 50p. (Span.). 1981. write for info. (ISBN 84-7075-197-2). Fundacion J March.

Vocabulario Politico Republicano y Franquista, 1931-1971. Miguel A. Rebollo Torio. 184p. (Span.). 1978. 13.95 (ISBN 84-7366-072-2, S-50122). French & Eur.

Vocabulario Popoluca de Sayula. Lawrence Clark & Nancy Clark. (Vocabularios Indigenas Ser.: No. 4). 165p. (Span.). 1960. pap. 3.00x (ISBN 0-88312-663-X); microfiche 2.25 (ISBN 0-88312-365-7). Summer Inst Ling.

Vocabulario Popular Sevillano. 2nd ed. Manual Gonzalez Salas. 182p. (Span.). 1982. pap. 550.00 ptas (ISBN 8-42870-515-1). Prensa Espanola.

Vocabulario Puertorriqueno. De Rosario. (Span.). 1966. 10.95 (ISBN 0-87751-010-5, Pub by Troutman Press). E Torres & Sons.

Vocabulario Quechua del Pastaza. Peter Landerman. (Peruvian Linguistic Ser.: No. 8). 165p. (Span.). 1973. pap. 2.50x (ISBN 0-88312-664-8); microfiche 2.25 (ISBN 0-88312-366-5). Summer Inst Ling.

Vocabulario Sonorense. Horacio Sobrrzo. (Span.). 25.95 (ISBN 0-686-56691-2, S-12361). French & Eur.

Vocabulario Superior. Gaston Fernandez De La Torriente. 176p. (Span.). 1975. pap. 8.75 (ISBN 84-359-0124-6). French & Eur.

Vocabulario superior. 7th ed. Gaston Fernandez de la Torriente. 176p. (Span.). 1982. pap. 350.00 ptas (ISBN 84-359-0124-6). Playor.

Vocabulario T. Frances. (Fr.). 40.00 ptas. Bruno.

Vocabulario Tecnico De Contabilidad Moderna. Abiud Ramos-Ramos. LC 77-11200. (Span.). 1978. pap. 8.75 (ISBN 0-8477-2629-0). U of PR Pr.

Vocabulario Tecnologico Aeronautico. 2nd ed. Instituto Americano. LC 77-556591. 77p. (Eng. & Span.). 1976. write for info. (ISBN 8-4353-0618-6). Inst Amer.

Vocabulario Teologico del Evangelio de Saint Juan. J. Mateos Alvarez. 310p. (Span.). 1980. pap. 13.95 (ISBN 84-7057-270-9, S-33107). French & Eur.

Vocabulario Totonaco de la Sierra. Herman P. Aschmann. (Vocabularios Indigenas Ser.: No. 7). 171p. (Span.). 1962. pap. 3.00x (ISBN 0-88312-666-4); 2.25 (ISBN 0-88312-568-4). Summer Inst Ling.

Vocabulario Trabalhista: Direito do Trabalho, Processo do Trabalho, Previdencia Socail. Gerson Valle. LC 76-463962. 288p. (Port.). 1975. Cr.$60.00. Rio Grafica.

Vocabulario Tzeltal de Bachajon. Florence Gerdel & Marianna Slocum. (Vocabularios Indigenas Ser.: No. 13). 215p. (Span.). 1965. 3.00 (ISBN 0-88312-589-7). Summer Inst Ling.

Vocabulario Vial. OAS General Secretariat. 368p. (Eng., Span., Fr. & Port.). 1979. text ed. 15.00 (ISBN 0-8270-1332-9). OAS.

Vocabulario vital e irracional en Azorin. Jose D. Perona Sanchez. 110p. (Span.). 1981. pap. write for info. (ISBN 84-00-04957-8). Consejo Superior.

Vocabulario y Refranero Criollo. Tito Saubidet. (Span.). 85.00 (ISBN 0-686-56666-1, S-33072). French & Eur.

Vocabularios Aleman-Espanol-Polaco. (Ger. , Span. & Pol.). 0.80; Mex.$10.00. Novaro.

Vocabularios Frances-Espanol-Ingles. (Fr. , Span. & Eng.). 0.80; Mex.$10.00. Novaro.

Vocabularios Japones-Espanol-Ruso. (Japanese, Span. & Rus.). 0.80; Mex.$10.00. Novaro.

Vocabularios Ocho Idiomas (Coleccion, 4 vols. (Span.). 0.80 ea.; Mex.$10.00 ea. Novaro.

Vocabularios Portugues-Espanol-Italiano. (Port. , Span. & Ital.). 0.80; Mex.$10.00. Novaro.

Vocabularis Tematics. Antoni Lllllull Marti. LC 79-127295. ii, 117p. (Catalan.). 1979. write for info. (ISBN 8-450-03005-6). Organismos Ofic.

Vocabularium. Papias. 400p. (Ital.). 1968. L.30000.00. Bottega d'Erasmo.

Vocabularium Nocentium Florae. 4th ed. R. Kwizda. (Lat.). 1963. pap. 23.50 (ISBN 0-387-80646-6). Springer-Verlag.

Vocabularium Pharmaceuticum. 2nd ed. Ed. by Albert Graa. 125p. (Eng., Ger., Fr. & Ital.). 1964. text ed. 13.50x (ISBN 0-8002-3024-8). Intl Pubns Serv.

Vocabularium Polyglottum Vitae Silvarum. R. Litschauer. 126p. (Lat., Eng., Ger., Fr., Span. & Rumanian.). 1955. 21.50 (ISBN 0-686-56473-1, M-7679, Pub. by P. Parey). French & Eur.

Vocabularium Polyglottum Vitae Silvarum. R. Litschauer. 126p. (Lat., Eng., Ger., Fr., Span. & Romanian.). 1955. 21.50. Parey.

Vocabularium Saxonicum. L. Nowell. Ed. by A. Marckwardt. (Lat.). Repr. of 1952 ed. 15.00 (ISBN 0-527-67800-7). Kraus Repr.

Vocabularium syriacum. R. Kobert. v, 215p. (Lat.). 1956. L.7000.00; L.pap. 5000.00. Pont Ist Biblico.

Vocabularium vulgare. Nicola Valla. 95p. (Ital.). 1966. L.6000.00. Bottega d'Erasmo.

Vocabulary. Patricia Dunn-Rankin. (Illus.). 1978. pap. text ed. 13.95 (ISBN 0-07-018268-X, C). McGraw.

Vocabulary. 2nd ed. Patricia Dunn-Rankin. (Illus.). 224p. Date not set. pap. text ed. 13.95 (ISBN 0-07-018278-7, Pub. by C.); instr's. manual 12.50 (ISBN 0-07-018279-5). Mcgraw.

Vocabulary. Jack Rudman. (Teachers License Examination Ser.: G-5). (Cloth bdg. avail. on request). pap. 10.00 (ISBN 0-8373-8195-9). Natl Learning.

Vocabulary. (Manual of Petroleum Measurement Standards: Chap. 1). 1977. 5.00 (85225239). Am Petroleum.

Vocabulary & Composition Through Pleasurable Reading, Bk. 3. Harold Levine. (Orig.). (gr. 10-12). 1976. wkbk. 8.17 (ISBN 0-87720-306-7); pap. text ed. 7.17 (ISBN 0-87720-377-6). AMSCO Sch.

Vocabulary & Composition: Through Pleasurable Reading, Book 4. Harold Levine. (gr. 11-12). 1978. wkbk 8.17 (ISBN 0-87720-376-8); pap. text ed. 7.17 (ISBN 0-87720-378-4). AMSCO Sch.

Vocabulary & Composition Through Pleasurable Reading, Bk. 6. Harold Levine. (gr. 11-12). 1979. pap. text ed. 8.17 (ISBN 0-87720-388-1); wkbk. 7.17 (ISBN 0-87720-387-3). AMSCO Sch.

Vocabulary & Science Structure of Maori Children. I. H. Barham. (Maori.). 1.25. Nzcer.

Vocabulary & Syntax of the Old English Version in the Paris Psalter. John D. Tinkler. LC 68-29824. (Janua Linguarum, Ser. Practica: No. 67). (Illus.). 92p. (Orig., Old Eng.). 1971. pap. text ed. 16.00x (ISBN 90-2791-895-3). Mouton.

Vocabulary Arranged for the Instruction of the Deaf & Dumb. Wm. Vaughan. 69.95 (ISBN 0-8490-1265-1). Gordon Pr.

Vocabulary Builder & Guide to Verbal Tests. 5th ed. David R. Turner. LC 73-77242. 1973. pap. 7.95 (ISBN 0-668-00535-1). Arco.

Vocabulary Builder: The Practically Painless Way to a Larger Vocabulary. Judi Kesselman-Turkel & Franklynn Peterson. 192p. (Orig.). 1982. pap. 4.95 (ISBN 0-8092-5650-9). Contemp Bks.

Vocabulary Building & Word Study. Mary Lewick-Wallace. Ed. by Alton Raygor. (Communication Skills Ser.). 240p. (Orig.). 1981. pap. text ed. 11.95 (ISBN 0-07-067902-9, C). McGraw.

Vocabulary Building at the College Level. 2nd ed. Elton P. Henley. 1978. pap. text ed. 11.95 (ISBN 0-8403-1088-9). Kendall-Hunt.

Vocabulary Building: Syllabus, Level III. Diana C. Watson & Hernan Hurtado. 1973. pap. text ed. 5.25 (ISBN 0-89420-007-0, 270043); cassette recordings 69.20 (ISBN 0-89420-194-8, 270000). Natl Book.

Vocabulary Building: Syllabus, Level IV. Diana C. Watson & Malcom Watson. 1975. pap. text ed. 5.35 (ISBN 0-89420-039-9, 270053); cassette recordings 68.90 (ISBN 0-89420-195-6, 270200). Natl Book.

Vocabulary Change: A Study of Variation in Regional Words in Eight of the Southern States. Gordon R. Wood. LC 76-86183. 407p. 1971. 19.50x (ISBN 0-8093-0433-3). S Ill U Pr.

Vocabulary Control for Information Retrieval. F. Wilfrid Lancaster. LC 78-186528. (Illus.). xiv, 233p. 1972. text ed. 27.50 (ISBN 0-87815-006-4). Info Resources.

Vocabulary de la Fonderie, Francais-Anglais. (Fr. & Eng., French-English Vocabulary of Foundries). pap. 14.95 (ISBN 0-686-56719-6, M-6557). French & Eur.

Vocabulary de la Fonderie, Francais-Anglais. (Fr. & Eng., French-English Vocabulary of Foundries). pap. 12.50 (ISBN 0-686-56720-X, M-6556). French & Eur.

Vocabulary Development. Dale McMaster. (Language Arts Ser.). 24p. (gr. 6-9). 1976. wkbk. 5.00 (ISBN 0-8209-0312-4, VD-4). ESP.

Vocabulary Development Through Language Awareness. Kristbjorg E. O'Harra. (Illus.). 192p. 1984. pap. text ed. 11.95 (ISBN 0-13-150078-3). P-H.

Vocabulary Expansion I. Dorothy Rubin. 416p. 1982. pap. text ed. 9.95 (ISBN 0-02-404220-X). Macmillan.

Vocabulary Expansion II. Dorothy Rubin. 288p. 1982. pap. text ed. 9.95 (ISBN 0-02-404240-4). Macmillan.

Vocabulary for Adults. Jack S. Romine. LC 75-17660. (Self-Teaching Guides). 221p. 1975. pap. text ed. 5.95 (ISBN 0-471-73285-0, Pub. by Wiley Pr). Wiley.

Vocabulary for Annie Brigitte Gilles Tardos. Jackson MacLow. 1980. ltd. signed ed. 50.00 (ISBN 0-930794-73-7). Station Hill Pr.

Vocabulary for the College-Bound Student. Harold Levine. (Orig.). (gr. 9-12). 1964. text ed. 11.50 (ISBN 0-87720-367-9); pap. text ed. 6.17 (ISBN 0-87720-366-0); wkbk. o.p. 6.58 (ISBN 0-87720-312-1); with answers o.p. 4.20 (ISBN 0-87720-313-X). AMSCO Sch.

Vocabulary for the College-Bound Student. 2nd ed. Harold Levine. (Orig.). (gr. 11-12). 1982. text ed. 7.00 (ISBN 0-87720-442-X). AMSCO Sch.

Vocabulary for the High School Student. Harold Levine. 224p. (Orig.). (gr. 9-12). 1967. text ed. 11.50 (ISBN 0-87720-365-2); pap. text ed. 6.17 (ISBN 0-87720-364-4); wkbk. o.p. 6.58 (ISBN 0-87720-310-5); with answers o.p. 4.20 (ISBN 0-87720-311-3). AMSCO Sch.

Vocabulary for the High School Student. 2nd ed. Harold Levine. (gr. 10-12). 1982. wkbk. 7.00 (ISBN 0-87720-437-3). AMSCO Sch.

Vocabulary for the Spanish-Speaking Student of Shorthand. Maria Rivero Wood. 58p. (Span.). 1966. 0.85. U. Puerto Rico.

Vocabulary Foundations for the College Student. Harold Levine & Robert T. Levine. (Orig.). 1980. pap. text ed. 8.92 (ISBN 0-87720-962-6). AMSCO Sch.

Vocabulary Improvement. 3rd ed. Nancy Davis. 1978. pap. text ed. 14.50x (ISBN 0-07-015543-7, C). McGraw.

Vocabulary Improvement. Nancy B. Davis. (Eng.). Epap. 8.25. McGraw.

Vocabulary in Context. English Language Institute. (Intensive Course in English Ser.). 1964. pap. 5.95x (ISBN 0-472-08305-8). U of Mich Pr.

Vocabulary in Context: Getting the Precise Meaning. Walter Pauk. (Skill at a Time Ser). 64p. (gr. 9 up). 1975. pap. text ed. 3.20x (ISBN 0-89061-021-5, ST-1). Jamestown Pubs.

Vocabulary List-Key to Exercise for Practical Chinese Reader. Beijing Language Institute. (Practical Chinese Reader Ser.: No. 1 & 2). 75p. (Orig.). 1982. pap. 1.95 (ISBN 0-8351-1148-2). China Bks.

Vocabulary Made Easy. Visual Education Corporation. LC 83-9882. (Illus.). 136p. (gr. 9 up). 1983. wkbk. 6.00b (ISBN 0-07-039665-5, Pub. by G). McGraw.

Vocabulary Made Easy for Spanish Speakers. Muriel Hernandez De Prieto. LC 76-3732. 96p. (Orig., Prog. Bk.). 1976. pap. text ed. 3.75 (ISBN 0-8477-2622-3). U of PR Pr.

Vocabulary Made Easy for Spanish Speakers: Teacher's Guide. Muriel H. Prieto. LC 76-3732. 1978. pap. text ed. 3.00 (ISBN 0-8477-2635-5). U of PR Pr.

Vocabulary Magic. Imogene Forte & Mary A. Pangle. LC 77-89526. (Magic & Mastery Language Ser.). (Illus.). 112p. (gr. 2-6). 1977. pap. 5.95 (ISBN 0-913916-49-8, IP 49-8). Incentive Pubns.

Vocabulary Mastery. Scott Bornstein. (Illus.). 272p. (YA) (gr. 9-12). 1982. 19.95 (ISBN 0-9602610-1-X). Bornstein Memory.

Vocabulary Mastery. Imogene Forte & Mary A. Pangle. (Magic & Mastery Language Ser.). (Illus.). 1971. 3.95 (ISBN 0-913916-40-4, IP40-4). Incentive Pubns.

Vocabulary Norms for Deaf Children. George R. Guilfoyle & Toby Silverman-Dresner. LC 72-83498. (Lexington School Ser.: Book 7). 1972. softcover 8.00 (ISBN 0-88200-060-8, C2344). Alexander Graham.

Vocabulary of Anglo-Irish. James M. Clark. LC 73-12699. (Eng. & Irish.). 1917. lib. bdg. 15.00 (ISBN 0-8414-3394-1). Folcroft.

Vocabulary of Common Japanese Words. A. Rose-Innes. (Japanese). 3.00 (ISBN 0-88710-123-2). Far Eastern Pubns.

Vocabulary of First-Grade Children. Moe J. Alden et al. 136p. 1981. 21.50x (ISBN 0-398-04623-9). C C Thomas.
Vocabulary of High School Latin. Gonzalez Lodge. LC 73-177003. (Columbia University. Teachers College. Contributions to Education: No. 9). (Lat.). Repr. of 1912 ed. 17.50 (ISBN 0-404-55009-6). AMS Pr.
Vocabulary of Marble Playing. K. B. Harder. Bd. with Position of the Charleston Dialect. R. I. McDavid. (Publications of the American Dialect Society: No. 23). 61p. 1955. pap. 5.95 (ISBN 0-8173-0623-4). U of Ala Pr.
Vocabulary of Mental Aberration in Roman Comedy & Petronius. Dorothy M. Paschall. (Language Dissertations: No. 27). 1939. pap. 9.00 (ISBN 0-527-00773-0). Kraus Repr.
Vocabulary of Organic Chemistry. Milton Orchin et al. LC 79-25930. 1980. 43.50x (ISBN 0-471-04491-1, Pub. by Wiley-Interscience). Wiley.
Vocabulary of Science. Lancelot Hogben. LC 77-108314. 1971. pap. 3.95 (ISBN 0-8128-1394-4). Stein & Day.
Vocabulary of the Efik or Old Calabar Language. 2nd ed. Hope M. Waddell. 94p. 1972. Repr. of 1849 ed. 7.00x (ISBN 0-8002-1353-X). Intl Pubns Serv.
Vocabulary of the Eskimos of Point Barrow & Cape Smyth. facs. ed. P. N. Ray & John Murdoch. 13p. Repr. of 1885 ed. pap. 2.95 (ISBN 0-8466-0093-5, S93). Shorey.
Vocabulary of the Greek New Testament. James H. Moulton & George Milligan. (Gr.). 1949. 24.95 (ISBN 0-8028-2178-2). Eerdmans.
Vocabulary of the Hudailian Poems. Bernhard Lewin. (Acta Regiae Societatis Scientarum et Litterarum Goteborg, Humaniora: No. 13). 1978. pap. text ed. 28.00x (ISBN 91-85252-16-6). Humanities.
Vocabulary of the Language of San Antonio Mission, California. Buenaventura Sitjar. LC 10-26367. (Library of American Linguistics: No. 7). (Span.). Repr. of 1861 ed. 15.00 (ISBN 0-404-50987-8). AMS Pr.
Vocabulary of the Lau Language, Big Mala, Solomon Islands. Walter G. Ivens. LC 75-35127. (Lao.). Repr. of 1935 ed. 12.00 (ISBN 0-404-14143-9). AMS Pr.
Vocabulary of the Limbu Language of Eastern Nepal. Ed. by H. W. Senior. LC 78-908311. 86p. (Eng. & Limbu.). 1977. Repr. of 1908 ed. Rs.65.00. Radha.
Vocabulary of the Mangaian Language. F. W. Christian. (Mangaian.). Repr. of 1924 ed. pap. 8.00 (ISBN 0-527-02114-8). Kraus Repr.
Vocabulary One Thousand. Cronin. xi, 180p. (Eng.). Epap. 5.80. HarBraceJ.
Vocabulary One Thousand: With Words in Context. 2nd ed. Morton J. Cronin. 180p. 1981. pap. text ed. 9.95 (ISBN 0-15-594987-X, HC); instr's. manual 1.50 (ISBN 0-15-594988-8). HarBraceJ.
Vocabulary; or, Collection of Words & Phrases, Which Have Been Supposed to Be Peculiar to the United States of America; to Which Is Prefixed an Essay on the Present State of the English Language in the United States, 2 vols. in 1. John Pickering. Bd. with Letter to John Pickering on the Subject of His Vocabulary or Collection of Words & Phrases. Noah Webster. LC 70-178096. vii, 266p. 1972. Repr. of 1817 ed. lib. bdg. 24.00 (ISBN 0-8337-2752-4). B Franklin.
Vocabulary or Phrase Book of the Mutsun Language of Alta California. Felipe Arroyo De La Cuesta. (Library of American Linguistics: Vol. 8). (Catalan.). Repr. of 1862 ed. 17.50 (ISBN 0-404-50988-6). AMS Pr.
Vocabulary Resources for the College Student. Harold Levine & Robert Levine. (Orig.). 1980. pap. 8.92 (ISBN 0-87720-961-8). AMSCO Sch.
Vocabulary Skills, 3 Bks, Bks. D-F. pap. 1.59 ea.; Tchr's eds. 1.59 ea. Bk. D (ISBN 0-8372-3476-X). Tchr's ed (ISBN 0-8372-9210-7). Bk. E (ISBN 0-8372-3477-8). Tchr's ed (ISBN 0-8372-9211-5). Tchr's ed (ISBN 0-8372-3478-6) (ISBN 0-8372-9212-3). Bowmar-Noble.
Vocabulary, Spelling & Grammar. 10th ed. Walter J. Miller & Elizabeth Morsecluley. 256p. 1983. pap. 5.95 (ISBN 0-668-05806-4). Arco.
Vocabulary, Spelling & Grammar. 9th ed. David R. Turner. LC 70-153705. (Orig.). 1975. pap. 6.00 (ISBN 0-668-00077-5). Arco.
Vocabulary Study. Dale McMasters. (Language Arts Ser.). 24p. (gr. 5-7). 1976. wkbk. 5.00 (ISBN 0-8209-0311-6, VD-3). ESP.
Vocabulary: The Words Used to Express Ideas & Feelings. Joan Roloff-Stoddard et al. 1980. pap. text ed. 11.95x (ISBN 0-02-477440-5). Macmillan.
Vocabulary Through Pleasurable Reading, Bk. 1. Harold Levine. (Orig.). (gr. 7-10). 1974. pap. text ed. 7.17 (ISBN 0-87720-373-3); wkbk. 8.17 (ISBN 0-87720-368-7). AMSCO Sch.
Vocabulary Through Pleasurable Reading, Bk. 2. Harold Levine. (gr. 7-12). 1974. wkbk 8.17 (ISBN 0-87720-369-5); pap. text ed. 7.17 (ISBN 0-87720-374-1). AMSCO Sch.
Vocational Rehabilitation & the Employment of the Disabled. 182p. pap. 8.75 (ISBN 92-2-002571-X, ILO177, ILO). Unipub.
Voces Extranjeras en el Lengua Technologico. J. J. Alzugaray. (Span. & Eng.). 1980. pap. 9.95 (ISBN 0-686-92477-0, S-33100). French & Eur.
Voces Extranjeras en el Lenguaje Tecnologico. J. J. Alzugaray. 126p. (Span.). 1979. pap. write for info. (ISBN 84-205-0647-8). Edit Alhambra.
Voces Homofonas, Homografas & Homonimas Castellanas. Compiled by Alvaro J. Moreno. LC 77-457746. xxxiii, 315p. (Span.). 1975. write for info. Moreno Ed.
Vokabular der Psychoanalyse, 2 vols. Jean Laplanche. (Ger.). 1973. pap. 15.95 (ISBN 3-518-07607-8, M-7680, Pub. by Suhrkamp). French & Eur.
Vol. 10 see Theological Dictionary of the New Testament.
Volistaendiges Woerterbuch Ueber die Gedichte des Homores und der Homeriden. 9th ed. Carl Capelle. (Ger.). 1968. 48.00 (ISBN 3-534-03408-2, M-7681, Pub. by Wissenschaftl Buchgesells). French & Eur.
Volkssprache der Unteren Saar & der Obermosel: Ein Moselfrankisches Woerterbuch. Karl Conrath. LC 75-522113. xix, 308p. (Ger.). 1975. write for info. MG Schmitz.
Vollstaendiges Woerterbuch Zur Sogenannten Caedmonschen Genesis. Theodor Braasch. (Ger.). 1933. 17.95 (ISBN 3-533-00946-7, M-7682, Pub. by Carl Winter). French & Eur.
Vollstaendiges Woerterbuch Zur Sogenannten Caedmonschen Genesis. Theodor Braasch. (Ger.). 1933. 17.95 (ISBN 3-533-00946-7). Winter Univ.
Voltaire & His Portable Dictionary. William Trapnell. 75p. 1972. 15.00x (ISBN 3-465-00905-3). Intl Pubns Serv.
Von Bach zur Elektronik. Rudolf Brauner. LC 78-347055. 96p. (Ger.). 1977. S.60.00 (ISBN 3-853-85001-4). Prugg.
Von Praefigierten Verben Abgeleiteten Substantive in der Modernen Serbokroatischen Standartsprache. Klaus Koszinowski. LC 77-463046. 271p. (Serbo-Croatian.). 1976. DM.29.00 (ISBN 3-87690-112-X). Sagner.
Vorsilbe ver & Ihre Geschichte. Max Leopold. LC 77-562245. viii, 284p. (Ger.). 1977. DM.49.80 (ISBN 3-48706-181-3). Olms Verlag.
Vostochnoslavianskie Iazykovedy. M. G. Bulakhov. (Rus.). 1978. 15.75. Four Continent.
Vox--Diccionari Manual Ortografic. 552p. (Catalan.). 1975. leather 16.75 (ISBN 84-7153-327-8, S-31579). French & Eur.
Vox--Diccionario Abreviado Ortografico de la Lengua Espanola. 2nd ed. Prologue by Joaquin C. Sotelo. 416p. (Span.). 1978. leatherette 5.75 (ISBN 84-7153-227-1, S-12372). French & Eur.
Vox--Diccionario Conciso de la Lengua Espanola. 2nd ed. 464p. (Span.). 1977. pap. 3.25 (ISBN 84-7153-233-6, S-26963). French & Eur.
Vox--Diccionario de Sinonimos. Samuel Gili Gaya. 376p. (Span.). 1979. leatherette 10.95 (ISBN 84-7153-178-X, S-12324). French & Eur.
Vox--Diccionario Fundamental de la Lengua Espanola. 604p. (Span.). 1975. leatherette 10.50 (ISBN 84-7153-229-8, S-26961). French & Eur.
Vox--Diccionario Fundamental de la Lengua Espanola. 604p. (Span.). 1977. pap. 8.95 (ISBN 84-7153-230-1, S-50220). French & Eur.
Vox--Diccionario General Ilustrado de la Lengua Espanola. 3rd ed. 1752p. (Span.). 1978. leatherette 34.95 (ISBN 84-7153-109-7, S-12378). French & Eur.
Vox--Lexis-22, Diccionario Enciclopedia, 23 vols. 6704p. (Span.). 1977. Set. leatherette 250.00 (ISBN 84-7153-400-2, S-31569). French & Eur.
Vox--Vocabulari Basic Infantil i d'Adults. 112p. (Catalan.). 1977. pap. 5.50 (ISBN 84-7153-265-4, S-50216). French & Eur.
Vox Concise Spanish & English Dictionary. Biblograf. xxvi, 981p. (Span. & Eng.). E6.95 (ISBN 0-245-50989-5, Pub. by Biblograf S. A., Barcelona). Harrap.
Vox-Diccionari Manual de Sinonims. 2nd ed. 318p. (Catalan.). 1979. leatherette 12.95 (ISBN 84-7153-325-1, S-50217). French & Eur.
Vox-Diccionario Abreviado de la Lengua Espanola. 9th ed. 512p. (Span.). 1979. leatherette 4.75 (ISBN 84-7153-201-8, S-12371). French & Eur.
Vox-Diccionario Abreviado de Sinonimos. 3rd ed. 352p. (Span.). 1978. leatherette 5.75 (ISBN 84-7153-207-7, S-12370). French & Eur.
Vox-Diccionario Abreviado Frances-Espanol, Espanol-Frances. 8th ed. 672p. (Fr. & Span.). 1978. leatherette 7.25 (ISBN 84-7153-216-6, S-12414). French & Eur.
VOX-Diccionario basico frances-espanol, espanol-frances. 660p. (Fr. & Span.). 8.90. Imported Bks.
Vox-Diccionario Basico Latino-Espanol, Espanol-Latino. 8th ed. Eustaquio Echuari. 830p. (Lat. & Span.). 1978. leatherette 9.95 (ISBN 84-7153-223-9, S-12396). French & Eur.
Vox-Diccionario Compendiado de la Lengua Espanola. 2nd ed. 646p. (Span.). 1979. leatherette 4.95 (ISBN 84-7153-232-8, S-12373). French & Eur.
Vox-Diccionario Escolar de la Lengua Espanola. 5th ed. 884p. (Span.). 1978. leatherette 13.50 (ISBN 84-7153-172-0, S-12376). French & Eur.
Vox-Diccionario Ingles-Espanol, Espanol-Ingles. 4th ed. 1450p. (Eng. & Span.). 1978. leatherette 24.95 (ISBN 84-7153-151-8, S-12417). French & Eur.
Vox-Diccionario Inicial de la Lengua Espanola. 340p. (Span.). 1975. leatherette 6.95 (ISBN 0-686-57340-4, S-26962). French & Eur.
Vox-Diccionario Manual Griego-Espanol. 11th ed. Jose M. Pabon. 724p. (Gr. & Span.). 1979. leatherette 17.25 (ISBN 84-7153-192-5, S-12136). French & Eur.
Vox-Diccionario Manual Ilustrado de la Lengua Espanola. 4th ed. 1170p. (Span.). 1978. leatherette 13.95 (ISBN 84-7153-166-6, S-12379). French & Eur.
Vox-Diccionario Manual Ingles-Espanol, Espanol-Ingles. 8th ed. 1008p. (Eng. & Span.). 1979. leatherette 15.95 (ISBN 84-7153-181-X, S-12491). French & Eur.
Vox-Diccionario Tematico de la Lengua Espanola. 496p. (Span.). 1975. leatherette 26.25 (ISBN 84-7153-116-X, S-50219). French & Eur.
Vox New Compact Spanish & English Dictionary. Biblograf. 796p. (Span. & Eng.). E3.95 (ISBN 0-245-50990-9, Pub. by Biblograf, Barcelona). Harrap.
Vox Shorter Spanish & English Dictionary. Biblograf. 1448p. (Span. & Eng.). E20.00 (ISBN 0-245-50988-7, Pub. by Biblograf S. A., Barcelona). Harrap.
Vvedenie v Logiku. N. I. Kondakov. 465p. (Rus.). 1967. 6.85 (Pub. by Nauka). Four Continent.

W

Wafayat al-a yan: Ibn Khallikan's Biographical Dictionary, 4 vols. Tr. by Mac Guckin De Slane from Arabic. (Eng. & Arabic.). 110.00 set (129-1). Intl Bk Ctr.
Walker's Rhyming Dictionary of the English Language: In Which the Whole Language is Arranged According to its Terminations. rev. & enl. ed. J. Walker. 558p. 1979. Repr. of 1924 ed. 14.95 (ISBN 0-7100-2247-6). Routledge & Kegan.
Wall Street Thesauris. Paul Sarnoff. 1963. 12.95 (ISBN 0-8392-1127-9). Astor-Honor.
Walt Disney's Winnie-the-Pooh Dictionary. (Look-Look Bks.). (Illus.). (ps). 1981. 1.25 (ISBN 0-307-11868-1, Golden Pr); PLB 6.08 (ISBN 0-307-61868-4). Western Pub.
Ward's Natural Sign Language Thesaurus of Useful Signs N' Synonyms. Jill Ward. Ed. by John Joyce. LC 77-93547. (Illus.). 1978. 27.00 (ISBN 0-917002-18-0, 446). Joyce Media.
Warp & Weft: A Dictionary of Textile Terms. Dorothy K. Burnham. (Illus.). 240p. 1982. 35.00 (ISBN 0-684-17332-8, ScribT). Scribner.
Was Bedeuted Das? Duden. 444p. (Ger.). write for info (ISBN 91-24-20301-7). Esselte Studium.
Watch & Clockmakers' Handbook, Dictionary & Guide. F. J. Britten. (Illus.). 499p. 1978. Repr. of 1907 ed. 29.50 (ISBN 0-902028-46-4). Antique Collect.
Waverley Dictionary. May Rogers. 75.00 (ISBN 0-8490-1279-1). Gordon Pr.
Waverly Dictionary. 2nd ed. May Rogers. LC 66-27850. 1967. Repr. of 1885 ed. 37.00x (ISBN 0-8103-3222-1). Gale.
Webster Illustrated Contemporary Dictionary. Sidney Landau & Ronald Bogus. LC 82-45499. 1024p. 1982. 12.95 (ISBN 0-385-18306-2). Doubleday.
Webster's Collegiate Thesaurus. (Eng.). 1976. 11.95 (ISBN 0-87779-069-8, 72421). Merriam.
Webster's Concise Family Dictionary. Ed. by Merriam-Webster Editorial Staff. 848p. 1975. 7.95 (ISBN 0-87779-039-6). Merriam-Webster Inc.
Webster's Concise Family Dictionary. 1975. 6.95 (ISBN 0-87779-039-6, 72423). Merriam.
Webster's Dictionary for Everyday Use. Ed. by John G. Allee. 445p. 1971. pap. 3.25 (ISBN 0-06-463330-6, EH 330, EH). B&N NY.
Webster's Dictionary of Synonyms-Forty-One. (Eng.). 1978. 10.95 (ISBN 0-87779-241-0, 72410). Merriam.

Webster's Elementary Dictionary. Merriam-Webster Editorial Staff. (Illus.). (gr. 1-6). 1980. 9.95 (ISBN 0-87779-475-8). Merriam-Webster Inc.
Webster's Encyclopedia of Dictionaries: 1975 Large Print. 24.50x (ISBN 0-685-70713-X). Wehman.
Webster's Instant Word Guide. Ed. by Merriam-Webster Reference Editor. 384p. 1980. 3.95 (ISBN 0-87779-273-9). Merriam-Webster Inc.
Webster's Intermediate Dictionary. Ed. by Merriam Company. LC 70-38974. (Illus.). 960p. (gr. 7-9). 1977. 8.95 (ISBN 0-87779-279-8). Merriam-Webster Inc.
Webster's New Collegiate Dictionary. (Eng.). 1981. 14.95 (ISBN 0-87779-409-X, 72407). Merriam.
Webster's New Collegiate Dictionary. (Eng.). 1981. 13.95 (ISBN 0-87779-408-1, 72420). Merriam.
Webster's New Compact Dictionary. 1979. 2.95 (ISBN 0-8407-4081-6). Nelson.
Webster's New Dictionary of Synonyms. Merriam-Webster Editorial Staff. 942p. 1978. thumb-indexed 12.95 (ISBN 0-87779-241-0). Merriam-Webster Inc.
Webster's New Ideal Dictionary. Ed. by Merriam Company. (Illus.). 1978. 6.95 (ISBN 0-87779-249-6). Merriam-Webster Inc.
Webster's New Twentieth Century Dictionary. unabridged. 2nd ed. (Illus.). 1979. deluxe color ed., thumb indexed 59.95 (ISBN 0-529-04852-3, 86N-I). Collins Pubs.
Webster's New World Crossword Puzzle Dictionary. 1983. pap. write for info. (ISBN 0-671-46870-7). S&S.
Websters New World Crossword Puzzle Dictionary. Compiled by Jane S. Whitfield. LC 75-926. 7.95 (ISBN 0-529-05176-1, 190); thumb-indexed 8.95 (ISBN 0-529-05278-4, 190-I). Collins Pubs.
Webster's New World Dictionary. 1983. 16.95 (ISBN 0-671-47035-3). S&S.
Webster's New World Dictionary. 2nd ed. 1728p. 16.95 (ISBN 0-671-47035-3). S&S.
Webster's New World Dictionary: Basic School Edition. 3rd ed. (Eng.). 1983. 10.98. P-H.
Webster's New World Dictionary: Compact School & Office Edition. LC 76-58966. 1977. 3.49 (ISBN 0-529-05344-6, 134R). Collins Pubs.
Webster's New World Dictionary: Compact School & Office Edition. (Eng.). 3.93. P-H.
Webster's New World Dictionary for Young Readers: New Rev. Color Edition. Ed. by David B. Guralnik. LC 78-59178. (Illus.). (gr. 4-9). 9.95 (ISBN 0-529-05625-9, 103N). Collins Pubs.
Webster's New World Dictionary: Modern Desk Edition. Ed. by David B. Guralnik. LC 79-52089. (Illus.). 1979. gold-stamped hardcovers 4.95 (ISBN 0-529-05333-0, 166N); thumb indexed 5.95 (ISBN 0-529-05340-3, 166N-I). Collins Pubs.
Webster's New World Dictionary of Computer Terms. Date not set. 5.95 (ISBN 0-671-46866-9). S&S.
Webster's New World Dictionary of the American Language. David Guralnik. 704p. 1982. pap. 3.50 (ISBN 0-446-31192-8). Warner Bks.
Webster's New World Dictionary of the American Language. David B. Guralnik. 704p. 1983. pap. 8.95 (ISBN 0-446-37914-X). Warner Bks.
Webster's New World Dictionary of the American Language. second concise ed. LC 79-50954. 1979. 8.95 (ISBN 0-529-05267-9, 83N); thumb-indexed 9.95 (ISBN 0-529-05268-7, 83N-I); pap. 4.95 (ISBN 0-529-05281-4, M37ON). Collins Pubs.
Webster's New World Dictionary of the American Language: Second College Edition. Ed. by David B. Guralnik et al. (Illus.). 1980. 10.95 (ISBN 0-529-05324-1, 60B); thumb-indexed 11.95 (ISBN 0-529-05326-8, 60BI); lea. gift ed. 45.00 (ISBN 0-529-05329-2, 62BI); pap. 8.50 (ISBN 0-529-05327-6, 60BP). Collins Pubs.
Webster's New World Dictionary: Second College Ed. (Illus.). deluxe ed. 18.95 (ISBN 0-529-05328-4, 65B-I). Collins Pubs.
Webster's New World Dictionary: Second College Edition, Revised School Printing. Ed. by David B. Guralnik. (Eng.). 10.98; pap. 4.32. P-H.
Webster's New World Dictionary: Student Edition. Ed. by David B. Guralnik. (Eng.). 1983. 10.59; pap. 4.32. P-H.
Webster's New World Dictionary: Student's Edition. Ed. by David B. Gurainik. 1976. 17.28 (ISBN 0-13-944652-4). P-H.
Webster's New World Dictionary: Students Edition. LC 76-4634. 1976. 9.95 (ISBN 0-529-05375-6, 79). Collins Pubs.
Webster's New World Handy Pocket Dictionary. LC 76-48828. 1977. with slip-on vinyl jacket 1.95 (ISBN 0-529-05323-3, 171N); prepack of 20 39.00 (ISBN 0-529-05335-7, 171NP). Collins Pubs.
Webster's New World Quick Reference Dictionary. LC 70-147261. 1977. 1.00 (ISBN 0-529-03091-8, 172); prepack of 20 20.00 (ISBN 0-529-05336-5, 172P). Collins Pubs.
Webster's New World Thesaurus. Charles Laird. 544p. 1982. pap. 2.95 (ISBN 0-446-31203-7). Warner Bks.
Webster's New World Thesaurus. Charlton Laird. 544p. 1983. pap. 8.95 (ISBN 0-446-37053-3). Warner Bks.
Webster's New World Thesaurus. Charlton Laird. (Eng.). 12.93; pap. 8.94. P-H.
Webster's New World Thesaurus. Ed. by Charlton Laird. 688p. 8.95 (ISBN 0-529-03961-3, 2694N); thumb indexed 9.95 (ISBN 0-529-05187-7, 2694N-1); pap. 5.95 (ISBN 0-529-04805-1, M383). Collins Pubs.
Webster's New World Thesaurus. Ed. by Charlton Laird. pap. 8.95 (ISBN 0-452-00627-9, F627, Mer). NAL.
Webster's New World Vest Pocket Dictionary. LC 76-48830. 1977. imitation lea. 0.99 (ISBN 0-529-04686-5, 183N); 30-copy prepack 26.70 (ISBN 0-529-04804-3, 183NP). Collins Pubs.
Webster's Ninth New Collegiate Dictionary. 8th ed. Merriam-Webster Editorial Staff. 1568p. 1983. gray lexotone 15.95 (ISBN 0-87779-508-8); thumb-indexed red linen 14.95 (ISBN 0-87779-409-X); thumb-indexed brown skivertex 14.95 (ISBN 0-87779-509-6). Merriam-Webster Inc.
Webster's Official Crossword Puzzle Dictionary. Merriam Webster Editorial Staff. LC 81-38341. 757p. 1981. 12.95 (ISBN 0-87779-021-3). Merriam-Webster Inc.
Webster's Official Crossword Puzzle Dictionary. (Eng.). 1981. 12.95 (ISBN 0-87779-021-3, 72446). Merriam.
Webster's Red Seal Crossword Dictionary. Norman Hill. 272p. 1982. pap. 2.95 (ISBN 0-446-31186-3). Warner Bks.
Webster's Scholastic Dictionary. (gr. 9 up). pap. 2.95 (ISBN 0-8049-2001-X, D1). Airmont.
Webster's School Dictionary. Merriam-Webster Editorial Staff. (Illus.). (gr. 8-12). 1980. 10.95 (ISBN 0-87779-280-1). Merriam-Webster Inc.
Webster's School Thesaurus. Merriam-Webster Editorial Staff. 1978. 9.95 (ISBN 0-87779-178-3). Merriam-Webster Inc.
Webster's School Thesaurus. (Eng.). 1978. 8.95 (ISBN 0-87779-178-3, 72435). Merriam.
Websters Seventh New Collegiate Dictionary. (Eng.). 1976. 16.95 (ISBN 0-87779-314-X, 72406). Merriam.
Webster's Sports Dictionary. Ed. by Merriam-Webster Editorial Staff. 1976. 8.95 (ISBN 0-87779-067-1). Merriam-Webster Inc.
Webster's Super New School & Office Dictionary. 1978. pap. 2.50 (ISBN 0-449-23249-2, Crest). Fawcett.
Webster's Synonyms, Antonyms, Homonyms. pap. 1.99 (ISBN 0-671-41838-6). Dennison.
Webster's Third Interntaional Dictionary. (Eng.). 1981. 85.00 (ISBN 0-87779-206-2, 72449). Merriam.
Webster's Third New International Dictionary. (Illus.). 1981. 69.65 (ISBN 0-87779-201-1, 72448). Merriam.
Webster's Third New International Dictionary, Unabridged: The Great Library of the English Language. Ed. by Merriam Company. Incl. Regular-Paper Style. blue sturdite 69.95 (ISBN 0-87779-201-1); Tan Imperial Buckram. deluxe binding 79.95 (ISBN 0-87779-206-2). (Illus.). 2728p. (Sprinkled edges, indexed). 1981. Merriam-Webster Inc.
Webster's Third on Non-Standard Usage. Jean Malmstrom. Bd. with Social Aspects of Bilingualism in San Antonio, Texas. Janet B. Sawyer; Names in Gardening. Margaret M. Bryant. (Publications of the American Dialect Society: No. 41). 69p. 1964. pap. 5.00 (ISBN 0-8173-0641-2). U of Ala Pr.
Webster's Unafraid Dictionary. Leonard L. Levinson. (Orig.). 1967. pap. 2.95 (ISBN 0-02-040540-5, Collier). Macmillan.
Webster's Vest Pocket Dictionary. Merriam-Webster Editorial Staff. 380p. 1981. pap. 2.25 (ISBN 0-87779-190-2). Merriam-Webster Inc.
Welding Terms & Definitions. American Welding Society. 15.00. Am Welding.
Welsh-English, English-Welsh Dictionary. H. Meurig Evans & W. O. Thomas. (Welsh & Eng.). 20.50 (ISBN 0-87557-091-7, 091-7). Saphrograph.
Welt Von A-Z, 2 vols. (Illus.). 1264p. (Ger.). 66.70 (1102). Adler Bks.
Western Canadian Dictionary & Phrase-Book. John Sandilands. 1977. Can.$5.00 (ISBN 0-88864-021-8). U of Toronto Pr.
Western Lexikon. Joe Hembus. LC 79-396669. 816p. (Ger.). 1978. DM.12.80 (ISBN 3-453-00767-0). Heyne W Verlag.
Which I Which? A Manual of Homophones. S. F. Hagan. write for info. (ISBN 0-333-27235-8). Macmillan.
White-Hmong English Dictionary. Compiled by Ernest E. Heimbach. (Linguistic Ser.: No. IV). 497p. 1979. Repr. of 1969 ed. 6.50 (ISBN 0-87727-075-9, DP 75). Cornell SE Asia.
White Hmong-English Dictionary. rev. ed. Compiled by Ernest E. Heimbach. (Linguistics Ser.: No. IV). 497p. 1979. 6.50 (ISBN 0-686-89057-4). Cornell SE Asia.
Whitfield's University Rhyming Dictionary: English Language Rime. F. Stillman. 283p. 1964. pap. 3.95 (ISBN 0-8152-0080-3, M-9049). French & Eur.
Whitfield's University Rhyming Dictionary. Jane S. Whitfield. Ed. by Frances Stillman. 284p. 1981. pap. 4.95 (ISBN 0-06-463538-4, EH 538, EH). B&N NY.
Whitfield's University Rhyming Dictionary. Jane S. Whitfield. Ed. by Frances Stillman. (Apollo Eds.). pap. 3.95i (ISBN 0-8152-0080-3, A80). T Y Crowell.
Whittington's Dictionary of Plastics. 2nd rev. ed. Lloyd R. Whittington. LC 78-73776. 1978. 29.95 (ISBN 0-87762-267-1). Technomic.
Wielki Slownik Polsko-Angielski, 2 vols. Jan Stanislawski. LC 79-338334. (Pol. & Eng.). 1978. 1600.00 Zl. Wiedza Powszechna.
Wielki Slownik Polsko-Niemiecki: Grosswoerterbuch Polnische-Deutsch, 2 vols. Jan Piprek & Juliusz Ippoldt. LC 79-348368. (Pol. & Ger.). 1977. 650.00 Zl. Wiedza Powszechna.
Wielki Slownik Polsko-Rosyski (Polish-Russian Dictionary) Mirowicz. 1331p. (Pol. & Rus.). 1980. 70.00 (ISBN 0-686-87195-2, M-9131). French & Eur.
Winston Canadian Dictionary for Schools. 1965. 8.10 (ISBN 0-03-923504-1); pap. 4.50 (ISBN 0-03-923312-X). HRW.
Winston Dictionary for Schools. Holt Staff. (gr. 5-9). 1967. text ed. 4.84 (ISBN 0-03-063485-7); text ed. 5.36 indexed (ISBN 0-03-065960-4). HR&W.
Winston Dictionary of Canadian English. 1969. 11.14 (ISBN 0-03-923512-2). HRW.
Winston Dictionary of Canadian English. 1975. 8.91 (ISBN 0-03-923516-5). HRW.
Winston Primary Dictionary. 1972. 5.20 (ISBN 0-03-923500-9). HRW.
WIPO Glossary of the Terms of the Law of Copyright & Neighboring Rights. 281p. 1980. pap. 38.25 (ISBN 92-805-0016-3, WIPO69, WIPO). Unipub.
Wirtschafts-Woerterbuch. 4th ed. R. Eichborn. 2169p. (Ger. & Eng., Dictionary of Economics). write for info (M-7687, Pub. by Econ Vlg.). French & Eur.
Wirtschafts-Woerterbuch. 2nd ed. R. Eichborn & A. Fuentes. 2174p. (Ger. & Span.). 120.00 (ISBN 3-430-12388-7, M-7686, Pub. by Econ Vlg.). French & Eur.
Wirtschaftssprache Deutsch-Englisch, Englisch-Deutsch. R. Renner & R. Sachs. 544p. (Ger. & Eng.). 21.00. M Rosenberg.
Wirtschaftssprache Franzoesisch-Deutsch. G. Haensch & R. Renner. 540p. (Fr. & Ger.). 1975. 32.00 (ISBN 3-19-006202-1, M-7683, Pub. by M. Hueber). French & Eur.
Wirtschaftssprache Franzoesisch-Deutsch. G. Haensch & R. Renner. 540p. (Fr. & Ger.). 1975. 32.00 (ISBN 3-19-006202-1). Hueber.
Wirtschaftssprache Spanisch-Deutsch. G. Haensch & F. Casero. (Span. & Ger.). 1971. 32.00 (ISBN 3-19-006203-X, M-7684, Pub. by M. Hueber). French & Eur.
Wirtschaftssprache Spanisch-Deutsch. G. Haensch & F. Casero. (Span. & Ger.). 1971. 32.00 (ISBN 3-19-006203-X). Hueber.
Wirtschaftswoerterbuch Spanisch-Deutsch. Eichborn & Fuentes. (Span. & Ger.). 1974. 120.00 (ISBN 3-430-12390-9, M-7685, Pub. by Econ). French & Eur.
Wissen von A-Z: Ein Allgemeines Lexikon fur die Schule. Gisela Preuss. (Illus.). 568p. (Ger.). DM.write for info. (ISBN 3-411-01780-5). Biblio Inst.
Wissenschaftstheoretisches Lexikon. Edmund Braun. (Ger.). 1977. 79.95 (ISBN 3-222-10953-2, M-7688, Pub. by Styria). French & Eur.
Woerter & Gegenwoerter. 4th ed. C. Agricola & E. Agricola. 280p. (Ger.). 1982. M.9.80. Bibl Inst Leipzig.
Woerter & Wendungen. Ed. by E. Agricola et al. 818p. (Ger.). 1982. M.22.00. Bibl Inst Leipzig.
Woerter zur Valenz & Distribution der Substantive. 2nd ed. K. Sommerfeldt & H. Schreiber. 434p. (Ger.). 1980. M.22.00. Bibl Inst Leipzig.
Woerterbuch, 2 vols. Gross. (Ger.). DM.98.00 ea. Verlag Harri Deutsch.
Woerterbuch - Linguistische Grundbegriffe. 2nd ed. W. Ulrich. (Ger.). 1975. pap. 12.95 (ISBN 3-554-80336-7, M-6914). French & Eur.
Woerterbuch als Fehlerquelle. 48p. (Ger.). 1970. DM.4.80 (ISBN 3-87118-019-X). Buske.
Woerterbuch Bau: Ingenieurbau & Baumaschinen. 3rd ed. H. Bucksch. 934p. (Eng. & Ger.). 1965. DM.38.00 (ISBN 3-7625-1411-9). Bauverlag.

Woerterbuch Burmesisch-Deutsch. Annemarie Esche. LC 76-476865. 546p. (Ger. & Burmese.). 1976. M.65.00. VEB Verlag Enzyklopadie.

Woerterbuch Chemie & Chemische Technik, 2 vols. Gross. Incl. Vol. 1. 700p. (Eng. & Ger.). 1976 (ISBN 3-87144-141-4); Vol. 2. 700p. (Ger. & Eng.). 1980 (ISBN 3-87144-142-2). (Ger. & Eng.). DM.98.00 ea. Verlag Harri Deutsch.

Woerterbuch Chemie und Chemische Technik, Vol. 1. 1600p. (Ger.). 1975. 78.00 (ISBN 3-87144-141-4, M-6966). French & Eur.

Woerterbuch Chemie und Chemische Technik, Vol. 2. H. Gross. (Ger.). 68.00 (ISBN 0-686-56616-5, M-6965). French & Eur.

Woerterbuch christlicher Ethik. Bernhard Stoeckle. LC 75-520505. 284p. (Ger.). 1975. write for info. (ISBN 3-451-07533-4). Herder.

Woerterbuch Christlicher Ethik. Bernhard Stoeckle. 284p. (Ger.). 1975. DM.9.90 (ISBN 3-451-07533-4). Herder.

Woerterbuch Datenerfassung: Programmierung. Buerger. 386p. (Eng., Fr., Rus. & Ger.). 1976. DM.78.00 (ISBN 3-87144-264-X). Verlag Harri Deutsch.

Woerterbuch Datenerfassung-Programmierung. E. Buerger. (Eng., Ger., Fr. & Rus., Dictionary of Data Processing & Programming). 1976. 56.00 (ISBN 3-87144-265-8, M-6967). French & Eur.

Woerterbuch der Abkurzungen. Josef Werlin. 260p. (Ger.). 1979. pap. 8.00. Imported Bks.

Woerterbuch der Agrarpolitik. R. Bremer et al. 175p. (Ger.). 1961. DM.9.80 (ISBN 3-490-01315-8). Parey.

Woerterbuch der Altgermanischen Personen und Voelkernamen. 2nd ed. M. Schoenfeld. 309p. (Ger.). 1965. 32.00 (ISBN 3-533-00512-7, M-7045). French & Eur.

Woerterbuch der Amerikanismen. 3rd ed. Friedrich Koehler. (Ger.). 1972. 25.00 (ISBN 3-500-25340-7, M-7044). French & Eur.

Woerterbuch der Antike. 8th ed. Hans Lamer. (Ger.). 1976. 23.00 (ISBN 3-520-09608-0, M-7042). French & Eur.

Woerterbuch der Antike: Mit Beruecks Ihres Fortwirkens. Paul Kroh. Ed. by E. Bux & W. Schoene. LC 76-475045. 832p. (Ger.). 1976. DM.25.00 (ISBN 3-520-09608-0). Kroener.

Woerterbuch der Berufs & Wirtschaftspaedagogik. 320p. (Ger.). 1973. DM.9.90 (ISBN 3-451-09009-0). Herder.

Woerterbuch der Berufs und Wirtschaftspaedagogik. 320p. (Ger.). 1973. pap. 7.95 (ISBN 0-686-56645-9, M-7038). French & Eur.

Woerterbuch der Biochemie. Thielmann. 724p. (Eng., Span., Fr., Rus. & Ger.). 1978. DM.58.00 (ISBN 3-87144-346-8). Verlag Harri Deutsch.

Woerterbuch der Biochemie. K. Thielmann. 724p. (Ger., Eng., Fr., Rus. & Span., Dictionary of Biochemistry). 1978. 38.00 (ISBN 0-686-56646-7, M-7041). French & Eur.

Woerterbuch der Biochemie. K. Von Thielmann. LC 79-354449. 742p. (Eng., Fr., Rus., & Span.). 1977. M.48.00. VEB Verlag Enzyklopadie.

Woerterbuch der Biologie. Guenther Haensch. (Eng., Ger., Fr. & Span., Dictionary of Biology). 1976. pap. 78.00 (ISBN 3-405-10933-7, M-7040). French & Eur.

Woerterbuch der Biologie. Werner Jacobs. (Ger.). 1976. pap. 15.00 (ISBN 3-437-30195-0, M-7039). French & Eur.

Woerterbuch der Chemie, Vol. 1. I. Ernst & F. Ernst von Morgenstern. 891p. (Eng. & Ger., English-German Dictionary of Chemistry). 36.00 (ISBN 3-87097-011-1, M-7037). French & Eur.

Woerterbuch der Chemie, Vol. 2. I. Ernst & F. Ernst von Morgenstern. 892p. (Eng. & Ger., English-German Dictionary of Chemistry). 44.00 (ISBN 3-87097-012-X, M-7036). French & Eur.

Woerterbuch der Chemie: Band I, D - E. 727p. (Ger.). 1982. DM.45.00. Brandstetter.

Woerterbuch der Chemie: Band II, English-Deutsch. Ernst. 1056p. (Eng. & Ger.). 1982. DM.55.00. Brandstetter.

Woerterbuch der Chinesischen Revolution. P. Dittmar. 224p. (Ger.). 1975. pap. 5.95 (ISBN 0-686-56644-0, M-7035). French & Eur.

Woerterbuch der Dampferzeugungstechnik-Dictionary of Steam Generator Engineering. Ed. by Deutsche Babcock et al. 512p. (Ger., Eng., Span. Fr.). 1972. 29.50x (ISBN 3-8027-2471-2). Intl Pubns Serv.

Woerterbuch der Darstellenden Kuenste: Russiche-Deutsch. Gabriele Fischborn. LC 77-569863. 248p. (Ger. & Rus.). 1976. M.18.00. VEB Verlag Enzyklopadie.

Woerterbuch der Datentechnick. Joachim Schulz. LC 77-514536. 134p. (Eng., Rus. & Ger.). 1977. DM.50.00 (ISBN 3-87097-075-8). Brandstetter.

Woerterbuch der Datentechnik. Brinkmann & Schmidt. 733p. (Ger. & Eng.). 1982. DM.60.00. Brandstetter.

Woerterbuch der Datentechnik. Linse. 394p. (Ger. & Fr.). 1982. DM.50.00. Brandstetter.

Woerterbuch der Datentechnik: Russisch-Deutsch-Englisch. Schulz. 364p. (Rus., Ger. & Eng.). 1982. DM.50.00. Brandstetter.

Woerterbuch der Datenverarbeitung. 2nd ed. A. Oppermann. 343p. (Eng. & Ger., Dictionary of Dataprocessing). 1973. 28.00 (ISBN 3-7940-3099-0, M-7034). French & Eur.

Woerterbuch der DDR Paedagogik. Johannes Niermann. (Ger.). 1974. pap. 13.50 (ISBN 3-494-02036-1, M-7032). French & Eur.

Woerterbuch der Deutschen & Niederlaendischen Rechtssprache: Lexikon fuer Justiz, Verwaltung, Wirtschaft & Handel. Hans Langendorf. LC 78-376399. (Ger. & Dutch.). 1976. DM.55.00 (ISBN 3-406-06672-0). Kluwer Group.

Woerterbuch der Deutschen Aussprache. 2nd ed. Hans Krech. 549p. (Ger.). 1967. 19.95 (ISBN 0-686-56643-2, M-7033). French & Eur.

Woerterbuch der deutschen Gegenwartssprache, 6 vols. (Ger.). 1978. Vol. 1-5. 24.00 ea.; Vol. 6. 19.80 ea. M Rosenberg.

Woerterbuch der Deutschen Gegenwartssprache: Vol. 6. 480p. (Ger.). pap. 19.80. M Rosenberg.

Woerterbuch der Deutschen Gegenwartssprache: Vols. 1-5, 6 vols. 800p. (Ger.). pap. 24.00 ea. M Rosenberg.

Woerterbuch der Deutschen Pflanzennamen. Marzell. (Ger.). fascs. 1-22 550.00 (ISBN 0-686-56642-4, M-7031). French & Eur.

Woerterbuch der Deutschen Sprache mit Rechtschreiblehre. 256p. (Ger.). 1966. DM.3.80 (ISBN 3-8036-0251-3). Gebrueder Weiss.

Woerterbuch der Deutschen Umgangsprache: Vol. 3, Hochdeutsch-Umgangsdeutsch A-Z. (Ger.). 1983. 13.50. M Rosenberg.

Woerterbuch der Deutschen Umgangsprache: Vol. 4, Berufsschelten & Verwandtes. H. Keupper. (Ger.). 1983. 19.00. M Rosenberg.

Woerterbuch der Deutschen Umgangssprache: Vol. 5, 10000 neue Ausdruecke Sachschelten. H. Kuepper. (Ger.). 1983. 19.00. M Rosenberg.

Woerterbuch der Deutschen Umgangssprache: Vol. 6, Jugenddeutsch A-Z. H. Kuepper. (Ger.). 1983. 21.00. M Rosenberg.

Woerterbuch der Deutschen und Franzoesischen Rechtssprache, Vol. 1. 2nd ed. Michel Doucet. (Ger. & Fr.). 1966. 28.00 (ISBN 3-406-00969-7, M-7030). French & Eur.

Woerterbuch der Deutschen und Franzoesischen Rechtssprache, Vol. 2. 2nd ed. Michel Doucet. (Ger. & Fr.). 1977. 54.00 (ISBN 3-406-01196-9, M-7029). French & Eur.

Woerterbuch der Deutschen und Italienischen Wirtschafts und Rechtssprache, Vol. 1. 2nd ed. Giuseppe Conte. (Ital. & Ger.). 1971. 30.00 (ISBN 3-406-01195-0, M-7028). French & Eur.

Woerterbuch der Deutschen und Italienischen Wirtschafts und Rechtssprache, Vol. 2. 2nd ed. Giuseppe Conte. (Ger. & Ital.). 1969. 30.00 (ISBN 3-406-00887-9, M-7027). French & Eur.

Woerterbuch der Deutschen und Nierderlaendischen Rechtssprache, Vol. 1. Hans Langendorf. (Dutch & Ger.). 1976. 44.00 (ISBN 3-406-06672-0, M-7025). French & Eur.

Woerterbuch der Deutschen und Nierderlaendischen Rechtssprache, Vol. 2. Hans Langendorf. (Dutch & Ger.). 1976. 44.00 (ISBN 3-406-06673-9, M-7026). French & Eur.

Woerterbuch der Deutschen und Spanischen Sprache, Vol. 1. 3rd ed. Rudolf Slaby. (Ger. & Span.). 1975. 76.00 (ISBN 3-87097-067-7, M-7024). French & Eur.

Woerterbuch der Deutschen und Spanischen Sprache, Vol. 2. 2nd ed. Rudolf Slaby. (Ger. & Span.). 1973. 66.00 (ISBN 3-87097-040-5, M-7023). French & Eur.

Woerterbuch der Deutschen und Spanischen Rects und Wirtschaftssprache, Vol. 2. H. Becher. (Ger. & Span.). 1972. 79.95 (ISBN 3-406-00470-9, M-7022). French & Eur.

Woerterbuch der Elektronik. E. Knaeps & D. Zacharias. 104p. (Ger. & Fr.). 1976. pap. 9.95 (ISBN 3-7723-6231-1, M-7020). French & Eur.

Woerterbuch der Elektronik. Leonhard Schneider. (Ger. & Pol.). 1977. pap. 13.50 (ISBN 3-7723-6431-4, M-7021). French & Eur.

Woerterbuch der Elektrotechnik Fernmeldetechnik & Elektronik: Band I, Deutsch-Englisch-Franzoesisch. Goedecke. 908p. (Ger., Eng. & Fr.). 1982. DM.70.00. Brandstetter.

Woerterbuch der Elektrotechnik Fernmeldetechnik & Elektronik: Band II, Franzoesisch-Englisch-Deutsch. Goedecke. 908p. (Fr., Eng. & Ger.). 1982. DM.70.00. Brandstetter.

Woerterbuch der Elektrotechnik Fernmeldetechnik & Elektronik: Band III, Englisch-Deutsch-Franzoesisch. Goedecke. 1252p. (Eng., Ger. & Fr.). 1982. DM.80.00. Brandstetter.

Woerterbuch der Elektrotechnik, Fernmeldetechnik und Elektonik, Vol. 1. W. Goedecke. (Ger., Eng. & Fr., Dictionary of Electrical Engineering, Telecommunication Engineering & Electronics). 1966-68. 56.00 (ISBN 3-87097-013-8, M-7018). French & Eur.

Woerterbuch der Elektrotechnik, Fernmeldetechnik und Elektronik, Vol. 2. W. Goedecke. (Fr., Eng. & Ger., Dictionary of Electrical Engineering, Telecommuunications Engineering & Electronics). 1966-68. 56.00 (ISBN 3-87097-014-6, M-7019). French & Eur.

Woerterbuch der Elektrotechnik und Elektronik. Tomislav Miladinovic. (Ger. & Rus.). 1970. 92.00 (ISBN 3-7736-5285-2, M-7016). French & Eur.

Woerterbuch der Elsaessischen Mundarten. Ernst Martin & Hans Lienhart. (Ger.). 1974. DM.435.00 (ISBN 3-11-003338-0). De Gruyter.

Woerterbuch der Elsaessischen Mundarten, 2 vols. Ed. by Ernst Martin & Hans Lienhart. (Illus.). xxii, 1958p. (Ger.). 1974. Repr. of 1889 ed. 271.00x (ISBN 3-11-003338-0). De Gruyter.

Woerterbuch der Englischen und Deutschen Sprache, Vol. 1. Weis Schoeffler. (Ger. & Eng., Dictionary of the English & German Language). pap. 17.95 (ISBN 3-12-518100-3, M-7015). French & Eur.

Woerterbuch der Englischen und Deutschen Sprache, Vol. 2. Weis Schoeffler. (Ger. & Eng., Dictionary of the English & German Language). pap. 17.95 (ISBN 3-12-518200-X, M-7014). French & Eur.

Woerterbuch der Epilepsie. H. Gastaut. (Ger.). 1975. pap. 22.50 (ISBN 3-7773-0380-1, M-7013). French & Eur.

Woerterbuch der Erziehung. Christoph Wulf. 717p. (Ger.). 1976. DM.28.00 (ISBN 3-492-02098-4). Piper Co.

Woerterbuch der Forstwirtschaft. Johannes V. Weck. (Ger., Eng., Fr., Span. & Rus., Dictionary of Forestry). 1966. 99.50 (ISBN 3-405-10494-7, M-7005). French & Eur.

Woerterbuch der Forstwirtschaft Deutsch-Englisch-Franzoesisch-Spanisch-Russisch. Johannes Weck et al. (Ger., Eng., Fr., Span. & Rus.). 1966. DM.128.00 (ISBN 3-405-10494-7). BLV Verlag.

Woerterbuch der Franzoesischen und Deutschen Sprache, Vol. 1. E. Weis & H. Mattutat. (Fr. & Ger.). 18.95 (ISBN 3-215-01824-1, M-7004). French & Eur.

Woerterbuch der Franzoesischen und Deutschen Sprache, Vol. 2. E. Weis & H. Mattutat. (Ger. & Fr.). 18.95 (ISBN 3-215-01825-X, M-7003). French & Eur.

Woerterbuch der Handels, Finanz und Rechtssprache. 2nd ed. Robert Herbst. (Ger., Eng & Fr., Dictionary of Commercial, Fininancial & Legal Terms). 1975. 92.00 (ISBN 3-85942-001-1, M-7002). French & Eur.

Woerterbuch der Industriellen Technik: Band I, Deutsch-Englisch. ix, 1092p. (Ger & Eng.). 1983. DM.130.00. Brandstetter.

Woerterbuch der Industriellen Technik: Band III, Deutsch-Franzoesisch. Ernst. 1233p. (Ger. & Fr.). 1982. DM.130.00. Brandstetter.

Woerterbuch der Industriellen Technik: Band II, Englisch-Deutsch. ix, 1092p. (Eng. & Ger.). 1983. DM.140.00. Brandstetter.

Woerterbuch der Industriellen Technik: Band IV, Franzoesisch-Deutsch. Ernst. 1182p. (Fr. & Ger.). 1982. DM.130.00. Brandstetter.

Woerterbuch der Industriellen Technik: Band IX, Franzoesisch-Englisch. Ernst. 1085p. (Fr. & Eng.). 1982. DM.140.00. Brandstetter.

Woerterbuch der Industriellen Technik: Band VII, Deutsch-Portugiesisch. Ernst. 450p. (Ger. & Port.). 1983. DM.100.00. Brandstetter.

Woerterbuch der Industriellen Technik: Band V, Deutsch-Spanisch. Ernst. 1035p. (Ger. & Span.). 1982. DM.80.00. Brandstetter.

Woerterbuch der Industriellen Technik: Band VIII, Portugiesch-Deutsch. Ernst. 587p. (Port. & Ger.). 1982. DM.60.00. Brandstetter.

Woerterbuch der Industriellen Technik: Band VI, Spanisch-Deutschg) Ernst. 1073p. (Span. & Ger.). 1982. DM.80.00. Brandstetter.

Woerterbuch der Industriellen Technik, Vol. 1. R. Ernst. (Ger. & Eng., Dictionary of Industrial Engineering). 1974. 80.00 (ISBN 3-87097-060-X, M-7001). French & Eur.

Woerterbuch der Industriellen Technik, Vol. 2. R. Ernst. (Eng. & Ger., Dictionary of Industrial Engineering). 1975. 80.00 (ISBN 3-87097-068-5, M-7000). French & Eur.

Woerterbuch der Industriellen Technik, Vol. 3. R. Ernst. (Ger. & Fr.). 1965. 64.00 (ISBN 3-87097-005-7, M-6999). French & Eur.

Woerterbuch der Industriellen Technik, Vol. 4. R. Ernst. (Fr. & Ger.). 1968. 56.00 (ISBN 3-87097-006-5, M-6998). French & Eur.

Woerterbuch der Industriellen Technik, Vol. 5. 2nd ed. R. Ernst. (Ger. & Span.). 1973. 56.00 (ISBN 3-87097-069-3, M-6997). French & Eur.

Woerterbuch der Industriellen Technik, Vol. 7. R. Ernst. (Port. & Ger.). 1963. 48.00 (ISBN 3-87097-009-X, M-6995). French & Eur.

Woerterbuch der Industriellen Technik, Vol. 8. R. Ernst. (Port. & Ger.). 1967. 48.00 (ISBN 3-87097-010-3, M-6994). French & Eur.

Woerterbuch der Internationalen Beziehungen und der Politik. 2nd ed. Guenther Haensch. (Ger., Eng., Fr. & Span., Dictionary of International Relations & Politics). pap. 40.00 (ISBN 3-19-006211-0, M-6993). French & Eur.

Woerterbuch der Italienisch & Deutschen Sprache: Bd 1: Italienisch-Deutsch. (Ital. & Ger.). 1970. DM.280.00 (ISBN 3-87097-033-2). Brandstetter.

Woerterbuch der Italienisch & Deutschen Sprache: Bd 2: Deutsch-Italienisch. 1596p. (Ger. & Ital.). 1972. DM.280.00 (ISBN 3-87097-034-0). Brandstetter.

Woerterbuch der Italienischen und Deutschen Sprache, Vol. 1. (Ital. & Ger.). 1970. 225.00 (ISBN 3-87097-033-2, M-6992). French & Eur.

Woerterbuch der Italienischen und Deutschen Sprache, Vol. 2. (Ger. & Ital.). 1972. 225.00 (ISBN 3-87097-034-0, M-6991). French & Eur.

Woerterbuch der Jaegerei. 4th ed. W. Frevert. (Ger.). 1975. 12.00 (ISBN 3-490-05612-4, M-6990). French & Eur.

Woerterbuch der Jagel. Anne Kirchoff. (Ger., Eng. & Fr., Dictionary of Hunting). 1976. 27.50 (ISBN 3-405-11571-X, M-6989). French & Eur.

Woerterbuch der Kabeltechnik. Christel Richling. (Ger., Eng. & Fr., Dictionary of Cable Engineering). 1976. pap. 48.00 (ISBN 3-87097-072-3, M-6988). French & Eur.

Woerterbuch der Kabeltechnik. Christel Richling. LC 77-46358. 610p. (Eng., Fr. & Ger.). 1976. DM.60.00 (ISBN 3-87097-072-3). Brandstetter.

Woerterbuch der Kabeltechnik: Deutsch-Englisch-Franzoesisch. Drewitz Richling. 610p. (Ger., Eng. & Fr.). 1982. DM.60.00. Brandstetter.

Woerterbuch der Kerenergie. F. V. Franzen. (Eng. & Ger., Dictionary of Nuclear Energy). 1957. 20.00 (ISBN 0-686-56618-1, M-6987). French & Eur.

Woerterbuch der Kernenergie. F. Franzen & L. Hard. viii, 240p. (Ger.). 1957. DM.23.90 (ISBN 3-18-400034-6). Brandstetter.

Woerterbuch der Klassischen Arabischen: Bd 1. Joerg Kroemer et al. Ed. by Manfred Ullman. (Ger. & Arabic.). 1970. DM.178.00 (ISBN 3-447-01276-5). Harrassowitz.

Woerterbuch der Klassischen Arabischen: Bd 1, Lfg 7. Manfred Ullmann & Anton Spitaler. (Ger. & Arabic.). 1965. DM.18.00 (ISBN 3-447-01051-7). Harrassowitz.

Woerterbuch der Klassischen Arabischen Sprache: Bd 1, Lfg 2. Joerg Kraemer et al. (Ger. & Arabic.). 1960. DM.9.00 (ISBN 3-447-01046-0). Harrassowitz.

Woerterbuch der Klassischen Arabischen Sprache: Bd 1, Lfg 1. Anton Spitaler et al. (Ger. & Arabic.). 1957. DM.9.00 (ISBN 3-447-01045-2). Harrassowitz.

Woerterbuch der Klassischen Arabischen Sprache: Bd 1, Lfg 3. Manfred Ullmann & Anton Spitaler. (Ger. & Arabic.). 1962. DM.9.00 (ISBN 3-447-01047-9). Harrassowitz.

Woerterbuch der Klassischen Arabischen Sprache: Bd 1, Lfg 4. Manfred Ullmann & Anton Spitaler. (Ger. & Arabic.). 1962. DM.9.00 (ISBN 3-447-01048-7). Harrassowitz.

Woerterbuch der Klassischen Arabischen Sprache: Bd 1, Lfg 5. Manfred Ullmann & Anton Spitaler. (Ger. & Arabic.). 1964. DM.9.00 (ISBN 3-447-01049-5). Harrassowitz.

Woerterbuch der Klassischen Arabischen Sprache: Bd 1, Lfg 6. Manfred Ullmann & Anton Spitaler. (Ger. & Arabic.). 1964. DM.9.00 (ISBN 3-447-01050-9). Harrassowitz.

Woerterbuch der Klassischen Arabischen Sprache: Bd 1, Lfg 8. Manfred Ullmann & Anton Spitaler. (Ger. & Arabic.). 1966. DM.18.00 (ISBN 3-447-01052-5). Harrassowitz.

Woerterbuch der Klassischen Arabischen Sprache: Bd 1, Lfg 9-10. Manfred Ullmann & Anton Spitaler. (Ger. & Arabic.). 1970. DM.56.00 (ISBN 3-447-01053-3). Harrassowitz.

Woerterbuch der Klassischen Arabischen Sprache: Bd 2, Lfg 1. Manfred Ullmann. 64p. (Ger. & Arabic.). 1972. DM.28.00 (ISBN 3-447-01473-3). Harrassowitz.

Woerterbuch der Klassischen Arabischen Sprache: Bd 2, Lfg 4. Manfred Ullmann. 64p. (Ger. & Arabic.). 1976. DM.39.80 (ISBN 3-447-01789-9). Harrassowitz.

Woerterbuch der Klassischen Arabischen Sprache: Bd 2, Lfg 2. Manfred Ullmann & Rotraud Wojtowytsch-Wielandt. 64p. (Ger. & Arabic.). 1973. DM.28.00 (ISBN 3-447-01526-8). Harrassowitz.

Woerterbuch der Kraftuebertragungselemente-Deutsch-Spanisch-Franzoesisch-Englisch-Italienisch-Niederlandisch-Schwedisch-Finnisch: Bd 1, Zahnraeder. 116p. (Ger. , Span. , Fr. , Eng. , Ital. , Dutch, Swedish & Finnish.). 1976. DM.39.50 (ISBN 3-7830-0104-8). Krausskopf.

Woerterbuch der Kraftuebertragungselemente. (Ger. , Eng. , Fr. , Span. , Dutch, Swed. , Ital. & Finnish., Dictionary of Power Transmission Elements). 1976. 32.00 (ISBN 3-7830-0104-8, M-6985). French & Eur.

Woerterbuch der Kunst. 8th ed. Johannes Jahn. (Ger.). 1975. 20.00 (ISBN 3-520-16508-2, M-6986). French & Eur.

Woerterbuch der Kunst. 8th ed. Johannes Jahn. LC 76-463394. (Illus.). viii, 806p. (Ger.). 1975. write for info. (ISBN 3-520-16508-2). Kroener.

Woerterbuch der Kunst. 9th ed. Johannes Jahn. LC 80-473856. (Illus.). viii, 834p. (Ger.). 1979. write for info. (ISBN 3-520-16509-0). Kroener.

Woerterbuch der Landwirtschaft. 4th ed. Guenther Haensch. (Ger., Eng., Fr. & Span., Dictionary of Agriculture). 1975. pap. 99.50 (ISBN 3-405-10950-7, M-6984). French & Eur.

Woerterbuch der Lerntheorien & der Verhaltenstherapie. Hans Zeier. LC 76-482355. (Illus.). 189p. (Ger.). 1976. DM.14.80 (ISBN 3-463-00655-3). Kindler.

Woerterbuch der Logik. Nikolai I. Kondakov et al. LC 79-380114. 554p. (Ger.). 1978. M.22.00. Bibl Inst Leipzig.

Woerterbuch der Mathematik. Ralf Sube. 800p. (Eng., Ger., Fr. & Rus., Dictionary of Mathematics). 1979. 80.00 (ISBN 3-87144-445-6, M-6983). French & Eur.

Woerterbuch der Mathmetik, 2 vols. Eisenreich & Sube. 1458p. (Eng., Fr., Rus. & Ger.). 1982. DM.198.00 (ISBN 3-87144-445-6). Verlag Harri Deutsch.

Woerterbuch der Medizin und Pharmazeutik: Medical & Pharmaceutical Dictionary, 2 vols. Rev. ed. Werner E. Bunjes. (Eng. & Ger.). 1981. DM.75.00 ea. Thieme Verlag.

Woerterbuch der Modernen Technik. A. Oppermann. (Ger. & Eng., Dictionary of Modern Engineering). 112.00 (ISBN 3-7940-6001-6, M-6982). French & Eur.

Woerterbuch der Muenzkunde. 2nd ed. Ed. by Friedrich Von Schroetter. (Ger.). 1970. 75.00x (ISBN 3-11-001227-8). De Gruyter.

Woerterbuch der Optik & Feinmechanik: Band II, Englisch-Franzoesisch-Deutsch. Schulz. 124p. (Eng., Fr. & Ger.). 1982. DM.16.00. Brandstetter.

Woerterbuch der Optik & Feinmechanik: Band III, Franzoesisch-Deutsch-Englisch. Schulz. 109p. (Fr., Ger. & Eng.). 1982. DM.16.00. Brandstetter.

Woerterbuch der Optik und Feinmechanik: English-French-German Dictionary of Optics & Mechanical Engineering. E. Schulz. (Eng., Fr. & Ger.). 1961. write for info. (M-90925). French & Eur.

Woerterbuch der Optik und Feinmechanik, Vol. 1. Ernst Schulz. (Fr., Ger. & Eng., Dictionary of Optics & Mechanical Engineering). 1961. pap. 12.00 (ISBN 3-87097-036-7, M-6978). French & Eur.

Woerterbuch der Optik und Feinmechanik, Vol. 2. Ernst Schulz. (Fr., Ger. & Eng., Dictionary of Optics & Mechanical Engineering). 1961. pap. 12.00 (ISBN 3-87097-037-5, M-6977). French & Eur.

Woerterbuch der Paedagogik. 9th ed. Wilhelm Hehlmann. (Ger.). 1971. pap. 17.50 (ISBN 3-520-09409-6, M-6976). French & Eur.

Woerterbuch der Paedagogik. Willmann-Institut. 1150p. (Ger.). 1978. DM.128.00 (ISBN 3-451-17641-6). Herder.

Woerterbuch der Paedagogik, 3 vols. Willmann-Institut Muenchen. LC 78-355189. (Ger.). 1977. DM.98.00 (ISBN 3-451-17641-6). Herder.

Woerterbuch der Paedagogik, 3 vols, Vols. 1-3. (Ger.). 1977. Set. pap. 105.00 (ISBN 3-451-17641-6, M-6971). French & Eur.

Woerterbuch der Paedagogischen Psychologie: Lexikon der Paedagogik. 304p. (Ger.). 1974. 9.90 (ISBN 3-451-09016-3). Herder.

Woerterbuch der Paedagogischen Psychologie. 3rd ed. (Ger.). 1976. 7.95 (ISBN 0-686-56617-3, M-6970). French & Eur.

Woerterbuch der Parapsychologie. Hermann Schreiber. (Ger.). 1974. pap. 12.00 (ISBN 3-463-00660-X, M-6969). French & Eur.

Woerterbuch der Patentfachsprache. 4th ed. B. Klaften & F. C. Allison. (Eng. & Ger., Dictionary of Technical Terms of Patents). 1971. 54.00 (ISBN 3-87910-105-1, M-6974). French & Eur.

Woerterbuch der Patentfachsprache-Patent Terminological Dictionary: English-German & German-English. 4th ed. Berthold Klaften. LC 76-866071. 568p. (Eng. & Ger.). 1971. 32.50x (ISBN 3-87910-105-1). Intl Pubns Serv.

Woerterbuch der Patentpraxis. Detlev V. Uexkuell. (Ger. & Eng., Dictionary of Patent Practice). 1976. 57.00 (ISBN 3-452-18239-8, M-6973). French & Eur.

Woerterbuch der Photo, Film und Kinotechnik. Wolfgang Grau. (Ger., Eng. & Fr., Dictionary of Photo, Film & Cinematechniques). 1958. pap. 28.00 (ISBN 3-8101-0021-8, M-6968). French & Eur.

Woerterbuch der Psychiatrie und Medizinischen Psychologie. 2nd ed. Uwe H. Peters. (Ger., Eng. & Fr., Dictionary of Psychiatry & Medical Psychology). 1977. pap. 28.00 (ISBN 3-541-06552-4, M-6972). French & Eur.

Woerterbuch der Psychologie. Ed. by G. Clauss et al. (Illus.). 704p. (Ger.). 1981. write for info. Bibl Inst Leipzig.

Woerterbuch der Psychologie. Guenter Clauss. 596p. (Ger.). 1976. write for info. (ISBN 3-7609-0256-1). Pahl-Rugenstein.

Woerterbuch der Psychologie. Gunter Clauss. LC 77-458138. (Illus.). 596p. (Ger.). 1976. M.18.00. Biblio Inst.

Woerterbuch der Psychologie. 11th ed. Wilhelm Hehlmann. (Ger.). 1974. pap. 17.50 (ISBN 3-520-26911-2, M-6964). French & Eur.

Woerterbuch der Psychologie. Guenther V. Clauss. (Ger.). 1976. 22.50 (ISBN 3-7609-0256-1, M-6963). French & Eur.

Woerterbuch der Recht & Wirtschaftssprache: Teil I, Niederlandisch-Deutsch. Hans Langendorf & P. A. Stein. 365p. (Dutch & Ger.). 1976. DM.55.00. Recht & Wirtschaft.

Woerterbuch der Recht & Wirtshaftssprache: Teil II, Deutsch-Spanisch. Herbert J. Becher. viii, 814p. (Ger. & Span.). 1979. DM.148.00. Recht & Wirtschaft.

Woerterbuch der Rechts & Wirtschaftssprache: Teil II, Deutsch-Englisch. Alfred Romain. viii, 848p. (Ger. & Eng.). 1980. DM.138.00. Recht & Wirtschaft.

Woerterbuch der Rechts & Wirtschaftssprache: Teil II, Deutsch-Niederlaendisch. Hans Langendorf & P. A. Stein. 365p. (Ger. & Dutch.). 1976. DM.55.00. Recht & Wirtschaft.

Woerterbuch der Rechts & Wirtschaftssprache: Teil I, Deutsch-Russisch. Gyula Decsi & Sandor Karcsay. (Ger. & Rus.). write for info. Recht & Wirtschaft.

Woerterbuch der Rechts & Wirtschaftssprache: Teil I, Englisch-Deutsch. Alfred Romain. viii, 760p. (Eng & Ger.). 1979. DM.98.00. Recht & Wirtschaft.

Woerterbuch der Rechts & Wirtschaftssprache: Teil II, Russisch-Deutsch. Gyula Decsi & Sandor Karcsay. (Rus. & Ger.). write for info. Recht & Wirtschaft.

Woerterbuch der Rechts & Wirtschaftssprache: Teil I, Spanisch-Deutsch. Herbert J. Becher. viii, 933p. (Span. & Ger.). 1978. DM.175.00. Recht & Wirtschaft.

Woerterbuch der Regionalen Umgangssprache in Lateinamerika. Maria Schwauss. LC 77-562131. 692p. (Ger. & Span.). 1977. M.52.00. VEB Verlag Enzyklopadie.

Woerterbuch der Reinen und Angewandten Physik, Vol. 1. L. De Vries. (Ger. & Eng., Dictionary of Physics & Applied Physics). 1964. 38.00 (ISBN 3-486-30942-0, M-6954). French & Eur.

Woerterbuch der Reinen und Angewandten Physik, Vol. 2. L. De Vries. (Eng. & Ger., Dictionary of Physics & Applied Physics). 1964. 38.00 (ISBN 0-686-56615-7, M-6962). French & Eur.

Woerterbuch der Religionen. Alfred Bertholet. LC 76-483576. x, 659p. (Ger.). 1976. DM.25.00 (ISBN 3-520-12503-X). Kroener.

Woerterbuch der Reprographie. Deutsches Komitee fur Reprographie. LC 76-456115. 273p. (Eng., Fr. & Ger.). 1975. write for info. Aussant & Schrift.

Woerterbuch der Reprographie. 273p. (Ger.). 1976. write for info. (ISBN 3-7940-3259-4). Saur Verlag.

Woerterbuch der Reprographie: Begriffe und Definitionen. 3rd rev. ed. Deutsches Komittee fuer Reprographie. 273p. (Ger., Eng. & Fr., Dictionary of Reprography: Terms & Definitions). 1976. pap. 44.00 (ISBN 0-686-56614-9, M-6961). French & Eur.

Woerterbuch der Russichen Gewaessernamen: Lfg 1. (Ger.). 1961. DM.46.00 (ISBN 3-447-00976-4). Harrassowitz.

Woerterbuch der Russichen Gewaessernamen: Lfg 2. (Ger.). DM.46.00 (ISBN 3-447-00977-2). Harrassowitz.

Woerterbuch der Russichen Gewaessernamen: Bd 2, Z-K. (Ger. & Rus.). DM.154.00 (ISBN 3-447-00972-1). Harrassowitz.
Woerterbuch der Russichen Gewaessernamen: Lfg 4. (Ger. & Rus.). DM.46.00 (ISBN 3-447-00979-9). Harrassowitz.
Woerterbuch der Russischen Gewaessernamen: Bd 1, A-E. Max Vasmer. (Ger.). 1961. DM.168.00 (ISBN 3-447-00971-3). Harrassowitz.
Woerterbuch der Russischen Gewaessernamen: Bd 3, L-P. (Ger. & Rus.). DM.166.00 (ISBN 3-447-00973-X). Harrassowitz.
Woerterbuch der Russischen Gewaessernamen: Bd 4, R-U. (Ger. & Rus.). 1968. DM.132.00 (ISBN 3-447-00974-8). Harrassowitz.
Woerterbuch der Russischen Gewaessernamen: Bd 5, F-Ja. (Ger. & Rus.). 1969. DM.74.00 (ISBN 3-447-00975-6). Harrassowitz.
Woerterbuch der Russischen Gewaessernamen: Lfg 3. (Ger. & Rus.). DM.46.00 (ISBN 3-447-00978-0). Harrassowitz.
Woerterbuch der Russischen Gewaessernamen: Lfg 5. (Ger.). DM.46.00 (ISBN 3-447-00980-2). Harrassowitz.
Woerterbuch der Russischen Gewaessernamen: Lfg 6. (Ger. & Rus.). DM.32.00 (ISBN 3-447-00981-0). Harrassowitz.
Woerterbuch der Russischen Gewaessernamen: Lfg 7. (Ger. & Rus.). DM.46.00 (ISBN 3-447-00982-9). Harrassowitz.
Woerterbuch der Russischen Gewaessernamen: Lfg 8. (Ger. & Rus.). DM.46.00 (ISBN 3-447-00983-7). Harrassowitz.
Woerterbuch der Russischen Gewaessernamen: Lfg 9. (Ger. & Rus.). DM.74.00 (ISBN 3-447-00984-5). Harrassowitz.
Woerterbuch der Russischen Gewaessernamen: Lfg 10. (Ger. & Rus.). DM.44.00 (ISBN 3-447-00985-3). Harrassowitz.
WOerterbuch der Russischen Gewaessernamen: Lfg 11. (Ger. & Rus.). DM.44.00 (ISBN 3-447-00986-1). Harrassowitz.
Woerterbuch der Russischen Gewaessernamen: Lfg 12. (Ger. & Rus.). DM.44.00 (ISBN 3-447-00987-X). Harrassowitz.
Woerterbuch der Russischen Gewaessernamen: Lfg 13. (Ger. & Rus.). DM.44.00 (ISBN 3-447-00988-8). Harrassowitz.
Woerterbuch der Russischen Gewaessernamen: Lfg 14. (Ger. & Rus.). DM.30.00 (ISBN 3-447-00989-6). Harrassowitz.
Woerterbuch der Russischen Gewaessernamen: Lfg 15. iv, 190p. (Ger. & Rus.). DM.50.00 (ISBN 3-447-01494-6). Harrassowitz.
Woerterbuch der Schulpaedagogik. 4th ed. Arnold Schwendtke. (Ger.). 1976. pap. 10.95 (ISBN 3-451-09001-5, M-6960). French & Eur.
Woerterbuch der Schulpaedagogik. 384p. (Ger.). 1976. 12.90 (ISBN 3-451-09001-5). Herder.
Woerterbuch der Schweisstechnik. A. Kleiber. (Eng. & Ger., Dictionary of Welding). 1970. 38.00 (ISBN 3-87097-024-3, M-6959). French & Eur.
Woerterbuch der Seeschiffahrt, Vol. 1. 2nd ed. Hans Rinke. (Eng. & Ger., Dictionary of Merchant Shipping). 1975. 25.00 (ISBN 3-19-006294-3, M-6958). French & Eur.
Woerterbuch der Seeschiffahrt, Vol. 2. 2nd ed. Hans Rinke. (Ger. & Eng., Dictionary of Merchant Shipping). 27.50 (ISBN 3-19-006295-1, M-6957). French & Eur.
Woerterbuch der Sozialarbeit & Sozialpaedagogik. Arnold Schwendtke. 312p. (Ger.). 1977. DM.18.80 (ISBN 3-494-02072-8). Quelle & Meyer.
Woerterbuch der Sozialarbeit und der Sozialpaedagogik. Arnold Schwendtke. (Ger.). 1977. pap. write for info (ISBN 3-494-02072-8, M-6955). French & Eur.
Woerterbuch der Soziologie. Ed. by Wilhelm Bernsdorf. (Ger.). 1969. DM.78.00 (ISBN 3-432-80392-3). Enke.
Woerterbuch der Soziologie. Guenter Hartfiel. LC 77-458366. vi, 715p. (Ger.). 1976. DM.22.00 (ISBN 3-520-41002-8). Kroener.
Woerterbuch der Soziologie: Bd 1, 5 Aufl. Ed. by Wilhelm Bernsdorf. (Ger.). 1976. DM.6.80 (ISBN 3-596-26131-7). Fischer Taschen.
Woerterbuch der Soziologie: Bd 2, 4 Aufl. Ed. by Wilhelm Bernsdorf. (Ger.). 1975. DM.6.80 (ISBN 3-596-26132-5). Fischer Taschen.
Woerterbuch der Soziologie: Bd 3, 4 Aufl. Ed. by Wilhelm Bernsdorf. (Ger.). 1976. DM.6.80 (ISBN 3-596-26133-3). Fischer Taschen.
Woerterbuch der Spanischen & Deutschen Sprache. Guenther Haensch. LC 77-579293. 684p. (Span. & Ger.). 1977. M.22.80 (ISBN 3-125-17400-7). Klett.
Woerterbuch der Spanischen & Deutschen Sprache: Band II, Deutsch-Spanisch. Slaby & Grossmann. 1256p. (Ger. & Span.). 1982. DM.100.00. Brandstetter.
Woerterbuch der Spanischen & Deutschen Sprache: Band I, Spanisch-Deutsch. Slaby & Grossmann. 1188p. (Span. & Ger.). 1982. DM.100.00. Brandstetter.
Woerterbuch der Spanischen und Deutschen Rechts und Wirtschaftssprache, Vol. 1. H. Becher. (Span. & Ger.). 1971. 85.00 (ISBN 3-406-00469-5, M-6956). French & Eur.
Woerterbuch der Symbolik. Ed. by Manfred Lurker. LC 80-464096. xvi, 686p. (Ger.). 1979. write for info. (ISBN 3-520-46401-2). Kroener.
Woerterbuch der Technik. Karl H. Radde. LC 77-464498. 716p. (Span. & Ger.). 1977. DM.108.00 (ISBN 3-7736-5530-4). Girardet.
Woerterbuch der Technik. Rudolf Walther. (Eng. & Ger., Dictionary of Technology). 1974. 88.00 (ISBN 3-7736-5100-7, M-6952). French & Eur.
Woerterbuch der Technik, Vol. 1. Karl H. Radde. (Span. & Ger.). 1977. 86.00 (ISBN 3-7736-5530-4, M-6949). French & Eur.
Woerterbuch der Technik, Vol. 2. Karl H. Radde. (Span. & Ger.). 1977. 86.00 (ISBN 3-7736-5531-2, M-6950). French & Eur.
Woerterbuch der Textilindustrie, Vol. 2. Louis de Vries. (Eng. & Ger., Dictionary of Textile Industry). pap. 25.00 (ISBN 0-686-56612-2, M-6948). French & Eur.
Woerterbuch der Tiefenpsychologie. 2nd ed. Uwe H. Peters. LC 80-490459. 182p. (Eng. & Ger.). 1978. DM.18.00 (ISBN 3-463-00734-7). Kindler.
Woerterbuch der Ungarischen Rechts und Verwaltungssprache, Vol. 1. 2nd ed. Sandor Karcsay. (Ger. & Hungarian.). 1969. 38.00 (ISBN 3-406-03325-3, M-6947). French & Eur.
Woerterbuch der Ungarischen Rechts und Verwaltungssprache, Vol. 2. 2nd ed. (Ger. & Hungarian.). 1972. 38.00 (ISBN 3-406-03326-1, M-6946). French & Eur.
Woerterbuch der Verhaltensforschung. Klaus Immelmann. LC 78-342717. 133p. (Eng. & Ger.). 1975. DM.12.00 (ISBN 3-463-00616-2). Kindler.
Woerterbuch der Voelkerkunde. Walter Hirschberg. (Ger.). 1965. 17.50 (ISBN 3-520-20501-7, M-6945). French & Eur.
Woerterbuch der Vorschulerzeihung. 336p. (Ger.). 1976. DM.12.90 (ISBN 3-451-09035-X). Herder.
Woerterbuch der Vorschulerziehung. Ed. by Engelbert Schinzler. LC 76-470196. 335p. (Ger.). 1976. DM.12.90 (ISBN 3-451-09035-X). Herder.
Woerterbuch der Vorschulerziehung. (Ger.). 1976. pap. 10.50 (ISBN 0-686-56611-4, M-6944). French & Eur.
Woerterbuch der Weidmannssprache. Franz Kehrein. (Ger.). 1969. 36.00 (ISBN 3-500-26250-3, M-6943). French & Eur.
Woerterbuch der Werbung und des Marketing. Clemens Gruber. (Eng. & Ger.). 1977. pap. 15.00 (ISBN 3-19-006312-5, M-6942). French & Eur.
Woerterbuch der Wirkstoffprufung. Werner Goedecke. LC 80-475766. (Eng., Ger. & Fr.). 1979. write for info. (ISBN 3-18-400434-1). VDI-Verlag.
Woerterbuch der Wirtschaft. 7th ed. Horst C. Recktenwald. (Ger.). 1975. 20.00 (ISBN 3-520-11407-0, M-6941). French & Eur.
Woerterbuch der Wirtschaft. 7th ed. Horst C. Rektenwald. LC 76-454037. (Illus.). xvi, 555p. (Ger.). 1975. DM.25.00 (ISBN 3-520-11407-0). Kroener.
Woerterbuch des Arbeits & Sozialrechts: Deutsch-Franz Dictionnaire de Droit du Trava il & de Droit Social. Alexandre Bonnefoi. LC 76-469011. 395p. (Fr. & Ger.). 1975. DM.45.00 (ISBN 3-19-006293-5). Hueber.
Woerterbuch des Arbeits und Sozialrechtd. Alexandre Bonnefoi. (Ger. & Fr.). 1975. 55.00 (ISBN 3-19-006293-5, M-6938). French & Eur.
Woerterbuch des Buches. H. Helmut. (Ger.). 1976. pap. 15.95 (ISBN 3-465-00186-9, M-6937). French & Eur.
Woerterbuch Des Internationalen Verkehrs (Dictionary of International Traffic) Gerhard Bein. 233p. (Ger. & Eng.). 1968. 9.00x (ISBN 0-8002-1306-8). Intl Pubns Serv.
Woerterbuch des Italienisch-Deutschen Privat & Wirtschaftsrechts: Band I, Deutsch-Italienisch. H. Trioke-Strambaci & E. Helffrich-Mariani. xix, 1332p. (Ger. & Ital.). 1982. DM.148.00. Recht & Wirtschaft.
Woerterbuch des Italienisch-Deutschen Privat & Wirtschaftsrechts: Band II, Italienish-Deutsch. H. Troike-Strambaci & E. Helffrich-Mariani. xix, 1332p. (Ital. & Ger.). 1982. DM.148.00. Recht & Wirtschaft.
Woerterbuch des Kraftfahreugwesens. Otto Vollnhals. LC 75-515768. 618p. (Ital. & Ger.). 1975. DM.108.00 (ISBN 3-7736-5120-1). Girardet.
Woerterbuch des Kraftfahrzeugwesens. Otto Vollnhals. (Ger. & Ital.). 1975. 92.00 (ISBN 3-7736-5120-1, M-6936). French & Eur.
Woerterbuch des Pantentwesens in 5 Sprachen. Gyorgy L. Szendy. (Ger., Eng., Fr., Span. & Rus., Dictionary of Patents in Five Languages). 1974. 76.00 (ISBN 3-18-400269-1, M-6935). French & Eur.
Woerterbuch des Steuerrechts. Rudolf Roessler. (Ger.). 1971. 54.00 (ISBN 3-448-00204-6, M-6934). French & Eur.
Woerterbuch des Steuerrechts. Rudolf Roessler et al. (Ger.). 1973. write for info. (ISBN 3-448-00204-6). Haufe.
Woerterbuch des Verlagswesens in 20 Sprachen. 2nd ed. Imre Mora. (Ger., The Publisher's Practical Dictionary in 20 Languages). 1977. 96.00 (ISBN 3-7940-4112-7, M-6933). French & Eur.
Woerterbuch des Verlagswesens in 20 Sprachen. Imre Mora. 389p. (Ger.). 1977. write for info. (ISBN 3-7940-4112-7). Saur Verlag.
Woerterbuch des Voelkerrechts: Bd 1, Aachener Kongress-Hussar Fall. Ed. by Karl Strupp et al. (Ger.). 1960. DM.225.00 (ISBN 3-11-001030-5). De Gruyter.
Woerterbuch des Voelkerrechts: Bd 2, Ibero-Amerikanismus bis Quirin-Fall. Ed. by Hermann Mosler et al. (Ger.). 1961. DM.225.00 (ISBN 3-11-001031-3). De Gruyter.
Woerterbuch des Voelkerrechts: Bd 3, Rapollo-Vertrag bis Zypern. Ed. by Hermann Mosler et al. (Ger.). 1962. DM.50.00 (ISBN 3-11-001033-X). De Gruyter.
Woerterbuch des Wirtschafts, Rechts und Handelssprache. C. Dietl. (Eng. & Ger., Dictionary of Economic, Legal & Commercial Terms). 1970. 33.00 (ISBN 3-87527-003-7, M-6939). French & Eur.
Woerterbuch Deutsch-Hindi. Margot Gatzlaff-Halsig. LC 78-359321. 646p. (Ger. & Hindi.). 1977. M.60.00. VEB Verlag Enzyklopadie.
Woerterbuch Deutsch-Indonesisch. Gerhard Kahlo et al. LC 77-463622. xxiv, 400p. (Ger. & Indonesian.). 1975. M.38.00. VEB Verlag Enzyklopadie.
Woerterbuch Elektrotechnik & Elektronik. H. Schwenkhagen. LC 78-381882. 839p. (Eng. & Ger.). 1978. DM.160.00 (ISBN 3-7736-5072-8). Girardet.
Woerterbuch Elektrotechnik und Elektronik. 2nd ed. H. Schwenkhagen. (Ger. & Eng., Dictionary of Electrical Engineering and Electronics). 1967. 128.00 (ISBN 0-686-56610-6, M-6927). French & Eur.
Woerterbuch Elektrotechnik und Elektronik. H. F. Schwenkhagen & H. Meinhhold. (Ger. & Eng., Dictionary of Electrical Engineering and Electronics). 1978. 128.00 (ISBN 3-7736-5072-8, M-6928). French & Eur.
Woerterbuch Erdoelverarbeitung-Petrolchemie. W. Leipnitz. (Eng., Ger., Fr & Rus., Dictionary of Petroleum-processing). 1977. 48.00 (ISBN 0-686-56609-2, M-6925). French & Eur.
Woerterbuch fuer Aerzte. 2nd ed. Lejeune & Bunjes. (Ger., Dictionary for Physicians). 1968. pap. 55.00 (ISBN 3-13-370502-4, M-6924). French & Eur.
Woerterbuch fuer Architektur, Hochbau & Baustoffe. 2nd ed. H. Bucksch. 1137p. (Eng. & Ger.). 1976. DM.220.00 (ISBN 3-7625-0714-7). Bauverlag.
Woerterbuch fuer Architektur, Hochbau & Baustoffe. Herbert Buksch. LC 77-578817. (Ger. & Fr.). 1977. DM.29.00 (ISBN 3-762-50786-4). Bauverlag.
Woerterbuch fuer Architektur, Hochbau & Baustoffe: Band 1, Deutsch-Englisch. 2nd ed. H. Bucksch. 942p. (Ger. & Eng.). 1980. DM.220.00 (ISBN 3-7625-1399-6). Bauverlag.
Woerterbuch Fuer Architektur: Hochbau und Baustoffe. (Fr. & Ger.). 1979. 232.00 (ISBN 0-686-56608-4, M-6923). French & Eur.
Woerterbuch fuer Bautechnik & Baumaschinen: Band I, Deutsch-Englisch. H. Bucksch. 1184p. (Ger. & Eng.). 1982. DM.160.00 (ISBN 3-7625-2032-1). Bauverlag.
Woerterbuch fuer Bautechnik & Baumaschinen: Band II, Englisch-Deutsch. H. Bucksch. 1219p. (Eng. & Ger.). 1982. DM.160.00 (ISBN 3-7625-2034-8). Bauverlag.
Woerterbuch fuer Bautechnik und Baumaschinen. 4th ed. H. Bucksch. (Ger. & Fr.). 1976. pap. 112.00 (ISBN 0-686-56607-6, M-6922). French & Eur.
Woerterbuch fuer das Wasser und Abwasserfach. 2nd ed. Fritz Meinck. (Ger., Eng., Fr. & Ital., Dictionary of Water and Sewage Disposal Plants). 1977. 128.00 (ISBN 3-486-35352-7, M-6920). French & Eur.
Woerterbuch fuer den Hobbyelektroniker. Junge. 250p. (Ger.). 1983. DM.19.80 (ISBN 3-87144-676-9). Verlag Harri Deutsch.
Woerterbuch fuer die Grundschule. Erwin Schwartz et al. 96p. (Ger.). 1978. DM.5.90 (ISBN 3-14-190586-X). Westermann.
Woerterbuch fuer Erziehung & Unterricht. 2nd ed. Peter Koeck & Hans Ott. 656p. (Ger.). 1979. DM.44.80. Auer.
Woerterbuch fuer Metallurgie, Mineralogie, Geologie, Bergbau & die Oelindustrie. A. Cagnacci-Schwicker. 1530p. (Eng., Fr., Ger. & Ital.). 1970. DM.110.00 (ISBN 3-7625-0751-1). Bauverlag.

Woerterbuch fuer Metallurgie, Mineralogie, Geologie, Bergbau & die Oelindustrie Englische-Franzosisch-Deutsch-Italienisch. Angelo Cagnacci-Schwicker. 1530p. (Eng., Fr., Ger. & Ital.). 1970. DM.110.00 (ISBN 3-7625-0751-1). Bauverlag.

Woerterbuch fuer Metallurgie, Mineralogie, Geologie, Bergbau und die Oelindustrie. (Eng. , Fr. , Ger. & Ital., Dictionary of Metallurgy, Mineralogy, Geology, Mining and Oil Industry). 1970. 88.00 (ISBN 3-7625-0751-1, M-6912). French & Eur.

Woerterbuch fuer Recht, Wirtschaft & Politik: Teil II, Deutsch-Englisch. Clara E. Dietl & Egon Lorenz. (Ger. & Eng.). 1983. write for info. Recht & Wirtschaft.

Woerterbuch fuer Strassenbau und Strassenverkehe. Karl Steinig. (Fr. & Ger.). 1970. 92.00 (ISBN 3-7812-0560-6, M-6921). French & Eur.

Woerterbuch fuer Wirtschaft, Recht & Handel: Band I, Deutsch-Franzoesisch. Potonnier. 1616p. (Ger. & Fr.). 1982. DM.130.00. Brandstetter.

Woerterbuch fuer Wirtschaft, Recht & Handel: Band II, Franzoesisch-Deutsch. Potonnier. 1502p. (Fr. & Ger.). 1982. DM.100.00. Brandstetter.

Woerterbuch fuer Wirtschaft: Recht und Handel, Vol. 1. Georges Potonnier. (Ger. & Fr.). 1970. 56.00 (ISBN 3-87097-030-8, M-6919). French & Eur.

Woerterbuch fuer Wirtschaft: Recht und Handel, Vol. 2. Georges Potonnier. (Fr. & Ger.). 1970. 80.00 (ISBN 3-87097-031-6, M-6918). French & Eur.

Woerterbuch fuer Wirtschaft-Recht-Verkehr-Verwaltungs & Umgangssprache: Vol.I, Englisch-Deutsch. rev. ed. R. Eichborn. 1150p. (Eng. & Ger.). 1983. 124.00. M Rosenberg.

Woerterbuch fuer Wirtschaft-Recht-Verkehr-Verwaltungs & Umgangssprache: Vol. II, Deutch-Englisch. R. Eichborn. 1150p. (Ger. & Eng.). 1982. 124.00. M Rosenberg.

Woerterbuch fur Bau & Grundstucksrecht & Raumordnung. H. Bucksch. (Ger. & Eng.). 1982. write for info. (ISBN 3-7625-1413-5). Bauverlag.

Woerterbuch fur Baurecht, Grundstucksrecht & Raumordnung: Band I, Deutsch-Englisch. H. Bucksch. 1400p. (Ger. & Eng.). 1982. DM.380.00. Bauverlag.

Woerterbuch fur Baurecht, Grungstucksrecht & Raumordnung: Band II, Englisch-Deutsch. H. Bucksch. 1400p. (Eng. & Ger.). 1982. DM.380.00. Bauverlag.

Woerterbuch fur das Wasser & Abwasserfach. Fritz Meinck. LC 78-337966. 737p. (Eng., Fr. & Ital.). 1977. write for info. (ISBN 3-486-35352-7). Oldenbourg Verlag.

Woerterbuch fur den Hobby-Elektroniker Englisch-Deutsch. Hans D. Junge. 240p. (Eng. & Ger.). 1982. M.28.00. VEB Technik.

Woerterbuch Geowissenschaften. Watznauer. 400p. (Eng. & Ger.). 1982. DM.58.00 (ISBN 3-87144-635-1). Verlag Harri Deutsch.

Woerterbuch Geowissenschaften. Watznauer. 400p. (Ger. & Eng.). 1982. DM.58.00 (ISBN 3-87144-636-X). Verlag Harri Deutsch.

Woerterbuch Geowissenschaften, Vol. 1. A. Watznauer. (Eng. & Ger., English-German Dictionary of Geo-Sciences). 1973. 38.00 (ISBN 3-87144-139-2, M-6917). French & Eur.

Woerterbuch Geowissenschaften, Vol. 2. A. Watznauer. (Ger. & Eng., German-English Dictionary of Geo-Sciences). 1973. 45.00 (ISBN 3-87144-140-6, M-6916). French & Eur.

Woerterbuch Industrieofen & Indudtrielle Warmeanlagen. Josef Stepanek. LC 76-454323. viii, 444p. (Eng., Span. & Fr.). 1975. DM.78.00 (ISBN 3-8027-2484-4). Vulkan Verlag.

Woerterbuch Informationsverarbeitung. Buerger. 461p. (Eng., Fr., Rus. & Ger.). 1979. DM.98.00 (ISBN 3-87144-265-8). Verlag Harri Deutsch.

Woerterbuch Klima & Kaeltetechnik. Heinrich. 404p. (Eng., Fr., Rus. & Ger.). 1978. DM.85.00 (ISBN 3-87144-303-4). Verlag Harri Deutsch.

Woerterbuch Klima & Kaltetechnik. Gunter Heinrich. LC 79-349127. 404p. (Eng., Ger., Fr. & Rus.). 1978. 74.00 F (ISBN 3-87144-303-4). Verlag Harri Deutsch.

Woerterbuch Kristallografie. Backhaus. 132p. (Eng., Fr., Rus. & Ger.). 1983. DM.20.00 (ISBN 3-87144-744-7). Verlag Harri Deutsch.

Woerterbuch Kritische Erziehung. Eberhard Rauch & Wolfgang Anzinger. (Ger.). 1975. DM.7.80 (ISBN 3-596-26301-8). Fischer Taschen.

Woerterbuch Kybernetik. Alfred Oppermann. (Ger. & Eng., Dictionary of Cybernetics). 1969. pap. 22.50 (ISBN 3-7940-3258-6, M-6915). French & Eur.

Woerterbuch: Linguistische Grundbegriffe. 2nd ed. Winfried Ulrich. LC 77-460610. (Illus.). 173p. (Ger.). 1975. DM.13.80 (ISBN 3-554-80336-7). Hirt.

Woerterbuch Linguistische Grundbegriffe. Winfried Von Ulrich. 176p. (Ger.). 1975. DM.14.80 (ISBN 3-554-80336-7). Hirt.

Woerterbuch Medizin. Noehring. 640p. (Eng & Ger.). 1983. DM.89.00 (ISBN 3-87144-725-0). Verlag Harri Deutsch.

Woerterbuch Medizinischer Fachausdruecke. 2nd ed. Fachredaktion. (Ger.). 1973. 25.00 (ISBN 3-13-437802-7, M-6913). French & Eur.

Woerterbuch Medizinischer Fachausdruecke. (Ger.). 1973. DM.32.00 (ISBN 3-13-437802-7). Thieme Verlag.

Woerterbuch Medizinischer Grundbegriffe. Eduard Seidler. LC 80-470172. 367p. (Ger.). 1979. DM.12.90 (ISBN 3-451-07706-X). Herder.

Woerterbuch Musik. Horst Leuchtmann. (Ger. & Eng., Dictionary of Terms in Music). 1977. 38.00 (ISBN 3-7940-3186-5, M-6911). French & Eur.

Woerterbuch Musik. xvi, 493p. (Ger. & Eng.). 1977. DM.48.00 (ISBN 3-7940-3186-5). Saur Verlag.

Woerterbuch Pferd & Reiter. Zdzislaw Baronowski. 176p. (Ger.). 1976. DM.18.00 (ISBN 0-273-00937-0). Pitman Bks.

Woerterbuch Pferd und Reiter. Zdzislaw Baranowski. (Eng., Fr. & Ger., Dictionary of Horses and Horsemanship). 1977. 24.95 (ISBN 0-273-00937-0, M-6910). French & Eur.

Woerterbuch Physik, 3 vols. Eisenreich & Sube. 2895p. (Eng., Fr., Rus. & Ger.). 1983. DM.390.00 (ISBN 3-87144-143-0). Verlag Harri Deutsch.

Woerterbuch Physik, 3 vols. Ralf Sube & Gunther Eisenreich. (Eng., Ger., Fr & Rus., Dictionary of Physics). 1970. Set. 312.00 (ISBN 3-87144-143-0, M-6909). French & Eur.

Woerterbuch Programmierter Unterricht. (Ger.). 1964. DM.4.80 (ISBN 3-7863-0015-1). Manz.

Woerterbuch Sanskrit-Deutsch. Klaus Mylius. LC 76-506569. 583p. (Ger. & Sanskrit.). 1975. M.86.00. VEB Verlag Enzyklopadie.

Woerterbuch ser Pferdekunde. Hans G. Muhlmann. LC 77-554222. 383p. (Ger.). 1976. write for info. Verlag Sankt.

Woerterbuch Swahili-Deutsch. HIldegard Hoftmann et al. LC 79-384471. 402p. (Ger. & Swahili.). 1979. DM.42.00. VEB Verlag Enzyklopadie.

Woerterbuch Vietnamesisch-Deutsch. Winfried Boscher et al. LC 78-375203. 738p. (Ger. & Vietnamese.). 1978. M.48.00. VEB Verlag Enzyklopadie.

Woerterbuch Werkzeuge. 2nd ed. Henry G. Freeman. (Ger. & Eng., Dictionary of Tools). 1960. leatherette 92.00 (ISBN 3-7736-5052-3, M-6908). French & Eur.

Woerterbuch Werkzeuge und Werkzeugmaschinen. Kurt Stellhorn. (Ger. & Fr.). 1969. leatherette 56.00 (ISBN 3-7736-5260-7, M-6907). French & Eur.

Woerterbuch Wirtschaft. Noehring. 784p. (Eng. & Ger.). 1981. DM.29.80 (ISBN 3-87144-652-1). Verlag Harri Deutsch.

Woerterbuch Wirtschaft Recht Handel: Deutsch-Franzoesisch, Vol. 1. 2nd, rev. ed. Georges E. Potonnier & Brigitte Potonnier. 1616p. (Ger. & Fr.). 1982. 430.00 F. Maison Dictionnaire.

Woerterbuch Wirtschaft Recht Handel: Deutsch-Franzoesisch, Vol. 2. Georges E. Potonnier & Brigitte Potonnier. 1486p. (Fr. & Ger.). 1970. 330.00 F. Maison Dictionnaire.

Woerterbuch zum Deutschen Sprachgebrauch: Woerter & Wendungen. 818p. (Ger.). 1972. pap. 11.00. M Rosenberg.

Woerterbuch zur Geschichte. 3rd ed. Erich Bayer. (Ger.). 1974. pap. 19.95 (ISBN 3-520-28903-2, M-6905). French & Eur.

Woerterbuch zur Geschichte. Erich Bayer. (Ger.). 1974. DM.22.00 (ISBN 3-520-28903-2). Kroener.

Woerterbuch zur klinischen Psychologie, 2 vols. Hellmuth Benesch. (Ger.). DM.22.80. Deutscher Taschenbuch.

Woerterbuch zur Oberoesterreichischen Volksmundart. Ed. by Otto Jungmair. LC 80-487672. 351p. (Ger.). 1978. S.280.00. Selbstverlag Inst.

Woerterbuch zur Politik und Wirtschaftpolitik. Hans E. Zahn. (Ger., Eng & Fr.). 1976. 76.00 (ISBN 3-7819-2011-9, M-6904). French & Eur.

Woerterbuch zur Politischen Oekonomie. 2nd ed. Gert V. Eynern. (Ger.). 1977. pap. 19.95 (ISBN 3-531-21148-X, M-6902). French & Eur.

Woerterbuch zur Politischen Oekonomie. Ed. by Gert Von Eynern & Carl Boehret. LC 78-393797. 582p. (Ger.). 1977. DM.26.00 (ISBN 3-531-21148-X). Westdeutscher.

Woerterbuch zur Psychologie. Werner D. Froehlich & James Drever. (Ger.). DM.16.80. Deutscher Taschenbuch.

Woerterbuch zur Publizistik. K. Koszyk. (Ger.). 1970. 28.00 (ISBN 3-7940-4281-6, M-6901). French & Eur.

Woerterbuch zur Rechtschreibung. (Ger.). DM.5.20 (ISBN 3-12-216800-6). Klett.

Woerterbuch zur Sexualpolitik und ihren Grenzgebieten. (Ger.). pap. 22.50 (ISBN 3-7615-0016-5, M-6900). French & Eur.

Woerterbuch zur Valenz & Distribution Deutscher Adjektive. 3rd ed. K. E. Sommerfeldt & H. Schreiber. 435p. (Ger.). 1982. M.22.00. Bibl Inst Leipzig.

Woerterbuch zur Valenz & Distribution der Substantive. Karl-Ernst Sommerfeldt. LC 80-479437. 432p. (Ger.). 1977. M.16.00. Bibl Inst Leipzig.

Woerterbuch zur Valenz & Distribution Deutscher Verben. 6th ed. G. Helbig & W. Schenkel. 458p. (Ger.). 1982. M.22.00. Bibl Inst Leipzig.

Woerterbucher der Fertigungstechnik: Bd 1, Schmieden-Freiformschmieden & Gesenkschmieden. G. Pahlitzsch. 108p. (Ger.). 1962. DM.45.00 (ISBN 3-7736-5920-2). Girardet.

Woerterbucher der Fertigungstechnik Deutsch-Englisch-Franzoesisch: Bd 2, Schleifen Oberflaechenrauheit. G. Pahlitzsch. 139p. (Ger., Eng. & Fr.). 1963. DM.45.00 (ISBN 3-7736-5930-X). Girardet.

Woerterbucher der Fertigungstechnik Deutsch-Englisch-Franzoesisch: Bd 3, Blechbearbeitung. G. Pahlitzsch. 136p. (Ger., Eng. & Fr.). 1965. DM.45.00 (ISBN 3-7736-5940-7). Girardet.

Woerterbucher der Fertigungstechnik Deutsch-Englisch-Franzoesisch: Bd 4, Grundbegriffe des Spanens. G. Pahlitzsch. 123p. (Ger., Eng. & Fr.). 1969. DM.45.00 (ISBN 3-7736-5941-5). Girardet.

Woerterbucher der Fertigungstechnik Deutsch-Englisch-Franzoesisch: Bd 5, Kaltfliesspressen & Kaltstauchen. G. Pahlitzsch. 157p. (Ger., Eng. & Fr.). 1969. DM.45.00 (ISBN 3-7736-5945-8). Girardet.

Woerterbucher der Fertigungstechnik Deutsch-Englisch-Franzoesisch: Bd 6, Hobeln, Stassen, Raeumen, Drehen. G. Pahlitzsch. 194p. (Ger., Eng. & Fr.). 1972. DM.45.00 (ISBN 3-7736-5946-6). Girardet.

Woerterbucher der Fertigungstechnik Deutsch-Englisch-Franzoesisch: Bd 7, Bohren, Senken, Reiben, Gewindeschneiden. G. Pahlitzsch. 220p. (Ger., Eng. & Fr.). 1977. DM.45.00 (ISBN 3-7736-5947-4). Girardet.

Woerterbucher der Fertigungstechnik Daenisch-Norwegisch-Schwedisch-Finnisch: Bd 1N, Schmieden-Freiformschmeiden & Gesenkschmieden. G. Pahlitzsch. 148p. (Danish, Norwegian, Swedish & Finnish.). 1972. DM.45.00 (ISBN 3-7736-5851-6). Girardet.

Woerterbucher der Fertigungstechnik Deutsch-Spanisch-Italienisch-Portugiesisch: Bd 1R, Schmieden-Freiformschmieden & Gesenkschmieden. G. Pahlitzsch. 114p. (Ger., Span., Ital & Port.). 1967. DM.45.00 (ISBN 3-7736-5801-X). Girardet.

Woeter & Wendungen: Woerterbuch zum Deutschen Sprachgebrauch. 818p. (Ger.). 1972. 11.00. M Rosenberg.

Woleaian-English Dictionary. Ho-Min Sohn & Anthony F. Tawerilmang. (Pali Language Texts: Micronesia). 382p. (Pali & Eng.). 1976. pap. text ed. 14.00x (ISBN 0-8248-0415-5). UH Pr.

Woman's Day Dictionary of Furniture. Dina VonZweck. 1983. pap. 4.95 (ISBN 0-8065-0842-6). Citadel Pr.

Woman's Day Dictionary of Glass. Dina VonZweck. 1983. pap. 4.95 (ISBN 0-8065-0841-8). Citadel Pr.

Wood's New World Unabridged Rhyming Dictionary. Clement Wood. 1056p. 15.00 (ISBN 0-529-03390-9, 1084). Collins Pubs.

Woordenboek Hebreeuws-Nederlands. Jitschak Pimentel. LC 78-388662. 480p. (Hebrew & Dutch.). 1978. fl.49.00 (ISBN 9-0601-0322-X). Strengholt.

Woordenboek Hebreeuws-Nederlands. Jitschak Pimentel. LC 78-388662. 480p. (Hebrew & Dutch.). 1978. fl.49.00 (ISBN 9-06010-322-X). Strengholt.

Woordenboek van magic, okkultisme & parapsychologi. Nel Noordzij. LC 76-456275. 110p. (Dutch.). 1976. fl.12.50 (ISBN 9-02613-015-5). Fontein.

Woordenboek Welzijn. Marijke Van Hee. LC 79-391588. 266p. (Dutch.). 1979. fl.37.50 (ISBN 9-060-95489-0). VUGA.

Word Book. American Heritage. LC 76-698. 1976. 3.95 (ISBN 0-395-24521-4). HM.

Word Book II. (Eng.). 3.95. HM.

Word Count of Modern Arabic Prose. Jacob Landau. 485p. (Arabic & Eng.). 1959. 10.00x (275-4). Intl Bk Ctr.

Word Desk Set II. (Eng.). 12.95. HM.

Word for Word. Edward C. Pinkerton. LC 77-20391. xxxii, 432p. 1982. 39.95 (ISBN 0-930454-06-5). Verbatim.
Word Frequencies of Spoken American English. Hartvig Dahl. LC 80-116646. xii, 348p. 1980. 60.00 (ISBN 0-930454-07-3). Verbatim.
Word Game Winning Dictionary. Ed. by Bruce Wetterau. (Orig.). 1980. pap. 2.95 (ISBN 0-451-09214-7, E9214, Sig). NAL.
Word-Hoard: An Introduction to Old English Vocabulary. Stephen A. Barney et al. LC 76-47003. 1977. pap. 5.95x (ISBN 0-300-02110-0). Yale U Pr.
Word Meanings in the New Testament: I & II Corinthians, Galatians & Ephesians, Vol. 4. Ralph Earle. 1979. 9.95 (ISBN 0-8010-3349-7). Baker Bk.
Wordbook. Gilbert Kahn & Donald J. Mulkerne. 1975. pap. text ed. 6.95x (ISBN 0-02-474780-7, 47478). Glencoe.
Wordpower. Edward De Bono. 1977. pap. 4.95i (ISBN 0-06-090568-9, CN 568, CN). Har-Row.
Words & Arms: A Dictionary of Security & Defense Terms with Supplementary Data. Ed. by Wolfram F. Hanrieder & Larry V. Buel. 1979. lib. bdg. 35.00x (ISBN 0-89158-383-1). Westview.
Words As Definitions of Experience. Arnold Wesker & Richard Appignanesi. (Education Ser.). 48p. (Orig.). 1980. pap. 1.25 (ISBN 0-904613-26-7). Writers & Readers.
Words, Facts & Phrases: A Dictionary of Curious, Quaint, & Out-of-the-Way Matters. Eliezer E. Edwards. LC 68-21768. 1968. Repr. of 1881 ed. 42.00x (ISBN 0-8103-3087-3). Gale.
Words for the Wise: A Field Guide to Academic Terms. Mark Beach. LC 79-51616. (Illus., Orig.). 1979. pap. 4.95 (ISBN 0-9602664-0-2). Coast to Coast.
Words I Like to Read & Write: Grades 1-2 Picture Dictionary. O'Donnell & Townes. (Illus., Eng.). 5.46 (516324-9). Har-Row.
Words I Like to Read & Write: Grades 2-4 Picture Dictionary. O'Donnell & Townes. (Illus., Eng.). 8.22 (516425-7). Har-Row.
Words of Science. Isaac Asimov. (Illus.). (gr. 7 up). 1959. 10.95 (ISBN 0-395-06571-2). HM.
Words of Science & the History Behind Them. Isaac Asimov. (Illus.). (RL 7). 1969. pap. 1.95 (ISBN 0-451-61799-1, MJ1799, Ment). NAL.
Words Relating to Plants & Animals in the Mammoth Cave Region see Lexicon of the Sports & Racing Car Enthusiast.
Words That Mean Business: Three Thousand Terms for Access to Business Information. Warner-Eddison Associates. 235p. 1981. 49.95 (ISBN 0-918212-55-3). Neal-Schuman.
Words, Words, Words: A Dictionary for Writers & Others Who Care About Words. John B. Bremner. LC 80-256. 1980. 26.00x (ISBN 0-231-04492-5); pap. 10.95 (ISBN 0-231-04493-3). Columbia U Pr.
Wordsmanship. Claurene Du Gran. 95p. 1981. 9.95 (ISBN 0-930454-11-1). Verbatim.
Wordsworth & the Vocabulary of Emotion. Josephine Miles. 1965. lib. bdg. 18.00x (ISBN 0-374-95681-2). Octagon.
World Almanac Dictionary of Dates. Laurence Urdang. 320p. 1982. 8.95 (ISBN 0-911818-26-X). World Almanac.
World Almanac Dictionary of Dates. World Almanac Editors. Ed. by Laurence Urdang, Inc. LC 81-71772. 320p. 24.95x (ISBN 0-582-28372-8). Longman.
World Book Dictionary, 2 Vols. Ed. by Clarence L. Barnhart & Robert K. Barnhart. LC 82-45610. (Illus.). 2554p. (gr. 4-12). 1983. lib. bdg. write for info. (ISBN 0-7166-0283-0). World Bk.
World Dictionaries in Print, 1983. 450p. 1983. 99.50 (ISBN 0-8352-1615-2). Bowker.
World Dictionary. (Span. & Eng.). write for info. (608-37). Pan Amer Pub.
World Guide to Abbreviations of Organizations. 6th ed. Ed. by F. A. Buttress. 500p. 1980. 115.00x (ISBN 0-8103-2024-X). Gale.
World Mining: Glossary of Mining, Processing & Geological Terms. Wyllie & Argall. 432p. (Eng., Ger., Fr., Span. & Swedish.). 60.00. W H Freeman.
World Mining Glossary of Mining, Processing & Geological Terms. Ed. by R. J. Wyllie & George O. Argall, Jr. LC 74-20169. (A World Mining Book). 432p. 1975. 47.50 (ISBN 0-87930-031-0). Miller Freeman.
World-Wide French Dictionary. Ed. by Robert Switzer. (Fr.). 1978. pap. 2.95 (ISBN 0-449-30849-9, Prem). Fawcett.
World-Wide French Dictionary: Indexed. (Fr.). 7.95 (ISBN 0-8329-9681-5). New Century.
World Wide French Language Dictionary French-English. 512p. (Fr. & Eng.). 7.95; pap. 3.95 (ISBN 0-8329-9682-3). New Century.
World-Wide German Dictionary. Ed. by Paul H. Glucksman. (Ger.). 1978. pap. 2.50 (ISBN 0-449-30850-2, Prem). Fawcett.
World Wide German Language Dictionary German-English. 544p. (Ger. & Eng.). 7.95 (ISBN 0-8329-0144-X); pap. 3.95 (ISBN 0-8329-9687-4). New Century.
World-Wide Italian Dictionary. Ed. by Vittore E. Bocchetta. (Ital.). 1977. pap. 2.50 (ISBN 0-449-30840-5, Prem). Fawcett.
World Wide Italian Language Italian-English. 544p. (Ital. & Eng.). 7.95 (ISBN 0-8329-9696-3). New Century.
World-Wide Spanish. (Span. & Eng.). thumb index 7.95 (7736-3); pap. 3.95 (7735-5). Natl Textbk.
World-Wide Spanish Dictionary. Ed. by Emilio LeFort. (Span.). 1978. pap. 2.95 (ISBN 0-449-30851-0, Prem). Fawcett.
World Wide Spanish Language Dictionary Spanish-English. 640p. (Span. & Eng.). 7.95; pap. 3.95 (ISBN 0-8329-9712-9). New Century.
Worldwide Dictionary. 640p. (Span. & Eng.). pap. 3.95 (T05). Bilingual Ed Serv.
Wortabet's Pocket English-Arabic Dictionary. John Wortabet & Harvey Porter. 448p. (Eng. & Arabic.). pap. 5.50 (083-X). Intl Bk Ctr.
Wortbildung der Deutschen Gegenwartssprache. 4th ed. W. Fleischer. 363p. (Ger.). 1976. M.26.00. Bibl Inst Leipzig.
Wortbildung Diachron, Synchron. Osterreichisches Linguistisches Programm. Ed. by Oswald Panagl. LC 78-356489. (Illus.). 157p. (Ger.). 1976. S.200.00 (ISBN 3-851-24533-4). Inst Verg Sprach.
Worterbuch der Mikroelktronik, Dictionary Microelectronics: English-German, German-English. 218p. (Eng. & Ger.). 1980. pap. 39.95 (ISBN 3-88322-001-9, M-9219). French & Eur.
Worterbuch der Technik: Italienisch-Deutsch. A. Schlegelmich. 630p. (Ital. & Ger.). 1981. 95.00 (ISBN 3-7736-5110-4, M-122653). French & Eur.
Wortkonkordanz zu den Altmittel & Altniederfraenkischen Psalmen & Glossen. Arend Quak. 182p. (Dutch.). 1975. fl.25.00. Rodopi.
Wortschatz der Information und Dokumentation. G. Schmoll. 160p. (Ger.). 15.95 (ISBN 3-7940-4037-6, M-7690, Pub. by Vlg. Dokumentation). French & Eur.
Wortschatz des Juristen: Ein Lern & Lesebuch Juristischen Sprachausdrucks. Karl Luggauer. LC 76-465150. 206p. (Ger.). 1976. write for info. (ISBN 3-853-66138-6). Heyn.
Writer's Dictionary. new ed. A. G. Seaton. LC 77-166289. 1000p. 1973. 20.00 (ISBN 0-685-38709-7). St Martin.
Writer's Rhyming Dictionary. Langford Reed. 7.95 (ISBN 0-87116-044-7). Writer.
Writing Vocabulary of Elementary Children. Robert L. Hillerich. 316p. 1978. 15.25x (ISBN 0-398-03814-7). C C Thomas.
Written Word II. (Eng.). 4.95. HM.

X

Xerox Dictionary Thumb Index. Morris. 10.95 (ISBN 0-448-02905-7, G&D). Putnam Pub Group.
Xerox Intermediate Dictionary. Ed. by William Morris. (Illus.). 800p. (gr. 4-6). 1973. Repr. 9.95 (ISBN 0-448-02849-2, G&D). Putnam Pub Group.
Xhosa-English Dictionary. J. McLaren. Ed. by W. G. Bennie & J. J. Jolobe. (Xhosa & Eng.). 22.50 (ISBN 0-87559-069-1). Shalom.

Y

Y geiriadur mawr. 8th ed. Meurig Evans & W. O. Thomas. LC 79-337696. (Eng. & Welsh.). 1978. E4.95. Davies Dewi.
Y Geiriadur Mawr: The Complete Welsh-English, English-Welsh Dictionary. H. Meurig & W. O. Thomas. Ed. by S. J. Williams. 859p. (Welsh & Eng.). 1981. 35.00 (ISBN 0-686-97426-3, M-9434). French & Eur.
Yachting Dictionary. A. Tetsmann & H. Lind. 192p. 1980. 50.00x (ISBN 0-686-82331-1, Pub. by Collets). State Mutual Bk.
Yachtman's Eight Language Dictionary. 3rd ed. Barbara Webb. 1983. 8.95 (ISBN 0-8286-0092-9). De Graff.
Yachtsman's Eight Language Dictionary. Barbara Webb. (Illus.). 160p. 1973. 12.00x (ISBN 0-8464-0983-6). Beekman Pubs.
Yana Dictionary. Edward Sapir & Morris Swadesh. (U. C. Publ. in Linguistics: Vol. 22). 1960. pap. 14.00x (ISBN 0-520-09219-8). U of Cal Pr.
Yapese-English Dictionary. John T. Jensen et al. LC 76-47495. (Pali Language Texts: Micronesia). 202p. (Orig., Yapese & Eng.). 1977. pap. text ed. 10.00x (ISBN 0-8248-0517-8). UH Pr.
Yesterday & Today: A Dictionary of Recent American History. Stanley Hochman. LC 79-12265. (Illus.). 407p. 1979. 29.95 (ISBN 0-07-029103-9). McGraw.
Yiddish Alphabet Book. Frederica Postman. LC 78-78188. (Illus., Yiddish & Eng.). 1979. 8.95x (ISBN 0-9602402-0-9). PNye Pr.
Yiddish-English Dictionary. 22.50 (ISBN 0-87559-193-0). Shalom.
Yiddish Word Book for English Speaking People. Samuel Rosenbaum. 199p. (Yiddish & Eng.). 1980. pap. text ed. 6.95 (ISBN 0-442-21932-6). Van Nos Reinhold.
Yiddish Word Book for English-Speaking People. Samuel Rosenbaum. (Yiddish & Eng.). 1978. 9.95 (ISBN 0-442-27015-1). Van Nos Reinhold.
Yoga Illustrated Dictionary. Harvey Day. (Illus.). 1970. 9.95 (ISBN 0-87523-177-2). Emerson.
York Dictionary of English-French-German-Spanish Literary Terms & Their Origin. Saad Elkhadem. (Eng., Fr., Ger., & Span.). 1976. pap. 9.95 (ISBN 0-919966-04-7); pap. 6.95 (ISBN 0-919966-01-2). York Pr CA.
York Dictionary of English-French-German-Spanish Literary Terms & Their Origin. Saad Elkhaden. LC 77-364336. 154p. (Eng., Fr., Ger. & Span.). 1976. 6.95 (ISBN 0-919966-01-2). York Pr CA.
Young Canada Dictionary. Dan Leibman. (Illus.). 1980. pap. write for info. (ISBN 0-17-600751-2). Nelson & Sons Group.
Young People's Animal Encyclopedia, 24 vols. Ed. by Maurice Burton. LC 72-83306. (Illus.). 48p. (gr. 4-9). 1980. Set. PLB 226.60 (ISBN 0-516-00300-3). Childrens.
Young People's Science Dictionary, 2 vols. Young People's Science Encyclopedia Editors. LC 67-17925. (Illus.). (gr. 4 up). 1979. lib. bdg. 17.25 (ISBN 0-516-00274-0). Childrens.
Youngs Analytical Concordance to the Bible. Young. 18.50x (ISBN 0-686-12407-3); thumb-indexed 22.50 (ISBN 0-686-12408-1). Church History.
Young's Analytical Concordance to the Bible. Robert Young. 1955. 19.95 (ISBN 0-8028-8084-3); deluxe ed. 22.95 (ISBN 0-8028-8085-1). Eerdmans.
Your Jewish Lexicon. Edith Samuel. 192p. (Orig., Hebrew.). 1982. 10.00 (ISBN 0-8074-0054-8); pap. 5.95 (ISBN 0-8074-0061-0). UAHC.
Yugoslavian Dictionary: English-Serbocroatian. Z. Simic. 446p. (Eng. & Serbocroatian.). 1977. pap. text ed. 6.50x (ISBN 0-89918-784-6). Vanous.
Yugoslavian-English Slovene Dictionary. R. Skerlj et al. 1122p. (Eng. & Slovenian.). 1979. text ed. 35.00x (ISBN 0-89918-704-8, Y704). Vanous.
Yugoslavian Mining Dictionary: English-Serbo-English. S. Verbic. 527p. (Serbocroatian & Eng.). 1981. pap. text ed. 25.00x (ISBN 0-89918-783-8). Vanous.
Yugoslavian Pocket Dictionary: Slovene-English, English-Slovenski. Komac & Skerlj. (Eng. & Slovenian.). 1979. 15.00x (ISBN 0-89918-778-1, Y-778). Vanous.
Yugoslavic Deluxe Dictionary: English-Croation or Serbian. 11th ed. R. Filipuvic et al. 1436p. (Eng. & Serbocroatian.). 1980. 75.00x (ISBN 0-89918-779-X, Y-779). Vanous.
Yugoslavic Dictionary: English-Slovene. 3rd ed. A. Grad et al. 1124p. (Eng. & Slovenian.). 1979. 35.00x (ISBN 0-89918-704-8, Y-704). Vanous.
Yugoslavic Dictionary: Slovene-English. 7th ed. J. Kotnik. (Eng. & Serbocroatian.). 1978. 40.00x (ISBN 0-89918-708-0, Y-708). Vanous.
Yugoslavic Pocket Dictionary: English-Croation. R. Filipuvic et al. 564p. (Eng. & Croatian.). 1979. 20.00x (ISBN 0-89918-780-3, Y-780). Vanous.

Z

Z Ninety Four Industrial Engineering Terminology: 1972 Index. American Society of Mechanical Engineers. 11.00 (N00073); members 8.80. ASME.
Zahnarztliches aus dem Dictionnaire des Sciences Medicales. Werner H. Aeschlimann. LC 75-507852. 75p. (Fr.). 1975. 20.00 F (ISBN 3-260-03859-0). Juris Druckg.
Zeisberger's Indian Dictionary: English, German, Iroquois - the Onandaga & Algonquin - the Delaware. David Zeisberger. LC 76-43905. 248p. (Eng., Ger. & Iroquois.). Repr. of 1887 ed. 42.50 (ISBN 0-404-15802-1). AMS Pr.
Zement-Woerterbuch: Herstellung & Technologie. (Eng. & Ger.). write for info. (ISBN 3-7625-1341-4). Bauverlag.
Zen Dictionary. Ernest Wood. LC 72-77518. 1972. pap. 5.25 (ISBN 0-8048-1060-5). C E Tuttle.
Zenei Zseblexikon. Gabor Darvas. LC 79-380372. 341p. (Hungarian.). 1978. 26.00 Ft (ISBN 9-633-30265-X). Zenemukiado.
Zola Dictionary. J. G. Patterson. LC 68-27179. 1969. Repr. of 1912 ed. 34.00x (ISBN 0-8103-3173-X). Gale.
Zola Dictionary. J. G. Patterson. 75.00 (ISBN 0-8490-1350-X). Gordon Pr.

Zoologisches Woerterbuch - Palaearktische Tiere. Michael Klemm. 850p. (Ger., Lat. & Rus.). 1973. 160.00x (ISBN 3-489-71734-1). Intl Pubns Serv.

Zoologisches Woerterbuch Palaearktische Tiere. Michael Klemm. (Lat., Ger. & Rus.). 1973. 220.00 (ISBN 0-686-56474-X, M-7692, Pub. by Parey Berlin). French & Eur.

Zoologisches Woerterbuch Palaearktische Tiere. Michael Klemm. (Lat., Ger. & Rus.). 1973. 220.00. Parey.

Zulu-English & Zulu Dictionary. (Zulu & Eng.). 19.50 (ISBN 0-685-77569-0, 096-8). Saphrograph.

Zulu-English, English-Zulu Dictionary. rev. ed. Ed. by C. M. Doke. (Zulu & Eng.). pap. 20.00 (ISBN 0-85494-010-3). Heinman.

Zum Fachwortschatz. Sabine Kruger. LC 80-467779. vii, 523p. (Ger.). 1979. DM.90.00 (ISBN 3-18-150037-2). VDI Verlag.

Zwei Hundert Eins Spanische Verben. Henry Strutz. (Ger. & Span.). 1981. pap. 3.95 (ISBN 0-8120-0688-7). Barron.

Zweisprachiges Woerterbuch fuer Angenaeherte Operationelle Analyse. Gudrun Guckler. (Ger.). write for info. (ISBN 3-878-08053-0). Narr.

Zweisprachiges Woerterbuch Fuer Angenaeherte Operationelle Analyse Semantischer Entsprechungen Mittels EDV. G. Guckler. (Ger. & It.). 30.00 (ISBN 3-87808-053-0). French & Eur.

Author/Editor/Compiler Index

A

A, Peters J. Dictionary of Herpetology: Description of Words & Terms. Lubrecht & Cramer.

A Szotarszerk Bizottsag Vezetoje Toth Lajos. Magyar-Orosz Katonai Szotar. Akademiai Kiado.

Aarnes, Asbjorn. Litteraert Lekxikon. Tanum-Norli.

Abaev, V. I. Istoriko-Etimologicheskii Slovar Osetinskogo (Pub. by Nauka). Four Continent.

Abcarius, J. John. An English-Arabic Reader's Dictionary. Intl Bk Ctr.

Abcarius, John. An English-Arabic Readers' Dictionary. Intl Bk. Ctr.

Abdallah. Abdallah Dictionary of International Relations & Conference Terminology in English-Arabic. Intl Bk Ctr.

Abd Al-Monem, Mufid Al-Guindi. Diccionario Espanol-Arabe de Verbos, Gramatica y Temas de Conversacion. French & Eur.

Abdeen, Adnan. A Dictionary of Accounting & Finance. Intl Bk Ctr.

--English-Arabic Dictionary for Accounting & Finance (Pub. by Wiley-Interscience). Wiley.

--English-Arabic Dictionary of Accounting & Finance. Intl Bk Ctr.

Abd-El-Gawad, Tawfik. Technical Dictionary: Archtiecture & Building (Pub. by Collets). State Mutual Bk.

Abdel-Massih, Ernest T. A Computerized Lexicon of Tamazight: Berber Dialect of Ayt Seghrouchen. Ctr for NE & North African Stud.

--A Sample Lexicon of Pan-Arabic. Ctr for NE & North African Stud.

Abd-El-Wahed. Automotive Engineering Dictionary: English-French-German-Arabic. French & Eur.

--Radio & Television Dictionary. French & Eur.

--Refrigeration & Conditioning Dictionary. French & Eur.

Abd-El-Wahed, A. M. Chemical Technology Dictionary: English, French-German-Arabic. French & Eur.

--Iron & Steel Industry Dictionary. French & Eur.

--Machine Tools Dictionary: English-French-German-Arabic. French & Eur.

--Metal Forming Dictionary. French & Eur.

Abd-el-Washed, ed. see Zimaity, M. A.

Abel, Emily K. Terminal Degree: The Job Crisis in Higher Education. Praeger.

Abel, Ernest L. A Marihuana Dictionary: Words, Terms, Events & Persons Relating to Cannabis. Greenwood.

Abercrombie, M., et al. Diccionario De Biologia. French & Eur.

--Dicionario de Biologia. Pub Euro Am.

--The Penguin Dictionary of Biology. Viking Pr.

Aberlaitz & Buenaventura de Oreyegui, P. Diccionario Vasco-Castellano, Castellano-Vasco De Voces Comunes a Dos O Mas Dialectos Del Euskera. French & Eur.

Abhyankar, Kashinath V. & Shukla, J. M. A Dictionary of Sanskrit Grammar. Oriental Institute.

Abo, Takaji, et al. Marshallese-English Dictionary. UH Pr.

Abos Santabarbara, Angel L. & Marco Martinez, Antonio. Diccionario de terminos basicos para la historia. Alhambra.

Abraham, Samuel V. Real Estate Dictionary & Reference Guide. McFadden, S. Michele & Wilson-Fulkerson, Roberta, eds. Career Pub.

Abraham, Werner & Meno Blanco, Francisco. Diccionario de Terminologia Linguistica Actual. Gredos.

Abrahamian, R. Pekhleviisko-Persidsko-Armiano-Russko-Angliiskii Slovar (Pub. by Mitk). Four Continent.

Abrahams, Roger D. & Rankin, Lois, eds. Counting Out Rhymes: A Dictionary. U of Tex Pr.

Abramov, L. Ia., ed. Shakhmatnyi Slovar (Pub. by Fiz. & Sport). Four Continent.

Abrams, M. H. A Glossary of Literary Terms (HoltC). HR&W.

Academie International du Tourisme. Diccionario Turistico Internacional: Edition Espagnole. Acad Intl Tour.

Academie Internationale du Tourisme. Dictionar Turistic International: Edition Roumaine. Acad Intl Tour.

--Dictionnaire touristique international: Edition francaise. Acad Intl Tour.

--International Toeristisch Woordenboek: Edition Neerlandais. Acad Intl Tour.

Accattatis, Luigi. Dizionario del dialetto calabrese. Brenner.

--Vocabolario del dialetto calabrese. Pellegrini.

Accountants International Study Group. Comparative Glossary of Accounting Terms in Canada, the United Kingdom & the United States. Can Inst Chart Accts.

Achard, Claude F. Dictionnaire de la Provence & du Comte Venaissin. Slatkine.

--Vocabulaire Francois-Provencal. Slatkine.

Acharya, Prasanna K. A Dictionary of Hindu Architecture: Treating of Sanskrit Architectural Terms. Bharatiya Publishing House.

Achon, M. A., jt. auth. see Wittfoht, A.

Achterberg, E. & Lanz, K. Enzyklopadisches Lexikon Fur des Geld, Bank und Borsen Wesen (Pub. by Fritz Knapp Verlag). French & Eur.

ACI Committee 116. Cement & Concrete Terminology. ACI.

Adam, Gyorgy, jt. auth. see Straub, Ferene B.

Adam, J. H., ed. Longman Dictionary of Business English. Longman.

Adamicska, O., jt. auth. see Kerdel-Vegas, F.

Adams, I. H. Agrarian Landscape Terms: A Glossary for Historical Geography. Acad Pr.

Adams, James N. The Latin Sexual Vocabulary: Three Years of Confrontation. Johns Hopkins.

Adams, Jay E. Christian Counselor's Wordbook. Baker Bk.

Adams, R. F. English-Efik Dictionary. Shalom.

Adams, Ramon F. The Language of the Railroader. U of Okla Pr.

Addi, Al-Sayyid. Dictionary of Persian Loan Words in the Arabic Language. Intl Bk Ctr.

Adkins, Lesley & Adkins, Roy A. A Thesaurus of British Archaeology. B&N Imports.

Adkins, Roy A., jt. auth. see Adkins, Lesley.

Adler, J. A. Elsevier's Dictionary of Criminal Science. Elsevier.

Adloff, Richard, jt. auth. see Thompson, Virginia.

Adnani, Muhammad. Dictionary of Common Language Errors & Their Corrections: Arabic-Arabic. Intl Bk Ctr.

Adorno, Francesco, jt. auth. see Lamanna, Paolo E.

Adrian, J. & Legrand, G. Dictionnaire de Biochimie Alimentaire et de Nutruition. French & Eur.

Aedos. Diccionario Espanol de Sinonimos, Equivalencias & Ideas Alfines. Aedos.

Aeschilimann, Werner-Heinrich. Dictionnaire des Sciences Medicales, 1821-1822. Juris Druck.

Aeschlimann, E. & Ancono, Paolo. Dictionnaire des Miniaturistes du Moyan Age: La Renaissance dans les Differentes Contrees de l'Europa. Kraus.

Aeschlimann, Werner H. Zahnarztliches aus dem Dictionnaire des Sciences Medicales. Juris Druckg.

Afanaseva, I. N., et al. Anglo-russki i biologicheski i slovar. Russkii Iazyk.

Affre, Henri & Rodez. Dictionnaire des Institutions, Moeurs & Costumes du Rouergue. Lafitte Repr.

Afronin, N. P., et al. Russko-Angliiskii Voenno-Morskoi Slovar (Pub. by Voenizdat). Four Continent.

Agard, Frederick B., jt. auth. see Sola, Donald F.

Agence de Cooperation Culturelle & Technique. Vocabulaire de l'oceanologie. C. I. L. F.

Agnew, Irene, ed. Glossary of English & Russian Computer & Automated Control Systems Terminology. Agnew Tech-Tran.

Agricola, C. & Agricola, E. Woerter & Gegenwoerter. Bibl Inst Leipzig.

Agricola, E., jt. auth. see Agricola, C.

Agricola, E., et al, eds. Woerter & Wendungen. Bibl Inst Leipzig.

Aguayo, Carlos A. & Biaggi, Virgilio. Diccionario De Biologia Animal. U of PR Pr.

Aguilar, Peris & Jose-Aguilar Civera, J. Diccionario de Energia Solar. Alhambra.

Aguilera, F. Lexico Espanol-Kawesqar. Centro Invest.

Aguilera Cerni, Vincente, ed. Diccionario del Arte Moderno: Conceptos, Ideas, Tendencias. Toreres.

Aguirre de Carcer. Diccionario militar bilingue. Dossat.

Ahlberg, Axel W., et al. Latinsk-Svensk Ordbok. Esselte Studium.

Ahlhaus, Otto E., et al. Tachenlexikon Umweltschultz. Pr Univ Fr.

Ahlheim, Karl H. Die Biologie: Ein Lexikon der Gesamten Schulbiologie. Biblio Inst.
—Die Psychologie: Ein Sachlexikon fuer die Schule. Biblio Inst.

Ahlsved, Karl-Johan, et al. Lexicon Forestale. Suomen Standard.

Aichelburg, Ulrico Di see Di Aichelburg, Ulrico.

Ainsworth & Bisby. Dictionary of the Fungi (Pub. by CAB Bks England). State Mutual Bk.

Ainsworth & Bisby's. Dictionary of the Fungi. French & Eur.

Ainsworth, G. C. Ainsworth & Bisby's Dictionary of the Fungi, Including the Lichens. Intl Pubns Serv.

Aite, M. C. Dizionario di medicina. Zanichelli.

Ajvarado, Lisandro. Glosario de voces indigenas de Venezuela. Minist Ed Caracas.

Akademie Verlages Budapest, ed. Taschenlexikon Ungarn. Bibl Inst Leipzig.

Akerlung, Alfred. Svensk-Spansk Ordbok. Casa Novas, M. J. & Gronbarj, M., eds. Esselte Studium.

Akhmanova, et al. Russian-English Dictionary. Imported Bks.

Akhmanova, O. S. Russko-Angliiskii Slovar (Pub. by Russkii Iazyk). Four Continent.
—Slovar Omonimov Russkogo Iazyka (Pub. by Sov. Entsiklopediia). Four Continent.

Akhmanova, O. S. & Wilson, E. English-Russian Dictionary. French & Eur.

Akhmanova, O. S., ed. Anglo-Russkii Slovar (Pub. by Russkii Iazyk). Four Continent.
—Russko-Angliiskii Slovar (Kratkii (Pub. by Russkii Iazyk). Four Continent.

Akhmanova, Ol'ga S. Russko-Angliiskii. Russkii Iazyk.

Akhmanova, Olga S. & Wilson, Elizabeth A. Russko-Angliisku Slovar-Russian-English Dictionary. Russkii Iazyk.

Akhmanova, Ol'ga Sergeevna. Anglo-Russkii Slovar. Russkii Iazyk.

Akmanova, A. English-Russian Dictionary (Pub. by Collet's). State Mutual Bk.

Akoun, A., et al. Dictionnaire de Politique. Larousse FR.

Al-Ada, Samuhi Fouk see Fouk al-Ada, Samuhi.

Al-Adnani, Muhammad. A Dictionary of Common Language Errors & their Corrections. Intl Bk Ctr.

Al-Amir Al-Nasiruddin, Amin. Ar-Rafed. Intl Bk Ctr.

Alanne, V. S. Finnish Dictionary: Suomalais-Englantilainen. Vanous.
—Finnish-English General Dictionary. French & Eur.

Albanese, Joseph. The Nurses' Drug Reference. McGraw.

Albert, Roald & Hahnewald, Harry. Medizintechnik-Englisch-Deutsch-Franzoesisch-Russisch-Spanisch-Polnisch-Ungarisch-Slowakisch. VEB Technik.

Albert, Salich, jt. auth. see Harrison, Sheldon P.

Alberti & Santiago, Gubern. Diccionari castella-catala, catala-castella. Alberti.

Alberti, Santiago. Diccionari Castella-Catala, Catala-Castella Petit. Alberti.
—Diccionari Castella-Catala, Catala-Castella, Mitja. French & Eur.
—Diccionari De la Llengua Catalan. French & Eur.
—Diccionari de la Llengua Catalana. Alberti.
—Diccionario Castella-Catala, Catala-Castella Petit. French & Eur.
—Diccionario Castella-Catala, Catala-Castella Gran. French & Eur.

Albertini, Jean. Dictionnaire Francais-Corse. C. E. R. C.
—Dictionnaire Francais-Corse. French & Eur.

Albertus, F. Tysk-Dansk: Dansk-Tysk Ordbog. French & Eur.

Albertus, Flemming G. Gjellerups Gronne Ordbog. Gjellerup Forlag.

Albota, Mihail. Dictionar Poliglot de Geodezie: Fotogrammetrie si Cartografie. Editura Stiintifica.

Albrecht, Guenther. Lexikon Deutschsprachiger Schriftsteller. French & Eur.
—Lexikon Deutschsprachiger Schriftsteller. French & Eur.

Albrecht, Guenther, et al, eds. Lexikon Deutschsprachiger Schriftsteller: Bd 1. Scriptor Verlag.
—Lexikon Deutschsprachiger Schriftsteller: Bd 3. Scriptor Verlag.
—Lexikon Deutschsprachiger Schriftsteller: Bd 4. Scriptor Verlag.
—Lexikon Deutschsprachiger Schriftsteller: Bd 1. Scriptor Verlag.
—Lexikon Deutschsprachiger Schriftsteller: Bd 2. Scriptor Verlag.

Albrecht, Gunter E. & Reichardt, Hans D. Modellbahnlexikon. Alba Buchverlag.

Al-Bustani, Abdullah. Al-Wafi. Intl Bk Ctr.

Al-Bustani, Butros. Qutr Al-Muhit. Intl Bk Ctr.

Al-Bustani, Butrus. Arabic-Arabic Dictionary Muhit Al Muhit. Intl Bk Ctr.

Alcala, A. Vocabulario Andaluz. French & Eur.

Alcalay, Reuben. Complete English-Hebrew, Hebrew-English Dictionary. SBS Pub.
—The Massada English-Hebrew Student Dictionary. SBS Pub.

Alcalay, Rueben. The Complete English-Hebrew Dictionary. Massada Pr.
—The Complete Hebrew-English Dictionary. Massada Pr.
—The Massada Student Dictionary English-Hebrew. Massada Pr.

Alcala-Zamora. Alcala-Zamora, Diccionario Frances-Espanol, Espanol-Frances. French & Eur.
—Alcala-Zamora, Diccionario Frances-Espanol, Espanol-Frances. French & Eur.

Alcala Zamora. Diccionario bilingue frances-espanol-aleman. Sopena.

Alcala-Zamora & Antignac, T. Diccionario frances-espanol y espanol-frances. Imported Bks.

Alcantud, Adela. Diccionario Bilingue De Psicologia. Senda Nueva.

Alcedo, Antonio De see De Alcedo, Antonio.

Al-Chihabi, Emir. Dictionnaire des Termes Agricoles: Francais-Arabe. Intl Bk Ctr.

Alcover, Antoni M. & Moll, Francesc de B. Diccionari I Catala-Valencia-Balear. French & Eur.

Alcover Sureda, Antoni M. & Casasnoves, Moll. Diccionari catala-valencia-balear. Moll Edit.

Alden, Moe J., et al. The Vocabulary of First-Grade Children. C C Thomas.

Alderson, A. D., ed. The Oxford English-Turkish Dictionary. Iz, Fahir. Oxford U Pr.

Alderson, A. D. & Iz, Fahir, eds. Concise Oxford Turkish Dictionary. Oxford U Pr.

Alekhina, A. I. Kratikii Russko-Angliiskii i Anglo-Russkii Frazeologicheskii Slovar' Four Continent.

Aleksandrova, Z. E. Slovar Sinonimov Russkogo Iazyka (Pub. by Sov. Entsiklopediia). Four Continent.

Aleksandrova, Z. E., ed. see Cheshko.

Alekseev, M. P. Slovari Inostrannykh Iazykov v Russkom Azbukovnikeveka (Pub. by Nauka). Four Continent.

Alekseev, P. M. English-Russian Glossary of Physics Terms (Pub. by Collets). State Mutual Bk.

Alekseev, P. M., et al. Chastotnyi Anglo-Russkii Fizicheskii Slovar Minimum (Pub. by Voenizdat). Four Continent.

Alessandrino, Igino. Dizionario delle contravvenzioni. Patron.

Alessio, Giovanni. Lexicon etymologicum: Supplemento ai dizionario etimologici latini e romanzi. Licosa.

Alessio, Luigi. Vocabolario dell'argot. Petrini.

Alexandre, Charles, jt. auth. see Vernet, Pierre.

Alexandrian, Sarane. Dictionnaire de la Peinture Surrealiste (Pub. by Filipacchi). Hippocrene Bks.
—Dictionnaire de la Peinture Surrealiste. French & Eur.

Alexandrova. Dictionnaire des Synonymes de la Langue Russe. MIR.

Alexenberg, Melvin & Alexenberg, Miriam. Alef Bet Picture Dictionary. Shulsinger Sales.

Alexenberg, Miriam, jt. auth. see Alexenberg, Melvin.

Alfaro, Ricardo J. Diccionario de Anglicismos. French & Eur.

Alfaro Perez, Juan. Diccionario Maritimo y De Construccion Naval. French & Eur.

Al Faruqi, Lois I., ed. An Annotated Glossary of Arabic Musical Terms. Greenwood.

Alfaya, Javier, ed. Diccionario Santillana. Santillana.

Alford, M. H. & Alford, V. L. Russian-English Scientific & Technical Dictionary. Pergamon.

Alford, M. H. & Alford, V. L., eds. Russian-English, English-Russian Scientific & Technical Dictionary. Pergamon.

Alford, V. L., jt. auth. see Alford, M. H.

Alford, V. L., jt. ed. see Alford, M. H.

Algra, N. E., rev. by see Fockman, Andreae & Sybrandus, Johannes.

Alhambra. Diccionario Arabe-Espanol, Espanol-Arabe. French & Eur.

Alheim, Karl-Heinz, ed. Duden Woerterbuch Medizinischer Fachausdruecke. Thieme Verlag.

Aliandro, H. Dicionario Ingles-Portugues. French & Eur.
—Dicionario Portugues-Ingles. French & Eur.

Aliandro, Hygino. Portuguese-English Dictionary. Imported Bks.

Aliev, G. G. Persidsko-Russkii & Russko-Persidskii Voennyi Slovar (Pub. by Voenizdat). Four Continent.

Aliko, Hysni, jt. auth. see Kici, Gasper.

Alinei, M. Dizionario inverso italiano. Il Mulino.

Alisky, Marvin. Historical Dictionary of Peru. Scarecrow.

Alisky, Marvin, jt. auth. see Briggs, Donald C.

Al-Kasimi, Ali M. Linguistics & Bilingual Dictionaries. Humanities.

Al-Khatib, Ahmad S. A New Dictionary of Petroleum & the Oil Industry. Lib Liban.

Al-Khuli, Muhammad A. Dictionary of Theoretical Linguistics: English-Arabic with Arabic-English Glossary. Intl Bk Ctr.

Allaby, ed. Dictionary of the Environment. Macmillan.

Allaby, Michael. A Dictionary of the Environment. Van Nos Reinhold.

Allard, Guy & Granoble. Dictionnaire Historique, Chronologique, Geographique, Genealogique, Heraldique, Juridique, Politique & Botanographique du Daup. Slatkine.

Allee, John G., ed. Webster's Dictionary for Everyday Use (EH). B&N NY.

Allen, E. F. Dictionary of Abbreviations & Symbols. Shalom.

Allen, F. Sturges. Allen's Synonyms & Antonyms (EH). B&N NY.

Allen, Louis A. COMVOC, the Louis A. Allen Common Vocabulary of Professional Management. Palo Alto, Ca.

Allen, Robert D. & Wolfe, Thomas E. The Allen & Wolfe Illustrated Dictionary of Real Estate (Pub. by Wiley-Interscience). Wiley.

Allen, Sture. Svenska Ordlista. Esselte Studium.
—Vara Viktiga Ord: Basordlista Med Utbytesord. Esselte Studium.

Allen, Sture, et al. Svensk Baklaengesordbok. Esselte Studium.

Allen, Virginia F. Techniques in Teaching Vocabulary. Oxford U Pr.

Alletz, Pons Auguste. Dictionnaire des Richesses de la Langue Francoise: Neologisme qui s'y Introduit. Slatkine.

Allison, F. C., jt. auth. see Klaften, B.

Allison, F. C., jt. auth. see Klaften, E. B.

Allison, G. Mini English-Thai-English Dictionary. French & Eur.

Allison, Norman & Allison, Sonia. Drinks Dictionary. W Collins Sons.

Allison, Sonia, jt. auth. see Allison, Norman.

Allorto, Lily, et al. Nuovo dizionario Ricordi della musica e dei musicisti. Ricordi.

Allswede, Jerry L., jt. ed. see Heiser, Edward J.

Allyn, Rube. Dictionary of Fishes. Great Outdoors.

Almeida, Dauster C. Dicionario de Expressoes Idiomaticas Ingles-Portugues. Auer.

Almeida Costa, J. & Sampaio de Melo. Dicionario da Lingua Portuguesa. Imported Bks.

Almoyna, Julio Martinez see Martinez Almoyna, Julio.

Alonso, Martin. Diccionario del Espanol Moderno. French & Eur.
—Diccionario escolar del idioma espanol. Aguilar SP.
—Diccionario espanol moderno. Aguilar SP.
—Diccionario ortografico del idioma espanol. Aguilar SP.

Al-Sayyid'Addi Shir. A Dictionary of Persian Loan Words in the Arabic Language. Intl Bk Ctr.

Al-Sharif Al-Juriani. Kitab Al-Ta'rifat: Book of Definitions. Intl Bk Ctr.

Alsina, Claudi. Vocabulari Catala De Matematica Basica. French & Eur.

Alsina, R., jt. auth. see Perez, J.

Alsop, John R. An Index to Bauer Arndt, Gingrich Greek Lexicon. Zondervan.

Altemeyer, A., jt. auth. see Bucksch, H.

Altenberg. Dizionario italiano-tedesco. Vallardi A.

Altenberg, G. A. & Ubaldi, V. Dizionario Italiano-Tedesco, Tedesco-Italian. French & Eur.

Altfelder, Klaus. Lexikon der Unternehmensfuehrung. French & Eur.

Altfelder, Klaus, et al. Lexikon der Unternehmensfuehrung. Kiehl.

Althaus, H. P., et al, eds. Lexikon der Germanistischen. M Rosenberg.

Althaus, Hans. Lexikon der Grammatischen Linguistik. French & Eur.

Althaus, Hans P., et al, eds. Lexikon der Germanistischen Linguistik. Niemeyer.

Altieri de Barreto, Carmen G. El Lexico De la Delincuencia En Puerto Rico. U of PR Pr.

Altman, M. Dicionario Tecnico Contabil: Portugues-Ingles, Ingles-Portugues. French & Eur.

Altman, Philip L. & Katz, Dorothy D., eds. Inbred & Genetically Defined Strains of Laboratory Animals. Incl. Pt. 1. Mouse & Rat; Pt. 2. Hamster, Guinea Pig, Rabbit & Chicken. FASEB.

Altmeyer, A. P., jt. auth. see Bucksch, H.

Al Tulab, Munjid see Tulab, Munjid al & Mashreq, Dar el.

Alvarado, Lisandro. Glosario de bajo espanol en Venezuela. Minist Ed Caracas.

Alvarez, J. Mateos. Vocabulario Teologico del Evangelio de Saint Juan. French & Eur.

Alvarez de la Brana, Ramon. Siglas & Abreviaturas Latinas con su Significado por Orden Alfabetico de un Catalogo de las Abreviaturas. Olms Verlag.

Alvarez-Prada, Enrique. Langenscheidts Handwoerterbuch Spanisch: Teil II, Deutsch-Spanisch. Langenscheidt.

Alvaro Zamora, Maria Isabel. Lexico de Ceramica & Alfareria Aragonesas. Portico.

Alvey, Glenn, Jr. Dizionario dei termini cinematografici. Edizioni Mediterranee.
Alvey, P. J., jt. auth. see Farnfield, Carolyn A.
Alvisi & Arce. Vocabolario spagnolo-italiano e italiano-spagnolo. Malipiero.
Al-Wahab, Ibrahim. Law Dictionary (English-Arabic) Intl Bk Ctr.
Al-Yaziji, Ibrahim. Naj'ati Ur-Ra'id wa-Shar'Atu al-Warid fi al-Mutaradifi wa al-Mu tawarid. Intl Bk Ctr.
Alzugaray, J. J. Voces Extranjeras en el Lengua Technologico. French & Eur.
--Voces Extranjeras en el Lenguaje Tecnologico. Edit Alhambra.
Amador, E. F. Martinez. Diccionario Aleman-Espanol, Espanol-Aleman. French & Eur.
Amador, E. M. Martinez. Diccionario Frances-Espanol, Espanol-Frances. French & Eur.
--Diccionario Ingles-Espanol, Espanol-Ingles. French & Eur.
--Diccionario Italiano-Espanol, Espanol-Italiano. French & Eur.
--Diccionario Manual Aleman-Espanol, Spanisch-Deutsch. French & Eur.
--Diccionario Manual Amador Aleman-Espanol, Espanol-Aleman. French & Eur.
--Diccionario Manual Amador Frances-Espanol y Espanol-Frances. French & Eur.
Amalric, Jacques, et al. Lexico historico de Espana. Lajo, Rosina & Frigola, Victoria, trs. Taurus Ediciones SA.
Amankwaah, J. W. & Rytz, O., eds. Gonja-English Dictionary & Spelling Book. Inst Afr Stu.
Amato, Loredana Serafini see Serafini Amato, Loredana.
Ambruzzi, Lucio. Nuovo dizionario italiano-spagnolo. Paravia.
--Nuovo dizionario spagnolo-italiano. Paravia.
Amelin, B., jt. auth. see Pinkevich, A.
Amendola, Joao. Dictionario Italiano Portugues. Behar, Macim & Moretti, Mario, eds. Hemus-Livraria.
American Arbitration Association. Dictionary of Arbitration & Its Terms. Oceana.
American Association for State & Local History. Glossary of Legal Terminology: An Aid to Geneologists. AASLH.
--A Glossary of Old Lamps & Lighting Devices. AASLH.
American Association of Electromyography & Electrodiagnosis. Glossary of EMG Terms. Am Assn Electromyography.
American Association of Nurserymen. Technical Glossary of Horticultural & Landscape Terminology. Am Nurserymen.
American Bankers Association. Bank Card Standards Manual Glossary. Am Bankers.
American Classical League. The Golden Greek Glossary. Am Classical.
American Congress on Surveying & Mapping. Automation Terms in Cartography. Am Congrs Survey.
--Definitions of Surveying & Associated Terms. Am Congrs Survey.
American Fisheries Society, Fish Health Section see Post, G.
American Foundation for the Blind (New York) Dictionary Catalog of the M. C. Migel Memorial Library (Hall Library). G K Hall.
American Foundrymen Society. Metalcasting Dictionary. Am Foundrymen.
American Gas Association. Glossary for the Gas Industry. Am Gas Assn.
American Geological Institute. Dictionary of Geological Terms (Anchor Pr, Anch). Doubleday.
American Heritage. Diccionario Ingles. HM.
--Exercises to Accompany American Heritage Dictionary. HM.
--The Word Book. HM.
American Heritage Editors, ed. American Heritage School Dictionary. HM.
American Heritage Staff. Concise American Heritage Dictionary. HM.
American Hotel & Motel Association. Expense & Payroll Dictionary. Am Hotel & Motel Assn.
--Uniform System of Accounts & Expense Dictionary for Small Hotels & Motels. Educ Inst Am Hotel.
American Institute of Architects. Glossary of Construction Industry Terms. Am Inst Arch.
American Institute of Industrial Engineers. Industrial Engineering Terminology Index. Inst Indus Eng.
American Institute of Real Estate Appraisers. Real Estate Appraisal Terminology. Boyce, Byrl N., ed. Natl Assoc Realtors.
American Lung Association. A Glossary on Air Pollution. Am Lung Assn.
American Medical Association. Current Medical Information & Terminology. AMA.
--Physician's Current Procedural Terminology. AMA.
American Medical Record Association. Glossary of Hospital Terms. Healthcare Fin Man Assn.
--Glossary of Hospital Terms. Am Med Record Assn.
--Introduction to Medical Terminology for Nursing Home Personnel. Am Med Record Assn.
--Medical Terminology Outline: 1980. Am Med Record Assn.
American Meteorological Society. Glossary of Meteorology. Am Meteorological.
American National Standards Institute, jt. auth. see Conveyor Equipment Manufacturers Association.
American National Standards Institute & National Fluid Power Association. Glossary of Terms for Fluid Power (Includes Supplement B93.2a) ANSI-B93.2m. Natl Fluid Power.
--Supplement to the Glossary of Terms for Fluid Power: ANSI-B93.2a. Natl Fluid Power.
American National Standards Institute. Terms & Conveyors Definitions: ANSI-CEMA No. 102, ANSI MH4.1. Material Handling.
American Nuclear Society. Glossary of Terms in Nuclear Science & Technology: ANS-9, N1.1-1976. Am Nuclear Soc.
--Trial Use Nuclear Glossary. Am Nuclear Soc.
American Numismatic Society. Dictionary & Auction Catalogues of the Library of the American Numismatic Society, New York, 7 Vols (Hall Library). G K Hall.
American Numismatic Society, New York. Dictionary & Auction Catalogues of the Library of the American Numismatic Society: First Supplement 1962-67 (Hall Library). G K Hall.
--Dictionary & Auction Catalogues of the Library of the American Numismatic Society, Second Supplement (Hall Library). G K Hall.
American Occupational Therapy Association. Occupational Therapy Product Output Reporting Systems & Uniform Terminology for Reporting Occupational Therapy Services. Am Occup Therapy.
--Uniform Terminology System for Reporting Occupational Therapy Services. Am Occup Therapy.
American Osteopathic Association. Osteopathic Terminology. Am Osteopathic.
American Petroleum Institute. Thesaurus. Am Petroleum.
American Physiological Society. Glossary of Respiratory & Gas Exchange. Am Physiological.
--Glossary of Terms for Thermal Physiology. Am Physiological.
American Psychiatric Assn., ed. A Psychiatric Glossary. Little.
American Psychiatric Association. A Psychiatric Glossary. Am Psychiatric.
American Public Transit Association. Glossary of Reliability, Availability, & Maintainability Terminology for Rail Rapid Transit. Am Public Transit.
American Society for Metals. Thesaurus of Metallurgical Terms. ASM.
American Society for Quality Control. Glossary & Tables for Statistical Quality Control. Am Soc QC.
--Terms, Symbols & Definitions for Acceptance Sampling: ANSI-ASQC Standard a2-1978. Am Soc QC.
American Society of Civil Engineers, compiled By. Definitions of Surveying & Associated Terms. Am Soc Civil Eng.
American Society of Civil Engineers & American Water Works Association, eds. Glossary: Water & Wastewater Control Engineering. Am Soc Civil Eng.
American Society of Civil Engineers, compiled by. Prospects for Metropolitan Water Management. Am Soc Civil Eng.
American Society of Heating, Refrigerating & Air-Conditioning Engineers. Automatic Control Terminology for Heating, Ventilating, Air Conditioning & Refrigeration Equipment. Am Heat Ref & Air Eng.
American Society of Heating, Refrigeration & Air Conditioning Engineers. Refrigeration Terms & Definitions. Am Heat Ref & Air Eng.
American Society of Internal Medicine. Procedural Terminology for Internists. Am Soc Intern Med.
American Society of Lubrication Engineers. Glossary of Seal Terms. Am Lubrication Engs.
American Society of Mechanical Engineers. Diaphragm Actuated Control Valve Terminology: 1961-No.112. ASME.
--Dictionary of Terms for Computer-Aided Preparation of Product Definition Data (Including Engineering Drawings) Y14.26.3-1975. ASME.
--Glossary of Mechanical Press Terms: B5.49-1977. ASME.
--Glossary of Terms Concerning Letter Symbols: Y10.1-1972. ASME.
--Glossary of Terms for Mechanical Fasteners: B18.12-1962 (R1975) ASME.
--Glossary of Terms Used in the Measurement of Fluid Flow in Pipes: ANSI-ASME MFC-1M-1979. ASME.
--Pallet Definitions & Terminology: MH1.1.2-1978. ASME.
--Terminology for Automatic Control: MC85.1-1963. ASME.
--Terminology for Pressure Relief Devices: B95.1-1977. ASME.
--Z Ninety Four Industrial Engineering Terminology: 1972 Index. ASME.
American Spice Trade Association. Glossary of Spices. Am Spice Trade.
American Water Works Association. Glossary: Water & Wastewater Control Engineering. Am Water Wks Assn.
American Water Works Association, jt. ed. see American Society of Civil Engineers.
American Welding Society. Welding Terms & Definitions. Am Welding.
Amerlinck, Teodoro. Diccionario poligloto de nombres. UNAM.
Amery & Mila. First One Thousand Words-English (Usborne-Hayes). EDC.
Amery, et al. The First Thousand Words in German. Adler Bks.
Amey, jt. ed. see Coveney.
Amey, J., jt. auth. see Coveney, James.
Amey, Julian, jt. auth. see Conveney, James.
Amich, Julian. Diccionario maritimo. Juventud.
Amkreutz, Carl. Abreviation du traitement de l'informatique. Maison Dictionnaire.
--Dictionnaire du Traitement de l'information: Francais-Allemand-Anglais. Carl Amkreutz.
--Dictionnaire du traitement de l'informatique. Maison Dictionnaire.
Ammer, Christine. Harper's Dictionary of Music (HarpT). Har-Row.
--Harper's Dictionary of Music. B&N NY.
--Musician's Handbook of Foreign Terms. Assoc-Mus.
Ammer, Christine & Ammer, Dean. Dictionary of Business & Economics. Free Pr.
Ammer, Christine & Ammer, Dean S. Dictionary of Business & Economics. Free Pr.
Ammer, Dean, jt. auth. see Ammer, Christine.
Ammer, Dean S., jt. auth. see Ammer, Christine.
Amstutz, G. Glossary of Mining Geology. Enke.
--Glossary of Mining Geology (Pub. by F. Enke). French & Eur.
Amstutz, G. C., et al. Glossary of Mining Geology. Esser, F. & Park, Won C., eds. Enke.
Ancelin-Schutzenberger, Anne. Vocabulaire des Techniques de Groupe. Epi.
Ancilli, Ermanno. Diccionario de espiritualidad: Obra Completa. Llopis, Joan, tr. Herder SA.
--Diccionario de espiritualidad: Tomo 1. Llopis, Joan, tr. Herder SA.
Ancono, Paolo, jt. auth. see Aeschlimann, E.
Ander Egg, Ezequiel. Diccionario del Trabajo Social. Organ Ofic Adm.
--Diccionario Del Trabajo Social. French & Eur.
Anderla, Georges & Schmidt-Anderla, Georgette. Business Dictionary: English-French, French-English. Intl Pubns Serv.
Andersen, Francis I. & Forbes, A. Dean. A Linguistic Concordance of Ruth & Jonah: Hebrew Vocabulary & Idiom. Biblical Res Assocs.
Anderson, Anne. Little Beginner's Dictionary. U of Toronto Pr.
Anderson, Jean, jt. auth. see Kasten, Lloyd.
Anderson, K. & Mafera, G. Italiensk-Dansk Ordbog. French & Eur.
Anderson, N. C., jt. ed. see Rudler, G.
Anderson, Olov B. A Companion Volume to R. H. Mathews' Chinese-English Dictionary. Curzon Pr.
--A Concordance to Five Systems of Transcription for Standard Chinese (Pub. by Curzon Pr England). Apt Bks.
Anderson, R. Anglo-Scandinavian Law Dictionary (Dist. by Columbia U Pr). Universitet.
Anderson, R. G. Dictionary of Data Processing & Computer Terms. Intl Ideas.
Anderson, Ralph J. Anglo-Scandinavian Law Dictionary of Legal Terms. Universitets.
Anderson, Robert & Eckhard, Ronald. Lexicon of Literary Terms. Monarch Pr.
Anderson, William, ed. Ballentine's Law Dictionary with Pronunciations. Lawyers Co-Op.
Andover, James J., ed. see Berman, Ben.
Andrade, Candido T. Dicionario Professional de Relacoes Publicas & Comunicacao & Glossario. Saraiva SA.
Andras, L. T. & Murval, M. How to Say It in Hungarian: An English-Hungarian Phrase-Book with Lists of Words. Heinman.
Andre, Yvonne. Vocabulaire de Base du Chinois Moderne. Klincksieck.
Andreassen, A. T., jt. auth. see Ansteinsson, J.
Andreichina, K., et al. Russian-Bulgarian Phraseological Dictionary. Vlasova, ed. French & Eur.
Andres, F. Diccionario espanol de sinonimos y equivalencias. Aedos.
Andres, M. F. Diccionario Espanol de Sinonimos y Equivalencias. French & Eur.
Andresen, Carl, et al. Lexikon der Alten Welt. Artemis Verlag.
Andresen, Karl. Lexikon der Alten Welt. French & Eur.

Andrews. Dictionary of the Hawaiian Language. Iaconi.

Andrews, Edmund & Andrews, Irene D. A Comparative Dictionary of the Tahitian Language: Tahitian-English with an English-Tahitian Finding List. AMS Pr.

Andrews, Irene D., jt. auth. see Andrews, Edmund.

Andrews, James B. Vocabulaire Francais-Mentonnais. Lafitte Repr.

Andrews, Lorrin. A Dictionary of the Hawaiian Language. C E Tuttle.

Andrews, Robert C., jt. auth. see Bush, Clifford L.

Andrews Heath de Zapata, Dorothy. Vocabulario de Mayathan. Dorothy Andrews Heath de Zapata.

Andrianov, B. A., et al. Rumynsko-Russkii Politekhnicheskii (Pub. by Gostekhteorizdat). Four Continent.

Andronescu, Serban. Rumanian-English Dictionary. Saphrograph.

Andronescu, Serban C. English-Romanian Dictionary. Am Inst Writing Res.

Andronov, M. S. Russko-Tamil'Skii Slovar (Pub. by Sov. Entsiklopediia). Four Continent.

Andrue Aznar, Rafael, tr. see Maury, E. A.

Andrusyshen, C. H., ed. Ukrainian-English Dictionary. U of Toronto Pr.

Andujar, Julio I. Mastering Spanish Verbs. Camino Real.

Anell, Ivar. Vad Betyder Vaxtens Latinska Namn. Forum Bok.

Angela. Daffy Definitions of Medical Terms. Vantage.

Angele, H. Four-Language Technical Dictionary of Chromatography: English, German, French, Russian. Pergamon.

Angelini, Gino. Nuovo dizionario latino-italiano. Dante Alighieri.

Angelini, Gino, et al. Dizionario latino. Dante Alighieri.

Angelis, V. De see Papias, Gramarian.

Angelo, Joseph. The Dictionary of Space Technology (Pub. by Muller Ltd). State Mutual Bk.

Angelo, Joseph A., Jr. Dictionary of Space Technology. Facts on File.
--The Dictionary of Space Technology. Van Nos Reinhold.

Angerstein, Wilfried. Lexikon der Radiologischen Technik in der Mediazin. Thieme Verlag.

Angerstein, Winifred. Lexikon der Radiologischen Technik in der Medizin. Thieme Verlag.

Angiloini, Francesco. Vocabolario milanese-italiano. Imago Libri.

Angiolini, Francesco. Vocabolario milanese-italiano coi segni per la pronuncia. Forni.

Anglin, Donald L., jt. auth. see Crouse, William H.

Angstrom, M., jt. auth. see Ruben.

Anh-Viet, Tu Dien. English-Vietnamese Dictionary (Pub. by Collets). State Mutual Bk.

Ani, Moukhtar, jt. ed. see Stowasser, Karl.

Anikin, A. V., ed. Anglo-Russkii Eknomicheskii Slovar (Pub. by Russkii Iazyk). Four Continent.

Anisimova, T. I. Posobie Po Leksicheskoi Sochetaemosti Slov Russkogo Iazyka (Pub. by Vysheishaia Shkola). Four Continent.

Anisson du Perron, J., jt. auth. see Mai-Aru.

Anisson du Perron, J., jt. auth. see Mai-Aru, Mai-Arii.

Annaratone, Alessandro & La Magna, Giovanni. Vocabolario greco-italiano. Signorelli C.

Annett, Ross H., Jr. & Samuelson, G. Allen. Dictionary of Coleoptera Collections of North America: Canada Through Panama. World Natural Hist.

Anorga, J. Nuevo diccionario bilingue Minerva. Pan Amer Pub.

Anosova, N. N., et al. Bolsho i anglo-russki i slovar. Russkii Iazyk.

Anpilogova, B. G., et al. Foundation Dictionary of Russian: Three Thousand High Semantic Frequency Words. Dover.
--Essential Russian-English Dictionary. Four Continent.

Ansteinsson, J. Norwegian Technical Dictionary: English-Norwegian. Vanous.

Ansteinsson, J. & Andreassen, A. T. Norwegian-English, English-Norwegian Technical Dictionary. Heinman.

Ansteinsson, J., ed. Norwegian Technical Dictionary: Norwegian-English. Vanous.

Antelava, G. I. Kratkii Turetsko-Russkii Slovar "Novykh Slov" (Pub. by Metsniereba). Four Continent.

Antelava, H. G. Abbreviated Turkish-Russian Dictionary of New Words. French & Eur.

Anthony, Albert S., jt. ed. see Brinton, Daniel G.

Anthony, E., jt. auth. see Snelling, Henry H.

Anthony, John D. Historical & Cultural Dictionary of the Sultanate of Oman & the Emirates of Eastern Arabia. Scarecrow.

Antignac, T., jt. auth. see Alcala-Zamora.

Antique Collector's Club. The Dictionary of British Artists: 1880-1940. Antique Collect.

Antique Collectors' Club. Pictorial Dictionary of British Nineteenth Century Furniture Design. Antique Collect.

Antiseri, D., tr. see Wittgenstein, Ludwig.

Antolinez, Crescencio. Fachworterbuch Fur Recht und Verwaltung (Pub. by Carl Heymanns Verlag KG). French & Eur.

Anton, G. Haberkamp De see Haberkamp de Anton, G.

Anton, G. Haberkamp De see Haberkamp de Anton, G. & Willers, D. H.

Anton, Haberkamp De see Haensch, G.

Antoniu, George, et al. Dictionar Juridic Penal. Editura Stiintifica.

Anzinger, Wolfgang, jt. auth. see Rauch, Eberhard.

Apel & Daniel. Harvard Brief Dictionary of Music. PB.

Apel, Max & Luds, Peter. Philosophiches Woerterbuch. De Gruyter.

Apel, Willi. Harvard Dictionary of Music (Belknap Pr). Harvard U Pr.

Apel, Willi & Daniel, Ralph T., eds. The Harvard Brief Dictionary of Music. WSP.

Apelt, M. German-English Dictionary: Art History-Archaeology. Heinman.

Apelt, M. L. German-English Dictionary: Art History, Archaeology. M Rosenberg.

Appel, L. Lexique des Fruits et Legumes. French & Eur.

Appel, Louise. Lexique Anglais-Francais Des Fruits et Legumes. French & Eur.

Appel, Reinhold. Lexikon fur Tennisfreunde. Baumann, Ernst, ed. Bucher.

Apperson, G. L. Jane Austen Dictionary. Folcroft.

Appignanesi, Richard, jt. auth. see Wesker, Arnold.

APR Industries Division of Aero Products Research, Inc., ed. The Complete CB Dictionary. Aero Products.

Apte, V. S. Practical Sanskrit-English Dictionary. Orient Bk Dist.
--Sanskrit-English, English-Sanskrit Student's Dictionary. Heinman.
--The Student's English-Sanskrit Dictionary. Orient Bk Dist.
--Student's English-Sanskrit Dictionary. Verry.

Apte, Vaman S. Practical Sanskrit-English Dictionary. Verry.

Aquilar Pelaez, V. Diccionario Geografico de Guatemala. Intl Guatemala.

Aquino-Bermudez, et al. Mi Diccionario Ilustrado: Edicion Bilingue. Lothrop.

Aquistapace, Jean N. Diccionario de la politica. Magisterio Esp.

Aquistapace, Jean-Noel. Diccionario De la Politica. French & Eur.

Arakin, T. English-Russian Dictionary (Pub. by Collets). State Mutual Bk.

Arakin, V. D. English-Russian Dictionary. French & Eur.
--Norvezhsko-Russkii Slovar (Pub. by GINS). Four Continent.

Arakin, V. D., et al, eds. Anglo-Russkii Slovar (Pub. by Russkii Iazyk). Four Continent.

Arana, Evangelina & Swadesh, Mauricio. Diccionario analitico de Mampruli. INAH.

Arana Soto, Salvador. Diccionario de Temas Regionalistas En la Poesia Puertorriquena. French & Eur.

Araushkin, N. S., et al. Karmannyi Kitaisko-Russkii Slovar (Pub. by Russkii Iazyk). Four Continent.

Arbelaiz, Juan J. Diccionario Vasco-Castellano & Castellano-Vasco. Encicl Vasca.

Arbelaiz, Juan Jose. Diccionario Vasco-Castellano & Castellano-Vasco de Voces Comunes. Encicl Vasca.

Arcane Order. Encyclopedia of Arcane Wisdom. Arcane Order.

Arce, jt. auth. see Alvisi.

Archibald, E. H. Dictionary of Sea Painters. Antique Collect.
--Dictionary of Sea Painters. Apollo.

Ardener, Shirley, ed. Defining Females: The Nature of Women in Society. Halsted Pr.

Areisin, L. & Mueller-Hegemann, A., eds. Jugendlexikon Jugend zu Zweit. Bibl Inst Leipzig.

Aresin, L. & Mueller-Hegemann, A., eds. Jugendlexikon Junge Ehe. Bibl InstLeipzig.

Argall, jt. auth. see Wyllie.

Argall, George O., Jr., jt. ed. see Wyllie, R. J.

Argaw, Makonnen. Lexique Queze-Amharique. Publ. Orientalistes France.

Argentina, ed. Diccionario indice analitico. Ediar.

Arias Llamas, Inocencio F., et al. Diccionario periodistico de Futbol. Organ Ofic Adm.

Arias Truillo, Bernardo. Diccionario de emociones. Berout.

Arimany Coma, Miguel. Diccionari Catala General Usual. French & Eur.
--Diccionari Escolar Catala Arimany. French & Eur.
--Diccionari Manual Castella-Catala. French & Eur.
--Diccionari Manual Catala-Castella. French & Eur.
--Diccionari Manual Catala-Castella i Castella-Catala. French & Eur.
--Diccionari Practic Castella-Catala, Catala-Castella. French & Eur.
--Diccionari Practic Catala-Frances. French & Eur.
--Diccionari Usual Catala-Castella i Castella-Catala. French & Eur.

Arimany Coma, Miquel. Diccionari Basic Catala-Castella, Castella-Catala. French & Eur.

Arisi Rota, Umberto. Dizionario aziendale. Buffetti.

Aristos. Diccionario Ilustrado De la Lengua Espanola. French & Eur.

Arlt, Reiner, et al, eds. Lexikon Recht der Landwirtschaft der Deutschen Demokratischen Republik. Staatsdruk.

Armanet, J. & Becquer, A. Annales des Mines: Lexique Technique Allemand-Francais. French & Eur.

Armas Chitty, Jose. A. see De Armas Chitty, Jose A.

Armbruster, C. H. Dongolese Nubian: A Grammar. Cambridge U Pr.
--Dongolese Nubian, a Lexicon. Cambridge U Pr.

Armengol, Joseph, et al, eds. English-Spanish Guide for Medical Personnel. Med Exam.

Arms Control Association. A Glossary of Arms Control Terms. Arms Control.

Armstrong, Terry, et al, eds. A Reader's Hebrew-English Lexicon of the Old Testament: (Genesis-Deuteronomy) Zondervan.

Arnal, Jacques. L Argot de Police. Euredif.

Arnal Cavero, Pedro. Vocabulario del Alto-Aragones de Alquezar & Pueblos Proximos (CSIC). Inst. Antonio de Nebrija.

Arnaldi, G. Dizionario dei termini storiografici. Zanichelli.

Arnau, Frank. Universal Film Lexicon. Gordon Pr.

Arnaud, Jean F. Diccionario De la Electronica. French & Eur.
--Dictionnaire de l'electronique. Larousse.

Arnaud, Jean-Francois. Diccionario de la electronica. Plaza Janes.

Arnaudon, Jean-Claude. Dictionnaire du Blues. Filipacchi.

Arnold, Hans J. Stellwerksdienst. Transpress Verlag fur Verkehrswesen.

Arnold, Wilhelm, et al, eds. Lexikon der Psychologie. Herder.
--Lexikon der Psychologie: Bd 2, Graphologie-Prompling. Herder.
--Lexikon der Psychologie: Bd 3, Propaganda-Zz. Herder.
--Lexikon der Psychologie: Bd 1, A-Gewissen. Herder.

Arnold, Winifred H. Glossary of a Thousand & One Terms Used in Conchology. Shell Cab.

Arnould, M. & Zubini, F. English-French Petroleum Dictionary (Pub. by Graham & Trotman England). State Mutual Bk.

Arnould, Michel & Zubini, Fabio. English-French Petroleum Dictionary. Crane-Russak Co.

Arogones, Pablo. Diccionario basico. Mayfe.

Arrighi, Cletto. Dizionario milanese-italiano. Hoepli.

Arroyo De La Cuesta, Felipe. Vocabulary or Phrase Book of the Mutsun Language of Alta California. AMS Pr.

Arroyo Marcos, Gloria, tr. see Bergfeld, Rainer.

Arroyo Marcos, Gloria, tr. see Ottokar, Peter.

Arsenijevic, N. S. German-Serbocroatian Electrotechnical Dictionary. French & Eur.

Arslanian, G. T., et al. Russko-Arabskii Meditsinskii Slovar (Pub. by Russkii Iazyk). Four Continent.

Artella, Eduard. Vocabulari Catala-Castella. Barcino Edit.

Artells, Eduard. Vocabulari Castella-Catala. Barcino Edit.
--Vocabulari Castella-Catala. French & Eur.
--Vocabulari Catala-Castella. French & Eur.

Arthur, William. An Etymological Dictionary of Family Christian Names. Gordon Pr.

Artiukhov, M. G., et al. Bolgarsko-Russkii Voennyi Slovar (Pub. bu Voenizdat). Four Continent.

Artobolevskii, I. I., ed. Politekhnicheskii Slovar (Pub. by Sov Entsiklopediia). Four Continent.

Arturo del Hoyo, Asesor, ed. see Sainz de Robles, Federico C.

Arumaa, P., et al. Russko-Estonskii Slovar (Pub. by Valgus). Four Continent.

Arunabharathi, N. Glossary of Linguistics. Tamil Nuulagam.

Arundel De Conde, Gerard. Dictionnaire des Anoblis Normands. G. Arundel De Conde.

Arva, Gyorgy. Etlapiras. Kozgazdasagi.

Aschersleben, Karl. Handlexikon der Schulpaedogogik. Kohlhammer.

Aschiero, Hipolito F. Diccionario de Homofonos Castellaros. French & Eur.

Aschiero, Hipolito R. Diccionario de Homofonos Castellans: Repertorio Alfabetico de Adjetivos, Verbos & su Correcta Ortografia. Edit Victor Leru.

Aschmann, Bessie, jt. auth. see Aschmann, Herman.

Aschmann, Herman & Aschmann, Bessie. Diccionario Totonaco De Papantla. Summer Inst Ling.

Aschmann, Herman P. Vocabulario Totonaco de la Sierra. Summer Inst Ling.

Ashkharumov, R. T., et al. Russko-Armianskii Politekhnicheskii Slovar (Pub. by An Arm SSR). Four Continent.

Ashley, Richard & Duggal, Heidi. Dictionary of Nutrition. PB.

Asimov, Isaac. Words of Science. HM.
--Words of Science & the History Behind Them (Ment). NAL.

Askim, P. Norwegian-English, English-Norwegian Maritime-Technical Dictionary. Heinman.

Asmussen, H. Ordbog for Rensning Vask og Rengoring. Tek Inst.

Asrhants, Konstantin G., jt. auth. see Matveev, Vladimir S.

Assaran, Hassan. Arabic-English Dictionary of Basic Scientific & Technical Terms: "Al Mustalah". Intl Bk Ctr.
Assfalg, Julius & Krueger, P. Kleines Woerterbuch Des Christlichen Orients (Pub. by Harrassowitz). French & Eur.
Assiouly, E. Banking & Financial Dictionary: English-French-Arabic. French & Eur.
Association of Desk & Derrick Clubs of America. D & D Standard Oil Abbreviator. Pennwell Pub.
Association Technique de Traitement Thermique. Glossaire du Traitement Thermique. Pyc.
Ast, Friedrich. Lexicon Platonicum. B Franklin.
Astone, Nicholas A., jt. auth. see Martin, Julian A.
Atanassova, T., et al. Bulgarian-English Dictionary (Pub. by Collets). State Mutual Bk.
Athenstaedt, William. Elektrotechnik Elektronik. VEB Verlag Technik.
Atkins, B. T., et al, eds. Collins Robert Dictionary: French-English-English-French. Duval, A. & Milnet, R. C. Collins Pubs.
Atkins, Beryl, jt. auth. see McArthur, Tom.
Atkins, Beryl T., et al. Collins-Robert French-English, English-French dictionary. W Collins Sons.
--Collins-Robert French-English Dictionary. W Collins Pubs.
Atkinson, David. Menu French. Oxford Poly Pr.
Atnassova, T., et al. Bulgarian-English Dictionary. French & Eur.
Attal, Jean-Pierre. Business English Vocabulary. Edns Organisation.
Attiyate, Y. H. Lexique CN: Anglais-Allemand-Francais. Iron Age Metalworking Int.
Atwood, E. Bagby. The Regional Vocabulary of Texas. U of Tex Pr.
Atzeni, E. Vocabolario domestico sardo-italiano. Forni.
Auandani, Guy, jt. auth. see Laeng, Mauro.
Aubakirov, Z., et al. Russko-Kazakhskii Tolkovyi Geograficheskii Slovar (Pub. by Nauka). Four Continent.
Aubert, Henri. Diccionario de Mitologia. French & Eur.
Aubert, Roger & Van Cauwenberg. Dictionnaire d'histoire & de Geographie Ecclesiastiques. Letouzey & Ane.
--Dictionnaire d'Histoire et du Geographie Ecclesiastiques. French & Eur.
Aubert, Roger, et al. Dictionnaire d'histoire & de Geographie Ecclesiastiques. Letouzey & Ane.
Aubert de la Chenaye-Desbois, Francais. Dictionnaire de la Noblesse. French & Eur.
Aufrecht, Walter E. & Hurd, John. A Synoptic Concordance of Aramaic Inscriptions. Biblical Res Assocs.
Auger, Jules. Vocabulaire Architecturale. Montreal P. U.
Auger, Pierre & Rousseau, Louis-Jean. Lexique Anglais-Francais De L'industrie Miniere, 1. French & Eur.
Augst, Gerhard. Lexikon zur Wortbildung. Narr.
Auld, Douglas & Bannock, Graham. The American Dictionary of Economics. Facts on File.
Aulie, Evelyn W. De see Aulie, H. W. & De Aulie, Evelyn W.
Aulie, H. W. & De Aulie, Evelyn W. Diccionario Ch'ol-Espanol. Inst Ling Ver.
Aurenche, Oliver, ed. Dictionnaire Illustre Multilingue de l'Architecture du Proche Orient Ancien. Boccard.
Aureneche, Olivier. Dictionnaire Illustre Multilinque De L'architecture du Procher-Orient Ancien. French & Eur.
Aurigemma, L., tr. see Jung, C. Gustav.
Aurobindo. Glossary of Terms in Sri Aurobindo's Writings (Pub. by Sri Aurobindo Ashram Trust India, Pub. by Sri Aurobindo Ashram Trust India). Auromere.
Aurobindo, Sri. Dictionary of Sri Aurobindo's Yoga. Pandit, Sri M., ed. Lotus Light.
Aurousseau, Paul. International Hospital Vade Mecum & English, French, Spanish Glossary. Editions Sedip F.Galula.
Aurox, Sylvain & Weil, Yvonne. Nouveau vocabulaire des etudes philosophiques. Hachette-Jeunesse.
Austeda, Franz. Lexikon der Philosophie. Hollinek.
Austridan, Y., ed. Diccionario Hebreo-Castallano: Castellano-Hebreo. French & Eur.
Autenrieth, Georg. A Homeric Dictionary for Schools & Colleges. Flagg, Isaac, ed. Keep, Robert P., tr. U of Okla Pr.
Auvray, Louis, jt. auth. see De La Chavignerie, Emile B.
Averbach. Diccionario de electronica, proceso de datos. Iber Euro Edns.
Avery, Robert, et al, eds. Turkish, English-English, Turkish Dictionary (the Redhouse Portable Dictionary) Heinman.
Avis, Walter S. Canadian Intermediate Dictionary. U of Toronto Pr.
Avis, Walter S., et al. Canadian Junior Dictionary. U of Toronto Pr.
--A Dictionary of Canadianisms. U of Toronto Pr.
Avramenko, Boris I. Ital'iansko-Russkii i Rusko-Ital'ianskii Stroitel'nyi Slovar. Russkii Iazyk.
Avril, J. T. Dictionnaire Provencal-Francais. Slatkine.
--Vocabulaire Francais-Provencal: Dictionnaire Provencal-Francais. Slatkine.
Awang, Sudjai H. & Yusoff, Khan. Kamus Lengkap: Penyunting. Pustaka Antara.
Axelsen, J., jt. ed. see Vinterberg, H.
Ayala Lopez, Manuel, jt. auth. see Martinez Burgos, Matias.
Ayers, Donald M. Bioscientific Terminology. U of Ariz Pr.
Aymard Lapalu, Nicole. Safety at Work & Pollution Control. Elp.
Azevedo, Domingos De see De Azevedo, Domingos.
Azkue, Resurreccion M. Diccionario Vasco-Espanol-Frances. French & Eur.
Azzaretti, M. Dictionnaire International d'abreviations Scientifiques et Techniques. Maison Dictionnaire.
--Dictionnaire International d'abreviation Scientifiques et Techniques. Maison Dictionnaire.
Azzaretti, Michel. Dictionnaire International D'abreviations Scientigiques & Techniques. Maison Dictionnaire.
Azzolini, Giambattista. Vocabolario vernacolo-italiano pei destrette roveretano e trentino. Manfrini.

B

Ba'Alabaki, Munir. English-Arabic Pocket Dictionary: Al-Mawrid Al Quareb. Intl Bk Ctr.
Ba'Albaki, Munir. English-Arabic Dictionary: Al-Mawrid. Intl Bk Ctr.
--English-Arabic Dictionary: Al-Mawrid. Intl Bk Ctr.
--English-Arabic Dictionary: Al-Mawrid Al-Waset. Intl Bk Ctr.
--English-Arabic Pocket Dictionary: Al Mawrid. Intl Bk Ctr.
--English-Arabic Student Dictionary: Al-Muyassar. Intl Bk Ctr.
--A Modern English-Arabic Dictionary. Intl Bk Ctr.
Baar, A. Russisch Woordenboek. Coutinho.
Babcock, Deutsche, et al, eds. Woerterbuch der Dampferzeugungstechnik-Dictionary of Steam Generator Engineering. Intl Pubns Serv.
Babecki, Jerzy. Slownik Lekarski Lacinsko-Polski. Panstwowe Zaklad W.
--Slownik Tekarski Polsko-Lacinksi. Panstwowe Zaklad W.
Babecki, Jerzy & Maksys, Anna. Slownik Skrotow w Medycynie i Naukach Pokrewnych. Panstwowe Zaklad W.
Babeliowsky, J. K. Basiswoordenlijst Latijn. Staatsdruk.
Bach, H. & Florant, J. Luftartsteknisk Ordbog Engelsk-Dansk. French & Eur.
Bachellery, E., jt. auth. see Vendryes, Joseph.
Back, H., et al. Dictionary of Politics & Economics. French & Eur.
Backe, Torild, et al. Concise Swedish-English Glossary of Legal Terms. Rothman.
Backeberg, Curt. Cactus Lexicon (Pub. by RHS Ent England). State Mutual Bk.
Backhaus. Woerterbuch Kristallografie. Verlag Harri Deutsch.
Bacmeister, Arnold. Das Grosse Lexikon der Fischwaid (Pub. by Jfland). French & Eur.
Bacon, F., et al. Petit Lexique de la Manutentio n. Anglais-Francais. Chartrand, P., ed. French & Eur.
Bacquet, Paul. Le Vocabulaire Anglais. PUF.
Badawi, A. A Dictionary of the Social Sciences. Lib Liban.
Badawi, Zaki, compiled by. A Dictionary of the Social Sciences. Intl Bk Ctr.
Badellino, Oreste. Dizionario italiano-latino. Rosenberg & Sel.
--Dizionario italiano-latino: Edizione speciale. Rosenberg & Sel.
Bader, Oliver & Theret, Michel. Diccionario enciclopedico de metalurgia: Espanol-frances, frances-espanol y espanol-engles, engles-espanol. ETA.
--Diccionario Enciclopedico de Metalurgia. French & Eur.
Baeckbom, Roy, jt. auth. see Eriksson, Erick R.
Baeckmann, Walter G. von see Von Baeckmann, Walter G.
Baeckmann, Walter Von see Osteroth, Dieter & Von Baeckmann, Walter G.
Bagder, George P. An English-Arabic Lexicon. Intl Bk Ctr.
Bagma, jt. auth. see Bljach.
Bagma, B. T., jt. auth. see Bljach, I. S.
Bagma, L. T. Kratkii Nemetsko-Russkii Vneshnetorgovyi Slovar (Pub. by Vneshtorgizdat). Four Continent.
Bagonova-Sidlova, Milota. Dictionar Portrativ Roman-Slovac, Slovac-Roman. SNTC.
Bagster, Samuel. Bagster's Keyword Concordance. Revell.
Bahri, Hardev. Bahri's Law Dictionary. Haredeva Bahari.
--Comprehensive English-Hindi Dictionary. Intl Pubns Serv.
Baihaki, Achmad, et al. Dafoar islilah pertanian. Pustaka Antara.
Bailentyne, D. W. & Walker, L. E., trs. Diccionario de leyes y efectos cientificos. Leru.
Bailey, Eric V. A Glossary of Spanish Philatelic Terms. Intl Guatemala.
Bailey, Harold W. Dictionary of Khotan Saka. Cambridge U Pr.
Bailey, I. E. Dansk-Engelsk Handels-og Fagordbog. French & Eur.
Bailey, Nathan. Universal Etymological English Dictionary. Adler.
Bailie, J. M., ed. The Hamlyn Crossword dictionary. Hamlyn Pub.
Bailie, John, ed. The Crossword Dictionary. Newnes Bks.
--The Good Spelling Dictionary. Newnes Bks.
--Pocket Crossword Dictionary. Newnes Bks.
Bailleul, Charles. Petit Dictionnaire-Bambara-Francais Francais-Bambara (Pub. by Avebury England). Humanities.
Bailliere, et al. Dizionario medico. Edi Ermes.
Bailly, Anatole. Dictionnaire Abrege Grec-Francais. Hachette-Jeunesse.
--Dictionnaire Abrege Grec-Francais. French & Eur.
--Dictionnaire Grec-Francais. Hachette-Jeunesse.
--Dictionnaire Grec-Francais. French & Eur.
Bailly, R. Dictionnaire des synonymes. Larousse.
Bailly, Victor. Dictionnaire Orthographique. Plantyn Edns.
Baird, J. Arthur, ed. see Morton, A. Q., et al.
Baird, J. Arthur, ed. see Morton, A. Q. & Michaelson, Sidney.
Baird, J. Arthur, ed. see Radday, Yehuda T. & Leb, G. M.
Bajec, A. & Kalan, P. Dizionario Italian-Slovar. French & Eur.
Bajic, B., et al. Technical-Economical Dictionary for Business Purposes. French & Eur.
Bakalla. Dictionary of Modern Linguistic Terms: English-Arabic, Arabic-English. Intl Bk Ctr.
Baker, A. E. & Tennyson, Alfred. Concordance to the Devil & the Lady. Tennyson, Charles, ed. Kraus Repr.
Baker, H. H. A Classified French Vocabulary. Harrap.
Baker, Kenneth, jt. auth. see Brugger, Walter.
Baker, Th. Dictionary of Musical Terms: Containing an English-Italian Vocabulary for Composers & Students. Saphrograph.
Baker, Theodore. Dictionary of Musical Terms. AMS Pr.
--Dictionary of Musical Terms. Assoc-Mus.
--Schirmer Pronouncing Pocket Manual of Musical Terms. Assoc-Mus.
Baker, W. M. Bell's Acrostic Dictionary. Gale.
Bakos, Ferenc, et al. Idegen Szavak Szotara. Terra.
Bakos, Forenc & Fabian, Pal. Idegen Szavak Szotara. Terra.
Balaguer, Miguel. Diccionario Griego-Espanol. French & Eur.
Balagur, Miguel. Diccionario griego-espanol. Bibliografica.
Balay, Maurice. Lexique Informatique. Bordas-Dunod.
--Lexique Informatique. French & Eur.
Balbastre & Ferrer, Josep. Diccionari tecnic de l'automovil. Portic.
Baldelli, Ignazio & Mazzetti, Alberto. Vocabolario minimo della lingua italiana per stranieri. Monnier.
Baldelli, Ignazio, et al. Vocabolario minimo della lingua italiana per stranieri con dizionarietto somalo. Monnier.
Baldinger, Kurt. Dictionnaire Etymologique de l'ancien Francais. Laval P. U.
--Dictionnaire Etymologique de l'ancien Francais. Laval P. U.
Baldinger, Kurt & Straka, Georges. Dictionnaire Etymologique de l'ancien Francais, 1. Klincksieck.
Baldinger, Kurt, et al. Dictionnaire Etymologique de l'ancien Francais. Laval P. U.
Baldwin, James M. Dictionary of Philosophy & Psychology. Incl. Vols. 1 & 2; Vol. 3., 2 Pts. Bibliography of Philosophy, Psychology and Cognate Subjects. Peter Smith.
Baldwin, James M., et al. Dictionary of Philosophy & Psychology. Gordon Pr.
Balet, Robert, jt. auth. see Favre, Christophe.
Baleyte, Jean, ed. see Quemner, T. A.
Ball, Robert H., jt. auth. see Bowman, Walter P.
Balla, M. J., jt. auth. see Podveska, M. L.
Ballard, Edward B., et al, eds. A Technical Glossary of Horticultural & Landscape Terminology. Horticult Research.
Ballard, Richard. Talking Dictionary. Ulrich.
Ballarin Cornel, Angel. Vocabulario de Benasque. Fernando el Catolico.
Ballentyne, D. W. & Lovett, D. R. Dictionary of Named Effects: Laws in Chemistry, Physics & Mathematics (Pub. by Chapman & Hall England). Methuen Inc.
Ballentyne, D. W. & Walker, L. E. Diccionario de Leyes y Efectos Cientificos En Quimica-Fisica Matematicas. French & Eur.
Ballereau, Emile & Bouquet, Georges. Le Vocabulaire Vivant. SUDEL.
Ballesteros, Luis W. Diccionario Tecnico De Electromecanica: Ingles-Espanol. Intl Learn Syst.

Ballesteros Weis, L. Diccionario Tecnico de electromecanica: Ingles-espanol. Limusa.
Ballot, Marc M. & Fougerouse. Le Vocabulaire par la Vie des Mots. Lavauzelle.
Balmas, E. & Wagner, R. L. Vocabolario del francese moderno. Ist Geo Agostini.
Balmas, Enea. Dizionario pratico della lingua francese. Ist Geog Agostini.
--Dizionario pratico della lingua francese. Ghisetti & Corvi.
--Vocabolario del francese moderno. Ghisetti & Corvi.
Balter, Deborah J. Primary Aeronautical Language Manual. Aviation.
Banca Mas Sarda, Servicio de Estudios. Diccionario de Banca & Borsa: Catala-Castella-Diccionario de Banca & Bolsa. Alba.
Bander, Edward J. Dictionary of Selected Legal Terms & Maxims. Oceana.
Band-Kuzmany, K. R. Glossary of the Theatre. Elsevier.
Banerji, Sures C. Glossary of Smrti Literature. Verry.
Bang, Jorgen. Femmedordbog. Berlingske Forlag.
Baniecki, Henryk. Encyklopedia Techniki. Wydawnictwa Naukowo.
Banitt, Menahem. Le Glossaire de Bale. Brill.
Bank-Lexikon. Handwoerterbuch fur der Bank & Sparkassenwesen. Gabler.
Banker, John, et al. Bahnar Dictionary. Summer Inst Ling.
Banks, Charles E. Topographical Dictionary of Two Thousand Eighty-Five English Emigrants to New England, 1620-1650. Genealog Pub.
Bannock, Graham, et al. Dizionario di economia. Laterza.
Bannock, Graham, jt. auth. see Auld, Douglas.
Bantas, T., jt. auth. see Levitchi, V.
Banvard, Paul & Kuhn, Pierre. Vocabulaire Progressif de l'allemand. CDU.
Bar, E. Dictionnaire des Synonymes. Garnier.
Baraga, R. R. Dictionary of the Otchipwe Language. Ross.
Barakat, Gamal. English-Arabic Dictionary of Diplomacy & Related Terminology. Intl Bk Ctr.
Baranowski, Zdzislaw. The International Horseman's Dictionary (Dist. by Sporting Book Center). J A Allen.
--Woerterbuch Pferd und Reiter. French & Eur.
Barantsev, K. T. Anglo-Ukrainskii Frazeologicheskii Slovar (Pub. by Radianska Shkola). Four Continent.
Baravikas, V., et al. Kratkii Shkol'Nyi Anglo-Litovskii i Litovsko-Angliiskii Slovar (Pub. by Shviesa). Four Continent.
Baravykas, V., jt. auth. see Piesarskas, B.
Barbaud, Roger. Dictionnaire des Delais de Procedure. Dalloz.
Barbeau, Victor. Dictionnaire Bibliographique du Canada. Acad Can Fr.
Barber, Bruce T. Designer's Dictionary Two. Signs of Times.
Barber, Edward A. & Lockwood, Luke V. The Ceramic Furniture & Silver Collectors' Glossary. Da Capo.
Barber, Edwin A. The Ceramic Collectors' Glossary. Da Capo.
Barberousse, Michel. Dictionnaire de la Voile. Seuil.
--Dizionario della vela. Mursia S.
Barberousse, Michel, ed. Dictionnaire de la Voile. French & Eur.
Barbier. Dictionnaire Des Ouvrages Anonymes. French & Eur.
Barbier, et al. Diccionario tecnico ilustrado de edificacion y obras publicas. G Gili.
Barbier, Jean-Philippe & Hugues, Francois-Claude. Dictionnaire des Maladies. Heures de France.
Barbier, Maurice. Diccionario Tecnico Ilustrado De Edificacion y Obras Publicas. French & Eur.
--Dictionnaire Technique du Batiment & des Travaux Publics. Eyrolles.
Barbier, Maurice & Cadiergues, Roger. Dictionnaire Technique du Batiment & des Travaux Publics. Eyrolles.
Barbier, Paul. Lexique d'Erquinghem-Lys. Ste. Linguistique Picarde.
Barbier De Meynard, Achille. Dictionnaire Geographique, Historique & Literaire: La Perse & des Contrees Adjacentes. Philo Pr.
Barbudo Duarte, Enrique, jt. auth. see Garcia de Paredes y Castro, Jose.
Barca, Luciano. Dizionario di politica economica. Editori Riuniti.
Barcelo, J. L. Vocabulario de Estadistica. Hispano Europa.
Barcelo, J. R. Diccionario Terminologico de Quimica. Alhambra.
--Spanish-English, English-Spanish Chemical Vocabulary. Heinman.
Barcelo, Jose R. Diccionario Terminologico de Quimica. Edit Alhambra.
Barcelo Matutano, Jose. Diccionario terminologico de Quimaca. Alhambra.
Barcelo Matutano, Jose R. Diccionario Terminologico de Quimica. French & Eur.
Barcia, Roque. Diccionario de Sinonimos. Oasis SA.
--Sinonimus Castellanos. French & Eur.
Barczi, Geza. A Pesti Nyelv. Magyar Tarsasag.
Bardsley, C. W. A Dictionary of English & Welsh Surnames with Special American Instances (Pub.by Heraldry Today England). State Mutual Bk.
Bardsley, Charles W. A Dictionary of English & Welsh Surnames with Special American Instances. Genealog Pub.
Barella Campos, Ana G., jt. auth. see Barella Campos, Juana.
Barella Campos, Juana & Barella Campos, Ana G. Diccionario De Refranes. French & Eur.
Barfield, John, jt. auth. see Craven, Henry.
Barham, I. H. Vocabulary & Science Structure of Maori Children. Nzcer.
Baried, Baroroh, ed. Kamus Istilah Filologi. Universitas Gadjah Mada.
Baril, Jacques. Dictionnaire de Danse. French & Eur.
Barker, John. Dictionary of Soil Mechanics & Foundation Engineering. Longman.
Barker, M. A., et al. Urdu-English Vocabulary: Student's Dictionary. Spoken Lang Serv.
Barker, M. L. & Homeyer, H., eds. The Pocket Oxford German Dictionary. Incl. Pt. 1. German-English; Pt. 2. English-German. Carr, C. T., compiled by.. Oxford U Pr.
Barker, Ronnie. Fletcher's Book of Rhyming Slang (Pub. by Pan Bks). State Mutual Bk.
Barkhudarov, S. G., ed see Potikha, Z. A.
Barkhudarova. Dictionnaire Orthographique de la Langue Russe. Mir.
Barlow, A. R. English-Kikuyu Dictionary. Benson, T. G., tr. Oxford U Pr.
Barlow, Harold & Morgenstern, Sam, eds. Dictionary of Musical Themes. Crown.
--Dictionary of Opera & Song Themes. Crown.
Barme, Geremie, jt. auth. see Lee, Bennett.
Barnard, Helen. Advanced English Vocabulary. Newbury Hse.
--Advanced English Vocabulary. Newbury Hse.
--Advanced English Vocabulary. Newbury Hse.
--Advanced English Vocabulary. Newbury Hse.
Barnes, Robert J., jt. ed. see Hagelman, Charles W., Jr.
Barnett, Franklin. Dictionary of Prehistoric Indian Artifacts of the American Southwest. Northland.
Barney, Stephen A., et al. Word-Hoard: An Introduction to Old English Vocabulary. Yale U Pr.
Barnhart, Clarence. Dictionary of New English. Colin.
Barnhart, Clarence L., ed. Scott, Foresman Advanced Dictionary. Doubleday.
--Scott, Foresman Beginning Dictionary. Doubleday.
--Scott, Foresman Intermediate Dictionary. Doubleday.
--Thorndike Barnhart Handy Dictionary. Bantam.
Barnhart, Clarence L. & Barnhart, Robert K., eds. The World Book Dictionary. World Bk.
Barnhart, Clarence L., et al. Second Barnhart Dictionary of New English (HarpT). Har-Row.
Barnhart, Robert K., jt. ed. see Barnhart, Clarence L.
Baronowski, Zdzislaw. Woerterbuch Pferd & Reiter. Pitman Bks.
Barraine, Raymond. Nouveau Dictionnaire de Droit et de Sciences Economiques. French & Eur.
Barrera Vasquez, Alfredo. Diccionario Maya Cordemex Maya-Espanol. Porrua.
Barrett, A. J. Mammalian Proteases: A Glossary & Bibliography: Vol. 2, Exopeptidases. McDonald, J. K., ed. Acad Pr.
Barrett, Alan & McDonald, J. Ken. Mammalian Proteases: a Glossary & Bibliography: Vol. 1: Endopeptidases. Acad Pr.
Barrett, Paul, et al, eds. Concordance to Darwin's "Origin of Species". Cornell U Pr.
Barrett, W. A., jt. auth. see Stainer, J.
Barrett, W. A., jt. auth. see Stainer, John.
Barrillon, Raymond. Dictionnaire de la Constitution: Les Institutions de la Ve Republique. Cujas.
--Droit Administratif. Pr Univ Fr.
Barry, W. R., ed. Architectural, Construction, Manufacturing & Engineering Glossary of Terms. Am Assn Cost Engineers.
Bars, Alain le see Rassat, Patrick & Le Bars, Alain.
Bart, Pauline. Social Structure & Vocabularies of Discomfort: What Happened to Female Hysteria. Know Inc.
Barth, Heinrich, ed. Collection of Vocabularies of Central African Languages (F Cass Co). Biblio Dist.
Barthe, Roger. Lexique Francais-Occitan. Amis Langue.
--Lexique Francais-Occitan. R. Barthe.
--Lexique Occitan-Francais. Amis Langue.
--Lexique Occitan-Francais. Lemouzi.
Barthelemy, Adrien. Dictionnaire Arabe-Francais: Dialectes de Syrie. Geuthner.
Bartlett, John R. Dictionary of Americanism: A Glossary of Words & Phrases, Usually Regarded As Peculiar to the United States (Regency). Scholarly.
Bartminska, Izabela. Nazwiska Obce w Jezyku Polskim. Panstwowe Zaklad W.
Bartminska, Izabela, et al. Narwiska Obce w Jezyku Polskim. Panstwowe Zaklad W.
Bartnicka, Barbara & Sinielnikoff, Roxana. Slownik Podstawowy Jezyka Polskiego dia Cudzoziemcow. Wydaw-a U. W.
Bartnicka, Barbara, et al. Slownik Podstawowy Jezyka Polskiego dia Cudzoziemcow. Wydaw-a UW.
Barzun, Jacques, ed. see Follett, Wilson.
Basiaux, jt. auth. see Pierret, Albert.
Basin, O. I. Filatelisticheskii Slovar (Pub. by Sviaz). Four Continent.
Basinski, Antoni. Slownik Polskiej Terminologii Chemicznej. Wydawnictwa Naukowo.
Baskin, Wade. Dictionary of Satanism. Citadel Pr.
Baskin, Wade, jt. ed. see Wedeck, Harry E.
Bassegoda Muste, B. Diccionario poliglota de la arquitectura. Imported Bks.
Bassegoda Muste, Buenaventura. Nuevo Glosario, Diccionario Poliglota de la Arquitectura. French & Eur.
Basselman, James A., jt. auth. see Farrall, Arthur W.
Bassoli, jt. auth. see Gaft.
Bassoli, F., jt. auth. see Gareff, G.
Bastian, Hans D., ed. Lexikon fuer Junge Erwachsene. Kreuz Verlag.
Bastian, Hartmut. Ullstein Lexikon der Pflanzenwelt (Pub. by Ullstein Verlag VA). French & Eur.
--Ullstein Lexikon der Tierwelt (Pub. by Ullstein Verlag/VVA). French & Eur.
Bastin. Diccionario de psicologia sexual. Herder SA.
Bastin, G. Diccionario De Psicologia Sexual. French & Eur.
Bastin, Georges. Dizionario di psicologia sessuale. La Scuola.
Batarec, Evelyn. Lexique des Termes de Prothese Dentaire. Prelat.
--Lexique des Termes de Prothese Dentaire. French & Eur.
Bates, Natica I., ed. see Murray, G. W.
Bates, Robert L. & Jackson, Julia A., eds. Glossary of Geology. Am Geol.
Bates, Scott. Dictionnaire des Mots Libres d'Apollinaire. Filipacchi.
Bathe, Basel & Villiers, Alan. The Visual Encyclopedia of Nautical Terms Under Sail. Crown.
Battista, O. A. Dictionary of Quotoons. Research Servs Corp.
--Quotoons: A Speakers Dictionary (Perigee). Putnam Pub Group.
Battles, Ford L. & Miller, Charles. A Concordance to Calvin's Institutio. C E Barbour.
Battro, A. M. Dictionnaire d'Epistemologie Genetique (Pub. by Reidel Holland). Kluwer Academic.
Batz, Laila. Banking Language. Running Pr.
Baubec, A., et al. Dictionar Turc-Roman. Editura Stiintifica.
Baudoin, Anne-Marie. Vocabulaire Francais-Anglais De L'automobile: Le Moteur. French & Eur.
--Vocabulaire Francais-Anglais de l'automobile. Quebec Off.
Baudouin, Alphonse. Glossaire du Patois de la Foret de Clairvaux. Slatkine.
Baudry, Gerard H. Dictionnaire des Correspondants de Tellhard. G. Baudry.
Bauer. Diccionario De Teologia Biblica. French & Eur.
Bauer, Johannes B. Bibeltheologisches Woerterbuch (Pub. by Styria). French & Eur.
Bauer, Karl W. & Hengst, Heinz. Kritische Stichwoerter zur Kinderkultur. W Fink.
Bauer, Walter. Griechisch-Deutsches Woerterbuch zu den Schriften des Neuen Testaments und der uebrigen urchristlichen Literatur. De Gruyter.
Baulig, Henri. Vocabulaire Franco-Anglo-Allemand de Geomorphologie. Strasbourg, U.
Baumann, Ernst, ed. see Appel, Reinhold.
Baumgart, Arturo E. von see Von Baumgart, Arturo E.
Baumgartel. Diccionario de pedagogia. Paulinas.
Baumgartner, Walter, jt. auth. see Koehler, Ludwig.
Baus, Herbert M. The Experts Crossword Puzzle Dictionary (Dolp). Doubleday.
--The Master Crossword Puzzle Dictionary. Doubleday.
--Master Crossword Puzzle Dictionary: The Unabridged Wordbank. Doubleday.
Bautista, jt. auth. see Enriquez.
Bayard, Jean P. Dictionnaire Mytho-hermetique: La Symbolique du Feu. Payot.
Bayer, Erich. Woerterbuch zur Geschichte. Kroener.
--Woerterbuch zur Geschichte. French & Eur.
Bayle, Pierre. Dictionnaire Historique & Critique. Slatkine.
--Dictionnaire Historique & Critique. Sociales.
Bayod Serrat, Ramon. Diccionario Laboral. French & Eur.
Bazin, Jean de see De Bazin, Jean.
Bazzarelli, E. Dizionario Motta della lingua italiana. Motta.
Bazzetta de Vemenia, Nino. Dizionario del gergo milanese e lombardo. Forni.

B. D'Herbelot de Molainville, et al. Bibliotheque Orientale, ou Dictionnaire universel, contenant generalment tout ce qui regarde la connaissance des peuples de 'orient. Caratzas Pub Co.

Bea, L. de see Sandahl, P. & De Bea, L.

Bea, Louise de, jt. auth. see Sandahl, Pierre.

Bea, Luoise de see Sandahl, Pierre & De Bea, Louise.

Beach, Beatrice, jt. auth. see Hu, C. T.

Beach, Edward L., jt. auth. see Noel, John V., Jr.

Beach, Mark. Words for the Wise: A Field Guide to Academic Terms. Coast to Coast.

Beard, R. The Indo-European Lexicon: Synchronic Theory. Elsevier.

Beatty, B., jt. auth. see Ware, D.

Beau, A. E. Langenscheidts Taschenwoerterbuch Portugiesisch: Teil II, Deutsch-Portugiesisch. Langenscheidt.

Beau, A. E. & Irmen, F. Langenscheidts Taschenwoerterbuch Portugiesisch. Langenscheidt.

Beaucaire, Louis, jt. auth. see Lange-Kowal, Ernst E.

Beaucaire, Louis, ed. see Lange-Kowal, Ernst Erwin.

Beaud, Michel & Bellon, Bertrand. Dictionnaire des Groupes Industriels & Financiers en France. Seuil.

Beaudet, Albert. Dictionnaire Anglo-Francais des Nouveautes Linguistiques. Fides.

Beaujean, ed. see Littre.

Beaumont, Cyril W. A French-English Dictionary of Technical Terms Used in Classical Ballet. Imp Soc Tchrs Da.

Beaver, Frank. Dictionary of Film Terms (C). McGraw.

Becerra, Rosina, jt. auth. see Giovannoni, Jeanne M.

Becher, H. Woerterbuch der Deutschen und Spanischen Rects und Wirtschaftssprache. French & Eur.

--Woerterbuch der Spanischen und Deutschen Rechts und Wirtschaftssprache. French & Eur.

Becher, Herbert J. Woerterbuch der Recht & Wirtshaftssprache: Teil II, Deutsch-Spanisch. Recht & Wirtschaft.

--Woerterbuch der Rechts & Wirtschaftssprache: Teil I, Spanisch-Deutsch. Recht & Wirtschaft.

Beck, jt. auth. see Stoeckhert, Klaus.

Beck, Carl, et al, eds. Political Science Thesaurus. Am Political.

Beck, Isabel L., et al. The Rationale & Design of a Program to Teach Vocabulary to Fourth-Grade Students. Learn Res Dev.

Becker. Glossaire sur la T. V. A. Office Intern. Librairie.

Becker, Donald. Reverse Dictionary of Urdu (Pub. by Manohaar India). South Asia Bks.

Becker, Esther, ed. Dictionary of Personnel & Industrial Relations. Philos Lib.

Becker, Felix, jt. ed. see Thieme, Ulrich.

Becker, H. Dictionnaire trilingue du Droit des Affaires pour le Commerce & l'industrie: Allemand-Anglais-Francais & index. Maison Dictionnaire.

Becker, Idel. Dicionario Espanhol-Portugues & Portugues-Espanhol. Liv Nobel.

Becker, U. Herder - Lexikon Umwelt (Pub. by Herder). French & Eur.

--Herder-Lexikon Umwelt. Herder.

--Herder-Lexikon Weltaumphysik. Herder.

--Herder-Lexikon Weltaumphysik (Pub. by Herder). French & Eur.

Becker, Udo. Diccionario Rioduero: Ecologia. French & Eur.

--Diccionario Rioduero: Fisica Del Espacio. French & Eur.

--Herder-Lexikon. Herder.

Becker, Ursula. Rechtsworterbuch Fur Die Gewerbliche Wirtschaft (Pub. by Fritz Knapp Verlag). French & Eur.

Beckman, Erik. The Criminal Justice Dictionary. Pierian.

Beckman, Nat. Norsk-Svensk Ordbok. Maehle, Leif & Sigurd, Bengt, eds. Esselte Studium.

Beckman, Natanael. Norsk-Svensk Ordbok. Maehle, Lief & Sigurd, Bengt, eds. Esselte Studium.

Beckum, J. H. van see Van Beckum, J. H.

Beckum, J. H. Van see Van Beckum, J. H. & Wallis, H.

Becquer, A., jt. auth. see Armanet, J.

Bede, Jean-Albert & Edgerton, William, eds. Columbia Dictionary of Modern European Literature. Columbia U Pr.

Bedrossian, Mathias. Armenian-English Dictionary. Intl Bk Ctr.

Bedrossian, Matthias. New Dictionary of Armenian-English. Intl Bk Ctr.

Beebe, Brooke M. & Rosenblatt, Ruth Y. The Dictionary. Soc for Visual.

Beeching, Cyril L. A Dictionary of Eponyms (Pub. by Bingley England). Shoe String.

--A Dictionary of Eponyms (Pub. by Bingley England). Shoe String.

Beedell, Suzanne & Hargreaves, Barbara. The Complete Guide to Country Living. David & Charles.

Beene, Wayne, jt. ed. see Woodhead, Daniel.

Beer, Edith L. Monarch's Dictionary of Investment Terms. Monarch Pr.

Beersmans, Frans. Langenscheidts Taschenwoerterbuch Niederlaendisch: Teil II, Deutsch-Niederlaendisch. Langenscheidt.

Beersmans, Frans, jt. auth. see Van De Wiele, F. J. J.

Beeton, Douglas R. & Dorner, Helene T. A Dictionary of English Usage in Southern Africa. Oxford U Pr.

Begell, William, ed. Glossary of Terms in Heat Transfer, Fluid Flow & Related Topics. Hemisphere Pub.

Beguin, Andre. Dictionnaire Technique & Critique du Dessin. Vander Oyez.

--Dictionnaire Technique et Critique du Dessin. French & Eur.

Beguin, J., et al. Vocabulaire Technique des Assurances sur la Vie. French & Eur.

Beguin, L., et al. Vocabulaire Technique des Assurances sur la Vie, French & Eur.

Behar, Macim, ed. see Amendola, Joao.

Beigbeder, Olivier. Lexique des Symboles. Zodiaque.

Beigel. Dictionary of Psychology & Related Fields. Brandstetter.

Beigel, Hugo G. Dictionary of Psychology & Related Fields. Ungar.

Beijing Foreign Institute. The Pinyin Chinese-English Dictionary. Wu Jingrong, ed (Pub. by Wiley-Interscience). Wiley.

Beijing Language Institute. Vocabulary List-Key to Exercise for Practical Chinese Reader. China Bks.

Bein, G. German-English Dictionary of International Transport (Pub. by Collet's). State Mutual Bk.

Bein, Gerhard. Woerterbuch Des Internationalen Verkehrs (Dictionary of International Traffic) Intl Pubns Serv.

Beinhauer, Werner. Stilistisch-Phraseologisches Woerterbuch Spanisch-Deutsch. Hueber.

Beitler, L. & McDonald, B. English for the Medical Professions. McGraw.

Beker, T. E. Diccionario de primeros auxilios medico-veterinarios. Lib. del Colegio.

Bekmukhametov, E. Russko-Kazakhskii Terminologicheskii Slovar (Pub. by Izd. An Kaz. SSR). Four Continent.

Belfort, Anne Marie, jt. auth. see Camard, Jean Pierre.

Belic, Jaromir & Kamis, Adolf. Maly Starocesky Slovnik. S. P. N.

Belisle, Louis-Alexandre. Dictionnaire General de la Langue Francaise au Canada. Beauchemin.

Belkina, E. S. Russko-Indoneziiskii Slovar (Pub. by Sov. Entsiklopediia). Four Continent.

Bell, Francis L. Tanga-English, English-Tanga Dictionary. Univ Syd Aust Lang.

Bell, John. Dictionnaire Anglais-Francais. Garnier.

Bell, Robert E. Dictionary of Classical Mythology: Symbols, Attributes, & Associations. ABC Clio.

Bellegarde, Ida. Easy Steps to a Large Vocabulary. Bell Ent.

Belle-Isle, Gerald J. Dictionnaire Technique General: Anglais-Francais. Bordas-Dunod.

--Dictionnaire Technique General Anglais-Francais. Beauchemin.

Belle-Isle, J. English-French General Technical Dictionary. Routledge & Kegan.

Belle-Isle, J. G. Dictionnaire technique general. Imported Bks.

Belle Isle, J. Gerald. Dictionnaire Technique General: Anglais-Francais. French & Eur.

Bellenger, W. A. A Dictionary of Idioms, French & English. Telegraph Bks.

Bellini, Bernardo, jt. auth. see Tommaseo, Niccolo.

Bellini, L. Dizionario della lingua italiano. Rizzoli Edit.

Bellisco Hernandez, Manuel. Diccionario de Banca y Bolsa, Tomo I: Ingles-Espanol. French & Eur.

Bellon, Bertrand, jt. auth. see Beaud, Michel.

Belmont, Abel. Dictionnaire Historique & Artistique de la Rose. Lechevalier.

Belodvorskii, Iu. M. Kratkii Slovar Gazovika (Pub. by Ministertvo Kommun Khoz). Four Continent.

Belot, P. Dictionnaire Al-Fara-id Arabe-Francais. Dar El-Machreq.

Bels-Koning, H. C. & Van Kuijk, W. M. Mushroom Terms. Centre for Agricultural Pub. & Documentation.

Beltran. Diccionario de banca y bolsa. Labor.

Benac, Henri. Dictionnaire des Synonymes. Hachette.

--Dictionnaire des Synonymes. Renouveau Pedagogique.

Benacka, S. English-Slovak Technical Dictionary (Pub. by Collet's). State Mutual Bk.

Benacka, Stefan. Anglicko-Slovensky Technicky Slovnik. Alfa-Vydavatel.

Benarde, Melvin A. The Food Additives Dictionary (Wallaby). S&S.

Bender. Dictionary of Nutrition. Butterworth.

Bender, Arnold E. Dictionary of Nutrition & Food Technology. Butterworth.

Bender, Byron W. Spoken Marshallese. UH Pr.

Bender, James F. N. B. C. Handbook of Pronunciation. Crowell, Thomas, Jr., ed. T Y Crowell.

Bender, Todd K. A Concordance to Conrad's the Mirror of the Sea & the Inheritors. Garland Pub.

Bender, Todd K., jt. auth. see Higdon, David.

Bendezu Neyra, Guillermo E. Argo Limeno. Libreria.

Bendick, Jeanne & Levin, Marcia. Mathematics Illustrated Dictionary: Facts, Figures & People, Including the New Math (GB). McGraw.

Benedetti, Rinaldo de see De Benedetti, Rinaldo.

Benedetto, U. Spanish-English, English-Spanish Dictionary. Heinman.

Benedetto, Ubaldo di see Di Benedetto, Ubaldo.

Benedictines de la Congregation de Saint-Maur. Dictionnaire de l'art de Verifier les Dates. Migne, J. P., ed. Caratzas Pub Co.

Benes, Josef & Puba, Vaclay. Muzeologicky slovnik. SNTC.

Benesch, Hellmuth. Woerterbuch zur klinischen Psychologie. Deutscher Taschenbuch.

Benesova, Hana. Cesko-Italsky Slovnik na Cesty. SNTC.

Benezit. Dictionnaire Critique et Documentaire des Peintres, Sculpteurs, Dessinateurs, et Graveurs de Tous les Temps et de Tons les Pays. French & Eur.

Benezit, E. Dictionnaire des Peintres, Sculpteurs, Dessinateurs et Graveurs. Hacker.

Benezit, Emmanuel. Dictionnaire Critique & Documentaire: Peintres, Sculptres, Dessinateurs de Tous les Temps & de Tous les Pays. Grund.

Benito Bacho, Jose. Diccionario de la Construccion y Obras Publicas Ingles-Espanol. French & Eur.

--Diccionario de la Construccion y Obras Publicas, Tomo 2: Span. French & Eur.

--Diccionario de la Construcion y de Obras Publicas, Tomo I: Ingles. French & Eur.

Benito y Bacho, Jose de & Hernandez, Manuel B. Diccionario de la Constuccion & Obras Publicas. Lib Tec Bell.

Beniukh, O. P. Karmannyi Anglo-Russkii Slovar (Pub. by Sov Entsiklopediia). Four Continent.

--Karmannyi Anglo-Russkii Slovar (Pub. by Russkii Iazyk). Four Continent.

Beniukh, O. P., et al. Karmannyi Anglo-Russkii Slovar (Pub. by Russkii Iazyk). Four Continent.

--Karmannyi Anglo-Russkii Slovar' Four Continent.

--Karmannyi Russko-Angliiskii Slovar (Pub. by Sov Entsiklopediia). Four Continent.

Beniukh, O. P., et al, eds. Karmannyi Russko-Angliiskii Slovar' Four Continent.

Bennett, A. Y. Picture Dictionary, ABCs, Telling Time, Counting Rhymes, Riddles & Finger Plays (G&D). Putnam Pub Group.

Bennett, Archie. The New Color Picture Dictionary for Children. Childrens.

--The New Color Picture Dictionary for Children. Delair.

Bennett, Archie, ed. New Illustrated Grosset Dictionary (G&D). Putnam Pub Group.

Bennett, Harry, ed. Concise Chemical & Technical Dictionary. Chem Pub.

Bennett, John, et al, eds. Visual Display Terminal: Usability Issues & Health Concerns. P-H.

Bennett, Roger G. Naturgeografisk ordbok: Engelsk-Norsk. Berg Inst Sociol.

Bennett, Russell & Watson, James, eds. Stanley Gibbons Philatelic Terms Illustrated. StanGib Ltd.

Bennie, W. G., ed. see McLaren, J.

Bensch, Erhard. Schiffbau, Schiffahrt, Fischereitechnik-Russisch-Englisch-Deutsch. VEB Technk.

Bensch, Erhard, jt. auth. see Dipl-Ling, V.

Benseler, Frank, jt. auth. see Reifferscheid, Adolph.

Benson, M. English-Serbocroatian Dictionary. French & Eur.

--Serbocroatian-English Dictionary. French & Eur.

Benson, Morton. Englesko-srpskohrvatski Recnik. Beogradski.

--English - SerboCroatian Dictionary. U of Pa Pr.

Benson, Morton, ed. Dictionary of Russian Personal Names. U of Pa Pr.

--Serbocroatian-English Dictionary. U of Pa Pr.

Benson, T. G., tr. see Barlow, A. R.

Bentley, Harold W. A Dictionary of Spanish Terms in English, with Special Reference to the American Southwest. Octagon.

Bentolila, Alain, ed. see Nougayrol, Pierre, et al.

Bentot, Gaston, ed. see Sachs, Karl & Villatte, Cesaire.

Benveniste, Emile. Vocabolario delle istituzioni indoeuropee: Vol. 1, Economia-parentela-societa. Liborio, M. A., tr. Einaudi.

--Vocabulaire des Institutions Indo-Europeennes, 2. Minuit.

Ben-Yehuda, Eliezer, ed. Dictionary & Thesaurus of the Hebrew Language (Yoseloff). A S Barnes.

Benzon, Gorm R. Gyldendals Antikvitetshandbog. Gyldendal Norsk.

Berardi, Roberto. Dizionario di termini della critica letteraria. Monnier.

--Dizionario di termini storici, politici ed economici moderni. Monnier.

Berberi, Dilaver & Berberi, Edel A., eds. Cortina-Grosset Basic Dictionary: Italian (G&D). Putnam Pub Group.

Berberi, Dilaver, ed. see Laita, Luis M.

Berberi, Dilaver, ed. see Marcy, Teresa & Marcy, Michel.

Berberi, Edel A., jt. ed. see Berberi, Dilaver.

Berberi, Edel A., ed. see Laita, Luis M.

Berberi, Edel A., ed. see Marcy, Teresa & Marcy, Michel.

Berbrich, Joan D. One Hundred One Ways to Learn Vocabulary. AMSCO Sch.

Berdell, Dorothy K., ed. see Olivares, Dennis A.

Berenger, Jean. Lexique Historique de l'Europa Danublenne, XVIe.-XXe. Siecle. Colin.

Berenyi, John. The Modern American Business Dictionary: Including Reaganomics & an Appendix of Business Slang. Morrow.

--The Modern American Business Dictionary: Including Reagonomics & an Appendix of Business Slang. Quill NY.

Berg, Ragnar, jt. auth. see Hauser, Gaylord.

Berg, Sture. Olika Lika Ord: Svenskt Homograflexikon. Almqvist.

Berger. Dictionary of Psychology. Brandstetter.

Berger, Alfred H., ed. Dictionary of Psychology: English-German. Ungar.

Berger, K. Mykologisches Worterbuch. French & Eur.

Berger, Karl. Mycological Dictionary (Pub. by Collets). State Mutual Bk.

Berger, Karl Von see Von Berger, Karl.

Berger, Marshall D. Vest Pocket Russian (BN). B&N NY.

Bergeron, L. Dictionnaire de la Langue Quebecoise. French & Eur.

Bergeron, Leandre. The Quebecois Dictionary. Enslow Pubs.

Bergeson, Sandy. Dieter's Dictionary: Chubby Webster's. Print Mat.

Bergfeld, R. Herder-Lexikon Biologie. Herder.

--Herder-Lexikon Biologie (Pub. by Herder). French & Eur.

Bergfeld, Rainer. Diccionario Rioduero: Biologia. French & Eur.

--Diccionarios Rioduero: Biologia. Arroyo Marcos, Gloria, tr. Catolica Edit.

Bergflexner, Stuart, ed. Oxford American Dictionary. Avon.

Bergflexner, Stuart, et al, eds. The Oxford American Dictionary. Avon.

Berghe, Christian van den. Dictionnaire des Idees dans L'oeuvre de Simone de Beauvoir. Mouton.

Bergman, P. H. Concise Dictionary of Twenty-Six Languages in Simultaneous Translation (Sig). NAL.

Bergman, Peter. The Basic English-Chinese, Chinese-English Dictionary. Imported Bks.

Bergman, Peter, ed. The Basic English-Chinese, Chinese-English Dictionary with PINYIN Transliteration. Humanities.

Bergman, Peter M. Concise Dictionary of Twenty-Six Languages. Imported Bks.

Bergman, Peter M., compiled by. The Basic English-Chinese, Chinese-English Dictionary (Sig). NAL.

Bergquist, Sidney R., ed. New Webster's Dictionary of the English Language (Handy School & Office Edition) Delair.

--New Webster's Dictionary of the English Language (Modern Desk Edition) Delair.

Bergstrom, Mats & Carlson, Ingvar. Engelsk-Svensk Ordbog. Natur & Kultur.

Berindei, Mihai. Dictionar de Jazz. Editura Stiintifica.

Berke, jt. auth. see Gioello.

Berkebile, Don H. Carriage Terminology: An Historical Dictionary. Smithsonian.

Berkman, Al. Singers Glossary of Show Business Jargon. Melrose Pub Co.

Berlitz. Berlitz Pocket Dictionaries: Danish-English-Danish. Macmillan.

--Berlitz Pocket Dictionaries: Dutch-English-Dutch. Macmillan.

--Berlitz Pocket Dictionaries: Finnish-English-Finnish. Macmillan.

--Berlitz Pocket Dictionaries: French-English-French. Macmillan.

--Berlitz Pocket Dictionaries: German-English-German. Macmillan.

--Berlitz Pocket Dictionaries: Italian-English-Italian. Macmillan.

--Berlitz Pocket Dictionaries: Norwegian-English-Norwegian. Macmillan.

--Berlitz Pocket Dictionaries: Portuguese-English-Portuguese. Macmillan.

--Berlitz Pocket Dictionaries: Spanish-English-Spanish. Macmillan.

--Berlitz Pocket Dictionaries: Swedish-English-Swedish. Macmillan.

Berlitz Editors. Berlitz Arabic for Travellers (Berlitz). Macmillan.

--Berlitz French for Travellers (Berlitz). Macmillan.

--Berlitz Greek for Travellers (Berlitz). Macmillan.

--Berlitz Hebrew for Travellers (Berlitz). Macmillan.

--Berlitz Italian for Travellers (Berlitz). Macmillan.

--Berlitz Japanese for Travellers (Berlitz). Macmillan.

--Berlitz Latin-American Spanish for Travellers (Berlitz). Macmillan.

--Berlitz Pocket Dictionaries: Danish-English (Berlitz). Macmillan.

--Berlitz Pocket Dictionaries: Dutch-English (Berlitz). Macmillan.

--Berlitz Pocket Dictionaries: Finnish-English (Berlitz). Macmillan.

--Berlitz Pocket Dictionaries: French-English (Berlitz). Macmillan.

--Berlitz Pocket Dictionaries: German-English (Berlitz). Macmillan.

--Berlitz Pocket Dictionaries: Italian-English (Berlitz). Macmillan.

--Berlitz Pocket Dictionaries: Norwegian-English (Berlitz). Macmillan.

--Berlitz Pocket Dictionaries: Spanish-English (Berlitz). Macmillan.

--Berlitz Pocket Dictionaries: Swedish-English (Berlitz). Macmillan.

--Berlitz Portuguese for Travellers (Berlitz). Macmillan.

--Berlitz Spanish for Travellers (Berlitz). Macmillan.

--Portuguese-English Dictionary (Berlitz). Macmillan.

--Spanish-English Dictionary (Berlitz). Macmillan.

--Swedish-English, English-Swedish Pocket Dictionary (Berlitz). Macmillan.

Berman, Ben. The Dictionary of Business & Credit Terms. Andover, James J., ed. NACM.

Berna, Henri. Dictionnaire Technique & Administratif de la Navigation Interieure. Berger-Levrault.

--Dictionnaire Technique et Administratif De la Navigation Interieure. French & Eur.

Bernabo, M. & Picchi, F. Grande Dizionario di Marina: Inglese-Italiano, Italiano-Inglese. French & Eur.

Bernard, Jean-Louis. Dictionnaire de l'insolite & du Fantastique. Dauphin.

Bernard, Yves. Diccionario Economico & Financiero. Assn Prog Direc.

Bernard, Yves & Colli, Jean-Claude. Vocabulaire Economique & Financier. Seuil.

--Vocabulaire Economique et Financier: Coll. Points Economie. French & Eur.

Bernard, Yves & Suarez Campos, Jose M. Vocabulario Economico & Financiero. Assn Prog Direc.

Bernard, Yves, et al. Dictionnaire Economique et Financier. Lewandowski, Dominique, ed. French & Eur.

--Dictionnaire Economique & Financier. Seuil.

Bernardez, Enrique, tr. see Lewandowski, Theodor, et al.

Bernasconi, J. R. Collector's Glossary of Antiques & Fine Arts. Intl Pubns Serv.

Bernasconi, John R. Collector's Glossary. Transatlantic.

Bernice P. Bishop Museum - Honolulu. Dictionary Catalog of the Library of the Bernice P. Bishop Museum (Hall Library). G K Hall.

Bernsdorf, Wilhelm, ed. Woerterbuch der Soziologie. Enke.

--Woerterbuch der Soziologie: Bd 1, 5 Aufl. Fischer Taschen.

--Woerterbuch der Soziologie: Bd 2, 4 Aufl. Fischer Taschen.

--Woerterbuch der Soziologie: Bd 3, 4 Aufl. Fischer Taschen.

Bernshtein, L. B. Nemetsko-Russkii Gidrotekhnicheskii Slovar (Pub. by Fizmatgiz). Four Continent.

Bernstein, L. B. Deutsch-Russisches Worterbuch fur Wasserbau. French & Eur.

Bernstein, Theodore M. Bernstein's Reverse Dictionary. Times Bks.

Berr, Samuel. An Etymological Glossary to the Old Saxon Heliand. Intl Pubns Serv.

Berrios, Jose, jt. auth. see Sahai, Hardeo.

Berry, George R. Berry's Greek-English New Testament Lexicon with Synonyms: Numerically Coded to Strong's Exhaustive Concordance. Baker Bk.

--A Dictionary of New Testament Greek Synonyms. Zondervan.

Berry, Richard W., jt. auth. see Tver, David F.

Berset, F. Handelskorrenpondenz in Vier Sprachen. M Rosenberg.

Bersez, Jacques. Dictionnaire pratique & explicatif des produits magiques & articles usuels. Jacques Bersez.

--Dictionnaire Pratique & Explicatif des Produits Magiques & Articles Usuels. Bersez.

Bertaux. Dictionnaire Classique Francais-Allemand. Hachette.

Bertaux, Felix & Lepointe, Emile. Dictionnaire Redige en Caracteres Latins: Allemand-Francais. Hachette.

--Dictionnaire Redige en Caracteres Latins: Francais-Allemand. Hachette.

Bertaux, Pierre. Franzosisch-Deutsches, Deutsch-Franzosisches Woerterbuch. Brandstetter.

--Franzosisch-Deutsches, Deutsch-Franzosisches Woerterbuch. Brandstetter.

--Franzosisch-Deutsches, Deutsch-Franzosisches Woerterbuch (Pub. by Brandstetter). French & Eur.

Bertet, Amato, et al. Dizionario italiano-francese e francese-italiano. Paravia.

Berthe, Leon-Noel. Dictionnaire des Correspondants de l'academie. Eveche D'Arras.

Bertholet, Alfred. Woerterbuch der Religionen. Kroener.

Berton, C. Dictionnaire des Cardinaux. Migne, J. P., ed. Caratzas Pub Co.

Bertrand, P., jt. auth. see Jourbel, H.

Bertrand, P., jt. tr. see Joubrel, H.

Bertrand, P., et al. Dizionario di informazione sessuale. Gribaudi.

Bertrand, Paul. Diccionario de informacion sexual. Granica.

Bertrand Du Chazaud, Henri. Dictionnaire des Synonymes. Soc Nouveau.

Bertraux, Lepointe. Franzoesisch-Deutsches-Deutsch-Franzoesisches Woerterbuch: Band II, Deutsch-Franzoesisch. Brandstetter.

--Franzosisch-Deutsches-Deutsch-Franzosisches Woerterbuch: Band I, Franzoesisch-Deutsch. Brandstetter.

Berulfsen, B. Engelsk-Norsk Ordbok. French & Eur.

--English-Norsk Dictionary: Gyldendals. Vanous.

Berulfsen, B. & Berulfsen, T. English-Norwegian Dictionary. Kunnskapsforlaget.

--Norwegian Dictionary: Engelsk-Norwegina. Vanous.

Berulfsen, B. & Svenkerud, A. Norwegian Deluxe Dictionary: English-Norse. Vanous.

Berulfsen, B., jt. auth. see Kirkeby, W.

Berulfsen, B. & Scavenius, H., eds. McKay's Modern Norwegian-English & English-Norwegian Dictionary. McKay.

Berulfsen, T., jt. auth. see Berulfsen, B.

Bes, J. Chartering & Shipping Terms: Time-Sheet Supplements. Heinman.

--Fletamentos y Terminos de Embarque. Heineman.

Beseler, D. & Jacobs, B. Technical Dictionary of Anglo-American Legal Terminology (Pub. by de Gruyter). French & Eur.

Beseler, D. v. & Jacobs, B., eds. Law Dictionary: Technical Dictionary of Anglo-American Legal Terminology, German-English. De Gruyter.

Beseler, Dora Von & Jacobs, Barbara. Law Dictionary: Fachwoerterbuch der anglo-amerikanischen Rechtssprache, Englisch-Deutsch. De Gruyter.

Besse, B., et al. Lexique Anglais-Francais de L'Aciere Electrique. French & Eur.

Bessinger, J. B., Jr., ed. Concordance to Beowulf. Cornell U Pr.

--A Concordance to the "Anglo-Saxon Poetic Records". Cornell U Pr.

Betteridge, H. T. Cassell's German-English, English-German Dictionary. Imported bks.

Bevan, G. A., ed. see University of Wales Press.

Bevan, Stanley C., et al. A Concise Etymological Dictionary of Chemistry (Pub. by Applied Sci England). Elsevier.

Bevington, J. Macmillan Colour Dictionary. Macmillan.

Bezner. Elektromaschinen-Woerterbuch. Brandstetter.

Bezner, Heinrich. Electrical Machines Dictionary. Brandstetter.

Bhalddraithe, Tomas De see De Bhaldraithe, Tomas & Claithe, Baile A.

Bhaldraithe, Tomas de see De Bhaldraithe, Tomas.

Bhardraithe, T. De see De Bhardraithe, T.

Bhattacharya, Sachchidananda. A Dictionary of Indian History. Greenwood.

Bhola, Nath T., jt. auth. see Chaturvedi, Mahendra.

Biaggi, Virgilio, jt. auth. see Aguayo, Carlos A.

Biagi, Adele, jt. auth. see Ragazzini, Giuseppe.

Biagi, Adele, jt. ed. see Ragazzini, Giuseppe.

Bianchi, E., et al. Dizionario illustrato della lingua latina. Monnier.

--Dizionario illustrato della lingua latina. Monnier.

Bianchi, Raffaello. Il Vocabolario Latino-Italiano & Italiano-Latino. Monnier.

Bianchi, Raffaello & Lelli, Onorio. Vocabolario Latino-italiano, italiano-latino. Monnier.

Biard, Roland. Dictionnaire de L'Extreme-Gauche. Belfond.

--Dictionnaire de l'Extreme-Gauche: De 1945 a Nos Jours. Belfond.

--Dictionnaire de l'Extreme-Gauche: De 1945 a Nos Jours. French & Eur.

Biass-Ducroux, Francoise. Glossary of Genetics. Elsevier.

Biava. Dizionario italiano-portoghese. Vallardi A.

Biava, A. Dizionario Italiano-Portoghese, Portoghese-Italiano. French & Eur.

Bibelriether, Hans, et al, eds. Lexikon fuer Bergfreunde. Bucher.

Bibliographisches Institut. Meyers Lexikon A-Z. Bibl Inst Leipzig.

Biblograf. Vox Concise Spanish & English Dictionary (Pub. by Biblograf S. A., Barcelona). Harrap.

--Vox New Compact Spanish & English Dictionary (Pub. by Biblograf, Barcelona). Harrap.

--Vox Shorter Spanish & English Dictionary (Pub. by Biblograf S. A., Barcelona). Harrap.
Bichiacchi, Ada de see Maiocchi, Annamaria F. & De Bichiacchi, Ada.
Bickel, Walter, ed. Hering's Dictionary of Classical & Modern Cookery (Pub. by Virtuea Col Ltd. England). CBI Pub.
Bickel, Walter, tr. see Hering, Richard.
Biddle, Wayne. Coming to Terms: From Alpha to X-Ray, a Lexicon for the Science-Watcher. Avon.
--Coming to Terms: Lexicon for the Science Watcher. Viking Pr.
Bidoli, Emilio & Cosciani, Guido. Dizionario tedesco-italiano. Paravia.
Bieber, Doris M. Dictionary of Legal Abbreviations Used in American Law Books. W S Hein.
Biedermann, Hans. Handlexikon der magischen Kunste. Droemersche Knaur.
Bielas, Leon. Slownik Minimum Francusko-Polski. Wiedza Powszechna.
Bielecki, Tadeusz, ed. Maly Slownik Antropologiczny. Wiedza Powszechna.
Bielfeldt, Hans H. Deutsch-Russiches Woerterbuch: S-Z. Loetzsch, Ronald, ed. Akad Verl Ath.
--Deutsch-Russisches Woerterbuch: A-G. Loetzsch, R., et al, eds. Akad Verl Ath.
--Deutsch-Russisches Woerterbuch: H-R. Loetzsch, Ronald, ed. Akad Verl Ath.
Biella, Joan C. Dictionary of Old South Arabic: Sabaen Dialect. Scholars Pr CA.
Bierce, Ambrose. The Devil's Dictionary. Dover.
--The Devil's Dictionary. Stemmer Hse.
Bierens de Haan, Barthhold. Dictionnaire Critique de Psychiatrie. Hameau.
Bierfelder, W. Handwoerterbuch des Oeffentlichen Dienster: Das Personalwesen. Schmidt Verlag.
--Handwoerterbuch des Oeffentlichen Dienster: Das Personalwesen (Pub. by E. Schmidt). French & Eur.
Bierfelder, Wilhelm, ed. Handwoerterbuch des Oeffentlichen Dienstes. Schmidt Verlag.
Bierhorst, John. A Nahual-English Dictionary & Concordance to the "Cantares Mexicanos". With an Analytic Transcription & Grammatical Notes. Stanford U Pr.
Biffoli, T., jt. auth. see Sbrulli, G.
Biggs, Bruce, ed. The Complete English-Maori Dictionary. Oxford U Pr.
Bilancia, Philip R. Dictionary of Chinese Law & Government. Stanford U Pr.
Bilginer, Sadettin. Deutsch-Turkisches Woerterbuch fur Technische Berufe. Girardet.
--Deutsch-Turkisches Worterbuch Fur Technische Berufe (Pub. by Verlag W. Girardet). French & Eur.
Billet, F., jt. auth. see Fouchier, J.
Billip, K. English-Polish & Polish-English Minimum Dictionary. Wiedza Powszechna.
Billip, K., jt. auth. see Stanislawski, J.
Bilzer, B. Begriffslexikon der Bildenden Kuenste. French & Eur.
Binder, R., jt. auth. see Novak, J.
Bindmann, W. Fachwoerterbuch Optik und Optischer Geraetebau (Pub. by Dausien). French & Eur.
Bindmann, Werner. Fachwoerterbuch Optik & Optischer Geratebau: Deutsch-Englisch. W Dausien.
--Fachwoerterbuch Optik & Optischer Geratebau: Englisch-Deutsch. W Dausien.
--Optik & Optischer Geratebau Deutsch-Englisch. VEB Technik.
Bindoni, Vincenzo & Netto, G. Vocabolarietto del dialetto trevigiano 1884. Canova.
Binet, Agnes V., jt. auth. see Morei, Ferenc.
Bini, Edson. Dicionario Tecnico Industrial. Hemus-Livraria.
Bioy Casares, Adolfo. Breve Diccionario del Argentino Exquisito. French & Eur.
Birdmann, G. English-German, German, English Solid State Physics & Electronics Dictionary (Pub. by Collet's). State Mutual Bk.
Birgersson, Helge. Svensk-Tysk Affarsordlista. Esselte Studium.
Birkfellner, Gerhard, ed. Teutscher, & Reussischer, Dictionarium: Dictionarium Vindobonense. Akad Verl Ath.
Birkhauser-Boston Publishing. The Herbst-Readett Three-Language Dictionaries of Commerce, Finance & Law. Birkhauser.
--The Herbst-Readett Two-Language Dictionaries of Finance, Commerce & Law. Birkhauser.
Biro, Elizabeth De see De Biro, Elizabeth.
Biron, Alain. Vocabulaire Pratique des Sciences Sociales. Ouvrieres.
Birou, Alain. Lexico De Economia. French & Eur.
--Lexico De Sociologia. French & Eur.
--Vocabulaire Pratique des Sciences Sociales. French & Eur.
Birrell, Augustine. Emerson: A Lecture. Arden Lib.
Bisby, jt. auth. see Ainsworth.
Bisby's, jt. auth. see Ainsworth.
Bischoff, Joachim. Grundbegriffe der Marxistischen Theorie. VSA Verlag.
Bischoff, Walter. Das Kleine Bergbaulexikon. Verlag Glockauf.
--Das Kleine Bergbaulexikon. Verlag Gluckauf.
Bissanti, Andrea, et al. Diccionario medico. Blanco, Catala J., tr. Mas Ivars.
Bittner, Gerhard, jt. auth. see Zoepfl, Helmut.
Biundi, Giuseppe. Dizionario siciliano-italiano. Forni.
Biundi, Giuseppe & Rigoli, A. Dizionario siciliano-italiano. Il Vespro.
Bjerke, L. & Soraas, H., eds. Norwegian Dictionary: English-Norwegian. Vanous.
Blachere, Regis & Chouemi, Moustafa. Dictionnaire Arabe-Francais-Anglais. Maison & Larose.
--Dictionnaire Arabe-Francais-Anglais, 1. French & Eur.
--Dictionnaire Arabe-Francais-Anglais, 2. French & Eur.
Black, George, ed. see International Chain of Industrial & Technical Advertising Agencies.
Black, Henry C. Black's Law Dictionary. Nolan, Joseph R. & Connolly, Michael J., eds. West Pub.
--Black's Law Dictionary: Abridged Fifth Edition. Nolan, Joseph R., et al, eds. West Pub.
Blackburn, Graham. The Overlook Illustrated Dictionary of Nautical Terms. Overlook Pr.
Blackman, R. D. A Dictionary of Foreign Phrases & Classical Quotations. Quality Lib.
Blacque-Belair, Alain. Dictionnaire de Medecine Clinique Pharmacologique & Therapeutique. Maloine.
--Dictionnaire Medicine, Clinique, Pharmacologique et Therapeutique. French & Eur.
Blacque-Belair, Alain & Fossey, Bernard M. de. Dictionnaire de Diagnostic Clinique et Topographique. French & Eur.
Blain, Mireille. Trois Cent Cinquante Definitions Biologiques Raisonnees. Doc Univers.
Blair, Robert W., et al. Mayan Language Dictionary. Garland Pub.
Blake, R. E., jt. auth. see Ruttkowski, Wolfgang V.
Blanchard, E. Dictionnaire du Bon Langage. LIDEC.
Blanchet, Hector, jt. auth. see Charbot, Nicolas.
Blanco, Catala J., tr. see Bissanti, Andrea, et al.
Blanco Garcia, Vicente. Diccionario latino-espanol y espanol-latino. Aguilar SP.
Blanes Prieto, Joaquin. Diccionario de terminos contables. CECSA.
--Diccionario de Terminos Contables. French & Eur.
Blanquez. Diccionario Latino-Espanol, Espanol-Latino. French & Eur.
Blanquez Fraile, Agustin. Diccionario manual latino-espanol y espanol-latino. Sopena.
Blaschke, Karlheinz, et al. Lexikon Staedte & Wappen der Deutschen Demokratischen Republik. VEB Verlag Enzyklopadie.
Blattner, Karl. Langenscheidts Taschenwoerterbuecher Russisch. Langenscheidt.
--Russisch. Incl. Teil I. Russisch-Deutsch. Orschel, H., rev. by.; Teil II. Deutsch-Russisch. Braun, M. & Pollok, K., eds.. Langenscheidt.
Blattner, Karl & Orschel, H. Langenscheidts Taschenwoerterbuch Russisch: Teil I, Russisch-Deutsch. Langenscheidt.
Blattner, Karl, et al. Langenscheidts Taschenwoerterbuch Russisch. Langenscheidt.
Blaudin De The, Bernard, jt. auth. see Capot-Rey, Robert.
Blauvelt, Carolyn T. & Nelson, Fred. A Manual of Orthopaedic Terminology. Mosby.
Blazquez, Jose M. Diccionario de las religiones perromanas de Hispania. Istmo.
Bleandonu, Gerard. Dictionnaire de Psychiatrie Sociale. Payot.
Bleaudonu, Gerard. Dictionnaire de Psychiatrie Sociale. Payot.
Bleek, Dorothea F. A Bushman Dictionary. Am Orient Soc.
Bleiber, German. Diccionario de historia de Espana. Alianza Ed.
Bleiberg, German. Diccionario de Historia de Espana. Alianza Ed.
--Diccionario de Historia de Espana. Alianza Ed.
--Diccionario de Historia de Espana. Alianza Ed.
--Diccionario de Historia de Espana. French & Eur.
--Diccionario de Historia de Espana. French & Eur.
Blinkenberg, A. & Hoybye, P. Dansk-Fransk Ordbog. French & Eur.
Blinkenberg, A. P. & Hoybye, Poul. Dansk-Fransk Ordbog. Thiele, Margrethe, ed. Erhvervso.
Blinkert, B. Herder-Lexikon Soziologie. Herder.
--Herder-Lexikon Soziologie (Pub. by Herder). French & Eur.
Bliss, A. J. A Dictionary of Foreign Words & Phrases in Current English. Routledge & Kegan.
Bljach & Bagma. Deutsch-Russisches Oekonomisches Woerterbuch. Wissenschaftliche.
Bljach, I. S. & Bagma, B. T. Deutsch-Russisches Okonomisches Worterbuch: Dictionary German-Russian of Economics. French & Eur.
Bloch, Oscar & Von Wartburg, Walther. Dictionnaire Etymologique de la Langue Francaise. PUF.
Bloch, Oscar & Wartburg, Walther Von. Dictionnaire Etymologique de la Langue Francaise. French & Eur.
Block, C., et al. Geillustrrerd Woordenboek Voor de Autombieltechniek en Zes Talen. French & Eur.
Block, Karen K. & McCaslin, Ellen S. A Plan for Using CAI to Teach Vocabulary Concepts. Learn Res Dev.
Bloech, Juergen, ed. see Luecke, Wolfgang.
Blok, C. & Jezewski, W. Dictionnaire Illustre de l'Automobile "Kluwer," en 6 Langues. French & Eur.
Blok, Czesaw & Jezewski, Wiesaw. Automobily. Wydawnictwa.
Blok, Czeslaw. Ilustrowany Slownik Samochodowy. Wydawnictwa.
Blok, Czeslaw & Jezewski, Wieslaw. Illustrated Automobile Dictionary (Pub. by Kluwer Tech Netherlands). Kluwer Academic.
Blok, Jezewski. Diccionario tecnico ilustrado del automovil. Diorki, tr. Aneto Edns.
Blom, Eric. Diccionario de la musica. Claridad.
--Everyman's Dictionary of Music (Plume). NAL.
Blom-Dahl, C. Norwegian-Spanish Dictionary. Kunnskapsforlaget.
Blumenberg, Franz-Jurgen. Herder-Lexikon: Psychologie Sachwoerterbuch. Herder.
Blumenbrg & Kury. Herder - Lexikon Psychologie (Pub. by Herder). French & Eur.
--Herder-Lexikon Psychologie. Herder.
Blumner, Hugo. Technologie und Terminologie der Gewerbe und Kunste bei Griechen und Romern. Finley, Moses, ed. Ayer Co.
Bluth, John V. Concordance to the Doctrine & Covenants. Deseret Bk.
Bluvshtein, V. O. Slovar Angliishkikh & Amerikanskikh Sokrashchenii (Pub. by GINS). Four Continent.
--Slovar Nemetskikh Sokrashchenii (Pub. by GINS). Four Continent.
Bly, Robert W. A Dictionary of Computer Words (Banbury). Dell.
Board of Jewish Education. Miloni: Illustrated Dictionary for Children. Board Jewish Educ.
--My Little Dictionary. Board Jewish Educ.
Boas, Franz. Kwakiutl Grammar - with a Glossary of Suffixes. AMS Pr.
Boatner, ed. see Makkai, Adam.
Boatner, M., et al, eds. Dictionary of American Idioms for Deaf. Barron.
Boatner, M. T., et al, eds. Dictionary of American Idioms for the Deaf. Barron.
--Dictionary of American Idioms. Barron.
Boatner, Mark M., 3rd. The Civil War Dictionary. McKay.
Boatner, Maxine & Gates, John. Dictionary of Idioms for the Deaf. Natl Assn Deaf.
Bobbio, Norberto. Diccionario de politica: Obra completa. Crisafio, Raul, tr. Siglo XXI.
--Diccionario de politica: Tomo 1: A-J. Crisafio, Raul, tr. Siglo XXI.
Bobbio, Norberto & Matteuci, Nicola. Dizionario di politica. UTET.
Bobbio, Norberto & Matteuci, Nicola, eds. Dizionario di Politica. UTET.
Boccaccio, Giovanni. Dizionario geografico. Fogola.
Bocchetta, V., ed. Vest Pocket Italian Dictionary. New Century.
Bocchetta, Vittore & Young, Ruth E., eds. New Century Vest-Pocket Italian Dictionary. New Century.
Bocchetta, Vittore E., ed. New Century World-Wide Italian Dictionary: Italian-English, English-Italian. New Century.
--World-Wide Italian Dictionary (Prem). Fawcett.
Boch, Raol. Dizionario Francese Italiano, Italiano Francese. Zanichelli.
Boch, Raoul. Dizionario del francese fondamentale. Zanichelli.
--Dizionario francese-italiano italiano-francese. Zanichelli.
Bodel, Sen A., jt. auth. see Vinterberg, H.
Bodelsen, C. A., jt. auth. see Vinterberg, H.
Bodey, Jozsef. Magyar-Bolgar Szotar. Terra.
--Magyar-Bolgar Szotar. Terra.
Bodrogligeti. The Persian Vocabulary of the Codex Cumanicus (Pub. by Kaido Hungary). Heyden.
Bodson, Arthur. Vocabulaire Latin. Sciences Lettres.
Bodson, Dennis, ed. & frwd. by. Fiberoptics & Lightwave Communications Vocabulary. McGraw.
Boehm, Klaus, ed. see Sharman, Fay.
Boehret, Carl, jt. ed. see Von Eynern, Gert.
Boeing & Haeusgen. Herder-Lexikon Kunst. Herder.
--Herder-Lexikon Kunst (Pub. by Herder). French & Eur.
Boeing, G. Herder - Lexikon Wirtschaft (Pub. by Herder). French & Eur.
--Herder-Lexikon Wirtschaft. Herder.
Boeing-Haeusgen, Ursula. Diccionario Rioduero: Arte. French & Eur.

Boerhave Beekman, W., ed. Elsevier's Wood Dictionary. Elsevier.
Boerio, Giuseppe. Dizionario del dialetto veneziano. Giunti-Martello.
Boerner, F. Taschenwoerterbuch der Botanischen Pflanzennamem. Parey.
--Taschenwoerterbuch der Botanischen Pflanzennamem (Pub. by P. Parey). French & Eur.
Boetner, Maxine & Gates, John E. A Dictionary of American Idioms. Makkai, Adam, ed. Barron.
Bogadek, F. A. New English-Croatian & Croatian-English Dictionary. Hafner.
Bogadek, Francis A. New English-Croatian, Croatian-English Dictionary. Hafner.
Bogason, S. O. English-Icelandic Dictionary. Heinman.
Bogason, S. O., jt. auth. see Sigurdsson, A.
Bogdan, Istvan. Papirkeszltoink Mestersegszavai. MTESZ.
--Papirkeszltoink Mestersegszavai. MTESZ.
Bogenschuetz. Fachwoerterbuch fuer Batterien & Energie-Direktumwandlung. Brandstetter.
Bogenschuetz, A. Fachwoerterbuch fuer Batterien und Energie-Direktumwandlung. Brandstetter.
Boggs, R. S. & Dixon, J. I. Everyday Spanish Idioms. Regents Pub.
Bogoraz, Vladimir G. Koryak Texts. AMS Pr.
Bogus, Ronald, jt. auth. see Landau, Sidney.
Bogus, Ronald, jt. ed. see Landau, Sidney.
Bogusiawski, Andrzej. Illustrowany Slownik Rosyjsko-Polski. Wiedza Powszechna.
Boguslawski, Andrzej. Illustrowany Slownik Rosyjsko-Polski, Polsko-Rosyjski. Wiedza Poswzechna.
Bohigas Rosell, Mauricio. Diccionario Ingles-Espanol, Spanish-English. French & Eur.
Bohusch, Otmar. Lexikon der Grammatischen Terminologie. Auer.
--Lexikon der Grammatischen Terminologie. French & Eur.
Boije af Gennas, Fredrik C. Prinsessans ABC Bok. Rediviva.
Boisselier, Jackie, jt. auth. see Capron, Gustave.
Boixareu, jt. auth. see McGraw-Hill.
Bola Publications. Bola Glossary of Civil Procedural Law: Spanish-English & English-Spanish. Bola Pubns.
--Bola Glossary of Electronic Data Processing & Computer Terms English-Spanish & Spanish-English. Bola Pubns.
Bolado, Victor H. Management Terminology: English-Spanish & Spanish-English. Todd & Honeywell.
Bolander, B. O. Instant Medical Dictionary. Watts.
--The Instant Quotation Dictionary. Watts.
Bolander, Donald O., et al. Instant Medical Spelling Dictionary. Career Inst.
--Instant Quotation Dictionary. Career Inst.
Boleslaw, Adamczyk. Pieciojezyczny Slownik Gleboznawczy. Panstwowe Zaklad W.
Bolo, Helene & Cavrois, Philippe. Dictionnaire de l'offshore Petrole Gaz. S. C. M.
Bolz, Roger W., jt. auth. see Tver, David F.
Bomse, Marguerite D. Practical Spanish Dictionary & Phrasebook. Pergamon.
Bonaccorsi, Alfredo. Nuovo dizionario musicale Curci. Curci.
Bonaffe, Edmond. Dictionnaire des Amateurs Francais au 17 Siecle. Lenox.
Bonassies, F., jt. auth. see Bories, J.
Bonazzi, Benedetto. Dizionario greco-italiano. Morano.
Bond, Otto F., jt. auth. see Castillo, Carlos.
Bond, P. S., jt. auth. see Garber, Max B.
Bone, Hugh A. Party Committees & National Politics. U of Wash Pr.
Bones, R. A., ed. Dictionary of Telecommunications. Philos Lib.
Bongiovanni, Gail. Medical Spanish (HP). McGraw.
Boni, Luigi. Dizionario dell'enigmista. Mazziana.
Bonin, Werner F. Lexikon der Parapsychologie & ihrer Grenzgebiete. Scherz AG.
Bonnaffe, Edmond. Dictionnaire des Amateurs Francais au Dix-Septieme Siecle. B Franklin.
Bonnefoi, Alexandre. Woerterbuch des Arbeits & Sozialrechts: Deutsch-Franz Dictionnaire de Droit du Trava il & de Droit Social. Hueber.
--Woerterbuch des Arbeits und Sozialrechtd. French & Eur.
Bonnefoy, Claude, et al. Dictionnaire de Litterature Francais Contemporaine. French & Eur.
Bonnin Valls, Ignacio, et al. Lexico Dos. Vicens-Vives.
--Lexico Uno. Vicens-Vives.
Bono, Edward De see De Bono, Edward.
Bonvalot, Marie. Le Vocabulaire Medical de Base. Organisation Instruction Proger.
--Le Vocabulaire Medical de Base. Soc Etudes Tech.
--Le Vocabulaire Medical De Base. French & Eur.
Booij, G, et al. Lexikon van de Taalwetenschap. Spectrum NL.
Boone, Lalla P. The Petroleum Dictionary. U of Okla Pr.
Booth, K. M. Dictionary of Refrigeration & Air Conditioning (Pub. by Applied Science). Burgess-Intl Ideas.
Booth, K. M., ed. Dictionary of Refrigeration & Air Conditioning. Elsevier.
Bordeje Morencos, Fernando de see De Bordeje Morencos, Fernando.
Borden, Arthur R., Jr. A Comprehensive Old-English Dictionary. U Pr of Amer.
Borel, Pierre. Vocabulaire Systematique Francais-Allemand. Francke.
Borelli, A., et al. Dizionario inglese. Ist Geo Agostini.
Bories, J. & Bonassies, F. Dictionnaire Pratique de la Presse, de l'imprimerie & de la Librairie. Gregg.
Boris, Gilbert & Denizeau, M. Lexique du Parler des Marazig. Imprimerie Nat.
Borisov, et al. Diccionario De Economia Politica. French & Eur.
--Diccionario de Economia Politica. French & Eur.
Borisov, E. F., ed. Politekonomicheskii Slovar (Pub. by Politizdat). Four Continent.
Bork, E. & Kaper, E. Dansk-Tysk Ordbog. French & Eur.
--Tysk-Dansk Ordbog. French & Eur.
Bork, Egon & Kaper, Egon. Dansk-Tysk Ordbog. Gyldendal Norsk.
Borkowski, Pioter. English-Polish Dictionary of Idioms & Phrases. Hippocrene Bks.
Borkowski, Piotr. English-Polish Dictionary of Idioms & Phrases. Hippocrene Bks.
Born, Erhard. Lexikon Fuer Eisenbahnfreunde. French & Eur.
Born, Erhard Von see Von Born, Erhard, et al.
Born, Ernst. Lexikon Fuer Die Graphische Industrie. French & Eur.
Born, R., ed. see Broers, A. & Smit, J.
Bornecque, Henri & Cauet, Fernand. Dictionnaire Latin-Francais. French & Eur.
Bornemisza, Elemer, jt. auth. see Gavande, S. A.
Bornstein, Harry. The Signed English Dictionary. Gallaudet Coll.
Bornstein, Harry & Saulnier, Karen L., eds. The Comprehensive Signed English Dictionary. Gallaudet Coll.
Bornstein, Scott. Vocabulary Mastery. Bornstein Memory.
Borovski, Conrad. Active German Idioms. Hueber.
Borra, Edoardo. Dizionario di sessuologia o dell'armonia coniugale. Edizioni Paoline.
--Dizionario di sessuologia o dell'armonia coniugale. Edizioni Paoline.
Borra, Edoardo, et al. Sana Alimentazione. Edizioni Paoline.
Borrello, Alfred. An E. M. Forster Glossary. Scarecrow.
Borror, Donald J. Dictionary of Word Roots & Combining Forms. Mayfield Pub.
Borshch, A. T., et al, eds. Russko-Moldavskii Slovar (Pub. by Izd. Inostr. & Natsional Slovarei). Four Continent.
Bortnikov, V. B., et al. Russko-Moldavskii Ekonomicheskii Slovar (Pub. by Kartia Moldoveniaske). Four Continent.
Bortolan, D. Vocabolario dei dialetto antico vicentino. Forni.
--Vocabolario del dialetto antico vicentino. Forni.
Borucki, Hans, et al. Die Physik: Ein Lexikon der Gesamten Schulphysik. Biblio Inst.
--Die Chemie: Ein Lexikon der Gesamten Schulchemie. Biblio Inst.
Borum, Oscar A. & Von Eyben, W. E. Juridisk Ordbog. Gad Forlag.
Bos, Alphonse. Glossaire de la Langue d'Oll. Laffitte Reprints.
Bos, Aphonse. Glossaire de la Langue d'Oll. Slatkine.
Boscarol, M., tr. see Wiegelmann, Alfred.
Bosch. Fachwoerterbuch Kraftfahrtechnik (Pub. by VDI Verlag GMBH). French & Eur.
--Fachwoerterbuch Kraftfahrtechnik (Pub. by VDI Verlag GMBH). French & Eur.
Bosch, R., ed. Technical Dictionary for Automotive Engineering (Pub. by VDI W Germany). Heyden.
Bosch, Ten. Dutch-English-French-German Engineering Dictionary. Heinman.
Boscher, Winfried, et al. Woerterbuch Vietnamesisch-Deutsch. VEB Verlag Enzyklopadie.
Bossaglia, Rossana. Dizionario di terminologia di storia dell'arte. Bignami.
Bossicart, Claude. Dictionnaire de l'effusion. Dryadè.
Bossier, Rene. Dictionnaire Technique des Fabrications Mecaniques. Desforges.
Boston Public Library. Dictionary Catalog of the Music Collection, Boston Public Library (Hall Library). G K Hall.
Bosworth, Joseph. A Compendious Anglo-Saxon & English Dictionary. Longwood Pr.
Bosworth, Joseph, et al, eds. An Anglo-Saxon Dictionary. Oxford U Pr.
Botel, Morton. Primary Multi-Level Speller & First Dictionary. Penns Valley.
Botiakova, V. V., et al. Russko-Angliiskii Shkol'No-Pedagogicheskii Slovar (Pub. by Iaroslavsk. Knizhn. Izd.). Four Continent.
Bottero, A. Dizionario dell'infermiera. EIPS.
Botterweck, G. Johannes & Ringgren, Helmer, eds. Theological Dictionary of the Old Testament. Eerdmans.
--Theological Dictionary of the Old Testament. Incl. Vol. I; Vol. II; Vol. III. Eerdmans.
Bottiglioni, G. Dizionario delle parlate corse. Stem Mucchi.
Bottomore, Tom & Harris, Laurence, eds. A Dictionary of Marxist Thought. Harvard U Pr.
Bouckaert, J. J. Nieuwe Medische Winkler Prins. Elsevier Nederland.
Boudier, J. F. & Luquet, F. M. Dictionnaire Laitier: French-English-French. French & Eur.
Boudon, Raymond & Lazarsfeld, Paul. Vocabulaire Des Sciences Sociales: Concepts et Indices. Mouton.
Boughner, Howard. Dictionary of Things to Draw (G&D). Putnam Pub Group.
Boulay, J., jt. auth. see Desrosiers, G.
Bouquet, Georges, jt. auth. see Ballereau, Emile.
Bourasse, J. J. Dictionnaire d'Epigraphie Chretienne. Migne, J. P., ed. Caratzas Pub Co.
Bourbon Parma, Cecilia de see De Bourbon Parma, Cecilia.
Bourdet, Francoise. Understanding French Cookery: A Guide to French Recipes & Cooking Terms. Kingsmead Pr.
Bourke, D. O. French-English Horticultural Dictionary (Pub. by CAB Bks England). State Mutual Bk.
--Horticultural Dictionary: French-English. French & Eur.
Bourneuf, Jacques, jt. auth. see Domart, Andre.
Boursin, E. & Challamel, Auguste. Dictionnaire de la Revolution Francaise. Kraus.
Boursin, Jean-Louis. DEMO: Dictionnaire Elementaire de Mathematiques Modernes. French & Eur.
Bouscaren, Christian. Le Vocabulaire Anglais au Baccalaureat. Ophrys.
Boushahla, Jo J. & Reidel-Geubtner, Virginia. The Dream Dictionary: The Key to Your Unconscious. Pilgrim NY.
Boussinot, Roger. Dictionnaire des Synonymes, Analogies & Antonymes. Bordas-Dunod.
Boutet, Frederic. Dictionnaire des sciences occultes suivi d'un dictionnaire des songes. Pygmalion.
Bouvier-Ajam, Maurice, et al. Dictionnaire Economique & Social. Edns Sociales.
Bouyer, Louis. Diccionario De Teologia. French & Eur.
Bowman, Walter P. & Ball, Robert H. Theatre Language, a Dictionary. Theatre Arts.
Boxshall, G. A., jt. auth. see Lincoln, R. J.
Boyce, Byrl N., ed. Real Estate Appraisal Terminology. Ballinger Pub.
Boyce, Byrl N., ed. see American Institute of Real Estate Appraisers.
Boyd-Bowman, Peter. Lexico hispanoamericano del siglo XVIII. Hispanic Seminary.
Boyer, A. L. Dictionnaire de Physiologie. Migne, J. P., ed. Caratzas Pub Co.
Boyle, John A. Persian-English Dictionary, Romanized. Saphrograph.
Bozzano, Lily A., et al, eds. Nuovo Dizionario Ricordi Della Musica & dei Musicisti. G Ricordi.
Braasch, Theodor. Vollstaendiges Woerterbuch Zur Sogenannten Caedmonschen Genesis. Winter Univ.
--Vollstaendiges Woerterbuch Zur Sogenannten Caedmonschen Genesis (Pub. by Carl Winter). French & Eur.
Brace, Edward R. An Illustrated Dictionary of Chess. Newnes Bks.
Brace, G., jt. auth. see Moureau, M.
Brace, Gerald, jt. ed. see Moureau, Magdaleine.
Brache, Jose A. Cinco Mil Seiscientos Refranes & Frases de Uso Comun Entre los Dominicanos. Pichardo, Nicolas, ed. Galaxia.
Brachmann-Teubner, Elisabeth. Lexikon Archivwesen der DDR. Staatsdruk.
Bradley, John W. Dictionary of Miniaturists, Illustrators, Calligraphers, & Copyists, with References to Their Works, & Notices of Their Patrons, from the Establishment of Christianity to the 18th Century. B Franklin.
Bradley, William J. CB Fact Book & Language Dictionary. DMR Pubns.
Bragadir, Sabine, jt. auth. see Dioudonnat, Pierre-Marie.
Braier, Leon. Diccionario Enciclopedico de Medicino Jims. Jims.
Brain, James L. A Short Dictionary of Science Terms for Swahili Speakers. Syracuse U Foreign Comp.
--A Social Science Vocabulary of Swahili. Syracuse U Foreign Comp.
Brambilla, A., ed. see Castiglioni, Luigi.
Branca Ciocetti, M. A., tr. see Fatturosso, V. & Ritter, O.
Branch, Alan E. Dictionary of Shipping-International Trade Terms & Abbreviations. Witherby UK.

Branch, Michael, et al. A Student's Glossary of Finnish. Soderstrom.
Branciard, Michel. Dictionnaire Economique & Social: Dictionnaire Thomas Suavet. Ouvrieres.
Brand, John R. Handbook of Electronic Formulas, Symbols, & Definitions. Van Nos Reinhold.
Brandau, Carlos. Diccionario Aleman-Espanol. Mayfe.
--Diccionario Espanol-Aleman. Mayfe.
Brandenberger, E. & Stattmann, F. Nuclear Power Dictionary (Verlag Karl Thiemig). French & Eur.
Brandin, Louis, jt. auth. see Lambert, Mayer.
Brandon, S. G. F. Diccionario de Religiones Comparadas. French & Eur.
Branford, Jean. A Dictionary of South African English. Oxford U Pr.
Brannen, Noah, jt. auth. see Thorlin, Eldora.
Brasholz, Anton, et al. Lexikon der Anstrichtechnik: Bd 2. Callwey.
Brassine, J. Rechtskundig Woerdenboek: Dictionnaire Juridique. Bruylant.
Brassine, Jules. Dictionnaire Juridique Flammand-Francais. Bruylant.
Bratcher, R. G., et al. A New Testament Wordbook for Translators. United Bible.
Bratescu, Gheorghe. Dictionar Cronologie de Medicina si Farmacie. Editura Stiintifica.
Bratus, B. V., et al. Russian Word-Collocations: Learner's Dictionary. Four Continent.
Brau, Jean-Louis. Dictionnaire de l'astrologie. Larousse FR.
--Dictionnaire de l'astrologie. Larousse.
Brault, Gerard J. Early Blazon: Heraldic Terminology in the Twelfth & Thirteenth Centuries; with Special Reference to Arthurian Literature. Oxford U Pr.
Braun, Edmund. Wissenschaftstheoretisches Lexikon (Pub. by Styria). French & Eur.
Braun, M. & Pollok, K. Langenscheidts Taschenwoerterbuch Russisch: Teil II, Deutsch-Russisch. Langenscheidt.
Braun, M. see Blattner, Karl.
Brauner, Rudolf. Von Bach zur Elektronik. Prugg.
Brautigam, Kurt. So Werd bei uns Geredd. SVA Verlag.
Bray & Trump. Dictionary of Archaeology. Penguin.
Bray, J. W. A History of English Critical Terms. Gordon Pr.
--A History of English Critical Terms. Gordon Pr.
Bray, W. & Trump, D. Lexikon der Archaeologie. French & Eur.
Bray, Warwick & Trump, David. Diccionario De Arqueologia. French & Eur.
--Dizionario di archeologia. Mondadori.
Brazhdzhiunas, P. Litovsko-Russko-Anglo-Nemetskii Slovar Fizicheskikh Terminov (Pub. by Mokslas). Four Continent.
Brazol, D. Diccionario de terminos meterologicos: Ingles-espanol espanol-ingles. Hachette.
Breaban, M. Dictionar de Metalurgie Englez-Roman. Editura Stiintifica.
Breaban, M. L. Dictionar de Metalurgie Francez-Roman. Editura Stiintifica.
Breitsameter. Lexikon der Schulphysik: Elektrizitaet und Magnetismus A-K. French & Eur.
--Lexikon der Schulphysik: Elektrizitaet und Magnetismus L-Z. French & Eur.
Breitung, Eusebius. Deutsch-Japanisches Woerterbuch. Buske.
Bremer, R., et al. Woerterbuch der Agrarpolitik. Parey.
Bremner, John B. Words, Words, Words: A Dictionary for Writers & Others Who Care About Words. Columbia U Pr.
Brenesan, Janos. Orvosi Szotar. Terra.
Brenet, Michel. Diccionario de la musica. Iberia SA.
--Diccionario De la Musica: Historico y Tecnico. French & Eur.
Breton, Andre. Lexico Sucinto del Erotismo. French & Eur.
Breuer, Hans. Dictionary for Computer Languages. Acad Pr.
Breuer, K. German-English, English-German Technical Pocket Dictionary. Heinman.
Breuer, Karl. Pocket Dictionary of Technology & Science: Technischwissenschaftliches Taschenwoerte'buch: German-English & English-German. Intl Pubns Serv.
Breugger, Walter. Diccionario de Filosofia (French & Eur). French & Eur.
Brewer, Annie M., ed. Dictionaries, Encyclopedias, & Other Word-Related Books. Gale.
Brewer, E. C. The Dictionary of Phrase & Fable. Outlet Bk Co.
Brewer, E. Cobham. Brewer's Dictionary of Phrase & Fable: Centenary Edition. Evans, Ivor, pref. by. (HarpT). Har-Row.
--A Dictionary of Miracles, Imitative, Realistic, & Dogmatic. Gale.
Brewer, Ebenezer. A Dictionary of Miracles. Gordon Pr.
Brewer, Forrest & Brewer, Jean. Vocabulario Mexicano de Tetelcingo. Summer Inst Ling.
Brewer, Jean, jt. auth. see Brewer, Forrest.
Bridel, Philippe Cyriaque & Favrat, Louis. Glossaire du Patois de la Suisse Romande. Slatkine.
Bridger & Wolk. The New Jewish Encyclopedia. Behrman.
Briese, K. English-German Dictionary (Pub. by Collet's). State Mutual Bk.
Brigato, Giovanni & Pisano, Giorgio. Dizionario eponimico ostetrico-ginecologico. Piccin.
Briggs, Donald C. & Alisky, Marvin. Historical Dictionary of Mexico. Scarecrow.
Briggs, Geoffrey, ed. Civic & Corporate Heraldry: A Dictionary of Impersonal Arms of England, Wales, & Northern Ireland. Gale.
Brighenti, Eliseo. Dizionario greco moderno-italiano e italiano-greco moderno: Vol. 1, Greco moderno-italiano. Cisalpino.
Brinkmann & Schmidt. Woerterbuch der Datentechnik. Brandstetter.
Brinkmann, Karl H. Dictionary of Dataprocessing. French & Eur.
Brinkmann, Karl-Heinz, et al. Data Systems Dictionary. Brandstetter.
Brinton, Daniel G. Lenape-English Dictionary. Waletittin.
--A Lenape-English Dictionary. AMS Pr.
Brinton, Daniel G. & Anthony, Albert S., eds. A Lenape-English Dictionary. AMS Pr.
Brissiere, P. De see De Brissiere, P.
British Columbia, Ministry of Lands, Parks & Housing. Land Allocation Terminology. Minist Prov Sec.
Britten, F. J. Britten's Watch & Clock Maker's Handbook, Dictionary & Guide. Good, Richard, ed. Arco.
--Watch & Clockmakers' Handbook, Dictionary & Guide. Antique Collect.
Brkic, S. Serbocroatian-English Dictionary. French & Eur.
Broad, Lewis C. & Broad, Violet M. Dictionary to the Plays & Novels of Bernard Shaw. Folcroft.
Broad, Violet M., jt. auth. see Broad, Lewis C.
Broadbent, D. T. & Masubuchi, M. Multilingual Glossary of Automatic Control Technology: English-French-German-Russian-Italian-Spanish-Japanese. Pergamon.
Broadbent, K. Dictionary of China's Rural Economy. French & Eur.
Brocher, Tobias. Lexikon der Sozialerziehung. French & Eur.
Brockhaus. Diccionario popular de las ciencias y de la tecnica. Gill Gustavo.
Broeger, Achim. Meyers Grosses Kinderlexikon. Biblio Inst.
Broers, A. & Smit, J. English-Dutch Dictionary. Born, R., ed. French & Eur.
Bromberg, Murray, et al. Five Hundred & Four Absolutely Essential Words. Barron.
Brommer. Lexique Anglais-Francais des Termes Appartenant aux Techniques en Usage a I. G. N. I. G. N.
Brommer, ed. Lexique Anglais-Francais des Termes Appartenant Aux Techniques En Usage a I.G.N. French & Eur.
Bronstein, Arthur J. Pronunciation of American English. P-H.
Brooks, Hugh. Encyclopedia of Building & Construction Terms. P-H.
Brooks, J. R., jt. auth. see Whitten, D. G.
Brossard. Dictionary of Music. Gruber, Albion, ed. Inst Mediaeval Mus.
Brosse, La. Diccionario del Cristianismo. French & Eur.
Brosse, Olivier. Diccionario del Cristianismo. Herder SA.
Brosset, Raymond & Fondaneche, Pierre. Dictionnaire Memento d'electronique. Bordas-Dunod.
--Dictionnaire Memento D'electronique. French & Eur.
Broster, E. J. Glossary of Applied Management & Financial Statistics. Crane-Russak Co.
Brougham, A. E., jt. ed. see Reed, A. W.
Brousse, Guy. Dictionnaire Foucher de Stenographie. Foucher.
--Dictionnaire Foucher de Stenographie Prevost-Delauney. Foucher.
Brown, C. N. Modern English-Greek Dictionary. French & Eur.
Brown, Calvin S. A Glossary of Faulkner's South. Yale U Pr.
Brown, Charles P. Dictionary of Telugu & English: Explaining English Idioms & Phrases in Telugu. Ayer Co.
Brown, Frances A. Comprehensive Forkner Shorthand Dictionary. Forkner.
Brown, Francis, et al, eds. see Gesenius, William.
Brown, James I. Programmed Vocabulary. P-H.
Brown, John E. & Brown, Margaret H. The Crossworder's List Book. St Martin.
Brown, Joseph F. Diabetes Dictionary & Guide. Press West.
Brown, Lawrence K. A Thesaurus of Spanish Idioms & Everyday Language. Ungar.
Brown, Margaret H., jt. auth. see Brown, John E.
Brown, Philomena. A Basic Dictionary of Home Economics (Pub. by Bell & Hyman England). State Mutual Bk.
Brown, R. F. Diccionario Collins Contemporary English-Spanish Ingles-Espanol. Grijalbo.
Brown, R. F., ed. Spanish-English, English-Spanish Gem Dictionary. Collins Pubs.
Brown, R. H. Diccionario de terminos maritimos en seguros. Gonzalez Hevia, Raul, tr. Mapfre.
Brown University. Dictionary Catalog of the Harris Collection of American Poetry & Plays, Brown University (Hall Library). G K Hall.
Browning, D. S. Everyman's Dictionary of Literary Biography (Pub by J M Dent England). Biblio Dist.
Brownstone, David M. & Franck, Irene M. Dictionary of Publishing. Van Nos Reinhold.
--The VNR Investor's Dictionary. Van Nos Reinhold.
--The VNR Real Estate Dictionary. Van Nos Reinhold.
Brownstone, David M., et al. The VNR Dictionary of Business & Finance. Van Nos Reinhold.
Brozovic, Blanka & Gercan, Oktavija. English-Serbocroatian & Serbocroatian-English Dictionary. Intl Learn Syst.
Bruce, George. Harbottle's Dictionary of Battles. Van Nos Reinhold.
Bruggencate, K. T. Dutch-English Dictionary. Gerritsen, J., et al, eds. French & Eur.
--English-Dutch Dictionary. Gerritsen, J., et al, eds. French & Eur.
Bruggencate, K. Ten. Dutch-English, English-Dutch Dictionary. Heinman.
Brugger, Walter & Baker, Kenneth. Philosophical Dictionary. Guild Bks.
Bruguera Grane, Francisco. Diccionario Ingles-Espanol, Espanol-Ingles. French & Eur.
Brunacci, G., jt. auth. see Cusatelli, G.
Brunati, G. Dizionarietto degli uomini illustri della riviera di Sabo. Forni.
Brun-Durand, Justin. Dictionnaire Topographique & Historique de la Drome. Chantermerle.
Brunet, G. Dictionnaire des Apocryphes. Migne, J. P., ed. Caratzas Pub Co.
Brunhuber, E. Giesserei - Fachwoerterbuch (Pub. by Fachverlag, Schiele & Schon). French & Eur.
--Giesserei - Lexikon 1978 (Pub. by Fachverlag, Schiele & Schon). French & Eur.
--Giesserei-Fachwoerterbuch. Schiele & Schon.
--Giesserei-Lexikon 1978. Schiele & Schon.
Brunhuber, Ernst. Giesserei-Fachworterbuch. Schiele & Schon.
Brunius, Niklas. Teaterord. Nord Teater.
Brunner, Victor. Diccionario de Siglas en Comercio Exterior. Liv Nobel.
Bruno, Michael H., ed. Glossary of Paper Terms for Web & Sheet-Fed Offset Printing. TAPPI.
Brunoli, A. Dizionario Avicolo Internazionale. Ed Calderini.
Brunoli, Alberto. Dizionario avicolo internazionale. Edagricole.
Bruno Natlis, Elena. Estudio Comparativo de Vocabularios Tobas y Pilagas. French & Eur.
Brussel, James A. & Cantzlaar, George L. Diccionario de Psiquiatria. French & Eur.
Brussel, James A. & Cantzlaar, Geroge L., trs. Diccionario de psiquiatria. CECSA.
Bruttini, Alberto. Dictionnaire de Sylviculture: Francais-Allemand-Anglais-Espagnol-Italien. Lechevalier.
Bruun, Erik. Dansk Sprogbrug. Gyldendal Norsk.
Bruzelius, Anders, et al. Kortfattad Engelsk-svensk Juridisk Ordbok. Liber Gleerup.
Bruzelius, Andre, et al, eds. Concise English-Swedish Dictionary of Legal Terms. French & Eur.
Bryant, Al. New Compact Bible Dictionary. Zondervan.
Bryant, Margaret M; see Malmstrom, Jean.
Bryant, T. A., compiled by. Today's Dictionary of the Bible. Bethany Hse.
Bryson, William H. A Dictionary of Sigla & Abbreviations to & in Law Books Before 1607. U Pr of Va.
Brzeska, Wanda & Brzeski, Alojzy. Ilustrowany Slownik Niemiecko-Polski. Wiedza Powszechna.
Brzeska, Wanda, et al. Ilustrowany Slownik Niemiecko-Polski. Wiedza Powszechna.
Brzeski, Alojzy, jt. auth. see Brzeska, Wanda.
Buarque de Holanda Ferreira, Aurelio. Minidicionario da Lingua Portuguesa. Edit Atica.
Bubic, S. Dictionary of Economic Terms. French & Eur.
Bubnikova, M. Rusko-Sesky Chemicky Slovnik. Russkii Iazyk.
Buca, M., ed. Dictionar Analogic si de Sinonime al Limbii Romane. Editura Stiintifica.
Buchanan, Brian W. Glossary of Indexing Terms (Linnet). Shoe String.
Buchanan-Brown, John, jt. ed. see Kogan Page, Ltd.
Buchholz, W., et al. Iterated Inductive Definitions & Subsystems of Analysis: Recent Proof-Theoretical Studies. Springer-Verlag.
Buchkina, B. Z., et al. Slitno Ili Razdelno (Pub. by Russkii Iazyk). Four Continent.
Buchner, Greet. Milieuvriendelijk van A tot Z. Driehoek.

Buck, Carl D. Dictionary of Selected Synonyms in the Principal Indo-European Languages. U of Chicago Pr.

Buck, Dudley. Musical Pronouncing Dictionary. Scholarly.

--Pronouncing Musical Dictionary. Scholarly.

Buck, Frederick H. Glossary of Mongolian Technical Terms. Spoken Lang Serv.

Buck, Stuart H., ed. Tibetan-English Dictionary with Supplement. Cath U Pr.

Buckingham, J., et al, eds. Dictionary of Organic Compounds (Pub. by Chapman & Hall). Methuen Inc.

Buckingham, J. B., et al, eds. Dictionary of Organic Compounds: First Supplement (Pub. by Chapman & Hall). Methuen Inc.

Buckland, A. R. Diccionario Biblico: Broch. Life Pubs Intl.

--Diccionario Biblico: Enc. Life Pubs Intl.

Buckland, William K., jt. auth. see **Kendall, Maurice G.**

Buckland, William R. & Kendall, Maurice G. Diccionario de Estadistica. Piramide.

Bucksch. Diccionario Para Obras Publica, Edificacion y Maquinaria En Obra. French & Eur.

--Diccionario para obras publicas, edificacion y maquinaria en obra: Aleman-espanol, espanol-aleman. Herder SA.

--Dictionnaire pour l'Architecture le Batiment et les Materiaux de Construction: Allemand-Francais. Maison Dictionnaire.

--Dictionnaire pour l'architecture le Batiment et les Materiaux de Construction: Francais-Allemand. Maison Dictionnaire.

Bucksch, H. Dictionary of Civil Engineering & Construction Machinery & Equipment. Intl Pubns Serv.

--Dictionary of Mechanisms. French & Eur.

--Getriebe-Woerterbuch. Bauverlag.

--Holz-Woerterbuch: Band I, Deutsch-Englisch. Bauverlag.

--Woerterbuch Bau: Ingenieurbau & Baumaschinen. Bauverlag.

--Woerterbuch fuer Architektur, Hochbau & Baustoffe. Bauverlag.

--Woerterbuch fuer Architektur, Hochbau & Baustoffe: Band 1, Deutsch-Englisch. Bauverlag.

--Woerterbuch fuer Bautechnik & Baumaschinen: Band I, Deutsch-Englisch. Bauverlag.

--Woerterbuch fuer Bautechnik & Baumaschinen: Band II, Englisch-Deutsch. Bauverlag.

--Woerterbuch fuer Bautechnik und Baumaschinen. French & Eur.

--Woerterbuch fur Bau & Grundstucksrecht & Raumordnung. Bauverlag.

--Woerterbuch fur Baurecht, Grundstucksrecht & Raumordnung: Band I, Deutsch-Englisch. Bauverlag.

--Woerterbuch fur Baurecht, Grungstucksrecht & Raumordnung: Band II, Englisch-Deutsch. Bauverlag.

Bucksch, H. & Altemeyer, A. Dictionnaire des Canalisations a Grande Distance: Anglais-Francais-Allemand. French & Eur.

Bucksch, H. & Altmeyer, A. P. Pipeline Dictionary. Bauverlag.

--Pipeline Dictionary (Pub. by Bauverlag). French & Eur.

--Pipeline Dictionary. Intl Pubns Serv.

Bucksch, Hector. Dictionnaire Allemand-Francais pour les Travaux Publics: Le Batiement & l'equipement des Chantiers des Chantiers de Constuction. Eyrolles.

--Dictionnaire Anglais-Francais pour les Travaux Publics: Le Batiment & L'equipement des Chantiers de Construction. Eyrolles.

--Dictionnaire des Canalisations: Francais-Allemand. Eyrolles.

--Dictionnaire Francais-Allemand pour le Travaux Publics le Batiment & l'equipement des Chantiers de Construction. Eyrolles.

--Dictionnaire Francais-Anglais pour les Travaux Publics: Le Batiment & l'equipement des Chantiers de Construction. Eyrolles.

--Dictionnaire pour les Travaux Publics, le Batiment et l'Equipement des Chantiers de Construction. French & Eur.

Bucksch, Herbert. Dental dictionary. Verlag Neuer.

--Dictionary of Architecture, Building Construction & Materials. French & Eur.

--Dictionary of Architecture, Building Construction & Materials. French & Eur.

--Dictionary of Architecture, Building Construction & Materials. Intl Pubns Serv.

--Dictionary of Civil Engineering & Construction Machinery & Equipment. French & Eur.

--Dictionary of Civil Engineering & Construction Machinery & Equipment. French & Eur.

--Dictionary of Civil Engineering & Construction Machinery & Equipment. French & Eur.

--Dictionary of Civil Engineering & Construction Machinery & Equipment. French & Eur.

--Dictionary of Mechanisms-Getriebeworterbuch: German-English, English-German. Intl Pubns Serv.

--Dictionary of Wood & Woodworking Practice. Intl Pubns Serv.

--Dictionary of Wood & Woodworking Practice. Intl Pubns Serv.

--Holz Woerterbuch. Bauverlag.

--Holz Woerterbuch. Bauverlag.

--Holz Woerterbuch (Pub. by Bauverlag). French & Eur.

--Holz Woerterbuch (Pub. by Bauverlag). French & Eur.

Bucksch, Herbert & Galan e Hidalgo, Arturo. Diccionario frances-espanol de la construccion y obras publicas. ETA.

Bucksch, Herbert & Galan e Hildalgo, Arturo. Diccionario Frances-Espanol de la Construccion y Obras Publicas. French & Eur.

Bucur, Marin, ed. see **Eminescu, Mihail.**

Budd Hadatta Mahathera, A. Pali-English Dictionary. Saphrograph.

Budenz, Jozsef. Comparative Dictionary of the Finno-Ugric Elements in the Hungarian Vocabulary. Res Ctr Lang Semiotic.

Budgay. Dizionario turco-italiano. Vallardi A.

Budge, E. Wallis. Egyptian Hieroglyphic Dictionary, Vols. 1 & 2. Dover.

Budge, Ernest A. A Hieroglyphic Vocabulary to the Theban Recension of the Book of the Dead. AMS Pr.

Budic, D. W. Diccionario del comercia exterior. Ergon.

Budig, Peter K. Elektrotechnik Elektronik. VEB Verlag Technik.

--Elektrotechnik Elektronik Deutsch-Englisch. VEB Technik.

--Fachwoerterbuch Elektrotechnik, Elektronik (Pub. by Huethig). French & Eur.

Budig, Peter-Klaus, ed. Electricity & Electronics Technical Dictionary. Intl Pubns Serv.

Buel, Larry V., jt. ed. see **Hanrieder, Wolfram F.**

Buenaventura de Oreyegui, P., jt. auth. see **Aberlaitz.**

Buerger. Woerterbuch Datenerfassung: Programmierung. Verlag Harri Deutsch.

--Woerterbuch Informationsverarbeitung. Verlag Harri Deutsch.

Buerger, E. Woerterbuch Datenerfassung-Programmierung. French & Eur.

Bueschgen, Hans E., ed. Handwoerterbuch der Finanzwirtschaft. Poeschel.

Bugday, M. Celalettin. Dizionario Italiano-Turco, Turco-Italiano. French & Eur.

Buhler, Alain & Didier, J. Dictionnaire de la revolution Etudiante. Controverses.

Buhr, M., jt. auth. see **Klaus, G.**

Buhr, M., jt. ed. see **Klaus, G.**

Buhr, Manfred, jt. auth. see **Klaus, Georg.**

Building Industry & Civil Engineering Society. Dictionary of Technical Information (Pub. by Collet's). State Mutual Bk.

Buissonnier, Solange. Vocabulaire & Elocution les Debutants. Hachette.

Buksch, Herbert. Woerterbuch fuer Architektur, Hochbau & Baustoffe. Bauverlag.

Bulakhov, M. G. Vostochnoslavianskie Iazykovedy. Four Continent.

Bulas, Kazimierz, et al. The Kosciuszko Foundation English-Polish, Polish-English Dictionary. Kosciuszko.

Bulgakov. Diccionario militar espanol-ruso. Pueblos Unidos.

Bulke. English Hindi Dictionary. Auromere.

Bullas, K. & Whitfield, F. J. Dictionary English-Polish, Polish-English. Adler.

Bullock, Alan & Stallybrass, Oliver, eds. The Harper Dictionary of Modern Thought (HarpT). Har-Row.

Bullokar, John. English Expositor: Teaching the Interpretation of the Hardest Words Used in Our Language. Adler.

Bulygin, N. F. Karmannyi Indoneziisko-Russkii Slovar (Pub. by GINS). Four Continent.

Bulygin, N. F., et al. Karmannyi Russko-Indoneziiskii Slovar (Pub. by GINS). Four Continent.

Bumpus, John S. Dictionary of Ecclesiastical Terms: Being a History & Explanation of Certain Terms Used in Architecture, Ecclesiology, Liturgiology, Music, Ritual, Cathedral, Constitution, Etc. Gale.

Bunin, D. A. Nemetsko-Russkii Zheleznodorozhnyi Slovar (Pub. by Gosizdat Tekhn.-Teoret. Lit.). Four Continent.

Bunin, D. A., et al. Deutsch-Russisches Worterbuch fur Eisenbahnwessen. French & Eur.

Bunjes, jt. auth. see **Lejeune.**

Bunjes, W. E., jt. auth. see **Lejeune, F.**

Bunjes, Werner E. Woerterbuch der Medizin und Pharmazeutik: Medical & Pharmaceutical Dictionary. Thieme Verlag.

Bunnell, Peter, ed. see **Snelling, Henry H. & Anthony, E.**

Bunnell, Peter C., ed. see **Guerronnan, Anthony.**

Bunye, Maria V., jt. auth. see **Yap, Elsa P.**

Buracas, A. English-Lithuanian Dictionary of Economic Terms (Pub. by Mokslas). Four Continent.

Burbidge, R. A Dictionary of British Flower, Fruit & Still Life Painters: Vol. 2, 1850-1950 (Pub. by A & C Black England). Humanities.

Burchfield, R. W. A Supplement to the Oxford English Dictionary, Volume 2 H-N. Oxford U Pr.

Burchfield, R. W., ed. Supplement to the Oxford English Dictionary Vol. 1: A-G. Oxford U Pr.

Burchfield, Robert W., ed. A Supplement to the Oxford English Dictionary. Oxford U Pr.

Bureau de l'Information Scientifique & Technique. Thesaurus Genie Chimique. Doc Scient.

Bureau International de Documentation de Chemin de Fer. Chemins de Fer Glossary. Elsevier.

Bureau, Jacques. Dictionnaire de l'informatique. Larousse.

--Dictionnaire de l'Informatique. French & Eur.

Burfeindt-Moral, H. & Moral-Arroyo, J. A. Langenscheidts Satz-Lexikon des Spanischen Geschaeftsbriefes. Langenscheidt.

Burger, Andre. Lexique Complet de la Langue de Villon. Droz.

Burger, E. Technical Dictionary of Data Processing, Computers & Office Machines, English, German, French, Russian. Pergamon.

Burger, E., ed. Technical Dictionary of Automatization & Programming: English, French, German, Russian,- Slovene. French & Eur.

--Technical Reference Dictionary. French & Eur.

Burger, Erich. Automatizovany Zber Dat Programovanie. Alfa-Vydavatel.

--Datenerfassung Programmierung. VEB Verlag Technik.

--Datenerfassung Programmierung-Englisch-Deutsch-Franzoesisch-Russisch. VEB Technik.

--Informationsverarbeitung-Englisch-Deutsch-Franzoesisch-Russisch. VEB Technik.

Burger, Habil E. Dictionary of Automatic Data Processing (Pub. by Collet's). State Mutual Bk.

Burger, Ing H. Dictionary of Automatic Data Processing (Pub. by Collets). State Mutual Bk.

Burgess, Francis H. A Dictionary for Yachtsmen. David & Charles.

Burke, John. Osborne's Concise Law Dictionary. Sweet Max.

Burkett, Eva M. American Dictionaries of the English Language Before 1861. Scarecrow.

Burnand, Tony. Dictionnaire Chasse. Larousse.

--Dictionnaire de la chasse. Larousse.

--Dictionnaire de la Chasse (Pub. by Larousse). French & Eur.

Burnett, Joseph W., jt. auth. see **Robinson, Harry M., Jr.**

Burnham, Dorothy K. Warp & Weft: A Dictionary of Textile Terms (ScribT). Scribner.

Burningham, Robin. Illustrated Hawaiian Word Book. Bess Pr.

Burridge, Shirley, ed. Oxford Elementary Learner's Dictionary of English. Oxford U Pr.

Burrow, Thomas & Emeneau, Murray B. Dravidian Etymological Dictionary. Oxford U Pr.

Burtin Vinholes, S., et al. Dicionario Frances-Portugues, Portugues-Frances. Editora Globo.

Burton, Maurice. Le Dictionnaire en Couleurs des Animaux. Elsevier Sequoia.

--Le Dictionnaire En Couleurs Des Animaux. French & Eur.

Burton, Maurice, ed. Young People's Animal Encyclopedia. Childrens.

Burton, Philip E. A Dictionary of Minicomputing & Microcomputing. Garland Pub.

Burton, William C. Legal Thesaurus. Macmillan.

Burton, William C. & DeCosta, Steven E. The Legal Thesaurus. Free Pr.

Busa, Vittorio. Dizionario italiano di vocaboli e modi usati in poesia: Per le Scuole superiori. Mori.

Busch, Karl F., jt. auth. see **Steiger, Eduard.**

Bush, Clifford L. & Andrews, Robert C. Dictionary of Reading & Learning Disabilities. Western Psych.

Bussi, Luciano & Cognazzo, Maria. Nuovo Dizionario Inglese-Italiano Delle Science Mediche. S F Vanni.

Bussy, J. H. Diccionario tecnico de terminos ferroviarios: Espanol-frances-aleman-ingles-italiano-holandes. G Gili.

Bustamente, Agustin, tr. see **Pevsner, Nikolaus,** et al.

Bustani, Butros. Muhit al-Muhit. Intl Bk Ctr.

Bustani, Butros, jt. auth. see **Wafi, Al.**

Busto, M. Pequeno Diccionario Tecnologico: Farmacia, Quimica, Fisica, Medicina y Ciencias Naturales. French & Eur.

Busturia, Daniel. Diccionario terminoligico de la Comunidades Europeas. Assn Prog Direc.

Butler, Bill. Dictionary of the Tarot. Schocken.

Butler, Montagu C. Esperanto-English Dictionary. Esperanto League North Am.

Butterfield, Arthur. Practical Spanish-English, English-Spanish Dictionary. Hippocrene Bks.

Butterworth, Neil. A Dictionary of American Composers. Garland Pub.

Butterworth, Rod & Flodin, Mickey. The Perigee Visual Dictionary of Signing (G&D). Putnam Pub Group.

Buttress, F. A., ed. World Guide to Abbreviations of Organizations. Gale.

Buttrick, George A. & Crim, Keith R., eds. The Interpreter's Dictionary of the Bible. Abingdon.

Butzmann, G., ed. Jugendlexikon UdSSR. Bibl Inst Leipzig.

Butzmann, G., et al, eds. Jugendlexikon A-Z. Bibl Inst Leipzig.

Bux, E., ed. see Kroh, Paul.

Buxtorf, Johann. Lexicon Chaldaicum Talmudicum & Rabbinicum. Olms Verlag.

Buydens, John. Groot Systematisch en Klankalfabetisch Rijmwoordenboek. Nederlandse Boek.

Byers, Edward E. Ten Thousand Medical Words, Spelled & Divided for Quick Reference (G). McGraw.

Byers, John R., Jr. & Owen, James J. A Concordance to the Five Novels of Nathaniel Hawthorne. Garland Pub.

Byington, Cyrus. A Dictionary of the Choctaw Language. Scholarly.

Bykova, E. M., et al. Bengal'sko-Russkii Slovar (Pub. by Gosizdat Inostr. Natsion. Slovarei). Four Continent.

Byl, Simon. Vocabulaire Grec de Base. Dessain & Tolra.

Bynum, W. F., et al. Dictionary of the History of Science. Macmillan London.

Bynum, William F., et al, eds. Dictionary of the History of Science. Princeton U Pr.

Byrne, Josefa H. Mrs. Byrne's Dictionary of Unusual, Obscure, & Preposterous Words, Gathered from Numerous & Diverse Authoritative Sources. Byrne, Robert, ed. & intro. by. Univ Bks.

Byrne, Josefa Heifetz. Mrs. Byrne's Dictionary of Unusual, Obscure, & Preposterous Words. Byrne, Robert, ed. & intro. by. Citadel Pr.

Byrne, Robert, ed. & intro. by see Byrne, Josefa H.

Byrne, Robert, ed. & intro. by see Byrne, Josefa Heifetz.

Bysiewicz, Shirley R. Monarch's Dictionary of Legal Terms. Monarch Pr.

Bystrova, E., jt. auth. see Shansky, N.

Bzdega, A., et al. Podreczny Slownik Polsko-Niemiecki (Manual Dictionary Polish-German) French & Eur.

C

Cabanne, Pierre. Dictionnaire International des Arts. Bordas.
--Dictionnaire International des Arts (Dist. by Continental Bk Co). Bordas.

Cabourdin, Guy & Viard, Georges. Lexique historique de la France d'Ancien regime. A Colin.

Cabral, Antonio C. Emprestimos Linguisticos nas Linguas Mocambicanas. Lourenco Marques.

Caccianotti, Luigi. Dizionario metodico del commercio laniero. Edit Laniera.

Caceres Freire, Julian. Diccionario de Regionalismos de la Provincia de la Rioja. French & Eur.

Cadenas y Vicent, Vicente de. Diccionario heraldico. Consejo Superior.

Cadiergues, Roger, jt. auth. see Barbier, Maurice.

Cadiz, Javier Gomez De see Gomez de Cadiz, Javier.

Cafagna, C. & Gangi, M. Dizionario chitarristico italiano. Berben.

Caffarena de Jiles, Elena. Diccionario de jurisprudencia chilena: Recopilacionde conceptos y definiciones. Juridica-Andres Belio.

Cage, William, jt. auth. see Duong Thanh Binh.

Cagnacci-Schwicker, A. Woerterbuch fuer Metallurgie, Mineralogie, Geologie, Bergbau & die Oelindustrie. Bauverlag.

Cagnacci-Schwicker, Angelo. Dictionnaire International de Metallurgie, Mineralogie, Geologie et Industries Extractives. French & Eur.

--Woerterbuch fuer Metallurgie, Mineralogie, Geologie, Bergbau & die Oelindustrie Englische-Franzosisch-Deutsch-Italienisch. Bauverlag.

Cagnat, Rene & Goyau, G. Lexique des Antiquites Romaines. Boccard.

Caha, J. & Kramsky, J. English-Czech Dictionary (Pub. by Collet's). State Mutual Bk.

Caha, J., ed. English-Czech Dictionary (Pub. by State Pedag. Publ. House). Four Continent.

Cahen, Jacques-Gabriel. Vocabulaire de Racine. Slatkine.

Cahill, P. Joseph, tr. see Leon-Dufour, Xavier.

Cahn, Sammy. The Songwriter's Rhyming Dictionary. Facts on File.

Cailleux, E. Elements de Geologie En Six Langues. French & Eur.

Caillon, Octave. Dictionnaire Etymologique. Ligel.

Cairo, G. Dizionario ragionato dei simboli. Forni.

Calamante, Mario. Dizionario illustrato e commentato delle norme di circolazione previste dal nuovo codice della strada. Ateneo & Bizzarri.

Calamegriaule, Genevieve. Dictionnaire Dogon: Ethnologique & Linguistique. S. E. L. A. F.

Calasibetta, Charlotte M. Fairchild's Dictionary of Fashion. Davis, Lorraine & Goble, Ermina S., eds. Fairchild.

Calbet Corbella, Josep Maria. Diccionari de metjes catalans. Dalmau.

Calbet Sequi, Juan. Terminos & Conceptos Mas Usuales en Mecanizacion Administrativa. Limusa.

Caldwell, Pablo. Diccionario de Modismos Ingleses. French & Eur.

Calfa, Ambroise. Dictionnaire Armenien-Francais. Klincksieck.
--Dictionnaire Armenien-Francais. French & Eur.

Callaham, Ludmila I. Russian-English Chemical & Polytechnical Dictionary. Wiley.
--Russian-English Chemical & Polytechnical Dictionary (Pub. by Wiley-Interscience). Wiley.

Calmann-Levy, jt. auth. see Noctuel.

Calmet, A. Dictionnaire Historique, Archeologique, Philologique, Chronologique Geographique et Literal de la Bible. Migne, J. P., ed. Caratzas Pub Co.

Calonghi, et al, eds. Dizionario della lingua latina: Latino-italiano e italiano-latino. Rosenberg & Sellier.

Calonghi, Ferruccio. Dizionario latino-italiano. Rosenberg & Sel.

Calonja, Juan R., jt. auth. see Pey, Santiago.

Calsat, Jean-Henri. Vocabulaire International des Termes d'urbanisme & d'architecture: Francais-Allemand-Anglais. Eyrolles.

Calsat, Jean-Henri & Sydler, Jean P. Vocabulaire International des Termes d'Urbanisme et d'Architecture. French & Eur.

Calsat, Jean-Henri & Sydler, Jean-Pierre. Vocabulaire International des Termes d'urbanisme et d'architecture: Francais-Allemand-Anglais. Ste. Diff. Tech. Bat. T. P.

Calvert, Brigadier M., jt. auth. see Young, Brigadier P.

Calvert, G. H. Cortina Handy Spanish-English, English-Spanish Dictionary. B&N NY.
--Spanish Dictionary. Routledge & Kegan.

Calvert, G. H., ed. Cortina Handy Spanish-English Dictionary. Cortina.

Calvin, Jean. Glossaire Dictionnaire des Locutions Obscures & des Mots Vieillis: Recontrent dans les Oeuvres de Calvin. Slatkine.

Camarao, P. C. & Serra, M. A. Great Technical Dictionary: Dicionario Tecnico English-Portuguese. French & Eur.

Camarao, Paulo C., et al. Great technical dictionary. Ao Livro Tecnico.

Camard, Jean Pierre & Belfort, Anne Marie. Dictionnaire des Peintres et Sculpteurs Provencaux. French & Eur.

Camard, Jean-Pierre, jt. auth. see Fondation Paul Richard.

Cambridge Book Editors. Increase Your Vocabulary. Cambridge Bk.

Camden, William G. A Descriptive Dictionary: Bislama to English. Camden Aus.

Cameron, Angus, jt. auth. see Frank, Roberta.

Cameron, Angus, jt. ed. see Frank, Roberta.

Cameron, D. Arabic-English Dictionary. Intl Bk Ctr.

Camille, Cl. & Dehaine, M. Dictionnaire de l'Informatique, Francais-Anglais. French & Eur.

Camille, Claude & Dehaine, Michael. Harrap's French & English Dictionary of Data Processing. Harrap.

Camille, Claude & Dehaine, Michel. Dictionnaire de l'informatique: Francais-Anglais. Bordas-Dunod.
--Harrap's English-French Dictionary of Data Processing. Harrap.

Camilleri, Charles. Camilleri's Dictionary of Musical Terms. Waterloo.

Campagna, G., ed. see Castiglioni, Luigi.

Campanini, Giuseppe, et al. Vocabolario latino-italiano-latino. Paravia.

Campbell, Robert J., ed. Psychiatric Dictionary. Oxford U Pr.

Campos, Geir. Pequeno Dicionario de Arte Poetica. Editora Cultrix.

Canadian Institute of Chartered Accountants. Terminology for Accountants. Canadian Inst Chart.

Canadian Pulp & Paper Association. Glossary of Printing Terms for the Papermaker. CN Pulp & Paper.
--Paper Defect Terminology - Coated Papers & Boards. CN Pulp & Paper.

Canadian Securities Institute. Investment Terms & Definitions. Can Securities Inst.

Canadian Society of Petroleum Geologists. Lexicon of Canadian Stratigraphy Arctic Archipelago. Can Soc Petro Geo.
--Lexicon of Canadian Stratigraphy Yukon-MacKenzie. Can Soc Petro Geo.

Canal, J. De La see De La Canal, J.

Canal, Julio de la. Diccionario de sinonimos e ideas afines. CECSA.

Canal, Julio De La see De La Canal, Julio.

Canavaggio, Pierre. Dictionnaire Raisonne Des Superstitions et Des Croyances Populaires. French & Eur.

Cande, Roland de. Dictionnaire Des Musiciens. French & Eur.

Cande, Roland de see De Cande, Roland.

Canestrari, R., tr. see Pieron, Henri.

Cannelin, Aulis, et al. Suomalais-Ruotsalainen Suursanakirja. Werner Soderstrom.

Cannelin, Knut, et al. Finsk-Swensk Storordbok. Esselte Studium.

Cannistraro, Philip V., ed. Historical Dictionary of Fascist Italy. Greenwood.

Cano Gonzalez, Ana M. Vocabulario del Bable de Somiedo. Consejo Superior.

Cantamessa, Giuseppe & Messina, Giuseppe. Dizionario della lingua italiana. Signorelli C.

Cantizar, George L., jt. auth. see Brussel, James A.

Cantizar, Geroge L., jt. tr. see Brussel, James A.

Capdevila Font, Juan. Diccionario Actualizado de la Lengua Espanola. French & Eur.
--Diccionario Actualizado De Sinonimos y Contrarios De la Lengua Espanola. French & Eur.
--Diccionario de Citas. French & Eur.
--Diccionario de la Lengua Espanola y Enciclopedia Escolar. French & Eur.
--Diccionario de la Lengua Espanola y Enciclopedia Escolar Distein. French & Eur.
--Diccionario de la Literatura Universal. French & Eur.
--Diccionario de la Vida Sexual. French & Eur.
--Diccionario De Matematicas. French & Eur.

--Diccionario Escolar De Sinonimos y Contrarios De la Lengua Espanola. French & Eur.
--Diccionario Ideologico Manual de la Lengua Espanola. French & Eur.
--Diccionario Practico Escolar de la Lengua Espanola. French & Eur.
--Diccionario Simultaneo en 6 Idiomas. French & Eur.

Capdevilla Font, Juan. Diccionario Basico Escolar de la Lengua Espanola. French & Eur.
--Diccionario Basico Escolar de la Lengua Espanola. French & Eur.
--Diccionario De la Lengua Espanola y Enciclopedia Escolar. French & Eur.
--Diccionario Simultaneo en 21 Idiomas. French & Eur.

Capelle, Carl. Volistaendiges Woerterbuch Ueber die Gedichte des Homores und der Homeriden (Pub. by Wissenschaftl Buchgesells). French & Eur.

Capelli. Dizionario di Abbreviature Latine & Italiane. Hoepli.

Capelli, A. Dizionario di abbreviature latine ed italiane. Hoepli.

Capitant, H. Vocabulario Juridico. Depalma.

Capone, Federico. Dizionario astrologico. Capone C.

Capot-Rey, Robert & Blaudin De The, Bernard. Glossaire des Principaux Termes Geographiques & Logiques Sahariens. Sahariennes Inst. Rech.

Capou, Gerard. Le Dictionnaire des Mots Cles du Dessin de la Peinture, de l'Estampe. Capou.

Caprile, Jean P. Lexique Tumak-Francais Tchad. Reimer.

Capron, Gustave & Boisselier, Jackie. Dictionnaire de Prevention. Soc Corp Hygiene.

Caput, J., jt. auth. see Caput, J. P.

Caput, J. P. & Caput, J. Dictionnaire des Verbe Francais (Dist. by Continental Bk Co). Larousse.
--Dictionnaire des verbes francais. Larousse.

Caput, Jean & Caput, Josette. Dictionnaire des Verbes Francais. Larousse.

Caput, Josette, jt. auth. see Caput, Jean.

Caradec, Francois. Dictionnaire Du Francais Argotique et Populaire. French & Eur.

Carbonell, Basset D. Diccionario de Modismos Ingleses. Dos Continentes.

Carbonell, Sebastiano. Dizionario fraseologico completo italiano-spagnolo e spagnolo-italiano: Parte italiana-spagnola. Hoepli.
--Dizionario fraseologico completo italiano-spagnolo e spagnolo-italiano: Parte spagnola-italiana. Hoepli.

Carboni, Paolo. Dizionario tecnico-scientifico: Italiano-tedesco. Patron.
--Dizionario tecnico-scientifico: Tedesco-italiano. Patron.

Carcamo, L. Dictionnaire pour Ingenieurs et Techniciens: Francais-Espagnol, Espagnol-Francais. French & Eur.

Cardenas, Eduardo, ed. Diccionario Moderno. Edit Norma.

Cardenas Nannetti, Jorge. Diccionario Mininorma. Norma Edit.
--Diccionario Norma: El Lexico de Nuestro Tiempo. Norma.

Cardoso, Ersilio. Dictionnaire Portugais-Francais. Garnier.
--Grande Dicionario Frances-Portugues. Difel Difusao.

Cardoso, Ersilo. Dictionnaire Portugais-Francais. Garnier.
--Dictionnaire Poucet Allemand-Francais. Hatier.

Carena, A. Dizionario di agricoltura. UTET.

Cariere, G., ed. Dictionary of Surface-Active Agents, Cosmetics & Toiletries. Elsevier.

Carillon, Annie & Goutel, Beatrice. Dictionnaire du Scrabble. Hachette.

Carl, W. H. Dictionnaire de poche du teletraitement des donnees. Maison Dictionnaire.

Carletti, Ernesto. Dizionario tascabile illustrato. Citta Nuova.

Carlson, Don, ed. Automation in Housing & Systems Building News: Dictionary of Industrialized Manufactured Housing. Automation in Housing Mag.
Carlson, G. E., jt. auth. see Putnam, R. E.
Carlson, G. E., jt. auth. see Putnam, Robert.
Carlson, Ingvar, jt. auth. see Bergstrom, Mats.
Carlut, Charles. A Concordance to Flaubert's Bouvard et Pecuchet. Garland Pub.
Carmara Oficial de Comercio, Industria y Navegacion Barcelona. Diccionari d'Informatica. Organ Ofic Adm.
Carnelutti, Daniel. Dictionnaire Technique de l'automobile. Spes SA.
Carnoy, Albert. Dictionnaire Etymologique des noms Grecs de Plantes. Peeters.
Carpovich, Eugene A. Russian-English Atomic Dictionary: Physics, Mathematics, Nucleonics. Tech Dict.
--Russian-English Biological & Medical Dictionary. Tech Dict.
--Russian-English Chemical Dictionary. Tech Dict.
--Russian-English Metals & Machines Dictionary. Tech Dict.
Carpovich, Vera V. Solzhenitsyn's Peculiar Vocabulary, Russian-English Glossary. Tech Dict.
Carr, C. T. see Barker, M. L. & Homeyer, H.
Carr, W. L., jt. ed. see Schaeffer, Randolph F.
Carrasco, Castulo. Diccionario de Medicina Farmacia Veterinaria & Quimica. Garsi Edit.
Carrasco Martinez, Castulo. Diccionario De Medicina, Farmacia Veterinaria y Quimica. French & Eur.
Carrere, Jean & Dessaigne, Jacques. Lexique des Termes Usuels de Psychiatrie. Berger-Levrault.
--Lexique des Termes Usuels de Psychiatrie. French & Eur.
Carreter, Fernando L. Diccionario de Terminos Filologicos (French & Eur). French & Eur.
--Diccionario de Terminos Filologicos (French & Eur). French & Eur.
Carriere, Anne-Marie. Le Dictionnaire des Hommes. Pensee Moderne.
Carriere, G. Dictionary of Surface Active Agents, Cosmetics & Toiletries. Elsevier.
Carroll, David. The Dictionary of Foreign Terms in the English Language (Hawthorn). Dutton.
Carroll, Vern & Soulik, Tobias. Nukuoro Lexicon. UH Pr.
Cartailhac, Emile. Dictionnaire Archeologique de la Gaul. Nationale.
--Dictionnaire Archeologique de la Gaule. Biblio Nationale.
Carter, F. T., jt. ed. see Leschonski, K.
Carter, Harley. Diccionario de Electronica. French & Eur.
Carter, Harley, tr. Diccionario de electronica. Leru.
Carter, Henry H. Dictionary of Middle English Musical Terms. Gerhard, George B., et al, eds. Kraus Repr.
Carton, J. B. Glossaire Picard du Parler de Long. Eklitra.
Caruth, Donald L., jt. auth. see Filkins, James H.
Carvalho Neto, Paulo de. Diccionario d Teoria Folklorica. Intl Guatemala.
Carver, D. J., et al, eds. Collins English Learner's Dictionary (Pub. by Collins ELT Scotland). State Mutual Bk.
Casa Aruta. Diccionario de la industria textil. Labor SA.
Casaccia, G. Dizionario genovese-italiano. Brenner.
Casalis, Jacques. Dictionnaire Laitier: Francais-Allemand-Anglais. Litec.
--Dictionnaire Laitier: Francais, Allemand, Anglais. French & Eur.
Casa Novas, M. J., ed. see Akerlung, Alfred.
Casares, Julio. Diccionario ideologico de la lengua espanola. G Gili.
--Diccionario Ideologico de la Lengua Espanola (GIL). Lectorum Pubns.
--Novedades en el Diccionario Academico (AGL). Lectorum Pubns.
Casares Sanchez, Julio. Diccionario Ideologico de la Lengua Espanola. G Gili.
Casasanta, Mario, jt. auth. see Spinelli, Vincenzo.
Casasnoves, Moll, jt. auth. see Alcover Sureda, Antoni M.
Cascianni, L., tr. see Wiegelmann, Alfred.
Caselli, G., jt. auth. see Grimod, Francesco.
Casero, F., jt. auth. see Haensch, G.
Casesnovas, Dario Maravall see Maravall Casesnovas, Dario.
Cassart, C. & Moirant, R. Dictionnaire du Cheval et du Chevalier. French & Eur.
Cassell. Cassell's Colloquial French. Macmillan.
--Cassell's Colloquial German. Macmillan.
--Cassell's Colloquial Italian. Macmillan.
--Cassell's Colloquial Spanish. Macmillan.
--Cassell's Dutch Dictionary: English-Dutch Dutch-English. Macmillan.
--Cassell's French Dictionary: Concise French-English English-French. Macmillan.
--Cassell's French Dictionary: Standard French-English English-French. Macmillan.
--Cassell's French Dictionary: Thumb-indexed French-English English-French. Macmillan.
--Cassell's Italian Dictionary: Standard Italian-English English-Italian. Macmillan.
--Cassell's Italian Dictionary: Thumb-indexed Italian-English English-Italian. Macmillan.
--Cassell's Latin Dictionary: Concise Latin-English English-Latin. Macmillan.
--Cassell's Latin Dictionary: Latin-English, English Latin. Simpson, D. P., ed. Macmillan.
--Cassell's Latin Dictionary: Standard Latin-English English-Latin. Macmillan.
--Cassell's New Dutch Dictionary: English-Dutch, Dutch-English. Macmillan.
--Cassell's Spanish Dictionary: Concise Spanish-English English-Spanish. Macmillan.
--Cassell's Spanish Dictionary: Spanish-English, English-Spanish. Peers, Edqan A., ed. Macmillan.
--Cassell's Spanish Dictionary: Thumb-indexed Spanish-English English-Spanish. Macmillan.
Cassells. French Concise Dictionary. Macmillan.
--Italian-English Dictionary. Macmillan.
--Latin Concise Dictionary. Macmillan.
--Latin-English Dictionary. Macmillan.
--Spanish Concise Dictionary. Macmillan.
--Spanish-English Dictionary. Macmillan.
Cassells, et al. Cassell's Italian Dictionary: Italian-English, English-Italian. Macmillan.
Cassiani, Ernesto. Dizionario moderno italiano-francese e francese-italiano. SEI.
Cassidy, Frederic G. The ADS Dictionary - How Soon? Bd. with The Linguistic Atlas of New England Revisited. U of Ala Pr.
Cassidy, Frederick G. & Le Page, R. B., eds. Dictionary of Jamaican English. Cambridge U Pr.
Cassin, Barbara & Solomon, Sheila. Dictionary of Eye Terminology. Triad Pub FL.
Casso-Cervera. Diccionario de derecho privado. Labor.
Cassone, F. Vocabolario italiano-francese-italiano (CEB). Capitol-Dischi.
Castagno, Margaret F. Historical Dictionary of Somalia. Scarecrow.
Castan, Pascual. Los Terminos Judiciales. Dist. Anfora.
--Los Terminos Judiciales. Dist. Arenzadi.
Castany, G. Dictionnaire Francais d'Hydrogeologie. Bureau Recherches.
Castelbajac, Bernadette de see De Castelbajac, Bernadette.
Castell, Edmund. Lexicon Heptaglotton. Intl Pubns Serv.
Castellana, Georges. Dictionnaire Francais-Nicois. Serre.
--Dictionnaire Francais Nicois. Serre.
Castellanos Alentorn, Prado, jt. auth. see Guisset Poch, Consuelo.
Castellanos i Llorenc, Carlos. Diccionari Catala-Frances, Frances-Catala. Encic Catalan.
Castellanos Llorenc, Carles & Castellanos Llorenc, Rafael. Diccionario Catala-Frances, Frances-Catala. French & Eur.
Castellanos Llorenc, Rafael, jt. auth. see Castellanos Llorenc, Carles.
Castell Blanch, Emilio. Claves de la Masoneria. Dopesa.
Castellini, A., jt. auth. see Mazzaglia, E.
Castelo Matran, Julio. Diccionario Basico de Seguros. Mapfre.
--Diccionario Basico De Seguros. French & Eur.
Castelo Matran, Julio, jt. auth. see Mueller Lutz, H.
Castiglioni, Luigi. Vocabolario Della Lingua Latina. Brambilla, A. & Campagna, G., eds. Loescher.
Castiglioni, Luigi & Mariotti, Scevola. Vocabolario della lingua latina: Latino-italiano e italiano-latino. Loescher.
Castillo, Bond. University of Chicago Spanish-English Dictionary. Iaconi.
Castillo, Carlos & Bond, Otto F. Spanish-English Dictionary. PB.
--University of Chicago Dictionary. Camino Real.
--University of Chicago Spanish Dictionary. Lincoln Canfield, D., rev. by. Natl Textbk.
--University of Chicago Spanish Dictionary (Phoen). U of Chicago Pr.
Castillo, Carlos & Garcia, Barbara M. The University of Chicago Spanish Dictionary. U of Chicago Pr.
Castillo, Felix Quesada see Quesada Castillo, Felix.
Castillo, Gonzalo. Diccionario de Similes & Analogias (BCA). Lectorum Pubns.
--Diccionario de similes y analogias. Costa Amic.
--Diccionario de similes y analogias. EDIMEX.
Castillo Mathieu, Micolas De see De Castillo Mathieu, Micolas.
Castonguay, Jacques. Dictionnaire Francais-Anglais de la Psychologie & des Sciences Connexes. Maloine.
Casullo, Fernando. Diccionario de voces lunfardas y vulgares. Freeland.
Casullo, Fernando H. Diccionario de Voces Lunfardas & Vulgares. Plus Ultra SA.
Catalan Lafuente, Jose. Diccionario Tecnico Del Agua. French & Eur.
Cattell, Ann. Dictionary of Esoteric Words. Citadel Pr.
Cauberghe, J. R., jt. auth. see Verhoeff-Schot, E.
Cauet, Fernand, jt. auth. see Bornecque, Henri.
Cauhe, Joana Raspall De see Raspall de Cauhe, Joana, et al.
Caulfield, Sophia F. & Saward, Blanche C. Dictionary of Needlework. Gale.
Cavaletto, M., et al. Dizionario Italiano-Bulgaro. French & Eur.
Cavallaro, Giovanni. Dizionario siciliano-italiano. Bonanno.
Cavero, David Ortega see Ortega Cavero, David & Da Conceica, Julio.
Cavinato, Joseph L., ed. Transportation-Logistics Dictionary. Traffic Serv.
Cavrois, Philippe, jt. auth. see Bolo, Helene.
Cawdrey, Robert. A Table Alphabeticall of English Wordes. Walter J Johnson.
Cazzaroli, Gianni. Dictionnaire de la Mer & de la Navigation. Denoel.
--Dictionnaire de la Navication. French & Eur.
Ceadel, Eric B. Japanese-English Dictionary. Saphrograph.
Cebrian, Llerrero J. Diccionario de Radio & Television (II) Alhambra.
Cebrian Herreros, Mariano. Diccionario Internacional de Radio & Television. Organ Ofic Adm.
Ceccald, Mathieu. Dictionnaire Corse-Francais, Pierre d'Evisa. Klincksieck.
--Dictionnaire Corse-Francais (Pierre d'Evisa) CNRS.
Ceccaldi, Mathieu. Dictionnaire Corse-Francais, Pierre d'Evisa. French & Eur.
Cecchetti, Bartolomeo. Saggio di un dizionario del linguaggio archivistico veneto. Forni.
Cecchini, Norma. Dizionario sinottico di iconologia. Patron.
Cecchini, Norma & Plessi, Giuseppe. Dizionario Sinottico di Iconologia. Patron.
Cecioni, C. G. Vocabolario inglese-italiano e italiano-inglese. Malipiero.
Cederholm, jt. auth. see Peralta.
CEI. Dizionario della strumentazione nucleare. AEEI.
Cejador & Frauca, Julio. Vocabulario Medieval Castellano. Las Americas.
Cela, Camilo J. Diccionario Secreto (ALFA). Lectorum Pubns.
Cela, Camilo J. & Margarit, Badia A. M. Diccionari Manual Castella-Catala Catala-Castella. Biblograf SP.
Cela Trulock, Camilo J. Diccionario Secreto. French & Eur.
Celerier, P. & Maillard, J. P. Dictionnaire des Structures Fondamentales du Francais (Dist. by Continental Bk Co). Cle International.
Cellard, J. & Key, A. Dictionnaire du Francais non Conventionnel. French & eur.
Cenac, Arnaud, jt. auth. see Perlemuter, Leon.
Cenacmoncaut, Justin E. Dictionnaire Gascon-Francais du Departement du Gers. Slatkine.
Center for Applied Linguistics, Washington D.C. Dictionary Catalog of the Library of the Center for Applied Linguistics, Washington, D. C (Hall Library). G K Hall.
Centre Culturel Occitan Pais Nissart. Glossari Ilustrat. Centre Cult. Pais Nissart.
Centre de Documentation de L'armement. Lexique des Mots-cles, Descripteurs & Identificateurs, Francais-Anglais: Utiliser pour la Recherche Documentaire. Centre Documentation Armement.
--Lexique Thematique des Descripteurs et Identificateurs. French & Eur.
Centre de Formation et de Perfectionnement des Journalistes. Petit Lexique des Termes Judiciares: A l'Usage des Journalistes. Centre Formation.
Centre International Du Droit Des Affaires (CIDA) Lexique Pratique Commercial. Marlin.
Centre National De la Recherche Scientifique & Imbs, Paul, eds. Tresor De la Langue Francaise: Dictionnaire De la Langue Du 19th et Du 20th Siecle (1789-1960) Intl Pubns Serv.
Centre Technique des Industries de la Fonderie. Vocabulaire de Fonderie Anglais-Francais. Ed Tech Ind.
--Vocabulaire de Fonderie Francais-Allemand. Ed Tech Ind.
Centre de Documentatio de. Lexique Thematique des Des Descripteurs & Identificateurs. Centre Documentation.
Centro Studi Filosofici di Gallarate. Dizionario delle idee. Sansoni.
Ceppellini, Vincenzo. Dizionario grammaticale. Ist Geo Agostini.
Cerda, et al. Vocabulario Espanol de Tejas. Camino Real.
Cerlogne, Jean B. Dictionnaire du Patols Valdotain. Slatkine.
Cerny, Jaroslav. Coptic Etymological Dictionary. Cambridge U Pr.
Cerron-Palomino, Rodolfo. Diccionario Quechua Junin-Huanca. Minist Ed Caracas.
Cervantes Gimeno, Fernando, ed. see Laplanche, Jean & Pontalis, Jean-Bertrand.

Cervantes Gimeno, Fernando, tr. see Laplanche, Jean, et al.
Cesana, Gianni. Dizionario ragionato di sinonimi e dei contrari. De Vecchi Italy.
Cesarman, Carlos. Diccionario de sinonimos OMNIA. Pax.
Chaballe, L. Y. & Masuy, L. Elsevier's Oil & Gas Field Dictionary. Elsevier.
Chaballe, L. Y. & Vandenberghe, J. P. Elsevier's Dictionary of Building Tools & Materials. Elsevier.
Chaballe, L. Y., jt. ed. see Vandenberghe, J. P.
Chabaud, N., jt. auth. see Planque, B.
Chabrol, G. M. Dictionnaire Historique des Fiefs: Chateilenies & Paroisses de la Haute & de la Basse Auvergne. Guenegaud.
Chadsey, Charles P. & Wentworth, Harold, eds. The Grosset Webster Large-Type Dictionary (G&D). Putnam Pub Group.
Chadwick, Brian, ed. see Sharman, Fay.
Chaffurin, L. & Mergault, J. Dictionnaire Bilingue Larousse, Francais-Anglais, Anglais-Francais. Larousse.
Chaffurin, Louis & Mergault, Jean. Dictionnaire Bilingue Apollo Francais-Anglais. Larousse.
Chalaguina, I. Dicionario de Bolso Portugues-Russo. French & Eur.
Challamel, Auguste, jt. auth. see Boursin, E.
Challinor, John. A Dictionary of Geology. Oxford U Pr.
--A Dictionary of Geology. Verry.
Chambadal, L. L. Dizionario di matematica moderna. Mursia.
Chambadal, Lucien. Diccionario de las matematicas modernas. Plaza Janes.
--Diccionario De las Matematicas Modernas. French & Eur.
--Dictionnaire des Mathematiques Modernes. Larousse.
--Dictionnaire des Mathematiques Modernes. French & Eur.
Chamberlain, Paul, jt. auth. see Jordana, Ricard.
Chamberlain, Paul, jt. auth. see Jordana, Ricardo.
Chambers. Dictionary of Science & Technology. Brandstetter.
--Dictionary of Science & Technology. Brandstetter.
Chambure, Eugene de see De Chambure, Eugene.
Chamfort, Nicolas De see De Chamfort, Nicolas.
Champeval, J. B. Dictionnaire des Familles Nobles & Notables de la Correze. Lafitte Repr.
Champion, Sara. Dictionary of Terms & Techniques in Archaeology (An Everest House Book). Dodd.
Champion, Sarah. A Dictionary of Terms & Techniques in Archaeology. Facts on File.
Chan, Shau Wing. Concise English-Chinese Dictionary. Stanford U Pr.
Chandler, Alfred D., jt. ed. see Lee, John.
Chandna, K., jt. ed. see Tayyeb, R.
Chandor, Anthony. Diccionario de Computadores. French & Eur.
--Dizionario di informatica. Rapelli, G., tr. Zanichelli.
--The Facts on File Dictionary of Micro Computers. Facts on File.
--The Facts on File Dictionary of Microcomputers. Facts on File.
--The Penguin Book of Microprocessors. Penguin.
--The Penguin Dictionary of Microprocessors. Penguin.
Chandor, Anthony, et al. The Penguin Dictionary of Computers. Penguin.
Chandra Das, S. Tibetan-English Dictionary: With Sanskrit Synonyms. Sanberg, Graham & Heyde, A. William, eds. Lancaster-Miller.
Chandrasekhara, M. S., ed. see Pillai, T. R.
Chang, S. Chinese-English Dictionary of Physical Terms (Pub. by Harrassowitz). French & Eur.
Chang-Rodriquez, E., jt. auth. see Juilland, Alphonse.
Chanlett, Eliska. A Glossary of Selected Demographic Terms. Intl Program Labs.
Channazaroff-Waganoff. Diccionario basico de fudicion ingles-castellano. Mitre.
Chanski, N. Dictionnaire Etymologique de la Langue Russe, 1, A-J. MIR.
--Dictionnaire Etymologique de la Langue Russe. MIR.
Chantraine, Pierre. Dictionnaire Etymologique de la Langue Grecque. Klincksieck.
--Dictionnaire Etymologique de la Langue Grecque, 2. Klincksieck.
--Dictionnaire Etymologique de la Langue Grecque, 3. Klincksieck.
--Dictionnaire Etymologique de la Langue Grecque, 4. Klincksieck.
Chao, Yuen R. & Yang, Lien-Sheng. Concise Dictionary of Spoken Chinese. Harvard U Pr.
Chaplin, J. P. Dictionary of Psychology (LE). Dell.
--The Dictionary of the Occult & Paranormal (LE). Dell.
Chapman. Medical Dictionary for the Lay Person. Barron.
Chappat, Djenane. Diccionario de la Limpieza. French & Eur.
Chappat, Djenane, tr. Diccionario de limpieza. Alianza Ed.
Chapple, Richard. A Dostoevsky Dictionary. Ardis Pubs.
Charbot, Nicolas & Blanchet, Hector. Dictionnaire des Patols du Dauphine. Lafitte Repr.
--Dictionnaire des Patols du Dauphine. Slatkine.
Chardana, J. L. & Vega, V. Diccionario ilustrado de trucos. G Gili.
Chardans, J. L. & Vega, Vicente. Diccionario Ilustrado de Trucos. French & Eur.
Charles, Bernard H. Pottery & Porcelain: A Glossary of Terms. Hippocrene Bks.
Charles, Marie C., jt. auth. see Ducroz, Jean M.
Charles, Victorin. Diccionario Atomico. French & Eur.
Charles, Victorin, tr. Diccionario atomico. Leru.
Charmet, Raymond. Dictionnaire de l'art Contemporain. Larousse.
Charron, Jacqueline. Dictionnaire Raisonne des Mots-Croises. Homme.
Chartrand, P., ed. see Bacon, F., et al.
Chartrand, P., ed. see Fortin, A., et al.
Chassant, A. & Tausin, H. Dictionnaire des Devises Historiques & Heraldiques. Slatkine.
Chassant, Alphonse A. Dictionnaire des Abbreviations Latines et Francaises Usitees dans les Inscriptions Lapidaires et Metalliques, les Manuscrits et les Chartes de Moyen Age. B Franklin.
Chassant, Louis A. Dictionnaire des Abreviations Latines & Francaise: Usitees dans les Inscriptions du Moyen-Age. Lenox.
--Dictionnaire des Abreviations Latines & Francaises: Usitees dans les Inscriptions du Moyen Age. Olms Verlag.
Chassant, Louis A. & Delbarre, P. J. Dictionnaire de Sigillographie Pratique. Olms Verlag.
Chassant, Louis A. & Tausin, Henri. Dictionnaire des Devises Heraldiques. Olms Verlag.
Chassany, Jean-Philippe. Dictionnaire de Meteorologie Populaire. Maison & Larose.
--Dictionnaire de Meteorologie Populaire. French & Eur.
Chassard, Jean & Weil, Gonthier. Vocabulaire Allemand. Hachette.
Chastel, Pierre. Lexique des Dieux. Delpire.
Chatain, Yves. Terminologia Anatomica. Norma.
Chatelanat, Charles & Henzi, Theodor. Vocabulaire de Base Allemand-Francais. Hachette.
Chaturvedi, Mahendra & Bhola, Nath T. A Practical Hindi-English Dictionary. South Asia Bks.
Chaudenson, Robert. Le Lexique du Parler Creole de la Reunion. Champion.
Chaudhary, Abdul G. The Law Latin Lexicon. Khyber Law Publishers.
Chauffurin, L. Petit Dictionnaire bilingue Larousse, francais-anglais et English-French. Larousse.
Chaumuzeau, P., et al. Dictionnaire de Medecine. Flammarion.
Chavignerie, Emile B. De La see De La Chavignerie, Emile B. & Auvray, Louis.
Chayne, G. J. Classified Spanish Vocabulary. Intl Ideas.
Chazaud, Henri Bertrand Du see Bertrand Du Chazaud, Henri.
Cheadle, John R. Basic Greek Vocabulary. St Martin.
Chebotarev, A. I. Gidrologicheskii Slovar (Pub. by GIdrometeoizdat). Four Continent.
Chebotarev, L. Gidrologicheskii Slovar (Pub. by Gidrometeorologich Izd.). Four Continent.
Chekhranov, V. D. Russko-Ukrainskii Metallurgicheskii Slovar (Pub. by Naukova Dumka). Four Continent.
Chen, Janet. A Practical English-Chinese Pronouncing Dictionary. Iaconi.
Chen, Janey. Practical English-Chinese Pronouncing Dictionary. C E Tuttle.
Chen, Janey & Simms, Ena. A Practical English-Chinese Pronouncing Dictionary. C E Tuttle.
Cheneviere, Adolphe & Frank, Felix. Lexique de la Langue de Bonaventure Des Periers. Slatkine.
Cherbonneau, Auguste. Arabic-French Dictionary. Intl Bk Ctr.
--Dictionnaire Arabe-Francais: Langue ecrite. Intl Bk Ctr.
Chermak, A. Czech-English, English-Czech Dictionary. Saphrograph.
--English-Czech, Czech-English Dictionary. Saphrograph.
Chernukhin, A. E. English-Russian Polytechnical Dictionary. Pergamon.
Chernukhin, A. E., ed. English-Russian Polytechnical Dictionary (Pub. by Collets). State Mutual Bk.
Cherry, R. L., ed. see Saxton, Dean & Saxton, Lucille.
Cherubini, Francesco. Vocabolario milanese-italiano. Brenner.
Cherukhina, A. E. Anglo-russki i politekhnicheski. Russky Yazyk.
Cheshko. Slovar' Sinonimov Russkogo Iazyka. Aleksandrova, Z. E., ed. Four Continent.
Chesnel De La Charbouclais, L. P. Dictionnaire de Geologie... et Dictionnaire de Chronologie Universelle par M. Champagnac. Migne, J. P., ed. Caratzas Pub Co.
--Dictionnaire de Technologie. Migne, J. P., ed. Caratzas Pub Co.
--Dictionnaire des Merveilles et Curiosites de Nature et De Art. Migne, J. P., ed. Caratzas Pub Co.
Chesnokov, L. A., et al. Parusny i sport. Russkii Iazyk.
Chetwynd, Tom. Le Dictionnaire des Reves. Seghers.
Chevalier, Jean & Gheerbrant, Alain. Dictionnaire des Symboles. Seghers.
--Dictionnaire des Symboles. French & Eur.
Chevallier, J. Precis De Terminologie Medicale. French & Eur.
Cheve, C. F. Dictionnaire des Apologistes Involontaires. Migne, J. P., ed. Caratzas Pub Co.
--Dictionnaire des Conversions. Migne, J. P., ed. Caratzas Pub Co.
Chiang Ker-Chiu. Practical English-Cantonese Dictionary. Colton Bk.
Chihabi. Agriculture, Forestry, & Allied Terminology Dictionary: English-Arabic with Arabic Glossary. Khatib, A., ed. Intl Bk Ctr.
Childers, Robert. A Dictionary of the Pali language. Orient Bk Dist.
Chinese-English Translation Assistance Group, ed. Chinese Dictionaries: An Extensive Bibliography of Dictionaries in Chinese & Other Languages. Greenwood.
Chinese Language Division of Home Affairs Department. An English-Chinese Glossary of Terms Commonly Used in Government. Govt Printer.
Chiranky, Gary, ed. see Colletti, Anthony B.
Chitty, Jose. A. Armas see De Armas Chitty, Jose A.
Chiu, Hong-Yee, ed. Chinese-English & English-Chinese Astronomical Dictionary (Consultants). Plenum Pub.
Chiu, Kwong Ki see Kwong Ki Chaou.
Chi Wen-Shun, ed. Chinese-English Dictionary of Contemporary Usage. U of Cal Pr.
Chodera & Kubica, eds. Langenscheidts Handwoerterbuecher Deutsch-Polnisch. Langenscheidt.
Cholvis, F. Diccionario de Contabilidad. Ateneo Edit.
--Diccionario de Contabilidad. French & Eur.
Cholvis, Francisco. Diccionario de contabilidad. Contabilidad Moderna.
Choppy, Jacques. Dictionnaire de l'Industrie Routiere. Eyrolles.
Chouemi, M. & Pellat, C. H. Al-Kamil Dictionnaire Arabe-Francais-Anglais. French & Eur.
Chouemi, Moustafa, jt. auth. see Blachere, Regis.
Choy, Rita Mei-Wah see Mei-Wah Choy, Rita.
Christ, Jean-Frederic. Dictionnaire des Monogrammes. Minkoff Repr.
Christensen, Sven. Engelskt-Svenskt Flyglexikon. Esselte Studium.
Christian, F. W. Vocabulary of the Mangaian Language. Kraus Repr.
Christie, George A., jt. auth. see Fisher, Richard B.
Christophensen, Scavenius. Norwegian Dictionary: Norsk-English. Kirkeby, Willie, ed. Vanous.
Christy, Thomas, jt. auth. see Leonard, C. Henri.
Chrysler Corporation. Glossary of Automotive Terminology: French-English English-French. Soc Auto Engineers.
--Glossary of Automotive Terminology: Spanish-English English-Spanish. Soc Auto Engineers.
Chtchoukine, Anatoll. Dictionnaire Illustre de la Langue Russe: Francais-Espagnol-Russe. Mir.
Chu, Hsiu-Feng, et al. English-Chinese Chinese-English Dictionary of Business Terms (Pub. by Chih-Wen Pub Co China). Cheng & Tsui.
Chu-Chi, W. English-Chinese Dictionary of Physical Terms. French & Eur.
Chukalov, S. K. Russko-Bolgarskii Slovar (Pub. by Sov. Entsiklopediia). Four Continent.
Churchward, Clerk M. Rotuman Grammar & Dictionary. AMS Pr.
Ciani, Maria G. Lexikon zu Lycophron. Olms Verlag.
Ciardi, John. A Browser's Dictionary (HarpT). Har-Row.
--A Second Browser's Dictionary: Native's Guide to the Unknown American Language (HarpT). Har-Row.
Ciardi Dupre, Giovanni & Escher, Angelica. Dizionario italiano-tedesco e tedesco-italiano. SEI.
Cicchini, Joelle, ed. Thesaurus Hydrologie. Serv Doc Cart.
C.I.D.A. Lexique Commercial: Tout le vocabulaire des affaires. Maison Dictionnaire.
Cihui, Y. Dongwuxue. English-Chinese Biology Dictionary. French & Eur.
C.I.L.F. Vocabulaire de la geomorphologie. Maison Dictionniare.
--Vocabulaire de la radiographie. Maison Dictionnaire.
--Vocabulaire de la topographie. Maison Dictionnaire.
--Vocabulaire de l'Hydrologie et de la meteorologie. Maison Dictionnaire.
--Vocabulaire de sciences et techniques spatiales. Maison Dictionnaire.
Cinti, Decio. Dizionario dei sinonimi e dei contrari. Ist Geo Agostini.
Cirlot. Diccionario de simbolos. Labor SA.
Cirlot, J. Diccionario de Simbolos. French & Eur.
Cirlot, Juan E. Diccionario de los Ismos (ARG). Lectorum Pubns.
--Diccionario de Simbolismos. Labor SA.

--Diccionario de simbolos. Labor SA.
--Diccionario de Simbolos. Editorial Labor SA.
--Diccionario de simbolos. Labor.
Cirlot, Juan-Eduardo. Diccionario Universal del Arte y los Artistas. French & Eur.
Civil Engineering Society, jt. auth. see Building Industry.
Cizevska, Tatjana. Glossary of the Igor Tale. Mouton.
Claessens, Dieter. Jugendlexikon Gesellschaft: Einfache Antworten afu Schwierige Fragen. Rowohlt.
Clair, Colin. Dictionnaire des Herbes & des Epices. Denoel.
--Dictionnaire des Herbes et des Epices. French & Eur.
Clairmont, Leonard. Tahitian-English, English Tahitian Dictionary. Shalom.
Claithe, Baile A., jt. auth. see De Bhaldraithe, Tomas.
Clapin, Sylva. Dictionnaire Canadien-Francais. Soc Dev Liv.
--Dictionnaire Canadien-Francais. Laval.
--Dictionnaire Canadien-Francais. French & Eur.
Clapin, Sylvia. New Dictionary of Americanisms. Gale.
Clara, Cenni. Dizionarietto fraseologico commerciale italiano-inglese. Trevisini.
Clara, Cenni & Clotilde, Sandri. Dizionarietto fraseologico commerciale italiano-francese. Trevisini.
Claraso, Noel. Diccionario humoristico. Sintes.
Claraso, V. Diccionario Humoristico. French & Eur.
Clarity, B. A Dictionary of Iraqi Arabic. Intl Bk Ctr.
Clark, Charlotte & Davies, Cornelia Oakes. Standard Rebus Glossary. Am Guidance.
Clark, Donald T. & Gottfried, Bert A., eds. University Dictionary of Business & Finance. T Y Crowell.
Clark, J. M., ed. German-English, English-German Gem Dictionary. Collins Pubs.
Clark, James M. The Vocabulary of Anglo-Irish. Folcroft.
Clark, Lawrence & Clark, Nancy. Vocabulario Popoluca de Sayula. Summer Inst Ling.
Clark, Mary Cowden see Cowden-Clark, Mary.
Clark, Nancy, jt. auth. see Clark, Lawrence.
Clark, Steve. Illustrated Basketball Dictionary for Young People. Harvey.
Clarke, Hugh A. Pronouncing Dictionary of Musical Terms, Giving the Meaning Derivation & Pronunciation of Italian, German, French & Other Words. Scholarly.
Clarke, John H. A Dictionary of Practical Materia Medica (Pub. by Daniel Co England). State Mutual Bk.
Clason, ed. Elsevier's Dictionary of Tools & Ironware. Elsevier.
Clason, W. Elsevier's Dictionary of Chemical Engineering. Elsevier.
--Elsevier's Dictionary of Television, & Video Recording. Elsevier.
Clason, W., ed. Dictionary of Library Science Information & Documentation. Elsevier.
--Electronics Dictionary: Russian Supplement. Elsevier.
--Electronics Dictionary: Swedish Supplement. Elsevier.
--Elsevier's Dictionary of Amplification Modulation Reception & Transmission. Elsevier.
--Elsevier's Dictionary of Automatic Control. Elsevier.
Clason, W. E. Dizionario di metallurgia. Etas Libri.
--Elsevier's Dictionary of Cinema, Sound & Music. Elsevier.
--Elsevier's Dictionary of Computers, Automatic Control & Data Processing. Elsevier.
--Elsevier's Dictionary of Electronics & Waveguides. Elsevier.
--Elsevier's Dictionary of General Physics. Elsevier.
--Elsevier's Dictionary of Metallurgy & Metal Working. Elsevier.
--Elsevier's Dictionary of Nuclear Science & Technology. Elsevier.
--Elsevier's Electrotechnical Dictionary. Elsevier.
--Elsevier's Telecommunication Dictionary. Elsevier.
Clason, W. E., jt. auth. see De Vries, L.
Classon, Sigvard. Socialfoersaekringslexikon. LiberFoerlag.
Clauser. Diccionario de materiales y procesos de ingenieria. Labor SA.
Clauser, H. R. Diccionario De Materiales y Procesos De Ingenieria. French & Eur.
Clauson, Gerard. An Etymological Dictionary of Pre-Thirteenth Century Turkish. Oxford U Pr.
Clauss, G., et al, eds. Woerterbuch der Psychologie. Bibl Inst Leipzig.
Clauss, Guenter. Woerterbuch der Psychologie. Pahl-Rugenstein.
Clauss, Gunter. Woerterbuch der Psychologie. Biblio Inst.
Clave, Margara. Diccionario de Sinonimos & Antonimos. Porrua.
Claviez, Wolfram. Seemaennisches Woerterbuch (Pub. by Delius, Klaving & Co.). French & Eur.
Clayton, Peter, jt. auth. see Gammond, Peter.
Cleasby, Richard & Vigfusson, Gudbrand, eds. Icelandic-English Dictionary. Oxford U Pr.
Clebert, Jean Paul. Dictionnaire du Symbolisme Animal. Albin-Michel.
Clediere, Jean, et al. Dictionnaire Francais-Allemand. Larousse FR.
Clegg, Joan. Dictionary of Social Services: Policy & Practice. Intl Pubns Serv.
Clement, Felix & Larousse, Pierre. Dictionnaire Des Operas. Da Capo.
Clement, Jean M. Dictionnaire des Industries Alimentaires. Masson & Cie.
Clement, Jean-Michel. Dictionnaire des Industries Alimentaires. French & Eur.
Clemente, Zamora & Juan-Guitart, Jorge. Dialectologia Hispanoamericana. Almar Edns.
Cleveland, Charles D. Complete Concordance to the Poetical Works of John Milton. Folcroft.
Clifford, C. R., ed. Lace Dictionary: Including Historic & Commercial Terms, Technical Terms, Native & Foreign. Gale.
Clifford, James L. Dictionary Johnson (GB). McGraw.
--Dictionary Johnson: The Middle Years of Samuel Johnson (GB). McGraw.
Clifford, Mary E., et al, eds. News Dictionary 1976. Facts on File.
Clifford Vaughn, F. Glossary of Economics. Elsevier.
Clifton, Ebenezer & Mac Laughlin, Horace J. Dictionnaire Anglais-Francais. Garnier.
Cline, David, et al. Dictionary of Visual Science. Chilton.
Clotilde, Sandri, jt. auth. see Clara, Cenni.
Cloutier, Francois. Dictionnaire des Parents. Edns Du Jour.
Cluny, Claude-Michel. Dictionnaire des Nouveaux Cinemas Arabes. Sindbad.
Cobos, Ruben. A Dictionary of New Mexico & Southern Colorado Spanish. Museum NM Pr.
Cockeram, Henry. English Dictionary: An Interpreter of Hard English Words. Adler.
Codera Martin, J. M. Diccionario de Derecho Mercantil. Piramide.
Codera Martin, Jose. Diccionario De Derecho Mercantil. French & Eur.
Codera Martin, Jose M. Diccionario de Calculo Mercantil. Piramide.
--Diccionario de Contabilidad. Piramide.
--Diccionario de contabilidad. Piramide.
--Diccionario De Contabilidad. French & Eur.
Coetzee, A. African-English, English-African Dictionary. Shalom.
Coeuroy, Andre. Dictionnaire Critique de la Musique Ancienne & Moderne. Payot.
Coghlan, Ronan. Dictionary of Irish Myth & Legend. Donard Pub Co.
Cognazzo, Maria, jt. auth. see Bussi, Luciano.
Cognia, Raymond & Elgar, Frank. Illustrated Dictionary of Impressionism. Barron.
Cogo, Robert, ed. see Lawrence, Erma.
Cohen, Andre. Dictionnaire Medical Illustre de Semiologie Patronymique. Maloine.
Cohen, David. Dictionnaire des Racines Semitiques. Mouton De Gruyter.
--Dictionnaire Des Racines Semitiques Ou Attestees Dans les Langues Semitiques: Comprenant un Fichier Comparatif De Jean Cantineau. Mouton.
--Dictionnaire Des Racines Semitiques: Ou Attestees Dans les Langues Semitiques. Mouton.
--Dictionnaire des Racines Semitiques, 2. Mouton De Gruyter.
Cohen, Jean & Dourlen-Rollier, Anne Marie. Dictionnaire de la Vie Affective et Sexuelle. French & Eur.
Cohen, Viviane. Dictionnaire des Couleurs. Paris Livre de Odege.
--Dictionnaire des Couleurs. Livre de Paris.
Cohn, M. M. Dictionnaire francais-hebreu. Larousse.
Cohn, Marc M. Dictionnaire Francais-Hebreu. Larousse.
--Dictionnaire Francais-Hebreu. French & Eur.
--Nouveau Dictionnaire Hebreu-Francais. French & Eur.
Colas, Rene. Dictionnaire Technique de l'eau & des Questions Connexes. Le Prat.
Colasse. Lexique de Comptabilite & de Gestion. Ecole Electricite.
--Lexique de Comptabilite et de Gestion. French & Eur.
Colby, Roy. Communism-English Dictionary. Western Islands.
Colcord, Joanna C. Sea Language Comes Ashore. Dorsen, Richard M., ed. Ayer Co.
--Sea Language Comes Ashore. Cornell Maritime.
Colella, A. Nuovo Dizionario di Elettrotecnic e di Elettronica: Italiano-Inglese, Inglese-Italiano. French & Eur.
Colella, Antonio. Nuovo Dizionario di Elettrotecnica & di elettronica. Il Rostro.
--Nuovo dizionario di elettrotecnica e elettronica italiano-inglese, inglese-italiano. Il Rostro.
Coleman, F. Guide to Surgical Terminology. Med Economics.
Coleman, Francis. Guide to Surgical Terminology. Van Nos Reinhold.
Coler, Christfried. Diccionario por Fechas de Historia Universal. French & Eur.
Coles, E. An English Dictionary. Adler.
Coletti Gruenbaum, Hanne. Dizionario persiano-italiano classico, moderno, familiare. Coletti.
Colin, Francoise, et al. Harrap's French & English Business Dictionary. Imported Bks.
Colinari, John, jt. auth. see Lipton, Gladys.
Collard, Elizabeth, jt. auth. see Collard, Howard.
Collard, Howard & Collard, Elizabeth. Vocabulario Mayo. Summer Inst Ling.
Collazo, Javier L. English-Spanish, Spanish-English Encyclopedic Dictionary of Technical Terms. McGraw.
--English-Spanish Spanish-English Encyclopedic Dictionary of Technical Terms. McGraw.
Collet, K., ed. Polygraph Dictionary for the Graphic Industries in Six Languages. Intl Pubns Serv.
Colletti, Anthony B. Dictionary of Cosmetology & Related Sciences. Sheridan.
--A Dictionary of Cosmetology & Related Services. Chiranky, Gary, ed. Keystone Pubns.
Coll Garcia, Jose L. El Diccionario de Coll. Planeta SA.
Colli, G. Dizionario italiano illustrato per l'uso essenziale della lingua. SEI.
Colli, Jean-Claude, jt. auth. see Bernard, Yves.
Colligan, Louise. How to Use the Thesaurus. Scholastic Inc.
Collin, Francoise, et al, eds. Harrap's French & English Business Dictionary. Natl Textbk.
Collin, P. H., ed. Harrap's Easy English Dictionary. Harrap.
--Harrap's English Dictionary. Harrap.
--Harrap's Two Thousand Word English Dictionary. Harrap.
Collin, P. H., ed. see Forbes, Patricia & Smith, Muriel H.
Collin, P. H., et al. Harrap's Shorter French & English Dictionary. Harrap.
Collin, P. H., et al, eds. see Mansion, J. E.
Collin, Paul. Vocabulaire Grec. Dessain & Tolra.
Collin de Pianci, Santiago. Diccionario de los infiernos. Rueda.
Collinder, Bjorn. Fenno-Ugric Vocabulary: An Etymologic Dictionary of the Uralic Languages. Buske.
--Fenno-Ugric Vocabulary: An Etymological Dictionary of the Uralic Languages (Pub. by Helmut Buske Verlag Hamburg). Benjamins North Am.
--Ordhandboken. Fyris.
Collins. Diccionario castellano-ingles. Albatros.
Collins, John. A Dictionary of Spanish Proverbs. Folcroft.
Collins, Robert. French-English Dictionary. Iaconi.
--French-English English-French Dictionary. U of Toronto Pr.
Collison, Mary, jt. auth. see Collison, Robert.
Collison, R. L. Dictionaries of English & Foreign Languages. Hafner.
Collison, Robert. A History of Foreign-Language Dictionaries (Pub. by A Deutsch England). State Mutual Bk.
Collison, Robert & Collison, Mary. Dictionary of Foreign Quotations. Facts on File.
Collison, Robert L., ed. Dictionary of Dates. Greenwood.
Collocott, T. C. Diccionario Cientifico y Tecnologico Espanol, Ingles, Frances, Aleman. Imported Bks.
Collocott, T. C., ed. Chambers' English Dictionary. Littlefield.
Collocott, T. C., jt. ed. see Thorne, J. O.
Coloma, Jose M. Leico De Politica. French & Eur.
--Lexico de Politica. Laia.
Colombo, P. Vocabolario della lingua italiana (CEB). Capitol-Dischi.
--Vocabolario della lingua italiana (CEB). Capitol-Dischi.
Colomer del Castillo, Jordi. Diccionari Angles-Catala. Portic.
--Diccionari Ingles-Catala, Catala-Ingles. French & Eur.
Colpron, Gilles. Les Anglicismes au Quebec. French & Eur.
Coluccio, Felix. Diccionario de Voces & Expresiones Argentinas. Plus Ultra S. A.
Columbia University. Dictionary Catalog of the Library of the School of Library Service (Hall Library). G K Hall.
--Dictionary Catalog of the Library of the School of Library Service, 1st Suppl (Hall Library). G K Hall.
--Dictionary Catalog of the Teachers College Library (Hall Library). G K Hall.
--Dictionary Catalog of the Teachers College Library, First Supplement (Hall Library). G K Hall.
--Dictionary Catalog of the Teachers College Library, Second Supplement (Hall Library). G K Hall.
Columbia University Law Library, New York. Dictionary Catalog of the Columbia University Law Library (Hall Library). G K Hall.
--Dictionary Catalog of the Columbia University Law Library, First Supplement (Hall Library). G K Hall.
Columbia University, Teachers College Library. Dictionary Catalog of the Teachers College Library, Columbia University, Third Supplement (Hall Library). G K Hall.

Colussi. Dizionario italiano-finlandese. Vallardi A.
Colussi, G. Finnish-Italian Dictionary. French & Eur.
--Finnish-Italian-Finnish Dictionary. French & Eur.
Colussi, G., ed. Dizionario Italiano-Finlandes, Finlandes-Italiano. French & Eur.
Colvin, Lucie G. Historical Dictionary of Senegal. Scarecrow.
Combes, Steve. Dictionary of Cuisine French. Intl Pubns Serv.
Combs, C. Murphy, ed. Illustrated Medical Dictionary. Delair.
Comitato Del Folklore Cremonese. Dizionario del dialetto cremonese. Libreria Convegno.
Commissariat a l'Energie Atomique. Dictionnaire des Sciences & Techniques Nucleaires. Brandstetter.
--Dictionnaire des Sciences & Techniques Nucleaires. Eyrolles.
Commission of the European Communities, Directorate-General for Research, Science & Education, ed. Agricultural Economics & Rural Sociology: Multilingual Thesaurus. Incl. Vol. 1. German; Vol. 2. English; Vol. 3. French; Vol. 4. Italian; Vol. 5. Quadrilingual Index. Pub. by K G Saur). Gale.
Commission of the European Communities, Directorate-General for Scientific & Technical Information & Information Management, ed. Food: Multilingual Thesaurus. Incl. Vol. 1. German; Vol. 2. English; Vol. 3. French; Italian; Vol. 5. Quadrilingual Index. Pub. by K G Saur). Gale.
Commission of the European Communities, ed. Veterinary Multilingual Thesaurus (Pub. by K G Saur). Gale.
Commisssion of the European Communities. Oil & Gas Multilingual Glossary (Pub. by Graham & Trotman England). State Mutual Bk.
Committee on Animal Nutrition, National Research Council. Nutritional Energetics of Domestic Animals & Glossary of Energy Terms. Natl Acad Pr.
Committee on Developments in Business Financing of the Section of Corporation, et al. Term Loan Handbook. HarBraceJ.
Committee on the Medical Aspects of Sports, jt. ed. see Subcommittee on Classification of Sports in Injuries.
Compagnol, Marcello G. Dizionario Merli geografico, storico, economico: Vol. 1, Lettera AZ. ERGA.
Comte, Edward Le see Le Comte, Edward.
Comte, Edward S. Le see Le Comte, Edward S.
Comte Jaubert. Glossaire du Centre de la France. Slatkine.
Comte, R. & Pernin, A. Lexique des Industries Graphiques. French & Eur.
Comte, Rene & Pernin, Andre. Lexique des Industries Graphiques. Comp Fr Edns.
Conceica, Julio da see Ortega Cavero, David & Da Conceica, Julio.
Conceicao Fernandes, Julio Da. Diccionario Manual Espanol-Portugues, Portugues-Espanol. French & Eur.
--Diccionario Portugues-Espanol. French & Eur.
Condal, Elias. Dizionario dell'intellettuale di sinistra. Savelli.
Condrea-Derer, Doina. Dictionar Roman-Italian: Pentru uzul Elevilor. Editura Stiintifica.
Condruc, Mihai. Dictionar de Electrotehnica. Editura Stiintifica.
--Dictionar de Electrotehnik. Editura Stiintifica.
Conea, Ana. Dictionar de Stinta Solului. Editura Stiintifica.
Congar, Yves & Siegwalt, Gerard. Vocabulaire Oecumenique. Cerf.
Congdon, TIm, et al. Diccionario de economia. Menduina, Antonio, tr. Grijalbo.
Congrat-Butlar, Stefan, ed. Russian Vest Pocket Dictionary. Random.
Congres International de la Preparation des Minerais. Lexique Quadrilingue de la Preparation des Minerals: Allemand-Anglais-Francais-Russe. Ste. Industrie Minerale.
Congres International de la Preparation des Minerais, ed. Lexique Quadrilinque de la Preparation des Minerais. French & Eur.
Congressional Information Service, Inc. Staff, ed. CIS Online User Guide & Thesaurus. Cong Info.
Connolly, Michael J., ed. see Black, Henry C.
Connolly, William E. The Terms of Political Discourse. Princeton U Pr.
Connors, Tracy D. Longman Dictionary of the Mass Media & Communication. Longman.
Conrad, R., ed. Kleines Woerterbuch Sprachwissenschaftlicher Termini. Bibl Inst Leipzig.
Conrad, W. BI-Taschenlexikon Elektronik-Funktechnik. Biblio Inst.
Conrad, W., et al. BI-Taschenlexikon Energie. Bibl Inst Leipzig.
Conrath, Karl. Die Volkssprache der Unteren Saar & der Obermosel: Ein Moselfrankisches Woerterbuch. MG Schmitz.
Conseil International de la Language Francaise. Vocabulaire de l'Hydrologie et de la Meteorologie. Maison Dictionnaire.
Conseil International de la Langue Francaise. Vocabulaire de la Chasse & de la Venerie. Hachette.
--Vocabulaire de la Publicite. Hachette.
Conseil International De la Langue Francaise, ed. Vocabulaire De la Publicite. French & Eur.
Conseil International de la Langue Francaise. Vocabulaire de la Radiodifussion. Hachette.
--Vocabulaire de l'environnement. Hachette.
Conseil International de la Langue Fran c04aise, ed. Vocabulaire de L'Environnement. French & Eur.
Conseil International de la Langue Francaise. Vocabulaire d'ecologie. Hachette.
--Vocabulaire du Beton. Eyrolles.
Conseil International De la Langue Francais. Vocabulaire Du Beton. French & Eur.
Consejo Superior de Esenanza. Vocabulario Ortografico: Sugerencias para su Enserianza. U. Puerto Rico.
Considine, Tim. The Language of Sport. Doering, Henry & Fisher, Patricia, eds. World Almanac.
Conso, P., et al. Dictionnaire du Francais Vivant: Collection "Dunod Entreprise" (Dist. by Continental Bk Co). Bordas.
Constantin, Aime & Desormaux, Joseph. Dictionnaire Savoyard. Slatkine.
Constantin, Aime & Desormeaux, Joseph. Dictionnaire Savoyard. Lafitte Repr.
Constantinescu, Silviu. Mic Dictionar de Cuvinte Perechi. Albatros.
Constantinescu-Dobridor, G. Mic Dictionar de Terminologie Lingvistica. Albatros.
Constantino. Ilokano Dictionary. Iaconi.
Constantino, Ernesto. Ilokano Dictionary. McKaughan, Howard P., ed. UH Pr.
Constantinon, P. English-Spanish Dictionary. Shalom.
Constantinou, P., ed. Spanish-English Dictionary. Shalom.
Conte, Giuseppe. Dizionario giuridico-economico: Vol. 1, Italiano-tedesco. Giuffre.
--Dizionario giuridico-economico: Vol. 2, Tedesco-italiano. Giuffre.
--Woerterbuch der Deutschen und Italienischen Wirtschafts und Rechtssprache. French & Eur.
--Woerterbuch der Deutschen und Italienischen Wirtschafts und Rechtssprache. French & Eur.
Conti, Elio. Vocabolario metaurense. Forni.
Conveney, James & Amey, Julian. Glossary of Spanish & English Management Terms. Biling Rev Pr.
Conveney, James & Moore, Shiela J. Lexique De Termes Anglais-Francais De Gestion: Les Cycle Au Superieur, Ecoles Superieures De Gestion. French & Eur.
Conveyor Equipment Manufacturers Association & American National Standards Institute. Conveyor Terms & Definitions. Conveyor Equip Mfrs.
Cook, Albert S. Concordance to Beowulf. Folcroft.
--A Concordance to English Poems of Thomas Gray. Folcroft.
Cook, Chris. Dictionary of Historical Terms. Macmillan London.
Cook, J. Gordon. ABC of Plant Terms (Pub. by Meadowfield Pr England). State Mutual Bk.
Cooke, E. I. & Cooke, R. W. Gardner's Chemical Synonyms & Trade Names: A Dictionary & Commercial Handbook Containing Over 35,500 Definitions & Identifications (Pub. by Tech Pr). State Mutual Bk.
Cooke, R. W., jt. auth. see Cooke, E. I.
Coon, ed. Dictionary of Useful Plants: The Use, History & Folklore of More Than 500 Plant Species. Rodale Pr Eng.
Cooper, Hellen H. Vocabulario Ingles-Espanol para Servicio Clinico. Pax.
Cooper, Richard & Uden, Grant. British Ships & Seamen. St Martin.
Cooper, W. R. An Archaic Dictionary. Gordon Pr.
Cooper, William R. Archaic Dictionary. Gale.
Copeland, Robert M. & Susskind, Nathan, eds. The Language of Herz's "Esther". A Study in Judeo-German Dialectology. U of Ala Pr.
Copperud, Roy H. Dicionario de Ingles Coloquial. Difel Editorial, S. A.
Corballis, R. & Harding, J. M. John Webster Concordance. Humanities.
Corbett, Tom, jt. auth. see Robinson, Stearn.
Corbiere, A. & Lautier. Dictionnaire Espagnol-Francais. Dessain & Tolra.
Corbiere, Lautier. Dictionnaire Francais-Espagnol. Dessain & Tolra.
Corblet, Jules. Glossaire Etymologique & Comparatif du Patois Picard Ancien & Moderne. Slatkine.
Cordier, Henri. Bibliotheca Indosinica. Dictionnaire bibliographique des ouvrages relatifs a la peninsule indo-chinoise. B Franklin.
--Bibliotheca Sinica, dictionnaire bibliographique des ouvrages relatifs a l'Empire chinois. B Franklin.
Cordignano, F. Dizionario Italiano-Albanese. Forni.
Coripio Perez, Fernando. Diccionario Etimologico Abreviado. French & Eur.
Corkhill, Thomas. The Complete Dictionary of Wood. Stein & Day.
--The Complete Dictionary of Wood. Stein & Day.
Cormier, France-Pauline. Vocabulaire de la Radio & de la Television. Quebec Off.
--Vocabulaire de l'electroacoustique de l'acoustique. Quebec Off.
Corning, Howard M., ed. Dictionary of Oregon History. Binford.
Cornubert, Raymond. Dictionnaire Chimique. Intl Pubns Serv.
--Dictionnaire de Chimie Allemand-Francais. French & Eur.
Corominas, Joan. Breve Diccionario Etimologico de la Lengua Castellana (GRD). Lectorum Pubns.
--Breve Diccionario Etimologico de la Lengua Espanola. French & Eur.
--Diccionario Critico Etimologico De la Lengua Espanola. French & Eur.
Corominas, Joan & Pascual, J. A. Diccionario Critico Etimologico Castellano & Hispanico. Gredos.
Coromines i Vegneaux, Joan. Diccionari etimologie i complementari de la llengua catalana. Curial.
Coromines i Vigneaux, Joan. Diccionari etimologic i complementari de la llengua catalana. Curial.
Coromines i Vigneaux, Joan & Pascual, J. A. Diccionario critico etimologico castellano & hispanico. Gredos.
Corriente Cordoba, Federico. Diccionario espanol-arabe. Inst Hispano-Arabe.
--Diccionario Espanol-Arabe. French & Eur.
Corripio, Fernando. Diccionario Abreviado de Sinonimos (BRG). Lectorum Pubns.
--Diccionario de Incorrecciones, Dudas & Normas Gramaticales. Edit Bruguera.
--Diccionario Etimologico Abreviado. Bruguera.
--Diccionario Etimologico Abreviado (BRG). Lectorum Pubns.
--Diccionario Etimologico General de la Lengua Castellana. Bruguera.
Corripio Perez, Fernando. Diccionario Abreviado de Sinonimos. French & Eur.
--Diccionario Etimologico General de la Lengua Espanola (French & Eur). French & Eur.
Corson, Betty M., ed. The New Secretary's Deskbook. HR&W Canada.
Cortada, Francisco J. Diccionario medico Labor. Labor SA.
Cortada, James W., ed. Historical Dictionary of the Spanish Civil War, 1936-1939. Greenwood.
Corte, Della & Gatti, trs. Diccionario de la musica. Ricordi.
Cortelazzo, Manlio & Zolli, Paolo. Dizionario etimologico della lingua italiana: Vol. 1, A-C. Zanichelli.
Cortes, Lia, jt. auth. see Fuentes, Jordi.
Cortiella Martret, Aureli. Vocabulari de Barbarismes & Castellanismes. Organ Ofic Adm.
Cortina. Cortina-Ace Basic French Dictionary. Ace Bks.
--Cortina-Ace Basic German Dictionary. Ace Bks.
--Cortina-Ace Basic Italian Dictionary. Ace Bks.
--Cortina-Ace Basic Spanish Dictionary. Ace Bks.
Cortina & Grosset. Basic Spanish Dictionary: English-Spanish, Spanish-English. Pan Amer Pub.
Corwin, Charles, et al. A Dictionary of Japanese & English Idiomatic Equivalents. Kodansha.
Cosciani, Guido. Dizionario italiano-tedesco. Paravia.
Cosciani, Guido, jt. auth. see Bidoli, Emilio.
Cossarini, M. G., tr. see Morice, Eugene.
Costa, J. Almeida see Almeida Costa, J. & Sampaio de Melo.
Costa, Jean. Vocabulaire Analogique de la Langue Corse. C. E. R. C.
Costa, Vasco & Frances, Osvald. Diccionario De Unidadaes y Tablas De Conversion. French & Eur.
Costa, Vasco & Frances, Osvaldo. Diccionario de unidades y tablas de conversion. G Gili.
Costanzo, Maurizio. Dizionario delle idee correnti. Bompiani.
Costaz, Louis. Dictionnaire Syriaque-Francais-Anglais. Dar El-Machreq.
Coste, D., jt. ed. see Galisson, R.
Costello, Nancy A. Katu Vocabulary. Summer Inst Ling.
Coston, Henry. Dictionnaire de la Politique Francaise. Coston.
--Dictionnaire de la Politique Francaise. Francaise Lib.
--Dictionnaire de la Politique Francaise, 3. Coston.
--Dictionnaire des Dynasties Bourgeoises & du Monde des Affaires. A. Moreau.
Cote, N. & Gaumond, J. Nomenclature des Appelations d'emploi dans L' Industrie Papetiere Quebecoise: Anglais-Francais. French & Eur.
Cote-Prefont, Gisele, jt. auth. see Prefontaine, Robert.
Cotgrave, Randle. A Dictionarie of the French & English Tongues. Walter J Johnson.
--Dictionary of the French & English Tongues. Adler.

Cotolulis, Socratis. Dictionar Roman-Grec. Editura Stiintifica.
Cotta, Alain. Dictionnaire de la Science Economique. Delarge.
--Dictionnaire de la Science Economique. French & Eur.
Cotti-Cometti, G. & George, P. Dizionario della geografica: Geografica umana. CESVIET.
Cotton, Gerard. Vocabulaire Raisonne Latin-Francais. Dessain & Tolra.
Coudereau, Henri. Vocabulaires Methodiques Ouayana, Apari, Oyampal, Emerillon. Kraus.
Coudray, Leandre. Lexique des Sciences de l'education. E. S. F.
Coughlin, George G. Dictionary of Law. Har-Row.
Coulet du Gard, Rene. Dictionary of Spanish Place Names of the Northwest Coast of America: California. Edns Des Deux Mondes.
--Dictionary of Spanish Place Names of the Northwest Coast of America: Oregon, Washington State, British Columbia, Alaska. Edns Des Deux Mondes.
Coulombe, Victor, jt. auth. see Rolland-Thomas, Paule.
Coulson, J., ed. The Pocket Oxford Russian-English Dictionary. Oxford U Pr.
Coulson, J., et al, eds. The Oxford Illustrated Dictionary. Oxford U Pr.
Coulson, Jessie, et al, eds. The Pocket Oxford Russian Dictionary: Russian-English - English-Russian. Oxford U Pr.
Coulson, Jessie S. The Pocket Oxford Russian-English Dictionary. Imprint of Oxford U Pr.
Counihan, Martin. A Dictionary of Energy. Routledge & Kegan.
Couro, Ted & Hutcheson, Christina. Dictionary of Mesa Grande Diegueno. Malki Mus Pr.
Course, A. G. & Oram, R. B. Glossary of Cargo Handling Terms (Pub. by Nautical England). State Mutual Bk.
--Glossary of Cargo Handling Terms. Sheridan.
Courtes, Joseph, jt. auth. see Greimas, Algirdas J.
Courtine, Robert H. Dictionnaire des Fromages. Larousse.
--Dictionnaire des Fromages. French & Eur.
Courtis, S. A., jt. auth. see Watters, Garnette.
Courtois, Jean. Lexiques de Termes de Pathologie Dentaire. Prelat.
Cousin, Jean. Vocabulaire Grec de la Terminologie Rhetorique: Dans; Etudes sur Quintillen (Pub. by B R Gruner Netherlands). Humanities.
Cousineau, Rene, jt. auth. see Ricour, Pierre.
Couvreur. Dictionnaire Classique de la Langue Chinoise. Mason & Larose.
Couvveur, F. S. Dictionnaire Classique de la Langue Chinoise. French & Eur.
Couzinie, J. Dictionnaire de la Langue Romano-Casteaise & des Contrees Limitrophes. Lafitte Repr.
Covarrubias Horozco, Sebastian De see De Covarrubias Horozco, Sebastian.
Coveney & Moore. Glossary of French & English Management Terms. Imported Bks.
--Glossary of French & English Management Terms. Longman.
Coveney & Amey, eds. Glossary of Spanish & English Management Terms. Longman.
Coveney, James. Glossary of English & German Management Terms. Longman.
Coveney, James & Amey, J. Glossary of Spanish & English Management Terms. Longman.
Coveney, James & Moore, Sheila J. Lexique de Termes Anglais-Francais de Gestion. Colin.
Coveney, James & Moore, Shelia J., eds. Glossary of French & English Management Terms. Longman.
Coveny, James & Degens, Christina. Glossary of German & English Management Terms. Longman.
Cowan, Henry J. A Dictionary of Architectural Science. Halsted Pr.
Cowan, J. M., jt. auth. see Wehr, Hans.
Cowan, J. M., ed. see Wehr, Hans.
Cowan, J. Milton, ed. Dictionary of Modern Written Arabic. Intl Pubns Serv.
Cowan, J Milton, ed. see Wehr, Hans.
Cowan, J. Milton, ed. see Wehr, Hans.
Cowan, Milton J., ed. see Wehr, Hans.
Cowan, S. T. A Dictionary of Microbial Taxonomic Usage. Lubrecht & Cramer.
--A Dictionary of Microbial Taxonomy. Hill, L. R., ed. Cambridge U Pr.
Cowden-Clark, Mary. Complete Concordance to Shakespeare. Folcroft.
Cowie, A. P. & Mackin, Ronald. Oxford Dictionary of Current Idiomatic English: Verbs with Prepositions & Particles. Oxford U Pr.
Cowles, Roy T. The Cantonese Speaker's Dictionary. Paragon.
Coysh, A. W. The Dictionary of Blue & White Pottery. Antique Collect.
Craciun, Teofil. Mic Dictionar de Biologie. Albatros.
Craeybeckx, A. S. Elsevier's Dictionary of Photography. Elsevier.
Cragg, Dan, jt. auth. see Elting, John R.
Craig, Robert D. & King, Frank P., eds. Historical Dictionary of Oceania. Greenwood.
Craig, Ruth P. Diccionario de Dos Cientos Uno Verbos Ingleses. Barron.
Craigie, William A. & Hulbert, James R., eds. Dictionary of American English on Historical Principles. U of Chicago Pr.
Cramer, Dettmar. Lexikon fuer Fussballfreunde: Fachliche Beratung. Bucher.
Crane, Dale, jt. auth. see Foye, James.
Crane, Dale, et al. Aircraft Technical Dictionary. Aviation Maintenance.
Crane, David. A Dictionary of Canadian Economics. Hurtig.
--A Dictionary of Canadian Economics. Hurtig.
Crane, Helen, jt. auth. see Reid, Hale.
Craven, Henry & Barfield, John. English-Congo & Congo-English Dictionary. Ayer Co.
Cree, A. Cree's Dictionary of Latin Quotations. Newbury Bks.
Creedman, Theodore S. Historical Dictionary of Costa Rica. Scarecrow.
--Historical Dictionary of Costa Rica. Intl Guatemala.
Crespi, Irene & Ferrario, Jorge. Lexico tecnico de las artes plasticas. EUDEBA.
Crespo Rodriguez, Rafael. Vocabulario de Construccion Naval. Universidades & Acad.
Creswell, Thomas J. Usage in Dictionaries & Dictionaries of Usage. NCTE.
Criado de Val, Manuel. Diccionario de espanol equivoco. Edi-Seis.
Crim, Keith, et al, eds. Abingdon Dictionary of Living Religions. Abingdon.
Crim, Keith R., jt. ed. see Buttrick, George A.
Crisafio, Raul, tr. see Bobbio, Norberto.
Cristea, Petre. Dictionar Tehnic Auto de Buzunar in Sapte Limbi. Editura Stiintifica.
Criswell, E. H; see King, A. T.
Critchley, Macdonald, ed. Butterworths Medical Dictionary. Butterworth.
--Butterworths Medical Dictionary. Butterworth.
Croft, K. Science Readings for Students of English As a Second Language, with Exercises for Vocabulary Development (I). McGraw.
Cronin. Vocabulary One Thousand. HarBraceJ.
Cronin, Morton J. Vocabulary One Thousand: With Words in Context (HC). HarBraceJ.
Crosbie, John S. Crosbie's Dictionary of Puns (Harmony). Crown.
--Crosbie's Dictionary of Riddles (Harmony). Crown.
Crosby, Cynthia A. Historical Dictionary of Malawi. Scarecrow.
Crosland, Andrew. A Concordance to The Complete Poetry of Stephen Crane. Bruccoli.
Cross, F. L. & Livingstone, Elizabeth A. The Oxford Dictionary of the Christian Church. Oxford U Pr.
Cross, Frank M., Jr. & Freedman, David N. Early Hebrew Orthography: A Study of the Epigraphic Evidence. Am Orient Soc.
Crouse, William H. & Anglin, Donald L. Pocket Automotive Dictionary, with Metric Conversion Table (G). McGraw.
Crout, Robert R., jt. auth. see Heggoy, Alf A.
Crowdis, David, jt. auth. see Crowdis, Kay.
Crowdis, Kay & Crowdis, David. Designing & Building Your Own Home. Reston.
Crowell. Diccionario espanol-ingles, ingles-espanol. Hachette.
Crowell, Thomas, Jr., ed. see Bender, James F.
Crowley, Ellen, ed. Acronyms, Initialisms & Abbreviations Dictionary. Gale.
--Reverse Acronyms, Initialisms, & Abbreviations Dictionary. Gale.
Cruden, Alexander. Cruden's Concordance: Handy Reference Edition. Baker Bk.
--Cruden's Pocket Dictionary of Bible Terms. Baker Bk.
--Cruden's Unabridged Concordance. Baker Bk.
--Cruden's Unabridged Concordance. Broadman.
Cruikshank, Eleanor P. French-English Instant Vocabulary. Cruikshank.
Crum, Walter E., ed. Coptic Dictionary. Oxford U Pr.
Cruz, M. & Ignashev, S. P. Tagalog-Russian Dictionary. French & Eur.
Crystal, David. A First Dictionary of Linguistics & Phonetics (Pub. by Andre Deutsch). Westview.
Csoma de Koros, Alexander. A Dictionary of Tibetan & English (Pub. by Cosmo Pubns India). Orient Bk Dist.
Cuartas, Augusto, jt. auth. see Santamaria, Antonio.
Cuartas, Augusto, jt. auth. see Santamarie, Andres.
Cuddon, J. A. A Dictionary of Literary Terms. Doubleday.
--The International Dictionary of Sports & Games. Schocken.
Cuervo. Diccionario de construccion y regimen de la lengue castellano. Herder SA.
Cuervo, R. J. Diccionario de construccion y regimen de la lengua castellana. Inst Caro y Cuervo.
Cuervo, Rufino J. Diccionario de Construccion & Regimen de la Lengua Castellana. Inst Caro y Cuervo.
Cuervo, Rufino J., prologue by see Gagini, Carlos & Soto, Victor M.
Cuesta, Felip Arroyo De La see Arroyo De La Cuesta, Felipe.
Cuisin, Michel. Dictionnaire des Oiseaux. Larousse.
--Dictionnaire oiseaux. Larousse.
Cummings, David, jt. auth. see Pipkin, Bernard.
Cunliffe, Richard J. A Lexicon of the Homeric Dialect. U of Okla Pr.
--A New Shakespearean Dictionary. AMS Pr.
--New Shakespearean Dictionary. Folcroft.
Cunningham, P. J., jt. auth. see Riley, P. A.
Curcio, Michele. Dictionnaire de l'astrologie. Casterman.
Curl, Michael. The Anagram Dictionary (Pub. by Robert Hale England). State Mutual Bk.
Curme, George O. A Grammar of the English Language. Verbatim.
--A Grammar of the English Language: Parts of Speech. Verbatim.
--A Grammar of the English Language: Syntax. Verbatim.
Curzon, L. B. A Dictionary of Law (Pub. by Macdonald & Evans England). Intl Ideas.
Cusatelli, G. Dizionario Garzanti della Lingua Italiana. French & Eur.
--Dizionario Garzanti della Lingua Italiana. French & Eur.
Cusatelli, G. & Brunacci, G. Dizionario Garzanti: Francese-Italiano, Italiano-Francese. Salati, U. & Dominicis, F., eds. French & Eur.
Cusatelli, G., ed. Dizionario Garzanti della Lingua Italiana. French & Eur.
Cushing, William. Initials & Pseudonyms: A Dictionary of Literary Disguises. Gale.
Cusihuaman, Antonio G. Diccionario Quechua Cuzco-Collao. Minist Ed Caracas.
Cusset, Francis. English-French & French-English Technical Dictionary. Chem Pub.
--Vocabulaire Technique Allemand-Francais. Berger-Levrault.
--Vocabulaire Technique Allemand-Francais, Francais-Allemand. French & Eur.
--Vocabulaire Technique Anglais-Francais, Francais-Anglais. French & Eur.
--Vocabulaire Technique Anglais-Francais. Berger-Levrault.
Cuthbertson, John. Complete Glossary to the Poetry & Prose of Robert Burns. B Franklin.
Cutolo, Alessandro. Vocabolario della lingua italiana. Euro Co.
Cuvillier, Armand. Diccionario de Filosofia. French & Eur.
Cuyas, A., ed. New Appleton's Cuyas English-Spanish & Spanish-English Dictionary. P-H.
Cuyas, Arturo. English-Spanish to Spanish-English Dictionary. P-H.
Cuyas Armengol, Arturo. Diccionario De Bolsillo Frances-Espanol, Espagnol-Francais. French & Eur.
--Diccionario Manual Frances-Espanol, Espagnol-Francais. French & Eur.
--Diccionario Manual Ingles-Espanol, Spanish-English. French & Eur.
--Diccionario Manual Ingles-Espanol, Spanish-English. French & Eur.
--Gran Diccionario Cuyas Ingles-Espanol, Spanish-English. French & Eur.
Cvetanovic, Ratimir J. English-Serbocroatian, Serbocroatian-English Dictionary. Saphrograph.
Cvrcek, Jarom. Slovnik Zakladnich Odbornych Rusko-Ceskych Vyrazu ze Silnicni a Mestske Dopravy. SNTC.
Czerni & Skrzynka. Polish-English Dictionary of Science & Technology (Pub. by Collets). State Mutual Bk.
Czerni, S. & Skrzynska, M. Polish Science & Technology Dictionary: English-Polish. Vanous.
--Polish Science & Technology Dictionary: Polish-English. Vanous.
Czerni, Sergiusz & Skrzynska, Maria, eds. Polish-English Dictionary of Science & Technology. Intl Learn Syst.

D

Daae, E. English-Norwegian, Norwegian-English, Lommeordbok. French & Eur.
--Francais-Norvegien-Francais Lommerorbok. French & Eur.
Dabac, Ulatko. Technisches Woerterbuch. Bauverlag.
--Technisches Woerterbuch (Pub. by Bauverlag). French & Eur.
Dabbs, Jack A. Glossary of Agricultural Terms, English-Bengali. Dabbs.
--Short Bengali-English, English-Bengali Dictionary. Dabbs.
--Short Bengali-English, English-Bengali Dictionary. Dabbs.
Dabout, E., ed. Diccionario de Medicina. French & Eur.
Dacio, Juan. Diccionario de los Papas. French & Eur.
Da Conceica, Julio, jt. auth. see Ortega Cavero, David.

Daehler, David J., ed. English-Chinese Glossary for Elementary Chinese. Cheng & Tsui.
Da Fonseca, F. Peixoto. Dictionnaire Bilingue Larousse, Francais-Portugais et Portugais-Francais. Larousse.
Daglish, R. C., ed. see Taube, A. M., et al.
Dagneaud, Robert. Le Vocabulaire Grammatical. CDU.
D'Agostino, Francisco J. Vocabulario Ingles-Espanol de Electronica. ARBO.
Dahdah, Antoine. Dictionary of Arabic Grammar, in Charts & Tables. Intl Bk Ctr.
Dahl, C. Food & Menu Dictionary. CBI Pub.
Dahl, Hartvig. Word Frequencies of Spoken American English. Verbatim.
Dahl, Richard C. & Whelan, John F., eds. The Military Law Dictionary. Oceana.
Dahlgren, Sven, ed. see Wrete, Martin.
Dahlhaus, Carl & Eggebrecht, Hans H. Brockhaus Riemann Musiklexikon. Eur-Am Music.
--Brockhaus-Riemann-Musiklexikon in Zwei Baenden: Band 1, A-K. F A Brockhaus.
--Brockhaus-Riemann-Musiklexikon in Zwei Baenden: Band 2, L-Z. F A Brockhaus.
Daintith, John. A Dictionary of Physical Sciences (Pica Pr). Universe.
Daintith, John, ed. Dictionary of Chemistry. Har-Row.
--Dictionary of Chemistry. B&N NY.
--A Dictionary of Physical Sciences. Rowman & Allanheld.
--Dictionary of Physics. Har-Row.
--The Facts on File Dictionary of Chemistry. Facts on File.
--The Facts on File Dictionary of Physics. Facts on File.
Dal', V. Tolkovyi Slovar' Zhivogo Velikorusskogo Iazyka. Four Continent.
Dalal-Clayton, D. B., ed. Black's Agricultural Dictionary. B&N Imports.
Dale, D. A. The New Zealand Commercial Dictionary. Intl Pubns Serv.
Dale, Edgar & O'Rourke, Joseph. The Living Word Vocabulary. World Bk.
Dale, Johan H. van see Van Dale, Johan H.
D'Alembert, jt. ed. see Diderot, Denis.
Dale Moral, Jose, jt. auth. see Morel, Hector.
Dalgado, Sebastiao R. Glossario Luso-Asiatico (Pub. by Helmut Buske Verlag Hamburg). Benjamins North Am.
Dalgish, Gerard M. A Dictionary of Africanisms: Contributions of Sub-Saharan Africa to the English Language. Greenwood.
Dalla Volta, Amedeo. Dizionario di psicologia. Giunti-Barbera.
Daly, Kathleen N. The Macmillan Picture Wordbook. Macmillan.
D'Ambra, R. Vocabolario napolitano-toscano. Forni.
Dana, Bill. Cowboy-English, English-Cowboy Dictionary. Ballantine.
Danger, Eric P. Dicionario de Plantas Oteis do Brasil. Difel Difusao.
Daniel, jt. auth. see Apel.
Daniel, A. R. Baker's Dictionary. Elsevier.
Daniel, Becky, jt. auth. see Daniel, Charlie.
Daniel, Charlie & Daniel, Becky. My Very Own Dictionary. Good Apple.
Daniel, Ralph T., jt. ed. see Apel, Willi.
Daniels, F. J. Basic English: Writer's Japanese-English Word Book (Pub. by Hokuseido Pr). Heian Intl.
Danielsson, B. Modern English-Swedish Dictionary. French & Eur.
Danielsson, Bror. Engelsk-Svensk Ordbok (Prisma Modern) Vanous.
Dansel, Michel. Dictionnaire des Inconnus aux Noms Communs. Encre.
Daoud, Hesham O. Daoud's Aviation Dictionary (Pub. by Daouds). Aviation.
Da Parigi, Tomaso, jt. auth. see De Sommevoire, Alexis.
D'Arbela, Edmondo, et al. Vocabolario latino-italiano e italiano-latino. Signorelli C.
Darcy, H. L., ed. Luftfahrtechisches Worterbuch, Deutsch-English (Pub. by Walter de Gruyter, Inc.). French & Eur.
Dar el Mashreq. Arabic-English Dictionary. Intl Bk Ctr.
--Arabic-English Students Dictionary. Intl Bk Ctr.
--Munjid al Tulab. Intl Bk Ctr.
--Student Arabic-English Dictionary. Intl Bk Ctr.
Daremberg, Charles & Saglio, E. Dictionnaire des Antiquites Grecques & Romaines. Akadem Druck-U Verlagsanstalt.
Darlington, C. D. & Heider, Karl G. Bild der Voelker. F A Brockhaus.
Darmesteter, Arsene. Le Glosses & Glossaires Hebreux-Francais. Champion.
Darmesteter, Arsene, jt. auth. see Hatzfeld, Adolphe.
Darmesteter, Arsene, jt. auth. see Hatzfeld, Adophe.
Dartmouth College Library, Hanover, N. H. Dictionary Catalog of the Stefansson Collection on the Polar Regions (Hall Library). G K Hall.
Darton, Harvey. Plates Illustrative of the Vocabulary for the Deaf & Dumb. Gordon Pr.
Darton, Michael, ed. A Modern Concordance to the New Testament. Doubleday.
Darvas, Gabor. Zenei Zseblexikon. Zenemukiado.
Das, S. C. Tibetan-English Dictionary. Orientalia.
Das, S. C. & Kazi, I. D. Tibetan-English, English-Tibetan Dictionary. Heinman.
Das, S. Chandra see Chandra Das, S.
Das, Sarat C. Tibetan-English Dictionary, with Sanskrit Synonyms. Sandberg, G. & Heyde, A. W., eds. Intl Pubns Serv.
Dass, S. C. Tibetan-English Dictionary. Orient Bk Dist.
Daudet, Yves, jt. auth. see Debbasch, Charles.
Daughters of St. Paul. ABC's Dictionary. Dghtrs St Paul.
Daum, E. & Schenk, W. A Directory of Russian Verbs. Hippocrene Bks.
Daum, E., ed. see Ruzicka, R.
Daum, Edmund & Schenk, W. Deutsch-Russisches Woerterbuch. Hueber.
--Deutsch-Russisches Woerterbuch (Pub. by Max Hueber). French & Eur.
--Russich-Deutsches Woerterbuch. Hueber.
--Russich-Deutsches Woerterbuch (Pub. by Max Hueber). French & Eur.
Daum, V. & Schenk. Dictionary of Russian Verbs (Russian-English (Pub. by Collet's). State Mutual Bk.
Dauzat, A., et al. Nouveau Dictionnaire etymologique. Larousse.
Dauzat, Albert. Dictionnaire des noms de famille et prenoms de France. Larousse.
--Nouveau Dictionnaire Etymologique. French & Eur.
Dauzat, Albert, et al. Dictionnaire Etymologique. Larousse.
Davary, Gholam D. Baktrisch: Ein Woerterbuch. Groos Verlag.
Davau, M. R., et al, eds. Dictionnaire Bordas: Dictionnaire du Francais Vivant. Harrap.
Davaux, M., et al. Dictionnaire du Francais Vivant: Nouvelle Edition (Dist. by Continental Bk Co). Bordas.
Davenport, Peter, jt. ed. see Thompson, Philip.
David. Definitions & Divisions of Philosophy. Kendall, Bridget & Thomson, Robert W., trs. Scholars Pr CA.
David, S. Vocabolario italiano-tedesco-italiano (CEB). Capitol-Dischi.
--Vocabolario italiano-tedesco-italiano (CEB). Capitol-Dischi.
David, Sante, ed. Vocabolario Italiano-Tedesco, Tedesco-Italiano. Capitol Edit.
David Ben Abraham. The Hebrew-Arabic Dictionary of the Bible, Known As Kitab Jami al-Alfaz (Agron) Skoss, Solomon L., ed. AMS Pr.
Davidenko, R. A. An Explanatory Dictionary for Students of English (Pub. by Ganatleba). Four Continent.
--An Explanatory Dictionary for Students of English (Pub by Ganatleba). Four Continent.
Davidova, A. A., et al. Karmannyi Russko-Urdu Slovar (Pub. by GINS). Four Continent.
Davids, L. E. Instant Business Dictionary. Watts.
Davids, Lewis E. Dictionary of Banking & Finance. Littlefield.
--Dictionary of Banking & Finance. Rowman.
--Dictionary of Insurance. Littlefield.
--Dictionary of Insurance. Rowman & Allanheld.
--Instant Business Dictionary. Career Inst.
Davids, T. Rhys. The Pali Text Society's Pali-English Dictionary. Intl Pubns Serv.
Davidson, Alan, tr. see Dumas, Alexandre.
Davidson, Benjamin. Analytical Hebrew & Chaldee Lexicon (Pub. by Bagster). Zondervan.
Davidson, Hugh M. & Dube, Pierre H., eds. A Concordance to the Pascal's Pensees. Cornell U Pr.
Davidson, Jane, tr. see Dumas, Alexandre.
Davidson, Jessica. How to Improve Your Spelling & Vocabulary. Watts.
Davidson, K., ed. Russko-Shvedskii Slovar (Pub. by Russkii Iazyk). Four Continent.
Davies, Adriana, ed. see Ormond, Richard & Rogers, Malcolm.
Davies, Cornelia Oakes, jt. auth. see Clark, Charlotte.
Davies, John. A Tahitian & English Dictionary. AMS Pr.
Davies, T. L. A Supplementary English Glossary. R West.
Davies, T. Lewis. English Glossary: A Supplementary. Arden Lib.
Davies, Thomas L. Supplementary English Glossary. Gale.
Davis. Davis Dictionary of the Bible. Broadman.
Davis, Hunter. Book of British Lists. Hamlyn Pub.
Davis, John D. Davis Dictionary of the Bible. Baker Bk.
Davis, Lorraine, ed. see Calasibetta, Charlotte M.
Davis, Nancy. Vocabulary Improvement (C). McGraw.
Davis, Nancy B. Vocabulary Improvement. McGraw.
Davis, P. E., jt. auth. see Smith, G. L.
Davis, Phyllis E., jt. auth. see Smith, Genevieve L.
Davis, Robert R., Jr. Lexicon of Historical & Political Terms. Monarch Pr.
--Lexicon of Historical & Political Terms. Reed, R., ed. R & E Res Assoc.
Davitz, Joel R., et al. Terminology & Concepts in Mental Retardation. Tchrs Coll.
Davrout, L., tr. see Wieger, L.
Davrout, L., tr. see Wieger, Leon.
Dawydoff, W. Technical Dictionary of High Polymers: English, French, German, Russian. Pergamon.
Day, Harvey. Occult Illustrated Dictionary. Oxford U Pr.
--Yoga Illustrated Dictionary. Emerson.
Daykin, Vernon. Technical Arabic (Pub. by Lund Humphries England). State Mutual Bk.
Dayre De Mailhol, C. P. Dictionnaire Historique & Heraldique. Slatkine.
Deak, Etienne. Grand Dictionnaire d'Americanismes: Contenant les Principaux Termes Americains avec Leur Equivalent Exact en Francais. Intl Pubns Serv.
Deak, Etienne & Deak, Simone. Dictionnaire des Americanismes. Dauphin.
--Dictionnaire des Americanismes. French & Eur.
Deak, Simone, jt. auth. see Deak, Etienne.
De Alcedo, Antonio. Geographical & Historical Dictionary of America & the West Indies. Thompson, George A., tr. B Franklin.
De Andrea. Diccionario manual latino-castellano y castellano-latino. Sopena.
Deane, Samuel. The New England Farmer; or, Georgical Dictionary. Ayer Co.
De Angelis, V., ed. see Papias, Gramarian.
De Anton, G. Haberkamp see Haberkamp de Anton, G.
De Anton, G. Haberkamp see Haberkamp de Anton, G. & Willers, D. H.
De Anton, Haberkamp G., ed. see Haensch, G.
De Armas Chitty, Jose A. Vocabulario del Hato. U. Central Ven.
Deaton, Donald B., ed. Glossary of Printing Terms. AATCC.
De Aulie, Evelyn W., jt. auth. see Aulie, H. W.
De Azevedo, Domingos. Dictionnaire Francais-Portugais. Garnier.
--Dictionnaire Portugais-Francais. Garnier.
--Grande Dicionario Portugues-Frances. Difel Difusao.
Debahy, M. Dictionary Hebrew Verbs. Intl Bk Ctr.
--Dictionary of Hebrew Verbs. Intl Bk Ctr.
De Bazin, Jean. Vocabulaire de la Princesse de Cleves. Nizet.
Debbasch, Charles & Daudet, Yves. Lexique des Termes Politiques. Dalloz.
--Lexique des Termes Politiques. French & Eur.
De Bea, L., jt. auth. see Sandahl, P.
De Bea, Louise, jt. auth. see Sandahl, Pierre.
De Benedetti, Rinaldo. Dizionario rapido di scienze pure ed applicate. UTET.
Debenjak, D. Modern Dictionary Slovene-German-Slovene. French & Eur.
De Bhaldraithe, Tomas. English-Irish Dictionary. Oifig An Tsolathair.
De Bhaldraithe, Tomas & Claithe, Baile A. English-Irish Dictionary: Terminological Additions & Corrections. Govt Publications Sale Office.
De Bhardraithe, T. English-Irish Dictionary. Colton Bk.
De Bichiacchi, Ada, jt. auth. see Maiocchi, Annamaria F.
De Biro, Elizabeth. Hungarian Cooking. Saphrograph.
Deblock, Nick J. Elsevier's Dictionary of Public Health. Elsevier.
De Bonnefoux, Pierre M. & Paris, Edmund. Le Dictionnaire de la Marine a Voile. Courtille.
De Bono, Edward. Wordpower (CN). Har-Row.
De Bordeje Morencos, Fernando. Diccionario militar estrategico y politico. San Martin.
De Bourbon Parma, Cecilia. Diccionario del Carlismo. Dopesa.
Debrie, Rene. Lexique Picard des Parlers Ouest-Amienois. Univers Picardie.
--Lexique Picard du Berger. Eklitra.
--Lexiques Picards du Cidrier & du Meunier. Eklitra.
De Brissiere, P. Caribbean Cookery. Saphrograph.
Debuigne, Gerard. Dictionnaire des Plantes qui Guerissent. Larousse.
--Dictionnaire des Plantes Qui Guerissent. French & Eur.
--Dictionnaire des Vins. Larousse.
--Dictionnaire vins. Larousse.
De Cadiz, Javier Gomez see Gomez de Cadiz, Javier.
De Cahors, Jean E. Dictionnaire Hatier-Beauchemin: Francais-Latin. Beauchemin.
Decahors, Jean-Elie. Dictionnaire Francais-Latin. Hatier.
Decalo, Samuel. Historical Dictionary of Chad. Scarecrow.
--Historical Dictionary of Dahomey. Scarecrow.
--Historical Dictionary of Niger. Scarecrow.
--Historical Dictionary of Togo. Scarecrow.
De Cande, Roland. Diccionare de la musica. EDNS Sesenti Dos.
--Dizionario dei musicisti. Bompiani.

--Dizionario della musica. Bompiani.
De Casasnovas, F. Vocabulari Mallorqui-Castella. Moll Edit.
De Castelbajac, Bernadette. Qui a dit Quoi? Dictionanaire des Mots & des Phrases qui Ont Une Historire. Tallandier.
De Castillo Mathieu, Micolas. Lexico Caribe en el Caribe Negro de Honduras Britanica. Instituto Caro & Cuervo.
De Cauhe, Joana Raspall see Raspall de Cauhe, Joana, et al.
De Chambure, Eugene. Glossaire du Morvan. Taverdet, Gerard, pref. by. Lafitte Repr.
De Chamfort, Nicolas. Dictionnaire Dramatique. Slatkine.
De Chtcherba. Dictionnaire Russe-Francais. Mir.
DeCosta, Steven E., jt. auth. see Burton, William C.
DeCoster, Jean. Dictionary for Automotive Engineering (Pub. by K G Saur). Shoe String.
Decour, Armand. Vocabulaire du Patols de Bettant, 2. Decour.
De Covarrubias Horozco, Sebastian. Tesoro De la Lengua Castellana, O Espanola. Hispanic Soc.
Decsi, Gyula & Karcsay, Sandor. Woerterbuch der Rechts & Wirtschaftssprache: Teil I, Deutsch-Russisch. Recht & Wirtschaft.
--Woerterbuch der Rechts & Wirtschaftssprache: Teil II, Russisch-Deutsch. Recht & Wirtschaft.
Dedichen, L. Fransk-Norsk Ordbok. French & Eur.
Dedichen, Line. French-Norwegian Dictionary. Kunnskapsforlaget.
De Dony, Ivon P. Lexico de lenguaje figurado. Club de Lectores.
De Felice, Emido & Duro, Aldo. Dizionario della lingua e della civita italiana contemporanea. Palumbo.
De Figueiredo, Candido. Grande Dicionario da Lingua Portuguesa. Difel Difusao.
De Fiore, E., tr. see Gastaut, H.
De Fiore, Gaspare. Dizionario del disegno. La Scuola.
De Fleurian, Dominique, et al. Dictionnaire National des Communes de France. Albin-Michel.
De Fontenay, Louis-Abel. Dictionnaire des Artistes ou Notice Historique: Raisonnee des Architectes, Peintres & Graveurs. Minkoff.
De Foucauld, Charles. Dictionnaire Touareg-Francais. Imprimerie Nat.
De Francis, J., compiled by. A Chinese-English Glossary of the Mathematical Sciences. Am Math.
De Galiana, Thomas. Diccionario de la astronautica. Plaza Janes.
--Diccionario de los descubrimientos cientificos. Plaza Janes.
De Galiana Mingot, Tomas see Mingot, Tomas De Galiana.
De Gamez, Tana, ed. Simon & Schuster's Concise International Dictionary. S & S.
De Garmendia Miangolarra, J. Ignacio. Diccionario de bolsa. Piramide.
Degens, Christina, jt. auth. see Coveny, James.
De Gil, Beatriz Massa see Massa De Gil, Beatriz.
De Gil, Beatriz Massa see Massa de Gil, Beatriz, et al.
De Goma, F. S., jt. auth. see Marole, L. T.
De Gorog, Ralph. Dictionnaire inverse de l'ancien francais. Medieval & Renaissance NY.
--Lexique Francais Moderne - Ancien Francais. U of Ga Pr.
De Grandpre, Jean-Paul. Vocabulaire Bilingue des Assurances sur la Vie. Quebec Off.
DeGross, Katherine, jt. auth. see Probst, Lester A.
Dehaine, M., jt. auth. see Camille, Cl.
Dehaine, Michael, jt. auth. see Camille, Claude.
Dehaine, Michel, jt. auth. see Camille, Claude.
De Haro Vera, Andres, tr. see Heymer, A.
Dehn-Nielsen, Henning. Fogtdals et-binds leksikon i farver. Sejersen, Gorm, ed. Fogtdals Boger.
Deidda, A. Vocabolario tedesco-italiano e italiano-tedesco. Malipiero.
Dejnozka, Edward L. Educational Administration Glossary. Greenwood.
DeJoia, Alex & Stenton, Adrian. Terms in Systemic Linguistics. St Martin.
De Jong, Frits J., et al, eds. Quadrilingual Economics Dictionary (Pub. by Martinus Nijhoff Netherlands). Kluwer Academic.
De Kerchove, R. Small Craft Dictionary. Van Nos Reinhold.
De Koros, Alexander Csoma see Csoma de Koros, Alexander.
De Laborde, Leon. Glossaire Francais du Moyen Age: L'usage de l'archeologue & de l'amateur des Arts. Slatkine.
De LaBrosse, Olivier see Henry, Antonir Marie & LaBrosse, Olivier De.
De la Camara, Maximino San Miguel see San Miguel de la Camara, Maximino.
De La Canal, J. Diccionario ortografico. EDIMEX.
De La Canal, Julio. Diccionario Ortografico. MEX.
De la Canal, Julio see Canal, Julio de la.
De La Chavignerie, Emile B. & Auvray, Louis. Dictionnaire General. Rosenblum, Robert, ed. Garland Pub.
De la Cierva, Patronato J. Diccionario Ruso-Espanol de la Ciencia y la Tecnica. French & Eur.
Delacour, Jean. Dictionnaire des Mots d'esprit. Albin Michel.
De La Cuesta, Felip Arroyo see Arroyo De La Cuesta, Felipe.
Delamare, J. & Delamare, Th. Dictionnaire Francais-Anglais et Anglais-Francais des Termes Techniques de Medecine. French & Eur.
Delamare, Jean & Delamareriche, Marie-Therese. Dictionnaire Francais-Anglais des Termes Techniques de Medecine. Maloine.
Delamare, Jean, jt. auth. see Garnier, Marcel.
Delamare, Th., jt. auth. see Delamare, J.
Delamareriche, Marie-Therese, jt. auth. see Delamare, Jean.
Delamarre. Dictionnaire Francais-Anglais et Anglais-Francais des Termes Techniques De Medecine. French & Eur.
De Landberg, C. & Zettersteen, K. V. Glossaire Datinois. Brill.
De Landsheere, Gilbert. Dictionnaire de l'Evaluation et de la Recherche en Education. French & Eur.
Delattre, J. & DeVernisy, G. Vocabulaire Barometre Dans le Langage Economique. French & Eur.
Delattre, J. & Vernisy, G. Le Vocabulaire Barometre dans le Langage Economique. Georg.
De Launay, Jacques & Lousse, Emile. Dictionnaire d'Histoire Contemporaine 1776-1969. Rencontre.
Delbarre, P. J., jt. auth. see Chassant, Louis A.
Delboulle, Achille. Glossaire de la Vallee d'Yeres. Slatkine.
De Leon, G. F. Diccionario de derecho romano. Plus Ultra.
Delgaty, Alfa & Sanchez, Augustin R. Diccionario Tzotzil De San Andres Con Variaciones Dialectales. Summer Inst Ling.
Del Giacco, G. S. Glossario di immunologia. Minerva Medica.
Delmas-Harrap. Dictionnaire des Affaires Francais-Anglais, Anglais-Francais. French & Eur.
Delorme, Jean. Vocabulaire Technique Bilingue. Quebec Off.
Delporte, Jacques, jt. auth. see Saint Riquier, Marc.
Del Riego, Francisco Fernandez see Fernandez del Riego, Francisco.
Del Riego, Francisco Fernandez see Franco Grande, Xose L. & Fernandez del Riego, Francisco.
Delson, Donn. The Dictionary of Marketing & Related Terms in the Motion Picture Industry. Bradson.
Delson, Donn & Hurst, Walter E. Delson's Dictionary of Radio & Records Industry Terms. Posner, Neil, ed. Bradson.
Delson, Donn & Michalove, Ed. Delson's Dictionary of Cable, Video & Satellite Terms. Posner, Neil, ed. Bradson.
Dels Prats, Alfonso T. Diccionario de Dificultades del Ingles. Editorial Juventud.
--Diccionario de Modismos Ingleses & Norteamericanos. Editorial Juventud.
Dels Prats, Alfonso Torrents see Torrents dels Prats, Alfonso.
Delvalle, Juan. Diccionario bilinque para la juventud. Dist. Comuneros.
Del Vasto, Lanza. Definitions of Nonviolence. Sidgwick, Jean, tr. Greenlf Bks.
Delvau, Alfred. Dictionnaire de la Langue Verte. Slatkine.
Del Vecchio, Alfred, ed. Concise Dictionary of Atomics. Philos Lib.
De Maesschalck, A., jt. auth. see Van Gemert, G. A.
De Mailhol, D. Dictionnaire Historique & Heraldique. Fac.
Demaison, H. Dictionnaire Technologique: Aeronautique. Maison Dictionnaire.
De Marsy, Francois-Marie. Dictionnaire Abrege de Peinture & d'Architecture. Minkoff.
De Melo, Sampaio see Almeida Costa, J. & Sampaio de Melo.
De Mertzenfeld, R. Mertz see Mertz De Mertzenteld, R., et al.
De Meude-Monpas, Jean J. see Meude-Monpas, Jean J. de.
De Michele, Vincenzo. Diccionario: Atlas De Mineralogia. French & Eur.
De Morais, A., ed. see Ferreira, J. Albino.
De Morais, Armando. Dicionario De Ingles-Portugues. Intl Learn Syst.
--Dicionario de Ingles-Portugues "Editora". Porto Editora.
De Morais, O., ed. see Ferreira, J. Albino.
De Nebrija, Antonio. Vocabulario de Romance: El Latin. Castalia Edit.
De Nebruja, Elio de. Vocabulario de romance en latin. Macdonald, Gerald J., tr. Castalia Edit.
Deneubourg, Debleser M. Vocabulaire, Orthographe, Conjugaison, Analyse. Wesmael-Charlier.
Deneubourg, N. Vocabulaire, Orthographe, Conjugalson, Analyse. Wesmael-Charlier.
--Vocabulaire, Orthographe, Conlugalson, Analyse. Wesmael-Charlier.
Denis, S. & Maraval, M. Diccionario espanol-frances. Hachette.
--Diccionario frances-espanol. Hachette.
Denis, Serge & Maraval, M. Dictionnaire Espagnol-Francais. Hachette.
Denis, Serge & Maraval, Marcel. Dictionnaire Espagnol-Francais. French & Eur.
Denis, Serge, et al. Le Dictionnaire Espagnol-Francais. Hachette Jeunesse.
--Le Dictionnaire Espagnol-Francais et Francais-Espagnol. French & Eur.
Denison, T. S. A Mexican-Aryan Comparative Vocabulary. Gordon Pr.
Denisov, A. I., ed. Trudovoe Pravo: Entsiklopedicheskii Slovar (Pub. by Sov. Entsiklopediia). Four Continent.
Denisov, P. N., et al. Uchebnyi Slovar' Sochetaenosti Slov Russkogo Iazyka. Four Continent.
Denisova, M. A. Lingvisticheskii Slovar (Pub. by Russkii Iazyk). Four Continent.
--Lingvostranovedcheskii Slovar' Four Continent.
Denis-Papin, Maurice. Dictionnaire Analogique et de Synonymes Pour la Resolution des Problemes des Mots Croises (Pub. by Albin Michel). French & Eur.
--Dictionnaire Analoqique & de Synonymes pour la Resolution des Problemes des Mots Croises. Albin Michel.
--Dictionnaire des Mots Croises. Albin Michel.
--Dictionnaire Des Mots Croises. French & Eur.
--Dictionnaire des Mots Croises & Jeux Divers. Albin Michel.
Denissov, A. I., ed. see Voronine, V. V., et al.
Denizeau, Claude. Dictionnaire des Parlers Arabes de Syrie, Libyan & Palestine. Maison & Larose.
--Dictionnaire des Parlers Arabes de Syrie, Liban et Palestine. French & Eur.
Denizeau, M., jt. auth. see Boris, Gilbert.
Denney, R. C. A Dictionary of Chromatography. Macmillan London.
--A Dictionary of Spectroscopy. Macmillan London.
--Dictionary of Spectroscopy (Pub. by Wiley-Interscience). Wiley.
Denney, Roland C. Dictionary of Chromatography (Pub. by Wiley-Interscience). Wiley.
Dennis, J. G., ed. International tectonic lexicon. Schweizerbart.
Denoeu, F., et al. French & English Idioms. Barron.
De Noter, R. & Vuillermoz, P. Dictionnaire des Synonymes. PUF.
Densmore, Dana. Speech Is the Form of Though - With a New Glossary. Know Inc.
Denti, Renzo. Dizionario italiano-inglese e inglese-italiano tecnico. Hoepli.
--Dizionario Tecnico Francese-Italiano. Hoepli.
--Dizionario tecnico francese-italiano e italiano-francese. Hoepli.
--Dizionario Tecnico Italiano-Inglese. Hoepli.
--Dizionario Tecnico Italiano-Inglese, Inglese-Italiano. S F Vanni.
De Pando y Villarroya, Jose L. Diccionario de Marina. Autores-Editores.
De Parada, Alejandro Gomez see Gomez de Parada, Alejandro.
De Pianci, Santiago Collin see Collin de Pianci, Santiago.
De Pina, Araujo A. Portuguese-English, English-Portuguese Technical Dictionary. Heinman.
De Pina, Rafael. Diccionario de Derecho. Porrua.
De Pina Araujo, Avelino. De Pina's Technical Dictionary. McGraw.
De Poorter, Wim. Filmlexikon. Nygh Ditmar.
Deputatova, N. F., et al. Nemetsko-Russkii Slovar Po Metalloobrabotke (Pub. by Gosizdat Tekhnich Teoretich. Lit.). Four Continent.
De Regnier, Henri. Lexique de la Langue de Jean de La Fontaine. Lenox.
--Lexique de la Langue de La Rochefoucauld. Olms.
De Renty, Ivan. The Businessman's Everyday English to Spanish Dictionary: El Mundo De Negocios. Larousse.
--Lexique de l'Anglais des affaires. Imported Bks.
--Lexique de l'anglais des Affaires. L. G. F.
--Lexique Quadrilingue des Affaires: Anglais-Francais-Allemand-Espagnol. Hachette.
De Rochefort, Cesar. Dictionnaire General & Curieux Contenant les Principaux Mots: Les Plus Usitez en la Langue Francoise. Slatkine.
De Roquefort, Jean-Baptiste B. Glossaire de la Langue Romane. Slatkine.
De Rosario. Vocabulario Puertorriqueno (Pub by Troutman Press). E Torres & Sons.
De Ruggiero, Ettore. Dizionario epigrafico di antichita romane. L'Erma.
Derveer, Paul D. Van see Van Derveer, Paul D. & Haas, Leonard E.
Derveer, Van see Van Derveer & Haas.
De Sacy, Samuel S., jt. auth. see Serand, Pierre.
De Salzade, M. Dictionnaire historique des monnoies tant anciennes que modernes. Thimonier.
Desbrandes, R., jt. auth. see Ketchian, S.

Deschamps, Pierre. Dictionnaire de Geographie Ancienne et Moderne. French & Eur.
De Seyn, Eugene. Dictionnaire de L'histoire de Belgique. Halbart Wahle.
Desfeuilles, Arthur. Lexique de la Langue de Moliere. Lenox.
--Lexique de la Langue de Moliere avec une. B Franklin.
Desfeuilles, Paul. Dictionnaire de Rimes. Garnier.
Deshpande, P. G. A Modern English-Gujarati Dictionary. Oxford U Pr.
Desilets, Antoine. La Photo de A & Z. Edns Homme.
De Silva, Dharmasena. Kalamanakarana Paribhasika Sabda Sangrahaya. Kojamba.
De Sivry, L. Dictionnaire Geographique, Historique, Descriptif, Archeologique des Pelegrinages. Migne, J. P., ed. Caratzas Pub Co.
Des Mas-Latrie, L. Dictionnaire de Statistique Religieuse. Migne, J. P., ed. Caratzas Pub Co.
Desmond, Ray. Dictionary of British & Irish Botanists & Horticulturists: Including Plant Collectors & Botanical Artists. Rowman.
Desmond, Ray, ed. Dictionary of British & Irish Botanists & Horticulturists. Taylor & Francis.
De Sola, R. Abbreviations Dictionary. Elsevier.
De Sola, Ralph. Crime Dictionary. Facts on File.
De Somaize, Antoine B. Le Dictionnaire des Precleuses. Kraus.
De Sommevoire, Alexis & Da Parigi, Tomaso. Tesoro Della Linqua Greca-Volgare Ed Italiana, cioe Ricchissimo dizzionario greco-volgare et italiano. Caratzas Pub Co.
Desormaux, Joseph, jt. auth. see Constantin, Aime.
Desormeaux, Joseph, jt. auth. see Constantin, Aime.
De Sousa Vieira, Jose. Dicionario de Frances-Portugues: Com Transcicao Fonetica. Porto Ed.
Desov. Concise English-Russian Technical Dictionary. Imported Bks.
Desov, A. English-Bulgarian Concise Technical Dictionary. Heinman.
Desrat, G. Dictionnaire de la Danse, Historique, Theorique, Pratique & Bibliographique. Olms Verlag.
Desrosiers, G. & Boulay, J. Vocabulaire des assurances Sociales. French & Eur.
Desruisseaux, Pierre. Dictionnaire de Meteorologie Populaire au Quebec. Edns Laurore.
Des Ruisseaux, Pierre. Dictionnaire de Meteorologie Populaire au Quebec. Aurore.
Dessaigne, Jacques, jt. auth. see Carrere, Jean.
De Togore, Roca. Diccionario de economia y dissiplinas a fines, aleman-espanol. InterCiencia.
De Toro, Gisbert, jt. auth. see De Toro, Miguel.
De Toro, M. & Gisbert. Dictionnaire Bilingue Larousse, Francais-Espagnol, Espanol-Frances. Larousse.
De Toro, Miguel & De Toro, Gisbert. Dictionnaire Bilingue Apollo Francais-Espagnol. Larousse.
De Toro Gisbert, M. Dictionnaire Bilingue: Francais-Espagnol, Espagnol-Francais. French & Eur.
De Traversay, Yves, jt. auth. see Renouil, Yves.
Dettner, H. Fachwoerterbuch fuer der Metalloberflaechenveredelung. Siemens AG.
Deursen, A. Van see Van Deursen, A.
Deutsch, Babette. Poetry Handbook: A Dictionary of Terms (EH). B&N NY.
Deutsch-Franz Jugendwerk. Glossar der Jugendarbeit: Deutsch Jugend & Ihr Soziales Umfeld. H Luchterhand.
Deutscher, Ruth, et al, eds. Lexikon der Sozialen Arbeit. Kohlhammer.
Deutsches Komitee fur Reprographie. Woerterbuch der Reprographie. Aussant & Schrift.
Deutsches Komittee fuer Reprographie. Woerterbuch der Reprographie: Begriffe und Definitionen. French & Eur.
Deutsches Kommitee Fur Reprographie, ed. Dictionary of Reprography: Terms & Definitions (Pub. by K G Saur). Gale.
Devambez, Pierre. Diccionario de la Civilizacion Griega. French & Eur.
Devecchi, ed. see Zainqui Erro, Jose M.
DeVernisy, G., jt. auth. see Delattre, J.
Devigne, Paul. Glossaire du Patois Thierachien. Ste. Linguistique Picarde.
De Villiers-Sidani, Maria E. Lexique de la Prevention des Accidents. Quebec Off.
De Villiers-Sidani, Maria E., et al. Lexique de Prevention des Accidents. French & Eur.
De Vincentiis, D. L. Vocabolario del dialetto tarantino in corrispondenza della lingua italiana. Forni.
De Vinols De Montfleury, Jules-Gabriel. Vocabulaire Patois Vellavien-Francais. Lafitte Repr.
DeVito, Albert. Chord Dictionary. Kenyon.
De Vito, Albert. Pocket Dictionary of Music Terms. Kenyon.
Devlin. A Dictionary of Synonyms & Antonyms. Warner Bks.
De Vogue, Melchior & Oousel, Raymond. Glossaire de Termes Techniques: L'usage des Lecteurs de la Nuit des Temps. Zodiaque.
Devoto. Avviamento All'Etimologia Italiana: Dizionario Etimologico. Oscar.
Devoto, G. & Oli, G. C., eds. Dizionario della Lingua Italiano. French & Eur.
Devoto, Giacomo & Oli, Giancarlo. Dizionario della lingua italiana. Monnier.
--Vocabolario della lingua italiana. Monnier.
--Vocabolario ilustrato della lingua italiana. Sel Rdrs Digest.
De Vries & Herrmann. Technical & Engineering Dictionary: Band II, English-German. Brandstetter.
--Technical & Engineering Dictionary: Band I, German-English. Brandstetter.
De Vries, A. Dictionary of Symbols & Imagery (North-Holland). Elsevier.
De Vries, Geerte. Van Goor's Deens Woordenboek. Goor.
De Vries, L. Woerterbuch der Reinen und Angewandten Physik. French & Eur.
--Woerterbuch der Reinen und Angewandten Physik. French & Eur.
De Vries, L. & Clason, W. E. Dictionary of Pure & Applied Physics. Elsevier.
De Vries, Louis. French-English Science & Technology Dictionary. Hochman, Stanley, rev. by. McGraw.
--French-English Science Dictionary. McGraw.
--German-English Science Dictionary. McGraw.
DeVries, Louis. German-English Technical & Engineering Dictionary (P&RB). McGraw.
De Vries, Louis & Hermann, Theo M. German-English Technical & Engineering Dictionary. McGraw.
De Vries, Louis & Hochman, Stanley. French-English Science & Technology Dictionary. McGraw.
De Vries, Louis & Jacolev, Leon. German-English Science Dictionary. McGraw.
--German-English Science Dictionary. McGraw.
DeVries, Louis & Jacolev, Leon. German-English Science Dictionary (P&RB). McGraw.
DeVries, Louis & Kolb, Helga. Dictionary of Chemistry & Chemical Engineering. Incl. Vol. 1. German-English; Vol. 2. English-German. Verlag Chemie.
Dewan Bahasa dan Pustaka. Istilah Senibina, Perancangan dan Ukur Kuantiti. Dewan Bahasa.
--Kamus dwibahasa, bahasa Inggeris-bahasa Malaysia. Dewan Bahasa.
Deweerdt, Jacques. Vocabulaire Fondamental de Technologie. Gamma.
--Vocabulaire Fondamental de Technologie. French & Eur.
Dey, Nano Lal see Lal Dey, Nando.
Dey, Nundo Lal. The Geographical Dictionary of Ancient & Mediaeval India. Intl Pubns Serv.
--Geographical Dictionary of Ancient & Mediaeval India. Verry.
Dhamotharau, A. Tamil dictionaries. Steiner Verlag.
Dheilly, Joseph. Dictionnaire Biblique. French & Eur.
D'Iachkov, A. I., et al, eds. Kratkii Defektologicheskii Slovar (Pub. by Prosveschchenie). Four Continent.
Di Aichelburg, Ulrico. Dizionario di medicina: Enciclopedia degli alimenti. UTET.
--Dizionario di medicina per le famiglie. UTET.
Diakova, G. A. Fitopatologicheskii Slovar Spravochnik (Pub. by Nauka). Four Continent.
Diamant, Lincoln, ed. The Broadcast Communications Dictionary. Hastings.
Diaz Mateo, Felix & Hochleitner, Frida. Diccionario manual frances-espanol, espanol-frances. Espasa Calpe.
Diaz-Retg, E. Diccionario de Dificultades de la Lengua Espanola. French & Eur.
Diaz Velazquiz, Mariano. Diccionario basico de matematicas. Anaya.
Di Benedetto, Ubaldo, ed. New Comprehensive English-Spanish, Spanish-English Dictionary. Intl Pubns Serv.
Di Cesare, Mario A. & Fogel, Ephim, eds. A Concordance to the Poems of Ben Jonson. Cornell U Pr.
Di Cesare, Mario A. & Mignani, Rigo, eds. A Concordance to the Complete Writings of George Herbert. Cornell U Pr.
Dick, Esther A., jt. auth. see Snell, Walter.
Dickinson, Colin & Lucas, John. Van Nostrand Reinhold Color Dictionary of Mushrooms. Van Nos Reinhold.
Dider, Marcel. Mes Dix Mille Mots. Harrap.
Diderot, Denis & D'Alembert, eds. Encyclopedie ou dictionnaire raisonne des sciences, des arts et des metiers. Adler.
Didier, J., jt. auth. see Buhler, Alain.
Didier, Marcel. Mes dix millet mots. Barron.
Didler, M. Le Dictionnaire Pour L'Ecole: Mes 10,000 Mots. Barron.
Diego Hernandez, Juan. Diccionario de Formularios Generales. Coleccion Nereo.
--Diccionario de Formularios Generales: Tomo 7. Coleccion Nereo.
Diego Hernandez, Juan & Rodriguez Segui, Alejandro. Diccionario de Formularios Generales. Coleccion Nereo.
Dieterich, Genoveva. Pequeno Diccionario De Teatro Mundial. French & Eur.
Dietl, C. Woerterbuch des Wirtschafts, Rechts und Handelssprache. French & Eur.
Dietl, Clara E. & Lorenz, Egon. Woerterbuch fuer Recht, Wirtschaft & Politik: Teil II, Deutsch-Englisch. Recht & Wirtschaft.
Dietrich, G. & Mueller-Hegemann, A., eds. Jugendlexikon Biologie. Bibl Inst Leipzig.
Dietrichson, Jan W. & Verland, Orm. English-Norwegian, Norwegian-English. Kunnskapsforlaget.
Diez Mateo, Felix. Diccionario castellano ilustrado. Neguri.
--Diccionario Espanol Etimologico (CANT). Lectorum Pubns.
--Diccionario Espanol Etimologico. French & Eur.
--Diccionario espanol etimologico: El pequeno academico. Cantabrica.
--Diccionario Manual Aleman-Espanol, Espanol-Aleman. French & Eur.
Diez Mateo, Felix & Hochleitner, Frida. Diccionario Manual Frances-Espanol, Espanol-Frances. French & Eur.
--Diccionario manual ingles-espanol, espanol-ingles. Espasa Calpe.
--Diccionario Manual Ingles-Espanol, Espanol-Ingles. French & Eur.
Diez-Picazo, Luis. Dictamenes Juridicos. Civitas.
Difel. Dicionario Frances-Portuques. Difel Editorial, S. A.
Dijk, G. Economische Begrippen. NIB.
Dijk, Marcel Van see Van Dijk, Marcel & Sandeau, Georges.
Dijkhoff, Mario. Bokabulario Papiamentu-Ulandes. Walburg Pers.
Dikepa, Kalio H., jt. auth. see Lieber, Michael D.
Dillard, J. L. Lexicon of Black English. Continuum.
Dillon, Michael. A Dictionary of Chinese History (F Cass Co). Biblio Dist.
Dills, Lanie. The Official CB Slanguage Language Dictionary. Burrows & Baker.
Dinkel, John. The Road & Track Illustrated Auto Dictionary. Norton.
Dinneen. Irish-English Dictionary. Colton Bk.
Dinneen, Patrick S. English-Irish Dictionary. Murcava, L. O., ed. Shalom.
Dinneen, Patrick S., rev. by. Irish-English Dictionary. Shalom.
Dion, Gerard. Dictionnaire Canadien des Relations du Travall Francais-Anglais. Laval P. U.
--Dictionnaire Canadien des Relations du Travail: Francais-Anglais. French & Eur.
--Glossary of Terms Used in Industrial Relations. Univ Laval.
--Vocabulaire Francais-Anglais des Relations Professionnelles. Laval P. U.
Diorki, tr. see Blok, Jezewski.
Dioudonnat, Pierre-Marie & Bragadir, Sabine. Dictionnaire des 10,000 Dirigeants Politiques Francais. French & Eur.
Dipl-Ling, V. & Bensch, Erhard. Dictionary of Shipbuilding, Shipping & Fisheries (Pub. by Collet's). State Mutual Bk.
Disney, Walt. Diccionario Disney. French & Eur.
--Dictionnaire Magique. Nathan.
Dissing, Borge & Lave, Rud. Dansk-Tysk Ordbog. Gyldendal Norsk.
Distein. Diccionario de la Lengua Espanola. Distein.
Dittmar, P. Woerterbuch der Chinesischen Revolution. French & Eur.
Divers. Dictionnaire de la presse ecrite et audiovisuelle. Maison Dictionnaire.
Divry, D. C. Divry's Spanish English Dictionary. Camino Real.
Divry, G. C. Modern English-Greek-English Desk Dictionary with Thumb Index. French & Eur.
--New English-Greek-English Handy Dictionary. French & Eur.
Divry, George C., ed. Divry's New Modern Greek-English & English-Greek Handy Dictionary. Divry.
Dixon, J. I., jt. auth. see Boggs, R. S.
Dixson & Fox. Meu Primeiro Dicionario Ilustrado de Ingles. Imported Bks.
Dixson, et al. My First English-Japanese Picture Dictionary. Regents Pub.
Dixson, Robert J., jt. auth. see Whitford, Harold C.
Dlugi, D. A., et al. Karmannyi Cheshsko-Russkii i Russko-Cheshskii Slovar (Pub. by Sov Entsiklopediia). Four Continent.
Dluhy, Robert, ed. Dictionary for Marine Technology. Adler.
Dobbs, Annie C. Dictionnaire Abrege du Surrealisme. Corti.
--Dictionnaire Abrege du Surrealisme. French & Eur.
Dobel, Richard, ed. Lexikon der Goethe-Zitate. Artemis Verlag.
Dobovskaia, I. K. Frantsuzsko-Russkii Geologicheskii Slovar (Pub. by Gosfizmat). Four Continent.

Dobriansky, A. F., ed. see Pinkevich, A. & Amelin, B.

Dobrovolny, Bohumil. Piirucni Slovnik Vedy a Techniky. Prace.

Dobrovolskaia, I. A. Karmannyi Ital'iansko-Russkii Slovar (Pub. by GINS). Four Continent.

Dobrovolskaia, I. A., et al. Karmannyi Russko-Ital'ianskii Slovar (Pub. by Sov Entsiklopediia). Four Continent.

DObson, W. A. A Dictionary of the Chinese Particles. U of Toronto Pr.

--Dictionary of the Chinese Particles, with a Prolegomenon in Which the Problems of the Particles are Considered & They are Classified by Their Grammaticel Functions. U of Toronto Pr.

Docte, E. Le see Le Docte, E.

Dodin, Lucien. Dictionnaire du Petit Offset. Prismes.

Doering, Henry, ed. see Considine, Tim.

Doherty, J. E., jt. auth. see Hickey, D. J.

Doherty, Robert E. Industrial & Labor Relations Terms: A Glossary. ILR Pr.

Doke, C. M. English & Zulu Dictionary: English-Zulu, Zulu-English. Intl Learn Syst.

Doke, C. M., ed. Zulu-English, English-Zulu Dictionary. Heinman.

Doke, Clement M. English-Lamba Dictionary. Shalom.

Dolgopolova. Dictionnaire de Poche Russe-Francais. MIR.

Dollinger, A., ed. Dictionary of Metallurgy. French & Eur.

Dollinger, Alfred. Six Language Dictionary of Welding Technique. Intl Pubns Serv.

Dolman, Bernard. The Dictionary of Contemporary British Artists, 1929. Antique Collect.

Domanski, Jerzy. Tysiac Slow o Samolocie i Lotnictwie. Wydaw. Min. Obrony Narodowej.

Domart, Andre. Petit Larousse de la Medecine. Larousse.

Domart, Andre & Bourneuf, Jacques. Larousse de la Medecine. French & Eur.

Dominicis, F., ed. see Cusatelli, G. & Brunacci, G.

Domininghaus, Hans. Lexikon der Kunststoffe. Heyne W Verlag.

Domville, Eric, ed. A Concordance to the Plays of W. B. Yeats. Cornell U Pr.

Donadini, G., jt. auth. see Donadini, Jean-Claude.

Donadini, Jean-Claude & Donadini, G. Lexique Technique des Produits Chimiques. Rous.

Donaldson, David, ed. see Jamieson, John.

Donati, G. Dizionario dei motti e leggende delle monete italiane. La Vela.

Donati, Mario, jt. auth. see Grandis, Valentino.

Doniach, N. S., ed. Oxford English-Arabic Dictionary of Current Usage. Oxford U Pr.

Donker, Marjorie & Muldrow, George M. Dictionary of Literary-Rhetorical Conventions of the English Renaissance. Greenwood.

Donow, Herbert S., ed. A Concordance to the Poems of Sir Philip Sidney. Cornell U Pr.

Dony, Ivon P. De see De Dony, Ivon P.

Doolin, Dennis & Ridley, Charles. A Chinese-English Dictionary of Communist Chinese Terminology. Hoover Inst Pr.

Dorais, Louis J. Lexique Analytique du Vocabulaire Inuit Moderne au Quebec-Labrador (Dist. by Four Continent Bk). Univ Laval.

Dordillon, Ildefonse. Dictionnaire de la Langue des Iles Marquises. French & Eur.

Dorfman, John R. Stock Market Dictionary. Doubleday.

Dorian, A. & Osenton, J. Fachwoerterbuch der Luftfahrt (Pub. by R. Oldenbourg). French & Eur.

Dorian, A. F., compiled by. Dictionary of Science & Technology. Elsevier.

Dorian, A. F., ed. Dictionary of Science & Technology. Elsevier.

Dorian, Angelo F. Dictionary of Science & Technology. Elsevier.

Dorin, E. Diccionario de psicologia abrangendo terminologia de ciencias correlatas. Edicoes Melhoramentos.

Doring, G. & Rudolphi. Tiefkuhl Lexikon (Pub. by Deutscher Fachverlag). French & Eur.

Dorion, Henri & Poirier, Jean. Lexique des Termes Utiles a l'etude des Noms de Lieux. Laval P.U.

--Lexique Des Termes Utiles a L'etude Des Noms De Lieux. French & Eur.

Dorland Newman, W. A. Dizionario medico. CEA.

Dorner, Helene T., jt. auth. see Beeton, Douglas R.

Dornette, William H. L. Stedman's Medical Dictionary: Fifth Unabridged Lawyers' Edition. Anderson Pub Co.

Dornseiff, F. & Hansen, Bernard. Reverse Lexicon of Greek Proper Names. Ares.

Doroszewski, W., ed. Slownik Poprawnej Polszczyzny (Pub. by Panstwowe Wydawnictwo Naukowe). Four Continent.

Dorsch, F. Psychologisches Woerterbuch. Huber.

--Psychologisches Woerterbuch (Pub. by H. Huber). French & Eur.

Dorsch, Friedrich. Diccionario De Psicologia. French & Eur.

--Psychologisches Woerterbuch. H Huber.

Dorsen, Richard M., ed. see Colcord, Joanna C.

D'Ortigue, M. J. Dictionnaire Liturgique, Historique et Theorique de Plainchant et de Musique d'Eglise. Da Capo.

Doskoboinik, D. I., et al, eds. Anglo-Russkii Iadernyi Slovar (Pub. by Glav. Red. Inostr. Nauchn. Tekhn. Slovarei Fizmatgiza). Four Continent.

Dottin, Georges & Langouet, J. Glossaire du Parler de Piechatel. Slatkine.

Dottrens, Robert & Massarenti, Dino. Vocabulaire Fondamentale du Francais. Delachaux.

Doty, Richard G. The Macmillan Encyclopedic Dictionary of Numismatics. Macmillan.

Douai, jt. auth. see Vermesse, Louis.

Doucet. Dictionnaire Juridique et Economique: Anglais-Francais Francais-Anglais. Maison Dictionnaire.

Doucet, Friedrich W. Diccionario de Psicoanalisis Clasico. Labor.

---Diccionario De Psicoanalisis Clasico. French & Eur.

Doucet, M. Dictionnaire Juridique & Economique Francais-Allemand & Allemand-Francais. Fleck, K., ed. Bruylant.

--Dictionnaire Juridique & Economique Francias-Allemand & Allemand-Francais. Fleck, K., ed. Bruylant.

--Dictionnaire Juridique & Economique Francais-Allemand & Allemand Francais. Klaus, E. W., ed. Bruylant.

Doucet, Michel. Woerterbuch der Deutschen und Franzoesischen Rechtssprache. French & Eur.

--Woerterbuch der Deutschen und Franzoesischen Rechtssprache. French & Eur.

Dougherty, Margaret M., et al. Instant Spelling Dictionary. Career Inst.

Dougherty, Margaret M., et al, eds. Instant Spelling Dictionary. Watts.

Douglas, J. H., et al, eds. Cassell's Concise French-English, English-French Dictionary. Macmillan.

Douglas, J. M. & Lomo, A., eds. Divry's New Spanish-English & English-Spanish Handy Dictionary. Divry.

Douglas, W. H. Illustrated Topical Dictionary of the Western Desert Language: 1959. Humanities.

Douglas-Young, John. Illustrated Encyclopedic Dictionary of Electronic Circuits. P-H.

Doujat, Jean. Dictionnaire de la Langue Toulousaine. Lafitte Repr.

Douret, Michel. Dictionnaire Juridique et Economique, 1: Francais-Allemand. French & Eur.

Dourlen-Rollier, Anne Marie, jt. auth. see Cohen, Jean.

Dournon, Jean-Yves. Dictionnaire des 1001 Tournures: La Correspondance Pratique. L. G. F.

--Dictionnaire Pratique d'orthographe & des Difficultes du Francais. Hachette.

Dov Ben Abba. The Signet Hebrew-English - English-Hebrew Dictionary (Sig). NAL.

Dovnar-Zapolskaia, N. M. Nemetsko-Russkii Mekhaniko-Matematicheskii Slovar (Pub. by MGU). Four Continent.

Dow, Francis D. Partially Naturalised French Words in Modern English. Dow.

--Partially Naturalised French Words in Modern English. Dow.

Dowling, Noel. Dictionary of Economic Definitions for the Leaving Certificate. Educ Co Ire.

Downard, William L. Dictionary of the History of the American Brewing & Distilling Industries. Greenwood.

Dox, Ida, et al. Melloni's Illustrated Medical Dictionary. Williams & Wilkins.

Dozorov, N. I. Dopolnenie K Anglo-Russkomu Slovariu Po Radioelektrike & Sviazi (Pub. by Izd. Glav. upravl. Po Ispol'z. Atomn. Energii). Four Continent.

Dozy, R. Dictionaire Detaille des Noms de Vetements Chez Les Arabes. Intl Bk Ctr.

--Dictionnaire detaille des noms des vetements chez les Arabes. Intl Bk Ctr.

--Glossaire des mots Espagnols derives de l'Arabe. Intl Bk Ctr.

--Glossaire des Mots Espagnols et Portugais Derives De L'arabe. Intl Bk Ctr.

--Supplement Aux Dictionnaire Arabe (Arabic-French) Intl Bk Ctr.

--Supplement aux dictionnaires Arabes. Intl Bk Ctr.

Dragnev, M. V. & Rosov, Victor. Dictionnaire Francais-Russe de Mathematique. MIR.

Dragovic, J. English-Russian-Serbocroatian Aviations Dictionary. French & Eur.

Drazil. Dictionary of Quantities & Units of Measurement. Brandstetter.

Dreniasova, T. N. Karmannyi Niderlandsko-Russkii Slovar (Pub. by Russkii Iazyk). Four Continent.

Dreschler, Hanno, et al. Gesellschaft & Staat: Lexikon der Politik. Signal-Verlag.

Dreuihe. Dictionnaire Anglais-Francais et Lexique Francais-Anglais des termes Politiques Juridiques et Economiques. French & Eur.

Drever, James. A Dictionary of Psychology. Gannon.

--Dictionary of Psychology. Penguin.

Drever, James, jt. auth. see Froehlich, Werner D.

Drewes, J. B., jt. auth. see Koenen, Matthijs J.

Drieux, Jean P. & Jarlaud, Alain. Let's Talk D. P. Computer Lexicon. French & Eur.

Drieux, Jean-Pierre & Jarlaud, Alain. Let's Talk D. P. Lexique D'informatique. Bordas.

Drill, Douglas D. Doubtful Dictionary. Wilson-Fulkerson, Roberta, ed. Career Pub.

Drizari, Nelo. Albanian-English, English-Albanian Dictionary. Ungar.

Drosdowski, Gunther. Fremdwoerterbuch: Herkunft & Bedeutung der Fremdwoerter. Biblio Inst.

D'Rovira, Eugenio. Glosari. Ediciones Sesent Dos.

Drozd & Seibicke. Deutsche Fach & Wissenschaftssprache. Brandstetter.

Drummond, David A. & Perkins, G. Dictionary of Russian Obscenities. Berkeley Slavic.

Drvodelic, M. Serbocroatian-English Dictionary. French & Eur.

Drvodelic, Milan. English-Croatian or Serbian Dictionary. Intl Learn Syst.

Dubac, R. Vocabulaire de gestion. Maison Dictionnaire.

Dube, Pierre H., jt. ed. see Davidson, Hugh M.

Dubois & Dubois-Charlier, F. Dictionnaire du Francais Langue Etrangere: Niveau I (Dist. by Continental Bk Co). Larousse.

Dubois, C. Pluri Dictionnaire. Larousse.

Dubois, Charlier F. Dictionnaire Francais-Anglais des Debutantes (Dist. by Continental Bk Co). Larousse.

Dubois, F. & Werny, P. Dictionnaire Francais-Allemand des Locutions. French & Eur.

Dubois, J. Dictionnaire du Francais Contemporain (Dist. by Continental Bk Co). Larousse.

--Dictionnaire du Francais Contemporain. French & Eur.

--Dictionnaire du Francais Langue Etrangere. Larousse.

--Larousse de la Langue Francaise Lexis, Illustre (Dist. by Continental Bk Co). Larousse.

Dubois, J. & Dubois-Charlier, F. Dictionnaire du Francais Langue Etrangere: Niveau II (Dist. by Continental Bk Co). Larousse.

Dubois, J. & Giacomo, M. Dictionnaire de Linguistique. Larousse.

Dubois, J., et al. Dictionnaire de Linguistique (Dist. by Continental Bk Co). Larousse.

Dubois, Jean. Diccionario de Linguistica. French & Eur.

--Vocabulaire Politique & Social en France de 1869 a 1872. Larousse FR.

Dubois, Jean & Lagane, Rene. Dictionnaire du Francais Classique. Larousse.

--Dictionnaire du Francais Classique. French & Eur.

--Dictionnaire du Francais Contemporain. Larousse.

Dubois, Jean, ed. Lexis: Dictionnaire De la Langue Francaise. French & Eur.

--Lexis-Dictionnaire de la langue francaise. Larousse.

--Lexis-Dictionnaire de la Langue Francaise. Larousse.

--Lexis: Dictionnaire de la Langue Frances. Larousse.

Dubois, Jean & Duboise-Charlier, Francoise, eds. Larousse de Base: Dictionnaire d'Apprentissage du Francais. Larousse FR.

Dubois, Jean, et al. Dictionnaire de Linguistique. Larousse.

Dubois, Jean, et al, eds. Dictionnaire du Francais Contemporain. Larousse FR.

Dubois, M. Dictionnaire de sigles nationaux et internationaux. Maison Dictionnaire.

Dubois, M. Claude. Petit Larousse en Couleur 1980 (Dist. by Continental Bk Co). Larousse.

--Petit Larousse 1980 (Dist. by Continental Bk Co). Larousse.

Dubois, M. M. Dictionnaire de Locutions (Dist. by Continental Bk Co). Larousse.

--Dictionnaire moderne Larousse francais-anglais et anglais-francais. Larousse.

--Dictionnaire Moderne "Saturne" (Dist. by Continental Bk Co). Larousse.

Dubois, Marguerite-Marie. Dictionnaire de Locutions: Francais-Anglais. Larousse.

--Dictionnaire de Locutions, Francais-Anglais. French & Eur.

Dubois, Marie M. Dictionnaire Moderne Saturne: Francais-Anglais. Larousse FR.

Dubois, Marie-Marguerite. Dictionnaire Moderne Saturne: Francais-Anglais, Anglais-Francais. French & Eur.

Dubois, Michel. Dictionnaire de Sigles Nationaux & Internationaux. Maison Dictionnaire.

--Dictionnaire de Sigles Nationaux et Internationaux. French & Eur.

Dubois Charlier, et al. Dictionnaire d'Anglais Niveau 1. Larousse.

Dubois-Charlier, F. Dictionnaire D'anglais. Larousse FR.

Dubois-Charlier, F., jt. auth. see Dubois.

Dubois-Charlier, F., jt. auth. see Dubois, J.

Dubois-Charlier, F., et al. Dictionnaire d'Anglais. Larousse.

Dubois-Charlier, Francois, et al. Dictionnaire d'anglais. Larousse.

Duboise-Charlier, Francoise, jt. ed. see Dubois, Jean.
Dubrovin, M. Russkie Frazeologizmy v Kartinkakh (Pub. by Russkii Iazyk). Four Continent.
Dubrovin, M. I. A Book of Russian Idioms. Four Continent.
Dubuc, R. Vocabulaire bilinque du theatre: Anglais-Francais Francais Anglais. Maison Dictionnaire.
Dubuc, Robert. Vocabulaire de Gestion. Radio-Canada.
Ducach, Juan. Nuevo Diccionario Castellano-Hebreo. Massada Pr.
Du Cange, Charles D. Glossarium ad Scriptores Mediae & Infimae Graecitatis. Akad Druck.
DuCange, Charles Du Fresne. Glossarium Ad Scriptores Mediae et Infimae Graecitatis. Intl Pubns Serv.
Duc-Goninaz, Michel. Vocabulaire Esperanto. Ophrys.
Du Chazaud, Henri Bertrand see Bertrand Du Chazaud, Henri.
Ducrot, Oswald & Todorov, Tzvetan. Encyclopedic Dictionary of the Sciences of Language. Porter, Catherine, tr. Johns Hopkins.
Ducroz, Jean M. & Charles, Marie C. Lexique Soncy Francais. Harmattan.
Dudavskii, V. I., et al. Russko-Pol'skii Politekhnicheskii Slovar (Pub. by Gosizdat Tekhn. Teoretich. Lit.). Four Continent.
Dudawaki, B., et al. Russian-Polish Political Dictionary. French & Eur.
Duden. Was Bedeuted Das? Esselte Studium.
Duden, Konrad. Sammlung Duden: Band I, Vollstaendiges Orthographisches Woerterbuch der Deutschen Sprache. Biblio Inst.
Duden, R. Duden-Stilwoerterbuch. Adler.
Dudenredaktion, jt. auth. see Harrap.
Dudenredaktion Manheim. Der Kleine Duden, Fremdenwoerterbuch. Biblio Inst.
Duelo, Gerardo. Diccionario De Grupos, Fuerzas, y Partidos Politicos Espanoles. French & Eur.
Duffy, Charles & Petit, Henry. Dictionary of Literary Terms. Brown Bk.
Dugast, Idelette. Lexique de la Langue Turen: Parler des Banen du sud-ouest du Cameroun. S. E. L. A. F.
Duggal, Heidi, jt. auth. see Ashley, Richard.
Du Gran, Claurene. Wordsmanship. Verbatim.
Duijker, Hubert C. & Van Rijswijk, Maria J. Dictionnaire de Psychologie en Trois Langues, 3: Allemand-Anglais-Francais. Editest.
Duijker, Hubert C. Dictionnaire de Psychologie en Trois Langues, Vol. 2. French & Eur.
Duijker, Hubert C. & Van Rijswijk, Maria J. Dictionnaire de Psychologie en Trois Langues: Anglais-Francais-Allemand. Editest.
--Dictionnaire de Psychologie en Trois Langues, 2: Francais-Allemand-Anglais. Editest.
Duijker, Hubert C. & Van Sijswijk, Maria. Dictionnaire de Psychologie en 3 Langues. French & Eur.
Dulong. Dictionnaire Correctif du Francais au Canada. Laval P. U.
Dumas, Alexandre. Dumas on Food. Davidson, Alan & Davidson, Jane, trs. U Pr of Va.
Dumeril, E. Dictionnaire du Patols Normand. Slatkine.
Dumortier, J. Le Vocabulaire Medical d'Eschyle & les Ecrits Hippocratiques. Belles Lettres.
Duncan, A. S., et al, eds. Dictionary of Medical Ethics. Crossroad NY.
Duncan, Helen A. Duncan's Dictionary for Nurses. Springer Pub.
Dunmore, Charles W. & Fleischer, Rita M. Medical Terminology: Exercise in Etymology. Davis Co.
Dunn, Charles W., ed. The Actors' Analects. Columbia U Pr.
Dunn, George E. A Gilbert & Sullivan Dictionary. Folcroft.
Dunn, John A. A Practical Dictionary of the Coast Tsimshian Language. Natl Mus Can.
Dunn, Oscar. Glossaire Franco-Canadien. Univ Laval.
--Glossaire Franco-Canadien: Vocabulaire de Locutions Vicieuses Usitees au Canada. Laval P. U.
Dunn-Rankin, Patricia. Vocabulary (C). McGraw.
--Vocabulary (Pub. by C.). Mcgraw.
Duong Thanh Binh & Cage, William. Vietnamese-English Phrasebook with Useful Word List. Ctr Appl Ling.
Duong Thanh Binh, jt. auth. see Gage, William.
DuPlessis, E. Die Kennis Gids tot Moderne Afrikaans. Human & Rousseau.
DuPont, Marcella M. Definitions & Criteria. Swallow.
Dupre, Celine, jt. auth. see Lanecki, Francois.
Dupuis, H., et al. Lexique de la Fabrication du Refrigerateur: Francais-Anglais. French & Eur.
Dupuis, Hector. Dictionnaire des Synonymes & des Antonymes. Fides.
--Dictionnaire des synonymes et des antonymes. Legare, Romain, rev. by. Soc Dev Liv.
Dupuis, Hector & Legare, Romain. Dictionnaire des Synonymes & des Antonymes. Ecole.
--Dictonnaire des Synonymes et des Antonymes. French & Eur.
Du Puitspelu, Nizier. Dictionnaire Etymologique du Patols Lyonnais. Slatkine.
Duquesne, J. Dictionnaires des Plantes Medicinales. Chiron.
Duraffour, Antonin. Glossaire des Patois Franco-Provencaux. CNRS.
--Glossaire des Patois Franco-Provencaux. CNRS.
Durand, Roger H. & Greco, Salvatore. Vocabulaire Italien par l'image. Bordas-Dunod.
Durante, Dino & Turato, Gianfranco. Dizionario etimologico veneto-italiano. Erredici.
Duranteau. Dizionario medico. Newton Compton.
Durante Avellanal, Ciro. Diccionario odontologico. Mundi.
Duro, Aldo, jt. auth. see De Felice, Emido.
Duroux, Paul-Emile. Dictionnaire des Anthropologistes. Delarge.
--Dictionnaire des Anthropologistes. French & Eur.
Duse, Ada. Dizionario commerciale fraseologico italiano-inglese, inglese-italiano. Bignami.
--Dizionario fraseologico commerciale italiano-francese e francese-italiano. Bignami.
Dusseau, John L., jt. auth. see Sloane, Sheila B.
Dutch, R. A., ed. see Roget, Peter M.
Dutton, Brian, et al. Diccionario esencial Ingles-espanol, Espanol-Ingles. Diafora.
Duval, A. see Atkins, B. T., et al.
Duval, C. Dictionnaire de la Chimie et de Ses Applications. French & Eur.
Duy-Tu, Tran, et al. Polytechnisches Woerterbuch Deutsch-Vietnamesisch. VEB Technik.
Dwelly. Illustrated Gaelic-English Dictionary. Colton Bk.
Dybovskaia, V. & Kirillova, I. Dictionnaire Geologique: Francais-Russe. French & Eur.
Dyche, Thomas. A New General English Dictionary. Adler.
Dykstra, J. K. Op 't Aljemint. AFUK-LEARMIDDELFUNS.
Dyller, Fran, jt. auth. see Mason, David.
Dymshits, Z. M., et al. Karmannyi Russko-Khindi Slovar (Pub. by GINS). Four Continent.
Dzenit, S. I. Telugu-Russkii Slovar (Pub. by Sov. Entsiklopediia). Four Continent.
Dzhouiz, D. Slovar Angliiskogo Proiznosheniia (Pub. by GINS). Four Continent.

E

Eaglefield-Hull, A., ed. Dictionary of Modern Music & Musicians. Da Capo.
Earle, Ralph. Word Meanings in the New Testament: I & II Corinthians, Galatians & Ephesians. Baker Bk.
Earnshaw, Pat. A Dictionary of Lace (Pub. by Shire Pubns England). Seven Hills Bks.
Eastman, P. D. Cat in the Hat Beginner Book Dictionary. Beginner.
--Cat in the Hat Beginner Book Dictionary in English & Spanish. Beginner.
--Cat in the Hat Beginner Book Dictionary in French & English. Beginner.
Eastwood, J. & Wright, W. Aldis. A Glossary of the English Bible Words. Telegraph Bks.
Eberle, jt. auth. see Zavada.
Ebner, Jakob. Rechtschreibung & Wortkunde: Ein Woerterbuch fur die Schule. Biblio Inst.
Echanova, Carlos T. Diccionario de sociologia. Calica.
Echauri Martinez, Eustaquio. Diccionario Basico Latino-Espanol, Espanol-Latino. Biblo Sp.
Echols, John M. & Shadily, Hassan. An English-Indonesian Dictionary. Cornell U Pr.
--An Indonesian-English Dictionary. Cornell U Pr.
Echuari, Eustaquio. Vox-Diccionario Basico Latino-Espanol, Espanol-Latino. French & Eur.
Eckardt, Andre. Chinesisch-Koreanisch-Deutsch Woerterbuch. Groos Verlag.
--Deutsch-Koreanisches Woerterbuch. Groos Verlag.
--Koreanisch-Deutsches Woerterbuch. Groos Verlag.
Eckel, Denis & Hofer, Manfred. Dictionnaire Allemand-Francais. Garnier.
Eckel, Denis & Manfred, Hofer. Dictionnaire Allemand-Francais et Francais-Allemand. French & Eur.
Eckert, Werner. Einfuehrung in die Deutsche Wortbildungslehre. Schmidt Verlag.
Eckhard, Ronald, jt. auth. see Anderson, Robert.
Eckhardt, S. Dictionnaire de Poche Francais-Hongrois. Terra.
--Dictionnaire Usuel Hongrois-Francais. Terra.
--Hungarian-French Concise Dictionary. French & Eur.
Eckhardt, Sandor. Magyar-Francia Szotar. Akademiai Kiado.
--Magyar-Francia Szotar. Akademiai Kiado.
Eckinger, Ludwig, ed. see Maier, Karl E.
Eddison, John. Dictionary of Bible Words. Scripture Union.
Eden, P., ed. Dictionary of Land Surveyors & Local Cartographers of Great Britain & Ireland (Pub. by Dawson). State Mutual Bk.
Edenso, Christine, ed. see Lawrence, Erma.
Edgerton, F. Buddhist Hybrid Sanskrit Dictionary & Grammar. Orientalia.
--Buddhist Hybrid Sanskrit Grammer & Dictionary. Orient Bk Dist.
Edgerton, Franklin. Buddhist Hybrid Sanskrit Grammar & Dictionary. Incl. Vol. 1. Grammar; Vol. 2. Dictionary. Intl Pubns Serv.
--Buddhist Hybrid Sanskrit Grammar & Dictionary. Verry.
Edgerton, William, jt. ed. see Bede, Jean-Albert.
Edicoes Melhoramentos. Dicionario Basico do Ingles Moderno. Edicoes Melhoramentos.
Edison Electric Institute. Glossary of Electric Utility Terms. Edison Electric.
Editions Berlitz. German-English, English-German Dictionary: Woerterbuch Deutsch-Englisch, Englisch-Deutsch (Pub. by Berlitz). Macmillan.
--Spanish-English, English-Spanish Dictionary. Macmillan.
Editions Berlitz S. A. English-French Dictionary (Pub by Berlitz). Macmillan.
Editions Technip. Glossary of Onshore & Offshore Pipelines. Graham & Trotman.
Editura Tehnica. Dictionar Tehnic Poliglot. Irvington.
Edler, Florence. Glossary of Mediaeval Terms of Business, 1200-1600. Kraus Repr.
Edon, Georges. Dictionnaire Francais-Latin. Belin.
--Dictionnaire Francais-Latin. French & Eur.
Eduardo, H. Diccionario Estudios de Castellano sec. Castagnino. Leru.
Edward, Wm., jt. auth. see Qamus, Madd A.
Edwards, Eliezer E. Words, Facts & Phrases: A Dictionary of Curious, Quaint, & Out-of-the-Way Matters. Gale.
Edwards, Nancy M., et al, eds. Office Automation: A Glossary and Guide. Knowledge Indus.
Edwards, R. J., compiled by. Crossword Anagram Dictionary (Mayflower Bks). Smith Pubs.
Edwards, Ralph. The Shorter Dictionary of English Furniture. Newnes Bks.
Edwards, Tryon, ed. New Dictionary of Thoughts. Doubleday.
E.G.B., ed. Diccionario del lenguaje usual. Santilana SA.
Egbert, Lawrence D. Multilingual Law Dictionary: English, French, Spanish, German. Oceana.
Egerod, Soren. Atayal-English Dictionary (Pub. by Curzon Pr England). Humanities.
Eggebrecht, H., jt. auth. see Gurlitt, W.
Eggebrecht, Hans H., jt. auth. see Dahlhaus, Carl.
Eggeling, H. F. Dictionary of Modern German Prose Usage. Oxford U Pr.
Egidius, Henry. Uppslagsbok i Psykoterapi och Medicinsk Psykologi. Natur & Kultur.
Egli, Jakob. Etymologisch Geographisches Lexikon (Pub. by Saendig-Walluf). French & Eur.
Ehresmann, Julia M., ed. Pocket Dictionary of Art Terms. NYGS.
Ehrlich, Ann. Cavity Classification & Related Terminology. Colwell Co.
--Introduction to Dental Terminology. Colwell Co.
Ehrlich, Eugene & Murphy, Daniel. Basic Vocabulary Builder (SP). McGraw.
Ehrlich, Eugene, et al, eds. Oxford American Dictionary. Oxford U Pr.
Ehrlich, Ida L. Instant Vocabulary. PB.
Eichborn & Fuentes. Wirtschaftswoerterbuch Spanisch-Deutsch (Pub. by Econ). French & Eur.
Eichborn, R. Kleine Eichborn, Taschenwoerterbuch der Wirtschaftssprache (Pub. by Siebenpunkt Vlg.). French & Eur.
--Kleine Eichborn, Taschenwoerterbuch der Wirtschaftssprache (Pub. by Siebenpunkt Vlg.). French & Eur.
--Wirtschafts-Woerterbuch (Pub. by Econ Vlg.). French & Eur.
--Woerterbuch fuer Wirtschaft-Recht-Verkehr-Verwaltungs & Umgangssprache: Vol.I, Englisch-Deutsch. M Rosenberg.
--Woerterbuch fuer Wirtschaft-Recht-Verkehr-Verwaltungs & Umgangssprache: Vol. II, Deutch-Englisch. M Rosenberg.
Eichborn, R. & Fuentes, A. Wirtschafts-Woerterbuch (Pub. by Econ Vlg.). French & Eur.
Eichborn, R. V. Dictionary of Economics. Incl. Vol. 1. English & German; Vol. 2. German & English. Adler.
Eigenmann, G., jt. auth. see Villavecchia, G. V.
Eiguren, Joe V. English-Basque Dictionary. L Fereday Schol.
Eikeland, I., jt. auth. see Vogt, J.
Eimert, Herbert. Das Lexikon der Elektronischen Musik. French & Eur.
Einarsson, Stefan. Icelandic Grammar, Text & Glossary. Johns Hopkins.

Einspahr, Bruce, compiled by. Index to the Brown, Driver & Briggs Hebrew Lexicon. Moody.
Eisenreich & Sube. Woerterbuch der Mathmetik. Verlag Harri Deutsch.
--Woerterbuch Physik. Verlag Harri Deutsch.
Eisenreich, G. & Sube, R. Dictionary of Mathematics. Elsevier.
Eisenreich, G., jt. auth. see Sube, R.
Eisenreich, G., jt. ed. see Sube, R.
Eisenreich, Gunther, jt. auth. see Sube, Ralf.
Eitel, Ernes J. Chinese Dictionary: Cantonese Dialect. Ayer Co.
Eitzen, K. Military Eitzen (Pub. by Vlg. Offene Worte). French & Eur.
Ekbo, Sven & Loman, Bengt. Vaegledning till Svenska Akademiens Ordbok. Esselte Studium.
Ekwall, Eilert. Shakespeare's Vocabulary: Its Etymological Elements. AMS Pr.
El-Baz, Farouk. Say It in Arabic. Gannon.
Elbert, Samuel H. Dictionary of the Language of Rennell & Bellona: Part One: Rennellese & Bellonese to English. UH Pr.
Elbert, Samuel H., jt. auth. see Pukui, Mary K.
El-Desouti, H. Y. Plastic Technology Dictionary. French & Eur.
Electrical Generating Systems Marketing Association. Glossary of Department of Defense Configuration Management Terminology & Definitions. Elec Gen Syst.
--Glossary of Standard Industry Terminology & Definitions. Elec Gen Syst.
Elerick, Charles, tr. see Elerick, Marisa Luz E.
Elerick, Marisa Luz E. Annotated Bibliography of Technical & Specialized Dictionaries. Elerick, Charles & Teschner, Richard V., trs. Whitston Pub.
Elgar, Frank, jt. auth. see Cognia, Raymond.
Elgin, Peter. Talk & Taxonomy. Benjamins.
Elgin, Suzette H. More on the Gentle Art of Verbal Self-Defense. P-H.
Elias. Arabic-English Collegiate Dictionary. Colton Bk.
--Elias Arabic-English Modern Dictionary. Kazi Pubns.
--Elias English-Arabic & Arabic-English Pocket Dictionary. Kazi Pubns.
--Elias English-Arabic Modern Dictionary. Kazi Pubns.
--English-Arabic Collegiate Dictionary. Colton Bk.
Elias, ed. English Arabic, Arabic-English Pocket Dictionary. Colton Bk.
Elias, A. E. English Arabic, Arabic-English Dictionary. Intl Bk Ctr.
Elias, E. Elias Pocket Dictionary: English, Arabic. French & Eur.
Elias, E. A. Arabic-English, English-Arabic Dictionary. Heinman.
--English-Arabic; Arabic-English Dictionary. Intl Bk Ctr.
Elias, E. A., ed. Arabic-English, English-Arabic Collegiate Dictionary. Heinman.
--Arabic-English, English-Arabic School Dictionary. Heinman.
Elias, Edward. English-Arabic Dictionary, Romanized. Shalom.
Elias, Elias. Arabic-English Modern Dictionary. Intl Bk Ctr.
--Elias' English-Arabic Dictionary. Intl Bk Ctr.
--Elias English-Arabic Practical Dictionary of the Colloquial Arabic of the Middle East. Intl Bk Ctr.
--Modern Arabic-English Dictionary. Intl Bk Ctr.
Elias, M. Elias' Pocket Dictionary Arabic-English. French & Eur.
Eliasov, L. E. Slovar Russkikh Govorov Zabaikalia (Pub. by Nauka). Four Continent.
Elies I Busqueta, Pere. Canigo: Dicionario Catalan-Castellano, Castellano-Catalan. Sopena.
Elihai, Yohanan. Dictionnaire de l'Arabe Parle Palestinien. French & Eur.
--Dictionnaire de L'arabe Parte Palestinien: Francais-Arabe. Klincksieck.
Eliot, T. S. Notes Towards the Definition of Culture. HarBraceJ.
Eliseev, I. S. Karmannyi Russko-Finskii Slovar (Pub. by Russkii Iazyk). Four Continent.
Elkhadem, Saad. The York Dictionary of English-French-German-Spanish Literary Terms & Their Origin. York Pr CA.
Elkhaden, Saad. The York Dictionary of English-French-German-Spanish Literary Terms & Their Origin. York Pr CA.
Elkins, Richard E. Manobo-English Dictionary. UH Pr.
Elliot. Diccionario de politica. Labor SA.
Elliott, Francis E., jt. auth. see Fischer, Eric.
Ellis, Frederick S. Lexical Concordance to the Poetical Works of Percy Bysshe Shelley. B Franklin.
Ellison, Al. Ellison's French Menu Reader. Ellison Ent.
--Ellison's Latin American Menu Reader. Ellison Ent.
Ellyson, Louise. A Dictionary of Homonyms: New Word Patterns. Amereon Ltd.
El Mashreq, Dar. Arabic Dictionary: Al Munjid fi al-Lugha Wal 'Alam. Intl Bk Ctr.
El Mashreq, Dar see Tulab, Munjid al & Mashreq, Dar el.
Eloy, N. F. Dictionnaire Historique de la Medecine Ancienne & Moderne. Olms.
Else, Gerald F. Basic Latin Vocabulary Along Etymological Lines. Am Classical.
Elson, Louis C. Elson's Music Dictionary. Gale.
Elting, John R. & Cragg, Dan. A Dictionary of Soldier Talk (ScribT). Scribner.
Embacher, F. Lexikon der Reisen und Entdeckungen. Humanities.
Emberson, Frances G. Mark Twain's Vocabulary. Arden Lib.
--Mark Twain's Vocabulary. Darby Bks.
--Mark Twain's Vocabulary. Folcroft.
Emde, Heiner. Das Lexikon der Politik. Heyne W Verlag.
Emeneau, Murray B., jt. auth. see Burrow, Thomas.
Emert, Phyllis R. Illustrated Track & Field Dictionary for Young People. Harvey.
--Illustrated Track & Field Dictionary for Young People. P-H.
Emery, Donald W. Variant Spellings in Modern American Dictionaries. NCTE.
Eminescu, Mihail. Dictionar de Rime. Bucur, Marin & Tausan, Victoria A., eds. Albatros.
Emolumento, V. Dizionario Commerciale Francese-Italiano. French & Eur.
Emolumento, Vincenzo. Dizionario commerciale francese-italiano. Editrice Bibliografica.
--Dizionario commerciale italiano-francese. Bibliografica.
Endicott, J. G., jt. auth. see West, M. P.
Endres, Edmund. Moselfraenkische Mundart. Rheinland Verlag.
Engen, Rodney K. Dictionary of Victorian Engravers, Print Publishers & Their Works. Somerset Hse.
Engeroff, K. & Lovelace-Kaeufer, C. English-German Dictionary of Idioms. Adler.
Engert, M. & Stephan, H., eds. Lexikon RGW. Bibl Inst Leipzig.
Engineering Index, Inc. Engineering Index Thesaurus. Macmillan Info.
Engineers Joint Council Editors. Thesaurus of Engineering & Scientific Terms. AAES.
Englert, Sebastian. Diccionario Rapanui-Espanol, Redactado en la Isla de Pascua. AMS Pr.
English Language Institute. Vocabulary in Context. U of Mich Pr.
English Language Services. Key to English Vocabulary. Macmillan.
Engstroem, Ake & Toernblom, H. Bonniers Musiklexikon. Bonnier Forlag.
Engstroem, E. Swedish-English, English-Swedish Technical Dictionary. Heinman.
Enrile, E. Dizionario dello sport. Edizioni Paoline.
Enriquez & Bautista. English-Tagalog-Visayan Pocket Dictionary. Colton Bk.
Enriquez & Guzman. English-Tagalog, Tagalog-English Pocket Dictionary. Colton Bk.
Enriquez & Quimba. English-Tagalog-Ilocano Pocket Dictionary. Colton Bk.
Enriquez Palomic, R. Lexico basico del contador. Trillas.
Epstein, Howard M. & Kanner, Gerald B., eds. News Dictionary: Vol. 5, 1968. Facts on File.
Equipo Reactor de Ceac. Diccionario de la Construccion. French & Eur.
--Diccionario de la Decoracion. French & Eur.
--Manual del Automovil en 5 Idiomas: Diccionario Idiomatico del Automovil. French & Eur.
Equipo Reactor de CEAC, ed. Diccionario del Automovil. French & Eur.
Erbse, Hartmut, jt. auth. see Snell, Bruno.
Ercolani, Libero. Vocabolario romagnolo-italiano, italiano-romagnolo. Edn Girasole.
Erdfly-Markovics, L. Hungarian Kitchen Parade. Saphrograph.
Erdman, David V., ed. Concordance to the Writings of William Blake. Cornell U Pr.
Erdsneker, Barbara & Haller, Margaret. Civil Service Arithmetic & Vocabulary. Arco.
Ergo, A. B., jt. auth. see Henry, J. M.
Ergo, A. B., et al. Thesaurus des Symboles Agrobioclimatiques, Geographiques & Techniques, 4. Centre Informatique Develop.
Eriksson, Erick R. & Baeckbom, Roy. Modernt Foertagsekonomiskt Lexikon. Prisma.
Ernault, Emile. Glossaire Moyen-Breton. Slatkine.
Ernault, Emile Jean M. Glossaire Moyen-Breton. Lafitte Repr.
Ernout, Alfred & Meillet, Antoine. Dictionnaire Etymologique de la Langue Latine. Klincksieck.
Ernst. Woerterbuch der Chemie: Band II, English-Deutsch. Brandstetter.
--Woerterbuch der Industriellen Technik: Band III, Deutsch-Franzoesisch. Brandstetter.
--Woerterbuch der Industriellen Technik: Band IV, Franzoesisch-Deutsch. Brandstetter.
--Woerterbuch der Industriellen Technik: Band IX, Franzoesisch-Englisch. Brandstetter.
--Woerterbuch der Industriellen Technik: Band VII, Deutsch-Portugiesisch. Brandstetter.
--Woerterbuch der Industriellen Technik: Band V, Deutsch-Spanisch. Brandstetter.
--Woerterbuch der Industriellen Technik: Band VIII, Portugiesch-Deutsch. Brandstetter.
--Woerterbuch der Industriellen Technik: Band VI, Spanisch-Deutschg) Brandstetter.
Ernst, E., jt. auth. see Lange-Kowal.
Ernst, I. & Ernst von Morgenstern, F. Woerterbuch der Chemie. French & Eur.
--Woerterbuch der Chemie. French & Eur.
Ernst, R. Diccionario tecnico industrial: Vol. 1, Espanol-aleman. G Gili.
--Dictionary of Chemical Terms. Adler.
--Dictionnaire de la Technique Industrielle: Allemand-Francais. Maison Dictionnaire.
--German-English, English-German Dictionary of Industrial Technics. Heinman.
--Woerterbuch der Industriellen Technik. French & Eur.
--Woerterbuch der Industriellen Technik. French & Eur.
--Woerterbuch der Industriellen Technik. French & Eur.
--Woerterbuch der Industriellen Technik. French & Eur.
--Woerterbuch der Industriellen Technik. French & Eur.
--Woerterbuch der Industriellen Technik. French & Eur.
--Woerterbuch der Industriellen Technik. French & Eur.
Ernst, Richard. Dictionary of Chemistry. French & Eur.
--Dictionary of Chemistry. French & Eur.
--Dictionary of Engineering & Technology. Oxford U Pr.
--Dictionary of Engineering & Technology: With Extensive Treatment of the Most Modern Techniques & Processes. Oxford U Pr.
--Dictionnaire General de la Technique Industrielle: Francais-Anglais. Maison Dictionnaire.
Ernst, Richard, ed. Dictionary of Engineering & Technology. Oxford U Pr.
Ernst von Morgenstern, F., jt. auth. see Ernst, I.
Eroles, Emili. Diccionario Historico del Libro. Milla Lib.
Ersov, N. N. & Komarov, A. N., eds. Projet de Lexique Minier Russe-Francais. French & Eur.
Escarpanter, Jose A. Ortografia Moderna. Playor.
Escarpit, Denise. Press, Radio & Television. Elp.
Escarpit, Robert. Dictionnaire International des Termes Literaires. Mouton-De.
Esche, Annemarie. Woerterbuch Burmesisch-Deutsch. VEB Verlag Enzyklopadie.
Escher, Angelica, jt. auth. see Ciardi Dupre, Giovanni.
Escobar, Guillermo. Vocabulario Lengua General Quichua. U. San Marcos.
Esnault. Dictionnaire des Argots Francais. French & Eur.
Espersen, Johan C. Bornholmsk Ordbog. Rosenkilde.
Espina Perez, Dario. Diccionario de cubanismos. Dist. Universal.
Espinosa, Aurelio M. & Gambetta, Leon. Spanish for Doctors & Nurses. Camino Real.
Espiru, Salvador. Diccionari Manual de Sinonims. Biblograf SP.
Esser, F., ed. see Amstutz, G. C., et al.
Esser, William L. Dictionary of Man's Foods. Natural Hygiene.
--Dictionary of Natural Foods. Natural Hygiene.
Estes, Ralph W. A Dictionary of Accounting. MIT Pr.
Estienne, Henri. Thesaurus Graecae Linguae. Akad Druck.
Estienne, Robert. Dictionariolum Puerorum Tribus Linguis: Lat., Ang. & Gall. Conscriptum. Walter J Johnson.
--Dictionnaire Francais-Latin. Slatkine.
Estornes Lasa, Bernardo, et al. Diccionario Aunamendi Espanol-Vasco: Tomo 7, Conch-Corr. Aunamendi Edit.
Estrany, Santiago. Vocabulari de Barbarismes. Teide.
Ethier-Blais, Jean. Dictionnaire de Moi-Meme. Presse.
Etter, Lewis E. Glossary of Words & Phrases Used in Radiology, Nuclear Medicine & Ultrasound. C C Thomas.
Ettinger, David. Hebrew-English Pictorial Dictionary. Shalom.
European Brewery Convention. Elsevier's Dictionary of Brewing. Elsevier.
European Coal & Steel Community, Luxembourg, ed. Ergonomics Glossary: Terms Commonly Used in Ergonomics. Intl Pubns Serv.
European Committee of Associations of Gear & Transmission Element Manufacturers (EUROTRANS), ed. Glossary of Transmission Elements: Gears. Marlin.
European Directories, ed. The Dictionary of Toiletry & Cosmetic Manufacturers in Western Europe (Pub. by European Directories England). State Mutual Bk.
European Heating & Ventilating Associations, ed. The International Dictionary of Heating, Ventilating, & Air Conditioning (E&FN Spon England). Methuen Inc.
European Parliament - Translation Division. Terminology of Environmental Hygiene. Intl Pubns Serv.

European Society for Opinion & Marketing Research. Glossary of Technical Terms for Market Researchers: English-German-Spanish-French-Italian-Dutch. Intl Pubns Serv.
Evanoff, Philip C. & Gerlach, Werner, eds. Surface Strength Terminology. TAPPI.
Evans, Christopher R. Psychology: ADictionary of the Mind, Brain & Behavior. Arrow Bks.
Evans, Frank B., et al. A Basic Glossary for Archivists, Manuscript Curators, & Records Managers. Soc Am Archivists.
Evans, H. Meurig & Thomas, W. O. The Complete Welsh-English, English-Welsh Dictionary. Y Geiriadur Mawr. Humanities.
--Welsh-English, English-Welsh Dictionary. Saphrograph.
Evans, Ivor, pref. by see Brewer, E. Cobham.
Evans, Ivor H., ed. Brewer's Dictionary of Phrase & Fable (Pub. by Cassell England). State Mutual Bk.
Evans, Meurig & Thomas, W. O. Y geiriadur mawr. Davies Dewi.
Evarts, Prescott. Essential Words for a Perfect Vocabulary. Arco.
Even-Shoshan, Abraham, ed. The Complete Hebrew Dictionary in Seven Volumes. K Sefer.
--The Complete Hebrew Dictionary in Three Volumes. K Sefer.
--Condensed Hebrew Dictionary. K Sefer.
--The Student's Dictionary. K Sefer.
Evered, H. & Wallnig, G. Duits voor Bouwkundigen-Saksaa Rakentajille. Bauverlag.
Evered, H., jt. auth. see Wallnig, G.
Evered, H., jt. auth. see Wallnig, Gunter.
Evered, Harry, jt. auth. see Wallnig, Gunter.
Everest. Diccionario Vertice Everest: Frances-Espanol, Espanol-Frances. Everest.
Everhart, Jim. Illustrated Texas Dictionary of the English Language. Cliffs.
Evgueniev. Dictionnaire des Synonymes de la Langue Russe. MIR.
Evjen, H. Norwegian-Spanish Dictionary of Commerce. Kunnskapsforlaget.
Ewald, Peter K. Encyclopedia of Finance & Investment Terms. Barron.
Ewart, Ron. Fuchsia Lexicon. Van Nos Reinhold.
Eyben, W. E. von see Borum, Oscar A. & Von Eyben, W. E.
Eynern, Gert V. Woerterbuch zur Politischen Oekonomie. French & Eur.
Eynern, Gert von see Von Eynern, Gert & Boehret, Carl.

F

Fabian, Pal, jt. auth. see Bakos, Forenc.
Fabra, Pompeu. Diccionari General de la Llengua Catalana. Edhasa.
--Diccionario General de la Lengua Catalana. Edhasa.
Fabra Poch, Pompeu. Diccionario General de la Lengua Catalana. French & Eur.
--Diccionario general de llengua catalana. Edhasa.
Fabre, Antonin. Lexique de la Langue de Chapelain. Slatkine.
Fabrega, P. Diccionario moderno frances-espanol y espanol-frances. Bosch Casa.
Fabri, M. A Bibliography of Hispanic Dictionaries: Catalan, Galician, Spanish, Spanish in Latin America & the Philippines. Heinman.
Facco, Giannina & Facco, Maria. Vocabolarietto figurato. Edipem.
Facco, Maria, jt. auth. see Facco, Giannina.
Fachredaktion. Woerterbuch Medizinischer Fachausdruecke. French & Eur.
Fachredaktionen des Bibliographischen Instituts, ed. Duden-Rechnen & Mathematik. Biblio Inst.
Fadanelli. Dizionario italiano-russo. Vallardi A.
Fadanelli, R. Dizionario Italiano-Russo, Russo-Italiane. French & Eur.
Fages, Jean B. & Pagano, Christian. Dictionnaire des Media. Hurtubise H. M. H.
Fages, Jean-Baptiste. Diccionario de los Medios de Comunicacion: Tecnica, Semiologia, Linguistica. French & Eur.
Fages, Jean Baptiste & Pagano, Christian. Dictionnaire des Media. Delarge.
--Dictionnaire des Media. French & Eur.
Fagnan, E. Additions Aux Dictionnaires Arabes (Arabic-French) Intl Bk Ctr.
Faine. Dictionnaire Francais-Creole. Maison Dictionnaire.
Faine, Jules. Dictionnaire Francais-Creole. Lemeac.
--Dictionnaire Francais-Creole. French & Eur.
Fairchild, H. P., et al. Diccionario de sociologia. Fondo Cult.
Fairchild, Henry P. Dictionary of Sociology & Related Sciences. Greenwood.
--Dictionary of Sociology & Related Sciences. Littlefield.
Fairholt, Frederick W. A Dictionary of Terms in Art. Gordon Pr.
Fairholt, Frederick W., ed. Dictionary of Terms in Art. Gale.
Fairholt, Fredrick W. A Glossary of Costume in England. Charles River Bks.
Falcon, C., et al. Diccionario de la Mitologia Clasica. French & Eur.
Falconer, William. Universal Dictionary of the Marine. Kelley.
Falcon Martinez, Constantino, et al. Diccionario de la mitologia clasica: A-H. Alianza Ed.
--Diccionario de la mitologia clasica: I-Z. Alianza Ed.
Falcucci, F. D. Vocabolario dei dialetti della Corsica. Licosa.
--Vocabolario dei dialetti della Corsica. Licosa.
Falk, Bernard & Wolf, Jakob. Handlexikon fuer Handel & Absatz. Verlag Moderne Industrie.
Falk, H. S. & Torp, Alf. Norwegisch-Daenisches Etymologisches Woerterbuch. Winter Univ.
--Norwegisch-Daenisches Etymologisches Woerterbuch. Winter Univ.
--Norwegisch-Daenisches Etymologisches Woerterbuch (Pub. by Carl Winter). French & Eur.
--Norwegisch-Daenisches Etymologisches Woerterbuch (Pub. by Carl Winter). French & Eur.
--Norwegisch Daenisches Etymologisches Woerterbuch: Mit Literatur-Nachweisen Strittiger Etymologien Sowie Deutschem und Altnordischen Woerterverzeichnis (Dist. by Columbia U Pr). Universitet.
Fanfani, Pietro. Vocabolario dell'uso toscano. Le Lettere.
Fang, Chaoying, jt. ed. see Goodrich, L. Carrington.
Fann, William E. & Goshen, Charles E. The Language of Mental Health. Mosby.
Farbregd & Kamarainen. Finnish-Norwegian Norwegian-Finnish Pocket Dictionary. Kunnskapsforlaget.
Farbregd, T., et al. Finnish-Norwegian-Finnish Dictionary (Suomi-Noria-Suomi) French & Eur.
Farbregd, Turid & Kamarainen, Aili. Suomi-Norja-Suomi: Taskusanakirja. Soderstrom.
Fargher, Douglas. Fargher's English-Manx Dictionary (Pub. by Shearwater England). State Mutual Bk.
Fargher, Douglas C. Fargher's English Manx Dictionary. Humanities.
Faries, R. & Watkins, E. A. A Dictionary of the Cree Language. Anglican Church.
Farizov, I. O. Russko-Kurdskii Slovar (Pub. by GINS). Four Continent.
Farmer, Johns. The Public School Word-Book. R West.
Farnfield, Carolyn A. & Alvey, P. J. Textile Terms & Definitions. State Mutual Bk.
Farr, Kenneth R. Historical Dictionary of Puerto Rico & the U.S. Virgin Islands. Scarecrow.
Farrall, Arthur W. & Basselman, James A. Dictionary of Agricultural & Food Engineering. Interstate.
Farrell, R. B. Dictionary of German Synonyms. Cambridge U Pr.
Farrell, Ralph B. Dictionary of German Synonyms. Cambridge U Pr.
Farsi, S. Kamusi Vocabulaire. Edns St Paul.
Faruqi, Harith. Law Dictionary (Arabic-English) Intl Bk Ctr.
--Law Dictionary (English-Arabic) Intl Bk Ctr.
Faruqi, Lois I. Al see Al Faruqi, Lois I.
Fatturosso, V. & Ritter, O. Dizionario di farmacologia clinica. Branca Ciocetti, M. A., tr. Edipem.
Faulkner, R. O. A Concise Dictionary of Middle Egyptian (Pub. by Griffith Inst). State Mutual Bk.
Faure, Robert. Le Dictionnaire de L'agriculture. Doc Univers.
Faus, Agustin. Diccionario de la montana. Juventud.
Favata, Angelo. Dizionario dei termini giuridici. La Tribuna.
Favati, F. Dizionario di Agricoltura. Ed Calderini.
Favati, Franco. Dizionario di agricoltura: English-italian e italiano-inglese. Edagricole.
Favrat, Louis, jt. auth. see Bridel, Philippe Cyriaque.
Favre, Christophe & Balet, Robert. Lexique du Parler de Saviese. Champion.
Favre, Henri. Larousse Dictionary of the Fresh-Water Aquarium. Vevers, Gwynne, tr. Barron.
Favre, Yves-Alain A. Dictionnaire des Auteurs de Langue Francais. Flammarion.
Fazl-i-Ali. Dictionary of Persian & English Languages (Pub. by Cosmo Pubns India). Orient Bk Dist.
Federation Internationale de la Precontrainte. Multi-Lingual Dictionary of Concrete. Elsevier.
Federation of Societies for Coatings Technology, Definitions Committee, ed. Glossary of Color Terms. Fed Soc Coat Tech.
Federation of Societies on Coatings Technology. Paint-Coatings Dictionary. Fed Soc Coat Tech.
Fedida, P. Diccionario de Psicoanalisis. French & European.
Fedida, Pierre. Diccionario de Psicoanalisis. Alianza Ed.
--Dictionnaire de la Psychanalyse. Larousse.
Fedirko, J. V., jt. auth. see Gorner, Horst.
Fedou, R. Lexique Histoire du Moyen-Age. French & Eur.
Fehrenbach, Robert J., et al, eds. A Concordance to the Plays, Poems, & Translations of Christopher Marlowe. Cornell U Pr.
Feierabend, K. Langenscheidts Taschenwoerterbuecher Hebraeisch-Deutsch. Langenscheidt.
Feigl, Josef. Anglicko-Cesky a Cesko-Anglicky Slovnik por Televizni Pracovniky a Prekladatele. SNTC.
Feijoo, Guillermo M. Ortografia Functional: Atlas de la Aparatologia Ortopedica. Mundi.
Feijoo Zollern, Inocencio. Diccionario infantil: La lupa magica. Lopez Paco.
Feinberg, H. Cosmetics-Perfumery Thesaurus. Macmillan Info.
Feinstein, George W. Programmed College Vocabulary Three Thousand Six Hundred. P-H.
Feinstein, Paul T., jt. auth. see Rosenberg, Kenyon C.
Fejto, Francois. Dictionnaire des Partis Communistes & des Mouvements Revolutionnaires. Casterman.
Fekete, Ivan. Epuletgepeszet. Akademiai Kiado.
Felber, Helmut, compiled by. International Bibliography of Standardized Vocabularies (Pub. by K G Saur). Gale.
Feldbausch, F. Bankwoerterbuch Englisch-Deutsch, Deutsch-Englisch (Pub. by Vlg. Moderne Industrie). French & Eur.
Feldbausch, Friedrich K. Banking Dictionary: German-English & English-German. Intl Pubns Serv.
Feldman-Konrad, N. I. Iaponsko-Russkii Uchebnyi Slovar Ieroglifov (Pub. by Russkii Iazyk). Four Continent.
Felice, Emido de see De Felice, Emido & Duro, Aldo.
Felitsyna, V. P. & Prokhorov, Iu. E. Russkie Poslovitsy, Pogovorki i Krylatye Vyrazheniia (Pub. by Russkii Iazyk). Four Continent.
Felitsyna, Vera P. Russkie Poslovitsy, Pogovorki & Krylatye Vyrazheniia. Russkii Iazyk.
Felix, Jiri. Cesko-Rumunsky & Rumunsko-Cesky Slovnik na Cesty. SNTC.
Fenn, Courtenay H., ed. Five Thousand Dictionary: A Chinese-English Pocket Dictionary & Index to the Character Cards of the College of Chinese Studies. Harvard U Pr.
Fenwick, Sara I., ed. see University Of Chicago - Graduate Library School - 24th Conference.
Feoktistov, A. P. Russko-Mordovskii Slovar (Pub. by Nauka). Four Continent.
Ferland, M. G., jt. auth. see Villeneuve, G. O.
Ferland, Michel G., jt. auth. see Villeneuve, Georges O.
Ferlov, Niels, ed. see Molde, Bertil.
Fernald, James C. Funk & Wagnall's Standard Handbook of Synonyms, Antonyms & Prepositions. T y Crowell.
Fernandes. Diccionario de Verbos e Regimes. French & Eur.
Fernandes, F. Diccionario Brasileiro Contemporaneo. French & Eur.
--Dicionario da Lingua Portuguesa. French & Eur.
Fernandes, F. & Luft, C. P. Dicionario de Sinonimos e Antonimos da Lingua Portuguesa. French & Eur.
Fernandez Armesto, Fermin. Vocabulario castelan-galego. Castro Edns.
Fernandez de la Torriente, Gaston. Vocabulario superior. Playor.
--Vocabulario Superior. French & Eur.
Fernandez de la Vega & Hernandez Miyares. Ortografia Activa: Letras & Acentos. Gale.
Fernandez del Riego, Francisco. Vocabulario Castellano-Gallego. Galaxia.
Fernandez del Riego, Francisco, jt. auth. see Franco Grande, Xose L.
Fernandez de Miranda, Maria T. Diccionario ixcateco. INAH.
Fernandez Galiano, M., jt. auth. see Pabon, Jose M.
Fernandez Gandia, J. M. Diccionario escolar ilustrado. CECSA.
Fernandez-Martinez, F. Diccionario Tecnico de Aeronautica. Paraninfo.
Fernandez Naranjo, Nicolas. Diccionario de Bolivianismos. Cochabamba.
Fernandez Pareja, Francisco. Vocabulario de Priego de Cordoba & su Comarca. Autores-Editores.
Ferrar, H., et al. The Concise Oxford French Dictionary: French-English, English-French. Imported Bks.
Ferrar, H., et al, eds. The Concise Oxford French Dictionary. Oxford U Pr.
Ferrari, G. B. Vocabolario reggiano-italiano. Forni.
Ferrario, E. V., tr. see Gomez, Joan.
Ferrario, Jorge, jt. auth. see Crespi, Irene.
Ferraris, E. Dictionnaire de l'Industrie des matieres plastiques. Maison Dictionnaire.
Ferraris, Enrico & Istituto Italiano dei Plastici. Dizionario per l'industria delle materie plastiche: Definizioni italiane e termini corrispondenti in francese, inglese e tedesco. SAPIL.
Ferraro, Alfredo. Dizionario di metrologia generale. Zanichelli.

Ferraro, Giuseppe. Dizionario monferrino. Forni.
Ferrater, Mora. Diccionario de Filosofia. French & Eur.
Ferrater Mora, Jose. Diccionario de Filosofia. French & Eur.
--Diccionario de Filosofia Abreviado. French & Eur.
Ferreira, J. A. Portuguese-English, English-Portuguese Dictionary. Heinman.
Ferreira, J. Albino. English-Portuguese Dictionary. De Morais, O., ed. Shalom.
--Portuguese-English Dictionary. De Morais, A., ed. Shalom.
Ferrer, Josep, jt. auth. see Balbastre.
Ferrer Mir, Jaime, et al. Ortografia Castellano. S M Edns.
Ferrer Pastor, Francesc. Diccionari de la Rima. Piquenas Edit.
--Vocabulari Castella-Valencia. Sicania.
--Vocabulari Castella-Valencia. Sicania.
Ferrer-Pastor, Francesc. Vocabulari Castella-Valencia & Valencia-Castella. Estel Edit.
Ferrer Pastor, Francesc. Vocabulari Valencia-Castella. Fermar.
Ferrer Santalo, Joan. Diccionari practic de comerc exterior Catala-Angles Angles-Catala. Organ Ofic Adm.
Ferri, L. Vocabolario ferrarese-italiano. Forni.
Ferval, L., jt. auth. see Lange, K.
Fest, Wilfried. Dictionary of German History 1806-1945. St Martin.
Fetscher, Iring. Lexikon des Marxismus. French & Eur.
Fetz, Friedrich, ed. Lexikon des Alpinen Schifahrens. Inn Verlag.
Feuillet, L. Lexique Francais-Grec. Belin.
Feutry, Michel. Dictionnaire Technologique, 1: Anglais-Francais-Allemand. Maison Dictionnaire.
--Technological Dictionary. Maison Dictionnaire.
Feutry, Michel, et al. Dictionnaire Technologique, 1: Anglais-Francais-Allemand. Maison Dictionnaire.
Feutry, Michel, et al, eds. Dictionary of Industrial Technology: English-French-German-Portuguese-Spanish. Heinman.
--Technological Dictionary: Mechanics, Metalurgy, Hydraulics & Related Industries. Marlin.
Feyerabend, K. Hebraisch-Deutsch: Zum Alten Testament. Langenscheidt.
--Langenscheidts Taschenwoerterbuch Hebraisch. Langenscheidt.
Feyerabend, Karl, ed. Langenscheidt's Pocket Greek Dictionary, Classical Greek-English. Am Map.
--Langenscheidt's Pocket Hebrew Dictionary, Hebrew-English. Am Map.
Feys, R. & Fitch, F., eds. Dictionary of Symbols of Mathematical Logic (North Holland). Elsevier.
Fiandaca, G. Dizionario di elettronica: Tedesco-italiano. Il Rostro.
Fiedler, F. & Gurst, G., eds. Jugendlexikon Philosophie. Bibl Inst Leipzig.
Field, Claud. Dictionary of Arabic-Persian Quotes. Intl Bk Ctr.
--Dictionary of Arabic-Persian Quotes. Intl Bk Ctr.
--A Dictionary of Oriental Quotations. Gordon Pr.
Field, Claud H. Dictionary of Oriental Quotations. Gale.
Field, John. English Field-Names: A Dictionary. Gale.
Field, R. M. A Glossary of Office Automation Terms. Soc Tech Comm.
Fielding, Mantle. Dictionary of American Painters, Sculptors & Engravers: Enlarged. Assoc Bk.
Figueiredo, Candido de see De Figueiredo, Candido.
Filbee, Marjorie. The Connoisseur Dictionary of Country Furniture. Hearst Bks.
--Dictionary of Country Furniture (Pub. by Ebury Pr England). State Mutual Bk.
Filbert, Pierre, jt. auth. see Schmitt, Roger.
Filin, F. P., ed. Russkii Iazyk: Entsiklopediia. Four Continent.
Filipovic, R. Croatian-English, English-Croatian Small Pocket Dictionary. Vanous.
Filipovic, Rudolf. English-Croatian or Serbian Dictionary (Pub. by Collets). State Mutual Bk.
Filipovic, Rudolf, et al. English-Serbocroatian Dictionary. Intl Learn Syst.
Filippi & La Tour. Dizionario francese-italiano e italiano-francese. Giunti-Martello.
Filipuvic, R., et al. Yugoslavic Deluxe Dictionary: English-Croation or Serbian. Vanous.
--Yugoslavic Pocket Dictionary: English-Croation. Vanous.
Filkins, James H. & Caruth, Donald L. Lexicon of American Business Terms. Monarch Pr.
Fillenbaum, Samuel & Rapoport, Amnon. Structures in the Subjective Lexicon: An Experimental Approach to the Study of Semantic Fields. Acad Pr.
Filler, Louis. Dictionary of American Social Change. Krieger.
--Dictionary of American Social Reform. Greenwood.
Finamore, G. Vocabolario dell'uso abruzzese. Dante Alighieri.
--Vocabolario dell'uso abruzzese. Forni.
Findeisen, Barbara. A Course in Miracles Concordance. Coleman Graphics.
Findling, John E. Dictionary of American Diplomatic History. Greenwood.
Fine, Bernard D., jt. ed. see Moore, Burness E.
Finke, K. & Goock, R. Das Moderne Kinder-Lexikon in Farbe.Unsere Welt in Wort Und Bild: Unsere Welt in Wort & Bild. Adler Bks.
Finkenstaedt, Thomas. A Chronological English Dictionary. Listing 80,000 Words in Order of Their Earliest Known Occurrence. Intl Pubns Serv.
Finley, Moses, ed. see Blumner, Hugo.
Finley, Moses, ed. see Korver, Jan.
Finnegan, Edward G., ed. New Webster's Crossword Puzzle Dictionary: Vest Pocket Edition. Delair.
--New Webster's Dictionary of the English Language (College Edition) Delair.
--New Webster's Dictionary (Vest Pocket Edition) Delair.
--New Webster's English-Spanish Dictionary: Vest Pocket Edition. Delair.
--New Webster's Law for Everyone: Vest Pocket Edition. Delair.
--New Webster's Medical Dictionary: Vest Pocket Edition. Delair.
--New Webster's Vest Pocket Thesaurus. Delair.
--New Webster's Word Divider: Vest Pocket Edition. Delair.
Finney, Frederick M. Dictionary of Syngraphics & Associated Terms. Challenge Pr.
Finnie, W. Bruce. Topographic Terms in the Ohio Valley 1748-1800. U of Ala Pr.
Fiore, E. de see Gastaut, H.
Fiore, Gaspare de see De Fiore, Gaspare.
Fischborn, Gabriele. Woerterbuch der Darstellenden Kuenste: Russiche-Deutsch. VEB Verlag Enzyklopadie.
Fischer, A. Lumko English-Xhosa Dictionary. Oxford U Pr.
Fischer, Eric & Elliott, Francis E. A German & English Glossary of Geographical Terms. Greenwood.
Fischer, Rossi K. Glosario de mercadeo. Limusa.
Fishbein, Morris. Modern Home Dictionary of Medical Words: With Descriptions, Uses & Standards of Commonly Used Tests (Dolp). Doubleday.
Fisher, J. Patrick. Basic Medical Terminology. Bobbs.
--Basic Medical Terminology. Bobbs.
Fisher, Patricia, ed. see Considine, Tim.
Fisher, R. & Krchten, P. English-French Dictionary of Computer Science. Heinman.
Fisher, Richard B. & Christie, George A. A Dictionary of Drugs: The Medicines You Use. Schocken.
Fisk University Library (Nashville) Dictionary Catalog of the Negro Collection of the Fisk University Library (Hall Library). G K Hall.
Fitch, F., jt. ed. see Feys, R.
Fitzgerald, E. M., ed. Chambers Mini Dictionary (Pub. by W. R. Chambers). Hippocrene Bks.
Fitzgerald, Edward. Dictionary of Madame De Sevigne. Kerrich, Mary E., ed. B Franklin.
Fitzgerald, Percy. The Pickwickian Dictionary & Cyclopedia. Folcroft.
Fitzgerald, Percy H. The Pickwickian Dictionary & Cyclopaedia. AMS Pr.
Flagg, Isaac, ed. see Autenrieth, Georg.
Fleche, Francis La see La Fleche, Francis.
Fleck, K., ed. see Doucet, M.
Fleischer, Rita M., jt. auth. see Dunmore, Charles W.
Fleischer, W. Wortbildung der Deutschen Gegenwartssprache. Bibl Inst Leipzig.
Fleischmann, Gunther, jt. auth. see Schmieder, Christian.
Fleming, John, jt. auth. see Honour, Hugh.
Fleming, John, et al. The Penguin Dictionary of Architecture. Penguin.
Fleming-Mitchell, Leslie. Astrology Terms. Running Pr.
Fleming-Redish. The McMaster Glossary of Fortran Seventy-Seven. Kendall-Hunt.
Flemion, Philip F. Historical Dictionary of El Salvador. Scarecrow.
--Historical Dictionary of El Salvador. Intl Guatemala.
Fletcher, Leonard, et al. Construction Contract Dictionary (Pub. by E & Fn. Spon England). Methuen Inc.
Fleurian, Dominique de. Dictionnaire National des Communes de France. Simond, Jacques & Frenay, Jacques, eds. French & Eur.
Fleury, Paul & Roy, E. Dictionnaire de Stenographie. Estoup.
Flew, Antony. A Dictionary of Philosophy. St Martin.
Flew, Antony, ed. Dictionary of Philosophy. St Martin.
Flexner, Stuart B., jt. auth. see Wentworth, Harold.
Flodin, Mickey, jt. auth. see Butterworth, Rod.
Florance, A. Geographical Lexicon of Greek Coin Inscriptions. Ares.
Florant, J., jt. auth. see Bach, H.
Flores de Vega. Diccionario ortografico hispanoamericano. Peisa.
Florez, L. Lexico de la casa popular urbano en Bolivar, Colombia. Inst Caro y Cuervo.
--Lexico del cuerpo humano en Colombia. Inst Caro y Cuervo.
Florez, Luis. Del Espanol Hablado en Colombia: Seis Muestras de Lexico. Instituto Caro & Cuervo.
Flumiana, Carlo M. The New Expanded Dictionary of Stock Market Charts. Inst Econ Finan.
Flumiani, C. M. The New Dictionary of Strange & Ingenious Stock Market Tricks the Experts Follow in Their Search for Wealth. Am Classical Coll Pr.
--The New Expanded Dictionary of Stock Market Charts. Am Classical Coll Pr.
Flumiani, Carlo M. The New Expanded Dictionary of Stock Market Charts. Inst Econ Finan.
Flynn & Montoto. Spanish for Urban Workers. Camino Real.
Fockman, Andreae & Sybrandus, Johannes. Fockema Andreae's Rechtsgeleerd Handwoordenboek. Algra, N. E., rev. by. Tjeenk Willinik.
Fodor, N. & Gaynor, F. Dizionario di psicoanalisi tratto dalle opere di Sigmund Freud. Feltrinelli.
Fogarty, Robert S. Dictionary of American Communal & Utopian History. Greenwood.
Fogel, Ephim, jt. ed. see Di Cesare, Mario A.
Fohrer, Georg, et al, eds. Hebrew & Aramaic Dictionary of the Old Testament. Johnstone, W. A., tr. from Ger. De Gruyter.
Folb, Edith A. Black Vernacular Vocabulary: A Study of Intra-Inter-Cultural Concerns & Usage. Ctr Afro-Am Stud.
Foldes, Istvan & Makai, Gyoergy. Politikai Kissotar: A Szocikkek Szerzoi. Kos Kony.
Folena, G., ed. see Palazzi, F.
Folkman, D. & Folkman, E. Dictionary of Races or Peoples. Gordon Pr.
Folkman, E., jt. auth. see Folkman, D.
Follett, Wilson. Modern American Usage: A Guide. Barzun, Jacques, ed. Hill & Wang.
Folley, T. Spanish Aide-Memoire: English-Spanish Vocabulary (SpS). Sportshelf.
Folliet, jt. auth. see Watson.
Folomkina, A. & Weiser, H. The Learner's English-Russian Dictionary. Russki Iazyk.
Folomkina, S. & Weiser, H. Learner's English-Russian Dictionary. MIT Pr.
--The Learner's English-Russian Dictionary. French & Eur.
Folomkina, S. K., et al. Anglo-Russkii Uchebnyi Slovar' Four Continent.
Folomkina, V. & Weiser, T. Learner's English-Russian Dictionary (Pub. by Collet's). State Mutual Bk.
Fonda Publicaciones U. P. T. C., ed. Diccionario de paronimos. U. Pedagogica y Tec.
Fondaneche, Pierre, jt. auth. see Brosset, Raymond.
Fondation Paul Richard & Camard, Jean-Pierre. Dictionnaire des Peintres & Sculpteurs Provencaux: 1880-1950. Bendor.
Fonseca, F. Peixoto Da see Da Fonseca, F. Peixoto.
Fonteneau, M. & Theureau, S. Mon Dictionnaire Francais-Anglais (Dist. by Continental Bk Co). Larousse.
Fontoynont, Victor. Vocabulaire Grec. Picard.
Fontoynont-Ribot. Vocabulario Griego. Sal Terrae.
Font Quer. Diccionario de botanica. Labor.
Font Quer, Pio. Diccionario de Botanico. Labor SA.
Foort, Jean. Glossaire des Rues de Dunkerque. Foort.
Foote, ed. Thesaurus of Entomology. Entomol Soc.
Foray, Cyril P. Historical Dictionary of Sierra Leone. Scarecrow.
Forbes, A. Dean, jt. auth. see Andersen, Francis I.
Forbes, Patricia & Smith, Muriel H. Harrap's Concise French & English Dictionary. Collin, P. H., ed. Harrap.
Forbes, Patricia & Ledesert, Margaret, eds. Harrap's Mini Pocket French & English Dictionary. Harrap.
--Harrap's New Pocket French & English Dictionary. Harrap.
Forbes, Patricia, ed. see Mansion, J. E.
Forcellini, Egidio. Lexicon totius latinitatus. Lib Edit Greg.
Forest Products Research Society. Glossary of Terms Related to the Drying of Wood. Forest Prod.
--Thesaurus of Forest Products Terms. Forest Prod.
Fornas Prat, Jordi. Diccionari Italia-Catala Catala-Italia. Portic.
Forney, Matthias, ed. The Car Builder's Dictionary. N K Gregg.
Forney, Matthias N. The Railroad Car Builders Pictorial Dictionary. Peter Smith.
Forster, Klaus. Pronouncing Dictionary of English-Place Names. Routledge & Kegan.
Forstmann, Wilfried, et al. Die Geschichte: Ein Sachlexikon fuer die Schule. Biblio Inst.
Forsythe, Elizabeth, ed. see Riley, P. A. & Cunningham, P. J.
Forte, Imogene & MacKenzie, Joy. Dictionary Dynamite. Incentive Pubns.
Forte, Imogene & Pangle, Mary A. Vocabulary Magic. Incentive Pubns.

--Vocabulary Mastery. Incentive Pubns.

Forth, E. & Schewitzer, E., eds. Meyers Taschenlexikon Bionik. Bibl Inst Leipzig.

Fortin, A., et al. Petit Lexique du Soudage. Anglais-Francais. Chartrand, P., ed. French & Eur.

Foscue, Virginia O. A Preliminary Survey of the Vocabulary of White Alabamians (Am Dialect Soc). U of Ala Pr.

Fossey, Bernard M. de, jt. auth. see Blacque-Belair, Alain.

Foster, David W., ed. Dictionary of Contemporary Latin American Authors. ASU Lat Am St.

Foster, Ethel M., ed. see Foster, Joshua J.

Foster, John, compiled by. Shakespeare Word-Book, Being a Glossary of Archaic Forms & Varied Usages of Words Employed by Shakespeare. Russell.

Foster, Joshua J. A Dictionary of Painters of Miniatures, 1525-1850 with Some Account of Exhibitions, Collections, Sales, Etc. Foster, Ethel M., ed. B Franklin.

Foucauld, Charles de see De Foucauld, Charles.

Fouchier, J. & Billet, F. Chemical Dictionary. Elsevier.

Fougerouse, jt. auth. see Ballot, Marc M.

Fouk al-Ada, Samuhi. A Dictionary of Diplomacy & International Affairs. Intl Bk Ctr.

Foulquie, Paul. Diccionario De Pedagogia. French & Eur.

--Diccionario De Pedogogia. French & Eur.

--Diccionario Del Lenguaje Filosofico. French & Eur.

--Dictionnaire de la Langue Pedagogique. PUF.

Fournier, J. & Laborde, G. Le Mot et L'idee, Francais-Portugais, Portugais-Francais. French & Eur.

Fournier, J., jt. auth. see Jarnier, R.

Fournier, Robert. Diccionario ilustrado de alfareria practica. Torres, Elena, tr. Omega SA.

--Illustrated Dictionary of Pottery Form. Van Nos Reinhold.

--Illustrated Dictionary of Practical Pottery. Van Nos Reinhold.

Fowler, George L., ed. Locomotive Dictionary. N K Gregg.

Fowler, H. W. A Dictionary of Modern English Usage (GB). Oxford U Pr.

Fowler, Henry W. Dictionary of Modern English Usage. Gowers, Ernest, ed. Oxford U Pr.

Fowler, Jennifer. Heinemann Modern Dictionary for Dental Students. French & Eur.

Fowler, Roger, ed. A Dictionary of Modern Critical Terms. Routledge & Kegan.

Fowler, W. S. Dictionary of Idioms. Nelson & Sons Group.

Fox, jt. auth. see Dixson.

Fox, Charles E. Arosi Dictionary. Linguistic Circle.

Fox, Charles El. Dictionary of Nggela. Anthro AucMus.

Foye, James & Crane, Dale. Aviation Technical Dictionary. Aviation Maint.

Fracass, E. A. Terminologia Musical: Texto del Conservatorio "Fracassi". Ricordi.

Fraenkel, B. Dicionario de termos tecnicos Ingles-Portugues, Portugues-Ingles. Imported Bks.

Fraenkel, B. B. Dicionario de Expressoes Idiomaticas da Lingua Inglesa. Imported Bks.

Fraenkel, Ernst. Litauisches Etymologisches Woerterbuch (Pub. by Westdeutscher Verlag/VVA). French & Eur.

--Litauisches Etymologisches Woerterbuch (Pub. by Westdeutscher Verlag/VVA). French & Eur.

Fraga, C. P., jt. auth. see Quintanilla, R. H.

Frager, Ruth L., jt. auth. see Paternoster, Lewis M.

Frances, Osvald, jt. auth. see Costa, Vasco.

Frances, Osvaldo, jt. auth. see Costa, Vasco.

Francis, J. De see De Francis, J.

Francis, James J. The New English Astrological Thesaurus. CSA Pr.

Franciscan Fathers. Ethnologic Dictionary of the Navaho Language. St Michaels.

Franciscans, Saint Michaels, Arizona. An Ethnologic Dictionary of the Navaho Language. AMS Pr.

Francisco, Padill. Diccionario de anglicismos, barbaricismos, pachuquismos & otras locuci o01nes. Iaconi.

Franck, Irene M., jt. auth. see Brownstone, David M.

Franco Arias, Froilan. El Vocabulario Politico de Alguno Periodicos de Mexico D. F. Fundacion J March.

Franco Grande, X. L. Diccionario galego-castelan. Galaxia.

Franco Grande, Xose L. Diccionario galego-castelan. Galaxia.

--Diccionario Galego-Castelan e Vocabulario Castelan-Galego. French & Eur.

--Vocabulario Galego-Castelan. Galaxia.

--Vocabulario Galego-Castelan. French & Eur.

Franco Grande, Xose L. & Fernandez del Riego, Francisco. Vocabulario Galego-Castelan Castellano-Gallego. Galaxia.

Francois, Dom Jean. Dictionnaire Roman, Wallon, Celtique & Tudesque: Servir a l'intelligence des Anciennes lois & Contrats, des Chartes. Slatkine.

Frangos, Eftychia, jt. auth. see Valmin, Natan.

Frangos, Eftychia, ed. see Mystakidis, Antonis.

Frank, Felix, jt. auth. see Cheneviere, Adolphe.

Frank, Roberta & Cameron, Angus. A Plan for the Dictionary of Old English. U of Toronto Pr.

Frank, Roberta & Cameron, Angus, eds. A Plan for the Dictionary of Old English. U of Toronto Pr.

Franke, tr. Diccionario de fisica. Labor SA.

Frankl, F. Dictionnaire de Droit Social Francais-Allemand. French & Eur.

Franklin, Afred L. Dictionnaire Historique Des Arts, Metiers & Professions Exerces Dans Paris Depuis Le Treizieme Siecle. B Franklin.

Franklin, Alfred. Dictionnaire Historique des Arts, Metlers & Professions Exerces dans Paris Depuis le Treizieme Siecle. Lenox.

--Dictionnaire Historique des Arts: Metiers & Professions Exerces dans Paris, Depuis 13 Siecle. Lafitte Repr.

Franklin, Alfred L. Dictionnaire Historique des Arts, Metiers & Professions: Exercees dans Paris Depuis le 13 Siecle. Ohm Verlag.

Franklin, K. J., et al. A Kewa Dictionary with Supplementary Grammatical & Anthropological Materials. Linguistic Circle.

Franklyn, Julian. A Dictionary of Rhyming Slang. Routledge & Kegan.

Franklyn, Julian, ed. A Dictionary of the Occult. Gale.

Franks. Simplified Medical Dictionary. Van Nos Reinhold.

Franquesa, Manuel. Diccionari De Sinonims. French & Eur.

Franquesa, Miquel. Diccionari de sinonims. Portic.

Franquesa Lluelles, Manuel. Diccionario de Sinonimos. Portic.

Franz, Georg I. Fachworter der Elektronik. Franzis Verlag.

Franz, L. Lexikon Zur - und Fruehgeschichtlicher Fundstaetten Oesterreichs. French & Eur.

Franz, L. & Neumann, A. R., eds. Lexikon Zur & Freuhgeschictlicher Fundstaetten Oesterreichs. Habelt.

Franzen, F. & Hard, L. Woerterbuch der Kernenergie. Brandstetter.

Fraser, Edward & Gibbons, John. Soldier & Sailor Words & Phrases. Gale.

Frauca, Julio, jt. auth. see Cejador.

Frazer, Joan, et al. Thirty-Thousand Selected Words Organized by Letter, Sound & Syllable. Communication Skill.

Frederic i Ricart, Antoni, jt. auth. see Merenciano.

Frederick Muller, Ltd., ed. Multilingual Computer Dictionary (Pub. by Muller Ltd). State Mutual Bk.

--Multilingual Dictionary of Printing & Publishing (Pub. by Muller Ltd). State Mutual Bk.

--Multilingual Energy Dictionary (Pub. by Muller Ltd). State Mutual Bk.

Frederick, Richard G., jt. auth. see Roe, Keith E.

Fredoville, Jean C. Dictionnaire civilisation Romaine. Larousse.

Freedman, Alan. The Computer Glossary: It's Not Just a Glossary. Computer Lang.

Freedman, Alan & Morrison, Irma L. The Computer Glossary: It's Not Just a Glossary. P-H.

Freedman, David, ed. see Morton, A. Q., et al.

Freedman, David N., jt. auth. see Cross, Frank M., Jr.

Freedman, David Noel, ed. see Morton, A. Q. & Michaelson, Sidney.

Freedman, David Noel, ed. see Radday, Yehuda T. & Leb, G. M.

Freedman, Matt, jt. auth. see Hoffman, Paul.

Freeman, H. A Glossary of Technical Concepts Containing 4300 Din Definitions (Pub. by Din Verlag). Heyden.

--Taschenwoerterbuch Eisen und Stahl. Hueber.

--Taschenwoerterbuch Eisen und Stahl (Pub. by M. Hueber). French & Eur.

--Taschenwoerterbuch Kraftfahrzeugtechnik. Hueber.

--Taschenwoerterbuch Kraftfahrzeugtechnik (Pub. by M. Hueber). French & Eur.

--Technisches Taschenwoerterbuch. Heuber.

--Technisches Taschenwoerterbuch (Pub. by M. Hueber). French & Eur.

Freeman, H. G. Special Dictionary Machinery. Adler.

Freeman, Henry. Technisches Taschen Woerterbuch: Deutsch-Englisch, Englisch-Deutsch. Hueber.

Freeman, Henry G. Dictionary of Mechanical Engineering. Intl Pubns Serv.

--Dictionary of Metal-Cutting Machine Tools. Adler.

--Dictionary of Metal-Cutting Machine Tools. French & Eur.

--Fachenglisch Fur Technik und Industrie (Pub. by Carl Heymanns Verlag KG). French & Eur.

--Fachwoerterbuch Spanende Werkzeugmaschinen. Girardet.

--Fachwoerterbuch Spanende Werkzeugmaschinen (Pub. by Verlag W. Gerardet). French & Eur.

--Pocket Dictionary Iron & Steel. Intl Pubns Serv.

--Pocket Dictionary of Automotive Engineering: Taschenwoerterbuch Kraftfahrzuegtechnik. Intl Pubns Serv.

--Spanende Werkzeugmaschinen, Deutsch-Englische Begriffserlauterungen und Kommentare. Girardet.

--Spanende Werkzeugmaschinen, Deutsch-Englische Begriffserlauterungen und Kommentare (Pub. by Verlag W. Girardet). French & Eur.

--Spezialwoerterbuch Maschinenwesen. Girardet.

--Spezialwoerterbuch Maschinenwesen (Pub. by Verlag W. Girardet). French & Eur.

--Technical Pocket Dictionary, English-German, German-English. Adler.

--Technical Pocket Dictionary-Technisches Taschenwoerterbuch. Intl Pubns Serv.

--Technisches Englisch (Pub. by Girardet). French & Eur.

--Technishes Englisch. Girardet.

--Tool Dictionary. Adler.

--Woerterbuch Werkzeuge. French & Eur.

Freeman, Henry G., compiled by. DIN Definitions: German-English with an English-German Vocabulary. Heinman.

Freeman, Roger L. English-Spanish, Spanish-English Dictionary of Communications & Electronic Terms. Cambridge U Pr.

Freeman, William. Concise Dictionary of English Idioms. Writer.

Freiberger, Nancy & Vy Thi Be. Nung Fan Slihng Vocabulary. Summer Inst Ling.

Frenay, Agnes C. Understanding Medical Terminology. Cath Health.

Frenay, Jacques, ed. see Fleurian, Dominique de.

French, Hollis. Silver Collector's Glossary & a List of Early American Silversmiths & Their Marks. Da Capo.

French Language Bureau. Lexique Anglais-Francais des Petits Appareils Electromenagers. Edit Quebec.

Frenzel, Herbert & Frenzel, Walter. Langenscheids Handwoerterbuch Italienisch: Teil II, Deutsch-Italienisch. Macchi, Vladimiro, ed. Langenscheidt.

Frenzel, Herbert & Frenzel, Walter, eds. Langenscheids Handwoerterbuecher: Tl 2, Deutsch-Italienisch. Langenscheidt.

Frenzel, W. Langenscheids Taschenwoerterbuch Italienisch: Teil II, Deutsch-Italienisch. Langenscheidt.

Frenzel, W., jt. auth. see Macchi, V.

Frenzel, W. & Macchi, V., eds. Langenscheids Taschenwoerterbuch der Italienischen & Deutschen Sprache. Langenscheidt.

Frenzel, Walter, jt. auth. see Frenzel, Herbert.

Frenzel, Walter, jt. auth. see Giovannelli, Paolo.

Frenzel, Walter, jt. ed. see Frenzel, Herbert.

Freshman, Samuel K. Real Estate Finance & Syndication Glossary. Law & Cap Dynamics.

Frevert, W. Woerterbuch der Jaegerei. French & Eur.

Frey, A. R. Dictionary of Numismatic Names (Pub by Spink & Son England). S J Durst.

Frey, Hans. Das Grosse Lexikon der Aquaristik. Neumann-Neudamm.

Freyberger, G. Abkurzungen der Kernkraftwerkstechnik. Thiemeg.

Freyberger, G. H. Abbreviations of Nuclear Power Plant Engineering (Pub. by Verlag Karl Thiemig). French & Eur.

Freyd-Wadham, H. Englisches Wirtschaftsalphabet (Pub. by Th. Grossmann). French & Eur.

Freyha, Anis. A Dictionary of Modern Lebanese Proverbs. Intl Bk Ctr.

--Dictionary of Modern Lebanese Proverbs. Intl Bk Ctr.

--Dictionary of Non-Classical Vocables in Spoken Arabic. Intl Bk Ctr.

--A Dictionary of the Names of Towns & Villages in Lebanon. Intl Bk Ctr.

Freyha, Annis. Arabic-Arabic Dictionary of the Names of Towns & Villages in Lebanon. Intl Bk Ctr.

Freytag, George W. Lexicon Arabico-Latinum. Intl Bk Ctr.

--Lexicon Arabico-Latinum. Intl Bk Ctr.

Frias, A. Diccionario comercial: Espanol-ingles e ingles-espanol. Juventud.

Frias-Sucre, Alejandro. Diccionario comercial Ingles-Espanol, Espanol-Ingles. Fed Gremios.

Frias-Sucre Girard, Alejandro. Diccionario Comercial Ingles-Espanol. Lectorum Pubns.

Frias-Sucre Giraud, A. Spanish-English, English-Spanish Commercial Dictionary: "the Secretary". Heinman.

Frias-Sucre Giraud, Alejandro. Diccionario Comercial Espanol-Ingles: El Secretario. Juventud.

--Diccionario Comercial Espanol-Ingles y Ingles-Espanol. French & Eur.

Frick, G. William. Environmental Glossary. Gov Insts.

Frid, Lena. Dataordbok. EC Print AB.

Fried, Jerome, compiled by. The Bantam Crossword Dictionary. Bantam.
Friederich, Wolf von see Von Friederich, Wolf.
Friedmann, jt. auth. see Grossmann.
Friedmann, G., jt. auth. see Grossmann, T.
Friedreich, W. Taschenwoerterbuch des Fremdenverkehrs. Hueber.
Friedrich, Gerhard, jt. ed. see Kittel, Gerhard.
Friedrich, Johannes & Kammenhuber, Annelies. Hethitisches Woerterbuch. Winter Univ.
Friedrich, W. Taschenwoerterbuch des Fremdenverkehrs (Pub. by M. Hueber). French & Eur.
Friedrich, Wolf. Dictionary of Tourism: German-English & English-German. Intl Pubns Serv.
Frigola, Victoria, tr. see Amalric, Jacques, et al.
Frisk, Hjalmar. Griechiesches Etymologisches Woerterbuch. Winter Univ.
--Griechisches Etymologiches Woerterbuch. Winter Univ.
--Griechisches Etymologisches Woerterbuch (Pub. by Carl Winter). French & Eur.
--Griechisches Etymologisches Woerterbuch (Pub. by Carl Winter). French & Eur.
--Griechisches Etymologisches Woerterbuch (Pub. by Carl Winter). French & Eur.
--Griechishes Etymologishes Woerterbuch. Winter Univ.
Frisoni, Gaetano. Dizionario moderno italiano-spagnolo e spagnolo-italiano: Vol. 1, Italiano-spagnolo. Hoepli.
--Dizionario moderno italiano-spagnolo e spagnolo-italiano: Vol. 2, Spagnolo-italiano. Hoepli.
--Dizionario Moderno Spagnuolo-Italiano, Italiano-Spagnuolo. S F Vanni.
Frisoni, Giuseppe. Dizionario moderno genovese-italiano e italiano-genovese. Forni.
Frizzi, Giuseppe. Dizionario dei Frizzetti Popolari Firoentini. Multigrafica.
Frizzi, Graziano. Dizionarietto di informatica. Bucalo.
Froehlich, Werner D. & Drever, James. Woerterbuch zur Psychologie. Deutscher Taschenbuch.
Frohlich, Gerd, et al. Phytopathologie & Pflanzenschutz. Fischer Verlag.
Froimont, J. Dictionnaire de Poche Explicatif. Erasme.
--Dictionnaire des Synonymes: Francais-Neerlandais. Erasme.
Frolov, Ivant, ed. Dictionary of Philosophy. Intl Pub Co.
Fromherz, H. & King, A. English-German Chemical Terminology: An Introduction to Chemistry in English & German. Verlag Chemie.
--English-German Chemical Terminology: An Introduction to Chemistry in English & German (Pub. by Vlg. Chemie). French & Eur.
--Franzoesische und Deutsche Chemische Fachuasdruecke. Verlag Chemie.
--French-English Chemical Terminology: An Introduction to Chemistry in French & English. Verlag Chemie.
--French-English Chemical Terminology: An Introduction to Chemistry in French & English (Pub. by Vlg. Chemie). French & Eur.
Fromherz, Hans & King, Alexander. English-German Chemical Terminology: An Introduction to Chemistry in English & German. Verlag Chemie.
--French-English Chemical Terminology: An Introduction to Chemistry in French & English. Verlag Chemie.
--French-German Chemical Terminology: An Introduction to Chemistry in French & German. Verlag Chemie.
Frommer, Harvey. Sports Lingo: A Dictionary of the Language of Sports. Atheneum.
Frommhold, Hanns. Bauworterbuch. Werner Verlag.
Froundiian-Dirair. Armenisch-Deutsches Woerterbuch. Oldenbourg Verlag.
--Armenisch-Deutsches Woerterbuch (Pub. by Oldenbourg). French & Eur.
Fryd, E. Tysk-Dansk Dansk-Tysk Special Ordbog. French & Eur.
Fryd, Ejnar. Tysk-Dansk, Dansk-Tysk Specialordbog. For Stat Rev.
Fryd, Ejnar, ed. Fransk-Dansk, Dansk-Fransk Specialordbog. For Stat Rev.
Fuchs, Maximilien. Lexique du Journal des Goncourt. Slatkine.
Fuchs, W. Lexikon Zur Soziologie. French & Eur.
Fuchs, Werner, et al, eds. Lexikon zur Soziologie: Bd 1. Rowohlt.
--Lexikon zur Soziologie: Bd 2. Rowohlt.
Fuentes, jt. auth. see Eichborn.
Fuentes, A., jt. auth. see Eichborn, R.
Fuentes, D. & Lopez, J. A. Barrio Language Dictionary. Borden.
Fuentes, Dagaberto & Lopez, Jose A. Barrio Language Dictionary. Camino Real.
Fuentes, Jordi & Cortes, Lia. Diccionario politico de Chile. Orbe Edns.
Fuentes Aguilar, Luis, jt. auth. see Soto Mora, Consuelo.
Fuentes Estanol, Maria J. Vocabulario fenicio. Consejo Superior.
Fuentes Franco, Jordi. Diccionario y gramatica de la lengua de la isla de Pascua: Pascuense-castellano, castellano-pascuense, pascuense-ingles, ingles-pascuense. Juridica-Andres Bello.
Fueyo Cuesta, Laureano. Diccionario Terminologico De Minas, Canteras y Mineralurgia. French & Eur.
Fullana Llompart, Miguel. Diccionario De L'art I Els Oficis De la Construccion. French & Eur.
Fulvi, Fulvio. Dizionario di termini della geografia umana. Patron.
--Dizionario di Terminini Della Geografia Umana. Patron.
Fumagalli, Giuseppe. Lexicon typographicum Italiae. Olschki.
Funk And Wagnalls Dictionary Staff, jt. ed. see Hayakawa, S. I.
Funk And Wagnalls Editors. Funk & Wagnalls Standard College Dictionary. T Y Crowell.
Funk, Wilfred & Lewis, Norman. Thirty Days to a More Powerful Vocabulary. T Y Crowell.
Funk, Wilfred, jt. auth. see Lewis, Norman.
Furetiere, Antoine. Dictionnaire Universel. Slatkine.
--Dictionnaire Universel: Contenant Generalement tous les Mots Francois, 2. Olms.
--Dictionnaire Universel: Contenant Generalement tous les Mots Francois, 3. Olms.
--Dictionnaire Universel: Contenant Generalement tous les Mots Francois, 4. Olms.
--Dictionnaire Universel d'Antoine Furetiere. Ste. Nouv. Littre.
Furetiere, Antoine & La Haye. Dictionnaire Universel: Contenant Generalement tous les Mots Francois, 1. Olms.
Furness, Mrs. Horace H. Concordance to Shakespeare's Poems: An Index to Every Word Therein Contained. Ayer Co.
Furst, Gesenius. Hebrew-English Dictionary: Hebrew & Chaldee Lexicon to the Old Testament. Mitchell, Edward C., ed. Shalom.
Furstenau, Eugenio. Dicionario de termos tecnicos Ingles-Portugues. Editora Globo.
Fusari, Alberto. Dizionario di Terminologia Ortopedica & Traumatologia. Gaggi.
Fusella, L. & Girace, A. Dizionario pratico e frasario per conversazione italiano-amarica. Ist Univers Orient.
Fuster Ortells, Joan. Diccionari Pera Ociosos. French & Eur.
Fuzellier, Etienne. Dictionnaire des Oeuvres & des Themes du Cinema Mondial. Hachette-Jeunesse.
Fyle, Clifford N., compiled by. A Krio-English Dictionary. Oxford U Pr.

G

Gaal, Robert A. The Diamond Dictionary. Gemological.
Gaballi Prat, P. Diccionario De Terminos Comerciales. French & Eur.
Gabillon, Aime. Dictionnaire des Mots, des Phrases, des Images. RST.
Gabrielli, Aldo. Dizionario dei sinonimi e dei contrari. Ist Edit Ital.
--Dizionario dei verbi italiani regolari ed irregolari. Ist Edit Ital.
--Dizionario linguistico moderno. Edn Scol Mond.
Gabrielsen, Daae. Norwegian-English Dictionary of Commerce. Kunnskapsforlaget.
--Norwegian-French Dictionary of Commerce. Kunnskapsforlaget.
--Norwegian-German Dictionary of Commerce. Kunnskapsforlaget.
Gache, Roberto. Glosario de la farsa urbana. Centro Ed.
Gack & Jahn. Herder - Lexikon Tiere (Pub. by Herder). French & Eur.
--Herder-Lexikon Tiere. Herder.
Gaden, Henri. Lexique Poular-Francais: Le Poular Dialecte Peul du Fouta Senegalais. Gregg.
Gaffiot, F. Dizionario illustrato latino-italiano. Piccin.
Gaffiot, Felix. Dictionnaire Abrege Latin-Francais. Hachette Jeunesse.
--Dictionnaire Abrege Latin-Francais. French & Eur.
--Dictionnaire Abrege Latin-Francais Illustre. Renouveau Pedagogique.
--Dictionnaire Latin-Francais. Hachette.
--Dictionnaire Latin-Francais. French & Eur.
Gaft & Bassoli. Dizionario italiano-svedese. Vallardi A.
Gage, William & Duong Thanh Binh. Vietnamese-English Phrasebook with Useful Word List: For English Speakers. Ctr Appl Ling.
Gagini, Carlos & Soto, Victor M. Diccionario de Costarriquenismos. Cuervo, Rufino J., prologue by. Costa Rica.
Gagliardelli, jt. auth. see Ragazzini.
Gagnacci-Schwicker, A. & Schwicker. International Dictionary of Metallurgey, Mineralogy, Geology & the Mining & Oil Industries. Bauverlag.
--International Dictionary of Metallurgy, Mineralogy, Geology & the Mining & Oil Industries (Pub. by Bauverlag). French & Eur.
Gailey, Harry A. Historical Dictionary of the Gambia. Scarecrow.
Gaimaro, Oscar. Diccionario de los ingenios. Alonso Edns.
Galan e Hidalgo, Arturo, jt. auth. see Bucksch, Herbert.
Galan e Hildalgo, Arturo, jt. auth. see Bucksch, Herbert.
Galant, Armando. Diccionario Espanol-Frances. Mayfe.
--Diccionario Espanol-Frances. Mayfe.
--Diccionario Frances-Espanol. Mayfe.
Galdi, Laszlo. Orosz-Magyar Szotar. Akademiai Kiado.
Galfridus Anglicus. Promptorium Parvulorum Sive Clericorum, Dictionarius Anglolatinus Princeps. Johnson Repr.
Galfridus, Anglicus. Promptorium Parvulorum Sive Clericorum, Lexicon Anglo-Latinum Princeps. AMS Pr.
Galiana, Thomas De see De Galiana, Thomas.
Galiano, M. Fernandez see Pabon, Jose M. & Fernandez Galiano, M.
Gali I Herrera, Jordi, prologue by see Vox.
Galisson. La Banalisation Lexicale (Dist. by Continental Bk Co). Lib. Fernand Nathan.
Galisson, R. & Coste, D., eds. Dictionnaire de Didactique des Langues. Hachette-Jeunesse.
--Dictionnaire de Didactique des Largues. French & Eur.
Galland, Frank J., ed. Dictionary of Computing: Data Communications, Hardware & Software Basics, Digital Electronics (Pub. by Wiley-Interscience). Wiley.
Gallaudet College Library, Washington, D. C. Dictionary Catalog on Deafness & the Deaf (Hall Library). G K Hall.
Gallego Tribaldos, Juan J. Ortografia Practica del Espanol. Ave Maria.
Galler, Meyer. Soviet Prison Camp Speech: Supplement. Soviet Studies.
Galler, Meyer & Marquess, Harlan E., eds. Soviet Prison Camp Speech: A Survivor's Glossary. U of Wis Pr.
Gallet, Francois. Dictionnaire Phonetique d'Orthographe. PenseeUniv.
Galley, Samuel. Dictionnaire Francais-Fang. Messeiller.
Galliano, Luciano. Dizionario di sociologia. UTET.
Gallo, Cristine. Language of the Puerto Rican Street. C Gallo.
Galperin, I. R., ed. Bolshoi Anglo-Russkii Slovar (Pub. by Russkii Iazyk). Four Continent.
--Bol'Shoi Anglo-Russkii Slovar. Four Continent.
--A Supplement to the New English-Russian Dictionary. Four Continent.
Galvan, Roberto A. & Teschner, Richard V. El Diccionario Del Espanol Chicano. Inst Mod Lang.
--El Diccionario del Espanol de Tejas. Edicoes Melhoramentos.
Gamber, Ortwin, et al, eds. Glossarium Armorum: Bd 6 Texthefte in Deutsch, Englisch, Franzoesisch, Italienisch, Daenisch, Tschechisch. Verlag der Buchhaendler-Vereinigung GmbH.
Gambetta, Leon, jt. auth. see Espinosa, Aurelio M.
Gamchina, K. Dictionnaire Francais-Russe. French & Eur.
Gamez, Tana De see De Gamez, Tana.
Gamillscheg, Ernst. Etymologisches Woerterbuch der Franzoesischen Sprache. Winter Univ.
--Etymologisches Woerterbuch der Franzoesischen Sprache (Pub. by Carl Winter). French & Eur.
Gammond, Peter & Clayton, Peter. Dictionary of Popular Music. Scholarly.
Gamrekeli, N., et al. Nemetsko-Gruzinsko-Russkii Frazeologicheskii Slovar (Pub. by Ganatleba). Four Continent.
Ganchina, K. A. Dictionnaire Francais-Russe. MIR.
Gangi, M., jt. auth. see Cafagna, C.
Ganich, D. I., et al. Russko-Ukrainskii Slovar (Pub. by Sov. Entsiklopediia). Four Continent.
Gankin, E. B. Akhmarsko-Russkii Slovar (Pub. by Sov Entsiklopediia). Four Continent.
--Russko-Amkharskii Slovar (Pub. by Sov. Entsiklopediia). Four Continent.
Gannett, Henry. A Geographic Dictionary of Connecticut & Rhode Island. Genealog Pub.
--A Geographic Dictionary of Massachusetts. Genealog Pub.
--A Geographic Dictionary of New Jersey. Genealog Pub.
Ganning, London. A Dictionary of Bad Manners. HM.
Garber, Max B. & Bond, P. S. A Modern Military Dictionary: Ten Thousand Technical & Slang Terms of Military Usage. Gale.
Garcia. Dizionario italiano-spagnolo. Vallardi A.
Garcia, A. Dizionario Italiano-Spagnolo, Spagnolo-Italiano. French & Eur.
Garcia, Barbara M., jt. auth. see Castillo, Carlos.
Garcia, Hoz, tr. Diccionario de pedagogia Labor. Labor SA.
Garcia, M. Luz, tr. see Lewandowski, Theodor, et al.
Garcia, Mercadel. Diccionario ilustrado de lengua espanola. Mayfe.
Garcia, W. Joseph. Medical Sign Language: Easily Understood Definitions of Commonly Used Medical, Dental & First Aid Terms. C C Thomas.

Garcia Becerra, Manuel. Diccionario escolar americano. Iztaccihuatl.
Garcia de Diego. Diccionario de voces naturales. Aguilar SP.
Garcia de Diego, Vicenete. Diccionario de Voces Naturales. French & Eur.
Garcia de Diego, Vicente. Diccionario etimologica espanol e hispanico. SAETA.
Garcia de Paredes, Angel, jt. auth. see Gooch, Anthony.
Garcia de Paredes y Castro, Jose & Barbudo Duarte, Enrique. Diccionario maritimo ingles-espanol y espanol-ingles. Fragata.
Garcia Hoz, Victor. Diccionario de Pedagogia Labor. French & Eur.
--Diccionario escolar etimologica. Magisterio Esp.
--Diccionario Escolar Etimologico. Magisterio Esp.
--Diccionario Escolar Etimologico. French & Eur.
--Vocabulario General de Orientacion Cientifica y Sus Estratos. French & Eur.
Garcia Merayo, F. Glosario de informatica. Urmo.
--Glosario De Informatica: Terminologia Ordenada Segun el Vocablo Ingles y Su Acepcion En Espanol. French & Eur.
Garcia Mercadal, Jose. Diccionario Espanol Ilustrado. Mayfe.
--Diccionario Lengua Espanola Forja. French & Eur.
Garcia Morente, Manuel, jt. auth. see Larrieu, Roberto.
Garcia Patier, Carlos. Diccionario Taurino Ilustrado. Cometa SA.
Garcia-Pelayo, R. Dictionnaire Moderne "Saturne" (Dist. by Continental Bk Co). Larousse.
Garcia-Pelayo, R. & Testas, J. Dictionnaire moderne Larousse, francais-espagnol et espagnol-francais. Larousse.
Garcia-Pelayo, R., ed. Dictionnaire Moderne: Francaise-Espagnol, Espagnol-Francais. French & Eur.
Garcia-Pelayo, Ramon. Diccionario Larousse Del Espanol Moderno (Sig). NAL.
--Diccionario Moderno Espanol-Ingles, English-Spanish. French & Eur.
Garcia-Pelayo, Ramon & Testas, Jean. Dictionnaire Moderne Saturne: Francais-Espagnol. Larousse FR.
Garcia Soriano, Justo. Vocabulario del dialecto murciano. Organ Ofic Adm.
Garcia Tous, M. R., jt. auth. see Rabassa Asenjo, B.
Garcia Tous, M. R., jt. auth. see Rabassa Asenjo, Bernardo.
Garcin, E. Dictionnaire Historique & Topographique de la Ancienne & Moderne. Chantemerle.
Gardinier, David E. Historical Dictionary of Gabon. Scarecrow.
Gardner, A. Ward. Good Housekeeping Dictionary of Symptoms. Ace Bks.
Gardner, Elizabeth F. & Martin, Samuel E. An Introduction to Modern Japanese Orthography: Kana. Far Eastern Pubns.
Gardner, James. Illustrated Soccer Dictionary for Young People. Harvey.
--Illustrated Soccer Dictionary for Young People (Pub. by Treehouse). P-H.
Gareff, G. & Bassoli, F. Dizionario Italiano-Svedese, Svedese-Italiano. French & Eur.
Garfield, E. Transliterated Dictionary of the Russian Language. ISI Pr.
Garibian, A. Russko-Armianskii Slovar (Pub. by Hayastan). Four Continent.
Garibian, A. S. Russko-Armianskii Slovar (Pub. by Hayastan). Four Continent.
Gariel, A. Dictionnaire Hatier-Beauchemin: Latin-Francais. Beauchemin.
Garilovets, A. V. English-Russian Dictionary of Sports Terms & Phrases (Pub. by Collets). State Mutual Bk.
Garland, Ken. Illustrated Graphics Glossary (Pub. by Barrie & Jenkins England). State Mutual Bk.
Garlock, Trisha. Glossary of Papermaking Terms. World Print Coun.
Garmendia Miangolarra, I. Diccionario de Bolsa. Piramide.
Garmendia Miangolarra, J. Ignacio de. Diccionario De Bolsa. French & Eur.
Garmendia Miangolarra, J. Ignacio de see De Garmendia Miangolarra, J. Ignacio.
Garmendia y Berasategui, Ignacio de. Diccionario Maritimo Ilustrado Vasco-Castellano, Castellano-Vasco. French & Eur.
Garmonsway, G. N., ed. The Penquin English Dictionary. Lane.
Garnier, J. C., jt. auth. see Poussin, J. C.
Garnier, M., et al. Dizionario dei termini tecnici di medicina. DEMI.
Garnier, Marcel & Delamare, Jean. Dictionnaire des Termes Techniques de Medecine. Maloine.
--Dictionnaire des Termes Techniques De Medecine. French & Eur.
Garnier, Marcel, et al. Diccionario de los terminos tecnicos de Medicina. Llido Blasco, Julio, tr. Norma.
Garrett, John. Classical Dictionary of India. B Franklin.
Garrido, J. A. Diccionario Ingles-Espanol para Medicos y Estudiantes de Medicina. French & Eur.
Garrido, Juan A. Diccionario ingles-espanol para medicos y estudiantes de medicina. Pediatrica.
Garrido y Comas. Diccionario practico de seguros. Rev. Mex. de Seguros.
Garrido y Comas, Juan J. Diccionario practico de seguros. Ariel.
Garriga, Teresa. Lexica (II) Jaimes Libros.
Garro, Joaquin. Habla Que el Tiempo se Lleva? Costa Rica.
Gartshore, Linda. The Machine Knitter's Dictionary. St Martin.
Gary, Leger. Dictionnaire Patois-Francais a l'usage du Departement du Tarn & des Departements Circonvoisins. Lafitte Repr.
Gary, M., et al. Glossary of Geology. French & Eur.
Garza Bores, Jaime. Diccionario tecnico de terminologia comercial, contable y bancaria: Espanol-Ingles, Ingles-Espanol. Diana.
--Diccionario Tecnico de Terminologia Comercial Cantable y Bancaria. French & Eur.
Garzena, B. Dizionario delle arti figurative. Zanichelli.
Gasselin, E. Dictionnaire Francais-Arabe(Arabe Parle-Arabe Grammatical) Verry.
Gastaut, H. Dictionary of Epilepsy: Part I - Definitions. World Health.
--Dizionario dell'epilessia. De Fiore, E. & Vizioli, R., trs. Il Pensiero.
--Woerterbuch der Epilepsie. French & Eur.
Gastmann, Albert. Historical Dictionary of the French & Netherlands Antilles. Scarecrow.
Gates, ed. see Makkai, Adam.
Gates, John, jt. auth. see Boatner, Maxine.
Gates, John E., jt. auth. see Boetner, Maxine.
Gates, William. An Outline Dictionary of Maya Glyphs. Dover.
Gatin, Charles Louis. Dictionnaire Aide Memoire de Botanique (Pub. by Lechevalier). French & Eur.
Gatin, Charles-Louis. Dictionnaire Alde-Memoire de Botanique. Lechevalier.
Gatin, Charles Louis. Dictionnaire de Botanique. Kraus.
Gatti, jt. tr. see Corte, Della.
Gatti, Guido. Dizionario di musica. UTET.
Gatto, Massimo. Dizionario fraseologico e grammaticale italiano-francese. Sandron.
--Dizionario fraseologico e grammaticale italiano-inglese. Sandron.
Gatzlaff-Halsig, Margot. Woerterbuch Deutsch-Hindi. VEB Verlag Enzyklopadie.
Gaudilat, Louis. Lexique Officiel des lampes Radios. French & Eur.
Gaudillat, Louis. Lexique Officiel des Lampes Radio. Radio.
Gaugler, Eduard, ed. Handwoerterbuch des Personalwesens. Poeschel Verlag.
Gaultier, Claude, jt. auth. see Pinty, Jean-Jacques.
Gaumond, J., jt. auth. see Cote, N.
Gautier, jt. auth. see Panassie, Hugues.
Gautier, Madeleine, jt. auth. see Panassie, Hugues.
Gautier, T. F. Dictionnaire des Confreries & Corporations d'Arts & Metiers. Migne, J. P., ed. Caratzas Pub Co.
Gautrat, Jacques. Dictionnaire de la Montagne. French & Eur.
--Dictionnaire du Ski. Seuil.
--Dictionnaire du Ski. French & Eur.
Gavande, S. A. & Bornemisza, Elemer. Terminologia Moderna de Energia de Agua en el Sistema Suelo-Planta Atmosfera. IICA.
Gavray-Baty, P. Le Vocabulaire Toponymique du Ban de Fronville. Liege, Fac Lettres.
Gavrilovets, A. V. Russian-English Dictionary of Sports Terms & Phrases (Pub. by Collets). State Mutual Bk.
--Russko-Angliiskii Slovar-Razgovornik: Letnie Olimpiiskie Vidy Sporta (Pub. by Russkii Iazyk). Four Continent.
Gavuzzi, G. Vocabolario italiano-piemontese. Bottega d'Erasmo.
Gaward, Abd El. Architecture & Building Dictionary: English-French-German-Arabic. French & Eur.
Gay. Glossaire archeologique du moyer age et de la Renaissance. French & Eur.
Gay, Victor. Glossaire Archeologique du Moyen-Age & de la Renaissance. Kraus.
--Glossaire Archeologique du Moyen-Age & de la Renaissance. Picard.
Gaya, S. D. Gili see Gili Gaya, S. D.
Gaya, Samuel D. Gili see Menendez Pidal, Ramon D.
Gaya, Samuel Gili see Gili Gaya, Samuel.
Gaya Nuno, Benito. Lexicon Creticum: Estudios sobre Escritura & lengua cretense; inscripciones monumentales; faistos, arkolochori, mallia (CSIC). Inst. Antonio de Nebrija.
Gaynor, F., jt. auth. see Fodor, N.
Gaynor, Frank. Dictionary of Mysticism. Citadel Pr.
Gaynor, Frank, jt. auth. see Pei, Mario.
Gaynor, Frank, ed. New Military & Naval Dictionary. Greenwood.
Gaynor, Frank, jt. ed. see Pei, Mario.
Gaytan, C. Diccionario Mitologico. French & Eur.
Gazes, Anthimos, ed. Lexikon tes Hellenikes Glosses Tritomon: Lexicon of the Greek Language in Three Volumes. Caratzas Pub Co.
Geach, P. T., ed. see Prior, Arthur N.
Gebert, Erika, jt. auth. see Schock, Sarina.
Gee, Ralph C., jt. auth. see Townley, Helen M.
Geigant, Friedrich. Lexikon der Volkswirtschaft. French & Eur.
Geigant, Friedrich, et al. Lexikon der Volkswirtschaft. Verlag Moderne Industrie.
Geiler, L. B., et al, eds. Anglo-Russkii Elektrotekhnicheskii Slovar (Pub. by Gosizdat Tekhn. Teoret.). Four Continent.
Geissler, E. A. & Wolff, Lise. Legal Dictionary (Pub. by Collets). State Mutual Bk.
Gelb, Barbara L. The Dictionary of Food & What's in It for You. Ballantine.
Gelb, Ignace J. Glossary of Old Akkadian. U of Chicago Pr.
Gelber, Leonard, jt. auth. see Martin, Michael.
Gelderen, I. van see Van Gelderen, I. & Wallis, W. H.
Gelderen, Van see Van Gelderen.
Gelis, D. N., ed. Greek-English, English-Greek Medical Dictionary. Heinman.
Gellert, W., et al, eds. Lexikon der Mathematik. Bibl Inst Leipzig.
Gellinek, Christian. Hugo Grotius Drama Concordance. Camden Hse.
Gemert, G. A. van see Van Gemert, G. A. & De Maesschalck, A.
Gemoll, Guglielmo. Vocabolario greco-italiano. Sandron.
Genaust, Helmut. Etymologisches Woertenbuch der Botanischen Pflanzennamen (Pub. by Birkhaeuser). French & Eur.
Gendrel, M. Dictionnaire des Principaux Sigles Utilises dans le Monde Juridique de A-Z. Bruylant.
Genette, Francis. Dictionnaire du Bricolage & du Depannage. Sequoia.
--Dictionnaire Marabout du Bricolage. Marabout.
Genouvrier, E. Dictionnaire des Synonymes de Poche (Dist. by Continental Bk Co). Larousse.
Genouvrier, Emile, et al. Nouveau Dictionnaire des Synonymes. French & Eur.
Genovard. Diccionario de Psicologia. Jims.
Genovard Rossello, Candid. Vocabulario basico trilingue de psicologia cientifica: Ingles-castellano. Fontanella.
Genovart Rosello, C., ed. see Laeng, Mauro.
Gentle, E. J. & Reithmaier, L. W. Aviation-Space Dictionary. Aero.
Geoffroy. Dictionnaire Francais-Latin. Delalain.
--Dictionnaire Latin-Francais. Delalain.
Geoffroy Rivas, Pedro. La Lengua Salvadorena. Direccion de Publicaciones.
George, P., jt. auth. see Cotti-Cometti, G.
George, Pierre. Dictionnaire de la Geographie. French & Eur.
Georgin. Dictionnaire Grec-Francais. Hatier.
Georgin, Ch. Dictionnaire Grec-Francais. French & Eur.
Georr, Khalil. Dictionnaire Arabe Moderne Larousse. Larousse.
--Dictionnaire Arabe moderne Larousse. Larousse.
Gerard-Marchant, Remi. Glossaire d'histopathologia des Tumeurs Humaines. Masson & Cie.
Geraud-Venzac, ed. see Littre.
Gerber, Barbara & Storzer, Gerald. French Idioms on the Way. Barron.
Gerber, Barbara L. & Storzer, Gerald H. Dictionary of Modern French Idioms. Garland Pub.
Gercan, Oktavija, jt. auth. see Brozovic, Blanka.
Gerdel, Florence & Slocum, Marianna. Vocabulario Tzeltal de Bachajon. Summer Inst Ling.
Gerds, Peter, ed. see Rosenthal, Hans J.
Gere, S. V., et al. Italiansko-Russkii Slovar (Pub. by Gosizdat Inostr. Natsional Slovarei). Four Continent.
Gerecke, Klaus. Arzneimttel-Verzeichnis. VEB Verlag Technik.
Gerescher, Konrad. Politik Aufgespiesst: Heiteres Lexikon der Politischen Missbildung. Gauke.
Gerhard, George B., et al, eds. see Carter, Henry H.
Geri, M., ed. Tolkovyi Slovar' Angliskikh Geologicheskikh Terminov (Pub. by Prosveshchenie). Four Continent.
Gerlach, Werner, jt. ed. see Evanoff, Philip C.
Germa, Pierre. Depuis Quand? Les Origines des Choses de la Vie Quotidienne (Dist. by Continental Bk Co). Berger-Levrault.
--Larousse des Citations: Francaises et Etrangeres (Dist. by Continental Bk Co). Larousse.
German-Prozorova, L. P., et al. Anglo-Russkii Slovar Po Televideniiu (Pub. by Glav. Red. Fizmatgiza). Four Continent.
German-Prozorova, L. P., et al, eds. Anglo-Russkii Radiotekhnicheskii Slovar (Pub. by Gosizdat. Inostr. Slovarei). Four Continent.
Gerow, Edwin. A Glossary of Indian Figures of Speech. Mouton.
Gerrish, Howard H. Technical Dictionary. Goodheart.
Gerritsen, J., et al, eds. see Bruggencate, K. T.

Gersov, A. S. Finnish-Danish-Finnish Dictionary: Suomi-Tanska-Suomi. French & Eur.
Gerteiny, Alfred G. Historical Dictionary of Mauritania. Scarecrow.
Gervasi, Teresa, jt. auth. see Scardigli, Piergiuseppe.
Gerwick, Ben C., Jr. & Peters, V. P., eds. Russian-English Dictionary of Prestressed Concrete & Concrete Construction. Gordon.
Gesenius, Freiedrich H. Guilielmi Gesenii Thesaurus Philologicus Linguae Hebraeae. Biblio-Verlag.
Gesenius, Wilhelm. Hebrew & Chaldee Lexicon: Keyed to Strong's Exhaustive Concordance. Tregelles, Samuel P., tr. Baker Bk.
Gesenius, William. Hebrew & Chaldee Lexicon, Tregelles Translation. Eerdmans.
--Hebrew & English Lexicon to the Old Testament. Brown, Francis, et al, eds. Robinson, Edward, tr. Oxford U Pr.
Gester, Michel, jt. auth. see Michel, J.
Gettings, Fred. Dictionary of Occult, Hermetic & Alchemical Sigils. Routledge & Kegan.
Geytenbeek, Brian & Geytenbeek, Helen. Gidabal Grammar & Dictionary. Humanities.
Geytenbeek, Helen, jt. auth. see Geytenbeek, Brian.
Ghaleb, Edouard. Dictionnaire des Sciences de la Nature (Dictionary of the Natural Sciences) Intl Pubns Serv.
--Dictionnaire des Sciences de la Nature, 1. Dar El-Machreq.
--Dictionnaire des Sciences de la Nature, 2. Dar El-Machreq.
--Dictionnaire des Sciences de la Nature, 3. Dar El-Machreq.
Ghali, Magdi, jt. ed. see Wahba, Magdi.
Ghali, Wagdi R., jt. auth. see Wahba, Magdi.
Ghattas, Nabih. Dictionary of Economic Business & Finance. Intl Bk Ctr.
--Dictionary of Economics, Business & Finance: English-Arabic with Arabic Glossary. Intl Bk Ctr.
Gheerbrant, Alain, jt. auth. see Chevalier, Jean.
Ghelfi, R. A., et al. Glosario de terminos nucleares. EUDEBA.
Gheorghita, Stefan. Dictionar Poliglot de Matematica, Mecanica si Astronomie. Editura Stiintifica.
Ghiotti, et al. Dictionnaire Italien-Francais, Francais-Italien de la Langue d'Aujourd'hui. French & Eur.
Ghiotto, Candido, et al. Dizionario italiano-francese francese-italiano della lingua d'oggi. Petrini.
Ghitescu, Micaela. Dictionar Roman-Spaniol: Pentru uzul Elevilor. Editura Stiintifica.
--Dictionar Spaniol-Roman: Pentru uzul Elevilor. Editura Stiintifica.
Giacchi, Pirro. Dizionario del vernacolo fiorentino. Multigrafica.
Giacco, G. S. del see Del Giacco, G. S.
Giacomo, M., jt. auth. see Dubois, J.
Giammarco, Ernesto. Dizionario abruzzese e molisano: A-E. Ateneo & Bizzarri.
--Dizionario abruzzese e molisano: F-M. Ateneo & Bizzarri.
--Dizionario abruzzese e molisano: N-R. Ateneo & Bizzarri.
Giampaolo, Barosso. Dizionarietto della lingua italiana lussuosa. Rizzoli Edit.
Giannelli, Ciro. Un Lexique Macedonien du XV Siecle. Inst Etudes Slaves.
Giarratano, Joseph C. Timex-Sinclair One Thousand Pocket Dictionary. Que Corp.
Gibbons, John, jt. auth. see Fraser, Edward.
Gibbs, C. R. Dictionnaire Technique du Cinema: Anglais-Francais. Film Et Technique.
Gibbs, George. Alphabetical Vocabularies of the Clallam & Lumni. AMS Pr.
--Alphabetical Vocabulary of the Chinook Language. AMS Pr.
--Dictionary of the Chinook Jargon, or Trade Languages of Oregon. AMS Pr.
--Dictionary of the Nisqually Indian Language of Western Washington. Shorey.
Gibney, Frank, jt. ed. see Timmons, Christine.
Gibson, Carol, ed. The Facts on File Dictionary of Mathematics. Facts on File.
Gibson, Haldo. Svensk Slangordbok. Esselte Studium.
Gidmark, Jill B. Melville Sea Dictionary: A Glossed Concordance & Analysis of the Sea Language in Melville's Nautical Novels. Greenwood.
Gieber, Robert L. An English-French Glossary of Educational Terminology. U Pr of Amer.
Gifis, Steven H. Law Dictionary. Barron.
Gignoux, Phillipe. Glossaire des Inscriptions Pehlevies et Parthes. Intl Pubns Serv.
Gil, Beatriz Massa De see Massa De Gil, Beatriz.
Gil, Beatriz Massa De see Massa de Gil, Beatriz, et al.
Gil, Francisco, tr. see Tosco, Uberto.
Gil, L. S. Diccionario Tecnico-Maritimo Ingles-Espanol & Espanol-Ingles. Edit Alhambra.
Gil, L. Suarez, ed. Diccionario Tecnico Maritimo: Ingles-Espanol, Espanol-Ingles. French & Eur.
Gilbert, Allan H. A Geographical Dictionary of Milton. Arden Lib.
--Geographical Dictionary of Milton. Russell.
Gilbert, Jayne, jt. auth. see Rose, Jim.
Gilbert, Pierre. Dictionnaire des Mots Nouveaux. Tchou.
Gilbertson, G. Harrap's German & English Glossary of Terms in International Law. Harrap.
Gilboy, Robert C. Spell It Fast! The Quick Way to Spell Using Sixty Stimualting Word Lists. Acropolis.
Gil Esteban, Rafael. English-Spanish Banking Dictionary. Autores Propias.
Gili Gaya, S. D. Diccionario De Sinonimos. Colton Bk.
Gili Gaya, Samuel. Diccionario Abreviado de Sinonimos. Biblograf SP.
--Diccionario de Sinonimos. Biblograf SP.
--Diccionario de sinonimos. Natl Textbk.
--Diccionario Escolar de la Lengua Espanola. Biblograf SP.
--Ortografia Practica Espanola Vox. Biblo SP.
--Tesoro Lexicografico 1492-1726. CSIS.
--Vox--Diccionario de Sinonimos. French & Eur.
Gili Gaya, Samuel, rev. by. Diccionario Fundamental de la Lengua Espanola. Biblograf SP.
Gili Gaya, Samuel D., ed. see Menendez Pidal, Ramon D.
Gilissen, Theodor, jt. auth. see Thole, B. L.
Gilkey, Robert, ed. & intro. by. The Chinese Unicorn & Other Conceits from a Chinese Dictionary. Noname Pr.
Gilmer, Wesley. Cochran's Law Lexicon. Anderson Pub Co.
--The Law Dictionary (ScribT). Scribner.
Gilmore, William, ed. see Technical Association of the Pulp & Paper Industry Winding Committee.
Gilot, Michel, jt. auth. see Sgard, Jean.
Gilpin, Alan. Dictionary of Environmental Terms. U of Queensland Pr.
Gil-Robles, Jose M. Diccionario De Terminos Electrorales y Parlamentarios. French & Eur.
Gil-Robles y Quinones, Jose M. Diccionario de Terminos Electorales & Parlamentarios. Taurus Ediciones SA.
Gil Suarez, L. see Suarez Gil, L.
Gimenez Sales, Miguel. Diccionario Espanol-Frances, Espagnol-Francais. French & Eur.
Gimeno, E. Diccionario Lexicon Frances-Espanol, Espanol-Frances. French & Eur.
Gingrich, F. Wilbur, ed. Shorter Lexicon of the Greek New Testament. U of Chicago Pr.
Ginguay. Diccionario de informatica. Toray-Masson.
Ginguay, M. Dictionnaire d'Informatique: Anglais-Francais. French & Eur.
Ginguay, Michael. Diccionario De Informatica. French & Eur.
Ginguay, Michel. Dictionnaire D'informatique Anglais-Francais. Masson & Cie.
Ginguay, Michel & Lauret, Annette. Lexique d'informatique. Masson & Cie.
--Lexique d'Informatique. French & Eur.
Ginzburg, M. L., et al. Nemetsko-Russkii Elektrotekhnicheskii Slovar (Pub. by Gosizdat Fizmatlit). Four Continent.
Gioello & Berke. Fashion Production Terms. Fairchild.
Giomot, Sylvain. Dictionnaire de la Publicite et du Marketing: Anglais-Francais Francais-Anglais. Maison Dictionnaire.
Giordano, Albert G. Concise Dictionary of Business Terminology (Spec). P-H.
Giordano, Eduardo, tr. see Vani, Paule.
Giovannelli. Dizionario italiano-tedesco e tedesco-italiano. Signorelli C.
Giovannelli, Paolo & Frenzel, Walter. Langenscheidts Handwoerterbuch Italienisch-Deutsch. Langenscheidt.
--Langenscheidts Handwoerterbuch Italienisch: Teil I, Italienisch-Deutsch. Langenscheidt.
Giovannelli, Paolo, ed. Langenscheidts Handwoerterbuecher: Tl 1, Italienisch-Deutsch. Langenscheidt.
Giovannelli, Paolo, ed. see Storni, Bruno.
Giovanni, Boccali. Concordantiae verbales opuscolorum S. Francisci et S. Clarae Assisiensium. LIEF.
Giovannoni, Jeanne M. & Becerra, Rosina. Defining Child Abuse. Free Pr.
Girace, A., jt. auth. see Fusella, L.
Giraldi, Giovanni. Dizionario di estetica & di linguistica generale. Pergamena.
Girard, Denis. Dictionnaire Francais-Anglais. Garnier.
--Dictionnaire Francais-Anglais et Anglais-Francais. French & Eur.
Girard, Denis, et al. Cassell's French Dictionary: French-English, English-French. Imported Bks.
Girard, Denis, et al, eds. Cassell's French Dictionary. Macmillan.
Giraud, Alejandro F. S. Diccionario Comercial Ingles-Espanol, Espanol-Ingles. Editorial Juventud.
Giraudeau & Gore, Francis. Dictionnaire Francais-Tibetain. Maisonneuve, A.
Giraudeau, A. & Gore, Francis. Dictionnaire Francais-Tibetain (Tibet Oriental) French & Eur.
Girodet, J. Dictionnaire du Bon Francais. French & Eur.
Girodet, Jean. Logos: Grand Dictionnaire de la Langue Francaise. Bordas.
Girodet, Jean, ed. Logos-Grand Dictionnaire de la Langue Francaise. Harrap.
Girolami-Boulinier, Andree. Vocabulaire & Language. Delachaux.
Giroux, S., jt. auth. see Maurais, J.
Gisbert. Diccionario manual espanol-ruso. Pueblos Unidos.
Gisbert, jt. auth. see De Toro, M.
Gisbert, M. Toro de see De Toro Gisbert, M.
Giteau, Cecile. Dictionnaire des Arts du Spectacle. Bordas-Dunod.
--Dictionnaire des Arts du Spectacle: Theatre, Cinema, Cirque, Danse, Radio... French & Eur.
Giua, Michele, jt. auth. see Giua Lollini, Clara.
Giua Lollini, Clara & Giua, Michele. Dizionario tedesco-italiano per le scienze chimiche e affini. Rosenberg & Sel.
Giurdzhian, A. A., et al, eds. Anglo-Russkii Slovar Po Aviatsionno-Kosmicheskoi Meditsine (Pub. by Voenizdat). Four Continent.
Gives, L., et al. Dizionario inglese-italiano-francese-tedesco. De Bono.
--Dizionario italiano-inglese-francese-tedesco. De Bono.
Gladstone. Vocabulaire De Medecine & Des Sciences Connexes Anglais-Francais-Anglais. French & Eur.
Gladstone, W. J. Dictionnaire Anglais-Francais des Sciences Medicales & Paramedicales. Edisem.
--Dictionnaire Anglais-Francais des Sciences Medicales et Paramedicales. Maloine.
--Dictionnaire Anglais-Francais des Sciences Medicales et Paramedicales. French & Eur.
--Dictionnaire Anglais-Francais: Sciences Medicales & Paramedicales. Maloine.
--Vocabulaire de Medecine & des Sciences Connexes: Francais-Anglais. Masson & Cie.
Gladstone, William J. Dictionnaire Anglais-Francais des Sciences Medicales & Paramedicales. Maloine.
Glaister, Geoffrey. Glaister's Glossary of the Book: Terms Used in Paper-Making, Printing, Bookbinding, & Publishing. U of Cal Pr.
Glanze, Walter D. Longman Dictionary of Psychology & Psychoanalysis. Longman.
Glare, G. P., ed. Oxford Latin Dictionary, Fascicle 4. Gorgonia-Libero. Oxford U Pr.
Glare, P. G. Oxford Latin Dictionary: Fascicle 8. Oxford U Pr.
Glare, P. G., ed. Oxford Latin Dictionary. Oxford U Pr.
--Oxford Latin Dictionary: Fascicle 1, a-Calcitro. Oxford U Pr.
--Oxford Latin Dictionary: Fascicle 2, Calcitro-Demitto. Oxford U Pr.
--Oxford Latin Dictionary, Fascicle 3: Demiurgus-Gorgoneus. Oxford U Pr.
--Oxford Latin Dictionary: Fascicle 7. Oxford U Pr.
Glare, P. G. W., ed. Oxford Latin Dictionary: Fascicle 6-a-Calcitro. Oxford U Pr.
Glass, G. Englische Rechtssprache: Mustertexte & Fachausdruecke unter Einbeziehung von Amerikanismen. Bauverlag.
Glass, Stuart. A Divorce Dictionary: A Book for You & Your Children. Little.
Glazebrook, Richard, ed. A Dictionary of Applied Physics. Peter Smith.
Glazer, Edward, jt. ed. see Pyle, Ian.
Glazier. Least You Should Know About Vocabulary. HR&W.
Gleasner, Diana C. Illustrated Swimming, Diving & Surfing Dictionary for Young People. Harvey.
Gloag, John. A Short Dictionary of Furniture. Allen Unwin.
Glucksman, Paul H., ed. World-Wide German Dictionary (Prem). Fawcett.
Glucksmann, A., et al. Meyers Taschenlexikon Urheberrecht. Bibl Inst Leipzig.
Gluskina, A. E., et al. Kratkii Russko-Iaponskii Slovar (Pub. by GINS). Four Continent.
Glustrom, Simon. Language of Judaism. Ktav.
Glut, Donald F. The Dinosaur Dictionary. Citadel Pr.
--The Dinosaur Dictionary. Citadel Pr.
--The New Dinosaur Dictionary. Citadel Pr.
Gluzman, I. S. Anglo-Russkii Slovar Zheleznodorozhnoi Automatike, Telemekhanike & Sviazi (Pub. by Gosizdat Fizmat. Lit.). Four Continent.
Gobel, Marianne T. Szlovak-Magyar Szotar. Terra.
Gobello, Jose. Diccionario Lunfardo & de Otros Terminos Antiguos & Modernos Usuales. Pena Lillo.
--Diccionario Lunfardo Ilustrado. French & Eur.
Goble, Ermina S., ed. see Calasibetta, Charlotte M.
Gochberg, Herbert S., jt. ed. see Switzer, Richard.
Goddard, Ives. Delaware Verbal Morphology: A Descriptive & Comparative Study. Hankamer, Jorge, ed. Garland Pub.
Gode, P. K., et al, eds. Practical Sanskrit-English Dictionary. Prasarnmitr.

Godefroy, Frederic. Dictionnaire de L'ancienne Langue Francaise. Kraus.
--Lexique Compare de la Langue de Corneille. Kraus.
--Lexique de l'ancien Francais. Champion.
--Lexique de l'ancien Francais. Olms.
--Lexique de l'ancien Francais. French & Eur.
Godman, Arthur. Barnes & Noble Thesaurus of Chemistry. B&N NY.
--Barnes & Noble Thesaurus of Science. B&N NY.
--Illustrated Dictionary of Chemistry. Longman.
Goedecke. Woerterbuch der Elektrotechnik Fernmeldetechnik & Elektronik: Band I, Deutsch-Englisch-Franzoesisch. Brandstetter.
--Woerterbuch der Elektrotechnik Fernmeldetechnik & Elektronik: Band II, Franzoesisch-Englisch-Deutsch. Brandstetter.
--Woerterbuch der Elektrotechnik Fernmeldetechnik & Elektronik: Band III, Englisch-Deutsch-Franzoesisch. Brandstetter.
Goedecke, W. Woerterbuch der Elektrotechnik, Fernmeldetechnik und Elektonik. French & Eur.
--Woerterbuch der Elektrotechnik, Fernmeldetechnik und Elektronik. French & Eur.
Goedecke, Werner. Woerterbuch der Wirkstoffprufung. VDI-Verlag.
Goehler, Erich. Lexikon des Nebenstrafrechts. French & Eur.
Goehler, Erich, et al. Lexikon des Nebenstrafrechts. Beck Verlag.
Goelzer, Henri. Dictionnaire Francais-Latin. Garnier-Flammarion.
--Dictionnaire Francais-Latin. Garnier.
--Dictionnaire Latin-Francais. Garnier.
--Dictionnaire Latin-Francais. Garnier.
--Dictionnaire Latin-Francais. Garnier.
Goerlitz. Handlexikon zur Politikwissenschaft. Rowohlt.
--Handlexikon Zur Politikwissenschaft (Pub. by Rowohlt). French & Eur.
Goerner, H. & Kempcke, G., eds. Synonymwoerterbuch. Bibl Inst Leipzig.
Goerner, Horst, jt. auth. see Hueter, Paul.
Goeschel, H. & Zwahr, A., eds. Meyers Universal Lexikon. Bibl Inst Leipzig.
--Meyers Universal Lexikon. Bibl Inst Leipzig.
--Meyers Universal Lexikon. Bibl Inst Leipzig.
--Meyers Universal Lexikon. Bibl Inst Leipzig.
Goetze, Alfred. Fruehneuhochdeutsches Glossar. De Gruyter.
Goetze, Alfred & Mitzka, Walther, eds. Truebners Deutsches Woerterbuch. De Gruyter.
Goldberg, Nathan. New Functional Hebrew-English, English-Hebrew Dictionary. Ktav.
--New Illustrated Hebrew-English Dictionary for Young Readers. Ktav.
Goldhahn, Irmgard. Kleines Medizinisches Fremdworterbuch. Thieme Verlag.
Goldman, Alex J. Child's Dictionary of Jewish Symbols. Feldheim.
Goldstein, et al. Lexico de la Sexualidad. Loguez Edns.
Goldstein, Melvyn C. Tibetan-English Dictionary of Modern Tibetan. Himalaya Hse.
Goldstein, Sam. The Birdicide of Cock Robin, & Other Murderous Words Ending in Cide. Winds World Pr.
Goldstein-Jackson, Kevin, compiled by. The Dictionary of Essential Quotations. B&N Imports.
Goliakova, N. V., et al. Russko-Frantsuzskii Shkol'No-Pedagogicheskii Slovar (Pub. by Sov. Entsiklopediia). Four Continent.
Golian, Milan. L'aspect Verbal en Francais (Pub. by Helmut Buske Verlag Hamburg). Benjamins North Am.

Goliard, Roy. Scholar's Glossary of Sex. Heineman.
Goma, Eulalia. Diccionario Magico Infantil. Vilamala.
--Diccionario Magico Infantil. Vilamala.
--Diccionario Magico Infantil. French & Eur.
--Diccionario Magico Infantil En Seis Lenguas. French & Eur.
Goma, F. S. De see Marole, L. T. & De Goma, F. S.
Gomer, E. Swedish Modern Pocket Dictionary: Svensk-Engelsk, Engelsk-Svensk Grammatik Parlor. Vanous.
Gomez, Joan. Diccionario de Sintomas. Acervo.
--Diccionario de Sintomas. French & Eur.
--A Dictionary of Symptoms. Stein & Day.
--Dizionario dei sintomi. Ferrario, E. V., tr. Garzanti Edit.
Gomez de Cadiz, Javier. Diccionario de Siglas. Alas.
--Diccionario de Sigles de Organismos Nacionales e Internacionales. French & Eur.
Gomez de Parada, Alejandro. Diccionario Porrua Ingles-Espanol. Porrua.
--Diccionario Porrua Ingles-Espanol. Porrua.
--Diccionario Porrua ingles-espanol, espanol-ingles. Porrua.
Gomez de Segura Beaumont, Angel J. Diccionario Infantil Fher. French & Eur.
Gonfroy, Gerard. Dictionnaire Normatif Limousin-Francais. Lemouzi.
--Dictionnaire Normatif Limousin-Francais. Lemouzi.
Gonsalvo Mainar, Gonzalo. Diccionario De Metologia Estadistica. French & Eur.
Gonzalez Bonorino, Gonzalo. Lexico sedimentologico. Museo Arg. Ciencias Nat.
Gonzalez Gutierrez, O. Diccionario de expresiones idiomaticas y modismos ingleses. EUDEBA.
Gonzalez Gutierrez, Orlando. Diccionario de Expresiones Idiomaticas y Modismo Ingleses. French & Eur.
Gonzalez Hevia, Raul, tr. see Brown, R. H.
Gonzalez Marimon, Blanca. Diccionario de falsos amigos, frances-espanol. Alhambra.
Gonzalez Salas, Manual. Vocabulario Popular Sevillano. Prensa Espanola.
Gooch, Anthony & Garcia de Paredes, Angel. Diccionario Major Ingles-Espanol, Espanol-Ingles. Diafora.
Goock, R., jt. auth. see Finke, K.
Goock, Roland. Neues Taschenlexikon. Prae Heinz.
Good, Claude. Diccionario Triqui de Chicahuaxtla. French & Eur.
Good, Richard, ed. see Britten, F. J.
Goodenough, Ward H. & Sugita, Hiroshi. Trukese-English Dictionary. Am Philos.
Goodier, J. H. Dictionary of Painting & Decorating (Pub. by Griffin England). State Mutual Bk.
Goodrich, L. Carrington & Fang, Chaoying, eds. Dictionary of Ming Biography, 1364-1644. Columbia U Pr.
Goodrick, Edward W. & Kohlenberger, John R., III. The NIV Handy Concordance. Zondervan.
Goodspeed, Edgar J., jt. auth. see Owen, William B.
Gora, Zielona, jt. auth. see Kania, Stanislaw.
Gorbachevich, S., et al. Slovar Epitetov Russkogo Literaturnogo Iazyka (Pub. by Nauka). Four Continent.
Gordo-Guarinos, Francisco. Diccionario De Sinonimos y Antonimos. French & Eur.
Gordo Guarinos, Francisco. Diccionario Escolar Roble. French & Eur.
Gordo-Guarinos, Francisco. Diccionario Manual De la Lengua Espanol a-Z. French & Eur.
--Diccionario Manual De la Lengua Espanol A-Z. French & Eur.

Gordon, Bonnie. The Anatomy of the Image Maps According to Merriam-Webster's Third International Dictionary of the English Language: Unabridged. Visual Studies.
Gordon, Frank S. & Hemnes, Thomas. The Legal Word Book. HM.
Gore, Francis, jt. auth. see Giraudeau.
Gore, Francis, jt. auth. see Giraudeau, A.
Goretti, Maria, jt. auth. see Lamanna, Paolo E.
Gorgoni, G. Vocabolario agronomico nel dialetto della provincia de Lecce. Forni.
Gori, Roland-Claude & Poinso, Yves. Dictionnaire Pratique de Psychopathologie. Delarge.
Gorina, R. Russian Fare. Saphrograph.
Gorlitz, Axel. Diccionario de Ciencia Politica. Alianza Ed.
--Diccionario de Ciencia Politica. French & Eur.
Gorner, Horst. Kleines Polytechnisches Woerterbuch Russisch-Deutsch. VEB Technik.
Gorner, Horst & Fedirko, J. V. Kleines Polytechnisches Woerterbuch. VEB Verlag Technik.
Gorochow, P. K. Russisch-Deutsches Worterbuch der Funkechnik. French & Eur.
Gorog, Ralph De see De Gorog, Ralph.
Gorokhov, P. K. Russko-Nemetskii Radiotekhnicheskii Slovar (Pub. by Glav. Red. Inostr. Nauchno-Tekhn. Slovarei Fizmata). Glav. Red. Inostr. Nauchno-Tekhn. Slovarei Fizmata.
Gorski, N. N., et al. Deutsch-Russisches Worterbuch fur Ozeanographie. French & Eur.
Gorskii, D. P., ed see Kondakov, N. I.
Gorskii, N. N., et al. Nemetsko-Russkii Okeanograficheskii Slovar (Pub. by GINS). Four Continent.
Gorys, Erhard. Heimerans Kuchenlexikon. Kochbuch Verlag.
Gosetti, Fernanda. Dizinari dei Formaggi: Tutte le Notizie le Ricette come & con che Cosa Servirli. Marietti.
--Dizionario dei formaggi. Marietti.
--Dizionario dei formaggi. AMZ.
Goshen, Charles E., jt. auth. see Fann, William E.
Goshen-Gottstein, Moshe H. A Syriac-English Glossary: With Etymological Notes, Based on Brockelmann's Syriac Chrestomathy. Intl Pubns Serv.
Gostony, Colman G. Dictionnaire d'etymologie Sumerienne & Grammaire Comparee. Boccard.
--Dictionnaire d'Etymologie Sumerienne et Grammaire Comparee. French & Eur.
Gotch, A. F. Birds: Their Latin Names Explained (Pub. by Blandford Pr England). Sterling.
--Mammals: Their Latin Names Explained (Pub. by Blandford Pr England). Sterling.
Gottfredson, Gary D. & Holland, John L. Dictionary of Holland Occupational Codes. Consulting Psychol.
Gottfried, Bert A., jt. ed. see Clark, Donald T.
Gottschalg, J. & Just, K., eds. Jugendlexikon Politische Okonomie. Bibl Inst Leipzig.
Gottschalg, J. & Wolter, G., eds. Jugendlexikon Wissenschaftlicher Kommunismus. Bibl Inst Leipzig.
Gottschalk, Herbert. Lexikon der Mythologie der Eurpaeischen Voelker. French & Eur.
Gottschalk, W., jt. auth. see Taylor, Ronald J.
Gottschalk, Walter, ed. see Sachs, Karl & Villatte, Cesaire.
Gotze, Alfred. Trubners Deutsches Woerterbuch (Pub. by de Gruyter). French & Eur.
Gouchou, Henry J. Le Dictionnaire Astrologique. Dervy Livres.
--Le Dictionnaire Astrologique. French & Eur.
Gougenheim, G. Dictionnaire du Francais Fondamental (Dist. by Continental Bk Co). Didier.

Gougenheim, Georges. Dictionnaire Fondamental. Didier.
Gough, H. A Glossary of Terms Used in Heraldry. Gordon Pr.
Gould. IFIP Sachwoerterbuch der Datenverarbeitung. Verlag Harri Deutsch.
Gould Editorial Dept. Dictionary of Criminal Justice Terms. Gould.
Gould, I. IFIP-Sach Worterbuch der Datenverarbeitung (Pub. by Verlag Harri Deutsch). French & Eur.
Gould, Julius & Kolb, W. J. UNESCO Dictionary of the Social Sciences. Free Pr.
Gould, L. Harry. Marxist Glossary. Proletarian Pubs.
Gould, S. H. & Obreanu, P. E., eds. Romanian-English Dictionary & Grammar for the Mathematical Sciences. Am Math.
Goutel, Beatrice, jt. auth. see Carillon, Annie.
Governa, Mario. Dizionario di termini medici di uso comune. ERI.
Gowers, Ernest, ed. see Fowler, Henry W.
Goyau, G., jt. auth. see Cagnat, Rene.
Goyoaga, Ricardo, jt. auth. see Regueiro, Marina.
Gozmany, L., et al, eds. Septemlingual Dictionary of the Names of European Animal (Pub. by Kiado Hungary). Heyden.
Gozmany, Laslo. Septemligual Dictionary of the Names of European Animals (Pub. by Collet's). State Mutual Bk.
Gozmany, Laszlo, ed. Septemlingual Dictionary of the Names of European Animals. Intl Pubns Serv.
Graa, Albert, ed. Vocabularium Pharmaceuticum. Intl Pubns Serv.
Grabbe, Hans J. Bauherren-Lexikon. Vieweg.
Grabmueller, Klaus, pref. by. Vocabulaius Teutonico-Latinus. Olms Verlag.
Grad, A. Dictionary French-Slovene. French & Eur.
--Dictionnaire Moderne: Slovene-French-Slovene. French & Eur.
--Dizionario Moderno Slovene-Italian-Slovene. French & Eur.
Grad, A., jt. auth. see Kotnik, J.
Grad, A., ed. Diccionario Esloveno-Espanol. French & Eur.
Grad, A., et al. English-Slovene Dictionary. French & Eur.
--Yugoslavic Dictionary: English-Slovene. Vanous.
Graesse, Johann G. Orbis Latinus: Lexikon lateinischer geographischer Namen des Mittelalters und der Neuzeit. Plechl, Helmut, ed. Intl Pubns Serv.
Graham, John. Facts on File Dictionary of Telecommunications. Facts on File.
Graham, Peter. El Diccionario del cine. Novaro.
Graham, William. The Scots Word Book. Ramsay Head Pr.
Grahame-White, G. K., ed. see Horner, J. G.
Grallert, V., et al, eds. Filatelisticheskii Slovar (Pub. by Sviaz). Four Continent.
Gran, Claurene du see Du Gran, Claurene.
Grandgagnage, Charles-Marie. Dictionnaire Etymologique de la Langue Wallonne. Slatkine.
Grandis, Valentino & Donati, Mario. Dizionario tedesco-italiano di biologia e medicina. Rosenberg & Sel.
Grandpre, Jean-Paul. Vocabulaire des Assurances Sur la Vie. Quebec Off.
Grandpre, Jean-Paul de see De Grandpre, Jean-Paul.
Granoble, jt. auth. see Allard, Guy.
Grant, Bruce K. A Guide to Korean Characters: Reading & Writing Hangul & Hanja. Hollym Corp.
--A Guide to Korean Characters: Reading & Writing Hangul & Hanja. Hollym Intl.
Grant, Gail. Technical Manual & Dictionary of Classical Ballet. Dover.
Grant, Julius. Hackh's Chemical Dictionary (P&RB). McGraw.

Grant, Maurice. A Dictionary of British Landscape Painters: From the 16th Century to the Early 20th Century (Pub. by A & C Black England). Humanities.
Grant, Maurice H. A Dictionary of British Landscape Painters: From the 16th to the 20th Century. Intl Pubns Serv.
Grant, W. Parks. Handbook of Music Terms. Scarecrow.
Granville, Wilfred. Theater Dictionary: British & American Terms in the Drama, Opera, and Ballet. Greenwood.
Grapp, Valera. Paralegal's Encyclopedic Dictionary. P-H.
Grappin, P. Dictionnaire moderne Larousse, francais-allemand et allemand-francais. Larousse.
--Dictionnaire Moderne Saturne: Francais-Allemand. Larousse FR.
Gras, Louis-Pierre. Dictionnaire du Patols Forezien. Slatkine.
Grassi. Vocabolario della lingua italiana. Vallardi A.
Grassi, C. Vocabolarietto della Lingua Italiana. French & Eur.
Grassi, Luigi & Pepe, Mario. Dizionario della critica d'arte. UTET.
Grates. Diccionario de sinonimos castellanos. Sopena.
--Diccionario de Sinonimos Castellanos. Sopena.
--Diccionario de Sinonimos Castellanos (SPA). Lectorum Pubns.
Grau, Wolfgang. Woerterbuch der Photo, Film und Kinotechnik. French & Eur.
Graur, Alexandru. Dictionar de Cuvinte Calatoare. Albatros.
Graves, Algernon. Dictionary of Artists: London Exhibitions 1760-1893. Newbury Bks.
--The Royal Academy of Arts, a Complete Dictionary of Contributors & Their Work from Its Foundation in 1769 to 1904, Compiled with the Sanction of the President & Council of the Royal Academy. B Franklin.
Graves, B., jt. auth. see Schmidt-Joos, S.
Graves, Donald E. French Military Terminology, 1670-1815. New Bruns Mus.
Gray, H. J. & Isaacs, A., eds. A New Dictionary of Physics. Longman.
Gray, Peter. Dictionary of the Biological Sciences. Van Nos Reinhold.
Gray, Peter, ed. Student Dictionary of Biology. Van Nos Reinhold.
Grebe, Paul. Bedeutungswoerterbuch: Bedeutung & Gebrauch der Woerter. Biblio Inst.
--Sammlung Duden: Band III, Akten zur Geschichte der Deutschen Einheitsschreibung. Biblio Inst.
Grebenshchikov, O. S. Geobotanic Dictionary. Lubrecht & Cramer.
Greco, Salvatore, jt. auth. see Durand, Roger H.
Grecu, Mitica, et al. Dictionar Roman-Turc. Editura Stiintifica.
Green, Thomas E. & Osler, Robert W. Glossary of Insurance Terms. Merritt Co.
Greenberg, Milton, jt. auth. see Plano, Jack C.
Greene, Lawrence G., jt. ed. see Radin, Max.
Greenman, Robert. Captive Vocabulary. NY Times.
Greenough, J. B., ed. see Virgil.
Greenslade-Moore, Dianne, ed. see Kosbab, William H.
Greenstein, Carol. Dictionary of Logical Terms & Symbols. Van Nos Reinhold.
--Dictionary of Logical Terms & Symbols. Van Nos Reinhold.
Greenwald, Douglas, et al. The McGraw-Hill Dictionary of Modern Economics (P&RB). McGraw.
Greer, R. Dictionary of One Thousand Dreams. Stein Pub.
Gregg, J. R. & Leslie, L. A. Gregg Shorthand Dictionary. Mcgraw.
Gregorich, Barbara. Dictionary Skills. EDC.
--Expanding Your Vocabulary. Soc for Visual.
Greimas, Algirdas J. & Courtes, Joseph. Seminotique: Dictionnaire Raisonne de la Theorie du Language. Hachette-Jeunesse.
Greimas, Julien A. Dictionnaire de l'Ancien Francais. Larousse.
Greiner-Mai, H., jt. ed. see Steiner, G.
Grenier, Jean Guy. Dictionnaire Anglais-Francais D'electrotechnique. Lanaudiere.
Greutyner, jt. auth. see Johnson.
Gribanova, E. P. Karmannyi Russko-Norvezhskii Slovar (Pub. by GINS). Four Continent.
Gribble, Charles E. Russian Root List with a Sketch of Russian Word Formation. Slavica.
--Short Dictionary of Eighteenth Century Russian. Slavica.
Grieffenberg, C. R. von see Moeller, Hilke.
Grieken, J. E. Van see Van Grieken, J. E.
Grigg, Carolyn D., compiled by. Music Translation Dictionary: An English, Czech, Danish, Dutch, French, German, Hungarian, Italian, Polish, Portuguese, Russian, Spanish, Swedish Vocabulary of Music. Greenwood.
Grignon, Jean. Lexique Mathematique. F. I. C.
--Lexique Mathematique, Symboles, Vocabulaire, Tables. Centre Psych.
Grigorian, V. Z., et al. Russko-Armianskii Tolkovyi Slovar (Pub. by An Arm SSR). Four Continent.
Grigorovich, M. V., et al. Slovar Po Mineral Nomu Syriu Dlia Promyshlennosti Stroitelnykh Materialov (Pub. by Nedra). Four Continent.
Grimal, Pierre. Dictionnaire de la Mythologie Grecque et Romaine. French & Eur.
Grimal, Pierre & Payarois, Francisco. Diccionario de Mitologia Griega & Romana. Paidos Iberica.
Grimm, J. & Grimm, W. Deutsches Woerterbuch. Herzel Verlag.
Grimm, Jacob & Grimm, Wilhelm. Deutsches Woerterbuch. Adler.
Grimm, W., jt. auth. see Grimm, J.
Grimm, Wilhelm, jt. auth. see Grimm, Jacob.
Grimod, Francesco & Caselli, G. Vocabolario italiano-francese e francese-italiano. Dante Alighieri.
Grischen, N. Deutsch-Russische Wirtschaftssprache. Hueber.
--Deutsch-Russische Wirtschaftssprache (Pub. by M. Hueber). French & Eur.
Gritschneder, Otto. Ullstein Lexikon des Rechts (Pub. by Ullstein Verlag/VVA). French & Eur.
Groff, Lionello. Dizionario trentino-italiano. Monauni.
Gronbarj, M., ed. see Akerlung, Alfred.
Grootaers, Ludovic. Dictionnaire Classique Francais-Neerlandais. Vander.
--Dictionnaire Classique: Francais-Neerlandais, Neerlandais-Francais. French & Eur.
--Le Nouveau Dictionnaire Francais-Neerlandais, Nederlands-Francais. French & Eur.
Groothoff, Hans. Lexikon Fuer Eltern und Erzieher. French & Eur.
Groothoff, Hans H., et al, eds. Lexikon fuer Eltern & Erzieher. Gutersloher V.
--Lexikon fuer Eltern & Erzieher. Kreuz Verlag.
Grose, Frances. Dictionary of Vulgar Tongue, 1811. Macmillan London.
Grose, Francis. A Classical Dictionary of the Vulgar Tongue. Partridge, E., ed. Ayer Co.
Gross. Woerterbuch. Verlag Harri Deutsch.
--Woerterbuch Chemie & Chemische Technik. Incl. Vol. 1; Vol. 2. Verlag Harri Deutsch.
Gross & Hildebrand. Kleines Woerterbuch Chemie & Chemische Technik. Verlag Harri Deutsch.
--Kleines Woerterbuch Chemie & Chemische Technik. Verlag Harri Deutsch.
Gross, H. Woerterbuch Chemie und Chemische Technik. French & Eur.
Gross, H. & Hildebrand, H. Kleines Worterbuch der Chemie und Chem. Technik (Pub. by Verlag Harri Deutsch). French & Eur.
Gross, Helmut. Chemie & Chemische Technik Russisch-Deutsch. VEB Technik.
--Elektrotechnik Elektronik Russisch-Deutsch. VEB Technik.
--Kleines Woerterbuch der Chemie & Chemischen Technik. VEB Verlag Technik.
--Kleines Woerterbuch der Chemie & Chemischen Technik Russisch-Deutsch. VEB Technik.
--Kleines Woerterbuch der Elektrotechnik Elektronik Russisch-Deutsch. VEB Technik.
--Korrosion & Korrosionsschutz Deutsch-Russisch. VEB Technik.
Gross, Helmut & Hildebrand, Helmut. Chemie & Chemische Technik. VEB Verlag Technik.
Grosse, E. Dictionnaire d'Antiphilosophisme ou Refutation des Erreurs du 18e Siecle. Migne, J. P., ed. Caratzas Pub Co.
Grosse, Walter G., et al, eds. Versicherungsenzykolpaedie. Gabler.
Grosset, jt. auth. see Cortina.
Grossman, Herbert J., ed. Manual on Terminology & Classification in Mental Retardation. Am Assn Mental.
Grossman, Paul & Lang, Viktor, eds. Kleines Lexikon zur Politischen Bildung. Hornung-Verlag.
Grossman, R., jt. ed. see Slaby, R. J.
Grossmann. Englisches Handelsvokabularium Nach Sachgebieten (Pub. by Th. Grossmann). French & Eur.
Grossmann & Friedmann. Kaufmannisches Grundworte Buch Fur Schule und Praxis (Pub. by Fachverlag Th. Grossmann). French & Eur.
Grossmann, jt. auth. see Slaby.
Grossmann, T. & Friedmann, G. Kaufmaenisches Grundwoerterbuch fuer Schule & Praxis: Part I, Deutsch-Englisch. M. Rosenberg.
--Kaufmannisches Grundwoerterbuch fuer Schule und Praxis: Deutsch-Englisch. M Rosenberg.
Grotpeter, John J. Historical Dictionary of Swaziland. Scarecrow.
--Historical Dictionary of Zambia. Scarecrow.
Groves, Donald G., jt. auth. see Hunt, Lee M.
Gruber, Albion, ed. see Brossard.
Gruber, Clemens. Dictionary of Advertising & Marketing. Adler.
--Woerterbuch der Werbung und des Marketing. French & Eur.
Grue-Sorensen, K. & Winther-Jensen, Thyge, eds. Paedagogikkens Hvem Hvad Hvor. Politikens Forlag.
Grujic, B. Dictionnaire Serbocrate-Francais, Francais-Serbocroate, suivi d'une courte grammaire de Langue Francaise. French & Eur.
--Serbocroatian-English, English-Serbocroatian Dictionary. Heinman.
--Serbocroatian-English-Serbocroatian Dictionary: Short Grammar. Vanous.
Grujic, J. English-Serbo-Croat & Serbo-Croat-English Dictionary (Pub. by Collet's). State Mutual Bk.
Grujic, V. C. English-Serbocroat & Serbocroat-English Dictionary (Pub. by Collets). State Mutual Bk.
Grund. Benezit Dictionary of Artists. Apollo.
Grundman, jt. auth. see Pulliam.
Grundman, Claire, jt. ed. see Pulliam, Tom.
Grunwald-Beyer, A. Technisches Taschenwoerterbuch (Pub. by Georg Siemens Verlagsbuchhandlung). French & Eur.
Grunwedal, Albert, jt. ed. see Mainwaring, G. B.
Gruss, Robert. Dictionnaire de Marine. Maritimes Outre mer.
--Dictionnaire de Marine, Francais et Anglais. French & Eur.
Grzebieniowski, T. Concise English-Polish & Polish-English Dictionary. Barron.
--Illustrated English-Polish Polish-English Dictionary (Pub. by Wiedza Powszechna). Four Continent.
Grzebieniowski, Tadeusz, ed. Illustrated English-Polish Polish-English Dictionary. Intl Pubns Serv.
Grzebieniowski, Takeusz. Ilustrowany slownik angielsko-polski, polsko-angielski. Wiedza Powszechna.
Grzebienowski, Tadeus Z. Polish-English, English-Polish Dictionary. Hippocrene Bks.
Grzywaczewski, Zbigniew. Okrety i Zegluga. Wydawnictwa Naukowo.
Gual Camarena, Miguel. Vocabulario del Comercio Medieval. French & Eur.
Gualtieri, jt. auth. see Lysle.
Gualtieri, F. M. Dizionario italiano-inglese e inglese-italiano. Casanova F & C.
Gualtieri, Franceso M. Dizionario inglese moderno. Trevisini.
Guardia Mayarga, Cesar. Diccionario Kechwa-Castellano. Studium.
Guardia Mayorga, Cesar. Diccionario kechua-castellano, castellano-kechua. Peisa.
Guarino, Giuseppe. Dizionario Amministrativo. Giuffre.
--Dizionario amministrativo. Giuffre.
Guarnieri, M. & Guarnieri, O. Dizionario Tecnico Tedesco-Italiano, Italiano-Tedesco Garzanti. French & eur.
Guarnieri, O., jt. auth. see Guarnieri, M.
Guarnieri, Orazio, jt. auth. see Marolli, Giorgio.
Guasch, Antonio. Diccionario castellano-guarani, guarani-castellano. Dist. Comuneros.
Guasp, Ignacio. Diccionario de la Lengua Mechada. French & Eur.
Guaspare, Blanche, jt. auth. see Pommier, Agatha-Marguerite.
Gubba, W. Jurdisk Ordbog. Guba.
--Juridisk Ordbog, Dansk-Tysk: Supplement & Forkortelsesliste. Guba.
Guckler, G. Zweisprachiges Woerterbuch Fuer Angenaeherte Operationelle Analyse Semantischer Entsprechungen Mittels EDV (Pub. by G. Narr). French & Eur.
Guckler, Gudrun. Zweisprachiges Woerterbuch fuer Angenaeherte Operationelle Analyse. Narr.
Guell, Francisco. Malas Hierbas, Diccionario Clasificatorio Ilustrado. French & Eur.
Guenter, H. Jugendlexikon Wirtschaft (Pub. by Rowohlt). French & Eur.
--Jugenlexikon Wirtschaft. Rowohlt.
Guerber, R. Diccionario del automovil. G Gili.
Guerber, Robert. Dictionnaire de l'automobile. Flammarion.
--Dictonnaire de L'Automobile. French & Eur.
Guerber, Roger. Diccionario del Automovil. French & Eur.
Guerin, L. F. Dictionnaire de l'Histoire Universelle de l'Eglise. Migne, J. P., ed. Caratzas Pub Co.
Guerra y Gomez, Manuel. Diccionario Morfologico del Nuevo Testamento. Aldecoa.
Guerronnan, Anthony. Dictionnaire Synonymique. Bunnell, Peter C. & Sobieszek, Robert A., eds. Ayer Co.
Guethling, jt. auth. see Menge.
Guethling, Otto, jt. auth. see Menge, Hermann.
Guglielmotti, Alberto. Vocabolario marino e militare. Mursia.
Guha, Elisabeta S. Norsk-Rumensk Lommeordbok med Liten Parloer. Universitetsforlaget.
Guidos, Barbara & Hamilton, Betty. MASA: Medical Acronyms, Symbols & Abbreviations. Neal-Schuman.
Guignard, Theodore. Dictionnaire Laotien Francais. Gregg.
Guilbert. Le Vocabulaire de L'astronautique: Enquete Linguistique a travers la Presse d'information a L'occasion De Cinq Exploits de Cosmonautes. French & Eur.
Guilbert, L. Le Vocabulaire De L'astronautique. French & Eur.

Guilbert, L., et al. Grand Larousse de la Langue Francaise: Tome I (Dist. by Continental Bk Co). Larousse.
--Grand Larousse de la Langue Francaise: Tome VII (Dist. by Continental Bk Co). Larousse.
Guilbert, Louis. La Creativite lexicale. Larousse.
--La Formation du Vocabulaire de L'Aviation. French & Eur.
--Grand Larousse de la Langue Francaise. French & Eur.
Guilfoyle, George R. & Silverman-Dresner, Toby. Vocabulary Norms for Deaf Children. Alexander Graham.
Guilhaumou, Jean. Lexique de l'informatique. E. M. E.
Guillemaut, Lucien. Dictionnaire Patois. Slatkine.
Guillen, Raymond & Vincent, Jean, eds. Lexique de Termes Juridiques. Dalloz.
Guillien, Raymond & Vincent, Jean. Lexique de Termes Juridiques. Dalloz.
--Lexique des Termes Juridiques. French & Eur.
Guinagh, Kevin, tr. & compiled by. Dictionary of Foreign Phrases & Abbreviations. Wilson.
Guinle, R. L. A Modern Spanish-English & English-Spanish Technical & Engineering Dictionary. Routledge & Kegan.
Guinot, Jean P., jt. auth. see Romeuf, Jean.
Guiraud, Pierre. Dictionnaire Erotique. French & Eur.
--Dictionnaire Historique, Stylistique, Rhetorique, Etomologique, de la Litterature Erotique. Payot.
Guisset Poch, Consuelo & Castellanos Alentorn, Prado. Diccionario Infantil Ilustrado Bruguera. French & Eur.
Gulbransen, Egil. Juridisk Leksikon. Tanum-Norli.
Gulik, R. H. Van see Uhlenbeck, Christianus C. & Van Gulik, R. H.
Gullberg, Ingvar E. Swedish-English Dictionary of Technical Terms Used in Business, Industry, Administration, Education & Research. Heinman.
--Swedish-English Fact Ordbok (Technical Terms) Vanous.
Gullino Kuhn, A. Dizionario italiano-tedesco e tedesco-italiano. Casanova F & C.
Gulsoy, Joseph. El Diccionario valenciano-castellano de Manuel Josquin Savelo. Soc. Castellonenca de Cultura.
Guner, Musa. Svensk-Turkisk Ordbok. Studentlitt.
Gunston, Bill. Jane's Aerospace Dictionary. Jane's Pub Inc.
Gunston, C. A. Deutsch-Englishes Glossarium (Pub. by Fritz Knapp Verlag). French & Eur.
Guraedy, Ila. Illustrated Gymnastics Dictionary for Young People. Harvey.
Gurainik, David B., ed. Webster's New World Dictionary: Student's Edition. P-H.
Guralnik, David. Webster's New World Dictionary of the American Language. Warner Bks.
Guralnik, David B. Webster's New World Dictionary of the American Language. Warner Bks.
Guralnik, David B., ed. Webster's New World Dictionary for Young Readers: New Rev. Color Edition. Collins Pubs.
--Webster's New World Dictionary: Modern Desk Edition. Collins Pubs.
--Webster's New World Dictionary: Second College Edition, Revised School Printing. P-H.
--Webster's New World Dictionary: Student Edition. P-H.
Guralnik, David B., et al, eds. Webster's New World Dictionary of the American Language: Second College Edition. Collins Pubs.
Gurdjian, E. S., et al, eds. Glossary of Neurotraumatology. Springer-Verlag.
Gurlitt, W. & Eggebrecht, H. Riemann Musiklexikon (Pub. by Schatt's Soehne). French & Eur.
Gurst, G., jt. ed. see Fiedler, F.
Gurst, G., et al, eds. Kleines Fremdwoerterbuch. Bibl Inst Leipzig.
Gurung, Deu B., et al. Gurung-Nepali-English Glossary. Summer Inst Ling.
Gusmani, Roberto. Lydisches Woerterbuch. Winter Univ.
--Lydisches Woerterbuch (Pub. by Carl Winter). French & Eur.
Gustafsson, Uwe. English-Kotiya Oriya, Kotiya Oriya-English Glossary. Summer Inst Ling.
Gustason, Gerilee, et al. Signing Exact English. Modern Signs.
Guterbock, Hans G., jt. ed. see Hoffner, Harry A., Jr.
Guthling, jt. auth. see Menge.
Guthling, O. Langenscheidts Taschenwoerterbuch Altgriechisch: Teil II, Deutsch-Altgriechisch. Langenscheidt.
Guthling, O., jt. auth. see Menge, H.
Guthrie, Edwin R., jt. auth. see Smith, Stevenson.
Gutu, T. Riksmalsordboken: Norwegian Dictionary. Kunnskapsforlaget.
Guy, W. & Messell, J. Norsk-Engelsk Ordbok Praktisk. French & Eur.
Guyard, Marie-Renee. Le Vocabulaire Politique de Paul Eluard. Klincksieck.
Guzman, jt. auth. see Enriquez.
Guzman, Maria O. Tagalog-English - English-Tagalog Dictionary. Heinman.
Gyldendals. Norwegian Pocket Dictionary: English-Norwegian. Vanous.
Gylys, Barbara A. & Wedding, Mary E. Medical Terminology: A Systems Approach. Davis Co.

H

Haag, Herbert. Diccionario De la Biblia. French & Eur.
Haas, jt. auth. see Van Derveer.
Haas, Leonard E., jt. ed. see Van Derveer, Paul D.
Haas, Mary R. Thai Vocabulary. Spoken Lang Serv.
Haas, Mary R., ed. Thai-English Student's Dictionary. Stanford U Pr.
Haas, Peter. Management-Taschenlexikon. Verlag Moderne Industrie.
Haas, Roland. Dictionary of Psychology & Psychiatry. Hogrefe.
Haas, Roland, ed. Dictionary of Psychology & Psychiatry: English-German. C J Hogrefe.
Haberfellner, Eva, jt. auth. see Weis, Erich.
Haberkamp, Gisela, jt. auth. see Haensch, Gunther.
Haberkamp de Anton, G. Langenscheidts Taschenwoerterbuch Spanisch: Teil I, Spanisch-Deutsch. Langenscheidt.
Haberkamp de Anton, G. & Willers, D. H. Langenscheidts Taschenwoerterbuch Spanisch. Langenscheidt.
Haberkamp De Anton, G., jt. auth. see Haensch, G.
Haberle, Gregor D. & Haberle, Heinz O. Kurzlexikon der Elektrotechnik. Frankfurt Fachverlag.
Haberle, Heinz O., jt. auth. see Haberle, Gregor D.
Habert, R., et al. Lexique de l'Industrie Textile: Francais-Anglais. French & Eur.
Habibi, B. Deutsch-Persisches Fachwoerterbuch Fuer Naturwissenschaft, Medezin und Landwirtschaft (Pub. by Harrassowitz). French & Eur.
Hadar, Joseph. Dictionnaire Hebrau-Francais. Massada Pr.
Hadatta Mahathera, A Budd see Budd Hadatta Mahathera, A.
Hadderingh, H. Drents Woordenboek. Interbk Intl.
Haddon, Ernest B. Learn Swahili for English Speakers. Saphrograph.
Hadik, Laszlo, jt. auth. see Schwarz, Urs.
Hadrovics, Galdi, jt. auth. see Hadrovics, Laszlo.
Hadrovics, Laszlo. Magyar-Szerbhorvat Szotar. Terra.
--Orosz-Magyar Szotar. Akademiai Kiado.
--Szerbhorvat-Magyar Szotar. Terra.
Hadrovics, Laszlo & Hadrovics, Galdi. Magyar-Orosz Keziszotar. Akademiai Kiado.
Hadrovics, Laszlo, et al. Magyar-Orosz Kez Iszotar. Akademiai Kiado.
--Magyar-Szerbhorvat Szotar. Terra.
--Szerbhorvat-Magyar Szotar. Terra.
Haeder, Walter & Reichow, Guenther. Lexikon der Heizungs, Lueftungs & Klimatechnik. Langenscheidt.
Haefner, jt. auth. see Roepke.
Haenel, G. F. Dictionnaire des Manuscrits, Ou Recueil De Catalogues De Manuscrits Existants Dans les Pri Cipales Bibliotheques D'europe. Migne, J. P., ed. Caratzas Pub Co.
Haensch, G. Dictionary of Agriculture. Elsevier.
--Dictionary of Agriculture in German, French, Spanish, & Russian. De Anton, Haberkamp G., ed. Elsevier.
Haensch, G. & Casero, F. Wirtschaftssprache Spanisch-Deutsch. Hueber.
--Wirtschaftssprache Spanisch-Deutsch (Pub. by M. Hueber). French & Eur.
Haensch, G. & Haberkamp De Anton, G. Dictionary of Biology in English, French, German & Spanish. Elsevier.
Haensch, G. & Renner, R. Wirtschaftssprache Franzoesisch-Deutsch. Hueber.
--Wirtschaftssprache Franzoesisch-Deutsch (Pub. by M. Hueber). French & Eur.
Haensch, Guenther. Diccionario Ingles. Herder SA.
--Dictionary of Biology. French & Eur.
--Woerterbuch der Biologie. French & Eur.
--Woerterbuch der Internationalen Beziehungen und der Politik. French & Eur.
--Woerterbuch der Landwirtschaft. French & Eur.
--Woerterbuch der Spanischen & Deutschen Sprache. Klett.
Haensch, Guenther, jt. ed. see Mueller, Heinz.
Haensch, Gunther. Diccionario Manual Herder Frances-Espanol, Espanol-Frances. French & Eur.
--Diccionario Moderno Herder Aleman-Espanol, Espanol-Aleman. French & Eur.
--Diccionario moderno Herder Aleman-Espanol. Herder SA.
--Dictionnaire Agricole Allemand-Anglais-Francais-Espagnol-Russe. Maison Rustique.
--Dictionnaire de la Biologie. BLV Verlag.
Haensch, Gunther & Haberkamp, Gisela. Diccionario de Biologia en Quatre Lenguas: Aleman, Ingles, Frances y Espanol. French & Eur.
--Dictionnaire agricole Allemand, Anglais, Francais, Espanol, Russe. Maison Rustique.
--Dictionnaire Agricole Allemand, Anglais, Francais, Espagnol, Russe (Pub. by Maison Rust). French & Eur.
Haensch, Gunther, jt. auth. see Muller, Heinz.
Haesendock, Francois M. Judo: Encyclopedie in Beeld. Standard.
Haeusgen, jt. auth. see Boeing.
Haferkorn, R. Technisches Woerterbuch Deutsch-Esperanto. U of Toronto Pr.
Haffner, Friedrich. Grundbegriffe der Marxistischen Politischen Oekonomie des Kapitalismus. Colloguium Verlag.
Hagan, S. F. Which I Which? A Manual of Homophones. Macmillan.
Hagelman, Charles W., Jr. & Barnes, Robert J., eds. Concordance to Byron's Don Juan. Cornell U Pr.
Hagford, Edvin & Sundelin, Seppo. Dictionnaire Scolaire Francais-Finnois. Soderstrom.
Hagfors, E., et al. French-Finnish Dictionary. French & Eur.
Hahn, Lorna. Historical Dictionary of Libya. Scarecrow.
Hahnewald, Harry, jt. auth. see Albert, Roald.
Hahnewald, Harry, jt. auth. see Von Roald, Albert.
Haile, Berard. A Stem Vocabulary of the Navaho Language. AMS Pr.
Haim, S. Persian-English, English-Persian Shorter Dictionary. Heinman.
Hais, K. Czechoslovakian Pocket Dictionary: Czech-English-Czech. Vanous.
--English-Czech & Czech-English Pocket Dictionary (Pub. by State Pedag. Publ. House). Four Continent.
Hais, Karel. Anglico-Cesko a Cesko-Anglico Kapesni-Slovnik: English-Czech, Czech-English Dictionary. Imported Bks.
Haisch, Heinrich, ed. see Hochrain, Helmut.
Haisman & Muller. Glossay of Clinical Chemistry Terms. Butterworth.
Haisman, P. & Muller, B. R. Glossary of Clinical Chemistry Terms. Butterworth.
Haissinsky, M. Radiochemisches Lexikon der Elemente und Ihrer Isotope (Pub. by Duemmler). French & Eur.
Hakki, Mamdouh. Dictionnaire des termes juridiques et commerciaux. Intl Bk Ctr.
--Dictionnaire Des Terms Juridiques et Commerciaux (Francais-Arabe) Intl Bk Ctr.
Halasz, ed. Langenscheidts Handwoerterbuecher: Tl 2, Deutsch-Ungarisch. Langenscheidt.
Halbauer, S. Russisch-Deutsches Woerterbuch Fuer Naturwissenschaftler und Ingenieure. Hueber.
--Russisch-Deutsches Woerterbuch Fuer Naturwissenschaftler und Ingenieure (Pub. by M. Hueber). French & Eur.
Halder, jt. auth. see Mueller.
Haley, Gessner G. Diccionario de quimica y de productos quimicos. Omega SA.
Haliburton, Gordon. Historical Dictionary of Lesotho. Scarecrow.
Halikas, Coraline E. Just Words. Ili-Cor Pubns.
Halkett & Laing. A Dictionary of Anonymous & Pseudonymous Publications in the English Language: Vol. 1, 1475-1640. Horden, John, ed. Longman.
Hall. Dictionary of Drying. Dekker.
--Dictionary of Energy. Dekker.
Hall, Benjamin H. Collection of College Words & Customs. Gale.
Hall, F., jt. auth. see Hall, R.
Hall, Frances A., jt. auth. see Hall, Robert R., Jr.
Hall, Harold A. A Partial Vocabulary of the Ngalooma Aboriginal Tribe. Humanities.
Hall, James. Dictionary of Subjects & Symbols in Art (HarpT, HarpT). Har-Row.
Hall, John R. & Meritt, Herbert D. Concise Anglo-Saxon Dictionary. Cambridge U Pr.
Hall, R. & Hall, F. Italian & English Idioms. Barron.
Hall, Robert A., ed. The Random House Basic Dictionary Italian. Ballantine.
Hall, Robert A., et al, eds. Haitian Creole Grammar, Texts, Vocabulary. Kraus Repr.
Hall, Robert A., Jr. Italian Vest Pocket Dictionary. Random.
Hall, Robert A., Jr. & Langbaum, Francesca V. French Vest Pocket Dictionary. Random.
Hall, Robert A., Jr., jt. auth. see Linguistic Society of America.
Hall, Robert R., Jr. & Hall, Frances A. Two Thousand & One Italian & English Idioms: 2001 Locuzione Italiane e Inglese. Barron.
Haller, Margaret, jt. auth. see Erdsneker, Barbara.
Haller, Margaret A. Essential Vocabulary for College-Bound Students. Arco.
Halliday, W. J. Glossary of Immunological Terms. Butterworth.

Halliwell-Phillipps, James O. Dictionary of Archaic & Provincial Words, Obsolete Phrases, Proverbs, & Ancient Customs, from the Fourteenth Century. AMS Pr.

--Dictionary of Archaic & Provincial Words, Obsolete Phrases, Proverbs, & Ancient Customs, from the Fourteenth Century. Gale.

Halliwell-Phillipps, James O., ed. Dictionary of Archaic & Provincial Words, Obsolete Phrases, Proverbs, & Ancient Customs from the 14th Century. Johnson Repr.

Hamblock, Dieter. Englisch in Wirtschaft und Handel. Girardet.

--Englische in Wirtschaft und Handel. Girardet.

Hameed Khan, A., ed. Ferozsons Concise Dictionary. Ferozsons.

Hamel, Bernard. Dictionnaire de Poche, 1: Francais-Polonais. Polonaises.

--Dictionnaire de Poche, 2: Polonais-Francais. Polonaises.

Hamer, Frank. Potter's Dictionary of Materials & Techniques. Watson-Guptill.

Hamilton, Betty, jt. auth. see Guidos, Barbara.

Hamilton, David R., ed. see Ulrich, George.

Hamline Huniversity. Long Term Care & the Law. Hamline Law.

Hamlyn. French Dictionary. Hamlyn-Amer.

Hammar, Thekla. Svensk-Fransk Ordbok. Esselte Studium.

Hammond, N. G. & Scullard, H. H., eds. Oxford Classical Dictionary. Oxford U Pr.

Hamori, Laszlo. Varldspolitiskt lexikon. Natur & kultur.

Hamp, Eric L. Glossary of American Technical Linguistic Usage, 1925-1950. Intl Pubns Serv.

Hampel, Clifford & Hawley, Gessner. Glossary of Chemical Terms. Van Nos Reinhold.

Hampel, Clifford A. & Hawley, Gessner G. Glossary of Chemical Terms. Van Nos Reinhold.

Hampl, Zdenek. Portugalsko-Cesky Slovnik. SNTC.

Hampl, Zdenek & Holsan, Jiri. Portugalsko-Cesko-Portugalsky Kapesni Slovnik. SNTC.

Handel, S. Diccionario De Electronica. French & Eur.

--Dizionario di Elettronica Italiano-Inglese, Inglese-Italiano. French & Eur.

Handel, Saul. Dizionario di elettronica. Suriani, E., tr. Zanichelli.

--Dizionario di elettronica. Suriani, E., tr. Zanichelli.

Handford, S. A. & Herberg, M., eds. Langenscheidt's Pocket Latin Dictionary, Latin-English, English-Latin. Am Map.

Handoo, Jawaharlal & Handoo, Lalita. Hindu-Kashmiri Common Vocabulary. Ctr Inst Ind Lang.

Handoo, Lalita, jt. auth. see Handoo, Jawaharlal.

Hangin, John G. A Concise English-Mongolian Dictionary. Res Ctr Lang Semiotic.

Hanifi, M. Jamil. Historical & Cultural Dictionary of Afghanistan. Scarecrow.

Hankamer, Jorge, ed. see Goddard, Ives.

Hanle, Adolf. Die Geographie: Ein Lexikon der Gesamten Schul-Erdkunde. Biblio Inst.

--Meyers Neues Lexikon Weltatlas. Biblio Inst.

Hano & Robertson, Andrew B., trs. Diccionario de management. Oikos Tau.

Hanrieder, Wolfram F. & Buel, Larry V., eds. Words & Arms: A Dictionary of Security & Defense Terms with Supplementary Data. Westview.

Hansen, Bernard, jt. auth. see Dornseiff, F.

Hansen, Jeffrey N., jt. auth. see Hansen, Merrily P.

Hansen, Mamdouh. A Dictionary of Economics & Commerce. Intl Bk Ctr.

Hansen, Merrily P. & Hansen, Jeffrey N. High Action Reading for Vocabulary: Level B. Modern Curr.

Hanson, D. P. & Penrod, D. A. A Desk Reference of Legal Terms for School Psychologists & Special Educators. C C Thomas.

Hanson, J. L. Dictionary of Economics & Commerce. Intl Ideas.

Hanusova, S. Stary, jt. auth. see Rozkovcova, L. Z.

Har, R. & Synge, P. M. Diccionario Ilustrado en Color de Plantas de Jardin con Plantas de Interior y de Invernadero. French & Eur.

Harber, K., ed. Heinemann Australian Dictionary. Heinemann Ed.

Harbottle, T. B. Dictionary of Battles. Gordon Pr.

Harbottle, Thomas B. Dictionary of Battles. Gale.

--Dictionary of Historical Allusions. Gale.

Hard, L., jt. auth. see Franzen, F.

Harder, Hermann Von see Von Harder, Hermann, et al.

Harder, Herrmann. Lexikon Fuer Mineralien - und Gesteins Freunde. French & Eur.

Harder, K. B. The Vocabulary of Marble Playing. Bd. with The Position of the Charleston Dialect. McDavid, R. I. U of Ala Pr.

Harding, J. M., jt. auth. see Corballis, R.

Hardon, John A. Modern Catholic Dictionary. Doubleday.

Hargous, Henri. Vocabulario Fundamental de la Lengua Francesa. UNAM.

Hargreaves, Barbara, jt. auth. see Beedell, Suzanne.

Hargreaves, Roger. Mr. Men Picture Dictionary. Price Stern.

Harkavy, Alexander. Harkavy's Complete Dictionary. Hebrew Pub.

Harkins, William E. Dictionary of Russian Literature. Greenwood.

Harkovy, A. English-Yiddish Dictionary. Shalom.

--Spanish-English Technical Dictionary. Shalom.

Harlakova, Ivanka & Stankova, Elena. English-Bulgarian Dictionary (Pub. by Collets). State Mutual Bk.

Haro Tecglen, Eduardo. Diccionario del Democrata. Dopesa.

--Diccionario Politico. Planeta SA.

--Diccionario Politico. French & Eur.

Haro Vera, Andres de see Heymer, A.

Harper, Frederick D. Dictionary of Counseling Techniques & Terms. Douglass Pubs.

Harrap & Dudenredaktion. Duden-Was Bedeutet Das? Kleines Bedeutungswoerterbuch der Deutschen Sprache. Harrap.

Harrell, Richard S. & Sobelman, Harvey, eds. A Dictionary of Moroccan Arabic: Moroccan-Arabic English-Moroccan. Georgetown U Pr.

Harriman, Philip L. Dictionary of Psychology. Citadel Pr.

--Handbook of Psychological Terms. Littlefield.

Harrington, Arnoldo. Diccionario de terminos medicos: Ingles-espanol, espanol-ingles. Gnosis Edit.

Harris, Cyril M. Dictionary of Architecture & Construction (P&RB). McGraw.

Harris, John. Lexicon Techicum, or, a Universal English Dictionary of Arts & Sciences. Johnson Repr.

Harris, John & Lever, Jill. Illustrated Glossary of Architecture: Eight Fifty to Eighteen Thirty. Faber & Faber.

Harris, Laurence, jt. ed. see Bottomore, Tom.

Harris, Paul. A Concise Dictionary of Scottish Painters. Intl Pubns Serv.

Harrison, Everett F., ed. Baker's Dictionary of Theology. Baker Bk.

Harrison, Francis. The English & Low-Dutch School-Master. AMS Pr.

--English & Low-Dutch Schoolmaster. AMS Pr.

Harrison, Sheldon P. & Albert, Salich. Mokilese-English Dictionary. UH Pr.

Harrison, W. & LeFlemming, Svetlana. Russian-English & English-Russian Dictionary. Routledge & Kegan.

Harrison, William & Le Fleming, Svetlana. Russian-English, English-Russian Dictionary. Routledge & Kegan.

Harrod, L. M. The Librarians' Glossary & Reference Book: Of Terms Used in Librarianship Documentation & the Book Trade. Lexington Bks.

Hart, jt. auth. see Huskisson.

Hart, Clive. A Concordance to Finnegans Wake. Appel.

Hart, Gerry V. A Dictionary of Tax Definitions. Marchmont Pub.

Hart, Gerry V., ed. Dictionary of Taxation. Butterworth.

Hart, Norman A. & Stapleton, John. Glossary of Marketing Terms (Pub. by Heinemann England). State Mutual Bk.

--Glossary of Marketing Terms (Pub. by W Heinemann England). David & Charles.

Hartfiel, Guenter. Woerterbuch der Soziologie. Kroener.

Hartgenbush, jt. auth. see Zavada.

Hartig, Paul, jt. auth. see Lange-Kowal, Ernst E.

Hartman, Robert S. Terminos Fundamentales en Etica. Univ Aut Nuevo.

Hartmann, R. R., ed. Dictionaries & Their Users. Heinman.

Hartmann, R. R. & Stork, F. C., eds. Dictionary of Language & Linguistics. Halsted Pr.

Hartong, Bernard D. Elsevier's Dictionary of Barley, Malting, & Brewing. Elsevier.

Harvard University Dumbarton Oaks Research Library. Dictionary Catalogue of the Byzantine Collection of the Dumbarton Oaks Research Library (Hall Library). G K Hall.

Harvey, Herbert. Terminos del Parentesco en el Otomangue. INAH.

Harwood, Mary. Photography Language. Running Pr.

Haskell, Ann S. The Lexicon of the Sports & Racing Car Enthusiast. Bd. with Words Relating to Plants & Animals in the Mammoth Cave Region. Wilson, Gordon; Terms of Abuse for Some Chicago Social Groups. Pederson, Lee A. U of Ala Pr.

Hassan, Irene. Tausug-English Dictionary. Jolu, Sulu.

Hasselfeldt, Othmar. Internationes Kaselexikon. Fischer Taschen.

Hastrup, T. Latin-Dansk Ordbog. French & Eur.

Hatje, G. Diccionario ilustrado de la arquitectura contemporanes. G Gili.

Hatje, Gerd. Diccionario ilustrado de la arquitectura contemporanea. Mantero, Jose M., tr. G Gili.

--Diccionario Ilustrado De la Arquitectura Contemporanea. Sabater, Gerd, ed. French & Eur.

Hatzfeld, Adolphe & Darmesteter, Arsene. Dictionnaire General de la Langue Francaise: Commencement du 17 Siecle Jusqu'a nos Jours. Delagrave.

Hatzfeld, Adophe & Darmesteter, Arsene. Dictionnaire General de la Langue Francaise du Commencement du 17e Siecle Jusqu' a Nos Jours. French & Eur.

Haugen, G. Norwegian Dictionary: Norwegian-English. Vanous.

Haukoy & Zickfeldt. German-Norwegian Dictionary. Kunnskapsforlaget.

Hauser, Gaylord & Berg, Ragnar. Dictionary of Foods. Lust.

Hausmann, F. J., frwd. by. New Diesterweg-Larousse: Dictionnaire du Francais Langue Etrangere. Diesterweg.

--Newu Diesterweg-Larousse: Dictionnaire du Francais Langue Etrangere. Diesterweg.

Hausmann, Franz J. Einfuehrung in die Benutzung der Neufranzoesischen Woerterbucher. Niemeyer Verlag.

Haust, Jean. Dictionnaire Francais-Liegois. Vaillant-Carmanne.

--Dictionnaire Liegeois. Vaillant-Carmanne.

Hava, J. Al-Faraid: Arabic-English Dictionary. Intl Bk Ctr.

Hava, J. G. Al-Faraid Arabic-English Dictionary. Intl Pubns Serv.

Havas, L. Dictionnaire de Tourisme Francais-Hongrois. Terra.

Havlicek, jt. auth. see Wanke.

Hawes, Gene R. & Hawes, Lynne S. The Concise Dictionary of Education. Van Nos Reinhold.

Hawes, Lynne S., jt. auth. see Hawes, Gene R.

Hawkins, ed. Oxford Paperback Dictionary. Oxford U Pr.

Hawkins, Joyce M., compiled by. The Oxford Minidictionary. Oxford U Pr.

Hawley, Gessner. Condensed Chemical Dictionary. Van Nos Reinhold.

Hawley, Gessner, jt. auth. see Hampel, Clifford.

Hawley, Gessner G., jt. auth. see Hampel, Clifford A.

Hay, R., jt. auth. see Synge, P.

Hay, Roy & Synge, Patrick M. The Color Dictionary of Flowers & Plants for Home & Garden. Crown.

Hay, Roy, et al. Diccionario Ilustrado en Color De Plantas De Interior. French & Eur.

Hayakawa, S. I. & Funk And Wagnalls Dictionary Staff, eds. Funk & Wagnalls Modern Guide to Synonyms & Related Words. T Y Crowell.

Haydn, Joseph T. Dictionary of Names & Universal Information. Scholarly.

--Haydn's Dictionary of Dates & Universal Information Relating to All Ages & Nations. Scholarly.

Hayes, Sherman, ed. Primer of Business Terms & Phrases Related to Libraries. Library Admin.

Haygood, James D. Le Vocabulaire Fondamentale du Francais. Droz.

Hayward, Arthur L. & McFarlane, C. Learn Italian for English Speakers. Saphrograph.

Hazlewood, David. A Fijian & English & an English & Fijian Dictionary. AMS Pr.

Hazon. Dizionario Garzanti Italiano-Inglese & Inglese-Italiano. Speedimpex.

--Dizionario Garzanti Italiano-Inglese & Inglese-Italiano. Speedimpex.

Hazon, M. Dizionario Garzanti: Italiano-Inglese, Inglese-Italiano. French & Eur.

--Grande Dizionario Hazon Garzanti Inglese-Italiano, Italiano-Inglese. French & Eur.

--Italian-English, English-Italian (Grande) Dictionary. Heinman.

Hazon, M., ed. Dizionario Hazon Garzanti: Inglese-Italiano, Italiano-Inglese. French & Eur.

Hazon, Mario. Dizionario inglese-italiano e italiano-inglese: Edizione scholastica. Garzanti Edit.

Headley, R. Cambodian-English Dictionary. Iaconi.

Headley, Robert K. Cambodian-English Dictionary. Cath U Pr.

Heath, Dwight D. Historical Dictionary of Bolivia. Scarecrow.

Heath, Jeffrey. Basic Material in Ritarungu. Linguistic Circle.

Heck, Hans. Knaurs Lexikon der Technik (Pub. by Druckenmueller). French & Eur.

Heckman, Carol, et al, eds. GeoRef Thesaurus & Guide to Indexing. Am Geol.

Hee, Marijke van see Van Hee, Marijke.

Heggoy, Alf A. & Crout, Robert R. Historical Dictionary of Algeria. Scarecrow.

Hehlmann, Wilhelm. Woerterbuch der Paedagogik. French & Eur.

--Woerterbuch der Psychologie. French & Eur.

Heidenreich, Charles A. Dictionary of General Psychology: Basic Terminology & Key Concepts. Heidenreich.

Heider, Karl G., jt. auth. see Darlington, C. D.

Heiler, T. Diccionario tecnico ilustrado de herramientas de corte para el trabajo de metales: Espanol-aleman-ingles-frances-italiano. G Gili.

Heiler, Toni. Dictionnaire Technique Illustre des Outlis Coupants: L'usinage des Metaux; Francais-Allemand-Anglais-Italien-Espagnol. Eyrolles.

--Dictionnaire Technique Illustre Des Outils Coupants Pour L'usinage Des Metaux. French & Eur.
Heimanson, Rudolph. Dictionary of Political Science & Law. Oceana.
Heimbach, Ernest E., compiled by. White-Hmong English Dictionary. Cornell SE Asia.
--White Hmong-English Dictionary. Cornell SE Asia.
Hein, W. Lexikon der Schulphysik: Waerme und Wetter. French & Eur.
Heinecken, Karl H. Von see Von Heinecken, Karl H.
Heinisch, Kurt F. Kautschuk-Lexikon. Gentner.
Heinl, Robert D., Jr., ed. Dictionary of Military & Naval Quotations. Naval Inst Pr.
--Dictionary of Military & Naval Quotations. US Naval Inst.
Heinrich. Woerterbuch Klima & Kaeltetechnik. Verlag Harri Deutsch.
Heinrich, Gunter. Woerterbuch Klima & Kaltetechnik. Verlag Harri Deutsch.
Heinrichs, Heribert. Lexikon der Audio-Visuellen Bildungsmittel. French & Eur.
Heinrichs, Heribert, ed. Lexikon der Audio-Visuellen Bildungsmittel. Koesel.
Heinze. Fachwoerterbuch des Versicherungswesen. Brandstetter.
--Fachwoerterbuch des Versicherungswesen (Pub. by Brandstetter). French & Eur.
Heinze, S. Fachwoerterbuch des Transportwesens. Brandstetter.
--Fachwoerterbuch des Transportwesens (Pub. by Brandstetter). French & Eur.
--Fachwoerterbuch des Versicherungswesen (Pub. by Brandstetter). French & Eur.
--Fachwoerterbuch des Vesicherungswesen. Brandstetter.
Heinze, Siegfried. Dictionary of Transport Terms & Phrases. Intl Pubns Serv.
Heise, Jeanne, ed. see Sahai, Hardeo & Berrios, Jose.
Heiser, Edward J. & Allswede, Jerry L., eds. Blade Coating Defect Terminology. TAPPI.
Heitman, Francis B. Historical Register & Dictionary of the U. S. Army 1789-1903. Gordon Pr.
--Historical Register & Dictionary of the United States Army, from Its Organization, September 29, 1789, to March 2, 1903. U of Ill Pr.
Helbig, G. & Schenkel, W. Woerterbuch zur Valenz & Distribution Deutscher Verben. Bibl Inst Leipzig.
Helbig, W. Ray. Let's Learn a Little Hawaiian. Hawaiian Serv.
Helck, Wolfgang & Otto, Eberhard. Kleines Woerterbuch der Aegyptologie (Pub. by Harrassowitz). French & Eur.
--Lexikon der Aegyptologie. Harrassowitz.
--Lexikon der Aegyptologie: Bd II, Lfg 10. Harrassowitz.
--Lexikon der Aegyptologie: Bd II, Lfg 11. Harrassowitz.
--Lexikon der Aegyptologie: Bd II, Lfg 12. Harrassowitz.
--Lexikon der Aegyptologie: Bd II, Lfg 13. Harrassowitz.
--Lexikon der Aegyptologie: Bd II, Lfg 14. Harrassowitz.
--Lexikon der Aegyptologie: Bd II, Lfg 9. Harrassowitz.
--Lexikon der Aegyptologie: Bd 1, Lfg 1. Harrassowitz.
--Lexikon der Aegyptologie: Bd 1, Lfg. 2. Harrassowitz.
--Lexikon der Aegyptologie: Bd 1, Lfg. 3. Harrassowitz.
--Lexikon der Aegyptologie: Bd 1, Lfg 4. Harrassowitz.
--Lexikon der Aegyptologie: Bd 1, Lfg 6. Langenscheidt.
--Lexikon der Aegyptologie: Bd 1, Lfg 7. Harrassowitz.
--Lexikon der Aegyptologie: Bd 1, Lfg 8. Harrassowitz.
Helffrich-Mariani, E., jt. auth. see Trioke-Strambaci, H.
Helffrich-Mariani, E., jt. auth. see Troike-Strambaci, H.
Hellegouarch, Jean. Le Vocabulaire Latin des Relations & des Partis Politiques sous la Republique. Belles Lettres.
Hellegouarc'H, Jean. Le Vocabulaire Latin Des Relations Et Des Partis Politiques Sous la Republique. French & Eur.
Heller. Diccionario de economia politica. Labor.
Heller, C. Dictionary of Engineering Mechanics. Elsevier.
Helmlinger, Paul. Dictionnaire Duala-Francais. S. E. L. A. F.
--Lexique Francais-Duala: Dictionnaire Duala-Francais. S. E. L. A. F.
Helmut, H. Woerterbuch des Buches. French & Eur.
Hembus, Joe. Western Lexikon. Heyne W Verlag.
Hemeling, Karl E. English-Chinese Dictionary: Standard Chinese. Ayer Co.
Hemnes, Thomas, jt. auth. see Gordon, Frank S.
Hemphill, Charles F., Jr. & Hemphill, Phyllis. Dictionary of Practical Law (Spec). P-H.
Hemphill, Phyllis, jt. auth. see Hemphill, Charles F., Jr.
Hemstead, Hemel, jt. ed. see Logie, Gordon.
Hench, Atcheson L. The Use of the Dictionary of American English & the Dictionary of Americanisms. Bd. with Bilingualism Among American Slovaks: Analysis of Loans. Meyerstein, Goldie P; A Cleburne County, Arkansas Word List. Skillman, Billy G; Low German in Mexico. Moelleken, Wolfgang W. U of Ala Pr.
Henderson, L. Orthography & Word Recognition in Reading. Acad Pr.
Hendrix, Melvin K. An International Bibliography of African Lexicons. Scarecrow.
Hengst, Heinz, jt. auth. see Bauer, Karl W.
Henley, Elton P. Vocabulary Building at the College Level. Kendall-Hunt.
Henni, Mustapha. Dictionaire Des Termes Economiques et Commerciaux: Francais-Arabe. Intl Bk Ctr.
--Dictionary Des Terms Economiques et Commerciaux (French-English-Arabic) Intl Bk Ctr.
--Dictionnaire des termes economiques et commerciaux. Intl Bk Ctr.
Henni, Mustapha, compiled by. Dictionnaire des Termes Techniques et Commerciaux. INtl Bk Ctr.
Hennigsen, H. Danisch. Langenscheidt.
Henning, W. B. Fragment of a Khwarezmian Dictionary. MacKenzie, D. N., ed. Intl Pubns Serv.
Henningsen, H. Langenscheidts Taschenwoerterbuch Danisch. Langenscheidt.
--Langenscheidt's Taschenwoerterbuch Danisch: Teil I, Danisch-Deutsch. Langenscheidt.
--Langenscheidts Taschenwoerterbuch Danisch: Teil II, Deutsch-Danisch. Langenscheidt.
--Langenscheidts Taschenwoerterbuecher Daenisch. Langenscheidt.
Henry, Antonir Marie & LaBrosse, Olivier De, eds. Dictionnaire de la Foi Chretienne. French & Eur.
Henry, J. M. & Ergo, A. B. Thesaurus des Symboles Agrobioclimatiques, Geographiques & Techniques, 3. Centre Informatique Develop.
Henry, Louis. Dictionnaire Aerotechnique Anglais-Francais. Petit.
Henschel, E. & Pretzel, U., eds. Lexers Mittlehochdeutsches Taschenwoerterbuch: Mit Bearbeiteten & Erweiterten Nachtraegen. Hirzel Verlag.
Henstock, Colin. Dictionnaire Fondamental Harrap: Francais-Anglais. Bordas-Dunod.
--Harrap's First French Dictionary. Harrap.
Hentschel, Erwin. Tiernamen & Zoologische Fachworter. Fischer Verlag.
Henzi, Theodor, jt. auth. see Chatelanat, Charles.
Hepburn, James C. A Japanese & English Dictionary with an English & Japanese Index. C E Tuttle.
Herberg, M., jt. ed. see Handford, S. A.
Herbert. Dictionnaire Pittoresque & Historique: Ou Description d'architecture, Peinture, Sculpture, Gravure. Minkoff Repr.
Herbert, J. Conference Terminology in English, Spanish, Russian, Italian, German & Hungarian. Elsevier.
Herbert, W. J. & Wilkinson, P. C. Diccionario de Inmunologia. Jims.
--Diccionario De Inmunologia. French & Eur.
Herbin, Pierre. Vocabulaire de la Publicite. Bourdine.
Herbst, R. Dictionary of Commercial, Financial & Legal Terms. Adler.
--Dictionary of Commercial, Financial & Legal Terms. Heinman.
--Dictionary of Commericial, Financial & Legal Terms in Two Languages. Adler.
Herbst, Robert. Dictionary of Commerce, Finance & Law. French & Eur.
--Woerterbuch der Handels, Finanz und Rechtssprache. French & Eur.
Herbst, Robert & Readett, Alan G. The Herbst Dictionaries of Commercial, Financial & Legal Terms: English-German. Birkhauser.
--The Herbst Dictionaries of Commercial, Financial & Legal Terms Vol. I. Birkhauser.
Herbst, Robert & Readett, Alan G., eds. The Herbst Dictionaries of Commercial, Financial & Legal Terms: Deutsch-Englisch. Birkhauser.
--The Herbst Dictionaries of Commercial, Financial & Legal Terms Vol. 2. Birkhauser.
--Herbst Dictionary of Commercial, Financial & Legal Terms. Birkhauser.
--Herbst Dictionay of Commercial, Financial & Legal Terms. Birkhauser.
Herczeg, Gyula. Magyar-Olasz Szotar. Terra.
--Magyar-Olasz Szotar. Terra.
--Olasz-Magyar Szotar. Akademiai Kiado.
--Olasz-Magyar-Szotar. Terra.
--Olasz-Magyar Szotar: Vocabolario Italiano-Ungherese. Kolttay-Kastner, Jeno, ed. Akademiai Kiado.
Herder, tr. see Schoeck, Helmut.
Hereaucourt, jt. auth. see Wildhagen.
Hering, R. Hering's Dictionary of Classical & Modern Cookery. Corner.
Hering, Richard. Hering's Dictionary of Classical & Modern Cookery. Bickel, Walter, tr. from Ger. Radio City.
Herland. Dictionary of Mathematical Sciences: Band II, Englisch-German. Brandstetter.
--Dictionary of Mathematical Sciences: Band I, German-English. Brandstetter.
Herland, Leo. Dictionary of Mathematical Sciences. Incl. Vol. 1. German-English; Vol. 2. English-German. Ungar.
Herlitz, G., ed. Juedisches Lexikon. M. Rosenberg.
Herman, Louis J. A Dictionary of Slavic Word Families. Columbia U Pr.
Hermann, A. Lexikon der Schulphysik: Geschichte der Physik. French & Eur.
--Lexikon der Schulphysik: Geschichte der Physik. French & Eur.
Hermann, E. R., et al, eds. Piaget: Dictionary of Terms. Pergamon.
Hermann, Theo M., jt. auth. see De Vries, Louis.
Hernadi, Miklos. Koezhelyszotar. Gondolat.
--Kozhelyszotar. Gondolat.
Hernandez, Juan D. Diccionario de Formularios Generales. Nereo.
Hernandez, Manuel B., jt. auth. see Benito y Bacho, Jose de.
Hernandez Aquino, Luis. Diccionario de Voces Indigenas de Puerto Rico. French & Eur.
Hernandez De Prieto, Muriel. Vocabulary Made Easy for Spanish Speakers. U of PR Pr.
Hernandez Miyares, jt. auth. see Fernandez de la Vega.
Heron, Patricia A. Russian-English Integrated Dictionary. Univ Aston.
Heroux, M., et al. Lexique de l'Industrie Petroliere Ra Finage: Anglais-Francais. French & Eur.
Herrero, V. J. Diccionario de Expresiones y Frases Latinas. French & Eur.
Herring, J. A. The Foursquare Dictionary (Pub. by Mei Ya China). Intl Schol Bk Serv.
Herrmann, jt. auth. see De Vries.
Herrmann, Joachim. Meyers Grosses Sternbuch fur Kinder. Biblio Inst.
Herschelmann, Ferdinand. Meyers Grosses Jahreslexikon: Berichtszeitraum. Biblio Inst.
Herscu, G. F., ed. Elsevier's Dictionary of Rolling Mill Terminology. Elsevier.
Herselin, Jacqueline. Dictionnaire Italien-Francais. Garnier.
Hershey, Douglas M. The Ultimate Crossword Puzzle Index. A S Barnes.
Herstig, David. Deutsch-Hebraeisches Woerterbuch. Hueber.
--Deutsch-Hebraeische Woerterbuch (Pub. by Max Hueber). French & Eur.
--Hebraeisch-Deutches Woerterbuch. Hueber.
--Hebraeisch-Deutsches Woerterbuch (Pub. by Max Hueber). French & Eur.
Hertz, Leah. In Search of a Small Business Definition: An Exploration of the Small-Business Definitions of the U. S., the U.K., Israel, & the People's Republic of China. U Pr of Amer.
Hess, Thom. A Dictionary of Puget Salish. U of Wash Pr.
Hessmann, Pierre. Namenforschung im Ostniederlandisch-Westfalischen Grengebiet. Rodopi.
Heupel, Carl. Linguistisches Woerterbuch. Deutscher Taschenbuch.
Hewitt, A., jt. auth. see Sturgess, H.
Hexner, Erwin. Studies in Legal Terminology. Rothman.
Heyde, A. W., ed. see Das, Sarat C.
Heyde, A. William, ed. see Chandra Das, S.
Heylli, Edmond G. Dictionnaire des Racines Semitiques. Slatkine.
Heymer, A. Diccionario de Etologia. De Haro Vera, Andres, tr. Omega SA.
--Ethnologisches Woerterbuch. Parey.
--Ethnologisches Woerterbuch (Pub. by P. Parey). French & Eur.
Heymer, Armin. The Ethological Dictionary: In English, French & German (Garland STPM Pr). Garland Pub.
--Vocabulaire Ethnologique. French & Eur.
--Vocabulaire Ethologique: Allemand-Anglais-Francais. PUF.
Heyne, Moritz. Deutsche Woerterbuch. Hirzel Verlag.
--Deutsches Woerterbuch (Pub. by Hirzel). French & Eur.
Hibbard, A., jt. auth. see Thrall, W. F.
Hibbert, Tom. Delilah's International Dictionary of Rock Terms. Delilah Bks.
Hickey, D. J. & Doherty, J. E. Dictionary of Irish History Since 1800. B&N Imports.
Hickie, W. J. Greek-English Lexicon of the New Testament. Baker Bk.
Hidalgo, Dionisio. Diccionario De Bibliografia Espanola. B Franklin.
Hiebeler, Toni. Lexikon der Aero & Astronautik Einschliesslich Raketentechnik: Lexikon der Alpen. Sokoll.
Hieu, Nguyen-Trung, ed. Practical English-Vietnamese Idioms for Teachers & Students. Vantage.
Higdon, David & Bender, Todd K. A Concordance to Conrad's Under Western Eyes. Garland Pub.
Hildebrand, jt. auth. see Gross.

Hildebrand, H., jt. auth. see Gross, H.

Hildebrand, Helmut, jt. auth. see Gross, Helmut.

Hill, L. R., ed. see Cowan, S. T.

Hill, Norman. Webster's Red Seal Crossword Dictionary. Warner Bks.

Hill, R., rev. by see Wood, F. T.

Hill, Robert, jt. auth. see Wood, F. T.

Hill, Robert, ed. Dictionary of Difficult Words. Philos Lib.

Hill, Robert H. Dictionary of Difficult Words (Sig). NAL.

Hillerich, Robert L. A Writing Vocabulary of Elementary Children. C C Thomas.

Hillier, H. G. The Hillier Color Dictionary of Trees & Shrubs. Van Nos Reinhold.

Hillier, Mary. Pollock's Dictionary of English Dolls. Crown.

Hills, A. Swedish-English-Swedish Pocket Dictionary. Vanous.

Hiltunen, A. Finnish-Russian-Finnish Dictionary (Suomi-Venaja-Suomi) French & Eur.

Hincu, Dumitru. Dictionar Scolar. Editura Didactica.

Hinojosa, Ida, ed. Vest Pocket Spanish Dictionary. New Century.

Hinojosa, Ida N., ed. New Century World-Wide Spanish Dictionary: Spanish: Spanish-English, English-Spanish. New Century.

Hioki, Kojiro, jt. auth. see Seiler, Hansjakob.

Hionides, H. T. Greek-English, English-Greek Technical Dictionary. Heinman.

Hirschberg, Walter. Woerterbuch der Voelkerkunde. French & Eur.

Hirschelmann, Ferdinand. Meyers Grosses Jahreslexikon. Biblio Inst.

--Meyers Grosses Jahreslexikon. Biblio Inst.

Hirschhorn, Howard H. Spanish-English, English-Spanish Medical Guide. Regents Pub.

Hirst, T. O. A Grammar of the Dialect of Kendal (Wesmoreland) Descriptive & Historical with Specimens & a Glossary. Intl Pubns Serv.

Hirvensalo, L. Finnish-German-Finnish Dictionary (Suomi-Saksa-Suomi) French & Eur.

Hitchcock. An English-Hawaiian Dictionary. Iaconi.

Hitchcock, Harvey R. English-Hawaiian Dictionary. C E Tuttle.

Hitti, Jusuf. Medical English-Arabic Dictionary. Intl Bk Ctr.

Hitti, Yusuf K. English-Arabic Medical Dictionary. Intl Bk Ctr.

--Hitti's English-Arabic Medical Dictionary (Am U Beirut). Syracuse U Pr.

Hixson, Sandra, jt. auth. see Mathias, J.

Hoa. Essential English-Vietnamese Dictionary. Iaconi.

Hoa, Dinh Nguyen. Vietnamese-English Dictionary. Iaconi.

Hobar, Donald, ed. Papers of the Dictionary Society of North America, 1977. Ind St Univ.

--Papers of the Dictionary Society of North America 1977. Dict Soc NA.

Hochleitner, Frida & Mateo, Felix D. Diccionario Manual Frances-Espanol. Espasa Calpe.

Hochleitner, Frida, jt. auth. see Diaz Mateo, Felix.

Hochleitner, Frida, jt. auth. see Diez Mateo, Felix.

Hochleitner, Frida, jt. ed. see Mateo, Felix D.

Hochman, ed. Kettridge's English-French - French-English Dictionary (Sig). NAL.

Hochman, Stanley. Yesterday & Today: A Dictionary of Recent American History. McGraw.

Hochman, Stanley, jt. auth. see De Vries, Louis.

Hochman, Stanley, rev. by see De Vries, Louis.

Hochrain, Helmut. Das ABC des Pfeifenrauchers. Haisch, Heinrich, ed. Heyne W Verlag.

Hocquenghem, Alexis. Vocabulaire Elementaire des Ensembles. Masson & Cie.

Hodges, Tony. Historical Dictionary of Western Sahara. Scarecrow.

Hodous, L., jt. auth. see Soothill, W. E.

Hodous, L., jt. ed. see Soothill, William E.

Hoefling, O. Lexikon der Schulphysik: Atomphysik. French & Eur.

Hoefling, Oskar, ed. Lexikon der Schulphysik: Bd 1, Mechanik & Akustik. Aulis Verlag.

--Lexikon der Schulphysik: Bd 3, Elektrizitaet & Magnetismus-1.Tlbd, A-K. Aulis Verlag.

--Lexikon der Schulphysik: Bd 3, Elektrizitaet & Magnetismus-2.Tlbd, L-Z. Aulis Verlag.

--Lexikon der Schulphysik: Bd 4, Optik & Relativitaet. Aulis Verlag.

--Lexikon der Schulphysik: Bd 5, Atomphysik. Aulis Verlag.

--Lexikon der Schulphysik: Bd 6, Geschichte der Physik. Aulis Verlag.

--Lexikon der Schulphysik: Bd 7, Geschichte der Physik. Aulis Verlag.

--Lexikon der Schulphysik: Waerme & Wetter. Aulis Verlag.

Hoeftmann, Hildegard. The Structure of Lelemi Language. Intl Pubns Serv.

Hoequist, Charles, Jr., jt. ed. see Urdang, Lawrence.

Hoermann, Karl. Diccionario De Moral Cristiana. French & Eur.

--Diccionario De Moral Cristiana. French & Eur.

Hofer, Alfons. Illustriertes Textil und Mode - Lexikon (Pub. by Deutscher Fachverlag). French & Eur.

Hofer, Manfred, jt. auth. see Eckel, Denis.

Hoffe, Otfried. Lexikon der Ethik. Beck Verlag.

Hoffman, Alfred. Glosar der Wichtigsten Saugetiere Chinas. Harrassowitz.

Hoffman, E. Fachwoerterbuch fuer die Glasindustriel. Springer-Verlag.

Hoffman, Horace Addison. Everyday Greek: Greek Words in English, Including Scientific Terms. U of Chicago Pr.

Hoffman, Jeanne, jt. auth. see Prizzi, Elaine.

Hoffman, Johannes P. Dictionary of Packaging: German-English-French. Intl Pubns Serv.

Hoffman, Paul & Freedman, Matt. Dictionary, Schmictionary. Quill NY.

Hoffman, Peter. Fertigungsmesstechnik-Russischer-Deutsch: Deutsch-Russicherr. VEB Verlag Technik.

Hoffmann, Alfred. Glossar der Heute Chinesischen Vogelnamen. Harrassowitz.

--Neue Chinesische Vogelnamen. Harrassowitz.

Hoffmann, E. Dictionary for the Glass Industry: Fachwoerterbuch fuer die Glasindustrie. Springer-Verlag.

--Fachwoerterbuch Fuer die Glasindustriel (Pub. by Springer). French & Eur.

Hoffmann, Peter D. Fertigungsmesstechnik. VEB Verlag Technik.

Hoffner, Harry A., Jr. An English-Hittite Glossary. Intl Pubns Serv.

Hoffner, Harry A., Jr. & Guterbock, Hans G., eds. The Hittite Dictionary of the Oriental Institute of the University of Chicago. Oriental Inst.

Hofinger, M. Lexicon Hesiodeum: Cum Indice Inverso. Brill Verlag.

Hofmann, Egon. Dictionary of Dataprocessing. French & Eur.

Hoftmann, HIldegard, et al. Woerterbuch Swahili-Deutsch. VEB Verlag Enzyklopadie.

Hogben, Lancelot. Vocabulary of Science. Stein & Day.

Hohenadel & Relton. Textilwoerterbuch: Band II, Deutsch-English. Brandstetter.

Hohenadel, P. & Relton, J. A Modern Textile Dictionary: English-German. French & Eur.

Hohenadel, P. & Relton, V. A Modern Textile Dictionary. French & Eur.

Hohenadel, Paul & Relton, Jonathan. Textil-Worterbuch. Brandstetter.

Hohenadel, Relton & Relton. Textilwoerterbuch: Band I, English-Deutsch. Brandstetter.

Holladay, William L. A Concise Hebrew & Aramaic Lexicon of the Old Testament. Eerdmans.

Holland, John L., jt. auth. see Gottfredson, Gary D.

Hollander, N., et al. Lexico Marinero: Six Idiomas. French & Eur.

Holli, Melvin G. & Jones, Peter d'A, eds. Biographical Dictionary of American Mayors, 1820 to 1980. Greenwood.

Holly, David. A Complete Categorized Greek-English New Testament Vocabulary. Attic Pr.

--A Complete Categorized Greek-English New Testament Vocabulary. Baker Bk.

Holm, John A. & Shilling, Alison W. The Dictionary of Bahamian English. Lexik Hse.

Holmboe, Henrik. Dansk Retrogradordbog. Akademisk Forlag.

Holmes, Keith D. Seventy Steps to Vocabulary Power. Educ Serv Pub.

Holmes, Sandra. Henderson's Dictionary of Biological Terms. Van Nos Reinhold.

Holsan, Jiri, jt. auth. see Hampl, Zdenek.

Holt, Alfred H. Phrase & Word Origins: A Study of Familiar Expressions. Dover.

Holt Staff. Holt Intermediate Dictionary of American English. HR&W.

--Winston Dictionary for Schools. HR&W.

Holum, John R. Topics & Terms in Environmental Problems (Pub. by Wiley-Interscience). Wiley.

Homeyer, H., jt. ed. see Barker, M. L.

Honegger, M. Dictionnaire de la Musique: Science de la Musique. French & Eur.

Honegger, Marc. Dictionnaire de la Musique. Bordas-Dunod.

Honegger, Marc, ed. Dictionnaire de la Musique. French & Eur.

Honnorat, Simon-Jude. Dictionnaire Provencal-Francais ou Dictionnaire de la Langue D'oc Ancienne & Moderne. Slatkine.

Honour, Hugh & Fleming, John. Dictionary of the Decorative Arts (HarpT). Har-Row.

Hony, H. C. Turkish-English Dictionary. Oxford U Pr.

Hony, H. C., jt. auth. see Iz, Fahir.

Hood, W. A-Z of Clinical Chemistry. Halsted Pr.

Hook, J. N. The Grand Panjandrum: And 1999 Other Rare & Delightful Words & Expressions. Macmillan.

Hooson, William. The Miners Dictionary. IMM North Am.

Hooton, E. A., ed. see Murray, G. W.

Hope, Robert C. Glossary of Dialectal Place-Nomenclature. Gale.

Hopke, William E., ed. Encyclopedia of Career & Vocational Guidance (Anch). Doubleday.

Hopkins, Jeanne, ed. Glossary of Astronomy & Astrophysics. U of Chicago Pr.

--Glossary of Astronomy & Astrophysics. U of Chicago Pr.

Horalek, Karel. Skolni Rusko-Cesky Slovnik. SNTC.

Horden, John, ed. see Halkett & Laing.

Hordeski, Michael. Illustrated Dictionary of Microcomputer Terminology. TAB Bks.

Horlacher, Friedrich W. Piccolo Dizionario Americano Italiano. Nuova Vallecchi.

Hornberger, Esteban S. & Hornberger, H. N. Diccionario Tri-lingue. LCA.

Hornberger, H. N., jt. auth. see Hornberger, Esteban S.

Hornburger. African Countries & Cultures. McKay.

Hornby. The Advanced Learner's Dictionary of Current English with Chinese Translation. Iaconi.

Hornby, A. S. Oxford Advanced Learner's Dictionary of Current English. Oxford U Pr.

--Oxford Student's Dictionary of American English. Oxford U Pr.

--Oxford Student's Dictionary of American English. Oxford U Pr.

--Oxford Student's Dictionary of Current English. Ruse, Christina, ed. Oxford U Pr.

Hornby, A. S. & Parnwell, E. C. The Oxford English-Reader's Dictionary. Langenscheidt.

Hornby, A. S., compiled by. Oxford Student's Dictionary of Current English. Oxford U Pr.

Hornby, A. S. & Parnwell, E. C., eds. The Progressive English Dictionary. Oxford U Pr.

Hornby, A. S., et al. The Advanced Learner's Dictionary of Current English with Chinese Translation. Imported Bks.

--Oxford Advanced Learner's Dictionary of Current English with Chinese Translations. Oxford U Pr.

--Oxford student's dictionary of Current English. Oxford U Pr.

Hornby, Albert S. Kamus pembaca, Inggeris-Malayu. Oxford U Pr.

Hornby, Albert S. & Parnwell, E. C., eds. English-Reader's Dictionary. Oxford U Pr.

Horne, Elinor C. Javanese-English Dictionary. Yale U Pr.

Horner, C. F. & Liebster, L. M. THe Hamlyn Pocket Dictionary of Business Terms. Hamlyn Pub.

Horner, Colin, jt. auth. see Liebster, Leo.

Horner, J. G. Dictionary of Mechanical Engineering Terms. Grahame-White, G. K., ed. Heinman.

Horny. Oxford Advanced Learner's Dictionary of Current English. Iaconi.

Horozco, Sebastian De Covarrubias see De Covarrubias Horozco, Sebastian.

Horta. Diccionario de Sinonimos & Ideas Afines & de la Rima. Paraninfo.

Horta Massanes, Joaquin. Diccionario de Sinonimos e Ideas Afines & de la Rima (PAR). Lectorum Pubns.

--Diccionario de sinonimos e ideas afines y de la rima. Paraninfo.

Horta Massanet, Joaquin. Diccionario de Sinonimos e Ideas Afines & de la Rima. Paraninfo.

--Diccionario De Sinonimos E Ideas Afines y De la Rima. French & Eur.

Horwill, H. W. An Anglo-American Interpreter: A Vocabulary & Phrase Book. Folcroft.

Host. Danish Pocket Dictionary. Vanous.

Hostettler, R. Printer's Terms Dictionary. Heinman.

Houaiss, Antonio. Dicionario Basico Escolar Koogan-Larousse. Edit Atica.

Houaiss, Antonio, ed. Pequeno Dicionario Enciclopedico Koogan Larouse. Larousse.

Houfe, Simon. The Dictionary of British Book Illustrators & Caricaturists: 1800-1914. Antique Collect.

Houghton, Diane & Wallace, Ralph G. Students' Accounting Vocabulary. Gower Pub Ltd.

Houle, Michel & Julien, Alain. Dictionnaire du Cinema Quebecois. Fides.

Hoult, Thomas F. Dictionary of Modern Sociology. Rowman.

Hourcastagne, Andre. Lexique du Secourisme & de la Plongee Autonome. France Selection.

Howard University Library, Washington, D.C. Dictionary Catalog of the Arthur B. Spingarn Collection of Negro Authors (Hall Library). G K Hall.

--Dictionary Catalog of the Jesse E. Moorland Collection of Negro Life & History (Hall Library). G K Hall.

--Dictionary Catalog of the Jesse E. Moorland Collection of Negro Life & History, First Supplement (Hall Library). G K Hall.

Howard W. Sams Editorial Staff. Dictionary of Audio & Hi-Fi. Sams.

Howe, Robin, jt. auth. see Simon, Andre L.

Howell, G. & Perez Y Sabido, J. Spanish-English Handbook. Med Economics.

Howes, F. N. Dictionary of Useful & Everyday Plants & Their Common Names. Cambridge U Pr.

Howson, A. G. A Handbook of Terms Used in Algebra & Analysis. Cambridge U Pr.
Howson, G., jt. ed. see Soule, Richard.
Hoybye, P., jt. auth. see Blinkenberg, A.
Hoybye, Poul, jt. auth. see Blinkenberg, A. P.
Hoyer-Kreuter. Technological Dictionary in Three Languages. Schlomann, Alfred, ed. Incl. Vol. 1. German-English-French; Vol. 2. English-German-French; Vol. 3. French-German-English. Ungar.
Hoyle, John. Dictionarium Musica, Being a Complete Dictionary, or, Treasury of Music. Broude.
Hrabcowa, Stanislawa, et al. Slownik Jezyka Polskiego dia Cudzoziemcow. Wydaw-a UW.
Hu, C. T. & Beach, Beatrice. Russian-Chinese-English Glossary of Education. Tchrs Coll.
Huang, Parker P. Cantonese Dictionary: Cantonese-English, English-Cantonese. Yale U Pr.
Huang, Parker Po-fei. Cantonese Dictionary: Cantonese-English, English-Cantonese. Yale U Pr.
Huart, Pierre. Vocabulaire de l'analyse Psychologique dans l'oeuvre de Thucydide. Klincksieck.
Hubbard, L. Ron. Dianetics & Scientology Technical Dictionary. Church Scient NY.
--Dianetics & Scientology Technical Dictionary. Bridge Pubns Inc.
Hubbard, Stuart W. The Computer Graphics Glossary. Oryx Pr.
Huber, Rudolf & Rieth, Renate, eds. Glossarium Artis: Deutsch-Franzoesisches Woerterbuch zur Kunst. Max Niemeyer.
--Glossarium Artis: Fasz 1, Burgen & Feste Plaetze. Max Niemeyer.
--Glossarium Artis: Fasz 2, Liturgische Geraete-Objets Liturgiques. Max Niemeyer.
--Glossarium Artis: Fasz 3, Bogen & Arkaden-Arcs et Arcades. Max Niemeyer.
--Glossarium Artis: Fasz 4, Paramente & Buecher der Christlichen Kirchen. Max Niemeyer.
--Glossarium Artis: Fasz 6, Gewoelbe & Kuppeln-Voutes et Coupoles. Niemeyer.
Hubert, J., jt. auth. see Stein, Henri.
Hubert, J., ed. see Stein, Henri.
Hucker, Charles O. A Dictionary of Official Titles in Imperial China: Governmental Nomenclature from Antiquity to 1850. Stanford U Pr.
Hudson, Kenneth. The Dictionary of Even More Diseased English. MacMillan London.
--The Dictionary of Even More Diseased English. Macmillan.
--Dictionary of the Teenage Revolution & its Aftermath. Macmillan London.
Huerlimann, Ernst. Lexikon Feurden Bauherrn. French & Eur.
Huerta, Fernando, et al. Diccionario ingles-espanol espanol-ingles. Circulo Lect.
Huertas Garcia, Alfredo. Ortografia metodica de la lengua espanola. Porrua.
Hueter, Paul & Goerner, Horst. Polytechnisches Woerterbuch Russisch-Deutsch. VEB Technik.
Huffman, Franklin E. Cambodian English. Yale U Pr.
Huffman, Franklin E. & Proum, Im. Cambodian-English Glossary. Yale U Pr.
--English-Khmer Dictionary. Yale U Pr.
Huffman, Ray. Nuer English Dictionary. Shalom.
Hughes. Dictionary of Islam. Kazi Pubns.
Hughes, Charles A. Ace's French Phrase Book & Dictionary. Ace Bks.
--Ace's Italian Phrase Book & Dictionary. Ace Bks.
--Ace's Scandinavian Phrase Book & Dictionary. Ace Bks.
--Ace's Spanish Phrase Book & Dictionary. Ace Bks.
--Aces's Italian Phrase Book & Dictionary. Ace Bks.
--Grosset's Italian Phrase Book & Dictionary for Travelers (G&D). Putnam Pub Group.
Hughes, Dom A., compiled by. Liturgical Terms for Music Students: A Dictionary. Scholarly.
Hughes, Edward C. Obsteric-Gynecological Terminology. Davis Co.
Hughes, Harold H. Dictionary of Abbreviations in Medicine & the Health Sciences. Lexington Bks.
Hughes, L. E., jt. auth. see Tweney, C. F.
Hughes, Thomas P. A Dictionary of Islam. Gordon Pr.
--Dictionary of Islam. Intl Pubns Serv.
--A Dictionary of Islam. South Asia Bks.
Hugo, Latzko. Angol Nyelvkonyv: English Language Book for Self-Learners & Student with Teachers. Saphrograph.
Hugon, Paul D. The Modern Word-Finder: A Living Guide to Modern Usage, Spelling, Synonyms, Pronunciation, Grammar, Word Origins, & Authorship. Gale.
Hugues, Francois-Claude, jt. auth. see Barbier, Jean-Philippe.
Hugues, Michel, jt. auth. see Sumpf, Joseph.
Huihua, Jianyi H. Simple Chinese Conversation. Saphrograph.
Hulbert, James R., jt. ed. see Craigie, William A.
Hull, Arthur E., ed. Dictionary of Modern Music & Musicians. AMS Pr.
--A Dictionary of Modern Music & Musicians. Scholarly.
Humberdrotz, R., jt. auth. see Schukry, K.
Humphreys, Fisher & Wise, Philip. A Dictionary of Doctrinal Terms. Broadman.
Hung, W. S. A New English-Chinese Law Dictionary. French & Eur.
Hung, William. A New English-Chinese Law Dictionary. M Stevenson.
Hunger, H. Lexikon der Griechischen und Roemischen Mythologie. French & Eur.
Hunsberger, I. Moyer. The Quintessential Dictionary. A & W Pubs.
Hunt, Cecil. A Dictionary of Word Makers: Pen Pictures of the People Behind Our Language. Folcroft.
Hunt, Daniel V. Conservation & Solar Energy Dictionary. Van Nos Reinhold.
Hunt, Lee M. & Groves, Donald G. Glossary of Ocean Science & Undersea Technology Terms. Compass Va.
Hunt, V. Daniel. Energy Dictionary. Van Nos Reinhold.
--The Solar Energy Dictionary. Indus Pr.
Hunter, Alfred C. Lexique de la Langue de Jean Chapelain. Droz.
Hunter, Samuel D. The Dictionary of Anagrams. Routledge & Kegan.
Hunter, W. W. A Comparative Dictionary of the Languages of India & High Asia. Orient Bk Dist.
Huntington Free Library & Reading Room. Dictionary Catalog of the American Indian Collection (Hall Library). G K Hall.
Hurd, John, jt. auth. see Aufrecht, Walter E.
Hurlimann, Ernst. Lexikon fur den Bauherrn. Verlag Moderne.
Hurme, R. & Pesonen, M. Finnish Deluxe Dictionary: English-Finnish. Vanous.
Hurme, R., et al. English-Finnish General Dictionary. French & Eur.
Hurme, Raija & Pesonen, Maritta. Englantilais-suomalainen Suursanakirja: English-Finnish General Dictionary. Soderstrom.
Hurrle, Karl, et al. Technical Dictionary of Vacuum Physics & Vacuum Technology (English, French, German, Russian) Pergamon.
Hurst, Walter E., jt. auth. see Delson, Donn.
Hurtado, Hernan, jt. auth. see Watson, Diana C.
Hurtaut, Magny. Dictionnaire Historique de la Ville de Paris & de ses Environs. Minkoff Repr.
Huskisson & Hart. Joint Disease. Wright-PSG.
Husson, Roger. Dictionnaire de Biologie Animale. Gauthier-Villars.
Hutar, Laddie F. Job Success Dictionary: A Hutar Guide to Becoming a More Valuable Employee & Earning More. Hutar.
Hutcheson, Christina, jt. auth. see Couro, Ted.
Hyamson, Albert M. Dictionary of English Phrases: Phraseological Allusions, Catchwords, Stereotyped Modes of Speech & Metaphors, Nicknames, Sobriquets, Derivations from Personal Names. Gale.
Hyman, Charles J. German-English, English-German Astronautics Dictionary (Consultants). Plenum Pub.
--German-English, English-German Electronics Dictionary (Consultants). Plenum Pub.
Hyman, Charles J., ed. Dictionary of Physics & Allied Sciences: German-English. Ungar.
Hyman, Robin, jt. auth. see Trevaskis, John.

I

Iakovlev, B. E. Cheshsko-Russkii Radiotekhnicheskii Slovar (Pub. by Glav. Red. Inostr. Nauchn. Tekhn. Slovarei Fizmata). Four Continent.
I.A.R.R. Abair faclan. Mingulay.
Iashunskaia, F. I., et al, eds. Anglo-Russkii Slovar Po Kauchuku, Rezine & Khimicheskim Voloknam (Pub. by Glav. Red. Inostr. Nauchn. Tekhn. Slovrei Fizmatgiza). Four Continent.
Iasulovich, N. I. Tolkovyi Slovar Terminov, Primeniaemykh & Sudovom Mashinostroenii (Pub. by Sudostroenie). Four Continent.
Ibanez, Esteban. Diccionario espanol-senhayi: Dialecto bereber de Senhay de Serair. Inst. de Estudios Africanos CSIC.
Ibarra, Francisco. Look & Learn Spanish. Camino Real.
Ibeas, F. F. Diccionario Tecnologico Ingles-Espanol. Edit Alhambra.
--English-Spanish Technical Dictionary. Heinman.
Ibeas, Franco. Diccionario Tecnologico Ingles-Espanol: Electricidad, Electronica, Telecomunicacion, & Materias Afinas con la Fisica, Optica & Quimica. Alhambra.
--Diccionario tecnologico Ingl e01s-Espa n13ol. Fed Gremios.
Ibero, Ramon. Diccionario de Ajedrez. French & Eur.
IBM. Diccionario De Siglas Relacionadas Con la Informatica. French & Eur.
--Glossario della Elabarione dei Dati: Inglese-Italiano, Italiono-Inglese. French & Eur.
Icard, S. Dictionary of Greek Coin Inscriptions. Obol Intl.
Icard, Severin. Dictionary of Greek Coin Inscriptions. S J Durst.
Icart, Antoine. Je Sais Tout Sur le Monde & la Nature. Hachette-Jeunesse.
ICG. Dictionary of Glass Making. Elsevier.
Idlin, Ralph, ed. Dictionary of Physics & Allied Sciences: English-German. Ungar.
IFIP. IFIP Fachtworterbuch der Informationsverabeitung (North Holland). Elsevier.
Ignashev, S. P., jt. auth. see Cruz, M.
Igoe, Robert S. The Dictionary of Food Ingredients. Van Nos Reinhold.
Ilg, G. Proverbes Francais: In French with Equivalents in English, German, Dutch, Italian, Spanish, Latin. Elsevier.
Iliev, A., et al. Russko-Uigurskii Slovar (Pub. by Gosizdat Natsional Inostr Slovarei). Four Continent.
Illingworth, Valerie. The Anchor Dictionary of Astronomy (Anch). Doubleday.
Illingworth, Valerie, ed. Facts on File: Dictionary of Astronomy. Facts on File.
Ilmberger, Josef. Die Bairische Fibel. B. L. V.
Imbs, Paul, jt. ed. see Centre National De la Recherche Scientifique.
IML-Institute of Modern Languages. Dictionary of the Spanish in Texas. Camino Real.
Immelmann, Klaus. Woerterbuch der Verhaltensforschung. Kindler.
Imperato, Pascal J., ed. Historical Dictionary of Mali. Scarecrow.
Indiana University, Institute for Sex Research. Sexual Nomenclature: A Thesaurus (Hall Library). G K Hall.
Inghult, Goran. Die Semantische Struktur Desubstantivischer Bildungen auf Maessig. Almqvist.
Inglis, James. Topical Dictionary of Bible Texts. Baker Bk.
Inoue, Jukichi. Inoue's Smaller Japanese-English Dictionary. C E Tuttle.
Institut de Ceramique Francaise. Thesaurus Ceramique. Francaise, Institut Ceramique.
Institut Dominicain d'Etudes Orientales du Caire, ed. Melanges: Tables generales (1954-1977) Intl Bk Ctr.
Institut Francais D'Archeologie Orientale, jt. auth. see Jomier, Jacques.
Institut Francais du Petrole. Thesaurus Economie de l'energie. Technip.
Institut fur Angewandte Sprachwissenschaft. Russisch-Deutsches Woerterbuch der Chemie & Chemischen. VEB Verlag Technik.
Institut fur Grafische Technik. Lexikon der Grafischen Technik. Saur Verlag.
Institut International de Terminologie Juridique & Administrative. Glossaire Europeen de Terminologie Juridique & Administrative, 1. Bordas-Dunod.
--Glossaire Europeen de Terminologie Juridique & Administrative, 3. Bordas-Dunod.
--Glossaire Europeen de Terminologie Juridique & Administrative, 5. Bordas-Dunod.
--Glossaire Europeen de Terminologie Juridique & Administrative, 6. Bordas-Dunod.
--Glossaire Europeen de Terminologie Juridique & Administrative, 8. Bordas-Dunod.
--Niederlassungsrecht. Langen AG.
Institute for Language Study. Vest Pocket Arabic (BN). B&N NY.
--Vest Pocket English (BN). B&N NY.
--Vest Pocket French (BN). B&N NY.
--Vest Pocket German (BN). B&N NY.
--Vest Pocket Italian (BN). B&N NY.
--Vest Pocket Japanese (BN). B&N NY.
--Vest Pocket Modern Greek (BN). B&N NY.
--Vest Pocket Spanish (BN). B&N NY.
Institute for Power System. Europump Terminology: Pump Applications. State Mutual Bk.
--Hydraulic Standards, Lexicon & Data. State Mutual Bk.
--Pneumatic Power Glossary. State Mutual Bk.
Institute of Business Appraiser. Glossary of Value Terms. Inst Busn Appraisers.
Institute of Electrical & Electronics Engineers, Inc. IEEE Standard Dictionary of Electrical & Electronics Terms (Pub. by Wiley-Interscience). Wiley.
Institute of Environmental Science. Glossary of Computer Controlled Environmental Testing Terminology. Inst Environ Sci.
Institute of Financial Education. Glossary of Savings Association Terminology. Inst Finan Educ.
Institute of Industrial Launderers. Glossary of Commonly Used Terms. Inst Indus Launderer.
Institute of Marine Engineers. Glossary of Marine Technology Terms. Sheridan.
--Glossary of Marine Technology Terms (Pub. by Heinemann England). State Mutual Bk.

Institute of Modern Language. Dictionary of the Spanish in Texas. Camino Real.
Institute of Signage Research. Glossary (ISR). Natl Elec Sign.
Institution of Fire Engineers. Dictionary of Fire Technology. Inst Fire Eng.
Instituto Americano. Vocabulario Tecnologico Aeronautico. Inst Amer.
Instituto da Lingua Galega. Dicionario Basico da Lingua Galega. Xerais de Galicia.
International Cartographic Association. Glossary of Terms in Computer Assisted Cartography. Am Congrs Survey.
International Chain of Industrial & Technical Advertising Agencies. Dictionary of Advertising & Marketing Terms in Six Languages: English-Spanish-French-German-Italian-Japanese. Black, George, ed. Marlin.
International Council of Ophthalmology, ed. Perimetric Standards & Perimetric Glossary (Pub. by Junk Pubs Netherlands). Kluwer Academic.
International Council of Opthalmology, ed. Perimetric Standards & Perimetric Glossary (Pub. by Junk Pubs Netherlands). Kluwer Academic.
International Electrotechnical Com. Vocabulario Electronico Internacional. French & Eur.
International Fabricare Institute. Chemical Terms for Washroom Procedures. Intl Fabricare Inst.
--Knit Terms. Intl Fabricare Inst.
--Terms-Mill Defects. Intl Fabricare Inst.
--Terms-Mill Defects. Intl Fabricare Inst.
--Terms Related to Soap & Detergents. Intl Fabricare Inst.
International Federation of Surveyors. Multilingual Dictionary of the International Federation of Surveyors. Elsevier.
International Gas Union, ed. Elsevier's Dictionary of the Gas Industry. Elsevier.
International Gas Union, compiled by. Supplement to Elsevier's Dictionary of the Gas Industry: Polygot. Elsevier.
International Graphoanalysis Society. Dictionary of Stroke Structures in Graphoanalysis. Intl Graphoanalysis.
International Information Centre for Terminology, ed. see Wuster, Eugen, et al.
International Institute of Refrigeration. New International Dictionary of Refrigeration (IIR). Unipub.
International Institution for Production Engineering Research. Dictionary of Production Engineering: German-English-French. Incl. Vol. 1. Forging & Drop Forging; Vol. 2. Grinding - Surface Roughness; Vol. 3. Sheet Metal Forming; Vol. 4. Fundamental Terms of Cutting; Vol. 5. Cold Extrusion & Upsetting; Vol. 6. Planing, Slotting, Broaching, Turning; Vol. 7; Milling, Sawing, Gear Manufacturing. Intl Pubns Serv.
International Masonry Institute. Masonry Glossary. CBI Pub.
International Monetary Fund, Bureau of Language Services. IMF Glossary: English-French-Spanish. Intl Monetary.
International Planned Parenthood Federation, ed. Defining Family Health Needs, Standards of Care & Priorities: With Particular Reference to Family Planning (Pub. by Intl Planned Parent). State Mutual Bk.
Introito & Porta. Vocabolario italiano-tedesco. Bottega d'Erasmo.
Investment Funds Institute of Canada-L' Institut Des Fonds D' Investissement Du Canada. Glossary of Mutual Fund Terms. Inv Funds Inst CN.
Ioannidia, A. A. Russko-Novogrecheskii Slovar (Pub. by Sov. Entsiklopediia). Four Continent.
Ioudine, P., jt. auth. see Rosenthal, M.
Ippoldt, J., jt. auth. see Piprek, J.
Ippoldt, Juliusz, jt. auth. see Piprek, Jan.
Ireland Department of Education. Focloir Modulach. Le Ceannach Direach on Oifig Dhiolta Foilseachan Rialtais.
Irey, Eugene F. A Concordance to Melville's Moby Dick. Garland Pub.
Iribarren Reta, Mercedes. Diccionario Humano. French & Eur.
Irmen, F. Langenscheidts Taschenwoerterbuch Portugiesisch: Teil I, Portugiesisch-Deutsch. Langenscheidt.
--Langenscheidts Taschenwoerterbuecher Portugiesisch-Deutsch. Langenscheidt.
Irmen, F., jt. auth. see Beau, A. E.
Iron & Steel Institute. Iron & Steel Dictionary: German-English & English-German. Intl Pubns Serv.
--Iron & Steel Dictionary: German-French & French-German. Intl Pubns Serv.
--Iron & Steel Dictionary: German-Italian & Italian-German. Intl Pubns Serv.
--Iron & Steel Dictionary: German-Spanish & Spanish-German. Intl Pubns Serv.
Irwin, Stevens. Dictionary of Electronic Organ Stops. Assoc-Mus.
--Dictionary of Hammond Organ Stops. Assoc-Mus.
--Dictionary of Pipe Organ Stops. Assoc-Mus.
Isaacs, A., jt. ed. see Gray, H. J.
Isaacs, Alan. The Multilingual Commercial Dictionary. Facts on File.
--The Multilingual Computer Dictionary. Facts on File.
Isaacs, Alan, ed. Dictionary of Music. Newnes Bks.
--Multilingual Commercial Dictionary. Facts on File.
--Multilingual Computer Dictionary. Facts on File.
--The Multilingual Computer Dictionary. Facts on File.
--The Multilingual Dictionary of Printing & Publishing. Facts on File.
--The Multilingual Energy Dictionary. Facts on File.
Isaacs, Alan & Martin, Elizabeth, eds. Dictionary of Music. Facts on File.
Isambaev, M. Russko-Latino-Kazakhskii Terminologicheskii Slovar (Pub. by Izd. An Kaz. SSR). Four Continent.
Isham, Norman M. Early American Houses & a Glossary of Colonial Architectural Terms. Da Capo.
Isler, C. Isler's Pocket Dictionary of Diagnostic Tests, Procedures & Terms. Med Economics.
Ismat, Shafiq. The Police Dictionary. Intl Bk Ctr.
--Police Dictionary: English-Arabic Dictionary. Intl Bk Ctr.
Isopel, May, ed. Italian-English, English-Italian Gem Dictionary. Collins Pubs.
Israelevich, E. E. English-Russian Dictionary of Finance & World Trade. Imported Bks.
Istituto Italiano dei Plastici, jt. auth. see Ferraris, Enrico.
Istituto per l'Enciclopedia della Banca e della Borsa. Dizionario di banca e di borsa: Vol. 1, A-D. Giuffre.
Iudakhin, K. K., ed. Russko-Kirgizskii Slovar (Pub. by GINS). Four Continent.
Ivamy, ed. Dictionary of Taxation. Butterworth.
Ivens, H., et al, eds. Jugendlexikon Weltpolitik. Bibl Inst Leipzig.
Ivens, Walter G. A Dictionary of the Language of Bugotu, Santa Isabel Island, Solomon Islands. AMS Pr.
--A Vocabulary of the Lau Language, Big Mala, Solomon Islands. AMS Pr.
Iwamura, Susan. The Verbal Games of Pre-School Children. St Martin.
IWT Verlag Editors. Microelectronics Dictionary (Pub. by VDI W Germany). Heyden.
Iz, Fahir & Hony, H. C. The Oxford English-Turkish Dictionary. Oxford U Pr.
Iz, Fahir see Alderson, A. D.
Iz, Fahir, jt. ed. see Alderson, A. D.
Izak, Miklos. Hiradastechnikai Kislexikon. Mueszaki Konyv.
Izbicki. Education A-Z. W Collins Sons.

J

Jaba, Auguste. Dictionnaire Kurde-Francais. Biblio-Verlag.
Jacks, G. V. & Tavernier, R. Vocabulaire Multilingue de la Science du Sol: Anglais-Francais-Espagnol-Allemand-Portugais-Italien-Neerlandais-Suedois-Russe. F. A. O.
Jackson, Benjamin D. Glossary of Botanic Terms, with Their Derivation & Accent. Hafner.
Jackson, Herbert L., jt. auth. see Jacob, Alphons.
Jackson, Julia A., jt. ed. see Bates, Robert L.
Jackson, Lenli. One Hundred Simple Chinese Recipes. Saphrograph.
Jacob, Alphons & Jackson, Herbert L. Dictionary of Radiologic Terminology. Green.
Jacob, Henry. Pocket Dictionary of Publishing Terms. Beekman Pubs.
Jacob, J. Concise Cambodian-English Dictionary. Iaconi.
Jacob, Judith. A Concise Cambodian-English Dictionary. Oxford U Pr.
Jacob, Nina, jt. auth. see Oftedal, Laura.
Jacob, U. & Petersein, G. T. BI-Taschenlexikon Heimtiere. Bibl Inst Leipzig.
Jacobi, C. Vocabulaire Forestier Francais-Allemand-Danois. Picard.
Jacobi, Charles T. The Printers' Vocabulary. Gale.
Jacobs, Arthur. Diccionario de Musica. French & Eur.
--New Dictionary of Music. Penguin.
Jacobs, Arthur, tr. Diccionario de musica. Leru.
Jacobs, B., jt. auth. see Beseler, D.
Jacobs, B., jt. ed. see Beseler, D. v.
Jacobs, Barbara, jt. auth. see Beseler, Dora Von.
Jacobs, George J. Dictionary of Vertebrate Zoology, Russian-English: English-Russian. Smithsonian.
Jacobs, Michael. Complete CB Slang Dictionary (Success). Merit Pubns.
Jacobs, Sidney J. The Jewish Word Book. Jonathan David.
Jacobs, Werner. Systematische Zoologie Insekten. Fischer Verlag.
--Woerterbuch der Biologie. French & Eur.
Jacobsen, Hermann. The Lexicon of Succulent Plants (Pub by Blandford Pr England). Sterling.
Jacobson, Howard B., ed. Mass Communications Dictionary. Philos Lib.
--Mass Communications Dictionary: A Reference Work of Common Terminologies for Press, Print, Broadcast, Film, Advertising & Communications Research. Greenwood.
Jacolev, Leon, jt. auth. see DeVries, Louis.
Jacolev, Leon, jt. auth. see De Vries, Louis.
Jacolev, Leon, jt. auth. see De Vries, louis.
Jaeger, Edmund C. A Dictionary of Greek & Latin Combining Forms Used in Zoological Names. C C Thomas.
Jaensch, Dean & Teichmann, Max E. The Macmillan Dictionary of Australian Politics. Macmillan Aust.
Jaffe, Evan. Illustrated Ballet Dictionary. Harvey.
Jaffs, Julian. Dictionary of World Wines, Liqueurs, & Other Drinks. Pagurian.
Jago, Frederick W. An English-Cornish Dictionary. AMS Pr.
Jahn, jt. auth. see Gack.
Jahn, H. Herder-Lexikon Pflanzen. Herder.
--Herder-Lexikon Pflanzen (Pub. by Herder). French & Eur.
Jahn, Johannes. Woerterbuch der Kunst. Kroener.
--Woerterbuch der Kunst. Kroener.
--Woerterbuch der Kunst. French & Eur.
Jakob, Ludwig. Lexikon der Onologie. Meininger.
Jakobsen, Jakob. An Etymological Dictionary of the Norn Language in Shetland. AMS Pr.
Jakosci, Slownik. Glossary of Terms Used in Quality Control (Pub. by Collets). State Mutual Bk.
Jakubke, H. D. Lexikon Biochemie. French & Eur.
Jakubke, Hans D. & Jeschkeit, Hans. Lexikon biochemie. Verlag Chemie.
Jal, Augustin. Nouveau Glossaire Nautique. Mouton.
--Nouveau Glossaire Nautique, Lettre C: Revision De L'edition Publiee En 1848. Mouton.
James, Arthur M. A Dictionary of Thermodynamics. Halsted Pr.
James, Glenn. Mathematics Dictionary. Van Nos Reinhold.
James, Simon, compiled by. A Dictionary of Economic Quotations. B&N Imports.
Jameson, E. W., Jr. A Short Dictionary of Simplified Chinese Characters. E W Jameson Jr.
Jameson, J. Franklin. Dictionary of United States History: Alphabetical, Chronological, Statistical. McKinley, Albert E., ed. Gale.
Jamieson, John. Etymological Dictionary of the Scottish Language. Longmuir, John & Donaldson, David, eds. AMS Pr.
Jane, Albert. Diccionari calala de simonims. Aedos.
--Diccionari Catala de Sinonims. French & Eur.
Janicot, Aime. Vocabulaire Anglais par l'image. Bordas-Dunod.
Janis, J. Harold. Modern Business Language & Usage in Dictionary Form. Doubleday.
Jannaris, A. N. A Concise Dictionary of the English & Modern Greek Languages. Caratzas Pub Co.
Jannini Pasquale, A. Vocabolario commerciale italiano-francese e francese-italiano, Caputo Cataldo. Monnier.
Jannota, Elpidio. Dizionario italiano-arabo moderno. Ist Poligrafico.
Janson, H. W. An Iconographic Index to Stanislas Lami's Dictionnaire des Sculpteurs de l'Ecole Francaise au Dix-Neuvieme Siecle. Garland Pub.
Jansonius, H. Dutch-English (Only) New Great Dictionary. Heinman.
Jarlaud, Alain, jt. auth. see Drieux, Jean P.
Jarlaud, Alain, jt. auth. see Drieux, Jean-Pierre.
Jarnier, R. & Fournier, J. Dictionnaire Bordas: Cahier de Travaux Diriges. Harrap.
Jarnier, Robert. Dictionnaire Bordas. Bordas-Dunod.
Jaschke, H. A. Tibetan-English Dictionary. Orient Bk Dist.
Jaschke, R. English Arabic Conversational Dictionary. Iaconi.
Jaschke, Richard. English-Arabic Conversational Dictionary. Intl Bk Ctr.
Jaschke, Richard, ed. English-Arabic Conversational Dictionary, with Supplement. Ungar.
Jastrow, Marcus. Hebrew-Aramaic-English Dictionary, a Dictionary of Talmud Babli & Talmud Yerushalmi Targum & Midrash. Shalom.
Jaubert, Hippolyte-Francois. Glossaire du Centre de la France. Slatkine.
Jay, E. Pictorial Dictionary of Nineteeth Century Furniture Design. Apollo.
Jean-Charles, Jehanne. Le Lexique des Bons Petits Plats. Presses Cite.
Jeanne, Pierre-Charles. Dictionnaire du Cinema Universal, 6. Laffont.
Jedlicka, Alois. Dictionary of Slavic Linquistic Terminology (Pub. by Helmut Buske Verlag Hamburg). Benjamins North Am.
--Dictionary of Slavonic Linquistc Terminology (Pub. by Helmut Buske Verlag Hamburg). Benjamins North am.

Jedraszko, Sabian. Slownik Lekarski Polsko-Angielski. Panstwowy Zaklad W.
Jeffrey, Charles. Biological Nomenclature. Crane-Russak Co.
Jefkins, Frank. Dictionary of Marketing & Communication. Intl Ideas.
Jehan, L. F. Dictionnaire d'Anthropologie ou Histoire Naturelle del'Homme et des Races Humaines. Migne, J. P., ed. Caratzas Pub Co.
--Dictionnaire d'Apologetique. Migne, J. P., ed. Caratzas Pub Co.
--Dictionnaire de Botanique. Migne, J. P., ed. Caratzas Pub Co.
--Dictionnaire de Chimie et de Mineralogie. Migne, J. P., ed. Caratzas Pub Co.
--Dictionnaire De Cosmogonie et De Paleontologie. Migne, J. P., ed. Caratzas Pub Co.
--Dictionnaire de Linguistique et de Philologie Comparee. Migne, J. P., ed. Caratzas Pub Co.
--Dictionnaire de Zoologie. Migne, J. P., ed. Caratzas Pub Co.
--Dictionnaire des Controverses Historiques. Migne, J. P., ed. Caratzas Pub Co.
--Dictionnaire Historique des Sciences Physiques et Naturelles. Migne, J. P., ed. Caratzas Pub Co.
Jeharned. Medical Terminology Made Easy. Physicians Rec.
Jenkins, William A. & Schiller, Andrew. My First Picture Dictionary. Lothrop.
Jenkins, William A., jt. auth. see Schiller, Andrew.
Jensen, John T., et al. Yapese-English Dictionary. UH Pr.
Jerrard, G. & Neill, D. B. Diccionario de Unidades Cientificas. Bellaterra.
Jerrard, H. G. & McNeill, D. B. Diccionario de Unidades Cientificas. French & Eur.
--Dictionary of Scientific Units. Halsted Pr.
Jeschkeit, Hans, jt. auth. see Jakubke, Hans D.
Jesperson, Otto. International Dictionary. Winter Univ.
--International Dictionary (Pub. by Carl Winter). French & Eur.
Jesse, A. Physics Terminology. French & Eur.
--Physik-Fachsprache Englisch-Franzosisch-Deutsch. Bauverlag.
--Terminologie de la physique: Anglais-Allemand-Francais. Maison Dictionnaire.
Jetikov. Dictionnaire Russe-Francais de l'automobile & du Tracteur. Mir.
Jezewski, W., jt. auth. see Blok, C.
Jezewski, Wiesaw, jt. auth. see Blok, Czesaw.
Jezewski, Wieslaw, jt. auth. see Blok, Czeslaw.
Jimenez Ortega, Javier. Diccionario de Biologia. Porrua.
Joan-Pascual, J. A. Diccionario Critico Etimologico Castellano & Hispanico. Gredos.
Johannesson, Alex. Islaendisches Etymologisches Woerterbuch (Pub. by Francke). French & Eur.
Johannisson, Ture & Ljunggren, K. G., eds. Svensk Handordbok: Kronstruktioner & Fraseologi. Esselte Studium.
Johannsen, H. Management Glossary: (English-Arabic) Intl Bk Ctr.
Johannsen, H. & Page, G. T., eds. International Dictionary of Management (Pub by Kogan Pg). Nichols Pub.
Johannsen, H., et al. Diccionario de Management. French & Eur.
Johannsen, Hano & Page, G. Terry. The International Dictionary of Business. P-H.
John M. Wing Foundation, Newberry Library. Dictionary Catalogue of the History of Printing from the John M. Wing Foundation, Second Supplement (Hall Library). G K Hall.
Johndro. Astrological Dictionary. Am Fed Astrologers.
Johnsich, John R., intro. By. Real Estate Securities & Title Insurance Terminology. Real Estate Pub.
--Title Insurance & Real Estate Securities Terminology. Real Estate Pub.
Johnson & Greutyner. The Dictionary of British Artists Eighteen Eighty to Nineteen Forty. Apollo.
Johnson, jt. auth. see Teitelbaum.
Johnson, Arta F. How to Read German Church Records Without Knowing Much German. Johnson.
Johnson, Charles B., jt. auth. see Marks, Georgette A.
Johnson, D. D, jt. auth. see Pearson, P. D.
Johnson, F. Swahili-English Dictionary. Saphrograph.
Johnson, Frederick, ed. Standard Swahili-English Dictionary. Oxford U Pr.
Johnson, Samuel. A Dictionary of the English Language. Intl Bk Ctr.
--Dictionary of the English Language. AMS Pr.
--A Dictionary of the English Language. Ayer Co.
--Dictionary of the English Language. Intl Bk Ctr.
--Dictionary of the English Language: In Which the Words Are Deduced from Their Originals & Illustrated in Their Different Significations by Examples from the Best Writers. Adler.
Johnson, Victor. An Advanced Modern German Vocabulary. Harrap Co.
Johnston, Grahame, ed. The Australian Pocket Oxford Dictionary. Oxford U Pr.
Johnstone, Thomas M. Harsusi Lexicon & English-Harsusi Word-list. Oxford U Pr.
Johnstone, W. A., tr. see Fohrer, Georg, et al.
Joint Association of Classical Teachers. Greek Vocabulary. Cambridge U Pr.
Jolivet, A., jt. auth. see Pinloche, A.
Jolly, Jean. Dictionnaire des Parlementaires Francais: Vol. 3, 1889-1940. PUF.
--Dictionnaire des Parlementaires Francais: Vol. 4, 1889-1940. PUF.
Jolobe, J. J., ed. see McLaren, J.
Jomier, Jacques & Institut Francais D'Archeologie Orientale. Lexique Pratique Francais-Arabe. Francais, Inst. Archeo. Orient.
Jones, B. J. English-Korean Dictionary for Practical Conversation. Hollym Corp.
--Standard English-Korean Dictionary for Foreigners. Hollym Intl.
Jones, B. J., ed. Standard English-Korean Dictionary: For Foreigners. Hollym Corp.
Jones, B. J., ed. see Pong Kook Lee.
Jones, C. E., jt. auth. see Little, R. J.
Jones, Daniel, ed. Everyman's English Pronouncing Dictionary: Completely Revised (Pub. by J. M. Dent England). Biblio Dist.
Jones, David J., ed. The Australian Dictionary of Acronyms & Abbreviations. Second Back Row.
--The Australian Dictionary of Acronyms & Abbreviations. Second Back Row.
Jones, Hugh P., ed. Dictionary of Foreign Phrases & Classical Quotations. Longwood Pr.
--Dictionary of Foreign Phrases & Classical Quotations. Tanager Bks.
--A New Dictionary of Foreign Phrases & Classical Quotations. Century Bookbindery.
Jones, Peter d'A, jt. ed. see Holli, Melvin G.
Jones, Stephen. Practical English-German, German-English Dictionary. Hippocrene Bks.
Jones, William J. Lexicon of French Borrowings in the German Vocabulary. De Gruyter.
Jong, F. J. Economisch Woorden Boek: Engels-Frans-Duits-Nederlands. French & Eur.
Jong, Frits J. De see De Jong, Frits J., et al.
Jongerius, A. & Rutherford, G. K., eds. Glossary of Soil Micromorphology. Pudoc.
Jorda, Ernest, tr. see Trimmer, Eric.
Jorda, L. Diccionario Ingles-Espanol. Omega SA.
Jordana, Ricard. Mi Primer Diccionario Ingles-Espanol. Edns Nauta.
--Mi primer diccionario Ingles-Espanol. Fed Gremios.
Jordana, Ricard & Chamberlain, Paul. Diccionario Ingles-Espanol, Espanol-Ingles. Edns Nauta.
--Diccionario Ingles-Espanol, Espanol-Ingles. Fed Gremios.
Jordana, Ricardo & Chamberlain, Paul. Diccionario ingles-espanol espanol-ingles. Nauta SA.
Jordana de Pozas, Luis & Merlin, Olivier. Dictionnaire Juridique, Francais-Espagnol, Espagnol-Francais. French & Eur.
Jorgensen, V. Tams. Snaak Friisk: Interfriisk Leksikon. Verein Nord.
Jose, V., jt. auth. see Peers, E. A.
Jose, V., jt. ed. see Peers, E. A.
Jose, Victor, jt. auth. see Peers, Edgar A.
Jose-Aguilar Civera, J., jt. auth. see Aguilar, Peris.
Josselson, Harry H., ed. Russian-English Plastics Dictionary: Reversed from an English-Russian Dictionary by Computer Processing. Wayne St U Pr.
Jossier, Sophie. Dictionnaire des Patols de l'Yonne. Slatkine.
Jota, Zelio dos Santos. Dicionarios de Linguistica. Prensa Acad.
Joubrel, H. & Bertrand, P., trs. Diccionario de educacion infantil. Leru.
Jouffroy, A. Dictionnaire des Erreurs Sociales. Migne, J. P., ed. Caratzas Pub Co.
--Dictionnaire des Inventions et Decouvertes Anciennes et Modernes. Migne, J. P., ed. Caratzas Pub Co.
Jouhanneaud, P. Dictionnaire d'Anecdotes Chretiennes. Migne, J. P., ed. Caratzas Pub Co.
Jourbel, H. & Bertrand, P. Diccionario de Educacion Infantil. French & Eur.
Jourcin, Albert. Dictionnaire des Femmes Celebres. Larousse.
Jouve, E. G. Dictionnaire d'Esthetique Chretienne ou Theorie du Beau dans l'Art Chretien. Migne, J. P., ed. Caratzas Pub Co.
Jover Peralta, A & Ozuna, T. Diccionario guarani-espanol, espanol-guarani. Dist. Comuneros.
Jowitt, William A. Jowitt's Dictionary of English Law. Sweet & Maxwell.
Joy, Edward. Pictorial Dictionary of British Nineteenth Century Furniture Designs. Hacker.
Joyce, John, ed. see Ward, Jill.
Jozwicki, J. Minimum-Worterbuch: Deutsch-Polnisch, Polnisch-Deutsch. French & Eur.
Juan-Guitart, Jorge, jt. auth. see Clemente, Zamora.
Judd, Henry P. The Hawaiian Language & Hawaiian-English Dictionary. Hawaiian Serv.
Juhasz, Jozsef. Magyar Ertelmezo Keziszotar. Akademiai Kiado.
Juhasz, Jozsef, et al, eds. Magyar Ertelmezo Keziszotar. Akademiai Kiado.
Juilland, Alphonse. Dictionnaire Inverse De la Langue Francaise. Mouton.
Juilland, Alphonse & Chang-Rodriquez, E. Frequency Dictionary of Spanish Words. Mouton.
Juilland, Ileana. Dictionnaire Des Idees Dans L'oeuvre D'andre Malraux. French & Eur.
Julian, J., ed. A Dictionary of Hymnology: Origin & History of Christian Hymns. Gordon Pr.
Julien, Alain, jt. auth. see Houle, Michel.
Julland, Ileana. Dictionnaire Des Idees Dans L'oeuvre D'Andre Malraux: Collection Dictionaries Des Idees Dans les Litteratures Occidentales, Litterature Francaise: Dictionnnaires D'auteurs. Mouton.
July, Fortune, jt. auth. see Olmi, Andre.
Juncker. Junckers Worterbuch German-American Slang. Seiffhart, Arthur, ed. Assoc Bk.
Jung, C. Gustav. Dizionario di psicologia analitica. Musatti, C. L. & Aurigemma, L., trs. Boringhieri.
Jung, Fernand & Weil, Georg. Der Horror-Film. Roloff.
Junge. Woerterbuch fuer den Hobbyelektroniker. Verlag Harri Deutsch.
Junge, Hans D. Brockhaus ABC Elektronik. R Brockhaus.
--Brockhaus ABC Elektrotechnik. F A Brockhaus.
--Technische Kybernetik Grundlagen & Anwendungen Deutsch-Englisch. VEB Technik.
--Woerterbuch fur den Hobby-Elektroniker Englisch-Deutsch. VEB Technik.
Jungmair, Otto, ed. Woerterbuch zur Oberoesterreichischen Volksmundart. Selbstverlag Inst.
Jurancic. Dictionary Slovene-Serbocroatian-Slovene. French & Eur.
Jurancic, J. Serbocroatian-Slovene Dictionary. French & Eur.
Jurjani, Al Sharif. Kitab al-Ta Rifat (Book of Definitions) Arabic-Arabic Dictionary. Intl Bk Ctr.
Just, K., jt. ed. see Gottschalg, J.
Justus, Fred. Jumbo Vocabulary Development Yearbook: Grade 1. ESP.
--Jumbo Vocabulary Development Yearbook: Grade 2. ESP.
--Jumbo Vocabulary Fun Yearbook. ESP.

K

Kabesch, Friedrich. Langenscheidts Taschenwoerterbuch Tschechisch: Teil II, Deutsch-Tschechisch. Langenscheidt.
--Langenscheidts Taschenwoerterbuecher Deutsch-Tschechisch. Langenscheidt.
Kabesch, Friedrich, jt. auth. see Ulbrich, Rolf.
Kaczmarski, Stanisaw P. A Glossary of Polish & English Verb Forms. Panstwowy Zaklad W.
Kaczmarski, Stanislaw P. A Glossary of Polish & English Verb Forms. Panstwowe Zaklad W.
Kadar, I. & Ratz, O. Langenscheidts Handwoerterbuch Ungarisch HALASZ: Teil II, Deutsch-Ungarisch. Langenscheidt.
Kadic, Ante. Croation Reader with Vocabulary. Mouton.
Kaerre, Karl K., jt. auth. see Santesson, R.
Kafitz, Franz. Lexikon des Wirtschaftsrechnens. French & Eur.
Kagaine, Elga & Rage, S. Ergemes Izloksnes Vardnica. Zinatne.
Kahane, Henry, et al. Glossario degli antichi portolani italiani. Olschki.
Kahla, Martti. Kirjastotermien Sanakirja. Neuvost.
Kahlmann, Andre. Petit Dictionnaire du Francais gue l'on n'Apprend pas a l'Ecole. Esselte Studium.
--Petit Dictionnaire du Francais que l'on n'Apprend Pas a l'Ecole. Esselte Studium.
Kahlo, Gerhard, et al. Woerterbuch Deutsch-Indonesisch. VEB Verlag Enzyklopadie.
Kahn, Gilbert & Mulkerne, Donald J. The Wordbook. Glencoe.
Kai. All Romanized English-Japanese Dictionary. Iaconi.
Kai, Hyojun R. All-Romanized English-Japanese Dictionary. C E Tuttle.
Kairov, I. A., ed. Pedagogicheskii Slovar (Pub. by Izd. Akademii Ped. Nauk). Four Continent.
Kaiser. Kleines Kriminologisches Woerterbuch (Pub. by Herder). French & Eur.
--Kleines Kriminologishes Woerterbuch. Herder.
Kaiser, Ulrich. Lexikon Fuer Tennisfreunde. French & Eur.
Kaiser, Ulrich, et al. Lexikon fuer Tennisfreunde. Bucher Verlag.
Kalan, P., jt. auth. see Bajec, A.
Kalck, Pierre. Historical Dictionary of the Central African Republic. O'Toole, Thomas, tr. Scarecrow.
Kaliske, G. Dictionary of Plastics Technology in English, German, French & Russian. Elsevier.
Kaliske, Gisbert. Plasttechnik-Englisch-Deutsch-Franzoesisch-Russisch. VEB Technik.
Kalquist, Eskil, et al. Ordlistan Fran Natur & Kultur. Natur & Kultur.
Kaltenborn, Arthur L., jt. auth. see Ward, Kendall K.

Kaluza, B. Herder - Lexikon Paedagogik (Pub. by Herder). French & Eur.

--Herder-Lexikon Paedagogik. Herder.

Kaluza, Bjorn, ed. Herder Lexikon Paedogogik. Herder.

Kaluzhnin, L. A., et al. Nemetsko-Russkii Matematicheskii Slovar (Pub. by Fizmatgiz). Four Continent.

Kamarainen, jt. auth. see Farbregd.

Kamarainen, Aili, jt. auth. see Farbregd, Turid.

Kamenetz, Georgette, jt. auth. see Kamenetz, Herman L.

Kamenetz, Herman L. Dictionary of Rehabilitation Medicine. Springer Pub.

--Physiatric Dictionary: Glossary of Physical Medicine & Rehabilitation. C C Thomas.

Kamenetz, Herman L. & Kamenetz, Georgette. Dictionnaire de Medecine Physique de Reeducation et Readaptation Fonctionelles. French & Eur.

--Dictionnaire Francais-Anglais de Medecine Physique de Reeducation & de Readaptation Fonctionhelles. Maloine.

Kamenetz, Herman L. & Kamentz, Georgette. Dictionnaire de Medecine Physique de Reeducation & Readaptation. Maloine.

Kamentz, Georgette, jt. auth. see Kamenetz, Herman L.

Kamis, Adolf, jt. auth. see Belic, Jaromir.

Kammenhuber, Annelies, jt. auth. see Friedrich, Johannes.

Kampen, V. van see Van Kampen, V.

Kamrat, Mordechai & Samuel, Edwin, eds. Roots: A Hebrew-English Word List. K Sefer.

Kania, Stanislaw & Gora, Zielona. Polska Gwara Konspiracyjno-Partyzancka Czasu Okupacji Hitlerowskiej. Wyzsza Szkola.

Kanner, Gerald B., jt. ed. see Epstein, Howard M.

Kantrowitz, Joanne, jt. auth. see Kantrowitz, Nathan.

Kantrowitz, Martin P. Que Paso? Camino Real.

Kantrowitz, Nathan & Kantrowitz, Joanne. Stateville Names: A Prison Vocabulary. Maledicta.

Kaper, E., jt. auth. see Bork, E.

Kaper, Egon, jt. auth. see Bork, Egon.

Kappes, Matthias. Aristoteles-Lexikon. B Franklin.

Kaps, Urban. Medizinisches Woerterbuch (Pub. by Bruno Wilkens). French & Eur.

Karaalioglu, Seyit K. Cagdas Ozturce Sozlugu. Inkilap ve Aka Kitabevleri.

Karasaev, Aisash T., et al. Russko-Chechenskii Slovar. Russkii Iazyk.

Karaulov, Iu. N., ed. Chastotnyi Slovar Semanticheskikh Mnozhitelei Russkogo Iazyka (Pub. by Nauka). Four Continent.

Karcsay, Sandor. Ungarisch-Deutsches Woerterbuch der Rechts & Verwaltungssprache: Teil I, Ungarisch-Deutsch. Recht & Wirtschaft.

--Ungarisch-Deutsches Woerterbuch der Rechts & Verwaltungssprache: Teil II, Deutsch-Ungarisch. Recht & Wirtschaft.

--Woerterbuch der Ungarischen Rechts und Verwaltungssprache. French & Eur.

Karcsay, Sandor, jt. auth. see Decsi, Gyula.

Kardanov, B. M., et al. Russko-Kabardinsko-Cherkesskii Slovar (Pub. by GINS). Four Continent.

Karim, A. Common English Words & Idioms with Their Equivalents in Bahasa Indonesia. C E Tuttle.

Karim, A. & Lucy, T. A Dictionary of English Bahasa Malaysia Idiomatic Phrases. Jaya Ciencia.

Karimova, G. R. Russko-Bashkirskii Slovar (Pub. by GINS). Four Continent.

Karin, Thomas. Diccionario del Arte Actual. French & Eur.

Karlgren, Bernhard. Analytic Dictionary of Chinese & Sino-Japanese. Peter Smith.

--Analytical Dictionary of Chinese & Sino-Japanese. Dover.

--Schrift & Sprache der Chinesen. Springer-Verlag.

Karlsruhe. Diccionario tecnico del seguro de vida. Rev. Mex. de Seguros.

Karmi, Hasan. English-Arabic Dictionary: Al-Manar. Intl Bk Ctr.

Karmi, Hassan. Al Manar: English-Arabic Dictionary. Intl Bk Ctr.

Karre, K. Swedish Karre Dictionary, Vol. 1: Svensk-Engelsk. Vanous.

--Swedish Karre Dictionary, Vol. 2: Engelsk-Svensk. Vanous.

Karttunen, Frances. An Analytical Dictionary of Nahuatl. U of Tex Pr.

Karttunen, Kaarina. Nykyslangin Sanakirja. Soderstrom.

Kase, Francis J., ed. Dictionary of Industrial Property, Legal & Related Terms: English, Spanish, French & German. Sijthoff & Noordhoff.

Kasher, M. M. Encyclopedia of Biblical Interpretation. Ktav.

Kassel, Hans. Lexikon Datens & Datensicherung. Siemens AG.

Kasten, Lloyd & Anderson, Jean. Concordance to the Celestina (1499) Hispanic Seminary.

Kasten, Lloyd & Nitti, John. Concordances & Texts of the Royal Scriptorium Manuscripts of Alfonso X, el Sabio. Hispanic Seminary.

Kasten, Lloyd, jt. auth. see Nitti, John.

Katara, P., et al. Finnish-German Great Dictionary. French & Eur.

Katayama, Hiroshi, jt. auth. see Nishiyama, Kazuo.

Katona, Lorant. Magyar-Orosz Muszaki Szotar. Akademiai Kiado.

Kato Yda, Manuel M., jt. auth. see Martinez Duenas, Luis M.

Katz, Dorothy D., jt. ed. see Altman, Philip L.

Katz, Eliezer. A Classified Concordance. Incl. Vol. 1. The Torah; Vol. 2. The Early Prophets; Vol. 3. The Later Prophets. Bloch.

Katz, Eliezer, ed. Classified Concordance: To the Bible & Its Various Subjects. Bloch.

Kauffman, Donald T., ed. Baker's Pocket Dictionary of Religious Terms. Baker Bk.

Kaupert, W., ed. Dictionary of Waste Disposal & Public Cleansing. Elsevier.

Kaushik, P. D. Congress Ideology & Programme. Paragon.

Kawamoto, Shigeo & Nishiwaki, Junzaburo, eds. The Kodansha English-Japanese Dictionary. Narita, Shigehisa & Shimizu, Mamoru, trs. Kodansha.

Kay, Margarita. Southwestern Medical Dictionary: Spanish-English & English-Spanish. U of Ariz Pr.

Kaye, Alan S. A Dictionary of Nigerian Arabic. Undena Pubns.

Kazachenok, T. G. Farmakologicheskii Slovar: Latinsko-Russkii & Russko-Latinskii (Pub. by Vysheishaia). Four Continent.

Kazi, I. D., jt. auth. see Das, S. C.

Kazimirski, A. B. Dictionnaire Arabe-Francais. Intl Bk Ctr.

Kazirmski, A. Arabe Francais Dictionnaire. Intl Bk Ctr.

Kedrinskii, Vsevolod V. Anglo-Russkii Slovar po Khimii i Pererabotke Nefti. Russkii Iazyk.

Keep, Robert P., tr. see Autenrieth, Georg.

Kehler. Surface Treatment of Aluminum--A Glossary of Technical Terms. Heyden.

Kehrein, Franz. Woerterbuch der Weidmannssprache. French & Eur.

Keim, Marianne. Insurance Language. Running Pr.

Kelin, F. V., ed. Ispansko-Russkii Slovar (Pub. by Gosizdat Inostr Natsional Slovarei). Four Continent.

Kelina. Diccionario espanol-ruso. Pueblos Unidos.

Keller, Howard H. German Root Lexicon. U of Miami Pr.

--A German Word Family Dictionary: Together with English Equivalents. U of Cal Pr.

Keller, M., et al. A Dictionary of Words About Alcohol. Rutgers Ctr Al.

Keller, Sally. English-Khmer Medical Dictionary. Summer Inst Ling.

Kelley, John W., jt. ed. see Wells, Roger.

Kelley, Thomas M., jt. auth. see Seitzinger, Jack M.

Kelly, John W., tr. see Wells, Roger, Jr.

Kelly-Bootle, Stan. The Devil's DP Dictionary (P&RB). McGraw.

Kemp, J. Alan, ed. see Lepsius, Richard.

Kempcke, G., jt. ed. see Goerner, H.

Kendall, Bridget, tr. see David.

Kendall, Maurice G. & Buckland, William K. Dictionary of Statistical Terms. Longman.

Kendall, Maurice G., jt. auth. see Buckland, William R.

Kendris. Dictionnaire De Deux Cent Un Verbes Anglais Conjugues Completement a Tous les Temps & a Toutes les Personnes. Barron.

Kendris, C. Dictionary of Five-Hundred-One French Verbs Fully Conjugated. Barron.

Kendris, Christopher. Diccionario De Dos Cientos Uno Verbos Franceses Conjugados en Todos sus Tiempos & Personas. Barron.

--Dictionary of Five Hundred One Spanish Verbs. Camino Real.

--Dictionnaire de Docientos Uno Verboes Espagnols Conjugues a Toutes les Personnes. Barron.

--Two Thousand & One Words You Need to Know to Pass Any Spanish Test. Barron.

Kenesbaev, S., et al. Russko-Kazakhsii Slovar Lingvisticheskikh Terminov (Pub. by An Arm SSR). Four Continent.

Kenigsberg, jt. auth. see Petroni.

Kennedy, George A. Minimum Vocabularies of Written Chinese. Far Eastern Pubns.

Kennedy, John. Stem Dictionary of the English Language. Gale.

--A Stem Dictionary of the English Language. R West.

Kennedy, Michael, ed. The Concise Oxford Dictionary of Music. Oxford U Pr.

Kennedy, W. G. & Silva, Maria. Expressoes Idiomaticas Inglesas: English Idioms. Imported Bks.

Kennon, L. H. Tests of Literary Vocabulary for Teachers of English. AMS Pr.

Kenny, A. J., ed. see Prior, Arthur N.

Kent, Roland G. Old Persian Grammar Texts Lexicon. Am Orient Soc.

Kent, Rosalind. Reading the Russian Language: A Guide for Librarians & Other Professionals. Dekker.

Kent, Ruth. Language of Journalism: A Glossary of Print-Communications Terms. Kent St U Pr.

Kenyon, J. P., ed. A Dictionary of British History. Stein & Day.

Kenyon, John S. & Knott, Thomas A. Pronouncing Dictionary of American English. Merriam-Webster Inc.

Kercheville, F. M. A Preliminary Glossary of New Mexican Spanish. Borgo Pr.

Kerchuville, F. M. Practical Spoken Spanish. Camino Real.

Kerdel-Vegas, F. & Adamicska, O. Diccionario de sindromes. Cientifico Med.

Kerler, Richard. Begriffe des Managements. Humboldt Taschen.

Kerr, Allen. Comprehensive Lao-English Dictionary. Iaconi.

--Lao-English Dictionary. Cath U Pr.

Kerr, Avice H. Medical Hieroglyphs. Enterprise Calif.

Kerrich, Mary E., ed. see Fitzgerald, Edward.

Kersey, J. A New English Dictionary. Adler.

Kershaw, F. & Russon, S. German for Business Studies. French & Eur.

Kersley, Leo & Sinclair, Janet. A Dictionary of Ballet Terms. Da Capo.

Kesselman-Turkel, Judi & Peterson, Franklynn. The Vocabulary Builder: The Practically Painless Way to a Larger Vocabulary. Contemp Bks.

Ketchian, S. & Desbrandes, R. Technical Petroleum Dictionary of Well-Logging, Drilling & Production Terms (Pub. by Graham & Trotman England). State Mutual Bk.

Ketchian, S., et al, eds. Technical Petroleum Dictionary of Well-Logging Drilling, & Production Terms. Gordon.

Ketchian, Sonia. Dictionnaire Petrolier des Techniques de Diagraphie, Forage & Production: Russe-Francais-Anglais-Allemand. Technip.

--Dictionnaire Petrolier des Techniques de Diagraphique, Forage et Production. French & Eur.

Ketchian, Sonia, ed. Technical Petroleum Dictionary of Well-Logging, Drilling & Production Terms. Intl Pubns Serv.

Kettridge. French-English, English-French Dictionary of Commercial & Financial Terms. French & Eur.

Kettridge, J. O. Dictionary of Technical Terms. Routledge & Kegan.

--French-English & English-French Dictionary of Commercial & Financial Terms. Routledge & Kegan.

--French-English & English-French Dictionary of Commercial & Financial Terms, Phrases & Practice. Routledge & Kegan.

--French-English & English-French Dictionary of Financial & Mercantile Terms, Phrases & Practice. Routledge & Kegan.

--French-English & English-French Dictionary of Technical Terms & Phrases. Incl. Vol. 1. French-English; Vol. 2. English-French. Routledge & Kegan.

--French for English Idioms & Figurative Phrases. Routledge & Kegan.

--French Idioms & Figurative Phrases. Saphrograph.

Kettridge, Julius O. Dictionary of Technical Terms. French & Eur.

--Financial & Mercantile Dictionary. French & Eur.

Keupper, H. Woerterbuch der Deutschen Umgangsprache: Vol. 4, Berufsschelten & Verwandtes. M Rosenberg.

Key, A., jt. auth. see Cellard, J.

Keyes, W. Noel. Keyes Encyclopedic Dictionary of Procurement Law: Definitions of Legal Terms & Concepts in Private Procurement & Public Procurement of Federal, State & Local Governments, Their Contractors & Subcontractors. Oceana.

Kgasa, Morulaganyi. Thanodi ya Setswana ya Dikole. Longman S Africa.

Khaikin, Ia. B. Anglo-Russkii Slovar Dorozhnika (Pub. by Izd. Avtotrnsport. Lit.). Four Continent.

Khatib, A., ed. see Chihabi.

Khatib, Ahmad. Arabic-English Dictionary of Agricultural Terms & Allied Terminology. Intl Bk Ctr.

--A Dictionary of Agricultural & Allied Terminology. Intl Bk Ctr.

--A Dictionary of Natural Environment. Intl Bk Ctr.

--A Dictionary of Petroleum & the Oil Industry. Intl Bk Ctr.

--Dictionary of the Natural Environment: English-Arabic. Intl Bk Ctr.

--A New Dictionary of Scientific & Technical Terms. Intl Bk Ctr.

Khatib, Ahmad S. Al see Al-Khatib, Ahmad S.

Khatib, Ahmed. Chihabi's Dictionary of Agricultural & Forestry Terms. Intl Bk Ctr.

--English-Arabic Dictionary of Petroleum Terms & the Oil Industry. Intl Bk Ctr.

Khin, Yvonne M. The Collector's Dicionary of Quilt Names & Patterns. Acropolis.

Khopkar, M. B., compiled by. Dictionary of Political Terminology. Ind-US Inc.

Khorikov, I. P. Novogrechesko-Russkii Slovar (Pub. by Russkii Iazyk). Four Continent.

Khramov, A. V., ed. Russko-Anglo-Nemetsko-Frantsuzskii Slovar Terminov Po Avtomaticheskomu Upravleniiu (Pub. by An Arm SSR). Four Continent.
Khromov, S. P. Meteorologicheskii Slovar (Pub. by Gidrometeoizdat). Four Continent.
Kibirkshtis, L. B., et al. Karmannyi Urdu-Russkii Slovar (Pub. by GINS). Four Continent.
Kici, Gasper. Albanian-English Dictionary. G Kici.
Kici, Gasper & Aliko, Hysni. English-Albanian Dictionary. G Kici.
Kidd, D. A. Latin-English, English-Latin Dictionary. Saphrograph.
Kiefer, Ferenc, ed. Morphologie & Generative Grammatik. Akad Verl Ath.
Kiel, Cornelis. Dictionarium Teutonicolatinum. Olms Verlag.
Kielitoimisto. Udissanasto Kahdeksankymmenta. Soderstorm.
Kielski, B., jt. auth. see Kupisz, K.
Kierst. Polish-English - English-Polish Dictionary. Saphrograph.
Kierst, W. English-Polish, Polish-English Dictionary. Saphrograph.
Kikuoka, Tadashi, ed. Japanese Newspaper Compounds: The One Thousand Most Important in Order of Frequency. C E Tuttle.
Killer, W. K. Bautechnisches Englisch im Bild: Illustrated Technical German for Builders. Bauverlag.
--Illustrated Technical German for Builders. Bauverlag.
--Illustrated Technical German for Builders (Pub. by Bauverlag). French & Eur.
Kilmurray, Elaine, ed. see Ormond, Richard & Rogers, Malcolm.
Kimball, Richard L. China Beginner's Traveler's Dictionary. China Bks.
--China Beginner's Traveler's Dictionary. Eurasia Pr NY.
King, A., jt. auth. see Fromherz, H.
King, A. T. Oil Refinery Terms in Oklahoma. Bd. with State-Wide Dialect Collecting. Criswell, E. H; Problems Confronting the Investigator of Gullah. Turner, L. D. U of Ala Pr.
King, Alexander, jt. auth. see Fromherz, Hans.
King, Copland. A Grammar & Dictionary of the Binandere Language, Mamba River...Papua. Bd. with A Grammar & Dictionary of the Wedau Language. AMS Pr.
King, Frank P., jt. ed. see Craig, Robert D.
King, Robert C. Dizionario di genetica. ISEDI.
Kingdon, Roger, jt. auth. see West, Michael P.
Kinsman, Donald M. International Meat Science Dictionary. American Pr.
Kintana, Xabier. Euskal Histegi Modernoa. Cinsa Coord.
Kintana, Xabier, et al, eds. Euskal Histegi Modernoa. Coord Iniciat.
Kiraly, R. Portuguese-Hungarian Concise Dictionary. French & Eur.
Kiraly, Rudolf. Portugal-Magyar Szotar. Akademiai Kiado.
Kirchner, Joachim, ed. Lexicon des Buchwesen: Bd 4, Bilderatlas zum Buchwesen Teil 2. Hiersemann.
--Lexikon des Buchwesens. Hiersemann.
--Lexikon des Buchwesens: Bd 1, Text A-K. Hiersemann.
--Lexikon des Buchwesens: Bd 2, Text L-Z. Hiersemann.
--Lexikon des Buchwesens: Bd 3, Bilderatlas zum Buchwesen Teil 1. Hiersemann.
Kirchoff, Anne. Woerterbuch der Jagel. French & Eur.
Kirillova, I., jt. auth. see Dybovskaia, V.
Kirkeby, W. & Berulfsen, B. Norwegian-English, English-Norwegian Dictionary. Heinman.
Kirkeby, W. A. Norwegian-English Dictionary. Kunnskapsforlaget.
--Norwegian-English Dictionary. Kunnskapsforlaget.
Kirkeby, W. A. & Utgabes, S. Norsk-Engelsk Ordbok. French & Eur.
Kirkeby, Willie, ed. see Christophensen, Scavenius.
Kirkeby, Willy. Bil-og Trafikkteknisk Ordbok. Kunnskapsforlaget.
--Norsk-Engelsk Ordbok. Kunnskapsforlaget.
Kirkely, Willie. Norsk-Engelsk Ordbok. Vanous.
Kirkpatrick, E. M., ed. Chambers Universal Learners' Dictionary (Pub. by W & R Chambers Scotland). State Mutual Bk.
Kirkpatrick, E. M., et al, eds. Chambers Second Learners' Dictionary. W & R Chambers.
Kirwin, W. J see Story, G. M.
Kittel, Gerhard & Friedrich, Gerhard, eds. Theological Dictionary of the New Testament. Incl. Vol. 1; Vol. 2; Vol. 3; Vol. 4; Vol. 5; Vol. 6; Vol. 7; Vol. 8; Vol. 9; Vol. 10. Eerdmans.
Kittredge, G. L., ed. see Virgil.
Kiwanis-Club. Le Dictionnaire Franco-Montcellien. Kiwanis-Club.
Kjaer, L. Ove. Dansk-Latinsk: Ordbog. French & Eur.
Klaften, B. & Allison, F. C. Woerterbuch der Patentfachsprache. French & Eur.
Klaften, Berthold. Mathematisches Vokabular (Pub. by Wila). French & Eur.
--Woerterbuch der Patentfachsprache-Patent Terminological Dictionary: English-German & German-English. Intl Pubns Serv.
Klaften, E. B. German-English, English-German Mathematical Dictionary. Heinman.
Klaften, E. B. & Allison, F. C. German-English, English-German Patent Terminological Dictionary. Heinman.
Klapper, Marvin. Textile Glossary. Fairchild.
Klar, J., jt. ed. see Nagy, E.
Klar, Janos, jt. auth. see Nagy, Erno.
Klatt, E. & Klatt, G. Langenscheidts Taschenwoerterbuch Englisch: Teil II, Deutsch-Englisch. Langenscheidt.
Klatt, E. & Roy, D. Langenscheidts Taschenwoerterbuch Englisch: Teil I, Englisch-Deutsch. Langenscheidt.
--Langenscheidts Taschenwoerterbuecher Englisch-Deutsch. Langenscheidt.
Klatt, E., et al. Langenscheidts Taschenwoerterbuch Englisch. Langenscheidt.
Klatt, Edmund. Langenscheidt's Standard Dictionary. Imported Bks.
Klatt, Edmund, et al. Langenscheidt's Standard German Dictionary: German-English, English-German. Am Map.
Klatt, Edmund, et al, eds. Langenscheidt's Taschenworterbuch. Am Map.
Klatt, G., jt. auth. see Klatt, E.
Klatzkin. Thesaurus Philosophicus Linguae Hebraica. Feldheim.
Klaus, E. W., ed. see Doucet, M.
Klaus, G. & Buhr, M. Marxistisch-Leninistisches Woerterbuch der Philosophie. Rowohlt.
--Marxistisch-Leninistisches Woerterbuch der Philosophie (Pub. by Rowohlt). French & Eur.
Klaus, G. & Buhr, M., eds. Philosophisches Woerterbuch. Bibl Inst Leipzig.
Klaus, Georg & Buhr, Manfred. Philosophisches Worterbuch. Bibl Inst Leipzig.
Klaus, Hans. Banking Dictionary of English-American & German Terms. Intl Ideas.
Klaus, Hans A. Franzoesische Fachausdruecke im Bankgeschaeft: Franzoesisch-Deutsch, Deutsch-Franzoesisch. Haupt Verlag.
Kleczek, Josip. Astronomical Dictionary: In Six Languages. Acad Pr.
Kleemann, Axel. Pharmazeutische. Thieme Verlag.
Kleiber, A. Dictionary of Welding. Adler.
--English-German, German-English Welding Engineering Dictionary (Pub. by Collets). State Mutual Bk.
--Woerterbuch der Schweisstechnik. French & Eur.
Klein, Ernest. Comprehensive Etymological Dictionary of the English Language. Elsevier.
Klein, Heijo. DuMont's Kleines Sachworterbuch der Druektechnik & Grafischen Kunst. DuMont Buch.
--DuMont's Kleines Sachworterbuch der Drucktechnik & Grafischen Kunst. DuMont Buchverlag.
Klein, J. Herder-Lexikon Geologie und Mineralogie. Herder.
--Herder-Lexikon Geologie und Mineralogie (Pub. by Herder). French & Eur.
Klein, J. R. Vocabulaire des Moeurs de la Vie Parisienne Sous le Second Empire. Vander.
Klein, Johannes. Diccionario Rioduero: Paises De la Tierra. French & Eur.
Klein, Johannes, jt. auth. see Klein, Margit.
Klein, M. Herder - Lexikon Gemeinschaftskunde (Pub. by Herder). French & Eur.
--Herder - Lexikon Geographie (Pub. by Herder). French & Eur.
--Herder-Lexikon Gemeinschaftskunde. Herder.
--Herder-Lexikon Geographie. Herder.
Klein, Margit & Klein, Johannes. Diccionario Rioduero: Geografia. French & Eur.
Klein, Sanford L. Glossary of Anesthesia. Med Exam.
Klemm, Michael. Zoologisches Woerterbuch - Palaearktische Tiere. Intl Pubns Serv.
--Zoologisches Woerterbuch Palaearktische Tiere. Parey.
--Zoologisches Woerterbuch Palaearktische Tiere (Pub. by Parey Berlin). French & Eur.
Kleper, Michael L. Illustrated Dictionary of Typographic Communication. Tech & Ed Ctr Graph Arts RIT.
--The Illustrated Dictionary of Typographic Communication. Graphic Dimensions.
Klimek, Adolf. Polovodicove Soucastky. SNTL.
Klimke, Reiner & Savelsberg, Jorg. Lexikon fur Pferdefreunde. Bucher.
Klishov, A. A. Kratkii Tsitologicheskii Slovar (Pub. by Meditsina). Four Continent.
Kloe, Donald R. A Dictionary of Onomatopoeic Sounds, Tones, & Noises in English & Spanish. Ethridge.
Klos, J., jt. auth. see Wittman, A.
Klost, Walter. Arbeitsschutzlexikon. Verlag Moderne.
Kluber, Louis, jt. auth. see Lelu, Adolphe.
Klunzinger, Karl B. Upper Egypt: Its People & Its Products. AMS Pr.
Knaeps, E. & Zacharias, D. Woerterbuch der Elektronik. French & Eur.
Knauer, Karl. Bertelsmann Woerterbuch Deutsch-Franzoesisch, Franzoesisch-Deutsch. C Bertelsmann.
--Bertelsmann Woerterbuch Deutsch-Franzoesisch, Franzoesisch-Deutsch (Pub. by Bertelsmann Lexikon VVA). French & Eur.
Knebel, Gerhard. Technical Dictionary for the Shoe Industry (Pub. by Huethig). French & Eur.
Knell, Heiner. Ullstein Lexikon der Kunst und Architektur (Pub. by Ullstein Verlag/VVA). French & Eur.
Knerr, Richard. Lexikon der Mathematik. Fischer Taschen.
Kniepkamp, H. P. Legal Dictionary. Adler.
Knoch, A. E., ed. Concordant Literal New Testament with Keyword Concordance. Concordant.
Knoll, Ludwig. Lexikon der praktischen Psychologie. Luebbe.
Knott, Thomas A., jt. auth. see Kenyon, John S.
Knowles, James H. A Dictionary of Kashmiri Proverbs & Sayings. Gordon Pr.
Knox, Alexander. Glossary of Geographical & Topographical Terms. Gale.
Knutsen, Knut J. Engelsk-Norsk Teknisk Ordliste. Tapir.
Kobert, R. Vocabularium syriacum. Pont Ist Biblico.
Koblischke, H. Grosses Abkuerzungsbuch. Bibl Inst Leipzig.
--Kleines Abkuerzungsbuch. Bibl Inst Leipzig.
Kobo Orts Kh., et al. Kratkii Ispansko-Russkii & Russko-Ispanskii Nauchno-Tekhnicheskii Slovar (Pub. by An Arm SSR). Four Continent.
Kobylkova, Andela. Anglicko-Cesky Lekarsky Slovnik. SNTC.
Koch, Harry W. An Easy Guide to English Grammar & Vocabulary. Ken-Bks.
Koch, Willi A. Musisches Lexikon. Kroener.
Koch, Z. J. Polnisch-Deutsches Wissenschaftlich-Technishes Worterbuch. French & Eur.
Koeck, Peter & Ott, Hans. Woerterbuch fuer Erziehung & Unterricht. Auer.
Koegler, Horst. The Concise Oxford Dictionary of Ballet. Oxford U Pr.
Koehler, Friedrich. Woerterbuch der Amerikanismen. French & Eur.
Koehler, Ludwig & Baumgartner, Walter. Lexicon in Veteris Testamenti Libros: Hebrew-Aramaic Lexicon, Incl. Supplement. Eerdmans.
Koelle, Sigismund W. Polyglotta Africana. Intl Pubns Serv.
Koelver, Bernhard. Verschiffene Praefixe im Altindischen. Steiner Verlag.
Koenen, Matthijs J. & Drewes, J. B. Verklarend Handwoordenboek der Nederlandse Taal. Academia Edms.
Koester, Rudolf. Ullstein Lexikon der Deutschen Sprache (Pub. by Ullstein Verlag/VVA). French & Eur.
Kogan Page, Ltd. & Buchanan-Brown, John, eds. Le Mot Juste: A Dictionary of Classical & Foreign Words & Phrases (Vin). Random.
Kogos, Fred. Dictionary of Yiddish Slang. Lyle Stuart.
Kohlenberger, John R., III, jt. auth. see Goodrick, Edward W.
Kohler, Friedrich. Ro Ro Ro Woerterbuch: Deutsch-Englisch, Englisch-Deutsch. Rowohlt.
Kohler, Rolf & Mayr, Ernst. EDV-Abkurzungen. Siemens AG.
Kohls, S. Oekonomisches Woerterbuch Aussenwirtschaft (Pub. by Ruceken Vlg). French & Eur.
Kohls, S., ed. Dictionary of International Economics: German, Russian, English, French, Spanish. Sijthoff & Noordhoff.
Kohls, Siegfried, ed. Oekonomisches Woerterbuch Aussenwirtschaft (Dictionary of External Exonomic Relations & Trade) Intl Pubns Serv.
Kohls, V. Economics & Foreign Trade Dictionary (Pub. by Collet's). State Mutual Bk.
Koichubaev, E. Kratkii Tolkovyi Slovar Toponimov Kazakhstana (Pub. by Nauka). Four Continent.
Koistinen, R. M. Finnish-French-Finnish Dictionary (Suomi-Ranska-Suomi) French & Eur.
Koistinen, Raila-Maarit & Lasslo, Helene. Dictionnaire Finnois-Francais-Finnois. Soderstrom.
Kolafova, V. & Slaba, D. Czech-English-Czech Dictionary. Vanous.
Kolatch, Alfred J. The Dictionary of First Names (Perigee). Putnam Pub Group.
Kolb, Helga, jt. auth. see DeVries, Louis.
Kolb, W. J., jt. auth. see Gould, Julius.
Kolesnikov, N. P. Slovar' Omonimov Russkogo Iazyka. Four Continent.
Kolesnikova, A. & Lulchak, L. Dictionnaire Illustre: Francais-Russe. French & Eur.
Kolesnikova, A. D., et al. Frantsuzsko-Russkii Illiustrirovannyi Slovar (Pub. by Sov Entsiklopediia). Four Continent.
Koliadenkov, M. N., et al. Erziansko-Russkii Slovar (Pub. by Gosizdat Inostr Natsional Slovarei). Four Continent.
Koliadenkov, M. N., et al, eds. Russko-Erzianskii Slovar (Pub. by GINS). Four Continent.
Kollar, D., et al. Slovak-Russian Dictionary. French & Eur.

Kollnig, Karl Rudolf. Politisch-Soziologisches Woerterbuch. Kamp Verlag.

Kolpakov, B. T., ed. Kratkii Vneshnetorgovyi Slovar (Pub. by Vneshtorgizdat). Four Continent.

Kolpas, Norman. The Gourmet's Lexicon (Perigee). Putnam Pub Group.

Kolttay-Kastner, Jeno, ed. see Herczeg, Gyula.

Kolver, Bernhard. Verschliffene Prafixe im Altindischen. Steiner Verlag.

Komac & Skeri, J. Modern Dictionary Slovene-English, English-Slovene. French & Eur.

Komac & Skerlj. Yugoslavian Pocket Dictionary: Slovene-English, English-Slovenski. Vanous.

Komarov, A. N., jt. ed. see Ersov, N. N.

Konarski, M. M. Russian-English Dictionary of Modern Terms in Aeronautics & Rocketry. Pergamon.

--Russian-English Space Technology Dictionary. Pergamon.

Kondakov, N. I. Logicheskii Slovar. Gorskii, D. P., ed (Pub. by Nauka). Four Continent.

--Vvedenie v Logiku (Pub. by Nauka). Four Continent.

Kondakov, Nikolai I., et al. Woerterbuch der Logik. Bibl Inst Leipzig.

Kondo, K. Elsevier's Dictionary of Automobile Engineering. Elsevier.

Konig. Diccionario De las Religiones. French & Eur.

Koning, Frederick. Diccionario de Demonologia. French & Eur.

Konrad, Roselinde. Reviewing German Grammar & Building Vocabulary. U Pr of Amer.

Kopeckeho, L. V., ed. Skolni Rusko-Cesky Slovnik. SNTC.

Kopetskov, L. V., et al. Russko-Cheshskii Slovar (Pub. by Russkii Iazyk). Four Continent.

Koprulu, Cemal, jt. auth. see Steuerwald, K.

Korigodskii, V. N., et al. Indoneziisko-Russkii Slovar (Pub. by Gosizdat Inostr Natsional Slovarei). Four Continent.

Korigodsky, R. N., et al. Indonesian-Russian Dictionary. French & Eur.

Korina, N. B., et al. Frantsuzsko-Russkii Uchebnyi Slovar (Pub. by Russkii Iazyk). Four Continent.

Korneev, L. A. Russko-Malagasiiskii Slovar (Pub. bu Sov. Entsiklopediia). Four Continent.

Kornitzky, H. Langenscheidts Taschenwoerterbuch Schwedisch. Langenscheidt.

--Langenscheidts Taschenwoerterbuch Schwedisch: Teil II, Deutsch-Schwedisch. Langenscheidt.

--Langenscheidts Taschenwoerterbuch Schwedisch: Teil I, Schwedisch-Deutsch. Langenscheidt.

--Langenscheidts Taschenwoerterbuecher Schwedisch. Langenscheidt.

--Schwedisch. Langenscheidt.

Kornrumpf, H. J. Dictionnaire Europa Francais-Turc. Larousse.

Koros, Alexander Csoma De see Csoma de Koros, Alexander.

Korver, Jan. De Terminologie van het Crediet-Wezen in het Grieksch. Finley, Moses, ed. Ayer Co.

Kosbab, William H. Motorcycle Dictionary. Greenslade-Moore, Dianne & Lamont, Daveta, eds. Career Pub.

Kosik, Vaclav. Cesko, Slovensko, Latinsko, Anglicko, Nemecko, Rusky, Slovnik Plevelu. SNTC.

Kossel, Hans. Herder Lexikon. Herder.

Kossmann, H., jt. auth. see Schibsbye, K.

Kostallari, A. Karmannyi Russko-Albanskii Slovar. Four Continent.

Kostic. Medicinski Leksikon. French & Eur.

Koszinowski, Klaus. Die Von Praefigierten Verben Abgeleiteten Substantive in der Modernen Serbokroatischen Standartsprache. Sagner.

Koszyk, K. Woerterbuch zur Publizistik. French & Eur.

Kotapish, Carl & Kotapish, Sharon. A Darai-English, English-Darai Glossary. Summer Inst Abor.

Kotapish, Sharon, jt. auth. see Kotapish, Carl.

Kotet, I. Hungarian-Vietnamese Dictionary. French & Eur.

Kotik, M. G. Anglo-Russkii Slovar Po Aerogidrodinamike (Pub. by Glav. Red. Inostr. Tekhn. Slovrei Fizmatgiza). Four Continent.

Kotimaisten Kielten Tutkimuskekus. Uudissanasto Kahdeksankymmenta. Soderstrom.

Kotnick, J. Slovene-English Dictionary. Shalom.

Kotnik, J. Slovene-English Dictionary. French & Eur.

--Yugoslavic Dictionary: Slovene-English. Vanous.

Kotnik, J. & Grad, A. Slovene-English, English-Slovene Dictionary. Heinman.

Kotoleva, N. Z., ed. Novoe V Russkoi Leksike (Pub. by Russkii Iazyk). Four Continent.

Kotov, A. V. Kitaisko-Russkii Slovar-Minimum (Pub. by Russkii Iazyk). Four Continent.

Kotz, Samuel. Russian-English Dictionary & Reader in the Cybernetical Sciences. Acad Pr.

Koubourlis, Demetrius J. & Parrish, Stephen M., eds. A Concordance to the Poems of Osip Mandelstam. Cornell U pr.

Koushakdjian, M. Armenian-English - English-Armenian Dictionary. Heinman.

Kovacs, Magdolna. Angol-Magyar Mikroelektronikai. KG Informatik.

Kovalenko, Y. G. English-Russian Dictionary of Reliability & Quality Control. Pergamon.

Kovel, Ralph M. & Kovel, Terry H. Dictionary of Marks: Pottery & Porcelain. Crown.

Kovel, Terry H., jt. auth. see Kovel, Ralph M.

Kowalski, Kazlmierz. Maly Slownik Zoologiczny. Wiedza Powszechna.

Kowit, Steve. Cross Word Dictionary (Success). Merit Pubns.

Kozaklewicz, Stefana. Slownik Terminologiczny Sztuk Pieknych. Panstwowe Wydawnicto Iskry.

Kozelka, Paul. A Glossary to the Plays of Bernard Shaw. Folcroft.

Kozlov, G. A., et al, eds. Kratkii Ekonomicheskii Slovar (Pub. by Politizdat). Four Continent.

Kraemer, Joerg, et al. Woerterbuch der Klassischen Arabischen Sprache: Bd 1, Lfg 2. Harrassowitz.

Kramer. Van Goor's Concise Indonesian Dictionary. Iaconi.

Kramer, A. L., Sr. English-Indonesian, Indonesian-English Dictionary. Shalom.

--Van Goor's Concise Indonesian Dictionary: English-Indonesian Indonesian-English. C E Tuttle.

Kramer, K. Erdoel-Lexikon (Crude Oil Dictionary) Intl Pubns Serv.

Kramer, Karlheinz. Erdoel Lexicon (Pub. by Heuthig). French & Eur.

Kramers. Dutch-English, English-Dutch Dictionary. Heinman.

Kramsky, J., jt. auth. see Caha, J.

Krapf, Ludwig, ed. Dictionary of the Suahili Language (Pub. by Negro U Pr). Greenwood.

Krasowski, J. Owen. Dictionary & Reference Guide for Respiratory Therapy. Year Bk Med.

Kraus, Barbara. Barbara Kraus Dictionary of Protein (Sig). NAL.

--The Dictionary of Sodium, Fats, & Cholesterol (Perigee). Putnam Pub Group.

Krawczykiewicz, A. Suomi-Poula Suomi Dictionary: Finnish-Polish-Finnish. French & Eur.

Krchten, P., jt. auth. see Fisher, R.

Krech, Hans. Woerterbuch der Deutschen Aussprache. French & Eur.

Kreiser, Klaus, et al, eds. Lexikon der Islamischen Welt. Kohlhammer.

--Lexikon der Islamischen Welt: Bd 2, Gram-Nom. Kohlhammer.

--Lexikon der Islamischen Welt: Bd 3, Nor-Z. Kohlhammer.

--Lexikon der Islamischen Welt: Bd 1, A-Grab. Kohlhammer.

Kreivsky, Joseph & Linfield, Jordon L. The Bad Spellers Dictionary. Random.

Kreizer, V. L., jt. auth. see Prosorova, L. P.

Kremnitz, Walter A. Lexikon der Mythologie Aegyptens, Persiens & des Orients. Ambro Lacus.

Krichbaum, Jorg. Dumonts Kleines Lexikon der Phantastischen Malerei. DuMont Buchverlag.

Krichbaum, Jorg & Zondergeld, Rein. Dictionary of Fantastic Art. Barron.

Kriel, T. Popular Northern Sotho Dictionary. Van Schaik.

Krishan Rao, V. S. Dictionary of Bharatnatya (Orient Longman). South Asia Bks.

Krishna, N. V., rev. by see Pillai, T. Ramalingam.

Krishtofovich, A. N. Geologicheskii Slovar (Pub. by Gos. Nauch. Tekhn. Izd. Lit. Po Geologii & Okhrane Nedr.). Four Continent.

Krist, Thomas. Taschen-Lexikon Internationale Abkurzungen & Kurzzeichen. Technik Tabel.

Kritzinger, M. S. Afrikaans-English, English-Afrikaans Dictionary. Heinman.

Kroeger-Jannetti, A. Technisches Taschenwoerterbuch (Pub. by Georg Siemens Verlagsbuchhandlung). French & Eur.

Kroemer, Joerg, et al. Woerterbuch der Klassischen Arabischen: Bd 1. Ullman, Manfred, ed. Harrassowitz.

Kroh, Paul. Woerterbuch der Antike: Mit Beruecks Ihres Fortwirkens. Bux, E. & Schoene, W., eds. Kroener.

Kroha, Tyll. Lexikon der Numismatik. French & Eur.

Krolkoff, Georg. Langenscheidts Taschenwoerterbuecher Arabisch-Deutsch. Langenscheidt.

Kropacek, Lubos. Arabsko-Cesky Cesko-Arabsky Slovnik. SNTC.

Krotkoff, G. Langenscheidts Taschenwoerterbuch Arabisch: Teil I, Arabisch-Deutsch. Langenscheidt.

Krotkoff, G., et al. Langenscheidts Taschenwoerterbuch Arabisch. Langenscheidt.

Krueger, John R. The Kalmyk-Mongolian Vocabulary in Stralenberg's Geography of 1730. Almqvist.

--Materials for an Oirat-Mongolian to English Citation Dictionary, Pt. 1. Mongolia.

Krueger, P., jt. auth. see Assfalg, Julius.

Kruger, Fritz, tr. El lexico rural del noroeste iberico (CSIC). Inst. Antonio de Nebrija.

Kruger, Sabine. Zum Fachwortschatz. VDI Verlag.

Krus, M. Tagal'sko-Russkii Slovar (Pub. by GINS). Four Continent.

Krus, M., et al. Russko-Tagal'skii Slovar (Pub. by Sov. Entsiklopediia). Four Continent.

--Tagal sko Russkii Slovar. Four Continent.

Krusche, Dieter & Labenskt, Jurgen. Reclams Filmfuhrer. Reclam.

Kruyskamp, C., ed. see Van Dale, Johan H.

Krymova, N. I., et al. Russko-Datskii Slovar (Pub. by GINS). Four Continent.

Kryt, D. Dictionary of Chemical Terminology. Elsevier.

Kryt, Dobromila & Semniuk, Bazyli, eds. English-Polish Polish-English Chemical Dictionary. Intl Pubns Serv.

Krywalski, Diether. Knaurs Lexikon der Weltliteratur. Droemersche Knaur.

Kubica, jt. ed. see Chodera.

Kucera. The Compact Dictionary of Exact Science & Technology: Band I, English-German. Brandstetter.

--The Compact Dictionary of Exact Science & Technology: Band II, German-English. Brandstetter.

--Technisches Woerterbuch: Band I, Russisch-Deutsch. Brandstetter.

--Technisches Woerterbuch: Band II, Deutsch-Russisch. Brandstetter.

Kucera, A. The Compact Dictionary of Exact Science & Technology. Harrap.

--The Compact Dictionary of Exact Science & Technology: English-German. French & Eur.

Kucera, Antonin. Technisches Woerterbuch. Brandstetter.

--Technisches Woerterbuch. Brandstetter.

--Technisches Woerterbuch (Pub. by Brandstetter). French & Eur.

--Technisches Woerterbuch (Pub. by Brandstetter). French & Eur.

Kuentz, Eugene. Dictionnaire Anglais-Francais. Ecole.

Kuentz, Eugene & Saillens, Emile. Dictionnaire Anglais-Francais. Licet.

--Dictionnaire Anglais-Francais. Magnard.

Kuepper, H. Woerterbuch der Deutschen Umgangssprache: Vol. 5, 10000 neue Ausdruecke Sachschelten. M Rosenberg.

--Woerterbuch der Deutschen Umgangssprache: Vol. 6, Jugenddeutsch A-Z. M Rosenberg.

Kuepper, Heinz. ABC-Komiker bis Zwitschergemuese. Deutsche Sprache.

Kuhn, Peter. Deutsche Woerterbucher. Niemeyer.

Kuhn, Pierre, jt. auth. see Banvard, Paul.

Kuhner, Hans. Dictionnaire des Papes. Buchet Chastel.

--Dictionnaire des Papes. French & Eur.

Kuipers, A. H. A Dictionary of Proto-Circassian Roots. Humanities.

Kuipers, A. H., jt. ed. see Rainich, Gabrielle.

Kuipers, Aert H. Squamish Language. Mouton.

Kulier, Ignac. Englesko-Hrvatska ili Srpska Tehnicko-Tehnoloska. Prehrambeno-Tehnoloski.

Kunin, A. V., et al. Anglo-Russkii Frazeologicheskii Slovar. Four Continent.

Kunitskaya-Peterson, Christina. International Dictionary of Obscenities: A Guide to Dirty Words & Indecent Expressions in Spanish, Italian, French, German, & Russian. Berkeley Slavic.

Kunst, H. Evangelisches Staatslexikon. Kreuz.

--Evangelisches Staatslexikon (Pub. by Kreuz Vlg.). French & Eur.

Kunze, H. & Rueckl, G., eds. Lexikon des Bibliothekswesens. Bibl Inst Leipzig.

Kunze, Horst. Lexikon des Bibliothekswesens. French & Eur.

Kunze, Horst & Rueckl, Gotthard, eds. Lexikon des Bibliothekswesens. Saur Verlag.

Kunzer, Paul E. Caesar Vocabularies. Am Classical.

--Cicero Vocabularies. Am Classical.

--Vergil Vocabularies. Am Classical.

Kupisz, K. & Kielski, B. Dictionnaire Pratique Francais-Polonais. French & Eur.

Kupisz, Kazimierz, et al. Podreczny Slownik Polsko-Francuski. Wiedza Powszechna.

Kurgansky, Alexander, ed. see Quemner, T. A.

Kurian, George. Dictionary of Biography (LE). Dell.

Kurian, George T. Historical & Cultural Dictionary of India. Scarecrow.

Kurochkin, V. D., et al. Slovar Spravochnik Nazvanii Obraztsov Vooruzheniia & Boevoi Tekhniki Kapitalisticheskikh Stran & Osnovnykh Firm Proizvodiashikh Vooruzhenie (Pub. by Voenizdat). Four Continent.

Kurowski, Ulrich. Lexikon des Internationalen Films. Hanser.

Kurth, Hanns. Diccionario de los suenos. Rada, Carmen, tr. Circulo Lect.

--Lexikon der Modernen Konservation. French & Eur.

Kurtz, Laura S. Historical Dictionary of Tanzania. Scarecrow.

Kurtz, M., et al. Ten Thousand Legal Words (G). McGraw.

Kury, jt. auth. see Blumenbrg.

Kuscinski, A. Dictionnaire des Conventionnels. Francais, Ed. Du Vexin.

Kut, David. Dictionary of Applied Energy Conservation: An Illustrated Dictionary of Terms. Nichols Pub.

Kutuzov, A. I. Kratkii Suakhili-Russkii & Russko-Suakhili Slovar (Pub. by Sov Entsiklopediia). Four Continent.
--Russian-Swahili, Swahili-Russian Dictionary. French & Eur.
--Slovar Russko-Suakhili Gazetnoi Leksiki (Pub. by In-Tut Mezhdunarod. Otnoshenii). Four Continent.
Kuusiena, M. E., et al, eds. Russko-Finskii Slovar (Pub. by GINS). Four Continent.
Kuvshinoff, B. W., et al, eds. Fire Sciences Dictionary (Pub. by Wiley-Interscience). Wiley.
Kuzmin, B. S., ed. Kratkii Topografo-Geodezicheskii Slovar (Pub. by Nedra). Four Continent.
Kuznetsov, B., ed. Russian-English Polytechnical Dictionary. Pergamon.
Kuznetsova. Russko-Angliiskii Politekhnicheskii Slovar (Pub. by Russkii Iazyk). Four Continent.
Kwiatkowski, Gerhard. Die Musik: Ein Sachlexikon. Biblio Inst.
Kwizda, R. Vocabularium Nocentium Florae. Springer-Verlag.
Kwon, Hyogmyou. Basic Chinese-Korean Character Dictionary. Harrassowitz.
Kwong Ki Chaou. Dictionary of English Phrases with Illustrative Sentences. Gale.
Kykkotis, I. Modern English-Greek & Greek-English Dictionary (Pub. by Lund Humphries England). State Mutual Bk.

L

Laanpere, H. Finnish-Estonian-Finnish Dictionary: Suomi-Eesti-s. French & Eur.
Labenskt, Jurgen, jt. auth. see Krusche, Dieter.
Laborde, G., jt. auth. see Fournier, J.
Laborde, Leon de see De Laborde, Leon.
Labourasse, Henri A. Glossaire Abrege Patois de la Meuse. Slatkine.
LaBrosse, Olivier De, jt. ed. see Henry, Antonir Marie.
La Canal, J. De see De La Canal, J.
La Canal, Julio De see De La Canal, Julio.
Lacey, A. R. A Dictionary of Philosophy. Routledge & Kegan.
--A Dictionary of Philosophy (ScribC). Scribner.
La Chavignerie, Emile B. De see De La Chavignerie, Emile B. & Auvray, Louis.
Laclotte, Michel & Smith, Alistair, eds. Larousse Dictionary of Painters. Larousse.
Lacombe, Francois. Dictionnaire de la Langue Romane ou du Vieux Langue Francois. Slatkine.
Lacroix, M., jt. auth. see Magnien, Victor.
Ladbury, Ann. The Dressmaker's Dictionary. Arco.
Ladero Sanchez, Lazaro. Basico Sopena: Diccionario Ilustrado de la Lengua Espanla (SOP). Lectorum Pubns.
Laeng. Vocabulario de Pedagogia. Herder SA.
Laeng, Mauro. Vocabulario de Pedagogia. Genovart Rosello, C., ed. Herder SA.
Laeng, Mauro & Auandani, Guy. Vocabulaire de Pedagogie Moderne. Centurion.
Laffal, Julius. Concept Dictionary of English. Gallery Pr.
La Fleche, Francis. A Dictionary of the Osage Language. Scholarly.
Lafleur, Bruno. Dictionnaire des locutions idiomatiques Fran c04aises. Soc Dev Liv.
Lafon, Robert. Vocabulaire de Psychopedagogic et de Psychiatrie de l'Enfant. Pr Univ Fr.
--Vocabulaire De Psychopedagogie et De Psychiatrie De L'enfant. French & Eur.
Laframbois, Yves. L' Architecture Traditionnelle au Quebec: Glossaire Illustre de la Maison aux 17e & 18e Siecles. Edns Homme.
Lagane, Rene, jt. auth. see Dubois, Jean.

Lagrenade, Marcel. Lexique Aborite. Dotmar.
--Lexique Forestier: Anglais-Francais. Dotmar.
--Vocabulaire Technique. Dotmar.
Laguna de la Vera, Francisco, jt. auth. see Radde, Karl H.
La Haye, jt. auth. see Furetiere, Antoine.
Laing, jt. auth. see Halkett.
Laird, Charles. Webster's New World Thesaurus. Warner Bks.
Laird, Charlton. Webster's New World Thesaurus. P-H.
--Webster's New World Thesaurus. Warner Bks.
Laird, Charlton, ed. Webster's New World Thesaurus. Collins Pubs.
--Webster's New World Thesaurus (Mer). NAL.
Laita, Luis M. Cortina-Grosset Basic Spanish Dictionary. Berberi, Dilaver & Berberi, Edel A., eds. (G&D). Putnam Pub Group.
Laita, Luis M., ed. Cortina-Grosset Basic Spanish Dictionary (G&D). Putnam Pub Group.
Laitier, Gabriel. Dictionnaire de Physique. Maloine.
--Dictionnaire de Physique. French & Eur.
Lajo, Rosina, tr. see Amalric, Jacques, et al.
Lalanne, Charles C. Glossaire du Patois Poitavin. Lafitte Repr.
Lalanne, Ludovic. Dictionnaire Historique de la France. Slatkine.
--Dictionnaire Historique de la France. Slatkine.
--Dictionnaire Historique De la France. B Franklin.
--Dictionnaire Historique de la France Contenant l'histoire Civile, Politique. Lenox.
Lal Dey, Nando. The Geographical Dictionary of Ancient & Medieval India. Orient Bk Dist.
La Magna, Giovanni. Dizionario sintattico latino: Italiano-latino e latino-italiano. Signorelli C.
La Magna, Giovanni, jt. auth. see Annaratone, Alessandro.
Laman, Karl Edward. Dictionnaire Kikongo-Francais. Gregg.
Lamanna, Paolo E. & Adorno, Francesco. Dizionario di termini filosofici. Monnier.
Lamanna, Paolo E. & Goretti, Maria. Dizionario di pedagogia, psicologia, storia dell'educazione. Monnier.
Lamb, Geoffrey. Illustrated Magic Dictionary. Lodestar Bks.
Lambard, Neil. Pocket Dictionary of Banjo Chords. Kenyon.
Lambdin, William. Doublespeak Dictionary. Pinnacle Bks.
Lambert, Denis-Clair. Dictionnaire Francais-Anglais de l'economie Monetaire. Ouvrieres.
--Dictionnaire Francais-Anglais de l'economie. Ouvrieres.
Lambert, Marcus. Pennsylvania German Dictionary. Schiffer.
Lambert, Marcus B. A Dictionary of Non-English Words of the Pennsylvania German Dialect. Penn German Soc.
Lambert, Mayer & Brandin, Louis. Glossaire Hebreu-Francais. Slatkine.
--Glossaire Hebreu-Francais du XIIIe. Siecle. Slatkine.
Lamblin, L. Le Larousse des Enfants (Dist. by Continental Bk Co). Larousse.
Lambton, Ann K. Persian Vocabulary. Cambridge U Pr.
Lamer, Hans. Woerterbuch der Antike. French & Eur.
Lamizet, Bernard. Dictionnaire des Synonymes & Antonymes. Garnier-Flammarion.
Lamizet, Bernard, jt. auth. see Lamizet, Bojana.
Lamizet, Bojana. Dictionnaire Orthographique Suivi d'Une Liste des Verbes Irreguliers. Garnier.
Lamizet, Bojana & Lamizet, Bernard. Dictionnaire Orthographique. Garnier.
Lammar, Jutta. Der Grosse Ravensburger Werkkunstbuch. Maier Verlag.
Lamming, Anne, compiled by. A Co-operator's Dictionary: Basic List of Co-operative & Commercial Terms for Use at Primary Level in Developing Countries. Intl Coop All.

Lamont, Daveta, ed. see Kosbab, William H.
Lampe, G. W., ed. A Patristic Greek Lexicon. Brepols.
--Patristic Greek Lexicon. Oxford U Pr.
--Patristic Greek Lexicon Nineteen Sixty-One to Sixty-Eight. Oxford U Pr.
Lampen, Av Lea. Finsk-Svensk & Svensk-Finsk Fickordbok. Esselte Studium.
Lampen, L. Finnish-Swedish Dictionary. French & Eur.
--Finnish-Swedish-Finnish Dictionary (Suomi-Ruotsi-Suomi) French & Eur.
--Swedish-Finnish Dictionary. French & Eur.
Lampen, Lea. Finsk-Svensk Skolordbok. Esselte Studium.
--Svensk-Finsk Storordbok. Esselte Studium.
Lampeu, Lea. Ruotsalais-Suomalaines. WSOY.
Lamsa, George M. Idioms in the Bible Explained. Aramaic Bible.
Lana, Italo. Vocabolario Della Lingua Latina: Italiano-Latino, Latino-Italiano. Paravia.
--Vocabolario latino. Paravia.
Lancaster, F. Wilfrid. Vocabulary Control for Information Retrieval. Info Resources.
Lancombe, Michel & Monceaux, Jean-Pierre. Lexique Etymologique des Termes Medicaux. Lamarre Poinot.
Landau, Jacob. A Word Count of Modern Arabic Prose. Intl Bk Ctr.
Landau, Sidney & Bogus, Ronald. Webster Illustrated Contemporary Dictionary. Doubleday.
Landau, Sidney & Bogus, Ronald, eds. Doubleday Dictionary: For Home, School & Office. Doubleday.
--Doubleday Roget's Thesaurus in Dictionary Form. Doubleday.
Landberg, C. de see De Landberg, C. & Zettersteen, K. V.
Landerman, Peter. Vocabulario Quechua del Pastaza. Summer Inst Ling.
Landshut, Siegfried. Politisches Woerterbuch (Pub. by Hochschule Fuer Wirtschaft U. Politik). French & Eur.
Landy, Marc, ed. Environmental Impact Statement Glossary: A Reference Source for EIS Writers, Reviewers & Citizens (IFI Plenum). Plenum Pub.
Lane, Edward W., ed. Arabic-English Lexicon. Ungar.
Lane, Edward W., compiled by. An Arabic-English Lexicon: Madd al Qamus. Intl Bk Ctr.
Lanecki, Francois & Dupre, Celine. Vocabulaire Francais-Anglais de la Machine a Coudre Industrielle. Quebec Off.
--Vocabulaire Francais-Anglais De la Machine a Coudre Industrielle. French & Eur.
Lang, Viktor, jt. ed. see Grossman, Paul.
Langbaum, Francesca L., ed. The Random House Basic Dictionary French. Ballantine.
Langbaum, Francesca V., jt. auth. see Hall, Robert A., Jr.
Langdon, David. How to Talk Golf: David Langdon's A-Z of Golfing Terms. Spon Ltd.
Lange, K. & Ferval, L. International Construction Terminology. Bauverlag.
--International Construction Terminology (Pub. by Bauverlag). French & Eur.
Lange, K., et al. Englische & Franzoesisch Fachsprache im Auslandsbau. Bauverlag.
Lange-Koval, Ernst E. & Wilhelm, Kurt. Dictionnaire Pratique Mercure: Francais-Allemand, Allemand-Francais. French & Eur.
--Dictionnaire Pratique Mercure Francais-Allemand. Larousse.
Lange-Kowal & Ernst, E. Langenscheidts Taschenwoerterbuecher Franzoesisch-Deutsch. Langenscheidt.
Lange-Kowal, E. E. Langenscheidts Taschenwoerterbuch Franzoesisch: Teil I, Franzoesisch-Deutsch. Langenscheidt.

Lange-Kowal, E. E., et al. Langenscheidts Taschenwoerterbuch Franzoesisch. Langenscheidt.
Lange-Kowal, Ernst E. Langenscheidts Grosse Schulwoerterbuch Deutsch-Franzoesisch. Langenscheidt.
--Langenscheidts Grosse Schulwoerterbuecher Franzoesisch-Deutsch. Langenscheidt.
--Langenscheidts Handwoerterbuch: Teil II, Deutsch-Franzoesisch. Langenscheidt.
Lange-Kowal, Ernst E. & Beaucaire, Louis. Langenscheidts Grosse Schulwoerterbuch Franzoesisch-Deutsch. Langenscheidt.
--Langenscheidts Handwoerterbuch: Franzoesisch-Deutsch Deutsch-Franzoesisch. Langenscheidt.
--Langenscheidts Handwoerterbuch: Teil I, Franzoesisch-Deutsch. Langenscheidt.
Lange-Kowal, Ernst E. & Hartig, Paul. Langenscheidts Schulwoerterbuch Franzoesisch-Deutsch. Langenscheidt.
Lange-Kowal, Ernst E., jt. auth. see Pertsch, Erich.
Lange-Kowal, Ernst E., ed. Langenscheidts Handwoerterbuecher: Tl 1, Franzoesisch-Deutsch. Langenscheidt.
Lange-Kowal, Ernst Erwin. Langenscheidts Handwoerterbuch: Franzoesisch. Beaucaire, Louis, ed. Langenscheidt.
Langenbucher, W. R., ed. Kulturpolitisches Woerterbuch. M Rosenberg.
Langendorf, Hans. Legal Dictionary: Part 1, Dutch-German. Kluwer Academic.
--Woerterbuch der Deutschen & Niederlaendischen Rechtssprache: Lexikon fuer Justiz, Verwaltung, Wirtschaft & Handel. Kluwer Group.
--Woerterbuch der Deutschen und Niederlaendischen Rechtssprache. French & Eur.
--Woerterbuch der Deutschen und Niederlaendischen Rechtssprache. French & Eur.
Langendorf, Hans & Stein, P. A. Woerterbuch der Recht & Wirtschaftssprache: Teil I, Niederlandisch-Deutsch. Recht & Wirtschaft.
--Woerterbuch der Rechts & Wirtschaftssprache: Teil II, Deutsch-Niederlaendisch. Recht & Wirtschaft.
Langenkamp, R. D. Handbook of Oil Industry Terms & Phrases. Pennwell Pub.
Langenkamp, Robert D., ed. Illustrated Petroleum: Reference Dictionary. Pennwell Pub.
Langenscheidt. Diccionario moderno: Aleman-espanol, espanol-aleman. Herder SA.
--Dizionario italiano-tedesco tedesco-italiano. Signorelli C.
--Dizionario pratico tedesco-italiano italiano-tedesco. Signorelli C.
Langenscheidt-Redaktion. Langenscheidts Schulwoerterbuch Englisch-Deutsch. Langenscheidt.
Langenscheidt Staff, ed. Langenscheidt's New Pocket French Dictionary: French-English, English-French. Am Map.
--Langenscheidt's New Pocket German Dictionary: German-English, English-German. Am Map.
Langenssheidt. Diccionario moderno: Ingles-espanol, espanol-ingles. Herder SA.
Langford, jt. auth. see Perreau.
Langker, R. Flash in New South Wales, 1788-1850. Univ Syd Aust Lang.
Langland, William. Piers Plowman Glossary. Skeat, W. W., ed. Kraus Repr.
Langle, Arturo. Vocabulario, Apodos, Seudonimos, Sobrenombres & Hemerografia de la Revolucion. UNAM.
Langnas, Isaac A. Dictionary of Discoveries. Greenwood.
Langouet, J., jt. auth. see Dottin, Georges.

Language Services Division of the Foreign Office of the Federal Republic of Germany, ed. Disarmament Terminology: English, German, French, Spanish, Russian. De Gruyter.
Languirand, Jacques. Le Dictionnaire Insolite. Jour, Ed. Du.
Lanham, Richard A. A Handlist of Rhetorical Terms: A Guide for Students of English Literature. U of Cal Pr.
Lantz, Louise K. Dictionary & Price Guide to Kitchenware Collectibles. Everybodys Pr.
Lanz, K., jt. auth. see Achterberg, E.
Lanzara, A. Dizionario tedesco-italiano. Forni.
Lanzone, R. V. Dizionario Di Mitologia Egizia. Benjamins North Am.
Lapauri, A. A., et al, eds. Kratkii Fotograficheskii Slovar (Pub. by Iskusstvo). Four Continent.
Lapedes. Dictionary of Scientific & Technical Terms. McGraw.
Lapedes, D. Dizionario Enciclopedico Scientifico e Tecnico: Inglese-Italiano, Italiano-Inglese. French & Eur.
Lapidus, A., et al. The Learner's Russian-English Dictionary: For Foreign Students of Russian. Four Continent.
Lapidus, B. A. & Shevisova, S. V. Learner's Russian-English Dictionary for Foreign Students of Russian. Russica.
Lapidus, B. A. & Shevtsoka, S. V. The Learner's Russian-English Dictionary. French & Eur.
Lapidus, B. A. & Shevtsova, S. V. Learner's Russian-English Dictionary. MIT Pr.
Lapidus, B. A., et al. The Learner's Russian-English Dictionary (Pub. by Russkii Iazyk). Four Continent.
Laplanche, Jean. Vocabulaire de la Psychanalyse. PUF.
--Das Vokabular der Psychoanalyse (Pub. by Suhrkamp). French & Eur.
Laplanche, Jean & Pontalis, Jean-Bertrand. Diccionario Del Psicoanalisis. Cervantes Gimeno, Fernando, ed. French & Eur.
Laplanche, Jean, ed. Vocabulaire de la Psychanalyse. Pontalis, Jean-Baptiste. French & Eur.
Laplanche, Jean, et al. Diccionario de psicoanalisis. Cervantes Gimeno, Fernando, tr. Labor SA.
Laplanche Pontalis. Diccionario del psicoanalisis. Labor SA.
Lapoulide, J. Diccionario Grafico de Arte y Oficios Artisticos. French & Eur.
Laprusa, Mariana. Leksykon Wiedzy Wojskowej. Wydaw Min. Obrony Narodowej.
Laptukhin, V. V. Russko-Khausa Slovar (Pub. by Sov. Entsiklopediia). Four Continent.
Lapuente, F. A., jt. auth. see Rogers, P. P.
Laqueur, Walter. Dictionary of Politics. Free Pr.
Lara, Jesus. Diccionario de Ro de Qheshwa-Espanol, Espanol-Qheshwa. French & Eur.
--Diccionario Qheshwa-Castellano. Amigos del Libro.
--Diccionaro de Qheshwa-Espanol, Espanol-Qheshwa. French & Eur.
LaRoche, Nancy & Urdang, Laurence, eds. Picturesque Expressions: A Thematic Dictionary. Gale.
Larousse & Co. Dictionnaire Complet des Mots Croises. Larousse.
--Dictionnaire du vocabulaire essentiel. Larousse.
--Larousse de poche. Larousse.
--Larousse de poche, francais-allemand et allemand-francais. Larousse.
Larousse And Co. Larousse de poche francais-espagnol, & espanol-frances. Larousse.
Larousse & Co. Larousse de poche, francais-italien et italien-francais. Larousse.
--Larousse de poche French-English & English-French. Larousse.
--Larousse des debutants. Larousse.
Larousse And Co. Mon Premier Larousse francais-anglais, anglais-francais en couleurs. Larousse.
Larousse & Co. Nouveau Larousse Eementaire. Larousse.
Larousse And Co. Nouveau Petit Larousse en couleurs. Larousse.
--Petit Dictionnaire bilingue Larousse, francais-espagnol, espanol-frances. Larousse.
--Petit Dictionnaire francais Larousse. Larousse.
Larousse, G. Vocabulario Juridico Frances-Espanol. Abeledo Perrot.
Larousse, Pierre, jt. auth. see Clement, Felix.
Larrauri, A. Dictionary of Oto-Rhino-Laryngology in Five Languages. Intl Pubns Serv.
Larreula, Frederic. Diccionari Catala-Castella-Castellano-Catalan. Bruguera.
Larrieu, Robert. Dictionnaire Espagnol-Francais. Garnier.
--Dictionnaire Espagnol-Francais. Garnier-Flammarion.
Larrieu, Robert, jt. auth. see Salva, Vicente.
Larrieu, Robert, jt. ed. see Salva, Vicente.
Larrieu, Roberto & Garcia Morente, Manuel. Diccionario Major Frances-Espanol, Espanol-Frances. Diafora.
Larson, Mildred L. Vocabulario Aguaruna de Amazonas. Summer Inst Ling.
Larson, Randy. Illustrated Backpacking & Hiking Dictionary for Young People. P-H.
Larsson, Lars G. & Lorveberg, Sven. Karnkraft Fran A til O. Ingenjorsforlaget.
La Rue, Andre. Dictionnaire d'argot. Flammarion.
La Rue, Jean. Dictionnaire d'Argot et des Principales Locutions Populaires. French & Eur.
LaSalle, Herbert J., jt. auth. see Riese, Alan W.
Lasnier, Paul. Dictionnaire des Mots Croises: Noms Communs. Homme.
Lass, Abraham & Lass, Betty. Dictionary of Pronunciation. Times Bks.
Lass, Betty, jt. auth. see Lass, Abraham.
Lasslo, Helene, jt. auth. see Koistinen, Raila-Maarit.
Lasso de La Vega, Javier & Rubert Candau, Jose M., eds. Diccionario Enciclopedias Labor. French & Eur.
Last, J. T. Polyglotta Africana Orientalis. Intl Pubns Serv.
Laszlo, Orszagh. A Concise English-Hungarian Dictionary. Akademiai Kiado.
Lates, Ernest M., et al. Dictionar Poliglot. Editura Stiintifica.
Latham, Edward. Dictionary of Names, Nicknames, & Surnames. Gale.
Latham, R. E., compiled by. Dictionary of Medieval Latin from British Sources: Fascicule I, A-B. Oxford U Pr.
Latouche, Robert, jt. auth. see Vallee, Eugene.
La Tour, jt. auth. see Filippi.
Laucka, A., et al. English-Lithuanian Dictionary (Pub. by Mokslas). Four Continent.
Launay, Michel. Le Vocabulaire Politique de J. J. Rousseau. Slatkine.
Laureilhe, Marie T. Le Thesaurus: Son Role, sa Structure, son Elaboration. Assoc Biblio.
Laureilhe, Marie-Therese. Le Thesaurus. Ecole Biblio.
Laurence Urdang Associates. Hamlyn French Dictionary. Hamlyn-Amer.
Laurence Urdang Associates, Ltd. The Penguin Dictionary of Proverbs. Penguin.
Laurence Urdang Associates, Ltd., compiled by. Hamlyn German Dictionary: German-English, English-German. Hamlyn-Amer.
Laurence Urdang Associates Under the Editorial Supervision of the Longman Dictionary Department. Longman Dictionary of English Idioms. Longman.
Laurence Urdang, Inc., ed. see World Almanac Editors.
Laurendeau, F., et al, eds. Harrap's French & English Business Dictionary. Harrap.
Laurent, Claire. Dizionario italiano-francese. Vallardi A.
Laurent, G. Dizionario Italiano-Francese, Francese-Italiano. French & Eur.
Lauret, Annette, jt. auth. see Ginguay, Michel.
Lauricella, Emanuele. Dizionario medico. USES.
Lautier, jt. auth. see Corbiere, A.
Lauzel, Pierre. Lexique de la Gestion. E. M. E.
Lave, Rud, jt. auth. see Dissing, Borge.
Lavy, Jaacom. Langenscheidt's Hebrew-German Dictionary. Am Map.
Lavy, Jaacov. Hebraisch. Langenscheidt.
--Langenscheidts Handwoerterbuch Hebraisch: Teil II, Deutsch-Hebraisch. Langenscheidt.
--Langenscheidts Handwoerterbuch Hebraisch: Teil I, Hebraisch-Deutsch. Langenscheidt.
Law, J. & Oliver, H. J. Glossary of Histopathological Terms. Butterworth.
Lawes, William G. Grammar & Vocabulary of Language Spoken by Motu Tribe (New Guinea) AMS Pr.
Lawrence, Erma. Haida Dictionary. Edenso, Christine & Cogo, Robert, eds. Society for the Preservation of Haida Language & Literature.
Lawrence, Marjorie K., et al. Grammar & Orthography. Smeeth, William B., ed (Pub. by Lawrence). Borden.
Laycock, Donald C. The Complete Enochian Dictionary. Askin Pub.
Layman, Dale P. The Terminology of Anatomy & Physiology: A Programmed Approach (Pub. by Wiley Med). Wiley.
Layton, C. W. Dictionary of Nautical Words & Terms (Pub. by Nautical England). State Mutual Bk.
--Dictionary of Nautical Words & Terms. Sheridan.
--Harbord's Glossary of Navigation (Pub. by Nautical England). State Mutual Bk.
Lazarsfeld, Paul. Vocabulaire des Sciences Sociales. Mouton De Gruyter.
Lazarsfeld, Paul, jt. auth. see Boudon, Raymond.
Lazarus, Arnold & Smith, H. Wendell. A Glossary of Literature & Composition. NCTE.
Lazzati. Diccionario de paronimos castellanos. Sopena.
--Diccionario del verbo castellano. Sopena.
Lazzati, Santiago. Diccionario del Verbo Castellano (SPA). Lectorum Pubns.
--Diccionario del Verbo Castellano: Como Se Conjugan los Verbos Americanos. French & Eur.
Lea, J. Terminology & Communication Skills in the Health Sciences. Reston.
Leach, R. Musical Thesaurus: A Dictionary of Musical Language. Newbury Bks.
Leach, Robert. Musical Thesaurus: A Dictionary of Musical Language. J Hannon.
Leal. Diccionario Naval. Paraninfo.
Leal, L. Diccionario naval: Ingles-espanol y espanol-ingles. Paraninfo.
Leal, Luis. Diccionario Naval Ingles-Espanol. Paraninfo.
Leal y Leal, Luis. Diccionario naval ingles-espanol espanol-ingles. Paraninfo.
Leb, G. M., jt. auth. see Radday, Yehuda T.
Lebaigue, Charles. Dictionnaire Latin-Francais. French & Eur.
Le-Ba-Khanh, jt. ed. see Le-Ba-Kong.
Le-Ba-Kong & Le-Ba-Khanh, eds. Vietnamese-English, English Vietnamese Dictionary. Ungar.
Le Bars, Alain, jt. ed. see Rassat, Patrick.
Lebedev, K. A. Karmannyi Afgansko-Russkii Slovar (Pub. by Gosizdat Natsional Slovarei). Four Continent.
Lebedev, K. A., et al. Russko-Afganskii Slovar (Pub. by Sov Entsiklopediia). Four Continent.
Lebel, Wilfrid. Le Dictionnaire des Affaires. Homme.
Le Berre, Yves, jt. auth. see Le Du, Jean.
Le Boeuf, Christine. Vocabulaire en Images, 1. Ecole.
--Vocabulaire en Images, 2. Ecole.
LeBreton, Auguste. L Argot Chez les Vrais de Vrais. Presses Cite.
Le Comte, Edward. Dictionary of Puns in Milton's English Poetry. Columbia U Pr.
Le Comte, Edward S. Milton Dictionary. AMS Pr.
Ledesert, D. H., ed. see Mansion, J. E.
Ledesert, D. M., ed. see Mansion, J. E.
Ledesert, Margaret, jt. ed. see Forbes, Patricia.
Ledesert, Margaret, ed. see Mansion, J. E.
Ledesert, R. L., ed. see Mansion, J. E.
Ledesert, R. P., ed. see Mansion, J. E.
Ledesma, S. Diccionario ortografico: Libro del maestro. Barreiro Ramos.
Le Docte, E. Dictionnaire des Termes Juridique en Quartre Langues: Francais, Neerlandais, Anglais, Allemand. French & Eur.
--Dictionnaire des Termes Juridiques en Quatre Langues: Francais-Neerlandais-Anglais-Allemand. Vander Oyez.
LeDocte, E. Dictionnaire les termes juridiques en quatre langues: Francais-Neerlandais-Anglais-Allemand. Maison Dictionnaire.
Le Docte, E., ed. Legal Dictionary in Four Languages. Oyez.
--Legal Dictionary in Four Languages. Rothman.
Le Du, Jean & Le Berre, Yves. Dictionnaire Pratique Francais-Breton. Rennes, C. R. D. P.
Lee, Bennett & Barme, Geremie. China Traveler's Phrasebook. China Bks.
Lee, Charles A. Aleutian Indian & English Dictionary. Shorey.
Lee, Donald W. Harbrace Vocabulary Guide (HC, HC). HarBraceJ.
Lee, Frederick G. A Glossary of Liturgical & Ecclesiastical Terms. Gale.
Lee, John & Chandler, Alfred D., eds. Pitman's Dictionary of Industrial Administration: A Comprehensive Encyclopedia of the Organization, Administration, & Management of Modern Industry. Ayer Co.
Lee, Kee-Dong. Kusaiean-English Dictionary. UH Pr.
Lee, W. R. Study Dictionary of Social English. Newson, B., ed. Pergamon.
Leecraft, Jodie, ed. A DIctionary of Petroleum Terms. PETEX.
Lee-Delisle, Dora. English-Hungarian, Hungarian-English Medical Dictionary. Saphrograph.
Leenhardt, Maurice. Vocabulaire & Grammaire de la Langue Houailou. Inst Ethnol.
Lees, Gene. A Modern Rhyming Dictionary. Cherry Lane.
Lefebvre, Jean-Jacques. Dictionnaire Beauchemin Canadien. Beauchemin.
Lefebvre, M. Nouveau Dictionnaire du Batiment: Anglais-Francais Francais-Anglais. Maison Dictionnaire.
Lefebvre, Marcel. Dictionnaire du Batiment: Francais-Anglais. LEMEAC.
--Glossaire de la Finance. Lemeac.
--Nouveau Dictionnaire Du Batiment. French & Eur.
Le Fevre, Jean. Dictionnaire de Rimes Francaises. Slatkine.
Le Fleming, Svetlana, jt. auth. see Harrison, William.
LeFlemming, Svetlana, jt. auth. see Harrison, W.
LeFort, Emilio, ed. World-Wide Spanish Dictionary (Prem). Fawcett.
Leftwich, A. W. A Dictionary of Entomology. Crane-Russak Co.
--A Dictionary of Zoology. Crane-Russak Co.
--Dizionario di zoologia. Newton-Compton.
Legare, Romain, jt. auth. see Dupuis, Hector.
Legare, Romain, rev. by see Dupuis, Hector.
Le Garff, Andre. Dictionnaire de l'informatique. PUF.

Leger, Albault A. Dictionnaire Francais-Esperanto. Esperanto.
Legrand, G., jt. auth. see Adrian, J.
Legrand, Gerard, jt. auth. see Maillard, Robert.
Lehmann, Arnold O. Lehmann's Little Dictionary of Liturgical Terms. Northwest Pub.
Lehmann, Ulrich. Palaeontologisches Woerterbuch. Enke.
--Palaeontologisches Woerterbuch (Pub. by Dtv). French & Eur.
--Palaeontologisches Woerterbuch (Pub. by F. Enke). French & Eur.
--Palaontologisches Woerterbuch. Enke.
Lehnert, Martin. Altenglisches Elementarbuch Einfuehrung, Grammatik, Texte Mit Uebersetzung und Woerterbuch. De Gruyter.
Lehtipuu, Irma. Englantilais-Suomalainen Asunto ja Rakennusalan Sanasto. Otava.
Leibman, Dan. Young Canada Dictionary. Nelson & Sons Group.
Leipnitz. Erdoelverarbeitung-Petrolchemie. Brandstetter.
Leipnitz, E. Dictionary of Petroleum-Industry & Petroleum Chemistry. Adler.
Leipnitz, W. Technical Dictionary of Petrochemistry (Pub. by Vlg. Technik). French & Eur.
--Woerterbuch Erdoelverarbeitung-Petrolchemie. French & Eur.
Leipnitz, Walter. Erdolverarbeitung und Petrolchemie: A Dictionary of Crude Oil Processing & Petroleum Chemistry English-German-French-Russian. Intl Learn Syst.
Leirie, Michel. Glossaire: Mots sans Memoire. Gallimard.
Leitch, Barbara A. A Concise Dictionary of Indian Tribes of North America. LePoer, Kendall, ed. Ref Pubns.
Leite, Yara M. Dicionario Juridico Brasileiro: Contendo Termos, Expressoes Idiomaticas & Brocardos Usuais em Direito. Saraiva SA.
Leite, Yara Muller. Dicionario de Acoes & de Procedimentos Judiciais. Saraiva SA.
Lejeune & Bunjes. Woerterbuch fuer Aerzte. French & Eur.
Lejeune, F. & Bunjes, W. E. Dictionary for Physicians. French & Eur.
Lekhin, I. V., et al. Slovar' Inostrannykh Slov. Four Continent.
Lelama, Homero. Diccionario de Mitologia. French & Eur.
Leland, Louis S. Kiwi: Yankee Dictionary. Bradt Ent.
Leland, Louis S., Jr. A Personal Kiwi-Yankee Dictionary. Pelican.
Le Lionnais, Francois. Dictionnaire des Echecs. PUF.
Lelli, Onorio, jt. auth. see Bianchi, Raffaello.
Lelu, Adolphe & Kluber, Louis. Vocabulaire & Exercices Francais. Hatier.
--Vocabulaire & Exercices Francais. Hatier.
--Vocabulaire & Exercices Francais. Hatier.
--Vocabulaire & Exercises Francais. Hatier.
--Vocabulaire & Exercises Francais. Hatier.
Le Maistre. Dictionnaire Jersias-Francais. French & Eur.
Lemaitre, Yves. Lexique du Tahitien Contemporain: Tahitien-Francais. Orstom.
Lembke, R. Langenscheidts Sportwoerterbuch (Pub. by Langenscheidt). French & Eur.
Lemee, Albert. Dictionnaire Descriptif & Synonymique des Genres de Plantes Phanerogmes, 7. Lechevalier.
--Dictionnaire Descriptif & Synonymique des Genres de Plantes Phanerogmes, 8. Lechevalier.
--Dictionnaire Descriptif & Synonymique des Genres de Plantes Phanerogames, 9. Lechevalier.
--Dictionnaire Descriptif & Synonymique des Genres de Plantes Phanerogames, 10. Lechevalier.
Lemmons, Reuel G., et al, eds. see Smith, William.
Lemon. Glossary for the Study of English. Oxford U Pr.
Lempereur, Agnes, jt. auth. see Thines, Georges.
Lempriere, J. A. A Classical Dictionary. Gordon Pr.
Lenczewska, Bronislawa. Slownik Terminow z Zakresu Informatyki. Politekens Forlag.
Lender, T., et al. Diccionario de Biologia. Serrano, Merce & Vallespinos, Ferran, trs. Grijalbo.
Lenier, Minnette & Maker, Janet. Keys to a Powerful Vocabulary: Level I. P-H.
LeNoir, C. P. Dictionnaire des Droits et de la Raison. Migne, J. P., ed. Caratzas Pub Co.
--Dictionnaire des Harmonies de la Raison et de la Foi. Migne, J. P., ed. Caratzas Pub Co.
Lenzi, Mario. Dizionario di giornalismo. Mursia.
Leo. Complete Dictionary of Astrology (Inner Traditions). Am Fed Astrologers.
Leo, Alan & Robson. Alan Leo's Dictionary of Astrology (Pub. by Sun Pub). Am Fed Astrologers.
Leo, Alan & Robson, Vivian E. Alan Leo's Dictionary of Astrology. Sun Pub.
Leon, Leon G. F. de see De Leon, G. F.
Leon, V. Diccionario del Argot Espanol. French & Eur.
Leon, Victor. Diccionario de Argot Espanol. Alianza Ed.
Leonard, C. Henri & Christy, Thomas. Dictionary of Materia Medica & Therapeutics. Gordon Pr.
Leonard, P. Vocabulaire Pratique du Grec. Duculot.
Leon-Dufour, Xavier. Diccionario del Nuevo Testamento. French & Eur.
Leon-Dufour, Xavier, ed. Dictionary of Biblical Theology. Cahill, P. Joseph, tr. from Fr. Seabury.
Leong-Hong, Belkis W. & Plagman, Bernard K. Data Dictionary-Directory Systems: Administration Implementation & Usage (Pub. by Wiley-Interscience). Wiley.
--Data Dictionary-Directory Systems: Administration Implementation & Usage. Data Process Mgmt.
--Data Dictionary-Directory Systems: Aministration, Implementation & Usage. Data Process Mgmt.
Leonhardt, J. BI-Taschenlexikon Radioaktivitaet. Bibl Inst Leipzig.
Leonidova. Russian-Bulgarian Dictionary. French & Eur.
Leonidova, M. A. Karmannyi Bolgarsko-Russkii Slovar (Pub. by Gosizdat Inostr. & Natsional). Four Continent.
--Karmannyi Russko-Bolgarskii Slovar. Four Continent.
Leon Nunez, Victor. Diccionario de argot espanol. Alianza Ed.
Leontev, A. A. Slovar Assotsiativnykh Norm Russkogo Iazyka (Pub. by MGU). Four Continent.
Leopold, Max. Die Vorsilbe ver & Ihre Geschichte. Olms Verlag.
Le Page, R., jt. auth. see O'Dwyer, R.
Le Page, R. B., jt. ed. see Cassidy, Frederick G.
Le Pennec, Marie F. Petit Glossaire du Language Erotique aux XVIIe & XVIIIe Siecles. Borderie.
Lepine, Pierre. Dictionnaire Francais-Anglais des Termes Medicaux & Biologiques. Flammarion.
--Dictionnaire Francais-Anglais et Anglais-Francais des Termes Medicaux et Biologiques. French & Eur.
Leping, A. A., ed. Russko-Nemetskii Slovar (Pub. by GINS). Four Continent.
Leping, E. I., ed. Russko-Nemetskii Slovar (Pub. by Russkii Iazyk). Four Continent.
LePoer, Kendall, ed. see Leitch, Barbara A.
Lepointe, Emile, jt. auth. see Bertaux, Felix.
Lepsius, Richard. Standard Alphabet for Reducing Unwritten Languages & Foreign Graphic Systems to a Uniform Orthography in European Letters. Kemp, J. Alan, ed. Benjamins North Am.
Lerche, Mario R. Deutsch-Spanisches Glossarium (Pub. by Fritz Knapp Verlag). French & Eur.
--Deutsch-Spanisches Glossarium Finanzieller & Wirtschaftlicher Fachausdrueck. Knapp Verlag.
Lerond, A. Dictionnaire de la Prononciation (Dist. by Continental Bk Co). Larousse.
--Dictionnaire de la Prononciation. French & Eur.
Le Roux, Hubert. Dictionnaire de Poitiers, Ville d'art & d'histoire. H. Le Roux.
Le Sage, Laurent. Dictionnaire des Critiques Litteraires. Pa St U Pr.
Leschonski, K. & Carter, F. T., eds. Elsevier's Dictionary of Particle Technology. Elsevier.
Lesko, Leonard H., ed. Dictionary of Late Egyptian. B C Scribe.
Leskova, T. & Plisek, V. Czech-English Technical Textile Dictionary (Pub. by Collet's). State Mutual Bk.
Leslau, Wolf. Concise Amharic Dictionary. U of Cal Pr.
Leslie, L. A., jt. auth. see Gregg, J. R.
Lesobre, J. & Sommer, H. Vocabulaire Technique Des Assurances: Anglais-Francais, Francais-Anglais. French & Eur.
Lesoil, M. Norsk-Fransk Ordbok. French & Eur.
--Norwegian-French Dictionary. Kunnskapsforlaget.
Lespy, Jean-Desire & Raymond, Paul. Dictionnaire Bearnais Ancien & Moderne. Slatkine.
Lessing, F. D. Mongolian-English Dictionary. Mongolia.
Leuchtmann, H., ed. Dictionary of Musical Terms in Seven Languages. Heinman.
Leuchtmann, Horst. Dictionary of Terms in Music (Pub. by K G Saur). Shoe String.
--Woerterbuch Musik. French & Eur.
Leutzeler, H. Bildwoerterbuch der Kunst (Pub. by F. Duemmlers). French & Eur.
Levarie, Siegmund & Levy, Ernst. A Dictionary of Musical Morphology. Inst Mediaeval Mus.
--Musical Morphology: A Discourse & a Dictionary. Kent St U Pr.
Levens, Peter. Manipulus Vocabulorum. AMS Pr.
Levenston, Edward A. & Sivan, Reuven. The New Bantam-Megiddo Hebrew Dictionary. Bantam.
Levenston, Edward A., jt. auth. see Sivan, Reuben.
Levenston, Edward A., jt. auth. see Sivan, Reuven.
Levenston, Edward A. & Sivan, Reuban, eds. The Megiddo Modern Dictionary: English-Hebrew, Hebrew-English. Carta Pub Co.
--The Megiddo Modern Dictionary: English-Hebrew, Hebrew-English (Carta Maps & Guides Pub Israel). Hippocrene Bks.
Lever, Jill, jt. auth. see Harris, John.
Levesque, Pierre-Charles, jt. auth. see Watelet, Claude-Henre.
Levesque, Pierre-Charles, jt. auth. see Watelet, Claude-Henri.
Levin, Marcia, jt. auth. see Bendick, Jeanne.
Levine, Harold. Vocabulary & Composition Through Pleasurable Reading. AMSCO Sch.
--Vocabulary & Composition Through Pleasurable Reading. AMSCO Sch.
--Vocabulary & Composition: Through Pleasurable Reading. AMSCO Sch.
--Vocabulary for the College-Bound Student. AMSCO Sch.
--Vocabulary for the College-Bound Student. AMSCO Sch.
--Vocabulary for the High School Student. AMSCO Sch.
--Vocabulary for the High School Student. AMSCO Sch.
--Vocabulary Through Pleasurable Reading. AMSCO Sch.
--Vocabulary Through Pleasurable Reading. AMSCO Sch.
Levine, Harold & Levine, Robert. Vocabulary Resources for the College Student. AMSCO Sch.
Levine, Harold & Levine, Robert T. Vocabulary Foundations for the College Student. AMSCO Sch.
Levine, Robert, jt. auth. see Levine, Harold.
Levine, Robert M. Historical Dictionary of Brazil. Scarecrow.
--Race & Ethnic Relations in Latin America & the Caribbean: An Historical Dictionary & Bibliography. Scarecrow.
Levine, Robert T., jt. auth. see Levine, Harold.
Le Vine, Victor T. & Nye, Roger. Historical Dictionary of Cameroon. Scarecrow.
Levinsky, Otto. Francouzsko-Cesky a Cesko-Francouzsky Slovnik pro Televizni Pracovniky a Prekladatele. SNTC.
Levinson, Leonard L. Left-Handed Dictionary (Collier). Macmillan.
--Webster's Unafraid Dictionary (Collier). Macmillan.
Levitchi, V. & Bantas, T. English-Romanian Dictionary (Pub. by Collet's). State Mutual Bk.
Levy, Ernst, jt. auth. see Levarie, Siegmund.
Lewandowski, Dominique, ed. see Bernard, Yves, et al.
Lewandowski, Theodor, et al. Diccionario de linguistica. Bernardez, Enrique & Garcia, M. Luz, trs. Edns Catedra.
Lewick-Wallace, Mary. Vocabulary Building & Word Study. Raygor, Alton, ed (C). McGraw.
Lewin, B. Kleines Woerterbuch der Japanologie (Pub. by Harrassowitz). French & Eur.
Lewin, Bernhard. A Vocabulary of the Hudailian Poems. Humanities.
Lewis, Carolyn D. Medical Latin. M Jones.
Lewis, Charlton T. Elementary Latin Dictionary. Oxford U Pr.
Lewis, Charlton T. & Short, Charles. Latin Dictionary: Founded on Andrews Edition of Freund's Latin Dictionary. Oxford U Pr.
Lewis, Frank. A Dictionary of British Historical Painters (Pub. by A & C Black England). Humanities.
Lewis, George C. Remarks on the Use & Abuse of Some Political Terms. U of Mo Pr.
Lewis, Norman. Roget's Thesaurus in Dictionary Form (Medallion). Berkley Pub.
Lewis, Norman & Funk, Wilfred. Thirty Days to a More Powerful Vocabulary. PB.
Lewis, Norman, jt. auth. see Funk, Wilfred.
Lewis, Samuel. Topographical Dictionary of Ireland (Pub by Kennikat). Assoc Faculty Pr.
Lewis, Terence, et al, eds. Harrap's English-Brazilian Portuguese Business Dictionary. Harrap.
Lewis, Walter H. Ecology Field Glossary: A Naturalist's Vocabulary. Greenwood.
Lexikographischen Institut Sansoni, ed. Langenscheidts Grosswoerterbuch: Teil II, Deutsch-Italiensch. Macchi, Vladimiro. Langenscheidt.
--Langenscheidts Grosswoerterbuch: Teil I, Italienisch-Deutsch. Langenscheidt.
Lexikon-Institut Bertelsmann. Lexikon der Medizin & Gesundheit. C Bertelsmann.
Lexikonredaktion. BI-Handlexikon. Bibl Inst Leipzig.
Lexikonredaktion, ed. BI-Handlexikon. Bibl Inst Leipzig.
--Meyers Grosses Handlexikon in Farbe. Biblio Inst.
Lexikonredaktion des Bibliographischen Instituts, ed. Duden-Lexikon in Drei Banden. Biblio Inst.
--Meyers Grosses Standardlexikon in 3 Banden. Biblio Inst.
Lhande, Pierre. Dictionnaire Basque Francais. Beauchesne.
--Dictionnaire Basque Francais. French & Eur.

L'Heritier, Philippe. Dictionnaire de Genetique. Masson & Cie.
L'Heureux, Mother Aloysius G. Mystical Vocabulary of Venerable Mere Marie De L'Incarnation & Its Problems. AMS Pr.
Li, P. K., ed. A Text of Chinese Military Terms. French & Eur.
Liang, Shi-Chiu. A New Practical Chinese-English Dictionary (Pub. by Far East Bk Co China). Cheng & Tsui.
--A New Practical Chinese-English Dictionary (Pub. by Far East Bk Co China). Cheng & Tsui.
Liang, Shi-Chiu, ed. A New Practical Chinese-English Dictionary (Pub. by Far East Bk Co China). Cheng & Tsui.
--A New Practical English-Chinese Dictionary (Pub. by Far East Bk Co China). Cheng & Tsui.
Liban, Libr d. ABC Dictionary I: Arabic & Span. Intl Bk Ctr.
Liborio, M. A., tr. see Benveniste, Emile.
Libr. du Liban. ABC Dictionary I: Arabic & Fr. Intl Bk Ctr.
--ABC Dictionary I: Arabic & Ger. Intl Bk Ctr.
Libr du Liban. ABC Dictionary Tamhidi: Arabic & Eng. Intl Bk Ctr.
--ABC Dictionary Tamhidi: Arabic & Fr. Intl Bk Ctr.
--ABC Dictionary Tamhidi: Arabic & Ital. Intl Bk Ctr.
--ABC Dictionary Tamhidi: Arabic Ger. Intl Bk Ctr.
--ABC Dictionary Tamhidi: Arabic-Spanish. Intl Bk Ctr.
--My Illustrated Dictionary: Arabic & Fr. Intl Bk Ctr.
--My Illustrated Dictionary: Arabic & Ger. Intl Bk Ctr.
--My Illustrated Dictionary: Arabic & Ital. Intl Bk Ctr.
--My Illustrated Dictionary: Arabic & Span. Intl Bk Ctr.
--My Illustrated Dictionary: Arabic Eng. Intl Bk Ctr.
Libr. du Liban, ed. A Dictionary of Economics & Commerce. Intl Bk Ctr.
Librairie A. Quillet. Dictionnaire Quillet de la Langue Francaise. Librairie Aritide.
Librairie Larousse. Larousse de Poche: Precis de Grammaire. Lib Gen Fr.
Lichtenstern, Hermann. Duden-Das Woerterbuch Medizinischer Fachausdruecke. Biblio Inst.
Licklider, Patricia. Building a College Vocabulary. Little.
Liddell & Scott. An Intermediate Greek-English Lexicon. Oxford U Pr.
Liddell, H. G. & Scott, Robert, eds. Abridged Greek-English Lexicon. Oxford U Pr.
--Intermediate Greek-English Lexicon. Oxford U Pr.
Liddell, H. G., et al. Dizionario illustrato greco-italiano. Monnier.
Liddell, Henry G. & Scott, Robert, eds. Greek-English Lexicon. Oxford U Pr.
Lieber, Michael D. & Dikepa, Kalio H. Kapingamarangi Lexicon. UH Pr.
Lieberman, J. E. Enriching Vocabulary Concept in The Classroom. Assn Child & Adult Learn.
Lieberman, Leo, ed. see Martin, Michael & Gelber, Leonard.
Liebling, Emil, jt. auth. see Mathews, William S.
Liebster, L. M., jt. auth. see Horner, C. F.
Liebster, Leo & Horner, Colin. Pocket Dictionary of Business Terms. Newnes Bks.
Lienhart, Hans, jt. auth. see Martin, Ernst.
Lienhart, Hans, jt. ed. see Martin, Ernst.
Ligou, Daniel. Dictionnaire Universel de la Franc-Maconnerie. Prisme.
Lille, jt. auth. see Vermesse, Louis.
Lima, Robert F., ed. Arco Motor Vehicle Dictionary: English & Spanish. Arco.
Lincoln, Abraham. Lincoln Dictionary. Winn, Ralph, ed (WL). Citadel Pr.
Lincoln, R. J. & Boxshall, G. A. A Dictionary of Ecology, Evolution & Systematics. Cambridge U Pr.
Lincoln Canfield, D., rev. by see Castillo, Carlos & Bond, Otto F.
Lind, H., jt. auth. see Tetsmann, A.
Lindberg, G. U. Multilingual Dictionary of Names of Marine Food-Dishes of World Fauna (Pub. by Collets). State Mutual Bk.
Lindeke, Wolfgang. Dictionary of Ventilation & Health (Pub. by Collet's). State Mutual Bk.
--Technical Veterinary Dictionary. French & Eur.
Lindemann, G. Lexikon der Kunststile. French & Eur.
Linder, Bernhard & Paltorp, Adam S. Lademanns Rejseleksikon Danmark. Lademann Forlag.
Lindlar, H. Rororo Musikhandbuch. Rowohlt.
--Rororo Musikhandbuch (Pub. by Rowohlt). French & Eur.
Lindner, K. & Neumann, K. H. Jugendlexikon Astronomie & Raumfahrt. Bibl Inst Leipzig.
Linfield, Jordon L., jt. auth. see Kreivsky, Joseph.
Ling, Agnes H., jt. auth. see Ling, Daniel.
Ling, Daniel & Ling, Agnes H. Basic Vocabulary & Language Thesaurus for Hearing-Impaired Children. Alexander Graham.
Ling, T. O. A Dictionary of Buddhism (ScribT). Scribner.
Ling, Trevor. A Dictionary of Buddhism: Indian & South-East Asia (Pub. by K P Bagchi India). Humanities.
Lingeman, Richard R. Drugs from A to Z: A Dictionary (SP). McGraw.
Linguistic Society of America & Hall, Robert A., Jr. Melanesian Pidgin Phase-Book & Vocabulary. Linguistic Soc Am.
Linguistic Society of America & Sturtevant, E. H. Hittite Glossary. Linguistic Soc Am.
Linguistic Society of America & Woodard, C. M. Census of French & Provencal Dialect Dictionaries in American Libraries. Linguistic Soc Am.
Lini, L. Dizionario italo-indonesiano. EMI.
Liniger-Goumaz, Max. Historical Dictionary of Equatorial Guinea. Scarecrow.
Linnapuomi, Kalervo. Ruotsin Kielen Perus ja Taydennyssanasto. Otava.
Linnard, W. Russian-English Forestry & Wood Dictionary (Pub. by CAB Bks England). State Mutual Bk.
Linnert, Peter. Lexikon Angloamerikanischer und Deutscher Managementbegriffe. French & Eur.
Linse. Woerterbuch der Datentechnik. Brandstetter.
Linton, George E. The Modern Textile & Apparel Dictionary. Textile Bk.
--The Modern Textile & Apparel Dictionary (Pub. by Meadowfield Pr England). State Mutual Bk.
Lionnais, Francois Le see Le Lionnais, Francois.
Lipparini, L. Vocabolario latino-italiano e italiano-latino. Malipiero.
Lipperheide, Manfred, et al. Fachbegriffe der Versicherungwirtschaft. Deutsch Spark.
Lippman, Peter. One & Only Wacky Wordbook (Golden Pr). Western Pub.
Lipsik, Frank. Le Dictionnaire des Varietes, A-Z. Menges.
Lipton & Munoz. Spanish Bilingual Dictionary. Camino Real.
Lipton, G. French Bilingual Dictionary: A Beginner's Guide in Words & Pictures. Barron.
Lipton, G. & Munoz, O. Spanish Bilingual Dictionary: Diccionario Espanol-Ingles-Ingles-Espanol. Barron.
Lipton, Gladys. French Bilingual Dictionary. Barron.
--French Bilingual Dictionary: A Beginner's Guide in Words & Pictures. Barron.
--French Bilingual Dictionary: Compact Ed. Barron.
Lipton, Gladys & Colinari, John. Italian Bilingual Dictionary: A Beginner's Guide in Words & Pictures. Barron.
Lipton, Gladys & Munoz, Olivia. Spanish Bilingual Dictionary: A Beginners Guide in Words & Pictures. Barron.
--Spanish Bilingual Dictionary: Compact Guide. Barron.
Lipton, Gladys C. French Bilingual Dictionary: A Beginner's Guide in Words & Pictures. Barron.
Lipton, Munoz. Spanish Bilingual Dictionary. Camino Real.
Litero. Diccionario De Crucigramas. French & Eur.
Lithgow, Daphne, jt. auth. see Lithgow, David.
Lithgow, David & Lithgow, Daphne. Muyuw Dictionary. Summer Inst Ling.
Litschauer, R. Vocabularium Polyglottum Vitae Silvarum. Parey.
--Vocabularium Polyglottum Vitae Silvarum (Pub. by P. Parey). French & Eur.
Little, R. J. & Jones, C. E. A Dictionary of Botany. Van Nos Reinhold.
Litton. Russko-Bengal'skii Slovar (Pub. by Sov. Entsiklopediia). Four Continent.
Litton, D. Karmannyi Bengal'sko-Russkii Slovar (Pub. by Gosizdat Natsional Slovarei). Four Continent.
Littre. Dictionnaire de la Langue Francaise. Beaujean & Geraud-Venzac, eds. French & Eur.
Littre, Emile. Dictionnaire de La Langue Francaise. French & Eur.
Liu, Eric S. Frequency Dictionary of Chinese Words. Mouton.
Liu, F. & L. Yan Mau. Chinese Medical Terminology: English to Chinese. French & Eur.
Livadic. Dizionario Italiano-Serbo Croato. Vallardi A.
Livadic, P., ed. Dizionario Italiano-Serbocroato, Serbocroato-Italiano. French & Eur.
Livescu, Jean & Savin, Emilia. Dictionar Roman-German: Pentru uzul Elevilor. Editura Stiintifica.
Livet, Charles L. Lexique de la Langue de Moliere, 1. Olms.
--Lexique de la Langue de Moliere, 2. Olms.
--Lexique de la Langue de Moliere, 3. Olms.
Livingstone, E. A., ed. The Concise Oxford Dictionary of the Christian Church. Oxford U Pr.
Livingstone, Elizabeth A., jt. auth. see Cross, F. L.
Lizarraga, Francisco. Diccionario tecnico militar ingles-espanol y espanol-ingles para uso de los ejercitos de tierra, mar y aire. Bibliografica.
Lizaso, Domingo. Diccionario onomastico y heraldico vasco: Tomo 7. Encicl Vasca.
Ljunggren, K. G., jt. ed. see Johannisson, Ture.
Llauro Padrosa, J. Diccionario latino-espanol. SAETA.
Llauro Padrose, J. & Marques Casanovas, J. Diccionario espanol-latino. SAETA.
Llido Blasco, Julio, tr. see Garnier, Marcel, et al.
Llllull Marti, Antoni. Vocabularis Tematics. Organismos Ofic.
Llopis, Joan, tr. see Ancilli, Ermanno.
Lluelles Cardona, Victor. Diccionari Politic De Catalunya. French & Eur.
Lluis. Diccionario Terminologico. Fondo Educativo.
Loane, George G. Short Handbook of Literary Terms. Folcroft.
Lobban, Richard. Historical Dictionary of the Republics of Guinea-Bissau & Cape Verde. Scarecrow.
Lockard, L. Desk Reference for Neuroanatomy: A Guide to Essential Terms. Springer-Verlag.
Lockwood, J. L., jt. ed. see Smith, William.
Lockwood, Laura E. Lexicon to the English Poetical Works of John Milton. Folcroft.
Lockwood, Luke V. Furniture Collector's Glossary. Da Capo.
Lockwood, Luke V., jt. auth. see Barber, Edward A.
Lodge, Gonzalez. The Vocabulary of High School Latin. AMS Pr.
Lodhi, Abdulaziz, et al. Korfattad Svensk-Swahili Ordbok. Nord Afrik.
Loebel & Mueller. Lexikon der Datenverarbeitung. French & Eur.
Loechel, William E. Pictorial Medical Terminology. C C Thomas.
Loennecken, S. Spanish-Norwegian Dictionary. Kunnskapsforlaget.
--Spansk-Norsk Ordbok. French & Eur.
Loetzsch, R., et al, eds. see Bielfeldt, Hans H.
Loetzsch, Ronald, ed. see Bielfeldt, Hans H.
Logie, G. Glossary of Employment & Industry. Elsevier.
--Glossary of Populations & Housing. Elsevier.
--Glossary of Transport. Elsevier.
Logie, Gordon & Hemstead, Hemel, eds. International Planning Glossary. Intl Plan Glos.
Lohwater, A. J. Russian-English Dictionary of the Mathematical Sciences. Am Math.
Loi, I., jt. auth. see Rosiello, L.
Lokotsch, Karl. Etymologisches Woerterbuch der Europaeischen Woerter Orientalischen Ursprungs. Winter Univ.
--Etymologisches Woerterbuch der Europaeischen Woerter Orientalischen Ursprungs (Pub. by Carl Winter). French & Eur.
Lokshina, S. M. Kratkii Slovar Inostrannykh Slov (Pub. by Russkii Iazyk). Four Continent.
Loland, Stale & Thorsen, Arnold. Norsk Forkortingsbok. J W Cappelens.
Loman, Bengt, jt. auth. see Ekbo, Sven.
Lomax, J. D. Data Dictionary Systems. Intl Pubns Serv.
Lombardero, O. J. Glosario de terminos parasitologicos. EUDEBA.
Lomo, A., jt. ed. see Douglas, J. M.
Long, Karen, ed. see Lucas, Caroline & Turner, Carann.
Long, William H. A Dictionary of the Isle of Wight Dialect, & of Provincialisms Used in the Island, with Illustrative Anecdotes & Tales. Folcroft.
Longan, Tang & Zenglian, Ni. English-Chinese Dictionary of Metals & Their Heat Treatment. Indus Pr.
Longley, D., jt. auth. see Shain, M.
Longley, David, jt. auth. see Shain, Michael.
Longley, Dennis & Shain, Michael. Dictionary of Information Technology. Macmillan London.
--Dictionary of Information Technology (Pub. by Wiley-Interscience). Wiley.
Longmuir, John, ed. see Jamieson, John.
Longnon, Auguste. Dictionnaire Topographique de la France. Biblio Nationale.
Lopatnikov, L. I. Kratkii Ekonomiko-Matematicheskii Slovar (Pub. by Nauka). Four Continent.
--Populiarnyi Ekonomiko-Matematicheskii Slovar (Pub. by Znanie). Four Continent.
Lope Blanch, J. M. El Lexico indigena en el espanol de Mexico. Col. de Mexico.
Lope Blanch, Juan M. Vocabulario Mexicano Relativo a la Muerte. UNAM.
Lopez, Issac M. Basque-Spanish Dictionary. Revisionist Pr.
Lopez, J. A., jt. auth. see Fuentes, D.
Lopez, Jesus. Ortografia programada. Del Castillo.
Lopez, Jose A., jt. auth. see Fuentes, Dagaberto.
Lopez de Haro, Carlos. Diccionario de Reglas, Alforismos & Principios de Derecho. Reus SA.
Lopez de Zuazo, A. Diccionario del Periodismo. Piramide.
Lopez de Zuazo Algar, Antonio. Diccionario del periodismo. Piramide.
--Diccionario del Periodismo. French & Eur.
Lopez Dominguez, Mario. Diccionario de las Artes Marciales. Ramos-Majos.

Lopez Mendizabal, Isaac. La Lengua Vasca. Aunamendi Edit.

--La Lengua Vasca: Gramatica, Conversacion, Diccionario Vasco-Castellano, Castellano-Vasco. Aunamendi Edit.

Lopez Mendizabal, Isaak. Diccionario Vasco-Castellano. French & Eur.

Lordkipanidze, A. G., et al. Russko-Indoneziiskii Uchebnyi Slovar (Pub. by GINS). Four Continent.

Lorenz, Egon, jt. auth. see Dietl, Clara E.

Lorinczy, Eva B. Uj Magyar Tajszotar. Akademiai Kiado.

Lorinczy, Eva B., ed. see Magyar Tudomanyos Akademia Nyelvtudomany Intezeteben.

Lorton, David. The Juridical Terminology of International Relations in Egyptian Texts Through Dynasty XVIII. Johns Hopkins.

Lorveberg, Sven, jt. auth. see Larsson, Lars G.

Losique, Serge. Dictionnaire Etymologique des Noms de Pays & de Peuples. Klincksieck.

Loth, Joseph. Vocabulaire du Vieux Breton. Champion.

Lo-Tien, F. Beginner's Translation Handbook: English-Chinese. French & Eur.

Loughead, Flora H. Dictionary of Given Names. A H Clark.

Lousse, Emile, jt. auth. see De Launay, Jacques.

Love, P. Terminologia de la Danza Moderna. EUDEBA.

Lovelace-Kaeufer, C., jt. auth. see Engeroff, K.

Lovett, D. R., jt. auth. see Ballentyne, D. W.

Loving, Dick. Awa Dictionary. Linguistic Circle.

Lowe, Joseph D. Dictionary of Political Terms: Chinese-English, English-Chinese. Lowe Pub.

Luangpraseut, Kamchong, tr. English-Lao Phrasebook with Useful Word List: For Laotians. Ctr Appl Ling.

Lucas, Caroline & Turner, Carann. Population-Family Planning Thesaurus: An Alphabetical & Hierarchical Display of Terms Drawn from Population-Related Literature in the Social Sciences. Long, Karen & Turner, Carann, eds. Carolina Pop Ctr.

Lucas, D. J., et al. A First Science Dictionary: College Edition. Crane-Russak Co.

Lucas, David. A First Science Dictionary. Intl Bk Ctr.

Lucas, John, jt. auth. see Dickinson, Colin.

Lucchesi, M. Dizionario Medico Ragionato Inglese-Italiano. French & Eur.

Lucchesi, Mario. Dizionario Medico Ragionato Inglese-Italiano: Termini, Abbreviazioni, Sigle, Eponimi e Sinonimi Medici, Medico-Biologici e Delle Specializzazioni Mediche. S F Vanni.

Lucchesi, U. M. Dizionario medico ragionato per le scienze mediche inglese-italiano. Cortina M.

Luciano, L. & Traina, A. Vocabolario fraseologico italiano-latino. Patron.

Lucy, T., jt. auth. see Karim, A.

Luds, Peter, jt. auth. see Apel, Max.

Luecke, Wolfgang. Investigationslexikon. Bloech, Juergen, ed. Vahlen.

Luft, Anita. Diccionario de Palabras Anticuadas y en Desuso. French & Eur.

Luft, C. P., jt. auth. see Fernandes, F.

Luggauer, Karl. Der Wortschatz des Juristen: Ein Lern & Lesebuch Juristischen Sprachausdrucks. Heyn.

Lugo-Guernelli, A., et al. Manuel De Gramatica Comercial. French & Eur.

Lukianenkov, K. F. Chastotnyi Anglo-Russkii Slovar Minimum Po Sudovozhdeniiu (Pub. by Voenizdat). Four Continent.

Lulchak, L., jt. auth. see Kolesnikova, A.

Lumeka, Placide-Raphael. Vocabulaire Alphabetique & Analogique Destine aus Ecollers Africains Francophones. Lang, H.

Luna de la Fuente. Vocabulario de Terminos: Criollos Tipicos Relacionados con el Caballo de Paso. U. Agraria.

Lund, Morten. The Real Skiers' Dictionary. S&S.

Lupandin, K. A., jt. auth. see Rabinowitch, Z. E.

Luquet, F. M., jt. auth. see Boudier, J. F.

Lurker, Manfred, ed. Woerterbuch der Symbolik. Kroener.

Luzuriaga, Lorenzo. Diccionario de pedagogia. Losada.

L'Vov, M. R. Slovar' Antonimov Russkogo Iazyka. Four Continent.

L. Yan Mau, jt. auth. see Liu, F.

Lyman, Thomas A. Dictionary of Mong Njua: A Miao (Meo) Language of Southeast Asia. Mouton.

Lysaght, T. Dictionary, Material Towards the Compilation of a Concise Old Church Slavonic English. VicUni.

--Material Towards the Compilation of a Concise Old Church Slavonic-English Dictionary. Victoria University Press.

Lysaght, T. A. Material Towards the Compilation of a Concise Old Church Slavonic-English Dictionary. Price Milburn.

Lyse, Peter. Attved Tyrifjorden. Universitetsforlaget.

Lysle & Gualtieri. Dizionario delle lingue italiana e inglese. Casanova F & C.

Lysle & Pontevideo. Dizionario italiano-tedesco e tedesco-italiano. Casanova F & C.

M

McAdam, E. L. & Milne, G., eds. Johnson's Dictionary: A Modern Selection. Macmillan London.

McAllister, J. Vocabolario italiano-inglese, inglese-italiano (CEB). Capitol-Dischi.

MacAndrew, Ronald, ed. see Patterson, William R.

McArthur, Tom & Atkins, Beryl. Dictionary of English Phrasal Verbs & Their Idioms. Pan Pacific Bk.

--Dictionary of English Phrasal Verbs & Their Idioms (Pub. by Collins ELT Scotland). State Mutual Bk.

Macarulla, D. Diccionario Lexicon Ingles-Espanol, Espanol-Ingles. French & Eur.

Macazaga Ordono, Cesar. Diccionario de la Lengua Nahuatl. Innovacion.

--Diccionario de la Lengua Nahuatl. Innovacion.

McCarren, V. P., ed. A Critical Concordance to Catullus. Humanities.

McCaslin, Ellen S., jt. auth. see Block, Karen K.

Macchi, L. Diccionario latino. Don Bosco Ed.

Macchi, V. Langenscheidts Taschenwoerterbuch Italienisch: Teil I, Italienisch-Deutsch. Langenscheidt.

Macchi, V. & Frenzel, W. Langenscheidts Taschenwoerterbuch Italienisch-Deutsch. Langenscheidt.

Macchi, V., jt. ed. see Frenzel, W.

Macchi, Vladimiro see Lexikographischen Institut Sansoni.

Macchi, Vladimiro, ed. Inglese-italiano, italiano-inglese. Sansoni.

--Langenscheidts Grossworterbucher Italienisch. Langenscheidt.

--Tedesco-Italiano, Italiano-Tedesco. Sansoni.

Macchi, Vladimiro, ed. see Frenzel, Herbert & Frenzel, Walter.

Macchi, Vladimiro Von see Von Macchi, Vladimiro.

MacClelland. Vocabulaire de Lais de Marie de France. Ottawa U.

Mac Cragh, Esteban. Nuevo Diccionario Ingles-Espanol y Espanol-Ingles. French & Eur.

McCrea, Barbara P. & Plano, Jack C. The Soviet & East European Political Dictionary. ABC-Clio.

McDavid, R. I; see Harder, K. B.

MacDonald. Dictionary of Canadian Artists. Apollo.

McDonald, B., jt. auth. see Beitler, L.

MacDonald, Gerald, ed. Vocabulario De Romance En Latin: Antonio De Nebrija. Temple U Pr.

Macdonald, Gerald J., tr. see De Nebruja, Elio de.

McDonald, J. K., ed. see Barrett, A. J.

McDonald, J. Ken, jt. auth. see Barrett, Alan.

McDonald, Marianne. Terms for happiness in Euripides. Vandenhoeck.

MacDonald-Taylor, Margaret. Dictionary of Marks (Hawthorn). Dutton.

--A Dictionary of Marks (Pub. by Ebury Pr England). State Mutual Bk.

MacDonnell, Arthur A. Practical Sanskrit Dictionary: With Transliteration Accentuation & Etymological Analysis Throughout. Oxford U Pr.

Macedo, Horacio. Dicionario Escolar de Quimica. Edit Atica.

McElrath, Ruth G., tr. see McElrath, William N.

McElrath, William N. Bible Dictionary for Young Readers. Broadman.

--Mi Primer Diccionario Biblico. McElrath, Ruth G., tr. from Eng. Casa Bautista.

McFadden, S. Michele, ed. see Abraham, Samuel V.

McFarland, Daniel M. Historical Dictionary of Upper Volta. Scarecrow.

McFarland, George B. Thai-English Dictionary. Stanford U Pr.

McFarlane, C., jt. auth. see Hayward, Arthur L.

McGill University, Blacker - Wood Library of Zoology & Ornithology. A Dictionary Catalogue of the Blacker - Wood Library of Zoology & Ornithology (Hall Library). G K Hall.

MacGowan, J. English & Chinese Dictionary of the Amoy Dialect. Oriental Bk Store.

McGraw Hill. McGraw Hill Dictionary of Scientific & Technical Terms. Parker, Sybil P., ed (Pub by P & RB). McGraw.

McGraw-Hill & Boixareu. Diccionario de Terminos Cientificos & Tecnicos. Marcombo.

McGraw-Hill Editors. Dictionary of the Life Sciences (P&RB). McGraw.

Mac Guckin De Slane, tr. from Arabic. Wafayat al-a yan: Ibn Khallikan's Biographical Dictionary. Intl Bk Ctr.

Machado, D. Diccionario Tecnico de la Construccion, Edificacion & Obras Publicas. Paraninfo.

Machado, Antonio N. Dicionario Conciso da Lingua Portuguesa. Difel Editorial, S. A.

Machado, Antonio N., ed. Dicionario Conciso da Lingua Portuguesa. Didel Difusao.

Machado, M. Diccionario tecnico de la construccion: Edificacion y obras publicas; francesa-espanol y espanol-frances. Paraninfo.

--Diccionario Tecnico De la Construccion, Edificacion y Obras Publicas Frances-Espanol y Espanol-Frances. French & Eur.

MacIver, D. Chinese-English Dictionary: Hakka-Dialect. Oriental Bk Store.

Mack, R. Russian-English Veterinary Dictionary (Pub. by CAB Bks England). State Mutual Bk.

--Veterinary Dictionary: Russian-English. French & Eur.

McKaskill, S. G. Dictionary of Good English. Macmillan London.

McKaughan, Howard P., ed. see Constantino, Ernesto.

McKaughan, Howard P., ed. see Yap, Elsa P. & Bunye, Maria V.

Mackay, Charles. Dictionary of Lowland Scotch. Gale.

Mackay, E. & Williams, G. M. Typewriting Dictionary. Pitman Bks.

Mackay, Edith. Typewriting Dictionary. Beekman Pubs.

Mackay, James. Dictionary of Western Sculptors in Bronze. Antique Collect.

McKenna, Michael. Stein & Day Dictionary of Definitive Quotations. Stein & Day.

Mackensen, Lutz. Deutsches Woerterbuch. Suedwest.

--Deutsches Woerterbuch (Pub. by Suedwest). French & Eur.

MacKenzie, D. N., ed. see Henning, W. B.

Mackenzie, David. A Manual of Manuscript Transcription for the Dictionary of the Old Spanish Language. Hispanic Seminary.

McKenzie, John L. & Maggioni, B. Dizionario biblico. Cittadella.

MacKenzie, Joy, jt. auth. see Forte, Imogene.

Mackey, James. Dictionary of Western Sculptors in Bronze. Apollo.

Mackey, William Francis & Savard, J. G. Vocabulaire Disponible du Francais en France & en Acadie. Didier.

McKibben-Stockwell. Nuevo Lexico Griego Espanol (Edit Mundo). Casa Bautista.

Mackin, Ronald, jt. auth. see Cowie, A. P.

McKinley, Albert E., ed. see Jameson, J. Franklin.

McLaren, J. Dictionary of Austrialian Education. U of Queensland Pr.

--Xhosa-English Dictionary. Bennie, W. G. & Jolobe, J. J., eds. Shalom.

McLaughlin, Charles. Space Age Dictionary. Van Nos Reinhold.

Mac Laughlin, Horace J., jt. auth. see Clifton, Ebenezer.

MacLaurin, Lois M. Franklin's Vocabulary. R West.

MacLennan, Malcolm. Gaelic Dictionary: Gaelic-English English-Gaelic. Pergamon.

--A Pronouncing & Etymological Dictionary of the Gaelic Language. Aberdeen U Pr.

MacLeod, Malcolm L. A Concordance to the Poems of Robert Herrick. Folcroft.

MacLow, Jackson. A Vocabulary for Annie Brigitte Gilles Tardos. Station Hill Pr.

McManus, Edwin G., et al. Palauan-English Dictionary. UH Pr.

McMaster, Dale. Vocabulary Development. ESP.

McMasters, Dale. Beginning Vocabulary. ESP.

--The Dictionary. ESP.

--Everyday Vocabulary. ESP.

--Vocabulary Study. ESP.

Macmillan Pub. Co. Macmillan Dictionary. Macmillan.

--Macmillan School Dictionary. Macmillan.

McMurtray, Frances. Allied Health Reading Vocabulary Workbook. American Pr.

McNaughton, William. Reading & Writing Chinese: A Guide to the Chinese Writing System. C E Tuttle.

McNeil, Donald S., ed. Jewelers' Dictionary. Jewelers Circular.

McNeil, Donald S., compiled by. The Jewelers' Dictionary. Jewelers Circular.

McNeill, D. B., jt. auth. see Jerrard, H. G.

Macura, P. Dictionary of Botany. Elsevier.

--Elsevier's Dictionary of Botany, Vol. 1: Plant Names. Elsevier.

Macura, Paul. Russian-English Botanical Dictionary. Slavica.

Maddison, Robert. A Dictionary of Astronomy. Newnes Bks.

Madrigal, Margarita. See it-Say it in Spanish. Camino Real.

Maehle, Leif, ed. see Beckman, Nat.

Maehle, Lief, ed. see Beckman, Natanael.

Maesschalck, A. de see Van Gemert, G. A. & De Maesschalck, A.

Mafera, G., jt. auth. see Anderson, K.

Magalini, Sergio. Dizionario delle sindromi mediche. DEMI.

413

Magalini, Sergio I. & Scrascia, Euclide. Dictionary of Medical Syndromes (Lippincott Medical). Lippincott.
Mager, N. H. & Mager, S. K. The Morrow Book of New Words: 8500 Terms Not Yet in Standard Dictionaries. Morrow.
Mager, Nathan H. & Mager, Sylvia K. Encyclopedic Dictionary of English Usage (Reward). P-H.
Mager, S. K., jt. auth. see Mager, N. H.
Mager, Sylvia K., jt. auth. see Mager, Nathan H.
Maget, E. Dictionnaire de Echecs. French & Eur.
Maggioni, B., jt. auth. see McKenzie, John L.
Maggs, Carol V., jt. auth. see Neff, Ivan C.
Magni, Mauro. Dizionario degli errori. Edit Vecchi.
Magnien, Victor & Lacroix, M. Dictionnaire Grec-Francais. Belin.
--Dictionnaire Grec-Francais. French & Eur.
Magy, Tamas. Utiszotar, Angol-Magyar. Terra.
Magyar Tudomanyos Akademia Nyelvtudomany Intezeteben. Magyar Tajszotar. Lorinczy, Eva B., ed. Akademiai Kiado.
Mahathera, A Budd Hadatta see Budd Hadatta Mahathera, A.
Mahmoudi, Jalil. A Concordance to the Hidden Words of Baha'u'llah. Baha'i.
Mai-Aru & Anisson du Perron, J. Dictionnaire Francais-Tahitien et Tahitien-Francais. French & Eur.
Mai-Aru, Mai-Arii & Anisson du Perron, J. Dictionnaire Francais-Tahitien. Pensee Moderne.
Maier, Johann & Schaefer, Peter. Kleinnes Lexikon des Judentums. F Bahn.
Maier, Karl E. Paedagogisches Taschenlexikon. Eckinger, Ludwig, ed. Wolf Verlag.
Mailhol, D. de see De Mailhol, D.
Maillard, J. P., jt. auth. see Celerier, P.
Maillard, Robert & Legrand, Gerard. Dictionnaire Universel de la Peinture. Ste. Nouv. Littre.
Maillard, Robert, ed. Dictionnaire Universal de la Peinture. Soc Nouveau.
Maine, jt. auth. see Manset.
Mainwaring, G. B. & Grunwedal, Albert, eds. Dictionary of the Lepcha language. Radha.
Maiocchi, Annamaria F. & De Bichiacchi, Ada. Harrap's Compact Italian & English Dictionary. Harrap.
Maizel, jt. auth. see Skvorzova.
Major, Alan. A New Dictionary of Kent Dialect (Pub. by Meresborough England). State Mutual Bk.
Major, Clarence. Dictionary of Afro-American Slang. Intl Pub Co.
Makai, Gyoergy, jt. auth. see Foldes, Istvan.
Maker, Janet, jt. auth. see Lenier, Minnette.
Makkai, Adam. A Dictionary of American Idioms in Chinese. Gates & Boatner, eds. Barron.
Makkai, Adam, ed. see Boetner, Maxine & Gates, John E.
Maksys, Anna, jt. auth. see Babecki, Jerzy.
Malagoli, Giuseppe. Vocabolarietto del vernacolo pisano. Nistri-Lischi.
Malara, G. Vocabolario dialettale calabro-reggino-italiano. Forni.
Malaret, A. Lexicon de fauna y flora. Inst Caro y Cuervo.
Malaret, Augusto. Diccionario De Americanismos. Gordon Pr.
--Vocabulario de Puerto Rico. Las Americas.
Malaspina, Carlo. Vocabolario parmigiano-italiano. Forni.
Malchiori, G. Battista. Vocabolario bresciano-italiano. Forni.
Malcoux, M. Diccionario humoristico. Grijalbo.
Malczewski, J. Szkolny Slownik Terminow Nauki i Jezyku (Pub. by Wydaw. Szkolne & Pedagogiczne). Four Continent.
Maldonado, Tomas. Universita la Sperimentazione Dipartimentale. Guaraldi.
Malgorn. Diccionario Tecnico Espanol-Ingles. Paraninfo.
--Diccionario Tecnico Frances-Espanol. Paraninfo.
--Diccionario Tecnico Ingles-Espanol. Paraninfo.
Malgorn, G. Dictionnaire Technique Anglais-Francais. French & Eur.
--Dictionnaire Technique Francais-Anglais. French & Eur.
Malgorn, Guy. Diccionario Tecnico Espanol-Frances. French & Eur.
--Diccionario Tecnico Espanol-Ingles. Paraninfo.
--Diccionario Tecnico Espanol-Ingles. French & Eur.
--Diccionario tecnico Espa n13ol-Ingl e01s. Fed Gremios.
--Diccionario tecnico frances-espanol y espanol-frances. Paraninfo.
--Diccionario Tecnico Ingles-Espanol. French & Eur.
--Dictionnaire Technique Francais-Espagnol. French & Eur.
--Dictionnaire technique Anglais-Francais. Imported Bks.
--Dictionnaire Technique Francais-Anglais. Gauthier-Villars.
--Dictionnaire Technique Francais-Espagnol. Gauthier-Villars.
Malgorn, Guy M. Dictionnaire Technique Francais-Anglai. Bordas.
Malignon, J. Dictionnaire des Ecrivains Francais. French & Eur.
Malignon, Jean. Dictionnaire de Politique. Cujas.
--Dictionnaire de Politique. French & Eur.
Malka, Elle. Dictionnaire Pratique des Termes Juridiques: Francais-Arabe. France Selection.
Malkiel, Yakov. Etymological Dictionaries: A Tentative Typology. U of Chicago Pr.
Mallalien, H. L. The Dictionary of Watercolors Artists. Apollo.
--The Dictionary of Watercolors Artists. Apollo.
Mallalieu, H. L. The Dictionary of Watercolour Artists up to 1920: Vol. 1, The Text. Antique Collect.
--The Dictionary of Watercolour Artists up to 1920: Vol. 2, The Plates. Antique Collect.
Mallement De Messanges, Claude. Dictionnaire de Halles. Slatkine.
Malmstrom, Jean. Webster's Third on Non-Standard Usage. Bd. with Social Aspects of Bilingualism in San Antonio, Texas. Sawyer, Janet B; Names in Gardening. Bryant, Margaret M. U of Ala Pr.
Malof, Joseph. A Manual of English Meters. Greenwood.
Maloux, M. Dictionnaire des proverbes, sentences et maximes. Larousse.
Maloux, Maurice. Dictionnaire Humoristique. Albin-Michel.
Malstrom, Robert C. SRA Data Processing Glossary. SRA.
Malta, Christovao P. Dicionario de Direito do Trabalho. Rio Grafica.
Malthus, Thomas R. Definitions in Political Economy. Kelley.
Malvezin, Pierre. Glossaire de la Langue d'Oc. Laffitte Reprints.
--Glossaire de la Langue d'Oc. Slatkine.
Malzac, R. P. Dictionnaire Francais-Malgache. Maritimes Outremer.
--Dictionnaire Francais-Malgache. French & Eur.
--Vocabulaire Francais-Malgache. Maritimes Outremer.
Mancera. Terminologia del Contador. Banca Comercio.
Mandel, Oscar. A Definition of Tragedy. U Pr of Amer.
Manfred, Hofer, jt. auth. see Eckel, Denis.
Mangada, J., jt. auth. see Santamaria, Cuartas.
Mann, Cameron. Concordance to the English Poems of George Herbert. Folcroft.
Mann, David D., ed. A Concordance to the Plays of William Congreve. Cornell U Pr.
Mann, Michael, ed. The International Dictionary of Sociology. Continuum.
Mansat, Andre. Vocabulaire d'anglais Commercial. Didier.
Manser, jt. ed. see Urdang.
Manser, M. H., ed. Pocket Thesaurus of English Words. Hamlyn-Amer.
--Thesaurus of English Words. Hamlyn-Amer.
Manser, Martin H. That's What People Say! A Dictionary of Common Speech Idioms. Macmillan.
Manset & Maine. The Learning Inc. Dictionary of Learning Handicaps. Assn Child & Adult Learn.
Mansion, J. E. Harrap's Concise Student French & English Dictionary. Collin, P. H., et al, eds. Natl Textbk.
--Harrap's New Collegiate French & English Dictionary. Ledesert, D. H., ed. Natl Textbk.
--Harrap's New Standard French & English Dictionary. Imported Bks.
--Harrap's New Standard French & English Dictionary. Clarke Ltd.
--Harrap's New Standard French & English Dictionary: A-I, French-English. Ledesert, D. M. & Ledesert, R. P., eds. Harrap.
--Harrap's New Standard French & English Dictionary: A-K, English-French. Ledesert, D. M. & Ledesert, R. L., eds. Harrap.
--Harrap's New Standard French & English Dictionary: J-Z, French-English. Ledesert, D. M. & Ledesert, R. P., eds. Harrap.
--Harrap's New Standard French & English Dictionary: L-Z, English-French. Ledesert, D. M. & Ledesert, R. P., eds. Harrap.
--Harrap's New Standard French & English Dictionary, Part One, French-English (A-I) Ledesert, D. H. & Ledesert, R. P., eds. Natl Textbk.
--Harrap's New Standard French & English Dictionary, Part One, French-English (J-Z) Ledesert, D. H. & Ledesert, R. P., eds. Natl Textbk.
--Harrap's Standard French & English Dictionary. Harrap.
--Harrap's Standard French & English Dictionary, Part 2, English-French (A-Z) Natl Textbk.
--Harrap's Super-Mini French & English Dictionary. Forbes, Patricia & Ledesert, Margaret, eds. Natl Textbk.
Mansion, J. E., et al. Harrap's Shorter French & English Dictionary. Harrap Co.
Mansoor. Introduction, Key to Text, Vocabularies. E J Brill.
Mantero, Jose M., tr. see Hatje, Gerd.
Manuila, A & Nicole, M. Dictionnaire Francais de Medicine el de Biologie. French & Eur.
Manuila, A. & Nicole, M. Dictionnaire Francais de Medicine et de Biologie, Vol. 1. French & Eur.
Manuila, A., et al. Dictionnaire Francais de Medicine el de Biologie. French & Eur.
Manuila, L., et al. Petit Dictionnaire Medical. French & Eur.
Manuila, Nicole A. Dictionnaire Francais de Medecine & de Biologie, 1 A-D. Masson.
--Le Dictionnaire Francais de Medecine & de Biologie, 2. Masson.
--Dictionnaire Francais de Medecine & de Biologie, 3 N-Z. Masson.
--Dictionnaire Francais de Medecine & de Biologie, 4. Masson.
Manzano, M. Orta. Diccionario de Sinonimos y Antonimos. French & Eur.
Manzhigeev, I. A. Buriatskie Shamanisticheskie i Doshamanisticheskie Terminy (Pub. by Nauka). Four Continent.
Manzoni, M., tr. see Monkhouse, F. J.
Manzoni, Marcello. Dizionario di geologia. Zanichelli.
Maquet, Charles. Dictionnaire Analogique. Larousse.
--Dictionnaire Analogique. Larousse.
Mara, Thalia. The Language of Ballet. Dance Horiz.
Maragliano, Alessandro. Dizionario Dialettale Vogherese. Patron.
Maranesi, Ernesto & Papini, P. Vocabolario modenese-italiano. Forni.
Maraval, M., jt. auth. see Denis, S.
Maraval, M., jt. auth. see Denis, Serge.
Maraval, Marcel, jt. auth. see Denis, Serge.
Maravall Casesnovas, Dario. Diccionario de Matematica Moderna. Nacional Editora.
Maravall Casesnoves, Dario. Diccionario de matematica moderna. Nacional Editora.
--Diccionario De Matematica Moderna. French & Eur.
March, Benjamin. Some Technical Terms of Chinese Painting. Paragon.
March, Francis, et al. March's Thesaurus & Dictionary of the English Language. Abbeville Pr.
March, Robert T. Accounting Language. Running Pr.
Marchais, Pierre. Glossaire De Psychiatrie. French & Eur.
Marchand. Premier Dictionnaire Nathan (Dist. by Continental Bk Co). Lib. Fernand Nathan.
Marchand, Frank. Dictionnaire Actif Nathan. Nathan.
Marchand, Prosper. Dictionnaire Historique. Olms.
Marchand-Ennery, Rabbin. Dictionnaire Hebreu-Francais. Colbo.
Marchesan, Marco. Dizionario di ipnopsicologia. Ist. Indagini Psicologiche.
Marchese, Angelo. Dizionario di Retorica & di Stilistica. Mondadori.
Marck, Louis, jt. auth. see Rechtschaffen, Bernard.
Marckwardt, A., ed. see Nowell, L.
Marco Martinez, Antonio, jt. auth. see Abos Santabarbara, Angel L.
Marconi, R. & Zino, E. Dizionario inglese-italiano per le scienze mediche. Minerva Medica.
Marcovecchio, E. Dizionario tedesco-italiano per le scienze mediche. Minerva Medica.
Marcu, Marinca. Dictionar Elementar de Stiinte. Editura Stiintifica.
Marcus, Irving. The Portable Dictionary of Real Estate Terminology. Branden.
Marcus, Russell. English-Lao, Lao-English Dictionary. C E Tuttle.
Marcy, Michel, jt. auth. see Marcy, Teresa.
Marcy, Michel, jt. auth. see Nutting, Teresa.
Marcy, Teresa & Marcy, Michel. Cortina-Grosset Basic French Dictionary. Berberi, Dilaver & Berberi, Edel A., eds. (G&D). Putnam Pub Group.
Marec, Eugene. Dictionnaire de l'electricien Praticien. Bailliere.
Marei, H. Basic Technical Dictionary: French-English-German-Arabic. French & Eur.
Margarit, Badia A. M., jt. auth. see Cela, Camilo J.
Mariani, John F. The Dictionary of American Food & Drink. Ticknor & Fields.
Mariano, Cosimo. Nuovo dizionario italiano-latino. Dante Alighieri.
Mariconda, Barbara & Puccio, Denise. Muppet Music Dictionary. Cherry Lane.
Mariel, Pierre. Dictionnaire des Societes Secretes En Occident. French & Eur.
Mariners Museum Library - Newport News - Virginia. Dictionary Catalog of the Library of the Mariners Museum (Hall Library). G K Hall.
Maring, Ester G., jt. auth. see Maring, Joel M.
Maring, Joel M. & Maring, Ester G. Historical & Cultural Dictionary of Burma. Scarecrow.
Marion, Marcel. Dictionnaire des Institutions de la France aux XVII & XVIII Siecles. Lenox.
--Dictionnaire des Institutions de la France aux 17 & 18 Siecles. Picard.
Marion, Marcel, ed. Dictionnaire Des Institutions De la France Aux Dix-Septieme et Dix-Huitieme Siecles. B Franklin.
Mariotti, Scevola, jt. auth. see Castiglioni, Luigi.
Mariotti, Wilson, ed. see Pietzschke, Fritz.
Markowitz, Endel. Encyclopedia Yiddishanica. Haymark.
Marks, G. Harrap's Dictionnaire d'argot: French to English, English to French Slang Dictionary. French & Eur.

Marks, Georgette A. The New English-French Dictionary of Slang & Colloquialisms. Dutton.
Marks, Georgette A. & Johnson, Charles B. Harrap's English-French Dictionary of Slang & Colloquialisms. Harrap.
Marks, Georgette A., jt. auth. see Marks, Joseph.
Marks, Georgette A., rev. by see Marks, Joseph & Marks, Georgette A.
Marks, Joseph & Marks, Georgette A. Harrap's French & English Dictionary of Slang & Colloquialisms. Marks, Georgette A., rev. by. Harrap.
Marks, Robert W. Diccionario & Manual de las Nuevas Matematicas. Editors Pr Serv.
--Diccionario y manual de la nueva fisica y quimica. Edit Pr Serv.
--Diccionario y manual de las nuevas matematicas. Edit Pr Serv.
Markus, John. Diccionario de Electronica & Tecnica Nuclear. Marcombo.
--Diccionario de Electronica y Tecnica Nuclear. French & Eur.
--Vocabulario Ingles-Espanol de Electronica & Tecnica Nuclear. Marcombo.
--Vocabulario Ingles-Espanol de Electronica y Tecnica Nuclear. French & Eur.
Markus, John, tr. Diccionario de electronica y tecnica nuclear. Marcombo.
Marler, E. E., compiled by. Pharmacological & Chemical Synonyms: A Collection of Names of Drugs, Pesticides & Other Compounds Drawn from the Medical Literature of the World. Elsevier.
Marmol, F. Dictionnaire des Filigranes Classes en Groupe Alphabetique. Olms Verlag.
Marois, Roger. Vocabulaire Francais-Anglais d'archeologie Prehistorique. Quebec P. U.
Marole, L. T. & De Goma, F. S. English-Venda Dictionary. Shalom.
Marolli, G. Dizionario Tecnico Italiano-Inglese, Inglese-Italiano. French & Eur.
--Italian-English, English-Italian Technical Dictionary. Heinman.
Marolli, Giorgio. Dizionario tecnico inglese-italiano e italiano-inglese. Monnier.
Marolli, Giorgio & Guarnieri, Orazio. Dizionario Tecnico Tedesco-Italiano. Garzanti Edit.
--Dizionario tecnico tedesco-italiano italiano-tedesco. Garzanti Edit.
Maronski, J. & Rupinska, M. Computer Networks Terminology. French & Eur.
Marouzeau, Jules. Lexique De la Terminologie Linguistique. Intl Pubns Serv.
Marques Casanovas, J., jt. auth. see Llauro Padrose, J.
Marquess, Harlan E., jt. ed. see Galler, Meyer.
Marquet, Lluis. Diccionari d'electronica. Portic.
Marquet, Luis. Diccionari d'Electronica. French & Eur.
Marquez Bessa, Antonio. Diccionario Politico Para Occidente. French & Eur.
Marquez Villagas, Luis. Un Lexico de la artesania (CSIC). Univ Granada.
Marquez Villegas, Luis. Vocabulario Del Espanol Hablado. French & Eur.
Marri, Fabio. Glossario al milanese di Bonvesin. Patron.
Marsden, William. Malay-English Dictionary. Ayer Co.
Marsico, Vincenzo. Dizionario delle malattie, sindromi e sintori oculari. Minerva Medica.
Marsy, Francois-Marie De see De Marsy, Francois-Marie.
Marthaler, Andre. Le Vocabulaire Vivant. Payot.
--Le Vocabulaire Vivant, 1. Payot.
--Le Vocabulaire Vivant, 3. Payot.
Marti, A. & Marti, J. Pequeno Diccionario Espanol-Polaco, Polaco-Espanol. French & Eur.
Marti, J., jt. auth. see Marti, A.
Marti Ballester, Jesus. Diccionario del pensamiento de Santa Teresa de Jesus. Edicep.
Marti Marca, Antonio, et al. Maly Slownik Hispansko-Polski & Polsko-Hiszpanski. Wiedza Powszechna.
Martin, B. W. The Dictionary of the Occult. Hutch Pub Co.
Martin, E. A. Dictionary of Life Sciences. Macmillan London.
Martin, Elizabeth, jt. ed. see Isaacs, Alan.
Martin, Ernst & Lienhart, Hans. Woerterbuch der Elsaessischen Mundarten. De Gruyter.
Martin, Ernst & Lienhart, Hans, eds. Woerterbuch der Elsaessischen Mundarten. De Gruyter.
Martin, Helmut, et al. Vocabulaire Usuel du Chinois Moderne. Langen Kommand.
Martin, Jaime. Diccionario De Expresiones Malsonantes Del Espanol. French & Eur.
Martin, Joan M. The Nurse's Dictionary. Faber & Faber.
Martin, Julian A. Law Enforcement Vocabulary. C C Thomas.
Martin, Julian A. & Astone, Nicholas A. Criminal Justice Vocabulary. C C Thomas.
Martin, M. W. A Concise Dictionary of Medicine. Jonathan David.
Martin, Michael & Gelber, Leonard. Dictionary of American History. Lieberman, Leo, ed. Rowman.
Martin, Phyllis M. Historical Dictionary of Angola. Scarecrow.
Martin, R. A. Syntactical & Critical Concordance to the Greek Text of Baruch & the Epistle of Jeremiah. Biblical Res Assocs.
Martin, S. Basic Japanese Conversation Dictionary. Iaconi.
Martin, Samuel. Basic Japanese Conversation Dictionary: English-Japanese & Japanese-English. C E Tuttle.
Martin, Samuel E., jt. auth. see Gardner, Elizabeth F.
Martin, Samuel E., et al. Korean-English Dictionary. Yale U Pr.
Martin, Sue. Dictionary of the Life Sciences. Universe.
Martin-Doisy, F. Dictionnaire d'Economic Charitable. Migne, J. P., ed. Caratzas Pub Co.
Martinet, Andre & Walter, Henriette. Dictionnaire de la Prononciation Francaise dans son Usage Reel. France Expansion.
--Dictionnaire de la Prononciation Francaise Dans Son Usage Reel. French & Eur.
Martinez Almoyna, Julio. Dicionario de Portugues-Espanol. Porto Editora.
Martinez Burgos, Matias & Ayala Lopez, Manuel. Diccionario escolar latino-espanol y espanol-latino. Bibliografica.
Martinez Cachero, Luis A. Diccionario de Hacienda & Derecho Fiscal. Piramide.
Martinez Calvo, L. Diccionario Espanol-Ruso. Sopena.
Martinez Calvo, Lorenzo. Diccionario Espanol-Ruso. French & Eur.
--Diccionario Ruso-Espanol. French & Eur.
Martinez Cerezo, A. Diccionario de Banca. Piramide.
Martinez Cerezo, Antonio. Diccionario de banca (Dist. Grupo Editorial). Piramide.
--Diccionario De Banca. French & Eur.
Martinez Cruz, Abelardo. Lexico De Antropologia. French & Eur.
Martinez de Sousa, J. Diccionario de Tipografia & del Libro. Paraninfo.
--Diccionario General de Periodismo. Paraninfo.
--Diccionario Internacional de Siglas. Piramide.
Martinez de Sousa, Jose. Diccionario de Tipografia & del Libro. Labor SA.
--Diccionario de tipografia y del libro. Paraninfo.
--Diccionario General del Periodismo. Paraninfo.
--Diccionario Internacional de Siglas. French & Eur.
Martinez Duenas, Luis M. & Kato Yda, Manuel M. Diccionario espanol-japones. Edi-Seis.
Martinez Hidalgo Teran, Jose M. Diccionario Nautico. French & Eur.
Martinot Lagarde. Lexique de Sylviculture Allemand-Francais. Genie Rural.
Martins, Joaquim A. Dicionario Tecnico Ingles-Portugues. Pub Euro Am.
Martins, M. J. Portuguese-English, English-Portuguese Dictionary. Heinman.
Martius, T. Dictionary of International Trade Fairs (Pub. by Collet's). State Mutual Bk.
Martschenko, W. G. Deutsch-Russisches Meteorologisches Wörterbuch. French & Eur.
Marty-Lavezux, Charles J. Lexique de la Langue de Pierre Corneille. Lenox.
Marvan, Jiri. Reverse Dictionary of Czech. Pa St U Pr.
Marwick, Arthur, et al, eds. The Illustrated Dictionary of British History. Thames Hudson.
Marwick, Lawrence. A Glossary of Current Terminology. Govt Print.
Marx, Roland. Lexique Historique de la Grande-Bretagne XVIe. & XXe. Siecle. Colin.
Marzell. Woerterbuch der Deutschen Pflanzennamen. French & Eur.
Masanov, I. F. Slovar PsevdonimovRusskikh Pisatelei: Uchenykh & Obshchestvennykh Deiatelei (Pub. by Izd. Vsesoiuzn Knizhn Palaty). Four Continent.
Masciotta, Michelangelo. Dizionario di termini artistici. Monnier.
Mascitelli. Diccionario De Terminos Marxistos. French & Eur.
Masendorf, Friedrich, jt. auth. see Reinartz, Erika.
Mashreq, Dar El see El Mashreq, Dar.
Mashreq, Dar el, jt. auth. see Tulab, Munjid al.
Masica, Colin P. Defining a Linquistic Area: South Asia. U of Chicago Pr.
Mas-Latrie, L. des see Des Mas-Latrie, L.
Mason, David & Dyller, Fran. Pharmaceutical Dictionary & Reference for Prescriptions Drugs (Playboy). Putnam Pub Group.
--Pharmaceutical Dictionary & Reference 1982. Berkley Pub.
Mason, I. L. A Dictionary of Livestock Breeds (Pub. by CAB Bks England). State Mutual Bk.
Masquet, Georges. Dictionnaire des Grands Evenements de l'histoire. Hachette.
--Dictionnaire des Grands Evenements de l'Historie. Hachette-Jeunesse.
--Dictionnaire des Grands Evenements de L'histoire (Pub. by Hachette). French & Eur.
Massachusetts Horticultural Society, Boston. Dictionary Catalog of the Library of the Massachusetts Horticultural Society (Hall Library). G K Hall.
--Dictionary Catalog of the Library of the Massachusetts Horticultural Society, First Supplement (Hall Library). G K Hall.
Massa De Gil, Beatriz. Diccionario Tecnico de Biblioteconomia. Trillas.
Massa de Gil, Beatriz, et al. Diccionario tecnico de biblioteconomia espanol-ingles, ingles-espanol. Trillas.
Massanes, Joaquin H. Diccionario de Sinonimos e Ideas Afines y de la Rima. Paraninfo.
Massarenti, Dino, jt. auth. see Dottrens, Robert.
Masson, Andre, jt. auth. see Moreau, Pierre.
Masson, Arthur. Vocabulaire. Hachette.
Masson, Herre. Dictionnaire Initiatique. French & Eur.
Masson, Herve. Dictionnaire Initiatique. Belfond.
Masson, Philippe. Dictionnaire de la Seconde Guerre mondiale. Larousse.
Massor Gimeno, Juan, tr. see Mommsen, H., et al.
Masterton, William L., et al. Chemistry (CBS C). SCP.
Mastropasqua, V. Dizionario Tecnico Nautico: Italiano-Inglese, Inglese-Italiano. French & Eur.
Masubuchi, M., jt. auth. see Broadbent, D. T.
Masuda, M., ed. Dictionary of Marine Engineering Terms: Japanese-English, English-Japanese. French & Eur.
Masuy, L., jt. auth. see Chaballe, L. Y.
Mataix, M. Diccionario de eletronica y energia nuclear ingles-espanol. Danae.
Mataix, Mariano. Diccionario de Electronica, Informatica & Centrales Nucleares. Marcombo.
Mataix Lord, Mariano. Diccionario De Electronica, Informatica y Centrales Nucleares. French & Eur.
Mateo, Felix D., jt. auth. see Hochleitner, Frida.
Mateo, Felix D. & Hochleitner, Frida, eds. Diccionario Manual Aleman-Espanol, Espanol-Aleman. Espasa Calpe.
Mateos, Fernando, et al. Diccionario Espanol de la Lengua China. French & Eur.
Material Handling Institute. Glossary of Automatic Identification Terms. Material Handling.
Mateu Sancho, Pedro. Diccionario de la astronomia y astronautica. Destino.
--Diccionario de la Astronomica y Astronautica. French & Eur.
Mathews, B. English-Chinese Picture Dictionary. G Brash.
Mathews, Mitford M., ed. Americanisms: A Dictionary of Selected Americanisms on Historical Principles (Phoen). U of Chicago Pr.
Mathews, Robert H. Chinese-English Dictionary: A Chinese-English Dictionary Compiled for the China Inland Mission. Harvard U Pr.
Mathews, Shailer & Smith, Gerald B., eds. Dictionary of Religion & Ethics. Gale.
Mathews, William S. & Liebling, Emil. Pronouncing & Defining Dictionary of Music. AMS Pr.
Mathias, J. & Hixson, Sandra. A Compilation of Chinese Dictionaries. Far Eastern Pubns.
Mathiassen, Therkel. Report on the Expedition. AMS Pr.
Mathieu, Gilbert. Vocabulaire de l'economie. Delarge.
--Vocabulaire De L'economie. French & Eur.
Mathieu, Gustave. La Sante Grace a la Dietetique. Doc Scient.
Mathieu, Micolas De Castillo see De Castillo Mathieu, Micolas.
Mathiot, Madeleine. A Dictionary of Papago Usage: Vol. I, B-K. Mouton.
Matore, Geneve, jt. auth. see Matore, Georges.
Matore, Georges. Dictionnaire du Vocabulaire Essentiel. Larousse.
--Dictionnaire du Vocabulaire Essentiel. French & Eur.
Matore, Georges & Matore, Geneve. Le Vocabulaire & la Societe Sous Louis Phillippe. Slatkine.
Matteucci, M. Dictionnaire Juridique. French & Eur.
Matteuci, Nicola, jt. auth. see Bobbio, Norberto.
Matteuci, Nicola, jt. ed. see Bobbio, Norberto.
Matthes, Max. Textil-Fachwoerterbuch. Schiele & Schon.
Matthews, B. English-Chinese Picture Dictionary. Hippocrene Bks.
Matthews, B. & Tan, K. English-Chinese Picture Dictionary. Iaconi.
Matthews, C. M. Health & Culture in a South Indian village. Orient Bk Dist.
Matthews, Washington. Ethnography & Philology of the Hidatsa Indians: U. S. Geological & Geographical Survey of the Territories, Miscellaneous Publication. Johnson Repr.
--Grammar & Dictionary of the Language of the Hidatsa. AMS Pr.
Mattutat, H., jt. auth. see Weis, E.
Mattutat, Heinrich, jt. auth. see Weis, Erich.
Mattutat, Heinrich, jt. ed. see Weis, Erich.
Mattutat, Heinrich, ed. see Weiss, Erich.

Matuschek, Herbert. Einwortlexeme & Wortgruppenlexeme in der Technischen Terminologie des Polnscheni. Sagner.
Matveev, Vladimir S. & Asrhants, Konstantin G. Portuagalsko-Russkil Politekhnicheskil Slovar. Russkii Iazyk.
Mauila, A., et al. Dictionnaire Francais de Medicine el de Biologie. French & Eur.
Maulmier, Thierrey. Diccionario Terminos. French & Eur.
Maupoix, Edy. Svensk-Fransk Affaersordlista. Esselte Studium.
Maurais, J. Lexique des Epices et Assaisonnements: Anglais-Francais. French & Eur.
Maurais, J. & Giroux, S. Lexiques des Boissons Gazeuses. French & Eur.
Maurel, Rosie. Dictionnaire des Aliments. Table Ronde.
Maurino, Ferdinando D. Modern Language Dictionary. S & S.
Mauroy, L. N. Dictionnaire d'Agriculture. Migne, J. P., ed. Caratzas Pub Co.
Maury, E. A. Diccionario familiar de homeopatia. Santos, Domingo, tr. Pomaire.
--Diccionario familiar de las medicinas naturales. Andrue Aznar, Rafael, tr. Martinez Roca.
Maury, E. A. & Rudder, C. Diccionario Familiar de Mediciana Natural. French & Eur.
Maury, Emmerick A. Dictionnaire Familial des Medecines Naturelies. Delarge.
--Dictionnaire Familial d'homeopathie. Delarge.
--Dictionnaire Familial D'homoeopathie. Edns Univers.
Mawson, C. O. Dictionary of Foreign Terms. B&N NY.
Mawson, C. Sylvester, ed see Roget, Peter M.
Maxwell, Christine. The Children's Dictionary. Wheaton.
Maxwell, Stuart P. Studies in Greek Colour Terminology (Pub. by E J Brill Holland). Humanities.
Mayer, E. Dictionnaire des Valeurs de Meubles & Objets d'art. Fischbacher.
Mayer, Enrique. Le Dictionnaire des Meubles & Objets D'art 1965 & 1966. Mayer.
--Le Dictionnaire des Meubles & Objets d'art, 1963 & 1964. Mayer Ed.
Mayer, G. Dizionario di economia. Bulzoni.
Mayer, JoAnne C. & Sippl, Charles J. Essential Computer Dictionary & Speller for Secretaries, Managers, & Office Personnel (Spec). P-H.
Mayer, Ralph. A Dictionary of Art Terms & Techniques (EH). B&N NY.
--A Dictionary of Art Terms & Techniques (Pub. by Lewis Pubs). State Mutual Bk.
--Dictionary of Art Terms & Techniques. T Y Crowell.
Mayers, Keith. A Dictionary of Locksmithing. Mayers-Joseph.
Mayhew, A. I. & Skeat, Walter W. Concise Dictionary of Middle English from A.D. 1150 to 1580. Norwood Edns.
Mayhew, A. L. & Skeat, W. W. Concise Dictionary of Middle English from A. D. 1150-1580. Folcroft.
Maynard. Dictionary of Data Processing. Butterworth.
Mayr, Ernst, jt. auth. see Kohler, Rolf.
Mayrand, Albert. Dictionnaire de Maximes & Locutions Latines Utilisees en Droit Quebecois. Guerin.
Mayrhofer, Manfred. Kurzgefasstes Etymologisches Des Altindischen. Winter Univ.
--Kurzgefasstes Etymologisches Woerterbuch Des Altindischen. Winter Univ.
--Kurzgefasstes Etymologisches Woerterbuch Des Altindischen (Pub. by Carl Winter). French & Eur.
--Kurzgefasstes Etymologisches Woerterbuch Des Altindischen (Pub. by Carl Winter). French & Eur.
Mazur, I. N. Kratkii Russko-Koreiskii Slovar (Pub. by GINS). Four Continent.
Mazzaglia, E. & Castellini, A. Dizionario delle nuove scienze: Astronautica, electronica, fiscia nucleare. Edizioni Paoline.
Mazzetti, Alberto, jt. auth. see Baldelli, Ignazio.
Mazzucato, Fluffy M. Dizionario delle buone maniere. Bietti.
Mazzucchi, P. Dizionario polesano-italiano. Forni.
Meadows, A. J., et al. Dictionary of New Information Technology (Pub. by Century Pub Co). State Mutual Bk.
Medina, G. Diccionario ideografico poligloto. Aguilar SP.
Medina, Jose T. Diccionario de Anonimos y Seudonimos Hispanoamericanos. Ethridge.
Meerhaeghe, Marcel A. van see Van Meerhaeghe, Marcel A.
Meier, Matt S. & Rivera, Feliciano, eds. Dictionary of Mexican American History. Greenwood.
Meikleham, Robert. A Dictionary of Architecture. Gordon Pr.
Meillet, Antoine, jt. auth. see Ernout, Alfred.
Meinck, F. & Mohle, K. Dictionary of Water & Sewage Engineering. Elsevier.
Meinck, Fritz. Woerterbuch fuer das Wasser und Abwasserfach. French & Eur.
--Woerterbuch fur das Wasser & Abwasserfach. Oldenbourg Verlag.
Meinhhold, H., jt. auth. see Schwenkhagen, H. F.
Meinikov, O. English-Russian Astronomical Dictionary (Pub. by Collet's). State Mutual Bk.
Mei-Wah Choy, Rita. Read & Write Chinese: A Simplified Guide to the Chinese Characters. China West.
Melillo, Michelle. Concordanze dei dialetti di Puglia. Atlantica.
Mellerio, Louis. Lexique de Ronsard. Kraus.
--Lexique de Ronsard. Olms.
Melloni, B., et al. Diccionario de Medicina Ilustrado. Reverte SA.
Mellor, Allec. Dictionnaire de la Franc-Maconnerie et des Francs-Macons. French & Eur.
Melnicove, Betty F. Crossword Puzzle Dictionary. B&N NY.
Melnicove, Bettye F. New Webster's Crossword Puzzle Dictionary (Crest). Fawcett.
Melnikov, N. V., et al. Gornoe Delo: Terminologicheskii Slovar (Pub. by Nedra). Four Continent.
Melnikov, O. A., et al, eds. Anglo-Russkii Astronomicheskii Slovar (Pub. by Sov Entsiklopediia). Four Continent.
Melnikova, M. M. & Smirnov, I. P. English-Russian Dictionary of Electrochemistry & Corrosion. French & Eur.
Melnikova, M. M., et al, eds. Anglo-Russkii Slovar Po Elektrokhimii i Korrozii (Pub. by Russkii Iazyk). Four Continent.
Melo, Sampaio De see Almeida Costa, J. & Sampaio de Melo.
Melzi, Robert C. The Bantam New College Italian & English Dictionary. Bantam.
--The New College Italian & English Dictionary. AMSCO Sch.
Menacho, Mary. A Practical Dictionary of Crosswords. Academy Pr-Santa.
Menage, Gilles. Dictionnaire Etymologique de la Langue Francaise avec les Origines Francaises. Slatkine.
Mencken, Henry L., ed. New Dictionary of Quotations on Historical Principles from Ancient & Modern Sources. Knopf.
Mendelkern, Solomon. Concordance of the Bible. Feldheim.
Mendes Campos, Aluizio. Dicionario Frances-Portugues de Locucoes. Edit Atica.
Mendez. Diccionario Basico de la Industria del Petroleo & Derivados. Paraninfo.
Mendez, ed. Diccionario Tecnico de la Industria del Petroleo y Derivados. French & Eur.
Mendez Manzano, Augustin. Basic Dictionary of the Petroleum Industry. Imported Bks.
--Diccionario basico de la industria del petroleo. Paraninfo.
Mendizabal, Isaac Lopez see Lopez Mendizabal, Isaac.
Menduina, Antonio, tr. see Congdon, TIm, et al.
Menendez Pidal, Ramon D. Diccionario General Ilustrado de la Lengua Espanola. Gili Gaya, Samuel D., ed. Biblograf SP.
Menge & Guethling. Langenscheidts Grosswoerterbuch Deutsch-Lateinisch. Langenscheidt.
--Langenscheidts Grosswoerterbuch Lateinisch-Deutsch. Langenscheidt.
Menge & Guthling. Langenscheidts Grosswoerterbuch Altgriechisch-Deutsch. Langenscheidt.
Menge, H. Langenscheidts Taschenwoerterbuch Altgriechisch: Teil I, Altgriechisch-Deutsch. Langenscheidt.
--Langenscheidts Taschenwoerterbuecher Lateinisch. Langenscheidt.
--Langenscheidts Taschenwoerterbuecher Altgriechisch-Deutsch. Langenscheidt.
Menge, H. & Guthling, O. Langenscheidts Taschenwoerterbuch Altgriechisch. Langenscheidt.
Menge, H. & Pertsch, E. Langenscheidts Taschenwoerterbuch Lateinisch. Langenscheidt.
--Langenscheidts Taschenwoerterbuch Lateinisch: Teil I, Lateinisch-Deutsch. Langenscheidt.
Menge, Hermann. Langenscheidts Taschenwoerterbuch Lateinisch: Teil II, Deutsch-Lateinisch. Langenscheidt.
--Lateinisch. Pertsch, E., rev. by. Langenscheidt.
Menge, Hermann & Guethling, Otto. Langenscheidts Grosswoerterbuch: Lateinisch-Deutsch. Langenscheidt.
Menge, R. & Preuss, S. Lexicon Caesarianum. French & Eur.
Mengel, J. Dansk-Italiensk Ordborg. French & Eur.
Menghi, A. Nuovo dizionario di terminologia giuridica. Cortina M.
--Nuovo Dizionario di Terminologia Giuridica. French & Eur.
Meno Blanco, Francisco, jt. auth. see Abraham, Werner.
Menon, K. P. A Dictionary of Kathakali (Orient Longman). South Asia Bks.
--Dictionary of Kathakali (Orient Longman). South Asia Bks.
Mensier, Paul H. Dictionnaire des Hulles Vegetales. Lechevalier.
Mentzel, Wolfgang & Wittlesberger, Helmut. Kleines Wirtschafts-Woerterbuch. Herder.
Merani, Alberto L. Diccionario de psicologia. Grijalbo.
Meras, Albert A. & Miller, Maud. Kleiner Wortschatz. Ridgeway, W. R., rev. by. Harrap.
Mercer. Glossary of Film Terms. Univ Film & Video.
Mercier, Jean. Lexique Anglais-Francais Des Appareils De Mesures Electriques. French & Eur.
--Lexique Anglais-Francais du Compteur d'electricite. Quebec Off.
--Lexique Anglais-Francais Du Compteur D'electricite: Principes et Pieces Composantes. French & Eur.
--Lexique Anglais-Francais du Programmateur de Cuisiniere. Quebec Off.
--Lexique Anglais-Francais Du Programmateur De Cuisiniere: Fonctionnement et Pieces Composantes. French & Eur.
Mercier, L. S. Dictionnaire d'un Polygraphe. U. G. E.
Merenciano & Frederic i Ricart, Antoni. Vocabulari Automobilistic. Claret.
Mergault, J. Nouveau Larousse "Mars" (Dist. by Continental Bk Co). Larousse.
Mergault, J., jt. auth. see Chaffurin, L.
Mergault, Jean, jt. auth. see Chaffurin, Louis.
Merino. Diccionario de Dudas Ingles-Espanol. Paraninfo.
--Diccionario Tematico Ingles-Espanol & Espanol-Ingles. Paraninfo.
Merino, Jose. Diccionario de Dudas Ingles-Espanol. Paraninfo.
--Diccionario de dudas Ingles-Espanol. Fed Gremios.
--Diccionario Tematico Ingles-Espanol & Espanol-Ingles. Paraninfo.
--Diccionario tematico Ingles-Espanol & Espanol-Ingles. Fed Gremios.
--Diccionario Tematico Ingles-Espanol, Espanol-Ingles. French & Eur.
Merino Bustamante, Jose. Diccionario auxiliar de traductor: Espanol-Ingles. CEEI.
--Diccionario Auxiliar del Traductor Espanol-Ingles. CEEI.
--Diccionario Auxiliar del Traductor Espanol-Ingles. French & Eur.
--Diccionario De Dudas Ingles-Espanol. French & Eur.
--Vocabulario Ingles-Espanol, Espanol-Ingles. French & Eur.
Merino Bustamente, Jose. Diccionario de dudas: Ingles-espanol. Paraninfo.
Merino-Rodriguez, M., ed. Lexicon of International & National Units. Elsevier.
Merino-Rodriguez, Manuel, ed. Lexicon of Plant Pests & Diseases. Elsevier.
Meritt, Herbert D., jt. auth. see Hall, John R.
Merlin, Olivier. Dictionnaire Juridique: Francais-Espagnol. Navarre.
Merlin, Olivier, jt. auth. see Jordana de Pozas, Luis.
Merlo Pick, Vittorio. Vocabolario italiano-kiswahili. EMI.
--Vocabolario kiswahili-italiano. EMI.
--Vocabolario swahili-italiano e italiano-swahili. EMI.
Merrani, Alberto L. Diccionario De Psicologia. French & Eur.
Merriam Company, ed. Webster's Intermediate Dictionary. Merriam-Webster Inc.
--Webster's New Ideal Dictionary. Merriam-Webster Inc.
--Webster's Third New International Dictionary, Unabridged: The Great Library of the English Language. Incl. Regular-Paper Style; Tan Imperial Buckram. Merriam-Webster Inc.
Merriam, Kendall A. Illustrated Dictionary of Lobstering. Cumberland Pr.
Merriam-Webster Editorial Staff. Webster's Elementary Dictionary. Merriam-Webster Inc.
--Webster's New Dictionary of Synonyms. Merriam-Webster Inc.
--Webster's Ninth New Collegiate Dictionary. Merriam-Webster Inc.
Merriam Webster Editorial Staff. Webster's Official Crossword Puzzle Dictionary. Merriam-Webster Inc.
Merriam-Webster Editorial Staff. Webster's School Dictionary. Merriam-Webster Inc.
--Webster's School Thesaurus. Merriam-Webster Inc.
--Webster's Vest Pocket Dictionary. Merriam-Webster Inc.
Merriam Webster Editorial Staff, ed. Six Thousand Words: A Supplement to Webster's Third New International Dictionary. Merriam-Webster Inc.
Merriam-Webster Editorial Staff, ed. Webster's Concise Family Dictionary. Merriam-Webster Inc.
--Webster's Sports Dictionary. Merriam-Webster Inc.
Merriam-Webster Reference Editor, ed. Webster's Instant Word Guide. Merriam-Webster Inc.
Mertz De Mertzenteld, R., et al. Dictionnaire Technologique Feutry: Mecanique-Metallurgie-Hydraulique. Maison Dictionnaire.
--Dictionnaire Technologique Feutry: Supplement Espagnol. Maison Dictionnaire.
--Dictionnaire Technologique: Supplement Portugais. Maison Dictionnaire.
Mertzenfeld, R. Mertz De see Mertz De Mertzenteld, R., et al.
Meschiari, E. Vocabolario mirandolese-italiano. La Vela.

Messell, J., jt. auth. see Guy, W.
Messina, Giuseppe, jt. auth. see Cantamessa, Giuseppe.
Messinger, H. Langenscheidts Grosswoerterbuch: Englisch-Deutsch. Langenscheidt.
Messinger, H. & Ruedenberger, H. Langenscheidts Grosse Schulwoerterbuecher Englisch-Deutsch. Langenscheidt.
Messinger, Heinz. Der Kleine Muret-Sanders: Deutsch-Englisch. Langenscheidt.
--Langenscheidt Grosswoerterbuch: Englisch-Deutsch. Langenscheidt.
--Langenscheidt's Comprehensive English-German Dictionary. Imported Bks.
--Langenscheidts Grosse Schulwoerterbuch Deutsch-Englisch. Langenscheidt.
--Langenscheidts Grosswoerterbuch Englisch-Deutsch. Langenscheidt.
--Langenscheidts Handwoerterbuch: Teil II, Deutsch-Englisch. Langenscheidt.
--Langenscheidts Handwoerterbuecher: Tl 2, Deutsch-Englisch. Langenscheidt.
--Langenscheidt's New College German Dictionary: German-English, English-German. Imported Bks.
Messinger, Heinz & Rudenberg, Werner. Langenscheidts Grosse Schulwoerterbuch Englisch-Deutsch. Langenscheidt.
--Langenscheidt's New College German Dictionary (German-English, English-German) Am Map.
Messinger, Heinz & Ruedenberg, Werner. Langenscheidts Handwoerterbuch: Englisch-Deutsch Deutsch-Englisch. Langenscheidt.
--Langenscheidts Handwoerterbuch: Teil I, Englisch-Deutsch. Langenscheidt.
--Langenscheidts Handwoerterbuecher: Tl 1, Englisch-Deutsch. Langenscheidt.
Messinger, Heinz, ed. Condensed Muret-Sanders German-English Dictionary. Gale.
Messinger, Heinz & Rudenberg, Werner, eds. Englisch. Langenscheidt.
Messinger, Heinz & Ruedenberg, Werner, eds. Langenscheidts Handwoerterbuecher Englisch. Langenscheidt.
--Langenscheidts Handwoerterbuecher Franzoesisch. Langenscheidt.
--Langenscheidts Handwoerterbuecher Italienisch. Langenscheidt.
--Langenscheidts Handwoerterbuecher Russisch. Langenscheidt.
--Langenscheidts Handwoerterbuecher Spanisch. Langenscheidt.
Metelka, Charles J., ed. The Dictionary of Tourism. Merton Hse.
Metro, Andre. Dictionnaire Forestier Multilingue. C. I. L. F.
--Dictionnaire Forestier Multilingue. French & Eur.
Meude-Monpas, Jean J. de. Dictionnaire de Musique dans Lequel on Simplifie les Expressions et Les Definitions Mathematiques et Physiques qui ont Rapport a cet Art. AMS Pr.
Meurig, H. & Thomas, W. O. Y Geiriadur Mawr: The Complete Welsh-English, English-Welsh Dictionary. Williams, S. J., ed. French & Eur.
Meyer & Orlando. Technisches Woerterbuch: Band I, Italienisch-Deutsch. Brandstetter.
--Technisches Woerterbuch: Band II, Deutsch-Italienisch. Brandstetter.
Meyer, A. & Orlando, S. Dizionario tecnico italiano-tedesco e tedesco-italiano. Hoepli.
Meyer, Alice. Dizionario Tecnico Italiano-Tedesco. Brandstetter.
Meyer, George A. The Two Word Verb: A Dictionary of the Verb Preposition Phrases in American English. Mouton.
Meyer, Harvey K. Historical Dictionary of Honduras. Intl Guatemala.
Meyer, Karl H. Altkirchenslavisch-Griechisches Woerterbuch Des Codex Supraliensis. J J Augustin.
Meyer, Peter K. Taschenlexikon der Verhaltenskunde. Schoningh.
Meyer, Rudolph. Explosives. Verlag Chemie.
Meyer-Camberg, Ernst. Das Praktische Lexikon der Naturheilkunde (Pub. by Mosaik/VVA). French & Eur.
Meyer-Luebke, Wilhelm. Romanisches Etymologisches Woerterbuch (Pub. by Carl Winter). French & Eur.
--Romanishes Etymologisches Woerterbuch. Winter Univ.
Meyerstein, Goldie P; see Hench, Atcheson L.
Meynen, E. Multilingual Dictionary of Technical Terms in Cartography (Pub. by F. Steiner). French & Eur.
Mezer, A. V. Slovarnyi Ukazatel Po Knigovedeniiu (Pub. by Kolos). Four Continent.
Mezzera, Umberto. Glossario di tecnologia meccanica. Etas Libri.
Mialaret, Gaston. Vocabulaire De L'Education. French & Eur.
Mialaret, Gaston, ed. Vocabulaire de l'Education. Pr Univ Fr.
Michaelis. Concise Dictionary Portuguese-English. Iaconi.
--Portuguese-English, English-Portuguese Basic Dictionary. Heinman.
--Portuguese Pocket Dictionary. Heinman.
Michaelson, Sidney, jt. auth. see Morton, A. Q.
Michalove, Ed, jt. auth. see Delson, Donn.
Michauz, Jean P. Dictionnaire de L'outillage et de la Machine-Outil. Ophrys.
Michea, Rene. Vocabulaire Allemand Progressif & livret d'exercices. Didier.
Michel, Christian & Novak, Felix. Kleines Psychologisches Woerterbuch. Herder.
Michel, J. & Gester, Michel. Lexique de base du Latin. Sikkel.
Michel, Raoul & Pardel-Lans, Humbert. Dictionnaire-Formulaire Commercial. Foucher.
Michelin Guides & Maps. Dictionnaire des Communes de France (Guide to French Townships) Michelin.
Michell, Edward B. Siamese-English Dictionary. Ayer Co.
Michell, Gillian, ed. Papers of the Dictionary Society of North America 1979. Ind St Univ.
--Papers of the Dictionary Society of North America 1979. Dict Soc NA.
Michelon, Oscar. Diccionario de San Francisco. Akademische Druck Verlagt.
Michelsen, Kari, et al, eds. Cappelens Musikkeleksikon. J W Cappelens.
Michelson, Derrick O. Fachworterbuch Textil (Pub. by Deutscher Fachuerlag). French & Eur.
--Textile Terminology: German-English & English-German. Intl Pubns Serv.
Michigan State University,(East Lansing) Dictionary Catalog of the G. Robert Vincent Library (Hall Library). G K Hall.
Midoux, Marcel. Vocabulaire Usuel du Chinois Moderne. Pubns Orient.
--Vocabulaire Usuel du Chinois Moderne, 2: Chinois-Francais. Geuthner.
--Vocabulaire Usuel du Chinois Moderne, 3: Chinois-Francais. Geuthner.
Miers, Horst E. Lexikon des Geheimwissens. Goldmann.
--Lexikon des Geheimwissens. French & Eur.
Miettinen, Liisa. Toimitustyon Terminologiaa. Otava.
Migliori, Enrico. Dizionario spagnolo-italiano e italiano-spagnolo. Giunti-Martello.
Migliorini, Bruno. Parole & Storia. Rizzoli Edit.
--Vocabolario della lingua italiana. Paravia.
Migliorini, Bruno & Pellegrini, G. Dizionario del feltrino rustico. Liviana.
Mignani, Rigo, jt. ed. see Di Cesare, Mario A.
Mignard, Thomas. Vocabulaire Raisonne & Compare du Dialecte & du Patols de la Province de Bourgogne. Slatkine.
Migne, J. P., ed. Dictionnaire de Paleographie, de Cryptographie, de Dactylologie. Caratzas Pub Co.
--Dictionnaire des Muses ou Description des Principaux Musees d'Europe... Suivi Notions sur la Photographie par X. Caratzas Pub Co.
--Dictionnaire d'Ethnographie. Caratzas Pub Co.
Migne, J. P., ed. see Benedictines de la Congregation de Saint-Maur.
Migne, J. P., ed. see Berton, C.
Migne, J. P., ed. see Bourasse, J. J.
Migne, J. P., ed. see Boyer, A. L.
Migne, J. P., ed. see Brunet, G.
Migne, J. P., ed. see Calmet, A.
Migne, J. P., ed. see Chesnel De La Charbouclais, L. P.
Migne, J. P., ed. see Chesnel De la Charbouclais, L. P.
Migne, J. P., ed. see Cheve, C. F.
Migne, J. P., ed. see De Sivry, L.
Migne, J. P., ed. see Des Mas-Latrie, L.
Migne, J. P., ed. see Gautier, T. F.
Migne, J. P., ed. see Grosse, E.
Migne, J. P., ed. see Guerin, L. F.
Migne, J. P., ed. see Haenel, G. F.
Migne, J. P., ed. see Jehan, L. F.
Migne, J. P., ed. see Jouffroy, A.
Migne, J. P., ed. see Jouhanneaud, P.
Migne, J. P., ed. see Jouve, E. G.
Migne, J. P., ed. see LeNoir, C. P.
Migne, J. P., ed. see Martin-Doisy, F.
Migne, J. P., ed. see Mauroy, L. N.
Migne, J. P., ed. see Morin, F.
Migne, J. P., ed. see Nadal, J. C.
Migne, J. P., ed. see Ott, A.
Migne, J. P., ed. see Peltier, A. C.
Migne, J. P., ed. see Petin, L. M.
Migne, J. P., ed. see Pinard, C.
Migne, J. P., ed. see Pluquet, F. A.
Migne, J. P., ed. see Poujol, F. A.
Migne, J. P., ed. see Poussin, J. C. & Garnier, J. C.
Migne, J. P., ed. see Prompsault, J. H.
Migne, J. P., ed. see Quantin, M.
Migne, J. P., ed. see Raymond, D.
Migne, J. P., ed. see Sevestre, A.
Miguel i Verges, Jose Maria. Diccionario de Insurgentes. Porrua.
Mihailescu, Nicolae. Lexikon Geologie Geografie Mine Petrol. Editura Stiintifica.
Mikhailov, A. I., et al, eds. Terminologicheskii Slovar Po Nauchnoi Informatsii (Pub. by Vsesoiuznyi in-tut Nauchin & Tekhn. Imformatsii). Four Continent.
Miklosich, Franz. Dictionnaire Abrege de Six Langues Slaves. Philo Pr.
Miksa, Frances. Subject in the Dictionary Catalog From Cutter to the Present. ALA.
Mila, jt. auth. see Amery.
Miladinovic, Tomislav. Woerterbuch der Elektrotechnik und Elektronik. French & Eur.
Milanova, D. Swedish-Russian Dictionary. French & Eur.
Miles, Josephine. Coming to Terms. U of Ill Pr.
--Wordsworth & the Vocabulary of Emotion. Octagon.
Milioni, B., jt. auth. see Toledo, F.
Millan Contreras. Diccionario Internacional Abreviado de Siglas, Contracciones & Abreviaturas. Paraninfo.
Millan Contreras, Donato. Diccionario Internacional Abreviado De Siglas Contracciones y Abreviaturas. French & Eur.
--Diccionario Internacional de Siglas, Contracciones & Abreviaturas. Paraninfo.
Millar. Diccionario en Color de Arbustos. French & Eur.
Millar Gault, S. Diccionario Ilustrado En Color De Arbustos. French & Eur.
Miller, B. D. Local Warning System Definition. Mgmt Info Serv.
Miller, Carolyn H. Illustrated T.V. Dictionary. Harvey.
Miller, Charles, jt. auth. see Battles, Ford L.
Miller, Maud, jt. auth. see Meras, Albert A.
Miller, P. The Gardener's Dictionary. Lubrecht & Cramer.
Miller, P. R. & Pollard, H. L. Multilingual Compendium of Plant Diseases. Am Phytopathol Soc.
Miller, Walter J. & Morsecluley, Elizabeth. Vocabulary, Spelling & Grammar. Arco.
Miller, Wick R. Newe Natekwinappeh: Shoshoni Stories & Dictionary. AMS Pr.
Millers, Antonia. Grammar, Vocabulary, Exercises of the Latvian Language for the Use of Students. Echo Pubs.
Millet, Kenneth C. Piecewise Linear Concordances & Isotopies. Am Math.
Millet, Robert. Dictionnaire de la Loi. Homme.
Millidge, Edward A. Esperanto-English Dictionary. Saphrograph.
Milligan, George, jt. auth. see Moulton, James H.
Millington, T. Alaric, jt. auth. see Millington, William.
Millington, William & Millington, T. Alaric. Dictionary of Mathematics (EH). B&N NY.
Mills, Dorothy H., et al. Spanish Vocabulary & Structure for the Health Professional. Mills Pub Co.
Mills, Lawrence H. Dictionary of the Gathic Language. AMS Pr.
Mills, Roger F., ed. see Wojowasito, Soewojo.
Milne, G., jt. ed. see McAdam, E. L.
Milnet, R. C. see Atkins, B. T., et al.
Milne-Thomson, L. M. Russian-English Mathematical Dictionary. U of Wis Pr.
Milovanov, E. L. & Veistman, E. A., eds. English-Russian Dictionary of Environmental Control. Pergamon.
Milovanov, E. L., et al. Anglo-russki i slovar po okhrane okruzha i ushche i sredy. Russki Iazyk.
Mineau, Robert & Racinoux, Lucien. Glossaire des Vieux Parlers du Departement de la Vilenne. Quiniste.
Mingot, Tomas De Galiana. Pequeno Larousse de ciencias y tecnicas. Larousse.
Ministere de L'education. Lexique de L'education au Nouveau-Brunswick. Ministere de L'education.
Ministere des Communications Assemblee Nationale. Lexique du Journal des Debats. Quebec Off.
--Lexique du Journal des Debats. Quebec Off.
--Lexique du Journal des Debats. Quebec Off.
Ministere du Travail Et du la Main-D'oeuvre. Vocabulaire Francais-Anglais des Relations Professionnelles. Quebec Off.
Ministry of Agriculture & Fisheries-Netherlands & Nijdam, J., eds. Elsevier's Dictionary of Horticulture. Elsevier.
Ministry of Education. Scientific Terms, Aeronautics: Japanese-English, English-Japanese. French & Eur.
--Scientific Terms, Chemistry: Japanese-English, English-Japanese. French & Eur.
--Scientific Terms Mathematics: Japanese-English, English-Japanese. French & Eur.
--Scientific Terms Meteorology: Japanese-English, English-Japanese. French & Eur.
--Scientific Terms Physics: Japanese-English, English-Japanese. French & Eur.
--Scientific Terms Spectroscopy: Japanese-English, English-Japanese. French & Eur.
Ministry of Education Science & Culture. Scientific Terms Electrical Engineering. French & Eur.
Mink, tr. Diccionario tecnico espanol-aleman. Bluma.
Mink, Auteur H. Dictionnaire Technique Francais-Espagnol. French & Eur.
Mink, H. Diccionario Tecnico Aleman-Espanol, Espanol-Aleman. French & Eur.
--Diccionario Tecnico: Suplemento. French & Eur.

--Diccionario Tecnico: Suplemento al Tomo II, Espanol-Aleman. Herder SA.
--Diccionario Tecnico, Tomo 1: Aleman-Espanol (French & Eur). French & Eur.
--Diccionario Tecnico, Tomo 2: Espanol-Aleman (French & Eur). French & Eur.
Mink, Hermann. Diccionario Tecnico. Blume Edit.
--Diccionario Tecnico Frances-Espanol. French & Eur.
--Technisches Fachwoerterbuch. Gustavo Gili.
Minor, Dorothy, jt. auth. see Minor, Eugene E.
Minor, Eugene E. & Minor, Dorothy. Vocabulario Huitoto Muinane. Summer Inst Ling.
Minsheu, John. Ductor in Linguas: The Guide into Tongues. Schol Facsimiles.
Mintz, Patricia. Dictionary of Graphic Arts Terms: A Communication Tool for People Who Buy Type & Printing. Van Nos Reinhold.
Miquel I Verges, Jose Maria. Diccionario de Insurgentes. French & Eur.
Mira, Giuseppe M. Bibliografia Siciliana, Ovvero Gran Dizionario Bibliografico Delle Opere Editi E Inedite, Antiche E Moderne Di Autori Siciliani O Di Argomento Siciliano Stampate in Sicilia. B Franklin.
Miracle, Josep. Diccionari Catala-Castella, Castella-Catala. Poseidon SA.
--Diccionari catala-castella, castella-catala. Edhasa.
Miracle Montserrat, Josep. Diccionari Manual de la Llengua Catalana. French & Eur.
Mirambel, Andre. Petit Dictionnaire Francais-Grec Moderne et Grec Moderne-Francais. French & Eur.
Miranda, Hernany. Diccionario Popular Matematico. Direc Pubns.
Miranda, Jose, jt. auth. see Yanguas.
Miravitlles Serradell, Joan. Diccionari general de barbarismes i altres incorreccions. Claret Edit.
Miremont, Pierre. Glossaire del Perigord Negre. P. Miremont.
Mireur, H. Dictionnaire des Ventes d'art Faites en France & a l'etranger, 1. Olms Verlag.
--Dictionnaire des Ventes d'art Faites en France & a l'etranger, 2. Olms Verlag.
--Dictionnaire des Ventes d'art Faites en France & a l'etranger, 3. Olms Verlag.
--Dictionnaire des Ventes d'art Faites en France & a l'etranger, 4. Olms Verlag.
--Dictionnaire des Ventes d'art Faites en France & a l'etranger, 5. Olms Verlag.
--Dictionnaire des Ventes d'art Faites en France & a l'etranger, 6. Olms Verlag.
Miri, Hector F. Diccionario Bachiller. Claridad.
Miroglio, Abel & Miroglio, Yvonne D. L'Europe & ses population. Nyhoff.
Miroglio, Yvonne D., jt. auth. see Miroglio, Abel.
Mironova, Inessa N. Slownik Kieszonkowy Polsko-Rosyjski. Russkii Iazyk.
Mirowicz. Wielki Slownik Polsko-Rosyski (Polish-Russian Dictionary) French & Eur.
Misra, Bal G., jt. auth. see National Conference on Dictionary Making in Indian Languages.
Missionary Research Library. New York Dictionary Catalog of the Missionary Research Library (Hall Library). G K Hall.
Missir, Emile. Dictionnaire Francais-Romaneique. Klincksieck.
Mistral, Frederic. Le Tresor de Felibridge: Dictionnaire Provencal-Francais. French & Eur.
Mitchell, Edward C., ed. see Furst, Gesenius.
Mitchell, G. Duncan. Dizionario di sociologia. Newton-Compton.
Mitchell, G. Duncan, ed. A New Dictionary of the Social Sciences. Aldine Pub.
Mitchell Library, the Library of New South Wales. (Sydney, Australia) Dictionary Catalog of Printed Books (Hall Library). G K Hall.
Mitra, Ashok. Terms of Trade & Class Relations: An Essay in Political Economy (F Cass Co). Biblio Dist.
Mitronova, I. N., jt. auth. see Sinitsyna, G. V.
Mitronova, I. N., et al. Karmannyi Pol'Sko-Russkii & Russko-Polskii Slovar (Pub. by Russkii Iazyk). Four Continent.
Mitry, Jean. Diccionario del cine. Plaza Janes.
Mitton, Jacqueline. Key Definitions in Astronomy. Littlefield.
Mitzka, Walther, jt. ed. see Goetze, Alfred.
Miuller, V. K., ed. Anglo-Russkii Slovar. Four Continent.
Miura, Akira. English Loanwords in Japanese: A Selection. C E Tuttle.
Miyayama, H., et al. A Glossary of Agricultural Terms. French & Eur.
Modglin, Nel. The Rhymer & Other Helps for Poets. Dorrance.
Modica, Enzo. Dizionario delle Autonomie Locali. Editori Riuniti.
Modica, Enzo & Triva, Rubes. Dizionario delle autonomie locali. Editori Riuniti.
Moechel, G. Oekonomisches Woerterbuch Russisch-Deutsch (Pub. by Vlg. Die Wirtschaft). French & Eur.
Moelleken, Wolfgang W; see Hench, Atcheson L.
Moeller, Hilke. Thraenen-Samen & Steckdosenschnauze. Von Grieffenberg, C. R. & Schnurres, Wolfdietrich, eds. Jurisdruck.
Moellerke, Georg. Concise Electronics Dictionary. A T Fachverlag.
Mohle, K., jt. auth. see Meinck, F.
Moirant, R., jt. auth. see Cassart, C.
Moiseev, A. V. Ekonomicheskii Slovar Spravochnik Rabochego (Pub. by Politizdat). Four Continent.
Moiseev, Anatolii V. Ekonomicheskii Slovar-Spravochnik Rabochego. Politizdat.
Moisy, Henri. Dictionnaire du Patois Normand. Slatkine.
Mokri, M. Al-Hadiyati 'I-Hamidiyah. Intl Bk Ctr.
--Kurdish-Arabic Dictionary: Al-Hadiyati 'l-Hamidiyah. Intl Bk Ctr.
Molde, Bertil. Dansk-Svensk Ordbok. Ferlov, Niels, ed. Esselte Studium.
Moldenhauer, Janice. Developing Dictionary Skills. Good Apple.
Molesworth, James T. A Dictionary-Marathi & English. Intl Pubns Serv.
Molho, Emanuel. The Dictionary Catalogue. French & Eur.
Molina Aranda, Fernando. Diccionario Tecnico Hostelero. French & Eur.
Moliner, Maria. Diccionario de uso de espanol: Tomo 1. Gredos.
--Diccionario de uso de espanol: Tomo 2. Gredos.
--Diccionario de uso del espanol. Gredos.
--Diccionario de uso del espanol: Obra completa. Gredos.
--Diccionario de uso del espanol: Tomo 1. Gredos.
--Diccionario de uso del espanol: Tomo 2. Gredos.
--Diccionario del Uso del Espanol. GRD.
--Diccionario Del Uso Del Espanol. French & Eur.
Moll, Francesc de B., jt. auth. see Alcover, Antoni M.
Moll, Francisco de B. Diccionario manual italiano-espanol. Moll Edit.
Moll Casanovas, Fransesc de B. Diccionari Catala-Castella I Castella-Catala. French & Eur.
Moll Y Cassanovas, Francisco de. Diccionari Catala-Castella. Moll Edit.
Molnar. Diccionario de seguros. Rev. Mex. de Seguros.
Molossi, L. Vocabolario topografico dei ducati di Parma, Piacenza e Guastalla. Forni.
Molotkova, A. I. Frazeologicheskii Slovar Russkogo Iazyka (Pub. by Russkii Iazyk). Four Continent.
Mommsen. Diccionario medico Labor para la familia. Labor SA.
--Diccionario Medico Labor Para la Familia. French & Eur.
Mommsen, H. Diccionario Medico Labor para la Familia. French & Eur.
Mommsen, H., et al. Diccionario Medico Labor para la Familia. Massor Gimeno, Juan & Vilahur Pedrals, J., trs. Labor SA.
Monceaux, Jean-Pierre, jt. auth. see Lancombe, Michel.
Monier-Williams. Sanskrit-English Dictionary. South Asia Bks.
Monier-Williams, Monier. English Sanskrit Dictionary. Auromere.
--English-Sanskrit Dictionary. Humanities.
--English-Sanskrit Dictionary. Intl Pubns Serv.
Monier-Williams, Monier, et al. Sanskrit-English Dictionary. Oxford U Pr.
Monkhouse & Small. Dictionary of the Natural Environment. E. Arnold.
Monkhouse, F. Dictionary of Natural Environment with English-Arabic Glossary. Intl Bk Ctr.
--A Dictionary of the Natural Environment. Intl Bk Ctr.
Monkhouse, F. J. Diccionario De Terminos Geograficos. French & Eur.
--Dizionario di geografia. Manzoni, M., tr. Zanichelli.
Monkhouse, F. J. & Small, John. Dictionary of Natural Environment. E Arnold.
Montagnet, Desgoses. Dictionnaire de Medecine Amusante. De Rache.
Montanaro, John S. Chinese-English Phrase Book for Travellers (Pub. by Wiley Pr). Wiley.
Monterde, Francisco, ed. see Raluy Pondevida, Antonio.
Monterde, Francisco, rev. by see Raluy Poudevida, Antonio.
Monterde, Francisco, ed. see Raluy Poudevila, Antonio.
Montgomery, Hugh. A Dictionary of Political Phrases & Allusions. Gordon Pr.
--Dictionary of Political Phrases & Allusions with a Short Bibliography. Gale.
Monti, Pietro. Vocabolario dei dialette della citta e diocesi di Como. Forni.
Montoto, jt. auth. see Flynn.
Moor, Lise. English-French-German Glossary for Psychiatry, Child Psychiatry & Abnormal Psychology. Intl Pubns Serv.
--Glossaire de Psychiatrie. Masson.
--Glossaire De Psychiatrie. French & Eur.
Moore. Diccionario de geografia. Dossat.
--Dizionario di geografia. Newton-Compton.
Moore, jt. auth. see Coveney.
Moore, Burness E. & Fine, Bernard D., eds. A Glossary of Psychoanalytic Terms & Concepts. Am Psychoanalytic.
Moore, Byron C., et al. A Dictionary of Special Education Terms. C C Thomas.
--Introduction to Mental Retardation Syndromes & Terminology. C C Thomas.
Moore, John W. A Dictionary of Musical Information. AMS Pr.
--Dictionary of Musical Information. B Franklin.
Moore, Lillian. A Child's First Picture Dictionary (G&D). Putnam Pub Group.
Moore, Norman D. Dictionary of Business, Finance, & Investment. Investor's Syst.
Moore, Richard A. Historical Dictionary of Guatemala. Intl Guatemala.
Moore, Sheila J., jt. auth. see Coveney, James.
Moore, Shelia J., jt. ed. see Coveney, James.
Moore, Shiela J., jt. auth. see Conveney, James.
Moore, Thurston. The Original Word Game Dictionary. Stein & Day.
Moore, W. C. Diccionario de Geografia. French & Eur.
Moore, W. G. Dictionary of Geography. Penguin.
--A Dictionary of Geography: Definitions & Explanations of Terms Used in Physical Geography. B&N Imports.
Mora, Imra. The Publishers Practical Dictionary (Pub. by K G Saur). Shoe String.
Mora, Imre. Husznyelvu Kiadoi Szotar. Akademiai Kiado.
--Woerterbuch des Verlagswesens in 20 Sprachen. Saur Verlag.
--Woerterbuch des Verlagswesens in 20 Sprachen. French & Eur.
Morais, A. De see Ferreira, J. Albino.
Morais, Armando de see De Morais, Armando.
Morais, O. De see Ferreira, J. Albino.
Moral-Arroyo, J. A., jt. auth. see Burfeindt-Moral, H.
Morales Marin, Jose L. Diccionario de terminos artisticos. Unali.
Moreau, Joseph. Dictionnaire de Geographie Historique de la Gaule et de la France. French & Eur.
Moreau, Pierre & Masson, Andre. Vocabulaire Redaction. Hachette.
Moreau, Pierre F., jt. auth. see Mousseau, Jacques.
Morehead, Albert H., et al, eds. New American Roget's College Thesaurus in Dictionary Form (G&D). Putnam Pub Group.
Morehead, Andrew T., jt. auth. see Morehead, Philip D.
Morehead, Loy, jt. auth. see Wilson, Tom.
Morehead, Philip D. & Morehead, Andrew T. The New American Webster Handy College Dictionary. NAL.
Morei, Ferenc & Binet, Agnes V. Ablak-Zsir Kepes Gyermeklexikon. Adler Bks.
Morel, Hector & Dale Moral, Jose. Diccionario de parapsicologia. Kier.
Morelli, Marcello. Dizionario di informatica e degli elaboratori elettronici. Angeli.
Moreno, Alvaro J., compiled by. Voces Homofonas, Homografas & Homonimas Castellanas. Moreno Ed.
Moreno, Daniel. Diccionario de politica. Porrua.
Moreno, Miguel Pacheco see Pacheco Moreno, Miguel.
Moreno Castro, Pablo-Carrillo & Reyes, Juan R. Diccionario Gitano. Piquenas Edit.
Moreno Pacheo, Miguel. Economic Terminology. Adler.
Moreschi, Xavier. Lexique Francais-Corse. Corses.
Moretti, Giovanni. Vocabolario del dialetto de Magione. Univ Perugia.
Moretti, Mario, ed. see Amendola, Joao.
Moreu-Rey, E. Vocabulario Basico Frances. Teide.
Moreu Rey, Enrico. Vocabulario Basico Frances. Teide.
Morev, L. N. Taisko-Ruskii Slovar (Pub. by Sov. Entsiklopediia). Four Continent.
Morgan, Bayard, jt. auth. see Wadepuhl, Walter.
Morgan, Joyce L. & Wilbur, Beverley. Dent's Primary Dictionary. Dent.
Morgenstern, Sam, jt. ed. see Barlow, Harold.
Morice, E. Diccionario de Estadistica. French & Eur.
Morice, Eugene. Dizionario di statistica. Cossarini, M. G., tr. ISEDI.
Morier, Henri. Dictionnaire de Poetique & de Rhetorique. Pr Univ Fr.
Morilla, Abad I. Diccionario de Ingenieria de Caminos. Piramide.
Morilla Abad, I. Diccionario de Ingenieria de Caminos. Piramide.
Morin, F. Dictionnaire de Philosophie et de Theologie Scolastiques. Migne, J. P., ed. Caratzas Pub Co.
Morinigo, Marcos A. Diccionario de americanismos. Teide.
--Diccionario de Americanismos. SEI.
--Diccionario de Americanismos. French & Eur.

Moritz, H. & Torok, T. Technical Dictionary of Spectroscopy & Spectral Analysis: English, German, French, Russian. Pergamon.

Moritz, R. E., ed. Knaurs Musiklexikon. M Rosenberg.

Morley, Neil, jt. auth. see Verbov, Julian.

Mormile, Mario. Dictionnaire Commercial: Italien-Francais Francais-Italien. Maison Dictionnaire.

--Dizionario commerciale italiano-francese e francese-italiano. Bulzoni.

--Dizionario Commerciale Italiano-Francese, Francese-Italiano. Maison Dictionnaire.

Morri, A. Vocabolario romagnolo-italiano. Forni.

Morris. Xerox Dictionary Thumb Index (G&D). Putnam Pub Group.

Morris, Edward E. Austral English. Gale.

Morris, John, ed. Descartes Dictionary. Philos Lib.

Morris, Mary, jt. auth. see Morris, William.

Morris, William. The Ginn Beginning Dictionary. Ginn.

--It's Easy to Increase Your Vocabulary. Penguin.

Morris, William & Morris, Mary. Harper Dictionary of Contemporary Usage (HarpT). Har-Row.

--Morris Dictionary of Word & Phrase Origins (HarpT). Har-Row.

Morris, William, ed. Xerox Intermediate Dictionary (G&D). Putnam Pub Group.

Morrison, Irma L., jt. auth. see Freedman, Alan.

Morsecluley, Elizabeth, jt. auth. see Miller, Walter J.

Mortgage Bankers Association of America. Mortgage Banking Terms: A Working Glossary. Mortgage Bankers.

Mortillaro, Vincenzo. Nuovo dizionario siciliano-italiano. Soc St Catanese.

--Nuovo dizionario siciliano-italiano. Forni.

Morton, A. Q. & Michaelson, Sidney. A Critical Concordance to the Acts of the Apostles. Biblical Res Assocs.

--Critical Concordance to the Letter of Paul to the Romans. Baird, J. Arthur & Freedman, David Noel, eds. Biblical Res Assocs.

Morton, A. Q., et al. Critical Concordance to the Letter of Paul to the Colossians. Baird, J. Arthur & Freedman, David, eds. Biblical Res Assocs.

--Critical Concordance to the Letter of Paul to the Philippians. Baird, J. Arthur & Freedman, David, eds. Biblical Res Assocs.

--A Critical Concordance to I & II Corinthians. Biblical Res Assocs.

--A Critical Concordance to the Epistle of Paul to the Galatians. Baird, J. Arthur & Freedman, David, eds. Biblical Res Assocs.

--A Critical Concordance to the Letter of Paul to the Ephesians. Baird, J. Arthur & Freedman, David, eds. Biblical Res Assocs.

Morton, C., jt. auth. see Morton, Ian.

Morton, Ian & Morton, C. Elsevier's Dictionary of Food Science & Technology. Elsevier.

Mory, Ludwig, et al. Brukmanns' Zinn-Lexikon. Bruckmann KG.

Mosler, Hermann, et al, eds. Woerterbuch des Voelkerrechts: Bd 2, Ibero-Amerikanismus bis Quirin-Fall. De Gruyter.

--Woerterbuch des Voelkerrechts: Bd 3, Rapollo-Vertrag bis Zypern. De Gruyter.

Mosse, Walter M. Theological German Vocabulary. Octagon.

Mossman, Jennifer, ed. Pseudonyms & Nicknames Dictionary. Gale.

Mostaert, Antoine. Dictionnaire Ordos. Johnson Repr.

Motta, Giuseppe. Dizionario Commerciale Inglese-Italiano, Italiano-Inglese: Economia, Legge, Finanza, Banca, Etc. S F Vanni.

--Dizionario italiano-inglese e inglese-italiano. Signorelli C.

Moulis, Adelin. Dictionnaire Languedocien-Francais. Moulis, Ad.

Moulton, Harold K., ed. The Analytical Greek Lexicon Revised. Zondervan.

Moulton, James H. & Milligan, George. Vocabulary of the Greek New Testament. Eerdmans.

Moulton, Jenni H., ed. The Random House Basic Dictionary German. Ballantine.

Mounin, Georges. Diccionario de linguistica. Pochtar, Ricardo, tr. Labor SA.

--Dictionnaire de la Linguistique. PUF.

Moureau, M. & Brace, G. Dictionary of Petroleum Technology: English-French, French-English. Imported Bks.

Moureau, Madeleine & Rouge, Janine. Dictionnaire Technique des Termes Utilises dans l'industrie du Petrole: Anglais-Francais. Technip.

Moureau, Magdeleine & Brace, Gerald, eds. Dictionary of Petroleum Technology-Dictionnaire Technique Du Petrol: English-French - French-English. Intl Pubns Serv.

Moureau, Magdeleine. Dictionnaire Technique du Petrole. Technip.

Moureau, Magdeleine & Rouge, Janine. Dictionnaire Technique des Termes Utilises Dans l'Industrie du Petrole, Anglais-Francais, Francais-Anglais. French & Eur.

Mourre, Michel. Dizionario Mondadori di storia universale. Mondadori.

Mousseau, Jacques & Moreau, Pierre F. L'Inconscient. Retz.

Mouthany, J. R. English Without Teacher & Dictionary: English-Arabic. Intl Bk Ctr.

Mrazek, Jindrich. Slovnik Zakladnich Odbornych Cesko-Nemeckych Vyrazu ze Silnicni a Mestske Dopravy. SNTL.

Muchow, Helmut. Festkorperelektronik. VEB Technik.

Mudge, Isadore G. & Sears, Minnie E. George Eliot Dictionary. Folcroft.

Mudrov, B. G., ed. Kitaisko-Russkii Slovar (Pub. by Russkii Iazyk). Four Continent.

Mudrov, V. G. Karmannyi Russko-Kitaiskii Slovar (Pub. by Russkii Iazyk). Four Continent.

Mueller & Halder. Kleines Philosophisches Woerterbuch. Herder.

--Kleines Philosophisches Woerterbuch (Pub. by Herder). French & Eur.

Mueller, jt. auth. see Loebel.

Mueller, A., ed. Lexikon der Kybernetik. Quickborner Team.

Mueller, C. Lexikon der Psychiatrie. Springer-Verlag.

Mueller, Heinz & Haensch, Guenther, eds. Langenscheidts Handwoerterbuecher: Tl 1, Spanisch-Deutsch. Langenscheidt.

Mueller, Peter. Lexikon der Datenverarbeitung. French & Eur.

Mueller, Peter B. German-English, English-German: A Dictionary of Professional Terminology of Speech Pathology & Audiology. C C Thomas.

Mueller-Hegemann, A., jt. ed. see Areisin, L.

Mueller-Hegemann, A., jt. ed. see Aresin, L.

Mueller-Hegemann, A., jt. ed. see Dietrich, G.

Mueller Lutz, H. & Castelo Matran, Julio. Diccionario de Seguros. Mapfre.

Mueller-Lutz, H. L. Diccionario De Seguros. French & Eur.

Mugica. Diccionario manual latino-espanol y espanol-latino. Razon y Fe.

Mugica Berrondo, Placido. Diccionario Vasco-Castellano: Tomo 1. Mensajero Edns.

--Diccionario Vasco-Castellano: Tomo 2. Mensajero Edns.

Mugica Betrondo, Placido. Diccionario Vasco-Castellano: Obra completa. Mensajero Edns.

Mugica Urdangarin, Luis M. Diccionario General y Tecnico: Hiztegi Orokor-Teknikoa. French & Eur.

Mugika, Placido. Diccionario Castellano-Vasco. French & Eur.

Mugler, Charles. Dictionnaire Historique de la Terminologique Optique des Grecs. Klincksieck.

--Dictionnaire Historique de la Terminologique Optique des Grecs. French & Eur.

Muhandes, Kamel, jt. auth. see Wahba, Magdi.

Muhlhausler, Peter. Growth & Structure of the Lexicon of New Guinea Pidgin. Linguistic Circle.

Muhlmann, Hans G. Woerterbuch ser Pferdekunde. Verlag Sankt.

Mujica Herzog, Enrique. Diccionario del Socialismo. Dopesa.

Mukhel, V. Kratkii Estonsko-Russkii Slovar (Pub. by Tallinn). Four Continent.

--Russko-Estonskii Slovar (Pub. by Estonsk. Gos. Izd.). Four Continent.

Muldrow, George M., jt. auth. see Donker, Marjorie.

Mulhall, Michael G. Dictionary of Statistics. Gordon Pr.

Mulkerne, Donald J., jt. auth. see Kahn, Gilbert.

Mullen, William B. Dictionary of Scientific Word Elements. Littlefield.

Muller. Diccionario Aleman-Espanol, Espanol-Aleman. French & Eur.

Muller, jt. auth. see Haisman.

Muller, B. R., jt. auth. see Haisman, P.

Muller, F. Atheneum Worterbuch: Aleman-Espanol, Espanol-Aleman. French & Eur.

Muller, Franz. Diccionario Aleman-Espanol-Aleman. Imported Bks.

--Diccionario bilingue aleman-espanol y espanol-aleman. Sopena.

Muller, Hanns. Pocket Dictionary of Horseman's Terms in English, German, French & Spanish. Transatlantic.

Muller, Hans. Diccionario Lexicon Aleman-Espanol, Espanol-Aleman. French & Eur.

Muller, Heinz & Haensch, Gunther. Langenscheidts Handwoerterbuch Spanisch: Teil I, Spanisch-Deutsch. Langenscheidt.

Muller, Heinz, et al. Langenscheidts Handwoerterbuch Spanisch-Deutsch. Langenscheidt.

Muller, Jean. Dictionnaire Abrege des Imprimeurs-Editeurs du 16 Siecle. Koerner.

Muller, Joseph-Emile. Illustrated Dictionary of Expressionism. Barron.

Muller, Peter Von see Schmid, Hans & Von Muller, Peter.

Muller, V. English-Russian Dictionary (Pub. by Collet's). State Mutual Bk.

Muller, V. K., ed. English-Russian Dictionary. Dutton.

Muller, Vaclav. Maly Divadelni Slovnik. Kultura.

Muller, Vladimir K. English-Russian Dictionary. Saphrograph.

Muller, W., ed. Dictionary of the Graphic Arts Industry. Elsevier.

Muller, Wilhelm. Customs Dictionary: German-English-French-Italian. Intl Pubns Serv.

Muller, Wolfgang. Polygrafie-Englisch-Deutsch-Franzoesisch-Russisch-Spanisch-Polnisch-Ungarisch-Solwakisch. VEB Technik.

--Die Richtige Wortwahl: Ein Vergleichendes Woerterbuch Sinnverwandter Ausdruecke. Biblio Inst.

Muller-Halder. Breve Diccionario Philosofia. French & Eur.

Muller-Reuter, Theodor. Lexikon der Deutschen Konzertliteratur. Da Capo.

Munnik, Eulalie. Afrikaanse Verklarende Woordeboek vir Biologie. Knaggs Assoc.

Munniksma, F., ed. International Business Dictionary in Nine Languages. Esperanto League North Am.

Munoz, jt. auth. see Lipton.

Munoz, O., jt. auth. see Lipton, G.

Munoz, Olivia, jt. auth. see Lipton, Gladys.

Munso, J. Diccionario Turistico de Cataluna, Baleares y Andora. French & Eur.

Munsterberg, Hugo. Dictionary of Chinese & Japanese Art. Hacker.

Munte Vila, Josep. Diccionari Catala-Castella: Vocabulari Basic. Blume Edit.

Munz, Max & Winkel, Harald. Lexikon der Kostenrechnung. Kiehl.

Murashkevich, A. M. Anglo-Russkii Slovar Po Raketnoi Tekhnike (Pub. by Gosizdat. Literatury). Four Continent.

--Slovar Anglo-Amerikanskikh Sokrashchenii Po Aviatsionnoi & Raketno-Kosmicheskoi Tekhnike (Pub. by Voenizdat). Four Continent.

Murashkevich, A. M. & Vladimirov, O. N. English-Russian Aviation & Space Abbreviations Dictionary (Pub. by Collets). State Mutual Bk.

Murawski, H. Geologisches Woerterbuch. Deutscher Taschenbuch Verlag.

--Geologisches Woerterbuch. Deutscher Taschenbuch Verlag.

Murcava, L. O., ed. see Dinneen, Patrick S.

Murdoch, John, jt. auth. see Ray, P. N.

Murphy, B. Dictionary of Australian History. McGraw.

Murphy, Daniel, jt. auth. see Ehrlich, Eugene.

Murphy, John D. Luganda-English Dictionary. Cath U Pr.

Murphy, John J. The Book of Pidgin English. AMS Pr.

Murray, Carol, jt. auth. see Shalhoub, Judy.

Murray, G. W. English-Nubian Comparative Dictionary. Hooton, E. A. & Bates, Natica I., eds. Kraus Repr.

Murray, Joan. A CB Picture Dictionary. Doubleday.

Murray, John. The Media Law Dictionary. U Pr of Amer.

Murray, Joseph P. Selective English Old-French Glossary As a Basis for Studies in Old French Onomatology & Synonymics. AMS Pr.

Murray, Linda, jt. auth. see Murray, Peter.

Murray, Peter & Murray, Linda. Diccionario De Artes y Artistas. French & Eur.

--The Penguin Dictionary of Art & Artists. Gannon.

Murval, M., jt. auth. see Andras, L. T.

Musatti, C. L., tr. see Jung, C. Gustav.

Muschinsky, Lars J. & Schnack, Karsten, eds. Paedagogisk Opslangsbog: Alfabetisk Ordnet. Ejlers Forlag.

Musmarra, Alfio. Dizionario botanico. Edagricole.

Muss-Arnolt, William. A Concise Dictionary of the Assyrian Languages. AMS Pr.

Musset, Georges. Glossaire des Patois & des Parlers de l'Aunis & de la Saintonge. Lafitte Repr.

Muste, B. Bassegoda see Bassegoda Muste, B.

Musu, Boy. Dizionario italiano-inglese. Vallardi A.

Musu-Boy, R. Dizionario Italiano-Inglese, Inglese-Italiano. French & Eur.

Mutinelli, Fabio. Lessico Vento. Forni.

Myers, Patricia A. A Glossary for Radiologic Technologists. Praeger.

Myklestad, J. Meyer & Soras, H. English-Norwegian, Norwegian-English Dictionary. Saphrograph.

Mylius, Klaus. Woerterbuch Sanskrit-Deutsch. VEB Verlag Enzyklopadie.

Mystakidis, Antonis. Nygrekisk-Svensk Ordbok. Frangos, Eftychia, ed. Esselte Studium.

N

Nabel, H. L., et al. Shuter's New Basic English Dictionary for Xhosa Speakers. Shuter & Shooter.
Nadal, J. C. Dictionnaire d'Eloquence Sacree. Migne, J. P., ed. Caratzas Pub Co.
Nagel, Kurt. Lexikon EDV und Rechnungswesen. French & Eur.
Naggary-Bey, M. Dictionnaire Francais-Arabe. Verry.
Nagy, E. & Klar, J., eds. English-Hungarian Technical Dictionary (Pub. by Collet's). State Mutual Bk.
Nagy, Erno & Klar, Janos. Magyar-Angol Muszaki Szotar. Akademiai Kiado.
Nagy, Gabor O., et al. Magyar Szinonimaszotar. Akademiai Kiado.
Nagy, Istvan G. Haditechnikai Kislexikon. Zrinyikatunai.
Nagy, Sandor, ed. Pedagogiai Lexikon. Akademiai Kiado.
Nagy, T. Hungarian-English Technical Dictionary (Pub. by Collet's). State Mutual Bk.
Najjar. Law Dictionary French-Arabic: Dictionnaire Juridique. Intl Bk Ctr.
Nakhimovsky, A. D. & Paperno, V. A. An English-Russian Dictionary of Nabokov's "Lolita". Ardis Pubs.
Nania, G. Dictionnaire d'informatique: Francais-Anglais-Italien-Espagnol-Portugais. Maison Dictionnaire.
Nania, Georges. Dictionnaire d'informatique. Maison Dictionnaire.
Nanooch, Henry, et al. Plains Cree Dictionary. U of Toronto Pr.
Nanxe, Aline de. Diccionario Del Amor. French & Eur.
Napalis, I., et al. Orfograficheskii Slovar Litovskogo Iazyka Dlia Shkol (Pub. by Izd Pedag Lit). Four Continent.
Napoleoni, Claudio. Diccionario de Economia Politica. Ortells Ferriz.
--Diccionario de economia politicia. Castilla.
Nardin, Pierre. Lexique Compare des Fabilaux de Jean Bedel. Slatkine.
Narita, Shigehisa, tr. see Kawamoto, Shigeo & Nishiwaki, Junzaburo.
Nash. Multinlingual Lexicon of Linguistics & Philology. French & Eur.
Nash, Rose. Multilingual Lexicon of Linguistics & Philology: English, Russian, German, French. U of Miami Pr.
Nasr, Raja. Colloquial Arabic: An Oral Approach. Intl Bk Ctr.
--An English-Colloquial Arabic Dictionary. Intl Bk Ctr.
--English Colloquial Arabic Dictionary. Intl Bk Ctr.
Nasr, Raja T. An English Colloquial Arabic Dictionary in Phonetic Script. Transatlantic.
Nasr, Zacharia, ed. A Dictionary of Economics & Commerce. Macmillan London.
Nassir, Abdilahi. A Concise Dictionary of English-Swahili Idioms. Shungways Publishers.
Nassiruddin, Amin Al-Amir see Al-Amir Al-Nasiruddin, Amin.
National Association of Broadcasters. Standard Definition of Broadcast Research Terms. Natl Assn Broadcasters.
National Association of Corrosion Engineers. Glossary of Terms Used in Maintenance Painting. Natl Corrosion Eng.
National Computing Centre, ed. Thesaurus of Computing Terms. Intl Pubns Serv.
National Conference on Dictionary Making in Indian Languages & Misra, Bal G. Lexicography in India. Central Institute of Indian Languages.
National Fire Protection Association. Fire Terms: A Guide to Their Meaning & Use. Natl Fire Prot.
National Fluid Power Association. Glossary of Terms for Compressed Air Dryers (Included in Supplement to the Glossary of Terms, ANSI-B93.2a-1978) NFPA-T3.27.1. Natl Fluid Power.
--Glossary of Terms for Fluid Power Quick Disconnect Couplings (Included in Supplement to the Glossary of Terms) NFPA-T3.20.1. Natl Fluid Power.
--Glossary of Terms for Hydraulic Fluid Power Filters & Separator: NFPA-T3.10.3m. Natl Fluid Power.
National Fluid Power Association, jt. auth. see American National Standards Institute.
National Heart, Lung & Blood Institute. A Handbook of Heart Terms. Enslow Pubs.
National Information Center for Educational Media. NICSEM Special Education Thesaurus. Univ SC Natl Info.
National Knitted Outerwear Association. Knitting Dictionary. Natl Knit Outwear.
National Research Council. Glossary of Urban Public Transportation Terms. Natl Acad Pr.
National Shorthand Reporters Association. A Systematic Guide to Medical Terminology. Natl Shorthand Rptr.
National Woman's Christian Temperance Union. Key Terms & Phrases. WCTU.
Natta, F. Vocabolario sallustiano. L'Erma.
Naugle, Helen H., ed. A Concordance to the Poems of Samuel Johnson. Cornell U Pr.
Nauman, St. Elmo, Jr. The New Dictionary of Existentialism. Citadel Pr.
Nauton, P., ed. Vocabulaire du Cantal du Nord & de la Margeride Auvergnate d'Apres l'ALMC. Cercle Occitan.
Navarrete Luft, Anita. Diccionario de Terminos Anticuados & en Desuso. PLY.
Navarro Dagnino, J. Vocabulario Maritimo Ingles-Espanol. G Gili.
Navarro Dagnino, Juan. Vocabulario maritimo ingles-espanol y espanol-ingles. G Gili.
--Vocabulario Maritimo Ingles-Espanol y Espanol-Ingles. French & Eur.
Navarro Garcia, Felipe. Diccionario del Pasota. Planeta SA.
Naxerova. Technisches Woerterbuch: Band I, Tschechisch-Deutsch. Brandstetter.
Naxerova, A. Technisches Woerterbuch. Brandstetter.
--Technisches Woerterbuch. Brandstetter.
--Technisches Woerterbuch (Pub. by Brandstetter). French & Eur.
--Technisches Woerterbuch (Pub. by Brandstetter). French & Eur.
Nayler, G. H., jt. auth. see Nayler, J. L.
Nayler, J. L. & Nayler, G. H. Dictionary of Mechanical Engineering. Butterworth.
Naz, R. Dictionnaire de Droit Canonique. French & Eur.
Nebrija, Antonio de see De Nebrija, Antonio.
Nebruja, Elio A. de see De Nebruja, Elio de.
Nechas, James W. Synonomy, Repitition & Restatement in the Vocabulary of Herman Melville's Moby Dick. Folcroft.
Neff, Ivan C. & Maggs, Carol V. Dictionary of Oriental Rugs: With a Monograph on Identification by Weave. Van Nos Reinhold.
Neffgen, H. Grammar & Vocabulary of the Samoan Language. Stock, Arnold B., tr. from Ger. AMS Pr.
Neggers, Gladys. Vocabulario culto. Playor.
--Vocabulario Culto. French & Eur.
Negre, Herve. Dictionnaire des Histoires Droles. Fayard.
--Dictionnaire des Histoires Droles, 1. L. G. F.
--Dictionnaire des Histoires Droles, 2. L. G. F.
Neiger, E. Terminologia Turistico Alberghiera. Ed Calderini.
Neiger, Elisabetta. Dizionario gastronomico. Buffetti.
--Terminologia turistico alberghiera: L'albergatore poliglotta. Ed Calderini.
Neil, Charles, jt. ed. see Wright, Charles.
Neill, D. B., jt. auth. see Jerrard, G.
Neill, S. E. Lexikon Zur Weltmission. French & Eur.
Nekriach, E. F. Russko-Ukrainskii Khimicheskii Slovar (Pub. by An Arm SSR). Four Continent.
Nelida, Caffarello. Dizionario di antichita classiche. Olschki.
Neliubin, L. D. Illiustrirovannyi Voenno-Tekhnicheskii Slovar (Pub. by Voenizdat). Four Continent.
Nelli, Bruno. Dizionario sintattico latino. Giardini Pisa.
Nelli, Rene. Dictionnaire des Heresies Meridionales. Privat.
--Dictionnaire Des Heresies Meridionales. French & Eur.
Nelson, Andrew. Modern Reader's Japanese-English Character Dictionary. C E Tuttle.
Nelson, Andrew N. The Modern Reader's Japanese-English Character Dictionary. C E Tuttle.
Nelson, Fred, jt. auth. see Blauvelt, Carolyn T.
Nelson, Robert V. Understanding Basic Energy Terms. Ide Hse.
Nelson, Wilton M., ed. Diccionario Ilustrado de la Biblia. Edit Caribe.
Nelvik, Nikolai. Norsk Landbruksordbok. Samlaget.
Neri, A. Vocabolario del dialetto modenese. Forni.
Nesheim, Asbjorn, jt. ed. see Nielsen, Konrad.
Nettleship, ed. see Seyffert, Oskar.
Netto, G., jt. auth. see Bindoni, Vincenzo.
Neubert, G. Dictionary of Hydraulics & Pneumatics: English-German-Russian-Slovene. French & Eur.
Neubert, Gunter. Dictionary of Hydraulics & Pneumatics (Pub. by Collet's). State Mutual Bk.
Neubert, Gunter, ed. Technical Dictionary of Hydraulics & Pneumatics. Pergamon.
Neuder, Gustav F. & Ullrich, Heinz M. Dictionary of Radiological Engineering. De Gruyter.
Neuman, Maur. Dictionnaire des Medicaments. Heures de France.
Neuman, Maurice. Dictionnaire des Medicaments. French & Eur.
Neumann, A. R., jt. ed. see Franz, L.
Neumann, Guenther, ed. see Tischler, Johann.
Neumann, Hugo. Dictionnaire Juridique Francais-Allemand, Allemand-Francais. Quemner, Thomas A., ed. French & Eur.
Neumann, K. H., jt. auth. see Lindner, K.
Neuvonen, E. K. Finnish-Spanish-Finnish Dictionary. French & Eur.
Neve, John. Concordance to the Poetical Works of William Cowper. B Franklin.
Neve, Richard. City & Country Purchaser & Builder's Dictionary. Kelley.
Neverov, S. Ispansko-Russkii Razgovornik (Pub. by Izd. Lit. Na Inostr. Iaz.). Four Continent.
Neves, Alfredo N. Diccionario de Americanismos. SPA.
New World Dictionary Editors. Misspeller's Dictionary. S&S.
New York Public Library. Dictionary Catalog of the Schomburg Collection of Negro Literature & History, Supplement 1974 (Hall Library). G K Hall.
New York Public Library, Research Libraries. Dictionary Catalog & Shelf List of the Spencer Collection of Illustrated Books & Manuscripts & Fine Bindings (Hall Library). G K Hall.
--Dictionary Catalog of Jewish Collection (Pub. by Hall Library). G K Hall.
--Dictionary Catalog of the Albert A. & Henry W. Berg Collection of English & American Literature, First Supplement (Hall Library). G K Hall.
New York Public Library Research Libraries. Dictionary Catalog of the Art & Architecture Division, The Research Libraries of The New York Public Library (Hall Library). G K Hall.
New York Public Library, Research Libraries. Dictionary Catalog of the Dance Collection, Performing Arts Research Center (Hall Library). G K Hall.
--Dictionary Catalog of the Henry W. & Albert A. Berg Collection of English & American Literature (Hall Library). G K Hall.
--Dictionary Catalog of the History of the Americas Collection (Hall Library). G K Hall.
--Dictionary Catalog of the History of the Americas Collection, First Supplement (Hall Library). G K Hall.
--Dictionary Catalog of the Jewish Collection, First Supplement (Hall Library). G K Hall.
--Dictionary Catalog of the Local History & Genealogy Division (Hall Library). G K Hall.
--Dictionary Catalog of the Manuscript Division (Hall Library). G K Hall.
--Dictionary Catalog of the Map Division (Hall Library). G K Hall.
--Dictionary Catalog of the Music Collection (Hall Library). G K Hall.
--Dictionary Catalog of the Music Collection, Supplement II (Hall Library). G K Hall.
--Dictionary Catalog of the Oriental Collection: First Supplement (Hall Library). G K Hall.
--Dictionary Catalog of the Oriental Collection (Hall Library). G K Hall.
--The Dictionary Catalog of the Prints Division (Hall Library). G K Hall.
--Dictionary Catalog of the Rare Book Division: First Supplement (Hall Library). G K Hall.
--Dictionary Catalog of the Rare Book Division (Hall Library). G K Hall.
New York Public Library, the Research Libraries. Dictionary Catalog of the Slavonic Collection (Hall Library). G K Hall.
New York Times. The New York Times Everyday Dictionary. Paikeday, Thomas M., ed. Times Bks.
Newberry Library - Chicago. Dictionary Catalog of the Edward E. Ayer Collection of Americana & American Indians, First Supplement (Hall Library). G K Hall.
--Dictionary Catalog of the Edward E. Ayer Collection of Americana & American Indians (Hall Library). G K Hall.
--Dictionary Catalogue of the History of Printing from the John M. Wing Foundation (Hall Library). G K Hall.
--Dictionary Catalogue of the History of Printing from the John M. Wing Foundation, First Supplement (Hall Library). G K Hall.
Newell, Leonard E. A Batad Ifugao Vocabulary. HRAFP.
Newhouse, Dora. The Encyclopedia of Homonyms 'Sound-Alikes' Newhouse Pr.
--Homonyms. Newhouse Pr.
--Homonyms-Homonimos: Sound-Alikes. Newhouse Pr.
Newman, Frank E. New Practical Dictionary for Crossword Puzzles. Doubleday.
Newman, Frank Eaton. New Practical Dictionary for Crossword Puzzles. Doubleday.
Newman, Harold. An Illustrated Dictionary of Glass. Thames Hudson.
--An Illustrated Dictionary of Jewelry. Thames Hudson.
Newman, Harold, jt. auth. see Savage, George.
Newman, Paul. Sabon Kamus na Hausa Zuwa Turanci. Oxford U Pr.
Newman-Gordon, Pauline, ed. Dictionnaire Des Idees Dans L'oeuvre De Marcel Proust: Collection Dictionnaires Des Idees Dans les Litteratures Occidentales, Litterature Francaise. Mouton.
Newmark, Maxim. Dictionary of Foreign Words & Phrases. Greenwood.
Newson, B., ed. see Lee, W. R.
Ngata, Apirana N. Complete Manual of Maori Grammar & Conversation, with Vocabulary. AMS Pr.

Nguyen-Dinh-Hoa. Essential English-Vietnamese Dictionary. C E Tuttle.
--Vietnamese-English Dictionary. C E Tuttle.
--Vietnamese Phrase Book. C E Tuttle.
Nguyen-Dinh-Hoa, ed. Vietnamese-English Dictionary. C E Tuttle.
Nguyen Hy Quang. English-Vietnamese Phrasebook with Useful Word List: For Vietnamese Speakers. Ctr Appl Ling.
Nicchi, E. Dizionario dei comuni. La Tribuna.
Nichea, Niccolo. Vocabolario croato serbo-italiano de M. Deanovic e J. Jerej. Del Bianco.
Nichil, P. Lexique Francais-Anglais et Anglais-Francais des Termes d'usage Courant En Hydraulique et Pneumatique. French & Eur.
Nichols, Peter & Vibes, Pierre. Vocabulaire Anglais-Francais de Terminologie, Economique & Juridique. L. G. D. J.
Nicol, Karl Ludwig, ed. Herder-Lexikon Musik: Sachwoerterbuch. Herder.
Nicole, M., jt. auth. see Manuila, A.
Nicolosi, Lucille. Terminology of Communication Disorders: Speech, Language, & Hearing. Williams & Wilkins.
Nicolosi, Lucille, et al. Terminology of Communication Disorders: Speech, Language, Hearing. Williams & Wilkins.
Nicolson, Iain, ed. Dictionary of Astronomy. B&N NY.
Nicotra, V. Dizionario siciliano-italiano. Forni.
Nielsen, B. K., et al. Engelsk-Dansk-Ordbog. French & Eur.
Nielsen, Konrad & Nesheim, Asbjorn, eds. Lapp Dictionary. Universitet.
Nieri, I. Vocabolario lucchese. Forni.
Niermann, Johannes. Woerterbuch der DDR Paedagogik. French & Eur.
Niermeyer, J. F. Lexique Latin Medieval-Francais-Anglais. Brill.
Nierop, Maarten van see Van Nierop, Maarten.
Niewerth, Hans. Lexikon der Planun und Organisation. French & Eur.
Niewwerth, Hans, et al, eds. Lexikon der Planung & Organisation. Quickborner Team.
Nijdam, J., jt. ed. see Ministry of Agriculture & Fisheries-Netherlands.
Nikitin, V. T. Kratkii Ekonomicheskii Slovar-Spravochnik Mastera i Nachal'nika Tsekha (Pub. by Ekonomika). Four Continent.
Niklis, Werner S., ed. Handwoerterbuch der Schulpaedagogik. Klinkhardt.
Nilsson, Kare. Norsk-Portugisisk Ordbok. Universitetsforlaget.
Niobey. Dictionnaire Analogique de Poche (Dist. by Continental Bk Co). Larousse.
Nishiwaki, Junzaburo, jt. ed. see Kawamoto, Shigeo.
Nishiyama, Kazuo & Katayama, Hiroshi. Hawaii's Real Estate Industry & Technical Terminology in English & Japanese. Honolulu Japanese.
Nitronowa, I., et al. Polish-Russian, Russian-Polish Dictionary. French & Eur.
Nitti, John & Kasten, Lloyd. Complete Concordances & Texts of the Fourteenth-Century Aragonese Manuscripts of Juan Fernandez de Heredia. Hispanic Seminary.
Nitti, John, jt. auth. see Kasten, Lloyd.
Nixon, P. J. A Glossary of Virginia Words. U of Ala Pr.
Njoku, John E. A Dictionary of Igbo Names, Culture & Proverbs. U Pr of Amer.
Nobel, jt. auth. see Veillon.
Nobel, A., jt. auth. see Veillon, E.
Nobel, Albert, jt. auth. see Veillon, Emmanuel.
Nobel, John V. Naval Terms Dictionary. Gordon Pr.
Noble, Albert, jt. auth. see Veillon, Emile.
Noble, C. E. Australian Economic Terms. Longman.
Noctuel & Calmann-Levy. Dictionnaire Francais-Russe. Labiche.
Noehring. Woerterbuch Medizin. Verlag Harri Deutsch.
--Woerterbuch Wirtschaft. Verlag Harri Deutsch.
Noejd, Rubin. Engelsk-Svensk Ordbok. Esselte Studium.
Noel, Bernard. Dictionnaire de la Commune. French & Eur.
Noel, John V. The Boating Dictionary: Sail & Power. Van Nos Reinhold.
Noel, John V., Jr. The VNR Dictionary of Ships & the Sea. Van Nos Reinhold.
Noel, John V., Jr. & Beach, Edward L. Naval Terms Dictionary. US Naval Inst.
Noel-Henrard, L. & Noel-Henrard, M. Dictionnaire Marabout des Mots Croises, 1. Marabout.
--Dictionnaire Marabout des Mots Croises, 2. Marabout.
Noel-Henrard, M., jt. auth. see Noel-Henrard, L.
Nogueira, J. & Turover, G. Diccionario Ruso-Espanol. French & Eur.
Noguer More, Jesus. Diccionario Enciclopedico De la Vida Sexual. French & Eur.
Noid, Ruben. Svensk-Fransk & Fransk-Svensk Ordbok. Esselte Studium.
Nojd, Ruben. English-Swedish Dictionary. Saphrograph.
--Fransk-Svensk Ordbok. Esselte Studium.
Nojd, Ruben & Tornberg, Astrid. McKay's Modern English-Swedish, Swedish-English Dictionary. Imported Bks.
Nolan, Joseph R., ed. see Black, Henry C.
Nolan, Joseph R., et al, eds. see Black, Henry C.
Noonan, Larry. The Basic-BASIC English Dictionary. Dilithium Pr.
--Basic BASIC-English Dictionary for the Apple, PET & TRS-80. TAB Bks.
Noordzij, Nel. Woordenboek van magic, okkultisme & parapsychologi. Fontein.
Noory, Samuel. Dictionary of Pronunciation. Cornwall Bks.
Norback, C. & Norback, P. The Must Words: The Six Thousand Most Important Words for a Successful & Profitable Vocabulary (GB). McGraw.
Norback, Craig & Norback, Peter. The Must Words: The Six Thousand Most Important Words for a Successful & Profitable Vocabulary. McGraw.
Norback, P., jt. auth. see Norback, C.
Norback, Peter, jt. auth. see Norback, Craig.
Norman, Jerry. A Concise Manchu-English Lexicon. U of Wash Pr.
Normandeau, Lucien. Lexique de Mecanique d'ajustage. Quebec Off.
Norsk Sprakrad. Norsk Dataordbok. Universitetsforlaget.
Norton-Kyshe, J. W. Dictionary of Legal Quotations. Gordon Pr.
Norton-Kyshe, James W. Dictionary of Legal Quotations. Gale.
Nosova, O. P. Kratkii Lugunda-Russkii & Russko-Lugunda Slovar (Pub. by Sov Entsiklopediia). Four Continent.
Noter, R. De see De Noter, R. & Vuillermoz, P.
Nougayrol, Pierre, et al. Dictionnaire Elementaire Creole Haitien-Francais. Bentolila, Alain, ed. French & Eur.
Novak, Felix, jt. auth. see Michel, Christian.
Novak, J. & Binder, R. A Concise English-Slovak & Slovak-English Technical Dictionary (Pub. by Collet's). State Mutual Bk.
--A Concise English-Slovak & Slovak-English Technical Dictionary (Pub. by Collets). State Mutual Bk.
Noveannu, Eugen P. Dictionar-Rus-Roman: Pentru uzual Elevilor. Editura Stiintifica.
Novelli, Tina. Dizionario Etnologico Africano. Jaca Bk.
--Etnologico africano. Jaca Bk.
Novikov, N. N., et al. Russko-Birmanskii Slovar (Pub. by Sov. Entsiklopediia). Four Continent.
Novo, G. Diccionario General de Turismo. French & Eur.
Novodvorkis, A. I. Anglo-Litovskii Politekhnicheskii Slovar (Pub. by Gospolitnauchizdat). Four Continent.
Novozhilov, S. N., et al. Velosipeday i sport. Russky Yazyk.
Nowell, L. Vocabularium Saxonicum. Marckwardt, A., ed. Kraus Repr.
Nowitschkowa, A. L., jt. auth. see Scharow, W. A.
Noyes, Sybil, et al. Genealogical Dictionary of Maine & New Hampshire. Genealog Pub.
Nuessel, Frank H., Jr., ed. Linguistic Approaches to the Romance Lexicon. Georgetown U Pr.
Nugue, Christian, ed. see Weiss, Erich.
Nunberg, Geoffrey, ed. The American Heritage Dictionary. HM.
Nunes, C. Dicionario de Bolso Russo-Portuguese. French & Eur.
Nunez, Benjamin. Dictionary of Afro-Latin American Civilization. Greenwood.
--Terminos Topograficos en la Argentina Colonial, 1516-1810. Inst. Pan. Georg.
Nunez, Estuardo, jt. auth. see Paz Soldan Y Unanue, Pedro.
Nurigiani, Giorgio. Vocabolario italiano-macedone. Lint.
Nurmela, T. Finnish-French Dictionary. French & Eur.
Nurmela, Tauno. Dictionnaire Finnois-Francais. Soderstrom.
Nurnberg & Rosenblum. Adult Approach to Vocabulary Building. Mentor Bks.
Nuss, A. M. Export for Marketing French. French & Eur.
Nusser, Peter, ed. Anzeigenwerbung: Ein Reader fuer Studenten & Lehrer der Deutscher Sprache & Literatur. Fink Verlag.
Nutting, Teresa & Marcy, Michel. Cortina-Grosset Basic French Dictionary. G&D.
Nuzzo, Mario. Dizionario della lingua italiana. Marotta.
Nyanatiloka. Buddhist Dictionary. AMS Pr.
Nyblom, Ake. Engelsk-Svensk Elteknisk Forkortningslista. Ingenjorsforlaget.
Nye, Roger, jt. auth. see Le Vine, Victor T.
Nyirkos, I. Finnish-Hungarian-Finnish Dictionary (Suomi-Unkari-Suomi) French & Eur.
Nyirkos, Istvan. Suomi-Unkari-Suomi: Taskusanakirja. Soderstrom.
--Unkarilais-Suomalainen Sanakirja. Suoma Kirja.
Nykysuomen Laitos. Nykysuomen Sivistyssankirja: Vierasperaiset Sanat. Suoma Kirja.
Nyssen, Hubert. Lexique du Marketing. Delpire.
--Lexique du Marketing. French & Eur.

O

Oakey, Virginia. Dictionary of Film & Television Terms. B&N NY.
OAS General Secretariat. Vocabulario Vial. OAS.
O'Bannon, Loran. Dictionary of Ceramic Science & Engineering (Plenum Pr). Plenum Pub.
Obermayer, H. Kleines Stuttgarter-Bibellexikon (Pub. by Vlg. Katholisches Bibelwerk). French & Eur.
Obermayer, Heinz. Diccionario Biblico Manual. French & Eur.
Obraska, P., ed. see Perlemuter, L.
Obraska, Paul, jt. auth. see Perlemuter, Leon.
Obreanu, P. E., jt. ed. see Gould, S. H.
O'Brien. New Russian-English & English-Russian Dictionary. Imported Bks.
Ocampo de Gomez, Aurora & Prado Velazquez, Ernesto. Diccionario de Escritores Mexicanos. French & Eur.
Ockham, William. Ockham's Theory of Terms. Loux, Michael J., tr. U of Notre Dame Pr.
Octavo, M. S., ed. see Pillai, T. Ramalingam.
Odhner, Einer. Svenskt Rimlexikon. Forum Bok.
Odhner, John D. English-Lingala Manual. U Pr of Amer.
O'Donaill. Foclair Gaeilge Bearla (Irish-English Dictionary) Colton Bk.
O'Donnell. Dictionary Real Estate Terms. Dryden Pr.
O'Donnell & Townes. Words I Like to Read & Write: Grades 1-2 Picture Dictionary. Har-Row.
--Words I Like to Read & Write: Grades 2-4 Picture Dictionary. Har-Row.
O'Donoghue, Michael. Van Nostrand Reinhold Color Dictionary of Minerals & Gemstones. Van Nos Reinhold.
O'Dwyer, R. & Le Page, R. Glossary of Modern Art (WL). Citadel Pr.
OECD. Chemical Control Legislation Glossary. OECD.
--Multilingual Dictionary of Fish & Fish Products. State Mutual Bk.
OECD, ed. Multilingual Dictionary of Fish & Fish Products. Intl Pubns Serv.
Oesterby, M., ed. Dictionary of the Russian Academy. A Wofsy Fine Arts.
Oestling, Sven E. Foerkortningslexikon. Utrikespolitiska.
Oeter, D. Herder - Lexikon Medizin (Pub. by Herder). French & Eur.
--Herder-Lexikon Medizin. Herder.
Office de la Langue Francaise. Lexique Anglais-Francais du Compteur d'electricite. Quebec Off.
Oftedal, Laura & Jacob, Nina. My First Dictionary (G&D). Putnam Pub Group.
Ogden, C. K., ed. The General Basic English Dictionary. Rowman.
Ogden, Shelia J., jt. auth. see Radcliff, Ruth K.
Ogee, Jean, et al. Dictionnaire Historique & Geographique de la Province de Bretagne. Floch.
Ogilvie, Mardel. Terminology & Definitions of Speech Defects. AMS Pr.
Ogot, Bethwell A. Historical Dictionary of Kenya. Scarecrow.
O'Harra, Kristbjorg E. Vocabulary Development Through Language Awareness. P-H.
Oirschot, Anton van. Het Stoelenboek. Helmond.
Ol'dal, G. I. Russko-Vengerskii Slovar (Pub. by Gosizdat Inostr Natsional Slovarei). Four Continent.
Ol'Dal, G. I., et al. Karmannyi Vengersko-Russkii Slovar (Pub. by GINS). Four Continent.
Olev, Kulno. English-Estonian-Russian Maritime Dictionary (Pub. by Collets). State Mutual Bk.
--Maritime Dictionary (Pub. by Collets). State Mutual Bk.
Olgin, Joseph. Illustrated Football Dictionary for Young People. Harvey.
Oli, G. C., jt. ed. see Devoto, G.
Oli, Giancarlo, jt. auth. see Devoto, Giacomo.
Oliphant, Robert. Harley Latin-Old English Glossary. Mouton.
Olivares, Dennis A. The Spelling Helper Dictionary. Berdell, Dorothy K., ed. Denco Intl.
Oliver, H. J., jt. auth. see Law, J.
Olivera. Diccionario de economia y cooperativismo. Albatros.
Olivera, J. Diccionario de economia y cooperativismo. Hachette-Jeunesse.
Olivetti. Diccionario de Informatica Ingles-Espanol: Edicion Corregida. Paraninfo.
--Diccionario de Informatica Ingles-Espanol. Paraninfo.
Olmi, Andre & July, Fortune. Lexique du Calcul Economique & de l'econometrie. E. M. E.
Olney, Ross R. Illustrated Auto Racing Dictionary for Young People. Harvey.
--Illustrated Auto Racing Dictionary for Young People. P-H.
Olson, Wilson W. The Fern Dictionary. LA Intl Fern.

Olton, Roy, jt. auth. see Plano, Jack C.

Onatskyj, E. Vocabolario ucraino-italiano. Ist Univers Orient.

Onega, Pedro L., ed. Diccionario de la Vida Sexual. Distein.

Onieva. Diccionario Multiple: Nueve Diccionarios en un Solo Volumen. Paraninfo.

Onieva, Antonio J. Dicciqnario multiple: Nueve diccionarios en un volumen. Paraninfo.

Onieva, J. A. Diccionario Multiple. Paraninfo.

Onillon, Rene, jt. auth. see Verrier, A. J.

Onions, Charles T., et al, eds. Oxford Dictionary of English Etymology. Oxford U Pr.

Onofrio, Jean B. Essai d'un Glossaire des Patois de Lyonnais, Forez & Beaujolais. Horvath.

--Glossaire de Patois: Lyonnais, Forez & Beaujolais. Horvath.

Oousel, Raymond, jt. auth. see De Vogue, Melchior.

Opie, Iona & Opie, Peter, eds. Oxford Dictionary of Nursery Rhymes. Oxford U Pr.

Opie, Peter, jt. ed. see Opie, Iona.

Oppenheim, A. Leo, ed. The Assyrian Dictionary of the Oriental Institute of the University of Chicago. Oriental Inst.

--The Assyrian Dictionary of the Oriental Institute of the University of Chicago. Oriental Inst.

Oppenheim, A. Leo & Reiner, Erica, eds. Assyrian Dictionary of the Oriental Institute of the University of Chicago. Incl. Vol. 1, A, Pt. 2; Vol. 3, D; Vol. 4, E; Vol. 7, I-J; Vol. 9, L; Vol. 10, M, Pts 1 & 2; Vol. 16, S. Oriental Inst.

--The Assyrian Dictionary of the Oriental Institute of the University of Chicago. Oriental Inst.

Oppenheim, A. Leo, et al, eds. The Assyrian Dictionary of the Oriental Institute of the University of Chicago. Oriental Inst.

Opperman, Alfred. Dictionary of Electronics (K G Saur). Gale.

Oppermann, A. Woerterbuch der Datenverarbeitung. French & Eur.

--Woerterbuch der Modernen Technik. French & Eur.

Oppermann, Alfred. Dictionary of Dataprocessing. French & Eur.

--Dictionary of Modern Engineering. French & Eur.

--Dictionary of Modern Engineering. French & Eur.

--Woerterbuch Kybernetik. French & Eur.

Oppermann, Alfred, ed. Dictionary of Modern Engineering. Incl. Vol. 1. English-German; Vol. 2. German-English. Pub. by K G Saur). Gale.

Oram, R. B., jt. auth. see Course, A. G.

Oran, Daniel. Oran's Dictionary of the Law. West Pub.

--Oran's Dictionary of the Law. West Pub.

Oran, Daniel & Shafritz, Jay M. The MBA's Dictionary. P-H.

Orchin, Milton, et al. The Vocabulary of Organic Chemistry (Pub. by Wiley-Interscience). Wiley.

Ordang, Laurence. The Bantam Medical Dictionary. Bantam.

Ordman. The New Zealand Dictionary (Pub. by Heinemann Pubs New Zealand). Intl Schol Bk Serv.

Ordono, Cesar Macazaga see Macazaga Ordono, Cesar.

O'Reilly, Edward. An Irish-English Dictionary. Gordon Pr.

Orellana, E. Diccionario ingles-espanol de las ciencias de la tierra. Interciencia.

Orellana, Marina. Glosario internacional: Ingles-espanol. Universitaria.

Orlandi, Giuseppe. Dizionario italiano-inglese e inglese-italiano: Edizione minore. Signorelli C.

Orlando, jt. auth. see Meyer.

Orlando, S., jt. auth. see Meyer, A.

Orlando-Meyer, Salvatore. Technisches Woerterbuch. Brandstetter.

--Technisches Woerterbuch. Brandstetter.

--Technisches Woerterbuch (Pub. by Brandstetter). French & Eur.

--Technisches Woerterbuch (Pub. by Brandstetter). French & Eur.

Orlov, F. M. Kratkii Veterinarnyi Slovar Klinicheskikh Terminov (Pub. by Khozizdat). Four Continent.

Ormond, Richard & Rogers, Malcolm. Dictionary of British Portraiture: Vol. 1, the Middle Ages to the Early Georgian; Historical Figures Born Before 1700. Davies, Adriana, ed. Oxford U Pr.

--Dictionary of British Portraiture: Vol. 2, the Later Georgians to the Early Victorians; Historical Figures Born Between 1700 & 1800. Kilmurray, Elaine, ed. Oxford U Pr.

Ormond, Richard & Rogers, Malcolm, eds. Dictionary of British Portraiture. Oxford U Pr.

Ornato, Monique. Dictionnaire des Charges, Emplois & Metiers Relevant des Institutions. CNRS.

--Dictionnaires des Charges, Emplois & Metiers XIVe. & XVe. Siecles: Relevant des Institutions Monarchiques en France. CNRS.

Orne, Jerrold. Language of the Foreign Book Trade: Abbreviations, Terms, Phrases. ALA.

O'Rourke, Joseph, jt. auth. see Dale, Edgar.

O'Rourke, Terrence J. A Basic Vocabulary of American Sign Language for Parents & Children. Natl Assn Deaf.

Orozco, C. R. Spanish-English, English-Spanish Commercial Dictionary. Pergamon.

Orschel, H. Langenscheidts Taschenwoerterbuecher Russisch-Deutsch. Langenscheidt.

Orschel, H., jt. auth. see Blattner, Karl.

Orschel, H. see Blattner, Karl.

Orsman, H. W., ed. Heinemann New Zealand Dictionary. Heinemann Ed Bks.

--Heinemann New Zealand Dictionary. Heinemann Ed.

Orszagh. Hungarian Deluxe Dictionary: English-Hungarian. Vanous.

--Hungarian Deluxe Dictionary: Hungarian-English. Vanous.

Orszagh, I. Pocket English-Hungarian Dictionary (Pub. by Collet's). State Mutual Bk.

--Pocket Hungarian-English Dictionary (Pub. by Collet's). State Mutual Bk.

Orszagh, L. English-Hungarian Dictionary. Saphrograph.

--Hungarian-English Dictionary. Saphrograph.

--Hungarian-English, English-Hungarian Concise Dictionary (1976-79) Heinman.

Orszagh, L., ed. Magyar-Angol Szotar, Hungarian-English Dictionary. Saphrograph.

Orszagh, Laszlo. Hungarian Concise Dictionary: English-Hungarian. Vanous.

--Hungarian Concise Dictionary: Hungarian-English. Vanous.

--Hungarian-English: English Hungarian Dictionary. Heinman.

--Hungarian Pocket Dictionary: Hungarian-English. Vanous.

Orszagh, Laszlo, ed. English-Hungarian Dictionary. Intl Pubns Serv.

Orszagh, V. A Concise English-Hungarian Dictionary (Pub. by Collet's). State Mutual Bk.

--A Concise Hungarian-English Dictionary (Pub. by Collet's). State Mutual Bk.

--English-Hungarian Dictionary (Pub. by Collet's). State Mutual Bk.

--Hungarian-English Dictionary (Pub. by Collet's). State Mutual Bk.

Orszagn, L. Angol-Magyar Szotar English-Hungarian Dictionary. Saphrograph.

Ortega Cavero, David. Diccionario Portugues-Espanol, Espanol-Portugues. French & Eur.

Ortega Cavero, David & Da Conceica, Julio. Diccionario portugues-espanol, espanol-portugues. Sopena.

Ortega Garcia, Luiz Miguel. Diccionario Tecnico-Comercial y Profesional de Automocion. Tecnipublicaciones.

Ortencio, B. W. Dicionario do Brasil Central. Edit Atica.

Ortiz De Burgos, Jose. Diccionario Manual Italiano-Espanol, Spagnuolo-Italiano. French & Eur.

Ortiz Oderigo. Diccionario del jazz. Ricordi.

Orts, J. C., et al. Breve Diccionario Espanol-Ruso: Ruso-Espanol de Terminos Cientificos & Tecnicos. French & Eur.

Ortutay, Gyula, ed. Magyar Neprajzi Lexikon. Akademiai Kiado.

Orudzhev, A. Azerbaidzhansko-Russkii Frazeogicheskii (Idiomaticheskii) Slovar (Pub. by Elm). Four Continent.

Osborne, Charles. The Dictionary of the Opera. S&S.

Osborne, Harold, ed. The Oxford Companion to Twentieth-Century Art. Oxford U Pr.

Osenton, J. Fachwoerterbuch der Luftfahrt. Oldenbourg Verlag.

Osenton, J., jt. auth. see Dorian, A.

Osicka, V. & Poldauf, I., eds. English-Czech Dictionary (Pub. by Collet's). State Mutual Bk.

Osipov, M. I. Kratkii Taisko-Russkii Slovar (Pub. by LGU). Four Continent.

Osler, Robert W., jt. auth. see Green, Thomas E.

Osmowej, M. N. Polish-Russian Dictionary of Economics. French & Eur.

Ostapenko. Dictionnaire Francais-Russe Militaire. Mir.

Osterberg, Richard F. & Smith, Betty. Silver Flatware Dictionary. A S Barnes.

Osteroth, Dieter & Von Baeckmann, Walter G. Chemisch-Technisches Lexikon. Springer-Verlag.

Osterreichisches Linguistisches Programm. Wortbildung Diachron, Synchron. Panagl, Oswald, ed. Inst Verg Sprach.

Ostrowski, Roza & Trojanwska, Izabela. Bedekr Kaszubski. Wydawn.

O'Sullivan, James N., ed. Lexicon to Achilles Tatius. De Gruyter.

Otero, Anibal. Vocabulario de San Jorge de Piquin. Univers Santiago.

Othon, jt. auth. see Plano.

O'Toole, Thomas, tr. see Kalck, Pierre.

O'Toole, Thomas E. Historical Dictionary of Guinea: Republic of Guinea-Conakry. Scarecrow.

Ott, A. Dictionnaire des Sciences Politiques et Sociales. Migne, J. P., ed. Caratzas Pub Co.

Ott, Hans, jt. auth. see Koeck, Peter.

Ottenheimer. New Rhyming Dictionary of One & Two Syllable Rhymes (BN). B&N NY.

Ottenheimer. ed. German-English, English-German Dictionary (BN). B&N NY.

Otto, Eberhard, jt. auth. see Helck, Wolfgang.

Otto, Norbert & Wojtecki, Dieter. Glossar zur Fruehmittelalterlichen Geschichte im Oestlichen Europa. Buch Vertrieb.

--Glossar zur Fruehmittelalterlichen Geschichte im Oestlichen Europa: Lfg 7, Baioariae Marcha-Behin Redaktion. Buch Vertrieb.

Ottokar, Peter. Diccionario Rioduero: Quimica. Arroyo Marcos, Gloria, tr. Catolica Edit.

--Diccionario Rioduero: Quimica. French & Eur.

Oudin, Bernard. Dizionario degli architetti. ISEDI.

Ouseg, H. L. Twenty-One Language Dictionary: International Dictionary. Philos Lib.

Oweida, A. M. The New Medical-Pharmaceutical Dictionary. French & Eur.

Owen, James J., jt. auth. see Byers, John R., Jr.

Owen, William B. & Goodspeed, Edgar J. Homeric Vocabularies: Greek & English Word-Lists for the Study of Homer. U of Okla Pr.

Oyeregui, Buenaventura de. Diccionario Vasco-Castellano, Castellano-Vasco De Voces Comunes a Dos O Mas Dialectos Del Euskera. French & Eur.

Ozhegov. Diccionario de lengua rusa. Pueblos Unidos.

Ozhegov, S. I. Slovar Russkogo Iazyka (Pub. by Russkii Iazyk). Four Continent.

Ozuna, T., jt. auth. see Jover Peralta, A.

P

Paardekooper, Petrus C. ABN-Uitspraakgids. Heideland-Orbis.

Paasch, Henri. Dictionnaire Anglais-Francais Des Termes & Locutions Maritimes. Maritimes Outre mer.

--Dictionnaire Anglais-Francais et Francais-Anglais des Termes et Locutions Maritimes. French & Eur.

Pabon, Jose M. Vox-Diccionario Manual Griego-Espanol. French & Eur.

Pabon, Jose M. & Fernandez Galiano, M. Diccionario Manual Griego-Espanol. Biblograf SP.

Pabst, Martin. Technologisches Woerterbuch Franzoisisch. Girardet.

--Technologisches Woerterbuch Franzoisisch (Pub. by Verlag W. Girardet). French & Eur.

Pacheco, M. Economic Terminology: English-Spanish. Hueber.

Pacheco Moreno, Miguel. Economic Terminology. Hueber.

Pacheo, Miguel Moreno see Moreno Pacheo, Miguel.

Padelford, Frederick M. Old English Musical Terms. Longwood Pr.

Padilla, Francisco. Bilingual Dictionary of Anglicismos, Barbarismos, Pachuquismos y Otras Locuciones En el Barrio. Padilla.

Padovani, G. & Silvestri, R. Dictionnaire Bilingue Larousse, Francais-Italien et Italien-Francais. Larousse.

Padovani, Giuseppe & Silvestri, Richard. Dictionnaire Bilingue Apollo Francais-Italien. Larousse.

Paenson, I. Manual of the Terminology of Public International Law & International Organizations. Kluwer Academic.

Paenson, Isaac. Systematic Glossary of the Terminology of Statistical Methods: English, French, Spanish, Russian. Pergamon.

Paganini, A. Vocabolario domestico genovese-italiano. Forni.

Paganini, Angelo. Vocabolario Domestico Genovese-Italiano. Forni.

Pagano, Christian, jt. auth. see Fages, Jean B.

Pagano, Christian, jt. auth. see Fages, Jean Baptiste.

Page, A. A Dictionary of Photographic Terms. Heinman.

Page, Dominique. Petit Dictionnaire de Droit Quebecois & Canadien. Fides.

Page, G. T., jt. ed. see Johannsen, H.

Page, G. Terry, jt. auth. see Johannsen, Hano.

Page, R. Le see O'Dwyer, R. & Le Page, R.

Pahlitzsch, G. Woerterbucher der Fertigungstechnik: Bd 1, Schmieden-Freiformschmieden & Gesenkschmieden. Girardet.

--Woerterbucher der Fertigungstechnik Deutsch-Englisch-Franzoesisch: Bd 2, Schleifen Oberflaechenrauheit. Girardet.

--Woerterbucher der Fertigungstechnik Deutsch-Englisch-Franzoesisch: Bd 3, Blechbearbeitung. Girardet.

--Woerterbucher der Fertigungstechnik Deutsch-Englisch-Franzoesisch: Bd 4, Grundbegriffe des Spanens. Girardet.

--Woerterbucher der Fertigungstechnik Deutsch-Englisch-Franzoesisch: Bd 5, Kaltfliesspressen & Kaltstauchen. Girardet.

--Woerterbucher der Fertigungstechnik Deutsch-Englisch-Franzoesisch: Bd 6, Hobeln, Stassen, Raeumen, Drehen. Girardet.

--Woerterbucher der Fertigungstechnik Deutsch-Englisch-Franzoesisch: Bd 7, Bohren, Senken, Reiben, Gewindeschneiden. Girardet.
--Woerterbucher der Fertigungstechnik Daenisch-Norwegisch-Schwedisch-Finnisch: Bd 1N, Schmieden-Freiformschmeiden & Gesenkschmieden. Girardet.
--Woerterbucher der Fertigungstechnik Deutsch-Spanisch-Italienisch-Portugiesisch: Bd 1R, Schmieden-Freiformschmeiden & Gesenkschmieden. Girardet.
Paikeday, Thomas. Compact Dictionary of Canadian English. HRW.
Paikeday, Thomas M., ed. see New York Times.
Painter, James A., jt. ed. see Parrish, Stephen M.
Pakistani. English-Urdu Dictionary. Kazi Pubns.
Palacios. Diccionario de la legislacion de seguros. Rev. Mex. de Seguros.
Palay, Simin. Dictionnaire du Bernais & du Gascon Modernes. CNRS.
Palay, Simon. Dictionnaire du Bearnais & du Gascon Modernes. CNRS.
Palazzi, F. Novissimo Dizionario della Lingua Italiana. Folena, G., ed. French & Eur.
Palermo, Antonio & Palermo, Carlo. Dizionario giuridico del lavoro e delle assicurazioni sociali. La Tribuna.
Palermo, Carlo, jt. auth. see Palermo, Antonio.
Palevskaia, M. F. Materialy Frazeologicheskogo Slovaria Russkogo Iazka XVIII Veka (Pub. by Shtiintsa). Four Continent.
Palgrave, Robert H. Dictionary of Political Economy. Gale.
Pallares, Eduardo. Diccionario de Derecho Procesal Civil. Porrua.
--Diccionario de Derecho Procesal Civil. French & Eur.
--Diccionario Teorico y Practico del Juicio de Amparo. French & Eur.
--Dixcionario de Filosofia. French & Eur.
Pallas, Peter S. Linguarum Totius Orbis Vocabularia Comparativa. Buske.
--Linquarum Totius Orbis Vocabularia Comparativa (Pub. by Helmut Buske Verlag Hamburg). Benjamins North Am.
--Linquarum Totius Orbis Vocabularia Comparativa (Pub. by Helmut Buske Verlag Hamburg). Benjamins North Am.
Pallegoix, Jean-Baptiste. Dictionarium Linguae Thai Slve Slamensis Interpretatione Latina, Gallica & Anglica. Gregg.
Pallini, L. Dizionario sintetico da tavolo. Vallardi F.
Pallotta, Gino. Dizionario politico e parlamentare. Newton Compton.
--Dizionario Politico e Parlamentare Italiano. Newton Compton.
--Dizionario Storico Della Mafia. Newton Compton.
Palm, Goran. Konsten Att Veta Bast Fran ABBA til Ovre Slummen. Norstedt Soner.
Palmer. Diccionario de historia moderna. Labor SA.
Palmer, A. Smythe, ed. see Trench, Richard C.
Palmer, Abram. Folk-Etymology: A Dictionary of Verbal Corruptions or Words Perverted in Form. Haskell.
Palmer, Abram S. Folk-Etymology, a Dictionary of Verbal Corruptions or Words Perverted in Form or Meaning, by False Derivation or Mistaken Analogy. Greenwood.
Palmer, Alan. Facts on File Dictionary of Twentieth Century History. Facts on File.
--The Penguin Dictionary of Twentieth Century History: Nineteen Hundred to Nineteen Seventy-Eight. Penguin.
Palmer, Alan W. Dictionary of Modern History. Penguin.
Palmer, Joseph, compiled by. Jane's Dictionary of Naval Terms. Hippocrene Bks.
Palmer, Susan R., ed. Petroleum Industry Glossary. Inst Energy.
Palmer, Susan Reeves, ed. Petroleum Industry Glossary Handbook. Inst Energy.
Palmieri, G. Giuseppe. Dizionario di terminologia medica. Vallardi F.
Palomino, Rodolfo Cerron see Cerron-Palomino, Rodolfo.
Paltorp, Adam S., jt. auth. see Linder, Bernhard.
Pan American Institute of Geography & History. Glosario de Terminos Mareograficos. Instituto Panamericano.
Panagl, Oswald, ed. see Osterreichisches Linguistisches Programm.
Panassie, Hugues & Gautier. Dictionnaire du Jazz. Albin Michel.
Panassie, Hugues & Gautier, Madeleine. Dictionnaire du Jazz. French & Eur.
Pandit, Sri M., ed. see Aurobindo, Sri.
Pando, J. L. Diccionario maritimo. Dossat.
Pandosy, Marie C. Grammar & Dictionary of the Yakama Language. AMS Pr.
Paneth, Donald. News Dictionary 1980. Facts on File.
Paneth, Donald, ed. News Dictionary Nineteen Seventy-Eight. Facts on File.
Panganiban. Concise English-Tagalog Dictionary. Iaconi.
Panganiban, J. Villar. Concise English-Tagalog Dictionary. C E Tuttle.
Panganiban, Jose Villa see Villa Panganiban, Jose.
Pangle, Mary A., jt. auth. see Forte, Imogene.
Paniagua, J. R. Vocabulario Basico de la Arquitectura. French & Eur.
Panoff & Perrin. Dizionario di etnologia. Newton-Compton.
Panoff, Michel & Perrin, Michel. Dictionnaire de l'ethnologie. Payot.
Panovf, Irina. Dictionar englez-roman. Editura Stiintificia.
Panwolf, Wilhelm. Kleines Weinlexikon. Goldmann.
Panzini, Alfredo, et al. Dizionario moderno. Hoepli.
Paoli, Bruno A. Dizionario moderno italiano-francese e francese-italiano. Edn Scol Mond.
Paolo, Marchi G. Concordanze verghiane. Fiorini.
Papahagi, Tache. Mic Dictionar Folkloric: Spicuiri Folklorice si Etnografice Comparate. Minerva Yugo.
Papa-Sotir, Mihai. Dictionar Poliglot de Industrie Alimentara. Editura Stiintifica.
Paperno, V. A., jt. auth. see Nakhimovsky, A. D.
Papi, Giuseppe U. Dizionario di economia. UTET.
Papias. Vocabularium. Bottega d'Erasmo.
Papias, Gramarian. Papiae Elementarium. De Angelis, V., ed. Cisalpino.
Papini, P., jt. auth. see Maranesi, Ernesto.
Papinot, E. Historical & Geographical Dictionary of Japan. C E Tuttle.
Papok, K. K. & Ragozin, N. A. Tekhnicheskii Slovar Spravochnik Po Toplivu & Maslam (Pub. by Gostoptekhizdat). Four Continent.
--Tekhnicheskii Slovar Spravochnik po Toplivu i Maslam (Pub. by Gostoptekhizda r). Four Continent.
Pappalardo, Armando. Dizionario di scienze occulte. Cisalpino.
Parada, Alejandro Gomez De see Gomez de Parada, Alejandro.
Parashkevov, Boris, et al. Bulgarialais-Suomalainen Sanakirja. Gaudeamus.
Pardel-Lans, Humbert, jt. auth. see Michel, Raoul.
Paredes, Luis. Diccionario de Sinonimos, Antonimos & Ideas Afines. Gabriela Mistral.
Parenti, Francesco. Dizionario ragionato di psicologia individuale. Cortina M.
Parenti, U. Dizionario di zoologia: A-L. Ist Geo Agostini.
--Dizionario di zoologia: M-Z. Ist Geo Agostino.
Parenti, Umberto. Diccionario De Zoologia. French & Eur.
--Dictionnaire de Zoologie: Vol. 1, A-J. Atlas.
--Dictionnaire de Zoologie: Vol. 2, K-Z. Atlas.
Parfaict, Claude. Dictionnaire des Theatres de Paris. Slatkine.
Paris, Edmund, jt. auth. see De Bonnefoux, Pierre M.
Paris, Pierre. Dictionnaire des Antiquites Grecques. Boccard.
--Lexique Des Antiquites Grecques. French & Eur.
Park, Marinell & Weber, Nancy. Diccionario Quechua San Martin. Ministerio de Educacion.
Park, Won C., ed. see Amstutz, G. C., et al.
Parke, Davis & Company. Medical Word Building. Van Nos Reinhold.
Parker, B., jt. ed. see Parker, G.
Parker, Bertha M. The New Golden Dictionary (Golden Pr). Western Pub.
Parker, G. & Parker, B., eds. Dictionary of the European Communities. Butterworth.
Parker, Gary J. Diccionario Polilectal del Quechua de Ancash. Centro Invest.
--Diccionario Quechua. Minist Ed Caracas.
Parker, James. Glossary of Terms Used in Heraldry. C E Tuttle.
Parker, John Henry. A Concise Glossary of Terms Used in Grecian, Roman, Italian, & Gothic Architecture. Longwood Pr.
Parker, K. Vocabulario de la Cronica Troyana. U de Salamanca.
Parker, Sybil P., ed see McGraw Hill.
Parkhurst. Greek & English Lexicon. AMG Pubs.
Parks, Anton. Anglicko-slovensk y lekarsky slovnik. Univerzita Komenskeho.
Parlagreco. Dizionario portoghese-italiano. Vallardi A.
Parlagreco, C. Dizionario Portoghese-Italiano, Italiano-Portoghese. French & Eur.
Parlier, Jaki, jt. auth. see Parlier, Jim.
Parlier, Jim & Parlier, Jaki. Managalasi Language: Managalasi Dictionary. Summer Inst Abor.
Parma, Cecilia de Bourbon see De Bourbon Parma, Cecilia.
Parnaso. Diccionario Sopena De Literatura. French & Eur.
Parnwell, E. Oxford Picture Dictionary of American English & Spanish. Iaconi.
Parnwell, E. C. English-Spanish picture dictionary. Fondo Educativo.
--Oxford Picture Dictionary of American English: English-Japanese Edition. Oxford U Pr.
--Oxford Picture Dictionary of American English: English-Japanese Edition. Oxford U Pr.
--Oxford Picture Dictionary of American English. Oxford U Pr.
Parnwell, E. C., jt. auth. see Hornby, A. S.
Parnwell, E. C., jt. ed. see Hornby, A. S.
Parnwell, E. C., jt. ed. see Hornby, Albert S.
Parrish, Carl, tr. see Tinctoris, Johannes.
Parrish, Stephen M. & Painter, James A., eds. Concordance to the Poems of W. B. Yeats. Cornell U Pr.
Parrish, Stephen M., jt. ed. see Koubourlis, Demetrius J.
Parrish, Stephen M., jt. ed. see Tyler, J. Allen.
Parsenow, Gunther. Fachwoerterbuch Fur Recht und Wirtschaft (Pub. by Carl Heymanns Verlag KG). French & Eur.
Parsons, C., jt. auth. see Wilson, John.
Parsons, Charles. Russian-English Dictionary of...(a,e,i,ya) tel' Words. Translation Research.
--Russian-English Dictionary of irovat' Verbs. Translation Research.
--Russian-English Dictionary of....ost' Words. Translation Research.
Partridge, A. C. Orthography in Shakespeare & Elizabethan Drama: A Study of Colloquial Contractions, Elision, Prosody, & Punctuation. U of Nebr Pr.
Partridge, E., ed. see Grose, Francis.
Partridge, Eric. A Dictionary of Catch Phrases. Stein & Day.
--A Dictionary of Cliches. Routledge & Kegan.
--Dictionary of Slang & Unconventional English. Macmillan.
--Smaller Slang Dictionary. Routledge & Kegan.
Paruit, Bernard. Illustrated Glossary of Process Equipment: Chinese-English-French Edition. Gulf Pub.
--Illustrated Glossary of Process Equipment: English-French-Spanish Edition. Gulf Pub.
Pascenkova, N. A., et al. Czechoslovakian-Russian Dictionary of Geology. French & Eur.
Paschall, Dorothy M. Vocabulary of Mental Aberration in Roman Comedy & Petronius. Kraus Repr.
Pascual, J. A., jt. auth. see Corominas, Joan.
Pascual, J. A., jt. auth. see Coromines i Vigneaux, Joan.
Pascual, Recuero. Diccionario Basico Latino-Espanol. Ameller Edic.
Pashchenko, N. A., et al. Kratkii Cheshsko-Russkii Geofizicheskii Slovar (Pub. by Glav. Red. Nauchn. Tekhn. Slovarei Fizmata). Four Continent.
Pasini, Frassoni F. Dizionario storico araldico dell'antico ducato di Ferrara. Forni.
Pasquali, Maurizio. Dizionario tascabile delle tecniche ambientale: Italiano, francese, inglese, tedesco. SAPIL.
Passebecq, Andre. L'argile pour votre Sante. Dangles.
Passeron, Rene. Lexikon des Surrealismus. French & Eur.
Passeron, Rene, ed. Lexikon des Surrealismus. Wissenschaftliche.
Pastor Petit, Domingo. Diccionario del espionaje. Plaza Janes.
Paternoster, Lewis M. & Frager, Ruth L. Three Dimensions of Vocabulary Growth. AMSCO Sch.
Paterson, John. The Pocket Dictionary of Wines. Newnes Bks.
Pathak, R. C. Concise English Hindi Dictionary. Auromere.
--Concise Hindi-English Dictionary. Auromere.
--Hindi English Dictionary. Auromere.
Pathak, R. C., ed. Hindi-English - English-Hindi Standard Illustrated Dictionary. Heinman.
Patit, Charles & Savage, William. Dictionnaire Classique Anglais-Francais. Hac.
Patkar, Madhukar M. History of Sanskrit Lexicography (Pub. by Munshiram Manoharlal India). Humanities.
Patockova, Vlasta. Technickoekonomicky Rusko-Cesky Slovnik. SNTL.
Paton, John. Knowledge Encyclopedia. Windward.
Patronato Juan de la Cierva. Diccionario ruso-espanol de la ciencia y de la tecnica. Dossat.
Patsis, C. Greek-English, English-Greek Dictionary. Heinman.
Patterson, A. M. German-English Dictionary for Chemists (Pub. by Wiley-Interscience). Wiley.
Patterson, J. G. Zola Dictionary. Gale.
--A Zola Dictionary. Gordon Pr.
Patterson, W. R. Learn French for English Speakers. Saphrograph.
Patterson, William R. Learn Spanish for English Speakers. MacAndrew, Ronald, ed. Saphrograph.
Paufique, Robert. Vocabulaire Espagnol par l'image. Bordas-Dunod.
Pauk, Walter. Vocabulary in Context: Getting the Precise Meaning. Jamestown Pubs.
Paul, H. Deutsches Woerterbuch Tuebingen. M Rosenberg.
Paul, Hermann. Deutsches Woerterbuch. Niemeyer.
--Deutsches Woerterbuch (Pub. by Max Niemeyer). French & Eur.
Pauliat, P. Dictionnaire russe-francais. Larousse.

Pauliat, Paul. Dictionnaire Bilingue Apollo. Larousse.

--Dictionnaire Francais-Russe. Larousse.

Paulik, Helmut. Lexikon der Ausbildungspraxis. French & Eur.

Paulik, Helmut, ed. Lexikon der Ausbildungspraxis. Verlag Mod Ind.

Paulik, Helmut, et al, eds. Lexikon der Ausbildungspraxis. Verlag Moderne Industrie.

Paulsen, G. Norsk-Tysk Ordbok. French & Eur.

Paulsen, Gerd. Norwegian-German Dictionary. Kunnskapsforlaget.

Paviere, Sydney. A Dictionary of British Sporting Painters (Pub. by A & C Black England). Humanities.

Pavlov, Ernst A. & Semenova, Olga I. Nemetsko-Russkii Slovar po Lesnomu Khoziaistvu. Russkii Iazyk.

Pavoncello, Nello. Elef Millim. Carucci.

--Mille Parole Fondamentali. Carucci.

Pawlow, E. A. & Semjonowa, O. I. Deutsch-Russisches Worterbuch der Forstund Holzwirtschaft. French & Eur.

Paxton, ed. Dictionary of the European Community. Macmillan.

Paxton, John. A Dictionary of the European Communities. Macmillan LOndon.

--A Dictionary of the European Communities. St Martin.

Paxton, John, ed. Dictionary of Abbreviations. Rowman.

--A Dictionary of the European Economic Community. Facts on File.

--Everyman's Dictionary of Abbreviations: With Supplement. Rowman.

Payarois, Francisco, jt. auth. see Grimal, Pierre.

Pay-Costa, M. Dictionnaire Pratique Mercure: Francais-Espagnol, Espagnol-Francais. French & Eur.

Pay Estrany, S. Diccionari de sinonims i antonims. Teide.

Payne, J. Barton. Hebrew Vocabularies. Baker Bk.

Payne, Lynette R. Created Fables for Vocabulary Growth: A Classroom Project. Vantage.

Payne Smith, J., ed. see Smith, R. Payne.

Paz Soldan Y Unanue, Pedro & Nunez, Estuardo. Diccionario de Peruanismos. Edns Peisa.

Pearce, D. W. The Dictionary of Modern Economics. Macmillan London.

--The Macmillan Dictionary of Modern Economics. Macmillan London.

Pearce, Evelyn. Pearce's Medical & Nursing Dictionary & Encyclopedia. Faber & Faber.

Pearson, P. D. & Johnson, D. D. Teaching Reading Vocabulary & Teaching Reading Comprehension (HoltC). HR&W.

Pearson, Roger. Dictionary of Anthropology. Krieger.

Peck, Michael A., jt. auth. see Ratcliff, Ronald E.

Pecorella, Giusto. Vocabolario numerico siciliano-italiano. Bietti.

Pecorini, Giorgio. Dizionario della scuola democratica. Emme.

Pederson, Lee A; see Haskell, Ann S.

Pedio, Tommaso. Dizionario dei patrioti lucani artefici ed oppositori (1700-1870) Vol. 1, A-C. Soc Bari.

--Dizionario dei patrioti lucani artefici ed oppositori (1700-1870) Vol. 2, D-I. Soc Bari.

Peek, H. Standaard Nederlands-Engels Technisch Woordenboek. Standaard Uitgeverij.

Peers, E. A. & Jose, V. Diccionario Cassell Espanol-Ingles, Ingles-Espanol. Salvat Editores.

--Diccionario Cassell Espanol-Ingles, Ingles-Espanol. Salvat Editores.

--Diccionario Cassell Espanol-Ingles, Ingles-Espanol. Salvat Editores.

--Diccionario Cassell Espanol-Ingles,Ingles-Espanol. Salvat Editores.

Peers, E. A. & Jose, V., eds. Diccionario Cassell Espanol-Ingles, Ingles Espanol. Salvat Editores.

Peers, Edgar A. Diccionario Cassell espanol-ingles, ingles-espanol: Tomo 1. Salvat Editores.

--Diccionario Cassell espanol-ingles, ingles-espanol: Tomo 2. Salvat Editores.

--Diccionario Cassell espanol-ingles, ingles-espanol: Tomo 3. Salvat Editores.

--Diccionario Cassell espanol-ingles, ingles-espanol: Tomo 4. Salvat Editores.

--Diccionario Cassell espanol-ingles, ingles-espanol: Tomo 5. Salvat Editores.

--Diccionario Cassell espanol-ingles, ingles-espanol: Tomo 6. Salvat Editores.

Peers, Edgar A. & Jose, Victor. Diccionario Cassell Espanol-Ingles, Ingles-Espanol. Salvat Editores.

Peers, Edgar A., ed. Cassell's Spanish Dictionary: Spanish-English, English-Spanish. Macmillan.

Peers, Edgar Allison. Diccionario Cassell espanol-ingles, ingles-espanol: Obra completa. Salvat Editores.

Peers, Edqan A., ed. see Cassell.

Pegler, Martin M. Dictionary of Interior Design. Fairchild.

Pegna, Vera. Dizionario Italiano-Francese e Francese-Italiano di termini in uso in economia, borsa, finanza. Etas Libri.

Pei, Mario & Gaynor, Frank. Dictionary of Linguistics. Littlefield.

Pei, Mario & Gaynor, Frank, eds. Dictionary of Linguistics. Philos Lib.

Pei, Mario A. Glossary of Linguistic Terminology. Columbia U Pr.

Peisikov, L. S., et al. Kratkii Voennyi Persidsko-Russkii Slovar (Pub. by Voenizdat Inostr & Natsional' Slovarei). Four Continent.

Peixoto da Fonseca, Fernando V. Dictionnaire Bilingue Apollo Francais-Portugais. Larousse.

Pelayo, R. Garcia see Garcia-Pelayo, R.

Pelayo, Ramon G. see Garcia-Pelayo, Ramon.

Pellat, C. H., jt. auth. see Chouemi, M.

Pellegrini, G., jt. auth. see Migliorini, Bruno.

Pelletier, Andre. Lexique d'antiquites Romaines. Colin.

Peltier, A. C. Dictionnaire Universel et Complet des Conciles. Migne, J. P., ed. Caratzas Pub Co.

Pena, Aurelio. Diccionario ingles-espanol y espanol-ingles. Bibliografica.

Penalosa, Joaquin Antonio. Vocabulario & Refranero Religioso de Mexico. Jus.

Pennak, Robert W. Collegiate Dictionary of Zoology (Pub. by Wiley-Interscience). Wiley.

Pennance, F. G., jt. auth. see Seldon, Arthur.

Pennanee, F. G., jt. tr. see Seldon, Arthur.

Pennec, Marie F. le see Le Pennec, Marie F.

Penrice, John. Dictionary & Glossary of the Koran. Intl Bk Ctr.

--A Dictionary & Glossary of the Koran (Pub. by Curzon Pr England). Apt Bks.

--Dictionary & Glossary of the Koran. Intl Bk Ctr.

--Dictionary & Glossary of the Koran, with Copious Grammatical References & Explanations. Biblo.

--A Dictionary & Glossary of the Koran with Grammatical References & Explanations. Gordon Pr.

Penrod, D. A., jt. auth. see Hanson, D. P.

Pensinger, Brenda. Diccionario Mixteco del Este De Jamiltepec. Summer Inst Ling.

Pepe, Mario, jt. auth. see Grassi, Luigi.

Pepper, W. H. Diccionario de terminos periodisticos y graficos. Sudamer.

Peppin, Brigid. Book Illustrators of the Twentieth Century. Arco.

Peralta & Cederholm. Svensk-Spansk Affaersordlista. Esselte Studium.

Peraux, Henry. Diccionario general de acustica y electroacustica. Paraninfo.

Percy Badger, George. An English-Arabic Lexicon. Intl Bk Ctr.

Pereira, jt. auth. see Richardson.

Pereira, Maria S., jt. ed. see Pereira, Milton S.

Pereira, Milton S. & Pereira, Maria S., eds. Harrap's Modern Portuguese & English Dictionary. Harrap.

Perello, Jorge. Lexicon de Comunicologia. Augusta SA.

--Lexicon de Comunicologia: Diccinario para Audiologos, Audioprotesistas, Foniatras, Logopedas, Profesores De Sordos y Psicolinguistas. French & Eur.

Perevod, A. S., jt. auth. see Stamp, L.

Perez, J. & Alsina, R. Diccionario de vinos espanoles. Teide.

Perez Caballero, Arelio. Diccionario juridico peruano. Mejia.

Perez Calvo, Carlos E. Diccionario Ilustrado de Arquitectura. Plaza Janes.

Perez Cuadrado, Cosme. Diccionario General de Sinonimos & Antonimos. Coculsa.

Perez Rioja, J. A. Diccionario de simbolos y mitos: Las ciencias y las artes en su expresion figurada. Tecnos SA.

Perez Rioja, Jose A. Diccionario de Simbolos y Mitos: Las Ciencias y las Artes en Su Expresion Figurada. French & Eur.

Perez-Rioja, Jose A. Diccionario Literario Universal. Tecnos SA.

Perez Y Sabido, J., jt. auth. see Howell, G.

Peri, A. Vocabolario cremonese-italiano. Forni.

Periaux. Dictionnaire Indicateur des Rues & Places. Lafitte Repr.

Perkins, G., jt. auth. see Drummond, David A.

Perlemuter, L. Dictionnaire Pratique De Therapeutique Medicale, 3. Obraska, P., ed. French & Eur.

Perlemuter, Leon & Cenac, Arnaud. Dictionnaire Pratique de Medecine Clinique. Masson.

--Dictionnaire Pratique De Medecine Clinique. French & Eur.

Perlemuter, Leon & Obraska, Paul. Dictionnaire Pratique de Theraeutique Medicale. Masson.

Perlemuter, Leon, jt. auth. see Touitou, Yvan.

Permartin, Julio, ed. Diccionario del vino de Jerez. Jerez Industrial.

Pernety, Antoine J. Le Dictionnaire Mytho-Hermetique. Retz.

--Le Dictionnaire Mytho-Hermetique. French & Eur.

--Dictionnaire Mythohermetique. Denoel.

Pernety, Antoine Joseph. Dictionnaire Portatif de Peinture, Sculpture & Gravure. Minkoff Repr.

Pernin, A., jt. auth. see Comte, R.

Pernin, Andre, jt. auth. see Comte, Rene.

Pernot, Hubert. Dictionnaire Grec Moderne Francais. Garnier.

Peron. A Dictionary of Business Terms. Larousse.

Peron, Michel & Withnell, William. Dictionnaire des Affaires: Francais-Anglais. Larousse.

Peron, Michel, et al. Dictionnaire Francais-Anglais, Anglais-Francais des affaires. Larousse.

--Dictionnaire francais-anglais, anglais-francais des affaires: A French-English English-French Dictionary of Business Terms. Larousse.

Perona Sanchez, Jose D. El Vocabulario vital e irracional en Azorin. Consejo Superior.

Perreau & Langford. Concise French-American Dictionary of Figurative & Idiomatic Language. French & Eur.

Perrin, jt. auth. see Panoff.

Perrin, Michel, jt. auth. see Panoff, Michel.

Perrot, D. V. Swahili Dictionary. McKay.

Perry, Day & Wolfe, Josephine B., eds. Dictionary of Basic Words. Childrens.

Perry, F. E. A Dictionary of Banking (Pub. by Macdonald & Evans England). Intl Ideas.

Pertsch, Dietrich. Lateinisch-Deutsch. Langenscheidt.

Pertsch, E., jt. auth. see Menge, H.

Pertsch, E., rev. by see Menge, Hermann.

Pertsch, Erich. Langenscheidts Grosses Schulwoerterbuch Lateinisch-Deutsch. Langenscheidt.

--Langenscheidts Handwoerterbuch Lateinisch-Deutsch. Langenscheidt.

--Langenscheidts Schulwoerterbuecher Lateinisch-Deutsch. Langenscheidt.

Pertsch, Erich & Lange-Kowal, Ernst E. Langenscheidts Schulwoerterbuch Lateinisch-Deutsch. Langenscheidt.

Pertsch, Erich, compiled by. Lateinisch-Deutsch. Langenscheidt.

Perucca, Eligio. Dizionario d'ingegneria. UTET.

--Dizionario d'ingegneria. UTET.

--Dizionario d'ingegneria. UTET.

--Dizionario d'ingegneria. UTET.

--Dizionario d'ingegneria. UTET.

--Dizionario d'ingegneria. UTET.

--Dizionario d'ingegneria. UTET.

--Dizionario d'ingegneria. UTET.

--Dizionario d'ingegneria. UTET.

--Dizionario d'ingeneria. UTET.

Perugini, Angelo. Dizionario Italiano-Latino. Libr Ed Vat.

--Dizionario italiano-latino. Libr Ed Vat.

Perusse, Roland I. Historical Dictionary of Haiti. Scarecrow.

Pesonen, M., jt. auth. see Hurme, R.

Pesonen, Maritta, jt. auth. see Hurme, Raija.

Pesonen, Niilo. Laaketieteen Sanairja. Werner Soderstrom.

Pesonen, Pentti. Ranskalais-Suomalainen-Sanakirja. Otava.

Pessis-Pasternak, Guitta. Dictionnaire de l'audio-Visual. Flammarion.

--Dictionnaire de l'audio-Visual: Francais-Anglais. Flammarion.

--Dictionnaire de l'Audio-Visuel: Francais-Anglais, Anglais-Francais. French & Eur.

Pessoneaux, Emile. Dictionnaire Grec-Francais. French & Eur.

Pessonneaux, Emile. Dictionnaire Grec-Francais. Belin.

Peter, O. Herder-Lexikon Chemie. Herder.

--Herder-Lexikon Chemie (Pub. by Herder). French & Eur.

Peteraitis, Vilius. Lithuanian-English Dictionary. Shalom.

Peters, Jean, ed. The Bookman's Glossary. Bowker.

Peters, Uwe H. Woerterbuch der Psychiatrie und Medizinischen Psychologie. French & Eur.

--Woerterbuch der Tiefenpsychologie. Kindler.

Peters, V. P., jt. ed. see Gerwick, Ben C., Jr.

Petersein, G. T., jt. auth. see Jacob, U.

Peterson, Franklyn, jt. auth. see Kesselman-Turkel, Judi.

Petin, L. M. Dictionnaire Hagiographique. Migne, J. P., ed. Caratzas Pub Co.

Petinis, Lambros. Dictionar Grec-Roman. Editura Stiintifica.

Petit, Charles & Savage, William. Dictionnaire Classique Anglais-Francais et Francais-Anglais. French & Eur.

Petit, Henry, jt. auth. see Duffy, Charles.

Petit, J. L., et al. Thesaurus des Symboles Agrobioclimatiques, Geographiques & Techniques. Centre Informatique Develop.

Petit, Karl. Le Dictionnaire des Citations. Bout.

Petrenko, O. Anglo-Russkii Slovar Po Iadernym Vzryvam (Pub. by Voenizdat). Four Continent.

Petroni & Kenigsberg. Diccionario de urbanismo. Cesarini.

Petrov, V. S. & Tulin, S. A. Russian-Czechoslovakian Polytechnical Dictionary. French & Eur.

Pettijohn, F. J. & Potter, P. E. Atlas & Glossary of Primary Sedimentary Structures. Springer-Verlag.

Pettman, Charles. Africanderisms. Gale.

Pettoello, Pietro. Vocabolario per le favole de Fedro. Loescher.

Petzold, Armin. Silikatova Technika. Alfa-Vydavatel.

Pevesner, Nikolaus. Diccionario de Arquitectura. Alianza Ed.

Pevsner, N. Lexikon der Weltarchitektur. French & Eur.

Pevsner, Nikolaus, et al. Diccionario de arquitectura. Bustamante, Agustin, tr. Alianza Ed.
--Diccionario de Arquitectura. French & Eur.
--A Dictionary of Architecture. Overlook Pr.
Pevsner, Nikolaus, et al, eds. Lexikon der Weltarchitektur. Prestel-Verlag.
--Lexikon der Weltgeschichte. Englisch Verlag.
Pey. Pequeno Diccionario de Sinonimos. Edit Teide.
Pey, Santiago. Diccionario de Sinonimos, Ideas Afines & Contrarios (TEI). Lectorum Pubns.
Pey, Santiago & Calonja, Juan R. Pequeno Diccionario de Sinonimos, Ideas Afines & Contrarios (Pub. by Biblograf S. A., Barcelona). Harrap.
Pey, Santiago, jt. auth. see Ruiz Calonja, J.
Pey Estrany, Santiago. Diccionari De Sinonimos I Antonimos. French & Eur.
--Diccionari de sinonims i antonims: Edicio economica. Teide.
--Diccionario de Sinonimos Ideas Afines & Contrarios. Teide.
Pey Estrany, Santiago & Ruiz Calonja, J. Diccionario De Sinonimos Ideas Afines y Contrarios. French & Eur.
Peytard, Jean. Recherches sur la Prefixation en Francais Contemporain. Klincksieck.
Pfahlberg, B. Herder - Lexikon Politik (Pub. by Herder). French & Eur.
--Herder-Lexikon Politik. Herder.
Pfahlberg, Bernard, ed. Politik: Mit 1800 Stichwoertern. Herder.
Pfannkuch, Hans-Olaf. Elsevier's Dictionary of Hydrogeology. Elsevier.
Pfeffer, M. Kleines Woerterbuch Zur Arbeits und Sozialpolitik. Herder.
--Kleines Woerterbuch Zur Arbeits und Sozialpolitik (Pub. by Herder). French & Eur.
Pheby, J. A., ed. The Oxford-Duden Pictorial English Dictionary. Oxford U Pr.
Phelizon, Jean F. Lexique des Termes Economiques. Tech Vulgar.
Phelizon, Jean-Francois. Lexique des Termes Economiques. Tech Vulgar.
Philatelic Foundation. Philatelic Vocabulary in Five Languages. Philatelic Found.
Philbert, Christophe. Petit Lexique Somali-Francais. Klincksieck.
Phillips, Claude S. The African Political Dictionary. ABC-Clio.
Phillips, Louis. The Official Funnybones Flaky Dictionary. Wanderer Bks.
Phythian, B. A., ed. A Concise Dictionary of Correct English. Littlefield.
--Concise Dictionary of Correct English. Rowman.
--A Concise Dictionary of Foreign Expressions. B&N Imports.
Pianci, Santiago Collin De see Collin de Pianci, Santiago.
Piasek, Martin. Chinesisch-Deutsches Woerterbuch. Hueber.
--Chinesisch-Deutsches Woerterbuch (Pub. by Max Heuber). French & Eur.
Piat. Dictionnaire Francais-Langue. Ramoun.
--Dictionnaire Francais-Langue d'Oc. French & Eur.
Piat, L. Dictionnaire Francais-Occitanien. Berenguie.
Picard, R. French Dishes, Easy & Delicious. Saphrograph.
Picchi, F., jt. auth. see Bernabo, M.
Piccioni, M. Diccionario de alimentacion animal. Acribia.
Piccioni, Marcello. Dictionnaire des Aliments pour les Animaux. Maison Rustique.
--DIzionario degli alimenti per il bestiame. Edagricole.
Picciony, M., ed. Diccionario de Alimentacion Animal. French & Eur.
Picconi, Marcello. Dictionnaire des Aliments pour les Animaux. French & Eur.
Picerno, Vincent J. Dictionary of Musical Terms. Haskell.

Pichardo, Nicolas, ed. see Brache, Jose A.
Pick, Albert. Papiergeld-Lexikon. Mosaik Verlag.
Pickering, John. A Vocabulary; or, Collection of Words & Phrases, Which Have Been Supposed to Be Peculiar to the United States of America; to Which Is Prefixed an Essay on the Present State of the English Language in the United States. Bd. with A Letter to John Pickering on the Subject of His Vocabulary or Collection of Words & Phrases. Webster, Noah. B Franklin.
Picoche. La Lexicologie (Dist. by Continental Bk Co). Lib. Fernand Nathan.
Pidal, Ramon D. Menendez see Menendez Pidal, Ramon D.
Piernas, J. Vocabulario de Economia. Espasa Calpe.
Piero, Guelfi C. Dizionario araldico. Forni.
Pieron, Henri. Dizionario di psicologia. Canestrari, R., tr. La Nuova Italia.
--Vocabulaire de la psychologie. Pr Univ Fr.
--Vocabulaire de la Psychologie. PUF.
--Vocabulaire De la Psychologie. French & Eur.
Pieron, Henri, et al, trs. Lexicon Kapelusz: Psicologia. Kapelusz.
Pierrard, Pierre. Dictionnaire de la Troisieme Republique. Larousse.
--Dictionnaire des Prenoms & des Saints. Larousse.
Pierre, Jose. An Illustrated Dictionary of Pop Art. Barron.
--An Illustrated Dictionary of Surrealism. Barron.
Pierret, Albert & Basiaux. Vocabulaire, Phraseologie, Lecture, Informations. Wesmael-Charlier.
--Vocabulaire, Phraseologie, Lecture Mentale. Wesmael-Charlier.
Pierret, Albert, et al. Vocabulaire, Phraseologie, Lecture, Informations. Wesmael-Charlier.
Pierson, Raymond H. Guia de modismos espanoles. Natl Textbk.
Piesarskas, B. & Baravykas, V. Lithuanian-English, English-Lithuanian Dictionary. Heinman.
Piesarskas, B., et al. Lithuanian-English Dictionary (Pub. by Vilnius). Four Continent.
Pieterse, Liberius. English-Urdu Dictionary of Christian Terminology. Slomp, Jan, ed. Christian Study Centre.
Pietzschke, F., ed. Portuguese-English, English-Portuguese Illustrated Dictionary: The New Michaelis. Heinman.
Pietzschke, Fritz. Novo Michaelis, Dicionario Ilustrado. Mariotti, Wilson, ed. Edicoes Melhoramentos.
Pigatti Ranzoli, M., jt. auth. see Ranzoli, Cesare.
Pihkala, Juhani, jt. auth. see Pihkala, Liisa.
Pihkala, Liisa & Pihkala, Juhani. Englandtilais-Suomalainen Laboratorio- ja Prosessialan Sanasto. Otava.
Pilla, T. Ramalingam. Sailee Nihantu: Dictionary of Idioms & Phrases. DC Bks.
Pillai, C. Madhavan. Abhinava Malayala Nikhantu: New Malayalam Dictionary. DC Bks.
Pillai, T. R. English-Malayalam Dictionary. Chandrasekhara, M. S., ed. DC Bks.
Pillai, T. Ramalingam. English-English-Malayalam Dictionary. Krishna, N. V., rev. by. DC Bks.
--English-English-Malayalam Dictionary. Octavo, M. S., ed. DC Bks.
Pimentel, Jitschak. Woordenboek Hebreeuws-Nederlands. Strengholt.
--Woordenboek Hebreeuws-Nederlands. Strengholt.
Pina, Rafael de. Diccionario de Derecho. French & Eur.
Pina, Rafael de see De Pina, Rafael.
Pina Araujo, Avelino De see De Pina Araujo, Avelino.
Pinard, C. Dictionnaire des Objections Populaires contre le Dogme, la Morale, la Discipline et L'histoire de Eglise Catholique. Migne, J. P., ed. Caratzas Pub Co.

Pine, L. G. A Dictionary of Mottoes. Routledge & Kegan.
Pinedo Peydro, Felix-Jesus. Diccionario mimico espanol. Organ Ofic Adm.
Pineiro, J. Compendio de Dificultades de la Lengua Inglesa. Biblograf SP.
Pineiro, Jaime. Compendio de dificultades de la lengua inglesa. Fed Gremios.
Pinelli, Stefano. Piccolo Dizionario del Dialetto Bresciano. Grafo.
Pinguentini, Gianni. Nuovo dizionario del dialetto triestino. Nuova Cappelli.
Pink, M. Alderton. A Dictionary of Correct English. R West.
Pinkerton, Edward C. Word for Word. Verbatim.
Pinkevich, A. & Amelin, B. Diccionario Espanol-Ruso de le Prospeccion y Refinacion del Petroleo. Dobriansky, A. F., ed. French & Eur.
Pinkevich, A. A., et al. Ispansko-Russkii Slovar Po Dobyche i Pererabotke Nefti (Pub. by Lenizdat). Four Continent.
Pinloche, A. Dictionnaire Francais-Allemand, Deutsch-Franzosisch. French & Eur.
Pinloche, A. & Jolivet, A. Dictionnaire Bilingue Larousse, Francais-Alemand et Allemand-Francais. Larousse.
Pinney, Edward L., Jr. & Slipp, Samuel. Glossary of Group & Family Therapy. Brunner-Mazel.
Pinoche, Jacqueline. Le Vocabulaire Psychologique dans les Chroniques de Froissart, 1. Klincksieck.
Pinoche, Jolivet A. Dictionnaire Bilingue Apollo Francais-Allemand. Larousse.
Pinty, Jean-Jacques & Gaultier, Claude. Dictionnaire Pratique de Statistiques en Sciences Humaines. Delarge.
Pipics, Z. The Librarian's Practical Dictionary in Twenty-Two Languages (Pub. by Collet's). State Mutual Bk.
Pipics, Zoltan. Librarians Practical Dictionary in 22 Languages (Worterbuch Des Bibliothekars in 22 Sprachen (Pub by Verlag Dokumentation). Bowker.
Pipitone, Francesco. Dizionario fraseologico e grammaticale della lingua inglese. Galeati.
Pipkin, Bernard & Cummings, David. Environmental Geology: Practical Exercises. Star Pub CA.
Piprek, J. & Ippoldt, J. Grobworterbuch Polnisch-Deutsch. French & Eur.
Piprek, Jan & Ippoldt, Juliusz. Wielki Slownik Polsko-Niemiecki: Grosswoerterbuch Polnische-Deutsch. Wiedza Powszechna.
Piquette, Robert, et al. Dictionnaire des Mots Croises. Homme.
Piraux. Diccionario General de Acustica & Electroacustica. Paraninfo.
--Dictionnaire Francais-Anglais d'electro-technique et d'electronique. French & Eur.
Piraux, H. Dictionnaire des termes relatifs a electrotechnique, l'electronique et aux applications connexes. Eyrolles.
--Dizionario Inglese-Italiano dei Termini Relativi All'Elettronica: All'Elettrotecnica e Alle Applicazioni Connesse. French & Eur.
--French-Eng., Eng-French Dictionary of Electrotechnic Electronics & Allied Fields. Heinman.
Piraux, H., et al. Diccionario ingles-espanol de electrotecnia y electronica. ETA.
Piraux, Henri. Diccionario General De Acustica y Electro Acustica. French & Eur.
--Dictionnaire Allemand-Francais des Termes Relatifs a l'electrotechnique: L'electrotechnique & aux Applications Connexes. Eyrolles.
--Dictionnaire Allemand-Francais des Termes Relatifs a l'Electrorechnique, l'Electronique, et aux Applications Connexes. French & Eur.

--Dictionnaire Anglais-Francis des Termes Relatifs a L'electrotechnique: l'ectrotechnique & aux Applications Connexes. Eyrolles.
--Dictionnaire Francais-Anglais des Termes Relatifs a l'electronique: L'electronique & aux Applications Connexes. Eyrolles.
Piraux, Henry. Dizionario inglese-italiano dei termini relativi all'eiettrotecnica. Signorelli C.
Piriou-Vandamme, M., jt. auth. see Schuurmans, Stekhoven G.
Pirog, Zh. I., et al. Karmannyi Russko-Niderlandskii Slovar (Pub. by Russkii Iazyk). Four Continent.
Pirot, Z. I. Russko-Gollandskii Slovar (Pub. by GINS). Four Continent.
Pisano, Giorgio, jt. auth. see Brigato, Giovanni.
Pisarek, W. Slownik Jezyka Niby-Polskiego, Czyli Bledy Jezykowe (Pub. by Ossolineum). Four Continent.
Piscitelli, N. Dizionario di anatomia e fisiologia umana. Ist Geo Agostini.
Piscitelli, Nicola. Diccionario Atlas De Anatomia Humana. French & Eur.
Piskunova, I. A. Nemetsko-Russkii Geodezicheskii Slovar (Pub. by Nedra). Four Continent.
Pitkin, ed. Index to the Theological Dictionary to the New Testament. Eerdmans.
Pitman, Isaac. Pitman Dictionary of English & Shorthand. Pitman Learning.
Pitt, Valerie H., ed. The Penguin Dictionary of Physics. Penguin.
Pittano, Giuseppe. Dizionario elementare. Edipem.
--Dizionario elementare: Per la Scuola elementare. Edipem.
--Dizionario elementare: Per la Scuola elementare. Edipem.
--Dizionario latino-italiano e italiano-latino. Edn Scol Mond.
Plagman, Bernard K., jt. auth. see Leong-Hong, Belkis W.
Plaisance, George. Lexique Pedologique Trilingue. French & Eur.
Plaisance, Georges. Dictionnaire des Forets. G. Plaisance.
--Dictionnaire Des Forets. French & Eur.
--Lexique Pedologique Trilingue. CDU.
Plaja, Aurora D., prologue by. Diccionario Inicial de la Lengua Espanola. Biblo Sp.
Planells Cardona, Mariano. Diccionario de secretos de Ibiza. Obelisco.
Plano & Othon. Diccionario de relaciones internacionales. Limusa.
Plano, Jack C. Political Science Dictionary (HoltC). HR&W.
Plano, Jack C. & Greenberg, Milton. The American Political Dictionary. HR&W.
Plano, Jack C. & Olton, Roy. The International Relations Dictionary. ABC-Clio.
Plano, Jack C., jt. auth. see Rossi, Ernest E.
Plano, Jack C., et al. Political Science Directory (HIS). HR&W.
--The Dictionary of Political Analysis. ABC-Clio.
Plano, Jack C., jt. auth. see McCrea, Barbara P.
Planque, B. & Chabaud, N. La Pratique d'un Dictionnaire (Dist. by Continental Bk Co). Larousse.
Plans y De Gabriel Sanz De Bremond, Fructuoso. Diccionario Ortografico Mikron. French & Eur.
Plans Sanz de Bremond, Fructuoso. Diccionario Ingles-Espanol. Mayfe.
--Diccionario ortografico. Mayfe.
Plans Sanz De Bremond, Jose M. Diccionario Practico: Asesor De la Propiedad & Copropiedad Inmobiliaria. French & Eur.
Platts, John T. A Dictionary of Urdu Classical Hindi & English. Intl Pubns Serv.
--Dictionary of Urdu, Classical Hindi, & English. Oxford U Pr.
Playfair, A. S. The Pocket Medical Dictionary. Newnes Bks.
Pleasants, Jeanne V. Phonetic French Dictionary: Contrasting French-English Sounds. Playette Corp.

Plechl, Helmut, ed. see Graesse, Johann G.
Plessi, Giuseppe, jt. auth. see Cecchini, Norma.
Plisek, V., jt. auth. see Leskova, T.
Plomteux, Hugo. I Dialetti della Liguria Orientale Odierna. Patron.
Ploquin, Max. Dictionnaire de l'Enfantement. French & Eur.
Pluquet, F. A. Dictionnaire des Heresies des Erreurs et des Schismes. Migne, J. P., ed. Caratzas Pub Co.
Poblete, Carlos. Diccionario de la Musica. U. de Valparaiso.
Poblete Varas, Carlos. Diccionario de la musica. Universitarias Valparaiso.
Pochertsova, L. D., et al, eds. English-Russian Phrase Book. Four Continent.
Pochtar, Ricardo, tr. see Mounin, Georges.
Podhradsky, Gerhard. New Dictionary of the Liturgy. Alba.
Podiko, M. V. Russko-Moldavskii Slovar (Pub. by Kartia Moldoveniaske). Four Continent.
Podolskaia, N. V. Slovar Russkoi Onomasticheskoi Terminologii (Pub. by Nauka). Four Continent.
Podveska, M. L. & Balla, M. J. English-Ukrainian Dictionary (Pub. by Collet's). State Mutual Bk.
Podvesko, M. L., ed. English-Ukrainian Dictionary. Saphrograph.
--Ukrainian-English Dictionary. Saphrograph.
Podvesko, M. L., compiled by. Ukrainian-English, English-Ukrainian Dictionary. Heinman.
Poerwadarminta, W. Kamus Umum Bahasa Indonesia. P N Balai Pustaka.
Pognowski, Iwo. The New Polish-English Dictionary. Hippocrene Bks.
Pogonowski, Iwo. Concise Polish-English-English-Polish Dictionary. Hippocrene Bks.
--Dictionary, Polish-English, English-Polish: Contemporary Usage American & Polish. Hippocrene Bks.
--Dictionary Polish-English, English-Polish Slovnik. Hippocrene Bks.
--Practical Polish-English Dictionary: Polish-English; English-Polish. Hippocrene Bks.
Poidras, Henri. Critical & Documentary Dictionary of Violin Makers Old & Modern. Scholarly.
Poinso, Yves. Diccionario Practico De Psicopatologia. French & Eur.
Poinso, Yves, jt. auth. see Gori, Roland-Claude.
Poinsotte, J. P. Dictionnaire des Sigles Medicaux. French & Eur.
Poirier, Jean, jt. auth. see Dorion, Henri.
Poirion, Daniel. Lexique de Charles d'Orleans dans les Ballades. Droz.
Poitevin, F. Beer. Diccionario Medico. French & Eur.
Pokorny, Julius. Indogermanisches Etymologisches Woerterbuch (Pub. by Francke). French & Eur.
Pokorny, Julius, ed. see Walde, Alois.
Poldauf, I., ed. Czech-English Dictionary (Pub. by Collet's). State Mutual Bk.
--Czech-English, English Czech Dictionary. Heinman.
Poldauf, I., jt. ed. see Osicka, V.
Poldauf, J. Czech-English-Czech Dictionary. Vanous.
Poli, G. A., jt. auth. see Segatore, L.
Poli, Gianangelo, jt. auth. see Segatore, Luigi.
Pollak, Kurt. Knaurs Lexikon der Modernen Medizin (Pub. by Druckenmueller). French & Eur.
Pollard, H. L., jt. auth. see Miller, P. R.
Pollet, Gilbert, jt. auth. see Sleeman, J. H.
Pollet, R. Lexique de la photographie d'Amateur: Anglais-Francais Francais-Anglais. Maison Dictionnaire.
--Lexique du cinema d'Amateur: Anglais-Francais Francais-Anglais. Maison Dictionnaire.
Pollet, R. J. Lexique de termes techniques: Anglais-Francais & index Francais. Maison Dictionnaire.
Pollet, Ray J. Lexique de la Photographie d'amateur: Francais-Anglais. Lemeac.
--Lexique de Termes Techniques: Un Lexique Anglais-Francais. Lemeac.
--Lexique de Termes Techniques: Un Lexique Anglais-Francais. French & Eur.
Pollin, Alice M. & Smith, Philip H., eds. A Concordance to the Plays & Poems Federico Garcia Lorca. Cornell U Pr.
Pollmann, Friedrich. Macmillan Lensing New Basic Dictionary. Macmillan London.
Pollok, K., jt. auth. see Braun, M.
Pollok, K. see Blattner, Karl.
Poltoratzky, Marianna, jt. auth. see Wolkonsky, Catherine.
Pommier, Agatha-Marguerite & Guaspare, Blanche. Dictionnaire de Stenographie Duploye. Foucher.
Pompili, G. Glossario di medicina nucleare. Minerva Medica.
Pomponas, Giannes K. Lexiko tes Mykenaikes Hellenikes. Ekdoseis Filon.
Pong Kook Lee. Standard English-Korean Dictionary for Foreigners. Jones, B. J., ed. Hollym Intl.
Ponomareva, B. N., ed. Politicheskii Slovar (Pub. by Politizdat). Four Continent.
Pons. Global Woerterbuch: English-German, German-English. M Rosenberg.
Pons, Teofilo. Dizionario del dialetto valdese della Val Germanasca. Soc Studi Valdesi.
Pontalis, Jean-Baptiste see Laplanche, Jean.
Pontalis, Jean-Bertrand, jt. auth. see Laplanche, Jean.
Pontevideo, jt. auth. see Lysle.
Pontifical Institute of Mediaeval Studies, Toronto. Dictionary Catalog of the Library of the Pontifical Institute of Mediaeval Studies: First Supplement (Hall Library). G K Hall.
Pontifical Institute of Medieval Studies, Ontario. Dictionary Catalogue of the Library of the Pontifical Institute of Medieval Studies (Hall Library). G K Hall.
Ponting, Ken. A Dictionary of Dyes & Dyeing (Pub. by Bell & Hyman England). State Mutual Bk.
Pont Mestres, Magin. Politica & Politiqueria: Diccionario Para el Hombre de la Calle. Edns Acervo.
Pont Quer, Pio. Diccionario De Botanica. French & Eur.
Pooch, H. Fachwoerterbuch des Nachrichtenwese. Schiele & Schon.
--Fachwoerterbuch des Nachrichtenwesens (Pub. by Fachvlg. Schiele & Schoen). French & Eur.
Poole, Adrian, jt. auth. see Walsh, Dermot.
Poolman & Scott, Christopher. New Basic Dictionary. Macmillan London.
Poorter, Wim De see De Poorter, Wim.
Pope, Lillie. Learning Disabilities Glossary. Book-Lab.
Pope, Patricia. Dictionary of Sharks. Great Outdoors.
Popelar, Inge. Das Akademiewoerterbuch von 1694: Das Woerterubch des Honnete Homme? Niemeyer.
Popescu-Neveanu, Paul. Dictionar de psihologie. Albatros.
Popic, R., et al. Scientific Technological Dictionary. French & Eur.
Popovici, Calin. Dictionar de Astronomie Astronautica. Editura Stiintifica.
Porat. Diccionario de psiquiatria. Labor SA.
Poretskaia, R. E. Orfograficheskii Morskoi Slovar (Pub. by Voenizdat). Four Continent.
Porot, Antoine. Diccionario De Psiquiatria. French & Eur.
Porot, Antoine, ed. Manuel Alphabetique De Psychiatrie Clinique et Therapeutique. French & Eur.
Porro, Maurizio & Turroni, Giuseppe. Il Cinema Vuol Dire. Garzanti Edit.
Porta, jt. auth. see Introito.
Porter, Catherine, tr. see Ducrot, Oswald & Todorov, Tzvetan.
Porter, H., jt. ed. see Wortabet, J.
Porter, Harvey, jt. auth. see Wortabet, John.
Porter, Harvey, jt. ed. see Wortabet, William.
Porter, J. W. & Rolls, B. A., eds. Proteins in Human Nutrition. Acad Pr.
Posener, Georges. Dictionnaire de la Civilisation Egytienne. French & Eur.
Posner, Neil, ed. see Delson, Donn & Hurst, Walter E.
Posner, Neil, ed. see Delson, Donn & Michalove, Ed.
Post, G., ed. Glossary of Fish Health Terms. American Fisheries Society, Fish Health Section. Am Fisheries Soc.
Postlethwayt, Malachy. Universal Dictionary of Trade & Commerce. Kelley.
Postman, Frederica. The Yiddish Alphabet Book. PNye Pr.
Potapova, N. Learn Russian. Saphrograph.
Pothion, Jean. Dictionnaire des Bureaux de Poste Francais. Poste Aux Lettres.
Potikha, Z. A. Shkol' Nyi Slovoobrazovatel Nyi' Slovar' Four Continent.
--Shkol'nyi Slovoobrazovatel'Nyi Slovar. Barkhudarov, S. G., ed (Pub. by Proveschchenie). Four Continent.
Potlog, Alexe. S. Dictionar Practic de Agronomie. Editura Stiintifica.
Potonnier. Woerterbuch fuer Wirtschaft, Recht & Handel: Band I, Deutsch-Franzoesisch. Brandstetter.
--Woerterbuch fuer Wirtschaft, Recht & Handel: Band II, Franzoesisch-Deutsch. Brandstetter.
Potonnier, Brigitte, jt. auth. see Potonnier, Georges E.
Potonnier, Georges. Woerterbuch fuer Wirtschaft: Recht und Handel. French & Eur.
--Woerterbuch fuer Wirtschaft: Recht und Handel. French & Eur.
Potonnier, Georges E. & Potonnier, Brigitte. Woerterbuch Wirtschaft Recht Handel: Deutsch-Franzoesisch. Maison Dictionnaire.
--Woerterbuch Wirtschaft Recht Handel: Deutsch-Franzoesisch. Maison Dictionnaire.
Pototskaia, V. V., et al. Russko-Frantsuzskii Slovar (Pub. by Sov. Entsiklopediia). Four Continent.
Potozkaia, Varvara. Dictionnaire Francais-Russe. MIR.
--Dictionnaire Russe-Francais. Mir.
Potter, P. E., jt. auth. see Pettijohn, F. J.
Poujol, F. A. Dictionnaire de Medecine Pratique. Migne, J. P., ed. Caratzas Pub Co.
--Dictionnaire des Facultes Intellectuelles et Affectives de l'ame ou l'on Traite des Passions, des Vertus, des Vices, Des Defauts. Migne, J. P., ed. Caratzas Pub Co.
Poulbriere, Jean-Baptiste. Dictionnaire des Paroisses de la Correze, 3. Correze, Ste Scientifique.
Pouletti, J., et al. Dictionnaire Pratique de Droit Medicale. French & Eur.
Poulsen, O. Dansk-Tysk Ordbog for Korrespondenter. French & Eur.
Poulsen, Sven-Olaf. Ordbog for Korrespondenter, Dansk-Tysk. Kjaer Bogtryk.
Poussin, J. C. & Garnier, J. C. Dictionnaire de la Tradition Pontificale, Patristique et Conciliaire. Migne, J. P., ed. Caratzas Pub Co.
Powell, J. Quileute Dictionary. Univ Idaho.
Powell-Froissard, Lily. The Spanish-English, English-Spanish Crossword Puzzle Book. Citadel Pr.
Pozniak, G. I., ed. Dictionary of Helminthology & Plant Nematology. French & EUr.
Pozniak, G. J. Russian-English Dictionary of Helminthology & Plant Nematology (Pub. by CAB Bks England). State Mutual Bk.
Pozsonyi, Gabor. Filmgyartas es Filmtechnika. Akademiai Kiado.
Prada Becares, Juan. Diccionario Terminologia Medica Explicada. Autores-Editores.
--Diccionario Terminologia Medica Explicada. French & Eur.
Prado Velazquez, Ernesto, jt. auth. see Ocampo de Gomez, Aurora.
Prano, A. V. Russko-Litovskii Sel'Skokhoziaistvennyi Slovar (Pub. by Mintis). Four Continent.
Prather-Moses, Alice I. The International Dictionary of Women Workers in the Decorative Arts: A Historical Survey from the Distant Past to the Early Decades of the Twentieth Century. Scarecrow.
Prati, Angelico. Dizionario etimologico italiano. Multigrafica.
--Vocabolari delle parlate italiante. Forni.
--Vocabolario etimologico italiano. Garzanti Edit.
Prats, Alfonso T. Diccionario De Dificultades Del Ingles: Difficulties of English Idioms for Spanish Speaking People. Heinman.
Prats, Alfonso T. Dels see Dels Prats, Alfonso T.
Prats, Alfonso Torrents Dels see Torrents dels Prats, Alfonso.
Prazak, Josef M. Latinsko-Cesky Slovnik. SNTC.
Prefontaine, Robert & Cote-Prefont, Gisele. Dictionnaire. Beauchemin.
Prehl, Hede, et al. Politik & Gesellschaft: Ein Lexikon zur Politischen Bildung. Biblio Inst.
Preisigke, Friedrich. Fachwoerter des Oeffentlichen Verwaltungsdienstes Aegyptens in den Griechischen Papyrusurkunden der Ptolemaeisch-Romischen Zeit. Olms Verlag.
Prendergast, Alice. Medical Terminology: A Text-Workbook (Med-Nurse). A-W.
Prenis, John. Computer Terms. Running Pr.
--The Running Press Glossary of Computer Terms: An Insider's Guide to the Language of the Experts. Running Pr.
Prenis, John, ed. The Computer Dictionary: A User-Friendly Guide to Language, Terms, & Jargon. Running Pr.
Press, Charles & VerBerg, Kenneth. State & Community Governments in the Federal System. Wiley.
Press, Margaret L. Chemehuevi: A Grammar & Lexicon. U of Cal Pr.
Pressat, Roland. Dictionnaire de Demographie. Pr Univ Fr.
Pressot, Marcel. Vocabulaire des Quinze Joles du Mariage. Slatkine.
Preston, Dennis. Bituminous Coal Mining Vocabulary of the Eastern United States. U of Ala Pr.
Pretorius, Stanley H. Svensk-Engelsk Affarsordlists. Esselte Studium.
Pretz, Bernhard. Dictionary of Military Technological Abbreviations & Acronyms. Routledge & Kegan.
Pretzel, U., jt. ed. see Henschel, E.
Preuschen, Erwin. Griechisch-Deutsches Taschenwoerterbuch zum Neuen Testament. De Gruyter.
Preuss, Gisela. Das Grosse Duden-Schulerlexikon: Ein Nachschlagewerk fuer Jeden Schueler. Biblio Inst.
--Das Wissen von A-Z: Ein Allgemeines Lexikon fur die Schule. Biblio Inst.
Preuss, S., jt. auth. see Menge, R.
Prevot, Floriane. Dictionnaire de la Beaute Feminine. French & Eur.
--Dictionnaire du Savoir-Vivre Moderne. Casterman.
Price, A. Rae. Developing Your Vocabulary. Wm C Brown.
Price, Pamela V. Dictionary of Wines & Spirits (Pub. by Northwood Bks). State Mutual Bk.
Price, Thomas. English-Nyanja Dictionary. Shalom.
Prichard, Robert W. & Robinson, Robert E. Twenty Thousand Medical Words (HP). McGraw.
Pride, Kitty, jt. auth. see Pride, Leslie.
Pride, Leslie & Pride, Kitty. Vocabulario Chatino de Tataltepec. Summer Inst Ling.
Prieto, Muriel H. Vocabulary Made Easy for Spanish Speakers: Teacher's Guide. U of PR Pr.

Princeton University. Dictionary Catalog of the Princeton University Plasma Physics Laboratory Library (Hall Library). G K Hall.
--Dictionary Catalog of the Princeton University Plasma Physics Laboratory Library, First Supplement (Hall Library). G K Hall.
Pring, J. T., ed. The Oxford Dictionary of Modern Greek: English-Greek. Oxford U Pr.
--The Oxford Dictionary of Modern Greek: Greek-English, English-Greek. Oxford U Pr.
Prior, Arthur N. The Doctrine of Propositions & Terms. Geach, P. T. & Kenny, A. J., eds. U of Mass Pr.
Prisma-Lagersson, R. Swedish-English Modern Dictionary. Vanous.
Prisma-Lagersson, Rolf. Svensk-Engelsk Modern Ordbok. Vanous.
Pritchard, H. Wayne, pref. by. Resource Conservation Glossary. Soil Conservation.
Prizzi, Elaine & Hoffman, Jeanne. Diction Harry's Magical, Marvelous, Motivational Dictionary Kit. Pitman Learning.
Probst, Lester A. & DeGross, Katherine. Transportation Dictionary. Data Tactics.
Proctor, Paul, ed. Longman Dictionary of Contemporary English. Longman.
Profor. Initiation Au Vocabulaire Du Batiment et Des Travaux Publics. French & Eur.
Prokhorov, I. G., et al, eds. Russkie Poslovitsy, Pogovorki i Krylatye Slovar: Lingvostranovedcheskii Slovar. Four Continent.
Prokhorov, Iu. E., jt. auth. see Felitsyna, V. P.
Prompsault, J. H. Dictionnaire Raisonne de Droit et de Jurisprudence en Matiere Civile Ecclesiastique. Migne, J. P., ed. Caratzas Pub Co.
Pronin, Alex. Russian Vocabulary Builder, Seven Verbs a Day (Pub. by Lawrence). Borden.
Prosorova, L. P. & Kreizer, V. L. English-Russian Televisions Dictionary. French & Eur.
Prost, Antoine. Vocabulaire des Proclamations Electorales de 1881, 1885. PUF.
Proulx, G. J. Dictionnaire D'electronique & Tele-Communication: Anglais-Francais. Beauchemin.
--Dictionnaire d'Electronique et Tele-Communication: Anglais-Francais. French & Eur.
Proum, Im, jt. auth. see Huffman, Franklin E.
Prouty, Chris & Rosenfeld, Eugene. Historical Dictionary of Ethiopia. Scarecrow.
Provenzal, Dino. Dizionario dei dubbi linguistici. Hoepli.
--Dizionario delle immagini. Hoepli.
--Dizionario delle voci. Hoepli.
--Dizionario umoristico. Cisalpino-La Goliardica.
Provincial Archives & Victoria, British Columbia. Dictionary Catalogue of the Library of the Provincial Archives of British Columbia (Hall Library). G K Hall.
Pryce, D. K. Les Idiotismes du Francais Fondamental, Premier Degre. Harrap.
Pschyrembel, Willibald. Klinisches Woerterbuch Mit Klinischen Syndromen. De Gruyter.
Puba, Vaclay, jt. auth. see Benes, Josef.
Puccio, Denise, jt. auth. see Mariconda, Barbara.
Puchner, Guenter. Sprechen Sie Rotwelsch. Heimeran.
Puertas Gallego, M. J., tr. see Rieger, R., et al.
Pugh, Eric. Third Dictionary of Acronyms & Abbreviations: More Abbreviations in Management, Technology, & Information Science (Linnet). Shoe String.
Pugh, Eric, compiled by. Pugh's Dictionary of Acronyms & Abbreviations. Oryx Pr.
Pujol, R. Dictionnaire du Consommateur. Gonthier.

Pujolle, Jean. Lexique Guide D'acoustique Architecturale. Eyrolles.
Pukui, Mary K. & Elbert, Samuel H. Hawaiian Dictionary. UH Pr.
Pukui, Mary K., et al. The Pocket Hawaiian Dictionary: With a Concise Hawaiian Grammar. UH Pr.
Pulgram, Ernst. Italic, Latin, Italian. C Winter.
Pulliam & Grundman. The New York Times Crossword Puzzle Dictionary. Times Bks.
Pulliam, Tom & Grundman, Claire, eds. The New York Times Crossword Puzzle Dictionary. Warner Bks.
Pulver, Jeffrey. A Dictionary of Old English Music & Musical Instruments. Gordon Pr.
Purves, J. Italian-English, English-Italian Pocket Dictionary. French & Eur.
Purves, John. Italian Dictionary. Routledge & Kegan.
Putnam, R. E. & Carlson, G. E. Architectural & Building Trades Dictionary. Van Nos Reinhold.
Putnam, Robert & Carlson, G. E. Architectural & Building Trades Dictionary. Am Technical.
Puttock, A. G. Dictionary of Heraldry & Related Subjects. Genealog Pub.
Puy-Costa, M. Dictionnaire Pratique Mercure Francais-Espagnol. Larousse.
Pyle, Ian & Glazer, Edward, eds. Dictionary of Computing. Oxford U Pr.
Pyles, Donald W. Dictionary of Synergetics. Synergetics WV.

Q

Qamus, Madd A. & Edward, Wm. An Arabic-English Lexicon. Intl Bk Ctr.
Qazi, M. A. Concise Dictionary of Islamic Terms. Intl Bk Ctr.
Quadros, Janio. Novo Dicionario Pratico da Lingua Portuguesa. Editora Rideet.
Quak, Arend. Wortkonkordanz zu den Altmittel & Altniederfrankischen Psalmen & Glossen. Rodopi.
Quantin, M. Dictionnaire Raisonne de Diplomatie Chretienne. Migne, J. P., ed. Caratzas Pub Co.
Quemner. Dictionaire Juridique Francais-Anglais, Anglais-Francais. French & Eur.
Quemner, T. A. French-English, English-French Legal Dictionary. Baleyte, Jean & Kurgansky, Alexander, eds. Heinman.
Quemner, Thomas A. Dictionnaire Juridique: Frances-Allemand. Navarre.
--Legal Dictionary: French-English & English-French. Intl Pubns Serv.
Quemner, Thomas A., ed. see Neumann, Hugo.
Querexeta Gallostequi, Jaime. Diccionario Onomastico y Heraldico Vasco. French & Eur.
Quesada Castillo, Felix. Diccionario Quechua Cajamarca-Canaris. Minist Ed Caracas.
--Lexico Quechua de Cajamarca. Centro Invest.
Queval, Jean. Lexique de la Musique. Delpire.
--Lexique de la Musique. French & Eur.
Quicherat, Louis. Dictionnaire Francais-Latin. Hachette-Jeinesse.
Quick, John. Dictionary of Weapons & Military Terms (P&RB). McGraw.
Quimba, jt. auth. see Enriquez.
Quintana Cabanas, Jose M. La Pedagogia Moderna. Noguer SA.
Quintanilla, R. H. & Fraga, C. P. Glosario de terminos entomologicos. EUDEBA.
Quintano Heilpern. Diccionario juridico aleman-espanol de derecho comparado: Con vocabulario juridico espanol-aleman. Rev Derecho Pri.
Quiroga Flores, Miguel Angel. Diccionario Kollasuyo, Espanol-Quechua. Cochabamba.

Quitard, Pierre-Marie. Dictionnaire Etymologique: Historique & Anecdotique des Proverbes & des Locutions Proverbiales de la Langue Francaise. Slatkine.
Quo, J. C. English-Chinese Dictionary Romanized. French & Eur.
Quo, James. Concise Chinese-English Dictionary Romanized. Iaconi.
--Concise English-Chinese Dictionary Romanized. Iaconi.
Quo, James C. Concise Chinese - English Dictionary Romanized. C E Tuttle.
--Concise Chinese-English Dictionary, Romanized. C E Tuttle.
--Concise English-Chinese Dictionary. C E Tuttle.
--Concise English-Chinese Dictionary, Romanized. Imported Bks.
--English-Chinese Dictionary, Romanized. Saphrograph.

R

R. Diccionario Escolar de la Lengua Espanola. Sopena.
Rabassa Asenjo, B. & Garcia Tous, M. R. Diccionario de Marketing. Piramide.
Rabassa Asenjo, Bernardo & Garcia Tous, M. R. Diccionario de Marketing. French & Eur.
Rabinovich, I. S. Nepal'Sko-Russkii Slovar (Pub. by Sov Entsiklopediia). Four Continent.
--Pandzhabsko-Russkii Slovar (Pub. by GINS). Four Continent.
Rabinowitch, Z. E. & Lupandin, K. K. English-Russian Textile Dictionary. French & Eur.
Rabotin, Maurice. Le Vocabulaire Politique & Socio-Ethnique a Montreal de 1839 a 1842. Didier-Canada.
Rachet, G. & Rachet, M. F. Dictionnaire civilisation Grecque. Larousse.
Rachet, M. F., jt. auth. see Rachet, G.
Racine, Pierre. Lexique Historique de l'Italie XVIe.-XXe. Siecle. Colin.
Racinoux, Lucien, jt. auth. see Mineau, Robert.
Rack, Guenter. Mathematisch-Naturwissenschaftliches Woerterbuch Deutsch-Dari. Groos Verlag.
Racquet & Tennis Club New York. Dictionary Catalogue of the Library of Sports in the Racquet & Tennis Club with Special Collections on Tennis, Lawn Tennis, & Early American Sports (Hall Library). G K Hall.
Rada, Carmen, tr. see Kurth, Hanns.
Radcliff, Ruth K. & Ogden, Shelia J. Nursing & Medical Terminology: A Workbook. Mosby.
Radday, Yehuda T. An Analytical Linguistic Concordance to the Book of Isaiah. Biblical Res Assocs.
--An Analytical, Linguistic Key-Word-in-Context Concordance to the Book of Judges. Biblical Res Assocs.
Radday, Yehuda T. & Leb, G. M. An Analytical, Linguistic, Key-Word-in-Context Concordance to Esther, Ruth, Canticles, Ecclesiastes & Lamentations. Baird, J. Arthur & Freedman, David Noel, eds. Biblical Res Assocs.
Radde, Karl H. Polytechnisches Woerterbuch Deutsch-Spanisch. VEB Technik.
--Woerterbuch der Technik. Girardet.
--Woerterbuch der Technik. French & Eur.
--Woerterbuch der Technik. French & Eur.
Radde, Karl H. & Laguna de la Vera, Francisco. Polytechnisches Woerterbuch. VEB Technik.
Raddi, Renzo. A Firenze si Parla Cosi: Frasario Moderno del Vernacolo Fiorentino. Libreria.

Radet for Teknisk Terminologi. Ordbok for Automatiseringsteknikk. Universitesforlaget.
Radic, S., ed. Technological Engineering Dictionary German-Serbocroatian. French & Eur.
Radin, Max & Greene, Lawrence G., eds. Law Dictionary. Oceana.
Rafael. Diccionario pedagogico. Min. Educ.
Rafael, G. Diccionario para un macuto. Nacional Editora.
Rafferty, Kathleen, ed. The Dell Crossword Dictionary (Dell Trade Pbks). Dell.
--Dell Crossword Puzzle Dictionary. Dell.
Ragazzini & Gagliardelli. Italian-English, English-Italian Commercial Dictionary. Heinman.
Ragazzini, Giuseppe. Dizionario inglese-italiano e italiano-inglese con glossario bilingue di tecnica navale. Zanichelli.
--Dizionario inglese-italiano e italiano-inglese. Zanichelli.
Ragazzini, Giuseppe & Biagi, Adele. Dizionario inglese-italiano. Zanichelli.
Ragazzini, Giuseppe & Biagi, Adele, eds. Concise English-Italian Italian-English Dictionary. Longman.
Rage, S., jt. auth. see Kagaine, Elga.
Ragozin, N. A., jt. auth. see Papok, K. K.
Ragueau, Francois. Glossaire du Droit Francais. Slatkine.
Rahinantti, K. Finnish-Portuguese-Finnish Dictionary. French & Eur.
Rahinantti, Kristina, et al. Suomi-Portugali-Suomi. Werner Soderstrom.
Rahmanoba. German-Russian Dictionary. French & Eur.
Rahner, K. Herders Theologisches Taschenlexikon (Pub. by Herder). French & Eur.
--Herders Theologishes Taschenlexikon. Herder.
Rahner, Karl & Vorgrimler, Herbert. Dictionary of Theology. Crossroad NY.
Railsearch Publishing, Inc., ed. The New Dictionary of Railroad Working Terminology. Railsearch.
Rainich, Gabrielle & Kuipers, A. H., eds. Russian-English Vocabulary with Grammatical Sketch. Am Math.
Rakhmanov, I. V., ed. Nemetsko-Russkii Slovar (Pub. by GINS). Four Continent.
--Nemetsko-Russkii Slovar (Pub. by GINS). Four Continent.
--Slovar Naibolee Upotrebitel'Nykh Slov Anglii-Skogo, Nemetskogo & Frantsuzskogo Iazykov (Pub. by Izd. Inostr. & Natsional'Nal'Nykh Slovarei). Four Continent.
Rall, Dietrich, et al. Diccionario de Valencias Verbales. Aleman-Espanol. Benjamins North Am.
Raluy Pondevida, Antonio. Diccionario Porrua de la lengua espanola: Contiene las palabras basicas del idioma, con abundantes exicanismos & americanismos, tecnicismos, verbos & notas ortograficas. Monterde, Francisco, ed. Porrua.
Raluy Poudevida, Antonio. Breve Diccionario Porrua de la Lengua Espanola. Lectorum Pubns.
--Breve diccionario Porrua de la lengua espanola. Monterde, Francisco, rev. by. Porrua.
--Diccionario Porrua de la Espanola. Porrua.
--Diccionario Porrua de la lengua espanola. Porrua.
--Diccionario Porrua de la lengua espanola. Monterde, Francisco, rev. by. Porrua.
Raluy Poudevila, Antonio. Diccionario Forrua de la Lengua Espanola. Monterde, Francisco, ed. French & Eur.
--Diccionario Porrua de la Lengua Espanola Para Escuelas Primarias. Monterde, Francisco, ed. French & Eur.
Rama, Louis. Dictionnaire Technique de la Maroquinerie. Centre Technique.
Ramalingom, T. Dictionary of Instrument Science (Pub. by Wiley-Interscience). Wiley.

Ramirez, Hector. Ortografia Practica: Acentuacion, Consonantes, Vocabulario (Dist. Lib. Studium). Gale.
Ramirez Gronda, J. D. Diccionario juridico. Claridad.
Ramirez Villareal, Humberto. Diccionario Ilustrado de Electronica. French & Eur.
Ramirez Villarreal, Humberto. Diccionario ilustrado de electronica: Espanol-ingles e ingles-espanol. Diana.
Ramondino, Salvatore, ed. New World Spanish-English & English-Spanish Dictionary. Collins Pubs.
--New World Spanish-English, English-Spanish Dictionary (Sig). NAL.
Ramos, T. Tagalog Dictionary. Iaconi.
Ramos, Teresita V. Tagalog Dictionary. UH Pr.
Ramos-Ramos, Abiud. Vocabulario Tecnico De Contabilidad Moderna. U of PR Pr.
Rampa, Lobsang T. Dictionnaire de Rampa. Presse.
Rampini, Gino. Dizionario della sicurezza sociale. Giuffre.
Ranby, Peter. Nanumea Lexicon. Linguistic Circle.
Rances, Atilano. Diccionario Ilustrado De la Lengua Espanola. French & Eur.
Rand, Silas T. Dictionary of the Languages of the Micmac Indians, Who Reside in Nova Scotia, New Brunswick, Prince Edward Island, Cape Breton & Newfoundland. Johnson Repr.
Rand, W. W. Diccionario De la Santa Biblia. Edit Caribe.
Randel, Don M. Harvard Concise Dictionary of Music (Belknap Pr, Belknap Pr). Harvard U Pr.
Random House, Inc. The Random House Dictionary: Concise Edition. Random.
Rankin, Lois, jt. ed. see Abrahams, Roger D.
Rankin, N. A. The Pocket Oxford English-Russian Dictionary. Oxford U Pr.
Ranzoli, Cesare & Pigatti Ranzoli, M. Dizionario di scienze filosofiche. Hoepli.
Rao, Krishna. A Dictionary of Bharata Natya (Pub. by Orient Longman Ltd India). Apt Bks.
Rapelli, G., tr. see Chandor, Anthony.
Rapetti, Sergio, et al. Piccolo lessico universale. Nuova Vallecchi.
Rapoport, Amnon, jt. auth. see Fillenbaum, Samuel.
Rappoport, Angelo S. Dictionary of Socialism. Gordon Pr.
Raskevics, J., et al. English-Latvian-Russian Dictionary (Pub. by Collets). State Mutual Bk.
Rasmussen, R. Kent. Historical Dictionary of Rhodesia-Zimbabwe. Scarecrow.
Raspall de Cauhe, Joana, et al. Diccionari Usual de Sinonims Catalans: Mots i Frases. French & Eur.
Rassat, Patrick & Le Bars, Alain, eds. La Fiscalite. Hachette L.
Rastorguev, P. A. Slovar Narodnykh Govorov Zapadnoi Brianshchiny (Pub. by Nauka). Four Continent.
Rat, M. Dictionnaire des Locutions Francaises. Larousse.
Rat, Maurice. Dictionnaire des Locutions Francaises. Larousse.
--Dictionnaire Orthographique Garnier. Garnier.
Ratcliff, Ronald E. & Peck, Michael A. Dictionary of Naval Terminology-Dictionnaire de Terminologie Navale: English-French; Anglais-Francais (Pub. by Technique Doc France). Sheridan.
Ratz, O., jt. auth. see Kadar, I.
Rauch, Eberhard & Anzinger, Wolfgang. Woerterbuch Kritische Erziehung. Fischer Taschen.
Rauk, M. English-Estonian Dictionary for Schools (Pub. by Valgus). Four Continent.
Ravazzini, Giacomo. Dizionario di architettura. Cisalpino.
Raven, F. A. Die Schwachen Verben des Althochdeutschen. U of Ala Pr.
Raventos, M. H. Spanish Dictionary. McKay.
Rawson, Hugh. A Dictionary of Euphemisms & Other Double Talk. Crown.
Ray, A., ed. see Robert, Paul.
Ray, P. N. & Murdoch, John. Vocabulary of the Eskimos of Point Barrow & Cape Smyth. Shorey.
Ray, Sidney H. & Riley, E. B. A Grammar of the Kiwai Language, Fly Delta, Papua, with a Kiwai Vocabulary. AMS Pr.
Raygor, Alton, ed see Lewick-Wallace, Mary.
Raylor, R., ed. see Schibsbye, K. & Kossmann, H.
Raymond, D. Dictionnaire d'Education. Migne, J. P., ed. Caratzas Pub Co.
Raymond, Paul, jt. auth. see Lespy, Jean-Desire.
Raymond, Walter J. Dictionary of Politics. Brunswick Pub.
Razso, Imre. English-Hungarian Technical Dictionary-Angol-Magyar Muszaki Szotar. Saphrograph.
Razzaqi, Abd A. Dictionary of Sufi Technical Terms. Safwat, Nabil, tr (Pub. by Octagon Pr England). Ins Study Human.
Read. Dictionary of Gemmology. Butterworth.
Read, Gardner. Thesaurus of Orchestral Devices. Greenwood.
Readers Digest Editors. Family Word Finder. RD Assn.
Readett, Alan G., jt. auth. see Herbst, Robert.
Readett, Alan G., jt. ed. see Herbst, Robert.
Reading, Hugo F. A Dictionary of the Social Sciences. Routledge & Kegan.
Real Academia de la Historia. Diccionario Historico Geografico Ilustrado Del Pais Vasco. French & Eur.
Real Academia de la Lengua Espanol. Diccionario de la Lengua Espanol. French & Eur.
Real Academia Espanola. Diccionario De la Lengua Espanola. Colton Bk.
--Diccionario Manual y Illustrado De La Lengua Espanola. Colton Bk.
Real Academie de la Lengua Espanol. Diccionario Manual e Ilustrado de la Lengua Espanol. French & Eur.
Reaney, P. H. A Dictionary of British Surnames. Routledge & Kegan.
Reau, L. Diccionario poligloto de terminos de Arte y Arquitectura. Fondo Cult.
Reavis, Marshall W. Handbook of Insurance Terms & Concepts. Develop Sys Corp.
Rebollo Torio, Miguel A. Vocabulario Politico Republicano y Franquista, 1931-1971. French & Eur.
Rebora, Piero, et al. Cassell's Italian Dictionary: Italian-English, English-Italian. Imported bks.
Reboul, P., jt. auth. see Wordingham, J. A.
Reboul, P., jt. tr. see Wordingham, J. A.
Rebourgeon, P., et al, eds. Dictionnaire de Tennis. French & Eur.
Rechenbach, Charles W. Swahili-English Dictionary. Cath U Pr.
Rechtschaffen, Bernard & Marck, Louis. Two Thousand & One German & English Idioms: 2001 Deutsche und Englische Idiome. Barron.
Reck, J. Herder-Lexikon Mathematik. Herder.
--Herder-Lexikon Mathematik (Pub. by Herder). French & Eur.
Reck, Jurgen. Diccionario Rioduero Matematica. French & Eur.
--Diccionarios Rioduero: Matematicas. Strobl, Walter, tr. Catolica Edit.
Recktenwald, Horst C. Woerterbuch der Wirtschaft. French & Eur.
Redden, Kenneth R. & Veron, Enid L. Modern Legal Glossary. Michie Co.
Redgrave, Samuel. Dictionary of Artists of the English School. Newbury Bks.
--A Dictionary of Artists of the English School. Saifer.
Redhouse, James W. Turkish-English Dictionary. Ayer Co.
Reeb, Georg. Thesaurus Philosophorum Seu Distinctiones et Axiomata Philosophica. Clearwater Pub.
Reece, Laurie. Dictionary of the Walbiri (Walpiri) Language of Central Australia. Univ Syd Aust Lang.
Reed, A. W. & Brougham, A. E., eds. The Concise Maori Handbook. Reed Ltd.
Reed, Langford. Writer's Rhyming Dictionary. Writer.
Reed, R., ed. see Davis, Robert R., Jr.
Reese, William L. Dictionary of Philosophy & Religion: Eastern & Western Thought. Humanities.
Regnier, Adolphe. Lexique de la Langue de la Bruyere. Olms.
--Lexique de la Langue du Cardinal de Retz. Olms.
Regueiro, Marina & Goyoaga, Ricardo. Vocabulario de las lenguas ibericas. Nuestra Cultura.
Rehg, Kenneth L. & Sohl, Damian G. Ponapean-English Dictionary. UH Pr.
Reich, H. J., jt. auth. see Vuexkull, J.
Reichardt, Hans D., jt. auth. see Albrecht, Gunter E.
Reichardt, L. Dictionary of Technical Acoustics. Adler.
Reichardt, W. Acoustics Dictionary (Pub. by Martinus Nijhoff Netherlands). Kluwer Academic.
--Dictionary of Acoustics: English-German-French-Russian-Spanish-Polish-Madarsko-Slovene. French & Eur.
Reichardt, Walter. Technicka Akustika. VEB Verlat Technik.
--Technische Akustik. VEB Verlag Technik.
Reichow, Guenther, jt. auth. see Haeder, Walter.
Reid, et al. Diccionario Totonaco de Xicotepec de Juarez. Summer Inst Ling.
Reid, Cornelius L. A Dictionary of Vocal Terminology: An Analysis. J Patelson Music.
Reid, Hale & Crane, Helen. My Picture Dictionary. Ginn.
--My Second Picture Dictionary. Ginn.
Reid, J. B. Complete Word & Phrase Concordance to the Poems & Songs of Robert Burns. B Franklin.
Reidel-Geubtner, Virginia, jt. auth. see Boushahla, Jo J.
Reiff, Filipp. Novye Parallel'nye Slovari Iazykov Russkago, Frantsuzskago, Nemetskago i Angliiskago. Incl. Vol. 1. Russkii Slovar; Vol. 2. Dictionnaire Francais; Vol. 3. Deutsches Woerterbuch; Vol. 4. English Dictionary. Four Continent.
Reifferscheid, Adolph & Benseler, Frank. Lexikon des Rechts. H Luchterhand.
Reilly, Elizabeth C. Dictionary of Colonial American Printers' Ornaments & Illustrations (Dist. by U Pr of Va). Am Antiquarian.
Reilly, Robin & Savage, George. The Dictionary of Wedgwood. Antique Collect.
Reinartz, Erika & Masendorf, Friedrich. Kleines Woerterbuch der Sonderpaedagogik: Englisch-Deutsche. Marhold.
Reiner, Erica, jt. ed. see Oppenheim, A. Leo.
Reinhorm, Marc. Dictionnaire Laotien-Francais. C. N. R. S.
Reinhorn, Marc. Dictionnaire Laotien-Francais. CNRS.
--Dictionnaire Laotien-Francais. French & Eur.
Reisner, Thomas A. A Dictionary of Superseded Accentuations in 18th Century English. P Lang Pubs.
Reissner, Albert & Wade, Carlson. Dictionary of Sexual Terms. Assoc Bk.
Reithmaier, L. W., jt. auth. see Gentle, E. J.
Reitsak, A. Russko-Estonskii Razgovornik (Pub. by Valgus). Four Continent.
Rektenwald, Horst C. Woerterbuch der Wirtschaft. Kroener.
Relton, jt. auth. see Hohenadel.
Relton, jt. auth. see Hohenadel, Relton.
Relton, J., jt. auth. see Hohenadel, P.
Relton, Jonathan, jt. auth. see Hohenadel, Paul.
Relton, V., jt. auth. see Hohenadel, P.
Remmers, Mary. Little League Baseball Lingo. Hart Graphics.
Remy, Maurice. Dictionnaire du Francais Moderne. Hatier.
Renier, Fernand. Dutch-English Dictionary. Routledge & Kegan.
Renier, Fernand G. Dutch-English, English-Dutch Dictionary. Saphrograph.
Renner, et al. Economic Terminology German-English. Adler.
Renner, R. & Sachs, R. Wirtschaftssprache Deutsch-Englisch, Englisch-Deutsch. M Rosenberg.
Renner, R. & Tooth, J. Rechtssprache Englisch-Deutsch. Hueber.
--Rechtssprache Englisch-Deutsch (Pub. by M. Hueber). French & Eur.
Renner, R., jt. auth. see Haensch, G.
Renner, Ruediger & Tooth, Jeffery. Legal Terminology English & German. Adler.
--Legal Terminology English-German. Intl Pubns Serv.
Renouil, Yves & De Traversay, Yves. Dictionnaire du Vin. Feret.
Renouil, Yves & Traversay, Yves de. Dictionnaire du Vin. French & Eur.
Renoux, Y. & Yates, J. Glossary of International Treaties. Elsevier.
Renty, Ivan de. Lexique de L'Anglais des Affaires. French & Eur.
--Lexique Quadrilingue Des Affaires. French & Eur.
Renty, Ivan De see De Renty, Ivan.
Renty, Ivan de see De Renty, Ivan.
Rentzmann, Wilhelm. Numismatisches Wappen-Lexicon. Transpress Verlag fur Verkehrswesen.
Reouven, Rene. Diccionario de los Asesinos. French & Eur.
Research & Education Association. Technical Dictionary for Civil Engineers. Res & Educ.
Research Libraries of the New York Public Library. Dictionary Catalog of Materials on New York City (Hall Library). G K Hall.
--Dictionary Catalog of the Art & Architecture Division, Supplement 1974 (Hall Library). G K Hall.
--Dictionary Catalog of the Music Collection, Supplement 1974 (Hall Library). G K Hall.
--Second Edition of the Dictionary Catalog of the Music Collection (Hall Library). G K Hall.
Retsker, I. I., ed. Frantsuzsko-Russkii Frazeologicheskii Slovar (Pub. by Gosizdat Inostr Natsional Lit). Four Continent.
Retzlaff, Ewald. Kurzzeichen-Lexikon fur Kabel & Isoierte Leitungen Nach VDE IEC & CEE. VDE Verlag.
Reuters Ltd. Reuters Glossary of International Economic & Financial Terms (Coward). Putnam Pub Group.
Reventos, Margaret H. Diccionario moderno espanol-ingles, ingles-espanol. CECSA.
Rey, Jean. Dictionnaire Selectif & Commente des Difficultes de la Version Anglais. Ophrys.
Rey-Debove, G. Dictionnaire des Anglicismes. French & Eur.
ReyDebove, J., ed. see Robert, Paul.
Reyes, Juan R., jt. auth. see Moreno Castro, Pablo-Carrillo.
Reynolds, Barbara. Cambridge Italian Dictionary. Cambridge U Pr.
--Concise Cambridge Italian Dictionary. Cambridge U Pr.
--The Concise Cambridge Italian Dictionary. Penguin.
Reynolds, Kimberley & Seddon, Richard. Illustrated Dictionary of Art Terms: A Handbook for the Artist & Art Lover (Pub. by Ebury Pr England). State Mutual Bk.
Rezasco, G. Dizionario del linguaggio italiano storico e amministrativo. Forni.

Rhae, Kenneth & Southern, Richard. Lexique International des Termes Techniques de Theatre en 8 Langues. Meddens.
--Lexique International Des Termes Techniques De Theatre, en 8 Langues. French & Eur.

Ricart Matas, Jose. Diccionario de la Musica, Historico & Tecnico. Iberia SA.

Ricart Matas, Juan. Diccionario Biografico de la Musica. French & Eur.

Riccardi, Mario. Glossario geografico. Japadre.

Ricci, J. Elsevier's Banking Dictionary. Elsevier.

Ricci, V. Vocabolario trentino-italiano. Forni.

Rice. Introduction to Dental Terminology. Year Bk Med.

Rice, Edward. Eastern Definitions (Anch). Doubleday.

Rice, Michael D. Prentice-Hall Dictionary of Business, Finance & Law. P-H.

Richards, A. J., ed. An Iban-English Dictionary. Oxford U Pr.

Richards, Ruth M. Concordance to the Sonnets of Gongora. Hispanic Seminary.

Richardson & Pereira. McKay's Modern Portuguese-English, English-Portuguese Dictionary. Imported Bks.

Richardson, Elbert L., et al, eds. McKay's Modern Portuguese-English & English-Portuguese Dictionary. McKay.

Richardson, Henry B. Etymological Vocabulary to the Libro De Buen Amor of Juan Ruiz, Arcipreste De Hita. AMS Pr.
--Outline of French Grammar with Vocabularies. Irvington.

Richardson, Leonard T. Lexique de la Langue des Oeuvres Burlesques de Scarron. Olms.

Richelet, Pierre. Dictionnaire Francois. Olms.
--Dictionnaire Francois. Slatkine.

Richey, Jim. Drugstore Language. Janus Bks.
--Supermarket Language. Janus Bks.

Richling, Christel. Woerterbuch der Kabeltechnik. Brandstetter.
--Woerterbuch der Kabeltechnik. French & Eur.

Richling, Drewitz. Woerterbuch der Kabeltechnik: Deutsch-Englisch-Franzoesisch. Brandstetter.

Richter, G., ed. Dictionary of Optics Photography & Photogrammetry: German-English & English-German. Elsevier.

Rickards, Ralph. Understanding Medical Terms: A Self-Instructional Course. Churchill.

Ricour, Pierre. Lexique Anglais-Francais De la Banque et De la Monnaie. French & Eur.

Ricour, Pierre & Cousineau, Rene. Lexique de la Banque & de la Monnaie. Edit Quebec.

Rico y Amat, Juan. Diccionario de los Politicos. Narcea SA.
--Diccionario de los Politicos, 1855. Narcea SA.

Ridgeway, W. R., rev. by see Meras, Albert A. & Miller, Maud.

Ridley, Charles, jt. auth. see Doolin, Dennis.

Ridout, Ronald, ed. Nelson ELT Pocket Dictionary. Nelson & Sons Group.

Rieger, R., et al. Glosario de Genetica y Citogenetica II. Puertas Gallego, M. J., tr. Alhambra.
--Glossary & Genetics & Cytogenetics. Springer-Verlag.

Riego, Francisco Fernandez Del see Fernandez del Riego, Francisco.

Riego, Francisco Fernandez Del see Franco Grande, Xose L. & Fernandez del Riego, Francisco.

Rielly & Savage. Dictionary of Wedgewood. Apollo.

Riemann, Hugo. Dictionary of Music. Da Capo.
--Dictionary of Music. Scholarly.

Riese, Alan W. & LaSalle, Herbert J. All About the Dictionary. AMSCO Sch.

Rieth, Renate, jt. ed. see Huber, Rudolf.

Rietstap, Johannes B. Armorial general precede d'un dictionnaire des termes du Blason. Olms Verlag.
--Armorial general precede d'un dictionnaire des termes du Blason. Olms Verlag.
--Armorial General Precede d'un Dictionnaire des Termes du Blason (Pub. by Olms). French & Eur.
--Armorial General Precede d'un Dictionnaire des Termes du Blason (Pub. by Olms). French & Eur.

Rigal, Waldo A. The Inverted Medical Dictionary. Technomic.

Riggs, Stephen R. Dakota-English Dictionary. Ross.

Rigoli, A., jt. auth. see Biundi, Giuseppe.

Rigsbibliotekareembedet. Bibliotekskoder. Bibliotekscentralen.

Rigutini, G., jt. auth. see Tommaseo, Niccolo.

Riikon, E. & Tuomikowski, A. Finnish Dictionary: English-Finnish. Vanous.

Rijswijk, Maria J. Van see Duijker, Hubert C. & Van Rijswijk, Maria J.

Rijswijk, Maria J. Van see Duijker, Hubert C. & Van Rijswijk, Maria J.

Riland, George. New Steinerbooks Dictionary of the Paranormal. Garber Comm.
--The New Steinerbooks Dictionary of the Paranormal. Garber Comm.

Riley, E. B., jt. auth. see Ray, Sidney H.

Riley, P. A. & Cunningham, P. J. The Faber Pocket Medical Dictionary. Forsythe, Elizabeth, ed. Faber & Faber.

Riley, Sharon J., ed. GeoRef Thesaurus & Guide to Indexing. Am Geol.

Ringgren, Helmer, jt. ed. see Botterweck, G. Johannes.

Rinke, Hans. Woerterbuch der Seeschiffahrt. French & Eur.
--Woerterbuch der Seeschiffahrt. French & Eur.

Rinzler, Carol A. The Dictionary of Medical Folklore. T Y Crowell.

Risatti, Howard. New Music Vocabulary: A Guide to Notational Signs for Contemporary Music. U of Ill Pr.

Rischer, Klaus. Lexikon fuer Berufs & Arbeitspaedagogik: Ueber 2400 Haupt- & Hinweisstichworte. Kiehl.

Ristic, Svetomir & Simic, Zivojin. English-Serbocroatian Dictionary. Intl Learn Syst.

Ristic, Syetomir & Simic, Zivojin, eds. Englesko-srpskohrvatski Recnik. Prosveta.

Ritter, O., jt. auth. see Fatturosso, V.

Ritter, U. P. & Zinn, K. G. Grundwortschatz wirtschaftswissenshcaftlicher Begriffe: Deutsch- Englisch, Englisch-Deutsch. M Rosenberg.

Rittershofer, Werner. Das Lexikon Wirtschaft, Gesellschaft, Gewerkschaften. Bund.

Rittmann, Herbert. Deutsches Munzsammler-Lexikon. Battenberg.

Rivera, Feliciano, jt. ed. see Meier, Matt S.

Rivero Wood, Maria. Vocabulary for the Spanish-Speaking Student of Shorthand. U. Puerto Rico.

Riviere, Lindsay. Historical Dictionary of Mauritius. Scarecrow.

Roald, Albert von see Von Roald, Albert & Hahnewald, Harry.

Roback, A. A. A Dictionary of International Slurs. Maledicta.

Robb. Diccionario de terminos legales. Rev. Mex. de Seguros.

Robb, Louis. Dictionary of Modern Business. Anderson Kramer.

Robb, Louis A. Diccionario de terminos legales espanol-ingles e ingles-espanol. Limusa.
--Diccionario de Terminos Legales Espanol-Ingles e Ingles-Espanol: Spanish-English, English-Spanish Dictionary of Legal Terms. Larousse.
--Diccionario de Terminos Legales, Espanol-Ingles. Limusa.
--Diccionario de Terminos Legales Espanol-Ingles (LIM). Lectorum Pubns.
--Diccionario para Ingenieros Espanol-Ingles, Ingles-Espanol. French & Eur.
--Diccionario para ingenieros: Ingles-espanol, espanol-ingles. CECSA.
--Dictionary of Legal Terms, Spanish-English & English-Spanish (Pub. by Wiley-Interscience). Wiley.
--Dictionary of Legal Terms: Spanish-English,English-Spanish. Intl Learn Syst.
--Engineers' Dictionary, Spanish-English, English-Spanish (Pub. by Wiley-Interscience). Wiley.

Robelo, Cecilio A. Diccionario de mitologia Nahuatl. Innovacion.

Roberston, Ricardo. Diccionario bilingue ingles-espanol y espanol-ingles. Sopena.

Robert. Dictionnaire Alphabetique et Analogique de la Langue Francaise. French & Eur.

Robert, Paul. Dictionnaire Alphabetique & Analogique de la Langue Francais. Ray, A. & ReyDebove, J., eds. Soc Nouveau.
--Dictionnaire Alphabetique & Analogique de la Langue Francais. Ste. Nouv. Littre.
--Dictionnaire Alphabetique & Analogique de la Langue Francais. Ste. Nouv. Littre.
--Dictionnaire Alphabetique & Analogique de la Langue Francais. Ste. Nouv. Littre.
--Le Micro-Robert: Dictionnaire Du Francais Primordial. French & Eur.

Robert, Paul, ed. The Robert Dictionaries. Incl. Le Micro Robert en Poche; Le Micro Robert; Le Petit Robert; Le Grand Robert; Dictionnaire Universel des Noms Propres. Scribner.

Roberts, G. K. Dictionary of Political Analysis. St Martin.

Roberts, Harold S. Roberts' Dictionary of Industrial Relations. BNA.

Robertson. Diccionario Ingles-Espanol, Espanol-Ingles. French & Eur.

Robertson, Andrew B., jt. tr. see Hano.

Robertson, Richard G., ed. Robertson's Practical English-Thai Dictionary. C E Tuttle.

Robertson, S. Practical English-Thai Dictionary. Iaconi.

Robinson, David F. Lithuanian Reverse Dictionary. Slavica.

Robinson, Dow F. Manual for Bilingual Dictionaries. Summer Inst Ling.

Robinson, Edward, tr. see Gesenius, William.

Robinson, Harry M., Jr. & Burnett, Joseph W. A Dictionary of Dermatologic Therapy. Yorke Med.

Robinson, Robert E., jt. auth. see Prichard, Robert W.

Robinson, Stearn. Dreamer's Dictionary. Warner Bks.

Robinson, Stearn & Corbett, Tom. Dreamer's Dictionary: Complete Guide to Interpreting Your Dreams. Taplinger.

Robinson, Wm. J. Medical Sex Dictionary. Truth Seeker.

Robson, jt. auth. see Leo, Alan.

Robson, Leonard V. Vocabulario consultivo por secciones: Espanol-ingles. Confed Espanola.

Robson, Vivian E., jt. auth. see Leo, Alan.

Roca Muntanola, Julio. Diccionario de Parapsicologia. Alas.
--Diccionario de Parapsicologia. French & Eur.

Roccella, Remingio. Vocabolario della lingua parlata in Piazza Armerina. Forni.

Rocci, Lorenzo. Vocabolario greco-italiano. Dante Alighieri.

Roche, Elizabeth, jt. auth. see Roche, Jerome.

Roche, Francois. Lexique du Marketing. E. M. E.

Roche, Jerome & Roche, Elizabeth. A Dictionary of Early Music. Oxford U Pr.

Rochefort, Cesar de see De Rochefort, Cesar.

Rockey, D. Phonetic Lexicon of Monosyllabic & Some Disyllabic Words, with Homophones, Arranged According to Their Phonetic Structure (Wiley Heyden). Wiley.

Rodale, J. I. Synonym Finder. Rodale Pr Inc.

Rodd, Louis. Diccionario de terminos legales. Iaconi.

Rodero, Jose M. Diccionario de caza. Juventud.

Rodez, jt. auth. see Affre, Henri.

Rodgers, Harold R., et al, eds. Arlington Dictionary of Electronics. Beekman Pubs.

Rodriguez, Joaquin O. Diccionario textil panamericano: English-Spanish Dictionary of Textile Terms. W R C Smith.

Rodriguez, Rafael Crespo see Crespo Rodriguez, Rafael.

Rodriguez, Zorobabel. Diccionario de Chilenismos. Universidad & Acad.

Rodriguez Lapa, M. Vocabulario Galego-Portugues. Galaxia.

Rodriguez Monino, Antonio. Diccionario Bibliografico De Liegos Sueltos Poeticos, Siglo XVI. French & Eur.

Rodriguez Segui, Alejandro, jt. auth. see Diego Hernandez, Juan.

Roe, Keith E. & Frederick, Richard G. Dictionary of Theoretical Concepts in Biology. Scarecrow.

Roehrich, L. Lexikon der Sprichwoertlichen Redensarten. M Rosenberg.

Roemer, Theo. Dictionary of Welding - Fachwoerterbuch der Schweisstechnik: German-English & English-German. Intl Pubns Serv.

Roepke & Haefner. Deutsch-Franzoesisches Glossarium: Finanzieller und Wirtschaftlicher Fachausdrueke. Maison Dictionnaire.

Roepke, F. Deutsch-Franzosisches Glossarium (Pub. by Fritz Knapp Verlag). French & Eur.
--Franzoesisch-Deutsches Glossarium (Pub. by Fritz Knapp Verlag). French & Eur.

Roessler, Rudolf. Woerterbuch des Steuerrechts. French & Eur.

Roessler, Rudolf, et al. Woerterbuch des Steuerrechts. Haufe.

Rofe, Leslie G. Behind the Headlines. Belin.

Rofer, F. Diccionario de sinonimos espanoles. EDIMEX.

Rofer, Francisco. Diccionario de Sinonimos Espanoles. Edit Mex U.

Rogers, Malcolm, jt. auth. see Ormond, Richard.

Rogers, Malcolm, jt. ed. see Ormond, Richard.

Rogers, May. The Waverley Dictionary. Gordon Pr.
--Waverly Dictionary. Gale.

Rogers, P. P. & Lapuente, F. A. Diccionario De Seudonimos Literarios Espanoles, Con Algunas Iniciales. French & Eur.

Rogers, Thomas. Greek Word Roots: A Practical List with Greek & English Derivatives. Baker Bk.

Rogers, Walter T. Dictionary of Abbreviations. Gale.

Roget, John L., ed. see Roget, Peter M.

Roget, Peter M. Roget's International Thesaurus. T y Crowell.
--Roget's Thesaurus of English Words & Phrases. Dutch, R. A., ed. St Martin.
--Roget's Thesaurus of Words & Phrases (G&D). Putnam Pub Group.
--Roget's University Thesaurus. Mawson, C. Sylvester, ed (EH). B&N NY.
--Thesaurus of English Words & Phrases. Roget, John L. & Roget, Samuel R., eds. Shalom.

Roget, Samuel R., ed. see Roget, Peter M.

Rogger, M. R., tr. Dizionario dell'antichita classica. Zanichelli.

Rohlfs, Gerhard. Nuovo Dizionario Dialettale Della Calabria. Longo A.
--Nuovo dizionario dialettale della Calabria. Longo A.
--Vocabolario dei dialette salentini. Congedo.

Rohr, B. & Wiele, H., eds. Lexikon der Technik. Bibl Inst Leipzig.

Rolland-Thomas, Paule & Coulombe, Victor. Vocabulaire Technique de la Bibliotheconomie. Assoc. Canad. Biblio. Lang. Fr.

Rollin, Jack. The Guinness Book of Soccer Facts & Feats. Guinness Super.

--The Guinness Book of Soccer Facts & Feats. Guinness Super.
Rolls, B. A., jt. ed. see Porter, J. W.
Roloff-Stoddard, Joan, et al. Vocabulary: The Words Used to Express Ideas & Feelings. Macmillan.
Romain, Alfred. Dictionary of German & English Legal & Economic Terminology. French & Eur.
--Dictionary of German & English Legal & Economic Terminology. French & Eur.
--Woerterbuch der Rechts & Wirtschaftssprache: Teil II, Deutsch-Englisch. Recht & Wirtschaft.
--Woerterbuch der Rechts & Wirtschaftssprache: Teil I, Englisch-Deutsch. Recht & Wirtschaft.
Roman, J. Dictionnaire Topographique de la France. Biblio Nationale.
Romand, Didier. Dictionnaire du Marche de l'Art: Meubles, Objects, Curiosities. Amateur.
Romand, Didier & Schurr, Gerald. Le Dictionnaire du Marche de l'Art. French & Eur.
Romand, Didier & Schurr, Gerard. Dictionnaire du Marche de l'art. Amateur.
Roman de Bera, P. Diccionario Castellano-Vasco. French & Eur.
Roman del Cerro, Juan L. El Lexico base del castellano: Analisis estadistico y de contenido. Confed Espanola.
Romanov, A., jt. ed. see Wedel, E.
Romanov, A. S. Romanov Russian-English Dictionary. PB.
Rome, Franca. Atlante Della Sessualita. A Mondadi.
Romeo, Luigi. Ecce Homo! A Lexicon of Man. Benjamins North Am.
Romero, J. L. Diccionario de historia universal. Atlantida.
Romero Gualda, Maria V. Vocabulario De Cine y Television En Espana. French & Eur.
Romeu, Xavier. Brei Diccionari Ideologic: Amb Vocabulari Catala-Castella & Castella-Catala. Edit Teide.
--Vocabulari Ideologic Catala. Teide.
Romeuf, Jean & Guinot, Jean P. Diccionario del Jefe de Empresa. French & Eur.
Romine, Jack S. Vocabulary for Adults (Pub. by Wiley Pr). Wiley.
Rona, G., ed. see Schibsbye, K. & Kossmann, H.
Ronart, Nandy. Lexikon der Arabischen Welt. French & Eur.
Ronart, Nandy Von see Von Ronart, Nandy & Ronart, Stephan.
Ronart, Stephan, jt. auth. see Von Ronart, Nandy.
Roncalla, P. Ortografia Practica: Ejercicios & Ensayos Sobre Ortografia Castellano. Gale.
Room, Adrian. Dictionary of Cryptic Crossword Clues. Routledge & Kegan.
--Dictionary of Trade Name Origins. Routledge & Kegan.
--Room's Classical Dictionary. Routledge & Kegan.
--Room's Dictionary of Confusibles. Routledge & Kegan.
--Room's Dictionary of Distinguishables. Routledge & Kegan.
Roper, Nancy. The New American Pocket Medical Dictionary. Churchill.
--New American Pocket Medical Dictionary (ScribT). Scribner.
Roquefort, Jean-Baptiste B. De see De Roquefort, Jean-Baptiste B.
Rosa, Manuel A., ed. Corrugating Defect Terminology: Fabrication Manuel for Corrugated Box Plants. TAPPI.
Rosa, U. Glossario storico popolare piemontese. Forni.
Rosamani, Enrico. Vocabolario Marinaresco Giuliano-Dalmata. Olschki.
--Vocabolario marinaresco giuliano-dalmata. Olschki.
Rosario. Diccionario de Terminos Aerauticos. French & Eur.
Rosario, et al. Diccionario de Terminos Aeronauticos: Ingles-Espanol & Espanol-Ingles. Paraninfo.
Rose, Howard N. A Thesaurus of Slang. Gale.
Rose, Jim & Gilbert, Jayne. Dietetic Policies & Procedures Manual for Long Term Care Facilities. Aspen Systems.
Rose-Innes, A. Vocabulary of Common Japanese Words. Far Eastern Pubns.
Rose-Innes, Arthur. Beginner's Dictionary of Chinese-Japanese Characters. Dover.
--Beginners Dictionary of Chinese-Japanese Characters. Peter Smith.
--Beginners' Dictionary of Chinese-Japanese Characters & Compounds. Dover.
Rosenbaum, Samuel. A Yiddish Word Book for English Speaking People. Van Nos Reinhold.
--A Yiddish Word Book for English-Speaking People. Van Nos Reinhold.
Rosenbaum, Stanford P., ed. Concordance to the Poems of Emily Dickinson. Cornell U Pr.
Rosenberg, Jerry M. Dictionary of Banking & Finance (Pub. by Wiley-Interscience). Wiley.
--Dictionary of Banking & Finance (Pub. by Wiley-Interscience). Wiley.
--Dictionary of Business & Management. Wiley.
--Dictionary of Business & Management (Pub. by Wiley-Interscience). Wiley.
Rosenberg, Kenyon C. & Feinstein, Paul T. Dictionary of Library & Educational Technology. Libs Unl.
Rosenberg, M. B. English-Russian Dictionary of Refrigerating & Cryogenic Engineering. French & Eur.
Rosenberg, Paul, ed. The Urban Information Thesaurus: A Vocabulary for Social Documentation. Greenwood.
Rosenblatt, Ruth Y., jt. auth. see Beebe, Brooke M.
Rosenbloom, Joseph. A Dictionary of Dinosaurs. Messner.
--Doctor Knock-Knock's Official Knock-Knock Dictionary. Sterling.
--Doctor Knock-Knock's Official Knock-Knock Dictionary. Sterling.
Rosenblum, jt. auth. see Nurnberg.
Rosenblum, Robert, ed. see De La Chavignerie, Emile B. & Auvray, Louis.
Rosendahl, Fritz. Handbuch der Namensverfahren in der Chemischen Technik. Vulkan Verlag.
Rosendorfsky, Jaroslav. Dizionario ceco-italiano. Ist Univers Orient.
--Dizionario italiano-ceco. Ist Univers Orient.
Rosenfeld, Eugene, jt. auth. see Prouty, Chris.
Rosenfeld, V. Kleines Fachwoerterbuch Geologie (Pub. by Borntaeger). French & Eur.
Rosenstein, E., ed. Diccionario De Especialidades Farmaceuticas. Drug Intl Pubns.
Rosentahl, A., et al. Deutsch-Finnisches Schulworterbuch. French & Eur.
Rosental, M. Diccionario De Philosofia. French & Eur.
Rosenthal. Dictionnaire d'accentuation pour les Travailleurs de la Radio & de la Television. MIR.
Rosenthal, Hans J. Schluesselwoerter zur Berufsbildung. Gerds, Peter, ed. Beltz & Co.
Rosenthal, Harold & Warrack, John. Dictionnaire de l'opera. Fayard.
--Dictionnaire de L'opera. French & Eur.
Rosenthal, Harold & Warrack, John, eds. The Concise Oxford Dictionary of Opera. Oxford U Pr.
--The Concise Oxford Dictionary of Opera. Oxford U Pr.
Rosenthal, M. & Ioudine, P. Petit Dictionnaire Philosophique. French & Eur.
Roshton, M. Legal Secretary's Concise Dictionary. Claitors.
Rosiello, L. & Loi, I. Dizionario di linguistica. Zanichelli.
Rosner, Fred. Moses Maimonides Glossary of Drug Names. Am Philos.
Rosov, Victor, jt. auth. see Dragnev, M. V.
Ross, Jeffrey S., jt. auth. see Ross, Martin J.
Ross, Louis A. Diccionario de Terminos Legales Espanol-Ingles. Camino Real.
--Diccionario de t e01rminos legalese. Camino Real.
Ross, Martin J. & Ross, Jeffrey S. New Encyclopedic Dictionary of Business Law: With Forms (Busn). P-H.
Ross, Peter. Practical Italian-English, English-Italian Dictionary. Hippocrene Bks.
Ross, Ronald G. Data Dictionaries & Data Administration: Concepts & Practices for Data Resource Management. Am Mgmt.
Rossdale, Peter D. & Wreford, Susan M. Horses' Health A to Z. Arco.
Rossi, A. Dizionario italiano moderno. Malipiero.
Rossi, Ernest E. & Plano, Jack C. The Latin American Political Dictionary. ABC-Clio.
Rossi, Gualtiero. Dizionario inglese-italiano e italiano-inglese con glossario bilingue di economia e organizzazione aziendale. Zanichelli.
Rossi, Luigi. Dizionario di balletto. Edizioni Della Danza.
Rostan, Edwin. Vocabolario francese-italiano e italiano-francese. Malipiero.
Rosten, Leo. Joys of Yiddish (GB). McGraw.
Roth, Leo, ed. Handlexikon zur Erziehungswissenschaft. Ehrenwirth.
Roth, Rainer. Lexikon der Arbeits und Soziallehre. French & Eur.
Roth, Rainer A. & Selzer, Helmut M., eds. Lexikon zur Arbeits & Soziallehre. Habelt.
Roth, Reiner A. & Selzer, Helmut M. Lexikon zur Arbeits & Soziallehre. Schmidt, Jurgen, ed. Auer.
Rothenberg, Robert. New American Medical Dictionary & Health Manual (Sig). NAL.
--The Plain-Language Law Dictionary. Penguin.
Roth-Laly, Arlette. Lexique des Parlers Arabes-Tchado-Soudanais. Editions du CNRS.
--Lexique des Parlers Arabes-Tchado-Soudanais: K-Y. CNRS.
--Lexique des Parlers Arabes-Tchado-Soudanais. CNRS.
--Lexique des Parlers Arabes-Tchado-Soudanais. CNRS.
--Lexique des Parlers Arabes-Tchado-Soudanais, 3. CNRS.
Rothman, Raymond C. Notary Public Practices & Glossary. Natl Notary.
Rott, N. V., ed. Malaiziisko-Russko-Angliiskii Slovar (Pub. by Russkii Iazyk). Four Continent.
Rotteck. Dictionnaire Allemand-Francais. Garnier.
Rotteck, ed. Dictionnaire Allemand-Francais, Francais-Allemand. French & Eur.
Rouaix, Paul. Dictionnaire des Idees Suggerees par les Mots. Colin.
Roubakine. Dictionnaire Francais-Russe de Mathematique. MIR.
--Dictionnaire Francais-Russe de Medecine. MIR.
Roucka, Bohuslav. Pracovni Heslar Ceskeho Pravnehistorickeho Terminologickeho Slovniku. Ustav Statu a Prava Ceskoslovenske Akademie Ved.
Roucoules, Leon. Terminologie Fondamentale en Odonto-Stomatologie. Maloine.
Rouede, Denis. Dictionnaire Italien-Francais. Garnier.
Rouede, Denise, jt. auth. see Rouede, Pierre.
Rouede, Pierre & Rouede, Denise. Dictionnaire Italien-Francais et Francais-Italien. French & Eur.
Rouet, Marcel. Dictionnaire de la Culture Physique. French & Eur.
Rouge, Janine, jt. auth. see Moureau, Madeleine.
Rouge, Janine, jt. auth. see Moureau, Magdeleine.
Rouillard, Dom P. Diccionario De los Santos De Cada Dia. French & Eur.
Rousmaniere, John. A Glossary of Modern Sailing Terms. Dodd.
Rousseau, Jean J. A Complete Dictionary of Music. AMS Pr.
--Dictionnaire De Musique. Johnson Repr.
Rousseau, Jean Jacques. Dictionnaire de Musique. Johnson.
Rousseau, Jean-Jacques. Dictionnaire de Musique. Olms.
Rousseau, Louis-Jean, jt. auth. see Auger, Pierre.
Rousselet, Blanc P. Dictionnaire des Animaux. French & Eur.
Rousselet-Blanc, Josette, jt. auth. see Rousselet-Blanc, Pierre.
Rousselet-Blanc, Pierre & Rousselet-Blanc, Josette. Dictionnaire du Chien. Laffont.
--Dictionnaire du Chien. French & Eur.
Rousselet-Blanc, Pierre, ed. Larousse du chat. Larousse.
Rousset, A. Dictionnaire Geographique, Historique & Statistique des Communes: Franche-Comte & des Hameaux qui en Dependent. Guenegaud.
Roux, Genevieve. Dictionnaire Intime de la Femme. Privat.
Roux, Hubert Le see Le Roux, Hubert.
Rouzet, Anne. Dictionnaire des Imprimeurs. De Graaf.
Rover, M. French for Business Studies. French & Eur.
Rowntree, Derek. A Dictionary of Education. B&N Imports.
Rowson, K., et al. A Dictionary of Virology. Mosby.
Roy, D., jt. auth. see Klatt, E.
Roy, E., jt. auth. see Fleury, Paul.
Royal-Dawson, Warren, compiled by. Miscellaneous Papers by or Concerning John Ruskin. Darby Bks.
Royuela, Alberto. Diccionario de la Ultra Derecha. Dopesa.
Rozanova, V. V., ed. Kratkii Tolkovyi Slovar' Russkogo Iazyka: Dlia Inostransev. Four Continent.
--Kratkii Tolkovyi Slovar Russkogo Iazyka (Pub. by Russkii Iazyk). Four Continent.
Rozenberg, M. B. English-Russian Dictionary of Refrigeration & Low Temperature Technology. Pergamon.
Rozental, D. E. Russko-Ital'ianskii Ucxhebnyi Slovar (Pub. by Sov. Entsiklopediia). Four Continent.
Rozental, D. E., et al. Slovar-Spravochni k Lingvisticheskikh Terminov (Pub. by Prosveschchenie). Four Continent.
--Slovar Trudnostei Russkogo Iazyka. Four Continent.
Rozkovcova, L. Z. & Hanusova, S. Stary. Rustina pro Vedecke a Odborne Pracovniky. Academia.
Ruben & Angstrom, M. Swedish-English Dictionary. Saphrograph.
Rubert Candau, Jose M., jt. ed. see Lasso de La Vega, Javier.
Rubin, A., jt. auth. see Wittfoht, A.
Rubin, B. Dictionnaire Technique Hongrois-Francais. Terra.
Rubin, Barbara B., tr. from Latin. The Dictionaries of John de Garlande. Coronado Pr.
Rubin, Dorothy. Vocabulary Expansion I. Macmillan.
--Vocabulary Expansion II. Macmillan.
Rudakova, I. F. Uchebny Slovar Obschetekhnich: Leksiki (Pub. by Russkii Iazyk). Four Continent.
Rudakova, I. F., et al. Uchebnyi Slovar Obshchetekhnich: Russko-Anglo-Frantsuzsko-Nemetskii (Pub. by Russkii Iazyk). Four Continent.
Rudder, C., jt. auth. see Maury, E. A.
Rudenberg, Werner. Chinesisch-Deutsches Woerterbuch. De Gruyter.
Rudenberg, Werner, jt. auth. see Messinger, Heinz.
Rudenberg, Werner, jt. ed. see Messinger, Heinz.
Rudler, G. & Anderson, N. C., eds. French-English, English-French Gem Dictionary. Collins Pubs.
Rudman, Jack. Civil Service Vocabulary. Natl Learning.
--Handbook of the Stock Market (HOS) Natl Learning.
--Vocabulary. Natl Learning.
Rudnyckyj, J. B. An Etymological Dictionary of the Ukrainian Language. Ukrainian Acad.
Rudolphi, jt. auth. see Doring, G.
Rueckl, G., jt. ed. see Kunze, H.

Rueckl, Gotthard, jt. ed. see Kunze, Horst.

Ruedenberg, Werner, jt. auth. see Messinger, Heinz.

Ruedenberg, Werner, jt. ed. see Messinger, Heinz.

Ruedenberger, H., jt. auth. see Messinger, Heinz.

Ruelle, Pierre. Le Vocabulaire Professional du Houilleur Borain. Acad Royale.

Ruffner, Frederick G., Jr. & Thomas, Robert C., eds. Code Names Dictionary: A Guide to Code Names, Slang, Nicknames, Journalese, & Similar Terms. Gale.

Ruffner, James, et al, eds. Eponyms Dictionaries Index: A Compilation of Terms Based on Names of Actual or Legendary Persons. Gale.

Ruggiero, Ettore De see De Ruggiero, Ettore.

Ruhland, Jean. Dictionnaire Francais-Allemand-Anglais pour le Commerce Exterieur. Ruhland.

--Dictionnaire Technique Bilingue. Ruhland.

--Dictionnaire Trilingue. Ruhland.

Ruisseaux, Pierre Des see Des Ruisseaux, Pierre.

Ruiz, Clodoaldo Soto see Soto Ruiz, Clodoaldo.

Ruiz, Torres. Diccionario de terminos medicos. Iaconi.

Ruiz Calonja, J. & Pey, Santiago. Diccionario de sininimos, ideas afines y contrarios. Teide.

Ruiz Calonja, J., jt. auth. see Pey Estrany, Santiago.

Ruiz Fernandez, Ciriaco. El Lexico del Teatro de Valle Inclan. Univ Salamanca.

Ruiz Jodar, Carlos. Diccionario Espanol-Aleman, Aleman-Espanol Militar. French & Eur.

Ruiz Torres, F. Diccionario aleman-espanol de medicina. MMW Verlag.

--Diccionario aleman-espanol de medicina. Alhambra.

--Diccionario aleman-espanol y espanol-aleman de medicina. Alhambra.

--Diccionario de terminos medicos Ingles-Espanol & Espanol-Ingles. Fed Gremios.

--Diccionario de terminos medicos ingles-espanol espanol-ingles. Larousse.

--Diccionario de Terminos Medicos Ingles-Espanol. Alhambra.

--Diccionario Ingles-Espanol de Medicina. Alhambra.

Ruiz Torres, Francisco. Diccionario Aleman-Espanol, Espanol-Aleman de Medicina. French & Eur.

--Diccionario de terminos medicos: Ingles-Espanol, espanol-ingles. Alhambra.

--Diccionario Espanol-Ingles, Ingles-Espanol. French & Eur.

--Vocabulario Ingles-Espanol, Espanol-Ingles de Medicina. French & Eur.

Runes, Dagobert D. Diccionario De Filosofia. French & Eur.

--Dictionary of Judaism. Citadel Pr.

Runes, Dagobert D., ed. Concise Dictionary of Judaism. Greenwood.

--Dictionary of Philosophy. Philos Lib.

Running Press, ed. The Scrabble Trade Mark Crossword Games Scorebook. Running Pr.

Runyon, Harry. Faulkner Glossary. Citadel Pr.

Rupinska, M., jt. auth. see Maronski, J.

Ruse, Christina, ed. see Hornby, A. S.

Russek, P. R., jt. auth. see Zlatovski, George.

Russek, P. R. see Zlatovski, George.

Russell, Bertrand. Diccionario del hombre contemporaneo. Rueda.

--Diccionario del Hombre Contemporaneo. French & Eur.

Russell, James. Marx-Engels Dictionary. Greenwood.

Russell, Marcus. English-Lao, Lao-English Dictionary. Iaconi.

Russell, Percy, jt. auth. see Tver, David.

Russev, R. Bulgarian-English Dictionary. Saphrograph.

Russev, Rusi, ed. Bulgarian-English Dictionary. Ungar.

Russo. Vocabulario Logico, Historico & Positivo. Coop. Der.

Russo, Eduardo Angel. Vocabulario Logico. Coop. Der.

Russo-Alesi, Anthony I. Martyrology Pronouncing Dictionary. Gale.

Russon, S., jt. auth. see Kershaw, F.

Ruth, W. Lexikon der Schulphysik: Optik und Relativitaet. French & Eur.

Rutherford, G. K., jt. ed. see Jongerius, R.

Ruttkowski, Wolfgang V. & Blake, R. E. Glossaire de Termes Litteraires. Francke.

Ruysch, W. A. Elsevier's Multilingual Dictionary of Insurance Technology. Elsevier.

Ruzicka, R. A Dictionary of Russian Verbs. Daum, E. & Schenk, W., eds. Hippocrene Bks.

Ruzicka, Rudolf. A Dictionary of Russian Verbs (Dist. by Four Continent). Hippocrene Bks.

Ryan, P. New Dictionary of Modern Maori. Hein.

Ryan, P. M., ed. New Dictionary of Modern Maori (Pub. by Heinemann Pub New Zealand). Intl Schol Bk Serv.

Rybicki, Stephen A., ed. Abbreviations: A Reverse Guide to Standard & Generally Accepted Abbreviated Forms. Pierian.

Rycroft, Charles. A Critical Dictionary of Psychoanalysis. Littlefield.

--Dizionario critico di psicoanalisi. Astrolabio.

Rytz, O., jt. ed. see Amankwaah, J. W.

S

Saagpakk, Paul F. Estonian-English Dictionary. Yale U Pr.

Saarikoski, Lea. Englantilais-Suomaainen Elektromikka ja Instrumentointisanasto. Otava.

--Englantilais-Suomalainen Moottorialan Sanasto. Otava.

--Englantilais-Suomalainen Tekstiili-ja Vaatetusalan Sanasto. Otava Kust.

Saario, Hilkka. Timber Trade Terminology. Gaudeamus.

Sabater, Gerd, ed. see Hatje, Gerd.

Sabatier, Robert. Diccionario Ilustrado de la Muerte. French & Eur.

Sabek, Jerwan. English-French-Arabic Trilingual Dictionary. Intl Bk Ctr.

Sabrie, A. M. & Scharaf, R. S., eds. Textile Industry Dictionary. French & Eur.

Sacerdote, Gustavo. Langenscheidts Taschenwoerterbuecher Italienisch. Langenscheidt.

Sacerdoti. Dizionario italiano-latino. Vallardi A.

Sacerdoti, N. Dizionario Italiano-Latino, Latino-Italiano. French & Eur.

Sachs & Villatte. Langenscheidts Grosswoerterbuch Franzoesisch: Tl 1, Franzoesisch-Deutsch. Langenscheidt.

Sachs, Karl & Villatte, Cesaire. Langenscheidts Grosswoerterbuch: Teil II, Deutsch-Franzoesisch. Gottschalk, Walter & Bentot, Gaston, eds. Langenscheidt.

--Langenscheidts Grosswoerterbuch: Teil I, Franzoesisch-Deutsch. Langenscheidt.

Sachs, R., jt. auth. see Renner, R.

Sachs, Rudolf. British & American Business in Key Words (Pub. by Fritz Knapp Verlag). French & Eur.

--British & American Business in Keywords. Knapp Verlag.

--British & American Business in Keywords. Knapp Verlag.

--British & American Business Terms (Pub. by Macdonald & Evans England). Intl Ideas.

Sacleux, Charles. Dictionnaire Francais-Swahili. Institut Ethnologie.

--Dictionnaire Swahili-Francais. Inst Ethnol.

Sacy, Samuel S. De see Serand, Pierre & De Sacy, Samuel S.

Sadie, Stanley, ed. The New Grove Dictionary of Music & Musicians. Groves Dict Music.

Sadoul, George. Dicccionario del Cine. French & Eur.

Sadoul, Georges. Dictionnaire des Cineastes. French & Eur.

--Dictionnaire des Films. Seuil.

--Dictionnaire des Films. French & Eur.

Saeeed, M. A Dictionary of Muslim Philosophy. Kazi Pubns.

Safire, William. Safire's Political Dictionary. Ballantine.

--Safire's Political Dictionary: The New Language of Politics. Random.

Safwat, Nabil, tr see Razzaqi, Abd A.

Saglio, E., jt. auth. see Daremberg, Charles.

Sahai, Hardeo & Berrios, Jose. A Dictionary of Statistical, Scientific & Technical Terms: English-Spanish, Spanish-English. Smith, Richard A. & Heise, Jeanne, eds. (Pub. by Wadsworth Internacional Iberoamerica). Wadsworth Pub.

Saillens, Emile, jt. auth. see Kuentz, Eugene.

Sainsbury, Diana, jt. auth. see Singleton, Paul.

Sainsbury, John S., ed. A Dictionary of Musicians: From the Earliest Times. Da Capo.

St. Elmo Naumann, Jr. Dictionary of Asian Philosophies. Citadel Pr.

St. Germain. The Palmistic Dictionary. Found Class Reprints.

Saint Riquier, Marc & Delporte, Jacques. Lexique de l'homme a Cheval. Amphora.

Saint-Riquier, Marc de. Lexique de l'homme a Cheval. French & Eur.

Saint-Simon, F. Dictionnaire de la Noblesse Francais. Contrepoint.

Saint-Simon, F. de, jt. auth. see Sereville, Etienne De.

Saint-Simon, Fernand de, jt. auth. see Sereville, Etienne de.

Sainz de Robles, F. Diccionario espanol de sinonimos y antonimos. Iaconi.

Sainz de Robles, F. C. Diccionario espanol de sinonimos y antonimos. Aguilar SP.

Sainz de Robles, Federico C. Diccionario Espanol de Sinonimos y Antonimos. Arturo del Hoyo, Asesor, ed. French & Eur.

Saisse, Louis. Dictionaire Francais-Arabe. Intl Bk Ctr.

--Dictionnaire Francais-Arabe. Intl Bk Ctr.

Saiz, M. Diccionario de Electronica, Radio & TV: Ingles-Espanol. Lectorum Pubns.

--Diccionario de Mecanica Ingles-Espanola. Lectorum Pubns.

Sak, Ziya. English-Turkish, Turkish-English Dictionary. Saphrograph.

Sakharov. Dictionnaire Francais-Russe du Batiment. MIR.

Salamaa, Elsa. Maly Slownik Finsko-Polski & Polski-Finski. Kirjayhtyma.

Salaman. Dictionary of Tools. Bennett IL.

Salaman, R. A. Dictionary of Tools Used in the Woodworking & Allied Trades c. 1700-1970 (ScribT). Scribner.

Salas, Rodrigo. Los Mil Quinientos. Edit Vecchi.

Salati, U., ed. see Cusatelli, G. & Brunacci, G.

Salazar Lopez, Jose M. Diccionario legislativo de cinematografia y teatro. Nacional Editora.

Salmone, Anthony. An Advanced Learner's Arabic-English Dictionary. Intl Bk Ctr.

--Arabic-English Advanced Learners Dictionary. Intl Bk Ctr.

Sal'nov, N. Al. Russko-Novogrecheskii Karmannyi Slovar (Pub. by Sov. Entsiklopediia). Four Continent.

Salon, A. Vocabulaire Critique des relations culturelles internationales. Maison Dictionnaire.

Saltikoff, Boris. Mineraalinimisanasto. Geo Tutkim.

Salto Dolla, Angel. Diccionario De Terminos De Proceso De Datos: Con Vocabulario Espanol-Ingles, Ingles-Espanol. French & Eur.

--Diccionario de terminos de proceso de datos: Definicion de 2500 terminos de informatica y vocabulario completo espanol-ingles e ingles-espanol. Paraninfo.

Salva, Vicente. Dictionnaire Espagnol-Francais. Garnier-Flammarion.

Salva, Vicente & Larrieu, Robert. Dictionnaire Espagnol-Francais. Garnier.

Salva, Vicente & Larrieu, Robert, eds. Dictionnaire Espagnol-Francais et Francais-Espagnol. French & Eur.

Salzade, M. de see De Salzade, M.

Samarani, B. Vocabulario cremasco-italiano. Forni.

Sambor, Jadwiga. O Slownictwie Statystycznie Rzadkim. Panstwowe Zaklad W.

Samilov, Michael. A Lexicon to the Glory of God Greek-Russian (18th Century) Facsimile Edition Paris Ms. Suppl. grec 1117 (Pub. by Variorum). State Mutual Bk.

Sampaio de Melo, jt. auth. see Almeida Costa, J.

Samson, P. Glossary of Hematological & Seriological Terms. Butterworth.

Samuel, Albert. Petit Vocabulire Politique. Chronique Sociale.

Samuel, Edith. Your Jewish Lexicon. UAHC.

Samuel, Edwin, jt. ed. see Kamrat, Mordechai.

Samuelson, G. Allen, jt. auth. see Annett, Ross H., Jr.

Sanberg, Graham, ed. see Chandra Das, S.

Sanchez, Augustin R., jt. auth. see Delgaty, Alfa.

Sanchez Benedito, Francisco. Diccionario Conciso de Modismos Ingles-Espanol, Espanol-Ingles. French & Eur.

--Diccionario consico de modiamos. Alhambra.

Sanchez-Boudy, Jose. Diccionario De Cubanismos Mas Usuales. Ediciones.

Sanchez Carrate, Juan A. Diccionario de la Izquierda Comunista. Dopesa.

Sanchez Monge y Parellada, Enrique. Diccionario de Plantas Agricolas. Minist Agricultura.

Sanchez Ordonez, Angel. Diccionario Penal: Libro del Opositor C. G. P. Lemos.

Sanchez Sivori, Amalia. Diccionario de Payadores. Plus Ultra S. A.

Sanchez y Pascual, Enrique. Diccionario de la Vida Sexual. Prod Edit.

Sandahl, P. & De Bea, L. Dictionnaire Politique & Diplomatique. Bruylant.

Sandahl, Pierre & Bea, Louise de. Dictionnaire Politique et Diplomatique. French & Eur.

Sandahl, Pierre & De Bea, Louise. Dictionnaire Politique & Diplomatique. Litec.

Sandberg, G., ed. see Das, Sarat C.

Sandeau, Georges, jt. auth. see Van Dijk, Marcel.

Sandefur, John R. & Sandefur, Joy L., eds. Beginnings of a Ngukurr-Bamyili Creole Dictionary: Work Papers of SIL-AAB, Series B; vol. 4. Summer Inst Abor.

Sandefur, Joy L., jt. auth. see Sandefur, John R.

Sandilands, John. Western Canadian Dictionary & Phrase-Book. U of Toronto Pr.

Sandir-White, Alex. Dictionary of French Slang. Aurea.

Sandoval, Lisandro. Semantica Guatemala O Diccionario De Guatemaltequisma. Intl Guatemala.

Sandri-White, Alex. Boobytraps of the German Language. Aurea.

--Dictionary of Hungarian Slang. Aurea.

Sandvei, Marius. Svensk-Norsk Ordbok. Fabritius.

Sanguinetti, C. S., ed. Mi primer diccionario Larousse en colores. Larousse.

Sani, Luciano. Vocabolario inglese-italiano e italiano-inglese. Dante Alighieri.

--Vocabolario inglese-italiano, italiano-inglese. Dante Alighieri.

San Juan Rubio, Roman. Terminos Internacionales en la Gestion de Compras & Ventas. APD.

San Martin Unamuno, Jose M. Diccionario de parapsicologia. Don Bosco Ed.
San Miguel de la Camara, Maximino. Diccionario petrografico: Vol 1, Rocas eruptivas (CSIC). Inst. Jose Acosta y Lucas Mallada.
Sanna, Carlo. Il Gergo della Camorra. Il Vespro.
Sanquiao, O. J. Diccionario Politico: Los Ministros Nacionales. Platero.
Sansoni. Das Grosse Woerterbuch der Italienischen & Deutschen Sprache: Band I, Italienisch-Deutsch. Brandstetter.
--Das Grosse Woerterbuch der Italienischen & Deutschen Sprache: Band II, Deutsch-Italienisch. Brandstetter.
Santamaria, A. Diccionario de sinonimos y antonimos. Sopena.
Santamaria, Antonio. Diccionario de Sinonimos, Antonimos & Ideas Afines (SOP). Lectorum Pubns.
Santamaria, Antonio & Cuartas, Augusto. Diccionario de Incorrecciones & Particularidades & Curiosidades del Lenguaje (PAR). Lectorum Pubns.
Santamaria, Cuartas & Mangada, J. Diccionario de Incorreciones & Particularidades del Lenguaje. Paraninfo.
Santamaria, Francisco. Diccionario de Mejicanismos. Porrua.
Santamaria, Francisco J. Diccionario De Mejicanismos. Colton Bk.
--Diccionario de Mejicanismos. French & Eur.
Santamarie, Andres & Cuartas, Augusto. Diccionario de Incorreciones y Particularidades del Lenguaje. French & Eur.
Santano. Diccionario de Electronica. Paraninfo.
--Diccionario de Gentilicios & Toponimos. Paraninfo.
Santano y Leon, Daniel. Diccionario de gentilicios y toponimos. Paraninfo.
Santesson, R. & Kaerre, Karl K. Swedish-English, English-Swedish Dictionary. Heinman.
Santiago, Gubern, jt. auth. see Alberti.
Santillan, Diego Abad de. Diccionario de Argentinismos de Ayer y de Hoy. French & Eur.
Santos, Agustin A. Diccionarior Nuclear. Organ Ofic Adm.
Santos, Domingo, tr. see Maury, E. A.
Santos, F. N. Dicionario Ingles-Portugues de Economia. Pub Euro Am.
Sapir, Edward & Swadesh, Morris. Yana Dictionary. U of Cal Pr.
Saponaro, A. Diccionario de los Sintomas: Los Testa de su Salud. French & Eur.
Saras, Marcel. Dictionar Francez-Roman: Pentru uzul Elevilor. Editura Stiintifica.
Sarkany, Pal, ed. Nemzetkozi Kutya Enciklopedia. Terra.
Sarnoff, Paul. Wall Street Thesauris. Astor-Honor.
Sarrazin, Gregor, ed. see Schmidt, Alexander.
Sarumpaet, J. Modern Usage in Bahasa Indonesia. Pitman Ltd.
Sattler, Helen R. The Illustrated Dinosaur Dictionary. Lothrop.
Sattler, Helen Roney. The Illustrated Dinosaur Dictionary. Lothrop.
Saubidet, Tito. Vocabulario y Refranero Criollo. French & Eur.
Sauer, Hans. Relais Lexikon. Vertrieb.
Sauermost, R. Herder-Lexikon Physik. Herder.
--Herder-Lexikon Physik (Pub. by Herder). French & Eur.
Sauermost, Rolf. Diccionario Rioduero: Fisica. French & Eur.
Saukkonen, Pauli. Nykysuomen Saneiston Yleisyystilastoa Sanennloppuisessa Aakkosjarjestykessa. Oulun Yliopisto.
Saulnier, Karen L., jt. ed. see Bornstein, Harry.
Saunier, Joannes. Vocabulaire Grec. Gigord.
Saur, Karl O. Klipp & Klar. Biblio Inst.
Sau Sanchez, Victoria. Un Diccionario ideoligico feminista. Icaria Edit.
--Un Diccionario Ideologico Feminista. Icaria Edit.
Sava, Iosif & Vartolomei, Luminita. Dictionar de Muzica. Editura Stiintifica.
Savage, jt. auth. see Rielly.
Savage, George. Dictionary of Antiques (Mayflower Bks). Smith Pubs.
Savage, George & Newman, Harold. Illustrated Dictionary of Ceramics. Van Nos Reinhold.
Savage, George, jt. auth. see Reilly, Robin.
Savage, James. A Genealogical Dictionary of the First Settlers of New England. Genealog Pub.
--A Genealogical Dictionary of the First Settlers of New England. Gordon Pr.
Savage, William. Dictionary of the Art of Printing. B Franklin.
--A Dictionary of the Art of Printing. Intl Pubns Serv.
Savage, William, jt. auth. see Patit, Charles.
Savage, William, jt. auth. see Petit, Charles.
Savaiano, E. & Wing, L. Spanish & English Idioms: 2001 Modismos Espanoles & Ingleses. Barron.
Savaiano, E. & Winget, L. Modismos en Ingles. Barron.
--Spanish-English Idioms: 2001 Modisomos Espanoles & Ingleses (Pocket Size) Barron.
Savard, J. G., jt. auth. see Mackey, William Francis.
Savelsberg, Jorg, jt. auth. see Klimke, Reiner.
Saverien, Alexandre. Dictionnaire Universel de Mathematique & de Physique, 1. Olms.
--Dictionnaire Universel de Mathematique & de Physique, 2. Olms.
Savin, Emilia, jt. auth. see Livescu, Jean.
Savonius, M. Scandinavian Smorgasbord, Soups, Savouries & Sweets. Saphrograph.
Savory, Theodore. Latin & Greek for Biologists (Pub. by Meadowfield Pr England). State Mutual Bk.
Saward, Blanche C., jt. auth. see Caulfield, Sophia F.
Sawers, Robin, ed. Harrap's Concise German & English Dictionary. Harrap.
Sawyer, Janet B; see Malmstrom, Jean.
Saxton, Dean & Saxton, Lucille. Papago & Pima to English, English to Papago & Pima Dictionary. Cherry, R. L., ed. U of Ariz Pr.
Saxton, Lucille, jt. auth. see Saxton, Dean.
Saylor, Henry H. Dictionary of Architecture. Wiley.
Sbrulli, G. & Biffoli, T. Dizionario italiano-francese-italiano. Valmartina.
Scale Manufacturers Association. Terms & Definitions for the Weighing Industry. Scale Mfrs.
Scanlan, George. Harrap's Russian Vocabulary. Harrap Co.
Scardigli, Piergiuseppe & Gervasi, Teresa. Avviamento All'etimologia Inglese e Tedesca: Dizionario Comparativo dell'Elemento Germanico Commune ad Entrabe le Lingue. Monnier.
Scarry. Dictionnaire Animaux. French & Eur.
Scarry, Huck, illus. My First Picture Dictionary (BYR). Random.
Scarry, R. Min Forste Ordbok: English & Norwegian. Vanous.
Scarry, Richard. Mein Allerschoenstes Woerterbuch. Adler Bks.
--Mi Primer Gran Diccionario Infantil. French & Eur.
--Primo Dizionario. Intl Learn Syst.
--Richard Scarry's Storybook Dictionary (Golden Pr). Western Pub.
Scavenius, H., jt. ed. see Berulfsen, B.
Scavnicky, Gary E., jt. auth. see Stahl, Fred A.
Schaefer, Michael. Die Adjektive auf Isch in der Deutschen Gegenwartssprache. Winter Univ.
Schaefer, Peter & Wiczorke, Martin. Lexikon der Prozessrechnertechnik. Siemens AG.
Schaefer, Peter, jt. auth. see Maier, Johann.
Schaeffer, Randolph F. & Carr, W. L., eds. Latin English Derivative Dictionary. Am Classical.
Schaeffer, Rudolph F., ed. Greek English Derivative Dictionary. Am Classical.
Schaffer, jt. auth. see Tuazon.
Schaffer, jt. auth. see Tuazon, Redentor M.
Schaffran, Emerich, ed. Dictionary of European Art. Philos Lib.
Schafritz, Jay M. Dictionary of Personnel Management & Labor Relations. Moore Pub IL.
Schaldach, Herbert von see Von Schaldach, Herbert.
Schapera, I. Kinship Terminology in Jane Austen's Novels. Humanities.
Scharaf, R. S., jt. ed. see Sabrie, A. M.
Scharf, T. & Shetty, M. C. Dictionary of Development Banking: A Compilation of Terms in English, French, & German with Definitions in English. Elsevier.
Scharnow, Ulrich. Transpress Lexikon Seefahrt. Transpress Verlag fur Verkehrswesen.
Scharow, W. A. & Nowitschkowa, A. L. Deutsch-Russisches Worterbuch der Rechentechnik und Datenverarbeitung. French & Eur.
Schattner, Friedrich. Dictionar de Electrotehnica. Editura Stiintifica.
--Dictionar de Electrotehnica. Editura Stiintifica.
--Dictionar Tehnic Polon-Roman si Roman-Polon. Wydawnictwa Naukowo.
Scheengluth, Carlos. Diccionario Ilustrado De Terminologia Textil Aleman-Espanol, Espanol-Aleman. French & Eur.
Scheid, Harald, et al. Die Mathematik II: Ein Lexikon zur Schulmathematik Sekundarstufe II. Biblio Inst.
--Die Mathematik I: Ein Lexikon zur Schulmathematik Sekundarstufe. Biblio Inst.
Scheid, O. N. Vocabulaire Allemand par l'image. Bordas-Dunod.
Scheler, Auguste. Glossaire Philologique de la Geste de Liege. Slatkine.
Schenck, A. Kuenstlerlexikon. Rowohlt.
--Kuenstlerlexikon (Pub. by Rowohlt). French & Eur.
Schenk, jt. auth. see Daum, V.
Schenk, W., jt. auth. see Daum, E.
Schenk, W., jt. auth. see Daum, Edmund.
Schenk, W., ed. see Ruzicka, R.
Schenkel, W., jt. auth. see Helbig, G.
Schepisi, Givanna, ed. Diccionario Abreviado Italiano-Espanol Espanol-Italiano. Biblograf SP.
Scherath, Bernfried. Sanskrit vocabulary. Brill.
Schewitzer, E., jt. ed. see Forth, E.
Schibsbye, K. & Kossmann, H. Danish-English Dictionary. Rona, G. & Raylor, R., eds. Shalom.
Schierbaum, Wilfried, ed. Bekleidungslexikon. Schiele & Schoen.
Schildt, Bengt. Rysk-Svensk Teknisk Ordbok. Esselte Studium.
Schiller, Andrew & Jenkins, William A. Junior Thesaurus: In Other Words II. Lothrop.
Schiller, Andrew, jt. auth. see Jenkins, William A.
Schimitzek, S., et al. Kleinworterbuch Deutsch-Polnisch (Handy German-Polish Dictionary) French & Eur.
Schimpff, Jill W. Open Sesame Picture Dictionary: Featuring Jim Henson's Sesame Street Muppets, Children's Television Workshop. Oxford U Pr.
--Oxford Picture Dictionary of American English Workbook. Oxford U Pr.
Schinzler, Engelbert, ed. Woerterbuch der Vorschulerziehung. Herder.
Schlegelmich, A. Worterbuch der Technik: Italienisch-Deutsch. French & Eur.
Schlegelmilch, Alibert. Polytechnisches Woerterbuch (Pub. by Veb Verlag Technik). French & Eur.
--Polytechnisches Woerterbuch (Pub. by Veb Verlag Technik). French & Eur.
Schlegelmilch, Aribert. Polytechnisches Woerterbuch. VEB Verlag Technik.
--Polytechnisches Woerterbuch Italienisch-Deutsch. VEB Technik.
--Polytechnisches Worterbuch. Hueber.
Schlerath, B. Sanskrit Vocabulary Arranged According to Word Families with Meanings in English, German & Spanish. Heinman.
Schlomann, A. Illustrierte Technische Woerterbucher: Eisenbahnmaschinenwesen. Oldenbourg Verlag.
--Illustrierte Technische Woerterbucher: Eisenbahnmaschinenwesen (Pub. by R. Oldenbourg). French & Eur.
--Illustrierte Technische Woerterbucher: Eisenbahnbau und Betrieb. Oldenbourg Verlag.
--Illustrierte Technische Woerterbucher: Eisenbahnbau und Betrieb (Pub. by R. Oldenbourg). French & Eur.
--Illustrierte Technische Woerterbucher: ELektrotechnik und Elektrochemie. Oldenbourg Verlag.
--Illustrierte Technische Woerterbucher: Elektrotechnik und Elektrochemie (Pub. by R. Oldenbourg). French & Eur.
--Illustrierte Technische Woerterbucher: Maschinenelemente. Oldenbourg Verlag.
--Illustrierte Technische Woerterbucher: Maschinenelemente (Pub. by R. Oldenbourg). French & Eur.
--Illustrierter Technische Woerterbucher: Luffahrts. Oldenbourg Verlag.
--Illustrierter Technische Woerterbucher: Luffahrts (Pub. by R. Oldenbourg). French & Eur.
Schlomann, Alfred, ed. Illustrated Technical Dictionaries-Illustrierte Technische Woerterbuechen: In Six Languages. Incl. Vol. 1. Machinenelemante-Elements of Machinery & Tools; Vol. 2. Elektrotechnik & Elektrochemie-Electrical Engineering, Incl. Telegraphy & Telephony; Vol. 5. Eisenbahnbau und Betreib-Railway Construction & Operation; Vol. 14. Faserrohnstoffe - Raw Materials of the Textile Industry; Vol. 16. Webereiund Gewelbe - Weaving & Woven Fabrics; Vol. 17. Luftfahrt-Aeronautics. Intl Pubns Serv.
Schlomann, Alfred, ed. see Hoyer-Kreuter.
Schmalz, Larry C. & Sippl, Charles J. Computer Glossary for Students & Teachers. T Y Crowell.
Schmid, Hans & Von Muller, Peter. EDV-Taschenlexikon: In Zusammenarbeit Mit Guido Lobel. Verlag Moderne Industrie.
Schmidgall-Tellings, A. Ed. & Stevens, Alan. Contemporary Indonesian-English Dictionary. Ohio U Pr.
Schmidt, jt. auth. see Brinkmann.
Schmidt, Alexander. Shakespeare - Lexicon: A Complete Dictionary of All the English Words, Phrases & Constructions in the Works of the Poet. Sarrazin, Gregor, ed. De Gruyter.
--Shakespeare Lexicon: A Complete Dictionary of All the English Words, Phrases & Constructions in the Work of the Poet. Sarrazin, Gregor, ed. Ayer Co.
Schmidt, Heinrich. Philosophisches Woerterbuch. Kroener.
Schmidt, Helmut. Bergbautechnik & Aufbereitung Deutsch-Englisch. VEB Technik.
Schmidt, J. Dictionnaire mythologie grecque et romaine. Larousse.
--Vocabulaire d'Arabe Moderne: Economie-Politique-Actualite. Maison Dictionnaire.
--Vocabulaire d'Arabe moderne: Economie-Politique-Actualite. Maison Dictionnaire.
Schmidt, J. E. English Word Power for Physicians & Other Professionals: A Vigorous & Cultured Vocabulary. C C Thomas.

--Index of Paramedical Vocabulary. C C Thomas.
--Police Medical Dictionary. C C Thomas.
Schmidt, J. J. Vocabulaire Francais-Arabe de l'ingenieur & du Technicien, 1. Maisonneuve & Larose.
Schmidt, Jurgen, ed. see Roth, Reiner A. & Selzer, Helmut M.
Schmidt, Karl A. Easy Ways to Enlarge Your German Vocabulary. Dover.
Schmidt, Michael, ed. Diccionario Aleman-Espanol Espanol-Aleman. Biblograf SP.
Schmidt, Walter. Taschenworterbuch. VEB Verlag Enzyklopadie.
Schmidt, Walter, ed. Taschenwoerterbuch Englisch-Deutsch. VEB Verlag Enzyklopadie.
Schmidt-Anderla, Georgette, jt. auth. see Anderla, Georges.
Schmidt-Joos, S. & Graves, B. Rock Lexikon. Rowohlt.
--Rock Lexikon (Pub. by Rowohlt). French & Eur.
Schmieder, Christian & Fleischmann, Gunther. Schuelerlexikon fuer Arbeitslehre & Sozialkunde. Auer.
Schmitt, Roger & Filbert, Pierre. Vocabulaire & Style. Nathan.
Schmitt, Tilman. Fachworterbuch der Brauerei & Abfullpraxis. Carl KG.
Schmoll, G. Wortschatz der Information und Dokumentation (Pub. by Vlg. Dokumentation). French & Eur.
Schnack, Karsten, jt. ed. see Muschinsky, Lars J.
Schneeweiss, R. Dictionary of Cereal Processing & Cereal Chemistry. Elsevier.
Schneider, Hugo, et al, eds. Glossarium Amorum: Lfg 1, Schutzwaffen. Verlag der Buchhaendler-Vereinigung GmbH.
Schneider, Jan, ed. Langenscheidts Taschenwoerterbuecher Niederlandisch-Deutsch. Langenscheidt.
Schneider, Leonhard. Woerterbuch der Elektronik. French & Eur.
Schneider, Lucien. Dictionnaire des Infixes de l'esquimau de l'Ungava. Quebec Off.
--Dictionnaire Esquimau-Francais du Parler de l'Ungava & Contrees Limitrophes. Laval P. U.
--Dictionnaire Francais-Esquimau du Parier: l'Ungava & Contrees Limitrophes, 2. Laval P. U.
Schnitzlein, Gerhard. Lexikon Kraftfahrzeugtechnik. VEB Verlag Technik.
Schnitzler, Ilse. Lexikon Fuer Planetenbilder. French & Eur.
Schnurres, Wolfdietrich, ed. see Moeller, Hilke.
Schock, Sarina & Gebert, Erika. Fachworterbuch Textil (Pub. by Deutscher Fachverlag). French & Eur.
Schoeck. Diccionario de Sociologia. Herder SA.
Schoeck, H. Soziologisches Woerterbuch. Herder.
--Soziologisches Woerterbuch (Pub. by Herder). French & Eur.
Schoeck, Helmut. Diccionario de sociologia. Herder, tr. Herder SA.
--Diccionario de sociologia. Herder, tr. Herder AS.
--Diccionario De Sociologia. French & Eur.
Schoeffler, Weis. Woerterbuch der Englischen und Deutschen Sprache. French & Eur.
--Woerterbuch der Englischen und Deutschen Sprache. French & Eur.
Schoell, K. Dutch-Norwegian & Norwegian-Dutch Pocket Dictionary. Kunnskapsforlaget.
Schoene, W., ed. see Kroh, Paul.
Schoenfeld, Hanns-Martin, jt. auth. see Sommer, Werner.
Schoenfeld, Hans-Martin, jt. auth. see Sommer, Werner.
Schoenfeld, M. Woerterbuch der Altgermanischen Personen und Voelkernamen. French & Eur.
Schoenhals, Alvin & Schoenhals, Louise. Vocabulario Mixe de Totontepec. Summer Inst Ling.
Schoenhals, Louise, jt. auth. see Schoenhals, Alvin.
Schoffler & Weis. Pons Globalworterbuch. Klett.
Schoffler-Weiss. German-English, English-German Dictionary. M Rosenberg.
Scholes, P. A. Diccionario Oxford de la musica. Sudamer.
Schonberg, James. The Comparative Trilby Glossary, French-English. Century Bookbindery.
Schonfield, Hugh J. Popular Dictionary of Judaism. Citadel Pr.
Schonkron, M. Rumanian-English & Dictionary. Iaconi.
Schonkron, M., ed. Rumanian-English, English-Rumanian Dictionary, with Supplement. Ungar.
School of Social Work, Columbia University. Dictionary Catalog of the Whitney M. Young, Jr., Memorial Library of Social Work (Hall Library). G K Hall.
Schorb, Alfons O. Paedagogisches Taschenlexikon: A-Z. Kamp Verlag.
Schrader, Halwart. Oldtimer-Lexikon. BLV-Verlag.
Schraffl, jt. auth. see Zavada.
Schregle, Gotz. Deutsch-Arabisches Worterbuch. Lib Liban.
Schreiber, H., jt. auth. see Sommerfeldt, K.
Schreiber, H., jt. auth. see Sommerfeldt, K. E.
Schreiber, Hermann. Woerterbuch der Parapsychologie. French & Eur.
Schreiner, Jean, et al. Le Nouveau Dictionnaire de la Peche. French & Eur.
Schroetter, Friedrich Von, ed. Woerterbuch der Muenzkunde. De Gruyter.
Schubert, Delwyn G. A Dictionary of Terms & Concepts in Reading. C C Thomas.
Schuermans-Stekhoven, G. Dictionnaire Technique Universel Kluwer: Francais-Neerlandais. Kluwer-Deventer.
Schuermans Stekhoven, G. Dictionnaire Technique Universel Kluwer: Neerlandais-Francais. Kluwer-Deventer.
Schuh, Russell G. A Dictionary of Ngizim. U of Cal Pr.
Schukry, K. Langenscheidts Taschenwoerterbuecher Deutsch-Arabisch. Langenscheidt.
Schukry, K. & Humberdrotz, R. Langenscheidts Taschenwoerterbuch Arabisch: Teil II, Deutsch-Arabisch. Langenscheidt.
Schuler, A. Economics Dictionary (Pub. by Collets). State Mutual Bk.
Schulz. Woerterbuch der Datentechnik: Russisch-Deutsch-Englisch. Brandstetter.
--Woerterbuch der Optik & Feinmechanik: Band II, Englisch-Franzoesisch-Deutsch. Brandstetter.
--Woerterbuch der Optik & Feinmechanik: Band III, Franzoesisch-Deutsch-Englisch. Brandstetter.
Schulz, Charles M. The Charlie Brown Dictionary. Scholastic Inc.
Schulz, E. Woerterbuch der Optik und Feinmechanik: English-French-German Dictionary of Optics & Mechanical Engineering. French & Eur.
Schulz, Ernst. Woerterbuch der Optik und Feinmechanik. French & Eur.
--Woerterbuch der Optik und Feinmechanik. French & Eur.
Schulz, Joachim. Data Systems Dictionary. Brandstetter.
--Data Systems Dictionary: English-Russian-German (Pub. by Brandstetter Verlag). French & Eur.
--Woerterbuch der Datentechnick. Brandstetter.
Schulze, Hans H. Rororo-Lexikon zur Datenverarbeitung. Rowohlt.
Schur, Norman W. English English: A Descriptive Dictionary. Verbatim.
Schurr, Gerald, jt. auth. see Romand, Didier.
Schurr, Gerard, jt. auth. see Romand, Didier.
Schutzenberg. Diccionario de Tecnicas de Grupo. Soc Ed Atenas.
Schutzsenberger, Anne A. Diccionario De la Tecnicas De Grupo. French & Eur.
Schuurmang, G., ed. Elseviers Dictionary of Metal Cutting Tools. Elsevier.
Schuurmans, G. Kluwer's Universeel Technisch Woordenboek: Duits-Nederlands. French & Eur.
--Kluwer's Universeel Technisch Woordenboek, Nederlands-Engels. French & Eur.
--Kluwer's Universeel Technisch Woordenboek: Nederlands-Frans. French & Eur.
--Kluwer's Universeel Technish Woordenboek: Frans-Nederlands. French & Eur.
--Kluwer's Universel Technisch Woordenboek: Nederlands-Duits. French & Eur.
Schuurmans, G., ed. Elseviers Automobile Dictionary. Elsevier.
Schuurmans, Stekhoven G. & Piriou-Vandamme, M. Kluwer's Universeel Technisch Woordenboek Frans-Nederlands. Kluwer Technische.
Schuurmans, Stekhovenn G. Kluwer's Universeel Technisch Woorenboek Nederlands Frans. Kluwer Technische.
Schuurmans-Stekhoven, G. Dictionnaire Technique Universal Kluwer, Francais-Neerlandais. French & Eur.
--Dictionnaire Technique Universal Kluwer Neerlandais-Francais. French & Eur.
Schuurmans Stekhoven, G. Dutch-English, English-Dutch Engineering Dictionary. Heinman.
Schuwer, Philippe. Dictionnaire de l'Edition: Francais-Anglais, Anglais-Francais. French & Eur.
--Dictionnaire de l'edition: Francais-Anglais. Cercle Librairie.
Schwartz, Erwin, et al. Woerterbuch fuer die Grundschule. Westermann.
Schwartz, Robert J. Complete Dictionary of Abbreviations. T Y Crowell.
Schwarz, Urs & Hadik, Laszlo. Strategic Terminology. French & Eur.
Schwauss, Maria. Woerterbuch der Regionalen Umgangssprache in Lateinamerika. VEB Verlag Enzyklopadie.
Schwendtke, Arnold. Woerterbuch der Schulpaedagogik. French & Eur.
--Woerterbuch der Sozialarbeit & Sozialpaedagogik. Quelle & Meyer.
--Woerterbuch der Sozialarbeit und der Sozialpaedagogik. French & Eur.
Schwenkhagen, H. Woerterbuch Elektrotechnik & Elektronik. Girardet.
--Woerterbuch Elektrotechnik und Elektronik. French & Eur.
Schwenkhagen, H. F. & Meinhhold, H. Woerterbuch Elektrotechnik und Elektronik. French & Eur.
Schwesinger, Gladys C. The Social-Ethical Significance of Vocabulary. AMS Pr.
Schwicker, jt. auth. see Gagnacci-Schwicker, A.
Schwicker, Angelo C. International Dictionary of Building Construction: English-French-German-Italian. Scholium Intl.
Schwilling, Werner. Lexikon der Geldenlage. French & Eur.
Sciarone Abondio, Giuseppe. Vocabolario fondamentale della lingua italiana. Minerva Italica.
Scientific Apparatus Makers Association. Process Instrumentation Reliability Terminology: 32.1-1976. Sci Apparatus.
--Process Measurement & Control Terminology: 20.1-1973. Sci Apparatus.
Scneider, M. E. Semiiazychnyi Slovar Po Mekhanike Gruntov & Fundamentostroeniiu (Pub. by Gosizdat Fizmat. Lit.). Four Continent.
Scott & Smith. Dictionary of Waste & Water Treatment. Butterworth.
Scott, jt. auth. see Liddell.
Scott, A. F. Current Literary Terms: A Concise Dictionary of Their Origin & Use. Macmillan London.
Scott, A. F., ed. Current Literary Terms. St Martin.
Scott, Christopher. A Learner's First Dictionary. Macmillan London.
Scott, Christopher, jt. auth. see Poolman.
Scott, Henry L. Military Dictionary. Greenwood.
Scott, John S. Dictionary of Building. Penguin.
--Dictionary of Civil Engineering. Halsted Pr.
Scott, Robert, jt. ed. see Liddell, H. G.
Scott, Robert, jt. ed. see Liddell, Henry G.
Scott, Thomas. The Interpreter, Wherein Three Principal Terms of State Are Clearly Unfolded. Walter J Johnson.
Scott, Sir Walter. Complete Glossary for Sir Walter Scott's Novels & Romances. B Franklin.
Scouezec. Diccionario De Atres Adivinatorias. French & Eur.
Scrascia, Euclide, jt. auth. see Magalini, Sergio I.
Screen, J. E., jt. ed. see Walford, Alberto J.
Scremin. Diccionario de moral profesional medica. Garriga.
Scruton, Robert. A Dictionary of Political Thought (HarpT). Har-Row.
Scruton, ROger. A Dictionary of Political Thought. Macmillan London.
Scruton, Roger, ed. Dictionary of Political Thought. Macmillan London.
Scullard, H. H., jt. ed. see Hammond, N. G.
Seaburg, S. L., et al, eds. Paper Oriented Glossary Covering Advanced Process Control Terminology. TAPPI.
Sears, Minnie E., jt. auth. see Mudge, Isadore G.
Season, S. M. Chinese-English Idioms & Phrases. French & Eur.
Seaton, A. G. Writer's Dictionary. St Martin.
Sebastian Yarza, Florencio I. Diccionario griego-espanol. Sopena.
Seco, Manuel. Diccionario de Dudas & Dificultades de la Lengua Espanola. Aguilar SP.
--Diccionario de dudas de la lengua espanola. Aguilar.
--Diccionario de Dudas de la Lengua Espanola (AGL). Lectorum Pubns.
--Diccionario de dudas de la lengua espanola. Iaconi.
--Diccionario de Dudas de la Lengua Espanol. French & Eur.
Seddon, Richard, jt. auth. see Reynolds, Kimberley.
Sedira, Ben. Dictionnaire Arabe-Francais. French & Eur.
--Dictionnaire Francais-Arabe. French & Eur.
Seebold, Elmar. Vergleichendes und Etymologisches Worterbuch der Germanischen Starken Verben. Mouton.
Segal, Louis. English-Russian Dictionary. Beekman Pubs.
Segatore, L. & Poli, G. A. Dizionario medico. Ist Geog Agostini.
Segatore, Luigi & Poli, Gianangelo. Diccionario Medico. Teide.
--Diccionario Medico. French & Eur.
Segditsas, P., ed. Elseviers Nautical Dictionary. Elsevier.
Seguy, Eugene. Dictionnaire des Termes Techniques d'entomologie Elementaire. Lechevalier.
--Dictionnaire des Termes Techniques d'Entomologies Elementaire. French & Eur.
Seibicke, jt. auth. see Drozd.
Seidler, Eduard. Woerterbuch Medizinischer Grundbegriffe. Herder.
Seiffhart, Arthur, ed. see Juncker.
Seiler, Hansjakob & Hioki, Kojiro. Cahuilla Dictionary. Malki Mus Pr.
Seitzinger, Jack M. & Kelley, Thomas M. Police Terminology: Programmed Manual for Criminal Justice Personnel. C C Thomas.
Sejersen, Gorm, ed. see Dehn-Nielsen, Henning.
Seldon, Arthur & Pennance, F. G. Diccionario De Economia. French & Eur.

--Diccionario de Economia. French & Eur.
Seldon, Arthur & Pennanee, F. G., trs. Diccionario de economia. Oikos Tau.
Seleccione Reader's Digest. Diccionario Medico Familiar. French & Eur.
Sell. Diccionario para especialistas de seguros. Rev. Mex. de Seguros.
Sella, Pietro. Dizionario latino-italiano: Stato della Chiesa-Veneto-Abruzzi. Biblioteca Apostolica Vaticana.
--Glossario latino-emiliano. Biblio Apost.
Sellien, H., jt. ed. see Sellien, R.
Sellien, R. Dr. Gablers Wirtschafts - Lexikon (Pub. by Betriebswirtschaftlicher Vlg.). French & Eur.
Sellien, R. & Sellien, H., eds. Doktor Gabler's Wirtschafts-Lexikon. Gabler.
Selzer, Helmut M., jt. auth. see Roth, Reiner A.
Selzer, Helmut M., jt. ed. see Roth, Rainer A.
Semenova, Olga I., jt. auth. see Pavlov, Ernst A.
Semjonowa, O. I., jt. auth. see Pawlow, E. A.
Semniuk, Bazyli, jt. ed. see Kryt, Dobromila.
Sen, Chitrabhanu. A Dictionary of the Vedic rituals. Concept Pub. Co.
Senechal, jt. auth. see Tanguay, Cyprien.
Senior, H. W., ed. A Vocabulary of the Limbu Language of Eastern Nepal. Radha.
Senn, Alfred, jt. auth. see Williams, Edwin B.
Seone, Joaquin R. Diccionario de contabilidad, organizacion, administracion, control & ciencia afines. Difusion.
Serafini Amato, Loredana. La Distribuzione della Posposizione nel Lituano Antico. Ist Univers Orient.
Serand, Pierre & De Sacy, Samuel S. Dictionnaire des Citations Francaises. Larousse.
Sereville, Etienne De & Saint-Simon, F. de. Dictionnaire de la Noblesse Francais. French & Eur.
Sereville, Etienne de & Saint-Simon, Fernand de. Supplement au Dictionnaire de la Noblesse Francaise. French & Eur.
Serra, M. A., jt. auth. see Camarao, P. C.
Serrano, Merce, tr. see Lender, T., et al.
Serrano, Miguel G. Diccionario de Terminos Socio-politicos. Everest.
Serrano Laktaw, Pedro, ed. Diccionario hispano-tagalog y tagalog-hispano. Cultura Hispan.
Serrano Mesa, Eleesbaan. Diccionario espanol-ingles ingles-espanol. Mayfe.
--Diccionario Ingles-Espanol, Espanol-Ingles Forja. French & Eur.
--Diccionario Ingles-Espanol, Espanol-Ingles. French & Eur.
Serre, Robert. Dictionnaire Contextuel Anglais-Francais de l'energie Solaire. Serre.
Serullaz, Maurice. Lexikon des Impressionismus. French & Eur.
Servi, Vera. Cookbook Dictionary. Camaro Pub.
Servolini, L. L. Dizionario illustrato degli incisori italiani. Goerlich.
Servotte, Josef V. Dictionnaire Commercial & Financier en Quatre Langues: Francais-Neerlandais-Anglais-Allemand. Erasme.
--Dictionnaire Commercial & Financier: Francais-Anglais. Marabout.
Servotte, Jozef V. Commercial & Financial Dictionary in Four Languages. Intl Pubns Serv.
Sese, Bernard. Vocabulaire de la Langue Espagnole Classique: XVIe & XVIIe Siecles. Doc Univers.
--Vocabulaire de la Langue Espagnole Classique: XVIe. & XVIIe. Siecles. CDU.
Sethaputra, So, compiled by. New Model English - Thai Dictionary. Intl Pubns Serv.
Settimj, L. Dizionario merceologico per la pratica applicazione della nuova tariffa doganale italiana. Hoepli.
Setton, C., et al. Dictionnaire Hachette de la Langue Francaise. French & Eur.
Sevestre, A. Dictionnaire de Patrologie. Migne, J. P., ed. Caratzas Pub Co.
Sevortian, E. V. Etimologicheskii Slovar Tiurkskikh Iazykov (Pub. by Nauka). Four Continent.
--Etimologicheskii Slovar Tiurkskikh Iazykov (Pub. by Nauka). Four Continent.
Seyffert, Oskar. Dictionary of Classical Antiquities. Nettleship, ed. Peter Smith.
Sezepesi, G & Szekely, B. Systems Analysis & Operations Research Dictionary (Pub. by Collets). State Mutual Bk.
Sgard, Jean. Dictionnaire des Journalistes. Club Livre Select.
Sgard, Jean & Gilot, Michel. Dictionnaire des Journalistes, 1600-1789. French & Eur.
Shaaban, Robert. Adili Na Nduguze. Macmillan London.
Shadily, Hassan, jt. auth. see Echols, John M.
Shafritz, Jay M., jt. auth. see Oran, Daniel.
Shagirov, A. K. Etimologicheskii Slovar Adygskikh (Cherkesskikh (Pub. by Nauka). Four Continent.
Shain, M. & Longley, D. A Dictionary of Information Technology (Pub. by Macmillan England). State Mutual Bk.
Shain, Michael & Longley, David. Dictionary of Information Technology. Macmillan London.
Shain, Michael, jt. auth. see Longley, Dennis.
Shaldach, Herbert Von see Von Schaldach, Herbert.
Shalhoub, Judy & Murray, Carol. Clinical Spanish for Dietitians. Plycon Pr.
Shann, C. D., ed. The Pipeline Glossary & Directory. Scientific Surveys.
Shanney, A. T. Hindi-English Dictionary: With Pronounciations Romanized. Shalom.
Shanskii, N. M. Chetyre Tys Acha Naibolee Upotrebitel Nykh Slov Russkogo Iazyka. Four Continent.
--Etimologicheskii Slovar Russkogo Iazyka: Tom. 1, Vyp. 4 (G (Pub. by MGU). Four Continent.
--Etimologicheskii Slovar Russkogo Iazyka: Tom. 1, Vyp. 5 (D, E, Zh (Pub. by MGU). Four Continent.
--Etimologicheskii Slovar Russkogo Iazyka: Tom. 2, Vyp. 6 (Z (Pub. by MGU). Four Continent.
--Etimologichesskii Slovar Russkogo Iazyka: Tom. 2, Vyp. 7 (I (Pub. by MGU). Four Continent.
Shanskii, N. M., ed. Etimologicheskii Slovar Russkogo Iazyka: Tom. 1, Vyp. 3 (V (Pub. by MGU). Four Continent.
Shanskii, N. M., et al. Kratkii Etimologicheskii Slovar Russkogo Iazyka (Pub. by Proveschchenie). Four Continent.
Shansky, N. & Bystrova, E. Seven Hundred Russian Idioms & Set Phrases. Four Continent.
Shapiro, Amy. Martial Arts Language. Running Pr.
Shapiro, Irving J. Dictionary of Marketing Terms. Littlefield.
--Dictionary of Marketing Terms. Rowman.
Sharbatov, G. Sh. Russko-Arabskii Uchebnyi Slovar (Pub. by Russki Iazyk). Four Continent.
Sharma, Jagdish S. The National Geographical Dictionary of India. Intl Pubns Serv.
Sharman, Fay. The Taste of France: A Dictionary of French Food & Wine. Chadwick, Brian & Boehm, Klaus, eds. HM.
Sharov, V., et al. Nemetsko-Russkii Slovar Po Vychislitelnoi Tekhnike (Pub. by Russkii Iazyk). Four Continent.
Sharp, D. W., ed. Miall's Dictionary of Chemistry. Longman.
Shaw, Arnold. A Dictionary of American Pop-Rock. Assoc-Mus.
Shaw, Frank. Dictionary of Automotive Engineering. Newnes Bks.
Shaw, Harry. Concise Dictionary of Literary Terms (SP). McGraw.
--Dictionary of Problem Words & Expressions (P&RB). McGraw.
Shaw, Janet, jt. auth. see Shaw, John R.
Shaw, John R. & Shaw, Janet. The New Horizon Ladder Dictionary of the English Language for Young Readers (Sig). NAL.
Shaw, Marie-Jose. The Dictionary. ESP.
--Jumbo Vocabulary Development Yearbook: Grade 3. ESP.
--Jumbo Vocabulary Development Yearbook: Grade 4. ESP.
--Jumbo Vocabulary Development Yearbook: Grade 5. ESP.
Shchukin, M. Chetyrekhiazychnyi Entsiklopedicheskii Slovar Terminov Po Fizicheskoi Geografii (Pub. by Russkii Iaxyknt Bk). Four Continent.
Shea, John D. French-Onondaga Dictionary, from a Manuscript of the Seventeenth Century. AMS Pr.
Shearer, Howard E., ed. Glossary of Textile Terminology for the Paper Manufacturer. TAPPI.
Shefski, Bill. Football Language. Running Pr.
--Running Press Glossary of Football Language. Running Pr.
Shemakin, Iu. I., ed. Tezaurus Nauchno-Tekhnicheskikh Terminov (Pub. by Voenizdat). Four Continent.
Shepherd, James F. College Vocabulary Skills. HM.
Shetty, M. C., jt. auth. see Scharf, T.
Shevchenko, V. S., et al. Kratkii Cheshsko-Russkii i Russko-Cheshskii Vneshnetorgovyi Slovar (Pub. by Vneshtorgizdat). Four Continent.
Shevisova, S. V., jt. auth. see Lapidus, B. A.
Shevtsoka, S. V., jt. auth. see Lapidus, B. A.
Shevtsova, S. V., jt. auth. see Lapidus, B. A.
Shilling, Alison W., jt. auth. see Holm, John A.
Shimizu, Mamoru, tr. see Kawamoto, Shigeo & Nishiwaki, Junzaburo.
Shinagel, Michael, ed. A Concordance to the Poems of Jonathan Swift. Cornell U Pr.
Shipley, Joseph T. Diccionario de la Literatura Mundial. French & Eur.
--Dictionary of Early English. Littlefield.
--Dictionary of Word Origins. Greenwood.
--Dictionary of Word Origins. Littlefield.
Shipley, Joseph T., ed. Dictionary of World Literary Terms. Writer.
Shipley, Robert M. Dictionary of Gems & Gemology. Gemological.
Shipp, G. P. Modern Greek Evidence for the Ancient Greek Vocabulary (Pub. by Sydney U Pr). Intl Schol Bk Serv.
Shipp, James F. Russian-English Dictionary of Abbreviations & Initialisms. Translation Research.
--Russian-English Dictionary of Surnames: Important Names from Science & Technology. Translation Research.
--Russian-English Index to Scientific Apparatus Nomenclature. Trans Res Inst.
Shiratori, F., jt. auth. see Tamura, S.
Shiratori, T. Chinese-English-Japanese Glossary of Chemical Terms. French & Eur.
Shishmarev, A. I. & Zamorin, A. P. Explanatory Dictionary of Computing Machinery & Data Processing (Pub. by Collets). State Mutual Bk.
Shismarev, A. I. & Zamorin, A. P. Explanatory Dictionary of Computing Machinery & Data Processing. French & Eur.
Shnitnikov, Boris N. Kazakh-English Dictionary. Mouton.
Short, Charles, jt. auth. see Lewis, Charlton T.
Shoshan, A. Even & Yarden, Dov, eds. Milon Kis: A Hebrew Pocket Dictionary. Board Jewish Educ.
Shoshan, Abraham E., ed. The Complete Hebrew Dictionary Supplement to the 3 Volume Set. K Sefer.
--The Complete Hebrew Dictionary Supplement Volume to Seven Volume Set. K Sefer.
Shosteck, Patti. A Lexicon of Jewish Cooking. Contemp Bks.
Shuhan, Zhao, ed. see Xinglian, Zhang.
Shukla, J. M., jt. auth. see Abhyankar, Kashinath V.
Shukla, Lalit K. Study of Hindu Art & Architecture with Special Reference to Terminology. Verry.
Shumaker, David, ed. Seven Language Dictionary. Crown.
Shumway, Eric B. Intensive Course in Tongan. UH Pr.
Shuurmans, G. Kluwer's Universeel Technisch Woordenboek: Engels-Nederlands. French & Eur.
Shvarts, V. V. The Concise Illustrated Russian-English Dictionary of Mechanical Engineering. Pergamon.
--Kratkii Illiustrirovannyi Russko-Angliiskii Slovar Po Mashinostroeniu (Pub. by Russkii Iazyk). Four Continent.
Shvarts, Vladimir. The Concise Illustrated Russian-English Dictionary of Mechanical Engineering (Pub. by Collets). State Mutual Bk.
Sidgwick, Jean, tr. see Del Vasto, Lanza.
Sidou, J. Vocabulario do Cheque. Editora Revista.
Sieferl, Fritz, ed. Das Lexikon der Deutschen Staedte & Gemeinden. Fackelverlag.
Siefert, Fritz. Das Lexikon der Deutschen Staedt und Gemeinden. French & Eur.
Siefert, Fritz, ed. Das Lexikon der Deutschen Staedte & Gemeinden. Suedwest.
Siegwalt, Gerard, jt. auth. see Congar, Yves.
Siekmann, Rob. Prisma Voetbalwoordenboek. Spectrum NL.
Siemens. Quantities, Formulae, Definitions (Wiley Heyden). Wiley.
Sieny, Mahmoud. Syntax of Urban Hijazi Arabic. Intl Bk Ctr.
Sierra, Jose A. English-Spanish Sports Dictionary for Soccer (Pub. by Wolfhound Pr Ireland). State Mutual Bk.
Sigurd, Bengt, ed. see Beckman, Nat.
Sigurd, Bengt, ed. see Beckman, Natanael.
Sigurdsson, A. Icelandic-English Dictionary. Heinman.
Sigurdsson, A. & Bogason, S. O. Icelandic-English - English-Icelandic Dictionary. Heinman.
Sigurdsson, Arngrimur. Icelandic-English Dictionary. Shalom.
Sikora, G. Technical Automotive Dictionary: Russian-English-German-French-Bulgarian. French & Eur.
Sikorski, Lech. Maly Slownik Polsko-Swedzki. Plastik.
--Maly Slownik Szwedzko-Polski. Wiedza Powszechna.
Silberling, E. Dictionnaire De Sociologie Phalansterienne: Guide Des Oeuvres Completes De Charles Fourier. B Franklin.
Sil'ianov, V. V., et al. Anglo-Russkaia Terminologiia Po Organizatsii & Bezopasnosti Dorozhnogo Divizheniia (Pub. by Viniti). Four Continent.
Sillamy, N. Dictionnaire psychologie. Larousse.
Sillamy, Norbert. Diccionario de la psicologia. Plaza Janes.
--Dictionnaire de la Psychologie. Larousse.
--Dictionnaire de Psychologie. Larousse.
Sillamy, Norberth. Diccionario de la Psicologia. French & Eur.
Silva, Dharmasena de see De Silva, Dharmasena.
Silva, Maria, jt. auth. see Kennedy, W. G.
Silverman-Dresner, Toby, jt. auth. see Guilfoyle, George R.
Silverstein, et al. Spanish Now. Camino Real.
Silvert, J. Estonian-English Dictionary. Shalom.
Silvestri, R., jt. auth. see Padovani, G.

Silvestri, Richard, jt. auth. see Padovani, Giuseppe.
Silvestrov, P. V. Dictionnaire Meteorologique: Francais-Russe. French & Eur.
Silvy, Antoine. Dictionnaire Montagnais Francais. Quebec P. U.
Simeon, Remi. Diccionario de la Lengua Nahuatl o Mexicana. Siglo Veintiuno.
Simic, Z. English-Serbocroatian Dictionary. French & Eur.
--Yugoslavian Dictionary: English-Serbocroatian. Vanous.
Simic, Zivojin, jt. auth. see Ristic, Svetomir.
Simic, Zivojin, jt. ed. see Ristic, Syetomir.
Simin. Dictionnaire du Bearnais & du Gascon Moderne. CNRS.
Simko, P. English-Slovak Dictionary (Pub. by Collet's). State Mutual Bk.
Simms, Ena, jt. auth. see Chen, Janey.
Simon, Alfred. Dictionnaire du Theatre Francais Contemporain. Larousse.
--Dictionnaire Du Theatre Francais Contemporain. French & Eur.
--Dictionnaire theatre francais contemporain. Larousse.
Simon & Schuster. Diccionario Espanol-Ingles Pocket Dictionary. Camino Real.
--Diccionario Espa n13ol -- Ingl e01s Pocket Dictionary. Camino Real.
Simon, Andre L. & Howe, Robin. Dictionary of Gastronomy. Overlook Pr.
Simon, W. A Beginner's Chinese English Dictionary of the National Language (Gwpyeu (Pub. by Lund Humphries England). State Mutual Bk.
Simond, Jacques, ed. see Fleurian, Dominique de.
Simone, R. Dizionario italiano-francese e francese-italiano. La Nuova Italia.
Simoneau, Francois N. Vocabulaire Suedois. Ophrys.
Simonet, Francisco J. Glosario de voces Ibericas y Latinas. Intl Bk Ctr.
--Glosario de voces ibericas y latinas: Tomo 1. Atlas Edns.
--Glosario de voces ibericas y latinas: Tomo 2. Atlas Edns.
--Glosario de voces ibericas y latinas: Obras completa. Atlas Edns.
Simons, Eric N. A Dictionary of Machining. Philos Lib.
Simpson, D. P. Cassell's Latin Dictionary: Latin-English, English-Latin. Imported Bks.
Simpson, D. P., compiled by. Cassell's Concise Latin-English, English-Latin Dictionary. Macmillan.
Simpson, D. P., ed. Cassell's Latin Dictionary: Latin-English, English-Latin. Macmillan.
Simpson, D. P., ed. see Cassell.
Sinclair, Janet, jt. auth. see Kersley, Leo.
Singleton, Paul & Sainsbury, Diana. Dictionary of Microbiology (Pub. by Wiley-Interscience). Wiley.
Sinielnikoff, Roxana, jt. auth. see Bartnicka, Barbara.
Sinitsyna, G. V. & Mitronova, I. N. Karmannyi Polsko-Russkii & Russko-Polskii Slovar. Russkii Iazyk.
Sinsoilliez, Robert. Lexique des Termes de Parodontologie de Microbiologie Parodontale et Buccale et de Sciences Fondamentales. French & Eur.
--Lexique des Termes Parodontologie de Microbiologie: Parodontale & Buccale & de Sciences Fondamentales. Prelat.
Sintas, J. Diccionario De Maximas Pensamientos y Sentacias. French & Eur.
Sintes. Diccionario de Aforismos, Proverbios & Refranes (SOP). Lectorum Pubns.
--Diccionario de aforismos, proverbios y refranes. Sintes.
Sintes, J. Diccionario de Aforismos: Proverbios Refranes. French & Eur.
--Diccionario de la Felicidad. French & Eur.
--Diccionario Humoristico. French & Eur.
Sintes Pros, Jorge. Diccionario de aforismos, proverbios y refrances. Sintes.
Sintes Pros, Jorge, ed. Diccionario de maximas, pensamientos y sentencias. Sintes.
--Diccionario humoristico. Sintes.
Sippl, Charles. Microcomputer Dictionary. Sams.
Sippl, Charles J. Data Communications Dictionary. Van Nos Reinhold.
Sippl, Charles J. & Sippl, Roger J. Computer Dictionary. Sams.
Sippl, Charles J., jt. auth. see Mayer, JoAnne C.
Sippl, Charles J., jt. auth. see Schmalz, Larry C.
Sippl, Roger J., jt. auth. see Sippl, Charles J.
Sirages, H. Elsevier's Football Dictionary. Elsevier.
Sircar, D. C. Indian Epigraphical Glossary. Orient Bk Dist.
Siregar, A. Hamid. Kamus Inggeris Indonesia: Dictionary English-Indonesia for School, Office & Home. Pustaka Antara.
Sisson, A. F. Unabridged Crossword Puzzle Dictionary. Doubleday.
Sitjar, Buenaventura. Vocabulary of the Language of San Antonio Mission, California. AMS Pr.
Sitzmann, Edourd. Dictionnaire de Biographie des Hommes Celebres: Despuis les Temps les Plus Recules Jusqu'a nos Jours. Berger Levrault.
Siunchev, Kh. I, et al, eds. Russko-Karachaevo-Balkarskii Slovar (Pub. by Sov. Entsiklopediia). Four Continent.
Sivan, Reuban, jt. ed. see Levenston, Edward A.
Sivan, Reuben & Levenston, Edward A. The New Bantam-Meggido Hebrew & English Dictionary. Bantam.
Sivan, Reuven & Levenston, Edward A. The New Bantam-Megiddo Hebrew & English Dictionary. Schocken.
Sivan, Reuven, jt. auth. see Levenston, Edward A.
Sivry, L. De see De Sivry, L.
Sizaire, P. Dictionnaire Technique De la Construction Electrique. French & Eur.
Sizaire, Pierre. Dictionnaire Technique de la Construction Electrique. Eyrolles.
Skadberg, Kare & Ulset, Tor. Merknader til en dell Norrone Tekster. Univers Oslo.
Skeat, W. W., jt. auth. see Mayhew, A. L.
Skeat, W. W., ed. see Langland, William.
Skeat, Walter W., jt. auth. see Mayhew, A. I.
Skeat, Walter W., ed. Concise Etymological Dictionary of the English Language. Oxford U Pr.
--Etymological Dictionary of the English Language. Oxford U Pr.
Skeri, J., jt. auth. see Komac.
Skerlj, jt. auth. see Komac.
Skerlj, R., et al. Yugoslavian-English Slovene Dictionary. Vanous.
Skey, Malcolm, ed. English-Italian, Italian-English Dictionary. Oxford U Pr.
Skillman, Billy G; see Hench, Atcheson L.
Skoss, Solomon, ed. Hebrew-Arabic Dictionary of the Bible Known As Kitab Jami-Al-Alfaz. Elliots Bks.
Skoss, Solomon L., ed. see David Ben Abraham.
Skripecz, Ratz S., et al. Langenscheidts Handwoerterbuch Ungarisch HALASZ: Teil I, Ungarisch-Deutsch. Langenscheidt.
Skrzynka, jt. auth. see Czerni.
Skrzynska, M., jt. auth. see Czerni, S.
Skrzynska, Maria, jt. ed. see Czerni, Sergiusz.
Skvorzova & Maizel. Dizionario italiano-russo. Editori Riuniti.
Slaba, D., jt. auth. see Kolafova, V.
Slaby & Grossmann. Woerterbuch der Spanischen & Deutschen Sprache: Band II, Deutsch-Spanisch. Brandstetter.
--Woerterbuch der Spanischen & Deutschen Sprache: Band I, Spanisch-Deutsch. Brandstetter.
Slaby, R. J. & Grossman, R., eds. Spanish & German Dictionary. Incl. Vol. 1. Spanish-German; Vol. 2. German-Spanish. Ungar.
Slaby, Rudolf. Diccionario De las Lenguas Espanola y Alemana. French & Eur.
--Woerterbuch der Deutschen und Spanischen Sprache. French & Eur.
--Woerterbuch der Deutschen und Spanischen Sprache. French & Eur.
Slaby, Rudolf, et al. Diccionario de la lengua espanola y alemana: Tomo 1. Herder SA.
--Diccionario de las lenguas espanola alemana. Herder SA.
Slaby-Grossmann. Diccionario de las lenguas espanola y alemana: Aleman-espanol. Herder.
Slagmolen, Gerrit. Muzieklexicon. Bruna.
Slater, William J., ed. Lexicon to Pindar. De Gruyter.
Sleeman, J. H. & Pollet, Gilbert. Lexicon Plotinianum. Leuven U Pr.
Slesser, Malcolm. Dictionary of Energy. Macmillan London.
--The Dictionary of Energy. Schocken.
Slesser, Malcom, et al, eds. Dictionary of Energy. Macmillan London.
Slette, T. Norwegian-English Dictionary. Vanous.
Sliosberg, A. Elsevier's Dictionary of Pharmaceutical Science & Techniques. Incl. Vol. 1: Pharmaceutical Technology; Vol. 2: Materia Medica. Elsevier.
--Elsevier's Medical Dictionary in Five Languages. Elsevier.
Slipp, Samuel, jt. auth. see Pinney, Edward L., Jr.
Sloan, Harold S. & Zurcher, Arnold J. Dictionary of Economics. B&N Imports.
--Dictionary of Economics (EH). B&N NY.
Sloane, Sheila B. & Dusseau, John L. The Legal Speller with Useful Medical Terms. West Pub.
Slocum, Marianna, jt. auth. see Gerdel, Florence.
Slomp, Jan, ed. see Pieterse, Liberius.
Slonimsky, Nicholas. Thesaurus of Scales & Melodic Patterns (ScribT). Scribner.
Slonimsky, Nicolas. Lexicon of Musical Invective: Critical Assaults on Composers Since Beethoven's Time. U of Wash Pr.
Slopek, Stefan. Slownik Immunologiczny Ilustrowany. Panstowy Zaklad W.
Small, jt. auth. see Monkhouse.
Small, John, jt. auth. see Monkhouse, F. J.
Smalley, W. A., et al. Orthography Studies. Am Bible.
--Orthography Studies. United Bible.
Smeeth, William B., ed see Lawrence, Marjorie K., et al.
Smejkalova, J., et al. Czechoslovakian Dictionary: English-Slovak & Slovak-English. Vanous.
--Slovak-English-Slovak Pocket Dictionary. Vanous.
Smiddy, F. G. Dictionary of General Pathology. Beekman Pubs.
--Dictionary of General Pathology (Pub. by Pitman Bks England). State Mutual Bk.
Smirnitskii, A. I. Russko-Angliiskii Slovar. Four Continent.
Smirnitskii, T. Russian-English Dictionary (Pub. by Collet's). State Mutual Bk.
Smirnitsky, A. I. Russian English Dictionary. Dutton.
--Russian-English Dictionary. Saphrograph.
Smirnov, I. P., jt. auth. see Melnikova, M. M.
Smirnova, L. A. Russko-Angliiskii Razgovornik Dlia Fizikov (Pub. by Sov Entsiklopediia). Four Continent.
--Russko-Angliiskii Razgovornik Dlia Fizikov (Pub. by Russkii Iazyk). Four Continent.
Smit, J., jt. auth. see Broers, A.
Smith, jt. auth. see Scott.
Smith, Alistair, jt. ed. see Laclotte, Michel.
Smith, Betty, jt. auth. see Osterberg, Richard F.
Smith, C. C., et al, eds. Langenscheidt's Standard Spanish Dictionary: Spanish-English, English-Spanish. Am Map.
Smith, Charles J. Synonyms Discriminated. Smith, Percy H., ed. Gale.
Smith, Colin. Diccionario Collins Ingles-Espanol. Grijalbo.
Smith, Edward C. & Zurcher, Arnold J. Dictionary of American Politics. B&N Imports.
--Dictionary of American Politics (EH). B&N NY.
Smith, Elliott. Contemporary Vocabulary. St Martin.
Smith, Eric. A Dictionary of Classical Allusion in English Literature. B&N Imports.
Smith, Forrest G. Dictionary of Freshman Composition. Littlefield.
Smith, G. L. & Davis, P. E. Medical Terminology (Pub. by Wiley Med). Wiley.
Smith, Genevieve L. & Davis, Phyllis E. Quick Medical Terminology (Pub. by Wiley Pr). Wiley.
Smith, George. A Universal Military Dictionary. U of Toronto Pr.
Smith, Gerald B., jt. ed. see Mathews, Shailer.
Smith, H. Wendell, jt. auth. see Lazarus, Arnold.
Smith, Henry P. Glossary of Terms & Phrases. Gale.
Smith, Jacob B., ed. Greek-English Concordance. Herald Pr.
Smith, Josefa J., et al, eds. Cortina-Grosset Basic German Dictionary (G&D). Putnam Pub Group.
Smith, Muriel H., jt. auth. see Forbes, Patricia.
Smith, Percy H., ed. see Smith, Charles J.
Smith, Philip H., jt. ed. see Pollin, Alice M.
Smith, R. Payne. Compendious Syriac Dictionary Founded Upon the Thesaurus Syriacus of R. Payne Smith. Payne Smith, J., ed. Oxford U Pr.
Smith, Richard A., ed. see Sahai, Hardeo & Berrios, Jose.
Smith, Richard H. A Concise Coptic-English Lexicon. Eerdmans.
Smith, Robert W. Dictionary of English Word-Roots. Rowman.
--Dictionary of English Word-Roots: English-Roots & Roots-English with Examples & Exercises. Littlefield.
Smith, Roge T. Gothic Architecture in England with an Illustrated Glossary of Technical Terms. Gloucester Art.
Smith, Stevenson & Guthrie, Edwin R. General Psychology in Terms of Behavior. Johnson Repr.
Smith, V. J. Dictionary of Synonyms & Antonyms. Shalom.
Smith, W. B. De la Toponymie Bretonne, Dictionnaire Etymologique. Kraus Repr.
Smith, William. Dictionary of Greek & Roman Antiquities. Longwood Pr.
--New Smith's Bible Dictionary. Lemmons, Reuel G., et al, eds. Doubleday.
--New Smith's Bible Dictionary (Galilee). Doubleday.
--Smith's Dictionary of the Bible. Baker Bk.
Smith, William, ed. Dictionary of Greek & Roman Biography & Mythology. AMS Pr.
--Dictionary of Greek & Roman Geography. AMS Pr.
Smith, William & Lockwood, J. L., eds. Chambers Murray Latin-English Dictionary. B&N Imports.
Smith Colinbermego, Manuel. Diccionario Collins Spanish-English Ingles-Espanol. Grijalbo.
Smith-Davis. Terminologia Medica: Texto Programado. Limusa.
Smithsonian Institution, Washington, D. C. Dictionary Catalog of the Library of the Freer Gallery of Art (Hall Library). G K Hall.
Smolik, H. Tierlexikon. Rowohlt.
--Tierlexikon (Pub. by Rowohlt). French & Eur.
Smolin, Ronald P., ed. High Technology Glossary: Nineteen Eighty-Three. Intl Edns.
Snell, Bruno & Erbse, Hartmut. Lexikon des Fruehgriechischen Epos: Lfg 1. Vandenhoeck.

--Lexikon des Fruehgriechischen Epos: Lfg 2. Vandenhoeck.
--Lexikon des Fruehgriechischen Epos: Lfg 3. Vandenhoeck.
--Lexikon des Fruehgriechischen Epos: Lfg 4. Vandenhoeck.
--Lexikon des Fruehgriechischen Epos: Lfg 5. Vandenhoeck.
--Lexikon des Fruehgriechischen Epos: Lfg 6. Vandenhoeck.
--Lexikon des Fruehgriechischen Epos: Lfg 7. Vandenhoeck.
--Lexikon des Fruehgriechischen Epos: Lfg 8. Vandenhoeck.
Snell, Walter & Dick, Esther A. Glossary of Mycology. Harvard U Pr.
Snelling, Henry H. & Anthony, E. A Dictionary of the Photographic & a Comprehensive & Systematic Catalogue of Photographic Apparatus Material: Manufactured, Imported & Sold by E. Anthony. Bunnell, Peter & Sobieszek, Robert A., eds. Ayer Co.
S.N.F.R. Les Ressorts: Francais-Allemand-Anglais-Espagnol. Maison Dictionnaire.
Snyckers, Alexandre, jt. auth. see Werny, Paul.
Soap & Detergent Association. A Handbook of Industry Terms. Soap & Detergent.
Sobecka, Z., et al, eds. Dictionary of Chemistry & Chemical Technology in Six Languages. Pergamon.
Sobel, Lester A., ed. News Dictionary: 1973. Facts on File.
Sobel, Lester A., et al. News Dictionary: Vol. 1, 1964. Facts on File.
Sobel, Lester A., et al, eds. News Dictionary: Vol. 2, 1965. Facts on File.
--News Dictionary: Vol. 3, 1966. Facts on File.
--News Dictionary: Vol. 4, 1967. Facts on File.
Sobelman, Harvey, jt. ed. see Harrell, Richard S.
Sobieszek, Robert A., ed. see Guerronnan, Anthony.
Sobieszek, Robert A., ed. see Snelling, Henry H. & Anthony, E.
Sobrrzo, Horacio. Vocabulario Sonorense. French & Eur.
Societe du Paler Francais au Canada. Glossaire du Parler Francais au Canada. French & Eur.
Societe du Parler Francais au Canada. Glossaire du Parler Francais au Canada. Laval P. U.
Societe Nationale Industrielle Aerospatiale, ed. Dictionnaire Des Techniques Aeronautiques et Spatiales. Intl Pubns Serv.
Society for Range Management Glossary Committee. A Glossary of Terms Used in Range Management. Soc Range Mgmt.
Society for Technical Communication. Glossary of Automated Text Processing Terms. Soc Tech Comm.
--Glossary of Graphics & Technical Art Terms. Soc Tech Comm.
Society of American Foresters. Terminology of Forest Science, Technology, Practice & Products (with 1978 Addendum) Soc Am Foresters.
Society of American Registered Architects. Obtaining a Computer & Computer Terminology. Soc Am Reg Architects.
Society of Automotive Engineers. Glossary of Automotive Electronic Terms. Soc Auto Engineers.
--SAE Motor Vehicle, Safety & Environmental Terminology. Soc Auto Engineers.
--Society of Vehicle Safety & Environmental Terminology Handbook. Soc Auto Engineers.
--Vehicle Dynamics Terminology. Soc Auto Engineers.
Society of Glass Decorations. Glossary of Decorating Terminology. Soc Glass Decorators.
Society of Motion Picture & Television Engineers. Magnetic Video Tape Recording Glossary. Soc Motion Pic & TV Engrs.
Society of Naval Architects & Marine Engineers. Glossary for High Speed Surface Craft. Soc Naval Arch.
Society of the Plastics Industry. Plastic Bottle Glossary. Soc Plastic Ind.
--Recommendations for Labeling Plastics Microwave Cookware & Glossary. Soc Plastic Ind.
Soeur, Samnang, tr. English-Khmer Phrasebook with Useful Word List: For Cambodians. Ctr Appl Ling.
Sohl, Damian G., jt. auth. see Rehg, Kenneth L.
Sohn, Ho-Min & Tawerilmang, Anthony F. Woleaian-English Dictionary. UH Pr.
Soja, Stanislaw, et al. Maly Slownik Wlosko-Polski. Wiedza Powszechna.
--Maly Slownik Wlosko-Polski & Polsko-Wloski. Wiedza Powszechna.
Sokolowska, M. & Szarski, J. Maly Slownik Techniczny Niemiecko i Polski-Niemiecki. Wydawnictwa Naukowo.
Sola, Donald F. & Agard, Frederick B. Spanish Pocket Dictionary. Random.
Sola, Donald P., ed. The Random House Basic Dictionary Spanish. Ballantine.
Sola, Ralph de see De Sola, Ralph.
Sole Tura, Jorge. Diccionario del Comunismo. French & Eur.
Solomon, Boris. Dictionnaire de la Technologie des Corps Gras. Inst Corps Gras.
Solomon, Sheila, jt. auth. see Cassin, Barbara.
Solov'ev, V. Moldavsko-Russkii Frazeologicheskii Slovar (Pub. by Lumina). Four Continent.
Somaize, Antoine De see De Somaize, Antoine B.
Sommer, Edouard. Lexique Francais-Latin. Hachette-Jeunesse.
--Lexique Latin-Francais. Hachette.
Sommer, H., jt. auth. see Lesobre, J.
Sommer, Henri. Vocabulaire Technique des Assurances & Reassurances Anglais-Francais. Berger-Levrault.
Sommer, Jean E. Lexique de la Langue de Mme de Sevigne. Lenox.
--Lexique de la Langue de Mme de Sevigne, 1. Olms.
--Lexique de la Langue de Mme de Sevigne, 2. Olms.
Sommer, Werner & Schoenfeld, Hanns-Martin. Management Dictionary. De Gruyter.
Sommer, Werner & Schoenfeld, Hans-Martin. Management Dictionary: Fachwoerterbuch fuer Betriebswirtschaft, Wirtschafts und Steuerrecht und Datenverarbeitung. De Gruyter.
Sommerau, E. F. Nemetsko-Russkii Meditsinskii Slovar (Pub. by Medgiz). Four Continent.
Sommerfeldt, K. & Schreiber, H. Woerter zur Valenz & Distribution der Substantive. Bibl Inst Leipzig.
Sommerfeldt, K. E. & Schreiber, H. Woerterbuch zur Valenz & Distribution Deutscher Adjektive. Bibl Inst Leipzig.
Sommerfeldt, Karl-Ernst. Woerterbuch zur Valenz & Distribution der Substantive. Bibl Inst Leipzig.
Sommerville, Paul. Dictionary of Geotechnics. Butterworth.
Song, M. E. English Korean Dictionary Romanized. Shalom.
Sontheimer, W., jt. ed. see Ziegler, K.
Soothill, W. E. & Hodous, L. A Dictionary of Chinese Buddhist Terms (Pub. by Motilal Banarsidass India). Orient Bk Dist.
Soothill, William E. & Hodous, L., eds. Dictionary of Chinese Buddhist Terms, with Sanskrit & English Equivalents & a Sanskrit-Pali Index. Verry.
Sopena. Diccionario Iter Ortografico. Lectorum Pubns.
Soper, J. H., ed. Hawaiian Phrase Book. C E Tuttle.
Soraas, H., jt. ed. see Bjerke, L.
Soras, H., jt. auth. see Myklestad, J. Meyer.
Sorensen, N. C. Dansk-Fransk Ordbog. French & Eur.
Sorensen, Niels C. Dansk-Fransk Ordbog. Gyldendal Norsk.
Soroa. Diccionario de agricultura. Labor.
So Sethaputra, compiled by. New Model Thai-English Dictionary. Thai Watana.
Sota Aburto, Manuel de. Diccionario Retana De Autoridades De la Lengua Vasca. French & Eur.
Sotelo, Joaquin C., prologue by. Vox--Diccionario Abreviado Ortografico de la Lengua Espanola. French & Eur.
Sotir, Mihai Papa see Papa-Sotir, Mihai.
Soto, Victor M., jt. auth. see Gagini, Carlos.
Soto Mora, Consuelo. Vocabulario Geomortologico. UNAM.
Soto Mora, Consuelo & Fuentes Aguilar, Luis. Glosario de terminos geograficos. UNAM.
Soto Ruiz, Clodoaldo. Diccionario Quechua Ayacucho-Chanca. Minist Ed Caracas.
Soule, Richard. Soule's Dictionary of English Synonyms. Bantam.
Soule, Richard & Howson, G., eds. Dictionary of English Synonyms & Synonymous Parallel Expressions. Shalom.
Soulik, Tobias, jt. auth. see Carroll, Vern.
Sournia, Jean-Charles. Dictionnaire des Assurances Sociales. French & Eur.
Sousa Vieira, Jose de see De Sousa Vieira, Jose.
Southern, Richard, jt. auth. see Rhae, Kenneth.
Sozanskiej, Ewa. Slownik Elektroniczny Polsko-Angielsko-Rosyjski. Wydawnictwa Naukowo.
Spaltro, Enzo. Dizionario di psicologia del lavoro. Ghisoni.
Spano, Giovanni. Vocabolario sardo-italiano e italiano-sardo. Forni.
Sparkes, Ivan G., ed. A Dictionary of Collective Nouns & Group Terms (Pub. by White Lion Publishers). Gale.
Spazhev, Iu. A., et al. Russko-Rumynskii Voennyi Slovar (Pub. by Voenizdat). Four Continent.
Spears, Richard A. Slang & Euphemism: Abridged Edition (Sig). NAL.
Speck, E. G. Diccionario cientifico ilustrado. Editors Pr Serv.
Speichert, H. Kritisches Lexikon der Erzeihungswissenschaft und Bildungspolitik. Rowohlt.
--Kritisches Lexikon der Erzeihungswissenschaft und Bildungspolitik (Pub. by Rowohlt). French & Eur.
Speichert, Horst, ed. Kritisches Lexikon der Erziehungswissenschaft & Bildungspolitik. Verlag.
Spencer, D. A. Focal Dictionary of Photographic Technologics. Focal Pr.
Spencer, Donald. Computer Dictionary for Everyone (ScribT). Scribner.
Spencer, Donald D. Computer Dictionary. Camelot Pub.
--Computer Dictionary for Everyone (ScribT). Scribner.
--The Illustrated Computer Dictionary. Merrill.
--Illustrated Computer Dictionary for Young People. Camelot Pub.
--Microcomputers at a Glance. Camelot Pub.
Spencer, William. Historical Dictionary of Morocco. Scarecrow.
Spenger, O. A. Gidrologicheskii Slovar na Inostrannykh Iazykakh (Pub. by Gidrometeoizdat). Four Continent.
Sperber, Hans & Trittschuh, Travis. American Political Terms: An Historical Dictionary. Wayne St U Pr.
Speroni, Miguel Angel. Diccionario Subversivo. Hachette Jeunesse.
Spiller. Vocabolario del milanese d'oggi. Rizzoli Edit.
Spillner, P. Internationales Woerterbuch der Abkuerzungen Von Organisationen (Pub. by Vlg. Dokumentation). French & Eur.
Spillner, Paul. International Dictionary of Abbreviations of Organizations (Pub. by Verlag Dokumentation SVK). French & Eur.
Spinelli, Vincenzo & Casasanta, Mario. Dizionario completo italiano-portoghese (brasiliano) e portoghese (brasiliano)-italiano. Hoepli.
--Dizionario completo italiano-portoghese (brasiliano) e portoghese (brasiliano)-italiano. Hoepli.
Spira, Harold R. Canine Terminology. Howell Bk.
Spiro, Socrates. Arabic-English Dictionary: Colloquial Arabic of Egypt. Intl Bk Ctr.
--An Arabic-English Dictionary of the Colloquial Arabic of Egypt. Intl Bk Ctr.
--English-Arabic Dictionary: Colloquial Arabic of Egypt. Intl Bk Ctr.
--An English-Arabic Dictionary of the Colloquial Arabic of Egypt. Intl Bk Ctr.
Spirolazzi, Giancarlo. Dizionario di psicologia forense. Giuffre.
Spitaler, Anton, jt. auth. see Ullmann, Manfred.
Spitaler, Anton, et al. Woerterbuch der Klassischen Arabischen Sprache: Bd 1, Lfg 1. Harrassowitz.
Sponzel, Kurt. Lexikon der Anstrichtechnik. French & Eur.
Sponzel, Kurt & Wallenfang, Wilhelm. Lexikon der Anstrichtechnik: Bd 1. Callwey.
Spreutels, Marcel. Dictionnaire du Style et des Usages Administratifs. French & Eur.
Springer, O. New Muret-Sanders Encyclopedic Dictionary: Part II, German-English. M Rosenberg.
Springer, O., ed. New Muret-Sanders Encyclopedic Dictionary: Part I, English-German. M Rosenberg.
Springer, Otto. Der Grosse Muret-Sanders: Teil I, Englisch-Deutsch. Langenscheidt.
--Der Grosse Muret-Sanders: Teil II, Deutsch-Englisch. Langenscheidt.
Springer, Otto, ed. Langenscheidt's New Muret-Sanders English-German Dictionary. Incl. Vol. 1. A-M; Vol. 2. N-Z. Hippocrene Bks.
--Langenscheidt's New Muret-Sanders German-English Encyclopedic Dictionary: Part 2, Vol. 2, L-Z. Am Map.
--Der Neue Muret-Sanders. Incl. Teil I. Englisch-Deutsch; Teil II. Deutsch-Englisch. Langenscheidt.
Springhetti, Emilio. Lexicon linguisticae et philologiae. Univ Gregoriana.
Sprudzs, Adolf. Benelux Abbreviations & Symbols: Law & Related Subjects. Oceana.
--Italian Abbreviations & Symbols: Law & Related Subjects. Oceana.
Sri Aurobindo. Glossary of Terms in Sri Aurobindo's Writings. Matagiri.
Stahl, Fred A. & Scavnicky, Gary E. Reverse Dictionary of the Spanish Language. U of Ill Pr.
Stainer, Cecie. Dictionary of Violin Makers. Longwood Pr.
Stainer, J. & Barrett, W. A. A Dictionary of Musical Terms. Gordon Pr.
Stainer, John & Barrett, W. A. Dictionary of Musical Terms. Scholarly.
Stallybrass, Oliver, jt. ed. see Bullock, Alan.
Stamp, L. & Perevod, A. S. Slovar Obshchegeo graficheskikh Terminov (Pub. by Progress). Four Continent.
Stancin, Nicolae. Dictionar Tehnic de Radio si Televiziune. Editura Stiintifica.
Stanciulescu-Cuza, Mariana. Dictionar Frazeologic Italian-Roman. Editura Stiintifica.
Standards Council, Society for Technical Communication. Abbreviations & Symbols for Terms Used in Electronics. Soc Tech Comm.
Standke, Wolfgang, compiled by. Foundry Dictionary: German-English & English-German. Intl Pubns Serv.
Stanford, G. McGraw-Hill Vocabulary. McGraw.
Stanford, Gene. McGraw-Hill Vocabulary. McGraw.

--McGraw-Hill Vocabulary. McGraw.
--McGraw-Hill Vocabulary. Weeden, Hester E., ed. McGraw.
Stanford, W. J. McGraw-Hill Vocabulary. McGraw.
Stang, David J. & Wrightman, Lawrence S. Dictionary of Social Behavior & Social Research Methods. Brooks-Cole.
Stanislawski, J. English-Polish & Polish-English Dictionary. McKay.
--The Great English-Polish Dictionary. French & Eur.
--The Great Polish-English Dictionary. French & Eur.
--Polish-English & English-Polish Dictionary. McKay.
--Polish-English, English-Polish Dictionary (1975) Heinman.
--Polish-English, English-Polish Practical Dictionary. Heinman.
--A Practical Polish-English Dictionary. French & Eur.
Stanislawski, J. & Billip, K. Polish Practical Dictionary (English-Polish) Vanous.
Stanislawski, J., ed. The Great English-Polish Dictionary (Pub. by Collet's). State Mutual Bk.
--The Great Polish-English Dictionary (Pub. by Collet's). State Mutual Bk.
Stanislawski, J., et al. A Practical English-Polish Dictionary. French & Eur.
Stanislawski, Jan. Polish Great Dictionary, Vol. 1: English-Polish. Vanous.
--A Practical English-Polish Dictionary. Intl Pubns Serv.
--A Practical Polish-English Dictionary. Intl Pubns Serv.
--Wielki Slownik Polsko-Angielski. Wiedza Powszechna.
Stanislawski, Jan, ed. Great English-Polish Dictionary. Intl Pubns Serv.
Stanisljawski, J., et al. Polish-English Practical Dictionary. Vanous.
Stanislowski, J. Polish Great Dictionary, Vol. 2: Polish-English. Vanous.
Stankova, Elena, jt. auth. see Harlakova, Ivanka.
Stanley, John. The Creature Features Movie Guide or An A to Z Encyclopedia to Fantastic Films or Is There a Mad Doctor in the House? Creatures at Large.
Stano, Mikulas. Polsko -Slovensky a Slovensko-Polsky Slovnik. SNTC.
Stano, Mikulas, et al. Pol'sko-Slovensky a Slovensko-Polsky Slovnik. SNTC.
Stanway, ed. Dictionary of Operations. Paladin.
Stapleton, John, jt. auth. see Hart, Norman A.
Starets, S., jt. auth. see Voinova, N.
Stark, Frederick. Phrase Dictionaries for the American Tourist. Incl. German for the American Tourist; Spanish for the English-Speaking Tourist; French for the English-Speaking Tourist; Italian for the English-Speaking Tourist; Greek for the English-Speaking Tourist; Russian for the English-Speaking Tourist. Delair.
Starnes, DeWitt T. & Talbert, Ernest W. Classical Myth & Legend in Renaissance Dictionaries. Greenwood.
Statt, D. Dictionary of Human Behavior (Pub. by Har-Row Ltd England). Har-Row.
Statt, David. Dictionary of Psychology. Har-Row.
Stattmann, F. Dictionary of Power Plant Engineering: Conventional Steam Power Plants. French & Eur.
--Dictionary of Power Plant Engineering: Nuclear Power Plants. French & Eur.
Stattmann, F., jt. auth. see Brandenberger, E.
Stearn, William T. Botanical Latin: History, Grammar, Syntax, Terminology & Vocabulary. Hafner.
Stedman. Stedman's Medical Dictionary (Pub. by Williams & Wilkins). Krieger.
Steele, Guy L. The Hacker's Dictionary (CN). Har-Row.
Steen, Edwin B. Abbreviations in Medicine (Pub. by Bailliere-Tindall). Saunders.
--Dictionary of Biology (EH). B&N NY.
--Dictionary of Biology. B&N Imports.
Steenwyk, Elizabeth Van see Van Steenwyk, Elizabeth.
Stefanelli, Renzo. Capire l'Economiea: Dizionario Critico del Capitalismo Contemporaneo. De Donato.
Steffanides, George F. The Scientist's Thesaurus. Steffanides.
Stegeman, Wilson. Medical Terms Simplified. West Pub.
Stegenga, J. Greek-English Analytical Concordance of the Greek-English New Testament. Hellenes.
Steible, Daniel J., ed. Concise Handbook of Linguistics. Philos Lib.
Steiger, Eduard & Busch, Karl F. Bautechnik. Bibl Inst Leipzig.
Stein, Harold A., et al. Manual of Opthalmic Terminology. Mosby.
Stein, Henri. Dictionnaire Topographique de la France. Hubert, J., ed. French & Eur.
Stein, Henri & Hubert, J. Dictionnaire Topographique de la France. Biblio Nationale.
Stein, Jess, ed. The Random House Basic Speller-Divider. Ballantine.
--The Random House Dictionary. Ballantine.
--Student's Webster Dictionary. Sharon Pubns.
Stein, P. A., jt. auth. see Langendorf, Hans.
Steiner, G. & Greiner-Mai, H., eds. BI-Taschenlexikon Fremdsprachige Schriftsteller. Bibl Inst Leipzig.
Steiner, G., et al, eds. Lexikon Fremdsprachiger Schriftsteller. Bibl Inst Leipzig.
Steiner, Roger, ed. Bantam New College French & English Dictionary. Bantam.
Steiner, Roger J. The Bantam New College French & English Dictionary. Bantam.
--The New College French & English Dictionary. AMSCO Sch.
Steinfeldt, E. Russian Word Count. Four Continent.
Steingass. Persian-English Dictionary. Iaconi.
Steingass, F. Arabic-English Learners Dictionary. Intl Bk Ctr.
--Comprehensive Persian-English Dictionary. Intl Bk Ctr.
--A Comprehensive Persian-English Dictionary. South Asia Bks.
--English-Arabic Dictionary. Orient Bk Dist.
--English-Arabic Learner's Dictionary. Intl Bk Ctr.
--A Learner's Arabic-English Dictionary. Intl Bk Ctr.
--A Learner's Arabic-English Dictionary. South Asia Bks.
--A Learner's English-Arabic Dictionary. Intl Bk Ctr.
Steinig, Karl. Woerterbuch fuer Strassenbau und Strassenverkehe. French & Eur.
Steinmetz, A. Langenscheidts Taschenwoerterbuch Neugriechisch: Teil II, Deutsch-Neugriechisch. Langenscheidt.
Stellhorn, Kurt. Technologisches Woerterbuch Franzoisisch. Girardet.
--Technologisches Woerterbuch Franzoisisch (Pub. by Verlag W. Girardet). French & Eur.
--Woerterbuch Werkzeuge und Werkzeugmaschinen. French & Eur.
Stenesh, J. Dictionary of Biochemistry (Pub. by Wiley-Interscience). Wiley.
Stenton, Adrian, jt. auth. see DeJoia, Alex.
Stepanek, Josef. Woerterbuch Industrieofen & Indudtrielle Warmeanlagen. Vulkan Verlag.
Stepanets, A. T. Illiustrirovannyi Aviatsionnyi Slovar Dlia Molodezhi (Pub. by Dosaaf). Four Continent.
Stephan, H., jt. ed. see Engert, M.
Stephanova, L., et al. Dictionnaire Bulgare-Francais. French & Eur.
Stephanus, Charles. Dictionarium Historicum, Geographicum, Poeticum. Garland Pub.
Stephens, R. W., ed. Sound: In Eight Languages. Halsted Pr.
Stephens, Roy. Yr Odliadur. Lewis Ltd.
Sterkenburg, P. Een Glossarium van Zeventiende-Eeuws Nederlands. Tjeenk Willinik.
Sternberg, Jacques. Dictionnaire du Mepris. Calmann Levy.
Steuerwald, K. Langenscheidts Taschenwoerterbuch Tuerkisch: Teil I, Tuerkisch-Deutsch. Langenscheidt.
Steuerwald, K. & Koprulu, Cemal. Langenscheidts Taschenwoerterbuch Tuerkisch-Deutsch. Langenscheidt.
--Langenscheidts Taschenwoerterbuch Tuerkisch: Teil II, Deutsch-Tuerkisch. Langenscheidt.
Steuerwald, Karl. Langenscheidts Taschenwoerterbuecher Tuerkisch. Langenscheidt.
--Langenscheidts Taschenwoerterbuecher Tuerkisch-Deutsch. Langenscheidt.
Stevens, Alan, jt. auth. see Schmidgall-Tellings, A. Ed.
Stevens, Richard P. Historical Dictionary of the Republic of Botswana. Scarecrow.
Stevenson. Dictionary Roman Coins (Pub. by B A Seaby England). S J Durst.
Stiegeler, Stella E. A Dictionary of Earth Sciences (Pica Pr). Universe.
Stiehl, Ulrich. Dictionary of Book Publishing (Pub. by K G Saur). Gale.
Stiller, Richard. Illustrated Sex Dictionary. Assoc Bk.
Stillman, F. Whitfield's University Rhyming Dictionary: English Language Rime. French & Eur.
Stillman, Frances & Whitfield, Jane S. Poet's Manual & Rhyming Dictionary. T Y Crowell.
Stillman, Frances, ed see Whitfield, Jane S.
Stillman, Frances, ed. see Whitfield, Jane S.
Stimson, Hugh M. T'ang Poetic Vocabulary. Far Eastern Pubns.
Stock, Arnold B., tr. see Neffgen, H.
Stockhammer, Morris. Kant Dictionary. Philos Lib.
Stoeckhert, Klaus & Beck. Kunststofflexikon. Hanser.
Stoeckle, Bernard, ed. The Concise Dictionary of Christian Ethics. Crossroad NY.
Stoeckle, Bernhard. Woerterbuch christlicher Ethik. Herder.
--Woerterbuch Christlicher Ethik. Herder.
Stoehr, W. Lexikon der Voelker und Kulturen. French & Eur.
Stoetzer, U., ed. Grosses Woerterbuck der Deutschen Aussprache. Bibl Inst Leipzig.
Stoicovici, Elena, et al. Dictionar Roman-Vietnamez. Tipografia.
Stokes, Adrian V. Concise Encyclopedia of Computer Terminology. Gower Pub Ltd.
Stoliarov, D. E., ed. Russian-English Oil-Field Dictionary. Pergamon.
Stoltzfus, N. Unraveling the Integral Knot Concordance Group. Am Math.
Stone, Louise W., et al, eds. An Anglo-Norman Dictionary. Modern Humanities Res.
Stone, R. G., et al. A Glossary of English Equivalents of Terms Commonly Used in French Auctions, Catalogues, & Stamp Trade. France & Col Philatelist.
Stork, F. C., jt. ed. see Hartmann, R. R.
Storni, Bruno. Schwierigkeiten des Deutsch-Italienischen Wortschatzes. Giovannelli, Paolo, ed. Klett.
Story, G. M., ed. Dictionary of Newfoundland English. Kirwin, W. J & Widdowson, J. D. U of Toronto Pr.
Storzer, Gerald, jt. auth. see Gerber, Barbara.
Storzer, Gerald H., jt. auth. see Gerber, Barbara L.
Stoudt, Betty. Vocabulario Mixteco de San Miguel el Grande. Summer Inst Ling.
Stoutenburgh, John L., ed. Dictionary of Arts & Crafts. Philos Lib.
Stowasser, Karl & Ani, Moukhtar, eds. A Dictionary of Syrian Arabic: English-Arabic. Georgetown U Pr.
Straka, Georges, jt. auth. see Baldinger, Kurt.
Strakhova, A. A., et al, eds. Russko-Nemetskii Slovar (Pub. by GINS). Four Continent.
Strasak & Sulek. Technisches Deutsch fuer Auslaender. Brandstetter.
Strasak, Jaroslav. Technisches Deutschfuer Auslaender. French & Eur.
Stratmann, Francis H. A Dictionary of the Old English Language: Compiled from Writings of the XII, XIII, XIV, & XV Centuries. Folcroft.
Stratmann, Franz H. A Supplement of the Dictionary of the English Language of the XII, XIII, XIV, & XV Centuries. R West.
--A Supplement to the Dictionary of the English Language of the 12th, 13th, 14th, & 15th Centuries. Folcroft.
Stratton, Clarence. Handbook of English. Gale.
Straub, Ferene B. & Adam, Gyorgy. Biologiai Lexikon. Akademiai Kiado.
Strauss, Eduard. Medizinische Fachsprache Verstandlich Gemacht. Froehlich Verlag.
Strayer, Joseph R., ed. Dictionary of the Middle Ages (ScribR). Scribner.
--Dictionary of the Middle Ages (ScribR). Scribner.
Strickland, Walter G. Dictionary of Irish Artists (Pub. by Irish Academic Pr Ireland). Biblio Dist.
Strmberg, Alva. Stora Synonymordboken. Strombergs.
Strobl, Walter, tr. see Reck, Jurgen.
Stroebel, Leslie & Todd, Hollis. Dictionary of Contemporary Photography. Morgan.
Stroebel, Leslie & Todd, Hollis N. Dictionary of Contemporary Photography. Morgan.
Strom, D. & Strom, J. A. German-Norwegian Dictionary of Technical Terms. Kunnskapsforlaget.
--Norwegian-German Dictionary of Technical Terms. Kunnskapsforlaget.
Strom, J. A., jt. auth. see Strom, D.
Strong, James. Strong's Exhaustive Concordance. Baker Bk.
--Strong's Exhaustive Concordance. Broadman.
Strong, William. Basic Usage & Vocabulary (RanC). Random.
Strumilin, S. G., ed. Slovar Semiletki (Pub. by Politizdat). Four Continent.
Strupp, Karl, et al, eds. Woerterbuch des Voelkerrechts: Bd 1, Aachener Kongress-Hussar Fall. De Gruyter.
Strutz. Five Hundred & One German Verbs: Written in Japanese. Barron.
Strutz, H. Dictionary of Five Hundred One German Verbs Fully Conjugated. Barron.
Strutz, Henry. Zwei Hundert Eins Spanische Verben. Barron.
Stuart, Malcolm. Van Nostrand Reinhold Color Dictionary of Herbs & Herbalism. Van Nos Reinhold.
Stuart, Maxwell P. Studies in Greek Colour Terminology (Pub. by E J Brill Holland). Humanities.
Stultz, Russell A. The Illustrated CPM-Wordstar Dictionary with Mailmerge & Spellstar Operations. P-H.
--The Illustrated Word Processing Dictionary. P-H.
Sturgess, H. & Hewitt, A. A Dictionary of Legal Terms & Citations. Gordon Pr.
Sturgis, R. A Dictionary of Architecture & Building. Gordon Pr.
Sturgis, Russell. Dictionary of Architecture & Building, Biographical & Descriptive. Gale.
Sturtevant, E. H., jt. auth. see Linguistic Society of America.
Stypula, Ryszard, et al. Slownik Polsko-Rosyjski. Wiedza Powszechna.
--Podreczny Slownik Polsko-Rosyjski. Wiedza Powszechna.

Suares, Jean-Claude. The Devil's Dictionary (TYC-T). T Y Crowell.
Suarez, Andres Santiago. Diccionario Economico De la Empresa. French & Eur.
Suarez, L. Gil see Suarez Gil, L.
Suarez Campos, Jose M., jt. auth. see Bernard, Yves.
Suarez Gil, L. Diccionario tecnico-maritimo Ingles-Espanol & Espanol-Ingles. Fed Gremios.
Suarez Suarez, A. S., et al. Diccionario Economico de la Empresa. Piramide.
Suariz Gil, L. Diccionario tecnico maritimo: Ingles-espanol espanol-ingles. Alhambra.
Suarvet, Thomas H. Dictionnaire Economique et Social. French & Eur.
Suavet, Thomas. Dictionnaire Economique & Social. Ouvrieres.
Subcommittee on Classification of Sports in Injuries & Committee on the Medical Aspects of Sports, eds. Standard Nomenclature of Athletic Injuries. AMA.
Sube, jt. auth. see Eisenreich.
Sube, R. & Eisenreich, G. Physics Dictionary (Pub. by Collet's). State Mutual Bk.
Sube, R., jt. auth. see Eisenreich, G.
Sube, R. & Eisenreich, G., eds. Physics Dictionary. Adler.
Sube, Ralf. Woerterbuch der Mathematik. French & Eur.
Sube, Ralf & Eisenreich, Gunther. Mathematik Englisch-Deutsch-Franzoesisch-Russisch. VEB Technik.
--Woerterbuch Physik. French & Eur.
Suess, Jared H. Central European Geneological Terminology. Everton Pubs.
Sugita, Hiroshi, jt. auth. see Goodenough, Ward H.
Sulek, jt. auth. see Strasak.
Sulima-Samujillo, A. P., et al. Deutsch-Russisches Worterbuch fur Eisenbahnwesen. French & Eur.
Sullivan Assoc. Reading Vocabulary. Learning Line.
Sullivan, George. The Complete Sports Dictionary. Scholastic Inc.
Sumpf, Joseph & Hugues, Michel. Dictionnaire de Sociologie. Larousse.
--Dictionnaire de Sociologie. French & Eur.
Sundby, Dag, ed. Den Nye Forkortningsordboken. Schibsted.
Sundelin, Seppo, jt. auth. see Hagford, Edvin.
Suomen Standardisoimislitto. Sahkotieteellinen Sanasto. Suomen Standard.
Suppa, Giuseppe. Glossario italiano tessile in cinque lingue. Tec Tessile.
Suriani, E., tr. see Handel, Saul.
Suryakanta. Sanskrit-Hindi-English Dictionary. Intl Pubns Serv.
Susskind, Nathan, jt. ed. see Copeland, Robert M.
Svenkerud, A., jt. auth. see Berulfsen, B.
Sveriges Standardiseringskommission. Dataordboken. Standard Sver.
Swadesh, Mauricio, jt. auth. see Arana, Evangelina.
Swadesh, Morris, jt. auth. see Sapir, Edward.
Swanfeldt, Andrew. Apollo Crossword Puzzle Dictionary. T y Crowell.
--Crossword Puzzle Dictionary. T y Crowell.
--The Swanfeldt Famous Crossword Puzzle Dictionary (EH). B&N NY.
Swanljung, Ritva. Rakennusalan Sanastot ja Sanastohankkeet Suomessa. Valtion.
Swannell, Julia, ed. Little Oxford Dictionary. Oxford U Pr.
Sweeney, Karen. Illustrated Tennis Dictionary for Young People. Harvey.
Sweet, Henry. Student's Dictionary of Anglo-Saxon. Oxford U Pr.
Switzer, Richard & Gochberg, Herbert S., eds. New Century Vest Pocket French Dictionary. New Century.
Switzer, Robert, ed. World-Wide French Dictionary (Prem). Fawcett.
Sybertz, Gustav. Technical Dictionary for Weaponry (Pub. by Neumann-Neudamm). French & Eur.
Sybex Staff & Zaks, Rodnay. International Microcomputer Dictionary. Sybex.
Sybrandus, Johannes, jt. auth. see Fockman, Andreae.
Sydler, Jean P., jt. auth. see Calsat, Jean-Henri.
Sydler, Jean-Pierre, jt. auth. see Calsat, Jean-Henri.
Sydow, A. Cibernetical Dictionary: E-G-F-R-Slovene. French & Eur.
--Dictionary of Cybernetics (Pub. by Collet's). State Mutual Bk.
Sydow, Achim. Kybernetik. VEB Verlag Technik.
Sykes, Egerton. Everyman's Dictionary of Non-Classical Mythology (Pub. by J. M. Dent England). Biblio Dist.
Sykes, J. B., ed. The Concise Oxford Dictionary of Current English. Oxford U Pr.
--The Pocket Oxford Dictionary of Current English. Oxford U Pr.
Sykora, Jiri. Automatizacna Technika. Alfa-Vydavatel.
--Dictionary of Automation Techniques (Pub. by Collet's). State Mutual Bk.
--Dictionary of Automation Techniques (Pub. by Collets). State Mutual Bk.
Sykora, Jiri, ed. Dictionary of Automatical Technique. French & Eur.
Sylvain, Fernand. Dictionnaire de la comptabilite. Can Inst Chart Accts.
Synge, P. & Hay, R. Dictionary of Garden Plants & Flowers in Colour: May 1981 (Pub. by RHS Ent England). State Mutual Bk.
Synge, P. M., jt. auth. see Har, R.
Synge, Patrick M., jt. auth. see Hay, Roy.
Synge, Patrick M., ed. Dictionary of Gardening - Supplement. Oxford U Pr.
Systems Research Institute Staff. Dictionary of Administration & Management. Systems Res.
Szabo, Miklos. Orosz-Magyar Szotar Iskolak Szamara. Akademiai Kiado.
Szarski, J., jt. auth. see Sokolowska, M.
Szczesniak, Lenny, tr. see Zanzucchi, Anne M.
Szekely, B., jt. auth. see Sezepesi, G.
Szendy, Gyorgy L. Woerterbuch des Pantentwesens in 5 Sprachen. French & Eur.
Szolginia, Witold. Architektura & Budownictwo. Wydawnictwa Naukowo.
Szwykowski, Ludwik, et al. Maly Slownik Francusko-Polski. Wiedza Powszechna.

T

Taddey, Gerhard. Lexikon der Deutschen Geschichte. French & Eur.
Taddey, Gerhard, ed. Lexikon der Deutschen Geschichte. Kroener.
Talamo. The Real Estate Dictionary. Caroline Hse.
Talamo, John. The Real Estate Dictionary. Contemp Bks.
Talbert, Ernest W., jt. auth. see Starnes, DeWitt T.
Talvitie, Jyrki K. Ranskalais-Suomalainen Tekniikan ja Kaupan Sanakirja. Tietoteos.
Tamas, Magay. Hungarian Dictionary for Tourists. Vanous.
Tamburin, Vincenzo M. Dizionario del dialetto di Cortina d'Ampezzo. Pozza.
Tames, R. Mungo Park. Newbury Bks.
Tamm, J. Estonsko-Russkii Slovar (Pub. by Valgus). Four Continent.
Tamura, S. & Shiratori, F. Chinese-English-Japanese Glossary of Chemical Terms. French & Eur.
Tan, K., jt. auth. see Matthews, B.
Tan, K. T. Chinese-English Dictionary: Taiwan Dialect. Oriental Bk Store.
Tanguay, Cyprien & Senechal. Dictionnaire Genealogique des Familles Canadiennes: Depuls la Fondation de la Colonie Jusqu'a nos Jours. Elysee.
Tardy. Dictionnaire des Horlogers Francais. Tardy-Lengelle.
Tarrants, William E., ed. Dictionary of Terms Used in the Safety Profession. ASSE.
Taspinar. Technisches Woerterbuch. Brandstetter.
Taspinar, Adnan H. Taspinar's Technical Dictionary. Taspinar's Technical Publications.
Taube, A. M. Frantsuzsko-Russkii Voennyi Slovar (Pub. by Voenizdat). Four Continent.
--Russian-English Dictionary (Pub. by Collet's). State Mutual Bk.
--Russko-Angliiskii Slovar (Pub. by Russkii Iazyk). Four Continent.
Taube, A. M., et al. Russian-English Dictionary. Daglish, R. C., ed. French & Eur.
Taubes, Frederic. Painter's Dictionary of Materials & Methods. Watson-Guptill.
Taupiac, Jacme. Pichon Diccionari Frances-Occitan. Inst Occit Tlse.
Tausan, Victoria A., ed. see Eminescu, Mihail.
Tausin, H., jt. auth. see Chassant, A.
Tausin, Henri, jt. auth. see Chassant, Louis A.
Tautz, G. BI-Taschenlexikon Orden, Preise & Medaillen Staatliche Auszeichnungen der DDR. Bibl Inst Leipzig.
Taverdet, Gerard, pref. by see De Chambure, Eugene.
Tavernier, R., jt. auth. see Jacks, G. V.
Tawerilmang, Anthony F., jt. auth. see Sohn, Ho-Min.
Taylor, A. Icelandic-English-Icelandic, Pocket Dictionary. Vanous.
Taylor, Hugh. Golf Dictionary (SpS). Sportshelf.
Taylor, James L. Dicionario Metalurgico Ingles-Portugues, Portugues-Ingles. Imported Bks.
--English-Portuguese Metallurgical Dictionary. Imported Bks.
--Harrap Portuguese-English Dictionary. Harrap.
--A Portuguese-English Dictionary. Stanford U Pr.
Taylor, Richard S., ed. Beacon Dictionary of Theology. Beacon Hill.
Taylor, Ronald J. & Gottschalk, W. German-English Dictionary of Idioms. Adler.
Tayyeb, R. & Chandna, K., eds. Dictionary of Acronyms & Abbreviations in Library & Information Science. CLA.
Tebben, Joseph. Medical & Technical Terminology. Collegiate Pub.
Technical Association of the Pulp & Paper Industry Winding Committee. Roll Defect Terminology: Paper Finishing & Converting. Gilmore, William, ed. TAPPI.
Technical Committee on Computer Controlled Environmental Testing of the Inst. of Environ. Sciences. Glossary of Computer Controlled Environmental Testing Terminology. Inst Environ Sci.
Technische Universitat Dresden, ed. German-English Dictionary of Chemistry & Chemical Technology-Chemie und Chemische Technik: Deutsch-Englisch. Intl Pubns Serv.
Technishe Universitaet, Dresden, ed. English-German Dictionary of Chemistry & Chemical Technology. Intl Pubns Serv.
Tedjini, Abulgacim. Dictionnaire Francais-Marocain. Maritimes Outre-Mer.
Tedjini, Abulqacim. Dictionnaire. Maritimes Outremer.
Teichmann, Max E., jt. auth. see Jaensch, Dean.
Teitelbaum & Johnson. Mangled Medicine Definitions We Doubt You Learned in School. Van Nos Reinhold.
Tekniska Nomenklaturcentralen. Byggordsamling. Tek Nomen.
--Komunalteknisk Ordlista. Tek Nomen.
--Plan och Byggtermer. Tek Nomen.
--Skogsordlista. Tek Nomen.
Telegin, A. I., et al. Frantsuzsko-Russkii Slovar Po Sudostroeniiu i Sudokhodstvu (Pub. by Glav. Red. Nauchn. Tekhn. Slovarei Fizmatgiza). Four Continent.
Tembrock, Gunter. Verhaltensbiologie. Fischer Verlag.
Tennyson, Alfred, jt. auth. see Baker, A. E.
Tennyson, Charles, ed. see Baker, A. E. & Tennyson, Alfred.
Teppe, Julien. Vocabulaire de la Vie Amoureuse. Pavillon.
Terblanche, H. Engels-Afrikaanse Tegniese Woordeboek. Nasou.
Terceiro, J. B. Diccionario de economia. Zyx.
Terrel, P., et al. Collins German-English, English-German Dictionary. French & Eur.
Terrell, Peter, et al. Collins German Dictionary: German-English, English-Ger. Imported Bks.
Terry, Edward M. A Richard Wagner Dictionary. Greenwood.
Ters, Francois. Vocabulaire Orthographique de Base. OCDL.
Ters, Francois, et al. Vocabulaire Orthographique de Base. Messeiller.
Tertulia Edipica. Dicionario de Sinonimos. Porto Editora.
Tescher & Bills. Spanish & English of the United States Hispanos. Camino Real.
Teschner, Richard V., jt. auth. see Galvan, Roberto A.
Teschner, Richard V., tr. see Elerick, Marisa Luz E.
Teselkin, A. S., et al. Indoneziisko-Russkii Uchebnyi Slovar (Pub. by Sov Entsiklopediia). Four Continent.
Testas, J., jt. auth. see Garcia-Pelayo, R.
Testas, Jean, jt. auth. see Garcia-Pelayo, Ramon.
Testi, Gino. Dizionario di alchimia e di chimica antiquaria. Edizioni Mediterranee.
Tetsmann, A. & Lind, H. Yachting Dictionary (Pub. by Collets). State Mutual Bk.
Tewes, U. Lexikon der Medizinischen Psychologie. French & Eur.
Tezenas Du Montcel, Henri. Dictionnaire des Sciences de la Gestion. Delarge.
--Dictionnaire des Sciences de la Gestion. Hurtubise H. M. H.
Thalbourne, Michael A. A Glossary of Terms Used in Parapsychology (Pub. by W Heinemann). David & Charles.
Thanh Nghi. Dictionnaire Vietnamien-Francais. Asiatheque.
Tharp, James A. A Rhade-English Dictionary with English-Rhade Finder List. Linguistic Circle.
Thayer, Joseph H. Greek-English Lexicon of the New Testament: A Dictionary Numerically Coded to Strong's Exhaustive Concordance. Baker Bk.
--Thayer's Greek-English Lexicon of the New Testament. Broadman.
The, Liang G. Kamus Logika. Nur Cahaya.
Theilman, K. Dictionary of Biochemistry (Pub. by Collets). State Mutual Bk.
Theimer, Walter. Lexikon der Politik: Politik Grundbegriffe & Grundgedanken. Francke.
Theimer, Walter, tr. Diccionario de poltica mundial. Ariel.
Theodorakis, Mikis. Lexique de la Resistance Grecque: Journal de Resistance. Flammarion.
Theodorson, Achilles A., jt. auth. see Theodorson, George A.
Theodorson, George A. & Theodorson, Achilles A. A Modern Dictionary of Sociology. B&N NY.
Theophilakis, E. Greek-Norwegian Norwegian-Greek Pocket Dictionary. Kunnskapsforlaget.
Theret, Michel, jt. auth. see Bader, Oliver.
Theureau, S., jt. auth. see Fonteneau, M.
Thewlis, J. Concise Dictionary of Physics: And Related Subjects. Pergamon.
Thibault, Adrien. Glossaire du Pays Biaiaois. Slatkine.
Thibert, A. Eskimo-English, English-Eskimo Dictionary. Heinman.

Thiele, Margrethe, ed. see Blinkenberg, A. P. & Hoybye, Poul.

Thielmann. Woerterbuch der Biochemie. Verlag Harri Deutsch.

Thielmann, K. Dictionary of Biochemistry. French & Eur.

--Woerterbuch der Biochemie. French & Eur.

Thielmann, K. Von see Von Thielmann, K.

Thieme, Ulrich & Becker, Felix, eds. Allegemeines Lexikon der Bildenden Kunstler von der Antike bis zur Gegenwart. Somerset Pub.

Thies, Werner. Modellflug-Lexikon. Verlag Technik.

Thiess, Gunter, et al, eds. Training von A bis Z: Kleines Worterbuch fuer der Theorie & Praxis der Sportl Trainings. Sportverlag.

Thiessen, Jack, jt. auth. see Thiessen, John.

Thiessen, John & Thiessen, Jack. Mennonite Low-German Dictionary. Elwert.

Thines, Georges & Lempereur, Agnes. Diccionario General de Ciencias Humanas. French & Eur.

--Dictionnaire General des Sciences Humaines. Delarge.

--Dictionnaire General des Sciences Humaines. French & Eur.

Thoburn, et al. Mon Premier Dictionnaire en 2000 mots & 2000 Images (Dist. by Continental Bk Co). Casterman.

Thole, B. L. & Gilissen, Theodor. Dictionary of Stock Market Terms in Four Languages. Shalom.

Thomas, A. V. Dictionnaire des Difficultes de la Langue Francaise (Dist. by Continental Bk Co) Larousse.

--Dictionnaire des Difficultes de la Langue Francaise. Larousse.

Thomas, Clayton L., ed. Taber's Cyclopedic Medical Dictionary. Davis Co.

Thomas, Denis. Dictionary of Fine Arts. Newnes Bks.

Thomas, Joseph. Universal Pronouncing Dictionary of Biography & Mythology. AMS Pr.

Thomas, Raymond. Diccionario del Budo: Artes Marciales. French & Eur.

Thomas, Robert C., jt. ed. see Ruffner, Frederick G., Jr.

Thomas, W. O., jt. auth. see Evans, H. Meurig.

Thomas, W. O., jt. auth. see Evans, Meurig.

Thomas, W. O., jt. auth. see Meurig, H.

Thomik, Rudolf. Fachwoerterbuch fuer Wirtschaft, Handel & Finanzen. Heymanns Verlag.

--Fachwoerterbuch Fur Wirtschaft, Handel und Finanzen (Pub. by Carl Heymanns Verlag KG). French & Eur.

Thompson, George A., tr. see De Alcedo, Antonio.

Thompson, George J. Verbal Judo: Words for Street Survival. C C Thomas.

Thompson, Philip & Davenport, Peter, eds. Dictionary of Graphic Cliches. St Martin.

--The Dictionary of Graphic Images. St Martin.

Thompson, Reginald C. A Dictionary of Assyrian Botany. AMS Pr.

--A Dictionary of Assyrian Chemistry & Geology. AMS Pr.

Thompson, Virginia & Adloff, Richard. Historical Dictionary of the People's Republic of the Congo (Congo-Brazzaville) Scarecrow.

Thomson. Dictionary of Medical Ethics & Practice. Wright-PSG.

Thomson, F. J. Elsevier's Dictionary of Financial Terms. Elsevier.

Thomson, Robert W., tr. see David.

Thomson, William A., ed. Black's Medical Dictionary. B&N Imports.

Thorlin, Eldora & Brannen, Noah. Everyday Japanese. Weatherhill.

Thorlin, Eldora S. Japanese Word & Phrase Book for Tourists. C E Tuttle.

Thorndike, Edward L. A Teacher's Word Book of the Twenty Thousand Words Found Most Frequently & Widely in General Reading for Children & Young People. Gale.

Thorne, J. O. & Collocott, T. C., eds. Chambers Biographical Dictionary (Pub. by Two Continents). Am Map.

Thorsen, Arnold, jt. auth. see Loland, Stale.

Thrall, W. F. & Hibbard, A. A Handbook to Literature. Darby Bks.

Thuillier. Lexique Anglais-Francais des Termes Appartenant Aux Technques En Usage I.G.N. French & Eur.

Thuiluer. Lexique Anglais-Francais: Termes Appartenant aux Techniques en Usage a I. G. N. Premiere Partie. I. G. N.

Tikhonov, A. N. Shkol' Nyi Slovoobrazovatel Nyi' Slovar' Russkogo Iazyka: Posobie dlia Uchaschikhsia. Four Continent.

--Shkolnyi Slovo-Obrazovatel'Nyislovar Russkogo Iazyka (Pub. by Prosveschchenie). Four Continent.

Tilander, Gunnar. Lexique du Roman de Renart. Champion.

Timmons, Christine & Gibney, Frank, eds. Britannica Book of English Usage. Doubleday.

Timms, Noel & Timms, Rita. Dictionary of Social Welfare. Routledge & Kegan.

Timms, Rita, jt. auth. see Timms, Noel.

Timofeev, L. I., et al, eds. Kratkii Slovar' Literaturovedcheskikh Terminov. Four Continent.

Timofeev, Leonid I. & Turev, S. V. Kratkii Slovar Literaturovedcheskikh Terminov (Pub. by Proveschchenie). Four Continent.

Tinctoris, Johannes. Dictionary of Musical Terms. Parrish, Carl, tr. Da Capo.

Tinkler, John D. Vocabulary & Syntax of the Old English Version in the Paris Psalter. Mouton.

Tiraboschi, Antonio. Vocabolario dei dealetti bergamashi. Forni.

--Vocabolario dei deatetti bergamashi. Forni.

Tireman, Loyd S. Spanish Vocabulary of Four Native Spanish-Speaking Pre-First-Grade Children. Borgo Pr.

Tischler, Johann. Hethitisches Etymologisches Glossar. Neumann, Guenther, ed. Inst Verg Sprach.

--Kleinasiatische Hydronymie: Semantik & Morphologie Analyse der Geichicher Gewaessernamen. Reichert.

Tischler, Wolfgang. Okologie. Fischer Verlag.

Tisserant, C. Dictionnaire Banda-Francais. Institut Ethnologie.

Tisserant, Ch. Dictionnaire Banda-Francais (Pub. by Institut Ethnologie). French & Eur.

Tissier, Jean. Dictionnaire Berrichon. Slatkine.

--Dictionnaire Berrichon avec Citations Litteraires. Lafitte Repr.

Tissot, Livio. Dizionario primierotto. Manfrini.

Titone, Virgilio. Dizionario delle idee comuni. Pan Italy.

Titova, I. A. Polsko-Ruskii Khimicheskii Slovar (Pub. by Sov Entsiklopedija). Four Continent.

Todd, A. H. Lexicon of Terms Relating to the Assessment & Classification of Coal Resources (Pub. by Graham & Trotman England). State Mutual Bk.

--Lexicon of Terms Relating to the Assessment & Classification of Coal Resources. Crane-Russak Co.

Todd, Hollis, jt. auth. see Stroebel, Leslie.

Todd, Hollis N., jt. auth. see Stroebel, Leslie.

Todorov, Tzvetan, jt. auth. see Ducrot, Oswald.

Toernblom, H., jt. auth. see Engstroem, Ake.

Toesca, Maurice. Dictionnaire de la Contradiction. French & Eur.

Togore, Roca De see De Togore, Roca.

Tokarev, S. A., et al, eds. Frantsuzsko-Russkii Obshchestvenno-Politisheskii Slovar (Pub. by Izd. In-ta Mezhdunarod. Otnoshenii). Four Continent.

Toledo, F. & Milioni, B. Dicionario de Administracao de Recursos Humanos com Termos: Ingles-Portugues, Portugues-Ingles. French & Eur.

Tollet, Gustav. Atk-Sanakirja. Tietojen.

Tolstoi, D. M. English-Russian Physics Dictionary (Pub. by Collets). State Mutual Bk.

Tolstoi, D. M., ed. Anglo-Russkii Fizicheskii Slovar (Pub. by Russkii Iazyk). Four Continent.

--English-Russian Physics Dictionary. Pergamon.

Tomba, Silvia. Svensk-Italiensk Ordbok. Esselte Studium.

Tommaseo, Niccolo. Dizionario dei sinonimi della lingua italiana. Nuova Vallecchi.

Tommaseo, Niccolo & Bellini, Bernardo. Dizionario della lingua italiana. Rizzoli Edit.

Tommaseo, Niccolo & Rigutini, G. Dizionario dei sinonimi della lingua italiana. Vallardi F.

Tomsic, F. German-Slovene Dictionary. French & Eur.

--Slovene-German Dictionary. French & Eur.

Tonetti, F. Dizionario del dialetto valsesiano. Forni.

Tooley, R. V. Tooley's Dictionary of Mapmakers. A R Liss.

--Tooley's Dictionary of Mapmakers. A R Liss.

Tooth, J., jt. auth. see Renner, R.

Tooth, Jeffery, jt. auth. see Renner, Ruediger.

Tootil, Elizabeth, ed. Dictionary of Biology. Intl Bk Ctr.

Tootill, Elizabeth, ed. The Facts on File Dictionary of Biology. Facts on File.

Toporov, V. N. Prusskii Iazyk Slovar: E-H (Pub. by Nauka). Four Continent.

Topping, Donald. Spoken Chamorro: With Gramatical Notes & Glossary. UH Pr.

Topping, Donald M., et al. Chamorro-English Dictionary. UH Pr.

Toprov, V. N. Prusskii Iazyk Slovar: I-L (Pub. by Nauka). Four Continent.

Tornberg, et al. Svensk-Engelsk & Engelsk-Svensk Ordbok. Esselte Studium.

Tornberg, Astrid, jt. auth. see Nojd, Ruben.

Tornberg, Astrid, et al. McKay's Modern Swedish-English & English-Swedish Dictionary. McKay.

Toro, Gisbert De see De Toro, Miguel & De Toro, Gisbert.

Toro, M. De see De Toro, M. & Gisbert.

Toro, Miguel De see De Toro, Miguel & De Toro, Gisbert.

Torok, T., jt. auth. see Moritz, H.

Torp, Alf, jt. auth. see Falk, H. S.

Torre-Bueno, J. R. dela. A Glossary of Entomology. Lubrecht & Cramer.

Torrens dels Prats, A. Diccionario de modismos ingleses y norteamericanos. Juventud.

Torrens dels Prats, Alfonso. Diccionario de dificultades del Ingles. Fed Gremios.

--Diccionario de modismos ingleses y norteamericanos. Fed Gremios.

Torrents dels Prats, Alfonso. Diccionario de Dificultades del Ingles. Lectorum Pubns.

--Diccionario de dificultades del ingles (JUV). Lectorum Pubns.

--Diccionario De Dificultades Del Ingles. French & Eur.

--Diccionario de ingles-americano. Juventud.

--Diccionario de Modismos Inglese y Norteamericanos. French & Eur.

Torres, Elena, tr. see Fournier, Robert.

Torres, F. R. Diccionario de Terminos Medicos Ingles-Espanol & Espanol-Ingles. Edit Alhambra.

Torres, Rosa E. Terminologia de la Education. Minist Ed La Paz.

Torres Calvo, Angel. Diccionario de textos sociales pontificios. Bibliografica.

Torrinha, Francisco. Dicionario Latino-Portuges. Porto Ed.

Tortora, Giovanni. Dictionnaire Juridique: Italien-Francais Francais-Italien. Maison Dictionnaire.

Tosco, U. Dizionario di botanica: A-L. Ist Geo Agostini.

--Dizionario di Botanica: M-Z. Ist Geo Agostini.

Tosco, Uberto. Diccionario de botanica. Gil, Francisco, tr. Teide.

--Dictionnaire de Botanique: Vol. 1, A-H. Atlas.

--Dictionnaire de Botanique: Vol. 2, I-Z. Atlas.

Tosi, Carlo P. Dizionario della lingua italiana. Principato.

Toth, Lajos. Orosz-Magyar Katonai Szotar. Akademiai Kiado.

Toth, Lajos, et al. Katonai Ertelmezo Szotar. Zrinyi Katonai.

Toth, Rudolf. Terminoloski Komparativni Srpskohrvatsko. Ekonomski Fakultet.

Touati, Maurice A. Lexique Francais de la Reparation Juridique du Dommage Corporel. Maloine.

--Lexique Francais De la Reparation Juridique Du Dommage Corporel. French & Eur.

--Lexique Francais Des Abreviations et Formules Medico-Chirurgicales Courantes. French & Eur.

--Lexique Francais des Abreviations: Formules Medico-Chirugicales Courantes. Maloine.

--Lexique Francais: La Reparation Juridique du Dommage Corporel. Maloine.

Touitou, Yvan & Perlemuter, Leon. Dictionnaire Pratique de Pharmacologie Clinique. Masson & Cie.

--Dictionnaire Pratique de Pharmacologie Clinique. Masson.

--Dictionnaire Pratique de Pharmacologie: Clinique. French & Eur.

Tovar, Enrique D. Vocabulario del Oriente Peruano. U. San Marcos.

Towers, John. Dictionary-Catalogue of Operas & Operettas. Da Capo.

Townes, jt. auth. see O'Donnell.

Townley, Helen M. & Gee, Ralph C. Thesaurus-Making: Grow Your Own Word-Stock. Westview.

Townsend, W. C. Handbook of Homophones. Summer Inst Ling.

Tozzetti, Ottaviano T. Dizionario botanico italiano. Forni.

Trade & Technical Pr.Ltd., ed. Europump Terminology: Pump Applications (Pub. by Trade & Tech). State Mutual Bk.

Traina, A., jt. auth. see Luciano, L.

Transportation Research Board. Glossary of Urban Public Transportation Terms. Transport Res Bd.

Trapnell, William. Voltaire & His Portable Dictionary. Intl Pubns Serv.

Traupman, John C. New College German & English Dictionary. AMSCO Sch.

--New College Latin & English Dictionary. AMSCO Sch.

Traupman, John C., ed. The Bantam New College German & English Dictionary. Bantam.

--New College Latin & English Dictionary. Bantam.

Travers, Milton A. One of the Keys: The Wampanoag Contribution. Chris Mass.

Traversay, Yves de, jt. auth. see Renouil, Yves.

Travlos, John. Pictorial Dictionary of Ancient Athens. Hacker.

Tregelles, Samuel P., tr. see Gesenius, Wilhelm.

Trejo, Arnulfo D. Diccionario etimologica latinoamericano de lexico de la delincuencia. UTEHA.

Trempe, Jean-Pierre. Lexique de la Psychanalyse. Quebec P. U.

Trench, Richard C. A Select Glossary of English Words Used Formerly in Senses Different from Their Present. Palmer, A. Smythe, ed. Arden Lib.

Trenel, Jacques. Lexique Francais-Latin. Belin.

Trevaskis, John & Hyman, Robin. Boys & Girls First Dictionary. U of Toronto Pr.

Triadu, Joan. Diccionari Ortografic. Biblograf SP.

Trimmer, Eric. Diccionario visual del sexo. Jorda, Ernest, tr. Circulo Lect.

Trimmer, Eric J. The Visual Dictionary of Sex. A & W Pubs.
Trimmer, Eric J., ed. The Visual Dictionary of Sex (A & W Visual Library). A & W Pubs.
Trioke-Strambaci, H. & Helffrich-Mariani, E. Woerterbuch des Italienisch-Deutschen Privat & Wirtschaftsrechts: Band I, Deutsch-Italienisch. Recht & Wirtschaft.
Tripp, Rhoda T., ed. International Thesaurus of Quotations. T Y Crowell.
Trittschuh, Travis, jt. auth. see Sperber, Hans.
Triva, Rubes, jt. auth. see Modica, Enzo.
Troike-Strambaci, H. & Helffrich-Mariani, E. Woerterbuch des Italienisch-Deutschen Privat & Wirtschaftsrechts: Band II, Italienish-Deutsch. Recht & Wirtschaft.
Trojanwska, Izabella, jt. auth. see Ostrowski, Roza.
Troskolanski, A. T. Dictionary of Hydraulic Machinery. Elsevier.
Trotsky, Judith, ed. News Dictionary 1974. Facts on File.
--News Dictionary 1975. Facts on File.
Troupeau, Gerard. Lexique Index du Kitab de Sibawayhl. Klincksieck.
Truck Trailer Manufacturers Association. Nomenclature & Terminology of Tank Trailers & Containers. Truck Trailer Mfrs.
Trump, jt. auth. see Bray.
Trump, D., jt. auth. see Bray, W.
Trump, David. The Penguin Dictionary of Archaeology. Penguin.
Trump, David, jt. auth. see Bray, Warwick.
Tschamler, Herbert, ed. see Zoepfl, Helmut & Bittner, Gerhard.
Tsintsius, V. I. Russko-Evenskii Slovar (Pub. by GINS). Four Continent.
Tsirpanlis, Constantine N. Modern Greek Idiom & Phrase Book. Barron.
Tsyganenko. Dictionnaire Etymologique de la Langue Russe. MIR.
Tuazon & Schaffer. The New Comprehensive A-Z Crossword Dictionary. Avon.
Tuazon, Redentor M. & Schaffer. The New Comprehensive A-Z Crossword Dictionary (G&D). Putnam Pub Group.
Tubella, Imma. Diccionari del Nacionalisme. French & Eur.
Tucker, T. G. Etymological Dictionary of Latin. Ares.
Tu-Dien Tieu-Chuan Anh-Viet. Hoa's Essential English-Vietnamese Dictionary. Iaconi.
--Standard Pronouncing English-Vietnamese Dictionary. Iaconi.
Tu-Dien Tuie-Chuan Viet-Anh. Standard Pronouncing Vietnamese English Dictionary. Iaconi.
Tuke, Daniel H. A Dictionary of Psychological Medicine. Ayer Co.
Tulab, Munjid al & Mashreq, Dar el. Arabic Student Dictionary. Intl Bk Ctr.
Tulin, S. A., jt. auth. see Petrov, V. S.
Tuomikowski, A., jt. auth. see Riikon, E.
Turato, Gianfranco, jt. auth. see Durante, Dino.
Turchin, P. E. Russko-Frantsuzskii Aviatsionno-Tekhnicheskii Slovar (Pub. by Sov. Entsiklopedia). Four Continent.
Turell, Baldovi F. Diccionario Auxiliar del Crucigramista. Bruguera MX.
Turell Baldovi, Fausto. Diccionario Auxiliar del Crucigramista. French & Eur.
--Diccionario auxiliar del crucigramista II. Bruguera.
Turev, S. V., jt. auth. see Timofeev, Leonid I.
Turkina, Phil E. Latvian-English Dictionary. Saphrograph.
Turner, Carann, jt. auth. see Lucas, Caroline.
Turner, Carann, ed. see Lucas, Caroline & Turner, Carann.
Turner, David R. Vocabulary Builder & Guide to Verbal Tests. Arco.
--Vocabulary, Spelling & Grammar. Arco.
Turner, L. D. Notes on the Sounds & Vocabulary of Gullah. U of Ala Pr.
Turner, L. D; see King, A. T.
Turner, Paul & Turner, Shirley. Dictionary of Chontal to Spanish-English, & Spanish to Chontal. U of Ariz Pr.
Turner, Sir Ralph. A Comparative Dictionary of the Indo-Aryan Languages. Oxford U Pr.
Turner, Shirley, jt. auth. see Turner, Paul.
Turover, G., jt. auth. see Nogueira, J.
Turroni, Giuseppe, jt. auth. see Porro, Maurizio.
Turtoi, Dumitru, et al. Dictionar de Chimie si Inginerie Chimica Rus-Roman. Editura Stiintifica.
Turvey, B., compiled by. Kwanyama-English Dictionary. Witwatersrand.
Tutin, John R. Concordance to FitzGerald's Translation of the Rubaiyat of Omar Khayyam. B Franklin.
Tutsch, D. Lexikon der Medizinischen Fachsprache. French & Eur.
Tutsch, Dagobert. Lexikon der Medizin. French & Eur.
--Taschenlexikon Medizin. Urban & Schwarzen.
Tutsch, Dagobert, ed. Lexikon der Medizinischen Fachsprache: Bd 1, A-L. Rowohlt.
--Lexikon der Medizinischen Fachsprache: Bd 2, M-Z. Rowohlt.
Tutzaver, Ingrid M., jt. auth. see Tutzaver, Otto E.
Tutzaver, Otto E. & Tutzaver, Ingrid M. Dictionary of environmental protection. Heymanns Verlag.
Tuxen, S. L., ed. Taxonomist's Glossary of Genitalia in Insects. Lubrecht & Cramer.
Tver, David & Russell, Percy. The Nutrition Dictionary. Van Nos Reinhold.
Tver, David F. Dictionary of Astronomy, Space & Atmospheric Phenomena. Van Nos Reinhold.
--Dictionary of Dangerous Pollutants, Ecology & Environment. Indus Pr.
--Ocean & Marine Dictionary. Cornell Maritime.
Tver, David F. & Berry, Richard W. The Petroleum Dictionary. Van Nos Reinhold.
--Petroleum Dictionary. Van Nos Reinhold.
Tver, David F. & Bolz, Roger W. Robotics Sourcebook & Dictionary. Indus Pr.
Tver, David F., compiled by. Dictionary of Business & Science. Gulf Pub.
Tver, David F., et al. Dictionary of Astronomy, Space & Atmospheric Phenomena. Van Nos Reinhold.
Tweney, C. F. & Hughes, L. E. Diccionario tecnologico Chambers: Espanol-ingles-frances-aleman. Omega SA.
Twitchell, Paul. Eckankar Dictionary. IWP Pub.
Tyler, J. Allen & Parrish, Stephen M., eds. A Concordance to the Fables & Tales of Jean De la Fontaine. Cornell U Pr.
Tymchuk, Alexander J. The Mental Retardation Dictionary. Western Psych.
Tyrkiel, E. F. Dictionary of Physical Metallurgy. Elsevier.
Tyrrell, William B. Medical Terminology for Medical Students. C C Thomas.

U

Ubaldi, V., jt. auth. see Altenberg, G. A.
Ubanou. Diccionario de eiencias. Dossat.
Ubarov, Chapman. Diccionario de Ciencias. French & Eur.
U Chin Vei, et al. Karmannyi Russko-Birmanskii Slovar (Pub. by GINS). Four Continent.
Uden, Grant, jt. auth. see Cooper, Richard.
Ugo, Monetti. Dizionarietto di tecnica bancaria, mercantile con appendice trilingue. RIREA.
Ugolini, Luigi. Dizionario del cacciatore italiano. Bietti.
Uhlenbeck, Christianus C. & Van Gulik, R. H. A Blackfoot-English Vocabulary. AMS Pr.
--An English-Blackfoot Vocabulary. AMS Pr.
Uhlig, Siegfried. Einfuhrung in das Technische Russisch Maschinenbau: Lehrmaterial fuer den Fremdsprachenunterricht. VEB Technik.
Ulbrich, Rolf. Langenscheidts Taschenwoerterbuch Tschechisch: Teil I, Tschechisch-Deutsch. Langenscheidt.
--Langenscheidts Taschenwoerterbuecher Tschechisch-Deutsch. Langenscheidt.
Ulbrich, Rolf & Kabesch, Friedrich. Langenscheidts Taschenwoerterbuch Tschechisch-Deutsch. Langenscheidt.
Ulleland, M. Italian-Norwegian Dictionary. Kunnskapsforlaget.
--Italiensk-Norsk Ordbok. French & Eur.
Ullman, Manfred, ed. see Kroemer, Joerg, et al.
Ullmann, Manfred. Woerterbuch der Klassischen Arabischen Sprache: Bd 2, Lfg 1. Harrassowitz.
--Woerterbuch der Klassischen Arabischen Sprache: Bd 2, Lfg 4. Harrassowitz.
Ullmann, Manfred & Spitaler, Anton. Woerterbuch der Klassischen Arabischen: Bd 1, Lfg 7. Harrassowitz.
--Woerterbuch der Klassischen Arabischen Sprache: Bd 1, Lfg 3. Harrassowitz.
--Woerterbuch der Klassischen Arabischen Sprache: Bd 1, Lfg 4. Harrassowitz.
--Woerterbuch der Klassischen Arabischen Sprache: Bd 1, Lfg 5. Harrassowitz.
--Woerterbuch der Klassischen Arabischen Sprache: Bd 1, Lfg 6. Harrassowitz.
--Woerterbuch der Klassischen Arabischen Sprache: Bd 1, Lfg 8. Harrassowitz.
--Woerterbuch der Klassischen Arabischen Sprache: Bd 1, Lfg 9-10. Harrassowitz.
Ullmann, Manfred & Wojtowytsch-Wielandt, Rotraud. Woerterbuch der Klassischen Arabischen Sprache: Bd 2, Lfg 2. Harrassowitz.
Ullrich, Heinz M., jt. auth. see Neuder, Gustav F.
Ulrich, George. Beginning Dictionary. Hamilton, David R., ed. HM.
--Children's Dictionary. HM.
Ulrich, Gertrude A. One Hundred Eleven Viennese Dishes. Saphrograph.
Ulrich, W. Woerterbuch - Linguistische Grundbegriffe. French & Eur.
Ulrich, Winfried. Woerterbuch: Linguistische Grundbegriffe. Hirt.
Ulrich, Winfried Von see Von Ulrich, Winfried.
Ulset, Tor, jt. auth. see Skadberg, Kare.
Ul'Tsiferov, O. G. Khindi-Russkii Uchebnyi Slovar (Pub. by GINS). Four Continent.
Umbral Perez, Francisco. Diccionario Para Pobres. French & Eur.
Unbegaun, B. O., jt. ed. see Wheeler, Marcus.
Undersea Medical Society, Inc. Glossary of Diving & Hyperbaric Terms. Undersea Med.
Underwood. Concise English-Korean Dictionary Romanized. Iaconi.
Underwood, Joan V. Concise English-Korean Dictionary Romanized. C E Tuttle.
Underwood, Peter. Dictionary of the Supernatural: An A to Z of Hauntings, Possession, Witchcraft, Demonology & Other Occult Phenomena. Harrap.
UNESCO. Diccionario De Ciencias Sociales. French & Eur.
Ungarelli, Gaspare. Vocabolario del dialetto bolognese. Multigrafica.
Union Europeenne Des Experts Compatables, Economiques et Financiers. Accounting Dictionary - U.E.C. Lexicon: American-French-German-Spanish-Dutch. Intl Pubns Serv.
U. S. Armed Forces. Dictionary of Spoken Spanish Words, Phrases, Sentences. Doubleday.
U. S. Army Natick Laboratories. Glossary of Environmental Terms (Terrestrial) Gale.
U. S. Department of Housing & Urban Development, Washington, D. C. Dictionary Catalog of the United States Department of Housing & Urban Development Library & Information Division (Hall Library). G K Hall.
U. S. Department of Housing and Urban Development, Washington, D. C. Dictionary Catalog of the United States Department of Housing & Urban Development Library & Information Division, First Supplement (Hall Library). G K Hall.
U. S. Department of the Interior, Washington, D. C. Dictionary Catalog of the Department Library (Hall Library). G K Hall.
U. S. Department of the Interior Washington D.C. Dictionary Catalog of the Department Library, Fourth Suppl (Hall Library). G K Hall.
United States Golf Association. Dictionary of Turfgrass Terms. US Golf Assn.
United States League of Savings Associations. Housing-Planning Glossary. US League Savings Assns.
U. S. War Department. Dictionary of Spoken Russian: Russian-English: English-Russian. Dover.
--Dictionary of Spoken Spanish: Spanish-English, English-Spanish. Dover.
--A Phrase & Sentence Dictionary of Spoken Spanish. Gannon.
Universidad de Chicago. Diccionario ingles-espanol y espanol-ingles. Aguilar SP.
University of California - Berkeley. Dictionary Catalog of the Giannini Foundation of Agricultural Economics Library (Hall Library). G K Hall.
--Dictionary Catalog of the Water Resources Center Archives (Hall Library). G K Hall.
University of California, Berkeley. Dictionary Catalog of the Water Resources Center Archives, Fourth Suppl (Hall Library). G K Hall.
University of California, Berkeley, Water Resources Center. Dictionary Catalog of the Water Resources Center Archives: Sixth Supplement (Hall Library). G K Hall.
University Of Chicago - Graduate Library School - 24th Conference. New Definitions of School-Library Service: Proceedings. Fenwick, Sara I., ed. U of Chicago Pr.
University of London. Dictionary Catalogue of the London School of Hygiene & Tropical Medicine (Hall Library). G K Hall.
University of the State of New York, State Education Department. Iontenwennaweienstahkhwa. State U NY Pr.
University of Wales Press. A Dictionary of the Welsh Language: Part 31. Bevan, G. A., ed. Verry.
University of Washington at Seattle. The Dictionary Catalog of the Pacific Northwest Collection of the University of Washington Libraries (Hall Library). G K Hall.
Unseld, D. Medizinisches Woerterbuch der Deutschen und Englischen Sprache (Pub. by Wissenschaftlicher Vlg.). French & Eur.
Unseld, D. W. German-English, English-German Medical Dictionary. Heinman.
--Medical Dictionary. Adler.
Unseld, Dieter. Medical Dictionary of the English & German Languages: Medizinisches Worterbuch der Deutschen und Englischen Sprache. Intl Pubns Serv.
Unseld, Dieter W. Medical Dictionary of the English & German Languages. Wissenschaftliche.
Unstead, R. J. Dictionary of History (Pub. by Two Continents). Hippocrene Bks.

Unwin, Kenneth. Langenscheidt's Standard French Dictionary: French-English, English-French. Am Map.
Uphof, J. C. Dictionary of Economic Plants. Lubrecht & Cramer.
Urdang. Urdang Dictionary of Current Medical Terms (Pub. by Wiley Med). Wiley.
Urdang & Manser, eds. Dictionary of Synonyms & Antonyms. Pan Bks.
Urdang, Laurance, ed. Allusions, Cultural, Literary, Biblical, & Historical: A Thematic Dictionary. Gale.
Urdang, Laurence. The Basic Book of Synonyms & Antonyms (Sig). NAL.
--A Basic Dictinary of Synonyms & Antonyms. Lodestar Bks.
--A Basic Dictionary of Synonyms & Antonyms. Lodestar Bks.
--The World Almanac Dictionary of Dates. World Almanac.
Urdang, Laurence, ed. Dictionary of Advertising Terms. Crain Bks.
--The New York Times Everyday Reader's Dictionary of Misunderstood, Misused, Mispronounced Words. Times Bks.
--Suffixes: And Other Word-Final Elements of English. Gale.
Urdang, Laurence, jt. ed. see LaRoche, Nancy.
Urdang, Lawrence & Hoequist, Charles, Jr., eds. Ologies & Isms: A Thematic Dictionary. Gale.
Urdung, Lawrence, ed. The Random House Basic Dictionary-Synonyms & Antonyms. Ballantine.
Urech, Edouard. Dictionnaire des Symboles Chretiens. Delachaux.
--Lexikon Christlicher Symbole. F Bahn.
Urwin, Kenneth. Dictionnaire Pratique Mercure: Francais-Anglais, Anglais-Francais. French & Eur.
Urwin, Kenneth, ed. A Short Old French Dictionary for Students (Pub. by Basil Blackwell). Biblio Dist.
U.S. Department of the Interior, Washington D.C. Dictionary Catalog of the Department Library, Third Sup (Hall Library). G K Hall.
US Pharmacoepial Convention. USAN & the USP Dictionary. US Pharmacopeia.
U.S. War Dept., ed. A Phrase & Sentence Dictionary of Spoken Russian. Imported bks.
U.S.Department of Housing & Urban Development, Washington, D.C. Dictionary Catalog of the United States Department of Housing & Urban Development, Library & Information Division Second Suppl (Hall Library). G K Hall.
Usha, Brahmacharini, ed. Ramakrishna-Vedanta Wordbook: A Brief Dictionary of Hinduism. Vedanta Pr.
Ushakov, D. N., ed. Tolkovyi Slovar Russkogo Iazyka. Four Continent.
Ushakov, D. N., et al. Orfograficheskii Slovar (Pub. by Prosveschchenie). Four Continent.
--Orfograficheskii Slovar' Four Continent.
Ushakova, L. I., et al. Indioneziisko-Russkii Uchebnyi Razgovornik (Pub. by Gosizdat Inostr Natsional Slovarei). Four Continent.
Usher, George. A Dictionary of Botany. Crane-Russak Co.
Utgabes, S., jt. auth. see Kirkeby, W. A.
Uvarov, E. B., et al. Dicionario de ciencia. Pub Euro Am.

V

Vaccaro, Gennaro. Dizionario delle parole nuovissime e dificili. Romana Libri ALfabeto.
--Vocabolario romanesco-belliano e italiano-romanesco. Romana Libri.
--Vocabolario romanesco-trilussiano e italiano-romanesco. Romana Libri.
Vacchi, G. Dizionario di musica. Zanichelli.
Vaillancourt, J. Lexique Anglais-Francais. Edns Ottawa.
Vaillancourt, Jean. Lexique Anglais-Francais: Termes Techniques a l'usage des Biologistes. U of Toronto Pr.
Vaillancourt, Pauline M. International Directory of Acronyms in Library, Information & Computer Sciences. Bowker.
Vaitkiavichiute, V. A. Polsko-Litovskii Slovar (Pub. by Mokslas). Four Continent.
Vajda, Georges. Le Dictionnaire des Autorites. CNRS.
--Le Dictionnaire des Autorites. French & Eur.
Vakharos, I., et al. Finsko-Russkii Slovar (Pub. by Russkii Iazyk). Four Continent.
Valderrama Martinez, Fernando. Glosario Espanol-Arabe. Albir.
--Glosario Espanol-Arabe y Arabe-Espanol. Albir.
Valenius, A. P. Kratkii Russko-Shvedskii Slovar (Pub. by GINS). Four Continent.
Valensi, Serge. Lexique Usuel d'informatique. S. C. M.
Valensin, Georges. Dictionnaire de la Sexualite. French & Eur.
Valla, Nicola. Vocabularium vulgare. Bottega d'Erasmo.
Valla Gorina, Manuel. Diccionario de la Musica. Alianza.
Valle, Gerson. Vocabulario Trabalhista: Direito do Trabalho, Processo do Trabalho, Previdencia Socail. Rio Grafica.
Valle, Guglielmo. Vocabolario dei piccoli. La Scuola.
Vallee, Eugene & Latouche, Robert. Dictionnaire Topographique de la France, 1. Biblio Nationale.
Vallespinos, Ferran, tr. see Lender, T., et al.
Vallieres, P., et al. Lexique des Produits de la Peche: Anglais-Francais. French & Eur.
Valls Gorina, Manual. Diccionario de la Musica. Alianza Ed.
Valls Gorina, Manuel. Diccionario de la musica. Alianza Ed.
Valmin, Natan & Frangos, Eftychia. Svensk-Nygrekisk Ordbok. Esselte Studium.
Van Amerongen, C. Dictionary of Cement. French & Eur.
Van Baars & Van der Schoot. Engels-Nederlands Woodenboek. Spectrum Pub.
Van Beckum, J. H., ed. Langenscheidts Handwoerterbuecher: Tl 1, Gelderen, 1 van: Niederlandisch-Deutsch. Langenscheidt.
Van Beckum, J. H. & Wallis, H., eds. Langenscheidts Handwoerterbuecher: Tl 2, Gelderen, 1 van, Deutsch-Niederlandisch. Langenscheidt.
Van Cappen. Dizionario italiano-olandese. Vallardi A.
Van Cauwenberg, jt. auth. see Aubert, Roger.
Van Dale, Johan H. Groot Woordenboek der Nederlandse Taal. Kruyskamp, C., ed. Nyhoff.
Vandelli, Canzio. Dizionario fraseologico di Inglese Tecnico. Mondini Siccardi.
--Dizionario fraseologico di russo-italiano e viceversa. Mondini Siccardi.
Vandenberghe, J. P., jt. auth. see Chaballe, L. Y.
Vandenberghe, J. P., compiled by. Elsevier's Nautical Dictionary. Elsevier.
Vandenberghe, J. P. & Chaballe, L. Y., eds. Elsevier's Nautical Dictionary in Six Languages. Elsevier.
Van der Schoot, jt. auth. see Van Baars.
Van Derveer & Haas. International Glossary of Technical Terms for the Pulp & Paper Industry. Imported Bks.
Van Derveer, Paul D. & Haas, Leonard E., eds. International Glossary of Technical Terms for the Pulp & Paper Industry. Miller Freeman.
Van Deursen, A. Illustrated Dictionary of Bible Manners & Customs. Citadel Pr.
Van De Wiele, F. J. Langenscheidts Taschenwoerterbuch Niederlaendisch: Teil I, Niederlaendisch-Deutsch. Langenscheidt.
Van De Wiele, F. J. J. & Beersmans, Frans. Langenscheidts Taschenwoerterbuch Niederlandisch-Deutsch. Langenscheidt.
Van Dijk, Marcel & Sandeau, Georges. Thesaurus du Management & de l'economie. M. Van Dijk.
Van Gelderen, ed. Duits-Neederland Woordenboek. French & Eur.
Van Gelderen, I. & Wallis, W. H. Langenscheidts Handwoerterbuch Niederlaendisch Wolters: Teil I, Niederlaendisch-Deutsch. Langenscheidt.
Van Gemert, G. A. & De Maesschalck, A. Geneesmiddelenzakboekje. Agon Elsevier.
Vangmark, H. Dansk-Russik Ordborg. French & Eur.
Vangmark, Helge. Dansk-Russik Ordbog. Grafisk Forlag.
Van Grieken, J. E. Dictionnaire du Traducteur: Francais-Neerlandais. Administratives.
Van Gulik, R. H., jt. auth. see Uhlenbeck, Christianus C.
Van Hee, Marijke. Woordenboek Welzijn. VUGA.
Vani, Paule. Diccionario de trucos. Giordano, Eduardo, tr. Granica.
Van Kampen, V. Dizionario Italiano-Olandese, Olandese-Italiano. French & Eur.
Van Kuijk, W. M., jt. auth. see Bels-Koning, H. C.
Van Meerhaeghe, Marcel A. Lexicon Van de Economie. Stenfert Kroese.
Van Nierop, Maarten. Nieuwe Woorden. Scheltens.
Vanoverbergh, Morice. Isneg-English Vocabulary. UH Pr.
Van Rijswijk, Maria J., jt. auth. see Duijker, Hubert C.
Van Rijswijk, Maria J., jt. auth. see Duijker, Hubert C.
Van Sijswijk, Maria, jt. auth. see Duijker, Hubert C.
Van Steenwyk, Elizabeth. Illustrated Riding Dictionary for Young People. Harvey.
Vansteenwyk, Elizabeth Van. Illustrated Horseback Riding Dictionary for Young People. P-H.
Van Voss, M. Heerma. Agypten, die 21: Dynastie. E J Brill.
Van Wagoner, Merrill. English-Arabic Vocabulary. Intl Bk Ctr.
Van Wagoner, Merrill Y., et al. English-Arabic Vocabulary: Students Pronouncing Dictionary. Spoken Lang Serv.
Van Wely, F. P. Cassell's Dutch Dictionary: English-Dutch, Dutch-English. Macmillan.
Varela Colmeiro, G. Diccionario comercial y economico moderno: Ingles-espanol. Inter-Ciencia.
Varios. Diccionario Enciclopedico De las Ciencias Del Lenquaje. French & Eur.
Varios, tr. Diccionario A R V E: Obra completa. Argos-Vergara.
--Diccionario A R V E: Tomo 1; Ingles-Espanol. Argos-Vergara.
--Diccionario A R V E: Tomo 2; Espanol-Ingles. Argos-Vergara.
--Diccionario de terminos cientificos y tecnicos: Tomo 5 II. Marcombo.
Varma, B. Kanti. Bulgarian-Hindi Dictionary. French & Eur.
Varnai, Peter. Operalexikon. Zenemukiado.
Varsanyi, Istvan. Lengyel-Magyar Szotar. Terra.
--Magyar-Lengyel Szotar. Terra.
--Magyar-Lengyel Szotar. Terra.
Vartolomei, Luminita, jt. auth. see Sava, Iosif.
Vascenco, Victor. Dictionar de Buzunar Roman-Rus. Editura Stiintifica.
Vasil'Eva, A. S. Russkikh Glagolov. Four Continent.
Vasmer, Max. Russich Elymologisches Woerterbuch (Pub. by Carl Winter). French & Eur.
--Russich Etymologishes Woerterbuch. Winter Univ.
--Russisch Etymologisches Woerterbuch. Winter Univ.
--Russisch Etymologisches Woerterbuch. Winter Univ.
--Russisch Etymologisches Woerterbuch (Pub. by Carl Winter). French & Eur.
--Russisch Etymologisches Woerterbuch (Pub. by Carl Winter). French & Eur.
--Woerterbuch der Russischen Gewaessernamen: Bd 1, A-E. Harrassowitz.
Vasquez, Librado & Vasquez, Maria E. Regional Dictionary of Chicano Slang. Camino Real.
Vasquez, Librado K. & Vasquez, Maria E. Regional Dictionary of Chicano Slang. Jenkins.
Vasquez, Maria E., jt. auth. see Vasquez, Librado.
Vasquez, Maria E., jt. auth. see Vasquez, Librado K.
Vassiliades, G., ed. Penguin-Hellenews English-Greek Dictionary. Caratzas Pub Co.
Vassilieva. Dictionnaire Russe-Francais Polytechnique. Mir.
Vasto, Lanza Del see Del Vasto, Lanza.
Vaughan, Wm. A Vocabulary Arranged for the Instruction of the Deaf & Dumb. Gordon Pr.
Vaughn, Jim. Jumbo Vocabulary Development Yearbook: Grade 7. ESP.
--Jumbo Vocabulary Development Yearbook: Grade 10. ESP.
Vautherin, Auguste. Glossaire du Patois de Chatenois avec Vocables des Autres: Localites du Territoire de Belfort & des Environs. Slatkine.
Vayssier, Aime R. Dictionnaire Patois-Francais du Departement de l'Aveyron. Slatkine.
V. Clauss, Guenther. Woerterbuch der Psychologie. French & Eur.
Veb. Inst. Leipzig. Bi-Lexikon A-Z. Bibl Inst Leipzig.
Vebel, C. Diccionario del perfecto automobilista. Grijalbo.
Vebel, Christian. Dictionnaire du Parfait Automobiliste. Pensee Moderne.
Vega, V. Diccionario ilustrado de anecdotas. G Gili.
--Diccionario ilustrado de efemerides. G Gili.
Vega, V., jt. auth. see Chardana, J. L.
Vega, Vicente. Diccionario Ilustrado de Rarezas, Inverosimilitudes y Curiosidades. French & Eur.
Vega, Vicente, jt. auth. see Chardans, J. L.
Vega, Vincente. Diccionario Ilustrado de Efemerides. French & Eur.
Veh, Otto, ed. Lexikon der Roemischen Kaiser. Artemis Verlag.
Veillon & Nobel. Dizionario Medico Poliglotta. French & Eur.
--Dizionario medico poliglotta: Inglese-tedesco-francese. Piccin.
Veillon, E. & Nobel, A. Medizinisches Woerterbuch. Huber.
--Medizinisches Woerterbuch (Pub. by H. Huber). French & Eur.
--Spanisches Supplement Zu Medizinisches Woerterbuch. Huber.
--Spanisches Supplement Zu Medizinisches Woerterbuch (Pub. by H. Huber Vlg.). French & Eur.
Veillon, Emile & Noble, Albert. Dictionnaire Medical. Masson.
Veillon, Emmanuel & Nobel, Albert. Dictionnaire Medical. Hans.
Veillon, Emmanuel, jt. auth. see Lovasy, Ernest.
Veillon-Nobel. Diccionario Medico & su Suplemento Espanol. Cientifico Med.
Veistman, E. A., jt. ed. see Milovanov, E. L.
Velazquez, et al, eds. The Spanish & English, English & Spanish Dictionary - Self Pronouncing. P-H.
Velazquez, Mariana. Velazquez Spanish & English Dictionary. New Century.
Velazquez, Mariano. Diccionario Velazquez: Espanol e ingles. Follett.
Velco, G. Textile Dictionary (Pub. by Collets). State Mutual Bk.
Velden, F. J. Beknopt Juridisch Woordenboek Frans-Nederlands. Kluwer Group.
Vels. Diccionario de grafologia. Cedel.
Vels, Augusto. Diccionario de Grafologia y Terminos Psicologicos Afines. French & Eur.

Velte, Herbert. Budo-Lexikon: 1500 Fachausdruecke Fernoestl. Falken Verlag.
Vencovska, Marta. Cesko-Rusky Slovnik na Cesty. SNTC.
Vendryes, Joseph. Lexique Etymologique de L'Irlandais Ancien: Fascicule R-S. CNRS.
--Lexique Etymologique de L'Irlandais Ancien: Fascicule T-U. CNRS.
--Lexique Etymologique de l'Irlandais Ancien. CNRS.
--Lexique Etymologique de l'Irlandais Ancien, 1. CNRS.
Vendryes, Joseph & Bachellery, E. Lexique Etymologique de L'Irlandais Ancien: Lettre B. CNRS.
Venezky, Richard L. Structure of English Orthography. Mouton.
Venturino, B. Dizionario borana-italiano. EMI.
Venturoli, Marcello & Zangrandi, Ruggero. Dizionario della paura. Nistri-Lischi.
Vera, Andres de Haro see Heymer, A.
Vera, Francisco. Lexicon Kapelusz: Matematica. Kapelusz.
Verbeke, Ronald. Un Dictionnaire Critique des Drogues. Bourgois.
--Un Dictionnaire Critique des Drogues. French & Eur.
VerBerg, Kenneth, jt. auth. see Press, Charles.
Verbic, Ing S. English-Serbocroat & Serbocroat-English Geological & Mining Dictionary (Pub. by Collets). State Mutual Bk.
Verbic, S. Yugoslavian Mining Dictionary: English-Serbo-English. Vanous.
Verbov, Julian & Morley, Neil. Color Atlas of Pediatric Dermatology (Lippincott Medical). Lippincott.
Verhoeff, Schot E. Standaard Nieuw Engels-Nederlands Woordenboek. Standaard Uitgeverij.
Verhoeff-Schot, E. & Cauberghe, J. R. Standard Niew Engels-Nederlands, Nederlands-Engels Woordenboek. Standaard Uitgeverij.
Verland, Orm, jt. auth. see Dietrichson, Jan W.
Verma, M. K. Structure of the Noun Phrase in English & Hindi. Orient Bk Dist.
Vermesse, Louis & Douai. Dictionnaire du Patois de la Flandre Francaise. Slatkine.
Vermesse, Louis & Lille. Vocabulaire du Patois Lillois. Lafitte Repr.
--Vocabulaire du Patois Lillois. Slatkine.
Verneaux, Roger. Le Vocabulaire de Kant, 1. Aubier-Montaigne.
Vernet, Pierre & Alexandre, Charles. Dictionnaire Elementaire Creole Haitien-Francais. Hatier.
Vernisy, G., jt. auth. see Delattre, J.
Veron, Enid L., jt. auth. see Redden, Kenneth R.
Veronese, Ugo. Dizionario del pescatore italiano di acqua dolce. Bietti.
Verplanck, William. Dictionary of Psychology: With Thesaurus. Irvington.
Verrier, A. J. & Onillon, Rene. Glossaire Etymologique & Historique des Patois & des Parlers de l'Anjou. Slatkine.
Versini, Georges. Dictionnaire du Bridge. PUF.
Verzhikovskii, A. P., et al. Kratkii Slovar Po Radioelektronike (Pub. by Voenizdat). Four Continent.
Vesikansa, Jouko. Tasmennyssanasto. Werner Soderstrom.
Vetrini, T., jt. auth. see Zanobini, L.
Vetrini, Trentino. Dizionario della pubblica istruzione: Legislazione e pratica amministrativa sulla istruzione primaria. Giuffre.
Vevers, Gwynne, tr. see Favre, Henri.
V. Franzen, F. Woerterbuch der Kerenergie. French & Eur.
Vial, Claude. Lexique d'antiquites Grecques. Colin.
Vianello, Natale. Vocabolario latino-italiano, italiano-latino. Dante Alighieri.
Viard, Georges, jt. auth. see Cabourdin, Guy.
Vibes, Pierre, jt. auth. see Nichols, Peter.
Vicens Carrio, J. Lexicon comercial internacional: Espanol, frances, ingles, italiano, portugues y aleman. Reverte SA.
Victoria, British Columbia, jt. auth. see Provincial Archives.
Victorica, Ricardo. Errores y Omisiones del Diccionario de Anonimos y Seudonimos Hispanoamericanos de Jose Toribio Medina. Ethridge.
--Nueva Epanortosis al Diccionario de Anonimos Seudonimos de J. T. Medina. Ethridge.
Vidal, Jean P. Diccionario esencial frances-espanol, espanol-frances. Diafora.
Vidari, Giovanni, et al. Vocabolario del dialetto di Vigevano. Olschki.
Vieillefosse, Roger. Dictionnaire de Pharmacologie Dentaire. Maloine.
Vieira, Jose de Sousa see De Sousa Vieira, Jose.
Viellefosse, Roger. Dictionnaire de Pharmacologie Dentaire. French & Eur.
Viera Clavijo, Jose. Diccionario de historia natural de las Islas Canarias. Muralla.
Viet, Jean. Thesaurus for Information Processing in Sociology. Mouton.
--Thesaurus pour le Traitement de l'information en Sociologie. Mouton de Gruyter.
Viet, Jean, ed. Eudised Multilingual Thesaurus for Information Processing in the Field of Education. Mouton.
Vigfusson, Gudbrand, jt. ed. see Cleasby, Richard.
Vigram, George V. The Englishman's Greek Concordance of the New Testament. Broadman.
Viktorov, D. P. Kratkii Slovar Botanicheskikh Terminov (Pub. by Sov. Nauka). Four Continent.
--Kratkii Slovar Botanicheskikh Terminov (Pub. by Nauka). Four Continent.
Vilahur Pedrals, J., tr. see Mommsen, H., et al.
Vilaro, Josep, et al. Diccionario Religioso Para los Hombres De Hoy. French & Eur.
Vilikovska. Slovak-English Dictionary. Vanous.
Vilikovska, J. & Vilikovsky, P. Slovak-English Dictionary (Pub. by Collet's). State Mutual Bk.
Vilikovska, J. & Vilkovsky, Jan. Slovak-English Dictionary. Shalom.
Vilikovsky, P., jt. auth. see Vilikovska, J.
Viljoen, Johannes J. Ndonga, Afrikaans, English: Dreitalige Woordeboek. Van Schaik.
Vilkovsky, Jan, jt. auth. see Vilikovska, J.
Villafuerte, Carlos. Diccionario de Toponimos Indigenas de Catamarca. Plus Ultra S. A.
Villain, Siefried P. Dictionnaire Allemand-Francais. Garnier-Flammarion.
Villain, Siegfried P. Dictionnaire Allemand-Francais. Garnier-Flammarion.
Villa Panganiban, Jose. Concise English-Tagalog Dictionary. Imported Bks.
Villarroel, Raul. Vocabulario Griego-Argentino. Castellvi.
Villate, Jose T. Dictionary of Environmental Engineering & Related Sciences. Edns Universal.
--Dictionary of Environmental Engineering & Related Sciences. Ediciones.
Villatte, jt. auth. see Sachs.
Villatte, Cesaire, jt. auth. see Sachs, Karl.
Villavecchia, G. V. & Eigenmann, G. Nuovo dizionario di merceologia e chimia applicata. Hoepli.
Villavecchia, G. V., et al. Dizionario di merceologia e chimica applicata. Hoepli.
--Nuovo dizionario di merceologia e chimica applicata. Hoepli.
--Nuovo dizionario di merceologia e chimica applicata. Hoepli.
--Nuovo dizionario di merceologia e chimica applicata. Hoepli.
--Nuovo dizionario di merceologia e chimica applicata. Hoepli.
--Nuovo dizionario di merceologia e chimica applicata. Hoepli.
Villeirs-Sidani, Maria E. see De Villiers-Sidani, Maria E.
Villemin, Martial. Dictionnaire des Termes Veterinaires & Zootechniques. Vigot.
Villeneuve, G. O. & Ferland, M. G. Glossaire De Meteorologie et De Climatologie. French & Eur.
Villeneuve, Georges O. & Ferland, Michel G. Glossaire de Meteorologie & de Climatologie. Laval P. U.
Villers, M. Vocabulaire de l'Informatique de Gestion: Anglais-Francais. French & Eur.
Villey-Desmeserets, Pierre L. Lexique de la Langue des Essais de Michel de Montaigne. Lenox.
Villiers, Alan, jt. auth. see Bathe, Basel.
Villiers, M., et al. Vocabulaire de la Vente Promotionelle: Anglais-Francais. French & Eur.
Vinay, Jean-Paul, et al. The Canadian Dictionary-French-English. McClelland.
Vincent, Jean. Dictionnaire Anglais-Francais. Garnier-Flammarion.
--Dictionnaire Anglais-Francais. Garnier-Flammarion.
Vincent, Jean, jt. auth. see Guillien, Raymond.
Vincent, Jean, jt. ed. see Guillen, Raymond.
Vincent, P. Dictionnaire de la Virilite. French & Eur.
Vincent, Paul. Dictionnaire de la Virilite. Maloine.
Vincenzo, Coratelli. Dizionarietto del costume della moda e dell'acconciatura. San Marco.
Vinoly, A. & Vinoly, J. Diccionario-guia de redaccion. Teide.
Vinoly, A. J. Diccionario-Guia de Redaccion. French & Eur.
Vinoly, A. J., et al. Pequeno Diccionario De Sinonimos y Sus Contrarios. French & Eur.
Vinoly, Alberto, ed. Pequeno diccionario de sinonimos, ideas afines y contrarios. Larousse.
Vinoly, J., jt. auth. see Vinoly, A.
Vinterberg, H. & Bodel, Sen A. Danish Dictionary Deluxe. Vanous.
Vinterberg, H. & Bodelsen, C. A. Dansk-Engelsk Ordbog. French & Eur.
Vinterberg, H. & Axelsen, J., eds. Danish-English, English-Danish Dictionary. Heinman.
Vinterberg, H., et al. Danish Dictionary: Rode Ordbog-Gyldendals, Danish-English. Vanous.
--Danish Dictionary: Rode Ordbog-Gyldendals, English-Danish. Vanous.
--Dansk-Engelsk Ordboger. French & Eur.
Violette, Louis. Dictionnaire Samoa-Francais-Anglais et Francais-Samoa-Anglais. AMS Pr.
Viollet-Le-Duc. Dictionnaire Raisonne de l'Architecture Francaise, du XIe au Siecles. French & Eur.
Viollet-Le-Duc, Eugene E. Dictionnaire Raisonne Du Mobilier Francais De L'epoque Carlovingienne a la Renaissance. AMS Pr.
Vira, Raghu. A Comprehensive English-Hindi Dictionary of Governmental & Educational Words & Phrases. Intl Pubns Serv.
Virel, Andre. Vocabulaire des Psychotherapies. Fayard.
Virgil. Virgil Eclogues & a Special Vocabulary to Virgil. Greenough, J. B. & Kittredge, G. L., eds. Caratzas Pub Co.
Vischer, Ruediger. Lateinische Wortkunde fuer Anfaenger & Fortgeschrittene. Teubner.
Vising, Johan. Fransk-Svensk Ordbok. Esselte Studium.
Visser, A., ed. Dictionary of Soil Mechanics. Elsevier.
Visser, G. J. Nederlands-Engels Woordenboek. Spectrum Pub.
Visual Education Corporation. Vocabulary Made Easy (Pub. by G). McGraw.
Viterbo, E. Vocabolario della lingua oromonica. Hoepli.
Vito, Albert De see De Vito, Albert.
Vitu, Auguste C. Le Jargon du XVe Siecle: Etude Philologique. Slatkine.
Vives. Diccionario de bolsillo latino-espanol & espanol-latino. Coculsa.
Vizcaino Casas, Fernando. Diccionario del cine espanol 1896-1968. Nacional Editora.
Vizetelly, Frank H. Desk-Book of Errors in English. Gale.
Vizioli, R., tr. see Gastaut, H.
Vladimirov, O. N., jt. auth. see Murashkevich, A. M.
Vlasova, ed. see Andreichina, K., et al.
Vlchek. Russian-Czechoslovakian Dictionary. French & Eur.
Vogely, Maxine A. A Proust Dictionary. Whitston Pub.
Vogt, J. & Eikeland, I. Swedish-Norwegian Dictionary. Kunnskapsforlaget.
Vogue, Melchior de see De Vogue, Melchior & Oousel, Raymond.
Voinov, M. Latin-Bulgarian Dictionary. French & Eur.
Voinova, L. A., et al, eds. Frazeologicheskii Slovar' Russkogo Iazyka. Four Continent.
Voinova, N. & Starets, S. Diccionario Pratico Russo-Portugues. French & Eur.
Volcher, R. Dizionario di sessuologia. Cittadella.
Volkart, K. Gips - Woerterbuch (Pub. by Bauverlag). French & Eur.
--Gips-Woerterbuch. Bauverlag.
Volkart, K. H. Gips-Woerterbuch. Bauverlag.
--Gypsum & Plaster Dictionary. Bauverlag.
--Gypsum & Plaster Dictionary (Pub. by Bauverlag). French & Eur.
--Gypsum & Plaster Dictionary. Intl Pubns Serv.
Volkell, Randolph Z. Quick Legal Terminology (Pub. by Wiley Pr). Wiley.
Volker, R. Dizionario si sessuologia. Cittadella.
Voll, John. Historical Dictionary of the Sudan. Scarecrow.
Vollnhals, Otto. Woerterbuch des Kraftfahreugwesens. Girardet.
--Woerterbuch des Kraftfahrzeugwesens. French & Eur.
Volodin, N. V. Anglo-Russkii Voenno-Inzhenernyi Slovar (Pub. by Voenizdat). Four Continent.
Volpe, P. P. Vocabolario napolitano-italiano. Forni.
Voltaire. Diccionario Filosofico. French & Eur.
--Diccionario Filosofico. French & Eur.
--Diccionario Filosofico. French & Eur.
Vomackova, Libuse. Cesko-Francouzsky Technicky Slovnik. SNTC.
--Francouzsko-Cesky Technicky Slovnik. SNTC.
Von Allmen, J. Vocabolario biblico. AVE.
Von Baeckmann, Walter G. Lexikon der Gastechnik. Vulkan Verlag.
Von Baeckmann, Walter G., jt. auth. see Osteroth, Dieter.
Von Bahder, Egon. Technologisches Woerterbuch. Girardet.
--Technologisches Woerterbuch (Pub. by Girardet). French & Eur.
Von Baumgart, Arturo E. Langenscheidts Fachwoerterbuecher Deutsch-Spanisch. Langenscheidt.
Von Berger, Karl. Mykologisches Worterbuch. Fischer Verlag.
Von Born, Erhard, et al. Lexikon fuer Eisenbahnfreunde. Bucher Verlag.
Von Eyben, W. E., jt. auth. see Borum, Oscar A.
Von Eynern, Gert & Boehret, Carl, eds. Woerterbuch zur Politischen Oekonomie. Westdeutscher.
Von Friederich, Wolf. Dictionary of English Words in Context. Lensing Verlag.
Von Grieffenberg, C. R., ed. see Moeller, Hilke.
Von Harder, Hermann, et al. Lexikon fuer Mineralien & Gesteinfreunde. Bucher Verlag.
Von Heinecken, Karl H. Dictionnaire Des Artistes, Dont Nous Avons Des Estampes, Avec une Notice Detailee De Leurs Ouvrages Graves. Johnson Repr.
Von Linnert, et al. Lexikon der Managementbegriffe. Heyne W Verlag.

Von Macchi, Vladimiro. Langenscheidts Grosswoerterbuch Italienisch. Langenscheidt.
--Langenscheidts Grosswoerterbuch Italienisch. Langenscheidt.
Von Muller, Peter, jt. auth. see Schmid, Hans.
Von Roald, Albert & Hahnewald, Harry. Medizintechnik. VEB Verlag Technik.
Von Ronart, Nandy & Ronart, Stephan. Lexikon der Arabischen Welt. Artemis Verlag.
Von Schaldach, Herbert. DTV Woerterbuch der Medizin. Deutscher Taschenbuch Verlag.
--DTV Woerterbuch der Medizin. Deutscher Taschenbuch Verlag.
--DTV Woerterbuch der Medizin. Deutscher Taschenbuch Verlag.
--DTV Woerterbuch der Medizin (Pub. by DTV Deutscher Taschenbuch Vlg.). French & Eur.
--DTV Woerterbuch der Medizin (Pub. by DTV Deutscher Taschenbuch Vlg.). French & Eur.
--DTV Woerterbuch der Medizin (Pub. by DTV Deutscher Taschenbuch Vlg.). French & Eur.
Von Thielmann, K. Woerterbuch der Biochemie. VEB Verlag Enzyklopadie.
Von Trygue Alsos. Deutsch-Norwegisch-Deutsch. French & Eur.
Von Ulrich, Winfried. Woerterbuch Linguistische Grundbegriffe. Hirt.
Von Wartburg, Walther, jt. auth. see Bloch, Oscar.
Von Wartburg, Walther see Bloch, Oscar & Wartburg, Walther Von.
VonZweck, Dina. Woman's Day Dictionary of Furniture. Citadel Pr.
--Woman's Day Dictionary of Glass. Citadel Pr.
Voorhees, David W. Concise Dictionary of American History (ScribR). Scribner.
Vorgrimler, Herbert, jt. auth. see Rahner, Karl.
Voronin, V. V., et al. Russko-Frantsuzskii Stroitelnyi Slovar (Pub. by Russkii Iazyk). Four Continent.
Voronine, V. V., et al. Dictionnaire Russe-Francais du Batiment. Denissov, A. I., ed. French & Eur.
Voropaev, N. Anglo-Russkii Slovar po Kvantovoi Elektronike i Golografii. Russkii Iazyk.
Voros, Arpad. Onteszet. Akademiai Kiado.
Voss, M. Heerma Van see Van Voss, M. Heerma.
Vox. Diccionari Fondamental de la Llengua Catalana. Gali I Herrera, Jordi, prologue by. Biblo Sp.
--Diccionari Manual Castella-Catala, Catala-Castella. Biblo Sp.
--Diccionario de Sinonimos. Brandstetter.
--Diccionario General-Ilustrado la Lengau Espanola. Brandstetter.
--Diccionario Manual Ilustrado de la Lengua Espanola. Brandstetter.
--Diccionario Monografico de Bellas Artes. French & Eur.
--Diccionario Superior Frances-Espanol, Espanol-Frances. Biblo Sp.
--Diccionario Tematico de la Lengua Espanola. Biblo Sp.
Vox, ed. Diccionario Monografico de Matematicas. French & Eur.
--Diccionario Monografico de Medicina y Salud. French & Eur.
--Diccionario Monografico de Technologia. French & Eur.
Vries, A. De see De Vries, A.
Vries, Geerte de see De Vries, Geerte.
Vries, L. de see De Vries, L.
Vries, L. De see De Vries, L. & Clason, W. E.
Vries, Louis de. Dictionary of Chemistry & Chemical Engineering. French & Eur.
--Dictionary of Chemistry & Chemical Engineering. French & Eur.
--Woerterbuch der Textilindustrie. French & Eur.
Vries, Louis de see De Vries, Louis.
Vries, Louis de see De Vries, Louis & Hermann, Theo M.
Vries, Louis de see De Vries, Louis & Hochman, Stanley.
Vries, Louis de see De Vries, Louis & Jacolev, Leon.
Vries, Louis de see De Vries, louis & Jacolev, Leon.
V. Uexkuell, Detlev. Woerterbuch der Patentpraxis. French & Eur.
Vuexkull, J. & Reich, H. J. Dictionary of Patent Practice. French & Eur.
Vuillermoz, P., jt. auth. see De Noter, R.
Vuitton, Jacques & Vuitton, Philippe. Nouveau Lexique d'Economie: Economie, Droit, Gestion, Finance. Doc Univers.
Vuitton, Philippe, jt. auth. see Vuitton, Jacques.
Vukicevic, B., ed. Dictionary of Construction Industries. French & Eur.
Vulcanescu, Romulus. Dictionar de Etnologie. Albatros.
Vuolle, Aino. Suomalais-Englantilainen Sanakirja. Femi Suuri.
Vuorela, Toivo. Kansanperinteen Sanakirja. Soderstrom.
V. Weck, Johannes. Woerterbuch der Forstwirtschaft. French & Eur.
Vydava Treti Trida Ceske Akademie Ved a Umeni. Prirucni Slovnik Jazyka Ceskeho. Statni.
Vygodskaia, K. S. Karmannyi Frantsuzsko-Russkii Slovar (Pub. by GINS). Four Continent.
Vygodskaia, K. S., et al. Kratkii Frantsuzsko-Russkii i Russko-Frantsuzskii Slovar (Pub. by Sov Entsiklopediia). Four Continent.
Vy Thi Be, jt. auth. see Freiberger, Nancy.

W

Wacker, Wilhelm H., ed. Steuerlexikon. Vahlen.
Waddell, Hope M. A Vocabulary of the Efik or Old Calabar Language. Intl Pubns Serv.
Wade, Carlson, jt. auth. see Reissner, Albert.
Wadepuhl, Walter & Morgan, Bayard. Minimum Standard German Vocabulary. Irvington.
Wafi, Al & Bustani, Butros. A Concise Arabic Dictionary. Intl Bk Ctr.
Waggoner, Merrill Van Y. see Van Wagoner, Merrill Y., et al.
Wagner, R. L., jt. auth. see Balmas, E.
Wagner, Rene L. Le Vocabulaire Francais, 1. Didier Erudition.
--Le Vocabulaire Francais, 2. Didier Erudition.
Wagoner, Merrill van see Van Wagoner, Merrill.
Wahba, Magdi. A Dictionary of Literary Terms (English-French-Arabic) Intl Bk Ctr.
--A Dictionary of Modern Political Idiom. Lib Liban.
--English-French-Arabic Dictionary of Political Idioms. Intl Bk Ctr.
Wahba, Magdi & Ghali, Wagdi R. A Dictionary of Modern Political Idiom: English-French-Arabic. Lib Liban.
Wahba, Magdi & Muhandes, Kamel. A Dictionary of Literary & Linguistic Terms. Intl Bk Ctr.
Wahba, Magdi, compiled by. A Dictionary of Literary Terms. Intl Bk Ctr.
Wahba, Magdi & Ghali, Magdi, eds. A Dictionary of Political Idioms. Intl Bk Ctr.
Wahed, Abd El. Agricultural Engineering Dictionary: English-French-German-Arabic. French & Eur.
Wahrig. DTV Woerterbuch der deutschen Sprache. Imported Bks.
Wahrig, G. Deutsches Woerterbuch und Lexicon der deutsches Sprachlehre. M Rosenberg.
--German-English Dictionary (Pub. by Collet's). State Mutual Bk.
Wahrig, G., ed. DTV-Woerterbuch der deutschen Sprache. M Rosenberg.
Wahrig, Gerhard. Deutsches Woerterbuch. Imported Bks.
--Deutsches Woerterbuch. C Bertelsmann.
--Deutsches Woerterbuch (Pub. by Bertelsmann Lexikon VVA). French & Eur.
Wahrig, Gerhard, et al. Brockhaus-Wahrig Deutsches Woerterbuch in Sechs Baenden: Band 1-3. F A Brockhaus.
Wahrig-Gerhard. Fremdwoerter Lexikon. C Bertelsmann.
Wahrmund, Adolf. Handworterbuch der neu Arabischen und Deutschen Sprache. Intl Bk Ctr.
--Handworterbuch der Neu-Arabischen und Deutschen Sprache. Verry.
Wain, Harry. The Story Behind the Word: Some Interesting Origins of Medical Terms. C C Thomas.
Wait, John C., ed. Freight & Passenger Cars from the 1898 Car Builder's Dictionary: Part 1. N K Gregg.
--Freight & Passenger Cars from the 1898 Car Builder's Dictionary: Part 2. N K Gregg.
--Freight & Passenger Cars from the 1898 Car Builder's Dictionary: Part 3. N K Gregg.
Walde, Alois. Vergleichendes Woerterbuch der Indogermanischen Sprachen. Pokorny, Julius, ed. De Gruyter.
Waldhorn, Arthur, ed. Concise Dictionary of American Language. Philos Lib.
Waldman, Harry, ed. Dictionary of Indians of North America. Scholarly.
Waldstein, A. Hebrew-English, English-Hebrew Dictionary. Shalom.
Walega, Stanislaw. Slownik Finsko-Polski. Wiedza Powszechna.
Wales University. Dictionary of the Welsh Language. Verry.
Walewski, Stanislaw. Langenscheidts Taschenwoerterbuch Polnisch. Langenscheidt.
--Langenscheidts Taschenwoerterbuch Polnisch: Teil II, Deutsch-Polnisch. Langenscheidt.
--Langenscheidts Taschenwoerterbuch Polnisch: Teil I, Polnisch-Deutsch. Langenscheidt.
--Polnisch. Langenscheidt.
Walford, Alberto J. & Screen, J. E., eds. A Guide to Foreign Language Courses & Dictionaries. Greenwood.
Walker, Henry. Illustrated Baseball Dictionary for Young People. Harvey.
Walker, J. Walker's Rhyming Dictionary of the English Language: In Which the Whole Language is Arranged According to its Terminations. Routledge & Kegan.
Walker, John A. Glossary of Art, Architecture, & Design Since 1945 (Linnet). Shoe String.
Walker, L. E., jt. auth. see Ballentyne, D. W.
Walker, L. E., jt. tr. see Bailentyne, D. W.
Walker, Mort. The Lexicon of Comicana. Comicana.
Walker, W. G., et al. Glossary of Educational Terms: Usage in Five English Speaking Countries. U of Queensland Pr.
Wallace, Grocet. The New York Historical Society's Dictionary of Artists in America, 1564-1860. Apollo.
Wallace, Michael J. Dictionary of English Idioms (Pub. by Collins ELT Scotland). State Mutual Bk.
Wallace, Ralph G., jt. auth. see Houghton, Diane.
Wallace, Tom. Dictionary. Am Prod & Inventory.
Wallenfang, Wilhelm, jt. auth. see Sponzel, Kurt.
Wallis, H., jt. ed. see Van Beckum, J. H.
Wallis, John E. Doctor Johnson & His English Dictionary. Arden Lib.
Wallis, W. H. Neederland-Duits: Wolter's Woorden Boek. French & Eur.
Wallis, W. H., jt. auth. see Van Gelderen, I.
Wallnig, G. & Evered, H. L' Anglais Dans le Batiment: Text En Anglais Avec un Glossaire Illustre. French & Eur.
--Deutsch fuer Baufachleute. Bauverlag.
--Deutsch fur Baufachleute fuer Daenen, Norweger & Sshweden. Bauverlag.
--Dictionnaire Technique du Bois, en Quatre Langues. French & Eur.
--Engels voor Bouwkundigen-Englantia Rakentajille. Bauverlag.
--Englisch fuer Baufachleute: Band 1. Bauverlag.
--Englisch fur Baufachleute: Band 2. Bauverlag.
--German for Building Specialists: L'Allemand dans le Batiment, el Aleman en la construccion. Bauverlag.
--German for Building Specialists, (L'allemand Dans le Batiment, el Aleman En la Construccion (Pub. by Bauverlag). French & Eur.
Wallnig, G., jt. auth. see Evered, H.
Wallnig, Gunter & Evered, H. L' Anglais Dans le Batiment: Texte En Anglais Avec un Glossaire Illustre, 2. French & Eur.
Wallnig, Gunter & Evered, Harry. El Ingles en la Construccion. French & Eur.
Walmsley, Julian. Dictionary of International Finance. Macmillan London.
--A Dictionary of International Finance. Greenwood.
Walsh, Dermot & Poole, Adrian. A Dictionary of Criminology. Routledge & Kegan.
Walter, Claire. Illustrated Skiing Dictionary for Young People. P-H.
Walter, Frank K. Abbreviations & Technical Terms Used in Book Catalogues & in Bibliographies. Longwood Pr.
Walter, Henriette, jt. auth. see Martinet, Andre.
Walther, Johann. Musikalisches Lexikon (Pub. by Baerenreiter). French & Eur.
Walther, Johann L. Lexicon Diplomaticum Abbreviationes Syllabarum et Vocum in Diplomatibus et Codicibus a Seculo Octo a Sextum-Decimum Usque Occurentes Exponens. B Franklin.
Walther, R. Technical Dictionary of Production Engineering: Vol. 2, German-English. Pergamon.
Walther, Rudolf. Polytechnic Dictionary: German-English, English-German. Adler.
--Polytechnisches Woerterbuch. VEB Verlag Technik.
--Polytechnisches Woerterbuch (Pub. by Veb Verlag Technik). French & Eur.
--Polytechnisches Woerterbuch (Pub. by Veb Verlag Technik). French & Eur.
--Polytechnisches Woerterbuch Deutsch-Englisch. VEB Technik.
--Woerterbuch der Technik. French & Eur.
Walther, Rudolph. Technical Dictionary of Production Engineering (English-German) Pergamon.
Wang, W. The Lexicon in Phonological Change. Mouton.
Wanke & Havlicek. English Fuer Elektrotechniker & Elektroniker. Brandstetter.
Wapnick, Ken. Glossary Index for a Course in Miracles. Coleman Graphics.
Ward, Jill. Ward's Natural Sign Language Thesaurus of Useful Signs N' Synonyms. Joyce, John, ed. Joyce Media.
Ward, Kendall K. & Kaltenborn, Arthur L. Guides for American-English Pronunciation. C C Thomas.
Ward, Philip. A Dictionary of Common Fallacies. Oleander Pr.
Ware, D. & Beatty, B. Diccionario de Arquitectura. G Gili.
Warman, Adolfo I. Vaughan. Diccionario trilingue miskito-ingles-espanol. Imp. Nac. Manugua EDUCA.
Warnant, Leon. Dictionnaire de la Prononciation Francais. Duculot.
--Dictionnaire de la Prononciation Francais. Duculot.
--Dictionnaire de la Prononciation Francais. Renouveau Pedagogique.
--Dictionnaire de la Prononciation Francaise. French & Eur.
--Dictionnaire des Rimes Orales & Ecrites. Larousse.

--Dictionnaire des rimes orales et ecrites. Larousse.
Warneck, Johannes G. Toba-Batak-Deutsches Worterbuch. Nyhoff.
Warner-Eddison Associates. Words That Mean Business: Three Thousand Terms for Access to Business Information. Neal-Schuman.
Warner Educational Services, ed. The Super Dictionary. HR&W.
Warrack, A. Scots Dictionary. U of Ala Pr.
Warrack, Alexander. Chambers Scots Dictionary (Pub. by Two Continents). Am Map.
Warrack, John, jt. auth. see Rosenthal, Harold.
Warrack, John, jt. ed. see Rosenthal, Harold.
Warren, A. Dansk-Tysk Teknisk Ordborg. French & Eur.
--Engelsk-Dansk Teknisk Ordbog. French & Eur.
Warren, H. C. Diccionario de psicologia. Fondo Cult.
Warren Spring Laboratory, ed. Thesaurus of Terms for Indexing the Literature of Minerals Processing & Metals Extraction, 1974 (Pub. by W Spring England). State Mutual Bk.
Warrern, A. Danish-English, English-Danish Technical Dictionary. Heinman.
--Tysk-Dansk Teknisk Ordbog. French & Eur.
Warrington, John. Everyman's Classical Dictionary (Pub. by J. M. Dent England). Biblio Dist.
Warshaw, Thayer S. Abingdon Glossary of Religious Terms. Abingdon.
Wartburg, Walter von. Franzoesisch Etymologisches Woerterbuch (Pub. by Francke). French & Eur.
Wartburg, Walther Von, jt. auth. see Bloch, Oscar.
Wartburg, Walther Von see Bloch, Oscar & Von Wartburg, Walther.
Warusfel, Andre. Diccionario razonado de matematicas: De las matematicas clasicas a la matematica moderna. Tecnos SA.
--Dictionnaire Raisonne de Mathematiques. Seuil.
--Dictionnaire Raisonne De Mathematiques. French & Eur.
Watelet, Claude-Henre & Levesque, Pierre-Charles. Dictionnaire des Arts de Peinture, Sculpture & Gravure. Olms Verlag.
Watelet, Claude-Henri & Levesque, Pierre-Charles. Dictionnaire des Arts de Peinture & Gravure. Minkoff Repr.
--Dictionnaire des Arts de Peinture, Sculpture & Gravure. Olms Verlag.
--Dictionnaire des Arts de Peinture, Sculpture & Gravure. Olms Verlag.
--Dictionnaire des Arts de Peinture, Sculpture & Gravure. Olms Verlag.
--Dictionnaire des Arts de Peinture, Sculpture & Gravure. Olms Verlag.
Water Pollution Control Federation, et al. Glossary: Water & Wastewater Control Engineering. Water Pollution.
Waterhouse, Ellis. The Dictionary of British Eighteenth Century Painters. Antique Collect.
Waterson, Natalie. Uzbeck-English Dictionary. Oxford U Pr.
Watkins, E. A., jt. auth. see Faries, R.
Watson & Folliet. Round the World-English (Usborne-Hayes). EDC.
Watson, Diana C. & Hurtado, Hernan. Vocabulary Building: Syllabus, Level III. Natl Book.
Watson, Diana C. & Watson, Malcom. Vocabulary Building: Syllabus, Level IV. Natl Book.
Watson, James, jt. ed. see Bennett, Russell.
Watson, Malcom, jt. auth. see Watson, Diana C.
Watson, Owen, ed. Longman's Modern English Dictionary. Longman England.
Watson, T. J. An Illustrated Vocabulary for the Use of the Deaf & Dumb. Gordon Pr.
Watt, Alec. Barnes & Noble Thesaurus of Geology. B&N NY.
Watt, George. A Dictionary of the Economic Products of India. Intl Pubns Serv.
--A Dictionary of the Economic Products of India (Pub. by Intl Bk Dist). Intl Schol Bk Serv.
Watters, David & Watters, Nancy. An English-Kham, Kham-English Glossary. Summer Inst Ling.
Watters, Garnette & Courtis, S. A. Picture Dictionary for Children (G&D). Putnam Pub Group.
Watters, Nancy, jt. auth. see Watters, David.
Watts, John D. Lists of Words Occurring Frequently in the Hebrew Bible. Eerdmans.
Watts, Peter. A Dictionary of the Old West. Knopf.
Watznauer. Woerterbuch Geowissenschaften. Verlag Harri Deutsch.
--Woerterbuch Geowissenschaften. Verlag Harri Deutsch.
Watznauer, A. Dictionary of Geosciences. Elsevier.
--Woerterbuch Geowissenschaften. French & Eur.
--Woerterbuch Geowissenschaften. French & Eur.
Watznauer, Adolf. Geowissenschaften Deutsch-Englisch. VEB Technik.
--Geowissenschaften Englisch-Deutsch. VEB Technik.
Wawrzyniak, Marka. Mianownictwo Histologiczne. Panstowy Zaklad W.
Weaver, Peter. The Birdwatcher's Dictionary (Pub. by T & A D Poyser England). Buteo.
Webb, Augustus D. New Dictionary of Statistics: A Complement to the Fourth Edition of Mulhall's Dictionary of Statistics. Gale.
Webb, Barbara. Dictionnaire a l'usage des Plaisanciers. Maritimes Outre mer.
--Dizionario dello yachting in otto lingue. Mursia S.
--Yachtman's Eight Language Dictionary. De Graff.
--Yachtsman's Eight Language Dictionary. Beekman Pubs.
Webel, A. A German-English Dictionary of Technical, Scientific & General Terms. Routledge & Kegan.
Weber, Albert. Grammatiken und Woerterbuecher des Schweizer Deutschen (Pub. by Hans Rohr). French & Eur.
Weber, David J. Los Sufijos Posesivos en el Quechua del Huallaga. Inst Ling Ver.
Weber, Erich, et al. Kleines Sozial Wissenschaftliches Woerterbuch fuer Paedagogen. Auer.
Weber, Fritz W. Elsevier's Dictionary of High Vacuum Science & Technology. Elsevier.
Weber, Nancy, jt. auth. see Park, Marinell.
Webster, Donald H. & Zibell, Wilfried. Inupiat Eskimo Dictionary. Summer Inst Ling.
Webster, Noah. American Dictionary of the English Language. Found Am Christ.
--An American Dictionary of the English Language: To Which Are Prefixed, an Introductory Dissertation of the Origin, History & Connection of the Language of Western Asia & Europe & A...Grammar of the English Language. Johnson Repr.
Webster, Noah see Pickering, John.
Weck, J. Dictionary of Forestry. Elsevier.
Weck, Johannes, et al. Woerterbuch der Forstwirtschaft Deutsch-Englisch-Franzoesisch-Spanisch-Russisch. BLV Verlag.
Wedding, Mary E., jt. auth. see Gylys, Barbara A.
Wedeck, H. E. Dictionary of Astrology. Citadel Pr.
Wedeck, Harry E., ed. Dictionary of Aphrodisiacs. Philos Lib.
Wedeck, Harry E & Baskin, Wade, eds. Dictionary of Spiritualism. Philos Lib.
Wedel, E. & Romanov, A., eds. Langenscheidt's Pocket Russian Dictionary: Russian-English, English-Russian. Am Map.
Wedertz, Bill, ed. Dictionary of Naval Abbreviations. Naval Inst Pr.
--Dictionary of Naval Abbreviations. US Naval Inst.
Weeden, Hester E., ed. see Stanford, Gene.
Weekley, E. Etymological Dictionary of Modern English. Peter Smith.
Weekley, Ernest. Etymological Dictionary of Modern English. Dover.
Weeterau, Bruce. Complete Word-Finder Crossword Dictionary (Sig). NAL.
Wehlen, Rainer. Regeln & Sprache des Sports 1. Biblio Inst.
--Regeln & Sprache des Sports 2. Biblio Inst.
Wehr, H. Arabic-English Dictionary. Iaconi.
Wehr, Hans. Arabic-English Dictionary. Cowan, J Milton, ed. Spoken Lang Serv.
--A Dictionary of Modern Written Arabic. Cowan, Milton J., ed. Spoken Lang Serv.
--A Dictionary of Modern Written Arabic. Cowan, J. M., ed. Harrap.
--A Dictionary of Modern Written Arabic. Cowan, J. Milton, ed. Harrassowitz.
--A Dictionary of Modern Written Arabic. Cowan, J. M., ed. Spoken Lang Serv.
Wehr, Hans & Cowan, J. M. Arabic-English Dictionary. Imported Bks.
Wehr, Hans, compiled by. A Dictionary of Modern Written Arabic. Intl Bk Ctr.
Wei, S. Practical Dictionary of Chinese Idioms, English Idioms, English Synonyms. Iaconi.
Wei, S. S. Chinese Idioms, English Idioms, English Synonyms Practical Dictionary. Heinman.
Weigand, Karl. Deutsches Woerterbuch. De Gruyter.
Weik, Martin H. Communications Standard Dictionary. Van Nos Reinhold.
--Fiber Optics & Lightwave Communications Standard Dictionary. Van Nos Reinhold.
--Standard Dictionary of Computers & Information Processing. Hayden.
Weil, Georg, jt. auth. see Jung, Fernand.
Weil, Gonthier, jt. auth. see Chassard, Jean.
Weil, Yvonne, jt. auth. see Aurox, Sylvain.
Weinreich, Uriel. Modern English-Yiddish, Yiddish-English Dictionary (P&RB). McGraw.
--Modern English-Yiddish Yiddish-English Dictionary. Schocken.
--Modern English-Yiddish, Yiddish-English Dictionary. Yivo Inst.
Weinstein, Warren. Historical Dictionary of Burundi. Scarecrow.
Weinzierl, Emil. Begriffswoerterbuch zur Betriebswirtschafts & Managementlehre. Industrieverlag.
Weis, jt. auth. see Schoffler.
Weis, jt. auth. see Zavada.
Weis, E. & Mattutat, H. Woerterbuch der Franzoesischen und Deutschen Sprache. French & Eur.
--Woerterbuch der Franzoesischen und Deutschen Sprache. French & Eur.
Weis, E., et al. Pons Schoffler Weis English-German, German-English Dictionary. French & Eur.
Weis, Erich & Haberfellner, Eva. Vocabulaire Commercial Francais-Allemand. Klett.
Weis, Erich & Mattutat, Heinrich. Dictionnaire Allemand-Francais. Bordas-Dunod.
--Dictionnaire Allemand-Francais. French & Eur.
--Dictionnaire Francais-Allemand. Bordas-Dunod.
--Dictionnaire Francais-Allemand. Bordas-Dunod.
--Dictionnaire Francais-Allemand et Allemand-Francais. French & Eur.
Weis, Erich & Mattutat, Heinrich, eds. Harrap's Schoeffler-Weis German & English Dictionary. Harrap.
Weiser, H., jt. auth. see Folomkina, A.
Weiser, H., jt. auth. see Folomkina, S.
Weiser, T., jt. auth. see Folomkina, V.
Weiss, Erich. Pons-Grosswoerterbuch. Mattutat, Heinrich & Nugue, Christian, eds. Klett.
Weiss-Ballesteros. Diccionario ingles-espanol, tecnico-electromecanico. Index.
Weissling, Heinrich. Taschenworterbuch Deutsch-Ungarisch. VEB Verlag Enzyklopadie.
Weissling, Heinrich, ed. Taschenwoerterbuch Deutsch-Ungarisch. VEB Verlag Enzyklopaedie.
Weitzel, Wolfgang. Technical Dictionary Pulp & Paper. Incl. Vol. 1. English-German; Vol. 2. German-English. Intl Pubns Serv.
Welk, Martin H. Standard Dictionary of Computers & Information Processing. Telecom Lib.
Welles, E. R. The Learning Incorporated Dictionary of Learning Handicaps. Learning Inc.
Welling, Manfred S. German-English Glossary of Plastics Machiney Terms (Pub. by Hanser International). Macmillan.
Wells, J. C. Esperanto Dictionary. McKay.
Wells, Roger & Kelley, John W., eds. English-Eskimo & Eskimo-English Vocabularies. AMS Pr.
Wells, Roger, Jr., compiled by. English-Eskimo & Eskimo-English Vocabularies. Kelly, John W., tr. C E Tuttle.
Wells, Roy A. Some Royal Arch Terms Examined. Lewis Ltd.
Wendt, H. F. Langenscheidts Taschenwoerterbuch Neugriechisch: Teil I, Neugriechisch-Deutsch. Langenscheidt.
Wendt, H. F., ed. Langenscheidts Taschenwoerterbuecher Neugriechisch-Deutsch. Langenscheidt.
Wennrich, P. Anglo-Amerikanische Abkuerzungen und Kurzwoerter der Elektrotechnik (Pub. by Vlg. Dokumentation). French & Eur.
Wennrich, Peter. Anglo-American & German Abbreviations in Environmental Protection (Pub. by K G Saur). Gale.
--Anglo-American & German Abbreviations in Science & Technology. Bowker.
Wennrich, Peter, compiled by. Anglo-American & German Abbreviations in Science & Technology: Part 4, Supplement. Bowker.
Wentworth, Harold & Flexner, Stuart B. Dictionary of American Slang. Langenscheidt.
--Dictionary of American Slang. T Y Crowell.
--Pocket Dictionary of American Slang. PB.
Wentworth, Harold, jt. ed. see Chadsey, Charles P.
Wentzel, Petrus J. Drietalige Elementere Woordeboek. U Sth Africa.
Werlin, Josef. Woerterbuch der Abkurzungen. Imported Bks.
Wernicke, H. Dictionary of Electronics, Communications & Electrical Engineering. Adler.
Werny, P., jt. auth. see Dubois, F.
Werny, Paul & Snyckers, Alexandre. Dictionnaire des Locutions Francais-Allemand. Larousse FR.
Weroniecki, T., ed. Diccionario Tecnico Espanol-Polaco. French & Eur.
Wesker, Arnold & Appignanesi, Richard. Words As Definitions of Experience. Writers & Readers.
Wessen, Elias. Vara Ord: Kortfattad Etymologisk Ordbok. Esselte Studium.
West, Geoffrey, ed. Black's Veterinary Dictionary. B&N Imports.
West, M. P. & Endicott, J. G. New Method Dictionary. Shalom.
West, Michael P. & Kingdon, Roger. An International Reader's Dictionary. Longman England.
Weston, John, compiled by. The Oxford Children's Dictionary in Colour. Oxford U Pr.
Wetterau, Bruce. The Macmillan Concise Dictionary of World History. Macmillan.
Wetterau, Bruce, ed. The Word Game Winning Dictionary (Sig). NAL.
Weymuth, E. Langenscheidts Taschenwoerterbuch Franzoesisch: Teil II, Deutsch-Franzoesisch. Langenscheidt.

Wezler, Albrecht. Bestimmung & Angabe der Funktion von Sekundar-Suffixen Durch Panini. Steiner Verlag.
Wharton, E. R. Etymological Lexicon of Classical Greek. Ares.
Wheatley, Henry B. A Dictionary of Reduplicated Words in the English Language. Folcroft.
Wheeler, Marcus & Unbegaun, B. O., eds. The Oxford Russian-English Dictionary. Oxford U Pr.
Wheeler, William. Concordance to the Spectator. Folcroft.
Whelan, John F., jt. ed. see Dahl, Richard C.
Whisker, James B. Dictionary of Concepts on American Politics. Wiley.
Whitehouse, Ruth, ed. The Macmillan Dictionary of Archaeology. Macmillan.
Whitfield, F. J., jt. auth. see Bullas, K.
Whitfield, Jane. Songwriters Rhyming Dictionary. Wilshire.
Whitfield, Jane S. Whitfield's University Rhyming Dictionary. Stillman, Frances, ed (EH). B&N NY.
--Whitfield's University Rhyming Dictionary. Stillman, Frances, ed. T Y Crowell.
Whitfield, Jane S., jt. auth. see Stillman, Frances.
Whitfield, Jane S., compiled by. Websters New World Crossword Puzzle Dictionary. Collins Pubs.
Whitford, Harold C. & Dixson, Robert J. Handbook of American Idioms & Idiomatic Usage. Regents Pub.
Whitney, A. H. Learn Hungarian for English Speakers. Saphrograph.
Whitten, D. G. & Brooks, J. R. Dizionario di geologia. Mondadori.
Whittington, Lloyd R. Whittington's Dictionary of Plastics. Technomic.
Wiczorke, Martin, jt. auth. see Schaefer, Peter.
Widdowson, J. D. see Story, G. M.
Widman, Karen. Dansk-Svensk Ordbok. Esselte Studium.
Wiebeck, E. Bi-Taschenlexikon Schiffbau-Schiffahrt. Bibl Inst Leipzig.
Wiedert, Alfons. Tai-Khamti Phonology & Vocabulary. Steiner Verlag.
Wiegelmann, Alfred. Dizionario dei semiconduttori. Cascianni, L. & Boscarol, M., trs. Muzzio.
Wieger, L. Chinese Characters, Their Origin, Etymology, History, Classification & Signification. Davrout, L., tr. Dover.
Wieger, Leon. Chinese Characters. Davrout, L., tr. Paragon.
Wiele, H., jt. ed. see Rohr, B.
Wiener, Philip P., ed. Dictionary of the History of Ideas (ScribR). Scribner.
--Dictionary of the History of Ideas (ScribR). Scribner.
Wieselgren, Per. Svensk-Estnisk Ordbok. Fyris.
Wiesner, E. & Willer, S. Lexikon der Genetik der Hundekrankheiten. S. Karger.
Wiezell, Richard. Ingles Al Dedillo: English at Your Fingertips. New Century.
Wijewardena, Hema. Kalamanakarana Paribhasika Sabda Sangrahaya. Dewan Bahasa.
Wilbur, Beverley, jt. auth. see Morgan, Joyce L.
Wilcox, R. Dictionary of Costume (Pub. by Batsford England). David & Charles.
Wilcox, R. Turner. Dictionary of Costume (ScribT). Scribner.
Wildhagen. Englisch-Deutsches, Deutsch-Englisches Woerterbuch. Brandstetter.
--Englisch-Deutsches, Deutsch-Englisches Woerterbuch. Brandstetter.
Wildhagen & Hereaucourt. English-German, German-English Dictionary. M Rosenberg.
Wildhagen, Heraucourt. Englisch-Deutsches Deutsch-Englisches Woerterbuch: Band II, Deutsch-Englisch. Brandstetter.
--Englisch-Deutsches Deutsch-Englisches Woerterbuch: Band I, Englisch-Deutsch. Brandstetter.
Wilds, Thomas. Glossary of Japanese Patent Law Terms: Japanese-English-Japanese. Marlin.
Wilhelm, Evelyne. Bien Manger dans Quinze Pays. Encre.
Wilhelm, Hellmut. German-Chinese Dictionary. Ayer Co.
Wilhelm, Kurt. Langenscheidts Grosse Schulwoerterbuecher Deutsch-Franzoesisch. Langenscheidt.
Wilhelm, Kurt, jt. auth. see Lange-Koval, Ernst E.
Wilhelm, Kurt, ed. Langenscheidts Handwoerterbuecher: Tl 2, Deutsch-Franzoesisch. Langenscheidt.
Wilken-Jensen, K. Lexikon Allergologicum. Pergamon.
Wilkes, G. A. A Dictionary of Australian Colloquialisms (Pub. by Sydney U Pr). Intl Schol Bk Serv.
Wilkin, Robert. Dictionnaire du Droit Public. Bruylant.
Wilkinson, P. C., jt. auth. see Herbert, W. J.
Willems, Emilio. Dictionnaire de Sociologie. Riviere.
--Dictionnaire de Sociologie. French & Eur.
Willemze, Theo. Spectrum Muzieklexicon. Spectrum NL.
Willer, S., jt. auth. see Wiesner, E.
Willerfest, Biro. English-Hungarian, Hungarian-English Dictionary-Angol-Magyar-Angol Szotar. Saphrograph.
Willers, D. H. Langenscheidts Taschenwoerterbuch Spanisch: Teil II, Deutsch-Spanisch. Langenscheidt.
Willers, D. H., jt. auth. see Haberkamp de Anton, G.
Willers, H. Langenscheidts Taschenwoerterbuecher Spanisch-Deutsch. Langenscheidt.
William, Raymond. Keywords: A Vocabulary of Culture & Society (GB). Oxford U Pr.
Williams, C. B. Style & Vocabulary: Numerical Studies. Lubrecht & Cramer.
Williams, E. N. Facts on File Dictionary of European History: 1485-1789. Facts on File.
--The Penguin Dictionary of English & European History 1485-1789. Penguin.
Williams, Edwin B. Diccionario Del Idioma Espanol. Lectorum Pubns.
--New College Spanish & English Dictionary. AMSCO Sch.
Williams, Edwin B. & Senn, Alfred. Diccionario multilingue. Edit Pr Serv.
Williams, Edwin B., ed. Bantam New College Spanish & English Dictionary. Bantam.
--The Scribner-Bantam English Dictionary. Bantam.
Williams, G. H. Dictionary of Weeds of Western Europe: Their Common Names & Importance. Elsevier.
Williams, G. M., jt. auth. see Mackay, E.
Williams, H. W. Dictionary of the Maori Language. Govern.
Williams, M. Sanskrit-English Dictionary. Orient Bk Dist.
Williams, M. Monier. Dictionary of English & Sanskrit. Intl Pubns Serv.
Williams, Mary. Dickens Concordance. Folcroft.
Williams, Monier. Sanskrit Manual (Enlarged) with a Vocabulary (English & Sanskrit) Verry.
Williams, Monier, ed. Sanskrit-English Dictionary: Etymologically & Philologically Arranged with Special Reference to Cognate Indo-European Languages. Intl Pubns serv.
Williams, Monier, et al. Sanskrit-English Dictionary. Lancaster-Miller.
Williams, Roger. Key into the Language of America. Gale.
Williams, Rosalind. Practical French-English, English-French Dictionary. Hippocrene Bks.
Williams, S. J., ed. see Meurig, H. & Thomas, W. O.
Williams, Samuel W. Chinese-English Dictionary. Ayer Co.
Williams, Vergil L. Dictionary of American Penology: An Introductory Guide. Greenwood.
Williamson, J. P. English-Dakota Dictionary. Ross.
Willis, J. C. A Dictionary of the Flowering Plants & Ferns Vol. 1: Generic & Family Names. Cambridge U Pr.
Willis, Jean. Historical Dictionary of Uruguay. Scarecrow.
Willmann-Institut. Woerterbuch der Paedagogik. Herder.
Willmann-Institut Muenchen. Woerterbuch der Paedagogik. Herder.
Wilmeth, Don B. The Language of American Popular Entertainment: A Glossary of Argot, Slang, & Terminology. Greenwood.
Wilpert, Gero von. Lexikon der Weltliteratur: Werke. French & Eur.
Wilson, A. Latin Dictionary. McKay.
Wilson, Arnold. A Dictionary of British Marine Painters (Pub. by A & C Black England). Humanities.
Wilson, Basil, jt. auth. see Wurm, Stefan A.
Wilson, E., jt. auth. see Akhmanova, O. S.
Wilson, E. A. The Modern Russian Dictionary for English Speakers: English-Russian. Pergamon.
Wilson, Elizabeth A., jt. auth. see Akhmanova, Olga S.
Wilson, Gordon see Haskell, Ann S.
Wilson, Howard. Glossary of Economic Terms. ARA.
Wilson, James. Dictionary of Astrology. Weiser.
--Dictionary of Astrology (Samuel Weiser Inc.). Am Fed Astrologers.
Wilson, John & Parsons, C. Basic Latin Vocabulary. St Martin.
Wilson, Tom & Morehead, Loy. New American Crossword Puzzle Dictionary (Sig). NAL.
Wilson-Fulkerson, Roberta, ed. see Abraham, Samuel V.
Wilson-Fulkerson, Roberta, ed. see Drill, Douglas D.
Wilstach, Frank J., ed. Dictionary of Similes. Gale.
Winburne, John N., et al, eds. Dictionary of Agricultural & Allied Terminology. Mich St U Pr.
Windsor, A. T., ed. Using the ICL Data Dictionary: Proceedings of the ICL DDS User Group. Birkhauser.
Wing, L., jt. auth. see Savaiano, E.
Wingate, Isabel B., ed. Fairchild's Dictionary of Textiles. Fairchild.
Winget, L., jt. auth. see Savaiano, E.
Winick, Charles. Dictionary of Anthropology. Greenwood.
--Dictionary of Anthropology. Littlefield.
Winick, Charles, tr. Diccionario de antropologia. Troquel.
Winkel, Harald, jt. auth. see Munz, Max.
Winkler, Werner. Technical Dictionary of Textile Chemistry - Fachwoerterbuch Chemiefasern: German-English-French, English-German-French, French-German-English. Intl Pubns Serv.
Winn, Ralph, ed see Lincoln, Abraham.
Winniczuk, Lida. Maly Slownik Kultury Antycznej. Wiedza Powszechna.
Winslow, Donald J. Life-Writing: A Glossary of Terms in Biography, Autobiography & Related Forms. UH Pr.
Winslow, M. Tamil-English, English-Tamil Dictionary. Heinman.
Winter, Ruth. The Consumer's Dictionary of Cosmetic Ingredients. Crown.
--A Consumer's Dictionary of Food Additives. Crown.
Winther-Jensen, Thyge, jt. ed. see Grue-Sorensen, K.
Wintz, E. Dictionnaire Francais-Dyola. Gregg.
Wise, Philip, jt. auth. see Humphreys, Fisher.
Withnell, William, jt. auth. see Peron, Michel.
Witkowski, Regine. Genetik Erblicher Syndrome & Missbildungen. Fischer Verlag.
Wittfoht. Dictionnaire des Matieres Plastiques. French & Eur.
--Dictionnaires des Matieres Plastiques. Francaise, Compagnie Edition.
Wittfoht, A. Kunststofftechnik Woerterbuch. Hanser.
--Kunststofftechnik Woerterbuch (Pub. by C. Hanser). French & Eur.
--Kunststofftechnisches Woerterbuch. Hanser.
--Kunststofftechnisches Woerterbuch. Hanser.
--Kunststofftechnisches Woerterbuch. Hanser.
--Kunststofftechnisches Woerterbuch (Pub. by C. Hanser). French & Eur.
--Kunststofftechnisches Woerterbuch (Pub. by C. Hanser). French & Eur.
--Kunststofftechnisches Woerterbuch (Pub. by C. Hanser). French & Eur.
--Kunststofftechnisches Woerterbuch. French & Eur.
Wittfoht, A. & Achon, M. A. Diccionario Tecnico De la Plasticos Aleman-Espanol. French & Eur.
Wittfoht, A & Achon, M. A. Diccionario tecnico de plasticos aleman-espanol. Urmo.
Wittfoht, A. & Rubin, A. Diccionario tecnico de plasticos: Espanol-aleman (Dist. Elcano, Mexico). Urmo.
Wittfoht, A. M. The Technical Terms in Plastics Engineering. Elsevier.
Wittfoht, A. M., ed. Plastics Technical Dictionary (Pub. by Hanser International). Macmillan.
--Plastics Technical Dictionary: Part 1: English-German (Pub. by Hanser International). Macmillan.
--Plastics Technical Dictionary: Part 2: German-English (Pub. by Hanser International). Macmillan.
--Plastics Technical Dictionary: Part 3: Reference Volume (Pub. by Hanser International). Macmillan.
Wittgenstein, Ludwig. Dizionario per le scuole elementari. Antiseri, D., tr. Armando.
Witthoeft, Hans. Lexikon der Deutschen Marinegeschichte. French & Eur.
Witthoeft, Hans J., ed. Lexikon der Deutschen Marinegeschichte. Koehlers Verlag.
Wittlesberger, Helmut, jt. auth. see Mentzel, Wolfgang.
Wittman, A. & Klos, J. Dictionary of Data Processing. Elsevier.
Wittman, Alfred. Fachwoerterbuch der Datenverarbeitung. Oldenbourg Verlag.
Wittmann, Alfred. Dictionary of Data Processing. Elsevier.
Witty, F. R. Nelson Canadian Elementary School Dictionary. Nelson & Sons Group.
--Pacific Junior Dictionary. Pan Pacific Bk.
Witty, F. R., ed. Nelson Canadian Elementary School Dictionary. Nelson & Sons Group.
Wllliams, Monier. A Dictionary, English & Sanskrit. Orient Bk Dist.
Wojowasito, Soewojo. A Kawi Lexicon. Mills, Roger F., ed. Ctr S&SE Asian.
Wojtecki, Dieter, jt. auth. see Otto, Norbert.
Wojtowytsch-Wielandt, Rotraud, jt. auth. see Ullmann, Manfred.
Wolf, Jakob, jt. auth. see Falk, Bernard.
Wolfe, Josephine B., jt. ed. see Perry, Day.
Wolfe, Lucienne V. English-French Glossary. Govt Print.
Wolfe, Thomas E., jt. auth. see Allen, Robert D.
Wolff, Hans. A Comparative Vocabulary of Aubuan Dialects. State Mutual Bk.
Wolff, John V. Dictionary of Cebuano Visayan. Cornell SE Asia.
Wolff, Lise, jt. auth. see Geissler, E. A.
Wolk, jt. auth. see Bridger.
Wolkonsky, Catherine & Poltoratzky, Marianna. Handbook of Russian Roots. Columbia U Pr.
Woll, Allen. Dictionary of the Black Theatre: Broadway, Off-Broadway, & Selected Harlem Theatre. Greenwood.
Wollaston, A. N. English Persian Dictionary (Pub. by Cosmo Pubns India). Orient Bk Dist.

--An English-Persian Dictionary Compiled from Original Sources. Humanities.

Wolman, Benjamin B. Dictionary of Behavioral Science. Van Nos Reinhold.

Wolman, Benjamin B., ed. Dictionary of Behavorial Science. Van Nos Reinhold.

Wolter, G., jt. ed. see Gottschalg, J.

Wood. Two Hundred One Persian Verbs - Arabic Script. Barron.

--Two Hundred One Persian Verbs - Romanization. Barron.

Wood, Christopher. The Dictionary of Victorian Painters. Antique Collect.

--Dictionary of Victorian Painters. Apollo.

Wood, Clement. Wood's New World Unabridged Rhyming Dictionary. Collins Pubs.

Wood, Clement, ed. Complete Rhyming Dictionary. Doubleday.

Wood, Donna, ed. Trade Names Dictionary: Company Index. Gale.

Wood, E. Diccionario Zen. Paido.

Wood, E., ed. Diccionario Zen. French & Eur.

Wood, Ernest. Zen Dictionary. C E Tuttle.

Wood, F. T. Dictionary of English Colloquial Idioms. Hill, R., rev. by. Macmillan.

Wood, F. T. & Hill, Robert. Dictionary of English Colloguial Idioms. Macmillan LOndon.

Wood, Gordon R. Vocabulary Change: A Study of Variation in Regional Words in Eight of the Southern States. S Ill U Pr.

Woodard, C. M., jt. auth. see **Linguistic Society of America.**

Woodcock, C. Dictionary of Contemporary Violin & Bow Makers. Heinman.

Woodhead, Daniel. A Dictionary of Modern Iraqi Arabic. Intl Bk Ctr.

Woodhead, Daniel & Beene, Wayne, eds. A Dictionary of Iraqi Arabic: Arabic-English. Georgetown U Pr.

Woodhouse, S. C., ed. Latin-English & English-Latin Dictionary. Routledge & Kegan.

Woodson, Linda. A Handbook of Modern Rhetorical Terms. NCTE.

Woolley, LeGrand H. Medical-Dental Terminology: Syllabus. Natl Book.

Wordingham, J. A. & Reboul, P. Diccionario del Plastico. French & Eur.

--Dictionary of Plastics. Littlefield.

Wordingham, J. A. & Reboul, P., trs. Diccionario plastico. Leru.

Worgt, Gerhard, ed. Taschenwoerterbuch Deutsch-Niederlaendisch. VEB Verlag Enzyklopadie.

World Almanac Editors. World Almanac Dictionary of Dates. Laurence Urdang, Inc., ed. Longman.

World Energy Conference. Standard Terms of the Energy Economy. Pergamon.

World Energy Conference, ed. Energy Terminology: A Multi-Lingual Glossary. Pergamon.

World Pub. Co. Prentice-Hall Students Edition of the Concise Webster's New World Dictionary of the American Language. P.-H.

Wortabet, J. & Porter, H., eds. English-Arabic, Arabic-English Dictionary. Ungar.

Wortabet, John. Arabic-English Pocket Dictionary. Intl Bk Ctr.

--English-Arabic, Arabic-English Dictionary. Intl Bk Ctr.

--English-Arabic; Arabic-English Dictionary. Intl Bk Ctr.

--English-Arabic; Arabic-English Pocket Dictionary. Intl Bk Ctr.

--English-Arabic Pocket Dictionary. Intl Bk Ctr.

Wortabet, John & Porter, Harvey. Wortabet's Pocket English-Arabic Dictionary. Intl Bk Ctr.

Wortabet, William. Arabic-English Dictionary. Intl Bk Ctr.

Wortabet, William & Porter, Harvey, eds. Arabic-English Dictionary. Intl Bk Ctr.

Wortman, Leon A. A Deskbook of Business Management Terms. Am Mgmt.

--A Deskbook of Business Management Terms. Am Mgmt.

Wotton, Tom S. A Dictionary of Foreign Musical Terms & Handbook of Orchestral Instruments. Scholarly.

Woyke, Wichard, ed. Handwoerterbuch Internationale Politik. Leske-Budrich.

Wragg, David. A Dictionary of Aviation. Fell.

Wragg, David W. Dictionary of Aviation. Beekman Pubs.

Wreford, Susan M., jt. auth. see **Rossdale, Peter D.**

Wrete, Martin. Kortfattad Medicinsk Ordbok. Dahlgren, Sven, ed. Esselte Studium.

Wright, Charles & Neil, Charles, eds. The Protestant Dictionary: Containing Articles on the History, Doctrines & Practices of the Christian Church. Gale.

Wright, F. A., ed. Lempriere's Classical Dictionary. Routledge & Kegan.

Wright, Graeme. Illustrated Dictionary of Sports. Rand.

Wright, John, ed. The English Dialect Dictionary: Being the Complete Vocabulary of All Dialect Words...During the Last Two Hundred Years. Oxford U Pr.

Wright, Peter. Language of British Industry. Verry.

Wright, Roy V., ed. Freight Cars from the 1919 Car Builder's Dictionary. N K Gregg.

--Freight Cars from the 1919 Car Builder's Dictionary. N K Gregg.

--Locomotives from the Nineteen Sixteen Locomotive Dictionary. N K Gregg.

--Passenger Cars from the 1999 Car Builder's Dictionary. N K Gregg.

Wright, T. Anglo-Saxon & English Vocabularies. Adler.

Wright, Thomas. Anglo-Saxon & Old English Vocabularies. Gordon Pr.

Wright, W. Aldis, jt. auth. see **Eastwood, J.**

Wright, Wendell W., ed. The Rainbow Dictionary for Young Reader. Collins Pubs.

Wrightman, Lawrence S., jt. auth. see **Stang, David J.**

Wu Jingrong, ed see **Beijing Foreign Institute.**

Wulf, Christoph. Woerterbuch der Erziehung. Piper Co.

Wuole, A. Finnish-English, English-Finnish Dictionary. Shalom.

Wuolle. Finnish-English-Finnish Dictionary. French & Eur.

Wuolle, A. English-Finnish Dictionary. French & Eur.

--Finnish-English, English-Finnish Dictionary. Heinman.

--Finnish-English, English-Finnish Dictionary. Heinman.

Wuolle, Aino. Finnish Small Dictionary: English-Finnish. Vanous.

--Finnish Small Dictionary: Finnish-English. Vanous.

Wurm, Stefan A. & Wilson, Basil. English Finderlist of Reconstructions in Austronesian Languages. Linguistic Circle.

Wurmser, Andre. Dictionnaire pour l'intelligence des Choses. Sagittaire.

Wuster, Eugen, et al. International Bibliography of Standardized Vocabularies. International Information Centre for Terminology, ed. K G Saur.

Wyld, Henry C., ed. The Universal Dictionary of the English Langauge. Routledge & Kegan.

Wyllie & Argall. World Mining: Glossary of Mining, Processing & Geological Terms. W H Freeman.

Wyllie, R. J. & Argall, George O., Jr., eds. World Mining Glossary of Mining, Processing & Geological Terms. Miller Freeman.

Wynne, R. C. English-Mbukusha dictionary. Avebury Pub Co.

--English-Mbukushu Dictionary (Pub. by Avebury England). Humanities.

Wynne, Ronald C. English-Mbukushu Dictionary. Avebury Pub Co.

Wypych, Konrad. Deutsch Lehnwoerter in der Polnischen Bergbausprache. MG Schmitz.

--Deutsche Lehnworter in der Polnischen Bergbausprache. MG Schmitz.

Wysinska, E. Slownik Wspolczesnego T Atru: Tworcy, Teatry, Teorie (Pub. by Wydaw. Artystyczne & Filmowe). Four Continent.

X

Xin Ying-Han-Cidian Editing Committee. A New English-Chinese Dictionary (Pub. by Joint Pub Co China). Cheng & Tsui.

Xinglian, Zhang. A Glossary of Chinese Archaeology. Shuhan, Zhao, ed. China Bks.

Xuriguera, J. B. Nou Diccionari de la Llengua Catalana. French & Eur.

Y

Yacobian, A. H. English-Armenian, Armenian English Dictionary. Shalom.

Yakubaitis, E. A. English-Russian Glossary of Computer Systems & Networks Terminology (Pub. by Collets). State Mutual Bk.

Yale University. Henry S. Graves Memorial Library. Dictionary Catalogue of the Yale Forestry Library (Hall Library). G K Hall.

Yamada, Hiroshi. Sanyo's Tri-Lingual Glossary of Chemical Terms. Sadtler Res.

Yamaguchi, M. Illustratred New Shipbuilding Dictionary: English-Japanese, Japanese-English. French & Eur.

Yancy, Wallace. The Dream Dictionary. Carlton.

Yang, Lien-Sheng, jt. auth. see **Chao, Yuen R.**

Yanguas & Miranda, Jose. Diccionario de los fueros & leyes de Navarra. Aranzadi Edit.

Yap, Elsa P. & Bunye, Maria V. Cebuano-Visayan Dictionary. McKaughan, Howard P., ed. UH Pr.

Yapp, Peter, ed. The Travellers' Dictionary of Quotation: Who Said What, about Where. Routledge & Kegan.

Yarden, Dov, jt. ed. see **Shoshan, A. Even.**

Yarwood, Doreen. Costume of the Western World. St Martin.

Yaselman. Diccionario ruso-espanol. Aguilar SP.

Yates, J., jt. auth. see **Renoux, Y.**

Yazyk, Russkii. Russian-English Dictionary of Sports Terms & Phrases (Pub. by Collet's). State Mutual Bk.

Yelland, H. L., et al. Handbook of Literary Terms. Writer.

Yerevan. Anglo-Armianskii Shkolnyi Slovar (Pub. by Luys). Four Continent.

Yerian, et al. Personal Shorthand Student Dictionary. Natl Book.

Yogis, John. Law Dictionary: The Canadian Edition. Barron.

Yorkey, Richard. Checklists for Vocabulary Study. Longman.

Yorston, Keith. The Australian Commercial Dictionary. Intl Pubns Serv.

Young. Youngs Analytical Concordance to the Bible. Church History.

Young, Brigadier P. Dictionary of Battles (Mayflower Bks). Smith Pubs.

Young, Brigadier P. & Calvert, Brigadier M. Dictionary of Battles (Mayflower Bks). Smith Pubs.

Young, Douglas. Concordance of Ugaritic. Pont Ist Biblico.

Young, Hartsill. A.L.A. Glossary of Library & Information Science. ALA.

Young People's Science Encyclopedia Editors. Young People's Science Dictionary. Childrens.

Young, Percy M. A Critical Dictionary of Composers & Their Music. Hyperion Conn.

Young, Robert. Young's Analytical Concordance to the Bible. Eerdmans.

Young, Ruth E., jt. ed. see **Bocchetta, Vittore.**

Younge, W. A. A Kipling Dictionary. Gordon Pr.

Younger, Maria. Diccionario Espanol-Ingles. Mayfe.

Younis. Dictionary of Folklore: English-Arabic. Intl Bk Ctr.

Yusoff, Khan, jt. auth. see **Awang, Sudjai H.**

Z

Zacharias, D., jt. auth. see **Knaeps, E.**

Zahn, H. Dictionary of Politics & Economic Policy. French & Eur.

Zahn, Hans E. Englisch-Deutsches Glossarium (Pub. by Fritz Knapp Verlag). French & Eur.

--English-German Glossary of Financial & Economic Terms. Intl Pubns Serv.

--Euro Dictionary of Economics & Business. Rothman.

--Euro-Wirtschafts Worterlrich in Drei Sprachen (Pub. by Fritz Knapp Verlag). French & Eur.

--Woerterbuch zur Politik und Wirtschaftpolitik. French & Eur.

Zaidenberg, Arthur. Dictionary of Drawing. Cornwall Bks.

Zaimovskii, S. G. Concise English-Russian, Russian-English Dictionary (Pub. by Collet's). State Mutual Bk.

--Kratkii Anglo-Russkii i Russko-Angliiskii Slovar' Four Continent.

Zaimovsky, S. G. Kratkii Anglo-Russkii i Russko-Angliiskii (Pub. by Russkii Iazyk). Four Continent.

--Russian-English, English-Russian Dictionary. Saphrograph.

Zainqui, Jose M. Diccionario Razonado de Sinonimos y Contrarios. French & Eur.

Zainqui Erro, Jose M. Ortografia Practica. Edit Vecchi.

--Ortografia Practica. Devecchi, ed. Edit Vecchi.

Zaks, Rodnay, jt. auth. see **Sybex Staff.**

Zalizniak, A. A., ed. Grammaticheskii Slovar' Russkogo Iazyka. Four Continent.

Zalucki, H. Dictionary of Russian Technical & Scientific Abbreviations. Elsevier.

Zambaldi, Francesco. Vocabolario etimologico italiano. Dante Alighieri.

Zamora, Antonio. Diccionario de sininimos espanoles. Claridad.

Zamora Vicente, Alfonso. Diccionario Moderno del Espanol Usual. Sader SA.

Zamorin, A. P., jt. auth. see **Shishmarev, A. I.**

Zamorin, A. P., jt. auth. see **Shismarev, A. I.**

Zampetti, Pietro. Dictionary of Venetian Painters. Incl. Vol. 1. Fourteenth to Fifteenth Centuries; Vol. 2. Sixteenth Century; Vol. 3. Seventeenth Century; Vol. 4. Eighteenth Century; Vol. 5. 19th & 20th Centuries. Intl Pubns Serv.

--A Dictionary of Venetian Painters: Vol. 1, 14th & 15th Centuries (Pub. by A & C Black England). Humanities.

--A Dictionary of Venetian Painters: Vol. 2, 16th Century (Pub. by A & C Black England). Humanities.

--A Dictionary of Venetian Painters: Vol. 4, 18th Century (Pub. by A & C Black England). Humanities.

--A Dictionary of Venetian Painters: Vol. 5, 19th & First Decade of the 20th Century (Pub. by A & C Black England). Humanities.

Zandreitere, I. Frantsuzsko-Russkii Illiustrirovannyi Slovar (Pub. by Latv Valstsnent Bk). Four Continent.

Zandreitere, I., et al. Frantsuzsko-Latviiskii Slovar (Pub. by Latv Valsts). Four Continent.

Zangrandi, Ruggero, jt. auth. see **Venturoli, Marcello.**

Zaniah. Diccionario Esoterico. French & Eur.

Zanobini, L. & Vetrini, T. Dizionario della publica istruzione. Giuffre.

--Dizionario della publica istruzione. Giuffre.

Zanzucchi, Anne M. Family Portrait, from a Mother's Diary. Szczesniak, Lenny, tr. from It. New City.

Zarubin, S. F. Russko-Iaponskii Slovar (Pub. by Sov. Entsiklopediia). Four Continent.

Zaunmuller, Wolfram. Bibliographisches Handbuch der Sprachworterbucher: Ein Internationales Verzeichnis Von 5600 Worterbuchern der Jahre 1460-1958 Fur Mehr Als 500 Sprachen und Dialekte. Intl Pubns Serv.

Zavada. Satzlexikon der Handelskorrespondenz. Brandstetter.

Zavada & Eberle. Diccionario Fraseologico Comercial. French & Eur.

--Satzlexikon der Handelskorrespondenz. Brandstetter.

Zavada & Hartgenbush. Satzlexikon der Handelskorrespondenz. Brandstetter.

Zavada & Schraffl. Satzlexikon der Handelskorrespondenz. Brandstetter.

Zavada & Weis. Satzlexikon der Handelskorrespondenz. Brandstetter.

Zavada, Dusan. Slovak-English Business Correspondence Dictionary (Pub. by Collet's). State Mutual Bk.

Zavala Cubillos, Armando. Diccionario Estudios de geografia. Leru.

Zedtwitz, Hans G. Jurdicia Lexikon: Das Kleine Oesterreicher Rechtswoerterbuch. Juridica Verlag.

Zeier, Hans. Woerterbuch der Lerntheorien & der Verhaltenstherapie. Kindler.

Zeisberger, David. Zeisberger's Indian Dictionary: English, German, Iroquois - the Onandaga & Algonquin - the Delaware. AMS Pr.

Zeliqzon, Leon. Dictionnaire des Patols Romans de la Moselle. Strasbourg, U.

Zellmer, Ernst. Die Lateinischen Woerter auf -Ura. Selbstverlag Inst.

Zellweger, Rudolf. Le Vocabulaire Allemand du Bachelier. Payot.

Zendrera, Concepcion. Mi Diccionario Ilustrado. French & Eur.

Zentner, Christian, ed. Lexikon des II. Weltkriegs. Suedwest.

Zentner, Cristian. Lexikon Des II Weltkriegs. French & Eur.

Zettersteen, K. V., jt. auth. see De Landberg, C.

Z'graggen, J. A. A Comparative Word List of the Mabuso Languages, Madang Province, Papua New Guinea. Linguistic Circle.

--A Comparative Word List of the Rai Coast Languages, Madang Province, Papua New Guinea. Linguistic Circle.

--A Comparative Word List of the Southern Adelbert Range Languages, Madang Province, Papua New Guinea. Linguistic Circle.

Z'graggon, J. A. A Comparative Word List of the Northern Adelbert Range Languages, Madang Province, Papua New Guinea. Linguistic Circle.

Zhamin, V. A., ed. Politicheskaia Ekonomiia Slovar (Pub. by Politizdat). Four Continent.

Zhitomirskii, M. M. Nemetsko-Russkii Arkhitekturnyi Slovar (Pub. by GINS). Four Continent.

Zhluktenko, I. O., ed. English-Ukrainian Dictionary. Four Continent.

Zhong Wai Publishing Company. An English-Chinese Dictionary of Engineering & Technology. Wiley.

Zhou Long Ru. English-Chinese Dictionary of Abbreviation & Acronyms. China Bks.

Zhuchkevich, V. A. Kratkii Toponimicheskii Slovar Belorussii (Pub. by MGU). Four Continent.

Zickfeldt, jt. auth. see Haukoy.

Ziefle, Helmut W. Dictionary of Modern Theological German. Baker Bk.

Ziegler. Grammatisches Worterbuch der Gebrauchlichsten Spanischer Verben (Pub. by Fachverlag Th. Grossman). French & Eur.

Ziegler, K. & Sontheimer, W., eds. Lexikon der Antike. M Rosenberg.

Ziervogel, D. Groot Noord-Sotho-Woordeboek. Van Schaik.

Zimaity, M. A. Aeronautic Engineering Dictionary: English-French-German-Arabic. Abd-el-Washed, ed. French & Eur.

Zimmerman. Dictionary of Classical Mythology. Bantam.

Zimmerman, John E. Dictionary of Classical Mythology (HarpT). Har-Row.

Zimmerman, M. G. Russian-English Scientific & Technical Dictionary of Useful Combinations & Expressions. Shalom.

Zimmerman, Mikhail G. Russian-English Translators Dictionary: A Guide to Scientific & Technical Usage (Plenum Pr). Plenum Pub.

Zimmermann, Ralf. Dictionary of Lighting (Pub. by Collet's). State Mutual Bk.

Zingarelli, Nicola. Vocabolario della lingua italiana. Zanichelli.

--Vocabolario della lingua italiana. Zanichelli.

Zingitis, A. Russko-Latyshskii Politekhnicheskii Slovar (Pub. by Liesma). Four Continent.

Zinn, K. G., jt. auth. see Ritter, U. P.

Zino, E., jt. auth. see Marconi, R.

Ziring, Lawrence. The Middle East Political Dictionary. ABC-Clio.

Zita, K. Lexikon der Schulphysik: Mechanik und Akustik. French & Eur.

Zlatovski, George. Dictionnaire Technique de L'Automobile. Russek, P. R., ed. French & Eur.

Zlatovski, George & Russek, P. R. Dictionnaire Technique de l'automobile. Bordas-Dunod.

Zlotnicki, B. Lexicon Medicum: Medizinisches Woerterbuch in 6 Sprachen; Englisch, Russisch, Franzoesisch, Deutsch, Latein, Polnisch. Langenscheidt.

--Lexikon Medicum. French & Eur.

Zlotnicki, Boleslaw. Slownik Lekarski Polsko-Niemiecki. Panstwowe Zaklad W.

Zlotnicki, T. Lexicon Medicum (Pub. by Collet's). State Mutual Bk.

Zlotnickiego, Boleslaw. Lexicon Medicum. French & Eur.

Zoega, Geir T. Concise Dictionary of Old Icelandic.

Zoepfl, Helmut & Bittner, Gerhard. Kleines Lexikon der Paedagogik & Didaktik. Tschamler, Herbert, ed. Auer.

Oxford U Pr.

Zoepfl, Helmut, ed. Kleines Lexikon der Paedagogik & Didaktik. Auer.

Zoepfl, Herbert. Kleines Lexikon der Paedagogik und Didaktik. Auer.

--Kleines Lexikon der Paedagogik und Didaktik (Pub. by Auer). French & Eur.

Zolli, Paolo, jt. auth. see Cortelazzo, Manlio.

Zoltnicki, B. Medical Dictionary (Pub. by Schattauer). French & Eur.

Zondergeld, Rein, jt. auth. see Krichbaum, Jorg.

Zorin, I. N. Russko-Kitaiskii Obschcheekonomicheskii i Vneshnetorgovyi Slovar (Pub. by Vneshtorgizdat). Four Continent.

Zotter, Josefa. Cortina-Grosset Basic German Dictionary. G&D.

Zotter, Josefa, ed. Cortina-Grosset Basic German Dictionary (G&D). Putnam Pub Group.

Zubini, Fabio, jt. auth. see Arnould, Michel.

Zudin, P. B. Russko-Afganskii Slovar (Pub. by GINS). Four Continent.

Zupko, Ronald E. French Weights & Measures before the Revolution: A Dictionary of Provincial & Local Units. Ind U Pr.

Zurcher, Arnold J., jt. auth. see Sloan, Harold S.

Zurcher, Arnold J., jt. auth. see Smith, Edward C.

Zurita Ruiz, Jose. Diccionario basico de la construccion. Ceac.

--Diccionario Basico de la Construccion. French & Eur.

--Diccionario basico de la construccion II. Ceac.

Zvarich, V. V. Numizmaticheskii Slovar (Pub. by Izd. L'Vovsk. Unta.). Four Continent.

Zvidadze, Givi. A Dictionary of Contemporary English. Humanities.

Zwahr, A., jt. ed. see Goeschel, H.

Zwanenburg, Wiecher. Ambiguite Dans le Lexique. Humanities.

Zweck, Dina Von see VonZweck, Dina.

Zwemer, Thomas J. Boucher's Clinical Dental Terminology: A Glossary of Accepted Terms in All Disciplines of Dentistry. Mosby.

Zykina, M. I., et al. Chastotnyi Slovar Obschenauchnoi Leksiki (Pub. by MGU). Four Continent.

LANGUAGE INDEX

AFGHANI

Karmannyi Afgansko-Russkii Slovar.
K. A. Lebedev. (Pub. by Gosizdat
Natsional Slovarei). Four
Continent.
Russko-Afganskii Slovar. P. B. Zudin.
(Pub. by GINS). Four Continent.
Russko-Afganskii Slovar. K. A.
Lebedev et al. (Pub. by Sov
Entsiklopediia). Four Continent.

AFRICAN

African-English, English-African
Dictionary. A. Coetzee. Shalom.

AFRIKAANS

Afrikaans-English, English-Afrikaans
Dictionary. M. S. Kritzinger.
Heinman.
Afrikaanse Verklarende Woordeboek
vir Biologie. Eulalie Munnik.
Knaggs Assoc.
Die Kennis Gids tot Moderne
Afrikaans. E. DuPlessis. Human &
Rousseau.

Drietalige Elementere Woordeboek.
Petrus J. Wentzel. U Sth Africa.
Engels-Afrikaanse Tegniese
Woordeboek. H. Terblanche.
Nasou.
Ndonga, Afrikaans, English:
Dreitalige Woordeboek. Johannes J.
Viljoen & P. Amakali. Van Schaik.

ALBANIAN

Albanian-English & English Albanian
Dictionary. Saphrograph.
Albanian-English Dictionary. Gasper
Kici. G Kici.
Albanian-English, English-Albanian
Dictionary. Nelo Drizari. Ungar.
Dizionario Italiano-Albanese. F.
Cordignano. Forni.
English-Albanian Dictionary. Gasper
Kici & Hysni Aliko. G Kici.
Karmannyi Russko-Albanskii Slovar.
A. Kostallari. Four Continent.

ALEUTIAN

Aleutian Indian & English Dictionary.
Charles A. Lee. Shorey.

AMHARIC

Concise Amharic Dictionary. Wolf
Leslau. U of Cal Pr.

ARABIC

ABC Dictionary I: Arabic & Fr. Libr.
du Liban. Intl Bk Ctr.
ABC Dictionary I: Arabic & Ger. libr.
du Liban. Intl Bk Ctr.
ABC Dictionary I: Arabic & Span.
Libr d. Liban. Intl Bk Ctr.
ABC Dictionary I, Arabic Italian. Intl
Bk Ctr.
ABC Dictionary I, Arabic-Spanish.
Intl Bk Ctr.
ABC Dictionary Tamhidi: Arabic &
Eng. Libr du Liban. Intl Bk Ctr.

ABC Dictionary Tamhidi: Arabic &
Fr. Libr du Liban. Intl Bk Ctr.
ABC Dictionary Tamhidi: Arabic &
Ital. Libr du Liban. Intl Bk Ctr.

ABC Dictionary Tamhidi: Arabic
Ger. Libr du Liban. Intl Bk Ctr.
ABC Dictionary Tamhidi: Arabic-
Spanish. Libr du Liban. Intl Bk Ctr.

Abdallah Dictionary of International
Relations & Conference
Terminology in English-Arabic.
Abdallah. Intl Bk Ctr.

Additions Aux Dictionnaires Arabes
(Arabic-French) E. Fagnan. Intl Bk
Ctr.

An Advanced Learner's Arabic-
English Dictionary. Anthony
Salmone. Intl Bk Ctr.

Aeronautic Engineering Dictionary:
English-French-German-Arabic. M.
A. Zimaity. Ed. by Abd-el-Washed.
French & Eur.

Agricultural Engineering Dictionary:
English-French-German-Arabic.
Abd El Wahed. French & Eur.

Agriculture, Forestry, & Allied
Terminology Dictionary: English-
Arabic with Arabic Glossary.
Chihabi. Ed. by A. Khatib. Intl Bk
Ctr.

Al-Faraid Arabic-English Dictionary.
J. G. Hava. Intl Pubns Serv.

Al-Faraid: Arabic-English Dictionary.
J. Hava. Intl Bk Ctr.

Al-Hadiyati 'I-Hamidiyah. M. Mokri.
Intl Bk Ctr.

Al-Kamil Dictionnaire Arabe-
Francais-Anglais. M. Chouemi & C.
H. Pellat. French & Eur.

Al Manar: English-Arabic Dictionary.
Hassan Karmi. Intl Bk Ctr.

Al-Wafi. Abdullah Al-Bustani. Intl Bk
Ctr.
An Annotated Glossary of Arabic
Musical Terms. Ed. by Lois I. Al
Faruqi. Greenwood.

Ar-Rafed. Amin Al-Amir Al-
Nasiruddin. Intl Bk Ctr.
Arabe Francais Dictionnaire. A.
Kazirmski. Intl Bk Ctr.

Arabic-Arabic Dictionary Muhit Al
Muhit. Butrus Al-Bustani. Intl Bk
Ctr.
Arabic Dictionary: Al Munjid fi al-
Lugha Wal 'Alam. Dar El Mashreq.
Intl Bk Ctr.

Arabic-English Advanced Learners
Dictionary. Anthony Salmone. Intl
Bk Ctr.

Arabic-English Collegiate Dictionary. Elias. Colton Bk.

Arabic-English Dictionary. D. Cameron. Intl Bk Ctr.

Arabic-English Dictionary. William Wortabet. Intl Bk Ctr.

Arabic-English Dictionary. Saphrograph.

Arabic-English Dictionary. Hans Wehr. Ed. by J Milton Cowan. Spoken Lang Serv.

Arabic-English Dictionary. Dar el Mashreq. Intl Bk Ctr.

Arabic-English Dictionary. Ed. by William Wortabet & Harvey Porter. Intl Bk Ctr.

Arabic-English Dictionary. Hans Wehr & J. M. Cowan. Imported Bks.

Arabic-English Dictionary. H. Wehr. Iaconi.

Arabic-English Dictionary: Colloquial Arabic of Egypt. Socrates Spiro. Intl Bk Ctr.

Arabic-English Dictionary: Hava's Al-Faraid. Intl Bk Ctr.

Arabic-English Dictionary of Agricultural Terms & Allied Terminology. Ahmad Khatib. Intl Bk Ctr.

An Arabic-English Dictionary of the Colloquial Arabic of Egypt. Socrates Spiro. Intl Bk Ctr.

Arabic-English, English-Arabic Collegiate Dictionary. Ed. by E. A. Elias. Heinman.

Arabic-English, English-Arabic Dictionary. E. A. Elias. Heinman.

Arabic-English, English-Arabic School Dictionary. Ed. by E. A. Elias. Heinman.

Arabic-English, English-Arabic Student's Dictionary. Heinman.

Arabic-English Learners Dictionary. F. Steingass. Intl Bk Ctr.

An Arabic-English Lexicon. Madd A. Qamus & Wm. Edward. Intl Bk Ctr.

Arabic-English Lexicon. Ed. by Edward W. Lane. Ungar.

An Arabic-English Lexicon: Madd al Qamus. Compiled by Edward W. Lane. Intl Bk Ctr.

Arabic-English Modern Dictionary. Elias Elias. Intl Bk Ctr.

Arabic-English Students Dictionary. Dar El Mashreq. Intl Bk Ctr.

Arabic-French Dictionary. Auguste Cherbonneau. Intl Bk Ctr.

Arabic Pocket Dictionary. Heinman.

Arabic Student Dictionary. Munjid al Tulab & Dar el Mashreq. Intl Bk Ctr.

Arabisch. Incl. Langenscheidt.

Arabsko-Cesky Cesko-Arabsky Slovnik. Lubos Kropacek. SNTC.

Architecture & Building Dictionary: English-French-German-Arabic. Abd El Gaward. French & Eur.

Automotive Engineering Dictionary: English-French-German-Arabic. Abd-El-Wahed. French & Eur.

Banking & Financial Dictionary: English-French-Arabic. E. Assiouly. French & Eur.

Basic Technical Dictionary: French-English-German-Arabic. H. Marei. French & Eur.

Berlitz Arabic for Travellers. Berlitz Editors. (Berlitz). Macmillan.

Chaldean Arabic, English Picture Dictionary. Intl Bk Ctr.

Chemical Technology Dictionary: English, French-German-Arabic. A. M. Abd-El-Wahed. French & Eur.

Chihabi's Dictionary of Agricultural & Forestry Terms. Ahmed Khatib. Intl Bk Ctr.

Colloquial Arabic: An Oral Approach. Raja Nasr. Intl Bk Ctr.

A Concise Arabic Dictionary. Al Wafi & Butros Bustani. Intl Bk Ctr.

Concise Dictionary of Islamic Terms. M. A. Qazi. Intl Bk Ctr.

Deutsch-Arabisches Worterbuch. Gotz Schregle. Lib Liban.

Diccionario Arabe-Espanol. French & Eur.

Diccionario Arabe-Espanol, Espanol-Arabe. Alhambra. French & Eur.

Diccionario Espanol-Arabe. Federico Corriente Cordoba. French & Eur.

Diccionario espanol-arabe. Federico Corriente Cordoba. Inst Hispano-Arabe.

Diccionario Espanol-Arabe de Verbos, Gramatica y Temas de Conversacion. Mufid Al-Guindi Abd Al-Monem. French & Eur.

Dictionaire Des Termes Economiques et Commerciaux: Francais-Arabe. Mustapha Henni. French & Eur.

Dictionaire Detaille des Noms de Vetements Chez Les Arabes. R. Dozy. Intl Bk Ctr.

Dictionaire Francais-Arabe. Louis Saisse. Intl Bk Ctr.

A Dictionary & Glossary of the Koran. John Penrice. (Pub. by Curzon Pr England). Apt Bks.

Dictionary & Glossary of the Koran. John Penrice. Intl Bk Ctr.

Dictionary & Glossary of the Koran. John Penrice. Intl Bk Ctr.

Dictionary & Glossary of the Koran, with Copious Grammatical References & Explanations. John Penrice. Biblio.

Dictionary Arabic-Chinese. French & Eur.

Dictionary Des Terms Economiques et Commerciaux (French-English-Arabic) Mustapha Henni. Intl Bk Ctr.

A Dictionary of Accounting & Finance. Adnan Abdeen. Intl Bk Ctr.

A Dictionary of Agricultural & Allied Terminology. Ahmad Khatib. Intl Bk Ctr.

A Dictionary of Arab Grammatical Terms: The Monitor. Intl Bk Ctr.

Dictionary of Arabic Grammar, in Charts & Tables. Antoine Dahdah. Intl Bk Ctr.

Dictionary of Arabic-Persian Quotes. Claud Field. Intl Bk Ctr.

Dictionary of Arabic-Persian Quotes. Claud Field. Intl Bk Ctr.

A Dictionary of Common Language Errors & their Corrections. Muhammad Al-Adnani. Intl Bk Ctr.

Dictionary of Common Language Errors & Their Corrections: Arabic-Arabic. Muhammad Adnani. Intl Bk Ctr.

A Dictionary of Diplomacy & International Affairs. Samuhi Fouk al-Ada. Intl Bk Ctr.

Dictionary of Economic Business & Finance. Nabih Ghattas. Intl Bk Ctr.

A Dictionary of Economics & Commerce. Ed. by Zacharia Nasr. Macmillan London.

A Dictionary of Economics & Commerce. Mamdouh Hansen. Intl Bk Ctr.

A Dictionary of Economics & Commerce. Ed. by Libr. du Liban. Intl Bk Ctr.

Dictionary of Economics, Business & Finance: English-Arabic with Arabic Glossary. Nabih Ghattas. Intl Bk Ctr.

Dictionary of Folklore: English-Arabic. Younis. Intl Bk Ctr.

Dictionary of Hebrew Verbs. M. Debahy. Intl Bk Ctr.

A Dictionary of Iraqi Arabic. B. Clarity. Intl Bk Ctr.

A Dictionary of Iraqi Arabic: Arabic-English. Ed. by Daniel Woodhead & Wayne Beene. Georgetown U Pr.

Dictionary of Library Science Information & Documentation. Ed. by W. Clason. Elsevier.

A Dictionary of Literary & Linguistic Terms. Magdi Wahba & Kamel Muhandes. Intl Bk Ctr.

A Dictionary of Literary Terms. Compiled by Magdi Wahba. Intl Bk Ctr.

A Dictionary of Modern Iraqi Arabic. Daniel Woodhead. Intl Bk Ctr.

Dictionary of Modern Lebanese Proverbs. Anis Freyha. Intl Bk Ctr.

A Dictionary of Modern Lebanese Proverbs. Anis Freyha. Intl Bk Ctr.

Dictionary of Modern Linguistic Terms (English-Arabic) Intl Bk Ctr.

Dictionary of Modern Linguistic Terms: English-Arabic, Arabic-English. Bakalla. Intl Bk Ctr.

A Dictionary of Modern Political Idiom. Magdi Wahba. Lib Liban.

A Dictionary of Modern Political Idiom: English-French-Arabic. Magdi Wahba & Wagdi R. Ghali. Lib Liban.

A Dictionary of Modern Written Arabic. Hans Wehr. Ed. by J. M. Cowan. Spoken Lang Serv.

Dictionary of Modern Written Arabic. Ed. by J. Milton Cowan. Intl Pubns Serv.

A Dictionary of Modern Written Arabic. Hans Wehr. Ed. by Milton J. Cowan. Spoken Lang Serv.

A Dictionary of Modern Written Arabic. Hans Wehr. Ed. by J. M. Cowan. Harrap.

A Dictionary of Modern Written Arabic. Compiled by Hans Wehr. Intl Bk Ctr.

A Dictionary of Modern Written Arabic. Hans Wehr. Ed. by J. Milton Cowan. Harrassowitz.

A Dictionary of Moroccan Arabic: Moroccan-Arabic English-Moroccan. Ed. by Richard S. Harrell & Harvey Sobelman. Georgetown U Pr.

A Dictionary of Natural Environment. Ahmad Khatib. Intl Bk Ctr.

A Dictionary of Nigerian Arabic. Alan S. Kaye. Undena Pubns.

Dictionary of Non-Classical Vocables in Spoken Arabic. Anis Freyha. Intl Bk Ctr.

Dictionary of Old South Arabic: Sabaen Dialect. Joan C. Biella. Scholars Pr CA.

Dictionary of Persian Loan Words in the Arabic Language. Al-Sayyid Addi. Intl Bk Ctr.

A Dictionary of Persian Loan Words in the Arabic Language. Al-Sayyid'Addi Shir. Intl Bk Ctr.

A Dictionary of Petroleum & the Oil Industry. Ahmad Khatib. Intl Bk Ctr.

A Dictionary of Political Idioms. Ed. by Magdi Wahba & Magdi Ghali. Intl Bk Ctr.

Dictionary of Sufi Technical Terms. Abd A. Razzaqi. Tr. by Nabil Safwat. (Pub. by Octagon Pr England). Ins Study Human.

A Dictionary of Syrian Arabic: English-Arabic. Ed. by Karl Stowasser & Moukhtar Ani. Georgetown U Pr.

A Dictionary of the Names of Towns & Villages in Lebanon. Anis Freyha. Intl Bk Ctr.

A Dictionary of the Natural Environment. F. Monkhouse. Intl Bk Ctr.

A Dictionary of the Social Sciences. Compiled by Zaki Badawi. Intl Bk Ctr.

A Dictionary of the Social Sciences. A. Badawi. Lib Liban.

Dictionary of Theoretical Linguistics (English-Arabic) Arabic-English Glossary. Intl Bk Ctr.

Dictionary of Theoretical Linguistics: English-Arabic with Arabic-English Glossary. Muhammad A. Al-Khuli. Intl Bk Ctr.

Dictionnaire Al-Fara-id Arabe-Francais. P. Belot. Dar El-Machreq.

Dictionnaire Arabe-Francais. Ben Sedira. French & Eur.

Dictionnaire Arabe-Francais. N'Damena Tchad.

Dictionnaire Arabe-Francais. A. B. Kazimirski. Intl Bk Ctr.

Dictionnaire Arabe-Francais-Anglais, 1. Regis Blachere & Moustafa Chouemi. French & Eur.

Dictionnaire Arabe-Francais-Anglais, 2. Regis Blachere & Moustafa Chouemi. French & Eur.

Dictionnaire Arabe-Francais: Dialectes de Syrie. Adrien Barthelemy. Geuthner.

Dictionnaire Arabe-Francais: Langue ecrite. Auguste Cherbonneau. Intl Bk Ctr.

Dictionnaire Arabe Moderne Larousse. Khalil Georr. Larousse.

Dictionnaire de l'Arabe Parle Palestinien. Yohanan Elihai. French & Eur.

Dictionnaire de L'arabe Parte Palestinien: Francais-Arabe. Yohanan Elihai. Klincksieck.

Dictionnaire des Nouveaux Cinemas Arabes. Claude-Michel Cluny. Sindbad.

Dictionnaire des Parlers Arabes de Syrie, Libyan & Palestine. Claude Denizeau. Maison & Larose.

Dictionnaire des Parlers Arabes de Syrie, Liban et Palestine. Claude Denizeau. French & Eur.

Dictionnaire des Sciences de la Nature (Dictionary of the Natural Sciences) Edouard Ghaleb. Intl Pubns Serv.

Dictionnaire des Termes Agricoles: Francais-Arabe. Emir Al-Chihabi. Intl Bk Ctr.

Dictionnaire des termes economiques et commerciaux. Mustapha Henni. Intl Bk Ctr.

Dictionnaire des termes juridiques et commerciaux. Mamdouh Hakki. Intl Bk Ctr.

Dictionnaire des Termes Techniques et Commerciaux. Compiled by Mustapha Henni. INtl Bk Ctr.

Dictionnaire detaille des noms des vetements chez les Arabes. R. Dozy. Intl Bk Ctr.

Dictionnaire Francais-Arabe. M. Naggary-Bey. Verry.

Dictionnaire Francais-Arabe. Ben Sedira. French & Eur.

Dictionnaire Francais-Arabe. Louis Saisse. Intl Bk Ctr.

Dictionnaire Francais-Arabe(Arabe Parle-Arabe Grammatical) E. Gasselin. Verry.

Dictionnaire Juridique. Intl Bk Ctr.

Dictionnaire Moderne Francais-Arabe. French & Eur.

Dictionnaire Pratique des Termes Juridiques: Francais-Arabe. Elle Malka. France Selection.

Dizionario italiano-arabo moderno. Elpidio Jannota. Ist Poligrafico.

Elias Arabic-English Modern Dictionary. Elias. Kazi Pubns.

Elias English-Arabic & Arabic-English Pocket Dictionary. Elias. Kazi Pubns.

Elias' English-Arabic Dictionary. Elias Elias. Intl Bk Ctr.

Elias English-Arabic Modern Dictionary. Elias. Kazi Pubns.

Elias English-Arabic Practical Dictionary of the Arabic of the Middle East. Intl Bk Ctr.

Elias English-Arabic Practical Dictionary of the Colloquial Arabic of the Middle East. Elias Elias. Intl Bk Ctr.

Elias' Pocket Dictionary Arabic-English. M. Elias. French & Eur.

Elias Pocket Dictionary: English, Arabic. E. Elias. French & Eur.

English-Arabic; Arabic-English Dictionary. E. A. Elias. Intl Bk Ctr.

English-Arabic; Arabic-English Dictionary. John Wortabet. Intl Bk Ctr.

English-Arabic, Arabic-English Dictionary. Ed. by J. Wortabet & H. Porter. Ungar.

English-Arabic, Arabic-English Dictionary. A. E. Elias. Intl Bk Ctr.

English-Arabic, Arabic-English Dictionary. John Wortabet. Intl Bk Ctr.

English Arabic, Arabic-English Pocket Dictionary. Ed. by Elias. Colton Bk.

English-Arabic; Arabic-English Pocket Dictionary. John Wortabet. Intl Bk Ctr.

English-Arabic Collegiate Dictionary. Elias. Colton Bk.

English Arabic Conversational Dictionary. Richard Jaschke. Intl Bk Ctr.

English Arabic Conversational Dictionary. R. Jaschke. Iaconi.

English-Arabic Conversational Dictionary, with Supplement. Ed. by Richard Jaschke. Ungar.

English-Arabic Dictionary. F. Steingass. Orient Bk Dist.

English-Arabic Dictionary. Saphrograph.

English-Arabic Dictionary: Al-Manar. Hasan Karmi. Intl Bk Ctr.

English-Arabic Dictionary: Al-Mawrid. Munir Ba'Albaki. Intl Bk Ctr.

English-Arabic Dictionary: Al-Mawrid Al-Waset. Munir Ba'Albaki. Intl Bk Ctr.

English-Arabic Dictionary: Colloquial Arabic of Egypt. Socrates Spiro. Intl Bk Ctr.

English-Arabic Dictionary for Accounting & Finance. Adnan Abdeen. (Pub. by Wiley-Interscience). Wiley.

English-Arabic Dictionary of Diplomacy & Related Terminology. Gamal Barakat. Intl Bk Ctr.

An English-Arabic Dictionary of the Colloquial Arabic of Egypt. Socrates Spiro. Intl Bk Ctr.

English-Arabic Dictionary, Romanized. Edward Elias. Shalom.

English-Arabic Learner's Dictionary. F. Steingass. Intl Bk Ctr.

An English-Arabic Lexicon. George Percy Badger. Intl Bk Ctr.

English-Arabic Medical Dictionary. Yusuf K. Hitti. Intl Bk Ctr.

English-Arabic Pocket Dictionary. John Wortabet. Intl Bk Ctr.

English-Arabic Pocket Dictionary. Intl Bk Ctr.

English-Arabic Pocket Dictionary: Al-Mawrid Al Quareb. Munir Ba'Alabki.

English-Arabic Pocket Dictionary: Al Mawrid. Munir Ba'Albaki. Intl Bk Ctr.

An English-Arabic Readers' Dictionary. John Abcarius. Intl Bk Ctr.

English-Arabic Student Dictionary: Al-Muyassar. Munir Ba'Albaki. Intl Bk Ctr.

English-Arabic Student Dictionary: Dar el Mashreq. Intl Bk Ctr.

English-Arabic Vocabulary. Merrill Van Wagoner. Intl Bk Ctr.

English-Arabic Vocabulary: Students Pronouncing Dictionary. Merrill Y. Van Wagoner et al. Spoken Lang Serv.

An English-Colloquial Arabic Dictionary. Raja Nasr. Intl Bk Ctr.

English-French-Arabic Trilingual Dictionary. Jerwan Sabek. Intl Bk Ctr.

First Picture Dictionary - English-Arabic. Intl Bk Ctr.

Glosario de voces Ibericas y Latinas. Francisco J. Simonet. Intl Bk Ctr.

Glosario Espanol-Arabe. Fernando Valderrama Martinez. Albir.

Glosario Espanol-Arabe y Arabe-Espanol. Fernando Valderrama Martinez. Albir.

Glossaire des mots Espagnols derives de l'Arabe. R. Dozy. Intl Bk Ctr.

Glossaire des Mots Espagnols et Portugais Derives De L'arabe. R. Dozy. Intl Bk Ctr.

Glossary of Conference Terms: Arabic, French, English. (UNESCO). Unipub.

Glossary of Conference Terms, English, French, Arabic. (UNESCO). Unipub.

Glossary of Conference Terms: English, French, Arabic. (UNESCO). Unipub.

Handworterbuch der Neu-Arabischen und Deutschen Sprache. Adolf Wahrmund. Verry.

Handworterbuch der neu Arabischen und Deutschen Sprache. Adolf Wahrmund. Intl Bk Ctr.

The Hebrew-Arabic Dictionary of the Bible, Known As Kitab Jami al-Alfaz (Agron) David Ben Abraham. Ed. by Solomon L. Skoss. AMS Pr.

Hebrew-Arabic Dictionary of the Bible Known As Kitab Jami-Al-Alfaz. Ed. by Solomon Skoss. Elliots Bks.

Hitti's English-Arabic Medical Dictionary. Yusuf K. Hitti. (Am U Beirut). Syracuse U Pr.

Iron & Steel Industry Dictionary. A. M. Abd-El-Wahed. French & Eur.

Kitab al-Ta Rifat (Book of Definitions) Arabic-Arabic Dictionary. Al Sharif Jurjani. Intl Bk Ctr.

Kitab Al-Ta'rifat: Book of Definitions. Al-Sharif Al-Juriani. Intl Bk Ctr.

Kurdish-Arabic Dictionary: Al-Hadiyati 'l-Hamidiyah. M. Mokri. Intl Bk Ctr.

Langenscheidts Taschenwoerterbuch Arabisch: Teil II, Deutsch-Arabisch. K. Schukry & R. Humberdrotz. Langenscheidt.

Langenscheidts Taschenwoerterbuecher Arabisch-Deutsch. Georg Krolkoff. Langenscheidt.

Langenscheidts Taschenwoerterbuecher Deutsch-Arabisch. K. Schukry. Langenscheidt.

Larousse Arab Dictionary. Intl Bk Ctr.

Law Dictionary (Arabic-English) Harith Faruqi. Intl Bk Ctr.

Law Dictionary (English-Arabic) Ibrahim Al-Wahab. Intl Bk Ctr.

Law Dictionary French-Arabic: Dictionnaire Juridique. Najjar. Intl Bk Ctr.

Learn Arabic for English Speakers. Saphrograph.

A Learner's Arabic-English Dictionary. F. Steingass. South Asia Bks.

A Learner's Arabic-English Dictionary. F. Steingass. Intl Bk Ctr.

A Learner's English-Arabic Dictionary. F. Steingass. Intl Bk Ctr.

Lexicon Arabico-Latinum. George W. Freytag. Intl Bk Ctr.

Lexicon Arabico-Latinum. George W. Freytag. Intl Bk Ctr.

Lexique des Parlers Arabes-Tchado-Soudanais. Arlette Roth-Laly. Editions du CNRS.

Lexique des Parlers Arabes-Tchado-Soudanais: K-Y. Arlette Roth-Laly. CNRS.

Lexique des Parlers Arabes-Tchado-Soudanais. Arlette Roth-Laly. CNRS.

Lexique des Parlers Arabes-Tchado-Soudanais. Arlette Roth-Laly. CNRS.

Lexique des Parlers Arabes-Tchado-Soudanais, 3. Arlette Roth-Laly. CNRS.

Lexique Francais-Arabe de la Protection Civile & du Secourisme. France Selection.

Lexique Pratique Francais-Arabe. Jacques Jomier & Institut Francais D'Archeologie Orientale. Francais, Inst. Archeo. Orient.

Machine Tools Dictionary: English-French-German-Arabic. A. M. Abd-El-Wahed. French & Eur.

Management Glossary: (English-Arabic) H. Johannsen. Intl Bk Ctr.

Melanges: Tables generales (1954-1977) Ed. by Institut Dominicain d'Etudes Orientales du Caire. Intl Bk Ctr.

Metal Forming Dictionary. A. M. Abd-El-Wahed. French & Eur.

Modern Arab Dictionary. Larousse.

Modern Arab Dictionary. Pan Amer Pub.

Modern Arabic-English Dictionary. Elias Elias. Intl Bk Ctr.

A Modern English-Arabic Dictionary. Munir Ba'Albaki. Intl Bk Ctr.

Muhit al-Muhit. Butros Bustani. Intl Bk Ctr.

Munjid al Tulab. Dar el Mashreq. Intl Bk Ctr.

Munjid fi al Lugha wal A'Alam. Intl Bk Ctr.

My Illustrated Dictionary: Arabic & Fr. Libr du Liban. Intl Bk Ctr.

My Illustrated Dictionary: Arabic & Ger. Librairie du Liban. Intl Bk Ctr.

My Illustrated Dictionary: Arabic & Ital. Libr du Liban. Intl Bk Ctr.

My Illustrated Dictionary: Arabic & Span. Libr du Liban. Intl Bk Ctr.

My Illustrated Dictionary: Arabic Eng. Libr du Liban. Intl Bk Ctr.

Naj'ati Ur-Ra'id wa-Shar'Atu al-Warid fi al-Mutaradifi wa al-Mu tawarid. Ibrahim Al-Yaziji. Intl Bk Ctr.

A New Dictionary of Petroleum & the Oil Industry. Ahmad S. Al-Khatib. Lib Liban.

A New Dictionary of Scientific & Technical Terms. Ahmad Khatib. Intl Bk Ctr.

The New Medical-Pharmaceutical Dictionary. A. M. Oweida. French & Eur.

Oxford English-Arabic Dictionary of Current Usage. Ed. by N. S. Doniach. Oxford U Pr.

Plastic Technology Dictionary. H. Y. El-Desouti. French & Eur.

The Police Dictionary. Shafiq Ismat. Intl Bk Ctr.

Police Dictionary: English-Arabic Dictionary. Shafiq Ismat. Intl Bk Ctr.

Qutr Al-Muhit. Butros Al-Bustani. Intl Bk Ctr.

Radio & Television Dictionary. Abd-El-Wahed. French & Eur.

Refrigeration & Conditioning Dictionary. Abd-El-Wahed. French & Eur.

Russian-Arabic Dictionary. French & Eur.

Russko-Arabskii Meditsinskii Slovar. G. T. Arslanian et al. (Pub. by Russkii Iazyk). Four Continent.

Russko-Arabskii Uchebnyi Slovar. G. Sh. Sharbatov. (Pub. by Russki Iazyk). Four Continent.

A Sample Lexicon of Pan-Arabic. Ernest T. Abdel-Massih. Ctr for NE & North African Stud.

Say It in Arabic. Farouk El-Baz. Gannon.

Student Arabic-English Dictionary. Dar el Mashreq. Intl Bk Ctr.

Supplement Aux Dictionnaire Arabe (Arabic-French) R. Dozy. Intl Bk Ctr.

Supplement aux dictionnaires Arabes. R. Dozy. Intl Bk Ctr.

Syntax of Urban Hijazi Arabic. Mahmoud Sieny. Intl Bk Ctr.

Technical Arabic. Vernon Daykin. (Pub. by Lund Humphries England). State Mutual Bk.

Technical Dictionary: Archtiecture & Building. Tawfik Abd-El-Gawad. (Pub. by Collets). State Mutual Bk.

Technical Dictionary: Refrigeration & Air Conditioning. (Pub. by Collets). State Mutual Bk.

Technical Dictionary: The Textile Industry. (Pub. by Collets). State Mutual Bk.

Textile Industry Dictionary. Ed. by A. M. Sabrie & R. S. Scharaf et al. French & Eur.

Two Hundred One Persian Verbs - Arabic Script. Wood. Barron.

Vest Pocket Arabic. Institute for Language Study. Illus. by Winston Roeth. (BN). B&N NY.

Vocabulaire d'Arabe Moderne: Economie-Politique-Actualite. J. Schmidt. Maison Dictionnaire.

Vocabulaire d'Arabe moderne: Economie-Politique-Actualite. J. Schmidt. Maison Dictionnaire.

Vocabulaire des Conferences: Francais-Anglais-Arabe: Francais-Anglais-Arabe. Unesco.

Vocabulaire Francais-Arabe de l'ingenieur & du Technicien, 1. J. J. Schmidt. Maisonneuve & Larose.

Wafayat al-a yan: Ibn Khallikan's Biographical Dictionary. Tr. by Mac Guckin De Slane. from Arabic Intl Bk Ctr.

Woerterbuch der Klassischen Arabischen: Bd 1. Joerg Kroemer et al. Ed. by Manfred Ullman. Harrassowitz.

Woerterbuch der Klassischen Arabischen: Bd 1, Lfg 7. Manfred Ullmann & Anton Spitaler. Harrassowitz.

Woerterbuch der Klassischen Arabischen Sprache: Bd 1, Lfg 1. Anton Spitaler et al. Harrassowitz.

Woerterbuch der Klassischen Arabischen Sprache: Bd 1, Lfg 2. Joerg Kraemer et al. Harrassowitz.

Woerterbuch der Klassischen Arabischen Sprache: Bd 1, Lfg 3. Manfred Ullmann & Anton Spitaler. Harrassowitz.

Woerterbuch der Klassischen Arabischen Sprache: Bd 1, Lfg 4. Manfred Ullmann & Anton Spitaler. Harrassowitz.

Woerterbuch der Klassischen Arabischen Sprache: Bd 1, Lfg 5. Manfred Ullmann & Anton Spitaler. Harrassowitz.

Woerterbuch der Klassischen Arabischen Sprache: Bd 1, Lfg 6. Manfred Ullmann & Anton Spitaler. Harrassowitz.

Woerterbuch der Klassischen Arabischen Sprache: Bd 1, Lfg 8. Manfred Ullmann & Anton Spitaler. Harrassowitz.

Woerterbuch der Klassischen Arabischen Sprache: Bd 1, Lfg 9-10. Manfred Ullmann & Anton Spitaler. Harrassowitz.

Woerterbuch der Klassischen Arabischen Sprache: Bd 2, Lfg 1. Manfred Ullmann. Harrassowitz.

Woerterbuch der Klassischen Arabischen Sprache: Bd 2, Lfg 2. Manfred Ullmann & Rotraud Wojtowytsch-Wielandt. Harrassowitz.

Woerterbuch der Klassischen Arabischen Sprache: Bd 2, Lfg 4. Manfred Ullmann. Harrassowitz.

A Word Count of Modern Arabic Prose. Jacob Landau. Intl Bk Ctr.

Wortabet's Pocket English-Arabic Dictionary. John Wortabet & Harvey Porter. Intl Bk Ctr.

ARAMAIC

A Concise Hebrew & Aramaic Lexicon of the Old Testament. William L. Holladay. Eerdmans.

Hebrew & Aramaic Dictionary of the Old Testament. Ed. by Georg Fohrer et al. Tr. by W. A. Johnstone. from Ger De Gruyter.

Hebrew-Aramaic-English Dictionary, a Dictionary of Talmud Babli & Talmud Yerushalmi Targum & Midrash. Marcus Jastrow. Shalom.

Lexicon Chaldaicum Talmudicum & Rabbinicum. Johann Buxtorf. Olms Verlag.

Lexicon in Veteris Testamenti Libros: Hebrew-Aramaic Lexicon, Incl. Supplement. Ludwig Koehler & Walter Baumgartner. Eerdmans.

ARMENIAN

Anglo-Armianskii Shkolnyi Slovar. Yerevan. (Pub. by Luys). Four Continent.
Armenian-English - English-Armenian Dictionary. M. Koushakdjian. Heinman.
Armenian-English Dictionary. Mathias Bedrossian. Intl Bk Ctr.
Armenisch-Deutsches Woerterbuch. Froundiian-Dirair. (Pub. by Oldenbourg). French & Eur.
Armenisch-Deutsches Woerterbuch. Froundiian-Dirair. Oldenbourg Verlag.
Dictionnaire Armenien-Francais. Ambroise Calfa. French & Eur.
Dictionnaire Armenien-Francais. Ambroise Calfa. Klincksieck.
English-Armenian, Armenian English Dictionary. A. H. Yacobian. Shalom.
New Dictionary of Armenian-English. Matthias Bedrossian. Intl Bk Ctr.
Pekhleviisko-Persidsko-Armiano-Russko-Angliiskii Slovar. R. Abrahamian. (Pub. by Mitk). Four Continent.
Russko-Armianskii Frazeologicheskii Slovar. (Pub. by Gos. Un-Tet). Four Continent.
Russko-Armianskii Politekhnicheskii Slovar. R. T. Ashkharumov et al. (Pub. by An Arm SSR). Four Continent.
Russko-Armianskii Slovar. A. S. Garibian. (Pub. by Hayastan). Four Continent.
Russko-Armianskii Slovar. A. Garibian. (Pub. by Hayastan). Four Continent.
Russko-Armianskii Tolkovyi Slovar. V. Z. Grigorian et al. (Pub. by An Arm SSR). Four Continent.

ASSYRIAN

The Assyrian Dictionary of the Oriental Institute of the University of Chicago. Ed. by A. Leo Oppenheim. Oriental Inst.
The Assyrian Dictionary of the Oriental Institute of the University of Chicago. Ed. by A. Leo Oppenheim. Oriental Inst.
Assyrian Dictionary of the Oriental Institute of the University of Chicago. Ed. by A. Leo Oppenheim & Erica Reiner. Incl. Oriental Inst.
The Assyrian Dictionary of the Oriental Institute of the University of Chicago. Ed. by A. Leo Oppenheim & Erica Reiner. Oriental Inst.
The Assyrian Dictionary of the Oriental Institute of the University of Chicago. Ed. by A. Leo Oppenheim et al. Oriental Inst.
A Concise Dictionary of the Assyrian Languages. William Muss-Arnolt. AMS Pr.
A Dictionary of Assyrian Botany. Reginald C. Thompson. AMS Pr.
A Dictionary of Assyrian Chemistry & Geology. Reginald C. Thompson. AMS Pr.

ATAYAL

Atayal-English Dictionary. Soren Egerod. (Pub. by Curzon Pr England). Humanities.

AZERBAIJANI

Russko-Azerbaidzhanskii Slovar. (Pub. by Elm). Four Continent.
Slovar Terminov PoElektroprovodu & Avtomatizatsii Promyshlennykh Ustanovo. (Pub. by Izd. An Az. SSR). Four Continent.

AZTEC

Diccionario de la Lengua Nahuatl. Cesar Macazaga Ordono. Innovacion.
Diccionario de la Lengua Nahuatl o Mexicana. Remi Simeon. Siglo Veintiuno.

BAHASA

A Dictionary of English Bahasa Malaysia Idiomatic Phrases. A. Karim & T. Lucy. Jaya Ciencia.

BAHNAR

Bahnar Dictionary. John Banker et al. Summer Inst Ling.

BAMBARA

Petit Dictionnaire-Bambara-Francais Francais-Bambara. Charles Bailleul. (Pub. by Avebury England). Humanities.

BANDA

Dictionnaire Banda-Francais. C. Tisserant. Institut Ethnologie.

BANGALA

English-Lingala Manual. John D. Odhner. U Pr of Amer.

BASHKIR

Russko-Bashkirskii Slovar. G. R. Karimova. (Pub. by GINS). Four Continent.

BASQUE

Basque-Spanish Dictionary. Issac M. Lopez. Revisionist Pr.
Dictionnaire Basque Francais. Pierre Lhande. French & Eur.
English-Basque Dictionary. Joe V. Eiguren. L Fereday Schol.
Euskal Histegi Modernoa. Xabier Kintana. Cinsa Coord.
Euskal Histegi Modernoa. Ed. by Xabier Kintana et al. Coord Iniciat.
La Lengua Vasca. Isaac Lopez Mendizabal. Aunamendi Edit.
La Lengua Vasca: Gramatica, Conversacion, Diccionario Vasco-Castellano, Castellano-Vasco. Isaac Lopez Mendizabal. Aunamendi Edit.
Natur Zientziak. Aranzazu.

BENGALI

Bengali-English Dictionary. Saphrograph.
Bengal'sko-Russkii Slovar. E. M. Bykova et al. (Pub. by Gosizdat Inostr. Natsion. Slovarei). Four Continent.
English-Bengali Dictionary. Saphrograph.
Glossary of Agricultural Terms, English-Bengali. Jack A. Dabbs. Dabbs.
Karmannyi Bengal'sko-Russkii Slovar. D. Litton. (Pub. by Gosizdat Natsional Slovarei). Four Continent.
Learn Bengali: For English Speakers. Saphrograph.
Russko-Bengal'skii Slovar. Litton. (Pub. by Sov. Entsiklopediia). Four Continent.
Short Bengali-English, English-Bengali Dictionary. Jack A. Dabbs. Dabbs.

BERBER

A Computerized Lexicon of Tamazight: Berber Dialect of Ayt Seghrouchen. Ernest T. Abdel-Massih. Ctr for NE & North African Stud.

BINANDERE

A Grammar & Dictionary of the Binandere Language, Mamba River. ..Papua. Copland King. Bd. with AMS Pr.

BISLAMA

A Descriptive Dictionary: Bislama to English. William G. Camden. Camden Aus.

BLACKFOOT

A Blackfoot-English Vocabulary. Christianus C. Uhlenbeck & R. H. Van Gulik. AMS Pr.
An English-Blackfoot Vocabulary. Christianus C. Uhlenbeck & R. H. Van Gulik. AMS Pr.

BOHEMIAN

Masarykuv Slovnik Naucny. Pergamon.

BRETON

Dictionnaire Breton-Francais, Francais-Breton. French & Eur.

BULGARIAN

Bolgarsko-Russkii Voennyi Slovar. M. G. Artiukhov et al. (Pub. bu Voenizdat). Four Continent.
Bulgarialais-Suomalainen Sanakirja. Boris Parashkevov et al. Gaudeamus.
Bulgarian-English Dictionary. R. Russev. Saphrograph.
Bulgarian-English Dictionary. Ed. by Rusi Russev. Ungar.
Bulgarian-English Dictionary. T. Atnassova et al. French & Eur.
Bulgarian-English Dictionary. T. Atanassova et al. (Pub. by Collets). State Mutual Bk.
Bulgarian-Hindi Dictionary. B. Kanti Varma. French & Eur.
Bulgarian-Russian Dictionary (M-9095) French & Eur.
Dictionnaire Bulgare-Francais. L. Stephanova et al. French & Eur.
Dizionario Italiano-Bulgaro. M. Cavaletto et al. French & Eur.
English-Bulgarian Concise Technical Dictionary. A. Desov. Heinman.
English-Bulgarian Dictionary. Ivanka Harlakova & Elena Stankova. (Pub. by Collets). State Mutual Bk.
Karmannyi Bolgarsko-Russkii Slovar. M. A. Leonidova. (Pub. by Gosizdat Inostr. & Natsional). Four Continent.
Karmannyi Russko-Bolgarskii Slovar. (Pub. by Russkii Iazyk). Four Continent.
Karmannyi Russko-Bolgarskii Slovar. M. A. Leonidova. Four Continent.
Kratkii Terminologicheskii Spravochnik po Ekonomike Geologorazvedochnykh Rabot. Wydawnictwa.
Langenscheidts Universal-Woerterbuch Bulgarisch. Langenscheidt.
Langenscheidts Universal-Woerterbuecher Bulgarisch-Deutsch. Langenscheidt.
Landwirtschaftliches Woerterbuch in Acht Sprachen. (Pub. by BLV). French & Eur.
Latin-Bulgarian Dictionary. M. Voinov. French & Eur.
Magyar-Bolgar Szotar. Jozsef Bodey. Terra.
Magyar-Bolgar Szotar. Jozsef Bodey. Terra.
Russian-Bulgarian Dictionary. Leonidova. French & Eur.
Russian-Bulgarian Phraseological Dictionary. K. Andreichina et al. Ed. by Vlasova. French & Eur.
Russko-Bolgarskii Slovar. S. K. Chukalov. (Pub. by Sov. Entsiklopediia). Four Continent.
Technical Automotive Dictionary: Russian-English-German-French-Bulgarian. G. Sikora. French & Eur.
Textile Dictionary. G. Velco. (Pub. by Collets). State Mutual Bk.

BURMESE

Karmannyi Russko-Birmanskii Slovar. U Chin Vei et al. (Pub. by GINS). Four Continent.
Russsko-Birmanskii Slovar. N. N. Novikov et al. (Pub. by Sov. Entsiklopediia). Four Continent.
Woerterbuch Burmesisch-Deutsch. Annemarie Esche. VEB Verlag Enzyklopadie.

CAMBODIAN

Cambodian English. Franklin E. Huffman. Yale U Pr.
Cambodian-English Dictionary. Robert K. Headley. Cath U Pr.
Cambodian-English Dictionary. R. Headley. Iaconi.
Cambodian-English, English-Cambodian Dictionary. Iaconi.
Concise Cambodian-English Dictionary. J. Jacob. Iaconi.
English-Khmer Phrasebook with Useful Word List: For Cambodians. Tr. by Samnang Soeur. Ctr Appl Ling.

CANTONESE

Practical English-Cantonese Dictionary. Chiang Ker-Chiu. Colton Bk.

CARIB

Lexico Caribe en el Caribe Negro de Honduras Britanica. Micolas De Castillo Mathieu. Instituto Caro & Cuervo.

CASTILIAN

Diccionari Castella-Catala, Catala-Castella, Mitja. Santiago Alberti. French & Eur.
Diccionari Kechwa-Castellano. Cesar Guardia Mayarga. Studium.
Diccionari Manual Castella-Catala. Miguel Arimany Coma. French & Eur.
Diccionari Manual Catala-Castella. Miguel Arimany Coma. French & Eur.
Diccionari Manual Catala-Castella i Castella-Catala. Miguel Arimany Coma. French & Eur.
Diccionari Practic Castella-Catala, Catala-Castella. Miguel Arimany Coma. French & Eur.
Diccionari Usual Catala-Castella i Castella-Catala. Miguel Arimany Coma. French & Eur.
Diccionario Castella-Catala, Catala-Castella Petit. Santiago Alberti. French & Eur.
Diccionario Castella-Catala, Catala-Castella Gran. Santiago Alberti. French & Eur.
Diccionario Castellano-Vasco. Placido Mugika. French & Eur.
Diccionario Vasco-Castellano. Isaak Lopez Mendizabal. French & Eur.

Diccionario Vasco-Castellano, Castellano-Vasco De Voces Comunes a Dos O Mas Dialectos Del Euskera. Buenaventura de Oyeregui. French & Eur.
Nuevo Diccionario Castellano-Hebreo. Juan Ducach. Massada Pr.

CATALAN

Brei Diccionari Ideologic: Amb Vocabulari Catala-Castella & Castella-Catala. Xavier Romeu. Edit Teide.
Brew Vocabulari Catala-Castella-Angles de Comerc Exterior. French & Eur.
Canigo Diccionari Castella-Catala, Catala-Castella. French & Eur.
Diccionari Basic Catala-Castella, Castella-Catala. Miguel Arimany Coma. French & Eur.
Diccionari Catala-Castella I Castella-Catala. Fransesc de B. Moll Casanovas. French & Eur.
Canigo: Diccionari Catalan-Castellano, Castellano-Catalan. Pere Elies I Busqueta. Sopena.
Diccionari Castella-Catala, Catala-Castella, Mitja. Santiago Alberti. French & Eur.
Diccionari Castella-Catala, Catala-Castella Petit. Santiago Alberti. Alberti.
Diccionari Catala-Castella. Francisco de Moll Y Cassanovas. Moll Edit.
Diccionari Catala-Castella, Castella-Catala. Josep Miracle. Poseidon SA.
Diccionari Catala de Sinonims. Albert Jane. French & Eur.
Diccionari Catala-Frances, Frances-Catala. Carlos Castellanos i Llorenc. Encic Catalan.
Diccionari Catala General Usual. Miguel Arimany Coma. French & Eur.
Diccionari De la Llengua Catalan. Santiago Alberti. French & Eur.
Diccionari De Sinonims I Antonims. Santiago Pey Estrany. French & Eur.
Diccionari De Sinonims. Manuel Franquesa. French & Eur.
Diccionari del Nacionalisme. Imma Tubella. French & Eur.
Diccionari d'Electronica. Luis Marquet. French & Eur.
Diccionari Escolar Catala Arimany. Miguel Arimany Coma. French & Eur.
Diccionari Fondamental de la Llengua Catalana. Vox. Prologue by Jordi Gali I Herrera. Biblo Sp.
Diccionari Fondamental de la Llengua Catalana. Biblograf SP.
Diccionari General de la Llengua Catalana. Pompeu Fabra. Edhasa.
Diccionari I Catala-Valencia-Balear. Antoni M. Alcover & Francesc de B. Moll. French & Eur.
Diccionari Ingles-Catala, Catala-Ingles. Jordi Colomer del Castillo. French & Eur.
Diccionari Manual Castella-Catala. Miguel Arimany Coma. French & Eur.
Diccionari Manual Castella-Catala, Catala-Castella. Vox. Biblo Sp.
Diccionari Manual Castella-Catala Catala-Castella. Camilo J. Cela & Badia A. M. Margarit. Biblograf SP.
Diccionari Manual Catala-Castella. Miguel Arimany Coma. French & Eur.
Diccionari Manual Catala-Castella i Castella-Catala. Miguel Arimany Coma. French & Eur.
Diccionari Manual de la Llengua Catalana. Josep Miracle Montserrat. French & Eur.

Diccionari Manual de Sinonims. Salvador Espiru. Biblograf SP.
Diccionari Ortografic. Joan Triadu. Biblograf SP.
Diccionari Pera Ociosos. Joan Fuster Ortells. French & Eur.
Diccionari Politic De Catalunya. Victor Lluelles Cardona. French & Eur.
Diccionari Practic Castella-Catala, Catala-Castella. Miguel Arimany Coma. French & Eur.
Diccionari Practic Catala-Frances. Miguel Arimany Coma. French & Eur.
Diccionari Practic de Sinonims Catalans: Mots i Frases. French & Eur.
Diccionari Usual Catala-Castella i Castella-Catala. Miguel Arimany Coma. French & Eur.
Diccionari Usual de Sinonims Catalans: Mots i Frases. Joana Raspall de Cauhe et al. French & Eur.
Diccionario Castella-Catala, Catala-Castella Petit. Santiago Alberti. French & Eur.
Diccionario Castella-Catala, Catala-Castella Gran. Santiago Alberti. French & Eur.
Diccionario Catala-Frances, Frances-Catala. Carles Castellanos Llorenc & Rafael Castellanos Llorenc. French & Eur.
Diccionario de Banca & Borsa: Catala-Castella-Diccionario de Banca & Bolsa. Banca Mas Sarda, Servicio de Estudios. Alba.
Diccionario De L'art I Els Oficis De la Construccion. Miguel Fullana Llompart. French & Eur.
Diccionario General de la Lengua Catalana. Pompeu Fabra Poch. French & Eur.
Diccionario Magico Infantil En Seis Lenguas. Eulalia Goma. French & Eur.
Diccionario Simultaneo en 21 Idiomas. Juan Capdevilla Font. French & Eur.
Nou Diccionari de la Llengua Catalana. J. B. Xuriguera. French & Eur.
Nuevo Glosario, Diccionario Poliglota de la Arquitectura. Buenaventura Bassegoda Muste. French & Eur.
Vocabulari Castella-Catala. Eduard Artells. French & Eur.
Vocabulari Castella-Valencia & Valencia-Castella. Francesc Ferrer-Pastor. Estel Edit.
Vocabulari Catala-Castella. Eduard Artells. French & Eur.
Vocabulari Catala De Matematica Basica. Claudi Alsina. French & Eur.
Vocabularis Tematics. Antoni Lllllull Marti. Organismos Ofic.
Vocabulary or Phrase Book of the Mutsun Language of Alta California. Felipe Arroyo De La Cuesta. AMS Pr.
Vox--Diccionari Manual Ortografic. French & Eur.
Vox--Vocabulari Basic Infantil i d'Adults. French & Eur.
Vox-Diccionari Manual de Sinonims. French & Eur.

CELTIC

An Etymological Dictionary of the Norn Language in Shetland. Jakob Jakobsen. AMS Pr.

CHALDEE

Hebrew & Chaldee Lexicon: Keyed to Strong's Exhaustive Concordance. Wilhelm Gesenius. Tr. by Samuel P. Tregelles. Baker Bk.
Hebrew & Chaldee Lexicon, Tregelles Translation. William Gesenius. Eerdmans.

CHAMORRO

Chamorro-English Dictionary. Donald M. Topping et al. UH Pr.
Spoken Chamorro: With Gramatical Notes & Glossary. Donald Topping. UH Pr.

CHEYENNE

English-Cheyenne Dictionary: A Dictionary of the Cheyenne Language. MT Coun Indian.

CHINESE

The Advanced Learner's Dictionary of Current English with Chinese Translation. A. S. Hornby et al. Imported Bks.
The Advanced Learner's Dictionary of Current English with Chinese Translation. Hornby. Iaconi.
Analytic Dictionary of Chinese & Sino-Japanese. Bernhard Karlgren. Peter Smith.
Analytical Dictionary of Chinese & Sino-Japenese. Bernhard Karlgren. Dover.
Basic Chinese-Korean Character Dictionary. Hyogmyou Kwon. Harrassowitz.
The Basic English-Chinese, Chinese-English Dictionary with PINYIN Transliteration. Ed. by Peter Bergman. Humanities.
The Basic English-Chinese, Chinese-English Dictionary. Compiled by Peter M. Bergman. (Sig). NAL.
The Basic English-Chinese, Chinese-English Dictionary. Peter Bergman. Imported Bks.
A Beginner's Chinese English Dictionary of the National Language (Gwpyeu) W. Simon. (Pub. by Lund Humphries England). State Mutual Bk.
Beginners Dictionary of Chinese-Japanese Characters. Arthur Rose-Innes. Peter Smith.
Beginner's Dictionary of Chinese-Japanese Characters. Arthur Rose-Innes. Dover.
Beginners' Dictionary of Chinese-Japanese Characters & Compounds. Arthur Rose-Innes. Dover.
Bibliotheca Sinica, dictionnaire bibliographique des ouvrages relatifs a l'Empire chinois. Henri Cordier. B Franklin.
Cantonese Dictionary: Cantonese-English, English-Cantonese. Parker P. Huang. Yale U Pr.
Cantonese Dictionary: Cantonese-English, English-Cantonese. Parker Po-fei Huang. Yale U Pr.
The Cantonese Speaker's Dictionary. Roy T. Cowles. Paragon.
Caribbean Cookery. P. De Brissiere. Saphrograph.
China Beginner's Traveler's Dictionary. Richard L. Kimball. China Bks.
China Traveler's Phrasebook. Bennett Lee & Geremie Barme. China Bks.
Chinese Characters. Leon Wieger. Tr. by L. Davrout. Paragon.

Chinese Characters, Their Origin, Etymology, History, Classification & Signification. L. Wieger. Tr. by L. Davrout. Dover.

Chinese Dictionaries: An Extensive Bibliography of Dictionaries in Chinese & Other Languages. Ed. by Chinese-English Translation Assistance Group. Greenwood.

Chinese Dictionary: Cantonese Dialect. Ernes J. Eitel. Ayer Co.

Chinese-English & English-Chinese Astronomical Dictionary. Ed. by Hong-Yee Chiu. (Consultants). Plenum Pub.

Chinese-English Dictionary. Samuel W. Williams. Ayer Co.

The Chinese-English Dictionary. French & Eur.

Chinese-English Dictionary. Ungar.

Chinese-English Dictionary. (Pub. by Collets). State Mutual Bk.

Chinese-English Dictionary: Hakka-Dialect. D. MacIver. Oriental Bk Store.

A Chinese-English Dictionary of China's Rural Economy. (CAB). Unipub.

A Chinese-English Dictionary of Communist Chinese Terminology. Dennis Doolin & Charles Ridley. Hoover Inst Pr.

Chinese-English Dictionary of Contemporary Usage. Ed. by Chi Wen-Shun. U of Cal Pr.

Chinese-English Dictionary of Current Affairs. French & Eur.

Chinese-English Dictionary of Military Terms. French & Eur.

Chinese-English Dictionary of Military Technical Terms. S.N.

Chinese-English Dictionary: Taiwan Dialect. K. T. Tan. Oriental Bk Store.

Chinese-English, English-Chinese Dictionary. Heinman.

Chinese-English Expressions for Travellers. Ungar.

A Chinese-English Glossary of the Mathematical Sciences. Compiled by J. De Francis. Am Math.

Chinese-English Idioms & Phrases. S. M. Season. French & Eur.

Chinese-English-Japanese Glossary of Chemical Terms. T. Shiratori. French & Eur.

Chinese-English-Japanese Glossary of Chemical Terms. S. Tamura & F. Shiratori. French & Eur.

Chinese-English Phrase Book for Travellers. John S. Montanaro. (Pub. by Wiley Pr). Wiley.

Chinese Idioms, English Idioms, English Synonyms Practical Dictionary. S. S. Wei. Heinman.

Chinese Medical Terminology: English to Chinese. F. Liu & L. Yan Mau. French & Eur.

Chinese Pocket Dictionary. Heinman.

Chinese-Russian Phonetic Dictionary. French & Eur.

The Chinese Unicorn & Other Conceits from a Chinese Dictionary. Ed. by Robert Gilkey. Noname Pr.

Chinesisch-Deutsches Woerterbuch. Werner Rudenberg. De Gruyter.

Chinesisch-Deutsches Woerterbuch. Martin Piasek. (Pub. by Max Heuber). French & Eur.

Chinesisch-Deutsches Woerterbuch. Martin Piasek. Hueber.

Chinesisch-Koreanisch-Deutsch Woerterbuch. Andre Eckardt. Groos Verlag.

A Companion Volume to R. H. Mathews' Chinese-English Dictionary. Olov B. Anderson. Curzon Pr.

A Compilation of Chinese Dictionaries. J. Mathias & Sandra Hixson. Far Eastern Pubns.

Concise Chinese - English Dictionary Romanized. James C. Quo. C E Tuttle.

Concise Chinese-English Dictionary, Romanized. James C. Quo. C E Tuttle.

Concise Chinese-English Dictionary Romanized. James Quo. Iaconi.

Concise Chinese-English Dictionary. James C. Quo. C E Tuttle.

Concise English-Chinese Dictionary. Shau Wing Chan. Stanford U Pr.

A Concise English-Chinese Dictionary. French & Eur.

Concise English-Chinese Dictionary, Romanized. James C. Quo. Imported Bks.

Concise English-Chinese Dictionary Romanized. James Quo. Iaconi.

A Concordance to Five Systems of Transcription for Standard Chinese. Olov B. Anderson. (Pub. by Curzon Pr England). Apt Bks.

Deutsch-Chinesisches Handworterbuch. French & Eur.

Deutsch-Chinesisches Standard Handworterbuch. French & Eur.

Diccionario Abreviado Espanol-Chino. French & Eur.

Diccionario del Budo: Artes Marciales. Raymond Thomas. French & Eur.

Diccionario Espanol de la Lengua China. Fernando Mateos et al. French & Eur.

Dictionary Arabic-Chinese. French & Eur.

Dictionary Industrial Chemistry: English-Chinese. French & Eur.

Dictionary Korean-Chinese. French & Eur.

Dictionary of Aerodynamics. French & Eur.

A Dictionary of American Idioms in Chinese. Adam Makkai. Ed. by Gates & Boatner. Barron.

Dictionary of Astronomy. French & Eur.

Dictionary of China's Rural Economy. K. Broadbent. French & Eur.

A Dictionary of Chinese Buddhist Terms. W. E. Soothill & L. Hodous. (Pub. by Motilal Banarsidass India). Orient Bk Dist.

Dictionary of Chinese Buddhist Terms, with Sanskrit & English Equivalents & a Sanskrit-Pali Index. Ed. by William E. Soothill & L. Hodous. Verry.

Dictionary of Chinese Law & Government. Philip R. Bilancia. Stanford U Pr.

Dictionary of Electrical Circuits. French & Eur.

Dictionary of Electronics Engineering. French & Eur.

Dictionary of Forestry. French & Eur.

Dictionary of Gas Turbine Installation. French & Eur.

Dictionary of High Polymer Macromolecule. French & Eur.

Dictionary of Industrial Chemistry. French & Eur.

Dictionary of Industrial Chemistry. French & Eur.

Dictionary of Industrial Organic Chemistry. French & Eur.

Dictionary of Mathematics. French & Eur.

Dictionary of Measurement Technology for Computers. French & Eur.

Dictionary of Meteorology. French & Eur.

Dictionary of Physics. French & Eur.

Dictionary of Physics: English-Chinese. French & Eur.

Dictionary of Political Terms: Chinese-English, English-Chinese. Joseph D. Lowe. Lowe Pub.

Dictionary of Science & Technology. French & Eur.

Dictionary of Science & Technology. French & Eur.

Dictionary of Science & Technology: Eng. & Chinese. French & Eur.

Dictionary of Spice Technology. French & Eur.

Dictionary of Telecommunications: English-Chinese. French & Eur.

A Dictionary of the Chinese Particles. W. A. DObson. U of Toronto Pr.

Dictionary of the Chinese Particles, with a Prolegomenon in Which the Problems of the Particles are Considered & They are Classified by Their Grammaticel Functions. W. A. Dobson. U of Toronto Pr.

Dictionary of Zoology: English-Chinese. French & Eur.

Dictionnaire Chinois-Francais. French & Eur.

Dictionnaire Chinois-Francais des Locutions et Proverbes. French & Eur.

Dictionnaire Classique de la Langue Chinoise. F. S. Couvreur. French & Eur.

Dictionnaire Classique de la Langue Chinoise. Couvreur. Mason & Larose.

Dictionnaire de Poche Francais-Chinois. French & Eur.

Dictionnaire de Poche Francais-Chinois. Pekin.

Dictionnaire Francais-Chinois. French & Eur.

Dictionnaire Francais-Chinois. French & Eur.

English & Chinese Dictionary of the Amoy Dialect. J. MacGowan. Oriental Bk Store.

English-Chinese & Chinese-English Dictionary. China Bks.

English-Chinese Architectural Engineering Dictionary. French & Eur.

English-Chinese Biology Dictionary. Y. Dongwuxue Cihui. French & Eur.

English-Chinese Dictionary of Abbreviation & Acronyms. Zhou Long Ru. China Bks.

An English-Chinese Dictionary of Abreviations & Acronyms. French & Eur.

English-Chinese Dictionary of Aeronautical Engineering. French & Eur.

English-Chinese Dictionary of Chemistry & Chemical Engineering. French & Eur.

English-Chinese Dictionary of Civil & Architectural Engineering Terms. French & Eur.

English-Chinese Dictionary of Construction Engineering. French & Eur.

An English-Chinese Dictionary of Engineering & Technology. Zhong Wai Publishing Company. Wiley.

English-Chinese Dictionary of Mathematical Terms. French & Eur.

English-Chinese Dictionary of Medicine. China Bks.

English-Chinese Dictionary of Physical Geography. French & Eur.

English-Chinese Dictionary of Physical Terms. W. Chu-Chi. French & Eur.

English-Chinese Dictionary of Railway Terms. French & Eur.

English-Chinese Dictionary of Scientific & Technology Abreviations. French & Eur.

An English-Chinese Dictionary of Technology. French & Eur.

English-Chinese Dictionary, Romanized. James C. Quo. Saphrograph.

English-Chinese Dictionary Romanized. J. C. Quo. French & Eur.

English-Chinese Dictionary: Standard Chinese. Karl E. Hemeling. Ayer Co.

English-Chinese Glossary for Elementary Chinese. Ed. by David J. Daehler. Cheng & Tsui.

English-Chinese Glossary of Electronic & Electrical Engineering. French & Eur.

An English-Chinese Glossary of Social Sciences & Education. French & Eur.

An English-Chinese Glossary of Terms Commonly Used in Government. Chinese Language Division of Home Affairs Department. Govt Printer.

English-Chinese Maritime Dictionary. French & Eur.

English-Chinese Medical Dictionary. French & Eur.

English-Chinese Medical Dictionary. French & Eur.

English-Chinese Microbiological Dictionary. French & Eur.

English-Chinese Picture Dictionary. B. Matthews. Hippocrene Bks.

English-Chinese Picture Dictionary. B. Mathews. G Brash.

English-Chinese Picture Dictionary. B. Matthews & K. Tan. Iaconi.

English-Chinese Textile Dictionary. French & Eur.

Frequency Dictionary of Chinese Words. Eric S. Liu. Mouton.

General Chinese-English Dictionary. French & Eur.

German-Chinese Dictionary. Hellmut Wilhelm. Ayer Co.

Glosar der Wichtigsten Saugetiere Chinas. Alfred Hoffman. Harrassowitz.

Glossar der Heute Chinesischen Vogelnamen. Alfred Hoffmann. Harrassowitz.

A Glossary of Chinese Archaeology. Zhang Xinglian. Ed. by Zhao Shuhan. China Bks.

Glossary of Current Chinese-English Phrases. China Bks.

Japanese-Chinese Dictionary. French & Eur.

Japanese-Chinese Dictionary. French & Eur.

Japanese-Chinese Loanword Dictionary (M-9259) French & Eur.

Japanese-Chinese Science & Technology Dictionary. French & Eur.

Japanese-English-Chinese Radio Technology Dictionary. French & Eur.

A Junior English-Chinese Dictionary. French & Eur.

Learn Chinese: For English Speakers. Saphrograph.

Learner's Chinese-English Dictionary. China Bks.

Learner's Chinese-English Dictionary. China Bks.

Learner's Chinese-English Dictionary. Iaconi.

Minimum Vocabularies of Written Chinese. George A. Kennedy. Far Eastern Pubns.

Model English-Chinese Dictionary with Illustrative Examples. French & Eur.

Neue Chinesische Vogelnamen. Alfred Hoffmann. Harrassowitz.

A New Chinese-English Dictionary. French & Eur.

New English-Chinese Dictionary. French & Eur.

A New English-Chinese Dictionary. Ungar.

A New English-Chinese Dictionary. French & Eur.

A New English-Chinese Dictionary. French & Eur.

A New English-Chinese Dictionary. China Bks.

A New English-Chinese Law Dictionary. W. S. Hung. French & Eur.

A New English-Chinese Law Dictionary. William Hung. M Stevenson.

A New Practical English-Chinese Dictionary. French & Eur.

Nouveau Dictionnaire: Francais-Chinois. French & Eur.

Nouveau Dictionnaire Francais-Chinois. French & Eur.

Oxford Advanced Learner's Dictionary of Current English. Horny. Iaconi.

Oxford Advanced Learner's Dictionary of Current English with Chinese Translations. A. S. Hornby et al. Oxford U Pr.

Un Petit Dictionnaire Francais-Chinois. French & Eur.

The Pinyin Chinese-English Dictionary. Beijing Foreign Institute. Ed. by Wu Jingrong. (Pub. by Wiley-Interscience). Wiley.

The Pinyin Chinese-English Dictionary. Iaconi.

A Pocket Chinese-English Dictionary: Zhong Hua Edition. China Bks.

A Pocket Concise Chinese-English Dictionary. French & Eur.

A Pocket English-Chinese Dictionary. China Bks.

A Pocket English-Chinese Dictionary. French & Eur.

A Pocket English-Chinese Dictionary. China Bks.

A Pocket English-Chinese Dictionary. Iaconi.

Practical Dictionary of Chinese Idioms, English Idioms, English Synonyms. S. Wei. Iaconi.

A Practical English-Chinese Dictionary. French & Eur.

Practical English-Chinese Pronouncing Dictionary. Janey Chen. C E Tuttle.

A Practical English-Chinese Pronouncing Dictionary. Janey Chen & Ena Simms. C E Tuttle.

A Practical English-Chinese Pronouncing Dictionary. Janet Chen. Iaconi.

Read & Write Chinese: A Simplified Guide to the Chinese Characters. Rita Mei-Wah Choy. China West.

Reading & Writing Chinese: A Guide to the Chinese Writing System. William McNaughton. C E Tuttle.

Russian-Chinese Dictionary of Export & Economics. French & Eur.

Schrift & Sprache der Chinesen. Bernhard Karlgren. Springer-Verlag.

A Short Dictionary of Simplified Chinese Characters. E. W. Jameson, Jr. E W Jameson Jr.

Simple Chinese Conversation. Jianyi H. Huihua. Saphrograph.

A Student English-Chinese Dictionary. Hippocrene Bks.

Supplementary Indexes to Lin Yutang's Chinese-English Dictionary of Modern Usage. Chinese U Pr.

A Text of Chinese Military Terms. Ed. by P. K. Li. French & Eur.

The Trictionary. Bilingual Pubns.

Vocabulaire de Base du Chinois Moderne. Yvonne Andre. Klincksieck.

Vocabulaire Methodique Chinois-Francais a l'usage des Interpretes. Asie-Orientale Cent. Pub.

Vocabulaire Usuel du Chinois Moderne. Helmut Martin et al. Langen Kommand.

Vocabulaire Usuel du Chinois Moderne. Marcel Midoux. Pubns Orient.

Vocabulaire Usuel du Chinois Moderne, 2: Chinois-Francais. Marcel Midoux. Geuthner.

Vocabulaire Usuel du Chinois Moderne, 3: Chinois-Francais. Marcel Midoux. Geuthner.

CHINOOKAN

Alphabetical Vocabulary of the Chinook Language. George Gibbs. AMS Pr.

Dictionary of the Chinook Jargon, or Trade Languages of Oregon. George Gibbs. AMS Pr.

CHIPPWA

Dictionary of the Otchipwe Language. R. R. Baraga. Ross.

CHOCTAW

A Dictionary of the Choctaw Language. Cyrus Byington. Scholarly.

CHONTAL

Dictionary of Chontal to Spanish-English, & Spanish to Chontal. Paul Turner & Shirley Turner. U of Ariz Pr.

CONGO

English-Congo & Congo-English Dictionary. Henry Craven & John Barfield. Ayer Co.

CORNISH

Cornish-English Dictionary. British Am Bks.

An English-Cornish Dictionary. Frederick W. Jago. AMS Pr.

CORSE

Dictionnaire Francais-Corse. Jean Albertini. French & Eur.

CORSICAN

Dictionnaire Corse-Francais, Pierre d'Evisa. Mathieu Ceccaldi. French & Eur.

CREE

A Dictionary of the Cree Language. R. Faries & E. A. Watkins. Anglican Church.

Plains Cree Dictionary. Henry Nanooch et al. U of Toronto Pr.

CREOLE

Beginnings of a Ngukurr-Bamyili Creole Dictionary: Work Papers of SIL-AAB, Series B; vol. 4. Ed. by John R. Sandefur & Joy L. Sandefur. Summer Inst Abor.

Dictionnaire Francais-Creole. Jules Faine. French & Eur.

Dictionnaire Francais-Creole. Faine. Maison Dictionnaire.

Haitian Creole Grammar, Texts, Vocabulary. Ed. by Robert A. Hall et al. Kraus Repr.

Le Lexique du Parler Creole de la Reunion. Robert Chaudenson. Champion.

CROATIAN

Croatian-English, English-Croatian Small Pocket Dictionary. R. Filipovic. Vanous.

Croatian-English, English-Croatian Pocket Dictionary. Heinman.

Croation Reader with Vocabulary. Ante Kadic. Mouton.

Dictionnaire Francais-Serbo-Croate. French & Eur.

New English-Croatian & Croatian-English Dictionary. F. A. Bogadek. Hafner.

New English-Croatian, Croatian-English Dictionary. Francis A. Bogadek. Hafner.

Yugoslavic Pocket Dictionary: English-Croation. R. Filipuvic et al. Vanous.

CZECH

Anglicko-Cesky Lekarsky Slovnik. Andela Kobylkova. SNTC.

Anglicko-Cesky a Cesko-Anglicky Slovnik por Televizni Pracovniky a Prekladatele. Josef Feigl. SNTC.

Anglico-Cesko a Cesko-Anglico Kapesni-Slovnik: English-Czech, Czech-English Dictionary. Karel Hais. Imported Bks.

Arabsko-Cesky Cesko-Arabsky Slovnik. Lubos Kropacek. SNTC.

Astronomical Dictionary: In Six Languages. Josip Kleczek. Acad Pr.

Astronautical Multilingual Dictionary: International Academy of Astronautics. Elsevier.

Cesko-Francouzsky Technicky Slovnik. Libuse Vomackova. SNTC.

Cesko-Italsky Slovnik na Cesty. Hana Benesova. SNTC.

Cesko-Rumunsky & Rumunsko-Cesky Slovnik na Cesty. Jiri Felix. SNTC.

Cesko-Rusky Slovnik na Cesty. Marta Vencovska. SNTC.

Cesko, Slovensko, Latinsko, Anglicko, Nemecko, Rusky, Slovnik Plevelu. Vaclav Kosik. SNTC.

Cesky a Sovensky Terminologicky Slovnik z Fytopatologie a Ochrany Rostlin. SNTC.

Cheshsko-Russkii Radiotekhnicheskii Slovar. B. E. Iakovlev. (Pub. by Glav. Red. Inostr. Nauchn. Tekhn. Slovarei Fizmata). Four Continent.

Czech-English-Czech Dictionary. V. Kolafova & D. Slaba. Vanous.

Czech-English-Czech Dictionary. J. Poldauf. Vanous.

Czech-English Dictionary. Ed. by I. Poldauf. (Pub. by Collet's). State Mutual Bk.

Czech-English, English Czech Dictionary. Ed. by I. Poldauf. Heinman.

Czech-English, English-Czech Dictionary. A. Chermak. Saphrograph.

Czech-English, English-Czech Pocket Dictionary. Heinman.

Czech-English, English-Czech Pocket Dictionary. (Pub. by Artia Czechoslovakia). Hippocrene Bks.

Czech-English, English-Czech Pocket Dictionary. Artia.

Czech-English Technical Dictionary. (Pub. by SNTL). Four Continent.

Czech-English Technical Textile Dictionary. T. Leskova & V. Plisek. (Pub. by Collet's). State Mutual Bk.

Czechoslovakian Dictionary: English-Slovak & Slovak-English. J. Smejkalova et al. Vanous.

Czechoslovakian Pocket Dictionary: Czech-English-Czech. K. Hais. Vanous.

Czechoslovakian-Russian Dictionary of Geology. N. A. Pascenkova et al. French & Eur.

Diccionario Simultaneo en 21 Idiomas. Juan Capdevilla Font. French & Eur.

A Dictionary of Slavic Word Families. Louis J. Herman. Columbia U Pr.

Dizionario ceco-italiano. Jaroslav Rosendorfsky. Ist Univers Orient.

Dizionario italiano-ceco. Jaroslav Rosendorfsky. Ist Univers Orient.

English-Czech, Czech-English Dictionary. A. Chermak. Saphrograph.

English-Czech & Czech-English Pocket Dictionary. K. Hais. (Pub. by State Pedag. Publ. House). Four Continent.

English-Czech Dictionary. J. Caha & J. Kramsky. (Pub. by Collet's). State Mutual Bk.

English-Czech Dictionary. Ed. by V. Osicka & I. Poldauf. (Pub. by Collet's). State Mutual Bk.

English-Czech Dictionary. Ed. by J. Caha. (Pub. by State Pedag. Publ. House). Four Continent.

English-Czech Technical Dictionary. (Pub. by SNTL). Four Continent.

Etlapiras. Gyorgy Arva. Kozgazdasagi.

Francouzsko-Cesky a Cesko-Francouzsky Slovnik pro Televizni Pracovniky a Prekladatele. Otto Levinsky. SNTC.

Francouzsko-Cesky Technicky Slovnik. Libuse Vomackova. SNTC.

Glossarium Armorum: Bd 6 Texthefte in Deutsch, Englisch, Franzoesisch, Italienisch, Daenisch, Tschechisch. Ed. by Ortwin Gamber et al. Verlag der Buchhaendler-Vereinigung GmbH.

Karmannyi Cheshsko-Russkii i Russko-Cheshskii Slovar. D. A. Dlugi et al. (Pub. by Sov Entsiklopediia). Four Continent.

Kratkii Cheshsko-Russkii Geofizicheskii Slovar. N. A. Pashchenko et al. (Pub. by Glav. Red. Nauchn. Tekhn. Slovarei Fizmata). Four Continent.

Kratkii Cheshsko-Russkii i Russko-Cheshkii Vneshnetorgovyi Slovar. V. S. Shevchenko et al. (Pub. by Vneshtorgizdat). Four Continent.

Landwirtschaftliches Woerterbuch in Acht Sprachen. (Pub. by BLV). French & Eur.

Langenscheidts Taschenwoerterbuch Tschechisch-Deutsch. Rolf Ulbrich & Friedrich Kabesch. Langenscheidt.

Langenscheidts Taschenwoerterbuch Tschechisch: Teil II, Deutsch-Tschechisch. Friedrich Kabesch. Langenscheidt.

Langenscheidts Taschenwoerterbuch Tschechisch: Teil I, Tschechisch-Deutsch. Rolf Ulbrich. Langenscheidt.

Langenscheidts Taschenwoerterbuecher Tschechisch. Langenscheidt.

Langenscheidts Taschenwoerterbuecher Deutsch-Tschechisch. Friedrich Kabesch. Langenscheidt.

Langenscheidts Taschenwoerterbuecher Tschechisch-Deutsch. Rolf Ulbrich. Langenscheidt.

Langenscheidts Universal-Woerterbuch Tschechisch. Langenscheidt.

Langenscheidts Universal-Woerterbuecher Tschechisch-Deutsch. Langenscheidt.

Latinsko-Cesky Slovnik. Josef M. Prazak. SNTC.

Learn Czech for English Speakers. Saphrograph.

Maly Divadelni Slovnik. Vaclav Muller. Kultura.

Maly Starocesky Slovnik. Jaromir Belic & Adolf Kamis et al. S. P. N.

Music Translation Dictionary: An English, Czech, Danish, Dutch, French, German, Hungarian, Italian, Polish, Portuguese, Russian, Spanish, Swedish Vocabulary of Music. Compiled by Carolyn D. Grigg. Greenwood.

Muzeologicky slovnik. Josef Benes & Vaclay Puba. SNTC.

Mykologicky slovnik. K. Berger. French & Eur.

Mykologisches Worterbuch. Karl Von Berger. Fischer Verlag.

Piirucni Slovnik Vedy a Techniky. Bohumil Dobrovolny. Prace.

Polovodicove Soucastky. Adolf Klimek. SNTL.

Polygrafie-Englisch-Deutsch-Franzoesisch-Russisch-Spanisch-Polnisch-Ungarisch-Solwakisch. Wolfgang Muller. VEB Technik.

Portugalsko-Cesko-Portugalsky Kapesni Slovnik. Zdenek Hampl & Jiri Holsan. SNTC.

Portugalsko-Cesky Slovnik. Zdenek Hampl. SNTC.

Pracovni Heslar Ceskeho Pravnehistorickeho Terminologickeho Slovniku. Bohuslav Roucka. Ustav Statu a Prava Ceskoslovenske Akademie Ved.

Pirucni Slovnik Jazyka Ceskeho. Vydava Treti Trida Ceske Akademie Ved a Umeni. Statni.

Pirucni Slovnik Jazyka Ceskeho: Zarabcty-Zzonka. Statni.

Pirucni Slovnik Naucny. Pergamon.

Recueil Terminologique Multilingue du Soudage et des Techniques Connexes. French & Eur.

Reverse Dictionary of Czech. Jiri Marvan. Pa St U Pr.

Russko-Chechenskii Slovar. Aisash T. Karasaev et al. Russkii Iazyk.

Rusko-Sesky Chemicky Slovnik. M. Bubnikova. Russkii Iazyk.

Russian-Czechoslovakian Dictionary.
Vlchek. French & Eur.
Russian-Czechoslovakian
Polytechnical Dictionary. V. S.
Petrov & S. A. Tulin. French &
Eur.
Rustina pro Vedecke a Odborne
Pracovniky. L. Z. Rozkovcova & S.
Stary Hanusova. Academia.
Skolni Rusko-Cesky Slovnik. Ed. by
L. V. Kopeckeho. SNTC.
Skolni Rusko-Cesky Slovnik. Karel
Horalek. SNTC.
Slovnik Zakladnich Odbornych
Cesko-Nemeckych Vyrazu ze
Silnicni a Mestske Dopravy.
Jindrich Mrazek. SNTL.
Slovnik Zakladnich Odbornych
Rusko-Ceskych Vyrazu ze Silnicni
a Mestske Dopravy. Jarom Cvrcek.
SNTC.
Technickoekonomicky Rusko-Cesky
Slovnik. Vlasta Patockova. SNTL.
Technisches Woerterbuch. A.
Naxerova. (Pub. by Brandstetter).
French & Eur.
Technisches Woerterbuch. A.
Naxerova. (Pub. by Brandstetter).
French & Eur.
Technisches Woerterbuch. A.
Naxerova. Brandstetter.
Technisches Woerterbuch. A.
Naxerova. Brandstetter.
Technisches Woerterbuch: Band I,
Tschechisch-Deutsch. Naxerova.
Brandstetter.
Tschechisch. Incl. Langenscheidt.

DAKOTA

Dakota-English Dictionary. Stephen
R. Riggs. Ross.
English-Dakota Dictionary. J. P.
Williamson. Ross.

DANISH

Berlitz Pocket Dictionaries: Danish-
English. Berlitz Editors. (Berlitz).
Macmillan.
Berlitz Pocket Dictionaries: Danish-
English-Danish. Berlitz. Macmillan.
Bibliotekskoder.
Rigsbibliotekareembedet.
Bibliotekscentralen.
Bornholmsk Ordbog. Johan C.
Espersen. Rosenkilde.
Danisch. H. Henningsen.
Langenscheidt.
Danish Dictionary Deluxe. H.
Vinterberg & Sen A. Bodel. Vanous.
Danish Dictionary: Rode Ordbog-
Gyldendals, Danish-English. H.
Vinterberg et al. Vanous.
Danish Dictionary: Rode Ordbog-
Gyldendals, English-Danish. H.
Vinterberg et al. Vanous.
Danish-English-Danish Ser.
Macmillan.
Danish-English Dictionary. K.
Schibsbye & H. Kossmann. Ed. by
G. Rona & R. Raylor. Shalom.
Danish-English, English-Danish
Dictionary. Ed. by H. Vinterberg &
J. Axelsen. Heinman.
Danish-English, English-Danish
Technical Dictionary. A. Warrern.
Heinman.
Danish Pocket Dictionary. Heinman.
Danish Pocket Dictionary. Host.
Vanous.
Dansk-Engelsk Handels-og
Fagordbog. I. E. Bailey. French &
Eur.
Dansk-Engelsk Ordbog. H. Vinterberg
& C. A. Bodelsen. French & Eur.
Dansk-Engelsk Ordboger. H.
Vinterberg et al. French & Eur.
Dansk-Fransk Ordbog. A.
Blinkenberg & P. Hoybye. French
& Eur.
Dansk-Fransk Ordbog. A. P.
Blinkenberg & Poul Hoybye. Ed. by
Margrethe Thiele. Erhvervso.
Dansk-Fransk Ordbog. N. C.
Sorensen. French & Eur.
Dansk-Fransk Ordbog. Niels C.
Sorensen. Gyldendal Norsk.

Dansk-Italiensk Ordborg. J. Mengel.
French & Eur.
Dansk-Latinsk: Ordbog. L. Ove Kjaer.
French & Eur.
Dansk Retrogradordbog. Henrik
Holmboe. Akademisk Forlag.
Dansk-Russik Ordbog. Helge
Vangmark. Grafisk Forlag.
Dansk-Russik Ordborg. H. Vangmark.
French & Eur.
Dansk-Spansk Ordborg. French &
Eur.
Dansk Sprogbrug. Erik Bruun.
Gyldendal Norsk.
Dansk-Svensk Ordbok. Bertil Molde.
Ed. by Niels Ferlov. Esselte
Studium.
Dansk-Svensk Ordbok. Karen
Widman. Esselte Studium.
Dansk-Tysk Ordbog. E. Bork & E.
Kaper. French & Eur.
Dansk-Tysk Ordbog. Borge Dissing &
Rud Lave. Illus. by L. Taaning.
Gyldendal Norsk.
Dansk-Tysk Ordbog. Egon Bork &
Egon Kaper. Gyldendal Norsk.
Dansk-Tysk Ordbog for
Korrespondenter. O. Poulsen.
French & Eur.
Dansk-Tysk Teknisk Ordborg. A.
Warren. French & Eur.
Deutsch fur Baufachleute fuer
Daenen, Norweger & Sshweden. G.
Wallnig & H. Evered. Bauverlag.
Diccionario Lexicon Espanol-Danes
& Espanol-Danes. French & Eur.
Diccionario Simultaneo en 21
Idiomas. Juan Capdevilla Font.
French & Eur.
Dictionnaire Danois-Francais.
Larousse.
Dictionnaire de Poche Francais-
Danois. Berlitz.
Dictionnaire Lilliput Bilingue
Francais-Danois. Larousse FR.
Dizionario danese-italiano e italiano-
danese. Malipiero.
Dizionario italiano-danese. Malipiero.
Elsevier's Dictionary of Barley,
Malting, & Brewing. Bernard D.
Hartong. Elsevier.
Elsevier's Dictionary of Horticulture.
Ed. by Ministry of Agriculture &
Fisheries- Netherlands & J. Nijdam.
Elsevier.
Engelsk-Dansk-Ordbog. B. K. Nielsen
et al. French & Eur.
Engelsk-Dansk Teknisk Ordbog. A.
Warren. French & Eur.
Femmedordbog. Jorgen Bang.
Berlingske Forlag.
Finnish-Danish-Finnish Dictionary:
Suomi-Tanska-Suomi. A. S. Gersov.
French & Eur.
Fogtdals et-binds leksikon i farver.
Henning Dehn-Nielsen. Ed. by
Gorm Sejersen. Fogtdals Boger.
Fransk-Dansk, Dansk-Fransk
Specialordbog. Ed. by Ejnar Fryd.
For Stat Rev.
Gjellerups Gronne Ordbog. Flemming
G. Albertus. Gjellerup Forlag.
Glossarium Armorum: Bd 6 Texthefte
in Deutsch, Englisch, Franzoesisch,
Italienisch, Daenisch, Tschechisch.
Ed. by Ortwin Gamber et al. Verlag
der Buchhaendler-Vereinigung
GmbH.
Gyldendals Antikvitetshandbog.
Gorm R. Benzon. Gyldendal
Norsk.
International Planning Glossary. Ed.
by Gordon Logie & Hemel
Hemstead. Intl Plan Glos.
Italiensk-Dansk Ordbog. K. Anderson
& G. Mafera. French & Eur.
Jurdisk Ordbog. W. Gubba. Guba.
Juridisk Ordbog. Oscar A. Borum &
W. E. Von Eyben. Gad Forlag.
Juridisk Ordbog, Dansk-Tysk:
Supplement & Forkortelsesliste. W.
Gubba. Guba.
Komunalteknisk Ordlista. Tekniska
Nomenklaturcentralen. Tek
Nomen.
Lademanns Leksikon. Pergamon.
Lademanns Rejseleksikon Danmark.
Bernhard Linder & Adam S.
Paltorp. Lademann Forlag.
Langenscheidt Danish-English Lilliput
Dictionary. Langenscheidt.
Langenscheidt English-Danish Lilliput
Dictionary. Langenscheidt.

Langenscheidt's Lilliput Danish-
English Dictionary. Am Map.
Langenscheidt's Lilliput English-
Danish Dictionary. Am Map.
Langenscheidts Taschenwoerterbuch
Danisch. H. Henningsen.
Langenscheidt.
Langenscheidts Taschenwoerterbuch
Danisch: Teil I, Danisch-Deutsch.
H. Henningsen. Langenscheidt.
Langenscheidts Taschenwoerterbuch
Danisch: Teil II, Deutsch-Danisch.
H. Henningsen. Langenscheidt.
Langenscheidts
Taschenwoerterbuecher Daenisch.
H. Henningsen. Langenscheidt.
Langenscheidts
Taschenwoerterbuecher Deutsch-
Daenisch. Langenscheidt.
Langenscheidts Universal-
Woerterbuch Danisch.
Langenscheidt.
Langenscheidts Universal-
Woerterbuecher Daenisch-Deutsch.
Langenscheidt.
Latin-Dansk Ordbog. T. Hastrup.
French & Eur.
Lexicon Sopena: Diccionario de
bolsillo, danes-espanol y espanol-
danes. Sopena.
Lilliput Dictionary. Langenscheid-
Hachette.
Lilliput Dictionary. Langenscheidt.
Luftartsteknisk Ordbog Engelsk-
Dansk. H. Bach & J. Florant.
French & Eur.
Music Translation Dictionary: An
English, Czech, Danish, Dutch,
French, German, Hungarian,
Italian, Polish, Portuguese, Russian,
Spanish, Swedish Vocabulary of
Music. Compiled by Carolyn D.
Grigg. Greenwood.
New International Dictionary of
Refrigeration. International Institute
of Refrigeration. (IIR). Unipub.
Norwegisch-Daenisches
Etymologisches Woerterbuch. H. S.
Falk & Alf Torp. (Pub. by Carl
Winter). French & Eur.
Norwegisch-Daenisches
Etymologisches Woerterbuch. H. S.
Falk & Alf Torp. (Pub. by Carl
Winter). French & Eur.
Norwegisch-Daenisches
Etymologisches Woerterbuch. H. S.
Falk & Alf Torp. Winter Univ.
Norwegisch-Daenisches
Etymologisches Woerterbuch. H. S.
Falk & Alf Torp. Winter Univ.
Norwegisch Daenisches
Etymologisches Woerterbuch: Mit
Literatur-Nachweisen Strittiger
Etymologien Sowie Deutschem und
Altnordischen Woerterverzeichnis.
H. S. Falk & Alf Torp. (Dist. by
Columbia U Pr). Universitet.
Ordbog for Korrespondenter, Dansk-
Tysk. Sven-Olaf Poulsen. Kjaer
Bogtryk.
Paedagogikkens Hvem Hvad Hvor.
Ed. by K. Grue-Sorensen & Thyge
Winther-Jensen. Politikens Forlag.
Paedagogisk Opslangsbog: Alfabetisk
Ordnet. Ed. by Lars J. Muschinsky
& Karsten Schnack. Illus. by Claus
Fenger. Ejlers Forlag.
Teaterord. Niklas Brunius. Nord
Teater.
Tysk-Dansk: Dansk-Tysk Ordbog. F.
Albertus. French & Eur.
Tysk-Dansk Dansk-Tysk Special
Ordbog. E. Fryd. French & Eur.
Tysk-Dansk, Dansk-Tysk
Specialordbog. Ejnar Fryd. For Stat
Rev.
Tysk-Dansk Ordbog. E. Bork & E.
Kaper. French & Eur.
Tysk-Dansk Teknisk Ordbog. A.
Warrern. French & Eur.
Vad Betyder Vaxtens Latinska Namn.
Ivar Anell. Forum Bok.
Van Goor's Deens Woordenboek.
Geerte De Vries. Goor.
Vocabulaire Forestier Francais-
Allemand-Danois. C. Jacobi.
Picard.
Woerterbucher der Fertigungstechnik
Daenisch-Norwegisch-Schwedisch-
Finnisch: Bd 1N, Schmieden-
Freiformschmieden &
Gesenkschmieden. G. Pahlitzsch.
Girardet.

DANSIH

Dansk-Engelsk Teknisk Ordbog.
French & Eur.

DARAI

A Darai-English, English-Darai
Glossary. Carl Kotapish & Sharon
Kotapish. Summer Inst Abor.

DARI

Mathematisch-
Naturwissenschaftliches
Woerterbuch Deutsch-Dari.
Guenter Rack. Groos Verlag.

DUTCH

ABN-Uitspraakgids. Petrus C.
Paardekooper. Heideland-Orbis.
Accounting Dictionary - U.E.C.
Lexicon: American-French-
German-Spanish-Dutch. Union
Europeenne Des Experts
Compatables, Economiques et
Financiers. Intl Pubns Serv.
Athenum Woordenboek: Espanol-
Holandes, Holandes-Espanol.
French & Eur.
Basiswoordenlijst Latijn. J. K.
Babeliowsky. Staatsdruk.
Beknopt Juridisch Woordenboek
Frans-Nederlands. F. J. Velden.
Kluwer Group.
Berlitz Pocket Dictionaries: Dutch-
English. Berlitz Editors. (Berlitz).
Macmillan.
Berlitz Pocket Dictionaries: Dutch-
English-Dutch. Berlitz. Macmillan.
Bokabulario Papiamentu-Ulandes.
Mario Dijkhoff. Walburg Pers.
Capitol's Concise Dictionary. French
& Eur.
Cassell's Dutch Dictionary: English-
Dutch, Dutch-English. Macmillan.
Cassell's Dutch Dictionary: English-
Dutch Dutch-English. Cassell.
Macmillan.
Cassell's New Dutch Dictionary:
English-Dutch, Dutch-English.
Cassell. Macmillan.
Commercial & Financial Dictionary
in Four Languages. Jozef V.
Servotte. Intl Pubns Serv.
Diccionario espanol, ingles, frances,
italiano, aleman y holandes. Rev.
Mex. de Seguros.
Diccionario Lexicon Holandes-
Espanol y Espanol-Holandes.
French & Eur.
Diccionario Simultaneo en 21
Idiomas. Juan Capdevilla Font.
French & Eur.
Diccionario tecnico de terminos
ferroviarios: Espanol-frances-
aleman-ingles-italiano-holandes. J.
H. Bussy. G Gili.

Diccionario Universal Herder Holandes-Espanol, Espanol-Holandes. French & Eur.

Dictionary of Library Science Information & Documentation. Ed. by W. Clason. Elsevier.

Dictionary of Soil Mechanics. Ed. by A. Visser. Elsevier.

Dictionary of Stock Market Terms in Four Languages. B. L. Thole & Theodor Gilissen. Shalom.

Dictionary of Surface-Active Agents, Cosmetics & Toiletries. Ed. by G. Cariere. Elsevier.

Dictionary of Surface Active Agents, Cosmetics & Toiletries. G. Carriere. Elsevier.

Dictionnaire Classique Francais-Neerlandais. Ludovic Grootaers. Vander.

Dictionnaire Classique: Francais-Neerlandais, Neerlandais-Francais. Ludovic Grootaers. French & Eur.

Dictionnaire Commercial & Financier en Quatre Langues: Francais-Neerlandais-Anglais-Allemand. Josef V. Servotte. Erasme.

Dictionnaire de Poche Francais-Neerlandais. Berlitz.

Dictionnaire de Poche: Francais-Neerlandias. Erasme.

Dictionnaire des Synonymes: Francais-Neerlandais. J. Froimont. Erasme.

Dictionnaire des Termes Juridique en Quatre Langues: Francais, Neerlandais, Anglais, Allemand. E. Le Docte. French & Eur.

Dictionnaire des Termes Juridiques en Quatre Langues: Francais-Neerlandais-Anglais-Allemand. E. Le Docte. Vander Oyez.

Dictionnaire du Traducteur: Francais-Neerlandais. J. E. Van Grieken. Administratives.

Dictionnaire Illustre de l'Automobile "Kluwer," en 6 Langues. C. Blok & W. Jezewski. French & Eur.

Dictionnaire International du Tourisme: Allemand-Anglais-Espagnol-Italien-Neerlandai. Acad Intl Tour.

Dictionnaire International Electrotechnique: Francais-Russe-Anglais-Allemand-Italien-Suedois-Hollandais-Polonais. Mir.

Dictionnaire International Electrotechnique: Francais-Russe-Anglais-Allemand-Espagnol-Suedois-Hollandais-Polonais. Mir.

Dictionnaire les termes juridiques en quatre langues: Francais-Neerlandais-Anglais-Allemand. E. LeDocte. Maison Dictionnaire.

Dictionnaire Lilliput Bilingue Francais-Neerlandais. Larousse FR.

Dictionnaire Neerlandais-Francais. Larousse FR.

Dictionnaire Technique Francais-Neerlandais. Voutquenne, C.

Dictionnaire Technique Universal Kluwer, Francais-Neerlandais. G. Schuurmans-Stekhoven. French & Eur.

Dictionnaire Technique Universal Kluwer Neerlandais-Francais. G. Schuurmans-Stekhoven. French & Eur.

Dictionnaire Technique Universel Kluwer: Francais-Neerlandais. G. Schuermans-Stekhoven. Kluwer-Deventer.

Dictionnaire Technique Universel Kluwer: Neerlandais-Francais. G. Schuermans Stekhoven. Kluwer-Deventer.

Dizionario italiano-olandese. Malipiero.

Dizionario italiano-olandese. Van Cappen. Vallardi A.

Dizionario Italiano-Olandese, Olandese-Italiano. V. Van Kampen. French & Eur.

Dizionario olandese-italiano e italiano. Malipiero.

Drents Woordenboek. H. Hadderingh. Interbk Intl.

Duits voor Bouwkundigen-Saksaa Rakentajille. H. Evered & G. Wallnig. Bauverlag.

Dutch-English Dictionary. K. T. Bruggencate. Ed. by J. Gerritsen et al. French & Eur.

Dutch-English Dictionary. Fernand Renier. Routledge & Kegan.

Dutch-English-Dutch. Macmillan.

Dutch-English, English-Dutch Dictionary. K. Ten Bruggencate. Heinman.

Dutch-English, English-Dutch Dictionary. Kramers. Heinman.

Dutch-English, English-Dutch Dictionary. Fernand G. Renier. Saphrograph.

Dutch-English, English-Dutch Engineering Dictionary. G Schuurmans Stekhoven. Heinman.

Dutch-English-French-German Engineering Dictionary. Ten Bosch. Heinman.

Dutch-English (Only) New Great Dictionary. H. Jansonius. Heinman.

Dutch-Norwegian & Norwegian-Dutch Pocket Dictionary. K. Schoell. Kunnskapsforlaget.

Economisch Woorden Boek: Engels-Frans-Duits-Nederlands. F. J. Jong. French & Eur.

Economische Begrippen. G. Dijk. NIB.

Elsevier's Banking Dictionary. J. Ricci. Elsevier.

Elsevier's Dictionary of Building Tools & Materials. L. Y. Chaballe & J. P. Vandenberghe. Elsevier.

Elsevier's Dictionary of Chemical Engineering. W. Clason. Elsevier.

Elsevier's Dictionary of Cinema, Sound & Music. W. E. Clason. Elsevier.

Elsevier's Dictionary of Criminal Science. J. A. Adler. Elsevier.

Elsevier's Dictionary of Electronics & Waveguides. W. E. Clason. Elsevier.

Elsevier's Dictionary of Financial Terms. F. J. Thomson. Elsevier.

Elsevier's Dictionary of General Physics. W. E. Clason. Elsevier.

Elsevier's Dictionary of Horticulture. Ed. by Ministry of Agriculture & Fisheries- Netherlands & J. Nijdam. Elsevier.

Elseviers Dictionary of Metal Cutting Tools. Ed. by G. Schuurmang. Elsevier.

Elsevier's Dictionary of Metallurgy & Metal Working. W. E. Clason. Elsevier.

Elsevier's Dictionary of Nuclear Science & Technology. W. E. Clason. Elsevier.

Elsevier's Dictionary of Public Health. Nick J. Deblock. Elsevier.

Elsevier's Dictionary of Television, & Video Recording. W. Clason. Elsevier.

Elsevier's Dictionary of Tools & Ironware. Ed. by Clason. Elsevier.

Elsevier's Electrotechnical Dictionary. W. E. Clason. Elsevier.

Elsevier's Geneesmiddelengids. Elsevier Nederland.

Elsevier's Multilingual Dictionary of Insurance Technology. W. A. Ruysch. Elsevier.

Elsevier's Nautical Dictionary in Six Languages. Ed. by J. P. Vandenberghe & L. Y. Chaballe. Elsevier.

Elseviers Rubber Dictionary. Elsevier.

Elsevier's Telecommunication Dictionary. W. E. Clason. Elsevier.

Elsevier's Wood Dictionary. Ed. by W. Boerhave Beekman. Elsevier.

Engels-Nederlands Woodenboek. Van Baars & Van der Schoot. Spectrum Pub.

Engels voor Bouwkundigen-Englantia Rakentajille. G. Wallnig & H. Evered. Bauverlag.

The English & Low-Dutch School-Master. Francis Harrison. AMS Pr.

English & Low-Dutch Schoolmaster. Francis Harrison. AMS Pr.

English-Dutch Dictionary. K. T. Bruggencate. Ed. by J. Gerritsen et al. French & Eur.

English-Dutch Dictionary. A. Broers & J. Smit. Ed. by R. Born. French & Eur.

Filmlexikon. Wim De Poorter. Nygh Ditmar.

Fockema Andreae's Rechtsgeleerd Handwoordenboek. Andreae Fockman & Johannes Sybrandus. Rev. by N. E. Algra. Tjeenk Willink.

Geillustrrerd Woordenboek Voor de Autombieltechniek en Zes Talen. C. Block et al. French & Eur.

Geneesmiddelenzakboekje. G. A. Van Gemert & A. De Maesschalck. Agon Elsevier.

Glossaire d'organes de Transmission, 1: Les Engrenages Allemand-Espagnol-Francais-Anglais-Italien-Neerlandais-Suedois-Finnois. Maison Dictionnaire.

Een Glossarium van Zeventiende-Eeuws Nederlands. P. Sterkenburg. Tjeenk Willink.

Glossary of International Treaties. Y. Renoux & J. Yates. Elsevier.

Glossary of Populations & Housing. G. Logie. Elsevier.

Glossary of Technical Terms for Market Researchers: English-German-Spanish-French-Italian-Dutch. European Society for Opinion & Marketing Research. Intl Pubns Serv.

Groot Systematisch en Klankalfabetisch Rijmwoordenboek. John Buydens. Nederlandse Boek.

Groot Woordenboek der Nederlandse Taal. Johan M. Van Dale. Ed. by C. Kruyskamp. Nyhoff.

International Planning Glossary. Ed. by Gordon Logie & Hemel Hemstead. Intl Plan Glos.

International Toeristisch Woordenboek: Edition Neerlandais. Academie Internationale du Tourisme. Acad Intl Tour.

Judo: Encyclopedie in Beeld. Francois M. Haesendock. Standard.

Karmannyi Niderlandsko-Russkii Slovar. T. N. Dreniasova. (Pub. by Russkii Iazyk). Four Continent.

Karmannyi Russko-Niderlandskii Slovar. Zh. I. Pirog et al. (Pub. by Russkii Iazyk). Four Continent.

Kluwer's Universeel Technisch Woordenboek: Engels-Nederlands. G. Shuurmans. French & Eur.

Kluwer's Universeel Technisch Woordenboek Frans-Nederlands. Stekhoven G. Schuurmans & M. Piriou-Vandamme. Kluwer Technische.

Kluwer's Universeel Technisch Woordenboek, Nederlands-Engels. G. Schuurmans. French & Eur.

Kluwer's Universeel Technisch Woordenboek: Nederlands-Frans. G. Schuurmans. French & Eur.

Kluwer's Universeel Technisch Woorenboek Nederlands Frans. Stekhovenn G. Schuurmans. Kluwer Technische.

Kluwer's Universeel Technish Woordenboek: Frans-Nederlands. G. Schuurmans. French & Eur.

Kluwer's Universel Technisch Woordenboek: Nederlands-Duits. G. Schuurmans. French & Eur.

Kramer's Engels Woordenboek. Elsevier.

Langenscheidt Dutch-English Lilliput Dictionary. Langenscheidt.

Langenscheidt English-Dutch Lilliput Dictionary. Langenscheidt.

Langenscheidts Handwoerterbuch Niederlandisch Wolters: Teil I, Niederlaendisch-Deutsch. I. Van Gelderen & W. H. Wallis. Langenscheidt.

Langenscheidts Handwoerterbuecher: Tl 1, Gelderen, 1 van: Niederlaendisch-Deutsch. Ed. by J. H. Van Beckum. Langenscheidt.

Langenscheidts Handwoerterbuecher: Tl 2, Gelderen, 1 van, Deutsch-Niederlandisch. Ed. by J. H. Van Beckum & H. Wallis. Langenscheidt.

Langenscheidt's Lilliput Dutch-English Dictionary. Am Map.

Langenscheidt's Lilliput English-Dutch Dictionary. Am Map.

Langenscheidts Taschenwoerterbuch Niederlandisch-Deutsch. F. J. J. Van De Wiele & Frans Beersmans. Langenscheidt.

Langenscheidts Taschenwoerterbuch Niederlaendisch: Teil II, Deutsch-Niederlaendisch. Frans Beersmans. Langenscheidt.

Langenscheidts Taschenwoerterbuch Niederlaendisch: Teil I, Niederlaendisch-Deutsch. F. J. Van De Wiele. Langenscheidt.

Langenscheidts Taschenwoerterbuecher Niederlandisch-Deutsch. Ed. by Jan Schneider. Langenscheidt.

Langenscheidts Universal-Woerterbuch Niederlaendisch. Langenscheidt.

Legal Dictionary: Part 1, Dutch-German. Hans Langendorf. Kluwer Academic.

Lexicon of International & National Units. Ed. by M. Merino-Rodriguez. Elsevier.

Lexicon Sopena: Diccionario de bolsillo, holandes-espanol y espanol-holandes. Sopena.

Lexicon Van de Economie. Marcel A. Van Meerhaeghe. Stenfert Kroese.

Lexikon van de Taalwetenschap. G Booij et al. Spectrum NL.

Lilliput Dictionary. Langenscheidt.

Lilliput Dictionary. Langenscheidt.

Milieuvriendelijk van A tot Z. Greet Buchner. Driehoek.

Multilingual Vocabulary of Educational Radio & Television Terms. Intl Pubns Serv.

Music Translation Dictionary: An English, Czech, Danish, Dutch, French, German, Hungarian, Italian, Polish, Portuguese, Russian, Spanish, Swedish Vocabulary of Music. Compiled by Carolyn D. Grigg. Greenwood.

Muzieklexicon. Gerrit Slagmolen. Bruna.

Namenforschung im Ostniederlandisch-Westfalischen Grengebiet. Pierre Hessmann. Rodopi.

Nederlands-Engels Woordenboek. G. J. Visser. Spectrum Pub.

Niederlaendisch. Incl. Langenscheidt.

Nieuwe Medische Winkler Prins. J. J. Bouckaert. Elsevier Nederland.

Nieuwe Woorden. Maarten Van Nierop. Scheltens.

Norsk-Nederlansk-Norsk. French & Eur.

Le Nouveau Dictionnaire Francais-Neerlandais, Nederlandais-Francais. Ludovic Grootaers. French & Eur.

Ordbog for Rensning Vask og Rengoring. H. Asmussen. Tek Inst.

Ordbok for Automatiseringsteknikk. Radet for Teknisk Terminologi. Universitesforlaget.

Printer's Terms Dictionary. R. Hostettler. Heinman.

Prisma Voetbalwoordenboek. Rob Siekmann. Spectrum NL.

Proverbes Francais: In French with Equivalents in English, German, Dutch, Italian, Spanish, Latin. G. Ilg. Elsevier.

Russisch Woordenboek. A. Baar. Coutinho.

Semiiazychnyi Slovar Po Elektrosviazi. (Pub. by Sov. Entsiklopediia). Four Continent.

Spectrum Muzieklexicon. Theo Willemze. Spectrum NL.

Standaard Nederlands-Engels Technisch Woordenboek. H. Peek. Standaard Uitgeverij.

Standaard Nieuw Engels-Nederlands Woordenboek. Schot E. Verhoeff. Standaard Uitgeverij.

Standard Niew Engels-Nederlands, Nederlands-Engels Woordenboek. E. Verhoeff-Schot & J. R. Cauberghe. Standaard Uitgeverij.

Het Stoelenboek. Anton van Oirschot. Helmond.

Taschenwoerterbuch Deutsch-Niederlaendisch. Ed. by Gerhard Worgt. VEB Verlag Enzyklopadie.

Ten Bosch's Quadralingual Engineering Dictionary. Imported Bks.

De Terminologie van het Crediet-Wezen in het Grieksch. Jan Korver. Ed. by Moses Finley. Ayer Co.

Terminology of Environmental Hygiene. European Parliament - Translation Division. Intl Pubns Serv.

Van Goor's Deens Woordenboek. Geerte De Vries. Goor.

Verklarend Handwoordenboek der Nederlandse Taal. Matthijs J. Koenen & J. B. Drewes. Academia Edms.

EFIK (continued)

Vocabulaire des Termes: Essentiels Utilises pour la Transmissien Ligne; Francais-Espagnol-Russe-Allemand-Italien-Neerlandais-Polonais-Portugais-Suedois. U. I. T.

Vocabulaire Multilingue de la Science du Sol: Anglais-Francais-Espagnol-Allemand-Portugais-Italien-Neerlandais-Suedois-Russe. G. V. Jacks & R. Tavernier. F. A. O.

Woerterbuch der Deutschen & Niederlaendischen Rechtssprache: Lexikon fuer Justiz, Verwaltung, Wirtschaft & Handel. Hans Langendorf. Kluwer Group.

Woerterbuch der Deutschen und Nierderlaendischen Rechtssprache. Hans Langendorf. French & Eur.

Woerterbuch der Deutschen und Nierderlaendischen Rechtssprache. Hans Langendorf. French & Eur.

Woerterbuch der Kraftuebertragungselemente-Deutsch-Spanisch-Franzoesisch-Englisch-Italienisch-Niederlandisch-Schwedisch-Finnisch: Bd 1, Zahnraeder. Krausskopf.

Woerterbuch der Kraftuebertragungselemente. French & Eur.

Woerterbuch der Recht & Wirtschaftssprache: Teil I, Niederlandisch-Deutsch. Hans Langendorf & P. A. Stein. Recht & Wirtschaft.

Woerterbuch der Rechts & Wirtschaftssprache: Teil II, Deutsch-Niederlaendisch. Hans Langendorf & P. A. Stein. Recht & Wirtschaft.

Woordenboek Hebreeuws-Nederlands. Jitschak Pimentel. Strengholt.

Woordenboek Hebreeuws-Nederlands. Jitschak Pimentel. Strengholt.

Woordenboek van magic, okkultisme & parapsychologi. Nel Noordzij. Fontein.

Woordenboek Welzijn. Marijke Van Hee. VUGA.

Wortkonkordanz zu den Altmittel & Altniederfraenkischen Psalmen & Glossen. Arend Quak. Rodopi.

EFIK

English-Efik Dictionary. R. F. Adams. Shalom.

EGYPTIAN

A Concise Dictionary of Middle Egyptian. R. O. Faulkner. (Pub. by Griffith Inst). State Mutual Bk.

Dictionary of Late Egyptian. Ed. by Leonard H. Lesko. B C Scribe.

ENOCHIAN

The Complete Enochian Dictionary. Donald C. Laycock. Askin Pub.

ESKIMO

Dictionnaire Francais-Esquimau du Parier: l'Ungava & Contrees Limitrophes, 2. Lucien Schneider. Laval P. U.

English-Eskimo & Eskimo-English Vocabularies. Ed. by Roger Wells & John W. Kelley. AMS Pr.

English-Eskimo & Eskimo-English Vocabularies. Compiled by Roger Wells, Jr. Tr. by John W. Kelly. C E Tuttle.

English-Eskimo, Eskimo-English Dictionary. Shalom.

Eskimo-English, English-Eskimo Dictionary. A. Thibert. Heinman.

Inupiat Eskimo Dictionary. Donald H. Webster & Wilfried Zibell. Summer Inst Ling.

Lexique Analytique du Vocabulaire Inuit Moderne au Quebec-Labrador. Louis J. Dorais. (Dist. by Four Continent Bk). Univ Laval.

ESPERANTO

Diccionario Lexicon Esperanto-Espanol, Espanol-Esperanto. French & Eur.

Dictionnaire Francais-Esperanto. Albault A. Leger. Esperanto.

Diccionario Simultaneo en 21 Idiomas. Juan Capdevilla Font. French & Eur.

Esperanto Dictionary. J. C. Wells. McKay.

Esperanto-English Dictionary. Montagu C. Butler. Esperanto League North Am.

Esperanto-English Dictionary. Edward A. Millidge. Saphrograph.

Learn Esperanto for English Speakers. Saphrograph.

Lexicon Sopena: Diccionario de bolsillo, esperanto-espanol y espanol-esperanto. Sopena.

Technisches Woerterbuch Deutsch-Esperanto. R. Haferkorn. U of Toronto Pr.

Vocabulaire Esperanto. Michel Duc-Goninaz. Ophrys.

ESTONIAN

English-Estonian Dictionary for Schools. M. Rauk. (Pub. by Valgus). Four Continent.

English-Estonian-Russian Maritime Dictionary. Kulno Olev. (Pub. by Collets). State Mutual Bk.

Estonian-English Dictionary. J. Silvert. Shalom.

Estonian-English Dictionary. Paul F. Saagpakk. Yale U Pr.

Estonsko-Russkii Slovar. J. Tamm. (Pub. by Valgus). Four Continent.

Finnish-Esthonian-Finnish Dictionary: Suomi-Eesti-s. H. Laanpere. French & Eur.

Kratkii Estonsko-Russkii Slovar. V. Mukhel. (Pub. by Tallinn). Four Continent.

Maritime Dictionary. Kulno Olev. (Pub. by Collets). State Mutual Bk.

Russko-Estonskii Razgovornik. A. Reitsak. (Pub. by Valgus). Four Continent.

Russko-Estonskii Slovar. V. Mukhel. (Pub. by Estonsk. Gos. Izd.). Four Continent.

Russko-Estonskii Slovar. P. Arumaa et al. (Pub. by Valgus). Four Continent.

Svensk-Estnisk Ordbok. Per Wieselgren. Fyris.

FIJIAN

A Fijian & English & an English & Fijian Dictionary. David Hazlewood. AMS Pr.

FINNISH

Atk-Sanakirja. Gustav Tollet. Tietojen.

Berlitz Pocket Dictionaries: Finnish-English-Finnish. Berlitz. Macmillan.

Berlitz Pocket Dictionaries: Finnish-English. Berlitz Editors. (Berlitz). Macmillan.

Comparative Dictionary of the Finno-Ugric Elements in the Hungarian Vocabulary. Jozsef Budenz. Res Ctr Lang Semiotic.

Deutsch-Finnisches Schulworterbuch. A. Rosentahl et al. French & Eur.

Diccionario Lexicon Finlandes-Espanol, Espanol-Finlandes. French & Eur.

Diccionario Simultaneo en 21 Idiomas. Juan Capdevilla Font. French & Eur.

Dictionnaire de Poche Francais-Finnois. Berlitz.

Dictionnaire Finnois-Francais. Tauno Nurmela. Soderstrom.

Dictionnaire Finnois-Francais-Finnois. Raila-Maarit Koistinen & Helene Lasslo et al. Soderstrom.

Dictionnaire Scolaire Francais-Finnois. Edvin Hagford & Seppo Sundelin. Soderstrom.

Dizionario Italiano-Finlandes, Finlandes-Italiano. Ed. by G. Colussi. French & Eur.

Dizionario italiano-finlandese. Colussi. Vallardi A.

Duits voor Bouwkundigen-Saksaa Rakentajille. H. Evered & G. Wallnig. Bauverlag.

Engels voor Bouwkundigen-Englantia Rakentajille. G. Wallnig & H. Evered. Bauverlag.

Englandtilais-Suomalainen Laboratorio- ja Prosessialan Sanasto. Liisa Pihkala & Juhani Pihkala. Otava.

Englantilais-Suomaainen Elektromikka ja Instrumentointisanasto. Lea Saarikoski. Otava.

Englantilais-Suomalainen Asunto ja Rakennusalan Sanasto. Irma Lehtipuu. Otava.

Englantilais-Suomalainen Moottorialan Sanasto. Lea Saarikoski. Otava.

Englantilais-Suomalainen Tekstiili-ja Vaatetusalan Sanasto. Lea Saarikoski. Otava Kust.

Englantilais-suomalainen Suursanakirja: English-Finnish General Dictionary. Raija Hurme & Maritta Pesonen. Soderstrom.

English-Finnish Dictionary. A. Wuolle. French & Eur.

English-Finnish General Dictionary. R. Hurme et al. French & Eur.

Fenno-Ugric Vocabulary: An Etymological Dictionary of the Uralic Languages. Bjorn Collinder. Benjamins North Am.

Finnish-Danish-Finnish Dictionary: Suomi-Tanska-Suomi. A. S. Gersov. French & Eur.

Finnish Deluxe Dictionary: English-Finnish. R. Hurme & M. Pesonen. Vanous.

Finnish Dictionary: English-Finnish. E. Riikon & A. Tuomikowski. Vanous.

Finnish Dictionary: Suomalais-Englantilainen. V. S. Alanne. Vanous.

Finnish-English, English-Finnish Dictionary. A. Wuolle. Heinman.

Finnish-English, English-Finnish Dictionary. A. Wuole. Shalom.

Finnish-English, English-Finnish Dictionary. A. Wuolle. Heinman.

Finnish-English-Finnish. Macmillan.

Finnish-English-Finnish Dictionary. Wuolle. French & Eur.

Finnish-English General Dictionary. V. S. Alanne. French & Eur.

Finnish-Esthonian-Finnish Dictionary: Suomi-Eesti-s. H. Laanpere. French & Eur.

Finnish-French Dictionary. T. Nurmela. French & Eur.

Finnish-French-Finnish Dictionary (Suomi-Ranska-Suomi) R. M. Koistinen. French & Eur.

Finnish-German-Finnish Dictionary (Suomi-Saksa-Suomi) L. Hirvensalo. French & Eur.

Finnish-German Great Dictionary. P. Katara et al. French & Eur.

Finnish-Hungarian-Finnish Dictionary (Suomi-Unkari-Suomi) I. Nyirkos. French & Eur.

Finnish-Italian Dictionary. G. Colussi. French & Eur.

Finnish-Italian-Finnish Dictionary. G. Colussi. French & Eur.

Finnish-Norwegian-Finnish Dictionary (Suomi-Noria-Suomi) T. Farbregd et al. French & Eur.

Finnish-Norwegian Norwegian-Finnish Pocket Dictionary. Farbregd & Kamarainen. Kunnskapsforlaget.

Finnish Pocket Dictionary. Heinman.

Finnish Pocket Dictionary, Finnish-English - English-Finnish. Vanous.

Finnish-Portuguese-Finnish Dictionary. K. Rahinantti. French & Eur.

Finnish-Russian-Finnish Dictionary (Suomi-Venaja-Suomi) A. Hiltunen. French & Eur.

Finnish Small Dictionary: English-Finnish. Aino Wuolle. Vanous.

Finnish Small Dictionary: Finnish-English. Aino Wuolle. Vanous.

Finnish-Spanish-Finnish Dictionary. E. K. Neuvonen. French & Eur.

Finnish-Swedish Dictionary. L. Lampen. French & Eur.

Finnish-Swedish-Finnish Dictionary. French & Eur.

Finnish-Swedish-Finnish Dictionary (Suomi-Ruotsi-Suomi) L. Lampen. French & Eur.

Finsk-Svensk & Svensk-Finsk Fickordbok. Av Lea Lampen. Esselte Studium.

Finsk-Svensk Skolordbok. Lea Lampen. Esselte Studium.

Finsk-Swensk Storordbok. Knut Cannelin et al. Esselte Studium.

Finsko-Russkii Slovar. I. Vakharos et al. (Pub. by Russkii Iazyk). Four Continent.

French-Finnish Dictionary. E. Hagfors et al. French & Eur.

Glossaire d'organes de Transmission, 1: Les Engrenages Allemand-Espagnol-Francais-Anglais-Italien-Neerlandais-Suedois-Finnois. Maison Dictionnaire.

Graafinen Sanakirja. Soderstrom.

International Planning Glossary. Ed. by Gordon Logie & Hemel Hemstead. Intl Plan Glos.

Kansanperinteen Sanakirja. Toivo Vuorela. Soderstrom.

Karmannyi Russko-Finskii Slovar. I. S. Eliseev. (Pub. by Russkii Iazyk). Four Continent.

Kirjastotermien Sanakirja. Martti Kahla. Neuvost.

Komunalteknisk Ordlista. Tekniska Nomenklaturcentralen. Tek Nomen.

Kratkii Russko-Finskii Slovar. (Pub. by GINS). Four Continent.

Laaketieteen Sanairja. Niilo Pesonen. Werner Soderstrom.

Langenscheidts Universal-Woerterbuch Finnisch. Langenscheidt.

Learn Finnish for English Speakers. Saphrograph.

Lexicon Forestale. Karl-Johan Ahlsved et al. Suomen Standard.

Lexicon Sopena: Diccionario de bolsillo, finlandes-espanol y espanol-finlandes. Sopena.

Maly Slownik Finsko-Polski & Polski-Finski. Elsa Salamaa. Kirjayhtyma.

Mineraalinimisanasto. Boris Saltikoff. Geo Tutkim.

Nykvsuomen Saneiston Yleisyystilastoa Sanennloppuisessa Aakkosjarjestykessa. Pauli Saukkonen. Oulun Yliopisto.

Nykyslangin Sanakirja. Kaarina Karttunen. Soderstrom.

Nykysuomen Sivistyssankirja: Vierasperaiset Sanat. Nykysuomen Laitos. Suoma Kirja.

Rakennusalan Sanastot ja Sanastohankkeet Suomessa. Ritva Swanljung. Valtion.

Ranskalais-Suomalainen-Sanakirja. Pentti Pesonen. Otava.

Ranskalais-Suomalainen Tekniikan ja Kaupan Sanakirja. Jyrki K. Talvitie. Tietoteos.

Ravitsemusalan Sanastro. Otava.

Ruotsalais-Suomalaines. Lea Lampeu. WSOY.

Ruotsin Kielen Perus ja Taydennyssanasto. Kalervo Linnapuomi. Otava.

Russko-Finskii Slovar. Ed. by M. E. Kuusiena et al. (Pub. by GINS). Four Continent.

Sahkotieteellinen Sanasto. Suomen Standardisoimislitto. Suomen Standard.

Slownik Finsko-Polski. Stanislaw Walega. Wiedza Powszechna.

A Student's Glossary of Finnish. Michael Branch et al. Soderstrom.

Suomalais-Englantilainen Sanakirja. Aino Vuolle. Femi Suuri.

Suomalais-Ruotsalainen Suursanakirja. Aulis Cannelin et al. Werner Soderstrom.

Suomi-Norja-Suomi: Taskusanakirja. Turid Farbregd & Aili Kamarainen. Soderstrom.

Suomi-Portugali-Suomi. Kristina Rahinantti et al. Werner Soderstrom.

Suomi-Poula Suomi Dictionary: Finnish-Polish-Finnish. A. Krawczykiewicz. French & Eur.

Suomi-Unkari-Suomi: Taskusanakirja. Istvan Nyirkos. Soderstrom.

Svensk-Finsk Storordbok. Lea Lampen. Esselte Studium.

Swedish-Finnish Dictionary. L. Lampen. French & Eur.

Tasmennyssanasto. Jouko Vesikansa. Werner Soderstrom.

Teaterord. Niklas Brunius. Nord Teater.

Timber Trade Terminology. Hilkka Saario. Gaudeamus.

Toimitustyon Terminologiaa. Liisa Miettinen. Otava.

Udissanasto Kahdeksankymmenta. Kielitoimisto. Soderstorm.

Unkarilais-Suomalainen Sanakirja. Istvan Nyirkos. Suoma Kirja.

Uudissanasto. Soderstrom.

Uudissanasto Kahdeksankymmenta. Kotimaisten Kielten Tutkimuskekus. Soderstrom.

Vad Betyder Vaxtens Latinska Namn. Ivar Anell. Forum Bok.

Woerterbuch der Kraftuebertragungselemente-Deutsch-Spanisch-Franzoesisch-Englisch-Italienisch-Niederlandisch-Schwedisch-Finnisch: Bd 1, Zahnraeder. Krausskopf.

Woerterbuch der Kraftuebertragungselemente. French & Eur.

Woerterbucher der Fertigungstechnik Daenisch-Norwegisch-Schwedisch-Finnisch: Bd 1N, Schmieden-Freiformschmieden & Gesenkschmieden. G. Pahlitzsch. Girardet.

FLEMISH

Dictionnaire Juridique Flammand-Francais. Jules Brassine. Bruylant.

FRENCH

ABC Dictionary I: Arabic & Fr. Libr. du Liban. Intl Bk Ctr.

ABC Dictionary Tamhidi: Arabic & Fr. Libr du Liban. Intl Bk Ctr.

Abreviation du traitement de l'informatique. Carl Amkreutz. Maison Dictionnaire.

Accounting Dictionary - U.E.C. Lexicon: American-French-German-Spanish-Dutch. Union Europeenne Des Experts Compatables, Economiques et Financiers. Intl Pubns Serv.

Ace's French Phrase Book & Dictionary. Charles A. Hughes. Ace Bks.

Additions Aux Dictionnaires Arabes (Arabic-French) E. Fagnan. Intl Bk Ctr.

Aeronautic Engineering Dictionary: English-French-German-Arabic. M. A. Zimaity. Ed. by Abd-el-Washed. French & Eur.

Agricultural Engineering Dictionary: English-French-German-Arabic. Abd El Wahed. French & Eur.

Das Akademiewoerterbuch von 1694: Das Woerterubch des Honnete Homme? Inge Popelar. Niemeyer.

Al-Kamil Dictionnaire Arabe-Francais-Anglais. M. Chouemi & C. H. Pellat. French & Eur.

Alcala-Zamora, Diccionario Frances-Espanol, Espanol-Frances. Alcala-Zamora. French & Eur.

Alcala-Zamora, Diccionario Frances-Espanol, Espanol-Frances. Alcala-Zamora. French & Eur.

Ambiguite Dans le Lexique. Wiecher Zwanenburg. Humanities.

Amglo-Russko-Nemetsko-Frantsuzskii Tolkovyi Slovar Po Vychislitel Noi Tekhnike & Obrabotke Dannykh. (Pub. by Russkii Iazyk). Four Continent.

L' Anglais Dans le Batiment: Text En Anglais Avec un Glossaire Illustre. G. Wallnig & H. Evered. French & Eur.

L' Anglais Dans le Batiment: Texte En Anglais Avec un Glossaire Illustre, 2. Gunter Wallnig & H. Evered. French & Eur.

Les Anglicismes au Quebec. Gilles Colpron. French & Eur.

Anglo-Ispano-Russko-Frantsuzskii Slovar Nauchnykh & Tekhnicheskikh Terminov Po Atomnoi Energii. (Pub. by United Nations Publications). Four Continent.

Anglo-Russkii Slovar Po Fizike Vysokikh Energii. (Pub. by Russkii Iazyk). Four Continent.

Annales des Mines: Lexique Technique Allemand-Francais. J. Armanet & A. Becquer. French & Eur.

Applied Technical Dictionary: Air Conditioning & Refrigeration. (Pub. by Collets). State Mutual Bk.

Applied Technical Dictionary: Oil Processing & Petrochemistry. (Pub. by Collets). State Mutual Bk.

Applied Technical Dictionary: Silicate Technology. (Pub. by Collets). State Mutual Bk.

Arabe Francais Dictionnaire. A. Kazirmski. Intl Bk Ctr.

Arabic-French Dictionary. Auguste Cherbonneau. Intl Bk Ctr.

Architecture & Building Dictionary: English-French-German-Arabic. Abd El Gaward. French & Eur.

L' Architecture Traditionelle au Quebec: Glossaire Illustre de la Maison aux 17e & 18e Siecles. Yves Laframbois. Edns Homme.

L Argot Chez les Vrais de Vrais. Auguste LeBreton. Presses Cite.

L Argot de Police. Jacques Arnal. Euredif.

Armorial General Precede d'un Dictionnaire des Termes du Blason. Johannes B. Rietstap. (Pub. by Olms). French & Eur.

Armorial General Precede d'un Dictionnaire des Termes du Blason. Johannes B. Rietstap. (Pub. by Olms). French & Eur.

Armorial general precede d'un dictionnaire des termes du Blason. Johannes B. Rietstap. Olms Verlag.

Armorial general precede d'un dictionnaire des termes du Blason. Johannes B. Rietstap. Olms Verlag.

Astronautical Multilingual Dictionary: International Academy of Astronautics. Elsevier.

Astronomical Dictionary: In Six Languages. Josip Kleczek. Acad Pr.

Atlas & Glossary of Primary Sedimentary Structures. F. J. Pettijohn & P. E. Potter. Springer-Verlag.

Automatizacna Technika. Jiri Sykora. Alfa-Vydavatel.

Automatizovany Zber Dat Programovanie. Erich Burger. Alfa-Vydavatel.

Automobily. Czesaw Blok & Wiesaw Jezewski. Wydawnictwa.

Automotive Engineering Dictionary: English-French-German-Arabic. Abd-El-Wahed. French & Eur.

Avfallsordlista. Tek Nomen.

La Banalisation Lexicale. Galisson. (Dist. by Continental Bk Co). Lib. Fernand Nathan.

Banking & Financial Dictionary: English-French-Arabic. E. Assiouly. French & Eur.

Bantam New College French & English Dictionary. Ed. by Roger Steiner. Bantam.

The Bantam New College French & English Dictionary. Roger J. Steiner. Bantam.

Basic Dictionary of the Petroleum Industry. Augustin Mendez Manzano. Imported Bks.

Basic Technical Dictionary: French-English-German-Arabic. H. Marei. French & Eur.

Behind the Headlines. Leslie G. Rofe. Belin.

Beknopt Juridisch Woordenboek Frans-Nederlands. F. J. Velden. Kluwer Group.

Berlitz French for Travellers. Berlitz Editors. (Berlitz). Macmillan.

Berlit.. Pocket Dictionaries: French-English. Berlitz Editors. (Berlitz). Macmillan.

Berlitz Pocket Dictionaries: French-English-French. Berlitz. Macmillan.

Bertelsmann Woerterbuch Deutsch-Franzoesisch, Franzoesisch-Deutsch. Karl Knauer. (Pub. by Bertelsmann Lexikon VVA). French & Eur.

Bertelsmann Woerterbuch Deutsch-Franzoesisch, Franzoesisch-Deutsch. Karl Knauer. C Bertelsmann.

Bibliotheca Sinica, dictionnaire bibliographique des ouvrages relatifs a l'Empire chinois. Henri Cordier. B Franklin.

Bibliotheque Orientale, ou Dictionnaire universel, contenant generalment tout ce qui regarde la connaissance des peuples de 'orient. B. D'Herbelot de Molainville et al. Caratzas Pub Co.

Bien Manger dans Quinze Pays. Evelyne Wilhelm. Encre.

Bildwoerterbuch Deutsch-Englisch-Franzosisch. Biblio Inst.

Brockhaus Bildwoerterbuecher in vier Sprachen. F A Brockhaus.

Business Dictionary: English-French, French-English. Georges Anderla & Georgette Schmidt-Anderla. Intl Pubns Serv.

Business English Vocabulary. Jean-Pierre Attal. Edns Organisation.

The Canadian Dictionary-French-English. Jean-Paul Vinay et al. McClelland.

Cassell's Colloquial French. Cassell. Macmillan.

Cassell's Compact French-English, English-French Dictionary. (LE). Dell.

Cassell's Concise French-English, English-French Dictionary. Ed. by J. H. Douglas et al. Macmillan.

Cassell's French Dictionary. Ed. by Denis Girard et al. Macmillan.

Cassell's French Dictionary: Concise French-English English-French. Cassell. Macmillan.

Cassell's French Dictionary: French-English, English-French. Denis Girard et al. Imported Bks.

Cassell's French Dictionary: French-English, English-French. Macmillan.

Cassell's French Dictionary: Standard French-English English-French. Cassell. Macmillan.

Cassell's French Dictionary: Thumb-indexed French-English English-French. Cassell. Macmillan.

Cat in the Hat Beginner Book Dictionary in French & English. P. D. Eastman. Beginner.

Cesko-Francouzsky Technicky Slovnik. Libuse Vomackova. SNTC.

Chemical Dictionary. J. Fouchier & F. Billet. Elsevier.

Chemical Technology Dictionary: English, French-German-Arabic. A. M. Abd-El-Wahed. French & Eur.

Chemins de Fer Glossary. Bureau International de Documentation de Chemin de Fer. Elsevier.

Cibernetical Dictionary: E-G-F-R-Slovene. A. Sydow. French & Eur.

A Classified French Vocabulary. H. H. Baker. Harrap.

Collins French-English English-French Dictionary. Berkley Pub.

Collins-Robert Concise French-English & English-French Dictionary. S&S.

Collins Robert Dictionary: French-English-English-French. A. Duval & R. C. Milnet. Ed. by B. T. Atkins et al. Collins Pubs.

Collins Robert French-English & English-French Dictionary. S&S.

Collins-Robert French-English Dictionary. Beryl T. Atkins et al. W Collins Pubs.

Collins Robert French-English, English-French Dictionary. Imported Bks.

Collins-Robert French-English, English-French dictionary. Beryl T. Atkins et al. W Collins Sons.

Commercial & Financial Dictionary in Four Languages. Jozef V. Servotte. Intl Pubns Serv.

The Comparative Trilby Glossary, French-English. James Schonberg. Century Bookbindery.

Concise French-American Dictionary of Figurative & Idiomatic Language. Perreau & Langford. French & Eur.

The Concise Oxford French Dictionary. Ed. by H. Ferrar et al. Oxford U Pr.

The Concise Oxford French Dictionary: French-English, English-French. H. Ferrar et al. Imported Bks.

A Concordance to the Fables & Tales of Jean De la Fontaine. Ed. by J. Allen Tyler & Stephen M. Parrish. Cornell U Pr.

Cortina-Ace Basic French Dictionary. Cortina. Ace Bks.

Cortina-Grosset Basic French Dictionary. Teresa Marcy & Michel Marcy. Ed. by Dilaver Berberi & Edel A. Berberi. (G&D). Putnam Pub Group.

Cortina-Grosset Basic French Dictionary. Teresa Nutting & Michel Marcy. G&D.

La Creativite lexicale. Louis Guilbert. Larousse.

Customs Dictionary: German-English-French-Italian. Wilhelm Muller. Intl Pubns Serv.

Dansk-Fransk Ordbog. A. Blinkenberg & P. Hoybye. French & Eur.

Dansk-Fransk Ordbog. N. C. Sorensen. French & Eur.

Dansk-Fransk Ordbog. A. P. Blinkenberg & Poul Hoybye. Ed. by Margrethe Thiele. Erhvervso.

Dansk-Fransk Ordbog. Niels C. Sorensen. Gyldendal Norsk.

Dataordboken. Sveriges Standardiseringskommission. Standard Sver.

Datenerfassung Programmierung. Erich Burger. VEB Verlag Technik.

Datenerfassung Programmierung-Englisch-Deutsch-Franzoesisch-Russisch. Erich Burger. VEB Technik.

De la Toponymie Bretonne, Dictionnaire Etymologique. W. B. Smith. Kraus Repr.

DEMO: Dictionnaire Elementaire de Mathematiques Modernes. Jean-Louis Boursin. French & Eur.

Depuis Quand? Les Origines des Choses de la Vie Quotidienne. Pierre Germa. (Dist. by Continental Bk Co.) Berger-Levrault.

Deutsch-Franzoesisches Glossarium: Finanzieller und Wirtschaftlicher Fachausdruecke. Roepke & Haefner. Maison Dictionnaire.

Deutsch-Franzosisches Glossarium. F. Roepke. (Pub. by Fritz Knapp Verlag). French & Eur.

Deutsch fuer Baufachleute. G. Wallnig & H. Evered. Bauverlag.

Les Dialectes Romans de France a la Lumiere des Atlas Regionaux. CNRS.

Diccionari Catala-Frances, Frances-Catala. Carlos Castellanos i Llorenc. Encic Catalan.

Diccionari practic catala-frances. M. Arimany.

Diccionari practic frances-catala. M. Arimany.

Diccionari practic frances-catala, catala-frances. M. Arimany.

Diccionario Abreviado Frances-Espanol Espanol-Frances. Biblograf SP.

Diccionario Basico de la Industria del Petroleo & Derivados. Mendez. Paraninfo.

Diccionario Basico Frances-Espanol Espanol-Frances. Biblograf SP.

Diccionario bilingue frances-espanol-aleman. Alcala Zamora. Sopena.

Diccionario Brevis duplex: frances-castellano y castellano-frances. Sopena.

Diccionario Catala-Frances, Frances-Catala. Carles Castellanos Llorenc & Rafael Castellanos Llorenc. French & Eur.

Diccionario Cientifico y Tecnologico Espanol, Ingles, Frances, Aleman. T. C. Collocott. Imported Bks.

Diccionario Compendiado, Frances-Espanol, Espanol-Frances. Biblograf SP.

Diccionario Cuyas: Spanish-French, French-Spanish. Colton Bk.

Diccionario de Biologia en Quatre Lenguas: Aleman, Ingles, Frances y Espanol. Gunther Haensch & Gisela Haberkamp. French & Eur.

Diccionario De Bolsillo Frances-Espanol, Espagnol-Francais. Arturo Cuyas Armengol. French & Eur.

Diccionario De Dos Cientos Uno Verbos Franceses Conjugados en Todos sus Tiempos & Personas. Christopher Kendris. Barron.

Diccionario De Electronica, Informatica y Centrales Nucleares. Mariano Mataix Lord. French & Eur.

Diccionario de falsos amigos, frances-espanol. Blanca Gonzalez Marimon. Alhambra.

Diccionario de la Decoracion. Equipo Reactor De Ceac. French & Eur.

Diccionario de Seguros. H. L. Mueller-Lutz. French & Eur.

Diccionario del Automovil. Roger Guerber. French & Eur.

Diccionario Enciclopedia Universal. French & Eur.

Diccionario Enciclopedias Labor. Ed. by Javier Lasso de La Vega & Jose M. Rubert Candau. French & Eur.

Diccionario enciclopedico de metalurgia: Espanol-frances, frances-espanol y espanol-engles, engles-espanol. Oliver Bader & Michel Theret. ETA.

Diccionario Enciclopedico de Metalurgia. Oliver Bader & Michel Theret. French & Eur.

Diccionario esencial frances-espanol, espanol-frances. Jean P. Vidal. Diafora.

Diccionario Espanol-Frances. Armando Galant. Mayfe.

Diccionario espanol-frances. Mayfe.

Diccionario espanol-frances. Zeus.

Diccionario espanol-frances. S. Denis & M. Maraval. Hachette.

Diccionario Espanol-Frances. Armando Galant. Mayfe.

Diccionario Espanol-Frances, Espagnol-Francais. Miguel Gimenez Sales. French & Eur.

Diccionario espanol, ingles, frances, italiano, aleman y holandes. Rev. Mex. de Seguros.

Diccionario Everest Cuspide frances-espanol, espanol-frances. Everest.

Diccionario Everest Cuspide: Frances-Espanol y espanol-frances. Everest.

Diccionario Everest 'Cuspide' frances-espanol y espanol-frances: Anonimas y colectivas. Everest.

Diccionario Everest Vertice Frances-Espanol, Espano-Frances. Imported Bks.

Diccionario Everest 10. Larousse.

Diccionario frances-espanol. Mayfe.

Diccionario frances-espanol. Zeus.

Diccionario frances-espanol. S. Denis & M. Maraval. Hachette.

Diccionario Frances-Espanol. Armando Galant. Mayfe.

Diccionario Frances-Espanol de la Construccion y Obras Publicas. Herbert Bucksch & Arturo Galan e Hildalgo. French & Eur.

Diccionario frances-espanol de la construccion y obras publicas. Herbert Bucksch & Arturo Galan e Hidalgo. ETA.

Diccionario Frances-Espanol, Espanol-Frances. E. M. Martinez Amador. French & Eur.

Diccionario frances-espanol, espanol-frances. Tesoro.

Diccionario frances-espanol espanol-frances. Zeus.

Diccionario frances-espanol y espanol-frances. Alcala-Zamora & T. Antignac. Imported Bks.

Diccionario frances-espanol y espanol-frances. Mayfe.

Diccionario frances-espanol y espanol-frances. Mayfe.

Diccionario Lexicon Frances-Espanol, Espanol-Frances. E. Gimeno. French & Eur.

Diccionario Magico Infantil En Seis Lenguas. Eulalia Goma. French & Eur.

Diccionario Major Frances-Espanol, Espanol-Frances. Roberto Larrieu & Manuel Garcia Morente. Diafora.

Diccionario Manual Amador Frances-Espanol y Espanol-Frances. E. M. Martinez Amador. French & Eur.

Diccionario Manual Frances-Espanol. Frida Hochleitner & Felix D. Mateo. Espasa Calpe.

Diccionario Manual Frances-Espanol, Espagnol-Francais. Arturo Cuyas Armengol. French & Eur.

Diccionario Manual Frances-Espanol, Espanol-Frances. Felix Diez Mateo & Frida Hochleitner. French & Eur.

Diccionario Manual Frances-Espanol Espanol-Frances. Biblograf SP.

Diccionario manual frances-espanol, espanol-frances. Felix Diaz Mateo & Frida Hochleitner. Espasa Calpe.

Diccionario Manual Frances-Espanol Espanol-Frances Vox. Biblo SP.

Diccionario Manual Herder Frances-Espanol, Espanol-Frances. Gunther Haensch. French & Eur.

Diccionario moderno: Frances-espanol, espanol-frances. Herder SA.

Diccionario moderno frances-espanol y espanol-frances. P. Fabrega. Bosch Casa.

Diccionario Modernos Herder Frances-Espanol. Herder SA.

Diccionario Nautico. Jose M. Martinez Hidalgo Teran. French & Eur.

Diccionario Parvus duplex: Frances-castellano y castellano-frances. Sopena.

Diccionario poliglota de la arquitectura. B. Bassegoda Muste. Imported Bks.

Diccionario Simultaneo en 21 Idiomas. Juan Capdevilla Font. French & Eur.

Diccionario Simultaneo en 6 Idiomas. Juan Capdevila Font. French & Eur.

Diccionario Superior Frances-Espanol, Espanol-Frances. Vox. Biblo Sp.

Diccionario Superior Frances-Espanol Espanol-Frances. Biblograf SP.

Diccionario superior Frances-Espanol Espanol-Frances 'Vox' Biblo SP.

Diccionario Tecnico. Hermann Mink. Blume Edit.

Diccionario Tecnico de la Construccion, Edificacion & Obras Publicas. Machado. Paraninfo.

Diccionario Tecnico De la Construccion, Edificacion y Obras Publicas Frances-Espanol y Espanol-Frances. M. Machado. French & Eur.

Diccionario tecnico de la construccion: Edificacion y obras publicas; francesa-espanol y espanol-frances. M. Machado. Paraninfo.

Diccionario tecnico de terminos ferroviarios: Espanol-frances-aleman-ingles-italiano-holandes. J. H. Bussy. G Gili.

Diccionario Tecnico Espanol-Frances. Guy Malgorn. French & Eur.

Diccionario tecnico espanol-frances; frances-espanol. EDAF.

Diccionario Tecnico Frances-Espanol. French & Eur.

Diccionario Tecnico Frances-Espanol. Hermann Mink. French & Eur.

Diccionario Tecnico Frances-Espanol. Malgorn. Paraninfo.

Diccionario tecnico frances-espanol y espanol-frances. Guy Malgorn. Paraninfo.

Diccionario tecnico ilustrado de herramientas de corte para el trabajo de metales: Espanol-aleman-ingles-frances-italiano. T. Heiler. G Gili.

Diccionario tecnologico Chambers: Espanol-ingles-frances-aleman. C. F. Tweney & L. E. Hughes. Omega SA.

Diccionario universal: Frances-espanol, espanol-frances. Herder SA.

Diccionario Universal Herder Frances-Espanol, Espanol-Frances. French & Eur.

Diccionario Vasco-Espanol-Frances. Resurreccion M. Azkue. French & Eur.

Diccionario Vertice Everest: Frances-Espanol, Espanol-Frances. Everest.

Diccionario Nuclear. Agustin A. Santos. Organ Ofic Adm.

Dicionario de Bolso Portugues-Frances. Difel Difusao.

Dicionario de Frances-Portugues. Porto Ed.

Dicionario de Frances-Portugues. Porto Ed.

Dicionario de Frances-Portugues: Com Transcicao Fonetica. Jose De Sousa Vieira. Porto Ed.

Dicionario Frances-Portugues de Locucoes. Aluizio Mendes Campos. Edit Atica.

Dicionario Frances-Portugues, Portugues-Frances. S. Burtin Vinholes et al. Editora Globo.

Dicionario Frances-Portugues. Difel. Difel Editorial, S. A.

Dictionaire Des Termes Economiques et Commerciaux: Francais-Arabe. Mustapha Henni. Intl Bk Ctr.

Dictionaire Detaille des Noms de Vetements Chez Les Arabes. R. Dozy. Intl Bk Ctr.

Dictionaire Francais-Anglais d'electro-technique et d'electronique. Piraux. French & Eur.

Dictionaire Francais-Arabe. Louis Saisse. Intl Bk Ctr.

Dictionaire Juridique Francais-Anglais, Anglais-Francais. Quemner. French & Eur.

Dictionaire Technique Francais-Espagnol. Guy Malgorn. French & Eur.

Dictionanaire Francais-Breton. French & Eur.

Dictionar de Electrotehnica. Mihai Condruc. Editura Stiintifica.

Dictionar de Electrotehnik. Mihai Condruc. Editura Stiintifica.

Dictionar de Metalurgie Francez-Roman. M. L. Breaban. Editura Stiintifica.

Dictionar Francez-Roman: Pentru uzul Elevilor. Marcel Saras. Editura Stiintifica.

Dictionar Poliglot. Ernest M. Lates et al. Editura Stiintifica.

Dictionar Poliglot de Geodezie: Fotogrammetrie si Cartografie. Mihail Albota. Editura Stiintifica.

Dictionar Poliglot de Industrie Alimentara. Mihai Papa-Sotir. Editura Stiintifica.

Dictionar Poliglot de Matematica, Mecanica si Astronomie. Stefan Gheorghita. Editura Stiintifica.

Dictionar Tehnic Auto de Buzunar in Sapte Limbi. Petre Cristea. Editura Stiintifica.

A Dictionarie of the French & English Tongues. Randle Cotgrave. Walter J Johnson.

Dictionario de Portugues-Frances. Porto Ed.

Dictionariolum Puerorum Tribus Linguis: Lat., Ang. & Gall. Conscriptum. Robert Estienne. Walter J Johnson.

Dictionarium Linguae Thai Sive Slamensis Interpretatione Latina, Gallica & Anglica. Jean-Baptiste Pallegoix. Gregg.

Dictionarium Tetraglotten Seu Voces Latinae Omnes, et Graecae Eis Respondentes, Cum Gallica & Teutonica (Quam Passim Flandricam Vocant) Earum Interpretatione: Dictionarum Tetraglotten A.D. MDLXII Ed. Mouton.

Dictionary Des Terms Economiques et Commerciaux (French-English-Arabic) Mustapha Henni. Intl Bk Ctr.

Dictionary for the Graphic Arts in Eight Languages: German-English-French-Spanish-Russian-Hungarian-Polish-Slowak. Perfect Graphic.

Dictionary French-Slovene. A. Grad. French & Eur.

Dictionary of Acoustics: English-German-French-Russian-Spanish-Polish-Madarsko-Slovene. W. Reichardt. French & Eur.

Dictionary of Agriculture in German, French, Spanish, & Russian. G. Haensch. Ed. by Haberkamp G. De Anton. Elsevier.

Dictionary of Automatic Data Processing. Ing H. Burger. (Pub. by Collets). State Mutual Bk.

Dictionary of Automatical Technique. Ed. by Jiri Sykora. French & Eur.

Dictionary of Automobile Terms. Massada Pr.

Dictionary of Biochemistry. K. Thielmann. French & Eur.

Dictionary of Biology. Guenther Haensch. French & Eur.

Dictionary of Biology in English, French, German & Spanish. G. Haensch & G. Haberkamp De Anton. Elsevier.

A Dictionary of Business Terms. Peron. Larousse.

Dictionary of Cereal Processing & Cereal Chemistry. R. Schneeweiss. Elsevier.

Dictionary of Chemical Terminology. D. Kryt. Elsevier.

Dictionary of Chemical Terminology. (Pub. by Vyd. Naukowo-Techniczne). Four Continent.

Dictionary of Civil Engineering & Construction Machinery & Equipment. Herbert Bucksch. French & Eur.

Dictionary of Civil Engineering & Construction Machinery & Equipment. Herbert Bucksch. French & Eur.

Dictionary of Commercial, Financial & Legal Terms. R. Herbst. Adler.

Dictionary of Concrete Terms. Massada Pr.

Dictionary of Dairy Terminology. Elsevier.

Dictionary of Dams. Massada Pr.

Dictionary of Data Processing. Alfred Wittmann. Elsevier.

Dictionary of Development Banking: A Compilation of Terms in English, French, & German with Definitions in English. T. Scharf & M. C. Shetty. Elsevier.

A Dictionary of Diplomacy & International Affairs. Samuhi Fouk al-Ada. Intl Bk Ctr.

A Dictionary of Economics & Commerce. Ed. by Zacharia Nasr. Macmillan London.

Dictionary of Engineering Metrology Terms. Massada Pr.

Dictionary of environmental protection. Otto E. Tutzaver & Ingrid M. Tutzaver. Heymanns Verlag.

Dictionary of Five-Hundred-One French Verbs Fully Conjugated. C. Kendris. Barron.

Dictionary of Floor, Wall & Ceiling Covering. Massada Pr.

Dictionary of Forestry. J. Weck. Elsevier.

Dictionary of Foundry Terms. Massada Pr.

Dictionary of French Slang. Alex Sandir-White. Aurea.

Dictionary of German & English Legal & Economic Terminology. Alfred Romain. French & Eur.

Dictionary of Glass Making. ICG. Elsevier.

Dictionary of Hydraulic Machinery. A. T. Troskolanski. Elsevier.

Dictionary of Hydrology Terms. Massada Pr.

A Dictionary of Idioms, French & English. W. A. Bellenger. Telegraph Bks.

Dictionary of Idioms French-English: Dictionnaire des locutions. Larousse.

Dictionary of Industrial Property, Legal & Related Terms: English, Spanish, French & German. Ed. by Francis J. Kase. Sijthoff & Noordhoff.

Dictionary of International Economics: German, Russian, English, French, Spanish. Ed. by S. Kohls. Sijthoff & Noordhoff.

Dictionary of Joinery Terms: Doors, Windows, Shutters. Massada Pr.

Dictionary of Library Science Information & Documentation. Ed. by W. Clason. Elsevier.

Dictionary of Library Terms. Massada Pr.

A Dictionary of Literary Terms. Compiled by Magdi Wahba. Intl Bk Ctr.

Dictionary of Maritime Terms. Massada Pr.

Dictionary of Mathematics. G. Eisenreich & R. Sube. Elsevier.

Dictionary of Metallurgy. Ed. by A. Dollinger. French & Eur.

Dictionary of Meteorological Terms. Massada Pr.

Dictionary of Modern French Idioms. Barbara L. Gerber & Gerald H. Storzer. Garland Pub.

A Dictionary of Modern Political Idiom. Magdi Wahba. Lib Liban.

A Dictionary of Modern Political Idiom: English-French-Arabic. Magdi Wahba & Wagdi R. Ghali. Lib Liban.

Dictionary of Musical Terms in Seven Languages. Ed. by H. Leuchtmann. Heinman.

Dictionary of Oto-Rhino-Laryngology in Five Languages. A. Larrauri. Intl Pubns Serv.

Dictionary of Packaging: German-English-French. Johannes P. Hoffman. Intl Pubns Serv.

Dictionary of Petroleum Technology-Dictionnaire Technique Du Petrol: English-French - French-English. Ed. by Magdaleine Moureau & Gerald Brace. Intl Pubns Serv.

Dictionary of Petroleum Technology: English-French, French-English. M. Moureau & G. Brace. Imported Bks.

Dictionary of Photograhy. Massada Pr.

Dictionary of Physical Metallurgy. E. F. Tyrkiel. Elsevier.

Dictionary of Physics: No. 1, Mechanics. Massada Pr.

Dictionary of Physics: No. 2, Electricity & Magnetism. Massada Pr.

Dictionary of Physics: No. 3, Optics. Massada Pr.

Dictionary of Plastics Technology in English, German, French & Russian. G. Kaliske. Elsevier.

A Dictionary of Political Idioms. Ed. by Magdi Wahba & Magdi Ghali. Intl Bk Ctr.

Dictionary of Politics & Economic Policy. H. Zahn. French & Eur.

Dictionary of Politics & Economics. H. Back et al. French & Eur.

Dictionary of Power Plant Engineering: Conventional Steam Power Plants. F. Stattmann. French & Eur.

Dictionary of Power Plant Engineering: Nuclear Power Plants. F. Stattmann. French & Eur.

Dictionary of Production Engineering: German-English-French. International Institution for Production Engineering Research. Incl. Intl Pubns Serv.

Dictionary of Pump Terms. Massada Pr.

Dictionary of Quantities & Units of Measurement. Drazil. Brandstetter.

Dictionary of Reprography: Terms & Definitions. Ed. by Deutsches Kommittee Fur Reprographie. (Pub. by K G Saur). Gale.

Dictionary of Science & Technology. Angelo F. Dorian. Elsevier.

Dictionary of Sea Waves & Currents Terms. Massada Pr.

Dictionary of Sewage & Sanitary Installation Terms. Massada Pr.

Dictionary of Soil Mechanics. Ed. by A. Visser. Elsevier.

Dictionary of Soil Science & Soil Engineering Terms. Massada Pr.

Dictionary of Stock Market Terms in Four Languages. B. L. Thole & Theodor Gilissen. Shalom.

Dictionary of Strength of Materials. Massada Pr.

Dictionary of Surface-Active Agents, Cosmetics & Toiletries. Ed. by G. Cariere. Elsevier.

Dictionary of Surface Active Agents, Cosmetics & Toiletries. G. Carriere. Elsevier.

Dictionary of Technical Acoustics. L. Reichardt. Adler.

Dictionary of Technical Drawing. Massada Pr.

Dictionary of Technical Terms. Julius O. Kettridge. French & Eur.

Dictionary of Technical Terms. J. O. Kettridge. Routledge & Kegan.

Dictionary of the French & English Tongues. Randle Cotgrave. Adler.

Dictionary of the Graphic Arts Industry. Ed. by W. Muller. Elsevier.

A Dictionary of the Social Sciences. Compiled by Zaki Badawi. Intl Bk Ctr.

A Dictionary of the Social Sciences. A. Badawi. Lib Liban.

Dictionary of Waste Disposal & Public Cleansing. Ed. by W. Kaupert. Elsevier.

Dictionary of Water & Sewage Engineering. F. Meinck & K. Mohle. Elsevier.

Dictionnaire. Robert Prefontaine & Gisele Cote-Prefont. Beauchemin.

Dictionnaire. Abulqacim Tedjini. Maritimes Outremer.

Dictionnaire a l'Usage des Plaisanciers. French & Eur.

Dictionnaire a l'usage des Plaisanciers. Barbara Webb. Maritimes Outre mer.

Dictionnaire Abrege de Peinture & d'Architecture. Francois-Marie De Marsy. Minkoff.

Dictionnaire Abrege de Six Langues Slaves. Franz Miklosich. Philo Pr.

Dictionnaire Abrege des Imprimeurs-Editeurs du 16 Siecle. Jean Muller. Koerner.

Dictionnaire Abrege du Surrealisme. Annie C. Dobbs. French & Eur.

Dictionnaire Abrege du Surrealisme. Annie C. Dobbs. Corti.

Dictionnaire Abrege Grec-Francais. Anatole Bailly. French & Eur.

Dictionnaire Abrege Grec-Francais. Anatole Bailly. Hachette-Jeunesse.

Dictionnaire Abrege Latin-Francais. Felix Gaffiot. French & Eur.

Dictionnaire Abrege Latin-Francais. Felix Gaffiot. Hachette Jeunesse.

Dictionnaire Abrege Latin-Francais Illustre. Felix Gaffiot. Renouveau Pedagogique.

Dictionnaire Actif Nathan. (Dist. by Continental Bk Co). Lib. Fernand Nathan.

Dictionnaire Actif Nathan. Frank Marchand. Nathan.

Dictionnaire Aerotechnique Anglais-Francais. Louis Henry. Petit.

Dictionnaire Agricole Allemand, Anglais, Francais, Espagnol, Russe. Gunther Haensch & Gisela Haberkamp. (Pub. by Maison Rust). French & Eur.

Dictionnaire Agricole Allemand-Anglais-Francais-Espagnol-Russe. Gunther Haensch. Maison Rustique.

Dictionnaire agricole Allemand, Anglais, Francais, Espanol, Russe. Gunther Haensch & Gisela Haberkamp. Maison Rustique.

Dictionnaire Aide Memoire de Botanique. Charles Louis Gatin. (Pub. by Lechevalier). French & Eur.

Dictionnaire Al-Fara-id Arabe-Francais. P. Belot. Dar El-Machreq.

Dictionnaire Alde-Memoire de Botanique. Charles-Louis Gatin. Lechevalier.

Dictionnaire Allemand-Francais. Erich Weis & Heinrich Mattutat. French & Eur.

Dictionnaire Allemand-Francais. Larousse.

Dictionnaire Allemand-Francais. Erich Weis & Heinrich Mattutat. Bordas-Dunod.

Dictionnaire Allemand-Francais. Denis Eckel & Manfred Hofer. Garnier.

Dictionnaire Allemand-Francais. Rotteck. Garnier.

Dictionnaire Allemand-Francais. Siegfried P. Villain. Garnier-Flammarion.

Dictionnaire Allemand-Francais. Siefried P. Villain. Garnier-Flammarion.

Dictionnaire Allemand-Francais des Termes Relatifs a l'Electrorechnique, l'Electronique, et aux Applications Connexes. Henri Piraux. French & Eur.

Dictionnaire Allemand-Francais des Termes Relatifs a l'electrotechnique: L'electrotechnique & aux Applications Connexes. Henri Piraux. Eyrolles.

Dictionnaire Allemand-Francais et Francais-Allemand. Denis Eckel & Hofer Manfred. French & Eur.

Dictionnaire Allemand-Francais, Francais-Allemand. Ed. by Rotteck. French & Eur.

Dictionnaire Allemand-Francais pour les Travaux Publics: Le Batiement & l'equipement des Chantiers des Chantiers de Constuction. Hector Bucksch. Eyrolles.

Dictionnaire Alphabetique & Analogique de la Langue Francais. Paul Robert. Ed. by A. Ray & J. ReyDebove. Soc Nouveau.

Dictionnaire Alphabetique & Analogique de la Langue Francais. Paul Robert. Ste. Nouv. Littre.

Dictionnaire Alphabetique & Analogique de la Langue Francais. Paul Robert. Ste. Nouv. Littre.

Dictionnaire Alphabetique & Analogique de la Langue Francais. Paul Robert. Ste. Nouv. Littre.

Dictionnaire Alphabetique et Analogique de la Langue Francaise. Robert. French & Eur.

Dictionnaire Analogique. Charles Maquet. Larousse.

Dictionnaire Analogique. Charles Maquet. Larousse.

Dictionnaire Analogique de Poche. Niobey. (Dist. by Continental Bk Co). Larousse.

Dictionnaire Analogique et de Synonymes Pour la Resolution des Problemes des Mots Croises. Maurice Denis-Papin. (Pub. by Albin Michel). French & Eur.

Dictionnaire Analoqique & de Synonymes pour la Resolution des Problemes des Mots Croises. Maurice Denis-Papin. Albin Michel.

Dictionnaire Anglais Chambers: Junior Learners' Dictionary. (Dist. by Continental Bk Co). Lib. Fernand Nathan.

Dictionnaire Anglais-Francais. John Bell. Garnier.

Dictionnaire Anglais-Francais. Larousse.

Dictionnaire Anglais-Francais. Ebenezer Clifton & Horace J. Mac Laughlin. Garnier.

Dictionnaire Anglais-Francais. Eugene Kuentz. Ecole.

Dictionnaire Anglais-Francais. Eugene Kuentz & Emile Saillens. Licet.

Dictionnaire Anglais-Francais. Eugene Kuentz & Emile Saillens. Magnard.

Dictionnaire Anglais-Francais. Jean Vincent. Garnier-Flammarion.

Dictionnaire Anglais-Francais. Jean Vincent. Garnier-Flammarion.

Dictionnaire Anglais-Francais D'electrotechnique. Jean Guy Grenier. Lanaudiere.

Dictionnaire Anglais-Francais des Sciences Medicales & Paramedicales. William J. Gladstone. Maloine.

Dictionnaire Anglais-Francais des Sciences Medicales & Paramedicales. W. J. Gladstone. Edisem.

Dictionnaire Anglais-Francais des Sciences Medicales et Paramedicales. W. J. Gladstone. French & Eur.

Dictionnaire Anglais-Francais des Sciences Medicales et Paramedicales. W. J. Gladstone. Maloine.

Dictionnaire Anglais-Francais Des Termes & Locutions Maritimes. Henri Paasch. Maritimes Outre mer.

Dictionnaire Anglais-Francais et Francais-Anglais des Termes et Locutions Maritimes. Henri Paasch. French & Eur.

Dictionnaire Anglais-Francais et Lexique Francais-Anglais des termes Politiques Juridiques et Economiques. Dreuihe. French & Eur.

Dictionnaire Anglais-Francais pour les Travaux Publics: Le Batiment & L'equipement des Chantiers de Construction. Hector Bucksch. Eyrolles.

Dictionnaire Anglais-Francais: Sciences Medicales & Paramedicales. W. J. Gladstone. Maloine.

Dictionnaire Anglais-Francis des Termes Relatifs a L'electrotechnique: l'ectrotechnique & aux Applications Connexes. Henri Piraux. Eyrolles.

Dictionnaire Anglo-Francais des Nouveautes Linguistiques. Albert Beaudet. Fides.

Dictionnaire Animaux. Scarry. French & Eur.

Dictionnaire-Annuaire de l'agriculture. Faure.

Dictionnaire Arabe-Francais. Ben Sedira. French & Eur.

Dictionnaire Arabe-Francais. N'Damena Tchad.

Dictionnaire Arabe-Francais. A. B. Kazimirski. Intl Bk Ctr.

Dictionnaire Arabe-Francais-Anglais. Regis Blachere & Moustafa Chouemi. Maison & Larose.

Dictionnaire Arabe-Francais-Anglais, 1. Regis Blachere & Moustafa Chouemi. French & Eur.

Dictionnaire Arabe-Francais-Anglais, 2. Regis Blachere & Moustafa Chouemi. French & Eur:

Dictionnaire Arabe-Francais: Dialectes de Syrie. Adrien Barthelemy. Geuthner.

Dictionnaire Arabe-Francais: Langue ecrite. Auguste Cherbonneau. Intl Bk Ctr.

Dictionnaire Archeologique de la Gaul. Emile Cartailhac. Nationale.

Dictionnaire Archeologique de la Gaule. Emile Cartailhac. Biblio Nationale.

Dictionnaire Armenien-Francais. Ambroise Calfa. French & Eur.

Dictionnaire Armenien-Francais. Ambroise Calfa. Klincksieck.

Le Dictionnaire Astrologique. Henry J. Gouchou. French & Eur.

Le Dictionnaire Astrologique. Henry J. Gouchou. Dervy Livres.

Dictionnaire Banda-Francais. C. Tisserant. Institut Ethnologie.

Dictionnaire Basque Francais. Pierre Lhande. French & Eur.

Dictionnaire Basque Francais. Pierre Lhande. Beauchesne.

Dictionnaire Bearnais Ancien & Moderne. Jean-Desire Lespy & Paul Raymond. Slatkine.

Dictionnaire Beauchemin Canadien. Jean-Jacques Lefebvre. Beauchemin.

Dictionnaire Berrichon. Jean Tissier. Slatkine.

Dictionnaire Berrichon avec Citations Litteraires. Jean Tissier. Lafitte Repr.

Dictionnaire Bibliographique du Canada. Victor Barbeau. Acad Can Fr.

Dictionnaire Biblique. Joseph Dheilly. French & Eur.

Dictionnaire Bilingue "Apollo". (Dist. by Continental Bk Co). Larousse.

Dictionnaire Bilingue Apollo. Paul Pauliat. Larousse.

Dictionnaire Bilingue Apollo Francais-Allemand. Jolivet A. Pinoche. Larousse.

Dictionnaire Bilingue Apollo Francais-Anglais. Louis Chaffurin & Jean Mergault. Larousse.

Dictionnaire Bilingue Apollo Francais-Espagnol. Miguel De Toro & Gisbert De Toro. Larousse.

Dictionnaire Bilingue Apollo Francais-Italien. Giuseppe Padovani & Richard Silvestri. Larousse.

Dictionnaire Bilingue Apollo Francais-Portugais. Fernando V. Peixoto da Fonseca. Larousse.

Dictionnaire Bilingue: Francais-Espagnol, Espagnol-Francais. M. De Toro Gisbert. French & Eur.

Dictionnaire Bilingue Francais-Russe et Russe-Francais. (Apollo). Larousse.

Dictionnaire Bilingue Larousse, Francais-Anglais, Anglais-Francais. L. Chaffurin & J. Mergault. Larousse.

Dictionnaire Bilingue Larousse, Francais-Alemand et Allemand-Francais. A. Pinloche & A. Jolivet. Larousse.

Dictionnaire Bilingue Larousse, Francais-Espagnol, Espanol-Frances. M. De Toro & Gisbert. Larousse.

Dictionnaire Bilingue Larousse, Francais-Italien et Italien-Francais. G. Padovani & R. Silvestri. Larousse.

Dictionnaire Bilingue Larousse, Francais-Portugais et Portugais-Francais. F. Peixoto Da Fonseca. Larousse.

Dictionnaire Bordas. Robert Jarnier. Bordas-Dunod.

Dictionnaire Bordas: Cahier de Travaux Diriges. R. Jarnier & J. Fournier. Harrap.

Dictionnaire Bordas: Dictionnaire du Francais Vivant. Ed. by M. R. Davau et al. Harrap.

Dictionnaire Breton-Francais, Francais-Breton. French & Eur.

Dictionnaire Bulgare-Francais. L. Stephanova et al. French & Eur.

Dictionnaire Canadien des Relations du Travail: Francais-Anglais. Gerard Dion. French & Eur.

Dictionnaire Canadien des Relations du Travall Francais-Anglais. Gerard Dion. Laval P. U.

Dictionnaire Canadien-Francais. Sylva Clapin. French & Eur.

Dictionnaire Canadien-Francais. Sylva Clapin. Soc Dev Liv.

Dictionnaire Canadien-Francais. Sylva Clapin. Laval.

Dictionnaire Chasse. Tony Burnand. Larousse.

Dictionnaire Chimique. Raymond Cornubert. Intl Pubns Serv.

Dictionnaire Chinois-Francais. French & Eur.

Dictionnaire Chinois-Francais des Locutions et Proverbes. French & Eur.

Dictionnaire civilisation Grecque. G. Rachet & M. F. Rachet. Larousse.

Dictionnaire civilisation Romaine. Jean C. Fredoville. Larousse.

Dictionnaire Classique Anglais-Francais. Charles Patit & William Savage. Hac.

Dictionnaire Classique Anglais-Francais et Francais-Anglais. Charles Petit & William Savage. French & Eur.

Dictionnaire Classique de la Langue Chinoise. F. S. Couvveur. French & Eur.

Dictionnaire Classique Francais-Allemand. Bertaux. Hachette.

Dictionnaire Classique Francais-Neerlandais. Ludovic Grootaers. Vander.

Dictionnaire Classique: Francais-Neerlandais, Neerlandais-Francais. Ludovic Grootaers. French & Eur.

Dictionnaire Commente de l'oeuvre de General de Gaulle. French & Eur.

Dictionnaire Commercial & Financier en Quatre Langues: Francais-Neerlandais-Anglais-Allemand. Josef V. Servotte. Erasme.

Dictionnaire Commercial & Financier: Francais-Anglais. Josef V. Servotte. Marabout.

Dictionnaire Commercial: Italien-Francais Francais-Italien. Mario Mormile. Maison Dictionnaire.

Dictionnaire Commerciale. French & Eur.

Dictionnaire Complet des Mots Croises. French & Eur.

Dictionnaire Complet des Mots Croises. Larousse & Co. Larousse.

Dictionnaire Contextuel Anglais-Francais de l'energie Solaire. French & Eur.

Dictionnaire Contextuel Anglais-Francais de l'energie Solaire. Robert Serre. Serre.

Dictionnaire Correctif du Francais au Canada. Dulong. Laval P. U.

Dictionnaire Corse-Francais, Pierre d'Evisa. Mathieu Ceccaldi. French & Eur.

Dictionnaire Corse-Francais, Pierre d'Evisa. Mathieu Ceccald. Klincksieck.

Dictionnaire Corse-Francais (Pierre d'Evisa) Mathieu Ceccald. CNRS.

Dictionnaire Critique & Documentaire: Peintres, Sculptres, Dessinateurs de Tous les Temps & de Tous les Pays. Emmanuel Benezit. Grund.

Dictionnaire Critique de la Musique Ancienne & Moderne. Andre Coeuroy. Payot.

Dictionnaire Critique de Psychiatrie. Barthhold Bierens de Haan. Hameau.

Un Dictionnaire Critique des Drogues. Ronald Verbeke. French & Eur.

Un Dictionnaire Critique des Drogues. Ronald Verbeke. Bourgois.

Dictionnaire Critique et Documentaire des Peintres, Sculpteurs, Dessinateurs, et Graveurs de Tous les Temps et de Tons les Pays. Benezit. French & Eur.

Dictionnaire d'accentuation pour les Travailleurs de la Radio & de la Television. Rosenthal. MIR.

Dictionnaire d'Agriculture. L. N. Mauroy. Ed. by J. P. Migne. Caratzas Pub Co.

Dictionnaire d'Agriculture. French & Eur.

Dictionnaire d'agriculture. C. I. L. F.

Dictionnaire d'Anecdotes Chretiennes. P. Jouhanneaud. Ed. by J. P. Migne. Caratzas Pub Co.

Dictionnaire d'Anglais. F. Dubois-Charlier et al. Larousse.

Dictionnaire D'anglais. F. Dubois-Charlier. Larousse FR.

Dictionnaire d'anglais. Francois Dubois-Charlier et al. Larousse.

Dictionnaire d'Anglais Niveau 1. Dubois Charlier et al. Larousse.

Dictionnaire Danois-Francais. Larousse.

Dictionnaire d'Anthropologie ou Histoire Naturelle del'Homme et des Races Humaines. L. F. Jehan. Ed. by J. P. Migne. Caratzas Pub Co.

Dictionnaire d'Antiphilosophisme ou Refutation des Erreurs du 18e Siecle. E. Grosse. Ed. by J. P. Migne. Caratzas Pub Co.

Dictionnaire d'Apologetique. L. F. Jehan. Ed. by J. P. Migne. Caratzas Pub Co.

Dictionnaire d'argot. Andre La Rue. Flammarion.

Dictionnaire d'Argot et des Principales Locutions Populaires. Jean La Rue. French & Eur.

Dictionnaire de Ballet Moderne. French & Eur.

Dictionnaire de Biochimie Alimentaire et de Nutruition. J. Adrian & G. Legrand et al. French & Eur.

Dictionnaire de Biographie des Hommes Celebres: Despuis les Temps les Plus Recules Jusqu'a nos Jours. Edourd Sitzmann. Berger Levrault.

Dictionnaire de Biologie Animale. Roger Husson. Gauthier-Villars.

Dictionnaire de Botanique. L. F. Jehan. Ed. by J. P. Migne. Caratzas Pub Co.

Dictionnaire de Botanique. Charles Louis Gatin. Kraus.

Dictionnaire de Botanique: Vol. 1, A-H. Uberto Tosco. Atlas.

Dictionnaire de Botanique: Vol. 2, I-Z. Uberto Tosco. Atlas.

Dictionnaire de Chimie Allemand-Francais. Raymond Cornubert. French & Eur.

Dictionnaire de Chimie et de Mineralogie. L. F. Jehan. Ed. by J. P. Migne. Caratzas Pub Co.

Dictionnaire De Cosmogonie et De Paleontologie. L. F. Jehan. Ed. by J. P. Migne. Caratzas Pub Co.

Dictionnaire de Danse. Jacques Baril. French & Eur.

Dictionnaire de Demographie. Roland Pressat. Pr Univ Fr.

Dictionnaire De Deux Cent Un Verbes Anglais Conjuges Completement a Tous les Temps & a Toutes les Personnes. Kendris. Barron.

Dictionnaire de Deux Cent un Verbes Allemandes. Barron.

Dictionnaire de Diagnostic Clinique et Topographique. Alain Blacque-Belair & Bernard M. de Fossey. French & Eur.

Dictionnaire de Didactique des Langues. Ed. by R. Galisson & D. Coste. Hachette-Jeunesse.

Dictionnaire de Didactique des Largues. Ed. by R. Galisson & D. Coste. French & Eur.

Dictionnaire de Droit. French & Eur.

Dictionnaire de Droit Canonique. R. Naz. French & Eur.

Dictionnaire de Droit Social Francais-Allemand. F. Frankl. French & Eur.

Dictionnaire de Echecs. E. Maget. French & Eur.

Dictionnaire de Franglais. French & Eur.

Dictionnaire de Genetique. Philippe L'Heritier. Masson & Cie.

Dictionnaire de Geographie Ancienne et Moderne. Pierre Deschamps. French & Eur.

Dictionnaire de Geographie Historique de la Gaule et de la France. Joseph Moreau. French & Eur.

Dictionnaire de Geologie... et Dictionnaire de Chronologie Universelle par M. Champagnac. L. P. Chesnel De La Charbouclais. Ed. by J. P. Migne. Caratzas Pub Co.

Dictionnaire de Halles. Claude Mallement De Messanges. Slatkine.

Dictionnaire de la Beaute Feminine. Floriane Prevot. French & Eur.

Dictionnaire de la Biologie. Gunther Haensch. BLV Verlag.

Dictionnaire de la Biologie--B.L.V. French & Eur.

Dictionnaire de la Chasse. Tony Burnand. (Pub. by Larousse). French & Eur.

Dictionnaire de la chasse. Tony Burnand. Larousse.

Dictionnaire de la Chimie et de Ses Applications. C. Duval. French & Eur.

Dictionnaire de la Civilisation Egyptienne. Georges Posener. French & Eur.

Dictionnaire de la Civilisation Grecque. French & Eur.

Dictionnaire de la Commune. Bernard Noel. French & Eur.

Dictionnaire de la comptabilite. Fernand Sylvain. Can Inst Chart Accts.

Dictionnaire de la Constitution: Les Institutions de la Ve Republique. Raymond Barrillon. French & Eur.

Dictionnaire de la Contradiction. Maurice Toesca. French & Eur.

Dictionnaire de la Culture Physique. Marcel Rouet. French & Eur.

Dictionnaire de la Danse, Historique, Theorique, Pratique & Bibliographique. G. Desrat. Olms Verlag.

Dictionnaire de la Foi Chretiene. Ed. by Antonir Marie Henry & Olivier De LaBrosse. French & Eur.

Dictionnaire de la Franc-Maconnerie et des Francs-Macons. Allec Mellor. French & Eur.

Dictionnaire de la Geographie. Pierre George. French & Eur.

Dictionnaire de la Langue des Iles Marquises. Ildefonse Dordillon. French & Eur.

Dictionnaire de la Langue Francaise. Littre. Ed. by Beaujean & Geraud-Venzac. French & Eur.

Dictionnaire de La Langue Francaise. Emile Littre. French & Eur.

Dictionnaire de la Langue Pedagogique. Paul Foulquie. PUF.

Dictionnaire de la Langue Quebecoise. L. Bergeron. French & Eur.

Dictionnaire de la Langue Romane ou du Vieux Langue Francois. Francois Lacombe. Slatkine.

Dictionnaire de la Langue Romano-Casteaise & des Contrees Limitrophes. J. Couzinie. Lafitte Repr.

Dictionnaire de la Langue Toulousaine. Jean Doujat. Lafitte Repr.

Dictionnaire de la Langue Verte. Alfred Delvau. Slatkine.

Dictionnaire de la Linguistique. Georges Mounin. PUF.

Dictionnaire de la Loi. Robert Millet. Homme.

Le Dictionnaire de la Marine a Voile. Pierre M. De Bonnefoux & Edmund Paris. Courtille.

Dictionnaire de la Mer & de la Navigation. Gianni Cazzaroli. Denoel.

Dictionnaire de la Montagne. Jacques Gautrat. French & Eur.

Dictionnaire de la Musique. Ed. by Marc Honegger. French & Eur.

Dictionnaire de la Musique. Marc Honegger. Bordas-Dunod.

Dictionnaire de la Musique: Science de la Musique. M. Honegger. French & Eur.

Dictionnaire de la Mythologie Grecque et Romaine. Pierre Grimal. French & Eur.

Dictionnaire de la Navication. Gianni Cazzaroli. French & Eur.

Dictionnaire de la Noblesse. Francais Aubert de la Chenaye-Desbois. French & Eur.

Dictionnaire de la Noblesse Francais. Etienne De Sereville & F. de Saint-Simon. French & Eur.

Dictionnaire de la Noblesse Francais. F. Saint-Simon. Contrepoint.

Dictionnaire de la Peinture Italienne. French & Eur.

Dictionnaire de la Peinture Surrealiste. Sarane Alexandrian. French & Eur.

Dictionnaire de la Peinture Surrealiste. Sarane Alexandrian. (Pub. by Filipacchi). Hippocrene Bks.

Dictionnaire de la Politique Francaise. Henry Coston. Coston.

Dictionnaire de la Politique Francaise. Henry Coston. Francaise Lib.

Dictionnaire de la Politique Francaise, 3. Henry Coston. Coston.

Dictionnaire de la presse ecrite et audiovisuelle. Divers. Maison Dictionnaire.

Dictionnaire de la Prononciation. A. Lerond. French & Eur.

Dictionnaire de la Prononciation. A. Lerond. (Dist. by Continental Bk Co). Larousse.

Dictionnaire de la Prononciation Francaise Dans Son Usage Reel. Andre Martinet & Henriette Walter. French & Eur.

Dictionnaire de la Prononciation Francaise dans son Usage Reel. Andre Martinet & Henriette Walter. France Expansion.

Dictionnaire de la Prononciation Francaise. Leon Warnant. French & Eur.

Dictionnaire de la Prononciation Francais. Leon Warnant. Duculot.

Dictionnaire de la Prononciation Francais. Leon Warnant. Duculot.

Dictionnaire de la Prononciation Francais. Leon Warnant. Renouveau Pedagogique.

Dictionnaire de la Provence & du Comte Venaissin. Claude F. Achard. Slatkine.

Dictionnaire de la Psychanalyse. Pierre Fedida. Larousse.

Dictionnaire de la Psychologie. Norbert Sillamy. Larousse.

Dietionnaire de la Publicite et du Marketing: Anglais-Francais Francais-Anglais. Sylvain Giomot. Maison Dictionnaire.

Dictionnaire de la revolution Etudiante. Alain Buhler & J. Didier. Controverses.

Dictionnaire de la Revolution Francaise. E. Boursin & Auguste Challamel. Kraus.

Dictionnaire de la Science Economique. Alain Cotta. French & Eur.

Dictionnaire de la Science Economique. Alain Cotta. Delarge.

Dictionnaire de la Seconde Guerre mondiale. Philippe Masson. Larousse.

Dictionnaire de la Sexualite. Georges Valensin. French & Eur.

Dictionnaire de la Technique Industrielle: Allemand-Francais. R. Ernst. Maison Dictionnaire.

Dictionnaire de la Technologie des Corps Gras. Boris Solomon. Inst Corps Gras.

Dictionnaire de la Tradition Pontificale, Patristique et Conciliaire. J. C. Poussin & J. C. Garnier. Ed. by J. P. Migne. Caratzas Pub Co.

Dictionnaire de la Troisieme Republique. Pierre Pierrard. Larousse.

Dictionnaire de la Vie Affective et Sexuelle. Jean Cohen & Anne Marie Dourlen-Rollier et al. French & Eur.

Dictionnaire de la Virilite. P. Vincent. French & Eur.

Dictionnaire de la Virilite. Paul Vincent. Maloine.

Dictionnaire de la Voile. Ed. by Michel Barberousse. French & Eur.

Dictionnaire de la Voile. Michel Barberousse. Seuil.

Dictionnaire de l'academie Francois. Slatkine.

Le Dictionnaire de L'agriculture. Robert Faure. Doc Univers.

Dictionnaire de l'Ancien Francais. Julien A. Greimas. Larousse.

Dictionnaire de L'ancienne Langue Francaise. Frederic Godefroy. Kraus.

Dictionnaire de l'Arabe Parle Palestinien. Yohanan Elihai. French & Eur.

Dictionnaire de L'arabe Parte Palestinien: Francais-Arabe. Yohanan Elihai. Klincksieck.

Dictionnaire de l'art Contemporain. Raymond Charmet. Larousse.

Dictionnaire de l'art de Verifier les Dates. Benedictines de la Congregation de Saint-Maur. Ed. by J. P. Migne. Caratzas Pub Co.

Dictionnaire de l'astrologie. Jean-Louis Brau. Larousse FR.

Dictionnaire de l'astrologie. Michele Curcio. Casterman.

Dictionnaire de l'astrologie. Jean-Louis Brau. Larousse.

Dictionnaire de l'audio-Visual. Guitta Pessis-Pasternak. Flammarion.

Dictionnaire de l'audio-Visual: Francais-Anglais. Guitta Pessis-Pasternak. Flammarion.

Dictionnaire de l'Audio-Visuel: Francais-Anglais, Anglais-Francais. Guitta Pessis-Pasternak. French & Eur.

Dictionnaire de l'automobile. Robert Guerber. Flammarion.

Dictionnaire de l'Edition: Francais-Anglais, Anglais-Francais. Philippe Schuwer. French & Eur.

Dictionnaire de l'edition: Francais-Anglais. Philippe Schuwer. Cercle Librairie.

Dictionnaire de l'effusion. Claude Bossicart. Dryade.

Dictionnaire de l'electricien Praticien. Eugene Marec. Bailliere.

Dictionnaire de l'electronique. Jean F. Arnaud. Larousse.

Dictionnaire de l'Enfantement. Max Ploquin. French & Eur.

Dictionnaire de l'ethnologie. Michel Panoff & Michel Perrin. Payot.

Dictionnaire de l'Evaluation et de la Recherche en Education. Gilbert De Landsheere. French & Eur.

Dictionnaire de L'Extreme-Gauche. Roland Biard. Belfond.

Dictionnaire de l'Extreme-Gauche: De 1945 a Nos Jours. Roland Biard. French & Eur.

Dictionnaire de l'Extreme-Gauche: De 1945 a Nos Jours. Roland Biard. Belfond.

Dictionnaire de L'histoire de Belgique. Eugene De Seyn. Halbart Wahle.

Dictionnaire de l'Histoire Universelle de l'Eglise. L. F. Guerin. Ed. by J. P. Migne. Caratzas Pub Co.

Dictionnaire de l'Industrie des matieres plastiques. E. Ferraris. Maison Dictionnaire.

Dictionnaire de l'industrie Francaise. U. F. A. P.

Dictionnaire de l'Industrie Routiere. Jacques Choppy. Eyrolles.

Dictionnaire de l'Informatique. Jacques Bureau. French & Eur.

Dictionnaire de l'informatique. Jacques Bureau. Larousse.

Dictionnaire de l'informatique. Andre Le Garff. PUF.

Dictionnaire de l'Informatique, Francais-Anglais. Cl. Camille & M. Dehaine. French & Eur.

Dictionnaire de l'Informatique: Francais-Anglais. Claude Camille & Michel Dehaine. Bordas-Dunod.

Dictionnaire de Linguistique. J. Dubois & M. Giacomo et al. Larousse.

Dictionnaire de Linguistique. J. Dubois et al. (Dist. by Continental Bk Co). Larousse.

Dictionnaire de Linguistique. Jean Dubois et al. Larousse.

Dictionnaire de Linguistique et de Philologie Comparee. L. F. Jehan. Ed. by J. P. Migne. Caratzas Pub Co.

Dictionnaire de l'insolite & du Fantastique. Jean-Louis Bernard. Dauphin.

Dictionnaire de Litterature Francais Contemporaine. Claude Bonnefoy et al. French & Eur.

Dictionnaire de Locutions. M. M. Dubois. (Dist. by Continental Bk Co). Larousse.

Dictionnaire de Locutions, Francais-Anglais. Marguerite-Marie Dubois. French & Eur.

Dictionnaire de Locutions: Francais-Anglais. Marguerite-Marie Dubois. Larousse.

Dictionnaire de l'offshore Petrole Gaz. Helene Bolo & Philippe Cavrois. S. C. M.

Dictionnaire de L'opera. Harold Rosenthal & John Warrack. French & Eur.

Dictionnaire de l'opera. Harold Rosenthal & John Warrack. Fayard.

Dictionnaire de L'outillage et de la Machine-Outil. Jean P. Michauz. Ophrys.

Dictionnaire de Marine. Robert Gruss. Maritimes Outre mer.

Dictionnaire de Marine, Francais et Anglais. Robert Gruss. French & Eur.

Dictionnaire de Maximes & Locutions Latines Utilisees en Droit Quebecois. Albert Mayrand. Guerin.

Dictionnaire de Medecine. P. Chaumuzeau et al. Flammarion.

Dictionnaire de Medecine Amusante. Desgoses Montagnet. De Rache.

Dictionnaire de Medecine Clinique Pharmacologique & Therapeutique. Alain Blacque-Belair. Maloine.

Dictionnaire de Medecine Flammarion. French & Eur.

Dictionnaire de Medecine Flammarion. Flammarion.

Dictionnaire de Medecine Physique de Reeducation & Readaptation. Herman L. Kamenetz & Georgette Kamentz. Maloine.

Dictionnaire de Medecine Physique de Reeducation et Readaptation Fonctionelles. Herman L. Kamenetz & Georgette Kamenetz. French & Eur.

Dictionnaire de Medecine Pratique. F. A. Poujol. Ed. by J. P. Migne. Caratzas Pub Co.

Dictionnaire de Meteorologie Populaire. Jean-Philippe Chassany. French & Eur.

Dictionnaire de Meteorologie Populaire. Jean-Philippe Chassany. Maison & Larose.

Dictionnaire de Meteorologie Populaire au Quebec. Pierre Desruisseaux. Edns Laurore.

Dictionnaire de Meteorologie Populaire au Quebec. Pierre Des Ruisseaux. Aurore.

Dictionnaire de Minerologie. Atlas.

Dictionnaire de Moi-Meme. Jean Ethier-Blais. Presse.

Dictionnaire de Mots Croises. Larousse.

Dictionnaire de Musique. Jean Jacques Rousseau. Johnson.

Dictionnaire de Musique. Jean-Jacques Rousseau. Olms.

Dictionnaire de Musique dans Lequel on Simplifie les Expressions et Les Definitions Mathematiques et Physiques qui ont Rapport a cet Art. Jean J. de Meude-Monpas. AMS Pr.

Dictionnaire de Paleographie, de Cryptographie, de Dactylologie. Ed. by J. P. Migne. Caratzas Pub Co.

Dictionnaire de Patrologie. A. Sevestre. Ed. by J. P. Migne. Caratzas Pub Co.

Dictionnaire de Pharmacologie Dentaire. Roger Viellefosse. French & Eur.

Dictionnaire de Pharmacologie Dentaire. Roger Vieillefosse. Maloine.

Dictionnaire de Philosophie et de Theologie Scolastiques. F. Morin. Ed. by J. P. Migne. Caratzas Pub Co.

Dictionnaire de Physiologie. A. L. Boyer. Ed. by J. P. Migne. Caratzas Pub Co.

Dictionnaire de Physique. Gabriel Laitier. French & Eur.

Dictionnaire de Physique. Gabriel Laitier. Maloine.

Dictionnaire de poche du teletraitement des donnees. W. H. Carl. Maison Dictionnaire.

Dictionnaire de Poche Explicatif. J. Froimont. Erasme.

Dictionnaire de Poche Francais-Allemand. Berlitz.

Dictionnaire de Poche Francais-Anglais. Berlitz.

Dictionnaire de Poche Francais-Chinois. French & Eur.

Dictionnaire de Poche Francais-Chinois. Pekin.

Dictionnaire de Poche Francais-Danois. Berlitz.

Dictionnaire de Poche Francais-Espagnol. Berlitz.

Dictionnaire de Poche Francais-Finnois. Berlitz.

Dictionnaire de Poche Francais-Hongrois. S. Eckhardt. Terra.

Dictionnaire de Poche Francais-Italien. Berlitz.

Dictionnaire de Poche Francais-Neerlandais. Berlitz.

Dictionnaire de Poche: Francais-Neerlandias. Erasme.

Dictionnaire de Poche Francais-Norvegien. Berlitz.

Dictionnaire de Poche Francais-Suedois. Berlitz.

Dictionnaire de Poche Russe-Francais. Dolgopolova. MIR.

Dictionnaire de Poche, 1: Francais-Polonais. Bernard Hamel. Polonaises.

Dictionnaire de Poche, 2: Polonais-Francais. Bernard Hamel. Polonaises.

Dictionnaire de Poetique & de Rhetorique. Henri Morier. Pr Univ Fr.

Dictionnaire de Poitiers, Ville d'art & d'histoire. Hubert Le Roux. H. Le Roux.

Dictionnaire de Politique. Jean Malignon. French & Eur.

Dictionnaire de Politique. A. Akoun et al. Larousse FR.

Dictionnaire de Politique. Jean Malignon. Cujas.

Dictionnaire de Politique: Coll. le Present en Question. French & Eur.

Dictionnaire de Politique: Collection le Present en Question. (Dist. by Continental Bk Co). Larousse.

Dictionnaire de Prevention. Gustave Capron & Jackie Boisselier. Soc Corp Hygiene.

Dictionnaire de Psychiatrie Sociale. Gerard Bleaudonu. Payot.

Dictionnaire de Psychiatrie Sociale. Gerard Bleandonu. Payot.

Dictionnaire de Psychologie. Norbert Sillamy. Larousse.

Dictionnaire de Psychologie en Trois Langues: Anglais-Francais-Allemand. Hubert C. Duijker & Maria J. Van Rijswijk. Editest.

Dictionnaire de Psychologie en Trois Langues, Vol. 2. Hubert C. Duijker. French & Eur.

Dictionnaire de Psychologie en Trois Langues, 2: Francais-Allemand-Anglais. Hubert C. Duijker & Maria J. Van Rijswijk. Editest.

Dictionnaire de Psychologie en Trois Langues, 3: Allemand-Anglais-Francais. Hubert C. Duijker & Maria J. Van Rijswijk. Editest.

Dictionnaire de Psychologie en 3 Langues. Hubert C. Duijker & Maria Van Sijswijk. French & Eur.

Dictionnaire de Rampa. Lobsang T. Rampa . Presse.

Dictionnaire de Rimes. Paul Desfeuilles. Garnier.

Dictionnaire de Rimes Francaises. Jean Le Fevre. Slatkine.

Dictionnaire de Sigillographie Pratique. Louis A. Chassant & P. J. Delbarre. Olms Verlag.

Dictionnaire de Sigles Nationaux & Internationaux. Michel Dubois. Maison Dictionnaire.

Dictionnaire de Sigles Nationaux et Internationaux. Michel Dubois. French & Eur.

Dictionnaire de sigles nationaux et internationaux. M. Dubois. Maison Dictionnaire.

Dictionnaire de Sociologie. Joseph Sumpf & Michel Hugues. French & Eur.

Dictionnaire de Sociologie. Emilio Willems. French & Eur.

Dictionnaire de Sociologie. Joseph Sumpf & Michel Hugues. Larousse.

Dictionnaire de Sociologie. Emilio Willems. Riviere.

Dictionnaire De Sociologie Phalansterienne: Guide Des Oeuvres Completes De Charles Fourier. E. Silberling. B Franklin.

Dictionnaire de Statistique Religieuse. L. Des Mas-Latrie. Ed. by J. P. Migne. Caratzas Pub Co.

Dictionnaire de Stenographie. Paul Fleury & E. Roy. Estoup.

Dictionnaire de Stenographie Duploye. Agatha-Marguerite Pommier & Blanche Guaspare. Foucher.

Dictionnaire de Sylviculture: Francais-Allemand-Anglais-Espagnol-Italien. Alberto Bruttini. Lechevalier.

Dictionnaire de Technologie. L. P. Chesnel De la Charbouclais. Ed. by J. P. Migne. Caratzas Pub Co.

Dictionnaire de Tennis. Ed. by P. Rebourgeon et al. French & Eur.

Dictionnaire de Tourisme Francais-Hongrois. L. Havas. Terra.

Dictionnaire de Zoologie. L. F. Jehan. Ed. by J. P. Migne. Caratzas Pub Co.

Dictionnaire de Zoologie: Vol. 1, A-J. Umberto Parenti. Atlas.

Dictionnaire de Zoologie: Vol. 2, K-Z. Umberto Parenti. Atlas.

Dictionnaire d'Economic Charitable. F. Martin-Doisy. Ed. by J. P. Migne. Caratzas Pub Co.

Dictionnaire d'Education. D. Raymond. Ed. by J. P. Migne. Caratzas Pub Co.

Dictionnaire D'electronique & Tele-Communication: Anglais-Francais. G. J. Proulx. Beauchemin.

Dictionnaire d'Electronique et Tele-Communication: Anglais-Francais. G. J. Proulx. French & Eur.

Dictionnaire d'Eloquence Sacree. J. C. Nadal. Ed. by J. P. Migne. Caratzas Pub Co.

Dictionnaire d'Epigraphie Chretienne. J. J. Bourasse. Ed. by J. P. Migne. Caratzas Pub Co.

Dictionnaire d'Epistemologie Genetique. A. M. Battro. (Pub. by Reidel Holland). Kluwer Academic.

Dictionnaire des Abbreviations Latines et Francaises Usitees dans les Inscriptions Lapidaires et Metalliques, les Manuscrits et les Chartes de Moyen Age. Alphonse A. Chassant. B Franklin.

Dictionnaire des Abreviations Latines & Francaise: Usitees dans les Inscriptions du Moyen-Age. Louis A. Chassant. Lenox.

Dictionnaire des Abreviations Latines & Francaises: Usitees dans les Inscriptions du Moyen Age. Louis A. Chassant. Olms Verlag.

Le Dictionnaire des Affaires. Wilfrid Lebel. Homme.

Dictionnaire des Affaires Francais-Anglais, Anglais-Francais. Delmas-Harrap. French & Eur.

Dictionnaire des Affaires: Francais-Anglais. Michel Peron & William Withnell. Larousse.

Dictionnaire des Aliments. Rosie Maurel. Table Ronde.

Dictionnaire des Aliments pour les Animaux. Marcello Picconi. French & Eur.

Dictionnaire des Aliments pour les Animaux. Marcello Piccioni. Maison Rustique.

Dictionnaire des Amateurs Francais au Dix-Septieme Siecle. Edmond Bonnaffe. B Franklin.

Dictionnaire des Amateurs Francais au 17 Siecle. Edmond Bonnaffe. Lenox.

Dictionnaire des Americanismes. Etienne Deak & Simone Deak. French & Eur.

Dictionnaire des Americanismes. Etienne Deak & Simone Deak. Dauphin.

Dictionnaire des Anglicismes. G. Rey-Debove. French & Eur.

Dictionnaire des Animaux. Blanc P. Rousselet. French & Eur.

Dictionnaire des Animaux. Deux Coqs.

Dictionnaire des Anoblis Normands. Gerard Arundel De Conde. G. Arundel De Conde.

Dictionnaire des Anthropologistes. Paul-Emile Duroux. French & Eur.

Dictionnaire des Anthropologistes. Paul-Emile Duroux. Delarge.

Dictionnaire des Antiquites Grecques. Pierre Paris. Boccard.

Dictionnaire des Antiquites Grecques & Romaines. Charles Daremberg & E. Saglio. Akadem Druck-U Verlagsanstalt.

Dictionnaire des Apocryphes. G. Brunet. Ed. by J. P. Migne. Caratzas Pub Co.

Dictionnaire des Apologistes Involontaires. C. F. Cheve. Ed. by J. P. Migne. Caratzas Pub Co.

Dictionnaire des Argots Francais. Esnault. French & Eur.

Dictionnaire des Artistes ou Notice Historique: Raisonnee des Architectes, Peintres & Graveurs. Louis-Abel De Fontenay. Minkoff.

Dictionnaire des Arts de Peinture & Gravure. Claude-Henri Watelet & Pierre-Charles Levesque. Minkoff Repr.

Dictionnaire des Arts de Peinture, Sculpture & Gravure. Claude-Henre Watelet & Pierre-Charles Levesque. Olms Verlag.

Dictionnaire des Arts de Peinture, Sculpture & Gravure. Claude-Henri Watelet & Pierre-Charles Levesque. Olms Verlag.

Dictionnaire des Arts de Peinture, Sculpture & Gravure. Claude-Henri Watelet & Pierre-Charles Levesque. Olms Verlag.

Dictionnaire des Arts de Peinture, Sculpture & Gravure. Claude-Henri Watelet & Pierre-Charles Levesque. Olms Verlag.

Dictionnaire des Arts de Peinture, Sculpture & Gravure. Claude-Henri Watelet & Pierre-Charles Levesque. Olms Verlag.

Dictionnaire des Arts du Spectacle. Cecile Giteau. Bordas-Dunod.

Dictionnaire des Arts du Spectacle: Theatre, Cinema, Cirque, Danse, Radio... Cecile Giteau. French & Eur.

Dictionnaire des Assurances Sociales. Jean-Charles Sournia. French & Eur.

Dictionnaire des Assurances Sociales. Masson.

Dictionnaire des Auteurs de Langue Francais. Yves-Alain A. Favre. Flammarion.

Le Dictionnaire des Autorites. Georges Vajda. French & Eur.

Le Dictionnaire des Autorites. Georges Vajda. CNRS.

Dictionnaire des Bureaux de Poste Francais. Jean Pothion. Poste Aux Lettres.

Dictionnaire des Canalisations a Grande Distance: Anglais-Francais-Allemand. H. Bucksch & A. Altemeyer. French & Eur.

Dictionnaire des Canalisations: Francais-Allemand. Hector Bucksch. Eyrolles.

Dictionnaire des Cardinaux. C. Berton. Ed. by J. P. Migne. Caratzas Pub Co.

Dictionnaire des Changements de Noms. Lib.

Dictionnaire des Charges, Emplois & Metiers Relevant des Institutions. Monique Ornato. CNRS.

Dictionnaire des Chateaux de France. Larousse.

Dictionnaire des Cineastes. Georges Sadoul. French & Eur.

Le Dictionnaire des Citations. Karl Petit. Bout.

Dictionnaire des Citations Francaises. French & Eur.

Dictionnaire des Citations Francaises. Pierre Serand & Samuel S. De Sacy. Larousse.

Dictionnaire des Communes. Larousse.

Dictionnaire des Communes (de France) French & Eur.

Dictionnaire des Communes de France (Guide to French Townships) Michelin Guides & Maps. Michelin.

Dictionnaire des Communes de la Haute-Saone, 3. M. Bon.

Dictionnaire des Communes de la Haute-Saone, 4. M. Bon.

Dictionnaire des Communes de la Haute-Saone, 1. M. Bon.

Dictionnaire des Communes de la Haute-Saone, 2. M. Bon.

Dictionnaire des Communes de la Haute-Saone, 5. M. Bon.

Dictionnaire des Communes de la Haute-Saone, 6. M. Bon.

Dictionnaire des Confreries & Corporations d'Arts & Metiers. T. F. Gautier. Ed. by J. P. Migne. Caratzas Pub Co.

Dictionnaire des Controverses Historiques. L. F. Jehan. Ed. by J. P. Migne. Caratzas Pub Co.

Dictionnaire des Conventionnels. A. Kuscinski. Francais, Ed. Du Vexin.

Dictionnaire des Conversions. C. F. Cheve. Ed. by J. P. Migne. Caratzas Pub Co.

Dictionnaire des Correspondants de l'academie. Leon-Noel Berthe. Eveche D'Arras.

Dictionnaire des Correspondants de Tellhard. Gerard H. Baudry. G. Baudry.

Dictionnaire des Costumes, Croyances & Langages. Reprints.

Dictionnaire des Couleurs. Viviane Cohen. Paris Livre de Odege.

Dictionnaire des Couleurs. Viviane Cohen. Livre de Paris.

Dictionnaire des Critiques Litteraires. Laurent Le Sage. Pa St U Pr.

Dictionnaire des Delais de Procedure. Roger Barbaud. Dalloz.

Dictionnaire des Devises Heraldiques. Louis A. Chassant & Henri Tausin. Olms Verlag.

Dictionnaire des Devises Historiques & Heraldiques. A. Chassant & H. Tausin. Slatkine.

Dictionnaire des Difficultes de la Langue Francaise. A. V. Thomas. Larousse.

Dictionnaire des Difficultes de la Langue Francaise. A. V. Thomas. (Dist. by Continental Bk Co). Larousse.

Dictionnaire des Difficultes Grammaticale & Lexicologiques. Scientifiques & Litteraires.

Dictionnaire des Difficultes Grammaticales & Lecicologiques. Samson, CED.

Dictionnaire des Droits et de la Raison. C. P. LeNoir. Ed. by J. P. Migne. Caratzas Pub Co.

Dictionnaire des Dynasties Bourgeoises & du Monde des Affaires. Henry Coston. A. Moreau.

Dictionnaire des Echecs. Francois Le Lionnais. PUF.

Dictionnaire des Ecrivains Francais. J. Malignon. French & Eur.

Dictionnaire des Erreurs Sociales. A. Jouffroy. Ed. by J. P. Migne. Caratzas Pub Co.

Dictionnaire des Facultes Intellectuelles et Affectives de l'ame ou l'on Traite des Passions, des Vertus, des Vices, Des Defauts. F. A. Poujol. Ed. by J. P. Migne. Caratzas Pub Co.

Dictionnaire des Familles Nobles & Notables de la Correze. J. B. Champeval. Lafitte Repr.

Le Dictionnaire des Femmes. Pensee Moderne.

Dictionnaire des Femmes Celebres. Albert Jourcin. Larousse.

Dictionnaire des Filigranes Classes en Groupe Alphabetique. F. Marmol. Olms Verlag.

Dictionnaire des Films. Georges Sadoul. French & Eur.

Dictionnaire des Films. Georges Sadoul. Seuil.

Dictionnaire Des Forets. Georges Plaisance. French & Eur.

Dictionnaire des Forets. Georges Plaisance. G. Plaisance.

Dictionnaire des Frequences de Mots dans le Russe. Steinfeld.

Dictionnaire des Frequences: Vocabulaire Literaire des 19 & 20 Siecles, 1. Klincksieck.

Dictionnaire des Frequences: Vocabulaire Literaire des 19 & 20 Siecles, 2. Klincksieck.

Dictionnaire des Frequences: Vocabulaire Literaire des 19 & 20 Siecles, 3. Klincksieck.

Dictionnaire des Frequences: Vocabulaire Literaire des 19 & 20 Siecle, 4. Klincksieck.

Dictionnaire des Fromages. Robert H. Courtine. French & Eur.

Dictionnaire des Fromages. Robert H. Courtine. Larousse.

Dictionnaire des Grands Evenements de L'histoire. Georges Masquet. (Pub. by Hachette). French & Eur.

Dictionnaire des Grands Evenements de l'histoire. Georges Masquet. Hachette.

Dictionnaire des Grands Evenements de l'Historie. Georges Masquet. Hachette-Jeunesse.

Dictionnaire des Groupes Industriels & Financiers en France. French & Eur.

Dictionnaire des Groupes Industriels & Financiers en France. Michel Beaud & Bertrand Bellon. Seuil.

Dictionnaire des Harmonies de la Raison et de la Foi. C. P. LeNoir. Ed. by J. P. Migne. Caratzas Pub Co.

Dictionnaire des Herbes & des Epices. Colin Clair. Denoel.

Dictionnaire des Herbes et des Epices. Colin Clair. French & Eur.

Dictionnaire des Heresies des Erreurs et des Schismes. F. A. Pluquet. Ed. by J. P. Migne. Caratzas Pub Co.

Dictionnaire Des Heresies Meridionales. Rene Nelli. French & Eur.

Dictionnaire des Heresies Meridionales. Rene Nelli. Privat.

Dictionnaire des Histoires Droles. Herve Negre. Fayard.

Dictionnaire des Histoires Droles, 1. Herve Negre. L. G. F.

Dictionnaire des Histoires Droles, 2. Herve Negre. L. G. F.

Le Dictionnaire des Hommes. Anne-Marie Carriere. Pensee Moderne.

Dictionnaire des Horlogers Francais. Tardy. Tardy-Lengelle.

Dictionnaire des Hulles Vegetales. Paul H. Mensier. Lechevalier.

Dictionnaire Des Idees Dans L'oeuvre D'andre Malraux. Ileana Juilland. French & Eur.

Dictionnaire Des Idees Dans L'oeuvre D'Andre Malraux: Collection Dictionaries Des Idees Dans les Litteratures Occidentales, Litterature Francaise: Dictionnnaires D'auteurs. Ileana Julland. Mouton.

Dictionnaire Des Idees Dans L'oeuvre De Marcel Proust: Collection Dictionnaires Des Idees Dans les Litteratures Occidentales, Litterature Francaise. Ed. by Pauline Newman-Gordon. Mouton.

Dictionnaire des Idees dans L'oeuvre de Simone de Beauvoir. Christian van den Berghe. Mouton.

Dictionnaire des Idees Suggerees par les Mots. Paul Rouaix. Colin.

Dictionnaire des Imprimeurs. Anne Rouzet. De Graaf.

Dictionnaire des Inconnus aux Noms Communs. Michel Dansel. Encre.

Dictionnaire des Industries Alimentaires. Jean-Michel Clement. French & Eur.

Dictionnaire des Industries Alimentaires. Jean M. Clement. Masson & Cie.

Dictionnaire des Infixes de l'esquimau de l'Ungava. Lucien Schneider. Quebec Off.

Dictionnaire Des Institutions De la France Aux Dix-Septieme et Dix-Huitieme Siecles. Ed. by Marcel Marion. B Franklin.

Dictionnaire des Institutions de la France aux XVII & XVIII Siecles. Marcel Marion. Lenox.

Dictionnaire des Institutions de la France aux 17 & 18 Siecles. Marcel Marion. Picard.

Dictionnaire des Institutions, Moeurs & Costumes du Rouergue. Henri Affre & Rodez. Lafitte Repr.

Dictionnaire des Inventions et Decouvertes Anciennes et Modernes. A. Jouffroy. Ed. by J. P. Migne. Caratzas Pub Co.

Dictionnaire des Journalistes. Jean Sgard. Club Livre Select.

Dictionnaire des Journalistes, 1600-1789. Jean Sgard & Michel Gilot. French & Eur.

Dictionnaire des Locutions Francais-Allemand. Paul Werny & Alexandre Snyckers. Larousse FR.

Dictionnaire des Locutions Francaises. M. Rat. Larousse.

Dictionnaire des Locutions Francaises. Maurice Rat. Larousse.

Dictionnaire des locutions idiomatiques Françaises. Bruno Lafleur. Soc Dev Liv.

Dictionnaire des Maladies. Jean-Philippe Barbier & Francois-Claude Hugues. Heures de France.

Dictionnaire des Manuscrits, Ou Recueil De Catalogues De Manuscrits Existants Dans les Pri Cipales Bibliotheques D'europe. G. F. Haenel. Ed. by J. P. Migne. Caratzas Pub Co.

Dictionnaire des Mathematiques Modernes. Lucien Chambadal. French & Eur.

Dictionnaire des Mathematiques Modernes. Lucien Chambadal. Larousse.

Dictionnaire des Matieres Plastiques. Wittfoht. French & Eur.

Dictionnaire des Media. Jean Baptiste Fages & Christian Pagano. French & Eur.

Dictionnaire des Media. Jean Baptiste Fages & Christian Pagano. Delarge.

Dictionnaire des Media. Jean B. Fages & Christian Pagano. Hurtubise H. M. H.

Dictionnaire des Medicaments. Maurice Neuman. French & Eur.

Dictionnaire des Medicaments. Maur Neuman. Heures de France.

Dictionnaire des Merveilles et Curiosites de Nature et De Art. L. P. Chesnel De la Charbouclais. Ed. by J. P. Migne. Caratzas Pub Co.

Le Dictionnaire des Meubles & Objets D'art 1965 & 1966. Enrique Mayer. Mayer.

Le Dictionnaire des Meubles & Objets d'art, 1963 & 1964. Enrique Mayer. Mayer Ed.

Dictionnaire des Miniaturistes du Moyan Age: La Renaissance dans les Differentes Contrees de l'Europa. E. Aeschlimann & Paolo Ancono. Kraus.

Dictionnaire des Monogrammes. Jean-Frederic Christ. Minkoff Repr.

Le Dictionnaire des Mots Cles du Dessin de la Peinture, de l'Estampe. Gerard Capou. Capou.

Dictionnaire des Mots Contemporains. French & Eur.

Dictionnaire Des Mots Croises. Maurice Denis-Papin. French & Eur.

Dictionnaire des Mots Croises. Larousse.

Dictionnaire des Mots Croises. Maurice Denis-Papin. Albin Michel.

Dictionnaire des Mots Croises. Robert Piquette et al. Homme.

Dictionnaire des Mots Croises & Jeux Divers. Maurice Denis-Papin. Albin Michel.

Dictionnaire des Mots Croises: Noms Communs. Paul Lasnier. Homme.

Dictionnaire des Mots, des Phrases, des Images. Aime Gabillon. RST.

Dictionnaire des Mots d'esprit. Jean Delacour. Albin Michel.

Dictionnaire des Mots Libres d'Apollinaire. Scott Bates. Filipacchi.

Dictionnaire des Mots Nouveaux. Pierre Gilbert. Tchou.

Dictionnaire des Muses ou Description des Principaux Musees d'Europe... Suivi Notions sur la Photographie par X. Ed. by J. P. Migne. Caratzas Pub Co.

Dictionnaire Des Musiciens. Roland de Cande. French & Eur.

Dictionnaire des Nouveaux Cinemas Arabes. Claude-Michel Cluny. Sindbad.

Dictionnaire des Objections Populaires contre le Dogme, la Morale, la Discipline et L'histoire de Eglise Catholique. C. Pinard. Ed. by J. P. Migne. Caratzas Pub Co.

Dictionnaire des Oeuvres & des Themes du Cinema Mondial. Etienne Fuzellier. Hachette-Jeunesse.

Dictionnaire des Oeuvres: Index. French & Eur.

Dictionnaire des Oiseaux. Michel Cuisin. Larousse.

Dictionnaire Des Operas. Felix Clement & Pierre Larousse. Da Capo.

Dictionnaire Des Ouvrages Anonymes. Barbier. French & Eur.

Dictionnaire des Papes. Hans Kuhner. French & Eur.

Dictionnaire des Papes. Hans Kuhner. Buchet Chastel.

Dictionnaire Des Paralleles, Concordances et Analogies Bibliques. Clearwater Pub.

Dictionnaire des Parents. Francois Cloutier. Edns Du Jour.

Dictionnaire des Parlementaires Francais: Vol. 3, 1889-1940. Jean Jolly. PUF.

Dictionnaire des Parlementaires Francais: Vol. 4, 1889-1940. Jean Jolly. PUF.

Dictionnaire des Parlers Arabes de Syrie, Liban et Palestine. Claude Denizeau. French & Eur.

Dictionnaire des Paroisses de la Correze, 3. Jean-Baptiste Poulbriere. Correze, Ste Scientifique.

Dictionnaire des Partis Communistes & des Mouvements Revolutionnaires. Francois Fejto. Casterman.

Dictionnaire des Patols de l'Yonne. Sophie Jossier. Slatkine.

Dictionnaire des Patols du Dauphine. Nicolas Charbot & Hector Blanchet. Lafitte Repr.

Dictionnaire des Patols du Dauphine. Nicolas Charbot & Hector Blanchet. Slatkine.

Dictionnaire des Patols Romans de la Moselle. Leon Zeliqzon. Strasbourg, U.

Dictionnaire des Peintres & Sculpteurs Provencaux: 1880-1950. Fondation Paul Richard & Jean-Pierre Camard. Bendor.

Dictionnaire des Peintres et Sculpteurs Provencaux. Jean Pierre Camard & Anne Marie Belfort. French & Eur.

Dictionnaire des Peintres, Sculpteurs, Dessinateurs et Graveurs. E. Benezit. Hacker.

Dictionnaire des Personnages. French & Eur.

Dictionnaire des Personnages de Tous les Temps & de Tous les Pays. French & Eur.

Dictionnaire des Plantes Qui Guerissent. Gerard Debuigne. French & Eur.

Dictionnaire des Plantes qui Guerissent. Gerard Debuigne. Larousse.

Dictionnaire des Poincons de l'Orfevrerie Provinciale Francaise. Droz.

Le Dictionnaire des Precieuses. Antoine B. De Somaize. Kraus.

Dictionnaire des Prenoms & des Saints. Pierre Pierrard. Larousse.

Dictionnaire des Principaux Sigles Utilises dans le Monde Juridique de A-Z. M. Gendrel. Bruyant.

Dictionnaire des proverbes, sentences et maximes. M. Maloux. Larousse.

Dictionnaire des Racines Semitiques. Edmond G. Heylli. Slatkine.

Dictionnaire des Racines Semitiques. David Cohen. Mouton De Gruyter.

Dictionnaire Des Racines Semitiques Ou Attestees Dans les Langues Semitiques: Comprenant un Fichier Comparatif De Jean Cantineau. David Cohen. Mouton.

Dictionnaire Des Racines Semitiques: Ou Attestees Dans les Langues Semitiques. David Cohen. Mouton.

Dictionnaire des Racines Semitiques, 2. David Cohen. Mouton De Gruyter.

Le Dictionnaire des Reves. Tom Chetwynd. Seghers.

Dictionnaire des Richesses de la Langue Francoise: Neologisme qui s'y Introduit. Pons Auguste Alletz. Slatkine.

Dictionnaire des Rimes Orales & Ecrites. Leon Warnant. Larousse.

Dictionnaire des rimes orales et ecrites. Leon Warnant. Larousse.

Dictionnaire des Sciences & Techniques Nucleaires. Commissariat a l'Energie Atomique. Brandstetter.

Dictionnaire des Sciences & Techniques Nucleaires. PUF.

Dictionnaire des Sciences & Techniques Nucleaires. Commissariat a L'energie Atomique. Eyrolles.

Dictionnaire des Sciences de la Gestion. Henri Tezenas Du Montcel. Delarge.

Dictionnaire des Sciences de la Gestion. Henri Tezenas Du Montcel. Hurtubise H. M. H.

Dictionnaire des Sciences de la Nature (Dictionary of the Natural Sciences) Edouard Ghaleb. Intl Pubns Serv.

Dictionnaire des Sciences de la Nature, 1. Edouard Ghaleb. Dar El-Machreq.

Dictionnaire des Sciences de la Nature, 2. Edouard Ghaleb. Dar El-Machreq.

Dictionnaire des Sciences de la Nature, 3. Edouard Ghaleb. Dar El-Machreq.

Dictionnaire des Sciences Medicales, 1821-1822. Werner-Heinrich Aeschilmann. Juris Druck.

Dictionnaire des sciences occultes suivi d'un dictionnaire des songes. Frederic Boutet. Pygmalion.

Dictionnaire des Sciences Politiques et Sociales. A. Ott. Ed. by J. P. Migne. Caratzas Pub Co.

Dictionnaire des Sigles Economiques & Sociaux. Liaisons Sociales.

Dictionnaire des Sigles Medicaux. J. P. Poinsotte. French & Eur.

Dictionnaire des Societes Secretes En Occident. Pierre Mariel. French & Eur.

Dictionnaire des Structures Fondamentales du Francais. P. Celerier & J. P. Maillard. (Dist. by Continental Bk Co). Cle International.

Dictionnaire des Symboles. Jean Chevalier & Alain Gheerbrant. French & Eur.

Dictionnaire des Symboles. Jean Chevalier & Alain Gheerbrant. Seghers.

Dictionnaire des Symboles Chretiens. Edouard Urech. Delachaux.

Dictionnaire des Symptomes. Edito Serv.

Dictionnaire des synonymes. R. Bailly. Larousse.

Dictionnaire des Synonymes. Henri Bertrand Du Chazaud. Soc Nouveau.

Dictionnaire des Synonymes. Larousse.

Dictionnaire des Synonymes. E. Bar. Garnier.

Dictionnaire des Synonymes. Henri Benac. Hachette.

Dictionnaire des Synonymes. Henri Benac. Renouveau Pedagogique.

Dictionnaire des Synonymes. R. De Noter & P. Vuillermoz. PUF.

Dictionnaire des Synonymes, Analogies & Antonymes. Roger Boussinot. Bordas-Dunod.

Dictionnaire des Synonymes & Antonymes. Bernard Lamizet. Garnier-Flammarion.

Dictionnaire des Synonymes & des Antonymes. Hector Dupuis & Romain Legare. Ecole.

Dictionnaire des Synonymes & des Antonymes. Hector Dupuis. Fides.

Dictionnaire des Synonymes de Poche. E. Genouvrier. (Dist. by Continental Bk Co). Larousse.

Dictionnaire des synonymes et des antonymes. Hector Dupuis. Rev. by Romain Legare. Soc Dev Liv.

Dictionnaire des Synonymes: Francais-Neerlandais. J. Froimont. Erasme.

Dictionnaire des Techniques Aeronautiques & Spatiales. Bordas.

Dictionnaire Des Techniques Aeronautiques et Spatiales. Ed. by Societe Nationale Industrielle Aerospatiale. Intl Pubns Serv.

Dictionnaire Des Techniques Aeronautiques et Spatiales--Trilingue: Francais, Anglais, Allemand: 24,000 Entrees Dans Chaque Langue. French & Eur.

Dictionnaire des Termes Agricoles: Francais-Arabe. Emir Al-Chihabi. Intl Bk Ctr.

Dictionnaire des Termes d'anatomie, d'embryologie & d'histologie. Ernest Lovasy & Emmanuel Veillon. Maloine.

Dictionnaire des Termes d'Anatomie, d'Embryologie et d'Histologie. Ernst Lovasy. French & Eur.

Dictionnaire des termes economiques et commerciaux. Mustapha Henni. Intl Bk Ctr.

Dictionnaire des Termes Juridique en Quartre Langues: Francais, Neerlandais, Anglais, Allemand. E. Le Docte. French & Eur.

Dictionnaire des Termes Juridiques en Quatre Langues: Francais-Neerlandais-Anglais-Allemand. E. Le Docte. Vander Oyez.

Dictionnaire des termes juridiques et commerciaux. Mamdouh Hakki. Intl Bk Ctr.

Dictionnaire des termes relatifs a electrotechnique, l'electronique et aux applications connexes. H. Piraux. Eyrolles.

Dictionnaire des Termes Techniques d'Entomologies Elementaire. Eugene Seguy. French & Eur.

Dictionnaire des Termes Techniques d'entomologie Elementaire. Eugene Seguy. Lechevalier.

Dictionnaire des Termes Techniques De Medecine. Marcel Garnier & Jean Delamare. French & Eur.

Dictionnaire des Termes Techniques de Medecine. Marcel Garnier & Jean Delamare. Maloine.

Dictionnaire des Termes Techniques et Commerciaux. Compiled by Mustapha Henni. INtl Bk Ctr.

Dictionnaire des Termes Veterinaires & Zootechniques. Martial Villemin. Vigot.

Dictionnaire des Theatres de Paris. Claude Parfaict. Slatkine.

Dictionnaire des Valeurs de Meubles & Objets d'art. E. Mayer. Fischbacher.

Dictionnaire des Vanites, 1. Contrepoint.

Dictionnaire des Vanites, 2. Contrepoint.

Le Dictionnaire des Varietes, A-Z. Frank Lipsik. Menges.

Dictionnaire des Ventes d'art Faites en France & a l'etranger, 1. H. Mireur. Olms Verlag.

Dictionnaire des Ventes d'art Faites en France & a l'etranger, 2. H. Mireur. Olms Verlag.

Dictionnaire des Ventes d'art Faites en France & a l'etranger, 3. H. Mireur. Olms Verlag.

Dictionnaire des Ventes d'art Faites en France & a l'etranger, 4. H. Mireur. Olms Verlag.

Dictionnaire des Ventes d'art Faites en France & a l'etranger, 5. H. Mireur. Olms Verlag.

Dictionnaire des Ventes d'art Faites en France & a l'etranger, 6. H. Mireur. Olms Verlag.

Dictionnaire des Verbe Francais. J. P. Caput & J. Caput. (Dist. by Continental Bk Co). Larousse.

Dictionnaire des verbes francais. J. P. Caput & J. Caput. Larousse.

Dictionnaire des Verbes Francais. Jean Caput & Josette Caput. Larousse.

Dictionnaire des Vins. Gerard Debuigne. Larousse.

Dictionnaire des 10,000 Dirigeants Politiques Francais. Pierre-Marie Dioudonnat & Sabine Bragadir. French & Eur.

Dictionnaire des 1001 Tournures: La Correspondance Pratique. Jean-Yves Dournon. L. G. F.

Dictionnaire Descriptif & Synonymique des Genres de Plantes Phanerogmes, 7. Albert Lemee. Lechevalier.

Dictionnaire Descriptif & Synonymique des Genres de Plantes Phanerogmes, 8. Albert Lemee. Lechevalier.

Dictionnaire Descriptif & Synonymique des Genres de Plantes Phanerogames, 9. Albert Lemee. Lechevalier.

Dictionnaire Descriptif & Synonymique des Genres de Plantes Phanerogames, 10. Albert Lemee. Lechevalier.

Dictionnaire d'Esthetique Chretienne ou Theorie du Beau dans l'Art Chretien. E. G. Jouve. Ed. by J. P. Migne. Caratzas Pub Co.

Dictionnaire detaille des noms des vetements chez les Arabes. R. Dozy. Intl Bk Ctr.

Dictionnaire d'Ethnographie. Ed. by J. P. Migne. Caratzas Pub Co.

Dictionnaire d'etymologie Sumerienne & Grammaire Comparee. Colman G. Gostony. Boccard.

Dictionnaire d'Etymologie Sumerienne et Grammaire Comparee. Colman G. Gostony. French & Eur.

Dictionnaire d'Histoire & de Geographie Ecclesiastiques. Letouzey & Ane.

Dictionnaire d'histoire & de Geographie Ecclesiastiques. Roger Aubert & Van Cauwenberg. Letouzey & Ane.

Dictionnaire d'histoire & de Geographie Ecclesiastiques. Roger Aubert et al. Letouzey & Ane.

Dictionnaire d'Histoire Contemporaine 1776-1969. Jacques De Launay & Emile Lousse. Rencontre.

Dictionnaire d'Histoire et du Geographie Ecclesiastiques. Roger Aubert & Van Cauwenberg. French & Eur.

Dictionnaire d'informatique. Georges Nania. Maison Dictionnaire.

Dictionnaire d'Informatique: Anglais-Francais. M. Ginguay. French & Eur.

Dictionnaire D'informatique Anglais-Francais. Michel Ginguay. Masson & Cie.

Dictionnaire d'informatique: Anglais-Francais. Masson.

Dictionnaire d'informatique: Francais-Anglais-Italien-Espagnol-Portugais. G. Nania. Maison Dictionnaire.

Dictionnaire d'informatique: Francais-Anglais. Masson.

Dictionnaire Dogon: Ethnologique & Linguistique. Genevieve Calamegriaule. S. E. L. A. F.

Dictionnaire d'oto-rhino-laryngologie: Francais-Anglais-Espagnol-Allemand-Italien. Maloine.

Dictionnaire Dramatique. Nicolas De Chamfort. Slatkine.

Dictionnaire du Batiment: Francais-Anglais. Marcel Lefebvre. LEMEAC.

Dictionnaire du Bearnais & du Gascon Modernes. Simon Palay. CNRS.

Dictionnaire du Bearnais & du Gascon Moderne. Simin. CNRS.

Dictionnaire du Bernais & du Gascon Modernes. Simin Palay. CNRS.

Dictionnaire du Blues. Jean-Claude Arnaudon. Filipacchi.

Dictionnaire du Bon Francais. J. Girodet. French & Eur.

Dictionnaire du Bon Langage. E. Blanchard. LIDEC.

Dictionnaire du Bricolage & du Depannage. Francis Genette. Sequoia.

Dictionnaire du Bridge. Georges Versini. PUF.

Dictionnaire du Cheval et du Chevalier. C. Cassart & R. Moirant. French & Eur.

Dictionnaire du Chien. Pierre Rousselet-Blanc & Josette Rousselet-Blanc. French & Eur.

Dictionnaire du Chien. Pierre Rousselet-Blanc & Josette Rousselet-Blanc. Laffont.

Dictionnaire du Cinema Quebecois. French & Eur.

Dictionnaire du Cinema Quebecois. Michel Houle & Alain Julien. Fides.

Dictionnaire du Cinema Universal, 6. Pierre-Charles Jeanne. Laffont.

Dictionnaire du Consommateur. R. Pujol. Gonthier.

Dictionnaire du Droit des Societes Anonymes. Joly.

Dictionnaire du Droit des Societes a Responsabille. JolY.

Dictionnaire du Droit des Societes a Responsabille. Joly.

Dictionnaire du Droit Public. Robert Wilkin. Bruylant.

Dictionnaire du Francais Argotique & Populaire. Larousse.

Dictionnaire du Francais Classique. Jean Dubois & Rene Lagane. French & Eur.

Dictionnaire du Francais Classique. Jean Dubois & Rene Lagane. Larousse.

Dictionnaire du francais contemporain: Manuel et travaux pratique. Larousse.

Dictionnaire du Francais Contemporain. J. Dubois. French & Eur.

Dictionnaire du Francais Contemporain. Ed. by Jean Dubois et al. Larousse FR.

Dictionnaire du Francais Contemporain. J. Dubois. (Dist. by Continental Bk Co). Larousse.

Dictionnaire du Francais Contemporain. Jean Dubois & Rene Lagane. Larousse.

Dictionnaire du Francais Contemporain (DFC) Larousse-Langenscheidt.

Dictionnaire du Francais Facile. Hachette.

Dictionnaire du Francais Fondamental. G. Gougenheim. (Dist. by Continental Bk Co). Didier.

Dictionnaire du Francais Fondamental pour l'Afrique. Didier.

Dictionnaire du Francais Langue Etrangere. J. Dubois. Larousse.

Dictionnaire du Francais Langue Etrangere: Niveau I. Dubois & F. Dubois-Charlier. (Dist. by Continental Bk Co). Larousse.

Dictionnaire du Francais Langue Etrangere: Niveau II. J. Dubois & F. Dubois-Charlier. (Dist. by Continental Bk Co). Larousse.

Dictionnaire du Francais Moderne. Maurice Remy. Hatier.

Dictionnaire du Francais non Conventionnel. J. Cellard & A. Key. French & eur.

Dictionnaire du Francais Vivant. Biblograf SP.

Dictionnaire du Francais Vivant: Collection "Dunod Entreprise". P. Conso et al. (Dist. by Continental Bk Co). Bordas.

Dictionnaire du Francais Vivant: Nouvelle Edition. M. Davaux et al. (Dist. by Continental Bk Co). Bordas.

Dictionnaire du Jazz. Hugues Panassie & Madeleine Gautier. French & Eur.

Dictionnaire du Jazz. Hugues Panassie & Gautier. Albin Michel.

Dictionnaire du Marche Commun. French & Eur.

Dictionnaire du Marche Commun. Joly.

Le Dictionnaire du Marche de l'Art. Didier Romand & Gerald Schurr. French & Eur.

Dictionnaire du Marche de l'art. Didier Romand & Gerard Schurr. Amateur.

Dictionnaire du Marche de l'Art: Meubles, Objects, Curiosities. Didier Romand. Amateur.

Dictionnaire du Mepris. Jacques Sternberg. Calmann Levy.

Dictionnaire du Parfait Automobiliste. Christian Vebel. Pensee Moderne.

Dictionnaire du Patois Normand. Henri Moisy. Slatkine.

Dictionnaire du Patois de la Flandre Francaise. Louis Vermesse & Douai. Slatkine.

Dictionnaire du Patois du Bas-Limousin. Slatkine.

Dictionnaire du Patois Forezien. Louis-Pierre Gras. Slatkine.

Dictionnaire du Patois Normand. E. Dumeril. Slatkine.

Dictionnaire du Patois Valdotain. Jean B. Cerlogne. Slatkine.

Dictionnaire du Petit Offset. Lucien Dodin. Prismes.

Dictionnaire du Savoir-Vivre Moderne. Floriane Prevot. Casterman.

Dictionnaire du Scrabble. Annie Carillon & Beatrice Goutel. Hachette.

Dictionnaire du Ski. Jacques Gautrat. French & Eur.

Dictionnaire du Ski. Jacques Gautrat. Seuil.

Dictionnaire du Style & des Usages Administratifs. Sodi.

Dictionnaire du Style et des Usages Administratifs. Marcel Spreutels. French & Eur.

Dictionnaire du Symbolisme Animal. Jean Paul Clebert. Albin-Michel.

Dictionnaire Du Theatre Francais Contemporain. Alfred Simon. French & Eur.

Dictionnaire du Theatre Francais Contemporain. Alfred Simon. Larousse.

Dictionnaire du Traducteur: Francais-Neerlandais. J. E. Van Grieken. Administratives.

Dictionnaire du Traitement de l'information: Francais-Allemand. Pioton.

Dictionnaire du Traitement de l'information: Francais-Allemand-Anglais. Carl Amkreutz. Carl Amkreutz.

Dictionnaire du traitement de l'informatique. Carl Amkreutz. Maison Dictionnaire.

Dictionnaire du Vin. Yves Renouil & Yves de Traversay. French & Eur.

Dictionnaire du Vin. Yves Renouil & Yves De Traversay. Feret.

Dictionnaire du Vocabulaire Essentiel. Georges Matore. French & Eur.

Dictionnaire du vocabulaire essentiel. Larousse & Co. Larousse.

Dictionnaire du Vocabulaire Essentiel. Georges Matore. Larousse.

Dictionnaire du Vocabulaire Orthographique. Larousse.

Dictionnaire Duala-Francais. Paul Helmlinger. S. E. L. A. F.

Dictionnaire Duden-Larousse: Tout Allemand. Larousse.

Dictionnaire d'un Polygraphe. L. S. Mercier. U. G. E.

Dictionnaire Economique & Financier. Yves Bernard et al. Seuil.

Dictionnaire Economique & Financier. Homme.

Dictionnaire Economique & Social. Maurice Bouvier-Ajam et al. Edns Sociales.

Dictionnaire Economique & Social. Thomas Suavet. Ouvrieres.

Dictionnaire Economique & Social: Dictionnaire Thomas Suavet. Michel Branciard. Ouvrieres.

Dictionnaire Economique et Financier. Yves Bernard et al. Ed. by Dominique Lewandowski. French & Eur.

Dictionnaire Economique et Social. Thomas H. Suarvet. French & Eur.

Dictionnaire Elementaire Creole Haitien-Francais. Pierre Nougayrol et al. Ed. by Alain Bentolila. French & Eur.

Dictionnaire Elementaire Creole Haitien-Francais. Pierre Vernet & Charles Alexandre. Hatier.

Le Dictionnaire En Couleurs Des Animaux. Maurice Burton. French & Eur.

Le Dictionnaire en Couleurs des Animaux. Maurice Burton. Elsevier Sequoia.

Dictionnaire Erotique. Pierre Guiraud. French & Eur.

Dictionnaire Espagnol-Francais. Serge Denis & Marcel Maraval. French & Eur.

Le Dictionnaire Espagnol-Francais. Serge Denis et al. Hachette Jeunesse.

Dictionnaire Espagnol-Francais. Robert Larrieu. Garnier.

Dictionnaire Espagnol-Francais. Vicente Salva. Garnier-Flammarion.

Dictionnaire Espagnol-Francais. Vicente Salva & Robert Larrieu. Garnier.

Dictionnaire Espagnol-Francais. Robert Larrieu. Garnier-Flammarion.

Dictionnaire Espagnol-Francais. A. Corbiere & Lautier. Dessain & Tolra.

Dictionnaire Espagnol-Francais. Larousse.

Dictionnaire Espagnol-Francais. Serge Denis & M. Maraval. Hachette.

Le Dictionnaire Espagnol-Francais et Francais-Espagnol. Serge Denis et al. French & Eur.

Dictionnaire Espagnol-Francais et Francais-Espagnol. Ed. by Vicente Salva & Robert Larrieu. French & Eur.

Dictionnaire Esquimau-Francais du Parler de l'Ungava & Contrees Limitrophes. Lucien Schneider. Laval P. U.

Dictionnaire Etymologiqe du Moyen-Breton. Slatkine.

Dictionnaire Etymologique. Octave Caillon. Ligel.

Dictionnaire Etymologique. Albert Dauzat et al. Larousse.

Dictionnaire Etymologique de la Langue Francaise avec les Origines Francaises. Gilles Menage. Slatkine.

Dictionnaire Etymologique de la Langue Francaise. Oscar Bloch & Walther Von Wartburg. French & Eur.

Dictionnaire Etymologique de la Langue Francaise. Oscar Bloch & Walther Von Wartburg. PUF.

Dictionnaire Etymologique de la Langue Wallonne. Charles-Marie Grandgagnage. Slatkine.

Dictionnaire Etymologique de l'ancien Francais, 1. Kurt Baldinger & Georges Straka. Klincksieck.

Dictionnaire Etymologique de l'ancien Francais. Kurt Baldinger. Laval P. U.

Dictionnaire Etymologique de l'ancien Francais. Kurt Baldinger et al. Laval P. U.

Dictionnaire Etymologique de l'ancien Francais. Kurt Baldinger. Laval P. U.

Dictionnaire Etymologique des Noms de Pays & de Peuples. Serge Losique. Klincksieck.

Dictionnaire Etymologique des noms Grecs de Plantes. Albert Carnoy. Peeters.

Dictionnaire Etymologique du Patois Lyonnais. Nizier Du Puitspelu. Slatkine.

Dictionnaire Etymologique: Historique & Anecdotique des Proverbes & des Locutions Proverbiales de la Langue Francaise. Pierre-Marie Quitard. Slatkine.

Dictionnaire Europa: Francais-Allemand. Larousse.

Dictionnaire Europa Francais-Anglais. Larousse.

Dictionnaire Europa Francais-Espagnol. Larousse.

Dictionnaire Europa Francais-Italien. Larousse.

Dictionnaire Europa Francais-Portugais. Larousse.

Dictionnaire Europa Francais-Turc. H. J. Kornrumpf. Larousse.

Dictionnaire Familial des Medecines Naturelies. Emmerick A. Maury. Delarge.

Dictionnaire Familial d'homeopathie. Emmerick A. Maury. Delarge.

Dictionnaire Familial D'homoeopathie. Emmerick A. Maury. Edns Univers.

Dictionnaire Finnois-Francais. Tauno Nurmela. Soderstrom.

Dictionnaire Finnois-Francais-Finnois. Raila-Maarit Koistinen & Helene Lasslo et al. Soderstrom.

Dictionnaire Fondamental. Georges Gougenheim. Didier.

Dictionnaire Fondamental Harrap: Francais-Anglais. Colin Henstock. Bordas-Dunod.

Dictionnaire Forestier Multilingue. Andre Metro. French & Eur.

Dictionnaire Forestier Multilingue. Andre Metro. C. I. L. F.

Dictionnaire-Formulaire Commercial. Raoul Michel & Humbert Pardel-Lans. Foucher.

Dictionnaire Foucher de Stenographie. Guy Brousse. Foucher.

Dictionnaire Foucher de Stenographie Prevost-Delauney. Guy Brousse. Foucher.

Dictionnaire Francais-Allemand. Jean Clediere et al. Larousse FR.

Dictionnaire Francais-Allemand. Erich Weis & Heinrich Mattutat. Bordas-Dunod.

Dictionnaire Francais-Allemand. Erich Weis & Heinrich Mattutat. Bordas-Dunod.

Dictionnaire Francais-Allemand-Anglais pour le Commerce Exterieur. Jean Ruhland. Ruhland.

Dictionnaire Francais-Allemand des Locutions. F. Dubois & P. Werny. French & Eur.

Dictionnaire Francais-Allemand, Deutsch-Franzosisch. A. Pinloche. French & Eur.

Dictionnaire Francais-Allemand et Allemand-Francais. Erich Weis & Heinrich Mattutat. French & Eur.

Dictionnaire Francais-Allemand pour le Travaux Publics le Batiment & l'equipement des Chantiers de Construction. Hector Bucksch. Eyrolles.

Dictionnaire Francais-Anglais. Denis Girard. Garnier.

Dictionnaire Francais-Anglais, Anglais-Francais des affaires. Michel Peron et al. Larousse.

Dictionnaire francais-anglais, anglais-francais des affaires: A French-English English-French Dictionary of Business Terms. Michel Peron et al. Larousse.

Dictionnaire Francais-Anglais, Anglais-Francais des Termes et Locutions de la Marine Marchande. French & Eur.

Dictionnaire Francais-Anglais de la Psychologie & des Sciences Connexes. Jacques Castonguay. Maloine.

Dictionnaire Francais-Anglais de l'economie Monetaire. Denis-Clair Lambert. Ouvrieres.

Dictionnaire Francais-Anglais de l'Economie. French & Eur.

Dictionnaire Francais-Anglais de l'economie. Denis-Clair Lambert. Ouvrieres.

Dictionnaire Francais-Anglais de Medecine Physique de Reeducation & de Readaptation Fonctionnelles. Herman L. Kamenetz & Georgette Kamenetz. Maloine.

Dictionnaire Francais-Anglais des Debutantes. Charlier F. Dubois. (Dist. by Continental Bk Co). Larousse.

Dictionnaire Francais-Anglais des Termes & Locutions de la Marine Marchande. Maritimes Outremer.

Dictionnaire Francais-Anglais des Termes Medicaux & Biologiques. Pierre Lepine. Flammarion.

Dictionnaire Francais-Anglais des Termes Relatifs a l'electronique: L'electronique & aux Applications Connexes. Henri Piraux. Eyrolles.

Dictionnaire Francais-Anglais des Termes Techniques de Medecine. Jean Delamare & Marie-Therese Delamareriche. Maloine.

Dictionnaire Francais-Anglais et Anglais-Francais des Termes Medicaux et Biologiques. Pierre Lepine. French & Eur.

Dictionnaire Francais-Anglais et Anglais-Francais des Termes Techniques de Medecine. J. Delamare & Th. Delamare. French & Eur.

Dictionnaire Francais-Anglais et Anglais-Francais des Termes Techniques De Medecine. Delamarre. French & Eur.

Dictionnaire Francais-Anglais et Anglais-Francais. Denis Girard. French & Eur.

Dictionnaire Francais-Anglais pour les Travaux Publics: Le Batiment & l'equipement des Chantiers de Construction. Hector Bucksch. Eyrolles.

Dictionnaire Francais-Arabe. M. Naggary-Bey. Verry.

Dictionnaire Francais-Arabe. Ben Sedira. French & Eur.

Dictionnaire Francais-Arabe. Louis Saisse. Intl Bk Ctr.

Dictionnaire Francais-Arabe(Arabe Parle-Arabe Grammatical) E. Gasselin. Verry.

Dictionnaire Francais Azed. Hatier.

Dictionnaire Francais-Chinois. French & Eur.

Dictionnaire Francais-Chinois. French & Eur.

Dictionnaire Francais-Corse. Jean Albertini. French & Eur.

Dictionnaire Francais-Corse. Jean Albertini. C. E. R. C.

Dictionnaire Francais-Creole. Jules Faine. French & Eur.

Dictionnaire Francais-Creole. Jules Faine. Lemeac.

Dictionnaire Francais-Creole. Faine. Maison Dictionnaire.

Dictionnaire Francais de Medecine & de Biologie, 1 A-D. Nicole A. Manuila. Masson.

Le Dictionnaire Francais de Medecine & de Biologie, 2. Nicole A. Manuila. Masson.

Dictionnaire Francais de Medecine & de Biologie, 3 N-Z. Nicole A. Manuila. Masson.

Dictionnaire Francais de Medecine & de Biologie, 4. Nicole A. Manuila. Masson.

Dictionnaire Francais de Medecine el de Biologie. A Manuila & M. Nicole. French & Eur.

Dictionnaire Francais de Medecine el de Biologie. A. Manuila et al. French & Eur.

Dictionnaire Francais de Medecine el de Biologie. A. Mauila et al. French & Eur.

Dictionnaire Francais de Medecine et de Biologie, Vol. 1. A. Manuila & M. Nicole. French & Eur.

Dictionnaire Francais d'Hydrogeologie. G. Castany. Bureau Recherches.

Dictionnaire Francais-Dyola. E. Wintz. Gregg.

Dictionnaire Francais-Espagnol. Lautier Corbiere. Dessain & Tolra.

Dictionnaire Francais-Esperanto. Albault A. Leger. Esperanto.

Dictionnaire Francais-Esquimau du Parier: l'Ungava & Contrees Limitrophes, 2. Lucien Schneider. Laval P. U.

Dictionnaire Francais-Fang. Samuel Galley. Messeiller.

Dictionnaire Francais-Francais des Mots Rare et Precieux. French & Eur.

Dictionnaire Francais-Hebreu. Marc M. Cohn. French & Eur.

Dictionnaire francais-hebreu. M. M. Cohn. Larousse.

Dictionnaire Francais-Hebreu. Marc M. Cohn. Larousse.

Dictionnaire Francais-Langue. Piat. Ramoun.

Dictionnaire Francais-Langue d'Oc. Piat. French & Eur.

Dictionnaire Francais-Latin. Georges Edon. French & Eur.

Dictionnaire Francais-Latin. Jean-Elie Decahors. Hatier.

Dictionnaire Francais-Latin. Georges Edon. Belin.

Dictionnaire Francais-Latin. Geoffroy. Delalain.

Dictionnaire Francais-Latin. Henri Goelzer. Garnier-Flammarion.

Dictionnaire Francais-Latin. Henri Goelzer. Garnier.

Dictionnaire Francais-Latin. Louis Quicherat. Hachette-Jeinesse.

Dictionnaire Francais-Latin. Robert Estienne. Slatkine.

Dictionnaire Francais-Liegois. Jean Haust. Vaillant-Carmanne.

Dictionnaire Francais-Malgache. R. P. Malzac. French & Eur.

Dictionnaire Francais-Malgache. R. P. Malzac. Maritimes Outremer.

Dictionnaire Francais-Marocain. Abulgacim Tedjini. Maritimes Outre-Mer.

Dictionnaire Francais-Nicois. Georges Castellana. Serre.

Dictionnaire Francais Nicois. Georges Castellana. Serre.

Dictionnaire Francais-Occitanien. L. Piat. Berenguie.

Dictionnaire Francais-Polonais. Vander.

Dictionnaire Francais-Portugais. Domingos De Azevedo. Garnier.

Dictionnaire Francais-Romaneique. Emile Missir. Klincksieck.

Dictionnaire Francais-Russe. K. Gamchina. French & Eur.

Dictionnaire Francais-Russe. K. A. Ganchina. MIR.

Dictionnaire Francais-Russe. Noctuel & Calmann-Levy. Labiche.

Dictionnaire Francais-Russe. Paul Pauliat. Larousse.

Dictionnaire Francais-Russe. Varvara Potozkaia. MIR.

Dictionnaire Francais-Russe de Mathematique. Roubakine. MIR.

Dictionnaire Francais-Russe de Mathematique. M. V. Dragnev & Victor Rosov. MIR.

Dictionnaire Francais-Russe de Medecine. Roubakine. MIR.

Dictionnaire Francais-Russe du Batiment. Sakharov. MIR.

Dictionnaire Francais-Russe Militaire. Ostapenko. Mir.

Dictionnaire Francais-Serbo-Croate. French & Eur.

Dictionnaire Francais-Serbo-Croate. Vander.

Dictionnaire Francais-Swahili. Charles Sacleux. Institut Ethnologie.

Dictionnaire Francais-Tahitien. Mai-Arii Mai-Aru & J. Anisson du Perron. Pensee Moderne.

Dictionnaire Francais-Tahitien et Tahitien-Francais. Mai-Aru & J. Anisson du Perron. French & Eur.

Dictionnaire Francais-Tibetain. Giraudeau & Francis Gore. Maisonneuve, A.

Dictionnaire Francais-Tibetain (Tibet Oriental) A. Giraudeau & Francis Gore. French & Eur.

Dictionnaire Francais-Vietnamien. Maison Dictionnaire.

Dictionnaire Franco-Hongrois. Voyages.

Le Dictionnaire Franco-Montcellien. Kiwanis-Club. Kiwanis-Club.

Dictionnaire Francois. Pierre Richelet. Olms.

Dictionnaire Francois. Pierre Richelet. Slatkine.

Dictionnaire Garzanti Francais-Italien. Bordas-Dunod.

Dictionnaire Garzanti Francais-Italien, Italien-Francais. French & Eur.

Dictionnaire Gascon-Francais du Departement du Gers. Justin E. Cenacmoncaut. Slatkine.

Dictionnaire Gastronomique. Union Helvi.

Dictionnaire Gemeaux Francais-Allemand. Hatier.

Dictionnaire Gemeaux: Francais-Anglais. Hatier.

Dictionnaire Gemeaux: Francais-Espagnol. Hatier.

Dictionnaire Gemeaux: Francais-Italien. Hatier.

Dictionnaire Genealogique des Familles Canadiennes: Depuls la Fondation de la Colonie Jusqu'a nos Jours. Cyprien Tanguay & Senechal. Elysee.

Dictionnaire General & Curieux Contenant les Principaux Mots: Les Plus Usitez en la Langue Francoise. Cesar De Rochefort. Slatkine.

Dictionnaire General de la Langue Francaise au Canada. Louis-Alexandre Belisle. Beauchemin.

Dictionnaire General de la Langue Francaise: Commencement du 17 Siecle Jusqu'a nos Jours. Adolphe Hatzfeld & Arsene Darmesteter. Delagrave.

Dictionnaire General de la Langue Francaise du Commencement du 17e Siecle Jusqu' a Nos Jours. Adophe Hatzfeld & Arsene Darmesteter. French & Eur.

Dictionnaire General de la Technique Industrielle: Francais-Anglais. Richard Ernst. Maison Dictionnaire.

Dictionnaire General des Sciences Humaines. Georges Thines & Agnes Lempereur. French & Eur.

Dictionnaire General des Sciences Humaines. Georges Thines & Agnes Lempereur. Delarge.

Dictionnaire Geographique, Historique & Literaire: La Perse & des Contrees Adjacentes. Achille Barbier De Meynard. Philo Pr.

Dictionnaire Geographique, Historique & Statistique des Communes: Franche-Comte & des Hameaux qui en Dependent. A. Rousset. Guenegaud.

Dictionnaire Geographique, Historique, Descriptif, Archeologique des Pelegrinages. L. De Sivry. Ed. by J. P. Migne. Caratzas Pub Co.

Dictionnaire Geologique: Francais-Russe. V. Dybovskaia & I. Kirillova. French & Eur.

Dictionnaire Grec-Francais. Ch. Georgin. French & Eur.

Dictionnaire Grec-Francais. Victor Magnien & M. Lacroix. French & Eur.

Dictionnaire Grec-Francais. Emile Pessoneaux. French & Eur.

Dictionnaire Grec-Francais. Anatole Bailly. Hachette-Jeunesse.

Dictionnaire Grec-Francais. Anatole Bailly. French & Eur.

Dictionnaire Grec-Francais. Victor Magnien & M. Lacroix. Belin.

Dictionnaire Grec-Francais. Emile Pessonneaux. Belin.

Dictionnaire Grec Moderne Francais. Hubert Pernot. Garnier.

Dictionnaire Hachette de la Langue Francaise. C. Setton et al. French & Eur.

Dictionnaire Hagiographique. L. M. Petin. Ed. by J. P. Migne. Caratzas Pub Co.

Dictionnaire Hatier-Beauchemin: Francais-Latin. Jean E. De Cahors. Beauchemin.

Dictionnaire Hatier-Beauchemin: Latin-Francais. A. Gariel. Beauchemin.

Dictionnaire Hebrau-Francais. Joseph Hadar. Massada Pr.

Dictionnaire Hebreu-Francais. Rabbin Marchand-Ennery. Colbo.

Dictionnaire Historique. Prosper Marchand. Olms.

Dictionnaire Historique & Artistique de la Rose. Abel Belmont. Lechevalier.

Dictionnaire Historique & Critique. Pierre Bayle. Slatkine.

Dictionnaire Historique & Critique. Pierre Bayle. Sociales.

Dictionnaire Historique & Geographique de la Province de Bretagne. Jean Ogee et al. Floch.

Dictionnaire Historique & Heraldique. C. P. Dayre De Mailhol. Slatkine.

Dictionnaire Historique & Heraldique. D. De Mailhol. Fac.

Dictionnaire Historique & Topographique de la Ancienne & Moderne. E. Garcin. Chantemerle.

Dictionnaire Historique, Archeologique, Philologique, Chronologique Geographique et Literal de la Bible. A. Calmet. Ed. by J. P. Migne. Caratzas Pub Co.

Dictionnaire Historique, Chronologique, Geographique, Genealogique, Heraldique, Juridique, Politique & Botanographique du Daup. Guy Allard & Granoble. Slatkine.

Dictionnaire Historique De la France. Ludovic Lalanne. B Franklin.

Dictionnaire Historique de la France. Ludovic Lalanne. Slatkine.

Dictionnaire Historique de la France. Ludovic Lalanne. Slatkine.

Dictionnaire Historique de la France Contenant l'histoire Civile, Politique. Ludovic Lalanne. Lenox.

Dictionnaire Historique de la Medecine Ancienne & Moderne. N. F. Eloy. Olms.

Dictionnaire Historique de la Terminologie Optique des Grecs. Charles Mugler. French & Eur.

Dictionnaire Historique de la Ville de Paris & de ses Environs. Magny Hurtaut. Minkoff Repr.

Dictionnaire Historique Des Arts, Metiers & Professions Exerces Dans Paris Depuis Le Treizieme Siecle. Afred L. Franklin. B Franklin.

Dictionnaire Historique des Arts, Metiers & Professions: Exercees dans Paris Depuis le 13 Siecle. Alfred L. Franklin. Olms Verlag.

Dictionnaire Historique des Arts, Metlers & Professions Exerces dans Paris Depuis le Treizieme Siecle. Alfred Franklin. Lenox.

Dictionnaire Historique des Arts: Metiers & Professions Exerces dans Paris, Depuis 13 Siecle. Alfred Franklin. Lafitte Repr.

Dictionnaire Historique des Fiefs: Chatelenies & Paroisses de la Haute & de la Basse Auvergne. G. M. Chabrol. Guenegaud.

Dictionnaire historique des monnoies tant anciennes que modernes. M. De Salzade. Thimonier.

Dictionnaire Historique des Sciences Physiques et Naturelles. L. F. Jehan. Ed. by J. P. Migne. Caratzas Pub Co.

Dictionnaire Historique, Literaire & Statistique. Lafitte Repr.

Dictionnaire Historique, Stylistique, Rhetorique, Etomologique, de la Litterature Erotique. Pierre Guiraud. Payot.

Dictionnaire Homeopatheque d'Urgerce. French & Eur.

Dictionnaire Homeopathique d'urgence. Ste. Ind. D'imprimere.

Dictionnaire Humoristique. Maurice Maloux. Albin-Michel.

Dictionnaire Iconologique. Minkoff Repr.

Dictionnaire Illustre de la Langue Russe: Francais-Espagnol-Russe. Anatoll Chtchoukine. Mir.

Dictionnaire Illustre de l'Automobile "Kluwer," en 6 Langues. C. Blok & W. Jezewski. French & Eur.

Dictionnaire Illustre des Merveliles Naturelles. Reader's Digest.

Dictionnaire Illustre des Petites Voitures. Rossel Edns.

Dictionnaire Illustre: Francais-Russe. A. Kolesnikova & L. Lulchak. French & Eur.

Dictionnaire Illustre Multilingue de l'Architecture du Proche Orient Ancien. Ed. by Oliver Aurenche. Illus. by Oliver Callot. Boccard.

Dictionnaire Illustre Multilingue De L'architecture du Procher-Orient Ancien. Olivier Aureneche. French & Eur.

Dictionnaire Image d'enfants. Mesure.

Dictionnaire Imaginaire de Queiques Poetes Reels. De Feu.

Dictionnaire Indicateur des Rues & Places. Periaux. Lafitte Repr.

Dictionnaire Initiatique. Herre Masson. French & Eur.

Dictionnaire Initiatique. Herve-Masson.

Dictionnaire Initiatique. Herve Masson. Belfond.

Le Dictionnaire Insolite. Jacques Languirand. Jour, Ed. Du.

Dictionnaire International D'abreviations Scientigiques & Techniques. Michel Azzaretti. Maison Dictionnaire.

Dictionnaire International d'abreviations Scientifiques et Techniques. M. Azzaretti. Maison Dictionnaire.

Dictionnaire International d'abreviation Scientifiques et Techniques. M. Azzaretti. Maison Dictionnaire.

Dictionnaire International de Metallurgie, Mineralogie, Geologie et Industries Extractives. Angelo Cagnacci-Schwicker. French & Eur.

Dictionnaire International de Science. E. M. E.

Dictionnaire International des Arts. Pierre Cabanne. Bordas.

Dictionnaire International des Arts. Pierre Cabanne. (Dist. by Continental Bk Co). Bordas.

Dictionnaire International des Termes Literaires. Robert Escarpit. Mouton-De.

Dictionnaire International Electrotechnique: Francais-Russe-Anglais-Allemand-Italien-Suedois-Hollandais-Polonais. Mir.

Dictionnaire International Electrotechnique: Francais-Russe-Anglais-Allemand-Espagnol-Suedois-Hollandais-Polonais. Mir.

Dictionnaire Intime de la Femme. Genevieve Roux. Privat.

Dictionnaire Inverse De la Langue Francaise. Alphonse Juilland. Mouton.

Dictionnaire Inverse de la Langue Francais. Mouton-De.

Dictionnaire Inverse de la Langue Russe. Mir.

Dictionnaire inverse de l'ancien francais. Ralph De Gorog. Medieval & Renaissance NY.

Dictionnaire Italien-Francais. Larousse FR.

Dictionnaire Italien-Francais. Denis Rouede. Garnier.

Dictionnaire Italien-Francais. Jacqueline Herselin. Garnier.

Dictionnaire Italien-Francais et Francais-Italien. Pierre Rouede & Denise Rouede. French & Eur.

Dictionnaire Italien-Francais, Francais-Italien de la Langue d'Aujourd'hui. Ghiotti et al. French & Eur.

Dictionnaire Jersias-Francais. Le Maistre. French & Eur.

Dictionnaire Juridique. M. Matteucci. French & Eur.

Dictionnaire Juridique. Intl Bk Ctr.

Dictionnaire Juridique & Economique Francais-Allemand & Allemand-Francais. M. Doucet. Ed. by K. Fleck. Bruylant.

Dictionnaire Juridique & Economique Francias-Allemand & Allemand-Francais. M. Doucet. Ed. by K. Fleck. Bruylant.

Dictionnaire Juridique & Economique Francais-Allemand & Allemand Francais. M Doucet. Ed. by E. W. Klaus. Bruylant.

Dictionnaire Juridique & Economique, 1: Francais-Allemand. Litec.

Dictionnaire Juridique et Economique: Anglais-Francais Francais-Anglais. Doucet. Maison Dictionnaire.

Dictionnaire Juridique et Economique, 1: Francais-Allemand. Michel Douret. French & Eur.

Dictionnaire Juridique Flammand-Francais. Jules Brassine. Bruylant.

Dictionnaire Juridique Francais-Allemand, Allemand-Francais. Hugo Neumann. Ed. by Thomas A. Quemner. French & Eur.

Dictionnaire Juridique, Francais-Espagnol, Espagnol-Francais. Luis Jordana de Pozas & Olivier Merlin. French & Eur.

Dictionnaire Juridique: Francais-Espagnol. Olivier Merlin. Navarre.

Dictionnaire Juridique: Francais-Italien. Navarre.

Dictionnaire Juridique: Frances-Allemand. Thomas A. Quemner. Navarre.

Dictionnaire Juridique: Italien-Francais Francais-Italien. Giovanni Tortora. Maison Dictionnaire.

Dictionnaire Kikongo-Francais. Karl Edward Laman. Gregg.

Dictionnaire Kurde-Francais. Auguste Jaba. Biblio-Verlag.

Dictionnaire Laitier: Francais, Allemand, Anglais. Jacques Casalis. French & Eur.

Dictionnaire Laitier: Francais-Allemand-Anglais. Jacques Casalis. Litec.

Dictionnaire Laitier: French-English-French. J. F. Boudier & F. M. Luquet. French & Eur.

Dictionnaire Languedocien-Francais. Adelin Moulis. Moulis, Ad.

Dictionnaire Laotien-Francais. Marc Reinhorn. French & Eur.

Dictionnaire Laotien-Francais. Marc Reinhorn. CNRS.

Dictionnaire Laotien Francais. Theodore Guignard. Gregg.

Dictionnaire Laotien-Francais. Marc Reinhorm. C. N. R. S.

Dictionnaire Laotien-Francais de Poche. (Dist. by Continental Bk Co). Larousse.

Dictionnaire Larousse Bilingue de Poche: Francais-Allemand. Larousse FR.

Dictionnaire Larousse Bilingue de Poche: Francais-Anglais. Larousse FR.

Dictionnaire Larousse Bilingue de Poche: Francais-Espagnol. Larousse FR.

Dictionnaire Larousse Bilingue de Poche: Francais-Italien. Larousse FR.

Dictionnaire Larousse de Poche. L. G. F.

Dictionnaire Larousse de Poche. Larousse FR.

Dictionnaire Larousse: Francais-Allemand. L. G. F.

Dictionnaire Larousse: Francais-Anglais. L. G. F.

Dictionnaire Larousse: Francais-Espagnol. L. G. F.

Dictionnaire Larousse: Francais-Italien. L. G. F.

Dictionnaire Larousse Moderne Francais-Anglais. Edns Francaises.

Dictionnaire Latin-Francais. Henri Bornecque & Fernand Cauet. French & Eur.

Dictionnaire Latin-Francais. Felix Gaffiot. French & Eur.

Dictionnaire Latin-Francais. Charles Lebaigue. French & Eur.

Dictionnaire Latin-Francais. Felix Gaffiot. Hachette.

Dictionnaire Latin-Francais. Geoffroy. Delalain.

Dictionnaire Latin-Francais. Henri Goelzer. Garnier.

Dictionnaire Latin-Francais. Henri Goelzer. Garnier.

Dictionnaire Latin-Francais. Henri Goelzer. Garnier.

Dictionnaire les termes juridiques en quatre langues: Francais-Neerlandais-Anglais-Allemand. E. LeDocte. Maison Dictionnaire.

Dictionnaire Lilliput Bilingue Francais-Allemand. Larousse FR.

Dictionnaire Lilliput Bilingue Francais-Anglais. Larousse FR.

Dictionnaire Lilliput Bilingue Francais-Danois. Larousse FR.

Dictionnaire Lilliput Bilingue Francais-Espagnol. Larousse FR.

Dictionnaire Lilliput Bilingue Francais-Italien. Larousse FR.

Dictionnaire Lilliput Bilingue Francais-Portugais. Larousse FR.

Dictionnaire Lilliput Bilingue Francais-Neerlandais. Larousse FR.

Dictionnaire Liturgique, Historique et Theorique de Plainchant et de Musique d'Eglise. M. J. D'Ortigue. Da Capo.

Dictionnaire Magique. Walt Disney. Nathan.

Dictionnaire Marabout des Mots Croises, 1. L. Noel-Henrard & M. Noel-Henrard. Marabout.

Dictionnaire Marabout des Mots Croises, 2. L. Noel-Henrard & M. Noel-Henrard. Marabout.

Dictionnaire Marabout du Bricolage. Francis Genette. Marabout.

Dictionnaire Marabout Universite. Marabout.

Dictionnaire Marabout Universite. Marabout.

Dictionnaire Marabout Universite: La Sociologie. Marabout.

Dictionnaire Marabout Universite: La Sociologie. Marabout.

Dictionnaire Marabout Universite: La Sociologie. Marabout.

Dictionnaire Medical. Emile Veillon & Albert Noble. Masson.

Dictionnaire Medical. Emmanuel Veillon & Albert Nobel. Hans.

Dictionnaire Medical Illustre De Semiologie Patronymique. French & Eur.

Dictionnaire Medical Illustre de Semiologie Patronymique. Andre Cohen. Maloine.

Dictionnaire Medicine, Clinique, Pharmacologique et Therapeutique. Alain Blacque-Belair. French & Eur.

Dictionnaire Memento D'electronique. Raymond Brosset & Pierre Fondaneche. French & Eur.

Dictionnaire Memento d'electronique. Raymond Brosset & Pierre Fondaneche. Bordas-Dunod.

Dictionnaire Meteorologique: Francais-Russe. P. V. Silvestrov. French & Eur.

Dictionnaire Minier Russe-Francais. French & Eur.

Dictionnaire Minier Russe-Francais. France, Centre Et. Charbonnage.

Dictionnaire Moderne Francais-Arabe. French & Eur.

Dictionnaire Moderne: Francaise-Espagnol, Espagnol-Francais. Ed. by R. Garcia-Pelayo. French & Eur.

Dictionnaire moderne Larousse francais-anglais et anglais-francais. M. M. Dubois. Larousse.

Dictionnaire moderne Larousse, francais-allemand et allemand-francais. P. Grappin. Larousse.

Dictionnaire moderne Larousse, francais-espagnol et espagnol-francais. R. Garcia-Pelayo & J. Testas. Larousse.

Dictionnaire Moderne "Saturne". M. M. Dubois. (Dist. by Continental Bk Co). Larousse.

Dictionnaire Moderne Saturne: Francais-Anglais, Anglais-Francais. Marie-Marguerite Dubois. French & Eur.

Dictionnaire Moderne Saturne: Francais-Allemand. P. Grappin. Larousse FR.

Dictionnaire Moderne Saturne: Francais-Anglais. Marie M. Dubois. Larousse FR.

Dictionnaire Moderne Saturne: Francais-Espagnol. Ramon Garcia-Pelayo & Jean Testas. Larousse FR.

Dictionnaire Moderne: Slovene-French-Slovene. A. Grad. French & Eur.

Dictionnaire Montagnais Francais. Antoine Silvy. Quebec P. U.

Le Dictionnaire Mytho-Hermetique. Antoine J. Pernety. French & Eur.

Le Dictionnaire Mytho-Hermetique. Antoine J. Pernety. Retz.

Dictionnaire Mytho-hermetique: La Symbolique du Feu. Jean P. Bayard. Payot.

Dictionnaire Mythohermetique. Antoine J. Pernety. Denoel.

Dictionnaire mythologie grecque et romaine. J. Schmidt. Larousse.

Dictionnaire National des Communes de France. Dominique de Fleurian. Ed. by Jacques Simond & Jacques Frenay. French & Eur.

Dictionnaire National des Communes de France. Albin-Michel.

Dictionnaire Neerlandais-Francais. Larousse FR.

Dictionnaire Normatif Limousin-Francais. Gerard Gonfroy. Lemouzi.

Dictionnaire oiseaux. Michel Cuisin. Larousse.

Dictionnaire Orthographique. Victor Bailly. Plantyn Edns.

Dictionnaire Orthographique. Bojana Lamizet & Bernard Lamizet. Garnier.

Dictionnaire Orthographique du Vocabulaire de Base. Desoer.

Dictionnaire Orthographique Garnier. Maurice Rat. Garnier.

Dictionnaire Orthographique Suivi d'Une Liste des Verbes Irreguliers. Bojana Lamizet. Garnier.

Dictionnaire Patois. Lucien Guillemaut. Slatkine.

Dictionnaire Patois-Francais a l'usage du Departement du Tarn & des Departements Circonvoisins. Leger Gary. Lafitte Repr.

Dictionnaire Patois-Francais du Departement de l'Aveyron. Aime R. Vayssier. Slatkine.

Dictionnaire Petrolier des Techniques de Diagraphie, Forage & Production: Russe-Francais-Anglais-Allemand. Sonia Ketchian. Technip.

Dictionnaire Petrolier des Techniques de Diagraphique, Forage et Production. Sonia Ketchian. French & Eur.

Dictionnaire Phonetique d'Orthographe. Francois Gallet. PenseeUniv.

Dictionnaire Pittoresque & Historique: Ou Description d'architecture, Peinture, Sculpture, Gravure. Herbert. Minkoff Repr.

Dictionnaire Politique & Diplomatique. P. Sandahl & L. De Bea. Bruylant.

Dictionnaire Politique & Diplomatique. Pierre Sandahl & Louise De Bea. Litec.

Dictionnaire Politique et Diplomatique. Pierre Sandahl & Louise de Bea. French & Eur.

Dictionnaire Polonais-Francais. Vander.

Dictionnaire Portatif de Peinture, Sculpture & Gravure. Antoine Joseph Pernety. Minkoff Repr.

Dictionnaire Portugais-Francais. Domingos De Azevedo. Garnier.

Dictionnaire Portugais-Francais. Ersilio Cardoso. Garnier.

Dictionnaire Portugais-Francais. Larousse.

Dictionnaire Portugais-Francais. Ersilio Cardoso. Garnier.

Dictionnaire Poucet Allemand-Francais. Ersillo Cardoso. Hatier.

Dictionnaire Poucet Anglais-Francais. Hatier.

Dictionnaire Poucet Espagnol-Francais. Hatier.

Dictionnaire Poucet Francais-Allemand. Hatier.

Dictionnaire Poucet Francais-Anglais. Hatier.

Dictionnaire pour Ingenieurs et Techniciens: Francais-Espagnol, Espagnol-Francais. L. Carcamo. French & Eur.

Dictionnaire Pour l'Architecture, le Batiment et les Materiaux de Construction. French & Eur.

Dictionnaire Pour l'Architecture, le Batiment et les Materiaux de Construction. French & Eur.

Dictionnaire pour L'Architecture, le Batiment et les Mateaux de Construction: Band I, Deutsch-Franzosisch. Bauverlag.

Dictionnaire pour l'Architecture, le Batiment et les Materiaux de Constrction: Band II, Franzosisch-Deutsch. Bauverlag.

Dictionnaire pour l'Architecture le Batiment et les Materiaux de Construction: Allemand-Francais. Bucksch. Maison Dictionnaire.

Dictionnaire pour l'architecture le Batiment et les Materiaux de Construction: Francais-Allemand. Bucksch. Maison Dictionnaire.

Le Dictionnaire Pour L'Ecole: Mes 10,000 Mots. M. Didler. Barron.

Dictionnaire pour les Travaux Publics & l'equipement des Chantiers de Construction. Bauverlag.

Dictionnaire pour les Travaux Publics & l'equipement des Chantiers de Construction. Bauverlag.

Dictionnaire Pour les Travaux Publics et l'Equipement des Chartiers de Construction. French & Eur.

Dictionnaire Pour les Travaux Publics et l'Equipement des Chartiers de Construction. French & Eur.

Dictionnaire pour les Travaux Publics, le Batiment et l'Equipement des Chantiers de Construction. Hector Bucksch. French & Eur.

Dictionnaire pour l'intelligence des Choses. Andre Wurmser. Sagittaire.

Dictionnaire pratique & explicatif des produits magiques & articles usuels. Jacques Bersez. Jacques Bersez.

Dictionnaire Pratique & Explicatif des Produits Magiques & Articles Usuels. Jacques Bersez. Bersez.

Dictionnaire Pratique de Droit Medicale. J. Pouletti et al. French & Eur.

Dictionnaire Pratique de la Presse, de l'imprimerie & de la Librairie. J. Bories & F. Bonassies. Gregg.

Dictionnaire Pratique De Medecine Clinique. Leon Perlemuter & Arnaud Cenac. French & Eur.

Dictionnaire Pratique de Medecine Clinique. Leon Perlemuter & Arnaud Cenac. Masson.

Dictionnaire Pratique de Pharmacologie: Clinique. Yvan Touitou & Leon Perlemuter. French & Eur.

Dictionnaire Pratique de Pharmacologie Clinique. Yvan Touitou & Leon Perlemuter. Masson & Cie.

Dictionnaire Pratique de Pharmacologie Clinique. Yvan Touitou & Leon Perlemuter. Masson.

Dictionnaire Pratique de Psychopathologie. Roland-Claude Gori & Yves Poinso. Delarge.

Dictionnaire Pratique de Statistiques en Sciences Humaines. Jean-Jacques Pinty & Claude Gaultier. Delarge.

Dictionnaire Pratique de Theraeutique Medicale. Leon Perlemuter & Paul Obraska. Masson.

Dictionnaire Pratique De Therapeutique Medicale, 3. L. Perlemuter. Ed. by P. Obraska. French & Eur.

Dictionnaire Pratique des Termes Juridiques: Francais-Arabe. Elle Malka. France Selection.

Dictionnaire Pratique d'orthographe & des Difficultes du Francais. Jean-Yves Dournon. Hachette.

Dictionnaire Pratique Francais-Breton. Jean Le Du & Yves Le Berre. Rennes, C. R. D. P.

Dictionnaire Pratique Francais-Polonais. K. Kupisz & B. Kielski. French & Eur.

Dictionnaire Pratique Mercure: Francais-Allemand, Allemand-Francais. Ernst E. Lange-Koval & Kurt Wilhelm. French & Eur.

Dictionnaire Pratique Mercure: Francais-Anglais, Anglais-Francais. Kenneth Urwin. French & Eur.

Dictionnaire Pratique Mercure: Francais-Espagnol, Espagnol-Francais. M. Pay-Costa. French & Eur.

Dictionnaire Pratique Mercure Francais-Allemand. Ernst E. Lange-Koval & Kurt Wilhelm. Larousse.

Dictionnaire Pratique Mercure Francais-Espagnol. M. Puy-Costa. Larousse.

Dictionnaire Pratique Quillet. Quillet.

Dictionnaire prehistoire. Larousse.

Dictionnaire Provencal-Francais. J. T. Avril. Slatkine.

Dictionnaire Provencal-Francais ou Dictionnaire de la Langue D'oc Ancienne & Moderne. Simon-Jude Honnorat. Slatkine.

Dictionnaire psychologie. N. Sillamy. Larousse.

Dictionnaire Quillet De la Langue Francais. French & Eur.

Dictionnaire Quillet de la Langue Francaise. Librairie A. Quillet. Librairie Aritide.

Dictionnaire Quillet de la Langue Francaise. Quillet.

Dictionnaire Raisonne de Diplomatie Chretienne. M. Quantin. Ed. by J. P. Migne. Caratzas Pub Co.

Dictionnaire Raisonne de Droit et de Jurisprudence en Matiere Civile Ecclesiastique. J. H. Prompsault. Ed. by J. P. Migne. Caratzas Pub Co.

Dictionnaire Raisonne de l'Architecture Francaise, du XIe au Siecles. Viollet-Le-Duc. French & Eur.

Dictionnaire Raisonne de Mathematiques. Andre Warusfel. French & Eur.

Dictionnaire Raisonne de Mathematiques. Andre Warusfel. Seuil.

Dictionnaire Raisonne des Mots-Croises. Jacqueline Charron. Homme.

Dictionnaire Raisonne Des Superstitions et Des Croyances Populaires. Pierre Canavaggio. French & Eur.

Dictionnaire Raisonne Du Mobilier Francais De L'epoque Carlovingienne a la Renaissance. Eugene E. Viollet-Le-Duc. AMS Pr.

Dictionnaire Redige en Caracteres Latins: Allemand-Francais. Felix Bertaux & Emile Lepointe. Hachette.

Dictionnaire Redige en Caracteres Latins: Francais-Allemand. Felix Bertaux & Emile Lepointe. Hachette.

Dictionnaire Roman, Wallon, Celtique & Tudesque: Servir a l'intelligence des Anciennes lois & Contrats, des Chartes. Dom Jean Francois. Slatkine.

Dictionnaire russe-francais. P. Pauliat. Larousse.

Dictionnaire Russe-Francais. De Chtcherba. Mir.

Dictionnaire Russe-Francais. Varvara Potozkaia. Mir.

Dictionnaire Russe-Francais de l'automobile & du Tracteur. Jetikov. Mir.

Dictionnaire Russe-Francais du Batiment. V. V. Voronine et al. Ed. by A. I. Denissov. French & Eur.

Dictionnaire Russe-Francais Polytechnique. Vassilieva. Mir.

Dictionnaire Samoa-Francais-Anglais et Francais-Samoa-Anglais. Louis Violette. AMS Pr.

Dictionnaire Savoyard. Aime Constantin & Joseph Desormeaux. Lafitte Repr.

Dictionnaire Savoyard. Aime Constantin & Joseph Desormaux. Slatkine.

Dictionnaire Scolaire du Francais. Langenscheidt.

Dictionnaire Scolaire Francais-Finnois. Edvin Hagford & Seppo Sundelin. Soderstrom.

Dictionnaire Selectif & Commente des Difficultes de la Version Anglais. Jean Rey. Ophrys.

Dictionnaire Serbocrate-Francais, Francais-Serbocroate, suivi d'une courte grammaire de Langue Francaise. B. Grujic. French & Eur.

Dictionnaire Swahili-Francais. Charles Sacleux. Inst Ethnol.

Dictionnaire Synonymique. Anthony Guerronnan. Ed. by Peter C. Bunnell & Robert A. Sobieszek. Ayer Co.

Dictionnaire Technique & Administratif de la Navigation Interieure. Henri Berna. Berger-Levrault.

Dictionnaire Technique & Critique du Dessin. Andre Beguin. Vander Oyez.

Dictionnaire Technique Anglais-Francais. G. Malgorn. French & Eur.

Dictionnaire technique Anglais-Francais. Guy Malgorn. Imported Bks.

Dictionnaire Technique Anglais-Francais d'electronique. Chiron.

Dictionnaire Technique Bilingue. Jean Ruhland. Ruhland.

Dictionnaire Technique De la Construction Electrique. P. Sizaire. French & Eur.

Dictionnaire Technique de la Construction Electrique. Pierre Sizaire. Eyrolles.

Dictionnaire Technique de la Maroquinerie. Louis Rama. Centre Technique.

Dictionnaire Technique de la Mecanisation Agricole. French & Eur.

Dictionnaire Technique de la Mecanisation Agricole: Francais-Anglais-Allemand-Espagnol-Italien. Centre Nat. Et. Machin Agricole.

Dictionnaire Technique de L'Automobile. George Zlatovski. Ed. by P. R. Russek. French & Eur.

Dictionnaire Technique de l'automobile. Daniel Carnelutti. Spes SA.

Dictionnaire Technique de l'automobile. George Zlatovski & P. R. Russek. Bordas-Dunod.

Dictionnaire Technique de L'Eau. French & Eur.

Dictionnaire Technique de l'eau. Grund.

Dictionnaire Technique de l'eau & des Questions Connexes. Rene Colas. Le Prat.

Dictionnaire Technique des Fabrications Mecaniques. Rene Bossier. Desforges.

Dictionnaire Technique des Termes Utilises Dans l'Industrie du Petrole, Anglais-Francais, Francais-Anglais. Magdeleine Moureau & Janine Rouge. French & Eur.

Dictionnaire Technique des Termes Utilises dans l'industrie du Petrole: Anglais-Francais. Madeleine Moureau & Janine Rouge. Technip.

Dictionnaire Technique du Batiment & des Travaux Publics. Maurice Barbier. Eyrolles.

Dictionnaire Technique du Batiment & des Travaux Publics. Maurice Barbier & Roger Cadiergues. Eyrolles.

Dictionnaire Technique du Bois, en Quatre Langues. G. Wallnig & H. Evered. French & Eur.

Dictionnaire Technique du Bois en Quatre Langues: Allemand-Russe-Anglais-Francais. Vander.

Dictionnaire Technique du Bois en 4 Langues. French & Eur.

Dictionnaire Technique du Bois: Texte en Allemand-Anglais-Francais-Russe. Eyrolles.

Dictionnaire Technique du Cinema: Anglais-Francais. C. R. Gibbs. Film Et Technique.

Dictionnaire Technique du Petrole. Magdeleine Moureau. Technip.

Dictionnaire Technique et Administratif De la Navigation Interieure. Henri Berna. French & Eur.

Dictionnaire Technique et Critique du Dessin. Andre Beguin. French & Eur.

Dictionnaire Technique Francais-Anglai. Guy M. Malgorn. Bordas.

Dictionnaire Technique Francais-Anglais. G. Malgorn. French & Eur.

Dictionnaire Technique Francais-Anglais. Guy Malgorn. Gauthier-Villars.

Dictionnaire Technique Francais-Espagnol. Auteur H. Mink. French & Eur.

Dictionnaire Technique Francais-Espagnol. Guy Malgorn. Gauthier-Villars.

Dictionnaire Technique: Francais-Neerlandais. Voutquenne, C.

Dictionnaire technique general. J. G. Belle-Isle. Imported Bks.

Dictionnaire Technique General: Anglais-Francais. J. Gerald Belle Isle. French & Eur.

Dictionnaire Technique General: Anglais-Francais. Gerald J. Belle-Isle. Bordas-Dunod.

Dictionnaire Technique General Anglais-Francais. Gerald J. Belle-Isle. Beauchemin.

Dictionnaire Technique Generale Anglais-Francais. French & Eur.

Dictionnaire Technique Hongrois-Francais. B. Rubin. Terra.

Dictionnaire Technique Illustre des Outlis Coupants: L'usinage des Metaux; Francais-Allemand-Anglais-Italien-Espagnol. Toni Heiler. Eyrolles.

Dictionnaire Technique Illustre Des Outils Coupants Pour L'usinage Des Metaux. Toni Heiler. French & Eur.

Dictionnaire Technique Russe-Francais de la Preparation. French & Eur.

Dictionnaire Technique Russe-Francais: La Preparation Mecanique des Charbons. France, Centre Et Charbonnage.

Dictionnaire Technique Universal Kluwer, Francais-Neerlandais. G. Schuurmans-Stekhoven. French & Eur.

Dictionnaire Technique Universal Kluwer Neerlandais-Francais. G. Schuurmans-Stekhoven. French & Eur.

Dictionnaire Technique Universel Kluwer: Francais-Neerlandais. G. Schuermans-Stekhoven. Kluwer-Deventer.

Dictionnaire Technique Universel Kluwer: Neerlandais-Francais. G. Schuermans Stekhoven. Kluwer-Deventer.

Dictionnaire Technologique: Aeronautique. H. Demaison. Maison Dictionnaire.

Dictionnaire Technologique Feutry: Mecanique-Metallurgie-Hydraulique. R. Mertz De Mertzenteld et al. Maison Dictionnaire.

Dictionnaire Technologique, 1: Anglais-Francais-Allemand. Michel Feutry. Maison Dictionnaire.

Dictionnaire Technologique, 1: Anglais-Francais-Allemand. Michel Feutry et al. Maison Dictionnaire.

Dictionnaire theatre francais contemporain. Alfred Simon. Larousse.

Dictionnaire Topographique & Historique de la Drome. Justin Brun-Durand. Chantermerle.

Dictionnaire Topographique de la France. Henri Stein. Ed. by J. Hubert. French & Eur.

Dictionnaire Topographique de la France. Auguste Longnon. Biblio Nationale.

Dictionnaire Topographique de la France. Biblio Nationale.

Dictionnaire Topographique de la France. J. Roman. Biblio Nationale.

Dictionnaire Topographique de la France. Henri Stein & J. Hubert. Biblio Nationale.

Dictionnaire Topographique de la France, 1. Eugene Vallee & Robert Latouche. Biblio Nationale.

Dictionnaire Touareg-Francais. Charles De Foucauld. Imprimerie Nat.

Dictionnaire touristique international: Edition francaise. Academie Internationale du Tourisme. Acad Intl Tour.

Dictionnaire Trilingue. Jean Ruhland. Ruhland.

Dictionnaire trilingue du Droit des Affaires pour le Commerce & l'industrie: Allemand-Anglais-Francais & index. H. Becker. Maison Dictionnaire.

Dictionnaire Universal de la Peinture. Ed. by Robert Maillard. Soc Nouveau.

Dictionnaire Universal de l'Art et des Artistes. French & Eur.

Dictionnaire Universel. Antoine Furetiere. Slatkine.

Dictionnaire Universel: Contenant Generalement tous les Mots Francois, 1. Antoine Furetiere & La Haye. Olms.

Dictionnaire Universel: Contenant Generalement tous les Mots Francois, 2. Antoine Furetiere. Olms.

Dictionnaire Universel: Contenant Generalement tous les Mots Francois, 3. Antoine Furetiere. Olms.

Dictionnaire Universel: Contenant Generalement tous les Mots Francois, 4. Antoine Furetiere. Olms.

Dictionnaire Universel d'Antoine Furetiere. Antoine Furetiere. Ste. Nouv. Littre.

Dictionnaire Universel de la Franc-Maconnerie. Daniel Ligou. Prisme.

Dictionnaire Universel de la Peinture. Robert Maillard & Gerard Legrand. Ste. Nouv. Littre.

Dictionnaire Universel de Mathematique & de Physique, 1. Alexandre Saverien. Olms.

Dictionnaire Universel de Mathematique & de Physique, 2. Alexandre Saverien. Olms.

Dictionnaire Universel et Complet des Conciles. A. C. Peltier. Ed. by J. P. Migne. Caratzas Pub Co.

Dictionnaire Usuel Hongrois-Francais. S. Eckhardt. Terra.

Dictionnaire Vidal. O. V. P.

Dictionnaire Vidal, 1982. Intl Pubns Serv.

Dictionnaire Vietnamien-Francais. Thanh Nghi. Asiatheque.

Dictionnaire vins. Gerard Debuigne. Larousse.

Dictionnaires. I. P. E. C.

Dictionnaires Bilingues Francais-Anglais. (Dist. by Continental Bk Co). Larousse.

Dictionnaires Bilingues Larousse Francais-Anglais. (Dist. by Continental Bk Co). Larousse.

Dictionnaires des Cathedrales de France. Larousse.

Dictionnaires des Charges, Emplois & Metiers XIVe. & XVe. Siecles: Relevant des Institutions Monarchiques en France. Monique Ornato. CNRS.

Dictionnaires des Comediens Francais. Slatkine.

Dictionnaires des Communes. Berger Levrault.

Dictionnaires des Matieres Plastiques. Wittfoht. Francaise, Compagnie Edition.

Dictionnaires des Parfums de France & de Lignes pour Hommes. Ed.

Dictionnaires des Plantes Medicinales. J. Duquesne. Chiron.

Dictionnaires Marabout Universite: La Sociologie. Marabout.

Dictionnaires Modernes Larousse Francais-Anglais. (Dist. by Continental Bk Co). Larousse.

Dictonnaire de L'Automobile. Robert Guerber. French & Eur.

Dictonnaire des Synonymes et des Antonymes. Hector Dupuis & Romain Legare. French & Eur.

Dictonnaire Du Francais Argotique et Populaire. Francois Caradec. French & Eur.

Dizionarietto fraseologico commerciale italiano-francese. Cenni Clara & Sandri Clotilde. Trevisini.

Dizionario assicurativo: Tedesco-francese-inglese-italiano. Centro St Assic.

Dizionario Commerciale Francese-Italiano. V. Emolumento. French & Eur.

Dizionario commerciale francese-italiano. Vincenzo Emolumento. Editrice Bibliografica.

Dizionario commerciale italiano-francese. Vincenzo Emolumento. Bibliografica.

Dizionario commerciale italiano-francese e francese-italiano. Mario Mormile. Bulzoni.

Dizionario Commerciale Italiano-Francese, Francese-Italiano. Mario Mormile. Maison Dictionnaire.

Dizionario del francese fondamentale. Raoul Boch. Zanichelli.

Dizionario francese-italiano e italiano-francese. Garzanti Edit.

Dizionario francese-italiano e italiano-francese. Garzanti Edit.

Dizionario francese-italiano e italiano-francese. Malipiero.

Dizionario francese-italiano e italiano-francese. Filippi & La Tour. Giunti-Martello.

Dizionario Francese Italiano, Italiano Francese. Raol Boch. Zanichelli.

Dizionario francese-italiano italiano-francese. La Mondadori.

Dizionario francese-italiano italiano-francese. Raoul Boch. Zanichelli.

Dizionario fraseologico commerciale italiano-francese e francese-italiano. Ada Duse. Bignami.

Dizionario fraseologico e grammaticale italiano-francese. Massimo Gatto. Sandron.

Dizionario Garzanti: Francese-Italiano, Italiano-Francese. G. Cusatelli & G. Brunacci. Ed. by U. Salati & F. Dominicis et al. French & Eur.

Dizionario Garzantil Italiano-Francese, Francese-Italiano. French & Eur.

Dizionario inglese-italiano-francese-tedesco. L. Gives et al. De Bono.

Dizionario italiano-francese. Malipiero.

Dizionario italiano-francese. Mondadori.

Dizionario italiano-francese. Claire Laurent. Vallardi A.

Dizionario italiano-francese e francese-italiano. Garzanti Edit.

Dizionario italiano-francese e francese-italiano. Garzanti Edit.

Dizionario italiano-francese e francese-italiano. R. Simone. La Nuova Italia.

Dizionario italiano-francese e francese-italiano. Amato Bertet et al. Paravia.

Dizionario Italiano-Francese e Francese-Italiano di termini in uso in economia, borsa, finanza. Vera Pegna. Etas Libri.

Dizionario Italiano-Francese, Francese-Italiano. G. Laurent. French & Eur.

Dizionario italiano-francese francese-italiano della lingua d'oggi. Candido Ghiotto et al. Petrini.

Dizionario italiano-francese-italiano. G. Sbrulli & T. Biffoli. Valmartina.

Dizionario italiano-inglese-francese-tedesco. L. Gives et al. De Bono.

Dizionario Medico Poliglotta. Veillon & Nobel. French & Eur.

Dizionario medico poliglotta: Inglese-tedesco-francese. Veillon & Nobel. Piccin.

Dizionario moderno italiano-francese e francese-italiano. Ernesto Cassiani. SEI.

Dizionario moderno italiano-francese e francese-italiano. Bruno A. Paoli. Edn Scol Mond.

Dizionario per l'industria delle materie plastiche: Definizioni italiane e termini corrispondenti in francese, inglese e tedesco. Enrico Ferraris & Istituto Italiano dei Plastici. SAPIL.

Dizionario pratico della lingua francese. Enea Balmas. Ist Geog Agostini.

Dizionario pratico della lingua francese. Enea Balmas. Ghisetti & Corvi.

Dizionario tascabile delle tecniche ambientale: Italiano, francese, inglese, tedesco. Maurizio Pasquali. SAPIL.

Dizionario Tecnico Francese-Italiano. Renzo Denti. Hoepli.

Dizionario tecnico francese-italiano e italiano-francese. Renzo Denti. Hoepli.

Dreisprachiges Woerterbuch der Soziologie. (Pub. by A. Hain). French & Eur.

Droit Administratif. Raymond Barrillon. Pr Univ Fr.

Duden Francais Bildworterbuch Deutsch & Franzoesisch. Biblio Inst.

Dumas on Food. Alexandre Dumas. Tr. by Alan Davidson & Jane Davidson. U Pr of Va.

Dutch-English-French-German Engineering Dictionary. Ten Bosch. Heinman.

Economisch Woorden Boek: Engels-Frans-Duits-Nederlands. F. J. Jong. French & Eur.

Einfuehrung in die Benutzung der Neufranzoesischen Woerterbucher. Franz J. Hausmann. Niemeyer Verlag.

Elements de Geologie En Six Langues. E. Cailleux. French & Eur.

Ellison's French Menu Reader. Al Ellison. Ellison Ent.

Elseviers Automobile Dictionary. Ed. by G. Schuurmans. Elsevier.

Elsevier's Banking Dictionary. J. Ricci. Elsevier.

Elsevier's Dictionary of Amplification Modulation Reception & Transmission. Ed. by W. Clason. Elsevier.

Elsevier's Dictionary of Automatic Control. Ed. by W. Clason. Elsevier.

Elsevier's Dictionary of Barley, Malting, & Brewing. Bernard D. Hartong. Elsevier.

Elsevier's Dictionary of Building Tools & Materials. L. Y. Chaballe & J. P. Vandenberghe. Elsevier.

Elsevier's Dictionary of Chemical Engineering. W. Clason. Elsevier.

Elsevier's Dictionary of Cinema, Sound & Music. W. E. Clason.

Elsevier's Dictionary of Computers, Automatic Control & Data Processing. W. E. Clason. Elsevier.

Elsevier's Dictionary of Criminal Science. J. A. Adler. Elsevier.

Elsevier's Dictionary of Electronics & Waveguides. W. E. Clason. Elsevier.

Elsevier's Dictionary of Financial Terms. F. J. Thomson. Elsevier.

Elsevier's Dictionary of General Physics. W. E. Clason. Elsevier.

Elsevier's Dictionary of High Vacuum Science & Technology. Fritz W. Weber. Elsevier.

Elsevier's Dictionary of Horticulture. Ed. by Ministry of Agriculture & Fisheries- Netherlands & J. Nijdam. Elsevier.

Elsevier's Dictionary of Hydrogeology. Hans-Olaf Pfannkuch. Elsevier.

Elseviers Dictionary of Metal Cutting Tools. Ed. by G. Schuurmang. Elsevier.

Elsevier's Dictionary of Metallurgy & Metal Working. W. E. Clason. Elsevier.

Elsevier's Dictionary of Nuclear Science & Technology. W. E. Clason. Elsevier.

Elsevier's Dictionary of Photography. A. S. Craeybeckx. Elsevier.

Elsevier's Dictionary of Public Health. Nick J. Deblock. Elsevier.

Elsevier's Dictionary of Rolling Mill Terminology. Ed. by G. F. Herscu. Elsevier.

Elsevier's Dictionary of Television, & Video Recording. W. Clason. Elsevier.

Elsevier's Dictionary of Tools & Ironware. Ed. by Clason. Elsevier.

Elsevier's Electrotechnical Dictionary. W. E. Clason. Elsevier.

Elsevier's Medical Dictionary in Five Languages. A. Sliosberg. Elsevier.

Elsevier's Multilingual Dictionary of Insurance Technology. W. A. Ruysch. Elsevier.

Elseviers Nautical Dictionary. Ed. by P. Segditsas. Elsevier.

Elsevier's Nautical Dictionary in Six Languages. Ed. by J. P. Vandenberghe & L. Y. Chaballe. Elsevier.

Elseviers Rubber Dictionary. Elsevier.

Elsevier's Telecommunication Dictionary. W. E. Clason. Elsevier.

Elsevier's Wood Dictionary. Ed. by W. Boerhave Beekman. Elsevier.

Enciclopedia simultanea de correspondencia comercial en seis idiomas. Distein.

Englisch fuer Baufachleute: Band 1. G. Wallnig & H. Evered. Bauverlag.

Englisch fur Baufachleute: Band 2. G. Wallnig & H. Evered. Bauverlag.

Englische & Franzoesisch Fachsprache im Auslandsbau. K. Lange et al. Bauverlag.

English-French & French-English Technical Dictionary. Francis Cusset. Chem Pub.

English-French-Arabic Trilingual Dictionary. Jerwan Sabek. Intl Bk Ctr.

English-French Dictionary. Saphrograph.

English-French Dictionary. Editions Berlitz S. A. (Pub by Berlitz). Macmillan.

English-French Dictionary of Computer Science. R. Fisher & P. Krchten. Heinman.

English-French, French-English Dictionary. B&N.

English-French General Technical Dictionary. J. Belle-Isle. Routledge & Kegan.

English-French-German Glossary for Psychiatry, Child Psychiatry & Abnormal Psychology. Lise Moor. Intl Pubns Serv.

English-French Glossary. Lucienne V. Wolfe. Govt Print.

An English-French Glossary of Educational Terminology. Robert L. Gieber. U Pr of Amer.

English-French Petroleum Dictionary. M. Arnould & F. Zubini. (Pub. by Graham & Trotman England). State Mutual Bk.

English-French Petroleum Dictionary. Michel Arnould & Fabio Zubini. Crane-Russak Co.

English-German -- German-English Welding Engineering Dictionary. (Pub. by Collet's). State Mutual Bk.

Erdoelverarbeitung-Petrolchemie. Leipnitz. Brandstetter.

Erdolverarbeitung und Petrolchemie: A Dictionary of Crude Oil Processing & Petroleum Chemistry English-German-French-Russian. Walter Leipnitz. Intl Learn Syst.
Ergonomics Glossary: Terms Commonly Used in Ergonomics. Ed. by European Coal & Steel Community, Luxembourg. Intl Pubns Serv.
Essai d'un Glossaire des Patois de Lyonnais, Forez & Beaujolais. Jean B. Onofrio. Horvath.
Essential French Vocabulary. Longman.
Ethnologisches Woerterbuch. A. Heymer. (Pub. by P. Parey). French & Eur.
Ethnologisches Woerterbuch. A. Heymer. Parey.
The Ethological Dictionary: In English, French & German. Armin Heymer. (Garland STPM Pr). Garland Pub.
Etymologisches Woerterbuch der Franzoesischen Sprache. Ernst Gamillscheg. (Pub. by Carl Winter). French & Eur.
Etymologisches Woerterbuch der Franzoesischen Sprache. Ernst Gamillscheg. Winter Univ.
Euro Dictionary of Economics & Business. Hans E. Zahn. Rothman.
Euro-Wirtschafts Worterlrich in Drei Sprachen. Hans E. Zahn. (Pub. by Fritz Knapp Verlag). French & Eur.
Export for Marketing French. A. M. Nuss. French & Eur.
Fachwoerterbuch der Datenverarbeitung. Alfred Wittman. Oldenbourg Verlag.
Fachwoerterbuch der Luftfahrt. A. Dorian & J. Osenton. (Pub. by R. Oldenbourg). French & Eur.
Fachwoerterbuch der Luftfahrt. J. Osenton. Oldenbourg Verlag.
Fachwoerterbuch Fur Wirtschaft, Handel und Finanzen. Rudolf Thomik. (Pub. by Carl Heymanns Verlag KG). French & Eur.
Fachworterbuch Polygrafie: English-Deutsch-French-Russian-Spanish-Polish-Hungarian-Slowakian. French & Eur.
Fachwoerterbuch Textil. Sarina Schock & Erika Gebert. (Pub. by Deutscher Fachverlag). French & Eur.
Filmgyartas es Filmtechnika. Gabor Pozsonyi. Akademiai Kiado.
Financial & Mercantile Dictionary. Julius O. Kettridge. French & Eur.
Finnish-French Dictionary. T. Nurmela. French & Eur.
Finnish-French-Finnish Dictionary (Suomi-Ranska-Suomi) R. M. Koistinen. French & Eur.
La Fiscalite. Ed. by Patrick Rassat & Alain Le Bars. Hachette L.
Fitopatologicheskii Slovar Spravochnik. G. A. Diakova. (Pub. by Nauka). Four Continent.
Five Thousand French Words. S&S.
La Formation du Vocabulaire de L'Aviation. Louis Guilbert. French & Eur.
Four Language Culinary Dictionary: French, Hungarian, English, German. Saphrograph.
Four-Language Technical Dictionary of Chromatography: English, German, French, Russian. H. Angele. Pergamon.
Four Languages Dictionary of Geological Terms. French & Eur.
Francais-Norvegien-Francais Lommerorbok. E. Daae. French & Eur.
Francouzsko-Cesky a Cesko-Francouzsky Slovnik pro Televizni Pracovniky a Prekladatele. Otto Levinsky. SNTC.
Francouzsko-Cesky Technicky Slovnik. Libuse Vomackova. SNTC.
Fransk-Dansk, Dansk-Fransk Specialordbog. Ed. by Ejnar Fryd. For Stat Rev.
Fransk-Norsk Ordbok. L. Dedichen. French & Eur.
Fransk-Svensk Ordbok. Johan Vising. Esselte Studium.
Fransk-Svensk Ordbok. Ruben Nojd. Esselte Studium.
Frantsuzsko-Latviiskii Slovar. I. Zandreitere et al. (Pub. by Latv Valsts). Four Continent.
Frantsuzsko-Russkii Frazeologicheskii Slovar. Ed. by I. I. Retsker. (Pub. by Gosizdat Inostr Natsional Lit). Four Continent.
Frantsuzsko-Russkii Geologicheskii Slovar. I. K. Dobovskaia. (Pub. by Gosfizmat). Four Continent.
Frantsuzsko-Russkii Illiustrirovannyi Slovar. A. D. Kolesnikova et al. (Pub. by Sov Entsiklopediia). Four Continent.
Frantsuzsko-Russkii Illiustrirovannyi Slovar. I. Zandreitere. (Pub. by Latv Valstsnent Bk). Four Continent.
Frantsuzsko-Russkii Obshchestvenno-Politisheskii Slovar. Ed. by S. A. Tokarev et al. (Pub. by Izd. In-ta Mezhdunarod. Otnoshenii). Four Continent.
Frantsuzsko-Russkii Slovar Po Sudostroeniiu i Sudokhodstvu. A. I. Telegin et al. (Pub. by Glav. Red. Nauchn. Tekhn. Slovarei Fizmatgiza). Four Continent.
Frantsuzsko-Russkii Uchebnyi Slovar. N. B. Korina et al. (Pub. by Russkii Iazyk). Four Continent.
Frantsuzsko-Russkii Voennyi Slovar. A. M. Taube. (Pub. by Voenizdat). Four Continent.
Franzoesisch. Incl. Langenscheidt.
Franzoesisch-Deutsches Glossarium. F. Roepke. (Pub. by Fritz Knapp Verlag). French & Eur.
Franzoesisch Etymologisches Woerterbuch. Walter von Wartburg. (Pub. by Francke). French & Eur.
Franzoesische Fachausdruecke im Bankgeschaeft: Franzoesisch-Deutsch, Deutsch-Franzoesisch. Hans A. Klaus. Haupt Verlag.
Franzoesische und Deutsche Chemische Fachuasdruecke. H. Fromherz & A. King. Verlag Chemie.
Franzosisch. Incl. Langenscheidt.
Franzosisch. Incl. Langenscheidt.
Franzosisch-Deutsch, Deutsch-Franzosisch. Langenscheidt.
Franzosisch-Deutsches, Deutsch-Franzosisches Woerterbuch. Pierre Bertaux. (Pub. by Brandstetter). French & Eur.
Franzosisch-Deutsches, Deutsch-Franzosisches Woerterbuch. Pierre Bertaux. Brandstetter.
Franzosisch-Deutsches, Deutsch-Franzosisches Woerterbuch. Pierre Bertaux. Brandstetter.
Franzosisch-Deutsches-Deutsch-Franzosisches Woerterbuch: Band I, Franzoesisch-Deutsch. Lepointe Bertraux. Brandstetter.
Frazeologicheskii Slovar Russkogo Iazyka. A. I. Molotkova. (Pub. by Russkii Iazyk). Four Continent.
French & English Idioms. F. Denoeu et al. Barron.
French Bilingual Dictionary. Gladys Lipton. Barron.
French Bilingual Dictionary: A Beginner's Guide in Words & Pictures. Gladys Lipton. Barron.
French Bilingual Dictionary: A Beginner's Guide in Words & Pictures. Gladys C. Lipton. Barron.
French Bilingual Dictionary: A Beginner's Guide in Words & Pictures. G. Lipton. Barron.
French Bilingual Dictionary: Compact Ed. Gladys Lipton. Barron.
French Dictionary. McKay.
French Dictionary. Hamlyn. Hamlyn-Amer.
French-Eng., Eng-French Dictionary of Electrotechnic Electronics & Allied Fields. H. Piraux. Heinman.
French-English & English-French Dictionary. Dennison.
French-English & English-French Dictionary of Commercial & Financial Terms, Phrases & Practice. J. O. Kettridge. Routledge & Kegan.
French-English & English-French Dictionary of Commercial & Financial Terms. J. O. Kettridge. Routledge & Kegan.
French-English & English-French Dictionary of Financial & Mercantile Terms, Phrases & Practice. J. O. Kettridge. Routledge & Kegan.
French-English & English-French Dictionary of Technical Terms & Phrases. J. O. Kettridge. Incl. Routledge & Kegan.
French-English Chemical Terminology: An Introduction to Chemistry in French & English. H. Fromherz & A. King. (Pub. by Vlg. Chemie). French & Eur.
French-English Chemical Terminology: An Introduction to Chemistry in French & English. Hans Fromherz & Alexander King. Verlag Chemie.
French-English Chemical Terminology: An Introduction to Chemistry in French & English. H. Fromherz & A. King. Verlag Chemie.
French-English Dictionary. Saphrograph.
French-English Dictionary. Robert Collins. Iaconi.
A French-English Dictionary of Technical Terms Used in Classical Ballet. Cyril W. Beaumont. Imp Soc Tchrs Da.
French-English English-French Dictionary. Robert Collins. U of Toronto Pr.
French-English, English-French Dictionary of Commercial & Financial Terms. Kettridge. French & Eur.
French-English, English-French Gem Dictionary. Ed. by G. Rudler & N. C. Anderson. Collins Pubs.
French-English, English-French Legal Dictionary. T. A. Quemner. Ed. by Jean Baleyte & Alexander Kurgansky. Heinman.
French-English Instant Vocabulary. Eleanor P. Cruikshank. Cruikshank.
French-English Science & Technology Dictionary. Louis De Vries & Stanley Hochman. McGraw.
French-English Science & Technology Dictionary. Louis De Vries. Rev. by Stanley Hochman. McGraw.
French-English Science Dictionary. Louis De Vries. McGraw.
French-Finnish Dictionary. E. Hagfors et al. French & Eur.
French for Business Studies. M. Rover. French & Eur.
French for English Idioms & Figurative Phrases. J. O. Kettridge. Routledge & Kegan.
French-German Chemical Terminology: An Introduction to Chemistry in French & German. Hans Fromherz & Alexander King. Verlag Chemie.
French Idioms & Figurative Phrases. J. O. Kettridge. Saphrograph.
French Idioms on the Way. Barbara Gerber & Gerald Storzer. Barron.
French Military Terminology, 1670-1815. Donald E. Graves. New Bruns Mus.
French-Norwegian Dictionary. Line Dedichen. Kunnskapsforlaget.
French-Onondaga Dictionary, from a Manuscript of the Seventeenth Century. John D. Shea. AMS Pr.
French-Swedish-French Dictionary. French & Eur.
French Vest Pocket Dictionary. Robert A. Hall, Jr. & Francesca V. Langbaum. Random.
Gem Language Dictionaries: French-English & English-French. S&S.
Gem Language Dictionaries: French-German & German-French. S&S.
Geobotanic Dictionary. O. S. Grebenshchikov. Lubrecht & Cramer.
Geowissenschaften. Schweizerbart.
German-English Dictionary for Chemists. A. M. Patterson. (Pub. by Wiley-Interscience). Wiley.
German for Building Specialists: L'Allemand dans le Batiment, el Aleman en la construccion. G. Wallnig & H. Evered. Bauverlag.
Giesserei - Fachwoerterbuch. E. Brunhuber. (Pub. by Fachverlag, Schiele & Schon). French & Eur.
Giesserei-Fachwoerterbuch. E. Brunhuber. Schiele & Schon.
Giesserei-Fachworterbuch. Ernst Brunhuber. Schiele & Schon.
Gips-Woerterbuch. K. H. Volkart. Bauverlag.
Glossaire Abrege Patois de la Meuse. Henri A. Labourasse. Slatkine.
Glossaire Anglais-Francais de l'industrie petroliere. Imported Bks.
Glossaire Anglais-Francais des Termes Miniers & du Vocabulaire Connexe. Centre D'edition.
Glossaire Archeologique du Moyen-Age & de la Renaissance. Victor Gay. Kraus.
Glossaire Archeologique du Moyen-Age & de la Renaissance. Victor Gay. Picard.
Glossaire archeologique du moyer age et de la Renaissance. Gay. French & Eur.
Glossaire Datinois. C. De Landberg & K. V. Zettersteen. Brill.
Le Glossaire de Bale. Menahem Banitt. Brill.
Glossaire de la Finance. French & Eur.
Glossaire de la Finance. Marcel Lefebvre. Lemeac.
Glossaire de la Langue d'Oc. Pierre Malvezin. Laffitte Reprints.
Glossaire de la Langue d'Oc. Pierre Malvezin. Slatkine.
Glossaire de la Langue d'Oll. Alphonse Bos. Laffitte Reprints.
Glossaire de la Langue d'Oll. Aphonse Bos. Slatkine.
Glossaire de la Langue Romane. Jean-Baptiste B. De Roquefort. Slatkine.
Glossaire de la Vallee d'Yeres. Achille Delboulle. Slatkine.
Glossaire de Meteorologie & de Climatologie. Georges O. Villeneuve & Michel G. Ferland. Laval P. U.
Glossaire De Meteorologie et De Climatologie. G. O. Villeneuve & M. G. Ferland. French & Eur.
Glossaire de Patois: Lyonnais, Forez & Beaujolais. Jean B. Onofrio. Horvath.
Glossaire de Pedologie. Biosphere.
Glossaire De Psychiatrie. Pierre Marchais. French & Eur.
Glossaire De Psychiatrie. Lise Moor. French & Eur.
Glossaire de Psychiatrie. Lise Moor. Masson.
Glossaire de Termes Litteraires. Wolfgang V. Ruttkowski & R. E. Blake. Francke.
Glossaire de Termes Relatifs aus Pratiques Commerciales Restrictes. O. C. D. E.
Glossaire de Termes Techniques: L'usage des Lecteurs de la Nuit des Temps. Melchior De Vogue & Raymond Ousel. Zodiaque.
Glossaire del Perigord Negre. Pierre Miremont. P. Miremont.
Glossaire des Inscriptions Pehlevies et Parthes. Phillipe Gignoux. Intl Pubns Serv.
Glossaire des mots Espagnols derives de l'Arabe. R. Dozy. Intl Bk Ctr.
Glossaire des Patois & des Parlers de l'Aunis & de la Saintonge. Georges Musset. Lafitte Repr.
Glossaire des Patois de la Suisse Romande. Droz.
Glossaire des Patois Franco-Provencaux. Antonin Duraffour. CNRS.
Glossaire des Patois Franco-Provencaux. Antonin Duraffour. CNRS.
Glossaire des Principaux Termes Geographiques & Logiques Sahariens. Robert Capot-Rey & Bernard Blaudin De The. Sahariennes Inst. Rech.
Glossaire des Rues de Dunkerque. Jean Foort. Foort.
Glossaire des Termes & Symboles en Matiere de Conversion Thermoelectronique. O. C. D. E.
Glossaire des Termes d'usage Courant en Commande Numerique. Ste. Publications Mecaniques.
Glossaire des Vieux Parlers du Departement de la Vilenne. Robert Mineau & Lucien Racinoux. Quiniste.
Glossaire d'histopathologia des Tumeurs Humaines. Remi Gerard-Marchant. Masson & Cie.
Glossaire Dictionnaire des Locutions Obscures & des Mots Vieillis: Recontrent dans les Oeuvres de Calvin. Jean Calvin. Slatkine.

Glossaire d'organes de Transmission, 1: Les Engrenages Allemand-Espagnol-Francais-Anglais-Italien-Neerlandais-Suedois-Finnois. Maison Dictionnaire.

Glossaire du Centre de la France. Hippolyte-Francois Jaubert. Slatkine.

Glossaire du Centre de la France. Le Comte Jaubert. Slatkine.

Glossaire du Droit Francais. Francois Ragueau. Slatkine.

Glossaire du Morvan. Eugene De Chambure. Pref. by Gerard Taverdet. Lafitte Repr.

Glossaire du Parler de Piechatel. Georges Dottin & J. Langouet. Slatkine.

Glossaire du Parler Francais au Canada. Societe du Paler Francais au Canada. French & Eur.

Glossaire du Parler Francais au Canada. Societe du Parler Francais au Canada. Laval P. U.

Glossaire du Patois de Chatenois avec Vocables des Autres: Localites du Territoire de Belfort & des Environs. Auguste Vautherin. Slatkine.

Glossaire du Patois de la Foret de Clairvaux. Alphonse Baudouin. Slatkine.

Glossaire du Patois de la Suisse Romande. Philippe Cyriaque Bridel & Louis Favrat. Slatkine.

Glossaire du Patois Poitavin. Charles C. Lalanne. Lafitte Repr.

Glossaire du Patois Thierachien. Paul Devigne. Ste. Linguistique Picarde.

Glossaire du Pays Biaiaois. Adrien Thibault. Slatkine.

Glossaire du Traitement Thermique. Association Technique de Traitement Thermique. Pyc.

Glossaire Etymologique & Comparatif du Patois Picard Ancien & Moderne. Jules Corblet. Slatkine.

Glossaire Etymologique & Historique des Patois & des Parlers de l'Anjou. A. J. Verrier & Rene Onillon. Slatkine.

Glossaire Europeen de Terminologie Juridique & Administrative: No. 15 Termes de Droit Anglais des Obligations, Anglais-Francais. French & Eur.

Glossaire Europeen de Terminologie Juridique & Administrative, 1. Institut International de Terminologie Juridique & Administrative. Bordas-Dunod.

Glossaire Europeen de Terminologie Juridique & Administrative, 2. Bordas-Dunod.

Glossaire Europeen de Terminologie Juridique & Administrative, 3. Institut International de Terminologie Juridique & Administrative. Bordas-Dunod.

Glossaire Europeen de Terminologie Juridique & Administrative, 5. Institut International de Terminologie Juridique & Administrative. Bordas-Dunod.

Glossaire Europeen de Terminologie Juridique & Administrative, 6. Institut International de Terminologie Juridique & Administrative. Bordas-Dunod.

Glossaire Europeen de Terminologie Juridique & Administrative, 8. Institut International de Terminologie Juridique & Administrative. Bordas-Dunod.

Glossaire Europeen de Terminologie Juridique et Administrative. French & Eur.

Glossaire Europeen de Terminologie Juridique et Administrative: Amenagement du Territiore. French & Eur.

Glossaire Europeen de Terminologie Juridique et Administrative: Budget. French & Eur.

Glossaire Europeen de Terminologie Juridique et Administratif. French & Eur.

Glossaire Europeen de Terminologie Juridique et Administrative: Droits D'Etablissement. French & Eur.

Glossaire Europeen de Terminologie Juridique et Administrative: Droit du Mariage. French & Eur.

Glossaire Europeen de Terminologie Juridique et Administrative: Driot de al Fonction Publique. French & Eur.

Glossaire Europeen de Terminologie Juridiqe et Administrative: Droits des Collectivites Locales. French & Eur.

Glossaire Europeen de Terminologie Juridique et Administrative: Eductions et Enseignment. French & Eur.

Glossaire Europeen de Terminologie Juridique et Administrative: Jeunesse. French & Eur.

Glossaire Europeen de Terminologie Juridique et Administrative: Law of Establishment. French & Eur.

Glossaire Europeen de Terminologie Juridique et Administrative: Marches Publics. French & Eur.

Glossaire Europeen de Terminologie Juridique et Administrative: Renumeration. French & Eur.

Glossaire Europeen de Terminologie Juridique et Administrative: Regional Policy. French & Eur.

Glossaire Europeen de Terminologie Juridique et Administrative: Terminologie Administrative et Secretariat. French & Eur.

Glossaire Europeen en Quatre Langues: Francais-Italien-Allemand-Anglais. L. G. D. J.

Glossaire Francais du Moyen Age: L'usage de l'archeologue & de l'amateur des Arts. Leon De Laborde. Slatkine.

Glossaire Franco-Canadien. Oscar Dunn. Univ Laval.

Glossaire Franco-Canadien: Vocabulaire de Locutions Vicieuses Usitees au Canada. Oscar Dunn. Laval P. U.

Glossaire Hebreu-Francais. Mayer Lambert & Louis Brandin. Slatkine.

Glossaire Hebreu-Francais du XIIIe. Siecle. Mayer Lambert & Louis Brandin. Slatkine.

Glossaire International d'Hydrologie. French & Eur.

Glossaire International d'hydrologie. Unesco.

Glossaire: Mots sans Memoire. Michel Leirie. Gallimard.

Glossaire Moyen-Breton. Emile Jean M. Ernault. Lafitte Repr.

Glossaire Moyen-Breton. Emile Ernault. Slatkine.

Glossaire Philologique de la Geste de Liege. Auguste Scheler. Slatkine.

Glossaire Picard du Parler de Long. J. B. Carton. Eklitra.

Glossaire sur la T. V. A. Becker. Office Intern. Librairie.

Glossar der Jugendarbeit: Deutsch Jugend & Ihr Soziales Umfeld. Deutsch-Franz Jugendwerk. H Luchterhand.

Glossari Ilustrat. Centre Culturel Occitan Pais Nissart. Centre Cult. Pais Nissart.

Glossarium Armorum: Bd 6 Texthefte in Deutsch, Englisch, Franzoesisch, Italienisch, Daenisch, Tschechisch. Ed. by Ortwin Gamber et al. Verlag der Buchhaendler-Vereinigung GmbH.

Glossarium Artis: Deutsch-Franzoesisches Woerterbuch zur Kunst. Ed. by Rudolf Huber & Renate Rieth. Max Niemeyer.

Glossary of Automotive Terminology: French-English English-French. Chrysler Corporation. Soc Auto Engineers.

Glossary of Conference Terms: Arabic, French, English. (UNESCO). Unipub.

Glossary of Conference Terms, English, French, Arabic. (UNESCO). Unipub.

Glossary of Conference Terms: English, French, Arabic. (UNESCO). Unipub.

Glossary of Economics. F. Clifford Vaughn. Elsevier.

A Glossary of English Equivalents of Terms Commonly Used in French Auctions, Catalogues, & Stamp Trade. R. G. Stone et al. France & Col Philatelist.

Glossary of Fiber Optics Terms. Info Gatekeepers.

Glossary of French & English Management Terms. Ed. by James Coveney & Shelia J. Moore. Longman.

Glossary of French & English Management Terms. Coveney & Moore. Imported Bks.

Glossary of French & English Management Terms. Coveney & Moore. Longman.

Glossary of Genetics. Francoise Biass-Ducroux. Elsevier.

Glossary of International Treaties. Y. Renoux & J. Yates. Elsevier.

Glossary of Mining Geology. G. Amstutz. (Pub. by F. Enke). French & Eur.

Glossary of Mining Geology. G. C. Amstutz et al. Ed. by F. Esser & Won C. Park. Enke.

Glossary of Neurotraumatology. Ed. by E. S. Gurdjian et al. Springer-Verlag.

Glossary of Onshore & Offshore Pipelines. Editions Technip. Graham & Trotman.

Glossary of Physiological Terms. (Pub. by Collets). State Mutual Bk.

Glossary of Populations & Housing. G. Logie. Elsevier.

Glossary of Soil Micromorphology. Ed. by A. Jongerius & G. K. Rutherford. Pudoc.

Glossary of Technical Terms for Market Researchers: English-German-Spanish-French-Italian-Dutch. European Society for Opinion & Marketing Research. Intl Pubns Serv.

Glossary of Terms in Heat Transfer, Fluid Flow & Related Topics. Ed. by William Begell. Hemisphere Pub.

Glossary of Terms Used in Industrial Relations. Gerard Dion. Univ Laval.

Glossary of the Theatre. K. R. Band-Kuzmany. Elsevier.

Le Glosses & Glossaires Hebreux-Francais. Arsene Darmesteter. Champion.

Grand Dictionnaire d'Americanismes: Contenant les Principaux Termes Americains avec Leur Equivalent Exact en Francais. Etienne Deak. Intl Pubns Serv.

Grand Larousse de la Langue Francaise. Louis Guilbert. French & Eur.

Grand Larousse de la Langue Francaise: Tome I. L. Guilbert et al. (Dist. by Continentai Bk Co). Larousse.

Grand Larousse de la Langue Francaise: Tome VII. L. Guilbert et al. (Dist. by Continental Bk Co). Larousse.

Grande Dicionario Frances-Portugues. Ersilio Cardoso. Difel Difusao.

Grande Dicionario Portugues-Frances. Domingos De Azevedo. Difel Difusao.

Grande Encyclopedie Larousse. Pergamon.

Grundwortschatz: Deutsch Essential German-Allemand. M Rosenberg.

Gypsum & Plaster Dictionary. K. H. Volkart. (Pub. by Bauverlag). French & Eur.

Gypsum & Plaster Dictionary. K. H. Volkart. Intl Pubns Serv.

Gypsum & Plaster Dictionary. K. H. Volkart. Bauverlag.

Hamlyn French Dictionary. Laurence Urdang Associates. Hamlyn-Amer.

Hamlyn French-English Dictionary. Larousse.

Handelskorrenpondenz in Vier Sprachen. F. Berset. M Rosenberg.

Harrap's Concise French & English Dictionary. Patricia Forbes & Muriel H. Smith. Ed. by P. H. Collin. Harrap.

Harrap's Concise Student French & English Dictionary. J. E. Mansion. Ed. by P. H. Collin et al. Natl Textbk.

Harrap's Dictionnaire d'argot: French to English, English to French Slang Dictionary. G. Marks. French & Eur.

Harrap's English-French Dictionary of Data Processing. Claude Camille & Michel Dehaine. Harrap.

Harrap's English-French Dictionary of Slang & Colloquialisms. Georgette A. Marks & Charles B. Johnson. Harrap.

Harrap's First French Dictionary. Colin Henstock. Harrap.

Harrap's French & English Business Dictionary. Ed. by Francoise Collin et al. Natl Textbk.

Harrap's French & English Business Dictionary. Ed. by F. Laurendeau et al. Harrap.

Harrap's French & English Business Dictionary. Francoise Colin et al. Imported Bks.

Harrap's French & English Dictionary of Data Processing. Claude Camille & Michel Dehaine. Harrap.

Harrap's French & English Dictionary of Slang & Colloquialisms. Joseph Marks & Georgette A. Marks. Rev. by Georgette A. Marks. Harrap.

Harrap's French-English Dictionary of Slang & Colloquialisms. French & Eur.

Harrap's Mini Pocket French & English Dictionary. Ed. by Patricia Forbes & Margaret Ledesert. Harrap.

Harrap's New Collegiate French & English Dictionary. J. E. Mansion. Ed. by D. H. Ledesert. Natl Textbk.

Harrap's New Collegiate French Dictionary: English-French, French-English. Imported Bks.

Harrap's New Pocket French & English Dictionary. Ed. by Patricia Forbes & Margaret Ledesert. Harrap.

Harrap's New Standard Francais-Anglais, 1: A-I. French & Eur.

Harrap's New Standard Francais-Anglais, 2: J-Z. French & Eur.

Harrap's New Standard French & English Dictionary. J. E. Mansion. Imported Bks.

Harrap's New Standard French & English Dictionary. J. E. Mansion. Clarke Ltd.

Harrap's New Standard French & English Dictionary: A-I, French-English. J. E. Mansion. Ed. by D. M. Ledesert & R. P. Ledesert. Harrap.

Harrap's New Standard French & English Dictionary: A-K, English-French. J. E. Mansion. Ed. by D. M. Ledesert & R. L. Ledesert. Harrap.

Harrap's New Standard French & English Dictionary: J-Z, French-English. J. E. Mansion. Ed. by D. M. Ledesert & R. P. Ledesert. Harrap.

Harrap's New Standard French & English Dictionary: L-Z, English-French. J. E. Mansion. Ed. by D. M. Ledesert & R. P. Ledesert. Harrap.

Harrap's New Standard French & English Dictionary, Part One, French-English (A-I) J. E. Mansion. Ed. by D. H. Ledesert & R. P. Ledesert. Natl Textbk.

Harrap's New Standard French & English Dictionary, Part One, French-English (J-Z) J. E. Mansion. Ed. by D. H. Ledesert & R. P. Ledesert. Natl Textbk.

Harrap's Shorter French & English Dictionary. P. H. Collin et al. Harrap.

Harrap's Shorter French & English Dictionary. J. E. Mansion et al. Harrap Co.

Harrap's Standard Anglais-Francais. French & Eur.

Harrap's Standard French & English Dictionary. J. E. Mansion. Harrap.

Harrap's Standard French & English Dictionary, Part 2, English-French (A-Z) J. E. Mansion. Natl Textbk.

Harrap's Super-Mini French & English Dictionary. J. E. Mansion. Ed. by Patricia Forbes & Margaret Ledesert. Natl Textbk.

Heinemann Modern Dictionary for Dental Students. Jennifer Fowler. French & Eur.

The Herbst Dictionaries of Commercial, Financial & Legal Terms Vol. I. Robert Herbst & Alan G. Readett. Birkhauser.

The Herbst Dictionaries of Commercial, Financial & Legal Terms Vol. 2. Ed. by Robert Herbst & Alan G. Readett. Birkhauser.

Herbst Dictionary of Commercial, Financial & Legal Terms. Ed. by Robert Herbst & Alan G. Readett. Birkhauser.

The Herbst-Readett Three-Language Dictionaries of Commerce, Finance & Law. Birkhauser-Boston Publishing. Birkhauser.

Horticultural Dictionary: French-English. D. O. Bourke. French & Eur.

Hugo Pocket Dictionary: French-English, English-French. Littlefield.

Hungarian-French Concise Dictionary. S. Eckhardt. French & Eur.

Les Idiotismes du Francais Fondamental, Premier Degre. D. K. Pryce. Illus. by Raymond Fishwick. Harrap.

Illiustrirovannyi Voenno-Tekhnicheskii Slovar. L. D. Neliubin. (Pub. by Voenizdat). Four Continent.

Illustrierte Technische Woerterbucher: Eisenbahnmaschinenwesen. A. Schlomann. (Pub. by R. Oldenbourg). French & Eur.

Illustrierte Technische Woerterbucher: Eisenbahnmaschinenwesen. A. Schlomann. Oldenbourg Verlag.

Illustrierte Technische Woerterbucher: Eisenbahnbau und Betrieb. A. Schlomann. (Pub. by R. Oldenbourg). French & Eur.

Illustrierte Technische Woerterbucher: Eisenbahnbau und Betrieb. A. Schlomann. Oldenbourg Verlag.

Illustrierte Technische Woerterbucher: Elektrotechnik und Elektrochemie. A. Schlomann. (Pub. by R. Oldenbourg). French & Eur.

Illustrierte Technische Woerterbucher: ELektrotechnik und Elektrochemie. A. Schlomann. Oldenbourg Verlag.

Illustrierte Technische Woerterbucher: Maschinenelemente. A. Schlomann. (Pub. by R. Oldenbourg). French & Eur.

Illustrierte Technische Woerterbucher: Maschinenelemente. A. Schlomann. Oldenbourg Verlag.

Illustrierter Technische Woerterbucher: Luffahrts. A. Schlomann. (Pub. by R. Oldenbourg). French & Eur.

Illustrierter Technische Woerterbucher: Luffahrts. A. Schlomann. Oldenbourg Verlag.

Illustriertes Woerterbuch. (Pub. by Gebrueder Weiss). French & Eur.

Ilustrowany Slownik Samochodowy. Czeslaw Blok. Wydawnictwa.

IMF Glossary: English-French-Spanish. International Monetary Fund, Bureau of Language Services. Intl Monetary.

Informationsverarbeitung-Englisch-Deutsch-Franzoesisch-Russisch. Erich Burger. VEB Technik.

Initiation Au Vocabulaire Du Batiment et Des Travaux Publics. Profor. French & Eur.

International Bibliography of Standardized Vocabularies. Eugen Wuster et al. Ed. by International Information Centre for Terminology. K G Saur.

International Construction Terminology. K. Lange & L. Ferval et al. (Pub. by Bauverlag). French & Eur.

International Construction Terminology. K. Lange & L. Ferval et al. Bauverlag.

International Dictionary. Otto Jesperson. (Pub. by Carl Winter). French & Eur.

International Dictionary. Otto Jesperson. Winter Univ.

International Dictionary of Building Construction: English-French-German-Italian. Angelo C. Schwicker. Scholium Intl.

International Dictionary of Metallurgy, Mineralogy, Geology & the Mining & Oil Industries. A. Gagnacci-Schwicker & Schwicker. (Pub. by Bauverlag). French & Eur.

International Dictionary of Metallurgey, Mineralogy, Geology & the Mining & Oil Industries. A. Gagnacci-Schwicker & Schwicker. Bauverlag.

International Dictionary of Obscenities: A Guide to Dirty Words & Indecent Expressions in Spanish, Italian, French, German, & Russian. Christina Kunitskaya-Peterson. Berkeley Slavic.

International Electrotechnical Vocabulary: Electronics. French & Eur.

International Electrotechnical Vocabulary, Machines & Transformers. French & Eur.

International Glossary of Technical Terms for the Pulp & Paper Industry. Van Derveer & Haas. Imported Bks.

International Hospital Vade Mecum & English, French, Spanish Glossary. Paul Aurousseau. Editions Sedip F.Galula.

International Planning Glossary. Ed. by Gordon Logie & Hemel Hemstead. Intl Plan Glos.

International Vocabulary of Town Planning & Architecture. Intl Pubns Serv.

Interpretes de Bolsillo Espanol-Frances. Biblograf SP.

Interpretes de Bolsillo Frances-Espanol. Biblograf SP.

Iron & Steel Dictionary: German-French & French-German. Iron & Steel Institute. Intl Pubns Serv.

Iron & Steel Industry Dictionary. A. M. Abd-El-Wahed. French & Eur.

Japanese-Latin-English-German-French Medical Terminology. French & Eur.

Le Jargon du XVe Siecle: Etude Philologique. Auguste C. Vitu. Slatkine.

Je Sais Tout Sur le Monde & la Nature. Antoine Icart. Hachette-Jeunesse.

Jean's Pocket Dictionaries: French-English. Hammond Inc.

Kamusi Vocabulaire. S. Farsi. Edns St Paul.

Karmannyi Frantsuzsko-Russkii Slovar. K. S. Vygodskaia. (Pub. by GINS). Four Continent.

Karmannyi Russko-Frantsuzskii Slovar. Four Continent.

Kettridge's English-French - French-English Dictionary. Ed. by Hochman. (Sig). NAL.

Kettridge's French-English, English-French Dictionary. NAL.

Kluwer's Universeel Technisch Woordenboek Frans-Nederlands. Stekhoven G. Schuurmans & M. Piriou-Vandamme. Kluwer Technische.

Kluwer's Universeel Technisch Woordenboek: Nederlands-Frans. G. Schuurmans. French & Eur.

Kluwer's Universeel Technisch Woorenboek Nederlands Frans. Stekhovenn G. Schuurmans. Kluwer Technische.

Kluwer's Universeel Technish Woordenboek: Frans-Nederlands. G. Schuurmans. French & Eur.

Kratkii Frantsuzsko-Russkii i Russko-Frantsuzskii Slovar. K. S. Vygodskaia et al. (Pub. by Sov Entsiklopediia). Four Continent.

Kratkii Russko-Frantsuzskii Uchebnyi Slovar. (Pub. by Sov Entsiklopediia). Four Continent.

Kunststofftechnisches Woerterbuch. A. Wittfoht. (Pub. by C. Hanser). French & Eur.

Kunststofftechnisches Woerterbuch. A. Wittfoht. (Pub. by C. Hanser). French & Eur.

Kunststofftechnisches Woerterbuch. A. Wittfoht. Hanser.

Kunststofftechnisches Woerterbuch. A. Wittfoht. Hanser.

Langenscheidt English-French Lilliput Dictionary. Langenscheidt.

Langenscheidt French-English Lilliput Dictionary. Langenscheidt.

Langenscheidt Grossworterbucher Franzosisch. Incl. Langenscheidt.

Langenscheidts Grosse Schulwoerterbuch Deutsch-Franzoesisch. Ernst E. Lange-Kowal. Langenscheidt.

Langenscheidts Grosse Schulwoerterbucher Deutsch-Franzoesisch. Kurt Wilhelm. Langenscheidt.

Langenscheidts Grosse Schulwoerterbuch Franzoesisch-Deutsch. Ernst E. Lange-Kowal & Louis Beaucaire. Langenscheidt.

Langenscheidts Grosse Schulwoerterbuch Franzoesisch-Deutsch. Ernst E. Lange-Kowal. Langenscheidt.

Langenscheidts Grosse Schulwoerterbuecher Franzoesisch-Deutsch. Ernst E. Lange-Kowal. Langenscheidt.

Langenscheidts Grosswoerterbuch Franzoesisch: Tl 1, Franzoesisch-Deutsch. Sachs & Villatte. Langenscheidt.

Langenscheidts Grosswoerterbuch Franzoesisch: Tl 2, Deutsch-Franzoesisch. Langenscheidt.

Langenscheidts Grosswoerterbuch: Teil II, Deutsch-Franzoesisch. Karl Sachs & Cesaire Villatte. Ed. by Walter Gottschalk & Gaston Bentot. Langenscheidt.

Langenscheidts Grosswoerterbuch: Teil I, Franzoesisch-Deutsch. Karl Sachs & Cesaire Villatte. Langenscheidt.

Langenscheidts Handwoerterbuch: Franzoesisch-Deutsch Deutsch-Franzoesisch. Ernst E. Lange-Kowal & Louis Beaucaire. Langenscheidt.

Langenscheidts Handwoerterbuch: Franzoesisch. Ernst Erwin Lange-Kowal. Ed. by Louis Beaucaire. Langenscheidt.

Langenscheidts Handwoerterbuch: Teil II, Deutsch-Franzoesisch. Ernst E. Lange-Kowal. Langenscheidt.

Langenscheidts Handwoerterbuch: Teil I, Franzoesisch-Deutsch. Ernst E. Lange-Kowal & Louis Beaucaire. Langenscheidt.

Langenscheidts Handwoerterbuecher Franzoesisch. Ed. by Heinz Messinger & Werner Ruedenberg. Langenscheidt.

Langenscheidts Handwoerterbuecher: Franzoesisch, 2 Teile in 1. Langenscheidt.

Langenscheidts Handwoerterbuecher: Tl 1, Franzoesisch-Deutsch. Ed. by Ernst E. Lange-Kowal. Langenscheidt.

Langenscheidts Handwoerterbuecher: Tl 2, Deutsch-Franzoesisch. Ed. by Kurt Wilhelm. Langenscheidt.

Langenscheidt's Lilliput English-French Dictionary. Am Map.

Langenscheidt's Lilliput French-English Dictionary. Am Map.

Langenscheidts Lilliput-Woerterbuch Deutsch-Franzoesisch. Langenscheidt.

Langenscheidts Lilliput-Woerterbuch Franzoesisch-Deutsch. Langenscheidt.

Langenscheidts Lilliput-Woerterbucher Franzoesisch-Deutsch. Langenscheidt.

Langenscheidts Lilliput-Woerterbuecher Deutsch-Franzoesisch. Langenscheidt.

Langenscheidt's New Pocket French Dictionary: French-English, English-French. Ed. by Langenscheidt Staff. Am Map.

Langenscheidts Satz-Lexikon des Franzoesischen Geschaeftsbriefes. Langenscheidt.

Langenscheidts Schulwoerterbuch Franzoesisch-Deutsch. Ernst E. Lange-Kowal & Paul Hartig. Langenscheidt.

Langenscheidts Schulwoerterbuecher Franzoesisch-Deutsch. Langenscheidt.

Langenscheidts Sportwoerterbuch. R. Lembke. (Pub. by Langenscheidt). French & Eur.

Langenscheidts Sportwoerterbuch Deutsch-Englisch-Franzoesisch-Spanisch. Langenscheidt.

Langenscheidt's Standard French Dictionary: French-English, English-French. Kenneth Unwin. Am Map.

Langenscheidts Taschenwoerterbuch Franzoesisch. E. E. Lange-Kowal et al. Langenscheidt.

Langenscheidts Taschenwoerterbuch Franzoesisch: Teil II, Deutsch-Franzoesisch. E. Weymuth. Langenscheidt.

Langenscheidts Taschenwoerterbuch Franzoesisch: Teil I, Franzoesisch-Deutsch. E. E. Lange-Kowal. Langenscheidt.

Langenscheidts Taschenwoerterbuecher Franzoesisch-Deutsch. Lange-Kowal & E. Ernst. Langenscheidt.

Langenscheidt's Universal French-English, English-French Dictionary. Am Map.

Langenscheidts Universal-Woerterbuch Franzoesisch. Langenscheidt.

Langenscheidts Universal-Woerterbuecher Franzoesisch-Deutsch. Langenscheidt.

L'argile pour votre Sante. Andre Passebecq. Dangles.

Larouse de la Langue Francaise. Pergamon.

Larousse Bi-Lingual French-English, English French Dictionary. Larousse.

Larousse de Base: Dictionnaire d'Apprentissage du Francais. Ed. by Jean Dubois & Francoise Duboise-Charlier. Larousse FR.

Larousse de la Langue Francaise. Pergamon.

Larousse de la Langue Francaise Lexis, Illustre. J. Dubois. (Dist. by Continental Bk Co). Larousse.

Larousse de poche. Larousse & Co. Larousse.

Larousse De Poche. PB.

Larousse de poche, francais-allemand et allemand-francais. Larousse & Co. Larousse.

Larousse de poche francais-espagnol, & espanol-frances. Larousse And Co. Larousse.

Larousse de poche, francais-italien et italien-francais. Larousse & Co. Larousse.

Larousse de poche French-English & English-French. Larousse & Co. Larousse.

Larousse de Poche: Precis de Grammaire. Librairie Larousse. Lib Gen Fr.

Larousse des Citations: Francaises et Etrangeres. Pierre Germa. (Dist. by Continental Bk Co). Larousse.

Larousse des debutants. Larousse & Co. Larousse.

Le Larousse des Enfants. L. Lamblin. (Dist. by Continental Bk Co). Larousse.

Larousse du chat. Ed. by Pierre Rousselet-Blanc. Larousse.

Larousse French-English Dictionary. PB.

Larousse French-English Dictionary. Larousse.

Larousse Modern French-English, English-French Dictionary. Larousse.

L'aspect Verbal en Francais. Milan Golian. (Pub. by Helmut Buske Verlag Hamburg). Benjamins North Am.

Law Dictionary French-Arabic: Dictionnaire Juridique. Najjar. Intl Bk Ctr.

Learn French for English Speakers. W. R. Patterson. Saphrograph.

Legal Dictionary: French-English & English-French. Thomas A. Quemner. Intl Pubns Serv.

Let's Talk D. P: Computer Lexicon. Jean P. Drieux & Alain Jarlaud. French & Eur.

Let's Talk D. P: Lexique D'informatique. Jean-Pierre Drieux & Alain Jarlaud. Bordas.

L'Europe & ses population. Abel Miroglio & Yvonne D. Miroglio. Nyhoff.

Lexico de Ceramica & Alfareria Aragonesas. Maria Isabel Alvaro Zamora. Portico.

Lexico De Terminos Nucleares: Diccionario Vocabulario Triligue. French & Eur.

La Lexicologie. Picoche. (Dist. by Continental Bk Co). Lib Fernand Nathan.

Lexicologie & Lexicographie Francaises & Romanes. CNRS.

Lexicon comercial internacional: Espanol, frances, ingles, italiano, portugues y aleman. J. Vicens Carrio. Reverte SA.

Lexicon de Comunicologia: Diccinario para Audiologos, Audioprotesistas, Foniatras, Logopedas, Profesores De Sordos y Psicolinguistas. Jorge Perello. French & Eur.

Lexicon Medicum. Boleslaw Zlotnickiego. French & Eur.

Lexicon Medicum: Medizinisches Woerterbuch in 6 Sprachen; Englisch, Russisch, Franzoesisch, Deutsch, Latein, Polnisch. B. Zlotnicki. Langenscheidt.

Lexicon of French Borrowings in the German Vocabulary. William J. Jones. De Gruyter.

Lexicon of International & National Units. Ed. by M. Merino-Rodriguez. Elsevier.

Lexicon of Plant Pests & Diseases. Ed. by Manuel Merino-Rodriguez. Elsevier.

Lexicon Sopena: Diccionario de bolsillo, frances-espanol y espanol-frances. Sopena.

Lexicue Trilingue des Termes d'usage Courant En Machines Outils; les Tours. French & Eur.

Lexikon der Geschaeftsbriefe in Vier Sprachen. French & Eur.

Lexikon Medicum. B. Zlotnicki. French & Eur.

Lexique Aborite. Marcel Lagrenade. Dotmar.

Lexique Analytique du Vocabulaire Inuit Moderne au Quebec-Labrador. Louis J. Dorais. (Dist. by Four Continent Bk). Univ Laval.

Lexique Anglais-Francais. J. Vaillancourt. Edns Ottawa.

Lexique Anglais-Francais De la Banque et De la Monnaie. Pierre Ricour. French & Eur.

Lexique Anglais-Francais de L'Aciere Electrique. B. Besse et al. French & Eur.

Lexique Anglais-Francais De L'industrie Miniere, 1. Pierre Auger & Louis-Jean Rousseau. French & Eur.

Lexique Anglais-Francais Des Appareils De Mesures Electriques. Jean Mercier. French & Eur.

Lexique Anglais-Francais Des Fruits et Legumes. Louise Appel. French & Eur.

Lexique Anglais-Francais des Petits Appareils Electromenagers. French Language Bureau. Edit Quebec.

Lexique Anglais-Francais des Termes Appartenant Aux Techniques En Usage a I.G.N. Ed. by Brommer. French & Eur.

Lexique Anglais-Francais des Termes Appartenant Aux Technques En Usage I.G.N. Thuillier. French & Eur.

Lexique Anglais-Francais des Termes Appartenant aux Techniques en Usage a I. G. N. Brommer. I. G. N.

Lexique Anglais-Francais du Compteur d'electricite. Jean Mercier. Quebec Off.

Lexique Anglais-Francais du Compteur d'electricite. Office de la Langue Francaise. Quebec Off.

Lexique Anglais-Francais Du Compteur D'electricite: Principes et Pieces Composantes. Jean Mercier. French & Eur.

Lexique Anglais-Francais du Programmateur de Cuisiniere. Jean Mercier. Quebec Off.

Lexique Anglais-Francais Du Programmateur De Cuisiniere: Fonctionnement et Pieces Composantes. Jean Mercier. French & Eur.

Lexique Anglais-Francais: Termes Appartenant aux Techniques en Usage a I. G. N. Premiere Partie. Thuiluer. I. G. N.

Lexique Anglais-Francais: Termes Techniques a l'usage des Biologistes. Jean Vaillancourt. U of Toronto Pr.

Lexique CN: Anglais-Allemand-Francais. Y. H. Attiyate. Iron Age Metalworking Int.

Lexique Commente de la Douane & du Commerce Exterieur. Editorial Office.

Lexique Commercial: Tout le vocabulaire des affaires. C.I.D.A. Maison Dictionnaire.

Lexique Compare de la Langue de Corneille. Frederic Godefroy. Kraus.

Lexique Compare des Fabilaux de Jean Bedel. Pierre Nardin. Slatkine.

Lexique Complet de la Langue de Villon. Andre Burger. Droz.

Lexique d'amenagement du Territoire. C. N. I. P. E.

Lexique d'antiquites Grecques. Claude Vial. Colin.

Lexique d'antiquites Romaines. Andre Pelletier. Colin.

Lexique de base du Latin. J. Michel & Michel Gester. Sikkel.

Lexique de Charles d'Orleans dans les Ballades. Daniel Poirion. Droz.

Lexique de Comptabilite & de Gestion. Colasse. Ecole Electricite.

Lexique de Comptabilite & de Gestion. Colasse. French & Eur.

Lexique de la Banque & de la Monnaie. Pierre Ricour & Rene Cousineau. Edit Quebec.

Lexique de la Fabrication du Refrigerateur: Francais-Anglais. H. Dupuis et al. French & Eur.

Lexique de la Gestion. Pierre Lauzel. E. M. E.

Lexique de la Langue de Bonaventure Des Periers. Adolphe Cheneviere & Felix Frank. Slatkine.

Lexique de la Langue de Chapelain. Antonin Fabre. Slatkine.

Lexique de la Langue de Jean Chapelain. Alfred C. Hunter. Droz.

Lexique de la Langue de Jean de La Fontaine. Henri De Regnier. Lenox.

Lexique de la Langue de la Bruyere. Adolphe Regnier. Olms.

Lexique de la Langue de La Rochefoucauld. Henri De Regnier. Olms.

Lexique de la Langue de Mme de Sevigne. Jean E. Sommer. Lenox.

Lexique de la Langue de Mme de Sevigne, 1. Jean E. Sommer. Olms.

Lexique de la Langue de Mme de Sevigne, 2. Jean E. Sommer. Olms.

Lexique de la Langue de Moliere. Arthur Desfeuilles. Lenox.

Lexique de la Langue de Moliere avec une. Arthur Desfeuilles. B Franklin.

Lexique de la Langue de Moliere, 1. Charles L. Livet. Olms.

Lexique de la Langue de Moliere, 2. Charles L. Livet. Olms.

Lexique de la Langue de Moliere, 3. Charles L. Livet. Olms.

Lexique de la Langue de Pierre Corneille. Charles J. Marty-Lavezux. Lenox.

Lexique de la Langue des Essais de Michel de Montaigne. Pierre L. Villey-Desmeserets. Lenox.

Lexique de la Langue des Oeuvres Burlesques de Scarron. Leonard T. Richardson. Olms.

Lexique de la Langue du Cardinal de Retz. Adolphe Regnier. Olms.

Lexique de la Langue Turen: Parler des Banen du sud-ouest du Cameroun. Idelette Dugast. S. E. L. A. F.

Lexique de la Musique. Jean Queval. French & Eur.

Lexique de la Musique. Jean Queval. Delpire.

Lexique de la photographie d'Amateur: Anglais-Francais Francais-Anglais. R. Pollet. Maison Dictionnaire.

Lexique de la Photographie d'amateur: Francais-Anglais. Ray J. Pollet. Lemeac.

Lexique de la Prevention des Accidents. Maria E. De Villiers-Sidani. Quebec Off.

Lexique de la Psychanalyse. Jean-Pierre Trempe. Quebec Off.

Lexique de la Resistance Grecque: Journal de Resistance. Mikis Theodorakis. Flammarion.

Lexique De la Terminologie Linguistique. Jules Marouzeau. Intl Pubns Serv.

Lexique de l'ancien Francais. Frederic Godefroy. French & Eur.

Lexique de l'ancien Francais. Frederic Godefroy. Champion.

Lexique de l'ancien Francais. Frederic Godefroy. Olms.

Lexique de L'Anglais des Affaires. Ivan de Renty. French & Eur.

Lexique de l'Anglais des affaires. Ivan De Renty. Imported Bks.

Lexique de l'anglais des Affaires. Ivan De Renty. L. G. F.

Lexique de l'economie Suisse. Baconniere.

Lexique de L'education au Nouveau-Brunswick. Ministere de L'education. Ministere de L'education.

Lexique de l'homme a Cheval. Marc de Saint-Riquier. French & Eur.

Lexique de l'homme a Cheval. Marc Saint Riquier & Jacques Delporte. Amphora.

Lexique de l'Industrie Petroliere Ra Finage: Anglais-Francais. M. Heroux et al. French & Eur.

Lexique de l'Industrie Textile: Francais-Anglais. R. Habert et al. French & Eur.

Lexique de l'informatique. Jean Guilhaumou. E. M. E.

Lexique de Mecanique d'ajustage. Lucien Normandeau. Quebec Off.

Lexique de Prevention des Accidents. Maria E. De Villiers-Sidani et al. French & Eur.

Lexique de Psychologie & de Psychiatrie. Medicales Univ.

Lexique de Psychologie & de Psychiatrie. Medicales Univ.

Lexique de Ronsard. Louis Mellerio. Kraus.

Lexique de Ronsard. Louis Mellerio. Olms.

Lexique de Sylviculture Allemand-Francais. Martinot Lagarde. Genie Rural.

Lexique de Termes Anglais-Francais de Gestion. James Coveney & Sheila J. Moore. Colin.

Lexique De Termes Anglais-Francais De Gestion: Les Cycle Au Superieur, Ecoles Superieures De Gestion. James Conveney & Shiela J. Moore. French & Eur.

Lexique de Termes Juridiques. Ed. by Raymond Guillen & Jean Vincent. Dalloz.

Lexique de Termes Juridiques. Bruylant.

Lexique de Termes Juridiques. Raymond Guillien & Jean Vincent. Dalloz.

Lexique de Termes Politiques. Bruylant.

Lexique de termes techniques: Anglais-Francais & index Francais. R. J. Pollet. Maison Dictionnaire.

Lexique de Termes Techniques: Un Lexique Anglais-Francais. Ray J. Pollet. French & Eur.

Lexique de Termes Techniques: Un Lexique Anglais-Francais. Ray J. Pollet. Lemeac.

Lexique d'Erquinghem-Lys. Paul Barbier. Ste. Linguistique Picarde.

Lexique Des Antiquites Grecques. Pierre Paris. French & Eur.

Lexique Des Antiquites Romaines. Rene Cagnat & G. Goyau. Boccard.

Le Lexique des Bons Petits Plats. Jehanne Jean-Charles. Presses Cite.

Lexique des Dieux. Pierre Chastel. Delpire.

Lexique des Epices et Assaisonnements: Anglais-Francais. J. Maurais. French & Eur.

Lexique des Fruits et Legumes. L. Appel. French & Eur.

Lexique des Industries Graphiques. R. Comte & A. Pernin. French & Eur.

Lexique des Industries Graphiques. Rene Comte & Andre Pernin. Comp Fr Edns.

Lexique des Lettres Commerciales en Quatre Langues. Multi Ling Verlag A. G.

Lexique des Mots-cles, Descripteurs & Identificateurs, Francais-Anglais: Utiliser pour la Recherche Documentaire. Centre de Documentation de L'armement. Centre Documentation Armement.

Lexique des Parlers Arabes-Tchado-Soudanais. Arlette Roth-Laly. CNRS.

Lexique des Parlers Arabes-Tchado-Soudanais. Arlette Roth-Laly. CNRS.

Lexique des Parlers Arabes-Tchado-Soudanais, 3. Arlette Roth-Laly. CNRS.

Lexique des Pipelines a Terre et en Mer. Technip.

Lexique des Produits de la Peche: Anglais-Francais. P. Vallieres et al. French & Eur.

Lexique des Sciences de l'education. Leandre Coudray. E. S. F.

Lexique des Sciences Sociales. Bruylant.

Lexique des Symboles. Olivier Beigbeder. Zodiaque.

Lexique des Termes de Parodontologie de Microbiologie Parodontale et Buccale et de Sciences Fondamentales. Robert Sinsoilliez. French & Eur.

Lexique des Termes de Prothese Dentaire. Evelyn Batarec. French & Eur.

Lexique des Termes de Prothese Dentaire. Evelyn Batarec. Prelat.

Lexique Des Termes Du Batiment. French & Eur.

Lexique des Termes du Batiment. Massin.

Lexique des Termes Economiques. Jean F. Phelizon. Tech Vulgar.

Lexique des Termes Economiques. Jean-Francois Phelizon. Tech Vulgar.

Lexique des Termes Juridiques. Raymond Guillien & Jean Vincent. French & Eur.

Lexique des Termes Medicaux. French & Eur.

Lexique des Termes Medicaux. Lamarre Poinot.

Lexique des Termes Parodontologie de Microbiologie: Parodontale & Buccale & de Sciences Fondamentales. Robert Sinsoilliez. Prelat.

Lexique des Termes Politiques. Charles Debbasch & Yves Daudet. French & Eur.

Lexique des Termes Politiques. Charles Debbasch & Yves Daudet. Dalloz.

Lexique des Termes Techniques Concernant le Material d'Une Usine d'Acetylene Dissous. French & Eur.

Lexique des Termes Techniques Concernant le Material d'une Usine d'oxygene. Soudure Autogene.

Lexique des Termes Usuels de Psychiatrie. Jean Carrere & Jacques Dessaigne. French & Eur.

Lexique des Termes Usuels de Psychiatrie. Jean Carrere & Jacques Dessaigne. Berger-Levrault.

Lexique Des Termes Utiles a L'etude Des Noms De Lieux. Henri Dorion & Jean Poirier. French & Eur.

Lexique des Termes Utiles a l'etude des Noms de Lieux. Henri Dorion & Jean Poirier. Laval P. U.

Lexique d'Informatique. Michel Ginguay & Annette Lauret. French & Eur.

Lexique d'informatique. Michel Ginguay & Annette Lauret. Masson & Cie.

Lexique Du Batiment. French & Eur.

Lexique du Boeuf. Edit Quebec.

Lexique du Calcul Economique & de l'econometrie. Andre Olmi & Fortune July. E. M. E.

Lexique du cinema d'Amateur: Anglais-Francais Francais-Anglais. R. Pollet. Maison Dictionnaire.

Lexique du Journal des Debats. Ministere des Communications Assemblee Nationale. Quebec Off.

Lexique du Journal des Debats. Ministere des Communications Assemblee Nationale. Quebec Off.

Lexique du Journal des Debats. Ministere des Communications Assemblee Nationale. Quebec Off.

Lexique du Journal des Goncourt. Maximilien Fuchs. Slatkine.

Lexique du Marketing. Hubert Nyssen. French & Eur.

Lexique du Marketing. Hubert Nyssen. Delpire.

Lexique du Marketing. Francois Roche. E. M. E.

Le Lexique du Parler Creole de la Reunion. Robert Chaudenson. Champion.

Lexique du Parler de Saviese. Christophe Favre & Robert Balet. Champion.

Lexique du Parler des Marazig. Gilbert Boris & M. Denizeau. Imprimerie Nat.

Lexique du Roman de Renart. Gunnar Tilander. Champion.

Lexique du Secourisme & de la Plongee Autonome. Andre Hourcastagne. France Selection.

Lexique du Tahitien Contemporain: Tahitien-Francais. Yves Lemaitre. Orstom.

Lexique Etymologique de L'Irlandais Ancien: Fascicule R-S. Joseph Vendryes. CNRS.

Lexique Etymologique de L'Irlandais Ancien: Fascicule T-U. Joseph Vendryes. CNRS.

Lexique Etymologique de L'Irlandais Ancien: Lettre B. Joseph Vendryes & E. Bachellery et al. CNRS.

Lexique Etymologique de l'Irlandais Ancien. Joseph Vendryes. CNRS.

Lexique Etymologique de l'Irlandais Ancien, 1. Joseph Vendryes. CNRS.

Lexique Etymologique des Termes Medicaux. Michel Lancombe & Jean-Pierre Monceaux. Lamarre Poinot.

Lexique Forestier: Anglais-Francais. Marcel Lagrenade. Dotmar.

Lexique Francais-Anglais et Anglais-Francais des Termes d'usage Courant en Machines Outils et Machines Similaires. French & Eur.

Lexique Francais-Anglais et Anglais-Francais des Termes d'usage Courant En Hydraulique et Pneumatique. P. Nichil. French & Eur.

Lexique Francais-Anglais: Termes d'usage Courant en Hydraulique & Pneumatique. Ste. Publications Mecaniques.

Lexique Francais-Anglais: Termes d'usage Courant en Machines-Outlis & Machines Similaires. Ste. Publications Mecaniques.

Lexique Francais-Arabe de la Protection Civile & du Secourisme. France Selection.

Lexique Francais-Corse. Xavier Moreschi. Corses.

Lexique Francais De la Reparation Juridique Du Dommage Corporel. Maurice A. Touati. French & Eur.

Lexique Francais de la Reparation Juridique du Dommage Corporel. Maurice A. Touati. Maloine.

Lexique Francais Des Abreviations et Formules Medico-Chirurgicales Courantes. Maurice A. Touati. French & Eur.

Lexique Francais des Abreviations: Formules Medico-Chirugicales Courantes. Maurice A. Touati. Maloine.

Lexique Francais-Duala: Dictionnaire Duala-Francais. Paul Helmlinger. S. E. L. A. F.

Lexique Francais-Grec. L. Feuillet. Belin.

Lexique Francais: La Reparation Juridique du Dommage Corporel. Maurice A. Touati. Maloine.

Lexique Francais-Latin. Edouard Sommer. Hachette-Jeunesse.

Lexique Francais-Latin. Jacques Trenel. Belin.

Lexique Francais Moderne - Ancien Francais. Ralph De Gorog. U of Ga Pr.

Lexique Francais-Occitan. Roger Barthe. Amis Langue.

Lexique Francais-Occitan. Roger Barthe. R. Barthe.

Lexique General. (UN). Unipub.

Lexique Guide D'acoustique Architecturale. Jean Pujolle. Eyrolles.

Lexique Histoire du Moyen-Age. R. Fedou. French & Eur.

Lexique historique de la France d'Ancien regime. Guy Cabourdin & Georges Viard. A Colin.

Lexique Historique de la Grande-Bretagne XVIe. & XXe. Siecle. Roland Marx. Colin.

Lexique Historique de l'Espagne XVIe. & XXe. Siecle. Colin.

Lexique Historique de l'Europa Danublenne, XVIe.-XXe. Siecle. Jean Berenger. Colin.

Lexique Historique de l'Italie XVIe.-XXe. Siecle. Pierre Racine. Colin.

Lexique Index du Kitab de Sibawayhl. Gerard Troupeau. Klincksieck.

Lexique Informatique. Maurice Balay. French & Eur.

Lexique Informatique. Maurice Balay. Bordas-Dunod.

Lexique International De Petrographie Des Charbons. French & Eur.

Lexique International de Petrographie des Charbons. CNRS.

Lexique International de Petrographie des Charbons. CNRS.

Lexique International De Petrographie Des Charbon: Supplement. French & Eur.

Lexique International Des Termes Techniques De Theatre, en 8 Langues. Kenneth Rhae & Richard Southern. French & Eur.

Lexique International des Termes Techniques de Theatre en 8 Langues. Kenneth Rhae & Richard Southern. Meddens.

Lexique Latin-Francais. Edouard Sommer. Hachette.

Lexique Latin Medieval-Francais-Anglais. J. F. Niermeyer. Brill.

Un Lexique Macedonien du XV Siecle. Ciro Giannelli. Inst Etudes Slaves.

Lexique Mathematique. Jean Grignon. F. I. C.

Lexique Mathematique, Symboles, Vocabulaire, Tables. Jean Grignon. Centre Psych.

Lexique Methodique Illustre du Machinisme Agricole, 1. Centre Nat. & Machin Agricole.

Lexique Occitan-Francais. Roger Barthe. Amis Langue.

Lexique Occitan-Francais. Roger Barthe. Lemouzi.

Lexique Officiel des Lampes Radio. Louis Gaudillat. Radio.

Lexique Officiel des lampes Radios. Louis Gaudilat. French & Eur.

Lexique Patois-Francais du Parler de Vaux-Bugey, 1919-1940. Klincksieck.

Lexique Pedologique Trilingue. George Plaisance. French & Eur.

Lexique Pedologique Trilingue. Georges Plaisance. CDU.

Lexique Photo-Cinema. C. I. L. F.

Lexique Picard des Parlers Ouest-Amienois. Rene Debrie. Univers Picardie.

Lexique Picard du Berger. Rene Debrie. Eklitra.

Lexique Poular-Francais: Le Poular Dialecte Peul du Fouta Senegalais. Henri Gaden. Gregg.

Lexique Pratique Commercial. Centre International Du Droit Des Affaires (CIDA). Marlin.

Lexique Pratique Francais-Arabe. Jacques Jomier & Institut Francais D'Archeologie Orientale. Francais, Inst. Archeo. Orient.

Lexique Psychologique. Vie et Action.

Lexique Quadrilingue de la Preparation des Minerals: Allemand-Anglais-Francais-Russe. Congres International de la Preparation des Minerais. Ste. Industrie Minerale.

Lexique Quadrilingue Des Affaires. Ivan de Renty. French & Eur.

Lexique Quadrilingue des Affaires: Anglais-Francais-Allemand-Espagnol. Ivan De Renty. Hachette.

Lexique Quadrilingue de la Preparation des Minerais. Ed. by Congres International de la Preparation des Minerais. French & Eur.

Lexique Queze-Amharique. Makonnen Argaw. Publ. Orientalistes France.

Lexique Soncy Francais. Jean M. Ducroz & Marie C. Charles. Harmattan.

Lexique Stratigraphique International. French & Eur.

Lexique Technique des Produits Chimiques. Officielles, Ed. Vente Publ.

Lexique Technique des Produits Chimiques. Jean-Claude Donadini & G. Donadini. Rous.

Lexique Thematique des Des Descripteurs & Identificateurs. Centre de Documentatio de. Centre Documentation.

Lexique Thematique des Descripteurs et Identificateurs. Centre De Documentation De L'Armement. French & Eur.

Lexique Trilingue des Termes d'usage Courant: Electrotechnique, Electronique, Acoustique, Optique, Controle. Ste. Publications Mecaniques.

Lexique Trilingue des Termes D'Usage Courant En Electrotechnique, Electronique, Acoustique, Optique et Controle Par Ultrasons. French & Eur.

Lexique Trilinque des Termes de l'Eau. French & Eur.

Lexique Trilingue des Termes d'Usage Courant En Machines Outils, les Perceuses. French & Eur.

Lexique Trillingue des Termes d'usage Courant en Machines. Ste. Publications.

Lexique Trillingue des Termes d'usage Courant en Machines: Les Perceuses. Ste. Publications Mecaniques.

Lexique Tumak-Francais Tchad. Jean P. Caprile. Reimer.

Lexique Usuel d'informatique. Serge Valensi. S. C. M.

Lexiques de Termes de Pathologie Dentaire. Jean Courtois. Prelat.

Lexiques Des Boissons Gazeuses. J. Maurais & S. Giroux. French & Eur.

Lexiques Picards du Cidrier & du Meunier. Rene Debrie. Eklitra.

Lexis: Dictionnaire De la Langue Francaise. Ed. by Jean Dubois. French & Eur.

Lexis-Dictionnaire de la langue francaise. Ed. by Jean Dubois. Larousse.

Lexis-Dictionnaire de la Langue Francaise. Ed. by Jean Dubois. Larousse.

Lexis: Dictionnaire de la Langue Frances. Ed. by Jean Dubois. Larousse.

Lilliput Dictionary. Langenscheidt.

Lilliput Dictionary. Langenscheidt.

L'Inconscient. Jacques Mousseau & Pierre F. Moreau. Retz.

Logos: Grand Dictionnaire de la Langue Francaise. Jean Girodet. Bordas.

Logos-Grand Dictionnaire de la Langue Francaise. Ed. by Jean Girodet. Harrap.

Machine Tools Dictionary: English-French-German-Arabic. A. M. Abd-El-Wahed. French & Eur.

Magyar-Francia Szotar. Sandor Eckhardt. Akademiai Kiado.

Magyar-Francia Szotar. Sandor Eckhardt. Akademiai Kiado.

Maly Slownik Francusko-Polski. Ludwik Szwykowski et al. Wiedza Powszechna.

Manual del Automovil en 5 Idiomas: Diccionario Idiomatico del Automovil. Equipo Reactor de Ceac. French & Eur.

Manual of the Terminology of Public International Law & International Organizations. I. Paenson. Kluwer Academic.

Manuel Alphabetique De Psychiatrie Clinique et Therapeutique. Ed. by Antoine Porot. French & Eur.

Mathematics Dictionary. Glenn James. Van Nos Reinhold.

Mathematik Englisch-Deutsch-Franzoesisch-Russisch. Ralf Sube & Gunther Eisenreich. VEB Technik.

Medical Dictionary. B. Zoltnicki. (Pub. by Schattauer). French & Eur.

Medizinisches Woerterbuch. E. Veillon & A. Nobel. (Pub. by H. Huber). French & Eur.

Medizinisches Woerterbuch. E. Veillon & A. Nobel. Huber.

Medizintechnik. Albert Von Roald & Harry Hahnewald. VEB Verlag Technik.

Medizintechnik-Englisch-Deutsch-Franzoesisch-Russisch-Spanisch-Polnisch-Ungarisch-Slowakisch. Roald Albert & Harry Hahnewald. VEB Technik.

Mein Allerschoenstes Woerterbuch. Richard Scarry. Adler Bks.

Melanges: Tables generales (1954-1977) Ed. by Institut Dominicain d'Etudes Orientales du Caire. Intl Bk Ctr.

Menu French. David Atkinson. Oxford Poly Pr.

Mes Dix Mille Mots. Marcel Dider. Harrap.

Mes dix millet mots. Marcel Didier. Barron.

Metal Forming Dictionary. A. M. Abd-El-Wahed. French & Eur.

Le Micro-Robert: Dictionnaire Du Francais Primordial. Paul Robert. French & Eur.

Mon Dictionnaire Francais-Anglais. M. Fonteneau & S. Theureau. (Dist. by Continental Bk Co). Larousse.

Mon Grand Dictionnaire Francais-Anglais. French & Eur.

Mon Premier Dictionnaire en 2000 mots & 2000 Images. Thoburn et al. (Dist. by Continental Bk Co). Casterman.

Mon Premier Larousse francais-anglais, anglais-francais en couleurs. Larousse And Co. Larousse.

Le Mot et L'idee, Francais-Portugais, Portugais-Francais. J. Fournier & G. Laborde. French & Eur.

Le Mot Juste. Longman.

Mots croises. Larousse.

Multilengua Diccionario de Cartas Comerciales en Cuatro Idiomas. French & Eur.

Multilingual Computer Dictionary. Ed. by Alan Isaacs. Facts on File.

The Multilingual Computer Dictionary. Alan Isaacs. Facts on File.

Multilingual Glossary of Automatic Control Technology: English-French-German-Russian-Italian-Spanish-Japanese. D. T. Broadbent & M. Masubuchi. Pergamon.

Multilingual Law Dictionary: English, French, Spanish, German. Lawrence D. Egbert. Oceana.

Multilingual Lexicon of Linguistics & Philology: English, Russian, German, French. Rose Nash. U of Miami Pr.

Multilingual Technical Dictionary on Irrigation & Drainage. US Comm Irrigation.

Multilingual Vocabulary of Educational Radio & Television Terms. Intl Pubns Serv.

Music Translation Dictionary: An English, Czech, Danish, Dutch, French, German, Hungarian, Italian, Polish, Portuguese, Russian, Spanish, Swedish Vocabulary of Music. Compiled by Carolyn D. Grigg. Greenwood.

Musical Thesaurus: A Dictionary of Musical Language. Robert Leach. J Hannon.

My Illustrated Dictionary: Arabic & Fr. Libr du Liban. Intl Bk Ctr.

Mykologisches Worterbuch. K. Berger. French & Eur.

Mykologisches Worterbuch. Karl Von Berger. Fischer Verlag.

Mystical Vocabulary of Venerable Mere Marie De L'Incarnation & Its Problems. Mother Aloysius G. L'Heureux. AMS Pr.

New Century Vest Pocket French Dictionary. Ed. by Richard Switzer & Herbert S. Gochberg. New Century.

The New College French & English Dictionary. Roger J. Steiner. AMSCO Sch.

New Diesterweg-Larousse: Dictionnaire du Francais Langue Etrangere. Frwd. by F. J. Hausmann. Diesterweg.

The New English-French Dictionary of Slang & Colloquialisms. Georgette A. Marks. Dutton.

New International Dictionary of Refrigeration. International Institute of Refrigeration. (IIR). Unipub.

Newu Diesterweg-Larousse: Dictionnaire du Francais Langue Etrangere. Frwd. by F. J. Hausmann. Diesterweg.

Niederlassungsrecht. Institut International de Terminologie Juridique & Administrative. Langen AG.

Nomenclature des Appelations d'emploi dans L' Industrie Papetiere Quebecoise: Anglais-Francais. N. Cote & J. Gaumond. French & Eur.

Norsk-Fransk Ordbok. M. Lesoil. French & Eur.

Norwegian-French Dictionary. M. Lesoil. Kunnskapsforlaget.

Norwegian-French Dictionary of Commerce. Daae Gabrielsen. Kunnskapsforlaget.

Nouveau Dictionnaire de Droit et de Sciences Economiques. Raymond Barraine. French & Eur.

Le Nouveau Dictionnaire de la Peche. Jean Schreiner et al. French & Eur.

Nouveau Dictionnaire de la Peinture Moderne. French & Eur.

Nouveau Dictionnaire de la Sculpture Moderne. French & Eur.

Nouveau Dictionnaire des Synonymes. Emile Genouvrier et al. French & Eur.

Nouveau Dictionnaire Du Batiment. Marcel Lefebvre. French & Eur.

Nouveau Dictionnaire du Batiment: Anglais-Francais Francais-Anglais. M. Lefebvre. Maison Dictionnaire.

Nouveau Dictionnaire du Francais Contemporain Illustre. (Dist. by Continental Bk Co). Larousse.

Nouveau Dictionnaire Etymologique. Albert Dauzat. French & Eur.

Nouveau Dictionnaire etymologique. A. Dauzat et al. Larousse.

Nouveau Dictionnaire: Francais-Chinois. French & Eur.

Nouveau Dictionnaire Francais-Chinois. French & Eur.

Nouveau Dictionnaire Francais-Hebreu. Larousse.

Le Nouveau Dictionnaire Francais-Neerlandais, Nederlands-Francais. Ludovic Grootaers. French & Eur.

Nouveau Dictionnaire Hebreu-Francais. Marc M. Cohn. French & Eur.

Nouveau Dictionnaire hebreu-francais. Larousse.

Nouveau Dictionnaire International du Froid. French & Eur.

Nouveau Glossaire Nautique. Augustin Jal. Mouton.

Nouveau Glossaire Nautique, Lettre C: Revision De L'edition Publiee En 1848. Augustin Jal. Mouton.

Nouveau Larousse Eementaire. Larousse & Co. Larousse.

Nouveau Larousse Elementaire. (Dist. by Continental Bk Co) Larousse.

Nouveau Larousse Francais-Anglais, English-French. Larousse.

Nouveau Larousse "Mars". J. Mergault. (Dist. by Continental Bk Co). Larousse.

Nouveau Lexique d'Economie: Economie, Droit, Gestion, Finance. Jacques Vuitton & Philippe Vuitton. Doc Univers.

Nouveau Petit Larousse en couleurs. Larousse And Co. Larousse.

Nouveau vocabulaire des etudes philosophiques. Sylvain Aurox & Yvonne Weil. Hachette-Jeunesse.

Novye Parallel'nye Slovari Iazykov Russkago, Frantsuzskago, Nemetskago i Angliiskago. Filipp Reiff. Incl. Four Continent.

Nuevo Glosario, Diccionario Poliglota de la Arquitectura. Buenaventura Bassegoda Muste. French & Eur.

Oekonomisches Woerterbuch Aussenwirtschaft (Dictionary of External Exonomic Relations & Trade) Ed. by Siegfried Kohls. Intl Pubns Serv.

Oekonomisches Woerterbuch Aussenwirtschaft. S. Kohls. (Pub. by Ruceken Vlg). French & Eur.

Oekonomisches Woerterbuch Aussenwirtschaft. Wissenschaftliche.

Onteszet. Arpad Voros. Akademiai Kiado.

Outline of French Grammar with Vocabularies. Henry B. Richardson. Irvington.

The Oxford-Duden Pictorial French-English Dictionary. Oxford U Pr.

Oxford Picture Dictionary of American English. Oxford U Pr.

Partially Naturalised French Words in Modern English. Francis D. Dow. Dow.

Partially Naturalised French Words in Modern English. Francis D. Dow. Dow.

Parusny i sport. L. A. Chesnokov et al. Russkii Iazyk.

Petit Dictionnaire-Bambara-Francais Francais-Bambara. Charles Bailleul. (Pub. by Avebury England). Humanities.

Petit Dictionnaire Bilingue "Adonis". (Dist. by Continental Bk Co). Larousse.

Petit Dictionnaire bilingue Larousse, francais-anglais et English-French. L. Chauffurin. Larousse.

Petit Dictionnaire bilingue Larousse, francais-espagnol, espanol-frances. Larousse And Co. Larousse.

Petit Dictionnaire de Droit Quebecois & Canadien. Dominique Page. Fides.

Petit Dictionnaire du Francais gue l'on n'Apprend pas a l'Ecole. Andre Kahlmann. Esselte Studium.

Petit Dictionnaire du Francais que l'on n'Apprend Pas a l'Ecole. Andre Kahlmann. Esselte Studium.

Petit Dictionnaire Francais. (Dist. by Continental Bk Co). Larousse.

Un Petit Dictionnaire Francais-Chinois. French & Eur.

Petit Dictionnaire Francais-Grec Moderne et Grec Moderne-Francais. Andre Mirambel. French & Eur.

Petit Dictionnaire francais Larousse. Larousse And Co. Larousse.

Petit Dictionnaire Francais: Nouvelle Edition. (Dist. by Continental Bk Co). Larousse.

Petit Dictionnaire Medical. L. Manuila et al. French & Eur.

Petit Dictionnaire Moderne: Nouvelle Edition. (Dist. by Continental Bk Co). Larousse.

Petit Dictionnaire Philosophique. M. Rosenthal & P. Ioudine. French & Eur.

Petit Glossaire du Language Erotique aux XVIIe & XVIIIe Siecles. Marie F. Le Pennec. Borderie.

Petit Larousse de la Medecine. Andre Domart. Larousse.

Petit Larousse en Couleur 1980. M. Claude Dubois. (Dist. by Continental Bk Co). Larousse.

Petit Larousse 1980. M. Claude Dubois. (Dist. by Continental Bk Co). Larousse.

Petit Lexique de la Manutentio n. Anglais-Francais. F. Bacon et al. Ed. by P. Chartrand. French & Eur.

Petit Lexique des Termes Judiciares: A l'Usage des Journalistes. Centre de Formation et de Perfectionnement des Journalistes. Centre Formation.

Petit Lexique du Soudage. Anglais-Francais. A. Fortin et al. Ed. by P. Chartrand. French & Eur.

Petit Lexique Somali-Francais. Christophe Philbert. Klincksieck.

Petit Vocabulire Politique. Albert Samuel. Chronique Sociale.

Petits Dictionnaires Bilingues Larousse Francais-Anglais. (Dist. by Continental Bk Co). Larousse.

Philatelic Vocabulary in Five Languages. Philatelic Foundation. Philatelic Found.

Phonetic French Dictionary: Contrasting French-English Sounds. Jeanne V. Pleasants. Playette Corp.

La Photo de A & Z. Antoine Desilets. Edns Homme.

Phrase Dictionaries for the American Tourist. Frederick Stark. Incl. Delair.

Physics Dictionary. Ed. by R. Sube & G. Eisenvarich. Adler.

Physics Terminology. A. Jesse. French & Eur.

Physik-Fachsprache Englisch-Franzosisch-Deutsch. A. Jesse. Bauverlag.

Pichon Diccionari Frances-Occitan. Jacme Taupiac. Inst Occit Tlse.

Pieciojezyczny Slownik Gleboznawczy. Adamczyk Boleslaw. Panstwowe Zaklad W.

Pipeline Dictionary. H. Bucksch & A. P. Altmeyer. (Pub. by Bauverlag). French & Eur.

Pipeline Dictionary. H. Bucksch & A. P. Altmeyer. Intl Pubns Serv.

Pipeline Dictionary. H. Bucksch & A. P. Altmeyer. Bauverlag.

Plastic Technology Dictionary. H. Y. El-Desouti. French & Eur.

Plasttechnik-Englisch-Deutsch-Franzoesisch-Russisch. Gisbert Kaliske. VEB Technik.

Pluri Dictionnaire. C. Dubois. Larousse.

Pocket Dictionary of Horseman's Terms in English, German, French & Spanish. Hanns Muller. Transatlantic.

Pocket-Shorter Dictionary. Langenscheidt.

Podreczny Slownik Polsko-Francuski. Kazimierz Kupisz et al. Wiedza Powszechna.

Polygrafie-Englisch-Deutsch-Franzoesisch-Russisch-Spanisch-Polnisch-Ungarisch-Solwakisch. Wolfgang Muller. VEB Technik.

Polygraph Dictionary for the Graphic Industries in Six Languages. Ed. by K. Collet. Intl Pubns Serv.

Polytechnisches Woerterbuch. Alibert Schlegelmilch. (Pub. by Veb Verlag Technik). French & Eur.

Polytechnisches Woerterbuch. Alibert Schlegelmilch. (Pub. by Veb Verlag Technik). French & Eur.

Polytechnisches Woerterbuch. Aribert Schlegelmilch. VEB Verlag Technik.

Polytechnisches Woerterbuch Deutsch-Franzoesisch. Veb Technik.

Polytechnisches Woerterbuch Franzoesisch-Deutsch. VEB Technik.

Polytechnisches Worterbuch. Aribert Schlegelmilch. Hueber.

Pons-Grosswoerterbuch. Erich Weiss. Ed. by Heinrich Mattutat & Christian Nugue. Klett.

Practical Dictionary for Press & Advertising. Intl Pubns Serv.

Practical French-English, English-French Dictionary. Rosalind Williams. Hippocrene Bks.

La Pratique d'un Dictionnaire. B. Planque & N. Chabaud. (Dist. by Continental Bk Co). Larousse.

Precis De Terminologie Medicale. J. Chevallier. French & Eur.

Premier Dictionnaire Nathan. Marchand. (Dist. by Continental Bk Co). Lib. Fernand Nathan.

Press, Radio & Television. Denise Escarpit. Elp.

Printer's Terms Dictionary. R. Hostettler. Heinman.

Projet de Lexique Minier Russe-Francais. Ed. by N. N. Ersov & A. N. Komarov. French & Eur.

Proverbes Francais: In French with Equivalents in English, German, Dutch, Italian, Spanish, Latin. G. Ilg. Elsevier.

Quadrilingual Business Dictionary. (Pub. by European Schoolbks England). State Mutual Bk.

Qui a dit Quoi? Dictionanaire des Mots & des Phrases qui Ont Une Historire. Bernadette De Castelbajac. Tallandier.

Radio & Television Dictionary. Abd-El-Wahed. French & Eur.

The Random House Basic Dictionary French. Ed. by Francesca L. Langbaum. Ballantine.

Ranskalais-Suomalainen-Sanakirja. Pentti Pesonen. Otava.

Ranskalais-Suomalainen Tekniikan ja Kaupan Sanakirja. Jyrki K. Talvitie. Tietoteos.

Recherches sur la Prefixation en Francais Contemporain. Jean Peytard. Klincksieck.

Rechtskundig Woerdenboek: Dictionnaire Juridique. J. Brassine. Bruylant.

Rechtsworterbuch Fur Die Gewerbliche Wirtschaft. Ursula Becker. (Pub. by Fritz Knapp Verlag). French & Eur.

Recueil de Terminologie Multilinque du Soudage et des Techniques Connexes, French & Eur.

Recueil de Terminologie Multilinque du Soudage et des Techniques Connexes, Soudage Electrique a l'Arc. French & Eur.

Recueil Terminologique Multilingue de Soudage et des Techniques Connexes: Soudage Electrique a l'Arc. French & Eur.

Recueil Terminologique Multilinque du Soudage et des Techniques Connexes. French & Eur.

Recueil Terminologique Multilinque de Soudage et des Techniques Connexes: Projection a Chaud. French & Eur.

Recueil Terminologique Multilinque du Soudage et des Techniques Connexes: Coupage Thermique. French & Eur.

Recueil Terminologique Multilinque du Soudage et des Techniques Connexes: Soudage Electrique Par Resistance. French & Eur.

Refrigeration & Conditioning Dictionary. Abd-El-Wahed. French & Eur.

Les Ressorts: Francais-Allemand-Anglais-Espagnol. S.N.F.R. Maison Dictionnaire.

The Robert Dictionaries. Ed. by Paul Robert. Incl. Scribner.

Russkikh Glagolov. A. S. Vasil'Eva. Four Continent.

Russko-Anglo-Nemetsko-Frantsuzskii Slovar Terminov Po Avtomaticheskomu Upravleniiu. Ed. by A. V. Khramov. (Pub. by An Arm SSR). Four Continent.

Russko-Frantsuzskii Aviatsionno-Tekhnicheskii Slovar. P. E. Turchin. (Pub. by Sov. Entsiklopedia). Four Continent.

Russko-Frantsuzskii Shkol'No-Pedagogicheskii Slovar. N. V. Goliakova et al. (Pub. by Sov. Entsiklopediia). Four Continent.

Russko-Frantsuzskii Slovar. V. V. Pototskaia et al. (Pub. by Sov. Entsiklopediia). Four Continent.

Russko-Frantsuzskii Stroitelnyi Slovar. V. V. Voronin et al. (Pub. by Russkii Iazyk). Four Continent.

Safety at Work & Pollution Control. Nicole Aymard Lapalu. Elp.

Sahkotieteellinen Sanasto. Suomen Standardisoimislitto. Suomen Standard.

La Sante Grace a la Dietetique. Gustave Mathieu. Doc Scient.

Satzlexikon der Handelskorrespondenz. Zavada & Hartgenbush. Brandstetter.

Selective English Old-French Glossary As a Basis for Studies in Old French Onomatology & Synonymics. Joseph P. Murray. AMS Pr.

Semiiazychnyi Slovar Po Elektrosviazi. (Pub. by Sov. Entsiklopediia). Four Continent.

Semiiazychnyi Slovar Po Mekhanike Gruntov & Fundamentostroeniiu. M. E. Scneider. (Pub. by Gosizdat Fizmat. Lit.). Four Continent.

Seminotique: Dictionnaire Raisonne de la Theorie du Language. Algirdas J. Greimas & Joseph Courtes. Hachette-Jeunesse.

Septemlingual Dictionary of the Names of European Animal. Ed. by L. Gozmany et al. (Pub. by Kiado Hungary). Heyden.

Seven Language Dictionary. Ed. by David Shumaker. Crown.

Seven Languages Dictionary. Imported Bks.

A Short Old French Dictionary for Students. Ed. by Kenneth Urwin. (Pub. by Basil Blackwell). Biblio Dist.

Slovar Naibolee Upotrebitel'Nykh Slov Anglii-Skogo, Nemetskogo & Frantsuzskogo Iazykov. Ed. by I. V. Rakhmanov. (Pub. by Izd. Inostr. & Natsional'Nal'Nykh Slovarei). Four Continent.

Slownik Minimum Francusko-Polski. Leon Bielas. Wiedza Powszechna.

Standard French Dictionary. Langenscheidt.

Strategic Terminology. Urs Schwarz & Laszlo Hadik. French & Eur.

Supplement au Dictionnaire de la Noblesse Francaise. Etienne de Sereville & Fernand de Saint-Simon. French & Eur.

Supplement Aux Dictionnaire Arabe (Arabic-French) R. Dozy. Intl Bk Ctr.

Supplement aux dictionnaires Arabes. R. Dozy. Intl Bk Ctr.

Surface Treatment of Aluminum: Glossary of Technical Terms. Aluminum Verlag.

Svensk-Fransk Affaersordlista. Edy Maupoix. Esselte Studium.

Svensk-Fransk & Fransk-Svensk Ordbok. Ruben Noid. Esselte Studium.

Svensk-Fransk Ordbok. Thekla Hammar. Esselte Studium.

Svensk-Fransk Ordbok. Esselte Studium.

Systematic Glossary of the Terminology of Statistical Methods: English, French, Spanish, Russian. Isaac Paenson. Pergamon.

Systems Analysis & Operations Research Dictionary. G Sezepesi & B. Szekely. (Pub. by Collets). State Mutual Bk.

Technical Automotive Dictionary: Russian-English-German-French-Bulgarian. G. Sikora. French & Eur.

Technical Dictionary: Archtiecture & Building. Tawfik Abd-El-Gawad. (Pub. by Collets). State Mutual Bk.

Technical Dictionary of Automatization & Programming: English, French, German, Russian,-Slovene. Ed. by E. Burger. French & Eur.

Technical Dictionary of Data Processing, Computers & Office Machines, English, German, French, Russian. E. Burger. Pergamon.

Technical Dictionary of Petrochemistry. W. Leipnitz. (Pub. by Vlg. Technik). French & Eur.

Technical Dictionary of Textile Chemistry - Fachwoerterbuch Chemiefasern: German-English-French, English-German-French, French-German-English. Werner Winkler. Intl Pubns Serv.

Technical Dictionary: Refrigeration & Air Conditioning. (Pub. by Collets). State Mutual Bk.

Technical Dictionary: The Textile Industry. (Pub. by Collets). State Mutual Bk.

Technical-Economical Dictionary for Business Purposes. B. Bajic et al. French & Eur.

Technical Petroleum Dictionary of Well-Logging, Drilling & Production Terms. Ed. by Sonia Ketchian. Intl Pubns Serv.

Technische Akustik. Walter Reichardt. VEB Verlag Technik.

Technisches Taschenwoerterbuch. A. Grunwald-Beyer. (Pub. by Georg Siemens Verlagsbuchhandlung). French & Eur.

Technological Dictionary. Michel Feutry. Maison Dictionnaire.

Technological Dictionary in Three Languages. Hoyer-Kreuter. Ed. by Alfred Schlomann. Incl. Ungar.

Technologisches Woerterbuch Franzoisisch. Kurt Stellhorn. (Pub. by Verlag W. Girardet). French & Eur.

Technologisches Woerterbuch Franzoisisch. Kurt Stellhorn. Girardet.

Ten Bosch's Quadralingual Engineering Dictionary. Imported Bks.

Terminologia turistico alberghiera: L'albergatore poliglotta. Elisabetta Neiger. Ed Calderini.

Terminologie de la physique: Anglais-Allemand-Francais. A. Jesse. Maison Dictionnaire.

Terminologie et Lexicographie Medicales. French & Eur.

Terminologie Fondamentale En Odonto-Stomatologie et Lexique: Francais-Anglais, Anglais-Francais. French & Eur.

Terminologie Fondamentale en Odonto-Stomatologie. Leon Roucoules. Maloine.

Terminology of Documentation: A Selection of 1200 Basic Terms Published in English, French, German, Spanish & Russian. (UNESCO). Unipub.

Terminology of Environmental Hygiene. European Parliament - Translation Division. Intl Pubns Serv.

Terminology of Malaria & of Malaria Eradication: Report of a Drafting Committee. World Health.

Textile Dictionary. Elsevier.

Textile Dictionary. G. Velco. (Pub. by Collets). State Mutual Bk.

Textile Industry Dictionary. Ed. by A. M. Sabrie & R. S. Scharaf et al. French & Eur.

Le Thesaurus. Marie-Therese Laureilhe. Ecole Biblio.

Thesaurus Ceramique. Institut de Ceramique Francaise. Francaise, Institut Ceramique.

Thesaurus de l'education de l'Unesco: Francais-Anglais. Unesco.

Thesaurus des Symboles Agrobioclimatiques, Geographiques & Techniques. J. L. Petit et al. Centre Informatique Develop.

Thesaurus des Symboles Agrobioclimatiques, Geographiques & Techniques, 3. J. M. Henry & A. B. Ergo. Centre Informatique Develop.

Thesaurus des Symboles Agrobioclimatiques, Geographiques & Techniques, 4. A. B. Ergo et al. Centre Informatique Develop.

Thesaurus des Termes Geographiques. Technip.

Thesaurus di Scienze della Terra. Patron.

Thesaurus Doctrine Catholicae: Documentis Magisteri Ecceslasticae, Ordine Methodico. Beauchesne.

Thesaurus du Management & de L'economie. Bureau Marcel.

Thesaurus du Management & de l'economie. Marcel Van Dijk & Georges Sandeau. M. Van Dijk.

Thesaurus Economie de l'energie. Institut Francais du Petrole. Technip.

Thesaurus Genie Chimique. Bureau de l'Information Scientifique & Technique. Doc Scient.

Thesaurus Hydrologie. Ed. by Joelle Cicchini. Serv Doc Cart.

Thesaurus I. R. S. I. D. Francais, (Comptor) Siderurg.

Thesaurus Normalisation, 2: Index Bilingue Francais-Anglais par Mots Vedettes. A. F. N. O. R.

Thesaurus Normalisation, 3: Table de Correspondance Anglais-Francais. A. F. N. O. R.

Thesaurus Petrole. Technip.

Thesaurus Pollution Atmospherique. I. F. C. E.

Thesaurus pour le Traitement de l'information en Sociologie. Jean Viet. Mouton de Gruyter.

Le Thesaurus: Son Role, sa Structure, son Elaboration. Marie T. Laureilhe. Assoc Biblio.

Thesaurus Verrier. Inst Verre.

Thesaurus, 3: Liste Alphabetique. E. D. F.

Le Tresor de Felibridge: Dictionnaire Provencal-Francais. Frederic Mistral. French & Eur.

Tresor De la Langue Francaise: Dictionnaire De la Langue Du 19th et Du 20th Siecle (1789-1960) Ed. by Centre National De la Recherche Scientifique & Paul Imbs. Intl Pubns Serv.

Tresor de la Langue Francaise: Dictionnaire de la langue du 19e & du 20e siecle. (Dist. by Continental Bk Co) Klincksieck.

Trois Cent Cinquante Definitions Biologiques Raisonnees. Mireille Blain. Doc Univers.

Tu Dien Mien Dich Hoc. Y Hoc.

Uchebny Slovar Obschetekhnich: Leksiki. I. F. Rudakova. (Pub. by Russkii Iazyk). Four Continent.

Uchebnyi Slovar Obshcheteknich: Russko-Anglo-Frantsuzsko-Nemetskii. I. F. Rudakova et al. (Pub. by Russkii Iazyk). Four Continent.

Understanding French Cookery: A Guide to French Recipes & Cooking Terms. Francoise Bourdet. Kingsmead Pr.

Universal French Dictionary. Langenscheidt.

Vad Betyder Vaxtens Latinska Namn. Ivar Anell. Forum Bok.

Velosipeday i sport. S. N. Novozhilov et al. Russky Yazyk.

Vest Pocket French. Institute for Language Study. (BN). B&N NY.

Vest-Pocket French. New Century.

Vest Pocket French Dictionary. New Century.

Vocabolario commerciale italiano-francese e francese-italiano, Caputo Cataldo. A. Jannini Pasquale. Monnier.

Vocabolario del francese moderno. Enea Balmas. Ghisetti & Corvi.

Vocabolario del francese moderno. E. Balmas & R. L. Wagner. Ist Geo Agostini.

Vocabolario francese-italiano e italiano-francese. Edwin Rostan. Malipiero.

Vocabolario italiano-francese e francese-italiano. Francesco Grimod & G. Caselli. Dante Alighieri.

Vocabolario italiano-francese e francese-italiano. F. Cassone. (CEB). Capitol-Dischi.

Vocabulaire. Arthur Masson. Hachette.

Le Vocabulaire Allemand du Bachelier. Rudolf Zellweger. Payot.

Vocabulaire Allemand Progressif & livret d'exercices. Rene Michea. Didier.

Vocabulaire Alphabetique & Analogique Destine aux Ecollers Africains Francophones. Placide-Raphael Lumeka. Lang, H.

Vocabulaire Analogique de la Langue Corse. Jean Costa. C. E. R. C.

Vocabulaire & Elocution les Debutants. Solange Buissonnier. Hachette.

Vocabulaire & Exercices Francais. Adolphe Lelu & Louis Kluber. Hatier.

Vocabulaire & Exercices Francais. Adolphe Lelu & Louis Kluber. Hatier.

Vocabulaire & Exercices Francais. Adolphe Lelu & Louis Kluber. Hatier.

Vocabulaire & Exercises Francais. Adolphe Lelu & Louis Kluber. Hatier.

Vocabulaire & Exercices Francais. Adolphe Lelu & Louis Kluber. Hatier.

Le Vocabulaire & la Societe Sous Louis Phillippe. Georges Matore & Geneve Matore. Slatkine.

Vocabulaire & Language. Andree Girolami-Boulinier. Delachaux.

Vocabulaire & Redaction. Ligel.

Vocabulaire & Redaction. Ligel.

Vocabulaire & Style. Roger Schmitt & Pierre Filbert. Nathan.

Le Vocabulaire Anglais. Paul Bacquet. PUF.

Le Vocabulaire Anglais au Baccalaureat. Christian Bouscaren. Ophrys.

Vocabulaire Anglais-Francais de Terminologie, Economique & Juridique. Peter Nichols & Pierre Vibes. L. G. D. J.

Vocabulaire Architecturale. Jules Auger. Montreal P. U.

Vocabulaire Barometre Dans le Langage Economique. J. Delattre & G. DeVernisy. French & Eur.

Le Vocabulaire Barometre dans le Langage Economique. J. Delattre & G. Vernisy. Georg.

Vocabulaire Bilingue des Assurances sur la Vie. Jean-Paul De Grandpre. Quebec Off.

Vocabulaire bilinque du theatre: Anglais-Francais Francais Anglais. R. Dubuc. Maison Dictionnaire.

Vocabulaire Commercial Francais-Allemand. Erich Weis & Eva Haberfellner. Klett.

Vocabulaire Critique des relations culturelles internationales. A. Salon. Maison Dictionnaire.

Vocabulaire d'anglais Commercial. Andre Mansat. Didier.

Vocabulaire, Dans: Larousse pour Tous. Larousse FR.

Vocabulaire d'Arabe Moderne: Economie-Politique-Actualite. J. Schmidt. Maison Dictionnaire.

Vocabulaire d'Arabe moderne: Economie-Politique-Actualite. J. Schmidt. Maison Dictionnaire.

Vocabulaire d'Astronomie. French & Eur.

Vocabulaire d'astronomie: Francais-Anglais-Allemand. C. I. L. F.

Vocabulaire de Base Allemand-Francais. Charles Chatelanat & Theodor Henzi. Hachette.

Vocabulaire de Fonderie Anglais-Francais. Centre Technique des Industries de la Fonderie. Ed Tech Ind.

Vocabulaire de Fonderie Francais-Allemand. Centre Technique des Industries de la Fonderie. Ed Tech Ind.

Vocabulaire de gestion. R. Dubac. Maison Dictionnaire.

Vocabulaire de Gestion. Robert Dubuc. Radio-Canada.

Le Vocabulaire de Kant, 1. Roger Verneaux. Aubier-Montaigne.

Vocabulaire de la Chasse & de la Veneric. Conseil International de la Langue Francaise. Hachette.

Vocabulaire de la Fonderie: Anglais-Francais. Techniques Fonderie.

Vocabulaire de la Fonderie: Francais-Anglais. Techniques Fonderie.

Vocabulaire de la geomorphologie. C.I.L.F. Maison Dictionniare.

Vocabulaire de la Langue Espagnole Classique: XVIe & XVIIe Siecles. Bernard Sese. Doc Univers.

Vocabulaire de la Princesse de Cleves. Jean De Bazin. Nizet.

Vocabulaire de la Psychanalyse. Jean-Baptiste Pontalis. Ed. by Jean Laplanche. French & Eur.

Vocabulaire de la Psychanalyse. Jean Laplanche. PUF.

Vocabulaire De la Psychologie. Henri Pieron. French & Eur.

Vocabulaire de la psychologie. Henri Pieron. Pr Univ Fr.

Vocabulaire de la Psychologie. Henri Pieron. PUF.

Vocabulaire De la Publicite. Ed. by Conseil International De la Langue Francaise. French & Eur.

Vocabulaire de la Publicite. Conseil International de la Langue Francaise. Hachette.

Vocabulaire de la Publicite. Pierre Herbin. Bourdine.

Vocabulaire de la Radio & de la Television. French & Eur.

Vocabulaire de la Radio & de la Television. France-Pauline Cormier. Quebec Off.

Vocabulaire de la Radiodiffusion. Conseil International de la Langue Francaise. Hachette.

Vocabulaire de la radiographie. C.I.L.F. Maison Dictionnaire.

Vocabulaire de la topographie. C.I.L.F. Maison Dictionnaire.

Vocabulaire de la Vente Promotionelle: Anglais-Francais. M. Villiers et al. French & Eur.

Vocabulaire de la Vie Amoureuse. Julien Teppe. Pavillon.

Vocabulaire de Lais de Marie de France. MacClelland. Ottawa U.

Vocabulaire de l'analyse Psychologique dans l'oeuvre de Thucydide. Pierre Huart. Klincksieck.

Le Vocabulaire De L'astronautique. L. Guilbert. French & Eur.

Le Vocabulaire de L'astronautique: Enquete Linguistique a travers la Presse d'information a L'occasion De Cinq Exploits de Cosmonautes. Guilbert. French & Eur.

Vocabulaire De L'economie. Gilbert Mathieu. French & Eur.

Vocabulaire de L'economie. Edit Quebec.

Vocabulaire de l'economie. Gilbert Mathieu. Delarge.

Vocabulaire De L'Education. Gaston Mialaret. French & Eur.

Vocabulaire de l'Education. Ed. by Gaston Mialaret. Pr Univ Fr.

Vocabulaire de l'electroacoustique de l'acoustique. France-Pauline Cormier. Quebec Off.

Vocabulaire de L'Environnement. Ed. by Conseil International de la Langue Française. French & Eur.

Vocabulaire de l'environnement. Conseil International de la Langue Francaise. Hachette.

Vocabulaire de l'Hydrologie et de la Meteorologie. Conseil International de la Language Francaise. Maison Dictionnaire.

Vocabulaire de l'Hydrologie et de la meteorologie. C.I.L.F. Maison Dictionnaire.

Vocabulaire de l'Informatique de Gestion: Anglais-Francais. M. Villers. French & Eur.

Vocabulaire de l'oceanologie. Hachette-Jeunesse.

Vocabulaire de l'oceanologie. Agence de Cooperation Culturelle & Technique. C.I.L.F.

Vocabulaire de l'urbanisme. C.N.I.P.E.

Vocabulaire De Medecine & Des Sciences Connexes Anglais-Francais-Anglais. Gladstone. French & Eur.

Vocabulaire de Medecine & des Sciences Connexes: Francais-Anglais. W. J. Gladstone. Masson & Cie.

Vocabulaire De Medecine et Des Sciences Connexes: Francais-Anglais, Anglais-Francais. French & Eur.

Vocabulaire de Pedagogie Moderne. Mauro Laeng & Guy Auandani. Centurion.

Vocabulaire de Psychopedagogie et de Psychiatrie de l'Enfant. Robert Lafon. Pr Univ Fr.

Vocabulaire de Psychopedagogie & de Psychiatrie de l'enfant. PUF.

Vocabulaire De Psychopedagogie et De Psychiatrie De L'enfant. Robert Lafon. French & Eur.

Vocabulaire de Racine. Jacques-Gabriel Cahen. Slatkine.

Vocabulaire d'ecologie. Conseil International de la Langue Francaise. Hachette.

Vocabulaire des Animaux Marins en Latin Classique. Klincksieck.

Vocabulaire des assurances Sociales. G. Desrosiers & J. Boulay. French & Eur.

Vocabulaire des Assurances Sur la Vie. Jean-Paul Grandpre. Quebec Off.

Vocabulaire des Conferences: Francais-Anglais-Arabe: Francais-Anglais-Arabe. Unesco.

Vocabulaire des Finances Locales. C.N.I.P.E.

Vocabulaire des Institutions Indo-Europeennes, 2. Emile Benveniste. Minuit.

Vocabulaire des Moeurs de la Vie Parisienne Sous le Second Empire. J. R. Klein. Vander.

Vocabulaire des Proclamations Electorales de 1881, 1885. Antoine Prost. PUF.

Vocabulaire des Psychotherapies. Andre Virel. Fayard.

Vocabulaire des Quinze Joles du Mariage. Marcel Pressot. Slatkine.

Vocabulaire des Sciences Sociales. Paul Lazarsfeld. Mouton de Gruyter.

Vocabulaire Des Sciences Sociales: Concepts et Indices. Raymond Boudon & Paul Lazarsfeld. Mouton.

Vocabulaire des Techniques de Groupe. Anne Ancelin-Schutzenberger. Epi.

Vocabulaire des Termes: Essentiels Utilises pour la Transmissien Ligne; Francais-Espagnol-Russe-Allemand-Italien-Neerlandais-Polonais-Portugais-Suedois. U.I.T.

Vocabulaire d'initation aux Etudes Agronomiques. C.R.E.D.I.F.

Vocabulaire Disponible du Francais en France & en Acadie. William Francis Mackey & J. G. Savard. Didier.

Vocabulaire Du Beton. Conseil International De la Langue Francais. French & Eur.

Vocabulaire du Beton. Conseil International de la Langue Francaise. Eyrolles.

Vocabulaire du Cantal du Nord & de la Margeride Auvergnate d'Apres l'ALMC. Ed. by P. Nauton. Cercle Occitan.

Vocabulaire du Patois Lillois. Louis Vermesse & Lille. Lafitte Repr.

Vocabulaire du Patois Lillois. Louis Vermesse & Lille. Slatkine.

Vocabulaire du Patols de Bettant, 2. Armand Decour. Decour.

Vocabulaire du Vieux Breton. Joseph Loth. Champion.

Vocabulaire Economique & Financier. Yves Bernard & Jean-Claude Colli. Seuil.

Vocabulaire Economique et Financier: Coll. Points Economie. Yves Bernard & Jean-Claude Colli. French & Eur.

Vocabulaire Elementaire des Ensembles. Alexis Hocquenghem. Masson & Cie.

Vocabulaire en Images, 1. Christine Le Boeuf. Ecole.

Vocabulaire en Images, 2. Christine Le Boeuf. Ecole.

Vocabulaire Esperanto. Michel Duc-Goninaz. Ophrys.

Vocabulaire Ethnologique. Armin Heymer. French & Eur.

Vocabulaire Ethologique: Allemand-Anglais-Francais. Armin Heymer. PUF.

Vocabulaire Fondamental de Technologie. Jacques Deweerdt. French & Eur.

Vocabulaire Fondamental de Technologie. Jacques Deweerdt. Gamma.

Vocabulaire Fondamentale du Francais. Robert Dottrens & Dino Massarenti. Delachaux.

Le Vocabulaire Fondamentale du Francais. James D. Haygood. Droz.

Vocabulaire Forestier Francais-Allemand-Danois. C. Jacobi. Picard.

Vocabulaire Francais-Anglais d'archeologie Prehistorique. Roger Marois. Quebec P. U.

Vocabulaire Francais-Anglais De la Machine a Coudre Industrielle. Francois Lanecki & Celine Dupre. French & Eur.

Vocabulaire Francais-Anglais de la Machine a Coudre Industrielle. Francois Lanecki & Celine Dupre. Quebec Off.

Vocabulaire Francais-Anglais De L'automobile: Le Moteur. Anne-Marie Baudoin. French & Eur.

Vocabulaire Francais-Anglais de l'automobile. Anne-Marie Baudoin. Quebec Off.

Vocabulaire Francais-Anglais des Relations Professionnelles. Gerard Dion. Laval P. U.

Vocabulaire Francais-Anglais des Relations Professionnelles. Ministere du Travail Et du la Main-D'oeuvre. Quebec Off.

Vocabulaire Francais-Arabe de l'ingenieur & du Technicien, 1. J. J. Schmidt. Maisonneuve & Larose.

Vocabulaire Francais-Malgache. R. P. Malzac. Maritimes Outremer.

Vocabulaire Francais-Mentonnais. James B. Andrews. Lafitte Repr.

Vocabulaire Francais-Provencal: Dictionnaire Provencal-Francais. J. T. Avril. Slatkine.

Le Vocabulaire Francais, 1. Rene L. Wagner. Didier Erudition.

Le Vocabulaire Francais, 2. Rene L. Wagner. Didier Erudition.

Vocabulaire Franco-Anglo-Allemand de Geomorphologie. Henri Baulig. Strasbourg, U.

Vocabulaire Francois-Provencal. Claude F. Achard. Slatkine.

Vocabulaire General d'orientation Scientifique. Didier.

Le Vocabulaire Grammatical. Robert Dagneaud. CDU.

Vocabulaire Illustre des Emballages: Destines au Transport des Marchandises Dangereuses. O. N. U.

Vocabulaire International des Termes d'urbanisme & d'architecture: Francais-Allemand-Anglais. Jean-Henri Calsat. Eyrolles.

Vocabulaire International des Termes d'urbanisme & d'architecture: Francais-Allemand-Anglais. Jean-Henri Calsat & Jean-Pierre Sydler. Ste. Diff. Tech. Bat. T. P.

Vocabulaire International des Termes d'Urbanisme et d'Architecture. Jean-Henri Calsat & Jean P. Sydler. French & Eur.

Le Vocabulaire Latin Des Relations et Des Partis Politiques Sous la Republique. Jean Hellegouarc'H. French & Eur.

Le Vocabulaire Medical De Base. Marie Bonvalot. French & Eur.

Le Vocabulaire Medical de Base. Marie Bonvalot. Organisation Instruction Proger.

Le Vocabulaire Medical de Base. Marie Bonvalot. Soc Etudes Tech.

Le Vocabulaire Medical d'Eschyle & les Ecrits Hippocratiques. J. Dumortier. Belles Lettres.

Vocabulaire Meteorologique International: Quadrilingue (Anglais-Francais-Espagnol-Russe) O. M. M.

Vocabulaire Methodique Chinois-Francais a l'usage des Interpretes. Asie-Orientale Cent. Pub.

Vocabulaire Multilingue de la Science du Sol: Anglais-Francais-Espagnol-Allemand-Portugais-Italien-Neerlandais-Suedois-Russe. G. V. Jacks & R. Tavernier. F. A. O.

Vocabulaire Occitan. Lagarde.

Vocabulaire Oecumenique. Yves Congar & Gerard Siegwalt. Cerf.

Vocabulaire, Orthographe, Conjugaison, Analyse. Debleser M. Deneubourg. Wesmael-Charlier.

Vocabulaire, Orthographe, Conjugaison, Analyse. N. Deneubourg. Wesmael-Charlier.

Vocabulaire, Orthographe, Conlugaison, Analyse. N. Deneubourg. Wesmael-Charlier.

Vocabulaire Orthographique de Base. Francois Ters et al. Messeiller.

Vocabulaire Orthographique de Base. Francois Ters. OCDL.

Le Vocabulaire par la Vie des Mots. Marc M. Ballot & Fougerouse. Lavauzelle.

Vocabulaire Patois Vellavien-Francais. Jules-Gabriel De Vinols De Montfleury. Lafitte Repr.

Vocabulaire, Phraseologie, Lecture, Informations. Albert Pierret & Basiaux. Wesmael-Charlier.

Vocabulaire, Phraseologie, Lecture, Informations. Albert Pierret et al. Wesmael-Charlier.

Vocabulaire, Phraseologie, Lecture Mentale. Albert Pierret & Basiaux. Wesmael-Charlier.

Vocabulaire Politique & Social en France de 1869 a 1872. Jean Dubois. Larousse FR.

Le Vocabulaire Politique & Socio-Ethnique a Montreal de 1839 a 1842. Maurice Rabotin. Didier-Canada.

Le Vocabulaire Politique de J. J. Rousseau. Michel Launay. Slatkine.

Le Vocabulaire Politique de Paul Eluard. Marie-Renee Guyard. Klincksieck.

Vocabulaire Pratique des Sciences Sociales. Alain Birou. French & Eur.

Vocabulaire Pratique des Sciences Sociales. Alain Biron. Ouvrieres.

Le Vocabulaire Professional du Houilleur Borain. Pierre Ruelle. Acad Royale.

Le Vocabulaire Psychologique dans les Chroniques de Froissart, 1. Jacqueline Pinoche. Klincksieck.

Vocabulaire Raisonne & Compare du Dialecte & du Patols de la Province de Bourgogne. Thomas Mignard. Slatkine.

Vocabulaire Raisonne Latin-Francais. Gerard Cotton. Dessain & Tolra.

Vocabulaire Redaction. Pierre Moreau & Andre Masson. Hachette.

Vocabulaire Systematique Francais-Allemand. Pierre Borel. Francke.

Vocabulaire Technique. Marcel Lagrenade. Dotmar.

Vocabulaire Technique Allemand-Francais. Francis Cusset. Berger-Levrault.

Vocabulaire Technique Allemand-Francais, Francais-Allemand. Francis Cusset. French & Eur.

Vocabulaire Technique Anglais-Francais, Francais-Anglais. Francis Cusset. French & Eur.

Vocabulaire Technique Anglais-Francais. Francis Cusset. Berger-Levrault.

Vocabulaire Technique Bilingue. Jean Delorme. Quebec Off.

Vocabulaire Technique de la Bibliotheconomie. Paule Rolland-Thomas & Victor Coulombe. Assoc. Canad. Biblio. Lang. Fr.

Vocabulaire Technique des Assurances sur la Vie, L. Beguin et al. French & Eur.

Vocabulaire Technique des Assurances & Reassurances Anglais-Francais. Henri Sommer. Berger-Levrault.

Vocabulaire Technique Des Assurances: Anglais-Francais, Francais-Anglais. J. Lesobre & H. Sommer. French & Eur.

Le Vocabulaire Toponymique du Ban de Fronville. P. Gavray-Baty. Liege, Fac Lettres.

Vocabulaire Usuel du Chinois Moderne, 2: Chinois-Francais. Marcel Midoux. Geuthner.

Vocabulaire Usuel du Chinois Moderne, 3: Chinois-Francais. Marcel Midoux. Geuthner.

Le Vocabulaire Vivant. Emile Ballereau & Georges Bouquet. SUDEL.

Le Vocabulaire Vivant, 1. Andre Marthaler. Payot.

Le Vocabulaire Vivant, 3. Andre Marthaler. Payot.

Vocabulaires Methodiques Ouayana, Apari, Oyampal, Emerillon. Henri Coudereau. Kraus.

Vocabular Latina. Esselte Studium.

Vocabulario Basico Frances. E. Moreu-Rey. Teide.

Vocabulario Basico Frances. Enrico Moreu Rey. Teide.

Vocabulario Fundamental de la Lengua Francesa. Henri Hargous. UNAM.

Vocabulario Juridico Frances-Espanol. G. Larousse. Abeledo Perrot.

Vocabulario T. Frances. Bruno.

Vocabulario Vial. OAS General Secretariat. OAS.

Vocabularios Frances-Espanol-Ingles. Novaro.

Vocabularium Pharmaceuticum. Ed. by Albert Graa. Intl Pubns Serv.

Vocabularium Polyglottum Vitae Silvarum. R. Litschauer. (Pub. by P. Parey). French & Eur.

Vocabularium Polyglottum Vitae Silvarum. R. Litschauer. Parey.

Vocabulary de la Fonderie, Francais-Anglais. French & Eur.

Vocabulary de la Fonderie, Francais-Anglais. French & Eur.

Vox-Diccionario Abreviado Frances-Espanol, Espanol-Frances. French & Eur.

VOX-Diccionario basico frances-espanol, espanol-frances. Imported Bks.

Wirtschaftssprache Franzoesisch-Deutsch. G. Haensch & R. Renner. (Pub. by M. Hueber). French & Eur.

Wirtschaftssprache Franzoesisch-Deutsch. G. Haensch & R. Renner. Hueber.

Woerterbuch Datenerfassung-Programmierung. E. Buerger. French & Eur.

Woerterbuch Datenerfassung: Programmierung. Buerger. Verlag Harri Deutsch.

Woerterbuch der Biochemie. K. Thielmann. French & Eur.

Woerterbuch der Biochemie. K. Von Thielmann. VEB Verlag Enzyklopadie.

Woerterbuch der Biochemie. Thielmann. Verlag Harri Deutsch.

Woerterbuch der Biologie. Guenther Haensch. French & Eur.

Woerterbuch der
Dampferzeugungstechnik-
Dictionary of Steam Generator
Engineering. Ed. by Deutsche
Babcock et al. Intl Pubns Serv.
Woerterbuch der Datentechnik. Linse.
Brandstetter.
Woerterbuch der Deutschen und
Franzoesischen Rechtssprache.
Michel Doucet. French & Eur.
Woerterbuch der Deutschen und
Franzoesischen Rechtssprache.
Michel Doucet. French & Eur.
Woerterbuch der Elektronik. E.
Knaeps & D. Zacharias. French &
Eur.
Woerterbuch der Elektrotechnik
Fernmeldetechnik & Elektronik:
Band I, Deutsch-Englisch-
Franzoesisch. Goedecke.
Brandstetter.
Woerterbuch der Elektrotechnik
Fernmeldetechnik & Elektronik:
Band II, Franzoesisch-Englisch-
Deutsch. Goedecke. Brandstetter.
Woerterbuch der Elektrotechnik
Fernmeldetechnik & Elektronik:
Band III, Englisch-Deutsch-
Franzoesisch. Goedecke.
Brandstetter.
Woerterbuch der Elektrotechnik,
Fernmeldetechnik und Elektonik.
W. Goedecke. French & Eur.
Woerterbuch der Elektrotechnik,
Fernmeldetechnik und Elektronik.
W. Goedecke. French & Eur.
Woerterbuch der Forstwirtschaft.
Johannes V. Weck. French & Eur.
Woerterbuch der Forstwirtschaft
Deutsch-Englisch-Franzoesisch-
Spanisch-Russisch. Johannes Weck
et al. BLV Verlag.
Woerterbuch der Franzoesischen und
Deutschen Sprache. E. Weis & H.
Mattutat. French & Eur.
Woerterbuch der Franzoesischen und
Deutschen Sprache. E. Weis & H.
Mattutat. French & Eur.
Woerterbuch der Handels, Finanz und
Rechtssprache. Robert Herbst.
French & Eur.
Woerterbuch der Industriellen
Technik: Band III, Deutsch-
Franzoesisch. Ernst. Brandstetter.
Woerterbuch der Industriellen
Technik: Band IV, Franzoesisch-
Deutsch. Ernst. Brandstetter.
Woerterbuch der Industriellen
Technik: Band IX, Englisch-
Englisch. Ernst. Brandstetter.
Woerterbuch der Industriellen
Technik. R. Ernst. French & Eur.
Woerterbuch der Industriellen
Technik. R. Ernst. French & Eur.
Woerterbuch der Internationalen
Beziehungen und der Politik.
Guenther Haensch. French & Eur.
Woerterbuch der Jagel. Anne
Kirchoff. French & Eur.
Woerterbuch der Kabeltechnik.
Christel Richling. French & Eur.
Woerterbuch der Kabeltechnik.
Christel Richling. Brandstetter.
Woerterbuch der Kabeltechnik:
Deutsch-Englisch-Franzoesisch.
Drewitz Richling. Brandstetter.
Woerterbuch der
Kraftuebertragungselemente-
Deutsch-Spanisch-Franzoesisch-
Englisch-Italienisch-Niederlandisch-
Schwedisch-Finnisch: Bd 1,
Zahnraeder. Krausskopf.
Woerterbuch der
Kraftuebertragungselemente.
French & Eur.
Woerterbuch der Landwirtschaft.
Guenther Haensch. French & Eur.
Woerterbuch der Mathematik. Ralf
Sube. French & Eur.
Woerterbuch der Mathmetik.
Eisenreich & Sube. Verlag Harri
Deutsch.
Woerterbuch der Optik &
Feinmechanik: Band II, Englisch-
Franzoesisch-Deutsch. Brandstetter.
Woerterbuch der Optik &
Feinmechanik: Band III,
Franzoesisch-Deutsch-Englisch.
Schulz. Brandstetter.
Woerterbuch der Optik und
Feinmechanik: English-French-
German Dictionary of Optics &
Mechanical Engineering. E. Schulz.
French & Eur.

Woerterbuch der Optik und
Feinmechanik. Ernst Schulz.
French & Eur.
Woerterbuch der Optik und
Feinmechanik. Ernst Schulz.
French & Eur.
Woerterbuch der Photo, Film und
Kinotechnik. Wolfgang Grau.
French & Eur.
Woerterbuch der Psychiatrie und
Medizinischen Psychologie. Uwe H.
Peters. French & Eur.
Woerterbuch der Reprographie.
Deutsches Komitee fur
Reprographie. Aussant & Schrift.
Woerterbuch der Reprographie:
Begriffe und Definitionen.
Deutsches Komitee fuer
Reprographie. French & Eur.
Woerterbuch der Wirkstoffprufung.
Werner Goedecke. VDI-Verlag.
Woerterbuch des Arbeits &
Sozialrechts: Deutsch-Franz
Dictionnaire de Droit du Trava il &
de Droit Social. Alexandre
Bonnefoi. Hueber.
Woerterbuch des Arbeits und
Sozialrechtd. Alexandre Bonnefoi.
French & Eur.
Woerterbuch des Pantentwesens in 5
Sprachen. Gyorgy L. Szendy.
French & Eur.
Woerterbuch Erdoelverarbeitung-
Petrolchemie. W. Leipnitz. French
& Eur.
Woerterbuch fuer Architektur,
Hochbau & Baustoffe. Herbert
Buksch. Bauverlag.
Woerterbuch Fuer Architektur:
Hochbau und Baustoffe. French &
Eur.
Woerterbuch fuer Bautechnik und
Baumaschinen. H. Bucksch. French
& Eur.
Woerterbuch fuer das Wasser und
Abwasserfach. Fritz Meinck.
French & Eur.
Woerterbuch fuer Metallurgie,
Mineralogie, Geologie, Bergbau &
die Oelindustrie. A.
Cagnacci-Schwicker. Bauverlag.
Woerterbuch fuer Metallurgie,
Mineralogie, Geologie, Bergbau &
die Oelindustrie Englische-
Franzosisch-Deutsch-Italienisch.
Angelo Cagnacci-Schwicker.
Bauverlag.
Woerterbuch fuer Metallurgie,
Mineralogie, Geologie, Bergbau und
die Oelindustrie. French & Eur.
Woerterbuch fuer Strassenbau und
Strassenverkehe. Karl Steinig.
French & Eur.
Woerterbuch fuer Wirtschaft, Recht &
Handel: Band I, Deutsch-
Franzoesisch. Potonnier.
Brandstetter.
Woerterbuch fuer Wirtschaft, Recht &
Handel: Band II, Franzoesisch-
Deutsch. Potonnier. Brandstetter.
Woerterbuch fuer Wirtschaft: Recht
und Handel. Georges Potonnier.
French & Eur.
Woerterbuch fuer Wirtschaft: Recht
und Handel. Georges Potonnier.
French & Eur.
Woerterbuch fur das Wasser &
Abwasserfach. Fritz Meinck.
Oldenbourg Verlag.
Woerterbuch Industrieofen &
Indudtrielle Warmeanlagen. Josef
Stepanek. Vulkan Verlag.
Woerterbuch
Informationsverarbeitung. Buerger.
Verlag Harri Deutsch.
Woerterbuch Klima & Kaeltetechnik.
Heinrich. Verlag Harri Deutsch.
Woerterbuch Klima & Kaltetechnik.
Gunter Heinrich. Verlag Harri
Deutsch.
Woerterbuch Kristallografie.
Backhaus. Verlag Harri Deutsch.
Woerterbuch Pferd und Reiter.
Zdzislaw Baranowski. French &
Eur.
Woerterbuch Physik. Ralf Sube &
Gunther Eisenreich. French & Eur.
Woerterbuch Physik. Eisenreich &
Sube. Verlag Harri Deutsch.
Woerterbuch Werkzeuge und
Werkzeugmaschinen. Kurt
Stellhorn. French & Eur.

Woerterbuch Wirtschaft Recht
Handel: Deutsch-Franzoesisch.
Georges E. Potonnier & Brigitte
Potonnier. Maison Dictionnaire.
Woerterbuch Wirtschaft Recht
Handel: Deutsch-Franzoesisch.
Georges E. Potonnier & Brigitte
Potonnier. Maison Dictionnaire.
Woerterbuch zur Politik und
Wirtschaftpolitik. Hans E. Zahn.
French & Eur.
Woerterbucher der Fertigungstechnik
Deutsch-Englisch-Franzoesisch: Bd
2, Schleifen Oberflaechenrauheit.
G. Pahlitzsch. Girardet.
Woerterbucher der Fertigungstechnik
Deutsch-Englisch-Franzoesisch: Bd
3, Blechbearbeitung. G. Pahlitzsch.
Girardet.
Woerterbucher der Fertigungstechnik
Deutsch-Englisch-Franzoesisch: Bd
4, Grundbegriffe des Spanens. G.
Pahlitzsch. Girardet.
Woerterbucher der Fertigungstechnik
Deutsch-Englisch-Franzoesisch: Bd
5, Kaltfliesspressen & Kaltstauchen.
G. Pahlitzsch. Girardet.
Woerterbucher der Fertigungstechnik
Deutsch-Englisch-Franzoesisch: Bd
6, Hobeln, Stassen, Raeumen,
Drehen. G. Pahlitzsch. Girardet.
Woerterbucher der Fertigungstechnik
Deutsch-Englisch-Franzoesisch: Bd
7, Bohren, Senken, Reiben,
Gewindeschneiden. G. Pahlitzsch.
Girardet.
World Mining: Glossary of Mining,
Processing & Geological Terms.
Wyllie & Argall. W H Freeman.
World-Wide French Dictionary. Ed.
by Robert Switzer. (Prem). Fawcett.
World-Wide French Dictionary:
Indexed. New Century.
World Wide French Language
Dictionary French-English. New
Century.
The York Dictionary of English-
French-German-Spanish Literary
Terms & Their Origin. Saad
Elkhaden. York Pr CA.
The York Dictionary of English-
French-German-Spanish Literary
Terms & Their Origin. Saad
Elkhadem. York Pr CA.
Zahnarztliches aus dem Dictionnaire
des Sciences Medicales. Werner H.
Aeschlimann. Juris Druckg.

FRIESIAN

Op 't Aljemint. J. K. Dykstra. AFUK-
LEARMIDDELFUNS.

GAELIC

Abair faclan. I.A.R.R. Mingulay.
Chambers Scots Dictionary.
Alexander Warrack. (Pub. by Two
Continents). Am Map.
Dictionary of Irish Myth & Legend.
Ronan Coghlan. Donard Pub Co.
Dictionary of the Gathic Language.
Lawrence H. Mills. AMS Pr.
Dictionary of the Irish Language.
(Pub by Royal Irish Ireland). State
Mutual Bk.
English-Irish Dictionary. Tomas De
Bhaldraithe. Oifig An Tsolathair.

English-Irish Dictionary:
Terminological Additions &
Corrections. Tomas De Bhaldraithe
& Baile A. Claithe. Govt
Publications Sale Office.

Etymological Dictionary of the
Scottish Language. John Jamieson.
Ed. by John Longmuir & David
Donaldson. AMS Pr.

Focloir Modulach. Ireland
Department of Education. Le
Ceannach Direach on Oifig Dhiolta
Foilseachan Rialtais.

Gaelic Dictionary: Gaelic-English
English-Gaelic. Malcolm
MacLennan. Pergamon.

Illustrated Gaelic-English Dictionary.
Dwelly. Colton Bk.

Léxique Etymologique de l'Irlandais
Ancien. Joseph Vendryes. CNRS.

Lexique Etymologique de l'Irlandais
Ancien, 1. Joseph Vendryes.
CNRS.

A Pronouncing & Etymological
Dictionary of the Gaelic Language.
Malcolm Maclennan. Aberdeen U
Pr.

GERMAN

Abbreviations of Nuclear Power Plant
Engineering. G. H. Freyberger.
(Pub. by Verlag Karl Thiemig).
French & Eur.
Das ABC des Pfeifenrauchers. Helmut
Hochrain. Ed. by Heinrich Haisch.
Heyne W Verlag.
ABC Dictionary I: Arabic & Ger. libr.
du Liban. Intl Bk Ctr.
ABC Dictionary Tamhidi: Arabic
Ger. Libr du Liban. Intl Bk Ctr.
ABC-Komiker bis Zwitschergemuese.
Heinz Kuepper. Deutsche Sprache.
Abkeurzungen & Kurzwoerter aus
Technik & Naturwissenschaften:
E-D. Brandstetter.
Abkurzungen & Kurzwoerter aus
Technik & Naturwissenschaften.
Brandstetter.
Abkurzungen der
Kernkraftwerkstechnik. G.
Freyberger. Thiemeg.
Abreviation du traitement de
l'informatique. Carl Amkreutz.
Maison Dictionnaire.
Accounting Dictionary - U.E.C.
Lexicon: American-French-
German-Spanish-Dutch. Union
Europeenne Des Experts
Compatables, Economiques et
Financiers. Intl Pubns Serv.
Active German Idioms. Conrad
Borovski. Hueber.
Die Adjektive auf Isch in der
Deutschen Gegenwartssprache.
Michael Schaefer. Winter Univ.
An Advanced Modern German
Vocabulary. Victor Johnson. Harrap
Co.
Aeronautic Engineering Dictionary:
English-French-German-Arabic. M.
A. Zimaity. Ed. by Abd-el-Washed.
French & Eur.
Agricultural Engineering Dictionary:
English-French-German-Arabic.
Abd El Wahed. French & Eur.
Agypten, die 21: Dynastie. M.
Heerma Van Voss. E J Brill.
Allegemeines Lexikon der Bildenden
Kunstler von der Antike bis zur
Gegenwart. Ed. by Ulrich Thieme
& Felix Becker. Somerset Pub.
Altenglisches Elementarbuch
Einfuehrung, Grammatik, Texte
Mit Uebersetzung und
Woerterbuch. Martin Lehnert. De
Gruyter.

Altgriechisch. Incl. Langenscheidt.

Amglo-Russko-Nemetsko-Frantsuzskii Tolkovyi Slovar Po Vychislitel Noi Tekhnike & Obrabotke Dannykh. (Pub. by Russkii Iazyk). Four Continent.

L' Anglais Dans le Batiment: Text En Anglais Avec un Glossaire Illustre. G. Wallnig & H. Evered. French & Eur.

L' Anglais Dans le Batiment: Texte En Anglais Avec un Glossaire Illustre, 2. Gunter Wallnig & H. Evered. French & Eur.

Anglo-American & German Abbreviations in Environmental Protection. Peter Wennrich. (Pub. by K G Saur). Gale.

Anglo-American & German Abbreviations in Science & Technology: Part 4, Supplement. Compiled by Peter Wennrich. Bowker.

Anglo-American & German Abbreviations in Science & Technology. Peter Wennrich. Bowker.

Anglo-Amerikanische Abkuerzungen und Kurzwoerter der Elektrotechnik. P. Wennrich. (Pub. by Vlg. Dokumentation). French & Eur.

Annales des Mines: Lexique Technique Allemand-Francais. J. Armanet & A. Becquer. French & Eur.

Anzeigenwerbung: Ein Reader fuer Studenten & Lehrer der Deutscher Sprache & Literatur. Ed. by Peter Nusser. Fink Verlag.

Applied Technical Dictionary: Air Conditioning & Refrigeration. (Pub. by Collets). State Mutual Bk.

Applied Technical Dictionary: Oil Processing & Petrochemistry. (Pub. by Collets). State Mutual Bk.

Applied Technical Dictionary: Silicate Technology. (Pub. by Collets). State Mutual Bk.

Arabisch. Incl. Langenscheidt.

Arbeitsschutzlexikon. Walter Klost. Verlag Moderne.

Architecture & Building Dictionary: English-French-German-Arabic. Abd El Gaward. French & Eur.

Armenisch-Deutsches Woerterbuch. Froundiian-Dirair. (Pub. by Oldenbourg). French & Eur.

Armenisch-Deutsches Woerterbuch. Froundiian-Dirair. Oldenbourg Verlag.

Arzneimittel-Verzeichnis. Klaus Gerecke. VEB Verlag Technik.

Astronautical Multilingual Dictionary: International Academy of Astronautics. Elsevier.

Astronomical Dictionary: In Six Languages. Josip Kleczek. Acad Pr.

Atheneum Worterbuch: Aleman-Espanol, Espanol-Aleman. F. Muller. French & Eur.

Atlas & Glossary of Primary Sedimentary Structures. F. J. Pettijohn & P. E. Potter. Springer-Verlag.

Automobily. Czesaw Blok & Wiesaw Jezewski. Wydawnictwa.

Automotive Engineering Dictionary: English-French-German-Arabic. Abd-El-Wahed. French & Eur.

Avviamento All'etimologia Inglese e Tedesca: Dizionario Comparativo dell'Elemento Germanico Commune ad Entrabe le Lingue. Piergiuseppe Scardigli & Teresa Gervasi. Monnier.

Die Bairische Fibel. Josef Ilmberger. B. L. V.

Baktrisch: Ein Woerterbuch. Gholam D. Davary. Groos Verlag.

Banking Dictionary: German-English & English-German. Friedrich K. Feldbausch. Intl Pubns Serv.

Banking Dictionary of English-American & German Terms. Hans Klaus. Intl Ideas.

Bankwoerterbuch Englisch-Deutsch, Deutsch-Englisch. F. Feldbausch. (Pub. by Vlg. Moderne Industrie). French & Eur.

The Bantam New College German & English Dictionary. Ed. by John C. Traupman. Bantam.

Basic German-English Dictionary & Grammar. EMC.

Basic Technical Dictionary: French-English-German-Arabic. H. Marei. French & Eur.

Bauherren-Lexikon. Hans J. Grabbe. Vieweg.

Bautechnik. Eduard Steiger & Karl F. Busch. Bibl Inst Leipzig.

Bautechnisches Englisch im Bild: Illustrated Technical German for Builders. W. K. Killer. Bauverlag.

Bauworterbuch. Hanns Frommhold. Werner Verlag.

Bedeutungswoerterbuch: Bedeutung & Gebrauch der Woerter. Paul Grebe. Biblio Inst.

Begriffe des Managements. Richard Kerler. Humboldt Taschen.

Begriffslexikon der Bildenden Kuenste. B. Bilzer. French & Eur.

Begriffswoerterbuch zur Betriebswirtschafts & Managementlehre. Emil Weinzierl. Industrieverlag.

Bekleidungslexikon. Ed. by Wilfried Schierbaum. Schiele & Schoen.

Bergbautechnik & Aufbereitung Deutsch-Englisch. Helmut Schmidt. VEB Technik.

Berlitz Pocket Dictionaries: German-English. Berlitz Editors. (Berlitz). Macmillan.

Berlitz Pocket Dictionaries: German-English-German. Berlitz. Macmillan.

Bertelsmann Dictionary English-German, German-English. (Pub. by Bertelsmann Lexikon/VVA). French & Eur.

Bertelsmann Dictionary: English-German, German-English. C Bertelsmann.

Bertelsmann Lexikon. (Pub. by Bertelsmann). French & Eur.

Das Bertelsmann Lexikon. Pergamon.

Bertelsmann Lexikon. C Bertelsmann.

Bertelsmann Woerterbuch Deutsch-Franzoesisch, Franzoesisch-Deutsch. Karl Knauer. (Pub. by Bertelsmann Lexikon VVA). French & Eur.

Bertelsmann Woerterbuch Deutsch-Franzoesisch, Franzoesisch-Deutsch. Karl Knauer. C Bertelsmann.

BI-Handlexikon. Lexikonredaktion. Bibl Inst Leipzig.

BI-Handlexikon. Ed. by Lexikonredaktion. Bibl Inst Leipzig.

Bi-Lexikon A-Z. Veb. Inst. Leipzig. Bibl Inst Leipzig.

BI-Taschenlexikon Elektronik-Funktechnik. W. Conrad. Biblio Inst.

BI-Taschenlexikon Energie. W. Conrad et al. Bibl Inst Leipzig.

BI-Taschenlexikon Fremdsprachige Schriftsteller. Ed. by G. Steiner & H. Greiner-Mai. Bibl Inst Leipzig.

BI-Taschenlexikon Heimtiere. U. Jacob & G. T. Petersein. Bibl Inst Leipzig.

BI-Taschenlexikon Orden, Preise & Medaillen Staatliche Auszeichnungen der DDR. G. Tautz. Bibl Inst Leipzig.

BI-Taschenlexikon Radioaktivitaet. J. Leonhardt. Bibl Inst Leipzig.

Bi-Taschenlexikon Schiffbau-Schiffahrt. E. Wiebeck. Bibl Inst Leipzig.

Bibeltheologisches Woerterbuch. Johannes B. Bauer. (Pub. by Styria). French & Eur.

Bibliographisches Handbuch der Sprachworterbucher: Ein Internationales Verzeichnis Von 5600 Worterbuchern der Jahre 1460-1958 Fur Mehr Als 500 Sprachen und Dialekte. Wolfram Zaunmuller. Intl Pubns Serv.

Bild der Voelker. C. D. Darlington & Karl G. Heider. F A Brockhaus.

Bilder-Conversations-Lexikon fur das Deutsche Volk. F A Brockhaus.

Bildwoerterbuch der Kunst. H. Leutzeler. (Pub. by F. Duemmlers). French & Eur.

Bildwoerterbuch Deutsch-Englisch. M Rosenberg.

Bildwoerterbuch Deutsch-Englisch-Franzosisch. Biblio Inst.

Bildwoerterbuch Italienisch: Dizionario Figurato. Biblio Inst.

Bildwoerterbuch Schwedisch: Bildlexikon. Biblio Inst.

Bildwoerterbuch Spanisch: Diccionario por la Imagen. Biblio Inst.

Die Biologie: Ein Lexikon der Gesamten Schulbiologie. Karl H. Ahlheim. Biblio Inst.

Boobytraps of the German Language. Alex Sandri-White. Aurea.

British & American Business in Key Words. Rudolf Sachs. (Pub. by Fritz Knapp Verlag). French & Eur.

British & American Business in Keywords. Rudolf Sachs. Knapp Verlag.

Brockhaus ABC Elektronik. Hans D. Junge. R Brockhaus.

Brockhaus ABC Elektrotechnik. Hans D. Junge. F A Brockhaus.

Brockhaus Bildwoerterbuch Englisch-Deutsch. M Rosenberg.

Brockhaus Bildwoerterbuecher. F A Brockhaus.

Brockhaus Bildwoerterbuecher in vier Sprachen. F A Brockhaus.

Brockhaus der Naturwissenschaften & der Technik. F A Brockhaus.

Brockhaus der Naturwissenschaften und der Technik. (Pub. by Wiesbaden). French & Eur.

Brockhaus Illustrated Dictionary: English-German, German-English. Imported Bks.

Der Brockhaus in Zwei Baenden. F A Brockhaus.

Brockhaus Riemann Musiklexikon. Carl Dahlhaus & Hans H. Eggebrecht. Eur-Am Music.

Brockhaus-Riemann-Musiklexikon in Zwei Baenden: Band 1, A-K. Carl Dahlhaus & Hans H. Eggebrecht. F A Brockhaus.

Brockhaus-Riemann-Musiklexikon in Zwei Baenden: Band 2, L-Z. Carl Dahlhaus & Hans H. Eggebrecht. F A Brockhaus.

Brockhaus-Wahrig Deutsches Woerterbuch in Sechs Baenden: Band 1-3. Gerhard Wahrig et al. F A Brockhaus.

Brukmanns' Zinn-Lexikon. Ludwig Mory et al. Bruckmann KG.

Budo-Lexikon: 1500 Fachausdruecke Fernoestl. Herbert Velte. Falken Verlag.

Bueromaschinen Lexikon. (Pub. by Goeller Verlag). French & Eur.

Capitol's Concise Dictionary. French & Eur.

Cassell's Colloquial German. Cassell. Macmillan.

Cassell's Concise Latin-English, English-Latin Dictionary. Compiled by D. P. Simpson. Macmillan.

Cassell's German Dictionary: German-English, English-German. Macmillan.

Cassell's German-English, English-German Dictionary. H. T. Betteridge. Imported bks.

Cassell's New Compact German Dictionary. (LE). Dell.

Cassell's New Compact German-English, English-German Dictionary. Dell.

Cesko, Slovensko, Latinsko, Anglicko, Nemecko, Rusky, Slovnik Plevelu. Vaclav Kosik. SNTC.

Chemical Dictionary. J. Fouchier & F. Billet. Elsevier.

Chemical Technology Dictionary: English, French-German-Arabic. A. M. Abd-El-Wahed. French & Eur.

Chemie & Chemische Technik. Helmut Gross & Helmut Hildebrand. VEB Verlag Technik.

Chemie & Chemische Technik Englisch-Deutsch. VEB Technik.

Chemie & Chemische Technik Russisch-Deutsch. Helmut Gross. VEB Technik.

Die Chemie: Ein Lexikon der Gesamten Schulchemie. Hans Borucki et al. Biblio Inst.

Chemins de Fer Glossary. Bureau International de Documentation de Chemin de Fer. Elsevier.

Chemisch-Technisches Lexikon. Dieter Osteroth & Walter G. Von Baeckmann. Springer-Verlag.

Chinese-English Dictionary of Physical Terms. S. Chang. (Pub. by Harrassowitz). French & Eur.

Chinesisch-Deutsches Woerterbuch. Werner Rudenberg. De Gruyter.

Chinesisch-Deutsches Woerterbuch. Martin Piasek. (Pub. by Max Heuber). French & Eur.

Chinesisch-Deutsches Woerterbuch. Martin Piasek. Hueber.

Chinesisch-Koreanisch-Deutsch Woerterbuch. Andre Eckardt. Groos Verlag.

Cibernetical Dictionary: E-G-F-R-Slovene. A. Sydow. French & Eur.

Collins German Dictionary: German-English, English-Ger. Peter Terrell et al. Imported Bks.

Collins German-English & English-German Dictionary. S&S.

Collins German-English, English-German Dictionary. P. Terrel et al. French & Eur.

Collins German-English English-German Dictionary. Berkley Pub.

Commercial & Financial Dictionary in Four Languages. Jozef V. Servotte. Intl Pubns Serv.

The Compact Dictionary of Exact Science & Technology: Band I, English-German. Kucera. Brandstetter.

The Compact Dictionary of Exact Science & Technology: Band II, German-English. Kucera. Brandstetter.

The Compact Dictionary of Exact Science & Technology: English-German. A. Kucera. French & Eur.

Comprehensive German Dictionary. Langenscheidt.

Concise Electronics Dictionary. Georg Moellerke. A T Fachverlag.

Condensed Muret-Sanders German-English Dictionary. Ed. by Heinz Messinger. Gale.

Conference Terminology in English, Spanish, Russian, Italian, German & Hungarian. J. Herbert. Elsevier.

Cortina-Grosset Basic German Dictionary. Ed. by Josefa J. Smith et al. (G&D). Putnam Pub Group.

Cortina-Grosset Basic German Dictionary. Ed. by Josefa Zotter. (G&D). Putnam Pub Group.

Cortina-Grosset Basic German Dictionary. Josefa Zotter. G&D.

Customs Dictionary: German-English-French-Italian. Wilhelm Muller. Intl Pubns Serv.

Danisch. H. Hennigsen. Langenscheidt.

Dansk-Tysk Ordbog. E. Bork & E. Kaper. French & Eur.

Dansk-Tysk Ordbog. Borge Dissing & Rud Lave. Illus. by L. Taaning. Gyldendal Norsk.

Dansk-Tysk Ordbog. Egon Bork & Egon Kaper. Gyldendal Norsk.

Dansk-Tysk Ordbog for Korrespondenter. O. Poulsen. French & Eur.

Dansk-Tysk Teknisk Ordborg. A. Warren. French & Eur.

Das Grosse Lexikon der Aquaristik. Hans Frey. Neumann-Neudamm.

Data Systems Dictionary. Karl-Heinz Brinkmann et al. Brandstetter.

Data Systems Dictionary. Joachim Schulz. Brandstetter.

Data Systems Dictionary: English-Russian-German. Joachim Schulz. (Pub. by Brandstetter Verlag). French & Eur.

Dataordboken. Sveriges Standardiseringskommission. Standard Sver.

Datenerfassung Programmierung. Erich Burger. VEB Verlag Technik.

Datenerfassung Programmierung-Englisch-Deutsch-Franzoesisch-Russisch. Erich Burger. VEB Technik.

Dental dictionary. Herbert Bucksch. Verlag Neuer.

Der Duden in 10 Baenden das Standardwerk zur Deutschen Sprache. Incl. Bibliographisches Institut.

Der Horror-Film. Fernand Jung & Georg Weil. Roloff.

Deutsch-Arabisches Worterbuch. Gotz Schregle. Lib Liban.

Deutsch-Chinesisches Handworterbuch. French & Eur.

Deutsch-Chinesisches Standard Handworterbuch. French & Eur.

Deutsch-Englisch, Englisch-Deutsch. Langenscheidt.

Deutsch-Englishes Glossarium. C. A. Gunston. (Pub. by Fritz Knapp Verlag). French & Eur.

Deutsch-Finnisches Schulworterbuch. A. Rosentahl et al. French & Eur.

Deutsch-Franzoesisches Glossarium: Finanzieller und Wirtschaftlicher Fachausdrueke. Roepke & Haefner. Maison Dictionnaire.

Deutsch-Franzosisches Glossarium. F. Roepke. (Pub. by Fritz Knapp Verlag). French & Eur.

Deutsch fuer Baufachleute. G. Wallnig & H. Evered. Bauverlag.

Deutsch fur Baufachleute fuer Daenen, Norweger & Sshweden. G. Wallnig & H. Evered. Bauverlag.

Deutsch-Hebraeisches Woerterbuch. David Herstig. (Pub. by Max Hueber). French & Eur.

Deutsch-Hebraeisches Woerterbuch. David Herstig. Hueber.

Deutsch-Japanisches Woerterbuch. Eusebius Breitung. Buske.

Deutsch-Koreanisches Woerterbuch. Andre Eckardt. Groos Verlag.

Deutsch Lehnwoerter in der Polnischen Bergbausprache. Konrad Wypych. MG Schmitz.

Deutsch-Norwegisch-Deutsch. Von Trygue Alsos. French & Eur.

Deutsch-Persisches Fachwoerterbuch Fuer Naturwissenschaft, Medezin und Landwirtschaft. B. Habibi. (Pub. by Harrassowitz). French & Eur.

Deutsch-Russisches Woerterbuch: S-Z. Hans H. Bielfeldt. Ed. by Ronald Loetzsch. Akad Verl Ath.

Deutsch-Russische Wirtschaftssprache. N. Grischen. (Pub. by M. Hueber). French & Eur.

Deutsch-Russische Wirtschaftssprache. N. Grischen. Hueber.

Deutsch-Russisches Meteorologisches Worterbuch. W. G. Martschenko. French & Eur.

Deutsch-Russisches Oekonomisches Woerterbuch. Bljach & Bagma. Wissenschaftliche.

Deutsch-Russisches Okonomisches Worterbuch: Dictionary German-Russian of Economics. I. S. Bljach & B. T. Bagma. French & Eur.

Deutsch-Russisches Woerterbuch. Edmund Daum & W. Schenk. (Pub. by Max Hueber). French & Eur.

Deutsch-Russisches Woerterbuch. Edmund Daum & W. Schenk. Hueber.

Deutsch-Russisches Woerterbuch: A-G. Hans H. Bielfeldt. Ed. by R. Loetzsch et al. Akad Verl Ath.

Deutsch-Russisches Woerterbuch: H-R. Hans H. Bielfeldt. Ed. by Ronald Loetzsch. Akad Verl Ath.

Deutsch-Russisches Worterbuch der Forstund Holzwirtschaft. E. A. Pawlow & O. I. Semjonowa. French & Eur.

Deutsch-Russisches Worterbuch der Rechentechnik und Datenverarbeitung. W. A. Scharow & A. L. Nowitschkowa. French & Eur.

Deutsch-Russisches Worterbuch fur Eisenbahnwessen. D. A. Bunin et al. French & Eur.

Deutsch-Russisches Worterbuch fur Eisenbahnwesen. A. P. Sulima-Samujillo et al. French & Eur.

Deutsch-Russisches Worterbuch fur Ozeanographie. N. N. Gorski et al. French & Eur.

Deutsch-Russisches Worterbuch fur Wasserbau. L. B. Bernstein. French & Eur.

Deutsch-Spanisches Glossarium. Mario R. Lerche. (Pub. by Fritz Knapp Verlag). French & Eur.

Deutsch-Spanisches Glossarium Finanzieller & Wirtschaftlicher Fachausdrueck. Mario R. Lerche. Knapp Verlag.

Deutsch-Turkisches Woerterbuch fur Technische Berufe. Sadettin Bilginer. Girardet.

Deutsch-Turkisches Worterbuch Fur Technische Berufe. Sadettin Bilginer. (Pub. by Verlag W. Girardet). French & Eur.

Deutsch-Ungarisches Woerterbuch. Akademiai Kiado.

Deutsche Fach & Wissenschaftssprache. Drozd & Seibicke. Brandstetter.

Deutsche Lehnworter in der Polnischen Bergbausprache. Konrad Wypych. MG Schmitz.

Deutsche Woerterbuch. Moritz Heyne. Hirzel Verlag.

Deutsche Woerterbucher. Peter Kuhn. Niemeyer.

Deutsches Munzsammler-Lexikon. Herbert Rittmann. Battenberg.

Deutsches Woerterbuch. Jacob Grimm & Wilhelm Grimm. Adler.

Deutsches Woerterbuch. Karl Weigand. De Gruyter.

Deutsches Woerterbuch. (Bibliogr. Institut). French & Eur.

Deutsches Woerterbuch. Moritz Heyne (Pub. by Hirzel). French & Eur.

Deutsches Woerterbuch. Lutz Mackensen. (Pub. by Suedwest). French & Eur.

Deutsches Woerterbuch. Hermann Paul. (Pub. by Max Niemeyer). French & Eur.

Deutsches Woerterbuch. Gerhard Wahrig. (Pub. by Bertelsmann Lexikon VVA). French & Eur.

Deutsches Woerterbuch. J. Grimm & W. Grimm. Herzel Verlag.

Deutsches Woerterbuch. Gerhard Wahrig. Imported Bks.

Deutsches Woerterbuch. Biblio Inst.

Deutsches Woerterbuch. Lutz Mackensen. Suedwest.

Deutsches Woerterbuch. Hermann Paul. Niemeyer.

Deutsches Woerterbuch. Gerhard Wahrig. C Bertelsmann.

Deutsches Woerterbuch in 3 Banden: Band I, Deutsches Woerterbuch, A-F. Biblio Inst.

Deutsches Woerterbuch in 3 Banden: Band 2, Deutsches Woerterbuch. Biblio Inst.

Deutsches Woerterbuch in 3 Banden: Band 3, Deutsches Woerterbuch, O-Z. Biblio Inst.

Deutsches Woerterbuch Tuebingen. H. Paul. M Rosenberg.

Deutsches Woerterbuch und Lexicon der deutsches Sprachlehre. G. Wahrig. M Rosenberg.

Diccionario Abreviado Aleman-Espagnol. Biblo SP.

Diccionario aleman-espanol. Mayfe.

Diccionario Aleman-Espanol. Carlos Brandau. Mayfe.

Diccionario Aleman-Espanol-Aleman. Franz Muller. Imported Bks.

Diccionario aleman-espanol de medicina. F. Ruiz Torres. MMW Verlag.

Diccionario aleman-espanol de medicina. F. Ruiz Torres. Alhambra.

Diccionario Aleman-Espanol, Espanol-Aleman de Medicina. Francisco Ruiz Torres. French & Eur.

Diccionario Aleman-Espanol, Espanol-Aleman. E. F. Martinez Amador. French & Eur.

Diccionario Aleman-Espanol, Espanol-Aleman. Muller. French & Eur.

Diccionario Aleman-Espanol Espanol-Aleman. Ed. by Michael Schmidt. Biblograf SP.

Diccionario Aleman-Espanol Espanol-Aleman 'Vox' Biblo SP.

Diccionario aleman-espanol y espanol-aleman de medicina. F. Ruiz Torres. Alhambra.

Diccionario bilingue aleman-espanol y espanol-aleman. Franz Muller. Sopena.

Diccionario bilingue frances-espanol-aleman. Alcala Zamora. Sopena.

Diccionario Brevis duplex: aleman-castellano y castellano-aleman. Sopena.

Diccionario Cientifico y Tecnologico Espanol, Ingles, Frances, Aleman. T. C. Collocott. Imported Bks.

Diccionario Cuyas: Spanish-German, German-Spanish. Colton Bk.

Diccionario de Biologia en Quatre Lenguas: Aleman, Ingles, Frances y Espanol. Gunther Haensch & Gisela Haberkamp. French & Eur.

Diccionario de la Decoracion. Equipo Reactor De Ceac. French & Eur.

Diccionario de la lengua espanola y alemana: Tomo 1. Rudolf Slaby et al. Herder SA.

Diccionario de las lenguas espanola alemana. Rudolf Slaby et al. Herder SA.

Diccionario De las Lenguas Espanola y Alemana. Rudolf Slaby. French & Eur.

Diccionario de las lenguas espanola y alemana: Aleman-espanol. Slaby-Grossmann. Herder.

Diccionario De Seguros. H. L. Mueller-Lutz. French & Eur.

Diccionario de Valencias Verbales. Aleman-Espanol. Dietrich Rall et al. Benjamins North Am.

Diccionario del Automovil. Roger Guerber. French & Eur.

Diccionario Enciclopedia Universal. French & Eur.

Diccionario Enciclopedias Labor. Ed. by Javier Lasso de La Vega & Jose M. Rubert Candau. French & Eur.

Diccionario espanol-aleman. Mayfe.

Diccionario Espanol-Aleman. Carlos Brandau. Mayfe.

Diccionario Espanol-Aleman, Aleman-Espanol Militar. Carlos Ruiz Jodar. French & Eur.

Diccionario espanol, ingles, frances, italiano, aleman y holandes. Rev. Mex. de Seguros.

Diccionario Everest Vertice Aleman-Espanol, Spanisch-Deutsch. Imported bks.

Diccionario Everest 'Vertice' aleman-espanol y espanol-aleman. Everest.

Diccionario Fraseologico Comercial. Zavada & Eberle et al. French & Eur.

Diccionario Ilustrado De Terminologia Textil Aleman-Espanol, Espanol-Aleman. Carlos Scheengluth. French & Eur.

Diccionario Iter Aleman-Espanol, Espanol-Aleman. French & Eur.

Diccionario juridico aleman-espanol de derecho comparado: Con vocabulario juridico espanol-aleman. Quintano Heilpern. Rev Derecho Pri.

Diccionario Lexicon Aleman-Espanol, Espanol-Aleman. Hans Muller. French & Eur.

Diccionario Manual Aleman-Espanol, Espanol-Aleman. Felix Diez Mateo. French & Eur.

Diccionario Manual Aleman-Espanol, Espanol-Aleman. Ed. by Felix D. Mateo & Frida Hochleitner. Espasa Calpe.

Diccionario Manual Aleman-Espanol, Spanisch-Deutsch. E. M. Martinez Amador. French & Eur.

Diccionario Manual Amador Aleman-Espanol, Espanol-Aleman. E. M. Martinez Amador. French & Eur.

Diccionario moderno: Aleman-espanol, espanol-aleman. Langenscheidt. Herder SA.

Diccionario Moderno Herder Aleman-Espanol, Espanol-Aleman. Gunther Haensch. French & Eur.

Diccionario moderno Herder Aleman-Espanol. Gunther Haensch. Herder SA.

Diccionario Modernos Herder Aleman-Espanol. Herder SA.

Diccionario Para Obras Publica, Edificacion y Maquinaria En Obra. Bucksch. French & Eur.

Diccionario para Obras Publicas, Edificacion & Maquinaria en Obra. Bauverlag.

Diccionario Para Obras Publicas, Edificacion y Maquinaria en Obra. French & Eur.

Diccionario para obras publicas, edificacion y maquinaria en obra: Aleman-espanol, espanol-aleman. Bucksch. Herder SA.

Diccionario pervus duplex: Aleman-castellano y castellano-aleman. Sopena.

Diccionario poliglota de la arquitectura. B. Bassegoda Muste. Imported Bks.

Diccionario Simultaneo en 21 Idiomas. Juan Capdevilla Font. French & Eur.

Diccionario Simultaneo en 6 Idiomas. Juan Capdevila Font. French & Eur.

Diccionario Tecnico Aleman-Espanol, Espanol-Aleman. H. Mink. French & Eur.

Diccionario Tecnico De la Plasticos Aleman-Espanol. A. Wittfoht & M. A. Achon. French & Eur.

Diccionario tecnico de plasticos aleman-espanol. A Wittfoht & M. A. Achon. Urmo.

Diccionario tecnico de plasticos: Espanol-aleman. A. Wittfoht & A. Rubin. (Dist. Elcano, Mexico). Urmo.

Diccionario tecnico de terminos ferroviarios: Espanol-frances-aleman-ingles-italiano-holandes. J. H. Bussy. G Gili.

Diccionario tecnico espanol-aleman. Tr. by Mink. Bluma.

Diccionario tecnico ilustrado de herramientas de corte para el trabajo de metales: Espanol-aleman-ingles-frances-italiano. T. Heiler. G Gili.

Diccionario tecnico industrial: Vol. 1, Espanol-aleman. R. Ernst. G Gili.

Diccionario tecnico industrial: Vol. 2, Aleman-espanol. G Gili.

Diccionario Tecnico: Suplemento. H. Mink. French & Eur.

Diccionario Tecnico: Suplemento al Tomo II, Espanol-Aleman. H. Mink. Herder SA.

Diccionario Tecnico, Tomo 2: Espanol-Aleman. H. Mink. (French & Eur). French & Eur.

Diccionario tecnologico Chambers: Espanol-ingles-frances-aleman. C. F. Tweney & L. E. Hughes. Omega SA.

Diccionario Terminologico de Quimica. Jose R. Barcelo Matutano. French & Eur.

Diccionario universal: Aleman-espanol, espanol-aleman. Herder SA.

Diccionario Universal Herder Aleman-Espanol, Espanol-Aleman. French & Eur.

Dicionario de Alemao-Portugues. Porto Ed.

Dicionario de Bolso Portugues-Alemao. Difel Difusao.

Dicionario de Portugues-Alemao. Porto Ed.

Dictionar de Electrotehnica. Friedrich Schattner. Editura Stiintifica.

Dictionar de Electrotehnica. Friedrich Schattner. Editura Stiintifica.

Dictionar Frazeologic German-Roman. Editura Stiintifica.

Dictionar Poliglot. Ernest M. Lates et al. Editura Stiintifica.

Dictionar Poliglot de Geodezie: Fotogrammetrie si Cartografie. Mihail Albota. Editura Stiintifica.

Dictionar Poliglot de Industrie Alimentara. Mihai Papa-Sotir. Editura Stiintifica.

Dictionar Poliglot de Matematica, Mecanica si Astronomie. Stefan Gheorghita. Editura Stiintifica.

Dictionar Roman-German: Pentru uzul Elevilor. Jean Livescu & Emilia Savin. Editura Stiintifica.

Dictionar Tehnic Auto de Buzunar in Sapte Limbi. Petre Cristea. Editura Stiintifica.

Dictionarium Tetraglotten Seu Voces Latinae Omnes, et Graecae Eis Respondentes, Cum Gallica & Teutonica (Quam Passim Flandricam Vocant) Earum Interpretatione: Dictionarum Tetraglotten A.D. MDLXII Ed. Mouton.

Dictionary for Marine Technology. Ed. by Robert Dluhy. Adler.

Dictionary for Physicians. F. Lejeune & W. E. Bunjes. French & Eur.

Dictionary for the Graphic Arts: German-English, English-German. Perfect Graphic.

Dictionary for the Graphic Arts in Eight Languages: German-English-French-Spanish-Russian-Hungarian-Polish-Slowak. Perfect Graphic.

Dictionary of Acoustics: English-German-French-Russian-Spanish-Polish-Madarsko-Slovene. W. Reichardt. French & Eur.

Dictionary of Advertising & Marketing. Clemens Gruber. Adler.

Dictionary of Agriculture in German, French, Spanish, & Russian. G. Haensch. Ed. by Haberkamp G. De Anton. Elsevier.

Dictionary of Architecture, Building Construction & Materials. Herbert Bucksch. French & Eur.

Dictionary of Architecture, Building Construction & Materials. Herbert Bucksch. French & Eur.

Dictionary of Automatic Data Processing. Ing H. Burger. (Pub. by Collets). State Mutual Bk.

Dictionary of Automatical Technique. Ed. by Jiri Sykora. French & Eur.

Dictionary of Automobile Terms. Massada Pr.

Dictionary of Biochemistry. K. Thielmann. French & Eur.

Dictionary of Biology. Guenther Haensch. French & Eur.

Dictionary of Biology in English, French, German & Spanish. G. Haensch & G. Haberkamp De Anton. Elsevier.

Dictionary of Book Publishing. Ulrich Stiehl. (Pub. by K G Saur). Gale.

Dictionary of Cement. C. Van Amerongen. French & Eur.

Dictionary of Cereal Processing & Cereal Chemistry. R. Schneeweiss. Elsevier.

Dictionary of Chemical Terminology. D. Kryt. Elsevier.

Dictionary of Chemical Terminology. (Pub. by Vyd. Naukowo-Techniczne). Four Continent.

Dictionary of Chemistry. Richard Ernst. French & Eur.

Dictionary of Chemistry. Richard Ernst. French & Eur.

Dictionary of Chemistry & Chemical Engineering. Louis de Vries. French & Eur.

Dictionary of Chemistry & Chemical Engineering. Louis de Vries. French & Eur.

Dictionary of Chemistry & Chemical Engineering. Louis DeVries & Helga Kolb. Incl. Verlag Chemie.

Dictionary of Civil Engineering & Construction Machinery & Equipment. Herbert Bucksch. French & Eur.

Dictionary of Civil Engineering & Construction Machinery & Equipment. Herbert Bucksch. French & Eur.

Dictionary of Commerce, Finance & Law. Robert Herbst. French & Eur.

Dictionary of Commercial, Financial & Legal Terms. R. Herbst. Adler.

Dictionary of Commercial, Financial & Legal Terms. R. Herbst. Heinman.

Dictionary of Commericial, Financial & Legal Terms in Two Languages. R. Herbst. Adler.

Dictionary of Concrete Terms. Massada Pr.

Dictionary of Dairy Terminology. Elsevier.

Dictionary of Dams. Massada Pr.

Dictionary of Dataprocessing. Karl H. Brinkmann. French & Eur.

Dictionary of Dataprocessing. Egon Hofmann. French & Eur.

Dictionary of Dataprocessing. Alfred Oppermann. French & Eur.

Dictionary of Development Banking: A Compilation of Terms in English, French, & German with Definitions in English. T. Scharf & M. C. Shetty. Elsevier.

Dictionary of Economics. R. V. Eichborn. Incl. Adler.

Dictionary of Electronics. Alfred Opperman. (K G Saur). Gale.

Dictionary of Engineering & Technology. Richard Ernst. Oxford U Pr.

Dictionary of Engineering & Technology: With Extensive Treatment of the Most Modern Techniques & Processes. Richard Ernst. Oxford U Pr.

Dictionary of Engineering Metrology Terms. Massada Pr.

Dictionary of environmental protection. Otto E. Tutzaver & Ingrid M. Tutzaver. Heymanns Verlag.

Dictionary of Five Hundred One German Verbs Fully Conjugated. H. Strutz. Barron.

Dictionary of Floor, Wall & Ceiling Covering. Massada Pr.

Dictionary of Forestry. J. Weck. Elsevier.

Dictionary of Foundry Terms. Massada Pr.

Dictionary of Geosciences. A. Watznauer. Elsevier.

Dictionary of German & English Legal & Economic Terminology. Alfred Romain. French & Eur.

Dictionary of German & English Legal & Economic Terminology. Alfred Romain. French & Eur.

Dictionary of German Synonyms. R. B. Farrell. Cambridge U Pr.

Dictionary of German Synonyms. Ralph B. Farrell. Cambridge U Pr.

Dictionary of Glass Making. ICG. Elsevier.

Dictionary of Hydraulic Machinery. A. T. Troskolanski. Elsevier.

Dictionary of Hydraulics & Pneumatics: English-German-Russian-Slovene. G. Neubert. French & Eur.

Dictionary of Hydrology Terms. Massada Pr.

Dictionary of Industrial Property, Legal & Related Terms: English, Spanish, French & German. Ed. by Francis J. Kase. Sijthoff & Noordhoff.

Dictionary of Information Technology. Michael Shain & David Longley. Macmillan London.

Dictionary of International Economics: German, Russian, English, French, Spanish. Ed. by S. Kohls. Sijthoff & Noordhoff.

Dictionary of Joinery Terms: Doors, Windows, Shutters. Massada Pr.

Dictionary of Library Science Information & Documentation. Ed. by W. Clason. Elsevier.

Dictionary of Library Terms. Massada Pr.

Dictionary of Maritime Terms. Massada Pr.

Dictionary of Mathematical Sciences. Leo Herland. Incl. Ungar.

Dictionary of Mathematical Sciences: Band II, Englisch-German. Herland. Brandstetter.

Dictionary of Mathematical Sciences: Band I, German-English. Herland. Brandstetter.

Dictionary of Mathematics. G. Eisenreich & R. Sube. Elsevier.

Dictionary of Mechanical Engineering. Henry G. Freeman. Intl Pubns Serv.

Dictionary of Mechanisms. H. Bucksch. French & Eur.

Dictionary of Mechanisms-Getriebeworterbuch: German-English, English-German. Herbert Bucksch. Intl Pubns Serv.

Dictionary of Metal-Cutting Machine Tools. Henry G. Freeman. Adler.

Dictionary of Metal-Cutting Machine Tools. Henry G. Freeman. French & Eur.

Dictionary of Metallurgy. Ed. by A. Dollinger. French & Eur.

Dictionary of Meteorological Terms. Massada Pr.

Dictionary of Modern Engineering. Alfred Oppermann. French & Eur.

Dictionary of Modern Engineering. Alfred Oppermann. French & Eur.

Dictionary of Modern German Prose Usage. H. F. Eggeling. Oxford U Pr.

Dictionary of Modern Theological German. Helmut W. Ziefle. Baker Bk.

Dictionary of Musical Terms in Seven Languages. Ed. by H. Leuchtmann. Heinman.

Dictionary of Optics Photography & Photogrammetry: German-English & English-German. Ed. by G. Richter. Elsevier.

Dictionary of Oto-Rhino-Laryngology in Five Languages. A. Larrauri. Intl Pubns Serv.

Dictionary of Packaging: German-English-French. Johannes P. Hoffman. Intl Pubns Serv.

Dictionary of Patent Practice. J. Vuexkull & H. J. Reich. French & Eur.

Dictionary of Photograhy. Massada Pr.

Dictionary of Physical Metallurgy. E. F. Tyrkiel. Elsevier.

Dictionary of Physics & Allied Sciences: English-German. Ed. by Ralph Idlin. Ungar.

Dictionary of Physics & Allied Sciences: German-English. Ed. by Charles J. Hyman. Ungar.

Dictionary of Physics: No. 1, Mechanics. Massada Pr.

Dictionary of Physics: No. 2, Electricity & Magnetism. Massada Pr.

Dictionary of Physics: No. 3, Optics. Massada Pr.

Dictionary of Plastics Technology in English, German, French & Russian. G. Kaliske. Elsevier.

Dictionary of Politics & Economic Policy. H. Zahn. French & Eur.

Dictionary of Politics & Economics. H. Back et al. French & Eur.

Dictionary of Power Plant Engineering: Conventional Steam Power Plants. F. Stattmann. French & Eur.

Dictionary of Power Plant Engineering: Nuclear Power Plants. F. Stattmann. French & Eur.

Dictionary of Production Engineering: German-English-French. International Institution for Production Engineering Research. Incl. Intl Pubns Serv.

Dictionary of Psychology & Psychiatry: English-German. Ed. by Roland Haas. C J Hogrefe.

Dictionary of Psychology & Psychiatry. Roland Haas. Hogrefe.

Dictionary of Psychology & Related Fields. Hugo G. Beigel. Ungar.

Dictionary of Psychology: English-German. Ed. by Alfred H. Berger. Ungar.

Dictionary of Pump Terms. Massada Pr.

Dictionary of Quantities & Units of Measurement. Drazil. Brandstetter.

Dictionary of Radio & Television Terms. (Pub. by Wiley Heyden). Wiley.

Dictionary of Reprography: Terms & Definitions. Ed. by Deutsches Kommitee Fur Reprographie. (Pub. by K G Saur). Gale.

Dictionary of Russian Technical & Scientific Abbreviations. H. Zalucki. Elsevier.

Dictionary of Science & Technology. Compiled by A. F. Dorian. Elsevier.

Dictionary of Science & Technology. Chambers. Brandstetter.

Dictionary of Sea Waves & Currents Terms. Massada Pr.

Dictionary of Sewage & Sanitary Installation Terms. Massada Pr.

Dictionary of Soil Mechanics. Ed. by A. Visser. Elsevier.

Dictionary of Soil Science & Soil Engineering Terms. Massada Pr.

Dictionary of Stock Market Terms in Four Languages. B. L. Thole & Theodor Gilissen. Shalom.

Dictionary of Strength of Materials. Massada Pr.

Dictionary of Surface-Active Agents, Cosmetics & Toiletries. Ed. by G. Cariere. Elsevier.

Dictionary of Surface Active Agents, Cosmetics & Toiletries. G. Carriere. Elsevier.

Dictionary of Technical Acoustics. L. Reichardt. Adler.

Dictionary of Technical Drawing. Massada Pr.

Dictionary of the Graphic Arts Industry. Ed. by W. Muller. Elsevier.

Dictionary of Tourism: German-English & English-German. Wolf Friedrich. Intl Pubns Serv.

Dictionary of Transport Terms & Phrases. Siegfried Heinze. Intl Pubns Serv.

Dictionary of Waste Disposal & Public Cleansing. Ed. by W. Kaupert. Elsevier.

Dictionary of Water & Sewage Engineering. F. Meinck & K. Mohle. Elsevier.

Dictionary of Welding. A. Kleiber. Adler.

Dictionary of Welding - Fachwoerterbuch der Schweisstechnik: German-English & English-German. Theo Roemer. Intl Pubns Serv.

Dictionary of Wood & Woodworking Practice. Herbert Bucksch. Intl Pubns Serv.

Dictionary of Wood & Woodworking Practice. Herbert Bucksch. Intl Pubns Serv.

Dictionnaire Agricole Allemand, Anglais, Francais, Espagnol, Russe. Gunther Haensch & Gisela Haberkamp. (Pub. by Maison Rust). French & Eur.

Dictionnaire Agricole Allemand-Anglais-Francais-Espagnol-Russe. Gunther Haensch. Maison Rustique.

Dictionnaire agricole Allemand, Anglais, Francais, Espanol, Russe. Gunther Haensch & Gisela Haberkamp. Maison Rustique.

Dictionnaire Allemand-Francais. Erich Weis & Heinrich Mattutat. French & Eur.

Dictionnaire Allemand-Francais. Larousse.

Dictionnaire Allemand-Francais. Erich Weis & Heinrich Mattutat. Bordas-Dunod.

Dictionnaire Allemand-Francais. Denis Eckel & Manfred Hofer. Garnier.

Dictionnaire Allemand-Francais. Rotteck. Garnier.

Dictionnaire Allemand-Francais. Siegfried P. Villain. Garnier-Flammarion.

Dictionnaire Allemand-Francais. Siefried P. Villain. Garnier-Flammarion.

Dictionnaire Allemand-Francais des Termes Relatifs a l'Electrorechnique, l'Electronique, et aux Applications Connexes. Henri Piraux. French & Eur.

Dictionnaire Allemand-Francais des Termes Relatifs a l'electrotechnique: L'electrotechnique & aux Applications Connexes. Henri Piraux. Eyrolles.

Dictionnaire Allemand-Francais et Francais-Allemand. Denis Eckel & Hofer Manfred. French & Eur.

Dictionnaire Allemand-Francais, Francais-Allemand. Ed. by Rotteck. French & Eur.

Dictionnaire Allemand-Francais pour les Travaux Publics: Le Batiement & l'equipement des Chantiers des Chantiers de Constuction. Hector Bucksch. Eyrolles.

Dictionnaire Bilingue Apollo Francais-Allemand. Jolivet A. Pinoche. Larousse.

Dictionnaire Bilingue Larousse, Francais-Alemand et Allemand-Francais. A. Pinloche & A. Jolivet. Larousse.

Dictionnaire Classique Francais-Allemand. Bertaux. Hachette.

Dictionnaire Commercial & Financier en Quatre Langues: Francais-Neerlandais-Anglais-Allemand. Josef V. Servotte. Erasme.

Dictionnaire de Chimie Allemand-Francais. Raymond Cornubert. French & Eur.

Dictionnaire de Deux Cent un Verbes Allemandes. Barron.

Dictionnaire de Droit Social Francais-Allemand. F. Frankl. French & Eur.

Dictionnaire de la Biologie. Gunther Haensch. BLV Verlag.

Dictionnaire de la Biologie--B.L.V. French & Eur.

Dictionnaire de la Technique Industrielle: Allemand-Francais. R. Ernst. Maison Dictionaire.

Dictionnaire de la Technologie des Corps Gras. Boris Solomon. Inst Corps Gras.

Dictionnaire de l'Industrie des matieres plastiques. E. Ferraris. Maison Dictionnaire.

Dictionnaire de poche du teletraitement des donnees. W. H. Carl. Maison Dictionnaire.
Dictionnaire de Poche Francais-Allemand. Berlitz.
Dictionnaire de Psychologie en Trois Langues: Anglais-Francais-Allemand. Hubert C. Duijker & Maria J. Van Rijswijk. Editest.
Dictionnaire de Psychologie en Trois Langues, Vol. 2. Hubert C. Duijker. French & Eur.
Dictionnaire de Psychologie en Trois Langues, 2: Francais-Allemand-Anglais. Hubert C. Duijker & Maria J. Van Rijswijk. Editest.
Dictionnaire de Psychologie en Trois Langues, 3: Allemand-Anglais-Francais. Hubert C. Duijker & Maria J. Van Rijswijk. Editest.
Dictionnaire de Psychologie en 3 Langues. Hubert C. Duijker & Maria Van Sijswijk. French & Eur.
Dictionnaire de Sylviculture: Francais-Allemand-Anglais-Espagnol-Italien. Alberto Bruttini. Lechevalier.
Dictionnaire des Arts du Spectacle. Cecile Giteau. Bordas-Dunod.
Dictionnaire des Arts du Spectacle: Theatre, Cinema, Cirque, Danse, Radio... Cecile Giteau. French & Eur.
Dictionnaire des Canalisations a Grande Distance: Anglais-Francais-Allemand. H. Bucksch & A. Altemeyer. French & Eur.
Dictionnaire des Canalisations: Francais-Allemand. Hector Bucksch. Eyrolles.
Dictionnaire des Locutions Francais-Allemand. Paul Werny & Alexandre Snyckers. Larousse FR.
Dictionnaire des Sciences de la Nature (Dictionary of the Natural Sciences) Edouard Ghaleb. Intl Pubns Serv.
Dictionnaire des Techniques Aeronautiques & Spatiales. Bordas.
Dictionnaire Des Techniques Aeronautiques et Spatiales. Ed. by Societe Nationale Industrielle Aerospatiale. Intl Pubns Serv.
Dictionnaire des Techniques Aeronautiques et Spatiales--Trilingue: Francais, Anglais, Allemand: 24,000 Entrees Dans Chaque Langue. French & Eur.
Dictionnaire des Termes Juridique en Quatre Langues: Francais, Neerlandais, Anglais, Allemand. E. Le Docte. French & Eur.
Dictionnaire des Termes Juridiques en Quatre Langues: Francais-Neerlandais-Anglais-Allemand. E. Le Docte. Vander Oyez.
Dictionnaire d'oto-rhino-laryngologie: Francais-Anglais-Espagnol-Allemand-Italien. Maloine.
Dictionnaire du Traitement de l'information: Francais-Allemand. Pioton.
Dictionnaire du Traitement de l'information: Francais-Allemand-Anglais. Carl Amkreutz. Carl Amkreutz.
Dictionnaire du traitement de l'informatique. Carl Amkreutz. Maison Dictionnaire.
Dictionnaire Duden-Larousse: Tout Allemand. Larousse.
Dictionnaire Economique & Financier. Yves Bernard et al. Seuil.
Dictionnaire Europa: Francais-Allemand. Larousse.
Dictionnaire Francais-Allemand. Jean Clediere et al. Larousse FR.
Dictionnaire Francais-Allemand. Erich Weis & Heinrich Mattutat. Bordas-Dunod.
Dictionnaire Francais-Allemand. Erich Weis & Heinrich Mattutat. Bordas-Dunod.
Dictionnaire Francais-Allemand-Anglais pour le Commerce Exterieur. Jean Ruhland. Ruhland.
Dictionnaire Francais-Allemand des Locutions. F. Dubois & P. Werny. French & Eur.
Dictionnaire Francais-Allemand, Deutsch-Franzosisch. A. Pinloche. French & Eur.
Dictionnaire Francais-Allemand et Allemand-Francais. Erich Weis & Heinrich Mattutat. French & Eur.

Dictionnaire Francais-Allemand pour le Travaux Publics le Batiment & l'equipement des Chantiers de Construction. Hector Bucksch. Eyrolles.
Dictionnaire Gemeaux Francais-Allemand. Hatier.
Dictionnaire Illustre de l'Automobile "Kluwer," en 6 Langues. C. Blok & W. Jezewski. French & Eur.
Dictionnaire International d'abreviations Scientifiques et Techniques. M. Azzaretti. Maison Dictionnaire.
Dictionnaire International d'abreviation Scientifiques et Techniques. M. Azzaretti. Maison Dictionnaire.
Dictionnaire International du Tourisme: Allemand-Anglais-Espagnol-Italien-Neerlandai. Acad Intl Tour.
Dictionnaire International Electrotechnique: Francais-Russe-Anglais-Allemand-Italien-Suedois-Hollandais-Polonais. Mir.
Dictionnaire International Electrotechnique: Francais-Russe-Anglais-Allemand-Espagnol-Suedois-Hollandais-Polonais. Mir.
Dictionnaire Juridique & Economique Francais-Allemand & Allemand-Francais. M. Doucet. Ed. by K. Fleck. Bruylant.
Dictionnaire Juridique & Economique Francias-Allemand & Allemand-Francais. M. Doucet. Ed. by K. Fleck. Bruylant.
Dictionnaire Juridique & Economique Francais-Allemand & Allemand Francais. M Doucet. Ed. by E. W. Klaus. Bruylant.
Dictionnaire Juridique & Economique, 1: Francais-Allemand. Litec.
Dictionnaire Juridique et Economique, 1: Francais-Allemand. Michel Douret. French & Eur.
Dictionnaire Juridique: Frances-Allemand. Thomas A. Quemner. Navarre.
Dictionnaire Laitier: Francais, Allemand, Anglais. Jacques Casalis. French & Eur.
Dictionnaire Laitier: Francais-Allemand-Anglais. Jacques Casalis. Litec.
Dictionnaire Larousse Bilingue de Poche: Francais-Allemand. Larousse FR.
Dictionnaire Larousse: Francais-Allemand. L. G. F.
Dictionnaire des termes juridiques en quatre langues: Francais-Neerlandais-Anglais-Allemand. E. LeDocte. Maison Dictionnaire.
Dictionnaire Lilliput Bilingue Francais-Allemand. Larousse FR.
Dictionnaire Medical. Emile Veillon & Albert Noble. Masson.
Dictionnaire moderne Larousse, francais-allemand et allemand-francais. P. Grappin. Larousse.
Dictionnaire Moderne Saturne: Francais-Allemand. P. Grappin. Larousse FR.
Dictionnaire Petrolier des Techniques de Diagraphie, Forage & Production: Russe-Francais-Anglais-Allemand. Sonia Ketchian. Technip.
Dictionnaire Petrolier des Techniques de Diagraphique, Forage et Production. Sonia Ketchian. French & Eur.
Dictionnaire Poucet Allemand-Francais. Ersillo Cardoso. Hatier.
Dictionnaire Poucet Francais-Allemand. Hatier.
Dictionnaire Pour l'Architecture, le Batiment et les Materiaux de Construction. French & Eur.
Dictionnaire Pour l'Architecture, le Batiment et les Materiaux de Construction. French & Eur.
Dictionnaire pour L'Architecture, le Batiment et les Meteiaux de Construction: Band I, Deutsch-Franzosisch. Bauverlag.
Dictionnaire pour l'Architecture, le Batiment et les Materiaux de Constrction: Band II, Franzosisch-Deutsch. Bauverlag.

Dictionnaire pour l'Architecture le Batiment et les Materiaux de Construction: Allemand-Francais. Bucksch. Maison Dictionnaire.
Dictionnaire pour l'architecture le Batiment et les Materiaux de Construction: Francais-Allemand. Bucksch. Maison Dictionnaire.
Dictionnaire Pour les Travaux Publics et l'Equipement des Chantiers de Construction. French & Eur.
Dictionnaire Pour les Travaux Publics et l'Equipement des Chantiers de Construction. French & Eur.
Dictionnaire Pratique Mercure: Francais-Allemand, Allemand-Francais. Ernst E. Lange-Koval & Kurt Wilhelm. French & Eur.
Dictionnaire Pratique Mercure Francais-Allemand. Ernst E. Lange-Koval & Kurt Wilhelm. Larousse.
Dictionnaire Redige en Caracteres Latins: Allemand-Francais. Felix Bertaux & Emile Lepointe. Hachette.
Dictionnaire Redige en Caracteres Latins: Francais-Allemand. Felix Bertaux & Emile Lepointe. Hachette.
Dictionnaire Technique de la Mecanisation Agricole. French & Eur.
Dictionnaire Technique de la Mecanisation Agricole: Francais-Anglais-Allemand-Espagnol-Italien. Centre Nat. Et. Machin Agricole.
Dictionnaire Technique de L'Automobile. George Zlatovski. Ed. by P. R. Russek. French & Eur.
Dictionnaire Technique du Bois, en Quatre Langues. G. Wallnig & H. Evered. French & Eur.
Dictionnaire Technique du Bois en Quatre Langues: Allemand-Russe-Anglais-Francais. Vander.
Dictionnaire Technique du Bois en 4 Langues. French & Eur.
Dictionnaire Technique du Bois: Texte en Allemand-Anglais-Francais-Russe. Eyrolles.
Dictionnaire Technique Illustre des Outlis Coupants: L'usinage des Metaux; Francais-Allemand-Anglais-Italien-Espagnol. Toni Heiler. Eyrolles.
Dictionnaire Technique Illustre Des Outils Coupants Pour L'usinage Des Metaux. Toni Heiler. French & Eur.
Dictionnaire Technologique Feutry: Mecanique-Metallurgie-Hydraulique. R. Mertz De Mertzenteld et al. Maison Dictionnaire.
Dictionnaire Technologique, 1: Anglais-Francais-Allemand. Michel Feutry. Maison Dictionnaire.
Dictionnaire Technologique, 1: Anglais-Francais-Allemand. Michel Feutry et al. Maison Dictionnaire.
Dictionnaire Trilingue. Jean Ruhland. Ruhland.
Dictionnaire trilingue du Droit des Affaires pour le Commerce & l'industrie: Allemand-Anglais-Francais & index. H. Becker. Maison Dictionnaire.
DIN Definitions: German-English with an English-German Vocabulary. Compiled by Henry G. Freeman. Heinman.
Dizionario assicurativo: Tedesco-francese-inglese-italiano. Centro St Assic.
Dizionario di elettronica: Tedesco-italiano. G. Fiandaca. Il Rostro.
Dizionario giuridico-economico: Vol. 1, Italiano-tedesco. Giuseppe Conte. Giuffre.
Dizionario giuridico-economico: Vol. 2, Tedesco-italiano. Giuseppe Conte. Giuffre.
Dizionario illustrato italiano-tedesco. Longanesi.
Dizionario illustrato tedesco-italiano. Longanesi.
Dizionario inglese-italiano-francese-tedesco. L. Gives et al. De Bono.
Dizionario inglese-italiano-francese-tedesco. L. Gives et al. De Bono.
Dizionario italiano-tedesco. Malipiero.
Dizionario italiano-tedesco. Mondadori.

Dizionario italiano-tedesco. Altenberg. Vallardi A.
Dizionario italiano-tedesco. Guido Cosciani. Paravia.
Dizionario italiano-tedesco e tedesco-italiano. Giovannelli. Signorelli C.
Dizionario italiano-tedesco e tedesco-italiano. A. Gullino Kuhn. Casanova F & C.
Dizionario italiano-tedesco e tedesco-italiano. Giovanni Ciardi Dupre & Angelica Escher. SEI.
Dizionario italiano-tedesco e tedesco-italiano. Lysle & Pontevideo. Casanova F & C.
Dizionario Italiano-Tedesco, Tedesco-Italian. G. A. Altenberg & V. Ubaldi. French & Eur.
Dizionario italiano-tedesco tedesco-italiano. Langenscheidt. Signorelli C.
Dizionario Medico Poliglotta. Veillon & Nobel. French & Eur.
Dizionario medico poliglotta: Inglese-tedesco-francese. Veillon & Nobel. Piccin.
Dizionario per l'industria delle materie plastiche: Definizioni italiane e termini corrispondenti in francese, inglese e tedesco. Enrico Ferraris & Istituto Italiano dei Plastici. SAPIL.
Dizionario pratico tedesco-italiano italiano-tedesco. Langenscheidt. Signorelli C.
Dizionario tascabile delle tecniche ambientale: Italiano, francese, inglese, tedesco. Maurizio Pasquali. SAPIL.
Dizionario Tecnico Italiano-Tedesco. Alice Meyer. Brandstetter.
Dizionario tecnico italiano-tedesco e tedesco-italiano. A. Meyer & S. Orlando. Hoepli.
Dizionario tecnico-scientifico: Italiano-tedesco. Paolo Carboni. Patron.
Dizionario tecnico-scientifico: Tedesco-italiano. Paolo Carboni. Patron.
Dizionario Tecnico Tedesco-Italiano. Giorgio Marolli & Orazio Guarnieri. Garzanti Edit.
Dizionario tecnico tedesco-italiano italiano-tedesco. Giorgio Marolli & Orazio Guarnieri. Garzanti Edit.
Dizionario Tecnico Tedesco-Italiano, Italiano-Tedesco Garzanti. M. Guarnieri & O. Guarnieri. French & eur.
Dizionario tedesco-italiano. Emilio Bidoli & Guido Cosciani. Paravia.
Dizionario tedesco-italiano. A. Lanzara. Forni.
Dizionario tedesco-italiano di biologia e medicina. Valentino Grandis & Mario Donati. Rosenberg & Sel.
Dizionario tedesco-italiano e italiano-tedesco. Malipiero.
Dizionario tedesco-italiano e italiano-tedesco. Sansoni.
Dizionario tedesco-italiano per le scienze chimiche e affini. Clara Giua Lollini & Michele Giua. Rosenberg & Sel.
Dizionario tedesco-italiano per le scienze mediche. E. Marcovecchio. Minerva Medica.
Dr. Gabler's die Sprache der Chefs. (Pub. by Betriebswirtschaftlicher Vlg.). French & Eur.
Dr. Gablers Wirtschafts - Lexikon. R. Sellien. (Pub. by Betriebswirtschaftlicher Vlg.). French & Eur.
Doktor Gabler's Wirtschafts-Lexikon. Ed. by R. Sellien & H. Sellien. Gabler.
Dreisprachiges Woerterbuch der Soziologie. (Pub. by A. Hain). French & Eur.
DTV Junior Lexikon. (Pub. by DTV/KNO). French & Eur.
DTV Junior Lexikon. Deutscher Taschenbuch Verlag.
DTV Woerterbuch der deutschen Sprache. Wahrig. Imported Bks.
DTV-Woerterbuch der deutschen Sprache. Ed. by G. Wahrig. M Rosenberg.
DTV Woerterbuch der Medizin. Herbert Von Schaldach. (Pub. by DTV Deutscher Taschenbuch Vlg.). French & Eur.

DTV Woerterbuch der Medizin.
Herbert Von Schaldach. (Pub. by
DTV Deutscher Taschenbuch Vlg.).
French & Eur.

DTV Woerterbuch der Medizin.
Herbert Von Schaldach. (Pub. by
DTV Deutscher Taschenbuch Vlg.).
French & Eur.

DTV Woerterbuch der Medizin.
Herbert Von Schaldach. Deutscher
Taschenbuch Verlag.

DTV Woerterbuch der Medizin.
Herbert Von Schaldach. Deutscher
Taschenbuch Verlag.

DTV Woerterbuch der Medizin.
Herbert Von Schaldach. Deutscher
Taschenbuch Verlag.

Duden-Das Grosse Woerterbuch der
Deutschen Sprache in 6 Baenden.
Biblio Inst.

Duden-Das Woerterbuch
Medizinischer Fachausdruecke.
Hermann Lichtenstern. Biblio Inst.

Duden Francais Bildworterbuch
Deutsch & Franzoesisch. Biblio
Inst.

Der Duden in 10 Banden Das
Standardwerk zur Deutschen
Sprache: Duden Band I, Die
Rechtschreibung der Deutschen
Sprache & der Fremdwoerter.
Biblio Inst.

Duden-Lexikon in Drei Banden.
Biblio Inst.

Duden-Lexikon in Drei Banden. Ed.
by Lexikonredaktion des
Bibliographischen Instituts. Biblio
Inst.

Duden-Rechnen & Mathematik. Ed.
by Fachredaktionen des
Bibliographischen Instituts. Biblio
Inst.

Duden-Stilwoerterbuch. R. Duden.
Adler.

Duden-Was Bedeutet Das? Kleines
Bedeutungswoerterbuch der
Deutschen Sprache. Harrap &
Dudenredaktion. Harrap.

Duden Woerterbuch Medizinischer
Fachausdruecke. Ed. by Karl-Heinz
Alheim. Thieme Verlag.

Duden-Woerterbuch Medizinischer
Fachausdrucke. Biblio Inst.

Duits-Neederland Woordenboek. Ed.
by Van Gelderen. French & Eur.

Duits voor Bouwkundigen-Saksaa
Rakentajille. H. Evered & G.
Wallnig. Bauverlag.

Dumonts Kleines Lexikon der
Phantastischen Malerei. Jorg
Krichbaum. DuMont Buchverlag.

DuMont's Kleines Sachworterbuch
der Druektechnik & Grafischen
Kunst. Heijo Klein. DuMont Buch.

DuMont's Kleines Sachworterbuch
der Drucktechnik & Grafischen
Kunst. Heijo Klein. DuMont
Buchverlag.

Dutch-English-French-German
Engineering Dictionary. Ten Bosch.
Heinman.

Easy Ways to Enlarge Your German
Vocabulary. Karl A. Schmidt.
Dover.

Economic Terminology German-
English. Renner et al. Adler.

Economisch Woorden Boek: Engels-
Frans-Duits-Nederlands. F. J. Jong.
French & Eur.

EDV-Abkurzungen. Rolf Kohler &
Ernst Mayr. Siemens AG.

EDV-Taschenlexikon: In
Zusammenarbeit Mit Guido Lobel.
Hans Schmid & Peter Von Muller.
Verlag Moderne Industrie.

Einfuehrung in die Benutzung der
Neufranzoesischen Woerterbucher.
Franz J. Hausmann. Niemeyer
Verlag.

Einfuehrung in die Deutsche
Wortbildungslehre. Werner Eckert.
Schmidt Verlag.

Einfuhrung in das Technische
Russisch Maschinenbau:
Lehrmaterial fuer den
Fremdsprachenunterricht. Siegfried
Uhlig. VEB Technik.

Electrical Machines Dictionary.
Heinrich Bezner. Brandstetter.

Electricity & Electronics Technical
Dictionary. Ed. by Peter-Klaus
Budig. Intl Pubns Serv.

Elektromaschinen-Woerterbuch.
Bezner. Brandstetter.

Elektrotechnik Elektronik. Peter K.
Budig. VEB Verlag Technik.

Elektrotechnik Elektronik. William
Athenstaedt. VEB Verlag Technik.

Elektrotechnik Elektronik Deutsch-
Englisch. Peter K. Budig. VEB
Technik.

Elektrotechnik Elektronik Russisch-
Deutsch. Helmut Gross. VEB
Technik.

Elements de Geologie En Six
Langues. E. Cailleux. French &
Eur.

Elseviers Automobile Dictionary. Ed.
by G. Schuurmans. Elsevier.

Elsevier's Banking Dictionary. J.
Ricci. Elsevier.

Elsevier's Dictionary of Automatic
Control. Ed. by W. Clason.
Elsevier.

Elsevier's Dictionary of Barley,
Malting, & Brewing. Bernard D.
Hartong. Elsevier.

Elsevier's Dictionary of Building
Tools & Materials. L. Y. Chaballe
& J. P. Vandenberghe. Elsevier.

Elsevier's Dictionary of Chemical
Engineering. W. Clason. Elsevier.

Elsevier's Dictionary of Cinema,
Sound & Music. W. E. Clason.
Elsevier.

Elsevier's Dictionary of Criminal
Science. J. A. Adler. Elsevier.

Elsevier's Dictionary of Electronics &
Waveguides. W. E. Clason.
Elsevier.

Elsevier's Dictionary of Financial
Terms. F. J. Thomson. Elsevier.

Elsevier's Dictionary of General
Physics. W. E. Clason. Elsevier.

Elsevier's Dictionary of High Vacuum
Science & Technology. Fritz W.
Weber. Elsevier.

Elsevier's Dictionary of Horticulture.
Ed. by Ministry of Agriculture &
Fisheries- Netherlands & J. Nijdam.
Elsevier.

Elsevier's Dictionary of
Hydrogeology. Hans-Olaf
Pfannkuch. Elsevier.

Elseviers Dictionary of Metal Cutting
Tools. Ed. by G. Schuurmang.
Elsevier.

Elsevier's Dictionary of Metallurgy &
Metal Working. W. E. Clason.
Elsevier.

Elsevier's Dictionary of Nuclear
Science & Technology. W. E.
Clason. Elsevier.

Elsevier's Dictionary of Particle
Technology. Ed. by K. Leschonski
& F. T. Carter. Elsevier.

Elsevier's Dictionary of Photography.
A. S. Craeybeckx. Elsevier.

Elsevier's Dictionary of Public
Health. Nick J. Deblock. Elsevier.

Elsevier's Dictionary of Rolling Mill
Terminology. Ed. by G. F. Herscu.
Elsevier.

Elsevier's Dictionary of Television, &
Video Recording. W. Clason.
Elsevier.

Elsevier's Dictionary of Tools &
Ironware. Ed. by Clason. Elsevier.

Elsevier's Electrotechnical
Dictionary. W. E. Clason. Elsevier.

Elsevier's Football Dictionary. H.
Sirages. Elsevier.

Elsevier's Medical Dictionary in Five
Languages. A. Sliosberg. Elsevier.

Elsevier's Multilingual Dictionary of
Insurance Technology. W. A.
Ruysch. Elsevier.

Elseviers Nautical Dictionary. Ed. by
P. Segditsas. Elsevier.

Elsevier's Nautical Dictionary in Six
Languages. Ed. by J. P.
Vandenberghe & L. Y. Chaballe.
Elsevier.

Elseviers Rubber Dictionary. Elsevier.

Elsevier's Telecommunication
Dictionary. W. E. Clason. Elsevier.

Elsevier's Wood Dictionary. Ed. by
W. Boerhave Beekman. Elsevier.

Enciclopedia simultanea de
correspondencia comercial en seis
idiomas. Distein.

Engels voor Bouwkundigen-Englantia
Rakentajille. G. Wallnig & H.
Evered. Bauverlag.

Englisch. Ed. by Heinz Messinger &
Werner Rudenberg. Langenscheidt.

Englisch. Incl. Langenscheidt.

Englisch. Incl. Langenscheidt.

Englisch-Deutsches, Deutsch-
Englisches Woerterbuch.
Wildhagen. Brandstetter.

Englisch-Deutsches, Deutsch-
Englisches Woerterbuch.
Wildhagen. Brandstetter.

Englisch-Deutsches Deutsch-
Englisches Woerterbuch: Band II,
Deutsch-Englisch. Heraucourt
Wildhagen. Brandstetter.

Englisch-Deutsches Deutsch-
Englisches Woerterbuch: Band I,
Englisch-Deutsch. Heraucourt
Wildhagen. Brandstetter.

Englisch-Deutsches Glossarium. Hans
E. Zahn. (Pub. by Fritz Knapp
Verlag) French & Eur.

Englisch fuer Baufachleute: Band 1.
G. Wallnig & H. Evered. Bauverlag.

Englisch fuer die Seewirtschaft
Aufbaukurs Stufe IIa.
Wissenschaftliche.

Englisch fur Baufachleute: Band 2. G.
Wallnig & H. Evered. Bauverlag.

Englisch in Wirtschaft und Handel.
Dieter Hamblock. Girardet.

Englische & Franzoesisch
Fachsprache im Auslandsbau. K.
Lange et al. Bauverlag.

Englische in Wirtschaft und Handel.
Dieter Hamblock. Girardet.

Englische Rechtssprache: Mustertexte
& Fachausdruecke unter
Einbeziehung von Amerikanismen.
G. Glass. Bauverlag.

Englisches Handelsvokabularium
Nach Sachgebieten. Grossmann.
(Pub. by Th. Grossmann). French &
Eur.

Englisches Wirtschaftsalphabet. H.
Freyd-Wadham. (Pub. by Th.
Grossmann). French & Eur.

English-French-German Glossary for
Psychiatry, Child Psychiatry &
Abnormal Psychology. Lise Moor.
Intl Pubns Serv.

English Fuer Elektrotechniker &
Elektroniker. Wanke & Havlicek.
Brandstetter.

English-German Chemical
Terminology: An Introduction to
Chemistry in English & German. H.
Fromherz & A. King. (Pub. by Vlg.
Chemie). French & Eur.

English-German Chemical
Terminology: An Introduction to
Chemistry in English & German.
Hans Fromherz & Alexander King.
Verlag Chemie.

English-German Chemical
Terminology: An Introduction to
Chemistry in English & German. H.
Fromherz & A. King. Verlag
Chemie.

English-German Dictionary.
Saphrograph.

English-German Dictionary. K.
Briese. (Pub. by Collet's). State
Mutual Bk.

English-German Dictionary of
Chemistry & Chemical Technology.
Ed. by Technishe Universitaet,
Dresden. Intl Pubns Serv.

English-German Dictionary of
Idioms. K. Engeroff & C.
Lovelace-Kaeufer. Adler.

English-German, German-English
Dictionary. Wildhagen &
Hereaucourt. M Rosenberg.

English-German, German, English
Solid State Physics & Electronics
Dictionary. G. Birdmann. (Pub. by
Collet's). State Mutual Bk.

English-German, German-English
Welding Engineering Dictionary. A.
Kleiber. (Pub. by Collets). State
Mutual Bk.

English-German Glossary of Financial
& Economic Terms. Hans E. Zahn.
Intl Pubns Serv.

Enzyklopadisches Lexikon Fur des
Geld, Bank und Borsen Wesen. E.
Achterberg & K. Lanz. (Pub. by
Fritz Knapp Verlag). French & Eur.

Epuletgepeszet. Ivan Fekete.
Akademiai Kiado.

Erdoel Lexicon. Karlheinz Kramer.
(Pub. by Heuthig). French & Eur.

Erdoelverarbeitung-Petrolchemie.
Leipnitz. Brandstetter.

Erdolverarbeitung und Petrolchemie:
A Dictionary of Crude Oil
Processing & Petroleum Chemistry
English-German-French-Russian.
Walter Leipnitz. Intl Learn Syst.

Ergonomics Glossary: Terms
Commonly Used in Ergonomics.
Ed. by European Coal & Steel
Community, Luxembourg. Intl
Pubns Serv.

Ethnologisches Woerterbuch. A.
Heymer. (Pub. by P. Parey). French
& Eur.

Ethnologisches Woerterbuch. A.
Heymer. Parey.

The Ethological Dictionary: In
English, French & German. Armin
Heymer. (Garland STPM Pr).
Garland Pub.

Etymologisch Geographisches
Lexikon. Jakob Egli. (Pub. by
Saendig-Walluf). French & Eur.

Etymologisches Woertenbuch der
Botanischen Pflanzennamen.
Helmut Genaust. (Pub. by
Birkhaeuser). French & Eur.

Etymologisches Woerterbuch der
Europaeischen Woerter
Orientalischen Ursprungs. Karl
Lokotsch. (Pub. by Carl Winter).
French & Eur.

Etymologisches Woerterbuch der
Europaeischen Woerter
Orientalischen Ursprungs. Karl
Lokotsch. Winter Univ.

Etymologisches Woerterbuch der
Franzoesischen Sprache. Ernst
Gamillscheg. (Pub. by Carl Winter).
French & Eur.

Etymologisches Woerterbuch der
Franzoesischen Sprache. Ernst
Gamillscheg. Winter Univ.

Euro Dictionary of Economics &
Business. Hans E. Zahn. Rothman.

Euro-Wirtschafts Worterlrich in Drei
Sprachen. Hans E. Zahn. (Pub. by
Fritz Knapp Verlag). French & Eur.

Evangelisches Staatslexikon. H.
Kunst. (Pub. by Kreuz Vlg). French
& Eur.

Evangelisches Staatslexikon. H.
Kunst. Kreuz.

Fach Lexikon ABC Automatisierung.
(Pub. by Verlag Harri Deutsch).
French & Eur.

Fachbegriffe der
Versicherungwirtschaft. Manfred
Lipperheide et al. Deutsch Spark.

Fachenglisch Fur Technik und
Industrie. Henry G. Freeman. (Pub.
by Carl Heymanns Verlag KG).
French & Eur.

Fachlexikon ABC Biologie. (Pub. by
Harri Deutsch). French & Eur.

Fachlexikon ABC Chemie. (Pub. by
Verlag Harri Deutsch). French &
Eur.

Fachlexikon ABC Mathematik. (Pub.
by Verlag Harri Deutsch). French
& Eur.

Fachlexikon ABC Mathematik. (Pub.
by Harri Deutsch). French & Eur.

Fachlexikon ABC Physik. (Pub. by
Verlag Harri Deutsch). French &
Eur.

Fachlexikon ABC Technik und
Naturwissenschaft. French & Eur.

Fachwoerter des Oeffentlichen
Verwaltungsdienstes Aegyptens in
den Griechischen Papyrusurkunden
der Ptolemaeisch-Romischen Zeit.
Friedrich Preisigke. Olms Verlag.

Fachwoerterbuch der
Datenverarbeitung. Alfred
Wittman. Oldenbourg Verlag.

Fachwoerterbuch der Luftfahrt. A.
Dorian & J. Osenton. (Pub. by R.
Oldenbourg). French & Eur.

Fachwoerterbuch der Luftfahrt. J.
Osenton. Oldenbourg Verlag.

Fachwoerterbuch des
Nachrichtenwese. H. Pooch.
Schiele & Schon.

Fachwoerterbuch des
Nachrichtenwesens. H. Pooch.
(Pub. by Fachvlg. Schiele &
Schoen). French & Eur.

Fachwoerterbuch des
Transportwesens. S. Heinze. (Pub.
by Brandstetter). French & Eur.

Fachwoerterbuch des
Transportwesens. S. Heinze.
Brandstetter.

Fachwoerterbuch des
Versicherungswesen. Heinze. (Pub.
by Brandstetter). French & Eur.

Fachwoerterbuch des
Versicherungswesen. S. Heinze.
(Pub. by Brandstetter). French &
Eur.

Fachwoerterbuch des Versicherungswesen. Heinze. Brandstetter.

Fachwoerterbuch des Vesicherungswesen. S. Heinze. Brandstetter.

Fachwoerterbuch Elektrotechnik, Elektronik. Peter K. Budig. (Pub. by Huethig). French & Eur.

Fachwoerterbuch fuer Batterien & Energie-Direktumwandlung. Bogenschuetz. Brandstetter.

Fachwoerterbuch fuer Batterien und Energie-Direktumwandlung. A. Bogenschuetz. Brandstetter.

Fachwoerterbuch fuer der Metalloberflaechenveredelung. H. Dettner. Siemens AG.

Fachwoerterbuch Fuer die Glasindustriel. E. Hoffmann. (Pub. by Springer). French & Eur.

Fachwoerterbuch fuer die Glasindustriel. E. Hoffman. Springer-Verlag.

Fachwoerterbuch fuer Wirtschaft, Handel & Finanzen. Rudolf Thomik. Heymanns Verlag.

Fachwoerterbuch Fur Recht und Wirtschaft. Gunther Parsenow. (Pub. by Carl Heymanns Verlag KG). French & Eur.

Fachwoerterbuch Fur Wirtschaft, Handel und Finanzen. Rudolf Thomik. (Pub. by Carl Heymanns Verlag KG). French & Eur.

Fachwoerterbuch Kraftfahrtechnik. Bosch. (Pub. by VDI Verlag GMBH). French & Eur.

Fachwoerterbuch Kraftfahrtechnik. Bosch. (Pub. by VDI Verlag GMBH). French & Eur.

Fachwoerterbuch Optik & Optischer Geraetebau: Deutsch-Englisch. Werner Bindmann. W Dausien.

Fachwoerterbuch Optik & Optischer Geraetebau: Englisch-Deutsch. Werner Bindmann. W Dausien.

Fachwoerterbuch Optik und Optischer Geraetebau. W. Bindmann. (Pub. by Dausien). French & Eur.

Fachwoerterbuch Spanende Werkzeugmaschinen. Henry G. Freeman. (Pub. by Verlag W. Gerardet). French & Eur.

Fachwoerterbuch Spanende Werkzeugmaschinen. Henry G. Freeman. Girardet.

Fachworter der Elektronik. Georg I. Franz. Franzis Verlag.

Fachworterbuch der Brauerei & Abfullpraxis. Tilman Schmitt. Carl KG.

Fachworterbuch Fur Recht und Verwaltung. Crescencio Antolinez. (Pub. by Carl Heymanns Verlag KG). French & Eur.

Fachworterbuch Textil. Derrick O. Michelson. (Pub. by Deutscher Fachuerlag). French & Eur.

Fachworterbuch Textil. Sarina Schock & Erika Gebert. (Pub. by Deutscher Fachverlag). French & Eur.

Fachwortschatz Mathematik. VEB Verlag Enzyklopadie.

Das Farbige Duden Schuelerlexikon. Adler Bks.

Fertigungsmesstechnik. Peter D. Hoffmann. VEB Verlag Technik.

Fertigungsmesstechnik-Russischer-Deutsch: Deutsch-Russicherr. Peter Hoffman. VEB Verlag Technik.

Festkorperelektronik. Helmut Muchow. VEB Technik.

Filmgyartas es Filmtechnika. Gabor Pozsonyi. Akademiai Kiado.

Finnish-German-Finnish Dictionary (Suomi-Saksa-Suomi) L. Hirvensalo. French & Eur.

Finnish-German Great Dictionary. P. Katara et al. French & Eur.

The First Thousand Words in German. Amery et al. Adler Bks.

Fitopatologicheskii Slovar Spravochnik. G. A. Diakova. (Pub. by Nauka). Four Continent.

Five Hundred & One German Verbs: Written in Japanese. Strutz. Barron.

Five Thousand German Words. S&S.

Foundry Dictionary: German-English & English-German. Intl Pubns Serv.

Four Language Culinary Dictionary: French, Hungarian, English, German. Saphrograph.

Four-Language Technical Dictionary of Chromatography: English, German, French, Russian. H. Angele. Pergamon.

Four Languages Dictionary of Geological Terms. French & Eur.

Franzoesisch. Incl. Langenscheidt.

Franzoesisch-Deutsches-Deutsch-Franzoesisches Woerterbuch: Band II, Deutsch-Franzoesisch. Lepointe Bertraux. Brandstetter.

Franzoesisch-Deutsches Glossarium. F. Roepke. (Pub. by Fritz Knapp Verlag). French & Eur.

Franzoesische Fachausdruecke im Bankgeschaeft: Franzoesisch-Deutsch, Deutsch-Franzoesisch. Hans A. Klaus. Haupt Verlag.

Franzoesische und Deutsche Chemische Fachuasdruecke. H. Fromherz & A. King. Verlag Chemie.

Franzoesisch. Incl. Langenscheidt.

Franzoesisch. Incl. Langenscheidt.

Franzoesisch-Deutsch, Deutsch-Franzosisch. Langenscheidt.

Franzosisch-Deutsches, Deutsch-Franzosisches Woerterbuch. Pierre Bertaux. (Pub. by Brandstetter). French & Eur.

Franzosisch-Deutsches, Deutsch-Franzosisches Woerterbuch. Pierre Bertaux. Brandstetter.

Franzosisch-Deutsches, Deutsch-Franzosisches Woerterbuch. Pierre Bertaux. Brandstetter.

Franzosisch-Deutsches-Deutsch-Franzosisches Woerterbuch: Band I, Franzoesisch-Deutsch. Lepointe Bertraux. Brandstetter.

Fremdwoerter Lexikon. Wahrig-Gerhard. C Bertelsmann.

Fremdwoerterbuch: Herkunft & Bedeutung der Fremdwoerter. Gunther Drosdowski. Biblio Inst.

French-English Chemical Terminology: An Introduction to Chemistry in French & English. H. Fromherz & A. King. (Pub. by Vlg. Chemie). French & Eur.

French-English Chemical Terminology: An Introduction to Chemistry in French & English. H. Fromherz & A. King. Verlag Chemie.

French-German Chemical Terminology: An Introduction to Chemistry in French & German. Hans Fromherz & Alexander King. Verlag Chemie.

Fruehneuhochdeutsches Glossar. Alfred Goetze. De Gruyter.

Gablers Wirtschaftslexikon. Gabler.

Geillustrrerd Woordenboek Voor de Autombieltechniek en Zes Talen. C. Block et al. French & Eur.

Gem Language Dictionaries: French-German & German-French. S&S.

Gem Language Dictionaries: German-English & English-German. S&S.

Genetik Erblicher Syndrome & Missbildungen. Regine Witkowski. Fischer Verlag.

Geobotanic Dictionary. O. S. Grebenshchikov. Lubrecht & Cramer.

Die Geographie: Ein Lexikon der Gesamten Schul-Erdkunde. Adolf Hanle. Biblio Inst.

Geologisches Woerterbuch. H. Murawski. Deutscher Taschenbuch Verlag.

Geologisches Woerterbuch. H. Murawski. Deutscher Taschenbuch Verlag.

Geowissenschaften. Schweizerbart.

Geowissenschaften Deutsch-Englisch. Adolf Watznauer. VEB Technik.

Geowissenschaften Englisch-Deutsch. Adolf Watznauer. VEB Technik.

A German & English Glossary of Geographical Terms. Eric Fischer & Francis E. Elliott. Greenwood.

German-Chinese Dictionary. Hellmut Wilhelm. Ayer Co.

German Dictionary. Newnes Bks.

German Dictionary. Pan Amer Pub.

German-English & English-German Dictionary. Dennison.

German-English Dictionary. Saphrograph.

German-English Dictionary. G. Wahrig. (Pub. by Collet's). State Mutual Bk.

German-English Dictionary: Art History-Archaeology. M. Apelt. Heinman.

German-English Dictionary: Art History, Archaelogy. M. L. Apelt. M Rosenberg.

German-English Dictionary for Chemists. A. M. Patterson. (Pub. by Wiley-Interscience). Wiley.

German-English Dictionary of Chemistry & Chemical Technology-Chemie und Chemische Technik: Deutsch-Englisch. Ed. by Technische Universitat Dresden. Intl Pubns Serv.

German-English Dictionary of Idioms. Ronald J. Taylor & W. Gottschalk. Adler.

German-English Dictionary of International Transport. G. Bein. (Pub. by Collet's). State Mutual Bk.

A German-English Dictionary of Technical, Scientific & General Terms. A. Webel. Routledge & Kegan.

German-English, English-German: A Dictionary of Professional Terminology of Speech Pathology & Audiology. Peter B. Mueller. C C Thomas.

German-English, English-German Astronautics Dictionary. Charles J. Hyman. (Consultants). Plenum Pub.

German-English, English-German Dictionary. Ed. by Ottenheimer. (BN). B&N NY.

German-English, English-German Dictionary. Schoffler-Weiss. M Rosenberg.

German-English, English-German Dictionary of Industrial Technics. R. Ernst. Heinman.

German-English, English-German Dictionary: Woerterbuch Deutsch-Englisch, Englisch-Deutsch. Editions Berlitz. (Pub. by Berlitz). Macmillan.

German-English, English-German Electronics Dictionary. Charles J. Hyman. (Consultants). Plenum Pub.

German-English, English-German Gem Dictionary. Ed. by J. M. Clark. Collins Pubs.

German-English, English-German Mathematical Dictionary. E. B. Klaften. Heinman.

German-English, English-German Medical Dictionary. D. W. Unseld. Heinman.

German-English, English-German Patent Terminological Dictionary. E. B. Klaften & F. C. Allison. Heinman.

German-English, English-German Technical Pocket Dictionary. K. Breuer. Heinman.

German-English-German. Macmillan.

German-English Glossary of Plastics Machinery Terms. Manfred S. Welling. (Pub. by Hanser International). Macmillan.

German-English Science Dictionary. Louis DeVries & Leon Jacolev. (P&RB). McGraw.

German-English Science Dictionary. Louis De Vries. McGraw.

German-English Science Dictionary. Louis De Vries & Leon Jacolev. McGraw.

German-English Science Dictionary. louis De Vries & Leon Jacolev. McGraw.

German-English Technical & Engineering Dictionary. Louis DeVries. (P&RB). McGraw.

German-English Technical & Engineering Dictionary. Louis De Vries & Theo M. Hermann. McGraw.

German for Building Specialists, (L'allemand Dans le Batiment, el Aleman En la Construccion) G. Wallnig & H. Evered. (Pub. by Bauverlag). French & Eur.

German for Building Specialists: L'Allemand dans le Batiment, el Aleman en la construccion. G. Wallnig & H. Evered. Bauverlag.

German for Business Studies. F. Kershaw & S. Russon. French & Eur.

German-Norwegian Dictionary. Haukoy & Zickfeldt. Kunnskapsforlaget.

German-Norwegian Dictionary of Technical Terms. D. Strom & J. A. Strom. Kunnskapsforlaget.

German Root Lexicon. Howard H. Keller. U of Miami Pr.

German-Russian Dictionary. Rahmanoba. French & Eur.

German-Serbocroatian Electrotechnical Dictionary. N. S. Arsenijevic. French & Eur.

German-Slovene Dictionary. F. Tomsic. French & Eur.

German-Swedish-German Dictionary. French & Eur.

A German Word Family Dictionary: Together with English Equivalents. Howard H. Keller. U of Cal Pr.

Die Geschichte: Ein Sachlexikon fuer die Schule. Wilfried Forstmann et al. Biblio Inst.

Gesellschaft & Staat: Lexikon der Politik. Hanno Dreschler et al. Signal-Verlag.

Der Gesundheits-Brockhaus. F A Brockhaus.

Getriebe-Woerterbuch. H. Bucksch. Bauverlag.

Giesserei - Fachwoerterbuch. E. Brunhuber. (Pub. by Fachverlag, Schiele & Schon). French & Eur.

Giesserei - Lexikon 1978. E. Brunhuber. (Pub. by Fachverlag, Schiele & Schon). French & Eur.

Giesserei-Fachwoerterbuch. E. Brunhuber. Schiele & Schon.

Giesserei-Fachworterbuch. Ernst Brunhuber. Schiele & Schon.

Giesserei-Lexikon 1978. E. Brunhuber. Schiele & Schon.

Gips - Woerterbuch. K. Volkart. (Pub. by Bauverlag). French & Eur.

Gips-Woerterbuch. K. H. Volkart. Bauverlag.

Gips-Woerterbuch. K. Volkart. Bauverlag.

Global Woerterbuch: English-German, German-English. Pons. M Rosenberg.

Glosar der Wichtigsten Saugetiere Chinas. Alfred Hoffman. Harrassowitz.

Glossaire d'organes de Transmission, 1: Les Engrenages Allemand-Espagnol-Francais-Anglais-Italien-Neerlandais-Suedois-Finnois. Maison Dictionnaire.

Glossaire Europeen de Terminologie Juridque et Administrative. French & Eur.

Glossaire Europeen de Terminologie Juridique et Administrative: Amenagement du Territoire. French & Eur.

Glossaire Europeen de Terminologie Juridique et Administrative: Budget. French & Eur.

Glossaire Europeen de Terminologie Juridique et Administrative. Budgeting & Auditing. German-Italian. French & Eur.

Glossaire Europeen de Terminologie Juridique et Administrative: Civil Service Organizations. French & Eur.

Glossaire Europeen de Terminologie Juridique et Administrative: Driot Administratif. French & Eur.

Glossaire Europeen de Terminologie Juridique et Administrative: Droits D'Etablissement. French & Eur.

Glossaire Europeen de Terminologie Juridique et Administrative: Droit du Mariage. French & Eur.

Glossaire Europeen de Terminologie Juridique et Administrative: Driot de al Fonction Publique. French & Eur.

Glossaire Europeen de Terminologie Juridiqe et Administrative: Droits des Collectivites Locales. French & Eur.

Glossaire Europeen de Terminologie Juridique et Administrative: Eductions et Enseignment. French & Eur.

Glossaire Europeen de Terminologie Juridique et Administrative: Environment Policy Protection & Management of the Environment. French & Eur.

Glossaire Europeen de Terminologie Juridique et Administrative: Jeunesse. French & Eur.

Glossaire Europeen de Terminologie Juridique et Administrative: Local Government. French & Eur.

Glossaire Europeen de Terminologie Jurdique et Administrative. Motor, Insurance, German-Italian. French & Eur.

Glossaire Europeen de Terminologie Juridique et Administrative: Marches Publics. French & Eur.

Glossaire Europeen de Terminologie Juridique et Administrative. Office Terminology Procedure. German-Italina. French & Eur.

Glossaire Europeen de Terminologie Juridique et Administrative: Renumeration. French & Eur.

Glossaire Europeen de Terminologie Juridique et Administrative: Terminologie Administrative et Secretariat. French & Eur.

Glossaire Europeen de Terminologie Juridique et Administrative: Terminologie de Reunions. French & Eur.

Glossaire Europeen en Quatre Langues: Francais-Italien-Allemand-Anglais. L. G. D. J.

Glossar & Erlaeuterungen zur Grammatik Deutsch-Englisch. M Rosenberg.

Glossar der Heute Chinesischen Vogelnamen. Alfred Hoffmann. Harrassowitz.

Glossar der Jugendarbeit: Deutsch Jugend & Ihr Soziales Umfeld. Deutsch-Franz Jugendwerk. H Luchterhand.

Glossar Deutsch-Englisch. M Rosenberg.

Glossar zur Fruehmittelalterlichen Geschichte im Oestlichen Europa. Norbert Otto & Dieter Wojtecki. Buch Vertrieb.

Glossar zur Fruehmittelalterlichen Geschichte im Oestlichen Europa: Lfg 2, Quellensiglenverzeichnis, Aba-Alania. Buch Vertrieb.

Glossar zur Fruehmittelalterlichen Geschichte im Oestlichen Europa: Lfg 3, Alanorum Montes-Antes. Buch Vertrieb.

Glossar zur Fruehmittelalterlichen Geschichte im Oestlichen Europa: Lfg 5, Atto-Avari. Buch Vertrieb.

Glossar zur Fruehmittelalterlichen Geschichte im Oestlichen Europa: Lfg 6, Avari (Arabes)-Baioaria. Buch Vertrieb.

Glossar zur Fruehmittelalterlichen Geschichte im Oestlichen Europa: Lfg 7, Baioariae Marcha-Behin Redaktion. Norbert Otto & Dieter Wojtecki. Buch Vertrieb.

Glossar zur Fruehmittelalterlichen Geschichte im Oestlichen Europa: Lfg 1, Einleitung, Abkuerzungen & Literatursiglenverzeichnis. Buch Vertrieb.

Glossario Luso-Asiatico. Sebastiao R. Dalgado. (Pub. by Helmut Buske Verlag Hamburg). Benjamins North Am.

Glossarium Amorum: Lfg 1, Schutzwaffen. Ed. by Hugo Schneider et al. Verlag der Buchhaendler-Vereinigung GmbH.

Glossarium Armorum: Bd 6 Texthefte in Deutsch, Englisch, Franzoesisch, Italienisch, Daenisch, Tschechisch. Ed. by Ortwin Gamber et al. Verlag der Buchhaendler-Vereinigung GmbH.

Glossarium Artis: Deutsch-Franzoesisches Woerterbuch zur Kunst. Ed. by Rudolf Huber & Renate Rieth. Max Niemeyer.

Glossarium Artis: Fasz 1, Burgen & Feste Plaetze. Ed. by Rudolf Huber & Renate Rieth. Max Niemeyer.

Glossarium Artis: Fasz 2, Liturgische Geraete-Objets Liturgiques. Ed. by Rudolf Huber & Renate Rieth. Max Niemeyer.

Glossarium Artis: Fasz 3, Bogen & Arkaden-Arcs et Arcades. Ed. by Rudolf Huber & Renate Rieth. Max Niemeyer.

Glossarium Artis: Fasz 4, Paramente & Buecher der Christlichen Kirchen. Ed. by Rudolf Huber & Renate Rieth. Max Niemeyer.

Glossarium Artis: Fasz 6, Gewoelbe & Kuppeln-Voutes et Coupoles. Ed. by Rudolf Huber & Renate Rieth. Niemeyer.

Glossary of Economics. F. Clifford Vaughn. Elsevier.

Glossary of English & German Management Terms. James Coveney. Longman.

Glossary of Fiber Optics Terms. Info Gatekeepers.

Glossary of Genetics. Francoise Biass-Ducroux. Elsevier.

Glossary of German & English Management Terms. James Coveny & Christina Degens. Longman.

Glossary of German & English Management Terms. Imported Bks.

Glossary of Mining Geology. G. Amstutz. (Pub. by F. Enke). French & Eur.

Glossary of Mining Geology. G. C. Amstutz et al. Ed. by F. Esser & Won C. Park. Enke.

Glossary of Mining Geology. G. Amstutz. Enke.

Glossary of Neurotraumatology. Ed. by E. S. Gurdjian et al. Springer-Verlag.

Glossary of Physiological Terms. (Pub. by Collets). State Mutual Bk.

Glossary of Populations & Housing. G. Logie. Elsevier.

Glossary of Soil Micromorphology. Ed. by A. Jongerius & G. K. Rutherford. Pudoc.

Glossary of Technical Terms for Market Researchers: English-German-Spanish-French-Italian-Dutch. European Society for Opinion & Marketing Research. Intl Pubns Serv.

Glossary of Terms in Heat Transfer, Fluid Flow & Related Topics. Ed. by William Begell. Hemisphere Pub.

Glossary of the Theatre. K. R. Band-Kuzmany. Elsevier.

Glossary on Educational Technology. Saur Verlag.

Graafinen Sanakirja. Soderstrom.

Grammatiken und Woerterbuecher des Schweizer Deutschen. Albert Weber. (Pub. by Hans Rohr). French & Eur.

Grammatisches Worterbuch der Gebrauchlichsten Spanischer Verben. Ziegler. (Pub. by Fachverlag Th. Grossman). French & Eur.

Griechiesches Etymologisches Woerterbuch. Hjalmar Frisk. Winter Univ.

Griechisch-Deutsches Taschenwoerterbuch zum Neuen Testament. Erwin Preuschen. De Gruyter.

Griechisch-Deutsches Woerterbuch zu den Schriften des Neuen Testaments und der uebrigen urchristlichen Literatur. Walter Bauer. De Gruyter.

Griechisches Etymologiches Woerterbuch. Hjalmar Frisk. Winter Univ.

Griechisches Etymologisches Woerterbuch. Hjalmar Frisk. Winter Univ.

Griechisches Etymologisches Woerterbuch. Hjalmar Frisk. (Pub. by Carl Winter). French & Eur.

Griechisches Etymologisches Woerterbuch. Hjalmar Frisk. (Pub. by Carl Winter). French & Eur.

Griechisches Etymologisches Woerterbuch. Hjalmar Frisk. (Pub. by Carl Winter). French & Eur.

Griechishes Etymologishes Woerterbuch. Hjalmar Frisk. Winter Univ.

Grobworterbuch Polnisch-Deutsch. J. Piprek & J. Ippoldt. French & Eur.

Der Grosse Brockhaus. (Pub. by Brockhaus). French & Eur.

Der Grosse Brockhaus. Pergamon.

Der Grosse Brockhaus. F A Brockhaus.

Der Grosse Brockhaus: Band 14, Ergaenzungen A-Z. F A Brockhaus.

Der Grosse Brockhaus: Band 15. F A Brockhaus.

Der Grosse Brockhaus: Band 15-20. F A Brockhaus.

Der Grosse Duden. Bibl Inst Leipzig.

Das Grosse Duden-Schulerlexikon: Ein Nachschlagewerk fuer Jeden Schueler. Gisela Preuss. Biblio Inst.

Das Grosse Lexikon der Fischwaid. Arnold Bacmeister. (Pub. by Jfland). French & Eur.

Der Grosse Muret-Sanders: Teil I, Englisch-Deutsch. Otto Springer. Langenscheidt.

Der Grosse Muret-Sanders: Teil II, Deutsch-Englisch. Otto Springer. Langenscheidt.

Der Grosse Ravensburger Werkkunstbuch. Jutta Lammar. Maier Verlag.

Das Grosse Woerterbuch der Deutschen Sprache. M Rosenberg.

Das Grosse Woerterbuch der Italienischen & Deutschen Sprache: Band I, Italienisch-Deutsch. Sansoni. Brandstetter.

Das Grosse Woerterbuch der Italienischen & Deutschen Sprache: Band II, Deutsch-Italienisch. Sansoni. Brandstetter.

Grosses Abkuerzungsbuch. H. Koblischke. Bibl Inst Leipzig.

Grosses Fremdwoerterbuch. Bibl Inst Leipzig.

Grosses Schulwoerterbuch Englisch-German. M Rosenberg.

Grosses Woerterbuck der Deutschen Aussprache. Ed. by U. Stoetzer. Bibl Inst Leipzig.

Grosswoerterbuch der Englischen & Deutschen Sprache. M Rosenberg.

Grundbegriffe der Marxistischen Politischen Oekonomie des Kapitalismus. Friedrich Haffner. Colloquium Verlag.

Grundbegriffe der Marxistischen Theorie. Joachim Bischoff. VSA Verlag.

Grundwortschatz: Deutsch Essential German-Allemand. M Rosenberg.

Grundwortschatz wirtschaftswissenshcaftlicher Begriffe: Deutsch- Englisch, Englisch-Deutsch. U. P. Ritter & K. G. Zinn. M Rosenberg.

Gypsum & Plaster Dictionary. K. H. Volkart. (Pub. by Bauverlag). French & Eur.

Gypsum & Plaster Dictionary. K. H. Volkart. Intl Pubns Serv.

Gypsum & Plaster Dictionary. K. H. Volkart. Bauverlag.

Hamlyn German Dictionary: German-English, English-German. Compiled by Laurence Urdang Associates, Ltd. Hamlyn-Amer.

Hamlyn German-English Dictionary. Larousse.

Handbuch der Namensverfahren in der Chemischen Technik. Fritz Rosendahl. Vulkan Verlag.

Handelskorrenpondenz in Vier Sprachen. F. Berset. M Rosenberg.

Handlexikon der magischen Kunste. Hans Biedermann. Droemersche Knaur.

Handlexikon der Schulpaedogogik. Karl Aschersleben. Kohlhammer.

Handlexikon fuer Handel & Absatz. Bernard Falk & Jakob Wolf. Verlag Moderne Industrie.

Handlexikon zur Erziehungswissenschaft. Ed. by Leo Roth. Ehrenwirth.

Handlexikon Zur Politikwissenschaft. Goerlitz. (Pub. by Rowohlt). French & Eur.

Handlexikon zur Politikwissenschaft. Goerlitz. Rowohlt.

Handwoerterbuch der Finanzwirtschaft. Ed. by Hans E. Bueschgen. Poeschel.

Handwoerterbuch der Schulpaedagogik. Ed. by Werner S. Niklis. Klinkhardt.

Handwoerterbuch der Volkswirtschaft. Gabler.

Handwoerterbuch des Oeffentlichen Dienster: Das Personalwesen. W. Bierfelder. (Pub. by E. Schmidt). French & Eur.

Handwoerterbuch des Oeffentlichen Dienster: Das Personalwesen. W. Bierfelder. Schmidt Verlag.

Handwoerterbuch des Oeffentlichen Dienstes. Ed. by Wilhelm Bierfelder. Schmidt Verlag.

Handwoerterbuch des Personalwesens. Ed. by Eduard Gaugler. Poeschel Verlag.

Handwoerterbuch Deutsch-Englisch. M Rosenberg.

Handwoerterbuch fur der Bank & Sparkassenwesen. Bank-Lexikon. Gabler.

Handwoerterbuch Internationale Politik. Ed. by Wichard Woyke. Leske-Budrich.

Handworterbuch der Neu-Arabischen und Deutschen Sprache. Adolf Wahrmund. Verry.

Handworterbuch der neu Arabischen und Deutschen Sprache. Adolf Wahrmund. Intl Bk Ctr.

Harrap's Concise German & English Dictionary. Ed. by Robin Sawers. Harrap.

Harrap's German & English Glossary of Terms in International Law. G. Gilbertson. Harrap.

Harrap's Schoeffler-Weis German & English Dictionary. Ed. by Erich Weis & Heinrich Mattutat et al. Harrap.

Hebraeisch-Deutches Woerterbuch. David Herstig. Hueber.

Hebraeisch-Deutsches Woerterbuch. David Herstig. (Pub. by Max Hueber). French & Eur.

Hebraisch. Jaacov Lavy. Langenscheidt.

Hebraisch-Deutsch: Zum Alten Testament. K. Feyerabend. Langenscheidt.

Heimerans Kuchenlexikon. Erhard Gorys. Illus. by Peter Schimmel. Kochbuch Verlag.

The Herbst Dictionaries of Commercial, Financial & Legal Terms: Deutsch-Englisch. Ed. by Robert Herbst & Alan G. Readett. Birkhauser.

The Herbst Dictionaries of Commercial, Financial & Legal Terms: English-German. Robert Herbst & Alan G. Readett. Birkhauser.

The Herbst Dictionaries of Commercial, Financial & Legal Terms Vol. I. Robert Herbst & Alan G. Readett. Birkhauser.

The Herbst Dictionaries of Commercial, Financial & Legal Terms Vol. 2. Ed. by Robert Herbst & Alan G. Readett. Birkhauser.

Herbst Dictionary of Commercial, Financial & Legal Terms. Ed. by Robert Herbst & Alan G. Readett. Birkhauser.

Herbst Dictionay of Commercial, Financial & Legal Terms. Ed. by Robert Herbst & Alan G. Readett. Birkhauser.

The Herbst-Readett Three-Language Dictionaries of Commerce, Finance & Law. Birkhauser-Boston Publishing. Birkhauser.

The Herbst-Readett Two-Language Dictionaries of Finance, Commerce & Law. Birkhauser-Boston Publishing. Birkhauser.

Herder - Lexikon Gemeinschaftskunde. M. Klein. (Pub. by Herder). French & Eur.

Herder - Lexikon Geographie. M. Klein. (Pub. by Herder). French & Eur.

Herder - Lexikon Medizin. D. Oeter. (Pub. by Herder). French & Eur.

Herder - Lexikon Paedagogik. B. Kaluza. (Pub. by Herder). French & Eur.

Herder - Lexikon Politik. B. Pfahlberg. (Pub. by Herder). French & Eur.

Herder - Lexikon Psychologie. Blumenbrg & Kury. (Pub. by Herder). French & Eur.

Herder - Lexikon Tiere. Gack & Jahn. (Pub. by Herder). French & Eur.

Herder - Lexikon Umwelt. U. Becker. (Pub. by Herder). French & Eur.

Herder - Lexikon Wirtschaft. G. Boeing. (Pub. by Herder). French & Eur.

Herder Lexikon. Hans Kossel. Herder.

Herder-Lexikon. Udo Becker. Herder.

Herder-Lexikon Biologie. R. Bergfeld. (Pub. by Herder). French & Eur.

Herder-Lexikon Biologie. R. Bergfeld. Herder.

Herder-Lexikon Chemie. O. Peter. (Pub. by Herder). French & Eur.

Herder-Lexikon Chemie. O. Peter. Herder.

Herder-Lexikon Gemeinschaftskunde. M. Klein. Herder.

Herder-Lexikon Geographie. M. Klein. Herder.

Herder-Lexikon Geologie und Mineralogie. J. Klein. (Pub. by Herder). French & Eur.

Herder-Lexikon Geologie und Mineralogie. J. Klein. Herder.

Herder-Lexikon Kunst. Boeing & Haeusgen. (Pub. by Herder). French & Eur.

Herder-Lexikon Kunst. Boeing & Haeusgen. Herder.

Herder-Lexikon Mathematik. J. Reck. (Pub. by Herder). French & Eur.

Herder-Lexikon Mathematik. J. Reck. Herder.

Herder-Lexikon Medizin. D. Oeter. Herder.

Herder-Lexikon Musik: Sachwoerterbuch. Ed. by Karl Ludwig Nicol. Herder.

Herder-Lexikon Paedagogik. B. Kaluza. Herder.

Herder Lexikon Paedogogik. Ed. by Bjorn Kaluza. Herder.

Herder-Lexikon Pflanzen. H. Jahn. (Pub. by Herder). French & Eur.

Herder-Lexikon Pflanzen. H. Jahn. Herder.

Herder-Lexikon Physik. R. Sauermost. (Pub. by Herder). French & Eur.

Herder-Lexikon Physik. R. Sauermost. Herder.

Herder-Lexikon Politik. B. Pfahlberg. Herder.

Herder-Lexikon Psychologie. Blumenbrg & Kury. Herder.

Herder-Lexikon: Psychologie Sachwoerterbuch. Franz-Jurgen Blumenberg. Herder.

Herder-Lexikon Soziologie. B. Blinkert. (Pub. by Herder). French & Eur.

Herder-Lexikon Soziologie. B. Blinkert. Herder.

Herder-Lexikon Tiere. Gack & Jahn. Herder.

Herder-Lexikon Umwelt. U. Becker. Herder.

Herder-Lexikon Weltaumphysik. U. Becker. (Pub. by Herder). French & Eur.

Herder-Lexikon Weltaumphysik. U. Becker. Herder.

Herder-Lexikon Wirtschaft. G. Boeing. Herder.

Herders Theologisches Taschenlexikon. K. Rahner. (Pub. by Herder). French & Eur.

Herders Theologishes Taschenlexikon. K. Rahner. Herder.

Hethitisches Etymologisches Glossar. Johann Tischler. Ed. by Guenther Neumann. Inst Verg Sprach.

Hethitisches Woerterbuch. Johannes Friedrich & Annelies Kammenhuber. Winter Univ.

Holz Woerterbuch. Herbert Bucksch. (Pub. by Bauverlag). French & Eur.

Holz Woerterbuch. Herbert Bucksch. (Pub. by Bauverlag). French & Eur.

Holz Woerterbuch. Herbert Bucksch. Bauverlag.

Holz Woerterbuch. Herbert Bucksch. Bauverlag.

Holz-Woerterbuch: Band I, Deutsch-Englisch. H. Bucksch. Bauverlag.

Holz-Woerterbuch: Band II, Englisch-Deutsch. Bauverlag.

How to Read German Church Records Without Knowing Much German. Arta F. Johnson. Johnson.

Hugo Pocket Dictionary: German-English, English-German. Littlefield.

Husznyelvu Kiadoi Szotar. Imre Mora. Akademiai Kiado.

IFIP Fachworterbuch der Informationsverabeitung. IFIP. (North Holland). Elsevier.

IFIP-Sach Worterbuch der Datenverarbeitung. I. Gould. (Pub. by Verlag Harri Deutsch). French & Eur.

IFIP Sachwoerterbuch der Datenverarbeitung. Gould. Verlag Harri Deutsch.

Illiustrirovannyi Voenno-Tekhnicheskii Slovar. L. D. Neliubin. (Pub. by Voenizdat). Four Continent.

An Illustrated Dictionary of Chess. Edward R. Brace. Newnes Bks.

Illustrated Technical German for Builders. W. K. Killer. (Pub. by Bauverlag). French & Eur.

Illustrated Technical German for Builders. W. K. Killer. Bauverlag.

Illustrierte Technische Woerterbucher: Eisenbahnmaschinenwesen. A. Schlomann. (Pub. by R. Oldenbourg). French & Eur.

Illustrierte Technische Woerterbucher: Eisenbahnmaschinenwesen. A. Schlomann. Oldenbourg Verlag.

Illustrierte Technische Woerterbucher: Eisenbahnbau und Betrieb. A. Schlomann. (Pub. by R. Oldenbourg). French & Eur.

Illustrierte Technische Woerterbucher: Eisenbahnbau und Betrieb. A. Schlomann. Oldenbourg Verlag.

Illustrierte Technische Woerterbucher: Elektrotechnik und Elektrochemie. A. Schlomann. (Pub. by R. Oldenbourg). French & Eur.

Illustrierte Technische Woerterbucher: ELektrotechnik und Elektrochemie. A. Schlomann. Oldenbourg Verlag.

Illustrierte Technische Woerterbucher: Maschinenelemente. A Schlomann. (Pub. by R. Oldenbourg). French & Eur.

Illustrierte Technische Woerterbucher: Maschinenelemente. A. Schlomann. Oldenbourg Verlag.

Illustrierter Technische Woerterbucher: Luffahrts. A. Schlomann. (Pub. by R. Oldenbourg). French & Eur.

Illustrierter Technische Woerterbucher: Luffahrts. A. Schlomann. Oldenbourg Verlag.

Illustriertes Textil und Mode – Lexikon. Alfons Hofer. (Pub. by Deutscher Fachverlag). French & Eur.

Illustriertes Woerterbuch. (Pub. by Gebrueder Weiss). French & Eur.

Ilustrowany Slownik Niemiecko-Polski. Wanda Brzeska et al. Wiedza Powszechna.

Indogermanisches Etymologisches Woerterbuch. Julius Pokorny. (Pub. by Francke). French & Eur.

Informationsverarbeitung-Englisch-Deutsch-Franzoesisch-Russisch. Erich Burger. VEB Technik.

International Bibliography of Standardized Vocabularies. Eugen Wuster et al. Ed. by International Information Centre for Terminology. K G Saur.

International Dictionary. Otto Jesperson. (Pub. by Carl Winter). French & Eur.

International Dictionary. Otto Jesperson. Winter Univ.

International Dictionary of Abbreviations of Organizations. Paul Spillner. (Pub. by Verlag Dokumentation SVK). French & Eur.

International Dictionary of Building Construction: English-French-German-Italian. Angelo C. Schwicker. Scholium Intl.

International Dictionary of Metallurgy, Mineralogy, Geology & the Mining & Oil Industries. A. Gagnacci-Schwicker & Schwicker. (Pub. by Bauverlag). French & Eur.

International Dictionary of Metallurgey, Mineralogy, Geology & the Mining & Oil Industries. A. Gagnacci-Schwicker & Schwicker. Bauverlag.

International Dictionary of Obscenities: A Guide to Dirty Words & Indecent Expressions in Spanish, Italian, French, German, & Russian. Christina Kunitskaya-Peterson. Berkeley Slavic.

International Glossary of Technical Terms for the Pulp & Paper Industry. Van Derveer & Haas. Imported Bks.

International Microcomputer Dictionary. Sybex Staff & Rodnay Zaks. Sybex.

International Planning Glossary. Ed. by Gordon Logie & Hemel Hemstead. Intl Plan Glos.

International Vocabulary of Town Planning & Architecture. Intl Pubns Serv.

Internationales Woerterbuch der Abkuerzungen Von Organisationen. P. Spillner. (Pub. by Vlg. Dokumentation). French & Eur.

Internationes Kaselexikon. Othmar Hasselfeldt. Fischer Taschen.

Interpretes de Bolsillo Aleman-Espanols. Biblograf SP.

Interpretes de Bolsillo Espanol-Aleman. Biblograf SP.

Investigationslexikon. Wolfgang Luecke. Ed. by Juergen Bloech. Vahlen.

Iron & Steel Dictionary: German-French & French-German. Iron & Steel Institute. Intl Pubns Serv.

Iron & Steel Dictionary: German-Italian & Italian-German. Iron & Steel Institute. Intl Pubns Serv.

Iron & Steel Dictionary: German-Spanish & Spanish-German. Iron & Steel Institute. Intl Pubns Serv.

Iron & Steel Industry Dictionary. A. M. Abd-El-Wahed. French & Eur.

Islaendisches Etymologisches Woerterbuch. Alex Johannesson. (Pub. by Francke). French & Eur.

Italienisch. Incl. Langenscheidt.

Italienisch. Incl. Langenscheidt.

Japanese-Latin-English-German-French Medical Terminology. French & Eur.

Jean's Pocket Dictionaries: German-English. Hammond Inc.

Juedisches Lexikon. Ed. by G. Herlitz. M. Rosenberg.

Jugendlexikon A-Z. Ed. by G. Butzmann et al. Bibl Inst Leipzig.

Jugendlexikon Astronomie & Raumfahrt. K. Lindner & K. H. Neumann. Bibl Inst Leipzig.

Jugendlexikon Biologie. Ed. by G. Dietrich & A. Mueller-Hegemann. Bibl Inst Leipzig.

Jugendlexikon Gesellschaft: Einfache Antworten afu Schwierige Fragen. Dieter Claessens. Rowohlt.

Jugendlexikon Jugend zu Zweit. Ed. by L. Areisin & A. Mueller-Hegemann. Bibl Inst Leipzig.

Jugendlexikon Junge Ehe. Ed. by L. Aresin & A. Mueller-Hegemann. Bibl InstLeipzig.

Jugendlexikon Philosophie. Ed. by F. Fiedler & G. Gurst. Bibl Inst Leipzig.

Jugendlexikon UdSSR. Ed. by G. Butzmann. Bibl Inst Leipzig.

Jugendlexikon Weltpolitik. Ed. by H. Ivens et al. Bibl Inst Leipzig.

Jugendlexikon Wirtschaft. H. Guenter. (Pub. by Rowohlt). French & Eur.

Jugendlexikon Wissenschaftlicher Kommunismus. Ed. by J. Gottschalg & G. Wolter. Bibl Inst Leipzig.

Jugenlexikon Wirtschaft. H. Guenter. Rowohlt.

Junckers Worterbuch German-American Slang. Juncker. Ed. by Arthur Seiffhart. Assoc Bk.

Jurdicia Lexikon: Das Kleine Oesterreicher Rechtswoerterbuch. Hans G. Zedtwitz. Juridica Verlag.

Jurdisk Ordbog. W. Gubba. Guba.

Juridisk Ordbog, Dansk-Tysk: Supplement & Forkortelsesliste. W. Gubba. Guba.

Kaufmaenisches Grundwoerterbuch fuer Schule & Praxis: Part I, Deutsch-Englisch. T. Grossmann & G. Friedmann. M. Rosenberg.

Kaufmannisches Grundwoerterbuch fuer Schule und Praxis: Deutsch-Englisch. T. Grossmann & G. Friedmann. M Rosenberg.

Kaufmannisches Grundworte Buch Fur Schule und Praxis. Grossmann & Friedmann. (Pub. by Fachverlag Th. Grossmann). French & Eur.

Kautschuk-Lexikon. Kurt F. Heinisch. Gentner.

Kinder Duden: Mein Erster Duden. Adler Bks.

Kleinasiatische Hydronymie: Semantik & Morphologie Analyse der Geichlisor Gewaessernamen. Johann Tischler. Reichert.

Das Kleine Bergbaulexikon. Walter Bischoff. Verlag Glockauf.

Das Kleine Bergbaulexikon. Walter Bischoff. Verlag Gluckauf.

Der Kleine Duden: Deutsches Woerterbuch. Bibl io Inst.

Der Kleine Duden, Fremdenwoerterbuch. Dudenredaktion Manheim. Biblio Inst.

Der Kleine Duden: Fremdwoerterbuch. Biblio Inst.

Kleine Eichborn, Taschenwoerterbuch der Wirtschaftssprache. R. Eichborn. (Pub. by Siebenpunkt Vlg). French & Eur.

Kleine Eichborn, Taschenwoerterbuch der Wirtschaftssprache. R. Eichborn. (Pub. by Siebenpunkt Vlg). French & Eur.

Der Kleine Muret-Sanders: Deutsch-Englisch. Heinz Messinger. Langenscheidt.

Der Kleine Wahrig: Woerterbuch der deutschen Sprache. M Rosenberg.

Kleiner Wortschatz. Albert A. Meras & Maud Miller. Rev. by W. R. Ridgeway. Harrap.

Kleines Abkuerzungsbuch. H. Koblischke. Bibl Inst Leipzig.

Kleines Fachwoerterbuch Geologie. V Rosenfeld. (Pub. by Borntaeger). French & Eur.

Kleines Fremdwoerterbuch. Ed. by G. Gurst et al. Bibl Inst Leipzig.

Kleines Kriminologisches Woerterbuch. Kaiser. (Pub. by Herder). French & Eur.

Kleines Kriminologishes Woerterbuch. Kaiser. Herder.

Kleines Lexikon der Paedagogik & Didaktik. Ed. by Helmut Zoepfl. Auer.

Kleines Lexikon der Paedagogik & Didaktik. Helmut Zoepfl & Gerhard Bittner. Ed. by Herbert Tschamler. Auer.

Kleines Lexikon der Paedagogik und Didatik. Herbert Zoepfl. (Pub. by Auer). French & Eur.

Kleines Lexikon der Paedagogik und Didatik. Herbert Zoepfl. Auer.

Kleines Lexikon zur Politischen Bildung. Ed. by Paul Grossman & Viktor Lang. Hornung-Verlag.

Kleines Medizinisches Fremdworterbuch. Irmgard Goldhahn. Thieme Verlag.

Kleines Philosophisches Woerterbuch. Mueller & Halder. (Pub. by Herder). French & Eur.

Kleines Philosophisches Woerterbuch. Mueller & Halder. Herder.

Kleines Polytechnisches Woerterbuch. Horst Gorner & J. V. Fedirko. VEB ·Verlag Technik.

Kleines Polytechnisches Woerterbuch Russisch-Deutsch. Horst Gorner. VEB Technik.

Kleines Psychologisches Woerterbuch. Christian Michel & Felix Novak. Herder.

Kleines Sozial Wissenschaftliches Woerterbuch fuer Paedagogen. Erich Weber et al. Auer.

Kleines Stuttgarter-Bibellexikon. H. Obermayer. (Pub. by Vlg. Katholisches Bibelwerk). French & Eur.

Kleines Weinlexikon. Wilhelm Panwolf. Goldmann.

Kleines Wirtschafts-Woerterbuch. Wolfgang Mentzel & Helmut Wittlesberger. Herder.

Kleines Woerterbuch Chemie & Chemische Technik. Gross & Hildebrand. Verlag Harri Deutsch.

Kleines Woerterbuch Chemie & Chemische Technik. Gross & Hildebrand. Verlag Harri Deutsch.

Kleines Woerterbuch der Aegyptologie. Wolfgang Helck & Eberhard Otto. (Pub. by Harrassowitz). French & Eur.

Kleines Woerterbuch der Chemie & Chemische Technik. Helmut Gross. VEB Verlag Technik.

Kleines Woerterbuch der Chemie & Chemische Technik Deutsch-Englisch. VEB Technik.

Kleines Woerterbuch der Chemie & Chemische Technik Englisch-Deutsch. VEB Technik.

Kleines Woerterbuch der Chemie & Chemischen Technik Russisch-Deutsch. Helmut Gross. VEB Technik.

Kleines Woerterbuch der Elektrotechnik Elektronik Russisch-Deutsch. Helmut Gross. VEB Technik.

Kleines Woerterbuch der Japanologie. B. Lewin. (Pub. by Harrassowitz). French & Eur.

Kleines Woerterbuch der Sonderpaedagogik: Englisch-Deutsche. Erika Reinartz & Friedrich Masendorf. Marhold.

Kleines Woerterbuch Des Christlichen Orients. Julius Assfalg & P. Krueger. (Pub. by Harrassowitz). French & Eur.

Kleines Woerterbuch Des Hellenismus. (Pub. by Harrassowitz). French & Eur.

Kleines Woerterbuch Sprachwissenschaftlicher Termini. Ed. by R. Conrad. Bibl Inst Leipzig.

Kleines Woerterbuch Zur Arbeits und Sozialpolitik. M. Pfeffer. (Pub. by Herder). French & Eur.

Kleines Woerterbuch Zur Arbeits und Sozialpolitik. M. Pfeffer. Herder.

Kleines Worterbuch der Chemie und Chem. Technik. H. Gross & H. Hildebrand. (Pub. by Verlag Harri Deutsch). French & Eur.

Kleinnes Lexikon des Judentums. Johann Maier & Peter Schaefer. F Bahn.

Kleinworterbuch Deutsch-Polnisch (Handy German-Polish Dictionary) S. Schimitzek et al. French & Eur.

Klinisches Woerterbuch Mit Klinischen Syndromen. Willibald Pschyrembel. De Gruyter.

Klipp & Klar. Karl O. Saur. Biblio Inst.

Kluwer's Universeel Technisch Woordenboek: Duits-Nederlands. G. Schuurmans. French & Eur.

Kluwer's Universel Technisch Woordenboek: Nederlands-Duits. G. Schuurmans. French & Eur.

Knaura Lexikon, A-Z. (Pub. by Druckenmuellar). French & Eur.

Knaurs Lexicon A-Z. M Rosenberg.

Knaurs Lexicon der sinnverwandten Woerter. M Rosenberg.

Knaurs Lexikon A-Z. M Rosenberg.

Knaurs Lexikon der Modernen Medizin. Kurt Pollak. (Pub. by Druckenmueller). French & Eur.

Knaurs Lexikon der Technik. Hans Heck. (Pub. by Druckenmueller). French & Eur.

Knaurs Lexikon der Weltliteratur. Diether Krywalski. Droemersche Knaur.

Knaurs Musiklexikon. Ed. by R. E. Moritz. M Rosenberg.

Koreanisch-Deutsches Woerterbuch. Andre Eckardt. Groos Verlag.

Korrosion & Korrosionsschutz Deutsch-Russisch. Helmut Gross. VEB Technik.

Kratkii Nemetsko-Russkii Slovar Po Iadernoi Fizike i Iadernoi Tekhnike. Four Continent.

Kratkii Nemetsko-Russkii Vneshnetorgovyi Slovar. L. T. Bagma. (Pub. by Vneshtorgizdat). Four Continent.

Kratkii Russko-Nemetskii Frazeologicheskii Slovar. (Pub. by Russkii Iazyk). Four Continent.

Kritische Stichwoerter zur Kinderkultur. Karl W. Bauer & Heinz Hengst. W Fink.

Kritisches Lexikon der Erziehungswissenschaft und Bildungspolitik. H. Speichert. (Pub. by Rowohlt). French & Eur.

Kritisches Lexikon der Erziehungswissenschaft und Bildungspolitik. H. Speichert. Rowohlt.

Kritisches Lexikon der Erziehungswissenschaft & Bildungspolitik. Ed. by Horst Speichert. Verlag.

Kuenstlerlexikon. A. Schenck. (Pub. by Rowohlt). French & Eur.

Kuenstlerlexikon. A. Schenck. Rowohlt.

Kulturpolitisches Woerterbuch. Ed. by W. R. Langenbucher. M Rosenberg.

Kunststofflexikon. Klaus Stoeckhert & Beck. Hanser.

Kunststofftechnik Woerterbuch. A. Wittfoht. (Pub. by C. Hanser). French & Eur.

Kunststofftechnik Woerterbuch. A. Wittfoht. Hanser.

Kunststofftechnisches Woerterbuch. A. Wittfoht. (Pub. by C. Hanser). French & Eur.

Kunststofftechnisches Woerterbuch. A. Wittfoht. (Pub. by C. Hanser). French & Eur.

Kunststofftechnisches Woerterbuch. A. Wittfoht. French & Eur.

Kunststofftechnisches Woerterbuch. A. Wittfoht. Hanser.

Kunststofftechnisches Woerterbuch. A. Wittfoht. Hanser.

Kurzgefasstes Etymologisches Des Altindischen. Manfred Mayrhofer. Winter Univ.

Kurzgefasstes Etymologisches Woerterbuch Des Altindischen. Manfred Mayrhofer. (Pub. by Carl Winter). French & Eur.

Kurzgefasstes Etymologisches Woerterbuch Des Altindischen. Manfred Mayrhofer. (Pub. by Carl Winter). French & Eur.

Kurzgefasstes Etymologisches Woerterbuch Des Altindischen. Manfred Mayrhofer. Winter Univ.

Kurzlexikon der Elektrotechnik. Gregor D. Haberle & Heinz O. Haberle. Frankfurt Fachverlag.

Kurzzeichen-Lexikon fur Kabel & Isoierte Leitungen Nach VDE IEC & CEE. Ewald Retzlaff. VDE Verlag.

Kybernetik. Achim Sydow. VEB Verlag Technik.

Landwirtschaftliches Woerterbuch in Acht Sprachen. (Pub. by BLV). French & Eur.

Langenscheidt Comprehensive German Dictionary. Langenscheidt.

Langenscheidt Condensed Muret-Sanders German Dictionary. Langenscheidt.

Langenscheidt English-German Lilliput Dictionary. Langenscheidt.

Langenscheidt German-English Lilliput Dictionary. Langenscheidt.

Langenscheidt Grosswoerterbuch: Englisch-Deutsch. Heinz Messinger. Langenscheidt.

Langenscheidt Grosswoerterbucher Franzosisch. Incl. Langenscheidt.

Langenscheidt Modern Greek-English Lilliput Dictionary. Langenscheidt.

Langenscheidt New Muret-Sanders Encyclopedic Dictionary: German-English. Imported Bks.

Langenscheidt Taschenwoerterbuch Englisch komplett. Langenscheidt.

Langenscheidt's Comprehensive English-German Dictionary. Heinz Messinger. Imported Bks.

Langenscheidts Fachwoerterbuch Fernmeldewesen. (Pub. by Langenscheidt). French & Eur.

Langenscheidts Fachwoerterbuecher Deutsch-Spanish. Arturo E. Von Baumgart. Langenscheidt.

Langenscheidts Grosse Schulwoerterbuch Deutsch-Englisch. Heinz Messinger. Langenscheidt.

Langenscheidts Grosse Schulwoerterbuch Deutsch-Franzoesisch. Ernst E. Lange-Kowal. Langenscheidt.

Langenscheidts Grosse Schulwoerterbuecher Deutsch-Franzoesisch. Kurt Wilhelm. Langenscheidt.

Langenscheidts Grosse Schulwoerterbuch Englisch-Deutsch. Heinz Messinger & Werner Rudenberg. Langenscheidt.

Langenscheidts Grosse Schulwoerterbuecher Englisch-Deutsch. H. Messinger & H. Ruedenberger. Langenscheidt.

Langenscheidts Grosse Schulwoerterbuch Franzoesisch-Deutsch. Ernst E. Lange-Kowal & Louis Beaucaire. Langenscheidt.

Langenscheidts Grosse Schulwoerterbuecher Franzoesisch-Deutsch. Ernst E. Lange-Kowal. Langenscheidt.

Langenscheidts Grosses Schulwoerterbuch Lateinisch-Deutsch. Erich Pertsch. Langenscheidt.

Langenscheidts Grosswoerterbuch Altgriechisch: Tl 1, Altgriechisch-Deutsch. Langenscheidt.

Langenscheidts Grosswoerterbuch Deutsch-Lateinisch. Menge & Guethling. Langenscheidt.

Langenscheidts Grosswoerterbuch: Englisch-Deutsch. H. Messinger. Langenscheidt.

Langenscheidts Grosswoerterbuch Englisch-Deutsch. Heinz Messinger. Langenscheidt.

Langenscheidts Grosswoerterbuch Franzoesisch: Tl 1, Franzoesisch-Deutsch. Sachs & Villatte. Langenscheidt.

Langenscheidts Grosswoerterbuch Franzoesisch: Tl 2, Deutsch-Franzoesisch. Langenscheidt.

Langenscheidts Grosswoerterbuch Italienisch. Vladimiro Von Macchi. Langenscheidt.

Langenscheidts Grosswoerterbuch Italienisch. Vladimiro Von Macchi. Langenscheidt.

Langenscheidts Grosswoerterbuch: Lateinisch-Deutsch. Hermann Menge & Otto Guethling. Langenscheidt.

Langenscheidts Grosswoerterbuch Lateinisch-Deutsch. Menge & Guethling. Langenscheidt.

Langenscheidts Grosswoerterbuch Lateinisch: Tl 1, Lateinisch-Deutsch. Langenscheidt.

Langenscheidts Grosswoerterbuch Lateinisch: Tl 2, Deutsch-Lateinisch. Langenscheidt.

Langenscheidts Grosswoerterbuch: Teil II, Deutsch-Franzoesisch. Karl Sachs & Cesaire Villatte. Ed. by Walter Gottschalk & Gaston Bentot. Langenscheidt.

Langenscheidts Grosswoerterbuch: Teil II, Deutsch-Italienisch. Vladimiro Macchi. Ed. by Lexikographischen Institut Sansoni. Langenscheidt.

Langenscheidts Grosswoerterbuch: Teil I, Franzoesisch-Deutsch. Karl Sachs & Cesaire Villatte. Langenscheidt.

Langenscheidts Grosswoerterbuch: Teil I, Italienisch-Deutsch. Ed. by Lexikographischen Institut Sansoni. Langenscheidt.

Langenscheidts Grosswoerterbuch Altgriechisch-Deutsch. Menge & Guthling. Langenscheidt.

Langenscheidts Grosswoerterbucher Italienisch. Ed. by Vladimiro Macchi. Langenscheidt.

Langenscheidts Handwoerterbuch: Englisch-Deutsch Deutsch-Englisch. Heinz Messinger & Werner Ruedenberg. Langenscheidt.

Langenscheidts Handwoerterbuch: Franzoesisch-Deutsch Deutsch-Franzoesisch. Ernst E. Lange-Kowal & Louis Beaucaire. Langenscheidt.

Langenscheidts Handwoerterbuch: Franzoesisch-Deutsch. Ernst Erwin Lange-Kowal. Ed. by Louis Beaucaire. Langenscheidt.

Langenscheidts Handwoerterbuch Hebraisch: Teil II, Deutsch-Hebraisch. Jaacov Lavy. Langenscheidt.

Langenscheidts Handwoerterbuch Hebraisch: Teil I, Hebraisch-Deutsch. Jaacov Lavy. Langenscheidt.

Langenscheidts Handwoerterbuch Italienisch-Deutsch. Paolo Giovannelli & Walter Frenzel. Langenscheidt.

Langenscheidts Handwoerterbuch Italienisch: Teil II, Deutsch-Italienisch. Herbert Frenzel & Walter Frenzel. Ed. by Vladimiro Macchi. Langenscheidt.

Langenscheidts Handwoerterbuch Italienisch: Teil I, Italienisch-Deutsch. Paolo Giovannelli & Walter Frenzel. Langenscheidt.

Langenscheidts Handwoerterbuch Lateinisch-Deutsch. Erich Pertsch. Langenscheidt.

Langenscheidts Handwoerterbuch Niederlaendisch Wolters: Teil I, Niederlaendisch-Deutsch. I. Van Gelderen & W. H. Wallis. Langenscheidt.

Langenscheidts Handwoerterbuch Schwedisch PRISMA. Langenscheidt.

Langenscheidts Handwoerterbuch Spanisch-Deutsch. Heinz Muller et al. Langenscheidt.

Langenscheidts Handwoerterbuch Spanisch: Teil II, Deutsch-Spanisch. Enrique Alvarez-Prada. Langenscheidt.

Langenscheidts Handwoerterbuch Spanisch: Teil I, Spanisch-Deutsch. Heinz Muller & Gunther Haensch. Langenscheidt.

Langenscheidts Handwoerterbuch: Teil II, Deutsch-Englisch. Heinz Messinger. Langenscheidt.

Langenscheidts Handwoerterbuch: Teil II, Deutsch-Franzoesisch. Ernst E. Lange-Kowal. Langenscheidt.

Langenscheidts Handwoerterbuch: Teil I, Englisch-Deutsch. Heinz Messinger & Werner Ruedenberg. Langenscheidt.

Langenscheidts Handwoerterbuch: Teil I, Franzoesisch-Deutsch. Ernst E. Lange-Kowal & Louis Beaucaire. Langenscheidt.

Langenscheidts Handwoerterbuch Ungarisch HALASZ: Teil II, Deutsch-Ungarisch. I. Kadar & O. Ratz. Langenscheidt.

Langenscheidts Handwoerterbuch Ungarisch HALASZ: Teil I, Ungarisch-Deutsch. Ratz S. Skripecz et al. Langenscheidt.

Langenscheidts Handwoerterbuecher Deutsch-Polnisch. Ed. by Chodera & Kubica. Langenscheidt.

Langenscheidts Handwoerterbuecher Norwegisch-Deutsch. Langenscheidt.

Langenscheidts Handwoerterbuecher Polnisch-Deutsch. Langenscheidt.

Langenscheidts Handwoerterbuecher: Tl 1, Englisch-Deutsch. Heinz Messinger & Werner Ruedenberg. Langenscheidt.

Langenscheidts Handwoerterbuecher: Tl 1, Franzoesisch-Deutsch. Ed. by Ernst E. Lange-Kowal. Langenscheidt.

Langenscheidts Handwoerterbuecher: Tl 1, Gelderen, 1 van: Niederlandisch-Deutsch. Ed. by J. H. Van Beckum. Langenscheidt.

Langenscheidts Handwoerterbuecher: Tl 1, Italienisch-Deutsch.

Langenscheidts Handwoerterbuecher: Tl 1, Spanisch-Deutsch.

Langenscheidt.

Langenscheidts Handwoerterbuecher: Tl 2, Deutsch-Englisch. Heinz Messinger. Langenscheidt.

Langenscheidts Handwoerterbuecher: Tl 2, Deutsch-Franzoesisch. Ed. by Kurt Wilhelm. Langenscheidt.

Langenscheidts Handwoerterbuecher: Tl 2, Deutsch-Italienisch. Langenscheidt.

Langenscheidts Handwoerterbuecher: Tl 2, Deutsch-Ungarisch. Ed. by Halasz. Langenscheidt.

Langenscheidts Handwoerterbuecher: Tl 2, Gelderen, 1 van, Deutsch-Niederlandisch. Langenscheidt.

Langenscheidt's Hebrew-German Dictionary. Jaacom Lavy. Am Map.

Langenscheidt's Lilliput English-German Dictionary. Am Map.

Langenscheidt's Lilliput German-English Dictionary. Am Map.

Langenscheidt's Lilliput Modern Greek-English Dictionary. Am Map.

Langenscheidts Lilliput-Woerterbuch Deutsch-Englisch. Langenscheidt.

Langenscheidts Lilliput-Woerterbuch Deutsch-Franzoesisch. Langenscheidt.

Langenscheidts Lilliput-Woerterbuch Deutsch-Italienisch. Langenscheidt.

Langenscheidts Lilliput-Woerterbuch Deutsch-Lateinisch. Langenscheidt.

Langenscheidts Lilliput-Woerterbuch Deutsch-Spanisch. Langenscheidt.

Langenscheidts Lilliput-Woerterbuch
Englisch-Deutsch. Langenscheidt.

Langenscheidts Lilliput-Woerterbuch
Franzoesisch-Deutsch.
Langenscheidt.

Langenscheidts Lilliput-Woerterbuch
Italienisch-Deutsch. Langenscheidt.

Langenscheidts Lilliput-Woerterbuch
Lateinisch-Deutsch. Langenscheidt.

Langenscheidts Lilliput-Woerterbuch
Spanisch-Deutsch. Langenscheidt.

Langenscheidts Lilliput-
Woerterbucher Franzoesisch-
Deutsch. Langenscheidt.

Langenscheidts Lilliput-
Woerterbucher Altgriechisch-
Deutsch. Langenscheidt.

Langenscheidts Lilliput-
Woerterbucher Deutsch-Englisch.
Langenscheidt.

Langenscheidts Lilliput-
Woerterbucher Deutsch-
Franzoesisch. Langenscheidt.

Langenscheidts Lilliput-
Woerterbucher Deutsch-
Italienisch. Langenscheidt.

Langenscheidts Lilliput-
Woerterbucher Deutsch-
Lateinisch. Langenscheidt.

Langenscheidts Lilliput-
Woerterbucher Deutsch-Spanisch.
Langenscheidt.

Langenscheidts Lilliput-
Woerterbucher Englisch-Deutsch.
Langenscheidt.

Langenscheidts Lilliput-
Woerterbucher Italienisch-
Deutsch. Langenscheidt.

Langenscheidts Lilliput-
Woerterbucher Lateinisch-
Deutsch. Langenscheidt.

Langenscheidts Lilliput-
Woerterbucher Spanisch-Deutsch.
Langenscheidt.

Langenscheidt's New College
German Dictionary (German-
English, English-German) Heinz
Messinger & Werner Rudenberg.
Am Map.

Langenscheidt's New College
German Dictionary: German-
English, English-German. Heinz
Messinger. Imported Bks.

Langenscheidt's New Muret-Sanders
English-German Dictionary. Ed. by
Otto Springer. Incl. Hippocrene
Bks.

Langenscheidt's New Muret-Sanders
German-English Encyclopedic
Dictionary: Part 2, Vol. 2, L-Z. Ed.
by Otto Springer. Am Map.

Langenscheidt's New Pocket German
Dictionary: German-English,
English-German. Ed. by
Langenscheidt Staff. Am Map.

Langenscheidts Reisewoerterbucher
Spanisch-Deutsch. Langenscheidt.

Langenscheidts Satz-Lexikon des
Englischen Geschaeftsbriefes.
Langenscheidt.

Langenscheidts Satz-Lexikon des
Franzoesischen Geschaeftsbriefes.
Langenscheidt.

Langenscheidts Satz-Lexikon des
Spanischen Geschaeftsbriefes. H.
Burfeindt-Moral & J. A.
Moral-Arroyo. Langenscheidt.

Langenscheidts Schulwoerterbuch
Englisch-Deutsch.
Langenscheidt-Redaktion.
Langenscheidt.

Langenscheidts Schulwoerterbuch
Franzoesisch-Deutsch. Ernst E.
Lange-Kowal & Paul Hartig.
Langenscheidt.

Langenscheidts Schulwoerterbuch
Lateinisch-Deutsch. Erich Pertsch
& Ernst E. Lange-Kowal.
Langenscheidt.

Langenscheidts Schulwoerterbucher
Englisch-Deutsch. Langenscheidt.

Langenscheidts Schulwoerterbucher
Franzoesisch-Deutsch.
Langenscheidt.

Langenscheidts Schulwoerterbucher
Lateinisch-Deutsch. Langenscheidt.

Langenscheidts Schulwoerterbucher
Lateinisch-Deutsch. Erich Pertsch.
Langenscheidt.

Langenscheidts Sportwoerterbuch. R.
Lembke. (Pub. by Langenscheidt).
French & Eur.

Langenscheidts Sportwoerterbuch
Deutsch-Englisch-Franzoesisch-
Spanisch. Langenscheidt.

Langenscheidt's Standard Dictionary.
Edmund Klatt. Imported Bks.

Langenscheidt's Standard German
Dictionary: German-English,
English-German. Edmund Klatt et
al. Am Map.

Langenscheidts Taschenwoerterbuch
Altgriechisch. H. Menge & O.
Guthling. Langenscheidt.

Langenscheidts Taschenwoerterbuch
Altgriechisch: Teil I, Altgriechisch-
Deutsch. H. Menge. Langenscheidt.

Langenscheidts Taschenwoerterbuch
Altgriechisch: Teil II, Deutsch-
Altgriechisch. O. Guthling.
Langenscheidt.

Langenscheidts Taschenwoerterbuch
Arabisch. G. Krotkoff et al.
Langenscheidt.

Langenscheidts Taschenwoerterbuch
Arabisch: Teil I, Arabisch-Deutsch.
G. Krotkoff. Langenscheidt.

Langenscheidts Taschenwoerterbuch
Arabisch: Teil II, Deutsch-
Arabisch. K. Schukry & R.
Humberdrotz. Langenscheidt.

Langenscheidts Taschenwoerterbuch
Danisch. H. Henningsen.
Langenscheidt.

Langenscheidt's Taschenwoerterbuch
Danisch: Teil I, Danisch-Deutsch.
H. Henningsen. Langenscheidt.

Langenscheidts Taschenwoerterbuch
Danisch: Teil II, Deutsch-Danisch.
H. Henningsen. Langenscheidt.

Langenscheidts Taschenwoerterbuch
der Italienischen & Deutschen
Sprache. Ed. by W. Frenzel & V.
Macchi. Langenscheidt.

Langenscheidts Taschenwoerterbuch
Englisch. E. Klatt et al.
Langenscheidt.

Langenscheidts Taschenwoerterbuch
Englisch: Teil II, Deutsch-Englisch.
E. Klatt & G. Klatt. Langenscheidt.

Langenscheidts Taschenwoerterbuch
Englisch: Teil I, Englisch-Deutsch.
E. Klatt & D. Roy. Langenscheidt.

Langenscheidts Taschenwoerterbuch
Franzoesisch. E. E. Lange-Kowal et
al. Langenscheidt.

Langenscheidts Taschenwoerterbuch
Franzoesisch: Teil II, Deutsch-
Franzoesisch. E. Weymuth.
Langenscheidt.

Langenscheidts Taschenwoerterbuch
Franzoesisch: Teil I, Franzoesisch-
Deutsch. E. E. Lange-Kowal.
Langenscheidt.

Langenscheidts Taschenwoerterbuch
Hebraisch. K. Feyerabend.
Langenscheidt.

Langenscheidts Taschenwoerterbuch
Italienisch-Deutsch. V. Macchi &
W. Frenzel. Langenscheidt.

Langenscheidts Taschenwoerterbuch
Italienisch: Teil II, Deutsch-
Italienisch. W. Frenzel.
Langenscheidt.

Langenscheidts Taschenwoerterbuch
Italienisch: Teil I, Italienisch-
Deutsch. V. Macchi.
Langenscheidt.

Langenscheidts Taschenwoerterbuch
Lateinisch. H. Menge & E. Pertsch.
Langenscheidt.

Langenscheidts Taschenwoerterbuch
Lateinisch: Teil II, Deutsch-
Lateinisch. Hermann Menge.
Langenscheidt.

Langenscheidts Taschenwoerterbuch
Lateinisch: Teil I, Lateinisch-
Deutsch. H. Menge & E. Pertsch.
Langenscheidt.

Langenscheidts Taschenwoerterbuch
Neugriechisch: Teil II, Deutsch-
Neugriechisch. A. Steinmetz.
Langenscheidt.

Langenscheidts Taschenwoerterbuch
Neugriechisch: Teil I,
Neugriechisch-Deutsch. H. F.
Wendt. Langenscheidt.

Langenscheidts Taschenwoerterbuch
Niederlandisch-Deutsch. F. J. J.
Van De Wiele & Frans Beersmans.
Langenscheidt.

Langenscheidts Taschenwoerterbuch
Niederlaendisch: Teil II, Deutsch-
Niederlaendisch. Frans Beersmans.
Langenscheidt.

Langenscheidts Taschenwoerterbuch
Niederlaendisch: Teil I,
Niederlaendisch-Deutsch. F. J. Van
De Wiele. Langenscheidt.

Langenscheidts Taschenwoerterbuch
Polnisch. Stanislaw Walewski.
Langenscheidt.

Langenscheidts Taschenwoerterbuch
Polnisch: Teil II, Deutsch-Polnisch.
Stanislaw Walewski. Langenscheidt.

Langenscheidts Taschenwoerterbuch
Portugiesisch. A. E. Beau & F.
Irmen. Langenscheidt.

Langenscheidts Taschenwoerterbuch
Portugiesisch: Teil II, Deutsch-
Portugiesisch. A. E. Beau.
Langenscheidt.

Langenscheidts Taschenwoerterbuch
Polnisch: Teil I, Polnisch-Deutsch.
Stanislaw Walewski. Langenscheidt.

Langenscheidts Taschenwoerterbuch
Portugiesisch: Teil I, Portugiesisch-
Deutsch. F. Irmen. Langenscheidt.

Langenscheidts Taschenwoerterbuch
Russisch. Karl Blattner et al.
Langenscheidt.

Langenscheidts Taschenwoerterbuch
Russisch: Teil II, Deutsch-Russisch.
M. Braun & K. Pollok.
Langenscheidt.

Langenscheidts Taschenwoerterbuch
Russisch: Teil I, Russisch-Deutsch.
Karl Blattner & H. Orschel.
Langenscheidt.

Langenscheidts Taschenwoerterbuch
Schwedisch. H. Kornitzky.
Langenscheidt.

Langenscheidts Taschenwoerterbuch
Schwedisch: Teil II, Deutsch-
Schwedisch. H. Kornitzky.
Langenscheidt.

Langenscheidts Taschenwoerterbuch
Schwedisch: Teil I, Schwedisch-
Deutsch. H. Kornitzky.
Langenscheidt.

Langenscheidts Taschenwoerterbuch
Spanisch. G. Haberkamp de Anton
& D. H. Willers. Langenscheidt.

Langenscheidts Taschenwoerterbuch
Spanisch: Teil II, Deutsch-Spanisch.
D. H. Willers. Langenscheidt.

Langenscheidts Taschenwoerterbuch
Spanisch: Teil I, Spanisch-Deutsch.
G. Haberkamp de Anton.
Langenscheidt.

Langenscheidts Taschenwoerterbuch
Tschechisch-Deutsch. Rolf Ulbrich
& Friedrich Kabesch.
Langenscheidt.

Langenscheidts Taschenwoerterbuch
Tschechisch: Teil II, Deutsch-
Tschechisch. Friedrich Kabesch.
Langenscheidt.

Langenscheidts Taschenwoerterbuch
Tschechisch: Teil I, Tschechisch-
Deutsch. Rolf Ulbrich.
Langenscheidt.

Langenscheidts Taschenwoerterbuch
Tuerkisch-Deutsch. K. Steuerwald
& Cemal Koprulu. Langenscheidt.

Langenscheidts Taschenwoerterbuch
Tuerkisch: Teil II, Deutsch-
Tuerkisch. K. Steuerwald & Cemal
Koprulu. Langenscheidt.

Langenscheidts Taschenwoerterbuch
Tuerkisch: Teil I, Tuerkisch-
Deutsch. K. Steuerwald.
Langenscheidt.

Langenscheidts
Taschenwoerterbuecher
Altgriechisch-Deutsch. H. Menge.
Langenscheidt.

Langenscheidts
Taschenwoerterbuecher Arabisch-
Deutsch. Georg Krolkoff.
Langenscheidt.

Langenscheidts
Taschenwoerterbuecher Deutsch-
Arabisch. K. Schukry.
Langenscheidt.

Langenscheidts
Taschenwoerterbuecher Deutsch-
Daenisch. Langenscheidt.

Langenscheidts
Taschenwoerterbuecher Deutsch-
Lateinisch. Langenscheidt.

Langenscheidts
Taschenwoerterbuecher Deutsch-
Tschechisch. Friedrich Kabesch.
Langenscheidt.

Langenscheidts
Taschenwoerterbuecher Englisch-
Deutsch. E. Klatt & D. Roy.
Langenscheidt.

Langenscheidts
Taschenwoerterbuecher
Franzoesisch-Deutsch.
Lange-Kowal & E. Ernst.
Langenscheidt.

Langenscheidts
Taschenwoerterbuecher Hebraeisch-
Deutsch. K. Feierabend.
Langenscheidt.

Langenscheidts
Taschenwoerterbuecher Italienisch-
Deutsch. Langenscheidt.

Langenscheidts
Taschenwoerterbuecher
Neugriechisch-Deutsch. Ed. by H.
F. Wendt. Langenscheidt.

Langenscheidts
Taschenwoerterbuecher
Niederlandisch-Deutsch. Ed. by Jan
Schneider. Langenscheidt.

Langenscheidts
Taschenwoerterbuecher
Portugiesisch-Deutsch. F. Irmen.
Langenscheidt.

Langenscheidts
Taschenwoerterbuecher Russisch-
Deutsch. H. Orschel.
Langenscheidt.

Langenscheidts
Taschenwoerterbuecher
Schwedisch-Deutsch.
Langenscheidt.

Langenscheidts
Taschenwoerterbuecher Spanisch-
Deutsch. H. Willers. Langenscheidt.

Langenscheidts
Taschenwoerterbuecher
Tschechisch-Deutsch. Rolf Ulbrich.
Langenscheidt.

Langenscheidts
Taschenwoerterbuecher Tuerkisch-
Deutsch. Karl Steuerwald.
Langenscheidt.

Langenscheidt's Taschenworterbuch.
Ed. by Edmund Klatt et al. Am
Map.

Langenscheidt's Universal German-
English, English-German
Dictionary. Am Map.

Langenscheidts Universal-
Woerterbuch Bulgarisch.
Langenscheidt.

Langenscheidts Universal-
Woerterbuch Danisch.
Langenscheidt.

Langenscheidts Universal-
Woerterbuch Englisch.
Langenscheidt.

Langenscheidts Universal-
Woerterbuch Finnisch.
Langenscheidt.

Langenscheidts Universal-
Woerterbuch Franzoesisch.
Langenscheidt.

Langenscheidts Universal-
Woerterbuch Islaendisch.
Langenscheidt.

Langenscheidts Universal-
Woerterbuch Italienisch.
Langenscheidt.

Langenscheidts Universal-
Woerterbuch Japanisch.
Langenscheidt.

Langenscheidts Universal-
Woerterbuch Lateinisch.
Langenscheidt.

Langenscheidts Universal-
Woerterbuch Norwegisch.
Langenscheidt.

Langenscheidts Universal-
Woerterbuch Polnisch.
Langenscheidt.

Langenscheidts Universal-
Woerterbuch Rumaenisch.
Langenscheidt.

Langenscheidts Universal-
Woerterbuch Russisch.
Langenscheidt.

Langenscheidts Universal-
Woerterbuch Schwedisch.
Langenscheidt.

Langenscheidts Universal-
Woerterbuch Slowakisch.
Langenscheidt.

Langenscheidts Universal-
Woerterbuch Spanisch.
Langenscheidt.

Langenscheidts Universal-
Woerterbuch Tschechisch.
Langenscheidt.

Langenscheidts Universal-
Woerterbuch Tuerkisch.
Langenscheidt.

Langenscheidts Universal-
Woerterbuch Ungarisch.
Langenscheidt.

Langenscheidts Universal-
Woerterbuch Neugriechisch.
Langenscheidt.

Langenscheidts Universal-Woerterbuch Niederlaendisch. Langenscheidt.

Langenscheidts Universal-Woerterbuch Portugiesisch. Langenscheidt.

Langenscheidts Universal-Woerterbuch Serbokroatisch. Langenscheidt.

Langenscheidts Universal-Woerterbuecher Bulgarisch-Deutsch. Langenscheidt.

Langenscheidts Universal-Woerterbuecher Daenisch-Deutsch. Langenscheidt.

Langenscheidts Universal-Woerterbuch Englisch-Deutsch. Langenscheidt.

Langenscheidts Universal-Woerterbuch Franzoesisch-Deutsch. Langenscheidt.

Langenscheidts Universal-Woerterbuecher Islaendisch-Deutsch. Langenscheidt.

Langenscheidts Universal-Woerterbuecher Italienisch-Deutsch. Langenscheidt.

Langenscheidts Universal-Woerterbuecher Lateinisch-Deutsch. Langenscheidt.

Langenscheidts Universal-Woerterbuech Neugriechisch-Deutsch. Langenscheidt.

Langenscheidts Universal-Woerterbuch Norwegisch-Deutsch. Langenscheidt.

Langenscheidts Universal-Woerterbuecher Polnisch-Deutsch. Langenscheidt.

Langenscheidts Universal-Woerterbuecher Portugiesisch-Deutsch. Langenscheidt.

Langenscheidts Universal-Woerterbuecher Rumaenisch-Deutsch. Langenscheidt.

Langenscheidts Universal-Woerterbuecher Russisch-Deutsch. Langenscheidt.

Langenscheidts Universal-Woerterbuecher Serbokroatisch-Deutsch. Langenscheidt.

Langenscheidts Universal-Woerterbuecher Slowakisch-Deutsch. Langenscheidt.

Langenscheidts Universal-Woerterbuecher Spanisch-Deutsch. Langenscheidt.

Langenscheidts Universal-Woerterbuecher Tschechisch-Deutsch. Langenscheidt.

Langenscheidts Universal-Woerterbuecher Tuerkisch-Deutsch. Langenscheidt.

Langenscheidts Universal-Woerterbuecher Ungarisch-Deutsch. Langenscheidt.

Larousse de poche, francais-allemand et allemand-francais. Larousse & Co. Larousse.

Larousse Elementaire a L'usage des Allemand. Langenscheidt.

Lateinisch. Hermann Menge. Rev. by E. Pertsch. Langenscheidt.

Lateinisch-Deutsch. Compiled by Erich Pertsch. Langenscheidt.

Lateinisch-Deutsch. Dietrich Pertsch. Langenscheidt.

Lateinisch-Deutsch, Deutsch-Lateinisch. Langenscheidt.

Lateinische Wortkunde fuer Anfaenger & Fortgeschrittene. Ruediger Vischer. Teubner.

Die Lateinischen Woerter auf -Ura. Ernst Zellmer. Selbstverlag Inst.

Law Dictionary: Fachwoerterbuch der anglo-amerikanischen Rechtssprache, Englisch-Deutsch. Dora Von Beseler & Barbara Jacobs. De Gruyter.

Law Dictionary: Technical Dictionary of Anglo-American Legal Terminology, German-English. Ed. by D. v. Beseler & B. Jacobs. De Gruyter.

Legal Dictionary. H. P. Kniepkamp. Adler.

Legal Dictionary: Part 1, Dutch-German. Hans Langendorf. Kluwer Academic.

Legal Terminology English & German. Ruediger Renner & Jeffery Tooth. Adler.

Legal Terminology English-German. Ruediger Renner & Jeffery Tooth. Intl Pubns Serv.

Lexers Mittlehochdeutsches Taschenwoerterbuch: Mit Bearbeiteten & Erweiterten Nachtraegen. Ed. by E. Henschel & U. Pretzel. Hirzel Verlag.

Lexicon Caesarianum. R. Menge & S. Preuss. French & Eur.

Lexicon comercial internacional: Espanol, frances, ingles, italiano, portugues y aleman. J. Vicens Carrio. Reverte SA.

Lexicon de Comunicologia: Diccinario para Audiologos, Audioprotesistas, Foniatras, Logopedas, Profesores De Sordos y Psicolinguistas. Jorge Perello. French & Eur.

Lexicon des Buchwesen: Bd 4, Bilderatlas zum Buchwesen Teil 2. Ed. by Joachim Kirchner. Hiersemann.

Lexicon Forestale. Karl-Johan Ahlsved et al. Suomen Standard.

Lexicon Medicum. Boleslaw Zlotnickiego. French & Eur.

Lexicon Medicum: Medizinisches Woerterbuch in 6 Sprachen; Englisch, Russisch, Franzoesisch, Deutsch, Latein, Polnisch. B. Zlotnicki. Langenscheidt.

Lexicon of French Borrowings in the German Vocabulary. William J. Jones. De Gruyter.

Lexicon of International & National Units. Ed. by M. Merino-Rodriguez. Elsevier.

Lexicon of Plant Pests & Diseases. Ed. by Manuel Merino-Rodriguez. Elsevier.

Lexicon Sopena: Diccionario de bolsillo, aleman-espanol y espanol-aleman. Sopena.

Lexicon to Achilles Tatius. Ed. by James N. O'Sullivan. De Gruyter.

Lexikon Angloamerikanischer und Deutscher Managementbegriffe. Peter Linnert. French & Eur.

Lexikon Archivwesen der DDR. Elisabeth Brachmann-Teubner. Staatsdruk.

Lexikon Biochemie. H. D. Jakubke. French & Eur.

Lexikon biochemie. Hans D. Jakubke & Hans Jeschkeit. Verlag Chemie.

Lexikon Chemischer Kurzbezeichnungen Von Arzneistoffen. French & Eur.

Lexikon Chemischer Kurzbezeichnungen von Arzneistoffen. Govi Verlag.

Lexikon Christlicher Symbole. Edouard Urech. F Bahn.

Lexikon Datens & Datensicherung. Hans Kassel. Siemens AG.

Lexikon der Aegyptologie. Wolfgang Helck & Eberhard Otto. Harrassowitz.

Lexikon der Aegyptologie: Bd II, Lfg 10. Wolfgang Helck & Eberhard Otto. Harrassowitz.

Lexikon der Aegyptologie: Bd II, Lfg 11. Wolfgang Helck & Eberhard Otto. Harrassowitz.

Lexikon der Aegyptologie: Bd II, Lfg 12. Wolfgang Helck & Eberhard Otto. Harrassowitz.

Lexikon der Aegyptologie: Bd II, Lfg 13. Wolfgang Helck & Eberhard Otto. Harrassowitz.

Lexikon der Aegyptologie: Bd II, Lfg 14. Wolfgang Helck & Eberhard Otto. Harrassowitz.

Lexikon der Aegyptologie: Bd II, Lfg 9. Wolfgang Helck & Eberhard Otto. Harrassowitz.

Lexikon der Aegyptologie: Bd 1, Lfg 1. Wolfgang Helck & Eberhard Otto. Harrassowitz.

Lexikon der Aegyptologie: Bd 1, Lfg 2. Wolfgang Helck & Eberhard Otto. Harrassowitz.

Lexikon der Aegyptologie: Bd 1, Lfg 3. Wolfgang Helck & Eberhard Otto. Harrassowitz.

Lexikon der Aegyptologie: Bd 1, Lfg 4. Wolfgang Helck & Eberhard Otto. Harrassowitz.

Lexikon der Aegyptologie: Bd 1, Lfg 6. Wolfgang Helck & Eberhard Otto. Langenscheidt.

Lexikon der Aegyptologie: Bd 1, Lfg 7. Wolfgang Helck & Eberhard Otto. Harrassowitz.

Lexikon der Aegyptologie: Bd 1, Lfg 8. Wolfgang Helck & Eberhard Otto. Harrassowitz.

Lexikon der Aero & Astronautik Einschliesslich Raketentechnik: Lexikon der Alpen. Toni Hiebeler. Sokoll.

Lexikon der Aero und Astronautik Enischliesslich Raketentechnik. French & Eur.

Lexikon der Alten Welt. Karl Andresen. French & Eur.

Lexikon der Alten Welt. Carl Andresen et al. Artemis Verlag.

Lexikon der Anstrichtechnik. Kurt Sponzel. French & Eur.

Lexikon der Anstrichtechnik: Bd 1. Kurt Sponzel & Wilhelm Wallenfang. Callwey.

Lexikon der Anstrichtechnik: Bd 2. Anton Brasholz et al. Callwey.

Lexikon der Antike. Ed. by K. Ziegler & W. Sontheimer. M Rosenberg.

Lexikon der Arabischen Welt. Nandy Ronart. French & Eur.

Lexikon der Arabischen Welt. Nandy Von Ronart & Stephan Ronart. Artemis Verlag.

Lexikon der Arbeits und Soziallere. Rainer Roth. French & Eur.

Lexikon der Archaeologie. W. Bray & D. Trump. French & Eur.

Lexikon der Audio-Visuellen Bildungsmittel. Heribert Heinrichs. French & Eur.

Lexikon der Audio-Visuellen Bildungsmittel. Ed. by Heribert Heinrichs. Koesel.

Lexikon der Ausbildungspraxis. Helmut Paulik. French & Eur.

Lexikon der Ausbildungspraxis. Ed. by Helmut Paulik et al. Verlag Moderne Industrie.

Lexikon der Ausbildungspraxis. Ed. by Helmut Paulik. Verlag Mod Ind.

Lexikon der Datenverarbeitung. Loebel & Mueller. French & Eur.

Lexikon der Datenverarbeitung. Peter Mueller. French & Eur.

Lexikon der Deutschen Geschichte. Gerhard Taddey. French & Eur.

Lexikon der Deutschen Geschichte. Ed. by Gerhard Taddey. Kroener.

Lexikon der Deutschen Konzertliteratur. Theodor Muller-Reuter. Da Capo.

Lexikon der Deutschen Marinegeschichte. Hans Witthoeft. French & Eur.

Lexikon der Deutschen Marinegeschichte. Ed. by Hans J. Witthoeft. Koehlers Verlag.

Das Lexikon der Deutschen Staedt und Gemeinden. Fritz Siefert. French & Eur.

Das Lexikon der Deutschen Staedte & Gemeinden. Ed. by Fritz Sieferl. Fackelverlag.

Das Lexikon der Deutschen Staedte & Gemeinden. Ed. by Fritz Siefert. Suedwest.

Das Lexikon der Elektronischen Musik. Herbert Eimert. French & Eur.

Lexikon der Ethik. Otfried Hoffe. Beck Verlag.

Lexikon der Gastechnik. Walter G. Von Baeckmann. Vulkan Verlag.

Lexikon der Geldenlage. Werner Schwilling. French & Eur.

Lexikon der Genetik der Hundekrankheiten. E. Wiesner & S. Willer. S. Karger.

Lexikon der Germanistischen. Ed. by H. P. Althaus et al. M Rosenberg.

Lexikon der Germanistischen Linguistik. Ed. by Hans P. Althaus et al. Niemeyer.

Lexikon der Geschaeftsbriefe in Vier Sprachen. French & Eur.

Lexikon der Geschaeftsbriefe in vier Sprachen. Verlag Moderne.

Lexikon der Geschichte. Heyne W Verlag.

Lexikon der Geschicte. French & Eur.

Lexikon der Goethe-Zitate. Ed. by Richard Dobel. Artemis Verlag.

Lexikon der Grafischen Technik. Institut fur Grafische Technik. Saur Verlag.

Lexikon der Grafischen Technik. Saur Verlag.

Lexikon der Grammatischen Linguistik. Hans Althaus. French & Eur.

Lexikon der Grammatischen Terminologie. Otmar Bohusch. French & Eur.

Lexikon der Grammatischen Terminologie. Otmar Bohusch. Auer.

Lexikon der Graphischen Technik. French & Eur.

Lexikon der Griechischen und Roemischen Mythologie. H. Hunger. French & Eur.

Lexikon der Heizungs, Lueftungs & Klimatechnik. Walter Haeder & Guenther Reichow. Langenscheidt.

Lexikon der Islamischen Welt. Ed. by Klaus Kreiser et al. Kohlhammer.

Lexikon der Islamischen Welt: Bd 1, A-Grab. Ed. by Klaus Kreiser et al. Kohlhammer.

Lexikon der Islamischen Welt: Bd 2, Gram-Nom. Ed. by Klaus Kreiser et al. Kohlhammer.

Lexikon der Islamischen Welt: Bd 3, Nor-Z. Ed. by Klaus Kreiser et al. Kohlhammer.

Lexikon der Kostenrechnung. Max Munz & Harald Winkel. Kiehl.

Lexikon der Kunstslile: Bd 1, Von der Griechischen Archaik bis zur Renaissance. Rowohlt.

Lexikon der Kunststile. G. Lindemann. French & Eur.

Lexikon der Kunststile: Bd 2, Vom Barock bis zur Pop-art. Rowohlt.

Lexikon der Kunststoffe. Hans Dominighaus. Heyne W Verlag.

Lexikon der Kybernetik. (Pub. by Collets). State Mutual Bk.

Lexikon der Kybernetik. Ed. by A. Mueller. Quickborner Team.

Lexikon der Managementbegriffe. Von Linnert et al. Heyne W Verlag.

Lexikon der Mathematik. Richard Knerr. Fischer Taschen.

Lexikon der Mathematik. Ed. by W. Gellert et al. Bibl Inst Leipzig.

Lexikon der Medizin. Dagobert Tutsch. French & Eur.

Lexikon der Medizin & Gesundheit. Lexikon-Institut Bertelsmann. C Bertelsmann.

Lexikon der Medizinischen Fachsprache. D. Tutsch. French & Eur.

Lexikon der Medizinischen Fachsprache: Bd 1, A-L. Ed. by Dagobert Tutsch. Rowohlt.

Lexikon der Medizinischen Fachsprache: Bd 2, M-Z. Ed. by Dagobert Tutsch. Rowohlt.

Lexikon der Medizinischen Psychologie. U. Tewes. French & Eur.

Lexikon der Modernen Konservation. Hanns Kurth. French & Eur.

Lexikon der Mythologie Aegyptens, Persiens & des Orients. Walter A. Kremnitz. Ambro Lacus.

Lexikon der Mythologie der Eurpaeischen Voelker. Herbert Gottschalk. French & Eur.

Lexikon der Neuzeitlichen Landwirtschaft. French & Eur.

Lexikon der Neuzeitlichen Landwirtschaft. French & Eur.

Lexikon der Neuzeitlichen Landwirtschaft. French & Eur.

Lexikon der Neuzeitlichen Landwirtschaft. Girardet.

Lexikon der Neuzeitlichen Landwirtschaft: Bd 1, Tierernaehrung, Tierzucht, Tierhaltung. Girardet.

Lexikon der Neuzeitlichen Landwirtschaft: Bd 2, Ackerbau, Pflanzenbau, Gruenlandwirtschaft. Girardet.

Lexikon der Neuzeitlichen Landwirtschaft: Bd 3, Belriebswirtschaft, Markt, Recht. Girardet.

Lexikon der Numismatik. Tyll Kroha. French & Eur.

Lexikon der Numismatik. Umschau Verlag.

Lexikon der Onologie. Ludwig Jakob. Meininger.

Lexikon der Paedagogik: Bd 1, 3 Aubl. Herder.

Lexikon der Paedagogik: Bd 2, 3 Aufl. Herder.

Lexikon der Paedagogik: Bd 3, 3 Aufl. Herder.

Lexikon der Paedagogik: Bd 4, 3 Aufl. Herder.

Lexikon der Parapsychologie & ihrer Grenzgebiete. Werner F. Bonin. Scherz AG.

Lexikon der Philosophie. Franz Austeda. Hollinek.

Lexikon der Planun und Organisation. Hans Niewerth. French & Eur.

Lexikon der Planung & Organisation. Ed. by Hans Niewwwerth et al. Quickborner Team.

Das Lexikon der Politik. Heiner Emde. Heyne W Verlag.

Lexikon der Politik: Politik Grundbegriffe & Grundgedanken. Walter Theimer. Francke.

Lexikon der praktischen Psychologie. Ludwig Knoll. Luebbe.

Lexikon der Prozessrechnertechnik. Peter Schaefer & Martin Wiczorke. Siemens AG.

Lexikon der Psychiatrie. C. Mueller. Springer-Verlag.

Lexikon der Psychologie. Ed. by Wilhelm Arnold et al. Herder.

Lexikon der Psychologie: Bd 1, A-Gewissen. Ed. by Wilhelm Arnold et al. Herder.

Lexikon der Psychologie: Bd 2, Graphologie-Prompling. Ed. by Wilhelm Arnold et al. Herder.

Lexikon der Psychologie: Bd 3, Propaganda-Zz. Ed. by Wilhelm Arnold et al. Herder.

Lexikon der Radiologischen Technik in der Mediazin. Wilfried Angerstein. Thieme Verlag.

Lexikon der Radiologischen Technik in der Medizin. Winifred Angerstein. Thieme Verlag.

Lexikon der Reisen und Entdeckungen. F. Embacher. Humanities.

Lexikon der Roemischen Kaiser. Ed. by Otto Veh. Artemis Verlag.

Lexikon der Schulphysik: Atomphysik. O. Hoefling. French & Eur.

Lexikon der Schulphysik: Bd 1, Mechanik & Akustik. Ed. by Oskar Hoefling. Aulis Verlag.

Lexikon der Schulphysik: Bd 3, Elektrizitaet & Magnetismus-1. Tlbd, A-K. Ed. by Oskar Hoefling. Aulis Verlag.

Lexikon der Schulphysik: Bd 3, Elektrizitaet & Magnetismus-2. Tlbd, L-Z. Ed. by Oskar Hoefling. Aulis Verlag.

Lexikon der Schulphysik: Bd 4, Optik & Relativitaet. Ed. by Oskar Hoefling. Aulis Verlag.

Lexikon der Schulphysik: Bd 5, Atomphysik. Ed. by Oskar Hoefling. Aulis Verlag.

Lexikon der Schulphysik: Bd 6, Geschichte der Physik. Ed. by Oskar HOefling. Aulis Verlag.

Lexikon der Schulphysik: Bd 7, Geschichte der Physik. Ed. by Oskar Hoefling. Aulis Verlag.

Lexikon der Schulphysik: Elektrizitaet und Magnetismus A-K. Breitsameter. French & Eur.

Lexikon der Schulphysik: Elektrizitaet und Magnetismus L-Z. Breitsameter. French & Eur.

Lexikon der Schulphysik: Geschichte der Physik. A Hermann. French & Eur.

Lexikon der Schulphysik: Geschichte der Physik. A Hermann. French & Eur.

Lexikon der Schulphysik: Mechanik und Akustik. K. Zita. French & Eur.

Lexikon der Schulphysik: Optik und Relativitaet. W. Ruth. French & Eur.

Lexikon der Schulphysik: Waerme & Wetter. Ed. by Oskar Hoefling. Aulis Verlag.

Lexikon der Schulphysik: Waerme und Wetter. W. Hein. French & Eur.

Lexikon der Sozialen Arbeit. Ed. by Ruth Deutscher et al. Kohlhammer.

Lexikon der Sozialerziehung. Tobias Brocher. French & Eur.

Lexikon der Sprichwoertlichen Redensarten. L. Roehrich. M Rosenberg.

Lexikon der Technik. Ed. by B. Rohr & H. Wiele. Bibl Inst Leipzig.

Lexikon der Unternehmensfuehrung. Klaus Altfelder. French & Eur.

Lexikon der Unternehmensfuehrung. Klaus Altfelder et al. Kiehl.

Lexikon der Voelker & Kulturen: Bd 1. Rowohlt.

Lexikon der Voelker & Kulturen: Bd 2. Rowohlt.

Lexikon der Voelker & Kulturen: Bd 3. Rowohlt.

Lexikon der Voelker und Kulturen. W. Stoehr. French & Eur.

Lexikon der Volkswirtschaft. Friedrich Geigant. French & Eur.

Lexikon der Volkswirtschaft. Friedrich Geigant et al. Verlag Moderne Industrie.

Lexikon der Weltarchitektur. N. Pevsner. French & Eur.

Lexikon der Weltarchitektur. Ed. by Nikolaus Pevsner et al. Prestel-Verlag.

Lexikon der Weltgeschichte. French & Eur.

Lexikon der Weltgeschichte. Ed. by Nikolaus Pevsner et al. Englisch Verlag.

Lexikon der Weltliteratur: Werke. Gero von Wilpert. French & Eur.

Lexikon des Alpinen Schifahrens. Ed. by Friedrich Fetz. Inn Verlag.

Lexikon des Bibliothekswesens. Horst Kunze. French & Eur.

Lexikon des Bibliothekswesens. Ed. by H. Kunze & G. Rueckl. Bibl Inst Leipzig.

Lexikon des Bibliothekswesens. Ed. by Horst Kunze & Gotthard Rueckl. Saur Verlag.

Lexikon des Buchwesens. Ed. by Joachim Kirchner. Hiersemann.

Lexikon des Buchwesens: Bd 1, Text A-K. Ed. by Joachim Kirchner. Hiersemann.

Lexikon des Buchwesens: Bd 2, Text L-Z. Ed. by Joachim Kirchner. Hiersemann.

Lexikon des Buchwesens: Bd 3, Bilderatlas zum Buchwesen Teil 1. Ed. by Joachim Kirchner. Hiersemann.

Lexikon des Fruehgriechischen Epos: Lfg 1. Bruno Snell & Hartmut Erbse. Vandenhoeck.

Lexikon des Fruehgriechischen Epos: Lfg 2. Bruno Snell & Hartmut Erbse. Vandenhoeck.

Lexikon des Fruehgriechischen Epos: Lfg 3. Bruno Snell & Hartmut Erbse. Vandenhoeck.

Lexikon des Fruehgriechischen Epos: Lfg 4. Bruno Snell & Hartmut Erbse. Vandenhoeck.

Lexikon des Fruehgriechischen Epos: Lfg 5. Bruno Snell & Hartmut Erbse. Vandenhoeck.

Lexikon des Fruehgriechischen Epos: Lfg 6. Bruno Snell & Hartmut Erbse. Vandenhoeck.

Lexikon des Fruehgriechischen Epos: Lfg 7. Bruno Snell & Hartmut Erbse. Vandenhoeck.

Lexikon des Fruehgriechischen Epos: Lfg 8. Bruno Snell & Hartmut Erbse. Vandenhoeck.

Lexikon des Geheimwissens. Horst E. Miers. French & Eur.

Lexikon des Geheimwissens. Horst E. Miers. Goldmann.

Lexikon Des II Weltkriegs. Cristian Zentner. French & Eur.

Lexikon des II. Weltkriegs. Ed. by Christian Zentner. Suedwest.

Lexikon des Impressionismus. Maurice Serullaz. French & Eur.

Lexikon des Internationalen Films. Ulrich Kurowski. Hanser.

Lexikon des Marxismus. Iring Fetscher. French & Eur.

Lexikon des Mittelalters. French & Eur.

Lexikon des Mittelalters. Artemis Verlag.

Lexikon des Nebenstrafrechts. Erich Goehler. French & Eur.

Lexikon des Nebenstrafrechts. Erich Goehler et al. Beck Verlag.

Lexikon des Rechts. Adolph Reifferscheid & Frank Benseler. H Luchterhand.

Lexikon des Rechts. H Luchterhand.

Lexikon des Steuer & Wirtschaftsrechts. WRS Verlag.

Lexikon des Surrealismus. Rene Passeron. French & Eur.

Lexikon des Surrealismus. Ed. by Rene Passeron. Wissenschaftliche.

Lexikon des Wirtschaftsrechnens. Franz Kafitz. French & Eur.

Lexikon Deutschsprachiger Schriftsteller. Guenther Albrecht. French & Eur.

Lexikon Deutschsprachiger Schriftsteller. Guenther Albrecht. French & Eur.

Lexikon Deutschsprachiger Schriftsteller: Bd 1. Ed. by Guenther Albrecht et al. Scriptor Verlag.

Lexikon Deutschsprachiger Schriftsteller: Bd 2. Ed. by Guenther Albrecht et al. Scriptor Verlag.

Lexikon Deutschsprachiger Schriftsteller: Bd 3. Ed. by Guenther Albrecht et al. Scriptor Verlag.

Lexikon Deutschsprachiger Schriftsteller: Bd 4. Ed. by Guenther Albrecht et al. Scriptor Verlag.

Lexikon Deutschsprachiger Schriftsteller: Bd 1. Ed. by Guenther Albrecht et al. Scriptor Verlag.

Lexikon EDV und Rechnungswesen. Kurt Nagel. French & Eur.

Lexikon Feurden Bauherrn. Ernst Huerlimann. French & Eur.

Lexikon Fremdsprachiger Schriftsteller. Ed. by G. Steiner et al. Bibl Inst Leipzig.

Lexikon fuer Bergfreunde. Ed. by Hans Bibelriether et al. Bucher.

Lexikon fuer Berufs & Arbeitspaedagogik: Ueber 2400 Haupt- & Hinweisstichworte. Klaus Rischer. Kiehl.

Lexikon Fuer Die Graphische Industrie. Ernst Born. French & Eur.

Lexikon fuer Eisenbahnfreunde. Erhard Born. French & Eur.

Lexikon fuer Eisenbahnfreunde. Erhard Von Born et al. Bucher Verlag.

Lexikon fuer Eltern & Erzieher. Ed. by Hans H. Groothoff et al. Gutersloher V.

Lexikon fuer Eltern & Erzieher. Ed. by Hans H. Groothoff et al. Kreuz Verlag.

Lexikon Fuer Eltern und Erzieher. Hans Groothoff. French & Eur.

Lexikon fuer Fussballfreunde: Fachliche Beratung. Dettmar Cramer. Bucher.

Lexikon fuer Junge Erwachsene. Ed. by Hans D. Bastian. Kreuz Verlag.

Lexikon Fuer Mineralien - und Gesteins Freunde. Herrmann Harder. French & Eur.

Lexikon Fuer Mineralien & Gesteinfreunde. Hermann Von Harder et al. Bucher Verlag.

Lexikon Fuer Pferdefreunde. French & Eur.

Lexikon fuer Pferdefreunde. Bucher Verlag.

Lexikon Fuer Planetenbilder. Ilse Schnitzler. French & Eur.

Lexikon Fuer Tennisfreunde. Ulrich Kaiser. French & Eur.

Lexikon fuer Tennisfreunde. Ulrich Kaiser et al. Bucher Verlag.

Lexikon fur den Bauherrn. Ernst Hurlimann. Verlag Moderne.

Lexikon fur Pferdefreunde. Reiner Klimke & Jorg Savelsberg et al. Bucher.

Lexikon fur Tennisfreunde. Reinhold Appel. Ed. by Ernst Baumann. Bucher.

Lexikon in Farbe. Andreas & Andreas.

Lexikon Kraftfahrzeugtechnik. Gerhard Schnitzlein. VEB Verlag Technik.

Lexikon Medicum. B. Zlotnicki. French & Eur.

Lexikon Recht der Landwirtschaft der Deutschen Demokratischen Republik. Ed. by Reiner Arlt et al. Staatsdruk.

Lexikon RGW. Ed. by M. Engert & H. Stephan. Bibl Inst Leipzig.

Lexikon Staedte & Wappen der Deutschen Demokratischen Republik. Karlheinz Blaschke et al. VEB Verlag Enzyklopadie.

Das Lexikon Wirtschaft, Gesellschaft, Gewerkschaften. Werner Rittershofer. Bund.

Lexikon Zur - und Fruehgeschichtlicher Fundstaetten Oesterreichs. L. Franz. French & Eur.

Lexikon Zur & Freuhgeschictlicher Fundstaetten Oesterreichs. Ed. by L. Franz & A. R. Neumann. Habelt.

Lexikon zur Arbeits & Soziallehre. Reiner A. Roth & Helmut M. Selzer. Ed. by Jurgen Schmidt. Auer.

Lexikon zur Arbeits & Soziallehre. Ed. by Rainer A. Roth & Helmut M. Selzer. Habelt.

Lexikon Zur Soziologie. W. Fuchs. French & Eur.

Lexikon zur Soziologie: Bd 1. Ed. by Werner Fuchs et al. Rowohlt.

Lexikon zur Soziologie: Bd 2. Ed. by Werner Fuchs et al. Rowohlt.

Lexikon Zur Weltmission. S. E. Neill. French & Eur.

Lexikon zur Wortbildung. Gerhard Augst. Narr.

Lexikon 2000. (Pub. by Wissen). French & Eur.

Lexikothek: Bd 10, Torp-Z. C Bertelsmann.

Lexikothek: Bd 2, Bez-Dit. C Bertelsmann.

Lexikothek: Bd 3, Diu-Gass. C Bertelsmann.

Lexikothek: Bd 4, Gast-Hz. C Bertelsmann.

Lexikothek: Bd 5, I-Kreb. C Bertelsmann.

Lexikothek: Bd 6, Kred-Mit. C Bertelsmann.

Lexikothek: Bd 7, Miv-Phyo. C Bertelsmann.

Lexikothek: Bd 8, Phys-Schlo. C Bertelsmann.

Lexikothek: Bd 9, Schlu-Toro. C Bertelsmann.

Lexikothek: Das Bertelsmann Lexikon in 10 Baenden. C Bertelsmann.

Lexique CN: Anglais-Allemand-Francais. Y. H. Attiyate. Iron Age Metalworking Int.

Lexique De la Terminologie Linguistique. Jules Marouzeau. Intl Pubns Serv.

Lexique de Sylviculture Allemand-Francais. Martinot Lagarde. Genie Rural.

Lexique EUC Woerterbuch des Rechnungswesens. IdW Verlag.

Lexique Quadrilingue de la Preparation des Minerals: Allemand-Anglais-Francais-Russe. Congres International de la Preparation des Minerals. Ste. Industrie Minerale.

Lexique Quadrilingue Des Affaires. Ivan de Renty. French & Eur.

Lexique Quadrilingue des Affaires: Anglais-Francais-Allemand-Espagnol. Ivan De Renty. Hachette.

Lexique Quadrilinque de la Preparation des Minerals. Ed. by Congres International de la Preparation des Minerals. French & Eur.

Lilliput Dictionary. Langenscheidt.

Lilliput German-English Dictionary. Langenscheidt.

Linguistisches Woerterbuch. Carl Heupel. Illus. by Helmut Gattinger. Deutscher Taschenbuch.

Litauisches Etymologisches Woerterbuch. Ernst Fraenkel. (Pub. by Westdeutscher Verlag/VVA). French & Eur.

Litauisches Etymologisches Woerterbuch. Ernst Fraenkel. (Pub. by Westdeutscher Verlag/VVA). French & Eur.

Litovsko-Russko-Anglo-Nemetskii Slovar Fizicheskikh Terminov. P. Brazhdzhiunas. (Pub. by Mokslas). Four Continent.

Luftfahrtechnisches Worterbuch, Deutsch-English. Ed. by H. L. Darcy. (Pub. by Walter de Gruyter, Inc.). French & Eur.

Lydisches Woerterbuch. Roberto Gusmani. (Pub. by Carl Winter). French & Eur.

Lydisches Woerterbuch. Roberto Gusmani. Winter Univ.

Machine Tools Dictionary: English-French-German-Arabic. A. M. Abd-El-Wahed. French & Eur.

Maly Slownik Techniczny Niemiecko i Polski-Niemiecki. M. Sokolowska & J. Szarski. Wydawnictwa Naukowo.

Management Dictionary. De Gruyter.

Management Dictionary: Fachwoerterbuch fuer Betriebswirtschaft, Wirtschafts und Steuerrecht und Datenverarbeitung. Werner Sommer & Hans-Martin Schoenfeld. De Gruyter.

Management-Taschenlexikon. Peter Haas. Verlag Moderne Industrie.

Manual del Automovil en 5 Idiomas: Diccionario Idiomatico del Automovil. Equipo Reactor de Ceac. French & Eur.

Marxistisch-Leninistisches Woerterbuch der Philosophie. G. Klaus & M. Buhr. (Pub. by Rowohlt). French & Eur.

Marxistisch-Leninistisches Woerterbuch der Philosophie. G. Klaus & M. Buhr. Rowohlt.

Mathematics Dictionary. Glenn James. Van Nos Reinhold.

Mathematik Englisch-Deutsch-Franzoesisch-Russisch. Ralf Sube & Gunther Eisenreich. VEB Technik.

Mathematik Englisch-Deutsch-Franzoesisch-Russisch. Ralf Sube & Gunther Eisenreich. VEB Technik.

Die Mathematik I: Ein Lexikon zur Schulmathematik Sekundarstufe. Harald Scheid et al. Biblio Inst.

Die Mathematik II: Ein Lexikon zur Schulmathematik Sekundarstufe II. Harald Scheid et al. Biblio Inst.

Mathematisch-Naturwissenschaftliches Woerterbuch Deutsch-Dari. Guenter Rack. Groos Verlag.

Mathematisches Vokabular. Berthold Klaften. (Pub. by Wila). French & Eur.

Medical Dictionary. D. W. Unseld. Adler.

Medical Dictionary. B. Zoltnicki. (Pub. by Schattauer). French & Eur.

Medical Dictionary of the English & German Languages. Dieter W. Unseld. Wissenschaftliche.

Medical Dictionary of the English & German Languages: Medizinisches Worterbuch der Deutschen und Englischen Sprache. Dieter Unseld. Intl Pubns Serv.

Medizinische Fachsprache Verstandlich Gemacht. Eduard Strauss. Froehlich Verlag.

Medizinisches Woerterbuch. Urban Kaps. (Pub. by Bruno Wilkens). French & Eur.

Medizinisches Woerterbuch. E. Veillon & A. Nobel. (Pub. by H. Huber). French & Eur.

Medizinisches Woerterbuch. E. Veillon & A. Nobel. Huber.

Medizinisches Woerterbuch der Deutschen und Englischen Sprache. D. Unseld. (Pub. by Wissenschaftlicher Vlg.). French & Eur.

Medizintechnik-Englisch-Deutsch-Franzoesisch-Russisch-Spanisch-Polnisch-Ungarisch-Slowakisch. Roald Albert & Harry Hahnewald. VEB Technik.

Mein Allerschoenstes Woerterbuch. Richard Scarry. Adler Bks.

Mein Erster Brockhaus. F A Brockhaus.

Mennonite Low-German Dictionary. John Thiessen & Jack Thiessen. Elwert.

Metal Forming Dictionary. A. M. Abd-El-Wahed. French & Eur.

Metallurgisk Ordbok. Norsk Verkstedsindustris Standardiseringssentral.

Meyers grosses Handlexikon in Farbe. Biblio Inst.

Meyers Grosses Handlexikon in Farbe. Ed. by Lexikonredaktion. Biblio Inst.

Meyers Grosses Jahreslexikon. Ferdinand Hirschelmann. Biblio Inst.

Meyers Grosses Jahreslexikon. Ferdinand Hirschelmann. Biblio Inst.

Meyers Grosses Jahreslexikon: Berichtszeitraum. Ferdinand Herschelman. Biblio Inst.

Meyers Grosses Kinderlexikon. Achim Broeger. Illus. by Guenther Biste & Peter Freitag. Biblio Inst.

Meyers Grosses Personenlexikon. (Pub. by Bibliographisches Institut). French & Eur.

Meyers Grosses Personenlexikon. Biblio Inst.

Meyers Grosses Standardlexikon in 3 Banden. Ed. by Lexikonredaktion des Bibliographischen Instituts. Biblio Inst.

Meyers Grosses Sternbuch fur Kinder. Joachim Herrmann. Illus. by Harald Bukor & Ruth Bukor. Biblio Inst.

Meyers Grosses Taschenlexikon in 24 Banden. Biblio Inst.

Meyers Grosses Universallexikon-Jahrbucher. Biblio Inst.

Meyers Grosses Universallexikon-Jahrbucher. Biblio Inst.

Meyers Grosses Universallexikon-Jahrbucher. Biblio Inst.

Meyers Grosses Universallexikon-Jahrbucher: Luxusausgabe. Biblio Inst.

Meyers Illustrierte Weltgeschichte in 20 Banden: Band I, Die Vorgeschichte. Biblio Inst.

Meyers Kinderlexikon: Mein Erstes Lexikon. Adler Bks.

Meyers Kinderlexikon: Mein erstes Lexikon. Biblio Inst.

Meyers Lexikon A-Z. Bibliographisches Institut. Bibl Inst Leipzig.

Meyers Neues Lexikon. Pergamon.

Meyers Neues Lexikon Jahrbucher. Biblio Inst.

Meyers Neues Lexikon Weltatlas. Adolf Hanle. Biblio Inst.

Meyers Physik-Lexikon. (Pub. by Bibliographisches Institut). French & Eur.

Meyers Physik-Lexikon. Biblio Inst.

Meyers Standardlexikon Des Gesamten Wissens. (Pub. by Bibliographisches Institut). French & Eur.

Meyers Standardlexikon Des Gesamten Wissens. Biblio Inst.

Meyers Taschenlexikon Bionik. Ed. by E. Forth & E. Schewitzer. Bibl Inst Leipzig.

Meyers Taschenlexikon Urheberrecht. A. Glucksmann et al. Bibl Inst Leipzig.

Meyers Universal Lexikon. Ed. by H. Goeschel & A. Zwahr. Bibl Inst Leipzig.

Meyers Universal Lexikon. Ed. by H. Goeschel & A. Zwahr. Bibl Inst Leipzig.

Meyers Universal Lexikon. Ed. by H. Goeschel & A. Zwahr. Bibl Inst Leipzig.

Meyers Universal Lexikon. Ed. by H. Goeschel & A. Zwahr. Bibl Inst Leipzig.

Meyers Universallexikon. Bibl Inst Leipzig.

Microelectronics Dictionary. IWT Verlag Editors. (Pub. by VDI W Germany). Heyden.

Military Eitzen. K. Eitzen. (Pub. by Vlg. Offene Worte). French & Eur.

Mineralogy Dictionary, German-Russian. French & Eur.

Minimum Standard German Vocabulary. Walter Wadepuhl & Bayard Morgan. Irvington.

Minimum-Worterbuch: Deutsch-Polnisch, Polnisch-Deutsch. J. Jozwicki. French & Eur.

Modellbahnlexikon. Gunter E. Albrecht & Hans D. Reichardt et al. Alba Buchverlag.

Modellflug-Lexikon. Werner Thies. Verlag Technik.

Modern Dictionary Slovene-German-Slovene. D. Debenjak. French & Eur.

A Modern Textile Dictionary. P. Hohenadel & V. Relton. French & Eur.

A Modern Textile Dictionary: English-German. P. Hohenadel & J. Relton. French & Eur.

Das Moderne Kinder-Lexikon in Farbe.Unsere Welt in Wort Und Bild: Unsere Welt in Wort & Bild. K. Finke & R. Goock. Adler Bks.

Morphologie & Generative Grammatik. Ed. by Ferenc Kiefer. Akad Verl Ath.

Moselfraenkische Mundart. Edmund Endres. Rheinland Verlag.

Multilengua Diccionario de Cartas Comerciales en Cuatro Idiomas. French & Eur.

The Multilingual Computer Dictionary. Alan Isaacs. Facts on File.

Multilingual Dictionary of Technical Terms in Cartography. E. Meynen. (Pub. by F. Steiner). French & Eur.

Multilingual Glossary of Automatic Control Technology: English-French-German-Russian-Italian-Spanish-Japanese. D. T. Broadbent & M. Masubuchi. Pergamon.

Multilingual Law Dictionary: English, French, Spanish, German. Lawrence D. Egbert. Oceana.

Multilingual Lexicon of Linguistics & Philology: English, Russian, German, French. Rose Nash. U of Miami Pr.

Multilingual Technical Dictionary on Irrigation & Drainage. US Comm Irrigation.

Multilingual Vocabulary of Educational Radio & Television Terms. Intl Pubns Serv.

Music Translation Dictionary: An English, Czech, Danish, Dutch, French, German, Hungarian, Italian, Polish, Portuguese, Russian, Spanish, Swedish Vocabulary of Music. Compiled by Carolyn D. Grigg. Greenwood.

Musical Thesaurus: A Dictionary of Musical Language. Robert Leach. J Hannon.

Der Musik-Brockhaus. F A Brockhaus.

Die Musik: Ein Sachlexikon. Gerhard Kwiatkowski. Biblio Inst.

Musikalisches Lexikon. Johann Walther. (Pub. by Baerenreiter). French & Eur.

Musisches Lexikon. Willi A. Koch. Kroener.

My Illustrated Dictionary: Arabic & Ger. Libr du Liban. Intl Bk Ctr.

Mykologisches Worterbuch. K. Berger. French & Eur.

Namenforschung im Ostniederlandisch-Westfalischen Grengebiet. Pierre Hessmann. Rodopi.

Neederland-Duits: Wolter's Woorden Boek. W. H. Wallis. French & Eur.

Nemetsko-Gruzinsko-Russkii Frazeologicheskii Slovar. N. Gamrekeli et al. (Pub. by Ganatleba). Four Continent.

Nemetsko-Russkii Arkhitekturnyi Slovar. M. M. Zhitomirskii. (Pub. by GINS). Four Continent.

Nemetsko-Russkii Frazeologicheskii Slovar. (Pub. by GINS). Four Continent.

Nemetsko-Russkii Gidrotekhnicheskii Slovar. L. B. Bernshtein. (Pub. by Fizmatgiz). Four Continent.

Nemetsko-Russkii Matematicheskii Slovar. L. A. Kaluzhnin et al. (Pub. by Fizmatgiz). Four Continent.

Nemetsko-Russkii Meditsinskii Slovar. E. F. Sommerau. (Pub. by Medgiz). Four Continent.

Nemetsko-Russkii Mekhaniko-Matematicheskii Slovar. N. M. Dovnar-Zapolskaia. (Pub. by MGU). Four Continent.

Nemetsko-Russkii Okeanograficheskii Slovar. N. N. Gorskii et al. (Pub. by GINS). Four Continent.

Nemetsko-Russkii Slovar. Ed. by I. V. Rakhmanov. (Pub. by GINS). Four Continent.

Nemetsko-Russkii Slovar. Ed. by I. V. Rakhmanov. (Pub. by GINS). Four Continent.

Nemetsko-Russkii Slovar po Lesnomu Khoziaistvu. Ernst A. Pavlov & Olga I. Semenova. Russkii Iazyk.

Nemetsko-Russkii Slovar Po Metalloobrabotke. N. F. Deputatova et al. (Pub. by Gosizdat Tekhnich Teoretich. Lit.). Four Continent.

Nemetsko-Russkii Slovar Po Vychislitelnoi Tekhnike. V. Sharov et al. (Pub. by Russkii Iazyk). Four Continent.

Nemetsko-Russkii Zheleznodorozhnyi Slovar. D. A. Bunin. (Pub. by Gosizdat Tekhn.-Teoret. Lit.). Four Continent.

Der Neue Brockhaus. F A Brockhaus.

Der Neue Brockhaus Lexikon & Woerterbuch in funf Baenden & Einem Atlas: Band 1. F A Brockhaus.

Neue Chinesische Vogelnamen. Alfred Hoffmann. Harrassowitz.

Neue Herder. Incl. Pergamon.

Neue Herder: Lexikon. (Pub. by Herder). French & Eur.

Neue Herder: Lexikon. Herder.

Der Neue Muret-Sanders. Ed. by Otto Springer. Incl. Langenscheidt.

Neues Grosses Gartenlexikon. (Pub. by Suedwest). French & Eur.

Neues Grosses Gartenlexikon. Suedwest.

Neues Taschenlexikon. Roland Goock. Prae Heinz.

Neugriechisch. Incl. Langenscheidt.

New College Dictionary English-German. M Rosenberg.

New College German & English Dictionary. John C. Traupman. AMSCO Sch.

New College German Dictionary (Plain Edition) Langenscheidt.

New College German Dictionary (Thumb-Indexed) Langenscheidt-Hachette.

New Condensed Muret-Sanders German Dictionary. Langenscheidt.

New International Dictionary of Refrigeration. International Institute of Refrigeration. (IIR). Unipub.

New Muret-Sanders Encyclopedic Dictionary: Part I, English-German. Ed. by O. Springer. M Rosenberg.

New Muret-Sanders Encyclopedic Dictionary: Part II, German-English. O. Springer. M Rosenberg.

New Muret-Sanders Encyclopedic Dictionary: Pt. I, vol. 1, A-M. Langenscheidt.

New Muret-Sanders Encyclopedic Dictionary: Pt. II, vol. 1, A-K. Langenscheidt.

New Muret-Sanders Encyclopedic Dictionary: Pt. I, vol. 2, N-Z. Langenscheidt.

New Muret-Sanders Encyclopedic Dictionary: Pt. II, vol. 2, L-Z. Langenscheidt.

Niederlaendisch. Incl. Langenscheidt.

Niederlassungsrecht. Institut International de Terminologie Juridique & Administrative. Langen AG.

Norsk-Tysk Ordbok. G. Paulsen. French & Eur.

Norwegian-German Dictionary. Gerd Paulsen. Kunnskapsforlaget.

Norwegian-German Dictionary of Commerce. Daae Gabrielsen. Kunnskapsforlaget.

Norwegian-German Dictionary of Technical Terms. D. Strom & J. A. Strom. Kunnskapsforlaget.

Nouveau Dictionnaire International du Froid. French & Eur.

Novye Parallel'nye Slovari Iazykov Russkago, Frantsuzskago, Nemetskago i Angliiskago. Filipp Reiff. Incl. Four Continent.

Nuclear Power Dictionary. E. Brandenberger & F. Stattmann. (Verlag Karl Thiemig). French & Eur.

Nuevo Glosario, Diccionario Poliglota de la Arquitectura. Buenaventura Bassegoda Muste. French & Eur.

Numismatisches Wappen-Lexicon. Wilhelm Rentzmann. Transpress Verlag fur Verkehrswesen.

Oekonomisches Lexikon: A-G. Wissenschaftliche.

Oekonomisches Lexikon: H-P. Wissenschaftliche.

Oekonomisches Lexikon: Q-Z. Wissenschaftliche.

Oekonomisches Woerterbuch Aussenwirtschaft (Dictionary of External Exonomic Relations & Trade) Ed. by Siegfried Kohls. Intl Pubns Serv.

Oekonomisches Woerterbuch Aussenwirtschaft. S. Kohls. (Pub. by Ruceken Vlg). French & Eur.

Oekonomisches Woerterbuch Aussenwirtschaft. Wissenschaftliche.

Oekonomisches Woerterbuch Englisch-Deutsch. Wissenschaftliche.

Oekonomisches Woerterbuch Russisch-Deutsch. G. Moechel. (Pub. by Vlg. Die Wirtschaft). French & Eur.

Okologie. Wolfgang Tischler. Fischer Verlag.

Oldtimer-Lexikon. Halwart Schrader. BLV-Verlag.

Onteszet. Arpad Voros. Akademiai Kiado.

Optik & Optischer Geratebau Deutsch-Englisch. Werner Bindmann. VEB Technik.

Orbis Latinus: Lexikon lateinischer geographischer Namen des Mittelalters und der Neuzeit. Johann G. Graesse. Ed. by Helmut Plechl. Intl Pubns Serv.

Ordbog for Korrespondenter, Dansk-Tysk. Sven-Olaf Poulsen. Kjaer Bogtryk.

Oxford-Duden Bildwoerterbuch Deutsch & Englisch. Biblio Inst.

Oxford-Duden Bildwoerterbuch Englisch. Biblio Inst.

Paedagogisches Taschenlexikon. Karl E. Maier. Ed. by Ludwig Eckinger. Wolf Verlag.

Paedagogisches Taschenlexikon: A-Z. Alfons O. Schorb. Kamp Verlag.

Palaeontologisches Woerterbuch. Ulrich Lehmann. (Pub. by Dtv). French & Eur.

Palaeontologisches Woerterbuch. Ulrich Lehmann. (Pub. by F. Enke). French & Eur.

Palaeontologisches Woerterbuch. Ulrich Lehmann. Enke.

Palaontologisches Woerterbuch. Ulrich Lehmann. Enke.

Papiergeld-Lexikon. Albert Pick. Mosaik Verlag.

Parusny i sport. L. A. Chesnokov et al. Russkii Iazyk.

Pennsylvania German Dictionary. Marcus Lambert. Schiffer.

Pharmazeutische. Axel Kleemann. Thieme Verlag.

Philatelic Vocabulary in Five Languages. Philatelic Foundation. Philatelic Found.

Philosophiches Woerterbuch. Max Apel & Peter Luds. De Gruyter.

Philosophisches Woerterbuch. Heinrich Schmidt. Kroener.

Philosophisches Woerterbuch. Ed. by G. Klaus & M. Buhr. Bibl Inst Leipzig.

Philosophisches Worterbuch. Georg Klaus & Manfred Buhr. Bibl Inst Leipzig.

Phrase Dictionaries for the American Tourist. Frederick Stark. Incl. Delair.

Physics Dictionary. Ed. by R. Sube & G. Eisenreich. Adler.

Physics Terminology. A. Jesse. French & Eur.

Die Physik: Ein Lexikon der Gesamten Schulphysik. Hans Borucki et al. Biblio Inst.

Physik-Fachsprache Englisch-Franzosisch-Deutsch. A. Jesse. Bauverlag.

Phytopathologie & Pflanzenschutz. Gerd Frohlich et al. Fischer Verlag.

Pieciojezyczny Slownik Gleboznawczy. Adamczyk Boleslaw. Panstwowe Zaklad W.

Pipeline Dictionary. H. Bucksch & A. P. Altmeyer. (Pub. by Bauverlag). French & Eur.

Pipeline Dictionary. H. Bucksch & A. P. Altmeyer. Intl Pubns Serv.

Pipeline Dictionary. H. Bucksch & A. P. Altmeyer. Bauverlag.

Plast & Gummilexikon. EC Print AB.

Plastic Technology Dictionary. H. Y. El-Desouti. French & Eur.

Plastics Technical Dictionary: Part 1: English-German. Ed. by A. M. Wittfoht. (Pub. by Hanser International). Macmillan.

Plastics Technical Dictionary: Part 2: German-English. Ed. by A. M. Wittfoht. (Pub. by Hanser International). Macmillan.

Plasttechnik-Englisch-Deutsch-Franzoesisch-Russisch. Gisbert Kaliske. VEB Technik.

Pocket Dictionary Iron & Steel. Henry G. Freeman. Intl Pubns Serv.

Pocket Dictionary of Automotive Engineering: Taschenwoerterbuch Kraftfahrzeugtechnik. Henry G. Freeman. Intl Pubns Serv.

Pocket Dictionary of Technology & Science: Technischwissenschaftliches Taschenwoerte'buch: German-English & English-German. Karl Breuer. Intl Pubns Serv.

The Pocket Oxford German Dictionary. Ed. by M. L. Barker & H. Homeyer. Incl. German-English; English-German. Compiled by C. T. Carr. Oxford U Pr.

Pocket-Shorter Dictionary. Langenscheidt.

Podreczny Slownik Polsko-Niemiecki (Manual Dictionary Polish-German) A. Bzdega et al. French & Eur.

Politik & Gesellschaft: Ein Lexikon zur Politischen Bildung. Hede Prehl et al. Biblio Inst.

Politik Aufgespiesst: Heiteres Lexikon der Politischen Missbildung. Konrad Gerescher. Gauke.

Politik: Mit 1800 Stichwoertern. Ed. by Bernard Pfahlberg. Herder.

Politisch-Soziologisches Woerterbuch. Karl Rudolf Kollnig. Kamp Verlag.

Politisches Woerterbuch. Siegfried Landshut. (Pub. by Hochschule Fuer Wirtschaft U. Politik). French & Eur.

Polnisch. Stanislaw Walewski. Langenscheidt.

Polnisch-Deutsches Wissenschaftlich-Technishes Worterbuch. Z. J. Koch. French & Eur.

Polygrafie-Englisch-Deutsch-Franzoesisch-Russisch-Spanisch-Polnisch-Ungarisch-Solwakisch. Wolfgang Muller. VEB Technik.

Polygraph Dictionary for the Graphic Industries in Six Languages. Ed. by K. Collet. Intl Pubns Serv.

Polytechnic Dictionary: German-English, English-German. Rudolf Walther. Adler.

Polytechnisches Woerterbuch. Alibert Schlegelmilch. (Pub. by Veb Verlag Technik). French & Eur.

Polytechnisches Woerterbuch. Alibert Schlegelmilch. (Pub. by Veb Verlag Technik). French & Eur.

Polytechnisches Woerterbuch. Rudolf Walther. (Pub. by Veb Verlag Technik). French & Eur.

Polytechnisches Woerterbuch. Rudolf Walther. (Pub. by Veb Verlag Technik). French & Eur.

Polytechnisches Woerterbuch. Rudolf Walther. VEB Verlag Technik.

Polytechnisches Woerterbuch. Karl H. Radde & Francisco Laguna de la Vera. VEB Technik.

Polytechnisches Woerterbuch. Aribert Schlegelmilch. VEB Verlag Technik.

Polytechnisches Woerterbuch Deutsch-Englisch. Rudolf Walther. VEB Technik.

Polytechnisches Woerterbuch Deutsch-Franzoesisch. Veb Technik.

Polytechnisches Woerterbuch Deutsch-Spanisch. Karl H. Radde. VEB Technik.

Polytechnisches Woerterbuch Deutsch-Vietnamesisch. Tran Duy-Tu et al. VEB Technik.

Polytechnisches Woerterbuch Franzoesisch-Deutsch. VEB Technik.

Polytechnisches Woerterbuch Italienisch-Deutsch. Aribert Schlegelmilch. VEB Technik.

Polytechnisches Woerterbuch Russisch-Deutsch. Paul Hueter & Horst Goerner. VEB Technik.

Polytechnisches Woerterbuch Spanisch-Deutsch. VEB Technik.

Polytechnisches Worterbuch. Aribert Schlegelmilch. Hueber.

Pons Globalwoerterbuch Englisch-Deutsch. M Rosenberg.

Pons Globalworterbuch. Schoffler & Weis. Klett.

Pons-Grosswoerterbuch. Erich Weiss. Ed. by Heinrich Mattutat & Christian Nugue. Klett.

Pons Schoffler Weis English-German, German-English Dictionary. E. Weis et al. French & Eur.

Practical English-German, German-English Dictionary. Stephen Jones. Hippocrene Bks.

Practical Dictionary for Press & Advertising. Intl Pubns Serv.

Das Praktische Lexikon der Naturheilkunde. Ernst Meyer-Camberg. (Pub. by Mosaik/ VVA). French & Eur.

Press, Radio & Television. Denise Escarpit. Elp.

Printer's Terms Dictionary. R. Hostettler. Heinman.

Proverbes Francais: In French with Equivalents in English, German, Dutch, Italian, Spanish, Latin. G. Ilg. Elsevier.

Prusskii Iazyk Slovar: E-H. V. N. Toporov. (Pub. by Nauka). Four Continent.

Prusskii Iazyk Slovar: I-L. V. N. Toporov. (Pub. by Nauka). Four Continent.

Die Psychologie: Ein Sachlexikon fuer die Schule. Karl H. Ahlheim. Biblio Inst.

Psychologisches Woerterbuch. F. Dorsch. (Pub. by H. Huber). French & Eur.

Psychologisches Woerterbuch. Friedrich Dorsch. H Huber.

Putnam's Contemporary German Dictionary. Berkley Pub.

Quadrilingual Business Dictionary. (Pub. by European Schoolbks England). State Mutual Bk.

Radio & Television Dictionary. Abd-El-Wahed. French & Eur.

Radiochemisches Lexikon der Elemente und Ihrer Isotope. M. Haissinsky. (Pub. by Duemmler). French & Eur.

The Random House Basic Dictionary German. Ed. by Jenni H. Moulton. Ballantine.

Rechtschreibung & Wortkunde: Ein Woerterbuch fur die Schule. Jakob Ebner. Biblio Inst.

Rechtssprache Englisch-Deutsch. R. Renner & J. Tooth. (Pub. by M. Hueber). French & Eur.

Rechtssprache Englisch-Deutsch. R. Renner & J. Tooth. Hueber.

Rechtsworterbuch Fur Die Gewerbliche Wirtschaft. Ursula Becker. (Pub. by Fritz Knapp Verlag). French & Eur.

Reclams Filmfuhrer. Dieter Krusche & Jurgen Labenskt. Reclam.

Refrigeration & Conditioning Dictionary. Abd-El-Wahed. French & Eur.

Regeln & Sprache des Sports 1. Rainer Wehlen. Biblio Inst.

Regeln & Sprache des Sports 2. Rainer Wehlen. Biblio Inst.

Reisewoerrterbuch: German-English, English-German. M Rosenberg.

Reisewoerterbuch Deutsch-Englisch. M Rosenberg.

Relais Lexikon. Hans Sauer. Vertrieb.

Les Ressorts: Francais-Allemand-Anglais-Espagnol. S.N.F.R. Maison Dictionnaire.

Reviewing German Grammar & Building Vocabulary. Roselinde Konrad. U Pr of Amer.

Die Richtige Wortwahl: Ein Vergleichendes Woerterbuch Sinnverwandter Ausdruecke. Wolfgang Muller. Biblio Inst.

Riemann Musiklexikon. W. Gurlitt & H. Eggebrecht. (Pub. by Schatt's Soehne). French & Eur.

Ro Ro Ro Woerterbuch: Deutsch-Englisch, Englisch-Deutsch. Friedrich Kohler. Rowohlt.

Rock Lexikon. S. Schmidt-Joos & B. Graves. (Pub. by Rowohlt). French & Eur.

Rock Lexikon. S. Schmidt-Joos & B. Graves. Rowohlt.

Romanisches Etymologisches Woerterbuch. Wilhelm Meyer-Luebke. (Pub. by Carl Winter). French & Eur.

Romanishes Etymologisches Woerterbuch. Wilhelm Meyer-Luebke. Winter Univ.

Rororo-Lexikon zur Datenverarbeitung. Hans H. Schulze. Rowohlt.

Rororo Musikhandbuch. H. Lindlar. (Pub. by Rowohlt). French & Eur.

Rororo Musikhandbuch. H. Lindlar. Rowohlt.

Russian-German Dictionary. French & Eur.

Russisch-Deutsches Woerterbuch. Edmund Daum & W. Schenk. (Pub. by Max Hueber). French & Eur.

Russisch-Deutsches Woerterbuch. Edmund Daum & W. Schenk. Hueber.

Russisch-Deutsches Worterbuch der Funkechnik. P. K. Gorochow. French & Eur.

Russisch Elymologisches Woerterbuch. Max Vasmer. (Pub. by Carl Winter). French & Eur.

Russisch Etymologishes Woerterbuch. Max Vasmer. Winter Univ.

Russisch. Karl Blattner. Incl. Langenscheidt.

Russisch-Deutsches Woerterbuch der Chemie & Chemischen. Institut fur Angewandte Sprachwissenschaft. VEB Verlag Technik.

Russisch-Deutsches Woerterbuch Fuer Naturwissenschaftler und Ingenieure. S. Halbauer. (Pub. by M. Hueber). French & Eur.

Russisch-Deutsches Woerterbuch Fuer Naturwissenschaftler und Ingenieure. S. Halbauer. Hueber.

Russisch Etymologisches Woerterbuch. Max Vasmer. (Pub. by Carl Winter). French & Eur.

Russisch Etymologisches Woerterbuch. Max Vasmer. (Pub. by Carl Winter). French & Eur.

Russisch Etymologisches Woerterbuch. Max Vasmer. Winter Univ.

Russisch Etymologisches Woerterbuch. Max Vasmer. Winter Univ.

Russko-Anglo-Nemetsko-Frantsuzskii Slovar Terminov Po Avtomaticheskomu Upravleniiu. Ed. by A. V. Khramov. (Pub. by An Arm SSR). Four Continent.

Russko-Nemetskii Radioteknicheskii Slovar. P. K. Gorokhov. (Pub. by Glav. Red. Inostr. Nauchno-Tekhn. Slovarei Fizmata). Glav. Red. Inostr. Nauchno-Tekhn. Slovarei Fizmata.

Russko-Nemetskii Slovar. Ed. by E. I. Leping. (Pub. by Russkii Iazyk). Four Continent.

Russko-Novogrecheskii Karmannyi Slovar. N. Al. Sal'nov. (Pub. by Sov. Entsiklopediia). Four Continent.

Safety at Work & Pollution Control. Nicole Aymard Lapalu. Elp.

Sahkotieteellinen Sanasto. Suomen Standardisoimisliitto. Suomen Standard.

Sammlung Duden: Band I, Vollstaendiges Orthographisches Woerterbuch der Deutschen Sprache. Konrad Duden. Biblio Inst.

Sammlung Duden: Band II, Regeln & Woerterverzeichnis fuer die Deutsch Rechtschreibung. Biblio Inst.

Sammlung Duden: Band III, Akten zur Geschichte der Deutschen Einheitsschreibung. Paul Grebe. Biblio Inst.

Satzlexikon der Handelskorrespondenz. Zavada. Brandstetter.

Satzlexikon der Handelskorrespondenz. Zavada & Hartgenbush. Brandstetter.

Satzlexikon der Handelskorrespondenz. Zavada & Schraffl. Brandstetter.

Satzlexikon der Handelskorrespondenz. Zavada & Eberle. Brandstetter.

Satzlexikon der Handelskorrespondenz. Zavada & Weis. Brandstetter.

Schiffbau, Schiffahrt, Fischereitechnik-Russisch-Englisch-Deutsch. Erhard Bensch. VEB Technk.

Schluesselwoerter zur Berufsbildung. Hans J. Rosenthal. Ed. by Peter Gerds. Beltz & Co.

Schuelerlexikon fuer Arbeitslehre & Sozialkunde. Christian Schmieder & Gunther Fleischmann. Auer.

Die Schwachen Verben des Althochdeutschen. F. A. Raven. U of Ala Pr.

Schwedisch. H. Kornitzky. Langenscheidt.

Schwierigkeiten des Deutsch-Italienischen Wortschatzes. Bruno Storni. Ed. by Paolo Giovannelli. Klett.

Seemaennisches Woerterbuch. Wolfram Claviez. (Pub. by Delius, Klaving & Co.). French & Eur.

Die Semantische Struktur Desubstantivischer Bildungen auf Maessig. Goran Inghult. Almqvist.

Semiiazychnyi Slovar Po Elektrosviazi. (Pub. by Sov. Entsiklopediia). Four Continent.

Semiiazychnyi Slovar Po Mekhanike Gruntov & Fundamentostroeniiu. M. E. Scneider. (Pub. by Gosizdat Fizmat. Lit.). Four Continent.

Septemlingual Dictionary of the Names of European Animal. Ed. by L. Gozmany et al. (Pub. by Kiado Hungary). Heyden.

Seven Language Dictionary. Ed. by David Shumaker. Crown.

Seven Languages Dictionary. Imported Bks.

Siebenbuergisch-Saechsisches Woerterbuch. Incl. De Gruyter.

Slovar Naibolee Upotrebitel'Nykh Slov Anglii-Skogo, Nemetskogo & Frantsuzskogo Iazykov. Ed. by I. V. Rakhmanov. (Pub. by Izd. Inostr. & Natsional'Nal'Nykh Slovarei). Four Continent.

Slovene-German Dictionary. F. Tomsic. French & Eur.

Slovnik Zakladnich Odbornych Cesko-Nemeckych Vyrazu ze Silnicni a Mestske Dopravy. Jindrich Mrazek. SNTL.

Slownik Lekarski Polsko-Niemicki. Boleslaw Zlotnicki. Panstwowe Zaklad W.

So Werd bei uns Geredd. Kurt Brautigam. SVA Verlag.

Sommer-Schoenfeld, Management Dictionary, Deutsch-English: Fachwoerterbuch Fuer Betriebswirtschaft Wirtschafts-und Steuerrecht und Datenverarbeitung. De Gruyter.

Soziologisches Woerterbuch. H. Schoeck. (Pub. by Herder). French & Eur.

Soziologisches Woerterbuch. H. Schoeck. Herder.

Spanende Werkzeugmaschinen, Deutsch-Englische Begriffserlauterungen und Kommentare. Henry G. Freeman. (Pub. by Verlag W. Girardet). French & Eur.

Spanende Werkzeugmaschinen, Deutsch-Englische Begriffserlauterungen und Kommentare. Henry G. Freeman. Girardet.

Spanisch. Incl. Langenscheidt.

Spanisch. Incl. Langenscheidt.

Spanisches Supplement Zu Medizinisches Woerterbuch. E. Veillon & A. Nobel. (Pub. by H. Huber Vlg.). French & Eur.

Spanisches Supplement Zu Medizinisches Woerterbuch. E. Veillon & A. Nobel. Huber.

Spanish & German Dictionary. Ed. by R. J. Slaby & R. Grossman. Incl. Ungar.

Special Dictionary Machinery. H. G. Freeman. Adler.

Spezialwoerterbuch Maschinenwesen. Henry G. Freeman. (Pub. by Verlag W. Girardet). French & Eur.

Spezialwoerterbuch Maschinenwesen. Henry G. Freeman. Girardet.

Sport Brockhaus. (Pub. by Brockhaus). French & Eur.

Der Sport-Brockhaus. F A Brockhaus.

Der Sprach Brockhaus. Imported Bks.

Der Sprach-Brockhaus: Deutsches Bildwoerterbuch von A-Z. F A Brockhaus.

Sprechen Sie Rotwelsch. Guenter Puchner. Heimeran.

Standard German Dictionary. Langenscheidt.

Stellwerksdienst. Hans J. Arnold. Transpress Verlag fur Verkehrswesen.

Steuerlexikon. Ed. by Wilhelm H. Wacker. Vahlen.

Stilistisch-Phraseologisches Woerterbuch Spanisch-Deutsch. Werner Beinhauer. Hueber.

Strategic Terminology. Urs Schwarz & Laszlo Hadik. French & Eur.

Surface Treatment of Aluminum: Glossary of Technical Terms. Aluminum Verlag.

Svensk-Tysk Affarsordlista. Helge Birgersson. Esselte Studium.

Svensk-Tysk & Tysk-Svensk Standardlexikon. Esselte Studium.

Svensk-Tysk Ordbok. Esselte Studium.

Svensk-Tysk Ordbok: Supplement 78. Esselte Studium.

Svensk-Tysk Standardlexikon. Esselte Studium.

Svensk-Tyskt-Tyskt-Svenskt Standardlexikon. Esselte Studium.

Svenska Duden Bildlexikon. Imported Bks.

Synonymwoerterbuch. Ed. by H. Goerner & G. Kempcke. Bibl Inst Leipzig.

Systematische Zoologie Insekten. Werner Jacobs. Fischer Verlag.

Systems Analysis & Operations Research Dictionary. G Sezepesi & B. Szekely. (Pub. by Collets). State Mutual Bk.

Tachenlexikon Umweltschultz. Otto E. Ahlhaus et al. Pr Univ Fr.

Taschen-Lexikon International Abkurzungen & Kurzzeichen. Thomas Krist. Technik Tabel.

Taschenlexikon der Verhaltenskunde. Peter K. Meyer. Schoningh.

Taschenlexikon Elektronik, Funktechnik. (Pub. by Verlag Harri Deutsch). French & Eur.

Taschenlexikon Medizin. Dagobert Tutsch. Urban & Schwarzen.

Taschenwoerterbuch. Langenscheidt.

Taschenwoerterbuch der Botanischen Pflanzennamem. F. Boerner. (Pub. by P. Parey). French & Eur.

Taschenwoerterbuch der Botanischen Pflanzennamem. F. Boerner. Parey.

Taschenwoerterbuch des Fremdenverkehrs. W. Friedrich. (Pub. by M. Hueber). French & Eur.

Taschenwoerterbuch des Fremdenverkehrs. W. Friedreich. Hueber.

Taschenwoerterbuch Deutsch-Niederlaendisch. Ed. by Gerhard Worgt. VEB Verlag Enzyklopadie.

Taschenwoerterbuch Deutsch-Ungarisch. Ed. by Heinrich Weissling. VEB Verlag Enzyklopaedie.

Taschenwoerterbuch Eisen und Stahl. H. Freeman. (Pub. by M. Hueber). French & Eur.

Taschenwoerterbuch Eisen und Stahl. H. Freeman. Hueber.

Taschenwoerterbuch Englisch-Deutsch. Ed. by Walter Schmidt. VEB Verlag Enzyklopadie.

Taschenwoerterbuch Kraftfahrzeugtechnik. H. Freeman. (Pub. by M. Hueber). French & Eur.

Taschenwoerterbuch Kraftfahrzeugtechnik. H. Freeman. Hueber.

Taschenworterbuch. Walter Schmidt. VEB Verlag Enzyklopadie.

Taschenworterbuch Deutsch-Ungarisch. Heinrich Weissling. VEB Verlag Enzyklopadie.

Technical & Engineering Dictionary: Band II, English-German. De Vries & Herrmann. Brandstetter.

Technical & Engineering Dictionary: Band I, German-English. De Vries & Herrmann. Brandstetter.

Technical Automotive Dictionary: Russian-English-German-French-Bulgarian. G. Sikora. French & Eur.

Technical Dictionary: Archticture & Building. Tawfik Abd-El-Gawad. (Pub. by Collets). State Mutual Bk.

Technical Dictionary for Automotive Engineering. Ed. by R. Bosch. (Pub. by VDI W Germany). Heyden.

Technical Dictionary for the Shoe Industry. Gerhard Knebel. (Pub. by Huethig). French & Eur.

Technical Dictionary for Weaponry. Gustav Sybertz. (Pub. by Neumann-Neudamm). French & Eur.

Technical Dictionary of Anglo-American Legal Terminology. D. Beseler & B. Jacobs. (Pub. by de Gruyter). French & Eur.

Technical Dictionary of Automatization & Programming: English, French, German, Russian,-Slovene. Ed. by E. Burger. French & Eur.

Technical Dictionary of Data Processing, Computers & Office Machines, English, German, French, Russian. E. Burger. Pergamon.

Technical Dictionary of Petrochemistry. W. Leipnitz. (Pub. by Vlg. Technik). French & Eur.

Technical Dictionary of Production Engineering: Vol. 2, German-English. R. Walther. Pergamon.

Technical Dictionary of Textile Chemistry - Fachwoerterbuch Chemiefasern: German-English-French, English-German-French, French-German-English. Werner Winkler. Intl Pubns Serv.

Technical Dictionary Pulp & Paper. Wolfgang Weitzel. Incl. Intl Pubns Serv.

Technical Dictionary: Refrigeration & Air Conditioning. (Pub. by Collets). State Mutual Bk.

Technical Dictionary: The Textile Industry. (Pub. by Collets). State Mutual Bk.

Technical-Economical Dictionary for Business Purposes. B. Bajic et al. French & Eur.

Technical Petroleum Dictionary of Well-Logging, Drilling & Production Terms. Ed. by Sonia Ketchian. Intl Pubns Serv.

Technical Pocket Dictionary, English-German , German-English. Henry G. Freeman. Adler.

Technical Pocket Dictionary-Technisches Taschenwoerterbuch. Henry G. Freeman. Intl Pubns Serv.

Technical Veterinary Dictionary. Wolfgang Lindeke. French & Eur.

Technik-Worterbuch: Chemie & Chemische Technik. (Pub. by Collet's). State Mutual Bk.

Technisch Wissenschaftliches Taschenwoerterbuch. (Pub. by Georg Siemens Verlagsbuchhandlung). French & Eur.

Technische Akustik. Walter Reichardt. VEB Verlag Technik.

Technische Kybernetik Grundlagen & Anwendungen Deutsch-English. Hans D. Junge. VEB Technik.

Technisches Deutsch fuer Auslaender. Strasak & Sulek. Brandstetter.

Technisches Deutschfuer Auslaender. Jaroslav Strasak. French & Eur.

Technisches Englisch. Henry G. Freeman. (Pub. by Girardet). French & Eur.

Technisches Taschen Woerterbuch: Deutsch-Englisch, Englisch-Deutsch. Henry Freeman. Hueber.

Technisches Taschenwoerterbuch. H. Freeman. (Pub. by M. Hueber). French & Eur.

Technisches Taschenwoerterbuch. A. Grunwald-Beyer. (Pub. by Georg Siemens Verlagsbuchhandlung). French & Eur.

Technisches Taschenwoerterbuch. A. Kroeger-Jannetti. (Pub. by Georg Siemens Verlagsbuchhandlung). French & Eur.

Technisches Taschenwoerterbuch. H. Freeman. Heuber.

Technisches Woerterbuch. Ulatko Dabac. (Pub. by Bauverlag). French & Eur.

Technisches Woerterbuch. Antonin Kucera. (Pub. by Brandstetter). French & Eur.

Technisches Woerterbuch. Antonin Kucera. (Pub. by Brandstetter). French & Eur.

Technisches Woerterbuch. A. Naxerova. (Pub. by Brandstetter). French & Eur.

Technisches Woerterbuch. A. Naxerova. (Pub. by Brandstetter). French & Eur.

Technisches Woerterbuch. Salvatore Orlando-Meyer. (Pub. by Brandstetter). French & Eur.

Technisches Woerterbuch. Salvatore Orlando-Meyer. (Pub. by Brandstetter). French & Eur.

Technisches Woerterbuch. Taspinar. Brandstetter.

Technisches Woerterbuch. Ulatko Dabac. Bauverlag.

Technisches Woerterbuch. Antonin Kucera. Brandstetter.

Technisches Woerterbuch. Antonin Kucera. Brandstetter.

Technisches Woerterbuch. A. Naxerova. Brandstetter.

Technisches Woerterbuch. A. Naxerova. Brandstetter.

Technisches Woerterbuch. Salvatore Orlando-Meyer. Brandstetter.

Technisches Woerterbuch. Salvatore Orlando-Meyer. Brandstetter.

Technisches Woerterbuch: Band I, Italienisch-Deutsch. Meyer & Orlando. Brandstetter.

Technisches Woerterbuch: Band I, Russisch-Deutsch. Kucera. Brandstetter.

Technisches Woerterbuch: Band I, Tschechisch-Deutsch. Naxerova. Brandstetter.

Technisches Woerterbuch: Band II, Deutsch-Italienisch. Meyer & Orlando. Brandstetter.

Technisches Woerterbuch: Band II, Deutsch-Russisch. Kucera. Brandstetter.

Technisches Woerterbuch Deutsch-Esperanto. R. Haferkorn. U of Toronto Pr.

Technisches Woerterbuch Fuer Die Schuhindustrie: German-English & English-German. Intl Pubns Serv.

Technishes Englisch. Henry G. Freeman. Girardet.

Technological Dictionary. Michel Feutry. Maison Dictionnaire.

Technological Dictionary in Three Languages. Hoyer-Kreuter. Ed. by Alfred Schlomann. Incl. Ungar.

Technological Engineering Dictionary German-Serbocroatian. Ed. by S. Radic. French & Eur.

Technologie und Terminologie der Gewerbe und Kunste bei Griechen und Romern. Hugo Blumner. Ed. by Moses Finley. Ayer Co.

Technologisches Woerterbuch. Egon Von Bahder. (Pub. by Girardet). French & Eur.

Technologisches Woerterbuch. Egon Von Bahder. Girardet.

Technologisches Woerterbuch Franzoisisch. Martin Pabst. (Pub. by Verlag W. Girardet). French & Eur.

Technologisches Woerterbuch Franzoisisch. Kurt Stellhorn. (Pub. by Verlag W. Girardet). French & Eur.

Technologisches Woerterbuch Franzoisisch. Martin Pabst. Girardet.

Technologisches Woerterbuch
Franzoisisch. Kurt Stellhorn.
Girardet.
Technologisches Woerterbuch
Spanish. (Pub. by Verlag W.
Girardet). French & Eur.
Technologisches Woerterbuch
Spanish. Girardet.
Tedesco-Italiano, Italiano-Tedesco.
Ed. by Vladimiro Macchi. Sansoni.
Ten Bosch's Quadralingual
Engineering Dictionary. Imported
Bks.
Terminologia turistico alberghiera:
L'albergatore poliglotta. Elisabetta
Neiger. Ed Calderini.
Terminologie de la physique: Anglais-
Allemand-Francais. A Jesse.
Maison Dictionnaire.
Terminology of Documentation: A
Selection of 1200 Basic Terms
Published in English, French,
German, Spanish & Russian.
(UNESCO). Unipub.
Terminology of Environmental
Hygiene. European Parliament -
Translation Division. Intl Pubns
Serv.
Teutscher, & Reussischer,
Dictionarium: Dictionarium
Vindobonense. Ed. by Gerhard
Birkfellner. Akad Verl Ath.
Textil-Fachwoerterbuch. Max
Matthes. Schiele & Schon.
Textil-Worterbuch. Paul Hohenadel &
Jonathan Relton. Brandstetter.
Textile Dictionary. Elsevier.
Textile Dictionary. G. Velco. (Pub. by
Collets). State Mutual Bk.
Textile Industry Dictionary. Ed. by
A. M. Sabrie & R. S. Scharaf et al.
French & Eur.
Textile Terminology: German-English
& English-German. Derrick O.
Michelson. Intl Pubns Serv.
Textilwoerterbuch: Band I, English-
Deutsch. Relton Hohenadel &
Relton. Brandstetter.
Textilwoerterbuch: Band II, Deutsch-
English. Hohenadel & Relton.
Brandstetter.
Theological German Vocabulary.
Walter M. Mosse. Octagon.
Thesaurus di Scienze della Terra.
Patron.
Thraenen-Samen &
Steckdosenschnauze. Hilke Moeller.
Ed. by C. R. Von Grieffenberg &
Wolfdietrich Schnurres. Jurisdruck.
Tiefkuhl Lexikon. G. Doring &
Rudolphi. (Pub. by Deutscher
Fachverlag). French & Eur.
Tierlexikon. H. Smolik. (Pub. by
Rowohlt). French & Eur.
Tierlexikon. H. Smolik. Rowohlt.
Tiernamen & Zoologische
Fachworter. Erwin Hentschel.
Fischer Verlag.
Toba-Batak-Deutsches Worterbuch.
Johannes G. Warneck. Nyhoff.
Tool Dictionary. Henry G. Freeman.
Adler.
Torrent Control Terminology. (FAO).
Unipub.
Training von A bis Z: Kleines
Worterbuch fuer der Theorie &
Praxis der Sportl Trainings. Ed. by
Gunter Thiess et al. Sportverlag.
Transpress Lexikon Seefahrt. Ulrich
Scharnow. Transpress Verlag fur
Verkehrswesen.
Trubners Deutsches Woerterbuch.
Alfred Gotze. (Pub. by de Gruyter).
French & Eur.
Truebners Deutsches Woerterbuch.
Ed. by Alfred Goetze & Walther
Mitzka. De Gruyter.
Tschechisch. Incl. Langenscheidt.
Two Thousand & One German &
English Idioms: 2001 Deutsche und
Englische Idiome. Bernard
Rechtschaffen & Louis Marck.
Barron.
Tysk-Dansk: Dansk-Tysk Ordbog. F.
Albertus. French & Eur.
Tysk-Dansk Dansk-Tysk Special
Ordbog. E. Fryd. French & Eur.
Tysk-Dansk, Dansk-Tysk
Specialordbog. Ejnar Fryd. For Stat
Rev.
Tysk-Dansk Ordbog. E. Bork & E.
Kaper. French & Eur.
Tysk-Dansk Teknisk Ordbog. A.
Warrern. French & Eur.

Tysk-Svensk Ordbok. Esselte
Studium.
Tysk-Svensk Ordbok: Supplement 80.
Esselte Studium.
Uchebny Slovar Obschetekhnich:
Leksiki. I. F. Rudakova. (Pub. by
Russkii Iazyk). Four Continent.
Uchebnyi Slovar Obshchetekhnich:
Russko-Anglo-Frantsuzsko-
Nemetskii. I. F. Rudakova et al.
(Pub. by Russkii Iazyk). Four
Continent.
Ullstein Lexikon der Deutschen
Sprache. Rudolf Koester. (Pub. by
Ullstein Verlag/VVA). French &
Eur.
Ullstein Lexikon der Kunst und
Architektur. Heiner Knell. (Pub. by
Ullstein Verlag/VVA). French &
Eur.
Ullstein Lexikon der Medizin. (Pub.
by Ullstein Verlag/VVA). French &
Eur.
Ullstein Lexikon der Pflanzenwelt.
Hartmut Bastian. (Pub. by Ullstein
Verlag VA). French & Eur.
Ullstein Lexikon der Tierwelt.
Hartmut Bastian. (Pub. by Ullstein
Verlag/VVA). French & Eur.
Ullstein Lexikon des Rechts. Otto
Gritschneder. (Pub. by Ullstein
Verlag/VVA). French & Eur.
Ungarisch-Deutsches Woerterbuch
der Rechts & Verwaltungssprache:
Teil I, Ungarisch-Deutsch. Sandor
Karcsay. Recht & Wirtschaft.
Ungarisch-Deutsches Woerterbuch
der Rechts & Verwaltungssprache:
Teil II, Deutsch-Ungarisch. Sandor
Karcsay. Recht & Wirtschaft.
Universal German Dictionary.
Langenscheidt.
Universal Woerterbuch Englisch-
Deutsch. M Rosenberg.
Velosipeday i sport. S. N. Novozhilov
et al. Russky Yazyk.
Vergleichendes und Etymologisches
Worterbuch der Germanischen
Starken Verben. Elmar Seebold.
Mouton.
Vergleichendes Woerterbuch der
Indogermanischen Sprachen. Alois
Walde. Ed. by Julius Pokorny. De
Gruyter.
Verhaltensbiologie. Gunter Tembrock.
Fischer Verlag.
Versicherungsenzykolpaedie. Ed. by
Walter G. Grosse et al. Gabler.
Vest Pocket German. Institute for
Language Study. (BN). B&N NY.
Vest Pocket German Dictionary. New
Century.
Vocabolario italiano-tedesco. Introito
& Porta. Bottega d'Erasmo.
Vocabolario italiano-tedesco-italiano.
S. David. (CEB). Capitol-Dischi.
Vocabolario italiano-tedesco-italiano.
S. David. (CEB). Capitol-Dischi.
Vocabolario Italiano-Tedesco,
Tedesco-Italiano. Ed. by Sante
David. Capitol Edit.
Vocabolario tedesco-italiano e
italiano-tedesco. A. Deidda.
Malipiero.
Vocabulaire Allemand. Jean Chassard
& Gonthier Weil. Hachette.
Vocabulaire Allemand par l'image. O.
N. Scheid. Bordas-Dunod.
Vocabulaire d'Astronomie. French &
Eur.
Vocabulaire d'astronomie: Francais-
Anglais-Allemand. C. I. L. F.
Vocabulaire de Base Allemand-
Francais. Charles Chatelanat &
Theodor Henzi. Hachette.
Vocabulaire de Fonderie Francais-
Allemand. Centre Technique des
Industries de la Fonderie. Ed Tech
Ind.
Vocabulaire de la radiographie.
C.I.L.F. Maison Dictionnaire.
Vocabulaire de l'oceanologie.
Hachette-Jeunesse.
Vocabulaire de sciences et techniques
spatiales. C.I.L.F. Maison
Dictionnaire.
Vocabulaire des Termes: Essentiels
Utilises pour la Transmissien Ligne;
Francais-Espagnol-Russe-Allemand-
Italien-Neerlandais-Polonais-
Portugais-Suedois. U. I. T.
Vocabulaire Ethnologique. Armin
Heymer. French & Eur.

Vocabulaire Ethologique: Allemand-
Anglais-Francais. Armin Heymer.
PUF.
Vocabulaire Forestier Francais-
Allemand-Danois. C. Jacobi.
Picard.
Vocabulaire Franco-Anglo-Allemand
de Geomorphologie. Henri Baulig.
Strasbourg, U.
Vocabulaire International des Termes
d'urbanisme & d'architecture:
Francais-Allemand-Anglais. Jean-
Henri Calsat. Eyrolles.
Vocabulaire International des Termes
d'urbanisme & d'architecture:
Francais-Allemand-Anglais. Jean-
Henri Calsat & Jean-Pierre Sydler.
Ste. Diff. Tech. Bat. T. P.
Vocabulaire International des Termes
d'Urbanisme et d'Architecture.
Jean-Henri Calsat & Jean P. Sydler.
French & Eur.
Vocabulaire Multilingue de la Science
du Sol: Anglais-Francais-Espagnol-
Allemand-Portugais-Italien-
Neerlandais-Suedois-Russe. G. V.
Jacks & R. Tavernier. F. A. O.
Vocabulaire Progressif de l'allemand.
Paul Banvard & Pierre Kuhn. CDU.
Vocabulaire Systematique Francais-
Allemand. Pierre Borel. Francke.
Vocabulaire Technique Allemand-
Francais. Francis Cusset. Berger-
Levrault.
Vocabulaire Technique Allemand-
Francais, Francais-Allemand.
Francis Cusset. French & Eur.
Vocabulaire Technique Anglais-
Francais, Francais-Anglais. Francis
Cusset. French & Eur.
Vocabular Latina. Esselte Studium.
Vocabularios Aleman-Espanol-Polaco.
Novaro.
Vocabularium Pharmaceuticum. Ed.
by Albert Graa. Intl Pubns Serv.
Vocabularium Polyglottum Vitae
Silvarum. R. Litschauer. (Pub. by P.
Parey). French & Eur.
Vocabularium Polyglottum Vitae
Silvarum. R. Litschauer. Parey.
Das Vokabular der Psychoanalyse.
Jean Laplanche. (Pub. by
Suhrkamp). French & Eur.
Volistaendiges Woerterbuch Ueber die
Gedichte des Homores und der
Homeriden. Carl Capelle. (Pub. by
Wissenschaftl Buchgesells). French
& Eur.
Die Volkssprache der Unteren Saar &
der Obermosel: Ein
Moselfrankisches Woerterbuch.
Karl Conrath. MG Schmitz.
Vollstaendiges Woerterbuch Zur
Sogenannten Caedmonschen
Genesis. Theodor Braasch. (Pub. by
Carl Winter). French & Eur.
Vollstaendiges Woerterbuch Zur
Sogenannten Caedmonschen
Genesis. Theodor Braasch. Winter
Univ.
Von Bach zur Elektronik. Rudolf
Brauner. Prugg.
Die Vorsilbe ver & Ihre Geschichte.
Max Leopold. Olms Verlag.
Was Bedeutet Das? Duden. Esselte
Studium.
Die Welt Von A-Z. Adler Bks.
Western Lexikon. Joe Hembus. Heyne
W Verlag.
Wielki Slownik Polsko-Niemiecki:
Grosswoerterbuch Polnische-
Deutsch. Jan Piprek & Juliusz
Ippoldt. Wiedza Powszechna.
Wirtschafts-Woerterbuch. R.
Eichborn. (Pub. by Econ Vlg).
French & Eur.
Wirtschafts-Woerterbuch. R. Eichborn
& A. Fuentes. (Pub. by Econ Vlg).
French & Eur.
Wirtschaftssprache Deutsch-Englisch,
Englisch-Deutsch. R. Renner & R.
Sachs. M Rosenberg.
Wirtschaftssprache Franzoesisch-
Deutsch. G. Haensch & R. Renner.
(Pub. by M. Hueber). French &
Eur.
Wirtschaftssprache Franzoesisch-
Deutsch. G. Haensch & R. Renner.
Hueber.
Wirtschaftssprache Spanisch-Deutsch.
G. Haensch & F. Casero. (Pub. by
M. Hueber). French & Eur.
Wirtschaftssprache Spanisch-Deutsch.
G. Haensch & F. Casero. Hueber.

Wirtschaftswoerterbuch Spanisch-
Deutsch. Eichborn & Fuentes. (Pub.
by Econ). French & Eur.
Das Wissen von A-Z: Ein
Allgemeines Lexikon fur die Schule.
Gisela Preuss. Biblio Inst.
Wissenschaftstheoretisches Lexikon.
Edmund Braun. (Pub. by Styria).
French & Eur.
Woerter & Gegenwoerter. C. Agricola
& E. Agricola. Bibl Inst Leipzig.
Woerter & Wendungen. Ed. by E.
Agricola et al. Bibl Inst Leipzig.
Woerter zur Valenz & Distribution
der Substantive. K. Sommerfeldt &
H. Schreiber. Bibl Inst Leipzig.
Woerterbuch. Gross. Verlag Harri
Deutsch.
Woerterbuch - Linguistische
Grundbegriffe. W. Ulrich. French &
Eur.
Woerterbuch als Fehlerquelle. Buske.
Woerterbuch Bau: Ingenieurbau &
Baumaschinen. H. Bucksch.
Bauverlag.
Woerterbuch Burmesisch-Deutsch.
Annemarie Esche. VEB Verlag
Enzyklopadie.
Woerterbuch Chemie & Chemische
Technik. Gross. Incl; Verlag Harri
Deutsch.
Woerterbuch Chemie und Chemische
Technik. H. Gross. French & Eur.
Woerterbuch Chemie und Chemische
Technik. French & Eur.
Woerterbuch christlicher Ethik.
Bernhard Stoeckle. Herder.
Woerterbuch Christlicher Ethik.
Bernhard Stoeckle. Herder.
Woerterbuch Datenerfassung-
Programmierung. E. Buerger.
French & Eur.
Woerterbuch Datenerfassung:
Programmierung. Buerger. Verlag
Harri Deutsch.
Woerterbuch der Abkurzungen. Josef
Werlin. Imported Bks.
Woerterbuch der Agrarpolitik. R.
Bremer et al. Parey.
Woerterbuch der Altgermanischen
Personen und Voelkernamen. M.
Schoenfeld. French & Eur.
Woerterbuch der Amerikanismen.
Friedrich Koehler. French & Eur.
Woerterbuch der Antike. Hans
Lamer. French & Eur.
Woerterbuch der Antike: Mit
Beruecks Ihres Fortwirkens. Paul
Kroh. Ed. by E. Bux & W.
Schoene. Kroener.
Woerterbuch der Berufs &
Wirtschaftspaedagogik. Herder.
Woerterbuch der Berufs und
Wirtschaftspaedagogik. French &
Eur.
Woerterbuch der Biochemie. K.
Thielmann. French & Eur.
Woerterbuch der Biochemie.
Thielmann. Verlag Harri Deutsch.
Woerterbuch der Biologie. Guenther
Haensch. French & Eur.
Woerterbuch der Biologie. Werner
Jacobs. French & Eur.
Woerterbuch der Chemie. I. Ernst &
F. Ernst von Morgenstern. French
& Eur.
Woerterbuch der Chemie. I. Ernst &
F. Ernst von Morgenstern. French
& Eur.
Woerterbuch der Chemie: Band I, D -
E. Brandstetter.
Woerterbuch der Chemie: Band II,
English-Deutsch. Ernst.
Brandstetter.
Woerterbuch der Chinesischen
Revolution. P. Dittmar. French &
Eur.
Woerterbuch der
Dampferzeugungstechnik-
Dictionary of Steam Generator
Engineering. Ed. by Deutsche
Babcock et al. Intl Pubns Serv.
Woerterbuch der Darstellenden
Kuenste: Russische-Deutsch.
Gabriele Fischborn. VEB Verlag
Enzyklopadie.
Woerterbuch der Datentechnick.
Joachim Schulz. Brandstetter.
Woerterbuch der Datentechnik.
Brinkmann & Schmidt.
Brandstetter.
Woerterbuch der Datentechnik. Linse.
Brandstetter.

Woerterbuch der Datentechnik: Russisch-Deutsch-Englisch. Schulz. Brandstetter.

Woerterbuch der Datenverarbeitung. A. Oppermann. French & Eur.

Woerterbuch der DDR Paedagogik. Johannes Niermann. French & Eur.

Woerterbuch der Deutschen & Niederlaendischen Rechtssprache: Lexikon fuer Justiz, Verwaltung, Wirtschaft & Handel. Hans Langendorf. Kluwer Group.

Woerterbuch der Deutschen Aussprache. Hans Krech. French & Eur.

Woerterbuch der deutschen Gegenwartssprache. M Rosenberg.

Woerterbuch der Deutschen Gegenwartssprache: Vol. 6. M Rosenberg.

Woerterbuch der Deutschen Gegenwartssprache: Vols. 1-5. M Rosenberg.

Woerterbuch der Deutschen Pflanzennamen. Marzell. French & Eur.

Woerterbuch der Deutschen Sprache mit Rechtschreiblehre. Gebrueder Weiss.

Woerterbuch der Deutschen Umgangssprache: Vol. 3, Hochdeutsch-Umgangsdeutsch A-Z. M Rosenberg.

Woerterbuch der Deutschen Umgangssprache: Vol. 4, Berufsschelten & Verwandtes. H. Keupper. M Rosenberg.

Woerterbuch der Deutschen Umgangssprache: Vol. 5, 10000 neue Ausdruecke Sachschelten. H. Keupper. M Rosenberg.

Woerterbuch der Deutschen Umgangssprache: Vol. 6, Jugenddeutsch A-Z. H. Keupper. M Rosenberg.

Woerterbuch der Deutschen und Franzoesischen Rechtssprache. Michel Doucet. French & Eur.

Woerterbuch der Deutschen und Franzoesischen Rechtssprache. Michel Doucet. French & Eur.

Woerterbuch der Deutschen und Italienischen Wirtschafts und Rechtssprache. Giuseppe Conte. French & Eur.

Woerterbuch der Deutschen und Italienischen Wirtschafts und Rechtssprache. Giuseppe Conte. French & Eur.

Woerterbuch der Deutschen und Niederlaendischen Rechtssprache. Hans Langendorf. French & Eur.

Woerterbuch der Deutschen und Niederlaendischen Rechtssprache. Hans Langendorf. French & Eur.

Woerterbuch der Deutschen und Spanischen Sprache. Rudolf Slaby. French & Eur.

Woerterbuch der Deutschen und Spanischen Sprache. Rudolf Slaby. French & Eur.

Woerterbuch der Deutschen und Spanischen Rects und Wirtschaftssprache. H. Becher. French & Eur.

Woerterbuch der Elektronik. E. Knaeps & D. Zacharias. French & Eur.

Woerterbuch der Elektronik. Leonhard Schneider. French & Eur.

Woerterbuch der Elektrotechnik Fernmeldetechnik & Elektronik: Band I, Deutsch-Englisch-Franzoesisch. Goedecke. Brandstetter.

Woerterbuch der Elektrotechnik Fernmeldetechnik & Elektronik: Band II, Franzoesisch-Englisch-Deutsch. Goedecke. Brandstetter.

Woerterbuch der Elektrotechnik Fernmeldetechnik & Elektronik: Band III, Englisch-Deutsch-Franzoesisch. Goedecke. Brandstetter.

Woerterbuch der Elektrotechnik, Fernmeldetechnik und Elektonik. W. Goedecke. French & Eur.

Woerterbuch der Elektrotechnik, Fernmeldetechnik und Elektronik. W. Goedecke. French & Eur.

Woerterbuch der Elektrotechnik und Elektronik. Tomislav Miladinovic. French & Eur.

Woerterbuch der Elsaessischen Mundarten. Ed. by Ernst Martin & Hans Lienhart. De Gruyter.

Woerterbuch der Elsaessischen Mundarten. Ernst Martin & Hans Lienhart. De Gruyter.

Woerterbuch der Englischen und Deutschen Sprache. Weis Schoeffler. French & Eur.

Woerterbuch der Englischen und Deutschen Sprache. Weis Schoeffler. French & Eur.

Woerterbuch der Epilepsie. H. Gastaut. French & Eur.

Woerterbuch der Erziehung. Christoph Wulf. Piper Co.

Woerterbuch der Forstwirtschaft. Johannes V. Weck. French & Eur.

Woerterbuch der Forstwirtschaft Deutsch-Englisch-Franzoesisch-Spanisch-Russisch. Johannes Weck et al. BLV Verlag.

Woerterbuch der Franzoesischen und Deutschen Sprache. E. Weis & H. Mattutat. French & Eur.

Woerterbuch der Franzoesischen und Deutschen Sprache. E. Weis & H. Mattutat. French & Eur.

Woerterbuch der Handels, Finanz und Rechtssprache. Robert Herbst. French & Eur.

Woerterbuch der Industriellen Technik: Band I, Deutsch-Englisch. Brandstetter.

Woerterbuch der Industriellen Technik: Band III, Deutsch-Franzoesisch. Ernst. Brandstetter.

Woerterbuch der Industriellen Technik: Band II, Englisch-Deutsch. Brandstetter.

Woerterbuch der Industriellen Technik: Band IV, Franzoesisch-Deutsch. Ernst. Brandstetter.

Woerterbuch der Industriellen Technik: Band VII, Deutsch-Portugiesisch. Ernst. Brandstetter.

Woerterbuch der Industriellen Technik: Band V, Deutsch-Spanisch. Ernst. Brandstetter.

Woerterbuch der Industriellen Technik: Band VIII, Portugiesch-Deutsch. Ernst. Brandstetter.

Woerterbuch der Industriellen Technik: Band VI, Spanisch-Deutschg) Ernst. Brandstetter.

Woerterbuch der Industriellen Technik. R. Ernst. French & Eur.

Woerterbuch der Industriellen Technik. R. Ernst. French & Eur.

Woerterbuch der Industriellen Technik. R. Ernst. French & Eur.

Woerterbuch der Industriellen Technik. R. Ernst. French & Eur.

Woerterbuch der Industriellen Technik. R. Ernst. French & Eur.

Woerterbuch der Industriellen Technik. R. Ernst. French & Eur.

Woerterbuch der Internationalen Beziehungen und der Politik. Guenther Haensch. French & Eur.

Woerterbuch der Italienisch & Deutschen Sprache: Bd 1: Italienisch-Deutsch. Brandstetter.

Woerterbuch der Italienisch & Deutschen Sprache: Bd 2: Deutsch-Italienisch. Brandstetter.

Woerterbuch der Italienischen und Deutschen Sprache. Brandstetter.

Woerterbuch der Italienischen und Deutschen Sprache. French & Eur.

Woerterbuch der Jaegerei. W. Frevert. French & Eur.

Woerterbuch der Jagel. Anne Kirchoff. French & Eur.

Woerterbuch der Kabeltechnik. Christel Richling. French & Eur.

Woerterbuch der Kabeltechnik. Christel Richling. Brandstetter.

Woerterbuch der Kabeltechnik: Deutsch-Englisch-Franzoesisch. Drewitz Richling. Brandstetter.

Woerterbuch der Kerenergie. F. V. Franzen. French & Eur.

Woerterbuch der Kernenergie. F. Franzen & L. Hard. Brandstetter.

Woerterbuch der Klassischen Arabischen: Bd 1. Joerg Kroemer et al. Ed. by Manfred Ullman. Harrassowitz.

Woerterbuch der Klassischen Arabischen: Bd 1, Lfg 7. Manfred Ullmann & Anton Spitaler. Harrassowitz.

Woerterbuch der Klassischen Arabischen Sprache: Bd 1, Lfg 1. Anton Spitaler et al. Harrassowitz.

Woerterbuch der Klassischen Arabischen Sprache: Bd 1, Lfg 2. Joerg Kraemer et al. Harrassowitz.

Woerterbuch der Klassischen Arabischen Sprache: Bd 1, Lfg 3. Manfred Ullmann & Anton Spitaler. Harrassowitz.

Woerterbuch der Klassischen Arabischen Sprache: Bd 1, Lfg 4. Manfred Ullmann & Anton Spitaler. Harrassowitz.

Woerterbuch der Klassischen Arabischen Sprache: Bd 1, Lfg 5. Manfred Ullmann & Anton Spitaler. Harrassowitz.

Woerterbuch der Klassischen Arabischen Sprache: Bd 1, Lfg 6. Manfred Ullmann & Anton Spitaler. Harrassowitz.

Woerterbuch der Klassischen Arabischen Sprache: Bd 1, Lfg 8. Manfred Ullmann & Anton Spitaler. Harrassowitz.

Woerterbuch der Klassischen Arabischen Sprache: Bd 1, Lfg 9-10. Manfred Ullmann & Anton Spitaler. Harrassowitz.

Woerterbuch der Klassischen Arabischen Sprache: Bd 2, Lfg 1. Manfred Ullmann. Harrassowitz.

Woerterbuch der Klassischen Arabischen Sprache: Bd 2, Lfg 2. Manfred Ullmann & Rotraud Wojtowytsch-Wielandt. Harrassowitz.

Woerterbuch der Klassischen Arabischen Sprache: Bd 2, Lfg 4. Manfred Ullmann. Harrassowitz.

Woerterbuch der Kraftuebertragungselemente-Deutsch-Spanisch-Franzoesisch-Englisch-Italienisch-Niederlandisch-Schwedisch-Finnisch: Bd 1, Zahnraeder. Krausskopf.

Woerterbuch der Kraftuebertragungselemente. French & Eur.

Woerterbuch der Kunst. Johannes Jahn. French & Eur.

Woerterbuch der Kunst. Johannes Jahn. Kroener.

Woerterbuch der Kunst. Johannes Jahn. Kroener.

Woerterbuch der Landwirtschaft. Guenther Haensch. French & Eur.

Woerterbuch der Lerntheorien & der Verhaltenstherapie. Hans Zeier. Kindler.

Woerterbuch der Logik. Nikolai I. Kondakov et al. Bibl Inst Leipzig.

Woerterbuch der Mathematik. Ralf Sube. French & Eur.

Woerterbuch der Mathmetik. Eisenreich & Sube. Verlag Harri Deutsch.

Woerterbuch der Medizin und Pharmazeutik: Medical & Pharmaceutical Dictionary. Werner E. Bunjes. Thieme Verlag.

Woerterbuch der Modernen Technik. A. Oppermann. French & Eur.

Woerterbuch der Muenzkunde. Ed. by Friedrich Von Schroeter. De Gruyter.

Woerterbuch der Optik & Feinmechanik: Band II, Englisch-Franzoesisch-Deutsch. Schulz. Brandstetter.

Woerterbuch der Optik & Feinmechanik: Band III, Franzoesisch-Deutsch-Englisch. Schulz. Brandstetter.

Woerterbuch der Optik und Feinmechanik: English-French-German Dictionary of Optics & Mechanical Engineering. E. Schulz. French & Eur.

Woerterbuch der Optik und Feinmechanik. Ernst Schulz. French & Eur.

Woerterbuch der Optik und Feinmechanik. Ernst Schulz. French & Eur.

Woerterbuch der Paedagogik. Wilhelm Hehlmann. French & Eur.

Woerterbuch der Paedagogik. French & Eur.

Woerterbuch der Paedagogik. Willmann-Institut Muenchen. Herder.

Woerterbuch der Paedagogik. Willmann-Institut. Herder.

Woerterbuch der Paedagogischen Psychologie: Lexikon der Paedagogik. Herder.

Woerterbuch der Paedagogischen Psychologie. French & Eur.

Woerterbuch der Parapsychologie. Hermann Schreiber. French & Eur.

Woerterbuch der Patentfachsprache. B. Klaften & F. C. Allison. French & Eur.

Woerterbuch der Patentfachsprache-Patent Terminological Dictionary: English-German & German-English. Berthold Klaften. Intl Pubns Serv.

Woerterbuch der Patentpraxis. Detlev V. Uexkuell. French & Eur.

Woerterbuch der Photo, Film und Kinotechnik. Wolfgang Grau. French & Eur.

Woerterbuch der Psychiatrie und Medizinischen Psychologie. Uwe H. Peters. French & Eur.

Woerterbuch der Psychologie. Wilhelm Hehlmann. French & Eur.

Woerterbuch der Psychologie. Guenther V. Clauss. French & Eur.

Woerterbuch der Psychologie. Gunter Clauss. Biblio Inst.

Woerterbuch der Psychologie. Ed. by G. Clauss et al. Bibl Inst Leipzig.

Woerterbuch der Psychologie. Guenter Clauss. Pahl-Rugenstein.

Woerterbuch der Recht & Wirtschaftssprache: Teil I, Niederlandisch-Deutsch. Hans Langendorf & P. A. Stein. Recht & Wirtschaft.

Woerterbuch der Recht & Wirtshaftssprache: Teil II, Deutsch-Spanisch. Herbert J. Becher. Recht & Wirtschaft.

Woerterbuch der Rechts & Wirtschaftssprache: Teil II, Deutsch-Englisch. Alfred Romain. Recht & Wirtschaft.

Woerterbuch der Rechts & Wirtschaftssprache: Teil II, Deutsch-Niederlaendisch. Hans Langendorf & P. A. Stein. Recht & Wirtschaft.

Woerterbuch der Rechts & Wirtschaftssprache: Teil I, Deutsch-Russisch. Gyula Decsi & Sandor Karcsay. Recht & Wirtschaft.

Woerterbuch der Rechts & Wirtschaftssprache: Teil I, Englisch-Deutsch. Alfred Romain. Recht & Wirtschaft.

Woerterbuch der Rechts & Wirtschaftssprache: Teil II, Russisch-Deutsch. Gyula Decsi & Sandor Karcsay. Recht & Wirtschaft.

Woerterbuch der Rechts & Wirtschaftssprache: Teil I, Spanisch-Deutsch. Herbert J. Becher. Recht & Wirtschaft.

Woerterbuch der Regionalen Umgangssprache in Lateinamerika. Maria Schwauss. VEB Verlag Enzyklopadie.

Woerterbuch der Reinen und Angewandten Physik. L. De Vries. French & Eur.

Woerterbuch der Reinen und Angewandten Physik. L. De Vries. French & Eur.

Woerterbuch der Religionen. Alfred Bertholet. Kroener.

Woerterbuch der Reprographie. Deutsches Komitee fuer Reprographie. Aussant & Schrift.

Woerterbuch der Reprographie. Saur Verlag.

Woerterbuch der Reprographie: Begriffe und Definitionen. Deutsches Komitee fuer Reprographie. French & Eur.

Woerterbuch der Russichen Gewaessernamen: Lfg 1. Harrassowitz.

Woerterbuch der Russichen Gewaessernamen: Lfg 2. Harrassowitz.

Woerterbuch der Russichen Gewaessernamen: Bd 2, Z-K. Harrassowitz.

Woerterbuch der Russichen Gewaessernamen: Lfg 4. Harrassowitz.

Woerterbuch der Russichen Gewaessernamen: Bd 1, A-E. Max Vasmer. Harrassowitz.

Woerterbuch der Russischen Gewaessernamen: Bd 3, L-P. Harrassowitz.

Woerterbuch der Russischen Gewaessernamen: Bd 4, R-U. Harrassowitz.

Woerterbuch der Russischen Gewaessernamen: Bd 5, F-Ja. Harrassowitz.

Woerterbuch der Russischen Gewaessernamen: Lfg 3. Harrassowitz.

Woerterbuch der Russischen Gewaessernamen: Lfg 5. Harrassowitz.

Woerterbuch der Russischen Gewaessernamen: Lfg 6. Harrassowitz.

Woerterbuch der Russischen Gewaessernamen: Lfg 7. Harrassowitz.

Woerterbuch der Russischen Gewaessernamen: Lfg 8. Harrassowitz.

Woerterbuch der Russischen Gewaessernamen: Lfg 9. Harrassowitz.

Woerterbuch der Russischen Gewaessernamen: Lfg 10. Harrassowitz.

WOerterbuch der Russischen Gewaessernamen: Lfg 11. Harrassowitz.

Woerterbuch der Russischen Gewaessernamen: Lfg 12. Harrassowitz.

Woerterbuch der Russischen Gewaessernamen: Lfg 13. Harrassowitz.

Woerterbuch der Russischen Gewaessernamen: Lfg 14. Harrassowitz.

Woerterbuch der Russischen Gewaessernamen: Lfg 15. Harrassowitz.

Woerterbuch der Schulpaedagogik. Arnold Schwendtke. French & Eur.

Woerterbuch der Schulpaedagogik. Herder.

Woerterbuch der Schweisstechnik. A. Kleiber. French & Eur.

Woerterbuch der Seeschiffahrt. Hans Rinke. French & Eur.

Woerterbuch der Seeschiffahrt. Hans Rinke. French & Eur.

Woerterbuch der Sozialarbeit & Sozialpaedagogik. Arnold Schwendtke. Quelle & Meyer.

Woerterbuch der Sozialarbeit und der Sozialpaedagogik. Arnold Schwendtke. French & Eur.

Woerterbuch der Soziologie. Guenter Hartfiel. Kroener.

Woerterbuch der Soziologie. Ed. by Wilhelm Bernsdorf. Enke.

Woerterbuch der Soziologie: Bd 1, 5 Aufl. Ed. by Wilhelm Bernsdorf. Fischer Taschen.

Woerterbuch der Soziologie: Bd 2, 4 Aufl. Ed. by Wilhelm Bernsdorf. Fischer Taschen.

Woerterbuch der Soziologie: Bd 3, 4 Aufl. Ed. by Wilhelm Bernsdorf. Fischer Taschen.

Woerterbuch der Spanischen & Deutschen Sprache. Guenther Haensch. Klett.

Woerterbuch der Spanischen & Deutschen Sprache: Band II, Deutsch-Spanisch. Slaby & Grossmann. Brandstetter.

Woerterbuch der Spanischen & Deutschen Sprache: Band I, Spanisch-Deutsch. Slaby & Grossmann. Brandstetter.

Woerterbuch der Spanischen und Deutschen Rechts und Wirtschaftssprache. H. Becher. French & Eur.

Woerterbuch der Symbolik. Ed. by Manfred Lurker. Kroener.

Woerterbuch der Technik. Karl H. Radde. French & Eur.

Woerterbuch der Technik. Karl H. Radde. French & Eur.

Woerterbuch der Technik. Rudolf Walther. French & Eur.

Woerterbuch der Technik. Karl H. Radde. Girardet.

Woerterbuch der Textilindustrie. Louis de Vries. French & Eur.

Woerterbuch der Tiefenpsychologie. Uwe H. Peters. Kindler.

Woerterbuch der Ungarischen Rechts und Verwaltungssprache. Sandor Karcsay. French & Eur.

Woerterbuch der Ungarischen Rechts und Verwaltungssprache. French & Eur.

Woerterbuch der Verhaltensforschung. Klaus Immelmann. Kindler.

Woerterbuch der Voelkerkunde. Walter Hirschberg. French & Eur.

Woerterbuch der Vorschulerzeihung. Herder.

Woerterbuch der Vorschulerziehung. French & Eur.

Woerterbuch der Vorschulerziehung. Ed. by Engelbert Schinzler. Herder.

Woerterbuch der Weidmannssprache. Franz Kehrein. French & Eur.

Woerterbuch der Werbung und des Marketing. Clemens Gruber. French & Eur.

Woerterbuch der Wirkstoffprufung. Werner Goedecke. VDI-Verlag.

Woerterbuch der Wirtschaft. Horst C. Recktenwald. French & Eur.

Woerterbuch der Wirtschaft. Horst C. Rektenwald. Kroener.

Woerterbuch des Arbeits & Sozialrechts: Deutsch-Franz Dictionnaire de Droit du Trava il & de Droit Social. Alexandre Bonnefoi. Hueber.

Woerterbuch des Arbeits und Sozialrechtd. Alexandre Bonnefoi. French & Eur.

Woerterbuch des Buches. H. Helmut. French & Eur.

Woerterbuch Des Internationalen Verkehrs (Dictionary of International Traffic) Gerhard Bein. Intl Pubns Serv.

Woerterbuch des Italienisch-Deutschen Privat & Wirtschaftsrechts: Band I, Deutsch-Italienisch. H. Trioke-Strambaci & E. Helffrich-Mariani. Recht & Wirtschaft.

Woerterbuch des Italienisch-Deutschen Privat & Wirtschaftsrechts: Band II, Italienish-Deutsch. H. Troike-Strambaci & E. Helffrich-Mariani. Recht & Wirtschaft.

Woerterbuch des Kraftfahreugwesens. Otto Vollnhals. Girardet.

Woerterbuch des Kraftfahrzeugwesens. Otto Vollnhals. French & Eur.

Woerterbuch des Pantentwesens in 5 Sprachen. Gyorgy L. Szendy. French & Eur.

Woerterbuch des Steuerrechts. Rudolf Roessler. French & Eur.

Woerterbuch des Steuerrechts. Rudolf Roessler et al. Haufe.

Woerterbuch des Verlagswesens in 20 Sprachen. Imre Mora. French & Eur.

Woerterbuch des Verlagswesens in 20 Sprachen. Imre Mora. Saur Verlag.

Woerterbuch des Voelkerrechts: Bd 1, Aachener Kongress-Hussar Fall. Ed. by Karl Strupp et al. De Gruyter.

Woerterbuch des Voelkerrechts: Bd 2, Ibero-Amerikanismus bis Quirin-Fall. Ed. by Hermann Mosler et al. De Gruyter.

Woerterbuch des Voelkerrechts: Bd 3, Rapollo-Vertrag bis Zypern. Ed. by Hermann Mosler et al. De Gruyter.

Woerterbuch des Wirtschafts, Rechts und Handelssprache. C. Dietl. French & Eur.

Woerterbuch Deutsch-Hindi. Margot Gatzlaff-Halsig. VEB Verlag Enzyklopadie.

Woerterbuch Deutsch-Indonesisch. Gerhard Kahlo et al. VEB Verlag Enzyklopadie.

Woerterbuch Elektrotechnik & Elektronik. H. Schwenkhagen. Girardet.

Woerterbuch Elektrotechnik und Elektronik. H. Schwenkhagen. French & Eur.

Woerterbuch Elektrotechnik und Elektronik. H. F. Schwenkhagen & H. Meinhhold. French & Eur.

Woerterbuch Erdoelverarbeitung-Petrolchemie. W. Leipnitz. French & Eur.

Woerterbuch fuer Aerzte. Lejeune & Bunjes. French & Eur.

Woerterbuch fuer Architektur, Hochbau & Baustoffe. Herbert Buksch. Bauverlag.

Woerterbuch fuer Architektur, Hochbau & Baustoffe. H. Bucksch. Bauverlag.

Woerterbuch fuer Architektur, Hochbau & Baustoffe: Band 1, Deutsch-Englisch. H. Bucksch. Bauverlag.

Woerterbuch Fuer Architektur: Hochbau und Baustoffe. French & Eur.

Woerterbuch fuer Bautechnik & Baumaschinen: Band I, Deutsch-Englisch. H. Bucksch. Bauverlag.

Woerterbuch fuer Bautechnik & Baumaschinen: Band II, Englisch-Deutsch. H. Bucksch. Bauverlag.

Woerterbuch fuer Bautechnik und Baumaschinen. H. Bucksch. French & Eur.

Woerterbuch fuer das Wasser und Abwasserfach. Fritz Meinck. French & Eur.

Woerterbuch fuer den Hobbyelektroniker. Junge. Verlag Harri Deutsch.

Woerterbuch fuer die Grundschule. Erwin Schwartz et al. Westermann.

Woerterbuch fuer Erziehung & Unterricht. Peter Koeck & Hans Ott. Auer.

Woerterbuch fuer Metallurgie, Mineralogie, Geologie, Bergbau & die Oelindustrie. A. Cagnacci-Schwicker. Bauverlag.

Woerterbuch fuer Metallurgie, Mineralogie, Geologie, Bergbau & die Oelindustrie Englische-Franzosisch-Deutsch-Italienisch. Angelo Cagnacci-Schwicker. Bauverlag.

Woerterbuch fuer Metallurgie, Mineralogie, Geologie, Bergbau und die Oelindustrie. French & Eur.

Woerterbuch fuer Recht, Wirtschaft & Politik: Teil II, Deutsch-Englisch. Clara E. Dietl & Egon Lorenz. Recht & Wirtschaft.

Woerterbuch fuer Strassenbau und Strassenverkehe. Karl Steinig. French & Eur.

Woerterbuch fuer Wirtschaft, Recht & Handel: Band I, Deutsch-Franzoesisch. Potonnier. Brandstetter.

Woerterbuch fuer Wirtschaft, Recht & Handel: Band II, Franzoesisch-Deutsch. Potonnier. Brandstetter.

Woerterbuch fuer Wirtschaft: Recht und Handel. Georges Potonnier. French & Eur.

Woerterbuch fuer Wirtschaft: Recht und Handel. Georges Potonnier. French & Eur.

Woerterbuch fuer Wirtschaft-Recht-Verkehr-Verwaltungs & Umgangssprache: Vol.I, Englisch-Deutsch. R. Eichborn. M Rosenberg.

Woerterbuch fuer Wirtschaft-Recht-Verkehr-Verwaltungs & Umgangssprache: Vol. II, Deutsch-Englisch. R. Eichborn. M Rosenberg.

Woerterbuch fur Bau & Grundstucksrecht & Raumordnung. H. Bucksch. Bauverlag.

Woerterbuch fur Baurecht, Grundstucksrecht & Raumordnung: Band I, Deutsch-Englisch. H. Bucksch. Bauverlag.

Woerterbuch fur Baurecht, Grungstucksrecht & Raumordnung: Band II, Englisch-Deutsch. H. Bucksch. Bauverlag.

Woerterbuch fur den Hobby-Elektroniker Englisch-Deutsch. Hans D. Junge. VEB Technik.

Woerterbuch Geowissenschaften. A. Watznauer. French & Eur.

Woerterbuch Geowissenschaften. A. Watznauer. French & Eur.

Woerterbuch Geowissenschaften. Watznauer. Verlag Harri Deutsch.

Woerterbuch Geowissenschaften. Watznauer. Verlag Harri Deutsch.

Woerterbuch Informationsverarbeitung. Buerger. Verlag Harri Deutsch.

Woerterbuch Klima & Kaeltetechnik. Heinrich. Verlag Harri Deutsch.

Woerterbuch Klima & Kaltetechnik. Gunter Heinrich. Verlag Harri Deutsch.

Woerterbuch Kristallografie. Backhaus. Verlag Harri Deutsch.

Woerterbuch Kritische Erziehung. Eberhard Rauch & Wolfgang Anzinger. Fischer Taschen.

Woerterbuch Kybernetik. Alfred Oppermann. French & Eur.

Woerterbuch: Linguistische Grundbegriffe. Winfried Ulrich. Hirt.

Woerterbuch Linguistische Grundbegriffe. Winfried Von Ulrich. Hirt.

Woerterbuch Medizin. Noehring. Verlag Harri Deutsch.

Woerterbuch Medizinischer Fachausdruecke. Fachredaktion. French & Eur.

Woerterbuch Medizinischer Fachausdruecke. Thieme Verlag.

Woerterbuch Medizinischer Grundbegriffe. Eduard Seidler. Herder.

Woerterbuch Musik. Horst Leuchtmann. French & Eur.

Woerterbuch Musik. Saur Verlag.

Woerterbuch Pferd & Reiter. Zdzislaw Baronowski. Pitman Bks.

Woerterbuch Pferd und Reiter. Zdzislaw Baranowski. French & Eur.

Woerterbuch Physik. Ralf Sube & Gunther Eisenreich. French & Eur.

Woerterbuch Physik. Eisenreich & Sube. Verlag Harri Deutsch.

Woerterbuch Programmierter Unterricht. Manz.

Woerterbuch Sanskrit-Deutsch. Klaus Mylius. VEB Verlag Enzyklopadie.

Woerterbuch ser Pferdekunde. Hans G. Muhlmann. Verlag Sankt.

Woerterbuch Swahili-Deutsch. HIldegard Hoftmann et al. VEB Verlag Enzyklopadie.

Woerterbuch Vietnamesisch-Deutsch. Winfried Boscher et al. VEB Verlag Enzyklopadie.

Woerterbuch Werkzeuge. Henry G. Freeman. French & Eur.

Woerterbuch Werkzeuge und Werkzeugmaschinen. Kurt Stellhorn. French & Eur.

Woerterbuch Wirtschaft. Noehring. Verlag Harri Deutsch.

Woerterbuch Wirtschaft Recht Handel: Deutsch-Franzoesisch. Georges E. Potonnier & Brigitte Potonnier. Maison Dictionnaire.

Woerterbuch Wirtschaft Recht Handel: Deutsch-Franzoesisch. Georges E. Potonnier & Brigitte Potonnier. Maison Dictionnaire.

Woerterbuch zum Deutschen Sprachgebrauch: Woerter & Wendungen. M Rosenberg.

Woerterbuch zur Geschichte. Erich Bayer. French & Eur.

Woerterbuch zur Geschichte. Erich Bayer. Kroener.

Woerterbuch zur klinischen Psychologie. Hellmuth Benesch. Deutscher Taschenbuch.

Woerterbuch zur Oberoesterreichischen Volksmundart. Ed. by Otto Jungmair. Selbstverlag Inst.

Woerterbuch zur Politik und Wirtschaftpolitik. Hans E. Zahn. French & Eur.

Woerterbuch zur Politischen Oekonomie. Gert V. Eynern. French & Eur.

Woerterbuch zur Politischen Oekonomie. Ed. by Gert Von Eynern & Carl Boehret. Westdeutscher.

Woerterbuch zur Psychologie. Werner D. Froehlich & James Drever. Deutscher Taschenbuch.

Woerterbuch zur Publizistik. K. Koszyk. French & Eur.

Woerterbuch zur Rechtschreibung. Klett.

Woerterbuch zur Sexualpolitik und ihren Grenzgebieten. French & Eur.

Woerterbuch zur Valenz & Distribution Deutscher Adjektive. K. E. Sommerfeldt & H. Schreiber. Bibl Inst Leipzig.

Woerterbuch zur Valenz & Distribution der Substantive. Karl-Ernst Sommerfeldt. Bibl Inst Leipzig.

Woerterbuch zur Valenz & Distribution Deutscher Verben. G. Helbig & W. Schenkel. Bibl Inst Leipzig.

Woerterbucher der Fertigungstechnik: Bd 1, Schmieden-Freiformschmieden & Gesenkschmieden. G. Pahlitzsch. Girardet.

Woerterbucher der Fertigungstechnik Deutsch-Englisch-Franzoesisch: Bd 2, Schleifen Oberflaechenrauheit. G. Pahlitzsch. Girardet.

Woerterbucher der Fertigungstechnik Deutsch-Englisch-Franzoesisch: Bd 3, Blechbearbeitung. G. Pahlitzsch. Girardet.

Woerterbucher der Fertigungstechnik Deutsch-Englisch-Franzoesisch: Bd 4, Grundbegriffe des Spanens. G. Pahlitzsch. Girardet.

Woerterbucher der Fertigungstechnik Deutsch-Englisch-Franzoesisch: Bd 5, Kaltfliesspressen & Kaltstauchen. G. Pahlitzsch. Girardet.

Woerterbucher der Fertigungstechnik Deutsch-Englisch-Franzoesisch: Bd 6, Hobeln, Stassen, Raeumen, Drehen. G. Pahlitzsch. Girardet.

Woerterbucher der Fertigungstechnik Deutsch-Englisch-Franzoesisch: Bd 7, Bohren, Senken, Reiben, Gewindeschneiden. G. Pahlitzsch. Girardet.

Woerterbucher der Fertigungstechnik Deutsch-Spanisch-Italienisch-Portugiesisch: Bd 1R, Schmieden-Freiformschmieden & Gesenkschmieden. G. Pahlitzsch. Girardet.

Woeter & Wendungen: Woerterbuch zum Deutschen Sprachgebrauch. M Rosenberg.

World Mining: Glossary of Mining, Processing & Geological Terms. Wyllie & Argall. W H Freeman.

World-Wide German Dictionary. Ed. by Paul H. Glucksman. (Prem). Fawcett.

World Wide German Language Dictionary German-English. New Century.

Wortbildung der Deutschen Gegenwartssprache. W. Fleischer. Bibl Inst Leipzig.

Wortbildung Diachron, Synchron. Osterreichisches Linguistisches Programm. Ed. by Oswald Panagl. Inst Verg Sprach.

Worterbuch der Mikroelktronik, Dictionary Microelectronics: English-German, German-English. French & Eur.

Worterbuch der Technik: Italienisch-Deutsch. A. Schlegelmich. French & Eur.

Wortschatz der Information und Dokumentation. G. Schmoll. (Pub. by Vlg. Dokumentation). French & Eur.

Der Wortschatz des Juristen: Ein Lern & Lesebuch Juristischen Sprachausdrucks. Karl Luggauer. Heyn.

The York Dictionary of English-French-German-Spanish Literary Terms & Their Origin. Saad Elkhaden. York Pr CA.

The York Dictionary of English-French-German-Spanish Literary Terms & Their Origin. Saad Elkhadem. York Pr CA.

Zeisberger's Indian Dictionary: English, German, Iroquois - the Onandaga & Algonquin - the Delaware. David Zeisberger. AMS Pr.

Zement-Woerterbuch: Herstellung & Technologie. Bauverlag.

Zoologisches Woerterbuch - Palaearktische Tiere. Michael Klemm. Intl Pubns Serv.

Zoologisches Woerterbuch Palaearktische Tiere. Michael Klemm. (Pub. by Parey Berlin). French & Eur.

Zoologisches Woerterbuch Palaearktische Tiere. Michael Klemm. Parey.

Zum Fachwortschatz. Sabine Kruger. VDI Verlag.

Zwei Hundert Eins Spanische Verben. Henry Strutz. Barron.

Zweisprachiges Woerterbuch fuer Angenaeherte Operationelle Analyse. Gudrun Guckler. Narr.

Zweisprachiges Woerterbuch Fuer Angenaeherte Operationelle Analyse Semantischer Entsprechungen Mittels EDV. G. Guckler. (Pub. by G. Narr). French & Eur.

GONJA

Gonja-English Dictionary & Spelling Book. Ed. by J. W. Amankwaah & O. Rytz. Inst Afr Stu.

GREEK

Abridged Greek-English Lexicon. Ed. by H. G. Liddell & Robert Scott. Oxford U Pr.

Altgriechisch. Incl. Langenscheidt.

Altkirchenslavisch-Griechisches Woerterbuch Des Codex Supraliensis. Karl H. Meyer. J J Augustin.

The Analytical Greek Lexicon Revised. Ed. by Harold K. Moulton. Zondervan.

Basic Greek Vocabulary. John R. Cheadle. St Martin.

Berlitz Greek for Travellers. Berlitz Editors. (Berlitz). Macmillan.

Berry's Greek-English New Testament Lexicon with Synonyms: Numerically Coded to Strong's Exhaustive Concordance. George R. Berry. Baker Bk.

A Complete Categorized Greek-English New Testament Vocabulary. David Holly. Attic Pr.

A Complete Categorized Greek-English New Testament Vocabulary. David Holly. Baker Bk.

A Concise Dictionary of the English & Modern Greek Languages. A. N. Jannaris. Caratzas Pub Co.

Diccionario de Mitologia Griega & Romana. Pierre Grimal & Francisco Payarois. Paidos Iberica.

Diccionario Griego-Espanol. Miguel Balaguer. French & Eur.

Diccionario Griego-Espanol. French & Eur.

Diccionario griego-espanol. Miguel Balagur. Bibliografica.

Diccionario griego-espanol. Florencio I. Sebastian Yarza. Sopena.

Diccionario Manual Griego-Espanol. Jose M. Pabon & M. Fernandez Galiano. Biblograf SP.

Diccionario Manual Griego-Espanol Vox. Biblo SP.

Diccionario Simultaneo en 21 Idiomas. Juan Capdevilla Font. French & Eur.

Dictionar Grec-Roman. Lambros Petinis. Editura Stiintifica.

Dictionar Roman-Grec. Socratis Cotolulis. Editura Stiintifica.

A Dictionary of Greek & Latin Combining Forms Used in Zoological Names. Edmund C. Jaeger. C C Thomas.

Dictionary of Greek & Roman Biography & Mythology. Ed. by William Smith. AMS Pr.

Dictionary of Greek & Roman Geography. Ed. by William Smith. AMS Pr.

Dictionary of Greek Coin Inscriptions. S. Icard. Obol Intl.

Dictionary of Greek Coin Inscriptions. Severin Icard. S J Durst.

A Dictionary of New Testament Greek Synonyms. George R. Berry. Zondervan.

Dictionnaire Abrege Grec-Francais. Anatole Bailly. French & Eur.

Dictionnaire Abrege Grec-Francais. Anatole Bailly. Hachette-Jeunesse.

Dictionnaire Etymologique de la Langue Grecque. Pierre Chantraine. Klincksieck.

Dictionnaire Etymologique de la Langue Grecque, 2. Pierre Chantraine. Klincksieck.

Dictionnaire Etymologique de la Langue Grecque, 3. Pierre Chantraine. Klincksieck.

Dictionnaire Etymologique de la Langue Grecque, 4. Pierre Chantraine. Klincksieck.

Dictionnaire Etymologique des noms Grecs de Plantes. Albert Carnoy. Peeters.

Dictionnaire Grec-Francais. Anatole Bailly. French & Eur.

Dictionnaire Grec-Francais. Ch. Georgin. French & Eur.

Dictionnaire Grec-Francais. Victor Magnien & M. Lacroix. French & Eur.

Dictionnaire Grec-Francais. Emile Pessoneaux. French & Eur.

Dictionnaire Grec-Francais. Georgin. Hatier.

Dictionnaire Grec-Francais. Anatole Bailly. Hachette-Jeunesse.

Dictionnaire Grec-Francais. Victor Magnien & M. Lacroix. Belin.

Dictionnaire Grec-Francais. Emile Pessonneaux. Belin.

Dictionnaire Grec Moderne Francais. Hubert Pernot. Garnier.

Dictionnaire Historique de la Terminologie Optique des Grecs. Charles Mugler. Klincksieck.

Divry's Modern English-Greek & Greek-English Desk Dictionary. Divry.

Divry's New Modern Greek-English & English-Greek Handy Dictionary. Ed. by George C. Divry. Divry.

Dizionario greco-italiano. Benedetto Bonazzi. Morano.

Dizionario greco moderno-italiano e italiano-greco moderno: Vol. 1, Greco moderno-italiano. Eliseo Brighenti. Cisalpino.

Dizionario greco moderno-italiano e italiano-greco moderno: Vol. 2, Italiano-greco moderno. Cisalpino.

Dizionario greco moderno-italiano, italiano-greco moderno. Malipiero.

Dizionario illustrato greco-italiano. H. G. Liddell et al. Monnier.

Dizionario italiano-greco moderno. Malipiero.

English-Greek Pocket Dictionary. Saphrograph.

The Englishman's Greek Concordance of the New Testament. George V. Vigram. Broadman.

Englishman's Greek Concordance of the New Testament: Numerically Coded to Strong's Exhaustive Concordance. Baker Bk.

Etymological Lexicon of Classical Greek. E. R. Wharton. Ares.

Fachwoerter des Oeffentlichen Verwaltungsdienstes Aegyptens in den Griechischen Papyrusurkunden der Ptolemaeisch-Romischen Zeit. Friedrich Preisigke. Olms Verlag.

Geographical Lexicon of Greek Coin Inscriptions. A. Florance. Ares.

The Golden Greek Glossary. American Classical League. Am Classical.

Greek & English Lexicon. Parkhurst. AMG Pubs.

Greek-English Analytical Concordance of the Greek-English New Testament. J. Stegenga. Hellenes.

Greek-English Concordance. Ed. by Jacob B. Smith. Herald Pr.

Greek English Derivative Dictionary. Ed. by Rudolph F. Schaeffer. Am Classical.

Greek-English Dictionary "Modern". Saphrograph.

Greek-English, English-Greek Dictionary. C. Patsis. Heinman.

Greek-English, English-Greek Medical Dictionary. Ed. by D. N. Gelis. Heinman.

Greek-English, English-Greek Pocket Dictionary. Heinman.

Greek-English, English-Greek Technical Dictionary. H. T. Hionides. Heinman.

Greek-English Lexicon. Ed. by Henry G. Liddell & Robert Scott. Oxford U Pr.

Greek-English Lexicon of the New Testament: A Dictionary Numerically Coded to Strong's Exhaustive Concordance. Joseph H. Thayer. Baker Bk.

Greek-English Lexicon of the New Testament. W. J. Hickie. Baker Bk.

Greek-English Pocket Dictionary. Saphrograph.

Greek-Norwegian Norwegian-Greek Pocket Dictionary. E. Theophilakis. Kunnskapsforlaget.

Greek Vocabulary. Joint Association of Classical Teachers. Cambridge U Pr.

Greek Word Roots: A Practical List with Greek & English Derivatives. Thomas Rogers. Baker Bk.

Gresk-Norsk-Gresk Lommeordbok. French & Eur.

Griechiesches Etymologisches Woerterbuch. Hjalmar Frisk. Winter Univ.

Griechisch-Deutsches Taschenwoerterbuch zum Neuen Testament. Erwin Preuschen. De Gruyter.

Griechisch-Deutsches Woerterbuch zu den Schriften des Neuen Testamens und der uebrigen urchristlichen Literatur. Walter Bauer. De Gruyter.

Griechisches Etymologiches Woerterbuch. Hjalmar Frisk. Winter Univ.

Griechisches Etymologisches Woerterbuch. Hjalmar Frisk. (Pub. by Carl Winter). French & Eur.

Griechisches Etymologisches Woerterbuch. Hjalmar Frisk. (Pub. by Carl Winter). French & Eur.

Griechisches Etymologisches Woerterbuch. Hjalmar Frisk. (Pub. by Carl Winter). French & Eur.

Griechishes Etymologishes Woerterbuch. Hjalmar Frisk. Winter Univ.

Homeric Vocabularies: Greek & English Word-Lists for the Study of Homer. William B. Owen & Edgar J. Goodspeed. U of Okla Pr.

An Index to Bauer Arndt, Gingrich Greek Lexicon. John R. Alsop. Zondervan.

Intermediate Greek-English Lexicon. Ed. by H. G. Liddell & Robert Scott. Oxford U Pr.

An Intermediate Greek-English Lexicon. Liddell & Scott. Oxford U Pr.

Kleines Woerterbuch Des Hellenismus. (Pub. by Harrassowitz). French & Eur.

Langenscheidts Grosswoerterbuch Altgriechisch: Tl 1, Altgriechisch-Deutsch. Langenscheidt.

Langenscheidts Grossworterbuch Altgriechisch-Deutsch. Menge & Guthling. Langenscheidt.

Langenscheidts Lilliput-Woerterbuecher Altgriechisch-Deutsch. Langenscheidt.

Langenscheidt's Pocket Greek Dictionary, Classical Greek-English. Ed. by Karl Feyerabend. Am Map.

Langenscheidts Taschenwoerterbuch Altgriechisch. H. Menge & O. Guthling. Langenscheidt.

Langenscheidts Taschenwoerterbuch Altgriechisch: Teil I, Altgriechisch-Deutsch. H. Menge. Langenscheidt.

Langenscheidts Taschenwoerterbuch Altgriechisch: Teil II, Deutsch-Altgriechisch. O. Guthling. Langenscheidt.

Langenscheidts Taschenwoerterbuch Neugriechisch: Teil II, Deutsch-Neugriechisch. A. Steinmetz. Langenscheidt.

Langenscheidts Taschenwoerterbuch Neugriechisch: Teil I, Neugriechisch-Deutsch. H. F. Wendt. Langenscheidt.

Langenscheidts Taschenwoerterbuecher Altgriechisch-Deutsch. H. Menge. Langenscheidt.

Langenscheidts Taschenwoerterbuecher Neugriechisch. Langenscheidt.

Langenscheidts Taschenwoerterbuecher Neugriechisch-Deutsch. Ed. by H. F. Wendt. Langenscheidt.

Langenscheidts Universal-Woerterbuch Neugriechisch. Langenscheidt.

Langenscheidts Universal-Woerterbuecher Neugriechisch-Deutsch. Langenscheidt.

Latin & Greek for Biologists. Theodore Savory. (Pub. by Meadowfield Pr England). State Mutual Bk.

Learn Greek for English Speakers. Saphrograph.

Lexicon Hesiodeum: Cum Indice Inverso. M. Hofinger. Brill Verlag.

Lexicon Plotinianum. J. H. Sleeman & Gilbert Pollet. Leuven U Pr.

Lexiko tes Mykenaikes Hellenikes. Giannes K. Pomponas. Ekdoseis Filon.

Lexikon der Kunstslile: Bd 1, Von der Griechischen Archaik bis zur Renaissance. Rowohlt.

Lexikon des Fruehgriechischen Epos: Lfg 1. Bruno Snell & Hartmut Erbse. Vandenhoeck.

Lexikon des Fruehgriechischen Epos: Lfg 2. Bruno Snell & Hartmut Erbse. Vandenhoeck.

Lexikon des Fruehgriechischen Epos: Lfg 3. Bruno Snell & Hartmut Erbse. Vandenhoeck.

Lexikon des Fruehgriechischen Epos: Lfg 4. Bruno Snell & Hartmut Erbse. Vandenhoeck.

Lexikon des Fruehgriechischen Epos: Lfg 5. Bruno Snell & Hartmut Erbse. Vandenhoeck.

Lexikon des Fruehgriechischen Epos: Lfg 6. Bruno Snell & Hartmut Erbse. Vandenhoeck.

Lexikon des Fruehgriechischen Epos: Lfg 7. Bruno Snell & Hartmut Erbse. Vandenhoeck.

Lexikon des Fruehgriechischen Epos: Lfg 8. Bruno Snell & Hartmut Erbse. Vandenhoeck.

Lexikon tes Hellenikes Glosses Tritomon: Lexicon of the Greek Language in Three Volumes. Ed. by Anthimos Gazes. Caratzas Pub Co.

Lexikon zu Lycophron. Maria G. Ciani. Olms Verlag.

Lexique Francais-Grec. L. Feuillet. Belin.

Lilliput Dictionary. Langenscheidt.

Modern English-Greek & Greek-English Dictionary. I. Kykkotis. (Pub. by Lund Humphries England). State Mutual Bk.

Modern English-Greek Dictionary. C. N. Brown. French & Eur.

Modern English-Greek-English Desk Dictionary with Thumb Index. G. C. Divry. French & Eur.

Modern Greek Evidence for the Ancient Greek Vocabulary. G. P. Shipp. (Pub. by Sydney U Pr). Intl Schol Bk Serv.

Modern Greek Idiom & Phrase Book. Constantine N. Tsirpanlis. Barron.

Nemetsko-Gruzinsko-Russkii Frazeologicheskii Slovar. N. Gamrekeli et al. (Pub. by Ganatleba). Four Continent.

Neugriechisch. Incl. Langenscheidt.

New English-Greek-English Handy Dictionary. G. C. Divry. French & Eur.

Novogrechesko-Russkii Slovar. I. P. Khorikov. (Pub. by Russkii Iazyk). Four Continent.

Nygrekisk-Svensk Ordbok. Antonis Mystakidis. Ed. by Eftychia Frangos. Esselte Studium.

The Oxford Dictionary of Modern Greek: English-Greek. Ed. by J. T. Pring. Oxford U Pr.

The Oxford Dictionary of Modern Greek: Greek-English, English-Greek. Ed. by J. T. Pring. Oxford U Pr.

Patristic Greek Lexicon. Ed. by G. W. Lampe. Oxford U Pr.

A Patristic Greek Lexicon. Ed. by G. W. Lampe. Brepols.

Patristic Greek Lexicon Nineteen Sixty-One to Sixty-Eight. Ed. by G. W. Lampe. Oxford U Pr.

Penguin-Hellenews English-Greek Dictionary. Ed. by G. Vassiliades. Caratzas Pub Co.

Petit Dictionnaire Francais-Grec Moderne et Grec Moderne-Francais. Andre Mirambel. French & Eur.

Phrase Dictionaries for the American Tourist. Frederick Stark. Incl. Delair.

Pocket-Shorter Dictionary. Langenscheidt.

Reverse Lexicon of Greek Proper Names. F. Dornseiff & Bernard Hansen. Ares.

Russko-Novogrecheskii Slovar. A. A. Ioannidia. (Pub. by Sov. Entsiklopediia). Four Continent.

Svensk-Nygrekisk Ordbok. Natan Valmin & Eftychia Frangos. Esselte Studium.

Syntactical & Critical Concordance to the Greek Text of Baruch & the Epistle of Jeremiah. R. A. Martin. Biblical Res Assocs.

Tesoro Della Linqua Greca-Volgare Ed Italiana, cioe Ricchissimo dizzionary greco-volgare et italiano. Alexis De Sommevoire & Tomaso Da Parigi. Caratzas Pub Co.

Thayer's Greek-English Lexicon of the New Testament. Joseph H. Thayer. Broadman.

Thesaurus Graecae Linguae. Henri Estienne. Akad Druck.

Vest Pocket Modern Greek. Institute for Language Study. (BN). B&N NY.

Vocabolario greco-italiano. Guglielmo Gemoll. Sandron.

Vocabolario greco-italiano. Alessandro Annaratone & Giovanni La Magna. Signorelli C.

Vocabolario greco-italiano. Lorenzo Rocci. Dante Alighieri.

Vocabulaire Grec. Paul Collin. Dessain & Tolra.

Vocabulaire Grec. Victor Fontoynont. Picard.

Vocabulaire Grec. Joannes Saunier. Gigord.

Vocabulaire Grec de Base. Simon Byl. Dessain & Tolra.

Vocabulaire Grec de la Terminologie Rhetorique: Dans; Etudes sur Quintillen. Jean Cousin. (Pub. by B R Gruner Netherlands). Humanities.

Vocabulaire Pratique du Grec. P. Leonard. Duculot.

Vocabulario Griego-Argentino. Raul Villarroel. Castellvi.

Vocabulary of the Greek New Testament. James H. Moulton & George Milligan. Eerdmans.

Vox-Diccionario Manual Griego-Espanol. Jose M. Pabon. French & Eur.

GUARANI

Diccionario guarani-espanol, espanol-guarani. A Jover Peralta & T. Ozuna. Dist. Comuneros.

GUJARATI

A Modern English-Gujarati Dictionary. P. G. Deshpande. Oxford U Pr.

HAIDA

Haida Dictionary. Erma Lawrence. Ed. by Christine Edenso & Robert Cogo. Society for the Preservation of Haida Language & Literature.

HAITIAN

Dictionnaire Elementaire Creole Haitien-Francais. Pierre Nougayrol et al. Ed. by Alain Bentolila. French & Eur.

Haitian Creole Grammar, Texts, Vocabulary. Ed. by Robert A. Hall et al. Kraus Repr.

HARSUSI

Harsusi Lexicon & English-Harsusi Word-list. Thomas M. Johnstone. Oxford U Pr.

HAUSA

Sabon Kamus na Hausa Zuwa Turanci. Paul Newman & Roxana M. Newman. Oxford U Pr.

HAWAIIAN

A Dictionary of the Hawaiian Language. Lorrin Andrews. C E Tuttle.

Dictionary of the Hawaiian Language. Andrews. Iaconi.

English-Hawaiian Dictionary. Harvey R. Hitchcock. C E Tuttle.

An English-Hawaiian Dictionary. Hitchcock. Iaconi.

Hawaiian Dictionary. Mary K. Pukui & Samuel H. Elbert. UH Pr.

The Hawaiian Language & Hawaiian-English Dictionary. Henry P. Judd. Hawaiian Serv.

Hawaiian Phrase Book. Ed. by J. H. Soper. C E Tuttle.

Illustrated Hawaiian Word Book. Robin Burningham. Bess Pr.

Let's Learn a Little Hawaiian. W. Ray Helbig. Hawaiian Serv.

The Pocket Hawaiian Dictionary: With a Concise Hawaiian Grammar. Mary K. Pukui et al. UH Pr.

Vocabulaire & Grammaire de la Langue Houailou. Maurice Leenhardt. Inst Ethnol.

HEBREW

Analytical Hebrew & Chaldee Lexicon. Benjamin Davidson. (Pub. by Bagster). Zondervan.

Bantam Hebrew-English, English-Hebrew Dictionary. Bantam.

Berlitz Hebrew for Travellers. Berlitz Editors. (Berlitz). Macmillan.

Classified Concordance: To the Bible & Its Various Subjects. Ed. by Eliezer Katz. Bloch.

The Complete English-Hebrew Dictionary. Rueben Alcalay. Massada Pr.

Complete English-Hebrew, Hebrew-English Dictionary. Reuben Alcalay. SBS Pub.

The Complete Hebrew Dictionary in Seven Volumes. Ed. by Abraham Even-Shoshan. K Sefer.

The Complete Hebrew Dictionary in Three Volumes. Ed. by Abraham Even-Shoshan. K Sefer.

The Complete Hebrew Dictionary Supplement to the 3 Volume Set. Ed. by Abraham E. Shoshan. K Sefer.

The Complete Hebrew Dictionary Supplement Volume to Seven Volume Set. Ed. by Abraham E. Shoshan. K Sefer.

The Complete Hebrew-English Dictionary. Rueben Alcalay. Massada Pr.

A Concise Hebrew & Aramaic Lexicon of the Old Testament. William L. Holladay. Eerdmans.

Concordance of the Bible. Solomon Mendelkern. Feldheim.

Condensed Hebrew Dictionary. Ed. by Abraham Even-Shoshan. K Sefer.

Deutsch-Hebraeisches Woerterbuch. David Herstig. (Pub. by Max Hueber). French & Eur.

Deutsch-Hebraeisches Woerterbuch. David Herstig. Hueber.

Diccionario Hebreo-Castallano: Castellano-Hebreo. Ed. by Y. Austridan. French & Eur.

Diccionario hebreo-espanol. Perpetuo.

Dictionary of Automobile Terms. Massada Pr.

Dictionary of Concrete Terms. Massada Pr.

Dictionary of Dams. Massada Pr.

Dictionary of Engineering Metrology Terms. Massada Pr.

Dictionary of Floor, Wall & Ceiling Covering. Massada Pr.

Dictionary of Foundry Terms. Massada Pr.

Dictionary of Hebrew Verbs. M. Debahy. Intl Bk Ctr.

Dictionary of Hydrology Terms. Massada Pr.

Dictionary of Joinery Terms: Doors, Windows, Shutters. Massada Pr.

Dictionary of Library Terms. Massada Pr.

Dictionary of Maritime Terms. Massada Pr.

Dictionary of Mathematical Terms. Massada Pr.

Dictionary of Meteorological Terms. Massada Pr.

Dictionary of Photograhy. Massada Pr.

Dictionary of Physics: No. 1, Mechanics. Massada Pr.

Dictionary of Physics: No. 2, Electricity & Magnetism. Massada Pr.

Dictionary of Physics: No. 3, Optics. Massada Pr.

Dictionary of Pump Terms. Massada Pr.

Dictionary of Sea Waves & Currents Terms. Massada Pr.

Dictionary of Sewage & Sanitary Installation Terms. Massada Pr.

Dictionary of Soil Science & Soil Engineering Terms. Massada Pr.

Dictionary of Strength of Materials. Massada Pr.

Dictionary of Technical Drawing. Massada Pr.

Dictionary of Telecommunications & Electronics. Massada Pr.

Dictionary of Work Study Terms. Massada Pr.

Dictionnaire Francais-Hebreu. Marc M. Cohn. French & Eur.

Dictionnaire francais-hebreu. M. M. Cohn. Larousse.

Dictionnaire Francais-Hebreu. Marc M. Cohn. Larousse.

Dictionnaire Hebrau-Francais. Joseph Hadar. Massada Pr.

Dictionnaire Hebreu-Francais. Rabbin Marchand-Ennery. Colbo.

Early Hebrew Orthography: A Study of the Epigraphic Evidence. Frank M. Cross, Jr. & David N. Freedman. Am Orient Soc.

Elef Millim. Nello Pavoncello. Carucci.

Englishman's Hebrew & Chaldee Concordance of the Old Testament. Baker Bk.

The Englishman's Hebrew Chaldee Concordance of the Old Testament. Broadman.

Five Hundred Terms of Home Economic. Massada Pr.

Glossaire Hebreu-Francais. Mayer Lambert & Louis Brandin. Slatkine.

Glossaire Hebreu-Francais du XIIIe. Siecle. Mayer Lambert & Louis Brandin. Slatkine.

A Glossary of Current Terminology. Lawrence Marwick. Govt Print.

Le Glosses & Glossaires Hebreux-Francais. Arsene Darmesteter. Champion.

Guilielmi Gesenii Thesaurus Philologicus Linguae Hebraeae. Freidrich H. Gesenius. Biblio-Verlag.

Hebraeisch-Deutches Woerterbuch. David Herstig. Hueber.

Hebraeisch-Deutsches Woerterbuch. David Herstig. (Pub. by Max Hueber). French & Eur.

Hebraisch. Jaacov Lavy. Langenscheidt.

Hebraisch-Deutsch: Zum Alten Testament. K. Feyerabend. Langenscheidt.

Hebrew & Aramaic Dictionary of the Old Testament. Ed. by Georg Fohrer et al. Tr. by W. A. Johnstone. from Ger De Gruyter.

Hebrew & Chaldee Lexicon: Keyed to Strong's Exhaustive Concordance. Wilhelm Gesenius. Tr. by Samuel P. Tregelles. Baker Bk.

Hebrew & Chaldee Lexicon, Tregelles Translation. William Gesenius. Eerdmans.

Hebrew & English Lexicon to the Old Testament. William Gesenius. Ed. by Francis Brown et al. Tr. by Edward Robinson. Oxford U Pr.

The Hebrew-Arabic Dictionary of the Bible, Known As Kitab Jami al-Alfaz (Agron) David Ben Abraham. Ed. by Solomon L. Skoss. AMS Pr.

Hebrew-Arabic Dictionary of the Bible Known As Kitab Jami-Al-Alfaz. Ed. by Solomon Skoss. Elliots Bks.

Hebrew-Aramaic-English Dictionary, a Dictionary of Talmud Babli & Talmud Yerushalmi Targum & Midrash. Marcus Jastrow. Shalom.

Hebrew-English Dictionary: Hebrew & Chaldee Lexicon to the Old Testament. Gesenius Furst. Ed. by Edward C. Mitchell. Shalom.

Hebrew-English, English-Hebrew Dictionary. A. Waldstein. Shalom.

Hebrew-English Lexicon of the Bible. Schocken.

Hebrew-English Pictorial Dictionary. David Ettinger. Shalom.

Hebrew Nomenclature of Inorganic Chemistry. Massada Pr.

Hebrew Pocket Dictionary. Heinman.

Hebrew Vocabularies. J. Barton Payne. Baker Bk.

Index to the Brown, Driver & Briggs Hebrew Lexicon. Moody.

The Jewish Word Book. Sidney J. Jacobs. Jonathan David.

Langenscheidts Handwoerterbuch Hebraisch: Teil II, Deutsch-Hebraisch. Jaacov Lavy. Langenscheidt.

Langenscheidts Handwoerterbuch Hebraisch: Teil I, Hebraisch-Deutsch. Jaacov Lavy. Langenscheidt.

Langenscheidt's Hebrew-German Dictionary. Jaacom Lavy. Am Map.

Langenscheidt's Pocket Hebrew Dictionary, Hebrew-English. Ed. by Karl Feyerabend. Am Map.

Langenscheidts Taschenwoerterbuch Hebraisch. K. Feyerabend. Langenscheidt.

Langenscheidts Taschenwoerterbuecher Hebraeisch-Deutsch. K. Feierabend. Langenscheidt.

Learn Hebrew for English Speakers. Saphrograph.

Lexicon in Veteris Testamenti Libros: Hebraic-Aramaic Lexicon, Incl. Supplement. Ludwig Koehler & Walter Baumgartner. Eerdmans.

Lists of Words Occurring Frequently in the Hebrew Bible. John D. Watts. Eerdmans.

The Massada English-Hebrew Student Dictionary. Reuben Alcalay. SBS Pub.

The Massada Student Dictionary English-Hebrew. Rueben ALcalay. Massada Pr.

The Megiddo Modern Dictionary: English-Hebrew, Hebrew-English. Ed. by Edward A. Levenston & Reuban Sivan. (Carta Maps & Guides Pub Israel). Hippocrene Bks.

The Megiddo Modern Dictionary: English-Hebrew, Hebrew-English. Ed. by Edward A. Levenston & Reuban Sivan. Carta Pub Co.

The Megiddo Modern Dictionary: English-Hebrew to Hebrew-English. French & Eur.

Mille Parole Fondamentali. Nello Pavoncello. Carucci.

Milon Kis: A Hebrew Pocket Dictionary. Ed. by A. Even Shoshan & Dov Yarden. Board Jewish Educ.

Miloni: Illustrated Dictionary for Children. Board of Jewish Education. Board Jewish Educ.

My Little Dictionary. Board of Jewish Education. Board Jewish Educ.

The New Bantam-Meggido Hebrew & English Dictionary. Reuben Sivan & Edward A. Levenston. Bantam.

The New Bantam-Megiddo Hebrew & English Dictionary. Reuven Sivan & Edward A. Levenston. Schocken.

The New Bantam-Megiddo Hebrew Dictionary. Edward A. Levenston & Reuven Sivan. Bantam.

New Functional Hebrew-English, English-Hebrew Dictionary. Nathan Goldberg. Ktav.

New Illustrated Hebrew-English Dictionary for Young Readers. Nathan Goldberg. Ktav.

Nouveau Dictionnaire Francais-Hebreu. Larousse.

Nouveau Dictionnaire Hebreu-Francais. Marc M. Cohn. French & Eur.

Nouveau Dictionnaire hebreu-francais. Larousse.

Nuevo Diccionario Castellano-Hebreo. Juan Ducach. Massada Pr.

Pocket-Shorter Dictionary. Langenscheidt.

A Reader's Hebrew-English Lexicon of the Old Testament: (Genesis-Deuteronomy) Ed. by Terry Armstrong et al. Zondervan.

Roots: A Hebrew-English Word List. Ed. by Mordechai Kamrat & Edwin Samuel. Illus. by Yafa Talarek. K Sefer.

Seven Language Dictionary. Ed. by David Shumaker. Crown.

Seven Languages Dictionary. Imported Bks.

The Signet Hebrew-English - English-Hebrew Dictionary. Dov Ben Abba. (Sig). NAL.

Simon & Schuster Gem Ben-Yehuda's Hebrew-English & English-Hebrew Dictionary. S&S.

The Student's Dictionary. Ed. by Abraham Even-Shoshan. K Sefer.

Thesaurus Philosophicus Linguae Hebraica. Klatzkin. Feldheim.

Woordenboek Hebreeuws-Nederlands. Jitschak Pimentel. Strengholt.

Woordenboek Hebreeuws-Nederlands. Jitschak Pimentel. Strengholt.

Your Jewish Lexicon. Edith Samuel. UAHC.

HINDI

Bahri's Law Dictionary. Hardev Bahri. Haredeva Bahari.

Bulgarian-Hindi Dictionary. B. Kanti Varma. French & Eur.

A Comprehensive English-Hindi Dictionary of Governmental & Educational Words & Phrases. Raghu Vira. Intl Pubns Serv.

Comprehensive English-Hindi Dictionary. Hardev Bahri. Intl Pubns Serv.

Concise English Hindi Dictionary. R. C. Pathak. Auromere.

Concise Hindi-English Dictionary. R. C. Pathak. Auromere.

A Dictionary of Hindu Architecture: Treating of Sanskrit Architectural Terms. Prasanna K. Acharya. Bharatiya Publishing House.

A Dictionary of Urdu Classical Hindi & English. John T. Platts. Intl Pubns Serv.

Dictionary of Urdu, Classical Hindi, & English. John T. Platts. Oxford U Pr.

English Hindi Dictionary. Bulke. Auromere.

English-Hindi Dictionary. Saphrograph.

Hindi-English - English-Hindi Standard Illustrated Dictionary. Ed. by R. C. Pathak. Heinman.

Hindi English Dictionary. R. C. Pathak. Auromere.

Hindi-English Dictionary. Saphrograph.

Hindi-English Dictionary: With Pronounciations Romanized. A. T. Shanney. Shalom.

Hindi Pocket Dictionary. Heinman.

Hindu-Kashmiri Common Vocabulary. Jawaharlal Handoo & Lalita Handoo. Ctr Inst Ind Lang.

Meenakshi Hindi-English Dictionary. (Pub. by Meenakshi). South Asia Bks.

A Practical Hindi-English Dictionary. Mahendra Chaturvedi & Nath T. Bhola. South Asia Bks.

Sanskrit-Hindi-English Dictionary. Suryakanta. Intl Pubns Serv.

Structure of the Noun Phrase in English & Hindi. M. K. Verma. Orient Bk Dist.

Woerterbuch Deutsch-Hindi. Margot Gatzlaff-Halsig. VEB Verlag Enzyklopadie.

HINDUSTANI

English-Hindustani Dictionary. Saphrograph.

Learn Hindustani. Saphrograph.

HITTITE

The Hittite Dictionary of the Oriental Institute of the University of Chicago. Ed. by Harry A. Hoffner, Jr. & Hans G. Guterbock. Oriental Inst.

HUNGARIAN

Ablak-Zsir Kepes Gyermeklexikon. Ferenc Morei & Agnes V. Binet. Adler Bks.

Angol-Magyar Mikroelektronikai. Magdolna Kovacs. KG Informatik.

Angol-Magyar Szotar English-Hungarian Dictionary. L. Orszagn. Saphrograph.

Angol Nyelvkonyv: English Language Book for Self-Learners & Student with Teachers. Latzko Hugo. Saphrograph.

Biologiai Lexikon. Ferene B. Straub & Gyorgy Adam. Akademiai Kiado.

Comparative Dictionary of the Finno-Ugric Elements in the Hungarian Vocabulary. Jozsef Budenz. Res Ctr Lang Semiotic.

A Concise English-Hungarian Dictionary. V. Orszagh. (Pub. by Collet's). State Mutual Bk.

A Concise English-Hungarian Dictionary. Orszagh Laszlo. Akademiai Kiado.

A Concise Hungarian-English Dictionary. V. Orszagh. (Pub. by Collet's). State Mutual Bk.

Conference Terminology in English, Spanish, Russian, Italian, German & Hungarian. J. Herbert. Elsevier.

Deutsch-Ungarisches Woerterbuch. Akademiai Kiado.

Diccionario Simultaneo en 21 Idiomas. Juan Capdevilla Font. French & Eur.

Dictionary for the Graphic Arts in Eight Languages: German-English-French-Spanish-Russian-Hungarian-Polish-Slowak. Perfect Graphic.

Dictionary of Hungarian Slang. Alex Sandri-White. Aurea.

Dictionary of Musical Terms in Seven Languages. Ed. by H. Leuchtmann. Heinman.

Dictionary of Technical Acoustics. L. Reichardt. Adler.

Dictionary of the Graphic Arts
. Industry. Ed. by W. Muller. Elsevier.

Dictionnaire de Poche Francais-Hongrois. S. Eckhardt. Terra.

Dictionnaire de Tourisme Francais-Hongrois. L. Havas. Terra.

Dictionnaire Franco-Hongrois. Voyages.

Dictionnaire Technique Hongrois-Francais. B. Rubin. Terra.

Dictionnaire Usuel Hongrois-Francais. S. Eckhardt. Terra.

English-Hungarian Dictionary. L. Orszagh. Saphrograph.

English-Hungarian Dictionary. V. Orszagh. (Pub. by Collet's). State Mutual Bk.

English-Hungarian Dictionary. Ed. by Laszlo Orszagh. Intl Pubns Serv.

English-Hungarian, Hungarian-English Dictionary-Angol-Magyar-Angol Szotar. Biro Willerfest. Saphrograph.

English-Hungarian, Hungarian-English Medical Dictionary. Dora Lee-Delisle. Saphrograph.

English-Hungarian Technical Dictionary-Angol-Magyar Muszaki Szotar. Imre Razso. Saphrograph.

English-Hungarian Technical Dictionary. Ed. by E. Nagy & J. Klar. (Pub. by Collet's). State Mutual Bk.

Etlapiras. Gyorgy Arva. Kozgazdasagi.

Fachworterbuch Polygrafie: English-Deutsch-French-Russian-Spanish-Polish-Hungarian-Slowakian. French & Eur.

Fenno-Ugric Vocabulary: An Etymological Dictionary of the Uralic Languages. Bjorn Collinder. (Pub. by Helmut Buske Verlag Hamburg). Benjamins North Am.

Filmgyartas es Filmtechnika. Gabor Pozsonyi. Akademiai Kiado.

Finnish-Hungarian-Finnish Dictionary (Suomi-Unkari-Suomi) I. Nyirkos. French & Eur.

Four Language Culinary Dictionary: French, Hungarian, English, German. Saphrograph.

Haditechnikai Kislexikon. Istvan G. Nagy. Zrinyikatunai.

Hiradastechnikai Kislexikon. Miklos Izak. Mueszaki Konyv.

How to Say It in Hungarian: An English-Hungarian Phrase-Book with Lists of Words. L. T. Andras & M. Murval. Heinman.

Hungarian Concise Dictionary: English-Hungarian. Laszlo Orszagh. Vanous.

Hungarian Concise Dictionary: Hungarian-English. Laszlo Orszagh. Vanous.

Hungarian Deluxe Dictionary: English-Hungarian. Orszagh. Vanous.

Hungarian Deluxe Dictionary: Hungarian-English. Orszagh. Vanous.

Hungarian Dictionary for Tourists. Magay Tamas. Vanous.

Hungarian-English Dictionary. L. Orszagh. Saphrograph.

Hungarian-English Dictionary. V. Orszagh. (Pub. by Collet's). State Mutual Bk.

Hungarian-English, English-Hungarian Concise Dictionary (1976-79) L. Orszagh. Heinman.

Hungarian-English: English Hungarian Dictionary. Laszlo Orszagh. Heinman.

Hungarian-English Technical Dictionary. T. Nagy. (Pub. by Collet's). State Mutual Bk.

Hungarian-French Concise Dictionary. S. Eckhardt. French & Eur.

Hungarian Pocket Dictionary: Hungarian-English. Laszlo Orszagh. Vanous.

Hungarian-Vietnamese Dictionary. I. Kotet. French & Eur.

Husznyelvu Kiadoi Szotar. Imre Mora. Akademiai Kiado.

Idegen Szavak Szotara. Ferenc Bakos et al. Terra.

Idegen Szavak Szotara. Forenc Bakos & Pal Fabian. Terra.

Katonai Ertelmezo Szotar. Lajos Toth et al. Zrinyi Katonai.

Koezhelyszotar. Miklos Hernadi. Gondolat.

Kozhelyszotar. Miklos Hernadi. Gondolat.

Landwirtschaftliches Woerterbuch in Acht Sprachen. (Pub. by BLV). French & Eur.

Langenscheidts Handwoerterbuch Ungarisch HALASZ: Teil II, Deutsch-Ungarisch. I. Kadar & O. Ratz. Langenscheidt.

Langenscheidts Handwoerterbuch Ungarisch HALASZ: Teil I, Ungarisch-Deutsch. Ratz S. Skripecz et al. Langenscheidt.

Langenscheidts Handwoerterbuecher: Tl 2, Deutsch-Ungarisch. Ed. by Halasz. Langenscheidt.

Langenscheidts Universal-Woerterbuch Ungarisch. Langenscheidt.

Langenscheidts Universal-Woerterbuecher Ungarisch-Deutsch. Langenscheidt.

Learn Hungarian for English Speakers. A. H. Whitney. Saphrograph.

Lengyel-Magyar Szotar. Istvan Varsanyi. Terra.

Magyar-Angol Muszaki Szotar. Erno Nagy & Janos Klar et al. Akademiai Kiado.

Magyar-Angol Szotar, Hungarian-English Dictionary. Ed. by L. Orszagh. Saphrograph.

Magyar-Bolgar Szotar. Jozsef Bodey. Terra.

Magyar-Bolgar Szotar. Jozsef Bodey. Terra.

Magyar Ertelmezo Keziszotar. Jozsef Juhasz. Akademiai Kiado.

Magyar Ertelmezo Keziszotar. Ed. by Jozsef Juhasz et al. Akademiai Kiado.

Magyar-Francia Szotar. Sandor Eckhardt. Akademiai Kiado.

Magyar-Francia Szotar. Sandor Eckhardt. Akademiai Kiado.

Magyar-Lengyel Szotar. Istvan Varsanyi. Terra.

Magyar-Lengyel Szotar. Istvan Varsanyi. Terra.

Magyar Neprajzi Lexikon. Ed. by Gyula Ortutay. Akademiai Kiado.

Magyar-Olasz Szotar. Gyula Herczeg. Terra.

Magyar-Olasz Szotar. Gyula Herczeg. Terra.

Magyar-Orosz Katonai Szotar. A Szotarszerk Bizottsag Vezetoje Toth Lajos. Akademiai Kiado.

Magyar-Orosz Kez Iszotar. Laszlo Hadrovics et al. Akademiai Kiado.

Magyar-Orosz Keziszotar. Laszlo Hadrovics & Galdi Hadrovics. Akademiai Kiado.

Magyar-Orosz Muszaki Szotar. Lorant Katona. Akademiai Kiado.

Magyar-Szerbhorvat Szotar. Laszlo Hadrovics et al. Terra.

Magyar-Szerbhorvat Szotar. Laszlo Hadrovics. Terra.

Magyar Szinonimaszotar. Gabor O. Nagy et al. Akademiai Kiado.

Magyar Tajszotar. Magyar Tudomanyos Akademia Nyelvtudomany Intezeteben. Ed. by Eva B. Lorinczy. Akademiai Kiado.

Medizintechnik-Englisch-Deutsch-Franzoesisch-Russisch-Spanisch-Polnisch-Ungarisch-Slowakisch. Roald Albert & Harry Hahnewald. VEB Technik.

Music Translation Dictionary: An English, Czech, Danish, Dutch, French, German, Hungarian, Italian, Polish, Portuguese, Russian, Spanish, Swedish Vocabulary of Music. Compiled by Carolyn D. Grigg. Greenwood.

Nemzetkozi Kutya Enciklopedia. Ed. by Pal Sarkany. Terra.

Olasz-Magyar Szotar. Gyula Herczeg. Akademiai Kiado.

Olasz-Magyar-Szotar. Gyula Herczeg. Terra.

Olasz-Magyar Szotar: Vocabolario Italiano-Ungherese. Gyula Herczeg. Ed. by Jeno Kolttay-Kastner. Akademiai Kiado.

Onteszet. Arpad Voros. Akademiai Kiado.

Operalexikon. Peter Varnai. Zenemukiado.

Orosz-Magyar Katonai Szotar. Lajos Toth. Akademiai Kiado.

Orosz-Magyar Szotar. Laszlo Galdi. Akademiai Kiado.

Orosz-Magyar Szotar. Laszlo Hadrovics. Akademiai Kiado.

Orosz-Magyar Szotar Iskolak Szamara. Miklos Szabo. Akademiai Kiado.

Orvosi Szotar. Janos Brenesan. Terra.

Papirkeszltoink Mestersegszavai. Istvan Bogdan. MTESZ.

Papirkeszltoink Mestersegszavai. Istvan Bogdan. MTESZ.

Pedagogiai Lexikon. Ed. by Sandor Nagy. Akademiai Kiado.

A Pesti Nyelv. Geza Barczi. Magyar Tarsasag.

Pocket English-Hungarian Dictionary. I. Orszagh. (Pub. by Collet's). State Mutual Bk.

Pocket Hungarian-English Dictionary. I. Orszagh. (Pub. by Collet's). State Mutual Bk.

Politikai Kissotar: A Szocikkek Szerzoi. Istvan Foldes & Gyoergy Makai et al. Kos Kony.

Polygrafie-Englisch-Deutsch-Franzoesisch-Russisch-Spanisch-Polnisch-Ungarisch-Solwakisch. Wolfgang Muller. VEB Technik.

Portugal-Magyar Szotar. Rudolf Kiraly. Akademiai Kiado.

Portuguese-Hungarian Concise Dictionary. R. Kiraly. French & Eur.

Septemlingual Dictionary of the Names of European Animal. Ed. by L. Gozmany et al. (Pub. by Kiado Hungary). Heyden.

Suomi-Unkari-Suomi: Taskusanakirja. Istvan Nyirkos. Soderstrom.

Systems Analysis & Operations Research Dictionary. G Sezepesi & B. Szekely. (Pub. by Collets). State Mutual Bk.

Szerbhorvat-Magyar Szotar. Laszlo Hadrovics et al. Terra.

Szerbhorvat-Magyar Szotar. Laszlo Hadrovics. Terra.

Szlovak-Magyar Szotar. Marianne T. Gobel. Terra.

Taschenlexikon Ungarn. Ed. by Akademie Verlages Budapest. Bibl Inst Leipzig.

Taschenwoerterbuch Deutsch-Ungarisch. Ed. by Heinrich Weissling. VEB Verlag Enzyklopaedie.

Taschenworterbuch Deutsch-Ungarisch. Heinrich Weissling. VEB Verlag Enzyklopadie.

Technische Akustik. Walter Reichardt. VEB Verlag Technik.

Terminoloski Komparativni Srpskohrvatsko. Rudolf Toth. Ekonomski Fakultet.

UJ Magyar Lexikon. Pergamon.

Uj Magyar Tajszotar. Eva B. Lorinczy. Akademiai Kiado.

Ungarisch-Deutsches Woerterbuch der Rechts & Verwaltungssprache: Teil I, Ungarisch-Deutsch. Sandor Karcsay. Recht & Wirtschaft.

Ungarisch-Deutsches Woerterbuch der Rechts & Verwaltungssprache: Teil II, Deutsch-Ungarisch. Sandor Karcsay. Recht & Wirtschaft.

Unkarilais-Suomalainen Sanakirja. Istvan Nyirkos. Suoma Kirja.

Utiszotar, Angol-Magyar. Tamas Magy. Terra.

Woerterbuch der Ungarischen Rechts und Verwaltungssprache. Sandor Karcsay. French & Eur.

Woerterbuch der Ungarischen Rechts und Verwaltungssprache. French & Eur.

Zenei Zseblexikon. Gabor Darvas. Zenemukiado.

ICELANDIC

Concise Dictionary of Old Icelandic. Geir T. Zoega. Oxford U Pr.

English-Icelandic Dictionary. S. O. Bogason. Heinman.

Icelandic-English - English-Icelandic Dictionary. A. Sigurdsson & S. O. Bogason. Heinman.

Icelandic-English Dictionary. A. Sigurdsson. Heinman.

Icelandic-English Dictionary. Ed. by Richard Cleasby & Gudbrand Vigfusson. Oxford U Pr.

Icelandic-English Dictionary. Arngrimur Sigurdsson. Shalom.

Icelandic-English-Icelandic, Pocket Dictionary. A. Taylor. Vanous.

Icelandic Pocket Dictionary. Heinman.

Islaendisches Etymologisches Woerterbuch. Alex Johannesson. (Pub. by Francke). French & Eur.

Langenscheidts Universal-Woerterbuch Islaendisch. Langenscheidt.

Langenscheidts Universal-Woerterbuecher Islaendisch-Deutsch. Langenscheidt.

Merknader til en dell Norrone Tekster. Kare Skadberg & Tor Ulset. Univers Oslo.

Teaterord. Niklas Brunius. Nord Teater.

ILOKANO

Ilokano Dictionary. Constantino. Iaconi.

INDIC

Lexicography in India. National Conference on Dictionary Making in Indian Languages & Bal G. Misra. Central Institute of Indian Languages.

INDO-ARYAN

A Comparative Dictionary of the Indo-Aryan Languages. Sir Ralph Turner. Oxford U Pr.

INDONESIAN

Bibliotheca Indosinica. Dictionnaire bibliographique des ouvrages relatifs a la peninsule indo-chinoise. Henri Cordier. B Franklin.

Common English Words & Idioms with Their Equivalents in Bahasa Indonesia. A. Karim. C E Tuttle.

Contemporary Indonesian-English Dictionary. A. Ed. Schmidgall-Tellings & Alan Stevens. Ohio U Pr.

Dafoar islilah pertanian. Achmad Baihaki et al. Pustaka Antara.

Dizionario italo-indonesiano. L. Lini. EMI.

Elseviers Rubber Dictionary. Elsevier.

An English-Indonesian Dictionary. John M. Echols & Hassan Shadily. Cornell U Pr.

English-Indonesian, Indonesian-English Dictionary. A. L. Kramer, Sr. Shalom.

Indioneziisko-Russkii Uchebnyi Razgovornik. L. I. Ushakova et al. (Pub. by Gosizdat Inostr Natsional Slovarei). Four Continent.

An Indonesian-English Dictionary. John M. Echols & Hassan Shadily. Cornell U Pr.

Indonesian-Russian Dictionary. R. N. Korigodsky et al. French & Eur.

Indoneziisko-Russkii Slovar. V. N. Korigodskii et al. (Pub. by Gosizdat Inostr Natsional Slovarei). Four Continent.

Indoneziisko-Russkii Uchebnyi Slovar. A. S. Teselkin et al. (Pub. by Sov Entsiklopediia). Four Continent.

Kamus Inggeris Indonesia: Dictionary English-Indonesia for School, Office & Home. A. Hamid Siregar. Pustaka Antara.

Kamus Istilah Filologi. Ed. by Bararoh Baried. Universitas Gadjah Mada.

Kamus Logika. Liang G. The. Nur Cahaya.

Kamus Umum Bahasa Indonesia. W. Poerwadarminta. P N Balai Pustaka.

Karmannyi Indoneziisko-Russkii Slovar. N. F. Bulygin. (Pub. by GINS). Four Continent.

Karmannyi Russko-Indoneziiskii Slovar. N. F. Bulygin et al. (Pub. by GINS). Four Continent.

Modern Usage in Bahasa Indonesia. J. Sarumpaet. Pitman Ltd.

Peristilahan Kimia dan Farmasi. Penerbit Jaya.

Russko-Indoneziiskii Slovar. E. S. Belkina. (Pub. by Sov. Entsiklopediia). Four Continent.

Russko-Indoneziiskii Uchebnyi Slovar. A. G. Lordkipanidze et al. (Pub. by GINS). Four Continent.

Van Goor's Concise Indonesian Dictionary. Kramer. Iaconi.

Van Goor's Concise Indonesian Dictionary: English-Indonesian Indonesian-English. A. L. Kramer, Sr. C E Tuttle.

Woerterbuch Deutsch-Indonesisch. Gerhard Kahlo et al. VEB Verlag Enzyklopadie.

IRISH

English-Irish Dictionary. T. De Bhardraithe. Colton Bk.

English-Irish Dictionary. Patrick S. Dinneen. Ed. by L. O. Murcava. Shalom.

Foclair Gaeilge Bearla (Irish-English Dictionary) O'Donaill. Colton Bk.

Irish-English Dictionary. Dinneen. Colton Bk.

An Irish-English Dictionary. Edward O'Reilly. Gordon Pr.

Irish-English Dictionary. Shalom.

The Vocabulary of Anglo-Irish. James M. Clark. Folcroft.

IROQUOIS

Zeisberger's Indian Dictionary: English, German, Iroquois - the Onandaga & Algonquin - the Delaware. David Zeisberger. AMS Pr.

ISNEG

Isneg-English Vocabulary. Morice Vanoverbergh. UH Pr.

Dizionario di termini della critica letteraria. Roberto Berardi. Monnier.

Karmannyi Ital'iansko-Russkii Slovar. I. A. Dobrovolskaia. (Pub. by GINS). Four Continent.

Langenscheidts Grosswoerterbuch Italienisch. Vladimiro Von Macchi. Langenscheidt.

ITALIAN

ABC Dictionary I, Arabic Italian. Intl Bk Ctr.

ABC Dictionary Tamhidi: Arabic & Ital. Libr du Liban. Intl Bk Ctr.

Astronautical Multilingual Dictionary: International Academy of Astronautics. Elsevier.

Astronomical Dictionary: In Six Languages. Josip Kleczek. Acad Pr.

Atlante Della Sessualita. Franca Rome. A Mondadi.

Automobily. Czesaw Blok & Wiesaw Jezewski. Wydawnictwa.

Avviamento All'Etimologia Italiana: Dizionario Etimologico. Devoto. Oscar.

The Bantam New College Italian & English Dictionary. Robert C. Melzi. Bantam.

Berlitz Italian for Travellers. Berlitz Editors. (Berlitz). Macmillan.

Berlitz Pocket Dictionaries: Italien-English-Italian. Berlitz. Macmillan.

Berlitz Pocket Dictionaries: Italian-English. Berlitz Editors. (Berlitz). Macmillan.

Bibliografia Siciliana, Ovvero Gran Dizionario Bibliografico Delle Opere Editi E Inedite, Antiche E Moderne Di Autori Siciliani O Di Argomento Siciliano Stampate in Sicilia. Giuseppe M. Mira. B Franklin.

Bildwoerterbuch Italienisch: Dizionario Figurato. Biblio Inst.

Brockhaus Bildwoerterbuecher in vier Sprachen. F A Brockhaus.

Cambridge Italian Dictionary. Barbara Reynolds. Cambridge U Pr.

Capire l'Economiea: Dizionario Critico del Capitalismo Contemporaneo. Renzo Stefanelli. De Donato.

Capitol's Concise Dictionary. French & Eur.

Cassell's Colloquial Italian. Cassell. Macmillan.

Cassell's Italian Dictionary: Italian-English, English-Italian. Cassells et al. Macmillan.

Cassell's Italian Dictionary: Italian-English, English-Italian. Piero Rebora et al. Imported bks.

Cassell's Italian Dictionary: Standard Italian-English English-Italian. Cassell. Macmillan.

Cassell's Italian Dictionary: Thumb-indexed Italian-English English-Italian. Cassell. Macmillan.

Cesko-Italsky Slovnik na Cesty. Hana Benesova. SNTC.

Chemins de Fer Glossary. Bureau International de Documentation de Chemin de Fer. Elsevier.

Il Cinema Vuol Dire. Maurizio Porro & Giuseppe Turroni. Garzanti Edit.

Collins Italian-English English-Italian Dictionary. Berkley Pub.

Concise Cambridge Italian Dictionary. Barbara Reynolds. Cambridge U Pr.

The Concise Cambridge Italian Dictionary. Barbara Reynolds. Penguin.

Concise English-Italian Italian-English Dictionary. Ed. by Giuseppe Ragazzini & Adele Biagi. Longman.

Concordanze dei dialetti di Puglia. Michelle Melillo. Atlantica.

Concordanza verghiana. Marchi G. Paolo. Fiorini.

Conference Terminology in English, Spanish, Russian, Italian, German & Hungarian. J. Herbert. Elsevier.

Cortina-Grosset Basic Dictionary: Italian. Ed. by Dilaver Berberi & Edel A. Berberi. (G&D). Putnam Pub Group.

Customs Dictionary: German-English-French-Italian. Wilhelm Muller. Intl Pubns Serv.

Dansk-Italiensk Ordborg. J. Mengel. French & Eur.

I Dialetti della Liguria Orientale Odierna. Hugo Plomteux. Patron.

Diccionario Abreviado Italiano,-Espanol Espanol-Italiano. French & Eur.

Diccionario Abreviado Italiano-Espanol Espanol-Italiano. Ed. by Givanna Schepisi. Biblograf SP.

Diccionario Brevis duplex: Italiano-castellano y castellano-italiano. Sopena.

Diccionario Cuyas: Spanish-Italian, Italian-Spanish. Colton Bk.

Diccionario de la Decoracion. Equipo Reactor De Ceac. French & Eur.

Diccionario del Arte Moderno: Conceptos, Ideas, Tendencias. Ed. by Vincente Aguilera Cerni. Toreres.

Diccionario Enciclopedia Universal. French & Eur.

Diccionario espanol, ingles, frances, italiano, aleman y holandes. Rev. Mex. de Seguros.

Diccionario Everest Vertice Italian-Espanol, Spagnola-Italiano. Imported Bks.

Diccionario Italiano-Espanol, Espanol-Italiano. E. M. Martinez Amador. French & Eur.

Diccionario Italiano-Espanol Espanol-Italiano Vox. Biblo SP.

Diccionario Iter Italiano-Espanol, Espanol-Italiano. French & Eur.

Diccionario Lexicon Italiano-Espanol, Espanol-Italiano. French & Eur.

Diccionario manual italiano-espanol. Francisco de B. Moll. Moll Edit.

Diccionario Manual Italiano-Espanol, Spagnuolo-Italiano. Jose Ortiz De Burgos. French & Eur.

Diccionario Parvus duplex: Italiano-castellano y castellano-ingles. Sopena.

Diccionario poliglota de la arquitectura. B. Bassegoda Muste. Imported Bks.

Diccionario Simultaneo en 21 Idiomas. Juan Capdevilla Font. French & Eur.

Diccionario Simultaneo en 6 Idiomas. Juan Capdevila Font. French & Eur.

Diccionario Tecnico & Industrial Italiano-Espanol. L Carcamo.

Diccionario tecnico de terminos ferroviarios: Espanol-frances-aleman-ingles-italiano-holandes. J. H. Bussy & G Gili.

Diccionario tecnico ilustrado de herramientas de corte para el trabajo de metales: Espanol-aleman-ingles-frances-italiano. T. Heiler. G Gili.

Diccionario Universal Herder Italiano-Espanol, Espanol-Italiano. French & Eur.

Diccionario universal: Italiano-espanol, espanol-italiano. Herder SA.

Dictionar Frazeologic Italian-Roman. Mariana Stanciulescu-Cuza. Editura Stiintifica.

Dictionar Roman-Italian: Pentru uzul Elevilor. Doina Condrea-Derer. Editura Stiintifica.

Dictionar Tehnic Auto de Buzunar in Sapte Limbi. Petre Cristea. Editura Stiintifica.

Dictionary Italiano Portugues. Joao Amendola. Ed. by Macim Behar & Mario Moretti. Hemus-Livraria.

Dictionary of Hydraulic Machinery. A. T. Troskolanski. Elsevier.

Dictionary of Library Science Information & Documentation. Ed. by W. Clason. Elsevier.

Dictionary of Musical Terms: Containing an English-Italian Vocabulary for Composers & Students. Th. Baker. Saphrograph.

Dictionary of Musical Terms in Seven Languages. Ed. by H. Leuchtmann. Heinmann.

Dictionary of Oto-Rhino-Laryngology in Five Languages. A. Larrauri. Intl Pubns Serv.

Dictionary of Surface-Active Agents, Cosmetics & Toiletries. Ed. by G. Cariere. Elsevier.

Dictionary of Surface Active Agents, Cosmetics & Toiletries. G. Carriere. Elsevier.

Dictionary of Water & Sewage Engineering. F. Meinck & K. Mohle. Elsevier.

Dictionnaire Bilingue Apollo Francais-Italien. Giuseppe Padovani & Richard Silvestri. Larousse.

Dictionnaire Commercial: Italien-Francais Francais-Italien. Mario Mormile. Maison Dictionnaire.

Dictionnaire de la Peinture Italie. Hazan.

Dictionnaire de la presse ecrite et audiovisuelle. Divers. Maison Dictionnaire.

Dictionnaire de la Technologie des Corps Gras. Boris Solomon. Inst Corps Gras.

Dictionnaire de Poche Francais-Italien. Berlitz.

Dictionnaire de Sylviculture: Francais-Allemand-Anglais-Espagnol-Italien. Alberto Bruttini. Lechevalier.

Dictionnaire des Sciences de la Nature (Dictionary of the Natural Sciences) Edouard Ghaleb. Intl Pubns Serv.

Dictionnaire d'informatique. Georges Nania. Maison Dictionnaire.

Dictionnaire d'informatique: Francais-Anglais-Italien-Espagnol-Portugais. G. Nania. Maison Dictionnaire.

Dictionnaire d'oto-rhino-laryngologie: Francais-Anglais-Espagnol-Allemand-Italien. Maloine.

Dictionnaire Europa Francais-Italien. Larousse.

Dictionnaire Garzanti Francais-Italien. Bordas-Dunod.

Dictionnaire Garzanti Francais-Italien, Italien-Francais. French & Eur.

Dictionnaire Gemeaux: Francais-Italien. Hatier.

Dictionnaire Illustre de l'Automobile "Kluwer," en 6 Langues. C. Blok & W. Jezewski. French & Eur.

Dictionnaire International d'abreviations Scientifiques et Techniques. M. Azzaretti. Maison Dictionnaire.

Dictionnaire International du Tourisme: Allemand-Anglais-Espagnol-Italien-Neerlandai. Acad Intl Tour.

Dictionnaire International Electrotechnique: Francais-Russe-Anglais-Allemand-Italien-Suedois-Hollandais-Polonais. Mir.

Dictionnaire Italien-Francais. Larousse FR.

Dictionnaire Italien-Francais. Denis Rouede. Garnier.

Dictionnaire Italien-Francais. Jacqueline Herselin. Garnier.

Dictionnaire Italien-Francais et Francais-Italien. Pierre Rouede & Denise Rouede. French & Eur.

Dictionnaire Italien-Francais, Francais-Italien de la Langue d'Aujourd'hui. Ghiotti et al. French & Eur.

Dictionnaire Juridique. M. Matteucci. French & Eur.

Dictionnaire Juridique: Francais-Italien. Navarre.

Dictionnaire Juridique: Italien-Francais Francais-Italien. Giovanni Tortora. Maison Dictionnaire.

Dictionnaire Larousse Bilingue de Poche: Francais-Italien. Larousse FR.

Dictionnaire Larousse: Francais-Italien. L. G. F.

Dictionnaire Lilliput Bilingue Francais-Italien. Larousse FR.

Dictionnaire Technique de la Mecanisation Agricole. French & Eur.

Dictionnaire Technique de la Mecanisation Agricole: Francais-Anglais-Allemand-Espagnol-Italien. Centre Nat. Et. Machin Agricole.

Dictionnaire Technique Illustre des Outis Coupants: L'usinage des Metaux; Francais-Allemand-Anglais-Italien-Espagnol. Toni Heiler. Eyrolles.

Dictionnaire Technique Illustre Des Outils Coupants Pour L'usinage Des Metaux. Toni Heiler. French & Eur.

Dizionario italiano-spagnolo. Malipiero.

Dizionari dei Formaggi: Tutte le Notizie le Ricette come & con che Cosa Servirli. Fernanda Gosetti. Marietti.

Dizionarietto degli uomini illustri della riviera di Sabo. G. Brunati. Forni.

Dizionarietto del costume della moda e dell'acconciatura. Coratelli Vincenzo. San Marco.

Dizionarietto della lingua italiana lussuosa. Barosso Giampaolo. Rizzoli Edit.

Dizionarietto della malavita napoletana. Colonnese.

Dizionarietto di informatica. Graziano Frizzi. Bucalo.

Dizionarietto di tecnica bancaria, mercantile con appendice trilingue. Monetti Ugo. RIREA.

Dizionarietto fraseologico commerciale italiano-francese. Cenni Clara & Sandri Clotilde. Trevisini.

Dizionarietto fraseologico commerciale italiano-inglese. Cenni Clara. Trevisini.

Dizionarietto marinaro. Bianco.

Dizionario abruzzese e molisano: A-E. Ernesto Giammarco. Ateneo & Bizzarri.

Dizionario abruzzese e molisano: F-M. Ernesto Giammarco. Ateneo & Bizzarri.

Dizionario abruzzese e molisano: N-R. Ernesto Giammarco. Ateneo & Bizzarri.

Dizionario Amministrativo. Giuseppe Guarino. Giuffre.

Dizionario amministrativo. Giuseppe Guarino. Giuffre.

Dizionario araldico. Guelfi C. Piero. Forni.

Dizionario assicurativo: Tedesco-francese-inglese-italiano. Centro St Assic.

Dizionario astrologico. Federico Capone. Capone C.

Dizionario Avicolo Internazionale. A. Brunoli. Ed Calderini.

Dizionario avicolo internazionale. Alberto Brunoli. Edagricole.

Dizionario aziendale. Umberto Arisi Rota. Buffetti.

Dizionario biblico. John L. McKenzie & B. Maggioni. Cittadella.

Dizionario borana-italiano. B. Venturino. EMI.

Dizionario botanico. Alfio Musmarra. Edagricole.

Dizionario botanico italiano. Ottaviano T. Tozzetti. Forni.

Dizionario ceco-italiano. Jaroslav Rosendorfsky. Ist Univers Orient.

Dizionario chitarristico italiano. C. Cafagna & M. Gangi. Berben.

Dizionario Commerciale Francese-Italiano. V. Emolumento. French & Eur.

Dizionario commerciale francese-italiano. Vincenzo Emolumento. Editrice Bibliografica.

Dizionario commerciale fraseologico italiano-inglese, inglese-italiano. Ada Duse. Bignami.

Dizionario Commerciale Inglese-Italiano, Italiano-Inglese: Economia, Legge, Finanza, Banca, Etc. Giuseppe Motta. S F Vanni.

Dizionario commerciale italiano-francese. Vincenzo Emolumento. Bibliografica.

Dizionario commerciale italiano-francese e francese-italiano. Mario Mormile. Bulzoni.

Dizionario Commerciale Italiano-Francese, Francese-Italiano. Mario Mormile. Maison Dictionnaire.

Dizionario completo italiano-portoghese (brasiliano) e portoghese (brasiliano)-italiano. Vincenzo Spinelli & Mario Casasanta. Hoepli.

Dizionario completo italiano-portoghese (brasiliano) e portoghese (brasiliano)-italiano. Vincenzo Spinelli & Mario Casasanta. Hoepli.

Dizionario Completo Italiano-Portoghese (Brasiliano), Portoghese (Brasiliano)-Italiano: Con L'etimologia Delle Voci Italiane e Portoghesi (Brasiliane), la Loro Esatta Traduzione, Frasi e Modi Di Dire. S F Vanni.
Dizionario critico di psicoanalisi. Charles Rycroft. Astrolabio.
Dizionario danese-italiano e italiano-danese. Malipiero.
DIzionario degli alimenti per il bestiame. Marcello Piccioni. Edagricole.
Dizionario degli animali. Dami.
Dizionario degli architetti. Bernard Oudin. ISEDI.
Dizionario degli errori. Mauro Magni. Edit Vecchi.
Dizionario dei comuni. E. Nicchi. La Tribuna.
Dizionario dei comuni con le circoscrizioni guidiziarie. Giuffre.
Dizionario dei comuni e delle circoscrizioni amminstrative, delle frazioni e delle localita. La Tribuna.
Dizionario dei dubbi linguistici. Dino Provenzal. Hoepli.
Dizionario dei formaggi. Fernanda Gosetti. Marietti.
Dizionario dei formaggi. Fernanda Gosetti. AMZ.
Dizionario dei Frizzetti Popolari Firoentini. Giuseppe Frizzi. Multigrafica.
Dizionario dei giochi e degli sport. Zanichelli.
Dizionario dei motti e leggende delle monete italiane. G. Donati. La Vela.
Dizionario dei musicisti. Roland De Cande. Bompiani.
Dizionario dei patrioti lucani artefici ed oppositori (1700-1870) Vol. 1, A-C. Tommaso Pedio. Soc Bari.
Dizionario dei patrioti lucani artefici ed oppositori (1700-1870) Vol. 2, D-I. Tommaso Pedio. Soc Bari.
Dizionario dei piloti. Mondadori.
Dizionario dei semiconduttori. Alfred Wiegelmann. Tr. by L. Cascianni & M. Boscarol. Muzzio.
Dizionario dei sinonimi della lingua italiana. Niccolo Tommaseo. Nuova Vallecchi.
Dizionario dei sinonimi della lingua italiana. Niccolo Tommaseo & G. Rigutini. Vallardi F.
Dizionario dei sinonimi e dei contrari. Decio Cinti. Ist Geo Agostini.
Dizionario dei sinonimi e dei contrari. Aldo Gabrielli. Ist Edit Ital.
Dizionario dei sintomi. Joan Gomez. Tr. by E. V. Ferrario. Garzanti Edit.
Dizionario dei sogni e cabala del lotto. Malipiero.
Dizionario dei temi della fede. SEI.
Dizionario dei termini cinematografici. Glenn Alvey, Jr. Edizioni Mediterranee.
Dizionario dei termini giuridici. Angelo Favata. La Tribuna.
Dizionario dei termini storiografici. G. Arnaldi. Zanichelli.
Dizionario dei termini tecnici di medicina. M. Garnier et al. DEMI.
Dizionario dei verbi italiani regolari ed irregolari. Aldo Gabrielli. Ist Edit Ital.
Dizionario del cacciatore italiano. Luigi Ugolini. Bietti.
Dizionario del Concilio Ecumenico Vaticano Secondo. Scode.
Dizionario del dialetto calabrese. Luigi Accattatis. Brenner.
Dizionario del dialetto cremonese. Comitato Del Folklore Cremonese. Libreria Convegno.
Dizionario del dialetto di Cortina d'Ampezzo. Vincenzo M. Tamburin. Pozza.
Dizionario del dialetto valdese della Val Germanasca. Teofilo Pons. Soc Studi Valdesi.
Dizionario del dialetto valsesiano. F. Tonetti. Forni.
Dizionario del dialetto veneziano. Giuseppe Boerio. Giunti-Martello.
Dizionario del disegno. Gaspare De Fiore. La Scuola.
Dizionario del feltrino rustico. Bruno Migliorini & G. Pellegrini. Liviana.
Dizionario del francese fondamentale. Raoul Boch. Zanichelli.
Dizionario del gergo milanese e lombardo. Nino Bazzetta de Vemenia. Forni.
Dizionario del linguaggio italiano storico e amministrativo. G. Rezasco. Forni.
Dizionario del pescatore italiano di acqua dolce. Ugo Veronese. Bietti.
Dizionario del vernacolo fiorentino. Pirro Giacchi. Multigrafica.
Dizionario della critica d'arte. Luigi Grassi & Mario Pepe. UTET.
Dizionario della geografica: Geografica umana. G. Cotti-Cometti & P. George. CESVIET.
Dizionario della lingua e della civita italiana contemporanea. Emido De Felice & Aldo Duro. Palumbo.
Dizionario della lingua italiana. Garzanti Edit.
Dizionario della lingua italiana. Garzanti Edit.
Dizionario della lingua italiana. Garzanti Edit.
Dizionario della lingua italiana. Garzanti Edit.
Dizionario della lingua italiana. Bietti.
Dizionario della lingua italiana. Giuseppe Cantamessa & Giuseppe Messina. Signorelli C.
Dizionario della lingua italiana. Giacomo Devoto & Giancarlo Oli. Monnier.
Dizionario della lingua italiana. Mario Nuzzo. Marotta.
Dizionario della lingua italiana. Carlo P. Tosi. Principato.
Dizionario della lingua italiana. Niccolo Tommaseo & Bernardo Bellini. Rizzoli Edit.
Dizionario della lingua italiana. Garzanti Edit.
Dizionario della Lingua Italiano. Ed. by G. Devoto & G. C. Oli. French & Eur.
Dizionario della lingua italiano. L. Bellini. Rizzoli Edit.
Dizionario della lingua latina: Latino-italiano e italiano-latino. Ed. by Calonghi et al. Rosenberg & Sellier.
Dizionario della musica. Roland De Cande. Bompiani.
Dizionario della Natura. A Mondadi.
Dizionario della paura. Marcello Venturoli & Ruggero Zangrandi. Nistri-Lischi.
Dizionario della pubblica istruzione: Legislazione e pratica amministrativa sulla istruzione primaria. Trentino Vetrini. Giuffre.
Dizionario della publica istruzione. L. Zanobini & T. Vetrini. Giuffre.
Dizionario della publica istruzione. L. Zanobini & T. Vetrini. Giuffre.
Dizionario della scuola democratica. Giorgio Pecorini. Emme.
Dizionario della sicurezza sociale. Gino Rampini. Giuffre.
Dizionario della strumentazione nucleare. CEI. AEEI.
Dizionario della tecnica. Zanichelli.
Dizionario della vela. Michel Barberousse. Mursia S.
Dizionario dell'antichita classica. Tr. by M. R. Rogger. Zanichelli.
Dizionario dell'arte. Mondadori.
Dizionario delle arti figurative. B. Garzena. Zanichelli.
Dizionario delle Autonomie Locali. Enzo Modica. Editori Riuniti.
Dizionario delle autonomie locali. Enzo Modica & Rubes Triva. Editori Riuniti.
Dizionario delle buone maniere. Fluffy M. Mazzucato. Bietti.
Dizionario delle contravvenzioni. Igino Alessandrino. Patron.
Dizionario delle forniture grafiche, editoriale e cartotecniche. L'Ufficio Moderno.
Dizionario delle idee. Centro Studi Filosofici di Gallarate. Sansoni.
Dizionario delle idee comuni. Virgilio Titone. Pan Italy.
Dizionario delle idee correnti. Maurizio Costanzo. Bompiani.
Dizionario delle immagini. Dino Provenzal. Hoepli.
Dizionario delle lingue italiana e inglese. Lysle & Gualtieri. Casanova F & C.
Dizionario delle malattie, sindromi e sintori oculari. Vincenzo Marsico. Minerva Medica.
Dizionario delle nuove scienze: Astronautica, electronica, fiscia nucleare. E. Mazzaglia & A. Castellini. Edizioni Paoline.
Dizionario delle parlate corse. G. Bottiglioni. Stem Mucchi.
Dizionario delle parole nuovissime e dificili. Gennaro Vaccaro. Romana Libri ALfabeto.
Dizionario delle scienze fisiche e matematiche. Zanichelli.
Dizionario delle sindromi mediche. Sergio Magalini. DEMI.
Dizionario delle tecniche e delle scienze. Edizioni Paoline.
Dizionario delle tecniche pittoriche. Castel Caltan.
Dizionario delle voci. Dino Provenzal. Hoepli.
Dizionario dell'enigmista. Luigi Boni. Mazziana.
Dizionario dell'epilessia. H. Gastaut. Tr. by E. De Fiore & R. Vizioli. Il Pensiero.
Dizionario dell'infermiera. A. Bottero. EIPS.
Dizionario dell'intellettuale di sinistra. Elias Condal. Savelli.
Dizionario dello sport. E. Enrile. Edizioni Paoline.
Dizionario dello yachting in otto lingue. Barbara Webb. Mursia S.
Dizionario demografico multilingue. Giuffre.
Dizionario di Abbreviature Latine & Italiane. Capelli. Hoepli.
Dizionario di abbreviature latine ed italiane. A. Capelli. Hoepli.
Dizionario di Agricoltura. F. Favati. Ed Calderini.
Dizionario di agricoltura. A. Carena. UTET.
Dizionario di agricoltura: English-italian e italiano-inglese. Franco Favati. Edagricole.
Dizionario di alchimia e di chimica antiquaria. Gino Testi. Edizioni Mediterranee.
Dizionario di anatomia e fisiologia umana. N. Piscitelli. Ist Geo Agostini.
Dizionario di antichita classiche. Caffarello Nelida. Olschki.
Dizionario di archeologia. Warwick Bray & David Trump. Mondadori.
Dizionario di architettura. Giacomo Ravazzini. Cisalpino.
Dizionario di balletto. Luigi Rossi. Edizioni Della Danza.
Dizionario di banca e di borsa: Vol. 1, A-D. Istituto per l'Enciclopedia della Banca e della Borsa. Giuffre.
Dizionario di biologia. Zanichelli.
Dizionario di botanica: A-L. U. Tosco. Ist Geo Agostini.
Dizionario di Botanica: M-Z. U. Tosco. Ist Geo Agostini.
Dizionario di cultura universale. Vallardi F.
Dizionario di economia. Graham Bannock et al. Laterza.
Dizionario di economia. G. Mayer. Bulzoni.
Dizionario di economia. Giuseppe U. Papi. UTET.
Dizionario di elettronica. Saul Handel. Tr. by E. Suriani. Zanichelli.
Dizionario di elettronica. Saul Handel. Tr. by E. Suriani. Zanichelli.
Dizionario di Elettronica Italiano-Inglese, Inglese-Italiano. S. Handel. French & Eur.
Dizionario di elettronica: Tedesco-italiano. G. Fiandaca. Il Rostro.
Dizionario di estetica & di linguistica generale. Giovanni Giraldi. Pergamena.
Dizionario di etnologia. Panoff & Perrin. Newton-Compton.
Dizionario di farmacologia clinica. V. Fatturosso & O. Ritter. Tr. by M. A. Branca Ciocetti. Edipem.
Dizionario di genetica. Robert C. King. ISEDI.
Dizionario di geografia. F. J. Monkhouse. Tr. by M. Manzoni. Zanichelli.
Dizionario di geografia. Moore. Newton-Compton.
Dizionario di geologia. Marcello Manzoni. Zanichelli.
Dizionario di geologia. D. G. Whitten & J. R. Brooks. Mondadori.
Dizionario di giornalismo. Mario Lenzi. Mursia.
Dizionario di informatica. Anthony Chandor. Tr. by G. Rapelli. Zanichelli.
Dizionario di informatica e degli elaboratori elettronici. Marcello Morelli. Angeli.
Dizionario di informazione sessuale. P. Bertrand et al. Gribaudi.
Dizionario di ipnopsicologia. Marco Marchesan. Ist. Indagini Psicologiche.
Dizionario di linguistica. L. Rosiello & I. Loi. Zanichelli.
Dizionario di matematica moderna. L. L. Chambadal. Mursia.
Dizionario di medicina. M. C. Aite. Zanichelli.
Dizionario di medicina: Enciclopedia degli alimenti. Ulrico Di Aichelburg. UTET.
Dizionario di medicina per le famiglie. Ulrico Di Aichelburg. UTET.
Dizionario di merceologia e chimica applicata. G. V. Villavecchia et al. Hoepli.
Dizionario di metallurgia. W. E. Clason. Etas Libri.
Dizionario di metrologia generale. Alfredo Ferraro. Zanichelli.
Dizionario Di Mitologia Egizia. R. V. Lanzone. Benjamins North Am.
Dizionario di musica. G. Vacchi. Zanichelli.
Dizionario di musica. Guido Gatti. UTET.
Dizionario di pedagogia, psicologia, storia dell'educazione. Paolo E. Lamanna & Maria Goretti. Monnier.
Dizionario di Politica. Ed. by Norberto Bobbio & Nicola Matteuci. UTET.
Dizionario di politica. Norberto Bobbio & Nicola Matteuci. UTET.
Dizionario di politica economica. Luciano Barca. Editori Riuniti.
Dizionario di psichiatria. Newton-Compton.
Dizionario di psichiatria clinica & terapeutica. Edizioni Paoline.
Dizionario di psicoanalisi tratto dalle opere di Sigmund Freud. N. Fodor & F. Gaynor. Feltrinelli.
Dizionario di psicologia. Edizioni Paoline.
Dizionario di psicologia. Amedeo Dalla Volta. Giunti-Barbera.
Dizionario di psicologia. Henri Pieron. Tr. by R. Canestrari. La Nuova Italia.
Dizionario di psicologia analitica. C. Gustav Jung. Tr. by C. L. Musatti & L. Aurigemma. Boringhieri.
Dizionario di psicologia del lavoro. Enzo Spaltro. Ghisoni.
Dizionario di psicologia forense. Giancarlo Spirolazzi. Giuffre.
Dizionario di psicologia sessuale. Georges Bastin. La Scuola.
Dizionario di Retorica & di Stilistica. Angelo Marchese. Mondadori.
Dizionario di scienze filosofiche. Cesare Ranzoli & M. Pigatti Ranzoli. Hoepli.
Dizionario di scienze occulte. Armando Pappalardo. Cisalpino.
Dizionario di sessuologia. R. Volcher. Cittadella.
Dizionario di sessuologia o dell'armonia coniugale. Edoardo Borra. Edizioni Paoline.
Dizionario di sessuologia o dell'armonia coniugale. Edoardo Borra. Edizioni Paoline.
Dizionario di sociologia. Luciano Galliano. UTET.
Dizionario di sociologia. G. Duncan Mitchell. Newton-Compton.
Dizionario di statistica. Eugene Morice. Tr. by M. G. Cossarini. ISEDI.
Dizionario di termini artistici. Michelangelo Masciotta. Monnier.
Dizionario di termini della geografia umana. Fulvio Fulvi. Patron.
Dizionario di termini filosofici. Paolo E. Lamanna & Francesco Adorno. Monnier.
Dizionario di termini medici di uso comune. Mario Governa. ERI.
Dizionario di termini storici, politici ed economici moderni. Roberto Berardi. Monnier.

Dizionario di Terminini Della Geografia Umana. Fulvio Fulvi. Patron.

Dizionario di terminologia di storia dell'arte. Rossana Bossaglia. Bignami.

Dizionario di terminologia medica. G. Giuseppe Palmieri. Vallardi F.

Dizionario di Terminologia Ortopedica & Traumatologia. Alberto Fusari. Gaggi.

Dizionario di terminologia ortopedica e traumatologica. Gaggi.

Dizionario di zoologia. A. W. Leftwich. Newton-Compton.

Dizionario di zoologia: A-L. U. Parenti. Ist Geo Agostini.

Dizionario di zoologia: M-Z. U. Parenti. Ist Geo Agostino.

Dizionario Dialettale Vogherese. Alessandro Maragliano. Patron.

Dizionario d'ingegneria. Eligio Perucca. UTET.

Dizionario d'ingegneria. Eligio Perucca. UTET.

Dizionario d'ingegneria. Eligio Perucca. UTET.

Dizionario d'ingegneria. Eligio Perucca. UTET.

Dizionario d'ingegneria. Eligio Perucca. UTET.

Dizionario d'ingegneria. Eligio Perucca. UTET.

Dizionario d'ingegneria. Eligio Perucca. UTET.

Dizionario d'ingegneria. Eligio Perucca. UTET.

Dizionario d'ingeneria. Eligio Perucca. UTET.

Dizionario elementare. Giuseppe Pittano. Edipem.

Dizionario elementare: Per la Scuola elementare. Giuseppe Pittano. Edipem.

Dizionario elementare: Per la Scuola elementare. Giuseppe Pittano. Edipem.

Dizionario Enciclopedico Scientifico e Tecnico: Inglese-Italiano, Italiano-Inglese. D. Lapedes. French & Eur.

Dizionario epigrafico di antichita romane. Ettore De Ruggiero. L'Erma.

Dizionario eponimico ostetrico-ginecologico. Giovanni Brigato & Giorgio Pisano. Piccin.

Dizionario etimologico della lingua italiana: Vol. 1, A-C. Manlio Cortelazzo & Paolo Zolli. Zanichelli.

Dizionario etimologico italiano. Angelico Prati. Multigrafica.

Dizionario etimologico veneto-italiano. Dino Durante & Gianfranco Turato. Erredici.

Dizionario Etnologico Africano. Tina Novelli. Jaca Bk.

Dizionario francese-italiano e italiano-francese. Garzanti Edit.

Dizionario francese-italiano e italiano-francese. Garzanti Edit.

Dizionario francese-italiano e italiano-francese. Malipiero.

Dizionario francese-italiano e italiano-francese. Filippi & La Tour. Giunti-Martello.

Dizionario Francese Italiano, Italiano Francese. Raol Boch. Zanichelli.

Dizionario francese-italiano italiano-francese. La Mondadori.

Dizionario francese-italiano italiano-francese. Raoul Boch. Zanichelli.

Dizionario fraseologico commerciale italiano-francese e francese-italiano. Ada Duse. Bignami.

Dizionario fraseologico completo italiano-spagnolo e spagnolo-italiano: Parte italiana-spagnola. Sebastiano Carbonell. Hoepli.

Dizionario fraseologico completo italiano-spagnolo e spagnolo-italiano: Parte spagnola-italiana. Sebastiano Carbonell. Hoepli.

Dizionario fraseologico di Inglese Tecnico. Canzio Vandelli. Mondini Siccardi.

Dizionario fraseologico di russo-italiano e viceversa. Canzio Vandelli. Mondini Siccardi.

Dizionario fraseologico e grammaticale della lingua inglese. Francesco Pipitone. Galeati.

Dizionario fraseologico e grammaticale italiano-francese. Massimo Gatto. Sandron.

Dizionario fraseologico e grammaticale italiano-inglese. Massimo Gatto. Sandron.

Dizionario Garzanti della Lingua Italiana. G. Cusatelli. French & Eur.

Dizionario Garzanti della Lingua Italiana. G Cusatelli. French & Eur.

Dizionario Garzanti della Lingua Italiana. Ed. by G. Cusatelli. French & Eur.

Dizionario Garzanti Della Lingua Italiana. Speedimpex.

Dizionario Garzanti Della Lingua Italiana. Speedimpex.

Dizionario Garzanti: Francese-Italiano, Italiano-Francese. G. Cusatelli & G. Brunacci. Ed. by U. Salati & F. Dominicis et al. French & Eur.

Dizionario Garzanti Italiano-Inglese & Inglese-Italiano. Speedimpex.

Dizionario Garzanti Italiano-Inglese & Inglese-Italiano. Hazon. Speedimpex.

Dizionario Garzanti Italiano-Inglese & Inglese-Italiano. Hazon. Speedimpex.

Dizionario Garzanti: Italiano-Inglese, Inglese-Italiano. M. Hazon. French & Eur.

Dizionario Garzanti Italiano-Francese, Francese-Italiano. French & Eur.

Dizionario gastronomico. Elisabetta Neiger. Buffetti.

Dizionario genovese-italiano. G. Casaccia. Brenner.

Dizionario geografico. Giovanni Boccaccio. Fogola.

Dizionario giuridico del lavoro e delle assicurazioni sociali. Antonio Palermo & Carlo Palermo. La Tribuna.

Dizionario giuridico-economico: Vol. 1, Italiano-tedesco. Giuseppe Conte. Giuffre.

Dizionario giuridico-economico: Vol. 2, Tedesco-italiano. Giuseppe Conte. Giuffre.

Dizionario grammaticale. Vincenzo Ceppellini. Ist Geo Agostini.

Dizionario greco-italiano. Benedetto Bonazzi. Morano.

Dizionario greco moderno-italiano e italiano-greco moderno: Vol. 1, Greco moderno-italiano. Eliseo Brighenti. Cisalpino.

Dizionario greco moderno-italiano e italiano-greco moderno: Vol. 2, Italiano-greco moderno. Cisalpino.

Dizionario greco moderno-italiano, italiano-greco moderno. Malipiero.

Dizionario Hazon Garzanti: Inglese-Italiano, Italiano-Inglese. Ed. by M. Hazon. French & Eur.

Dizionario illustrato degli incisori italiani. L. L. Servolini. Goerlich.

Dizionario illustrato della lingua italiana. Sansoni.

Dizionario illustrato della lingua italiana. Ist Geo Agostini.

Dizionario illustrato della lingua italiana. Curcio.

Dizionario illustrato e commentato delle norme di circolazione previste dal nuovo codice della strada. Mario Calamante. Ateneo & Bizzarri.

Dizionario illustrato greco-italiano. H. G. Liddell et al. Monnier.

Dizionario illustrato italiano-tedesco. Longanesi.

Dizionario illustrato latino-italiano. F. Gaffiot. Piccin.

Dizionario illustrato tedesco-italiano. Longanesi.

Dizionario inglese-italiano. Giuseppe Ragazzini & Adele Biagi. Zanichelli.

Dizionario inglese-italiano dei termini relativi all'elettrotecnica. Henry Piraux. Signorelli C.

Dizionario Inglese-Italiano dei Termini Relativi All'Elettronica: All'Elettrotecnica e Alle Applicazioni Connesse. H. Piraux. French & Eur.

Dizionario inglese-italiano e italiano-inglese con glossario bilingue di economia e organizzazione aziendale. Gualtiero Rossi. Zanichelli.

Dizionario inglese-italiano e italiano-inglese con glossario bilingue di tecnica navale. Giuseppe Ragazzini. Zanichelli.

Dizionario inglese-italiano e italiano-inglese: Edizione scholastica. Mario Hazon. Garzanti Edit.

Dizionario inglese-italiano e italiano-inglese. Malipiero.

Dizionario inglese-italiano e italiano-inglese. Sansoni.

Dizionario inglese-italiano e italiano-inglese. Giuseppe Ragazzini. Zanichelli.

Dizionario inglese-italiano-francese-tedesco. L. Gives et al. De Bono.

Dizionario inglese-italiano, italiano-inglese: Adattamento e ristrutturazione dell'originale. SEI.

Dizionario inglese-italiano per le scienze mediche. R. Marconi & E. Zino. Minerva Medica.

Dizionario inverso italiano. M. Alinei. Il Mulino.

Dizionario Italian-Slovar. A. Bajec & P. Kalan. French & Eur.

Dizionario Italiano-Albanese. F. Cordignano. Forni.

Dizionario italiano-arabo moderno. Elpidio Jannota. Ist Poligrafico.

Dizionario Italiano-Bulgaro. M. Cavaletto et al. French & Eur.

Dizionario italiano-ceco. Jaroslav Rosendorfsky. Ist Univers Orient.

Dizionario italiano-danese. Malipiero.

Dizionario italiano di vocaboli e modi usati in poesia: Per le Scuole superiori. Vittorio Busa. Mori.

Dizionario Italiano-Finlandes, Finlandes-Italiano. Ed. by G. Colussi. French & Eur.

Dizionario italiano-finlandese. Colussi. Vallardi A.

Dizionario italiano-francese. Malipiero.

Dizionario italiano-francese. Mondadori.

Dizionario italiano-francese. Claire Laurent. Vallardi A.

Dizionario italiano-francese e francese-italiano. Garzanti Edit.

Dizionario italiano-francese e francese-italiano. Garzanti Edit.

Dizionario italiano-francese e francese-italiano. R. Simone. La Nuova Italia.

Dizionario italiano-francese e francese-italiano. Amato Bertet et al. Paravia.

Dizionario Italiano-Francese e Francese-Italiano di termini in uso in economia, borsa, finanza. Vera Pegna. Etas Libri.

Dizionario Italiano-Francese, Francese-Italiano. G. Laurent. French & Eur.

Dizionario italiano-francese francese-italiano della lingua d'oggi. Candido Ghiotto et al. Petrini.

Dizionario italiano-francese-italiano. G. Sbrulli & T. Biffoli. Valmartina.

Dizionario italiano-greco moderno. Malipiero.

Dizionario italiano illustrato. SEI.

Dizionario italiano illustrato. Ist Geog Agostini.

Dizionario italiano illustrato per l'uso essenziale della lingua. G. Colli. SEI.

Dizionario italiano-inglese. Mondadori.

Dizionario italiano-inglese. Malipiero.

Dizionario italiano-inglese. Boy Musu. Vallardi A.

Dizionario italiano-inglese e inglese-italiano. Giuseppe Motta. Signorelli C.

Dizionario italiano-inglese e inglese-italiano. Garzanti Edit.

Dizionario italiano-inglese e inglese-italiano. Garzanti Edit.

Dizionario italiano-inglese e inglese-italiano. F. M. Gualtieri. Casanova F & C.

Dizionario italiano-inglese e inglese-italiano: Edizione minore. Giuseppe Orlandi. Signorelli C.

Dizionario italiano-inglese e inglese-italiano tecnico. Renzo Denti. Hoepli.

Dizionario italiano-inglese-francese-tedesco. L. Gives et al. De Bono.

Dizionario Italiano-Inglese, Inglese-Italiano. R. Musu-Boy. French & Eur.

Dizionario italiano-inglese inglese-italiano. Mondadori.

Dizionario Italiano-Latino. Angelo Perugini. Libr Ed Vat.

Dizionario italiano-latino. Malipiero.

Dizionario italiano-latino. Oreste Badellino. Rosenberg & Sel.

Dizionario italiano-latino. Angelo Perugini. Libr Ed Vat.

Dizionario italiano-latino. Sacerdoti. Vallardi A.

Dizionario italiano-latino: Edizione speciale. Oreste Badellino. Rosenberg & Sel.

Dizionario Italiano-Latino, Latino-Italiano. N. Sacerdoti. French & Eur.

Dizionario italiano moderno. A. Rossi. Malipiero.

Dizionario italiano-olandese. Malipiero.

Dizionario italiano-olandese. Van Cappen. Vallardi A.

Dizionario Italiano-Olandese, Olandese-Italiano. V. Van Kampen. French & Eur.

Dizionario italiano-portoghese. Biava. Vallardi A.

Dizionario Italiano-Portoghese, Portoghese-Italiano. A. Biava. French & Eur.

Dizionario italiano-russo. Fadanelli. Vallardi A.

Dizionario italiano-russo. Skvorzova & Maizel. Editori Riuniti.

Dizionario Italiano-Russo, Russo-Italiane. R. Fadanelli. French & Eur.

Dizionario Italiano-Serbo Croato. Livadic. Vallardi A.

Dizionario Italiano-Serbocroato, Serbocroato-Italiano. Ed. by P. Livadic. French & Eur.

Dizionario italiano-serbocroato sloveno. Malipiero.

Dizionario italiano-spagnolo. Garcia. Vallardi A.

Dizionario Italiano-Spagnolo, Spagnolo-Italiano. A. Garcia. French & Eur.

Dizionario italiano-svedese. Malipiero.

Dizionario italiano-svedese. Gaft & Bassoli. Vallardi A.

Dizionario Italiano-Svedese, Svedese-Italiano. G. Gareff & F. Bassoli. French & Eur.

Dizionario italiano-tedesco. Malipiero.

Dizionario italiano-tedesco. Mondadori.

Dizionario italiano-tedesco. Altenberg. Vallardi A.

Dizionario italiano-tedesco. Guido Cosciani. Paravia.

Dizionario italiano-tedesco e tedesco-italiano. Giovannelli. Signorelli C.

Dizionario italiano-tedesco e tedesco-italiano. A. Gullino Kuhn. Casanova F & C.

Dizionario italiano-tedesco e tedesco-italiano. Giovanni Ciardi Dupre & Angelica Escher. SEI.

Dizionario italiano-tedesco e tedesco-italiano. Lysle & Pontevideo. Casanova F & C.

Dizionario Italiano-Tedesco, Tedesco-Italian. G. A. Altenberg & V. Ubaldi. French & Eur.

Dizionario italiano-tedesco tedesco-italiano. Langenscheidt. Signorelli C.

Dizionario Italiano-Turco, Turco-Italiano. M. Celalettin Bugday. French & Eur.

Dizionario italo-indonesiano. L. Lini. EMI.

Dizionario latino-italiano. Ferruccio Calonghi. Rosenberg & Sel.

Dizionario latino-italiano e italiano-latino. Malipiero.

Dizionario latino-italiano e italiano-latino. Giuseppe Pittano. Edn Scol Mond.

Dizionario latino-italiano: Stato della Chiesa-Veneto-Abruzzi. Pietro Sella. Biblioteca Apostolica Vaticana.

Dizionario linguistico moderno. Aldo Gabrielli. Edn Scol Mond.

Dizionario medico. Edizioni Paoline.

Dizionario medico. W. A. Dorland Newman. CEA.

Dizionario medico. Duranteau. Newton Compton.

Dizionario medico. Emanuele Lauricella. USES.

Dizionario medico. L. Segatore & G. A. Poli. Ist Geog Agostini.

Dizionario medico. Bailliere et al. Edi Ermes.

Dizionario Medico Poliglotta. Veillon & Nobel. French & Eur.

Dizionario Medico Ragionato Inglese-Italiano. M. Lucchesi. French & Eur.

Dizionario Medico Ragionato Inglese-Italiano: Termini, Abbreviazioni, Sigle, Eponimi e Sinonimi Medici, Medico-Biologici e Delle Specializzazioni Mediche. Mario Lucchesi. S F Vanni.

Dizionario medico ragionato per le scienze mediche inglese-italiano. U. M. Lucchesi. Cortina M.

Dizionario merceologico per la pratica applicazione della nuova tariffa doganale italiana. L. Settimj. Hoepli.

Dizionario Merli geografico, storico, economico: Vol. 1, Lettera AZ. Marcello G. Compagnol. ERGA.

Dizionario metodico del commercio laniero. Luigi Caccianotti. Edit Laniera.

Dizionario milanese-italiano. Cletto Arrighi. Hoepli.

Dizionario moderno. Alfredo Panzini et al. Hoepli.

Dizionario moderno genovese-italiano e italiano-genovese. Giuseppe Frisoni. Forni.

Dizionario moderno italiano-francese e francese-italiano. Ernesto Cassiani. SEI.

Dizionario moderno italiano-francese e francese-italiano. Bruno A. Paoli. Edn Scol Mond.

Dizionario moderno italiano-spagnolo e spagnolo-italiano: Vol. 1, Italiano-spagnolo. Gaetano Frisoni. Hoepli.

Dizionario moderno italiano-spagnolo e spagnolo-italiano: Vol. 2, Spagnolo-italiano. Gaetano Frisoni. Hoepli.

Dizionario Moderno Slovene-Italian-Slovene. A. Grad. French & Eur.

Dizionario Moderno Spagnuolo-Italiano, Italiano-Spagnuolo. Gaetano Frisoni. S F Vanni.

Dizionario Mondadori di storia universale. Michel Mourre. Mondadori.

Dizionario monferrino. Giuseppe Ferraro. Forni.

Dizionario Motta della lingua italiana. E. Bazzarelli. Motta.

Dizionario olandese-italiano e italiano. Malipiero.

Dizionario per le scuole elementari. Ludwig Wittgenstein. Tr. by D. Antiseri. Armando.

Dizionario per l'industria delle materie plastiche: Definizioni italiane e termini corrispondenti in francese, inglese e tedesco. Enrico Ferraris & Istituto Italiano dei Plastici. SAPIL.

Dizionario persiano-italiano classico, moderno, familiare. Hanne Coletti Gruenbaum. Coletti.

Dizionario polesano-italiano. P. Mazzucchi. Forni.

Dizionario politico e parlamentare. Gino Pallotta. Newton Compton.

Dizionario Politico e Parlamentare Italiano. Gino Pallotta. Newton Compton.

Dizionario portoghese-italiano. Parlagreco. Vallardi A.

Dizionario Portoghese-Italiano, Italiano-Portoghese. C. Parlagreco. French & Eur.

Dizionario pratico e frasario per conversazione italiano-amarica. L. Fusella & A. Girace. Ist Univers Orient.

Dizionario pratico tedesco-italiano italiano-tedesco. Langenscheidt. Signorelli C.

Dizionario primierotto. Livio Tissot. Manfrini.

Dizionario ragionato dei simboli. G. Cairo. Forni.

Dizionario ragionato di psicologia individuale. Francesco Parenti. Cortina M.

Dizionario ragionato di sinonimi e dei contrari. Gianni Cesana. De Vecchi Italy.

Dizionario rapido di scienze pure ed applicate. Rinaldo De Benedetti. UTET.

Dizionario Sandron della lingua italiana. Sandron.

Dizionario serbocroato-italiano e sloveno-italiano. Malipiero.

Dizionario si sessuologia. R. Volker. Cittadella.

Dizionario siciliano-italiano. Giuseppe Biundi & A. Rigoli. Il Vespro.

Dizionario siciliano-italiano. Giovanni Cavallaro. Bonanno.

Dizionario siciliano-italiano. V. Nicotra. Forni.

Dizionario siciliano-italiano. Giuseppe Biundi. Forni.

Dizionario Sinottico di Iconologia. Norma Cecchini & Giuseppe Plessi. Patron.

Dizionario sinottico di iconologia. Norma Cecchini. Patron.

Dizionario sintattico latino: Italiano-latino e latino-italiano. Giovanni La Magna. Signorelli C.

Dizionario sintetico da tavolo. L. Pallini. Vallardi F.

Dizionario spagnolo-italiano e italiano-spagnolo. Malipiero.

Dizionario spagnolo-italiano e italiano-spagnolo. Enrico Migliori. Giunti-Martello.

Dizionario storico araldico dell'antico ducato di Ferrara. Frassoni F. Pasini. Forni.

Dizionario Storico Della Mafia. Gino Pallotta. Newton Compton.

Dizionario svedes-italiano e italiano-svedese. Malipiero.

Dizionario tascabile delle tecniche ambientale: Italiano, francese, inglese, tedesco. Maurizio Pasquali. SAPIL.

Dizionario tascabile illustrato. Ernesto Carletti. Citta Nuova.

Dizionario Tecnico Francese-Italiano. Renzo Denti. Hoepli.

Dizionario tecnico francese-italiano e italiano-francese. Renzo Denti. Hoepli.

Dizionario tecnico inglese-italiano e italiano-inglese. Giorgio Marolli. Monnier.

Dizionario Tecnico Italiano-Inglese. Renzo Denti. Hoepli.

Dizionario Tecnico Italiano-Inglese, Inglese-Italiano. Renzo Denti. S F Vanni.

Dizionario Tecnico Italiano-Inglese, Inglese-Italiano. G. Marolli. French & Eur.

Dizionario Tecnico Italiano-Tedesco. Alice Meyer. Brandstetter.

Dizionario tecnico italiano-tedesco e tedesco-italiano. A. Meyer & S. Orlando. Hoepli.

Dizionario Tecnico Nautico: Italiano-Inglese, Inglese-Italiano. V. Mastropasqua. French & Eur.

Dizionario tecnico-scientifico: Italiano-tedesco. Paolo Carboni. Patron.

Dizionario tecnico-scientifico: Tedesco-italiano. Paolo Carboni. Patron.

Dizionario Tecnico Tedesco-Italiano. Giorgio Marolli & Orazio Guarnieri. Garzanti Edit.

Dizionario tecnico tedesco-italiano italiano-tedesco. Giorgio Marolli & Orazio Guarnieri. Garzanti Edit.

Dizionario Tecnico Tedesco-Italiano, Italiano-Tedesco Garzanti. M. Guarnieri & O. Guarnieri. French & eur.

Dizionario tedesco-italiano. Emilio Bidoli & Guido Cosciani. Paravia.

Dizionario tedesco-italiano. A. Lanzara. Forni.

Dizionario tedesco-italiano di biologia e medicina. Valentino Grandis & Mario Donati. Rosenberg & Sel.

Dizionario tedesco-italiano e italiano-tedesco. Malipiero.

Dizionario tedesco-italiano e italiano-tedesco. Sansoni.

Dizionario tedesco-italiano per le scienze chimiche e affini. Clara Giua Lollini & Michele Giua. Rosenberg & Sel.

Dizionario tedesco-italiano per le scienze mediche. E. Marcovecchio. Minerva Medica.

Dizionario teologico interdisciplinare. Marietti.

Dizionario trentino-italiano. Lionello Groff. Monauni.

Dizionario turco-italiano. Budgay. Vallardi A.

Dizionario umoristico. Dino Provenzal. Cisalpino-La Goliardica.

Elef Millim. Nello Pavoncello. Carucci.

Elsevier's Banking Dictionary. J. Ricci. Elsevier.

Elsevier's Dictionary of Barley, Malting, & Brewing. Bernard D. Hartong. Elsevier.

Elsevier's Dictionary of Chemical Engineering. W. Clason. Elsevier.

Elsevier's Dictionary of Cinema, Sound & Music. W. E. Clason. Elsevier.

Elsevier's Dictionary of Computers, Automatic Control & Data Processing. W. E. Clason. Elsevier.

Elsevier's Dictionary of Criminal Science. J. A. Adler. Elsevier.

Elsevier's Dictionary of Electronics & Waveguides. W. E. Clason. Elsevier.

Elsevier's Dictionary of Financial Terms. F. J. Thomson. Elsevier.

Elsevier's Dictionary of General Physics. W. E. Clason. Elsevier.

Elsevier's Dictionary of High Vacuum Science & Technology. Fritz W. Weber. Elsevier.

Elsevier's Dictionary of Horticulture. Ed. by Ministry of Agriculture & Fisheries- Netherlands & J. Nijdam. Elsevier.

Elsevier's Dictionary of Metallurgy & Metal Working. W. E. Clason. Elsevier.

Elsevier's Dictionary of Nuclear Science & Technology. W. E. Clason. Elsevier.

Elsevier's Dictionary of Public Health. Nick J. Deblock. Elsevier.

Elsevier's Dictionary of Television, & Video Recording. W. Clason. Elsevier.

Elsevier's Dictionary of Tools & Ironware. Ed. by Clason. Elsevier.

Elsevier's Electrotechnical Dictionary. W. E. Clason. Elsevier.

Elsevier's Medical Dictionary in Five Languages. A. Sliosberg. Elsevier.

Elsevier's Multilingual Dictionary of Insurance Technology. W. A. Ruysch. Elsevier.

Elseviers Nautical Dictionary. Ed. by P. Segditsas. Elsevier.

Elsevier's Nautical Dictionary in Six Languages. Ed. by J. P. Vandenberghe & L. Y. Chaballe. Elsevier.

Elseviers Rubber Dictionary. Elsevier.

Elsevier's Telecommunication Dictionary. W. E. Clason. Elsevier.

Elsevier's Wood Dictionary. Ed. by W. Boerhave Beekman. Elsevier.

Enciclopedia simultanea de correspondencia comercial en seis idiomas. Distein.

English-Italian, Italian-English Dictionary. Ed. by Malcolm Skey. Oxford U Pr.

English-Italian, Italian-English Dictionary. Saphrograph.

English-Italian, Italian-English Dictionary. Oxford U Pr.

Etnologico africano. Tina Novelli. Jaca Bk.

Fachwoerterbuch der Luftfahrt. A. Dorian & J. Osenton. (Pub. by R. Oldenbourg). French & Eur.

Fachwoerterbuch der Luftfahrt. J. Osenton. Oldenbourg Verlag.

Finnish-Italian Dictionary. G. Colussi. French & Eur.

Finnish-Italian-Finnish Dictionary. G. Colussi. French & Eur.

A Firenze si Parla Cosi: Frasario Moderno del Vernacolo Fiorentino. Renzo Raddi. Libreria.

Geillustrrerd Woordenboek Voor de Autombieltechniek en Zes Talen. C. Block et al. French & Eur.

Gem Language Dictionaries: Italian-English & English-Italian. S&S.

Il Gergo della Camorra. Carlo Sanna. Il Vespro.

Giesserei - Fachwoerterbuch. E. Brunhuber. (Pub. by Fachverlag, Schiele & Schon). French & Eur.

Giesserei-Fachwoerterbuch. E. Brunhuber. Schiele & Schon.

Giesserei-Fachworterbuch. Ernst Brunhuber. Schiele & Schon.

Glossaire d'organes de Transmission, 1: Les Engrenages Allemand-Espagnol-Francais-Anglais-Italien-Neerlandais-Suedois-Finnois. Maison Dictionnaire.

Glossaire Europeen de Terminologie Juridique et Administrative. Budgeting & Auditing. German-Italian. French & Eur.

Glossaire Europeen de Terminologie Juridique et Administrative: Local Government. French & Eur.

Glossaire Europeen de Terminologie Jurdique et Administrative. Motor, Insurance, German-Italian. French & Eur.

Glossaire Europeen de Terminologie Juridique et Administrative. Office Terminology Procedure. German-Italina. French & Eur.

Glossaire Europeen de Terminologie Juridique et Administrative: Terminologie de Reunions. French & Eur.

Glossaire Europeen en Quatre Langues: Francais-Italien-Allemand-Anglais. L. G. D. J.

Glossario al milanese di Bonvesin. Fabio Marri. Patron.

Glossario degli antichi portolani italiani. Henry Kahane et al. Olschki.

Glossario della Elabarione dei Dati: Inglese-Italiano, Italiano-Inglese. IBM. French & Eur.

Glossario di immunologia. G. S. Del Giacco. Minerva Medica.

Glossario di medicina nucleare. G. Pompili. Minerva Medica.

Glossario di tecnologia meccanica. Umberto Mezzera. Etas Libri.

Glossario geografico. Mario Riccardi. Japadre.

Glossario italiano tessile in cinque lingue. Giuseppe Suppa. Tec Tessile.

Glossario latino-emiliano. Pietro Sella. Biblio Apost.

Glossario storico popolare piemontese. U. Rosa. Forni.

Glossarium Armorum: Bd 6 Texthefte in Deutsch, Englisch, Franzoesisch, Italienisch, Daenisch, Tschechisch. Ed. by Ortwin Gamber et al. Verlag der Buchhaendler-Vereinigung GmbH.

Glossary of Genetics. Francoise Biass-Ducroux. Elsevier.

Glossary of International Treaties. Y. Renoux & J. Yates. Elsevier.

Glossary of Populations & Housing. G. Logie. Elsevier.

Glossary of Technical Terms for Market Researchers: English-German-Spanish-French-Italian-Dutch. European Society for Opinion & Marketing Research. Intl Pubns Serv.

Glossary of the Theatre. K. R. Band-Kuzmany. Elsevier.

Grande Dizionario di Marina: Inglese-Italiano, Italiano-Inglese. M. Bernabo & F. Picchi. French & Eur.

Grande Dizionario Hazon-Garzanti Inglese-Italiano Italiano-Inglese. Intl Learn Syst.

Grande Dizionario Hazon Garzanti Inglese-Italiano, Italiano-Inglese. M. Hazon. French & Eur.

Das Grosse Woerterbuch der Italienischen & Deutschen Sprache: Band I, Italienisch-Deutsch. Sansoni. Brandstetter.

Das Grosse Woerterbuch der Italienischen & Deutschen Sprache: Band II, Deutsch-Italienisch. Sansoni. Brandstetter.

Grosset's Italian Phrase Book & Dictionary for Travelers. Charles A. Hughes. (G&D). Putnam Pub Group.

Hamlyn Italian-English Dictionary. Larousse.

Harrap's Compact Italian & English Dictionary. Annamaria F. Maiocchi & Ada De Bichiacchi. Harrap.
Hugo Pocket Dictionary: Italian-English, English-Italian. Littlefield.
Illustrierte Technische Woerterbucher: Eisenbahnmaschinenwesen. A. Schlomann. (Pub. by R. Oldenbourg). French & Eur.
Illustrierte Technische Woerterbucher: Eisenbahnmaschinenwesen. A. Schlomann. Oldenbourg Verlag.
Illustrierte Technische Woerterbucher: Eisenbahnbau und Betrieb. A. Schlomann. (Pub. by R. Oldenbourg). French & Eur.
Illustrierte Technische Woerterbucher: Eisenbahnbau und Betrieb. A. Schlomann. Oldenbourg Verlag.
Illustrierte Technische Woerterbucher: Elektrotechnik und Elektrochemie. A. Schlomann. (Pub. by R. Oldenbourg). French & Eur.
Illustrierte Technische Woerterbucher: ELektrotechnik und Elektrochemie. A. Schlomann. Oldenbourg Verlag.
Illustrierte Technische Woerterbucher: Maschinenelemente. A. Schlomann. Oldenbourg Verlag.
Illustrierter Technische Woerterbucher: Luffahrts. A. Schlomann. Oldenbourg Verlag.
Inglese-italiano, italiano-inglese. Ed. by Vladimiro Macchi. Sansoni.
International Dictionary of Building Construction: English-French-German-Italian. Angelo C. Schwicker. Scholium Intl.
International Dictionary of Metallurgy, Mineralogy, Geology & the Mining & Oil Industries. A. Gagnacci-Schwicker & Schwicker. (Pub. by Bauverlag). French & Eur.
International Dictionary of Metallurgey, Mineralogy, Geology & the Mining & Oil Industries. A. Gagnacci-Schwicker & Schwicker. Bauverlag.
International Dictionary of Obscenities: A Guide to Dirty Words & Indecent Expressions in Spanish, Italian, French, German, & Russian. Christina Kunitskaya-Peterson. Berkeley Slavic.
International Microcomputer Dictionary. Sybex Staff & Rodnay Zaks. Sybex.
International Planning Glossary. Ed. by Gordon Logie & Hemel Hemstead. Intl Plan Glos.
Illustrierter Technische Woerterbucher: Luffahrts. A. Schlomann. (Pub. by R. Oldenbourg). French & Eur.
Interpretes de Bolsillo Italiano-Espanol. Biblograf SP.
Iron & Steel Dictionary: German-Italian & Italian-German. Iron & Steel Institute. Intl Pubns Serv.
Italian & English Idioms. R. Hall & F. Hall. Barron.
Italian Bilingual Dictionary: A Beginner's Guide in Words & Pictures. Gladys Lipton & John Colinari. Barron.
Italian Bilingual Dictionary: A Beginner's Guide in Words & Pictures. Barron.
Italian Dictionary. John Purves. Routledge & Kegan.
Italian Dictionary. Newnes Bks.
Italian-English Dictionary. Cassells. Macmillan.
Italian-English Dictionary.Saphrograph.
Concise English-Italian Italian-English Dictionary. Longman.
Italian-English, English-Italian Commercial Dictionary. Ragazzini & Gagliardelli. Heinman.
Italian-English, English-Italian Gem Dictionary. Ed. by May Isopel. Collins Pubs.
Italian-English, English-Italian (Grande) Dictionary. M. Hazon. Heinman.
Italian-English, English-Italian Pocket Dictionary. J. Purves. French & Eur.
Italian-English, English-Italian Technical Dictionary. G. Marolli. Heinman.
Italian-English-Italian. Macmillan.
Italian-Norwegian Dictionary. M. Ulleland. Kunnskapsforlaget.
Italian-Swedish-Italian Dictionary. French & Eur.
Italian Vest Pocket Dictionary. Robert A. Hall, Jr. Random.
Ital'iansko-Russkii i Rusko-Ital'ianskii Stroitel'nyi Slovar. Boris I. Avramenko. Russkii Iazyk.
Italiansko-Russkii Slovar. S. V. Gere et al. (Pub. by Gosizdat Inostr. Natsional Slovarei). Four Continent.
Italic, Latin, Italian. Ernst Pulgram. C Winter.
Italienisch. Incl. Langenscheidt.
Italienisch. Incl. Langenscheidt.
Italiensk-Dansk Ordbog. K. Anderson & G. Mafera. French & Eur.
Italiensk-Norsk Ordbok. M. Ulleland. French & Eur.
Italiensk-Svensk Ordbok. Esselte Studium.
Jean's Pocket Dictionaries: Italian-English. Hammond Inc.
Karmannyi Italiansko-Russkii Slovar. Four Continent.
Karmannyi Russko-Ital'ianskii Slovar. I. A. Dobrovolskaia et al. (Pub. by Sov Entsiklopediia). Four Continent.
Langenscheidt English-Italian Lilliput Dictionary. Langenscheidt.
Langenscheidt Italian-English Lilliput Dictionary. Langenscheidt.
Langenscheidts Grosswoerterbuch Italienisch. Vladimiro Von Macchi. Langenscheidt.
Langenscheidts Grosswoerterbuch: Teil II, Deutsch-Italiensch. Vladimiro Macchi. Ed. by Lexikographischen Institut Sansoni. Langenscheidt.
Langenscheidts Grosswoerterbuch: Teil I, Italienisch-Deutsch. Ed. by Lexikographischen Institut Sansoni. Langenscheidt.
Langenscheidts Grosswoerterbucher Italienisch. Ed. by Vladimiro Macchi. Langenscheidt.
Langenscheidts Handwoerterbuch Italienisch-Deutsch. Paolo Giovannelli & Walter Frenzel. Langenscheidt.
Langenscheidts Handwoerterbuch Italienisch: Teil II, Deutsch-Italienisch. Herbert Frenzel & Walter Frenzel. Ed. by Vladimiro Macchi. Langenscheidt.
Langenscheidts Handwoerterbuch Italienisch: Teil I, Italienisch-Deutsch. Paolo Giovannelli & Walter Frenzel. Langenscheidt.
Langenscheidts Handwoerterbuecher Italienisch. Ed. by Heinz Messinger & Werner Ruedenberg. Langenscheidt.
Langenscheidts Handwoerterbuecher: Italienisch, 2 Teile in 1. Langenscheidt.
Langenscheidts Handwoerterbuecher: Tl 1, Italienisch-Deutsch. Ed. by Paolo Giovannelli. Langenscheidt.
Langenscheidts Handwoerterbuecher: Tl 2, Deutsch-Italienisch. Ed. by Herbert Frenzel & Walter Frenzel. Langenscheidt.
Langenscheidt's Lilliput English-Italian Dictionary. Am Map.
Langenscheidt's Lilliput Italian-English Dictionary. Am Map.
Langenscheidts Lilliput-Woerterbuch Deutsch-Italienisch. Langenscheidt.
Langenscheidts Lilliput-Woerterbuch Italienisch-Deutsch. Langenscheidt.
Langenscheidts Lilliput-Woerterbuecher Deutsch-Italienisch. Langenscheidt.
Langenscheidts Lilliput-Woerterbuecher Italienisch-Deutsch. Langenscheidt.
Langenscheidts Taschenwoerterbuch der Italienischen & Deutschen Sprache. Ed. by W. Frenzel & V. Macchi. Langenscheidt.
Langenscheidts Taschenwoerterbuch Italienisch-Deutsch. V. Macchi & W. Frenzel. Langenscheidt.
Langenscheidts Taschenwoerterbuch Italienisch: Teil II, Deutsch-Italienisch. W. Frenzel. Langenscheidt.
Langenscheidts Taschenwoerterbuch Italienisch: Teil I, Italienisch-Deutsch. V. Macchi. Langenscheidt.
Langenscheidts Taschenwoerterbuecher Italienisch. Gustavo Sacerdote. Langenscheidt.
Langenscheidts Taschenwoerterbuecher Italienisch-Deutsch. Langenscheidt.
Langenscheidt's Universal Italian-English, English-Italian Dictionary. Am Map.
Langenscheidts Universal-Woerterbuch Italienisch. Langenscheidt.
Langenscheidts Universal-Woerterbuecher Italienisch-Deutsch. Langenscheidt.
Larousse de poche, francais-italien et italien-francais. Larousse & Co. Larousse.
Learn Italian for English Speakers. Arthur L. Hayward & C. McFarlane. Saphrograph.
Lessico Vento. Fabio Mutinelli. Forni.
Lexicologie & Lexicographie Francaises & Romanes. CNRS.
Lexicon comercial internacional: Espanol, frances, ingles, italiano, portugues y aleman. J. Vicens Carrio. Reverte SA.
Lexicon etymologicum: Supplemento ai dizionario etimologici latini e romanzi. Giovanni Alessio. Licosa.
Lexicon of International & National Units. Ed. by M. Merino-Rodriguez. Elsevier.
Lexicon of Plant Pests & Diseases. Ed. by Manuel Merino-Rodriguez. Elsevier.
Lexicon Sopena: Diccionario de bolsillo, italiano-espanol y espanol-italiano. Sopena.
Lexikon der Geschaeftsbriefe in Vier Sprachen. French & Eur.
Lexique De la Terminologie Linguistique. Jules Marouzeau. Intl Pubns Serv.
Lilliput Dictionary. Langenscheidt.
Magyar-Olasz Szotar. Gyula Herczeg. Terra.
Maly Slownik Wlosko-Polski & Polsko-Wloski. Stanislaw Soja et al. Wiedza Powszechna.
Manual del Automovil en 5 Idiomas: Diccionario Idiomatico del Automovil. Equipo Reactor de Ceac. French & Eur.
Mille Parole Fondamentali. Nello Pavoncello. Carucci.
Mondadori's Pocket Italian-English, English-Italian Dictionary. Imported Bks.
Multilingual Computer Dictionary. Ed. by Alan Isaacs. Facts on File.
The Multilingual Computer Dictionary. Isaacs. Facts on File.
Multilingual Glossary of Automatic Control Technology: English-French-German-Russian-Italian-Spanish-Japanese. D. T. Broadbent & M. Masubuchi. Pergamon.
Multilingual Vocabulary of Educational Radio & Television Terms. Intl Pubns Serv.
Music Translation Dictionary: An English, Czech, Danish, Dutch, French, German, Hungarian, Italian, Polish, Portuguese, Russian, Spanish, Swedish Vocabulary of Music. Compiled by Greenwood.
Musical Thesaurus: A Dictionary of Musical Language. J Hannon.
My Illustrated Dictionary: Arabic & Ital. Libr du Liban. Intl Bk Ctr.
New Century Vest-Pocket Italian Dictionary. Ed. by Vittore Bocchetta. New Century.
New Century World-Wide Italian Dictionary: Italian-English, English-Italian. Ed. by Vittore E. Bocchetta. New Century.
The New College Italian & English Dictionary. Robert C. Melzi. AMSCO Sch.
New International Dictionary of Refrigeration. International Institute of Refrigeration. (IIR). Unipub.
Nouveau Dictionnaire International du Froid. French & Eur.
Novissimo Dizionario della Lingua Italiana. F. Palazzi. Ed. by G. Folena. French & Eur.
Nuevo Glosario, Diccionario Poliglota de la Arquitectura. Buenaventura Bassegoda Muste. French & Eur.
Nuovo dizionario del dialetto triestino. Gianni Pinguentini. Nuova Cappelli.
Nuovo dizionario della lingua italiana. Curcio.
Nuovo Dizionario di Elettrotecnic e di Elettronica: Italiano-Inglese, Inglese-Italiano. A. Colella. French & Eur.
Nuovo Dizionario di Elettrotecnica & di elettronica. Antonio Colella. Il Rostro.
Nuovo dizionario di elettrotecnica e elettronica italiano-inglese, inglese-italiano. Antonio Colella. Il Rostro.
Nuovo dizionario di merceologia e chimica applicata. G. V. Villavecchia et al. Hoepli.
Nuovo dizionario di merceologia e chimica applicata. G. V. Villavecchia et al. Hoepli.
Nuovo dizionario di merceologia e chimica applicata. G. V. Villavecchia et al. Hoepli.
Nuovo dizionario di merceologia e chimica applicata. G. V. Villavecchia et al. Hoepli.
Nuovo dizionario di merceologia e chimica applicata. G. V. Villavecchia et al. Hoepli.
Nuovo dizionario di merceologia e chimia applicata. G. V. Villavecchia & G. Eigenmann et al. Hoepli.
Nuovo Dizionario di Terminologia Giuridica. A. Menghi. French & Eur.
Nuovo dizionario di terminologia giuridica. A. Menghi. Cortina M.
Nuovo Dizionario Dialettale Della Calabria. Gerhard Rohlfs. Longo A.
Nuovo dizionario dialettale della Calabria. Gerhard Rohlfs. Longo A.
Nuovo Dizionario Inglese-Italiano Delle Science Mediche. Luciano Bussi & Maria Cognazzo. S F Vanni.
Nuovo dizionario italiano-latino. Cosimo Mariano. Dante Alighieri.
Nuovo dizionario italiano-spagnolo. Lucio Ambruzzi. Paravia.
Nuovo dizionario latino-italiano. Gino Angelini. Dante Alighieri.
Nuovo dizionario musicale Curci. Alfredo Bonaccorsi. Curci.
Nuovo Dizionario Ricordi Della Musica & dei Musicisti. Ed. by Lily A. Bozzano et al. G Ricordi.
Nuovo dizionario Ricordi della musica e dei musicisti. Lily Allorto et al. Ricordi.
Nuovo dizionario siciliano-italiano. Vincenzo Mortillaro. Soc St Catanese.
Nuovo dizionario siciliano-italiano. Vincenzo Mortillaro. Forni.
Nuovo dizionario spagnolo-italiano. Lucio Ambruzzi. Paravia.
Olasz-Magyar Szotar. Gyula Herczeg. Akademiai Kiado.
Olasz-Magyar-Szotar. Gyula Herczeg. Terra.
Olasz-Magyar Szotar: Vocabolario Italiano-Ungherese. Gyula Herczeg. Ed. by Jeno Kolttay-Kastner. Akademiai Kiado.
Papiae Elementarium. Gramarian Papias. Ed. by V. De Angelis. Cisalpino.
Parole & Storia. Bruno Migliorini. Rizzoli Edit.
Philatelic Vocabulary in Five Languages. Philatelic Foundation. Philatelic Found.
Phrase Dictionaries for the American Tourist. Frederick Stark. Incl. Delair.
Piccolo Dizionario Americano Italiano. Friedrich W. Horlacher. Nuova Vallecchi.
Piccolo Dizionario del Dialetto Bresciano. Stefano Pinelli. Grafo.
Piccolo lessico universale. Sergio Rapetti et al. Nuova Vallecchi.
Polygraph Dictionary for the Graphic Industries in Six Languages. Ed. by K. Collet. Intl Pubns Serv.
Polytechnisches Woerterbuch Italienisch-Deutsch. Aribert Schlegelmilch. VEB Technik.
Practical Italian-English, English-Italian Dictionary. Peter Ross. Hippocrene Bks.
Primo Dizionario. Richard Scarry. Intl Learn Syst.

Printer's Terms Dictionary. R. Hostettler. Heinman.

Proverbes Francais: In French with Equivalents in English, German, Dutch, Italian, Spanish, Latin. G. Ilg. Elsevier.

Putnam's Contemporary Italian Dictionary. Berkley Pub.

The Random House Basic Dictionary. Pan Amer Pub.

The Random House Basic Dictionary Italian. Ed. by Robert A. Hall. Ballantine.

Romanisches Etymologisches Woerterbuch. Wilhelm Meyer-Luebke. (Pub. by Carl Winter). French & Eur.

Romanisches Etymologisches Woerterbuch. Wilhelm Meyer-Luebke. Winter Univ.

Russkikh Glagolov. A. S. Vasil'Eva. Four Continent.

Russko-Ital'ianskii Ucxhebnyi Slovar. D. E. Rozental. (Pub. by Sov. Entsiklopediia). Four Continent.

Saggio di un dizionario del linguaggio archivistico veneto. Bartolomeo Cecchetti. Forni.

Sana Alimentazione. Edoardo Borra et al. Edizioni Paoline.

Satzlexikon der Handelskorrespondenz. Zavada & Schraffl. Brandstetter.

Schwierigkeiten des Deutsch-Italienischen Wortschatzes. Bruno Storni. Ed. by Paolo Giovannelli. Klett.

Semiiazychnyi Slovar Po Elektrosviazi. (Pub. by Sov. Entsiklopediia). Four Continent.

Seven Language Dictionary. Ed. by David Shumaker. Crown.

Seven Languages Dictionary. Imported Bks.

Shogakukan Iwa Chujiten: Comprehensive Italian-Japanese Dictionary. Shogakukan.

Svensk-Italiensk Ordbok. Silvia Tomba. Esselte Studium.

Technisches Fachwoerterbuch. Hermann Mink. Gustavo Gili.

Technisches Woerterbuch. Salvatore Orlando-Meyer. (Pub. by Brandstetter). French & Eur.

Technisches Woerterbuch. Salvatore Orlando-Meyer. (Pub. by Brandstetter). French & Eur.

Technisches Woerterbuch. Salvatore Orlando-Meyer. Brandstetter.

Technisches Woerterbuch. Salvatore Orlando-Meyer. Brandstetter.

Technisches Woerterbuch: Band I, Italienisch-Deutsch. Meyer & Orlando. Brandstetter.

Technisches Woerterbuch: Band II, Deutsch-Italienisch. Meyer & Orlando. Brandstetter.

Tedesco-Italiano, Italiano-Tedesco. Ed. by Vladimiro Macchi. Sansoni.

Terminologia Turistico Alberghiera. E. Neiger. Ed Calderini.

Terminologia turistico alberghiera: L'albergatore poliglotta. Elisabetta Neiger. Ed Calderini.

Terminology of Environmental Hygiene. European Parliament - Translation Division. Intl Pubns Serv.

Tesoro Della Linqua Greca-Volgare Ed Italiana, cioe Ricchissimo dizzionario greco-volgare et italiano. Alexis De Sommevoire & Tomaso Da Parigi. Caratzas Pub Co.

Thesaurus di Scienze della Terra. Patron.

Torrent Control Terminology. (FAO). Unipub.

Two Thousand & One Italian & English Idioms: 2001 Locuzione Italiane e Inglese. Robert R. Hall, Jr. & Frances A. Hall. Barron.

Universal Italian Dictionary. Langenscheidt.

Universita la Sperimentazione Dipartimentale. Tomas Maldonado. Guaraldi.

Vest Pocket Italian. Institute for Language Study. (BN). B&N NY.

Vest Pocket Italian Dictionary. Ed. by V. Bocchetta. New Century.

Vocabolari delle parlate italiante. Angelico Prati. Forni.

Vocabolarietto del dialetto trevigiano 1884. Vincenzo Bindoni & G. Netto. Canova.

Vocabolarietto del vernacolo pisano. Giuseppe Malagoli. Nistri-Lischi.

Vocabolarietto della Lingua Italiana. C. Grassi. French & Eur.

Vocabolarietto figurato. Giannina Facco & Maria Facco. Edipem.

Vocabolario agronomico nel dialetto della provincia de Lecce. G. Gorgoni. Forni.

Vocabolario biblico. J. Von Allmen. AVE.

Vocabolario bresciano-italiano. G. Battista Malchiori. Forni.

Vocabolario commerciale italiano-francese e francese-italiano, Caputo Cataldo. A. Jannini Pasquale. Monnier.

Vocabolario cremasco-italiano. B. Samarani. Forni.

Vocabolario cremonese-italiano. A. Peri. Forni.

Vocabolario croato serbo-italiano de M. Deanovic & J. Jerej. Niccolo Nichea. Del Bianco.

Vocabolario degli accademici della Crusca. Licosa.

Vocabolario degli accademici della Crusca. Licosa.

Vocabolario dei dealetti bergamashi. Antonio Tiraboschi. Forni.

Vocabolario dei deatetti bergamashi. Antonio Tiraboschi. Forni.

Vocabolario dei dialette della citta e diocesi di Como. Pietro Monti. Forni.

Vocabolario dei dialette salentini. Gerhard Rohlfs. Congedo.

Vocabolario dei dialetti della Corsica. F. D. Falcucci. Licosa.

Vocabolario dei dialetti della Corsica. F. D. Falcucci. Licosa.

Vocabolario dei dialetto antico vicentino. D. Bortolan. Forni.

Vocabolario dei piccoli. Guglielmo Valle. La Scuola.

Vocabolario del dialetto antico vicentino. D. Bortolan. Forni.

Vocabolario del dialetto bolognese. Gaspare Ungarelli. Multigrafica.

Vocabolario del dialetto calabrese. Luigi Accattatis. Pellegrini.

Vocabolario del dialetto de Magione. Giovanni Moretti. Univ Perugia.

Vocabolario del dialetto de Vigevano. Giovanni Vidari et al. Olschki.

Vocabolario del dialetto modenese. A. Neri. Forni.

Vocabolario del dialetto tarantino in corrispondenza della lingua italiana. D. L. De Vincentiis. Forni.

Vocabolario del francese moderno. Enea Balmas. Ghisetti & Corvi.

Vocabolario del milanese d'oggi. Spiller. Rizzoli Edit.

Vocabolario della lingua italiana. P. Colombo. (CEB). Capitol-Dischi.

Vocabolario della lingua italiana. P. Colombo. (CEB). Capitol-Dischi.

Vocabolario della lingua italiana. Alessandro Cutolo. Euro Co.

Vocabolario della lingua italiana. Giacomo Devoto & Giancarlo Oli. Monnier.

Vocabolario della lingua italiana. Grassi. Vallardi A.

Vocabolario della lingua italiana. Bruno Migliorini. Paravia.

Vocabolario della lingua italiana. Nicola Zingarelli. Zanichelli.

Vocabolario della lingua italiana. Nicola Zingarelli. Zanichelli.

Vocabolario Della Lingua Latina. Luigi Castiglioni. Ed. by A. Brambilla & G. Campagna. Loescher.

Vocabolario Della Lingua Latina: Italiano-Latino, Latino-Italiano. Italo Lana. Paravia.

Vocabolario della lingua latina: Latino-italiano e italiano-latino. Luigi Castiglioni & Scevola Mariotti. Loescher.

Vocabolario della lingua oromonica. E. Viterbo. Hoepli.

Vocabolario della lingua parlata in Piazza Armerina. Remingio Roccella. Forni.

Vocabolario dell'argot. Luigi Alessio. Petrini.

Vocabolario delle istituzioni indoeuropee: Vol. 1, Economia-parentela-societa. Emile Benveniste. Tr. by M. A. Liborio. Einaudi.

Vocabolario dell'uso abruzzese. G. Finamore. Dante Alighieri.

Vocabolario dell'uso abruzzese. G. Finamore. Forni.

Vocabolario dell'uso toscano. Pietro Fanfani. Le Lettere.

Vocabolario dialettale calabro-reggino-italiano. G. Malara. Forni.

Vocabolario Domestico Genovese-Italiano. Angelo Paganini. Forni.

Vocabolario domestico genovese-italiano. A. Paganini. Forni.

Vocabolario domestico sardo-italiano. E. Atzeni. Forni.

Vocabolario etimologico italiano. Angelico Prati. Garzanti Edit.

Vocabolario etimologico italiano. Francesco Zambaldi. Dante Alighieri.

Vocabolario ferrarese-italiano. L. Ferri. Forni.

Vocabolario fondamentale della lingua italiana. Giuseppe Sciarone Abondio. Minerva Italica.

Vocabolario francese-italiano e italiano-francese. Edwin Rostan. Malipiero.

Vocabolario fraseologico italiano-latino. L. Luciano & A. Traina. Patron.

Vocabolario greco-italiano. Guglielmo Gemoll. Sandron.

Vocabolario greco-italiano. Alessandro Annaratone & Giovanni La Magna. Signorelli C.

Vocabolario greco-italiano. Lorenzo Rocci. Dante Alighieri.

Vocabolario ilustrato della lingua italiana. Giacomo Devoto & Giancarlo Oli. Sel Rdrs Digest.

Vocabolario inglese-italiano e italiano-inglese. C. G. Cecioni. Malipiero.

Vocabolario inglese-italiano e italiano-inglese. Luciano Sani. Dante Alighieri.

Vocabolario inglese-italiano, italiano-inglese. Luciano Sani. Dante Alighieri.

Vocabolario italiano-francese e francese-italiano. Francesco Grimod & G. Caselli. Dante Alighieri.

Vocabolario italiano-francese-italiano. F. Cassone. (CEB). Capitol-Dischi.

Vocabolario italiano-inglese, inglese-italiano. J. McAllister. (CEB). Capitol-Dischi.

Vocabolario italiano-kiswahili. Vittorio Merlo Pick. EMI.

Vocabolario italiano-macedone. Giorgio Nurigiani. Lint.

Vocabolario italiano-piemontese. G. Gavuzzi. Bottega d'Erasmo.

Vocabolario italiano-tedesco. Introito & Porta. Bottega d'Erasmo.

Vocabolario italiano-tedesco-italiano. S. David. (CEB). Capitol-Dischi.

Vocabolario italiano-tedesco-italiano. S. David. (CEB). Capitol-Dischi.

Vocabolario Italiano-Tedesco, Tedesco-Italiano. Ed. by Sante David. Capitol Edit.

Vocabolario kiswahili-italiano. Vittorio Merlo Pick. EMI.

Il Vocabolario Latino-Italiano & Italiano-Latino. Raffaello Bianchi. Monnier.

Vocabolario latino-italiano e italiano-latino. L. Lipparini. Malipiero.

Vocabolario Latino-italiano, italiano-latino. Raffaello Bianchi & Onorio Lelli. Monnier.

Vocabolario latino-italiano, italiano-latino. Natale Vianello. Dante Alighieri.

Vocabolario latino-italiano-latino. Giuseppe Campanini et al. Paravia.

Vocabolario lucchese. I. Nieri. Forni.

Vocabolario Marinaresco Giuliano-Dalmata. Enrico Rosamani. Olschki.

Vocabolario marinaresco giuliano-dalmata. Enrico Rosamani. Olschki.

Vocabolario marino e militare. Alberto Guglielmotti. Mursia.

Vocabolario metaurense. Elio Conti. Forni.

Vocabolario milanese-italiano. Francesco Angiolini. Imago Libri.

Vocabolario milanese-italiano. Francesco Cherubini. Brenner.

Vocabolario milanese-italiano coi segni per la pronuncia. Francesco Angiolini. Forni.

Vocabolario minimo della lingua italiana per stranieri. Ignazio Baldelli & Alberto Mazzetti. Monnier.

Vocabolario minimo della lingua italiana per stranieri con dizionarietto somalo. Ignazio Baldelli et al. Monnier.

Vocabolario mirandolese-italiano. E. Meschiari. La Vela.

Vocabolario modenese-italiano. Ernesto Maranesi & P. Papini. Forni.

Vocabolario napolitano-italiano. P. P. Volpe. Forni.

Vocabolario napolitano-toscano. R. D'Ambra. Forni.

Vocabolario numerico siciliano-italiano. Giusto Pecorella. Bietti.

Vocabolario parmigiano-italiano. Carlo Malaspina. Forni.

Vocabolario per le favole de Fedro. Pietro Pettoello. Loescher.

Vocabolario reggiano-italiano. G. B. Ferrari. Forni.

Vocabolario romagnolo-italiano. A. Morri. Forni.

Vocabolario romagnolo-italiano, italiano-romagnolo. Libero Ercolani. Edn Girasole.

Vocabolario romanesco-belliano e italiano-romanesco. Gennaro Vaccaro. Romana Libri.

Vocabolario romanesco-trilussiano e italiano-romanesco. Gennaro Vaccaro. Romana Libri.

Vocabolario sallustiano. F. Natta. L'Erma.

Vocabolario sardo-italiano e italiano-sardo. Giovanni Spano. Forni.

Vocabolario spagnolo-italiano e italiano-spagnolo. Alvisi & Arce. Malipiero.

Vocabolario swahili-italiano e italiano-swahili. Vittorio Merlo Pick. EMI.

Vocabolario tedesco-italiano e italiano-tedesco. A. Deidda. Malipiero.

Vocabolario topografico dei ducati di Parma, Piacenza e Guastalla. L. Molossi. Forni.

Vocabolario trentino-italiano. V. Ricci. Forni.

Vocabolario ucraino-italiano. E. Onatskyj. Ist Univers Orient.

Vocabolario vernacolo-italiano pei destrette roveretano e trentino. Giambattista Azzolini. Manfrini.

Vocabula amatoria. Le Lettere.

Vocabulaire des Termes: Essentiels Utilises pour la Transmissien Ligne; Francais-Espagnol-Russe-Allemand-Italien-Neerlandais-Polonais-Portugais-Suedois. U. I. T.

Vocabulaire Italien par l'image. Roger H. Durand & Salvatore Greco. Bordas-Dunod.

Vocabulaire Multilingue de la Science du Sol: Anglais-Francais-Espagnol-Allemand-Portugais-Italien-Neerlandais-Suedois-Russe. G. V. Jacks & R. Tavernier. F. A. O.

Vocabularios Portugues-Espanol-Italiano. Novaro.

Vocabularium. Papias. Bottega d'Erasmo.

Vocabularium Pharmaceuticum. Ed. by Albert Graa. Intl Pubns Serv.

Vocabularium vulgare. Nicola Valla. Bottega d'Erasmo.

Woerterbuch der Deutschen und Italienischen Wirtschafts und Rechtssprache. Giuseppe Conte. French & Eur.

Woerterbuch der Deutschen und Italienischen Wirtschafts und Rechtssprache. Giuseppe Conte. French & Eur.

Woerterbuch der Italienisch & Deutschen Sprache: Bd 1: Italienisch-Deutsch. Brandstetter.

Woerterbuch der Italienisch & Deutschen Sprache: Bd 2: Deutsch-Italienisch. Brandstetter.

Woerterbuch der Italienischen und Deutschen Sprache. French & Eur.

Woerterbuch der Italienischen und Deutschen Sprache. French & Eur.

Woerterbuch der Kraftuebertragungselemente-Deutsch-Spanisch-Franzoesisch-Englisch-Italienisch-Niederlandisch-Schwedisch-Finnisch: Bd 1, Zahnraeder. Krausskopf.

Woerterbuch der Kraftuebertragungselemente. French & Eur.

Woerterbuch des Italienisch-Deutschen Privat & Wirtschaftsrechts: Band I, Deutsch-Italienisch. H. Trioke-Strambaci & E. Helffrich-Mariani. Recht & Wirtschaft.

Woerterbuch des Italienisch-Deutschen Privat & Wirtschaftsrechts: Band II, Italienish-Deutsch. H. Troike-Strambaci & E. Helffrich-Mariani. Recht & Wirtschaft.

Woerterbuch des Kraftfahreugwesens. Otto Vollnhals. Girardet.

Woerterbuch des Kraftfahrzeugwesens. Otto Vollnhals. French & Eur.

Woerterbuch fuer das Wasser und Abwasserfach. Fritz Meinck. French & Eur.

Woerterbuch fuer Metallurgie, Mineralogie, Geologie, Bergbau & die Oelindustrie. A. Cagnacci-Schwicker. Bauverlag.

Woerterbuch fuer Metallurgie, Mineralogie, Geologie, Bergbau & die Oelindustrie Englische-Franzosisch-Deutsch-Italienisch. Angelo Cagnacci-Schwicker. Bauverlag.

Woerterbuch fuer Metallurgie, Mineralogie, Geologie, Bergbau und die Oelindustrie. French & Eur.

Woerterbuch fur das Wasser & Abwasserfach. Fritz Meinck. Oldenbourg Verlag.

Woerterbucher der Fertigungstechnik Deutsch-Spanisch-Italienisch-Portugiesisch: Bd 1R, Schmieden-Freiformschmieden & Gesenkschmieden. G. Pahlitzsch. Girardet.

World-Wide Italian Dictionary. Ed. by Vittore E. Bocchetta. (Prem). Fawcett.

World Wide Italian Language Italian-English. New Century.

Worterbuch der Technik: Italienisch-Deutsch. A. Schlegelmich. French & Eur.

Zweisprachiges Woerterbuch Fuer Angenaeherte Operationelle Analyse Semantischer Entsprechungen Mittels EDV. G. Guckler. (Pub. by G. Narr). French & Eur.

JAPANESE

All-Romanized English-Japanese Dictionary. Hyojun R. Kai. C E Tuttle.

All Romanized English-Japanese Dictionary. Kai. Iaconi.

Analytic Dictionary of Chinese & Sino-Japanese. Bernhard Karlgren. Peter Smith.

Basic English: Writer's Japanese-English Word Book. F. J. Daniels. (Pub. by Hokuseido Pr). Heian Intl.

Basic Japanese Conversation Dictionary: English-Japanese & Japanese-English. Samuel Martin. C E Tuttle.

Basic Japanese Conversation Dictionary. S. Martin. Iaconi.

Basic Words in Japanese. Pan Am Bk Co.

Beginners Dictionary of Chinese-Japanese Characters. Arthur Rose-Innes. Peter Smith.

Beginner's Dictionary of Chinese-Japanese Characters. Arthur Rose-Innes. Dover.

Beginners' Dictionary of Chinese-Japanese Characters & Compounds. Arthur Rose-Innes. Dover.

Berlitz Japanese for Travellers. Berlitz Editors. (Berlitz). Macmillan.

Chinese-English-Japanese Glossary of Chemical Terms. T. Shiratori. French & Eur.

Chinese-English-Japanese Glossary of Chemical Terms. S. Tamura & F. Shiratori. French & Eur.

Deutsch-Japanisches Woerterbuch. Eusebius Breitung. Buske.

Diccionario del Budo: Artes Marciales. Raymond Thomas. French & Eur.

Diccionario espanol-japones. Luis M. Martinez Duenas & Manuel M. Kato Yda. Edi-Seis.

Dictionary of Fishing Terms: Japanese-English, English-Japanese. French & Eur.

A Dictionary of Japanese & English Idiomatic Equivalents. Charles Corwin et al. Kodansha.

Dictionary of Marine Engineering Terms: Japanese-English, English-Japanese. Ed. by M. Masuda. French & Eur.

Dictionary of Shipping Terms. French & Eur.

Elseviers Automobile Dictionary. Ed. by G. Schuurmans. Elsevier.

Elseviers Rubber Dictionary. Elsevier.

English-Japanese Dictionary (Romanized) Saphrograph.

English-Japanese Marine Terms Dictionary. French & Eur.

English Loanwords in Japanese: A Selection. Akira Miura. C E Tuttle.

Everyday Japanese. Eldora Thorlin & Noah Brannen. Weatherhill.

Five Hundred & One German Verbs: Written in Japanese. Strutz. Barron.

A Glossary of Agricultural Terms. H. Miyayama et al. French & Eur.

Glossary of Terms in Heat Transfer, Fluid Flow & Related Topics. Ed. by William Begell. Hemisphere Pub.

Hawaii's Real Estate Industry & Technical Terminology in English & Japanese. Kazuo Nishiyama & Hiroshi Katayama. Honolulu Japanese.

Iaponsko-Russkii Politekhnicheskii Slovar. (Pub. by Russkii Iazyk). Four Continent.

Iaponsko-Russkii Uchebnyi Slovar Ieroglifov. N. I. Feldman-Konrad. (Pub. by Russkii Iazyk). Four Continent.

Illustrated New Shipbuilding Dictionary: English-Japanese, Japanese-English. M. Yamaguchi. French & Eur.

Inoue's Smaller Japanese-English Dictionary. Jukichi Inoue. C E Tuttle.

An Introduction to Modern Japanese Orthography: Kana. Elizabeth F. Gardner & Samuel E. Martin. Far Eastern Pubns.

A Japanese & English Dictionary with an English & Japanese Index. James C. Hepburn. C E Tuttle.

Japanese-Chinese Dictionary. French & Eur.

Japanese-Chinese Dictionary. French & Eur.

Japanese-Chinese Loanword Dictionary (M-9259) French & Eur.

Japanese-Chinese Science & Technology Dictionary. French & Eur.

Japanese-English-Chinese Radio Technology Dictionary. French & Eur.

Japanese-English Dictionary. Eric B. Ceadel. Saphrograph.

Japanese-English Dictionary: Romanized. Saphrograph.

Japanese-Latin-English-German-French Medical Terminology. French & Eur.

Japanese Newspaper Compounds: The One Thousand Most Important in Order of Frequency. Ed. by Tadashi Kikuoka. C E Tuttle.

Japanese Word & Phrase Book for Tourists. Eldora S. Thorlin. C E Tuttle.

Kleines Woerterbuch der Japanologie. B. Lewin. (Pub. by Harrassowitz). French & Eur.

The Kodansha English-Japanese Dictionary. Ed. by Shigeo Kawamoto & Junzaburo Nishiwaki et al. Tr. by Shigehisa Narita & Mamoru Shimizu. Kodansha.

The Kodansha English-Japanese Dictionary. Kodansha.

The Kodansha Japanese-English Dictionary. Kodansha.

The Kodansha Japanese-Russian Dictionary. Kodansha.

Kokugo Daijiten: Comprehensive Dictionary of the Japanese Language. Shogakukan.

Kotowaza Daijiten: Comprehensive Dictionary of Japanese Phrase, Fable & Proverb. Shogakukan.

Kratkii Iaponsko-Russkii Razgovornik. (Pub. by Iskra Revoliutsii). Four Continent.

Kratkii Russko-Iaponskii Slovar. A. E. Gluskina et al. (Pub. by GINS). Four Continent.

Langenscheidts Universal-Woerterbuch Japanisch. Langenscheidt.

Learn Japanese for English Speakers. Saphrograph.

Lexicon of International & National Units. Ed. by M. Merino-Rodriguez. Elsevier.

Modern Reader's Japanese-English Character Dictionary. Andrew Nelson. C E Tuttle.

The Modern Reader's Japanese-English Character Dictionary. Andrew N. Nelson. C E Tuttle.

Multilingual Glossary of Automatic Control Technology: English-French-German-Russian-Italian-Spanish-Japanese. D. T. Broadbent & M. Masubuchi. Pergamon.

My First English-Japanese Picture Dictionary. Dixson et al. Regents Pub.

New English-Japanese Dictionary. Kenkyusha.

New Japanese-English Dictionary of Economic Terms. French & Eur.

The Oxford-Duden Pictorial English-Japanese Dictionary. Oxford U Pr.

Oxford Picture Dictionary of American English: English-Japanese. Pan Amer Pub.

Oxford Picture Dictionary of American English: English-Japanese Edition. E. C. Parnwell. Oxford U Pr.

Practical Dictionary of Shipping Business: Japanese-English; English-Japanese. French & Eur.

Russko-Iaponskii Slovar. S. F. Zarubin. (Pub. by Sov. Entsiklopediia). Four Continent.

Scientific Terms, Aeronautics: Japanese-English, English-Japanese. Ministry of Education. French & Eur.

Scientific Terms, Chemistry: Japanese-English, English-Japanese. Ministry of Education. French & Eur.

Scientific Terms Electrical Engineering. Ministry of Education Science & Culture. French & Eur.

Scientific Terms Mathematics: Japanese-English, English-Japanese. Ministry of Education. French & Eur.

Scientific Terms Meteorology: Japanese-English, English-Japanese. Ministry of Education. French & Eur.

Scientific Terms Physics: Japanese-English, English-Japanese. Ministry of Education. French & Eur.

Scientific Terms Spectroscopy: Japanese-English, English-Japanese. Ministry of Education. French & Eur.

Shogakukan Iwa Chujiten: Comprehensive Italian-Japanese Dictionary. Shogakukan.

Shogakukan Random House Eiwa Daijiten. Shogakukan.

Vest Pocket Japanese. Institute for Language Study. (BN). B&N NY.

Vocabularios Japones-Espanol-Ruso. Novaro.

Vocabulary of Common Japanese Words. A. Rose-Innes. Far Eastern Pubns.

JAVANESE

Javanese-English Dictionary. Elinor C. Horne. Yale U Pr.

KALMYK

The Kalmyk-Mongolian Vocabulary in Stralenberg's Geography of 1730. John R Krueger. Almqvist.

KANJI

A New Dictionary of Kanji Usage. Barron.

KASHMIRI

Hindu-Kashmiri Common Vocabulary. Jawaharlal Handoo & Lalita Handoo. Ctr Inst Ind Lang.

KATU

Katu Vocabulary. Nancy A. Costello. Summer Inst Ling.

KAZAKH

Kazakh-English Dictionary. Boris N. Shnitnikov. Mouton.

KECHWA

Diccionario Kechwa-Castellano. Cesar Guardia Mayarga. Studium.

KEWA

A Kewa Dictionary with Supplementary Grammatical & Anthropological Materials. K. J. Franklin et al. Linguistic Circle.

KHAM

An English-Kham, Kham-English Glossary. David Watters & Nancy Watters. Summer Inst Ling.

KHAMTI

Tai-Khamti Phonology & Vocabulary. Alfons Wiedert. Steiner Verlag.

KHMER

Cambodian-English Glossary. Franklin E. Huffman & Im Proum. Yale U Pr.

A Concise Cambodian-English Dictionary. Judith Jacob. Oxford U Pr.

English-Khmer Dictionary. Franklin E. Huffman & Im Proum. Yale U Pr.

English-Khmer Medical Dictionary. Sally Keller. Summer Inst Ling.

English-Khmer Phrasebook with Useful Wordlist. Iaconi.

KHOSA

Lumko English-Xhosa Dictionary. A. Fischer. Oxford U Pr.

KIKUYU

English-Kikuyu Dictionary. A. R. Barlow. Tr. by T. G. Benson. Oxford U Pr.

KIWAI

A Grammar of the Kiwai Language, Fly Delta, Papua, with a Kiwai Vocabulary. Sidney H. Ray & E. B. Riley. AMS Pr.

KOREAN

Abbreviated Russian-Korean Dictionary. French & Eur.
Basic Chinese-Korean Character Dictionary. Hyogmyou Kwon. Harrassowitz.
Basic Words in Korean. Pan Amer Pub.
Chinesisch-Koreanisch-Deutsch Woerterbuch. Andre Eckardt. Groos Verlag.
Concise English-Korean Dictionary Romanized. Joan V. Underwood. C E Tuttle.
Concise English-Korean Dictionary Romanized. Underwood. Iaconi.
Deutsch-Koreanisches Woerterbuch. Andre Eckardt. Groos Verlag.
Diccionario del Budo: Artes Marciales. Raymond Thomas. French & Eur.
Dictionary Korean-Chinese. French & Eur.
English-Korean Dictionary for Practical Conversation. B. J. Jones. Hollym Corp.
English Korean Dictionary Romanized. M. E. Song. Shalom.
A Guide to Korean Characters: Reading & Writing Hangul & Hanja. Bruce K. Grant. Hollym Intl.
A Guide to Korean Characters: Reading & Writing Hangul & Hanja. Bruce K. Grant. Hollym Corp.
Korean Dictionary. (Dist. by Koryo Bks Importing, Inc) Sam-Sung Pub.
Korean-English Dictionary. Samuel E. Martin et al. Yale U Pr.
Koreanisch-Deutsches Woerterbuch. Andre Eckardt. Groos Verlag.
Kratkii Russko-Koreiskii Slovar. I. N. Mazur. (Pub. by GINS). Four Continent.
Standard English-Korean Dictionary for Foreigners. B. J. Jones. Hollym Intl.
Standard English-Korean Dictionary for Foreigners. Pong Kook Lee. Ed. by B. J. Jones. Hollym Intl.
Standard English-Korean Dictionary: For Foreigners. Ed. by B. J. Jones. Hollym Corp.

KRIO

A Krio-English Dictionary. Compiled by Clifford N. Fyle. Oxford U Pr.

KURDISH

Al-Hadiyati 'I-Hamidiyah. M. Mokri. Intl Bk Ctr.
Dictionnaire Kurde-Francais. Auguste Jaba. Biblio-Verlag.

KUSAIIEAN

Kusaiean-English Dictionary. Kee-Dong Lee. UH Pr.

KWANKIUTL

Kwakiutl Grammar - with a Glossary of Suffixes. Franz Boas. AMS Pr.

KWANYAMA

Kwanyama-English Dictionary. Compiled by B. Turvey. Witwatersrand.

LAMBA

English-Lamba Dictionary. Clement M. Doke. Shalom.

LAO

Comprehensive Lao-English Dictionary. Allen Kerr. Iaconi.
Dictionnaire Laotien-Francais. Marc Reinhorn. French & Eur.
Dictionnaire Laotien-Francais. Marc Reinhorn. CNRS.
Dictionnaire Laotien Francais. Theodore Guignard. Gregg.
English-Lao, Lao-English Dictionary. Marcus Russell. Iaconi.
English-Lao Phrasebook with Useful Word List: For Laotians. Tr. by Kamchong Luangpraseut. Ctr Appl Ling.
English-Lao, Lao-English Dictionary. Russell Marcus. C E Tuttle.
Lao-English Dictionary. Allen Kerr. Cath U Pr.
A Vocabulary of the Lau Language, Big Mala, Solomon Islands. Walter G. Ivens. AMS Pr.

LATIN

Basic Latin Vocabulary. John Wilson & C. Parsons. St Martin.
Basic Latin Vocabulary Along Etymological Lines. Gerald F. Else. Am Classical.
Basiswoordenlijst Latijn. J. K. Babeliowsky. Staatsdruk.
Botanical Latin: History, Grammar, Syntax, Terminology & Vocabulary. William T. Stearn. Hafner.
Cassell's Concise Latin-English, English-Latin Dictionary. Compiled by D. P. Simpson. Macmillan.
Cassell's Latin Dictionary: Concise Latin-English English-Latin. Cassell. Macmillan.
Cassell's Latin Dictionary: Latin-English, English-Latin. Ed. by D. P. Simpson. Macmillan.
Cassell's Latin Dictionary: Latin-English, English-Latin. D. P. Simpson. Imported Bks.
Cassell's Latin Dictionary: Latin-English, English Latin. Cassell. Ed. by D. P. Simpson. Macmillan.
Cassell's Latin Dictionary: Standard Latin-English English-Latin. Cassell. Macmillan.
Cassell's New Compact Latin Dictionary. (LE). Dell.

Cassell's New Latin-English, English-Latin Dictionary. Dell.
Cesko, Slovensko, Latinsko, Anglicko, Nemecko, Rusky, Slovnik Plevelu. Vaclav Kosik. SNTC.
Chambers Murray Latin-English Dictionary. Ed. by William Smith & J. L. Lockwood. B&N Imports.
Concordance of the Bible. Solomon Mendelkern. Feldheim.
Concordantiae verbales opusculorum S. Francisci et S. Clarae Assisiensium. Boccali Giovanni. LIEF.
Cree's Dictionary of Latin Quotations. A. Cree. Newbury Bks.
A Critical Concordance to Catullus. Ed. by V. P. McCarren. Humanities.
Dansk-Latinsk: Ordbog. L. Ove Kjaer. French & Eur.
Diccionario Abreviado Latino-Espanol Espanol-Latino. Biblograf SP.
Diccionario Abreviado Latino-Espanol Espanol-Latino 'Spes' Biblo SP.
Diccionario abreviado Latino-Espanol Espanol-Latino Vox. Biblo SP.
Diccionario Basico Latino-Espanol. Recuero Pascual. Ameller Edic.
Diccionario Basico Latino-Espanol. Biblo SP.
Diccionario Basico Latino-Espanol, Espanol-Latino. Eustaquio Echauri Martinez. Biblo Sp.
Diccionario Basico Latino-Espanol Espanol-Latino. Biblograf SP.
Diccionario basico latino-espanol, espanol-latino. Imported Bks.
Diccionario basico Latino-Espanol Espanol-Latino. Biblo SP.
Diccionario de bolsillo latino-espanol & espanol-latino. Vives. Coculsa.
Diccionario de Expresiones y Frases Latinas. V. J. Herrero. French & Eur.
Diccionario espanol-latino. J. Llauro Padrose & J. Marques Casanovas. SAETA.
Diccionario Everest Cima Latin. Everest.
Diccionario Everest Cima Latin-Espanol. Everest.
Diccionario Everest Cima Latin (II) Everest.
Diccionario Ilustrado Latino-Espanol Espanol-Latino. Biblograf SP.
Diccionario Ilustrado Latino-Espanol Espanol-Latino. Biblo SP.
Diccionario latino. L. Macchi. Don Bosco Ed.
Diccionario latino-espanol. J. Llauro Padrosa. SAETA.
Diccionario Latino-Espanol, Espanol-Latino. Blanquez. French & Eur.
Diccionario latino-espanol, espanol-latino: Serie Bachillerato Koel. Tesoro.
Diccionario manual latino-castellano y castellano-latino. De Andrea. Sopena.
Diccionario manual latino-espanol y espanol-latino. Agustin Blanquez Fraile. Sopena.
Diccionario manual latino-espanol y espanol-latino. Mugica. Razon y Fe.
Dicionario Latino-Portugues. Francisco Torrinha. Porto Ed.
Dictionariolum Puerorum Tribus Linguis: Lat., Ang. & Gall. Conscriptum. Robert Estienne. Walter J Johnson.
Dictionarium Linguae Thai Sive Slamensis Interpretatione Latina, Gallica & Anglica. Jean-Baptiste Pallegoix. Gregg.
Dictionarium Tetraglotten Seu Voces Latinae Omnes, et Graecae Eis Respondentes, Cum Gallica & Teutonica (Quam Passim Flandricam Vocant) Earum Interpretatione: Dictionarum Tetraglotten A.D. MDLXII Ed. Mouton.
Dictionarium Teutonicolatinum. Cornelis Kiel. Olms Verlag.
A Dictionary of Greek & Latin Combining Forms Used in Zoological Names. Edmund C. Jaeger. C C Thomas.
Dictionary of Greek & Roman Biography & Mythology. Ed. by William Smith. AMS Pr.

Dictionary of Medieval Latin from British Sources: Fascicule I, A-B. Oxford U Pr.
Dictionnaire Abrege Latin-Francais. Felix Gaffiot. French & Eur.
Dictionnaire Abrege Latin-Francais. Felix Gaffiot. Hachette Jeunesse.
Dictionnaire Abrege Latin-Francais Illustre. Felix Gaffiot. Renouveau Pedagogique.
Dictionnaire des Abreviations Latines & Francaise: Usitees dans les Inscriptions du Moyen-Age. Louis A. Chassant. Lenox.
Dictionnaire des Abreviations Latines & Francaises: Usitees dans les Inscriptions du Moyen Age. Louis A. Chassant. Olms Verlag.
Dictionnaire des Sciences de la Nature (Dictionary of the Natural Sciences) Edouard Ghaleb. Intl Pubns Serv.
Dictionnaire Etymologique de la Langue Latine. Alfred Ernout & Antoine Meillet. Klincksieck.
Dictionnaire Francais-Latin. Georges Edon. French & Eur.
Dictionnaire Francais-Latin. Jean-Elie Decahors. Hatier.
Dictionnaire Francais-Latin. Georges Edon. Belin.
Dictionnaire Francais-Latin. Geoffroy. Delalain.
Dictionnaire Francais-Latin. Henri Goelzer. Garnier-Flammarion.
Dictionnaire Francais-Latin. Henri Goelzer. Garnier.
Dictionnaire Francais-Latin. Louis Quicherat. Hachette-Jeinesse.
Dictionnaire Francais-Latin. Robert Estienne. Slatkine.
Dictionnaire Hatier-Beauchemin: Francais-Latin. Jean E. De Cahors. Beauchemin.
Dictionnaire Hatier-Beauchemin: Latin-Francais. A. Gariel. Beauchemin.
Dictionnaire Latin-Francais. Henri Bornecque & Fernand Cauet. French & Eur.
Dictionnaire Latin-Francais. Felix Gaffiot. French & Eur.
Dictionnaire Latin-Francais. Charles Lebaigue. French & Eur.
Dictionnaire Latin-Francais. Felix Gaffiot. Hachette.
Dictionnaire Latin-Francais. Geoffroy. Delalain.
Dictionnaire Latin-Francais. Henri Goelzer. Garnier.
Dictionnaire Latin-Francais. Henri Goelzer. Garnier.
Dictionnaire Latin-Francais. Henri Goelzer. Garnier.
Dizionario della lingua latina: Latino-italiano e italiano-latino. Ed. by Calonghi et al. Rosenberg & Sellier.
Dizionario di Abbreviature Latine & Italiane. Capelli. Hoepli.
Dizionario di abbreviature latine ed italiane. A. Capelli. Hoepli.
Dizionario illustrato della lingua latina. E. Bianchi et al. Monnier.
Dizionario illustrato della lingua latina. E. Bianchi et al. Monnier.
Dizionario illustrato latino-italiano. F. Gaffiot. Piccin.
Dizionario Italiano-Latino. Angelo Perugini. Libr Ed Vat.
Dizionario italiano-latino. Malipiero.
Dizionario italiano-latino. Oreste Badellino. Rosenberg & Sel.
Dizionario italiano-latino. Angelo Perugini. Libr Ed Vat.
Dizionario italiano-latino. Sacerdoti. Vallardi A.
Dizionario italiano-latino: Edizione speciale. Oreste Badellino. Rosenberg & Sel.
Dizionario Italiano-Latino, Latino-Italiano. N. Sacerdoti. French & Eur.
Dizionario latino. Gino Angelini et al. Dante Alighieri.
Dizionario latino-italiano. Ferruccio Calonghi. Rosenberg & Sel.
Dizionario latino-italiano e italiano-latino. Malipiero.
Dizionario latino-italiano e italiano-latino. Giuseppe Pittano. Edn Scol Mond.
Dizionario latino-italiano: Stato della Chiesa-Veneto-Abruzzi. Pietro Sella. Biblioteca Apostolica Vaticana.

Dizionario sintattico latino. Bruno Nelli. Giardini Pisa.

Dizionario sintattico latino: Italiano-latino e latino-italiano. Giovanni La Magna. Signorelli C.

Elementary Latin Dictionary. Charlton T. Lewis. Oxford U Pr.

Ellison's Latin American Menu Reader. Al Ellison. Ellison Ent.

Elsevier's Dictionary of Horticulture. Ed. by Ministry of Agriculture & Fisheries- Netherlands & J. Nijdam. Elsevier.

Etymological Dictionary of Latin. T. G. Tucker. Ares.

Farmakologicheskii Slovar: Latinsko-Russkii & Russko-Latinskii. T. G. Kazachenok. (Pub. by Vysheishaia). Four Continent.

Gem Language Dictionaries: Latin-English & English-Latin. S&S.

Glosario de voces ibericas y latinas: Tomo 1. Francisco J. Simonet. Atlas Edns.

Glosario de voces ibericas y latinas: Tomo 2. Francisco J. Simonet. Atlas Edns.

Glosario de voces ibericas y latinas: Obras completa. Francisco J. Simonet. Atlas Edns.

Glossarium ad Scriptores Mediae & Infimae Graecitatis. Charles D. Du Cange. Akad Druck.

Glossarium Ad Scriptores Mediae et Infimae Graecitatis. Charles Du Fresne DuCange. Intl Pubns Serv.

Guilielmi Gesenii Thesaurus Philologicus Linguae Hebraeae. Freiedrich H. Gesenius. Biblio-Verlag.

Harley Latin-Old English Glossary. Robert Oliphant. Mouton.

Italic, Latin, Italian. Ernst Pulgram. C Winter.

Japanese-Latin-English-German-French Medical Terminology. French & Eur.

Langenscheidt English-Latin Lilliput Dictionary. Langenscheidt.

Langenscheidts Grosses Schulwoerterbuch Lateinisch-Deutsch. Erich Pertsch. Langenscheidt.

Langenscheidts Grosswoerterbuch Deutsch-Lateinisch. Menge & Guethling. Langenscheidt.

Langenscheidts Grosswoerterbuch: Lateinisch-Deutsch. Hermann Menge & Otto Guethling. Langenscheidt.

Langenscheidts Grosswoerterbuch Lateinisch-Deutsch. Menge & Guethling. Langenscheidt.

Langenscheidts Grosswoerterbuch Lateinisch: Tl 1, Lateinisch-Deutsch. Langenscheidt.

Langenscheidts Grosswoerterbuch Lateinisch: Tl 2, Deutsch-Lateinisch. Langenscheidt.

Langenscheidts Handwoerterbuch Lateinisch-Deutsch. Erich Pertsch. Langenscheidt.

Langenscheidt's Lilliput English-Latin Dictionary. Am Map.

Langenscheidt's Lilliput Latin-English Dictionary. Am Map.

Langenscheidts Lilliput-Woerterbuch Deutsch-Lateinisch. Langenscheidt.

Langenscheidts Lilliput-Woerterbuch Lateinisch-Deutsch. Langenscheidt.

Langenscheidts Lilliput-Woerterbuecher Deutsch-Lateinisch. Langenscheidt.

Langenscheidts Lilliput-Woerterbuecher Lateinisch-Deutsch. Langenscheidt.

Langenscheidt's Pocket Latin Dictionary, Latin-English, English-Latin. Ed. by S. A. Handford & M. Herberg. Am Map.

Langenscheidts Schulwoerterbuch Lateinisch-Deutsch. Erich Pertsch & Ernst E. Lange-Kowal. Langenscheidt.

Langenscheidts Schulwoerterbuecher Lateinisch-Deutsch. Langenscheidt.

Langenscheidts Schulwoerterbuecher Lateinisch-Deutsch. Erich Pertsch. Langenscheidt.

Langenscheidts Taschenwoerterbuch Lateinisch. H. Menge & E. Pertsch. Langenscheidt.

Langenscheidts Taschenwoerterbuch Lateinisch: Teil II, Deutsch-Lateinisch. Hermann Menge. Langenscheidt.

Langenscheidts Taschenwoerterbuch Lateinisch: Teil I, Lateinisch-Deutsch. H. Menge & E. Pertsch. Langenscheidt.

Langenscheidts Taschenwoerterbuecher Lateinisch. H. Menge. Langenscheidt.

Langenscheidts Taschenwoerterbuecher Deutsch-Lateinisch. Langenscheidt.

Langenscheidt's Universal Latin-English, English-Latin Dictionary. Am Map.

Langenscheidts Universal-Woerterbuch Lateinisch. Langenscheidt.

Langenscheidts Universal-Woerterbuecher Lateinisch-Deutsch. Langenscheidt.

Lateinisch. Hermann Menge. Rev. by E. Pertsch. Langenscheidt.

Lateinisch-Deutsch. Compiled by Erich Pertsch. Langenscheidt.

Lateinisch-Deutsch. Dietrich Pertsch. Langenscheidt.

Lateinisch-Deutsch, Deutsch-Lateinisch. Langenscheidt.

Lateinische Wortkunde fuer Anfaenger & Fortgeschrittene. Ruediger Vischer. Teubner.

Latin & Greek for Biologists. Theodore Savory. (Pub. by Meadowfield Pr England). State Mutual Bk.

Latin-Bulgarian Dictionary. M. Voinov. French & Eur.

Latin Concise Dictionary. Cassells. Macmillan.

Latin-Dansk Ordbog. T. Hastrup. French & Eur.

Latin Dictionary. A. Wilson. McKay.

Latin Dictionary: Founded on Andrews Edition of Freund's Latin Dictionary. Charlton T. Lewis & Charles Short. Oxford U Pr.

Latin-English & English-Latin Dictionary. Dennison.

Latin-English & English-Latin Dictionary. Ed. by S. C. Woodhouse. Routledge & Kegan.

Latin English Derivative Dictionary. Ed. by Randolph F. Schaeffer & W. L. Carr. Am Classical.

Latin-English Dictionary. Cassells. Macmillan.

Latin-English, English-Latin. Inst Mod Lang.

Latin-English, English-Latin Dictionary. (BN). B&N NY.

Latin-English, English-Latin Dictionary. D. A. Kidd. Saphrograph.

Latinsk-Svensk Ordbok. Axel W. Ahlberg et al. Esselte Studium.

Latinsko-Cesky Slovnik. Josef M. Prazak. SNTC.

Latinsko-Russko-Latyshskii Slovar Meditsinskikh Terminov. (Pub. by Liesma). Four Continent.

The Law Latin Lexicon. Abdul G. Chaudhary. Khyber Law Publishers.

Lexicon Arabico-Latinum. George W. Freytag. Intl Bk Ctr.

Lexicon Arabico-Latinum. George W. Freytag. Intl Bk Ctr.

Lexicon Chaldaicum Talmudicum & Rabbinicum. Johann Buxtorf. Olms Verlag.

Lexicon Diplomaticum Abbreviationes Syllabarum et Vocum in Diplomatibus et Codicibus a Seculo Octo a Sextum-Decimum Usque Occurentes Exponens. Johann L. Walther. B Franklin.

Lexicon etymologicum: Supplemento ai dizionario etimologici latini e romanzi. Giovanni Alessio. Licosa.

Lexicon Latinitatis Medii Aevi: Praesertim ad res Ecclesiasticas Investigandas Pertinens. Brepols.

Lexicon linguisticae et philologiae. Emilio Springhetti. Univ Gregoriana.

Lexicon Medicum. Boleslaw Zlotnickiego. French & Eur.

Lexicon Medicum: Medizinisches Woerterbuch in 6 Sprachen; Englisch, Russisch, Franzoesisch, Deutsch, Latein, Polnisch. B. Zlotnicki. Langenscheidt.

Lexicon of Plant Pests & Diseases. Ed. by Manuel Merino-Rodriguez. Elsevier.

Lexicon Platonicum. Friedrich Ast. B Franklin.

Lexicon totius latinitatus. Egidio Forcellini. Lib Edit Greg.

Lexicon typographicum Italiae. Giuseppe Fumagalli. Olschki.

Lexikon Medicum. B. Zlotnicki. French & Eur.

Lexique de base du Latin. J. Michel & Michel Gester. Sikkel.

Lexique Francais-Latin. Edouard Sommer. Hachette-Jeunesse.

Lexique Francais-Latin. Jacques Trenel. Belin.

Lexique Latin Medieval-Francais-Anglais. J. F. Niermeyer. Brill.

Lilliput Dictionary. Langenscheidt.

Linguarum Totius Orbis Vocabularia Comparativa. Peter S. Pallas. Buske.

Malas Hierbas, Diccionario Clasificatorio Ilustrado. Francisco Guell. French & Eur.

Medical Dictionary. B. Zoltnicki. (Pub. by Schattauer). French & Eur.

Medical Latin. Carolyn D. Lewis. M Jones.

Mianownictwo Histologiczne. Marka Wawrzyniak. Panstowy Zaklad W.

Mykologisches Worterbuch. K. Berger. French & Eur.

Mykologisches Worterbuch. Karl Von Berger. Fischer Verlag.

New College Latin & English Dictionary. John C. Traupman. AMSCO Sch.

New College Latin & English Dictionary. Ed. by John C. Traupman. Bantam.

The New College Latin & English Dictionary. Bantam.

Nuovo dizionario italiano-latino. Cosimo Mariano. Dante Alighieri.

Nuovo dizionario latino-italiano. Gino Angelini. Dante Alighieri.

Orbis Latinus: Lexikon lateinischer geographischer Namen des Mittelalters und der Neuzeit. Johann G. Graesse. Ed. by Helmut Plechl. Intl Pubns Serv.

Oxford Latin Dictionary. Ed. by P. G. Glare. Oxford U Pr.

Oxford Latin Dictionary: Fascicle 1, a-Calcitro. Ed. by P. G. Glare. Oxford U Pr.

Oxford Latin Dictionary: Fascicle 2, Calcitro-Demitto. Ed. by P. G. Glare. Oxford U Pr.

Oxford Latin Dictionary, Fascicle 3: Demiurgus-Gorgoneus. Ed. by P. G. Glare. Oxford U Pr.

Oxford Latin Dictionary, Fascicle 4: Gorgonia-Libero. Ed. by G. P. Glare. Oxford U Pr.

Oxford Latin Dictionary: Fascicle 6-a-Calcitro. Ed. by P. G. W. Glare. Oxford U Pr.

Oxford Latin Dictionary: Fascicle 7. Ed. by P. G. Glare. Oxford U Pr.

Oxford Latin Dictionary: Fascicle 8. P. G. Glare. Oxford U Pr.

Papiae Elementarium. Gramarian Papias. Ed. by V. De Angelis. Cisalpino.

Pharmacological Dictionary. Latin-Russian, Russian-Latin. French & Eur.

Pocket-Shorter Dictionary. Langenscheidt.

Promptorium Parvulorum Sive Clericorum, Lexicon Anglo-Latinum Princeps. Anglicus Galfridus. AMS Pr.

Proverbes Francais: In French with Equivalents in English, German, Dutch, Italian, Spanish, Latin. G. Ilg. Elsevier.

Russko-Latino-Kazakhskii Terminologicheskii Slovar. M. Isambaev. (Pub. by Izd An Kaz. SSR). Four Continent.

Russko-Latinsko-Uzbekskii Slovar. (Pub. by Meditsina). Four Continent.

Septemlingual Dictionary of the Names of European Animal. Ed. by L. Gozmany et al. (Pub. by Kiado Hungary). Heyden.

Siglas & Abreviaturas Latinas con su Significado por Orden Alfabetico de un Catalogo de las Abreviaturas. Ramon Alvarez de la Brana. Olms Verlag.

Slownik Lekarski Lacinsko-Polski. Jerzy Babecki. Panstwowe Zaklad W.

Slownik Tekarski Polsko-Lacinksi. Jerzy Babecki. Panstwowe Zaklad W.

Spes--Diccionario Abreviado Latino-Espanol, Espanol-Latino. French & Eur.

Thesaurus Graecae Linguae. Henri Estienne. Akad Druck.

Thesaurus Philosophorum Seu Distinctiones et Axiomata Philosophica. Georg Reeb. Clearwater Pub.

Universal Latin Dictionary. Langenscheidt.

Vad Betyder Vaxtens Latinska Namn. Ivar Anell. Forum Bok.

Vocabolario Della Lingua Latina. Luigi Castiglioni. Ed. by A. Brambilla & G. Campagna. Loescher.

Vocabolario Della Lingua Latina: Italiano-Latino, Latino-Italiano. Italo Lana. Paravia.

Vocabolario della lingua latina: Latino-italiano e italiano-latino. Luigi Castiglioni & Scevola Mariotti. Loescher.

Vocabolario fraseologico italiano-latino. L. Luciano & A. Traina. Patron.

Il Vocabolario Latino-Italiano & Italiano-Latino. Raffaello Bianchi. Monnier.

Vocabolario latino-italiano e italiano-latino. Edmondo D'Arbela et al. Signorelli C.

Vocabolario latino-italiano e italiano-latino. L. Lipparini. Malipiero.

Vocabolario Latino-italiano, italiano-latino. Raffaello Bianchi & Onorio Lelli. Monnier.

Vocabolario latino-italiano, italiano-latino. Natale Vianello. Dante Alighieri.

Vocabolario latino-italiano-latino. Giuseppe Campanini et al. Paravia.

Vocabulaire Latin. Arthur Bodson. Sciences Lettres.

Le Vocabulaire Latin des Relations & des Partis Politiques sous la Republique. Jean Hellegouarch. Belles Lettres.

Vocabulaire Raisonne Latin-Francais. Gerard Cotton. Dessain & Tolra.

Vocabulaius Teutonico-Latinus. Pref. by Klaus Grabmueller. Olms Verlag.

Vocabular Latina. Esselte Studium.

Vocabulario De Romance En Latin: Antonio De Nebrija. Ed. by Gerald MacDonald. Temple U Pr.

Vocabularium Nocentium Florae. R. Kwizda. Springer-Verlag.

Vocabularium Polyglottum Vitae Silvarum. R. Litschauer. (Pub. by P. Parey). French & Eur.

Vocabularium Polyglottum Vitae Silvarum. R. Litschauer. Parey.

Vocabularium Saxonicum. L. Nowell. Ed. by A. Marckwardt. Kraus Repr.

Vocabularium syriacum. R. Kobert. Pont Ist Biblico.

The Vocabulary of High School Latin. Gonzalez Lodge. AMS Pr.

Vox-Diccionario Basico Latino-Espanol, Espanol-Latino. Eustaquio Echuari. French & Eur.

Zoologisches Woerterbuch - Palaearktische Tiere. Michael Klemm. Intl Pubns Serv.

Zoologisches Woerterbuch Palaearktische Tiere. Michael Klemm. (Pub. by Parey Berlin). French & Eur.

Zoologisches Woerterbuch Palaearktische Tiere. Michael Klemm. Parey.

LATVIAN

English-Latvian-Russian Dictionary. J. Raskevics et al. (Pub. by Collets). State Mutual Bk.
Ergemes Izloksnes Vardnica. Elga Kagaine & S. Rage. Zinatne.
Frantsuzsko-Latviiskii Slovar. I. Zandreitere et al. (Pub. by Latv Valsts). Four Continent.
Grammar, Vocabulary, Exercises of the Latvian Language for the Use of Students. Antonia Millers. Echo Pubs.
Latvian-English Dictionary. Phil E. Turkina. Saphrograph.
Slovar Terminov Pedagogiki. (Pub. by Liesma). Four Continent.

LENAPE

A Lenape-English Dictionary. Ed. by Daniel G. Brinton & Albert S. Anthony. AMS Pr.
Lenape-English Dictionary. Daniel G. Brinton. Waletittin.
A Lenape-English Dictionary. Daniel G. Brinton. AMS Pr.

LEPCHA

Dictionary of the Lepcha language. Ed. by G. B. Mainwaring & Albert Grunwedal. Radha.

LIMBU

A Vocabulary of the Limbu Language of Eastern Nepal. Ed. by H. W. Senior. Radha.

LITHUANIAN

Anglo-Litovskii Politekhnicheskii Slovar. A. I. Novodvorkis. (Pub. by Gospolitnauchizdat). Four Continent.
La Distribuzione della Posposizione nel Lituano Antico. Loredana Serafini Amato. Ist Univers Orient.
English-Lithuanian Dictionary. A. Laucka et al. (Pub. by Mokslas). Four Continent.
English-Lithuanian Dictionary of Economic Terms. A. Buracas. (Pub. by Mokslas). Four Continent.
Litauisches Etymologisches Woerterbuch. Ernst Fraenkel. (Pub. by Westdeutscher Verlag/VVA). French & Eur.
Litauisches Etymologisches Woerterbuch. Ernst Fraenkel. (Pub. by Westdeutscher Verlag/VVA). French & Eur.
Lithuanian-English Dictionary. Vilius Peteraitis. Shalom.
Lithuanian-English Dictionary. B. Piesarskas et al. (Pub. by Vilnius). Four Continent.
Lithuanian-English, English-Lithuanian Dictionary. B. Piesarskas & V. Baravykas. Heinman.
Lithuanian Reverse Dictionary. David F. Robinson. Slavica.
Litovsko-Russko-Anglo-Nemetskii Slovar Fizicheskikh Terminov. P. Brazhdzhiunas. (Pub. by Mokslas). Four Continent.
Polsko-Litovskii Slovar. V. A. Vaitkiavichiute. (Pub. by Mokslas). Four Continent.

LUGANDA

Kratkii Lugunda-Russkii & Russko-Lugunda Slovar. O. P. Nosova. (Pub. by Sov Entsiklopediia). Four Continent.
Luganda-English Dictionary. John D. Murphy. Cath U Pr.
Luganda-English Dictionary. Iaconi.

MABUSO

A Comparative Word List of the Mabuso Languages, Madang Province, Papua New Guinea. J. A. Z'graggen. Linguistic Circle.

MACEDONIAN

Vocabolario italiano-macedone. Giorgio Nurigiani. Lint.

MADANG

A Comparative Word List of the Northern Adelbert Range Languages, Madang Province, Papua New Guinea. J. A. Z'graggon. Linguistic Circle.
A Comparative Word List of the Rai Coast Languages, Madang Province, Papua New Guinea. J. A. Z'graggen. Linguistic Circle.
A Comparative Word List of the Southern Adelbert Range Languages, Madang Province, Papua New Guinea. J. A. Z'graggen. Linguistic Circle.

MADARSKO

Dictionary of Acoustics: English-German-French-Russian-Spanish-Polish-Madarsko-Slovene. W. Reichardt. French & Eur.
Dictionary of Automatical Technique. Ed. by Jiri Sykora. French & Eur.

MALAY

Diccionario Simultaneo en 21 Idiomas. Juan Capdevilla Font. French & Eur.
A Dictionary of English Bahasa Malaysia Idiomatic Phrases. A. Karim & T. Lucy. Jaya Ciencia.
Istilah biologi, bahasa Inggeris-bahasa Malaysia, bahasa Malaysia-Bahasa Inggeris. Dewan Bahasa.
Istilah geografi, Inggeris-Malaysia-Inggeris. Dewan Bahasa.
Istilah percetakan, penerbitan, dan komunikasi massa, Inggeris-Malaysia-Inggeris. Dewan Bahasa.
Istilah perpustakaan, Inggeris-Malaysia-Inggeris. Dewan Bahasa.
Istilah pertanian, bahasa Ingeris-bahas a Malaysia, bahasa Malaysia-bahasa Inggeris. Dewan Bahasa.
Istilah Senibina, Perancangan dan Ukur Kuantiti. Dewan Bahasa dan Pustaka. Dewan Bahasa.
Kamus dwibahasa, bahasa Inggeris-bahasa Malaysia. Dewan Bahasa dan Pustaka. Dewan Bahasa.
Kamus pembaca, Inggeris-Malayu. Albert S. Hornby. Oxford U Pr.
Malaiziisko-Russko-Angliiskii Slovar. Ed. by N. V. Rott. (Pub. by Russkii Iazyk). Four Continent.

Malay-English Dictionary. William Marsden. Ayer Co.
Senarai istilah seni lukis, bahasa Inggeris-bahasa Malaysia. Dewan Bahasa.

MALAYALAM

Abhinava Malayala Nikhantu: New Malayalam Dictionary. C. Madhavan Pillai. DC Bks.
English-English-Malayalam Dictionary. T. Ramalingam Pillai. Rev. by N. V. Krishna. DC Bks.
English-English-Malayalam Dictionary. T. Ramalingam Pillai. Ed. by M. S. Octavo. DC Bks.
English-Malayalam Dictionary. T. R. Pillai. Ed. by M. S. Chandrasekhara. DC Bks.
Sailee Nihantu: Dictionary of Idioms & Phrases. T. Ramalingam Pilla. DC Bks.

MALGACHE

Dictionnaire Francais-Malgache. R. P. Malzac. French & Eur.

MANAGALASI

Managalasi Language: Managalasi Dictionary. Jim Parlier & Jaki Parlier. Summer Inst Abor.

MANCHU

A Concise Manchu-English Lexicon. Jerry Norman. U of Wash Pr.

MANGAIAN

Vocabulary of the Mangaian Language. F. W. Christian. Kraus Repr.

MANOBO

Manobo-English Dictionary. Richard E. Elkins. UH Pr.

MAORI

The Complete English-Maori Dictionary. Ed. by Bruce Biggs. Oxford U Pr.
Complete Manual of Maori Grammar & Conversation, with Vocabulary. Apirana N. Ngata. AMS Pr.
The Concise Maori Handbook. Ed. by A. W. Reed & A. E. Brougham. Reed Ltd.
Dictionary of the Maori Language. H. W. Williams. Govern.
New Dictionary of Modern Maori. Ed. by P. M. Ryan. (Pub. by Heinemann Pub New Zealand). Intl Schol Bk Serv.
New Dictionary of Modern Maori. P. Ryan. Hein.
Vocabulary & Science Structure of Maori Children. I. H. Barham. Nzcer.

MARATHI

A Dictionary-Marathi & English. James T. Molesworth. Intl Pubns Serv.

MARQUISE

Dictionnaire de la Langue des Iles Marquises. Ildefonse Dordillon. French & Eur.

MARSHALLESE

Marshallese-English Dictionary. Takaji Abo et al. UH Pr.
Spoken Marshallese. Byron W. Bender. UH Pr.

MAYA

Diccionario de San Francisco. Oscar Michelon. Akademische Druck Verlagt.
Diccionario Maya Cordemex Maya-Espanol. Alfredo Barrera Vasquez. Porrua.
Vocabulario de Mayathan. Dorothy Andrews Heath de Zapata. Dorothy Andrews Heath de Zapata.

MAYLAY

Kamus Lengkap: Penyunting. Sudjai H. Awang & Khan Yusoff. Pustaka Antara.

MBUKUSHU

English-Mbukushu Dictionary. R. C. Wynne. (Pub. by Avebury England). Humanities.
English-Mbukushu Dictionary. Ronald C. Wynne. Avebury Pub Co.

MEDIEVAL

Dictionary of Medieval Latin from British Sources: Fascicule I, A-B. Oxford U Pr.

MELANESIAN

Melanesian Pidgin Phase-Book & Vocabulary. Linguistic Society of America & Robert A. Hall, Jr. Linguistic Soc Am.

511

MISKITO

Diccionario trilingue miskito-ingles-espanol. Adolfo I. Vaughan Warman. Imp. Nac. Manugua EDUCA.

MODERN

Lilliput Dictionary. Langenscheidt. Vest Pocket Modern Greek. Institute for Language Study. (BN). B&N NY.

MOHAWK

Iontenwennaweienstahkhwa. University of the State of New York, State Education Department. State U NY Pr.

MOKILESE

Mokilese-English Dictionary. Sheldon P. Harrison & Salich Albert. UH Pr.

MOLDAVIAN

Moldavsko-Russkii Frazeologicheskii Slovar. V. Solov'ev. (Pub. by Lumina). Four Continent.
Russko-Moldavskii & Moldavsko-Ruskii Shkolnyi Slovar. (Pub. by Lumina). Four Continent.
Russko-Moldavskii Ekonomicheskii Slovar. V. B. Bortnikov et al. (Pub. by Kartia Moldoveniaske). Four Continent.
Russko-Moldavskii Slovar. Ed. by A. T. Borshch et al. (Pub. by Izd. Inostr. & Natsional Slovarei). Four Continent.
Russko-Moldavskii Slovar. M. V. Podiko. (Pub. by Kartia Moldoveniaske). Four Continent.

MONGOLIAN

A Concise English-Mongolian Dictionary. John G. Hangin. Res Ctr Lang Semiotic.
Dictionary of Mong Njua: A Miao (Meo) Language of Southeast Asia. Thomas A. Lyman. Mouton.
Glossary of Mongolian Technical Terms. Frederick H. Buck. Spoken Lang Serv.
Mongolian-English Dictionary. F. D. Lessing. Mongolia.
Russko-Mongol'Skii Razgovornik. (Pub. by Russkii Iazyk). Four Continent.

MOPAN

Diccionario Bilingue Maya Mopan & Espanol. Inst Ling Ver.

MOROCCAN

A Dictionary of Moroccan Arabic: Moroccan-Arabic English-Moroccan. Ed. by Richard S. Harrell & Harvey Sobelman. Georgetown U Pr.

MOZAMBIQUE

Emprestimos Linguisticos nas Linguas Mocambicanas. Antonio C. Cabral. Lourenco Marques.

MUYUW

Muyuw Dictionary. David Lithgow & Daphne Lithgow. Summer Inst Ling.

NAVAHO

An Ethnologic Dictionary of the Navaho Language. Franciscans, Saint Michaels, Arizona. AMS Pr.
Ethnologic Dictionary of the Navaho Language. Franciscan Fathers. St Michaels.
A Stem Vocabulary of the Navaho Language. Berard Haile. AMS Pr.

NDONGA

Ndonga, Afrikaans, English: Dreitalige Woordeboek. Johannes J. Viljoen & P. Amakali. Van Schaik.

NEO-MELANESIAN

Growth & Structure of the Lexicon of New Guinea Pidgin. Peter Muhlhausler. Linguistic Circle.

NEPALESE

Gurung-Nepali-English Glossary. Deu B. Gurung et al. Summer Inst Ling.
Nepal'Sko-Russkii Slovar. I. S. Rabinovich. (Pub. by Sov Entsiklopediia). Four Continent.

NGGELA

Dictionary of Nggela. Charles El. Fox. Anthro AucMus.

NIGERIAN

A Dictionary of Nigerian Arabic. Alan S. Kaye. Undena Pubns.

NOR

Suomi-Norja-Suomi: Taskusanakirja. Turid Farbregd & Aili Kamarainen. Soderstrom.

NORSE

Merknader til en dell Norrone Tekster. Kare Skadberg & Tor Ulset. Univers Oslo.
Norsk-Fransk Ordbok. M. Lesoil. French & Eur.
Svensk-Norsk Ordbok. Marius Sandvei. Fabritius.

NORWEGIAN

Attved Tyrifjorden. Peter Lyse. Universitetsforlaget.
Berlitz Pocket Dictionaries: Norwegian-English-Norwegian. Berlitz. Macmillan.
Bil-og Trafikkteknisk Ordbok. Willy Kirkeby. Kunnskapsforlaget.

Cappelens Musikkeleksikon. Ed. by Kari Michelsen et al. J W Cappelens.
Den Nye Forkortningsordboken. Ed. by Dag Sundby. Schibsted.
Deutsch fur Baufachleute fuer Daenen, Norweger & Sshweden. G. Wallnig & H. Evered. Bauverlag.
Deutsch-Norwegisch-Deutsch. Von Trygue Alsos. French & Eur.
Diccionario Lexicon Noruego-Espanol, Espanol-Noruego. French & Eur.
Dictionnaire de Poche Francais-Norvegien. Berlitz.
Dutch-Norwegian & Norwegian-Dutch Pocket Dictionary. K. Schoell. Kunnskapsforlaget.
Engelsk-Norsk Teknisk Ordliste. Knut J. Knutsen. Tapir.
English-Norsk Dictionary: Gyldendals. B. Berulfsen. Vanous.
English-Norwegian Dictionary. B. Berulfsen & T. Berulfsen. Kunnskapsforlaget.
English-Norwegian, Norwegian-English. Jan W. Dietrichson & Orm Verland. Kunnskapsforlaget.
English-Norwegian, Norwegian-English Dictionary. J. Meyer Myklestad & H. Soras. Saphrograph.
English-Norwegian, Norwegian-English, Lommeordbok. E. Daae. French & Eur.
English-Norwegian Norwegian-English Pocket Dictionary. Hippocrene Bks.
Finnish-Norwegian-Finnish Dictionary (Suomi-Noria-Suomi) T. Farbregd et al. French & Eur.
Finnish-Norwegian Norwegian-Finnish Pocket Dictionary. Farbregd & Kamarainen. Kunnskapsforlaget.
Francais-Norvegien-Francais Lommerorbok. E. Daae. French & Eur.
French-Norwegian Dictionary. Line Dedichen. Kunnskapsforlaget.
German-Norwegian Dictionary. Haukoy & Zickfeldt. Kunnskapsforlaget.
German-Norwegian Dictionary of Technical Terms. D. Strom & J. A. Strom. Kunnskapsforlaget.
Greek-Norwegian Norwegian-Greek Pocket Dictionary. E. Theophilakis. Kunnskapsforlaget.
Gresk-Norsk-Gresk Lommeordbok. French & Eur.
International Planning Glossary. Ed. by Gordon Logie & Hemel Hemstead. Intl Plan Glos.
Italian-Norwegian Dictionary. M. Ulleland. Kunnskapsforlaget.
Italiensk-Norsk Ordbok. M. Ulleland. French & Eur.
Juridisk Leksikon. Egil Gulbransen. Tanum-Norli.
Karmannyi Russko-Norvezhskii Slovar. E. P. Gribanova. (Pub. by GINS). Four Continent.
Komunalteknisk Ordlista. Tekniska Nomenklaturcentralen. Tek Nomen.
Langenscheidts Handwoerterbuecher Norwegisch-Deutsch. Langenscheidt.
Langenscheidts Universal-Woerterbuch Norwegisch. Langenscheidt.
Langenscheidts Universal-Woerterbuecher Norwegisch-Deutsch. Langenscheidt.
Learn Norwegian for English Speakers. Saphrograph.
Lexicon Sopena: Diccionario de bolsillo, noruego-espanol y noruego-espanol. Sopena.
Litteraert Lekkikon. Asbjorn Aarnes. Tanum-Norli.
McKay's Modern Norwegian-English & English-Norwegian Dictionary. Ed. by B. Berulfsen & H. Scavenius. McKay.
Miljoleksikon. Norges Natur.
Min Forste Ordbok: English & Norwegian. R. Scarry. Vanous.
Naturgeografisk ordbok: Engelsk-Norsk. Roger G. Bennett. Berg Inst Sociol.
Norsk Dataordbok. Norsk Sprakrad. Universitetsforlaget.

Norsk-Engelsk Ordbok. Willie Kirkely. Vanous.
Norsk-Engelsk Ordbok. Willy Kirkeby. Kunnskapsforlaget.
Norsk-Engelsk Ordbok Praktisk. W. Guy & J. Messell. French & Eur.
Norsk Forkortingsbok. Stale Loland & Arnold Thorsen. J W Cappelens.
Norsk Landbruksordbok. Nikolai Nelvik. Samlaget.
Norsk-Nederlansk-Norsk. French & Eur.
Norsk-Portugisisk Ordbok. Kare Nilsson. Universitetsforlaget.
Norsk-Rumensk Lommeordbok med Liten Parloer. Elisabeta S. Guha. Universitetsforlaget.
Norsk-Svensk Ordbok. Nat. Beckman. Ed. by Leif Maehle & Bengt Sigurd. Esselte Studium.
Norsk-Svensk Ordbok. Natanael Beckman. Ed. by Lief Maehle & Bengt Sigurd. Esselte Studium.
Norsk-Tysk Ordbok. G. Paulsen. French & Eur.
Norvezhsko-Russkii Slovar. V. D. Arakin. (Pub. by GINS). Four Continent.
Norwegian Deluxe Dictionary: English-Norse. B. Berulfsen & A. Svenkerud. Vanous.
Norwegian Dictionary: Engelsk-Norwegina. B. Berulfsen & T. Berulfsen. Vanous.
Norwegian Dictionary: English-Norwegian. Ed. by L. Bjerke & H. Soraas. Vanous.
Norwegian Dictionary: Norsk-English. Scavenius Christophensen. Ed. by Willie Kirkeby. Vanous.
Norwegian Dictionary: Norwegian-English. G. Haugen. Vanous.
Norwegian-English Dictionary. T. Slette. Vanous.
Norwegian-English Dictionary. W. A. Kirkeby. Kunnskapsforlaget.
Norwegian-English Dictionary. W. A. Kirkeby. Kunnskapsforlaget.
Norwegian-English Dictionary of Commerce. Daae Gabrielsen. Kunnskapsforlaget.
Norwegian-English, English-Norwegian Dictionary. W. Kirkeby & B. Berulfsen. Heinman.
Norwegian-English, English-Norwegian Maritime-Technical Dictionary. P. Askim. Heinman.
Norwegian-English, English-Norwegian Technical Dictionary. J. Ansteinsson & A. T. Andreassen. Heinman.
Norwegian-English-Norwegian. Macmillan.
Norwegian-French Dictionary. M. Lesoil. Kunnskapsforlaget.
Norwegian-French Dictionary of Commerce. Daae Gabrielsen. Kunnskapsforlaget.
Norwegian-German Dictionary. Gerd Paulsen. Kunnskapsforlaget.
Norwegian-German Dictionary of Commerce. Daae Gabrielsen. Kunnskapsforlaget.
Norwegian-German Dictionary of Technical Terms. D. Strom & J. A. Strom. Kunnskapsforlaget.
Norwegian Pocket Dictionary. Heinman.
Norwegian Pocket Dictionary: English-Norwegian. Gyldendals. Vanous.
Norwegian-Spanish Dictionary. C. Blom-Dahl. Kunnskapsforlaget.
Norwegian-Spanish Dictionary of Commerce. H. Evjen. Kunnskapsforlaget.
Norwegian Technical Dictionary: English-Norwegian. J. Ansteinsson. Vanous.
Norwegian Technical Dictionary: Norwegian-English. Ed. by J. Ansteinsson. Vanous.
Norwegisch-Daenisches Etymologisches Woerterbuch. H. S. Falk & Alf Torp. (Pub. by Carl Winter). French & Eur.
Norwegisch-Daenisches Etymologisches Woerterbuch. H. S. Falk & Alf Torp. (Pub. by Carl Winter). French & Eur.
Norwegisch-Daenisches Etymologisches Woerterbuch. H. S. Falk & Alf Torp. Winter Univ.

Norwegisch-Daenisches
Etymologisches Woerterbuch. H. S.
Falk & Alf Torp. Winter Univ.
Norwegisch Daenisches
Etymologisches Woerterbuch: Mit
Literatur-Nachweisen Strittiger
Etymologien Sowie Deutschem und
Altnordischen Woerterverzeichnis.
H. S. Falk & Alf Torp. (Dist. by
Columbia U Pr). Universitet.
Riksmalsordboken: Norwegian
Dictionary. T. Gutu.
Kunnskapsforlaget.
Snaak Friisk: Interfriisk Leksikon. V.
Tams Jorgensen. Verein Nord.
Spanish-Norwegian Dictionary. S.
Loennecken. Kunnskapsforlaget.
Spansk-Norsk Ordbok. S.
Loennecken. French & Eur.
Teaterord. Niklas Brunius. Nord
Teater.
Vad Betyder Vaxtens Latinska Namn.
Ivar Anell. Forum Bok.
Woerterbucher der Fertigungstechnik
Daenisch-Norwegisch-Schwedisch-
Finnisch: Bd 1N, Schmieden-
Freiformschmeiden &
Gesenkschmieden. G. Pahlitzsch.
Girardet.

NORWEIGIAN

Norsk-Engelsk Ordbok. W. A.
Kirkeby & S. Utgabes. French &
Eur.

NUBIAN

English-Nubian Comparative
Dictionary. G. W. Murray. Ed. by
E. A. Hooton & Natica I. Bates.
Kraus Repr.

NYANJA

English-Nyanja Dictionary. Thomas
Price. Shalom.

OIRAT-MONGOLIAN

Materials for an Oirat-Mongolian to
English Citation Dictionary, Pt. 1.
John R. Krueger. Mongolia.

PALAUAN

Palauan-English Dictionary. Edwin G.
McManus et al. UH Pr.

PALI

A Dictionary of the Pali language.
Robert Childers. Orient Bk Dist.
Kapingamarangi Lexicon. Michael D.
Lieber & Kalio H. Dikepa. UH Pr.
Nukuoro Lexicon. Vern Carroll &
Tobias Soulik. UH Pr.
Pali-English Dictionary. A Budd
Hadatta Mahathera. Saphrograph.
The Pali Text Society's Pali-English
Dictionary. T. Rhys Davids. Intl
Pubns Serv.
Woleaian-English Dictionary. Ho-Min
Sohn & Anthony F. Tawerilmang.
UH Pr.

PAPAGO

A Dictionary of Papago Usage: Vol. I,
B-K. Madeleine Mathiot. Mouton.
Papago & Pima to English, English to
Papago & Pima Dictionary. Dean
Saxton & Lucille Saxton et al. Ed.
by R. L. Cherry. U of Ariz Pr.

PAPUAN

A Comparative Word List of the
Northern Adelbert Range
Languages, Madang Province,
Papua New Guinea. J. A.
Z'graggon. Linguistic Circle.
A Comparative Word List of the Rai
Coast Languages, Madang
Province, Papua New Guinea. J. A.
Z'graggon. Linguistic Circle.
A Comparative Word List of the
Southern Adelbert Range
Languages, Madang Province,
Papua New Guinea. J. A.
Z'graggon. Linguistic Circle.

PERSIAN

Abbreviated Military Dictionary.
French & Eur.
Abbreviated Russian-Persian
Technical Dictionary. French &
Eur.
Comprehensive Persian-English
Dictionary. F. Steingass. Intl Bk
Ctr.
A Comprehensive Persian-English
Dictionary. F. Steingass. South Asia
Bks.
Deutsch-Persisches Fachwoerterbuch
Fuer Naturwissenschaft, Medezin
und Landwirtschaft. B. Habibi.
(Pub. by Harrassowitz). French &
Eur.
Dictionary of Arabic-Persian Quotes.
Claud Field. Intl Bk Ctr.
Dictionary of Arabic-Persian Quotes.
Claud Field. Intl Bk Ctr.
Dictionary of Persian & English
Languages. Fazl-i-Ali. (Pub. by
Cosmo Pubns India). Orient Bk
Dist.
Dictionary of Persian Loan Words in
the Arabic Language. Al-Sayyid
Addi. Intl Bk Ctr.
A Dictionary of Persian Loan Words
in the Arabic Language.
Al-Sayyid'Addi Shir. Intl Bk Ctr.
Dizionario persiano-italiano classico,
moderno, familiare. Hanne Coletti
Gruenbaum. Coletti.
English Persian Dictionary. A. N.
Wollaston. (Pub. by Cosmo Pubns
India). Orient Bk Dist.
An English-Persian Dictionary
Compiled from Original Sources. A.
N. Wollaston. Humanities.
English-Persian Dictionary:
Romanized. Saphrograph.
Learn Persian for English Speakers.
Saphrograph.

Old Persian Grammar Texts Lexicon.
Roland G. Kent. Am Orient Soc.
Persian-English Dictionary. Steingass.
Iaconi.
Persian-English Dictionary,
Romanized. John A. Boyle.
Saphrograph.
Persian-English, English-Persian
Shorter Dictionary. S. Haim.
Heinman.
Persian Vocabulary. Ann K. Lambton.
Cambridge U Pr.
The Persian Vocabulary of the Codex
Cumanicus. Bodrogligeti. (Pub. by
Kaido Hungary). Heyden.
Persidsko-Russkii & Russko-Persidskii
Obshche-Ekonomicheskii &
Vneshnetorgovyi Slovar. (Pub. by
Vneshtorgizdat). Four Continent.
Persidsko-Russkii & Russko-Persidskii
Voennyi Slovar. G. G. Aliev. (Pub.
by Voenizdat). Four Continent.
Two Hundred One Persian Verbs -
Arabic Script. Wood. Barron.
Two Hundred One Persian Verbs -
Romanization. Wood. Barron.

PIDGIN

The Book of Pidgin English. John J.
Murphy. AMS Pr.

PIMA

Papago & Pima to English, English to
Papago & Pima Dictionary. Dean
Saxton & Lucille Saxton et al. Ed.
by R. L. Cherry. U of Ariz Pr.

POLISH

Architektura & Budownictwo. Witold
Szolginia. Wydawnictwa Naukowo.
Automatizacna Technika. Jiri Sykora.
Alfa-Vydavatel.
Bedekr Kaszubski. Roza Ostrowski &
Izabella Trojanwska. Wydawn.
Bolshoi Polsko-Russkii Slovar. (Pub.
by Russkii Iazyk). Four Continent.
Concise English-Polish & Polish-
English Dictionary. T.
Grzebieniowski. Barron.
Concise Polish-English-English-Polish
Dictionary. Iwo Pogonowski.
Hippocrene Bks.
Deutsch Lehnwoerter in der
Polnischen Bergbausprache. Konrad
Wypych. MG Schmitz.
Deutsche Lehnworter in der
Polnischen Bergbausprache. Konrad
Wypych. MG Schmitz.
Diccionario Simultaneo en 21
Idiomas. Juan Capdevilla Font.
French & Eur.
Diccionario Tecnico Espanol-Polaco.
Ed. by T. Weroniecki. French &
Eur.
Dictionar Tehnic Polon-Roman si
Roman-Polon. Friedrich Schattner.
Wydawnictwa Naukowo.
Dictionary English-Polish, Polish-
English. K. Bullas & F. J. Whitfield.
Adler.
Dictionary for the Graphic Arts in
Eight Languages: German-English-
French-Spanish-Russian-Hungarian-
Polish-Slowak. Perfect Graphic.
Dictionary of Acoustics: English-
German-French-Russian-Spanish-
Polish-Madarsko-Slovene. W.
Reichardt. French & Eur.
A Dictionary of Adam Mickiewicz's
Language: Vol. 1, A-C. (Pub. by
Ossolineum). Four Continent.
A Dictionary of Adam Mickiewicz's
Language: Vol. 2, D-6. (Pub. by
Ossolineum). Four Continent.
A Dictionary of Adam Mickiewicz's
Language: Vol. 3, H-K. (Pub. by
Ossolineum). Four Continent.
A Dictionary of Adam Mickiewicz's
Language: Vol. 4, L-M. (Pub. by
Ossolineum). Four Continent.
A Dictionary of Adam Mickiewicz's
Language: Vol. 5, N-O. (Pub. by
Ossolineum). Four Continent.

A Dictionary of Adam Mickiewicz's
Language: Vol. 6, P. (Pub. by
Ossolineum). Four Continent.
A Dictionary of Adam Mickiewicz's
Language: Vol. 7, P-R. (Pub. by
Ossolineum). Four Continent.
A Dictionary of Adam Mickiewicz's
Language: Vol. 8, S. (Pub. by
Ossolineum). Four Continent.
A Dictionary of Adam Mickiewicz's
Language: Vol. 9, T-W. (Pub. by
Ossolineum). Four Continent.
Dictionary of Automatical Technique.
Ed. by Jiri Sykora. French & Eur.
Dictionary of Chemical Terminology.
D. Kryt. Elsevier.
Dictionary of Chemical Terminology.
(Pub. by Vyd. Naukowo-
Techniczne). Four Continent.
Dictionary of Metallurgy. Ed. by A.
Dollinger. French & Eur.
Dictionary of Physical Metallurgy. E.
F. Tyrkiel. Elsevier.
Dictionary of Polish Pronunciation:
Slownik Wymomwy Polskiej PWN.
Hippocrene Bks.
A Dictionary of Slavic Word
Families. Louis J. Herman.
Columbia U Pr.
Dictionary of Surface-Active Agents,
Cosmetics & Toiletries. Ed. by G.
Cariere. Elsevier.
Dictionary of Surface Active Agents,
Cosmetics & Toiletries. G. Carriere.
Elsevier.
Dictionary of Technical Acoustics. L.
Reichardt. Adler.
Dictionary of the Graphic Arts
Industry. Ed. by W. Muller.
Elsevier.
Dictionary, Polish-English, English-
Polish: Contemporary Usage
American & Polish. Iwo
Pogonowski. Hippocrene Bks.
Dictionary Polish-English, English-
Polish Slovnik. Iwo Pogonowski.
Hippocrene Bks.
Dictionnaire de Poche, 1: Francais-
Polonais. Bernard Hamel.
Polonaises.
Dictionnaire de Poche, 2: Polonais-
Francais. Bernard Hamel.
Polonaises.
Dictionnaire Francais-Polonais.
Vander.
Dictionnaire International
Electrotechnique: Francais-Russe-
Anglais-Allemand-Italien-Suedois-
Hollandais-Polonais. Mir.
Dictionnaire International
Electrotechnique: Francais-Russe-
Anglais-Allemand-Espagnol-
Suedois-Hollandais-Polonais. Mir.
Dictionnaire Polonais-Francais.
Vander.
Dictionnaire Pratique Francais-
Polonais. K. Kupisz & B. Kielski.
French & Eur.
Dizionario polesano-italiano. P.
Mazzucchi. Forni.
Einwortlexeme & Wortgruppenlexeme
in der Technischen Terminologie
des Polnscheni. Herbert Matuschek.
Sagner.
Electronics Dictionary. (Pub. by
Collets). State Mutual Bk.
Encyklopedia Techniki. Henryk
Baniecki. Wydawnictwa Naukowo.
English-Polish & Polish-English
Compact Dictionary. Imported Bks.
English-Polish & Polish-English
Dictionary. J. Stanislawski. McKay.
English-Polish & Polish-English
Minimum Dictionary. K. Billip.
Wiedza Powszechna.
English-Polish Dictionary of Idioms &
Phrases. Pioter Borkowski.
Hippocrene Bks.
English-Polish Dictionary of Idioms &
Phrases. Piotr Borkowski.
Hippocrene Bks.
English-Polish Dictionary of Science
& Technology. (Pub. by Collets).
State Mutual Bk.
English-Polish Dictionary of Science
& Technology. (Pub. by Wydaw.
Naukowo-Techniczne). Four
Continent.
English-Polish-English Dictionary.
Saphrograph.
English-Polish Polish-English
Chemical Dictionary. Ed. by
Dobromila Kryt & Bazyli Semniuk.
Intl Pubns Serv.

English-Polish, Polish-English Dictionary. W. Kierst. Saphrograph.

Fachworterbuch Polygrafie: English-Deutsch-French-Russian-Spanish-Polish-Hungarian-Slowakian. French & Eur.

A Glossary of Polish & English Verb Forms. Stanislaw P. Kaczmarski. Panstwowe Zaklad W.

A Glossary of Polish & English Verb Forms. Stanisaw P. Kaczmarski. Panstwowy Zaklad W.

Glossary of Terms Used in Quality Control. Slownik Jakosci. (Pub. by Collets). State Mutual Bk.

Great English-Polish Dictionary. Ed. by Jan Stanislawski. Intl Pubns Serv.

The Great English-Polish Dictionary. Ed. by J. Stanislawski. (Pub. by Collet's). State Mutual Bk.

The Great English-Polish Dictionary. J. Stanislawski. French & Eur.

The Great Polish-English Dictionary. Ed. by J. Stanislawski. (Pub. by Collet's). State Mutual Bk.

The Great Polish-English Dictionary. J. Stanislawski. French & Eur.

Grobworterbuch Polnisch-Deutsch. J. Piprek & J. Ippoldt. French & Eur.

A Handy English-Polish Dictionary. (Pub. by Collet's). State Mutual Bk.

Illustrated English-Polish Polish-English Dictionary. Ed. by Tadeusz Grzebieniowski. Intl Pubns Serv.

Illustrated English-Polish Polish-English Dictionary. T. Grzebieniowski. (Pub. by Wiedza Powszechna). Four Continent.

Illustrowany Slownik Rosyjsko-Polski. Andrzej Bogusiawski. Wiedza Powszechna.

Illustrowany Slownik Rosyjsko-Polski, Polsko-Rosyjski. Andrzej Boguslawski. Wiedza Poswzechna.

Ilustrowany slownik angielsko-polski, polsko-angielski. Takeusz Grzebieniowski. Wiedza Powszechna.

Ilustrowany Slownik Niemiecko-Polski. Wanda Brzeska & Alojzy Brzeski. Wiedza Powszechna.

Ilustrowany Slownik Niemiecko-Polski. Wanda Brzeska et al. Wiedza Powszechna.

Ilustrowany Slownik Samochodowy. Czeslaw Blok. Wydawnictwa.

International Microcomputer Dictionary. Sybex Staff & Rodnay Zaks. Sybex.

Karmannyi Polsko-Russkii & Russko-Polskii Slovar. G. V. Sinitsyna & I. N. Mitronova. Russkii Iazyk.

Karmannyi Pol'Sko-Russkii & Russko-Polskii Slovar. I. N. Mitronova et al. (Pub. by Russkii Iazyk). Four Continent.

Karmannyi Polsko-Russkii i Russko-Polskii Slovar. Four Continent.

Kleinworterbuch Deutsch-Polnisch (Handy German-Polish Dictionary) S. Schimitzek et al. French & Eur.

The Kosciuszko Foundation English-Polish, Polish-English Dictionary. Kazimierz Bulas et al. Kosciuszko.

Landwirtschaftliches Woerterbuch in Acht Sprachen. (Pub. by BLV). French & Eur.

Langenscheidts Handwoerterbuecher Deutsch-Polnisch. Ed. by Chodera & Kubica. Langenscheidt.

Langenscheidts Handwoerterbuecher Polnisch-Deutsch. Langenscheidt.

Langenscheidts Taschenwoerterbuch Polnisch. Stanislaw Walewski. Langenscheidt.

Langenscheidts Taschenwoerterbuch Polnisch: Teil II, Deutsch-Polnisch. Stanislaw Walewski. Langenscheidt.

Langenscheidts Taschenwoerterbuch Polnisch: Teil I, Polnisch-Deutsch. Stanislaw Walewski. Langenscheidt.

Langenscheidts Universal-Woerterbuch Polnisch. Langenscheidt.

Langenscheidts Universal-Woerterbuecher Polnisch-Deutsch. Langenscheidt.

Leksykon Wiedzy Wojskowej. Mariana Laprusa. Wydaw Min. Obrony Narodowej.

Lengyel-Magyar Szotar. Istvan Varsanyi. Terra.

Lexicon Medicum. Boleslaw Zlotnickiego. French & Eur.

Lexicon Medicum: Medizinisches Woerterbuch in 6 Sprachen; Englisch, Russisch, Franzoesisch, Deutsch, Latein, Polnisch. B. Zlotnicki. Langenscheidt.

Lexicon of International & National Units. Ed. by M. Merino-Rodriguez. Elsevier.

Lexikon Medicum. B. Zlotnicki. French & Eur.

Magyar-Lengyel Szotar. Istvan Varsanyi. Terra.

Magyar-Lengyel Szotar. Istvan Varsanyi. Terra.

Maly Slownik Antropologiczny. Ed. by Tadeusz Bielecki. Wiedza Powszechna.

Maly Slownik Finsko-Polski & Polski-Finski. Elsa Salamaa. Kirjayhtyma.

Maly Slownik Francusko-Polski. Ludwik Szwykowski et al. Wiedza Powszechna.

Maly Slownik Hispansko-Polski & Polsko-Hiszpanski. Antonio Marti Marca et al. Wiedza Powszechna.

Maly Slownik Kultury Antycznej. Lida Winniczuk. Wiedza Powszechna.

Maly Slownik Polsko-Swedzki. Lech Sikorski. Plastik.

Maly Slownik Szwedzko-Polski. Lech Sikorski. Wiedza Powszechna.

Maly Slownik Techniczny Niemiecko i Polski-Niemiecki. M. Sokolowska & J. Szarski. Wydawnictwa Naukowo.

Maly Slownik Wlosko-Polski. Stanislaw Soja et al. Wiedza Powszechna.

Maly Slownik Wlosko-Polski & Polsko-Wloski. Stanislaw Soja et al. Wiedza Powszechna.

Maly Slownik Zoologiczny. Kazlmierz Kowalski. Wiedza Powszechna.

Medical Dictionary. B. Zoltnicki. (Pub. by Schattauer). French & Eur.

Medizintechnik. Albert Von Roald & Harry Hahnewald. VEB Verlag Technik.

Medizintechnik-Englisch-Deutsch-Franzoesisch-Russisch-Spanisch-Polnisch-Ungarisch-Slowakisch. Roald Albert & Harry Hahnewald. VEB Technik.

Mianownictwo Histologiczne. Marka Wawrzyniak. Panstowy Zaklad W.

Minimum-Worterbuch: Deutsch-Polnisch, Polnisch-Deutsch. J. Jozwicki. French & Eur.

Music Translation Dictionary: An English, Czech, Danish, Dutch, French, German, Hungarian, Italian, Polish, Portuguese, Russian, Spanish, Swedish Vocabulary of Music. Compiled by Carolyn D. Grigg. Greenwood.

Mykologisches Worterbuch. K. Berger. French & Eur.

Mykologisches Worterbuch. Karl Von Berger. Fischer Verlag.

Narwiska Obce w Jezyku Polskim. Izabela Bartminska et al. Panstwowe Zaklad W.

Nazwiska Obce w Jezyku Polskim. Izabela Bartminska. Panstwowe Zaklad W.

The New Polish-English Dictionary. Iwo Pognowski. Hippocrene Bks.

Okrety i Zegluga. Zbigniew Grzywaczewski. Wydawnictwa Naukowo.

Pequeno Diccionario Espanol-Polaco, Polaco-Espanol. A. Marti & J. Marti et al. French & Eur.

Pieciojezyczny Slownik Gleboznawczy. Adamczyk Boleslaw. Panstwowe Zaklad W.

Podreczny Slownik Polsko-Francuski. Kazimierz Kupisz et al. Wiedza Powszechna.

Podreczny Slownik Polsko-Niemiecki (Manual Dictionary Polish-German) A. Bzdega et al. French & Eur.

Podreczny Slownik Polsko-Rosyjski. Ryszard Stypula et al. Wiedza Powszechna.

Polish-English - English-Polish Dictionary. Kierst. Saphrograph.

Polish-English & English-Polish Dictionary. J. Stanislawski. McKay.

Polish-English Dictionary of Science & Technology. Ed. by Sergiusz Czerni & Maria Skrzynska. Intl Learn Syst.

Polish-English Dictionary of Science & Technology. Czerni & Skrzynka. (Pub. by Collets). State Mutual Bk.

Polish-English, English-Polish Dictionary (1975) J. Stanislawski. Heinman.

Polish-English, English-Polish Dictionary. Tadeus Z. Grzebienowski. Hippocrene Bks.

Polish-English, English-Polish Practical Dictionary. J. Stanislawski. Heinman.

Polish-English Practical Dictionary. J. Stanisljawski et al. Vanous.

Polish Great Dictionary, Vol. 1: English-Polish. Jan Stanislawski. Vanous.

Polish Great Dictionary, Vol. 2: Polish-English. J. Stanislowski. Vanous.

Polish Pocket Dictionary. Heinman.

Polish Practical Dictionary (English-Polish) J. Stanislawski & K. Billip. Vanous.

Polish-Russian Dictionary of Economics. M. N. Osmowej. French & Eur.

Polish-Russian, Russian-Polish Dictionary. I. Nitronowa et al. French & Eur.

Polish Science & Technology Dictionary: English-Polish. S. Czerni & M. Skrzynska. Vanous.

Polish Science & Technology Dictionary: Polish-English. S. Czerni & M. Skrzynska. Vanous.

Polnisch. Stanislaw Walewski. Langenscheidt.

Polnisch-Deutsches Wissenschaftlich-Technishes Worterbuch. Z. J. Koch. French & Eur.

Polska Gwara Konspiracyjno-Partyzancka Czasu Okupacji Hitlerowskiej. Stanislaw Kania & Zielona Gora et al. Wyzsza Szkola.

Polsko -Slovensky a Slovensko-Polsky Slovnik. Mikulas Stano. SNTC.

Polsko-Litovskii Slovar. V. A. Vaitkiavichiute. (Pub. by Mokslas). Four Continent.

Polsko-Ruskii Khimicheskii Slovar. I. A. Titova. (Pub. by Sov Entsiklopediia). Four Continent.

Polsko-Russkii Ekonomicheskii Slovar. (Pub. by Russkii Iazyk). Four Continent.

Polsko-Russkii Gornyi Slovar. (Pub. by Russkii Iazyk). Four Continent.

Polsko-Russkii Razgovornik Dlia Turistov. (Pub. by Russkii Iazyk). Four Continent.

Pol'sko-Slovensky a Slovensko-Polsky Slovnik. Mikulas Stano et al. SNTC.

Polygrafie-Englisch-Deutsch-Franzoesisch-Russisch-Spanisch-Polnisch-Ungarisch-Solwakisch. Wolfgang Muller. VEB Technik.

A Practical English-Polish Dictionary. Jan Stanislawski. Intl Pubns Serv.

A Practical English-Polish Dictionary. J. Stanislawski et al. French & Eur.

A Practical Polish-English Dictionary. Jan Stanislawski. Intl Pubns Serv.

A Practical Polish-English Dictionary. J. Stanislawski. French & Eur.

Practical Polish-English Dictionary: Polish-English; English-Polish. Iwo Pogonowski. Hippocrene Bks.

Recueil Terminologique Multilinque du Soudage et des Techniques Connexes. French & Eur.

Russian-Polish Political Dictionary. B. Dudawaki et al. French & Eur.

Russko-Pol'skii Politekhnicheskii Slovar. V. I. Dudavskii et al. (Pub. by Gosizdat Tekhn. Teoretich. Lit.). Four Continent.

Shorter Technological Dictionary: English-Polish, Polish-English. (Pub. by Wydaw. Naukowo-Tech.).

O Slownictwie Statystycznie Rzadkim. Jadwiga Sambor. Panstwowe Zaklad W.

Slownik Elektroniczny Polsko-Angielsko-Rosyjski. Ewa Sozanskiej. Wydawnictwa Naukowo.

Slownik Finsko-Polski. Stanislaw Walega. Wiedza Powszechna.

Slownik Immunologiczny Ilustrowany. Stefan Slopek. Panstwowe Zaklad W.

Slownik Informatyki Polsko-Angielsko-Rosyjski. Wydawnictwa Naukowo.

Slownik Jezyka Niby-Polskiego, Czyli Bledy Jezykowe. W. Pisarek. (Pub. by Ossolineum). Four Continent.

Slownik Jezyka Polskiego dia Cudzoziemcow. Stanislawa Hrabcowa et al. Wydaw-a UW.

Slownik Kieszonkowy Polsko-Rosyjski. Inessa N. Mironova. Russkii Iazyk.

Slownik Lekarski Lacinsko-Polski. Jerzy Babecki. Panstwowe Zaklad W.

Slownik Lekarski Polsko-Angielski. Sabian Jedraszko. Panstwowy Zaklad W.

Slownik Lekarski Polsko-Niemiecki. Boleslaw Zlotnicki. Panstwowe Zaklad W.

Slownik Minimum Francusko-Polski. Leon Bielas. Wiedza Powszechna.

Slownik Podstawowy Jezyka Polskiego dia Cudzoziemcow. Barbara Bartnicka & Roxana Sinielnikoff. Wydaw-a U. W.

Slownik Podstawowy Jezyka Polskiego dia Cudzoziemcow. Barbara Bartnicka et al. Wydaw-a UW.

Slownik Polskiej Terminologii Chemicznej. Antoni Basinski. Wydawnictwa Naukowo.

Slownik Polsko-Rosyjski. Ryszard Stypula et al. Wiedza Powszechna.

Slownik Poprawnej Polszczyzny. Ed. by W. Doroszewski. (Pub. by Panstwowe Wydawnictwo Naukowe). Four Continent.

Slownik Skrotow w Medycynie i Naukach Pokrewnych. Jerzy Babecki & Anna Maksys. Panstwowe Zaklad W.

Slownik Tekarski Polsko-Lacinksi. Jerzy Babecki. Panstwowe Zaklad W.

Slownik Terminologiczny Sztuk Pieknych. Stefana Kozaklewicz. Panstwowe Wydawnictwo Iskry.

Slownik Terminow z Zakresu Informatyki. Bronislawa Lenczewska. Politekens Forlag.

Slownik Wspolczesnego T Atru: Tworcy, Teatry, Teorie. E. Wysinska. (Pub. by Wydaw. Artystyczne & Filmowe). Four Continent.

Suomi-Poula Suomi Dictionary: Finnish-Polish-Finnish. A. Krawczykiewicz. French & Eur.

Szkolny Slownik Terminow Nauki i Jezyku. J. Malczewski. (Pub. by Wydaw. Szkolne & Pedagogiczne). Four Continent.

Technische Akustik. Walter Reichardt. VEB Verlag Technik.

Tysiac Slow o Samolocie i Lotnictwie. Jerzy Domanski. Wydaw. Min. Obrony Narodowej.

Vocabulaire des Termes: Essentiels Utilises pour la Transmissien Ligne; Francais-Espagnol-Russe-Allemand-Italien-Neerlandais-Polonais-Portugais-Suedois. U. I. T.

Vocabularios Aleman-Espanol-Polaco. Novaro.

Wielki Slownik Polsko-Angielski. Jan Stanislawski. Wiedza Powszechna.

Wielki Slownik Polsko-Niemiecki: Grosswoerterbuch Polnische-Deutsch. Jan Piprek & Juliusz Ippoldt. Wiedza Powszechna.

Wielki Slownik Polsko-Rosyski (Polish-Russian Dictionary) Mirowicz. French & Eur.

Woerterbuch der Elektronik. Leonhard Schneider. French & Eur.

PONAPEAN

Ponapean-English Dictionary.
Kenneth L. Rehg & Damian G.
Sohl. UH Pr.

PORTUGUESE

Basic Words in Portuguese. Pan Am
Bk Co.
Berlitz Pocket Dictionaries:
Portuguese-English-Portuguese.
Berlitz. Macmillan.
Berlitz Portuguese for Travellers.
Berlitz Editors. (Berlitz).
Macmillan.
Collins GEM Dictionary: Portuguese-
English, English-Portuguese.
Imported Bks.
Concise Dictionary Portuguese-
English. Michaelis. Iaconi.
De Pina's Technical Dictionary.
Avelino De Pina Araujo. McGraw.
Diccionario Biblico: Broch. A. R.
Buckland. Life Pubs Intl.
Diccionario Biblico: Enc. A. R.
Buckland. Life Pubs Intl.
Diccionario Brasileiro
Contemporaneo. F. Fernandes.
French & Eur.
Diccionario Brevis duplex: Portugues-
catellano y castellano-portugues.
Sopena.
Diccionario de Verbos e Regimes.
Fernandes. French & Eur.
Diccionario Enciclopedias Labor. Ed.
by Javier Lasso de La Vega & Jose
M. Rubert Candau. French & Eur.
Diccionario Fraseologico Comercial.
Zavada & Eberle et al. French &
Eur.
Diccionario Lexicon Portugues-
Espanol, Espanol-Portugues. French
& Eur.
Diccionario Manual Espanol-
Portugues, Portugues-Espanol. Julio
Da Conceicao Fernandes. French &
Eur.
Diccionario Parvus duplex: Portugues-
castellano y castellano-portugues.
Sopena.
Diccionario Portugues-Espanol. Julio
da Conceicao Fernandes. French &
Eur.
Diccionario Portugues-Espanol,
Espanol-Portugues. David Ortega
Cavero. French & Eur.
Diccionario portugues-espanol,
espanol-portugues. David Ortega
Cavero & Julio Da Conceica.
Sopena.
Diccionario portugues-espanol y
espanol-portugues. Mayfe.
Diccionario Pratico Russo-Portugues.
N. Voinova & S. Starets. French &
Eur.
Diccionario Simultaneo en 21
Idiomas. Juan Capdevilla Font.
French & Eur.
Diccionario Simultaneo en 6 Idiomas.
Juan Capdevila Font. French &
Eur.
Dicionario Basico do Ingles Moderno.
Edicoes Melhoramentos. Edicoes
Melhoramentos.
Dicionario Basico Escolar Koogan-
Larousse. Antonio Houaiss. Edit
Atica.
Dicionario Basico Michaelis.
Imported Bks.
Dicionario Conciso da Lingua
Portuguesa. Ed. by Antonio N.
Machado. Didel Difusao.
Dicionario Conciso da Lingua
Portuguesa. Antonio N. Machado.
Difel Editorial, S. A.
Dicionario da Lingua Portuguesa. F.
Fernandes. French & Eur.
Dicionario da Lingua Portuguesa. J.
Almeida Costa & Sampaio de Melo.
Imported Bks.

Dicionario de Acoes & de
Procedimentos Judiciais. Yara
Muller Leite. Saraiva SA.
Dicionario de Administracao de
Recursos Humanos com Termos:
Ingles-Portugues, Portugues-Ingles.
F. Toledo & B. Milioni. French &
Eur.
Dicionario de Alemao-Portugues.
Porto Ed.
Dicionario de Biologia. M.
Abercrombie et al. Pub Euro Am.
Dicionario de Bolso Portugues-
Alemao. Difel Difusao.
Dicionario de Bolso Portugues-
Frances. Difel Difusao.
Dicionario de Bolso Portugues-Russo.
I. Chalaguina. French & Eur.
Dicionario de Bolso Russo-
Portugues. C. Nunes. French &
Eur.
Dicionario de ciencia. E. B. Uvarov et
al. Pub Euro Am.
Dicionario de Direito do Trabalho.
Christovao P. Malta. Rio Grafica.
Dicionario de Eisica-Illustrado. Edit
Atica.
Dicionario de Expressoes Idiomaticas
da Lingua Inglesa. B. B. Fraenkel.
Imported Bks.
Dicionario de Expressoes Idiomaticas
Ingles-Portugues. Dauster C.
Almeida. Auer.
Dicionario de Frances-Portugues.
Porto Ed.
Dicionario de Frances-Portugues.
Porto Ed.
Dicionario de Frances-Portugues:
Com Transcicao Fonetica. Jose De
Sousa Vieira. Porto Ed.
Dicionario de Geografia do Brasil.
Imported Bks.
Dicionario de Historia do Brasil.
Imported Bks.
Dicionario de Ingles-Portugues. Porto
Ed.
Dicionario de Ingles-Portugues. Porto
Ed.
Dicionario de Ingles-Portugues
"Editora". Armando De Morais.
Porto Editora.
Dicionario de Ingles-Portugues
"Escolares". Porto Editora.
Dicionario de Plantas Oteis do Brasil.
Eric P. Danger. Difel Difusao.
Dicionario de Portugues-Alemao.
Porto Ed.
Dicionario de Portugues-Espanol.
Julio Martinez Almoyna. Porto
Editora.
Dicionario de Portugues-Ingles. Porto
Ed.
Dicionario de Portugues-Ingles. Porto
Ed.
Dicionario de Sinonimos. Tertulia
Edipica. Porto Editora.
Dicionario de Sinonimos e Antonimos
da Lingua Portuguesa. F. Fernandes
& C. P. Luft. French & Eur.
Dicionario de termos tecnicos Ingles-
Portugues. Eugenio Furstenau.
Editora Globo.
Dicionario de termos tecnicos Ingles-
Portugues, Portugues-Ingles. B.
Fraenkel. Imported Bks.
Dicionario do Brasil Central. B. W.
Ortencio. Edit Atica.
Dicionario Escolar de Quimica.
Horacio Macedo. Edit Atica.
Dicionario Espanhol-Portugues &
Portugues-Espanhol. Idel Becker.
Liv Nobel.
Dicionario Frances-Portugues de
Locucoes. Aluizio Mendes Campos.
Edit Atica.
Dicionario Frances-Portugues,
Portugues-Frances. S. Burtin
Vinholes et al. Editora Globo.
Dicionario Frances-Portugues. Difel.
Difel Editorial, S. A.
Dicionario Ingles-Portugues. H.
Aliandro. French & Eur.
Dicionario Ingles-Portugues de
Economia. F. N. Santos. Pub Euro
Am.
Dicionario Juridico Brasileiro:
Contendo Termos, Expressoes
Idiomaticas & Brocardos Usuais em
Direito. Yara M. Leite. Saraiva SA.
Dicionario Latino-Portugues.
Francisco Torrinha. Porto Ed.
Dicionario Melhoramentos da lingua
Portuguesa. Imported Bks.

Dicionario Metalurgico Ingles-
Portugues, Portugues-Ingles. James
L. Taylor. Imported Bks.
Dicionario Portugues-Ingles. Intl
Learn Syst.
Dicionario Portugues-Ingles. H.
Aliandro. French & Eur.
Dicionario pratico ilustrado. Lello &
Irmao.
Dicionario Professional de Relacoes
Publicas & Comunicacao &
Glossario. Candido T. Andrade.
Saraiva SA.
Dicionario Tecnico Contabil:
Portugues-Ingles, Ingles-Portugues.
M. Altman. French & Eur.
Dicionario Tecnico Industrial. Edson
Bini. Hemus-Livraria.
Dicionario Tecnico Ingles-Portugues.
Joaquim A. Martins. Pub Euro Am.
Dicionarios de Linguistica. Zelio dos
Santos Jota. Prensa Acad.
Dictionario de Portugues-Frances.
Porto Ed.
Dictionario Italiano Portugues. Joao
Amendola. Ed. by Macim Behar &
Mario Moretti. Hemus-Livraria.
Dictionnaire Bilingue Apollo
Francais-Portugais. Fernando V.
Peixoto da Fonseca. Larousse.
Dictionnaire Bilingue Larousse,
Francais-Portugais et Portugais-
Francais. F. Peixoto Da Fonseca.
Larousse.
Dictionnaire de la presse ecrite et
audiovisuelle. Divers. Maison
Dictionnaire.
Dictionnaire d'informatique. Georges
Nania. Maison Dictionnaire.
Dictionnaire d'informatique: Francais-
Anglais-Italien-Espagnol-Portugais.
G. Nania. Maison Dictionnaire.
Dictionnaire Europa Francais-
Portugais. Larousse.
Dictionnaire Francais-Portugais.
Domingos De Azevedo. Garnier.
Dictionnaire Lilliput Bilingue
Francais-Portugais. Larousse FR.
Dictionnaire Portugais-Francais.
Domingos De Azevedo. Garnier.
Dictionnaire Portugais-Francais.
Ersilio Cardoso. Garnier.
Dictionnaire Portugais-Francais.
Larousse.
Dictionnaire Portugais-Francais.
Ersillo Cardoso. Garnier.
Dictionnaire Technologique:
Supplement Portugais. R. Mertz De
Mertzenteld et al. Maison
Dictionnaire.
Dizionario completo italiano-
portoghese (brasiliano) e portoghese
(brasiliano)-italiano. Vincenzo
Spinelli & Mario Casasanta. Hoepli.
Dizionario completo italiano-
portoghese (brasiliano) e portoghese
(brasiliano)-italiano. Vincenzo
Spinelli & Mario Casasanta. Hoepli.
Dizionario Completo Italiano-
Portoghese (Brasiliano), Portoghese
(Brasiliano)-Italiano: Con
L'etimologia Delle Voci Italiane e
Portoghesi (Brasiliane), la Loro
Esatta Traduzione, Frasi e Modi Di
Dire. S F Vanni.
Dizionario italiano-portoghese. Biava.
Vallardi A.
Dizionario Italiano-Portoghese,
Portoghese-Italiano. A. Biava.
French & Eur.
Dizionario portoghese-italiano.
Parlagreco. Vallardi A.
Dizionario Portoghese-Italiano,
Italiano-Portoghese. C. Parlagreco.
French & Eur.
Elseviers Automobile Dictionary. Ed.
by G. Schuurmans. Elsevier.
Elsevier's Dictionary of Criminal
Science. J. A. Adler. Elsevier.
Elseviers Rubber Dictionary. Elsevier.
Enciclopedia simultanea de
correspondencia comercial en seis
idiomas. Distein.
English-Portuguese Dictionary. J.
Albino Ferreira. Ed. by O. De
Morais. Shalom.
English-Portuguese Metallurgical
Dictionary. James L. Taylor.
Imported Bks.
Expressoes Idiomaticas Inglesas:
English Idioms. W. G. Kennedy &
Maria Silva. Imported Bks.
Fachwoerterbuch der Luftfahrt. J.
Osenton. Oldenbourg Verlag.

Finnish-Portuguese-Finnish
Dictionary. K. Rahinantti. French
& Eur.
Gem Language Dictionaries:
Portuguese-English & English-
Portuguese. S&S.
Glossaire des Mots Espagnols et
Portugais Derives de L'arabe. R.
Dozy. Intl Bk Ctr.
Grande Dicionario da Lingua
Portuguesa. Candido De
Figueiredo. Difel Difusao.
Grande Dicionario Frances-Portugues.
Ersilio Cardoso. Difel Difusao.
Grande Dicionario Portugues-Frances.
Domingos De Azevedo. Difel
Difusao.
Great technical dictionary. Paulo C.
Camarao et al. Ao Livro Tecnico.
Great Technical Dictionary:
Dicionario Tecnico English-
Portuguese. P. C. Camarao & M. A.
Serra. French & Eur.
Harrap Portuguese-English
Dictionary. James L. Taylor.
Harrap.
Harrap's English-Brazilian Portuguese
Business Dictionary. Ed. by
Terence Lewis et al. Harrap.
Harrap's Modern Portuguese &
English Dictionary. Ed. by Milton
S. Pereira & Maria S. Pereira.
Harrap.
Langenscheidt English-Portuguese
Lilliput Dictionary. Langenscheidt.
Langenscheidt Portuguese-English
Lilliput Dictionary. Langenscheidt.
Langenscheidt's Lilliput English-
Portuguese Dictionary. Am Map.
Langenscheidt's Lilliput Portuguese-
English Dictionary. Am Map.
Langenscheidts Taschenwoerterbuch
Portugiesisch. A. E. Beau & F.
Irmen. Langenscheidt.
Langenscheidts Taschenwoerterbuch
Portugiesisch: Teil II, Deutsch-
Portugiesisch. A. E. Beau.
Langenscheidt.
Langenscheidts Taschenwoerterbuch
Portugiesisch: Teil I, Portugiesisch-
Deutsch. F. Irmen. Langenscheidt.
Langenscheidts
Taschenwoerterbuecher
Portugiesisch. Langenscheidt.
Langenscheidts
Taschenwoerterbuecher
Portugiesisch-Deutsch. F. Irmen.
Langenscheidt.
Langenscheidt's Universal
Portuguese-English, English-
Portuguese Dictionary. Am Map.
Langenscheidts Universal-
Woerterbuch Portugiesisch.
Langenscheidt.
Langenscheidts Universal-
Woerterbuecher Portugiesisch-
Deutsch. Langenscheidt.
Learn Portuguese for English Speakers.
Saphrograph.
Lello Popular: Novo Dicionario
Ilustrado Luso-Brasileiro. Lello &
Irmao.
Lexicon comercial internacional:
Espanol, frances, ingles, italiano,
portugues y aleman. J. Vicens
Carrio. Reverte SA.
Lexicon of International & National
Units. Ed. by M.
Merino-Rodriguez. Elsevier.
Lilliput Dictionary. Langenscheidt.
Lilliput Dictionary. Langenscheidt.
McKay's Modern Portuguese-English
& English-Portuguese Dictionary.
Ed. by Elbert L. Richardson et al.
McKay.
McKay's Modern Portuguese-English,
English-Portuguese Dictionary.
Richardson & Pereira. Imported
Bks.
Meu Primeiro Dicionario Ilustrado de
Ingles. Dixson & Fox. Imported
Bks.
Minidicionario da Lingua Portuguesa.
Aurelio Buarque de Holanda
Ferreira. Edit Atica.
Multilingual Computer Dictionary.
Ed. by Alan Isaacs. Facts on File.
The Multilingual Computer
Dictionary. Alan Isaacs. Facts on
File.

Music Translation Dictionary: An English, Czech, Danish, Dutch, French, German, Hungarian, Italian, Polish, Portuguese, Russian, Spanish, Swedish Vocabulary of Music. Compiled by Carolyn D. Grigg. Greenwood.

New Michaelis Illustrated Dictionary: English-Portuguese, Portuguese English. Imported Bks.

Norsk-Portugisisk Ordbok. Kare Nilsson. Universitetsforlaget.

Novo Dicionario Pratico da Lingua Portuguesa. Janio Quadros & Ubiratan Rosa. Editora Rideet.

Novo Michaelis, Dicionario Ilustrado. Fritz Pietzschke. Ed. by Wilson Mariotti. Edicoes Melhoramentos.

Pequeno Dicionario de Arte Poetica. Geir Campos. Editora Cultrix.

Pequeno Dicionario Enciclopedico Koogan Larouse. Ed. by Antonio Houaiss. Larousse.

Pequeno Dicionario Michaelis: English-Portuguese, Portuguese English. Imported Bks.

Pequeño diccionario Michaelis Inglés-Portuguese. Iaconi.

Portuagalsko-Russkil Politekhnicheskil Slovar. Vladimir S. Matveev & Konstantin G. Asrhants. Russkii Iazyk.

Portugal-Magyar Szotar. Rudolf Kiraly. Akademiai Kiado.

Portugalsko-Cesko-Portugalsky Kapesni Slovnik. Zdenek Hampl & Jiri Holsan. SNTC.

Portugalsko-Cesky Slovnik. Zdenek Hampl. SNTC.

Portugiesisch. Incl. Langenscheidt.

Portuguese-English Dictionary. J. Albino Ferreira. Ed. by A. De Morais. Shalom.

A Portuguese-English Dictionary. James L. Taylor. Stanford U Pr.

Portuguese-English Dictionary. Berlitz Editors. (Berlitz). Macmillan.

Portuguese-English Dictionary. Hygino Aliandro. Imported Bks.

Portuguese-English, English-Portuguese Basic Dictionary. Michaelis. Heinman.

Portuguese-English, English-Portuguese Dictionary. J. A. Ferreira. Heinman.

Portuguese-English, English-Portuguese Dictionary. M. J. Martins. Heinman.

Portuguese-English, English-Portuguese Illustrated Dictionary: The New Michaelis. Ed. by F. Pietzschke. Heinman.

Portuguese-English, English-Portuguese Technical Dictionary. Araujo A. De Pina. Heinman.

Portuguese-English-Portuguese. Macmillan.

Portuguese-Hungarian Concise Dictionary. R. Kiraly. French & Eur.

Portuguese Pocket Dictionary. Michaelis. Heinman.

Satzlexikon der Handelskorrespondenz. Zavada & Eberle. Brandstetter.

Seven Language Dictionary. Ed. by David Shumaker. Crown.

Seven Languages Dictionary. Imported Bks.

Suomi-Portugali-Suomi. Kristina Rahinantti et al. Werner Soderstrom.

Technologisches Woerterbuch Franzoisisch. Martin Pabst. (Pub. by Verlag W. Girardet). French & Eur.

Technologisches Woerterbuch Franzoisisch. Martin Pabst. Girardet.

Universal Portuguese Dictionary. Langenscheidt.

Vocabulaire des Termes: Essentiels Utilises pour la Transmissien Ligne; Francais-Espagnol-Russe-Allemand-Italien-Neerlandais-Polonais-Portugais-Suedois. U. I. T.

Vocabulaire Multilingue de la Science du Sol: Anglais-Francais-Espagnol-Allemand-Portugais-Italien-Neerlandais-Suedois-Russe. G. V. Jacks & R. Tavernier. F. A. O.

Vocabulario do Cheque. J. Sidou. Editora Revista.

Vocabulario Galego-Portugues. M. Rodriguez Lapa. Galaxia.

Vocabulario Trabalhista: Direito do Trabalho, Processo do Trabalho, Previdencia Socail. Gerson Valle. Rio Grafica.

Vocabulario Vial. OAS General Secretariat. OAS.

Vocabularios Portugues-Espanol-Italiano. Novaro.

Woerterbuch der Industriellen Technik: Band VII, Deutsch-Portugiesisch. Ernst. Brandstetter.

Woerterbuch der Industriellen Technik: Band VIII, Portugiesch-Deutsch. Ernst. Brandstetter.

Woerterbuch der Industriellen Technik. R. Ernst. French & Eur.

Woerterbuch der Industriellen Technik. R. Ernst. French & Eur.

Woerterbucher der Fertigungstechnik Deutsch-Spanisch-Italienisch-Portugiesisch: Bd 1R, Schmieden-Freiformschmieden & Gesenkschmieden. G. Pahlitzsch. Girardet.

PROTO-AUSTRONES

English Finderlist of Reconstructions in Austronesian Languages. Stefan A. Wurm & Basil Wilson. Linguistic Circle.

QHESHWA

Diccionario de Ro de Qheshwa-Espanol, Espanol-Qheshwa. Jesus Lara. French & Eur.

Diccionaro de Qheshwa-Espanol, Espanol-Qheshwa. Jesus Lara. French & Eur.

QUECHUA

Diccionario Kollasuyo, Espanol-Quechua. Miguel Angel Quiroga Flores. Cochabamba.

Diccionario Polilectal del Quechua de Ancash. Gary J. Parker. Centro Invest.

Diccionario Quechua. Gary J. Parker. Minist Ed Caracas.

Diccionario Quechua Ayacucho-Chanca. Clodoaldo Soto Ruiz. Minist Ed Caracas.

Diccionario Quechua Cajamarca-Canaris. Felix Quesada Castillo. Minist Ed Caracas.

Diccionario Quechua Cuzco-Collao. Antonio G. Cusihuaman. Minist Ed Caracas.

Diccionario Quechua Junin-Huanca. Rodolfo Cerron-Palomino. Minist Ed Caracas.

Diccionario Quechua San Martin. Marinell Park & Nancy Weber. Ministerio de Educacion.

Diccionario Tri-lingue. Esteban S. Hornberger & H. N. Hornberger. LCA.

Diccionario Triqui de Chicahuaxtla. Claude Good. Inst Ling Ver.

Lexico Quechua de Cajamarca. Felix Quesada Castillo. Centro Invest.

Los Sufijos Posesivos en el Quechua del Huallaga. David J. Weber. Inst Ling Ver.

QUILEUTE

Quileute Dictionary. J. Powell. Univ Idaho.

RADE

A Rhade-English Dictionary with English-Rhade Finder List. James A. Tharp. Linguistic Circle.

RAPANUI

Diccionario Rapanui-Espanol, Redactado en la Isla de Pascua. Sebastian Englert. AMS Pr.

RIGA

Ergemes Izloksnes Vardnica. Elga Kagaine & S. Rage. Zinatne.

RITARU

Basic Material in Ritarungu. Jeffrey Heath. Linguistic Circle.

ROMANIAN

Cesko-Rumunsky & Rumunsko-Cesky Slovnik na Cesty. Jiri Felix. SNTC.

Diccionario de Mitologia Griega & Romana. Pierre Grimal & Francisco Payarois. Paidos Iberica.

Dictionar Analogic si de Sinonime al Limbii Romane. Ed. by M. Buca. Editura Stiintifica.

Dictionar Cronologie de Medicina si Farmacie. Gheorghe Bratescu. Editura Stiintifica.

Dictionar de Astronomie Astronautica. Calin Popovici. Editura Stiintifica.

Dictionar de Buzunar Roman-Rus. Victor Vascenco. Editura Stiintifica.

Dictionar de Chimie si Inginerie Chimica Rus-Roman. Dumitru Turtoi et al. Editura Stiintifica.

Dictionar de Cuvinte Calatoare. Alexandru Graur. Albatros.

Dictionar de Electrotehnica. Mihai Condruc. Editura Stiintifica.

Dictionar de Electrotehnica. Friedrich Schattner. Editura Stiintifica.

Dictionar de Electrotehnica. Friedrich Schattner. Editura Stiintifica.

Dictionar de Electrotehnik. Mihai Condruc. Editura Stiintifica.

Dictionar de Etnologie. Romulus Vulcanescu. Albatros.

Dictionar de Jazz. Mihai Berindei. Editura Stiintifica.

Dictionar de Metalurgie Englez-Roman. M. Breaban. Editura Stiintifica.

Dictionar de Metalurgie Francez-Roman. M. L. Breaban. Editura Stiintifica.

Dictionar de Muzica. Iosif Sava & Luminita Vartolomei. Editura Stiintifica.

Dictionar de psihologie. Paul Popescu-Neveanu. Albatros.

Dictionar de Rime. Mihail Eminescu. Ed. by Marin Bucur & Victoria A. Tausan. Albatros.

Dictionar de Stinta Solului. Ana Conea. Editura Stiintifica.

Dictionar Elementar de Stiinte. Marinca Marcu. Editura Stiintifica.

Dictionar englez-roman. Irina Panovf. Editura Stiintifica.

Dictionar Francez-Roman: Pentru uzul Elevilor. Marcel Saras. Editura Stiintifica.

Dictionar Frazeologic German-Roman. Editura Stiintifica.

Dictionar Frazeologic Italian-Roman. Mariana Stanciulescu-Cuza. Editura Stiintifica.

Dictionar Grec-Roman. Lambros Petinis. Editura Stiintifica.

Dictionar Juridic Penal. George Antoniu et al. Editura Stiintifica.

Dictionar Poliglot. Ernest M. Lates et al. Editura Stiintifica.

Dictionar Poliglot de Geodezie: Fotogrammetrie si Cartografie. Mihail Albota. Editura Stiintifica.

Dictionar Poliglot de Industrie Alimentara. Mihai Papa-Sotir. Editura Stiintifica.

Dictionar Poliglot de Matematica, Mecanica si Astronomie. Stefan Gheorghita. Editura Stiintifica.

Dictionar Portrativ Roman-Slovac, Slovac-Roman. Milota Bagonova-Sidlova. SNTC.

Dictionar Practic de Agronomie. Alexe. S. Potlog. Editura Stiintifica.

Dictionar Roman-German: Pentru uzul Elevilor. Jean Livescu & Emilia Savin. Editura Stiintifica.

Dictionar Roman-Grec. Socratis Cotolulis. Editura Stiintifica.

Dictionar Roman-Italian: Pentru uzul Elevilor. Doina Condrea-Derer. Editura Stiintifica.

Dictionar Roman-Spaniol: Pentru uzul Elevilor. Micaela Ghitescu. Editura Stiintifica.

Dictionar Roman-Turc. Mitica Grecu et al. Editura Stiintifica.

Dictionar Roman-Vietnamez. Elena Stoicovici et al. Tipografia.

Dictionar-Rus-Roman: Pentru uzual Elevilor. Eugen P. Noveannu. Editura Stiintifica.

Dictionar Scolar. Editura Didactica.

Dictionar Spaniol-Roman: Pentru uzul Elevilor. Editura Stiintifica.

Dictionar Tecnic Rus-Roman. Editura Stiintifica.

Dictionar Tehnic Auto de Buzunar in Sapte Limbi. Editura Stiintifica.

Dictionar Tehnic de Radio si Televiziune. Nicolae Stancin. Editura Stiintifica.

Dictionar Tehnic Polon-Roman si Roman-Polon. Friedrich Schattner. Wydawnictwa Naukowo.

Dictionar Turc-Roman. A. Baubec et al. Editura Stiintifica.

Dictionar Turistic International: Edition Roumaine. Academie Internationale du Tourisme. Acad Intl Tour.

Diccionario Simultaneo en 21 Idiomas. Juan Capdevilla Font. French & Eur.

Dictionnaire de la presse ecrite et audiovisuelle. Divers. Maison Dictionnaire.

Dictionnaire Francais-Romaneique. Emile Missir. Klincksieck.

English-Romanian Dictionary. Serban C. Andronescu. Am Inst Writing Res.

English-Romanian Dictionary. V. Levitchi & T. Bantas. (Pub. by Collet's). State Mutual Bk.

Karmannyi Rumynsko-Russkii Slovar. Four Continent.

Langenscheidts Universal-Woerterbuch Rumaenisch. Langenscheidt.

Langenscheidts Universal-Woerterbuecher Rumaenisch-Deutsch. Langenscheidt.

Lexikon Geologie Geografie Mine Petrol. Nicolae Mihailescu. Editura Stiintifica.

Mic Dictionar de Biologie. Teofil Craciun. Albatros.

Mic Dictionar de Cuvinte Perechi. Silviu Constantinescu. Albatros.

Mic Dictionar de Terminologie Lingvistica. G. Constantinescu-Dobridor. Albatros.

Mic Dictionar Folkloric: Spicuiri Folklorice si Etnografice Comparate. Tache Papahagi. Minerva Yugo.

Norsk-Rumensk Lommeordbok med Liten Parloer. Elisabeta S. Guha. Universitetsforlaget.

Romanian-English Dictionary & Grammar for the Mathematical Sciences. Ed. by S. H. Gould & P. E. Obreanu. Am Math.

Rumanian-English & Dictionary. M. Schonkron. Iaconi.

Rumanian-English, English-Rumanian Dictionary, with Supplement. Ed. by M. Schonkron. Ungar.

Russian-Rumanian Military Dictionary. French & Eur.

Rumynsko-Russkii Politekhnicheskii. B. A. Andrianov et al. (Pub. by Gostekhteorizdat). Four Continent.

Russko-Rumynskii Voennyi Slovar. Iu. A. Spazhev et al. (Pub. by Voenizdat). Four Continent.

Vocabularium Polyglottum Vitae Silvarum. R. Litschauer. Parey.

Vocabolario romagnolo-italiano. A. Morri. Forni.

Vocabolario romagnolo-italiano, italiano-romagnolo. Libero Ercolani. Edn Girasole.

Vocabularium Polyglottum Vitae Silvarum. R. Litschauer. (Pub. by P. Parey). French & Eur.

RUSSIAN

Abbreviated Military Dictionary. French & Eur.

Abbreviated Russian-Korean Dictionary. French & Eur.

Abbreviated Russian-Persian Technical Dictionary. French & Eur.

Abbreviated Turkish-Russian Dictionary of New Words. H. G. Antelava. French & Eur.

Akhmarsko-Russkii Slovar. E. B. Gankin. (Pub. by Sov Entsiklopediia). Four Continent.

Amglo-Russko-Nemetsko-Frantsuzskii Tolkovyi Slovar Po Vychislitel Noi Tekhnike & Obrabotke Dannykh. (Pub. by Russkii Iazyk). Four Continent.

Anglo-Ispano-Russko-Frantsuzskii Slovar Nauchnykh & Tekhnicheskikh Terminov Po Atomnoi Energii. (Pub. by United Nations Publications). Four Continent.

Anglo-Latyshsko-Russkii Frazeologicheskii Slovar. (Pub. by Liesma). Four Continent.

Anglo-Russkaia Terminologiia Po Organizatsii & Bezopasnosti Dorozhnogo Divizheniia. V. V. Sil'ianov et al. (Pub. by Viniti). Four Continent.

Anglo-russki i biologicheski i slovar. I. N. Afanaseva et al. Russkii Iazyk.

Anglo-russki i politekhnicheski. A. E. Cherukhina. Russky Yazyk.

Anglo-russki i slovar po okhrane okruzha i ushche i sredy. E. L. Milovanov et al. Russki Iazyk.

Anglo-Russkii Astronomicheskii Slovar. Ed. by O. A. Melnikov et al. (Pub. by Sov Entsiklopediia). Four Continent.

Anglo-Russkii Biologicheskii Slovar. Russkii Iazyk.

Anglo-Russkii Biologischeskii Slovar. (Pub. by Russkii Iazyk). Four Continent.

Anglo-Russkii Eknomicheskii Slovar. Ed. by A. V. Anikin. (Pub. by Russkii Iazyk). Four Continent.

Anglo-Russkii Elektrotekhnicheskii Slovar. Ed. by L. B. Geiler et al. (Pub. by Gosizdat Tekhn. Teoret.). Four Continent.

Anglo-Russkii Fizicheskii Slovar. Ed. by D. M. Tolstoi. (Pub. by Russkii Iazyk). Four Continent.

Anglo-Russkii Frazeologicheskii Slovar. A. V. Kunin et al. Four Continent.

Anglo-Russkii Iadernyi Slovar. Ed. by D. I. Doskoboinik et al. (Pub. by Glav. Red. Inostr. Nauchn. Tekhn. Slovarei Fizmatgiza). Four Continent.

Anglo-Russkii Politekhnicheskii Slovar. Russki Iazyk.

Anglo-Russkii Radiotekhnicheskii Slovar. Ed. by L. P. German-Prozorova et al. (Pub. by Gosizdat. Inostr. Slovarei). Four Continent.

Anglo-Russkii Razgovornik Dlia Turistov. (Pub. by Russkii Iazyk). Four Continent.

Anglo-Russkii Razgovornik Dlia Turistov. (Pub. by Russkii Iazyk). Four Continent.

Anglo-Russkii Slovar. Ol'ga Sergeevna Akhmanova. Russkii Iazyk.

Anglo-Russkii Slovar. Ed. by V. D. Arakin et al. (Pub. by Russkii Iazyk). Four Continent.

Anglo-Russkii Slovar. Ed. by O. S. Akhmanova. (Pub. by Russkii Iazyk). Four Continent.

Anglo-Russkii Slovar. Ed. by V. K. Miuller. Four Continent.

Anglo-Russkii Slovar Dorozhnika. Ia. B. Khaikin. (Pub. by Izd. Avtotrnsport. Lit.). Four Continent.

Anglo-Russkii Slovar Po Aerogidrodinamike. M. G. Kotik. (Pub. by Glav. Red. Inostr. Tekhn. Slovrei Fizmatgiza). Four Continent.

Anglo-Russkii Slovar Po Aerogidrodinamike. (Pub. by Sov Entsiklopediia). Four Continent.

Anglo-Russkii Slovar Po Aviatsionno-Kosmicheskoi Meditsine. Ed. by A. A. Giurdzhian et al. (Pub. by Voenizdat). Four Continent.

Anglo-Russkii Slovar Po Avtomatike & Kontrol'noizmeritel'nym Priboram. (Pub. by Gosizdat Tekhnikoteoretich. Lit.). Four Continent.

Anglo-Russkii Slovar Po Elektrokhimii i Korrozii. Ed. by M. M. Melnikova et al. (Pub. by Russkii Iazyk). Four Continent.

Anglo-Russkii Slovar Po Iadernym Vzryvam. O. Petrenko. (Pub. by Voenizdat). Four Continent.

Anglo-Russkii Slovar Po Kauchuku, Rezine & Khimicheskim Voloknam. Ed. by F. I. Iashunskaia et al. (Pub. by Glav. Red. Inostr. Nauchn. Tekhn. Slovrei Fizmatgiza). Four Continent.

Anglo-Russkii Slovar Po Khimii & Tekhnologii Polimerov: Okolo 30000 Terminov. (Pub. by Russkii Iazyk). Four Continent.

Anglo-Russkii Slovar po Khimii i Pererabotke Nefti. Vsevolod V. Kedrinskii. Russki Iazyk.

Anglo-Russkii Slovar Po Kholodil Noi i Kriogennoi Tekhnike. (Pub. by Russkii Iazyk). Four Continent.

Anglo-Russkii Slovar po Kvantovoi Elektronike i Golografii. N. Voropaev. Russki Iazyk.

Anglo-Russkii Slovar'Po Kvantovoi Elektronike i Golografii. (Pub. by Russkii Iazyk). Four Continent.

Anglo-Russkii Slovar Po Okhrane Okruzhaiushchei Sredy. (Pub. by Russkii Iazyk). Four Continent.

Anglo-Russkii Slovar Po Radioelektronike i Sviazi. (Pub. by Soviete Ministrov). Four Continent.

Anglo-Russkii Slovar Po Raketnoi Tekhnike. A. M. Murashkevich. (Pub. by Gosizdat. Literatury). Four Continent.

Anglo-Russkii Slovar Po Televideniiu. L. P. German-Prozorova et al. (Pub. by Glav. Red. Fizmatgiza). Four Continent.

Anglo-Russkii Slovar Zheleznodorozhnoi Automatike, Telemekhanike & Sviazi. I. S. Gluzman. (Pub. by Gosizdat Fizmat. Lit.). Four Continent.

Anglo-Russkii Uchebnyi Slovar' S. K. Folomkina et al. Four Continent.

Anglo-Russkii Voenno-Inzhenernyi Slovar. N. V. Volodin. (Pub. by Voenizdat). Four Continent.

Applied Technical Dictionary: Air Conditioning & Refrigeration. (Pub. by Collets). State Mutual Bk.

Applied Technical Dictionary: Oil Processing & Petrochemistry. (Pub. by Collets). State Mutual Bk.

Astronautical Multilingual Dictionary: International Academy of Astronautics. Elsevier.

Astronomical Dictionary: In Six Languages. Josip Kleczek. Acad Pr.

Automatizacna Technika. Jiri Sykora. Alfa-Vydavatel.

Automatizovany Zber Dat Programovanie. Erich Burger. Alfa-Vydavatel.

Automobily. Czesaw Blok & Wiesaw Jezewski. Wydawnictwa.

Azerbaidzhansko-Russkii Frazeogicheskii (Idiomaticheskii) Slovar. A. Orudzhev. (Pub. by Elm). Four Continent.

Basic Dictionary Russian-English. Esselte Studium.

Basic Russian-English Dictionary. EMC.

Bengal'sko-Russkii Slovar. E. M. Bykova et al. (Pub. by Gosizdat Inostr. Natsion. Slovarei). Four Continent.

Bolgarsko-Russkii Voennyi Slovar. M. G. Artiukhov et al. (Pub. bu Voenizdat). Four Continent.

Bolsho i anglo-russki i slovar. N. N. Anosova et al. Russkii Iazyk.

Bolshoi Anglo-Russkii Slovar. Ed. by I. R. Galperin. (Pub. by Russkii Iazyk). Four Continent.

Bol'Shoi Anglo-Russkii Slovar. Ed. by I. R. Galperin. Four Continent.

Bolshoi Polsko-Russkii Slovar. (Pub. by Russkii Iazyk). Four Continent.

A Book of Russian Idioms. M. I. Dubrovin. Illus. by V. I. Tilman. Four Continent.

Breve Diccionario Espanol-Ruso: Ruso-Espanol de Terminos Cientificos & Tecnicos. J. C. Orts et al. French & Eur.

Bulgarian-Russian Dictionary (M-9095) French & Eur.

Buriatskie Shamanisticheskie i Doshamanisticheskie Terminy. I. A. Manzhigeev. (Pub. by Nauka). Four Continent.

Cesko-Rusky Slovnik na Cesty. Marta Vencovska. SNTC.

Cesko, Slovensko, Latinsko, Anglicko, Nemecko, Rusky, Slovnik Plevelu. Vaclav Kosik. SNTC.

Chastotnyi Slovar' Russkogo Iazyka. Four Continent.

Chastotnyi Anglo-Russkii Fizicheskii Slovar Minimum. P. M. Alekseev et al. (Pub. by Voenizdat). Four Continent.

Chastotnyi Anglo-Russkii Slovar Minimum Po Sudovozhdeniiu. K. F. Lukianenkov. (Pub. by Voenizdat). Four Continent.

Chastotnyi Slovar Obshchenauchnoi Leksiki. M. I. Zykina et al. (Pub. by MGU). Four Continent.

Chastotnyi Slovar Russkogo Iazyka. (Pub. by Russkii Iazyk). Four Continent.

Chastotnyi Slovar Semanticheskikh Mnozhitelei Russkogo Iazyka. Ed. by Iu. N. Karaulov. (Pub. by Nauka). Four Continent.

Chemie & Chemische Technik. Helmut Gross & Helmut Hildebrand. VEB Verlag Technik.

Chemie & Chemische Technik Russisch-Deutsch. Helmut Gross. VEB Technik.

Cheshsko-Russkii Radiotekhnicheskii Slovar. B. E. Iakovlev. (Pub. by Glav. Red. Inostr. Nauchn. Tekhn. Slovarei Fizmata). Four Continent.

Chetyre Tys Acha Naibolee Upotrebitel Nykh Slov Russkogo Iazyka. N. M. Shanskii. Four Continent.

Chetyrekhiazychnyi Entsiklopedicheskii Slovar Terminov Po Fizicheskoi Geografii. M. Shchukin. (Pub. by Russkii Iaxyknt Bk). Four Continent.

Chinese-Russian Phonetic Dictionary. French & Eur.

Cibernetical Dictionary: E-G-F-R-Slovene. A. Sydow. French & Eur.

Concise English-Russian, Russian-English Dictionary. S. G. Zaimovskii. (Pub. by Collet's). State Mutual Bk.

Concise English-Russian Technical Dictionary. Desov. Imported Bks.

The Concise Illustrated Russian-English Dictionary of Mechanical Engineering. V. V. Shvarts. Pergamon.

The Concise Illustrated Russian-English Dictionary of Mechanical Engineering. Vladimir Shvarts. (Pub. by Collets). State Mutual Bk.

A Concordance to the Poems of Osip Mandelstam. Ed. by Demetrius J. Koubourlis & Stephen M. Parrish. Cornell U pr.

Conference Terminology in English, Spanish, Russian, Italian, German & Hungarian. J. Herbert. Elsevier.

Czechoslovakian-Russian Dictionary of Geology. N. A. Pascenkova et al. French & Eur.

Dansk-Russik Ordbog. Helge Vangmark. Grafisk Forlag.

Dansk-Russik Ordborg. H. Vangmark. French & Eur.

Data Systems Dictionary. Joachim Schulz. Brandstetter.

Data Systems Dictionary: English-Russian-German. Joachim Schulz. (Pub. by Brandstetter Verlag). French & Eur.

Datenerfassung Programmierung. Erich Burger. VEB Verlag Technik.

Datenerfassung Programmierung-Englisch-Deutsch-Franzoesisch-Russisch. Erich Burger. VEB Technik.

Deutsch-Russisches Woerterbuch: S-Z. Hans H. Bielfeldt. Ed. by Ronald Loetzsch. Akad Verl Ath.

Deutsch-Russische Wirtschaftssprache. N. Grischen. (Pub. by M. Hueber). French & Eur.

Deutsch-Russische Wirtschaftssprache. N. Grischen. Hueber.

Deutsch-Russisches Meteorologisches Worterbuch. W. G. Martschenko. French & Eur.

Deutsch-Russisches Oekonomisches Woerterbuch. Bljach & Bagma. Wissenschaftliche.

Deutsch-Russisches Okonomisches Worterbuch: Dictionary German-Russian of Economics. I. S. Bljach & B. T. Bagma. French & Eur.

Deutsch-Russisches Woerterbuch. Edmund Daum & W. Schenk. (Pub. by Max Hueber). French & Eur.

Deutsch-Russisches Woerterbuch. Edmund Daum & W. Schenk. Hueber.

Deutsch-Russisches Woerterbuch: A-G. Hans H. Bielfeldt. Ed. by R. Loetzsch et al. Akad Verl Ath.

Deutsch-Russisches Woerterbuch: H-R. Hans H. Bielfeldt. Ed. by Ronald Loetzsch. Akad Verl Ath.

Deutsch-Russisches Worterbuch der Forstund Holzwirtschaft. E. A. Pawlow & O. I. Semjonowa. French & Eur.

Deutsch-Russisches Worterbuch der Rechentechnik und Datenverarbeitung. W. A. Scharow & A. L. Nowitschkowa. French & Eur.

Deutsch-Russisches Worterbuch fur Eisenbahnwesen. D. A. Bunin et al. French & Eur.

Deutsch-Russisches Worterbuch fur Eisenbahnwesen. A. P. Sulima-Samujillo et al. French & Eur.

Deutsch-Russisches Worterbuch fur Ozeanographie. N. N. Gorski et al. French & Eur.

Deutsch-Russisches Worterbuch fur Wasserbau. L. B. Bernstein. French & Eur.

Diccionari de agriculatura ruso-espanol. Cultura Popular.

Diccionario de agricultura ruso-espanol. Pueblos Unidos.

Diccionario de lengua rusa. Ozhegov. Pueblos Unidos.

Diccionario Espanol-Ruso. Lorenzo Martinez Calvo. French & Eur.

Diccionario Espanol-Ruso. French & Eur.

Diccionario Espanol-Ruso. L. Martinez Calvo. Sopena.

Diccionario espanol-ruso. Cultura Popular.

Diccionario espanol-ruso. (Mir) D'Ippolito.
Diccionario espanol-ruso. Kelina. Pueblos Unidos.
Diccionario Espanol-Ruso de le Prospeccion y Refinacion del Petroleo. A. Pinkevich & B. Amelin. Ed. by A. F. Dobriansky. French & Eur.
Diccionario espanol-ruso de terminos cientificos y tecnicos. Cultura Popular.
Diccionario ilustrado de la lengua rusa. Cultura Popular.
Diccionario ilustrado del idioma ruso. Pueblos Unidos.
Diccionario manual espanol-ruso. Gisbert. Pueblos Unidos.
Diccionario militar espanol-ruso. Bulgakov. Pueblos Unidos.
Diccionario Militar Espanol-Ruso, Ruso-Espanol. French & Eur.
Diccionario Pratico Russo-Portugues. N. Voinova & S. Starets. French & Eur.
Diccionario Ruso-Espanol. Lorenzo Martinez Calvo. French & Eur.
Diccionario Ruso-Espanol. J. Nogueira & G. Turover. French & Eur.
Diccionario ruso-espanol. Pueblos Unidos.
Diccionario ruso-espanol. Yaselman. Aguilar SP.
Diccionario ruso-espanol de la ciencia y de la tecnica. Patronato Juan de la Cierva. Dossat.
Diccionario ruso-espanol, espanol-ruso. Danae.
Diccionario Simultaneo en 21 Idiomas. Juan Capdevilla Font. French & Eur.
Dicionario de Bolso Portugues-Russo. I. Chalaguina. French & Eur.
Dicionario de Bolso Russo-Portuguese. C. Nunes. French & Eur.
Dictionar de Buzunar Roman-Rus. Victor Vascenco. Editura Stiintifica.
Dictionar de Chimie si Inginerie Chimica Rus-Roman. Dumitru Turtoi et al. Editura Stiintifica.
Dictionar Poliglot de Geodezie: Fotogrammetrie si Cartografie. Mihail Albota. Editura Stiintifica.
Dictionar Poliglot de Industrie Alimentara. Mihai Papa-Sotir. Editura Stiintifica.
Dictionar Poliglot de Matematica, Mecanica si Astronomie. Stefan Gheorghita. Editura Stiintifica.
Dictionar-Rus-Roman: Pentru uzual Elevilor. Eugen P. Noveannu. Editura Stiintifica.
Dictionar Tecnic Rus-Roman. Editura Stiintifica.
Dictionar Tehnic Auto de Buzunar in Sapte Limbi. Petre Cristea. Editura Stiintifica.
Dictionary for the Graphic Arts in Eight Languages: German-English-French-Spanish-Russian-Hungarian-Polish-Slowak. Perfect Graphic.
Dictionary of Acoustics: English-German-French-Russian-Spanish-Polish-Madarsko-Slovene. W. Reichardt. French & Eur.
Dictionary of Agriculture in German, French, Spanish, & Russian. G. Haensch. Ed. by Haberkamp G. De Anton. Elsevier.
Dictionary of Automatic Data Processing. Ing H. Burger. (Pub. by Collets). State Mutual Bk.
Dictionary of Automatical Technique. Ed. by Jiri Sykora. French & Eur.
Dictionary of Biochemistry. K. Thielmann. French & Eur.
Dictionary of Cereal Processing & Cereal Chemistry. R. Schneeweiss. Elsevier.
Dictionary of Chemical Terminology. D. Kryt. Elsevier.
Dictionary of Chemical Terminology. (Pub. by Vyd. Naukowo-Techniczne). Four Continent.
Dictionary of Engineering Mechanics. C. Heller. Elsevier.
Dictionary of Forestry. J. Weck. Elsevier.
Dictionary of Helminthology & Plant Nematology. Ed. by G. I. Pozniak. French & EUr.

Dictionary of Hydraulic Machinery. A. T. Troskolanski. Elsevier.
Dictionary of Hydraulics & Pneumatics: English-German-Russian-Slovene. G. Neubert. French & Eur.
Dictionary of International Economics: German, Russian, English, French, Spanish. Ed. by S. Kohls. Sijthoff & Noordhoff.
Dictionary of Mathematics. G. Eisenreich & R. Sube. Elsevier.
Dictionary of Metallurgy. Ed. by A. Dollinger. French & Eur.
Dictionary of Musical Terms in Seven Languages. Ed. by H. Leuchtmann. Heinman.
Dictionary of Physical Metallurgy. E. F. Tyrkiel. Elsevier.
Dictionary of Plastics Technology in English, German, French & Russian. G. Kaliske. Elsevier.
Dictionary of Russian Obscenities. David A. Drummond & G. Perkins. Berkeley Slavic.
A Dictionary of Russian Obscenities. Schoenhof.
Dictionary of Russian Technical & Scientific Abbreviations. H. Zalucki. Elsevier.
A Dictionary of Russian Verbs. Rudolf Ruzicka. (Dist. by Four Continent). Hippocrene Bks.
A Dictionary of Russian Verbs. R. Ruzicka. Ed. by E. Daum & W. Schenk. Hippocrene Bks.
Dictionary of Russian Verbs (Russian-English) V. Daum & Schenk. (Pub. by Collet's). State Mutual Bk.
A Dictionary of Slavic Word Families. Louis J. Herman. Columbia U Pr.
Dictionary of Spoken Russian: Russian-English: English-Russian. U. S. War Department. Dover.
Dictionary of Technical Acoustics. L. Reichardt. Adler.
Dictionary of the Graphic Arts Industry. Ed. by W. Muller. Elsevier.
Dictionary of the Russian Academy. Ed. by M. Oesterby. A Wofsy Fine Arts.
Dictionnaire Abrege de Six Langues Slaves. Franz Miklosich. Philo Pr.
Dictionnaire Agricole Allemand, Anglais, Francais, Espagnol, Russe. Gunther Haensch & Gisela Haberkamp. (Pub. by Maison Rust). French & Eur.
Dictionnaire Agricole Allemand-Anglais-Francais-Espagnol-Russe. Gunther Haensch. Maison Rustique.
Dictionnaire agricole Allemand, Anglais, Francais, Espanol, Russe. Gunther Haensch & Gisela Haberkamp. Maison Rustique.
Dictionnaire Bilingue Francais-Russe et Russe-Francais. (Apollo). Larousse.
Dictionnaire de la Langue Russe. Mir.
Dictionnaire de Poche Russe-Francais. Dolgopolova. MIR.
Dictionnaire des Frequences de Mots dans le Russe. Steinfeld.
Dictionnaire des Synonymes de la Langue Russe. Alexandrova. MIR.
Dictionnaire des Synonymes de la Langue Russe. Evgueniev. MIR.
Dictionnaire Etymologique de la Langue Russe, 1, A-J. N. Chanski. MIR.
Dictionnaire Etymologique de la Langue Russe. N. Chanski. MIR.
Dictionnaire Etymologique de la Langue Russe. Tsyganenko. MIR.
Dictionnaire Francais-Russe. K. Gamchina. French & Eur.
Dictionnaire Francais-Russe. K. A. Ganchina. MIR.
Dictionnaire Francais-Russe. Noctuel & Calmann-Levy. Labiche.
Dictionnaire Francais-Russe. Paul Pauliat. Larousse.
Dictionnaire Francais-Russe. Varvara Potozkaia. MIR.
Dictionnaire Francais-Russe de Mathematique. Roubakine. MIR.
Dictionnaire Francais-Russe de Mathematique. M. V. Dragnev & Victor Rosov. MIR.
Dictionnaire Francais-Russe de Medecine. Roubakine. MIR.

Dictionnaire Francais-Russe du Batiment. Sakharov. MIR.
Dictionnaire Francais-Russe Militaire. Ostapenko. Mir.
Dictionnaire Geologique: Francais-Russe. V. Dybovskaia & I. Kirillova. French & Eur.
Dictionnaire Illustre de la Langue Russe: Francais-Espagnol-Russe. Anatoll Chtchoukine. Mir.
Dictionnaire Illustre de l'Automobile "Kluwer," en 6 Langues. C. Blok & W. Jezewski. French & Eur.
Dictionnaire Illustre: Francais-Russe. A. Kolesnikova & L. Lulchak. French & Eur.
Dictionnaire International d'abreviation Scientifiques et Techniques. M. Azzaretti. Maison Dictionnaire
Dictionnaire International Electrotechnique: Francais-Russe-Anglais-Allemand-Italien-Suedois-Hollandais-Polonais. Mir.
Dictionnaire International Electrotechnique: Francais-Russe-Anglais-Allemand-Espagnol-Suedois-Hollandais-Polonais. Mir.
Dictionnaire Inverse de la Langue Russe. Mir.
Dictionnaire Meteorologique: Francais-Russe. P. V. Silvestrov. French & Eur.
Dictionnaire Minier Russe-Francais. French & Eur.
Dictionnaire Minier Russe-Francais. France, Centre Et. Charbonnage.
Dictionnaire Orthographique de la Langue Russe. Barkhudarova. Mir.
Dictionnaire Petrolier des Techniques de Diagraphie, Forage & Production: Russe-Francais-Anglais-Allemand. Sonia Ketchian. Technip.
Dictionnaire Petrolier des Techniques de Diagraphique, Forage et Production. Sonia Ketchian. French & Eur.
Dictionnaire russe-francais. P. Pauliat. Larousse.
Dictionnaire Russe-Francais. De Chtcherba. Mir.
Dictionnaire Russe-Francais. Varvara Potozkaia. Mir.
Dictionnaire Russe-Francais de l'automobile & du Tracteur. Jetikov. Mir.
Dictionnaire Russe-Francais du Batiment. V. V. Voronine et al. Ed. by A. I. Denissov. French & Eur.
Dictionnaire Russe-Francais Polytechnique. Vassiliev. Mir.
Dictionnaire Technique du Bois, en Quatre Langues. G. Wallnig & H. Evered. French & Eur.
Dictionnaire Technique du Bois en Quatre Langues: Allemand-Russe-Anglais-Francais. Vander.
Dictionnaire Technique du Bois en 4 Langues. French & Eur.
Dictionnaire Technique du Bois: Texte en Allemand-Anglais-Francais-Russe. Eyrolles.
Dictionnaire Technique Russe-Francais de la Preparation. French & Eur.
Dictionnaire Technique Russe-Francais: La Preparation Mecanique des Charbons. France, Centre Et Charbonnage.
A Dictionary of Russian Verbs. E. Daum & W. Schenk. Hippocrene Bks.
Dizionario fraseologico di russo-italiano e viceversa. Canzio Vandelli. Mondini Siccardi.
Dizionario italiano-russo. Fadanelli. Vallardi A.
Dizionario italiano-russo. Skvorzova & Maizel. Editori Riuniti.
Dizionario Italiano-Russo, Russo-Italiane. R. Fadanelli. French & Eur.
Dopolnenie K Anglo-Russkomu Slovariu Po Radioelektrike & Sviazi. N. I. Dozorov. (Pub. by Izd. Glav. upravl. Po Ispol'z. Atomn. Energii). Four Continent.
Einfuhrung in das Technische Russisch Maschinenbau: Lehrmaterial fuer den Fremdsprachenunterricht. Siegfried Uhlig. VEB Technik.

Ekonomicheskii Slovar-Spravochnik Rabochego. Anatolii V. Moiseev. Politizdat.
Ekonomicheskii Slovar Spravochnik Rabochego. A. V. Moiseev. (Pub. by Politizdat). Four Continent.
Eksportno-Importnyi Slovar. (Pub. by Vneshtorgizdat). Four Continent.
Electronics Dictionary. (Pub. by Collets). State Mutual Bk.
Elektrorazvedka: Spravochnik Geofizika. (Pub. by Nedra). Four Continent.
Elektrotechnik Elektronik. William Athenstaedt. VEB Verlag Technik.
Elektrotechnik Elektronik Russisch-Deutsch. Helmut Gross. VEB Technik.
Elements de Geologie En Six Langues. E. Cailleux. French & Eur.
Elseviers Automobile Dictionary. Ed. by G. Schuurmans. Elsevier.
Elsevier's Dictionary of Automatic Control. Ed. by W. Clason. Elsevier.
Elsevier's Dictionary of High Vacuum Science & Technology. Fritz W. Weber. Elsevier.
Elseviers Dictionary of Metal Cutting Tools. Ed. by G. Schuurmang. Elsevier.
English-Estonian-Russian Maritime Dictionary. Kulno Olev. (Pub. by Collets). State Mutual Bk.
English-Latvian-Russian Dictionary. J. Raskevics et al. (Pub. by Collets). State Mutual Bk.
English-Russian Astronomical Dictionary. O. Meinikov. (Pub. by Collet's). State Mutual Bk.
English-Russian Aviation & Space Abbreviations Dictionary. A. M. Murashkevich & O. N. Vladimirov. (Pub. by Collets). State Mutual Bk.
English-Russian Biological Dictionary. Pergamon.
English-Russian Dictionary. Louis Segal. Beekman Pubs.
English-Russian Dictionary. Ed. by V. K. Muller. Dutton.
English-Russian Dictionary. Vladimir K. Muller. Saphrograph.
English-Russian Dictionary. A. Akmanova. (Pub. by Collet's). State Mutual Bk.
English-Russian Dictionary. T. Arakin. (Pub. by Collets). State Mutual Bk.
English-Russian Dictionary. V. Muller. (Pub. by Collet's). State Mutual Bk.
English-Russian Dictionary. O. S. Akhmanova & E. Wilson. French & Eur.
English-Russian Dictionary. V. D. Arakin. French & Eur.
English-Russian Dictionary of Electrochemistry & Corrosion. M. M. Melnikova & I. P. Smirnov. French & Eur.
English-Russian Dictionary of Environmental Control. Ed. by E. L. Milovanov & E. A. Veistman. Pergamon.
English-Russian Dictionary of Finance & World Trade. E. E. Israelevich. Imported Bks.
English-Russian Dictionary of Minimum Physics. French & Eur.
An English-Russian Dictionary of Nabokov's "Lolita". A. D. Nakhimovsky & V. A. Paperno. Ardis Pubs.
English-Russian Dictionary of Nuclear Explosions. (Pub. by Collets). State Mutual Bk.
English-Russian Dictionary of Refrigerating & Cryogenic Engineering. M. B. Rosenberg. French & Eur.
English-Russian Dictionary of Reliability & Quality Control. Y. G. Kovalenko. Pergamon.
English-Russian Dictionary of Sports Terms & Phrases. A. V. Garilovets. (Pub. by Collets). State Mutual Bk.
English-Russian Dictionary of Sports Terms & Phrases: Summer Olympic Games & Sports. Four Continent.
English-Russian Glossary of Computer Systems & Networks Terminology. E. A. Yakubaitis. (Pub. by Collets). State Mutual Bk.

English-Russian Glossary of Physics Terms. P. M. Alekseev. (Pub. by Collets). State Mutual Bk.
English-Russian Phrase Book. Compiled by L. D. Pochertsova et al. Four Continent.
English-Russian Physics Dictionary. Ed. by D. M. Tolstoi. Pergamon.
English-Russian Physics Dictionary. D. M. Tolstoi. (Pub. by Collets). State Mutual Bk.
English-Russian Polytechnical Dictionary. Ed. by A. E. Chernukhin. (Pub. by Collets). State Mutual Bk.
English-Russian Polytechnical Dictionary. A. E. Chernukhin. Pergamon.
English-Russian, Russian-English Dictionary. French & Eur.
English-Russian-Serbocroatian Aviations Dictionary. J. Dragovic. French & Eur.
English-Russian Televisions Dictionary. L. P. Prosorova & V. L. Kreizer. French & Eur.
English-Russian Textile Dictionary. Z. E. Rabinowitch & K. K. Lupandin. French & Eur.
Epuletgepeszet. Ivan Fekete. Akademiai Kiado.
Erdoelverarbeitung-Petrolchemie. Leipnitz. Brandstetter.
Erdolverarbeitung und Petrolchemie: A Dictionary of Crude Oil Processing & Petroleum Chemistry English-German-French-Russian. Walter Leipnitz. Intl Learn Syst.
Erziansko-Russkii Slovar. M. N. Koliadenkov et al. (Pub. by Gosizdat Inostr Natsional Slovarei). Four Continent.
Essential Russian-English Dictionary. B. G. Anpilogova et al. Four Continent.
Estonsko-Russkii Slovar. J. Tamm. (Pub. by Valgus). Four Continent.
Etimologicheskii Slovar Adygskikh (Cherkesskikh) A. K. Shagirov. (Pub. by Nauka). Four Continent.
Etimologicheskii Slovar Russkogo Iazyka: Tom. 1, Vyp. 3 (V) Ed. by N. M. Shanskii. (Pub. by MGU). Four Continent.
Etimologicheskii Slovar Russkogo Iazyka: Tom. 1, Vyp. 4 (G) N. M. Shanskii. (Pub. by MGU). Four Continent.
Etimologicheskii Slovar Russkogo Iazyka: Tom. 1, Vyp. 5 (D, E, Zh) N. M. Shanskii. (Pub. by MGU). Four Continent.
Etimologicheskii Slovar Russkogo Iazyka: Tom. 2, Vyp. 6 (Z) N. M. Shanskii. (Pub. by MGU). Four Continent.
Etimologicheskii Slovar Slavianskikh Iazykov: Vyp. 4. (Pub. by Nauka). Four Continent.
Etimologicheskii Slovar Slavianskikh Iazykov: Vyp. 7. (Pub. by Nauka). Four Continent.
Etimologicheskii Slovar Tiurkskikh Iazykov. E. V. Sevortian. (Pub. by Nauka). Four Continent.
Etimologicheskii Slovar Tiurkskikh Iazykov. E. V. Sevortian. (Pub. by Nauka). Four Continent.
Etimologichesskii Slovar Russkogo Iazyka: Tom. 2, Vyp. 7 (I) N. M. Shanskii. (Pub. by MGU). Four Continent.
An Explanatory Dictionary for Students of English. R. A. Davidenko. (Pub. by Ganatleba). Four Continent.
Fachworterbuch Polygrafie: English-Deutsch-French-Russian-Spanish-Polish-Hungarian-Slowakian. French & Eur.
Farmakologicheskii Slovar: Latinsko-Russkii & Russko-Latinskii. T. G. Kazachenok. (Pub. by Vysheishaia). Four Continent.
Fertigungsmesstechnik. Peter D. Hoffmann. VEB Verlag Technik.
Fertigungsmesstechnik-Russischer-Deutsch: Deutsch-Russicherr. Peter Hoffman. VEB Verlag Technik.
Festkorperelektronik. Helmut Muchow. VEB Technik.
Filatelisticheskii Slovar. Ed. by V. Grallert et al. (Pub. by Sviaz). Four Continent.
Filmgyartas es Filmtechnika. Gabor Pozsonyi. Akademiai Kiado.
Finansovo-Kreditynyi Slovar. (Pub. by Finansy). Four Continent.
Finnish-Russian-Finnish Dictionary (Suomi-Venaja-Suomi) A. Hiltunen. French & Eur.
Finsko-Russkii Slovar. I. Vakharos et al. (Pub. by Russkii Iazyk). Four Continent.
Fitopatologicheskii Slovar Spravochnik. G. A. Diakova. (Pub. by Nauka). Four Continent.
Foundation Dictionary of Russian: Three Thousand High Semantic Frequency Words. B. G. Anpilogova et al. Dover.
Four-Language Technical Dictionary of Chromatography: English, German, French, Russian. H. Angele. Pergamon.
Four Languages Dictionary of Geological Terms. French & Eur.
Four Thousand Naibolee Upotrebitel'nykh Slov Russkogo Iazyka. (Pub. by Russkii Iazyk). Four Continent.
Frantsuzsko-Russkii Frazeologicheskii Slovar. Ed. by I. I. Retsker. (Pub. by Gosizdat Inostr Natsional Lit). Four Continent.
Frantsuzsko-Russkii Geologicheskii Slovar. I. K. Dobovskaia. (Pub. by Gosfizmat). Four Continent.
Frantsuzsko-Russkii Illiustrirovannyi Slovar. A. D. Kolesnikova et al. (Pub. by Sov Entsiklopediia). Four Continent.
Frantsuzsko-Russkii Illiustrirovannyi Slovar. I. Zandreitere. (Pub. by Latv Valstsnent Bk). Four Continent.
Frantsuzsko-Russkii Obshchestvenno-Politisheskii Slovar. Ed. by S. A. Tokarev et al. (Pub. by Izd. In-ta Mezhdunarod. Otnoshenii). Four Continent.
Frantsuzsko-Russkii Slovar Po Sudostroeniiu i Sudokhodstvu. A. I. Telegin et al. (Pub. by Glav. Red. Nauchn. Tekhn. Slovarei Fizmatgiza). Four Continent.
Frantsuzsko-Russkii Uchebnyi Slovar. N. B. Korina et al. (Pub. by Russkii Iazyk). Four Continent.
Frantsuzsko-Russkii Voennyi Slovar. A. M. Taube. (Pub. by Voenizdat). Four Continent.
Frazeologicheskii Slovar Russkogo Iazyka. A. I. Molotkova. (Pub. by Russkii Iazyk). Four Continent.
Frazeologicheskii Slovar' Russkogo Iazyka. Ed. by L. A. Voinova et al. Four Continent.
Geillustrrerd Woordenboek Voor de Autombieltechniek en Zes Talen. C. Block et al. French & Eur.
Gem Language Dictionaries: Russian-English & English-Russian. S&S.
Geobotanic Dictionary. O. S. Grebenshchikov. Lubrecht & Cramer.
Geologicheskii Slovar. A. N. Krishtofovich. (Pub. by Gos. Nauch. Tekhn. Izd. Lit. Po Geologii & Okhrane Nedr.). Four Continent.
Geologicheskii Slovar. (Pub. by Nedra). Four Continent.
German-Russian Dictionary. Rahmanoba. French & Eur.
Gidrologicheskii Slovar. L. Chebotarev. (Pub. by Gidrometeorologich Izd.). Four Continent.
Gidrologicheskii Slovar. A. I. Chebotarev. (Pub. by GIdrometeoizdat). Four Continent.
Gidrologicheskii Slovar na Inostrannykh Iazykakh. O. A. Spenger. (Pub. by Gidrometeoizdat). Four Continent.
Glossary of Economics. F. Clifford Vaughn. Elsevier.
Glossary of English & Russian Computer & Automated Control Systems Terminology. Ed. by Irene Agnew. Agnew Tech-Tran.
Glossary of Genetics. Francoise Biass-Ducroux. Elsevier.
Glossary of Geology. M. Gary et al. French & Eur.
Glossary of International Treaties. Y. Renoux & J. Yates. Elsevier.
Glossary of Physiological Terms. (Pub. by Collets). State Mutual Bk.
Glossary of Soil Micromorphology. Ed. by A. Jongerius & G. K. Rutherford. Pudoc.
Glossary of Terms in Heat Transfer, Fluid Flow & Related Topics. Ed. by William Begell. Hemisphere Pub.
Glossary of Terms Used in Quality Control. Slownik Jakosci. (Pub. by Collets). State Mutual Bk.
Gornoe Delo: Terminologicheskii Slovar. N. V. Melnikov et al. (Pub. by Nedra). Four Continent.
Gosudarstvennye Standarty SSSR. (Pub. by Izd Standartov). Four Continent.
Graafinen Sanakirja. Soderstrom.
Grammaticheskii Slovar' Russkogo Iazyka. Ed. by A. A. Zalizniak. Four Continent.
Handbook of Russian Roots. Catherine Wolkonsky & Marianna Poltoratzky. Columbia U Pr.
Harrap's Russian Vocabulary. George Scanlan. Harrap Co.
Hugo Pocket Dictionary: Russian-English, English-Russian. Littlefield.
Hugo Pocket Dictionary: Russian-English, English-Russian. French & Eur.
Iaponsko-Russkii Politekhnicheskii Slovar. (Pub. by Russkii Iazyk). Four Continent.
Iaponsko-Russkii Uchebnyi Slovar Ieroglifov. N. I. Feldman-Konrad. (Pub. by Russkii Iazyk). Four Continent.
IFIP Sachwoerterbuch der Datenverarbeitung. Gould. Verlag Harri Deutsch.
Illiustrirovannyi Aviatsionnyi Slovar Dlia Molodezhi. A. T. Stepanets. (Pub. by Dosaaf). Four Continent.
Illiustrirovannyi Voenno-Tekhnicheskii Slovar. L. D. Neliubin. (Pub. by Voenizdat). Four Continent.
Illustrierte Technische Woerterbucher: Eisenbahnmaschinenwesen. A. Schlomann. (Pub. by R. Oldenbourg). French & Eur.
Illustrierte Technische Woerterbucher: Eisenbahnmaschinenwesen. A. Schlomann. Oldenbourg Verlag.
Illustrierte Technische Woerterbucher: Eisenbahnbau und Betrieb. A. Schlomann. (Pub. by R. Oldenbourg). French & Eur.
Illustrierte Technische Woerterbucher: Eisenbahnbau und Betrieb. A. Schlomann. Oldenbourg Verlag.
Illustrierte Technische Woerterbucher: Elektrotechnik und Elektrochemie. A. Schlomann. (Pub. by R. Oldenbourg). French & Eur.
Illustrierte Technische Woerterbucher: ELektrotechnik und Elektrochemie. A. Schlomann. Oldenbourg Verlag.
Illustrierte Technische Woerterbucher: Maschinenelemente. A. Schlomann. (Pub. by R. Oldenbourg). French & Eur.
Illustrierte Technische Woerterbucher: Maschinenelemente. A. Schlomann. Oldenbourg Verlag.
Illustrierter Technische Woerterbucher: Luffahrts. A. Schlomann. (Pub. by R. Oldenbourg). French & Eur.
Illustrierter Technische Woerterbucher: Luffahrts. A. Schlomann. Oldenbourg Verlag.
Illustrowany Slownik Rosyjsko-Polski. Andrzej Bogusiawski. Wiedza Powszechna.
Illustrowany Slownik Rosyjsko-Polski, Polsko-Rosyjski. Andrzej Boguslawski. Wiedza Poswzechna.
Ilustrowany Slownik Samochodowy. Czeslaw Blok. Wydawnictwa.
Indioneziisko-Russkii Uchebnyi Razgovornik. L. I. Ushakova et al. (Pub. by Gosizdat Inostr Natsional Slovarei). Four Continent.
Indonesian-Russian Dictionary. R. N. Korigodsky et al. French & Eur.
Indoneziisko-Russkii Slovar. V. N. Korigodskii et al. (Pub. by Gosizdat Inostr Natsional Slovarei). Four Continent.
Indoneziisko-Russkii Uchebnyi Slovar. A. S. Teselkin et al. (Pub. by Sov Entsiklopediia). Four Continent.
Informationsverarbeitung-Englisch-Deutsch-Franzoesisch-Russisch. Erich Burger. VEB Technik.
Informatsionno-Poiskovyi Tezariius Po Informatike. (Pub. by Vsesoiuz). Four Continent.
International Dictionary of Obscenities: A Guide to Dirty Words & Indecent Expressions in Spanish, Italian, French, German, & Russian. Christina Kunitskaya-Peterson. Berkeley Slavic.
International Electrotechnical Vocabulary: Electronics. French & Eur.
International Electrotechnical Vocabulary, Machines & Transformers. French & Eur.
Ispansko-Russkii Razgovornik. S. Neverov. (Pub. by Izd. Lit. Na Inostr. Iaz.). Four Continent.
Ispansko-Russkii Slovar. Ed. by F. V. Kelin. (Pub. by Gosizdat Inostr Natsional Slovarei). Four Continent.
Ispansko-Russkii Slovar Po Dobyche i Pererabotke Nefti. A. A. Pinkevich et al. (Pub. by Lenizdat). Four Continent.
Istoriko-Etimologicheskii Slovar Osetinskogo. V. I. Abaev. (Pub. by Nauka). Four Continent.
Ital'iansko-Russkii i Rusko-Ital'ianskii Stroitel'nyi Slovar. Boris I. Avramenko. Russkii Iazyk.
Italiansko-Russkii Slovar. S. V. Gere et al. (Pub. by Gosizdat Inostr. Natsional Slovarei). Four Continent.
Karmannyi Afgansko-Russkii Slovar. K. A. Lebedev. (Pub. by Gosizdat Natsional Slovarei). Four Continent.
Karmannyi Anglo-Russkii Slovar. O. P. Beniukh. (Pub. by Sov Entsiklopediia). Four Continent.
Karmannyi Anglo-Russkii Slovar. O. P. Beniukh. (Pub. by Russkii Iazyk). Four Continent.
Karmannyi Anglo-Russkii Slovar. O. P. Beniukh et al. (Pub. by Russkii Iazyk). Four Continent.
Karmannyi Anglo-Russkii Slovar' O. P. Beniukh et al. Four Continent.
Karmannyi Bengal'sko-Russkii Slovar. D. Litton. (Pub. by Gosizdat Natsional Slovarei). Four Continent.
Karmannyi Bolgarsko-Russkii Slovar. M. A. Leonidova. (Pub. by Gosizdat Inostr. & Natsional). Four Continent.
Karmannyi Cheshsko-Russkii i Russko-Cheshskii Slovar. D. A. Dlugi et al. (Pub. by Sov Entsiklopediia). Four Continent.
Karmannyi Frantsuzsko-Russkii Slovar. K. S. Vygodskaia. (Pub. by GINS). Four Continent.
Karmannyi Indoneziisko-Russkii Slovar. N. F. Bulygin. (Pub. by GINS). Four Continent.
Karmannyi Ital'iansko-Russkii Slovar. I. A. Dobrovolskaia. (Pub. by GINS). Four Continent.
Karmannyi Italiansko-Russkii Slovar. Four Continent.
Karmannyi Kitaisko-Russkii Slovar. N. S. Araushkin et al. (Pub. by Russkii Iazyk). Four Continent.
Karmannyi Niderlandsko-Russkii Slovar. T. N. Dreniasova. (Pub. by Russkii Iazyk). Four Continent.
Karmannyi Polsko-Russkii & Russko-Polskii Slovar. G. V. Sinitsyna & I. N. Mitronova. Russkii Iazyk.
Karmannyi Pol'Sko-Russkii & Russko-Polskii Slovar. I. N. Mitronova et al. (Pub. by Russkii Iazyk). Four Continent.
Karmannyi Polsko-Russkii i Russko-Polskii Slovar. Four Continent.
Karmannyi Rumynsko-Russkii Slovar. Four Continent.
Karmannyi Russko-Albanskii Slovar. A. Kostallari. Four Continent.
Karmannyi Russko-Angliiskii Slovar. O. P. Beniukh et al. (Pub. by Sov Entsiklopediia). Four Continent.
Karmannyi Russko-Angliiskii Slovar' Ed. by O. P. Beniukh et al. Four Continent.

Karmannyi Russko-Birmanskii Slovar. U Chin Vei et al. (Pub. by GINS). Four Continent.
Karmannyi Russko-Bolgarskii Slovar. (Pub. by Russkii Iazyk). Four Continent.
Karmannyi Russko-Bolgarskii Slovar. M. A. Leonidova. Four Continent.
Karmannyi Russko-Finskii Slovar. I. S. Eliseev. (Pub. by Russkii Iazyk). Four Continent.
Karmannyi Russko-Frantsuzskii Slovar. Four Continent.
Karmannyi Russko-Indoneziiskii Slovar. N. F. Bulygin et al. (Pub. by GINS). Four Continent.
Karmannyi Russko-Ital'ianskii Slovar. I. A. Dobrovolskaia et al. (Pub. by Sov Entsiklopediia). Four Continent.
Karmannyi Russko-Khindi Slovar. Z. M. Dymshits et al. (Pub. by GINS). Four Continent.
Karmannyi Russko-Kitaiskii Slovar. V. G. Mudrov. (Pub. by Russkii Iazyk). Four Continent.
Karmannyi Russko-Niderlandskii Slovar. Zh. I. Pirog et al. (Pub. by Russkii Iazyk). Four Continent.
Karmannyi Russko-Norvezhskii Slovar. E. P. Gribanova. (Pub. by GINS). Four Continent.
Karmannyi Russko-Urdu Slovar. A. A. Davidova et al. (Pub. by GINS). Four Continent.
Karmannyi Slovar Ateista. (Pub. by Politizdat). Four Continent.
Karmannyi Slovatsko-Russkii i Russko-Slovatskii Slovar. (Pub. by Russkii Iazyk). Four Continent.
Karmannyi Urdu-Russkii Slovar. L. B. Kibirkshtis et al. (Pub. by GINS). Four Continent.
Karmannyi Vengersko-Russkii Slovar. G. I. Ol'Dal et al. (Pub. by GINS). Four Continent.
Khindi-Russkii Uchebnyi Slovar. O. G. Ul'Tsiferov. (Pub. by GINS). Four Continent.
Kirjastotermien Sanakirja. Martti Kahla. Neuvost.
Kitaisko-Russkii Slovar-Minimum. A. V. Kotov. (Pub. by Russkii Iazyk). Four Continent.
Kleines Polytechnisches Woerterbuch. Horst Gorner & J. V. Fedirko. VEB Verlag Technik.
Kleines Polytechnisches Woerterbuch Russisch-Deutsch. Horst Gorner. VEB Technik.
Kleines Woerterbuch der Chemie & Chemischen Technik. Helmut Gross. VEB Verlag Technik.
Kleines Woerterbuch der Chemie & Chemischen Technik Russisch-Deutsch. Helmut Gross. VEB Technik.
Kleines Woerterbuch der Elektrotechnik Elektronik Russisch-Deutsch. Helmut Gross. VEB Technik.
The Kodansha Japanese-Russian Dictionary. Kodansha.
Kompleksnyi Chastotnyi Slovar Russko Nauchnoi & Tekhnicheskoi Leksiki. (Pub. by Russkii Iazyk). Four Continent.
Korrosion & Korrosionsschutz Deutsch-Russisch. Helmut Gross. VEB Technik.
Kratikii Russko-Angliiskii i Anglo-Russkii Frazeologicheskii Slovar' A. I. Alekhina. Four Continent.
Kratkii Anglo-Gruzinskii Slovar. (Pub. by Metsniereba). Four Continent.
Kratkii Anglo-Russkii i Russko-Angliiskii. S. G. Zaimovsky. (Pub. by Russkii Iazyk). Four Continent.
Kratkii Anglo-Russkii i Russko-Angliiskii Slovar' S. G. Zaimovskii. Four Continent.
Kratkii Cheshsko-Russkii Geofizicheskii Slovar. N. A. Pashchenko et al. (Pub. by Glav. Red. Nauchn. Tekhn. Slovarei Fizmata). Four Continent.
Kratkii Cheshsko-Russkii i Russko-Cheshskii Vneshnetorgovyi Slovar. V. S. Shevchenko et al. (Pub. by Vneshtorgizdat). Four Continent.
Kratkii Defektologicheskii Slovar. Ed. by A. I. D'Iachkov et al. (Pub. by Prosveschchenie). Four Continent.
Kratkii Ekonomicheskii Slovar. Ed. by G. A. Kozlov et al. (Pub. by Politizdat). Four Continent.
Kratkii Ekonomicheskii Slovar Piatiletki Effektivnosti & Kachestva. (Pub. by Politizdat Ukrainy). Four Continent.
Kratkii Ekonomicheskii Slovar-Spravochnik Mastera i Nachal'nika Tsekha. V. T. Nikitin. (Pub. by Ekonomika). Four Continent.
Kratkii Ekonomiko-Matematicheskii Slovar. L. I. Lopatnikov. (Pub. by Nauka). Four Continent.
Kratkii Estonsko-Russkii Slovar. V. Mukhel. (Pub. by Tallinn). Four Continent.
Kratkii Etimologicheskii Slovar Russkogo Iazyka. N. M. Shanskii et al. (Pub. by Proveschchenie). Four Continent.
Kratkii Fotograficheskii Slovar. Ed. by A. A. Lapauri et al. (Pub. by Iskusstvo). Four Continent.
Kratkii Frantsuzsko-Russkii i Russko-Frantsuzskii Slovar. K. S. Vygodskaia et al. (Pub. by Sov Entsiklopediia). Four Continent.
Kratkii Iaponsko-Russkii Razgovornik. (Pub. by Iskra Revoliutsii). Four Continent.
Kratkii Illiustrirovannyi Russko-Angliiskii Slovar Po Mashinostroeniu. V. V. Shvarts. (Pub. by Russkii Iazyk). Four Continent.
Kratkii Ispansko-Russkii & Russko-Ispanskii Nauchno-Tekhnicheskii Slovar. Kbo Orts Kh. et al. (Pub. by An Arm SSR). Four Continent.
Kratkii Lugunda-Russkii & Russko-Lugunda Slovar. O. P. Nosova. (Pub. by Sov Entsiklopediia). Four Continent.
Kratkii Nemetsko-Russkii Vneshnetorgovyi Slovar. L. T. Bagma. (Pub. by Vneshtorgizdat). Four Continent.
Kratkii Politicheskii Slovar. (Pub. by Politizdat). Four Continent.
Kratkii Politicheskii Slovar. (Pub. by Politizdat). Four Continent.
Kratkii Russko-Finskii Slovar. (Pub. by GINS). Four Continent.
Kratkii Russko-Frantsuzskii Uchebnyi Slovar. (Pub. by Sov Entsiklopediia). Four Continent.
Kratkii Russko-Iaponskii Slovar. A. E. Gluskina et al. (Pub. by GINS). Four Continent.
Kratkii Russko-Koreiskii Slovar. I. N. Mazur. (Pub. by GINS). Four Continent.
Kratkii Russko-Nemetskii Frazeologicheskii Slovar. (Pub. by Russkii Iazyk). Four Continent.
Kratkii Russko-Shvedskii Slovar. A. P. Valenius. (Pub. by GINS). Four Continent.
Kratkii Shkol'Nyi Anglo-Litovskii i Litovsko-Angliiskii Slovar. V. Baravikas et al. (Pub. by Shviesa). Four Continent.
Kratkii Slovar Botanicheskikh Terminov. D. P. Viktorov. (Pub. by Sov. Nauka). Four Continent.
Kratkii Slovar Botanicheskikh Terminov. D. P. Viktorov. (Pub. by Nauka). Four Continent.
Kratkii Slovar Gazovika. Iu. M. Belodvorskii. (Pub. by Ministertvo Kommun Khoz). Four Continent.
Kratkii Slovar Inostrannykh Slov. S. M. Lokshina. (Pub. by Russkii Iazyk). Four Continent.
Kratkii Slovar Literaturovedcheskikh Terminov. Leonid I. Timofeev & S. V. Turev. (Pub. by Proveschchenie). Four Continent.
Kratkii Slovar' Literaturovedcheskikh Terminov. Ed. by L. I. Timofeev et al. Four Continent.
Kratkii Slovar Po Radioelektronike. A. P. Verzhikovskii et al. (Pub. by Voenizdat). Four Continent.
Kratkii Suakhili-Russkii & Russko-Suakhili Slovar. A. I. Kutuzov. (Pub. by Sov Entsiklopediia). Four Continent.
Kratkii Taisko-Russkii Slovar. M. I. Osipov. (Pub. by LGU). Four Continent.
Kratkii Terminologicheskii Spravochnik po Ekonomike Geologorazvedochnykh Rabot. Wydawnictwa.
Kratkii Tolkovyi Slovar' Russkogo Iazyka: Dlia Inostransev. Ed. by V. V. Rozanova. Four Continent.
Kratkii Tolkovyi Slovar Russkogo Iazyka. Ed. by V. V. Rozanova. (Pub. by Russkii Iazyk). Four Continent.
Kratkii Tolkovyi Slovar Russkogo Iazyka. (Pub. by Russkii Iazyk). Four Continent.
Kratkii Tolkovyi Slovar Toponimov Kazakhstana. E. Koichubaev. (Pub. by Nauka). Four Continent.
Kratkii Topografo-Geodezicheskii Slovar. Ed. by B. S. Kuzmin. (Pub. by Nedra). Four Continent.
Kratkii Toponimicheskii Slovar Belorussii. V. A. Zhuchkevich. (Pub. by MGU). Four Continent.
Kratkii Tsitologicheskii Slovar. A. A. Klishov. (Pub. by Meditsina). Four Continent.
Kratkii Turetsko-Russkii Slovar "Novykh Slov". G. I. Antelava. (Pub. by Metsniereba). Four Continent.
Kratkii Veterinarnyi Slovar Klinicheskikh Terminov. F. M. Orlov. (Pub. by Khozizdat). Four Continent.
Kratkii Vneshnetorgovyi Slovar. Ed. by B. T. Kolpakov. (Pub. by Vneshtorgizdat). Four Continent.
Kratkii Voennyi Persidsko-Russkii Slovar. L. S. Peisikov et al. (Pub. by Voenizdat Inostr & Natsional' Slovarei). Four Continent.
Landwirtschaftliches Woerterbuch in Acht Sprachen. (Pub. by BLV). French & Eur.
Langenscheidt Russian-English Lilliput Dictionary. Langenscheidt.
Langenscheidt Russian Pocket Dictionary. Langenscheidt.
Langenscheidts Handwoerterbuecher Russisch. Ed. by Heinz Messinger & Werner Ruedenberg. Langenscheidt.
Langenscheidt's Lilliput English-Russian Dictionary. Am Map.
Langenscheidt's Lilliput Russian-English Dictionary. Am Map.
Langenscheidt's Pocket Russian Dictionary: Russian-English, English-Russian. Ed. by E. Wedel & A. Romanov. Am Map.
Langenscheidts Taschenwoerterbuch Russisch. Karl Blattner et al. Langenscheidt.
Langenscheidts Taschenwoerterbuch Russisch: Teil II, Deutsch-Russisch. M. Braun & K. Pollok. Langenscheidt.
Langenscheidts Taschenwoerterbuch Russisch: Teil I, Russisch-Deutsch. Karl Blattner & H. Orschel. Langenscheidt.
Langenscheidts Taschenwoerterbuecher Russisch. Karl Blattner. Langenscheidt.
Langenscheidts Taschenwoerterbuecher Russisch-Deutsch. H. Orschel. Langenscheidt.
Langenscheidt's Universal Russian-English, English-Russian Dictionary. Am Map.
Langenscheidts Universal-Woerterbuch Russisch. Langenscheidt.
Langenscheidts Universal-Woerterbuecher Russisch-Deutsch. Langenscheidt.
Latinsko-Russko-Latyshskii Slovar Meditsinskikh Terminov. (Pub. by Liesma). Four Continent.
Learn Russian. N. Potapova. Saphrograph.
Learner's English-Russian Dictionary. S. Folomkina & H. Weiser. MIT Pr.
Learner's English-Russian Dictionary. V. Folomkina & T. Weiser. (Pub. by Collet's). State Mutual Bk.
The Learner's English-Russian Dictionary. S. Folomkina & H. Weiser. French & Eur.
The Learner's English-Russian Dictionary. A. Folomkina & H. Weiser. Russki Iazyk.
The Learner's English-Russian Dictionary: For English Speaking Students. Four Continent.
Learner's Russian-English Dictionary. B. A. Lapidus & S. V. Shevtsova. MIT Pr.
The Learner's Russian-English Dictionary. B. A. Lapidus & S. V. Shevtsoka. French & Eur.
The Learner's Russian-English Dictionary. B. A. Lapidus et al. (Pub. by Russkii Iazyk). Four Continent.
Learner's Russian-English Dictionary for Foreign Students of Russian. B. A. Lapidus & S. V. Shevisova. Russica.
The Learner's Russian-English Dictionary: For Foreign Students of Russian. A. Lapidus et al. Four Continent.
Lexico basico espanol-ruso. Cultura Popular.
Lexico basico espanol-ruso. D'Ippolito.
Lexicon Forestale. Karl-Johan Ahlsved et al. Suomen Standard.
Lexicon Medicum. Boleslaw Zlotnickiego. French & Eur.
Lexicon Medicum: Medizinisches Woerterbuch in 6 Sprachen; Englisch, Russisch, Franzoesisch, Deutsch, Latein, Polnisch. B. Zlotnicki. Langenscheidt.
Lexikon Medicum. B. Zlotnicki. French & Eur.
Lexique General. (UN). Unipub.
Lexique Quadrilingue de la Preparation des Minerals: Allemand-Anglais-Francais-Russe. Congres International de la Preparation des Minerais. Ste. Industrie Minerale.
Lexique Quadrilinque de la Preparation des Minerais. Ed. by Congres International de la Preparation des Minerais. French & Eur.
Lilliput Dictionary. Langenscheidt.
Linguarum Totius Orbis Vocabularia Comparativa. Peter S. Pallas. Buske.
Lingvisticheskii Slovar. M. A. Denisova. (Pub. by Russkii Iazyk). Four Continent.
Lingvostranovedcheskii Slovar' M. A. Denisova. Four Continent.
Linquarum Totius Orbis Vocabularia Comparativa. Peter S. Pallas. (Pub. by Helmut Buske Verlag Hamburg). Benjamins North Am.
Linquarum Totius Orbis Vocabularia Comparativa. Peter S. Pallas. (Pub. by Helmut Buske Verlag Hamburg). Benjamins North Am.
Litovsko-Russkii Slovar. (Pub. by Gosizdat Polit. & Nauchn.Lit. SSR.). Four Continent.
Litovsko-Russkii Slovar. (Pub. by Mintis). Four Continent.
Litovsko-Russko-Anglo-Nemetskii Slovar Fizicheskikh Terminov. P. Brazhdzhiunas. (Pub. by Mokslas). Four Continent.
Logicheskii Slovar. N. I. Kondakov. Ed. by D. P. Gorskii. (Pub. by Nauka). Four Continent.
Magyar-Orosz Katonai Szotar. A Szotarszerk Bizottsag Vezetoje Toth Lajos. Akademiai Kiado.
Magyar-Orosz Kez Iszotar. Laszlo Hadrovics et al. Akademiai Kiado.
Magyar-Orosz Keziszotar. Laszlo Hadrovics & Galdi Hadrovics. Akademiai Kiado.
Magyar-Orosz Muszaki Szotar. Lorant Katona. Akademiai Kiado.
Malaiziisko-Russko-Angliiskii Slovar. Ed. by N. V. Rott. (Pub. by Russkii Iazyk). Four Continent.
Manual of the Terminology of Public International Law & International Organizations. I. Paenson. Kluwer Academic.
Maritime Dictionary. Kulno Olev. (Pub. by Collets). State Mutual Bk.
Materialy Frazeologicheskogo Slovaria Russkogo Iazka XVIII Veka. M. F. Palevskaia. (Pub. by Shtiintsa). Four Continent.
Mathematics Dictionary. Glenn James. Van Nos Reinhold.
Medical Dictionary. B. Zoltnicki. (Pub. by Schattauer). French & Eur.

Medizintechnik. Albert Von Roald & Harry Hahnewald. VEB Verlag Technik.

Medizintechnik-Englisch-Deutsch-Franzoesisch-Russisch-Spanisch-Polnisch-Ungarisch-Slowakisch. Roald Albert & Harry Hahnewald. VEB Technik.

Meteorologicheskii Slovar. S. P. Khromov. (Pub. by Gidrometeoizdat). Four Continent.

Mezhdunarodnaia Anatomicheskaia Nomenklatura. (Pub. by Ganatleba). Four Continent.

Mezhdunarodnyi Elektrotekhnicheskii Slovar: Gruppa 07 (Elektronika) (Pub. by Gosizdat Fiziko-Matematich. Literatury). Four Continent.

Mezhdunarodnyi Elektrotekhnicheskii Slovar: Gruppa 10 (Mashiny & Transformatory) (Pub. by Gosizdat Fiziko Matematich. Literatury). Four Continent.

Mezhdunarodnyi Elektrotekhnicheskii Slovar: Gruppa 65 (Radiologiia & Radiologicheskaia Fizika) (Pub. by Sov Entsiklopediia). Four Continent.

Mineralogy Dictionary, German-Russian. French & Eur.

The Modern Russian Dictionary for English Speakers: English-Russian. E. A. Wilson. Pergamon.

Moldavsko-Russkii Frazeologicheskii Slovar. V. Solov'ev. (Pub. by Lumina). Four Continent.

Multilingual Glossary of Automatic Control Technology: English-French-German-Russian-Italian-Spanish-Japanese. D. T. Broadbent & M. Masubuchi. Pergamon.

Multilingual Lexicon of Linguistics & Philology: English, Russian, German, French. Rose Nash. U of Miami Pr.

Music Translation Dictionary: An English, Czech, Danish, Dutch, French, German, Hungarian, Italian, Polish, Portuguese, Russian, Spanish, Swedish Vocabulary of Music. Compiled by Carolyn D. Grigg. Greenwood.

Mykologisches Worterbuch. K. Berger. French & Eur.

Mykologisches Worterbuch. Karl Von Berger. Fischer Verlag.

Naibolee Upotrebitel'Nykh Slov Russkogo. (Pub. by Russkii Iazyk). Four Continent.

Nemetsko-Gruzinsko-Russkii Frazeologicheskii Slovar. N. Gamrekeli et al. (Pub. by Ganatleba). Four Continent.

Nemetsko-Russkii Arkhitekturnyi Slovar. M. M. Zhitomirskii. (Pub. by GINS). Four Continent.

Nemetsko-Russkii Elektrotekhnicheskii Slovar. M. L. Ginzburg et al. (Pub. by Gosizdat Fizmatlit). Four Continent.

Nemetsko-Russkii Frazeologicheskii Slovar. (Pub. by GINS). Four Continent.

Nemetsko-Russkii Geodezicheskii Slovar. I. A. Piskunova. (Pub. by Nedra). Four Continent.

Nemetsko-Russkii Gidrotekhnicheskii Slovar. L. B. Bernshtein. (Pub. by Fizmatgiz). Four Continent.

Nemetsko-Russkii Matematicheskii Slovar. L. A. Kaluzhnin et al. (Pub. by Fizmatgiz). Four Continent.

Nemetsko-Russkii Meditsinskii Slovar. E. F. Sommerau. (Pub. by Medgiz). Four Continent.

Nemetsko-Russkii Mekhaniko-Matematicheskii Slovar. N. M. Dovnar-Zapolskaia. (Pub. by MGU). Four Continent.

Nemetsko-Russkii Okeanograficheskii Slovar. N. N. Gorskii et al. (Pub. by GINS). Four Continent.

Nemetsko-Russkii Slovar. Ed. by I. V. Rakhmanov. (Pub. by GINS). Four Continent.

Nemetsko-Russkii Slovar. Ed. by I. V. Rakhmanov. (Pub. by GINS). Four Continent.

Nemetsko-Russkii Slovar po Lesnomu Khoziaistvu. Ernst A. Pavlov & Olga I. Semenova. Russkii Iazyk.

Nemetsko-Russkii Slovar Po Metalloobrabotke. N. F. Deputatova et al. (Pub. by Gosizdat Tekhnich Teoretich. Lit.). Four Continent.

Nemetsko-Russkii Slovar Po Vychislitelnoi Tekhnike. V. Sharov et al. (Pub. by Russkii Iazyk). Four Continent.

Nemetsko-Russkii Zheleznodorozhnyi Slovar. D. A. Bunin. (Pub. by Gosizdat Tekhn.-Teoret. Lit.). Four Continent.

Nepal'Sko-Russkii Slovar. I. S. Rabinovich. (Pub. by Sov Entsiklopediia). Four Continent.

New English-Russian Dictionary. (Pub. by Collet's). State Mutual Bk.

New International Dictionary of Refrigeration. International Institute of Refrigeration. (IIR). Unipub.

New Russian-English & English-Russian Dictionary. O'Brien. Imported Bks.

Norvezhsko-Russkii Slovar. V. D. Arakin. (Pub. by GINS). Four Continent.

Nouveau Dictionnaire International du Froid. French & Eur.

Novoe V Russkoi Leksike. Ed. by N. Z. Kotoleva. (Pub. by Russkii Iazyk). Four Continent.

Novogrechesko-Russkii Slovar. I. P. Khorikov. (Pub. by Russkii Iazyk). Four Continent.

Novye Parallel'nye Slovari Iazykov Russkago, Frantsuzskago, Nemetskago i Angliiskago. Filipp Reiff. Incl. Four Continent.

Numizmaticheskii Slovar. V. V. Zvarich. (Pub. by Izd. L'Vovsk. Unta.) Four Continent.

Oekonomisches Woerterbuch Aussenwirtschaft (Dictionary of External Exonomic Relations & Trade) Ed. by Siegfried Kohls. Intl Pubns Serv.

Oekonomisches Woerterbuch Aussenwirtschaft. S. Kohls. (Pub. by Ruceken Vlg). French & Eur.

Oekonomisches Woerterbuch Aussenwirtschaft. Wissenschaftliche.

Oekonomisches Woerterbuch Russisch-Deutsch. G. Moechel. (Pub. by Vlg. Die Wirtschaft). French & Eur.

Onteszet. Arpad Voros. Akademiai Kiado.

Orfograficheskii Morskoi Slovar. R. E. Poretskaia. (Pub. by Voenizdat). Four Continent.

Orfograficheskii Slovar. D. N. Ushakov et al. (Pub. by Prosveschchenie). Four Continent.

Orfograficheskii Slovar' D. N. Ushakov et al. Four Continent.

Orfograficheskii Slovar Russkogo Iazyka Dlia Shkol. I. Napalis et al. (Pub. by Izd Pedag Lit). Four Continent.

Orfograficheskii Slovar Russkogo Iazyka. (Pub. by Russkii Iazyk). Four Continent.

Orosz-Magyar Katonai Szotar. Lajos Toth. Akademiai Kiado.

Orosz-Magyar Szotar. Laszlo Galdi. Akademiai Kiado.

Orosz-Magyar Szotar. Laszlo Hadrovics. Akademiai Kiado.

Orosz-Magyar Szotar Iskolak Szamara. Miklos Szabo. Akademiai Kiado.

The Oxford Russian-English Dictionary. Ed. by Marcus Wheeler & B. O. Unbegaun. Oxford U Pr.

Pandzhabsko-Russkii Slovar. I. S. Rabinovich. (Pub. by GINS) Four Continent.

Parusny i sport. L. A. Chesnokov et al. Russkii Iazyk.

Pedagogicheskii Slovar. Ed. by I. A. Kairov. (Pub. by Izd. Akademii Ped. Nauk). Four Continent.

Pekhleviisko-Persidsko-Armiano-Russko-Angliiskii Slovar. R. Abrahamian. (Pub. by Mitk). Four Continent.

Persidsko-Russkii & Russko-Persidskii Obshche-Ekonomicheskii & Vneshnetorgovyi Slovar. (Pub. by Vneshtorgizdat). Four Continent.

Persidsko-Russkii & Russko-Persidskii Voennyi Slovar. G. G. Aliev. (Pub. by Voenizdat). Four Continent.

Pharmacological Dictionary. Latin-Russian, Russian-Latin. French & Eur.

A Phrase & Sentence Dictionary of Spoken Russian. Ed. by U.S. War Dept. Imported bks.

Phrase Dictionaries for the American Tourist. Frederick Stark. Incl. German for the American Tourist; Spanish for the English-Speaking Tourist; French for the English-Speaking Tourist; Italian for the English-Speaking Tourist; Greek for the English-Speaking Tourist; Russian for the English-Speaking Tourist. Delair.

Physics Dictionary. Ed. by R. Sube & G. Eisenreich. Adler.

Pieciojezyczny Slownik Gleboznawczy. Adamczyk Boleslaw. Panstwowe Zaklad W.

Plasttechnik-Englisch-Deutsch-Franzoesisch-Russisch. Gisbert Kaliske. VEB Technik.

The Pocket Oxford English-Russian Dictionary. N. A. Rankin. Oxford U Pr.

The Pocket Oxford Russian Dictionary: Russian-English - English-Russian. Ed. by Jessie Coulson et al. Oxford U Pr.

The Pocket Oxford Russian-English Dictionary. Ed. by J. Coulson. Oxford U Pr.

The Pocket Oxford Russian-English Dictionary. Jessie S. Coulson. Imprint of Oxford U Pr.

Pocket-Shorter Dictionary. Langenscheidt.

Podreczny Slownik Polsko-Rosyjski. Ryszard Stypula et al. Wiedza Powszechna.

Polish-Russian Dictionary of Economics. M. N. Osmowej. French & Eur.

Polish-Russian, Russian-Polish Dictionary. I. Nitronowa et al. French & Eur.

Politekhnicheskii Slovar. Ed. by I. I. Artobolevskii. (Pub. by Sov Entsiklopediia). Four Continent.

Politekonomicheskii Slovar. Ed. by E. F. Borisov. (Pub. by Politizdat). Four Continent.

Politicheskaia Ekonomiia Slovar. Ed. by V. A. Zhamin. (Pub. by Politizdat). Four Continent.

Politicheskii Slovar. Ed. by B. N. Ponomareva. (Pub. by Politizdat). Four Continent.

Polsko-Ruskii Khimicheskii Slovar. I. A. Titova. (Pub. by Sov Entsiklopediia). Four Continent.

Polsko-Russkii Ekonomicheskii Slovar. (Pub. by Russkii Iazyk). Four Continent.

Polsko-Russkii Gornyi Slovar. (Pub. by Russkii Iazyk). Four Continent.

Polsko-Russkii Razgovornik Dlia Turistov. (Pub. by Russkii Iazyk). Four Continent.

Polygrafie-Englisch-Deutsch-Franzoesisch-Russisch-Spanisch-Polnisch-Ungarisch-Solwakisch. Wolfgang Muller. VEB Technik.

Polytechnisches Woerterbuch Russisch-Deutsch. Paul Hueter & Horst Goerner. VEB Technik.

Populiarnyi Ekonomiko-Matematicheskii Slovar. L. I. Lopatnikov. (Pub. by Znanie). Four Continent.

Portugalsko-Russkii Politekhnicheskii Slovar. Vladimir S. Matveev & Konstantin G. Asrhants. Russkii Iazyk.

Posobie Po Leksicheskoi Sochetaemosti Slov Russkogo Iazyka. T. I. Anisimova. (Pub. by Vysheishaia Shkola). Four Continent.

Projet de Lexique Minier Russe-Francais. Ed. by N. N. Ersov & A. N. Komarov. French & Eur.

Prusskii Iazyk Slovar: E-H. V. N. Toporov. (Pub. by Nauka). Four Continent.

Prusskii Iazyk Slovar: I-L. V. N. Toprov. (Pub. by Nauka). Four Continent.

Pskovski Oblastnoi Slovar S Istoricheskimi Dannymi. (Pub. by LGU). Four Continent.

Pskovskii Oblastnoi Slovar S Istoricheskimi Dannymi. (Pub. by LGU). Four Continent.

Pskovskii Oblastnoi Slovar S Istorischeskmi Dannymi. (Pub. by LGU). Four Continent.

Razgovornik Dlia Avtoturistov: Anglo-Russkii. (Pub. by Russkii Iazyk). Four Continent.

Razoruzhenie: Spravochnik. (Pub. by Politizdat). Four Continent.

Reading the Russian Language: A Guide for Librarians & Other Professionals. Rosalind Kent. Dekker.

Recueil Terminologique Multilinque du Soudage et des Techniques Connexes. French & Eur.

Romanov Russian-English Dictionary. A. S. Romanov. PB.

Romanov's Pocket Russian-English, English-Russian Dictionary. Imported Bks.

Rumynsko-Russkii Politekhnicheskii. B. A. Andrianov et al. (Pub. by Gostekhteorizdat). Four Continent.

Rusko-Sesky Chemicky Slovnik. M. Bubnikova. Russkii Iazyk.

Russian-Arabic Dictionary. French & Eur.

Russian-Bulgarian Dictionary. Leonidova. French & Eur.

Russian-Bulgarian Phraseological Dictionary. K. Andreichina et al. Ed. by Vlasova. French & Eur.

Russian-Chinese Dictionary of Export & Economics. French & Eur.

Russian-Czechoslovakian Dictionary. Vlchek. French & Eur.

Russian-Czechoslovakian Polytechnical Dictionary. V. S. Petrov & S. A. Tulin. French & Eur.

Russian-English Atomic Dictionary: Physics, Mathematics, Nucleonics. Eugene A. Carpovich. Tech Dict.

Russian-English Biological & Medical Dictionary. Eugene A. Carpovich. Tech Dict.

Russian-English Botanical Dictionary. Paul Macura. Slavica.

Russian-English Chemical & Polytechnical Dictionary. Ludmilla I. Callaham. (Pub. by Wiley-Interscience). Wiley.

Russian-English Chemical & Polytechnical Dictionary. Ludmilla I. Callaham. Wiley.

Russian-English Chemical Dictionary. Eugene A. Carpovich. Tech Dict.

Russian English Dictionary. A. I. Smirnitsky. Dutton.

Russian-English Dictionary. T. Smirnitskii. (Pub. by Collet's). State Mutual Bk.

Russian-English Dictionary. A. M. Taube. (Pub. by Collet's). State Mutual Bk.

Russian-English Dictionary. A. M. Taube et al. Ed. by R. C. Daglish. French & Eur.

Russian-English Dictionary. Akhmanova et al. Imported Bks.

Russian-English Dictionary. Four Continent.

Russian-English Dictionary of Abbreviations & Initialisms. James F. Shipp. Translation Research.

Russian-English Dictionary of ...(a,e,i, ya) tel' Words. Charles Parsons. Translation Research.

Russian-English Dictionary of Data Processing Terminology. French & Eur.

Russian-English Dictionary of Helminthology & Plant Nematology. G. J. Pozniak. (Pub. by CAB Bks England). State Mutual Bk.

Russian-English Dictionary of irovat' Verbs. Charles Parsons. Translation Research.

Russian-English Dictionary of Modern Terms in Aeronautics & Rocketry. M. M. Konarski. Pergamon.

Russian-English Dictionary of ....ost' Words. Charles Parsons. Translation Research.

Russian-English Dictionary of Prestressed Concrete & Concrete Construction. Ed. by Ben C. Gerwick, Jr. & V. P. Peters. Gordon.

Russian-English Dictionary of Sports Terms & Phrases. Russkii Yazyk. (Pub. by Collet's). State Mutual Bk.

Russian-English Dictionary of Sports Terms & Phrases. A. V. Gavrilovets. (Pub. by Collets). State Mutual Bk.

Russian-English Dictionary of Surnames: Important Names from Science & Technology. James F. Shipp. Translation Research.

Russian-English Dictionary of the Mathematical Sciences. A. J. Lohwater. Am Math.

Russian-English, English-Russian Scientific & Technical Dictionary. Ed. by M. H. Alford & V. L. Alford. Pergamon.

Russian-English Forestry & Wood Dictionary. W. Linnard. (Pub. by CAB Bks England). State Mutual Bk.

Russian-English Glossary of Hydrobiology. (Consultants). Plenum Pub.

Russian-English Index to Scientific Apparatus Nomenclature. James F. Shipp. Trans Res Inst.

Russian-English Integrated Dictionary. Patricia A. Heron. Univ Aston.

Russian-English Mathematical Dictionary. L. M. Milne-Thomson. U of Wis Pr.

Russian-English Medical Dictionary. Pergamon.

Russian-English Metals & Machines Dictionary. Eugene A. Carpovich. Tech Dict.

Russian-English Monograph Series: Skorost' Translation Research.

Russian-English Oil-Field Dictionary. Ed. by D. E. Stoliarov. Pergamon.

Russian-English Plastics Dictionary: Reversed from an English-Russian Dictionary by Computer Processing. Ed. by Harry H. Josselson. Wayne St U Pr.

Russian-English Polytechnical Dictionary. Ed. by B. Kuznetsov. Pergamon.

Russian-English Scientific & Technical Dictionary. M. H. Alford & V. L. Alford. Pergamon.

Russian-English Scientific & Technical Dictionary of Useful Combinations & Expressions. M. G. Zimmerman. Shalom.

Russian-English Space Technology Dictionary. M. M. Konarski. Pergamon.

Russian-English Translators Dictionary: A Guide to Scientific & Technical Usage. Mikhail G. Zimmerman. (Plenum Pr). Plenum Pub.

Russian-English Veterinary Dictionary. R. Mack. (Pub. by CAB Bks England). State Mutual Bk.

Russian-English Vocabulary with Grammatical Sketch. Ed. by Gabrielle Rainich & A. H. Kuipers. Am Math.

Russian-German Dictionary. French & Eur.

Russian-Polish Political Dictionary. B. Dudawaki et al. French & Eur.

Russian Root List with a Sketch of Russian Word Formation. Charles E. Gribble. Slavica.

Russian-Rumanian Military Dictionary. French & Eur.

Russian-Swahili, Swahili-Russian Dictionary. A. I. Kutuzov. French & Eur.

Russian Vest Pocket Dictionary. Ed. by Stefan Congrat-Butlar. Random.

Russian Vocabulary Builder, Seven Verbs a Day. Alex Pronin. (Pub. by Lawrence). Borden.

Russian Word-Collocations: Learner's Dictionary. B. V. Bratus et al. Four Continent.

Russian Word Count. E. Steinfeldt. Four Continent.

Russich-Deutsches Woerterbuch. Edmund Daum & W. Schenk. (Pub. by Max Hueber). French & Eur.

Russich-Deutsches Woerterbuch. Edmund Daum & W. Schenk. Hueber.

Russisch-Deutsches Worterbuch der Funkechnik. P. K. Gorochow. French & Eur.

Russich Elymologisches Woerterbuch. Max Vasmer. (Pub. by Carl Winter). French & Eur.

Russich Etymologishes Woerterbuch. Max Vasmer. Winter Univ.

Russisch. Karl Blattner. Incl. Langenscheidt.

Russisch-Deutsches Woerterbuch der Chemie & Chemischen. Institut fur Angewandte Sprachwissenschaft. VEB Verlag Technik.

Russisch-Deutsches Woerterbuch Fuer Naturwissenschaftler und Ingenieure. S. Halbauer. (Pub. by M. Hueber). French & Eur.

Russisch-Deutsches Woerterbuch Fuer Naturwissenschaftler und Ingenieure. S. Halbauer. Hueber.

Russisch Etymologisches Woerterbuch. Max Vasmer. (Pub. by Carl Winter). French & Eur.

Russisch Etymologisches Woerterbuch. Max Vasmer. (Pub. by Carl Winter). French & Eur.

Russisch Etymologisches Woerterbuch. Max Vasmer. Winter Univ.

Russisch Etymologisches Woerterbuch. Max Vasmer. Winter Univ.

Russisch fuer Ingenieur & Fashschulen. Wissenschaftliche.

Russisch fuer Oekonomen: Lehrbuch fuer die Sprachkundigenausbildung IIb. Wissenschaftliche.

Russisch Woordenboek. A. Baar. Coutinho.

Russkie Frazeologizmy v Kartinkakh. M. Dubrovin. (Pub. by Russkii Iazyk). Four Continent.

Russkie Poslovitsy, Pogovorki & Krylatye Vyrazheniia. Vera P. Felitsyna. Russkii Iazyk.

Russkie Poslovitsy, Pogovorki i Krylatye Slovar: Lingvostranovedcheskii Slovar. Ed. by I. G. Prokhorov et al. Four Continent.

Russkie Poslovitsy, Pogovorki i Krylatye Vyrazheniia. V. P. Felitsyna & Iu. E. Prokhorov. (Pub. by Russkii Iazyk). Four Continent.

Russkii Iazyk: Entsiklopediia. Ed. by F. P. Filin. Four Continent.

Russkikh Glagolov. A. S. Vasil'Eva. Four Continent.

Russko-Afganskii Slovar. P. B. Zudin. (Pub. by GINS). Four Continent.

Russko-Afganskii Slovar. K. A. Lebedev et al. (Pub. by Sov Entsiklopediia). Four Continent.

Russko-Amkharskii Slovar. E. B. Gankin. (Pub. by Sov. Entsiklopediia). Four Continent.

Russko-Angliiskii. Ol'ga S. Akhmanova. Russkii Iazyk.

Russko-Angliiskii Politekhnicheskii Slovar. Kuznetsova. (Pub. by Russkii Iazyk). Four Continent.

Russko-Angliiskii Razgovornik Dlia Fizikov. L. A. Smirnova. (Pub. by Sov Entsiklopediia). Four Continent.

Russko-Angliiskii Razgovornik Dlia Fizikov. L. A. Smirnova. (Pub. by Russkii Iazyk). Four Continent.

Russko-Angliiskii Shkol'No-Pedagogicheskii Slovar. V. V. Botiakova et al. (Pub. by Iaroslavsk. Knizhn. Izd.). Four Continent.

Russko-Angliiskii Slovar. O. S. Akhmanova. (Pub. by Russkii Iazyk). Four Continent.

Russko-Angliiskii Slovar. A. M. Taube. (Pub. by Russkii Iazyk). Four Continent.

Russko-Angliiskii Slovar. A. I. Smirnitskii. Four Continent.

Russko-Angliiskii Slovar' - Razgovornik: Russian-English Dictionary of Sports Terms & Phrases - Olympic Summer. Four Continent.

Russko-Angliiskii Slovar (Kratkii) Ed. by O. S. Akhmanova. (Pub. by Russkii Iazyk). Four Continent.

Russko-Angliiskii Slovar-Razgovornik: Letnie Olimpiiskie Vidy Sporta. A. V. Gavrilovets. (Pub. by Russkii Iazyk). Four Continent.

Russko-Angliiskii Voenno-Morskoi Slovar. N. P. Afronin et al. (Pub. by Voenizdat). Four Continent.

Russko-Angliisku Slovar-Russian-English Dictionary. Olga S. Akhmanova & Elizabeth A. Wilson. Russkii Iazyk.

Russko-Anglo-Azerbaidzhansko-Kirgozsko-Turkmensko-Uzbekskii Terminologicheskii Slovar Po Avtomati cheskomu Upravleniiu. (Pub. by Elm). Four Continent.

Russko-Anglo-Nemetsko-Frantsuzskii Slovar Terminov Po Avtomaticheskomu Upravleniiu. Ed. by A. V. Khramov. (Pub. by An Arm SSR). Four Continent.

Russko-Arabskii Meditsinskii Slovar. G. T. Arslanian et al. (Pub. by Russkii Iazyk). Four Continent.

Russko-Arabskii Uchebnyi Slovar. G. Sh. Sharbatov. (Pub. by Russki Iazyk). Four Continent.

Russko-Armianskii Frazeologicheskii Slovar. (Pub. by Gos. Un-Tet). Four Continent.

Russko-Armianskii Politekhnicheskii Slovar. R. T. Ashkharumov et al. (Pub. by An Arm SSR). Four Continent.

Russko-Armianskii Slovar. A. S. Garibian. (Pub. by Hayastan). Four Continent.

Russko-Armianskii Slovar. A. Garibian. (Pub. by Hayastan). Four Continent.

Russko-Armianskii Tolkovyi Slovar. V. Z. Grigorian et al. (Pub. by An Arm SSR). Four Continent.

Russko-Azerbaidzhanskii Slovar. (Pub. by Elm). Four Continent.

Russko-Bashkirskii Slovar. G. R. Karimova. (Pub. by GINS). Four Continent.

Russko-Bengal'skii Slovar. Litton. (Pub. by Sov. Entsiklopediia). Four Continent.

Russko-Birmanskii Slovar. N. N. Novikov et al. (Pub. by Sov. Entsiklopediia). Four Continent.

Russko-Bolgarskii Slovar. S. K. Chukalov. (Pub. by Sov. Entsiklopediia). Four Continent.

Russko-Chechenskii Slovar. Aisash T. Karasaev et al. Russkii Iazyk.

Russko-Chechenskii Slovar. (Dist. by Four Continent Bk). Russkii Iazyk.

Russko-Cheshskii Slovar. L. V. Kopetskov et al. (Pub. by Russkii Iazyk). Four Continent.

Russko-Datskii Slovar. N. I. Krymova et al. (Pub. by GINS). Four Continent.

Russko-Erzianskii Slovar. Ed. by M. N. Koliadenkov et al. (Pub. by GINS). Four Continent.

Russko-Estonskii Razgovornik. A. Reitsak. (Pub. by Valgus). Four Continent.

Russko-Estonskii Slovar. V. Mukhel. (Pub. by Estonsk. Gos. Izd.). Four Continent.

Russko-Estonskii Slovar. P. Arumaa et al. (Pub. by Valgus). Four Continent.

Russko-Evenskii Slovar. V. I. Tsintsius. (Pub. by GINS). Four Continent.

Russko-Finskii Slovar. Ed. by M. E. Kuusiena et al. (Pub. by GINS). Four Continent.

Russko-Frantsuzskii Aviatsionno-Tekhnicheskii Slovar. P. E. Turchin. (Pub. by Sov. Entsiklopedia). Four Continent.

Russko-Frantsuzskii Shkol'No-Pedagogicheskii Slovar. N. V. Goliakova et al. (Pub. by Sov. Entsiklopediia). Four Continent.

Russko-Frantsuzskii Slovar. V. V. Pototskaia et al. (Pub. by Sov. Entsiklopediia). Four Continent.

Russko-Frantsuzskii Stroitelnyi Slovar. V. V. Voronin et al. (Pub. by Russkii Iazyk). Four Continent.

Russko-Gollandskii Slovar. Z. I. Pirot. (Pub. by GINS). Four Continent.

Russko-Iaponskii Slovar. S. F. Zarubin. (Pub. by Sov. Entsiklopediia). Four Continent.

Russko-Indoneziiskii Slovar. E. S. Belkina. (Pub. by Sov. Entsiklopediia). Four Continent.

Russko-Indoneziiskii Uchebnyi Slovar. A. G. Lordkipanidze et al. (Pub. by GINS). Four Continent.

Russko-Ital'ianskii Ucxhebnyi Slovar. D. E. Rozental. (Pub. by Sov. Entsiklopediia). Four Continent.

Russko-Kabardinsko-Cherkesskii Slovar. B. M. Kardanov et al. (Pub. by GINS). Four Continent.

Russko-Karachaevo-Balkarskii Slovar. Ed. by Kh. I Siunchev et al. (Pub. by Sov. Entsiklopediia). Four Continent.

Russko-Kazakhsii Slovar Lingvisticheskikh Terminov. S. Kenesbaev et al. (Pub. by An Arm SSR). Four Continent.

Russko-Kazakhskii Terminologicheskii Slovar. E. Bekmukhametov. (Pub. by Izd. An Kaz. SSR). Four Continent.

Russko-Kazakhskii Tolkovyi Geograficheskii Slovar. Z. Aubakirov et al. (Pub. by Nauka). Four Continent.

Russko-Khausa Slovar. V. V. Laptukhin. (Pub. by Sov. Entsiklopediia). Four Continent.

Russko-Kirgizskii Slovar. Ed. by K. K. Iudakhin. (Pub. by GINS). Four Continent.

Russko-Kitaiskii Obschcheekonomicheskii i Vneshnetorgovyi Slovar. I. N. Zorin. (Pub. by Vneshtorgizdat). Four Continent.

Russko-Kurdskii Slovar. I. O. Farizov. (Pub. by GINS). Four Continent.

Russko-Latino-Kazakhskii Terminologicheskii Slovar. M. Isambaev. (Pub. by Izd. An Kaz. SSR). Four Continent.

Russko-Latinsko-Uzbekskii Slovar. (Pub. by Meditsina). Four Continent.

Russko-Latyshskii Politekhnicheskii Slovar. A. Zingitis. (Pub. by Liesma). Four Continent.

Russko-Litovskii Sel'Skokhoziaistvennyi Slovar. A. V. Prano. (Pub. by Mintis). Four Continent.

Russko-Litovskii Slovar. (Pub. by Mintis). Four Continent.

Russko-Malagasiiskii Slovar. L. A. Korneev. (Pub. bu Sov. Entsiklopediia). Four Continent.

Russko-Moldavskii & Moldavsko-Ruskii Shkolnyi Slovar. (Pub. by Lumina). Four Continent.

Russko-Moldavskii Ekonomicheskii Slovar. V. B. Bortnikov et al. (Pub. by Kartia Moldoveniaske). Four Continent.

Russko-Moldavskii Slovar. Ed. by A. T. Borshch et al. (Pub. by Izd. Inostr. & Natsional Slovarei). Four Continent.

Russko-Moldavskii Slovar. M. V. Podiko. (Pub. by Kartia Moldoveniaske). Four Continent.

Russko-Mongol'Skii Razgovornik. (Pub. by Russkii Iazyk). Four Continent.

Russko-Mordovskii Slovar. A. P. Feoktistov. (Pub. by Nauka). Four Continent.

Russko-Nemetskii Radiotekhnicheskii Slovar. P. K. Gorokhov. (Pub. by Glav. Red. Inostr. Nauchno-Tekhn. Slovarei Fizmata). Glav. Red. Inostr. Nauchno-Tekhn. Slovarei Fizmata.

Russko-Nemetskii Slovar. Ed. by A. A. Leping. (Pub. by GINS). Four Continent.

Russko-Nemetskii Slovar. Ed. by A. A. Strakhova et al. (Pub. by GINS). Four Continent.

Russko-Nemetskii Slovar. Ed. by E. I. Leping. (Pub. by Russkii Iazyk). Four Continent.

Russko-Novogrecheskii Karmannyi Slovar. N. Al. Sal'nov. (Pub. by Sov. Entsiklopediia). Four Continent.

Russko-Novogrecheskii Slovar. A. A. Ioannidia. (Pub. by Sov. Entsiklopediia). Four Continent.

Russko-Pol'skii Politekhnicheskii Slovar. V. I. Dudavskii et al. (Pub. by Gosizdat Tekhn. Teoretich. Lit.). Four Continent.

Russko-Rumynskii Voennyi Slovar. Iu. A. Spazhev et al. (Pub. by Voenizdat). Four Continent.

Russko-Shvedskii Slovar. Ed. by K. Davidson. (Pub. by Russkii Iazyk). Four Continent.

Russko-Tagal'skii Slovar. M. Krus et al. (Pub. by Sov. Entsiklopediia). Four Continent.

Russko-Tamil'Skii Slovar. M. S. Andronov. (Pub. by Sov. Entsiklopediia). Four Continent.

Russko-Uigurskii Slovar. A. Iliev et al. (Pub. by Gosizdat Natsional Inostr Slovarei). Four Continent.

Russko-Ukrainskii Khimicheskii Slovar. E. F. Nekriach. (Pub. by An Arm SSR). Four Continent.

Russko-Ukrainskii Metallurgicheskii Slovar. V. D. Chekhranov. (Pub. by Naukova Dumka). Four Continent.

Russko-Ukrainskii Slovar. D. I. Ganich et al. (Pub. by Sov. Entsiklopediia). Four Continent.

Russko-Ukrainskii Slovar Sotsial'No-Ekonomicheskoi Terminologii. (Pub. by Ukr. Entsiklopediia). Four Continent.

Russko-Vengerskii Slovar. G. I. Ol'dal. (Pub. by Gosizdat Inostr Natsional Slovarei). Four Continent.

Russko-V'Etnamskii Slovar. (Pub. by Russkii Iazyk). Four Continent.

Rustina pro Vedecke a Odborne Pracovniky. L. Z. Rozkovcova & S. Stary Hanusova. Academia.

Rysk-Svensk Teknisk Ordbok. Bengt Schildt. Esselte Studium.

Sahkotieteellinen Sanasto. Suomen Standardisoimislitto. Suomen Standard.

Schiffbau, Schiffahrt, Fischereitechnik-Russisch-Englisch-Deutsch. Erhard Bensch. VEB Technk.

Semiazychnyi Slovar Po Elektrosviazi. (Pub. by Sov. Entsiklopediia). Four Continent.

Semiazychnyi Slovar Po Mekhanike Gruntov & Fundamentostroeniiu. M. E. Scneider. (Pub. by Gosizdat Fizmat. Lit.). Four Continent.

Septemlingual Dictionary of the Names of European Animal. Ed. by L. Gozmany et al. (Pub. by Kiado Hungary). Heyden.

Seven Hundred Russian Idioms & Set Phrases. N. Shansky & E. Bystrova. Four Continent.

Seven Language Dictionary. Ed. by David Shumaker. Crown.

Seven Languages Dictionary. Imported Bks.

Shakhmatnyi Slovar. Ed. by L. Ia. Abramov. (Pub. by Fiz. & Sport). Four Continent.

Shevchenkovskii Slovar: Na Ukrainskom Iazyke. (Pub. by Poligrafkniga). Four Continent.

Shkol' Nyi Slovoobrazovatel Nyi' Slovar' Z. A. Potikha. Four Continent.

Shkol' Nyi Slovoobrazovatel Nyi' Slovar' Russkogo Iazyka: Posobie dlia Uchaschikhsia. A. N. Tikhonov. Four Continent.

Shkolnyi Slovo-Obrazovatel'Nyislovar Russkogo Iazyka. A. N. Tikhonov. (Pub. by Prosveschchenie). Four Continent.

Shkol'nyi Slovoobrazovatel'Nyi Slovar. Z. A. Potikha. Ed. by S. G. Barkhudarov. (Pub. by Proveschchenie). Four Continent.

Short Dictionary of Eighteenth Century Russian. Charles E. Gribble. Slavica.

Silikatova Technika. Armin Petzold. Alfa-Vydavatel.

Skolni Rusko-Cesky Slovnik. Ed. by L. V. Kopeckeho. SNTC.

Skolni Rusko-Cesky Slovnik. Karel Horalek. SNTC.

Slaovosochetaniia Russkogo Iazyka. (Pub. by Russkii Iazyk). Four Continent.

Slitno Ili Razdelno. B. Z. Buchkina et al. (Pub. by Russkii Iazyk). Four Continent.

Slovak-Russian Dictionary. D. Kollar et al. French & Eur.

Slovar Angliishkikh & Amerikanskikh Sokrashchenii. V. O. Bluvshtein. (Pub. by GINS). Four Continent.

Slovar Anglo-Amerikanskikh Sokrashchenii Po Aviatsionnoi & Raketno-Kosmicheskoi Tekhnike. A. M. Murashkevich. (Pub. by Voenizdat). Four Continent.

Slovar Antonimov Russkogo Iazyka. (Pub. by Russkii Iazyk). Four Continent.

Slovar' Antonimov Russkogo Iazyka. M. R. L'Vov. Four Continent.

Slovar Assotsiativnykh Norm Russkogo Iazyka. A. A. Leontev. (Pub. by MGU). Four Continent.

Slovar Ekonomicheskikh Terminov. (Pub. by Liesma). Four Continent.

Slovar Epitetov Russkogo Literaturnogo Iazyka. S. Gorbachevich et al. (Pub. by Nauka). Four Continent.

Slovar Iazyka Pushkina. (Pub. by GINS). Four Continent.

Slovar Inostrannykh Slov. Russki Iazyk.

Slovar' Inostrannykh Slov. I. V. Lekhin et al. Four Continent.

Slovar Naibolee Upotrebitel'Nykh Slov Anglii-Skogo, Nemetskogo & Frantsuzskogo Iazykov. Ed. by I. V. Rakhmanov. (Pub. by Izd. Inostr. & Natsional'Nal'Nykh Slovarei). Four Continent.

Slovar Narodnykh Govorov Zapadnoi Brianshchiny. P. A. Rastorguev. (Pub. by Nauka). Four Continent.

Slovar Nemetskikh Sokrashchenii. V. O. Bluvshtein. (Pub. by GINS). Four Continent.

Slovar Obshchegeo graficheskikh Terminov. L. Stamp & A. S. Perevod. (Pub. by Progress). Four Continent.

Slovar Omonimov Russkogo Iazyka. O. S. Akhmanova. (Pub. by Sov. Entsiklopediia). Four Continent.

Slovar' Omonimov Russkogo Iazyka. N. P. Kolesnikov. Four Continent.

Slovar Osnovnykh Voennykh Terminov. (Pub. by Voenizdat). Four Continent.

Slovar Po Etike. (Pub. by Politizdat). Four Continent.

Slovar Po Kibernetike. (Pub. by Sov. Entsiklopediia). Four Continent.

Slovar Po Mineral Nomu Syriu Dlia Promyshlennosti Stroitelnykh Materialov. M. V. Grigorovich et al. (Pub. by Nedra). Four Continent.

Slovar PsevdonimovRusskikh Pisatelei: Uchenykh & Obshchestvennykh Deiatelei. I. F. Masanov. (Pub. by Izd. Vsesoiuzn Knizhn Palaty). Four Continent.

Slovar Russkikh Govorov Novosibirskoi Oblasti. (Pub. by Nauka). Four Continent.

Slovar Russkikh Govorov Zabaikalia. L. E. Eliasov. (Pub. by Nauka). Four Continent.

Slovar Russkikh Narodnykh Govorov. (Pub. by Nauka). Four Continent.

Slovar Russko-Suakhili Gazetnoi Leksiki. A. I. Kutuzov. (Pub. by In-Tut Mezhdunarod. Otnoshenii). Four Continent.

Slovar Russkogo Iazyka. S. I. Ozhegov. (Pub. by Russkii Iazyk). Four Continent.

Slovar Russkogo Iazyka XI-XVII: E-zinutie. (Pub. by Nauka). Four Continent.

Slovar Russkogo Iazyka XI-XVII: G-diatchiti. (Pub. by Nauka). Four Continent.

Slovar Russkogo Iazyka XI-XVII: Zipun-iianuarii. (Pub. by Nauka). Four Continent.

Slovar Russkogo Iazyka XVIII Veka. (Pub. by Nauka). Four Continent.

Slovar Russkoi Onomasticheskoi Terminologii. N. V. Podolskaia. (Pub. by Nauka). Four Continent.

Slovar Semiletki. Ed. by S. G. Strumilin. (Pub. by Politizdat). Four Continent.

Slovar Simonimov Russkogo Iazyka. (Pub. by Nauka). Four Continent.

Slovar Sinonimov Russkogo Iazyka. Z. E. Aleksandrova. (Pub. by Sov. Entsiklopediia). Four Continent.

Slovar' Sinonimov Russkogo Iazyka. Cheshko. Ed. by Z. E. Aleksandrova. Four Continent.

Slovar Sokrashchenii Po Informatike. (Pub. by Izd. Mexdunarod. Tsentral' Nauchin. & Tekhn. Informatsii). Four Continent.

Slovar Sovremennogo Russkogo Literaturnogo Iazyka: I-K. (Pub. by An Arm SSR). Four Continent.

Slovar Sovremennogo Russkogo Literaturnogo Iazyka: O. (Pub. by An Arm SSR). Four Continent.

Slovar Sovremennogo Russkogo Literaturnogo Iazyka: Zh-Z. (Pub. by An Arm SSR). Four Continent.

Slovar-Spravochni k Lingvisticheskikh Terminov. D. E. Rozental et al. (Pub. by Prosveschchenie). Four Continent.

Slovar Spravochnik Nazvanii Obraztsov Vooruzheniia & Boevoi Tekhniki Kapitalisticheskikh Stran & Osnovnykh Firm Proizvodiashikh Vooruzhenie. V. D. Kurochkin et al. (Pub. by Voenizdat). Four Continent.

Slovar' Spravochnik po Russkomu Iazyku Dlia Inostrantsev. Four Continent.

Slovar Terminov Pedagogiki. (Pub. by Liesma). Four Continent.

Slovar Terminov PoElektroprovodu & Avtomatizatsii Promyshlennykh Ustanovo. (Pub. by Izd. An Az. SSR). Four Continent.

Slovar Trudnostei Russkogo Iazyka. D. E. Rozental et al. Four Continent.

Slovari Inostrannykh Iazykov v Russkom Azbukovnikeveka. M. P. Alekseev. (Pub. by Nauka). Four Continent.

Slovarnyi Ukazatel Po Knigovedeniiu. A. V. Mezer. (Pub. by Kolos) Four Continent.

Slovnik Zakladnich Odbornych Rusko-Ceskych Vyrazu ze Silnicni a Mestske Dopravy. Jarom Cvrcek. SNTC.

Slovosochetaniia Russkogo Iazyka. (Pub. by Russkii Iazyk). Four Continent.

Slownik Elektroniczny Polsko-Angielsko-Rosyjski. Ewa Sozanskiej. Wydawnictwa Naukowo.

Slownik Informatyki Polsko-Angielsko-Rosyjski. Wydawnictwa Naukowo.

Slownik Kieszonkowy Polsko-Rosyjski. Inessa N. Mironova. Russki Iazyk.

Slownik Polsko-Rosyjski. Ryszard Stypula et al. Wiedza Powszechna.

Smolenskaia Oblast: Slovar Spravochnik Kraeveda. (Pub. by Rabochii). Four Continent.

Solzhenitsyn's Peculiar Vocabulary, Russian-English Glossary. Vera V. Carpovich. Tech Dict.

Soviet Prison Camp Speech: Supplement. Meyer Galler. Soviet Studies.

Sravnitelnyi Slovar Tunguso-Manchzhurskikh Iazykov: Materialy & Etimologicheskomu Slovariu. (Pub. by Nauka). Four Continent.

Stratigraficheskii Slovar SSSR. (Pub. by Nedra). Four Continent.

Stratigraficheskii Slovar SSSR. (Pub. by Nedra). Four Continent.

A Supplement to the New English-Russian Dictionary. Ed. by I. R. Galperin. Four Continent.

Swedish-Russian Dictionary. D. Milanova. French & Eur.

Systematic Glossary of the Terminology of Statistical Methods: English, French, Spanish, Russian. Isaac Paenson. Pergamon.

Systems Analysis & Operations Research Dictionary. G Sezepesi & B. Szekely. (Pub. by Collets). State Mutual Bk.

Tagal sko Russkii Slovar. M. Krus et al. Four Continent.

Tagalog-Russian Dictionary. M. Cruz & S. P. Ignashev. French & Eur.

Tagal'sko-Russkii Slovar. M. Krus. (Pub. by GINS). Four Continent.

Taisko-Ruskii Slovar. L. N. Morev. (Pub. by Sov. Entsiklopediia). Four Continent.

Technical Automotive Dictionary: Russian-English-German-French-Bulgarian. G. Sikora. French & Eur.

Technical Dictionary of Automatization & Programming: English, French, German, Russian,-Slovene. Ed. by E. Burger. French & Eur.

Technical Dictionary of Data Processing, Computers & Office Machines, English, German, French, Russian. E. Burger. Pergamon.

Technical Dictionary of Petrochemistry. W. Leipnitz. (Pub. by Vlg. Technik). French & Eur.

Technical Petroleum Dictionary of Well-Logging, Drilling & Production Terms. Ed. by Sonia Ketchian. Intl Pubns Serv.

Technical Veterinary Dictionary. Wolfgang Lindeke. French & Eur.

Technicka Akustika. Walter Reichardt. VEB Verlat Technik.

Technickoekonomicky Rusko-Cesky Slovnik. Vlasta Patockova. SNTL.

Technische Akustik. Walter Reichardt. VEB Verlag Technik.

Technisches Woerterbuch. Antonin Kucera. (Pub. by Brandstetter). French & Eur.

Technisches Woerterbuch. Antonin Kucera. (Pub. by Brandstetter). French & Eur.

Technisches Woerterbuch. Antonin Kucera. Brandstetter.

Technisches Woerterbuch. Antonin Kucera. Brandstetter.

Technisches Woerterbuch: Band I, Russisch-Deutsch. Kucera. Brandstetter.

Technisches Woerterbuch: Band II, Deutsch-Russisch. Kucera. Brandstetter.

Technologisches Woerterbuch. Egon Von Bahder. (Pub. by Girardet). French & Eur.

Technologisches Woerterbuch. Egon Von Bahder. Girardet.

Tekhnicheskaia Terminologiia. (Pub. by Metsniereeba). Four Continent.

Tekhnicheskii Slovar Spravochnik Po Toplivu & Maslam. K. K. Papok & N. A. Ragozin. (Pub. by Gostoptekhizdat). Four Continent.

Tekhnicheskii Slovar Spravochnik po Toplivu i Maslam. K. K. Papok & N. A. Ragozin. (Pub. by Gostoptekhizda r). Four Continent.

Telugu-Russkii Slovar. S. I. Dzenit. (Pub. by Sov. Entsiklopediia). Four Continent.

Terminologicheskii Slovar Po Informatike: Na 14-i Iazykakh. Four Continent.

Terminologicheskii Slovar Po Nauchnoi Informatsii. Ed. by A. I. Mikhailov et al. (Pub. by Vsesoiuznyi in-tut Nauchin & Tekhn. Imformatsii). Four Continent.

TerminologicheskiiSLovar Po Informatike. (Pub. by Izd. Mezhdunarod. Tsentra & Tekhn. Informatsii). Four Continent.

Terminology of Documentation: A Selection of 1200 Basic Terms Published in English, French, German, Spanish & Russian. (UNESCO). Unipub.

Terminology of Malaria & of Malaria Eradication: Report of a Drafting Committee. World Health.

Teutscher, & Reussischer, Dictionarium: Dictionarium Vindobonense. Ed. by Gerhard Birkfellner. Akad Verl Ath.

Textile Dictionary. G. Velco. (Pub. by Collets). State Mutual Bk.

Tezaurus Nauchno-Tekhnicheskikh Terminov. Ed. by Iu. I. Shemakin. (Pub. by Voenizdat). Four Continent.

Tezaurus Po Mineralam. (Pub. by Viniti). Four Continent.

Tezaurus Po Mineralm. (Pub. by Viniti). Four Continent.

Tolkovyi Slovar' Angliiskikh Geologicheskikh Terminov. Ed. by M. Geri. (Pub. by Prosveshchenie). Four Continent.

Tolkovyi Slovar Belorusskogo Iazyka. (Pub. by Glav. Red. Bel. Entsiklopedii). Four Continent.

Tolkovyi Slovar Moldavskogo Iazyka: A-M. (Pub. by Kartia Moldoveniaske). Four Continent.

Tolkovyi Slovar Russkogo Iazyka. Ed. by D. N. Ushakov. Four Continent.

Tolkovyi Slovar Terminov, Primeniaemykh & Sudovom Mashinostroenii. N. I. Iasulovich. (Pub. by Sudostroenie). Four Continent.

Tolkovyi Slovar Zhivogo Velikorusskogo Iazyka. (Pub. by Russkii Iazyk). Four Continent.

Tolkovyi Slovar' Zhivogo Velikorusskogo Iazyka. V. Dal'. Four Continent.

Transliterated Dictionary of the Russian Language. E. Garfield. ISI Pr.

Transpress Lexikon Seefahrt. Ulrich Scharnow. Transpress Verlag fur Verkehrswesen.

Trudovoe Pravo: Entsiklopedicheskii Slovar. Ed. by A. I. Denisov. (Pub. by Sov. Entsiklopediia). Four Continent.

Uchebny Slovar Obschetekhnich: Leksiki. I. F. Rudakova. (Pub. by Russkii Iazyk). Four Continent.

Uchebnyi Slovar Obshchetekhnich: Russko-Anglo-Frantsuzsko-Nemetskii. I. F. Rudakova et al. (Pub. by Russkii Iazyk). Four Continent.

Uchebnyi Slovar' Sochetaenosti Slov Russkogo Iazyka. P. N. Denisov et al. Four Continent.

Universal Russian Dictionary. Langenscheidt.

Velosipeday i sport. S. N. Novozhilov et al. Russky Yazyk.

Vest Pocket Russian. Marshall D. Berger. (BN). B&N NY.

Veterinary Dictionary: Russian-English. R. Mack. French & Eur.

Vocabulaire de l'oceanologie. Hachette-Jeunesse.

Vocabulaire des Termes: Essentiels Utilises pour la Transmissien Ligne; Francais-Espagnol-Russe-Allemand-Italien-Neerlandais-Polonais-Portugais-Suedois. U. I. T.

Vocabulaire Meteorologique International: Quadrilingue (Anglais-Francais-Espagnol-Russe) O. M. M.

Vocabulaire Multilingue de la Science du Sol: Anglais-Francais-Espagnol-Allemand-Portugais-Italien-Neerlandais-Suedois-Russe. G. V. Jacks & R. Tavernier. F. A. O.

Vocabularios Japones-Espanol-Ruso. Novaro.

Vostochnoslavianskie Iazykovedy. M. G. Bulakhov. Four Continent.

Vvedenie v Logiku. N. I. Kondakov. (Pub. by Nauka). Four Continent.

Wielki Slownik Polsko-Rosyski (Polish-Russian Dictionary) Mirowicz. French & Eur.

Woerterbuch Datenerfassung-Programmierung. E. Buerger. French & Eur.

Woerterbuch Datenerfassung: Programmierung. Buerger. Verlag Harri Deutsch.

Woerterbuch der Biochemie. K. Thielmann. French & Eur.

Woerterbuch der Biochemie. K. Von Thielmann. VEB Verlag Enzyklopadie.

Woerterbuch der Biochemie. Thielmann. Verlag Harri Deutsch.

Woerterbuch der Darstellenden Kuenste: Russiche-Deutsch. Gabriele Fischborn. VEB Verlag Enzyklopadie.

Woerterbuch der Datentechnick. Joachim Schulz. Brandstetter.

Woerterbuch der Datentechnik: Russisch-Deutsch-Englisch. Schulz. Brandstetter.

Woerterbuch der Elektrotechnik und Elektronik. Tomislav Miladinovic. French & Eur.

Woerterbuch der Forstwirtschaft. Johannes V. Weck. French & Eur.

Woerterbuch der Forstwirtschaft Deutsch-Englisch-Franzoesisch-Spanisch-Russisch. Johannes Weck et al. BLV Verlag.

Woerterbuch der Mathematik. Ralf Sube. French & Eur.

Woerterbuch der Mathmetik. Eisenreich & Sube. Verlag Harri Deutsch.

Woerterbuch der Rechts & Wirtschaftssprache: Teil I, Deutsch-Russisch. Gyula Decsi & Sandor Karcsay. Recht & Wirtschaft.

Woerterbuch der Rechts & Wirtschaftssprache: Teil II, Russisch-Deutsch. Gyula Decsi & Sandor Karcsay. Recht & Wirtschaft.

Woerterbuch der Russichen Gewaessernamen: Bd 2, Z-K. Harrassowitz.

Woerterbuch der Russischen Gewaessernamen: Lfg 4. Harrassowitz.

Woerterbuch der Russischen Gewaessernamen: Bd 3, L-P. Harrassowitz.

Woerterbuch der Russischen Gewaessernamen: Bd 4, R-U. Harrassowitz.

Woerterbuch der Russischen Gewaessernamen: Bd 5, F-Ja. Harrassowitz.

Woerterbuch der Russischen Gewaessernamen: Lfg 3. Harrassowitz.

Woerterbuch der Russischen Gewaessernamen: Lfg 6. Harrassowitz.

Woerterbuch der Russischen Gewaessernamen: Lfg 7. Harrassowitz.

Woerterbuch der Russischen Gewaessernamen: Lfg 8. Harrassowitz.

Woerterbuch der Russischen Gewaessernamen: Lfg 9. Harrassowitz.

Woerterbuch der Russischen Gewaessernamen: Lfg 10. Harrassowitz.

WOerterbuch der Russischen Gewaessernamen: Lfg 11. Harrassowitz.

Woerterbuch der Russischen Gewaessernamen: Lfg 12. Harrassowitz.

Woerterbuch der Russischen Gewaessernamen: Lfg 13. Harrassowitz.

Woerterbuch der Russischen Gewaessernamen: Lfg 14. Harrassowitz.

Woerterbuch der Russischen Gewaessernamen: Lfg 15. Harrassowitz.

Woerterbuch des Pantentwesens in 5 Sprachen. Gyorgy L. Szendy. French & Eur.

Woerterbuch Erdoelverarbeitung-Petrolchemie. W. Leipnitz. French & Eur.

Woerterbuch Informationsverarbeitung. Buerger. Verlag Harri Deutsch.

Woerterbuch Klima & Kaeltetechnik. Heinrich. Verlag Harri Deutsch.

Woerterbuch Klima & Kaltetechnik. Gunter Heinrich. Verlag Harri Deutsch.

Woerterbuch Kristallografie. Backhaus. Verlag Harri Deutsch.

Woerterbuch Physik. Ralf Sube & Gunther Eisenreich. French & Eur.

Woerterbuch Physik. Eisenreich & Sube. Verlag Harri Deutsch.

Zoologisches Woerterbuch - Palaearktische Tiere. Michael Klemm. Intl Pubns Serv.

Zoologisches Woerterbuch Palaearktische Tiere. Michael Klemm. (Pub. by Parey Berlin). French & Eur.

Zoologisches Woerterbuch Palaearktische Tiere. Michael Klemm. Parey.

SAMOAN

Grammar & Vocabulary of the Samoan Language. H. Neffgen. Tr. by Arnold B. Stock. from Ger. AMS Pr.

SANSKRIT

Bestimmung & Angabe der Funktion von Sekundar-Suffixen Durch Panini. Albrecht Wezler. Steiner Verlag.

Buddhist Hybrid Sanskrit Dictionary & Grammar. F. Edgerton. Orientalia.

Buddhist Hybrid Sanskrit Grammar & Dictionary. Franklin Edgerton. Incl. Intl Pubns Serv.

Buddhist Hybrid Sanskrit Grammer & Dictionary. F. Edgerton. Orient Bk Dist.

A Dictionary, English & Sanskrit. Monier Williams. Orient Bk Dist.

Dictionary of Chinese Buddhist Terms, with Sanskrit & English Equivalents & a Sanskrit-Pali Index. Ed. by William E. Soothill & L. Hodous. Verry.

Dictionary of English & Sanskrit. M. Monier Williams. Intl Pubns Serv.

A Dictionary of Sanskrit Grammar. Kashinath V. Abhyankar & J. M. Shukla. Oriental Institute.

A Dictionary of the Vedic rituals. Chitrabhanu Sen. Concept Pub. Co.

English Sanskrit Dictionary. Monier Monier-Williams. Auromere.

English-Sanskrit Dictionary. Monier Monier-Williams. Humanities.

English-Sanskrit Dictionary. Monier Monier-Williams. Intl Pubns Serv.

Kurzgefasstes Etymologisches Des Altindischen. Manfred Mayrhofer. Winter Univ.

Kurzgefasstes Etymologisches Woerterbuch Des Altindischen. Manfred Mayrhofer. (Pub. by Carl Winter). French & Eur.

Kurzgefasstes Etymologisches Woerterbuch Des Altindischen. Manfred Mayrhofer. (Pub. by Carl Winter). French & Eur.

Kurzgefasstes Etymologisches Woerterbuch Des Altindischen. Manfred Mayrhofer. Winter Univ.

Practical Sanskrit Dictionary: With Transliteration Accentuation & Etymological Analysis Throughout. Arthur A. MacDonnell. Oxford U Pr.

Practical Sanskrit-English Dictionary. V. S. Apte. Orient Bk Dist.

Practical Sanskrit-English Dictionary. Vaman S. Apte. Verry.

Practical Sanskrit-English Dictionary. Ed. by P. K. Gode et al. Prasarnmitr.

Sanskrit-English Dictionary. Monier Williams et al. Lancaster-Miller.

Sanskrit-English Dictionary. M. Williams. Orient Bk Dist.

Sanskrit-English Dictionary. Monier Monier-Williams et al. Oxford U Pr.

Sanskrit-English Dictionary. Monier-Williams. South Asia Bks.

Sanskrit-English Dictionary: Etymologically & Philologically Arranged with Special Reference to Cognate Indo-European Languages. Ed. by Monier Williams. Intl Pubns serv.

Sanskrit-English, English-Sanskrit Student's Dictionary. V. S. Apte. Heinman.

Sanskrit-Hindi-English Dictionary. Suryakanta. Intl Pubns Serv.

Sanskrit Manual (Enlarged) with a Vocabulary (English & Sanskrit) Monier Williams. Verry.

Sanskrit-Thai-English Dictionary. Intl Pubns Serv.

Sanskrit vocabulary. Bernfried Scherath. Brill.

The Student's English-Sanskrit Dictionary. V. S. Apte. Orient Bk Dist.

Student's English-Sanskrit Dictionary. V. S. Apte. Verry.

Tibetan-English Dictionary, with Sanskrit Synonyms. Sarat C. Das. Ed. by G. Sandberg & A. W. Heyde. Intl Pubns Serv.

Verschiffene Praefixe im Altindischen. Bernhard Koelver. Steiner Verlag.

Verschliffene Prafixe im Altindischen. Bernhard Kolver. Steiner Verlag.

Woerterbuch Sanskrit-Deutsch. Klaus Mylius. VEB Verlag Enzyklopadie.

SCOTTISH

Dictionary of Lowland Scotch. Charles Mackay. Gale.

SERBO-CROATIAN

Dictionary of Construction Industries. Ed. by B. Vukicevic. French & Eur.

Dictionary of Economic Terms. S. Bubic. French & Eur.

A Dictionary of Slavic Word Families. Louis J. Herman. Columbia U Pr.

Dictionary Slovene-Serbocroatian-Slovene. Jurancic. French & Eur.

Dictionnaire Francais-Serbo-Croate. Vander.

Dictionnaire Francais-Serbo-Croate. French & Eur.

Dictionnaire Serbocrate-Francais, Francais-Serbocroate, suivi d'une courte grammaire de Langue Francaise. B. Grujic. French & Eur.

Dizionario Italiano-Serbocroato, Serbocroato-Italiano. Ed. by P. Livadic. French & Eur.

Dizionario Italiano-Serbo Croato. Livadic. Vallardi A.

Dizionario italiano-serbocroato sloveno. Malipiero.

Dizionario serbocroato-italiano e sloveno-italiano. Malipiero.

Englesko-Hrvatska ili Srpska Tehnicko-Tehnoloska. Ignac Kulier. Prehrambeno-Tehnoloski.

English-Russian-Serbocroatian Aviations Dictionary. J. Dragovic. French & Eur.

Englesko-srpskohrvatski Recnik. Ed. by Syetomir Ristic & Zivojin Simic. Prosveta.

Englesko-srpskohrvatski Recnik. Morton Benson. Beogradski.

English - SerboCroatian Dictionary. Morton Benson. U of Pa Pr.

English-Croatian or Serbian Dictionary. Milan Drvodelic. Intl Learn Syst.

English-Croatian or Serbian Dictionary. Rudolf Filipovic. (Pub. by Collets). State Mutual Bk.

English-Serbo-Croat & Serbo-Croat-English Dictionary. J. Grujic. (Pub. by Collet's). State Mutual Bk.

English-Serbocroat & Serbocroat-English Dictionary. V. C. Grujic. (Pub. by Collets). State Mutual Bk.

English-Serbocroat & Serbocroat-English Geological & Mining Dictionary. Ing S. Verbic. (Pub. by Collets). State Mutual Bk.

English-Serbcroatian &
Serbocroatian-English Dictionary.
Blanka Brozovic & Oktavija
Gercan. Intl Learn Syst.
English-Serbocroatian Dictionary.
Rudolf Filipovic et al. Intl Learn
Syst.
English-Serbocroatian Dictionary.
Svetomir Ristic & Zivojin Simic.
Intl Learn Syst.
English-Serbocroatian Dictionary. Z.
Simic. French & Eur.
English-Serbocroatian Dictionary. M.
Benson. French & Eur.
English-Serbocroatian, Serbocroatian-
English Dictionary. Ratimir J.
Cvetanovic. Saphrograph.
German-Serbocroatian
Electrotechnical Dictionary. N. S.
Arsenijevic. French & Eur.
Learn Serbocroatian for English
Speakers. Saphrograph.
Langenscheidts Universal-
Woerterbuch Serbokroatisch.
Langenscheidt.
Langenscheidts Universal-
Woerterbuecher Serbokroatisch-
Deutsch. Langenscheidt.
Magyar-Szerbhorvat Szotar. Laszlo
Hadrovics et al. Terra.
Magyar-Szerbhorvat Szotar. Laszlo
Hadrovics. Terra.
Medicinski Leksikon. Kostic. French
& Eur.
Rjecnik Stranih Rijeci: Tudice &
Posudenice. Nakladni Zavod.
Scientific Technological Dictionary.
R. Popic et al. French & Eur.
Serbocroatian-English Dictionary. Ed.
by Morton Benson. U of Pa Pr.
Serbocroatian-English Dictionary. S.
Brkic. French & Eur.
Serbocroatian-English Dictionary. M.
Benson. French & Eur.
Serbocroatian-English Dictionary. M.
Drvodelic. French & Eur.
Serbocroatian-English, English-
Serbocroatian Dictionary. B. Grujic.
Heinman.
Serbocroatian-English-Serbocroatian
Dictionary: Short Grammar. B.
Grujic. Vanous.
Serbocroatian-Slovene Dictionary. J.
Jurancic. French & Eur.
Szerbhorvat-Magyar Szotar. Laszlo
Hadrovics et al. Terra.
Szerbhorvat-Magyar Szotar. Laszlo
Hadrovics. Terra.
Technical-Economical Dictionary for
Business Purposes. B. Bajic et al.
French & Eur.
Technisches Woerterbuch. Ulatko
Dabac. (Pub. by Bauverlag). French
& Eur.
Technisches Woerterbuch. Ulatko
Dabac. Bauverlag.
Technological Engineering Dictionary
German-Serbocroatian. Ed. by S.
Radic. French & Eur.
Vocabolario croato serbo-italiano de
M. Deanovic e J. Jerej. Niccolo
Nichea. Del Bianco.
Die Von Praefigierten Verben
Abgeleiteten Substantive in der
Modernen Serbokroatischen
Standartsprache. Klaus
Koszinowski. Sagner.
Yugoslavian Dictionary: English-
Serbocroatian. Z. Simic. Vanous.
Yugoslavian Mining Dictionary:
English-Serbo-English. S. Verbic.
Vanous.
Yugoslavic Deluxe Dictionary:
English-Croation or Serbian. R.
Filipuvic et al. Vanous.
Yugoslavic Dictionary: Slovene-
English. J. Kotnik. Vanous.

SHOSHONI

Newe Natekwinappeh: Shoshoni
Stories & Dictionary. Wick R.
Miller. AMS Pr.

SIAMESE

Siamese-English Dictionary. Edward
B. Michell. Ayer Co.

SINHALESE

Kalamanakarana Paribhasika Sabda
Sangrahaya. Hema Wijewardena.
Dewan Bahasa.

SINO-JAPANESE

Analytical Dictionary of Chinese &
Sino-Japenese. Bernhard Karlgren.
Dover.

SLAVIC

Langenscheidts Universal-
Woerterbuch Slowakisch.
Langenscheidt.
Langenscheidts Universal-
Woerterbuecher Slowakisch-
Deutsch. Langenscheidt.
Material Towards the Compilation of
a Concise Old Church Slavonic-
English Dictionary. T. Lysaght.
Victoria University Press.
Material Towards the Compilation of
a Concise Old Church Slavonic-
English Dictionary. T. A. Lysaght.
Price Milburn.
Medizintechnik-Englisch-Deutsch-
Franzoesisch-Russisch-Spanisch-
Polnisch-Ungarisch-Slowakisch.
Roald Albert & Harry Hahnewald.
VEB Technik.

SLOVAK

Anglicko-Slovensky Technicky
Slovnik. Stefan Benacka. Alfa-
Vydavatel.
Applied Technical Dictionary: Air
Conditioning & Refrigeration. (Pub.
by Collets). State Mutual Bk.
Applied Technical Dictionary: Oil
Processing & Petrochemistry. (Pub.
by Collets). State Mutual Bk.
Applied Technical Dictionary: Silicate
Technology. (Pub. by Collets). State
Mutual Bk.
Automatizacna Technika. Jiri Sykora.
Alfa-Vydavatel.
Cesko, Slovensko, Latinsko, Anglicko,
Nemecko, Rusky, Slovnik Plevelu.
Vaclav Kosik. SNTC.
Cesky a Sovensky Terminologicky
Slovnik z Fytopatologie a Ochrany
Rostlin. SNTC.
A Concise English-Slovak & Slovak-
English Technical Dictionary. J.
Novak & R. Binder. (Pub. by
Collet's). State Mutual Bk.
A Concise English-Slovak & Slovak-
English Technical Dictionary. J.
Novak & R. Binder. (Pub. by
Collets). State Mutual Bk.
Dictionar Portrativ Roman-Slovac,
Slovac-Roman. Milota
Bagonova-Sidlova. SNTC.
Dictionary for the Graphic Arts in
Eight Languages: German-English-
French-Spanish-Russian-Hungarian-
Polish-Slovak. Perfect Graphic.
Dictionary of Automatic Data
Processing. Ing H. Burger. (Pub. by
Collets). State Mutual Bk.
Dictionary of Slavic Linquistic
Terminology. Alois Jedlicka. (Pub.
by Helmut Buske Verlag Hamburg).
Benjamins North Am.

Dictionary of Slavonic Linquistc
Terminology. Alois Jedlicka. (Pub.
by Helmut Buske Verlag Hamburg).
Benjamins North am.
Dictionary of the Graphic Arts
Industry. Ed. by W. Muller.
Elsevier.
English-Slovak Dictionary. P. Simko.
(Pub. by Collet's). State Mutual Bk.
English-Slovak Technical Dictionary.
S. Benacka. (Pub. by Collet's).
State Mutual Bk.
Polsko -Slovensky a Slovensko-Polsky
Slovnik. Mikulas Stano. SNTC.
Pol'sko-Slovensky a Slovensko-Polsky
Slovnik. Mikulas Stano et al.
SNTC.
Silikatova Technika. Armin Petzold.
Alfa-Vydavatel.
Slovak-English Business
Correspondence Dictionary. Dusan
Zavada. (Pub. by Collet's). State
Mutual Bk.
Slovak-English Dictionary. J.
Vilikovska & Jan Vilkovsky.
Shalom.
Slovak-English Dictionary. J.
Vilikovska & P. Vilikovsky. (Pub.
by Collet's). State Mutual Bk.
Slovak-English Dictionary.
Vilikovska. Vanous.
Slovak-English, English-Slovak
Dictionary. (Pub. by Slovart
Czechoslovakia). Hippocrene Bks.
Slovak-English-Slovak Pocket
Dictionary. J. Smejkalova et al.
Vanous.
Slovak-Russian Dictionary. D. Kollar
et al. French & Eur.
Szlovak-Magyar Szotar. Marianne T.
Gobel. Terra.
Technicka Akustika. Walter
Reichardt. VEB Verlat Technik.
Technische Akustik. Walter
Reichardt. VEB Verlag Technik.

SLOVENIAN

Anglicko-slovensk y lekarsky slovnik.
Anton Parks. Univerzita
Komenskeho.
Dictionary of Automatical Technique.
Ed. by Jiri Sykora. French & Eur.
Cibernetical Dictionary: E-G-F-R-
Slovene. A. Sydow. French & Eur.
Dictionary French-Slovene. A. Grad.
French & Eur.
Dictionary of Acoustics: English-
German-French-Russian-Spanish-
Polish-Madarsko-Slovene. W.
Reichardt. French & Eur.
Dictionary of Hydraulics &
Pneumatics: English-German-
Russian-Slovene. G. Neubert.
French & Eur.
Dictionary of Metallurgy. Ed. by A.
Dollinger. French & Eur.
Dictionnaire Moderne: Slovene-
French-Slovene. A. Grad. French &
Eur.
Dictionary Slovene-Serbocroatian-
Slovene. Jurancic. French & Eur.
Dizionario Italian-Slovar. A. Bajec &
P. Kalan. French & Eur.
Dizionario serbocroato-italiano e
sloveno-italiano. Malipiero.
Dizionario Moderno Slovene-Italian-
Slovene. A. Grad. French & Eur.
English-Slovene Dictionary. A. Grad
et al. French & Eur.
German-Slovene Dictionary. F.
Tomsic. French & Eur.
Karmannyi Slovatsko-Russkii i
Russko-Slovatskii Slovar. (Pub. by
Russkii Iazyk). Four Continent.
Langenscheidts Universal-
Woerterbuch Slowenisch.
Langenscheidt.

Modern Dictionary Slovene-English,
English-Slovene. Komac & J. Skeri.
French & Eur.
Modèrn Dictionary Slovene-German-
Slovene. D. Debenjak. French &
Eur.
Recueil Terminologique Multilinque
du Soudage et des Techniques
Connexes. French & Eur.
Serbocroatian-Slovene Dictionary. J.
Jurancic. French & Eur.
Slovene-English Dictionary. J.
Kotnick. Shalom.
Slovene-English Dictionary. J. Kotnik.
French & Eur.
Slovene-English, English-Slovene
Dictionary. J. Kotnik & A. Grad.
Heinman.
Slovene-German Dictionary. F.
Tomsic. French & Eur.
Technical Dictionary English-Slovene.
French & Eur.
Technical Dictionary of
Automatization & Programming:
English, French, German, Russian,-
Slovene. Ed. by E. Burger. French
& Eur.
Technical Veterinary Dictionary.
Wolfgang Lindeke. French & Eur.
Yugoslavian-English Slovene
Dictionary. R. Skerlj et al. Vanous.
Yugoslavian Pocket Dictionary:
Slovene-English, English-Slovenski.
Komac & Skerlj. Vanous.
Yugoslavic Dictionary: English-
Slovene. A. Grad et al. Vanous.

SOMALI

Petit Lexique Somali-Francais.
Christophe Philbert. Klincksieck.

SOTHO

English Sotho-Sotho English
Dictionary. Shalom.
Groot Noord-Sotho-Woordeboek. D.
Ziervogel. Van Schaik.
Popular Northern Sotho Dictionary.
T. Kriel. Van Schaik.

SOUDANESE

Lexique des Parlers Arabes-Tchado-
Soudanais. Arlette Roth-Laly.
Editions du CNRS.

SPANISH

A Beginner's Bilingual Pictorial
Dictionary. Bilingual Ed Serv.
ABC Dictionary I: Arabic & Span.
Libr d. Liban. Intl Bk Ctr.
ABC Dictionary I, Arabic-Spanish.
Intl Bk Ctr.

ABC Dictionary Tamhidi: Arabic-Spanish. Libr du Liban. Intl Bk Ctr.

Accounting Dictionary - U.E.C. Lexicon: American-French-German-Spanish-Dutch. Union Europeenne Des Experts Compatables, Economiques et Financiers. Intl Pubns Serv.

Alcala-Zamora, Diccionario Frances-Espanol, Espanol-Frances. Alcala-Zamora. French & Eur.

Alcala-Zamora, Diccionario Frances-Espanol, Espanol-Frances. Alcala-Zamora. French & Eur.

Alevin sopena color. Iaconi.

Anglo-Ispano-Russko-Frantsuzskii Slovar Nauchnykh & Tekhnicheskikh Terminov Po Atomnoi Energii. (Pub. by United Nations Publications). Four Continent.

Appleton-Cuyas Dictionary: English-Spanish, Spanish-English. Pan Amer Pub.

Arco Motor Vehicle Dictionary: English & Spanish. Ed. by Robert F. Lima. Arco.

Argo Limeno. Guillermo E. Bendezu Neyra. Libreria.

Astronautical Multilingual Dictionary: International Academy of Astronautics. Elsevier.

Atheneum Worterbuch: Aleman-Espanol, Espanol-Aleman. F. Muller. French & Eur.

Athenum Woordenboek: Espanol-Holandes, Holandes-Espanol. French & Eur.

Atlas & Glossary of Primary Sedimentary Structures. F. J. Pettijohn & P. E. Potter. Springer-Verlag.

Bantam New College Dictionary: English-Spanish, Spanish-English. Pan Amer Pub.

Bantam New College Spanish & English Dictionary. Ed. by Edwin B. Williams. Bantam.

Barrio Language Dictionary. D. Fuentes & J. A. Lopez. Borden.

Barrio Language Dictionary. Dagaberto Fuentes & Jose A. Lopez. Camino Real.

Basic Dictionary of the Petroleum Industry. Augustin Mendez Manzano. Imported Bks.

Basic Spanish Dictionary: English-Spanish, Spanish-English. Cortina & Grosset. Pan Amer Pub.

Basic Words in Spanish. Pan Amer Pub.

Basico Sopena: Diccionario Ilustrado de la Lengua Espanla. Lazaro Ladero Sanchez. (SOP). Lectorum Pubns.

Basque-Spanish Dictionary. Issac M. Lopez. Revisionist Pr.

Beginner's Spanish-English Dictionary. Iaconi.

Berlitz Latin-American Spanish for Travellers. Berlitz Editors. (Berlitz). Macmillan.

Berlitz Pocket Dictionaries: Spanish-English. Berlitz Editors. (Berlitz). Macmillan.

Berlitz Pocket Dictionaries: Spanish-English-Spanish. Berlitz. Macmillan.

Berlitz Spanish for Travellers. Berlitz Editors. (Berlitz). Macmillan.

Bibliotheca Indosinica. Dictionnaire bibliographique des ouvrages relatifs a la peninsule indo-chinoise. Henri Cordier. B Franklin.

Bibliotheca Sinica, dictionnaire bibliographique des ouvrages relatifs a l'Empire chinois. Henri Cordier. B Franklin.

Bildwoerterbuch Spanisch: Diccionario por la Imagen. Biblio Inst.

Bilingual Dictionary of Anglicismos, Barbarismos, Pachuquismos y Otras Locuciones En el Barrio. Francisco Padilla. Padilla.

Bola Glossary of Civil Procedural Law: Spanish-English & English-Spanish. Bola Publications. Bola Pubns.

Bola Glossary of Electronic Data Processing & Computer Terms English-Spanish & Spanish-English. Bola Publications. Bola Pubns.

Bola Glossary of Electronic Data Processing & Computer Terms: English-Spanish & Spanish-English. Iaconi.

Breve Diccionario de Filosofia. French & Eur.

Breve Diccionario del Argentino Exquisito. Adolfo Bioy Casares. French & Eur.

Breve Diccionario Espanol-Ruso: Ruso-Espanol de Terminos Cientificos & Tecnicos. J. C. Orts et al. French & Eur.

Breve Diccionario Etimologico de la Lengua Castellana. Joan Corominas. (GRD). Lectorum Pubns.

Breve Diccionario Etimologico de la Lengua Espanola. Joan Corominas. French & Eur.

Breve Diccionario Philosofia. Muller-Halder. French & Eur.

Breve Diccionario Porrua de la Lengua Espanola. Antonio Raluy Poudevida. Lectorum Pubns.

Breve diccionario Porrua de la lengua espanola. Antonio Raluy Poudevida. Rev. by Francisco Monterde. Porrua.

Breve diccionario Porrua de la lengua espanola. Iaconi.

Brevis Diccionario Practico Castellano. French & Eur.

Brew Vocabulari Catala-Castella-Angles de Comerc Exterior. French & Eur.

The Businessman's Everyday English to Spanish Dictionary: El Mundo De Negocios. Ivan De Renty. Larousse.

Canigo Diccionari Castella-Catala, Catala-Castella. French & Eur.

Canigo: Dicionario Catalan-Castellano, Castellano-Catalan. Pere Elies I Busqueta. Sopena.

Capitol's Concise Dictionary. French & Eur.

Cassell's Colloquial Spanish. Cassell. Macmillan.

Cassell's Compact Spanish-English Dictionary. (LE). Dell.

Cassell's Concise Spanish-English English-Spanish Dictionary. Macmillan.

Cassell's Spanish Dictionary. Natl Textbk.

Cassell's Spanish Dictionary: Concise Spanish-English English-Spanish. Cassell. Macmillan.

Cassell's Spanish Dictionary: English-Spanish, Spanish-English. Pan Amer Pub.

Cassell's Spanish Dictionary: Spanish-English, English-Spanish. Ed. by Edgar A. Peers. Macmillan.

Cassell's Spanish Dictionary: Spanish-English, English-Spanish. Cassell. Ed. by Edgan A. Peers. Macmillan.

Cassell's Spanish Dictionary: Thumb-indexed Spanish-English English-Spanish. Cassell. Macmillan.

Cat in the Hat Beginner Book Dictionary in English & Spanish. P. D. Eastman. Beginner.

The Cat in the Hat Beginner Book Dictionary in Spanish & English. Lectorum Pubns.

Chemins de Fer Glossary. Bureau International de Documentation de Chemin de Fer. Elsevier.

Cinco Mil Seiscientos Refranes & Frases de Uso Comun Entre los Dominicanos. Jose A. Brache. Ed. by Nicolas Pichardo. Galaxia.

Claves de la Masoneria. Emilio Castell Blanch. Dopesa.

Collins Contemporary Dictionary: English-Spanish, Spanish-English. Pan Am Bk Co.

Collins English-Spanish & Spanish-English Dictionary. S&S.

Collins Spanish Dictionary: English-Spanish, Spanish-English. Pan Amer Pub.

Compacto Diccionario de la Lengua Espanola. Biblograf SP.

Compacto Diccionario de la Lengua Espanola "Vox". Biblograf.

Compacto Diccionario Ingles-Espanol Espanol-Ingles. Biblograf SP.

Compacto Diccionario Ingles-Espanol, Espanol-Ingles Vox. Biblograf.

Compendio de Dificultades de la Lengua Inglesa. J. Pineiro. Biblograf SP.

Compendio de dificultades de la lengua inglesa. Jaime Pineiro. Fed Gremios.

Compendios de Divulgacion Filologica. Incl. Biblograf.

Conciso Diccionario de la Lengua Espanola. Biblograf SP.

Conciso Diccionario de la Lengua Espanola "Vox". Biblograf.

Conciso Diccionario Ingles-Espanol, Espanol-Ingles Vox. Biblograf.

Conciso Diccionario Ingles-Espanol Espanol-Ingles. Biblograf SP.

Conference Terminology in English, Spanish, Russian, Italian, German & Hungarian. J. Herbert. Elsevier.

Cortina-Ace Basic Spanish Dictionary. Cortina. Ace Bks.

Cortina-Grosset Basic Spanish Dictionary. Ed. by Luis M. Laita. (G&D) Putnam Pub Group.

Cortina-Grosset Basic Spanish Dictionary. Luis M. Laita. Ed. by Dilaver Berberi & Edel A. Berberi. (G&D). Putnam Pub Group.

Cortina Handy Spanish-English Dictionary. Ed. by G. H. Calvert. Cortina.

Cortina Handy Spanish-English, English-Spanish Dictionary. G. H. Calvert. B&N NY.

Dansk-Spansk Ordborg. French & Eur.

Del Espanol Hablado en Colombia: Seis Muestras de Lexico. Luis Florez. Instituto Caro & Cuervo.

Deutsch fuer Baufachleute. G. Wallnig & H. Evered. Bauverlag.

Deutsch-Spanisches Glossarium. Mario R. Lerche. (Pub. by Fritz Knapp Verlag). French & Eur.

Deutsch-Spanisches Glossarium Finanzieller & Wirtschaftlicher Fachausdrueck. Mario R. Lerche. Knapp Verlag.

Dialectologia Hispanoamericana. Zamora Clemente & Jorge Juan-Guitart. Almar Edns.

Dicccionario del Cine. George Sadoul. French & Eur.

Diccionare de la musica. Roland De Cande. EDNS Seseni Dos.

Diccionari Angles-Catala. Jordi Colomer del Castillo. Portic.

Diccionari basic castella-catala i catala-castela. M. Arimany.

Diccionari Basic Catala-Castella, Castella-Catala. Miquel Arimany Coma. French & Eur.

Diccionari calala de simonims. Albert Jane. Aedos.

Diccionari Castella-Catala, Catala-Castella Petit. Santiago Alberti. Alberti.

Diccionari castella-catala, catala-castella. Alberti & Gubern Santiago. Alberti.

Diccionari Catala-Castella. Francisco de Moll Y Cassanovas. Moll Edit.

Diccionari Catala-Castella, Castella-Catala. Josep Miracle. Poseidon SA.

Diccionari catala-castella, castella-catala. Mateu.

Diccionari catala-castella, castella-catala. Josep Miracle. Edhasa.

Diccionari Catala-Castella-Castellano-Catalan. Frederic Larreula. Bruguera.

Diccionari Catala-Castella I Castella-Catala. Fransesc de B. Moll Casanovas. French & Eur.

Diccionari Catala-Castella: Vocabulari Basic. Josep Munte Vila. Blume Edit.

Diccionari catala general. M. Arimany.

Diccionari catala-valencia-balear. Antoni M. Alcover Sureda & Moll Casasnoves. Moll Edit.

Diccionari de agricultura ruso-espanol. Cultura Popular.

Diccionari de la Llengua Catalana. Santiago Alberti. Alberti.

Diccionari de la Rima. Francesc Ferrer Pastor. Piquenas Edit.

Diccionari de metjes catalans. Josep Maria Calbet Corbella. Dalmau.

Diccionari de sinonims i antonims. S. Pay Estrany. Teide.

Diccionari de sinonims. Miquel Franquesa. Portic.

Diccionari de sinonims i antonims: Edicio economica. Santiago Pey Estrany. Teide.

Diccionari d'electronica. Lluis Marquet. Portic.

Diccionari d'Informatica. Carmara Oficial de Comercio, Industria y Navegacion Barcelona. Organ Ofic Adm.

Diccionari escolar de la llengua catalana 'Vox'. Biblo SP.

Diccionari Escolarde la Llengua Catalana. Biblograf SP.

Diccionari etimologic i complementari de la llengua catalana. Joan Coromines i Vigneaux. Curial.

Diccionari etimologie i complementari de la llengua catalana. Joan Coromines i Vegneaux. Curial.

Diccionari general de barbarismes i altres incorreccions. Joan Miravitlles Serradell. Claret Edit.

Diccionari Italia-Catala Catala-Italia. Jordi Fornas Prat. Portic.

Diccionari Manual Castella-Catala, Catala-Castella. Vox. Biblo Sp.

Diccionari popular catala-castella. Milla Lib.

Diccionari Practic Catala-Frances. Miguel Arimany Coma. French & Eur.

Diccionari practic catala-frances. M. Arimany.

Diccionari practic catala general. M. Arimany.

Diccionari practic de comerc exterior Catala-Angles Angles-Catala. Joan Ferrer Santalo. Organ Ofic Adm.

Diccionari practic frances-catala. M. Arimany.

Diccionari practic frances-catala, catala-frances. M. Arimany.

Diccionari tecnic de l'automovil. Balbastre & Josep Ferrer. Portic.

Diccionario. Susaeta.

Diccionario A R V E: Obra completa. Tr. by Varios. Argos-Vergara.

Diccionario A R V E: Tomo 1; Ingles-Espanol. Tr. by Varios. Argos-Vergara.

Diccionario A R V E: Tomo 2; Espanol-Ingles. Tr. by Varios. Argos-Vergara.

Diccionario Abreviado Aleman-Espagnol. Biblo SP.

Diccionario Abreviado de la Lengua Espanola. Biblograf SP.

Diccionario abreviado de la Lengua Espanola Vox. Biblo SP.

Diccionario Abreviado de Sinonimos. Fernando Corripio Perez. French & Eur.

Diccionario Abreviado de Sinonimos. Samuel Gili Gaya. Biblograf SP.

Diccionario Abreviado de Sinonimos. Fernando Corripio. (BRG). Lectorum Pubns.

Diccionario abreviado de sinonimos 'Vox' Biblo SP.

Diccionario Abreviado Espanol-Chino. French & Eur.

Diccionario Abreviado Frances-Espanol Espanol-Frances. Biblograf SP.

Diccionario abreviado Ingles-Espanol Vox. Biblo SP.

Diccionario Abreviado Ingles-Espanol Espanol-Ingles. Biblograf SP.

Diccionario Abreviado Italiano,-Espanol Espanol-Italiano. French & Eur.

Diccionario Abreviado Italiano-Espanol Espanol-Italiano. Ed. by Givanna Schepisi. Biblograf SP.

Diccionario Abreviado Latino-Espanol Espanol-Latino. Biblograf SP.

Diccionario Abreviado Latino-Espanol Espanol-Latino 'Spes' Biblo SP.

Diccionario abreviado Latino-Espanol Espanol-Latino Vox. Biblo SP.

Diccionario Abreviado Ortografico de la Lengua Espanola. Biblograf SP.

Diccionario Academia. Fernandez.

Diccionario academia dos. Fernandez.

Diccionario Academico de la Lengua. Albir.

Diccionario Actualizado de la Lengua Espanola. Juan Capdevila Font. French & Eur.

Diccionario Actualizado De Sinonimos y Contrarios De la Lengua Espanola. Juan Capdevila Font. French & Eur.

Diccionario aleman-espanol. Mayfe.

Diccionario Aleman-Espanol. Carlos Brandau. Mayfe.

Diccionario Aleman-Espanol-Aleman. Franz Muller. Imported Bks.

Diccionario aleman-espanol de medicina. F. Ruiz Torres. MMW Verlag.

Diccionario aleman-espanol de medicina. F. Ruiz Torres. Alhambra.

Diccionario Aleman-Espanol, Espanol-Aleman de Medicina. Francisco Ruiz Torres. French & Eur.

Diccionario Aleman-Espanol, Espanol-Aleman. E. F. Martinez Amador. French & Eur.

Diccionario Aleman-Espanol, Espanol-Aleman. Muller. French & Eur.

Diccionario Aleman-Espanol Espanol-Aleman. Ed. by Michael Schmidt. Biblograf SP.

Diccionario Aleman-Espanol Espanol-Aleman 'Vox' Biblo SP.

Diccionario aleman-espanol y espanol-aleman de medicina. F. Ruiz Torres. Alhambra.

Diccionario Alevin Sopena Escolar de Iniciacion a la Lengua Espanola. Lectorum Pubns.

Diccionario Alienza ingles-espanol, espanol-ingles. Fernandez.

Diccionario analitico de Mampruli. Evangelina Arana & Mauricio Swadesh. INAH.

Diccionario Anaya de la Lengua. French & Eur.

Diccionario Anaya de la Lengua. Anaya.

Diccionario & Manual de las Nuevas Matematicas. Robert W. Marks. Editors Pr Serv.

Diccionario Arabe-Espanol. French & Eur.

Diccionario Arabe-Espanol, Espanol-Arabe. Alhambra. French & Eur.

Diccionario Aristos. Sopena.

Diccionario Aristos con perdanismos. Bruno.

Diccionario Atlas De Anatomia Humana. Nicola Piscitelli. French & Eur.

Diccionario: Atlas De Mineralogia. Vincenzo De Michele. French & Eur.

Diccionario Atomico. Victorin Charles. French & Eur.

Diccionario atomico. Tr. by Victorin Charles. Leru.

Diccionario Aunamendi Espanol-Vasco: Tomo 7, Conch-Corr. Bernardo Estornes Lasa et al. Aunamendi Edit.

Diccionario auxiliar de traductor: Espanol-Ingles. Jose Merino Bustamante. CEEI.

Diccionario Auxiliar del Crucigramista. Fausto Turell Baldovi. French & Eur.

Diccionario Auxiliar del Crucigramista. Baldovi F. Turell. Bruguera MX.

Diccionario auxiliar del crucigramista. Bruguera.

Diccionario auxiliar del crucigramista II. Fausto Turell Baldovi. Bruguera.

Diccionario Auxiliar del Traductor Espanol-Ingles. Jose Merino Bustamante. French & Eur.

Diccionario Auxiliar del Traductor Espanol-Ingles. Jose Merino Bustamante. CEEI.

Diccionario Axon de zoologia y botanica. Plus Ultra.

Diccionario Bachiller. Hector F. Miri. Claridad.

Diccionario basico. Sopena.

Diccionario basico. Pablo Arogones. Mayfe.

Diccionario Basico Anaya de la Lengua. Anaya.

Diccionario basico de fudicion ingles-castellano. Channazaroff-Waganoff. Mitre.

Diccionario Basico de la Construccion. Jose Zurita Ruiz. French & Eur.

Diccionario basico de la construccion. Jose Zurita Ruiz. Ceac.

Diccionario basico de la construccion II. Jose Zurita Ruiz. Ceac.

Diccionario basico de la industria del petroleo. Augustin Mendez Manzano. Paraninfo.

Diccionario Basico de la Industria del Petroleo & Derivados. Mendez. Paraninfo.

Diccionario basico de matematicas. Mariano Diaz Velazquiz. Anaya.

Diccionario Basico De Seguros. Julio Castelo Matran. French & Eur.

Diccionario Basico de seguros. Mex. de Seguros.

Diccionario Basico de Seguros. Julio Castelo Matran. Mapfre.

Diccionario basico escolar. Educar.

Diccionario basico escolar de la lengua castellana. Edit Nebrija.

Diccionario Basico Escolar de la Lengua Espanola. Juan Capdevilla Font. French & Eur.

Diccionario Basico Escolar de la Lengua Espanola. Juan Capdevilla Font. French & Eur.

Diccionario basico Espasa: Tomo 3. Espasa Calpe.

Diccionario Basico Frances-Espanol Espanol-Frances. Biblograf SP.

Diccionario Basico Ilustrado Espanol-Ingles. Mediterraneo.

Diccionario Basico Ilustrado Espanol Ingles. Mediterraneo.

Diccionario Basico Ilustrado Espanol-Ingles-Euskera: Obra Complete. Mediterraneo.

Diccionario Basico Ilustrado Espanol Ingles-Gallego. Mediterraneo.

Diccionario Basico Ilustrado Espanol Ingles-Gallego. Mediterraneo.

Diccionario Basico Ilustrado Espanol-Ingles: Obra Completa. Mediterraneo.

Diccionario Basico Ingles-Espanol Espanol-Ingles Vox. Biblo SP.

Diccionario Basico Ingles-Espanol Espanol-Ingles. Biblograf SP.

Diccionario Basico Latino-Espanol. Recuero Pascual. Ameller Edic.

Diccionario Basico Latino-Espanol. Biblo SP.

Diccionario Basico Latino-Espanol, Espanol-Latino. Eustaquio Echauri Martinez. Biblo Sp.

Diccionario Basico Latino-Espanol Espanol-Latino. Biblograf SP.

Diccionario basico latino-espanol, espanol-latino. Imported Bks.

Diccionario basico Latino-Espanol Espanol-Latino. Biblo SP.

Diccionario básico universal. Fernandez.

Diccionario Biblico Manual. Heinz Obermayer. French & Eur.

Diccionario Bibliografico De Liegos Sueltos Poeticos, Siglo XVI. Antonio Rodriguez Monino. French & Eur.

Diccionario Bilingue. Cruzada Span Pubns.

Diccionario bilingue aleman-espanol y espanol-aleman. Franz Muller. Sopena.

Diccionario Bilingue De Psicologia. Adela Alcantud. Senda Nueva.

Diccionario bilingue frances-espanol-aleman. Alcala Zamora. Sopena.

Diccionario bilingue ilustrado. Natl Textbk.

Diccionario bilingue ilustrado. Bilingual Ed Serv.

Diccionario bilingue ilustrado. Iaconi.

Diccionario bilingue ingles-espanol y espanol-ingles. Ricardo Roberston. Sopena.

Diccionario Bilingue Maya Mopan & Espanol. Inst Ling Ver.

Diccionario bilinque para la juventud. Juan Delvalle. Dist. Comuneros.

Diccionario Biografico de la Musica. Juan Ricart Matas. French & Eur.

Diccionario Brevis. Bruno.

Diccionario Brevis duplex: aleman-castellano y castellano-aleman. Sopena.

Diccionario Brevis duplex: frances-castellano y castellano-frances. Sopena.

Diccionario Brevis duplex: ingles-castellano y castellano-ingles. Sopena.

Diccionario Brevis duplex: Italiano-castellano y castellano-italiano. Sopena.

Diccionario Brevis duplex: Portugues-catellano y castellano-portugues. Sopena.

Diccionario Bursatil. French & Eur.

Diccionario Cassell espanol-ingles, ingles-espanol: Obra completa. Edgar Allison Peers. Salvat Editores.

Diccionario Cassell espanol-ingles, ingles-espanol: Tomo 1. Edgar A. Peers. Salvat Editores.

Diccionario Cassell espanol-ingles, ingles-espanol: Tomo 2. Edgar A. Peers. Salvat Editores.

Diccionario Cassell espanol-ingles, ingles-espanol: Tomo 3. Edgar A. Peers. Salvat Editores.

Diccionario Cassell espanol-ingles, ingles-espanol: Tomo 4. Edgar A. Peers. Salvat Editores.

Diccionario Cassell espanol-ingles, ingles-espanol: Tomo 5. Edgar A. Peers. Salvat Editores.

Diccionario Cassell espanol-ingles, ingles-espanol: Tomo 6. Edgar A. Peers. Salvat Editores.

Diccionario Cassell Espanol-Ingles, Ingles-Espanol. Edgar A. Peers & Victor Jose. Salvat Editores.

Diccionario Castella-Catala Catala-Castella. Biblo SP.

Diccionario castellano discolar. Castellana.

Diccionario castellano-guarani, guarani-castellano. Antonio Guasch. Dist. Comuneros.

Diccionario castellano illustrado. Fernandez.

Diccionario Castellano Ilustrado. French & Eur.

Diccionario castellano ilustrado. Felix Diez Mateo. Neguri.

Diccionario castellano ilustrado (Lexicon) Bilingual Ed Serv.

Diccionario castellano-ingles. Collins. Albatros.

Diccionario Castellano-Vasco. P. Roman de Bera. French & Eur.

Diccionario Ch'ol-Espanol. H. W. Aulie & Evelyn W. De Aulie. Inst Ling Ver.

Diccionario cientifico ilustrado. E. G. Speck. Editors Pr Serv.

Diccionario Cientifico y Tecnologico Espanol, Ingles, Frances, Aleman. T. C. Collocott. Imported Bks.

Diccionario Collins Contemporary English-Spanish Ingles-Espanol. R. F. Brown. Grijalbo.

Diccionario Collins Ingles-Espanol. Colin Smith. Grijalbo.

Diccionario Collins Spanish-English Ingles-Espanol. Manuel Smith Colinbermego. Grijalbo.

Diccionario comercial: Espanol-ingles e ingles-espanol. A. Frias. Juventud.

Diccionario Comercial Espanol-Ingles: El Secretario. Alejandro Frias-Sucre Giraud. Juventud.

Diccionario Comercial Espanol-Ingles y Ingles-Espanol. Alejandro Frias-Sucre Giraud. French & Eur.

Diccionario Comercial Ingles-Espanol. Alejandro Frias-Sucre Girard. Lectorum Pubns.

Diccionario Comercial Ingles-Espanol, Espanol-Ingles. Alejandro F. S. Giraud. Editorial Juventud.

Diccionario comercial Ingles-Espanol, Espanol-Ingles. Alejandro Frias-Sucre. Fed Gremios.

Diccionario comercial y economico moderno: Ingles-espanol. G. Varela Colmeiro. Inter-Ciencia.

Diccionario Compendiado de la Lengua Espanola. Biblograf SP.

Diccionario Compendiado de la Lengua Espanola 'Vox' Biblo SP.

Diccionario Compendiado, Frances-Espanol, Espanol-Frances. Biblograf SP.

Diccionario Compendiado Ingles-Espanol Espanol-Ingles. Biblograf SP.

Diccionario compendiado Ingles-Espanol, Espanol-Ingles. Fed Gremios.

Diccionario Compendiado Ingles-Espanol. Biblo SP.

Diccionario Conciso de Modismos Ingles-Espanol, Espanol-Ingles. Francisco Sanchez Benedito. French & Eur.

Diccionario consico de modiamos. Francisco Sanchez Benedito. Alhambra.

Diccionario Cordillera inglés-español, español-inglés. Bilingual Ed Serv.

Diccionario Corona Ingles. Everest.

Diccionario Critico Etimologico Castellano & Hispanico. Joan Corominas & J. A. Pascual. Gredos.

Diccionario critico etimologico castellano & hispanico. Joan Coromines i Vigneaux & J. A. Pascual. Gredos.

Diccionario Critico Etimologico Castellano & Hispanico. J. A. Joan-Pascual. Gredos.

Diccionario Critico Etimologico De la Lengua Espanola. Joan Corominas. French & Eur.

Diccionario Cuyas: Ingles-Espanol-Espanol-Ingles. Camino Real.

Diccionario Cuyas: Spanish-French, French-Spanish. Colton Bk.

Diccionario Cuyas: Spanish-German, German-Spanish. Colton Bk.

Diccionario Cuyas: Spanish-Italian, Italian-Spanish. Colton Bk.

Diccionario cuyás. Camino Real.

Diccionario d Teoria Folklorica. Paulo de Carvalho Neto. Intl Guatemala.

Diccionario de Aforismos, Proverbios & Refranes. Sintes. (SOP). Lectorum Pubns.

Diccionario de Aforismos: Proverbios Refranes. J. Sintes. French & Eur.

Diccionario de aforismos, proverbios y refrances. Sintes. Sintes.

Diccionario de aforismos, proverbios y refrances. Jorge Sintes Pros. Sintes.

Diccionario de agricultura. Soroa. Labor.

Diccionario de agricultura ruso-espanol. Pueblos Unidos.

Diccionario de Ajedrez. Ramon Ibero. French & Eur.

Diccionario de Alimentacion Animal. Ed. by M. Picciony. French & Eur.

Diccionario de alimentacion animal. M. Piccioni. Acribia.

Diccionario de Americanismos. Marcos A. Moringo. French & Eur.

Diccionario de americanismos. Tres Americas.

Diccionario de americanismos. Marcos A. Moringo. Teide.

Diccionario de Americanismos. Marcos A. Moringo. SEI.

Diccionario de Americanismos. Alfredo N. Neves. SPA.

Diccionario de Americanismos. Everest.

Diccionario de Anglicismos. Ricardo J. Alfaro. French & Eur.

Diccionario de anglicismos, barbaricismos, pachuquismos & otras locuciónes. Padill Francisco. Iaconi.

Diccionario de Anonimos y Seudonimos Hispanoamericanos. Jose T. Medina. Ethridge.

Diccionario de Antropologia. Bellaterra.

Diccionario de antropologia. Tr. by Charles Winick. Troquel.

Diccionario de Argentinismos de Ayer y de Hoy. Diego Abad de Santillan. French & Eur.

Diccionario de Argot Espanol. Victor Leon. Alianza Ed.

Diccionario de argot espanol. Victor Leon Nunez. Alianza Ed.

Diccionario De Arqueologia. Warwick Bray & David Trump. French & Eur.

Diccionario de Arquitectos de la Antiguedad a Nuestros Dias. G Gili.

Diccionario de Arquitectura. Nikolaus Pevsner et al. French & Eur.

Diccionario de Arquitectura. Tesoro Edit.

Diccionario de Arquitectura. D. Ware & B. Beatty. G Gili.

Diccionario de Arquitectura. Nikolaus
Pevsner. Alianza Ed.
Diccionario de arquitectura. Nikolaus
Pevsner et al. Tr. by Agustin
Bustamante. Alianza Ed.
Diccionario de Arte & Artistas.
Parramon Edns.
Diccionario de Arte & Artistas.
Parramon Edns.
Diccionario de Artes y Artistas.
Peter Murray & Linda Murray.
French & Eur.
Diccionario De Atres Adivinatorias.
Scouezec. French & Eur.
Diccionario de Autoridades. French &
Eur.
Diccionario De Banca. Antonio
Martinez Cerezo. French & Eur.
Diccionario de Banca. A. Martinez
Cerezo. Piramide.
Diccionario de banca. Antonio
Martinez Cerezo. (Dist. Grupo
Editorial). Piramide.
Diccionario de Banca & Borsa:
Catala-Castella-Diccionario de
Banca & Bolsa. Banca Mas Sarda,
Servicio de Estudios. Alba.
Diccionario de banca y bolsa. Beltran.
Labor.
Diccionario de Banca y Bolsa, Tomo
I: Ingles-Espanol. Manuel Bellisco
Hernandez. French & Eur.
Diccionario De Bibliografia Espanola.
Dionisio Hidalgo. B Franklin.
Diccionario de Bibliotecologia.
French & Eur.
Diccionario De Biologia. M.
Abercrombie et al. French & Eur.
Diccionario de Biologia. Javier
Jimenez Ortega. Porrua.
Diccionario de Biologia. T. Lender et
al. Tr. by Merce Serrano & Ferran
Vallespinos. Grijalbo.
Diccionario De Biologia Animal.
Carlos A. Aguayo & Virgilio Biaggi.
U of PR Pr.
Diccionario de Biologia en Quatre
Lenguas: Aleman, Ingles, Frances y
Espanol. Gunther Haensch &
Gisela Haberkamp. French & Eur.
Diccionario de Bolivianismos. Nicolas
Fernandez Naranjo. Cochabamba.
Diccionario de Bolsa. J. Ignacio de
Garmendia Miangolarra. French &
Eur.
Diccionario de Bolsa. I. Garmendia
Miangolarra. Piramide.
Diccionario de bolsa. J. Ignacio De
Garmendia Miangolarra. Piramide.
Diccionario De Bolsillo De la Lengua
Espanola: Mini Sopena. French &
Eur.
Diccionario De Bolsillo Frances-
Espanol, Espagnol-Francais. Arturo
Cuyas Armengol. French & Eur.
Diccionario De Bolsillo, Ingles-
Espanol y Spanish-English. French
& Eur.
Diccionario de bolsillo latino-espanol
& espanol-latino. Vives. Coculsa.
Diccionario de bolsillo: Spanish-
English English-Spanish. Follett.
Diccionario De Botanica. French &
Eur.
Diccionario De Botanica. Pio Pont
Quer. French & Eur.
Diccionario de botanica. Font Quer.
Labor.
Diccionario de botanica. Uberto
Tosco. Tr. by Francisco Gil. Teide.
Diccionario de Botanico. Pio Font
Quer. Labor SA.
Diccionario de Calculo Mercantil.
Jose M. Codera Martin. Piramide.
Diccionario de caza. Jose M. Rodero.
Juventud.
Diccionario De Celebridades
Musicales. French & Eur.
Diccionario de Chilenismos.
Zorobabel Rodriguez. Universidad
& Acad.
Diccionario de Ciencia Politica. Axel
Gorlitz. French & Eur.
Diccionario de Ciencia Politica. Axel
Gorlitz. Alianza Ed.
Diccionario de Ciencias. Chapman
Ubarov. French & Eur.
Diccionario de Ciencias Medicas
Dorland. Ateneo Edit.
Diccionario de Ciencias Medicas
Dorland (II) Ateneo Edit.
Diccionario De Ciencias Sociales.
UNESCO. French & Eur.
Diccionario de Citas. Juan Capdevila
Font. French & Eur.

Diccionario de cocina. Bruguera.
El Diccionario de Coll. Jose L. Coll
Garcia. Planeta SA.
Diccionario de Computadores.
Anthony Chandor. French & Eur.
Diccionario de Construccion &
Regimen de la Lengua Castellana.
Rufino J. Cuervo. Inst Caro y
Cuervo.
Diccionario de construccion y
regimen de la lengue castellano.
Cuervo. Herder SA.
Diccionario de construccion y
regimen de la lengua castellana. R.
J. Cuervo. Inst Caro y Cuervo.
Diccionario De Contabilidad. Jose M.
Codera Martin. French & Eur.
Diccionario de Contabilidad. F.
Cholvis. French & Eur.
Diccionario de contabilidad.
Francisco Cholvis. Contabilidad
Moderna.
Diccionario de Contabilidad. Jose M.
Codera Martin. Piramide.
Diccionario de Contabilidad. F.
Cholvis. Ateneo Edit.
Diccionario de contabilidad. Jose M.
Codera Martin. Piramide.
Diccionario de contabilidad,
organizacion, administracion,
control & ciencia afines. Joaquin R.
Seone. Difusion.
Diccionario de Costarriquenismos.
Carlos Gagini & Victor M. Soto.
Prologue by Rufino J. Cuervo.
Costa Rica.
Diccionario De Crucigramas. Litero.
French & Eur.
Diccionario de Crucigramas. G Gili.
Diccionario de cubanismos. Dario
Espina Perez. Dist. Universal.
Diccionario de Cubanismos Mas
Usuales. Jose Sanchez-Boudy.
Ediciones.
Diccionario de Demonologia.
Frederick Koning. French & Eur.
Diccionario de Derecho. Rafael de
Pina. French & Eur.
Diccionario de Derecho. Rafael De
Pina. Porrua.
Diccionario De Derecho Mercantil.
Jose Codera Martin. French & Eur.
Diccionario de Derecho Mercantil. J.
M. Codera Martin. Piramide.
Diccionario de derecho privado.
Casso-Cervera. Labor.
Diccionario de Derecho Procesal
Civil. Eduardo Pallares. French &
Eur.
Diccionario de Derecho Procesal
Civil. Eduardo Pallares. Porrua.
Diccionario de derecho romano. G. F.
De Leon. Plus Ultra.
Diccionario de Dificultades de la
Lengua Espanola. E. Diaz-Retg.
French & Eur.
Diccionario De Dificultades Del
Ingles: Difficulties of English
Idioms for Spanish Speaking
People. Alfonso T. Prats. Heinman.
Diccionario De Dificultades Del
Ingles. Alfonso Torrents dels Prats.
French & Eur.
Diccionario de Dificultades del Ingles.
Alfonso T. Dels Prats. Editorial
Juventud.
Diccionario de Dificultades del Ingles.
Alfonso Torrents dels Prats.
Lectorum Pubns.
Diccionario de dificultades del ingles.
Alfonso Torrents dels Prats. (JUV).
Lectorum Pubns.
Diccionario de dificultades del Ingles.
Alfonso Torrents dels Prats. Fed
Gremios.
Diccionario De Dos Cientos Uno
Verbos Franceses Conjugados en
Todos sus Tiempos & Personas.
Christopher Kendris. Barron.
Diccionario de Dos Cientos Uno
Verbos Ingleses. Ruth P. Craig.
Barron.
Diccionario de Dudas & Dificultades
de la Lengua Espanola. Manuel
Seco. Aguilar SP.
Diccionario de Dudas de la Lengua
Espanol. Manuel Seco. French &
Eur.
Diccionario de dudas de la lengua
espanola. Manuel Seco. Aguilar.
Diccionario de Dudas de la Lengua
Espanola. Manuel Seco. (AGL).
Lectorum Pubns.
Diccionario de dudas de la lengua
espanola. Manuel Seco. Iaconi.

Diccionario De Dudas Ingles-Espanol.
Jose Merino Bustamante. French &
Eur.
Diccionario de Dudas Ingles-Espanol.
Jose Merino. Paraninfo.
Diccionario de Dudas Ingles-Espanol.
Merino. Paraninfo.
Diccionario de dudas: Ingles-espanol.
Jose Merino Bustamante. Paraninfo.
Diccionario de dudas Ingles-Espanol.
Jose Merino. Fed Gremios.
Diccionario De Economia. Arthur
Seldon & F. G. Pennance. French
& Eur.
Diccionario de Economia. Arthur
Seldon & F. G. Pennance. French
& Eur.
Diccionario de economia. Tr. by
Arthur Seldon & F. G. Pennanee.
Oikos Tau.
Diccionario de economia. J. B.
Terceiro. Zyx.
Diccionario de economia. TIm
Congdon et al. Tr. by Antonio
Menduina. Grijalbo.
Diccionario De Economia Politica.
Borisov et al. French & Eur.
Diccionario de Economia Politica.
Borisov et al. French & Eur.
Diccionario de Economia Politica.
Autores-Editores.
Diccionario de Economia Politica.
Claudio Napoleoni. Ortells Ferriz.
Diccionario de economia politica.
Heller. Labor.
Diccionario de economia politica.
Claudio Napoleoni. Castilla.
Diccionario de economia y
cooperativismo. Olivera. Albatros.
Diccionario de economia y
cooperativismo. J. Olivera.
Hachette-Jeunesse.
Diccionario de economia y dissiplinas
a fines, aleman-espanol. Roca De
Togore. InterCiencia.
Diccionario de Educacion Infantil. H.
Jourbel & P. Bertrand. French &
Eur.
Diccionario de educacion infantil. Tr.
by H. Joubrel & P. Bertrand. Leru.
Diccionario de eiencias. Ubanou.
Dossat.
Diccionario de Electronica. Harley
Carter. French & Eur.
Diccionario De Electronica. S.
Handel. French & Eur.
Diccionario de Electronica. Santano.
Paraninfo.
Diccionario de electronica. Tr. by
Harley Carter. Leru.
Diccionario de Electronica & Tecnica
Nuclear. John Markus. Marcombo.
Diccionario de Electronica,
Informatica & Centrales Nucleares.
Mariano Mataix. Marcombo.
Diccionario de electronica, proceso de
datos. Averbach. Iber Euro Edns.
Diccionario de Electronica Radio &
TV. Minerva Bks.
Diccionario de Electronica, Radio &
TV: Ingles-Espanol. M. Saiz.
Lectorum Pubns.
Diccionario de electronica, radio y
TV. Afha Intl.
Diccionario de Electronica y Tecnica
Nuclear. John Markus. French &
Eur.
Diccionario de electronica y tecnica
nuclear. Tr. by John Markus.
Marcombo.
Diccionario de eletronica y energia
nuclear ingles-espanol. M. Mataix.
Danae.
Diccionario de emociones. Bernardo
Arias Truillo. Berout.
Diccionario de Energia Solar. Peris
Aguilar & J. Jose-Aguilar Civera.
Alhambra.
Diccionario de Escritores Mexicanos.
Aurora Ocampo de Gomez &
Ernesto Prado Velazquez. French &
Eur.
Diccionario de espanol equivoco.
Manuel Criado de Val. Edi-Seis.
Diccionario De Especialidades
Farmaceuticas. Ed. by E.
Rosenstein. Drug Intl Pubns.
Diccionario de espiritualidad: Obra
Completa. Ermanno Ancilli. Tr. by
Joan Llopis. Herder SA.
Diccionario de espiritualidad: Tomo
1. Ermanno Ancilli. Tr. by Joan
Llopis. Herder SA.
Diccionario de Estadistica. E. Morice.
French & Eur.

Diccionario de Estadistica. William R.
Buckland & Maurice G. Kendall.
Piramide.
Diccionario de Etologia. A. Heymer.
Tr. by Andres De Haro Vera.
Omega SA.
Diccionario de Expresiones
Idiomaticas y Modismo Ingleses.
Orlando Gonzalez Gutierrez.
French & Eur.
Diccionario de expresiones
idiomaticas y modismos ingleses. O.
Gonzalez Gutierrez. EUDEBA.
Diccionario de expresiones
idiomaticas y modismos ingleses. O.
Gonzalez Gutierrez. EUDEBA.
Diccionario De Expresiones
Malsonantes Del Espanol. Jaime
Martin. French & Eur.
Diccionario de Expresiones y Frases
Latinas. V. J. Herrero. French &
Eur.
Diccionario de falsos amigos, frances-
espanol. Blanca Gonzalez Marimon.
Alhambra.
Diccionario de Filosofia. Walter
Breugger. (French & Eur). French
& Eur.
Diccionario de Filosofia. Armand
Cuvillier. French & Eur.
Diccionario de Filosofia. Mora
Ferrater. French & Eur.
Diccionario de Filosofia. Jose Ferrater
Mora. French & Eur.
Diccionario De Filosofia. Dagobert D.
Runes. French & Eur.
Diccionario de Filosofia Abreviado.
Jose Ferrater Mora. French & Eur.
Diccionario de fisica. Tr. by Franke.
Labor SA.
Diccionario de Formularios
Generales. Juan Diego Hernandez.
Coleccion Nereo.
Diccionario de Formularios
Generales. Juan Diego Hernandez
& Alejandro Rodriguez Segui.
Coleccion Nereo.
Diccionario de Formularios
Generales. Juan D. Hernandez.
Nereo.
Diccionario de Formularios
Generales: Tomo 7. Juan Diego
Hernandez. Coleccion Nereo.
Diccionario de fotografia y cine.
Tesoro.
Diccionario de gemologia. Jover.
Diccionario de Gentilicios &
Toponimos. Santano. Paraninfo.
Diccionario de gentilicios y
toponimos. Daniel Santano y Leon.
Paraninfo.
Diccionario de Geografia. W. C.
Moore. French & Eur.
Diccionario de geografia. Moore.
Dossat.
Diccionario de grafologia. Vels. Cedel.
Diccionario de Grafologia y Terminos
Psicologicos Afines. Augusto Vels.
French & Eur.
Diccionario De Grupos, Fuerzas, y
Partidos Politicos Espanoles.
Gerardo Duelo. French & Eur.
Diccionario de habla inglesa: Ingles-
espanol, espanol-ingles. Edit Pr
Serv.
Diccionario de Hacienda & Derecho
Fiscal. Luis A. Martinez Cachero.
Piramide.
Diccionario de Historia de Espana.
German Bleiberg. French & Eur.
Diccionario de Historia de Espana.
German Bleiberg. French & Eur.
Diccionario de Historia de Espana.
German Bleiberg. Alianza Ed.
Diccionario de Historia de Espana.
German Bleiberg. Alianza Ed.
Alianza Ed.
Diccionario de Historia de Espana.
German Bleiberg. Alianza Ed.
Diccionario de Historia de Espana.
German Bleiberg. Alianza Ed.
Diccionario de historia moderna.
Palmer. Labor SA.
Diccionario de historia natural de las
Islas Canarias. Jose Viera Clavijo.
Muralla.
Diccionario de historia universal. J. L.
Romero. Atlantida.
Diccionario de Homofonos Castellans:
Repertorio Alfabetico de Adjetivos,
Verbos & su Correcta Ortografia.
Hipolito R. Aschiero. Edit Victor
Leru.

Diccionario de Homofonos Castellaros. Hipolito F. Aschiero. French & Eur.

Diccionario de Incorrecciones & Particularidades & Curiosidades del Lenguaje. Antonio Santamaria & Augusto Cuartas. (PAR). Lectorum Pubns.

Diccionario de Incorrecciones, Dudas & Normas Gramaticales. Fernando Corripio. Edit Bruguera.

Diccionario de Incorreciones & Particularidades del Lenguaje. Cuartas Santamaria & J. Mangada. Paraninfo.

Diccionario de Incorreciones, Dudas y Normas Gramaticales. French & Eur.

Diccionario de Incorreciones y Particularidades del Lenguaje. Andres Santamarie & Augusto Cuartas. French & Eur.

Diccionario de informacion sexual. Paul Bertrand. Granica.

Diccionario De Informatica. Michael Ginguay. French & Eur.

Diccionario de informatica. Ginguay. Toray-Masson.

Diccionario de Informatica Ingles-Espanol: Edicion Corregida. Olivetti. Paraninfo.

Diccionario de Informatica Ingles-Espanol. Olivetti. Paraninfo.

Diccionario de Ingenieria de Caminos. Abad I. Morilla. Piramide.

Diccionario de Ingenieria de Caminos. I. Morilla Abad. Piramide.

Diccionario de ingles-espanol, espanol-ingles. Bruguera.

Diccionario De Inmunologia. W. J. Herbert & P. C. Wilkinson. French & Eur.

Diccionario de Inmunologia. W. J. Herbert & P. C. Wilkinson. Jims.

Diccionario de Insurgentes. Jose Maria Miquel I Verges. French & Eur.

Diccionario de Insurgentes. Jose Maria Miguel i Verges. Porrua.

Diccionario de jurisprudencia chilena: Recopilacionde conceptos y definiciones. Elena Caffarena de Jiles. Juridica-Andres Belio.

Diccionario de la astronautica. Thomas De Galiana. Plaza Janes.

Diccionario de la astronomia y astronautica. Pedro Mateu Sancho. Destino.

Diccionario de la Astronomica y Astronautica. Pedro Mateu Sancho. French & Eur.

Diccionario De la Biblia. Herbert Haag. French & Eur.

Diccionario de la Civilizacion Griega. Pierre Devambez. French & Eur.

Diccionario de la cocina clasica americana y europea. Encicl Vasca.

Diccionario de la cocina clasica americana y europea. Encicl Vasca.

Diccionario de la cocina clasica american y europea. Encicl Vasca.

Diccionario de la cocina clasica americana y europea. Encicl Vasca.

Diccionario de la cocina clasica americana y europea. Encicl Vasca.

Diccionario de la cocina clasica americana y europea: Obra completa. Encicl Vasca.

Diccionario de la cocina clasica mejicana y europea: Obra completa. Encicl Vasca.

Diccionario de la cocina clasica mejicano y europea: Tomo 1. Encicl Vasca.

Diccionario de la cocina clasica mejicano y europea: Tomo 2. Encicl Vasca.

Diccionario de la cocina clasica mejicano y europea: Tomo 3. Encicl Vasca.

Diccionario de la cocina clasica mejicana y europea: Tomo 4. Encicl Vasca.

Diccionario de la cocina clasica mejicana y europea: Tomo 5. Encicl Vasca.

Diccionario de la Construccion. Equipo Reactor de Ceac. French & Eur.

Diccionario de la construccion. CEAC.

Diccionario de la Construccion y Obras Publicas Ingles-Espanol. Jose Benito Bacho. French & Eur.

Diccionario de la Construccion y Obras Publicas, Tomo 2: Span. Jose Benito Bacho. French & Eur.

Diccionario de la Construcion (II) Ceac.

Diccionario de la Construcion y de Obras Publicas, Tomo I: Ingles. Jose Benito Bacho. French & Eur.

Diccionario de la Constuccion & Obras Publicas. Jose de Benito y Bacho & Manuel B. Hernandez. Lib Tec Bell.

Diccionario de la Decoracion. Equipo Reactor De Ceac. French & Eur.

Diccionario De la Electronica. Jean F. Arnaud. French & Eur.

Diccionario de la electronica. Jean-Francois Arnaud. Plaza Janes.

Diccionario de la Felicidad. J. Sintes. French & Eur.

Diccionario de la industria textil. Casa Aruta. Labor SA.

Diccionario de la Izquierda Comunista. Juan A. Sanchez Carrate. Dopesa.

Diccionario de la legislacion de seguros. Palacios. Rev. Mex. de Seguros.

Diccionario de la Lengua. French & Eur.

Diccionario de la Lengua: A-B. Argos-Vergara.

Diccionario de la Lengua: C-CH. Argos-Vergara.

Diccionario de la Lengua: D-F. Argos-Vergara.

Diccionario de la Lengua Espanol. Real Academia de la Lengua Espanol. French & Eur.

Diccionario De la Lengua Espanola. Real Academia Espanola. Colton Bk.

Diccionario de la Lengua Espanola. French & Eur.

Diccionario De la Lengua Espanola. French & Eur.

Diccionario de la Lengua Espanola. Pergamon.

Diccionario de la Lengua Espanola. Distein. Distein.

Diccionario de la Lengua Espanola. Oceano.

Diccionario de la lengua espanola. Diana.

Diccionario de la lengua espanola. Real Academia Espasa.

Diccionario de la lengua espanola. Nauta SA.

Diccionario de la Lengua Espanola. Oceano.

Diccionario de la Lengua Espanola Novus. Oceano.

Diccionario de la Lengua Espanola: Obra Completa. Oceano.

Diccionario de la Lengua Espanola Real Academia Espanola. Lectorum Pubns.

Diccionario de la lengua espanola y alemana: Tomo 1. Rudolf Slaby et al. Herder SA.

Diccionario De la Lengua Espanola y Enciclopedia Escolar. Juan Capdevila Font. French & Eur.

Diccionario De la Lengua Espanola y Enciclopedia Escolar. Juan Capdevilla Font. French & Eur.

Diccionario de la Lengua Espanola y Enciclopedia Escolar Distein. Juan Capdevila Font. French & Eur.

Diccionario de la Lengua: G-M. Argos-Vergar.

Diccionario de la Lengua Mechada. Ignacio Guasp. French & Eur.

Diccionario de la Lengua: N-Q. Argos-Vergara.

Diccionario de la Lengua Nahuatl. Cesar Macazaga Ordono. Innovacion.

Diccionario de la Lengua Nahuatl. Cesar Macazaga Ordono. Innovacion.

Diccionario de la Lengua Nahuatl o Mexicana. Remi Simeon. Siglo Veintiuno.

Diccionario de la Lengua (Obra Completa) Argos-Vergara.

Diccionario de la Lengua: R-Z. Argos-Vergara.

Diccionario de la Limpieza. Djenane Chappat. French & Eur.

Diccionario de la Literatura Mundial. Joseph T. Shipley. French & Eur.

Diccionario de la Literatura Universal. Juan Capdevila Font. French & Eur.

Diccionario de la Mitologia Clasica. C. Falcon et al. French & Eur.

Diccionario de la mitologia clasica: A-H. Constantino Falcon Martinez et al. Alianza Ed.

Diccionario de la mitologia clasica: I-Z. Constantino Falcon Martinez et al. Alianza Ed.

Diccionario de la Mitologia Mundial. French & Eur.

Diccionario de la Mitologia Mundial. Edaf.

Diccionario de la montana. Agustin Faus. Juventud.

Diccionario de la mujer. Daimon.

Diccionario de la Musica. Manuel Valls Gorina. Alianza Ed.

Diccionario de la Musica. Carlos Poblete. U. de Valparaiso.

Diccionario de la musica. Eric Blom. Claridad.

Diccionario de la musica. Michel Brenet. Iberia SA.

Diccionario de la musica. Tr. by Della Corte & Gatti. Ricordi.

Diccionario de la musica. Carlos Poblete Varas. Universitarias Valparaiso.

Diccionario de la musica. Manuel Valls Gorina. Alianza Ed.

Diccionario de la Musica. Manuel Valla Gorina. Alianza.

Diccionario de la Musica, Historico & Tecnico. Jose Ricart Matas. Iberia SA.

Diccionario De la Musica: Historico y Tecnico. Michel Brenet. French & Eur.

Diccionario de la Politica. Jean-Noel Aquistapace. French & Eur.

Diccionario de la politica. Jean N. Aquistapace. Magisterio Esp.

Diccionario de la Psicologia. Norberth Sillamy. French & Eur.

Diccionario de la psicologia. Norbert Sillamy. Plaza Janes.

Diccionario De la Santa Biblia. W. W. Rand. Edit Caribe.

Diccionario De la Tecnicas De Grupo. Anne A. Schutzsenberger. French & Eur.

Diccionario de la Ultra Derecha. Alberto Royuela. Dopesa.

Diccionario de la Vida Sexual. Juan Capdevila Font. French & Eur.

Diccionario de la Vida Sexual. Ed. by Pedro L. Onega. Distein.

Diccionario de la Vida Sexual. Enrique Sanchez y Pascual. Prod Edit.

Diccionario de las Artes Marciales. Mario Lopez Dominguez. Ramos-Majos.

Diccionario de las lenguas espanola alemana. Rudolf Slaby et al. Herder SA.

Diccionario De las Lenguas Espanola y Alemana. Rudolf Slaby. French & Eur.

Diccionario de las lenguas espanola y alemana: Aleman-espanol. Slaby-Grossmann. Herder.

Diccionario De las Matematicas Modernas. Lucien Chambadal. French & Eur.

Diccionario de las matematicas modernas. Lucien Chambadal. Plaza Janes.

Diccionario De las Religiones. Konig. French & Eur.

Diccionario de las religiones perromanas de Hispania. Jose M. Blazquez. Istmo.

Diccionario de legislacion. Aranzadi Edit.

Diccionario de legislacion administrativa y fiscal de Navarra. Aranzadi Edit.

Diccionario De Legislacion de Navarra. Diput Foral.

Diccionario de lengua rusa. Ozhegov. Pueblos Unidos.

Diccionario de Leyes y Efectos Cientificos En Quimica-Fisica Matematicas. D. W. Ballentyne & L. E. Walker. French & Eur.

Diccionario de leyes y efectos cientificos. Tr. by D. W. Bailentyne & L. E. Walker. Leru.

Diccionario de limpieza. Tr. by Djenane Chappat. Alianza Ed.

Diccionario de Linguistica. Jean Dubois. French & Eur.

Diccionario de linguistica. Theodor Lewandowski et al. Tr. by Enrique Bernardez & M. Luz Garcia. Edns Catedra.

Diccionario de linguistica. Georges Mounin. Tr. by Ricardo Pochtar. Labor SA.

Diccionario de los alimentos. Cedel.

Diccionario de los Alimentos: Vitaminas, Calories, Coccion, Conservacion, Etc. French & Eur.

Diccionario de los Asesinos. Rene Reouven. French & Eur.

Diccionario de los descubrimientos cientificos. Thomas De Galiana. Plaza Janes.

Diccionario de los fueros & leyes de Navarra. Yanguas & Jose Miranda. Aranzadi Edit.

Diccionario de los infiernos. Santiago Collin de Pianci. Rueda.

Diccionario de los ingenios. Oscar Gaimaro. Alonso Eds.

Diccionario de los Ismos. Juan E. Cirlot. (ARG). Lectorum Pubns.

Diccionario de los Medios de Comunicacion: Tecnica, Semiologia, Linguistica. Jean-Baptiste Fages. French & Eur.

Diccionario de los Papas. Juan Dacio. French & Eur.

Diccionario de los Politicos. Juan Rico y Amat. Narcea SA.

Diccionario de los Politicos, 1855. Juan Rico y Amat. Narcea SA.

Diccionario De los Santos De Cada Dia. Dom P. Rouillard. French & Eur.

Diccionario de los Sintomas: Los Testa de su Salud. A. Saponaro. French & Eur.

Diccionario de los suenos. Hanns Kurth. Tr. by Carmen Rada. Circulo Lect.

Diccionario de los terminos tecnicos de Medicina. Marcel Garnier et al. Tr. by Julio Llido Blasco. Norma.

Diccionario de Management. H. Johannsen et al. French & Eur.

Diccionario de management. Tr. by Hano & Andrew B. Robertson. Oikos Tau.

Diccionario de Marina. Jose L. De Pando y Villarroya. Autores-Editores.

Diccionario de Marketing. Bernardo Rabassa Asenjo & M. R. Garcia Tous. French & Eur.

Diccionario de Marketing. B. Rabassa Asenjo & M. R. Garcia Tous. Piramide.

Diccionario De Matematica Moderna. Dario Maravall Casesnoves. French & Eur.

Diccionario de Matematica Moderna. Dario Maravall Casesnovas. Nacional Editora.

Diccionario de matematica moderna. Dario Maravall Casesnoves. Nacional Editora.

Diccionario De Matematicas. Juan Capdevila Font. French & Eur.

Diccionario De Materiales y Procesos De Ingenieria. H. R. Clauser. French & Eur.

Diccionario de materiales y procesos de ingenieria. Clauser. Labor SA.

Diccionario de maximas, pensamientos y sentencias. Ed. by Jorge Sintes Pros. Sintes.

Diccionario de mecanica. Minerva.

Diccionario de mecanica I y II. Minerva.

Diccionario de Mecanica Ingles-Espanola. M. Saiz. Lectorum Pubns.

Diccionario de Medicina. Ed. by E. Dabout. French & Eur.

Diccionario de Medicina de Urgencia. French & Eur.

Diccionario de medicina de urgencia. Cedel.

Diccionario de Medicina Farmacia Veterinaria & Quimica. Castulo Carrasco. Garsi Edit.

Diccionario De Medicina, Farmacia Veterinaria y Quimica. Castulo Carrasco Martinez. French & Eur.

Diccionario de Medicina Ilustrado. B. Melloni et al. Reverte SA.

Diccionario de Medicos Puertorriquenos Que Se Man Distinguico Fuera de la Medicina. French & Eur.

Diccionario De Mejicanismos. Francisco J. Santamaria. Colton Bk.

Diccionario de Mejicanismos. Francisco J. Santamaria. French & Eur.

Diccionario de Mejicanismos. Francisco Santamaria. Porrua.

Diccionario De Metologia Estadistica. Gonzalo Gonsalvo Mainar. French & Eur.

Diccionario de Mitologia. Henri Aubert. French & Eur.

Diccionario de Mitologia. Homero Lelama. French & Eur.

Diccionario de mitologia Nahuatl. Cecilio A. Robelo. Innovacion.

Diccionario de Modismos Inglese y Norteamericanos. Alfonso Torrents dels Prats. French & Eur.

Diccionario de Modismos Ingleses. Pablo Caldwell. French & Eur.

Diccionario de Modismos Ingleses. Basset D. Carbonell. Dos Continentes.

Diccionario de modismos ingleses. Sopena.

Diccionario de Modismos Ingleses & Norteamericanos. Alfonso T. Dels Prats. Editorial Juventud.

Diccionario de modismos ingleses y norteamericanos. Larousse.

Diccionario de modismos ingleses y norteamericanos. A. Torrens dels Prats. Juventud.

Diccionario de modismos ingleses y norteamericanos. Alfonso Torrens dels Prats. Fed Gremios.

Diccionario De Moral Cristiana. Karl Hoermann. French & Eur.

Diccionario De Moral Cristiana. Karl Hoermann. French & Eur.

Diccionario de moral profesional medica. Scremin. Garriga.

Diccionario de Musica. Arthur Jacobs. French & Eur.

Diccionario de musica. Tr. by Arthur Jacobs. Leru.

Diccionario de Palabras Anticuadas y en Desuso. Anita Luft. French & Eur.

Diccionario de Parapsicologia. Julio Roca Muntanola. French & Eur.

Diccionario de Parapsicologia. Julio Roca Muntanola. Alas.

Diccionario de parapsicologia. Hector Morel & Jose Dale Moral. Kier.

Diccionario de parapsicologia. Jose M. San Martin Unamuno. Don Bosco Ed.

Diccionario de paronimos. Ed. by Fonda Publicaciones U. P. T. C. U. Pedagogica y Tec.

Diccionario de Paronimos & Antonimos Castellanos. (SPA). Lectorum Pubns.

Diccionario de paronimos castellanos. Lazzati. Sopena.

Diccionario de Payadores. Amalia Sanchez Sivori. Plus Ultra S. A.

Diccionario De Pedagogia. Paul Foulque. French & Eur.

Diccionario de pedagogia. Baumgartel. Paulinas.

Diccionario de pedagogia. Lorenzo Luzuriaga. Losada.

Diccionario de Pedagogia Labor. Victor Garcia Hoz. French & Eur.

Diccionario de pedagogia Labor. Tr. by Hoz Garcia. Labor SA.

Diccionario De Pedogogia. Paul Foulque. French & Eur.

Diccionario de Peruanismos. Pedro Paz Soldan Y Unanue & Estuardo Nunez. Edns Peisa.

Diccionario De Philosofia. M. Rosental. French & Eur.

Diccionario de Pintura. Fasciculos Planeta.

Diccionario de pintura y dibujo. Tesoro.

Diccionario de Plantas Agricolas. Enrique Sanchez Monge y Parellada. Minist Agricultura.

Diccionario de politica. Elliot. Labor SA.

Diccionario de politica. Daniel Moreno. Porrua.

Diccionario de politica: Obra completa. Norberto Bobbio. Tr. by Raul Crisafio. Siglo XXI.

Diccionario de politica: Tomo 1: A-J. Norberto Bobbio. Tr. by Raul Crisafio. Siglo XXI.

Diccionario de poltica mundial. Tr. by Walter Theimer. Ariel.

Diccionario de primeros auxilios medico-veterinarios. T. E. Beker. Lib. del Colegio.

Diccionario de Psicoanalisis. P. Fedida. French & European.

Diccionario de Psicoanalisis. Pierre Fedida. Alianza Ed.

Diccionario de psicoanalisis. Jean Laplanche et al. Tr. by Fernando Cervantes Gimeno. Labor SA.

Diccionario De Psicoanalisis Clasico. Friedrich W. Doucet. French & Eur.

Diccionario de Psicoanalisis Clasico. Friedrich W. Doucet. Labor.

Diccionario De Psicologia. Friedrich Dorsch. French & Eur.

Diccionario De Psicologia. Alberto L. Merrani. French & Eur.

Diccionario de psicologia. Alberto L. Merani. Grijalbo.

Diccionario de Psicologia. Genovard. Jims.

Diccionario de psicologia. H. C. Warren. Fondo Cult.

Diccionario de Psicologia. Mensajero Edns.

Diccionario de psicologia abrangendo terminologia de ciencias correlatas. E. Dorin. Edicoes Melhoramentos.

Diccionario De Psicologia Sexual. G. Bastin. French & Eur.

Diccionario de psicologia sexual. Bastin. Herder SA.

Diccionario de Psiquiatria. James A. Brussel & George L. Cantzlaar. French & Eur.

Diccionario De Psiquiatria. Antoine Porot. French & Eur.

Diccionario de psiquiatria. Tr. by James A. Brussel & Geroge L. Cantzlaar. CECSA.

Diccionario de psiquiatria. Porat. Labor SA.

Diccionario de quimica y de productos quimicos. Gessner G. Haley. Omega SA.

Diccionario De Radio. French & Eur.

Diccionario De Radio & Television (II) Llerrero J. Cebrian. Alhambra.

Diccionario De Refranes. Juana Barella Campos & Ana G. Barella Campos. French & Eur.

Diccionario de Regionalismos de la Provincia de la Rioja. Julian Caceres Freire. French & Eur.

Diccionario de Reglas, Aforismos & Principios de Derecho. Carlos Lopez de Haro. Reus SA.

Diccionario de relaciones internacionales. Plano & Othon. Limusa.

Diccionario de Religiones Comparadas. S. G. F. Brandon. French & Eur.

Diccionario de Ro de Qheshwa-Espanol, Espanol-Qheshwa. Jesus Lara. French & Eur.

Diccionario de San Francisco. Oscar Michelon. Akademische Druck Verlagt.

Diccionario de secretos de Ibiza. Mariano Planells Cardona. Obelisco.

Diccionario De Seguros. H. L. Mueller-Lutz. French & Eur.

Diccionario de seguros. Molnar. Rev. Mex. de Seguros.

Diccionario de Seguros. H. Mueller Lutz & Julio Castelo Matran. Mapfre.

Diccionario De Seudonimos Literarios Espanoles, Con Algunas Iniciales. P. P. Rogers & F. A. Lapuente. French & Eur.

Diccionario de Siglas. Javier Gomez de Cadiz. Alas.

Diccionario de Siglas en Comercio Exterior. Victor Brunner. Liv Nobel.

Diccionario De Siglas Relacionadas Con la Informatica. IBM. French & Eur.

Diccionario de Sigles de Organismos Nacionales e Internacionales. Javier Gomez de Cadiz. French & Eur.

Diccionario de Simbolismos. Juan E. Cirlot. Labor SA.

Diccionario de Simbolos. J. Cirlot. French & Eur.

Diccionario de simbolos. Juan E. Cirlot. Labor SA.

Diccionario de Simbolos. Juan E. Cirlot. Editorial Labor SA.

Diccionario de simbolos. Cirlot. Labor SA.

Diccionario de simbolos. Juan E. Cirlot. Labor.

Diccionario de Simbolos y Mitos: Las Ciencias y las Artes en Su Expresion Figurada. Jose A. Perez Rioja. French & Eur.

Diccionario de simbolos y mitos: Las ciencias y las artes en su expresion figurada. J. A. Perez Rioja. Tecnos SA.

Diccionario de Similes & Analogias. Gonzalo Castillo. (BCA). Lectorum Pubns.

Diccionario de similes y analogias. Gonzalo Castillo. Costa Amic.

Diccionario de similes y analogias. Gonzalo Castillo. EDIMEX.

Diccionario de sindromes. F. Kerdel-Vegas & O. Adamicska. Cientifico Med.

Diccionario de sininimos espanoles. Antonio Zamora. Claridad.

Diccionario de sininimos, ideas afines y contrarios. J. Ruiz Calonja & Santiago Pey. Teide.

Diccionario De Sinonimos. S. D. Gili Gaya. Colton Bk.

Diccionario de Sinonimos. Samuel Gili Gaya. Biblograf SP.

Diccionario de Sinonimos. Samuel Gili Gaya. Natl Textbk.

Diccionario de Sinonimos. Roque Barcia. Oasis SA.

Diccionario de Sinonimos. Manuel Franquesa Lluelles. Portic.

Diccionario de Sinonimos & Antonimos. Margara Clave. Porrua.

Diccionario de Sinonimos & Ideas Afines & de la Rima. Horta. Paraninfo.

Diccionario de Sinonimos & Ideas Afines. CEC.

Diccionario De Sinonimos, Antonimcs y Paronimos. French & Eur.

Diccionario de Sinonimos-Antonimos. Cruzada Span Pubns.

Diccionario de Sinonimos, Antonimos & Ideas Afines. Andina.

Diccionario de Sinonimos, Antonimos & Ideas Afines. Luis Paredes. Gabriela Mistral.

Diccionario de Sinonimos, Antonimos & Ideas Afines. Antonio Santamaria. (SOP). Lectorum Pubns.

Diccionario de sinonimos, antonimos e ideas afines. Orbe Edns.

Diccionario de sinonimos castellanos. Grates. Sopena.

Diccionario de Sinonimos Castellanos. Grates. Sopena.

Diccionario de Sinonimos Castellanos. Grates. (SPA). Lectorum Pubns.

Diccionario de Sinonimos e Ideas Afines & de la Rima. Joaquin Horta Massanes. (PAR). Lectorum Pubns.

Diccionario de Sinonimos e Ideas Afines & de la Rima. Joaquin Horta Massanet. Paraninfo.

Diccionario de sinonimos e ideas afines. Andina.

Diccionario de sinonimos e ideas afines. Julio de la Canal. CECSA.

Diccionario De Sinonimos E Ideas Afines y De la Rima. Joaquin Horta Massanet. French & Eur.

Diccionario de Sinonimos e Ideas Afines y de la rima. Joaquin H. Massanes. Paraninfo.

Diccionario de sinonimos e ideas afines y de la rima. Natl Textbk.

Diccionario de sinonimos e ideas afines y de la rima. Joaquin Horta Massanes. Paraninfo.

Diccionario de Sinonimos Espanoles. French & Eur.

Diccionario de Sinonimos Espanoles. Francisco Rofer. Edit Mex U.

Diccionario de Sinonimos espanoles. F. Rofer. EDIMEX.

Diccionario de Sinonimos, Ideas Afines & Contrarios. Santiago Pey. (TEI). Lectorum Pubns.

Diccionario de Sinonimos Ideas Afines & Contrarios. Santiago Pey Estrany. Teide.

Diccionario De Sinonimos Ideas Afines y Contrarios. Santiago Pey Estrany & J. Ruiz Calonja. French & Eur.

Diccionario de sinonimos OMNIA. Carlos Cesarman. Pax.

Diccionario De Sinonimos y Antonimos. Francisco Gordo-Guarinos. French & Eur.

Diccionario de Sinonimos y Antonimos. M. Orta Manzano. French & Eur.

Diccionario de sinonimos y antonimos. A Santamaria. Sopena.

Diccionario de sinonimos y antonimos. Educar.

Diccionario de sinonimos y antonimos. Nauta SA.

Diccionario de Sintomas. Joan Gomez. French & Eur.

Diccionario de Sintomas. Joan Gomez. Acervo.

Diccionario De Sociologia. Helmut Schoeck. French & Eur.

Diccionario de Sociologia. Schoeck. Herder SA.

Diccionario de sociologia. Carlos T. Echanova. Calica.

Diccionario de sociologia. H. P. Fairchild et al. Fondo Cult.

Diccionario de sociologia. Helmut Schoeck. Tr. by Herder. Herder SA.

Diccionario de sociologia. Helmut Schoeck. Tr. by Herder. Herder AS.

Diccionario de Tecnicas de Grupo. Schutzenberg. Soc Ed Atenas.

Diccionario de tecnologia. Circulo Lect.

Diccionario de telecomunicaciones en siete idiomas. Cultura Popular.

Diccionario de Temas Regionalistas En la Poesia Puertorriquena. Salvador Arana Soto. French & Eur.

Diccionario De Teologia. Louis Bouyer. French & Eur.

Diccionario De Teologia Biblica. Bauer. French & Eur.

Diccionario de Terminologia Linguistica Actual. Werner Abraham & Francisco Meno Blanco. Gredos.

Diccionario de terminos administrativos. Pan Amer Pub.

Diccionario de Terminos Aerauticos. Rosario. French & Eur.

Diccionario de Terminos Aeronauticos: Ingles-Espanol & Espanol-Ingles. Rosario et al. Paraninfo.

Diccionario de Terminos Anticuados & en Desuso. Anita Navarrete Luft. PLY.

Diccionario de terminos artisticos. Jose L. Morales Marin. Unali.

Diccionario de terminos basicos para la historia. Angel L. Abos Santabarbara & Antonio Marco Martinez. Alhambra.

Diccionario de Terminos Cientificos & Tecnicos. McGraw.

Diccionario de Terminos Cientificos & Tecnicos. McGraw-Hill & Boixareu. Marcombo.

Diccionario de Terminos Cientificos & Tecnicos. Marcombo.

Diccionario de terminos cientificos y tecnicos: Obra completa. Marcombo.

Diccionario de terminos cientificos y tecnicos: Tomo 1 II. Marcombo.

Diccionario de terminos cientificos y tecnicos: Tomo 3 II. Marcombo.

Diccionario de terminos cientificos y tecnicos: Tomo 4 II. Marcombo.

Diccionario de terminos cientificos y tecnicos: Tomo 5 II. Tr. by Varios. Marcombo.

Diccionario De Terminos Comerciales. P. Gaballi Prat. French & Eur.

Diccionario de terminos comerciales. Hispano Europa.

Diccionario de Terminos Contables. Joaquin Blanes Prieto. French & Eur.

Diccionario de terminos contables. Joaquin Blanes Prieto. CECSA.

Diccionario De Terminos De Proceso De Datos: Con Vocabulario Espanol-Ingles, Ingles-Espanol. Angel Salto Dolla. French & Eur.

Diccionario de terminos de proceso de datos: Definicion de 2500 terminos de informatica y vocabulario completo espanol-ingles e ingles-espanol. Angel Salto Dolla. Paraninfo.

Diccionario de Terminos Electorales & Parlamentarios. Jose M. Gil-Robles y Quinones. Taurus Ediciones SA.

Diccionario De Terminos Electrorales y Parlamentarios. Jose M. Gil-Robles. French & Eur.

Diccionario de Terminos Filologicos. Fernando L. Carreter. (French & Eur). French & Eur.

Diccionario de Terminos Filologicos. Fernando L. Carreter. (French & Eur). French & Eur.

Diccionario De Terminos Geograficos. F. J. Monkhouse. French & Eur.

Diccionario de terminos legales. Robb. Rev. Mex. de Seguros.

Diccionario de terminos legales. Louis Rodd. Iaconi.

Diccionario de Terminos Legales Espanol-Ingles e Ingles-Espanol: Spanish-English, English-Spanish Dictionary of Legal Terms. Louis A. Robb. Larousse.

Diccionario de terminos legales espanol-ingles e ingles-espanol. Louis A. Robb. Limusa.

Diccionario de Terminos Legales Espanol-Ingles. Louis A. Ross. Camino Real.

Diccionario de Terminos Legales, Espanol-Ingles. Louis A. Robb. Limusa.

Diccionario de Terminos Legales Espanol-Ingles. Louis A. Robb. (LIM). Lectorum Pubns.

Diccionario de terminos maritimos en seguros. R. H. Brown. Tr. by Raul Gonzalez Hevia. Mapfre.

Diccionario De Terminos Marxistos. Mascitelli. French & Eur.

Diccionario de terminos medicos. Torres Ruiz. Iaconi.

Diccionario de Terminos Medicos Ingles-Espanol & Espanol-Ingles. F. R. Torres. Edit Alhambra.

Diccionario de terminos medicos Ingles-Espanol & Espanol-Ingles. F. Ruiz Torres. Fed Gremios.

Diccionario de terminos medicos: Ingles-espanol, espanol-ingles. Arnoldo Harrington. Gnosis Edit.

Diccionario de terminos medicos ingles-espanol espanol-ingles. F. Ruiz Torres. Larousse.

Diccionario de terminos medicos: Ingles-Espanol, espanol-ingles. Francisco Ruiz Torres. Alhambra.

Diccionario de Terminos Medicos Ingles-Espanol. F. Ruiz Torres. Alhambra.

Diccionario de terminos meterologicos: Ingles-espanol espanol-ingles. D. Brazol. Hachette.

Diccionario de terminos periodisticos y graficos. W. H. Pepper. Sudamer.

Diccionario de Terminos Socio-politicos. Miguel G. Serrano. Everest.

Diccionario de textos sociales pontificios. Angel Torres Calvo. Bibliografica.

Diccionario de términos legalese. Louis A. Ross. Camino Real.

Diccionario de Tipografia & del Libro. J. Martinez de Sousa. Paraninfo.

Diccionario de Tipografia & del Libro. Jose Martinez de Sousa. Labor SA.

Diccionario de tipografia y del libro. Jose Martinez de Sousa. Paraninfo.

Diccionario de Toponimos Indigenas de Catamarca. Carlos Villafuerte. Plus Ultra S. A.

Diccionario de trucos. Paule Vani. Tr. by Eduardo Giordano. Granica.

Diccionario de Unidadaes y Tablas De Conversion. Vasco Costa & Osvald Frances. French & Eur.

Diccionario de Unidades Cientificas. H. G. Jerrard & D. B. McNeill. French & Eur.

Diccionario de Unidades Cientificas. G. Jerrard & D. B. Neill. Bellaterra.

Diccionario de unidades, efectos y constantes. Tesoro.

Diccionario de unidades y tablas de conversion. Vasco Costa & Osvaldo Frances. G Gili.

Diccionario de urbanismo. Petroni & Kenigsberg. Cesarini.

Diccionario de uso de espanol: Tomo 1. Maria Moliner. Gredos.

Diccionario de uso de espanol: Tomo 2. Maria Moliner. Gredos.

Diccionario de uso del espanol. Maria Moliner. Gredos.

Diccionario de uso del espanol: Obra completa. Maria Moliner. Gredos.

Diccionario de uso del espanol: Tomo 1. Maria Moliner. Gredos.

Diccionario de uso del espanol: Tomo 2. Maria Moliner. Gredos.

Diccionario de Valencias Verbales. Aleman-Espanol. Dietrich Rall et al. Benjamins North Am.

Diccionario de vinos espanoles. J. Perez & R. Alsina. Teide.

Diccionario de Voces & Expresiones Argentinas. Felix Coluccio. Plus Ultra S. A.

Diccionario de Voces Indigenas de Puerto Rico. Luis Hernandez Aquino. French & Eur.

Diccionario de Voces Lunfardas & Vulgares. Fernando H. Casullo. Plus Ultra SA.

Diccionario de voces lunfardas y vulgares. Fernando Casullo. Freeland.

Diccionario de Voces Naturales. Vicenete Garcia de Diego. French & Eur.

Diccionario de voces naturales. Garcia de Diego. Aguilar SP.

Diccionario De Zoologia. Umberto Parenti. French & Eur.

Diccionario Del Amor. Aline de Nanxe. French & Eur.

Diccionario del Argot Espanol. V. Leon. French & Eur.

Diccionario del Arte Actual. Thomas Karin. French & Eur.

Diccionario del Automovil. Ed. by Equipo Reactor de CEAC. French & Eur.

Diccionario del Automovil. Roger Guerber. French & Eur.

Diccionario del automovil. CEAC.

Diccionario del automovil. R. Guerber. G Gili.

Diccionario del automovil II. Ceac.

Diccionario del Budo: Artes Marciales. Raymond Thomas. French & Eur.

Diccionario del Carlismo. Cecilia De Bourbon Parma. Dopesa.

El Diccionario del cine. Peter Graham. Novaro.

Diccionario del cine. Jean Mitry. Plaza Janes.

Diccionario Del Cine Espanol, 1896-1968. French & Eur.

Diccionario del cine espanol 1896-1968. Fernando Vizcaino Casas. Nacional Editora.

Diccionario del comercia exterior. D. W. Budic. Ergon.

Diccionario del Cristianismo. La. Brosse. French & Eur.

Diccionario del Cristianismo. Olivier Brosse. Herder SA.

Diccionario del Democrata. Eduardo Haro Tecglen. Dopesa.

El Diccionario del Espanol de Tejas. Roberto A. Galvan & Richard V. Teschner. Edices Melhoramentos.

Diccionario del Espanol Moderno. Martin Alonso. French & Eur.

Diccionario del espionaje. Domingo Pastor Petit. Plaza Janes.

Diccionario del Hogar Catolico. French & Eur.

Diccionario del Hombre Contemporaneo. Bertrand Russell. French & Eur.

Diccionario del hombre contemporaneo. Bertrand Russell. Rueda.

Diccionario Del Idioma Espanol. Edwin B. Williams. Lectorum Pubns.

Diccionario del Idioma Espanol Moderno. AGL.

Diccionario del jazz. Ortiz Oderigo. Ricordi.

Diccionario del Jefe de Empresa. Jean Romeuf & Jean P. Guinot. French & Eur.

Diccionario Del Lenguaje Filosofico. Paul Foulquie. French & Eur.

Diccionario del Lenguaje Usual. Santillana.

Diccionario del lenguaje usual. Ed. by E.G.B. Santilana SA.

Diccionario del Nuevo Testamento. Xavier Leon-Dufour. French & Eur.

Diccionario del Pasota. Felipe Navarro Garcia. Planeta SA.

Diccionario del pensamiento de Santa Teresa de Jesus. Jesus Marti Ballester. Edicep.

Diccionario del perfecto automobilista. C. Vebel. Grijalbo.

Diccionario del Periodismo. Antonio Lopez De Zuazo Algar. French & Eur.

Diccionario del Periodismo. A. Lopez de Zuazo. Piramide.

Diccionario del periodismo. Antonio Lopez de Zuazo Algar. Piramide.

Diccionario del Plastico. J. A. Wordingham & P. Reboul. French & Eur.

Diccionario del Psicoanalisis. Jean Laplanche & Jean-Bertrand Pontalis. Ed. by Fernando Cervantes Gimeno. French & Eur.

Diccionario del psicoanalisis. Laplanche Pontalis. Labor SA.

Diccionario del Socialismo. Enrique Mujica Herzog. Dopesa.

Diccionario Del Trabajo Social. Ezequiel Ander Egg. French & Eur.

Diccionario del Trabajo Social. Ezequiel Ander Egg. Organ Ofic Adm.

Diccionario Del Uso Del Espanol. Maria Moliner. French & Eur.

Diccionario del Uso del Espanol. Maria Moliner. GRD.

Diccionario del verbo castellano. Lazzati. Sopena.

Diccionario del Verbo Castellano. Santiago Lazzati. (SPA). Lectorum Pubns.

Diccionario del Verbo Castellano: Como Se Conjugan los Verbos Americanos. Santiago Lazzati. French & Eur.

Diccionario del vino de Jerez. Ed. by Julio Permartin. Jerez Industrial.

Diccionario demografico plurilingue. ONU.

Diccionario Didaktikon. Fernandez.

Diccionario Disney. Walt Disney. French & Eur.

Diccionario Durango: Enciclopédia regional. Fernandez.

Diccionario Durvan de la Lengua Espanola. French & Eur.

Diccionario Economico & Financiero. Yves Bernard. Assn Prog Direc.

Diccionario Economico De la Empresa. Andres Santiago Suarez. French & Eur.

Diccionario Economico de la Empresa. A. S. Suarez Suarez et al. Piramide.

Diccionario Edo. de México: Enciclopedia regional. Fernandez.

Diccionario el internacional. Fernandez.

Diccionario Electromecanico Ingles-Espanol. French & Eur.

Diccionario en Color de Arbustos. Millar. French & Eur.

Diccionario Enciclopedia Salvat Universal. French & Eur.

Diccionario Enciclopedia Universal. French & Eur.

Diccionario Enciclopedias Labor. Ed. by Javier Lasso de La Vega & Jose M. Rubert Candau. French & Eur.

Diccionario Enciclopedico. Natl Textbk.

Diccionario Enciclopedico Abreviado. French & Eur.

Diccionario Enciclopedico Bruguera. French & Eur.

Diccionario Enciclopedico Danae. French & Eur.

Diccionario Enciclopedico de la Masoneria. French & Eur.

Diccionario Enciclopedico De la Vida Sexual. Jesus Noguer More. French & Eur.

Diccionario Enciclopedico De las Ciencias Del Lenguaje. Varios. French & Eur.

Diccionario Enciclopedico de Medicina Jims. Leon Braier. Jims.

Diccionario enciclopedico de metalurgia: Espanol-frances, frances-espanol y espanol-engles, engles-espanol. Oliver Bader & Michel Theret. ETA.

Diccionario Enciclopedico de Metalurgia. Oliver Bader & Michel Theret. French & Eur.

Diccionario Enciclopedico Escolar Basico. French & Eur.

Diccionario Enciclopedico Escolar Basico. PlazaJanes.

Diccionario Enciclopedico Espasa. French & Eur.

Diccionario Enciclopedico Espasa. French & Eur.

Diccionario Enciclopedico: Gran Omeba. French & Eur.

Diccionario enciclopedico Hidalgo. Fernandez.

Diccionario enciclopedico Michoacán. Fernandez.

Diccionario enciclopedico Morelos. Fernandez.

Diccionario enciclopedico Nayarit. Fernandez.

Diccionario enciclopedico Nuevo-León. Fernandez.

Diccionario enciclopedico Oaxaca. Fernandez.

Diccionario enciclopedico Puebla. Fernandez.

Diccionario enciclopedico Querétaro. Fernandez.

Diccionario enciclopedico Quintana Roo. FErnandez.

Diccionario enciclopedico Sinaloa. Fernandez.

Diccionario enciclopedico Tlaxcala. Fernandez.

Diccionario Enciclopedico Tomo IX: Suplemento A-Z. Labor SA.

Diccionario enciclopedico Zacatecas. Fernandez.

Diccionario enciclopédico Aguascalientes. Fernandez.

Diccionario enciclopédico baja California norte. Fernandez.

Diccionario enciclopédico baja California sur. Fernandez.

Diccionario enciclopédico Campeche. Fernandez.

Diccionario enciclopédico Chiapas. Fernandez.

Diccionario enciclopédico Chihuahua: D. Fernandez.

Diccionario enciclopédico Colima. Fernandez.

Diccionario enciclopédico Distrito Federal ilustrado. Fernandez.

Diccionario Erotico De El y Ella. French & Eur.

Diccionario Escolar. Lectorum Pubns.

Diccionario escolar americano. Manuel Garcia Becerra. Iztaccihuatl.

Diccionario Escolar Billiken Ilustrado. Atlantida.

Diccionario Escolar de la Lengua Espanola. Sopena R. Sopena.

Diccionario Escolar de la Lengua Espanola. Samuel Gili Gaya. Biblograf SP.

Diccionario escolar de la Lengua Espanola Vox. Biblo SP.

Diccionario Escolar de la llengua Catalana 'Vox' Biblograf.

Diccionario Escolar de Sinonimos & Antonimos Vox. Biblo SP.

Diccionario Escolar de Sinonimos y Antonimas "Vox". Biblograf.

Diccionario Escolar De Sinonimos y Contrarios De la Lengua Espanola. Juan Capdevila Font. French & Eur.

Diccionario escolar del idioma espanol. Martin Alonso. Aguilar SP.

Diccionario escolar etimologico. Victor Garcia Hoz. Magisterio Esp.

Diccionario Escolar Etimologico. Victor Garcia Hoz. French & Eur.

Diccionario Escolar Etimologico. Victor Garcia Hoz. Magisterio Esp.

Diccionario Escolar Hispanoamericano. French & Eur.

Diccionario escolar hispanoamericano. EVA.

Diccionario escolar ilustrado. J. M. Fernandez Gandia. CECSA.

El Diccionario Escolar: La Escuela Alegro. Escuela Nueva.

Diccionario escolar latino-espanol y espanol-latino. Matias Martinez Burgos & Manuel Ayala Lopez. Bibliografica.

Diccionario Escolar Roble. Francisco Gordo Guarinos. French & Eur.

Diccionario Escolar Sopena Color De la Lengua Espanola. French & Eur.

Diccionario Escolar, 2. Santillana SA.

Diccionario Escuela. Fernandez.

Diccionario Esedal de la legislacion peruana. Esedal.

Diccionario esencial frances-espanol, espanol-frances. Jean P. Vidal. Diafora.

Diccionario esencial Ingles-espanol, Espanol-Ingles. Brian Dutton et al. Diafora.

Diccionario Esloveno-Espanol. Ed. by A. Grad. French & Eur.

Diccionario Esoterico. Zaniah. French & Eur.

Diccionario espanol-aleman. Mayfe.

Diccionario Espanol-Aleman. Carlos Brandau. Mayfe.

Diccionario Espanol-Aleman, Aleman-Espanol Militar. Carlos Ruiz Jodar. French & Eur.

Diccionario Espanol-Arabe. Federico Corriente Cordoba. French & Eur.

Diccionario espanol-arabe. Federico Corriente Cordoba. Inst Hispano-Arabe.

Diccionario Espanol-Arabe de Verbos, Gramatica y Temas de Conversacion. Mufid Al-Guindi Abd Al-Monem. French & Eur.

Diccionario Espanol de la Lengua China. Fernando Mateos et al. French & Eur.

Diccionario Espanol de Sinonimos, Equivalencias & Ideas Alfines. Aedos. Aedos.

Diccionario Espanol de Sinonimos y Antonimos. Federico C. Sainz de Robles. Ed. by Asesor Arturo del Hoyo. French & Eur.

Diccionario espanol de sinonimos y antonimos. F. C. Sainz de Robles. Aguilar SP.

Diccionario espanol de sinonimos y antonimos. F. Sainz de Robles. Iaconi.

Diccionario Espanol de Sinonimos y Equivalencias. M. F. Andres. French & Eur.

Diccionario espanol de sinonimos y equivalencias. F. Andres. Aedos.

Diccionario Espanol Etimologico. Felix Diez Mateo. French & Eur.

Diccionario Espanol Etimologico. Felix Diez Mateo. (CANT). Lectorum Pubns.

Diccionario espanol etimologico: El pequeno academico. Felix Diez Mateo. Cantabrica.

Diccionario Espanol-Frances. Armando Galant. Mayfe.

Diccionario espanol-frances. Mayfe.

Diccionario espanol-frances. Zeus.

Diccionario espanol-frances. S. Denis & M. Maraval. Hachette.

Diccionario Espanol-Frances. Armando Galant. Mayfe.

Diccionario Espanol-Frances, Espagnol-Francais. Miguel Gimenez Sales. French & Eur.

Diccionario Espanol Ilustrado. Jose Garcia Mercadal. Mayfe.

Diccionario Espanol-Ingles. Edns Nauta.

Diccionario Espanol-Ingles. Diana.

Diccionario espanol-ingles. Mayfe.

Diccionario espanol-ingles. Zeus.

Diccionario Espanol-Ingles. Maria Younger. Mayfe.

Diccionario Espanol-Ingles-Espanol. Oceano.

Diccionario Espanol-Ingles, Ingles-Espanol. French & Eur.

Diccionario Espanol-Ingles, Ingles-Espanol. Francisco Ruiz Torres. French & Eur.

Diccionario espanol-ingles, ingles-espanol. Crowell. Hachette.

Diccionario espanol-ingles ingles-espanol. Eleesbaan Serrano Mesa. Mayfe.

Diccionario Espanol-Ingles Pocket Dictionary. Simon & Schuster. Camino Real.

Diccionario espanol-japones. Luis M. Martinez Duenas & Manuel M. Kato Yda. Edi-Seis.

Diccionario espanol-latino. J. Llauro Padrose & J. Marques Casanovas. SAETA.

Diccionario espanol moderno. Martin Alonso. Aguilar SP.

Diccionario Espanol-Ruso. Lorenzo Martinez Calvo. French & Eur.

Diccionario Espanol-Ruso. French & Eur.

Diccionario Espanol-Ruso. L. Martinez Calvo. Sopena.

Diccionario espanol-ruso. Cultura Popular.

Diccionario espanol-ruso. (Mir) D'Ippolito.

Diccionario espanol-ruso. Kelina. Pueblos Unidos.

Diccionario Espanol-Ruso de le Prospeccion y Refinacion del Petroleo. A. Pinkevich & B. Amelin. Ed. by A. F. Dobriansky. French & Eur.

Diccionario espanol-ruso de terminos cientificos y tecnicos. Cultura Popular.

Diccionario espanol-senhayi: Dialecto bereber de Senhay de Serair. Esteban Ibanez. Inst. de Estudios Africanos CSIC.

Diccionario espanol Sol. Mayfe.

Diccionario Español -- Inglés Pocket Dictionary. Simon & Schuster. Camino Real.

Diccionario Estudiantil. French & Eur.

Diccionario estudiantil J. C y P.

Diccionario Estudios de Castellano sec. Castagnino. H. Eduardo. Leru.

Diccionario Estudios de geografia. Armando Zavala Cubillos. Leru.

Diccionario etimologica espanol e hispanico. Vicente Garcia de Diego. SAETA.

Diccionario etimologica latinoamericano de lexico de la delincuencia. Arnulfo D. Trejo. UTEHA.

Diccionario Etimologico Abreviado. Fernando Coripio Perez. French & Eur.

Diccionario Etimologico Abreviado. Fernando Corripio. Bruguera.

Diccionario Etimologico Abreviado. Fernando Corripio. (BRG). Lectorum Pubns.

Diccionario Etimologico General de la Lengua Castellana. Fernando Corripio. Bruguera.

Diccionario Etimologico General de la Lengua Espanola. Fernando Corripio Perez. (French & Eur). French & Eur.

Diccionario Euskera-Castellano. Sendoa.

Diccionario Everest "Cima". Lectorum Pubns.

Diccionario Everest Cima. Everest.

Diccionario Everest Cima: Espanol II. Everest.

Diccionario Everest Cima Latin-Espanol. Everest.

Diccionario Everest Cima latino-espanol, espanol-latino. Everest.

Diccionario Everest Corona. Everest.

Diccionario Everest 'Corona' Espanol II. Everest.

Diccionario Everest Corona ingles-espanol, espanol-ingles. Everest.

Diccionario Everest Cuarenta Lexico. Everest.

Diccionario Everest "Cumbre". Lectorum Pubns.

Diccionario Everest Cumbre. Everest.

Diccionario Everest Cumbre: Espanol II. Everest.

Diccionario Everest Cumbre, ingles-espanol, espanol-ingles. Everest.

Diccionario Everest 'Cumbre' Ingles-espanol y espanol-ingles. Everest.

Diccionario Everest Cupula. Everest.

Diccionario Everest Cupula: Espanol II. Everest.

Diccionario Everest Cupula, ingles-espanol, espanol-ingles. Everest.

Diccionario Everest 'Cuspide' Espanol II. Everest.

Diccionario Everest Cuspide frances-espanol, espanol-frances. Everest.

Diccionario Everest Cuspide: Frances-Espanol y espanol-frances. Everest.

Diccionario Everest 'Cuspide' frances-espanol y espanol-frances: Anonimas y colectivas. Everest.

Diccionario 'Everest Diez II. Everest.

Diccionario Everest "Punto". Lectorum Pubns.

Diccionario Everest Punto. Everest.

Diccionario Everest Punto English-Spanish Spanish-English. Larousse.

Diccionario Everest Punto: Espanol II. Everest.

Diccionario Everest Punto' Espanol II. Everest.

Diccionario Everest Punto. Ingles-Espanol. Everest.

Diccionario Everest 'Vertice' Everest.

Diccionario Everest "Vertice". Lectorum Pubns.

Diccionario Everest Vertice. Everest.

Diccionario Everest Vertice Aleman-Espanol, Spanisch-Deutsch. Imported bks.

Diccionario Everest 'Vertice' aleman-espanol y espanol-aleman. Everest.

Diccionario Everest-Vertice: English-Spanish, Spanish-English. Pan Amer Pub.

Diccionario Everest Vertice: Espanol II. Everest.

Diccionario Everest Vertice Frances-Espanol, Espano-Frances. Imported Bks.

Diccionario Everest Vertice ingles-espanol, espanol-ingles. Everest.

Diccionario Everest Vertice: Ingles-Espanol. Everest.

Diccionario Everest Vertice Italian-Espanol, Spagnolo-Italiano. Imported Bks.

Diccionario familiar de homeopatia. E. A. Maury. Tr. by Domingo Santos. Pomaire.

Diccionario familiar de las medicinas naturales. E. A. Maury. Tr. by Rafael Andrue Aznar. Martinez Roca.

Diccionario Familiar de Medicina Natural. E. A. Maury & C. Rudder et al. French & Eur.

Diccionario Filosofico. Voltaire. French & Eur.

Diccionario Filosofico. Voltaire. French & Eur.

Diccionario Filosofico. Voltaire. French & Eur.

Diccionario Forrua de la Lengua Espanola. Antonio Raluy Poudevila. Ed. by Francisco Monterde. French & Eur.

Diccionario frances-espanol. Mayfe.

Diccionario frances-espanol. Zeus.

Diccionario frances-espanol. S. Denis & M. Maraval. Hachette.

Diccionario Frances-Espanol. Armando Galant. Mayfe.

Diccionario Frances-Espanol de la Construccion y Obras Publicas. Herbert Bucksch & Arturo Galan e Hildalgo. French & Eur.

Diccionario frances-espanol de la construccion y obras publicas. Herbert Bucksch & Arturo Galan e Hidalgo. ETA.

Diccionario Frances-Espanol, Espanol-Frances. E. M. Martinez Amador. French & Eur.

Diccionario frances-espanol, espanol-frances. Tesoro.

Diccionario frances-espanol espanol-frances. Zeus.

Diccionario frances-espanol y espanol-frances. Alcala-Zamora & T. Antignac. Imported Bks.

Diccionario frances-espanol y espanol-frances. Mayfe.

Diccionario frances-espanol y espanol-frances. Mayfe.

Diccionario Fundamental de la Lengua Espanola. Rev. by Samuel Gili Gaya. Biblograf SP.

Diccionario Fundamental de la Lengua Espanola'Vox' Biblo SP.

Diccionario Fundamental de la Llengua Catalana 'Vox' Biblo SP.

Diccionario galego-castelan. X. L. Franco Grande. Galaxia.

Diccionario galego-castelan. Xose L. Franco Grande. Galaxia.

Diccionario Galego-Castelan e Vocabulario Castelan-Galego. Xose L. Franco Grande. French & Eur.

Diccionario General de Acustica & Electroacustica. Piraux. Paraninfo.

Diccionario general de acustica y electroacustica. Henry Peraux. Paraninfo.

Diccionario General de Ciencias Humanas. Georges Thines & Agnes Lempereur. French & Eur.

Diccionario General de la Lengua Catalana. Pompeu Fabra. Edhasa.

Diccionario general de llengua catalana. Pompeu Fabra Poch. Edhasa.

Diccionario General de Periodismo. J. Martinez de Sousa. Paraninfo.

Diccionario General de Sinonimos & Antonimos. Cosme Perez Cuadrado. Coculsa.

Diccionario General de Turismo. G. Novo. French & Eur.

Diccionario General del Periodismo. Jose Martinez de Sousa. Paraninfo.

Diccionario General Illustrado de la Lengua Espanol. French & Eur.

Diccionario general ilustrado. Marin.

Diccionario General Ilustrado de la Lengua Espanola. Ramon D. Menendez Pidal. Ed. by Samuel D. Gili Gaya. Biblograf SP.

Diccionario General Ilustrado de la Lengua. Albir.

Diccionario general ilustrado de la Lengua Espanola Vox. Biblo SP.

Diccionario General-Ilustrado la Lengau Espanola. Vox. Brandstetter.

Diccionario General y Tecnico: Hiztegi Orokor-Teknikoa. Luis M. Mugica Urdangarin. French & Eur.

Diccionario Geografico de Guatemala. V. Aquilar Pelaez. Intl Guatemala.

Diccionario Gitano. Pablo-Carrillo Moreno Castro & Juan R. Reyes. Piquenas Edit.

Diccionario Grafico de Arte y Oficios Artisticos. J. Lapoulide. French & Eur.

Diccionario Gramatical y de Dudas del Idioma. French & Eur.

Diccionario. Grandes Temas de la fe Cristiana. Don Bosco Ed.

Diccionario Griego-Espanol. Miguel Balaguer. French & Eur.

Diccionario Griego-Espanol. French & Eur.

Diccionario griego-espanol. Miguel Balagur. Bibliografica.

Diccionario griego-espanol. Florencio I. Sebastian Yarza. Sopena.

Diccionario Guanajuato: Enciplodia regional. Fernandez.

Diccionario guarani-espanol, espanol-guarani. A Jover Peralta & T. Ozuna. Dist. Comuneros.

Diccionario Guerrero: Enciplodia regional. Fernandez.

Diccionario-Guia de Redaccion. A. J. Vinoly. French & Eur.

Diccionario-guia de redaccion. A. Vinoly & J. Vinoly. Teide.

Diccionario Hebreo-Castallano: Castellano-Hebreo. Ed. by Y. Austridan. French & Eur.

Diccionario hebreo-espanol. Perpetuo.

Diccionario heraldico. Vicente de Cadenas y Vicent. Consejo Superior.

Diccionario hispano-tagalog y tagalog-hispano. Ed. by Pedro Serrano Laktaw. Cultura Hispan.

Diccionario Historico del Libro. Emili Eroles. Milla Lib.

Diccionario historico do la lengua espanola. (Real Academia) Espasa.

Diccionario Historico Geografico Ilustrado Del Pais Vasco. Real Academia de la Historia. French & Eur.

Diccionario Humano. Mercedes Iribarren Reta. French & Eur.

Diccionario Humoristico. J. Sintes. French & Eur.

Diccionario Humoristico. V. Claraso. French & Eur.

Diccionario humoristico. Sanchez Rodrigo.

Diccionario humoristico. Noel Claraso. Sintes.

Diccionario humoristico. M. Malcoux. Grijalbo.

Diccionario humoristico. Sintes.

Diccionario humoristico. Ed. by Jorge Sintes Pros. Sintes.

Diccionario ideografico poligloto. G. Medina. Aguilar SP.

Un Diccionario ideologico feminista. Victoria Sau Sanchez. Icaria Edit.

Diccionario Ideologico de la Lengua Espanola. Julio Casares Sanchez. G Gili.

Diccionario ideologico de la lengua espanola. Julio Casares. G Gili.

Diccionario Ideologico de la Lengua Espanola. Julio Casares. (GIL). Lectorum Pubns.

Un Diccionario Ideologico Feminista. Victoria Sau Sanchez. Icaria Edit.

Diccionario Ideologico Manual de la Lengua Espanola. Juan Capdevila Font. French & Eur.

Diccionario Ilustrado Basico. Cruzada Span Pubns.

Diccionario ilustrado Daimon. Daimon.

Diccionario Ilustrado Danae de la Lengua Espanola. French & Eur.

Diccionario ilustrado de alfareria practica. Robert Fournier. Tr. by Elena Torres. Omega SA.

Diccionario ilustrado de anecdotas. V. Vega. G Gili.

Diccionario Ilustrado de Arquitectura. Carlos E. Perez Calvo. Illus. by Ignacio V. Castro. Plaza Janes.

Diccionario Ilustrado de Efemerides. Vincente Vega. French & Eur.

Diccionario ilustrado de efemerides. V. Vega. G Gili.

Diccionario Ilustrado de Electronica. Humberto Ramirez Villareal. French & Eur.

Diccionario ilustrado de electronica: Espanol-ingles e ingles-espanol. Humberto Ramirez Villarreal. Diana.

Diccionario Ilustrado De Fotografia. French & Eur.

Diccionario Ilustrado De la Arquitectura Contemporanea. Gerd Hatje. Ed. by Gerd Sabater. French & Eur.

Diccionario ilustrado de la arquitectura contemporanes. G. Hatje. G Gili.

Diccionario ilustrado de la arquitectura contemporanea. Gerd Hatje. Tr. by Jose M. Mantero. G Gili.

Diccionario Ilustrado de la Biblia. Ed. by Wilton M. Nelson. Edit Caribe.

Diccionario Ilustrado De la Lengua Espanola. Aristos. French & Eur.

Diccionario Ilustrado De la Lengua Espanola. Atilano Rances. French & Eur.

Diccionario Ilustrado de la Lengua Espanola. Cruzada Span Pubns.

Diccionario ilustrado de la lengua rusa. Cultura Popular.

Diccionario Ilustrado de la Muerte. Robert Sabatier. French & Eur.

Diccionario ilustrado de las ciencias pura y aplicades. Mundi.

Diccionario ilustrado de lengua espanola. Mercadel Garcia. Mayfe.

Diccionario Ilustrado de Rarezas, Inverosimilitudes y Curiosidades. Vicente Vega. French & Eur.

Diccionario Ilustrado De Terminologia Textil Aleman-Espanol, Espanol-Aleman. Carlos Scheengluth. French & Eur.

Diccionario Ilustrado de Trucos. J. L. Chardans & Vicente Vega. French & Eur.

Diccionario ilustrado de trucos. J. L. Chardana & V. Vega. G Gili.

Diccionario ilustrado del idioma ruso. Pueblos Unidos.

Diccionario Ilustrado En Color De Arbustos. S. Millar Gauult. French & Eur.

Diccionario Ilustrado en Color De Plantas De Interior. Roy Hay et al. French & Eur.

Diccionario Ilustrado en Color de Plantas de Jardin con Plantas de Interior y de Invernadero. R. Har & P. M. Synge. French & Eur.

Diccionario Ilustrado Latino-Espanol Espanol-Latino. Biblograf SP.

Diccionario Ilustrado Latino-Espanol Espanol-Latino. Biblo SP.

Diccionario indice analitico. Ed. by Argentina. Ediar.

Diccionario indice de jurisprudencia civil 1947-1956. Bosch Casa.

El Diccionario Infantil de Palabras & Figuras. Escuela Nueva.

Diccionario Infantil Fher. Angel J. Gomez de Segura Beaumont. French & Eur.

Diccionario Infantil Ilustrado. French & Eur.

Diccionario Infantil Ilustrado. French & Eur.

Diccionario Infantil Ilustrado. Lectorum Pubns.

Diccionario infantil ilustrado. Mensajero Edns.

Diccionario infantil ilustrado. Plaza Janes.

Diccionario Infantil Ilustrado. Interediciones.

Diccionario Infantil Ilustrado Bruguera. Consuelo Guisset Poch & Prado Castellanos Alentorn. French & Eur.

Diccionario Infantil Ilustrado: Obra completa II. Plaza Janes.

Diccionario infantil: La lupa magica. Inocencio Feijoo Zollern. Lopez Paco.

Diccionario Ingles. Guenther Haensch. Herder SA.

Diccionario Ingles-Espanol. Edns Nauta.

Diccionario Ingles-Espanol. Mayfe.

Diccionario Ingles-Espanol. L. Jorda. Omega SA.

Diccionario ingles-espanol. Mayfe.

Diccionario ingles-espanol. Zeus.

Diccionario Ingles-Espanol. Oceano.

Diccionario Ingles-Espanol. Fructuoso Plans Sanz de Bremond. Mayfe.

Diccionario Ingles-Espanol & Espanol Ingles: Col. Forja de Idiomas. Mayfe.

Diccionario Ingles-Espanol & Espanol-Ingles. Mayfe.

Diccionario ingles-espanol de electrotecnia y electronica. H. Piraux et al. ETA.

Diccionario ingles-espanol de las ciencias de la tierra. E Orellana. Interciencia.

Diccionario Ingles-Espanol de Medicina. F. Ruiz Torres. Alhambra.

Diccionario Ingles-Espanol, Espanol-Ingles. E. M. Martinez Amador. French & Eur.

Diccionario Ingles-Espanol, Espanol-Ingles. Francisco Bruguera Grane. French & Eur.

Diccionario Ingles-Espanol, Espanol-Ingles. Robertson. French & Eur.

Diccionario Ingles-Espanol, Espanol-Ingles Forja. Eleesbaan Serrano Mesa. French & Eur.

Diccionario Ingles-Espanol, Espanol-Ingles. Eleesbaan Serrano Mesa. French & Eur.

Diccionario Ingles-Espanol Espanol-Ingles. Biblograf SP.

Diccionario Ingles-Espanol, Espanol-Ingles. Ricard Jordana & Paul Chamberlain. Edns Nauta.

Diccionario Ingles-Espanol, Espanol-Ingles. Tesoro.

Diccionario Ingles-Espanol Espanol-Ingles. Zeus.

Diccionario Ingles-Espanol, Espanol-Ingles. Ricard Jordana & Paul Chamberlain. Fed Gremios.

Diccionario ingles-espanol espanol-ingles. Fernando Huerta et al. Circulo Lect.

Diccionario Ingles-Espanol, Espanol-Ingles Novus. Oceano.

Diccionario Ingles-Espanol Espanol-Ingles. Sarpe.

Diccionario ingles-espanol espanol-ingles. Ricardo Jordana & Paul Chamberlain. Nauta SA.

Diccionario Ingles-Espanol-Ingles. Nauta SA.

Diccionario Ingles-Espanol para Medicos y Estudiantes de Medicina. J. A. Garrido. French & Eur.

Diccionario ingles-espanol para medicos y estudiantes de medicina. Juan A. Garrido. Pediatrica.

Diccionario Ingles-Espanol, Spanish-English. Mauricio Bohigas Rosell. French & Eur.

Diccionario ingles-espanol, tecnico-electromecanico. Weiss-Ballesteros. Index.

Diccionario Ingles-Espanol y Espanol-Ingles. French & Eur.

Diccionario ingles-espanol y espanol-ingles. Aurelio Pena. Bibliografica.

Diccionario ingles-espanol y espanol-ingles. Universidad de Chicago. Aguilar SP.

Diccionario Ingles: For Spanish Speakers. Natl Textbk.

Diccionario ingles. Iaconi.

Diccionario Inicial de la Lengua Espanola. Prologue by Aurora D. Plaja. Biblo Sp.

Diccionario Inicial de la Lengua Espanol. Biblograf SP.

Diccionario Inicial de la Lengua Espanola. Lectorum Pubns.

Diccionario Inicial de la Lengua Espanola. Biblo SP.

Diccionario Internacional Abreviado de Siglas, Contracciones & Abreviaturas. Millan Contreras. Paraninfo.

Diccionario Internacional Abreviado De Siglas Contracciones y Abreviaturas. Donato Millan Contreras. French & Eur.

Diccionario internacional de electronica. Cultura Popular.

Diccionario Internacional de Radio & Television. Mariano Cebrian Herreros. Organ Ofic Adm.

Diccionario Internacional de Siglas. Jose Martinez De Sousa. French & Eur.

Diccionario Internacional de Siglas. J. Martinez de Sousa. Piramide.

Diccionario Internacional de Siglas, Contracciones & Abreviaturas. Donato Millan Contreras. Paraninfo.

Diccionario internacional Simon & Schuster: Ingles-espanol y espanol-ingles. S & S.

Diccionario Italiano-Espanol, Espanol-Italiano. E. M. Martinez Amador. French & Eur.

Diccionario Italiano-Espanol Espanol-Italiano Vox. Biblo SP.

Diccionario Iter Aleman-Espanol, Espanol-Aleman. French & Eur.

Diccionario Iter Espanol-Ingles. Cruzada.

Diccionario Iter Italiano-Espanol, Espanol-Italiano. French & Eur.

Diccionario Iter Ortografico. Sopena. Lectorum Pubns.

Diccionario ixcateco. Maria T. Fernandez de Miranda. INAH.

Diccionario Jalisco ilustrado. Fernandez.

Diccionario juridico. J. D. Ramirez Gronda. Claridad.

Diccionario juridico aleman-espanol de derecho comparado: Con vocabulario juridico espanol-aleman. Quintano Heilpern. Rev Derecho Pri.

Diccionario juridico peruano. Arelio Perez Caballero. Mejia.

Diccionario Kapeluse de la Langua Espanola. French & Eur.

Diccionario Kapelusz de la Lengua Espanola. Kapelusz.

Diccionario Karten Ilustrado. French & Eur.

Diccionario kechua-castellano, castellano-kechua. Cesar Guardia Mayorga. Peisa.

Diccionario Kollasuyo, Espanol-Quechua. Miguel Angel Quiroga Flores. Cochabamba.

Diccionario Laboral. Ramon Bayod Serrat. French & Eur.

Diccionario Larousse De la Lengua Espanola-Nuevo Larousse Basico. Larousse.

Diccionario Larousse Del Espanol Moderno. Ramon Garcia-Pelayo. (Sig). NAL.

Diccionario Larousse moderno espanol-ingles. Iaconi.

Diccionario Larousse Moderno Espanol-Ingles, English-Spanish. Larousse.

Diccionario Larousse usual. Larousse.

Diccionario Larousse usual. Iaconi.

Diccionario latino-espanol. J. Llauro Padrosa. SAETA.

Diccionario Latino-Espanol, Espanol-Latino. Blanquez. French & Eur.

Diccionario latino-espanol, espanol-latino: Serie Bachillerato Koel. Tesoro.

Diccionario latino-espanol y espanol-latino. Vicente Blanco Garcia. Aguilar SP.

Diccionario legislativo de cinematografia y teatro. Jose M. Salazar Lopez. Nacional Editora.

Diccionario lengua espanola. Mayfe.

Diccionario Lengua Espanola Forja. Jose Garcia Mercadal. French & Eur.

Diccionario lexico basico espanol. Cultura Popular.

Diccionario Lexicon Aleman-Espanol, Espanol-Aleman. Hans Muller. French & Eur.

Diccionario Lexicon Espanol-Danes & Espanol-Danes. French & Eur.

Diccionario Lexicon Espanol-Esperanto-Espanol, Espanol-Esperanto. French & Eur.

Diccionario Lexicon Finlandes-Espanol, Espanol-Finlandes. French & Eur.

Diccionario Lexicon Frances-Espanol, Espanol-Frances. E. Gimeno. French & Eur.

Diccionario Lexicon Holandes-Espanol y Espanol-Holandes. French & Eur.

Diccionario Lexicon Ingles-Espanol, Espanol-Ingles. D. Macarulla. French & Eur.

Diccionario Lexicon Italiano-Espanol, Espanol-Italiano. French & Eur.

Diccionario Lexicon Noruego-Espanol, Espanol-Noruego. French & Eur.

Diccionario Lexicon Portugues-Espanol, Espanol-Portugues. French & Eur.

Diccionario Lexicon Sueco-Espanol, Espanol-Sueco. French & Eur.

Diccionario Lexikon. Fernandez.

Diccionario Literario Universal. Jose A. Perez-Rioja. Tecnos SA.

Diccionario Lunfardo & de Otros Terminos Antiguos & Modernos Usuales. Jose Gobello. Pena Lillo.

Diccionario Lunfardo Ilustrado. Jose Gobello. French & Eur.

Diccionario Magico Infantil. Eulalia Goma. French & Eur.

Diccionario Magico Infantil. Eulalia Goma. Vilamala.

Diccionario Magico Infantil. Eulalia Goma. Vilamala.

Diccionario Magico Infantil En Seis Lenguas. Eulalia Goma. French & Eur.

Diccionario Major Frances-Espanol, Espanol-Frances. Roberto Larrieu & Manuel Garcia Morente. Diafora.

Diccionario Major Ingles-Espanol, Espanol-Ingles. Anthony Gooch & Angel Garcia de Paredes. Diafora.

Diccionario Manual Aleman-Espanol, Espanol-Aleman. Felix Diez Mateo. French & Eur.

Diccionario Manual Aleman-Espanol, Espanol-Aleman. Ed. by Felix D. Mateo & Frida Hochleitner. Espasa Calpe.

Diccionario Manual Aleman-Espanol, Spanisch-Deutsch. E. M. Martinez Amador. French & Eur.

Diccionario Manual Amador Aleman-Espanol, Espanol-Aleman. E. M. Martinez Amador. French & Eur.

Diccionario Manual Amador Frances-Espanol y Espanol-Frances. E. M. Martinez Amador. French & Eur.

Diccionario Manual Amador Ingles-Espanol, Espanol-Ingles. French & Eur.

Diccionario Manual Auxiliar Basico. French & Eur.

Diccionario Manual de Bellas Artes. Biblograf.

Diccionario Manual De la Lengua Espanol a-Z. Francisco Gordo-Guarinos. French & Eur.

Diccionario Manual De la Lengua Espanol A-Z. Francisco Gordo-Guarinos. French & Eur.

Diccionario Manual de la Lengua Espanol: Real Academia Espanola. (ESP). Lectorum Pubns.

Diccionario manual de la lengua espanola: Real Academia Espanol. (ESP). Lectorum Pub.

Diccionario Manual de Medicina & Salud. Biblograf.

Diccionario Manual de Sinonimos, Antonimos e Ideas Afines. French & Eur.

Diccionario manual de sinonimos y antonimos. Biblograf.

Diccionario Manual e Ilustrado de la Lengua Espanol. Real Academie de la Lengua Espanol. French & Eur.

Diccionario manual e ilustrado de la lengua espanola. (Real Academia) Espasa.

Diccionario Manual Espanol-Portugues, Portugues-Espanol. Julio Da Conceicao Fernandes. French & Eur.

Diccionario manual espanol-ruso. Gisbert. Pueblos Unidos.

Diccionario Manual Frances-Espanol. Frida Hochleitner & Felix D. Mateo. Espasa Calpe.

Diccionario Manual Frances-Espanol, Espagnol-Francais. Arturo Cuyas Armengol. French & Eur.

Diccionario Manual Frances-Espanol, Espanol-Frances. Felix Diez Mateo & Frida Hochleitner. French & Eur.

Diccionario Manual Frances-Espanol Espanol-Frances. Biblograf SP.

Diccionario manual frances-espanol, espanol-frances. Felix Diaz Mateo & Frida Hochleitner. Espasa Calpe.

Diccionario Manual Frances-Espanol Espanol-Frances Vox. Biblo SP.

Diccionario Manual Griego-Espanol. Jose M. Pabon & M. Fernandez Galiano. Biblograf SP.

Diccionario Manual Griego-Espanol Vox. Biblo SP.

Diccionario Manual Herder Frances-Espanol, Espanol-Frances. Gunther Haensch. French & Eur.

Diccionario Manual Ilustrado de la Lengua Espanola. Biblograf SP.

Diccionario Manual Ilustrado de la Lengua Espanola. Vox. Brandstetter.

Diccionario Manual Ilustrado de la Lengua Espanola Vox. Biblo SP.

Diccionario manual ilustrado espanol A-Z. Universal Medinacelli.

Diccionario Manual Ingles-Espanol Espanol-Ingles Vox. Biblo SP.

Diccionario Manual Ingles-Espanol, Espanol-Ingles. Felix Diez Mateo & Frida Hochleitner. French & Eur.

Diccionario Manual Ingles-Espanol Espanol-Ingles. Biblograf SP.

Diccionario manual ingles-espanol, espanol-ingles. Felix Diez Mateo & Frida Hochleitner. Espasa Calpe.

Diccionario Manual Ingles-Espanol, Spanish-English. Arturo Cuyas Armengol. French & Eur.

Diccionario Manual Ingles-Espanol, Spanish-English. Arturo Cuyas Armengol. French & Eur.

Diccionario manual italiano-espanol. Francisco de B. Moll. Moll Edit.

Diccionario Manual Italiano-Espanol, Spagnuolo-Italiano. Jose Ortiz De Burgos. French & Eur.

Diccionario manual latino-castellano y castellano-latino. De Andrea. Sopena.

Diccionario manual latino-espanol y espanol-latino. Agustin Blanquez Fraile. Sopena.

Diccionario manual latino-espanol y espanol-latino. Mugica. Razon y Fe.

Diccionario Manual y Illustrado De La Lengua Espanola. Real Academia Espanola. Colton Bk.

Diccionario Marin de la Lengua Espanola: Obra Completa. Marin.

Diccionario Marin de la Lengua Espanola. Marin.

Diccionario maritimo. Julian Amich. Juventud.

Diccionario maritimo. J. L. Pando. Dossat.

Diccionario Maritimo Ilustrado Vasco-Castellano, Castellano-Vasco. Ignacio de Garmendia y Berasategui. French & Eur.

Diccionario maritimo ingles-espanol y espanol-ingles. Jose Garcia de Paredes y Castro & Enrique Barbudo Duarte. Fragata.

Diccionario Maritimo y De Construccion Naval. Juan Alfaro Perez. French & Eur.

Diccionario Maya Cordemex Maya-Espanol. Alfredo Barrera Vasquez. Porrua.

Diccionario Medico. Luigi Segatore & Gianangelo Poli. French & Eur.

Diccionario Medico. F. Beer Poitevin. French & Eur.

Diccionario Medico. Salvat Editores.

Diccionario Medico. Luigi Segatore & Gianangelo Poli. Teide.

Diccionario medico. Andrea Bissanti et al. Tr. by Catala J. Blanco. Mas Ivars.

Diccionario Medico. Salvat Editores.

Diccionario Medico & su Suplemento Espanol. Veillon-Nobel. Cientifico Med.

Diccionario medico de bolsillo. Salvat Editores.

Diccionario Medico: De Bosillo. French & Eur.

Diccionario Medico Familiar. Seleccione Reader's Digest. French & Eur.

Diccionario Medico Familiar II. Sel Rdrs Digest.

Diccionario medico Labor. Francisco J. Cortada. Labor SA.

Diccionario Medico Labor Para la Familia. Mommsen. French & Eur.

Diccionario Medico Labor para la Familia. H. Mommsen. French & Eur.

Diccionario medico Labor para la familia. Mommsen. Labor SA.

Diccionario Medico Labor para la Familia. H. Mommsen et al. Tr. by Juan Massor Gimeno & J. Vilahur Pedrals. Labor SA.

Diccionario medico para la familia moderna. Gaisa.

Diccionario mi amigo: Diccionario escolar de bolsillo. Fernandez.

Diccionario militar bilingue. Aguirre de Carcer. Dossat.

Diccionario militar espanol-ruso. Bulgakov. Pueblos Unidos.

Diccionario Militar Espanol-Ruso, Ruso-Espanol. French & Eur.

Diccionario militar estrategico y politico. Fernando De Bordeje Morencos. San Martin.

Diccionario mimico espanol. Felix-Jesus Pinedo Peydro. Organ Ofic Adm.

Diccionario Mini Sopena Ingles-Espanol. French & Eur.

Diccionario Mininorma. Jorge Cardenas Nannetti. Norma Edit.

Diccionario Mitologico. C. Gaytan. French & Eur.

Diccionario Mixteco del Este De Jamiltepec. Brenda Pensinger. Summer Inst Ling.

Diccionario Moderno. Ed. by Eduardo Cardenas. Edit Norma.

Diccionario moderno: Aleman-espanol, espanol-aleman. Langenscheidt. Herder SA.

Diccionario Moderno del Espanol Usual. Alfonso Zamora Vicente. Sader SA.

Diccionario Moderno Espanol-Ingles, English-Spanish. Ramon Garcia-Pelayo. French & Eur.

Diccionario moderno espanol-ingles, ingles-espanol. Margaret H. Reventos. CECSA.

Diccionario moderno: Frances-espanol, espanol-frances. Herder SA.

Diccionario moderno frances-espanol y espanol-frances. P. Fabrega. Bosch Casa.

Diccionario Moderno Herder Aleman-Espanol, Espanol-Aleman. Gunther Haensch. French & Eur.

Diccionario moderno Herder Aleman-Espanol. Gunther Haensch. Herder SA.

Diccionario moderno: Ingles-espanol, espanol-ingles. Langenssheidt. Herder SA.

Diccionario moderno Larousse. Pan Am Bk co.

Diccionario Modernos Herder Aleman-Espanol. Herder SA.

Diccionario Modernos Herder Frances-Espanol. Herder SA.

Diccionario Monografico de Bellas Artes. Vox. French & Eur.

Diccionario Monografico de Bellas Artes. Biblograf SP.

Diccionario Monografico de Matematicas. Ed. by Vox. French & Eur.

Diccionario Monografico de Matematicas. Biblograf SP.

Diccionario Monografico de Matematicas. Biblo SP.

Diccionario Monografico de Medicina & Salud. Biblograf SP.

Diccionario Monografico de Medicina y Salud. Ed. by Vox. French & Eur.

Diccionario Monografico de Reino Mineral 'Vox' Biblo SP.

Diccionario Monografico de Technologia. Ed. by Vox. French & Eur.

Diccionario Monografico de Tecnologia. Biblograf SP.

Diccionario Monografico de Tecnologia. Biblograf.

Diccionario Monografico del Reino Animal. French & Eur.

Diccionario Monografico del Reino Animal. Biblograf SP.

Diccionario Monografico del Reino Mineral. Biblograf SP.

Diccionario Monografico del Reino Mineral. Biblograf.

Diccionario Monografico del Reino Vegetal. Biblograf SP.

Diccionario Monografico del Reino Vegetal. Biblograf.

Diccionario Monografico del Reino Vegetal 'Vox' Biblo SP.

Diccionario Morfologico del Nuevo Testamento. Manuel Guerra y Gomez. Aldecoa.

Diccionario multilingue. Edwin B. Williams & Alfred Senn. Edit Pr Serv.

Diccionario Multiple. J. A. Onieva. Paraninfo.

Diccionario Multiple: Nueve Diccionarios en un Solo Volumen. Onieva. Paraninfo.

Diccionario multiple: Nueve diccionarios en un volumen. Antonio J. Onieva. Paraninfo.

Diccionario Mundo hispano. Fernandez.

Diccionario Nautico. Jose M. Martinez Hidalgo Teran. French & Eur.

Diccionario Naval. Leal. Paraninfo.

Diccionario Naval Ingles-Espanol. Luis Leal. Paraninfo.

Diccionario naval ingles-espanol espanol-ingles. Luis Leal y Leal. Paraninfo.

Diccionario naval: Ingles-espanol y espanol-ingles. L. Leal. Paraninfo.

Diccionario Norma: El Lexico de Nuestro Tiempo. Jorge Cardenas Nannetti. Norma.

Diccionario nuevo Larousse manual ilustrado. Larousse.

Diccionario Oceano de la Lengua Espanola. Oceano.

Diccionario Oceano Espanol-Ingles. Oceano.

Diccionario odontologico. Ciro Durante Avellanal. Mundi.

Diccionario Onomastico y Heraldico Vasco. Jaime Querexeta Gallostequi. French & Eur.

Diccionario onomastico y heraldico vasco: Tomo 7. Domingo Lizaso. Encicl Vasca.

Diccionario "Oriente". French & Eur.

Diccionario: Oriente. French & Eur.

Diccionario Ortografico. Mayfe.

Diccionario Ortografico. Julio De La Canal. MEX.

Diccionario ortografico. Mayfe.

Diccionario ortografico. J. De La Canal. EDIMEX.

Diccionario ortografico. Fructuoso Plans Sanz de Bremond. Mayfe.

Diccionario Ortografico del Idioma Espanol Moderno. AGL.

Diccionario ortografico del idioma espanol. Martin Alonso. Aguilar SP.

Diccionario ortografico hispanoamericano. Flores de Vega. Peisa.

Diccionario Ortografico Iter. French & Eur.

Diccionario ortografico: Libro del maestro. S. Ledesma. Barreiro Ramos.

Diccionario Ortografico Mikron. Plans y De Gabriel Sanz De Bremond, Fructuoso. French & Eur.

Diccionario Oxford de la musica. P. A. Scholes. Sudamer.

Diccionario para especialistas. Minerva.

Diccionario para especialistas de seguros. Sell. Rev. Mex. de Seguros.

Diccionario para Ingenieros Espanol-Ingles, Ingles-Espanol. Louis A. Robb. French & Eur.

Diccionario para ingenieros: Ingles-espanol, espanol-ingles. Louis A. Robb. CECSA.

Diccionario Para Obras Publica, Edificacion y Maquinaria En Obra. Bucksch. French & Eur.

Diccionario para Obras Publicas, Edificacion & Maquinaria en Obra. Bauverlag.

Diccionario Para Obras Publicas, Edificacion y Maquinaria en Obra. French & Eur.

Diccionario para obras publicas, edificacion y maquinaria en obra: Aleman-espanol, espanol-aleman. Bucksch. Herder SA.

Diccionario Para Pobres. Francisco Umbral Perez. French & Eur.

Diccionario para resolver palabras cruzadas. Cosmopolita.

Diccionario para un macuto. G. Rafael. Nacional Editora.

Diccionario Parvus duplex: Frances-castellano y castellano-frances. Sopena.

Diccionario Parvus duplex: Ingles-castellano y castellano-ingles. Sopena.

Diccionario Parvus duplex: Italiano-castellano y castellano-ingles. Sopena.

Diccionario Parvus duplex: Portugues-castellano y castellano-portugues. Sopena.

Diccionario pedagogico. Rafael. Min. Educ.

Diccionario Penal: Libro del Opositor C. G. P. Angel Sanchez Ordonez. Lemos.

Diccionario Pequeno Nebrija de la lengua castellana. Edit Nebrija.

Diccionario periodistico de Futbol. Inocencio F. Arias Llamas et al. Organ Ofic Adm.

Diccionario pervus duplex: Aleman-castellano y castellano-aleman. Sopena.

Diccionario petrografico: Vol 1, Rocas eruptivas. Maximino San Miguel de la Camara. (CSIC). Inst. Jose Acosta y Lucas Mallada.

Diccionario Planeta Abreviado de la Lengua Espanola Usual. Planeta SA.

Diccionario plastico. Tr. by J. A. Wordingham & P. Reboul. Leru.

Diccionario Plaza y Janes: Obra completa II. Plaza Janes.

Diccionario Plaza y Janes, S.A: Tomo 2 II. Plaza Janes.

Diccionario Plaza y Janes: Tomo 1 II. Plaza Janes.

Diccionario poliglota de la arquitectura. B. Bassegoda Muste. Imported Bks.

Diccionario poligloto de nombres. Teodoro Amerlinck. UNAM.

Diccionario poligloto de terminos de Arte y Arquitectura. L. Reau. Fondo Cult.

Diccionario Polilectal del Quechua de Ancash. Gary J. Parker. Centro Invest.

Diccionario politecnico de las lenguas espanola e inglesa. Castilla.

Diccionario Politico. Eduardo Haro Tecglen. French & Eur.

Diccionario Politico. Eduardo Haro Tecglen. Planeta SA.

Diccionario politico de Chile. Jordi Fuentes & Lia Cortes. Orbe Edns.

Diccionario Politico: Los Ministros Nacionales. O. J. Sanquiao. Platero.

Diccionario Politico Para Occidente. Antonio Marquez Bessa. French & Eur.

Diccionario popular castellano-catalan. Milla Lib.

Diccionario popular de las ciencias y de la tecnica. Brockhaus. Gill Gustavo.

Diccionario Popular Matematico. Hernany Miranda. Direc Pubns.

Diccionario por Fechas de Historia Universal. Christfried Coler. French & Eur.

Diccionario Porrua de Historia, Biografia y Geografia de Mexico. French & Eur.

Diccionario Porrua de la Espanola. Antonio Raluy Poudevida. Porrua.

Diccionario Porrua de la Lengua espanola: Contiene las palabras basicas del idioma, con abundantes exicanismos & americanismos, tecnicismos, verbos & notas ortograficas. Antonio Raluy Pondevida. Ed. by Francisco Monterde. Porrua.

Diccionario Porrua de la lengua espanola. Antonio Raluy Poudevida. Porrua.

Diccionario Porrua de la lengua espanola. Antonio Raluy Poudevida. Rev. by Francisco Monterde. Porrua.

Diccionario Porrua de la lengua espanola. Iaconi.

Diccionario Porrua de la Lengua Espanola Para Escuelas Primarias. Antonio Raluy Poudevila. Ed. by Francisco Monterde. French & Eur.

Diccionario Porrua Ingles-Espanol. Alejandro Gomez de Parada. Porrua.

Diccionario Porrua Ingles-Espanol. Alejandro Gomez de Parada. Porrua.

Diccionario Porrua ingles-espanol, espanol-ingles. Alejandro Gomez de Parada. Porrua.

Diccionario Portugues-Espanol. Julio da Conceicao Fernandes. French & Eur.

Diccionario Portugues-Espanol, Espanol-Portugues. David Ortega Cavero. French & Eur.

Diccionario portugues-espanol, espanol-portugues. David Ortega Cavero & Julio Da Conceica. Sopena.

Diccionario portugues-espanol y espanol-portugues. Mayfe.

Diccionario Practico: Asesor De la Propiedad & Copropiedad Inmobiliaria. Jose M. Plans Sanz De Bremond. French & Eur.

Diccionario Practico De Psicopatologia. Yves Poinso. French & Eur.

Diccionario practico de seguros. Juan J. Garrido y Comas. Ariel.

Diccionario practico de seguros. Garrido y Comas. Rev. Mex. de Seguros.

Diccionario Practico Escolar de la Lengua Espanola. Juan Capdevila Font. French & Eur.

Diccionario Punto. Larousse.

Diccionario Qheshwa-Castellano. Jesus Lara. Amigos del Libro.

Diccionario Quechua. Gary J. Parker. Minist Ed Caracas.

Diccionario Quechua Ayacucho-Chanca. Clodoaldo Soto Ruiz. Minist Ed Caracas.

Diccionario Quechua Cajamarca-Canaris. Felix Quesada Castillo. Minist Ed Caracas.

Diccionario Quechua Cuzco-Collao. Antonio G. Cusihuaman. Minist Ed Caracas.

Diccionario Quechua Junin-Huanca. Rodolfo Cerron-Palomino. Minist Ed Caracas.

Diccionario Quechua San Martin. Marinell Park & Nancy Weber. Ministerio de Educacion.

Diccionario Rances. Sopena.

Diccionario Rapanui-Espanol, Redactado en la Isla de Pascua. Sebastian Englert. AMS Pr.

Diccionario razonado de matematicas: De las matematicas clasicas a la matematica moderna. Andre Warusfel. Tecnos SA.

Diccionario Razonado de Sinonimos y Contrarios. Jose M. Zainqui. French & Eur.

Diccionario Real de la Lengua Espanola. Oceano.

Diccionario Real de la Lengua Espanola. Oceano.

Diccionario Real de la Lengua Espanola. Oceano.

Diccionario Real de la Lengua Espanola. Oceano.

Diccionario Real Espanol-Ingles. Oceano.

Diccionario Real Espanol-Ingles Ingles-Espanol. Oceano.

Diccionario Religioso Para los Hombres De Hoy. Josep Vilaro et al. French & Eur.

Diccionario Retana De Autoridades De la Lengua Vasca. Manuel de Sota Aburto. French & Eur.

Diccionario Rioduero: Arte. Ursula Boeing-Haeusgen. French & Eur.

Diccionario Rioduero: Biologia. Rainer Bergfeld. French & Eur.

Diccionario Rioduero: Ecologia. Udo Becker. French & Eur.

Diccionario Rioduero: Fisica. Rolf Sauermost. French & Eur.

Diccionario Rioduero: Fisica Del Espacio. Udo Becker. French & Eur.

Diccionario Rioduero: Geografia. Margit Klein & Johannes Klein. French & Eur.

Diccionario Rioduero: Geologia y Mineralogia. French & Eur.

Diccionario Rioduero Matematica. Jurgen Reck. French & Eur.

Diccionario Rioduero: Paises De la Tierra. Johannes Klein. French & Eur.

Diccionario Rioduero: Quimica. Peter Ottokar. French & Eur.

Diccionario Rioduero: Quimica. Peter Ottokar. Tr. by Gloria Arroyo Marcos. Catolica Edit.

Diccionario Rioduero: Zoologia. French & Eur.

Diccionario Ruso-Espanol. Lorenzo Martinez Calvo. French & Eur.

Diccionario Ruso-Espanol. J. Nogueira & G. Turover. French & Eur.

Diccionario ruso-espanol. Pueblos Unidos.

Diccionario ruso-espanol. Yaselman. Aguilar SP.

Diccionario ruso-espanol de la ciencia y de la tecnica. Patronato Juan de la Cierva. Dossat.

Diccionario Ruso-Espanol de la Ciencia y la Tecnica. Patronato J. De la Cierva. French & Eur.

Diccionario ruso-espanol, espanol-ruso. Danae.

Diccionario Saber miniatura. Fernandez.

Diccionario San Luis Potosi: Enciclopedia regional. Fernandez.

Diccionario Santillana. Ed. by Javier Alfaya. Santillana.

Diccionario Secreto. Camilo J. Cela Trulock. French & Eur.

Diccionario Secreto. Camilo J. Cela. (ALFA). Lectorum Pubns.

Diccionario Simultaneo en 21 Idiomas. Juan Capdevilla Font. French & Eur.

Diccionario simultaneo en 21 idiomas. Pan Amer Pub.

Diccionario Simultaneo en 6 Idiomas. Juan Capdevila Font. French & Eur.

Diccionario Sopena de Dudas & Dificultades del Idioma. Sopena.

Diccionario Sopena De Literatura. Parnaso. French & Eur.

Diccionario Subversivo. Miguel Angel Speroni. Hachette Jeunesse.

Diccionario Superior Frances-Espanol, Espanol-Frances. Vox. Biblo Sp.

Diccionario Superior Frances-Espanol Espanol-Frances. Biblograf SP.

Diccionario superior Frances-Espanol Espanol-Frances 'Vox' Biblo SP.

Diccionario Tabasco: Enciclopedia regional. Fernandez.

Diccionario Taurino Ilustrado. Carlos Garcia Patier. Cometa SA.

Diccionario Tecnic Aeronautico Espanol-Ingles: Tomo 2. Autor.

Diccionario Tecnico. Hermann Mink. Blume Edit.

Diccionario Tecnico Aeronautico Espanol-Ingles-Espanol. Autor.

Diccionario Tecnico Aeronautico Espanol-Ingles. Autor.

Diccionario Tecnico Aleman-Espanol, Espanol-Aleman. H. Mink. French & Eur.

Diccionario Tecnico & Industrial Italiano-Espanol. L Carcamo.

Diccionario tecnico automovilismo, mecanica automotriz: Espanol-Ingles. Cosmopolita.

Diccionario tecnico, automovilismo, mecanica automotriz: Ingles-espanol. Cosmopolita.

Diccionario Tecnico-Comercial y Profesional de Automocion. Luiz Miguel Ortega Garcia. Tecnipublicaciones.

Diccionario Tecnico de Aeronautica. F. Fernandez-Martinez. Paraninfo.

Diccionario tecnico de biblioteconomia espanol-ingles, ingles-espanol. Beatriz Massa de Gil et al. Trillas.

Diccionario Tecnico de Biblioteconomia. Beatriz Massa De Gil. Trillas.

Diccionario Tecnico de electromecanica: Ingles-espanol. L. Ballesteros Weis. Limusa.

Diccionario Tecnico De la Construccion, Edificacion y Obras Publicas Frances-Espanol y Espanol-Frances. M. Machado. French & Eur.

Diccionario tecnico de la construccion: Edificacion y obras publicas; francesa-espanol y espanol-frances. M. Machado. Paraninfo.

Diccionario Tecnico de la Industria del Petroleo y Derivados. Ed. by Mendez. French & Eur.

Diccionario Tecnico De la Plasticos Aleman-Espanol. A. Wittfoht & M. A. Achon. French & Eur.

Diccionario tecnico de plasticos aleman-espanol. A Wittfoht & M. A. Achon. Urmo.

Diccionario tecnico de plasticos: Espanol-aleman. A. Wittfoht & A. Rubin. (Dist. Elcano, Mexico). Urmo.

Diccionario Tecnico de Terminologia Comercial Cantable y Bancaria. Jaime Garza Bores. French & Eur.

Diccionario tecnico de terminologia comercial, contable y bancaria: Espanol-Ingles, Ingles-Espanol. Jaime Garza Bores. Diana.

Diccionario tecnico de terminos ferroviarios: Espanol-frances-aleman-ingles-italiano-holandes. J. H. Bussy. G Gili.

Diccionario Tecnico Del Agua. Jose Catalan Lafuente. French & Eur.

Diccionario tecnico del seguro de vida. Karlsruhe. Rev. Mex. de Seguros.

Diccionario tecnico electrotecnia; luminotecnia; espanol-ingles. Cosmopolita.

Diccionario tecnico, electrotecnia, luminotecnia: Ingles-espanol. Cosmopolita.

Diccionario tecnico espanol-aleman. Tr. by Mink. Bluma.

Diccionario Tecnico Espanol-Frances. Guy Malgorn. French & Eur.

Diccionario Tecnico espanol-frances; frances-espanol. EDAF.

Diccionario Tecnico Espanol-Ingles. Guy Malgorn. French & Eur.

Diccionario Tecnico Espanol-Ingles. Guy Malgorn. Paraninfo.

Diccionario Tecnico Espanol-Ingles. Malgorn. Paraninfo.

Diccionario Tecnico Espanol-Polaco. Ed. by T. Weroniecki. French & Eur.

Diccionario tecnico Español-Inglés. Guy Malgorn. Fed Gremios.

Diccionario Tecnico Frances-Espanol. French & Eur.

Diccionario Tecnico Frances-Espanol. Hermann Mink. French & Eur.

Diccionario Tecnico Frances-Espanol. Malgorn. Paraninfo.

Diccionario tecnico frances-espanol y espanol-frances. Guy Malgorn. Paraninfo.

Diccionario tecnico-grafico del automovil. Bluma.

Diccionario Tecnico Hostelero. Fernando Molina Aranda. French & Eur.

Diccionario Tecnico Ilustrado De Edificacion y Obras Publicas. Maurice Barbier. French & Eur.

Diccionario tecnico ilustrado de edificacion y obras publicas. Barbier et al. G Gili.

Diccionario tecnico ilustrado de herramientas de corte para el trabajo de metales: Espanol-aleman-ingles-frances-italiano. T. Heiler. G Gili.

Diccionario tecnico ilustrado del automovil. Jezewski Blok. Tr. by Diorki. Aneto Edns.

Diccionario tecnico industrial: Vol. 1, Espanol-aleman. R. Ernst. G Gili.

Diccionario tecnico industrial: Vol. 2, Aleman-espanol. G Gili.

Diccionario Tecnico Ingles-Espanol. Guy Malgorn. French & Eur.

Diccionario Tecnico Ingles-Espanol. Malgorn. Paraninfo.

Diccionario Tecnico-Maritimo Ingles-Espanol & Espanol-Ingles. L. S. Gil. Edit Alhambra.

Diccionario tecnico-maritimo Ingles-Espanol & Espanol-Ingles. L. Suarez Gil. Fed Gremios.

Diccionario Tecnico Maritimo: Ingles-Espanol, Espanol-Ingles. Ed. by L. Suarez Gil. French & Eur.

Diccionario tecnico maritimo: Ingles-espanol espanol-ingles. L. Suariz Gil. Alhambra.

Diccionario tecnico militar ingles-espanol y espanol-ingles para uso de los ejercitos de tierra, mar y aire. Francisco Lizarraga. Bibliografica.

Diccionario tecnico, radio, antenas, video, radar: Espanol-ingles. Cosmopolita.

Diccionario Tecnico: Suplemento. H. Mink. French & Eur.

Diccionario Tecnico: Suplemento al Tomo II, Espanol-Aleman. H. Mink. Herder SA.

Diccionario tecnico, television: Espanol-Ingles. Cosmopolita.

Diccionario tecnico, television: Ingles-Espanol. Cosmopolita.

Diccionario Tecnico, Tomo 1: Aleman-Espanol. H. Mink. (French & Eur). French & Eur.

Diccionario Tecnico, Tomo 2: Espanol-Aleman. H. Mink. (French & Eur). French & Eur.

Diccionario tecnologico Chambers: Espanol-ingles-frances-aleman. C. F. Tweney & L. E. Hughes. Omega SA.

Diccionario Tecnologico Del Plasticos. French & Eur.

Diccionario Tecnologico Ingles-Espanol: Electricidad, Electronica, Telecomunicacion, & Materias Afinas con la Fisica, Optica & Quimica. Franco Ibeas. Alhambra.

Diccionario Tecnologico Ingles-Espanol. French & Eur.

Diccionario Tecnologico Ingles-Espanol. F. F. Ibeas. Edit Alhambra.

Diccionario tecnologico Inglés-Español. Franco Ibeas. Fed Gremios.

Diccionario Tematico de la Lengua Espanola. Vox. Biblo Sp.

Diccionario Tematico de la Lengua Espanola. Biblograf SP.

Diccionario Tematico de la Lengua Espanola 'Vox' Biblo SP.

Diccionario Tematico de Sinonimos & Antonimos. Everest.

Diccionario Tematico Ingles-Espanol & Espanol-Ingles. Jose Merino. Paraninfo.

Diccionario Tematico Ingles-Espanol & Espanol-Ingles. Merino. Paraninfo.

Diccionario tematico Ingles-Espanol & Espanol-Ingles. Jose Merino. Fed Gremios.

Diccionario Tematico Ingles-Espanol, Espanol-Ingles. Jose Merino. French & Eur.

Diccionario Teorico y Practico del Juicio de Amparo. Eduardo Pallares. French & Eur.

Diccionario terminlogico de ciencias medicas. Salvat Editores.

Diccionario terminoligico de Ciencias Medicas II. Salvat Editores.

Diccionario terminoligico de la Comunidades Europeas. Daniel Busturia. Assn Prog Direc.

Diccionario Terminologia Medica Explicada. Juan Prada Becares. French & Eur.

Diccionario Terminologia Medica Explicada. Juan Prada Becares. Autores-Editores.

Diccionario Terminologico. Lluis. Fondo Educativo.

Diccionario Terminologico De Ciencias Medicas. French & Eur.

Diccionario Terminologico de Ciencias Medicas. Salvat Editores.

Diccionario Terminologico De Minas, Canteras y Mineralurgia. Laureano Fueyo Cuesta. French & Eur.

Diccionario terminologico de Quimaca. Jose Barcelo Matutano. Alhambra.

Diccionario Terminologico de Quimica. Jose R. Barcelo Matutano. French & Eur.

Diccionario Terminologico de Quimica. Jose R. Barcelo. Edit Alhambra.

Diccionario Terminologico de Quimica. J. R. Barcelo. Alhambra.

Diccionario Terminos. Thierrey Maulmier. French & Eur.

Diccionario textil panamericano: English-Spanish Dictionary of Textile Terms. Joaquin O. Rodriguez. W R C Smith.

Diccionario Totonaco De Papantla. Herman Aschmann & Bessie Aschmann. Summer Inst Ling.

Diccionario Totonaco de Xicotepec de Juarez. Reid et al. Summer Inst Ling.

Diccionario Tri-lingue. Esteban S. Hornberger & H. N. Hornberger. LCA.

Diccionario trilingue miskito-ingles-espanol. Adolfo I. Vaughan Warman. Imp. Nac. Manugua EDUCA.

Diccionario Triqui de Chicahuaxtla. Claude Good. Inst Ling Ver.

Diccionario Turistico de Cataluna, Baleares y Andora. J. Munso. French & Eur.

Diccionario Turistico Internacional: Edition Espagnole. Academie International du Tourisme. Acad Intl Tour.

Diccionario Tzotzil De San Andres Con Variaciones Dialectales. Alfa Delgaty & Augustin R. Sanchez. Summer Inst Ling.

Diccionario universal: Aleman-espanol, espanol-aleman. Herder SA.

Diccionario Universal del Arte. Argos-Vergara.

Diccionario Universal del Arte: A-CH. Argos-Vergara.

Diccionario Universal del Arte: D-H. Argos-Vergara.

Diccionario Universal del Arte: I-M. Argos-Vergara.

Diccionario Universal del Arte: N-R. Argos-Vergara.

Diccionario Universal del Arte: S-Z. Argos-Vergara.

Diccionario Universal del Arte y De los Artistas: Arquitectos. French & Eur.

Diccionario Universal del Arte y De los Artistas: Arte Occidental y del Proximo Oriente, II. French & Eur.

Diccionario Universal del Arte y De los Artistas: Arte Occidental y del Proximo Oriente, I. French & Eur.

Diccionario Universal del Arte y De los Artistas: Arte Oriental, Precolombino y De los Pueblos Primitivos. French & Eur.

Diccionario Universal del Arte y De los Artistas: Escultores. French & Eur.

Diccionario Universal del Arte y De los Artistas: Estilos y Tendencias En el Arte Occidental. French & Eur.

Diccionario Universal del Arte y De los Artistas: Pintores. French & Eur.

Diccionario Universal del Arte y los Artistas. Juan-Eduardo Cirlot. French & Eur.

Diccionario universal: Frances-espanol, espanol-frances. Herder SA.

Diccionario Universal Herder Aleman-Espanol, Espanol-Aleman. French & Eur.

Diccionario Universal Herder De la Lengua Espanola. French & Eur.

Diccionario Universal Herder Frances-Espanol, Espanol-Frances. French & Eur.

Diccionario Universal Herder Holandes-Espanol, Espanol-Holandes. French & Eur.

Diccionario Universal Herder Ingles-Espanol, Espanol-Ingles. French & Eur.

Diccionario Universal Herder Italiano-Espanol, Espanol-Italiano. French & Eur.

Diccionario universal: Ingles-espanol, espanol-ingles. Herder SA.

Diccionario universal: Italiano-espanol, espanol-italiano. Herder SA.

Diccionario universal Langenscheidt. Buena Prensa.

El Diccionario valenciano-castellano de Manuel Josquin Savelo. Joseph Gulsoy. Soc. Castellonenca de Cultura.

Diccionario Vasco-Castellano & Castellano-Vasco. Juan J. Arbelaiz. Encicl Vasca.

Diccionario Vasco-Castellano & Castellano-Vasco de Voces Comunes. Juan Jose Arbelaiz. Encicl Vasca.

Diccionario Vasco-Castellano, Castellano-Vasco de Voces Comunes a Dos O Mas Dialectos Del Euskera. Aberlaitz & P. Buenaventura de Oreyegui. French & Eur.

Diccionario Vasco-Castellano: Obra completa. Placido Mugica Betrondo. Mensajero Edns.

Diccionario Vasco-Castellano: Tomo 1. Placido Mugica Berrondo. Mensajero Edns.

Diccionario Vasco-Castellano: Tomo 2. Placido Mugica Berrondo. Mensajero Edns.

Diccionario Vasco-Espanol-Frances. Resurreccion M. Azkue. French & Eur.

Diccionario Velazquez: Espanol e ingles. Mariano Velazquez. Follett.

Diccionario Veracruz ilustrado. Fernandez.

Diccionario Vertice Everest: Frances-Espanol, Espanol-Frances. Everest. Everest.

Diccionario Visual Del Sexo. French & Eur.

Diccionario visual del sexo. Nauta SA.

Diccionario visual del sexo. Eric Trimmer. Tr. by Ernest Jorda. Circulo Lect.

Diccionario y gramatica de la lengua de la isla de Pascua: Pascuense-castellano, castellano-pascuense, pascuense-ingles, ingles-pascuense. Jordi Fuentes Franco. Juridica-Andres Bello.

Diccionario y manual de la nueva fisica y quimica. Robert W. Marks. Edit Pr Serv.

Diccionario y manual de las nuevas matematicas. Robert W. Marks. Edit Pr Serv.

Diccionario y tablas electronicas. Minerva.

Diccionario Yucatán: Enciclopedia regional. Fernandez.

Diccionario Zen. Ed. by E. Wood. French & Eur.

Diccionario Zen. E. Wood. Paido.

Diccionarior Nuclear. Agustin A. Santos. Organ Ofic Adm.

Diccionarios mundiales. Follett.

Diccionarios Rioduero: Biologia. Rainer Bergfeld. Tr. by Gloria Arroyo Marcos. Catolica Edit.

Diccionarios Rioduero: Matematicas. Jurgen Reck. Tr. by Walter Strobl. Catolica Edit.

Diccionaris catala-castella i castella-catala: Tipus breu. M Arimany.

Diccionaris catala-castella i castella-catala: Tipus basic. M Arimany.

Diccionaris catala-castella i castella-catala: Tipus especial. M Arimany.

Diccionaris catala-castella i castella-catala: Tipus manual. M Arimany.

Diccionaris catala-castella i castella-catala: Tipus practic. M Arimany.

Diccionaro de Qheshwa-Espanol, Espanol-Qheshwa. Jesus Lara. French & Eur.

Diccionrio De Sinonimos. French & Eur.

Dicionario Basico da Lingua Galega. Instituto da Lingua Galega. Xerais de Galicia.

Dicionario de Portugues-Espanol. Julio Martinez Almoyna. Porto Editora.

Dicionario Espanhol-Portugues & Portugues-Espanhol. Idel Becker. Liv Nobel.

Dictamenes Juridicos. Luis Diez-Picazo. Civitas.

Dictionar Roman-Spaniol: Pentru uzul Elevilor. Micaela Ghitescu. Editura Stiintifica.

Dictionar Spaniol-Roman: Pentru uzul Elevilor. Micaela Ghitescu. Editura Stiintifica.

Dictionar Tehnic Auto de Buzunar in Sapte Limbi. Petre Cristea. Editura Stiintifica.

Dictionary for the Graphic Arts in Eight Languages: German-English-French-Spanish-Russian-Hungarian-Polish-Slowak. Perfect Graphic.

Dictionary of Acoustics: English-German-French-Russian-Spanish-Polish-Madarsko-Slovene. W. Reichardt. French & Eur.

Dictionary of Agriculture in German, French, Spanish, & Russian. G. Haensch. Ed. by Haberkamp G. De Anton. Elsevier.

Dictionary of Automatical Technique. Ed. by Jiri Sykora. French & Eur.

Dictionary of Biochemistry. K. Thielmann. French & Eur.

Dictionary of Biology. Guenther Haensch. French & Eur.

Dictionary of Biology in English, French, German & Spanish. G. Haensch & G. Haberkamp De Anton. Elsevier.

Dictionary of Chontal to Spanish-English, & Spanish to Chontal. Paul Turner & Shirley Turner. U of Ariz Pr.

Dictionary of Dairy Terminology. Elsevier.

Dictionary of Environmental Engineering & Related Sciences. Jose T. Villate. Ediciones.

Dictionary of Environmental Engineering & Related Sciences. Jose T. Villate. Edns Universal.

Dictionary of Five Hundred One Spanish Verbs. Christopher Kendris. Camino Real.

Dictionary of Forestry. J. Weck. Elsevier.

Dictionary of Hydraulic Machinery. A. T. Troskolanski. Elsevier.

Dictionary of Industrial Property, Legal & Related Terms: English, Spanish, French & German. Ed. by Francis J. Kase. Sijthoff & Noordhoff.

Dictionary of International Economics: German, Russian, English, French, Spanish. Ed. by S. Kohls. Sijthoff & Noordhoff.

Dictionary of Legal Terms. Lectorum Pubns.

Dictionary of Legal Terms, Spanish-English & English-Spanish. Louis A. Robb. (Pub. by Wiley-Interscience). Wiley.

Dictionary of Legal Terms: Spanish-English,English-Spanish. Louis A. Robb. Intl Learn Syst.

Dictionary of Library Science Information & Documentation. Ed. by W. Clason. Elsevier.

Dictionary of Modern Business. Louis Robb. Anderson Kramer.

Dictionary of Musical Terms in Seven Languages. Ed. by H. Leuchtmann. Heinman.

A Dictionary of New Mexico & Southern Colorado Spanish. Ruben Cobos. Museum NM Pr.

A Dictionary of Onomatopoeic Sounds, Tones, & Noises in English & Spanish. Donald R. Kloe. Ethridge.

Dictionary of Oto-Rhino-Laryngology in Five Languages. A. Larrauri. Intl Pubns Serv.

Dictionary of Spanish Place Names of the Northwest Coast of America: California. Rene Coulet du Gard. Edns Des Deux Mondes.

Dictionary of Spanish Place Names of the Northwest Coast of America: Oregon, Washington State, British Columbia, Alaska. Rene Coulet du Gard. Edns Des Deux Mondes.

A Dictionary of Spanish Proverbs. John Collins. Folcroft.

A Dictionary of Spanish Terms in English, with Special Reference to the American Southwest. Harold W. Bentley. Octagon.

Dictionary of Spoken Spanish. Pan Amer Pub.

Dictionary of Spoken Spanish: Spanish-English, English-Spanish. U. S. War Department. Dover.

Dictionary of Spoken Spanish Words & Sentences. Camino Real.

Dictionary of Spoken Spanish Words & Sentences. Camino Real.

Dictionary of Spoken Spanish Words, Phrases, Sentences. U. S. Armed Forces. Doubleday.

Dictionary of Spoken Spanish Words, Phrases, Sentences. Doubleday.

A Dictionary of Statistical, Scientific & Technical Terms: English-Spanish, Spanish-English. Hardeo Sahai & Jose Berrios. Ed. by Richard A. Smith & Jeanne Heise. Illus. by Pat Dunbar. (Pub. by Wadsworth Internacional Iberoamerica). Wadsworth Pub.

Dictionary of Surface-Active Agents, Cosmetics & Toiletries. Ed. by G. Cariere. Elsevier.

Dictionary of Surface Active Agents, Cosmetics & Toiletries. G. Carriere. Elsevier.

Dictionary of Technical Acoustics. L. Reichardt. Adler.

Dictionary of the Graphic Arts Industry. Ed. by W. Muller. Elsevier.

Dictionary of the Spanish in Texas. IML-Institute of Modern Languages. Camino Real.

Dictionary of the Spanish in Texas. Institute of Modern Language. Camino Real.

Dictionnaire Agricole Allemand, Anglais, Francais, Espagnol, Russe. Gunther Haensch & Gisela Haberkamp. (Pub. by Maison Rust). French & Eur.

Dictionnaire Agricole Allemand-Anglais-Francais-Espagnol-Russe. Gunther Haensch. Maison Rustique.

Dictionnaire agricole Allemand, Anglais, Francais, Espanol, Russe. Gunther Haensch & Gisela Haberkamp. Maison Rustique.

Dictionnaire Bilingue Apollo Francais-Espagnol. Miguel De Toro & Gisbert De Toro. Larousse.

Dictionnaire Bilingue: Francais-Espagnol, Espagnol-Francais. M. De Toro Gisbert. French & Eur.

Dictionnaire Bilingue Larousse, Francais-Espagnol, Espanol-Frances. M. De Toro & Gisbert. Larousse.

Dictionnaire de Docientos Uno Verbeos Espagnols Conjugues a Toutes les Personnes. Christopher Kendris. Barron.

Dictionnaire de la Biologie. Gunther Haensch. BLV Verlag.

Dictionnaire de la Biologie--B.L.V. French & Eur.

Dictionnaire de la presse ecrite et audiovisuelle. Divers. Maison Dictionnaire.

Dictionnaire de la Technologie des Corps Gras. Boris Solomon. Inst Corps Gras.

Dictionnaire de Poche Francais-Espagnol. Berlitz.

Dictionnaire de Sylviculture: Francais-Allemand-Anglais-Espagnol-Italien. Alberto Bruttini. Lechevalier.

Dictionnaire d'informatique. Georges Nania. Maison Dictionnaire.

Dictionnaire d'informatique: Francais-Anglais-Italien-Espagnol-Portugais. G. Nania. Maison Dictionnaire.

Dictionnaire d'oto-rhino-laryngologie: Francais-Anglais-Espagnol-Allemand-Italien. Maloine.

Le Dictionnaire Espagnol-Francais. Serge Denis et al. Hachette Jeunesse.

Dictionnaire Espagnol-Francais. Robert Larrieu. Garnier.

Dictionnaire Espagnol-Francais. Vicente Salva. Garnier-Flammarion.

Dictionnaire Espagnol-Francais. Vicente Salva & Robert Larrieu. Garnier.

Dictionnaire Espagnol-Francais. Robert Larrieu. Garnier-Flammarion.

Dictionnaire Espagnol-Francais. A. Corbiere & Lautier. Dessain & Tolra.

Dictionnaire Espagnol-Francais. Larousse.

Dictionnaire Espagnol-Francais. Serge Denis & M. Maraval. Hachette.

Le Dictionnaire Espagnol-Francais et Francais-Espagnol. Serge Denis et al. French & Eur.

Dictionnaire Europa Francais-Espagnol. Larousse.

Dictionnaire Francais-Espagnol. Lautier Corbiere. Dessain & Tolra.

Dictionnaire Gemeaux: Francais-Espagnol. Hatier.

Dictionnaire Illustre de la Langue Russe: Francais-Espagnol-Russe. Anatoll Chtchoukine. Mir.

Dictionnaire International d'abreviations Scientifiques et Techniques. M. Azzaretti. Maison Dictionnaire.

Dictionnaire International d'abreviation Scientifiques et Techniques. M. Azzaretti. Maison Dictionnaire.

Dictionnaire International du Tourisme: Allemand-Anglais-Espagnol-Italien-Neerlandai. Acad Intl Tour.

Dictionnaire International Electrotechnique: Francais-Russe-Anglais-Allemand-Espagnol-Suedois-Hollandais-Polonais. Mir.

Dictionnaire Juridique, Francais-Espagnol, Espagnol-Francais. Luis Jordana de Pozas & Olivier Merlin. French & Eur.

Dictionnaire Juridique: Francais-Espagnol. Olivier Merlin. Navarre.

Dictionnaire Larousse Bilingue de Poche: Francais-Espagnol. Larousse FR.

Dictionnaire Larousse: Francais-Espagnol. L. G. F.

Dictionnaire Lilliput Bilingue Francais-Espagnol. Larousse FR.

Dictionnaire Moderne: Francaise-Espagnol, Espagnol-Francais. Ed. by R. Garcia-Pelayo. French & Eur.

Dictionnaire moderne Larousse, francais-espagnol et espagnol-francais. R. Garcia-Pelayo & J. Testas. Larousse.

Dictionnaire Moderne "Saturne". R. Garcia-Pelayo. (Dist. by Continental Bk Co). Larousse.

Dictionnaire Moderne Saturne: Francais-Espagnol. Ramon Garcia-Pelayo & Jean Testas. Larousse FR.

Dictionnaire Poucet Espagnol-Francais. Hatier.

Dictionnaire pour Ingenieurs et Techniciens: Francais-Espagnol, Espagnol-Francais. L. Carcamo. French & Eur.

Dictionnaire Pratique Mercure: Francais-Espagnol, Espagnol-Francais. M. Pay-Costa. French & Eur.

Dictionnaire Pratique Mercure Francais-Espagnol. M. Puy-Costa. Larousse.

Dictionnaire Technique de la Mecanisation Agricole. French & Eur.

Dictionnaire Technique de la Mecanisation Agricole: Francais-Anglais-Allemand-Espagnol-Italien. Centre Nat. Et. Machin Agricole.

Dictionnaire Technique Francais-Espagnol. Guy Malgorn. Gauthier-Villars.

Dictionnaire Technique Illustre des Outlis Coupants: L'usinage des Metaux; Francais-Allemand-Anglais-Italien-Espagnol. Toni Heiler. Eyrolles.

Dictionnaire Technique Illustre Des Outils Coupants Pour L'usinage Des Metaux. Toni Heiler. French & Eur.

Dictionnaire Technologique: Aeronautique. H. Demaison. Maison Dictionnaire.

Dictionnaire Technologique Feutry: Supplement Espagnol. R. Mertz De Mertzenteld et al. Maison Dictionnaire.

Divry's New Spanish-English & English-Spanish Handy Dictionary. Ed. by J. M. Douglas & A. Lomo. Divry.

Divry's Spanish English Dictionary. D. C. Divry. Camino Real.

Dixcionario de Filosofia. Eduardo Pallares. French & Eur.

Dizinario italiano-spagnolo. Malipiero.

Dizionario fraseologico completo italiano-spagnolo e spagnolo-italiano: Parte italiana-spagnola. Sebastiano Carbonell. Hoepli.

Dizionario italiano-spagnolo. Garcia. Vallardi A.

Dizionario Italiano-Spagnolo, Spagnolo-Italiano. A. Garcia. French & Eur.

Dizionario Medico Poliglotta. Veillon & Nobel. French & Eur.

Dizionario moderno italiano-spagnolo e spagnolo-italiano: Vol. 1, Italiano-spagnolo. Gaetano Frisoni. Hoepli.

Dizionario moderno italiano-spagnolo e spagnolo-italiano: Vol. 2, Spagnolo-italiano. Gaetano Frisoni. Hoepli.

Dizionario Moderno Spagnuolo-Italiano, Italiano-Spagnuolo. Gaetano Frisoni. S F Vanni.

Dizionario spagnolo-italiano e italiano-spagnolo. Malipiero.

Dizionario spagnolo-italiano e italiano-spagnolo. Enrico Migliori. Giunti-Martello.

Ductor in Linguas: The Guide into Tongues. John Minsheu. Schol Facsimiles.

Economic Terminology. Miguel Moreno Pacheo. Adler.

Economic Terminology. Miguel Pacheco Moreno. Hueber.

Economic Terminology: English-Spanish. M. Pacheco. Hueber.

Elements de Geologie En Six Langues. E. Cailleux. French & Eur.

Elseviers Automobile Dictionary. Ed. by G. Schuurmans. Elsevier.

Elsevier's Banking Dictionary. J. Ricci. Elsevier.

Elsevier's Dictionary of Amplification Modulation Reception & Transmission. Ed. by W. Clason. Elsevier.

Elsevier's Dictionary of Barley, Malting, & Brewing. Bernard D. Hartong. Elsevier.

Elsevier's Dictionary of Building Tools & Materials. L. Y. Chaballe & J. P. Vandenberghe. Elsevier.

Elsevier's Dictionary of Chemical Engineering. W. Clason. Elsevier.

Elsevier's Dictionary of Cinema, Sound & Music. W. E. Clason. Elsevier.

Elsevier's Dictionary of Computers, Automatic Control & Data Processing. W. E. Clason. Elsevier.

Elsevier's Dictionary of Criminal Science. J. A. Adler. Elsevier.

Elsevier's Dictionary of Electronics & Waveguides. W. E. Clason. Elsevier.

Elsevier's Dictionary of Financial Terms. F. J. Thomson. Elsevier.

Elsevier's Dictionary of General Physics. W. E. Clason. Elsevier.

Elsevier's Dictionary of High Vacuum Science & Technology. Fritz W. Weber. Elsevier.

Elsevier's Dictionary of Horticulture. Ed. by Ministry of Agriculture & Fisheries- Netherlands & J. Nijdam. Elsevier.

Elseviers Dictionary of Metal Cutting Tools. Ed. by G. Schuurmang. Elsevier.

Elsevier's Dictionary of Metallurgy & Metal Working. W. E. Clason. Elsevier.

Elsevier's Dictionary of Nuclear Science & Technology. W. E. Clason. Elsevier.

Elsevier's Dictionary of Public Health. Nick J. Deblock. Elsevier.

Elsevier's Dictionary of Rolling Mill Terminology. Ed. by G. F. Herscu. Elsevier.

Elsevier's Dictionary of Television, & Video Recording. W. Clason. Elsevier.

Elsevier's Dictionary of Tools & Ironware. Ed. by Clason. Elsevier.

Elsevier's Electrotechnical Dictionary. W. E. Clason. Elsevier.

Elsevier's Medical Dictionary in Five Languages. A. Sliosberg. Elsevier.

Elsevier's Multilingual Dictionary of Insurance Technology. W. A. Ruysch. Elsevier.

Elseviers Nautical Dictionary. Ed. by P. Segditsas. Elsevier.

Elsevier's Nautical Dictionary in Six Languages. Ed. by J. P. Vandenberghe & L. Y. Chaballe. Elsevier.

Elseviers Rubber Dictionary. Elsevier.

Elsevier's Telecommunication Dictionary. W. E. Clason. Elsevier.

Elsevier's Wood Dictionary. Ed. by W. Boerhave Beekman. Elsevier.

Enciclopedia simultanea de correspondencia comercial en seis idiomas. Distein.

Engineers' Dictionary, Spanish-English, English-Spanish. Louis A. Robb. (Pub. by Wiley-Interscience). Wiley.

English-Spanish Banking Dictionary. Rafael Gil Esteban. Autores Propias.

English-Spanish Dictionary. Saphrograph.

English-Spanish Dictionary. P. Constantinon. Shalom.

English-Spanish Guide for Medical Personnel. Ed. by Joseph Armengol et al. Med Exam.

English-Spanish picture dictionary. E. C. Parnwell. Fondo Educativo.

English-Spanish, Spanish-English Dictionary of Communications & Electronic Terms. Roger L. Freeman. Cambridge U Pr.

English-Spanish Spanish-English Encyclopedic Dictionary of Technical Terms. Javier L. Collazo. McGraw.

English-Spanish Sports Dictionary for Soccer. Jose A. Sierra. (Pub. by Wolfhound Pr Ireland). State Mutual Bk.

English-Spanish Technical Dictionary. F. F. Ibeas. Heinman.

English-Spanish Technical Dictionary. Shalom.

English-Spanish to Spanish-English Dictionary. Arturo Cuyas. P-H.

Errores y Omisiones del Diccionario de Anonimos y Seudonimos Hispanoamericanos de Jose Toribio Medina. Ricardo Victorica. Ethridge.

Essential Spanish Vocabulary. Longman.

Estudio Comparativo de Vocabularios Tobas y Pilagas. Elena Bruno Natlis. French & Eur.

Etymological Vocabulary to the Libro De Buen Amor of Juan Ruiz, Arcipreste De Hita. Henry B. Richardson. AMS Pr.

Euskal Histegi Modernoa. Xabier Kintana. Cinsa Coord.

Everyday Dictionary. Times Bks.

Everyday Spanish Idioms. R. S. Boggs & J. I. Dixon. Regents Pub.

Fachwoerterbuch der Luftfahrt. A. Dorian & J. Osenton. (Pub. by R. Oldenbourg). French & Eur.

Fachwoerterbuch der Luftfahrt. J. Osenton. Oldenbourg Verlag.

Fachworterbuch Fur Recht und Verwaltung. Crescencio Antolinez. (Pub. by Carl Heymanns Verlag KG). French & Eur.

Fachworterbuch Polygrafie: English-Deutsch-French-Russian-Spanish-Polish-Hungarian-Slowakian. French & Eur.

Finnish-Spanish-Finnish Dictionary. E. K. Neuvonen. French & Eur.

Fletamentos y Terminos de Embarque. J. Bes. Heineman.

Follet World-Wide Dictionary. Pan Amer Pub.

Follet World Wide Dictionary: Spanish-English, English-Spanish. Pan Am Bk Co.

Follett-Velazquez Spanish & English Dictionary. Cruzada Span Pubns.

Follett World-Wide Spanish-English Dictionary. Cruzada Span Pubns.

Frequency Dictionary of Spanish Words. Alphonse Juilland & E. Chang-Rodriquez. Mouton.

Gem Language Dictionaries: Spanish-English & English-Spanish. S&S.

Glosari. Eugenio D'Rovira. Ediciones Sesent Dos.

Glosario de bajo espanol en Venezuela. Lisandro Alvarado. Minist Ed Caracas.

Glosario de Genetica y Citogenetica II. R. Rieger et al. Tr. by M. J. Puertas Gallego. Alhambra.

Glosario de informatica. F. Garcia Merayo. Urmo.

Glosario De Informatica: Terminologia Ordenada Segun el Vocablo Ingles y Su Acepcion En Espanol. F. Garcia Merayo. French & Eur.

Glosario de la farsa urbana. Roberto Gache. Centro Ed.

Glosario de mercadeo. Rossi K. Fischer. Limusa.

Glosario de Tecnologia Educativa. Organize Am States.

Glosario de terminos entomologicos. R. H. Quintanilla & C. P. Fraga. EUDEBA.

Glosario de terminos geograficos. Consuelo Soto Mora & Luis Fuentes Aguilar. UNAM.

Glosario de terminos hospitalarios. OPS.

Glosario de terminos linguisticos. Serv Pub Minist.

Glosario de Terminos Mareograficos. Pan American Institute of Geography & History. Instituto Panamericano.

Glosario de terminos nucleares. R. A. Ghelfi et al. EUDEBA.

Glosario de terminos parasitologicos. O. J. Lombardero. EUDEBA.

Glosario de voces Ibericas y Latinas. Francisco J. Simonet. Intl Bk Ctr.

Glosario de voces ibericas y latinas: Tomo 1. Francisco J. Simonet. Atlas Edns.

Glosario de voces ibericas y latinas: Tomo 2. Francisco J. Simonet. Atlas Edns.

Glosario de voces ibericas y latinas: Obras completa. Francisco J. Simonet. Atlas Edns.

Glosario de voces indigenas de Venezuela. Lisandro Ajvarado. Minist Ed Caracas.

Glosario Espanol-Arabe. Fernando Valderrama Martinez. Albir.

Glosario Espanol-Arabe y Arabe-Espanol. Fernando Valderrama Martinez. Albir.

Glosario internacional: Ingles-espanol. Marina Orellana. Universitaria.

Glossaire des Mots Espagnols et Portugais Derives de L'arabe. R. Dozy. Intl Bk Ctr.

Glossaire d'organes de Transmission, 1: Les Engrenages Allemand-Espagnol-Francais-Anglais-Italien-Neerlandais-Suedois-Finnois. Maison Dictionnaire.

Glossary of Automotive Terminology: Spanish-English English-Spanish. Chrysler Corporation. Soc Auto Engineers.

Glossary of Conference Terms: Arabic, French, English. (UNESCO). Unipub.

Glossary of Fiber Optics Terms. Info Gatekeepers.

Glossary of Genetics. Francoise Biass-Ducroux. Elsevier.

Glossary of International Treaties. Y. Renoux & J. Yates. Elsevier.

Glossary of Mining Geology. G. Amstutz. (Pub. by F. Enke). French & Eur.

Glossary of Mining Geology. G. C. Amstutz et al. Ed. by F. Esser & Won C. Park. Enke.

Glossary of Mining Geology. G. Amstutz. Enke.

Glossary of Neurotraumatology. Ed. by E. S. Gurdjian et al. Springer-Verlag.

Glossary of Soil Micromorphology. Ed. by A. Jongerius & G. K. Rutherford. Pudoc.

Glossary of Spanish & English Management Terms. James Coveney & J. Amey. Longman.

Glossary of Spanish & English Management Terms. James Conveney & Julian Amey. Biling Rev Pr.

Glossary of Spanish & English Management Terms. Longman.

Glossary of Spanish & English Management Terms. Ed. by Coveney & Amey. Longman.

A Glossary of Spanish Philatelic Terms. Eric V. Bailey. Intl Guatemala.

Glossary of Technical Terms for Market Researchers: English-German-Spanish-French-Italian-Dutch. European Society for Opinion & Marketing Research. Intl Pubns Serv.

Gran Diccionario & Gramatica Ingles-Espanol, Espanol-Ingles. Nauta SA.

Gran Diccionario Cuyas Ingles-Espanol. Camino Real.

Gran Diccionario Cuyas Ingles-Espanol, Spanish-English. Arturo Cuyas Armengol. French & Eur.

Gran Diccionario Cuyas Inglés-Español. Camino Real.

Gran Diccionario Infantil Marin. Marin.

Gran Diccionario Sopena. Sopena.

Gran diccionario y gramatica de la lengua espanola: Obra completa. Nauta SA.

Grandes diccionarios bilingues Amador. Bilingual Ed Serv.

Guia de modismos espanoles. Raymond H. Pierson. Natl Textbk.

Habla Que el Tiempo se Lleva? Joaquin Garro. Costa Rica.

Hamlyn Spanish-English Dictionary. Larousse.

Handelskorrenpondenz in Vier Sprachen. F. Berset. M Rosenberg.

Harper English-Spanish, Spanish-English Dictionary. Pan Amer Pub.

Homonyms. Dora Newhouse. Newhouse Pr.

Homonyms-Homonimos: Sound-Alikes. Dora Newhouse. Newhouse Pr.

Hugo Pocket Dictionary: Spanish-English, English-Spanish. Littlefield.

Idiomatic Expressions English-Spanish. Pan Amer Pub.

Illustrirovannyi Voenno-Tekhnicheskii Slovar. L. D. Neliubin. (Pub. by Voenizdat). Four Continent.

Illustrierte Technische Woerterbucher: Eisenbahnmaschinenwesen. A. Schlomann. (Pub. by R. Oldenbourg). French & Eur.

Illustrierte Technische Woerterbucher: Eisenbahnmaschinenwesen. A. Schlomann. Oldenbourg Verlag.

Illustrierte Technische Woerterbucher: Eisenbahnbau und Betrieb. A. Schlomann. (Pub. by R. Oldenbourg). French & Eur.

Illustrierte Technische Woerterbucher: Eisenbahnbau und Betrieb. A. Schlomann. Oldenbourg Verlag.

Illustrierte Technische Woerterbucher: Elektrotechnik und Elektrochemie. A. Schlomann. (Pub. by R. Oldenbourg). French & Eur.

Illustrierte Technische Woerterbucher: ELektrotechnik und Elektrochemie. A. Schlomann. Oldenbourg Verlag.

Illustrierte Technische Woerterbucher: Maschinenelemente. A. Schlomann. (Pub. by R. Oldenbourg). French & Eur.

Illustrierte Technische Woerterbucher: Maschinenelemente. A. Schlomann. Oldenbourg Verlag.

Illustrierter Technische Woerterbucher: Luffahrts. A. Schlomann. (Pub. by R. Oldenbourg). French & Eur.

Illustrierter Technische Woerterbucher: Luffahrts. A. Schlomann. Oldenbourg Verlag.

Illustriertes Woerterbuch. (Pub. by Gebrueder Weiss). French & Eur.

IMF Glossary: English-French-Spanish. International Monetary Fund, Bureau of Language Services. Intl Monetary.

International Dictionary of Obscenities: A Guide to Dirty Words & Indecent Expressions in Spanish, Italian, French, German, & Russian. Christina Kunitskaya-Peterson. Berkeley Slavic.

International Dictionary of Spanish & English. Iaconi.

International Dictionary Simon & Schuster. Pan Amer Pub.

International Glossary of Technical Terms for the Pulp & Paper Industry. Van Derveer & Haas. Imported Bks.

International Hospital Vade Mecum & English, French, Spanish Glossary. Paul Aurousseau. Editions Sedip F.Galula.

International Microcomputer Dictionary. Sybex Staff & Rodnay Zaks. Sybex.

Interpretes de Bolsillo Aleman-Espanols. Biblograf SP.

Interpretes de Bolsillo Espanol-Aleman. Biblograf SP.

Interpretes de Bolsillo Espanol-Frances. Biblograf SP.

Interpretes de Bolsillo Espanol-Ingles. Biblograf SP.

Interpretes de Bolsillo Espanol-Italiano. Biblograf SP.

Interpretes de Bolsillo Frances-Espanol. Biblograf SP.

Interpretes de Bolsillo Ingles-Espanol. Biblograf SP.

Interpretes de Bolsillo Italiano-Espanol. Biblograf SP.

Iron & Steel Dictionary: German-Spanish & Spanish-German. Iron & Steel Institute. Intl Pubns Serv.

Ispansko-Russkii Razgovornik. S. Neverov. (Pub. by Izd. Lit. Na Inostr. Iaz.). Four Continent.

Ispansko-Russkii Slovar. Ed. by F. V. Kelin. (Pub. by Gosizdat Inostr Natsional Slovarei). Four Continent.

Ispansko-Russkii Slovar Po Dobyche i Pererabotke Nefti. A. A. Pinkevich et al. (Pub. by Lenizdat). Four Continent.

Jean's Pocket Dictionaries: Spanish-English. Hammond Inc.

Kratkii Ispansko-Russkii & Russko-Ispanskii Nauchno-Tekhnicheskii Slovar. Kobo Orts Kh. et al. (Pub. by An Arm SSR). Four Continent.

Kunststofftechnisches Woerterbuch. A. Wittfoht. (Pub. by C. Hanser). French & Eur.

Kunststofftechnisches Woerterbuch. A. Wittfoht. French & Eur.

Kunststofftechnisches Woerterbuch. A. Wittfoht. Hanser.

Langenscheidt English-Spanish Lilliput Dictionary. Langenscheidt.

Langenscheidt Spanish-English Lilliput Dictionary. Langenscheidt.

Langenscheidts Fachwoerterbuch Fernmeldewesen. (Pub. by Langenscheidt). French & Eur.

Langenscheidts Fachwoerterbuch Deutsch-Spanisch. Arturo E. Von Baumgart. Langenscheidt.

Langenscheidts Handwoerterbuch Spanisch-Deutsch. Heinz Muller et al. Langenscheidt.

Langenscheidts Handwoerterbuch Spanisch: Teil II, Deutsch-Spanisch. Enrique Alvarez-Prada. Langenscheidt.

Langenscheidts Handwoerterbuch Spanisch: Teil I, Spanisch-Deutsch. Heinz Muller & Gunther Haensch. Langenscheidt.

Langenscheidts Handwoerterbuch Spanisch. Ed. by Heinz Messinger & Werner Ruedenberg. Langenscheidt.

Langenscheidts Handwoerterbuecher: Spanisch, 2 Teile in 1. Langenscheidt.

Langenscheidts Handwoerterbuecher: Tl 1, Spanisch-Deutsch. Ed. by Heinz Mueller & Guenther Haensch. Langenscheidt.

Langenscheidt's Lilliput English-Spanish Dictionary. Am Map.

Langenscheidt's Lilliput Spanish-English Dictionary. Am Map.

Langenscheidts Lilliput-Woerterbuch Deutsch-Spanisch. Langenscheidt.

Langenscheidts Lilliput-Woerterbuch Spanisch-Deutsch. Langenscheidt.

Langenscheidts Lilliput-Woerterbuecher Deutsch-Spanisch. Langenscheidt.

Langenscheidts Lilliput-Woerterbuecher Spanisch-Deutsch. Langenscheidt.

Langenscheidts Reisewoerterbuecher Spanisch-Deutsch. Langenscheidt.

Langenscheidts Satz-Lexikon des Spanischen Geschaeftsbriefes. H. Burfeindt-Moral & J. A. Moral-Arroyo. Langenscheidt.

Langenscheidts Sportwoerterbuch. R. Lembke. (Pub. by Langenscheidt). French & Eur.

Langenscheidts Sportwoerterbuch Deutsch-Englisch-Franzoesisch-Spanisch. Langenscheidt.

Langenscheidt's Standard Spanish Dictionary: Spanish-English, English-Spanish. Ed. by C. C. Smith et al. Am Map.

Langenscheidts Taschenwoerterbuch Spanisch. G. Haberkamp de Anton & D. H. Willers. Langenscheidt.

Langenscheidts Taschenwoerterbuch Spanisch: Teil II, Deutsch-Spanisch. D. H. Willers. Langenscheidt.

Langenscheidts Taschenwoerterbuch Spanisch: Teil I, Spanisch-Deutsch. G. Haberkamp de Anton. Langenscheidt.

Langenscheidts Taschenwoerterbuecher Spanisch. Langenscheidt.

Langenscheidts Taschenwoerterbuecher Spanisch-Deutsch. H. Willers. Langenscheidt.

Langenscheidt's Universal Spanish-English, English-Spanish Dictionary. Am Map.

Langenscheidts Universal-Woerterbuch Spanisch. Langenscheidt.

Langenscheidts Universal-Woerterbuecher Spanisch-Deutsch. Langenscheidt.

Language of the Puerto Rican Street. Cristine Gallo. C Gallo.

Larousse de poche francais-espagnol, & espagnol-frances. Larousse And Co. Larousse.

Learn Spanish for English Speakers. William R. Patterson. Ed. by Ronald MacAndrew. Saphrograph.

Leico De Politica. Jose M. Coloma. French & Eur.

La Lengua Salvadorena. Pedro Geoffroy Rivas. Direccion de Publicaciones.

La Lengua Vasca. Isaac Lopez Mendizabal. Aunamendi Edit.

Lexica (II) Teresa Garriga. Jaimes Libros.

El Lexico base del castellano: Analisis estadistico y de contenido. Juan L. Roman del Cerro. Confed Espanola.

Lexico basico del contador. R. Enriquez Palomic. Trillas.

Lexico basico espanol-ruso. Cultura Popular.

Lexico basico espanol-ruso. D'Ippolito.

Lexico De Antropologia. Abelardo Martinez Cruz. French & Eur.

Lexico De Economia. Alain Birou. French & Eur.

Un Lexico de la artesania. Luis Marquez Villagas. (CSIC). Univ Granada.

Lexico de la casa popular urbano en Bolivar, Colombia. L. Florez. Inst Caro y Cuervo.

El Lexico De la Delincuencia En Puerto Rico. Carmen G. Altieri de Barreto. U of PR Pr.

Lexico de la Sexualidad. Goldstein et al. Loguez Edns.

Lexico de lenguaje figurado. Ivon P. De Dony. Club de Lectores.

Lexico de Politica. Jose M. Coloma. Laia.

Lexico De Sociologia. Alain Birou. French & Eur.

Lexico De Terminos Nucleares: Diccionario Vocabulario Triligue. French & Eur.

Lexico del cuerpo humano en Colombia. L. Florez. Inst Caro y Cuervo.

El Lexico del Teatro de Valle Inclan. Ciriaco Ruiz Fernandez. Univ Salamanca.

Lexico Dos. Ignacio Bonnin Valls et al. Vicens-Vives.

Lexico Espanol-Kawesqar. F. Aguilera. Centro Invest.

Lexico hispanoamericano del siglo XVIII. Peter Boyd-Bowman. Hispanic Seminary.

Lexico historico de Espana. Jacques Amalric et al. Tr. by Rosina Lajo & Victoria Frigola. Taurus Ediciones SA.

El Lexico indigena en el espanol de Mexico. J. M. Lope Blanch. Col. de Mexico.

Lexico Marinero: Six Idiomas. N. Hollander et al. French & Eur.

Lexico Quechua de Cajamarca. Felix Quesada Castillo. Centro Invest.

El lexico rural del noroeste iberico. Tr. by Fritz Kruger. (CSIC). Inst Antonio de Nebrija.

Lexico sedimentologico. Gonzalez Bonorino. Museo Arg. Ciencias Nat.

Lexico Sucinto del Erotismo. Andre Breton. French & Eur.

Lexico tecnico de las artes plasticas. Irene Crespi & Jorge Ferrario. EUDEBA.

Lexico Uno. Ignacio Bonnin Valls et al. Vicens-Vives.

Lexicolabor: Diccionario Enciclopedico Ilustrado. French & Eur.

Lexicon comercial internacional: Espanol, frances, ingles, italiano, portugues y aleman. J. Vicens Carrio. Reverte SA.

Lexicon Creticum: Estudios sobre Escritura & lengua cretense; inscripciones monumentales; faistos, arkolochori, mallia. Benito Gaya Nuno. (CSIC). Inst. Antonio de Nebrija.

Lexicon de Comunicologia. Jorge Perello. Augusta SA.

Lexicon de Comunicologia: Diccinario para Audiologos, Audioprotesistas, Foniatras, Logopedas, Profesores De Sordos y Psicolinguistas. Jorge Perello. French & Eur.

Lexicon de fauna y flora. A. Malaret. Inst Caro y Cuervo.

Lexicon Kapelusz: Matematica. Francisco Vera. Kapelusz.

Lexicon Kapelusz: Psicologia. Tr. by Henri Pieron et al. Kapelusz.

Lexicon of International & National Units. Ed. by M. Merino-Rodriguez. Elsevier.

Lexicon of Plant Pests & Diseases. Ed. by Manuel Merino-Rodriguez. Elsevier.

Lexicon por una Comision de Trabajo del CIMAC: Conseil International des Machines a Combustion. Marcombo.

Lexicon Sopena: Diccionario de bolsillo, aleman-espanol y espanol-aleman. Sopena.

Lexicon Sopena: Diccionario de bolsillo, catalan-espanol y espanol-catalan. Sopena.

Lexicon Sopena: Diccionario de bolsillo, danes-espanol y espanol-danes. Sopena.

Lexicon Sopena: Diccionario de bolsillo, esperanto-espanol y espanol-esperanto. Sopena.

Lexicon Sopena: Diccionario de bolsillo, finlandes-espanol y espanol-finlandes. Sopena.

Lexicon Sopena: Diccionario de bolsillo, frances-espanol y espanol-frances. Sopena.

Lexicon Sopena: Diccionario de bolsillo, holandes-espanol y espanol-holandes. Sopena.

Lexicon Sopena: Diccionario de bolsillo, ingles-espanol y espanol-ingles. Sopena.

Lexicon Sopena: Diccionario de bolsillo, italiano-espanol y espanol-italiano. Sopena.

Lexicon Sopena: Diccionario de bolsillo, lengua espanol. Sopena.

Lexicon Sopena: Diccionario de bolsillo, noruego-espanol y noruego-espanol. Sopena.

Lexicon Sopena: Diccionario de bolsillo, sueco-espanol y espanol-sueco. Sopena.

Lexicon sopena diccionario espanola. Natl Textbk.

Lexique General. (UN). Unipub.

Lexique Quadrilingue Des Affaires. Ivan de Renty. French & Eur.

Lexique Quadrilingue des Affaires: Anglais-Francais-Allemand-Espagnol. Ivan De Renty. Hachette.

Lexis Veinte-dos: Apendice Botanica. Circulo Lect.

Lexis Veinte-dos: Apendice Botanica. Circulo Lect.

Lexis-Veinte-Dos: Gramatica, Lengua & Estilo. Biblograf.

Lexis Veinte-dos: Medicina y Salud. Circulo Lect.

Lexis Veinte-dos: Sinonimos y Antonimos. Circulo Lect.

Lexis Veinte-dos: Sinonimos y Antonimos. Circulo Lect.
Lexix Veinte-Dos: Apendice, Botanica. Circulo Lect.
Lilliput Dictionary. Langenscheidt.
Lilliput Dictionary. Langenscheidt.
Look & Learn Spanish. Francisco Ibarra. Camino Real.
Los Sufijos Posesivos en el Quechua del Huallaga. David J. Weber. Inst Ling Ver.
Malas Hierbas, Diccionario Clasificatorio Ilustrado. Francisco Guell. French & Eur.
Maly Slownik Hispansko-Polski & Polsko-Hiszpanski. Antonio Marti Marca et al. Wiedza Powszechna.
Management Terminology: English-Spanish & Spanish-English. Victor H. Bolado. Todd & Honeywell.
Manual del Automovil en 5 Idiomas: Diccionario Idiomatico del Automovil. Equipo Reactor de Ceac. French & Eur.
A Manual of Manuscript Transcription for the Dictionary of the Old Spanish Language. David Mackenzie. Hispanic Seminary.
Manual of the Terminology of Public International Law & International Organizations. I. Paenson. Kluwer Academic.
Manuel De Gramatica Comercial. A. Lugo-Guernelli et al. French & Eur.
Mastering Spanish Verbs. Julio I. Andujar. Camino Real.
Mathematics Dictionary. Glenn James. Van Nos Reinhold.
Medical Spanish. Gail Bongiovanni. (HP). McGraw.
Medizintechnik. Albert Von Roald & Harry Hahnewald. VEB Verlag Technik.
Medizintechnik-Englisch-Deutsch-Franzoesisch-Russisch-Spanisch-Polnisch-Ungarisch-Slowakisch. Roald Albert & Harry Hahnewald. VEB Technik.
A Mexican-Aryan Comparative Vocabulary. T. S. Denison. Gordon Pr.
Mi Diccionario Ilustrado. Concepcion Zendrera. French & Eur.
Mi Diccionario Ilustrado: Edicion Bilingue. Aquino-Bermudez et al. Illus. by Aquino-Bermudez et al. Lothrop.
Mi Diccionario Ilustrado: Edicion Bilingue. Lectorum Pubns.
Mi Primer Diccionario Biblico. William N. McElrath. Tr. by Ruth G. McElrath. from Eng. Illus. by Don Fields. Casa Bautista.
Mi Primer Diccionario Escolar. French & Eur.
Mi primer diccionario ilustrado. Bilingual Ed Serv.
Mi Primer Diccionario Ingles-Espanol. Ricard Jordana. Edns Nauta.
Mi primer diccionario Ingles-Espanol. Ricard Jordana. Fed Gremios.
Mi primer diccionario Larousse en colores. Ed. by C. S. Sanguinetti. Larousse.
Mi primer diccionario Sigmar. Pan Amer Pub.
Mi Primer Gran Diccionario Infantil. Richard Scarry. French & Eur.
Mi Primer Sopena. Cruzada Span Pubns.
Mi primer Sopena. Iaconi.
Mi Primer Sopena: Diccionario Infantil Ilustrado. Lectorum Pubns.
Los Mil Quinientos. Rodrigo Salas. Edit Vecchi.
Mini-Sopena Ingles-Espanol. Cruzada Span Pubns.
Modern Language Dictionary. Ferdinando D. Maurino. S & S.
A Modern Spanish-English & English-Spanish Technical & Engineering Dictionary. R. L. Guinle. Routledge & Kegan.
Modismos en Ingles. E. Savaiano & L. Winget. Barron.
Multidiccionario. French & Eur.
Multilengua Diccionario de Cartas Comerciales en Cuatro Idiomas. French & Eur.
Multilingual Computer Dictionary. Ed. by Alan Isaacs. Facts on File.
The Multilingual Computer Dictionary. Alan Isaacs. Facts on File.

Multilingual Glossary of Automatic Control Technology: English-French-German-Russian-Italian-Spanish-Japanese. D. T. Broadbent & M. Masubuchi. Pergamon.
Multilingual Law Dictionary: English, French, German, Spanish, German. Lawrence D. Egbert. Oceana.
Multilingual Vocabulary of Educational Radio & Television Terms. Intl Pubns Serv.
Music Translation Dictionary: An English, Czech, Danish, Dutch, French, German, Hungarian, Italian, Polish, Portuguese, Russian, Spanish, Swedish Vocabulary of Music. Compiled by Carolyn D. Grigg. Greenwood.
My Illustrated Dictionary: Arabic & Span. Libr du Liban. Intl Bk Ctr.
Mykologisches Worterbuch. K. Berger. French & Eur.
Mykologisches Worterbuch. Karl Von Berger. Fischer Verlag.
New Appleton's Cuyas English-Spanish & Spanish-English Dictionary. Ed. by A. Cuyas. P-H.
New Century Velazquez Spanish-English Dictionary. New Century.
New Century World-Wide Spanish Dictionary: Spanish: Spanish-English, English-Spanish. Ed. by Ida N. Hinojosa. New Century.
New College Spanish & English Dictionary. Edwin B. Williams. AMSCO Sch.
New Comprehensive English-Spanish, Spanish-English Dictionary. Ed. by Ubaldo Di Benedetto. Intl Pubns Serv.
New International Dictionary of Refrigeration. International Institute of Refrigeration. (IIR). Unipub.
New Mayer's Dictionary: English-Spanish, Spanish-English. Fernandez.
New Revised Velazquez Spanish & English Dictionary. Natl Textbk.
The New World English-Spanish, Spanish-English Dictionary. S&S.
The New World English-Spanish, Spanish-English Dictionary. Iaconi.
New World Spanish-English & English-Spanish Dictionary. Ed. by Salvatore Ramondino. Collins Pubs.
New World Spanish-English, English-Spanish Dictionary. Ed. by Salvatore Ramondino. (Sig). NAL.
Norwegian-Spanish Dictionary. C. Blom-Dahl. Kunnskapsforlaget.
Norwegian-Spanish Dictionary of Commerce. H. Evjen. Kunnskapsforlaget.
Nouveau Dictionnaire International du Froid. French & Eur.
Novedades en el Diccionario Academico. Julio Casares. (AGL). Lectorum Pubns.
Nueva Epanortosis al Diccionario de Anonimos Seudonimos de J. T. Medina. Ricardo Victorica. Ethridge.
Nuevo diccionario academia. Fernandez.
Nuevo diccionario bilingue Minerva. J. Anorga. Pan Amer Pub.
Nuevo Diccionario Ilustrado de la Lengua Espanola. French & Eur.
Nuevo Diccionario Ingles-Espanol y Espanol-Ingles. Esteban Mac Cragh. French & Eur.
Nuevo diccionario mundo hispano. Fernandez.
Nuevo Glosario, Diccionario Poliglota de la Arquitectura. Buenaventura Bassegoda Muste. French & Eur.
Nuevo Lexico Griego Espanol. McKibben-Stockwell. (Edit Mundo). Casa Bautista.
Nuovo dizionario italiano-spagnolo. Lucio Ambruzzi. Paravia.
Nuovo dizionario spagnolo-italiano. Lucio Ambruzzi. Paravia.
Oekonomisches Woerterbuch Aussenwirtschaft (Dictionary of External Exonomic Relations & Trade) Ed. by Siegfried Kohls. Intl Pubns Serv.
Oekonomisches Woerterbuch Aussenwirtschaft. S. Kohls. (Pub. by Ruceken Vlg). French & Eur.
Oekonomisches Woerterbuch Aussenwirtschaft. Wissenschaftliche.

Ortografia Activa: Letras & Acentos. Fernandez de la Vega & Hernandez Miyares. Gale.
Ortografia Castellano. Jaime Ferrer Mir et al. S M Edns.
Ortografia Functional: Atlas de la Aparatologia Ortopedica. Guillermo M. Feijoo. Mundi.
Ortografia metodica de la lengua espanola. Alfredo Huertas Garcia. Porrua.
Ortografia Moderna. Jose A. Escarpanter. Playor.
Ortografia Practica. Jose M. Zainqui Erro. Edit Vecchi.
Ortografia Practica. Jose M. Zainqui Erro. Ed. by Devecchi. Edit Vecchi.
Ortografia Practica: Acentuacion, Consonantes, Vocabulario. Hector Ramirez. (Dist. Lib. Studium). Gale.
Ortografia Practica del Espanol. Juan J. Gallego Tribaldos. Ave Maria.
Ortografia Practica: Ejercicios & Ensayos Sobre Ortografia Castellana. P. Roncalla. Gale.
Ortografia Practica Espanola Vox. Samuel Gili Gaya. Biblo SP.
Ortografia programada. Jesus Lopez. Del Castillo.
Oxford Picture Dictionary of American English & Spanish. E. Parnwell. Iaconi.
Oxford Picture Dictionary of American English: English-Spanish. Pan Amer Pub.
Oxford Picture Dictionary of American English: English-Spanish Edition. Oxford U Pr.
Parusny i sport. L. A. Chesnokov et al. Russkii Iazyk.
La Pedagogia Moderna. Jose M. Quintana Cabanas. Noguer SA.
Pequeno Diccionara Kapelusz de la Lenguna Espanola. French & Eur.
Pequeno Diccionario de Sinonimos. Pey. Edit Teide.
Pequeno Diccionario de Sinonimos. Camino Real.
Pequeno Diccionario de Sinonimos, Ideas Afines & Contrarios. Santiago Pey & Juan R. Calonja. (Pub. by Biblograf S. A., Barcelona). Harrap.
Pequeno diccionario de sinonimos, ideas afines y contrarios. Ed. by Alberto Vinoly. Larousse.
Pequeno Diccionario De Sinonimos y Sus Contrarios. A. J. Vinoly et al. French & Eur.
Pequeno Diccionario De Teatro Mundial. Genoveva Dieterich. French & Eur.
Pequeno Diccionario Espanol-Polaco, Polaco-Espanol. A. Marti & J. Marti et al. French & Eur.
Pequeno diccionario Kapelusz de la lengua espanola. Kapelusz.
Pequeno Diccionario Tecnologico: Farmacia, Quimica, Fisica, Medicina y Ciencias Naturales. M. Busto. French & Eur.
Pequeno Larousse de ciencias y tecnicas. Tomas De Galiana Mingot. Larousse.
Pequeno Larousse de ciencias y técnicas. Iaconi.
Pequeño Larousse ilustrado. Iaconi.
Petit Dictionnaire bilingue Larousse, francais-espagnol, espanol-frances. Larousse And Co. Larousse.
Philatelic Vocabulary in Five Languages. Philatelic Foundation. Philatelic Found.
A Phrase & Sentence Dictionary of Spoken Spanish. U. S. War Department. Gannon.
A Phrase & Sentence Dictionary Spanish-English. Pan Amer Pub.
Phrase Dictionaries for the American Tourist. Frederick Stark. Incl. Delair.
Pocket Crossword Dictionary. Ed. by John Bailie. Newnes Bks.
Politica & Politiqueria: Diccionario Para el Hombre de la Calle. Magin Pont Mestres. Edns Acervo.
Polygraphe-Englisch-Deutsch-Franzoesisch-Russisch-Spanisch-Polnisch-Ungarisch-Solwakisch. Wolfgang Muller. VEB Technik.
Polygraph Dictionary for the Graphic Industries in Six Languages. Ed. by K. Collet. Intl Pubns Serv.

Polytechnisches Woerterbuch. Karl H. Radde & Francisco Laguna de la Vera. VEB Technik.
Polytechnisches Woerterbuch Deutsch-Spanisch. Karl H. Radde. VEB Technik.
Polytechnisches Woerterbuch Spanisch-Deutsch. VEB Technik.
Practical Spanish Dictionary & Phrasebook. Marguerite D. Bomse. Pergamon.
Practical Spanish-English, English-Spanish Dictionary. Arthur Butterfield. Hippocrene Bks.
Practical Spoken Spanish. F. M. Kerchuville. Camino Real.
A Preliminary Glossary of New Mexican Spanish. F. M. Kercheville. Borgo Pr.
Press, Radio & Television. Denise Escarpit. Elp.
Proverbes Francais: In French with Equivalents in English, German, Dutch, Italian, Spanish, Latin. G. Ilg. Elsevier.
Putman's Contemporary Spanish Dictionary. Camino Real.
Putnam's Contemporary Spanish Dictionary. Berkley Pub.
Pyramid Primary Dictionary. Pan Amer Pub.
Quadrilingual Business Dictionary. (Pub. by European Schoolbks England). State Mutual Bk.
Que Paso? Martin P. Kantrowitz. Camino Real.
The Random House Basic Dictionary. Pan Amer Pub.
The Random House Basic Dictionary Spanish. Ed. by Donald P. Sola. Ballantine.
Regional Dictionary of Chicano Slang. Librado Vasquez & Maria E. Vasquez. Camino Real.
Les Ressorts: Francais-Allemand-Anglais-Espagnol. S.N.F.R. Maison Dictionnaire.
Reverse Dictionary of the Spanish Language. Fred A. Stahl & Gary E. Scavnicky. U of Ill Pr.
Revised-Velasquez Spanish English Dictionary. Camino Real.
Russkikh Glagolov. A. S. Vasil'Eva. Four Continent.
Safety at Work & Pollution Control. Nicole Aymard Lapalu. Elp.
Satzlexikon der Handelskorrespondenz. Zavada & Weis. Brandstetter.
See it-Say it in Spanish. Margarita Madrigal. Camino Real.
Semantica Guatemala O Diccionario De Guatemaltequisma. Lisandro Sandoval. Intl Guatemala.
Semiiazychnyi Slovar Po Elektrosviazi. (Pub. by Sov. Entsiklopediia). Four Continent.
Semiiazychnyi Slovar Po Mekhanike Gruntov & Fundamentostroeniiu. M. E. Schneider. (Pub. by Gosizdat Fizmat. Lit.). Four Continent.
Septemlingual Dictionary of the Names of European Animal. Ed. by L. Gozmany et al. (Pub. by Kiado Hungary). Heyden.
Seven Languages Dictionary. Imported Bks.
Simon & Schuster International Dictionary: English-Spanish, Spanish-English. S&S.
Simon & Schuster's Concise International Dictionary. Ed. by Tana De Gamez. S & S.
Simon & Schuster's International Dictionary English-Spanish. Lectorum Pubns.
Simon & Schuster's International Dictionary: English-Spanish & Spanish-English. S&S.
Sinonimus Castellanos. Roque Barcia. French & Eur.
Southwestern Medical Dictionary: Spanish-English & English-Spanish. Margarita Kay. U of Ariz Pr.
Spanisch. Incl. Langenscheidt.
Spanisch. Incl. Langenscheidt.
The Spanish & English, English & Spanish Dictionary - Self Pronouncing. Ed. by Velazquez et al. P-H.
Spanish & English Idioms: 2001 Modismos Espanoles & Ingleses. E. Savaiano & L. Wing. Barron.

Spanish & English of the United States Hispanos. Tescher & Bills. Camino Real.

Spanish & German Dictionary. Ed. by R. J. Slaby & R. Grossman. Incl. Ungar.

Spanish Bilingual Dictionary. Munoz Lipton. Camino Real.

Spanish Bilingual Dictionary. Iaconi.

Spanish Bilingual Dictionary. Pan Amer Pub.

Spanish Bilingual Dictionary. Lipton & Munoz. Camino Real.

Spanish Bilingual Dictionary: A Beginners Guide in Words & Pictures. Gladys Lipton & Olivia Munoz. Barron.

Spanish Bilingual Dictionary: Compact Guide. Gladys Lipton & Olivia Munoz. Barron.

Spanish Bilingual Dictionary: Diccionario Espanol-Ingles-Ingles-Espanol. G. Lipton & O. Munoz. Barron.

Spanish Dictionary. M. H. Raventos. McKay.

Spanish Dictionary. Newnes Bks.

Spanish-English & English-Spanish Dictionary. Dennison.

Spanish-English Dictionary. Cassells. Macmillan.

Spanish-English Dictionary. Carlos Castillo & Otto F. Bond. PB.

Spanish-English Dictionary. Ed. by P. Constantinou. Shalom.

Spanish-English Dictionary. Berlitz Editors. (Berlitz). Macmillan.

Spanish-English, English-Spanish. Inst Mod Lang.

Spanish-English, English-Spanish Chemical Vocabulary. J. R. Barcelo. Heinman.

Spanish-English, English-Spanish Commercial Dictionary. C. R. Orozco. Pergamon.

Spanish-English, English-Spanish Commercial Dictionary: "the Secretary". A. Frias-Sucre Giraud. Heinman.

The Spanish-English, English-Spanish Crossword Puzzle Book. Lily Powell-Froissard. Citadel Pr.

Spanish-English, English-Spanish Dictionary. (BN). B&N NY.

Spanish-English, English-Spanish Dictionary. U. Benedetto. Heinman.

Spanish-English, English-Spanish Dictionary. Editions Berlitz. Macmillan.

Spanish-English, English-Spanish Gem Dictionary. Ed. by R. F. Brown. Collins Pubs.

Spanish-English Idioms: 2001 Modisomos Espanoles & Ingleses (Pocket Size) E. Savaiano & L. Winget. Barron.

Spanish-English-Spanish. Macmillan.

Spanish for Doctors & Nurses. Aurelio M. Espinosa & Leon Gambetta. Camino Real.

Spanish for Urban Workers. Flynn & Montoto. Camino Real.

Spanish-Norwegian Dictionary. S. Loennecken. Kunnskapsforlaget.

Spanish Now. Silverstein et al. Camino Real.

Spanish Pocket Dictionary. Donald F. Sola & Frederick B. Agard. Random.

Spanish-Swedish-Spanish Dictionary. French & Eur.

Spanish Vocabulary & Structure for the Health Professional. Dorothy H. Mills et al. Mills Pub Co.

Spanish Vocabulary of Four Native Spanish-Speaking Pre-First-Grade Children. Loyd S. Tireman. Borgo Pr.

Spansk-Norsk Ordbok. S. Loennecken. French & Eur.

Spansk-Svensk Ordbok. Esselte Studium.

Spes--Diccionario Abreviado Latino-Espanol, Espanol-Latino. French & Eur.

Standard Spanish Dictionary. Langenscheidt.

Stilistisch-Phraseologisches Woerterbuch Spanisch-Deutsch. Werner Beinhauer. Hueber.

Suplemento a la Segunda Edicion Del Diccionario Pornua De Historia, Biografia y Geografia de Mexico. French & Eur.

Svensk-Spansk Affaersordlista. Peralta & Cederholm. Esselte Studium.

Svensk-Spansk Ordbok. Alfred Akerlung. Ed. by M. J. Casa Novas & M. Gronbarj. Esselte Studium.

Systematic Glossary of the Terminology of Statistical Methods: English, French, Spanish, Russian. Isaac Paenson. Pergamon.

Technicka Akustika. Walter Reichardt. VEB Verlat Technik.

Technische Akustik. Walter Reichardt. VEB Verlag Technik.

Technisches Fachwoerterbuch. Hermann Mink. Gustavo Gili.

Technisches Taschenwoerterbuch. A. Kroeger-Jannetti. (Pub. by Georg Siemens Verlagsbuchhandlung). French & Eur.

Technologisches Woerterbuch Spanisch. (Pub. by Verlag W. Girardet). French & Eur.

Technologisches Woerterbuch Spanisch. Girardet.

Terminologia Anatomica. Yves Chatain. Norma.

Terminologia cientifica medica en euskera: Obra completa. Autor.

Terminologia cientifica medica en euskera. Autor.

Terminologia cientifica medica en euskera. Autor.

Terminologia de la Danza Moderna. P. Love. EUDEBA.

Terminologia de la Education. Rosa E. Torres. Minist Ed La Paz.

Terminologia del Contador. Mancera. Banca Comercio.

Terminologia del Paludismo & de la Erradicacion del Paludismo. OMS.

Terminologia Fitogenetica & Citogenetica. Herrero.

Terminologia Gramatical para su Empleo en la E. G. B. Serv Pub Minist.

Terminologia Medica: Texto Programado. Smith-Davis. Limusa.

Terminologia Moderna de Energia de Agua en el Sistema Suelo-Planta Atmosfera. S. A. Gavande & Elemer Bornemisza. IICA.

Terminologia Musical: Texto del Conservatorio "Fracassi". E. A. Fracass. Ricordi.

Terminologia Usual de la Ciencia & en la Tecnica de la Telecomunicacion. Paraninfo.

Terminology of Documentation: A Selection of 1200 Basic Terms Published in English, French, German, Spanish & Russian. (UNESCO). Unipub.

Terminology of Malaria & of Malaria Eradication: Report of a Drafting Committee. World Health.

Terminos & Conceptos Mas Usuales en Mecanizacion Administrativa. Juan Calbet Sequi. Limusa.

Terminos del Parentesco en el Otomangue. Herbert Harvey. INAH.

Terminos Fundamentales en Etica. Robert S. Hartman. Univ Aut Nuevo.

Terminos Internacionales en la Gestion de Compras & Ventas. Roman San Juan Rubio. APD.

Los Terminos Judiciales. Pascual Castan. Dist. Anfora.

Los Terminos Judiciales. Pascual Castan. Dist. Arenzadi.

Terminos Topograficos en la Argentina Colonial, 1516-1810. Benjamin Nunez. Inst. Pan. Georg.

Tesoro De la Lengua Castellana, O Espanola. Sebastian De Covarrubias Horozco. Hispanic Soc.

Tesoro del Declamador Universal. EDIMEX.

Tesoro Lexicografico 1492-1726. Samuel Gili Gaya. CSIS.

Textile Dictionary. Elsevier.

A Thesaurus of Spanish Idioms & Everyday Language. Lawrence K. Brown. Ungar.

Torrent Control Terminology. (FAO). Unipub.

The Trictionary. Bilingual Pubns.

Two Thousand & One Spanish & English Idioms. Pan Amer Pub.

Two Thousand & One Words You Need to Know to Pass Any Spanish Test. Christopher Kendris. Barron.

Universal Spanish Dictionary. Langenscheidt.

University of Chicago Dictionary. Carlos Castillo & Otto F. Bond. Camino Real.

University of Chicago Dictionary. Pan Amer Pub.

University of Chicago Spanish Dictionary. Carlos Castillo & Otto F. Bond. (Phoen) U of Chicago Pr.

The University of Chicago Spanish Dictionary. Carlos Castillo & Barbara M. Garcia. U of Chicago Pr.

University of Chicago Spanish Dictionary. Carlos Castillo & Otto F. Bond. Rev. by D. Lincoln Canfield. Natl Textbk.

The University of Chicago Spanish-English Dictionary. PB.

University of Chicago Spanish-English Dictionary. Bond Castillo. Iaconi.

Updated Concordance for the Tariff Schedule of the United States (TSUS) with the Brussels Tariff Nomenclature (BTN) OAS.

Velasquez Dictionary: English-Spanish, Spanish-English. Pan Am Bk Co.

Velasquez Spanish-English Dictionary. Camino Real.

Velazquez Spanish & English Dictionary. Mariana Velazquez. New Century.

Velazquez Spanish-English Dictionary: Indexed. New Century.

Velazquez Spanish-English, English-Spanish Dictionary. Iaconi.

Velosipeday i sport. S. N. Novozhilov et al. Russky Yazyk.

Vest Pocket Spanish. Institute for Language Study. (BN). B&N NY.

Vest-Pocket Spanish. New Century.

Vest-Pocket Spanish. Natl Textbk.

Vest Pocket Spanish Dictionary. Ed. by Ida Hinojosa. New Century.

Vocabolario latino. Italo Lana. Paravia.

Vocabolario latino-italiano e italiano-latino. Edmondo D'Arbela et al. Signorelli C.

Vocabolario spagnolo-italiano e italiano-spagnolo. Alvisi & Arce. Malipiero.

Vocabulaire de la Langue Espagnole Classique: XVIe & XVIIe Siecles. Bernard Sese. Doc Univers.

Vocabulaire de la Langue Espagnole Classique: XVIe. & XVIIe. Siecles. Bernard Sese. CDU.

Vocabulaire des Termes: Essentiels Utilises pour la Transmissien Ligne; Francais-Espagnol-Russe-Allemand-Italien-Neerlandais-Polonais-Portugais-Suedois. U. I. T.

Vocabulaire Espagnol par l'image. Robert Paufique. Bordas-Dunod.

Vocabulaire Meteorologique International: Quadrilingue (Anglais-Francais-Espagnol-Russe) O. M. M.

Vocabulaire Multilingue de la Science du Sol: Anglais-Francais-Espagnol-Allemand-Portugais-Italien-Neerlandais-Suedois-Russe. G. V. Jacks & R. Tavernier. F. A. O.

Vocabulari Automobilistic. Merenciano & Antoni Frederic i Ricart. Claret.

Vocabulari Basic Infantil & d'Adults. Biblograf S. A.

Vocabulari basic infantil i d'Adults 'Vox' Biblo SP.

Vocabulari basic infantil i d'Adults 'Vox' Biblo SP.

Vocabulari Castella-Catala. Eduard Artells. French & Eur.

Vocabulari Castella-Catala. Salvat Editores.

Vocabulari Castella-Catala. Eduard Artells. Barcino Edit.

Vocabulari Castella-Valencia. Francesc Ferrer Pastor. Sicania.

Vocabulari Castella-Valencia. Francesc Ferrer Pastor. Sicania.

Vocabulari Castella-Valencia. Estel Edit.

Vocabulari Castella-Valencia & Valencia-Castella. Francesc Ferrer-Pastor. Estel Edit.

Vocabulari Catala-Castella. Eduard Artells. French & Eur.

Vocabulari Catala-Castella. Eduard Artella. Barcino Edit.

Vocabulari de Barbarismes. Santiago Estrany. Teide.

Vocabulari de Barbarismes & Castellanismes. Aureli Cortiella Martret. Organ Ofic Adm.

Vocabulari de Fusteria: Generalitat de Catalunya. Organ Ofic Adm.

Vocabulari Ideologic Catala. Xavier Romeu. Teide.

Vocabulari Mallorqui-Castella. F. De Casasnovas. Moll Edit.

Vocabulari Valencia-Castella. Francesc Ferrer Pastor. Fermar.

Vocabulario Aguaruna de Amazonas. Mildred L. Larson. Summer Inst Ling.

Vocabulario & Refranero Religioso de Mexico. Joaquin Antonio Penalosa. Jus.

Vocabulario Andaluz. A. Alcala. French & Eur.

Vocabulario, Apodos, Seudonimos, Sobrenombres & Hemerografia de la Revolucion. Arturo Langle. UNAM.

Vocabulario Basico de la Arquitectura. J. R. Paniagua. French & Eur.

Vocabulario Basico por Areas. Socusa Edit.

Vocabulario basico trilingue de psicologia cientifica: Ingles-castellano. Candid Genovard Rossello. Fontanella.

Vocabulario castelan-galego. Fermin Fernandez Armesto. Castro Edns.

Vocabulario Castellano-Gallego. Francisco Fernandez del Riego. Galaxia.

Vocabulario Chatino de Tataltepec. Leslie Pride & Kitty Pride. Summer Inst Ling.

Vocabulario con Ilustraciones. Novaro.

Vocabulario consultivo por secciones: Espanol-ingles. Leonard V. Robson. Confed Espanola.

Vocabulario Culto. Gladys Neggers. French & Eur.

Vocabulario culto. Gladys Neggers. Playor.

Vocabulario de Artes de la Madera, Arquitectura y Decoracion. French & Eur.

Vocabulario de Benasque. Angel Ballarin Cornel. Fernando el Catolico.

Vocabulario De Cine y Television En Espana. Maria V. Romero Gualda. French & Eur.

Vocabulario de Construccion Naval. Rafael Crespo Rodriguez. Universidades & Acad.

Vocabulario de Economia. J. Piernas. Espasa Calpe.

Vocabulario de Electronica. Inst Amer.

Vocabulario de Estadistica. J. L. Barcelo. Hispano Europa.

Vocabulario de la Cronica Troyana. K. Parker. U de Salamanca.

Vocabulario de las lenguas ibericas. Marina Regueiro & Ricardo Goyoaga. Nuestra Cultura.

Vocabulario de Mayathan. Dorothy Andrews Heath de Zapata. Dorothy Andrews Heath de Zapata.

Vocabulario de Pedagogia. Laeng. Herder SA.

Vocabulario de Pedagogia. Mauro Laeng. Ed. by C. Genovart Rosello. Herder SA.

Vocabulario de Priego de Cordoba & su Comarca. Francisco Fernandez Pareja. Autores-Editores.

Vocabulario de Puerto Rico. Augusto Malaret. Las Americas.

Vocabulario de Romance: El Latin. Antonio De Nebrija. Castalia Edit.

Vocabulario de romance en latin. Elio de De Nebruja. Tr. by Gerald J. Macdonald. Castalia Edit.

Vocabulario De Romance En Latin: Antonio De Nebrija. Ed. by Gerald MacDonald. Temple U Pr.

Vocabulario de San Jorge de Piquin. Anibal Otero. Univers Santiago.

Vocabulario de Terminos: Criollos Tipicos Relacionados con el Caballo de Paso. Luna de la Fuente. U. Agraria.

Vocabulario del Alto-Aragones de Alquezar & Pueblos Proximos. Pedro Arnal Cavero. (CSIC). Inst. Antonio de Nebrija.

Vocabulario del Bable de Somiedo. Ana M. Cano Gonzalez. Consejo Superior.

Vocabulario del Comercio Medieval. Miguel Gual Camarena. French & Eur.

Vocabulario del dialecto murciano. Justo Garcia Soriano. Organ Ofic Adm.

Vocabulario Del Espanol Hablado. Luis Marquez Villegas. French & Eur.

Vocabulario del Hato. Jose A. De Armas Chitty. U. Central Ven.

Vocabulario del Oriente Peruano. Enrique D. Tovar. U. San Marcos.

Vocabulario Economico & Financiero. Yves Bernard & Jose M. Suarez Campos. Assn Prog Direc.

Vocabulario Electronico Internacional. International Electrotechnical Com. French & Eur.

Vocabulario Espanol de Tejas. Cerda et al. Camino Real.

Vocabulario fenicio. Maria J. Fuentes Estanol. Consejo Superior.

Vocabulario Galego-Castelan. Xose L. Franco Grande. French & Eur.

Vocabulario Galego-Castelan. Xose L. Franco Grande. Galaxia.

Vocabulario Galego-Castelan Castellano-Gallego. Xose L. Franco Grande & Francisco Fernandez del Riego. Galaxia.

Vocabulario General de Orientacion Cientifica y Sus Estratos. Victor Garcia Hoz. French & Eur.

Vocabulario Geomortologico. Consuelo Soto Mora. UNAM.

Vocabulario Griego. Fontoynont-Ribot. Sal Terrae.

Vocabulario Griego-Argentino. Raul Villarroel. Castellvi.

Vocabulario Huitoto Muinane. Eugene E. Minor & Dorothy Minor. Summer Inst Ling.

Vocabulario Ingles-Espanol de Electronica & Tecnica Nuclear. John Markus. Marcombo.

Vocabulario Ingles-Espanol de Electronica. Francisco J. D'Agostino. ARBO.

Vocabulario Ingles-Espanol de Electronica y Tecnica Nuclear. John Markus. French & Eur.

Vocabulario Ingles-Espanol, Espanol-Ingles de Medicina. Francisco Ruiz Torres. French & Eur.

Vocabulario Ingles-Espanol, Espanol-Ingles. Jose Merino Bustamante. French & Eur.

Vocabulario Ingles-Espanol para Servicio Clinico. Hellen H. Cooper. Pax.

Vocabulario Juridico. H. Capitant. Depalma.

Vocabulario Juridico Frances-Espanol. G. Larousse. Abeledo Perrot.

Vocabulario Logico. Eduardo Angel Russo. Coop. Der.

Vocabulario Logico, Historico & Positivo. Russo. Coop. Der.

Vocabulario Maritimo Ingles-Espanol. J. Navarro Dagnino. G Gili.

Vocabulario Maritimo Ingles-Espanol y Espanol-Ingles. Juan Navarro Dagnino. French & Eur.

Vocabulario maritimo ingles-espanol y espanol-ingles. Juan Navarro Dagnino. G Gili.

Vocabulario Mayo. Howard Collard & Elizabeth Collard. Summer Inst Ling.

Vocabulario Medieval Castellano. Cejador & Julio Frauca. Las Americas.

Vocabulario Mexicano de Tetelcingo. Forrest Brewer & Jean Brewer. Summer Inst Ling.

Vocabulario Mexicano Relativo a la Muerte. Juan M. Lope Blanch. UNAM.

Vocabulario Mixe de Totontepec. Alvin Schoenhals & Louise Schoenhals. Summer Inst Ling.

Vocabulario Mixteco de San Miguel el Grande. Betty Stoudt. Summer Inst Ling.

Vocabulario Ortografico: Sugerencias para su Enserianza. Consejo Superior de Esenanza. U. Puerto Rico.

El Vocabulario Politico de Alguno Periodicos de Mexico D. F. Froilan Franco Arias. Fundacion J March.

Vocabulario Politico Republicano y Franquista, 1931-1971. Miguel A. Rebollo Torio. French & Eur.

Vocabulario Popoluca de Sayula. Lawrence Clark & Nancy Clark. Summer Inst Ling.

Vocabulario Popular Sevillano. Manuel Gonzalez Salas. Prensa Espanola.

Vocabulario Puertorriqueno. De Rosario. (Pub by Troutman Press). E Torres & Sons.

Vocabulario Quechua del Pastaza. Peter Landerman. Summer Inst Ling.

Vocabulario Sonorense. Horacio Sobrrzo. French & Eur.

Vocabulario Superior. Gaston Fernandez De La Torriente. French & Eur.

Vocabulario superior. Gaston Fernandez de la Torriente. Playor.

Vocabulario Tecnico De Contabilidad Moderna. Abiud Ramos-Ramos. U of PR Pr.

Vocabulario Tecnologico Aeronautico. Instituto Americano. Inst Amer.

Vocabulario Teologico del Evangelio de Saint Juan. J. Mateos Alvarez. French & Eur.

Vocabulario Totonaco de la Sierra. Herman P. Aschmann. Summer Inst Ling.

Vocabulario Tzeltal de Bachajon. Florence Gerdel & Marianna Slocum. Summer Inst Ling.

Vocabulario Vial. OAS General Secretariat. OAS.

El Vocabulario vital e irracional en Azorin. Jose D. Perona Sanchez. Consejo Superior.

Vocabulario y Refranero Criollo. Tito Saubidet. French & Eur.

Vocabularios Aleman-Espanol-Polaco. Novaro.

Vocabularios Frances-Espanol-Ingles. Novaro.

Vocabularios Japones-Espanol-Ruso. Novaro.

Vocabularios Ocho Idiomas (Coleccion) Novaro.

Vocabularios Portugues-Espanol-Italiano. Novaro.

Vocabularium Polyglottum Vitae Silvarum. R. Litschauer. (Pub. by P. Parey). French & Eur.

Vocabularium Polyglottum Vitae Silvarum. R. Litschauer. Parey.

Vocabulary for the Spanish-Speaking Student of Shorthand. Maria Rivero Wood. U. Puerto Rico.

Vocabulary of the Language of San Antonio Mission, California. Buenaventura Sitjar. AMS Pr.

Voces Extranjeras en el Lengua Technologico. J. J. Alzugaray. French & Eur.

Voces Extranjeras en el Lenguaje Tecnologico. J. J. Alzugaray. Edit Alhambra.

Voces Homofonas, Homografas & Homonimas Castellanas. Compiled by Alvaro J. Moreno. Moreno Ed.

Vox--Diccionario Abreviado Ortografico de la Lengua Espanola. French & Eur.

Vox--Diccionario Conciso de la Lengua Espanola. French & Eur.

Vox--Diccionario de Sinonimos. Samuel Gili Gaya. French & Eur.

Vox--Diccionario Fundamental de la Lengua Espanola. French & Eur.

Vox--Diccionario Fundamental de la Lengua Espanola. French & Eur.

Vox--Diccionario General Ilustrado de la Lengua Espanola. French & Eur.

Vox--Lexis-22, Diccionario Enciclopedia. French & Eur.

Vox Concise Spanish & English Dictionary. Biblograf. (Pub. by Biblograf S. A., Barcelona). Harrap.

Vox-Diccionario Abreviado de la Lengua Espanola. French & Eur.

Vox-Diccionario Abreviado de Sinonimos. French & Eur.

Vox-Diccionario Abreviado Frances-Espanol, Espanol-Frances. French & Eur.

VOX-Diccionario basico frances-espanol, espanol-frances. Imported Bks.

Vox-Diccionario Basico Latino-Espanol, Espanol-Latino. Eustaquio Echuari. French & Eur.

Vox-Diccionario Compendiado de la Lengua Espanola. French & Eur.

Vox-Diccionario Escolar de la Lengua Espanola. French & Eur.

Vox-Diccionario Ingles-Espanol, Espanol-Ingles. French & Eur.

Vox-Diccionario Inicial de la Lengua Espanola. French & Eur.

Vox-Diccionario Manual Griego-Espanol. Jose M. Pabon. French & Eur.

Vox-Diccionario Manual Ilustrado de la Lengua Espanola. French & Eur.

Vox-Diccionario Manual Ingles-Espanol, Espanol-Ingles. French & Eur.

Vox-Diccionario Tematico de la Lengua Espanola. French & Eur.

Vox New Compact Spanish & English Dictionary. Biblograf. (Pub. by Biblograf, Barcelona). Harrap.

Vox Shorter Spanish & English Dictionary. Biblograf. (Pub. by Biblograf S. A., Barcelona). Harrap.

Wirtschafts-Woerterbuch. R. Eichborn & A. Fuentes. (Pub. by Econ Vlg.). French & Eur.

Wirtschaftssprache Spanisch-Deutsch. G. Haensch & F. Casero. (Pub. by M. Hueber). French & Eur.

Wirtschaftssprache Spanisch-Deutsch. G. Haensch & F. Casero. Hueber.

Wirtschaftswoerterbuch Spanisch-Deutsch. Eichborn & Fuentes. (Pub. by Econ). French & Eur.

Woerterbuch der Biochemie. K. Thielmann. French & Eur.

Woerterbuch der Biochemie. K. Von Thielmann. VEB Verlag Enzyklopadie.

Woerterbuch der Biochemie. Thielmann. Verlag Harri Deutsch.

Woerterbuch der Biologie. Guenther Haensch. French & Eur.

Woerterbuch der Dampferzeugungstechnik-Dictionary of Steam Generator Engineering. Ed. by Deutsche Babcock et al. Intl Pubns Serv.

Woerterbuch der Deutschen und Spanischen Sprache. Rudolf Slaby. French & Eur.

Woerterbuch der Deutschen und Spanischen Sprache. Rudolf Slaby. French & Eur.

Woerterbuch der Deutschen und Spanischen Rects und Wirtschaftssprache. H. Becher. French & Eur.

Woerterbuch der Forstwirtschaft. Johannes V. Weck. French & Eur.

Woerterbuch der Forstwirtschaft Deutsch-Englisch-Franzoesisch-Spanisch-Russisch. Johannes Weck et al. BLV Verlag.

Woerterbuch der Industriellen Technik: Band V, Deutsch-Spanisch. Ernst. Brandstetter.

Woerterbuch der Industriellen Technik: Band VI, Spanisch-Deutschg). Ernst. Brandstetter.

Woerterbuch der Industriellen Technik. R. Ernst. French & Eur.

Woerterbuch der Internationalen Beziehungen und der Politik. Guenther Haensch. French & Eur.

Woerterbuch der Kraftuebertragungselemente-Deutsch-Spanisch-Franzoesisch-Englisch-Italienisch-Niederlandisch-Schwedisch-Finnisch: Bd 1, Zahnraeder. Krausskopf.

Woerterbuch der Kraftuebertragungselemente. French & Eur.

Woerterbuch der Landwirtschaft. Guenther Haensch. French & Eur.

Woerterbuch der Recht & Wirtshaftssprache: Teil II, Deutsch-Spanisch. Herbert J. Becher. Recht & Wirtschaft.

Woerterbuch der Rechts & Wirtschaftssprache: Teil I, Spanisch-Deutsch. Herbert J. Becher. Recht & Wirtschaft.

Woerterbuch der Regionalen Umgangssprache in Lateinamerika. Maria Schwauss. VEB Verlag Enzyklopadie.

Woerterbuch der Spanischen & Deutschen Sprache. Guenther Haensch. Klett.

Woerterbuch der Spanischen & Deutschen Sprache: Band II, Deutsch-Spanisch. Slaby & Grossmann. Brandstetter.

Woerterbuch der Spanischen & Deutschen Sprache: Band I, Spanisch-Deutsch. Slaby & Grossmann. Brandstetter.

Woerterbuch der Spanischen und Deutschen Rechts und Wirtschaftssprache. H. Becher. French & Eur.

Woerterbuch der Technik. Karl H. Radde. French & Eur.

Woerterbuch der Technik. Karl H. Radde. French & Eur.

Woerterbuch der Technik. Karl H. Radde. Girardet.

Woerterbuch des Pantentwesens in 5 Sprachen. Gyorgy L. Szendy. French & Eur.

Woerterbuch Industrieofen & Induttrielle Warmeanlagen. Josef Stepanek. Vulkan Verlag.

Woerterbucher der Fertigungstechnik Deutsch-Spanisch-Italienisch-Portugiesisch: Bd 1R, Schmieden-Freiformschmieden & Gesenkschmieden. G. Pahlitzsch. Girardet.

The World Dictionary. Pan Amer Pub.

World Mining: Glossary of Mining, Processing & Geological Terms. Wyllie & Argall. W H Freeman.

World-Wide Spanish. Natl Textbk.

World-Wide Spanish Dictionary. Ed. by Emilio LeFort. (Prem). Fawcett.

World Wide Spanish Language Dictionary Spanish-English. New Century.

Worldwide Dictionary. Bilingual Ed Serv.

The York Dictionary of English-French-German-Spanish Literary Terms & Their Origin. Saad Elkhaden. York Pr CA.

The York Dictionary of English-French-German-Spanish Literary Terms & Their Origin. Saad Elkhadem. York Pr CA.

Zwei Hundert Eins Spanische Verben. Henry Strutz. Barron.

SQUAWMISH

Squamish Language. Aert H. Kuipers. Mouton.

SUDANESE

Lexique des Parlers Arabes-Tchado-Soudanais: K-Y. Arlette Roth-Laly. CNRS.

Lexique des Parlers Arabes-Tchado-Soudanais. Arlette Roth-Laly. CNRS.

Lexique des Parlers Arabes-Tchado-Soudanais. Arlette Roth-Laly. CNRS.

Lexique des Parlers Arabes-Tchado-Soudanais, 3. Arlette Roth-Laly. CNRS.

SUECO

Diccionario Lexicon Sueco-Espanol, Espanol-Sueco. French & Eur.

SWAHILI

Adili Na Nduguze. Robert Shaaban. Macmillan London.

A Concise Dictionary of English-Swahili Idioms. Abdilahi Nassir. Shungways Publishers.

Dictionary of the Suahili Language. Ed. by Ludwig Krapf. (Pub. by Negro U Pr) Greenwood.

Dictionnaire Francais-Swahili. Charles Sacleux. Institut Ethnologie.

Dictionnaire Swahili-Francais. Charles Sacleux. Inst Ethnol.

Kamusi Vocabulaire. S. Farsi. Edns St Paul.

Korfattad Svensk-Swahili Ordbok. Abdulaziz Lodhi et al. Nord Afrik.
Kratkii Suakhili-Russkii & Russko-Suakhili Slovar. A. I. Kutuzov. (Pub. by Sov Entsiklopediia). Four Continent.
Learn Swahili for English Speakers. Ernest B. Haddon. Saphrograph.
Russian-Swahili, Swahili-Russian Dictionary. A. I. Kutuzov. French & Eur.
A Short Dictionary of Science Terms for Swahili Speakers. James L. Brain. Syracuse U Foreign Comp.
Slovar Russko-Suakhili Gazetnoi Leksiki. A. I. Kutuzov. (Pub. by In-Tut Mezhdunarod. Otnoshenii). Four Continent.
A Social Science Vocabulary of Swahili. James L. Brain. Syracuse U Foreign Comp.
Standard Swahili-English Dictionary. Ed. by Frederick Johnson. Oxford U Pr.
Swahili Dictionary. D. V. Perrot. McKay.
Swahili-English Dictionary. Charles W. Rechenbach. Cath U Pr.
Swahili-English Dictionary. F. Johnson. Saphrograph.
Swahili-English Dictionary. Iaconi.
Vocabolario italiano-kiswahili. Vittorio Merlo Pick. EMI.
Vocabolario kiswahili-italiano. Vittorio Merlo Pick. EMI.
Vocabolario swahili-italiano e italiano-swahili. Vittorio Merlo Pick. EMI.
Woerterbuch Swahili-Deutsch. HIldegard Hoftmann et al. VEB Verlag Enzyklopadie.

SWEDISH

Avfallsordlista. Tek Nomen.
Berlitz Pocket Dictionaries: Swedish-English. Berlitz Editors. (Berlitz). Macmillan.
Berlitz Pocket Dictionaries: Swedish-English-Swedish. Berlitz. Macmillan.
Bildwoerterbuch Schwedisch: Bildlexikon. Biblio Inst.
Bonniers Musiklexikon. Ake Engstroem & H. Toernblom. Bonnier Forlag.
Bonniers Trebandlexikon. Pergamon.
Bra Bockers Lexikon. Pergamon.
Bulgarialais-Suomalainen Sanakirja. Boris Parashkevov et al. Gaudeamus.
Byggordsamling. Tekniska Nomenklaturcentralen. Tek Nomen.
Capitol's Concise Dictionary. French & Eur.
Chemins de Fer Glossary. Bureau International de Documentation de Chemin de Fer. Elsevier.
Concise English-Swedish Dictionary of Legal Terms. Ed. by Andre Bruzelius et al. French & Eur.
Concise Swedish-English Glossary of Legal Terms. Torild Backe et al. Rothman.
Dansk-Svensk Ordbok. Bertil Molde. Ed. by Niels Ferlov. Esselte Studium.
Dansk-Svensk Ordbok. Karen Widman. Esselte Studium.
Dataordbok. Lena Frid. EC Print AB.
Dataordbok: Computers, Automatic, Control & Data Processing. EC Print AB.
Dataordboken. Sveriges Standardiseringskommission. Standard Sver.
Deutsch fur Baufachleute fuer Daenen, Norweger & Sshweden. G. Wallnig & H. Evered. Bauverlag.
Diccionario Simultaneo en 21 Idiomas. Juan Capdevila Font. French & Eur.
Dictionnaire de Poche Francais-Suedois. Berlitz.

Dictionnaire International Electrotechnique: Francais-Russe-Anglais-Allemand-Italien-Suedois-Hollandais-Polonais. Mir.
Dictionnaire International Electrotechnique: Francais-Russe-Anglais-Allemand-Espagnol-Suedois-Hollandais-Polonais. Mir.
Dizionario italiano-svedese. Malipiero.
Dizionario italiano-svedese. Gaft & Bassoli. Vallardi A.
Dizionario Italiano-Svedese, Svedese-Italiano. G. Gareff & F. Bassoli. French & Eur.
Dizionario svedes-italiano e italiano-svedese. Malipiero.
Elsevier's Dictionary of Criminal Science. J. A. Adler. Elsevier.
Elsevier's Dictionary of Horticulture. Ed. by Ministry of Agriculture & Fisheries- Netherlands & J. Nijdam. Elsevier.
Elseviers Rubber Dictionary. Elsevier.
Elsevier's Wood Dictionary. Ed. by W. Boerhave Beekman. Elsevier.
Engelsk-Svensk Elteknisk Forkortningslista. Ake Nyblom. Ingenjorsforlaget.
Engelsk-Svensk Ordbog. Mats Bergstrom & Ingvar Carlson. Natur & Kultur.
Engelsk-Svensk Ordbok. Esselte Studium.
Engelsk-Svensk Ordbok. Rubin Noejd. Esselte Studium.
Engelsk-Svensk Teknisk Ordbok. Esselte Studium.
Engelska Ordboksguiden. Esselte Studium.
Engelskt-Svenskt Flyglexikon. Sven Christensen. Esselte Studium.
English-Swedish Dictionary. Ruben Nojd. Saphrograph.
English-Swedish-English Dictionary. French & Eur.
Fachwoerterbuch Fur Recht und Wirtschaft. Gunther Parsenow. (Pub. by Carl Heymanns Verlag KG). French & Eur.
Finnish-Swedish Dictionary. L. Lampen. French & Eur.
Finnish-Swedish-Finnish Dictionary. French & Eur.
Finnish-Swedish-Finnish Dictionary (Suomi-Ruotsi-Suomi) L. Lampen. French & Eur.
Finsk-Svensk & Svensk-Finsk Fickordbok. Av Lea Lampen. Esselte Studium.
Finsk-Svensk Skolordbok. Lea Lampen. Esselte Studium.
Finsk-Swensk Storordbok. Knut Cannelin et al. Esselte Studium.
Foerkortningslexikon. Sven E. Oestling. Utrikespolitiska.
Fransk-Svensk Ordbok. Johan Vising. Esselte Studium.
Fransk-Svensk Ordbok. Ruben Nojd. Esselte Studium.
French-Swedish-French Dictionary. French & Eur.
German-Swedish-German Dictionary. French & Eur.
Glossaire d'organes de Transmission, 1: Les Engrenages Allemand-Espagnol-Francais-Anglais-Italien-Neerlandais-Suedois-Finnois. Maison Dictionnaire.
Glossary of Populations & Housing. G. Logie. Elsevier.
Graphic & Paper Industry. EC Print AB.
Hill's English-Swedish, Swedish-English Pocket Dictionary. (Pub. by Bailey & Swinfen South Africa). State Mutual Bk.
Hitta Ratt & Stora Ordlistan. Esselte Studium.
International Glossary of Technical Terms for the Pulp & Paper Industry. Van Derveer & Haas. Imported Bks.
International Planning Glossary. Ed. by Gordon Logie & Hemel Hemstead. Intl Plan Glos.
Italian-Swedish-Italian Dictionary. French & Eur.
Italiensk-Svensk Ordbok. Esselte Studium.
Karnkraft Fran A til O. Lars G. Larsson & Sven Lorveberg. Ingenjorsforlaget.

Konsten Att Veta Bast Fran ABBA til Ovre Slummen. Goran Palm. Illus. by Karl-Olov Bjork. Norstedt Soner.
Korfattad Svensk-Swahili Ordbok. Abdulaziz Lodhi et al. Nord Afrik.
Kortfattad Engelsk-svensk Juridisk Ordbok. Anders Bruzelius et al. Liber Gleerup.
Kortfattad Medicinsk Ordbok. Martin Wrete. Ed. by Sven Dahlgren. Esselte Studium.
Langenscheidts Handwoerterbuch Schwedisch PRISMA. Langenscheidt.
Langenscheidts Taschenwoerterbuch Schwedisch. H. Kornitzky. Langenscheidt.
Langenscheidts Taschenwoerterbuch Schwedisch: Teil II, Deutsch-Schwedisch. H. Kornitzky. Langenscheidt.
Langenscheidts Taschenwoerterbuch Schwedisch: Teil I, Schwedisch-Deutsch. H. Kornitzky. Langenscheidt.
Langenscheidts Taschenwoerterbuecher Schwedisch. H. Kornitzky. Langenscheidt.
Langenscheidts Taschenwoerterbuecher Schwedisch-Deutsch. Langenscheidt.
Langenscheidts Universal-Woerterbuch Schwedisch. Langenscheidt.
Latinsk-Svensk Ordbok. Axel W. Ahlberg et al. Esselte Studium.
Lexicon Forestale. Karl-Johan Ahlsved et al. Suomen Standard.
Lexicon Sopena: Diccionario de bolsilo, sueco-espanol y espanol-sueco. Sopena.
McKay's Modern English-Swedish, Swedish-English Dictionary. Ruben Nojd & Astrid Tornberg. Imported Bks.
McKay's Modern Swedish-English & English-Swedish Dictionary. Astrid Tornberg et al. McKay.
Maly Slownik Polsko-Swedzki. Lech Sikorski. Plastik.
Maly Slownik Szwedzko-Polski. Lech Sikorski. Wiedza Powszechna.
Modern English-Swedish Dictionary. B. Danielsson. French & Eur.
Modernt Foertagsekonomiskt Lexikon. Erick R. Eriksson & Roy Baeckbom. Prisma.
Multilingual Vocabulary of Educational Radio & Television Terms. Intl Pubns Serv.
Music Translation Dictionary: An English, Czech, Danish, Dutch, French, German, Hungarian, Italian, Polish, Portuguese, Russian, Spanish, Swedish Vocabulary of Music. Compiled by Carolyn D. Grigg. Greenwood.
Norsk-Svensk Ordbok. Nat. Beckman. Ed. by Leif Maehle & Bengt Sigurd. Esselte Studium.
Norsk-Svensk Ordbok. Natanael Beckman. Ed. by Lief Maehle & Bengt Sigurd. Esselte Studium.
Nygrekisk-Svensk Ordbok. Antonis Mystakidis. Ed. by Eftychia Frangos. Esselte Studium.
Olika Lika Ord: Svenskt Homograflexikon. Sture Berg. Almqvist.
Ordhandboken. Bjorn Collinder. Fyris.
Ordlistan Fran Natur & Kultur. Eskil Kalquist et al. Natur & Kultur.
Plan by Byggtermer. Tekniska Nomenklaturcentralen. Tek Nomen.
Plast & Gummilexikon. EC Print AB.
Prinsessans ABC Bok. Fredrik C. Boije af Gennas. Rediviva.
Ruotsalais-Suomalaines. Lea Lampeu. WSOY.
Ruotsin Kielen Perus ja Taydennyssanasto. Kalervo Linnapuomi. Otava.
Rysk-Svensk Teknisk Ordbok. Bengt Schildt. Esselte Studium.
Sahkotieteellinen Sanasto. Suomen Standardisoimislitto. Suomen Standard.
Schwedisch. H. Kornitzky. Langenscheidt.

Semiiazychnyi Slovar Po Mekhanike Gruntov & Fundamentostroeniiu. M. E. Schneider. (Pub. by Gosizdat Fizmat. Lit.). Four Continent.
Skogsordlista. Tekniska Nomenklaturcentralen. Tek Nomen.
Skolordlista. Esselte Studium.
Socialfoersaekringslexikon. Sigvard Classon. LiberFoerlag.
Spanish-Swedish-Spanish Dictionary. French & Eur.
Spansk-Svensk Ordbok. Esselte Studium.
Stora Engelsk-Svenska Ordboken: A Comprehensive English-Swedish Dictionary. Esselte Studium.
Stora Synonymordboken. Alva Strmberg. Stromberg.
Suomalais-Ruotsalainen Suursanakirja. Aulis Cannelin et al. Werner Soderstrom.
Svensk Baklaengesordbok. Sture Allen et al. Esselte Studium.
Svensk-Engelsk Affarsordlists. Stanley H. Pretorius. Esselte Studium.
Svensk-Engelsk & Engelsk-Svensk Ordbok. Tornberg et al. Esselte Studium.
Svensk-Engelsk Modern Ordbok. Rolf Prisma-Lagersson. Vanous.
Svensk-Engelsk Pocketordbok. Esselte Studium.
Svensk-Estnisk Ordbok. Per Wieselgren. Fyris.
Svensk-Finsk Storordbok. Lea Lampen. Esselte Studium.
Svensk-Fransk Affaersordlista. Edy Maupoix. Esselte Studium.
Svensk-Fransk & Fransk-Svensk Ordbok. Ruben Noid. Esselte Studium.
Svensk-Fransk Ordbok. Thekla Hammar. Esselte Studium.
Svensk-Fransk Ordbok. Esselte Studium.
Svensk Handordbok: Kronstruktioner & Fraseologi. Ed. by Ture Johannisson & K. G. Ljunggren. Esselte Studium.
Svensk-Italiensk Ordbok. Silvia Tomba. Esselte Studium.
Svensk-Norsk Ordbok. Marius Sandvei. Fabritius.
Svensk-Nygrekisk Ordbok. Natan Valmin & Eftychia Frangos. Esselte Studium.
Svensk Slangordbok. Haldo Gibson. Esselte Studium.
Svensk-Spansk Affaersordlista. Peralta & Cederholm. Esselte Studium.
Svensk-Spansk Ordbok. Alfred Akerlung. Ed. by M. J. Casa Novas & M. Gronbarj. Esselte Studium.
Svensk-Turkisk Ordbok. Musa Guner. Studentlitt.
Svensk-Tysk Affarsordlista. Helge Birgersson. Esselte Studium.
Svensk-Tysk & Tysk-Svenskt Standardlexikon. Esselte Studium.
Svensk-Tysk Ordbok. Esselte Studium.
Svensk-Tysk Ordbok: Supplement 78. Esselte Studium.
Svensk-Tysk Standardlexikon. Esselte Studium.
Svensk-Tyskt-Tyskt-Svenskt Standardlexikon. Esselte Studium.
Svenska Akademiens Ordlista Oever Svenska Spraket. Esselte Studium.
Svenska Duden Bildlexikon. Imported Bks.
Svenska Ordlista. Sture Allen. Esselte Studium.
Svenskt Rimlexikon. Einer Odhner. Forum Bok.
Swedish-English Dictionary. Ruben & M. Angstrom. Saphrograph.
Swedish-English Dictionary of Technical Terms Used in Business, Industry, Administration, Education & Research. Ingvar E. Gullberg. Heinman.
Swedish-English, English-Swedish Dictionary. R. Santesson & Karl K. Kaerre. Heinman.
Swedish-English, English-Swedish Pocket Dictionary. Berlitz Editors. (Berlitz). Macmillan.
Swedish-English, English-Swedish Technical Dictionary. E. Engstroem. Heinman.
Swedish-English Fact Ordbok (Technical Terms) Ingvar E. Gullberg. Vanous.

Swedish-English Modern Dictionary.
R. Prisma-Lagersson. Vanous.
Swedish-English-Swedish. Macmillan.
Swedish-English-Swedish Pocket
Dictionary. A. Hills. Vanous.
Swedish-Finnish Dictionary. L.
Lampen. French & Eur.
Swedish Karre Dictionary, Vol. 1:
Svensk-Engelsk. K. Karre. Vanous.
Swedish Karre Dictionary, Vol. 2:
Engelsk-Svensk. K. Karre. Vanous.
Swedish Modern Pocket Dictionary:
Svensk-Engelsk, Engelsk-Svensk
Grammatik Parlor. E. Gomer.
Vanous.
Swedish-Norwegian Dictionary. J.
Vogt & I. Eikeland.
Kunnskapsforlaget.
Swedish Pocket Dictionary. Heinman.
Swedish-Russian Dictionary. D.
Milanova. French & Eur.
Teaterord. Niklas Brunius. Nord
Teater.
Tysk-Svensk Ordbok. Esselte
Studium.
Tysk-Svensk Ordbok: Supplement 80.
Esselte Studium.
Uppslagsbok i Psykoterapi och
Medicinsk Psykologi. Henry
Egidius. Natur & Kultur.
Vad Betyder Vaxtens Latinska Namn.
Ivar Anell. Forum Bok.
Vaegledning till Svenska Akademiens
Ordbok. Sven Ekbo & Bengt
Loman. Esselte Studium.
Vara Ord: Kortfattad Etymologisk
Ordbok. Elias Wessen. Esselte
Studium.
Vara Viktiga Ord: Basordlista Med
Utbytesord. Sture Allen. Esselte
Studium.
Varldspolitiskt lexikon. Laszlo
Hamori. Natur & kultur.
Vocabulaire des Termes: Essentiels
Utilises pour la Transmissien Ligne;
Francais-Espagnol-Russe-Allemand-
Italien-Neerlandais-Polonais-
Portugais-Suedois. U. I. T.
Vocabulaire Multilingue de la Science
du Sol: Anglais-Francais-Espagnol-
Allemand-Portugais-Italien-
Neerlandais-Suedois-Russe. G. V.
Jacks & R. Tavernier. F. A. O.
Vocabulaire Suedois. Francois N.
Simoneau. Ophrys.
Woerterbuch der
Kraftuebertragungselemente-
Deutsch-Spanisch-Franzoesisch-
Englisch-Italienisch-Niederlandisch-
Schwedisch-Finnisch: Bd 1,
Zahnraeder. Krausskopf.
Woerterbucher der Fertigungstechnik
Daenisch-Norwegisch-Schwedisch-
Finnisch: Bd 1N, Schmieden-
Freiformschmieden &
Gesenkschmieden. G. Pahlitzsch.
Girardet.
World Mining: Glossary of Mining,
Processing & Geological Terms.
Wyllie & Argall. W H Freeman.

TAGALOG

Concise English-Tagalog Dictionary.
J. Villar Panganiban. C E Tuttle.
Concise English-Tagalog Dictionary.
Jose Villa Panganiban. Imported
Bks.
Concise English-Tagalog Dictionary.
Panganiban. Iaconi.
Diccionario hispano-tagalog y tagalog-
hispano. Ed. by Pedro Serrano
Laktaw. Cultura Hispan.
English-Tagalog-Ilocano Pocket
Dictionary. Enriquez & Quimba.
Colton Bk.
English-Tagalog, Tagalog-English
Pocket Dictionary. Enriquez &
Guzman. Colton Bk.
English-Tagalog-Visayan Pocket
Dictionary. Enriquez & Bautista.
Colton Bk.
Russko-Tagal'skii Slovar. M. Krus et
al. (Pub. by Sov. Entsiklopediia).
Four Continent.
Tagal sko Russkii Slovar. M. Krus et
al. Four Continent.
Tagalog Dictionary. Teresita V.
Ramos. UH Pr.
Tagalog Dictionary. T. Ramos. Iaconi.
Tagalog-English - English-Tagalog
Dictionary. Maria O. Guzman.
Heinman.
Tagalog-Russian Dictionary. M. Cruz
& S. P. Ignashev. French & Eur.
Tagal'sko-Russkii Slovar. M. Krus.
(Pub. by GINS). Four Continent.

TAHITIAN

A Comparative Dictionary of the
Tahitian Language: Tahitian-
English with an English-Tahitian
Finding List. Edmund Andrews &
Irene D. Andrews. AMS Pr.
Dictionnaire Francais-Tahitien. Mai-
Arii Mai-Aru & J. Anisson du
Perron. Pensee Moderne.
Dictionnaire Francais-Tahitien et
Tahitien-Francais. Mai-Aru & J.
Anisson du Perron. French & Eur.
Lexique du Tahitien Contemporain:
Tahitien-Francais. Yves Lemaitre.
Orstom.
A Tahitian & English Dictionary.
John Davies. AMS Pr.
Tahitian-English, English Tahitian
Dictionary. Leonard Clairmont.
Shalom.

TAI

Taisko-Ruskii Slovar. L. N. Morev.
(Pub. by Sov. Entsiklopediia). Four
Continent.

SYRIAC

A Syriac-English Glossary: With
Etymological Notes, Based on
Brockelmann's Syriac
Chrestomathy. Moshe H.
Goshen-Gottstein. Intl Pubns Serv.
Compendious Syriac Dictionary
Founded Upon the Thesaurus
Syriacus of R. Payne Smith. R.
Payne Smith. Ed. by J. Payne
Smith. Oxford U Pr.
Dictionnaire Syriaque-Francais-
Anglais. Louis Costaz. Dar El-
Machreq.

TAMIL

Glossary of Linguistics. N.
Arunabharathi. Tamil Nuulagam.
Health & Culture in a South Indian
village. C. M. Matthews. Orient Bk
Dist.
Russko-Tamil'Skii Slovar. M. S.
Andronov. (Pub. by Sov.
Entsiklopediia). Four Continent.
Tamil dictionaries. A. Dhamotharau.
Steiner Verlag.
Tamil-English, English-Tamil
Dictionary. M. Winslow. Heinman.

TANGA

Tanga-English, English-Tanga
Dictionary. Francis L. Bell. Univ
Syd Aust Lang.

TAUSUG

Tausug-English Dictionary. Irene
Hassan. Jolu, Sulu.

TELUGU

Dictionary of Telugu & English:
Explaining English Idioms &
Phrases in Telugu. Charles P.
Brown. Ayer Co.

THAI

Mini English-Thai-English Dictionary.
G. Allison. French & Eur.
New Model English - Thai
Dictionary. Compiled by So
Sethaputra. Intl Pubns Serv.
New Model Thai-English Dictionary.
Compiled by So Sethaputra. Thai
Watana.
Practical English-Thai Dictionary. S.
Robertson. Iaconi.
Robertson's Practical English-Thai
Dictionary. Ed. by Richard G.
Robertson. C E Tuttle.
Sanskrit-Thai-English Dictionary. Intl
Pubns Serv.
Thai-English Dictionary. George B.
McFarland. Stanford U Pr.
Thai-English Student's Dictionary.
Ed. by Mary R. Haas. Stanford U
Pr.
Thai Vocabulary. Mary R. Haas.
Spoken Lang Serv.

TIBETAN

A Dictionary of Tibetan & English.
Alexander Csoma de Koros. (Pub.
by Cosmo Pubns India). Orient Bk
Dist.
Dictionnaire Francais-Tibetain.
Giraudeau & Francis Gore.
Maisonneuve, A.
Dictionnaire Francais-Tibetain (Tibet
Oriental) A. Giraudeau & Francis
Gore. French & Eur.
Tibetan-English Dictionary. S. C.
Dass. Orient Bk Dist.
Tibetan-English Dictionary. H. A.
Jaschke. Orient Bk Dist.
Tibetan-English Dictionary. S. C.
Das. Orientalia.
Tibetan-English Dictionary. Iaconi.
Tibetan-English Dictionary of
Modern Tibetan. Melvyn C.
Goldstein. Himalaya Hse.
Tibetan-English Dictionary, with
Sanskrit Synonyms. Sarat C. Das.
Ed. by G. Sandberg & A. W.
Heyde. Intl Pubns Serv.
Tibetan-English Dictionary: With
Sanskrit Synonyms. S. Chandra
Das. Ed. by Graham Sanberg & A.
William Heyde. Lancaster-Miller.
Tibetan-English Dictionary with
Supplement. Ed. by Stuart H. Buck.
Cath U Pr.
Tibetan-English, English-Tibetan
Dictionary. S. C. Das & I. D. Kazi.
Heinman.

TOBA

Toba-Batak-Deutsches Worterbuch.
Johannes G. Warneck. Nyhoff.

TSIMSHIAN

A Practical Dictionary of the Coast
Tsimshian Language. John A.
Dunn. Natl Mus Can.

TSWANA

Thanodi ya Setswana ya Dikole.
Morulaganyi Kgasa. Longman S
Africa.

TUMAK

Lexique Tumak-Francais Tchad. Jean
P. Caprile. Reimer.

TURKISH

Abbreviated Turkish-Russian
Dictionary of New Words. H. G.
Antelava. French & Eur.
Cagdas Ozturce Sozlugu. Seyit K.
Karaalioglu. Inkilap ve Aka
Kitabevleri.
Concise Oxford Turkish Dictionary.
Ed. by A. D. Alderson & Fahir Iz.
Oxford U Pr.
Deutsch-Turkisches Woerterbuch fur
Technische Berufe. Sadettin
Bilginer. Girardet.
Deutsch-Turkisches Worterbuch Fur
Technische Berufe. Sadettin
Bilginer. (Pub. by Verlag W.
Girardet). French & Eur.
Diccionario Simultaneo en 21
Idiomas. Juan Capdevilla Font.
French & Eur.
Dictionar Roman-Turc. Mitica Grecu
et al. Editura Stiintifica.
Dictionar Turc-Roman. A. Baubec et
al. Editura Stiintifica.
Dictionnaire Europa Francais-Turc.
H. J. Kornrumpf. Larousse.
Dizionario Italiano-Turco, Turco-
Italiano. M. Celalettin Bugday.
French & Eur.
Dizionario turco-italiano. Budgay.
Vallardi A.
English-Turkish, Turkish-English
Dictionary. Ziya Sak. Saphrograph.
Etimologicheskii Slovar Tiurkskikh
Iazykov. E. V. Sevortian. (Pub. by
Nauka). Four Continent.
Etimologicheskii Slovar Tiurkskikh
Iazykov. E. V. Sevortian. (Pub. by
Nauka). Four Continent.
An Etymological Dictionary of Pre-
Thirteenth Century Turkish. Gerard
Clauson. Oxford U Pr.
Kratkii Turetsko-Russkii Slovar
"Novykh Slov". G. I. Antelava.
(Pub. by Metsniereba). Four
Continent.
Langenscheidt English-Turkish
Lilliput Dictionary. Langenscheidt.
Langenscheidt Turkish-English
Lilliput Dictionary. Langenscheidt.
Langenscheidt's Lilliput English-
Turkish Dictionary. Am Map.
Langenscheidt's Lilliput Turkish-
English Dictionary. Am Map.
Langenscheidts Taschenwoerterbuch
Tuerkisch-Deutsch. K. Steuerwald
& Cemal Koprulu. Langenscheidt.
Langenscheidts Taschenwoerterbuch
Tuerkisch: Teil II, Deutsch-
Tuerkisch. K. Steuerwald & Cemal
Koprulu. Langenscheidt.

Langenscheidts Taschenwoerterbuch Tuerkisch: Teil I, Tuerkisch-Deutsch. K. Steuerwald. Langenscheidt.

Langenscheidts Taschenwoerterbuecher Tuerkisch. Karl Steuerwald. Langenscheidt.

Langenscheidts Taschenwoerterbuecher Tuerkisch-Deutsch. Karl Steuerwald. Langenscheidt.

Langenscheidt's Universal Turkish-English, English-Turkish Dictionary. Am Map.

Langenscheidts Universal-Woerterbuch Tuerkisch. Langenscheidt.

Langenscheidts Universal-Woerterbuecher Tuerkisch-Deutsch. Langenscheidt.

Learn Turkish, for English Speaker. Saphrograph.

Lilliput Dictionary. Langenscheidt.

Lilliput Dictionary. Langenscheidt.

Meydan-Larousse. Pergamon.

Multilingual Technical Dictionary on Irrigation & Drainage. US Comm Irrigation.

The Oxford English-Turkish Dictionary. Fahir Iz. Ed. by A. D. Alderson. Oxford U Pr.

The Oxford English-Turkish Dictionary. Fahir Iz & H. C. Hony. Oxford U Pr.

Portable Redhouse Turkish-English, English-Turkish Dictionary. Intl Learn Syst.

Recueil Terminologique Multilinque du Soudage et des Techniques Connexes. French & Eur.

Redhouse Cagdas Turkce-Ingilizce. Redhouse Pr.

Redhouse Cagdas Turkee-Ingilizee Sozlugii. Redhouse Pr.

Redhouse English-Turkish Dictionary. Intl Learn Syst.

Redhouse Ingilizce-Turkce Sozlugu. Redhouse Pr.

Redhouse Ingilizce-Turkce, Turkce-Ingilizce elsozlugu. Redhouse Pr.

Redhouse Ingilizee-Turkee-Ingilizee Elsozlugu. Redhouse Pr.

Redhouse Ingilizee-Turkee Sozlugu. Redhouse Pr.

Redhouse Turkish-English Dictionary. Intl Learn Syst.

Redhouse Yeni Turkee-Ingilizee Sozlugu. Redhouse Pr.

Shorter Redhouse Turkish-English Dictionary. Intl Learn Syst.

Svensk-Turkisk Ordbok. Musa Guner. Studentlitt.

Taspinar's Technical Dictionary. Adnan H. Taspinar. Taspinar's Technical Publications.

Technisches Woerterbuch. Taspinar. Brandstetter.

Trukese-English Dictionary. Ward H. Goodenough & Hiroshi Sugita. Am Philos.

Turkish-English Dictionary. James W. Redhouse. Ayer Co.

Turkish-English Dictionary. H. C. Hony. Oxford U Pr.

Turkish-English, English-Turkish Dictionary: New Red House. Heinman.

Turkish, English-English, Turkish Dictionary (the Redhouse Portable Dictionary) Ed. by Robert Avery et al. Heinman.

Universal Turkish Dictionary. Langenscheidt.

TUVALU

Nanumea Lexicon. Peter Ranby. Linguistic Circle.

TZOTZIL

Diccionario Tzotzil De San Andres Con Variaciones Dialectales. Alfa Delgaty & Augustin R. Sanchez. Summer Inst Ling.

UGARITIC

Concordance of Ugaritic. Douglas Young. Pont Ist Biblico.

UKRAINIAN

Anglo-Ukrainskii Slovar. (Pub. by Radianska Shkola). Four Continent.

English-Ukrainian Dictionary. Ed. by M. L. Podvesko. Saphrograph.

English-Ukrainian Dictionary. M. L. Podveska & M. J. Balla. (Pub. by Collet's). State Mutual Bk.

English-Ukrainian Dictionary. Ed. by I. O. Zhluktenko. Four Continent.

An Etymological Dictionary of the Ukrainian Language. J. B. Rudnyckyj. Ukrainian Acad.

Russko-Ukrainskii Khimicheskii Slovar. E. F. Nekriach. (Pub. by An Arm SSR). Four Continent.

Russko-Ukrainskii Metallurgicheskii Slovar. V. D. Chekhranov. (Pub. by Naukova Dumka). Four Continent.

Russko-Ukrainskii Slovar. D. I. Ganich et al. (Pub. by Sov. Entsiklopediia). Four Continent.

Russko-Ukrainskii Slovar Sotsial'No-Ekonomicheskoi Terminologii. (Pub. by Ukr. Entsiklopediia). Four Continent.

Slovar Gidronimov Ukrainy. (Pub. by Naukova Dumka). Four Continent.

Slovnik Staroukrainskoi Movi XVI-XV. (Pub. by Naukova Dumka). Four Continent.

Slovnik Ukrainskoi Movi: I-M. (Pub. by Naukova Dumka). Four Continent.

Slovnik Ukrainskoi Movi: N-O. (Pub. by Naukova Dumka). Four Continent.

Slovnik Ukrainskoi Movi: P-Poiti. (Pub. by Naukova Dumka). Four Continent.

Slovnik Ukrainskoi Movi: Poikhati-Prirobliati. (Pub. by Naukova Dumka). Four Continent.

Slovnik Ukrainskoi Movi: Priroda-Riakhtlivii. (Pub. by Naukova Dumka). Four Continent.

Slovnik Ukrainskoi Movi: S. (Pub. by Naukova Dumka). Four Continent.

Slovnik Ukrainskoi: T-F. (Pub. by Naukova Dumka). Four Continent.

Slovnik Ukrainskoi Movi: Z. (Pub. by Naukova). Four Continent.

Ukrainian-English Dictionary. Ed. by C. H. Andrusyshen. U of Toronto Pr.

Ukrainian-English, English-Ukrainian Dictionary. Compiled by M. L. Podvesko. Heinman.

Ukrainian-English, English-Ukrainian Pocket Dictionary. Heinman.

Vocabolario ucraino-italiano. E. Onatskyj. Ist Univers Orient.

URALIC

Fenno-Ugric Vocabulary: An Etymologic Dictionary of the Uralic Languages. Bjorn Collinder. Buske.

URDU

Dictionary of Urdu, Classical Hindi, & English. John T. Platts. Oxford U Pr.

English-Urdu Dictionary. Pakistani. Kazi Pubns.

English-Urdu Dictionary of Christian Terminology. Liberius Pieterse. Ed. by Jan Slomp. Christian Study Centre.

Feroz-ul-Lughat (Urdu) Dictionary. Kazi Pubns.

Ferozsons Concise Dictionary. Ed. by A. Hameed Khan. Ferozsons.

Karmannyi Russko-Urdu Slovar. A. A. Davidova et al. (Pub. by GINS). Four Continent.

Karmannyi Urdu-Russkii Slovar. L. B. Kibirkshtis et al. (Pub. by GINS). Four Continent.

Reverse Dictionary of Urdu. Donald Becker. (Pub. by Manohaar India). South Asia Bks.

Urdu-English Dictionary. Kazi Pubns.

Urdu-English Dictionary, Romanized. Saphrograph.

Urdu-English Vocabulary: Student's Dictionary. M. A. Barker et al. Spoken Lang Serv.

UZBEK

Russko-Latinsko-Uzbekskii Slovar. (Pub. by Meditsina). Four Continent.

Uzbeck-English Dictionary. Natalie Waterson. Oxford U Pr.

VASCO

Diccionario Castellano-Vasco. Placido Mugika. French & Eur.

Diccionario Castellano-Vasco. P. Roman de Bera. French & Eur.

Diccionario General y Tecnico: Hiztegi Orokor-Teknikoa. Luis M. Mugica Urdangarin. French & Eur.

Diccionario Magico Infantil En Seis Lenguas. Eulalia Goma. French & Eur.

Diccionario Maritimo Ilustrado Vasco-Castellano, Castellano-Vasco. Ignacio de Garmendia y Berasategui. French & Eur.

VENDA

English-Venda Dictionary. L. T. Marole & F. S. De Goma. Shalom.

VIETNAMESE

Basic words in Vietnamese. Pan Am Bk Co.

Dictionar Roman-Vietnamez. Elena Stoicovici et al. Tipografia.

Dictionnaire Francais-Vietnamien. Maison Dictionnaire.

Dictionnaire Vietnamien-Francais. Thanh Nghi. Asiatheque.

English-Vietnamese Dictionary. Tu Dien Anh-Viet. (Pub. by Collets). State Mutual Bk.

English-Vietnamese Dictionary Romanized. Shalom.

English-Vietnamese Phrasebook with Useful Word List: For Vietnamese Speakers. Nguyen Hy Quang. Ctr Appl Ling.

English-Vietnamese Pocket Dictionary. Shalom.

English-Vietnamese Pocket Dictionary. Iaconi.

Essential English-Vietnamese Dictionary. Nguyen-Dinh-Hoa. C E Tuttle.

Essential English-Vietnamese Dictionary. Hoa. Iaconi.

Hoa's Essential English-Vietnamese Dictionary. Tu-Dien Tieu-Chuan Anh-Viet. Iaconi.

Hungarian-Vietnamese Dictionary. I. Kotet. French & Eur.

Polytechnisches Woerterbuch Deutsch-Vietnamesisch. Tran Duy-Tu et al. VEB Technik.

Practical English-Vietnamese Idioms for Teachers & Students. Ed. by Nguyen-Trung Hieu. Vantage.

Russko-V'Etnamskii Slovar. (Pub. by Russkii Iazyk). Four Continent.

Standard Pronouncing English-Vietnamese Dictionary. Tu-Dien Tieu-Chuan Anh-Viet. Iaconi.

Standard Pronouncing Vietnamese English Dictionary. Tu-Dien Tuie-Chuan Viet-Anh. Iaconi.

Tu-Dien Dictionary. Pan Amer Pub.

Tu Dien Mien Dich Hoc. Y Hoc.

Vietnamese Dictionaries. Georgetown U Bil Ed Serv.

Vietnamese English Conversational Dictionary. Iaconi.

Vietnamese-English Dictionary. Ed. by Nguyen-Dinh-Hoa. C E Tuttle.

Vietnamese-English Dictionary. Nguyen-Dinh-Hoa. C E Tuttle.

Vietnamese-English Dictionary. Dinh Nguyen Hoa. Iaconi.

Vietnamese-English Dictionary Romanized. Shalom.

Vietnamese-English, English Vietnamese Dictionary. Ed. by Le-Ba-Kong & Le-Ba-Khanh. Ungar.

Vietnamese-English Phrasebook with Useful Word List. Duong Thanh Binh & William Cage. Ctr Appl Ling.

Vietnamese-English Phrasebook with Useful Word List: For English Speakers. William Gage & Duong Thanh Binh. Ctr Appl Ling.

Vietnamese-English Pocket Dictionary. Shalom.

Vietnamese Phrase Book. Nguyen-Dinh-Hoa. C E Tuttle.

Woerterbuch Vietnamesisch-Deutsch. Winfried Boscher et al. VEB Verlag Enzyklopadie.

WALBIRI

Dictionary of the Walbiri (Walpiri) Language of Central Australia. Laurie Reece. Univ Syd Aust Lang.

WALLOON

Dictionnaire Etymologique de la Langue Wallonne. Charles-Marie Grandgagnage. Slatkine.

Dictionnaire Francais-Liegois. Jean Haust. Vaillant-Carmanne.

Dictionnaire Liegeois. Jean Haust. Vaillant-Carmanne.

WELSH

The Complete Welsh-English, English-Welsh Dictionary: Y Geiriadur Mawr. H. Meurig Evans & W. O. Thomas. Humanities.

Dictionary of the Welsh Language. Wales University. Verry.

A Dictionary of the Welsh Language: Part 31. University of Wales Press. Ed. by G. A. Bevan. Verry.

Learn Welsh for English Speakers. Saphrograph.

Yr Odliadur. Roy Stephens. Lewis Ltd.

Welsh-English, English-Welsh Dictionary. H. Meurig Evans & W. O. Thomas. Saphrograph.

Y geiriadur mawr. Meurig Evans &
W. O. Thomas. Davies Dewi.
Y Geiriadur Mawr: The Complete
Welsh-English, English-Welsh
Dictionary. H. Meurig & W. O.
Thomas. Ed. by S. J. Williams.
French & Eur.

XHOSA

Xhosa-English Dictionary. J.
McLaren. Ed. by W. G. Bennie &
J. J. Jolobe. Shalom.

YAKAMA

Grammar & Dictionary of the
Yakama Language. Marie C.
Pandosy. AMS Pr.

YAPESE

Yapese-English Dictionary. John T.
Jensen et al. UH Pr.

YIDDISH

Dictionary of Yiddish Slang. Fred
Kogos. Lyle Stuart.
Encyclopedia Yiddishanica. Endel
Markowitz. Haymark.
Modern English-Yiddish, Yiddish-
English Dictionary. Uriel
Weinreich. (P&RB). McGraw.
Modern English-Yiddish Yiddish-
English Dictionary. Uriel
Weinreich. Schocken.
Modern English-Yiddish, Yiddish-
English Dictionary. Uriel
Weinreich. Yivo Inst.
The Yiddish Alphabet Book.
Frederica Postman. Illus. by Bonnie
Stone. PNye Pr.

A Yiddish Word Book for English-
Speaking People. Samuel
Rosenbaum. Van Nos Reinhold.

ZULU

English & Zulu Dictionary: English-
Zulu, Zulu-English. C. M. Doke.
Intl Learn Syst.
Zulu-English & Zulu Dictionary.
Saphrograph.
Zulu-English, English-Zulu
Dictionary. Ed. by C. M. Doke.
Heinman.

Key To Publishers' And Distributors'

Abbreviations

A & W Pubs
A & W Pubs., Inc.
95 Madison Ave., New York, NY 10016
Tel 212-725-4970 (SAN 200-2418)
(ISBN Prefix 0-89479)
A & W Visual Library *Imprint of* **A & W Pubs**

A Colin
Colin, Armand, Editeur
103 Blvd. St. Michel, F75005 Paris, France
(ISBN Prefix 2-200)

A H Clark
Clark, Arthur H., Co.
P.O. Box 230, Glendale, CA 91209
Tel 213-245-9119 (SAN 201-2006)
(ISBN Prefix 0-87062)

A. Mondadi
Mondadi, Arnoldo
CP 1772, I-20100 Milan, Italy

A R Liss
Liss, Alan R., Inc.
150 Fifth Ave., New York, NY 10011
Tel 212-741-2515 (SAN 207-7558)
(ISBN Prefix 0-8451)

A S Barnes
Barnes, A.S., & Co., Inc.
9601 Aero Dr., San Diego, CA 92123
Tel 619-560-5163 (SAN 201-2030)
(ISBN Prefix 0-498)

A Wofsy Fine Arts
Wofsy, Alan, Fine Arts
P.O. Box 2210, San Francisco, CA 94126
Tel 415-986-3030 (SAN 207-6438)
(ISBN Prefix 0-915346)

AAES
American Association of Engineering Societies
345 E. 47th St., New York, NY 10017
Tel 212-705-7840 (SAN 201-386X)
(ISBN Prefix 0-87615)

AASLH
American Association for State & Local
History
708 Berry Rd., Nashville, TN 37204
(SAN 201-1972)
(ISBN Prefix 0-910050)

AATCC
American Association Textile Chemists &
Colorists
Box 12215, Rsrch Triangle Pk, NC 27709
Tel 919-549-8141 (SAN 225-2538)

Abbeville Pr
Abbeville Press, Inc.
505 Park Ave., New York, NY 10022
Tel 212-888-1969 (SAN 211-4755)
(ISBN Prefix 0-89659)

ABC-Clio
American Bibliographical Center-Clio Press
Riviera Campus 2040 Alameda Padre Serra,
Box 4397, Santa Barbara, CA 93103
Tel 805-963-4221 (SAN 301-5467)
(ISBN Prefix 0-87436)

Aberdeen U Pr
Aberdeen Univ. Pr.
Farmers Hall, Aberdeen, AB9 2XT,
United Kingdom
(ISBN Prefix 0-08)

Abingdon
Abingdon Press
Customer Service Dept., 201 Eight Ave. S.,
Nashville, TN 37202 Tel 615-749-6301
(SAN 201-0054)
(ISBN Prefix 0-687)

Acad Can Fr
Academie Canadienne Francaise
535, ave Viger, Montreal 132e, Quebec,
Canada

Acad Intl Tour
Academie Internationale de Tourisme
4 rue des Iris, Monte-Carlo, Monaco

Acad Pr
Academic Press, Inc.
111 Fifth Ave., New York, NY 10003
Tel 212-741-6865 (SAN 206-8990)
(ISBN Prefix 0-12)

Acad Royale
Academie Royale des Lettres d'Or de France
9, Rue F. Coppee, 01120 Lozere Palaiseau,
France
(ISBN Prefix 2-902027)

Academia
Academia Press
P.O. Box 125, Oshkosh, WI 54901
Tel 414-235-8362 (SAN 201-2146)
(ISBN Prefix 0-911880)

Academy Pr-Campbell
See Academy Pr-Santa

Academy Pr-Santa
Academy Press
5227 Stevens Point, Santa Clara, CA 95051
Tel 408-241-6799 (SAN 201-2162)
(ISBN Prefix 0-912314; ISBN Prefix
0-89733)

Ace Bks
Ace Bks, Div. of Charter Communications,
Inc.
c/o Berkley/Jove Pub., 200 Madison Ave.,
New York, NY 10016 Tel 212-686-9820
(SAN 169-5800); Dist. by: ICD, 250 W.
55th St., New York, NY 10019
Tel 212-262-7444 (SAN 270-885X)
(ISBN Prefix 0-441)

Acervo
Acervo
Julio Verne, 5-7, Barcelona 6, Spain

ACI
American Concrete Institute
22400 W. Seven Mile Rd., P.O. Box 19150,
Detroit, MI 48219 Tel 313-532-2600
(SAN 203-1450)
(ISBN Prefix 0-87031)

Acribia
Acribia
Royo, 23, Saragossa 6, Spain

Acropolis
Acropolis Books
2400 17th St. N.W., Washington, DC
20009 Tel 202-387-6805 (SAN 201-2227)
(ISBN Prefix 0-87491)

Adler
Adler's Foreign Books, Inc.
162 Fifth Ave., New York, NY 10010
Tel 212-691-5151 (SAN 201-2251)
(ISBN Prefix 0-8417)

Adler Bks
Adler's Foreign Books, Inc.
162 Fifth Ave., New York, NY 10010
Tel 212-691-5151

Admin Res
See ARA

Aedos
Aedos, S.A.
Consejo de Ciento, 391, Barcelona-9, Spain

AEEI
AEEI-Associazione Elettrotecnica ed
Elettronica Italiana
Viale Monza, 259-20126 Milan, Italy

Aeonian Pr
See Amereon Ltd

Aero
Aero Pubs., Inc.
329 W. Aviation Rd., Fallbrook, CA 92028
Tel 714-728-8456 (SAN 201-2308)
(ISBN Prefix 0-8168)

Aero Products
Aero Products Research, Inc.
11201 Hindry Ave., Los Angeles, CA
90045 Tel 213-641-7242 (SAN 205-5996)
(ISBN Prefix 0-912682)

Afha Intl
Afha Internacional, S.A.
Maestro Nicolau, 4, Barcelona-21, Spain

AFUK Learmiddelfuns
AFUK Learmiddelfuns, Stichting
Postbus 53, Leeuwarden, Netherlands

Agnew Tech-Tran
Agnew Tech-Tran, Inc.
P.O. Box 789, Woodland Hills, CA 91365
Tel 213-340-5147 (SAN 212-7202)

Aguilar SP
Aguilar, S.A. de Ediciones
Juan Bravo 38, Madrid 6, Spain

Airmont
Airmont Publishing Co., Inc.
22 E. 60th St., New York, NY 10022
(SAN 206-8710)
(ISBN Prefix 0-8049)

Akad Druck
Adademische Druck und Verlagsanstalt
Auerspergasse 12, Postfach 598, 8011 Graz,
(ISBN Prefix 3-201)

Akad Verl Ath
Akademische Verlagsgesellschaft Athenaion
Zweigniederlassung der Akademischen
Verlagsgesellschaft mBH
Bandhofstr. 39, Postfach 1107, 6200
Wiesbaden, Federal Republic of Germany
(ISBN Prefix 3-7997)

Akademiai Kiado
Akademiai Kiado
Pb 24, U, Alkotmany U. 21, 1363
Budapest, Hungary

Akademische Druck Verlag
Akademische Druck und Verlagsanstalt
Amerspergasse 12, Postfach 598, 8011
Graz, Austria
(ISBN Prefix 3-201)

Akademisk Forlag
Akademisk Forlag
Store Kannikestraede 6-8 1169 Copenhagen
K, Denmark

ALA
American Library Assn.
50 E. Huron St., Chicago, IL 60611
Tel 312-944-6780 (SAN 201-0062)
(ISBN Prefix 0-8389)

Alas
Alas
Valencia 234, Barcelona 7, Spain

Alba
Alba House, Div. of the Society of St. Paul
2187 Victory Blvd., Staten Island, NY
10314 Tel 212-761-0047 (SAN 201-2405)
(ISBN Prefix 0-8189)

Alba Buchverlag
Alba Buchverlag GmbH & Co, KG
Roemerstr 9, 4000 Dusseldorf 30,
Federal Republic of Germany
(ISBN Prefix 3-87094)

Albatros
Albatros
Prague 1, Na Perstyne 1, Czechoslovakia

Alberti
Alberti, Editor
Trafalgar, 76, Barcelona-10, Spain

Albin-Michel
Albin-Michel
22, Rue Huyghens, 75014 Paris, France
(ISBN Prefix 2-226)

Albir
Albir, S.A. el Ediciones
Angeles, 8, Barcelona-1, Spain

Aldecoa
Aldecoa, S.A. Ediciones
Diego De Siloe, 18, Burgos, Spain

Aldine Pub
Aldine Publishing Co., Inc, Div. of Walter De
Gruyter, Inc.
200 Saw Mill River Rd., Hawthorne, NY
10532 Tel 914-747-0115 (SAN 212-4726)
(ISBN Prefix 0-202)

Alexander Graham
Alexander Graham Bell Assn. for the Deaf,
The
3417 Volta Place N.W., Washington, DC
20007 Tel 202-337-5220 (SAN 203-6924)
(ISBN Prefix 0-88200)

Alfa-Vydavatel
Alfa-Vydavatel'stvo Technickej A
Ekonomickej Literatury
89331 Bratislava, Hurbanovo Nam 3,
Czechoslovakia

Alfred Pub
Alfred Publishing Co., Inc.
15335 Morrison St., Suite 235, Sherman
Oaks, CA 91403 Tel 213-995-8811 (SAN
201-243X)
(ISBN Prefix 0-88284)

Alhambra
Alhambra, S. A.
Claudio Coello, 76, Madrid 1, Spain

Alianza Ed
Alianza Editorial, S.A.
Milan, 38, Madrid-33, Spain

Allen Unwin
Allen & Unwin, Inc.
9 Winchester Terrace, Winchester, MA
01890 Tel 617-729-0830 (SAN 210-3362)
Orders to:
300 Ratitan Center, Edison, NJ 08818
Tel 201-225-5555 (SAN 210-3370)
(ISBN Prefix 0-04; ISBN Prefix 0-86861)

Almar Edns
Almar Ediciones, S.A.
Compania, 5, Salamanca, Spain

Almgvist
Almgvist och Wiksell Forlag AB
Brunnsgrand 4, POB 2120, S-103 13
Stockholm, Sweden

Alonso Edns
Alonso Ediciones
Esparteros, 4, Madrid-12, Spain

Aluminium Verlag
Aluminium Verlag GmbH
Konigs Allee 30, 4000 Dusseldorf 1,
Federal Republic of Germany
(ISBN Prefix 3-87017)

Am Antiquarian
American Antiquarian Society
185 Salisbury St., Worcester, MA 01609
Tel 617-755-5221 (SAN 206-474X)
Dist. by:
Univ. Press of Virginia, P.O. Box 3608,
University Sta., Charlottesville, VA 22903
(SAN 202-5361)
(ISBN Prefix 0-912296)

Am Assn Cost Engineers
American Association of Cost Engineers
308 Monogahela Bldg., Morgantown, WV
26505 (SAN 214-0942)

Am Assn Electromyography
American Association of Electromyography &
Electrodiagnosis
732 Marquette Bank Building 200 South
Broadway, Rochester, MN 55901
Tel 507-288-0100 (SAN 224-3679)

Am Assn Mental
American Association on Mental Deficiency
5101 Wisconsin Ave., N.W., Washington,
DC 20016 Tel 202-686-5400 (SAN
206-961X)
(ISBN Prefix 0-940898)

Am Bankers
American Bankers Assn.
1120 Connecticut Ave. N.W., Washington,
DC 20036 Tel 202-467-6660 (SAN
208-4554)
(ISBN Prefix 0-89982)

Am Bible
American Bible Society
1865 Broadway, New York, NY 10023
Tel 212-581-7400 (SAN 203-5189)
(ISBN Prefix 0-8267)

Am Classical Coll Pr
American Classical College Press
P.O. Box 4526, Albuquerque, NM 87106
Tel 505-843-7749 (SAN 201-2618)
(ISBN Prefix 0-913314; ISBN Prefix
0-89266)

Am Congrs Survey
American Congress on Surveying & Mapping
210 Little Falls St., Falls Church, VA 22046
Tel 703-241-2446 (SAN 225-1531)

Am Donkey
American Donkey & Mule Society
Rte 5 Box 65, Denton, TX 76201
Tel 817-382-6845 (SAN 224-9855)

Am Fed Astrologers
American Federation of Astrologers
Box 22040, Tempe, AZ 85282 (SAN
225-1396)

Am Fisheries Soc
American Fisheries Society
5410 Grosvenor Lane, Suite 110, Bethesda,
MD 20014 Tel 301-596-3458 (SAN
284-964X); P.O. Box 1150, 10588 Jason
Ct., Columbia, MD 21044 (SAN
284-9658)
(ISBN Prefix 0-913235)

Am Foundrymen
American Foundrymen's Society
Golf & Wolf Rds., Des Plaines, IL 60016
(SAN 224-0424)

Am Gas Assn
American Gas Association
1515 Wilson Blvd, Arlington, VA 22209
Tel 703-841-8400 (SAN 224-7623)

Am Geol
American Geological Institute
One Skyline Place, 5205 Leesburg Pike,
Falls Church, VA 22041 Tel 703-379-2480
(SAN 202-4543)
(ISBN Prefix 0-913312)

Am Guidance
American Guidance Service, Inc.
Publishers' Bldg., Circle Pines, MN 55014
Tel 612-786-4343 (SAN 201-694X)
(ISBN Prefix 0-913476; ISBN Prefix
0-88671)

Am Heat Ref & Air Eng
American Society of Heating Refrigerating and
Air Conditioning Engineers, Inc.
1791 Tullie Cirlce NE, Atlanta, GA 30329
Tel 404-636-8400 (SAN 223-9809)

Am Hospital
American Hospital Assn.
840 N. Lake Shore Dr., Chicago, IL 60611
Tel 312-280-6235 (SAN 201-1603)
Orders to:
P.O. Box 96003, Chicago, IL 60693
Tel 312-280-6000 (SAN 201-1611)
(ISBN Prefix 0-87258)

Am Hotel & Motel Assn
American Hotel & Motel Association
888 Seventh Ave, New York, NY 10019
Tel 212-265-4506 (SAN 224-7917)

Am Inst Arch
American Institute of Architects
1735 New York Ave., N.W., Washington,
DC 20006 United States (SAN 277-9536)
(ISBN Prefix 0-913962)

Am Inst Indus Eng
See Inst Indus Eng

Am Inst Writing Res
American Institute for Writing Research, Corp.
Box 1364, Grand Central Sta., New York,
NY 10163 Tel 212-266-4141 (SAN
210-0290)
(ISBN Prefix 0-917944)

Am Lubrication Engs
American Society of Lubrication Engineers
838 Busse Hwy, Park Ridge, IL 60068
Tel 312-825-5536 (SAN 225-2031)

Am Lung Assn
American Lung Assn.
1740 Broadway, New York, NY 10019
(SAN 211-3503)
(ISBN Prefix 0-915116)

Am Map
American Map Corp.
46-35 54th Rd., Maspeth, NY 11378
Tel 212-784-0055 (SAN 202-4624)
(ISBN Prefix 0-8416)

Am Math
American Mathematical Society
P.O. Box 6248, Providence, RI 02940
Tel 401-272-9500 (SAN 201-1654)
Orders to:
P.O. Box 1571, Annex Sta., Providence, RI
02901 (SAN 201-1662)
(ISBN Prefix 0-8218)

Am Med Record Assn
American Medical Record Association
P.O. Box 97349, Chicago, IL 60690
Tel 312-787-2672 (SAN 224-4489)

Am Meteorological
American Meteorological Society
45 Beacon St, Boston, MA 02108
Tel 617-227-2425 (SAN 225-2139)

Am Mgmt
A M A C O M, Div. of American
Management Associations
135 W. 50th St., New York, NY 10020
Tel 212-586-8100 (SAN 201-1670)
(ISBN Prefix 0-8144)

Am Nuclear Soc
American Nuclear Society
555 N. Kensington Ave., La Grange Park,
IL 60525 Tel 312-352-6611 (SAN
207-5172)
(ISBN Prefix 0-89448)

Am Nurserymen
American Association of Nurserymen
230 Southern Bldg, Washington, DC 20005
Tel 202-737-4060 (SAN 225-0462)

Am Occup Therapy
American Occupational Therapy Association
Inc.
1383 Piccard Dr., Rockville, MD 20850
Tel 301-948-9626 (SAN 224-4705)

Am Optometric
American Optometric Foundation
4715 Cordell Ave, Washington, DC 20014
(SAN 224-4012)

Am Orient Soc
American Oriental Society
329 Sterling Memorial Library, Yale Sta.,
New Haven, CT 06520 Tel 203-436-1040
(SAN 211-3082)

Am Osteopathic
American Osteopathic Association
212 E Ohio St, Chicago, IL 60611
Tel 312-944-2713 (SAN 224-4071)

Am Petroleum
American Petroleum Institute Pubns.
2101 "L" St., N.W., Washington, DC 20037
Tel 202-833-5790 (SAN 204-5141)
(ISBN Prefix 0-89364)

Am Philos
American Philosophical Society
104 S. Fifth St., Philadelphia, PA 19106
Tel 215-627-0706 (SAN 206-9016)
(ISBN Prefix 0-87169)

Am Physiological
American Physiological Society
9650 Rockville Pike, Bethesda, MD 20014
Tel 301-530-7164 (SAN 225-2341)

Am Phytopathol Soc
American Phytopathological Society
3340 Pilot Knob Rd., St. Paul, MN 55121
Tel 612-454-7250 (SAN 212-0704)
(ISBN Prefix 0-89054)

Am Plan Assn
American Planning Association
1313 E 60th St, Chicago, IL 60637 (SAN
267-176X)

Am Political Collect
American Political Items Collectors
1054 Sharpsburg Dr., Huntsville, AL 35803
(SAN 225-5308)

Am Prod & Inventory
American Production & Inventory Control
Society
500 W. Annandale Rd., Falls Church, VA
22046 Tel 703-237-8344 (SAN 213-7208)
(ISBN Prefix 0-935406)

Am Psychiatric
American Psychiatric Assn, Subs. of American
Psychiatric Assn.
1400 K. St. N. W., Washington, DC 20005
Tel 202-682-6269 (SAN 202-4691)
(ISBN Prefix 0-89042)

Am Psychoanalytic
American Psychoanalytic Association
One E 57 St, New York, NY 10022
Tel 212-752-0450 (SAN 224-4381)

Am Psychol
American Psychological Assn.
1200 17th St., N.W., Washington, DC
20036 Tel 202-833-7600 (SAN 202-4705)
(ISBN Prefix 0-912704)

Am Public Transit
American Public Transit Association
1225 Connecticut Ave., NW, Washington,
DC 20036 Tel 202-826-2800 (SAN
224-9677)

Am Soc Ag Eng
American Society of Agricultural Engineers
2950 Niles Rd., St. Joseph, MI 49085
(SAN 223-6087)
(ISBN Prefix 0-916150)

Am Soc Civil Eng
American Society of Civil Engineers
345 E. 47th St., New York, NY 10017
Tel 212-705-7518 (SAN 204-7594)
(ISBN Prefix 0-87262)

Am Soc Intern Med
American Society of Internal Medicine
2550 M St. Nw, Suite 620, Washington,
DC 20037 (SAN 223-9817)

Am Soc QC
American Society of Quality Control
161 W Wisconsin Ave, Milwaukee, WI
53203 (SAN 225-2406)

Am Spice Trade
American Spice Trade Association
Box 1267, Englewood Clf, NJ 07632
Tel 201-568-2163 (SAN 224-7380)

Am Technical
American Technical Pubs., Inc.
12235 S. Laramie Ave., Alsip, IL 60658
Tel 800-323-3471 (SAN 206-8141)
(ISBN Prefix 0-8269)

KEY TO PUBLISHERS' AND DISTRIBUTORS' ABBREVIATIONS

Am Vacuum Soc
American Vacuum Society
335 E 45th St, New York, NY 10017
Tel 212-661-9404 (SAN 233-0512)

Am Water Wks Assn
American Water Works Assn.
6666 W. Quincy Ave., Denver, CO 80235
Tel 303-794-7711 (SAN 212-8241)
(ISBN Prefix 0-89867)

Am Welding
American Welding Society
2501 N. W. Seventh St., Miami, FL 33125
Tel 305-642-7090 (SAN 201-1700)
(ISBN Prefix 0-87171)

Am West
See Crown

AMA
American Medical Association
535 N. Dearborn St., Chicago, IL 60610
Tel 312-751-6000 (SAN 206-8516)
(ISBN Prefix 0-89970)

Amateur
Amateur
8, Rue Milton, 75009 Paris, France
(ISBN Prefix 2-85917)

Ambro Lacus
Ambro Lacus Buch und Bil Verlag
Hurtenstr. 25, 8131 Andechs,
Federal Republic of Germany
(ISBN Prefix 3-921445)

Ameller Edic
Ameller-Ediciones
Plata, 4, Barcelona 2, Spain

Amereon Ltd
Amereon Ltd.
P.O. Box 1200, Mattituck, NY 11952
Tel 516-298-5100 (SAN 201-2413)
(ISBN Prefix 0-88411; ISBN Prefix 0-89190)

American Pr
American Press
520 Commonwealth Ave., No. 416, Boston, MA 02215 Tel 617-247-0022 (SAN 210-7007)
(ISBN Prefix 0-89641)

AMG Pubs
AMG Pubs.
6815 Shallowford Rd., Chattanooga, TN 37421 (SAN 211-3074)
(ISBN Prefix 0-89957)

Amis Langue
Amis de la Langue DOc
2, Rue Peclet, 75015 Paris, France
(ISBN Prefix 2-900062)

Amphora
Amphora Editions
14, Rue de l'Odeon, 75006 Paris, France
(ISBN Prefix 2-85180)

AMS Pr
AMS Press, Inc.
56 E. 13th St., New York, NY 10003
Tel 212-777-4700 (SAN 201-1743)
(ISBN Prefix 0-404)

AMSCO Sch
AMSCO School Pubns., Inc.
315 Hudson St., New York, NY 10013
Tel 212-675-7000 (SAN 201-1751)
(ISBN Prefix 0-87720)

AMZ
AMZ
Corso Di Porta Romana, 63-30122 Milan, Italy

Anaya
Anaya
Carretera de Madrid Km 202 Santa Marta, Spain

Anch Imprint of **Doubleday**

Anchor Pr Imprint of **Doubleday**

Anderson Kramer
Anderson Kramer Associates, Inc.
1722 "H" St., N.W., Washington, DC 20006
Tel 202-298-7867 (ISBN Prefix 0-910136)

Anderson Pub Co
Anderson Publishing Co.
646 Main St., Cincinnati, OH 45201
(SAN 208-2799)
(ISBN Prefix 0-87084)

Andina
Andina, S.A. Editorial
Poligono Industrial de Pinto, Madrid, Spain

Andreas & Andreas
Andreas & Andreas
Hans Seebach-Str. 10, 5020 Salzburg, Austria

Aneto Edns
Aneto Ediciones S.A.
Alegre de Dalt, 45, Barcelona-24, Spain

Angeli
Angeli
Viale Monza, 106, 20127 Milan, Italy
(ISBN Prefix 8-8204)

Anglican Church
Anglican Church of Canada
600 Jarris St., Toronto, Ont. M4Y 2J6, Canada
(ISBN Prefix 0-919030)

Antique Collect
Antique Collectors' Club
E9, Sevana Park, Ithaca, NY 14850 (SAN 208-5003)
(ISBN Prefix 0-902028)

Ao Livro Tecnico
Ao Livro Tecnico SA Industria e Comercio
R. Sa Freire, 40, 20930 Rio de Janeiro, France

Apollo
Apollo
391 South Rd., Poughkeepsie, NY 12601
(SAN 216-101X)
(ISBN Prefix 0-938290)

Appel
Appel, Paul P., Pub.
216 Washington St., Mt. Vernon, NY 10553 Tel 914-667-7365 (SAN 202-3253)
(ISBN Prefix 0-911858)

Apt Bks
Apt Books, Inc.
141 E. 44th St., Suite 511, New York, NY 10017 (SAN 215-7209)
(ISBN Prefix 0-86590)

ARA
Administrative Research Associates
Irvine Town Ctr., Box 4211, Irvine, CA 92716 Tel 714-499-3939 (SAN 201-1891)
(ISBN Prefix 0-910022)

Aramaic Bible
Aramaic Bible Society, Inc.
P.O. Box 15307, St. Petersburg, FL 33733
Tel 813-345-1636 (SAN 204-4900)

Aranzadi Edit
Aranzadi Editorial Biblioteca de Derecho Positivo
Avenida Carlos III,·32 Pamplona, Spain

Aranzazu
Aranzazu
Santuario de Aranzazu, Onate (Guipuzcoa), Spain

ARBO
ARBO S.A.C.
Avenida Martin Garcia 653, Buenos Aires, Argentina

Arc Bks
See Arco

Arcane Order
Arcane Order Studio of Contemplation
2904 Rosemary Ln, Falls Church, VA 22042 Tel 703-536-8863 (SAN 225-4743)

Arco
Arco Publishing, Inc, Div. of Prentice-Hall, Inc.
215 Park Ave., S., New York, NY 10003
Tel 212-777-6300 (SAN 201-0003)
(ISBN Prefix 0-668)

Arden Lib
Arden Library
Mill & Main Sts., Darby, PA 19023
Tel 215-726-5505 (SAN 207-477X)
(ISBN Prefix 0-8495)

Ardis Pubs
Ardis Pubs.
2901 Heatherway, Ann Arbor, MI 48104
Tel 313-971-2367 (SAN 201-1492)
(ISBN Prefix 0-88233)

Ares
Ares Pubs., Inc.
7020 N. Western Ave., Chicago, IL 60645
Tel 312-743-1405 (SAN 205-6011)
(ISBN Prefix 0-89005)

Argos-Vergara
Argos-Vergara, S.A.
Aragon, 390, Barcelona-13, Spain

Armando
Armando
Via della Gensola, 60-61 - 00153 Rome, Italy

Arms Control
Arms Control Association, The
11 Dupont Cirlce, N.W., Washington, DC 20036 Tel 202-797-6450 (SAN 224-053X)
(ISBN Prefix 0-934766)

Arrow Bks
Arrow Books
3 Fitzroy Square, London, W1P 6JD, United Kingdom
(ISBN Prefix 0-09)

Artemis Verlag
ARTEMIS Verlags-Gesellschaft mbH
Martisstr 8, 8000 Munich 40,
Federal Republic of Germany
(ISBN Prefix 3-7608)

Artia
Artia
11127 Prague 1, Ve Smeckach 30, P.O. Box 790, Czechoslovakia

Asiatheque
Asiatheque
6, Rue Christine, 75006 Paris, France

Askin Pub
Association de l'Ecole Nationale Superieure de Bibliothecaires
16 Ennismore Av, London, W4 1SF, United Kingdom
(ISBN Prefix 0-905919)

ASM
American Society for Metals
9275 Kinsman Rd., Metals Park, OH 44073
Tel 216-338-5151 (SAN 204-7586)
(ISBN Prefix 0-87170)

ASME
American Society of Mechanical Engineers
345 E. 47th St., New York, NY 10017
Tel 212-705-7712 (SAN 201-1379)
(ISBN Prefix 0-87053)

ASP
American Society of Photogrammetry
210 Little Falls St., Falls Church, VA 22046 Tel 703-534-6617 (SAN 204-5044)
(ISBN Prefix 0-937294)

Aspen Systems
Aspen Systems Corp.
1600 Research Blvd., Rockville, MD 20850
Tel 301-251-5000 (SAN 226-2126)
(ISBN Prefix 0-912862; ISBN Prefix 0-89443)

ASSE
American Society of Safety Engineers
850 Busse Hwy., Park Ridge, IL 60068
Tel 312-692-4121 (SAN 201-7032)
(ISBN Prefix 0-939874)

Assn Child & Adult Learn
Association for Children & Adults with Learning Disabilities
4156 Library Rd., Pittsburgh, PA 15234
Tel 412-341-1515 (SAN 224-2354)
(ISBN Prefix 0-942670)

Assn Inform Image
National Micrographics Assn.
8719 Colesville Rd., Silver Spring, MD 20910 Tel 301-587-8202 (SAN 202-1021)
(ISBN Prefix 0-89258)

Assn Prog Direc
Asociacion para el Progresso de la Direccion
Montalban 3, Madrid-14, Spain

Assoc Biblio
Association de 'Ecole Nationale Superieure de Bibliothecaires
17-21, Blvd. Du 11 Novembre, 69621
Villeu Banne, France
(ISBN Prefix 2-901119)

Assoc Bk
Associated Booksellers
147 McKinley Ave., P.O. Box 6361, Bridgeport, CT 06606 Tel 203-366-5494 (SAN 169-0655)
(ISBN Prefix 0-87497)

Assoc Faculty Pr
Associated Faculty Press
90 South Bayles Ave., Port Washington, NY 11050 Tel 914-332-4030 (SAN 281-2932); 110 W. 57th Street, New York, NY 10019 (SAN 281-2940)
(ISBN Prefix 0-86733)

Assoc Mus
Associated Music Publishers G. Schirmer, Inc, Subs. of G. Shirmer, Inc.
866 Third Ave., New York, NY 10022
(SAN 222-9544)
(ISBN Prefix 0-911320)

ASTM
American Society for Testing & Materials
1916 Race St., Philadelphia, PA 19103
Tel 215-299-5400 (SAN 201-1344)
(ISBN Prefix 0-8031)

Astor-Honor
Astor-Honor, Inc.
48 E. 43rd St., New York, NY 10017
(SAN 203-5022)
(ISBN Prefix 0-8392)

549

Astrolabio
Astrolabio
Via Guido d'Arezzo, 16-00198 Rome, Italy
ASU Lat Am St
Arizona State Univ., Center for Latin
American Studies
Tempe, AZ 85281 Tel 602-965-5127
(SAN 201-1336)
(ISBN Prefix 0-87918)
Ateneo & Bizzarri
Ateneo & Bizzarri
Via Nazionale, 246-00184 Rome, Italy
Ateneo Edit
Ateneo Editorial El
Patagones 2463 - 1282 Buenos Aires,
Argentina
Atheneum
Atheneum Pubs.
597 Fifth Ave., New York, NY 10017
Tel 212-486-2700 (SAN 201-0011); 122
E. 42nd St., New York, NY 10017 (SAN
209-3162)
Dist. by:
The Scribner Book Companies, 201
Willowbrook Blvd., Wayne, NJ 07470
(SAN 201-002X)
(ISBN Prefix 0-689)
Atlantica
Atlantica
Via Gramsci, 11a-71043 Manfredonia
(Foggia), Italy
Atlas Edns
Atlas Ediciones
Lope de Vega, 18, Madrid-14, Spain
Attic Pr
Attic Press
Stony Point, Rte. 2, Greenwood, SC 29646
Tel 803-374-3013 (SAN 201-1328)
(ISBN Prefix 0-87921)
Auer
Auer, Ludwig, Padagogische Stiftung Cassiane
um Verlag Buchhandlung Druckerei
Heilig-Kreuz Str. 12-16, D 8850
Donauworth,
Federal Republic of Germany
(ISBN Prefix 3-403)
Augusta SA
Augusta S. A.
Ntra. Sra. del Coll, 14, Barcelona 23, Spain
Aulis Verlag
Aulis Verlag Deubner & Co. KG
Antwerpener Str 6-12, 5000 Cologne 1,
Federal Republic of Germany
Aunamendi Edit
Aunamendi Editorial
Apartado 2 GN. Kutxatilla Donostia - San
Sebastian, Spain
Aurea
Aurea Pubns.
P.O. Box 176, Allenhurst, NJ 07711
Tel 201-531-4535 (SAN 203-5081)
(ISBN Prefix 0-87174)
Auromere
Auromere, Inc.
1291 Weber St., Pomona, CA 91768
Tel 714-629-8255 (SAN 169-0043)
(ISBN Prefix 0-89744)
Aurora Edns
Aurora Ediciones
Rafael Calvo, 30, Madrid-10, Spain
Aussant & Schrift
Aussant-und-Schriftenmissions-Verlag GmbH
Wittensteinstr 110-114 Postfach 200735,
D-5600 Wupperrtal 2,
Federal Republic of Germany
Automation in Housing Mag
Automation in Housing
P.O. Box 120, Carpinteria, CA 93014
Tel 805-684-7659 (SAN 239-1589)
(ISBN Prefix 0-9607408)
Autores-Editores
Autores-Editores de Obras Propias Madrid
Madrid, Spain
AVE
AVE-Anonima Vertias Editrice
Via Della Conciliazione, 1-00193 Rome,
Italy
Ave Maria
Ave Maria Press
Notre Dame, IN 46556 Tel 219-287-2831
(SAN 201-1255)
(ISBN Prefix 0-87793)
Avebury Pub Co
Avebury Publishing Co. Ltd.
Olympic House, 1 63 Woodside Rd.,
Amersham, Bucks. HP6 5AA,
United Kingdom
(ISBN Prefix 0-86127)

Aviation
Aviation Book Co.
1640 Victory Blvd., Glendale, CA 91201
Tel 213-240-1771 (SAN 120-1530); P.O.
Box 4187, Glendale, CA 91202 (SAN
213-4993)
(ISBN Prefix 0-911720; ISBN Prefix
0-911721)
Aviation Maintenance
Aviation Maintenance Pubs.
P.O. Box 890, Basin, WY 82410
Tel 307-568-2413 (SAN 209-3189)
(ISBN Prefix 0-89100)
Avon
Avon Books
1790 Broadway, New York, NY 10019
Tel 212-399-4500 (SAN 201-4009)
(ISBN Prefix 0-380)
Ayer Co
Ayer Co.
99 Main St., Salem, NY 03079
Tel 617-683-8741 (SAN 211-6936)
(ISBN Prefix 0-88143)
Ayer Pr
Ayer Pr.
1 Bala Ave., Bala Cynwyd, PA 19004
Tel 215-664-6203 (SAN 204-5427)
(ISBN Prefix 0-910190)
B C Scribe
Scribe, B. C., Pubns.
P.O. Box 2453, Providence, RI 02906-0453
Tel 401-831-5069 (SAN 212-1727)
(ISBN Prefix 0-930548)
B Costa-Amic
Costa-Amic, B.
Mesones 14, Mexico, DF, Mexico
B Franklin
Franklin, Burt, Pub.
Dist. by:
Lenox Hill Publishing & Distributing Corp.,
235 E. 44th St., New York, NY 10017
(SAN 282-597X)
(ISBN Prefix 0-89102)
Baha'i
Baha'i Publishing Trust
415 Linden Ave., Wilmette, IL 60091
Tel 312-251-1854 (SAN 213-7496)
(ISBN Prefix 0-87743)
Bailliere
Bailliere & Fils
19, Rue Hautefeuille, 75006 Paris, France
Bailliere-Tindall *Imprint of* **Saunders**
Baker Bk
Baker Book House
P.O. Box 6287, Grand Rapids, MI 49506
Tel 616-676-9186 (SAN 201-4041)
(ISBN Prefix 0-8010)
Ballantine
Ballantine Books, Inc, Div. of Random House,
Inc.
201 E. 50th St., New York, NY 10022
Tel 212-751-2600 (SAN 214-1175)
Orders to:
400 Hahn Rd., Westminster, MD 21157
(SAN 214-1183)
(ISBN Prefix 0-345)
Ballinger Pub
Ballinger Publishing Co, Subs. of Harper &
Row, Inc.
54 Church St., P.O. Box 281, Harvard
Square, Cambridge, MA 02138
Tel 617-492-0670 (SAN 201-4084)
(ISBN Prefix 0-88410; ISBN Prefix
0-88730)
Banbury *Imprint of* **Dell**
B&N
See B&N Imports
B&N Imports
Barnes & Noble Books-Imports, Div. of
Littlefield, Adams & Co.
81 Adams Dr., Totowa, NJ 07512
Tel 201-256-8600 (SAN 206-7803)
(ISBN Prefix 0-389)
B&N NY
Barnes & Noble Books, Div. of Harper & Row
10 E. 53rd St., New York, NY 10022
Tel 212-593-7000 (SAN 238-4906)
Bantam
Bantam Books, Inc.
666 Fifth Ave., New York, NY 10019
Tel 212-765-6500 (SAN 201-3975)
Orders to:
414 E. Golf Rd., Des Plaines, IL 60016
(SAN 201-3983)
(ISBN Prefix 0-553)
Baptist Span
See Casa Bautista

Barcino Edit
Barcino Editorial
Montseny, 9, Barcelona-12, Spain
Barreiro & Ramos
Barreiro y Ramos, S.A.
Juan Carlos Gomez 1430, Montevideo,
Uruguay
Barron
Barron's Educational Series, Inc.
113 Crossways Park Dr., Woodbury, NY
11797 Tel 516-921-8750 (SAN
201-453X)
(ISBN Prefix 0-8120)
Basil Blackwell
See Biblio Dist
Battenberg
Battenberg, Ernst, Verlag
Prinzregentenstr. 79, 8000 Munich 80,
Federal Republic of Germany
(ISBN Prefix 3-87045)
Baudry
Baudry, Gerard Henry
60, Boulevard Vauban, 59000 Lille, France
Bauverlag
Bauverlag GmbH
Wittesbacherstr 10, Postfach 1460, D-6200
Wiesbaden 1,
Federal Republic of Germany
(ISBN Prefix 3-7626)
Beacon
See Beacon Hill
Beacon Hill
Beacon Hill Pr. of Kansas City
Dist. by:
Nazarene Pub. Hse., P.O. Box 527, Kansas
City, MO 64141 Tel 816-931-1900 (SAN
202-9022)
(ISBN Prefix 0-8341)
Beauchesne
Beauchesne
72 Rue des Saint-Peres, 75007 Paris,
France
(ISBN Prefix 2-7010)
Beck Verlag
Beck, Oscar, Verlagsbuchhandlung
Wilhelmstr. 9, 8000 Munich 40,
Federal Republic of Germany
(ISBN Prefix 3-406)
Beekman Pubs
Beekman Pubs., Inc.
P.O. Box 888, Woodstock, NY 12498
Tel 914-679-2300 (SAN 201-4467)
(ISBN Prefix 0-8464)
Beginner
Beginner Books, Div. of Random House, Inc.
201 E. 50th St., New York, NY 10022
(SAN 202-3288)
Orders to:
400 Hahn Rd., Westminster, MD 21157
(SAN 202-3296)
Behavioral Re
See Learning Line
Behrman
Behrman House, Inc.
1261 Broadway, New York, NY 10001
Tel 212-689-2020 (SAN 201-4459)
(ISBN Prefix 0-87441)
Belfond
Belfond, Pierre
3 bis, Rue de la Petite-Boucherie, 75006
Paris, France
(ISBN Prefix 2-7144)
Belin
Belin
8, Rue Ferou, 75006 Paris, France
(ISBN Prefix 2-7011)
Bell Ent
Bell Enterprises, Inc.
P.O. Box 9054, Pine Bluff, AR 71611
Tel 501-247-1922 (SAN 209-1895)
(ISBN Prefix 0-918340)
Bellaterra
Bellaterra, S.A. Edicones
Felipe De Paz, 12, Barcelona 28, Spain
Belles Lettres
Belles Lettres
95, Blvd. Raspail, 75006, France
(ISBN Prefix 2-251)
Beltz & Co
Beltz, Julius, GmbH & Co. KG
Am Hauptbahnhof 10, Postfach 1120, 6940
Weinheim Bergstr.,
Federal Republic of Germany
(ISBN Prefix 3-407)
Benjamins
Benjamins, John B. V.
Amsteldyk 44, Amsterdam, Netherlands

Benjamins North Am
Benjamins, John, North America
One Buttonwood Sq-202, Philadelphia, PA
19130 Tel 215-564-6379   (SAN 219-7677)
(ISBN Prefix 90-272)

Bennett Co
See Bennett Il

Bennett Il
Bennett Publishing Co.
809 W. Detweiller Dr., Peoria, IL 61615
Tel 309-691-4454   (SAN 201-4440)
(ISBN Prefix 0-87002)

Benziger
See Glencoe

Beogradski
Beogradski Izdavacko-Graficki Zabod
YU-11000 Belgrade, Blvd. Vojode Misica
17, Postanski Fah 340, Yugoslavia

Berben
Berben
Via Redipuglia, 30-60100 Ancona, Italy

Berger Levrault
Berger-Levrault
5, Rue Auguste-Comte, 75006 Paris, France
(ISBN Prefix 2-7013)

Berkeley Slavic
Berkeley Slavic Specialities
P.O. Box 3034, Oakland, CA 94609
Tel 415-653-8048   (SAN 212-7245)
(ISBN Prefix 0-933884)

Berkley Pub
Berkley Publishing Corp, Affiliate of G. P.
Putnam's Sons
200 Madison Ave., New York, NY 10016
Tel 212-686-9820   (SAN 201-3991)
Dist. by:
ICD, 250 W. 55th St., New York, NY
10019 Tel 212-262-7444   (SAN 169-5800)
(ISBN Prefix 0-425)

Berlingske Forlag
Berlingske Forlag A-S
Antonigade 7, 1147 Copenhagen K,
Denmark

Berlitz
Berlitz
31, Boulevard des Italiens, 75002 Paris,
France

Berlitz *Imprint of* **Macmillan**

Bersez
Bersez, Jacques
24, Route de Melun, 77580 Voulangis
Crecy-En-Brie, France

Bess Pr
Bess Press
P.O. Box 22388, Honolulu, HI 96822
(SAN 239-4111)
(ISBN Prefix 0-935848)

Bethany Fell
See Bethany Hse

Bethany Hse
Bethany House Pubs.
6820 Auto Club Rd., Minneapolis, MN
55438 Tel 612-944-2121   (SAN 201-4416)
(ISBN Prefix 0-87123)

Bianco
Bianco
Via in Arctione, 71-00187 Rome, Italy

Biblical Res Assocs
Biblical Research Associates Inc.
The College of Wooster, Wooster, OH
44691 Tel 216-263-2000   (SAN 211-2876)
(ISBN Prefix 0-935106)

Biblio Apost
Biblioteca Apostolica Vaticana
Citta del Vaticano, Italy

Biblio Dist
Biblio Distribution Centre
81 Adams Dr., Totowa, NJ 07512
Tel 201-256-8600   (SAN 211-724X)

Biblio Inst
Bibliographisches Institut AG
Dudenstr 6, Postfach 311, D-6800
Mannheim 1,
Federal Republic of Germany

Biblio Nacional
Biblioteca Nacional
18 de Julio 1790 Montevideo, Uruguay

Biblio-Verlag
Biblio-Verlag GmbH & Co, KG
Jahnstr. 15, Postf 1949, 4500 Osnabruck,
Federal Republic of Germany
(ISBN Prefix 3-7648)

Bibliografica
Bibliografica
Viale Vittorio Veneto, 24, 20124, Milan,
Italy
(ISBN Prefix 8-87075)

Bibliotek AB
Biblioteksforlaget AB
P.O. Box 14143, S-104 41 Stockholm,
Sweden

Bibliotekscentralen
Bibliotekscentralen
Telegravej 5, 2750 Ballerup, Denmark
(ISBN Prefix 8-7552)

Biblo
Biblo & Tannen Booksellers & Pubs., Inc.
321 Sandbank Rd., P.O. Box 302, Cheshire,
CT 06410 Tel 203-272-2308   (SAN
202-4071)
(ISBN Prefix 0-8196)

Bietti
Bietti SPA
Via Crescenzio 58, I-00193 Rome, Italy

Bignami
Bignami
Via Balzaretti, 6-20133 Milan, Italy

Biling Rev Pr
Bilingual Review Press, Department of Foreign
Languages & Bilingual Studies
106 Ford Hall, Eastern Michigan
University, Ypsilanti, MI 48197
Tel 313-487-0042

Bilingual Ed Serv
Bilingual Educational Services, Inc.
2514 S. Grand Ave., Los Angeles, CA
90007   (SAN 218-4680)
(ISBN Prefix 0-86624)

Bilingual Pubns
Bilingual Publications & Cultural Services
14 Washington Pl., New York, NY 10003
Tel 212-986-4800   (SAN 208-5534)
(ISBN Prefix 0-916576)

Binford
Binford & Mort Pubs.
2536 S.E. 11th Ave., Portland, OR 97202
Tel 503-238-9666   (SAN 201-4386)
(ISBN Prefix 0-8323)

Bio Res Inst
See World Natural Hist

Birkhauser
Birkhauser Boston Inc.
380 Green St., Cambridge, MA 02139
Tel 617-876-2334   (SAN 213-2869)
(ISBN Prefix 0-8176)

Blaine Ethridge
See Ethridge

Bloch
Bloch Publishing Co.
19 W. 21st St., New York, NY 10010
Tel 212-989-9104   (SAN 214-204X)
(ISBN Prefix 0-8197)

Blume Edit
Blume Editorial
Malanesado, 21-23, Barceona-17, Spain

BLV Verlag
BLV Verlagsgesellschaft mbH
Lothstr. 29, 8000 Munich 40,
Federal Republic of Germany
(ISBN Prefix 3-405)

BNA
Bureau of National Affairs, Inc.
1231 25th St., N.W., Washington, DC
20037 Tel 202-452-4402   (SAN 201-4262)
(ISBN Prefix 0-87179)

Board Jewish Educ
Board of Jewish Education of Greater New
York
426 W. 58th St, New York, NY 10019
Tel 212-245-8200   (SAN 213-0165)

Bob Jones Univ Pr
Jones, Bob University Press
Greenville, SC 29614   (SAN 284-5490)
(ISBN Prefix 0-89084)

Bobbs
Bobbs-Merrill Co., Inc, A Thomas Audel Co.
630 Third Ave., New York, NY 10017
Tel 212-697-7050   (SAN 201-3959)
(ISBN Prefix 0-672)

Boccard
Boccard
11, Rue de Medicis, 75006 Paris, France
(ISBN Prefix 2-7018)

Bola Pubns
Bola Pubns
8769 Devon Ave., Hesperia, CA 92345
Tel 619-244-6050   (SAN 240-3439)
(ISBN Prefix 0-943118)

Bompiani
Bompiani
Via Mecenate 91, I-20138 Milan, Italy

Bonanno
Bonanno
Via Vittorio Emanuele, 188-95024 Acireale
(Catania), Italy

Bonnier Forlag
Bonnier, Albert, Forlag AB
Sveavagen 56, Box 3159, 10363 Stockholm
3, Sweden

Book-Lab
Book-Lab, Inc.
500 74 St., North Bergen, NJ 07047
Tel 201-861-6763   (SAN 201-422X)
(ISBN Prefix 0-87594)

Bordas
Bordas Dunod
24-26 Blvd. de l'Hopital, 75005 Paris,
France
(ISBN Prefix 2-04)

Bordas-Dunod
Bordas-Dunod Bruxelles, S.A.
44 rue Otlet, B-1070 Brussels, Belgium

Borden
Borden Publishing Co.
1855 W. Main St., Alhambra, CA 91801
Tel 213-283-5031   (SAN 201-419X)
(ISBN Prefix 0-87505)

Borderie
Borderie
B. P. 1 les Pilles, 26110 Nyons, France
(ISBN Prefix 2-86380)

Borgo Pr
Borgo Press
P.O. Box 2845, San Bernardino, CA 92406
Tel 714-884-5813   (SAN 208-9459)
(ISBN Prefix 0-89370)

Boringhieri
Boringhieri
Corso Vittorio Emanuele, 86-10124 Turin,
Italy

Bornstein Memory
Bornstein Memory Training Schools
11693 San Vicente Blvd., W. Los Angeles,
CA 90049 Tel 213-478-2056   (SAN
213-0181)
(ISBN Prefix 0-9602610)

Bornstein Memory Schls
See Bornstein Memory

Bosch Casa
Bosch Casa Editorial, S.A.
Urgel, 51 bis, Barcelona-11, Spain

Bottega de'Erasmo
Bottega de'Erasmo
Via Ferrari, 9-10124 Turin, Italy

Bourdeaus
Bourdeaus-Capelle, S.A.
69 rue Sax, B-5500 Dinant, Belgium

Bout
Bout, Pierre
27, Cottages des Paulines, 63100
Clermont-Ferrand, France

Bowker
Bowker, R. R., Co, A Xerox Information Co.
205 E. 42nd St., New York, NY 10017
Tel 212-916-1600   (SAN 214-1191)
Orders to:
P.O. Box 1807, Ann Arbor, MI 48106
(SAN 214-1205)
(ISBN Prefix 0-8352)

Bowmar
See Bowmar-Noble

Bowmar-Noble
Bowmar/Noble Pubs, Div. of The Economy
Company
4563 Colorado Blvd., Los Angeles, CA
90039 Tel 213-247-8995   (SAN 201-4157)
(ISBN Prefix 0-8372; ISBN Prefix 0-8107)

Bradson
Bradson Press
120 Longfellow St., Thousand Oaks, CA
91360 Tel 805-496-8212   (SAN 213-7267)
(ISBN Prefix 0-9603574)

Bradt Ent
Bradt Enterprises Pubns.
93 Harvey St., Apt. 8, Cambridge, MA
02140 Tel 617-492-8776   (SAN
169-328X)
(ISBN Prefix 0-933982; ISBN Prefix
0-9505797)

Branden
Branden Press, Inc.
Box 843, 21 Sta. St., Brookline Village, MA
02147 Tel 617-734-2045   (SAN 201-4106)
(ISBN Prefix 0-8283)

Brandstetter
Brandstetter, Oscar, Verlag
Stiftstr 30, Postfach 1708, D-6200
Wiesbaden, Federal Republic of Germany

Brepols
Brepols
6, Rue du Vieux Colombier, 75006 Paris,
France
(ISBN Prefix 2-85006)

Brick Inst Amer
Brick Institute of America
1750 Old Meadow Road, McLean, VA
22102 (SAN 241-3647)
Bridge Pub
Bridge Publishing Co.
2500 Hamilton Blvd., South Plainfield, NJ
08805 Tel 201-754-0745 (SAN 239-5061)
Bridge Pubns Inc
Bridge Pubns. Inc.
1414 N. Catalina St., Los Angeles, CA
90027 Tel 213-382-0382 (SAN 208-3884)
(ISBN Prefix 0-88404)
Brill
Brill
Dude Ryn 33a, Leiden, Netherlands
Brill Verlag
Brill, E. J., GmbH Buchhandel und Druckerel,
Verlag Orientbuchhandlung
Am Friesenlatz, Antwerpener Str. 6-12,
5000 Cologne 1,
Federal Republic of Germany
(ISBN Prefix 3-7652)
British Am Bks
British American Books
P. O. Box 302, Willits, CA 95490 (SAN
201-9353)
(ISBN Prefix 0-89979)
Broadman
Broadman Press
127 Ninth Ave., N., Nashville, TN 37234
Tel 615-251-2544 (SAN 281-3440)
(ISBN Prefix 0-8054)
Brooks-Cole
Brooks/Cole Publishing Co, Div. of
Wadsworth, Inc.
555 Abrego St., Monterey, CA 93940
Tel 408-373-0728 (SAN 202-3369)
Orders to:
Wadsworth, Inc., Customer Service Ctr.,
7625 Empire Dr., Florence, KY 41042
Tel 800-354-9706 (SAN 200-2213)
(ISBN Prefix 0-8185)
Broude
Broude Brothers Ltd., Music
170 Varick St., New York, NY 10013
Tel 212-242-7001 (SAN 281-3483); 141
White Oaks Rd., Williamstown, MA 01267
(SAN 281-3491)
(ISBN Prefix 0-8450)
Brown Bk
Brown Book Co.
120 Secatogue Ave., Farmingdale, NY
11735 Tel 516-293-6969 (SAN 202-4276)
(ISBN Prefix 0-910294)
Bruccoli
Bruccoli Clark Books
2006 Sumter St., Columbia, SC 29201
(SAN 209-3987)
(ISBN Prefix 0-89723)
Bruce Pub Co
See Glencoe
Bruckmann
Bruckmann, F., KG
Nymphenburger Str. 86, 8000 Munich 20,
Federal Republic of Germany
(ISBN Prefix 3-7654)
Bruguera
Bruguera, S.A. Editorial
Camps y Fabies, 5 Barcelona-6, Spain
Bruguera MX
Bruguera Mexicana de Ediciones S. A.
Popocatepetl No. 421-6 Col. Grad. Anaya,
Mexico 13, D.F., Mexico
Bruna
Bruna
Postbus 8181, 3526 Utrecht, Netherlands
Brunner-Mazel
Brunner, Mazel, Inc.
19 Union Square W., New York, NY 10003
Tel 212-924-3344 (SAN 164-9167)
(ISBN Prefix 0-87630)
Bruno Assoc
Bruno Associates
5811 Santa Catalina Ave., Garden Grove,
CA 92645 Tel 714-897-8204
Brunswick Pub
Brunswick Publishing Co.
P.O. Box 555, Lawrenceville, VA 23868
Tel 804-848-3865 (SAN 211-6332)
(ISBN Prefix 0-931494)
Bruylant
Bruylant, Emile
Bruxelles, Belgium
(ISBN Prefix 2-8027)

BSA
Boy Scouts of America
1325 Walnut Hill Lane, Irving, TX 75062
Tel 214-659-2285 (SAN 284-9798)
Orders to:
Eastern Distribution Ctr., 2109
Westinghouse Blvd., P.O. Box 7143,
Charlotte, NC 28217 Tel 704-588-4260
(SAN 284-9801)
(ISBN Prefix 0-8395)
Bucalo
Bucalo
Via Bixio, 8-04100 Latina, Italy
Buch Vertrieb
Buch Vertrieb Hager GmbH
Mainzelandstr 147, Postfach 119151,
D-6000 Frankfurt Am Main 2,
Federal Republic of Germany
(ISBN Prefix 3-88145)
Bucher
Bucher, C. J., Verlag GmbH
Borsigallee 17, 6000 Frankfurt am Main 60,
Federal Republic of Germany
(ISBN Prefix 3-7658)
Buchet Chastel
Buchet Chastel
18, Rue de Conde, 75006 Paris, France
Buchhandlung
Verlag der Francke Buchhandlung GmbH
Am Schwanhof 19, Postfach 640, D-3550
Marburg/Lahn,
Federal Republic of Germany
Buffetti
Buffetti
Via Paola, 41-00186 Rome, Italy
Bulzoni
Bulzoni
Via dei Liburni, 14-00185 Rome, Italy
Bund
Bund-Verlag GmbH
Deutz-Kalker Str 46, Postfach 210140,
D-5000 Cologne 21,
Federal Republic of Germany
Bureau Marcel
Bureau Marcel Van Dijk
57, Rue Sainte-Anne, 75002 Paris, France
(ISBN Prefix 2-9500203)
Bureau Recherches
Bureau de Recherches Geologiques et
Minerales
74, Rue de la Federation, 75015 Paris,
France
(ISBN Prefix 2-7159)
Burgess-Intl Ideas
Burgess, Jack K. Inc., -International Ideas Inc.
Orders to:
Jack K. Burgess, Inc., 2175 Lemoine Ave.,
Fort Lee, NJ 07024 Tel 201-592-0739
(SAN 220-1356); Orders to: International
Ideas Inc., 1627 Spruce St., Philadelphia,
PA 19103 Tel 215-546-0392 (SAN
210-6043)
Burrows & Baker
Burrows & Baker
201 E. 21st St., New York, NY 10010
(SAN 223-2618)
(ISBN Prefix 0-930414)
Buske
Buske, Helmut
Schluterstr. 14, 2000 Hamburg 13,
Federal Republic of Germany
(ISBN Prefix 3-87118)
Busn *Imprint of* **P-H**
Butterworth
Butterworth Pubs., Inc.
10 Tower Office Park, Woburn, MA 01801
Tel 617-933-8260 (SAN 206-3964)
Butterworths
See Butterworth
BYR *Imprint of* **Random**
C B Pub & Dist
See Caratzas Pub Co
C Bertelsmann
Bertelsmann, C., Verlag GmbH
Neumarkterstr 18, D-8000 Munich 80,
Federal Republic of Germany
C C Thomas
Thomas, Charles C., Pub.
2600 S. First St., Springfield, IL 62717
Tel 217-789-8980 (SAN 201-9485)
(ISBN Prefix 0-398)
C E Barbour
Barbour, Clifford E., Library
Pittsburgh Theological Seminary, 616 N.
Highland Ave., Pittsburgh, PA 15206
Tel 412-362-5610 (SAN 209-6560)
(ISBN Prefix 0-931222)

C E Tuttle
Tuttle, Charles E., Co., Inc.
P.O. Box 410, 28 S. Main St., Rutland, VT
05701 Tel 802-773-8229 (SAN 213-2621)
(ISBN Prefix 0-8048)
C Gallo
Gallo, Cristino
1107 E. Ocean View Ave. No. 9, Norfolk,
VA 23503 Tel 804-587-7744 (SAN
214-3062)
Dist. by:
Book Service of Puerto Rico, 102 Avenida
De Diego, Santurce, PR 00907 (SAN
214-3070)
(ISBN Prefix 0-9604174)
C J Hogrefe
Hogrefe, C. J., Inc.
P.O. Box 51, Lewiston, NY 14092 (SAN
240-8600)
(ISBN Prefix 0-88937)
Cahners
See CBI Pub
Callwey
Callwey, Georg D. W.
Streitfeldstr 35, 8000 Munich 80,
Federal Republic of Germany
(ISBN Prefix 3-7667)
Calmann Levy
Calmann Levy
3, Rue Auber, 75009 Paris, France
Camaro Pub
Camaro Publishing Co.
Worldway Postal Sta., P.O. Box 90430, Los
Angeles, CA 90009 Tel 213-837-7500
(SAN 201-7865)
(ISBN Prefix 0-913290)
Cambridge Bk
Cambridge Bk. Co, Div. of Esquire, Inc.
888 Seventh Ave., New York, NY 10022
Tel 212-957-5300 (SAN 169-5703)
(ISBN Prefix 0-8428)
Cambridge U Pr
Cambridge Univ. Press
32 E. 57th St., New York, NY 10022
Tel 212-688-8888 (SAN 281-3750)
Orders to:
510 North Ave., New Rochelle, NY 10801
Tel 914-235-0300 (SAN 281-3769)
(ISBN Prefix 0-521)
Camden Aus
Camden, W.
Eastwood, Australia
(ISBN Prefix 0-9596774)
Camden Hse
Camden House, Inc.
Drawer 2025, Columbia, SC 29202 (SAN
215-9376)
(ISBN Prefix 0-938100)
Camelot Pub
Camelot Publishing Co.
P.O. Box 1357, Ormond Beach, FL 32074
Tel 904-672-5672 (SAN 202-5035)
(ISBN Prefix 0-89218)
Camino Real
Camino Real Book Store
P.O. Box 25426 Denver Federal Center,
Building 41, Denver, CO 80225
Tel 303-233-7586
Can Inst Chart Accts
Canadian Institute of Chartered Accountants
250 Bloor St. E., Toronto, Ontario M4W
1G5, Canada Tel 416-962-1242
Can Securities Inst
Canadian Securities Institute
Commerce Ct. S., 2nd Flr., Box 225,
Toronto, Ontario M5L 1E8, Canada
Tel 416-364-9130
Can Soc Petro Geo
Canadian Society of Petroleum Geologists
612 Lougheed Bldg., Calgary, Alberta T2P
1M7, Canada
Canadian Inst Chart
Canadian Institute of Chartered Accountants
250 Bloor St. E Suite 1109, Toronto, Ont,
M4W 1G5, Canada
(ISBN Prefix 0-88800)
Canova
Canova
Via Pancera, 3b - 31100 Treviso, Italy
Cantabrica
Cantabrica, S.A. Editorial
Plaza Conde de Aresti, 5, Bilbao-9, Spain
Capital-Dischi
Capital-Dischi CEB
Via Minghetti, 17-19 - 40057 Cadriano di
Granarolo E. (Bo), Italy

Capitol Edit
Capitol Editrice Dischi CEB
CP 441 I-40100 Bologna, Italy

Capone C
Capone C.
Via Morazzone, 16- 10132 Turin, Italy

Capou
Capou, Gerard, Editions
81170 Cordes, France
(ISBN Prefix 2-903141)

Caratzas Bros
See Caratzas Pub Co

Caratzas Pub Co
Caratzas Publishing Co., Inc.
481 Main St. (P.O. Box 210), New
Rochelle, NY 10801 Tel 914-632-8487
(SAN 201-3134)
(ISBN Prefix 0-89241)

Career Inst
Career Institute, Inc, Div. of Singer
Communications Corp.
1500 Cardinal Dr., Little Falls, NJ 07424
Tel 201-256-4512 (SAN 202-5132)
(ISBN Prefix 0-911744)

Career Pub
Career Publishing, Inc.
931 N. Main St., P.O. Box 5486, Orange,
CA 92667 Tel 800-854-4014 (SAN
208-581X)
(ISBN Prefix 0-89262)

Carl KG
Carl, Hans, KG
Breite Gasse 58-60, Postfach 9110, 8500
Nuremberg 1,
Federal Republic of Germany
(ISBN Prefix 3-418)

Carlton
Carlton Press
84 Fifth Ave., New York, NY 10011
Tel 212-243-8800 (SAN 201-9655)
(ISBN Prefix 0-8062)

Carolina Pop Ctr
Carolina Population Center, The Univ. of
North Carolina at Chapel Hill
Population Pubns., University Sq. 300A,
Chapel Hill, NC 27514 Tel 919-966-2152
(SAN 201-7687)
(ISBN Prefix 0-89055)

Caroline Hse
Caroline Hse., Inc.
920 W. Industrial Dr., Aurora, IL 60506
Tel 312-897-2050 (SAN 211-2280)

Carta Pub Co
Carta, The Israel Map & Publishing Co.
Yad Harutzim St., P.O. Box 2500,
Jerusalem, Israel

Carucci
Carucci Beniamino
Via Banchi Nuovi, 39 00186 Roma, Italy

Casa Bautista
Casa Bautista De Publicaciones
P.O. Box 4255, 7000 Alabama St., El Paso,
TX 79914 Tel 915-566-9656 (SAN
220-0139)
(ISBN Prefix 0-311)

Cascade Bks
Cascade Books
985 S.W. Westwood Dr., Portland, OR
97201 (SAN 205-6089)
(ISBN Prefix 0-913704)

Castalia Edit
Castalia Editorial
Zurbano, 39, Madrid-10, Spain

Castell
Castell Ediciones S.A.
Consejo de Ciento, 341, Barcelona -11,
Spain

Castellana
Castellana Editorial
Avda. De Filipinas, 52, Madrid-3, Spain

Casterman
Casterman
66 Rue Bonaparte, 75006 Paris, France
(ISBN Prefix 2-203)

Castilla
Castilla, S. A.
Maestro Alonso, 21-23, Madrid 28, Spain

Castro Edns
Castro Ediciones Del
Sada (la Coruna), Spain

Cath Health
Catholic Health Association, The
4455 Woodson Rd., St. Louis, MO 63134
Tel 314-427-2500 (SAN 201-968X)
(ISBN Prefix 0-87125)

Cath Hospital
See Cath Health

Cath U Pr
Catholic Univ. of America Press
620 Michigan Ave., N.E., Washington, DC
20064 Tel 202-635-5052 (SAN 203-6290)
Orders to:
P.O. Box 4852, Hampden Sta., Baltimore,
MD 21211 Tel 301-338-7817 (SAN
203-6304)
(ISBN Prefix 0-8132)

Catolica Edit
Catolica Editorial
Mateo Inurria, 15, Madrid 16, Spain

CBI Pub
CBI Publishing Co. Inc, Division of the
International Thompson Organisation
51 Sleeper St., Boston, MA 02210
Tel 617-426-2224 (SAN 201-9515)
(ISBN Prefix 0-8436)

CDU
C. D. U.
Paris, France

CEA
CEA-Casa Editrice Ambrosiana
Via Frua, 6-20146 Milan, Italy

Ceac
Ceac, S. A.
Via Layetana, 17, Barcelona 3, Spain

Cedel
Cedel, Ediciones
Viladrau (Gerona), Spain

CEEI
C.E.E.I.
Montera, 24, Madrid-14, Spain

Centre Formation
Centre de Formation et de Perfectionnement
des Journalistes
33, Rue du Louvre, 7500 Paris, France
(ISBN Prefix 2-85900)

Centre Technique
Centre Technique du Cuir
181, Ave. Jean-Jaures, 69007 Lyon, France
(ISBN Prefix 2-900376)

Centro Invest
Centro De Investigaciones Regionales De
Mesoamerica
P.O. Box 38, S. Woodstock, VT 05071
(SAN 260-0269)
(ISBN Prefix 0-910443)

Centro St Assil
Centro Studi Assicurativa
Corso Venzia, 8-20121 Milan, Italy

Centurion
Centurion
17, Rue de Babylone, 75007 Paris, France

Century Bookbindery
Century Bookbindery
P.O. Box 6471, Philadelphia, PA 19145
(SAN 209-2441)
(ISBN Prefix 0-89984)

Century Twenty One
See R & E Res Assoc

Cercle Occitan
Cercle Occitan d'Auvergne
29, Blvd. Gergovia, 63037
Clermont-Ferrand, France
(ISBN Prefix 2-900520)

Cerf
Cerf
29, Boulevard de Latour-Maubourg, 75340
Paris, France

CESVIET
CESVIET-Centro Studio e Doccumenti sul
Vietnam e il Terzo Mundo
Via Bazzini, 7-24065 Lovere (Bergamo),
Italy

Challenge Pr
Challenge Press, Book Div. of Economic
Research Center, Inc.
1107 Lexington Ave., Dayton, OH 45407
Tel 513-275-8637 (SAN 210-0509)
(ISBN Prefix 0-89421)

Chantemerle
Chantemerle, Alain
31 rue Frederic Mistral, 26110, Lyons,
France

Charles River Bks
Charles River Books
1 Thompson Square, Boston, MA 02129
Tel 617-242-5111 (SAN 209-2530)
(ISBN Prefix 0-89182)

Chatto-Bodley-Jonathan
See Merrimack Pub Cir

Chem Pub
Chemical Publishing Co., Inc.
80 8th Ave., New York, NY 10014
Tel 212-255-1950 (SAN 203-6444)
(ISBN Prefix 0-8206)

Cheng & Tsui
Cheng & Tsui Co.
25-31 West St., Boston, MA 02111
Tel 617-277-1769 (SAN 169-3387)
(ISBN Prefix 0-917056; ISBN Prefix
0-88727)

Cherry Lane
Cherry Lane Music Co., Inc, Div. of Cherry
Lane Music Co., Inc.
110 Midland Ave., Port Chester, NY 10573
Tel 914-937-8601 (SAN 219-0788)
(ISBN Prefix 0-89524)

Childrens
Childrens Press
1224 W. Van Buren St., Chicago, IL 60607
Tel 312-666-4200 (SAN 201-9264)
(ISBN Prefix 0-516)

Chilton
Chilton Book Co.
Orders to:
School, Library Services, Chilton Way,
Radnor, PA 19089 Tel 215-964-4729
(SAN 202-1552)
(ISBN Prefix 0-8019)

China Bks
China Books & Periodicals, Inc.
2929 24th St., San Francisco, CA 94110
Tel 415-282-2994 (SAN 214-1213)
(ISBN Prefix 0-8351)

China West
China West Books
P.O. Box 2804, San Francisco, CA 94126
Tel 415-755-3715 (SAN 238-9231)
(ISBN Prefix 0-941340)

Chinese U Pr
Chinese University Press, Chinese University
of Hong Kong
Shatin, New Territories, Hong Kong

Chr Science
Christian Science Pub. Society
Pub & Media Dept., 1 Norway St., Boston,
MA 02115 Tel 617-262-2300 (SAN
203-6541)
Orders to:
P.O. Box 1875, Boston, MA 02117 (SAN
203-655X)
(ISBN Prefix 0-87510)

Chris Mass
Christopher Publishing House (Mass)
1405 Hanover St., Box 1014, West
Hanover, MA 02339 Tel 617-878-4656
(SAN 202-1625)
(ISBN Prefix 0-8158)

Chronique Sociale
Chronique Sociale de France
16, Rue du Plat, 69002 Lyon, France
(ISBN Prefix 2-85008)

Church History
Church History Research & Archives
220 Graystone Dr., Gallatin, TN 37066
Tel 615-452-7027 (SAN 211-7827)
(ISBN Prefix 0-935122)

Church Scient NY
Church of Scientology of New York, The
227 W. 46th St., New York, NY 10036
(SAN 211-786X)

Churchill
Churchill Livingstone Inc.
1560 Broadway, New York, NY 10036
Tel 212-921-0430 (SAN 281-501X)
Dist. by:
J.A. Majors Co., 3770 Zip Industrial Blvd.,
Atlanta, GA 30354 (SAN 169-8117);
Dist. by: Brown & Connolly, Inc., 2
Keithway, Hingham, MA 02043
Tel 617-749-8570 (SAN 169-3298); Dist.
by: Login Brothers Books Co, Inc., 1450 W.
Randolph St., Chicago, IL 60607 (SAN
169-183X); Dist. by: J.A. Majors Co., 2221
Walnut Hill Lane, Irving, TX 75061
(SAN 169-8117); Dist. by: J.A. Majors Co.,
1806 Southgate Blvd., Houston, TX 77025
(SAN 281-5060); Dist. by: Eliot Books,
Inc., 35-53 24th St., Long Island City, NY
11106 (SAN 281-5079); Dist. by: J.A.
Majors Co., 3909 Bienville St., New
Orleans, LA 70119 (SAN 169-2984);
Dist. by: Rittenhouse Book Distributors,
Inc., 251 S. 24th St., Philadelphia, PA
19103 (SAN 169-7560); Dist. by: Medical
& Technical Books, Inc., 11511 Tennessee
Ave., Los Angeles, CA 90064 (SAN
168-9800)
(ISBN Prefix 0-443)

Cientifico Med
Cientifico Medica Editorial
Via Layenta, 53m Barcelona-3, Spain

Cinsa Coord
Cinsa Coordinacion de Iniciativas, S.A.
Avda. del Ejercito, 18, Bilbao-14, Spain
Circulo Lect
Circulo De Lectores. S.A.
Valencia, 344, Barcelona-9, Spain
Cisalpino
Cisalpino-la Goliardica
Via Bassini, 17-2, 20133 Milan, Italy
Citadel Pr
Citadel Press, Subs. of Lyle Stuart, Inc.
120 Enterprise Ave., Secaucus, NJ 07094
Tel 212-736-0007 (SAN 202-1676)
(ISBN Prefix 0-8065)
Citizens Law
Citizens Law Library
6 W. Loudoun St., P.O. Box 1745,
Leesburg, VA 22075 (SAN 211-1543)
(ISBN Prefix 0-89648)
Citta Nuova
Citta Nuova Editrice
Via Degli Scipino 265, I-00192 Rome, Italy
Cittadella
Cittadella
Via Ancaiani, 3-06081 Assis (Perugia), Italy
Civitas
CIVITAS, Inc.
60 E. 42nd St., Suite 411, New York, NY
10165 Tel 212-752-4530 (SAN 268-5647)
(ISBN Prefix 0-9610016)
CLA
Canadian Library Assn
151 Sparks St., Ottowa, Ont., K1P 5E3,
Canada
(ISBN Prefix 0-88024)
Claitors
Claitors Publishing Division
3165 S. Acadian at Interstate 10, Box 239,
Baton Rouge, LA 70821 (SAN 206-8346)
(ISBN Prefix 0-87511)
Claret Edit
Claret Editorial
Roger de Lluria, 5, Barcelona-10, Spain
Clarke Ltd
Clarke, Irwin, & Co., Ltd
791 Clair Ave. West Toronto, Ontario M6C
1B8, Canada
(ISBN Prefix 0-7720)
Clearwater Pub
Clearwater Publishing Co.
1995 Broadway, New York, NY 10023
Tel 212-873-2100 (SAN 201-8969)
(ISBN Prefix 0-8287; ISBN Prefix 0-88354)
Cliffs
Cliff's Notes, Inc.
1701 "P" St., Lincoln, NE 68501
Tel 402-477-6971 (SAN 202-1706)
(ISBN Prefix 0-8220)
CN *Imprint of* **Har-Row**
CN Pulp & Paper
Canadian Pulp & Paper Association (Technical
Section)
2300 Sun Life Bldg., Montreal, Quebec
H3B 2X9, Canada Tel 514-866-6621
CNRS
C. N. R. S.
15, Quai Anatole-France, 75700 Paris,
France
(ISBN Prefix 2-222)
Coast to Coast
Coast to Coast Books
2934 N.E. 16th Ave., Portland, OR 97212
Tel 503-282-5891 (SAN 212-7334)
(ISBN Prefix 0-9602664)
Coculsa
Coculsa Editorial
Torregalindo, 5, Madrid-16, Spain
Colbo
Colbo
3, Rue Richier, 75009 Paris, France
(ISBN Prefix 2-85332)
Coleccion Nereo
Coleccion Nereo
Jonch, 5, Sabadell (Barcelona), Spain
Coleman Graphics
Coleman Graphics, Inc.
99 Milbar Blvd., Farmingdale, NY 11735
Tel 516-293-0383 (SAN 238-1508)
(ISBN Prefix 0-942494)
Coletti
Coletti
Via delle Aceutine, 145-00121 Rome, Italy
Collegiate Pub
Collegiate Publishing, Inc.
1010 Second Ave., Suite 1808, San Diego,
CA 92101 Tel 714-234-3231 (SAN
202-1730)
(ISBN Prefix 0-88429)

Collier *Imprint of* **Macmillan**
Collins Pubs
Collins, William, Pubs., Inc.
2080 W. 117th St., Cleveland, OH 44111
Tel 216-941-6930 (SAN 205-4930); 200
Madison Ave., Suite 1405, New York, NY
10016 (SAN 205-4949)
Collins-World
See Collins Pubs
Colloquium Verlag
Colloquium Verlag Otto H. Hess
Unter den Eichen 93, 1000 Berlin 45,
Federal Republic of Germany
(ISBN Prefix 3-7678)
Colonnese
Colonnese
Via S. Pietro a Majella, 33-80138 Naples,
Italy
Colton Bk
Colton Book Imports
P.O. Box 526, San Francisco, CA 94101
(SAN 204-7136)
Columbia U Pr
Columbia Univ. Press
562 W. 113th St., New York, NY 10025
Tel 212-678-6777 (SAN 212-2472)
Orders to:
136 S. Broadway, Irvington-on-Hudson, NY
10533 Tel 914-591-9111 (SAN 212-2480)
(ISBN Prefix 0-231)
Colwell Co
Colwell Co.
201 Kenyon Rd., Champaign, IL 61820
Tel 217-351-5400 (SAN 208-1431)
Cometa
Cometa, S.A.
Ctra. de Castellon Km. 3, 400, Zaragoza 13,
Spain
Comicana
Comicana Inc. Book Divison
Rfd 2 Box 242 Hickory Kingdom Rd.,
Bedford, NY 10506 (SAN 219-7782)
(ISBN Prefix 0-940420)
Commerce Pr
See Pennwell Pub
Communication Skill
Communication Skill Builders, Inc.
3130 N. Dodge Blvd., P.O. Box 42050,
Tucson, AZ 85733 Tel 602-323-7500
(SAN 201-7768)
(ISBN Prefix 0-88450)
Comp Fr Edns
Compagnie Francaise d'Editions
40, Rue du Colisee, 75008 Paris, France
Compass Va
Compass Pubns., Inc.
1117 N. 19th St., Arlington, VA 22209
Tel 703-524-3136 (SAN 203-5774)
(ISBN Prefix 0-910422)
Computer Lang
Computer Language Co., Inc., The
140 W. 30th St., New York, NY 10001
Tel 212-736-8364 (SAN 239-1864)
(ISBN Prefix 0-941878)
Concordant
Concordant Publishing Concern
15570 W. Knochaven Rd., Canyon
Country, CA 91351 Tel 805-252-2112
(SAN 203-5790)
(ISBN Prefix 0-910424)
Concordia
Concordia Publishing House
3558 S. Jefferson Ave., St. Louis, MO
63118 Tel 314-664-7000 (SAN 202-1781)
(ISBN Prefix 0-570)
Confed Espanola
Confederacion Espanola de Cajas de Ahorro
Alcala, 27, Madrid-14, Spain
Cong Info
Congressional Information Service, Inc, Subs.
of Elsevier US Holdings, Inc.
4520 East-West Hwy., Suite 800,
Washington, DC 20014 Tel 301-654-1550
(SAN 206-345X)
(ISBN Prefix 0-912380)
Congedo
Congedo
Via Marche, 24-73013 Galatina (Lecce),
Italy
Consejo Super
Consejo Superior de Investigaciones Cientificas
Vitruvio, 8, Madrid-6, Spain
Consulting Psychol
Consulting Psychologists Press, Inc.
577 College Ave., Palo Alto, CA 94306
Tel 415-857-1444 (SAN 201-7849)
(ISBN Prefix 0-89106)

Contemp Bks
Contemporary Books, Inc.
180 N. Michigan Ave., Chicago, IL 60601
Tel 312-782-9181 (SAN 202-5493)
(ISBN Prefix 0-8092)
Continuum
Continuum Publishing Co.
575 Lexinton Ave., New York, NY 10022
(SAN 213-8220)
Dist. by:
Crosroad/Continuum, 575 Lexington Ave.,
New York, NY 10017 Tel 212-421-4800
(SAN 282-602X)
(ISBN Prefix 0-8264)
Conveyor Equip Mfrs
Conveyor Equipment Manufacturers
Association
1000 Vermont Av Nw, Washington, DC
20005 (SAN 224-8492)
Coord Iniciat
Coordinacion de Iniciajivas, S. A.
Auda. del Ejercito, 18, Bilbao 14, Spain
Cornell Maritime
Cornell Maritime Press, Inc.
P.O. Box 456, Centreville, MD 21617
Tel 301-758-1075 (SAN 203-5901)
(ISBN Prefix 0-87033)
Cornell SE Asia
Cornell Univ., Southeast Asia Program
120 Uris Hall, Ithaca, NY 14853
Tel 607-256-2378 (SAN 206-6416)
(ISBN Prefix 0-87727)
Cornell U Pr
Cornell Univ. Pr.
124 Roberts Pl., P.O. Box 250, Ithaca, NY
14850 Tel 607-257-7000 (SAN 281-5672)
Orders to:
714 Cascadila St., Ithaca, NY 14850
Tel 607-277-2211 (SAN 281-5680)
(ISBN Prefix 0-8014)
Corner
Corner Book Shop
102 Fourth Ave., New York, NY 10003
Tel 212-254-7714 (SAN 203-5928)
(ISBN Prefix 0-910442)
Cornwall Bks
Cornwall Books
4 Cornwall Dr., East Brunswick, NJ 08816
(SAN 219-7804)
(ISBN Prefix 0-8453)
Coronado Pr
Coronado Press, Inc.
P.O. Box 3232, Lawrence, KS 66044
Tel 913-843-5988 (SAN 201-7776)
(ISBN Prefix 0-87291)
Corti
Corti
11, Rue de Medicis, 75006 Paris, France
(ISBN Prefix 2-7143)
Cortina
Cortina, R. D., Co., Inc.
136 W. 52nd St., New York, NY 10019
Tel 212-582-3845 (SAN 204-2711)
(ISBN Prefix 0-8327)
Cortina M
Cortina Milano
Largo Richini, 1-20122 Milan, Italy
Costa Rica
Costa Rica Editorial
Avenida 18 Calle 1, San Jose, Costa Rica
Coston
Coston, Henry
8 Boulevard Ornano, 75018 Paris, France
Courtille
Courtille
26, Rue de Gramont, 75002 Paris, France
Coutinho
Coutinho
Badlaan 2, 1399 Muiderberg, Netherlands
Crain Bks
Crain Books, Div. of Crain Communications,
Inc.
740 Rush St., Chicago, IL 60611
Tel 312-649-5250 (SAN 207-1967)
(ISBN Prefix 0-87251)
Crane-Russak Co
Crane, Russak & Co., Inc.
3 E. 44th St, New York, NY 10017
Tel 212-867-1490 (SAN 202-1978)
(ISBN Prefix 0-8448)
Creatures at Large
Creatures at Large
1082 Grand Teton Dr., Pacifica, CA 94044
Tel 415-359-4341 (SAN 281-577X); P.O.
Box 687, Pacifica, CA 94044 (SAN
281-5788)
(ISBN Prefix 0-940064)

Crossroad NY
Crossroad Publishing Co.
575 Lexington Ave., New York, NY 10022
Tel 212-421-4800   (SAN 220-1429)
(ISBN Prefix 0-8245)

Crown
Crown Pubs., Inc.
1 Park Ave., New York, NY 10016
Tel 212-532-9200   (SAN 213-4357); 419
Park Ave., New York, NY 10016   (SAN 282-6038)
(ISBN Prefix 0-517)

Cruikshank
Cruikshank, Eleanor P.
194 San Carlos Ave., Sausalito, CA 94965
(SAN 215-7489)

Cruzada
Cruzada Mariana Ediciones
Margallo, 12, Caceres, Spain

Cruzada Span Pubns
Cruzada Spanish Pubns.
P.O. Box 650909, Miami, FL 33165
(SAN 214-2376)
(ISBN Prefix 0-933648)

CSA Pr
CSA Press
Lakemont, GA 30552 Tel 404-782-3931
(SAN 207-7329)
(ISBN Prefix 0-87707)

Ctr Afro-Am Stud
Center for Afro-American Studies (UCLA)
3111 Campbell Hall, 405 Hilgard Ave., Los
Angeles, CA 90024 Tel 213-825-3528
(SAN 214-2899)
(ISBN Prefix 0-934934)

Ctr Appl Ling
Center for Applied Linguistics
3520 Prospect St. NW, Washington, DC
20007 Tel 202-298-9292   (SAN 281-3998)
P.O. Box 4866, Hampden Station,
Baltimore, MD 21211   (SAN 281-4005)
(ISBN Prefix 0-87281)

Ctr Edit
Centre d'Edition-et de Diffusion Africaines
04 BP 541, Abidjan 04 Plateau,
Ivory Coast

Ctr Edit Amer
Centro Editor de America Latina, S.A.
Cangallo 1228, 2 D, 1038 Buenos Aires,
Argentina

Ctr for NE & North African Stud
Univ. of Michigan Center for Near Eastern &
North African Studies
144 Lane Hall, Univ. of Michigan, Ann
Arbor, MI 48109 Tel 313-764-0350   (SAN 211-7150)
(ISBN Prefix 0-932098)

Ctr Inst Ind Lang
Central Institute of Indian Languages
Manasagangotri, Mysore 570006, India

Ctr S&SE Asian
Univ. of Michigan, Center for South &
Southeast Asian Studies
240 Lane Hall, Ann Arbor, MI 48109
Tel 313-763-9764   (SAN 206-491X)
(ISBN Prefix 0-89148)

Cujas
Cujas
4-6-8, Rue de la Maison-Blanche, 75013
Paris, France
(ISBN Prefix 2-254)

Cult Hispano
Culturales Hispano Americanos
Caspe, 139 1-1, Barcelona-13, Spain

Cultura Popular
Cultura Popular Ediciones
Floridablanca, 96, Barcelona 15, Spain

Cumberland Pr
Cumberland Press
136 Main St., Freeport, ME 04032
Tel 207-865-4951   (SAN 203-2090)
(ISBN Prefix 0-87027)

Curci
Curci
Galleria del Corso, 4-20122 Milan, Italy

Curcio
Curcio
Via Arno, 64-00198 Rome, Italy

Curial
Curial Ediciones Catalanes
Bruch, 144, Barcelona-37, Spain

Curzon Pr
Curzon Press, Ltd.
88 Gray's Inn Rd, London WC1,
United Kingdom
(ISBN Prefix 0-7007)

D Van Nostrand
See Van Nos Reinhold

Da Capo
Da Capo Press, Inc.
233 Spring St., New York, NY 10013
Tel 212-620-8000   (SAN 201-2944)
(ISBN Prefix 0-306)

Dabbs
Dabbs, Jack A.
2806 Cherry Lane, Austin, TX 78703
Tel 512-472-7463   (SAN 205-4248)
(ISBN Prefix 0-911494)

Daimon
Daimon Manuel Tayo, Ediciones
Provenza, 284, Barcelona-8, Spain

Dalloz
Dalloz
11, Rue Soufflot, 75246 Paris, France
(ISBN Prefix 2-247)

Dami
Dami
Piazza Velasca, 5-20122 Milan, Italy

Danae
Danae, S.A. Ediciones
Paseo De Gracia, 26, Barcelona-7, Spain

Dance Horiz
Dance Horizons
1801 E. 26th St., Brooklyn, NY 11229
Tel 212-627-0477   (SAN 201-2952)
(ISBN Prefix 0-87127)

Dangles
Dangles
18, Rue Lavoisier, 45800
Saint-Jean-de-Braye, France
(ISBN Prefix 2-7033)

Dante Alighieri
Dante Alighieri
Via Timauo, 3-00195 Rome, Italy

Dar el Machreq
Dar-el Machreq
Lebanon
c/o Librairie Orientale, BP 1986, Beirut,
(ISBN Prefix 2-7214)

Darby Bks
Darby Books
P.O. Box 148, Darby, PA 19023
Tel 215-583-4550   (SAN 204-2371)
(ISBN Prefix 0-89987)

Data Process Mgmt
Data Processing Management Association
505 Busse Hwy, Park Ridge, IL 60068
(SAN 230-0346)

Data Tactics
Data Tactics, Inc
P.O. Box 583, Gaithersburg, MD 20760

David & Charles
David & Charles, Inc.
P.O. Box 57, North Pomfret, VT 05053
Tel 802-457-1911   (SAN 213-8859)
(ISBN Prefix 0-7153)

Davis Co
Davis, F. A., Co.
1915 Arch St., Philadelphia, PA 19103
Tel 215-568-2270   (SAN 200-2078)
(ISBN Prefix 0-8036)

Davis Dewi
Davies (Dewi)
9 Cefn Melindwr, Capel Bangor, Aberyst
Wyth, Dyfed, United Kingdom

DC Bks
DC Books
P.O. Box 214, Kottayam 686001, India

De Bono
De Bono, Guiseppe
Via Masaccio 220, I-50132 Florence, Italy

De Donato
De Donato
Lungomare Sauro, 25-70121 Bari, Italy

De Graff
De Graff, John, Inc.
Clinton Corners, NY 12514   (SAN 201-3061)
Dist. by:
International Marine Publishing Co., 21
Elm St., Camden, ME 04843
Tel 207-236-4342   (SAN 202-716X)
(ISBN Prefix 0-8286)

De Gruyter
De Gruyter, Walter, Inc.
200 Saw Mill River Rd., Hawthorne, NY
10532 Tel 914-747-0110   (SAN 201-3088)
(ISBN Prefix 3-11; ISBN Prefix 0-89925)

De Rache
De Rache, Andre
Brussels, Belgium
(ISBN Prefix 2-8015)

De Vecchi
De Vecchi, S.A. Editorial
Balmes, 247, Barcelona-6, Spain

Dekker
Dekker, Marcel, Inc.
270 Madison Ave., New York, NY 10016
Tel 212-696-9000   (SAN 201-3118)
(ISBN Prefix 0-8247)

Del Bianco
Del Bianco
Via S. Daniele, 11-33100 Udine, Italy

Del Castillo
Del Castillo, S. A.
Marques de Monteagudo, 16, Madrid 28,
Spain

Delagrave
Delagrave
15, Rue Soufflot, 75005 Paris, France

Delair
Delair Publishing Co., Inc.
420 Lexington Ave., Rm. 1621, New York,
NY 10170 Tel 212-867-2255   (SAN 213-4349)
(ISBN Prefix 0-8326)

Delalain
Delalain Editions
128, Boulevard Auguste Blanqui, 75005
Paris, France
(ISBN Prefix 2-85285)

Delarge
Delarge, Jean-Pierre, S.A.
10 Rue Mayet, F-75006, Paris, France

Delilah Bks
Delilah Books
118 E. 25th St., New York, NY 10010
(SAN 238-9339)
Dist. by:
Putnam Publishing Group, 1050 Wall St.
W., Lyndhurst, NJ 07071   (SAN 202-554X)
(ISBN Prefix 0-933328)

Dell
Dell Publishing Co., Inc.
1 Dag Hammarskjold Plaza, 245 E. 47th
St., New York, NY 10017
Tel 212-605-3000   (SAN 201-0097)
(ISBN Prefix 0-440)

Dell Trade Pbks *Imprint of* **Dell**

DEMI
DEMI
Via Oceano Atlantico, 410-00144 Rome,
Italy

Denco Intl
Denco International
P.O. Box 2001, Hialeah, FL 33012
Tel 305-822-6666   (SAN 213-6171)

Dennison
Dennison Pubns.
Dist. by:
Borden Publishing Co., 1855 W. Main St.,
Alhambra, CA 91801   (SAN 201-419X)

Denoel
Denoel
19, Rue de l'Universite, 75007 Paris,
France

Dent
Dent, J. M., &Sons, Ltd.
Aldine House, 33 Welbeck St., London
W1M 8LX, United Kingdom
(ISBN Prefix 0-460)

Dervy Livres
Dervy Livres
6, Rue de Savoie, 75006 Paris, France

Deseret Bk
Deseret Book Co.
40 E. South Temple, P.O. Box 30178, Salt
Lake City, UT 84130 Tel 801-534-1515
(SAN 201-3185)
(ISBN Prefix 0-87747)

Dessain & Tolra
Dessain et Tolra, Lethielleux, le Seneve,
Editorial Bouret
10 Rue Cassette, F-75006 Paris, France
(ISBN Prefix 2-249)

Destino
Destino, S.L. Ediciones
Consejo De Ciento, 425, Barcelona-9, Spain

Deutsche Sprache
Verlag fuer Deutsche Sprache GmbH
Taunusstr 11, 6200 Wiesbaden,
Federal Republic of Germany
(ISBN Prefix 3-88228)

Deutscher Taschenbuch Verlag
DTV-Deutscher Taschenbuch Verlag GmbH &
Co. KG
Friedrichstr la, Postfach 400422, D-5000
Munich 40, Federal Republic of Germany

Deux Coqs
Deux Coqs d'Or
28, Rue de la Boetie, 75008 Paris, France

Develop Sys Corp
Development Systems Corporation, Div. of
Development Systems Corp.
500 N. Dearborn St., Chicago, IL 60610
Tel 312-836-0466 (SAN 201-3622)
(ISBN Prefix 0-88462)

Dewan Bahasa
Dewan Bahasa dan Pustaka
P.O. Box 803, Kuala Lumpur 08-08,
Malawi

Dghtrs St Paul
Daughters of St. Paul
50 St. Paul's Ave., Boston, MA 02130
Tel 617-522-8911 (SAN 203-8900)
(ISBN Prefix 0-8198)

Diafora
Diafora, S.A.
Lauria, 118, Barcelona-37, Spain

Diana
Editorial Diana
Apdo. Postal 144≠986, Mexico 12, D.F.,
Mexico

Dict Soc NA
Dictionary Society of North America
Indiana State Univ., Dept. of English, Terre
Hatue, IN 47809 Tel 812-232-6311 (SAN
233-4755)

Didier
Didier, John, Editions
1 Rue des Chailles, F-92500 Rueil
Malmaison, France

Diesterweg
Verlag Moritz Diesterweg
Hochstr 31, D-6000 Frankfurt am Main 1,
Federal Republic of Germany
(ISBN Prefix 3-425)

Difel Difusao
Difel Difusao Editorial, S.A.
Av. Vieira de Carvalho, 40-CEP 01210, Sao
Paulo, Brazil

Dilithium Pr
Dilithium Press
8285 S.W. Nimbus St., Suite 151,
Beaverton, OR 97005 Tel 503-646-2713
(SAN 210-0649)
Orders to:
P.O. Box 606, Beaverton, OR 97075
(SAN 210-0657)
(ISBN Prefix 0-918398; ISBN Prefix
0-88056)

Diput Foral
Diputacion Foral de Navarra
Avda. de San Ignacio, Pamplona., Spain

Direc Pubns
Direccion General de Publicaciones y
Bibliotecas, Secretaria de Educacion Publica
Administracion de Correos No. 46, Mexico
3, D.F., Mexico

Distein
Distein, S.A. Ediciones
Via Layenta, 17, Barcelona-3, Spain

Divry
Divry, D.C., Inc.
293 Seventh Ave., New York, NY 10001
Tel 212-255-2153 (SAN 201-3320)
(ISBN Prefix 0-910516)

DMR Pubns
D. M. R. Pubns., Inc.
1410 E. Capitol Dr., Milwaukee, WI 53211
Tel 414-961-0120 (SAN 205-325X)
(ISBN Prefix 0-89552)

Doc Scient
Centre d'Etudes et de Documentations
Scientifiques
95 bis, Av Foch B. P. 27 76290
Montivillers, France
(ISBN Prefix 2-85256)

Doc Univers
Centre de Documentation Universitaire et
Societe d'Edition d'Enseignement Superiuer
88, Blvd. Saint-Germain, 75005 Paris,
France
(ISBN Prefix 2-7181)

Dodd
Dodd, Mead & Co.
79 Madison Ave., New York, NY 10016
Tel 212-685-6464 (SAN 201-3339)
(ISBN Prefix 0-396)

Dolp *Imprint of* **Doubleday**

Don Bosco Ed
Don Bosco Ediciones
Paseo De San Juan Bosco, 62,
Barcelona-17, Spain

Donard Pub Co
Donard Publishing Co.
18 Fairview Gardens, Bangor, Co. Down,
Ireland

Dopesa
Dopesa
Cardenal Reig, S/N, Barcelona-28, Spain

Dorrance
Dorrance & Co.
828 Lancaster Ave., Bryn Mawr, PA 19010
Tel 215-527-7880 (SAN 201-3363)
(ISBN Prefix 0-8059)

Dos Continentes
Dos Continentes Editorial
Rios Rosas, 36, Madrid-3, Spain

Dossat
Dossat, S. A.
Plaza de Santa Ana, 9, Madrid 12, Spain

Dotmar
Dotmar Inc.
395 de Maisonneuve Blvd, W. Montreal,
Que. 43A 1L6, Canada

Doubleday
Doubleday & Co., Inc.
245 Park Ave., New York, NY 10017
(SAN 281-6075)
Orders to:
501 Franklin Ave., Garden City, NY 11530
(SAN 281-6083)
(ISBN Prefix 0-385)

Douglass Pubs
Douglass Publishers, Inc.
P.O. Box 3270, Alexandria, VA 22302
Tel 703-522-4000 (SAN 211-7037)
(ISBN Prefix 0-935392)

Dover
Dover Pubns., Inc.
180 Varick St., New York, NY 10014
Tel 212-255-3755 (SAN 201-338X)
(ISBN Prefix 0-486)

Driehoek
Driehoek
Keizersgracht 756, Amsterdam,
Netherlands

Droemersche Knaur
Droemersche Verlagsanstalt Th Knaur Nachf
Rauchsttr 9-11, Postfach 800480, D-8000
Munich 80, Federal Republic of Germany
(ISBN Prefix 3-426)

Droz
Droz S. A. Librairie
11, Rue Massot, Case 389, 1211 Geneva
12, Switzerland
(ISBN Prefix 2-600)

Drug Intl Pubns
Drug Intelligence Pubns.
7752 Woodmont Ave., Washington, DC
20814 Tel 301-654-8736 (SAN 201-2804)
Orders to:
1241 Broadway, Hamilton, IL 62341
Tel 217-847-2504 (SAN 201-2812)
(ISBN Prefix 0-914768)

Dryden Pr
Dryden Press, Div. of Holt, Rinehart &
Winston, Inc.
901 N. Elm, Hinsdale, IL 60521
Tel 312-325-2985 (SAN 281-613X)
Orders to:
CBS College Publishing, 383 Madison Ave.,
New York, NY 10017 Tel 212-872-2219
(SAN 281-6148)
(ISBN Prefix 0-8498)

Duculot
Duculot Editions
Gembloux, Belgium
(ISBN Prefix 2-8011)

DuMont Buch
DuMont Buchverlag GmbH & Co. KG
Apostelnkloster 21-25, 5000 Cologne 1,
Federal Republic of Germany
(ISBN Prefix 3-7701)

Dutton
Dutton, E. P.
2 Park Ave., New York, NY 10016
Tel 212-725-1818 (SAN 201-0070)
(ISBN Prefix 0-525)

E Arnold
Arnold, Edward, Publishers Ltd.
300 North Charles Street, Baltimore, MD
21201 Tel 301-539-1529 (SAN 263-9203)
(ISBN Prefix 0-7131)

E J Brill
Brill, E. J., Pubs.
Dist. by:
Expediters of the Printed Word, Ltd., P.O.
Box 1305, Long Island City, NY 11101
(SAN 282-6399)

E Torres
Torres, Eliseo
17 E. 22 St., New York, NY 10010

E W Jameson Jr
Jameson, E. W., Jr.
13 Oakside, Davis, CA 95616 (SAN
207-5148)

EC Print AB
EC Print
Kastellgatan 1, S-41307 Gothenburg,
Sweden

Echo Pubs
Echo Pubs.
P.O. Box 7130, West Menlo Park, CA
94025 Tel 415-524-1575 (SAN 201-3592)
(ISBN Prefix 0-912852)

Ecole Biblio
Ecole Nationale Superieure des Biblioteques
17-21, Boulevard du 11 Novembre 1918,
69621 Villeurbanne, France

Ecole Electricite
Ecole Superieure d'Electricite
10, Avenue Pierre-Larousse, 92240
Malakoff, France

Ed Calderini
Edizioni Calderini
Emilia Lev 31, I-40139 Bolgna, Italy

Ed Methods
See Develop Sys Corp

Ed Tech Ind
Editions Techniques des Industries de la
Fonderie
12, Ave. Raphael, 75016 Paris, France
(ISBN Prefix 2-7119)

Ed Tecnicos
See French & Eur

Edaf
Edaf, Ediciones, Disttribuciones, S.A.
Jorge Juan 30, Madrid-4, Spain

Edagricole
Edagricole
Via Emilia Levante, 31-2-4, Italy

EDC
EDC Publishing
8141 E. 44th St., Tulsa, OK 74145 (SAN
226-2134)
(ISBN Prefix 0-88110)

Edhasa
Edhasa
Diagonal, 519-521, Barcelona-29, Spain

Edi Ermes
Edi Ermes
Via Timavo, 12, 20124 Milan, Italy

Edi-Seis
Edi-Seis, S.A.
Panama, 4, Madrid-16, Spain

Edicep
Edicep. Comercial Editora de Publicaciones,
S.A.
Admirante Cadarso, 11, Valencia-5, Spain

Ediciones
Ediciones Universal
3090 S.W. 8th St., Miami, FL 33135
Tel 305-642-3355 (SAN 207-2203)
(ISBN Prefix 0-89729)

Edicoes Melhoramentos
Edicoes Melhoramentos
Caixa Postal 8120, Rua Tito 479-05051,
Sao Paulo, Brazil

Edipem
Edipem
Via Giovanni da Verrazzano, 15-28100
Novara, Italy

Edisem
Edisem
2475, rue Sylva-Clapin, St-Hyacinthe,
Quebec J2S 5T5, Canada
(ISBN Prefix 2-89130)

Edison Electric
Edison Electric Institute
111 Nineteenth St. NW, Washington, DC
20036 (SAN 224-7119)

Edit Alhambra
Editorial Alhambra, S.A.
Claudio Coello, 76, Madrid 1, Spain

Edit Atica
Editora Atica S. A
Rue Barao de Iguape, 110, Ciaxa Postal
8656, Sao Paulo, Spain

Edit Bruguera
Editorial Bruguera, SA
Camps y Fabres 5, Barcelona 6, Spain

Edit Caribe
Editorial Caribe
3934 S. W. 8th St., Suite 303, Miami, FL
33134 Tel 305-445-0564 (SAN 215-1421)
(ISBN Prefix 0-89922)

Edit Laniera
Editoriale Laniera
Via Mazzini, 3-13051 Biella (Vercelli), Italy

Edit Mex U
Editores Mexicanos Unidos
Luis Gonzalez Obregon 5-B, Mexico 1, D.
F., Mexico
Edit Mundo *Imprint of* **Casa Bautista**
Edit Nebrija
Editorial Nebrija
Republica Argentina, 35, Leon-391, Spain
Edit Norma
Editorial Norma y Cia, SCA
Calle 37 No. 13-08, Apdo. Aereo 53550
Bogota, Colombia
Edit Pr Serv
Editors Press Service, Inc, Div. of Charleston
Post Pub. Co.
60 E. 42nd St., New York, NY 10017
Tel 212-682-2888 (SAN 204-1715)
(ISBN Prefix 0-89971)
Edit Quebec
Editeur Official du Quebec Cite Parlementaire
675 est, Boul. St. Cyrille, Quebec, Que
G1R 4Y7, Canada
(ISBN Prefix 0-7754)
Edit Teide
Editorial Teide
Viladomat, 291, Barcelona-29, Spain
Edit Vecchi
Editorial de Vecchi
Balmes 247, Barcelona-6, Spain
Edit Victor Leru
Editorial Victor Leru S.A.
Don Bosco 3834, 1206 Buenos Aires,
Argentina
Editest
Editest
Brussels, Belgium
(ISBN Prefix 2-8000)
Edito Serv
Edito-Service, S.A.
9 ter chemin de Roches, Bp 307, Ch-1211
Geneva 6, Switzerland
Editora Cultrix
Editora Cultrix
Rua Conselheiro Furtdo 648-6 andar-sala
62, 01511 Sao Paulo Sp, Brazil
Editora Globo
Editora Globo, S.A.
CP 1520, 9000 Porto Alegre RS, Brazil
Editora Revista
Editora Revista dos Trbunais Ltda.
Rua Conde do Pinhal, 78, 01501 Sao Paulo,
Brazil
Editori Riuniti
Editori Riuniti
Via Serchio 9-11, I-00198 Rome, Italy
Editorial Justa
Editorial Justa Pubns. Inc.
2831 Seventh St., Berkeley, CA 94710
Tel 415-848-3628 (SAN 208-1962)
Orders to:
P.O. Box 2131-C, Berkeley, CA 94702
(SAN 208-1970)
(ISBN Prefix 0-915808)
Editura Didactica
Editura Didactica Si Pedagogica
Str Spiru Haret 12, R-70738, Spectorul 7,
Bucharest, Rumania
Editura Stiintifica
Editura Stiintifica Si Enciclopedica
Piata Scinteii 1, R-71341 Bucharest,
Rumania
Edizioni Danza
Edizioni della Danza
Via Gallardi 4-13100 Vercelli, Italy
Edizioni Medit
Edizioni Mediteranee
Via Flaminia, 158-00196 Rome, Italy
Edn Girasole
Edizioni del Girasole
Via Ricci, 35-48100 Ravenna, Italy
Edn Scol Mond
Edizioni Scolastiche Mondadori
Via Archimede, 23-20129 Milan, Italy
Edns Acervo
Ediciones Acervo
Julio Verne, 5-6 Barcelona- 6, Spain
Edns Catedra
Ediciones Catedra, S.A.
Don Ramon de la Cruz, 67, Madrid-1,
Spain
Edns Des Deux Mondes
Editions Des Deux Mondes
P.O. Box 56, Newark, DE 19711
Tel 301-398-2834 (SAN 216-373X)
(ISBN Prefix 0-939586)

Edns Du Jour
Editions Du Jour
6765, rue Marseille, Montreal, Quebec
H1N 1M4, Canada
Edns Francaise
Editions Francaises
192, rue Dorchester sud, Quebec, Que.
G1K 5K9, Canada
Edns Homme
Editions de l'Homme
955 Rue Amherst, Montreal, Quebec. H2L
3K4, Canada
(ISBN Prefix 0-7759)
Edns Laurore
Editions de Laurore Inc.
1651, Rue Saint-Denis, Montreal, Que. 42X
3K5, Canada
(ISBN Prefix 0-88532)
Edns Nauta
Ediciones Nauta, S.A.
Calle Loreto, 16, Barcelona-29, Spain
Edns Organisation
Les Editions de'Organisation
5, Rue Rousselet, 75007 Paris, France
Edns Ottawa
Editions de l'Universite d'Ottawa
65, Ave Hastey, Ottawa, Ont, K1N 6N5,
Canada
(ISBN Prefix 0-7766)
Edns Sesenti Dos
Ediciones Sesenti-Dos
Provenza, 278, Barcelona-8, Spain
Edns Sociales
Editions Sociales-Messidor
146 rue du Faubourg-Poissonniere, F-75010
Paris,
(ISBN Prefix 2-209)
Edns St Paul
Editions Saint Paul
Ave du Commerce 76, BP127,
Kinshasa-Limite, Zaire
Edns Univers
Editions Universitaires
10, Rue Mayet, 75006 Paris, France
(ISBN Prefix 2-7113)
Edns Universal
Ediciones Universal
3090 SW 8th St., Miami, FL 33135
(ISBN Prefix 0-89279)
Educ Co Ire
Educational Company of Ireland Ltd.
P.O. Box 43A, Ballymont Rd.,
Walkinstown, Dublin 12, Ireland
(ISBN Prefix 0-86167)
Educ Inst Am Hotel
Educational Institute of the American Hotel &
Motel Assn.
1407 S. Harrison Rd., East Lansing, MI
48823 Tel 517-353-5500 (SAN 215-8590)
(ISBN Prefix 0-86612)
Educ Serv
Educational Service, Inc.
P.O. Box 219, Stevensville, MI 49127
Tel 616-429-1451 (SAN 206-9423)
(ISBN Prefix 0-89273)
Educ Serv Pub
Educational Service Publications
Box 205, Boones Mill, VA 24065
Tel 703-334-2269 (SAN 240-3714)
(ISBN Prefix 0-9608250)
Educ Today
See Pitman Learning
Educar
Educar Editores Ltda.
Calle 44n. 15-28, Bogota, Colombia
Eerdmans
Eerdmans, Wm. B., Publishing Co.
255 Jefferson Ave., S.E., Grand Rapids, MI
49503 Tel 616-459-4591 (SAN 220-0058)
(ISBN Prefix 0-8028)
EH *Imprint of* **B&N NY**
Einaudi
Einaudi, Guilio
Via Umberto Biancamano, CP 245, I-10121
Turin, Italy
EIPS
EIPS-Edizioni Il Pio Samaritano
Via Nava, 31-20159 Milan, Italy
Ejlers Forlag
Ejlers Christian, Forlag
Brolaeggerstraede 4, 1211, Copenhagen K,
Denmark
Ekdoseis Filon
Ekdoseis Filon
Panepistimiou 10, Athens 135, Greece

Eklitra
Eklitra-Association Culturelle Picarde
88 bis, Rue Gauthier de Rumilly, 8000
Amiens, France
(ISBN Prefix 2-85706)
Elec Gen Syst
Electric Generating Systems Marketing
Association
435 N Michigan Ave, Chicago, IL 60611
(SAN 224-7127)
Elliots Bks
Elliot's Books
P.O. Box 6, Northford, CT 06472
Tel 203-484-2184 (SAN 204-1529)
(ISBN Prefix 0-911830)
Ellison Ent
Ellison Enterprises
1919 Purdy Ave., Miami Beach, FL 33139
Tel 305-534-4454 (SAN 211-0091)
(ISBN Prefix 0-930580)
Elp
Elp
17, Rue Saint-Severin, 7500 Paris, France
(ISBN Prefix 2-7213)
Elsevier
Elsevier Science Publishing Co., Inc, Div. of
Biomedical Division
52 Vanderbilt Ave., New York, NY 10017
Tel 212-867-9040 (SAN 200-2051)
(ISBN Prefix 0-444; ISBN Prefix 0-7204)
Elsevier-NDU Nv
Elsevier-NDU Nv
Jan Van Galenstr 335, 1061 AZ
Amsterdam, Netherlands
Elsevier-Nelson
See Lodestar Bks
Elsevier Sci
See Elsevier
Elsevier Sequoia
Elsevier Sequoia, S.A.
50 Ave. de la Gare, BP 851, CH 1001
Lausanne 1, Switzerland
(ISBN Prefix 2-8003)
Elwert
Elwert, N. G., Verlag Inh.
Reitgasse 7-9, Postf 1128, 3550 Marburg,
Federal Republic of Germany
(ISBN Prefix 3-7708)
EMC
EMC Pub.
300 York Ave., St. Paul, MN 55101
Tel 612-771-1555 (SAN 201-3800)
(ISBN Prefix 0-88436; ISBN Prefix
0-912022)
Emerson
Emerson Books, Inc.
Madelyn Ave., Verplanck, NY 10596
Tel 914-739-3506 (SAN 201-3819)
(ISBN Prefix 0-87523)
EMI
EMI-Editrice Missionaria-Italiana
Via Meloncello, 3-3-40135 Bologna, Italy
Emme
Emme Edizioni
Via San Maurilio 13, I-20123 Milan, Italy
Encic Catalan
Enciclopedia Catalan, S.A.
Avda. Diagonal, 357 Pral. Barcelona-37,
Spain
Encicl Vasca
Enciclopedia Vasca, Editorial la Gran
Calzadas de Mallona, 8, Bilbao-6, Spain
Encre
Encre Editions
9, Rue Duphot, 75001 Paris, France
(ISBN Prefix 2-86418)
Ency Brit Ed
Encyclopaedia Britannica Educational Corp,
Affiliate of Encyclopaedia Britannica, Inc.
425 N. Michigan Ave., Chicago, IL 60611
Tel 312-321-6800 (SAN 201-3851)
(ISBN Prefix 0-87827)
Eng Joint Coun
See AAES
Englisch Verlag
Englisch, F., GmbH & Co.
Verlags-Kommanditgesellschaft
Webergasse 12, Postf 2309, 6200
Wiesbaden, Federal Republic of Germany
Enke
Enke, Ferdinand
Herdweg 63, Postf 1304, 7000 Stuttgart 1,
Federal Republic of Germany
(ISBN Prefix 3-432)

Enslow Pubs
Enslow Pubs. Inc.
Bloy St. & Ramsey Ave., Box 777, Hillside, NJ 07205 Tel 201-964-4116 (SAN 213-7518); Box 301, Short Hills, NJ 07078 (SAN 209-0651)
(ISBN Prefix 0-89490)

Enterprise Calif
Enterprise Pubns.
P.O. Box 4001, Downey, CA 90241
(SAN 207-222X)
(ISBN Prefix 0-918558)

Entomol Soc
Entomological Society of America
4603 Calvert Rd., College Park, MD 20740 Tel 301-864-1334 (SAN 201-3940)

ERGA
ERGA-Edizioni Realizzazioni Grafiche Artigiana
Via Montebruno, 7-16139 Genoa, Italy

Erhvervso
Erhvervsokonomisk Forlag
Copenhagen, Denmark

ERI
ERI
Via Arsenale, 41-10121, Turin, Italy

Erredici
Erredici
Via della Provvidenza 125-35030 Rubano (Padua), Italy

Escuela Nueva
Escuela Nueva y Alinorma
Paseo De la Habana, 174, Madrid-16, Spain

ESP
ESP, Inc.
P.O. Drawer 5037, 1201 E. Johnson Ave., Jonesboro, AR 72401 Tel 800-643-0280 (SAN 241-497X)
(ISBN Prefix 0-8209)

Espasa Calpe
Espasa Calpe, S.A.
Carretera de Irun, Km 12,200, Madrid-34, Spain

Esperanto League North Am
Esperanto League for North America, Inc.
P.O. Box 1129, El Cerrito, CA 94530
Tel 415-653-0998 (SAN 201-8241)

Esselte Studium
Esselte Studium
Scheelegatan 24, 11285 Stockholm, Sweden

Estoup
Estoup
47, Rue du Chateau-des-Rentiers 75013 Paris, France
(ISBN Prefix 2-85016)

Etas Libri
Etas Libri
Via Mecenate 87-6-20138 Milan, Italy

Ethridge
Ethridge, Blaine, Books
13977 Penrod St., Detroit, MI 48223
Tel 313-838-3363 (SAN 201-4327)
(ISBN Prefix 0-87917)

Eur-Am Music
European American Music
11 West End Road, Totowa, NJ 07512
Tel 201-256-7100 (SAN 201-7393)
(ISBN Prefix 0-913574)

Eurasia Pr NJ
See Eurasia Pr NY

Eurasia Pr NY
Eurasia Press
302 Fifth Ave., New York, NY 10001
(SAN 222-7886)
(ISBN Prefix 0-932030)

Euredif
Euredif
2 bis, Rue de la Baume, 75008 Paris, France
(ISBN Prefix 2-7167)

Euro Bk Co
European Book Co.
925 Larkin St., San Francisco, CA 94109
Tel 415-474-0626

Everest
Everest
Ctra. Leon-Coruna, km. 5, Leon, Spain

Everton Pubs
Everton Pubs. Inc.
526 N. Main St., P.O. Box 368, Logan, UT 84321 Tel 801-752-6022 (SAN 204-1332)

Everybodys Pr
Everybody's Press
Fame Avenue, Hanover, PA 17331
Tel 717-632-3535 (SAN 237-949X)

Eyrolles
Eyrolles
61 Blvd. Saint-Germain 7500 Paris, France
(ISBN Prefix 2-212)

F A Brockhaus
Brockhaus, F. A.
Leberberg 25, Postfach 1709, D-6200 Wiesbaden 1, Federal Republic of Germany

F Bahn
Bahn, Friedrick, Verlag GMBH
Zasiusstr 8, Postfach 1186, D-7550 Konstanz, Federal Republic of Germany

F Cass Co
See Biblio Dist

F Nathan
Nathan, Fernand
9 Rue Mechain, F-75014 Paris, France

Faber & Faber
Faber & Faber, Inc.
39 Thompson St., Winchester, MA 01890 Tel 617-721-1427 (SAN 218-7256)
(ISBN Prefix 0-571)

Fabritius
Fabritius & Sonners
Brobekkvn, 80, Oslo 5, Norway

Fackelverlag
Fackelverlag Fackelversand G. Bowitz GmbH
Schockenriedstr 46, 7000 Stuttgart 80, Federal Republic of Germany
(ISBN Prefix 3-87220)

Facts on File
Facts on File, Inc.
460 Park Ave. S., New York, NY 10016 Tel 212-683-2244 (SAN 201-4696)
(ISBN Prefix 0-87196; ISBN Prefix 0-87103)

Fairchild
Fairchild Books & Visuals
7 E. 12th St., New York, NY 10003
Tel 212-741-4280 (SAN 201-470X)
(ISBN Prefix 0-87005)

Falken Verlag
Falken Verlag GmbH
Schone Aussicht 21, Postf 1120 6272 Niedernhausen Taunus, Federal Republic of Germany
(ISBN Prefix 3-8068)

FAO Imprint of Unipub

Far Eastern Pubns
Far Eastern Pubns.
Box 2505 A, 340 Edwards St., New Haven, CT 06520 Tel 203-436-1075 (SAN 219-0710)

FASEB
Federation of American Societies for Experimental Biology
9650 Rockville Pike, Bethesda, MD 20814 Tel 301-530-7030 (SAN 205-5767)
(ISBN Prefix 0-913822)

Fayard
Fayard
75, Rue des Saints-Peres, 75006 Paris, France
(ISBN Prefix 2-213)

Fearon-Pitman
See Pitman Learning

Fed Gremios
Federacion de Gremios de Editores de Espana
Paseo de la Castellana, 82 - Madrid-6, Spain

Fed Soc Coat Tech
Federation of Societies for Coatings Technology
1315 Walnut St., Suite 832, Philadelphia, PA 19107 Tel 215-545-1506 (SAN 212-9035)
(ISBN Prefix 0-934010)

Feldheim
Feldheim, Philipp, Inc.
96 E. Broadway, New York, NY 10002
Tel 212-925-3180 (SAN 164-9671)
(ISBN Prefix 0-87306)

Fell
Fell, Frederick, Pubs., Inc.
386 Park Ave. S., New York, NY 10016 Tel 212-685-9017 (SAN 208-2365)
(ISBN Prefix 0-8119)

Feltrinelli
Feltrinelli
Vian Andegari, 6-20121 Milan, Italy

Femi Suuri
Femi, Suuri Naistenkerbo
Koydenpunojankatu 2, 00180 Helsinki 18, Finland

Feret
Feret et Fils, Editions
9, Rue De Grassi, 33000 Bordeaux, France

Fernandez
Fernandez Editores, SA
Calzada Mexico Coynacan 321 Mexico 13, DF, Mexico

Ferozsons
Ferozsons, Ltd.
60 Shahrah-e-Quad-e-Azam, Lahore, Pakistan

Fides
Fides Pubs., Inc.

Field Ent
See World Bk

Fin Analysis
Financial Analysis & Publications
P. O. Box H 256, Australia Square, Sydney, N. S. W. 2000, Austria

Finan Pub
Financial Publishing Co.
82 Brookline Ave., Boston, MA 02215
Tel 617-262-4040 (SAN 205-5805)
(ISBN Prefix 0-87600)

Fiorini
Fiorini
Via Altichiero, 11-37100 Verona, Italy

First Church
First Church of Christ Scientist
1 Norway St., Boston, MA 02115
Tel 617-262-2300 (SAN 206-6467)

Fischbacher
Fischbacher
33, Rue de Seine, 75006 Paris, France

Fischer Taschen
Fischer Taschenbuch Verlag GmbH
Geleitsstr 25, 6000 Frankfurt am Main 70, Federal Republic of Germany
(ISBN Prefix 3-596)

Fischer Verlag
Fischer, Gustav, Verlag GmbH & Co. KG
Wollgrasweg 49, Postf 720143, 7000 Stuttgart, Federal Republic of Germany
(ISBN Prefix 3-437)

Fitzhenry
Fitzhenry & Whiteside
150 Lesmill Rd., Don Mills, Ontario M3B 2T5, Canada
(ISBN Prefix 0-88902)

Flammarion
Flammarion et Cie
26 Rue Rauine, F-75278 Paris Cedex 06, France

Floch
Floch, Joseph
8, Rue Charles de Blois, 53100 Mayenne, France

Fluid Controls
Fluid Controls Institute, Inc.
U.S. Hwy. One, Tequesta, FL 33458
(SAN 224-7976)

FNB Imprint of Unipub

Focal Pr
Focal Pr.
10 Tower Office Pk., Woburn, MA 01801
Tel 617-933-8260 (SAN 220-0066)

Fogola
Fogola
Piazza Carlo Felice, 19-10133 Turin, Italy

Fogtdals Boger
Fogtdals Boger
Norre Farimagsgade 49, 1364 Copenhagen, Denmark

Folcroft
Folcroft Library Editions
P.O. Box 182, Folcroft, PA 19032 (SAN 206-8362)
(ISBN Prefix 0-8414)

Follett
Follett Publishing Co, Div. of Follett Corp.
1010 W. Washington Blvd., Chicago, IL 60607 Tel 312-666-5858 (SAN 200-2035)
(ISBN Prefix 0-695)

Fondo Educativo
Fondo Educativo Interamericano, S.A.
Apdo, Aereo 29696, Bogota, Colombia

Fontanella
Fontanella, S.A. Editorial
Escorial, 50, Barcelona-24, Spain

Fontein
Fontein
Postbus 308, Baarn, Netherlands

For Stat Rev
Foreningen af Statsautoriserede Revisorer
Kronprnsessegade 8, 1306 Copenhagen K, Denmark

Forest Prod
Forest Products Research Society
2801 Marshall Court, Madison, WI 53705
Tel 608-231-1361 (SAN 211-4216)
(ISBN Prefix 0-935018)

KEY TO PUBLISHERS' AND DISTRIBUTORS' ABBREVIATIONS

Forkner
Forkner Publishing Corp, Subs. of Gage Publishing Ltd.
164 Commander Blvd.,Agincourt, Ontario, M1S 3C7, Canada Tel 416-298-8188
(SAN 206-426X)
(ISBN Prefix 0-912036)
Formur Intl
Formur International
4200 Laclede Ave., St. Louis, MO 63108
(SAN 207-5768)
(ISBN Prefix 0-89378)
Forni
Forni
Via Gramsci, 164-40010 Sala Bolognese (Bologna), Italy
Forum Bok
Forum, Bokforlaget, AB
Tegnergatan 40, 11359 Stockholm, Sweden
Foucher
Foucher
128, Rue de Rivoli, 75001 Paris, France
(ISBN Prefix 2-216)
Found Am Christ
Foundation for American Christian Education
2946 25th Ave., San Francisco, CA 94132
Tel 415-661-1775 (SAN 205-5856)
(ISBN Prefix 0-912498)
Found Class Reprints
Foundation for Classical Reprints, The
607 McKnight St. N.W., Albuquerque, NM 87102 (SAN 212-9051)
(ISBN Prefix 0-89901)
Found Class Rep
See Found Class Reprints
Four Continent
Four Continents Book Store
149 Fifth Ave., New York, NY 10010
Tel 212-523-0250
Fragata
Fragata Ediciones
Biuenos Aires, 15, Cadiz, Spain
France & Col Philatelist
France and Colonies Philatelic Society, Inc.
103 Spruce St., Bloomfield, NJ 07003
(SAN 235-3016)
France Selection
France Selection
11, Rue du Departement, 75019 Paris, France
Francke
Francke Verlag
Hochfeldstr. 113, 3000 Bern, Switzerland
(ISBN Prefix 3-7720)
Frankfurt Fachverlag
Frankfurter Fachverlag Michael Kohl GmbH & Co. KG
Emil-Sulzbach-Str. 12, 6000 Frankfurt am Main 90, Federal Republic of Germany
(ISBN Prefix 3-87234)
Franzis Verlag
Franzis-Verlag GmbH
Karlstr. 37 8000 Munich 2, Federal Republic of Germany
(ISBN Prefix 3-7723)
Free Pr
Free Press, Div. of Macmillan Publishing Co., Inc.
866 Third Ave., New York, NY 10022
Tel 212-935-2000 (SAN 201-6656)
Dist. by:
Macmillan Co., Front & Brown Sts., Riverside, NJ 08370 Tel 609-461-6500
(SAN 202-5582)
(ISBN Prefix 0-02)
French & Eur
French & European Pubns., Inc.
115 Fifth Ave., New York, NY 10003
Tel 212-673-7400 (SAN 206-8109)
(ISBN Prefix 0-8288)
Froehlich Verlag
Forehlich, Alwin, Verlag
Falkensteiner Str. 27, 6000 Frankfurt am Main, Federal Republic of Germany
(ISBN Prefix 3-87240)
Fundacion J March
Fundacion Juan March
Castello, 77, Madrid-6, Spain
Fyris
Fyris
Apelgatan 7 E, Box 3082, 75003 Uppsala, Sweden
G Brash
Brash, Graham, Pte., Ltd.
36-C Prinsep St., Singapore 0718, Singapore

G Kici
Kici, Gasper
P.O. Box 1855, Washington, DC 20013
Tel 703-560-6467 (SAN 203-4115)
G Ricordi
Ricordi, G.C., SPA
Via Berchet 2, I-20121 Milan, Italy
Gabler
Betriebswirthschaftlicher Verlag Dr. Th. Gabler GmbH
Taunusstr. 54, 6200 Wiesbaden 1, Federal Republic of Germany
(ISBN Prefix 3-409)
Gad Forlag
Gad Forlag, G. E. C.
Vimmelskaftet 32, 1161 Copenhagen K, Denmark
Gage Ed Pub
Gage Educational Publishers Ltd
164 Commander Blvd Agincourt, Ontario M1S 3C8, Canada
(ISBN Prefix 0-7715)
Gaggi
Gaggi
Via S. Stefano, 130-40125 Bologna, Italy
Gaisa
Gaisa, S. L.
Gran Via Marques de Turia, 64, Valencia 5, Spain
Galaxia
Galaxia, S.A. Editorial
Reconquista, 7, Vigo (Ponte Vedra), Spain
Gale
Gale Research Co.
Book Tower, Detroit, MI 48226
Tel 313-961-2242 (SAN 213-4373)
(ISBN Prefix 0-8103)
Galeati
Galeati
Via Selice, 189-40026 Imola (Bologna), Italy
Galilee *Imprint of* **Doubleday**
Gallaudet Coll
Gallaudet College Press
Kendall Green, Washington, DC 20002
Tel 202-651-5595 (SAN 205-261X)
(ISBN Prefix 0-913580)
Gallery Pr
Gallery Press
117 N. Main St., Essex, CT 06426
Tel 203-767-0313 (SAN 207-0936)
(ISBN Prefix 0-913622)
Gallimard
Editions Gallimard
5 rue Sebastien-Bottir, F-75007 Paris, France
(ISBN Prefix 2-07)
Gamma
Gamma
77, Rue de Vaugirard, 75006 Paris, France
Gannon
Gannon, William
143 Sombrio Dr., Santa Fe, NM 87501
Tel 505-983-1579 (SAN 201-5889)
(ISBN Prefix 0-88307)
Garber Comm
Garber Communications, Inc.
7 Garber Hill Rd., Blauvelt, NY 10913
Tel 914-359-9292 (SAN 226-2789)
(ISBN Prefix 0-89345)
Garganti Edit
Garzanti Editore
Via Senato 25, I-20121 Milan, Italy
Garland Pub
Garland Publishing, Inc.
136 Madison Ave., 2nd Floor, New York, NY 10016 Tel 212-686-7492 (SAN 201-5897)
(ISBN Prefix 0-8240)
Garnier
Garnier
19, Rue des Plantes, 75014 Paris, France
(ISBN Prefix 2-7050)
Garriga
Garriga, S.A. Ediciones
Paris, 1443, Barcelona-36, Spain
Garsi Edit
Garsi Editorial
Londres 17, Madrid-28, Spain
Gaudeamus
Gaudeamus
Mannerheimintie 5C, 00100 Helsinki 10, Finland
GB *Imprint of* **Oxford U Pr**

Gemological
Gemological Institute of America
1660 Stewart St., Santa Monica, CA 90404
Tel 213-829-2991 (SAN 203-4212)
(ISBN Prefix 0-87311)
Genealog Pub
Genealogical Publishing Co., Inc.
111 Water St., Baltimore, MD 21202
Tel 301-837-8271 (SAN 206-8370)
(ISBN Prefix 0-8063)
Gentner
Gentner, Alfons W., Verlag GmbH & Co. KG
Forststr. 131, Postf 688, 7000 Stuttgart 1, Federal Republic of Germany
(ISBN Prefix 3-87247)
Geo Tutkim
Geologinen Tutkimuslaitos
02150 Espoo 15, Finland
Georgetown U Pr
Georgetown Univ. Press
Intercultural Center, Room 111, Washington, DC 20057 Tel 202-625-4824
(SAN 203-4247)
(ISBN Prefix 0-87840)
Geuthner
Geuthner
12, Rue Vavin, 75006 Paris, France
Ghisetti & Corvi
Ghisetti & Corvi
Corso Concordia, 7-20129 Milan, Italy
Ghisoni
Ghisoni
Via Maestri Campionesi, 5-20135 Milan, Italy
Giardini Pisa
Giardini (Pisa)
Via S. Bibbiana, 28-56100 Pisa, Italy
Gigord
Gigord
15, Rue Cassette, 75006 Paris, France
Giligia
Giligia Press
P.O. Box 626, Aurora, OR 97002
Tel 503-651-2090 (SAN 203-4255)
(ISBN Prefix 0-87791)
Ginn
Ginn & Co, A Xerox Publishing Co.
191 Spring St., Lexington, MA 02173
Tel 617-861-1670 (SAN 201-6486)
Orders to:
P.O. Box 2649, 1250 Fairwood Ave., Columbus, OH 43216 Tel 614-253-8661
(SAN 201-6494)
(ISBN Prefix 0-663)
Girardet
Girardet Graphische Betriebe und Verlag
Girardetstr. 2-38, 4300 Essen 1, Federal Republic of Germany
(ISBN Prefix 3-7736)
Giuffre
Giuffre
Via Statuto, 2-20121 Milan, Italy
Giunti-Barbera
Giunti-Barbera
Via Ammirato, 37-50136 Florence, Italy
Giunti-Martello
Giunti-Martello
Via Gioberti, 34-50121 Florence, Italy
Gjellerup Forlag
Gjellerup's, Jul. Forlag A-S
Romersgade 11, 1362 Copenhagen K, Denmark
Glencoe
Glencoe Publishing Co., Inc.
c/o Macmillan Publishing Co., Inc., 866 Third Ave., New York, NY 10022
Tel 212-935-2000 (SAN 202-5574)
(ISBN Prefix 0-02)
Gloucester Art
Gloucester Art Press
P.O. Box 4526, Albuquerque, NM 87196
Tel 505-843-7749 (SAN 205-2865)
(ISBN Prefix 0-930582)
Gnosis Edit
Gnosis Editorial
Fernando Gabriel, 15-2 Izda., Madrid-17, Spain
Goerlich
Goerlich
Via Giovanni da Verrazzano, 15-28100 Novara, Italy
Goldmann
Goldmann, Wilhelm, Verlag GmbH
Neumarkter Str 18, Postfach 800709, D-8000 Munich 80, Federal Republic of Germany

559

Gondolat
Gondolat Konyvkiado
PB 225, VIII, Brody S V.16, 1368
Budapest, Hungary

Gonthier
Gonthier
19, Rue Amelie, 75340 Paris, France

Good Apple
Good Apple, Inc.
P.O. Box 299, Carthage, IL 62321
Tel 217-357-3981 (SAN 208-6646)
(ISBN Prefix 0-916456; ISBN Prefix
0-86653)

Goodheart
Goodheart-Willcox Co., Inc.
123 W. Taft Dr., South Holland, IL 60473
Tel 312-333-7200 (SAN 203-4387)
(ISBN Prefix 0-87006)

Goor
Goor
Postbus 70707, Amsterdam, Netherlands

Gordon
Gordon & Breach Science Pubs., Inc.
1 Park Ave., New York, NY 10016
Tel 212-689-0360 (SAN 201-6370)
(ISBN Prefix 0-677)

Gordon Pr
Gordon Press Pubs.
P.O. Box 459, Bowling Green Sta., New
York, NY 10004 (SAN 201-6362)
(ISBN Prefix 0-87968)

Gould
Gould Pubns.
199 State St., Binghamton, NY 13901
Tel 607-724-3000 (SAN 201-6354)
(ISBN Prefix 0-87526)

Gov Insts
Government Institutes, Inc.
966 Hungerford Dr., No. 24, Rockville,
MD 20850 (SAN 214-3801)
(ISBN Prefix 0-86587)

Govi Verlag
Govi-Verlag (Pharmazeutischer Verlag) GmbH
Beethovenplatz 1-3, 6000 Frankfurt am
Main, Federal Republic of Germany
(ISBN Prefix 3-7741)

Govt Printer
Government Printer
BP 58, Brazzaville, Congo (Brazzaville)

Gower Pub Ltd
Gower Publishing Ltd.
Old Post Rd., Brookfield, VT 05036
Tel 802-276-3355 (SAN 262-0308)
(ISBN Prefix 0-566)

Grade Finders
Grade Finders, Inc.
642 Lancaster Ave., Berwyn, PA 19312
Tel 215-644-4159 (SAN 208-2322)
Orders to:
P.O. Box 444, Bala-Cynwyd, PA 19004
(SAN 208-2330)

Grafisk Forlag
Grafisk Forlag A-S
Klosterrisvej 7, 2100 Copenhagen 0,
Denmark

Grafo
Grafo
Via Bassi, 20-25100 Brescia, Italy

Graham & Trotman
Graham & Trotman Ltd.
4th Flr. Bond St. Hse. 14 Clifford St.,
London, W1X 1RD, United Kingdom
(ISBN Prefix 0-86010)

Granica
Granica Editor
Muntaner, 460,Barcelona 6, Spain

Graph Arts Res RIT
See Tech & Ed Ctr Graph Arts RIT

Graphic Dimensions
Graphic Dimensions
8 Frederick Rd., Pittsford, NY 14534
Tel 716-381-3428 (SAN 213-067X)
(ISBN Prefix 0-930904)

Great Outdoors
Great Outdoors Publishing Co.
4747 28th St., N., St. Petersburg, FL 33714
Tel 813-525-6609 (SAN 201-6273)
(ISBN Prefix 0-8200)

Gredos
Gredos, S.A. Editorial
Sanchez Pacheco, 83, Madrid-2, Spain

Green
Green, Warren H., Inc.
8356 Olive Blvd., St. Louis, MO 63132
Tel 314-991-1335 (SAN 201-4939)
(ISBN Prefix 0-87527)

Greenlf Bks
Greenleaf Books
Weare, NH 03281 (SAN 203-4514)
(ISBN Prefix 0-934676)

Greenwood
Greenwood Press
88 Post Rd. W., P.O. Box 5007, Westport,
CT 06881 Tel 203-226-3571 (SAN
213-2028)
(ISBN Prefix 0-8371; ISBN Prefix 0-313)

Gribaudi
Gribaudi
Corso Ferraris, 67-10128 Turin, Italy

Grijalbo
Grijalbo, S.A. Ediciones
Aragon, 386, Barcelona-13, Spain

Groves Dict Music
Groves Dictionaries of Music, Inc.
15 E. 26th St., Suite 1503, New York, NY
10010 Tel 212-532-4811 (SAN
211-9579); Tel 800-221-2123
(ISBN Prefix 0-943818)

Grund
Grund
60, Rue Mazarine, 75006 Paris, France

Guaraldi
Guaraldi
Via Masaccio, 268-50132 Florence, Italy

Guba
Guba, W.
8320 Morselet, Denmark

Guenegaud
Guenegaud
10, Rue de l'Odeon,75006 Paris, France

Guerin
Guerin Editeur
4574, Rue St. Denis, Montreal, Quebec
H2J 2L3, Canada

Guild Bks
Guild Books, Catholic Polls, Inc.
86 Riverside Dr., New York, NY 10024
Tel 212-799-2600 (SAN 203-4646)
(ISBN Prefix 0-912080)

Guild Prof Trans
See Translation Research

Guiness Super
Guiness Superlatives Ltd.
2 Cecil Ct., London Rd. Enfield, Midds.
EN2 6DJ, United Kingdom

Gulf Pub
Gulf Publishing Co.
P.O. Box 2608, Houston, TX 77001
Tel 713-529-4301 (SAN 201-6125)
(ISBN Prefix 0-87201)

Gutersloher
Gutersloher Verlagshaus Gerd Mohn
Konigstr 23, Postfach 2368, D-4830
Gutersloh 1, Federal Republic of Germany
(ISBN Prefix 3-579)

Gyldendal Norsk
Gyldendal Norsk Forlag
Klareboderne 3, DK-1001 Copenhagen K,
Denmark

Gypsum Assn
Gypsum Association
1603 Orrington Ave., Suite 1210, Evanston,
IL 60201 (SAN 224-8808)

H Luchterhand
Luchterhand, Herman, Verlag GMBH & Co.,
KG
Heddesdorfer Str 31, Postfach 1780,
D-5450 Neuwied 1,
Federal Republic of Germany

Habelt
Habelt, Rudolf, Verlag GmbH
Am Buchenhang 1, 5300 Bonn 1,
Federal Republic of Germany

Hachette-Jeunesse
Hachette-Jeunesse
79 Blvd. St-Germain, BP 1506, F-75006
Paris, France

Hacker
Hacker Art Books
54 W. 57th St., New York, NY 10019
Tel 212-757-1450 (SAN 201-6052)
(ISBN Prefix 0-87817)

Hafner
Hafner Press, Div. of Macmillan Publishing
Co., Inc.
866 Third Ave., New York, NY 10022
Tel 212-935-7616 (SAN 201-6001);
Tel 800-343-2806
Dist. by:
Collier-Macmillan Distribution Ctr.,
Riverside, NJ 08075 (SAN 202-5582)
(ISBN Prefix 0-02)

Halbart Wahle
Halbart Wahle & Cie
11rue des Carmes, 4000 Liege, Belgium

Halsted Pr
Halsted Press, Div. of John Wiley & Sons, Inc.
605 Third Ave., New York, NY 10158
Tel 212-850-6418 (SAN 202-2680)

Hameau
Hameau
15, Rue Servandoni, 75006 Paris, France
(ISBN Prefix 2-7203)

Hamilton Pr
See Citizens Law

Hamline Law
Hamline University School of Law Advanced
Legal Education
1536 Hewitt Ave, St Paul, MN 55104
(SAN 227-2636)

Hamlyn-Amer
Hamlyn/American
(SAN 200-2418)
(ISBN Prefix 0-600)

Hamlyn Pub
Hamlyn Publishing Group, Ltd.
Astronaut Housee, Hounslow Rd., Feltham,
Middlesex TW14 3AR, United Kingdom
(ISBN Prefix 0-600)

Hammond Inc
Hammond, Inc.
515 Valley St., Maplewood, NJ 07040
Tel 201-763-6000 (SAN 202-2702)
(ISBN Prefix 0-8437)

Hanser
Hanser, Carl, GmbH & Co.
Kolbergerstr. 22, 8000 Munich 80,
Federal Republic of Germany
(ISBN Prefix 3-446)

Har-Row
Harper & Row Pubs., Inc.
10 E. 53rd St., New York, NY 10022
Tel 212-207-7000 (SAN 200-2086); 1700
Montgomery St., San Francisco, CA 94111
Tel 415-989-9000 (SAN 215-3734)
Orders to:
Keystone Industrial Park, Scranton, PA
18512 (SAN 215-3742)
(ISBN Prefix 0-06)

HarBraceJ
Harcourt Brace Jovanovich, Inc.
1250 Sixth Ave., San Diego, CA 92101
Tel 619-231-6616 (SAN 200-2736); 757
Third Ave., New York, NY 10017 (SAN
200-2299)
(ISBN Prefix 0-15)

Harmattan
L'Harmattan
18, Rue des Quatres Vents, 75006 Paris,
France

Harmony *Imprint of* **Crown**

HarpT *Imprint of* **Har-Row**

Harrap
Harrap, George G., & Co. Ltd.
182-184 High Holborn, London WC1V
7AX, United Kingdom
(ISBN Prefix 0-245)

Harrap Co
Harrap, George G., & Co. Ltd
182-184 High Holborn, London WC1V
7AA, United Kingdom
(ISBN Prefix 0-245)

Harrassowitz
Harrassowitz, Otto
Tanusstr 6 Postf 2929, 6200 Wiesbaden,
Federal Republic of Germany
(ISBN Prefix 3-447)

Hart Graphics
Hart Graphics
P.O. Box 968, Austin, TX 78767 (SAN
217-1074)
(ISBN Prefix 0-9605422)

Harvard U Pr
Harvard Univ. Press
79 Garden St., Cambridge, MA 02138
Tel 617-495-2600 (SAN 281-7721)
Orders to:
Customer Service, Harvard Univ. Press, 79
Garden St., Cambridge, MA 02138
Tel 617-495-2480 (SAN 281-773X)
(ISBN Prefix 0-674)

Harvey
Harvey House, Pubs.
20 Waterside Plaza, New York, NY 10010
Tel 212-889-9520 (SAN 202-2796)
Orders to:
128 W. River St., Chippewa Falls, WI
54729 Tel 715-723-2814 (SAN
202-280X)
(ISBN Prefix 0-8178)

Haskell
Haskell Booksellers, Inc.
P.O. Box FF, Blythebourne Sta., Brooklyn,
NY 11219 Tel 212-435-0500 (SAN
202-2818)
(ISBN Prefix 0-8383)

Hastings
Hastings House Pubs., Inc.
10 E. 40th St., New York, NY 10016
Tel 212-689-5400 (SAN 213-9561)
(ISBN Prefix 0-8038)

Hatier
Hatier
8, Rue d'assas, 75006 Paris, France
(ISBN Prefix 2-218)

Haufe
Haufe, Rudolf, Verlag GmbH & Co. KG
Hinderburgstr 64, Postf 740, 7800 Freiburg
im Breisgau, Federal Republic of Germany
(ISBN Prefix 3-448)

Haupt Verlag
Haupt, Paul, AG Verlag
Falkenplatz 14, 3001 Bern, Switzerland
(ISBN Prefix 3-258)

Hawaiian Serv
Hawaiian Service, Inc.
P.O. Box 2835, Honolulu, HI 96803
Tel 808-841-0134 (SAN 205-0463)
(ISBN Prefix 0-930492)

Hawthorn *Imprint of Dutton*

Hayden
Hayden Book Co., Inc.
50 Essex St., Rochelle Park, NJ 07662
Tel 201-843-0550 (SAN 200-2094)
(ISBN Prefix 0-8104)

Haymark
Haymark Pubns.
P.O. Box 243, Fredericksburg, VA 22401
Tel 703-373-1144 (SAN 213-2508)
(ISBN Prefix 0-933910)

HC *Imprint of HarBraceJ*

Healthcare Fin Man Assn
Healthcare Financial Management Assn.
1900 Spring Rd., Suite 500, Oak Brook, IL
60521 Tel 312-655-4600 (SAN 207-5911)
(ISBN Prefix 0-930228)

Hearst Bks
Hearst Books, Div. of the Hearst Corp.
224 W. 57th St., Rm. 307, New York, NY
10019 Tel 212-262-8605 (SAN 202-2842)
Orders to:
P.O. Box 1406, Radio City Sta., New York,
NY 10019 (SAN 202-2850)
(ISBN Prefix 0-910992; ISBN Prefix
0-87851; ISBN Prefix 0-910990)

Hebrew Pub
Hebrew Publishing Co.
100 Water St., Brooklyn, NY 11201
Tel 212-858-6928 (SAN 201-5404)
(ISBN Prefix 0-88482)

Heian Intl
Heian International Publishing, Inc.
P.O. Box 2402, South San Francisco, CA
94083-2402 Tel 415-467-0222 (SAN
213-2036)
(ISBN Prefix 0-89346)

Heidenreich
Heidenreich House
5012 Oak Point Way, Fair Oaks, CA 95628
Tel 916-961-3297 (SAN 204-0395)
(ISBN Prefix 0-9600428)

Heimeran
Heimeran-Verlag
Dietlindenstr. 14, 8000 Munich 40,
Federal Republic of Germany
(ISBN Prefix 3-7765)

Heineman
Heineman, James H., Inc., Pub.
475 Park Ave., New York, NY 10022
Tel 212-688-2028 (SAN 204-0409)
(ISBN Prefix 0-87008)

Heinemann Ed
Heinemann Educational Books Inc.
4 Front St., Exeter, NH 03833
Tel 603-778-0534 (SAN 210-5829)
(ISBN Prefix 0-435)

Heinman
Heinman, W.S., Imported Books
225 W. 57th St., Rm. 404, New York, NY
10019 Tel 212-757-7628 (SAN
121-6201); P.O. Box, Ansonia Sta., New
York, NY 10019 (SAN 121-6201)

Hellenes
Hellenes-English Biblical Foundation
P.O. Box 10412, Jackson, MS 39209
(SAN 204-0433)
(ISBN Prefix 0-910710)

Helmond
Helmond
Churchil-Laan 107, Postbus 23, Helmond,
Netherlands

Hemisphere Pub
Hemisphere Publishing Corp.
1025 Vermont Ave., N.W., Washington,
DC 20005 Tel 202-783-3958 (SAN
207-4001)
Orders to:
19 W. 44th St., New York, NY 10036
Tel 212-921-0606 (SAN 207-401X)
(ISBN Prefix 0-89116)

Hemus-Livraria
Hemus-Livraria Editora Ltda.
CP 9686, 01510 Sao Paulo SP, Brazil

Herald Pr
Herald Press
616 Walnut Ave., Scottdale, PA 15683
Tel 412-887-8500 (SAN 202-2915)
(ISBN Prefix 0-8361)

Herder
Herder GmbH & Co. KG, Verlag
Hermann-Herder-Str. 4, 7800 Freiburg im
Breisgau, Federal Republic of Germany
(ISBN Prefix 3-451)

Herder SA
Herder S. A.
Provenzo, 388, Barcelona 25, Spain

Herrero
Herrero, S. A. Editorial
Rio Amazonas 44, Mexico 5, D. F., Mexico

Heures de France
Heures de France
21, Boulevard Richard Lenoir, 75011 Paris,
France
(ISBN Prefix 2-85385)

Heyden
Heyden & Son, Inc.
247 S. 41st St., Philadelphia, PA 19104
Tel 215-382-6673 (SAN 213-2052)

Heydent
See Heyden

Heymanns Verlag
Heymanns, Carl, Verlag KG
Rechts und Staatswissenschaftliche
Verlagsbuchhandlung, Gereonstr. 18-32,
5000 Cologne 1,
Federal Republic of Germany
(ISBN Prefix 3-452)

Heyn
Heyn, Johannes, Verlag
Kramergasse 2-4, 9010 Klagenfurt, Austria
(ISBN Prefix 3-85366)

Heyne W Verlag
Heyne, Wilhelm, Verlag
Turkenstr 5-7, Postfach 201204, D-8000
Munich 2, Federal Republic of Germany
(ISBN Prefix 3-453)

Hiersemann
Hiersemann, Anton
Rosenbergstr 113, 7000 Stuttgart 1,
Federal Republic of Germany

Hill & Wang
Hill & Wang, Inc, Div. of Farrar, Straus &
Giroux, Inc.
19 Union Square W., New York, NY 10003
Tel 212-741-6900 (SAN 201-9299)
(ISBN Prefix 0-8090)

Himalaya Hse
Himalaya House
P.O. Box 792, Wheat Ridge, CO 80033
Tel 303-423-3170 (SAN 211-1969)
(ISBN Prefix 0-89654)

Hippocrene Bks
Hippocrene Books, Inc. B
171 Madison Ave., New York, NY 10016
Tel 212-685-4372 (SAN 213-2060)
(ISBN Prefix 0-88254)

Hirt
Hirt, Ferdinand
Schauenburgerstr. 36, Postf 2580 2300 Kiel,
1, Federal Republic of Germany
(ISBN Prefix 3-554)

Hirzel Verlag
Hirzel, S., , Verlag GmbH & Co.
Birkenwaldstr 44, Postf 347, 7000 Stuttgart
1, Federal Republic of Germany
(ISBN Prefix 3-7776)

HIS *Imprint of HR&W*

Hispanic Seminary
Hispanic Seminary of Medieval Studies
3734 Ross St., Madison, WI 53705 (SAN
207-9836)

Hispanic Soc
Hispanic Society of America
613 W. 155th St., New York, NY 10032
Tel 212-926-2234 (SAN 204-0573)
(ISBN Prefix 0-87535)

Hispano Europea
Hispano Europea Editorial
Bori y Fontesta, 6, Barcelona-21, Spain

HM
Houghton Mifflin Co.
2 Park St., Boston, MA 02107
Tel 617-725-5000 (SAN 200-2388)
Orders to:
Wayside Road, Burlington, MA 01803
Tel 617-272-1500 (SAN 215-3793)
(ISBN Prefix 0-395)

Hoepli
Hoepli
Via Hoepli, 5, 20121, Milan, Italy
(ISBN Prefix 8-8203)

Hogrefe
Hogrefe, C. J., Inc.
525 Eglinton Ave. East, Toronto, Ontario
M4P 1N5, Canada
(ISBN Prefix 0-88937)

Hollinek
Hollinek, Brueder Gesellschaftsbuchdruckerei
und Verlagsbuchhandlung
Landstrasser Hauptstrasse 163, 1130 Wien,
Austria
(ISBN Prefix 3-85119)

Hollym Corp
Hollym Corporation
14-5 Kwanchol-dong, Chongno-ku Seoul
110, Korea, South

Hollym Intl
Hollym International Corp.
18 Donald Place, Elizabeth, NJ 07208
(SAN 211-0172)
(ISBN Prefix 0-930878)

HoltC *Imprint of HR&W*

Honolulu Japanese
Honolulu Japanese Chamber of Commerce
2454 S Beretania St, Honolulu, HI 96826
(SAN 225-6215)

Hoover Inst Pr
Hoover Institution Press
Stanford University, Stanford, CA 94305
Tel 415-497-3373 (SAN 202-3024)
(ISBN Prefix 0-8179)

Hornung-Verlag
Hornung-Verlag Viktor Lang
Stolzingstr. 25, 8000 Munich 81, Postfach
810506, Federal Republic of Germany

Horticult Research
Horticultural Research Institute, Inc.
230 Southern Bldg., Washington, DC 20005
Tel 202-737-4060 (SAN 213-3210)
(ISBN Prefix 0-935336)

Horvath
Horvath Editions Diffusion
30, Rue Benoit-Malon, 42300 Roanne,
France
(ISBN Prefix 2-7171)

Hospital Finan
See Healthcare Fin Man Assn

Howell Bk
Howell Book House Inc.
Helmsley Bldg., 230 Park Ave., New York,
NY 10169 Tel 212-986-4488 (SAN
202-3075)
(ISBN Prefix 0-87605)

HRAFP
Human Relations Area Files Press, Inc.
P.O. Box 2015, Yale Sta., New Haven, CT
06520 Tel 203-777-2334 (SAN 202-3091)
(ISBN Prefix 0-87536)

HR&W
Holt, Rinehart & Winston, Inc.
383 Madison Ave., New York, NY 10017
Tel 212-872-2000 (SAN 200-2108)
(ISBN Prefix 0-03)

HR&W Canada
Holt, Rinehart & Winston of Canada, Ltd.
55 Horner Ave., Toronto, Ont. M8Z 4X6,
Canada
(ISBN Prefix 0-03)

Hse of Collectibles
House of Collectibles, Inc.
1900 Premier Row, Orlando, FL 32809
Tel 305-857-9095 (SAN 202-3113)
(ISBN Prefix 0-87637)

Huber
Huber, Hans
Langgassstr. 76, 3000 Bern, Switzerland
(ISBN Prefix 3-456)

Hueber
Hueber, Max, Verlag GmbH & Co. KG
Max-Hueber-Str. 4, 8045 Munich,
Federal Republic of Germany
(ISBN Prefix 3-19)

Human & Rousseau
Human & Rousseau Publishers (Pty.), Ltd.
State House 3-9 Rose St., P.O. Box 5050,
Capetown 8000, South Africa

Humanities
Humanities Press, Inc.
Atlantic Highlands, NJ 07716
Tel 201-872-1441 (SAN 201-9272)
(ISBN Prefix 0-391)

Humboldt Taschen
Humboldt-Taschenbuchverlag Jacobi KG
Neusser Str. 3, 8000 Munich 40,
Federal Republic of Germany
(ISBN Prefix 3-581)

Hurtig
Hurtig, M. G., Ltd
10560-105th Street, Edmonton, Alta. T54
2W7, Canada
(ISBN Prefix 0-88830)

Hutar
Hutar Growth Management Institute
1701 E. Lake Ave. Suite 270, Glenview, IL
60025 (SAN 210-4385)
(ISBN Prefix 0-918896)

Hutch Pub Co
Hutchinson Publishing Group Ltd.
3 Fitzroy Square, London W1P 6JD,
United Kingdom
(ISBN Prefix 0-09)

Hutchinson
See Merrimack Pub Cir

Hyperion Conn
Hyperion Press, Inc.
47 Riverside Ave., P.O. Box 591, Westport,
CT 06880 Tel 203-226-1091 (SAN
202-3148)
(ISBN Prefix 0-88355; ISBN Prefix 0-8305)

Iaconi
Iaconi Book Imports, A Family Business
300 Pennsylvania, San Francisco, CA
94107 Tel 415-285-7393

IAEA *Imprint of* **Unipub**

Iber Euro Edns
Iberico Europea De Ediciones, S.A.
Serrano, 44, Madrid-7, Spain

Iberia SA
Iberia, S. A.
Muntaner 180, Barcelona 36, Spain

Icaria Edit
Icaria Editorial, S.A.
Calle de la Torre, 14, Barcelona-6, Spain

Ide Hse
Ide House, Inc.
4631 Harvey Dr., Mesquite, TX 75150
(SAN 216-146X)
(ISBN Prefix 0-86663)

IDRC *Imprint of* **Unipub**

IdW Verlag
IdW-Verlag GmbH
Cecilienallee 36, 4000 Dusseldorf 30,
Federal Republic of Germany

IIR *Imprint of* **Unipub**

Il Mulino
Il Mulino
Via S. Stefano 6-40125 Bologna, Italy

Il Pensiero
Il Pensiero Scientifico
Via Panama, 48-00198 Rome, Italy

Il Rostro
Il Rostro
Via Monte Generoso, 6a-20155 Milan, Italy

Il Vespro
Il Vespro
Via degli Orti, 41-90143 Palermo, Italy

Ili-Cor Pubns
Ili-Cor Pubns.
53 Storz Rd., Sacramento, CA 95823
Tel 916-393-3021 (SAN 240-1525)

Illum Way Pr
See IWP Pub

ILR Pr
ILR Pr.
New York State School of Industrial
Relations, Cornell Univ., Box 1000, Ithaca,
NY 14853 Tel 607-256-3061 (SAN
270-8825)
(ISBN Prefix 0-87546)

Imago Libri
Imago Libri
Via Pito, 11-20129 Milan, Italy

IMM North Am
IMM/North American Pubns. Center
Old Post Rd., Brookfield, VT 05036
(SAN 219-791X)

Imp Soc Tchrs Da
Imperial Society of Teachers of Dancing
Euston Hall, Birkenhead St., London
WC1H 8BE, United Kingdom
(ISBN Prefix 0-900484)

Imported Bks
Imported Bks.
P.O. Box 4414, 2025 W. Clarendon St.,
Dallas, TX 75208 Tel 214-941-6497

Incentive Pubns
Incentive Pubns., Inc.
2400 Crestmoor Rd., Nashville, TN 37215
Tel 615-385-2934 (SAN 203-8005)
(ISBN Prefix 0-913916; ISBN Prefix
0-86530)

Ind St Univ
Indiana State Univ.
Stalker Hall, Rm. 300, Terre Haute, IN
47809 Tel 812-232-6311 (SAN 211-0202)
(ISBN Prefix 0-940100)

Ind U Pr
Indiana Univ. Press
Tenth & Morton Sts., Bloomington, IN
47405 Tel 812-335-8287 (SAN 202-5647)
(ISBN Prefix 0-253)

Ind-US Inc
Ind-US, Inc.
Box 56, East Glastonbury, CT 06025
Tel 203-633-0045 (SAN 213-5809)

Index
Index
Commandante Zorita, 13, Madrid 20, Spain

Indus Pr
Industrial Press Inc.
200 Madison Ave., New York, NY 10157
Tel 212-889-6330 (SAN 202-6945)
(ISBN Prefix 0-8311)

Industrieverlag
Industrieverlag Peter Linde, GmbH
Dominikaner Bastei 10, 1010 Vienna 1,
Austria
(ISBN Prefix 3-85122)

Info Gatekeepers
Information Gatekeepers, Inc.
167 Corey Road, Brookline, MA 02146
Tel 617-739-2022 (SAN 237-9597)

Info Resources
Information Resources Press, Div. of Herner &
Co.
1700 N. Moore St., Suite 700, Arlington,
VA 22209 Tel 703-558-8270 (SAN
202-6961)
(ISBN Prefix 0-87815)

Ingenjorsforlaget
Ingenjorsforlaget AB
Birger Jarlsgatan 20, Box 5703, 11487
Stockholm, Sweden

Inkilap Ve Aka Kitabevleri
Inkilap Ve Aka Kitabevleri
Ankara Cad 95, Istanbul, Turkey

Inn Verlag
Inn-Verlag, Driesslein & Co. OHG
Zollerstr 3, 6021 Innsbruck, Austria
(ISBN Prefix 3-85123)

Innovacion
Innovacion Asesores, S. A. de C. V. Ediciones
Francisco Marquez 27 Mexico 13, D. F.,
Mexico

Ins Study Human
Institute for the Study of Human Knowledge
P. O. Box 176, Los Altos, CA 94022
Tel 415-948-9428 (SAN 226-4536)

Inst Afr Stu
Institute of African Studies
University of Ghana, Legon, Ghana

Inst Amer
Instituto Americano
Mendivil 6 y 8, Madrid 18, Spain

Inst Busn Appraisers
Institute of Business Appraisers, Incorporated,
the
P.O. Box 1447, Boynton Beach, FL 33435
Tel 305-734-1075 (SAN 224-6244)

Inst Caro y Cuervo
Instituto Caro y Cuervo
Apartado Aero 51502, Bogota, Colombia

Inst Corps Gras
Institut des Corps Gras
5, Boulevard de Latour Maubourg 75007
Paris, France

Inst Econ Finan
Institute for Economic & Financial Research
Dist. by:
American Classical College Press, P.O. Box
4526, Albuquerque, NM 87196
Tel 505-843-7749 (SAN 201-2618)
(ISBN Prefix 0-918968)

Inst Energy
Institutes for Energy Development, Inc.
P.O. Box 19243, Oklahoma City, OK
76133 Tel 405-691-4449 (SAN 209-9322)
(ISBN Prefix 0-89419)

Inst Environ
Institute for Environmental Studies
3400 Walnut St, Philadelphia, PA 19104
(SAN 226-5648)

Inst Ethnol
Institut d'Ethnologie
Palais de Chaillot, 75016 Paris, France
(ISBN Prefix 2-85265)

Inst Etudes Slaves
Institut d'Etudes Slaves
9, Rue Michelet, 75006 Paris, France

Inst Finan Educ
Institute of Financial Education
111 East Wacker Dr., Chicago, IL 60601
(SAN 224-1382)

Inst Fire Eng
Institution of Fire Engineers
148 New Walk, Leicester LE1 7QB,
United Kingdom

Inst Hispano-Arabe
Instituto Hispano-Arabe de Cultura
Paseo Juan XXIII, 5, Madrid-3, Spain

Inst Indus Eng
Institute of Industrial Engineers
25 Technology Park-Atlanta, Norcross, GA
30092 Tel 404-449-0460 (SAN 213-2338)
(ISBN Prefix 0-89806)

Inst Indus Launderer
Institute of Industrial Launderers
1730 M St Nw Ste 613, Washington, DC
20036 (SAN 224-8441)

Inst Ling Ver
Instituto Linguistico de Verano A. C.
Hidalgo 166, Tlalpan, Mexico, 22 D. F.,
Mexico

Inst Mediaeval Mus
Institute of Mediaeval Music
(SAN 206-6955)
c/o L.A. Dittmer, P.O. Box 295,
Henryville, PA 18332 Tel 717-629-1278
(SAN 285-0311)
(ISBN Prefix 0-912024; ISBN Prefix
0-931902)

Inst Mod Lang
Institute of Modern Languages, Inc.
P.O. Box 1087, Silver Spring, MD 20910
Tel 301-565-2580 (SAN 206-9598)
(ISBN Prefix 0-88499)

Inst Occit Tlse
Institut d'Estudes Occitanes, Toulouse
11 bis, Rue de la Concorde, 3100 Toulouse,
France
(ISBN Prefix 2-85910)

Inst Verg Sprach
Institut fuer Vergleichende Sprachwissenschaft
der Universitaet
Innrain 30, 6020 Innsbruck, Austria
(ISBN Prefix 3-85124)

Inst Verre
Institut du Verre
34, Rue Michel-Ange, 75016 Paris, France

Instituto Panamericano
Instituto Panamericano De Geografia E
Historia
Ex-Arzobispado, 29, Mejico, Mexico

Interbk Intl
Interbook International
Lange Haven 97, Schiedam, Netherlands

Interciencia
Interciencia
Costanilla de Los Angeles, 15, Madrid 13,
Spain

Interediciones
Interediciones, J.M.
Marcenado, 21, Madrid-2, Spain

Interstate
Interstate
19-27 N. Jackson St., Danville, IL 61832
Tel 217-446-0500 (SAN 206-6548)
(ISBN Prefix 0-8134)

Intl Bk Ctr
International Book Centre
P.O. Box 295, Troy, MI 48099
Tel 313-879-8436 (SAN 208-7022)
(ISBN Prefix 0-917062; ISBN Prefix
0-86685)

Intl Coop All
International Cooperative Alliance
11 Upper Grosvenor St, London W1X
9PA, United Kingdom
(ISBN Prefix 0-904380)

Intl Fabricare Inst
International Fabricare Institute
12251 Tech Rd., Silver Spring, MD 20904
Tel 301-622-1900 (SAN 223-8918)

Intl Graphoanalysis
International Graphoanalysis Society
111 N Canal St, Chicago, IL 60606 (SAN
225-4018)

Intl Guatemala
International Society of Guatemala Collectors
P O Box 246, Troy, NY 12181 (SAN
225-5952)

Intl Ideas
International Ideas Inc.
1627 Spruce St., Philadelphia, PA 19103
Tel 215-546-0392 (SAN 210-6043)
(ISBN Prefix 0-89563)

Intl Labour Office
International Labour Office
Washington Branch, 1750 New York Ave.,
N.W., Suite 311, Washington, DC 20006
(SAN 203-817X)
(ISBN Prefix 92-2)

Intl Learn Syst
International Learning Systems, Inc.
1715 Connecticut Ave., N.W., Washington,
DC 20009 Tel 202-232-4111 (SAN
209-1615)

Intl Monetary
International Monetary Fund
700 19th St., N.W., Washington, DC 20431
Tel 202-477-3086 (SAN 203-8188)
(ISBN Prefix 0-939934)

Intl Plan Glos
International Planning Glossaries
23 Connaught Close, Hemel Hempstead,
Herts. HP2 7AB, United Kingdom
(ISBN Prefix 0-905864)

Intl Program Labs
International Program of Laboratories for
Population Statistics
NCNB Plaza, Suite 400, 136 E. Rosemary
St., Chapel Hill, NC 27514
Tel 919-966-1131 (SAN 211-0229)
(ISBN Prefix 0-89383)

Intl Pub Co
International Pubs. Co.
381 Park Ave., S., Suite 1301, New York,
NY 10016 Tel 212-685-2864 (SAN
202-5655)
(ISBN Prefix 0-7178)

Intl Pubns Serv
International Pubns. Service
114 E. 32nd St., New York, NY 10016
Tel 212-685-9351 (SAN 169-5819)
(ISBN Prefix 0-8002; ISBN Prefix 0-85066)

Intl Schol Bk Serv
International Scholarly Book Services, Inc.
(ISBS, Inc.)
P.O. Box 1632, Beaverton, OR 97075
Tel 503-292-2606 (SAN 169-7129)
(ISBN Prefix 0-89955)

Inv Funds Inst CN
Investment Funds Institute of Canada
8 King St. E., Suite 210, Toronto, Ontario
M5C 1B5, Canada Tel 416-363-2158

Investor's Syst
Investor's Systems, Inc.
P.O. Box 1422, Dayton, OH 45401
Tel 513-223-6870 (SAN 207-3420)
(ISBN Prefix 0-915610)

Irvington
Irvington Pubs.
551 Fifth Ave., New York, NY 10176
Tel 212-697-8100 (SAN 207-2408)
(ISBN Prefix 0-89197; ISBN Prefix 0-8290)

ISEDI
ISEPI-Istituto Editoriale Internazionale
Via Paleocapa, 6-20121 Milan, Italy

ISI Pr
ISI Press, Subs. of Institute for Scientific
Information
3501 Market St., University City Science
Ctr., Philadelphia, PA 19104
Tel 215-386-0100 (SAN 209-9349)
(ISBN Prefix 0-89495)

Ist Edit Ital
Istituto Editoriale Italiano
Via Passo Pordoi, 21-20139 Milan, Italy

Ist Geo Agostini
Istituto Geografico de Agostini
Via Giovanni da Verrazzano, 15-28100
Novara, Italy

Ist Poligrafico
Istituto Poligrafico dello Stato
Piazza Verdi 10-00198 Rome, Italy

Ist Univers Orient
Istituto Universitario Orientale
Piazza S. Giovanni Maggiore, 30-80134
Naples, Italy

Istmo
Istmo
General Pardinas, 26, Madrid 1, Spain

ITA
See Pitman Learning

IWP Pub
IWP Publishing
P.O. Box 2449, Menlo Park, CA 94025
Tel 415-321-4468 (SAN 203-798X)
(ISBN Prefix 0-914766)

Iztaccihuatl
Iztaccihuatl, S. A. Editorial
Miguel E. Schultz 21, Mexico 4 D.F.,
Mexico

J A Allen
Allen, J. A., & Co. Ltd.
Dist. by:
Sporting Book Center, Inc., Canaan, NY
12029 Tel 518-794-8998 (SAN 222-8734)
(ISBN Prefix 0-85131)

J De Graff
See De Graff

J Groos Verlag
Groos, Julius, Verlag KG
Hertzstr 6, Postfach 102423 D-6900
Heidelberg 1,
Federal Republic of Germany
(ISBN Prefix 3-87276)

J Hannon
Hannon, J., & Co.
36 Great Clarendon St., Oxford, OX2 6AT,
United Kingdom
(ISBN Prefix 0-904233)

J J Augustin
Augustin, J. J., Inc., Pub.
Locust Valley, NY 11560
Tel 516-676-1510 (SAN 204-5451)
(ISBN Prefix 0-87439)

J Patelson Mus
Patelson, Joseph, Music House , Ltd.
160 W. 56th St., New York, NY 10019
Tel 212-757-5587 (SAN 203-9028)
(ISBN Prefix 0-915282)

J W Cappelens
Cappelens, J. W., Forlag AS
Kirkegaten 16, Oslo 1, Norway

Jaca Bk
Jaca Book
Via Saffi, 19-20123 Milan, Italy

Jaimes Libros
Jaimes Libros, S.A.
Avda. de Jose Antonio, 754, Barcelona-13,
Spain

Jameson & Peeters
See E W Jameson Jr

Jamestown Pubs
Jamestown Pubs., Inc.
P.O. Box 6743, Providence, RI 02940
Tel 401-351-1915 (SAN 201-5196)
(ISBN Prefix 0-89061)

Jane's Pub Inc
Jane's Publishing Inc.
286 Congress St., Boston, MA 02210
Tel 617-542-6564 (SAN 286-357X)

Janus Bks
Janus Book Pubs.
2501 Industrial Pkwy. W., Hayward, CA
94545 Tel 415-887-7070 (SAN 208-0478)
(ISBN Prefix 0-915510)

Japadre
Japadre
Corso Federico Ii, 49,67100 l'Aquila, Italy

Jaya Ciencia
Jaya Ciencia SA
Bealtran, 107, Barcelona-23, Spain

Jenkins
Jenkins Publishing Co.
P.O. Box 2085, Austin, TX 78767
Tel 512-444-6616 (SAN 202-7321)
(ISBN Prefix 0-8363)

Jewelers Circular
Jewelers' Circular-Keystone
Chilton Way, Radnor, PA 19089
Tel 215-964-4480 (SAN 210-9050)
(ISBN Prefix 0-931744)

Jims
Jims
Regas, 7 y 9, Barcelona 6, Spain

John Wright-PSG
See Wright-PSG

Johns Hopkins
Johns Hopkins Univ. Press
Baltimore, MD 21218 Tel 301-338-7861
(SAN 202-7348)
(ISBN Prefix 0-8018)

Johnson Nyquist
Johnson Nyquist Productions, Inc.
23854 Via Fabricante, D-1, Mission Viejo,
CA 92691 Tel 714-770-5777

Johnson Repr
Johnson Reprint Corp, Subs. of Harcourt,
Brace & Jovanovich, Inc.
111 Fifth Ave., New York, NY 10003
Tel 212-741-6800 (SAN 285-0362)
Orders to:
757 Third Ave., New York, NY 10017
Tel 212-888-2925 (SAN 285-0370)
(ISBN Prefix 0-384)

Joly
Joly, Andre
21, Avenue George-V, 75008 Paris, France

Jonathan David
Jonathan David Pubs., Inc.
68-22 Eliot Ave., Middle Village, NY
11379 Tel 212-456-8611 (SAN 201-0321)
(ISBN Prefix 0-8246)

Jove Pubns
Jove Pubns., Inc, Div. of Berkley/Jove
Publishing Group
200 Madison Ave., New York, NY 10016
Tel 212-686-9820 (SAN 215-8817)
Dist. by:
ICD, 250 W. 55th St., New York, NY
10019 Tel 212-262-7444 (SAN 169-5800)
(ISBN Prefix 0-515)

Jover
Jover, S.A. Ediciones
San Pedro Martir, 18, Barcelona-12, Spain

Joyce Media
Joyce Media Inc.
8753 Shirley Ave., P.O. Box 458,
Northridge, CA 91328 Tel 213-885-7181
(SAN 208-7197)
(ISBN Prefix 0-917002)

Joyce Motion Pict
See Joyce Media

Juridica Verlag
Juridica-Verlag GmbH
Wimbergergasse 33, 1070 Vienna, Austria
(ISBN Prefix 3-85131)

Jurisdruck
Juris Druck u. Verlag AG
Basteiplatz 5, 8001 Zurich, Switzerland
(ISBN Prefix 3-260)

Jus
Jus, S.A. Editorial
Plaza de Abasolo 14, Mexico 3, D.F.,
Mexico

Juventud
Juventud, S. A.
Provenza, 101, Barcelona 29, Spain

K G Saur
Saur, K. G., Publishing, Inc.
45 N. Broad St., Ridgewood, NJ 07450
Tel 201-652-6360 (SAN 214-1264)
(ISBN Prefix 0-89664)

K Sefer
Kiryat Sefer, Ltd.
c/o Ridgefield Pub. Co., 6925 Canby Ave.,
Suite 104, Reseda, CA 91335
Tel 213-343-8811 (SAN 215-8035)
(ISBN Prefix 965-17)

Kamp Verlag
Kamp, Ferdinand, GmbH & Co. KG, Verlag
Widumstr. 6-8, 4630 Bochum 1,
Federal Republic of Germany
(ISBN Prefix 3-592)

Kapelusz
Kapelusz Mexicana, S.A. Editorial
Av. Morelos 64-1, Apartado postal 32-676,
Mexico 1, D. F., Mexico

Kazi Pubns
Kazi Pubns.
1215 W. Belmont Ave., Chicago, IL 60657
Tel 312-327-7598 (SAN 209-6676)
(ISBN Prefix 0-935782)

Kelley
Kelley, Augustus M., Pubs.
1140 Broadway, Room 901, New York, NY
10001 Tel 212-685-7202 (SAN
206-975X)
Orders to:
300 Fairfield Rd., P.O. Box 1308, Fairfield,
NJ 07006 (SAN 206-9768)
(ISBN Prefix 0-678)

Ken-Bks
Ken-Books
1932 Ocean Ave., San Francisco, CA
94127 Tel 415-584-0799 (SAN 201-0429)
(ISBN Prefix 0-913164)

Ken Kyushu
Kenkyusha, Ltd.
1-2 Kagurazaka, Shinjuku-ku, Tokyo 162,
Japan

Kendall-Hunt
Kendall/Hunt Publishing Co.
2460 Kerper Blvd., Dubuque, IA 52001
Tel 319-589-2870 (SAN 203-9184)
(ISBN Prefix 0-8403)

Kent St U Pr
Kent State Univ. Press
Kent, OH 44242 Tel 216-672-7913 (SAN
201-0437)
(ISBN Prefix 0-87338)

Kenyon
Kenyon Pubns.
361 Pir Oak Lane, Westbury, NY 11590
Tel 516-333-3236 (SAN 201-5072)
Dist. by:
G. Schirmer, Inc., 866 Third Ave., New
York, NY 10022 Tel 212-702-5500 (SAN
222-9544)
(ISBN Prefix 0-934286)

Keystone Pubns
Keystone Pubns., Inc.
1657 Broadway, 2nd Fl., New York, NY
10019 Tel 212-582-2254 (SAN 204-9708)
(ISBN Prefix 0-912126)

KG Informatik
KG-Informatik
PB 453, V, Arany J. u. 24, 1372 Budapest,
Hungary

Kiehl
Kiehl, Ferdinand, Verlag GmbH
Pfaustr 13, 6700 Ludwigshafen am Rhein,
Federal Republic of Germany
(ISBN Prefix 3-470)

Kindler
Kindler, Leonard
P.O. Box 12328, Philadelphia, PA 19119
Tel 215-843-4487 (SAN 240-6977)
(ISBN Prefix 0-943502)

Kingsmead Pr
Kingsmead Press
Rosewell House, Kingsmead Square, Bath,
Avon, United Kingdom
(ISBN Prefix 0-901571)

Kirjayhjyma
Kirjayhjyma Oy
Eerikinkatu 28, 00180 Helsinki 18, Finland

Kjaers Bogtryk
Kjaers, A. M. Bogtryk
Gronojvet 1, 8462 Harlevu, Denmark

Klett
Klett, Ernst
Rotebuhlstr. 75-77, 7000 Stuttgart 1,
Federal Republic of Germany
(ISBN Prefix 3-12)

Klincksieck
Klincksieck
11 Rue de Lille, 75007 Paris, France
(ISBN Prefix 2-252)

Klinkhardt
Klinkhardt, Julius
Ramsauer Weg 5, Postf 29, 8173 Bad
Heilbrunn, Federal Republic of Germany
(ISBN Prefix 3-7815)

Kluwer Academic
Kluwer Academic Publishers
190 Old Derby St., Hingham, MA 02043
Tel 617-749-5262 (SAN 211-481X)

Kluwer Boston
See Kluwer Academic

Kluwer Group
Kluwer Group
Postbus 23, 7400 GA Deventer,
Netherlands

Kluwer Technische
Kluwer Technische Boeken BV
Brink 25, Postbus 23, 7400 GA Deventer,
Netherlands

Knaggs Assoc.
Knaggs, Oliver, & Associates, Capetown
1201-3 High Rd. Chadwell Heath Romford,
RM6 4DH, United Kingdom
(ISBN Prefix 0-620)

Knapp Verlag
Knapp, Fritz GmbH Verlag
Neue Mainzer Str 60, 6000 Frankfurt am
Main 1, Federal Republic of Germany

Knopf
Knopf, Alfred A., Inc, Subs. of Random
House, Inc.
201 E. 50th St., New York, NY 10022
Tel 212-757-2600 (SAN 202-5825)
Orders to:
400 Hahn Rd., Westminster, MD 21157
(SAN 202-5833)
(ISBN Prefix 0-394)

Know Inc
Know, Inc.
P.O. Box 86031, Pittsburgh, PA 15221
Tel 412-241-2844 (SAN 201-050X)
(ISBN Prefix 0-912786)

Knowledge Indus
Knowledge Industry Pubns., Inc.
701 Westchester Ave., White Plains, NY
10604 Tel 914-328-9157 (SAN 214-2082)
(ISBN Prefix 0-914236; ISBN Prefix
0-86729)

Kochbuch Verlag
Kochbuch Verlag Heimeran KG
Dietlindenstr. 14, 8000 Munich 40,
Federal Republic of Germany
(ISBN Prefix 3-8063)

Kodansha
Kodansha International USA, Ltd.
C/O Harper & Row Pubs., 10 E. 53rd St.,
New York, NY 10022 Tel 212-593-7050
(SAN 201-0526)
Dist. by:
Harper & Row Pubs., Inc., Keystone
Industrial Park, Scranton, PA 18512
(SAN 215-3742)
(ISBN Prefix 0-87011)

Koehlers Verlag
Koehlers Verlagsgesellschaft mbH
Steintorwall 17, Postf 2352, 4900 Herford,
Federal Republic of Germany
(ISBN Prefix 3-7822)

Koesel
Koesel-Verlag GmbH & Co.
Fluggenstr 2, 8000 Munich 19,
Federal Republic of Germany
(ISBN Prefix 3-466)

Kohlhammer
Kohlhammer, W., GmbH
Hessbruhlstr. 69, 7000 Stuttgart 80,
Federal Republic of Germany
(ISBN Prefix 3-17)

Kosciuszko
Kosciuszko Foundation, Inc.
15 E. 65th St., New York, NY 10021
Tel 212-734-2130 (SAN 208-7251)
(ISBN Prefix 0-917004)

Kozgazdasagi
Kozgazdasagi Es Jogi Konyvkiado
H-1374 Budapest V, Wagy Sandor U 6,
Postfiok 578, Hungary

Kraus
Kraus, J.
79, Rue du Fauborg-St.-Honore, 75008
Paris, France

Kraus Repr
Kraus Reprint, A Div. of Kraus-Thomson
Organization, Ltd.
Rte. 100, Millwood, NY 10546
Tel 914-762-2200 (SAN 201-0542)
(ISBN Prefix 0-527; ISBN Prefix 3-601;
ISBN Prefix 3-262)

Krausskopf
Krausskopf-Verlag GmbH
Lessingstr 12, 6500 Mainz 1,
Federal Republic of Germany
(ISBN Prefix 3-7830)

Krieger
Krieger, Robert E., Pub. Co., Inc.
P.O. Box 9542, Melbourne, FL 32902-9542
Tel 305-724-9542 (SAN 202-6562)
(ISBN Prefix 0-88275; ISBN Prefix
0-89874)

Kroener
Kroener, Alfred, Verlag
Reuchlinstr. 4 B, Postf 1109, 7000 Stuttgart
1, Federal Republic of Germany
(ISBN Prefix 3-520)

Ktav
Ktav Publishing House, Inc.
75 Varick St., New York, NY 10013
Tel 212-966-6980 (SAN 201-0038)
(ISBN Prefix 0-87068)

Kultura
Kultura
YU-91000 Skopje, Bulevar JNA 68A,
Postanski Fah 298, Yugoslavia

Kunnskapsforlaget
Kunnskapsforlaget
Postboks 6736, Sankt Olavs Plass,
Sehestedsgt 4, Oslo 1, Norway

L Carcamo
Carcamo, Luis
San Raimundo, 58, Madrid-20, Spain

L Fereday Schol
Fereday, Lynne, Scholarship Memorial Inc.
6427 Randolph Dr., Boise, ID 83709
Tel 208-375-7656

LA Intl Fern
Los Angeles International Fern Society
586 Paokano Loop, Kailua, HI 96734
(SAN 225-5731)

La Nuova Italia
La Nuova Italia
Via Giacomini, 8-50132 Florence, Italy

La Scuola
La Scuola
Via Cadorna, 11-25100 Brescia, Italy

La Tribuna
La Tribuna
Via Don Minzoni, 51-29100 Piacenza, Italy

La Vela
La Vela
Viale Sturchi, 28-41100 Modena, Italy

Labor
Labor, S.A.
Calabria, 235-239, Barcelona-29, Spain

Lademann Forlag
Lademann Forlagsaktieselskab
Linnesgade 25, 1361 Copenhagen K, D,
Denmark

Laffont
Laffont
31, Rue Falguiere, 75725 Paris, France

Lafitte Repr
Lafitte Reprints
1, Place Francis Chirat, 13100 Marseille,
France
(ISBN Prefix 2-86276)

Laia
Laia S. A.
Constitucion, 18-20, Barcelona, 14, Spain

Lamarre Poinot
Lamarre Poinot
4, Rue Antoine-Dubois, 75006 Paris,
France

Lancaster-Miller
Lancaster-Miller Pubs.
P. O. Box 3056, Berkeley, CA 94703
Tel 415-845-3782 (SAN 213-6503)
(ISBN Prefix 0-89581)

Lane
Lane, Allen
536 Kings Rd., London SW10-0U4,
United Kingdom
(ISBN Prefix 0-7139)

Langen AG
Langenscheidt AG
Hardturmstr. 76, Postf. 130, 8021 Zurich,
Switzerland
(ISBN Prefix 3-269)

Langen Kommand
Langenscheidt Kommanditgesellschaft
Crellestr. 29-30, 1000 Berlin 62,
Federal Republic of Germany
(ISBN Prefix 3-468)

Langenscheidt
Langenscheidt Pubs.
46-35 54th Rd., Maspeth, NY 11378
Tel 212-784-0055 (SAN 276-9441)

Larousse
Larousse & Co., Inc.
572 Fifth Ave., New York, NY 10036
Tel 212-575-9515 (SAN 202-6643)
(ISBN Prefix 0-88332)

Larousse FR
Larousse
17, Rue du Montparnasse, 75006 Paris,
France
(ISBN Prefix 2-03)

Las Americas
Las Americas S.A., Editorial
Parque Industrial Coacalco, Mexico 19,
D.F., Mexico

Laterza
Laterza
Via de Villa Sacchetti, 17-00197 Rome,
Italy

Lavauzelle
Lavauzelle, Charles
20 Rue de Leningrad, 75008 Paris, France

Law & Cap Dynamics
Law & Capital Dynamics
700 S. Flower St. Suite 2600, Los Angeles,
CA 90017 Tel 213-629-1100 (SAN
213-7690)
(ISBN Prefix 0-9600708)

Lawyers Co-Op
Lawyers Co-Operative Publishing Co.
1 Graves St., Rochester, NY 14694
Tel 716-546-5530 (SAN 202-6678)

LE *Imprint of* **Dell**

Le Prat
Le Prat, Guy, Editions
5, Rue des Grands-Augustins, 75006 Paris,
France

Learn Res Dev
Learning Research and Development Center
University of Pittsburgh
3939 O'hara St., Pittsburgh, PA 15260
Tel 412-624-4829 (SAN 224-1811)

Learning Inc.
Learning Inc.
Learning Place, Manset, ME 04656
Tel 207-244-5015 (SAN 201-5714)
(ISBN Prefix 0-913692)

Learning Line
Learning Line, The
P.O. Box 577, Palo Alto, CA 94302
Tel 415-854-4400 (SAN 220-018X)
Orders to:
P.O. Box 1200, Palo Alto, CA 94302
(SAN 220-0198)
(ISBN Prefix 0-8449)

Lechevalier
Lechevalier
19,Rue Augereau, 75007 Paris, France
(ISBN Prefix 2-7205)

Lectorum Corp
See Lectorum Pubns

Lectorum Pubns
Lectorum Pubns.
137 W. 14th St., New York, NY 10011
(SAN 207-253X)

Lello & Irmao
Lello e Irmao
Rua Da Carmelitas 144, Oporto 4000,
Portugal

Lemos
Lemos
O'Donnell, 27, Madrid 9, Spain

Lemouzi
Lemouzi
13, Place Municipale, 19000 Tulle, France

Lenox Hill
Lenox Hill Press, Div. of Crown Publishing,
Inc.
235 E. 44th St., New York, NY 10017
Tel 212-687-5250 (SAN 201-0801)

Lensing Verlag
Lensing, Lambert, GmbH, Verlag
Kampstr 42, 4600 Dortmund 1,
Federal Republic of Germany

L'Erma
L'Erma
Via Cassiodoro, 19-00193 Rome, Italy

Leske-Budrich
Leske, C. W., Verlag & Budrich GmbH
Furstenbergstr. 23, Postf 300406, 5090
Leverkusen 3,
Federal Republic of Germany
(ISBN Prefix 3-8100)

Letouzey & Ane
Letouzey & Ane
87, Boulevard Raspail, 75006 Paris, France

Leuven U Pr
Leuven University Press
Krakenstraat 3, Leuven BE, NL,
New Caledonia

Lewis Ltd
Lewis, A., (Masonic Publishers) Ltd.
Terminal House, Shepperton, Middx.,
TW17 8AS, United Kingdom
(ISBN Prefix 0-85318)

Lexik Hse
Lexik House Pubs.
75 Main St., P.O. Box 247, Cold Spring,
NY 10516 Tel 914-265-2822 (SAN
214-3984)
(ISBN Prefix 0-936368)

Lexington Bks
Lexington Books, Div. of D. C. Heath & Co.
Dist. by:
D. C. Heath & Co., 125 Spring St.,
Lexington, MA 02173 Tel 617-862-6650
(SAN 213-7526)
(ISBN Prefix 0-669)

Lib Aritide
Librairie Aritide Quillet S.A.
278 ! Blvd. St-Germain, F-75006 Paris,
France
(ISBN Prefix 2-85041)

Lib Edit Greg
Libreria Editrice Gregoriana
Via Roma, 37-35100 Padua, Italy

Lib Gen Fr
Librairie Generale Francaise
12, Rue Francois-ler, 75008 Paris, France
(ISBN Prefix 2-253)

Lib Lanore
Librairie Fernand Lanore Sarl
L Rue Palatine, F-75006 Paris, France

Lib Liban
Librairie Du Liban
Riad Al-Solh Sq, P.O. Box 945 Beirut,
Lebanon

Lib Tec Belt
Libreria Tecnica Bellisco
Garcilasco, 3, Madrid 10, Spain

Liberfoerlag
Liberfoerlag
Sortergatan 23 Fack, 16289 Vaellinby,
Sweden

Libr Ed Vat
Libreria Editrice Vaticana
Vatican City, Italy

Library Admin
Library Administration and Management
Association
50 E Huron St, Chicago, IL 60611
Tel 312-944-6780 (SAN 233-4879)

Libreria
Libreria
248 E. 50th St., New York, NY 10022
Tel 212-752-7187

Libreria Convegno
Libreria del Convegno
Corso Campi, 72-26100 Cremona, Italy

Libs Unl
Libraries Unlimited, Inc.
P.O. Box 263, Littleton, CO 80160
Tel 303-770-1220 (SAN 202-6767)
(ISBN Prefix 0-87287)

Licosa
Licosa-Libreria Commissionaria Sansoni
Via Lamarmora, 45-50121 Florence, Italy

Lidel
Lidel
1083, rue Van Horne, Montreal, Que. H2V
1J6, Canada

LIEF
LIEF-Libreria Internazionale Edizioni
Francescane
Borgo S. Lucia, 38-49 -36100 Vicenza, Italy

Life Pubs Intl
Life Pubs. International
3360 N.W. 110th St., Miami, FL 33167
Tel 305-685-6334 (SAN 213-5817)
(ISBN Prefix 0-8297)

Ligel
Ligel
77, Rue de Vaugirard, 75006 Paris, France

Limusa
Limusa, S.A. Editorial
Arcos de Belen 75, Mexico 1, D.F., Mexico

Linguistic Soc Am
Linguistic Society of America
3520 Prospect St. NW, Washington, DC
20007 (SAN 225-8420)

Lingusitic Circle
Linguistic Circle of Canberra
P.O. Box 4, Canberra A.C.T. 2601,
Australia
(ISBN Prefix 0-85883)

Lint
Lint
Via di Romangna, 30-34134 Trieste, Italy

Little
Little, Brown & Co.
34 Beacon St., Boston, MA 02106
Tel 617-227-0730 (SAN 281-8884)
Orders to:
200 West St., Waltham, MA 02154
Tel 617-890-0250 (SAN 281-8892)
(ISBN Prefix 0-316)

Littlefield
Littlefield, Adams & Co.
81 Adams Dr., Box 327, Totowa, NJ 07512
Tel 201-256-8600 (SAN 202-6791)
(ISBN Prefix 0-8226)

Liv Nobel
Livraria Nobel, S.A.
CP 2376, Sao Paulo Sp, Brazil

Liviana
Liviana
Italy

Livre de Paris
Livre de Paris
3, Avenue de Garlande, 92220 Bagneux,
France

Lodestar Bks
Lodestar Books
2 Park Ave., New York, NY 10016
Tel 212-725-1818 (SAN 212-5013)
(ISBN Prefix 0-525)

Loescher
Loescher
Via Vittoria Amedeo Ii, 18, 10121 Turin,
Italy

Loguez Edns
Loguez Ediciones
Avda. de Alemania, 25, Salamanca, Spain

Longanesi
Longanesi
Via Borghetto, 5-20122 Milan, Italy

Longman
Longman Inc.
1560 Broadway, New York, NY 10036
Tel 212-764-3950 (SAN 202-6856)

Longman England
Longman Group, Ltd.
Longman House, Burnt Mill, Harlow,
Essex, United Kingdom

Longman S Africa
Longman Penguin South Africa (Pty.), Ltd.
P.O. Box 1616, Capetown 8000,
South Africa

Longo A
Longo A.
Via Rocca ai Fossi, 6-48100 Ravenna, Italy

Longwood Pr
Longwood Publishing Group, In c.
51 Washington St., Dover, NH 03820
Tel 603-742-4662 (SAN 209-3170)
(ISBN Prefix 0-89341)

Lopez Paco
Lopez de Paco, Manuel
Juan De Austria, 15, Madrid-10, Spain

Lothrop
Lothrop, Lee & Shepard Books, Div. of
William Morrow & Co., Inc.
105 Madison Ave., New York, NY 10016
Tel 212-889-3050 (SAN 201-1034)
Orders to:
William Morrow & Co., Inc., Wilmor
Warehouse, 6 Henderson Dr., West
Caldwell, NJ 07006 (SAN 202-5779)
(ISBN Prefix 0-688)

Lotus Light
Lotus Light Pubns.
P.O. Box 2, Wilmot, WI 53192
Tel 414-862-6968 (SAN 239-1120)
(ISBN Prefix 0-941524)

Lowe Pub
Lowe, Joseph D., Publisher
2518 Clement St. Apt. 6, San Fransico, CA
94121 Tel 415-221-1070 (SAN 240-0227)
(ISBN Prefix 0-9605506)

Lubrecht & Cramer
Lubrecht & Cramer
RFD 1, Box 227, Monticello, NY 12701
Tel 914-794-8539 (SAN 214-1256)

Luebbe
Luebbe, Gustav, Verlag GmbH
Scheidbachstr. 29-31, Postf 200127, 5060
Bergisch Gladbach 2,
Federal Republic of Germany
(ISBN Prefix 3-7857)

L'Ufficio Moderno
L'Ufficio Moderno
Via Foppa, 7-20144 Milan, Italy

Lust
Lust, Benedict, Pubns.
25 Dewart Rd., Greenwich, CT 06830
Tel 203-661-0980 (SAN 201-1107)
Orders to:
P.O. Box 404, New York, NY 10156
(SAN 201-1115)
(ISBN Prefix 0-87904)

Lyle Stuart
Stuart, Lyle, Inc.
120 Enterprise Ave., Secaucus, NJ 07094
Tel 201-866-0490 (SAN 201-1131)
(ISBN Prefix 0-8184)

M Arimany
Arimany, Miguel, ,S.A.
Plaza Dugue de Medinaceli, 7, Barcelona-2,
Spain

M Jones
Jones, Marshall, Co, Div. of Golden Quill
Press
Francestown, NH 03043 (SAN 206-8834)
(ISBN Prefix 0-8338)

M Robertson
See Biblio Dist

M Rosenberg
Rosenberg, Mary S., Inc.
17 W 60th St., New York, NY 10023

McClelland
McClelland & Stewart, Ltd.
25 Hollinger Rd., Toronto, Ontario, M4B
3G2, Canada Tel 416-751-4520

McGraw
McGraw-Hill Book Co.
1221 Ave. of the Americas, New York, NY
10020 Tel 212-997-1221 (SAN
200-2248); Manchester Rd., Manchester,
MO 63011 Tel 314-227-1600 (SAN
200-2558)
Orders to:
Hightstown, NJ Tel 609-426-5000 (SAN
200-254X); Orders to: 8171 Redwood
Hwy., Novato, CA 94947
Tel 415-897-5251 (SAN 200-2566)
(ISBN Prefix 0-07)

McKay
McKay, David, Co., Inc.
2 Park Ave., New York, NY 10016
Tel 212-340-9800 (SAN 285-046X)
Orders to:
Fodor's/McKay, O'Neill Hwy., Dunmore,
PA 18512 Tel 717-344-2614 (SAN
285-0478)
(ISBN Prefix 0-679)

Macmillan
Macmillan Publishing Co., Inc.
866 Third Ave., New York, NY 10022
Tel 212-935-2000 (SAN 202-5574)
Orders to:
Front & Brown Sts., Riverside, NJ 08370
(SAN 202-5582)
(ISBN Prefix 0-02)

Macmillan Aust
Macmillan Co. of Australia, Pty. Ltd.
107 Moray St., Melbourne Vic. 3205,
Australia

Macmillan Info
Macmillan Information, Div. of Macmillan
Publishing Co., Inc.
866 Third Ave., New York, NY 10022
Tel 212-935-2000 (SAN 202-599X)
(ISBN Prefix 0-02)

Macmillan London
Macmillan Press, Ltd.
4 Little Essex St., London WC2R 3LF,
United Kingdom
(ISBN Prefix 0-333)

Magisterio Esp
Magisterio Espanol, S.A. Editorial
Quevedo, 1, Madrid-14, Spain

Magnard
Editions Magnard Sarl, Les
122 Blvd. St-Germain, F-75279 Paris Cedex
06, France

Magyar Tarsasag
Magyar Nyelvtudomany; Tarsasag
V, Pesti Barna u. 1, 1052 Budapest,
Hungary

Maison & Larose
Maisonneuve & Larose
11, Rue Victor Cousin, 75005 Paris, France

Maison Dictionnarie
Maison du Dictionnarie, La
95 Bis Rue Legendre, F-75017 Paris,
France

Maison Rustique
Maison Rustique
26, Rue Jacob, 75006 Paris, France
(ISBN Prefix 2-7066)

Majors
See S Karger

Maledicta
Maledicta Press
331 S. Greenfield Ave., Waukesha, WI
53186 Tel 414-542-5853 (SAN 208-1083)
(ISBN Prefix 0-916500)

Malipiero
Malipiero SpA
Viale Liguria 12-14, CP 788, I-40064
Ozzana Emilia (Bologna), Italy

Malki Mus Pr
Malki Museum Press
Dept. of Linguistics, Univ. of California,
Los Angeles, CA 90024 Tel 213-474-0169
(SAN 281-9724)
Orders to:
11-795 Fields Rd., Morongo Indian
Reservation, Banning, CA 92220
Tel 714-849-7289 (SAN 281-9732)

Maloine
Maloine
27, Rue de l'Ecole-de-Medecine, 75006
Paris, France
(ISBN Prefix 2-224)

Mandala
See Irvington

Manfrini
Manfrini
Localita Compagnole, 38060 Calliano
(Trento), Italy

Manz
Manz, G. J., AG, Verlag und Druckerei
Anzinger Str 1, 8000 Munich 80,
Federal Republic of Germany
(ISBN Prefix 3-7863)

Mapfre
Mapfre, S.A. Editorial
Avda. Baviera, 10 Bajo, Madrid-28, Spain

Marchmont Pub
Marchmont Publications Ltd.
Longdene, Haslemere Surrey GU2t 2PH,
United Kingdom
(ISBN Prefix 0-905753)

Marcombo
Marcombo, S.A. de Boixareu Editores
Gran Via de les Corts Catalanes, 594,
Barcelona-7, Spain

Marhold
Marhold, Carl, Verlagsbuchhandlung
Hessenhallee 12, 1000 Berlin 19,
Federal Republic of Germany
(ISBN Prefix 3-7864)

Marietti
Marietti
Via Adam, 15, 15133 Casale Monferrato,
Italy
(ISBN Prefix 8-8211)

Marin
Marin, S.A. Editorial
Nicaragua, 85-95, Barcelona-29, Spain

Maritimes Outremer
Maritimes & D'Outremer
17, Rue Jacob, 75006 Paris, France
(ISBN Prefix 2-7070)

Marlin
Marlin Pubns. International, Inc.
485 Fifth Ave., New York, NY 10017
Tel 212-986-7752 (SAN 210-9824)
(ISBN Prefix 0-930624)

Marotta
Marotta
Via Giordani, 21-80122 Naples, Italy

Martinez Roca
Martinez Roca, S.A. Ediciones
Avda. Jose Antonio, 774-7 Planta,
Barcelona-13, Spain

Mas Ivars
Mas Ivars Editores, S.L.
G. V. Marques del Turia, 64, Valencia-5,
Spain

Mason Charter
See Van Nos Reinhold

Massada Pub
Massada Press, Ltd.
46 Beth Lehen Rd., Jerusalem, Israel

Massin
Massin
2, Rue de l'Echelle, 75039 Paris, France

Masson & Cie
Masson & Cie
120, Blvd. Saint-Germain, 75006 Paris,
France
(ISBN Prefix 2-225)

Matagiri
Matagiri Sri Aurobindo Center, Inc.
Mt. Tremper, NY 12457 Tel 914-679-8322
(SAN 214-2058)
(ISBN Prefix 0-89071)

Material Handling
Material Handling Institute, Inc.
1326 Freeport Rd, Pittsburgh, PA 15238
(SAN 224-7992)

Mayers-Joseph
Mayers, Joseph, & Co., Inc.
50 Park Place, Suite H, Newark, NJ 07102
Tel 201-622-7854 (SAN 214-4115)
(ISBN Prefix 0-9604860)

Mayfe
Mayfe, S. A. Editorial
Ferraz, 28, Madrid-8, Spain

Mayfield Pub
Mayfield Publishing Co.
285 Hamilton Ave., Palo Alto, CA 94301
Tel 415-326-1640 (SAN 202-8972)
(ISBN Prefix 0-87484)

Mazziana
Mazziana
Via S. Carlo, 5-37100 Verona, Italy

Med Economics
Medical Economics Books
680 Kinderkamack Rd., Oradell, NJ 07649
Tel 201-262-3030 (SAN 202-2613)
Orders to:
Box 157, Florence, KY 41042 (SAN
202-2621)
(ISBN Prefix 0-87489)

Med Exam
Medical Examination Publishing Co., Inc.
3003 New Hyde Park Rd., New Hyde
Park, NY 11042 Tel 516-328-6200 (SAN
206-7897)
(ISBN Prefix 0-87488)

Med Group Mgmt
Medical Group Management Assn.
4101 E. Louisiana Ave., Denver, CO 80222
Tel 303-753-1111 (SAN 216-2695)

Medallion *Imprint of* **Berkley Pub**

Meddens
Meddens, Alelier, d'art Graphique
141-143 Av. de Scheut, 1070 Brussels,
Belgium

Medieval & Renaissance NY
Medieval & Renaissance Texts & Studies
State Univ. of New York, Binghamton, NY
13901 (SAN 216-6119)
(ISBN Prefix 0-86698)

Mediterraneo
Mediterraneo, S.A. Ediciones
Conde De Roche, 5, Murcia, Spain

Meininger
Meininger, D., Verlag und Druckerei GmbH
Maximilianstr. 11-17, 6730 Neustadt an der
Weinstrasse 1,
Federal Republic of Germany
(ISBN Prefix 3-87524)

Melrose Pub Co
Melrose Publishing Co.
384 N. San Vicente Blvd., Los Angeles, CA
90048 Tel 213-655-5177 (SAN 211-7436)
(ISBN Prefix 0-934972)

Menges
Menges
22, Rue Sebastien-Mercier, 75015 Paris,
France

Mensajero Edns
Mensajero Ediciones
Avenida de las Universidades, 13, Bilbao-7,
Spain

Ment *Imprint of* **NAL**

Mer *Imprint of* **NAL**

Merit Pubns
Merit Pubns., Inc.
610 NE 124th St., N. Miami, FL 33161
(SAN 211-4380)
(ISBN Prefix 0-87803)

Merriam
See Merriam-Webster Inc

Merriam-Webster Inc
Merriam-Webster Inc, Subs. of Encyclopaedia
Britannica, Inc.
47 Federal St. P.O. Box 281, Springfield,
MA 01101 Tel 413-734-3134 (SAN
202-6244)
(ISBN Prefix 0-87779)

Merrill
Merrill, Charles E., Publishing Co, Div. of Bell
& Howell Co.
1300 Alum Creek Dr., Columbus, OH
43216 Tel 614-258-8441 (SAN 200-2116)
(ISBN Prefix 0-675)

Merrimack Bk Serv
See Merrimack Pub Cir

Merrimack Pub Cir
Merrimack Book Service, Inc.
458 Boston St., Topsfield, MA 01973
Tel 617-887-2440 (SAN 212-193X)
Orders to:
99 Main St., Salem, NH 03079
Tel 617-685-4636 (SAN 212-1948)

Merritt Co
Merritt Co.
1661 Ninth St., Santa Monica, CA 90406
(SAN 203-8110)
(ISBN Prefix 0-930868)

Merton Hse
Merton House Travel and Tourism Publishers, Inc.
937 W. Liberty Dr., Wheaton, IL 60187
Tel 312-668-7410   (SAN 207-9739)
(ISBN Prefix 0-916032)

Messeiller
Messeiller, H.
11, rue St-Nicolas, 2006 Neuchatel, Switzerland
(ISBN Prefix 2-8261)

Messner
Messner, Julian, A Simon & Schuster Div. of Gulf & Western Corp.
1230 Ave. of the Americas, New York, NY 10020 Tel 212-245-6400   (SAN 202-6260)
(ISBN Prefix 0-671)

Methuen Inc
Methuen Inc.
733 Third Ave, New York, NY 10017
Tel 212-922-3550   (SAN 213-196X)
Dist. by:
Transworld Distribution Services, Inc., 80 Northfield Ave., Raritan Center, Edison, NJ 08817   (SAN 213-1978)
(ISBN Prefix 0-416)

MG Schmitz
Schmitz, Manfred G.
Juhenplatz 1, Postf 2540, 4790 Paderborn, Federal Republic of Germany
(ISBN Prefix 3-922272)

Mgmt Info Ser
Management Information Services
19722 E. Nine Mile Rd., St. Clair Shores, MI 48080   (SAN 206-6564)

Mich St U Pr
Michigan State Univ. Press
1405 S. Harrison Rd., 25 Manly Miles Bldg., East Lansing, MI 48824
Tel 517-355-9543   (SAN 202-6295)
(ISBN Prefix 0-87013)

Michael Joseph
See Merrimack Pub Cir

Michelin
Michelin Guides & Maps, Dept. of Michelin Tire Corp.
P.O. Box 1007, New Hyde Park, NY 11042
Tel 212-895-2342   (SAN 202-6309)

Michelin Tire
See Michelin

Michie-Bobbs
See Michie Co

Michie Co
Michie Co., The
P.O. Box 7587, Charlottesville, VA 22906
Tel 804-295-6171   (SAN 202-6317)
(ISBN Prefix 0-87215; ISBN Prefix 0-672)

Milla Lib
Milla, Libreria Editorial-Arxiu Teatral
San Pablo, 21, Barcelona-7, Spain

Miller Freeman
Miller Freeman Pubns., Inc.
500 Howard St., San Francisco, CA 94105
Tel 415-397-1881   (SAN 213-6511)
(ISBN Prefix 0-87930)

Mills Pub Co
Mills Publishing Co.
King Sta., P.O. Box 6158, Santa Ana, CA 92706 Tel 714-541-5750   (SAN 272-4464)
(ISBN Prefix 0-935356)

Minerva Bks
Minerva Books, Ltd.
137 W 14th St., New York, NY 10011
Tel 212-929-2833

Minerva Italica
Minerva Italica
Via del Rame, 6-24100 Bergamo, Italy

Minerva Medica
Minerva Medica
Corso Bramante, 83-10126 Turin, Italy

Minerva Yugo
Minerva
Yu-24000 Subotica, trg 29 Novembra br 3, Postanski fah 116, Yugoslavia

Mingulay
Mingulay Publications
29 Waterloo St., Glasgow, G2 6B2, United Kingdom

Minist Agricultura
Ministerio De Agricultura. Srv. De Publicaciones
Paseo Infanta Isabel, 1, Madrid-7, Spain

Minist Cultura
Ministerio de Cultura Serv. de Publicaciones
Avda. Genealismo, 39, Madrid-16, Spain

Minist Ed Caracas
Ministerio de Educacion, Direccion General, Departamento de Publicaciones
Salvador de Leona Coiiseo 29, Caracas, 101, Venezuela

Minist Ed La Paz
Ministerio de Educacion y Cultura
Apartado 3860, La Paz, Bolivia

Minist Prov Sec
Government of British Colombia, Legislative Library, Ministry of Provincial Secretary & Government Services
878 Viewfield Rd., Victoria, BC. V8V 1X4, Canada

Minkoff Repr
Minkoff Reprints
46, chemin de la Mousse, 1225 Chene-Bourg, Switzerland
(ISBN Prefix 2-8266)

Minuit
Minuit
7, Rue Bernard Palissy, 75006 Paris, France

MIT Pr
MIT Press
28 Carleton St., Cambridge, MA 02142
Tel 617-253-2884   (SAN 202-6414)
(ISBN Prefix 0-262)

Mitzi Bks
Mitzi Books, Div. of Sinai-Christian Pubns.
P.O. Box 160452, Mobile, AL 36616
Tel 404-834-4044   (SAN 223-1948)
(ISBN Prefix 0-940958)

MMW Verlag
MMW Medizin Verlag GmbH Munich
Blumenstr 48, 8000 Munich 2, Federal Republic of Germany
(ISBN Prefix 3-8208)

Modern Curr
Modern Curriculum Press, Div. of Esquire, Inc.
13900 Prospect Rd., Cleveland, OH 44136
Tel 216-238-2222   (SAN 206-6572)
(ISBN Prefix 0-87895; ISBN Prefix 0-8136)

Modern Humanities Res
Modern Humanities Research Association
George Washington University, Washington, DC 20006   (SAN 225-3186)

Modern Signs
Modern Signs Press
3131 Walker Lee Dr., Rossmoor, CA 90720
(SAN 282-0048)
Orders to:
P.O. Box 1181, Los Alamitos, CA 90720
Tel 213-596-8548   (SAN 282-0056)
(ISBN Prefix 0-916708)

Moll Edit
Moll Editorial
Torres Del Aor, 6, Palmade Malorca, Spain

Monarch Pr
Monarch Press, Div. of Simon & Schuster, Inc.
1230 Ave. of the Americas, 12th Fl., New York, NY 10020 Tel 212-245-6400   (SAN 204-5621)
(ISBN Prefix 0-671)

Monauni
Monauni
Via Manci, 141-38100 Trento, Italy

Mondadori
Mondadori, A.
Via Marconi, 27, 20090 Segrate-(Milano), Italy

Mondini Siccardi
Mondini e Siccardi
Via Calroll, 39r-16124 Genoa, Italy

Mongolia
Mongolia Society, Inc., The
P.O. Drawer 606, Bloomington, IN 47402
Tel 812-335-2766   (SAN 204-000X)
(ISBN Prefix 0-910980)

Monnier
Monnier
Via Scipione Ammirato, 100, 50316 Florence, Italy

Moody
Moody Press
2101 W. Howard St., Chicago, IL 60645
Tel 312-973-7800   (SAN 202-5604)
(ISBN Prefix 0-8024)

Moore Pub IL
Moore Publishing Company, Inc. (Il)
P.O. Box 709, Oak Park, IL 60303   (SAN 222-643X)
(ISBN Prefix 0-935610)

Morano
Morano
Piazza S. Domenico Maggiore, 9-80134 Naples, Italy

Moreno Ed
Moreno Educational Co.
7050 Bell Glade Lane, San Diego, CA 92119 Tel 714-461-0565

Morgan
Morgan & Morgan, Inc.
145 Palisades St., Dobbs Ferry, NY 10522
Tel 914-693-9303   (SAN 202-5620)
(ISBN Prefix 0-87100)

Mori
Mori
Via Sampolo, 6-90143 Palermo, Italy

Morrow
Morrow, William, & Co., Inc.
105 Madison Ave., New York, NY 10016
Tel 212-889-3050   (SAN 202-5760)
Orders to:
Wilmor Warehouse, 6 Henderson Dr., West Caldwell, NJ 07006   (SAN 202-5779)
(ISBN Prefix 0-688)

Mortgage Bankers
Mortgage Bankers Association of America
1125 15 St Nw, Washington, DC 20005
(SAN 224-8212)

Mosaik Verlag
Mosaik Verlag GmbH
Neumarkter Str. 18, 8000 Munich 80, Federal Republic of Germany
(ISBN Prefix 3-573)

Mosby
Mosby, C. V., Co.
11830 Westline Industrial Dr., St. Louis, MO 63141 Tel 314-872-8370   (SAN 200-2280)
(ISBN Prefix 0-8016)

Motta
Motta
Via Govone, 16-20154 Milan, Italy

Mouton
Mouton Pubs, Div. of Walter De Gruyter, Inc.
200 Saw Mill River Rd., Hawthorne, NY 10532 Tel 914-747-0111   (SAN 210-9239)

MT Coun Indian
Montana Council for Indian Education
517 Rimrock Rd., Billings, MT 59102
Tel 406-252-1800   (SAN 202-2117)
(ISBN Prefix 0-89992)

MTESZ
Mtesz Papir-es Nyomdaipari Mueszaki Egyesuelet
V, Kossuth L. ter 6, 1055 Budapest, Hungary

Mueszaki Konyv
Mueszaki Konyvkiado
PB 581, V, Bajcsy-Zs. ut 22, 1374 Budapest, Hungary

Multi Matters
Multilingual Matters Ltd.
Bank House, 8a Hill Road, Clevedon, Avon BS21 7HH, United Kingdom

Multigrafica
Multigrafica
Viale del Quattro Venti, 52a-00152 Rome, Italy

Muralla
Muralla, la Editorial
Constancia, 33, Madrid-2, Spain

Mursia
Mursia
Via Tadino, 29-20124 Milan, Italy

Mursia S
Mursia S.
Corso Venezia, 8-20121 Milan, Italy

Museum NM Pr
Museum of New Mexico Press
P.O. Box 2087, Santa Fe, NM 87503
Tel 505-827-6457   (SAN 202-2575)
(ISBN Prefix 0-89013)

Museum of NM Pr
See Museum NM Pr

Muzzio
Muzzio
Piazza De Gasperi, 12, 35100 Padua, Italy
(ISBN Prefix 8-87021)

N K Gregg
Gregg, Newton K., Pub.
P.O. Box 1459, Rohnert Park, CA 94928
Tel 707-584-9446   (SAN 206-9709)
(ISBN Prefix 0-87962; ISBN Prefix 0-912318)

NA Heating & AC Wholesalers
North American Heating & Air Conditioning Wholesalers Association
1661 W. Henderson Rd., Columbus, OH 43220 Tel 614-459-2100   (SAN 223-940X)

Nacional Editora
Nacional Editora
Torregalindo, 10, Madrid-16, Spain
NACM
National Assn. of Credit Management
Book Edit Dept., 475 Park Ave., S., New
York, NY 10016 Tel 212-578-4431 (SAN
205-7573)
(ISBN Prefix 0-934914)
Nakladni Zavod
Nakladni Zavod Matice Hrvatske
YU-41000 Zagreb, Ul Matice Hrvatske 2,
Postanski Fah 515, Yugoslavia
NAL
New American Library
1633 Broadway, New York, NY 10019
Tel 212-397-8000 (SAN 206-8079)
Orders to:
120 Woodbine St., Bergenfield, NJ 07621
Tel 201-387-0600 (SAN 206-8087)
(ISBN Prefix 0-451; ISBN Prefix 0-452;
ISBN Prefix 0-453)
Narcea SA
Narcea S.A. de Ediciones
Dr. Federico Rubio y Gali, 89 Madrid-20,
Spain
Narr
Narr, Gunter
Stauffenbergstr. 42, 7400 Tubingen-1,
Federal Republic of Germany
(ISBN Prefix 3-87808)
NARUC
National Association of Regulatory Utility
Commissioners
1102 ICC Bldg., P.O. Box 684, Washington,
DC 20044 (SAN 260-339X)
Nasou
Nasou: Nasionale Opvoedkundige Uitgewery
Postbus 105, 1500 Parow, South Africa
(ISBN Prefix 0-625)
Natl Acad Pr
National Academy Press
2101 Constitution Ave., Washington, DC
20418 Tel 202-334-3113 (SAN 202-8891)
(ISBN Prefix 0-309)
Natl Acad Sci
See Natl Acad Pr
Natl Assn Broadcasters
National Association of Broadcasters
1771 N St. N.W, Washington, DC 20036
(SAN 224-1986)
Natl Assn Deaf
National Assn. of the Deaf
814 Thayer Ave., Silver Spring, MD 20910
Tel 301-587-1788 (SAN 203-7092)
(ISBN Prefix 0-913072)
Natl Assn Elect Dist
National Association of Electrical Distributors
600 Summer St, Stamford, CT 06901
(SAN 272-7889)
Natl Assoc Realtors
National Association of Realtors
430 N Michigan Ave, Chicago, IL 60611
(SAN 224-9294)
Natl Book
National Book Co, Div. of Educational
Research Associates
333 S.W. Park Ave., Portland, OR 97205
Tel 503-228-6345 (SAN 212-4661)
(ISBN Prefix 0-89420)
Natl Corrosion Eng
National Association of Corrosion Engineers
P.O. Box 218340, Houston, TX 77218
(SAN 224-2001)
Natl Elec Sign
National Electric Sign Association
2625 Butterfield Rd, Oak Brook, IL 60521
(SAN 224-7151)
Natl Fire Prot
National Fire Protection Assn.
Batterymarch Park, Quincy, MA 02269
Tel 617-482-8755 (SAN 202-8948)
(ISBN Prefix 0-87765)
Natl Fluid Power
National Fluid Power Association
3333 N Mayfair Rd, Milwaukee, WI 53222
Tel 414-259-0990 (SAN 224-800X)
Natl Juv & Family Ct Judges
National Council of Juvenile & Family Court
Judges
Box 8978 University of Nevada, Reno, NV
89507 (SAN 225-0942)
Natl Knit Outwear
National Knitwear & Sportswear Association
51 Madison Ave., New York, NY 10010
Tel 212-683-7520 (SAN 223-9124)

Natl Learning
National Learning Corp.
212 Michael Dr., Syosset, NY 11791
Tel 516-921-8888 (SAN 206-8869)
(ISBN Prefix 0-8373; ISBN Prefix 0-8293)
Natl Micrograph
See Assn Inform Image
Natl Mus Can
National Museums of Canada
Dist. by:
University of Chicago Press, 11030 S.
Langley Ave., Chicago, IL 60628
(ISBN Prefix 0-226)
Natl Notary
National Notary Assn.
23012 Ventura Blvd., Woodland Hills, CA
91364 Tel 213-347-2035 (SAN 202-8964)
(ISBN Prefix 0-9600158; ISBN Prefix
0-933134)
Natl Shorthand Rptr
National Shorthand Reporters Association
118 Park St Se, Vienna, VA 22180 (SAN
224-9588)
Natl Textbk
National Textbook Co.
4255 W. Touhy Ave., Lincolnwood, IL
60646 Tel 312-679-4210 (SAN 169-2208)
(ISBN Prefix 0-8442)
Natur & Kultur
Natur och Kultur, Bokfoerlaget
Torsgatan 31, Box 6408, 11382 Stockholm
6, Sweden
Natural Hygiene
Natural Hygiene Press, Div. of American
Natural Hygiene Society, Inc.
698 Brooklawn Ave., Bridgeport, CT 06604
Tel 203-366-6229 (SAN 202-4314)
(ISBN Prefix 0-914532)
Nauta SA
Nauta, S. A.
Loreto, 16, Barcelona 29, Spain
Naval Inst Pr
Naval Institute Press
Annapolis, MD 21402 Tel 301-268-6110
(SAN 202-9006)
(ISBN Prefix 0-87021)
Navarre
Navarre
3, Rue Saint-Fictor, 75005 Paris, France
NCTE
National Council of Teachers of English
1111 Kenyon Rd., Urbana, IL 61801
Tel 217-328-3870 (SAN 202-9049)
(ISBN Prefix 0-8141)
Neal-Schuman
Neal-Schuman Pubs., Inc.
23 Cornelia St., New York, NY 10014
Tel 212-620-5990 (SAN 210-2455)
(ISBN Prefix 0-918212)
Nederlandse Boek
Nederlandse Boekhandel
Kapelsestraat 222, Kapellen, BE,
Netherlands
Negro U Pr
See Greenwood
Neguri
Neguri Editorial, S.A.
Espartero, 10, Bilbao-9, Spain
Nelson
Nelson, Thomas, Publishers
P.O. Box 141000, Nelson Place at Elm Hill
Pike, Nashville, TN 37214
Tel 615-889-9000 (SAN 209-3820)
(ISBN Prefix 0-8407)
Nelson & Sons Group
Nelson, Thomas, & Sons, Ltd.
Nelson House, Mayfield Rd.,
Walton-on-Thames, Surrey KT12 5PL,
United Kingdom
Nereo
Nereo, Coleccion
Jonch, 5, Sabadell (Barcelona), Spain
Neumann-Neudamm
Neumann-Neudamm GmbH & Co. KG, Verlag
Muhlenstr. 9, Postf 320, 3508 Melsungen,
Federal Republic of Germany
(ISBN Prefix 3-7888)
Neuvost
Neuvostoliittoinstituuti
Armfeltintie 10, 00150 Helsinki 15, Finland
New Bruns Mus
New Brunswick Museum
277 Douglas Ave., Saint John, N. B. E3K
1E5, Canada

New Century
New Century Pubs., Inc.
220 Old New Brunswick Rd., Piscataway,
NJ 08854 Tel 201-981-0820 (SAN
217-1201)
(ISBN Prefix 0-8329)
New City
New City Press
206 Skillman Ave., Brooklyn, NY 11211
Tel 212-782-2844 (SAN 203-7335)
(ISBN Prefix 0-911782)
New Viewpoints
See Watts
Newbury Bks
Newbury Books
Box 29, Topsfield, MA 01983
Tel 617-887-5082 (SAN 203-7386)
(ISBN Prefix 0-912728; ISBN Prefix
0-912729)
Newbury Bks Inc
See Newbury Bks
Newbury Hse
Newbury House Pubs.
54 Warehouse Lane, Rowley, MA 01969
Tel 800-343-1240 (SAN 202-9146)
(ISBN Prefix 0-88377; ISBN Prefix
0-912066)
Newhouse Pr
Newhouse Press
146 N. Rampart Blvd., Los Angeles, CA
90042 Tel 213-383-1089 (SAN 209-2689)
Orders to:
P.O. Box 76145, Los Angeles, CA 90076
(SAN 209-2697)
(ISBN Prefix 0-918050)
Newnes Bks
Newnes Books
C/0 Butterworth & Co. Ltd Borough
Green, Sevenoaks Kent TN15 8PH,
United Kingdom
(ISBN Prefix 0-600)
Newton Compton
Newton Compton
Via Germanilo, 197-00192 Rome, Italy
NIB
N. I. B.
Postbus 144, Zeist, Netherlands
Nichols Pub
Nichols Publishing Co.
P.O. Box 96, New York, NY 10024
Tel 212-580-8079 (SAN 212-0291)
(ISBN Prefix 0-89397)
Niemeyer
Niemeyer, Max, Verlag
Pfrondorfer Str 4, Postf 2140, 7400
Tubingen, Federal Republic of Germany
(ISBN Prefix 3-484)
Nistri-Lischi
Nistri-Lischi
Piazza Castelletto, 7-56100 Pisa, Italy
Nizet
Nizet
3 bis, Place de la Sorbonne, 75005 Paris,
France
Noble
See Bowmar-Noble
Noguer SA
Noguer, S.A. Editorial
Paseo De Gracia, 96, Barcelona-8, Spain
Noname Pr
Noname Press
5200 Klingle St., N.W., Washington, DC
20016 Tel 202-244-6243 (SAN 203-1639)
Nord Afrik
Nordiska Afikainstitutet
Sysslomansgatan 7, Box 2126, 75002
Uppsala, Sweden
Nord Teater
Nordiska Teaterunionen
Birger Jarlsgatan 53, 11145 Stockholm,
Sweden
Norges Natur
Norges Naturvernforbund
Postboks, 8268, Hammenrsborg, Oslo 1,
Norway
Norma
Norma
Sancho Davila, 27, Madrid 28, Spain
Norma Edit
Norma Editorial
Calle 37 no. 13-08, Bogota Colombia,
Colombia
Norsk Verks
Norsk Verkstedsindustris
Standardiseringssentral
Postboks 7072, Oslo, Norway

Norstedt Soner
Nordstedt & Soner AB PA
Tryckerigatan 2, Box 2052, 10312
Stockholm 2, Sweden
North Holland *Imprint of* **Elsevier**
Northland
Northland Press
P.O. Box N, Flagstaff, AZ 86002
Tel 602-774-5251 (SAN 202-9251)
(ISBN Prefix 0-87358)
Northwest Pub
Northwestern Publishing House
3624 W. North Ave., Milwaukee, WI
53208 Tel 414-442-1810 (SAN 206-7943)
(ISBN Prefix 0-8100)
Norton
Norton, W. W., & Co., Inc.
500 Fifth Ave., New York, NY 10110
Tel 212-354-5500 (SAN 202-5795)
(ISBN Prefix 0-393)
Norwood
See Norwood Edns
Norwood Edns
Norwood Editions
P.O. Box 38, Norwood, PA 19074
Tel 215-583-4550 (SAN 206-8613)
(ISBN Prefix 0-88305; ISBN Prefix 0-8482)
Novaro SA
Novaro S.A. Organizacion Editorial
Pallaras, 85 al 91, Barcelona-18, Spain
Nuestra Cultura
Nuestra Cultura, S.A. Editorial
Santa Amalia, 9, Bajo, Madrid-18, Spain
Nuova Cappelli
Nuova Cappelli
Via Marsili, 9-40124 Bologna, Italy
Nuova Vallecchi
Nuova Vallecchi
Via Capponi, 26-50121 Florence, Italy
NY Sch Indus Rel
See ILR Pr
NY Times
New York Times
229 W. 43rd St., New York, NY 10036
Tel 212-556-1234 (SAN 208-3027)
NYGS
New York Graphic Society Books
34 Beacon St., Boston, MA 02106
Tel 617-227-0730 (SAN 202-5841)
Dist. by:
Little, Brown & Co., 200 West St.,
Waltham, MA 02154 (SAN 281-8892)
(ISBN Prefix 0-8212)
Nyhoff
Nyhoff
Postbus 269, S-Gravenhage, Netherlands
O Maier Verlag
Maier, Otto, Verlag
Markstr 22-26 & Robert Bosch Str 1,
Postfach 1860, D-7980 Revensburg,
Federal Republic of Germany
OAS
Organization of American States
Dept. of Publications, 6840 Industrial Rd.,
Springfield, VA 22151 Tel 703-941-1617
(SAN 206-8877)
(ISBN Prefix 0-8270)
Oasis SA
Oasis, S.A., Ediciones
Av. Oaxaca 28 Planta Baja, Mexico 7, D.F.,
Mexico
Obelisco
Obelisco, S. A. Ediciones
Farmaceutico Carbonell, 50, Barcelona 34,
Spain
Obol Intl
Obol International, Div. of Unigraphics Inc.
8 S. Michigan Ave., Chicago, IL 60603
Tel 312-267-3662 (SAN 282-0692)
Orders to:
4747 N. Spaulding, Chicago, IL 60625
(SAN 282-0706)
(ISBN Prefix 0-916710; ISBN Prefix 0-86723)
OCDL
O. C. D. L. (l'Office Central de Libraire) Paris
France
Oceana
Oceana Pubns.
75 Main St., Dobbs Ferry, NY 10522
Tel 914-693-5944 (SAN 202-5744)
(ISBN Prefix 0-379)
Oceano
Oceano-Exito, S.A. Ediciones
Paseo De Gracia, 24, Barcelona-7, Spain

Octagon
Octagon Books
19 Union Square W., New York, NY 10003
Tel 212-741-6961 (SAN 202-8123)
(ISBN Prefix 0-374)
OECD
Organization for Economic Cooperation &
Development
1750 Pennsylvania Ave., Suite 1207, N.W.,
Washington, DC 20006 Tel 202-724-1857
(SAN 202-1277)
Ohio U Pr
Ohio Univ. Press
Scott Quadrangle, Athens, OH 45701
Tel 614-594-5505 (SAN 282-0773)
Orders to:
Harper & Row Publishers, Inc, Keystone
Industrial Park, Scranton, PA 18512
Tel 800-233-4377 (SAN 282-0781)
(ISBN Prefix 0-8214)
Oifig an Tsolathair
Oifig an Tsolathair
Baile, Dublin, Ireland
Oikos Tau
Oikos Tau, S.A. Ediciones
Montserrat, 12-14, Villassar de Mar,
Barcelona, Spain
Oldenbourg Verlag
Oldenbourg, R., Verlag GmbH
Rosenheimer Str. 145, 8000 Munich 80,
Federal Republic of Germany
(ISBN Prefix 3-486)
Oleander Pr
Oleander Press
210 Fifth Ave., New York, NY 10010
(SAN 206-1031)
(ISBN Prefix 0-902675; ISBN Prefix
0-900891; ISBN Prefix 0-906672)
Olms Verlag
Olms, Georg, Verlag GmbH
Hagentorwall 6-7, 3200 Hildesheim,
Federal Republic of Germany
(ISBN Prefix 3-487)
Olschki
Olschki
Viuzzo del Pozzetto, 50126 Florence, Italy
Omega SA
Omega, S.A. Editorial
Casanova, 220, Barcelona-36, Spain
OMS
Office of Management Studies
1527 New Hampshire Ave Nw,
Washington, DC 20036 (SAN 260-3853)
Ophrys
Ophrys
39, Rue d'Amsterdam, 75008 Paris, France
(ISBN Prefix 2-7080)
Orbe Edns
Orbe Ediciones
Edifico Gaztelondo, 45, (Redcaldeberri)
Bilbao, Spain
Organ Ofic Adm
Organismos Oficiales de la Administracion
Madrid, Spain
Organize Am States
Organization of American States
1725 I Street, NW, Washington, DC 20006
Tel 202-381-8877
Orient Bk Dist
Orient Book Distributors
P.O. Box 100, Livingston, NJ 07039
Tel 201-992-6992 (SAN 211-819X)
(ISBN Prefix 0-89684)
Oriental Bk Store
Oriental Book Store, The
P.O. Box 177, South Pasadena, CA
91030-0177 Tel 213-577-2413 (SAN
285-0818); 630 E. Colorado Blvd.,
Pasadena, CA 91101 Tel 213-577-2413
(SAN 285-0826)
Oriental Inst
Oriental Institute of the Univ. of Chicago
1155 E. 58th St., Chicago, IL 60637
Tel 312-753-2478 (SAN 210-4784)
(ISBN Prefix 0-918986)
Orientalia
Orientalia Art, Ltd.
P.O. Box 597, New York, NY 10003
Tel 212-473-9837 (SAN 282-0919); 61
Fourth Ave., New York, NY 10003 (SAN
282-0927)
(ISBN Prefix 0-87902)
Ortells Ferriz
Ortells Ferriz, Alfredo
Sagunto, 5, Valencia 9, Spain

Oryx Pr
Oryx Press
2214 N. Central Ave., Phoenix, AZ 85004
Tel 602-254-6156 (SAN 220-0201)
(ISBN Prefix 0-912700; ISBN Prefix
0-89774)
Otava
Otava Kustannusosakeyhtio
Uudenmaankatu 8-12, P.O. Box 134,
SF-00120 Helsinki 12, Finland
Otava Kust
Otava Kustannusosakeyhtio
Uudenmaankatu 8-12, 00120 Helsinki 12,
Finland
Oulun Yliopisto
Oulun Yliopisto
Kasarmintie 7, 90100 Oulu 10, Finland
Outlet Bk Co
Outlet Book Company, Div. of Crown
Publishers, Inc.
One Park Ave., New York, NY 10016
(SAN 200-2620)
Ouvrieres
Ouvrieres
12, Av. Soeur-Rosalie, 75013 Paris, France
(ISBN Prefix 2-7082)
Overlook Pr
Overlook Press
667 Madison Ave., Suite 401A, New York,
NY 10021 Tel 212-688-0920 (SAN
202-8360)
c/o Viking Press, 40 W. 23 St., New York,
NY 10010 Tel 212-807-7300 (SAN
200-2469)
(ISBN Prefix 0-87951)
Oxford Poly Pr
Oxford Polytechnic Press
Headington, Oxford OX3 0BP,
United Kingdom
Oxford U Pr
Oxford Univ. Press, Inc.
200 Madison Ave., New York, NY 10016
Tel 212-679-7300 (SAN 202-5884)
Orders to:
16-00 Pollitt Dr., Fair Lawn, NJ 07410
Tel 201-796-8000 (SAN 202-5892)
(ISBN Prefix 0-19)
Oyez
Oyez
212 Colgate Ave., Kensington, CA 94707
(SAN 206-877X)
(ISBN Prefix 0-911088)
P Elek
See Merrimack Pub Cir
P-H
Prentice-Hall, Inc.
Rte. 9W, Englewood Cliffs, NJ 07632
Tel 201-592-2000 (SAN 200-2175)
Orders to:
Box 500, Englewood Cliffs, NJ 07632
(SAN 215-3939)
(ISBN Prefix 0-13)
P Lang Pubs
Lang, Peter, Publishing, Inc.
34 E. 39th St., New York, NY 10016
Tel 212-692-9009 (SAN 241-5534)
P N Balai Pustaka
Balai Pustaka, P. N.
J1 Dakter Wahidin No. 1, Jakarta,
Indonesia
Pa St U Pr
Pennsylvania State Univ. Press
215 Wagner Bldg., University Park, PA
16802 Tel 814-865-1327 (SAN 213-5760)
(ISBN Prefix 0-271)
Padilla
Padilla, Francisco
P.O. Box 517, Westminster, CO 80030
Tel 303-629-2425 (SAN 216-2814)
(ISBN Prefix 0-9605292)
Pagurian
Pagurian Press
Dist. by:
Baker & Taylor, 1515 Broadway, New
York, NY 10036 Tel 212-673-6600 (SAN
169-5606)
(ISBN Prefix 0-88932; ISBN Prefix
0-919364)
Pahl-Rugenstein
Pahl-Rugenstein Verlag, Inhaber Manfred
Pahl-Rugenstein
Gottesweg 54, 5000 Cologne 51,
Federal Republic of Germany
(ISBN Prefix 3-7609)
Paidos Iberia
Paidos Iberica, S. A.
Mariano Cubi, 92, Barcelona 21, Spain

Palumbo
Palumbo
Via Ricasoli, 59-90139 Palermo, Italy
Pan Am Bk
Pan American Book Co.
4362 Melrose Ave., Los Angeles, CA
90029 Tel 213-665-1241
Pan Bks
Pan Books (Australia) Pty., Ltd.
1 Castlereagh St., Sydney, NSW 2000,
Australia
(ISBN Prefix 0-330)
Pan Italy
Pan
Via Solferino, 32-20121 Milan, Italy
Pan Pacific
Pan Pacific Book Distributors (S) Pte., Ltd.
597 Havelock Rd., Singapore 0316,
Singapore
Panstwowe Wydawnict Iskry
Panstwowe Wydawnictwo Iskry
Ul Smolna 11-13 P.O. Box 897, 00-375
Warsaw, Poland
Panstwowy Zaklad W
Panstwowy Zaklad Wydawnictw Lekarskich
Dluga 38-40, P.O. Box 379, 00-238
Warsaw, Poland
Paperback Lib
See Warner Bks
Paragon
Paragon Book Reprint Corp.
14 E. 38th St., New York, NY 10016
Tel 212-532-4920   (SAN 213-1986)
(ISBN Prefix 0-8188)
Paraninfo
Paraninfo, S.A. Editorial
Magallanes, 25, Madrid-15, Spain
Paravia
Paravia
Corso Racconigi, 16-10139 Turin, Italy
Parey
Parey, Paul
Spitalerstr 12, 2000 Hamburg 1,
Federal Republic of Germany
(ISBN Prefix 3-489)
Parramon Edns
Parramon Ediciones, S.A.
Lepanto, 264, Barcelona-13, Spain
Patron
Patron
Via Badini, 12-40127 Quarto Inferiore
(Bologna), Italy
Paulinas
Paulinas Ediciones
Protasio Gomez, 15, Madrid-27, Spain
Pavillon
Pavillon
5, Rue Rollin, 75005 Paris, France
Payot
Payot
106, Blvd. Saint-Germain, 75006 Paris,
France
(ISBN Prefix 2-228)
PB
Pocket Books, Inc, Div. of Simon & Schuster,
Inc.
1230 Ave. of the Americas, New York, NY
10020 Tel 212-246-2121   (SAN 202-5922)
(ISBN Prefix 0-671)
Pediatrica
Pediatrica
Mayor de Gracia, 102 Barcelona 12, Spain
Peeters
Peeters
B. P. 41, 3000 Louvain, Belgium
Pelican
Pelican Publishing Co., Inc.
1101 Monroe St., P.O. Box 189, Gretna,
LA 70053 Tel 504-368-1175   (SAN
212-0623)
(ISBN Prefix 0-911116; ISBN Prefix
0-88289)
Pellegrini
Pellegrini (Cosenza)
Via Parisio, 4-87100 Cosenza, Italy
Pena Lillo
Pena Lillo, A.
Hipolito Yrigoyen 1394, Buenos Aires,
Argentina
Penerbit Jaya
Penerbit Jaya
P.O. Box 6103, Pudu PO, Kuala Lumpur,
Malawi
Penguin
Penguin Books, Inc.
40 W. 23rd St., New York, NY 10010
Tel 212-807-7300   (SAN 202-5914)
(ISBN Prefix 0-14)

Penn German Soc
Pennsylvania German Society
R.D. 4, Box 71, New Oxford, PA 17350
Tel 717-627-4106   (SAN 205-1958)
Orders to:
Box 97, Breinigsville, PA 18031   (SAN
205-1966)
(ISBN Prefix 0-911122)
Penns Valley
Penns Valley Pubs.
1298 S. 28th St., Harrisburg, PA 17111
Tel 717-232-5844   (SAN 202-1455)
(ISBN Prefix 0-931992)
Pennwell Book Division
See Pennwell Pub
Pennwell Pub
Pennwell Publishing Co, Div. of Pennwell
Books
P.O. Box 1260, Tulsa, OK 74101
Tel 918-663-4220   (SAN 282-1559)
Orders to:
P.O. Box 21288, Tulsa, OK 74121
Tel 918-663-4225   (SAN 282-1567)
(ISBN Prefix 0-87814)
Pensee Moderne
Pensee Moderne
98, Rue de Vaugirard, 75006 Paris, France
(ISBN Prefix 2-7146)
Perfect Graphic
Perfect Graphic Arts
14 Dearborn Dr., Old Tappan, NJ 07675
Tel 201-767-8575   (SAN 204-9430)
(ISBN Prefix 0-911126)
Pergamena
Pergamena
Viale Ezio, 7-20149 Milan, Italy
Pergamon
Pergamon Press, Inc.
Maxwell House, Fairview Park, Elmsford,
NY 10523 Tel 914-592-7700   (SAN
213-9022)
(ISBN Prefix 0-08)
Peter Smith
Smith, Peter, Publisher Inc.
6 Lexington Ave., Magnolia, MA 01930
Tel 617-525-3562   (SAN 206-8885)
(ISBN Prefix 0-8446)
PETEX
Petroleum Extension Service (PETEX)
Industrial & Busn. Training Bur., Univ. of
Texas at Austin, Box S, Univ. Sta., Austin,
TX 78712   (SAN 208-3892)
Petrocelli-Charter
See Van Nos Reinhold
Phaidon
See Dutton
Phiebig
See S Karger
Philatelic Found
Philatelic Foundation, The
270 Madison Ave, New York, NY 10016
Tel 212-889-6483   (SAN 235-3253)
(ISBN Prefix 0-911989)
Philo Pr
Philo Press
Box 277, Youngstown, NY 14174
Tel 716-285-2355   (SAN 239-2801)
(ISBN Prefix 0-941650)
Philos Document
Philosophy Documentation Center
Bowling Green State University, Bowling
Green, OH 43403 Tel 419-372-2419
(SAN 202-134X)
(ISBN Prefix 0-912632)
Philos Lib
Philosophical Library, Inc.
200 W. 57th St., New York, NY 10019
Tel 212-265-6050   (SAN 201-999X)
(ISBN Prefix 0-8022)
Physicians Rec
Physicians' Record Co.
3000 S. Ridgeland Ave., Berwyn, IL 60402
Tel 312-749-3111   (SAN 205-3853)
(ISBN Prefix 0-917036)
Picard
Picard
82, Rue Bonaparte, 75006 Paris, France
Piccin
Piccin
Via Brunacci, 12, 35100 Padua, Italy
(ISBN Prefix 8-8212)
Pierian
Pierian Press
P.O. Box 1808, Ann Arbor, MI 48106
Tel 313-434-5530   (SAN 204-8949)
(ISBN Prefix 0-87650)

Pilgrim NY
Pilgrim Press, The
132 W. 31st St., New York, NY 10001
Tel 212-594-8555   (SAN 212-601X)
Dist. by:
Seabury Service Center, Somers, CT 06071
Tel 800-243-0004   (SAN 202-5426)
(ISBN Prefix 0-8298)
Pinnacle Bks
Pinnacle Books
1430 Broadway, New York, NY 10018
Tel 212-719-5900   (SAN 200-2442)
(ISBN Prefix 0-523)
Piper Co
Piper, R., & Co.
Georgenstr 4, 8000 Munich 40,
Federal Republic of Germany
(ISBN Prefix 3-492)
Piquenas Edit
Piquenas Editoriales
Madrid, Spain
Piramide
Piramide, S.A. Ediciones
Villafianca, 22, Madrid-28, Spain
Pitman
See Pitman Learning
Pitman Bks
Pitman Books Ltd.
39 Parker St. London WC2B 5PB,
United Kingdom
(ISBN Prefix 0-273)
Pitman Learning
Pitman Learning, Inc.
19 Davis Dr., Belmont, CA 94002
Tel 415-592-7810   (SAN 212-775X)
(ISBN Prefix 0-8224)
Pitman Ltd
Pitman, Isaac, Pty. Ltd.
158-164 Bouverie St., Carlton, Vic. 3053,
Australia
(ISBN Prefix 0-85896)
Planeta SA
Planeta S.A.
Calvet, 51-53, Barcelona 21, Spain
Plantyn Edns
Plantyn Editions
1, Place Gabriel-Gaure, 74000
Annely-le-Vieux, France
Playette Corp
Playette Corp.
P.O. Box 5, Roslyn, NY 11576
Tel 516-883-2825   (SAN 203-1000)
Playor
Playor Editorial
Santa Polonia, 7 Apdo, Madrid-14, Spain
Plaza Janes
Plaza Janes, S.A. Editores
Virgen de Guadalupe 21-33, Esplugas de
Llobregat (Barcelona), Spain
Plume *Imprint of* **NAL**
Plus Ultra
Editorial Plus Ultra SAI & C
Viamonte 1755, 1055 Buenos Aires,
Argentina
Plus Ultra S. A.
Plus Ultra S.A.
Sanchez Pacheco, 51, Madrid 2, Spain
Plycon Pr
Plycon Press
P.O. Box 220, Redondo Beach, CA 90277
Tel 213-379-9725   (SAN 201-8829)
Dist. by:
Burgess Publishing Co., 7108 Ohms Lane,
Minneapolis, MN 55435   (SAN 212-6001)
(ISBN Prefix 0-916434)
P'Nye Pr
P'Nye Press
The Printers Shop, 4047 Transport, Palo
Alto, CA 94303 Tel 415-494-6802   (SAN
212-5463)
(ISBN Prefix 0-9602402)
Poeschel Verlag
Poeschel, C. E., Verlag
Kernerstr. 43, Postf 527, 7000 Stuttgart 1,
Federal Republic of Germany
(ISBN Prefix 3-7910)
Politikens Forlag
Politikens Forlag A/S
Vestergade 26, DK-1456 Copenhagen K,
Denmark
Pomaire
Pomaire, S.A. Editorial
Avda. Infanta Carlota, 114, Barcelona-29,
Spain
Pont Ist Biblico
Pontificio Istituto Biblico
Piazza Pilotta, 35-00187 Rome, Italy

Porrua
Porrua S. A. Editorial
Argentina 15, Altos Mexico 1, D.F.,
Mexico
Port-Am Fed
Portico Libros
Plaza de San Francisco, 17, Zaragoza-6,
Spain
Portic
Portic Editorial
Avda. Marques De l'Argentera, 17,
Barcelona-3, Spain
Porto Ed
Porto Editoria, Limitada
Rua de Restauracao 365 Porto, Portugal
Porto Editora
Porto Editora
Rua Da Fabrica, 84-90, Oporto, Portugal
Poseidon SA
Poseidon S. A.
Llansa, 51, Barcelona 15, Spain
Poste aux Lettres
Poste aux Lettres
17, Rue du Faubourg Montmarte, 75009
Paris, France
Powner
Powner, Charles T., Co., Inc.
407 S. Dearborn St., Chicago, IL 60605
(SAN 204-9082)
(ISBN Prefix 0-911164)
Pozza
Pozza
Contra Gazzolle, 6-36100 Vicenza, Italy
Pr Univ Fr
Presses Universitaires de France
108, Blvd. Saint-Germain, 75006 Paris,
France
(ISBN Prefix 2-13)
Prace
Prace
11258 Prague 1, Vaclavske Nam 17, Nove
Mesto, Czechoslovakia
Prae Heinz
Praesentverlag Heinz Peter
Kleiststr. 15, Postf 2720, 4830 Gutrsloh 1,
Federal Republic of Germany
(ISBN Prefix 3-87644)
Praeger
Praeger Pubs, Div. of Holt Rinehart &
Winston/CBS
521 Fifth Ave., New York, NY 10175
Tel 212-599-8413   (SAN 202-022X)
(ISBN Prefix 0-275)
Prasarnmitr
Prasarnmitr
3382 New Petchaburi Rd, Bangkok,
Thailand
Prensa Acad
Prensa Academica Latinoamericana Ltda.
Gaboto, 1385, Montevideo, Uruguay
Prensa Espanola
Prensa Espanola, S.A.
Padilla, 6, Madrid-6, Spain
Press West
Press West
4947 E. Tanqueray, St. Louis, MO 63129
Tel 314-982-2616   (SAN 202-988X)
(ISBN Prefix 0-914592)
Presses Cite
Presses de la Cite
8, Rue Garanciere, 75006 Paris, France
(ISBN Prefix 2-258)
Prestel Verlag
Prestel Verlag
Mandlstr 26, D-8000 Munich 40,
Federal Republic of Germany
(ISBN Prefix 3-7913)
Price Milburn
Price Milburn
POB 995, Wellington, New Zealand
(ISBN Prefix 0-7055)
Price Stern
Price, Stern, Sloan, Pubs., Inc.
410 N. La Cienega Blvd., Los Angeles, CA
90048 Tel 213-657-6100   (SAN 202-0246)
(ISBN Prefix 0-8431)
Princeton U Pr
Princeton Univ. Press
41 William St., Princeton, NJ 08540
Tel 609-452-4900   (SAN 202-0254)
(ISBN Prefix 0-691)
Principato
Principato
Via Fauche, 10-20154 Milan, Italy

Print Mat
Printed Matter Publishing Co., Inc.
15 N. Arlington Heights Rd., Arlington
Heights, IL 60004 Tel 312-870-8742
(SAN 169-5924)
(ISBN Prefix 0-943084)
Printed Matter Pub
See Print Mat
Prisma
Prisma Bokforlaget AB
Apelbergsgatan 56, Box 3192, 10363
Stockholm, Sweden
Prisme
Prisme
1, Place Gabriel-Faure, 74000
Annely-le-Vieux, France
Prismes
Prismes
284, Avenue Marechal Leclerc, 34000
Montpellier, France
Privat
Privat
14, Rue des Arts, 31000 Toulouse, France
Pro Golfers
Professional Golfers Association of America
Box 12458, Lake Park, FL 33403   (SAN
224-5655)
Prod Edit
Producciones Editoriales
Auda. Jose Antonio, 800 Barcelona 13,
Spain
Prod Intl
Productivity International, Inc.
Forest Central Dr., Suite 317, Dallas, TX
75243 Tel 214-341-9606   (SAN 217-2658)
Proletarian Pubs
Proletarian Pubs
P.O. Box 3925, Chicago, IL 60654   (SAN
209-2158)
Orders to:
Vanguard Books, P.O. Box 3566, Chicago,
IL 60654 Tel 312-342-3425   (SAN
213-8212)
(ISBN Prefix 0-89380)
Prosveta
Prosveta
YU-1100 Belgrade, Dobracina 30,
Yugoslavia
Prugg
Prugg Verlag
Rotenlowengasse 1a, 1090 Vienna, Austria
(ISBN Prefix 3-85385)
PSG Pub
See Wright-PSG
Pub Aff Pr
Public Affairs Press
419 New Jersey Ave., Washington, DC
20003 Tel 202-544-3024   (SAN 202-1471)
(ISBN Prefix 0-8183)
Pub Euro Am
Publicacao Europa-America
Estrada De Lisboa-Sintra, 14, Lisboa,
Portugal
Pubns Organization
See Bridge Pubns Inc
Pubns Orient
Publications Orientalistes de France
4 rue de la Lille, F-75007 Paris, France
(ISBN Prefix 2-7169)
Pudoc
Pudoc
Postbus 4, Wageningen, Netherlands
PUF
Presses universitaires de France
108 boulevard St. Germain, 75006 Paris,
France
(ISBN Prefix 2-13)
Pustaka Antara
Pustaka Antara
Jl Mgapahit No. 28, Jakarta, Indonesia
Pyc
Pyc Edition
254 Rue de Vaugirard, 75015 Paris, France
(ISBN Prefix 2-85330)
Pygmalion
Pygmalion
198, Blvd. Saint-Germain, 75007 Paris,
France
(ISBN Prefix 2-85704)
Quadrangle
See Times Bks
Quality Lib
Quality Library Editions
P.O. Box 148, Darby, PA 19023   (SAN
209-1186)

Que Corp
Que Corp.
7960 Castleway Dr., Indianapolis, IN 46250
Tel 317-842-7162   (SAN 219-6298)
(ISBN Prefix 0-88022)
Quelle & Meyer
Quelle & Meyer Verlag Gmbh & Co.
Schloss-Wolfsbrunnen-Weg 29, Postf
104480, 6900 Heidelberg 1,
Federal Republic of Germany
(ISBN Prefix 3-494)
Quickborner Team
Verlag Quickborner Team GmbH
Mittleweg 119, 2000 Hamburg 13,
Federal Republic of Germany
(ISBN Prefix 3-87715)
Quill NY
Quill
105 Madison Ave., New York, NY 10016
(SAN 239-4790)
(ISBN Prefix 0-688)
R & E Res Assoc
R & E Research Associates, Inc.
936 Industrial Ave., Palo Alto, CA 94303
Tel 415-494-1112   (SAN 204-6555)
(ISBN Prefix 0-88247)
R Brockhaus
Brockhaus, R., Verlag
Postfach 110197, D-5600 Wuppertal,
Federal Republic of Germany
R DeBoo
DeBoo, Richard, Ltd.
51 Wellington St, Toronto, Ont. M5T 1H2,
United Kingdom
(ISBN Prefix 0-88820)
R Enslow
See Enslow Pubs
R West
West, Richard
Box 6404, Philadelphia, PA 19145   (SAN
206-8907)
(ISBN Prefix 0-8492; ISBN Prefix 0-8274)
Radha
Radha Krishna Prakasha
2 Ansari Rd, Daryaganj New Delhi 110002,
India
Radio
Radio
9, Rue Jacob, 75006 Paris, France
Radio City
Radio City Book Store
324 W. 47th St., New York, NY 10036
Tel 212-245-5754   (SAN 204-6644)
(ISBN Prefix 0-911202)
Railsearch
Railsearch Publishing, Inc.
P.O. Box 84, Chalfont, PA 18914   (SAN
214-4549)
(ISBN Prefix 0-937060)
Ramos-Majos
Ramos-Majos Editorial
Muntaner 114-116, Barcelona-36, Spain
Ramsay Head Pr
Ramsay Headpress
36 North Castle St., Edinburgh, EH2 3BN,
United Kingdom
RanC *Imprint of* **Random**
Rand
Rand McNally & Co.
P.O. Box 7600, Chicago, IL 60680
Tel 312-673-9100   (SAN 203-3917)
(ISBN Prefix 0-528)
Random
Random House, Inc.
Random House Publicity (11-6), 201 E.
50th St., New York, NY 10022
Tel 212-751-2600   (SAN 202-5507)
Orders to:
400 Hahn Rd., Westminster, MD 21157
(SAN 202-5515)
(ISBN Prefix 0-394)
Razon y Fe
Razon y Fe, S.A. Editorial
Pablo Aranda, 3, Madrid-6, Spain
RD Assn
Reader's Digest Assn., Inc.
750 Third Ave., New York, NY
10017-2797 Tel 212-850-7100   (SAN
282-2083)
Orders to:
Customer Service, Pleasantville, NY 10570
Tel 914-769-7000   (SAN 282-2091)
(ISBN Prefix 0-89577)

Readers Digest Pr
Reader's Digest Press
200 Park Ave., New York, NY 10017
(SAN 203-3887)
Dist. by:
McGraw-Hill Book Co., 1221 Ave. of the
Americas, New York, NY 10020 (SAN
200-2248)
(ISBN Prefix 0-88349)

Readex Bks
Readex Books, Div. of Readex Microprint
Corp.
101 Fifth Ave., New York, NY 10003
Tel 212-243-3822 (SAN 209-9926)
(ISBN Prefix 0-918414)

Readex Microprint
See Readex Bks

Real Estate Pub
Real Estate Publishing Co.
P.O. Box 41177, Sacramento, CA 95841
Tel 916-677-3864 (SAN 202-9782)
(ISBN Prefix 0-914256)

Reclam
Reclam, Philippe
Siemensstr 32, Postf 1149, 7257 Ditzingen,
Federal Republic of Germany
(ISBN Prefix 3-15)

Redhouse Pr
Redhouse Press
PK 142, Istanbul, Turkey

Rediviva
Rediviva Facsimileforlaget Bokforlagt
Roslagsgatan 11, Fack, 10432 Stockholm
19, Sweden

Reed Ltd
Reed (A. H. & A. W.) Ltd.
182 Wakefield St., Wellington,
New Zealand
(ISBN Prefix 0-589)

Ref Pubns
Reference Pubns., Inc.
Box 344, 218 St. Clair River Dr., Algonac,
MI 48001 Tel 313-794-5722 (SAN
208-4392)
(ISBN Prefix 0-917256)

Regents Pub
Regents Publishing Co., Inc, Div. of Hachette
2 Park Ave., New York, NY 10016
Tel 212-889-2780 (SAN 203-3844)
(ISBN Prefix 0-88345)

Regnery
See Contemp Bks

Reichert
Reichert, Ludwig, Dr.
Reisstr 10, 6200 Wiesbaden-Dotzheim,
Federal Republic of Germany
(ISBN Prefix 3-88226)

Reidel Pub
See Kluwer Academic

Reilly & Lee
See Contemp Bks

Reimer
Reimer, Dietrich
Unter den Eichen 57, 1000 Berlin 45,
Federal Republic of Germany
(ISBN Prefix 3-496)

Res & Educ
Research & Education Assn.
505 Eighth Ave., New York, NY 10018
Tel 212-695-9487 (SAN 204-6814)
(ISBN Prefix 0-87891)

Res Ctr Lang Semiotic
Research Center for Language & Semiotic
Studies
Dist. by:
Humanities Press, Inc., Atlantic Highlands,
NJ 07716 (SAN 201-9272)
(ISBN Prefix 0-87750)

Reston
Reston Publishing Co., Inc.
11480 Sunset Hills Rd., Reston, VA 22090
Tel 703-437-8900 (SAN 200-2337)
Dist. by:
Prentice-Hall, Inc., Englewood Cliffs, NJ
07632 (SAN 215-3939)
(ISBN Prefix 0-87909; ISBN Prefix 0-8359)

Retz
Retz
114, Ave. des Champs-Elysees, 75008
Paris, France
(ISBN Prefix 2-7256)

Reus SA
Reus, S.A. Instituto Editorial
Preciados, 23, Madrid-13, Spain

Rev Derecho Pri
Revista de Derecho Privado
Madrid, Spain

Revell
Revell, Fleming H., Co.
184 Central Ave., Old Tappan, NJ 07675
Tel 201-768-8060 (SAN 203-3801)
(ISBN Prefix 0-8007)

Reverte SA
Reverte, S.A. Editorial
Encarnacion, 86-88, Barcelona-24, Spain

Revisionist Pr
Revisionist Press
P.O. Box 2009, Brooklyn, NY 11202
(SAN 203-378X)
(ISBN Prefix 0-87700)

Reward *Imprint of* P-H

Rheinland Verlag
Rheinland-Verlag GmbH
Abtei Braunweiler, 5024 Pulheim 2,
Federal Republic of Germany
(ISBN Prefix 3-7927)

Rio Grafica
Rio Grafica e Editora, S.A.
Rua Itapiru 1209-5 andar, Rio Comprido,
2000 Rio de Janeiro Rj, Brazil

RIREA
RIREA-Rivista Italiana di Ragioneria e di
Economia Aziendale
Via delle Isole, 30-00198 Rome, Italy

RIT Graph Arts Res
See Tech & Ed Ctr Graph Arts RIT

Rizzoli Edit
Rizzoli Editore SPA
Via Rizzoli 2, I-20132 Milan, Italy

Rodale Pr Eng
Rodale Press
Chestnut Close, Potten End, Berkhamsted,
Herts., HP4 2QL, United Kingdom

Rodale Pr Inc
Rodale Press, Inc.
33 E. Minor St., Emmaus, PA 18049
Tel 215-967-5171 (SAN 200-2477)
(ISBN Prefix 0-87857)

Rodopi
Rodopi
Keizersgracht 302-304, Amsterdam,
Netherlands

Roller Rink Ops
Roller Skating Rink Operators Association of
America
7700 A St, Lincoln, NE 68510
Tel 402-489-8811 (SAN 224-6325)

Roloff
Roloff, Bernhard
Buchenweg 1, 8919 Schondorf Ammersee,
Federal Republic of Germany
(ISBN Prefix 3-88144)

Romana Libri
Romana Libri Alfabeto
Piazza Paoli, 3-00186 Rome, Italy

Rosenberg & Sel
Rosenberg & Sellier
Via A. Doria, 14, 10123 Turin, Italy

Rosenkilde
Rosenkilde og Bagger's Forlag
Kronprinsensgade 3, 1114 Coppenhagen K,
Denmark

Ross
Ross & Haines Old Books Co.
639 E. Lake St., Wayzata, MN 55391
Tel 612-473-7551 (SAN 204-7004)
(ISBN Prefix 0-87018)

Rossel Edns
Rossel Edition
73 rue d'Anjou, F-75008 Paris, France

Rothman
Rothman, Fred B., & Co.
10368 W. Centennial Rd., Littleton, CO
80127 Tel 303-979-5657 (SAN 159-9437)
(ISBN Prefix 0-8377)

Rothman Repr
See Rothman

Routledge & Kegan
Routledge & Kegan Paul, Ltd.
9 Park St., Boston, MA 02108
Tel 617-742-5863 (SAN 202-5469)
(ISBN Prefix 0-7100)

Rowman
Rowman & Littlefield, Inc, Div. of Littlefield,
Adams, & Co.
81 Adams Dr., Box 327, Totowa, NJ 07511
Tel 201-256-8600 (SAN 203-3704)
(ISBN Prefix 0-87471; ISBN Prefix 0-8476)

Rowman & Allanheld
Rowman & Allanheld, Div. of Littlefield,
Adams & Co.
81 Adams Dr., Totowa, NJ 07512
Tel 201-256-8600 (SAN 282-7921)

Rowohlt
Rowohlt Taschenbuch Verlag GmbH
Hamburger Str 17, Postfach 1349, D-2057
Reinbeck Bei Hamburg,
Federal Republic of Germany

RST
R. S. T.
9, Rue des Haies, 75020 Paris, France

Ruhland
Ruhland, Jean
Le Patis-Malaise, 44430 Loroux-Bottereau,
France
(ISBN Prefix 2-85751)

Running Pr
Running Press
125 S. 22nd St., Philadelphia, PA 19103
Tel 215-567-5080 (SAN 204-5702)
(ISBN Prefix 0-89471)

Russell
Russell & Russell, Pubs, Div. of Atheneum
Pubs.
597 Fifth Ave., New York, NY 10017
Tel 212-486-2685 (SAN 282-2644)
Orders to:
Scribner Distribution Center, 201
Willowbrook Blvd., Wayne, NJ 07470
Tel 201-256-0700 (SAN 282-2652)
(ISBN Prefix 0-8462)

Russica
Russica Book Shop
80 E. 11th St., New York, NY 10003

Russki Iazyk
Russki Iazyk
Pushkinskaya Ul 23, Moscow 103009,
U S S R

Rutgers Ctr Alcohol
Rutgers Ctr. of Alcohol Studies Pubns.
Smithers Hall, Rutgers Univ., New
Brunswick, NJ 08903 Tel 201-932-3510
(SAN 203-3658)
Orders to:
P.O. Box 969, Piscataway, NJ 08854
Tel 201-932-2190 (SAN 203-3666)
(ISBN Prefix 0-911290)

S F Vanni
Vanni, S.F.
30 W. 12th St., New York, NY 10011
Tel 212-675-6336 (SAN 220-0031)
(ISBN Prefix 0-913298)

S Ill U Pr
Southern Illinois Univ. Press
P.O. Box 3697, Carbondale, IL 62901
Tel 618-453-2281 (SAN 203-3623)
(ISBN Prefix 0-8093)

S J Durst
Durst, Sanford J.
29-28 41st Ave., Long Island City, NY
11101 Tel 212-706-0303 (SAN 211-6987)
(ISBN Prefix 0-915262)

S Karger
Karger, S., AG
150 5th Ave., Suite 1103, New York, NY
10011 Tel 212-924-9222 (SAN 281-8531)
Dist. by:
Albert J. Phiebig, P. O. Box 352, White
Plains, NY 10602 (SAN 281-854X)
(ISBN Prefix 3-8055)

S M Edns
Ediciones S.M.
29 Mandri 41, Barcelona-6, Spain

Sader SA
Sader, S.A. De Editores Reunidos
Plaza Marina Espanola, 6, Madrid 13,
Spain

Sadtler Res
Sadtler Research Laboratories, Inc.
3316 Spring Garden St., Philadelphia, PA
19104 Tel 215-382-7800 (SAN 203-0063)
(ISBN Prefix 0-8456)

Sagner
Sagner, Otto
Hessstr. 39-41, 8000 Munich 40,
Federal Republic of Germany
(ISBN Prefix 3-87690)

Saifer
Saifer, Albert, Pub.
P.O. Box 239 W.O.B., West Orange, NJ
07052 (SAN 204-7225)
(ISBN Prefix 0-87556)

Sal Terrae
Sal Terrae Editorial
Guevara, 20, Santander, Spain

Salvat
Salvat Editores S.A.
Principe de Vergara, 32, Madrid-1, Spain

Sam-Sung Pub
Seorg, Sam, Publishing Co. Ltd.
43-7 Kwanchul-dong, Chonqno-ku, Seoul
110, Korea, South
Samlaget
Samlaget, Det Norske
Trondheim 15, Oslo 5, Norway
Sams
Sams, Howard W., & Co, Inc, Subs. of ITT
4300 W. 62nd St., Indianapolis, IN 46206
Tel 317-298-5400 (SAN 203-3577)
(ISBN Prefix 0-672)
San Marco
San Marco
Via Abbadia, 13-24069 Trescore Balneario
(Bergamo), Italy
San Martin
San Martin
Puerto del Sol, 6, Madrid 14, Spain
Sanchez Rodrigo
Sanchez Rodrigo, S.A. Editorial
Pl. Nun Perez Monroy, 3, Plasencia
(Caceres), Spain
Sandron
Sandron
Via Farini, 10-50121, Florence, Italy
S&S
Simon & Schuster, Inc.
1230 Ave. of the Americas, New York, NY
10020 Tel 212-245-6400 (SAN 200-2450)
(ISBN Prefix 0-671)
Sansoni
Sansoni
Via Varchi, 47-50132 Florence, Italy
Santillana
Santillana Publishing Co.
575 Lexington Ave., New York, NY 10022
Tel 212-371-4069 (SAN 205-1133)
(ISBN Prefix 0-88272)
Santillana SA
Santillana, S. A.
Ecfo, 32, Madrid 27, Spain
Saphrograph
Saphrograph Co.
4910 Fort Hamilton Parkway, Brooklyn,
NY 11219 Tel 212-925-7840 (SAN
204-7276)
(ISBN Prefix 0-87557)
SAPIL
SAPIL - Poligrafica Industriale Lombarda
Via Fatebene Fratelli, 12-20121 Milan, Italy
Saraiva SA
Saraiva S. A. Livreiros Editores
Av do Emissario, 1897, 01139 San Paulo,
Brazil
Sarpe
S.A.R.P.E.
Fernandez de 1a Hoz, 52, Madrid-10, Spain
Sat Rev Pr
See Dutton
Saunders
Saunders, W. B., Co, Subs. of Columbia
Broadcasting System
W. Washington Square, Philadelphia, PA
19105 Tel 215-574-4792 (SAN
203-266X)
(ISBN Prefix 0-7216)
Saur Verlag
Saur, K. G., Verlag KG
Possenbacher Str. 2b, 8000 Munich 71,
Federal Republic of Germany
(ISBN Prefix 3-7940)
Savelli
Savelli
Via Cicerone, 44-00193 Rome, Italy
SBS Pub
SBS Publishing, Inc.
14 W. Forest Ave., Englewood, NJ 07631
Tel 201-569-8700 (SAN 213-3695)
(ISBN Prefix 0-89961)
Scale Mfrs
Scale Manufacturers Association
1000 Vermont Ave, NW, Washington, DC
20005 Tel 202-628-4634 (SAN 224-9812)
Scarecrow
Scarecrow Press, Inc, Subs. of Grolier
Educational Corp.
52 Liberty St., Box 656, Metuchen, NJ
08840 Tel 201-548-8600 (SAN 203-2651)
(ISBN Prefix 0-8108)
Scheltens
Scheltens en Giltay
Domstraat 5-13, Utrecht, Netherlands
Scherz AG
Scherz Verlag AG
Marktgasse 25, 3011 Bern, Switzerland
(ISBN Prefix 3-502)

Schibsted
Schibsted Chr.
Postboks 415, Oslo 1, Norway
Schiele & Schon
Fachverlag Schielle & Schon GmbH
Markgrafenstr 11, 1000 Berlin 61,
Federal Republic of Germany
(ISBN Prefix 3-7949)
Schiffer
Schiffer Publishing Ltd.
P.O. Box E, Exton, PA 19341
Tel 215-363-6889 (SAN 208-8428)
(ISBN Prefix 0-916838)
Schirmer Bks
See Assoc Mus
Schmidt Verlag
Schmidt, E., Verlag
Genthiner Str. 30g, 1000 Berlin 30,
Federal Republic of Germany
(ISBN Prefix 3-503)
Schocken
Schocken Books, Inc.
200 Madison Ave., New York, NY 10016
Tel 212-685-6500 (SAN 213-7585)
(ISBN Prefix 0-8052)
Schoenhof
Schoenhof's Foreign Books, Inc.
1280 Massachusetts Ave., Cambridge, MA
02138 Tel 617-547-8855 (SAN 212-0062)
(ISBN Prefix 0-87774)
Schol Bk Serv
See Scholastic Inc
Schol Facsimiles
Scholars' Facsimiles & Reprints
P.O. Box 344, Delmar, NY 12054
Tel 518-439-5978 (SAN 203-2627)
(ISBN Prefix 0-8201)
Scholarly
Scholarly Press Inc.
P.O. Box 160, Saint Clair Shores, MI 48080
Tel 313-884-0400 (SAN 209-0473)
(ISBN Prefix 0-403)
Scholars Pr
See Scholars Pr CA
Scholars Pr CA
Scholars Press
101 Salem St. P.O. Box 2268, Chico, CA
95927 Tel 916-891-4541 (SAN
207-964X)
(ISBN Prefix 0-89130)
Scholars Pr MI
See Scholars Pr CA
Scholastic Inc
Scholastic Inc.
730 Broadway, New York, NY 10003
Tel 212-505-3000 (SAN 202-5442)
Orders to:
P.O. Box 7502, 2931 E. McCarty St.,
Jefferson City, MO 65102 (SAN
202-5450)
(ISBN Prefix 0-590)
Scholium Intl
Scholium International, Inc
265 Great Neck Rd., Great Neck, NY
11021 Canada Tel 516-466-5181 (SAN
212-8764)
(ISBN Prefix 0-87936)
Schoningh
Schaningh, Ferdinand
Juhenplatz 1, 2540,4790 Paderborn,
Federal Republic of Germany
(ISBN Prefix 3-506)
Schweizerbart
Schweizerbat'sche, E., Verlagsbuch Handlung
(Nagele u. Obermiller)
Johannesstr 3 A, 7000 Stuttgart 1,
Federal Republic of Germany
Sci Apparatus
Scientific Apparatus Makers Association
Suite 300, 1101 16th St. NW, Washington,
DC 20036 Tel 202-223-1360 (SAN
224-9499)
Sci of Mind
Science of Mind Pubns.
P.O. Box 75127, Los Angeles, CA 90075
Tel 213-388-2181 (SAN 203-2570)
Dist. by:
Devorss & Co., P.O. Box 550, Marina Del
Rey, CA 90291 (SAN 168-9886)
(ISBN Prefix 0-911336)
Scientific Surveys
Scientific Surveys Ltd.
P. O. Box 21, Beaconsfield, Bucks. 4P9
14W, United Kingdom
Scode
Scode
Via Ampere, 28a -20131 Milan, Italy

SCP
Saunders College Publishing, Div. of CBS
College Publishing
W. Washington Square, Philadelphia, PA
19105 (SAN 282-2768); 0-03,
Orders to:
383madison Ave., New York, NY 10017
Tel 212-750-1330 (SAN 282-2776)
Scribner
Scribner's, Charles, Sons
597 Fifth Ave., New York, NY 10017
Tel 212-486-2703 (SAN 282-2873)
Orders to:
Shipping & Service Ctr., Vreeland Ave.,
Totowa, NJ 07512 (SAN 282-6550)
(ISBN Prefix 0-684)
Scriptor Verlag
Scriptor Verlag GmbH
Adelheidstr 2, Postf 1220, 6240 Konigstein
im Taunus, Federal Republic of Germany
Scripture Union
Scripture Union
Scripture Union House, 130 City Rd.,
London 3C7V 2 NJ, United Kingdom
(ISBN Prefix 0-85421)
Seabury
Seabury Press, Inc.
815 Second Ave., New York, NY 10017
Tel 212-557-0500 (SAN 202-5418)
Orders to:
Seabury Service Center, Somers, CT 06071
Tel 800-243-0004 (SAN 202-5426)
(ISBN Prefix 0-8164)
Second Back Row
Second Back Row Press Pty., Ltd.
P. O. Box 43, Leura, NSW 2060, Australia
(ISBN Prefix 0-909325)
Security World
See Butterworth
Seghers
Seghers
31-33, Falguiere, 75015 Paris, France
SEI
SEI
Corso Regina Margherita, 176, 10152
Turin, Italy
Sel Rdrs Digest
Selecciones del Reader's Digest, S.A.
Telemaco, 3, Madrid-27, Spain
Selbstverlag
Selbstverlag Press
P.O. Drawer 606, Bloomington, IN 47402
Tel 812-335-2766 (SAN 204-5761)
(ISBN Prefix 0-911706)
Senda Nueva
Senda Nueva De Ediciones, Inc.
640 W. 231st St., Apt. 3-B, Bronx, NY
10463 (SAN 210-0061)
(ISBN Prefix 0-918454)
Sequoia
Sequoia
Paris, France
Serre
Serre, Romert
1057 Riviero Dr. Ottawa, Ont. K1K on7,
Canada
(ISBN Prefix 0-9690950)
Serv Doc Cart
Service de Documentation et de Cartographie
Geographhiques
191, Rue Saint-Jacques, 75005 Paris,
France
(ISBN Prefix 2-901560)
Serv Pub Minist
Servicio de Publicaciones, Ministerio de
Educacion y Ciencia, Ciudad Universitaria
Apartado 169 F.D., Madrid -3, Spain
Seuil
Seuil
27, Rue Jacob, 75006 Paris, France
(ISBN Prefix 2-02)
Seven Hills Bks
Seven Hills Books
519 W. Third St., Cincinnati, OH 45202
Tel 513-381-3881 (SAN 169-6629)
(ISBN Prefix 0-911403)
Shalom
Shalom, P., Pubns., Inc.
5409 18th Ave., Brooklyn, NY 11204
(SAN 204-5893)
(ISBN Prefix 0-87559)
Sharon Pubns
Sharon Pubns. Inc.
105 Union Ave., Cresslill, NJ 07626
Tel 201-568-8800 (SAN 210-4989)
(ISBN Prefix 0-89531)

Shell Cab
Shell Cabinet
P.O. Box 29, Falls Church, VA 22046
Tel 703-256-0707 (SAN 122-8455)
(ISBN Prefix 0-913792)
Shelter Pubns
See Random
Sheridan
Sheridan House, Inc.
175 Orawaupum St., White Plains, NY
10606 Tel 914-948-1806 (SAN 204-5915)
(ISBN Prefix 0-911378)
Shoe String
Shoe String Press, Inc.
P.O. Box 4327, 995 Sherman Ave.,
Hamden, CT 06514 Tel 203-248-6307
(SAN 213-2079)
(ISBN Prefix 0-208)
Shogakukan
Shogakukan Publishing Co., Ltd.
2-3 Hitotsubashi, Chiyoda-Ku, Tokyo 101,
Japan
Shorey
Shorey Pubns.
110 Union St., Seattle, WA 98101
Tel 206-624-0221 (SAN 204-5958)
(ISBN Prefix 0-8466)
Shulsinger Bros
See Shulsinger Sales
Shulsinger Sales
Shulsinger Sales, Inc.
50 Washington St., Brooklyn, NY 11201
Tel 212-852-0042 (SAN 205-9851)
(ISBN Prefix 0-914080)
Shuter & Shooter
Shuter & Shooter Pty Ltd.
P.O. Box 109, 3200 Piertermaritzburg,
South Africa
(ISBN Prefix 0-86985)
Siemens AG
Siemens AG, ZVW Five Verlag
Werner-von-Siemens-Str. 50, Postf 3240,
8520 Erlangen 2,
Federal Republic of Germany
(ISBN Prefix 3-8009)
Sig *Imprint of NAL*
Siglo Veintiuno
Siglo Veintiuno Editores
Cerro del Agua 248, Mexico 20, D.F.,
Mexico
Siglo XXI
Siglo XXI de Espana Editores, S.A.
Plaza, 5, Madrid-33, Spain
Signal-Verlag
Signal-Verlag Hans Frevert
Balger Hauptstr 8, Postfach 813, D-7570
Baden-Baden,
Federal Republic of Germany
Signorelli C
Signorelli C.
Via Siusi 7-20132 Milan, Italy
Signs of Times
Signs of the Times Publishing Co.
407 Gilbert Ave., Cincinnati, OH 45202
Tel 513-421-2050 (SAN 204-5974)
(ISBN Prefix 0-911380)
Sijthoff & Noordhoff
Sijthoff & Noordhoff International Publishing
Co.
1600 Research Blvd., Rockville, MD 20850
Tel 301-251-0950 (SAN 210-8542)
Sikkel
Sikkel
Kapelsetraat 222, Kapellen, Belgium
Sintes
Sintes, S.A Editorial
Santa Teresa S/N, Las Fontas de Tarrasa
(Barcelona), Spain
Slatkine
Slatkine
5, Rue de Chaudronniers, 1211 Geneve 3,
France
(ISBN Prefix 2-05)
Slavica
Slavica Publishers Inc.
P.O. Box 14388, Columbus, OH 43214
Tel 614-268-4002 (SAN 208-8576)
(ISBN Prefix 0-89357)
Small Motor Mfrs
Small Motor Manufacturers Association
435 N. Michigan Ave., 17th Fl., Chicago,
IL 60611 (SAN 224-7178)

Smithsonian
Smithsonian Institution Pr.
Rm. 2280, Arts & Industries Bldg.,
Washington, DC 20560 Tel 202-357-1912
(SAN 206-8044)
Orders to:
P.O. Box 1579, Washington, DC 20013
Tel 202-357-1793 (SAN 206-8052)
(ISBN Prefix 0-87474)
Soap & Detergent
Soap & Detergent Association
475 Park Ave. South at 32nd St., New
York, NY 10016 Tel 212-725-1262 (SAN
224-7089)
Soc Am Archivists
Society of American Archivists
330 S. Wells St., Suite 810, Chicago, IL
60606 Tel 312-922-0140 (SAN 211-7614)
(ISBN Prefix 0-931828)
Soc Am Foresters
Society of American Foresters
5400 Grosvenor Lane, Bethesda, MD
20014 Tel 301-897-8720 (SAN 216-8561)
(ISBN Prefix 0-939970)
Soc Auto Engineers
Society of Automotive Engineers
400 Commonwealth Dr, Warrendale, PA
15096 (SAN 232-5721)
Soc Bari
Societa Storia Patria Bari
Piazza Umberto, 2-70121 Bari, Italy
Soc Corp Hygiene
Societe Corporative d'Hygiene et de Securite,
Dans les Chantiers
53-55, Rue Desnouettes, 75015 Paris,
France
Soc Dev Liv
Societe de Developpement du Livre et du
Periodique
1151, rue Alexandrea- Deseve, Montreal,
Quebec, H2l 2t7, Canada
Soc Ed Atenas
Sociedad de Educacion Atenas, S. A.
Mayor, 31, Madrid 13, Spain
Soc Etudes Tech
Societe d'Etudes Techniques et Fiduciares
4, Rue de Stockholm, 75008 Paris, France
Soc for Visual
Society for Visual Education, Inc.
1345 W. Diversey Pkwy., Chicago, IL
60614 Tel 312-525-1500 (SAN 208-3930)
(ISBN Prefix 0-89290)
Soc Glass Decorators
Society of Glass Decorators
207 Grant St, Pt Jefferson, NY 11777
(SAN 224-7747)
Soc Motion Pic & TV Engrs
Society of Motion Picture and Television
Engineers
862 Scardale Ave., Scarsdale, NY 10583
Tel 914-472-6600 (SAN 224-0173)
Soc Naval Arch
Society of Naval Architects & Marine
Engineers
One World Trade Center, 1369, New York,
NY 10048 Tel 212-432-0310 (SAN
202-0572)
(ISBN Prefix 0-9603048)
Soc Nouveau
Societe du Nouveau Littre Dictionnaire "Le
Robert"
107, Avenue Parmentier, 75011 Paris,
France
(ISBN Prefix 2-85036)
Soc Plastic Ind
Society of the Plastic Industry, Inc
355 Lexington Ave, New York, NY 10017
(SAN 224-9162)
Soc Range Mgmt
Society for Range Management
2760 W Fifth Ave, Denver, CO 80204
(SAN 225-0586)
Soc St Catanese
Societa Storica Catanese
Via Etnea, 248-95131 Catania, Italy
Soc Studi Valdesi
Societa di Studi Valdesi Distr. by Claudiana
Via Principe Tommaso, 1-10125 Turin,
Italy

Soc Tech Comm
Society for Technical Communication
815 15th St. N.W., Suite 506, Washington,
DC 20005 Tel 202-737-0035 (SAN
206-569X)
Dist. by:
Univelt, Inc., P.O. Box 28130, San Diego,
CA 92128 Tel 714-746-4005 (SAN
204-8868)
(ISBN Prefix 0-914548)
Sociales
Sociales
Paris, France
Socusa Edit
Socusa. Editora. Social y Cultural
Jorge Juan, 32, Marid-1, Spain
Soderstrom
Soderstrom Osakeyhtio (WSOY)
Bulevardi 12, 00120 Helsinki 12, Finland
Soil Conservation
Soil Conservation Society of America
7515 N.E. Ankeny Rd., Ankeny, IA 50021
(SAN 213-6961)
(ISBN Prefix 0-935734)
Sokoll
Sokoll, Alfred
Johannisplatz 14, 8000 Munich 80,
Federal Republic of Germany
(ISBN Prefix 3-920902)
Somerset Hse
Somerset Hse.
206 N. Alfred St., Alexandria, VA 22314
Tel 703-549-7369 (SAN 282-3306)
Orders to:
623 Martense Ave., Teaneck, NJ 07666
Tel 201-692-1801 (SAN 282-3314)
(ISBN Prefix 0-914146; ISBN Prefix
0-89887; ISBN Prefix 0-85964)
Somerset Pub
Somerset Pubs, Div. of Scholarly Press, Inc.
200 Park Ave., Suite 303E, New York, NY
10017 Tel 313-884-0440 (SAN 204-6105)
Sopena
Sopena
Provenza, 95, Barcelona-15, Spain
Soudure Autogene
Soudure Autogene Francaise
32, Boulevard de la Chapelle, 75018 Paris,
France
South Asia Bks
South Asia Books
P.O. Box 502, Columbia, MO 65205
Tel 314-449-1359 (SAN 207-4044)
(ISBN Prefix 0-88386; ISBN Prefix 0-8364)
Soviet Studies
Soviet Studies
P.O. Box 16, Hayward, CA 94543 (SAN
210-6671)
(ISBN Prefix 0-930232)
Sparkassenverlag
Deutscher Sparkassenverlag GmbH
Am Wallgraben 115, 7000 Stuttgart 80,
Finland
(ISBN Prefix 3-09)
Spec *Imprint of P-H*
Spectrum
Spectrum
Park Voorn 4, De Meern, Netherlands
Speech & Hearing
See Press West
Spoken Lang Serv
Spoken Language Services, Inc.
P.O. Box 783, Ithaca, NY 14850
Tel 607-257-0500 (SAN 203-2279)
(ISBN Prefix 0-87950)
Spon Ltd.
Spon, E. & F. N., Ltd.
11 New Fetter Lane, London, EC4P 4EE,
United Kingdom
(ISBN Prefix 0-413)
Springer Pub
Springer Publishing Co., Inc.
200 Park Ave., S., New York, NY 10003
Tel 212-475-6580 (SAN 203-2236)
(ISBN Prefix 0-8261)
Springer-Verlag
Springer-Verlag New York, Inc.
175 Fifth Avenue, New York, NY 10010
Tel 212-460-1500 (SAN 203-2228)
(ISBN Prefix 0-387)

SRA
Science Research Associates, Inc, Subs. of
IBM
1540 Page Mill Rd, P.O. Box 10021, Palo
Alto, CA 94304 Tel 415-493-4700 (SAN
282-2849); 155 N. Wacker Dr., Chicago, IL
60606 Tel 800-621-0476 (SAN 282-2857)
Orders to:
155 N. Wacker Dr., Chicago, IL 60606
(SAN 282-2865)
(ISBN Prefix 0-574)

St Clair Pr
See Wiley

St Martin
St. Martin's Press, Inc.
175 Fifth Ave., New York, NY 10010
Tel 212-674-5151 (SAN 200-2132)
(ISBN Prefix 0-312)

St Michaels
St. Michaels Historical Museum
St. Michaels Mission, St. Michaels, AZ
86511 Tel 602-871-4171 (SAN 239-5290)

ST Pubns
See Signs of Times

Staatsdruk
Staatsdrukkery en Uitgeversbedryf
Chr. Plantynstraat 1-9, S-Gravenhage,
Netherlands

Stanaard Uitgeverij
Standaard Uitgeverij NV Scriptoria
Belgielei 147a, Postbus 212, B-2000
Antwerp, Belgium

Standard Sver
Standardiserings Kommissionen i Sverige
Box 3295, 10366, Stockholm 3, Sweden

Stanford U Pr
Stanford Univ. Press
Stanford, CA 94305 Tel 415-497-9434
(SAN 203-3526)
(ISBN Prefix 0-8047)

StanGib Ltd
StanGib Ltd.
601 Franklin Ave., Garden City, NY 11530
Tel 516-746-4666 (SAN 213-3784)
(ISBN Prefix 0-85259)

Star Pub CA
Star Publishing Co.
P.O. Box 68, Belmont, CA 94002 (SAN
212-6958)
(ISBN Prefix 0-89863)

State Mutual Bk
State Mutual Book & Periodical Service, Ltd.
521 Fifth Ave., 17th Floor, New York, NY
10017 Tel 212-682-5844 (SAN 169-5975)
(ISBN Prefix 0-89771)

State U NY Pr
State Univ. of New York Press
State University Plaza, Albany, NY 12246
Tel 518-473-7602 (SAN 203-3488)
Orders to:
300 Ratitan Center Pkwy., Edison, NJ
08818 Tel 201-225-5555 (SAN 203-3496)
(ISBN Prefix 0-87395; ISBN Prefix
0-88706)

Station Hill Pr
Station Hill Press, Div. of Open Books
Station Hill Rd., Barrytown, NY 12507
(SAN 214-1485)
(ISBN Prefix 0-930794)

Statni
Statni Pedagogicke Nakladatelstvi
11301 Prague 1, Nove Mesto, Ostrovni 30,
Czechoslovakia

Steffanides
Steffanides, George F.
66 Lourdes Dr., W.D., Fitchburg, MA
01420 Tel 617-342-1997 (SAN 204-6369)
(ISBN Prefix 0-9600114)

Stein & Day
Stein & Day
Scarborough House, Briarcliff Manor, NY
10510 Tel 914-762-2151 (SAN 203-3461)
(ISBN Prefix 0-8128)

Stein Pub
Stein Publishing House
526 S. State St., Chicago, IL 60605 (SAN
204-6377)
(ISBN Prefix 0-911440)

Steiner Verlag
Steiner, Franz, Verlag GmbH
Friedichstr, 24, Postf 5529, 6200
Wiesbaden, Federal Republic of Germany
(ISBN Prefix 3-515)

Stem Mucchi
Stem Mucchi
Via Tabboni, 4, 4100 Modena, Italy
(ISBN Prefix 8-87000)

Stemmer Hse
Stemmer House Pubs., Inc.
2627 Caves Rd., Owings Mills, MD 21117
Tel 301-363-3690 (SAN 207-9623)
(ISBN Prefix 0-916144)

Stenfert Kroese
Stenfert Kroese
Postbus 33 Leiden, Netherlands

Sterling
Sterling Pub. Co., Inc.
2 Park Ave., New York, NY 10016
Tel 212-532-7160 (SAN 211-6324)
(ISBN Prefix 0-8069)

Strengholt
Strengholt
Postbus 338, Bussum, Netherlands

Strombergs
Strombergs Bokforlag AB
Vittangigatan 27, Box 65, 16211 Vallingby
1, Sweden

Studentlitt
Studentlitteratur AB
Akergranden 1, Box 1719, 22101 Lund,
Sweden

Studium-Vita Nova
Studium-Vita Nova
Via Crescenzio, 63-00193 Rome, Italy

SUDEL
S. U. D. E. L. (Societe Universitaire d'Editions
et de Librairie)
20, Rue Corvisart, 75640 Paris, France

Suedwest
Suedwest Verlag GmbH & Co. KG
Goethestr 43, 8000 Munich 2,
Federal Republic of Germany
(ISBN Prefix 3-517)

Summer Inst Abor
Summer Institute of Linguistics Aborigines
Branch
P. O. Berrimah N. T. 5788 Australia,
Australia

Summer Inst Ling
Summer Institute of Linguistics
Academic Pubns., 7500 W. Camp Wisdom
Rd., Dallas, TX 75236 Tel 214-298-3331
(SAN 204-6466)
(ISBN Prefix 0-88312)

Sun Pub
Sun Publishing Co.
P.O. Box 4383, Albuquerque, NM 87196
Tel 505-255-6550 (SAN 206-1325)
(ISBN Prefix 0-914172; ISBN Prefix
0-89540)

Suoma Kirja
Suomalaisen Kirjallisuuden Seura
Hillituskatu 1, 00170 Helsinki 17, Finland

Suomen Standard
Suomen Standardsoimislitto
Bulevardi 5 A 7, 00120 Helsinki 12,
Finland

Susaeta
Susaeta
Apartado 13. 136, Madrid, Spain

SVA Verlag
SVA Sudwestdeutsche Verlagsanstalt GmbH &
Co. KG
R 1, 4-6, 6800 Mannheim 1,
Federal Republic of Germany
(ISBN Prefix 3-87804)

Swallow
Swallow Press
Ohio University Press, Scott Quadrangle,
Athens, OH 45701 Tel 614-594-5852
(SAN 202-5663)
Orders to:
Harper & Row Publishers, Inc., Order
Service Dept., Keystone Industrial Park,
Scranton, PA 18512 Tel 800-233-4175
(SAN 202-5671); Tel 800-982-4377
(ISBN Prefix 0-8040)

Sweet & Maxwell
Sweet & Maxwell Ltd, Member of the
Associated Book Publishers Group
11 New Fetter Lane London EC4P 4EE,
United Kingdom
(ISBN Prefix 0-421; ISBN Prefix 0-457)

Sweet Max
Sweet & Maxwell
54 the Terrace, POB 5043, Wellington 1,
New Zealand
(ISBN Prefix 0-457)

Sybex
Sybex, Inc.
2344 Sixth St., Berkeley, CA 94710
Tel 415-848-8233 (SAN 211-1667)
(ISBN Prefix 0-89588)

Synergetics WV
Synergetics Press, The
Box 2091, Parkersburg, WV 26102
Tel 304-485-0460 (SAN 241-4643)
(ISBN Prefix 0-910217)

Syracuse U Foreign Comp
Syracuse Univ., Foreign & Comparative
Studies Program
119 College Place, Syracuse, NY 13210
Tel 315-423-2552 (SAN 220-0082)
(ISBN Prefix 0-915984)

Systems Res
Systems Research Institute
Publications Dept., P.O. Box 4568, Los
Angeles, CA 90051 (SAN 202-7585)
(ISBN Prefix 0-912352)

T Y Crowell
Crowell, Thomas Y., Co.
10 E. 53rd St., New York, NY 10022
Tel 212-593-3900 (SAN 210-5918)
Dist. by:
Harper & Row Pubs., Keystone Industrial
Park, Scranton, PA 18512 (SAN
215-3742)
(ISBN Prefix 0-690)

TAB Bks
Tab Books, Inc.
Monterey Ave., Blue Ridge Summit, PA
17214 Tel 717-794-2191 (SAN
202-568X)
(ISBN Prefix 0-8306)

Table Ronde
Table Ronde
40, Rue du Bac, 75007 Paris, France

Tallandier
Tallandier
17. Rue Remy-Dumoncel, 75014 Paris,
France
(ISBN Prefix 2-235)

Tanager Bks
Tanager Books Inc, Div. of Longwood Pub.
Group
51 Washington St., Dover, NH 03820
Tel 603-522-6282 (SAN 238-2016)
Dist. by:
Flatiron Book Distributors, Inc., 175 Fifth
Ave., Suite 814, New York, NY 10010
Tel 212-228-0390 (SAN 240-9917)
(ISBN Prefix 0-88072)

Tanum-Norli
Tanum-Norli
Kr. Augustsgt. 7 A, Oslo 1, Norway

Tapir
Tapir
Norges Tekniske Hogskole, 7000
Trondheim, Norway

Taplinger
Taplinger Publishing Co., Inc.
132 W. 22nd St., New York, NY 10011
Tel 212-741-0801 (SAN 213-6821)
(ISBN Prefix 0-8008)

TAPPI
Technical Assn. of the Pulp & Paper Industry
1 Dunwoody Park, Atlanta, GA 30338
Tel 404-394-6130 (SAN 212-5714)
(ISBN Prefix 0-89852)

Taurus Ediciones SA
Taurus Ediciones, S.A.
Velazquez, 76-4, Madrid-1, Spain

Taylor & Friends
Taylor, Sally, & Friends
756 Kansas St., San Francisco, CA 94107
(SAN 216-1990)
(ISBN Prefix 0-9604904)

Tchou
Tchou
2, Rue du Pont-Neuf, 75001 Paris, France

Tchrs Coll
Teachers College Press, Columbia Univ.
1234 Amsterdam Ave., New York, NY
10027 Tel 212-678-3929 (SAN 282-3985)
Orders to:
Harper & Row, Keystone Industrial Park,
Scranton, PA 18512 Tel 800-233-4175
(SAN 282-3993)
(ISBN Prefix 0-8077)

Tec Tessile
Tecnologia Tessile
Via Delleani, 24-13051 Biella (Vercelli),
Italy

Tech & Ed Ctr Graph Arts RIT
Technical & Education Center of the Graphic
Arts, Rochester Institute of Technology (T&E
Center)
1 Lomb Memorial Dr., Rochester, NY
14623 Tel 716-475-2761 (SAN 205-2334)
(ISBN Prefix 0-89938)

Tech Dict
Technical Dictionaries Co.
P.O. Box 144, New York, NY 10031
(SAN 205-4191)
(ISBN Prefix 0-911484)

Tech Vulgar
Technique & Vulgarisation
21, Rue Claude-Bernard, 75013 Paris,
France
(ISBN Prefix 2-7109)

Technik Tabel
Technik-Tabellen-Verlag Fikentscher & Co.
Eschollbrucker Str. 39, Postf 4135, 6100
Darmstadt, Federal Republic of Germany
(ISBN Prefix 3-87807)

Technip
Technip
27, Rue Ginoux, 75015 Paris, France
(ISBN Prefix 2-7108)

Technomic
Technomic Publishing Co.
851 New Holland Ave., Box 3535,
Lancaster, PA 17604 Tel 717-291-5609
(SAN 202-764X)
(ISBN Prefix 0-87762)

Tecnos SA
Tecnos S. A.
O'Donnell, 27, Madrid 9, Spain

Teide
Teide, S. A.
Viladomat, 291, Barcelona 29, Spain

Tek Inst
Teknologisk Institut
Gregersensvej, 2630 Tastrup, Denmark

Tek Nomen
Tekniska Nomen Klaturcentralen
Liljeholmsvagen 32, Box 43041, 10072
Stockholm 43, Sweden

Telecom Lib
Telecom Library, The
205 W. 19th St., New York, NY 10011
Tel 212-691-8215 (SAN 211-9862)
(ISBN Prefix 0-936648)

Telegraph Bks
Telegraph Books
Box 38, Norwood, PA 19074
Tel 215-583-4550 (SAN 213-8042)
(ISBN Prefix 0-89760)

Temple U Pr
Temple Univ. Press
Philadelphia, PA 19122 Tel 215-787-8787
(SAN 202-7666)
(ISBN Prefix 0-87722)

Terra
Terra
Pb 24, V, Alkotmany u. 21, 1363 Budapest,
Hungary

Tesoro
Tesoro
Auda de Jose Antonio, 43, Madrid 13,
Spain

Tesoro Edit
Tesoro Editorial
Avda. De Jose Antonio, 43, Madrid-13,
Spain

Teubner
Teubner, B. G., GmbH
Industriestr 15, Postf 8701069, 7000
Stuttgart 80, Federal Republic of Germany
(ISBN Prefix 3-519)

Tex A & M Lang
See Dabbs

Textile Bk
Textile Book Service, Inc.
P.O. Box 25, Broadway, NJ 08808
Tel 201-689-2230 (SAN 206-7714)
(ISBN Prefix 0-87245)

Thai Watana
Thai Watana Panich
599 Maitrijit Rd, Bangkok, Thailand

Thames Hudson
Thames & Hudson
Dist. by:
W.W. Norton, & Co., Inc., 500 Fifth Ave.,
New York, NY 10110 Tel 212-354-3763
(SAN 202-5795)
(ISBN Prefix 0-500)

Theatre Arts
Theatre Arts Books
153 Waverly Place, New York, NY 10014
Tel 212-675-1815 (SAN 202-7763)
(ISBN Prefix 0-87830)

Thieme Verlag
Thieme, Georg, Verlag
Herdweg 63, Postf 732, 7000 Stuttgart 1,
Federal Republic of Germany
(ISBN Prefix 3-13)

Thiemeg
Thiemeg, Karl, Graphische Kunstanstalt und
Buchdruckerei AG
Abt. Verlag, Pilgersheimer Str. 38, 8000
Munich 90, Federal Republic of Germany
(ISBN Prefix 3-521)

Thimanier
Thimonier, Jean-Louis
10 Rue de la Treille, 63000
Clermont-Ferrand, France
(ISBN Prefix 2-900232)

Ticknor & Fields
Ticknor & Fields
52 Vanderbilt Ave., New York, NY 10017
Tel 212-687-8996 (SAN 282-4043); 383
Orange St., New Haven, CT 06511
Tel 203-776-1878 (SAN 282-4035)
Dist. by:
Houghton Mifflin Co., 2 Park St., Boston,
MA 02108 Tel 617-725-5000 (SAN
200-2388)
(ISBN Prefix 0-89919)

Tietojen
Tietojenkasittelyliitto r. y
Fredrikinkatu 77 A 26, 00100 Helsinki 10,
Finland

Tietoteos
Tietoteos Kustannusliike
Pl40, 02211 Espoo 21, Finland

Time Bks
See Times Bks

Times Bks
Times Books, Div. of The New York Times
Co.
3 Park Ave., New York, NY 10016
Tel 212-725-2050 (SAN 202-5558)
Dist. by:
Harper & Row, Keystone Industrial Park,
Scranton, PA 18512 (SAN 200-2086)
(ISBN Prefix 0-8129)

Tipografia
Tipografia Poliglotta Vaticana
Vatican City, Vatican City

Tjeenk Willink
Tjeenk Willink, W. E. J.
Postbus 25, Zwolle, Netherlands

Todd & Honeywell
Todd & Honeywell Inc.
10 Cuttermill Rd., Great Neck, NY 11021
Tel 516-487-9777 (SAN 213-179X)
(ISBN Prefix 0-89962)

Toray-Masson
Toray-Masson, S. A.
Balmes, 151 Barcelona 8, Spain

Traffic Serv
Traffic Service Corp.
1435 "G" St. N.W., Suite 815, Washington,
DC 20005 Tel 202-626-4535 (SAN
202-7917)
(ISBN Prefix 0-87408)

Trans Res Inst
Translation Research Institute
5914 Pulaski Ave., Philadelphia, PA 19144
(ISBN Prefix 0-917564)

Transatlantic
Transatlantic Arts
P.O. Box 6086, Albuquerque, NM 87197
Tel 505-898-2289 (SAN 202-7968)
(ISBN Prefix 0-693)

Translation Research
Translation Research Institute
5914 Pulaski Ave., Philadelphia, PA 19144
Tel 215-848-7084 (SAN 207-2319)
(ISBN Prefix 0-917564)

Transport Res Bd
Transportation Research Board
2101 Constitution Ave Nw, Washington,
DC 20418 (SAN 225-2554)
(ISBN Prefix 0-309)

Trevisini
Trevisini
Via Tito Livio, 10-12-20137 Milan, Italy

Triad Pub FL
Triad Pub. Co., Inc.
1110 NW Eighth Ave., Gainesville, FL
32601 Tel 904-373-5308 (SAN 205-4574)
(ISBN Prefix 0-9600472; ISBN Prefix
0-937404)

Triad Sci Pubs
See Triad Pub FL

Trillas
Trillas, S. A. Editorial
Av Cinco de Mayo 43-105, Mexico 1, D.
F., Mexico

Truck Trailer Mfrs
Truck Trailer Manufacturers Association
2430 Pennsylvania Ave. NW, Washington,
DC 20037 (SAN 224-8867)

Truth Seeker
Truth Seeker Company Inc.
P.O. Box 2832, San Diego, CA 92112
Tel 619-574-7600 (SAN 226-3645)

U of Ala Pr
Univ. of Alabama Press
Box 2877, University, AL 35486
Tel 205-348-5180 (SAN 202-5272)
(ISBN Prefix 0-8173)

U of Ariz Pr
Univ. of Arizona Press
1615 E. Speedway, Tucson, AZ 85719
Tel 602-621-1441 (SAN 205-468X)
(ISBN Prefix 0-8165)

U of Cal Pr
Univ. of California Press
2223 Fulton St., Berkeley, CA 94720
Tel 415-642-6683 (SAN 203-3046)
(ISBN Prefix 0-520)

U of Chicago Pr
Univ. of Chicago Press
5801 Ellis Ave., Chicago, IL 60637
Tel 312-962-7906 (SAN 202-5280)
Orders to:
11030 S. Langley Ave., Chicago, IL 60628
Tel 312-568-1550 (SAN 202-5299)
(ISBN Prefix 0-226)

U of Ga Pr
Univ. of Georgia Press
Terrell Hall, Athens, GA 30602
Tel 404-542-2830 (SAN 203-3054)
(ISBN Prefix 0-8203)

U of Ill Pr
Univ. of Illinois Press
54 E. Gregory Dr., Champaign, IL 61820
Tel 217-333-0957 (SAN 202-5310)
(ISBN Prefix 0-252)

U of Mass Pr
Univ. of Massachusetts Press
P.O. Box 429, Amherst, MA 01004
Tel 413-545-2217 (SAN 203-3089)
(ISBN Prefix 0-87023)

U of Miami Pr
Univ. of Miami Press
P.O. Box 4836, Hampden Sta., Baltimore,
MD 21211 Tel 301-338-7886 (SAN
203-3119)
(ISBN Prefix 0-87024)

U of Mich Pr
Univ. of Michigan Press
P.O. Box 1104, Ann Arbor, MI 48106
Tel 313-764-4330 (SAN 282-4884)
Orders to:
839 Greene St., Ann Arbor, MI 48106
Tel 313-764-4392 (SAN 282-4892)
(ISBN Prefix 0-472)

U of Mo Pr
Univ. of Missouri Press
200 Lewis, Columbia, MO 65211
Tel 314-882-7641 (SAN 203-3143)
(ISBN Prefix 0-8262)

U of Nebr Pr
Univ. of Nebraska Press
901 N. 17th St., Lincoln, NE 68588
Tel 402-472-3581 (SAN 202-5337)
(ISBN Prefix 0-8032)

U of Notre Dame Pr
Univ. of Notre Dame Press
P.O. Box L, Notre Dame, IN 46556
Tel 219-239-6346 (SAN 203-3178)
Dist. by:
Harper & Row Pubs., Keystone Industrial
Park, Scranton, PA 18512 (SAN
215-3742)
(ISBN Prefix 0-268)

U of Okla Pr
Univ. of Oklahoma Press
1005 Asp Ave., Norman, OK 73019
Tel 405-325-5111 (SAN 203-3194)
(ISBN Prefix 0-8061)

U of Pa Pr
Univ. of Pennsylvania Press
3933 Walnut St., Philadelphia, PA 19104
Tel 215-243-6261 (SAN 202-5345)
(ISBN Prefix 0-8122)

U of PR Pr
Univ. of Puerto Rico Press
P.O. Box X, U.P.R. Sta., Rio Piedras, PR
00931 Tel 809-763-0812 (SAN 208-1245)
(ISBN Prefix 0-8477)

U of Queensland Pr
Univ. of Queensland Press
P.O. Box 1365, New York, NY 10023
Tel 212-799-3854 (SAN 206-8540)
Orders to:
5 S. Union St., Lawrence, MA 01843
Tel 617-685-3306 (SAN 206-8559)

U of Tex Pr
Univ. of Texas Press
P.O. Box 7819, Austin, TX 78712
Tel 512-471-4278 (SAN 212-9876)
(ISBN Prefix 0-292)

U of Toronto Pr
Univ. of Toronto Press
33 E. Tupper St., Buffalo, NY 14203
Tel 416-978-2052 (SAN 214-2651)
(ISBN Prefix 0-8020)

U of TX
University of Texas, Petroleum Extension
Service
10100 Burnet Rd., Austin, TX 78758
Tel 512-835-3154

U of Wash Pr
Univ. of Washington Pr.
P.O. Box 85569, Seattle, WA 98105
Tel 206-543-4050 (SAN 212-2502)
(ISBN Prefix 0-295)

U of Wis Pr
Univ. of Wisconsin Press
114 North Murray St., Madison, WI 53715
Tel 608-262-4922 (SAN 203-3259)
(ISBN Prefix 0-299)

U Pr of Amer
University Press of America
4720 Boston Way, Lanham, MD 20706
Tel 301-459-3366 (SAN 200-2256)
(ISBN Prefix 0-8191)

U Pr of Hawaii
See UH Pr

U Pr of Va
Univ. Press of Virginia
P.O. Box 3608, University Sta.,
Charlottesville, VA 22903
Tel 804-924-3468 (SAN 202-5361)
(ISBN Prefix 0-8139)

UAHC
Union of American Hebrew Congregations
838 Fifth Ave., New York, NY 10021
Tel 212-249-0100 (SAN 203-3291)
(ISBN Prefix 0-8074)

UH Pr
Univ. of Hawaii Press, The
2840 Kolowalu St., Honolulu, HI 96822
Tel 808-948-8255 (SAN 202-5353)
(ISBN Prefix 0-8248)

Ukrainian Acad
Ukrainian Academic Press, Div. of Libraries
Unlimited, Inc.
P.O. Box 263, Littleton, CO 80160
Tel 303-770-1220 (SAN 203-3305)
(ISBN Prefix 0-87287)

Ulrich
Ulrich's Bks., Inc.
549 E. University Ave., Ann Arbor, MI
48104 Tel 313-662-3201 (SAN 100-2945)
(ISBN Prefix 0-914004)

Umschau Verlag
Umschau Verlag Breidenstein GmbH
Stuttgarter Str 18-24, 6000 Frankfurt am
Main 1, Federal Republic of Germany
(ISBN Prefix 3-524)

Undena Pubns
Undena Pubns.
P.O. Box 97, Malibu, CA 90265
Tel 213-366-1744 (SAN 203-1922)
(ISBN Prefix 0-89003)

Undersea Med
Undersea Medical Society
9650 Rockville Pike, Bethesda, MD 20014
(SAN 224-4764)

Unesco
Unesco
7 place de Fontenoy, 75700 Paris (France)
UN, France

UNESCO Imprint of Unipub

Ungar
Ungar, Frederick, Publishing Co., Inc.
250 Park Ave. S., New York, NY 10003
Tel 212-473-7885 (SAN 202-5256)
(ISBN Prefix 0-8044)

Unipub
Unipub, A Xerox Publishing Co.
1180 Ave. of the Americas, New York, NY
10036 Tel 212-764-2791 (SAN 202-5264)
(ISBN Prefix 0-89059)

United Bible
United Bible Societies
1865 Broadway, New York, NY 10023
(SAN 204-8787)

United Church Pr
See Pilgrim NY

Univ Aut Nuevo
Universidad Autonoma de Nuevo Leon
Mexico, Mexico

Univ Bks
University Books, Inc, Div. of Lyle Stuart, Inc.
120 Enterprise Ave., Secaucus, NJ 07094
Tel 201-866-0490 (SAN 203-3348)
(ISBN Prefix 0-8216)

Univ Film & Video
Univ. Film & Video Assn.
Southern Ill Univ, Carbondale, IL 62901
Tel 618-453-2365 (SAN 236-4859)

Univ Granada
Universidad De Granada. Secretariado De
Publicaciones
Hospital Real, Granada, Spain

Univ Gregoriana
Universita Gregoriana
Piazza della Pilotta, 4-00187 Rome, Italy

Univ Laval
Presses de l'Universite Laval
C. P. 2474, Quebec, G1K 7R4, Canada
(ISBN Prefix 0-7746)

Univ Perugia
Universita di Perugia-Istituto di Filogia
Romanza
Piazza Morlacchi, 11-06100 Perugia, Italy

Univ Salamanca
Universidad de Salamanca Ediciones
Patio Escuelas, 1, Salamanca, Spain

Univ SC Natl Info
University of Southern California National
Information Center for Educational Media
NICEM/USC, 3716 South Hope St.,
Research Annex-Suite 301, Los Angeles,
CA 90007 Tel 213-743-6681 (SAN
208-4570)
(ISBN Prefix 0-89320)

Univ Syd Aust Lang
University of Sydney, Australian Language
Sydney N. S. W. 2006, Australia
(ISBN Prefix 0-909669)

Univers Oslo
Universitetsbiblioteket i Oslo
Drammensvn. 42, Oslo 2, Norway

Univers Picardie
Universite de Picardie, Amiens, Centre
d'Etudies Medievales
Chemin du Thil, 8000 Amiens, France
(ISBN Prefix 2-901121)

Univers Santiago
Universidad de Santiago
Plaza de Espana Edificio San Jeronimo,
Santiago de Compostela, Spain

Universe
Universe Books, Inc.
381 Park Ave., S., New York, NY 10016
Tel 212-685-7400 (SAN 202-537X)
(ISBN Prefix 0-87663)

Universidad & Acad
Universidades y Academicas
Madrid, Spain

Universitet
Universitetsforlaget
C/O Columbia Univ. Press, 562 W. 113th
St., New York, NY 10025 (SAN
204-8876)
Dist. by:
Columbia Univ. Press, 136 S. Broadway,
Irvington-on-Hudson, NY 10533 (SAN
212-2480)
(ISBN Prefix 82-00)

Universitets
Universitetsforlaget
Postboks 2977, Toyen, Oslo 6, Norway
(ISBN Prefix 8-200)

Urban & Schwarzen
Urban & Schwarzenberg
Pettenkoferstr. 18, 8000 Munich 2,
Federal Republic of Germany
(ISBN Prefix 3-541)

Urmo
Urmo, S.A. de Ediciones
Ajuriaguerra, 10, Bilboa 9, Spain

US Comm Irrigation
United States Committee on Irrigation
Drainage & Flood Control
Box 15326, Denver, CO 80215 (SAN
225-0411)

US Golf Assn
U.S. Golf Assn.
Golf House, Far Hills, NJ 07931
Tel 201-234-2300 (SAN 206-1511)

US League Savings Assns
United States League of Savings Associations
111 E. Wacker Dr., Chicago, IL 60601
Tel 312-644-3100 (SAN 223-8497)

US Naval Inst
United States Naval Institute
Annapolis, MD 21402 (SAN 260-3357)

US Pharmacopeia
United States Pharmacopeial Convention
12601 Twinbrook Pky, Rockville, MD
20852 (SAN 224-4225)

USES
USES
Via Ricasoli, 48, 50122 Florence, Italy

USPC
United States Pharmacopeial Convention, Inc.
USP Publication Services Dept., 12601
Twinbrook Pkwy., Rockville, MD 20852
Tel 301-881-0666 (SAN 220-2794)

UTET
UTET
Corso Raffaello 28, CP 1166 Ferrovia,
I-10125 Turin, Italy

Utrikespolitiska
Utrikespolitiska Institutet
Lilla Nygatan 23, 11128 Stockholm,
Sweden

Vahlen
Vahlen, Franz, GmbH
Wilhelmstr. 9, 8000 Munich 40,
Federal Republic of Germany
(ISBN Prefix 3-8006)

Vaillant-Carmanne
Vaillant-Carmanne
17 Rue Sainte-Veronique, 4000 Liege,
Belgium
(ISBN Prefix 2-87021)

Vallardi A
Vallardi A
Via Senato, 25-20121 Milan, Italy

Vallardi F
Vallardi F.
Via Cesare de Sesto, 15-20123 Milan, Italy

Vallentine Mitchell
See Biblio Dist

Valmartina
Valmartina
Viale Gramsci, 42-50132 Florence, Italy

Valtion
Valtion Teknillinen Tutkimuskeskus
Vuorimiehentie 5, 02150 Espoo 15, Finland

Van Nos Reinhold
Van Nostrand Reinhold Co, Div. of Litton
Educational Publishing, Inc.
135 W. 50th St., New York, NY 10020
Tel 212-265-8700 (SAN 202-5183)
Orders to:
Lepi Order Processing, 7625 Empire Dr.,
Florence, KY 41042 (SAN 202-5191)
(ISBN Prefix 0-442)

Van Schaik
Van Schaik, J. L., Edms. Bpk.
Postbus 724, 0001 Pretoria, Zambia
(ISBN Prefix 0-627)

Vandenhoeck
Vandenhoeck & Ruprecht (GmbH & Co. KG)
Theaterstr 13 u. - Robert-Bosch-Breite 6,
Posft 77, 3400 Gottingen,
Federal Republic of Germany

Vander
Vander
Louvain, Belgium
(ISBN Prefix 2-8008)

Vanous
Vanous, Arthur, Co.
616 Kinderkamack Rd., River Edge, NJ
07661 Tel 201-265-7555 (SAN 202-9324)
Orders to:
P.O. Box A, River Edge, NJ 07661 (SAN
202-9332)
(ISBN Prefix 0-89918)

Vantage
Vantage Press, Inc.
516 W. 34th St., New York, NY 10001
Tel 212-736-1767 (SAN 206-8893)
(ISBN Prefix 0-533)

VDE Verlag
VDE Verlag GmbH
Bismarckstr. 33, 1000 Berlin 12,
Federal Republic of Germany
(ISBN Prefix 3-8007)

VDI Verlag
VDI Verlag GmbH
Graf-Recke-Str. 84, 4000 Dusseldorf 1,
Federal Republic of Germany
(ISBN Prefix 3-18)

VEB Technik
VEB Verlag Technik
Oranienburger Str 13-14, Postfache 293,
DDR-1020 Berlin,
German Democratic Republic

VEB Verlag Enzyklopadie
VEB Verlag Enzyklopadie
Gerichtsweg 26, Postfach 13, DDR-7010
Leipzig, German Democratic Republic

Vedanta Pr
 Vedanta Press
  1946 Vedanta Place, Hollywood, CA
  90068-3996 Tel 213-465-7114 (SAN
  202-9340)
  Orders to:
  P.O. Box 290, Hollywood, CA 90028
  (SAN 202-9359)
  (ISBN Prefix 0-87481)
Verbatim
 Verbatim
  Box 668, Essex, CT 06426
  Tel 203-767-8248 (SAN 211-1047)
  (ISBN Prefix 0-930454)
Verein Nord
 Verein Nordfriesisches Institut e. V
  Osterstr. 63, 2257 Bredstedt,
  Federal Republic of Germany
  (ISBN Prefix 3-88007)
Verlag Chemie
 Verlag Chemie International, Inc.
  1020 NW 6th St., Plaza Centre, Suite E,
  Deerfield Beach, FL 33441
  Tel 305-428-5566 (SAN 212-2421)
  (ISBN Prefix 0-89573)
Verlag Gluckhauf
 Verlag Gluckhauf, GmbH
  Franz-Fischer-Weg 61, 4300 Essen 13,
  Federal Republic of Germany
  (ISBN Prefix 3-7739)
Verlag Harri Deutsch
 Verlag Harri Deutsch
  Grafstr 47, D-6000 Frankfurt am Main 90,
  Federal Republic of Germany
  (ISBN Prefix 3-87144)
Verlag Moderne
 Verlag Moderne Industrie, Wolfgang Dummer
 & Co.
  Ehrenbreitsteiner Str. 36, 8000 Munich 50,
  Federal Republic of Germany
  (ISBN Prefix 3-478)
Verlag Neuer
 Verlag Neuer Merkur GmbH
  Ingolstaedter Str 63a, 8000 Munich 46,
  Federal Republic of Germany
Verlag Sankt
 Verlag Sankt Georg GmbH
  Oststr 119, 4000 Dusseldorf 1,
  Federal Republic of Germany
  (ISBN Prefix 3-87692)
Verlag Technik
 Verlag fuer Technik und Handwerk GmbH
  Fremersbergstr. 1, 7570 Baden-Baden 70,
  Federal Republic of Germany
  (ISBN Prefix 3-88180)
Verry
 Verry, Lawrence, Inc.
  Mystic, CT 06355 Tel 203-536-7373
  (SAN 202-5205)
  (ISBN Prefix 0-8426)
Vertrieb
 Vertrieb GmbH
  Postfach 1740, 8028 Taufkirchen bei
  Munchen, Federal Republic of Germany
Vicens-Vives
 Vicens Vives
  Avda. de Sarria, 130, Barcelona-17, Spain
Vida Pubs
 See Life Pubs Intl
Vie et Action
 Vie et Action
  388, Boulevard Ricord, 06140 Vence,
  France
Vieweg
 Vieweg, Friedr., & Sohn Verlagsgesellschaft
 mbH
  Faulbrunnenstr. 13, Postf 5829, 6200
  Wiesbaden 1,
  Federal Republic of Germany
  (ISBN Prefix 3-528)
Vigot
 Vigot
  23, Rue de l'Ecole-de-Medecine, 75006
  Paris, France
Viking Pr
 Viking Press, Inc.
  40 W. 23rd St., New York, NY 10010
  Tel 212-807-7300 (SAN 282-5066)
  Orders to:
  Viking/Penguin, Inc., 299 Murray Hill
  Pkwy., East Rutherford, NJ 07073 (SAN
  282-5074)
  (ISBN Prefix 0-670)
Vilamala
 Vilamala
  Valencia, 246, Barcelona 7, Spain
Vin *Imprint of* **Random**

Visual Studies
 Visual Studies Workshop
  31 Prince St., Rochester, NY 14607
  (SAN 218-1606)
Voyages
 Voyages Deux Mille
  10, Rue Diderot, 38000 Grenoble, France
  (ISBN Prefix 2-7183)
VSA Verlag
 VSA-Verlag fuer das Studium der
  Arbeiterbewegung GmbH
  Stresemannstr. 384a, 2000 Hamburg 50,
  Federal Republic of Germany
  (ISBN Prefix 3-87975)
Vuga
 Vuga
  Postbus 16063, S-Gravenhage, Netherlands
Vulkan Verlag
 Classen, Willi, Vulkan Verlag GmbH & Co.
  KG
  Hollestr. 1G, Postf 103962, 4300 Essen 1,
  Federal Republic of Germany
  (ISBN Prefix 3-8027)
W & R Chambers
 W & R Chambers, Ltd.
  11 Thistle St., Edinburgh EH2 1DG,
  United Kingdom
W Collins Pubs
 Collins, William, Publishers, Ltd.
  P.O. Box 7, Auckland, New Zealand
W Collins Sons
 Collins, William, Sons & Co., Ltd.
  14 St. James Pl., London SW1A 1PS,
  United Kingdom
W Dausien
 Dausien, Werner
  Postfach 1355, D-6450 Hanau Am Main,
  Federal Republic of Germany
W Fink
 Fink, Wilhelm, Verlag GmbH
  Nikolaistr 2, D-8000 Munich 40,
  Federal Republic of Germany
  (ISBN Prefix 3-7705)
W H Anderson
 See Anderson Pub Co
W H Freeman
 Freeman, W. H., & Co, Subs. Scientific
  American, Inc.
  41 Madison Ave., 37th Fl., New York, NY
  10010 Tel 212-532-7660 (SAN 200-2302)
  (ISBN Prefix 0-7167)
W J Johnson
 See Walter J Johnson
W R C Smith
 Smith, W. R. C., Publishing Co.
  1760 Peachtree Rd., N.W., Atlanta, GA
  30357 Tel 404-874-4462 (SAN 202-9391)
  (ISBN Prefix 0-912476)
W S Hein
 Hein, William S., & Co., Inc.
  Hein Bldg. 1285 Main St., Buffalo, NY
  14209 Tel 716-882-2600 (SAN 210-9212)
  (ISBN Prefix 0-89941; ISBN Prefix
  0-930342)
Wadsworth
 See Wadsworth Pub
Wadsworth Pub
 Wadsworth Publishing Co.
  10 Davis Dr., Belmont, CA 94002
  Tel 415-595-2350 (SAN 200-2213)
  (ISBN Prefix 0-534)
Walburg Pers
 Walburg Pers
  Postbus 222, Zutphin, Netherlands
Wallaby *Imprint of* **PB**
Wallaby *Imprint of* **S&S**
Walter J Johnson
 Johnson, Walter J., Inc.
  355 Chestnut St., Norwood, NJ 07648
  Tel 201-767-1303 (SAN 209-1828)
  (ISBN Prefix 0-8472)
Wanderer Bks
 Wanderer Books, Div. of Simon & Schuster
  1230 Ave. of the Americas, New York, NY
  10020 Tel 212-245-6400 (SAN 212-5803)
  (ISBN Prefix 0-671)
Warner Bks
 Warner Books, Inc.
  666 Fifth Ave., New York, NY 10103
  Tel 212-484-2900 (SAN 282-5368)
  Orders to:
  Warner Publisher Services, 666 Fith Ave.,
  New York, NY 10103 Tel 212-484-2900
  (SAN 282-5376)
  (ISBN Prefix 0-446)

Water Pollution
 Water Pollution Control Federation
  2626 Pennsylvania Ave., N.W.,
  Washington, DC 20037 Tel 202-337-2500
  (SAN 217-1406)
Waterloo
 Waterloo Music Company Limited
  3 Regina Street, North Waterloo, Ontario
  N2J 4A5, Canada
  (ISBN Prefix 0-88909)
Watson-Guptill
 Watson-Guptill Pubns., Inc., Div. Billboard
  Publications, Inc.
  1 Astor Plaza, 1515 Broadway, New York,
  NY 10036 Tel 212-764-7518 (SAN
  282-5384)
  Orders to:
  1695 Oak St., Lakewood, NJ 08701
  Tel 800-526-3641 (SAN 282-5392)
  (ISBN Prefix 0-8230; ISBN Prefix 0-8174;
  ISBN Prefix 0-87165)
Watts
 Watts, Franklin, Inc, Subs. of Grolier Inc.
  387 Park Ave. South, New York, NY
  10016 Tel 212-686-7070 (SAN
  285-1156); 730 Fifth Ave., New York, NY
  10019 Tel 212-757-4050 (SAN 285-1164)
  (ISBN Prefix 0-531)
Wayne St U Pr
 Wayne State Univ. Press
  The Leonard N. Simons Bldg., 5959
  Woodward Ave., Detroit, MI 48202
  Tel 313-577-4603 (SAN 202-5221)
  (ISBN Prefix 0-8143)
WCTU
 National Woman's Christian Temperance
  Union
  1730 Chicago Ave, Evanston, IL 60201
  (SAN 225-8935)
Weatherhill
 Weatherhill, John, Inc.
  6 E. 39th St., New York, NY 10016
  Tel 212-686-2857 (SAN 202-9529)
  Dist. by:
  Charles E. Tuttle, Co., Inc., 28 S. Main St.,
  Rutland, VT 05701 (SAN 213-2621)
  (ISBN Prefix 0-8348)
Wehman
 Wehman Brothers, Inc.
  Ridgedale Ave., Morris County Mall, Cedar
  Knolls, NJ 07927 Tel 201-539-6300
  (SAN 206-779X)
  (ISBN Prefix 0-911604)
Weills
 See Berkley Pub
Weiser
 Weiser, Samuel, Inc.
  P.O. Box 612, York Beach, ME 03910
  Tel 207-363-4393 (SAN 202-9588)
  (ISBN Prefix 0-87728)
Werner Soderstrom
 Soderstrom Osakeyhtio, Werner
  Bulevardi 12, P.O. Box 222, SF-00121
  Helsinki 12, Finland
Werner Verlag
 Werner Verlag GmbH
  Berliner Allee 11 a, 4000 Dusseldorf 1,
  Federal Republic of Germany
  (ISBN Prefix 3-8041)
Wesmael-Charlier
 Wesmael-Charlier Editions
  Paris, France
West Pub
 West Publishing Co.
  P.O. Box 3526, St. Paul, MN 55165
  Tel 612-228-2710 (SAN 202-9618)
  (ISBN Prefix 0-8299; ISBN Prefix 0-314)
Westdeutscher Vlg
 Westdeutscher Verlag GmbH
  Faulbrunnenstr 13, Postf 5829 , 6200
  Weisbaden 1,
  Federal Republic of Germany
  (ISBN Prefix 3-531)
Westermann
 Westermann, Georg, Verlag, Druckerei und
  Kartographische Gmb & Co.
  Georg-Westermann-Allee 66, Postf 3320,
  3300 Braunschweig,
  Federal Republic of Germany
  (ISBN Prefix 3-14)
Western Islands
 Western Islands
  395 Concord Ave., Belmont, MA 02178
  Tel 617-489-0606 (SAN 206-8435)
  (ISBN Prefix 0-88279)

Western Psych
Western Psychological Services, Div. of
Manson Western Corp.
12031 Wilshire Blvd., Los Angeles, CA
90025 Tel 213-478-2061   (SAN 202-9634)
(ISBN Prefix 0-87424)

Westview
Westview Press
5500 Central Ave., Boulder, CO 80301
Tel 303-444-3541   (SAN 219-970X)
(ISBN Prefix 0-89158; ISBN Prefix
0-86531; ISBN Prefix 0-8133)

Weybright
See McKay

Wheaton
A Wheaton & Co., Ltd.
Hennock Rd., Exeter, Devon EX2 8RP,
United Kingdom

Whitston Pub
Whitston Publishing Co., Inc.
P.O. Box 958, Troy, NY 12181
Tel 518-283-4363   (SAN 203-2120)
(ISBN Prefix 0-87875)

Wiedza Powszechna
Wiedza Powszechna Panstwowe Wydawnictwo
Ul Jasna 26, P.O. Box 162, 00-054 Warsaw,
Poland

Wiley
Wiley, John, & Sons, Inc.
605 Third Ave., New York, NY 10158
Tel 212-850-6418   (SAN 200-2272)
(ISBN Prefix 0-471)

Williams & Wilkins
Williams & Wilkins Co.
428 E. Preston St., Baltimore, MD 21202
Tel 301-528-4221   (SAN 202-5175)
(ISBN Prefix 0-683)

Wilshire
Wilshire Book Co.
12015 Sherman Rd., North Hollywood, CA
91605 Tel 213-875-1711   (SAN 168-9932)
(ISBN Prefix 0-87980)

Wilson
Wilson, H. W.
950 University Ave., Bronx, NY 10452
Tel 212-588-8400   (SAN 203-2961)
(ISBN Prefix 0-8242)

Winds World Pr
Winds of the World Press
35 Whittemore Rd., Framingham, MA
01701   (SAN 215-8310)
(ISBN Prefix 0-938338)

Windward
Windward
Burn House, 88-89 High Holborn, London,
W. C. 1, United Kingdom

Winter Univ
Winter, Carl, Universitatsverlag GmbH
Lutherstr. 59, Postf 106140, 6900
Heidelberg, Federal Republic of Germany
(ISBN Prefix 3-533)

WIPO *Imprint of* **Unipub**

Wissenschaftliche
Wissenschaftliche Verlagsgesellschaft MBH
Birkhenwaldstr 44, Postf 40, 7000 Stuttgart
1, Federal Republic of Germany

Witherby UK
Witherby & Co. Ltd.
S. Plantain Pl. Crosby Row, London, SE1
1YN, United Kingdom
(ISBN Prefix 0-900886)

Witwatersrand U
Witwatersrand Univ. Pr.
1 Jan Smuts Ave., 2000 Johannesburg,
South Africa
(ISBN Prefix 0-85494)

Wm C Brown
Brown, William C., Co., Pubs.
2460 Kerper Blvd., Dubuque, IA 52001
Tel 319-589-2822   (SAN 203-2864)
(ISBN Prefix 0-697)

Woburn Pr
See Biblio Dist

Wolf Verlag
Wolf Verlag GmbH
Haidplatz 2, Postf 112, 8400 Regensburg
11, Federal Republic of Germany
(ISBN Prefix 3-523)

Word Processing
Word Processing Society Inc
Box 92553, Milwaukee, WI 53202   (SAN
232-8356)

World Almanac
World Almanac
200 Park Ave., New York, NY 10017
Tel 212-557-9651   (SAN 211-7703)
(ISBN Prefix 0-911818)

World Bk
World Bk., Inc, A Scott Fetzer company
Merchandise Mart Plaza, Rm 510, Chicago,
IL 60654 Tel 312-245-3456   (SAN
201-4815)
(ISBN Prefix 0-7166)

World Bk-Childcraft
See World Bk

World Digest
See World Natural Hist

World Health
World Health Organization
Dist. by:
Q Corp., 49 Sheridan Ave., Albany, NY
12210 Tel 518-436-9686   (SAN 221-6310)

World Natural Hist
World Natural History Pubns.
P.O. Box 550, Marlton, NJ 08053
Tel 609-654-6500   (SAN 208-9297)
(ISBN Prefix 0-916846)

World Print Coun
World Print Council
P O Box 26010, San Francisco, CA 94126
(SAN 225-2724)

Wright-PSG
Wright, John, PSG, Inc.
P.O.Box Six, Littleton, MA 01460
Tel 617-486-8971   (SAN 201-8934)
(ISBN Prefix 0-88416; ISBN Prefix
0-7236)

Writer
Writer, Inc.
8 Arlington St., Boston, MA 02116
Tel 617-536-7420   (SAN 203-2791)
(ISBN Prefix 0-87116)

Writers & Readers
Writers & Readers
c/o W.W. Norton Co., 500 Fifth Ave.,
New York, NY 10110 Tel 212-228-0390

WRS Verlag
WRS Verlag Wirtschaft, Recht und Steuren
GmbH & Co., Fachverlag
Irmgardstr, 8000 Munich 71,
Federal Republic of Germany

WSP
Washington Square Press, Inc, Div. of Simon
& Schuster, Inc.
1230 Ave. of the Americas, New York, NY
10020 Tel 212-246-2121   (SAN 206-9784)

Yale U Pr
Yale Univ. Press
302 Temple St., New Haven, CT 06520
Tel 203-432-4920   (SAN 203-2740)
Orders to:
92A Yale Sta., New Haven, CT 06520
Tel 203-432-4969   (SAN 203-2759)
(ISBN Prefix 0-300)

Year Bk Med
Year Book Medical Pubs., Inc.
35 E. Wacker Dr., Chicago, IL 60601
Tel 800-621-9262   (SAN 205-5600)
(ISBN Prefix 0-8151)

Yivo Inst
Yivo Institute for Jewish Research
1048 Fifth Ave., New York, NY 10028
Tel 212-535-6700   (SAN 207-1614)
(ISBN Prefix 0-914512)

York Pr CA
York Press
96 Feadow Green Court, Frederiction, N.
B. E3B 5L 8, Canada
(ISBN Prefix 0-919966)

Yorke Med
Yorke Medical Books
875 Third Ave., New York, NY 10022
Tel 212-605-9620   (SAN 207-155X)
(ISBN Prefix 0-914316)

Youth Ed
Youth Education Systems, Inc.
3305 W. Warner Ave., Santa Ana, CA
92704 Tel 714-556-7130   (SAN 205-5635)
(ISBN Prefix 0-87738)

Zanichelli
Zanichelli, Nicola, Spa
Via Irnerio 34, I-40126 Bologna, Italy

Zenemukiado
Zenemukiado Vallalat
PB 322, V, Vorosmarty jer 1, 1370
Budapest, Hungary

Zodiaque
Zodiaque-Presses Monastiques
Paris, France

Zondervan
Zondervan Publishing House
1415 Lake Dr., S.E., Grand Rapids, MI
49506 Tel 616-459-6900   (SAN 203-2694)
(ISBN Prefix 0-310)

Zrinyikatunai
Zriny Katunai Kiado
PB 22, 1440 Budapest, Hungary